# THE OFFICIAL®
## 2010 PRICE GUIDE TO
# FOOTBALL CARDS

## DR. JAMES BECKETT

## TWENTY-NINTH EDITION

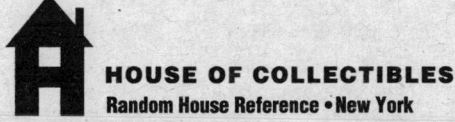

**HOUSE OF COLLECTIBLES**
Random House Reference • New York

Copyright © 2009 by James Beckett III

All rights reserved. Published in the United States by House of Collectibles, an imprint of The Random House Information Group, a division of Random House Inc., New York, and in Canada by Random House of Canada Limited, Toronto.

House of Collectibles and colophon are trademarks of Random House, Inc.

Random House is a registered trademark of Random House, Inc.

Please address inquiries about electronic licensing of any products for use on a network, in software, or on CD-ROM to the Subsidiary Rights Department, Random House Information Group, fax 212-572-6003
Visit the House of Collectibles Web site: www.houseofcollectibles.com

This book is available for special discounts for bulk purchases for sales promotions or premiums. Special editions, including personalized covers, excerpts of existing books, and corporate imprints, can be created in large quantities for special needs. For more information, write to:

Random House, Inc.,
Special Markets/Premium Sales
1745 Broadway, MD 6-2
New York, NY 10019

or e-mail specialmarket@randomhouse.com

Manufactured in the United States of America

ISSN: 0748-1365

ISBN: 978-0-375-72327-8

10 9 8 7 6 5 4 3 2 1

Twenty-Ninth Edition: August 2009

# Table of Contents

# Table of Contents

# Table of Contents

# Table of Contents

# Table of Contents

# Table of Contents

# Table of Contents

# Table of Contents

# About the Author

Jim Beckett, the leading authority on sportscard values in the United States, maintains a wide range of activities in the world of sports. He possesses one of the finest collections of sportscards and autographs in the world, has made numerous appearances on radio and television, and has been frequently cited in many national publications. He was awarded the first "Special Achievement Award for Contributions to the Hobby" by the National Sports Collectors Convention in 1980, the "Jock-Jaspersen Award for Hobby Dedication" in 1983, and the "Buck Barker, Spirit of the Hobby Award" in 1991.

Dr. Beckett is the author of *Beckett Baseball Card Price Guide, The Official Price Guide to Baseball Cards, Beckett Almanac of Baseball Cards and Collectibles, Beckett Football Card Price Guide, The Official Price Guide to Football Cards, Beckett Hockey Card Price Guide and Alphabetical Checklist, Beckett Basketball Card Price Guide, The Official Price Guide to Basketball Cards,* and *Beckett Baseball Card Alphabetical Checklist.* In addition, he is the founder and publisher of sports collectible magazines: *Beckett Baseball, Beckett Basketball, Beckett Football, Beckett Hockey,* and *Beckett Sports Card Monthly.*

Jim Beckett received his Ph.D. in Statistics from Southern Methodist University in 1975. Prior to starting Beckett Publications in 1984, Dr. Beckett served as an Associate Professor of Statistics at Bowling Green State University and as a Vice President of a consulting firm in Dallas, Texas. He currently resides in Dallas.

# How to Use This Book

Isn't it great? Every year this book gets better with all the new sets coming out. But even more exciting is that every year there are more attractive choices and, subsequently, more interest in the cards we love so much. This edition has been enhanced and expanded from the previous edition. The cards you collect—who appears on them, what they look like, where they are from, and (most important to most of you) what their current values are—are enumerated within. Many of the features contained in the other *Beckett Price Guides* have been incorporated into this volume since condition-grading, terminology, and many other aspects of collecting are common to the card hobby in general. We hope you find the book both interesting and useful in your collecting pursuits.

The Beckett Guide has been successful where other attempts have failed because it is complete, current, and valid. This price guide contains not just one but two price columns for all the football cards listed. These account for most of the major releases in existence. The prices were added to the card lists just prior to printing and reflect not the author's opinions or desires but the going retail prices for each card, based on the marketplace (sports memorabilia conventions and shows, sportscard shops, hobby papers, current mail-order catalogs, Internet sales, auction results, and other firsthand reporting of actually realized prices).

What is the best price guide available on the market today? Of course card sellers will prefer the price guide with the highest prices, while card buyers will naturally prefer the one with the lowest prices. Accuracy, however, is the true test. Use the price guide used by more collectors and dealers than all the others combined. Look for the Beckett name. I won't put my name on anything I won't stake my reputation on. Not the lowest and not the highest—but the most accurate, with integrity.

To facilitate your use of this book, read the complete introductory section on the following pages before going to the pricing pages. Every collectible field has its own terminology; we've tried to capture most of these terms and definitions in our glossary. Please read carefully the section on grading and the condition of your cards, as you will not be able to determine which price column is appropriate for a given card without first knowing its condition.

## Prices in This Guide

Prices found in this guide reflect current retail rates just prior to the printing of this book. They do not reflect the for-sale prices of the author, the publisher, the distributors, the advertisers, or any card dealers associated with this guide. No one is obligated in any way to buy, sell, or trade his or her cards based on these prices. The price listings were compiled by the author from actual buy/sell transactions at sports conventions, sportscard shops, buy/sell advertisements in the hobby papers, for-sale prices from dealer catalogs and price lists, and discussions with leading hobbyists in the U.S. and Canada. All prices are in U.S. dollars.

## Introduction

Welcome to the exciting world of sportscard collecting, one of America's most popular avocations. You have made a good choice in buying this book, since it will open up to you the entire panorama of this field in the simplest, most concise way.

The growth of *Beckett Baseball, Beckett Basketball, Beckett Football, Beckett Hockey,* and *Beckett Sports Card Monthly* is an indication of the unprecedented popularity of sportscards. Founded in 1984 by Dr. James Beckett, *Beckett Baseball* contains the most extensive and accepted monthly price guide, collectible glossy superstar covers, colorful feature articles, "Hot List," Convention Calendar, tips for beginners, "Readers Write" letters to and responses from the editor, information on errors and varieties, autograph collecting tips, and profiles of the sport's hottest stars. Published every month, *Beckett Baseball* is the hobby's largest paid circulation periodical. The other five magazines were built on the success of *Baseball*.

So collecting sportscards—while still pursued as a hobby with youthful exuberance by kids in the neighborhood—has also taken on the trappings of an industry, with thousands of full- and part-time card dealers, as well as vendors of supplies, clubs, and conventions. In fact, each year since 1980 thousands of hobbyists have assembled for a National Sports Collectors Convention, at which hundreds of dealers have displayed their wares, seminars have been conducted, autographs penned by sports notables, and millions of cards changed hands. The Beckett Guide is the best annual guide available to the exciting world of football cards. Read it and use it. May your enjoyment and your card collection increase in the coming months and years.

## How to Collect

Each collection is personal and reflects the individuality of its owner. There are no set rules on how to collect cards. Since card collecting is a hobby or leisure pastime, what you collect, how much you collect, and how much time and money you spend collecting are entirely up to you. The funds you have available for collecting and your own personal taste should determine how you collect. The information and ideas presented here are intended to help you get the most enjoyment from this hobby.

It is impossible to collect every card ever produced. Therefore, beginners as well as intermediate and advanced collectors usually specialize in some way. One of the reasons this hobby is popular is that individual collectors can define and tailor their collecting methods to match their own tastes. To give you some ideas of the various approaches to collecting, we will list some of the more popular areas of specialization.

Many collectors select complete sets from particular years. For example, they may concentrate on assembling complete sets from all the years since their birth or since they became avid sports fans. They may try to collect a card for every player during that specified period of time. Many others wish to acquire only certain players. Usually such players are the superstars of the sport, but occasionally collectors will specialize in all the cards of players who attended a particular college or came from a certain town. Some collectors are only interested in the first cards or Rookie Cards of certain players.

Another fun way to collect cards is by team. Most fans have a favorite team, and it is natural for that loyalty to be translated into a desire for cards of the players on that favorite team. For most of the recent years, team sets (all the cards from a given team for that year) are readily available at a reasonable price. See Beckett.com for searchable player checklists.

## Preserving Your Cards

Cards are fragile. They must be handled properly in order to retain their value. Careless handling can easily result in creased or bent cards. It is, however, not recommended that tweezers or tongs be used to pick up your cards since such utensils might mar or indent card surfaces and thus reduce those cards' conditions and values. In general, your cards should be handled directly as little as possible. This is sometimes easier to say than to do.

Although there are still many who use custom boxes, storage trays, or even shoe boxes, plastic sheets are the preferred method of many collectors for storing cards. A collection stored in plastic pages in a three-ring album allows you to view your collection at any time without the need to touch the card itself. Cards can also be kept in single holders (of various types and thicknesses) designed for the enjoyment of each card individually. For a large collection, some collectors may use a combination of the above methods. When purchasing plastic sheets for your cards, be sure that you find the pocket size that fits the cards snugly. Don't put your 1951 Bowman in a sheet designed to fit 1981 Topps.

Most hobby and collectibles shops and virtually all collectors' conventions will have these plastic pages available in quantity for the various sizes offered, or you can purchase them directly from the advertisers in this book. Also, remember that pocket size isn't the only factor to consider when looking for plastic sheets. Other factors such as safety, economy, appearance, availability, or personal preference also may indicate which types of sheets a collector may want to buy.

Damp, sunny, and/or hot conditions. No, this is not a weather forecast, but rather three elements to avoid in extremes if you are interested in preserving your collection. Too much (or too little) humidity can cause gradual deterioration of a card. Direct, bright sun (or fluorescent light) over time will bleach out the color of a card. Extreme heat accelerates the decomposition of the card. On the other hand, many cards have lasted more than 50 years without much scientific intervention. So be cautious, even if the above factors typically present a problem only when present in the extreme. It never hurts to be prudent.

# Terminology

Each hobby has its own language to describe its area of interest. The following list defines the most important terminology and abbreviations that may appear in this book:

**AS** - All-Star.

**CL** - Checklist card. A card that lists in order the cards and players in the set or series. Older checklist cards in mint condition that have not been checked off are very desirable and command large premiums.

**COMMON CARD** - The typical card of any set; it has no premium value accruing from subject matter, numerical scarcity, popular demand, or anomaly.

**COR** - Corrected card. A version of an error card that was fixed by the manufacturer.

**DIE-CUT** - A card with its stock partially cut. In some cases, after removal or appropriate folding, the remaining part of the card can be made to stand up.

**DP** - Double Print. A card that was printed in approximately double the quantity compared to other cards in the same series, or draft pick card.

**ERR** - Error card. A card with erroneous information, spelling, or depiction on either side of the card. Most errors are never corrected by the producing card company.

**FOIL** - A special type of sticker with a metallic-looking surface.

**HL** - Highlight card, for example from the 1978 Topps subset.

**HOF** - Hall of Fame, or Hall of Famer (also abbreviated HOFer).

**HOR** - Horizontal pose on a card as opposed to the standard vertical orientation found on most cards.

**IA** - In Action card. A special type of card depicting a player in an action photo, such as the 1982 Topps cards.

**LL** - League leader card. A card depicting the leader or leaders in a specific statistical category from the previous season. Not to be confused with team leader (TL).

**LOGO** - NFLPA logo on card.

**MVP** - Most Valuable Player.

**NO LOGO** - No NFLPA logo on card.

**NO TR** - No trade reference on card.

**NPO** - No position.

**OFF** - Officials cards.

**O-ROY** - Offensive Rookie of the Year.

**PARALLEL** - A card that is similar in design to its counterpart from a basic set, but offers a distinguishing quality.

**PB** - Pro Bowl.

**RB** - Record Breaker card or running back.

**RC** - Rookie Card. A player's first appearance on a regular issue card from one of the major card companies. With a few exceptions, each player has only one RC in any given set. A Rookie Card typically cannot be an All-Star, Highlight, In Action, league leader, Super Action, or team leader card. It can, however, be a coach card or draft pick card.

**REDEMPTION** - A program established by manufacturers that allows collectors to mail in a special card (usually a random insert) in return for special cards, sets, or other prizes not available through conventional channels.

**RET** - Retired.

**REV NEG** - Reversed or flopped photo side of the card. This is a major type of error card, but only some are corrected.

**ROY** - Rookie of the Year.

**SB** - Super Bowl.

**SET** - One each of an entire run of cards of the same type, produced by a particular manufacturer during a single season. In other words, if you have a complete set of 1975 Topps football cards, then you have every card from #1 up to and including #528; i.e., all the different cards that were produced.

**SP** - Single or Short Print. A card which was printed in lesser quantity compared to the other cards in the same series (also see DP). This term can only be used in a relative sense and in reference to one particular set. For instance, the 1989 Pro Set Pete Rozelle SP is less common than the other cards in that set, but it isn't necessarily scarcer than regular cards of any other set.

**TC** - Team card or team checklist card.

**TL** - Team leader card or Top Leader.

**UER** - Uncorrected error card.

**XRC** - Extended Rookie Card. A player's first appearance on a card, but issued in a set that was not distributed nationally or in packs. In football sets, this term generally refers to the 1984 and 1985 Topps USFL sets.

# Understanding Card Values

## Determining Value

Why are some cards more valuable than others? Obviously, the economic laws of supply and demand are applicable to card collecting just as they are to any other field where a commodity is bought, sold, or traded in a free, unregulated market.

Supply (the number of cards available on the market) is less than the total number of cards originally produced since attrition diminishes that original quantity. Each year a percentage of cards is typically thrown away, destroyed, or otherwise lost to collectors. This percentage is much, much smaller today than it was in the past because more and more people have become increasingly aware of the value of their cards.

For those who collect only mint condition cards, the supply of older cards can be quite small indeed. Until recently, collectors were not so conscious of the need to preserve the condition of their cards. For this reason, it is difficult to know exactly how many 1962 Topps are currently available, mint or otherwise. It is generally accepted that there are fewer 1962 Topps available than 1972, 1982, or 1992 Topps cards. If demand were equal for each of these sets, the law of supply and demand would increase the price for the least available sets.

Demand, however, is never equal for all sets, so price correlations can be complicated. The demand for a card is influenced by many factors. These include: (1) the age of the card; (2) the number of cards printed; (3) the player(s) portrayed on the card; (4) the attractiveness and popularity of the set; and (5) the physical condition of the card.

In general, (1) the older the card, (2) the fewer the number of the cards printed, (3) the more famous, popular, and talented the player, (4) the more attractive and popular the set, and (5) the better the condition of the card, the higher the value of the card will be. There are exceptions to all but one of these factors: the condition of the card. Given two cards similar in all respects except condition, the one in the better condition will always be valued higher.

While those guidelines help to establish the value of a card, the countless exceptions and peculiarities make any simple, direct mathematical formula to determine card values impossible.

## Regional Variation

Since the market varies from region to region, card prices of local players may be higher. This is known as a regional premium. How significant the premium is—and if there is any premium at all—depends on the local popularity of the team and the player.

The largest regional premiums usually do not apply to superstars, who often are so well known nationwide that the prices of their key cards are too high for local dealers to realize a premium.

Lesser stars often command the strongest premiums. Their popularity is concentrated in their home region, creating local demand that greatly exceeds overall demand.

Regional premiums can apply to popular retired players and sometimes can be found in the areas where the players grew up or starred in college.

A regional discount is the converse of a regional premium. Regional discounts occur when a player has been so popular in his region for so long that local collectors and dealers have accumulated quantities of his cards. The abundant supply may make the cards available in that area at the lowest prices anywhere.

### Set Prices

A somewhat paradoxical situation exists in the price of a complete set vs. the combined cost of the individual cards in the set. In nearly every case, the sum of the prices for the individual cards is higher than the cost for the complete set. This is prevalent especially in the cards of the past few years. The reasons for this apparent anomaly stem from the habits of collectors and from the carrying costs to dealers. Today, each card in a set normally is produced in the same quantity as all others in its set.

Many collectors pick up only stars, superstars, and particular teams. As a result, the dealer is left with a shortage of certain player cards and an abundance of others. He therefore incurs an expense in simply "carrying" these less desirable cards in stock. On the other hand, if he sells a complete set, he gets rid of large numbers of cards at one time. For this reason, he generally is willing to receive less money for a complete set. By doing this, he recovers all of his costs and also makes a profit.

Set prices do not include rare card varieties, unless specifically stated. Of course, the prices for sets do include one example of each type for the given set, but this is the least expensive variety.

# Grading Your Cards

Each hobby has its own grading terminology—stamps, coins, comic books, record collecting, etc. Collectors of sportscards are no exception. The one invariable criterion for determining the value of a card is its condition: the better the condition of the card, the more valuable it is. Condition grading, however, is subjective. Individual card dealers and collectors differ in the strictness of their grading, but the stated condition of a card should be determined without regard to whether it is being bought or sold.

No allowance is made for age. A 1952 card is judged by the same standards as a 1992 card. But there are specific sets and cards that are condition-sensitive because of their border color, consistently poor centering, etc. Such cards and sets sometimes command premiums above the listed percentages in mint condition.

# Condition Guide

### Grades

**Mint (Mt)** - A card with no flaws or wear. The card has four perfect corners, 55/45 or better centering from top to bottom and from left to right, original gloss, smooth edges, and original color borders. A mint card does not have print spots, color, or focus imperfections.

**Near Mint-Mint (NrMt-Mt)** - A card with one minor flaw. Any one of the following would lower a mint card to near mint-mint: one corner with a slight touch of wear, barely noticeable print spots, color or focus imperfections. The card must have 60/40 or better centering in both directions, original gloss, smooth edges, and original color borders.

**Near Mint (NrMt)** - A card with one minor flaw. Any one of the following would lower a mint card to near mint: one fuzzy corner or two to four corners with slight touches of wear, 70/30 to 60/40 centering, slightly rough edges, minor print spots, color or focus imperfections. The card must have original gloss and original color borders.

**Excellent-Mint (ExMt)** - A card with two or three fuzzy, but not rounded, corners and centering no worse than 80/20. The card may have no more than two of the following: slightly rough edges, very slightly discolored borders, minor print spots, color or focus imperfections. The card must have original gloss.

**Excellent (Ex)** - A card with four fuzzy but definitely not rounded corners and centering no worse than 80/20. The card may have a small amount of original gloss lost, rough edges, slightly discolored borders and minor print spots, color or focus imperfections.

**Very Good (Vg)** - A card that has been handled but not abused: slightly rounded corners with slight layering, slight notching on edges, a significant amount of gloss lost from the surface but no scuffing and moderate discoloration of borders. The card may have a few light creases.

**Good (G)**, **Fair (F)**, **Poor (P)** - A well-worn, mishandled, or abused card: badly rounded and layered corners, scuffing, most or all original gloss missing, seriously discolored borders, moderate or heavy creases, and one or more serious flaws. The grade of good, fair, or poor depends on the severity of wear and flaws. Good, fair, and poor cards generally are used only as fillers.

# Selling Your Cards

Just about every collector sells cards or will sell cards eventually. Someday you may be interested in selling your duplicates or maybe even your whole collection. You may sell to other collectors, friends, or dealers. You may even sell cards you purchased from a certain dealer back to that same dealer. In any event, it helps to know some of the mechanics of the typical transaction between buyer and seller.

Dealers will buy cards in order to resell them to other collectors who are interested in the cards. Dealers will always pay a higher percentage for items that (in their opinion) can be resold quickly, and a much lower percentage for those items that are perceived as having low demand and hence are slow moving. In either case, dealers must buy at a price that allows for the expense of doing business and a margin for profit.

If you have cards for sale, the best advice we can give is that you get several offers for your cards—either from card shops or at a card show—and take the best offer, all things considered. Note, the "best" offer may not be the one for the highest amount. And remember, if a dealer really wants your cards, he won't let you get away without making his best competitive offer. Another alternative is to place your cards in an auction as one or several lots.

Many people think nothing of going into a department store and paying $15 for an item of clothing for which the store paid $5. But if you were selling your $15 card to a dealer and he offered you $5 for it, you might think his markup unreasonable. To complete the analogy, most department stores (and card dealers) that consistently pay $10 for $15 items eventually go out of business. An exception is when the dealer has lined up a willing buyer for the item(s) you are attempting to sell, or if the cards are so hot that it's likely he'll have to hold the cards for only a short period of time.

In those cases, an offer of up to 75% of book value still will allow the dealer to make a reasonable profit considering the short time he will need to hold the merchandise. In general, however, most cards and collections will bring offers in the range of 25% to 50% of retail price. Also consider that most material from the past five to 20 years is plentiful. If that's what you're selling, don't be surprised if your best offer is well below that range.

## 2001 Absolute Memorabilia

|  |  | | |
|---|---|---|---|
| | COMP. SET w/o SP's (100) | 30.00 | 12.50 |
| 1 | David Boston | 1.25 | .50 |
| 2 | Jake Plummer | .75 | .30 |
| 3 | Thomas Jones | .75 | .30 |
| 4 | Jamal Anderson | 1.25 | .50 |
| 5 | Chris Redman | .50 | .20 |
| 6 | Jamal Lewis | 2.00 | .75 |
| 7 | Qadry Ismail | .75 | .30 |
| 8 | Ray Lewis | 1.25 | .50 |
| 9 | Shannon Sharpe | .75 | .30 |
| 10 | Travis Taylor | .75 | .30 |
| 11 | Trent Dilfer | .75 | .30 |
| 12 | Elvis Grbac | .75 | .30 |
| 13 | Eric Moulds | .75 | .30 |
| 14 | Rob Johnson | .75 | .30 |
| 15 | Muhsin Muhammad | .75 | .30 |
| 16 | Brian Urlacher | 2.00 | .75 |
| 17 | Cade McNown | .50 | .20 |
| 18 | Marcus Robinson | 1.25 | .50 |
| 19 | Akili Smith | .50 | .20 |
| 20 | Corey Dillon | 1.25 | .50 |
| 21 | Peter Warrick | 1.25 | .50 |
| 22 | Courtney Brown | .75 | .30 |
| 23 | Tim Couch | .75 | .30 |
| 24 | Emmitt Smith | 2.50 | 1.00 |
| 25 | Troy Aikman | 2.00 | .75 |
| 26 | Brian Griese | 1.25 | .50 |
| 27 | Ed McCaffrey | 1.25 | .50 |
| 28 | John Elway | 4.00 | 1.50 |
| 29 | Mike Anderson | 1.25 | .50 |
| 30 | Rod Smith | .75 | .30 |
| 31 | Terrell Davis | 1.25 | .50 |
| 32 | Barry Sanders | 2.50 | 1.00 |
| 33 | James Stewart | .75 | .30 |
| 34 | Ahman Green | 1.25 | .50 |
| 35 | Antonio Freeman | 1.25 | .50 |
| 36 | Brett Favre | 4.00 | 1.50 |
| 37 | Edgerrin James | 1.50 | .60 |
| 38 | Marvin Harrison | 1.25 | .50 |
| 39 | Peyton Manning | 3.00 | 1.25 |
| 40 | Fred Taylor | 1.25 | .50 |
| 41 | Jimmy Smith | .75 | .30 |
| 42 | Keenan McCardell | .50 | .20 |
| 43 | Mark Brunell | 1.25 | .50 |
| 44 | Sylvester Morris | .50 | .20 |
| 45 | Tony Gonzalez | .75 | .30 |
| 46 | Dan Marino | 4.00 | 1.50 |
| 47 | Jay Fiedler | 1.25 | .50 |
| 48 | Lamar Smith | .75 | .30 |
| 49 | Cris Carter | 1.25 | .50 |
| 50 | Daunte Culpepper | 1.25 | .50 |
| 51 | Randy Moss | 2.50 | 1.00 |
| 52 | Drew Bledsoe | 1.50 | .60 |
| 53 | Terry Glenn | .75 | .30 |
| 54 | Aaron Brooks | 1.25 | .50 |
| 55 | Joe Horn | .75 | .30 |
| 56 | Ricky Williams | 1.25 | .50 |
| 57 | Amani Toomer | .75 | .30 |
| 58 | Ike Hilliard | .75 | .30 |
| 59 | Kerry Collins | .75 | .30 |
| 60 | Ron Dayne | 1.25 | .50 |
| 61 | Tiki Barber | .75 | .30 |
| 62 | Chad Pennington | 2.00 | .75 |
| 63 | Curtis Martin | 1.25 | .50 |
| 64 | Laveranues Coles | 1.25 | .50 |
| 65 | Vinny Testaverde | .75 | .30 |
| 66 | Wayne Chrebet | .75 | .30 |
| 67 | Charles Woodson | .75 | .30 |
| 68 | Rich Gannon | 1.25 | .50 |
| 69 | Tim Brown | 1.25 | .50 |
| 70 | Tyrone Wheatley | .75 | .30 |
| 71 | Corey Simon | .75 | .30 |
| 72 | Donovan McNabb | 1.50 | .60 |
| 73 | Duce Staley | 1.25 | .50 |
| 74 | Jerome Bettis | 1.25 | .50 |
| 75 | Plaxico Burress | 1.25 | .50 |
| 76 | Doug Flutie | 1.25 | .50 |
| 77 | Junior Seau | .75 | .30 |
| 78 | Charlie Garner | .75 | .30 |
| 79 | Jeff Garcia | 1.25 | .50 |
| 80 | Jerry Rice | 2.50 | 1.00 |
| 81 | Steve Young | 1.25 | .50 |
| 82 | Terrell Owens | 1.25 | .50 |
| 83 | Darrell Jackson | .75 | .30 |
| 84 | Ricky Watters | .50 | .20 |
| 85 | Shaun Alexander | 1.50 | .60 |
| 86 | Isaac Bruce | 1.25 | .50 |
| 87 | Kurt Warner | 2.50 | 1.00 |
| 88 | Marshall Faulk | 1.50 | .60 |
| 89 | Torry Holt | 1.25 | .50 |
| 90 | Brad Johnson | 1.25 | .50 |
| 91 | Keyshawn Johnson | 1.25 | .50 |
| 92 | Mike Alstott | 1.25 | .50 |
| 93 | Shaun King | .50 | .20 |
| 94 | Warren Sapp | .75 | .30 |
| 95 | Warrick Dunn | 1.25 | .50 |
| 96 | Eddie George | 1.25 | .50 |
| 97 | Jevon Kearse | .75 | .30 |
| 98 | Steve McNair | 1.25 | .50 |
| 99 | Jeff George | .75 | .30 |
| 100 | Stephen Davis | 1.25 | .50 |
| 101 | Jason McKinley RC | 4.00 | 1.50 |
| 102 | Bobby Newcombe RC | 4.00 | 1.50 |
| 103 | Cedrick Wilson RC | 6.00 | 2.50 |
| 104 | Kevin Rambo RC | 4.00 | 1.50 |
| 105 | Kevin Kasper RC | 6.00 | 2.50 |
| 106 | Jamal Reynolds RC | 6.00 | 2.50 |
| 107 | Scotty Anderson RC | 4.00 | 1.50 |
| 108 | T.J. Houshmandzadeh RC | 8.00 | 3.00 |
| 109 | Chris Taylor RC | 4.00 | 1.50 |
| 110 | Vinny Sutherland RC | 4.00 | 1.50 |
| 111 | Jabari Holloway RC | 4.00 | 1.50 |
| 112 | Shad Meier RC | 4.00 | 1.50 |
| 113 | Correll Buckhalter RC | 8.00 | 3.00 |
| 114 | Dan Alexander RC | 6.00 | 2.50 |
| 115 | David Allen RC | 4.00 | 1.50 |
| 116 | LaMont Jordan RC | 12.00 | 5.00 |
| 117 | Nate Clements RC | 6.00 | 2.50 |
| 118 | Reggie White RC | 4.00 | 1.50 |
| 119 | Javon Green RC | 4.00 | 1.50 |
| 120 | Shaun Rogers RC | 6.00 | 2.50 |
| 121 | Heath Evans RC | 4.00 | 1.50 |
| 122 | Moran Norris RC | 2.50 | 1.00 |
| 123 | Ben Leard RC | 4.00 | 1.50 |
| 124 | David Rivers RC | 4.00 | 1.50 |
| 125 | A.J. Feeley RC | 6.00 | 2.50 |
| 126 | Boo Williams RC | 4.00 | 1.50 |
| 127 | Ronney Daniels RC | 2.50 | 1.00 |
| 128 | Alge Crumpler RC | 8.00 | 4.00 |
| 129 | Todd Heap RC | 6.00 | 2.50 |
| 130 | Tim Hasselbeck RC | 6.00 | 2.50 |
| 131 | Josh Booty RC | 6.00 | 2.50 |
| 132 | Jamie Winborn RC | 4.00 | 1.50 |
| 133 | Brian Allen RC | 2.50 | 1.00 |
| 134 | Sedrick Hodge RC | 2.50 | 1.00 |
| 135 | Tommy Polley RC | 6.00 | 2.50 |
| 136 | Torrance Marshall RC | 6.00 | 2.50 |
| 137 | Damione Lewis RC | 4.00 | 1.50 |
| 138 | Marcus Stroud RC | 6.00 | 2.50 |
| 139 | Aaron Schobel RC | 6.00 | 2.50 |
| 140 | DeLawrence Grant RC | 2.50 | 1.00 |
| 141 | Fred Smoot RC | 6.00 | 2.50 |
| 142 | Jamar Fletcher RC | 4.00 | 1.50 |
| 143 | Ken Lucas RC | 4.00 | 1.50 |
| 144 | Will Allen RC | 4.00 | 1.50 |
| 145 | Adam Archuleta RC | 6.00 | 2.50 |
| 146 | Derrick Gibson RC | 4.00 | 1.50 |
| 147 | Jarrod Cooper RC | 6.00 | 2.50 |
| 148 | Eddie Berlin RC | 4.00 | 1.50 |
| 149 | Steve Smith RC | 15.00 | 7.50 |
| 150 | Willie Middlebrooks RC | 4.00 | 1.50 |
| 151 | Michael Vick RPM RC | | |
| 152 | Drew Brees RPM RC | 50.00 | 20.00 |
| 153 | Chris Weinke RPM RC | 15.00 | 6.00 |
| 154 | Mar Tuiasosopo RPM RC | 15.00 | 6.00 |
| 155 | Mike McMahon RPM RC | 15.00 | 6.00 |
| 156 | Deuce McAllister RPM RC | 30.00 | 12.50 |
| 157 | Leonard Davis RPM RC | 10.00 | 4.00 |
| 158 | LaD Tomlinson RPM RC | 80.00 | 40.00 |
| 159 | Anthony Thomas RPM RC | 15.00 | 6.00 |
| 160 | Travis Henry RPM RC | 15.00 | 6.00 |
| 161 | James Jackson RPM RC | 15.00 | 6.00 |
| 162 | Michael Bennett RPM RC | 15.00 | 6.00 |
| 163 | Kevan Barlow RPM RC | 15.00 | 6.00 |
| 164 | Travis Minor RPM RC | 10.00 | 4.00 |
| 165 | David Terrell RPM RC | 15.00 | 6.00 |
| 166 | Santana Moss RPM RC | 25.00 | 10.00 |
| 167 | Rod Gardner RPM RC | 15.00 | 6.00 |
| 168 | Quincy Morgan RPM RC | 15.00 | 6.00 |
| 169 | Freddie Mitchell RPM RC | 15.00 | 6.00 |
| 170 | Reggie Wayne RPM RC | 30.00 | 12.50 |
| 171 | Koren Robinson RPM RC | 15.00 | 6.00 |
| 172 | Chad Johnson RPM RC | 40.00 | 15.00 |
| 173 | Chris Chambers RPM RC | 25.00 | 10.00 |
| 174 | Josh Heupel RPM RC | 15.00 | 6.00 |
| 175 | Andre Carter RPM RC | 15.00 | 6.00 |
| 176 | Justin Smith RPM RC | 15.00 | 6.00 |
| 177 | Richard Seymour RPM RC | 15.00 | 6.00 |
| 178 | Dan Morgan RPM RC | 15.00 | 6.00 |
| 179 | Gerard Warren RPM RC | 15.00 | 6.00 |
| 180 | Robert Ferguson RPM RC | 15.00 | 6.00 |
| 181 | Sage Rosenfels RPM RC | 15.00 | 6.00 |
| 182 | Rudi Johnson RPM RC | 30.00 | 12.50 |
| 183 | Snoop Minnis RPM RC | 15.00 | 6.00 |
| 184 | Jesse Palmer RPM RC | 15.00 | 6.00 |
| 185 | Quincy Carter RPM RC | 15.00 | 6.00 |

## 2002 Absolute Memorabilia

|  |  | | |
|---|---|---|---|
| | COMP.SET w/o SPs (150) | 30.00 | 12.50 |
| 1 | Aaron Brooks | 1.25 | .50 |
| 2 | Ahman Green | 1.25 | .50 |
| 3 | Alge Crumpler | .75 | .30 |
| 4 | Amani Toomer | .50 | .20 |
| 5 | Andre Carter | .50 | .20 |
| 6 | Anthony Thomas | 1.25 | .50 |
| 7 | Antonio Freeman | 1.25 | .50 |
| 8 | Antowain Smith | .75 | .30 |
| 9 | Az-Zahir Hakim | .50 | .20 |
| 10 | Bill Schroeder | .75 | .30 |
| 11 | Brad Johnson | .75 | .30 |
| 12 | Brett Favre | 3.00 | 1.25 |
| 13 | Brian Griese | 1.25 | .50 |
| 14 | Brian Urlacher | 2.00 | .75 |
| 15 | Chad Johnson | 1.25 | .50 |
| 16 | Chad Pennington | 1.50 | .60 |
| 17 | Champ Bailey | .75 | .30 |
| 18 | Charles Woodson | .75 | .30 |
| 19 | Charlie Batch | .75 | .30 |
| 20 | Charlie Garner | .75 | .30 |
| 21 | Chris Chambers | 1.25 | .50 |
| 22 | Chris Redman | .50 | .20 |
| 23 | Corey Dillon | .75 | .30 |
| 24 | Correll Buckhalter | .50 | .20 |
| 25 | Cris Carter | 1.25 | .50 |
| 26 | Cris Carter | 1.25 | .50 |

| | | |
|---|---|---|
| ❑ 27 Curtis Martin | 1.25 | .50 |
| ❑ 28 Danny Scott | .75 | .30 |
| ❑ 29 Darrell Jackson | .75 | .30 |
| ❑ 30 Daunte Culpepper | 1.25 | .50 |
| ❑ 31 David Boston | 1.25 | .50 |
| ❑ 32 David Terrell | .75 | .30 |
| ❑ 33 Derrick Alexander | .75 | .30 |
| ❑ 34 Derrick Mason | .75 | .30 |
| ❑ 35 Deuce McAllister | 1.50 | .60 |
| ❑ 36 Dominic Rhodes | 1.25 | .50 |
| ❑ 37 Donald Hayes | .50 | .20 |
| ❑ 38 Donovan McNabb | 1.50 | .60 |
| ❑ 39 Doug Flutie | 1.25 | .50 |
| ❑ 40 Drew Bledsoe | 1.50 | .60 |
| ❑ 41 Drew Brees | 1.25 | .50 |
| ❑ 42 Duce Staley | 1.25 | .50 |
| ❑ 43 Ed McCaffrey | 1.25 | .50 |
| ❑ 44 Eddie George | 1.25 | .50 |
| ❑ 45 Edgerrin James | 1.50 | .60 |
| ❑ 46 Elvis Joseph | .50 | .20 |
| ❑ 47 Emmitt Smith | 3.00 | 1.25 |
| ❑ 48 Eric Moulds | .75 | .30 |
| ❑ 49 Frank Sanders | .50 | .20 |
| ❑ 50 Fred Taylor | 1.25 | .50 |
| ❑ 51 Freddie Mitchell | .75 | .30 |
| ❑ 52 Garrison Hearst | .75 | .30 |
| ❑ 53 Gerard Warren | .50 | .20 |
| ❑ 54 Germane Crowell | .50 | .20 |
| ❑ 55 Isaac Bruce | 1.25 | .50 |
| ❑ 56 Jake Plummer | .75 | .30 |
| ❑ 57 Jamal Anderson | .75 | .30 |
| ❑ 58 Jamal Lewis | 1.25 | .50 |
| ❑ 59 James Allen | .75 | .30 |
| ❑ 60 James Jackson | .75 | .30 |
| ❑ 61 James Stewart | .75 | .30 |
| ❑ 62 Jason Brookins | .75 | .30 |
| ❑ 63 Jay Fiedler | .75 | .30 |
| ❑ 64 Jeff Garcia | 1.25 | .50 |
| ❑ 65 Jerome Bettis | 1.25 | .50 |
| ❑ 66 Jerry Rice | 2.50 | 1.00 |
| ❑ 67 Jevon Kearse | .75 | .30 |
| ❑ 68 Jim Miller | .50 | .20 |
| ❑ 69 Jimmy Smith | .75 | .30 |
| ❑ 70 Joe Horn | .75 | .30 |
| ❑ 71 Joey Galloway | .75 | .30 |
| ❑ 72 Jon Kitna | .75 | .30 |
| ❑ 73 Junior Seau | 1.25 | .50 |
| ❑ 74 Keenan McCardell | .50 | .20 |
| ❑ 75 Kendrell Bell | 1.25 | .50 |
| ❑ 76 Kerry Collins | .75 | .30 |
| ❑ 77 Kevan Barlow | .75 | .30 |
| ❑ 78 Kevin Dyson | .75 | .30 |
| ❑ 79 Kevin Johnson | .75 | .30 |
| ❑ 80 Kevin Kasper | .50 | .20 |
| ❑ 81 Keyshawn Johnson | 1.25 | .50 |
| ❑ 82 Kordell Stewart | .75 | .30 |
| ❑ 83 Koren Robinson | .75 | .30 |
| ❑ 84 Kurt Warner | 1.25 | .50 |
| ❑ 85 LaDainian Tomlinson | 2.50 | 1.00 |
| ❑ 86 Lamar Smith | .75 | .30 |
| ❑ 87 Laveranues Coles | .75 | .30 |
| ❑ 88 Mar'Tay Jenkins | .50 | .20 |
| ❑ 89 Mark Brunell | 1.25 | .50 |
| ❑ 90 Marshall Faulk | 1.25 | .50 |
| ❑ 91 Marty Booker | .75 | .30 |
| ❑ 92 Marvin Harrison | 1.25 | .50 |
| ❑ 93 Snoop Minnis | .50 | .20 |
| ❑ 94 Michael Bennett | .75 | .30 |
| ❑ 95 Michael Strahan | .75 | .30 |
| ❑ 96 Michael Vick | 2.50 | 1.00 |
| ❑ 97 Mike Alstott | 1.25 | .50 |
| ❑ 98 Mike Anderson | 1.25 | .50 |
| ❑ 99 Mike McMahon | .75 | .30 |
| ❑ 100 Muhsin Muhammad | .75 | .30 |
| ❑ 101 Nate Clements | .75 | .30 |
| ❑ 102 Oronde Gadsden | .75 | .30 |
| ❑ 103 Peter Warrick | .75 | .30 |
| ❑ 104 Peyton Manning | 2.50 | 1.00 |
| ❑ 105 Plaxico Burress | .75 | .30 |
| ❑ 106 Priest Holmes | 1.50 | .60 |
| ❑ 107 Quincy Carter | .75 | .30 |
| ❑ 108 Quincy Morgan | .75 | .30 |
| ❑ 109 Rocket Ismail | .75 | .30 |
| ❑ 110 Randy Moss | 2.50 | 1.00 |

| | | |
|---|---|---|
| ❑ 111 Ray Lewis | 1.25 | .50 |
| ❑ 112 Reggie Wayne | 1.25 | .50 |
| ❑ 113 Rich Gannon | 1.25 | .50 |
| ❑ 114 Rickey Dudley | .50 | .20 |
| ❑ 115 Ricky Watters | .75 | .30 |
| ❑ 116 Ricky Williams | 1.25 | .50 |
| ❑ 117 Rod Gardner | .75 | .30 |
| ❑ 118 Rod Smith | .75 | .30 |
| ❑ 119 Robert Ferguson | .50 | .20 |
| ❑ 120 Santana Moss | 1.25 | .50 |
| ❑ 121 Shaun Alexander | 1.50 | .60 |
| ❑ 122 Stephen Davis | .75 | .30 |
| ❑ 123 Steve McNair | 1.25 | .50 |
| ❑ 124 Steve Smith | 1.25 | .50 |
| ❑ 125 Terrell Davis | 1.25 | .50 |
| ❑ 126 Terrell Owens | 1.25 | .50 |
| ❑ 127 Terry Glenn | .75 | .30 |
| ❑ 128 Thomas Jones | .75 | .30 |
| ❑ 129 Tiki Barber | 1.25 | .50 |
| ❑ 130 Tim Brown | 1.25 | .50 |
| ❑ 131 Tim Couch | .75 | .30 |
| ❑ 132 Todd Heap | .75 | .30 |
| ❑ 133 Todd Pinkston | .75 | .30 |
| ❑ 134 Tom Brady | 3.00 | 1.25 |
| ❑ 135 Tony Boselli | .50 | .20 |
| ❑ 136 Tony Gonzalez | .75 | .30 |
| ❑ 137 Torry Holt | 1.25 | .50 |
| ❑ 138 Travis Henry | 1.25 | .50 |
| ❑ 139 Travis Taylor | .75 | .30 |
| ❑ 140 Trent Dilfer | .75 | .30 |
| ❑ 141 Trent Green | .75 | .30 |
| ❑ 142 Troy Brown | .75 | .30 |
| ❑ 143 Troy Hambrick | .50 | .20 |
| ❑ 144 Trung Canidate | .75 | .30 |
| ❑ 145 Vinny Testaverde | .75 | .30 |
| ❑ 146 Warren Sapp | .75 | .30 |
| ❑ 147 Warrick Dunn | 1.25 | .50 |
| ❑ 148 Wayne Chrebet | .75 | .30 |
| ❑ 149 Wesley Walls | .50 | .20 |
| ❑ 150 Zach Thomas | 1.25 | .50 |
| ❑ 151 Quentin Jammer RC | 6.00 | 2.50 |
| ❑ 152 Randy Fasani RC | 5.00 | 2.00 |
| ❑ 153 Kurt Kittner RC | 5.00 | 2.00 |
| ❑ 154 Chad Hutchinson RC | 6.00 | 2.50 |
| ❑ 155 Major Applewhite RC | 6.00 | 2.50 |
| ❑ 156 Wes Pate RC | 3.00 | 1.25 |
| ❑ 157 J.T. O'Sullivan RC | 8.00 | 3.00 |
| ❑ 158 Ryan Denney RC | 5.00 | 2.00 |
| ❑ 159 Ronald Curry RC | 6.00 | 2.50 |
| ❑ 160 Lamar Gordon RC | 6.00 | 2.50 |
| ❑ 161 Brian Westbrook RC | 10.00 | 5.00 |
| ❑ 162 Jonathan Wells RC | 6.00 | 2.50 |
| ❑ 163 Ricky Williams RC | 5.00 | 2.00 |
| ❑ 164 Verron Haynes RC | 6.00 | 2.50 |
| ❑ 165 Josh Scobey RC | 6.00 | 2.50 |
| ❑ 166 Larry Ned RC | 5.00 | 2.00 |
| ❑ 167 Adrian Peterson RC | 8.00 | 3.00 |
| ❑ 168 Chester Taylor RC | 12.00 | 5.00 |
| ❑ 169 Luke Staley RC | 5.00 | 2.00 |
| ❑ 170 Damien Anderson RC | 5.00 | 2.00 |
| ❑ 171 Lee Mays RC | 5.00 | 2.00 |
| ❑ 172 Deion Branch RC | 10.00 | 4.00 |
| ❑ 173 Terry Charles RC | 5.00 | 2.00 |
| ❑ 174 Woody Dantzler RC | 5.00 | 2.00 |
| ❑ 175 Jason McAddley RC | 5.00 | 2.00 |
| ❑ 176 Kelly Campbell RC | 5.00 | 2.00 |
| ❑ 177 Freddie Milons RC | 5.00 | 2.00 |
| ❑ 178 Kahlil Hill RC | 5.00 | 2.00 |
| ❑ 179 Brian Poli-Dixon RC | 5.00 | 2.00 |
| ❑ 180 Mike Echols RC | 3.00 | 1.25 |
| ❑ 181 Pete Rebstock RC | 3.00 | 1.25 |
| ❑ 182 Dwight Freeney RC | 10.00 | 4.00 |
| ❑ 183 Bryan Thomas RC | 5.00 | 2.00 |
| ❑ 184 Charles Grant RC | 6.00 | 2.50 |
| ❑ 185 Kalimba Edwards RC | 6.00 | 2.50 |
| ❑ 186 Ryan Sims RC | 6.00 | 2.50 |
| ❑ 187 John Henderson RC | 5.00 | 2.00 |
| ❑ 188 Wendell Bryant RC | 3.00 | 1.25 |
| ❑ 189 Albert Haynesworth RC | 6.00 | 2.50 |
| ❑ 190 Larry Tripplett RC | 3.00 | 1.25 |
| ❑ 191 Phillip Buchanon RC | 6.00 | 2.50 |
| ❑ 192 Lito Sheppard RC | 6.00 | 2.50 |
| ❑ 193 Mike Rumph RC | 6.00 | 2.50 |
| ❑ 194 Levar Fisher RC | 3.00 | 1.25 |

| | | |
|---|---|---|
| ❑ 195 Ed Reed RC | 12.00 | 5.00 |
| ❑ 196 Rocky Calmus RC | 6.00 | 2.50 |
| ❑ 197 Michael Lewis RC | 6.00 | 2.50 |
| ❑ 198 Napoleon Harris RC | 6.00 | 2.50 |
| ❑ 199 Robert Thomas RC | 6.00 | 2.50 |
| ❑ 200 Anthony Weaver RC | 5.00 | 2.00 |
| ❑ 201 Ladell Betts RPM RC | 12.00 | 6.00 |
| ❑ 202 Antonio Bryant RPM RC | 12.00 | 6.00 |
| ❑ 203 Reche Caldwell RPM RC | 12.00 | 6.00 |
| ❑ 204 David Carr RPM RC | 10.00 | 4.00 |
| ❑ 205 Tim Carter RPM RC | 6.00 | 3.00 |
| ❑ 206 Eric Crouch RPM RC | 12.00 | 6.00 |
| ❑ 207 Rohan Davey RPM RC | 12.00 | 5.00 |
| ❑ 208 Andre Davis RPM RC | 6.00 | 3.00 |
| ❑ 209 T.J. Duckett RPM RC | 12.00 | 5.00 |
| ❑ 210 DeShaun Foster RPM RC | 12.00 | 6.00 |
| ❑ 211 Jabar Gaffney RPM RC | 12.00 | 6.00 |
| ❑ 212 Daniel Graham RPM RC | 12.00 | 6.00 |
| ❑ 213 William Green RPM RC | 12.00 | 6.00 |
| ❑ 214 Joey Harrington RPM RC | 10.00 | 4.00 |
| ❑ 215 David Garrard RPM RC | 15.00 | 6.00 |
| ❑ 216 Ron Johnson RPM RC | 6.00 | 3.00 |
| ❑ 217 Ashley Lelie RPM RC | 25.00 | 10.00 |
| ❑ 218 Josh McCown RPM RC | 10.00 | 4.00 |
| ❑ 219 Maurice Morris RPM RC | 12.00 | 4.00 |
| ❑ 220 Julius Peppers RPM RC | 10.00 | 4.00 |
| ❑ 221 Clinton Portis RPM RC | 20.00 | 8.00 |
| ❑ 222 Patrick Ramsey RPM RC | 12.00 | 5.00 |
| ❑ 223 Antwaan Randle El RPM RC | 10.00 | 4.00 |
| ❑ 224 Josh Reed RPM RC | 12.00 | 6.00 |
| ❑ 225 Cliff Russell RPM RC | 6.00 | 3.00 |
| ❑ 226 Jeremy Shockey RPM RC | 12.00 | 5.00 |
| ❑ 227 Donte Stallworth RPM RC | 12.00 | 5.00 |
| ❑ 228 Travis Stephens RPM RC | 6.00 | 3.00 |
| ❑ 229 Javon Walker RPM RC | 12.00 | 5.00 |
| ❑ 230 Marquise Walker RPM RC | 6.00 | 3.00 |
| ❑ 231 Roy Williams RPM RC | 15.00 | 6.00 |
| ❑ 232 Mike Williams RPM RC | 6.00 | 3.00 |

## 2004 Absolute Memorabilia

| | | |
|---|---|---|
| ❑ COMP.SET w/o SP's (150) | 80.00 | 40.00 |
| ❑ 151-233 PRINT RUN 750 SER.#'d SETS | | |
| ❑ UNPRICED SPECTRUM PLATINUM #'d TO 1 | | |
| ❑ 1 Anquan Boldin | 3.00 | 1.25 |
| ❑ 2 Emmitt Smith | 6.00 | 3.00 |
| ❑ 3 Josh McCown | 2.50 | 1.00 |
| ❑ 4 Marcel Shipp | 2.50 | 1.00 |
| ❑ 5 Michael Vick | 3.00 | 1.25 |
| ❑ 6 Peerless Price | 2.50 | 1.00 |
| ❑ 7 T.J. Duckett | 2.50 | 1.00 |
| ❑ 8 Warrick Dunn | 2.50 | 1.00 |
| ❑ 9 Jamal Lewis | 2.50 | 1.00 |
| ❑ 10 Kyle Boller | 2.50 | 1.00 |
| ❑ 11 Ray Lewis | 3.00 | 1.25 |
| ❑ 12 Terrell Suggs | 2.00 | .75 |
| ❑ 13 Drew Bledsoe | 3.00 | 1.25 |
| ❑ 14 Eric Moulds | 2.50 | 1.00 |
| ❑ 15 Josh Reed | 3.00 | 1.00 |
| ❑ 16 Travis Henry | 2.50 | 1.00 |
| ❑ 17 DeShaun Foster | 2.50 | 1.00 |
| ❑ 18 Jake Delhomme | 2.50 | 1.00 |
| ❑ 19 Julius Peppers | 2.50 | 1.00 |
| ❑ 20 Muhsin Muhammad | 2.50 | 1.00 |
| ❑ 21 Stephen Davis | 2.50 | 1.00 |
| ❑ 22 Steve Smith | 3.00 | 1.25 |
| ❑ 23 Anthony Thomas | 2.50 | 1.00 |

|  |  | | |
|---|---|---|---|
| ❑ 24 | Brian Urlacher | 3.00 | 1.25 |
| ❑ 25 | Marty Booker | 2.50 | 1.00 |
| ❑ 26 | Rex Grossman | 3.00 | 1.25 |
| ❑ 27 | Carson Palmer | 4.00 | 1.50 |
| ❑ 28 | Chad Johnson | 2.50 | 1.00 |
| ❑ 29 | Corey Dillon | 2.50 | 1.00 |
| ❑ 30 | Peter Warrick | 2.50 | 1.00 |
| ❑ 31 | Rudi Johnson | 2.50 | 1.00 |
| ❑ 32 | Andre Davis | 2.00 | .75 |
| ❑ 33 | Dennis Northcutt | 2.00 | .75 |
| ❑ 34 | Lee Suggs | 3.00 | 1.25 |
| ❑ 35 | Tim Couch | 2.50 | 1.00 |
| ❑ 36 | Jeff Garcia | 3.00 | 1.25 |
| ❑ 37 | William Green | 2.00 | .75 |
| ❑ 38 | Antonio Bryant | 2.50 | 1.00 |
| ❑ 39 | Quincy Carter | 2.00 | .75 |
| ❑ 40 | Roy Williams S | 2.50 | 1.00 |
| ❑ 41 | Terence Newman | 2.50 | 1.00 |
| ❑ 42 | Keyshawn Johnson | 2.50 | 1.00 |
| ❑ 43 | Garrison Hearst | 2.50 | 1.00 |
| ❑ 44 | Champ Bailey | 2.50 | 1.00 |
| ❑ 45 | Ashley Lelie | 2.50 | 1.00 |
| ❑ 46 | Jake Plummer | 2.50 | 1.00 |
| ❑ 47 | Rod Smith | 2.50 | 1.00 |
| ❑ 48 | Shannon Sharpe | 2.50 | 1.00 |
| ❑ 49 | Charles Rogers | 2.50 | 1.00 |
| ❑ 50 | Joey Harrington | 2.50 | 1.00 |
| ❑ 51 | Ahman Green | 3.00 | 1.25 |
| ❑ 52 | Brett Favre | 8.00 | 3.00 |
| ❑ 53 | Donald Driver | 3.00 | 1.25 |
| ❑ 54 | Javon Walker | 2.50 | 1.00 |
| ❑ 55 | Robert Ferguson | 2.00 | .75 |
| ❑ 56 | Andre Johnson | 2.50 | 1.00 |
| ❑ 57 | David Carr | 2.50 | 1.00 |
| ❑ 58 | Domanick Davis | 3.00 | 1.25 |
| ❑ 59 | Edgerrin James | 3.00 | 1.25 |
| ❑ 60 | Marvin Harrison | 3.00 | 1.25 |
| ❑ 61 | Peyton Manning | 6.00 | 2.50 |
| ❑ 62 | Reggie Wayne | 2.50 | 1.00 |
| ❑ 63 | Byron Leftwich | 3.00 | 1.25 |
| ❑ 64 | Fred Taylor | 2.50 | 1.00 |
| ❑ 65 | Jimmy Smith | 2.50 | 1.00 |
| ❑ 66 | Dante Hall | 2.50 | 1.00 |
| ❑ 67 | Priest Holmes | 3.00 | 1.25 |
| ❑ 68 | Tony Gonzalez | 3.00 | 1.25 |
| ❑ 69 | Trent Green | 2.50 | 1.00 |
| ❑ 70 | Chris Chambers | 2.50 | 1.00 |
| ❑ 71 | Jay Fiedler | 2.00 | .75 |
| ❑ 72 | David Boston | 2.50 | 1.00 |
| ❑ 73 | Ricky Williams | 3.00 | 1.25 |
| ❑ 74 | Zach Thomas | 2.50 | 1.00 |
| ❑ 75 | Daunte Culpepper | 3.00 | 1.25 |
| ❑ 76 | Michael Bennett | 2.50 | 1.00 |
| ❑ 77 | Moe Williams | 2.00 | .75 |
| ❑ 78 | Randy Moss | 4.00 | 1.50 |
| ❑ 79 | David Givens | 2.50 | 1.00 |
| ❑ 80 | Deion Branch | 2.50 | 1.00 |
| ❑ 81 | Kevin Faulk | 2.50 | 1.00 |
| ❑ 82 | Richard Seymour | 2.00 | .75 |
| ❑ 83 | Tom Brady | 8.00 | 3.00 |
| ❑ 84 | Troy Brown | 2.50 | 1.00 |
| ❑ 85 | Ty Law | 2.50 | 1.00 |
| ❑ 86 | Aaron Brooks | 2.50 | 1.00 |
| ❑ 87 | Deuce McAllister | 3.00 | 1.25 |
| ❑ 88 | Donte Stallworth | 2.50 | 1.00 |
| ❑ 89 | Joe Horn | 2.50 | 1.00 |
| ❑ 90 | Amani Toomer | 2.50 | 1.00 |
| ❑ 91 | Jeremy Shockey | 2.50 | 1.00 |
| ❑ 92 | Kerry Collins | 2.50 | 1.00 |
| ❑ 93 | Michael Strahan | 2.50 | 1.00 |
| ❑ 94 | Tiki Barber | 3.00 | 1.25 |
| ❑ 95 | Chad Pennington | 3.00 | 1.25 |
| ❑ 96 | Curtis Martin | 3.00 | 1.25 |
| ❑ 97 | Santana Moss | 2.50 | 1.00 |
| ❑ 98 | Wayne Chrebet | 2.50 | 1.00 |
| ❑ 99 | Justin McCareins | 2.00 | .75 |
| ❑ 100 | Charles Woodson | 3.00 | 1.25 |
| ❑ 101 | Jerry Porter | 2.50 | 1.00 |
| ❑ 102 | Jerry Rice | 6.00 | 2.50 |
| ❑ 103 | Rich Gannon | 2.50 | 1.00 |
| ❑ 104 | Tim Brown | 3.00 | 1.25 |
| ❑ 105 | Warren Sapp | 2.50 | 1.00 |
| ❑ 106 | A.J. Feeley | 2.50 | 1.00 |
| ❑ 107 | Brian Westbrook | 3.00 | 1.25 |

|  |  | | |
|---|---|---|---|
| ❑ 108 | Correll Buckhalter | 2.50 | 1.00 |
| ❑ 109 | Donovan McNabb | 3.00 | 1.25 |
| ❑ 110 | Freddie Mitchell | 2.00 | .75 |
| ❑ 111 | Terrell Owens | 3.00 | 1.25 |
| ❑ 112 | Jevon Kearse | 2.50 | 1.00 |
| ❑ 113 | Todd Pinkston | 2.00 | .75 |
| ❑ 114 | Antwaan Randle El | 2.50 | 1.00 |
| ❑ 115 | Hines Ward | 3.00 | 1.25 |
| ❑ 116 | Jerome Bettis | 3.00 | 1.25 |
| ❑ 117 | Kendrell Bell | 2.00 | .75 |
| ❑ 118 | Plaxico Burress | 2.50 | 1.00 |
| ❑ 119 | Tommy Maddox | 2.50 | 1.00 |
| ❑ 120 | Duce Staley | 2.50 | 1.00 |
| ❑ 121 | Drew Brees | 3.00 | 1.25 |
| ❑ 122 | LaDainian Tomlinson | 5.00 | 2.00 |
| ❑ 123 | Keenan Barlow | 2.50 | 1.00 |
| ❑ 124 | Tai Streets | 2.00 | .75 |
| ❑ 125 | Tim Rattay | 2.00 | .75 |
| ❑ 126 | Darrell Jackson | 2.50 | 1.00 |
| ❑ 127 | Koren Robinson | 3.00 | 1.25 |
| ❑ 128 | Matt Hasselbeck | 3.00 | 1.25 |
| ❑ 129 | Shaun Alexander | 3.00 | 1.25 |
| ❑ 130 | Isaac Bruce | 2.50 | 1.00 |
| ❑ 131 | Kurt Warner | 3.00 | 1.25 |
| ❑ 132 | Marc Bulger | 2.50 | 1.00 |
| ❑ 133 | Marshall Faulk | 3.00 | 1.25 |
| ❑ 134 | Torry Holt | 3.00 | 1.25 |
| ❑ 135 | Derrick Brooks | 2.50 | 1.00 |
| ❑ 136 | Keenan McCardell | 2.00 | .75 |
| ❑ 137 | Mike Alstott | 2.50 | 1.00 |
| ❑ 138 | Thomas Jones | 2.50 | 1.00 |
| ❑ 139 | Charlie Garner | 2.50 | 1.00 |
| ❑ 140 | Derrick Mason | 2.50 | 1.00 |
| ❑ 141 | Drew Bennett | 2.50 | 1.00 |
| ❑ 142 | Eddie George | 3.00 | 1.25 |
| ❑ 143 | Keith Bulluck | 2.00 | .75 |
| ❑ 144 | Steve McNair | 3.00 | 1.25 |
| ❑ 145 | LaVar Arrington | 2.50 | 1.00 |
| ❑ 146 | Laveranues Coles | 2.50 | 1.00 |
| ❑ 147 | Patrick Ramsey | 2.50 | 1.00 |
| ❑ 148 | Rod Gardner | 2.00 | .75 |
| ❑ 149 | Clinton Portis | 3.00 | 1.25 |
| ❑ 150 | Mark Brunell | 2.50 | 1.00 |
| ❑ 151 | Craig Krenzel AU RC | 15.00 | 7.50 |
| ❑ 152 | Andy Hall AU RC | 12.00 | 6.00 |
| ❑ 153 | Josh Harris RC | 4.00 | 1.50 |
| ❑ 154 | Jim Sorgi AU RC | 15.00 | 7.50 |
| ❑ 155 | Jeff Smoker AU RC | 15.00 | 7.50 |
| ❑ 156 | John Navarre AU RC | 15.00 | 7.50 |
| ❑ 157 | Jared Lorenzen AU RC | 12.00 | 6.00 |
| ❑ 158 | Cody Pickett AU RC | 15.00 | 7.50 |
| ❑ 159 | Casey Bramlet RC | 4.00 | 1.50 |
| ❑ 160 | Matt Mauck AU RC | 15.00 | 7.50 |
| ❑ 161 | B.J. Symons AU RC | 15.00 | 7.50 |
| ❑ 162 | Bradlee Van Pelt RC | 5.00 | 2.00 |
| ❑ 163 | Ryan Dinwiddie RC | 4.00 | 1.50 |
| ❑ 164 | Michael Turner RC | 12.00 | 5.00 |
| ❑ 165 | Drew Henson RC | 4.00 | 1.50 |
| ❑ 166 | Troy Fleming RC | 4.00 | 1.50 |
| ❑ 167 | A. Echemandu RC | 5.00 | 2.00 |
| ❑ 168 | Quincy Wilson RC | 5.00 | 2.00 |
| ❑ 169 | Derrick Ward RC | 6.00 | 2.50 |
| ❑ 170 | Bruce Perry RC | 4.00 | 1.50 |
| ❑ 171 | Brandon Miree RC | 4.00 | 1.50 |
| ❑ 172 | Jarrett Payton RC | 12.00 | 5.00 |
| ❑ 173 | Ran Carthon RC | 4.00 | 1.50 |
| ❑ 174 | Carlos Francis AU RC | 12.00 | 6.00 |
| ❑ 175 | Samie Parker RC | 5.00 | 2.00 |
| ❑ 176 | Jerricho Cotchery RC | 6.00 | 2.50 |
| ❑ 177 | Ernest Wilford RC | 6.00 | 2.50 |
| ❑ 178 | Johnnie Morant RC | 5.00 | 2.00 |
| ❑ 179 | Maurice Mann AU RC | 15.00 | 7.50 |
| ❑ 180 | D.J. Hackett RC | 5.00 | 2.00 |
| ❑ 181 | Drew Carter RC | 6.00 | 2.50 |
| ❑ 182 | P.K. Sam RC | 4.00 | 1.50 |
| ❑ 183 | Jamaar Taylor RC | 4.00 | 1.50 |
| ❑ 184 | Ryan Krause RC | 4.00 | 1.50 |
| ❑ 185 | Triandos Luke RC | 4.00 | 1.50 |
| ❑ 186 | Jeris McIntyre RC | 4.00 | 1.50 |
| ❑ 187 | Clarence Moore AU RC | 15.00 | 7.50 |
| ❑ 188 | Mark Jones RC | 4.00 | 1.50 |
| ❑ 189 | Sloan Thomas AU RC | 12.00 | 6.00 |
| ❑ 190 | Sean Taylor RC | 6.00 | 2.50 |
| ❑ 191 | Derek Abney RC | 4.00 | 1.50 |
| ❑ 192 | Jonathan Vilma RC | 6.00 | 2.50 |

|  |  | | |
|---|---|---|---|
| ❑ 193 | Tommie Harris RC | 6.00 | 2.50 |
| ❑ 194 | D.J. Williams RC | 6.00 | 2.50 |
| ❑ 195 | Will Smith RC | 5.00 | 2.00 |
| ❑ 196 | Kenechi Udeze RC | 6.00 | 2.50 |
| ❑ 197 | Vince Wilfork RC | 6.00 | 2.50 |
| ❑ 198 | Ahmad Carroll RC | 5.00 | 2.00 |
| ❑ 199 | Jason Babin RC | 5.00 | 2.00 |
| ❑ 200 | Chris Gamble RC | 5.00 | 2.00 |
| ❑ 201 | Larry Fitzgerald RPM RC | 25.00 | 10.00 |
| ❑ 202 | DeAngelo Hall RPM RC | 8.00 | 3.00 |
| ❑ 203 | Matt Schaub RPM RC | 25.00 | 10.00 |
| ❑ 204 | Michael Jenkins RPM AU RC | 25.00 | 10.00 |
| ❑ 205 | Devard Darling RPM AU RC | 25.00 | 10.00 |
| ❑ 206 | J.P. Losman RPM RC | 10.00 | 4.00 |
| ❑ 207 | Lee Evans RPM RC | 10.00 | 4.00 |
| ❑ 208 | Keary Colbert RPM AU RC | 25.00 | 10.00 |
| ❑ 209 | Bernard Berrian RPM AU RC | 30.00 | 12.50 |
| ❑ 210 | Chris Perry RPM RC | 8.00 | 3.00 |
| ❑ 211 | Kellen Winslow RPM RC | 15.00 | 6.00 |
| ❑ 212 | Luke McCown RPM RC | 8.00 | 3.00 |
| ❑ 213 | Julius Jones RPM RC | 20.00 | 8.00 |
| ❑ 214 | Darius Watts RPM RC | 6.00 | 2.50 |
| ❑ 215 | Tatum Bell RPM AU RC | 25.00 | 10.00 |
| ❑ 216 | Kevin Jones RPM RC | 8.00 | 3.00 |
| ❑ 217 | Roy Williams RPM RC | 20.00 | 8.00 |
| ❑ 218 | Dunta Robinson RPM RC | 6.00 | 2.50 |
| ❑ 219 | Greg Jones RPM AU RC | 25.00 | 10.00 |
| ❑ 220 | Reggie Williams RPM RC | 8.00 | 3.00 |
| ❑ 221 | Mewelde Moore RPM RC | 8.00 | 3.00 |
| ❑ 222 | Ben Watson RPM RC | 8.00 | 3.00 |
| ❑ 223 | Cedric Cobbs RPM RC | 6.00 | 2.50 |
| ❑ 224 | Dev Henderson RPM AU RC | 25.00 | 10.00 |
| ❑ 225 | Eli Manning RPM RC | 50.00 | 20.00 |
| ❑ 226 | Robert Gallery RPM RC | 8.00 | 3.00 |
| ❑ 227 | Roethlisberger RPM RC | 60.00 | 25.00 |
| ❑ 228 | Philip Rivers RPM RC | 25.00 | 10.00 |
| ❑ 229 | Derrick Hamilton RPM RC | 5.00 | 2.00 |
| ❑ 230 | Rashaun Woods RPM RC | 5.00 | 2.00 |
| ❑ 231 | Steven Jackson RPM RC | 25.00 | 10.00 |
| ❑ 232 | Michael Clayton RPM RC | 8.00 | 3.00 |
| ❑ 233 | Ben Troupe RPM RC | 6.00 | 2.50 |

## 2005 Absolute Memorabilia

- ❑ 151-205 PRINT RUN 999 SER.#'d SETS
- ❑ 206-234 PRINT RUN 750 SER.#'d SETS
- ❑ UNPRICED PLATINUM PRINT RUN 1 SET
- ❑ HOBBY PRINTED ON HOLOFOIL STOCK

|  |  | | |
|---|---|---|---|
| ❑ 1 | Anquan Boldin | 2.50 | 1.00 |
| ❑ 2 | Kurt Warner | 3.00 | 1.25 |
| ❑ 3 | Josh McCown | 2.50 | 1.00 |
| ❑ 4 | Larry Fitzgerald | 3.00 | 1.25 |
| ❑ 5 | Alge Crumpler | 2.50 | 1.00 |
| ❑ 6 | Michael Vick | 3.00 | 1.25 |
| ❑ 7 | Peerless Price | 2.00 | .75 |
| ❑ 8 | T.J. Duckett | 2.00 | .75 |
| ❑ 9 | Warrick Dunn | 2.50 | 1.00 |
| ❑ 10 | Deion Sanders | 4.00 | 1.50 |
| ❑ 11 | Derrick Mason | 2.50 | 1.00 |
| ❑ 12 | Ed Reed | 2.50 | 1.00 |
| ❑ 13 | Jamal Lewis | 2.50 | 1.00 |
| ❑ 14 | Kyle Boller | 2.50 | 1.00 |
| ❑ 15 | Ray Lewis | 3.00 | 1.25 |
| ❑ 16 | Todd Heap | 2.50 | 1.00 |
| ❑ 17 | Eric Moulds | 2.50 | 1.00 |
| ❑ 18 | J.P. Losman | 3.00 | 1.25 |
| ❑ 19 | Lee Evans | 2.50 | 1.00 |

|  |  | | |
|---|---|---|---|
| ❏ 20 | Travis Henry | 2.50 | 1.00 |
| ❏ 21 | Willis McGahee | 3.00 | 1.25 |
| ❏ 22 | DeShaun Foster | 2.50 | 1.00 |
| ❏ 23 | Jake Delhomme | 3.00 | 1.25 |
| ❏ 24 | Julius Peppers | 2.50 | 1.00 |
| ❏ 25 | Keary Colbert | 2.00 | .75 |
| ❏ 26 | Stephen Davis | 2.50 | 1.00 |
| ❏ 27 | Steve Smith | 3.00 | 1.25 |
| ❏ 28 | Brian Urlacher | 3.00 | 1.25 |
| ❏ 29 | Muhsin Muhammad | 2.50 | 1.00 |
| ❏ 30 | Thomas Jones | 2.50 | 1.00 |
| ❏ 31 | Rex Grossman | 3.00 | 1.25 |
| ❏ 32 | Carson Palmer | 3.00 | 1.25 |
| ❏ 33 | Chad Johnson | 2.50 | 1.00 |
| ❏ 34 | Peter Warrick | 2.00 | .75 |
| ❏ 35 | Rudi Johnson | 2.50 | 1.00 |
| ❏ 36 | T.J. Houshmandzadeh | 2.50 | 1.00 |
| ❏ 37 | Antonio Bryant | 2.00 | .75 |
| ❏ 38 | Dennis Northcutt | 2.00 | .75 |
| ❏ 39 | Trent Dilfer | 2.50 | 1.00 |
| ❏ 40 | Kellen Winslow | 3.00 | 1.25 |
| ❏ 41 | Lee Suggs | 2.50 | 1.00 |
| ❏ 42 | Reuben Droughns | 2.00 | .75 |
| ❏ 43 | Drew Bledsoe | 3.00 | 1.25 |
| ❏ 44 | Jason Witten | 2.50 | 1.00 |
| ❏ 45 | Julius Jones | 3.00 | 1.25 |
| ❏ 46 | Keyshawn Johnson | 2.50 | 1.00 |
| ❏ 47 | Terrence Newman | 2.00 | .75 |
| ❏ 48 | Roy Williams S | 2.50 | 1.00 |
| ❏ 49 | Jake Plummer | 2.50 | 1.00 |
| ❏ 50 | Rod Smith | 2.50 | 1.00 |
| ❏ 51 | Ashley Lelie | 2.00 | .75 |
| ❏ 52 | Tatum Bell | 2.50 | 1.00 |
| ❏ 53 | Charles Rogers | 2.00 | .75 |
| ❏ 54 | Joey Harrington | 2.50 | 1.00 |
| ❏ 55 | Kevin Jones | 2.50 | 1.00 |
| ❏ 56 | Roy Williams WR | 3.00 | 1.25 |
| ❏ 57 | Ahman Green | 3.00 | 1.25 |
| ❏ 58 | Brett Favre | 8.00 | 3.00 |
| ❏ 59 | Donald Driver | 3.00 | 1.25 |
| ❏ 60 | Javon Walker | 2.50 | 1.00 |
| ❏ 61 | Andre Johnson | 2.50 | 1.00 |
| ❏ 62 | David Carr | 2.50 | 1.00 |
| ❏ 63 | Domanick Davis | 2.00 | .75 |
| ❏ 64 | Brandon Stokley | 2.00 | .75 |
| ❏ 65 | Dallas Clark | 2.50 | 1.00 |
| ❏ 66 | Edgerrin James | 2.50 | 1.00 |
| ❏ 67 | Marvin Harrison | 3.00 | 1.25 |
| ❏ 68 | Peyton Manning | 5.00 | 2.00 |
| ❏ 69 | Reggie Wayne | 2.50 | 1.00 |
| ❏ 70 | Reggie Williams | 2.50 | 1.00 |
| ❏ 71 | Byron Leftwich | 2.50 | 1.00 |
| ❏ 72 | Fred Taylor | 3.00 | 1.25 |
| ❏ 73 | Jimmy Smith | 2.50 | 1.00 |
| ❏ 74 | Priest Holmes | 3.00 | 1.25 |
| ❏ 75 | Tony Gonzalez | 2.50 | 1.00 |
| ❏ 76 | Dante Hall | 2.50 | 1.00 |
| ❏ 77 | Trent Green | 2.50 | 1.00 |
| ❏ 78 | Eddie Kennison | 2.00 | .75 |
| ❏ 79 | A.J. Feeley | 2.00 | .75 |
| ❏ 80 | Chris Chambers | 2.50 | 1.00 |
| ❏ 81 | Zach Thomas | 3.00 | 1.25 |
| ❏ 82 | Junior Seau | 3.00 | 1.25 |
| ❏ 83 | Marty Booker | 2.00 | .75 |
| ❏ 84 | Daunte Culpepper | 3.00 | 1.25 |
| ❏ 85 | Nate Burleson | 2.50 | 1.00 |
| ❏ 86 | Michael Bennett | 2.50 | 1.00 |
| ❏ 87 | Onterrio Smith | 2.00 | .75 |
| ❏ 88 | Corey Dillon | 2.50 | 1.00 |
| ❏ 89 | Deion Branch | 2.50 | 1.00 |
| ❏ 90 | Tom Brady | 6.00 | 2.50 |
| ❏ 91 | Troy Brown | 2.00 | .75 |
| ❏ 92 | Tedy Bruschi | 3.00 | 1.25 |
| ❏ 93 | Aaron Brooks | 2.50 | 1.00 |
| ❏ 94 | Donte Stallworth | 2.50 | 1.00 |
| ❏ 95 | Joe Horn | 2.50 | 1.00 |
| ❏ 96 | Deuce McAllister | 3.00 | 1.25 |
| ❏ 97 | Amani Toomer | 2.50 | 1.00 |
| ❏ 98 | Plaxico Burress | 3.00 | 1.25 |
| ❏ 99 | Jeremy Shockey | 3.00 | 1.25 |
| ❏ 100 | Eli Manning | 6.00 | 2.50 |
| ❏ 101 | Tiki Barber | 3.00 | 1.25 |
| ❏ 102 | Chad Pennington | 2.50 | 1.00 |
| ❏ 103 | Laveranues Coles | 2.50 | 1.00 |
| ❏ 104 | Curtis Martin | 3.00 | 1.25 |
| ❏ 105 | Justin McCareins | 2.00 | .75 |
| ❏ 106 | Wayne Chrebet | 2.50 | 1.00 |
| ❏ 107 | Jerry Porter | 2.50 | 1.00 |
| ❏ 108 | LaMont Jordan | 2.50 | 1.00 |
| ❏ 109 | Randy Moss | 3.00 | 1.25 |
| ❏ 110 | Kerry Collins | 2.50 | 1.00 |
| ❏ 111 | Charles Woodson | 2.50 | 1.00 |
| ❏ 112 | Brian Westbrook | 3.00 | 1.00 |
| ❏ 113 | Donovan McNabb | 3.00 | 1.25 |
| ❏ 114 | Jevon Kearse | 2.50 | 1.00 |
| ❏ 115 | Terrell Owens | 3.00 | 1.25 |
| ❏ 116 | Ben Roethlisberger | 8.00 | 3.00 |
| ❏ 117 | Hines Ward | 3.00 | 1.25 |
| ❏ 118 | Duce Staley | 2.50 | 1.00 |
| ❏ 119 | Jerome Bettis | 3.00 | 1.25 |
| ❏ 120 | Antonio Gates | 3.00 | 1.25 |
| ❏ 121 | Eric Parker | 2.00 | .75 |
| ❏ 122 | Keenan McCardell | 2.50 | 1.00 |
| ❏ 123 | Drew Brees | 3.00 | 1.25 |
| ❏ 124 | LaDainian Tomlinson | 5.00 | 2.00 |
| ❏ 125 | Brandon Lloyd | 2.00 | .75 |
| ❏ 126 | Kevan Barlow | 2.00 | .75 |
| ❏ 127 | Tim Rattay | 2.00 | .75 |
| ❏ 128 | Koren Robinson | 2.50 | 1.00 |
| ❏ 129 | Darrell Jackson | 2.50 | 1.00 |
| ❏ 130 | Jerry Rice | 6.00 | 2.50 |
| ❏ 131 | Matt Hasselbeck | 2.50 | 1.00 |
| ❏ 132 | Shaun Alexander | 3.00 | 1.25 |
| ❏ 133 | Isaac Bruce | 2.50 | 1.00 |
| ❏ 134 | Marc Bulger | 2.50 | 1.00 |
| ❏ 135 | Marshall Faulk | 3.00 | 1.25 |
| ❏ 136 | Steven Jackson | 3.00 | 1.50 |
| ❏ 137 | Torry Holt | 2.50 | 1.00 |
| ❏ 138 | Brian Griese | 2.50 | 1.00 |
| ❏ 139 | Michael Clayton | 2.50 | 1.00 |
| ❏ 140 | Michael Pittman | 2.00 | .75 |
| ❏ 141 | Mike Alstott | 2.50 | 1.00 |
| ❏ 142 | Chris Brown | 2.50 | 1.00 |
| ❏ 143 | Drew Bennett | 2.50 | 1.00 |
| ❏ 144 | Steve McNair | 3.00 | 1.25 |
| ❏ 145 | Clinton Portis | 3.00 | 1.25 |
| ❏ 146 | LaVar Arrington | 2.50 | 1.00 |
| ❏ 147 | Santana Moss | 2.50 | 1.00 |
| ❏ 148 | Patrick Ramsey | 2.00 | .75 |
| ❏ 149 | Rod Gardner | 2.00 | .75 |
| ❏ 150 | Sean Taylor | 2.50 | 1.00 |
| ❏ 151 | DeMarcus Ware RC | 10.00 | 4.00 |
| ❏ 152 | Shawne Merriman RC | 10.00 | 4.00 |
| ❏ 153 | Thomas Davis RC | 5.00 | 2.00 |
| ❏ 154 | Derrick Johnson RC | 6.00 | 2.50 |
| ❏ 155 | Travis Johnson RC | 4.00 | 1.50 |
| ❏ 156 | David Pollack RC | 5.00 | 2.00 |
| ❏ 157 | Erasmus James RC | 5.00 | 2.00 |
| ❏ 158 | Marcus Spears RC | 6.00 | 2.50 |
| ❏ 159 | Fabian Washington RC | 5.00 | 2.00 |
| ❏ 160 | Marlin Jackson RC | 5.00 | 2.00 |
| ❏ 161 | Cedric Benson RC | 6.00 | 2.50 |
| ❏ 162 | Matt Roth RC | 5.00 | 2.00 |
| ❏ 163 | Dan Cody RC | 6.00 | 2.50 |
| ❏ 164 | Bryant McFadden RC | 5.00 | 2.00 |
| ❏ 165 | Chris Henry RC | 6.00 | 2.50 |
| ❏ 166 | Brandon Jones RC | 5.00 | 2.00 |
| ❏ 167 | Marion Barber RC | 20.00 | 8.00 |
| ❏ 168 | Brandon Jacobs RC | 8.00 | 3.00 |
| ❏ 169 | Jerome Mathis RC | 6.00 | 2.50 |
| ❏ 170 | Craphonso Thorpe RC | 5.00 | 2.00 |
| ❏ 171 | Alvin Pearman RC | 5.00 | 2.00 |
| ❏ 172 | Darren Sproles RC | 8.00 | 3.00 |
| ❏ 173 | Fred Gibson RC | 5.00 | 2.00 |
| ❏ 174 | Roydell Williams RC | 5.00 | 2.00 |
| ❏ 175 | Airese Currie RC | 5.00 | 2.00 |
| ❏ 176 | Damien Nash RC | 5.00 | 2.00 |
| ❏ 177 | Dan Orlovsky RC | 6.00 | 2.50 |
| ❏ 178 | Adrian McPherson RC | 5.00 | 2.00 |
| ❏ 179 | Larry Brackins RC | 4.00 | 1.50 |
| ❏ 180 | Aaron Rodgers RC | 20.00 | 8.00 |
| ❏ 181 | Cedric Houston RC | 5.00 | 2.00 |
| ❏ 182 | Mike Williams RC | 6.00 | 2.50 |
| ❏ 183 | Heath Miller RC | 12.00 | 5.00 |
| ❏ 184 | Dante Ridgeway RC | 4.00 | 1.50 |
| ❏ 185 | Craig Bragg RC | 4.00 | 1.50 |
| ❏ 186 | Deandra Cobb RC | 5.00 | 2.00 |
| ❏ 187 | Derek Anderson RC | 10.00 | 4.00 |
| ❏ 188 | Paris Warren RC | 5.00 | 2.00 |
| ❏ 189 | David Greene RC | 5.00 | 2.00 |
| ❏ 190 | Lionel Gates RC | 4.00 | 1.50 |
| ❏ 191 | Anthony Davis RC | 5.00 | 2.00 |
| ❏ 192 | Noah Herron RC | 6.00 | 2.50 |
| ❏ 193 | Ryan Fitzpatrick RC | 6.00 | 2.50 |
| ❏ 194 | J.R. Russell RC | 4.00 | 1.50 |
| ❏ 195 | Jason White RC | 6.00 | 2.50 |
| ❏ 196 | Kay-Jay Harris RC | 5.00 | 2.00 |
| ❏ 197 | Steve Savoy RC | 4.00 | 1.50 |
| ❏ 198 | T.A. McLendon RC | 4.00 | 1.50 |
| ❏ 199 | Taylor Stubblefield RC | 4.00 | 1.50 |
| ❏ 200 | Josh Davis RC | 4.00 | 1.50 |
| ❏ 201 | Shaun Cody RC | 5.00 | 2.00 |
| ❏ 202 | Rasheed Marshall RC | 5.00 | 2.00 |
| ❏ 203 | Chad Owens RC | 6.00 | 2.50 |
| ❏ 204 | Tab Perry RC | 6.00 | 2.50 |
| ❏ 205 | James Kilian RC | 4.00 | 1.50 |
| ❏ 206 | Adam Jones RPM RC | 10.00 | 4.00 |
| ❏ 207 | Alex Smith QB RPM RC | 30.00 | 12.00 |
| ❏ 208 | Antrel Rolle RPM RC | 10.00 | 4.00 |
| ❏ 209 | Andrew Walter RPM RC | 10.00 | 4.00 |
| ❏ 210 | Braylon Edwards RPM RC | 30.00 | 12.00 |
| ❏ 211 | Cadillac Williams RPM RC | 25.00 | 10.00 |
| ❏ 212 | Carlos Rogers RPM RC | 10.00 | 4.00 |
| ❏ 213 | Charlie Frye RPM RC | 10.00 | 4.00 |
| ❏ 214 | Ciatrick Fason RPM RC | 8.00 | 3.00 |
| ❏ 215 | Courtney Roby RPM RC | 8.00 | 3.00 |
| ❏ 216 | Eric Shelton RPM RC | 8.00 | 3.00 |
| ❏ 217 | Frank Gore RPM RC | 25.00 | 10.00 |
| ❏ 218 | J.J. Arrington RPM RC | 10.00 | 4.00 |
| ❏ 219 | Kyle Orton RPM RC | 12.00 | 5.00 |
| ❏ 220 | Jason Campbell RPM RC | 20.00 | 8.00 |
| ❏ 221 | Mark Bradley RPM RC | 10.00 | 4.00 |
| ❏ 222 | Mark Clayton RPM RC | 10.00 | 4.00 |
| ❏ 223 | Matt Jones RPM RC | 15.00 | 6.00 |
| ❏ 224 | Maurice Clarett RPM | 8.00 | 3.00 |
| ❏ 225 | Reggie Brown RPM RC | 10.00 | 4.00 |
| ❏ 226 | Ronnie Brown RPM RC | 30.00 | 12.00 |
| ❏ 227 | Roddy White RPM RC | 12.00 | 5.00 |
| ❏ 228 | Ryan Moats RPM RC | 10.00 | 4.00 |
| ❏ 229 | Roscoe Parrish RPM RC | 8.00 | 3.00 |
| ❏ 230 | Stefan LeFors RPM RC | 8.00 | 3.00 |
| ❏ 231 | Terrence Murphy RPM RC | 6.00 | 2.50 |
| ❏ 232 | Troy Williamson RPM RC | 10.00 | 4.00 |
| ❏ 233 | Vernand Morency RPM RC | 10.00 | 4.00 |
| ❏ 234 | Vincent Jackson RPM RC | 10.00 | 4.00 |

## 2005 Absolute Memorabilia Retail

| | | | |
|---|---|---|---|
| ❏ COMPLETE SET (150) | | 30.00 | 15.00 |
| ❏ *VETERANS: .1X TO .25X BASIC CARDS | | | |
| ❏ *ROOKIES 151-205: .2X TO .5X BASIC CARDS | | | |
| ❏ RETAIL PRINTED ON WHITE STOCK | | | |

## 2006 Absolute Memorabilia

| | | | |
|---|---|---|---|
| ❏ 1 | Anquan Boldin | 2.50 | 1.00 |
| ❏ 2 | J.J. Arrington | 2.50 | 1.00 |
| ❏ 3 | Kurt Warner | 2.50 | 1.00 |
| ❏ 4 | Larry Fitzgerald | 3.00 | 1.25 |
| ❏ 5 | Marcel Shipp | 2.00 | .75 |
| ❏ 6 | Alge Crumpler | 2.50 | 1.00 |
| ❏ 7 | Michael Jenkins | 2.50 | 1.00 |
| ❏ 8 | Michael Vick | 3.00 | 1.25 |

|  |  | | |
|---|---|---|---|
| 9 | T.J. Duckett | 2.00 | .75 |
| 10 | Warrick Dunn | 2.50 | 1.00 |
| 11 | Derrick Mason | 2.50 | 1.00 |
| 12 | Jamal Lewis | 2.50 | 1.00 |
| 13 | Kyle Boller | 2.50 | 1.00 |
| 14 | Mark Clayton | 2.50 | 1.00 |
| 15 | Ray Lewis | 3.00 | 1.25 |
| 16 | Todd Heap | 2.50 | 1.00 |
| 17 | Eric Moulds | 2.50 | 1.00 |
| 18 | J.P. Losman | 2.50 | 1.00 |
| 19 | Josh Reed | 2.00 | .75 |
| 20 | Lee Evans | 2.50 | 1.00 |
| 21 | Willis McGahee | 2.50 | 1.25 |
| 22 | DeShaun Foster | 2.50 | 1.00 |
| 23 | Jake Delhomme | 2.50 | 1.00 |
| 24 | Julius Peppers | 2.50 | 1.00 |
| 25 | Keary Colbert | 2.50 | 1.00 |
| 26 | Stephen Davis | 2.50 | 1.00 |
| 27 | Steve Smith | 3.00 | 1.25 |
| 28 | Brian Urlacher | 3.00 | 1.25 |
| 29 | Cedric Benson | 2.50 | 1.00 |
| 30 | Rex Grossman | 3.00 | 1.25 |
| 31 | Thomas Jones | 2.50 | 1.00 |
| 32 | Muhsin Muhammad | 2.50 | 1.00 |
| 33 | Carson Palmer | 3.00 | 1.25 |
| 34 | Chad Johnson | 2.50 | 1.00 |
| 35 | Rudi Johnson | 2.50 | 1.00 |
| 36 | T.J. Houshmandzadeh | 2.50 | 1.00 |
| 37 | Charlie Frye | 2.50 | 1.00 |
| 38 | Dennis Northcutt | 2.00 | .75 |
| 39 | Reuben Droughns | 2.50 | 1.00 |
| 40 | Braylon Edwards | 3.00 | 1.25 |
| 41 | Drew Bledsoe | 2.50 | 1.00 |
| 42 | Jason Witten | 2.50 | 1.00 |
| 43 | Julius Jones | 2.50 | 1.00 |
| 44 | Keyshawn Johnson | 2.50 | 1.00 |
| 45 | Roy Williams S | 2.50 | 1.00 |
| 46 | Terry Glenn | 2.50 | 1.00 |
| 47 | Ashley Lelie | 2.50 | 1.00 |
| 48 | Jake Plummer | 2.50 | 1.00 |
| 49 | Rod Smith | 2.50 | 1.00 |
| 50 | Tatum Bell | 2.50 | 1.00 |
| 51 | Mike Anderson | 2.50 | 1.00 |
| 52 | Joey Harrington | 2.00 | .75 |
| 53 | Kevin Jones | 2.50 | 1.00 |
| 54 | Mike Williams | 3.00 | 1.25 |
| 55 | Roy Williams WR | 3.00 | 1.25 |
| 56 | Marcus Pollard | 2.00 | .75 |
| 57 | Aaron Rodgers | 3.00 | 1.25 |
| 58 | Brett Favre | 6.00 | 2.50 |
| 59 | Donald Driver | 2.50 | 1.00 |
| 60 | Javon Walker | 2.50 | 1.00 |
| 61 | Samkon Gado | 3.00 | 1.25 |
| 62 | Bubba Franks | 2.00 | .75 |
| 63 | Andre Johnson | 2.50 | 1.00 |
| 64 | Corey Bradford | 2.00 | .75 |
| 65 | David Carr | 2.50 | 1.00 |
| 66 | Domanick Davis | 2.50 | 1.00 |
| 67 | Jabar Gaffney | 2.00 | .75 |
| 68 | Edgerrin James | 2.50 | 1.00 |
| 69 | Dallas Clark | 2.50 | 1.00 |
| 70 | Marvin Harrison | 3.00 | 1.25 |
| 71 | Peyton Manning | 5.00 | 2.00 |
| 72 | Reggie Wayne | 2.50 | 1.00 |
| 73 | Brandon Stokley | 2.50 | 1.00 |
| 74 | Byron Leftwich | 2.50 | 1.00 |
| 75 | Fred Taylor | 2.50 | 1.00 |
| 76 | Jimmy Smith | 2.50 | 1.00 |
| 77 | Matt Jones | 2.50 | 1.00 |
| 78 | Ernest Wilford | 2.50 | 1.00 |
| 79 | Larry Johnson | 2.50 | 1.00 |
| 80 | Tony Gonzalez | 2.50 | 1.00 |
| 81 | Trent Green | 2.50 | 1.00 |
| 82 | Eddie Kennison | 2.00 | .75 |
| 83 | Dante Hall | 2.50 | 1.00 |
| 84 | Chris Chambers | 2.50 | 1.00 |
| 85 | Randy McMichael | 2.00 | .75 |
| 86 | Terrell Owens | 3.00 | 1.25 |
| 87 | Ronnie Brown | 3.00 | 1.25 |
| 88 | Zach Thomas | 3.00 | 1.25 |
| 89 | Marty Booker | 2.00 | .75 |
| 90 | Daunte Culpepper | 3.00 | 1.25 |
| 91 | Mewelde Moore | 2.00 | .75 |
| 92 | Nate Burleson | 2.50 | 1.00 |
| 93 | Troy Williamson | 2.50 | 1.00 |
| 94 | Corey Dillon | 2.50 | 1.00 |
| 95 | David Givens | 2.50 | 1.00 |
| 96 | Deion Branch | 2.50 | 1.00 |
| 97 | Tedy Bruschi | 3.00 | 1.25 |
| 98 | Tom Brady | 5.00 | 2.00 |
| 99 | Aaron Brooks | 2.50 | 1.00 |
| 100 | Deuce McAllister | 2.50 | 1.00 |
| 101 | Donte Stallworth | 2.50 | 1.00 |
| 102 | Joe Horn | 2.50 | 1.00 |
| 103 | Eli Manning | 4.00 | 1.50 |
| 104 | Jeremy Shockey | 3.00 | 1.25 |
| 105 | Plaxico Burress | 3.00 | 1.25 |
| 106 | Tiki Barber | 3.00 | 1.25 |
| 107 | Chad Pennington | 2.50 | 1.00 |
| 108 | Curtis Martin | 3.00 | 1.25 |
| 109 | Laveranues Coles | 2.00 | .75 |
| 110 | Justin McCareins | 2.00 | .75 |
| 111 | Kerry Collins | 2.50 | 1.00 |
| 112 | LaMont Jordan | 2.50 | 1.00 |
| 113 | Randy Moss | 3.00 | 1.25 |
| 114 | Jerry Porter | 2.50 | 1.00 |
| 115 | Brian Westbrook | 2.50 | 1.00 |
| 116 | Donovan McNabb | 3.00 | 1.25 |
| 117 | Reggie Brown | 2.50 | 1.00 |
| 118 | Ryan Moats | 2.50 | 1.00 |
| 119 | Antwaan Randle El | 2.50 | 1.00 |
| 120 | Ben Roethlisberger | 5.00 | 2.00 |
| 121 | Willie Parker | 4.00 | 1.50 |
| 122 | Hines Ward | 3.00 | 1.25 |
| 123 | Antonio Gates | 3.00 | 1.25 |
| 124 | Drew Brees | 3.00 | 1.25 |
| 125 | Keenan McCardell | 2.50 | 1.00 |
| 126 | LaDainian Tomlinson | 4.00 | 1.50 |
| 127 | Alex Smith QB | 3.00 | 1.25 |
| 128 | Brandon Lloyd | 2.50 | 1.00 |
| 129 | Frank Gore | 3.00 | 1.25 |
| 130 | Kevan Barlow | 2.50 | 1.00 |
| 131 | Darrell Jackson | 2.50 | 1.00 |
| 132 | Joe Jurevicius | 2.50 | 1.00 |
| 133 | Matt Hasselbeck | 2.50 | 1.00 |
| 134 | Shaun Alexander | 3.00 | 1.25 |
| 135 | Isaac Bruce | 2.50 | 1.00 |
| 136 | Marc Bulger | 2.50 | 1.00 |
| 137 | Steven Jackson | 3.00 | 1.25 |
| 138 | Torry Holt | 2.50 | 1.00 |
| 139 | Cadillac Williams | 3.00 | 1.25 |
| 140 | Chris Simms | 2.50 | 1.00 |
| 141 | Joey Galloway | 2.50 | 1.00 |
| 142 | Michael Clayton | 2.50 | 1.00 |
| 143 | Chris Brown | 2.50 | 1.00 |
| 144 | Drew Bennett | 2.50 | 1.00 |
| 145 | Steve McNair | 2.50 | 1.00 |
| 146 | Tyrone Calico | 2.00 | .75 |
| 147 | Clinton Portis | 3.00 | 1.25 |
| 148 | LaVar Arrington | 3.00 | 1.25 |
| 149 | Mark Brunell | 2.50 | 1.00 |
| 150 | Santana Moss | 2.50 | 1.00 |
| 151 | Greg Jennings RC | 10.00 | 4.00 |
| 152 | Joseph Addai RC | 20.00 | 8.00 |
| 153 | Erik Meyer RC | 5.00 | 2.00 |
| 154 | Drew Olson RC | 5.00 | 2.00 |
| 155 | Darrell Hackney RC | 5.00 | 2.00 |
| 156 | Paul Pinegar RC | 5.00 | 2.00 |
| 157 | Brandon Kirsch RC | 6.00 | 2.50 |
| 158 | Andre Hall RC | 6.00 | 2.50 |
| 159 | Taurean Henderson RC | 5.00 | 2.00 |
| 160 | Derrick Ross RC | 5.00 | 2.00 |
| 161 | Mike Bell RC | 6.00 | 2.50 |
| 162 | Wendell Mathis RC | 5.00 | 2.00 |
| 163 | Gerald Riggs RC | 6.00 | 2.50 |
| 164 | John David Washington RC | 5.00 | 2.00 |
| 165 | Devin Aromashodu RC | 5.00 | 2.00 |
| 166 | Ben Obomanu RC | 5.00 | 2.00 |
| 167 | David Anderson RC | 5.00 | 2.00 |
| 168 | Marques Colston RC | 15.00 | 6.00 |
| 169 | Kevin McMahan RC | 5.00 | 2.00 |
| 170 | Miles Austin RC | 6.00 | 2.50 |
| 171 | Martin Nance RC | 5.00 | 2.00 |
| 172 | Greg Lee RC | 5.00 | 2.00 |
| 173 | Hank Baskett RC | 6.00 | 2.50 |
| 174 | Anthony Mix RC | 5.00 | 2.00 |
| 175 | D'Brickashaw Ferguson RC | 6.00 | 2.50 |
| 176 | Kamerion Wimbley RC | 6.00 | 2.50 |
| 177 | Tamba Hali RC | 6.00 | 2.50 |
| 178 | Mathias Kiwanuka RC | 8.00 | 3.00 |
| 179 | Brodrick Bunkley RC | 6.00 | 2.50 |
| 180 | John McCargo RC | 5.00 | 2.00 |
| 181 | Claude Wroten RC | 4.00 | 1.50 |
| 182 | Gabe Watson RC | 5.00 | 2.00 |
| 183 | D'Qwell Jackson RC | 5.00 | 2.00 |
| 184 | Abdul Hodge RC | 6.00 | 2.50 |
| 186 | Chad Greenway RC | 6.00 | 2.50 |
| 187 | Bobby Carpenter RC | 6.00 | 2.50 |
| 188 | Manny Lawson RC | 6.00 | 2.50 |
| 189 | DeMeco Ryans RC | 8.00 | 3.00 |
| 190 | Rocky McIntosh RC | 6.00 | 2.50 |
| 191 | Thomas Howard RC | 6.00 | 2.50 |
| 192 | Jon Alston RC | 6.00 | 2.50 |
| 193 | A.J. Nicholson RC | 4.00 | 1.50 |
| 194 | Tye Hill RC | 6.00 | 2.50 |
| 195 | Antonio Cromartie RC | 6.00 | 2.50 |
| 196 | Johnathan Joseph RC | 5.00 | 2.00 |
| 197 | Kelly Jennings RC | 6.00 | 2.50 |
| 198 | Jimmy Williams RC | 6.00 | 2.50 |
| 199 | Ashton Youboty RC | 6.00 | 2.50 |
| 200 | Alan Zemaitis RC | 6.00 | 2.50 |
| 201 | Anwar Phillips RC | 5.00 | 2.00 |
| 202 | Jason Allen RC | 6.00 | 2.50 |
| 203 | Cedric Griffin RC | 6.00 | 2.50 |
| 204 | Ko Simpson RC | 6.00 | 2.50 |
| 205 | Pat Watkins RC | 6.00 | 2.50 |
| 206 | Donte Whitner RC | 6.00 | 2.50 |
| 207 | Bernard Pollard RC | 5.00 | 2.00 |
| 208 | Daniel Bing RC | 6.00 | 2.50 |
| 209 | De'Arrius Howard RC | 6.00 | 2.50 |
| 210 | Ethan Kilmer RC | 6.00 | 2.50 |
| 211 | Bennie Brazell RC | 5.00 | 2.00 |
| 212 | Haloti Ngata RC | 6.00 | 2.50 |
| 213 | Jeremy Bloom RC | 5.00 | 2.00 |
| 214 | Jay Cutler RC | 25.00 | 10.00 |
| 215 | Marcus Vick RC | 5.00 | 2.00 |
| 216 | Roman Harper RC | 5.00 | 2.00 |
| 217 | Anthony Smith RC | 6.00 | 2.50 |
| 218 | Daniel Bullocks RC | 6.00 | 2.50 |
| 219 | Eric Smith RC | 5.00 | 2.00 |
| 220 | Dusty Dvoracek RC | 6.00 | 2.50 |
| 221 | Brodie Croyle AU RC | 40.00 | 20.00 |
| 222 | Ingle Martin AU RC | 15.00 | 6.00 |
| 223 | Reggie McNeal AU RC | 12.00 | 5.00 |
| 224 | Bruce Gradkowski AU RC | 15.00 | 6.00 |
| 225 | D.J. Shockley AU RC | 15.00 | 6.00 |
| 226 | P.J. Daniels AU RC | 12.00 | 5.00 |
| 227 | Marques Hagans AU RC | 12.00 | 5.00 |
| 228 | Jerome Harrison RC | 12.00 | 5.00 |
| 229 | Wali Lundy AU RC | 12.00 | 5.00 |
| 230 | Cedric Humes AU RC | 12.00 | 5.00 |
| 231 | Quinton Ganther AU RC | 15.00 | 6.00 |
| 232 | Garrett Mills AU RC | 12.00 | 5.00 |
| 233 | Anthony Fasano AU RC | 15.00 | 6.00 |
| 234 | Tony Scheffler AU RC | 20.00 | 8.00 |
| 235 | Leonard Pope AU RC | 15.00 | 6.00 |
| 236 | David Thomas AU RC | 15.00 | 6.00 |
| 237 | Dominique Byrd AU RC | 12.00 | 5.00 |
| 238 | Jai Lewis AU/299 RC | 12.00 | 5.00 |
| 239 | Devin Hester AU RC | 50.00 | 30.00 |
| 240 | Willie Reid AU RC | 15.00 | 6.00 |
| 241 | Brad Smith AU RC | 15.00 | 6.00 |
| 242 | Cory Rodgers AU RC | 15.00 | 6.00 |
| 243 | Skyler Green AU RC | 15.00 | 6.00 |
| 244 | Domenik Hixon AU RC | 20.00 | 8.00 |
| 245 | Mike Hass AU RC | 15.00 | 6.00 |

| | | | |
|---|---|---:|---:|
| ❑ 246 | Jonathan Orr AU/299 RC | 12.00 | 5.00 |
| ❑ 247 | Delanie Walker AU/299 RC | 12.00 | 5.00 |
| ❑ 248 | Adam Jennings AU/299 RC | 12.00 | 5.00 |
| ❑ 249 | Jeff Webb AU/299 RC | 12.00 | 5.00 |
| ❑ 250 | Todd Watkins AU RC | 12.00 | 5.00 |
| ❑ 251 | Chad Jackson RPM RC | 8.00 | 3.00 |
| ❑ 252 | Laurence Maroney RPM RC | 25.00 | 10.00 |
| ❑ 253 | Tarvaris Jackson RPM RC | 10.00 | 4.00 |
| ❑ 254 | Michael Huff RPM RC | 10.00 | 4.00 |
| ❑ 255 | Mario Williams RPM RC | 15.00 | 6.00 |
| ❑ 256 | Marcedes Lewis RPM RC | 10.00 | 4.00 |
| ❑ 257 | Maurice Drew RPM RC | 20.00 | 8.00 |
| ❑ 258 | Vince Young RPM RC | 30.00 | 12.00 |
| ❑ 259 | LenDale White RPM RC | 20.00 | 8.00 |
| ❑ 260 | Reggie Bush RPM RC | 40.00 | 15.00 |
| ❑ 261 | Matt Leinart RPM RC | 30.00 | 12.00 |
| ❑ 262 | Michael Robinson RPM RC | 10.00 | 4.00 |
| ❑ 263 | Vernon Davis RPM RC | 10.00 | 4.00 |
| ❑ 264 | Brandon Williams RPM RC | 10.00 | 4.00 |
| ❑ 265 | Derek Hagan RPM RC | 10.00 | 4.00 |
| ❑ 266 | Jason Avant RPM RC | 10.00 | 4.00 |
| ❑ 267 | Brandon Marshall RPM RC | 12.00 | 5.00 |
| ❑ 268 | Omar Jacobs RPM RC | 8.00 | 3.00 |
| ❑ 269 | Santonio Holmes RPM RC | 25.00 | 10.00 |
| ❑ 270 | Jerious Norwood RPM RC | 12.00 | 5.00 |
| ❑ 271 | Demetrius Williams RPM RC | 10.00 | 4.00 |
| ❑ 272 | Sinorice Moss RPM RC | 10.00 | 4.00 |
| ❑ 273 | Leon Washington RPM RC | 10.00 | 4.00 |
| ❑ 274 | Kellen Clemens RPM RC | 12.00 | 5.00 |
| ❑ 275 | A.J. Hawk RPM RC | 20.00 | 8.00 |
| ❑ 276 | Maurice Stovall RPM RC | 10.00 | 4.00 |
| ❑ 277 | DeAngelo Williams RPM RC | 15.00 | 6.00 |
| ❑ 278 | Charlie Whitehurst RPM RC | 10.00 | 4.00 |
| ❑ 279 | Travis Wilson RPM RC | 10.00 | 4.00 |
| ❑ 280 | Joe Klopfenstein RPM RC | 8.00 | 3.00 |
| ❑ 281 | Brian Calhoun RPM RC | 8.00 | 3.00 |

## 2007 Absolute Memorabilia

| | | | |
|---|---|---:|---:|
| ❑ 1 | Tony Romo | 6.00 | 2.50 |
| ❑ 2 | Julius Jones | 2.50 | 1.00 |
| ❑ 3 | Terry Glenn | 2.50 | 1.00 |
| ❑ 4 | Terrell Owens | 3.00 | 1.25 |
| ❑ 5 | Marion Barber | 3.00 | 1.25 |
| ❑ 6 | Reuben Droughns | 2.50 | 1.00 |
| ❑ 7 | Eli Manning | 3.00 | 1.25 |
| ❑ 8 | Plaxico Burress | 2.50 | 1.00 |
| ❑ 9 | Jeremy Shockey | 2.50 | 1.00 |
| ❑ 10 | Brandon Jacobs | 2.50 | 1.00 |
| ❑ 11 | Donovan McNabb | 3.00 | 1.25 |
| ❑ 12 | Brian Westbrook | 2.50 | 1.00 |
| ❑ 13 | Reggie Brown | 2.50 | 1.00 |
| ❑ 14 | Hank Baskett | 2.50 | 1.00 |
| ❑ 15 | Jason Campbell | 2.50 | 1.00 |
| ❑ 16 | Clinton Portis | 2.50 | 1.00 |
| ❑ 17 | Santana Moss | 2.50 | 1.00 |
| ❑ 18 | Ladell Betts | 2.00 | .75 |
| ❑ 19 | Brandon Lloyd | 2.00 | .75 |
| ❑ 20 | Chris Cooley | 2.00 | .75 |
| ❑ 21 | Rex Grossman | 2.50 | 1.00 |
| ❑ 22 | Cedric Benson | 2.50 | 1.00 |
| ❑ 23 | Muhsin Muhammad | 2.50 | 1.00 |
| ❑ 24 | Bernard Berrian | 2.00 | .75 |
| ❑ 25 | Devin Hester | 3.00 | 1.25 |
| ❑ 26 | Brian Urlacher | 3.00 | 1.25 |
| ❑ 27 | Jon Kitna | 2.00 | .75 |
| ❑ 28 | Kevin Jones | 2.00 | .75 |

| | | | |
|---|---|---:|---:|
| ❑ 29 | Roy Williams | 2.50 | 1.00 |
| ❑ 30 | Mike Furrey | 2.50 | 1.00 |
| ❑ 31 | Ernie Sims | 2.00 | .75 |
| ❑ 32 | Tatum Bell | 2.00 | .75 |
| ❑ 33 | Brett Favre | 6.00 | 2.50 |
| ❑ 34 | Vernand Morency | 2.50 | 1.00 |
| ❑ 35 | Donald Driver | 2.50 | 1.00 |
| ❑ 36 | Greg Jennings | 2.50 | 1.00 |
| ❑ 37 | AJ Hawk | 3.00 | 1.25 |
| ❑ 38 | Tarvaris Jackson | 2.50 | 1.00 |
| ❑ 39 | Chester Taylor | 2.00 | .75 |
| ❑ 40 | Troy Williamson | 2.00 | .75 |
| ❑ 41 | Mewelde Moore | 2.00 | .75 |
| ❑ 42 | Michael Vick | 3.00 | 1.25 |
| ❑ 43 | Warrick Dunn | 2.50 | 1.00 |
| ❑ 44 | Joe Horn | 2.50 | 1.00 |
| ❑ 45 | Alge Crumpler | 2.50 | 1.00 |
| ❑ 46 | Jerious Norwood | 2.50 | 1.00 |
| ❑ 47 | Jake Delhomme | 2.50 | 1.00 |
| ❑ 48 | DeShaun Foster | 2.50 | 1.00 |
| ❑ 49 | Steve Smith | 2.50 | 1.00 |
| ❑ 50 | DeAngelo Williams | 3.00 | 1.25 |
| ❑ 51 | Drew Brees | 2.50 | 1.00 |
| ❑ 52 | Deuce McAllister | 2.50 | 1.00 |
| ❑ 53 | Marques Colston | 3.00 | 1.25 |
| ❑ 54 | Devery Henderson | 2.00 | .75 |
| ❑ 55 | Reggie Bush | 4.00 | 1.50 |
| ❑ 56 | Jeff Garcia | 2.50 | 1.00 |
| ❑ 57 | Cadillac Williams | 2.50 | 1.00 |
| ❑ 58 | Joey Galloway | 2.50 | 1.00 |
| ❑ 59 | Michael Clayton | 2.50 | 1.00 |
| ❑ 60 | Matt Leinart | 3.00 | 1.25 |
| ❑ 61 | Edgerrin James | 2.50 | 1.00 |
| ❑ 62 | Anquan Boldin | 2.50 | 1.00 |
| ❑ 63 | Larry Fitzgerald | 3.00 | 1.25 |
| ❑ 64 | Marc Bulger | 2.50 | 1.00 |
| ❑ 65 | Steven Jackson | 3.00 | 1.25 |
| ❑ 66 | Torry Holt | 2.50 | 1.00 |
| ❑ 67 | Isaac Bruce | 2.50 | 1.00 |
| ❑ 68 | Randy McMichael | 2.00 | .75 |
| ❑ 69 | Drew Bennett | 2.00 | .75 |
| ❑ 70 | Alex Smith | 3.00 | 1.25 |
| ❑ 71 | Frank Gore | 3.00 | 1.25 |
| ❑ 72 | Darrell Jackson | 2.50 | 1.00 |
| ❑ 73 | Ashley Lelie | 2.50 | 1.00 |
| ❑ 74 | Vernon Davis | 2.50 | 1.00 |
| ❑ 75 | Matt Hasselbeck | 2.50 | 1.00 |
| ❑ 76 | Shaun Alexander | 2.50 | 1.00 |
| ❑ 77 | Deion Branch | 2.50 | 1.00 |
| ❑ 78 | J.P. Losman | 2.00 | .75 |
| ❑ 79 | Lee Evans | 2.50 | 1.00 |
| ❑ 80 | Josh Reed | 2.00 | .75 |
| ❑ 81 | Daunte Culpepper | 2.50 | 1.00 |
| ❑ 82 | Ronnie Brown | 2.50 | 1.00 |
| ❑ 83 | Chris Chambers | 2.50 | 1.00 |
| ❑ 84 | Marty Booker | 2.00 | .75 |
| ❑ 85 | Zach Thomas | 2.50 | 1.00 |
| ❑ 86 | Tom Brady | 6.00 | 2.50 |
| ❑ 87 | Laurence Maroney | 3.00 | 1.25 |
| ❑ 88 | Randy Moss | 3.00 | 1.25 |
| ❑ 89 | Chad Jackson | 2.00 | .75 |
| ❑ 90 | Ben Watson | 2.00 | .75 |
| ❑ 91 | Donte' Stallworth | 2.50 | 1.00 |
| ❑ 92 | Chad Pennington | 2.50 | 1.00 |
| ❑ 93 | Thomas Jones | 2.50 | 1.00 |
| ❑ 94 | Laveranues Coles | 2.50 | 1.00 |
| ❑ 95 | Jerricho Cotchery | 2.00 | .75 |
| ❑ 96 | Leon Washington | 2.00 | .75 |
| ❑ 97 | Steve McNair | 2.50 | 1.00 |
| ❑ 98 | Willis McGahee | 2.50 | 1.00 |
| ❑ 99 | Derrick Mason | 2.00 | .75 |
| ❑ 100 | Demetrius Williams | 2.00 | .75 |
| ❑ 101 | Mark Clayton | 2.50 | 1.00 |
| ❑ 102 | Carson Palmer | 3.00 | 1.25 |
| ❑ 103 | Rudi Johnson | 2.50 | 1.00 |
| ❑ 104 | Chad Johnson | 3.00 | 1.25 |
| ❑ 105 | T.J. Houshmandzadeh | 2.50 | 1.00 |
| ❑ 106 | Charlie Frye | 2.50 | 1.00 |
| ❑ 107 | Braylon Edwards | 2.50 | 1.00 |
| ❑ 108 | Travis Wilson | 2.00 | .75 |
| ❑ 109 | Kellen Winslow | 2.50 | 1.00 |
| ❑ 110 | Jamal Lewis | 2.50 | 1.00 |
| ❑ 111 | Ben Roethlisberger | 4.00 | 1.50 |
| ❑ 112 | Willie Parker | 3.00 | 1.25 |

| | | | |
|---|---|---:|---:|
| ❑ 113 | Hines Ward | 3.00 | 1.25 |
| ❑ 114 | Santonio Holmes | 2.50 | 1.00 |
| ❑ 115 | Ahman Green | 2.50 | 1.00 |
| ❑ 116 | Andre Johnson | 2.50 | 1.00 |
| ❑ 117 | Matt Schaub | 2.50 | 1.00 |
| ❑ 118 | DeMeco Ryans | 2.50 | 1.00 |
| ❑ 119 | Owen Daniels | 2.00 | .75 |
| ❑ 120 | Peyton Manning | 5.00 | 2.00 |
| ❑ 121 | Joseph Addai | 3.00 | 1.25 |
| ❑ 122 | Marvin Harrison | 3.00 | 1.25 |
| ❑ 123 | Reggie Wayne | 2.50 | 1.00 |
| ❑ 124 | Dallas Clark | 2.00 | .75 |
| ❑ 125 | Byron Leftwich | 2.50 | 1.00 |
| ❑ 126 | Fred Taylor | 2.50 | 1.00 |
| ❑ 127 | Matt Jones | 2.50 | 1.00 |
| ❑ 128 | Reggie Williams | 2.50 | 1.00 |
| ❑ 129 | Marcedes Lewis | 2.00 | .75 |
| ❑ 130 | Maurice Jones-Drew | 3.00 | 1.25 |
| ❑ 131 | Vince Young | 3.00 | 1.25 |
| ❑ 132 | LenDale White | 2.50 | 1.00 |
| ❑ 133 | Brandon Jones | 2.00 | .75 |
| ❑ 134 | Jay Cutler | 3.00 | 1.25 |
| ❑ 135 | Travis Henry | 2.50 | 1.00 |
| ❑ 136 | Javon Walker | 2.50 | 1.00 |
| ❑ 137 | Rod Smith | 2.50 | 1.00 |
| ❑ 138 | Mike Bell | 2.50 | 1.00 |
| ❑ 139 | Brandon Marshall | 2.50 | 1.00 |
| ❑ 140 | Larry Johnson | 2.50 | 1.00 |
| ❑ 141 | Eddie Kennison | 2.00 | .75 |
| ❑ 142 | Tony Gonzalez | 2.50 | 1.00 |
| ❑ 143 | Brodie Croyle | 3.00 | 1.25 |
| ❑ 144 | LaMont Jordan | 2.50 | 1.00 |
| ❑ 145 | Ronald Curry | 2.50 | 1.00 |
| ❑ 146 | Philip Rivers | 3.00 | 1.25 |
| ❑ 147 | LaDainian Tomlinson | 4.00 | 1.50 |
| ❑ 148 | Vincent Jackson | 2.00 | .75 |
| ❑ 149 | Michael Turner | 2.50 | 1.00 |
| ❑ 150 | Antonio Gates | 2.50 | 1.00 |
| ❑ 151 | A.J. Davis RC | 8.00 | 3.00 |
| ❑ 152 | Aaron Rouse RC | 12.00 | 5.00 |
| ❑ 153 | Ahmad Bradshaw RC | 15.00 | 6.00 |
| ❑ 154 | Alonzo Coleman RC | 10.00 | 4.00 |
| ❑ 155 | Anthony Spencer RC | 12.00 | 5.00 |
| ❑ 156 | Brandon Siler RC | 10.00 | 4.00 |
| ❑ 157 | Buster Davis RC | 10.00 | 4.00 |
| ❑ 158 | Chris Houston RC | 10.00 | 4.00 |
| ❑ 159 | Dallas Baker RC | 10.00 | 4.00 |
| ❑ 160 | Dan Bazuin RC | 10.00 | 4.00 |
| ❑ 161 | Danny Ware RC | 10.00 | 4.00 |
| ❑ 162 | David Ball RC | 8.00 | 3.00 |
| ❑ 163 | David Irons RC | 8.00 | 3.00 |
| ❑ 164 | D'Juan Woods RC | 10.00 | 4.00 |
| ❑ 165 | Earl Everett RC | 10.00 | 4.00 |
| ❑ 166 | Eric Frampton RC | 10.00 | 4.00 |
| ❑ 167 | Eric Weddle RC | 10.00 | 4.00 |
| ❑ 168 | Eric Wright RC | 12.00 | 5.00 |
| ❑ 169 | Fred Bennett RC | 8.00 | 3.00 |
| ❑ 170 | Gary Russell RC | 12.00 | 5.00 |
| ❑ 171 | H.B. Blades RC | 10.00 | 4.00 |
| ❑ 172 | Jarrett Hicks RC | 10.00 | 4.00 |
| ❑ 173 | Jarvis Moss RC | 12.00 | 5.00 |
| ❑ 174 | Jason Snelling RC | 10.00 | 4.00 |
| ❑ 175 | Jerard Rabb RC | 10.00 | 4.00 |
| ❑ 176 | Jemaille Cornelius RC | 10.00 | 4.00 |
| ❑ 177 | Tyler Thigpen RC | 15.00 | 6.00 |
| ❑ 178 | Jon Beason RC | 12.00 | 5.00 |
| ❑ 179 | Jonathan Wade RC | 10.00 | 4.00 |
| ❑ 180 | Jordan Kent RC | 10.00 | 4.00 |
| ❑ 181 | Josh Gattis RC | 8.00 | 3.00 |
| ❑ 182 | Kenneth Darby RC | 12.00 | 5.00 |
| ❑ 183 | DeMarcus Tank Tyler RC | 10.00 | 4.00 |
| ❑ 184 | Levi Brown RC | 12.00 | 5.00 |
| ❑ 185 | Marcus McCauley RC | 10.00 | 4.00 |
| ❑ 186 | Tim Shaw RC | 10.00 | 4.00 |
| ❑ 187 | Michael Okwo RC | 10.00 | 4.00 |
| ❑ 188 | Mike Walker RC | 10.00 | 4.00 |
| ❑ 189 | Nate Ilaoa RC | 12.00 | 5.00 |
| ❑ 190 | Reggie Ball RC | 10.00 | 4.00 |
| ❑ 191 | Rhema McKnight RC | 10.00 | 4.00 |
| ❑ 192 | Zak DeOssie RC | 10.00 | 4.00 |
| ❑ 193 | Rufus Alexander RC | 12.00 | 5.00 |
| ❑ 194 | Ryan McBean RC | 12.00 | 5.00 |
| ❑ 195 | Ryne Robinson RC | 10.00 | 4.00 |
| ❑ 196 | Selvin Young RC | 20.00 | 8.00 |

| | | |
|---|---|---|
| ☐ 197 Steve Breaston RC | 12.00 | 5.00 |
| ☐ 198 Stewart Bradley RC | 12.00 | 5.00 |
| ☐ 199 Thomas Clayton RC | 10.00 | 4.00 |
| ☐ 200 Tim Crowder RC | 12.00 | 5.00 |
| ☐ 201 Aaron Ross AU RC | 15.00 | 6.00 |
| ☐ 202 Adam Carriker AU RC | 12.00 | 5.00 |
| ☐ 203 Alan Branch AU RC EXCH | 12.00 | 5.00 |
| ☐ 204 Amobi Okoye AU RC | 15.00 | 6.00 |
| ☐ 205 Aundrae Allison AU RC | 12.00 | 5.00 |
| ☐ 206 Ben Patrick AU RC | 12.00 | 5.00 |
| ☐ 207 Brandon Meriweather AU RC | 15.00 | 6.00 |
| ☐ 208 Chansi Stuckey AU RC | 12.00 | 5.00 |
| ☐ 209 Charles Johnson AU RC EXCH | 10.00 | 4.00 |
| ☐ 210 Chris Davis AU RC | 12.00 | 5.00 |
| ☐ 211 Chris Leak AU RC | 12.00 | 5.00 |
| ☐ 212 Courtney Taylor AU RC | 12.00 | 5.00 |
| ☐ 213 Craig Buster Davis AU RC EXCH | 13.00 | 6.00 |
| ☐ 214 Darius Walker AU RC | 15.00 | 6.00 |
| ☐ 215 Darrelle Revis AU RC | 15.00 | 6.00 |
| ☐ 216 David Clowney AU RC | 15.00 | 6.00 |
| ☐ 217 David Harris AU RC | 12.00 | 5.00 |
| ☐ 218 Daymeion Hughes AU RC | 12.00 | 5.00 |
| ☐ 219 DeShawn Wynn AU RC | 15.00 | 6.00 |
| ☐ 220 Dwayne Wright AU RC | 12.00 | 5.00 |
| ☐ 221 Ikaika Alama-Francis AU RC | 15.00 | 6.00 |
| ☐ 222 Isaiah Stanback AU RC | 15.00 | 6.00 |
| ☐ 223 Jacoby Jones AU RC | 15.00 | 6.00 |
| ☐ 224 Jamaal Anderson AU RC | 12.00 | 5.00 |
| ☐ 225 James Jones AU RC | 15.00 | 6.00 |
| ☐ 226 Jared Zabransky AU RC | 15.00 | 6.00 |
| ☐ 227 Jeff Rowe AU RC | 12.00 | 5.00 |
| ☐ 228 Joel Filani AU RC | 12.00 | 5.00 |
| ☐ 229 Jordan Palmer AU RC | 15.00 | 6.00 |
| ☐ 230 Josh Wilson AU RC | 12.00 | 5.00 |
| ☐ 231 Kenny Scott AU RC | 10.00 | 4.00 |
| ☐ 232 Kolby Smith AU RC | 15.00 | 6.00 |
| ☐ 233 LaMarr Woodley AU RC | 25.00 | 15.00 |
| ☐ 234 LaRon Landry AU RC | 20.00 | 8.00 |
| ☐ 235 Laurent Robinson AU RC | 12.00 | 5.00 |
| ☐ 236 Lawrence Timmons AU RC | 15.00 | 6.00 |
| ☐ 237 Leon Hall AU RC | 12.00 | 5.00 |
| ☐ 238 Matt Spaeth AU RC | 12.00 | 5.00 |
| ☐ 239 Michael Griffin AU RC | 15.00 | 6.00 |
| ☐ 240 Paul Posluszny AU RC | 20.00 | 8.00 |
| ☐ 241 Quentin Moses AU RC | 12.00 | 5.00 |
| ☐ 242 Ray McDonald AU RC | 12.00 | 5.00 |
| ☐ 243 Reggie Nelson AU RC | 12.00 | 5.00 |
| ☐ 244 Ronnie McGill AU RC | 12.00 | 5.00 |
| ☐ 245 Sabby Piscitelli AU RC | 15.00 | 6.00 |
| ☐ 246 Scott Chandler AU RC | 12.00 | 5.00 |
| ☐ 247 Toby Korrodi AU RC | 12.00 | 5.00 |
| ☐ 248 Tyler Palko AU RC | 12.00 | 5.00 |
| ☐ 249 Victor Abiamiri AU RC | 15.00 | 6.00 |
| ☐ 250 Zach Miller AU RC | 10.00 | 4.00 |
| ☐ 251 JaMarcus Russell RPM RC | 25.00 | 10.00 |
| ☐ 252 Calvin Johnson RPM RC | 25.00 | 10.00 |
| ☐ 253 Joe Thomas RPM RC | 10.00 | 4.00 |
| ☐ 254 Gaines Adams RPM RC | 10.00 | 4.00 |
| ☐ 255 Greg Olsen RPM RC | 12.00 | 5.00 |
| ☐ 256 Adrian Peterson RPM RC | 80.00 | 30.00 |
| ☐ 257 Ted Ginn RPM RC | 15.00 | 6.00 |
| ☐ 258 Patrick Willis RPM RC | 20.00 | 8.00 |
| ☐ 259 Marshawn Lynch RPM RC | 20.00 | 8.00 |
| ☐ 260 Brady Quinn RPM RC | 30.00 | 12.00 |
| ☐ 261 Dwayne Bowe RPM RC | 20.00 | 8.00 |
| ☐ 262 Robert Meachem RPM RC | 10.00 | 4.00 |
| ☐ 263 Anthony Gonzalez RPM RC | 15.00 | 6.00 |
| ☐ 264 Kevin Kolb RPM RC | 15.00 | 6.00 |
| ☐ 265 John Beck RPM RC | 10.00 | 4.00 |
| ☐ 266 Drew Stanton RPM RC | 10.00 | 4.00 |
| ☐ 267 Sidney Rice RPM RC | 10.00 | 4.00 |
| ☐ 268 Dwayne Jarrett RPM RC | 10.00 | 4.00 |
| ☐ 269 Kenny Irons RPM RC | 10.00 | 4.00 |
| ☐ 270 Chris Henry RPM RC | 10.00 | 4.00 |
| ☐ 271 Steve Smith RPM RC | 12.00 | 5.00 |
| ☐ 272 Brian Leonard RPM RC | 10.00 | 4.00 |
| ☐ 273 Brandon Jackson RPM RC | 10.00 | 4.00 |
| ☐ 274 Lorenzo Booker RPM RC | 10.00 | 4.00 |
| ☐ 275 Yamon Figurs RPM RC | 10.00 | 4.00 |
| ☐ 276 Jason Hill RPM RC | 10.00 | 4.00 |
| ☐ 277 Paul Williams RPM RC | 8.00 | 3.00 |
| ☐ 278 Tony Hunt RPM RC | 10.00 | 4.00 |
| ☐ 279 Trent Edwards RPM RC | 25.00 | 10.00 |
| ☐ 280 Garrett Wolfe RPM RC | 10.00 | 4.00 |

| | | |
|---|---|---|
| ☐ 281 Johnnie Lee Higgins RPM RC | 8.00 | 3.00 |
| ☐ 282 Michael Bush RPM RC | 10.00 | 4.00 |
| ☐ 283 Antonio Pittman RPM RC | 10.00 | 4.00 |
| ☐ 284 Troy Smith RPM RC | 12.00 | 5.00 |

## 2008 Absolute Memorabilia

| | | |
|---|---|---|
| ☐ 1 Anquan Boldin | 1.25 | .50 |
| ☐ 2 Edgerrin James | 1.25 | .50 |
| ☐ 3 Kurt Warner | 1.50 | .60 |
| ☐ 4 Larry Fitzgerald | 1.50 | .60 |
| ☐ 5 Matt Leinart | 1.25 | .60 |
| ☐ 6 Jerious Norwood | 1.25 | .50 |
| ☐ 7 Roddy White | 1.25 | .50 |
| ☐ 8 Michael Turner | 1.25 | .50 |
| ☐ 9 Joey Harrington | 1.25 | .50 |
| ☐ 10 Steve McNair | 1.50 | .60 |
| ☐ 11 Willis McGahee | 1.25 | .50 |
| ☐ 12 Derrick Mason | 1.00 | .40 |
| ☐ 13 Yamon Figurs | 1.00 | .40 |
| ☐ 14 Ray Lewis | 1.50 | .60 |
| ☐ 15 Trent Edwards | 1.50 | .60 |
| ☐ 16 Marshawn Lynch | 1.50 | .60 |
| ☐ 17 Fred Jackson RC | 1.50 | .60 |
| ☐ 18 Lee Evans | 1.25 | .50 |
| ☐ 19 Josh Reed | 1.00 | .40 |
| ☐ 20 Jake Delhomme | 1.25 | .50 |
| ☐ 21 DeAngelo Williams | 1.25 | .50 |
| ☐ 22 Steve Smith | 1.25 | .50 |
| ☐ 23 Jon Beason | 1.25 | .50 |
| ☐ 24 Rex Grossman | 1.25 | .50 |
| ☐ 25 Adrian Peterson | 1.25 | .50 |
| ☐ 26 Greg Olsen | 1.25 | .50 |
| ☐ 27 Devin Hester | 1.50 | .60 |
| ☐ 28 Brian Urlacher | 1.50 | .60 |
| ☐ 29 Carson Palmer | 1.50 | .60 |
| ☐ 30 Chad Johnson | 1.25 | .50 |
| ☐ 31 Rudi Johnson | 1.25 | .50 |
| ☐ 32 T.J. Houshmandzadeh | 1.25 | .50 |
| ☐ 33 Kenny Watson | 1.00 | .40 |
| ☐ 34 Derek Anderson | 1.25 | .50 |
| ☐ 35 Jamal Lewis | 1.25 | .50 |
| ☐ 36 Braylon Edwards | 1.25 | .50 |
| ☐ 37 Kellen Winslow | 1.25 | .50 |
| ☐ 38 Josh Cribbs | 1.25 | .50 |
| ☐ 39 Tony Romo | 2.50 | 1.00 |
| ☐ 40 Terrell Owens | 1.50 | .60 |
| ☐ 41 Jason Witten | 1.50 | .60 |
| ☐ 42 Marion Barber | 1.25 | .50 |
| ☐ 43 DeMarcus Ware | 1.25 | .50 |
| ☐ 44 Jay Cutler | 1.50 | .60 |
| ☐ 45 Brandon Marshall | 1.25 | .50 |
| ☐ 46 Selvin Young | 1.25 | .50 |
| ☐ 47 Brandon Stokley | 1.25 | .50 |
| ☐ 48 Tony Scheffler | 1.00 | .40 |
| ☐ 49 Jon Kitna | 1.25 | .50 |
| ☐ 50 Tatum Bell | 1.00 | .40 |
| ☐ 51 Roy Williams WR | 1.25 | .50 |
| ☐ 52 Calvin Johnson | 1.50 | .60 |
| ☐ 53 Shaun McDonald | 1.00 | .40 |
| ☐ 54 Aaron Rodgers | 1.50 | .60 |
| ☐ 55 Greg Jennings | 1.25 | .50 |
| ☐ 56 Donald Driver | 1.25 | .50 |
| ☐ 57 James Jones | 1.00 | .40 |
| ☐ 58 Ryan Grant | 1.50 | .60 |
| ☐ 59 Matt Schaub | 1.25 | .50 |
| ☐ 60 Ahman Green | 1.25 | .50 |

| | | |
|---|---|---|
| ☐ 61 Andre Johnson | 1.25 | .50 |
| ☐ 62 Kevin Walter | 1.00 | .40 |
| ☐ 63 Owen Daniels | 1.00 | .40 |
| ☐ 64 Peyton Manning | 2.50 | 1.00 |
| ☐ 65 Reggie Wayne | 1.25 | .50 |
| ☐ 66 Marvin Harrison | 1.50 | .60 |
| ☐ 67 Joseph Addai | 1.50 | .60 |
| ☐ 68 Anthony Gonzalez | 1.25 | .50 |
| ☐ 69 David Garrard | 1.25 | .50 |
| ☐ 70 Fred Taylor | 1.25 | .50 |
| ☐ 71 Maurice Jones-Drew | 1.25 | .50 |
| ☐ 72 Jerry Porter | 1.00 | .40 |
| ☐ 73 Reggie Williams | 1.25 | .50 |
| ☐ 74 Brodie Croyle | 1.50 | .60 |
| ☐ 75 Tony Gonzalez | 1.25 | .50 |
| ☐ 76 Larry Johnson | 1.50 | .60 |
| ☐ 77 Kolby Smith | 1.00 | .40 |
| ☐ 78 Dwayne Bowe | 1.25 | .50 |
| ☐ 79 John Beck | 1.00 | .40 |
| ☐ 80 Ted Ginn | 1.25 | .50 |
| ☐ 81 Ernest Wilford | 1.00 | .40 |
| ☐ 82 Ronnie Brown | 1.25 | .50 |
| ☐ 83 Tarvaris Jackson | 1.25 | .50 |
| ☐ 84 Adrian Peterson | 3.00 | 1.25 |
| ☐ 85 Chester Taylor | 1.00 | .40 |
| ☐ 86 Bernard Berrian | 1.25 | .50 |
| ☐ 87 Tom Brady | 2.50 | 1.00 |
| ☐ 88 Laurence Maroney | 1.25 | .50 |
| ☐ 89 Randy Moss | 1.50 | .60 |
| ☐ 90 Wes Welker | 1.50 | .60 |
| ☐ 91 Drew Brees | 1.50 | .60 |
| ☐ 92 Deuce McAllister | 1.25 | .50 |
| ☐ 93 Marques Colston | 1.25 | .50 |
| ☐ 94 Reggie Bush | 1.50 | .60 |
| ☐ 95 Devery Henderson | 1.00 | .40 |
| ☐ 96 Eli Manning | 1.25 | .50 |
| ☐ 97 Brandon Jacobs | 1.25 | .50 |
| ☐ 98 Derrick Ward | 1.00 | .40 |
| ☐ 99 Plaxico Burress | 1.25 | .50 |
| ☐ 100 Steve Smith | 1.25 | .50 |
| ☐ 101 Kellen Clemens | 1.25 | .50 |
| ☐ 102 Thomas Jones | 1.25 | .50 |
| ☐ 103 Laveranues Coles | 1.25 | .50 |
| ☐ 104 Jerricho Cotchery | 1.00 | .40 |
| ☐ 105 JaMarcus Russell | 1.50 | .60 |
| ☐ 106 Justin Fargas | 1.00 | .40 |
| ☐ 107 Michael Bush | 1.25 | .50 |
| ☐ 108 Javon Walker | 1.25 | .50 |
| ☐ 109 Zach Miller | 1.25 | .50 |
| ☐ 110 Donovan McNabb | 1.50 | .60 |
| ☐ 111 Brian Westbrook | 1.25 | .50 |
| ☐ 112 Kevin Curtis | 1.00 | .40 |
| ☐ 113 Reggie Brown | 1.25 | .50 |
| ☐ 114 Ben Roethlisberger | 2.00 | .75 |
| ☐ 115 Willie Parker | 1.25 | .50 |
| ☐ 116 Santonio Holmes | 1.25 | .50 |
| ☐ 117 Hines Ward | 1.50 | .60 |
| ☐ 118 Philip Rivers | 1.50 | .60 |
| ☐ 119 LaDainian Tomlinson | 2.00 | .75 |
| ☐ 120 Antonio Gates | 1.25 | .50 |
| ☐ 121 Vincent Jackson | 1.00 | .40 |
| ☐ 122 Alex Smith | 1.25 | .50 |
| ☐ 123 Frank Gore | 1.25 | .50 |
| ☐ 124 Vernon Davis | 1.00 | .40 |
| ☐ 125 Isaac Bruce | 1.25 | .50 |
| ☐ 126 Arnaz Battle | 1.00 | .40 |
| ☐ 127 Matt Hasselbeck | 1.25 | .50 |
| ☐ 128 Lofa Tatupu | 1.25 | .50 |
| ☐ 129 Deion Branch | 1.25 | .50 |
| ☐ 130 Nate Burleson | 1.00 | .40 |
| ☐ 131 Julius Jones | 1.25 | .50 |
| ☐ 132 Marc Bulger | 1.25 | .50 |
| ☐ 133 Steven Jackson | 1.50 | .60 |
| ☐ 134 Torry Holt | 1.25 | .50 |
| ☐ 135 Randy McMichael | 1.00 | .40 |
| ☐ 136 Jeff Garcia | 1.25 | .50 |
| ☐ 137 Cadillac Williams | 1.25 | .50 |
| ☐ 138 Warrick Dunn | 1.25 | .50 |
| ☐ 139 Joey Galloway | 1.25 | .50 |
| ☐ 140 Michael Clayton | 1.00 | .40 |
| ☐ 141 Vince Young | 1.50 | .60 |
| ☐ 142 LenDale White | 1.25 | .50 |
| ☐ 143 Alge Crumpler | 1.25 | .50 |
| ☐ 144 Justin Gage | 1.00 | .40 |

| # | Card | High | Low |
|---|------|------|-----|
| 145 | Roydell Williams | 1.00 | .40 |
| 146 | Jason Campbell | 1.25 | .50 |
| 147 | Clinton Portis | 1.25 | .50 |
| 148 | Chris Cooley | 1.25 | .50 |
| 149 | Santana Moss | 1.00 | .40 |
| 150 | Ladell Betts | 1.00 | .40 |
| 151 | Adrian Arrington AU RC | 4.00 | 1.50 |
| 152 | Alex Brink RC | 6.00 | 2.50 |
| 153 | Ali Highsmith RC | 4.00 | 1.50 |
| 154 | Allen Patrick AU RC | 12.00 | 5.00 |
| 155 | Andre Woodson AU RC | 15.00 | 6.00 |
| 156 | Anthony Alridge RC | 5.00 | 2.00 |
| 157 | Antoine Cason AU RC | 15.00 | 6.00 |
| 158 | Aqib Talib AU RC | 15.00 | 6.00 |
| 159 | Arman Shields RC | 5.00 | 2.00 |
| 160 | Brad Cottam AU RC | 15.00 | 6.00 |
| 161 | Brandon Flowers AU RC | 15.00 | 6.00 |
| 162 | Calais Campbell RC | 5.00 | 2.00 |
| 163 | Caleb Campbell RC | 6.00 | 2.50 |
| 164 | Chauncey Washington AU RC | 12.00 | 5.00 |
| 165 | Chevis Jackson RC | 5.00 | 2.00 |
| 166 | Chris Long AU RC | 20.00 | 8.00 |
| 167 | Colt Brennan AU RC | 60.00 | 30.00 |
| 168 | Cory Boyd AU RC | 12.00 | 5.00 |
| 169 | Craig Steltz RC | 5.00 | 2.00 |
| 170 | Curtis Lofton AU RC | 15.00 | 6.00 |
| 171 | Dan Connor AU RC | 15.00 | 6.00 |
| 172 | Dantrell Savage RC | 6.00 | 2.50 |
| 173 | Darius Reynaud RC | 5.00 | 2.00 |
| 174 | Darrell Strong RC | 5.00 | 2.00 |
| 175 | Davone Bess RC | 8.00 | 3.00 |
| 176 | Dennis Dixon AU RC | 15.00 | 6.00 |
| 177 | Derrick Harvey AU RC | 12.00 | 5.00 |
| 178 | DJ Hall RC | 6.00 | 2.50 |
| 179 | Dominique Rodgers-Cromartie AU RC | 15.00 | 6.00 |
| 180 | Erik Ainge AU RC | 15.00 | 6.00 |
| 181 | Erin Henderson RC | 5.00 | 2.00 |
| 182 | Ernie Wheelwright RC | 5.00 | 2.00 |
| 183 | Fred Davis AU RC | 15.00 | 6.00 |
| 184 | Joe Jon Finley RC | 5.00 | 2.00 |
| 185 | Jacob Hester AU RC | 15.00 | 6.00 |
| 186 | Jacob Tamme AU RC | 15.00 | 6.00 |
| 187 | Jalen Parmele RC | 5.00 | 2.00 |
| 188 | Jamar Adams RC | 5.00 | 2.00 |
| 189 | Jason Rivers RC | 6.00 | 2.50 |
| 190 | Jaymar Johnson RC | 5.00 | 2.00 |
| 191 | Jed Collins RC | 5.00 | 2.00 |
| 192 | Jermichael Finley AU RC | 15.00 | 6.00 |
| 193 | Jerod Mayo AU RC | 25.00 | 10.00 |
| 194 | John Carlson AU RC | 15.00 | 6.00 |
| 195 | Jonathan Hefney RC | 5.00 | 2.00 |
| 196 | Jordon Dizon AU RC | 15.00 | 6.00 |
| 197 | Josh Johnson AU RC | 15.00 | 6.00 |
| 198 | Josh Morgan AU RC | 15.00 | 6.00 |
| 199 | Justin Forsett AU RC | 15.00 | 6.00 |
| 200 | Justin Harper RC | 5.00 | 2.00 |
| 201 | Kalvin McRae RC | 5.00 | 2.00 |
| 202 | Keenan Burton AU RC | 12.00 | 5.00 |
| 203 | Keith Rivers AU RC | 15.00 | 6.00 |
| 204 | Kellen Davis RC | 4.00 | 1.50 |
| 205 | Kenneth Moore RC | 5.00 | 2.00 |
| 206 | Kenny Phillips AU RC | 20.00 | 8.00 |
| 207 | Kentwan Balmer AU RC | 12.00 | 5.00 |
| 208 | Kevin Robinson AU RC | 12.00 | 5.00 |
| 209 | Lavelle Hawkins AU RC | 12.00 | 5.00 |
| 210 | Lawrence Jackson AU RC | 12.00 | 5.00 |
| 211 | Leodis McKelvin AU RC | 15.00 | 6.00 |
| 212 | Marcus Henry RC | 5.00 | 2.00 |
| 213 | Marcus Monk RC | 6.00 | 2.50 |
| 214 | Marcus Smith AU RC | 12.00 | 5.00 |
| 215 | Marcus Thomas AU RC EXCH | 12.00 | 5.00 |
| 216 | Mark Bradford RC | 5.00 | 2.00 |
| 217 | Martellus Bennett AU RC | 15.00 | 6.00 |
| 218 | Martin Rucker AU RC | 12.00 | 5.00 |
| 219 | Matt Flynn AU RC | 20.00 | 8.00 |
| 220 | Mike Jenkins AU RC | 15.00 | 6.00 |
| 221 | Mike Hart AU RC | 20.00 | 8.00 |
| 222 | Owen Schmitt RC | 6.00 | 2.50 |
| 223 | Pat Sims RC | 5.00 | 2.00 |
| 224 | Paul Hubbard AU/91 RC | 12.00 | 5.00 |
| 225 | Paul Smith RC | 5.00 | 2.00 |
| 226 | Peyton Hillis RC | 8.00 | 3.00 |
| 227 | Phillip Merling RC | 5.00 | 2.00 |
| 228 | Pierre Garcon RC | 6.00 | 2.50 |
| 229 | Quentin Groves RC | 5.00 | 2.00 |
| 230 | Reggie Smith RC | 5.00 | 2.00 |
| 231 | Robert Killebrew RC | 5.00 | 2.00 |
| 232 | Ryan Grice-Mullen RC | 6.00 | 2.50 |
| 233 | Ryan Torain RC | 20.00 | 8.00 |
| 234 | Adarius Bowman RC | 5.00 | 2.00 |
| 235 | Sam Keller RC | 6.00 | 2.50 |
| 236 | Sedrick Ellis AU RC | 15.00 | 6.00 |
| 237 | Shawn Crable RC | 6.00 | 2.50 |
| 238 | Simeon Castille RC | 6.00 | 2.50 |
| 239 | Tashard Choice AU RC | 20.00 | 10.00 |
| 240 | Terrell Thomas RC | 5.00 | 2.00 |
| 241 | Dorien Bryant RC | 5.00 | 2.00 |
| 242 | Thomas Brown AU RC | 15.00 | 6.00 |
| 243 | Tim Hightower AU RC | 40.00 | 25.00 |
| 244 | Tracy Porter RC | 5.00 | 2.00 |
| 245 | Vernon Gholston AU RC | 15.00 | 6.00 |
| 246 | Bernard Morris RC | 5.00 | 2.00 |
| 247 | Will Franklin | 15.00 | 6.00 |
| 248 | Xavier Adibi RC | 5.00 | 2.00 |
| 249 | Xavier Omon RC | 6.00 | 2.50 |
| 250 | Zackary Bowman RC | 5.00 | 2.00 |
| 251 | Chad Henne RPM AU RC | 40.00 | 15.00 |
| 252 | Dustin Keller RPM AU RC | 20.00 | 10.00 |
| 253 | J.Stewart RPM AU RC | 50.00 | 25.00 |
| 254 | Steve Slaton RPM AU RC | 50.00 | 25.00 |
| 255 | Earl Bennett RPM AU RC | 15.00 | 6.00 |
| 256 | Brian Brohm RPM AU RC | 40.00 | 15.00 |
| 257 | Jamaal Charles RPM AU RC | 20.00 | 8.00 |
| 258 | M.Manningham RPM AU RC | 15.00 | 6.00 |
| 259 | Felix Jones RPM AU RC | 80.00 | 40.00 |
| 260 | DeS.Jackson RPM AU RC | 50.00 | 25.00 |
| 261 | Kevin O'Connell RPM AU RC | 30.00 | 12.00 |
| 262 | K.Smith RPM AU RC EXCH | 30.00 | 15.00 |
| 263 | Jerome Simpson RPM AU RC | 12.00 | 5.00 |
| 264 | D.McFadden RPM AU RC | 80.00 | 40.00 |
| 265 | H.Douglas RPM AU RC EXCH | 15.00 | 6.00 |
| 266 | J.D.Booty RPM AU RC | 20.00 | 10.00 |
| 267 | R.Mendenhall RPM AU RC | 50.00 | 25.00 |
| 268 | Malcolm Kelly RPM AU RC | 15.00 | 6.00 |
| 269 | Matt Ryan RPM AU RC | 120.00 | 60.00 |
| 270 | Joe Flacco RPM AU RC | 100.00 | 50.00 |
| 271 | E.Doucet RPM AU RC EXCH | 15.00 | 6.00 |
| 272 | Andre Caldwell RPM AU RC | 12.00 | 5.00 |
| 273 | James Hardy RPM AU RC | 15.00 | 6.00 |
| 274 | Jordy Nelson RPM AU RC | 30.00 | 12.00 |
| 275 | G.Dorsey RPM AU RC EXCH | 25.00 | 10.00 |
| 276 | Chris Johnson RPM AU RC | 60.00 | 30.00 |
| 277 | Eddie Royal RPM AU RC | 40.00 | 20.00 |
| 278 | Matt Forte RPM AU RC | 60.00 | 30.00 |
| 279 | Ray Rice RPM AU RC | 30.00 | 15.00 |
| 280 | Devin Thomas RPM AU RC | 15.00 | 6.00 |
| 281 | Limas Sweed RPM AU RC | 20.00 | 8.00 |
| 282 | Dexter Jackson RPM AU RC | 20.00 | 8.00 |
| 283 | Donnie Avery RPM AU RC | 25.00 | 10.00 |
| 284 | J.Long RPM AU RC EXCH | 20.00 | 8.00 |

## 2000 Aurora

| # | Card | High | Low |
|---|------|------|-----|
| | COMPLETE SET (150) | 30.00 | 12.50 |
| 1 | David Boston | .60 | .25 |
| 2 | Thomas Jones RC | 1.50 | .60 |
| 3 | Rob Moore | .40 | .15 |
| 4 | Jake Plummer | .40 | .15 |
| 5 | Frank Sanders | .40 | .15 |
| 6 | Jamal Anderson | .60 | .25 |
| 7 | Chris Chandler | .40 | .15 |
| 8 | Tim Dwight | .60 | .25 |
| 9 | Doug Johnson RC | 1.00 | .40 |
| 10 | Tony Banks | .40 | .15 |
| 11 | Qadry Ismail | .40 | .15 |
| 12 | Jamal Lewis RC | 2.50 | 1.00 |
| 13 | Chris Redman RC | .75 | .30 |
| 14 | Travis Taylor RC | 1.00 | .40 |
| 15 | Doug Flutie | .60 | .25 |
| 16 | Rob Johnson | .40 | .15 |
| 17 | Eric Moulds | .60 | .25 |
| 18 | Peerless Price | .40 | .15 |
| 19 | Antowain Smith | .40 | .15 |
| 20 | Steve Beuerlein | .40 | .15 |
| 21 | Tim Biakabutuka | .40 | .15 |
| 22 | Patrick Jeffers | .60 | .25 |
| 23 | Muhsin Muhammad | .40 | .15 |
| 24 | Curtis Enis | .25 | .08 |
| 25 | Cade McNown | .25 | .08 |
| 26 | Marcus Robinson | .60 | .25 |
| 27 | Dez White RC | 1.00 | .40 |
| 28 | Corey Dillon | .60 | .25 |
| 29 | Ron Dugans RC | .75 | .30 |
| 30 | Darnay Scott | .40 | .15 |
| 31 | Akili Smith | .25 | .08 |
| 32 | Peter Warrick RC | 1.00 | .40 |
| 33 | Tim Couch | .40 | .15 |
| 34 | JaJuan Dawson RC | .75 | .30 |
| 35 | Kevin Johnson | .60 | .25 |
| 36 | Dennis Northcutt RC | 1.00 | .40 |
| 37 | Travis Prentice RC | 1.00 | .40 |
| 38 | Troy Aikman | 1.25 | .50 |
| 39 | Rocket Ismail | .40 | .15 |
| 40 | Emmitt Smith | 1.25 | .50 |
| 41 | Jason Tucker | .25 | .08 |
| 42 | Terrell Davis | .60 | .25 |
| 43 | Olandis Gary | .60 | .25 |
| 44 | Brian Griese | .60 | .25 |
| 45 | Ed McCaffrey | .40 | .15 |
| 46 | Rod Smith | .40 | .15 |
| 47 | Charlie Batch | .60 | .25 |
| 48 | Germane Crowell | .25 | .08 |
| 49 | Reuben Droughns RC | 1.25 | .50 |
| 50 | Herman Moore | .40 | .15 |
| 51 | Barry Sanders | 1.50 | .60 |
| 52 | Brett Favre | 2.00 | .75 |
| 53 | Bubba Franks RC | 1.00 | .40 |
| 54 | Antonio Freeman | .60 | .25 |
| 55 | Dorsey Levens | .40 | .15 |
| 56 | Bill Schroeder | .40 | .15 |
| 57 | Marvin Harrison | .60 | .25 |
| 58 | Edgerrin James | 1.00 | .40 |
| 59 | Peyton Manning | 1.50 | .60 |
| 60 | Terrence Wilkins | .25 | .08 |
| 61 | Mark Brunell | .60 | .25 |
| 62 | Keenan McCardell | .40 | .15 |
| 63 | Jimmy Smith | .40 | .15 |
| 64 | R.Jay Soward RC | .75 | .30 |
| 65 | Shyrone Stith RC | 1.00 | .40 |
| 66 | Fred Taylor | .60 | .25 |
| 67 | Derrick Alexander | .40 | .15 |
| 68 | Donnell Bennett | .25 | .08 |
| 69 | Tony Gonzalez | .60 | .25 |
| 70 | Elvis Grbac | .40 | .15 |
| 71 | Sylvester Morris RC | .75 | .30 |
| 72 | Damon Huard | .60 | .25 |
| 73 | James Johnson | .25 | .08 |
| 74 | Dan Marino | 2.00 | .75 |
| 75 | Tony Martin | .40 | .15 |
| 76 | O.J. McDuffie | .40 | .15 |
| 77 | Quinton Spotwood RC | .75 | .30 |
| 78 | Cris Carter | .60 | .25 |
| 79 | Daunte Culpepper | .75 | .30 |
| 80 | Randy Moss | 1.25 | .50 |
| 81 | Robert Smith | .60 | .25 |
| 82 | Troy Walters RC | 1.00 | .40 |
| 83 | Drew Bledsoe | .75 | .30 |
| 84 | Tom Brady RC | 25.00 | 12.50 |
| 85 | Kevin Faulk | .40 | .15 |
| 86 | Terry Glenn | .40 | .15 |
| 87 | J.R. Redmond RC | .75 | .30 |
| 88 | Marc Bulger RC | 2.00 | .75 |
| 89 | Sherrod Gideon RC | .75 | .30 |
| 90 | Keith Poole | .25 | .08 |
| 91 | Ricky Williams | .60 | .25 |
| 92 | Kerry Collins | .40 | .15 |

| | | |
|---|---|---|
| 93 Ron Dayne RC | 1.00 | .40 |
| 94 Ike Hilliard | .40 | .15 |
| 95 Amani Toomer | .25 | .08 |
| 96 Wayne Chrebet | .40 | .15 |
| 97 Laveranues Coles RC | 1.25 | .50 |
| 98 Curtis Martin | .60 | .25 |
| 99 Chad Pennington RC | 2.50 | 1.00 |
| 100 Vinny Testaverde | .40 | .15 |
| 101 Tim Brown | .60 | .25 |
| 102 Rich Gannon | .60 | .25 |
| 103 Napoleon Kaufman | .40 | .15 |
| 104 Jerry Porter RC | 1.25 | .50 |
| 105 Tyrone Wheatley | .40 | .15 |
| 106 Charles Johnson | .40 | .15 |
| 107 Donovan McNabb | 1.00 | .40 |
| 108 Todd Pinkston RC | 1.00 | .40 |
| 109 Duce Staley | .60 | .25 |
| 110 Jerome Bettis | .60 | .25 |
| 111 Plaxico Burress RC | 2.00 | .75 |
| 112 Troy Edwards | .25 | .08 |
| 113 Richard Huntley | .25 | .08 |
| 114 Tee Martin RC | 1.00 | .40 |
| 115 Kordell Stewart | .40 | .15 |
| 116 Isaac Bruce | .60 | .25 |
| 117 Trung Canidate RC | .75 | .30 |
| 118 Marshall Faulk | .75 | .30 |
| 119 Torry Holt | .60 | .25 |
| 120 Kurt Warner | 1.25 | .50 |
| 121 Jermaine Fazande | .25 | .08 |
| 122 Trevor Gaylor RC | .75 | .30 |
| 123 Jim Harbaugh | .40 | .15 |
| 124 Junior Seau | .60 | .25 |
| 125 Giovanni Carmazzi RC | .75 | .30 |
| 126 Charlie Garner | .40 | .15 |
| 127 Terrell Owens | .60 | .25 |
| 128 Jerry Rice | 1.25 | .50 |
| 129 J.J. Stokes | .40 | .15 |
| 130 Steve Young | .75 | .30 |
| 131 Shaun Alexander RC | 3.00 | 1.25 |
| 132 Christian Fauria | .25 | .08 |
| 133 Jon Kitna | .60 | .25 |
| 134 Derrick Mayes | .40 | .15 |
| 135 Ricky Watters | .40 | .15 |
| 136 Mike Alstott | .60 | .25 |
| 137 Warrick Dunn | .60 | .25 |
| 138 Jacquez Green | .25 | .08 |
| 139 Joe Hamilton RC | .75 | .30 |
| 140 Shaun King | .25 | .08 |
| 141 Eddie George | .60 | .25 |
| 142 Jevon Kearse | .60 | .25 |
| 143 Steve McNair | .60 | .25 |
| 144 Yancey Thigpen | .25 | .08 |
| 145 Frank Wycheck | .25 | .08 |
| 146 Albert Connell | .25 | .08 |
| 147 Stephen Davis | .60 | .25 |
| 148 Toad Husak RC | 1.00 | .40 |
| 149 Brad Johnson | .60 | .25 |
| 150 Michael Westbrook | .40 | .15 |
| S1 Jon Kitna Sample | 1.00 | .40 |

### 1948 Bowman

| | | |
|---|---|---|
| COMPLETE SET (108) | 6000.00 | 4500.00 |
| COMMON 1/4/7/-/- | .60 | .25 |
| COMMON 2/5/8/-/- | 25.00 | 15.00 |
| COMMON SP 3/6/9 /-/- | 100.00 | 65.00 |
| WRAPPER (1-CENT) | 250.00 | 150.00 |
| 1 Joe Tereshinski RC ! | 150.00 | 80.00 |
| 2 Larry Olsonoski | 25.00 | 15.00 |
| 3 Johnny Lujack RC SP | 350.00 | 250.00 |
| 4 Ray Poole | 20.00 | 12.00 |

| | | |
|---|---|---|
| 5 Bill DeCorrevont RC | 25.00 | 15.00 |
| 6 Paul Briggs SP | 100.00 | 65.00 |
| 7 Steve Van Buren RC | 200.00 | 125.00 |
| 8 Kenny Washington RC | 60.00 | 40.00 |
| 9 Nolan Luhn SP | 100.00 | 65.00 |
| 10 Chris Iversen | 20.00 | 12.00 |
| 11 Jack Wiley | 25.00 | 15.00 |
| 12 Charley Conerly RC SP | 350.00 | 250.00 |
| 13 Hugh Taylor RC | 25.00 | 15.00 |
| 14 Frank Seno | 20.00 | 12.00 |
| 15 Gil Bouley SP | 100.00 | 65.00 |
| 16 Tommy Thompson RC | 35.00 | 20.00 |
| 17 Charley Trippi RC | 100.00 | 60.00 |
| 18 Vince Banonis SP | 100.00 | 65.00 |
| 19 Art Faircloth | 20.00 | 12.00 |
| 20 Clyde Goodnight | 25.00 | 15.00 |
| 21 Bill Chipley SP | 100.00 | 65.00 |
| 22 Sammy Baugh SP | 500.00 | 350.00 |
| 23 Don Kindt | 25.00 | 15.00 |
| 24 John Koniszewski SP | 100.00 | 65.00 |
| 25 Pat McHugh | 20.00 | 12.00 |
| 26 Bob Waterfield RC | 200.00 | 125.00 |
| 27 Tony Compagno SP | 100.00 | 65.00 |
| 28 Paul Governali RC | 25.00 | 15.00 |
| 29 Pat Harder RC | 60.00 | 40.00 |
| 30 Vic Lindskog SP | 100.00 | 65.00 |
| 31 Salvatore Rosato | 20.00 | 12.00 |
| 32 John Mastrangelo | 25.00 | 15.00 |
| 33 Fred Gehrke SP | 100.00 | 65.00 |
| 34 Bosh Pritchard | 25.00 | 15.00 |
| 35 Mike Micka | 20.00 | 12.00 |
| 36 Bulldog Turner RC SP | 250.00 | 150.00 |
| 37 Len Younce | 20.00 | 12.00 |
| 38 Pat West | 25.00 | 15.00 |
| 39 Russ Thomas SP | 100.00 | 65.00 |
| 40 James Peebles | 20.00 | 12.00 |
| 41 Bob Skoglund | 25.00 | 15.00 |
| 42 Walt Stickle SP | 100.00 | 65.00 |
| 43 Whitey Wistert RC | 25.00 | 15.00 |
| 44 Paul Christman RC | 60.00 | 40.00 |
| 45 Jay Rhodemyre SP | 100.00 | 65.00 |
| 46 Tony Minisi | 20.00 | 12.00 |
| 47 Bob Mann | 25.00 | 15.00 |
| 48 Mal Kutner RC SP | 110.00 | 70.00 |
| 49 Dick Poillon | 20.00 | 12.00 |
| 50 Charles Cherundolo | 25.00 | 15.00 |
| 51 Gerald Cowhig SP | 100.00 | 65.00 |
| 52 Neill Armstrong RC | 25.00 | 15.00 |
| 53 Frank Maznicki | 25.00 | 15.00 |
| 54 John Sanchez SP | 100.00 | 65.00 |
| 55 Frank Reagan | 25.00 | 15.00 |
| 56 Jim Hardy | 25.00 | 15.00 |
| 57 John Badaczewski SP | 100.00 | 65.00 |
| 58 Robert Nussbaumer | 20.00 | 12.00 |
| 59 Marvin Pregulman | 25.00 | 15.00 |
| 60 Elbie Nickel RC SP | 125.00 | 75.00 |
| 61 Alex Wojciechowicz RC | 150.00 | 90.00 |
| 62 Walt Schlinkman | 25.00 | 15.00 |
| 63 Pete Pihos RC | 225.00 | 150.00 |
| 64 Joseph Sulaitis | 20.00 | 12.00 |
| 65 Mike Holovak RC | 50.00 | 30.00 |
| 66 Cy Souders SP RC | 100.00 | 65.00 |
| 67 Paul McKee | 20.00 | 12.00 |
| 68 Bill Moore | 25.00 | 15.00 |
| 69 Frank Minini SP | 100.00 | 65.00 |
| 70 Jack Ferrante | 25.00 | 15.00 |
| 71 Les Horvath RC | 50.00 | 35.00 |
| 72 Ted Fritsch Sr. RC SP | 110.00 | 70.00 |
| 73 Tex Coulter RC | 25.00 | 15.00 |
| 74 Boley Dancewicz | 25.00 | 15.00 |
| 75 Dante Mangani SP | 100.00 | 65.00 |
| 76 James Hefti | 20.00 | 12.00 |
| 77 Paul Sarringhaus | 25.00 | 15.00 |
| 78 Joe Scott SP | 100.00 | 65.00 |
| 79 Bucko Kilroy RC | 25.00 | 15.00 |
| 80 Bill Dudley SP | 125.00 | 75.00 |
| 81 Mal Goldberg RC SP | 110.00 | 70.00 |
| 82 John Cannady | 20.00 | 12.00 |
| 83 Perry Moss | 25.00 | 15.00 |
| 84 Harold Crisler SP | 110.00 | 70.00 |
| 85 Bill Gray | 20.00 | 12.00 |
| 86 John Clement | 25.00 | 15.00 |
| 87 Dan Sandifer SP | 100.00 | 65.00 |
| 88 Ben Kish | 20.00 | 12.00 |

| | | |
|---|---|---|
| 89 Herbert Banta | 25.00 | 15.00 |
| 90 Bill Garnaas SP | 100.00 | 65.00 |
| 91 Jim White RC | 20.00 | 12.00 |
| 92 Frank Barzilauskas | 25.00 | 15.00 |
| 93 Vic Sears SP | 100.00 | 65.00 |
| 94 John Adams | 20.00 | 12.00 |
| 95 George McAfee RC | 150.00 | 90.00 |
| 96 Ralph Heywood SP | 100.00 | 65.00 |
| 97 Joe Muha | 20.00 | 12.00 |
| 98 Fred Enke | 25.00 | 15.00 |
| 99 Harry Gilmer RC SP | 175.00 | 100.00 |
| 100 Bill Miklich | 20.00 | 12.00 |
| 101 Joe Gottlieb | 25.00 | 15.00 |
| 102 Bud Angsman RC SP | 110.00 | 70.00 |
| 103 Tom Farmer | 20.00 | 12.00 |
| 104 Bruce Smith RC | 75.00 | 40.00 |
| 105 Bob Cifers SP | 100.00 | 65.00 |
| 106 Ernie Steele | 20.00 | 12.00 |
| 107 Sid Luckman RC SP | 300.00 | 175.00 |
| 108 Buford Ray RC SP ! | 400.00 | 250.00 |

### 1950 Bowman

| | | |
|---|---|---|
| COMPLETE SET (144) | 4000.00 | 3000.00 |
| WRAPPER (5-CENT) | 175.00 | 100.00 |
| 1 Doak Walker ! | 250.00 | 150.00 |
| 2 John Greene | 25.00 | 18.00 |
| 3 Bob Nowasky | 25.00 | 18.00 |
| 4 Jonathan Jenkins | 25.00 | 18.00 |
| 5 Y.A. Tittle RC | 250.00 | 175.00 |
| 6 Lou Groza RC | 175.00 | 100.00 |
| 7 Alex Agase RC | 30.00 | 20.00 |
| 8 Mac Speedie RC | 50.00 | 30.00 |
| 9 Tony Canadeo RC | 90.00 | 50.00 |
| 10 Larry Craig | 30.00 | 20.00 |
| 11 Ted Fritsch Sr. | 30.00 | 20.00 |
| 12 Joe Golding | 25.00 | 18.00 |
| 13 Martin Ruby | 25.00 | 18.00 |
| 14 George Taliaferro | 30.00 | 20.00 |
| 15 Tank Younger RC | 50.00 | 30.00 |
| 16 Glenn Davis RC | 125.00 | 75.00 |
| 17 Bob Waterfield | 125.00 | 75.00 |
| 18 Val Jansante | 25.00 | 18.00 |
| 19 Joe Geri | 25.00 | 18.00 |
| 20 Jerry Nuzum | 25.00 | 18.00 |
| 21 Elmer Bud Angsman | 25.00 | 18.00 |
| 22 Billy Dewell | 25.00 | 18.00 |
| 23 Steve Van Buren | 90.00 | 50.00 |
| 24 Cliff Patton | 25.00 | 18.00 |
| 25 Bosh Pritchard | 25.00 | 18.00 |
| 26 Johnny Lujack | 80.00 | 50.00 |
| 27 Sid Luckman | 125.00 | 75.00 |
| 28 Bulldog Turner | 60.00 | 35.00 |
| 29 Bill Dudley | 60.00 | 35.00 |
| 30 Hugh Taylor | 30.00 | 20.00 |
| 31 George Thomas | 25.00 | 18.00 |
| 32 Ray Poole | 25.00 | 18.00 |
| 33 Travis Tidwell | 25.00 | 18.00 |
| 34 Dick Bruce | 25.00 | 18.00 |
| 35 Joe Perry RC | 200.00 | 125.00 |
| 36 Frankie Albert RC | 50.00 | 30.00 |
| 37 Bobby Layne | 200.00 | 125.00 |
| 38 Leon Hart | 40.00 | 25.00 |
| 39 B.Hoernschemeyer RC | 30.00 | 20.00 |
| 40 Dick Barwegan RC | 25.00 | 18.00 |
| 41 Adrian Burk RC | 30.00 | 20.00 |
| 42 Barry French | 25.00 | 18.00 |
| 43 Marion Motley RC | 250.00 | 150.00 |
| 44 Jim Martin | 30.00 | 20.00 |
| 45 Otto Graham RC | 450.00 | 300.00 |
| 46 Al Baldwin | 25.00 | 18.00 |

| | | | |
|---|---|---:|---:|
| ❑ 47 | Larry Coutre | 30.00 | 20.00 |
| ❑ 48 | John Rauch | 25.00 | 18.00 |
| ❑ 49 | Sam Tamburo | 25.00 | 18.00 |
| ❑ 50 | Mike Swistowicz | 25.00 | 18.00 |
| ❑ 51 | Tom Fears RC | 150.00 | 90.00 |
| ❑ 52 | Elroy Hirsch RC | 225.00 | 125.00 |
| ❑ 53 | Dick Huffman | 25.00 | 18.00 |
| ❑ 54 | Bob Gage | 25.00 | 18.00 |
| ❑ 55 | Buddy Tinsley | 25.00 | 18.00 |
| ❑ 56 | Bill Blackburn | 25.00 | 18.00 |
| ❑ 57 | John Cochran | 25.00 | 18.00 |
| ❑ 58 | Bill Fischer | 25.00 | 18.00 |
| ❑ 59 | Whitey Wistert | 30.00 | 20.00 |
| ❑ 60 | Clyde Scott | 25.00 | 18.00 |
| ❑ 61 | Walter Barnes | 25.00 | 18.00 |
| ❑ 62 | Bob Perina | 25.00 | 18.00 |
| ❑ 63 | Bill Wightkin | 25.00 | 18.00 |
| ❑ 64 | Bob Goode | 25.00 | 18.00 |
| ❑ 65 | Al Demao | 25.00 | 18.00 |
| ❑ 66 | Harry Gilmer | 30.00 | 20.00 |
| ❑ 67 | Bill Austin | 25.00 | 18.00 |
| ❑ 68 | Joe Scott | 25.00 | 18.00 |
| ❑ 69 | Tex Coulter | 30.00 | 20.00 |
| ❑ 70 | Paul Salata | 25.00 | 18.00 |
| ❑ 71 | Emil Sitko RC | 30.00 | 20.00 |
| ❑ 72 | Bill Johnson C | 25.00 | 18.00 |
| ❑ 73 | Don Doll RC | 25.00 | 18.00 |
| ❑ 74 | Dan Sandifer | 25.00 | 18.00 |
| ❑ 75 | John Panelli | 25.00 | 18.00 |
| ❑ 76 | Bill Leonard | 25.00 | 18.00 |
| ❑ 77 | Bob Kelly | 25.00 | 18.00 |
| ❑ 78 | Dante Lavelli RC | 175.00 | 100.00 |
| ❑ 79 | Tony Adamle | 30.00 | 20.00 |
| ❑ 80 | Dick Wildung | 25.00 | 18.00 |
| ❑ 81 | Tobin Rote RC | 50.00 | 30.00 |
| ❑ 82 | Paul Burris | 25.00 | 18.00 |
| ❑ 83 | Lowell Tew | 25.00 | 18.00 |
| ❑ 84 | Barney Poole | 25.00 | 18.00 |
| ❑ 85 | Fred Naumetz | 25.00 | 18.00 |
| ❑ 86 | Dick Hoerner | 25.00 | 18.00 |
| ❑ 87 | Bob Reinhard | 25.00 | 18.00 |
| ❑ 88 | Howard Hartley RC | 25.00 | 18.00 |
| ❑ 89 | Darrell Hogan RC | 25.00 | 18.00 |
| ❑ 90 | Jerry Shipkey | 25.00 | 18.00 |
| ❑ 91 | Frank Tripucka | 30.00 | 20.00 |
| ❑ 92 | Buster Ramsey RC | 25.00 | 18.00 |
| ❑ 93 | Pat Harder | 30.00 | 20.00 |
| ❑ 94 | Vic Sears | 25.00 | 18.00 |
| ❑ 95 | Tommy Thompson QB | 30.00 | 20.00 |
| ❑ 96 | Bucko Kilroy | 30.00 | 20.00 |
| ❑ 97 | George Connor | 50.00 | 30.00 |
| ❑ 98 | Fred Morrison | 25.00 | 18.00 |
| ❑ 99 | Rookie | 25.00 | 18.00 |
| ❑ 100 | Sammy Baugh | 250.00 | 150.00 |
| ❑ 101 | Harry Ulinski | 25.00 | 18.00 |
| ❑ 102 | Frank Spaniel | 25.00 | 18.00 |
| ❑ 103 | Charley Conerly | 90.00 | 50.00 |
| ❑ 104 | Dick Hensley | 25.00 | 18.00 |
| ❑ 105 | Eddie Price | 25.00 | 18.00 |
| ❑ 106 | Ed Carr | 25.00 | 18.00 |
| ❑ 107 | Leo Nomellini | 75.00 | 45.00 |
| ❑ 108 | Verl Lillywhite | 25.00 | 18.00 |
| ❑ 109 | Wallace Triplett | 25.00 | 18.00 |
| ❑ 110 | Joe Watson | 25.00 | 18.00 |
| ❑ 111 | Cloyce Box RC | 30.00 | 20.00 |
| ❑ 112 | Billy Stone | 25.00 | 18.00 |
| ❑ 113 | Earl Murray | 25.00 | 18.00 |
| ❑ 114 | Chet Mutryn RC | 30.00 | 20.00 |
| ❑ 115 | Ken Carpenter | 25.00 | 18.00 |
| ❑ 116 | Lou Rymkus RC | 30.00 | 20.00 |
| ❑ 117 | Dub Jones RC | 30.00 | 20.00 |
| ❑ 118 | Clayton Tonnemaker | 25.00 | 18.00 |
| ❑ 119 | Walt Schlinkman | 25.00 | 18.00 |
| ❑ 120 | Billy Grimes | 25.00 | 18.00 |
| ❑ 121 | George Ratterman RC | 30.00 | 20.00 |
| ❑ 122 | Bob Mann | 25.00 | 18.00 |
| ❑ 123 | Buddy Young RC | 50.00 | 30.00 |
| ❑ 124 | Jack Zilly | 25.00 | 18.00 |
| ❑ 125 | Tom Kalmanir | 25.00 | 18.00 |
| ❑ 126 | Frank Sinkovitz | 25.00 | 18.00 |
| ❑ 127 | Elbert Nickel | 30.00 | 20.00 |
| ❑ 128 | Jim Finks RC | 75.00 | 40.00 |
| ❑ 129 | Charley Trippi | 60.00 | 35.00 |
| ❑ 130 | Tom Wham | 25.00 | 18.00 |

| | | | |
|---|---|---:|---:|
| ❑ 131 | Ventan Yablonski | 25.00 | 18.00 |
| ❑ 132 | Chuck Bednarik | 125.00 | 75.00 |
| ❑ 133 | Joe Muha | 25.00 | 18.00 |
| ❑ 134 | Pete Pihos | 80.00 | 45.00 |
| ❑ 135 | Washington Serini | 25.00 | 18.00 |
| ❑ 136 | George Gulyanics | 25.00 | 18.00 |
| ❑ 137 | Ken Kavanaugh | 30.00 | 20.00 |
| ❑ 138 | Howie Livingston | 25.00 | 18.00 |
| ❑ 139 | Joe Tereshinski | 25.00 | 18.00 |
| ❑ 140 | Jim White | 25.00 | 18.00 |
| ❑ 141 | Gene Roberts | 25.00 | 18.00 |
| ❑ 142 | Bill Swiacki | 30.00 | 20.00 |
| ❑ 143 | Norm Standlee | 25.00 | 18.00 |
| ❑ 144 | Knox Ramsey RC ! | 100.00 | 50.00 |

## 1951 Bowman

THOMAS LANDRY

| | | | |
|---|---|---:|---:|
| ❑ | COMPLETE SET (144) | 3500.00 | 2500.00 |
| ❑ | WRAPPER (1-CENT) | 250.00 | 150.00 |
| ❑ | WRAPPER (5-CENT) | 300.00 | 175.00 |
| ❑ 1 | Weldon Humble RC ! | 80.00 | 50.00 |
| ❑ 2 | Otto Graham | 250.00 | 150.00 |
| ❑ 3 | Mac Speedie | 35.00 | 20.00 |
| ❑ 4 | Norm Van Brocklin RC | 300.00 | 200.00 |
| ❑ 5 | Woodley Lewis RC | 25.00 | 15.00 |
| ❑ 6 | Tom Fears | 50.00 | 30.00 |
| ❑ 7 | George Musacco | 20.00 | 12.00 |
| ❑ 8 | George Taliaferro | 25.00 | 15.00 |
| ❑ 9 | Barney Poole | 20.00 | 12.00 |
| ❑ 10 | Steve Van Buren | 60.00 | 35.00 |
| ❑ 11 | Whitey Wistert | 25.00 | 15.00 |
| ❑ 12 | Chuck Bednarik | 80.00 | 50.00 |
| ❑ 13 | Bulldog Turner | 50.00 | 30.00 |
| ❑ 14 | Bob Williams | 20.00 | 12.00 |
| ❑ 15 | Johnny Lujack | 60.00 | 35.00 |
| ❑ 16 | Roy Rebel Steiner | 20.00 | 12.00 |
| ❑ 17 | Jug Girard | 25.00 | 15.00 |
| ❑ 18 | Bill Neal | 20.00 | 12.00 |
| ❑ 19 | Travis Tidwell | 20.00 | 12.00 |
| ❑ 20 | Tom Landry RC | 500.00 | 350.00 |
| ❑ 21 | Arnie Weinmeister RC | 60.00 | 35.00 |
| ❑ 22 | Joe Geri | 20.00 | 12.00 |
| ❑ 23 | Bill Walsh C RC | 30.00 | 15.00 |
| ❑ 24 | Fran Rogel | 20.00 | 12.00 |
| ❑ 25 | Doak Walker | 60.00 | 35.00 |
| ❑ 26 | Leon Hart | 35.00 | 20.00 |
| ❑ 27 | Thurman McGraw | 20.00 | 12.00 |
| ❑ 28 | Buster Ramsey | 20.00 | 12.00 |
| ❑ 29 | Frank Tripucka | 35.00 | 20.00 |
| ❑ 30 | Don Paul DB | 20.00 | 12.00 |
| ❑ 31 | Alex Loyd | 20.00 | 12.00 |
| ❑ 32 | Y.A.Tittle | 135.00 | 75.00 |
| ❑ 33 | Verl Lillywhite | 20.00 | 12.00 |
| ❑ 34 | Sammy Baugh | 175.00 | 110.00 |
| ❑ 35 | Chuck Drazenovich | 20.00 | 12.00 |
| ❑ 36 | Bob Goode | 20.00 | 12.00 |
| ❑ 37 | Horace Gillom RC | 25.00 | 15.00 |
| ❑ 38 | Lou Rymkus | 25.00 | 15.00 |
| ❑ 39 | Ken Carpenter | 20.00 | 12.00 |
| ❑ 40 | Bob Waterfield | 75.00 | 45.00 |
| ❑ 41 | Vitamin Smith RC | 25.00 | 15.00 |
| ❑ 42 | Glenn Davis | 60.00 | 35.00 |
| ❑ 43 | Dan Edwards | 20.00 | 12.00 |
| ❑ 44 | John Rauch | 20.00 | 12.00 |
| ❑ 45 | Cliff Toth | 20.00 | 12.00 |
| ❑ 46 | Pete Pihos | 60.00 | 35.00 |
| ❑ 47 | Russ Craft | 20.00 | 12.00 |
| ❑ 48 | Walter Barnes | 20.00 | 12.00 |
| ❑ 49 | Fred Morrison | 20.00 | 12.00 |

| | | | |
|---|---|---:|---:|
| ❑ 50 | Ray Bray | 20.00 | 12.00 |
| ❑ 51 | Ed Sprinkle RC | 25.00 | 15.00 |
| ❑ 52 | Floyd Reid | 20.00 | 12.00 |
| ❑ 53 | Billy Grimes | 20.00 | 12.00 |
| ❑ 54 | Ted Fritsch Sr. | 20.00 | 12.00 |
| ❑ 55 | Al DeRogatis | 25.00 | 15.00 |
| ❑ 56 | Charley Conerly | 75.00 | 45.00 |
| ❑ 57 | Jon Baker | 20.00 | 12.00 |
| ❑ 58 | Tom McWilliams | 20.00 | 12.00 |
| ❑ 59 | Jerry Shipkey | 20.00 | 12.00 |
| ❑ 60 | Lynn Chandnois RC | 25.00 | 15.00 |
| ❑ 61 | Don Doll | 20.00 | 12.00 |
| ❑ 62 | Lou Creekmur | 50.00 | 30.00 |
| ❑ 63 | Bob Hoernschemeyer | 25.00 | 15.00 |
| ❑ 64 | Tom Wham | 20.00 | 12.00 |
| ❑ 65 | Bill Fischer | 20.00 | 12.00 |
| ❑ 66 | Robert Nussbaumer | 20.00 | 12.00 |
| ❑ 67 | Gordy Soltau RC | 20.00 | 12.00 |
| ❑ 68 | Visco Grgich | 20.00 | 12.00 |
| ❑ 69 | John Strzykalski RC | 20.00 | 12.00 |
| ❑ 70 | Pete Stout | 20.00 | 12.00 |
| ❑ 71 | Paul Lipscomb | 20.00 | 12.00 |
| ❑ 72 | Harry Gilmer | 35.00 | 20.00 |
| ❑ 73 | Dante Lavelli | 50.00 | 30.00 |
| ❑ 74 | Dub Jones | 25.00 | 15.00 |
| ❑ 75 | Lou Groza | 75.00 | 45.00 |
| ❑ 76 | Elroy Hirsch | 75.00 | 45.00 |
| ❑ 77 | Tom Kalmanir | 20.00 | 12.00 |
| ❑ 78 | Jack Zilly | 20.00 | 12.00 |
| ❑ 79 | Bruce Alford | 20.00 | 12.00 |
| ❑ 80 | Art Weiner | 20.00 | 12.00 |
| ❑ 81 | Brad Ecklund | 20.00 | 12.00 |
| ❑ 82 | Bosh Pritchard | 20.00 | 12.00 |
| ❑ 83 | John Green | 20.00 | 12.00 |
| ❑ 84 | Ebert Van Buren | 20.00 | 12.00 |
| ❑ 85 | Julie Rykovich | 20.00 | 12.00 |
| ❑ 86 | Fred Davis | 20.00 | 12.00 |
| ❑ 87 | John Hoffman RC | 20.00 | 12.00 |
| ❑ 88 | Tobin Rote | 25.00 | 15.00 |
| ❑ 89 | Paul Burris | 20.00 | 12.00 |
| ❑ 90 | Tony Canadeo | 50.00 | 30.00 |
| ❑ 91 | Emlen Tunnell RC | 100.00 | 60.00 |
| ❑ 92 | Otto Schnellbacher RC | 20.00 | 12.00 |
| ❑ 93 | Ray Poole | 20.00 | 12.00 |
| ❑ 94 | Darrell Hogan | 20.00 | 12.00 |
| ❑ 95 | Frank Sinkovitz | 20.00 | 12.00 |
| ❑ 96 | Ernie Stautner | 75.00 | 45.00 |
| ❑ 97 | Elmer Bud Angsman | 20.00 | 12.00 |
| ❑ 98 | Jack Jennings | 20.00 | 12.00 |
| ❑ 99 | Jerry Groom | 20.00 | 12.00 |
| ❑ 100 | John Prohlik | 20.00 | 12.00 |
| ❑ 101 | J. Robert Smith | 20.00 | 12.00 |
| ❑ 102 | Bobby Layne | 135.00 | 75.00 |
| ❑ 103 | Frankie Albert | 35.00 | 20.00 |
| ❑ 104 | Gail Bruce | 20.00 | 12.00 |
| ❑ 105 | Joe Perry | 75.00 | 45.00 |
| ❑ 106 | Leon Heath | 20.00 | 12.00 |
| ❑ 107 | Ed Quirk | 20.00 | 12.00 |
| ❑ 108 | Hugh Taylor | 25.00 | 15.00 |
| ❑ 109 | Marion Motley | 100.00 | 60.00 |
| ❑ 110 | Tony Adamle | 20.00 | 12.00 |
| ❑ 111 | Alex Agase | 20.00 | 12.00 |
| ❑ 112 | Tank Younger | 35.00 | 20.00 |
| ❑ 113 | Bob Boyd | 20.00 | 12.00 |
| ❑ 114 | Jerry Williams | 20.00 | 12.00 |
| ❑ 115 | Joe Golding | 20.00 | 12.00 |
| ❑ 116 | Sherman Howard | 20.00 | 12.00 |
| ❑ 117 | John Wozniak | 20.00 | 12.00 |
| ❑ 118 | Frank Reagan | 20.00 | 12.00 |
| ❑ 119 | Vic Sears | 20.00 | 12.00 |
| ❑ 120 | Clyde Scott | 20.00 | 12.00 |
| ❑ 121 | George Gulyanics | 20.00 | 12.00 |
| ❑ 122 | Bill Wightkin | 20.00 | 12.00 |
| ❑ 123 | Chuck Hunsinger | 20.00 | 12.00 |
| ❑ 124 | Jack Cloud | 20.00 | 12.00 |
| ❑ 125 | Abner Wimberly | 20.00 | 12.00 |
| ❑ 126 | Dick Wildung | 20.00 | 12.00 |
| ❑ 127 | Eddie Price | 20.00 | 12.00 |
| ❑ 128 | Joe Scott | 20.00 | 12.00 |
| ❑ 129 | Jerry Nuzum | 20.00 | 12.00 |
| ❑ 130 | Jim Finks | 35.00 | 20.00 |
| ❑ 131 | Bob Gage | 20.00 | 12.00 |
| ❑ 132 | Bill Swiacki | 25.00 | 15.00 |
| ❑ 133 | Joe Watson | 20.00 | 12.00 |

| | Price | |
|---|---|---|
| ☐ 134 Ollie Cline | 20.00 | 12.00 |
| ☐ 135 Jack Lininger | 20.00 | 12.00 |
| ☐ 136 Fran Polsfoot | 20.00 | 12.00 |
| ☐ 137 Charley Trippi | 50.00 | 30.00 |
| ☐ 138 Ventan Yablonski | 20.00 | 12.00 |
| ☐ 139 Emil Sitko | 20.00 | 12.00 |
| ☐ 140 Leo Nomellini | 60.00 | 30.00 |
| ☐ 141 Norm Standlee | 20.00 | 12.00 |
| ☐ 142 Eddie Saenz | 20.00 | 12.00 |
| ☐ 143 Al Demao | 20.00 | 12.00 |
| ☐ 144 Bill Dudley ! | 150.00 | 75.00 |
| ☐ NNO Johnny Lujack Proof | 300.00 | 175.00 |
| ☐ NNO Bob Gage Proof | 125.00 | 75.00 |
| ☐ NNO Darrell Hogan Proof | 125.00 | 75.00 |

### 1952 Bowman Large

| | Price | |
|---|---|---|
| ☐ COMPLETE SET (144) | 12500.00 | 9500.00 |
| ☐ COMMON CARD (1-72) | 35.00 | 20.00 |
| ☐ COMMON CARD (73-144) | 40.00 | 25.00 |
| ☐ WRAPPER (5-CENT) | 60.00 | 30.00 |
| ☐ 1 Norm Van Brocklin SP ! | 500.00 | 350.00 |
| ☐ 2 Otto Graham | 300.00 | 200.00 |
| ☐ 3 Doak Walker | 100.00 | 60.00 |
| ☐ 4 Steve Owen RC CO | 80.00 | 50.00 |
| ☐ 5 Frankie Albert | 50.00 | 30.00 |
| ☐ 6 Laurie Niemi | 35.00 | 20.00 |
| ☐ 7 Chuck Hunsinger | 35.00 | 20.00 |
| ☐ 8 Ed Modzelewski | 50.00 | 30.00 |
| ☐ 9 Joe Spencer SP | 75.00 | 40.00 |
| ☐ 10 Chuck Bednarik SP | 350.00 | 200.00 |
| ☐ 11 Barney Poole | 35.00 | 20.00 |
| ☐ 12 Charley Trippi | 75.00 | 40.00 |
| ☐ 13 Tom Fears | 75.00 | 40.00 |
| ☐ 14 Paul Brown RC CO | 250.00 | 150.00 |
| ☐ 15 Leon Hart | 50.00 | 30.00 |
| ☐ 16 Frank Gifford RC | 500.00 | 350.00 |
| ☐ 17 Y.A.Tittle | 300.00 | 200.00 |
| ☐ 18 Charlie Justice SP | 175.00 | 100.00 |
| ☐ 19 George Connor SP | 175.00 | 100.00 |
| ☐ 20 Lynn Chandnois | 35.00 | 20.00 |
| ☐ 21 Billy Howton RC | 50.00 | 30.00 |
| ☐ 22 Kenneth Snyder | 35.00 | 20.00 |
| ☐ 23 Gino Marchetti RC | 250.00 | 150.00 |
| ☐ 24 John Karras | 35.00 | 20.00 |
| ☐ 25 Tank Younger | 50.00 | 30.00 |
| ☐ 26 Tommy Thompson SP | 35.00 | 20.00 |
| ☐ 27 Bob Miller SP RC! | 300.00 | 200.00 |
| ☐ 28 Kyle Rote SP | 175.00 | 100.00 |
| ☐ 29 Hugh McElhenny RC | 250.00 | 150.00 |
| ☐ 30 Sammy Baugh | 350.00 | 225.00 |
| ☐ 31 Jim Dooley RC | 45.00 | 25.00 |
| ☐ 32 Ray Mathews | 35.00 | 20.00 |
| ☐ 33 Fred Cone | 35.00 | 20.00 |
| ☐ 34 Al Pollard | 35.00 | 20.00 |
| ☐ 35 Brad Ecklund | 35.00 | 20.00 |
| ☐ 36 John Hancock RC SP! | 350.00 | 250.00 |
| ☐ 37 Elroy Hirsch SP | 200.00 | 125.00 |
| ☐ 38 Keever Jankovich | 35.00 | 20.00 |
| ☐ 39 Emlen Tunnell | 125.00 | 75.00 |
| ☐ 40 Steve Dowden | 35.00 | 20.00 |
| ☐ 41 Claude Hipps | 35.00 | 20.00 |
| ☐ 42 Norm Standlee | 35.00 | 20.00 |
| ☐ 43 Dick Todd CO | 35.00 | 20.00 |
| ☐ 44 Babe Parilli | 50.00 | 30.00 |
| ☐ 45 Steve Van Buren SP | 300.00 | 200.00 |
| ☐ 46 Art Donovan RC SP | 350.00 | 250.00 |
| ☐ 47 Bill Fischer | 35.00 | 20.00 |
| ☐ 48 George Halas RC CO | 275.00 | 160.00 |
| ☐ 49 Jerrell Price | 35.00 | 20.00 |
| ☐ 50 John Sandusky RC | 35.00 | 20.00 |
| ☐ 51 Ray Beck | 35.00 | 20.00 |
| ☐ 52 Jim Martin | 45.00 | 25.00 |
| ☐ 53 Joe Bach CO UER | 35.00 | 20.00 |
| ☐ 54 Glen Christian SP | 75.00 | 40.00 |
| ☐ 55 Andy Davis SP | 75.00 | 40.00 |
| ☐ 56 Tobin Rote | 45.00 | 25.00 |
| ☐ 57 Wayne Millner RC CO | 90.00 | 50.00 |
| ☐ 58 Zollie Toth | 35.00 | 20.00 |
| ☐ 59 Jack Jennings | 35.00 | 20.00 |
| ☐ 60 Bill McColl | 35.00 | 20.00 |
| ☐ 61 Les Richter RC | 45.00 | 25.00 |
| ☐ 62 Walt Michaels RC | 40.00 | -25.00 |
| ☐ 63 Charley Conerly SP | 700.00 | 400.00 |
| ☐ 64 Howard Hartley SP | 75.00 | 40.00 |
| ☐ 65 Jerome Smith | 35.00 | 20.00 |
| ☐ 66 James Clark | 35.00 | 20.00 |
| ☐ 67 Dick Logan | 35.00 | 20.00 |
| ☐ 68 Wayne Robinson | 35.00 | 20.00 |
| ☐ 69 James Hammond | 35.00 | 20.00 |
| ☐ 70 Gene Schroeder | 35.00 | 20.00 |
| ☐ 71 Tex Coulter | 45.00 | 25.00 |
| ☐ 72 John Schweder RC SP! | 600.00 | 400.00 |
| ☐ 73 Vitamin Smith SP | 150.00 | 90.00 |
| ☐ 74 Joe Campanella RC | 40.00 | 25.00 |
| ☐ 75 Joe Kuharich SP CO | 50.00 | 30.00 |
| ☐ 76 Herman Clark | 40.00 | 25.00 |
| ☐ 77 Dan Edwards | 40.00 | 25.00 |
| ☐ 78 Bobby Layne | 300.00 | 175.00 |
| ☐ 79 Bob Hoernschemeyer | 50.00 | 30.00 |
| ☐ 80 John Carr Blount | 40.00 | 25.00 |
| ☐ 81 John Kastan RC SP | 150.00 | 90.00 |
| ☐ 82 Harry Minarik RC SP | 150.00 | 90.00 |
| ☐ 83 Joe Perry | 125.00 | 75.00 |
| ☐ 84 Buddy Parker RC CO | 50.00 | 30.00 |
| ☐ 85 Andy Robustelli RC | 200.00 | 125.00 |
| ☐ 86 Dub Jones | 50.00 | 30.00 |
| ☐ 87 Mal Cook | 40.00 | 25.00 |
| ☐ 88 Billy Stone | 40.00 | 25.00 |
| ☐ 89 George Taliaferro | 50.00 | 30.00 |
| ☐ 90 Thomas Johnson RC SP | 150.00 | 90.00 |
| ☐ 91 Leon Heath SP | 100.00 | 60.00 |
| ☐ 92 Pete Pihos | 100.00 | 60.00 |
| ☐ 93 Fred Benners | 40.00 | 25.00 |
| ☐ 94 George Tarasovic | 40.00 | 25.00 |
| ☐ 95 Buck Shaw RC CO | 50.00 | 30.00 |
| ☐ 96 Bill Wightkin | 40.00 | 25.00 |
| ☐ 97 John Wozniak | 40.00 | 25.00 |
| ☐ 98 Bobby Dillon RC | 50.00 | 30.00 |
| ☐ 99 Joe Stydahar RC SP CO! | 650.00 | 450.00 |
| ☐ 100 Dick Alban RC SP | 150.00 | 90.00 |
| ☐ 101 Arnie Weinmeister | 60.00 | 35.00 |
| ☐ 102 Bobby Cross | 40.00 | 25.00 |
| ☐ 103 Don Paul DB | 40.00 | 25.00 |
| ☐ 104 Buddy Young | 60.00 | 35.00 |
| ☐ 105 Lou Groza | 125.00 | 75.00 |
| ☐ 106 Ray Pelfrey | 40.00 | 25.00 |
| ☐ 107 Maurice Nipp | 40.00 | 25.00 |
| ☐ 108 Hubert Johnston RC SP! | 650.00 | 450.00 |
| ☐ 109 Vol.Quinlan RC SP | 100.00 | 60.00 |
| ☐ 110 Jack Simmons | 40.00 | 25.00 |
| ☐ 111 George Ratterman | 50.00 | 30.00 |
| ☐ 112 John Badaczewski | 40.00 | 25.00 |
| ☐ 113 Bill Reichardt | 40.00 | 25.00 |
| ☐ 114 Art Weiner | 40.00 | 25.00 |
| ☐ 115 Keith Flowers | 40.00 | 25.00 |
| ☐ 116 Russ Craft | 40.00 | 25.00 |
| ☐ 117 J.O'Donahue RC SP | 150.00 | 90.00 |
| ☐ 118 Darrell Hogan SP | 100.00 | 60.00 |
| ☐ 119 Frank Ziegler | 40.00 | 25.00 |
| ☐ 120 Dan Towler | 60.00 | 35.00 |
| ☐ 121 Fred Williams | 40.00 | 25.00 |
| ☐ 122 Jimmy Phelan CO | 40.00 | 25.00 |
| ☐ 123 Eddie Price | 40.00 | 25.00 |
| ☐ 124 Chet Ostrowski | 40.00 | 25.00 |
| ☐ 125 Leo Nomellini | 100.00 | 60.00 |
| ☐ 126 S.Romanik RC SP! | 300.00 | 200.00 |
| ☐ 127 Ollie Matson RC SP | 300.00 | 200.00 |
| ☐ 128 Dante Lavelli | 90.00 | -50.00 |
| ☐ 129 Jack Christiansen RC | 175.00 | 100.00 |
| ☐ 130 Dom Moselle | 40.00 | 25.00 |
| ☐ 131 John Rapacz | 40.00 | 25.00 |
| ☐ 132 Chuck Ortmann UER | 40.00 | 25.00 |
| ☐ 133 Bob Williams | 40.00 | 25.00 |
| ☐ 134 Chuck Ulrich | 40.00 | 25.00 |
| ☐ 135 Gene Ronzani CO SP RC! | 650.00 | 450.00 |
| ☐ 136 Bert Rechichar SP | 100.00 | 60.00 |
| ☐ 137 Bob Waterfield | 125.00 | 75.00 |
| ☐ 138 Bobby Walston SP | 50.00 | 30.00 |
| ☐ 139 Jerry Shipkey | 40.00 | 25.00 |
| ☐ 140 Yale Lary SP | 200.00 | 125.00 |
| ☐ 141 Gordy Soltau | 40.00 | 25.00 |
| ☐ 142 Tom Landry | 600.00 | 450.00 |
| ☐ 143 John Papit | 40.00 | 25.00 |
| ☐ 144 Jim Lansford RC SP! | 3000.00 | 1800.00 |

### 1952 Bowman Small

| | Price | |
|---|---|---|
| ☐ COMPLETE SET (144) | 5000.00 | 3500.00 |
| ☐ COMMON CARD (1-72) | 25.00 | 15.00 |
| ☐ COMMON CARD (73-144) | 30.00 | 18.00 |
| ☐ WRAPPER (1-CENT) | 60.00 | 40.00 |
| ☐ 1 Norm Van Brocklin ! | 350.00 | 200.00 |
| ☐ 2 Otto Graham | 200.00 | 125.00 |
| ☐ 3 Doak Walker | 60.00 | 30.00 |
| ☐ 4 Steve Owen RC CO | 60.00 | 35.00 |
| ☐ 5 Frankie Albert | 35.00 | 20.00 |
| ☐ 6 Laurie Niemi | 25.00 | 15.00 |
| ☐ 7 Chuck Hunsinger | 25.00 | 15.00 |
| ☐ 8 Ed Modzelewski | 35.00 | 20.00 |
| ☐ 9 Joe Spencer | 25.00 | 15.00 |
| ☐ 10 Chuck Bednarik | 75.00 | 45.00 |
| ☐ 11 Barney Poole | 25.00 | 15.00 |
| ☐ 12 Charley Trippi | 60.00 | 35.00 |
| ☐ 13 Tom Fears | 60.00 | 35.00 |
| ☐ 14 Paul Brown RC CO | 150.00 | 90.00 |
| ☐ 15 Leon Hart | 35.00 | 20.00 |
| ☐ 16 Frank Gifford RC | 400.00 | 200.00 |
| ☐ 17 Y.A.Tittle | 125.00 | 75.00 |
| ☐ 18 Charlie Justice | 45.00 | 30.00 |
| ☐ 19 George Connor | 35.00 | 20.00 |
| ☐ 20 Lynn Chandnois | 25.00 | 15.00 |
| ☐ 21 Billy Howton RC | 40.00 | 25.00 |
| ☐ 22 Kenneth Snyder | 25.00 | 15.00 |
| ☐ 23 Gino Marchetti RC | 125.00 | 75.00 |
| ☐ 24 John Karras | 25.00 | 15.00 |
| ☐ 25 Tank Younger | 35.00 | 20.00 |
| ☐ 26 Tommy Thompson LB | 25.00 | 15.00 |
| ☐ 27 Bob Miller RC | 25.00 | 15.00 |
| ☐ 28 Kyle Rote RC | 50.00 | 30.00 |
| ☐ 29 Hugh McElhenny RC | 175.00 | 100.00 |
| ☐ 30 Sammy Baugh | 250.00 | 150.00 |
| ☐ 31 Jim Dooley RC | 30.00 | 18.00 |
| ☐ 32 Ray Mathews | 25.00 | 15.00 |
| ☐ 33 Fred Cone | 25.00 | 15.00 |
| ☐ 34 Al Pollard | 25.00 | 15.00 |
| ☐ 35 Brad Ecklund | 25.00 | 15.00 |
| ☐ 36 John Lee Hancock | 25.00 | 15.00 |
| ☐ 37 Elroy Hirsch | 60.00 | 35.00 |
| ☐ 38 Keever Jankovich | 25.00 | -15.00 |
| ☐ 39 Emlen Tunnell | 50.00 | 30.00 |
| ☐ 40 Steve Dowden | 25.00 | 15.00 |
| ☐ 41 Claude Hipps | 25.00 | 15.00 |
| ☐ 42 Norm Standlee | 25.00 | 15.00 |
| ☐ 43 Dick Todd CO | 25.00 | 15.00 |
| ☐ 44 Babe Parilli | 35.00 | 20.00 |
| ☐ 45 Steve Van Buren | 75.00 | 40.00 |
| ☐ 46 Art Donovan RC | 200.00 | 125.00 |
| ☐ 47 Bill Fischer | 25.00 | 15.00 |
| ☐ 48 George Halas RC CO | 250.00 | 150.00 |
| ☐ 49 Jerrell Price | 25.00 | 15.00 |
| ☐ 50 John Sandusky RC | 25.00 | 15.00 |

| | | |
|---|---|---|
| ❑ 51 Ray Beck | 25.00 | 15.00 |
| ❑ 52 Jim Martin | 30.00 | 18.00 |
| ❑ 53 Joe Bach CO UER | 25.00 | 15.00 |
| ❑ 54 Glen Christian | 25.00 | 15.00 |
| ❑ 55 Andy Davis | 25.00 | 15.00 |
| ❑ 56 Tobin Rote | 25.00 | 15.00 |
| ❑ 57 Wayne Millner RC CO | 50.00 | 30.00 |
| ❑ 58 Zollie Toth | 25.00 | 15.00 |
| ❑ 59 Jack Jennings | 25.00 | 15.00 |
| ❑ 60 Bill McColl | 25.00 | 15.00 |
| ❑ 61 Les Richter RC | 30.00 | 18.00 |
| ❑ 62 Walt Michaels RC | 30.00 | 18.00 |
| ❑ 63 Charley Conerly | 75.00 | 40.00 |
| ❑ 64 Howard Hartley | 25.00 | 15.00 |
| ❑ 65 Jerome Smith | 25.00 | 15.00 |
| ❑ 66 James Clark | 25.00 | 15.00 |
| ❑ 67 Dick Logan | 25.00 | 15.00 |
| ❑ 68 Wayne Robinson | 25.00 | 15.00 |
| ❑ 69 James Hammond | 25.00 | 15.00 |
| ❑ 70 Gene Schroeder | 25.00 | 15.00 |
| ❑ 71 Tex Coulter | 30.00 | 18.00 |
| ❑ 72 John Schweder | 25.00 | 15.00 |
| ❑ 73 Vitamin Smith | 35.00 | 20.00 |
| ❑ 74 Joe Campanella RC | 30.00 | 18.00 |
| ❑ 75 Joe Kuharich RC CO | 35.00 | 20.00 |
| ❑ 76 Herman Clark | 30.00 | 18.00 |
| ❑ 77 Dan Edwards | 30.00 | 18.00 |
| ❑ 78 Bobby Layne | 150.00 | 90.00 |
| ❑ 79 Bob Hoernschemeyer | 35.00 | 20.00 |
| ❑ 80 John Carr Blount | 30.00 | 18.00 |
| ❑ 81 John Kastan RC | 30.00 | 18.00 |
| ❑ 82 Harry Minarik | 30.00 | 18.00 |
| ❑ 83 Joe Perry | 75.00 | 40.00 |
| ❑ 84 Buddy Parker RC CO | 35.00 | 20.00 |
| ❑ 85 Andy Robustelli RC | 125.00 | 75.00 |
| ❑ 86 Dub Jones | 35.00 | 20.00 |
| ❑ 87 Mal Cook | 30.00 | 18.00 |
| ❑ 88 Billy Stone | 30.00 | 18.00 |
| ❑ 89 George Taliaferro | 35.00 | 20.00 |
| ❑ 90 Thomas Johnson RC | 30.00 | 18.00 |
| ❑ 91 Leon Heath | 30.00 | 18.00 |
| ❑ 92 Pete Pihos | 50.00 | 35.00 |
| ❑ 93 Fred Benners | 30.00 | 18.00 |
| ❑ 94 George Tarasovic | 30.00 | 18.00 |
| ❑ 95 Buck Shaw RC CO | 30.00 | 18.00 |
| ❑ 96 Bill Wightkin | 30.00 | 18.00 |
| ❑ 97 John Wozniak | 30.00 | 18.00 |
| ❑ 98 Bobby Dillon RC | 35.00 | 20.00 |
| ❑ 99 Joe Stydahar RC CO | 45.00 | 30.00 |
| ❑ 100 Dick Alban RC | 30.00 | 18.00 |
| ❑ 101 Arnie Weinmeister | 40.00 | 25.00 |
| ❑ 102 Bobby Cross | 30.00 | 18.00 |
| ❑ 103 Don Paul DB | 30.00 | 18.00 |
| ❑ 104 Buddy Young | 40.00 | 25.00 |
| ❑ 105 Lou Groza | 75.00 | 45.00 |
| ❑ 106 Ray Pelfrey | 30.00 | 18.00 |
| ❑ 107 Maurice Nipp | 30.00 | 18.00 |
| ❑ 108 Hubert Johnston | 30.00 | 18.00 |
| ❑ 109 Volney Quinlan RC | 30.00 | 18.00 |
| ❑ 110 Jack Simmons | 30.00 | 18.00 |
| ❑ 111 George Ratterman | 35.00 | 20.00 |
| ❑ 112 John Badaczewski | 30.00 | 18.00 |
| ❑ 113 Bill Reichardt | 30.00 | 18.00 |
| ❑ 114 Art Weiner | 30.00 | 18.00 |
| ❑ 115 Keith Flowers | 30.00 | 18.00 |
| ❑ 116 Russ Craft | 30.00 | 18.00 |
| ❑ 117 Jim O'Donahue RC | 30.00 | 18.00 |
| ❑ 118 Darrell Hogan | 30.00 | 18.00 |
| ❑ 119 Frank Ziegler | 30.00 | 18.00 |
| ❑ 120 Dan Towler | 40.00 | 25.00 |
| ❑ 121 Fred Williams | 30.00 | 18.00 |
| ❑ 122 Jimmy Phelan CO | 30.00 | 18.00 |
| ❑ 123 Eddie Price | 30.00 | 18.00 |
| ❑ 124 Chet Ostrowski | 30.00 | 18.00 |
| ❑ 125 Leo Nomellini | 75.00 | 40.00 |
| ❑ 126 Steve Romanik | 30.00 | 18.00 |
| ❑ 127 Ollie Matson RC | 125.00 | 75.00 |
| ❑ 128 Dante Lavelli | 60.00 | 35.00 |
| ❑ 129 Jack Christiansen RC | 80.00 | 50.00 |
| ❑ 130 Dom Moselle | 30.00 | 18.00 |
| ❑ 131 John Rapacz | 30.00 | 18.00 |
| ❑ 132 Chuck Ortmann UER | 30.00 | 18.00 |
| ❑ 133 Bob Williams | 30.00 | 18.00 |
| ❑ 134 Chuck Ulrich | 30.00 | 18.00 |

| | | |
|---|---|---|
| ❑ 135 Gene Ronzani RC CO | 30.00 | 18.00 |
| ❑ 136 Bert Rechichar | 35.00 | 20.00 |
| ❑ 137 Bob Waterfield | 75.00 | 45.00 |
| ❑ 138 Bobby Walston RC | 35.00 | 20.00 |
| ❑ 139 Jerry Shipkey | 30.00 | 18.00 |
| ❑ 140 Yale Lary RC | 80.00 | 50.00 |
| ❑ 141 Gordy Soltau | 30.00 | 18.00 |
| ❑ 142 Tom Landry | 400.00 | 250.00 |
| ❑ 143 John Papit | 30.00 | 18.00 |
| ❑ 144 Jim Lansford RC ! | 175.00 | 100.00 |

## 1953 Bowman

| | | |
|---|---|---|
| ❑ COMPLETE SET (96) | 3400.00 | 2200.00 |
| ❑ WRAPPER (5-CENT) | 150.00 | 90.00 |
| ❑ 1 Eddie LeBaron RC ! | 125.00 | 75.00 |
| ❑ 2 John Dottley | 30.00 | 18.00 |
| ❑ 3 Babe Parilli | 35.00 | 20.00 |
| ❑ 4 Bucko Kilroy | 35.00 | 20.00 |
| ❑ 5 Joe Tereshinski | 30.00 | 18.00 |
| ❑ 6 Doak Walker | 75.00 | 45.00 |
| ❑ 7 Fran Polsfoot | 30.00 | 18.00 |
| ❑ 8 Sisto Averno | 30.00 | 18.00 |
| ❑ 9 Marion Motley | 75.00 | 45.00 |
| ❑ 10 Pat Brady | 30.00 | 18.00 |
| ❑ 11 Norm Van Brocklin | 125.00 | 75.00 |
| ❑ 12 Bill McColl | 30.00 | 18.00 |
| ❑ 13 Jerry Groom | 30.00 | 18.00 |
| ❑ 14 Al Pollard | 30.00 | 18.00 |
| ❑ 15 Dante Lavelli | 50.00 | 30.00 |
| ❑ 16 Eddie Price | 50.00 | 30.00 |
| ❑ 17 Charley Trippi | 50.00 | 30.00 |
| ❑ 18 Elbert Nickel | 35.00 | 20.00 |
| ❑ 19 George Taliaferro | 35.00 | 20.00 |
| ❑ 20 Charley Conerly | 80.00 | 50.00 |
| ❑ 21 Bobby Layne | 125.00 | 75.00 |
| ❑ 22 Elroy Hirsch | 100.00 | 60.00 |
| ❑ 23 Jim Finks | 40.00 | 25.00 |
| ❑ 24 Chuck Bednarik | 75.00 | 45.00 |
| ❑ 25 Kyle Rote | 40.00 | 25.00 |
| ❑ 26 Otto Graham | 175.00 | 100.00 |
| ❑ 27 Harry Gilmer | 35.00 | 20.00 |
| ❑ 28 Tobin Rote | 35.00 | 20.00 |
| ❑ 29 Billy Stone | 30.00 | 18.00 |
| ❑ 30 Buddy Young | 35.00 | 20.00 |
| ❑ 31 Leon Hart | 40.00 | 25.00 |
| ❑ 32 Hugh McElhenny | 75.00 | 45.00 |
| ❑ 33 Dale Samuels | 30.00 | 18.00 |
| ❑ 34 Lou Creekmur | 50.00 | 30.00 |
| ❑ 35 Tom Catlin | 30.00 | 18.00 |
| ❑ 36 Tom Fears | 60.00 | 35.00 |
| ❑ 37 George Connor | 40.00 | 25.00 |
| ❑ 38 Bill Walsh C | 30.00 | 18.00 |
| ❑ 39 Leo Sanford SP | 30.00 | 18.00 |
| ❑ 40 Horace Gillom | 35.00 | 20.00 |
| ❑ 41 John Schweder SP | 45.00 | 30.00 |
| ❑ 42 Tom O'Connell | 30.00 | 18.00 |
| ❑ 43 Frank Gifford SP | 300.00 | 175.00 |
| ❑ 44 Frank Continetti SP | 45.00 | 30.00 |
| ❑ 45 John Olszewski SP | 45.00 | 30.00 |
| ❑ 46 Dub Jones | 35.00 | 20.00 |
| ❑ 47 Don Paul LB SP | 45.00 | 30.00 |
| ❑ 48 Gerald Weatherly SP | 45.00 | 30.00 |
| ❑ 49 Fred Bruney SP | 45.00 | 30.00 |
| ❑ 50 Jack Scarbath | 30.00 | 18.00 |
| ❑ 51 John Karras | 30.00 | 18.00 |
| ❑ 52 Al Conway SP | 45.00 | 30.00 |
| ❑ 53 Emlen Tunnell SP | 125.00 | 75.00 |
| ❑ 54 Gern Nagler SP | 45.00 | 30.00 |

| | | |
|---|---|---|
| ❑ 55 Kenneth Snyder SP | 45.00 | 30.00 |
| ❑ 56 Y.A.Tittle | 150.00 | 90.00 |
| ❑ 57 John Rapacz SP | 45.00 | 30.00 |
| ❑ 58 Harley Sewell SP | 45.00 | 30.00 |
| ❑ 59 Don Bingham | 30.00 | 18.00 |
| ❑ 60 Darrell Hogan | 30.00 | 18.00 |
| ❑ 61 Tony Curcillo | 30.00 | 18.00 |
| ❑ 62 Ray Renfro RC SP | 50.00 | 30.00 |
| ❑ 63 Leon Heath | 30.00 | 18.00 |
| ❑ 64 Tex Coulter SP | 45.00 | 30.00 |
| ❑ 65 Dewayne Douglas | 30.00 | 18.00 |
| ❑ 66 J. Robert Smith SP | 45.00 | 30.00 |
| ❑ 67 Bob McChesney SP | 45.00 | 30.00 |
| ❑ 68 Dick Alban SP | 45.00 | 30.00 |
| ❑ 69 Andy Kozar | 30.00 | 18.00 |
| ❑ 70 Merwin Hodel SP | 45.00 | 30.00 |
| ❑ 71 Thurman McGraw | 30.00 | 18.00 |
| ❑ 72 Cliff Anderson | 30.00 | 18.00 |
| ❑ 73 Pete Pihos | 60.00 | 35.00 |
| ❑ 74 Julie Rykovich | 30.00 | 18.00 |
| ❑ 75 John Kreamcheck SP | 45.00 | 30.00 |
| ❑ 76 Lynn Chandnois | 30.00 | 18.00 |
| ❑ 77 Cloyce Box SP | 45.00 | 30.00 |
| ❑ 78 Ray Mathews | 30.00 | 18.00 |
| ❑ 79 Bobby Walston | 35.00 | 20.00 |
| ❑ 80 Jim Dooley | 30.00 | 18.00 |
| ❑ 81 Pat Harder SP | 45.00 | 30.00 |
| ❑ 82 Jerry Shipkey | 30.00 | 18.00 |
| ❑ 83 Bobby Thomason RC | 30.00 | 18.00 |
| ❑ 84 Hugh Taylor | 35.00 | 20.00 |
| ❑ 85 George Ratterman | 35.00 | 20.00 |
| ❑ 86 Don Stonesifer | 30.00 | 18.00 |
| ❑ 87 John Williams SP RC | 45.00 | 30.00 |
| ❑ 88 Leo Nomellini | 50.00 | 30.00 |
| ❑ 89 Frank Ziegler | 30.00 | 18.00 |
| ❑ 90 Don Paul DB UER | 30.00 | 18.00 |
| ❑ 91 Tom Dublinski | 30.00 | 18.00 |
| ❑ 92 Ken Carpenter | 30.00 | 18.00 |
| ❑ 93 Ted Marchibroda RC | 40.00 | 25.00 |
| ❑ 94 Chuck Drazenovich | 30.00 | 18.00 |
| ❑ 95 Lou Groza SP | 125.00 | 75.00 |
| ❑ 96 William Cross RC SP ! | 100.00 | 50.00 |

## 1954 Bowman

| | | |
|---|---|---|
| ❑ COMPLETE SET (128) | 1800.00 | 1200.00 |
| ❑ COMMON CARD (1-64) | 5.00 | 3.00 |
| ❑ COMMON SP (65-96) | 25.00 | 15.00 |
| ❑ COMMON CARD (97-128) | 5.00 | 3.00 |
| ❑ WRAPPER (1-CENT) | 15.00 | 10.00 |
| ❑ WRAPPER (5-CENT) | 30.00 | 25.00 |
| ❑ 1 Ray Mathews ! | 30.00 | 15.00 |
| ❑ 2 John Huzvar | 5.00 | 3.00 |
| ❑ 3 Jack Scarbath | 5.00 | 3.00 |
| ❑ 4 Doug Atkins RC | 50.00 | 30.00 |
| ❑ 5 Bill Stits | 5.00 | 3.00 |
| ❑ 6 Joe Perry | 30.00 | 18.00 |
| ❑ 7 Kyle Rote | 15.00 | 7.50 |
| ❑ 8 Norm Van Brocklin | 50.00 | 25.00 |
| ❑ 9 Pete Pihos | 20.00 | 12.00 |
| ❑ 10 Babe Parilli | 8.00 | 4.00 |
| ❑ 11 Zeke Bratkowski RC | 25.00 | 15.00 |
| ❑ 12 Ollie Matson | 25.00 | 15.00 |
| ❑ 13 Pat Brady | 5.00 | 3.00 |
| ❑ 14 Fred Enke | 5.00 | 3.00 |
| ❑ 15 Harry Ulinski | 5.00 | 3.00 |
| ❑ 16 Bob Garrett | 5.00 | 3.00 |
| ❑ 17 Bill Bowman | 5.00 | 3.00 |
| ❑ 18 Leo Rucka | 5.00 | 3.00 |

| | | |
|---|---|---|
| ☐ 19 John Cannady | 5.00 | 3.00 |
| ☐ 20 Tom Fears | 25.00 | 15.00 |
| ☐ 21 Norm Willey | 5.00 | 3.00 |
| ☐ 22 Floyd Reid | 5.00 | 3.00 |
| ☐ 23 George Blanda RC | 175.00 | 100.00 |
| ☐ 24 Don Doheney | 5.00 | 3.00 |
| ☐ 25 Don Schweder | 5.00 | 3.00 |
| ☐ 26 Bert Rechichar | 5.00 | 3.00 |
| ☐ 27 Harry Dowda | 5.00 | 3.00 |
| ☐ 28 John Sandusky | 5.00 | 3.00 |
| ☐ 29 Les Bingaman RC | 15.00 | 7.50 |
| ☐ 30 Joe Arenas | 5.00 | 3.00 |
| ☐ 31 Ray Wietecha RC | 5.00 | 3.00 |
| ☐ 32 Elroy Hirsch | 30.00 | 18.00 |
| ☐ 33 Harold Giancanelli | 5.00 | 3.00 |
| ☐ 34 Billy Howton | 8.00 | 4.00 |
| ☐ 35 Fred Morrison | 5.00 | 3.00 |
| ☐ 36 Bobby Cavazos | 5.00 | 3.00 |
| ☐ 37 Darrell Hogan | 5.00 | 3.00 |
| ☐ 38 Buddy Young | 8.00 | 4.00 |
| ☐ 39 Charlie Justice | 20.00 | 12.00 |
| ☐ 40 Otto Graham | 80.00 | 50.00 |
| ☐ 41 Doak Walker | 35.00 | 20.00 |
| ☐ 42 Y.A. Tittle | 60.00 | 35.00 |
| ☐ 43 Buford Long | 5.00 | 3.00 |
| ☐ 44 Volney Quinlan | 5.00 | 3.00 |
| ☐ 45 Bobby Thomason | 5.00 | 3.00 |
| ☐ 46 Fred Cone | 5.00 | 3.00 |
| ☐ 47 Gerald Weatherly | 5.00 | 3.00 |
| ☐ 48 Don Stonesifer | 5.00 | 3.00 |
| ☐ 49A Lynn Chandnois ERR | 5.00 | 3.00 |
| ☐ 49B Lynn Chandnois COR | 5.00 | 3.00 |
| ☐ 50 George Taliaferro | 5.00 | 3.00 |
| ☐ 51 Dick Alban | 5.00 | 3.00 |
| ☐ 52 Lou Groza | 35.00 | 20.00 |
| ☐ 53 Bobby Layne | 60.00 | 35.00 |
| ☐ 54 Hugh McElhenny | 40.00 | 20.00 |
| ☐ 55 Frank Gifford | 100.00 | 60.00 |
| ☐ 56 Leon McLaughlin | 5.00 | 3.00 |
| ☐ 57 Chuck Bednarik | 40.00 | 20.00 |
| ☐ 58 Art Hunter | 5.00 | 3.00 |
| ☐ 59 Bill McColl | 5.00 | 3.00 |
| ☐ 60 Charley Trippi | 25.00 | 15.00 |
| ☐ 61 Jim Finks | 15.00 | 7.50 |
| ☐ 62 Bill Lange G | 5.00 | 3.00 |
| ☐ 63 Laurie Niemi | 5.00 | 3.00 |
| ☐ 64 Ray Renfro | 8.00 | 4.00 |
| ☐ 65 Dick Chapman | 25.00 | 15.00 |
| ☐ 66 Bob Hantla | 25.00 | 15.00 |
| ☐ 67 Ralph Starkey | 25.00 | 15.00 |
| ☐ 68 Don Paul LB | 25.00 | 15.00 |
| ☐ 69 Kenneth Snyder | 25.00 | 15.00 |
| ☐ 70 Tobin Rote SP | 30.00 | 18.00 |
| ☐ 71 Art DeCarlo | 25.00 | 15.00 |
| ☐ 72 Tom Keane SP | 25.00 | 15.00 |
| ☐ 73 Hugh Taylor SP | 30.00 | 18.00 |
| ☐ 74 Warren Lahr RC SP | 30.00 | 18.00 |
| ☐ 75 Jim Neal | 25.00 | 15.00 |
| ☐ 76 Leo Nomellini SP | 60.00 | 35.00 |
| ☐ 77 Dick Yelvington | 25.00 | 15.00 |
| ☐ 78 Les Richter SP | 30.00 | 18.00 |
| ☐ 79 Bucko Kilroy SP | 30.00 | 18.00 |
| ☐ 80 John Martinkovic | 25.00 | 15.00 |
| ☐ 81 Dale Dodrill RC SP | 25.00 | 15.00 |
| ☐ 82 Ken Jackson | 25.00 | 15.00 |
| ☐ 83 Paul Lipscomb | 25.00 | 15.00 |
| ☐ 84 John Bauer | 25.00 | 15.00 |
| ☐ 85 Lou Creekmur SP | 50.00 | 30.00 |
| ☐ 86 Eddie Price | 25.00 | 15.00 |
| ☐ 87 Kenneth Farragut | 25.00 | 15.00 |
| ☐ 88 Dave Hanner RC SP | 30.00 | 18.00 |
| ☐ 89 Don Boll | 25.00 | 15.00 |
| ☐ 90 Chet Hanulak | 25.00 | 15.00 |
| ☐ 91 Thurman McGraw | 25.00 | 15.00 |
| ☐ 92 Don Heinrich RC SP | 30.00 | 18.00 |
| ☐ 93 Dan McKown | 25.00 | 15.00 |
| ☐ 94 Bob Fleck | 25.00 | 15.00 |
| ☐ 95 Jerry Hilgenberg | 25.00 | 15.00 |
| ☐ 96 Bill Walsh C | 25.00 | 15.00 |
| ☐ 97A Tom Finnin ERR | 60.00 | 35.00 |
| ☐ 97B Tom Finnan COR | 8.00 | 4.00 |
| ☐ 98 Paul Barry | 5.00 | 3.00 |
| ☐ 99 Chick Jagade | 5.00 | 3.00 |
| ☐ 100 Jack Christiansen | 20.00 | 12.00 |

| | | |
|---|---|---|
| ☐ 101 Gordy Soltau | 5.00 | 3.00 |
| ☐ 102A Emlen Tunnell ERR | 20.00 | 12.00 |
| ☐ 102B Emlen Tunnell COR | 20.00 | 12.00 |
| ☐ 102C Emlen Tunnell COR | 20.00 | 12.00 |
| ☐ 103 Stan West | 5.00 | 3.00 |
| ☐ 104 Jerry Williams | 5.00 | 3.00 |
| ☐ 105 Veryl Switzer | 5.00 | 3.00 |
| ☐ 106 Billy Stone | 5.00 | 3.00 |
| ☐ 107 Jerry Watford | 5.00 | 3.00 |
| ☐ 108 Elbert Nickel | 8.00 | 4.00 |
| ☐ 109 Ed Sharkey | 5.00 | 3.00 |
| ☐ 110 Steve Meilinger | 5.00 | 3.00 |
| ☐ 111 Dante Lavelli | 20.00 | 12.00 |
| ☐ 112 Leon Hart | 15.00 | 7.50 |
| ☐ 113 Charley Conerly | 30.00 | 18.00 |
| ☐ 114 Richard Lemmon | 5.00 | 3.00 |
| ☐ 115 Al Carmichael | 5.00 | 3.00 |
| ☐ 116 George Connor | 20.00 | 12.00 |
| ☐ 117 John Olszewski | 5.00 | 3.00 |
| ☐ 118 Ernie Stautner | 25.00 | 15.00 |
| ☐ 119 Ray Smith | 5.00 | 3.00 |
| ☐ 120 Neil Worden | 5.00 | 3.00 |
| ☐ 121 Jim Dooley | 5.00 | 3.00 |
| ☐ 122 Arnold Galiffa | 5.00 | 3.00 |
| ☐ 123 Kline Gilbert | 5.00 | 3.00 |
| ☐ 124 Bob Hoernschemeyer | 8.00 | 4.00 |
| ☐ 125 Wilford White RC | 15.00 | 7.50 |
| ☐ 126 Art Spinney | 5.00 | 3.00 |
| ☐ 127 Joe Koch | 5.00 | 3.00 |
| ☐ 128 John Lattner RC ! | 80.00 | 40.00 |

## 1955 Bowman

| | | |
|---|---|---|
| ☐ COMPLETE SET (160) | 1600.00 | 1000.00 |
| ☐ COMMON CARD (1-64) | 5.00 | 3.00 |
| ☐ COMMON CARD (65-160) | 8.00 | 5.00 |
| ☐ WRAPPER (1-CENT) | 225.00 | 150.00 |
| ☐ WRAPPER (5-CENT) | 120.00 | 60.00 |
| ☐ 1 Doak Walker ! | 75.00 | 40.00 |
| ☐ 2 Mike McCormack RC | 30.00 | 18.00 |
| ☐ 3 John Olszewski | 5.00 | 3.00 |
| ☐ 4 Dorne Dibble | 5.00 | 3.00 |
| ☐ 5 Lindon Crow | 5.00 | 3.00 |
| ☐ 6 Hugh Taylor UER | 8.00 | 4.00 |
| ☐ 7 Frank Gifford | 75.00 | 45.00 |
| ☐ 8 Alan Ameche RC | 40.00 | 25.00 |
| ☐ 9 Don Stonesifer | 5.00 | 3.00 |
| ☐ 10 Pete Pihos | 15.00 | 7.50 |
| ☐ 11 Bill Austin | 5.00 | 3.00 |
| ☐ 12 Dick Alban | 5.00 | 3.00 |
| ☐ 13 Bobby Walston | 8.00 | 4.00 |
| ☐ 14 Len Ford RC | 40.00 | 25.00 |
| ☐ 15 Jug Girard | 5.00 | 3.00 |
| ☐ 16 Charley Conerly | 25.00 | 15.00 |
| ☐ 17 Volney Peters | 5.00 | 3.00 |
| ☐ 18 Max Boydston | 5.00 | 3.00 |
| ☐ 19 Leon Hart | 12.00 | 6.00 |
| ☐ 20 Bert Rechichar | 5.00 | 3.00 |
| ☐ 21 Lee Riley | 5.00 | 3.00 |
| ☐ 22 Johnny Carson | 5.00 | 3.00 |
| ☐ 23 Harry Thompson | 5.00 | 3.00 |
| ☐ 24 Ray Wietecha | 5.00 | 3.00 |
| ☐ 25 Ollie Matson | 25.00 | 15.00 |
| ☐ 26 Eddie LeBaron | 15.00 | 7.50 |
| ☐ 27 Jack Simmons | 5.00 | 3.00 |
| ☐ 28 Jack Christiansen | 15.00 | 7.50 |
| ☐ 29 Bucko Kilroy | 8.00 | 4.00 |
| ☐ 30 Tom Keane | 5.00 | 3.00 |
| ☐ 31 Dave Leggett | 5.00 | 3.00 |

| | | |
|---|---|---|
| ☐ 32 Norm Van Brocklin | 40.00 | 25.00 |
| ☐ 33 Harlon Hill RC | 8.00 | 4.00 |
| ☐ 34 Robert Haner | 5.00 | 3.00 |
| ☐ 35 Veryl Switzer | 5.00 | 3.00 |
| ☐ 36 Dick Stanfel RC | 12.00 | 6.00 |
| ☐ 37 Lou Groza | 25.00 | 15.00 |
| ☐ 38 Tank Younger | 12.00 | 6.00 |
| ☐ 39 Dick Flanagan | 5.00 | 3.00 |
| ☐ 40 Jim Dooley | 5.00 | 3.00 |
| ☐ 41 Ray Collins | 5.00 | 3.00 |
| ☐ 42 John Henry Johnson RC | 40.00 | 25.00 |
| ☐ 43 Tom Fears | 15.00 | 7.50 |
| ☐ 44 Joe Perry | 30.00 | 18.00 |
| ☐ 45 Gene Brito RC | 5.00 | 3.00 |
| ☐ 46 Bill Johnson C | 5.00 | 3.00 |
| ☐ 47 Dan Towler | 12.00 | 6.00 |
| ☐ 48 Dick Moegle | 8.00 | 4.00 |
| ☐ 49 Kline Gilbert | 5.00 | 3.00 |
| ☐ 50 Les Gobel | 5.00 | 3.00 |
| ☐ 51 Ray Krouse RC | 5.00 | 3.00 |
| ☐ 52 Pat Summerall ! | 70.00 | 35.00 |
| ☐ 53 Ed Brown RC | 12.00 | 6.00 |
| ☐ 54 Lynn Chandnois | 5.00 | 3.00 |
| ☐ 55 Joe Heap | 5.00 | 3.00 |
| ☐ 56 John Hoffman | 5.00 | 3.00 |
| ☐ 57 Howard Ferguson | 5.00 | 3.00 |
| ☐ 58 Bobby Watkins | 5.00 | 3.00 |
| ☐ 59 Charlie Ane RC | 5.00 | 3.00 |
| ☐ 60 Ken MacAfee E RC | 8.00 | 4.00 |
| ☐ 61 Ralph Guglielmi RC | 8.00 | 4.00 |
| ☐ 62 George Blanda | 60.00 | 35.00 |
| ☐ 63 Kenneth Snyder | 5.00 | 3.00 |
| ☐ 64 Chet Ostrowski | 5.00 | 3.00 |
| ☐ 65 Buddy Young | 15.00 | 7.50 |
| ☐ 66 Gordy Soltau | 8.00 | 5.00 |
| ☐ 67 Eddie Bell | 8.00 | 5.00 |
| ☐ 68 Ben Agajanian RC | 12.00 | 6.00 |
| ☐ 69 Tom Dahms | 8.00 | 5.00 |
| ☐ 70 Jim Ringo RC | 50.00 | 30.00 |
| ☐ 71 Bobby Layne | 75.00 | 45.00 |
| ☐ 72 Y.A.Tittle | 75.00 | 45.00 |
| ☐ 73 Bob Gaona | 8.00 | 5.00 |
| ☐ 74 Tobin Rote | 12.00 | 6.00 |
| ☐ 75 Hugh McElhenny | 30.00 | 18.00 |
| ☐ 76 John Kreamcheck | 8.00 | 5.00 |
| ☐ 77 Al Dorow | 12.00 | 6.00 |
| ☐ 78 Bill Wade | 15.00 | 7.50 |
| ☐ 79 Dale Dodrill | 8.00 | 5.00 |
| ☐ 80 Chuck Drazenovich | 8.00 | 5.00 |
| ☐ 81 Billy Wilson RC | 12.00 | 6.00 |
| ☐ 82 Les Richter | 12.00 | 6.00 |
| ☐ 83 Pat Brady | 8.00 | 5.00 |
| ☐ 84 Bob Hoernschemeyer | 12.00 | 6.00 |
| ☐ 85 Joe Arenas | 8.00 | 5.00 |
| ☐ 86 Len Szalaryn UER | 8.00 | 5.00 |
| ☐ 87 Rick Casares RC | 20.00 | 12.00 |
| ☐ 88 Leon McLaughlin | 8.00 | 5.00 |
| ☐ 89 Charley Toogood | 8.00 | 5.00 |
| ☐ 90 Tom Bettis | 8.00 | 5.00 |
| ☐ 91 John Sandusky | 8.00 | 5.00 |
| ☐ 92 Bill Wightkin | 8.00 | 5.00 |
| ☐ 93 Darrel Brewster | 8.00 | 5.00 |
| ☐ 94 Marion Campbell | 15.00 | 7.50 |
| ☐ 95 Floyd Reid | 8.00 | 5.00 |
| ☐ 96 Chick Jagade | 8.00 | 5.00 |
| ☐ 97 George Taliaferro | 8.00 | 5.00 |
| ☐ 98 Carlton Massey | 8.00 | 5.00 |
| ☐ 99 Fran Rogel | 8.00 | 5.00 |
| ☐ 100 Alex Sandusky | 8.00 | 5.00 |
| ☐ 101 Bob St.Clair RC | 35.00 | 20.00 |
| ☐ 102 Al Carmichael | 8.00 | 5.00 |
| ☐ 103 Carl Taseff RC | 8.00 | 5.00 |
| ☐ 104 Leo Nomellini | 25.00 | 15.00 |
| ☐ 105 Tom Scott | 8.00 | 5.00 |
| ☐ 106 Ted Marchibroda | 15.00 | 7.50 |
| ☐ 107 Art Spinney | 8.00 | 5.00 |
| ☐ 108 Wayne Robinson | 8.00 | 5.00 |
| ☐ 109 Jim Ricca | 8.00 | 5.00 |
| ☐ 110 Lou Ferry | 8.00 | 5.00 |
| ☐ 111 Roger Zatkoff | 8.00 | 5.00 |
| ☐ 112 Lou Creekmur | 15.00 | 7.50 |
| ☐ 113 Kenny Konz | 8.00 | 5.00 |
| ☐ 114 Doug Eggers | 8.00 | 5.00 |
| ☐ 115 Bobby Thomason | 8.00 | 5.00 |

| | | |
|---|---|---|
| ❏ 116 Bill McPeak | 8.00 | 5.00 |
| ❏ 117 William Brown | 8.00 | 5.00 |
| ❏ 118 Royce Womble | 8.00 | 5.00 |
| ❏ 119 Frank Gatski RC | 35.00 | 20.00 |
| ❏ 120 Jim Finks | 15.00 | 7.50 |
| ❏ 121 Andy Robustelli | 25.00 | 15.00 |
| ❏ 122 Bobby Dillon | 8.00 | 5.00 |
| ❏ 123 Leo Sanford | 8.00 | 5.00 |
| ❏ 124 Elbert Nickel | 12.00 | 6.00 |
| ❏ 125 Wayne Hansen | 8.00 | 5.00 |
| ❏ 126 Buck Lansford RC | 8.00 | 5.00 |
| ❏ 127 Gern Nagler | 8.00 | 5.00 |
| ❏ 128 Jim Salsbury | 8.00 | 5.00 |
| ❏ 129 Dale Atkeson RC | 8.00 | 5.00 |
| ❏ 130 John Schweder | 8.00 | 5.00 |
| ❏ 131 Dave Hanner | 12.00 | 6.00 |
| ❏ 132 Eddie Price | 8.00 | 5.00 |
| ❏ 133 Vic Janowicz | 30.00 | 15.00 |
| ❏ 134 Ernie Stautner | 25.00 | 15.00 |
| ❏ 135 James Parmer | 8.00 | 5.00 |
| ❏ 136 Emlen Tunnell UER | 20.00 | 12.00 |
| ❏ 137 Kyle Rote | 15.00 | 7.50 |
| ❏ 138 Norm Willey | 8.00 | 5.00 |
| ❏ 139 Charley Trippi | 20.00 | 12.00 |
| ❏ 140 Billy Howton | 12.00 | 6.00 |
| ❏ 141 Bobby Clatterbuck | 8.00 | 5.00 |
| ❏ 142 Bob Boyd | 8.00 | 5.00 |
| ❏ 143 Bob Toneff RC | 12.00 | 6.00 |
| ❏ 144 Jerry Helluin | 8.00 | 5.00 |
| ❏ 145 Adrian Burk | 8.00 | 5.00 |
| ❏ 146 Walt Michaels | 12.00 | 6.00 |
| ❏ 147 Zollie Toth | 8.00 | 5.00 |
| ❏ 148 Frank Varrichione RC | 8.00 | 5.00 |
| ❏ 149 Dick Bielski RC | 8.00 | 5.00 |
| ❏ 150 George Ratterman | 12.00 | 6.00 |
| ❏ 151 Mike Jarmoluk | 8.00 | 5.00 |
| ❏ 152 Tom Landry | 200.00 | 125.00 |
| ❏ 153 Ray Renfro | 12.00 | 6.00 |
| ❏ 154 Zeke Bratkowski | 12.00 | 6.00 |
| ❏ 155 Jerry Norton | 8.00 | 5.00 |
| ❏ 156 Maurice Bassett | 8.00 | 5.00 |
| ❏ 157 Volney Quinlan | 8.00 | 5.00 |
| ❏ 158 Chuck Bednarik | 30.00 | 18.00 |
| ❏ 159 Don Colo | 8.00 | 5.00 |
| ❏ 160 L.G. Dupre RC ! | 40.00 | 20.00 |

## 1991 Bowman

THURMAN THOMAS

| | | |
|---|---|---|
| ❏ COMPLETE SET (561) | 12.00 | 5.00 |
| ❏ COMP.FACT.SET (561) | 12.00 | 5.00 |
| ❏ 1 Jeff George RS | .25 | .08 |
| ❏ 2 Richmond Webb RS | .05 | .01 |
| ❏ 3 Emmitt Smith RS | 1.25 | .50 |
| ❏ 4 Mark Carrier DB RS UER | .05 | .01 |
| ❏ 5 Steve Christie RS | .05 | .01 |
| ❏ 6 Keith Sims RS | .05 | .01 |
| ❏ 7 Rob Moore RS UER | .25 | .08 |
| ❏ 8 Johnny Johnson RS | .05 | .01 |
| ❏ 9 Eric Green RS | .05 | .01 |
| ❏ 10 Ben Smith RS | .05 | .01 |
| ❏ 11 Tory Epps RS | .05 | .01 |
| ❏ 12 Andre Rison | .10 | .02 |
| ❏ 13 Shawn Collins | .05 | .01 |
| ❏ 14 Chris Hinton | .05 | .01 |
| ❏ 15 Deion Sanders | .40 | .15 |
| ❏ 16 Darion Conner | .05 | .01 |
| ❏ 17 Michael Haynes | .25 | .08 |
| ❏ 18 Chris Miller | .10 | .02 |
| ❏ 19 Jessie Tuggle | .05 | .01 |

| | | |
|---|---|---|
| ❏ 20 Scott Fulhage | .05 | .01 |
| ❏ 21 Bill Fralic | .05 | .01 |
| ❏ 22 Floyd Dixon | .05 | .01 |
| ❏ 23 Oliver Barnett | .05 | .01 |
| ❏ 24 Mike Rozier | .05 | .01 |
| ❏ 25 Tory Epps | .05 | .01 |
| ❏ 26 Tim Green | .05 | .01 |
| ❏ 27 Steve Broussard | .05 | .01 |
| ❏ 28 Bruce Pickens RC | .05 | .01 |
| ❏ 29 Mike Pritchard RC | .25 | .08 |
| ❏ 30 Andre Reed | .10 | .02 |
| ❏ 31 Darryl Talley | .05 | .01 |
| ❏ 32 Nate Odomes | .05 | .01 |
| ❏ 33 Jamie Mueller | .05 | .01 |
| ❏ 34 Leon Seals | .05 | .01 |
| ❏ 35 Keith McKeller | .05 | .01 |
| ❏ 36 Al Edwards | .05 | .01 |
| ❏ 37 Butch Rolle | .05 | .01 |
| ❏ 38 Jeff Wright RC | .05 | .01 |
| ❏ 39 Will Wolford | .05 | .01 |
| ❏ 40 James Williams | .05 | .01 |
| ❏ 41 Kent Hull | .05 | .01 |
| ❏ 42 James Lofton | .10 | .02 |
| ❏ 43 Frank Reich | .10 | .02 |
| ❏ 44 Bruce Smith | .25 | .08 |
| ❏ 45 Thurman Thomas | .25 | .08 |
| ❏ 46 Leonard Smith | .05 | .01 |
| ❏ 47 Shane Conlan | .05 | .01 |
| ❏ 48 Steve Tasker | .10 | .02 |
| ❏ 49 Ray Bentley | .05 | .01 |
| ❏ 50 Cornelius Bennett | .10 | .02 |
| ❏ 51 Stan Thomas | .05 | .01 |
| ❏ 52 Shaun Gayle | .05 | .01 |
| ❏ 53 Wendell Davis | .05 | .01 |
| ❏ 54 James Thornton | .05 | .01 |
| ❏ 55 Mark Carrier DB | .10 | .02 |
| ❏ 56 Richard Dent | .10 | .02 |
| ❏ 57 Ron Morris | .05 | .01 |
| ❏ 58 Mike Singletary | .10 | .02 |
| ❏ 59 Jay Hilgenberg | .05 | .01 |
| ❏ 60 Donnell Woolford | .05 | .01 |
| ❏ 61 Jim Covert | .05 | .01 |
| ❏ 62 Jim Harbaugh | .25 | .08 |
| ❏ 63 Neal Anderson | .10 | .02 |
| ❏ 64 Brad Muster | .05 | .01 |
| ❏ 65 Kevin Butler | .05 | .01 |
| ❏ 66 Trace Armstrong UER | .05 | .01 |
| ❏ 67 Ron Cox | .05 | .01 |
| ❏ 68 Peter Tom Willis | .05 | .01 |
| ❏ 69 Johnny Bailey | .05 | .01 |
| ❏ 70 Mark Bortz UER | .05 | .01 |
| ❏ 71 Chris Zorich RC | .25 | .08 |
| ❏ 72 Lamar Rogers RC | .05 | .01 |
| ❏ 73 David Grant UER | .05 | .01 |
| ❏ 74 Lewis Billups | .05 | .01 |
| ❏ 75 Harold Green | .10 | .02 |
| ❏ 76 Ickey Woods | .05 | .01 |
| ❏ 77 Eddie Brown | .05 | .01 |
| ❏ 78 David Fulcher | .05 | .01 |
| ❏ 79 Anthony Munoz | .10 | .02 |
| ❏ 80 Carl Zander | .05 | .01 |
| ❏ 81 Rodney Holman | .05 | .01 |
| ❏ 82 James Brooks | .10 | .02 |
| ❏ 83 Tim McGee | .05 | .01 |
| ❏ 84 Boomer Esiason | .10 | .02 |
| ❏ 85 Leon White | .05 | .01 |
| ❏ 86 James Francis UER | .05 | .01 |
| ❏ 87 Mitchell Price RC | .05 | .01 |
| ❏ 88 Ed King RC | .05 | .01 |
| ❏ 89 Eric Turner RC | .10 | .02 |
| ❏ 90 Rob Burnett RC | .10 | .02 |
| ❏ 91 Leroy Hoard | .10 | .02 |
| ❏ 92 Kevin Mack UER | .05 | .01 |
| ❏ 93 Thane Gash UER | .05 | .01 |
| ❏ 94 Gregg Rakoczy | .05 | .01 |
| ❏ 95 Clay Matthews | .10 | .02 |
| ❏ 96 Eric Metcalf | .10 | .02 |
| ❏ 97 Stephen Braggs | .05 | .01 |
| ❏ 98 Frank Minnifield | .05 | .01 |
| ❏ 99 Reggie Langhorne | .05 | .01 |
| ❏ 100 Mike Johnson | .05 | .01 |
| ❏ 101 Brian Brennan | .05 | .01 |
| ❏ 102 Anthony Pleasant | .05 | .01 |
| ❏ 103 Godfrey Myles RC UER | .05 | .01 |

| | | |
|---|---|---|
| ❏ 104 Russell Maryland RC | .25 | .08 |
| ❏ 105 James Washington RC | .05 | .01 |
| ❏ 106 Nate Newton | .10 | .02 |
| ❏ 107 Jimmie Jones | .05 | .01 |
| ❏ 108 Jay Novacek | .25 | .08 |
| ❏ 109 Alexander Wright | .05 | .01 |
| ❏ 110 Jack Del Rio | .10 | .02 |
| ❏ 111 Jim Jeffcoat | .05 | .01 |
| ❏ 112 Mike Saxon | .05 | .01 |
| ❏ 113 Troy Aikman | .75 | .30 |
| ❏ 114 Issiac Holt | .05 | .01 |
| ❏ 115 Ken Norton | .10 | .02 |
| ❏ 116 Kelvin Martin | .05 | .01 |
| ❏ 117 Emmitt Smith | 2.50 | 1.00 |
| ❏ 118 Ken Willis | .05 | .01 |
| ❏ 119 Daniel Stubbs | .05 | .01 |
| ❏ 120 Michael Irvin | .25 | .08 |
| ❏ 121 Danny Noonan | .05 | .01 |
| ❏ 122 Alvin Harper RC | .25 | .08 |
| ❏ 123 Reggie Johnson RC | .05 | .01 |
| ❏ 124 Vance Johnson | .05 | .01 |
| ❏ 125 Steve Atwater | .05 | .01 |
| ❏ 126 Greg Kragen | .05 | .01 |
| ❏ 127 John Elway | 1.25 | .50 |
| ❏ 128 Simon Fletcher | .05 | .01 |
| ❏ 129 Wymon Henderson | .05 | .01 |
| ❏ 130 Ricky Nattiel | .05 | .01 |
| ❏ 131 Shannon Sharpe | .50 | .20 |
| ❏ 132 Ron Holmes | .05 | .01 |
| ❏ 133 Karl Mecklenburg | .05 | .01 |
| ❏ 134 Bobby Humphrey | .05 | .01 |
| ❏ 135 Clarence Kay | .05 | .01 |
| ❏ 136 Dennis Smith | .05 | .01 |
| ❏ 137 Jim Juriga | .05 | .01 |
| ❏ 138 Melvin Bratton | .05 | .01 |
| ❏ 139 Mark Jackson UER | .05 | .01 |
| ❏ 140 Michael Brooks | .05 | .01 |
| ❏ 141 Alton Montgomery | .05 | .01 |
| ❏ 142 Mike Croel RC | .05 | .01 |
| ❏ 143 Mel Gray | .10 | .02 |
| ❏ 144 Michael Cofer | .05 | .01 |
| ❏ 145 Jeff Campbell | .05 | .01 |
| ❏ 146 Dan Owens | .05 | .01 |
| ❏ 147 Robert Clark UER | .05 | .01 |
| ❏ 148 Jim Arnold | .05 | .01 |
| ❏ 149 William White | .05 | .01 |
| ❏ 150 Rodney Peete | .10 | .02 |
| ❏ 151 Jerry Ball | .05 | .01 |
| ❏ 152 Bennie Blades | .05 | .01 |
| ❏ 153 Barry Sanders RC | 1.25 | .50 |
| ❏ 154 Andre Ware | .10 | .02 |
| ❏ 155 Lomas Brown | .05 | .01 |
| ❏ 156 Chris Spielman | .10 | .02 |
| ❏ 157 Kelvin Pritchett RC | .10 | .02 |
| ❏ 158 Herman Moore RC | .25 | .08 |
| ❏ 159 Chris Jacke | .05 | .01 |
| ❏ 160 Tony Mandarich | .05 | .01 |
| ❏ 161 Perry Kemp | .05 | .01 |
| ❏ 162 Johnny Holland | .05 | .01 |
| ❏ 163 Mark Lee | .05 | .01 |
| ❏ 164 Anthony Dilweg | .05 | .01 |
| ❏ 165 Scott Stephen RC | .05 | .01 |
| ❏ 166 Ed West | .05 | .01 |
| ❏ 167 Mark Murphy | .05 | .01 |
| ❏ 168 Darrell Thompson | .05 | .01 |
| ❏ 169 James Campen RC | .05 | .01 |
| ❏ 170 Jeff Query | .05 | .01 |
| ❏ 171 Brian Noble | .05 | .01 |
| ❏ 172 Sterling Sharpe UER | .25 | .08 |
| ❏ 173 Robert Brown | .05 | .01 |
| ❏ 174 Tim Harris | .05 | .01 |
| ❏ 175 LeRoy Butler | .10 | .02 |
| ❏ 176 Don Majkowski | .05 | .01 |
| ❏ 177 Vinnie Clark RC | .05 | .01 |
| ❏ 178 Esera Tuaolo RC | .05 | .01 |
| ❏ 179 Lorenzo White UER | .05 | .01 |
| ❏ 180 Warren Moon | .25 | .08 |
| ❏ 181 Sean Jones | .10 | .02 |
| ❏ 182 Curtis Duncan | .05 | .01 |
| ❏ 183 Al Smith | .05 | .01 |
| ❏ 184 Richard Johnson CB RC | .05 | .01 |
| ❏ 185 Tony Jones WR | .05 | .01 |
| ❏ 186 Bubba McDowell | .05 | .01 |
| ❏ 187 Bruce Matthews | .10 | .02 |

|  | | |
|---|---|---|
| ❑ 188 Ray Childress | .05 | .01 |
| ❑ 189 Haywood Jeffires | .10 | .02 |
| ❑ 190 Ernest Givins | .10 | .02 |
| ❑ 191 Mike Munchak | .10 | .02 |
| ❑ 192 Greg Montgomery | .05 | .01 |
| ❑ 193 Cody Carlson RC | .05 | .01 |
| ❑ 194 Johnny Meads | .05 | .01 |
| ❑ 195 Drew Hill UER | .05 | .01 |
| ❑ 196 Mike Dumas RC | .05 | .01 |
| ❑ 197 Darryll Lewis RC | .10 | .02 |
| ❑ 198 Rohn Stark | .05 | .01 |
| ❑ 199 Clarence Verdin UER | .05 | .01 |
| ❑ 200 Mike Prior | .05 | .01 |
| ❑ 201 Eugane Daniel | .05 | .01 |
| ❑ 202 Dean Biasucci | .05 | .01 |
| ❑ 203 Jeff Herrod | .05 | .01 |
| ❑ 204 Keith Taylor | .05 | .01 |
| ❑ 205 Jon Hand | .05 | .01 |
| ❑ 206 Pat Beach | .05 | .01 |
| ❑ 207 Duane Bickett | .05 | .01 |
| ❑ 208 Jessie Hester UER | .05 | .01 |
| ❑ 209 Chip Banks | .05 | .01 |
| ❑ 210 Ray Donaldson | .05 | .01 |
| ❑ 211 Bill Brooks | .05 | .01 |
| ❑ 212 Jeff George | .25 | .08 |
| ❑ 213 Tony Siragusa RC | .10 | .02 |
| ❑ 214 Albert Bentley | .05 | .01 |
| ❑ 215 Joe Valerio | .05 | .01 |
| ❑ 216 Chris Martin | .05 | .01 |
| ❑ 217 Christian Okoye | .05 | .01 |
| ❑ 218 Stephone Paige | .05 | .01 |
| ❑ 219 Percy Snow | .05 | .01 |
| ❑ 220 David Szott | .05 | .01 |
| ❑ 221 Derrick Thomas | .25 | .08 |
| ❑ 222 Todd McNair | .05 | .01 |
| ❑ 223 Albert Lewis | .05 | .01 |
| ❑ 224 Neil Smith | .25 | .08 |
| ❑ 225 Barry Word | .05 | .01 |
| ❑ 226 Robb Thomas | .05 | .01 |
| ❑ 227 John Alt | .05 | .01 |
| ❑ 228 Jonathan Hayes | .05 | .01 |
| ❑ 229 Kevin Ross | .05 | .01 |
| ❑ 230 Nick Lowery | .05 | .01 |
| ❑ 231 Tim Grunhard | .05 | .01 |
| ❑ 232 Dan Saleaumua | .05 | .01 |
| ❑ 233 Steve DeBerg | .05 | .01 |
| ❑ 234 Harvey Williams RC | .25 | .08 |
| ❑ 235 Nick Bell RC UER | .05 | .01 |
| ❑ 236 Mervyn Fernandez UER | .05 | .01 |
| ❑ 237 Howie Long | .25 | .08 |
| ❑ 238 Marcus Allen | .25 | .08 |
| ❑ 239 Eddie Anderson | .05 | .01 |
| ❑ 240 Ethan Horton | .05 | .01 |
| ❑ 241 Lionel Washington | .05 | .01 |
| ❑ 242 Steve Wisniewski UER | .05 | .01 |
| ❑ 243 Bo Jackson RC | .30 | .10 |
| ❑ 244 Greg Townsend | .05 | .01 |
| ❑ 245 Jeff Jaeger | .05 | .01 |
| ❑ 246 Aaron Wallace | .05 | .01 |
| ❑ 247 Garry Lewis | .05 | .01 |
| ❑ 248 Steve Smith | .05 | .01 |
| ❑ 249 Willie Gault UER | .05 | .01 |
| ❑ 250 Scott Davis | .05 | .01 |
| ❑ 251 Jay Schroeder | .05 | .01 |
| ❑ 252 Don Mosebar | .05 | .01 |
| ❑ 253 Todd Marinovich RC | .05 | .01 |
| ❑ 254 Irv Pankey | .05 | .01 |
| ❑ 255 Flipper Anderson | .05 | .01 |
| ❑ 256 Tom Newberry | .05 | .01 |
| ❑ 257 Kevin Greene | .10 | .02 |
| ❑ 258 Mike Wilcher | .05 | .01 |
| ❑ 259 Bern Brostek | .05 | .01 |
| ❑ 260 Buford McGee | .05 | .01 |
| ❑ 261 Cleveland Gary | .05 | .01 |
| ❑ 262 Jackie Slater | .05 | .01 |
| ❑ 263 Henry Ellard | .10 | .02 |
| ❑ 264 Alvin Wright | .05 | .01 |
| ❑ 265 Darryl Henley RC | .05 | .01 |
| ❑ 266 Damone Johnson RC | .05 | .01 |
| ❑ 267 Frank Stams | .05 | .01 |
| ❑ 268 Jerry Gray | .05 | .01 |
| ❑ 269 Jim Everett | .10 | .02 |
| ❑ 270 Pat Terrell | .05 | .01 |
| ❑ 271 Todd Lyght RC | .05 | .01 |
| ❑ 272 Aaron Cox | .05 | .01 |
| ❑ 273 Barry Sanders LL | .50 | .20 |
| ❑ 274 Jerry Rice LL | .40 | .15 |
| ❑ 275 Derrick Thomas LL | .25 | .08 |
| ❑ 276 Mark Carrier DB LL | .10 | .02 |
| ❑ 277 Warren Moon LL | .25 | .08 |
| ❑ 278 Randall Cunningham LL | .10 | .02 |
| ❑ 279 Nick Lowery LL | .05 | .01 |
| ❑ 280 Clarence Verdin LL | .05 | .01 |
| ❑ 281 Thurman Thomas LL | .25 | .08 |
| ❑ 282 Mike Horan LL | .05 | .01 |
| ❑ 283 Flipper Anderson LL | .05 | .01 |
| ❑ 284 John Offerdahl | .05 | .01 |
| ❑ 285 Dan Marino LL | 1.25 | .50 |
| ❑ 286 Mark Clayton | .10 | .02 |
| ❑ 287 Tony Paige | .05 | .01 |
| ❑ 288 Keith Sims | .05 | .01 |
| ❑ 289 Jeff Cross | .05 | .01 |
| ❑ 290 Pete Stoyanovich | .05 | .01 |
| ❑ 291 Ferrell Edmunds | .05 | .01 |
| ❑ 292 Reggie Roby | .05 | .01 |
| ❑ 293 Louis Oliver | .05 | .01 |
| ❑ 294 Jarvis Williams | .05 | .01 |
| ❑ 295 Sammie Smith | .05 | .01 |
| ❑ 296 Richmond Webb | .05 | .01 |
| ❑ 297 J.B. Brown | .05 | .01 |
| ❑ 298 Jim C.Jensen | .05 | .01 |
| ❑ 299 Mark Duper | .10 | .02 |
| ❑ 300 David Griggs | .05 | .01 |
| ❑ 301 Randal Hill RC | .10 | .02 |
| ❑ 302 Aaron Craver RC | .05 | .01 |
| ❑ 303 Keith Millard | .05 | .01 |
| ❑ 304 Steve Jordan | .05 | .01 |
| ❑ 305 Anthony Carter | .10 | .02 |
| ❑ 306 Mike Merriweather | .05 | .01 |
| ❑ 307 Audray McMillian RC UER | .05 | .01 |
| ❑ 308 Randall McDaniel | .10 | .02 |
| ❑ 309 Gary Zimmerman | .10 | .02 |
| ❑ 310 Carl Lee | .05 | .01 |
| ❑ 311 Reggie Rutland | .05 | .01 |
| ❑ 312 Hassan Jones | .05 | .01 |
| ❑ 313 Kirk Lowdermilk UER | .05 | .01 |
| ❑ 314 Herschel Walker | .10 | .02 |
| ❑ 315 Chris Doleman | .05 | .01 |
| ❑ 316 Joey Browner | .05 | .01 |
| ❑ 317 Wade Wilson | .10 | .02 |
| ❑ 318 Henry Thomas | .05 | .01 |
| ❑ 319 Rich Gannon | .25 | .08 |
| ❑ 320 Al Noga UER | .05 | .01 |
| ❑ 321 Pat Harlow RC | .05 | .01 |
| ❑ 322 Bruce Armstrong | .05 | .01 |
| ❑ 323 Maurice Hurst | .05 | .01 |
| ❑ 324 Brent Williams | .05 | .01 |
| ❑ 325 Chris Singleton | .05 | .01 |
| ❑ 326 Jason Staurovsky | .05 | .01 |
| ❑ 327 Marvin Allen | .05 | .01 |
| ❑ 328 Hart Lee Dykes | .05 | .01 |
| ❑ 329 Johnny Rembert | .05 | .01 |
| ❑ 330 Andre Tippett | .05 | .01 |
| ❑ 331 Greg McMurtry | .05 | .01 |
| ❑ 332 John Stephens | .05 | .01 |
| ❑ 333 Ray Agnew | .05 | .01 |
| ❑ 334 Tommy Hodson | .05 | .01 |
| ❑ 335 Ronnie Lippett | .05 | .01 |
| ❑ 336 Marv Cook | .05 | .01 |
| ❑ 337 Tommy Barnhardt RC | .05 | .01 |
| ❑ 338 Dalton Hilliard | .05 | .01 |
| ❑ 339 Sam Mills | .05 | .01 |
| ❑ 340 Morten Andersen | .05 | .01 |
| ❑ 341 Stan Brock | .05 | .01 |
| ❑ 342 Brett Maxie | .05 | .01 |
| ❑ 343 Steve Walsh | .05 | .01 |
| ❑ 344 Vaughan Johnson | .05 | .01 |
| ❑ 345 Rickey Jackson | .05 | .01 |
| ❑ 346 Renaldo Turnbull | .05 | .01 |
| ❑ 347 Joel Hilgenberg | .05 | .01 |
| ❑ 348 Toi Cook RC | .05 | .01 |
| ❑ 349 Robert Massey | .05 | .01 |
| ❑ 350 Pat Swilling | .10 | .02 |
| ❑ 351 Eric Martin | .05 | .01 |
| ❑ 352 Rueben Mayes UER | .05 | .01 |
| ❑ 353 Vince Buck | .05 | .01 |
| ❑ 354 Brett Perriman | .25 | .08 |
| ❑ 355 Wesley Carroll RC | .05 | .01 |
| ❑ 356 Jarrod Bunch RC | .05 | .01 |
| ❑ 357 Pepper Johnson | .05 | .01 |
| ❑ 358 Dave Meggett | .10 | .02 |
| ❑ 359 Mark Collins | .05 | .01 |
| ❑ 360 Sean Landeta | .05 | .01 |
| ❑ 361 Maurice Carthon | .05 | .01 |
| ❑ 362 Mike Fox UER | .05 | .01 |
| ❑ 363 Jeff Hostetler | .10 | .02 |
| ❑ 364 Phil Simms | .10 | .02 |
| ❑ 365 Leonard Marshall | .05 | .01 |
| ❑ 366 Gary Reasons | .05 | .01 |
| ❑ 367 Rodney Hampton | .25 | .08 |
| ❑ 368 Greg Jackson RC | .05 | .01 |
| ❑ 369 Jumbo Elliott | .05 | .01 |
| ❑ 370 Bob Kratch RC | .05 | .01 |
| ❑ 371 Lawrence Taylor | .25 | .08 |
| ❑ 372 Erik Howard | .05 | .01 |
| ❑ 373 Carl Banks | .05 | .01 |
| ❑ 374 Stephen Baker | .05 | .01 |
| ❑ 375 Mark Ingram | .10 | .02 |
| ❑ 376 Browning Nagle RC | .05 | .01 |
| ❑ 377 Jeff Lageman | .05 | .01 |
| ❑ 378 Ken O'Brien | .05 | .01 |
| ❑ 379 Al Toon | .10 | .02 |
| ❑ 380 Joe Prokop | .05 | .01 |
| ❑ 381 Tony Stargell | .05 | .01 |
| ❑ 382 Blair Thomas | .05 | .01 |
| ❑ 383 Erik McMillan | .05 | .01 |
| ❑ 384 Dennis Byrd | .05 | .01 |
| ❑ 385 Freeman McNeil | .05 | .01 |
| ❑ 386 Brad Baxter | .05 | .01 |
| ❑ 387 Mark Boyer | .05 | .01 |
| ❑ 388 Terance Mathis | .10 | .02 |
| ❑ 389 Jim Sweeney | .05 | .01 |
| ❑ 390 Kyle Clifton | .05 | .01 |
| ❑ 391 Pat Leahy | .05 | .01 |
| ❑ 392 Rob Moore | .25 | .08 |
| ❑ 393 James Hasty | .05 | .01 |
| ❑ 394 Blaise Bryant | .05 | .01 |
| ❑ 395A Jesse Campbell RC ERR | 1.00 | .40 |
| ❑ 395B Jesse Campbell RC COR | .05 | .01 |
| ❑ 396 Keith Jackson | .10 | .02 |
| ❑ 397 Jerome Brown | .05 | .01 |
| ❑ 398 Keith Byars | .05 | .01 |
| ❑ 399 Seth Joyner | .10 | .02 |
| ❑ 400 Mike Bellamy | .05 | .01 |
| ❑ 401 Fred Barnett | .25 | .08 |
| ❑ 402 Reggie Singletary RC | .05 | .01 |
| ❑ 403 Reggie White | .25 | .08 |
| ❑ 404 Randall Cunningham | .25 | .08 |
| ❑ 405 Byron Evans | .05 | .01 |
| ❑ 406 Wes Hopkins | .05 | .01 |
| ❑ 407 Ben Smith | .05 | .01 |
| ❑ 408 Roger Ruzek | .05 | .01 |
| ❑ 409 Eric Allen UER | .05 | .01 |
| ❑ 410 Anthony Toney UER | .05 | .01 |
| ❑ 411 Clyde Simmons | .05 | .01 |
| ❑ 412 Andre Waters | .05 | .01 |
| ❑ 413 Calvin Williams | .10 | .02 |
| ❑ 414 Eric Swann RC | .25 | .08 |
| ❑ 415 Eric Hill | .05 | .01 |
| ❑ 416 Tim McDonald | .05 | .01 |
| ❑ 417 Luis Sharpe | .05 | .01 |
| ❑ 418 Ernie Jones UER | .05 | .01 |
| ❑ 419 Ken Harvey | .10 | .02 |
| ❑ 420 Ricky Proehl | .05 | .01 |
| ❑ 421 Johnny Johnson | .05 | .01 |
| ❑ 422 Anthony Bell | .05 | .01 |
| ❑ 423 Timm Rosenbach | .05 | .01 |
| ❑ 424 Rich Camarillo | .05 | .01 |
| ❑ 425 Walter Reeves | .05 | .01 |
| ❑ 426 Freddie Joe Nunn | .05 | .01 |
| ❑ 427 Anthony Thompson UER | .05 | .01 |
| ❑ 428 Bill Lewis | .05 | .01 |
| ❑ 429 Jim Wahler RC | .05 | .01 |
| ❑ 430 Cedric Mack | .05 | .01 |
| ❑ 431 Mike Jones DE RC | .05 | .01 |
| ❑ 432 Ernie Mills RC | .10 | .02 |
| ❑ 433 Tim Worley | .05 | .01 |
| ❑ 434 Greg Lloyd | .25 | .08 |
| ❑ 435 Dermontti Dawson | .05 | .01 |
| ❑ 436 Louis Lipps | .05 | .01 |
| ❑ 437 Eric Green | .05 | .01 |
| ❑ 438 Donald Evans | .05 | .01 |

| | | |
|---|---|---|
| ❑ 439 D.J. Johnson | .05 | .01 |
| ❑ 440 Tunch Ilkin | .05 | .01 |
| ❑ 441 Bubby Brister | .05 | .01 |
| ❑ 442 Chris Calloway | .05 | .01 |
| ❑ 443 David Little | .05 | .01 |
| ❑ 444 Thomas Everett | .05 | .01 |
| ❑ 445 Carnell Lake | .05 | .01 |
| ❑ 446 Rod Woodson | .25 | .08 |
| ❑ 447 Gary Anderson K | .05 | .01 |
| ❑ 448 Merril Hoge | .05 | .01 |
| ❑ 449 Gerald Williams | .05 | .01 |
| ❑ 450 Eric Moten RC | .05 | .01 |
| ❑ 451 Marion Butts | .10 | .02 |
| ❑ 452 Leslie O'Neal | .10 | .02 |
| ❑ 453 Ronnie Harmon | .05 | .01 |
| ❑ 454 Gill Byrd | .05 | .01 |
| ❑ 455 Junior Seau | .25 | .08 |
| ❑ 456 Nate Lewis RC | .05 | .01 |
| ❑ 457 Leo Goeas | .05 | .01 |
| ❑ 458 Burt Grossman | .05 | .01 |
| ❑ 459 Courtney Hall | .05 | .01 |
| ❑ 460 Anthony Miller | .10 | .02 |
| ❑ 461 Gary Plummer | .05 | .01 |
| ❑ 462 Billy Joe Tolliver | .05 | .01 |
| ❑ 463 Lee Williams | .05 | .01 |
| ❑ 464 Arthur Cox | .05 | .01 |
| ❑ 465 John Kidd UER | .05 | .01 |
| ❑ 466 Frank Cornish | .05 | .01 |
| ❑ 467 John Carney | .05 | .01 |
| ❑ 468 Eric Bieniemy RC | .05 | .01 |
| ❑ 469 Don Griffin | .05 | .01 |
| ❑ 470 Jerry Rice | .75 | .30 |
| ❑ 471 Keith DeLong | .05 | .01 |
| ❑ 472 John Taylor | .10 | .02 |
| ❑ 473 Brent Jones | .25 | .08 |
| ❑ 474 Pierce Holt | .05 | .01 |
| ❑ 475 Kevin Fagan | .05 | .01 |
| ❑ 476 Bill Romanowski | .05 | .01 |
| ❑ 477 Dexter Carter | .05 | .01 |
| ❑ 478 Guy McIntyre | .05 | .01 |
| ❑ 479 Joe Montana | 1.25 | .50 |
| ❑ 480 Charles Haley | .10 | .02 |
| ❑ 481 Mike Cofer | .05 | .01 |
| ❑ 482 Jesse Sapolu | .05 | .01 |
| ❑ 483 Eric Davis | .05 | .01 |
| ❑ 484 Mike Sherrard | .05 | .01 |
| ❑ 485 Steve Young | .75 | .30 |
| ❑ 486 Darryl Pollard | .05 | .01 |
| ❑ 487 Tom Rathman | .05 | .01 |
| ❑ 488 Michael Carter | .05 | .01 |
| ❑ 489 Ricky Watters RC | 1.50 | .60 |
| ❑ 490 John Johnson RC | .05 | .01 |
| ❑ 491 Eugene Robinson | .05 | .01 |
| ❑ 492 Andy Heck | .05 | .01 |
| ❑ 493 John L. Williams | .05 | .01 |
| ❑ 494 Norm Johnson | .05 | .01 |
| ❑ 495 David Wyman | .05 | .01 |
| ❑ 496 Derrick Fenner UER | .05 | .01 |
| ❑ 497 Rick Donnelly | .05 | .01 |
| ❑ 498 Tony Woods | .05 | .01 |
| ❑ 499 Derrick Loville RC | .05 | .01 |
| ❑ 500 Dave Krieg | .10 | .02 |
| ❑ 501 Joe Nash | .05 | .01 |
| ❑ 502 Brian Blades | .10 | .02 |
| ❑ 503 Cortez Kennedy | .25 | .08 |
| ❑ 504 Jeff Bryant | .05 | .01 |
| ❑ 505 Tommy Kane | .05 | .01 |
| ❑ 506 Travis McNeal | .05 | .01 |
| ❑ 507 Terry Wooden | .05 | .01 |
| ❑ 508 Chris Warren | .25 | .08 |
| ❑ 509A Dan McGwire RC ERR | .05 | .01 |
| ❑ 509B Dan McGwire RC COR | .05 | .01 |
| ❑ 510 Mark Robinson | .05 | .01 |
| ❑ 511 Ron Hall | .05 | .01 |
| ❑ 512 Paul Gruber | .05 | .01 |
| ❑ 513 Harry Hamilton | .05 | .01 |
| ❑ 514 Keith McCants | .05 | .01 |
| ❑ 515 Reggie Cobb | .25 | .08 |
| ❑ 516 Steve Christie UER | .05 | .01 |
| ❑ 517 Broderick Thomas | .05 | .01 |
| ❑ 518 Mark Carrier WR | .25 | .08 |
| ❑ 519 Vinny Testaverde | .10 | .02 |
| ❑ 520 Ricky Reynolds | .05 | .01 |
| ❑ 521 Jesse Anderson | .05 | .01 |
| ❑ 522 Reuben Davis | .05 | .01 |
| ❑ 523 Wayne Haddix | .05 | .01 |
| ❑ 524 Gary Anderson RB UER | .05 | .01 |
| ❑ 525 Bruce Hill | .05 | .01 |
| ❑ 526 Kevin Murphy | .05 | .01 |
| ❑ 527 Lawrence Dawsey RC | .10 | .02 |
| ❑ 528 Ricky Ervins RC | .10 | .02 |
| ❑ 529 Charles Mann | .05 | .01 |
| ❑ 530 Jim Lachey | .05 | .01 |
| ❑ 531 Mark Rypien UER | .10 | .02 |
| ❑ 532 Darrell Green | .05 | .01 |
| ❑ 533 Stan Humphries | .25 | .08 |
| ❑ 534 Jeff Bostic UER | .05 | .01 |
| ❑ 535 Earnest Byner | .05 | .01 |
| ❑ 536 Art Monk UER | .10 | .02 |
| ❑ 537 Don Warren | .05 | .01 |
| ❑ 538 Darryl Grant | .05 | .01 |
| ❑ 539 Wilber Marshall | .05 | .01 |
| ❑ 540 Kurt Gouveia RC | .05 | .01 |
| ❑ 541 Markus Koch | .05 | .01 |
| ❑ 542 Andre Collins | .05 | .01 |
| ❑ 543 Chip Lohmiller | .05 | .01 |
| ❑ 544 Alvin Walton | .05 | .01 |
| ❑ 545 Gary Clark | .25 | .08 |
| ❑ 546 Ricky Sanders | .05 | .01 |
| ❑ 547 Redskins vs. Eagles | .05 | .01 |
| ❑ 548 Bengals vs. Oilers | .05 | .01 |
| ❑ 549 Dolphins vs. Chiefs | .05 | .01 |
| ❑ 550 Bears vs. Saints UER | .05 | .01 |
| ❑ 551 Playoffs/Thurman Thomas | .10 | .02 |
| ❑ 552 49ers vs. Redskins | .05 | .01 |
| ❑ 553 Giants vs. Bears | .05 | .01 |
| ❑ 554 Playoffs/Bo Jackson | .10 | .02 |
| ❑ 555 AFC Championship | .05 | .01 |
| ❑ 556 NFC Championship | .05 | .01 |
| ❑ 557 Super Bowl XXV | .05 | .01 |
| ❑ 558 Checklist 1-140 | .05 | .01 |
| ❑ 559 Checklist 141-280 | .05 | .01 |
| ❑ 560 Checklist 281-420 UER | .05 | .01 |
| ❑ 561 Checklist 421-561 UER | .05 | .01 |

## 1992 Bowman

| | | |
|---|---|---|
| ❑ COMPLETE SET (573) | 50.00 | 25.00 |
| ❑ 1 Reggie White | 1.00 | .40 |
| ❑ 2 Johnny Meads | .25 | .08 |
| ❑ 3 Chip Lohmiller | .25 | .08 |
| ❑ 4 James Lofton | .50 | .20 |
| ❑ 5 Ray Horton | .25 | .08 |
| ❑ 6 Rich Moran | .25 | .08 |
| ❑ 7 Howard Cross | .25 | .08 |
| ❑ 8 Mike Horan | .25 | .08 |
| ❑ 9 Erik Kramer | .50 | .20 |
| ❑ 10 Steve Wisniewski | .25 | .08 |
| ❑ 11 Michael Haynes | .50 | .20 |
| ❑ 12 Donald Evans | .25 | .08 |
| ❑ 13 Michael Irvin FOIL | 1.00 | .40 |
| ❑ 14 Gary Zimmerman | .25 | .08 |
| ❑ 15 John Friesz | .50 | .20 |
| ❑ 16 Mark Carrier WR | 1.00 | .40 |
| ❑ 17 Mark Duper | .25 | .08 |
| ❑ 18 James Thornton | .25 | .08 |
| ❑ 19 Jon Hand | .25 | .08 |
| ❑ 20 Sterling Sharpe | 1.00 | .40 |
| ❑ 21 Jacob Green | .25 | .08 |
| ❑ 22 Wesley Carroll | .25 | .08 |
| ❑ 23 Clay Matthews | .50 | .20 |
| ❑ 24 Kevin Greene | .50 | .20 |
| ❑ 25 Brad Baxter | .25 | .08 |
| ❑ 26 Don Griffin | .25 | .08 |
| ❑ 27 Robert Delpino | 1.50 | .60 |
| ❑ 28 Lee Johnson | .25 | .08 |
| ❑ 29 Jim Wahler | .25 | .08 |
| ❑ 30 Leonard Russell | .50 | .20 |
| ❑ 31 Eric Moore | .25 | .08 |
| ❑ 32 Dino Hackett | .25 | .08 |
| ❑ 33 Simon Fletcher | .25 | .08 |
| ❑ 34 Al Edwards | .25 | .08 |
| ❑ 35 Brad Edwards | .25 | .08 |
| ❑ 36 James Joseph | .25 | .08 |
| ❑ 37 Rodney Peete | .50 | .20 |
| ❑ 38 Ricky Reynolds | .25 | .08 |
| ❑ 39 Eddie Anderson | .25 | .08 |
| ❑ 40 Ken Clarke | .25 | .08 |
| ❑ 41 Tony Bennett | .50 | .20 |
| ❑ 42 Larry Brown DB | .25 | .08 |
| ❑ 43 Ray Childress | .25 | .08 |
| ❑ 44 Mike Kenn | .25 | .08 |
| ❑ 45 Vestee Jackson | .25 | .08 |
| ❑ 46 Neil O'Donnell | .50 | .20 |
| ❑ 47 Bill Brooks | .25 | .08 |
| ❑ 48 Kevin Butler | .25 | .08 |
| ❑ 49 Joe Phillips | .25 | .08 |
| ❑ 50 Cortez Kennedy | .50 | .20 |
| ❑ 51 Rickey Jackson | .25 | .08 |
| ❑ 52 Vinnie Clark | .25 | .08 |
| ❑ 53 Michael Jackson | .50 | .20 |
| ❑ 54 Ernie Jones | .25 | .08 |
| ❑ 55 Tom Newberry | .25 | .08 |
| ❑ 56 Pat Harlow | .25 | .08 |
| ❑ 57 Craig Taylor | .25 | .08 |
| ❑ 58 Joe Prokop | .25 | .08 |
| ❑ 59 Warren Moon FOIL SP | 2.00 | .75 |
| ❑ 60 Jeff Lageman | .25 | .08 |
| ❑ 61 Neil Smith | 1.00 | .40 |
| ❑ 62 Jim Jeffcoat | .25 | .08 |
| ❑ 63 Bill Fralic | .25 | .08 |
| ❑ 64 Mark Schlereth RC | .25 | .08 |
| ❑ 65 Keith Byars | .25 | .08 |
| ❑ 66 Jeff Hostetler | .50 | .20 |
| ❑ 67 Joey Browner | .25 | .08 |
| ❑ 68 Bobby Hebert FOIL SP | 1.50 | .60 |
| ❑ 69 Keith Sims | .25 | .08 |
| ❑ 70 Warren Moon | 1.00 | .40 |
| ❑ 71 Pio Sagapolutele RC | .25 | .08 |
| ❑ 72 Cornelius Bennett | .50 | .20 |
| ❑ 73 Greg Davis | .25 | .08 |
| ❑ 74 Ronnie Harmon | .25 | .08 |
| ❑ 75 Ron Hall | .25 | .08 |
| ❑ 76 Howie Long | 1.00 | .40 |
| ❑ 77 Greg Lewis | .25 | .08 |
| ❑ 78 Carnell Lake | .25 | .08 |
| ❑ 79 Ray Crockett | .25 | .08 |
| ❑ 80 Tom Waddle | .25 | .08 |
| ❑ 81 Vincent Brown | .25 | .08 |
| ❑ 82 Bill Brooks | .50 | .20 |
| ❑ 83 John L. Williams | .25 | .08 |
| ❑ 84 Floyd Turner | .25 | .08 |
| ❑ 85 Scott Radecic | .25 | .08 |
| ❑ 86 Anthony Munoz | .50 | .20 |
| ❑ 87 Lonnie Young | .25 | .08 |
| ❑ 88 Dexter Carter | .25 | .08 |
| ❑ 89 Tony Zendejas | .25 | .08 |
| ❑ 90 Tim Jorden | .25 | .08 |
| ❑ 91 LeRoy Butler | .25 | .08 |
| ❑ 92 Richard Brown RC | .25 | .08 |
| ❑ 93 Erric Pegram | .50 | .20 |
| ❑ 94 Sean Landeta | .25 | .08 |
| ❑ 95 Clyde Simmons | .25 | .08 |
| ❑ 96 Martin Mayhew | .25 | .08 |
| ❑ 97 Jarvis Williams | .25 | .08 |
| ❑ 98 Barry Word | .25 | .08 |
| ❑ 99 John Taylor FOIL | .50 | .20 |
| ❑ 100 Emmitt Smith | 8.00 | 3.00 |
| ❑ 101 Leon Seals | .25 | .08 |
| ❑ 102 Marion Butts | .25 | .08 |
| ❑ 103 Mike Merriweather | .25 | .08 |
| ❑ 104 Ernest Givins | .50 | .20 |
| ❑ 105 Wymon Henderson | .25 | .08 |
| ❑ 106 Robert Wilson | .25 | .08 |
| ❑ 107 Bobby Hebert | .25 | .08 |
| ❑ 108 Terry McDaniel | .25 | .08 |
| ❑ 109 Jerry Ball | .25 | .08 |

|  |  | | |
|---|---|---|---|
| 110 | John Taylor | .50 | .20 |
| 111 | Rob Moore | .50 | .20 |
| 112 | Thurman Thomas FOIL | 1.00 | .40 |
| 113 | Checklist 1-115 | .25 | .08 |
| 114 | Brian Blades | .50 | .20 |
| 115 | Larry Kelm | .25 | .08 |
| 116 | James Francis | .25 | .08 |
| 117 | Rod Woodson | 1.00 | .40 |
| 118 | Trace Armstrong | .25 | .08 |
| 119 | Eugene Daniel | .25 | .08 |
| 120 | Andre Tippett | .25 | .08 |
| 121 | Chris Jacke | .25 | .08 |
| 122 | Jessie Tuggle | .25 | .08 |
| 123 | Chris Chandler | 1.00 | .40 |
| 124 | Tim Johnson | .25 | .08 |
| 125 | Mark Collins | .25 | .08 |
| 126 | Aeneas Williams SP | 1.50 | .60 |
| 127 | James Jones DT | .25 | .08 |
| 128 | George Jamison | .25 | .08 |
| 129 | Deron Cherry | .25 | .08 |
| 130 | Mark Clayton | .50 | .20 |
| 131 | Keith DeLong | .25 | .08 |
| 132 | Marcus Allen | 1.00 | .40 |
| 133 | Joe Walter RC | .25 | .08 |
| 134 | Reggie Rutland | .25 | .08 |
| 135 | Kent Hull | .25 | .08 |
| 136 | Jeff Feagles | .25 | .08 |
| 137 | Ronnie Lott FOIL SP | 2.00 | .75 |
| 138 | Henry Rolling | .25 | .08 |
| 139 | Gary Anderson RB | .25 | .08 |
| 140 | Morten Andersen | .25 | .08 |
| 141 | Cris Dishman | .25 | .08 |
| 142 | David Treadwell | .25 | .08 |
| 143 | Kevin Gogan | .25 | .08 |
| 144 | James Hasty | .25 | .08 |
| 145 | Robert Delpino | .25 | .08 |
| 146 | Patrick Hunter | .25 | .08 |
| 147 | Gary Anderson K | .25 | .08 |
| 148 | Chip Banks | .25 | .08 |
| 149 | Dan Fike | .25 | .08 |
| 150 | Chris Miller | .50 | .20 |
| 151 | Hugh Millen | .25 | .08 |
| 152 | Courtney Hall | .25 | .08 |
| 153 | Gary Clark | .50 | .20 |
| 154 | Michael Brooks | .25 | .08 |
| 155 | Jay Hilgenberg | .25 | .08 |
| 156 | Tim McDonald | .25 | .08 |
| 157 | Andre Tippett | .50 | .20 |
| 158 | Doug Riesenberg | .25 | .08 |
| 159 | Bill Maas | .25 | .08 |
| 160 | Fred Barnett | .50 | .20 |
| 161 | Pierce Holt | .25 | .08 |
| 162 | Brian Noble | .25 | .08 |
| 163 | Harold Green | .50 | .20 |
| 164 | Joel Hilgenberg | .25 | .08 |
| 165 | Mervyn Fernandez | .25 | .08 |
| 166 | John Offerdahl | .25 | .08 |
| 167 | Shane Conlan | .25 | .08 |
| 168 | Mark Higgs FOIL SP | 1.50 | .60 |
| 169 | Bubba McDowell | .25 | .08 |
| 170 | Barry Sanders | 6.00 | 2.50 |
| 171 | Larry Roberts | .25 | .08 |
| 172 | Herschel Walker | .50 | .20 |
| 173 | Steve McMichael | .50 | .20 |
| 174 | Kelly Stouffer | .25 | .08 |
| 175 | Louis Lipps | .25 | .08 |
| 176 | Jim Everett | .50 | .20 |
| 177 | Tony Tolbert | .25 | .08 |
| 178 | Mike Baab | .25 | .08 |
| 179 | Eric Swann | .25 | .08 |
| 180 | Emmitt Smith FOIL SP | 12.00 | 5.00 |
| 181 | Tim Brown | 1.00 | .40 |
| 182 | Dennis Smith | .25 | .08 |
| 183 | Moe Gardner | .25 | .08 |
| 184 | Derrick Walker | .25 | .08 |
| 185 | Reyna Thompson | .25 | .08 |
| 186 | Esera Tuaolo | .25 | .08 |
| 187 | Jeff Wright | .25 | .08 |
| 188 | Mark Rypien | .25 | .08 |
| 189 | Quinn Early | .50 | .20 |
| 190 | Christian Okoye | .25 | .08 |
| 191 | Keith Jackson | .50 | .20 |
| 192 | Doug Smith | .25 | .08 |
| 193 | John Elway FOIL | 10.00 | 4.00 |
| 194 | Reggie Cobb | .25 | .08 |
| 195 | Reggie Roby | .25 | .08 |
| 196 | Clarence Verdin | .25 | .08 |
| 197 | Jim Breech | .25 | .08 |
| 198 | Jim Sweeney | .25 | .08 |
| 199 | Marv Cook | .25 | .08 |
| 200 | Ronnie Lott | .50 | .20 |
| 201 | Mel Gray | .50 | .20 |
| 202 | Maury Buford | .25 | .08 |
| 203 | Lorenzo Lynch | .25 | .08 |
| 204 | Jesse Sapolu | .25 | .08 |
| 205 | Steve Jordan | .25 | .08 |
| 206 | Don Majkowski | .25 | .08 |
| 207 | Flipper Anderson | .25 | .08 |
| 208 | Ed King | .25 | .08 |
| 209 | Tony Woods | .25 | .08 |
| 210 | Ron Heller | .25 | .08 |
| 211 | Greg Kragen | .25 | .08 |
| 212 | Scott Case | .25 | .08 |
| 213 | Tommy Barnhardt | .25 | .08 |
| 214 | Charles Mann | .25 | .08 |
| 215 | David Griggs | .25 | .08 |
| 216 | Kenneth Davis FOIL SP | 1.50 | .60 |
| 217 | Lamar Lathon | .25 | .08 |
| 218 | Nate Odomes | .25 | .08 |
| 219 | Vinny Testaverde | .50 | .20 |
| 220 | Rod Bernstine | .25 | .08 |
| 221 | Barry Sanders FOIL | 10.00 | 4.00 |
| 222 | Carlton Haselrig RC | .25 | .08 |
| 223 | Steve Beuerlein | .50 | .20 |
| 224 | John Alt | .25 | .08 |
| 225 | Pepper Johnson | .25 | .08 |
| 226 | Checklist 116-230 | .25 | .08 |
| 227 | Irv Eatman | .25 | .08 |
| 228 | Greg Townsend | .25 | .08 |
| 229 | Mark Jackson | .25 | .08 |
| 230 | Robert Blackmon | .25 | .08 |
| 231 | Terry Allen | 1.00 | .40 |
| 232 | Bennie Blades | .25 | .08 |
| 233 | Sam Mills | 1.00 | .40 |
| 234 | Richmond Webb | .25 | .08 |
| 235 | Richard Dent | .50 | .20 |
| 236 | Alonzo Mitz RC | .25 | .08 |
| 237 | Steve Young | 5.00 | 2.00 |
| 238 | Pat Swilling | .25 | .08 |
| 239 | James Campen | .25 | .08 |
| 240 | Earnest Byner | .25 | .08 |
| 241 | Pat Terrell | .25 | .08 |
| 242 | Carwell Gardner | .25 | .08 |
| 243 | Charles McRae | .25 | .08 |
| 244 | Vince Newsome | .25 | .08 |
| 245 | Eric Hill | .25 | .08 |
| 246 | Steve Young FOIL | 5.00 | 2.00 |
| 247 | Nate Lewis | .25 | .08 |
| 248 | William Fuller | .25 | .08 |
| 249 | Andre Waters | .25 | .08 |
| 250 | Dean Biasucci | .25 | .08 |
| 251 | Andre Rison | .50 | .20 |
| 252 | Brent Williams | .25 | .08 |
| 253 | Todd McNair | .25 | .08 |
| 254 | Jeff Davidson RC | .25 | .08 |
| 255 | Art Monk | .50 | .20 |
| 256 | Kirk Lowdermilk | .25 | .08 |
| 257 | Bob Golic | .25 | .08 |
| 258 | Michael Irvin | 1.00 | .40 |
| 259 | Eric Green | .25 | .08 |
| 260 | David Fulcher | .50 | .20 |
| 261 | Damone Johnson | .25 | .08 |
| 262 | Marc Spindler | .25 | .08 |
| 263 | Alfred Williams | .25 | .08 |
| 264 | Donnie Elder | .25 | .08 |
| 265 | Keith McKeller | .25 | .08 |
| 266 | Steve Bono RC | 1.00 | .40 |
| 267 | Jumbo Elliott | .25 | .08 |
| 268 | Randy Hilliard RC | .25 | .08 |
| 269 | Rufus Porter | .25 | .08 |
| 270 | Neal Anderson | .25 | .08 |
| 271 | Dalton Hilliard | .25 | .08 |
| 272 | Michael Zordich RC | .25 | .08 |
| 273 | Cornelius Bennett FOIL | .50 | .20 |
| 274 | Louie Aguiar RC | .25 | .08 |
| 275 | Aaron Craver | .25 | .08 |
| 276 | Tony Bennett | .25 | .08 |
| 277 | Terry Wooden | .25 | .08 |
| 278 | Mike Munchak | .50 | .20 |
| 279 | Chris Hinton | .25 | .08 |
| 280 | John Elway | 6.00 | 2.50 |
| 281 | Randall McDaniel | .25 | .08 |
| 282 | Brad Baxter | .50 | .20 |
| 283 | Wes Hopkins | .25 | .08 |
| 284 | Scott Davis | .25 | .08 |
| 285 | Mark Tuinei | .25 | .08 |
| 286 | Broderick Thompson | .25 | .08 |
| 287 | Henry Ellard | .50 | .20 |
| 288 | Adrian Cooper | .25 | .08 |
| 289 | Don Warren | .25 | .08 |
| 290 | Rodney Hampton | .50 | .20 |
| 291 | Kevin Ross | .25 | .08 |
| 292 | Mark Carrier DB | .25 | .08 |
| 293 | Ian Beckles | .25 | .08 |
| 294 | Gene Atkins | .25 | .08 |
| 295 | Mark Rypien FOIL | .50 | .20 |
| 296 | Eric Metcalf | .50 | .20 |
| 297 | Howard Ballard | .25 | .08 |
| 298 | Nate Newton | .25 | .08 |
| 299 | Dan Owens | .25 | .08 |
| 300 | Tim McGee | .25 | .08 |
| 301 | Greg McMurtry | .25 | .08 |
| 302 | Walter Reeves | .25 | .08 |
| 303 | Jeff Herrod | .25 | .08 |
| 304 | Darren Comeaux | .25 | .08 |
| 305 | Pete Stoyanovich | .25 | .08 |
| 306 | Johnny Holland | .25 | .08 |
| 307 | Jay Novacek | .50 | .20 |
| 308 | Steve Broussard | .25 | .08 |
| 309 | Darrell Green | .25 | .08 |
| 310 | Sam Mills | .25 | .08 |
| 311 | Tim Barnett | .25 | .08 |
| 312 | Steve Atwater | .25 | .08 |
| 313 | Tom Waddle FOIL | .50 | .20 |
| 314 | Felix Wright | .25 | .08 |
| 315 | Sean Jones | .25 | .08 |
| 316 | Jim Harbaugh | 1.00 | .40 |
| 317 | Eric Allen | .25 | .08 |
| 318 | Don Mosebar | .25 | .08 |
| 319 | Rob Taylor | .25 | .08 |
| 320 | Terance Mathis | .25 | .08 |
| 321 | Leroy Hoard | .50 | .20 |
| 322 | Kenneth Davis | .25 | .08 |
| 323 | Guy McIntyre | .25 | .08 |
| 324 | Deron Cherry | .50 | .20 |
| 325 | Tunch Ilkin | .25 | .08 |
| 326 | Willie Green | .25 | .08 |
| 327 | Darryl Henley | .25 | .08 |
| 328 | Shawn Jefferson | .25 | .08 |
| 329 | Greg Jackson | .25 | .08 |
| 330 | John Roper | .25 | .08 |
| 331 | Bill Lewis | .25 | .08 |
| 332 | Rodney Holman | .25 | .08 |
| 333 | Bruce Armstrong | .25 | .08 |
| 334 | Robb Thomas | .25 | .08 |
| 335 | Alvin Harper | .50 | .20 |
| 336 | Brian Jordan | .50 | .20 |
| 337 | Morten Andersen | .50 | .20 |
| 338 | Dermontti Dawson | .25 | .08 |
| 339 | Checklist 231-345 | .25 | .08 |
| 340 | Louis Oliver | .25 | .08 |
| 341 | Paul McJulien RC | .25 | .08 |
| 342 | Karl Mecklenburg | .25 | .08 |
| 343 | Lawrence Dawsey | .50 | .20 |
| 344 | Kyle Clifton | .25 | .08 |
| 345 | Jeff Bostic | .25 | .08 |
| 346 | Cris Carter | 1.50 | .60 |
| 347 | Al Smith | .25 | .08 |
| 348 | Mark Kelso | .25 | .08 |
| 349 | Art Monk FOIL | 1.00 | .40 |
| 350 | Michael Carter | .25 | .08 |
| 351 | Ethan Horton | .25 | .08 |
| 352 | Andy Heck | .25 | .08 |
| 353 | Gill Fenerty | .25 | .08 |
| 354 | David Brandon RC | .25 | .08 |
| 355 | Anthony Johnson | 1.00 | .40 |
| 356 | Mike Golic | .25 | .08 |
| 357 | Ferrell Edmunds | .25 | .08 |
| 358 | Dennis Gibson | .25 | .08 |
| 359 | Gill Byrd | .25 | .08 |
| 360 | Todd Lyght | .25 | .08 |
| 361 | Jayice Pearson RC | .25 | .08 |

| | | |
|---|---|---|
| ❏ 362 John Rade | .25 | .08 |
| ❏ 363 Keith Van Horne | .25 | .08 |
| ❏ 364 John Kasay | .25 | .08 |
| ❏ 365 Broderick Thomas | 1.50 | .60 |
| ❏ 366 Ken Harvey | .25 | .08 |
| ❏ 367 Nick Gannon | 1.00 | .40 |
| ❏ 368 Darrell Thompson | .25 | .08 |
| ❏ 369 Jon Vaughn | .25 | .08 |
| ❏ 370 Jesse Solomon | .25 | .08 |
| ❏ 371 Erik McMillan | .25 | .08 |
| ❏ 372 Bruce Matthews | .25 | .08 |
| ❏ 373 Wilber Marshall | .25 | .08 |
| ❏ 374 Brian Blades | 1.50 | .60 |
| ❏ 375 Vance Johnson | .25 | .08 |
| ❏ 376 Eddie Brown | .25 | .08 |
| ❏ 377 Don Beebe | .25 | .08 |
| ❏ 378 Brent Jones | .50 | .20 |
| ❏ 379 Matt Bahr | .25 | .08 |
| ❏ 380 Dwight Stone | .25 | .08 |
| ❏ 381 Tony Casillas | .25 | .08 |
| ❏ 382 Jay Schroeder | .25 | .08 |
| ❏ 383 Byron Evans | .25 | .08 |
| ❏ 384 Dan Saleaumua | .25 | .08 |
| ❏ 385 Wendell Davis | .25 | .08 |
| ❏ 386 Ron Holmes | .25 | .08 |
| ❏ 387 George Thomas RC | .25 | .08 |
| ❏ 388 Ray Berry | .25 | .08 |
| ❏ 389 Eric Martin | .25 | .08 |
| ❏ 390 Kevin Mack | .25 | .08 |
| ❏ 391 Natu Tuatagaloa RC | .25 | .08 |
| ❏ 392 Bill Romanowski | .25 | .08 |
| ❏ 393 Nick Bell FOIL SP | 1.50 | .60 |
| ❏ 394 Grant Feasel | .25 | .08 |
| ❏ 395 Eugene Lockhart | .25 | .08 |
| ❏ 396 Lorenzo White | .25 | .08 |
| ❏ 397 Mike Farr | .25 | .08 |
| ❏ 398 Eric Bieniemy | .25 | .08 |
| ❏ 399 Kevin Murphy | .25 | .08 |
| ❏ 400 Luis Sharpe | .25 | .08 |
| ❏ 401 Jessie Tuggle | 1.50 | .60 |
| ❏ 402 Cleveland Gary | .25 | .08 |
| ❏ 403 Tony Mandarich | .25 | .08 |
| ❏ 404 Bryan Cox | .50 | .20 |
| ❏ 405 Marvin Washington | .25 | .08 |
| ❏ 406 Fred Stokes | .25 | .08 |
| ❏ 407 Duane Bickett | .25 | .08 |
| ❏ 408 Leonard Marshall | .25 | .08 |
| ❏ 409 Barry Foster | .50 | .20 |
| ❏ 410 Thurman Thomas | 1.00 | .40 |
| ❏ 411 Willie Gault | .50 | .20 |
| ❏ 412 Vinson Smith RC | .25 | .08 |
| ❏ 413 Mark Bortz | .25 | .08 |
| ❏ 414 Johnny Johnson | .25 | .08 |
| ❏ 415 Rodney Hampton FOIL | 1.00 | .40 |
| ❏ 416 Steve Wallace | .25 | .08 |
| ❏ 417 Fuad Reveiz | .25 | .08 |
| ❏ 418 Derrick Thomas | .50 | .20 |
| ❏ 419 Jackie Harris RC | 1.00 | .40 |
| ❏ 420 Derek Russell | .25 | .08 |
| ❏ 421 David Grant | .25 | .08 |
| ❏ 422 Tommy Kane | .25 | .08 |
| ❏ 423 Stan Brock | .25 | .08 |
| ❏ 424 Haywood Jeffires | .50 | .20 |
| ❏ 425 Broderick Thomas | .25 | .08 |
| ❏ 426 John Kidd | .25 | .08 |
| ❏ 427 Mark McCarthy RC FOIL | .50 | .20 |
| ❏ 428 Jim Arnold | .25 | .08 |
| ❏ 429 Scott Fulhage | .25 | .08 |
| ❏ 430 Jackie Slater | .25 | .08 |
| ❏ 431 Scott Galbraith RC | .25 | .08 |
| ❏ 432 Roger Ruzek | .25 | .08 |
| ❏ 433 Irving Fryar | .50 | .20 |
| ❏ 434A D.Thomas FOIL ERR 494 | 1.00 | .40 |
| ❏ 434B D.Thomas FOIL COR | 1.00 | .40 |
| ❏ 435 D.J. Johnson | .25 | .08 |
| ❏ 436 Jim C.Jensen | .25 | .08 |
| ❏ 437 James Washington | .25 | .08 |
| ❏ 438 Phil Hansen | .25 | .08 |
| ❏ 439 Rohn Stark | .25 | .08 |
| ❏ 440 Jarrod Bunch | .25 | .08 |
| ❏ 441 Todd Marinovich | .25 | .08 |
| ❏ 442 Brett Perriman | 1.00 | .40 |
| ❏ 443 Eugene Robinson | .25 | .08 |
| ❏ 444 Robert Massey | .25 | .08 |
| ❏ 445 Nick Lowery | .25 | .08 |
| ❏ 446 Rickey Dixon | .25 | .08 |
| ❏ 447 Jim Lachey | .25 | .08 |
| ❏ 448 Johnny Hector | .50 | .20 |
| ❏ 449 Gary Plummer | .25 | .08 |
| ❏ 450 Robert Brown | .25 | .08 |
| ❏ 451 Gaston Green | .25 | .08 |
| ❏ 452 Checklist 346-459 | .25 | .08 |
| ❏ 453 Darion Conner | .25 | .08 |
| ❏ 454 Mike Cofer | .25 | .08 |
| ❏ 455 Craig Heyward | .50 | .20 |
| ❏ 456 Anthony Carter | .50 | .20 |
| ❏ 457 Pat Coleman RC | .25 | .08 |
| ❏ 458 Jeff Bryant | .25 | .08 |
| ❏ 459 Mark Gunn RC | .25 | .08 |
| ❏ 460 Stan Thomas | .25 | .08 |
| ❏ 461 Simon Fletcher | 1.50 | .60 |
| ❏ 462 Ray Agnew | .25 | .08 |
| ❏ 463 Jessie Hester | .25 | .08 |
| ❏ 464 Rob Burnett | .25 | .08 |
| ❏ 465 Mike Croel | .25 | .08 |
| ❏ 466 Mike Pitts | .25 | .08 |
| ❏ 467 Darryl Talley | .25 | .08 |
| ❏ 468 Rich Camarillo | .25 | .08 |
| ❏ 469 Reggie White FOIL | 1.00 | .40 |
| ❏ 470 Nick Bell | .25 | .08 |
| ❏ 471 Tracy Hayworth RC | .25 | .08 |
| ❏ 472 Eric Thomas | .25 | .08 |
| ❏ 473 Paul Gruber | .25 | .08 |
| ❏ 474 David Richards | .25 | .08 |
| ❏ 475 T.J. Turner | .25 | .08 |
| ❏ 476 Mark Ingram | .25 | .08 |
| ❏ 477 Tim Grunhard | .25 | .08 |
| ❏ 478 Marion Butts FOIL | .50 | .20 |
| ❏ 479 Tom Rathman | .25 | .08 |
| ❏ 480 Brian Mitchell | .50 | .20 |
| ❏ 481 Bryce Paup | 1.00 | .40 |
| ❏ 482 Mike Pritchard | .50 | .20 |
| ❏ 483 Ken Norton Jr. | .50 | .20 |
| ❏ 484 Roman Phifer | .25 | .08 |
| ❏ 485 Greg Lloyd | .50 | .20 |
| ❏ 486 Brett Maxie | .25 | .08 |
| ❏ 487 Richard Dent FOIL SP | 1.50 | .60 |
| ❏ 488 Curtis Duncan | .25 | .08 |
| ❏ 489 Chris Burkett | .25 | .08 |
| ❏ 490 Travis McNeal | .25 | .08 |
| ❏ 491 Carl Lee | .25 | .08 |
| ❏ 492 Clarence Kay | .25 | .08 |
| ❏ 493 Tom Thayer | .25 | .08 |
| ❏ 494 Erik Kramer FOIL SP | 2.00 | .75 |
| ❏ 495 Perry Kemp | .25 | .08 |
| ❏ 496 Jeff Jaeger | .25 | .08 |
| ❏ 497 Eric Sanders | .25 | .08 |
| ❏ 498 Burt Grossman | .25 | .08 |
| ❏ 499 Ben Smith | .25 | .08 |
| ❏ 500 Keith McCants | .25 | .08 |
| ❏ 501 John Stephens | .25 | .08 |
| ❏ 502 John Rienstra | .25 | .08 |
| ❏ 503 Jim Ritcher | .25 | .08 |
| ❏ 504 Harris Barton | .25 | .08 |
| ❏ 505 Andre Rison FOIL SP | 2.00 | .75 |
| ❏ 506 Chris Martin | .25 | .08 |
| ❏ 507 Freddie Joe Nunn | .25 | .08 |
| ❏ 508 Mark Higgs | .25 | .08 |
| ❏ 509 Norm Johnson | .25 | .08 |
| ❏ 510 Stephen Baker | .25 | .08 |
| ❏ 511 Ricky Sanders | .25 | .08 |
| ❏ 512 Ray Donaldson | .25 | .08 |
| ❏ 513 David Fulcher | .25 | .08 |
| ❏ 514 Gerald Williams | .25 | .08 |
| ❏ 515 Toi Cook | .25 | .08 |
| ❏ 516 Chris Warren | 1.00 | .40 |
| ❏ 517 Jeff Gossett | .25 | .08 |
| ❏ 518 Ken Lanier | .25 | .08 |
| ❏ 519 Haywood Jeffires FOIL SP | 2.00 | .75 |
| ❏ 520 Kevin Glover | .25 | .08 |
| ❏ 521 Mo Lewis | .25 | .08 |
| ❏ 522 Bern Brostek | .25 | .08 |
| ❏ 523 Bo Orlando RC | .25 | .08 |
| ❏ 524 Mike Saxon | .25 | .08 |
| ❏ 525 Seth Joyner | .25 | .08 |
| ❏ 526 John Carney | .25 | .08 |
| ❏ 527 Jeff Cross | .25 | .08 |
| ❏ 528 Gary Anderson K FOIL SP | 1.50 | .60 |
| ❏ 529 Chuck Cecil | .25 | .08 |
| ❏ 530 Tim Green | .25 | .08 |
| ❏ 531 Kevin Porter | .25 | .08 |
| ❏ 532 Chris Spielman | .50 | .20 |
| ❏ 533 Willie Drewrey | .25 | .08 |
| ❏ 534 Chris Singleton UER | .25 | .08 |
| ❏ 535 Matt Stover | .25 | .08 |
| ❏ 536 Andre Collins | .25 | .08 |
| ❏ 537 Erik Howard | .25 | .08 |
| ❏ 538 Steve Tasker | .50 | .20 |
| ❏ 539 Anthony Thompson | .25 | .08 |
| ❏ 540 Charles Haley | .50 | .20 |
| ❏ 541 Mike Merriweather | .50 | .20 |
| ❏ 542 Henry Thomas | .25 | .08 |
| ❏ 543 Scott Stephen | .25 | .08 |
| ❏ 544 Bruce Kozerski | .25 | .08 |
| ❏ 545 Tim McKyer | .25 | .08 |
| ❏ 546 Chris Doleman | .25 | .08 |
| ❏ 547 Riki Ellison | .25 | .08 |
| ❏ 548 Mike Prior | .25 | .08 |
| ❏ 549 Dwayne Harper | .25 | .08 |
| ❏ 550 Bubby Brister | .25 | .08 |
| ❏ 551 Dave Meggett | .50 | .20 |
| ❏ 552 Greg Montgomery | .25 | .08 |
| ❏ 553 Kevin Mack | .50 | .20 |
| ❏ 554 Mark Stepnoski | .50 | .20 |
| ❏ 555 Kenny Walker | .25 | .08 |
| ❏ 556 Eric Moten | .25 | .08 |
| ❏ 557 Michael Stewart | .25 | .08 |
| ❏ 558 Calvin Williams | .50 | .20 |
| ❏ 559 Johnny Hector | .25 | .08 |
| ❏ 560 Tony Paige | .25 | .08 |
| ❏ 561 Tim Newton | .25 | .08 |
| ❏ 562 Brad Muster | .25 | .08 |
| ❏ 563 Aeneas Williams | .50 | .20 |
| ❏ 564 Herman Moore | 1.00 | .40 |
| ❏ 565 Checklist 460-573 | .25 | .08 |
| ❏ 566 Jerome Henderson | .25 | .08 |
| ❏ 567 Danny Copeland | .25 | .08 |
| ❏ 568 Alexander Wright | .50 | .20 |
| ❏ 569 Tim Harris | .25 | .08 |
| ❏ 570 Jonathan Hayes | .25 | .08 |
| ❏ 571 Tony Jones T | .25 | .08 |
| ❏ 572 Carlton Bailey RC | .25 | .08 |
| ❏ 573 Vaughan Johnson | .25 | .08 |

## 1993 Bowman

| | | |
|---|---|---|
| ❏ COMPLETE SET (423) | 25.00 | 10.00 |
| ❏ 1 Troy Aikman FOIL | 3.00 | 1.50 |
| ❏ 2 John Parrella RC | .20 | .07 |
| ❏ 3 Dana Stubblefield RC | .75 | .30 |
| ❏ 4 Mark Higgs | .20 | .07 |
| ❏ 5 Tom Carter RC | .40 | .15 |
| ❏ 6 Nate Lewis | .20 | .07 |
| ❏ 7 Vaughn Hebron RC | .20 | .07 |
| ❏ 8 Ernest Givins | .40 | .15 |
| ❏ 9 Vince Buck | .20 | .07 |
| ❏ 10 Levon Kirkland | .20 | .07 |
| ❏ 11 J.J. Birden | .20 | .07 |
| ❏ 12 Steve Jordan | .20 | .07 |
| ❏ 13 Simon Fletcher | .20 | .07 |
| ❏ 14 Willie Green | .20 | .07 |
| ❏ 15 Pepper Johnson | .20 | .07 |
| ❏ 16 Roger Harper RC | .20 | .07 |
| ❏ 17 Rob Moore | .40 | .15 |
| ❏ 18 David Lang | .20 | .07 |
| ❏ 19 David Klingler | .20 | .07 |
| ❏ 20 Garrison Hearst RC FOIL | 2.00 | .75 |

|  |  | | |
|---|--------|---|---|
| ❏ 21 | Anthony Johnson | .40 | .15 |
| ❏ 22 | Eric Curry RC FOIL | .40 | .15 |
| ❏ 23 | Nolan Harrison | .20 | .07 |
| ❏ 24 | Earl Dotson RC | .20 | .07 |
| ❏ 25 | Leonard Russell | .40 | .15 |
| ❏ 26 | Doug Riesenberg | .20 | .07 |
| ❏ 27 | Dwayne Harper | .20 | .07 |
| ❏ 28 | Richard Dent | .40 | .15 |
| ❏ 29 | Victor Bailey RC | .20 | .07 |
| ❏ 30 | Junior Seau | .75 | .30 |
| ❏ 31 | Steve Tasker | .40 | .15 |
| ❏ 32 | Kurt Gouveia | .20 | .07 |
| ❏ 33 | Renaldo Turnbull UER | .20 | .07 |
| ❏ 34 | Dale Carter | .20 | .07 |
| ❏ 35 | Russell Maryland | .20 | .07 |
| ❏ 36 | Dana Hall | .20 | .07 |
| ❏ 37 | Marco Coleman | .20 | .07 |
| ❏ 38 | Greg Montgomery | .20 | .07 |
| ❏ 39 | Deon Figures RC | .20 | .07 |
| ❏ 40 | Troy Drayton RC | .40 | .15 |
| ❏ 41 | Eric Metcalf | .40 | .15 |
| ❏ 42 | Michael Husted RC | .20 | .07 |
| ❏ 43 | Harry Newsome | .20 | .07 |
| ❏ 44 | Kelvin Pritchett | .20 | .07 |
| ❏ 45 | Andre Rison FOIL | .75 | .30 |
| ❏ 46 | John Copeland RC | .40 | .15 |
| ❏ 47 | Greg Biekert RC | .20 | .07 |
| ❏ 48 | Johnny Johnson | .20 | .07 |
| ❏ 49 | Chuck Cecil | .20 | .07 |
| ❏ 50 | Rick Mirer RC FOIL | 1.50 | .60 |
| ❏ 51 | Rod Bernstine | .20 | .07 |
| ❏ 52 | Steve McMichael | .40 | .15 |
| ❏ 53 | Roosevelt Potts RC | .75 | .30 |
| ❏ 54 | Mike Sherrard | .20 | .07 |
| ❏ 55 | Terrell Buckley | .20 | .07 |
| ❏ 56 | Eugene Chung | .20 | .07 |
| ❏ 57 | Kimble Anders RC | .75 | .30 |
| ❏ 58 | Daryl Johnston | .75 | .30 |
| ❏ 59 | Harris Barton | .20 | .07 |
| ❏ 60 | Thurman Thomas FOIL | 1.50 | .60 |
| ❏ 61 | Eric Martin | .20 | .07 |
| ❏ 62 | Reggie Brooks RC FOIL | .40 | .15 |
| ❏ 63 | Eric Bieniemy | .20 | .07 |
| ❏ 64 | John Offerdahl | .20 | .07 |
| ❏ 65 | Wilber Marshall | .20 | .07 |
| ❏ 66 | Mark Carrier WR | .40 | .15 |
| ❏ 67 | Merril Hoge | .20 | .07 |
| ❏ 68 | Cris Carter | .75 | .30 |
| ❏ 69 | Marty Thompson RC | .20 | .07 |
| ❏ 70 | Randall Cunningham FOIL | 1.50 | .60 |
| ❏ 71 | Winston Moss | .20 | .07 |
| ❏ 72 | Doug Pelfrey RC | .20 | .07 |
| ❏ 73 | Jackie Slater | .20 | .07 |
| ❏ 74 | Pierce Holt | .20 | .07 |
| ❏ 75 | Hardy Nickerson | .40 | .15 |
| ❏ 76 | Chris Burkett | .20 | .07 |
| ❏ 77 | Michael Brandon | .20 | .07 |
| ❏ 78 | Tom Waddle | .20 | .07 |
| ❏ 79 | Walter Reeves | .20 | .07 |
| ❏ 80 | Lawrence Taylor FOIL | .75 | .30 |
| ❏ 81 | Wayne Simmons RC | .20 | .07 |
| ❏ 82 | Brent Williams | .20 | .07 |
| ❏ 83 | Shannon Sharpe | .75 | .30 |
| ❏ 84 | Robert Blackmon | .20 | .07 |
| ❏ 85 | Keith Jackson | .40 | .15 |
| ❏ 86 | A.J. Johnson | .20 | .07 |
| ❏ 87 | Ryan McNeil RC | .75 | .30 |
| ❏ 88 | Michael Dean Perry | .40 | .15 |
| ❏ 89 | Russell Copeland RC | .40 | .15 |
| ❏ 90 | Sam Mills | .20 | .07 |
| ❏ 91 | Courtney Hall | .20 | .07 |
| ❏ 92 | Gino Torretta RC | .40 | .15 |
| ❏ 93 | Artie Smith RC | .20 | .07 |
| ❏ 94 | David Whitmore | .20 | .07 |
| ❏ 95 | Charles Haley | .40 | .15 |
| ❏ 96 | Rod Woodson | .75 | .30 |
| ❏ 97 | Lorenzo White | .20 | .07 |
| ❏ 98 | Tom Scott OL RC | .20 | .07 |
| ❏ 99 | Tyji Armstrong | .20 | .07 |
| ❏ 100 | Boomer Esiason | .40 | .15 |
| ❏ 101 | Rocket Ismail FOIL | .75 | .30 |
| ❏ 102 | Mark Carrier DB | .20 | .07 |
| ❏ 103 | Broderick Thompson | .20 | .07 |
| ❏ 104 | Bob Whitfield | .20 | .07 |
| ❏ 105 | Ben Coleman RC | .20 | .07 |
| ❏ 106 | Jon Vaughn | .20 | .07 |
| ❏ 107 | Marcus Buckley RC | .20 | .07 |
| ❏ 108 | Cleveland Gary | .20 | .07 |
| ❏ 109 | Ashley Ambrose | .20 | .07 |
| ❏ 110 | Reggie White FOIL | 1.50 | .60 |
| ❏ 111 | Arthur Marshall RC | .20 | .07 |
| ❏ 112 | Greg McMurtry | .20 | .07 |
| ❏ 113 | Mike Johnson | .20 | .07 |
| ❏ 114 | Tim McGee | .20 | .07 |
| ❏ 115 | John Carney | .20 | .07 |
| ❏ 116 | Neil Smith | .75 | .30 |
| ❏ 117 | Mark Stepnoski | .20 | .07 |
| ❏ 118 | Don Beebe | .20 | .07 |
| ❏ 119 | Scott Mitchell | .75 | .30 |
| ❏ 120 | Randall McDaniel | .20 | .07 |
| ❏ 121 | Chidi Ahanotu RC | .20 | .07 |
| ❏ 122 | Ray Childress | .20 | .07 |
| ❏ 123 | Tony McGee RC | .40 | .15 |
| ❏ 124 | Marc Boutte | .20 | .07 |
| ❏ 125 | Ronnie Lott | .40 | .15 |
| ❏ 126 | Jason Elam RC | .75 | .30 |
| ❏ 127 | Martin Harrison RC | .20 | .07 |
| ❏ 128 | Leonard Renfro RC | .20 | .07 |
| ❏ 129 | Jessie Armstead RC | .40 | .15 |
| ❏ 130 | Quentin Coryatt | .40 | .15 |
| ❏ 131 | Luis Sharpe | .20 | .07 |
| ❏ 132 | Bill Maas | .20 | .07 |
| ❏ 133 | Jesse Solomon | .20 | .07 |
| ❏ 134 | Kevin Greene | .40 | .15 |
| ❏ 135 | Derek Brown RB RBK | .40 | .15 |
| ❏ 136 | Greg Townsend | .20 | .07 |
| ❏ 137 | Neal Anderson | .20 | .07 |
| ❏ 138 | John L. Williams | .20 | .07 |
| ❏ 139 | Vincent Brisby RC | .75 | .30 |
| ❏ 140 | Barry Sanders FOIL | 5.00 | 2.00 |
| ❏ 141 | Charles Mann | .20 | .07 |
| ❏ 142 | Ken Norton | .40 | .15 |
| ❏ 143 | Eric Moten | .20 | .07 |
| ❏ 144 | John Alt | .20 | .07 |
| ❏ 145 | Dan Footman RC | .40 | .15 |
| ❏ 146 | Bill Brooks | .20 | .07 |
| ❏ 147 | James Thornton | .20 | .07 |
| ❏ 148 | Martin Mayhew | .20 | .07 |
| ❏ 149 | Andy Harmon | .40 | .15 |
| ❏ 150 | Dan Marino FOIL | 6.00 | 2.50 |
| ❏ 151 | Micheal Barrow RC | .75 | .30 |
| ❏ 152 | Flipper Anderson | .20 | .07 |
| ❏ 153 | Jackie Harris | .20 | .07 |
| ❏ 154 | Todd Kelly RC | .20 | .07 |
| ❏ 155 | Dan Williams RC | .20 | .07 |
| ❏ 156 | Harold Green | .20 | .07 |
| ❏ 157 | David Treadwell | .20 | .07 |
| ❏ 158 | Chris Doleman | .20 | .07 |
| ❏ 159 | Eric Hill | .20 | .07 |
| ❏ 160 | Lincoln Kennedy RC | .20 | .07 |
| ❏ 161 | Devon McDonald RC | .20 | .07 |
| ❏ 162 | Natrone Means RC | .75 | .30 |
| ❏ 163 | Rick Hamilton RC | .20 | .07 |
| ❏ 164 | Kelvin Martin | .20 | .07 |
| ❏ 165 | Jeff Hostetler | .40 | .15 |
| ❏ 166 | Mark Brunell RC | 4.00 | 1.50 |
| ❏ 167 | Tim Barnett | .20 | .07 |
| ❏ 168 | Ray Crockett | .20 | .07 |
| ❏ 169 | William Perry | .40 | .15 |
| ❏ 170 | Michael Irvin | .75 | .30 |
| ❏ 171 | Marvin Washington | .20 | .07 |
| ❏ 172 | Irving Fryar | .40 | .15 |
| ❏ 173 | Scott Sisson RC | .20 | .07 |
| ❏ 174 | Gary Anderson K | .20 | .07 |
| ❏ 175 | Bruce Smith | .75 | .30 |
| ❏ 176 | Clyde Simmons | .20 | .07 |
| ❏ 177 | Russell White RC | .40 | .15 |
| ❏ 178 | Irv Smith RC | .20 | .07 |
| ❏ 179 | Mark Wheeler | .20 | .07 |
| ❏ 180 | Warren Moon | .75 | .30 |
| ❏ 181 | Del Speer RC | .20 | .07 |
| ❏ 182 | Henry Thomas | .20 | .07 |
| ❏ 183 | Keith Kartz | .20 | .07 |
| ❏ 184 | Ricky Ervins | .20 | .07 |
| ❏ 185 | Phil Simms | .40 | .15 |
| ❏ 186 | Tim Brown | .75 | .30 |
| ❏ 187 | Willis Peguese | .20 | .07 |
| ❏ 188 | Rich Moran | .20 | .07 |
| ❏ 189 | Robert Jones | .20 | .07 |
| ❏ 190 | Craig Heyward | .40 | .15 |
| ❏ 191 | Ricky Watters | .75 | .30 |
| ❏ 192 | Stan Humphries | .40 | .15 |
| ❏ 193 | Larry Webster | .20 | .07 |
| ❏ 194 | Brad Baxter | .20 | .07 |
| ❏ 195 | Randal Hill | .20 | .07 |
| ❏ 196 | Robert Porcher | .20 | .07 |
| ❏ 197 | Patrick Robinson RC | .20 | .07 |
| ❏ 198 | Ferrell Edmunds | .20 | .07 |
| ❏ 199 | Melvin Jenkins | .20 | .07 |
| ❏ 200 | Joe Montana FOIL | 6.00 | 2.50 |
| ❏ 201 | Marv Cook | .20 | .07 |
| ❏ 202 | Henry Ellard | .40 | .15 |
| ❏ 203 | Calvin Williams | .40 | .15 |
| ❏ 204 | Craig Erickson | .40 | .15 |
| ❏ 205 | Steve Atwater | .20 | .07 |
| ❏ 206 | Najee Mustafaa | .20 | .07 |
| ❏ 207 | Darryl Talley | .20 | .07 |
| ❏ 208 | Jarrod Bunch | .20 | .07 |
| ❏ 209 | Tim McDonald | .20 | .07 |
| ❏ 210 | Patrick Bates RC | .20 | .07 |
| ❏ 211 | Sean Jones | .20 | .07 |
| ❏ 212 | Leslie O'Neal | .40 | .15 |
| ❏ 213 | Mike Golic | .20 | .07 |
| ❏ 214 | Mark Clayton | .20 | .07 |
| ❏ 215 | Leonard Marshall | .20 | .07 |
| ❏ 216 | Curtis Conway RC | 1.50 | .60 |
| ❏ 217 | Andre Hastings RC | .40 | .15 |
| ❏ 218 | Barry Word | .20 | .07 |
| ❏ 219 | Will Wolford | .20 | .07 |
| ❏ 220 | Desmond Howard | .40 | .15 |
| ❏ 221 | Rickey Jackson | .20 | .07 |
| ❏ 222 | Alvin Harper | .40 | .15 |
| ❏ 223 | William White | .20 | .07 |
| ❏ 224 | Steve Broussard | .20 | .07 |
| ❏ 225 | Aeneas Williams | .20 | .07 |
| ❏ 226 | Michael Brooks | .20 | .07 |
| ❏ 227 | Reggie Cobb | .20 | .07 |
| ❏ 228 | Derrick Walker | .20 | .07 |
| ❏ 229 | Marcus Allen | .75 | .30 |
| ❏ 230 | Jerry Ball | .20 | .07 |
| ❏ 231 | J.B. Brown | .20 | .07 |
| ❏ 232 | Terry McDaniel | .20 | .07 |
| ❏ 233 | LeRoy Butler | .20 | .07 |
| ❏ 234 | Kyle Clifton | .20 | .07 |
| ❏ 235 | Henry Jones | .20 | .07 |
| ❏ 236 | Shane Conlan | .20 | .07 |
| ❏ 237 | Michael Bates RC | .20 | .07 |
| ❏ 238 | Vincent Brown | .20 | .07 |
| ❏ 239 | William Fuller | .20 | .07 |
| ❏ 240 | Ricardo McDonald | .20 | .07 |
| ❏ 241 | Gary Zimmerman | .20 | .07 |
| ❏ 242 | Fred Barnett | .40 | .15 |
| ❏ 243 | Elvis Grbac RC | 4.00 | 1.50 |
| ❏ 244 | Myron Baker RC | .20 | .07 |
| ❏ 245 | Steve Emtman | .20 | .07 |
| ❏ 246 | Mike Compton RC | .75 | .30 |
| ❏ 247 | Mark Jackson | .20 | .07 |
| ❏ 248 | Santo Stephens RC | .20 | .07 |
| ❏ 249 | Tommie Agee | .20 | .07 |
| ❏ 250 | Broderick Thomas | .20 | .07 |
| ❏ 251 | Fred Baxter RC | .20 | .07 |
| ❏ 252 | Andre Collins | .20 | .07 |
| ❏ 253 | Ernest Dye RC | .20 | .07 |
| ❏ 254 | Raylee Johnson RC | .40 | .15 |
| ❏ 255 | Rickey Dixon | .20 | .07 |
| ❏ 256 | Ron Heller | .20 | .07 |
| ❏ 257 | Joel Steed | .20 | .07 |
| ❏ 258 | Everett Lindsay RC | .20 | .07 |
| ❏ 259 | Tony Smith RB | .20 | .07 |
| ❏ 260 | Sterling Sharpe UER | .75 | .30 |
| ❏ 261 | Tommy Vardell | .20 | .07 |
| ❏ 262 | Morten Andersen | .20 | .07 |
| ❏ 263 | Eddie Robinson | .20 | .07 |
| ❏ 264 | Jerome Bettis RC | 8.00 | 4.00 |
| ❏ 265 | Alonzo Spellman | .20 | .07 |
| ❏ 266 | Harvey Williams | .40 | .15 |
| ❏ 267 | Jason Belser RC | .20 | .07 |
| ❏ 268 | Derek Russell | .20 | .07 |
| ❏ 269 | Derrick Lassic RC | .40 | .15 |
| ❏ 270 | Steve Young FOIL | 3.00 | 1.50 |
| ❏ 271 | Adrian Murrell RC | .75 | .30 |
| ❏ 272 | Lewis Tillman | .20 | .07 |

| | | |
|---|---|---|
| ❑ 273 O.J.McDuffie RC | .75 | .30 |
| ❑ 274 Marty Carter | .20 | .07 |
| ❑ 275 Ray Seals | .20 | .07 |
| ❑ 276 Earnest Byner | .20 | .07 |
| ❑ 277 Marion Butts | .20 | .07 |
| ❑ 278 Chris Spielman | .40 | .15 |
| ❑ 279 Carl Pickens | .40 | .15 |
| ❑ 280 Drew Bledsoe RC FOIL | 6.00 | 2.50 |
| ❑ 281 Mark Kelso | .20 | .07 |
| ❑ 282 Eugene Robinson | .20 | .07 |
| ❑ 283 Eric Allen | .20 | .07 |
| ❑ 284 Ethan Horton | .20 | .07 |
| ❑ 285 Greg Lloyd | .40 | .15 |
| ❑ 286 Anthony Carter | .40 | .15 |
| ❑ 287 Edgar Bennett | .75 | .30 |
| ❑ 288 Bobby Hebert | .20 | .07 |
| ❑ 289 Haywood Jeffires | .40 | .15 |
| ❑ 290 Glyn Milburn RC | .75 | .30 |
| ❑ 291 Bernie Kosar | .40 | .15 |
| ❑ 292 Jumbo Elliott | .20 | .07 |
| ❑ 293 Jessie Hester | .20 | .07 |
| ❑ 294 Brent Jones | .40 | .15 |
| ❑ 295 Carl Banks | .20 | .07 |
| ❑ 296 Brian Washington | .20 | .07 |
| ❑ 297 Steve Beuerlein | .40 | .15 |
| ❑ 298 John Lynch RC | 2.00 | .75 |
| ❑ 299 Troy Vincent | .20 | .07 |
| ❑ 300 Emmitt Smith FOIL | 5.00 | 2.50 |
| ❑ 301 Chris Zorich | .20 | .07 |
| ❑ 302 Wade Wilson | .20 | .07 |
| ❑ 303 Darrien Gordon RC | .20 | .07 |
| ❑ 304 Fred Stokes | .20 | .07 |
| ❑ 305 Nick Lowery | .20 | .07 |
| ❑ 306 Rodney Peete | .20 | .07 |
| ❑ 307 Chris Warren | .40 | .15 |
| ❑ 308 Herschel Walker | .40 | .15 |
| ❑ 309 Aundray Bruce | .20 | .07 |
| ❑ 310 Barry Foster FOIL | .40 | .15 |
| ❑ 311 George Teague RC | .40 | .15 |
| ❑ 312 Darryl Williams | .20 | .07 |
| ❑ 313 Thomas Smith RC | .40 | .15 |
| ❑ 314 Dennis Brown | .20 | .07 |
| ❑ 315 Marvin Jones RC FOIL | .40 | .15 |
| ❑ 316 Andre Tippett | .20 | .07 |
| ❑ 317 Demetrius DuBose RC | .20 | .07 |
| ❑ 318 Kirk Lowdermilk | .20 | .07 |
| ❑ 319 Shane Dronett | .20 | .07 |
| ❑ 320 Terry Kirby RC | .75 | .30 |
| ❑ 321 Qadry Ismail RC | .75 | .30 |
| ❑ 322 Lorenzo Lynch | .20 | .07 |
| ❑ 323 Willie Drewrey | .20 | .07 |
| ❑ 324 Jessie Tuggle | .20 | .07 |
| ❑ 325 Leroy Hoard | .40 | .15 |
| ❑ 326 Mark Collins | .20 | .07 |
| ❑ 327 Darrell Green | .20 | .07 |
| ❑ 328 Anthony Miller | .40 | .15 |
| ❑ 329 Brad Muster | .20 | .07 |
| ❑ 330 Jim Kelly FOIL | 1.50 | .60 |
| ❑ 331 Sean Gilbert | .40 | .15 |
| ❑ 332 Tim McKyer | .20 | .07 |
| ❑ 333 Scott Mersereau | .20 | .07 |
| ❑ 334 Willie Davis | .75 | .30 |
| ❑ 335 Brett Favre FOIL | 6.00 | 3.00 |
| ❑ 336 Kevin Gogan | .20 | .07 |
| ❑ 337 Jim Harbaugh | .75 | .30 |
| ❑ 338 James Trapp RC | .20 | .07 |
| ❑ 339 Pete Stoyanovich | .20 | .07 |
| ❑ 340 Jerry Rice FOIL | 3.00 | 1.50 |
| ❑ 341 Gary Anderson RB | .20 | .07 |
| ❑ 342 Carlton Gray RC | .20 | .07 |
| ❑ 343 Dermontti Dawson | .20 | .07 |
| ❑ 344 Ray Buchanan RC | .75 | .30 |
| ❑ 345 Derrick Fenner | .20 | .07 |
| ❑ 346 Dennis Smith | .20 | .07 |
| ❑ 347 Todd Rucci RC | .20 | .07 |
| ❑ 348 Seth Joyner | .20 | .07 |
| ❑ 349 Jim McMahon | .40 | .15 |
| ❑ 350 Rodney Hampton | .40 | .15 |
| ❑ 351 Al Smith | .20 | .07 |
| ❑ 352 Steve Everitt RC | .20 | .07 |
| ❑ 353 Vinnie Clark | .20 | .07 |
| ❑ 354 Eric Swann | .40 | .15 |
| ❑ 355 Brian Mitchell | .40 | .15 |
| ❑ 356 Will Shields RC | .75 | .30 |

| | | |
|---|---|---|
| ❑ 357 Cornelius Bennett | .40 | .15 |
| ❑ 358 Darrin Smith RC | .40 | .15 |
| ❑ 359 Chris Mims | .20 | .07 |
| ❑ 360 Blair Thomas | .20 | .07 |
| ❑ 361 Dennis Gibson | .20 | .07 |
| ❑ 362 Santana Dotson | .40 | .15 |
| ❑ 363 Mark Ingram | .20 | .07 |
| ❑ 364 Don Mosebar | .20 | .07 |
| ❑ 365 Ty Detmer | .75 | .30 |
| ❑ 366 Bob Christian RC | .20 | .07 |
| ❑ 367 Adrian Hardy | .20 | .07 |
| ❑ 368 Vaughan Johnson | .20 | .07 |
| ❑ 369 Jim Everett | .40 | .15 |
| ❑ 370 Ricky Sanders | .20 | .07 |
| ❑ 371 Jonathan Hayes | .20 | .07 |
| ❑ 372 Bruce Matthews | .20 | .07 |
| ❑ 373 Darren Drozdov RC | .75 | .30 |
| ❑ 374 Scott Brumfield RC | .20 | .07 |
| ❑ 375 Cortez Kennedy | .40 | .15 |
| ❑ 376 Tim Harris | .20 | .07 |
| ❑ 377 Neil O'Donnell | .75 | .30 |
| ❑ 378 Robert Smith RC | 3.00 | 1.25 |
| ❑ 379 Mike Caldwell RC | .20 | .07 |
| ❑ 380 Burt Grossman | .20 | .07 |
| ❑ 381 Corey Miller | .20 | .07 |
| ❑ 382 Kev.Williams WR FOIL RC | .40 | .15 |
| ❑ 383 Ken Harvey | .20 | .07 |
| ❑ 384 Greg Robinson RC | .20 | .07 |
| ❑ 385 Harold Alexander RC | .20 | .07 |
| ❑ 386 Andre Reed | .40 | .15 |
| ❑ 387 Reggie Langhorne | .20 | .07 |
| ❑ 388 Courtney Hawkins | .20 | .07 |
| ❑ 389 James Hasty | .20 | .07 |
| ❑ 390 Pat Swilling | .20 | .07 |
| ❑ 391 Chris Slade RC | .40 | .15 |
| ❑ 392 Keith Byars | .20 | .07 |
| ❑ 393 Dalton Hilliard | .20 | .07 |
| ❑ 394 David Williams | .20 | .07 |
| ❑ 395 Terry Obee RC | .20 | .07 |
| ❑ 396 Heath Sherman | .20 | .07 |
| ❑ 397 John Taylor | .40 | .15 |
| ❑ 398 Irv Eatman | .20 | .07 |
| ❑ 399 Johnny Holland | .20 | .07 |
| ❑ 400 John Elway FOIL | 6.00 | 2.50 |
| ❑ 401 Clay Matthews | .40 | .15 |
| ❑ 402 Dave Meggett | .20 | .07 |
| ❑ 403 Eric Green | .20 | .07 |
| ❑ 404 Bryan Cox | .20 | .07 |
| ❑ 405 Jay Novacek | .40 | .15 |
| ❑ 406 Kenneth Davis | .20 | .07 |
| ❑ 407 Lamar Thomas RC | .20 | .07 |
| ❑ 408 Lance Gunn RC | .20 | .07 |
| ❑ 409 Audray McMillian | .20 | .07 |
| ❑ 410 Derrick Thomas FOIL | 1.50 | .60 |
| ❑ 411 Rufus Porter | .20 | .07 |
| ❑ 412 Coleman Rudolph RC | .20 | .07 |
| ❑ 413 Mark Rypien | .20 | .07 |
| ❑ 414 Duane Bickett | .20 | .07 |
| ❑ 415 Chris Singleton | .20 | .07 |
| ❑ 416 Mitch Lyons RC | .20 | .07 |
| ❑ 417 Bill Fralic | .20 | .07 |
| ❑ 418 Gary Plummer | .20 | .07 |
| ❑ 419 Ricky Proehl | .20 | .07 |
| ❑ 420 Howie Long | .75 | .30 |
| ❑ 421 Willie Roaf RC FOIL | .75 | .30 |
| ❑ 422 Checklist 1-212 | .20 | .07 |
| ❑ 423 Checklist 213-423 | .20 | .07 |

## 1994 Bowman

| | | |
|---|---|---|
| ❑ COMPLETE SET (390) | 50.00 | 20.00 |
| ❑ 1 Dan Wilkinson RC | .40 | .15 |
| ❑ 2 Marshall Faulk RC | 15.00 | 6.00 |
| ❑ 3 Heath Shuler RC | .75 | .30 |
| ❑ 4 Willie McGinest RC | .75 | .30 |
| ❑ 5 Trent Dilfer RC | 3.00 | 1.25 |
| ❑ 6 Brent Jones | .40 | .15 |
| ❑ 7 Sam Adams RC | .40 | .15 |
| ❑ 8 Randy Baldwin | .20 | .07 |
| ❑ 9 Jamir Miller RC | .40 | .15 |
| ❑ 10 John Thierry RC | .20 | .07 |
| ❑ 11 Aaron Glenn RC | .75 | .30 |
| ❑ 12 Joe Johnson RC | .20 | .07 |
| ❑ 13 Bernard Williams RC | .20 | .07 |
| ❑ 14 Wayne Gandy RC | .20 | .07 |

| | | |
|---|---|---|
| ❑ 15 Aaron Taylor RC | .20 | .07 |
| ❑ 16 Charles Johnson RC | .75 | .30 |
| ❑ 17 Dew.Washington RC UER 309 | .40 | .15 |
| ❑ 18 Bernie Kosar | .40 | .15 |
| ❑ 19 Johnnie Morton RC | 2.50 | 1.00 |
| ❑ 20 Rob Fredrickson RC | .40 | .15 |
| ❑ 21 Shante Carver RC | .20 | .07 |
| ❑ 22 Thomas Lewis RC | .40 | .15 |
| ❑ 23 Greg Hill RC | .75 | .30 |
| ❑ 24 Cris Dishman | .20 | .07 |
| ❑ 25 Jeff Burris RC | .40 | .15 |
| ❑ 26 Isaac Davis RC | .20 | .07 |
| ❑ 27 Bert Emanuel RC | .75 | .30 |
| ❑ 28 Allen Aldridge RC | .20 | .07 |
| ❑ 29 Kevin Lee RC | .20 | .07 |
| ❑ 30 Chris Brantley RC | .20 | .07 |
| ❑ 31 Rich Braham RC | .20 | .07 |
| ❑ 32 Ricky Watters | .40 | .15 |
| ❑ 33 Quentin Coryatt | .20 | .07 |
| ❑ 34 Hardy Nickerson | .40 | .15 |
| ❑ 35 Johnny Johnson | .20 | .07 |
| ❑ 36 Ken Harvey | .20 | .07 |
| ❑ 37 Chris Zorich | .20 | .07 |
| ❑ 38 Chris Warren | .40 | .15 |
| ❑ 39 David Palmer RC | .75 | .30 |
| ❑ 40 Chris Miller | .20 | .07 |
| ❑ 41 Ken Ruettgers | .20 | .07 |
| ❑ 42 Joe Panos RC | .20 | .07 |
| ❑ 43 Mario Bates RC | .75 | .30 |
| ❑ 44 Harry Colon | .20 | .07 |
| ❑ 45 Barry Foster | .20 | .07 |
| ❑ 46 Steve Tasker | .40 | .15 |
| ❑ 47 Richmond Webb | .20 | .07 |
| ❑ 48 James Folston RC | .20 | .07 |
| ❑ 49 Erik Williams | .20 | .07 |
| ❑ 50 Rodney Hampton | .40 | .15 |
| ❑ 51 Derek Russell | .20 | .07 |
| ❑ 52 Greg Montgomery | .20 | .07 |
| ❑ 53 Anthony Phillips | .20 | .07 |
| ❑ 54 Andre Coleman RC | .20 | .07 |
| ❑ 55 Gary Brown | .20 | .07 |
| ❑ 56 Neil Smith | .40 | .15 |
| ❑ 57 Myron Baker | .20 | .07 |
| ❑ 58 Sean Dawkins RC | .75 | .30 |
| ❑ 59 Marvin Washington | .20 | .07 |
| ❑ 60 Steve Beuerlein | .40 | .15 |
| ❑ 61 Brentson Buckner RC | .20 | .07 |
| ❑ 62 William Gaines RC | .20 | .07 |
| ❑ 63 LeShon Johnson RC | .40 | .15 |
| ❑ 64 Errict Rhett RC | .75 | .30 |
| ❑ 65 Jim Everett | .40 | .15 |
| ❑ 66 Desmond Howard | .40 | .15 |
| ❑ 67 Jack Del Rio | .20 | .07 |
| ❑ 68 Isaac Bruce RC | 12.00 | 6.00 |
| ❑ 69 Van Malone RC | .20 | .07 |
| ❑ 70 Jim Kelly | .75 | .30 |
| ❑ 71 Leon Lett | .20 | .07 |
| ❑ 72 Greg Robinson | .20 | .07 |
| ❑ 73 Ryan Yarborough RC | .20 | .07 |
| ❑ 74 Terry Wooden | .20 | .07 |
| ❑ 75 Eric Allen | .20 | .07 |
| ❑ 76 Ernest Givins | .40 | .15 |
| ❑ 77 Marcus Spears RC | .20 | .07 |
| ❑ 78 Thomas Randolph RC | .20 | .07 |
| ❑ 79 Willie Clark RC | .20 | .07 |
| ❑ 80 John Elway | 4.00 | 1.50 |
| ❑ 81 Aubrey Beavers RC | .20 | .07 |
| ❑ 82 Jeff Cothran RC | .20 | .07 |

|  |  | | |
|---|--------|------|------|
| 83 | Norm Johnson | .20 | .07 |
| 84 | Donnell Bennett RC | .75 | .30 |
| 85 | Phillippi Sparks | .20 | .07 |
| 86 | Scott Mitchell | .40 | .15 |
| 87 | Bucky Brooks RC | .20 | .07 |
| 88 | Courtney Hawkins | .20 | .07 |
| 89 | Kevin Greene | .40 | .15 |
| 90 | Doug Nussmeier RC | .20 | .07 |
| 91 | Floyd Turner | .20 | .07 |
| 92 | Anthony Newman | .20 | .07 |
| 93 | Vinny Testaverde | .40 | .15 |
| 94 | Ronnie Lott | .40 | .15 |
| 95 | Troy Aikman | 2.00 | .75 |
| 96 | John Taylor | .40 | .15 |
| 97 | Henry Ellard | .40 | .15 |
| 98 | Carl Lee | .20 | .07 |
| 99 | Terry McDaniel | .20 | .07 |
| 100 | Joe Montana | 4.00 | 1.50 |
| 101 | David Klingler | .20 | .07 |
| 102 | Bruce Walker RC | .20 | .07 |
| 103 | Rick Cunningham RC | .20 | .07 |
| 104 | Robert Delpino | .20 | .07 |
| 105 | Mark Ingram | .20 | .07 |
| 106 | Leslie O'Neal | .20 | .07 |
| 107 | Darrell Thompson | .20 | .07 |
| 108 | Dave Meggett | .20 | .07 |
| 109 | Chris Gardocki | .20 | .07 |
| 110 | Andre Rison | .40 | .15 |
| 111 | Kelvin Martin | .20 | .07 |
| 112 | Marcus Robertson | .20 | .07 |
| 113 | Jason Gildon RC | 3.00 | 1.25 |
| 114 | Mel Gray | .20 | .07 |
| 115 | Tommy Vardell | .20 | .07 |
| 116 | Dexter Carter | .20 | .07 |
| 117 | Scottie Graham RC | .40 | .15 |
| 118 | Horace Copeland | .20 | .07 |
| 119 | Cornelius Bennett | .40 | .15 |
| 120 | Chris Maumalanga RC | .20 | .07 |
| 121 | Mo Lewis | .20 | .07 |
| 122 | Toby Wright RC | .20 | .07 |
| 123 | George Hegamin RC | .20 | .07 |
| 124 | Chip Lohmiller | .20 | .07 |
| 125 | Calvin Jones RC | .20 | .07 |
| 126 | Steve Shine | .20 | .07 |
| 127 | Chuck Levy RC | .20 | .07 |
| 128 | Sam Mills | .20 | .07 |
| 129 | Terance Mathis | .40 | .15 |
| 130 | Randall Cunningham | .75 | .30 |
| 131 | John Fina | .20 | .07 |
| 132 | Reggie White | .75 | .30 |
| 133 | Tom Waddle | .20 | .07 |
| 134 | Chris Calloway | .20 | .07 |
| 135 | Kevin Mawae RC | .75 | .30 |
| 136 | Lake Dawson RC | .40 | .15 |
| 137 | Alai Kalaniuabu | .20 | .07 |
| 138 | Tom Nalen RC | .75 | .30 |
| 139 | Cody Carlson | .20 | .07 |
| 140 | Dan Marino | 4.00 | 1.50 |
| 141 | Harris Barton | .20 | .07 |
| 142 | Don Mosebar | .20 | .07 |
| 143 | Romeo Bandison | .20 | .07 |
| 144 | Bruce Smith | .75 | .30 |
| 145 | Warren Moon | .75 | .30 |
| 146 | David Lutz | .20 | .07 |
| 147 | Dermontti Dawson | .20 | .07 |
| 148 | Ricky Proehl | .20 | .07 |
| 149 | Lou Benfatti RC | .20 | .07 |
| 150 | Craig Erickson | .20 | .07 |
| 151 | Sean Gilbert | .20 | .07 |
| 152 | Zefross Moss | .20 | .07 |
| 153 | Darnay Scott RC | 1.25 | .50 |
| 154 | Courtney Hall | .20 | .07 |
| 155 | Brian Mitchell | .20 | .07 |
| 156 | Joe Burch RC UER 333 | .20 | .07 |
| 157 | Terry Mickens | .20 | .07 |
| 158 | Jay Novacek | .40 | .15 |
| 159 | Chris Gedney | .20 | .07 |
| 160 | Bruce Matthews | .20 | .07 |
| 161 | Marlo Perry RC | .20 | .07 |
| 162 | Vince Buck | .20 | .07 |
| 163 | Michael Bates | .20 | .07 |
| 164 | Willie Davis | .40 | .15 |
| 165 | Mike Pritchard | .20 | .07 |
| 166 | Doug Riesenberg | .20 | .07 |
| 167 | Herschel Walker | .40 | .15 |
| 168 | Tim Ruddy RC | .20 | .07 |
| 169 | William Floyd RC | .75 | .30 |
| 170 | John Randle | .40 | .15 |
| 171 | Winston Moss | .20 | .07 |
| 172 | Thurman Thomas | .75 | .30 |
| 173 | Eric England RC | .20 | .07 |
| 174 | Vincent Brisby | .40 | .15 |
| 175 | Greg Lloyd | .40 | .15 |
| 176 | Paul Gruber | .20 | .07 |
| 177 | Brad Ottis RC | .20 | .07 |
| 178 | George Teague | .20 | .07 |
| 179 | Willie Jackson RC | .75 | .30 |
| 180 | Barry Sanders | 3.00 | 1.25 |
| 181 | Brian Washington | .20 | .07 |
| 182 | Michael Jackson | .40 | .15 |
| 183 | Jason Mathews RC | .20 | .07 |
| 184 | Chester McGlockton | .20 | .07 |
| 185 | Tydus Winans RC | .20 | .07 |
| 186 | Michael Haynes | .40 | .15 |
| 187 | Erik Kramer | .40 | .15 |
| 188 | Chris Doleman | .20 | .07 |
| 189 | Haywood Jeffires | .40 | .15 |
| 190 | Larry Whigham RC | .20 | .07 |
| 191 | Shawn Jefferson | .20 | .07 |
| 192 | Pete Stoyanovich | .20 | .07 |
| 193 | Rod Bernstine | .20 | .07 |
| 194 | William Thomas | .20 | .07 |
| 195 | Marcus Allen | .75 | .30 |
| 196 | Dave Brown | .40 | .15 |
| 197 | Harold Bishop RC | .20 | .07 |
| 198 | Lorenzo Lynch | .20 | .07 |
| 199 | Dwight Stone | .20 | .07 |
| 200 | Jerry Rice | 2.00 | .75 |
| 201 | Rocket Ismail | .40 | .15 |
| 202 | LeRoy Butler | .20 | .07 |
| 203 | Glenn Parker | .20 | .07 |
| 204 | Bruce Armstrong | .20 | .07 |
| 205 | Shane Conlan | .20 | .07 |
| 206 | Russell Maryland | .20 | .07 |
| 207 | Herman Moore | .75 | .30 |
| 208 | Eric Martin | .20 | .07 |
| 209 | John Friesz | .40 | .15 |
| 210 | Boomer Esiason | .40 | .15 |
| 211 | Jim Harbaugh | .75 | .30 |
| 212 | Harold Green | .20 | .07 |
| 213 | Perry Klein RC | .20 | .07 |
| 214 | Eric Metcalf | .40 | .15 |
| 215 | Steve Everitt | .20 | .07 |
| 216 | Victor Bailey | .20 | .07 |
| 217 | Lincoln Kennedy | .20 | .07 |
| 218 | Glyn Milburn | .40 | .15 |
| 219 | John Copeland | .20 | .07 |
| 220 | Drew Bledsoe | 2.00 | .75 |
| 221 | Kevin Williams WR | .40 | .15 |
| 222 | Roosevelt Potts | .20 | .07 |
| 223 | Troy Drayton | .20 | .07 |
| 224 | Terry Kirby | .75 | .30 |
| 225 | Ronald Moore | .20 | .07 |
| 226 | Tyrone Hughes | .40 | .15 |
| 227 | Wayne Simmons | .20 | .07 |
| 228 | Tony McGee | .20 | .07 |
| 229 | Derek Brown RBK | .20 | .07 |
| 230 | Jason Elam | .40 | .15 |
| 231 | Qadry Ismail | .75 | .30 |
| 232 | O.J. McDuffie | .75 | .30 |
| 233 | Mike Caldwell | .20 | .07 |
| 234 | Reggie Brooks | .40 | .15 |
| 235 | Rick Mirer | .75 | .30 |
| 236 | Steve Tovar | .20 | .07 |
| 237 | Patrick Robinson | .20 | .07 |
| 238 | Tom Carter | .20 | .07 |
| 239 | Ben Coates | .40 | .15 |
| 240 | Jerome Bettis | 1.25 | .50 |
| 241 | Garrison Hearst | .75 | .30 |
| 242 | Natrone Means | .75 | .30 |
| 243 | Dana Stubblefield | .40 | .15 |
| 244 | Willie Roaf | .40 | .15 |
| 245 | Cortez Kennedy | .40 | .15 |
| 246 | Todd Steussie RC | .40 | .15 |
| 247 | Pat Coleman | .20 | .07 |
| 248 | David Wyman | .20 | .07 |
| 249 | Jeremy Lincoln | .20 | .07 |
| 250 | Carlester Crumpler | .20 | .07 |
| 251 | Dale Carter | .20 | .07 |
| 252 | Corey Raymond RC | .20 | .07 |
| 253 | Bryan Cox | .20 | .07 |
| 254 | Charlie Garner RC | 3.00 | 1.25 |
| 255 | Jeff Hostetler | .40 | .15 |
| 256 | Shane Bonham RC | .20 | .07 |
| 257 | Thomas Everett | .20 | .07 |
| 258 | John Jackson T | .20 | .07 |
| 259 | Terry Irving RC | .20 | .07 |
| 260 | Corey Sawyer | .40 | .15 |
| 261 | Rob Waldrop | .20 | .07 |
| 262 | Curtis Conway | .75 | .30 |
| 263 | Winfred Tubbs RC | .40 | .15 |
| 264 | Sean Jones | .20 | .07 |
| 265 | James Washington | .20 | .07 |
| 266 | Lonnie Johnson RC | .20 | .07 |
| 267 | Rob Moore | .40 | .15 |
| 268 | Flipper Anderson | .20 | .07 |
| 269 | Jon Hand | .20 | .07 |
| 270 | Joe Patton RC | .20 | .07 |
| 271 | Howard Ballard | .20 | .07 |
| 272 | Fernando Smith RC | .20 | .07 |
| 273 | Jessie Tuggle | .20 | .07 |
| 274 | John Alt | .20 | .07 |
| 275 | Corey Miller | .20 | .07 |
| 276 | Gus Frerotte RC | 3.00 | 1.25 |
| 277 | Jeff Cross | .20 | .07 |
| 278 | Kevin Smith | .40 | .15 |
| 279 | Corey Louchiey RC | .20 | .07 |
| 280 | Micheal Barrow | .20 | .07 |
| 281 | Jim Flanigan RC | .40 | .15 |
| 282 | Calvin Williams | .40 | .15 |
| 283 | Jeff Jaeger | .20 | .07 |
| 284 | John Reece RC | .20 | .07 |
| 285 | Jason Hanson | .20 | .07 |
| 286 | Kurt Haws RC | .20 | .07 |
| 287 | Eric Davis | .20 | .07 |
| 288 | Maurice Hurst | .20 | .07 |
| 289 | Kirk Lowdermilk | .20 | .07 |
| 290 | Rod Woodson | .40 | .15 |
| 291 | Andre Reed | .40 | .15 |
| 292 | Vince Workman | .20 | .07 |
| 293 | Wayne Martin | .20 | .07 |
| 294 | Keith Lyle RC | .20 | .07 |
| 295 | Brett Favre | 4.00 | 1.50 |
| 296 | Doug Brien RC | .20 | .07 |
| 297 | Junior Seau | .75 | .30 |
| 298 | Randall McDaniel | .20 | .07 |
| 299 | Johnny Mitchell | .20 | .07 |
| 300 | Emmitt Smith | 3.00 | 1.25 |
| 301 | Michael Brooks | .20 | .07 |
| 302 | Steve Jackson | .20 | .07 |
| 303 | Jeff George | .75 | .30 |
| 304 | Irving Fryar | .40 | .15 |
| 305 | Derrick Thomas | .75 | .30 |
| 306 | Dante Jones | .20 | .07 |
| 307 | Darrell Green | .20 | .07 |
| 308 | Mark Bavaro | .20 | .07 |
| 309 | Eugene Robinson | .20 | .07 |
| 310 | Shannon Sharpe | .40 | .15 |
| 311 | Michael Timpson | .20 | .07 |
| 312 | Kevin Mitchell RC | .20 | .07 |
| 313 | Stevon Moore | .20 | .07 |
| 314 | Eric Swann | .40 | .15 |
| 315 | James Bostic RC | .75 | .30 |
| 316 | Robert Brooks | .75 | .30 |
| 317 | Pete Pierson RC | .20 | .07 |
| 318 | Jim Sweeney | .20 | .07 |
| 319 | Anthony Smith | .20 | .07 |
| 320 | Rohn Stark | .20 | .07 |
| 321 | Gary Anderson K | .20 | .07 |
| 322 | Robert Porcher | .20 | .07 |
| 323 | Darryl Talley | .20 | .07 |
| 324 | Stan Humphries | .40 | .15 |
| 325 | Shelly Hammonds RC | .20 | .07 |
| 326 | Jim McMahon | .40 | .15 |
| 327 | Lamont Warren RC | .20 | .07 |
| 328 | Chris Penn RC | .20 | .07 |
| 329 | Tony Woods | .20 | .07 |
| 330 | Raymont Harris RC | .75 | .30 |
| 331 | Mitch Davis RC | .20 | .07 |
| 332 | Michael Irvin | .75 | .30 |
| 333 | Kent Graham | .40 | .15 |
| 334 | Brian Blades | .40 | .15 |

|  |  | | |
|---|------|---|---|
| ❏ 335 | Lomas Brown | .20 | .07 |
| ❏ 336 | Willie Drewrey | .20 | .07 |
| ❏ 337 | Russell Freeman | .20 | .07 |
| ❏ 338 | Eric Zomalt RC | .20 | .07 |
| ❏ 339 | Santana Dotson | .40 | .15 |
| ❏ 340 | Sterling Sharpe | .40 | .15 |
| ❏ 341 | Ray Crittenden RC | .20 | .07 |
| ❏ 342 | Perry Carter RC | .20 | .07 |
| ❏ 343 | Austin Robbins | .20 | .07 |
| ❏ 344 | Mike Wells DT RC | .20 | .07 |
| ❏ 345 | Toddrick McIntosh RC | .20 | .07 |
| ❏ 346 | Mark Carrier WR | .40 | .15 |
| ❏ 347 | Eugene Daniel | .20 | .07 |
| ❏ 348 | Tre Johnson RC | .20 | .07 |
| ❏ 349 | D.J. Johnson | .20 | .07 |
| ❏ 350 | Steve Young | 1.50 | .60 |
| ❏ 351 | Jim Pyne RC | .20 | .07 |
| ❏ 352 | Jocelyn Borgella RC | .20 | .07 |
| ❏ 353 | Pat Carter | .20 | .07 |
| ❏ 354 | Sam Rogers RC | .20 | .07 |
| ❏ 355 | Jason Sehorn RC | 1.25 | .50 |
| ❏ 356 | Darren Carrington | .20 | .07 |
| ❏ 357 | Lamar Smith RC | 4.00 | 1.50 |
| ❏ 358 | James Burton RC | .20 | .07 |
| ❏ 359 | Darrin Smith | .20 | .07 |
| ❏ 360 | Marco Coleman | .20 | .07 |
| ❏ 361 | Webster Slaughter | .20 | .07 |
| ❏ 362 | Lewis Tillman | .20 | .07 |
| ❏ 363 | David Alexander | .20 | .07 |
| ❏ 364 | Bradford Banta RC | .20 | .07 |
| ❏ 365 | Enric Pegram | .20 | .07 |
| ❏ 366 | Mike Fox | .20 | .07 |
| ❏ 367 | Jeff Lageman | .20 | .07 |
| ❏ 368 | Kurt Gouveia | .20 | .07 |
| ❏ 369 | Tim Brown | .75 | .30 |
| ❏ 370 | Seth Joyner | .20 | .07 |
| ❏ 371 | Irv Eatman | .20 | .07 |
| ❏ 372 | Dorsey Levens RC | 4.00 | 1.50 |
| ❏ 373 | Anthony Pleasant | .20 | .07 |
| ❏ 374 | Henry Jones | .20 | .07 |
| ❏ 375 | Cris Carter | 1.00 | .40 |
| ❏ 376 | Morten Andersen | .20 | .07 |
| ❏ 377 | Neil O'Donnell | .75 | .30 |
| ❏ 378 | Tyronne Drakeford RC | .20 | .07 |
| ❏ 379 | John Carney | .20 | .07 |
| ❏ 380 | Vincent Brown | .20 | .07 |
| ❏ 381 | J.J. Birden | .20 | .07 |
| ❏ 382 | Chris Spielman | .40 | .15 |
| ❏ 383 | Mark Bortz | .20 | .07 |
| ❏ 384 | Ray Childress | .20 | .07 |
| ❏ 385 | Carlton Bailey | .20 | .07 |
| ❏ 386 | Charles Haley | .40 | .15 |
| ❏ 387 | Shane Dronett | .20 | .07 |
| ❏ 388 | Jon Vaughn | .20 | .07 |
| ❏ 389 | Checklist 1-195 | .20 | .07 |
| ❏ 390 | Checklist 196-390 | .20 | .07 |

## 1995 Bowman

|  |  | | |
|---|------|---|---|
| ❏ | COMPLETE SET (357) | 60.00 | 25.00 |
| ❏ 1 | Ki-Jana Carter RC | .75 | .30 |
| ❏ 2 | Tony Boselli RC | .75 | .30 |
| ❏ 3 | Steve McNair RC | 8.00 | 3.00 |
| ❏ 4 | Michael Westbrook RC | .60 | .25 |
| ❏ 5 | Kerry Collins RC | 5.00 | 2.00 |
| ❏ 6 | Kevin Carter RC | .75 | .30 |
| ❏ 7 | Mike Mamula RC | .20 | .07 |
| ❏ 8 | Joey Galloway RC | 4.00 | 1.50 |
| ❏ 9 | Kyle Brady RC | .75 | .30 |
| ❏ 10 | J.J. Stokes RC | .75 | .30 |
| ❏ 11 | Derrick Alexander DE RC | .20 | .07 |
| ❏ 12 | Warren Sapp RC | 4.00 | 1.50 |
| ❏ 13 | Mark Fields RC | .75 | .30 |
| ❏ 14 | Ruben Brown RC | .75 | .30 |
| ❏ 15 | Ellis Johnson RC | .20 | .07 |
| ❏ 16 | Hugh Douglas RC | .75 | .30 |
| ❏ 17 | Mike Pelton RC | .20 | .07 |
| ❏ 18 | Napoleon Kaufman RC | 3.00 | 1.25 |
| ❏ 19 | James O. Stewart RC | 2.50 | 1.00 |
| ❏ 20 | Luther Elliss RC | .20 | .07 |
| ❏ 21 | Rashaan Salaam RC | .40 | .15 |
| ❏ 22 | Tyrone Poole RC | .75 | .30 |
| ❏ 23 | Ty Law RC | 3.00 | 1.25 |
| ❏ 24 | Korey Stringer RC | .40 | .15 |
| ❏ 25 | Billy Milner RC | .20 | .07 |
| ❏ 26 | Devin Bush RC | .20 | .07 |
| ❏ 27 | Mark Bruener RC | .40 | .15 |
| ❏ 28 | Derrick Brooks RC | 4.00 | 1.50 |
| ❏ 29 | Blake Brockermeyer RC | .20 | .07 |
| ❏ 30 | Alundis Brice RC | .20 | .07 |
| ❏ 31 | Trezelle Jenkins RC | .20 | .07 |
| ❏ 32 | Craig Newsome RC | .20 | .07 |
| ❏ 33 | Fred Barnett | .30 | .10 |
| ❏ 34 | Ray Childress | .15 | .05 |
| ❏ 35 | Chris Miller | .15 | .05 |
| ❏ 36 | Charles Haley | .30 | .10 |
| ❏ 37 | Ray Crittenden | .15 | .05 |
| ❏ 38 | Gus Frerotte | .30 | .10 |
| ❏ 39 | Jeff George | .30 | .10 |
| ❏ 40 | Dan Marino | 3.00 | 1.25 |
| ❏ 41 | Shawn Lee | .15 | .05 |
| ❏ 42 | Herman Moore | .60 | .25 |
| ❏ 43 | Chris Calloway | .15 | .05 |
| ❏ 44 | Jeff Graham | .15 | .05 |
| ❏ 45 | Ray Buchanan | .15 | .05 |
| ❏ 46 | Doug Pelfrey | .15 | .05 |
| ❏ 47 | Lake Dawson | .30 | .10 |
| ❏ 48 | Glenn Parker | .15 | .05 |
| ❏ 49 | Terry McDaniel | .15 | .05 |
| ❏ 50 | Rod Woodson | .30 | .10 |
| ❏ 51 | Santana Dotson | .15 | .05 |
| ❏ 52 | Anthony Miller | .15 | .05 |
| ❏ 53 | Bo Orlando | .15 | .05 |
| ❏ 54 | David Palmer | .30 | .10 |
| ❏ 55 | William Floyd | .30 | .10 |
| ❏ 56 | Edgar Bennett | .30 | .10 |
| ❏ 57 | Jeff Blake RC | 2.50 | 1.00 |
| ❏ 58 | Anthony Pleasant | .15 | .05 |
| ❏ 59 | Quinn Early | .30 | .10 |
| ❏ 60 | Bobby Houston | .15 | .05 |
| ❏ 61 | Terrell Fletcher RC | .20 | .07 |
| ❏ 62 | Gary Brown | .15 | .05 |
| ❏ 63 | Dwayne Sabb | .15 | .05 |
| ❏ 64 | Roman Phifer | .15 | .05 |
| ❏ 65 | Sherman Williams RC | .20 | .07 |
| ❏ 66 | Roosevelt Potts | .15 | .05 |
| ❏ 67 | Darnay Scott | .30 | .10 |
| ❏ 68 | Charlie Garner | .60 | .25 |
| ❏ 69 | Bert Emanuel | .60 | .25 |
| ❏ 70 | Herschel Walker | .30 | .10 |
| ❏ 71 | Lorenzo Styles RC | .20 | .07 |
| ❏ 72 | Andre Coleman | .15 | .05 |
| ❏ 73 | Tyronne Drakelord | .15 | .05 |
| ❏ 74 | Jay Novacek | .30 | .10 |
| ❏ 75 | Raymont Harris | .15 | .05 |
| ❏ 76 | Tamarick Vanover RC | .75 | .30 |
| ❏ 77 | Tom Carter | .15 | .05 |
| ❏ 78 | Eric Green | .15 | .05 |
| ❏ 79 | Patrick Hunter | .15 | .05 |
| ❏ 80 | Jeff Hostetler | .30 | .10 |
| ❏ 81 | Robert Blackmon | .15 | .05 |
| ❏ 82 | Anthony Cook RC | .20 | .07 |
| ❏ 83 | Craig Erickson | .15 | .05 |
| ❏ 84 | Glyn Milburn | .15 | .05 |
| ❏ 85 | Greg Lloyd | .30 | .10 |
| ❏ 86 | Brent Jones | .15 | .05 |
| ❏ 87 | Barrett Brooks RC | .20 | .07 |
| ❏ 88 | Alvin Harper | .15 | .05 |
| ❏ 89 | Sean Jones | .15 | .05 |
| ❏ 90 | Cris Carter | .60 | .25 |
| ❏ 91 | Russell Copeland | .15 | .05 |
| ❏ 92 | Frank Sanders RC | .75 | .30 |
| ❏ 93 | Mo Lewis | .15 | .05 |
| ❏ 94 | Michael Haynes | .30 | .10 |
| ❏ 95 | Andre Rison | .30 | .10 |
| ❏ 96 | Jesse James RC | .20 | .07 |
| ❏ 97 | Stan Humphries | .30 | .10 |
| ❏ 98 | James Hasty | .15 | .05 |
| ❏ 99 | Ricardo McDonald | .15 | .05 |
| ❏ 100 | Jerry Rice | 1.50 | .60 |
| ❏ 101 | Chris Hudson RC | .20 | .07 |
| ❏ 102 | Dave Meggett | .15 | .05 |
| ❏ 103 | Brian Mitchell | .15 | .05 |
| ❏ 104 | Mike Johnson | .15 | .05 |
| ❏ 105 | Kordell Stewart RC | 4.00 | 1.50 |
| ❏ 106 | Michael Brooks | .15 | .05 |
| ❏ 107 | Steve Walsh | .15 | .05 |
| ❏ 108 | Eric Metcalf | .30 | .10 |
| ❏ 109 | Ricky Watters | .30 | .10 |
| ❏ 110 | Brett Favre | 3.00 | 1.25 |
| ❏ 111 | Aubrey Beavers | .15 | .05 |
| ❏ 112 | Brian Williams LB RC | .20 | .07 |
| ❏ 113 | Eugene Robinson | .15 | .05 |
| ❏ 114 | Matt O'Dwyer RC | .20 | .07 |
| ❏ 115 | Micheal Barrow | .15 | .05 |
| ❏ 116 | Rocket Ismail | .30 | .10 |
| ❏ 117 | Scott Gragg RC | .20 | .07 |
| ❏ 118 | Leon Lett | .15 | .05 |
| ❏ 119 | Reggie Roby | .15 | .05 |
| ❏ 120 | Marshall Faulk | 2.00 | .75 |
| ❏ 121 | Jack Jackson RC | .20 | .07 |
| ❏ 122 | Keith Byars | .15 | .05 |
| ❏ 123 | Eric Hill | .15 | .05 |
| ❏ 124 | Todd Sauerbrun RC | .20 | .07 |
| ❏ 125 | Dexter Carter | .15 | .05 |
| ❏ 126 | Vinny Testaverde | .30 | .10 |
| ❏ 127 | Shane Conlan | .15 | .05 |
| ❏ 128 | Terrance Shaw RC | .20 | .07 |
| ❏ 129 | Willie Roaf | .15 | .05 |
| ❏ 130 | Jim Kelly | .60 | .25 |
| ❏ 131 | Neil O'Donnell | .30 | .10 |
| ❏ 132 | Ray McElroy RC | .20 | .07 |
| ❏ 133 | Ed McDaniel | .15 | .05 |
| ❏ 134 | Brian Gelzheiser RC | .20 | .07 |
| ❏ 135 | Marcus Allen | .60 | .25 |
| ❏ 136 | Carl Pickens | .30 | .10 |
| ❏ 137 | Mike Verstegan RC | .20 | .07 |
| ❏ 138 | Chris Mims | .15 | .05 |
| ❏ 139 | Darryl Pounds RC | .20 | .07 |
| ❏ 140 | Emmitt Smith | 2.50 | 1.25 |
| ❏ 141 | Mike Frederick RC | .20 | .07 |
| ❏ 142 | Henry Ellard | .30 | .10 |
| ❏ 143 | Willie McGinest | .30 | .10 |
| ❏ 144 | Michael Roan RC | .20 | .07 |
| ❏ 145 | Chris Spielman | .30 | .10 |
| ❏ 146 | Darryl Talley | .15 | .05 |
| ❏ 147 | Randall Cunningham | .60 | .25 |
| ❏ 148 | Andrew Greene RC | .20 | .07 |
| ❏ 149 | George Teague | .15 | .05 |
| ❏ 150 | Tyrone Hughes | .30 | .10 |
| ❏ 151 | Ron Davis RC | .20 | .07 |
| ❏ 152 | Stevon Moore | .15 | .05 |
| ❏ 153 | Merton Hanks | .15 | .05 |
| ❏ 154 | Darren Perry | .15 | .05 |
| ❏ 155 | Dave Brown | .30 | .10 |
| ❏ 156 | Mike Morton RC | .20 | .07 |
| ❏ 157 | Seth Joyner | .15 | .05 |
| ❏ 158 | Bryan Cox | .15 | .05 |
| ❏ 159 | Corey Fuller RC | .20 | .07 |
| ❏ 160 | John Elway | 3.00 | 1.25 |
| ❏ 161 | Dewayne Washington | .30 | .10 |
| ❏ 162 | Chris Warren | .30 | .10 |
| ❏ 163 | Jeff Kopp RC | .20 | .07 |
| ❏ 164 | Sean Dawkins | .30 | .10 |
| ❏ 165 | Mark Carrier DB | .15 | .05 |
| ❏ 166 | Andre Hastings | .30 | .10 |
| ❏ 167 | Derek West RC | .20 | .07 |
| ❏ 168 | Glenn Montgomery | .15 | .05 |
| ❏ 169 | Trent Differ | .60 | .25 |
| ❏ 170 | Rob Johnson RC | 2.50 | 1.00 |
| ❏ 171 | Todd Scott | .15 | .05 |
| ❏ 172 | Charles Johnson | .30 | .10 |
| ❏ 173 | Kez McCorvey RC | .20 | .07 |
| ❏ 174 | Rob Fredrickson | .15 | .05 |
| ❏ 175 | Corey Sawyer | .15 | .05 |
| ❏ 176 | Brett Perriman | .30 | .10 |
| ❏ 177 | Ken Dilger RC | .75 | .30 |

| | | |
|---|---|---|
| ☐ 178 Dana Stubblefield | .30 | .10 |
| ☐ 179 Eric Allen | .15 | .05 |
| ☐ 180 Drew Bledsoe | 1.00 | .40 |
| ☐ 181 Tyrone Davis RC | .20 | .07 |
| ☐ 182 Reggie Brooks | .30 | .10 |
| ☐ 183 Dale Carter | .30 | .10 |
| ☐ 184 William Henderson RC | 3.00 | 1.25 |
| ☐ 185 Reggie White | .60 | .25 |
| ☐ 186 Lorenzo White | .15 | .05 |
| ☐ 187 Leslie O'Neal | .30 | .10 |
| ☐ 188 Stoney Case RC | .20 | .07 |
| ☐ 189 Jeff Burris | .15 | .05 |
| ☐ 190 Leroy Hoard | .15 | .05 |
| ☐ 191 Thomas Randolph | .15 | .05 |
| ☐ 192 Rodney Thomas RC | .40 | .15 |
| ☐ 193 Quentin Coryatt | .30 | .10 |
| ☐ 194 Terry Wooden | .15 | .05 |
| ☐ 195 David Sloan RC | .20 | .07 |
| ☐ 196 Bernie Parmalee | .30 | .10 |
| ☐ 197 Zack Crockett RC | .40 | .15 |
| ☐ 198 Troy Aikman | 1.50 | .60 |
| ☐ 199 Bruce Smith | .60 | .25 |
| ☐ 200 Eric Zeier RC | .75 | .30 |
| ☐ 201 Anthony Smith | .15 | .05 |
| ☐ 202 Jake Reed | .30 | .10 |
| ☐ 203 Hardy Nickerson | .15 | .05 |
| ☐ 204 Patrick Riley RC | .20 | .07 |
| ☐ 205 Bruce Matthews | .15 | .05 |
| ☐ 206 Larry Centers | .30 | .10 |
| ☐ 207 Troy Drayton | .15 | .05 |
| ☐ 208 John Burrough RC | .20 | .07 |
| ☐ 209 Jason Elam | .30 | .10 |
| ☐ 210 Donnell Woolford | .15 | .05 |
| ☐ 211 Sam Shade RC | .20 | .07 |
| ☐ 212 Kevin Greene | .30 | .10 |
| ☐ 213 Ronald Moore | .15 | .05 |
| ☐ 214 Shane Hannah RC | .20 | .07 |
| ☐ 215 Jim Everett | .15 | .05 |
| ☐ 216 Scott Mitchell | .30 | .10 |
| ☐ 217 Antonio Freeman RC | 3.00 | 1.25 |
| ☐ 218 Tony McGee | .15 | .05 |
| ☐ 219 Clay Matthews | .30 | .10 |
| ☐ 220 Neil Smith | .30 | .10 |
| ☐ 221 Mark Williams FOIL | .40 | .15 |
| ☐ 222 Derrick Graham FOIL | .40 | .15 |
| ☐ 223 Mike Hollis FOIL | .40 | .15 |
| ☐ 224 Darion Conner FOIL | .40 | .15 |
| ☐ 225 Steve Beuerlein FOIL | .40 | .15 |
| ☐ 226 Rod Smith DB FOIL | .40 | .15 |
| ☐ 227 James Williams LB FOIL | .40 | .15 |
| ☐ 228 Bob Christian FOIL | .40 | .15 |
| ☐ 229 Jeff Lageman FOIL | .40 | .15 |
| ☐ 230 Frank Reich FOIL | .40 | .15 |
| ☐ 231 Harry Colon FOIL | .40 | .15 |
| ☐ 232 Carlton Bailey FOIL | .40 | .15 |
| ☐ 233 Mickey Washington FOIL | .40 | .15 |
| ☐ 234 Shawn Bouwens FOIL | .40 | .15 |
| ☐ 235 Don Beebe FOIL | .40 | .15 |
| ☐ 236 Kelvin Pritchett FOIL | .40 | .15 |
| ☐ 237 Tommy Barnhardt FOIL | .40 | .15 |
| ☐ 238 Mike Dumas FOIL | .40 | .15 |
| ☐ 239 Brett Maxie FOIL | .40 | .15 |
| ☐ 240 Desmond Howard FOIL | .40 | .15 |
| ☐ 241 Sam Mills FOIL | .40 | .15 |
| ☐ 242 Keith Goganious FOIL | .40 | .15 |
| ☐ 243 Bubba McDowell FOIL | .40 | .15 |
| ☐ 244 Vinnie Clark FOIL | .40 | .15 |
| ☐ 245 Lamar Lathon FOIL | .40 | .15 |
| ☐ 246 Bryan Barker FOIL | .40 | .15 |
| ☐ 247 Darren Carrington FOIL | .40 | .15 |
| ☐ 248 Jay Barker RC | .20 | .07 |
| ☐ 249 Eric Davis | .15 | .05 |
| ☐ 250 Heath Shuler | .30 | .10 |
| ☐ 251 Donta Jones RC | .20 | .07 |
| ☐ 252 LeRoy Butler | .15 | .05 |
| ☐ 253 Michael Zordich | .15 | .05 |
| ☐ 254 Corey Harris RC | .30 | .10 |
| ☐ 255 Brian DeMarco RC | .20 | .07 |
| ☐ 256 Randal Hill | .15 | .05 |
| ☐ 257 Michael Irvin | .60 | .25 |
| ☐ 258 Natrone Means | .15 | .05 |
| ☐ 259 Linc Harden RC | .15 | .05 |
| ☐ 260 Jerome Bettis | .60 | .25 |
| ☐ 261 Tony Bennett | .15 | .05 |

| | | |
|---|---|---|
| ☐ 262 Dameian Jeffires RC | .20 | .07 |
| ☐ 263 Cornelius Bennett | .30 | .10 |
| ☐ 264 Chris Zorich | .15 | .05 |
| ☐ 265 Bobby Taylor RC | .75 | .30 |
| ☐ 266 Terrell Buckley | .15 | .05 |
| ☐ 267 Troy Dumas RC | .20 | .07 |
| ☐ 268 Rodney Hampton | .30 | .10 |
| ☐ 269 Steve Everitt | .15 | .05 |
| ☐ 270 Mel Gray | .15 | .05 |
| ☐ 271 Antonio Armstrong RC | .20 | .07 |
| ☐ 272 Jim Harbaugh | .30 | .10 |
| ☐ 273 Gary Clark | .15 | .05 |
| ☐ 274 Tau Pupua RC | .20 | .07 |
| ☐ 275 Warren Moon | .30 | .10 |
| ☐ 276 Corey Croom | .15 | .05 |
| ☐ 277 Tony Berti RC | .20 | .07 |
| ☐ 278 Shannon Sharpe | .30 | .10 |
| ☐ 279 Boomer Esiason | .30 | .10 |
| ☐ 280 Aeneas Williams | .15 | .05 |
| ☐ 281 Lethon Flowers RC | .20 | .07 |
| ☐ 282 Derek Brown TE | .15 | .05 |
| ☐ 283 Charlie Williams RC | .20 | .07 |
| ☐ 284 Dan Wilkinson | .30 | .10 |
| ☐ 285 Mike Sherrard | .15 | .05 |
| ☐ 286 Evan Pilgrim RC | .20 | .07 |
| ☐ 287 Kimble Anders | .30 | .10 |
| ☐ 288 Greg Jefferson RC | .20 | .07 |
| ☐ 289 Ken Norton | .30 | .10 |
| ☐ 290 Terance Mathis | .30 | .10 |
| ☐ 291 Torey Hunter RC | .20 | .07 |
| ☐ 292 Ken Harvey | .15 | .05 |
| ☐ 293 Irving Fryar | .30 | .10 |
| ☐ 294 Michael Reed RC | .20 | .07 |
| ☐ 295 Andre Reed | .30 | .10 |
| ☐ 296 Vencie Glenn | .15 | .05 |
| ☐ 297 Corey Swinson | .15 | .05 |
| ☐ 298 Harvey Williams | .30 | .10 |
| ☐ 299 Willie Davis | .30 | .10 |
| ☐ 300 Barry Sanders | 2.50 | 1.00 |
| ☐ 301 Curtis Martin RC | 8.00 | 3.00 |
| ☐ 302 Johnny Mitchell | .15 | .05 |
| ☐ 303 Daryl Johnston | .30 | .10 |
| ☐ 304 Lorenzo Lynch | .15 | .05 |
| ☐ 305 Christian Fauria RC | .40 | .15 |
| ☐ 306 Sean Gilbert | .30 | .10 |
| ☐ 307 Ray Zellars RC | .40 | .15 |
| ☐ 308 William Strong RC | .20 | .07 |
| ☐ 309 Jack Del Rio | .15 | .05 |
| ☐ 310 Junior Seau | .60 | .25 |
| ☐ 311 Justin Armour RC | .20 | .07 |
| ☐ 312 Eric Bjornson RC | .20 | .07 |
| ☐ 313 Vincent Brown | .15 | .05 |
| ☐ 314 Darius Holland RC | .20 | .07 |
| ☐ 315 Chad May RC | .20 | .07 |
| ☐ 316 Simon Fletcher | .15 | .05 |
| ☐ 317 Roell Preston RC | .30 | .10 |
| ☐ 318 John Thierry | .15 | .05 |
| ☐ 319 Orlando Thomas RC | .20 | .07 |
| ☐ 320 Zach Wiegert RC | .20 | .07 |
| ☐ 321 Derrick Alexander WR | .60 | .25 |
| ☐ 322 Chris Cowart RC | .20 | .07 |
| ☐ 323 Chris Sanders RC | .40 | .15 |
| ☐ 324 Robert Brooks | .60 | .25 |
| ☐ 325 Todd Collins RC | 2.50 | 1.00 |
| ☐ 326 Ken Irvin RC | .20 | .07 |
| ☐ 327 Erric Pegram | .30 | .10 |
| ☐ 328 Damien Covington RC | .20 | .07 |
| ☐ 329 Brendan Stai RC | .20 | .07 |
| ☐ 330 James A.Stewart RC | .20 | .07 |
| ☐ 331 Jessie Tuggle | .15 | .05 |
| ☐ 332 Marco Coleman | .15 | .05 |
| ☐ 333 Steve Young | 1.25 | .50 |
| ☐ 334 Greg Hill | .30 | .10 |
| ☐ 335 Darryl Williams | .15 | .05 |
| ☐ 336 Calvin Williams | .30 | .10 |
| ☐ 337 Cris Dishman | .15 | .05 |
| ☐ 338 Anthony Morgan | .15 | .05 |
| ☐ 339 Renaldo Turnbull | .15 | .05 |
| ☐ 340 Rick Mirer | .30 | .10 |
| ☐ 341 Tim Brown | .60 | .25 |
| ☐ 342 Dennis Gibson | .15 | .05 |
| ☐ 343 Brad Baxter | .15 | .05 |
| ☐ 344 Henry Jones | .15 | .05 |
| ☐ 345 Johnny Bailey | .15 | .05 |

| | | |
|---|---|---|
| ☐ 346 Rocket Ismail | .30 | .10 |
| ☐ 347 Richmond Webb | .15 | .05 |
| ☐ 348 Robert Jones | .15 | .05 |
| ☐ 349 Garrison Hearst | .60 | .25 |
| ☐ 350 Errict Rhett | .30 | .10 |
| ☐ 351 Steve Atwater | .15 | .05 |
| ☐ 352 Joe Cain | .15 | .05 |
| ☐ 353 Ben Coates | .30 | .10 |
| ☐ 354 Aaron Glenn | .15 | .05 |
| ☐ 355 Antonio Langham | .15 | .05 |
| ☐ 356 Eugene Daniel | .15 | .05 |
| ☐ 357 Tim Bowens | .15 | .05 |

## 1998 Bowman

| | | |
|---|---|---|
| ☐ COMPLETE SET (220) | 50.00 | 20.00 |
| ☐ 1 Peyton Manning RC | 25.00 | 10.00 |
| ☐ 2 Keith Brooking RC | 1.50 | .60 |
| ☐ 3 Duane Starks RC | .75 | .30 |
| ☐ 4 Takeo Spikes RC | 1.50 | .60 |
| ☐ 5 Andre Wadsworth RC | 1.25 | .50 |
| ☐ 6 Greg Ellis RC | .75 | .30 |
| ☐ 7 Brian Griese RC | 3.00 | 1.25 |
| ☐ 8 Germane Crowell RC | 1.25 | .50 |
| ☐ 9 Jerome Pathon RC | 1.25 | .60 |
| ☐ 10 Ryan Leaf RC | 1.50 | .60 |
| ☐ 11 Fred Taylor RC | 2.50 | 1.00 |
| ☐ 12 Robert Edwards RC | 1.25 | .50 |
| ☐ 13 Grant Wistrom RC | 1.25 | .50 |
| ☐ 14 Robert Holcombe RC | 1.25 | .50 |
| ☐ 15 Tim Dwight RC | 1.50 | .60 |
| ☐ 16 Jacquez Green RC | 1.25 | .50 |
| ☐ 17 Marcus Nash RC | .75 | .30 |
| ☐ 18 Jason Peter RC | .75 | .30 |
| ☐ 19 Anthony Simmons RC | 1.25 | .50 |
| ☐ 20 Curtis Enis RC | .75 | .30 |
| ☐ 21 John Avery RC | 1.25 | .50 |
| ☐ 22 Pat Johnson RC | 1.25 | .50 |
| ☐ 23 Joe Jurevicius RC | 1.50 | .60 |
| ☐ 24 Brian Simmons RC | 1.25 | .50 |
| ☐ 25 Kevin Dyson RC | 1.50 | .60 |
| ☐ 26 Skip Hicks RC | 1.25 | .50 |
| ☐ 27 Hines Ward RC | 8.00 | 3.00 |
| ☐ 28 Tavian Banks RC | 1.25 | .50 |
| ☐ 29 Ahman Green RC | 5.00 | 2.00 |
| ☐ 30 Tony Simmons RC | 1.25 | .50 |
| ☐ 31 Charles Johnson | .30 | .10 |
| ☐ 32 Freddie Jones | .30 | .10 |
| ☐ 33 Joey Galloway | .50 | .20 |
| ☐ 34 Tony Banks | .50 | .20 |
| ☐ 35 Jake Plummer | .75 | .30 |
| ☐ 36 Reidel Anthony | .50 | .20 |
| ☐ 37 Steve McNair | .50 | .20 |
| ☐ 38 Michael Westbrook | .50 | .20 |
| ☐ 39 Chris Sanders | .30 | .10 |
| ☐ 40 Isaac Bruce | .75 | .30 |
| ☐ 41 Charlie Garner | .75 | .30 |
| ☐ 42 Wayne Chrebet | .75 | .30 |
| ☐ 43 Michael Strahan | .50 | .20 |
| ☐ 44 Brad Johnson | .75 | .30 |
| ☐ 45 Mike Alstott | .75 | .30 |
| ☐ 46 Tony Gonzalez | .75 | .30 |
| ☐ 47 Johnnie Morton | .50 | .20 |
| ☐ 48 Darnay Scott | .50 | .20 |
| ☐ 49 Rae Carruth | .30 | .10 |
| ☐ 50 Terrell Davis | .75 | .30 |
| ☐ 51 Jermaine Lewis | .50 | .20 |
| ☐ 52 Frank Sanders | .50 | .20 |
| ☐ 53 Byron Hanspard | .30 | .10 |

**1999 Bowman**

| | | |
|---|---|---|
| ❏ 54 Gus Frerotte | .30 | .10 |
| ❏ 55 Terry Glenn | .75 | .30 |
| ❏ 56 J.J. Stokes | .50 | .20 |
| ❏ 57 Will Blackwell | .30 | .10 |
| ❏ 58 Keyshawn Johnson | .75 | .30 |
| ❏ 59 Tiki Barber | .75 | .30 |
| ❏ 60 Dorsey Levens | .75 | .30 |
| ❏ 61 Zach Thomas | .75 | .30 |
| ❏ 62 Corey Dillon | .75 | .30 |
| ❏ 63 Antowain Smith | .75 | .30 |
| ❏ 64 Michael Sinclair | .30 | .10 |
| ❏ 65 Rod Smith | .50 | .20 |
| ❏ 66 Trent Dilfer | .75 | .30 |
| ❏ 67 Warren Sapp | .50 | .20 |
| ❏ 68 Charles Way | .30 | .10 |
| ❏ 69 Tamarick Vanover | .30 | .10 |
| ❏ 70 Drew Bledsoe | 1.25 | .50 |
| ❏ 71 John Mobley | .30 | .10 |
| ❏ 72 Kerry Collins | .50 | .20 |
| ❏ 73 Peter Boulware | .30 | .10 |
| ❏ 74 Simeon Rice | .50 | .20 |
| ❏ 75 Eddie George | .75 | .30 |
| ❏ 76 Fred Lane | .30 | .10 |
| ❏ 77 Jamal Anderson | .75 | .30 |
| ❏ 78 Antonio Freeman | .75 | .30 |
| ❏ 79 Jason Sehorn | .50 | .20 |
| ❏ 80 Curtis Martin | .75 | .30 |
| ❏ 81 Bobby Hoying | .30 | .10 |
| ❏ 82 Garrison Hearst | .50 | .20 |
| ❏ 83 Glenn Foley | .50 | .20 |
| ❏ 84 Danny Kanell | .30 | .10 |
| ❏ 85 Kordell Stewart | .75 | .30 |
| ❏ 86 O.J. McDuffie | .50 | .20 |
| ❏ 87 Marvin Harrison | .75 | .30 |
| ❏ 88 Bobby Engram | .50 | .20 |
| ❏ 89 Chris Slade | .30 | .10 |
| ❏ 90 Warrick Dunn | .75 | .30 |
| ❏ 91 Ricky Watters | .50 | .20 |
| ❏ 92 Rickey Dudley | .30 | .10 |
| ❏ 93 Terrell Owens | .75 | .30 |
| ❏ 94 Karim Abdul-Jabbar | .75 | .30 |
| ❏ 95 Napoleon Kaufman | .75 | .30 |
| ❏ 96 Darrell Green | .50 | .20 |
| ❏ 97 Levon Kirkland | .30 | .10 |
| ❏ 98 Jeff George | .50 | .20 |
| ❏ 99 Andre Hastings | .30 | .10 |
| ❏ 100 John Elway | 3.00 | 1.25 |
| ❏ 101 John Randle | .50 | .20 |
| ❏ 102 Andre Rison | .50 | .20 |
| ❏ 103 Keenan McCardell | .50 | .20 |
| ❏ 104 Marshall Faulk | 1.00 | .40 |
| ❏ 105 Emmitt Smith | 2.50 | 1.00 |
| ❏ 106 Robert Brooks | .50 | .20 |
| ❏ 107 Scott Mitchell | .50 | .20 |
| ❏ 108 Shannon Sharpe | .50 | .20 |
| ❏ 109 Deion Sanders | .75 | .30 |
| ❏ 110 Jerry Rice | 1.50 | .60 |
| ❏ 111 Erik Kramer | .30 | .10 |
| ❏ 112 Michael Jackson | .30 | .10 |
| ❏ 113 Aeneas Williams | .30 | .10 |
| ❏ 114 Terry Allen | .75 | .30 |
| ❏ 115 Steve Young | 1.00 | .40 |
| ❏ 116 Warren Moon | .75 | .30 |
| ❏ 117 Junior Seau | .75 | .30 |
| ❏ 118 Jerome Bettis | .75 | .30 |
| ❏ 119 Irving Fryar | .50 | .20 |
| ❏ 120 Barry Sanders | 2.50 | 1.00 |
| ❏ 121 Tim Brown | .75 | .30 |
| ❏ 122 Chad Brown | .30 | .10 |
| ❏ 123 Ben Coates | .50 | .20 |
| ❏ 124 Robert Smith | .75 | .30 |
| ❏ 125 Brett Favre | 3.00 | 1.25 |
| ❏ 126 Derrick Thomas | .75 | .30 |
| ❏ 127 Reggie White | .75 | .30 |
| ❏ 128 Troy Aikman | 1.50 | .60 |
| ❏ 129 Jeff Blake | .50 | .20 |
| ❏ 130 Mark Brunell | .75 | .30 |
| ❏ 131 Curtis Conway | .50 | .20 |
| ❏ 132 Wesley Walls | .50 | .20 |
| ❏ 133 Thurman Thomas | .50 | .20 |
| ❏ 134 Chris Chandler | .50 | .20 |
| ❏ 135 Dan Marino | 3.00 | 1.25 |
| ❏ 136 Larry Centers | .30 | .10 |
| ❏ 137 Shawn Jefferson | .30 | .10 |
| ❏ 138 Andre Reed | .50 | .20 |
| ❏ 139 Jake Reed | .50 | .20 |
| ❏ 140 Cris Carter | .75 | .30 |
| ❏ 141 Elvis Grbac | .50 | .20 |
| ❏ 142 Mark Chmura | .50 | .20 |
| ❏ 143 Michael Irvin | .75 | .30 |
| ❏ 144 Carl Pickens | .50 | .20 |
| ❏ 145 Herman Moore | .50 | .20 |
| ❏ 146 Marvin Jones | .30 | .10 |
| ❏ 147 Terance Mathis | .50 | .20 |
| ❏ 148 Rob Moore | .50 | .20 |
| ❏ 149 Bruce Smith | .50 | .20 |
| ❏ 150 Rob Johnson CL | .30 | .10 |
| ❏ 151 Leslie Shepherd | .30 | .10 |
| ❏ 152 Chris Spielman | .30 | .10 |
| ❏ 153 Tony McGee | .30 | .10 |
| ❏ 154 Kevin Smith | .30 | .10 |
| ❏ 155 Bill Romanowski | .30 | .10 |
| ❏ 156 Stephen Boyd | .30 | .10 |
| ❏ 157 James Stewart | .50 | .20 |
| ❏ 158 Jason Taylor | .50 | .20 |
| ❏ 159 Troy Drayton | .30 | .10 |
| ❏ 160 Mark Fields | .30 | .10 |
| ❏ 161 Jessie Armstead | .30 | .10 |
| ❏ 162 James Jett | .50 | .20 |
| ❏ 163 Bobby Taylor | .30 | .10 |
| ❏ 164 Kimble Anders | .30 | .10 |
| ❏ 165 Jimmy Smith | .50 | .20 |
| ❏ 166 Quentin Coryatt | .30 | .10 |
| ❏ 167 Bryant Westbrook | .30 | .10 |
| ❏ 168 Neil Smith | .50 | .20 |
| ❏ 169 Darren Woodson | .30 | .10 |
| ❏ 170 Ray Buchanan | .30 | .10 |
| ❏ 171 Earl Holmes | .30 | .10 |
| ❏ 172 Ray Lewis | .75 | .30 |
| ❏ 173 Steve Broussard | .30 | .10 |
| ❏ 174 Derrick Brooks | .75 | .30 |
| ❏ 175 Ken Harvey | .30 | .10 |
| ❏ 176 Darryll Lewis | .30 | .10 |
| ❏ 177 Derrick Rodgers | .30 | .10 |
| ❏ 178 James McKnight | .30 | .10 |
| ❏ 179 Cris Dishman | .30 | .10 |
| ❏ 180 Hardy Nickerson | .30 | .10 |
| ❏ 181 Charles Woodson RC | 2.00 | .75 |
| ❏ 182 Randy Moss RC | 15.00 | 6.00 |
| ❏ 183 Stephen Alexander RC | 1.25 | .50 |
| ❏ 184 Samari Rolle RC | .75 | .30 |
| ❏ 185 James Duncan RC | .75 | .30 |
| ❏ 186 Lance Schulters RC | .75 | .30 |
| ❏ 187 Tony Parrish RC | 1.50 | .60 |
| ❏ 188 Corey Chavous RC | 1.50 | .60 |
| ❏ 189 Jammi German RC | .75 | .30 |
| ❏ 190 Sam Cowart RC | 1.25 | .50 |
| ❏ 191 Donald Hayes RC | 1.25 | .50 |
| ❏ 192 R.W. McQuarters RC | 1.25 | .50 |
| ❏ 193 Az-Zahir Hakim RC | 1.50 | .60 |
| ❏ 194 Chris Fuamatu-Ma'afala RC | 1.25 | .50 |
| ❏ 195 Allen Rossum RC | 1.25 | .50 |
| ❏ 196 Jon Ritchie RC | 1.25 | .50 |
| ❏ 197 Blake Spence RC | .75 | .30 |
| ❏ 198 Brian Alford RC | .75 | .30 |
| ❏ 199 Fred Weary RC | .75 | .30 |
| ❏ 200 Rod Rutledge RC | .75 | .30 |
| ❏ 201 Michael Myers RC | .75 | .30 |
| ❏ 202 Rashaan Shehee RC | 1.25 | .50 |
| ❏ 203 Donovin Darius RC | 1.25 | .50 |
| ❏ 204 E.G. Green RC | 1.25 | .50 |
| ❏ 205 Vonnie Holliday RC | 1.25 | .50 |
| ❏ 206 Charlie Batch RC | 1.50 | .60 |
| ❏ 207 Michael Pittman RC | 2.00 | .75 |
| ❏ 208 Artrell Hawkins RC | .75 | .30 |
| ❏ 209 Jonathan Quinn RC | 1.50 | .60 |
| ❏ 210 Kailee Wong RC | .75 | .30 |
| ❏ 211 DeShea Townsend RC | .75 | .30 |
| ❏ 212 Patrick Surtain RC | 1.50 | .60 |
| ❏ 213 Brian Kelly RC | 1.25 | .50 |
| ❏ 214 Tebucky Jones RC | .75 | .30 |
| ❏ 215 Pete Gonzalez RC | .75 | .30 |
| ❏ 216 Shaun Williams RC | 1.25 | .50 |
| ❏ 217 Scott Frost RC | .75 | .30 |
| ❏ 218 Leonard Little RC | 1.50 | .60 |
| ❏ 219 Alonzo Mayes RC | .75 | .30 |
| ❏ 220 Cordell Taylor RC | .30 | .10 |

| | | |
|---|---|---|
| ❏ COMPLETE SET (220) | 40.00 | 15.00 |
| ❏ 1 Dan Marino | 2.50 | 1.00 |
| ❏ 2 Michael Westbrook | .50 | .20 |
| ❏ 3 Yancey Thigpen | .30 | .10 |
| ❏ 4 Tony Martin | .50 | .20 |
| ❏ 5 Michael Strahan | .50 | .20 |
| ❏ 6 Dedric Ward | .30 | .10 |
| ❏ 7 Joey Galloway | .50 | .20 |
| ❏ 8 Bobby Engram | .50 | .20 |
| ❏ 9 Frank Sanders | .50 | .20 |
| ❏ 10 Jake Plummer | .50 | .20 |
| ❏ 11 Eddie Kennison | .50 | .20 |
| ❏ 12 Curtis Martin | .75 | .30 |
| ❏ 13 Chris Spielman | .30 | .10 |
| ❏ 14 Trent Dilfer | .50 | .20 |
| ❏ 15 Tim Biakabutuka | .50 | .20 |
| ❏ 16 Elvis Grbac | .50 | .20 |
| ❏ 17 Charlie Batch | .75 | .30 |
| ❏ 18 Takeo Spikes | .30 | .10 |
| ❏ 19 Tony Banks | .50 | .20 |
| ❏ 20 Doug Flutie | .75 | .30 |
| ❏ 21 Ty Law | .50 | .20 |
| ❏ 22 Isaac Bruce | .50 | .20 |
| ❏ 23 James Jett | .50 | .20 |
| ❏ 24 Kent Graham | .30 | .10 |
| ❏ 25 Derrick Mayes | .30 | .10 |
| ❏ 26 Amani Toomer | .30 | .10 |
| ❏ 27 Ray Lewis | .75 | .30 |
| ❏ 28 Shawn Springs | .30 | .10 |
| ❏ 29 Warren Sapp | .30 | .10 |
| ❏ 30 Jamal Anderson | .75 | .30 |
| ❏ 31 Byron Bam Morris | .30 | .10 |
| ❏ 32 Johnnie Morton | .30 | .10 |
| ❏ 33 Terance Mathis | .30 | .10 |
| ❏ 34 Terrell Davis | .75 | .30 |
| ❏ 35 John Randle | .50 | .20 |
| ❏ 36 Vinny Testaverde | .50 | .20 |
| ❏ 37 Junior Seau | .75 | .30 |
| ❏ 38 Riedel Anthony | .50 | .20 |
| ❏ 39 Brad Johnson | .50 | .20 |
| ❏ 40 Emmitt Smith | 1.50 | .60 |
| ❏ 41 Mo Lewis | .30 | .10 |
| ❏ 42 Terry Glenn | .75 | .30 |
| ❏ 43 Dorsey Levens | .75 | .30 |
| ❏ 44 Thurman Thomas | .50 | .20 |
| ❏ 45 Rob Moore | .50 | .20 |
| ❏ 46 Corey Dillon | .75 | .30 |
| ❏ 47 Jessie Armstead | .30 | .10 |
| ❏ 48 Marshall Faulk | 1.00 | .40 |
| ❏ 49 Charles Woodson | .75 | .30 |
| ❏ 50 John Elway | 2.50 | 1.00 |
| ❏ 51 Kevin Dyson | .50 | .20 |
| ❏ 52 Tony Simmons | .30 | .10 |
| ❏ 53 Keenan McCardell | .50 | .20 |
| ❏ 54 O.J. Santiago | .30 | .10 |
| ❏ 55 Jermaine Lewis | .50 | .20 |
| ❏ 56 Herman Moore | .50 | .20 |
| ❏ 57 Gary Brown | .30 | .10 |
| ❏ 58 Jim Harbaugh | .50 | .20 |
| ❏ 59 Mike Alstott | .75 | .30 |
| ❏ 60 Brett Favre | 2.50 | 1.00 |
| ❏ 61 Tim Brown | .75 | .30 |
| ❏ 62 Steve McNair | .75 | .30 |
| ❏ 63 Ben Coates | .50 | .20 |
| ❏ 64 Jerome Pathon | .30 | .10 |
| ❏ 65 Ray Buchanan | .30 | .10 |

| | | | | | | |
|---|---|---|---|---|---|---|
| 66 Troy Aikman | 1.50 | .60 | 150 Tiki Barber | .75 | .30 | |
| 67 Andre Reed | .50 | .20 | 151 David Boston RC | 2.00 | .75 | |
| 68 Bubby Brister | .30 | .10 | 152 Chris McAlister RC | 1.50 | .60 | |
| 69 Karim Abdul-Jabbar | .50 | .20 | 153 Peerless Price RC | 2.00 | .75 | |
| 70 Peyton Manning | 2.50 | 1.00 | 154 D'Wayne Bates RC | 1.50 | .60 | |
| 71 Charles Johnson | .30 | .10 | 155 Cade McNown RC | 1.50 | .60 | |
| 72 Natrone Means | .50 | .20 | 156 Akili Smith RC | 1.50 | .60 | |
| 73 Michael Sinclair | .30 | .10 | 157 Kevin Johnson RC | 2.00 | .75 | |
| 74 Skip Hicks | .30 | .10 | 158 Tim Couch RC | 2.00 | .75 | |
| 75 Derrick Alexander | .50 | .20 | 159 Sedrick Irvin RC | .75 | .30 | |
| 76 Wayne Chrebet | .50 | .20 | 160 Chris Claiborne RC | .75 | .30 | |
| 77 Rod Smith | .50 | .20 | 161 Edgerrin James RC | 8.00 | 3.00 | |
| 78 Cari Pickens | .50 | .20 | 162 Mike Cloud RC | 1.50 | .60 | |
| 79 Adrian Murrell | .50 | .20 | 163 Cecil Collins RC | .75 | .30 | |
| 80 Fred Taylor | .75 | .30 | 164 James Johnson RC | 1.50 | .60 | |
| 81 Eric Moulds | .75 | .30 | 165 Rob Konrad RC | 2.00 | .75 | |
| 82 Lawrence Phillips | .50 | .20 | 166 Daunte Culpepper RC | 8.00 | 3.00 | |
| 83 Marvin Harrison | .75 | .30 | 167 Kevin Faulk RC | 2.00 | .75 | |
| 84 Cris Carter | .75 | .30 | 168 Donovan McNabb RC | 10.00 | 4.00 | |
| 85 Ike Hilliard | .30 | .10 | 169 Troy Edwards RC | 1.50 | .60 | |
| 86 Hines Ward | .75 | .30 | 170 Amos Zereoue RC | 2.00 | .75 | |
| 87 Terrell Owens | .75 | .30 | 171 Karsten Bailey RC | 1.50 | .60 | |
| 88 Ricky Proehl | .30 | .10 | 172 Brock Huard RC | 2.00 | .75 | |
| 89 Bert Emanuel | .50 | .20 | 173 Joe Germaine RC | 1.50 | .60 | |
| 90 Randy Moss | 2.00 | .75 | 174 Torry Holt RC | 5.00 | 2.00 | |
| 91 Aaron Glenn | .30 | .10 | 175 Shaun King RC | 1.50 | .60 | |
| 92 Robert Smith | .75 | .30 | 176 Jevon Kearse RC | 3.00 | 1.25 | |
| 93 Andre Hastings | .30 | .10 | 177 Champ Bailey RC | 2.50 | 1.00 | |
| 94 Jake Reed | .50 | .20 | 178 Ebenezer Ekuban RC | 1.50 | .60 | |
| 95 Curtis Enis | .30 | .10 | 179 Andy Katzenmoyer RC | 1.50 | .60 | |
| 96 Andre Wadsworth | .30 | .10 | 180 Antoine Winfield RC | 1.50 | .60 | |
| 97 Ed McCaffrey | .50 | .20 | 181 Jermaine Fazande RC | 1.50 | .60 | |
| 98 Zach Thomas | .75 | .30 | 182 Ricky Williams RC | 4.00 | 1.50 | |
| 99 Kerry Collins | .50 | .20 | 183 Joel Makovicka RC | 2.00 | .75 | |
| 100 Drew Bledsoe | 1.00 | .40 | 184 Reginald Kelly RC | .75 | .30 | |
| 101 Germane Crowell | .30 | .10 | 185 Brandon Stokley RC | 2.50 | 1.00 | |
| 102 Bryan Still | .30 | .10 | 186 L.C. Stevens RC | .75 | .30 | |
| 103 Chad Brown | .30 | .10 | 187 Marty Booker RC | 2.00 | .75 | |
| 104 Jacquez Green | .30 | .10 | 188 Jerry Azumah RC | 2.00 | .75 | |
| 105 Garrison Hearst | .50 | .20 | 189 Ted White RC | .75 | .30 | |
| 106 Napoleon Kaufman | .75 | .30 | 190 Scott Covington RC | 2.00 | .75 | |
| 107 Ricky Watters | .50 | .20 | 191 Tim Alexander RC | .75 | .30 | |
| 108 O.J. McDuffie | .50 | .20 | 192 Darrin Chiaverini RC | 1.50 | .60 | |
| 109 Keyshawn Johnson | .75 | .30 | 193 Dat Nguyen RC | 2.00 | .75 | |
| 110 Jerome Bettis | .75 | .30 | 194 Wane McGarity RC | .75 | .30 | |
| 111 Duce Staley | .75 | .30 | 195 Al Wilson RC | 2.00 | .75 | |
| 112 Curtis Conway | .50 | .20 | 196 Travis McGriff RC | .75 | .30 | |
| 113 Chris Chandler | .50 | .20 | 197 Stacey Mack RC | 2.00 | .75 | |
| 114 Marcus Nash | .30 | .10 | 198 Antuan Edwards RC | .75 | .30 | |
| 115 Stephen Alexander | .30 | .10 | 199 Aaron Brooks RC | 4.00 | 1.50 | |
| 116 Darnay Scott | .30 | .10 | 200 De'Mond Parker RC | .75 | .30 | |
| 117 Bruce Smith | .50 | .20 | 201 Jed Weaver RC | .75 | .30 | |
| 118 Priest Holmes | 1.25 | .50 | 202 Madre Hill RC | .75 | .30 | |
| 119 Mark Brunell | .75 | .30 | 203 Jim Kleinsasser RC | 2.00 | .75 | |
| 120 Jerry Rice | 1.50 | .60 | 204 Michael Bishop RC | 2.00 | .75 | |
| 121 Randall Cunningham | .75 | .30 | 205 Michael Basnight RC | .75 | .30 | |
| 122 Scott Mitchell | .30 | .10 | 206 Sean Bennett RC | .75 | .30 | |
| 123 Antonio Freeman | .75 | .30 | 207 Dameane Douglas RC | 1.50 | .60 | |
| 124 Kordell Stewart | .50 | .20 | 208 Na Brown RC | 1.50 | .60 | |
| 125 Jon Kitna | .75 | .30 | 209 Patrick Kerney RC | 2.00 | .75 | |
| 126 Ahman Green | .75 | .30 | 210 Malcolm Johnson RC | .75 | .30 | |
| 127 Warrick Dunn | .75 | .30 | 211 Dre Bly RC | 2.00 | .75 | |
| 128 Robert Brooks | .50 | .20 | 212 Terry Jackson RC | 1.50 | .60 | |
| 129 Derrick Thomas | .75 | .30 | 213 Eugene Baker RC | .75 | .30 | |
| 130 Steve Young | 1.00 | .40 | 214 Autry Denson RC | .75 | .30 | |
| 131 Peter Boulware | .30 | .10 | 215 Darnell McDonald RC | 1.50 | .60 | |
| 132 Michael Irvin | .50 | .20 | 216 Charlie Rogers RC | 1.50 | .60 | |
| 133 Shannon Sharpe | .50 | .20 | 217 Joe Montgomery RC | 1.50 | .60 | |
| 134 Jimmy Smith | .50 | .20 | 218 Cecil Martin RC | 1.50 | .60 | |
| 135 John Avery | .30 | .10 | 219 Larry Parker RC | 2.00 | .75 | |
| 136 Fred Lane | .30 | .10 | 220 Mike Peterson RC | 2.00 | .75 | |
| 137 Trent Green | .50 | .20 | | | | |

## 2000 Bowman

| | | | | | | |
|---|---|---|---|---|---|---|
| 138 Andre Rison | .50 | .20 | COMPLETE SET (240) | 80.00 | 30.00 | |
| 139 Antowain Smith | .50 | .20 | 1 Eddie George | .60 | .25 | |
| 140 Eddie George | .75 | .30 | 2 Ike Hilliard | .40 | .15 | |
| 141 Jeff Blake | .50 | .20 | 3 Terrell Owens | .60 | .25 | |
| 142 Rocket Ismail | .30 | .10 | 4 James Stewart | .40 | .15 | |
| 143 Rickey Dudley | .30 | .10 | 5 Joey Galloway | .40 | .15 | |
| 144 Courtney Hawkins | .30 | .10 | 6 Jake Reed | .40 | .15 | |
| 145 Mikhael Ricks | .30 | .10 | 7 Derrick Alexander | .40 | .15 | |
| 146 J.J. Stokes | .50 | .20 | 8 Jeff George | .40 | .15 | |
| 147 Levon Kirkland | .30 | .10 | 9 Kerry Collins | .40 | .15 | |
| 148 Deion Sanders | .75 | .30 | 10 Tony Gonzalez | .40 | .15 | |
| 149 Barry Sanders | 2.50 | 1.00 | | | | |

| | | |
|---|---|---|
| 11 Marcus Robinson | .60 | .25 |
| 12 Charles Woodson | .40 | .15 |
| 13 Germane Crowell | .25 | .08 |
| 14 Yancey Thigpen | .25 | .08 |
| 15 Tony Martin | .40 | .15 |
| 16 Frank Sanders | .40 | .15 |
| 17 Napoleon Kaufman | .40 | .15 |
| 18 Jay Fiedler | .60 | .25 |
| 19 Patrick Jeffers | .60 | .25 |
| 20 Steve McNair | .40 | .15 |
| 21 Herman Moore | .40 | .15 |
| 22 Tim Brown | .60 | .25 |
| 23 Olandis Gary | .60 | .25 |
| 24 Corey Dillon | .60 | .25 |
| 25 Warren Sapp | .40 | .15 |
| 26 Curtis Enis | .25 | .08 |
| 27 Vinny Testaverde | .40 | .15 |
| 28 Tim Biakabutuka | .40 | .15 |
| 29 Kevin Johnson | .60 | .25 |
| 30 Charlie Batch | .60 | .25 |
| 31 Jermaine Fazande | .25 | .08 |
| 32 Shaun King | .60 | .25 |
| 33 Errict Rhett | .40 | .15 |
| 34 O.J. McDuffie | .40 | .15 |
| 35 Bruce Smith | .40 | .15 |
| 36 Antonio Freeman | .60 | .25 |
| 37 Tim Couch | .40 | .15 |
| 38 Duce Staley | .60 | .25 |
| 39 Jeff Blake | .40 | .15 |
| 40 Jim Harbaugh | .40 | .15 |
| 41 Jeff Graham | .25 | .08 |
| 42 Drew Bledsoe | .75 | .30 |
| 43 Mike Alstott | .60 | .25 |
| 44 Terance Mathis | .40 | .15 |
| 45 Antowain Smith | .40 | .15 |
| 46 Jerome Bettis | .60 | .25 |
| 47 Chris Chandler | .40 | .15 |
| 48 Keith Poole | .40 | .15 |
| 49 Ricky Watters | .40 | .15 |
| 50 Darnay Scott | .40 | .15 |
| 51 Damon Huard | .60 | .25 |
| 52 Peerless Price | .40 | .15 |
| 53 Brian Griese | .60 | .25 |
| 54 Frank Wycheck | .25 | .08 |
| 55 Kevin Dyson | .40 | .15 |
| 56 Junior Seau | .40 | .15 |
| 57 Curtis Conway | .40 | .15 |
| 58 Jamal Anderson | .60 | .25 |
| 59 Jim Miller | .25 | .08 |
| 60 Rob Johnson | .25 | .08 |
| 61 Mark Brunell | .60 | .25 |
| 62 Wayne Chrebet | .40 | .15 |
| 63 James Johnson | .25 | .08 |
| 64 Sean Dawkins | .25 | .08 |
| 65 Stephen Davis | .60 | .25 |
| 66 Daunte Culpepper | .75 | .30 |
| 67 Doug Flutie | .60 | .25 |
| 68 Pete Mitchell | .25 | .08 |
| 69 Bill Schroeder | .40 | .15 |
| 70 Terrence Wilkins | .25 | .08 |
| 71 Cade McNown | .25 | .08 |
| 72 Muhsin Muhammad | .40 | .15 |
| 73 E.G. Green | .25 | .08 |
| 74 Edgerrin James | 1.00 | .40 |
| 75 Troy Edwards | .25 | .08 |
| 76 Terry Glenn | .40 | .15 |
| 77 Tony Banks | .40 | .15 |
| 78 Derrick Mayes | .40 | .15 |

| | | |
|---|---|---|
| ❑ 79 Curtis Martin | .60 | .25 |
| ❑ 80 Kordell Stewart | .40 | .15 |
| ❑ 81 Amani Toomer | .40 | .15 |
| ❑ 82 Dorsey Levens | .40 | .15 |
| ❑ 83 Brad Johnson | .60 | .25 |
| ❑ 84 Ed McCaffrey | .60 | .25 |
| ❑ 85 Charlie Garner | .40 | .15 |
| ❑ 86 Brett Favre | 2.00 | .75 |
| ❑ 87 J.J. Stokes | .40 | .15 |
| ❑ 88 Steve Young | .75 | .30 |
| ❑ 89 Jonathan Linton | .25 | .08 |
| ❑ 90 Isaac Bruce | .60 | .25 |
| ❑ 91 Shawn Jefferson | .25 | .08 |
| ❑ 92 Rod Smith | .40 | .15 |
| ❑ 93 Champ Bailey | .40 | .15 |
| ❑ 94 Ricky Williams | .60 | .25 |
| ❑ 95 Priest Holmes | .75 | .30 |
| ❑ 96 Corey Bradford | .25 | .08 |
| ❑ 97 Eric Moulds | .60 | .25 |
| ❑ 98 Warrick Dunn | .60 | .25 |
| ❑ 99 Jevon Kearse | .60 | .25 |
| ❑ 100 Albert Connell | .25 | .08 |
| ❑ 101 Az-Zahir Hakim | .25 | .08 |
| ❑ 102 Marvin Harrison | .60 | .25 |
| ❑ 103 Qadry Ismail | .40 | .15 |
| ❑ 104 Oronde Gadsden | .40 | .15 |
| ❑ 105 Rob Moore | .40 | .15 |
| ❑ 106 Marshall Faulk | .75 | .30 |
| ❑ 107 Steve Beuerlein | .25 | .08 |
| ❑ 108 Torry Holt | .60 | .25 |
| ❑ 109 Donovan McNabb | 1.00 | .40 |
| ❑ 110 Rich Gannon | .60 | .25 |
| ❑ 111 Jerome Bettis | .60 | .25 |
| ❑ 112 Peyton Manning | 1.50 | .60 |
| ❑ 113 Cris Carter | .60 | .25 |
| ❑ 114 Jake Plummer | .40 | .15 |
| ❑ 115 Kent Graham | .25 | .08 |
| ❑ 116 Keenan McCardell | .40 | .15 |
| ❑ 117 Tim Dwight | .60 | .25 |
| ❑ 118 Fred Taylor | .60 | .25 |
| ❑ 119 Jerry Rice | 1.25 | .50 |
| ❑ 120 Michael Westbrook | .40 | .15 |
| ❑ 121 Kurt Warner | 1.25 | .50 |
| ❑ 122 Jimmy Smith | .40 | .15 |
| ❑ 123 Emmitt Smith | 1.25 | .50 |
| ❑ 124 Terrell Davis | .60 | .25 |
| ❑ 125 Randy Moss | 1.25 | .50 |
| ❑ 126 Akili Smith | .25 | .08 |
| ❑ 127 Rocket Ismail | .40 | .15 |
| ❑ 128 Jon Kitna | .60 | .25 |
| ❑ 129 Elvis Grbac | .40 | .15 |
| ❑ 130 Wesley Walls | .25 | .08 |
| ❑ 131 Torrance Small | .25 | .08 |
| ❑ 132 Tyrone Wheatley | .40 | .15 |
| ❑ 133 Carl Pickens | .40 | .15 |
| ❑ 134 Zach Thomas | .40 | .15 |
| ❑ 135 Jacquez Green | .25 | .08 |
| ❑ 136 Robert Smith | .60 | .25 |
| ❑ 137 Keyshawn Johnson | .60 | .25 |
| ❑ 138 Matthew Hatchette | .25 | .08 |
| ❑ 139 Troy Aikman | 1.25 | .50 |
| ❑ 140 Charles Johnson | .40 | .15 |
| ❑ 141 Terry Battle EP | .30 | .12 |
| ❑ 142 Pepe Pearson EP RC | .75 | .30 |
| ❑ 143 Cory Sauter EP | .30 | .12 |
| ❑ 144 Brian Shay EP | .30 | .12 |
| ❑ 145 Marcus Crandell EP RC | .50 | .20 |
| ❑ 146 Danny Wuerffel EP | .50 | .20 |
| ❑ 147 L.C. Stevens EP | .30 | .12 |
| ❑ 148 Ted White EP | .30 | .12 |
| ❑ 149 Matt Lytle EP RC | .50 | .20 |
| ❑ 150 Vershan Jackson EP RC | .30 | .12 |
| ❑ 151 Mario Bailey EP | .30 | .12 |
| ❑ 152 Darryl Daniel EP RC | .50 | .20 |
| ❑ 153 Sean Morey EP RC | .50 | .20 |
| ❑ 154 Jim Kubiak EP RC | .50 | .20 |
| ❑ 155 Aaron Stecker EP RC | .75 | .30 |
| ❑ 156 Damon Dunn EP RC | .50 | .20 |
| ❑ 157 Kevin Daft EP | .30 | .12 |
| ❑ 158 Corey Thomas EP | .30 | .12 |
| ❑ 159 Deon Mitchell EP RC | .30 | .12 |
| ❑ 160 Todd Floyd EP RC | .30 | .12 |
| ❑ 161 Norman Miller EP RC | .30 | .12 |
| ❑ 162 Jeremaine Copeland EP | .30 | .12 |

| | | |
|---|---|---|
| ❑ 163 Michael Blair EP | .30 | .12 |
| ❑ 164 Ron Powlus EP RC | .75 | .30 |
| ❑ 165 Pat Barnes EP | .50 | .20 |
| ❑ 166 Dez White RC | 1.00 | .40 |
| ❑ 167 Trung Canidate RC | .75 | .30 |
| ❑ 168 Thomas Jones RC | 1.50 | .60 |
| ❑ 169 Courtney Brown RC | 1.00 | .40 |
| ❑ 170 Jamal Lewis RC | 2.50 | 1.00 |
| ❑ 171 Chris Redman RC | .75 | .30 |
| ❑ 172 Ron Dayne RC | 1.00 | .40 |
| ❑ 173 Chad Pennington RC | 2.50 | 1.00 |
| ❑ 174 Plaxico Burress RC | 2.00 | .75 |
| ❑ 175 R.Jay Soward RC | .75 | .30 |
| ❑ 176 Travis Taylor RC | 1.00 | .40 |
| ❑ 177 Shaun Alexander RC | 3.00 | 1.25 |
| ❑ 178 Brian Urlacher RC | 4.00 | 1.50 |
| ❑ 179 Danny Farmer RC | .75 | .30 |
| ❑ 180 Tee Martin RC | 1.00 | .40 |
| ❑ 181 Sylvester Morris RC | .75 | .30 |
| ❑ 182 Curtis Keaton RC | .75 | .30 |
| ❑ 183 Peter Warrick RC | 1.00 | .40 |
| ❑ 184 Anthony Becht RC | 1.00 | .40 |
| ❑ 185 Travis Prentice RC | 1.00 | .40 |
| ❑ 186 J.R. Redmond RC | .75 | .30 |
| ❑ 187 Bubba Franks RC | 1.00 | .40 |
| ❑ 188 Ron Dugans RC | .50 | .20 |
| ❑ 189 Reuben Droughns RC | 1.25 | .50 |
| ❑ 190 Corey Simon RC | 1.00 | .40 |
| ❑ 191 Joe Hamilton RC | .75 | .30 |
| ❑ 192 Laveranues Coles RC | 1.25 | .50 |
| ❑ 193 Todd Pinkston RC | 1.00 | .40 |
| ❑ 194 Jerry Porter RC | 1.25 | .50 |
| ❑ 195 Dennis Northcutt RC | 1.00 | .40 |
| ❑ 196 Tim Rattay RC | 1.00 | .40 |
| ❑ 197 Giovanni Carmazzi RC | .50 | .20 |
| ❑ 198 Mareno Philyaw RC | .50 | .20 |
| ❑ 199 Avion Black RC | .75 | .30 |
| ❑ 200 Chafie Fields RC | .50 | .20 |
| ❑ 201 Rondell Mealey RC | .50 | .20 |
| ❑ 202 Troy Walters RC | 1.00 | .40 |
| ❑ 203 Frank Moreau RC | .75 | .30 |
| ❑ 204 Vaughn Sanders RC | .50 | .20 |
| ❑ 205 Sherrod Gideon RC | .50 | .20 |
| ❑ 206 Doug Chapman RC | .75 | .30 |
| ❑ 207 Marcus Knight RC | .75 | .30 |
| ❑ 208 Jamel White RC | .75 | .30 |
| ❑ 209 Windrell Hayes RC | .75 | .30 |
| ❑ 210 Reggie Germany RC | 1.00 | .40 |
| ❑ 211 Janious Jackson RC | .75 | .30 |
| ❑ 212 Ronney Jenkins RC | .75 | .30 |
| ❑ 213 Quinton Spotwood RC | .50 | .20 |
| ❑ 214 Rob Morris RC | .75 | .30 |
| ❑ 215 Gari Scott RC | .50 | .20 |
| ❑ 216 Kevin Thompson RC | .50 | .20 |
| ❑ 217 Trevor Insley RC | .50 | .20 |
| ❑ 218 Frank Murphy RC | .50 | .20 |
| ❑ 219 Patrick Pass RC | .75 | .30 |
| ❑ 220 Mike Anderson RC | 1.25 | .50 |
| ❑ 221 Derrius Thompson RC | 1.00 | .40 |
| ❑ 222 John Abraham RC | 1.00 | .40 |
| ❑ 223 Dante Hall RC | 2.00 | .75 |
| ❑ 224 Chad Morton RC | 1.00 | .40 |
| ❑ 225 Ahmed Plummer RC | .50 | .20 |
| ❑ 226 Julian Peterson RC | 1.00 | .40 |
| ❑ 227 Mike Green RC | .75 | .30 |
| ❑ 228 Michael Wiley RC | .75 | .30 |
| ❑ 229 Spergon Wynn RC | .75 | .30 |
| ❑ 230 Trevor Gaylor RC | .75 | .30 |
| ❑ 231 Doug Johnson RC | 1.00 | .40 |
| ❑ 232 Marc Bulger RC | 2.00 | .75 |
| ❑ 233 Ron Dixon RC | .75 | .30 |
| ❑ 234 Aaron Shea RC | .75 | .30 |
| ❑ 235 Thomas Hamner RC | .50 | .20 |
| ❑ 236 Tom Brady RC | 50.00 | 25.00 |
| ❑ 237 Deltha O'Neal RC | 1.00 | .40 |
| ❑ 238 Todd Husak RC | 1.00 | .40 |
| ❑ 239 Erron Kinney RC | 1.00 | .40 |
| ❑ 240 JaJuan Dawson RC | .50 | .20 |

## 2001 Bowman

| | | |
|---|---|---|
| ❑ COMPLETE SET (275) | 70.00 | 35.00 |
| ❑ 1 Emmitt Smith | 1.25 | .50 |
| ❑ 2 James Stewart | .40 | .15 |
| ❑ 3 Jeff Graham | .25 | .08 |

| | | |
|---|---|---|
| ❑ 4 Keyshawn Johnson | .60 | .25 |
| ❑ 5 Stephen Davis | .60 | .25 |
| ❑ 6 Chad Lewis | .25 | .08 |
| ❑ 7 Drew Bledsoe | .75 | .30 |
| ❑ 8 Fred Taylor | .60 | .25 |
| ❑ 9 Mike Anderson | .60 | .25 |
| ❑ 10 Tony Gonzalez | .40 | .15 |
| ❑ 11 Aaron Brooks | .60 | .25 |
| ❑ 12 Vinny Testaverde | .40 | .15 |
| ❑ 13 Jerome Bettis | .60 | .25 |
| ❑ 14 Marshall Faulk | .75 | .30 |
| ❑ 15 Jeff Garcia | .60 | .25 |
| ❑ 16 Terry Glenn | .40 | .15 |
| ❑ 17 Jay Fiedler | .60 | .25 |
| ❑ 18 Ahman Green | .60 | .25 |
| ❑ 19 Cade McNown | .25 | .08 |
| ❑ 20 Rob Johnson | .40 | .15 |
| ❑ 21 Jamal Anderson | .60 | .25 |
| ❑ 22 Corey Dillon | .40 | .15 |
| ❑ 23 Rod Smith | .40 | .15 |
| ❑ 24 Trent Green | .60 | .25 |
| ❑ 26 Ricky Williams | .60 | .25 |
| ❑ 27 Charlie Garner | .40 | .15 |
| ❑ 28 Shaun Alexander | .75 | .30 |
| ❑ 29 Jeff George | .40 | .15 |
| ❑ 30 Torry Holt | .60 | .25 |
| ❑ 31 James Thrash | .40 | .15 |
| ❑ 32 Rich Gannon | .60 | .25 |
| ❑ 33 Ron Dayne | .60 | .25 |
| ❑ 34 Dedric Ward | .25 | .08 |
| ❑ 35 Edgerrin James | .75 | .30 |
| ❑ 36 Cris Carter | .60 | .25 |
| ❑ 37 Derrick Mason | .40 | .15 |
| ❑ 38 Brad Johnson | .60 | .25 |
| ❑ 39 Charlie Batch | .60 | .25 |
| ❑ 40 Joey Galloway | .40 | .15 |
| ❑ 41 James Allen | .40 | .15 |
| ❑ 42 Tim Biakabutuka | .40 | .15 |
| ❑ 43 Ray Lewis | .60 | .25 |
| ❑ 44 David Boston | .60 | .25 |
| ❑ 45 Kevin Johnson | .40 | .15 |
| ❑ 46 Jimmy Smith | .40 | .15 |
| ❑ 47 Joe Horn | .40 | .15 |
| ❑ 48 Terrell Owens | .60 | .25 |
| ❑ 49 Eddie George | .60 | .25 |
| ❑ 50 Brett Favre | 2.00 | .75 |
| ❑ 51 Wayne Chrebet | .40 | .15 |
| ❑ 52 Hines Ward | .60 | .25 |
| ❑ 53 Warrick Dunn | .60 | .25 |
| ❑ 54 Matt Hasselbeck | .40 | .15 |
| ❑ 55 Tiki Barber | .60 | .25 |
| ❑ 56 Lamar Smith | .40 | .15 |
| ❑ 57 Tim Couch | .60 | .25 |
| ❑ 58 Eric Moulds | .40 | .15 |
| ❑ 59 Shawn Jefferson | .25 | .08 |
| ❑ 60 Donald Hayes | .25 | .08 |
| ❑ 61 Brian Urlacher | 1.00 | .40 |
| ❑ 62 Steve McNair | .60 | .25 |
| ❑ 63 Kurt Warner | 1.25 | .50 |
| ❑ 64 Tim Brown | .60 | .25 |
| ❑ 65 Troy Brown | .40 | .15 |
| ❑ 66 Albert Connell | .25 | .08 |
| ❑ 67 Peyton Manning | 1.50 | .60 |
| ❑ 68 Peter Warrick | .60 | .25 |
| ❑ 69 Elvis Grbac | .40 | .15 |
| ❑ 70 Chris Chandler | .40 | .15 |
| ❑ 71 Akili Smith | .25 | .08 |

|  |  | | |
|---|---|---|---|
| ❏ 72 | Keenan McCardell | .25 | .08 |
| ❏ 73 | Kerry Collins | .40 | .15 |
| ❏ 74 | Junior Seau | .60 | .25 |
| ❏ 75 | Donovan McNabb | .75 | .30 |
| ❏ 76 | Tony Banks | .40 | .15 |
| ❏ 77 | Steve Beuerlein | .25 | .08 |
| ❏ 78 | Daunte Culpepper | .60 | .25 |
| ❏ 79 | Darrell Jackson | .60 | .25 |
| ❏ 80 | Isaac Bruce | .60 | .25 |
| ❏ 81 | Tyrone Wheatley | .40 | .15 |
| ❏ 82 | Derrick Alexander | .40 | .15 |
| ❏ 83 | Germane Crowell | .25 | .08 |
| ❏ 84 | Jon Kitna | .40 | .15 |
| ❏ 85 | Jamal Lewis | 1.00 | .40 |
| ❏ 86 | Ed McCaffrey | .60 | .25 |
| ❏ 87 | Mark Brunell | .60 | .25 |
| ❏ 88 | Jeff Blake | .40 | .15 |
| ❏ 89 | Duce Staley | .60 | .25 |
| ❏ 90 | Doug Flutie | .60 | .25 |
| ❏ 91 | Kordell Stewart | .40 | .15 |
| ❏ 92 | Randy Moss | 1.25 | .50 |
| ❏ 93 | Marvin Harrison | .60 | .25 |
| ❏ 94 | Muhsin Muhammad | .40 | .15 |
| ❏ 95 | Brian Griese | .60 | .25 |
| ❏ 96 | Antonio Freeman | .60 | .25 |
| ❏ 97 | Amani Toomer | .40 | .15 |
| ❏ 98 | Oronde Gadsden | .40 | .15 |
| ❏ 99 | Curtis Martin | .60 | .25 |
| ❏ 100 | Jerry Rice | 1.25 | .50 |
| ❏ 101 | Michael Pittman | .25 | .08 |
| ❏ 102 | Shannon Sharpe | .40 | .15 |
| ❏ 103 | Peerless Price | .40 | .15 |
| ❏ 104 | Bill Schroeder | .40 | .15 |
| ❏ 105 | Ike Hilliard | .40 | .15 |
| ❏ 106 | Freddie Jones | .25 | .08 |
| ❏ 107 | Tai Streets | .25 | .08 |
| ❏ 108 | Ricky Watters | .40 | .15 |
| ❏ 109 | Az-Zahir Hakim | .25 | .08 |
| ❏ 110 | Jacquez Green | .25 | .08 |
| ❏ 111 | Bobby Shaw | .25 | .08 |
| ❏ 112 | Johnnie Morton | .40 | .15 |
| ❏ 113 | Laveranues Coles | .60 | .25 |
| ❏ 114 | Chad Pennington | 1.00 | .40 |
| ❏ 115 | Champ Bailey | .40 | .15 |
| ❏ 116 | Charles Woodson | .40 | .15 |
| ❏ 117 | Curtis Conway | .40 | .15 |
| ❏ 118 | Marcus Robinson | .60 | .25 |
| ❏ 119 | Michael Westbrook | .40 | .15 |
| ❏ 120 | Mike Alstott | .60 | .25 |
| ❏ 121 | Priest Holmes | .75 | .30 |
| ❏ 122 | Qadry Ismail | .40 | .15 |
| ❏ 123 | Rocket Ismail | .40 | .15 |
| ❏ 124 | Shawn Bryson | .25 | .08 |
| ❏ 125 | Jeff Lewis | .25 | .08 |
| ❏ 126 | Jeremy Mcdaniel | .25 | .08 |
| ❏ 127 | Terance Mathis | .25 | .08 |
| ❏ 128 | Travis Prentice | .25 | .08 |
| ❏ 129 | Warren Sapp | .40 | .15 |
| ❏ 130 | Jevon Kearse | .40 | .15 |
| ❏ 131 | George Layne RC | .75 | .30 |
| ❏ 132 | Correll Buckhalter RC | 1.50 | .60 |
| ❏ 133 | Tony Stewart RC | 1.25 | .50 |
| ❏ 134 | Chris Barnes RC | .75 | .30 |
| ❏ 135 | A.J. Feeley RC | 1.25 | .50 |
| ❏ 136 | Margin Hooks RC | .50 | .20 |
| ❏ 137 | Anthony Henry RC | 1.25 | .50 |
| ❏ 138 | Dwight Smith RC | .50 | .20 |
| ❏ 139 | Torrance Marshall RC | 1.25 | .50 |
| ❏ 140 | Gary Baxter RC | .75 | .30 |
| ❏ 141 | Derek Combs RC | .75 | .30 |
| ❏ 142 | Marcus Bell DT RC | .75 | .30 |
| ❏ 143 | Delawrence Grant RC | .75 | .30 |
| ❏ 144 | Jameel Cook RC | .75 | .30 |
| ❏ 145 | Eric Downing RC | .50 | .20 |
| ❏ 146 | Marlon McCree RC | .75 | .30 |
| ❏ 147 | Tay Cody RC | .50 | .20 |
| ❏ 148 | Mario Monds RC | .50 | .20 |
| ❏ 149 | Kenny Smith RC | .50 | .20 |
| ❏ 150 | Sedrick Hodge RC | .50 | .20 |
| ❏ 151 | Marcus Stroud RC | 1.25 | .50 |
| ❏ 152 | Steve Smith RC | 3.00 | 1.25 |
| ❏ 153 | Tyrone Robertson RC | .50 | .20 |
| ❏ 154 | James Reed RC | .50 | .20 |
| ❏ 155 | Kris Kocurek RC | .50 | .20 |
| ❏ 156 | Dan O'Leary RC | .75 | .30 |
| ❏ 157 | Harold Blackmon RC | .50 | .20 |
| ❏ 158 | Fred Smoot RC | 1.25 | .50 |
| ❏ 159 | Billy Baber RC | .50 | .20 |
| ❏ 160 | Jarrod Cooper RC | 1.25 | .50 |
| ❏ 161 | Travis Henry RC | 1.25 | .50 |
| ❏ 162 | David Terrell RC | 1.25 | .50 |
| ❏ 163 | Josh Heupel RC | 1.25 | .50 |
| ❏ 164 | Drew Brees RC | 5.00 | 2.00 |
| ❏ 165 | T.J. Houshmandzadeh RC | 1.50 | .60 |
| ❏ 166 | Rod Gardner RC | 1.25 | .50 |
| ❏ 167 | Richard Seymour RC | 1.25 | .50 |
| ❏ 168 | Koren Robinson RC | 1.25 | .50 |
| ❏ 169 | Scotty Anderson RC | .75 | .30 |
| ❏ 170 | Marques Tuiasosopo RC | 1.25 | .50 |
| ❏ 171 | John Capel RC | .75 | .30 |
| ❏ 172 | LaMont Jordan RC | 2.50 | 1.00 |
| ❏ 173 | James Jackson RC | 1.25 | .50 |
| ❏ 174 | Robby Newcombe RC | 1.25 | .50 |
| ❏ 175 | Anthony Thomas RC | 1.25 | .50 |
| ❏ 176 | Dan Alexander RC | 1.25 | .50 |
| ❏ 177 | Quincy Carter RC | 1.25 | .50 |
| ❏ 178 | Morton Greenwood RC | .75 | .30 |
| ❏ 179 | Robert Ferguson RC | 1.25 | .50 |
| ❏ 180 | Sage Rosenfels RC | 1.25 | .50 |
| ❏ 181 | Michael Stone RC | .50 | .20 |
| ❏ 182 | Chris Weinke RC | 1.25 | .50 |
| ❏ 183 | Travis Minor RC | .75 | .30 |
| ❏ 184 | Gerard Warren RC | 1.25 | .50 |
| ❏ 185 | Jamar Fletcher RC | .75 | .30 |
| ❏ 186 | Andre Carter RC | 1.25 | .50 |
| ❏ 187 | Deuce McAllister RC | 2.50 | 1.00 |
| ❏ 188 | Dan Morgan RC | 1.25 | .50 |
| ❏ 189 | Todd Heap RC | 1.25 | .50 |
| ❏ 190 | Snoop Minnis RC | .75 | .30 |
| ❏ 191 | Will Allen RC | .75 | .30 |
| ❏ 192 | Freddie Mitchell RC | 1.25 | .50 |
| ❏ 193 | Rudi Johnson RC | 2.50 | 1.00 |
| ❏ 194 | Kevan Barlow RC | 1.25 | .50 |
| ❏ 195 | Jamie Winborn RC | .75 | .30 |
| ❏ 196 | Onomo Ojo RC | .75 | .30 |
| ❏ 197 | Leonard Davis RC | .75 | .30 |
| ❏ 198 | Santana Moss RC | 2.00 | .75 |
| ❏ 199 | Chris Chambers RC | 2.00 | .75 |
| ❏ 200 | Michael Vick RC | 2.50 | 1.00 |
| ❏ 201 | Michael Bennett RC | 1.25 | .50 |
| ❏ 202 | Mike McMahon RC | .75 | .30 |
| ❏ 203 | Jonathan Carter RC | .75 | .30 |
| ❏ 204 | Jamal Reynolds RC | 1.25 | .50 |
| ❏ 205 | Justin Smith RC | 1.25 | .50 |
| ❏ 206 | Quincy Morgan RC | 1.25 | .50 |
| ❏ 207 | Chad Johnson RC | 3.00 | 1.25 |
| ❏ 208 | Jesse Palmer RC | 1.25 | .50 |
| ❏ 209 | Reggie Wayne RC | 2.50 | 1.00 |
| ❏ 210 | LaDainian Tomlinson RC | 25.00 | 10.00 |
| ❏ 211 | Andre Rison RC | .75 | .30 |
| ❏ 212 | Richmond Flowers RC | .75 | .30 |
| ❏ 213 | Derrick Blaylock RC | 1.25 | .50 |
| ❏ 214 | Cedrick Wilson RC | 1.25 | .50 |
| ❏ 215 | Zeke Moreno RC | 1.25 | .50 |
| ❏ 216 | Tommy Polley RC | 1.25 | .50 |
| ❏ 217 | Damione Lewis RC | .75 | .30 |
| ❏ 218 | Aaron Schobel RC | 1.25 | .50 |
| ❏ 219 | Alge Crumpler RC | 1.50 | .60 |
| ❏ 220 | Nate Clements RC | 1.25 | .50 |
| ❏ 221 | Quentin McCord RC | .75 | .30 |
| ❏ 222 | Ken-Yon Rambo RC | .75 | .30 |
| ❏ 223 | Milton Wynn RC | .75 | .30 |
| ❏ 224 | Derrick Gibson RC | .75 | .30 |
| ❏ 225 | Chris Taylor RC | .75 | .30 |
| ❏ 226 | Corey Hall RC | .50 | .20 |
| ❏ 227 | Vinny Sutherland RC | .75 | .30 |
| ❏ 228 | Kendrell Bell RC | 2.00 | .75 |
| ❏ 229 | Casey Hampton RC | .1.25 | .50 |
| ❏ 230 | Demetric Evans RC | .50 | .20 |
| ❏ 231 | Brian Allen RC | .50 | .20 |
| ❏ 232 | Rodney Bailey RC | .50 | .20 |
| ❏ 233 | Otis Leverette RC | .50 | .20 |
| ❏ 234 | Ron Edwards RC | .50 | .20 |
| ❏ 235 | Michael Jameson RC | .50 | .20 |
| ❏ 236 | Markus Steele RC | .75 | .30 |
| ❏ 237 | Jimmy Williams RC | .50 | .20 |
| ❏ 238 | Roger Knight RC | .50 | .20 |
| ❏ 239 | Randy Gamer RC | .50 | .20 |
| ❏ 240 | Raymond Perryman RC | .50 | .20 |
| ❏ 241 | Karon Riley RC | .50 | .20 |
| ❏ 242 | Adam Archuleta RC | 1.25 | .50 |
| ❏ 243 | Arnold Jackson RC | .75 | .30 |
| ❏ 244 | Ryan Pickett RC | .50 | .20 |
| ❏ 245 | Shad Meier RC | .75 | .30 |
| ❏ 246 | Reggie Germany RC | .75 | .30 |
| ❏ 247 | Justin McCareins RC | 1.25 | .50 |
| ❏ 248 | Idrees Bashir RC | .50 | .20 |
| ❏ 249 | Josh Booty RC | 1.25 | .50 |
| ❏ 250 | Eddie Berlin RC | .75 | .30 |
| ❏ 251 | Heath Evans RC | .75 | .30 |
| ❏ 252 | Alex Bannister RC | .50 | .20 |
| ❏ 253 | Corey Alston RC | .50 | .20 |
| ❏ 254 | Reggie White RC | .75 | .30 |
| ❏ 255 | Orlando Huff RC | .50 | .20 |
| ❏ 256 | Ken Lucas RC | .50 | .20 |
| ❏ 257 | Matt Stewart RC | .50 | .20 |
| ❏ 258 | Cedric Scott RC | .50 | .20 |
| ❏ 259 | Ronney Daniels RC | .50 | .20 |
| ❏ 260 | Kevin Kasper RC | 1.25 | .50 |
| ❏ 261 | Tony Driver RC | .75 | .30 |
| ❏ 262 | Kyle Vanden Bosch RC | 1.25 | .50 |
| ❏ 263 | T.J. Turner RC | .50 | .20 |
| ❏ 264 | Eric Westmoreland RC | .75 | .30 |
| ❏ 265 | Ronald Flemons RC | .50 | .20 |
| ❏ 266 | Eric Kelly RC | .50 | .20 |
| ❏ 267 | Moran Norris RC | .50 | .20 |
| ❏ 268 | Damerien McCants RC | .75 | .30 |
| ❏ 269 | James Boyd RC | .50 | .20 |
| ❏ 270 | Keith Adams RC | .50 | .20 |
| ❏ 271 | Brandon Manumaleuna RC | .75 | .30 |
| ❏ 272 | Dee Brown RC | 1.25 | .50 |
| ❏ 273 | Ross Kolodziej RC | .50 | .20 |
| ❏ 274 | Boo Williams RC | .75 | .30 |
| ❏ 275 | Patrick Chukwurah RC | .75 | .30 |

## 2002 Bowman

|  |  | | |
|---|---|---|---|
| | COMPLETE SET (275) | 50.00 | 20.00 |
| ❏ 1 | Emmitt Smith | 1.50 | .60 |
| ❏ 2 | Drew Brees | .60 | .25 |
| ❏ 3 | Duce Staley | .60 | .25 |
| ❏ 4 | Curtis Martin | .60 | .25 |
| ❏ 5 | Isaac Bruce | .60 | .25 |
| ❏ 6 | Stephen Davis | .40 | .15 |
| ❏ 7 | Darrell Jackson | .40 | .15 |
| ❏ 8 | James Stewart | .40 | .15 |
| ❏ 9 | Tim Couch | .40 | .15 |
| ❏ 10 | Travis Henry | .60 | .25 |
| ❏ 11 | Thomas Jones | .40 | .15 |
| ❏ 12 | Jamal Lewis | .60 | .25 |
| ❏ 13 | Chris Chambers | .60 | .25 |
| ❏ 14 | Jeff Blake | .40 | .15 |
| ❏ 15 | Plaxico Burress | .40 | .15 |
| ❏ 16 | Michael Pittman | .25 | .08 |
| ❏ 17 | Jeff Garcia | .60 | .25 |
| ❏ 18 | Tim Brown | .60 | .25 |
| ❏ 19 | Kent Graham | .25 | .08 |
| ❏ 20 | Shannon Sharpe | .40 | .15 |
| ❏ 21 | Corey Dillon | .40 | .15 |
| ❏ 22 | Muhsin Muhammad | .40 | .15 |
| ❏ 23 | Tony Gonzalez | .40 | .15 |
| ❏ 24 | Qadry Ismail | .40 | .15 |
| ❏ 25 | Mike McMahon | .60 | .25 |
| ❏ 26 | Edgerrin James | .75 | .30 |
| ❏ 27 | Daunte Culpepper | .60 | .25 |
| ❏ 28 | Deuce McAllister | .60 | .25 |
| ❏ 29 | Kerry Collins | .40 | .15 |

|  |  | | |
|---|--------|------|------|
| ☐ 30 | Eddie George | .60 | .25 |
| ☐ 31 | Terry Holt | .60 | .25 |
| ☐ 32 | Todd Pinkston | .40 | .15 |
| ☐ 33 | Quincy Carter | .40 | .15 |
| ☐ 34 | Rod Smith | .40 | .15 |
| ☐ 35 | Michael Vick | 1.25 | .50 |
| ☐ 36 | Jim Miller | .25 | .08 |
| ☐ 37 | Troy Brown | .40 | .15 |
| ☐ 38 | Wayne Chrebet | .40 | .15 |
| ☐ 39 | Curtis Conway | .25 | .08 |
| ☐ 40 | Reidel Anthony | .25 | .08 |
| ☐ 41 | Mark Brunell | .60 | .25 |
| ☐ 42 | Chris Weinke | .40 | .15 |
| ☐ 43 | Eric Moulds | .40 | .15 |
| ☐ 44 | Ike Hilliard | .25 | .08 |
| ☐ 45 | Jay Fiedler | .40 | .15 |
| ☐ 46 | Keyshawn Johnson | .60 | .25 |
| ☐ 47 | Rod Gardner | .40 | .15 |
| ☐ 48 | Chris Redman | .25 | .08 |
| ☐ 49 | James Allen | .40 | .15 |
| ☐ 50 | Kordell Stewart | .40 | .15 |
| ☐ 51 | Priest Holmes | .75 | .30 |
| ☐ 52 | Anthony Thomas | .40 | .15 |
| ☐ 53 | Peter Warrick | .40 | .15 |
| ☐ 54 | Jake Plummer | .40 | .15 |
| ☐ 55 | Jerry Rice | 1.25 | .50 |
| ☐ 56 | Joe Horn | .40 | .15 |
| ☐ 57 | Derrick Mason | .40 | .15 |
| ☐ 58 | Kurt Warner | .60 | .25 |
| ☐ 59 | Antowain Smith | .40 | .15 |
| ☐ 60 | Randy Moss | 1.25 | .50 |
| ☐ 61 | Warrick Dunn | .40 | .15 |
| ☐ 62 | Laveranues Coles | .40 | .15 |
| ☐ 63 | LaDainian Tomlinson | 1.00 | .40 |
| ☐ 64 | Michael Westbrook | .25 | .08 |
| ☐ 65 | Travis Taylor | .25 | .08 |
| ☐ 66 | Brian Griese | .60 | .25 |
| ☐ 67 | Bill Schroeder | .40 | .15 |
| ☐ 68 | Ahman Green | .60 | .25 |
| ☐ 69 | Jimmy Smith | .40 | .15 |
| ☐ 70 | Charlie Garner | .40 | .15 |
| ☐ 71 | Terrell Owens | .60 | .25 |
| ☐ 72 | Brad Johnson | .40 | .15 |
| ☐ 73 | James Thrash | .40 | .15 |
| ☐ 74 | Marvin Harrison | .60 | .25 |
| ☐ 75 | Brett Favre | 1.50 | .60 |
| ☐ 76 | Rocket Ismail | .40 | .15 |
| ☐ 77 | David Boston | .60 | .25 |
| ☐ 78 | Jermaine Lewis | .25 | .08 |
| ☐ 79 | Aaron Brooks | .60 | .25 |
| ☐ 80 | Shaun Alexander | .75 | .30 |
| ☐ 81 | Steve McNair | .60 | .25 |
| ☐ 82 | Marshall Faulk | .60 | .25 |
| ☐ 83 | Terrell Davis | .60 | .25 |
| ☐ 84 | Corey Bradford | .25 | .08 |
| ☐ 85 | David Terrell | .40 | .15 |
| ☐ 86 | Kevin Johnson | .40 | .15 |
| ☐ 87 | Jon Kitna | .25 | .08 |
| ☐ 88 | Az-Zahir Hakim | .25 | .08 |
| ☐ 89 | Drew Bledsoe | .75 | .30 |
| ☐ 90 | Garrison Hearst | .40 | .15 |
| ☐ 91 | Doug Flutie | .60 | .25 |
| ☐ 92 | Jerome Bettis | .60 | .25 |
| ☐ 93 | Vinny Testaverde | .40 | .15 |
| ☐ 94 | Tiki Barber | .60 | .25 |
| ☐ 95 | Johnnie Morton | .40 | .15 |
| ☐ 96 | Lamar Smith | .40 | .15 |
| ☐ 97 | Marcus Robinson | .40 | .15 |
| ☐ 98 | Fred Taylor | .60 | .25 |
| ☐ 99 | Tom Brady | 1.50 | .60 |
| ☐ 100 | Peyton Manning | 1.25 | .50 |
| ☐ 101 | Donovan McNabb | .75 | .30 |
| ☐ 102 | Rich Gannon | .60 | .25 |
| ☐ 103 | Hines Ward | .60 | .25 |
| ☐ 104 | Michael Bennett | .60 | .25 |
| ☐ 105 | Ricky Williams | .60 | .25 |
| ☐ 106 | Germane Crowell | .25 | .08 |
| ☐ 107 | Joey Galloway | .40 | .15 |
| ☐ 108 | Amani Toomer | .40 | .15 |
| ☐ 109 | Trent Green | .40 | .15 |
| ☐ 110 | Terry Glenn | .40 | .15 |
| ☐ 111 | Donte Stallworth RC | 2.50 | 1.00 |
| ☐ 112 | Mike Williams RC | 1.25 | .50 |
| ☐ 113 | Kurt Kittner RC | 1.25 | .50 |
| ☐ 114 | Josh Reed RC | 1.50 | .60 |
| ☐ 115 | Raonall Smith RC | 1.25 | .50 |
| ☐ 116 | David Garrard RC | 3.00 | 1.25 |
| ☐ 117 | Eric Crouch RC | 1.50 | .60 |
| ☐ 118 | Bryan Thomas RC | 1.25 | .50 |
| ☐ 119 | Levi Jones RC | 1.25 | .50 |
| ☐ 120 | Andre Davis RC | 1.25 | .50 |
| ☐ 121 | Herb Haygood RC | .75 | .30 |
| ☐ 122 | Josh McCown RC | 2.00 | .60 |
| ☐ 123 | Quentin Jammer RC | 1.50 | .60 |
| ☐ 124 | Cliff Russell RC | 1.25 | .50 |
| ☐ 125 | Jeremy Shockey RC | 2.50 | 1.00 |
| ☐ 126 | Jamin Elliott RC | .75 | .30 |
| ☐ 127 | Roy Williams RC | 3.00 | 1.25 |
| ☐ 128 | Marquise Walker RC | 1.25 | .50 |
| ☐ 129 | Kalimba Edwards RC | 1.50 | .60 |
| ☐ 130 | Daniel Graham RC | 1.50 | .60 |
| ☐ 131 | Freddie Milons RC | 1.25 | .50 |
| ☐ 132 | Anthony Weaver RC | 1.25 | .50 |
| ☐ 133 | Jake Schifino RC | 1.25 | .50 |
| ☐ 134 | Antonio Bryant RC | 1.50 | .60 |
| ☐ 135 | DeShaun Foster RC | 1.50 | .60 |
| ☐ 136 | Antwaan Randle El RC | 2.00 | .75 |
| ☐ 137 | William Green RC | 1.50 | .60 |
| ☐ 138 | Ed Reed RC | 4.00 | 1.50 |
| ☐ 139 | Maurice Morris RC | 1.50 | .60 |
| ☐ 140 | Joey Harrington RC | 2.00 | .60 |
| ☐ 141 | T.J. Duckett RC | 1.50 | .60 |
| ☐ 142 | Javon Walker RC | 2.50 | 1.00 |
| ☐ 143 | Albert Haynesworth RC | 1.50 | .60 |
| ☐ 144 | Julius Peppers RC | 3.00 | 1.25 |
| ☐ 145 | Clinton Portis RC | 5.00 | 2.00 |
| ☐ 146 | Craig Nall RC | 1.50 | .60 |
| ☐ 147 | Ashley Lelie RC | 3.00 | 1.25 |
| ☐ 148 | Reche Caldwell RC | 1.50 | .60 |
| ☐ 149 | Roshan Davey RC | 1.50 | .60 |
| ☐ 150 | Patrick Ramsey RC | 1.50 | .60 |
| ☐ 151 | Jabar Gaffney RC | 1.50 | .60 |
| ☐ 152 | Tank Williams RC | 1.25 | .50 |
| ☐ 153 | Ron Johnson RC | 1.25 | .50 |
| ☐ 154 | Ladell Betts RC | 1.50 | .60 |
| ☐ 155 | Brian Westbrook RC | 4.00 | 1.50 |
| ☐ 156 | Jamar Martin RC | 1.25 | .50 |
| ☐ 157 | Travis Stephens RC | 1.25 | .50 |
| ☐ 158 | Tim Carter RC | 1.25 | .50 |
| ☐ 159 | Darrell Hill RC | 1.50 | .60 |
| ☐ 160 | Luke Staley RC | 1.50 | .60 |
| ☐ 161 | Randy Fasani RC | 1.25 | .50 |
| ☐ 162 | Matt Schobel RC | 1.25 | .50 |
| ☐ 163 | Jon McGraw RC | .75 | .30 |
| ☐ 164 | Dwight Freeney RC | 2.50 | 1.00 |
| ☐ 165 | Chad Hutchinson RC | 1.25 | .50 |
| ☐ 166 | Adrian Peterson RC | 2.00 | .75 |
| ☐ 167 | Josh Scobey RC | 1.50 | .60 |
| ☐ 168 | Jonathan Wells RC | 1.50 | .60 |
| ☐ 169 | Sam Simmons RC | .75 | .30 |
| ☐ 170 | Jerramy Stevens RC | 1.50 | .60 |
| ☐ 171 | Jason McAddley RC | 1.25 | .50 |
| ☐ 172 | Ken Simonton RC | .75 | .30 |
| ☐ 173 | Chester Taylor RC | 3.00 | 1.25 |
| ☐ 174 | Brandon Doman RC | 1.25 | .50 |
| ☐ 175 | Javin Hunter RC | .75 | .30 |
| ☐ 176 | Eddie Drummond RC | 1.25 | .50 |
| ☐ 177 | Andre Lott RC | 1.50 | .60 |
| ☐ 178 | Travis Fisher RC | 1.50 | .60 |
| ☐ 179 | Jarvis Green RC | 1.25 | .50 |
| ☐ 180 | Ross Tucker RC | .75 | .30 |
| ☐ 181 | Lamont Brightful RC | .75 | .30 |
| ☐ 182 | Rocky Calmus RC | 1.50 | .60 |
| ☐ 183 | Wes Pate RC | .75 | .30 |
| ☐ 184 | Lamar Gordon RC | 1.50 | .60 |
| ☐ 185 | Terry Jones RC | 1.25 | .50 |
| ☐ 186 | Kyle Johnson RC | .75 | .30 |
| ☐ 187 | Daryl Jones RC | .75 | .30 |
| ☐ 188 | Tellis Redmon RC | 1.25 | .50 |
| ☐ 189 | Howard Green RC | 1.25 | .50 |
| ☐ 190 | Jarrod Baxter RC | 1.25 | .50 |
| ☐ 191 | Delvon Flowers RC | 1.25 | .50 |
| ☐ 192 | Kevin Curtis RC | .75 | .30 |
| ☐ 193 | Kelly Campbell RC | 1.25 | .50 |
| ☐ 194 | Eddie Freeman RC | .75 | .30 |
| ☐ 195 | Atrews Bell RC | .75 | .30 |
| ☐ 196 | Omar Easy RC | 1.50 | .60 |
| ☐ 197 | Jeremy Allen RC | .75 | .30 |
| ☐ 198 | Andra Davis RC | 1.25 | .50 |
| ☐ 199 | Jack Brewer RC | 1.25 | .50 |
| ☐ 200 | Mike Rumph RC | 1.50 | .60 |
| ☐ 201 | Seth Burford RC | 1.25 | .50 |
| ☐ 202 | Marquand Manuel RC | .75 | .30 |
| ☐ 203 | Marques Anderson RC | 1.50 | .60 |
| ☐ 204 | Ben Leber RC | 1.50 | .60 |
| ☐ 205 | Ryan Denney RC | 1.25 | .50 |
| ☐ 206 | Justin Peelle RC | .75 | .30 |
| ☐ 207 | Lito Sheppard RC | 1.50 | .60 |
| ☐ 208 | Damien Anderson RC | 1.25 | .50 |
| ☐ 209 | Lamont Thompson RC | 1.25 | .50 |
| ☐ 210 | David Priestley RC | 1.25 | .50 |
| ☐ 211 | Michael Lewis RC | 1.25 | .50 |
| ☐ 212 | Lee Mays RC | 1.25 | .50 |
| ☐ 213 | Alan Harper RC | .75 | .30 |
| ☐ 214 | Verron Haynes RC | 1.50 | .60 |
| ☐ 215 | Chris Hope RC | 1.50 | .60 |
| ☐ 216 | David Thornton RC | .75 | .30 |
| ☐ 217 | Derek Ross RC | 1.25 | .50 |
| ☐ 218 | Brett Keisel RC | 2.00 | 1.50 |
| ☐ 219 | Joseph Jefferson RC | 1.25 | .50 |
| ☐ 220 | Andre Goodman RC | 1.50 | .60 |
| ☐ 221 | Robert Royal RC | 1.25 | .50 |
| ☐ 222 | Sheldon Brown RC | 1.50 | .60 |
| ☐ 223 | DeVeren Johnson RC | 1.25 | .50 |
| ☐ 224 | Rock Cartwright RC | 2.00 | .60 |
| ☐ 225 | Quincy Monk RC | .75 | .30 |
| ☐ 226 | Nick Rogers RC | 1.25 | .50 |
| ☐ 227 | Kendall Simmons RC | 1.25 | .50 |
| ☐ 228 | Joe Burns RC | 1.25 | .50 |
| ☐ 229 | Wesly Mallard RC | 1.25 | .50 |
| ☐ 230 | Chris Cash RC | 1.25 | .50 |
| ☐ 231 | David Givens RC | 5.00 | 2.00 |
| ☐ 232 | John Owens RC | 1.25 | .50 |
| ☐ 233 | Jarrett Ferguson RC | 1.25 | .50 |
| ☐ 234 | Randy McMichael RC | 2.50 | 1.00 |
| ☐ 235 | Chris Baker RC | 1.25 | .50 |
| ☐ 236 | Rashad Bauman RC | 1.25 | .50 |
| ☐ 237 | Matt Murphy RC | 1.25 | .50 |
| ☐ 238 | LaVar Glover RC | .75 | .30 |
| ☐ 239 | Steve Bellisari RC | 1.25 | .50 |
| ☐ 240 | Chad Williams RC | 1.25 | .50 |
| ☐ 241 | Kevin Thomas RC | 1.25 | .50 |
| ☐ 242 | Carlos Hall RC | 1.50 | .60 |
| ☐ 243 | Nick Greisen RC | 1.25 | .50 |
| ☐ 244 | Justin Bannan RC | 1.25 | .50 |
| ☐ 245 | Charles Hill RC | .75 | .30 |
| ☐ 246 | Mark Anelli RC | .75 | .30 |
| ☐ 247 | Coy Wire RC | 1.50 | .60 |
| ☐ 248 | Darnell Sanders RC | 1.25 | .50 |
| ☐ 249 | Larry Foote RC | 4.00 | 1.50 |
| ☐ 250 | David Carr RC | 2.00 | .75 |
| ☐ 251 | Ricky Williams RC | 1.25 | .50 |
| ☐ 252 | Napoleon Harris RC | 1.50 | .60 |
| ☐ 253 | Ennis Haywood RC | 1.25 | .50 |
| ☐ 254 | Keyuo Craver RC | 1.25 | .50 |
| ☐ 255 | Kahlil Hill RC | 1.25 | .50 |
| ☐ 256 | J.T. O'Sullivan RC | 2.50 | 1.00 |
| ☐ 257 | Woody Dantzler RC | 1.25 | .50 |
| ☐ 258 | Phillip Buchanon RC | 1.50 | .60 |
| ☐ 259 | Charles Grant RC | 1.50 | .60 |
| ☐ 260 | Dusty Bonner RC | .75 | .30 |
| ☐ 261 | James Allen RC | .75 | .30 |
| ☐ 262 | Ronald Curry RC | 1.50 | .60 |
| ☐ 263 | Deion Branch RC | 2.50 | .60 |
| ☐ 264 | Larry Ned RC | 1.25 | .50 |
| ☐ 265 | Mel Mitchell RC | 1.25 | .50 |
| ☐ 266 | Kendall Newson RC | .75 | .30 |
| ☐ 267 | Shaun Hill RC | 2.50 | 1.00 |
| ☐ 268 | David Pugh RC | .75 | .30 |
| ☐ 269 | Dante Wesley RC | .75 | .30 |
| ☐ 270 | Josh Mallard RC | .75 | .30 |
| ☐ 271 | Akin Ayodele RC | .75 | .30 |
| ☐ 272 | Pete Hunter RC | 1.25 | .50 |
| ☐ 273 | Kevin McCadam RC | 1.25 | .50 |
| ☐ 274 | Jeff Kelly RC | 1.25 | .50 |
| ☐ 275 | John Henderson RC | 1.50 | .60 |

## 2004 Bowman

|  |  | | |
|---|--------|------|------|
| ☐ | COMPLETE SET (275) | 60.00 | 30.00 |
| ☐ 1 | Brett Favre | 2.00 | .75 |
| ☐ 2 | Jay Fiedler | .30 | .10 |
| ☐ 3 | Andre Davis | .30 | .10 |

|  |  | | |
|---|---|---|---|
| ❏ 4 | Travis Henry | .50 | .20 |
| ❏ 5 | Jimmy Smith | .50 | .20 |
| ❏ 6 | Santana Moss | .50 | .20 |
| ❏ 7 | Correll Buckhalter | .50 | .20 |
| ❏ 8 | Randy Moss | 1.00 | .40 |
| ❏ 9 | Edgerrin James | .75 | .30 |
| ❏ 10 | Marc Bulger | .75 | .30 |
| ❏ 11 | Derrick Mason | .50 | .20 |
| ❏ 12 | Mark Brunell | .50 | .20 |
| ❏ 13 | Donte' Stallworth | .50 | .20 |
| ❏ 14 | Deion Branch | .75 | .30 |
| ❏ 15 | Jake Plummer | .50 | .20 |
| ❏ 16 | Steve Smith | .50 | .20 |
| ❏ 17 | Jon Kitna | .50 | .20 |
| ❏ 18 | Andre Johnson | .75 | .30 |
| ❏ 19 | A.J. Feeley | .75 | .30 |
| ❏ 20 | Drew Bledsoe | .75 | .30 |
| ❏ 21 | Antonio Bryant | .50 | .20 |
| ❏ 22 | Reggie Wayne | .50 | .20 |
| ❏ 23 | Thomas Jones | .50 | .20 |
| ❏ 24 | Alge Crumpler | .50 | .20 |
| ❏ 25 | Anquan Boldin | .75 | .30 |
| ❏ 26 | Tim Rattay | .30 | .10 |
| ❏ 27 | Charlie Garner | .50 | .20 |
| ❏ 28 | James Thrash | .50 | .20 |
| ❏ 29 | Koren Robinson | .50 | .20 |
| ❏ 30 | Terrell Owens | .50 | .20 |
| ❏ 31 | Amani Toomer | .50 | .20 |
| ❏ 32 | Kelly Campbell | .30 | .10 |
| ❏ 33 | Patrick Ramsey | .50 | .20 |
| ❏ 34 | Plaxico Burress | .50 | .20 |
| ❏ 35 | Chad Pennington | .75 | .30 |
| ❏ 36 | Fred Taylor | .75 | .30 |
| ❏ 37 | Domanick Davis | .75 | .30 |
| ❏ 38 | DeShaun Foster | .50 | .20 |
| ❏ 39 | T.J. Duckett | .50 | .20 |
| ❏ 40 | Ahman Green | .75 | .30 |
| ❏ 41 | Lee Suggs | .75 | .30 |
| ❏ 42 | Tony Gonzalez | .50 | .20 |
| ❏ 43 | Rich Gannon | .50 | .20 |
| ❏ 44 | Kevan Barlow | .50 | .20 |
| ❏ 45 | Torry Holt | .75 | .30 |
| ❏ 46 | Aaron Brooks | .50 | .20 |
| ❏ 47 | Tyrone Calico | .50 | .20 |
| ❏ 48 | Keenan McCardell | .50 | .10 |
| ❏ 49 | Hines Ward | .75 | .30 |
| ❏ 50 | LaDainian Tomlinson | 1.25 | .50 |
| ❏ 51 | Dante Hall | .75 | .30 |
| ❏ 52 | Marcus Pollard | .50 | .20 |
| ❏ 53 | Corey Dillon | .50 | .20 |
| ❏ 54 | Justin McCareins | .30 | .10 |
| ❏ 55 | Stephen Davis | .50 | .20 |
| ❏ 56 | Jeff Garcia | .50 | .20 |
| ❏ 57 | Ashley Lelie | .50 | .20 |
| ❏ 58 | Javon Walker | .50 | .20 |
| ❏ 59 | Kyle Boller | .75 | .30 |
| ❏ 60 | Chad Johnson | .75 | .30 |
| ❏ 61 | Anthony Thomas | .50 | .20 |
| ❏ 62 | Byron Leftwich | 1.00 | .40 |
| ❏ 63 | David Boston | .50 | .20 |
| ❏ 64 | Onterrio Smith | .50 | .20 |
| ❏ 65 | Deuce McAllister | .75 | .30 |
| ❏ 66 | Antwaan Randle El | .75 | .30 |
| ❏ 67 | Justin Fargas | .50 | .20 |
| ❏ 68 | Laveranues Coles | .50 | .20 |
| ❏ 69 | Quincy Morgan | .50 | .20 |
| ❏ 70 | Priest Holmes | 1.00 | .40 |
| ❏ 71 | Robert Ferguson | .30 | .10 |
| ❏ 72 | Charles Rogers | .50 | .20 |
| ❏ 73 | Drew Brees | .75 | .30 |
| ❏ 74 | Matt Hasselbeck | .50 | .20 |
| ❏ 75 | Peyton Manning | 1.25 | .50 |
| ❏ 76 | Rudi Johnson | .50 | .20 |
| ❏ 77 | Jake Delhomme | .75 | .30 |
| ❏ 78 | Tiki Barber | .75 | .30 |
| ❏ 79 | Brad Johnson | .50 | .20 |
| ❏ 80 | Steve McNair | .75 | .30 |
| ❏ 81 | Willis McGahee | .75 | .30 |
| ❏ 82 | Josh McCown | .50 | .20 |
| ❏ 83 | Garrison Hearst | .50 | .20 |
| ❏ 84 | Quincy Carter | .50 | .20 |
| ❏ 85 | Ricky Williams | .75 | .30 |
| ❏ 86 | Trent Green | .50 | .20 |
| ❏ 87 | Curtis Martin | .75 | .30 |
| ❏ 88 | Jerry Porter | .50 | .20 |
| ❏ 89 | Brian Westbrook | .50 | .20 |
| ❏ 90 | Clinton Portis | .75 | .30 |
| ❏ 91 | Eric Moulds | .50 | .20 |
| ❏ 92 | Marcel Shipp | .50 | .20 |
| ❏ 93 | Joey Harrington | .75 | .30 |
| ❏ 94 | David Carr | .75 | .30 |
| ❏ 95 | Marvin Harrison | .75 | .30 |
| ❏ 96 | Joe Horn | .50 | .20 |
| ❏ 97 | Chris Chambers | .50 | .20 |
| ❏ 98 | Darrell Jackson | .50 | .20 |
| ❏ 99 | Eddie George | .50 | .20 |
| ❏ 100 | Donovan McNabb | 1.00 | .40 |
| ❏ 101 | Marshall Faulk | .75 | .30 |
| ❏ 102 | Rex Grossman | .75 | .30 |
| ❏ 103 | Tai Streets | .30 | .10 |
| ❏ 104 | Jeremy Shockey | .75 | .30 |
| ❏ 105 | Jamal Lewis | .75 | .30 |
| ❏ 106 | Tom Brady | 2.00 | .75 |
| ❏ 107 | Shaun Alexander | .75 | .30 |
| ❏ 108 | Carson Palmer | 1.00 | .40 |
| ❏ 109 | Daunte Culpepper | .75 | .30 |
| ❏ 110 | Michael Vick | 1.50 | .60 |
| ❏ 111 | Eli Manning RC | 12.00 | 5.00 |
| ❏ 112 | Kevin Jones RC | 1.50 | .60 |
| ❏ 113 | Philip Rivers RC | 5.00 | 2.00 |
| ❏ 114 | Ben Roethlisberger RC | 15.00 | 6.00 |
| ❏ 115 | Roy Williams RC | 4.00 | 1.50 |
| ❏ 116 | Tommie Harris RC | 1.50 | .60 |
| ❏ 117 | Vontez Duff RC | 1.00 | .40 |
| ❏ 118 | Karlos Dansby RC | 1.50 | .60 |
| ❏ 119 | Thomas Tapeh RC | 1.25 | .50 |
| ❏ 120 | Matt Schaub RC | 5.00 | 2.00 |
| ❏ 121 | Dexter Reid RC | 1.00 | .40 |
| ❏ 122 | Jonathan Smith RC | 1.00 | .40 |
| ❏ 123 | Ricardo Colclough RC | 1.50 | .60 |
| ❏ 124 | Jeff Dugan RC | 1.00 | .40 |
| ❏ 125 | Larry Fitzgerald RC | 5.00 | 2.00 |
| ❏ 126 | Gibril Wilson RC | 1.50 | .60 |
| ❏ 127 | Sean Taylor RC | 1.50 | .60 |
| ❏ 128 | Marquise Hill RC | 1.00 | .40 |
| ❏ 129 | Ernest Wilford RC | 1.50 | .60 |
| ❏ 130 | Cedric Cobbs RC | 1.50 | .60 |
| ❏ 131 | Rich Gardner RC | 1.25 | .50 |
| ❏ 132 | Chris Cooley RC | 1.50 | .60 |
| ❏ 133 | Kenechi Udeze RC | 1.50 | .60 |
| ❏ 134 | John Navarre RC | 1.25 | .50 |
| ❏ 135 | Ben Troupe RC | 1.50 | .60 |
| ❏ 136 | Dave Ball RC | 1.00 | .40 |
| ❏ 137 | Antwan Odom RC | 1.25 | .50 |
| ❏ 138 | Stuart Schweigert RC | 1.25 | .50 |
| ❏ 139 | Derek Abney RC | 1.00 | .40 |
| ❏ 140 | Keary Colbert RC | 1.50 | .60 |
| ❏ 141 | Jeris McIntyre RC | 1.00 | .40 |
| ❏ 142 | Matt Kranchick RC | 1.50 | .60 |
| ❏ 143 | Rodney Leisle RC | 1.00 | .40 |
| ❏ 144 | Vince Wilfork RC | 1.50 | .60 |
| ❏ 145 | Lee Evans RC | 2.00 | .75 |
| ❏ 146 | Darnell Dockett RC | 1.00 | .40 |
| ❏ 147 | Jeremy LeSueur RC | 1.00 | .40 |
| ❏ 148 | Gilbert Gardner RC | 1.00 | .40 |
| ❏ 149 | Amon Gordon RC | 1.00 | .40 |
| ❏ 150 | Darius Watts RC | 1.25 | .50 |
| ❏ 151 | Junior Siavii RC | 1.00 | .40 |
| ❏ 152 | Igor Olshansky RC | 1.50 | .60 |
| ❏ 153 | Courtney Watson RC | 1.25 | .50 |
| ❏ 154 | D.J. Williams RC | 1.50 | .60 |
| ❏ 155 | Mewelde Moore RC | 1.50 | .60 |
| ❏ 156 | Teddy Lehman RC | 1.50 | .60 |
| ❏ 157 | Nathan Vasher RC | 1.50 | .60 |
| ❏ 158 | Randy Starks RC | 1.00 | .40 |
| ❏ 159 | Isaac Sopoaga RC | 1.00 | .40 |
| ❏ 160 | Drew Henson RC | 1.00 | .40 |
| ❏ 161 | Erik Coleman RC | 1.25 | .50 |
| ❏ 162 | Robert Kent RC | 1.00 | .40 |
| ❏ 163 | Jammal Lord RC | 1.00 | .40 |
| ❏ 164 | Richard Seigler RC | 1.00 | .40 |
| ❏ 165 | Jeff Smoker RC | 1.25 | .50 |
| ❏ 166 | Niko Koutouvides RC | 1.00 | .40 |
| ❏ 167 | Adimchinobe Echemandu RC | 1.25 | .50 |
| ❏ 168 | Matt Mauck RC | 1.25 | .50 |
| ❏ 169 | Brandon Miree RC | 1.00 | .40 |
| ❏ 170 | Dunta Robinson RC | 1.50 | .60 |
| ❏ 171 | B.J. Symons RC | 1.50 | .60 |
| ❏ 172 | Courtney Anderson RC | 1.00 | .40 |
| ❏ 173 | Bruce Perry RC | 1.00 | .40 |
| ❏ 174 | Shaun Phillips RC | 1.00 | .40 |
| ❏ 175 | Greg Jones RC | 1.50 | .60 |
| ❏ 176 | Ryan Krause RC | 1.00 | .40 |
| ❏ 177 | Charlie Anderson RC | 1.00 | .40 |
| ❏ 178 | Tank Johnson RC | 1.25 | .50 |
| ❏ 179 | Dwan Edwards RC | 1.00 | .40 |
| ❏ 180 | Julius Jones RC | 4.00 | 1.50 |
| ❏ 181 | Chad Lavalais RC | 1.00 | .40 |
| ❏ 182 | Tim Anderson RC | 1.50 | .60 |
| ❏ 183 | Jarrett Payton RC | 1.50 | .60 |
| ❏ 184 | Matt Ware RC | 1.50 | .60 |
| ❏ 185 | DeAngelo Hall RC | 1.50 | .60 |
| ❏ 186 | Ben Hartsock RC | 1.50 | .60 |
| ❏ 187 | Bradlee Van Pelt RC | 1.50 | .60 |
| ❏ 188 | Michael Boulware RC | 1.50 | .60 |
| ❏ 189 | Keith Smith RC | 1.00 | .40 |
| ❏ 190 | Michael Jenkins RC | 1.50 | .60 |
| ❏ 191 | Quincy Wilson RC | 1.25 | .50 |
| ❏ 192 | Dontarrious Thomas RC | 1.25 | .50 |
| ❏ 193 | Sloan Thomas RC | 1.25 | .50 |
| ❏ 194 | Tony Hargrove RC | 1.00 | .40 |
| ❏ 195 | Ben Watson RC | 1.50 | .60 |
| ❏ 196 | Craig Krenzel RC | 1.50 | .60 |
| ❏ 197 | Jason Babin RC | 1.25 | .50 |
| ❏ 198 | Jim Sorgi RC | 1.50 | .60 |
| ❏ 199 | Triandos Luke RC | 1.00 | .40 |
| ❏ 200 | Kellen Winslow RC | 3.00 | 1.25 |
| ❏ 201 | Patrick Crayton RC | 2.00 | .75 |
| ❏ 202 | Michael Waddell RC | 1.00 | .40 |
| ❏ 203 | Chris Gamble RC | 1.25 | .50 |
| ❏ 204 | Josh Harris RC | 1.25 | .50 |
| ❏ 205 | Devard Darling RC | 1.25 | .50 |
| ❏ 206 | Shawntae Spencer RC | 1.00 | .40 |
| ❏ 207 | Will Smith RC | 1.25 | .50 |
| ❏ 208 | Samie Parker RC | 1.25 | .50 |
| ❏ 209 | Darrion Scott RC | 1.50 | .60 |
| ❏ 210 | Chris Perry RC | 1.50 | .60 |
| ❏ 211 | P.K. Sam RC | 1.00 | .40 |
| ❏ 212 | Wes Welker RC | 4.00 | 1.50 |
| ❏ 213 | Ryan Dinwiddie RC | 1.00 | .40 |
| ❏ 214 | Rod Davis RC | 1.00 | .40 |
| ❏ 215 | Casey Clausen RC | 1.25 | .50 |
| ❏ 216 | Clarence Moore RC | 1.25 | .50 |
| ❏ 217 | D.J. Hackett RC | 1.00 | .40 |
| ❏ 218 | Casey Bramlet RC | 1.00 | .40 |
| ❏ 219 | Jared Lorenzen RC | 1.25 | .50 |
| ❏ 220 | Devery Henderson RC | 1.50 | .60 |
| ❏ 221 | Sean Jones RC | 1.25 | .50 |
| ❏ 222 | Maurice Mann RC | 1.00 | .40 |
| ❏ 223 | Jared Allen RC | 2.00 | .75 |
| ❏ 224 | Bruce Thornton RC | 1.00 | .40 |
| ❏ 225 | Tatum Bell RC | 1.50 | .60 |
| ❏ 226 | Leon Joe RC | 1.00 | .40 |
| ❏ 227 | Tim Euhus RC | 1.00 | .40 |
| ❏ 228 | John Standeford RC | 1.00 | .40 |
| ❏ 229 | Reggie Torbor RC | 1.00 | .40 |
| ❏ 230 | Rashaun Woods RC | 1.50 | .60 |
| ❏ 231 | Jason Shivers RC | 1.00 | .40 |
| ❏ 232 | Jason Peters RC | 1.25 | .50 |
| ❏ 233 | Ahmad Carroll RC | 1.50 | .60 |
| ❏ 234 | Jason David RC | 1.50 | .60 |
| ❏ 235 | Keyaron Fox RC | 1.25 | .50 |
| ❏ 236 | Corey Williams RC | 1.25 | .50 |
| ❏ 237 | Raheem Orr RC | 1.00 | .40 |
| ❏ 238 | Carlos Francis RC | 1.00 | .40 |
| ❏ 239 | Von Hutchins RC | 1.00 | .40 |

| | | | |
|---|---|---|---|
| ❏ 240 Marcus Tubbs RC | 1.50 | .60 |
| ❏ 241 Daryl Smith RC | 1.50 | .60 |
| ❏ 242 Robert Gallery RC | 1.50 | .60 |
| ❏ 243 Sean Tufts RC | 1.00 | .40 |
| ❏ 244 Marquis Cooper RC | 1.50 | .60 |
| ❏ 245 Bernard Berrian RC | 1.50 | .60 |
| ❏ 246 Derrick Strait RC | 1.25 | .50 |
| ❏ 247 Travis LaBoy RC | 1.50 | .60 |
| ❏ 248 Johnnie Morant RC | 1.25 | .50 |
| ❏ 249 Caleb Miller RC | 1.00 | .40 |
| ❏ 250 Michael Clayton RC | 1.50 | .60 |
| ❏ 251 Will Poole RC | 1.50 | .60 |
| ❏ 252 Andy Hall RC | 1.25 | .50 |
| ❏ 253 Demorrio Williams RC | 1.50 | .60 |
| ❏ 254 Chris Thompson RC | 1.00 | .40 |
| ❏ 255 Derrick Hamilton RC | 1.00 | .40 |
| ❏ 256 Glenn Earl RC | 1.00 | .40 |
| ❏ 257 Jonathan Vilma RC | 1.50 | .60 |
| ❏ 258 Donnell Washington RC | 1.25 | .50 |
| ❏ 259 Drew Carter RC | 1.50 | .60 |
| ❏ 260 Steven Jackson RC | 5.00 | 2.00 |
| ❏ 261 Jamaar Taylor RC | 1.00 | .40 |
| ❏ 262 Nate Lawrie RC | 1.00 | .40 |
| ❏ 263 Cody Pickett RC | 1.25 | .50 |
| ❏ 264 Keiwan Ratliff RC | 1.00 | .40 |
| ❏ 265 Luke McCown RC | 1.50 | .60 |
| ❏ 266 Jerricho Cotchery RC | 1.50 | .60 |
| ❏ 267 Joey Thomas RC | 1.00 | .40 |
| ❏ 268 Shawn Andrews RC | 1.50 | .60 |
| ❏ 269 Derrick Ward RC | 1.50 | .60 |
| ❏ 270 Reggie Williams RC | 1.50 | .60 |
| ❏ 271 Rod Rutherford RC | 1.00 | .40 |
| ❏ 272 Michael Turner RC | 3.00 | 1.25 |
| ❏ 273 Michael Gaines RC | 1.00 | .40 |
| ❏ 274 Will Allen RC | 1.25 | .50 |
| ❏ 275 J.P. Losman RC | 2.00 | .75 |

## 2005 Bowman

| | | | |
|---|---|---|---|
| ❏ COMP.SET w/AU's (270) | 60.00 | 25.00 |
| ❏ 1 Peyton Manning | 1.25 | .50 |
| ❏ 2 Antonio Gates | .75 | .30 |
| ❏ 3 Priest Holmes | .75 | .30 |
| ❏ 4 Anquan Boldin | .60 | .25 |
| ❏ 5 Donovan McNabb | .75 | .30 |
| ❏ 6 Drew Bennett | .60 | .25 |
| ❏ 7 Michael Vick | .75 | .30 |
| ❏ 8 David Carr | .60 | .25 |
| ❏ 9 Drew Brees | .75 | .30 |
| ❏ 10 Trent Green | .60 | .25 |
| ❏ 11 Drew Bledsoe | .75 | .30 |
| ❏ 12 Randy Moss | .75 | .30 |
| ❏ 13 Terrell Owens | .75 | .30 |
| ❏ 14 Donte Stallworth | .60 | .25 |
| ❏ 15 Alge Crumpler | .60 | .25 |
| ❏ 16 Jake Plummer | .60 | .25 |
| ❏ 17 Curtis Martin | .75 | .30 |
| ❏ 18 Jason Witten | .60 | .25 |
| ❏ 19 Tom Brady | 1.50 | .60 |
| ❏ 20 Thomas Jones | .60 | .25 |
| ❏ 21 Tiki Barber | .75 | .30 |
| ❏ 22 Maurice Carthon CO | .50 | .20 |
| ❏ 23 Rex Grossman | .75 | .30 |
| ❏ 24 Brett Favre | 2.00 | .75 |
| ❏ 25 Marshall Faulk | .75 | .30 |
| ❏ 26 LaMont Jordan | .60 | .25 |
| ❏ 27 Kurt Warner | .75 | .30 |
| ❏ 28 Corey Dillon | .60 | .25 |
| ❏ 29 Julius Jones | .75 | .30 |

| | | | |
|---|---|---|---|
| ❏ 30 Ahman Green | .75 | .30 |
| ❏ 31 Jamal Lewis | .60 | .25 |
| ❏ 32 Ben Roethlisberger | 2.00 | .75 |
| ❏ 33 Keary Colbert | .50 | .20 |
| ❏ 34 Mike Nolan CO RC | .60 | .25 |
| ❏ 35 Joey Harrington | .75 | .30 |
| ❏ 36 Brian Westbrook | .75 | .30 |
| ❏ 37 Domanick Davis | .50 | .20 |
| ❏ 38 Carson Palmer | .75 | .30 |
| ❏ 39 Stephen Davis | .60 | .25 |
| ❏ 40 Eli Manning | 1.50 | .60 |
| ❏ 41 Edgerrin James | .60 | .25 |
| ❏ 42 Jonathan Vilma | .60 | .25 |
| ❏ 43 Brad Childress CO RC | .60 | .25 |
| ❏ 44 Willis McGahee | .75 | .30 |
| ❏ 45 Steve McNair | .75 | .30 |
| ❏ 47 Rudi Johnson | .60 | .25 |
| ❏ 48 Jerry Porter | .60 | .25 |
| ❏ 49 Chad Pennington | .75 | .30 |
| ❏ 50 Charles Rogers | .50 | .20 |
| ❏ 51 Patrick Ramsey | .60 | .25 |
| ❏ 52 Dwight Freeney | .60 | .25 |
| ❏ 53 Brian Griese | .60 | .25 |
| ❏ 54 Jerome Bettis | .75 | .30 |
| ❏ 55 Tim Lewis CO | .50 | .20 |
| ❏ 56 Aaron Brooks | .50 | .20 |
| ❏ 57 Matt Hasselbeck | .60 | .25 |
| ❏ 58 Chris Chambers | .60 | .25 |
| ❏ 59 Kyle Boller | .60 | .25 |
| ❏ 60 Brandon Lloyd | .50 | .20 |
| ❏ 61 Marc Bulger | .60 | .25 |
| ❏ 62 Isaac Bruce | .60 | .25 |
| ❏ 63 Jake Delhomme | .75 | .30 |
| ❏ 64 Chad Johnson | .60 | .25 |
| ❏ 65 Shaun Alexander | .75 | .30 |
| ❏ 66 Kevin Jones | .60 | .25 |
| ❏ 67 Eric Moulds | .60 | .25 |
| ❏ 68 Laveranues Coles | .60 | .25 |
| ❏ 69 A.J. Feeley | .50 | .20 |
| ❏ 70 Sean Taylor | .60 | .25 |
| ❏ 71 Romeo Crennel CO RC | .75 | .30 |
| ❏ 72 Ashley Lelie | .50 | .20 |
| ❏ 73 Nick Saban CO RC | .75 | .30 |
| ❏ 74 Deuce McAllister | .75 | .30 |
| ❏ 75 Kerry Collins | .60 | .25 |
| ❏ 76 Chris Brown | .60 | .25 |
| ❏ 77 Steven Jackson | 1.00 | .40 |
| ❏ 78 Nate Burleson | .60 | .25 |
| ❏ 79 LaDainian Tomlinson | 1.25 | .50 |
| ❏ 80 Darrell Jackson | .60 | .25 |
| ❏ 81 Torry Holt | .60 | .25 |
| ❏ 82 Lee Suggs | .60 | .25 |
| ❏ 83 Lee Evans | .60 | .25 |
| ❏ 84 Santana Moss | .60 | .25 |
| ❏ 85 Jeremy Shockey | .75 | .30 |
| ❏ 86 Hines Ward | .75 | .30 |
| ❏ 87 Muhsin Muhammad | .60 | .25 |
| ❏ 88 Daunte Culpepper | .75 | .30 |
| ❏ 89 Deion Branch | .60 | .25 |
| ❏ 90 DeShaun Foster | .60 | .25 |
| ❏ 91 Travis Henry | .60 | .25 |
| ❏ 92 Jerry Rice | 1.50 | .60 |
| ❏ 93 Reggie Wayne | .60 | .25 |
| ❏ 94 Roy Williams WR | .75 | .30 |
| ❏ 95 Michael Jenkins | .60 | .25 |
| ❏ 96 Tatum Bell | .60 | .25 |
| ❏ 97 Andre Johnson | .60 | .25 |
| ❏ 98 Dante Hall | .60 | .25 |
| ❏ 99 Javon Walker | .60 | .25 |
| ❏ 100 Larry Fitzgerald | .75 | .30 |
| ❏ 101 Joe Horn | .60 | .25 |
| ❏ 102 Marvin Harrison | .75 | .30 |
| ❏ 103 Fred Taylor | .75 | .30 |
| ❏ 104 Byron Leftwich | .60 | .25 |
| ❏ 105 Tony Gonzalez | .60 | .25 |
| ❏ 106 T.J. Houshmandzadeh | .60 | .25 |
| ❏ 107 J.P. Losman | .75 | .30 |
| ❏ 108 Michael Clayton | .60 | .25 |
| ❏ 109 Clinton Portis | .75 | .30 |
| ❏ 110 Ted Cottrell CO RC | .50 | .20 |
| ❏ 111 Braylon Edwards RC | 5.00 | 2.00 |
| ❏ 112 Aaron Rodgers RC | 5.00 | 2.00 |
| ❏ 113 Ronnie Brown RC | 5.00 | 2.00 |

| | | | |
|---|---|---|---|
| ❏ 114 Alex Smith QB RC | 2.50 | 1.00 |
| ❏ 115 Cadillac Williams RC | 3.00 | 1.25 |
| ❏ 116 Ciatrick Fason RC | 1.25 | .50 |
| ❏ 117 Derrick Johnson RC | 1.50 | .60 |
| ❏ 118 Carlos Rogers RC | 1.50 | .60 |
| ❏ 119 Ryan Moats RC | 1.50 | .60 |
| ❏ 120 Alvin Pearman RC | 1.25 | .50 |
| ❏ 121 Stefan LeFors RC | 1.25 | .50 |
| ❏ 122 Brandon Jacobs RC | 2.00 | .75 |
| ❏ 123 Kyle Orton RC | 2.00 | .75 |
| ❏ 124 Marion Barber RC | 5.00 | 2.00 |
| ❏ 125 Mark Bradley RC | 1.50 | .60 |
| ❏ 126 Travis Johnson RC | 1.00 | .40 |
| ❏ 127 Antrel Rolle RC | 1.50 | .60 |
| ❏ 128 Jason Campbell RC | 3.00 | 1.25 |
| ❏ 129 DeMarcus Ware RC | 2.50 | 1.00 |
| ❏ 130 Frank Gore RC | 4.00 | 1.50 |
| ❏ 131 Justin Miller RC | 1.25 | .50 |
| ❏ 132 J.J. Arrington RC | 1.50 | .60 |
| ❏ 133 Marcus Spears RC | 1.50 | .60 |
| ❏ 134 Roddy White RC | 2.00 | .75 |
| ❏ 135 Fabian Washington RC | 1.50 | .60 |
| ❏ 136 Vincent Jackson RC | 1.50 | .60 |
| ❏ 137 Erasmus James RC | 1.25 | .50 |
| ❏ 138 Roscoe Parrish RC | 1.50 | .60 |
| ❏ 139 Airese Currie RC | 1.25 | .50 |
| ❏ 140 Heath Miller RC | 3.00 | 1.25 |
| ❏ 141 Mike Patterson RC | 1.25 | .50 |
| ❏ 142 Troy Williamson RC | 1.50 | .60 |
| ❏ 143 Terrence Murphy RC | 1.00 | .40 |
| ❏ 144 Dan Orlovsky RC | 1.50 | .60 |
| ❏ 145 Eric Shelton RC | 1.25 | .50 |
| ❏ 146 Thomas Davis RC | 1.25 | .50 |
| ❏ 147 Cedric Benson RC | 1.50 | .60 |
| ❏ 148 Noah Herron RC | 1.50 | .60 |
| ❏ 149 Vernand Morency RC | 1.50 | .60 |
| ❏ 150 Darren Sproles RC | 2.00 | .75 |
| ❏ 151 Alex Smith TE RC | 1.50 | .60 |
| ❏ 152 Mark Clayton RC | 1.50 | .60 |
| ❏ 153 Craphonso Thorpe RC | 1.25 | .50 |
| ❏ 154 Mike Williams RC | 1.50 | .60 |
| ❏ 155 Anthony Davis RC | 1.25 | .50 |
| ❏ 156 Charlie Frye RC | 1.50 | .60 |
| ❏ 157 Fred Gibson RC | 1.25 | .50 |
| ❏ 158 Reggie Brown RC | 1.50 | .60 |
| ❏ 159 Andrew Walter RC | 1.50 | .60 |
| ❏ 160 Adam Jones RC | 1.50 | .60 |
| ❏ 161 David Greene RC | 1.25 | .50 |
| ❏ 162 Maurice Clarett RC | 1.25 | .50 |
| ❏ 163 Courtney Roby RC | 1.25 | .50 |
| ❏ 164 Derek Anderson RC | 2.50 | 1.00 |
| ❏ 165 Matt Jones RC | 2.50 | 1.00 |
| ❏ 166 Chris Henry RC | 1.50 | .60 |
| ❏ 167 Shaun Cody RC | 1.25 | .50 |
| ❏ 168 Khalif Barnes RC | 1.00 | .40 |
| ❏ 169 Matt Roth RC | 1.50 | .60 |
| ❏ 170 Lionel Gates RC | 1.00 | .40 |
| ❏ 171 Kevin Burnett RC | 1.25 | .50 |
| ❏ 172 Taylor Stubblefield RC | 1.00 | .40 |
| ❏ 173 Zach Tuiasosopo RC | 1.00 | .40 |
| ❏ 174 Alex Barron RC | 1.25 | .50 |
| ❏ 175 Mike Nugent RC | 1.25 | .50 |
| ❏ 176 Barrett Ruud RC | 1.50 | .60 |
| ❏ 177 Brock Berlin RC | 1.25 | .50 |
| ❏ 178 Kirk Morrison RC | 1.50 | .60 |
| ❏ 179 David Pollack RC | 1.25 | .50 |
| ❏ 180 Ryan Fitzpatrick RC | 1.50 | .60 |
| ❏ 181 Kay-Jay Harris RC | 1.25 | .50 |
| ❏ 182 Dan Cody RC | 1.50 | .60 |
| ❏ 183 Chad Owens RC | 1.50 | .60 |
| ❏ 184 Stanley Wilson RC | 1.25 | .50 |
| ❏ 185 Rasheed Marshall RC | 1.25 | .50 |
| ❏ 186 Bryant McFadden RC | 1.25 | .50 |
| ❏ 187 Joel Dreessen RC | 1.25 | .50 |
| ❏ 188 Donte Nicholson RC | 1.25 | .50 |
| ❏ 189 Scott Starks RC | 1.25 | .50 |
| ❏ 190 Walter Reyes RC | 1.00 | .40 |
| ❏ 191 Stanford Routt RC | 1.25 | .50 |
| ❏ 192 Lance Mitchell RC | 1.25 | .50 |
| ❏ 193 Rian Wallace RC | 1.25 | .50 |
| ❏ 194 Timmy Chang RC | 1.50 | .60 |
| ❏ 195 Oshiomogho Atogwe RC | 1.00 | .40 |
| ❏ 196 Larry Brackins RC | 1.00 | .40 |
| ❏ 197 Jovan Witherspoon RC | 1.00 | .40 |

| | | |
|---|---|---|
| ❏ 198 Boomer Grigsby RC | 1.50 | .60 |
| ❏ 199 Darryl Blackstock RC | 1.00 | .40 |
| ❏ 200 Jerome Mathis RC | 1.50 | .60 |
| ❏ 201 Ellis Hobbs RC | 1.50 | .60 |
| ❏ 202 Dante Ridgeway RC | 1.00 | .40 |
| ❏ 203 James Kilian RC | 1.00 | .40 |
| ❏ 204 Patrick Estes RC | 1.00 | .40 |
| ❏ 205 Justin Tuck RC | 2.00 | .75 |
| ❏ 206 Channing Crowder RC | 1.25 | .50 |
| ❏ 207 Dustin Fox RC | 1.50 | .60 |
| ❏ 208 Marlin Jackson RC | 1.25 | .50 |
| ❏ 209 Luis Castillo RC | 1.50 | .60 |
| ❏ 210 Paris Warren RC | 1.25 | .50 |
| ❏ 211 J.R. Russell RC | 1.00 | .40 |
| ❏ 212 Cedric Houston RC | 1.50 | .60 |
| ❏ 213 Corey Webster RC | 1.50 | .60 |
| ❏ 214 Craig Bragg RC | 1.00 | .40 |
| ❏ 215 Tab Perry RC | 1.50 | .60 |
| ❏ 216 Ryan Riddle RC | 1.00 | .40 |
| ❏ 217 Gino Guidugli RC | 1.00 | .40 |
| ❏ 218 Deandra Cobb RC | 1.25 | .50 |
| ❏ 219 Travis Daniels RC | 1.25 | .50 |
| ❏ 220 Marcus Maxwell RC | 1.00 | .40 |
| ❏ 221 Eric King RC | 1.00 | .40 |
| ❏ 222 Matt Cassel RC | 4.00 | 1.50 |
| ❏ 223 Justin Green RC | 1.50 | .60 |
| ❏ 224 Steve Savoy RC | 1.00 | .40 |
| ❏ 225 Shawne Merriman RC | 2.50 | 1.00 |
| ❏ 226 Damien Nash RC | 1.25 | .50 |
| ❏ 227 T.A. McLendon RC | 1.00 | .40 |
| ❏ 228 Vincent Fuller RC | 1.25 | .50 |
| ❏ 229 Jordan Beck RC | 1.25 | .50 |
| ❏ 230 Lofa Tatupu RC | 2.00 | .75 |
| ❏ 231 Will Peoples RC | 1.25 | .50 |
| ❏ 232 Chad Friehauf RC | 1.25 | .50 |
| ❏ 233 Brady Poppinga RC | 1.50 | .60 |
| ❏ 234 Anttaj Hawthorne RC | 1.25 | .50 |
| ❏ 235 Adrian McPherson RC | 1.25 | .50 |
| ❏ 236 Nick Collins RC | 1.50 | .60 |
| ❏ 237 Roydell Williams RC | 1.25 | .50 |
| ❏ 238 Craig Ochs RC | 1.25 | .50 |
| ❏ 239 Billy Bajema RC | 1.00 | .40 |
| ❏ 240 Jon Goldsberry RC | 1.50 | .40 |
| ❏ 241 Jared Newberry RC | 1.25 | .50 |
| ❏ 242 Odell Thurman RC | 1.50 | .60 |
| ❏ 243 Kelvin Hayden RC | 1.25 | .50 |
| ❏ 244 Jamaal Brimmer RC | 1.00 | .40 |
| ❏ 245 Jonathan Babineaux RC | 1.25 | .50 |
| ❏ 246 Bo Scaife RC | 1.25 | .50 |
| ❏ 247 Chris Spencer RC | 1.50 | .60 |
| ❏ 248 Manuel White RC | 1.25 | .50 |
| ❏ 249 Josh Davis RC | 1.00 | .40 |
| ❏ 250 Bryan Randall RC | 1.50 | .60 |
| ❏ 251 James Butler RC | 1.25 | .50 |
| ❏ 252 Harry Williams RC | 1.25 | .50 |
| ❏ 253 Leroy Hill RC | 1.50 | .60 |
| ❏ 254 Josh Bullocks RC | 1.50 | .60 |
| ❏ 255 Alfred Fincher RC | 1.25 | .50 |
| ❏ 256 Antonio Perkins RC | 1.25 | .50 |
| ❏ 257 Bobby Purify RC | 1.25 | .50 |
| ❏ 258 Rick Razzano RC | 1.00 | .40 |
| ❏ 259 Darrent Williams RC | 1.50 | .60 |
| ❏ 260 Darian Durant RC | 1.50 | .60 |
| ❏ 261 Fred Amey RC | 1.25 | .50 |
| ❏ 262 Ronald Bartell RC | 1.25 | .50 |
| ❏ 263 Kerry Rhodes RC | 1.50 | .60 |
| ❏ 264 Jerome Carter RC | 1.00 | .40 |
| ❏ 265 Marcus Randall RC | 1.25 | .50 |
| ❏ 266 Nehemiah Broughton RC | 1.25 | .50 |
| ❏ 267 Keron Henry RC | 1.00 | .40 |
| ❏ 268 Jerome Collins RC | 1.25 | .50 |
| ❏ 269 Trent Cole RC | 1.50 | .60 |
| ❏ 270 Alphonso Hodge RC | 1.00 | .40 |
| ❏ 271 Brandon Jones RC | 1.50 | .60 |
| ❏ 272 Chase Lyman RC | 1.00 | .40 |
| ❏ 273 Marviel Underwood RC | 1.25 | .50 |
| ❏ 274 Maurice Washington RC | 1.25 | .50 |
| ❏ 275 Madison Hedgecock RC | 1.50 | .60 |

## 2006 Bowman

| | | |
|---|---|---|
| ❏ 1 Plaxico Burress | .60 | .25 |
| ❏ 2 Lee Evans | .60 | .25 |
| ❏ 3 Shaun Alexander | .75 | .30 |
| ❏ 4 Muhsin Muhammad | .60 | .25 |

| | | |
|---|---|---|
| ❏ 5 Jamal Lewis | .60 | .25 |
| ❏ 6 Brett Favre | 1.50 | .60 |
| ❏ 7 Jake Plummer | .60 | .25 |
| ❏ 8 Clinton Portis | .75 | .30 |
| ❏ 9 Deuce McAllister | .60 | .25 |
| ❏ 10 Rod Marinelli CO RC | .50 | .20 |
| ❏ 11 Tom Brady | 1.25 | .50 |
| ❏ 12 Torry Holt | .60 | .25 |
| ❏ 13 T.J. Houshmandzadeh | .60 | .25 |
| ❏ 14 Rudi Johnson | .60 | .25 |
| ❏ 15 Priest Holmes | .60 | .25 |
| ❏ 16 Tatum Bell | .60 | .25 |
| ❏ 17 Carson Palmer | .75 | .30 |
| ❏ 18 Jeremy Shockey | .75 | .30 |
| ❏ 19 Willis McGahee | .75 | .30 |
| ❏ 20 Shawne Merriman | .60 | .25 |
| ❏ 21 Alge Crumpler | .60 | .25 |
| ❏ 22 Terrell Owens | .75 | .30 |
| ❏ 23 Marion Barber | .75 | .30 |
| ❏ 24 Fred Taylor | .60 | .25 |
| ❏ 25 Dante Hall | .60 | .25 |
| ❏ 26 Steve Smith | .75 | .30 |
| ❏ 27 Mike McCarthy CO RC | .50 | .20 |
| ❏ 28 Brad Johnson | .60 | .25 |
| ❏ 29 Reggie Wayne | .60 | .25 |
| ❏ 30 David Carr | .60 | .25 |
| ❏ 31 DeShaun Foster | .60 | .25 |
| ❏ 32 Julius Jones | .75 | .30 |
| ❏ 33 Tony Gonzalez | .60 | .25 |
| ❏ 34 Chad Johnson | .60 | .25 |
| ❏ 35 Javon Walker | .60 | .25 |
| ❏ 36 Curtis Martin | .75 | .30 |
| ❏ 37 Marc Bulger | .60 | .25 |
| ❏ 38 Peyton Manning | 1.25 | .50 |
| ❏ 39 LaMont Jordan | .60 | .25 |
| ❏ 40 LaDainian Tomlinson | 1.00 | .40 |
| ❏ 41 Tiki Barber | .75 | .30 |
| ❏ 42 Darrell Jackson | .60 | .25 |
| ❏ 43 Byron Leftwich | .60 | .25 |
| ❏ 44 J.P. Losman | .60 | .25 |
| ❏ 45 Dwight Freeney | .60 | .25 |
| ❏ 46 Kevin Jones | .75 | .30 |
| ❏ 47 Drew Brees | .75 | .30 |
| ❏ 48 Isaac Bruce | .60 | .25 |
| ❏ 49 Hines Ward | .75 | .30 |
| ❏ 50 Drew Bledsoe | .75 | .30 |
| ❏ 51 Randy Moss | .75 | .30 |
| ❏ 52 Roy Williams WR | .60 | .25 |
| ❏ 53 Edgerrin James | .60 | .25 |
| ❏ 54 Donte Stallworth | .60 | .25 |
| ❏ 55 Odell Thurman | .50 | .20 |
| ❏ 56 Chester Taylor | .60 | .25 |
| ❏ 57 Ahman Green | .60 | .25 |
| ❏ 58 Steven Jackson | .75 | .30 |
| ❏ 59 Randy McMichael | .50 | .20 |
| ❏ 60 Larry Fitzgerald | .75 | .30 |
| ❏ 61 Ben Roethlisberger | 1.25 | .50 |
| ❏ 62 Charlie Frye | .60 | .25 |
| ❏ 63 Daunte Culpepper | .75 | .30 |
| ❏ 64 Keary Colbert | .60 | .25 |
| ❏ 65 Santana Moss | .60 | .25 |
| ❏ 66 Patrick Ramsey | .60 | .25 |
| ❏ 67 Mark Clayton | .60 | .25 |
| ❏ 68 Jonathan Vilma | .60 | .25 |
| ❏ 69 Gary Kubiak CO | .50 | .20 |
| ❏ 70 Michael Jenkins | .60 | .25 |
| ❏ 71 Jake Delhomme | .60 | .25 |
| ❏ 72 Marvin Harrison | .75 | .30 |

| | | |
|---|---|---|
| ❏ 73 Aaron Rodgers | .75 | .30 |
| ❏ 74 Trent Green | .60 | .25 |
| ❏ 75 Andre Johnson | .60 | .25 |
| ❏ 76 Chris Chambers | .60 | .25 |
| ❏ 77 Matt Hasselbeck | .60 | .25 |
| ❏ 78 Chris Brown | .60 | .25 |
| ❏ 79 Reggie Brown | .60 | .25 |
| ❏ 80 Eli Manning | 1.00 | .40 |
| ❏ 81 Warrick Dunn | .60 | .25 |
| ❏ 82 Kurt Warner | .60 | .25 |
| ❏ 83 Corey Dillon | .60 | .25 |
| ❏ 84 Antonio Gates | .75 | .30 |
| ❏ 85 Anquan Boldin | .60 | .25 |
| ❏ 86 Terry Glenn | .60 | .25 |
| ❏ 87 Donovan McNabb | .75 | .30 |
| ❏ 88 Steve McNair | .60 | .25 |
| ❏ 89 Drew Bennett | .60 | .25 |
| ❏ 90 Jason Witten | .60 | .25 |
| ❏ 91 Alex Smith QB | .75 | .30 |
| ❏ 92 Joe Horn | .60 | .25 |
| ❏ 93 Eric Moulds | .60 | .25 |
| ❏ 94 Domanick Davis | .60 | .25 |
| ❏ 95 Billy Volek | .60 | .25 |
| ❏ 96 Deion Branch | .60 | .25 |
| ❏ 97 Chris Cooley | .60 | .25 |
| ❏ 98 Todd Heap UER | .60 | .25 |
| ❏ 99 Larry Johnson | .60 | .25 |
| ❏ 100 Chad Pennington | .60 | .25 |
| ❏ 101 Willie Parker | 1.00 | .40 |
| ❏ 102 Brandon Lloyd | .60 | .25 |
| ❏ 103 Cadillac Williams | .75 | .30 |
| ❏ 104 Rod Smith | .60 | .25 |
| ❏ 105 Philip Rivers | .75 | .30 |
| ❏ 106 Ronnie Brown | .75 | .30 |
| ❏ 107 Reuben Droughns | .60 | .25 |
| ❏ 108 Braylon Edwards | .75 | .30 |
| ❏ 109 Joey Galloway | .60 | .25 |
| ❏ 110 Michael Vick | .75 | .30 |
| ❏ 111 Reggie Bush RC | 6.00 | 2.50 |
| ❏ 112 Matt Leinart RC | 5.00 | 2.00 |
| ❏ 113 Vince Young RC | 5.00 | 2.00 |
| ❏ 114 Jay Cutler RC | 6.00 | 2.50 |
| ❏ 115 Santonio Holmes RC | 4.00 | 1.50 |
| ❏ 116 LenDale White RC | 3.00 | 1.25 |
| ❏ 117 DeAngelo Williams RC | 2.50 | 1.00 |
| ❏ 118 Mario Williams RC | 2.50 | 1.00 |
| ❏ 119 A.J. Hawk RC | 3.00 | 1.25 |
| ❏ 120 Joseph Addai RC | 5.00 | 2.00 |
| ❏ 121 Leonard Pope RC | 1.50 | .60 |
| ❏ 122 Tamba Hali RC | 1.50 | .60 |
| ❏ 123 Bruce Gradkowski RC | 1.50 | .60 |
| ❏ 124 Jerome Harrison RC | 1.50 | .60 |
| ❏ 125 Jason Allen RC | 1.50 | .60 |
| ❏ 126 Laurence Maroney RC | 4.00 | 1.50 |
| ❏ 127 Mathias Kiwanuka RC | 2.00 | .75 |
| ❏ 128 Brodrick Bunkley RC | 1.50 | .60 |
| ❏ 129 Brian Calhoun RC | 1.25 | .50 |
| ❏ 130 Bobby Carpenter RC | 1.50 | .60 |
| ❏ 131 Johnathan Joseph RC | 1.25 | .50 |
| ❏ 132 Maurice Stovall RC | 1.50 | .60 |
| ❏ 133 Anthony Fasano RC | 1.50 | .60 |
| ❏ 134 Travis Wilson RC | 1.50 | .60 |
| ❏ 135 Chad Jackson RC | 1.25 | .50 |
| ❏ 136 D'Brickashaw Ferguson RC | 1.50 | .60 |
| ❏ 137 Tarvaris Jackson RC | 1.50 | .60 |
| ❏ 138 Omar Jacobs RC | 1.25 | .50 |
| ❏ 139 Reggie McNeal RC | 1.25 | .50 |
| ❏ 140 Jerious Norwood RC | 2.00 | .75 |
| ❏ 141 Haloti Ngata RC | 1.50 | .60 |
| ❏ 142 Jason Avant RC | 1.50 | .60 |
| ❏ 143 Brandon Marshall RC | 2.00 | .75 |
| ❏ 144 Tye Hill RC | 1.50 | .60 |
| ❏ 145 Manny Lawson RC | 1.50 | .60 |
| ❏ 146 Brandon Williams RC | 1.50 | .60 |
| ❏ 147 Demetrius Williams RC | 1.50 | .60 |
| ❏ 148 Michael Huff RC | 1.50 | .60 |
| ❏ 149 Mike Hass RC | 1.50 | .60 |
| ❏ 150 Vernon Davis RC | 1.50 | .60 |
| ❏ 151 Donte Whitner RC | 1.50 | .60 |
| ❏ 152 Marcedes Lewis RC | 1.50 | .60 |
| ❏ 153 Michael Robinson RC | 1.50 | .60 |
| ❏ 154 Maurice Drew RC | 3.00 | 1.25 |
| ❏ 155 Sinorice Moss RC | 1.50 | .60 |
| ❏ 156 Brodie Croyle RC | 2.00 | .75 |

| | | |
|---|---|---|
| ☐ 157 Derek Hagan RC | 1.50 | .60 |
| ☐ 158 Chad Greenway RC | 1.50 | .60 |
| ☐ 159 Kellen Clemens RC | 2.00 | .75 |
| ☐ 160 Skyler Green RC | 1.50 | .60 |
| ☐ 161 Devin Hester RC | 3.00 | 1.25 |
| ☐ 162 Jeremy Bloom RC | 1.50 | .60 |
| ☐ 163 Ashton Youboty RC | 1.50 | .60 |
| ☐ 164 Kamerion Wimbley RC | 1.50 | .60 |
| ☐ 165 Charlie Whitehurst RC | 1.50 | .60 |
| ☐ 166 Devin Aromashodu RC | 1.25 | .50 |
| ☐ 167 Darnell Bing RC | 1.25 | .50 |
| ☐ 168 Adam Jennings RC | 1.25 | .50 |
| ☐ 169 Joe Klopfenstein RC | 1.25 | .50 |
| ☐ 170 Jeff Webb RC | 1.25 | .50 |
| ☐ 171 D.J. Shockley RC | 1.50 | .60 |
| ☐ 172 Daniel Bullocks RC | 1.50 | .60 |
| ☐ 173 Marcus Vick RC | 1.25 | .50 |
| ☐ 174 Greg Jennings RC | 2.50 | 1.00 |
| ☐ 175 David Thomas RC | 1.50 | .60 |
| ☐ 176 Thomas Howard RC | 1.50 | .60 |
| ☐ 177 Todd Watkins RC | 1.25 | .50 |
| ☐ 178 Leon Washington RC | 1.50 | .60 |
| ☐ 179 Winston Justice RC | 1.50 | .60 |
| ☐ 180 Lawrence Vickers RC | 1.25 | .50 |
| ☐ 181 Bernard Pollard RC | 1.25 | .50 |
| ☐ 182 Davin Joseph RC | 1.25 | .50 |
| ☐ 183 Abdul Hodge RC | 1.50 | .60 |
| ☐ 184 Pat Watkins RC | 1.50 | .60 |
| ☐ 185 Jon Alston RC | 1.50 | .60 |
| ☐ 186 Ernie Sims RC | 1.50 | .60 |
| ☐ 187 Jovon Bouknight RC | 1.25 | .50 |
| ☐ 188 D'Qwell Jackson RC | 1.50 | .60 |
| ☐ 189 Wali Lundy RC | 1.50 | .60 |
| ☐ 190 Corey Bramlet RC | 1.25 | .50 |
| ☐ 191 Jonathan Orr RC | 1.25 | .50 |
| ☐ 192 Gerald Riggs RC | 1.50 | .60 |
| ☐ 193 Antonio Cromartie RC | 1.50 | .60 |
| ☐ 194 Will Blackmon RC | 1.50 | .60 |
| ☐ 195 Chris Gocong RC | 1.25 | .50 |
| ☐ 196 David Pittman RC | 1.25 | .50 |
| ☐ 197 Quinn Sypniewski RC | 1.25 | .50 |
| ☐ 198 A.J. Nicholson RC | 1.00 | .40 |
| ☐ 199 Richard Marshall RC | 1.25 | .50 |
| ☐ 200 Kevin McMahan RC | 1.25 | .50 |
| ☐ 201 Cedric Humes RC | 1.50 | .60 |
| ☐ 202 J.D. Runnels RC | 1.25 | .50 |
| ☐ 203 Darryl Tapp RC | 1.25 | .50 |
| ☐ 204 Charles Davis RC | 1.25 | .50 |
| ☐ 205 Brad Smith RC | 1.50 | .60 |
| ☐ 206 Tim Massaquoi RC | 1.25 | .50 |
| ☐ 207 Nate Salley RC | 1.25 | .50 |
| ☐ 208 Matt Shelton RC | 1.50 | .60 |
| ☐ 209 Brett Basanez RC | 1.50 | .60 |
| ☐ 210 Demario Minter RC | 1.25 | .50 |
| ☐ 211 Marques Hagans RC | 1.25 | .50 |
| ☐ 212 Rocky McIntosh RC | 1.50 | .60 |
| ☐ 213 Anthony Mix RC | 1.25 | .50 |
| ☐ 214 Hank Baskett RC | 1.50 | .60 |
| ☐ 215 Jimmy Williams RC | 1.50 | .60 |
| ☐ 216 Andre Hall RC | 1.50 | .60 |
| ☐ 217 Cody Hodges RC | 1.25 | .50 |
| ☐ 218 Greg Lee RC | 1.25 | .50 |
| ☐ 219 Danieal Manning RC | 1.50 | .60 |
| ☐ 220 Jason Hatcher RC | 1.25 | .50 |
| ☐ 221 Ben Obomanu RC | 1.25 | .50 |
| ☐ 222 Dusty Dvoracek RC | 1.50 | .60 |
| ☐ 223 Ingle Martin RC | 1.50 | .60 |
| ☐ 224 Marcus McNeill RC | 1.25 | .50 |
| ☐ 225 DeMeco Ryans RC | 2.00 | .75 |
| ☐ 226 Dwayne Slay RC | 1.25 | .50 |
| ☐ 227 Domenik Hixon RC | 2.00 | .75 |
| ☐ 228 John David Washington RC | 1.25 | .50 |
| ☐ 229 P.J. Daniels RC | 1.25 | .50 |
| ☐ 230 Kelly Jennings RC | 1.50 | .60 |
| ☐ 231 Josh Betts RC | 1.25 | .50 |
| ☐ 232 Marques Colston RC | 4.00 | 1.50 |
| ☐ 233 John McCargo RC | 1.25 | .50 |
| ☐ 234 P.J. Pope RC | 1.50 | .60 |
| ☐ 235 Gabe Watson RC | 1.25 | .50 |
| ☐ 236 Paul Pinegar RC | 1.25 | .50 |
| ☐ 237 Ray Edwards RC | 1.50 | .60 |
| ☐ 238 Elvis Dumervil RC | 1.00 | .40 |
| ☐ 239 Travis Lulay RC | 1.25 | .50 |
| ☐ 240 Alan Zemaitis RC | 1.50 | .60 |
| ☐ 241 Bennie Brazell RC | 1.25 | .50 |
| ☐ 242 Jeff King RC | 1.25 | .50 |
| ☐ 243 Damien Rhodes RC | 1.50 | .60 |
| ☐ 244 Orien Harris RC | 1.25 | .50 |

| | | |
|---|---|---|
| ☐ 245 David Anderson RC | 1.25 | .50 |
| ☐ 246 Roman Harper RC | 1.25 | .50 |
| ☐ 247 Garrett Mills RC | 1.50 | .60 |
| ☐ 248 Anthony Schlegel RC | 1.25 | .50 |
| ☐ 249 David Kirtman RC | 1.25 | .50 |
| ☐ 250 Omar Gaither RC | 1.25 | .50 |
| ☐ 251 Freddie Keiaho RC | 1.25 | .50 |
| ☐ 252 J.J. Outlaw RC | 1.25 | .50 |
| ☐ 253 Willie Reid RC | 1.50 | .60 |
| ☐ 254 Tony Scheffler RC | 1.50 | .60 |
| ☐ 255 Dee Webb RC | 1.25 | .50 |
| ☐ 256 Drew Olson RC | 1.25 | .50 |
| ☐ 257 Tim Day RC | 1.25 | .50 |
| ☐ 258 Martin Nance RC | 1.25 | .50 |
| ☐ 259 Spencer Havner RC | 1.25 | .50 |
| ☐ 260 Ko Simpson RC | 1.25 | .50 |
| ☐ 261 Jesse Mahelona RC | 1.25 | .50 |
| ☐ 262 Owen Daniels RC | 1.50 | .60 |
| ☐ 263 Mike Bell RC | 1.50 | .60 |
| ☐ 264 Anwar Phillips RC | 1.25 | .50 |
| ☐ 265 Erik Meyer RC | 1.25 | .50 |
| ☐ 266 Delanie Walker RC | 1.25 | .50 |
| ☐ 267 Dominique Byrd RC | 1.25 | .50 |
| ☐ 268 Eric Smith RC | 1.25 | .50 |
| ☐ 269 Darrell Hackney RC | 1.25 | .50 |
| ☐ 270 Freddie Roach RC | 1.25 | .50 |
| ☐ 271 James Anderson RC | 1.00 | .40 |
| ☐ 272 Anthony Smith RC | 1.50 | .60 |
| ☐ 273 Quinton Ganther RC | 1.50 | .60 |
| ☐ 274 Nick Mangold RC | 1.25 | .50 |
| ☐ 275 Gerris Wilkinson RC | 1.00 | .40 |

**2007 Bowman**

| | | |
|---|---|---|
| ☐ 1 Matt Leinart | .75 | .30 |
| ☐ 2 Matt Schaub | .60 | .25 |
| ☐ 3 Jason Campbell | .60 | .25 |
| ☐ 4 Steve McNair | .60 | .25 |
| ☐ 5 J.P. Losman | .50 | .20 |
| ☐ 6 Jake Delhomme | .60 | .25 |
| ☐ 7 Rex Grossman | .60 | .25 |
| ☐ 8 Carson Palmer | .75 | .30 |
| ☐ 9 Tony Romo | 1.50 | .60 |
| ☐ 10 Jay Cutler | .75 | .30 |
| ☐ 11 Brett Favre | 1.50 | .60 |
| ☐ 12 Peyton Manning | 1.25 | .50 |
| ☐ 13 Trent Green | .60 | .25 |
| ☐ 14 Tom Brady | 1.50 | .60 |
| ☐ 15 Drew Brees | .75 | .30 |
| ☐ 16 Eli Manning | .75 | .30 |
| ☐ 17 Chad Pennington | .60 | .25 |
| ☐ 18 Donovan McNabb | .75 | .30 |
| ☐ 19 Ben Roethlisberger | 1.00 | .40 |
| ☐ 20 Philip Rivers | .75 | .30 |
| ☐ 21 Alex Smith QB | .75 | .30 |
| ☐ 22 Matt Hasselbeck | .60 | .25 |
| ☐ 23 Marc Bulger | .60 | .25 |
| ☐ 24 Vince Young | .75 | .30 |
| ☐ 25 Edgerrin James | .60 | .25 |
| ☐ 26 Warrick Dunn | .60 | .25 |
| ☐ 27 Jamal Lewis | .60 | .25 |
| ☐ 28 Willis McGahee | .60 | .25 |
| ☐ 29 DeShaun Foster | .60 | .25 |
| ☐ 30 DeAngelo Williams | .75 | .30 |
| ☐ 31 Cedric Benson | .60 | .25 |
| ☐ 32 Thomas Jones | .60 | .25 |
| ☐ 33 Rudi Johnson | .60 | .25 |
| ☐ 34 Julius Jones | .60 | .25 |
| ☐ 35 Dominic Rhodes | .60 | .25 |
| ☐ 36 Joseph Addai | .75 | .30 |
| ☐ 37 Fred Taylor | .60 | .25 |
| ☐ 38 Maurice Jones-Drew | .75 | .30 |

| | | |
|---|---|---|
| ☐ 39 Larry Johnson | .60 | .25 |
| ☐ 40 Ronnie Brown | .60 | .25 |
| ☐ 41 Chester Taylor | .50 | .20 |
| ☐ 42 Laurence Maroney | .75 | .30 |
| ☐ 43 Deuce McAllister | .60 | .25 |
| ☐ 44 Reggie Bush | 1.00 | .40 |
| ☐ 45 Brandon Jacobs | .60 | .25 |
| ☐ 46 Brian Westbrook | .60 | .25 |
| ☐ 47 Willie Parker | .75 | .30 |
| ☐ 48 LaDainian Tomlinson | 1.00 | .40 |
| ☐ 49 Frank Gore | .75 | .30 |
| ☐ 50 Shaun Alexander | .60 | .25 |
| ☐ 51 Steven Jackson | .60 | .25 |
| ☐ 52 Cadillac Williams | .60 | .25 |
| ☐ 53 Clinton Portis | .60 | .25 |
| ☐ 54 Michael Turner | .60 | .25 |
| ☐ 55 Anquan Boldin | .60 | .25 |
| ☐ 56 Larry Fitzgerald | .75 | .30 |
| ☐ 57 Derrick Mason | .60 | .25 |
| ☐ 58 Lee Evans | .60 | .25 |
| ☐ 59 Steve Smith | .60 | .25 |
| ☐ 60 Muhsin Muhammad | .60 | .25 |
| ☐ 61 Chad Johnson | .60 | .25 |
| ☐ 62 T.J. Houshmandzadeh | .60 | .25 |
| ☐ 63 Braylon Edwards | .60 | .25 |
| ☐ 64 Terrell Owens | .75 | .30 |
| ☐ 65 Terry Glenn | .60 | .25 |
| ☐ 66 Javon Walker | .60 | .25 |
| ☐ 67 Mike Furrey | .60 | .25 |
| ☐ 68 Roy Williams WR | .60 | .25 |
| ☐ 69 Donald Driver | .60 | .25 |
| ☐ 70 Greg Jennings | .60 | .25 |
| ☐ 71 Andre Johnson | .60 | .25 |
| ☐ 72 Reggie Wayne | .60 | .25 |
| ☐ 73 Marvin Harrison | .75 | .30 |
| ☐ 74 Matt Jones | .60 | .25 |
| ☐ 75 Chris Chambers | .60 | .25 |
| ☐ 76 Troy Williamson | .50 | .20 |
| ☐ 77 Devery Henderson | .60 | .25 |
| ☐ 78 Joe Horn | .60 | .25 |
| ☐ 79 Marques Colston | .75 | .30 |
| ☐ 80 Plaxico Burress | .60 | .25 |
| ☐ 81 Amani Toomer | .60 | .25 |
| ☐ 82 Jerricho Cotchery | .50 | .20 |
| ☐ 83 Laveranues Coles | .60 | .25 |
| ☐ 84 Randy Moss | .75 | .30 |
| ☐ 85 Donte Stallworth | .60 | .25 |
| ☐ 86 Reggie Brown | .60 | .25 |
| ☐ 87 Hines Ward | .75 | .30 |
| ☐ 88 Santonio Holmes | .60 | .25 |
| ☐ 89 Keenan McCardell | .50 | .20 |
| ☐ 90 Eric Parker | .50 | .20 |
| ☐ 91 Arnaz Battle | .60 | .25 |
| ☐ 92 Antonio Bryant | .60 | .25 |
| ☐ 93 Deion Branch | .60 | .25 |
| ☐ 94 Darrell Jackson | .60 | .25 |
| ☐ 95 Kevin Curtis | .60 | .25 |
| ☐ 96 Torry Holt | .60 | .25 |
| ☐ 97 Isaac Bruce | .60 | .25 |
| ☐ 98 Antwaan Randle El | .50 | .20 |
| ☐ 99 Santana Moss | .60 | .25 |
| ☐ 100 Alge Crumpler | .60 | .25 |
| ☐ 101 Kellen Winslow | .60 | .25 |
| ☐ 102 Tony Gonzalez | .60 | .25 |
| ☐ 103 Jeremy Shockey | .60 | .25 |
| ☐ 104 Antonio Gates | .60 | .25 |
| ☐ 105 Vernon Davis | .60 | .25 |
| ☐ 106 Tarvaris Jackson | .60 | .25 |
| ☐ 107 Travis Henry | .60 | .25 |
| ☐ 108 Drew Bennett | .50 | .20 |
| ☐ 109 Todd Heap | .50 | .20 |
| ☐ 110 Byron Leftwich | .60 | .25 |
| ☐ 111 JaMarcus Russell RC | 4.00 | 1.50 |
| ☐ 112 Brady Quinn RC | 5.00 | 2.00 |
| ☐ 113 Drew Stanton RC | 1.50 | .60 |
| ☐ 114 Troy Smith RC | 2.00 | .75 |
| ☐ 115 Kevin Kolb RC | 2.50 | 1.00 |
| ☐ 116 Trent Edwards RC | 4.00 | 1.50 |
| ☐ 117 John Beck RC | 1.50 | .60 |
| ☐ 118 Jordan Palmer RC | 1.50 | .60 |
| ☐ 119 Chris Leak RC | 1.25 | .50 |
| ☐ 120 Isaiah Stanback RC | 1.50 | .60 |
| ☐ 121 Tyler Palko RC | 1.50 | .60 |
| ☐ 122 Jared Zabransky RC | 1.50 | .60 |

| | | |
|---|---|---|
| 123 Jeff Rowe RC | 1.25 | .50 |
| 124 Zac Taylor RC | 1.50 | .60 |
| 125 Lester Ricard RC | 3.00 | 1.25 |
| 126 Adrian Peterson RC | 15.00 | 6.00 |
| 127 Marshawn Lynch RC | 3.00 | 1.25 |
| 128 Brandon Jackson RC | 1.50 | .60 |
| 129 Michael Bush RC | 1.50 | .60 |
| 130 Kenny Irons RC | 1.50 | .60 |
| 131 Antonio Pittman RC | 1.50 | .60 |
| 132 Tony Hunt RC | 1.50 | .60 |
| 133 Darius Walker RC | 1.50 | .60 |
| 134 Dwayne Wright RC | 1.25 | .50 |
| 135 Lorenzo Booker RC | 1.50 | .60 |
| 136 Kenneth Darby RC | 1.50 | .60 |
| 137 Chris Henry RB RC | 1.50 | .60 |
| 138 Selvin Young RC | 2.50 | 1.00 |
| 139 Brian Leonard RC | 1.50 | .60 |
| 140 Ahmad Bradshaw RC | 2.00 | .75 |
| 141 Gary Russell RC | 1.50 | .60 |
| 142 Kolby Smith RC | 1.50 | .60 |
| 143 Thomas Clayton RC | 1.25 | .50 |
| 144 Garrett Wolfe RC | 1.50 | .60 |
| 145 Calvin Johnson RC | 4.00 | 1.50 |
| 146 Ted Ginn Jr. RC | 2.50 | 1.00 |
| 147 Dwayne Jarrett RC | 1.50 | .60 |
| 148 Dwayne Bowe RC | 3.00 | 1.25 |
| 149 Sidney Rice RC | 1.50 | .60 |
| 150 Robert Meachem RC | 1.50 | .60 |
| 151 Anthony Gonzalez RC | 2.50 | 1.00 |
| 152 Craig Buster Davis RC | 1.25 | .50 |
| 153 Aundrae Allison RC | 1.25 | .50 |
| 154 Chansi Stuckey RC | 1.25 | .50 |
| 155 David Clowney RC | 1.25 | .50 |
| 156 Steve Smith USC RC | 2.00 | .75 |
| 157 Courtney Taylor RC | 1.25 | .50 |
| 158 Paul Williams RC | 1.25 | .50 |
| 159 Johnnie Lee Higgins RC | 1.25 | .50 |
| 160 Rhema McKnight RC | 1.25 | .50 |
| 161 Jason Hill RC | 1.50 | .60 |
| 162 Dallas Baker RC | 1.25 | .50 |
| 163 Greg Olsen RC | 2.00 | .75 |
| 164 Yamon Figurs RC | 1.50 | .60 |
| 165 Scott Chandler RC | 1.25 | .50 |
| 166 Matt Spaeth RC | 1.50 | .60 |
| 167 Ben Patrick RC | 1.25 | .50 |
| 168 Clark Harris RC | 1.25 | .50 |
| 169 Martrez Milner RC | 1.25 | .50 |
| 170 Joe Newton RC | 1.25 | .50 |
| 171 Alan Branch RC | 1.25 | .50 |
| 172 Amobi Okoye RC | 1.50 | .60 |
| 173 DeMarcus Tank Tyler RC | 1.25 | .50 |
| 174 Justin Harrell RC | 1.25 | .50 |
| 175 Brandon Mebane RC | 1.25 | .50 |
| 176 Gaines Adams RC | 1.50 | .60 |
| 177 Jamaal Anderson RC | 1.25 | .50 |
| 178 Adam Carriker RC | 1.25 | .50 |
| 179 Jarvis Moss RC | 1.50 | .60 |
| 180 Charles Johnson RC | 1.00 | .40 |
| 181 Anthony Spencer RC | 1.25 | .50 |
| 182 Quentin Moses RC | 1.25 | .50 |
| 183 LaMarr Woodley RC | 1.50 | .60 |
| 184 Victor Abiamiri RC | 1.50 | .60 |
| 185 Ray McDonald RC | 1.25 | .50 |
| 186 Tim Crowder RC | 1.50 | .60 |
| 187 Patrick Willis RC | 3.00 | 1.25 |
| 188 Brandon Siler RC | 1.25 | .50 |
| 189 David Harris RC | 1.25 | .50 |
| 190 Buster Davis RC | 1.25 | .50 |
| 191 Lawrence Timmons RC | 1.50 | .60 |
| 192 Paul Posluszny RC | 2.00 | .75 |
| 193 Jon Beason RC | 1.50 | .60 |
| 194 Rufus Alexander RC | 1.50 | .60 |
| 195 Earl Everett RC | 1.25 | .50 |
| 196 Stewart Bradley RC | 1.50 | .60 |
| 197 Prescott Burgess RC | 1.25 | .50 |
| 198 Leon Hall RC | 1.50 | .60 |
| 199 Darrelle Revis RC | 1.50 | .60 |
| 200 Aaron Ross RC | 1.50 | .60 |
| 201 Daymeion Hughes RC | 1.25 | .50 |
| 202 Marcus McCauley RC | 1.25 | .50 |
| 203 Chris Houston RC | 1.25 | .50 |
| 204 Tanard Jackson RC | 1.00 | .40 |
| 205 Jonathan Wade RC | 1.25 | .50 |
| 206 Josh Wilson RC | 1.25 | .50 |
| 207 Eric Wright RC | 1.50 | .60 |
| 208 A.J. Davis RC | 1.00 | .40 |
| 209 David Irons RC | 1.00 | .40 |
| 210 LaRon Landry RC | 2.00 | .75 |
| 211 Reggie Nelson RC | 1.25 | .50 |
| 212 Michael Griffin RC | 1.50 | .60 |
| 213 Brandon Meriweather RC | 1.50 | .60 |
| 214 Eric Weddle RC | 1.25 | .50 |
| 215 Aaron Rouse RC | 1.50 | .60 |
| 216 Josh Gattis RC | 1.00 | .40 |
| 217 Joe Thomas RC | 1.50 | .60 |
| 218 Levi Brown RC | 1.25 | .50 |
| 219 Tony Ugoh RC | 1.25 | .50 |
| 220 Ryart Kalil RC | 1.25 | .50 |
| 221 Joe Staley RC | 1.25 | .50 |
| 222 Steve Breaston RC | 1.50 | .60 |
| 223 Jacoby Jones RC | 1.50 | .60 |
| 224 Ryne Robinson RC | 1.25 | .50 |
| 225 Chris Davis RC | 1.25 | .50 |
| 226 Le'Ron McClain RC | 2.50 | 1.00 |
| 227 Joel Filani RC | 1.25 | .50 |
| 228 Gerald Alexander RC | 1.00 | .40 |
| 229 Justise Hairston RC | 1.25 | .50 |
| 230 Nate Ilaoa RC | 1.50 | .60 |
| 231 Brett Ratliff RC | 1.50 | .60 |
| 232 Kyle Steffes RC | 1.00 | .40 |
| 233 Jesse Pellot-Rosa RC | 1.00 | .40 |
| 234 Roy Hall RC | 1.50 | .60 |
| 235 Brannon Condren RC | 1.00 | .40 |
| 236 Clint Session RC | 1.25 | .50 |
| 237 Dan Bazuin RC | 1.25 | .50 |
| 238 Michael Okwo RC | 1.25 | .50 |
| 239 Kevin Payne RC | 1.00 | .40 |
| 240 Legedu Naanee RC | 1.50 | .60 |
| 241 Jarrett Hicks RC | 1.25 | .50 |
| 242 Sonny Shackelford RC | 1.25 | .50 |
| 243 Arron Sears RC | 1.25 | .50 |
| 244 Justin Durant RC | 1.25 | .50 |
| 245 Ikaika Alma-Francis RC | 1.50 | .60 |
| 246 Sabby Piscitelli RC | 1.50 | .60 |
| 247 Quincy Black RC | 1.25 | .50 |
| 248 Jay Alford RC | 2.50 | 1.00 |
| 249 Anthony Waters RC | 1.25 | .50 |
| 250 Laurent Robinson RC | 1.25 | .50 |
| 251 Brian Robison RC | 1.50 | .60 |
| 252 Jay Moore RC | 1.25 | .50 |
| 253 Stephen Nicholas RC | 1.00 | .40 |
| 254 John Bowie RC | 1.00 | .40 |
| 255 Brian Smith RC | 1.00 | .40 |
| 256 Marvin White RC | 1.00 | .40 |
| 257 Fred Bennett RC | 1.25 | .50 |
| 258 Kevin Kolb RC | 2.50 | 1.00 |
| 259 Dante Rosario RC | 1.25 | .50 |
| 260 Brent Celek RC | 1.25 | .50 |
| 261 Orenthal O'Neal RC | 1.25 | .50 |
| 262 Reagan Mauia RC | 1.00 | .40 |
| 263 Deon Anderson RC | 1.25 | .50 |
| 264 Tyler Ecker RC | 1.25 | .50 |
| 265 Michael Allan RC | 1.00 | .40 |
| 266 Jordan Kent RC | 1.25 | .50 |
| 267 John Broussard RC | 1.25 | .50 |
| 268 Chandler Williams RC | 1.25 | .50 |
| 269 Jason Snelling RC | 1.25 | .50 |
| 270 Derek Stanley RC | 1.25 | .50 |
| 271 Zach Miller RC | 1.00 | .40 |
| 272 Ramzee Robinson RC | 1.00 | .40 |
| 273 Michael Johnson RC | 1.25 | .50 |
| 274 Syndric Steptoe RC | 1.25 | .40 |
| 275 Tarell Brown RC | 1.00 | .40 |

## 2008 Bowman

| | | |
|---|---|---|
| 1 Drew Brees | .60 | .25 |
| 2 Tom Brady | 1.00 | .40 |
| 3 Peyton Manning | 1.00 | .40 |
| 4 Carson Palmer | .60 | .25 |
| 5 Ben Roethlisberger | .75 | .30 |
| 6 Eli Manning | .60 | .25 |
| 7 Tony Romo | .60 | .25 |
| 8 Vince Young | .60 | .25 |
| 9 Matt Hasselbeck | .50 | .20 |
| 10 David Garrard | .50 | .20 |
| 11 Jay Cutler | .60 | .25 |
| 12 Derek Anderson | .50 | .20 |
| 13 Philip Rivers | .60 | .25 |

| | | |
|---|---|---|
| 14 Donovan McNabb | .60 | .25 |
| 15 Matt Leinart | .60 | .25 |
| 16 Jason Campbell | .50 | .25 |
| 17 JaMarcus Russell | .50 | .20 |
| 18 Jeff Garcia | .50 | .20 |
| 19 Brodie Croyle | .50 | .20 |
| 20 Marc Bulger | .50 | .20 |
| 21 Trent Edwards | .60 | .25 |
| 22 Kyle Boller | .40 | .15 |
| 23 Tarvaris Jackson | .50 | .20 |
| 24 Matt Schaub | .50 | .20 |
| 25 Aaron Rodgers | .60 | .25 |
| 26 Steven Jackson | .60 | .25 |
| 27 Willie Parker | .50 | .20 |
| 28 Clinton Portis | .50 | .20 |
| 29 Adrian Peterson | 1.25 | .50 |
| 30 LaDainian Tomlinson | .75 | .30 |
| 31 Marion Barber | .60 | .25 |
| 32 Brian Westbrook | .50 | .20 |
| 33 Fred Taylor | .50 | .20 |
| 34 Marshawn Lynch | .60 | .25 |
| 35 Joseph Addai | .50 | .20 |
| 36 Willis McGahee | .50 | .20 |
| 37 Frank Gore | .50 | .20 |
| 38 Julius Jones | .50 | .20 |
| 39 Thomas Jones | .50 | .20 |
| 40 Cedric Benson | .40 | .15 |
| 41 LenDale White | .50 | .20 |
| 42 Ryan Grant | .60 | .25 |
| 43 Laurence Maroney | .50 | .20 |
| 44 Brandon Jacobs | .50 | .20 |
| 45 Jamal Lewis | .50 | .20 |
| 46 Larry Johnson | .50 | .20 |
| 47 Rudi Johnson | .50 | .20 |
| 48 Ahmad Bradshaw | .50 | .20 |
| 49 Justin Fargas | .40 | .15 |
| 50 Reggie Bush | .60 | .25 |
| 51 Maurice Jones-Drew | .50 | .20 |
| 52 Michael Turner | .50 | .20 |
| 53 Ronnie Brown | .50 | .20 |
| 54 DeAngelo Williams | .50 | .20 |
| 55 Edgerrin James | .50 | .20 |
| 56 Chad Johnson | .50 | .20 |
| 57 Reggie Wayne | .50 | .20 |
| 58 Anquan Boldin | .50 | .20 |
| 59 Randy Moss | .60 | .25 |
| 60 Plaxico Burress | .50 | .20 |
| 61 Terrell Owens | .60 | .25 |
| 62 Andre Johnson | .60 | .25 |
| 63 Larry Fitzgerald | .60 | .25 |
| 64 Braylon Edwards | .50 | .25 |
| 65 Steve Smith | .50 | .20 |
| 66 Greg Jennings | .50 | .20 |
| 67 Torry Holt | .50 | .20 |
| 68 T.J. Houshmandzadeh | .50 | .20 |
| 69 Jerricho Cotchery | .40 | .15 |
| 70 Joey Galloway | .50 | .20 |
| 71 Santonio Holmes | .50 | .20 |
| 72 Lee Evans | .50 | .20 |
| 73 Dwayne Bowe | .50 | .20 |
| 74 Laurent Robinson | .40 | .15 |
| 75 Wes Welker | .60 | .25 |
| 76 Roy Williams WR | .50 | .25 |
| 77 Brandon Marshall | .50 | .20 |
| 78 Hines Ward | .60 | .25 |
| 79 Donald Driver | .50 | .20 |
| 80 Calvin Johnson | .60 | .25 |
| 81 Marques Colston | .50 | .20 |

| | | |
|---|---|---|
| ❏ 82 Chris Chambers | .50 | .20 |
| ❏ 83 Amani Toomer | .50 | .20 |
| ❏ 84 Bernard Berrian | .50 | .20 |
| ❏ 85 Sidney Rice | .50 | .20 |
| ❏ 86 Anthony Gonzalez | .50 | .20 |
| ❏ 87 Steve Smith USC | .50 | .20 |
| ❏ 88 Ted Ginn Jr. | .50 | .20 |
| ❏ 89 Isaac Bruce | .50 | .20 |
| ❏ 90 Derrick Mason | .40 | .15 |
| ❏ 91 Roddy White | .50 | .20 |
| ❏ 92 Bobby Engram | .40 | .15 |
| ❏ 93 Reggie Williams | .50 | .20 |
| ❏ 94 Donte Stallworth | .50 | .20 |
| ❏ 95 Santana Moss | .50 | .20 |
| ❏ 96 Laveranues Coles | .50 | .20 |
| ❏ 97 Jerry Porter | .50 | .20 |
| ❏ 98 Shaun McDonald | .40 | .15 |
| ❏ 99 Dallas Clark | .50 | .20 |
| ❏ 100 Tony Gonzalez | .50 | .20 |
| ❏ 101 Kellen Winslow | .50 | .20 |
| ❏ 102 Antonio Gates | .50 | .20 |
| ❏ 103 Jason Witten | .50 | .20 |
| ❏ 104 Chris Cooley | .50 | .20 |
| ❏ 105 Brett Favre | 3.00 | 1.25 |
| ❏ 106 Bob Sanders | .50 | .20 |
| ❏ 107 John Harbaugh CO | .40 | .15 |
| ❏ 108 Jon Kitna | .40 | .15 |
| ❏ 109 Tony Sparano CO | .40 | .15 |
| ❏ 110 Mike Smith CO | .40 | .15 |
| ❏ 111 Ryan Clady RC | 1.50 | .60 |
| ❏ 112 Branden Albert RC | 1.50 | .60 |
| ❏ 113 Gosder Cherilus RC | 1.25 | .50 |
| ❏ 114 Duane Brown RC | 1.25 | .50 |
| ❏ 115 Brandon Flowers RC | 1.50 | .60 |
| ❏ 116 Quentin Groves RC | 1.50 | .60 |
| ❏ 117 Jason Jones RC | 1.50 | .60 |
| ❏ 118 Kendall Langford RC | 1.50 | .60 |
| ❏ 119 Brad Cottam RC | 1.50 | .60 |
| ❏ 120 Antwaun Molden RC | 1.25 | .50 |
| ❏ 121 Bryan Smith RC | 1.25 | .50 |
| ❏ 122 DaJuan Morgan RC | 1.25 | .50 |
| ❏ 123 Craig Stevens RC | 1.25 | .50 |
| ❏ 124 Tom Zbikowski RC | 2.00 | .75 |
| ❏ 125 Andre Fluellen RC | 1.25 | .50 |
| ❏ 126 Cliff Avril RC | 1.25 | .50 |
| ❏ 127 Tyvon Branch RC | 1.25 | .50 |
| ❏ 128 Justin King RC | 1.25 | .50 |
| ❏ 129 Jeremy Thompson RC | 1.00 | .40 |
| ❏ 130 William Hayes RC | 1.00 | .40 |
| ❏ 131 Will Franklin RC | 1.50 | .60 |
| ❏ 132 Marcus Smith RC | 1.25 | .50 |
| ❏ 133 Dwight Lowery RC | 1.00 | .40 |
| ❏ 134 Reggie Corner RC | 1.00 | .40 |
| ❏ 135 Kenny Iwebema RC | 1.00 | .40 |
| ❏ 136 Quintin Demps RC | 1.25 | .50 |
| ❏ 137 Jack Williams RC | 1.00 | .40 |
| ❏ 138 Craig Steltz RC | 1.25 | .50 |
| ❏ 139 Bryan Kehl RC | 1.25 | .50 |
| ❏ 140 Justin Tryon RC | 1.00 | .40 |
| ❏ 141 Arman Shields RC | 1.25 | .50 |
| ❏ 142 Paul Hubbard RC | 1.25 | .50 |
| ❏ 143 Jonathan Wilhite RC | 1.25 | .50 |
| ❏ 144 Thomas DeCoud RC | 1.00 | .40 |
| ❏ 145 Derek Fine RC | 1.25 | .50 |
| ❏ 146 Stanford Keglar RC | 1.00 | .40 |
| ❏ 147 Kenneth Moore RC | 1.25 | .50 |
| ❏ 148 Robert James RC | 1.00 | .40 |
| ❏ 149 Jalen Parmele RC | 1.25 | .50 |
| ❏ 150 Brandon Carr RC | 1.25 | .50 |
| ❏ 151 Gary Barnidge RC | 1.25 | .50 |
| ❏ 152 Zack Bowman RC | 1.25 | .50 |
| ❏ 153 Lex Hilliard RC | 1.00 | .40 |
| ❏ 154 Mario Urrutia RC | 1.25 | .50 |
| ❏ 155 Adrian Arrington RC | 1.25 | .50 |
| ❏ 156 Jerome Felton RC | 1.00 | .40 |
| ❏ 157 Chaz Schilens RC | 1.50 | .60 |
| ❏ 158 Steve Johnson RC | 1.50 | .60 |
| ❏ 159 Tim Hightower RC | 3.00 | 1.25 |
| ❏ 160 Alex Brink RC | 1.25 | .50 |
| ❏ 161 Brett Swain RC | 1.25 | .50 |
| ❏ 162 Matt Slater RC | 1.25 | .50 |
| ❏ 163 Justin Harper RC | 1.25 | .50 |
| ❏ 164 Marcus Monk RC | 1.50 | .60 |
| ❏ 165 Pierre Garcon RC | 1.50 | .50 |
| ❏ 166 Matt Ryan RC | 6.00 | 2.50 |
| ❏ 167 Brian Brohm RC | 2.00 | .75 |
| ❏ 168 Andre Woodson RC | 1.50 | .60 |
| ❏ 169 Chad Henne RC | 2.50 | 1.00 |
| ❏ 170 Joe Flacco RC | 5.00 | 2.00 |
| ❏ 171 John David Booty RC | 2.00 | .75 |
| ❏ 172 Colt Brennan RC | 4.00 | 1.50 |
| ❏ 173 Dennis Dixon RC | 1.50 | .60 |
| ❏ 174 Erik Ainge RC | 1.50 | .60 |
| ❏ 175 Josh Johnson RC | 1.50 | .60 |
| ❏ 176 Kevin O'Connell RC | 2.00 | .75 |
| ❏ 177 Matt Flynn RC | 2.00 | .75 |
| ❏ 178 Jaymar Johnson RC | 1.25 | .50 |
| ❏ 179 Marcus Thomas RC | 1.25 | .50 |
| ❏ 180 Darren McFadden RC | 4.00 | 1.50 |
| ❏ 181 Rashard Mendenhall RC | 3.00 | 1.25 |
| ❏ 182 Jonathan Stewart RC | 4.00 | 1.50 |
| ❏ 183 Felix Jones RC | 4.00 | 1.50 |
| ❏ 184 Jamaal Charles RC | 2.00 | .75 |
| ❏ 185 Chris Johnson RC | 4.00 | 1.50 |
| ❏ 186 Ray Rice RC | 2.00 | .75 |
| ❏ 187 Mike Hart RC | 2.00 | .75 |
| ❏ 188 Kevin Smith RC | 2.50 | 1.00 |
| ❏ 189 Steve Slaton RC | 3.00 | 1.25 |
| ❏ 190 Matt Forte RC | 4.00 | 1.50 |
| ❏ 191 Tashard Choice RC | 1.50 | .60 |
| ❏ 192 Cory Boyd RC | 1.25 | .50 |
| ❏ 193 Allen Patrick RC | 1.25 | .50 |
| ❏ 194 Thomas Brown RC | 1.50 | .60 |
| ❏ 195 Justin Forsett RC | 1.50 | .60 |
| ❏ 196 Harry Douglas RC | 1.50 | .60 |
| ❏ 197 DeSean Jackson RC | 3.00 | 1.25 |
| ❏ 198 Malcolm Kelly RC | 1.50 | .60 |
| ❏ 199 Limas Sweed RC | 2.00 | .75 |
| ❏ 200 Mario Manningham RC | 1.50 | .60 |
| ❏ 201 James Hardy RC | 1.50 | .60 |
| ❏ 202 Early Doucet RC | 1.50 | .60 |
| ❏ 203 Donnie Avery RC | 2.00 | .75 |
| ❏ 204 Dexter Jackson RC | 1.50 | .60 |
| ❏ 205 Devin Thomas RC | 1.50 | .60 |
| ❏ 206 Jordy Nelson RC | 2.00 | .75 |
| ❏ 207 Keenan Burton RC | 1.25 | .50 |
| ❏ 208 Earl Bennett RC | 1.50 | .60 |
| ❏ 209 Jerome Simpson RC | 1.25 | .50 |
| ❏ 210 Andre Caldwell RC | 1.25 | .50 |
| ❏ 211 Josh Morgan RC | 1.50 | .60 |
| ❏ 212 Eddie Royal RC | 3.00 | 1.25 |
| ❏ 213 Fred Davis RC | 1.50 | .60 |
| ❏ 214 John Carlson RC | 1.50 | .60 |
| ❏ 215 Martellus Bennett RC | 1.50 | .60 |
| ❏ 216 Martin Rucker RC | 1.25 | .50 |
| ❏ 217 Jermichael Finley RC | 1.50 | .60 |
| ❏ 218 Dustin Keller RC | 1.50 | .60 |
| ❏ 219 Jacob Tamme RC | 1.50 | .60 |
| ❏ 220 Kellen Davis RC | 1.00 | .40 |
| ❏ 221 Owen Schmitt RC | 1.50 | .60 |
| ❏ 222 Jacob Hester RC | 1.50 | .60 |
| ❏ 223 Chris Williams RC | 1.25 | .50 |
| ❏ 224 Jake Long RC | 2.00 | .75 |
| ❏ 225 Sam Baker RC | 1.00 | .40 |
| ❏ 226 Jeff Otah RC | 1.25 | .50 |
| ❏ 227 Glenn Dorsey RC | 2.00 | .75 |
| ❏ 228 Sedrick Ellis RC | 1.50 | .60 |
| ❏ 229 Kentwan Balmer RC | 1.25 | .50 |
| ❏ 230 Pat Sims RC | 1.25 | .50 |
| ❏ 231 Marcus Harrison RC | 1.50 | .60 |
| ❏ 232 Dre Moore RC | 1.25 | .50 |
| ❏ 233 Paul Smith RC | 1.25 | .50 |
| ❏ 234 Trevor Laws RC | 1.50 | .60 |
| ❏ 235 Chris Long RC | 2.00 | .75 |
| ❏ 236 Vernon Gholston RC | 1.50 | .60 |
| ❏ 237 Derrick Harvey RC | 1.50 | .60 |
| ❏ 238 Calais Campbell RC | 1.25 | .50 |
| ❏ 239 Phillip Merling RC | 1.25 | .50 |
| ❏ 240 Chris Ellis RC | 1.25 | .50 |
| ❏ 241 Lawrence Jackson RC | 1.25 | .50 |
| ❏ 242 Dan Connor RC | 1.50 | .60 |
| ❏ 243 Curtis Lofton RC | 1.50 | .60 |
| ❏ 244 Jerod Mayo RC | 2.50 | 1.00 |
| ❏ 245 Tavares Gooden RC | 1.25 | .50 |
| ❏ 246 Kyle Wright RC | 1.25 | .50 |
| ❏ 247 Philip Wheeler RC | 1.50 | .60 |
| ❏ 248 Marcus Monk RC | 1.50 | .60 |
| ❏ 249 Jonathan Goff RC | 1.25 | .50 |
| ❏ 250 Keith Rivers RC | 1.50 | .60 |
| ❏ 251 Lavelle Hawkins RC | 1.25 | .50 |
| ❏ 252 Xavier Adibi RC | 1.25 | .50 |
| ❏ 253 Chauncey Washington RC | 1.25 | .50 |
| ❏ 254 Bruce Davis RC | 1.25 | .50 |
| ❏ 255 Jordon Dizon RC | 1.50 | .60 |
| ❏ 256 Shawn Crable RC | 1.50 | .60 |
| ❏ 257 Geno Hayes RC | 1.00 | .40 |
| ❏ 258 Dominique Rodgers-Cromartie RC | 1.50 | .60 |
| ❏ 259 Chevis Jackson RC | 1.25 | .50 |
| ❏ 260 Terrence Wheatley RC | 1.25 | .50 |
| ❏ 261 Mike Jenkins RC | 1.50 | .60 |
| ❏ 262 Aqib Talib RC | 1.50 | .60 |
| ❏ 263 Leodis McKelvin RC | 1.50 | .60 |
| ❏ 264 Terrell Thomas RC | 1.25 | .50 |
| ❏ 265 Reggie Smith RC | 1.25 | .50 |
| ❏ 266 Antoine Cason RC | 1.50 | .60 |
| ❏ 267 Patrick Lee RC | 1.25 | .50 |
| ❏ 268 Tracy Porter RC | 1.25 | .50 |
| ❏ 269 Charles Godfrey RC | 1.50 | .60 |
| ❏ 270 Kenny Phillips RC | 1.50 | .60 |
| ❏ 271 Marcus Henry RC | 1.25 | .50 |
| ❏ 272 DJ Hall RC | 1.50 | .60 |
| ❏ 273 Xavier Omon RC | 1.50 | .60 |
| ❏ 274 Tyrell Johnson RC | 1.50 | .60 |
| ❏ 275 Ryan Torain RC | 1.50 | .60 |

### 1998 Bowman Chrome

| | | |
|---|---|---|
| ❏ COMPLETE SET (220) | 100.00 | 50.00 |
| ❏ 1 Peyton Manning RC | 40.00 | 15.00 |
| ❏ 2 Keith Brooking RC | 4.00 | 1.50 |
| ❏ 3 Duane Starks RC | 2.00 | .75 |
| ❏ 4 Takeo Spikes RC | 4.00 | 1.50 |
| ❏ 5 Andre Wadsworth RC | 3.00 | 1.25 |
| ❏ 6 Greg Ellis RC | 2.00 | .75 |
| ❏ 7 Brian Griese RC | 8.00 | 3.00 |
| ❏ 8 Germane Crowell RC | 3.00 | 1.25 |
| ❏ 9 Jerome Pathon RC | 4.00 | 1.50 |
| ❏ 10 Ryan Leaf RC | 4.00 | 1.50 |
| ❏ 11 Fred Taylor RC | 6.00 | 2.50 |
| ❏ 12 Robert Edwards RC | 3.00 | 1.25 |
| ❏ 13 Grant Wistrom RC | 3.00 | 1.25 |
| ❏ 14 Robert Holcombe RC | 3.00 | 1.25 |
| ❏ 15 Tim Dwight RC | 4.00 | 1.50 |
| ❏ 16 Jacquez Green RC | 3.00 | 1.25 |
| ❏ 17 Marcus Nash RC | 2.00 | .75 |
| ❏ 18 Jason Peter RC | 2.00 | .75 |
| ❏ 19 Anthony Simmons RC | 3.00 | 1.25 |
| ❏ 20 Curtis Enis RC | 2.00 | .75 |
| ❏ 21 John Avery RC | 3.00 | 1.25 |
| ❏ 22 Pat Johnson RC | 3.00 | 1.25 |
| ❏ 23 Joe Jurevicius RC | 3.00 | 1.25 |
| ❏ 24 Brian Simmons RC | 3.00 | 1.25 |
| ❏ 25 Kevin Dyson RC | 4.00 | 1.50 |
| ❏ 26 Skip Hicks RC | 3.00 | 1.25 |
| ❏ 27 Hines Ward RC | 15.00 | 7.50 |
| ❏ 28 Tavian Banks RC | 3.00 | 1.25 |
| ❏ 29 Ahman Green RC | 10.00 | 4.00 |
| ❏ 30 Tony Simmons RC | 3.00 | 1.25 |
| ❏ 31 Charles Johnson | .50 | .20 |
| ❏ 32 Freddie Jones | .50 | .20 |
| ❏ 33 Joey Galloway | .75 | .30 |
| ❏ 34 Tony Banks | .75 | .30 |
| ❏ 35 Jake Plummer | 1.25 | .50 |
| ❏ 36 Reidel Anthony | .75 | .30 |
| ❏ 37 Steve McNair | 1.25 | .50 |
| ❏ 38 Michael Westbrook | .75 | .30 |

| | | | |
|---|---|---|---|
| ❏ 39 Chris Sanders | .50 | .20 | |
| ❏ 40 Isaac Bruce | .50 | .20 | |
| ❏ 41 Charlie Garner | .75 | .30 | |
| ❏ 42 Wayne Chrebet | 1.25 | .50 | |
| ❏ 43 Michael Strahan | .75 | .30 | |
| ❏ 44 Brad Johnson | 1.25 | .50 | |
| ❏ 45 Mike Alstott | .50 | .20 | |
| ❏ 46 Tony Gonzalez | 1.25 | .50 | |
| ❏ 47 Johnnie Morton | .75 | .30 | |
| ❏ 48 Darnay Scott | .75 | .30 | |
| ❏ 49 Rae Carruth | .50 | .20 | |
| ❏ 50 Terrell Davis | 1.25 | .50 | |
| ❏ 51 Jermaine Lewis | .75 | .30 | |
| ❏ 52 Frank Sanders | .75 | .30 | |
| ❏ 53 Byron Hanspard | .50 | .20 | |
| ❏ 54 Gus Frerotte | .50 | .20 | |
| ❏ 55 Terry Glenn | 1.25 | .50 | |
| ❏ 56 J.J. Stokes | .75 | .30 | |
| ❏ 57 Will Blackwell | .50 | .20 | |
| ❏ 58 Keyshawn Johnson | 1.25 | .50 | |
| ❏ 59 Tiki Barber | 1.25 | .50 | |
| ❏ 60 Dorsey Levens | 1.25 | .50 | |
| ❏ 61 Zach Thomas | 1.25 | .50 | |
| ❏ 62 Corey Dillon | 1.25 | .50 | |
| ❏ 63 Antowain Smith | 1.25 | .50 | |
| ❏ 64 Michael Sinclair | .50 | .20 | |
| ❏ 65 Rod Smith | .75 | .30 | |
| ❏ 66 Trent Dilfer | 1.25 | .50 | |
| ❏ 67 Warren Sapp | .75 | .30 | |
| ❏ 68 Charles Way | .50 | .20 | |
| ❏ 69 Tamarick Vanover | .50 | .20 | |
| ❏ 70 Drew Bledsoe | 2.00 | .75 | |
| ❏ 71 John Mobley | .50 | .20 | |
| ❏ 72 Kerry Collins | .75 | .30 | |
| ❏ 73 Peter Boulware | .50 | .20 | |
| ❏ 74 Simeon Rice | .75 | .30 | |
| ❏ 75 Eddie George | 1.25 | .50 | |
| ❏ 76 Fred Lane | .50 | .20 | |
| ❏ 77 Jamal Anderson | 1.25 | .50 | |
| ❏ 78 Antonio Freeman | .75 | .30 | |
| ❏ 79 Jason Sehorn | .75 | .30 | |
| ❏ 80 Curtis Martin | 1.25 | .50 | |
| ❏ 81 Bobby Hoying | .75 | .30 | |
| ❏ 82 Garrison Hearst | 1.25 | .50 | |
| ❏ 83 Glenn Foley | .75 | .30 | |
| ❏ 84 Danny Kanell | .75 | .30 | |
| ❏ 85 Kordell Stewart | 1.25 | .50 | |
| ❏ 86 O.J. McDuffie | .75 | .30 | |
| ❏ 87 Marvin Harrison | 1.25 | .50 | |
| ❏ 88 Bobby Engram | .75 | .30 | |
| ❏ 89 Chris Slade | .50 | .20 | |
| ❏ 90 Warrick Dunn | 1.25 | .50 | |
| ❏ 91 Ricky Watters | .75 | .30 | |
| ❏ 92 Rickey Dudley | .50 | .20 | |
| ❏ 93 Terrell Owens | 1.25 | .50 | |
| ❏ 94 Karim Abdul-Jabbar | 1.25 | .50 | |
| ❏ 95 Napoleon Kaufman | 1.25 | .50 | |
| ❏ 96 Darrell Green | .75 | .30 | |
| ❏ 97 Levon Kirkland | .50 | .20 | |
| ❏ 98 Jeff George | .75 | .30 | |
| ❏ 99 Andre Hastings | .50 | .20 | |
| ❏ 100 John Elway | 5.00 | 2.00 | |
| ❏ 101 John Randle | .75 | .30 | |
| ❏ 102 Andre Rison | .75 | .30 | |
| ❏ 103 Keenan McCardell | .75 | .30 | |
| ❏ 104 Marshall Faulk | 1.50 | .60 | |
| ❏ 105 Emmitt Smith | 4.00 | 1.50 | |
| ❏ 106 Robert Brooks | .75 | .30 | |
| ❏ 107 Scott Mitchell | .75 | .30 | |
| ❏ 108 Shannon Sharpe | .75 | .30 | |
| ❏ 109 Deion Sanders | 1.25 | .50 | |
| ❏ 110 Jerry Rice | 2.50 | 1.00 | |
| ❏ 111 Erik Kramer | .50 | .20 | |
| ❏ 112 Michael Jackson | .50 | .20 | |
| ❏ 113 Aeneas Williams | .50 | .20 | |
| ❏ 114 Terry Allen | 1.25 | .50 | |
| ❏ 115 Steve Young | 1.50 | .60 | |
| ❏ 116 Warren Moon | 1.25 | .50 | |
| ❏ 117 Junior Seau | 1.25 | .50 | |
| ❏ 118 Jerome Bettis | 1.25 | .50 | |
| ❏ 119 Irving Fryar | .75 | .30 | |
| ❏ 120 Barry Sanders | 4.00 | 1.50 | |
| ❏ 121 Tim Brown | .50 | .20 | |
| ❏ 122 Chad Brown | .50 | .20 | |

| | | | |
|---|---|---|---|
| ❏ 123 Ben Coates | .75 | .30 | |
| ❏ 124 Robert Smith | 1.25 | .50 | |
| ❏ 125 Brett Favre | 5.00 | 2.00 | |
| ❏ 126 Derrick Thomas | 1.25 | .50 | |
| ❏ 127 Reggie White | 1.25 | .50 | |
| ❏ 128 Troy Aikman | 2.50 | 1.00 | |
| ❏ 129 Jeff Blake | .75 | .30 | |
| ❏ 130 Mark Brunell | 1.25 | .50 | |
| ❏ 131 Curtis Conway | .75 | .30 | |
| ❏ 132 Wesley Walls | .76 | .30 | |
| ❏ 133 Thurman Thomas | 1.25 | .50 | |
| ❏ 134 Chris Chandler | .75 | .30 | |
| ❏ 135 Dan Marino | 5.00 | 2.00 | |
| ❏ 136 Larry Centers | .50 | .20 | |
| ❏ 137 Shawn Jefferson | .50 | .20 | |
| ❏ 138 Andre Reed | .75 | .30 | |
| ❏ 139 Jake Reed | .75 | .30 | |
| ❏ 140 Cris Carter | 1.25 | .50 | |
| ❏ 141 Elvis Grbac | .75 | .30 | |
| ❏ 142 Mark Chmura | .75 | .30 | |
| ❏ 143 Michael Irvin | 1.25 | .50 | |
| ❏ 144 Carl Pickens | .75 | .30 | |
| ❏ 145 Herman Moore | .75 | .30 | |
| ❏ 146 Marvin Jones | .50 | .20 | |
| ❏ 147 Terance Mathis | .75 | .30 | |
| ❏ 148 Rob Moore | .75 | .30 | |
| ❏ 149 Bruce Smith | .75 | .30 | |
| ❏ 150 Rob Johnson CL | .50 | .20 | |
| ❏ 151 Leslie Shepherd | .50 | .20 | |
| ❏ 152 Chris Spielman | .50 | .20 | |
| ❏ 153 Tony McGee | .50 | .20 | |
| ❏ 154 Kevin Smith | .50 | .20 | |
| ❏ 155 Bill Romanowski | .50 | .20 | |
| ❏ 156 Stephen Boyd | .50 | .20 | |
| ❏ 157 James Stewart | .75 | .30 | |
| ❏ 158 Jason Taylor | .75 | .30 | |
| ❏ 159 Troy Drayton | .50 | .20 | |
| ❏ 160 Mark Fields | .50 | .20 | |
| ❏ 161 Jessie Armstead | .50 | .20 | |
| ❏ 162 James Jett | .75 | .30 | |
| ❏ 163 Bobby Taylor | .50 | .20 | |
| ❏ 164 Kimble Anders | .75 | .30 | |
| ❏ 165 Jimmy Smith | .75 | .30 | |
| ❏ 166 Quentin Coryatt | .50 | .20 | |
| ❏ 167 Bryant Westbrook | .50 | .20 | |
| ❏ 168 Neil Smith | .75 | .30 | |
| ❏ 169 Darren Woodson | .50 | .20 | |
| ❏ 170 Ray Buchanan | .50 | .20 | |
| ❏ 171 Earl Holmes | .50 | .20 | |
| ❏ 172 Ray Lewis | 1.25 | .50 | |
| ❏ 173 Steve Broussard | .50 | .20 | |
| ❏ 174 Derrick Brooks | 1.25 | .50 | |
| ❏ 175 Ken Harvey | .50 | .20 | |
| ❏ 176 Darryll Lewis | .50 | .20 | |
| ❏ 177 Derrick Rodgers | .50 | .20 | |
| ❏ 178 James McKnight | 1.25 | .50 | |
| ❏ 179 Cris Dishman | .50 | .20 | |
| ❏ 180 Hardy Nickerson | .50 | .20 | |
| ❏ 181 Charles Woodson RC | 5.00 | 2.00 | |
| ❏ 182 Randy Moss RC | 25.00 | 10.00 | |
| ❏ 183 Stephen Alexander RC | 3.00 | 1.25 | |
| ❏ 184 Samari Rolle RC | 2.00 | .75 | |
| ❏ 185 Jamie Duncan RC | 2.00 | .75 | |
| ❏ 186 Lance Schulters RC | 2.00 | .75 | |
| ❏ 187 Tony Parrish RC | 4.00 | 1.50 | |
| ❏ 188 Corey Chavous RC | 4.00 | 1.50 | |
| ❏ 189 Jammi German RC | 2.00 | .75 | |
| ❏ 190 Sam Cowart RC | 3.00 | 1.25 | |
| ❏ 191 Donald Hayes RC | 3.00 | 1.25 | |
| ❏ 192 R.W. McQuarters RC | 3.00 | 1.25 | |
| ❏ 193 Az-Zahir Hakim RC | 4.00 | 1.50 | |
| ❏ 194 Chris Fuamatu-Ma'afala RC | 3.00 | 1.25 | |
| ❏ 195 Allen Rossum RC | 2.00 | .75 | |
| ❏ 196 Jon Ritchie RC | 3.00 | 1.25 | |
| ❏ 197 Blake Spence RC | 2.00 | .75 | |
| ❏ 198 Brian Alford RC | 2.00 | .75 | |
| ❏ 199 Fred Weary RC | 2.00 | .75 | |
| ❏ 200 Rod Rutledge RC | 2.00 | .75 | |
| ❏ 201 Michael Myers RC | 2.00 | .75 | |
| ❏ 202 Rashaan Shehee RC | 3.00 | 1.25 | |
| ❏ 203 Donovin Darius RC | 3.00 | 1.25 | |
| ❏ 204 E.G. Green RC | 3.00 | 1.25 | |
| ❏ 205 Vonnie Holliday RC | 3.00 | 1.25 | |
| ❏ 206 Charlie Batch RC | 4.00 | 1.50 | |

| | | | |
|---|---|---|---|
| ❏ 207 Michael Pittman RC | 4.00 | 1.50 | |
| ❏ 208 Artrell Hawkins RC | 2.00 | .75 | |
| ❏ 209 Jonathan Quinn RC | 4.00 | 1.50 | |
| ❏ 210 Kailee Wong RC | 2.00 | .75 | |
| ❏ 211 Deshea Townsend RC | 2.00 | .75 | |
| ❏ 212 Patrick Surtain RC | 4.00 | 1.50 | |
| ❏ 213 Brian Kelly RC | 3.00 | 1.25 | |
| ❏ 214 Tebucky Jones RC | 2.00 | .75 | |
| ❏ 215 Pete Gonzalez RC | 2.00 | .75 | |
| ❏ 216 Shaun Williams RC | 3.00 | 1.25 | |
| ❏ 217 Scott Frost RC | 2.00 | .75 | |
| ❏ 218 Leonard Little RC | 4.00 | 1.50 | |
| ❏ 219 Alonzo Mayes RC | 2.00 | .75 | |
| ❏ 220 Cordell Taylor RC | 2.00 | .75 | |

## 1999 Bowman Chrome

RICKY WILLIAMS

| | | | |
|---|---|---|---|
| ❏ COMPLETE SET (220) | 80.00 | 40.00 | |
| ❏ 1 Dan Marino | 4.00 | 1.50 | |
| ❏ 2 Michael Westbrook | .75 | .30 | |
| ❏ 3 Yancey Thigpen | .50 | .20 | |
| ❏ 4 Tony Martin | .75 | .30 | |
| ❏ 5 Michael Strahan | .75 | .30 | |
| ❏ 6 Dedric Ward | .50 | .20 | |
| ❏ 7 Joey Galloway | .75 | .30 | |
| ❏ 8 Bobby Engram | .75 | .30 | |
| ❏ 9 Frank Sanders | .75 | .30 | |
| ❏ 10 Jake Plummer | .75 | .30 | |
| ❏ 11 Eddie Kennison | .75 | .30 | |
| ❏ 12 Curtis Martin | 1.25 | .50 | |
| ❏ 13 Chris Spielman | .50 | .20 | |
| ❏ 14 Trent Dilfer | .75 | .30 | |
| ❏ 15 Tim Biakabutuka | .75 | .30 | |
| ❏ 16 Elvis Grbac | .50 | .20 | |
| ❏ 17 Charlie Batch | 1.25 | .50 | |
| ❏ 18 Takeo Spikes | .50 | .20 | |
| ❏ 19 Tony Banks | .75 | .30 | |
| ❏ 20 Doug Flutie | 1.25 | .50 | |
| ❏ 21 Ty Law | .75 | .30 | |
| ❏ 22 Isaac Bruce | 1.25 | .50 | |
| ❏ 23 James Jett | .75 | .30 | |
| ❏ 24 Kent Graham | .50 | .20 | |
| ❏ 25 Derrick Mayes | .50 | .20 | |
| ❏ 26 Amani Toomer | .50 | .20 | |
| ❏ 27 Ray Lewis | 1.25 | .50 | |
| ❏ 28 Shawn Springs | .50 | .20 | |
| ❏ 29 Warren Sapp | .50 | .20 | |
| ❏ 30 Jamal Anderson | 1.25 | .50 | |
| ❏ 31 Byron Bam Morris | .50 | .20 | |
| ❏ 32 Johnnie Morton | .50 | .20 | |
| ❏ 33 Terance Mathis | .50 | .20 | |
| ❏ 34 Terrell Davis | 1.25 | .50 | |
| ❏ 35 John Randle | .75 | .30 | |
| ❏ 36 Vinny Testaverde | .75 | .30 | |
| ❏ 37 Junior Seau | 1.25 | .50 | |
| ❏ 38 Reidel Anthony | .50 | .20 | |
| ❏ 39 Brad Johnson | .50 | .20 | |
| ❏ 40 Emmitt Smith | 2.50 | 1.00 | |
| ❏ 41 Mo Lewis | .50 | .20 | |
| ❏ 42 Terry Glenn | 1.25 | .50 | |
| ❏ 43 Dorsey Levens | 1.25 | .50 | |
| ❏ 44 Thurman Thomas | .75 | .30 | |
| ❏ 45 Rob Moore | .75 | .30 | |
| ❏ 46 Corey Dillon | .75 | .30 | |
| ❏ 47 Jessie Armstead | .50 | .20 | |
| ❏ 48 Marshall Faulk | 1.25 | .60 | |
| ❏ 49 Charles Woodson | .50 | .20 | |
| ❏ 50 John Elway | 4.00 | 1.50 | |
| ❏ 51 Kevin Dyson | .75 | .30 | |

|  |  | | |
|---|--------|------|------|
| 52 | Tony Simmons | .50 | .20 |
| 53 | Keenan McCardell | .75 | .30 |
| 54 | O.J. Santiago | .50 | .20 |
| 55 | Jermaine Lewis | .75 | .30 |
| 56 | Herman Moore | .75 | .30 |
| 57 | Gary Brown | .50 | .20 |
| 58 | Jim Harbaugh | .75 | .30 |
| 59 | Mike Alstott | 1.25 | .50 |
| 60 | Brett Favre | 4.00 | 1.50 |
| 61 | Tim Brown | 1.25 | .50 |
| 62 | Steve McNair | .50 | .20 |
| 63 | Ben Coates | .50 | .20 |
| 64 | Jerome Pathon | .50 | .20 |
| 65 | Ray Buchanan | .50 | .20 |
| 66 | Troy Aikman | 2.50 | 1.00 |
| 67 | Andre Reed | .75 | .30 |
| 68 | Bubby Brister | .50 | .20 |
| 69 | Karim Abdul-Jabbar | .75 | .30 |
| 70 | Peyton Manning | 4.00 | 1.50 |
| 71 | Charles Johnson | .50 | .20 |
| 72 | Natrone Means | .75 | .30 |
| 73 | Michael Sinclair | .50 | .20 |
| 74 | Skip Hicks | .50 | .20 |
| 75 | Derrick Alexander | .50 | .20 |
| 76 | Wayne Chrebet | .75 | .30 |
| 77 | Rod Smith | .75 | .30 |
| 78 | Carl Pickens | .75 | .30 |
| 79 | Adrian Murrell | .50 | .20 |
| 80 | Fred Taylor | 1.25 | .50 |
| 81 | Eric Moulds | 1.25 | .50 |
| 82 | Lawrence Phillips | .75 | .30 |
| 83 | Marvin Harrison | 1.25 | .50 |
| 84 | Cris Carter | 1.25 | .50 |
| 85 | Ike Hilliard | .50 | .20 |
| 86 | Hines Ward | .75 | .30 |
| 87 | Terrell Owens | 1.25 | .50 |
| 88 | Ricky Proehl | .50 | .20 |
| 89 | Bert Emanuel | .75 | .30 |
| 90 | Randy Moss | 3.00 | 1.25 |
| 91 | Aaron Glenn | .50 | .20 |
| 92 | Robert Smith | 1.25 | .50 |
| 93 | Andre Hastings | .50 | .20 |
| 94 | Jake Reed | .75 | .30 |
| 95 | Curtis Enis | .75 | .30 |
| 96 | Andre Wadsworth | .50 | .20 |
| 97 | Ed McCaffrey | .75 | .30 |
| 98 | Zach Thomas | 1.25 | .50 |
| 99 | Kerry Collins | .75 | .30 |
| 100 | Drew Bledsoe | 1.50 | .60 |
| 101 | Germane Crowell | .50 | .20 |
| 102 | Bryan Still | .50 | .20 |
| 103 | Chad Brown | .50 | .20 |
| 104 | Jacquez Green | .50 | .20 |
| 105 | Garrison Hearst | .75 | .30 |
| 106 | Napoleon Kaufman | 1.25 | .50 |
| 107 | Ricky Watters | .75 | .30 |
| 108 | O.J. McDuffie | .75 | .30 |
| 109 | Keyshawn Johnson | 1.25 | .50 |
| 110 | Jerome Bettis | 1.25 | .50 |
| 111 | Duce Staley | .75 | .30 |
| 112 | Curtis Conway | .75 | .30 |
| 113 | Chris Chandler | .50 | .20 |
| 114 | Marcus Nash | .50 | .20 |
| 115 | Stephen Alexander | .50 | .20 |
| 116 | Darnay Scott | .75 | .30 |
| 117 | Bruce Smith | .75 | .30 |
| 118 | Priest Holmes | 2.00 | .75 |
| 119 | Mark Brunell | 1.25 | .50 |
| 120 | Jerry Rice | 2.50 | 1.00 |
| 121 | Randall Cunningham | 1.25 | .50 |
| 122 | Scott Mitchell | .50 | .20 |
| 123 | Antonio Freeman | 1.25 | .50 |
| 124 | Kordell Stewart | .75 | .30 |
| 125 | Jon Kitna | 1.25 | .50 |
| 126 | Ahman Green | 1.25 | .50 |
| 127 | Warrick Dunn | 1.25 | .50 |
| 128 | Robert Brooks | .75 | .30 |
| 129 | Derrick Thomas | 1.25 | .50 |
| 130 | Steve Young | 1.50 | .60 |
| 131 | Peter Boulware | .50 | .20 |
| 132 | Michael Irvin | .75 | .30 |
| 133 | Shannon Sharpe | .75 | .30 |
| 134 | Jimmy Smith | .75 | .30 |
| 135 | John Avery | .50 | .20 |
| 136 | Fred Lane | .50 | .20 |
| 137 | Trent Green | 1.25 | .50 |
| 138 | Andre Rison | .75 | .30 |
| 139 | Antowain Smith | 1.25 | .50 |
| 140 | Eddie George | 1.25 | .50 |
| 141 | Jeff Blake | .75 | .30 |
| 142 | Rocket Ismail | .75 | .30 |
| 143 | Rickey Dudley | .50 | .20 |
| 144 | Courtney Hawkins | .50 | .20 |
| 145 | Mikhael Ricks | .50 | .20 |
| 146 | J.J. Stokes | .75 | .30 |
| 147 | Levon Kirkland | .50 | .20 |
| 148 | Deion Sanders | 1.25 | .50 |
| 149 | Barry Sanders | 4.00 | 1.50 |
| 150 | Tiki Barber | 1.25 | .50 |
| 151 | David Boston RC | 2.00 | .75 |
| 152 | Chris McAlister RC | 1.25 | .50 |
| 153 | Peerless Price RC | 2.00 | .75 |
| 154 | D'Wayne Bates RC | 1.25 | .50 |
| 155 | Cade McNown RC | 1.25 | .50 |
| 156 | Akili Smith RC | 1.25 | .50 |
| 157 | Kevin Johnson RC | 2.00 | .75 |
| 158 | Tim Couch RC | 2.00 | .75 |
| 159 | Sedrick Irvin RC | 1.00 | .40 |
| 160 | Chris Claiborne RC | 1.00 | .40 |
| 161 | Edgerrin James RC | 10.00 | 4.00 |
| 162 | Mike Cloud RC | 1.25 | .50 |
| 163 | Cecil Collins RC | 1.00 | .40 |
| 164 | James Johnson RC | 1.25 | .50 |
| 165 | Rob Konrad RC | 2.00 | .75 |
| 166 | Daunte Culpepper RC | 10.00 | 4.00 |
| 167 | Kevin Faulk RC | 2.00 | .75 |
| 168 | Donovan McNabb RC | 12.00 | 5.00 |
| 169 | Troy Edwards RC | 1.25 | .50 |
| 170 | Amos Zereoue RC | 2.00 | .75 |
| 171 | Karsten Bailey RC | 1.25 | .50 |
| 172 | Brock Huard RC | 2.00 | .75 |
| 173 | Joe Germaine RC | 1.25 | .50 |
| 174 | Torry Holt RC | 6.00 | 2.50 |
| 175 | Shaun King RC | 1.25 | .50 |
| 176 | Jevon Kearse RC | 4.00 | 1.50 |
| 177 | Champ Bailey RC | 3.00 | 1.25 |
| 178 | Ebenezer Ekuban RC | 1.25 | .50 |
| 179 | Andy Katzenmoyer RC | 1.25 | .50 |
| 180 | Antoine Winfield RC | 1.25 | .50 |
| 181 | Jermaine Fazande RC | 1.25 | .50 |
| 182 | Ricky Williams RC | 5.00 | 2.00 |
| 183 | Joel Makovicka RC | 2.00 | .75 |
| 184 | Reginald Kelly RC | 1.25 | .50 |
| 185 | Brandon Stokley RC | 2.50 | 1.00 |
| 186 | L.C. Stevens RC | 1.00 | .40 |
| 187 | Marty Booker RC | 2.00 | .75 |
| 188 | Jerry Azumah RC | 1.25 | .50 |
| 189 | Ted White RC | 1.00 | .40 |
| 190 | Scott Covington RC | 2.00 | .75 |
| 191 | Tim Alexander RC | 1.00 | .40 |
| 192 | Darrin Chiaverini RC | 1.25 | .50 |
| 193 | Dat Nguyen RC | 2.00 | .75 |
| 194 | Wane McGarity RC | 1.00 | .40 |
| 195 | Al Wilson RC | 2.00 | .75 |
| 196 | Travis McGriff RC | 1.00 | .40 |
| 197 | Stacey Mack RC | 2.00 | .75 |
| 198 | Antuan Edwards RC | 1.00 | .40 |
| 199 | Aaron Brooks RC | 5.00 | 2.00 |
| 200 | De'Mond Parker RC | 1.00 | .40 |
| 201 | Jed Weaver RC | 1.00 | .40 |
| 202 | Madre Hill RC | 1.00 | .40 |
| 203 | Jim Kleinsasser RC | 2.00 | .75 |
| 204 | Michael Bishop RC | 2.00 | .75 |
| 205 | Michael Basnight RC | 1.00 | .40 |
| 206 | Sean Bennett RC | 1.25 | .50 |
| 207 | Dameane Douglas RC | 1.25 | .50 |
| 208 | Na Brown RC | 1.25 | .50 |
| 209 | Patrick Kerney RC | 2.00 | .75 |
| 210 | Malcolm Johnson RC | 1.00 | .40 |
| 211 | Dre Bly RC | 2.00 | .75 |
| 212 | Terry Jackson RC | 1.25 | .50 |
| 213 | Eugene Baker RC | 1.00 | .40 |
| 214 | Autry Denson RC | 1.25 | .50 |
| 215 | Damell McDonald RC | 1.25 | .50 |
| 216 | Charlie Rogers RC | 1.25 | .50 |
| 217 | Joe Montgomery RC | 1.25 | .50 |
| 218 | Cecil Martin RC | 1.25 | .50 |
| 219 | Larry Parker RC | 2.00 | .75 |
| 220 | Mike Peterson RC | 1.25 | .50 |

## 2000 Bowman Chrome

|  |  | | |
|---|--------|------|------|
| 1 | Eddie George | 1.00 | .40 |
| 2 | Ike Hilliard | .60 | .25 |
| 3 | Terrell Owens | 1.00 | .40 |
| 4 | James Stewart | .60 | .25 |
| 5 | Joey Galloway | .60 | .25 |
| 6 | Jake Reed | .40 | .15 |
| 7 | Derrick Alexander | .60 | .25 |
| 8 | Jeff George | .60 | .25 |
| 9 | Kerry Collins | .60 | .25 |
| 10 | Tony Gonzalez | .60 | .25 |
| 11 | Marcus Robinson | 1.00 | .40 |
| 12 | Charles Woodson | .60 | .25 |
| 13 | Germane Crowell | .40 | .15 |
| 14 | Yancey Thigpen | .40 | .15 |
| 15 | Tony Martin | .40 | .15 |
| 16 | Frank Sanders | .60 | .25 |
| 17 | Napoleon Kaufman | .60 | .25 |
| 18 | Jay Fiedler | 1.00 | .40 |
| 19 | Patrick Jeffers | 1.00 | .40 |
| 20 | Steve McNair | 1.00 | .40 |
| 21 | Herman Moore | .60 | .25 |
| 22 | Tim Brown | 1.00 | .40 |
| 23 | Olandis Gary | 1.00 | .40 |
| 24 | Corey Dillon | 1.00 | .40 |
| 25 | Warren Sapp | .60 | .25 |
| 26 | Curtis Enis | .40 | .15 |
| 27 | Vinny Testaverde | .60 | .25 |
| 28 | Tim Biakabutaka | .60 | .25 |
| 29 | Kevin Johnson | 1.00 | .40 |
| 30 | Charlie Batch | 1.00 | .40 |
| 31 | Jermaine Fazande | .60 | .25 |
| 32 | Shaun King | .40 | .15 |
| 33 | Errict Rhett | .60 | .25 |
| 34 | O.J. McDuffie | .60 | .25 |
| 35 | Bruce Smith | .60 | .25 |
| 36 | Antonio Freeman | 1.00 | .40 |
| 37 | Tim Couch | 3.00 | 1.25 |
| 38 | Duce Staley | 1.00 | .40 |
| 39 | Jeff Blake | .60 | .25 |
| 40 | Jim Harbaugh | .60 | .25 |
| 41 | Jeff Graham | .40 | .15 |
| 42 | Drew Bledsoe | 1.25 | .50 |
| 43 | Mike Alstott | 1.00 | .40 |
| 44 | Terance Mathis | .60 | .25 |
| 45 | Antowain Smith | .60 | .25 |
| 46 | Johnnie Morton | .60 | .25 |
| 47 | Chris Chandler | .60 | .25 |
| 48 | Keith Poole | .40 | .15 |
| 49 | Ricky Watters | .60 | .25 |
| 50 | Dorsey Levens | .40 | .15 |
| 51 | Damon Huard | 1.00 | .40 |
| 52 | Peerless Price | .60 | .25 |
| 53 | Brian Griese | 1.00 | .40 |
| 54 | Frank Wycheck | .60 | .25 |
| 55 | Kevin Dyson | .60 | .25 |
| 56 | Junior Seau | 1.00 | .40 |
| 57 | Curtis Conway | 1.00 | .40 |
| 58 | Jamal Anderson | 1.00 | .40 |
| 59 | Jim Miller | .40 | .15 |
| 60 | Rob Johnson | .60 | .25 |
| 61 | Mark Brunell | 1.00 | .40 |
| 62 | Wayne Chrebet | .60 | .25 |
| 63 | James Johnson | .40 | .15 |
| 64 | Sean Dawkins | .40 | .15 |
| 65 | Stephen Davis | 1.00 | .40 |
| 66 | Daunte Culpepper | 1.25 | .50 |

| □ | | | |
|---|---|---|---|
| 67 | Doug Flutie | 1.00 | .40 |
| 68 | Pete Mitchell | .40 | .15 |
| 69 | Bill Schroeder | .40 | .15 |
| 70 | Terrence Wilkins | .40 | .15 |
| 71 | Cade McNown | .40 | .15 |
| 72 | Muhsin Muhammad | .60 | .25 |
| 73 | E.G. Green | .40 | .15 |
| 74 | Edgerrin James | 1.50 | .60 |
| 75 | Troy Edwards | .40 | .15 |
| 76 | Terry Glenn | .60 | .25 |
| 77 | Tony Banks | .60 | .25 |
| 78 | Derrick Mayes | .60 | .25 |
| 79 | Curtis Martin | 1.00 | .40 |
| 80 | Kordell Stewart | .60 | .25 |
| 81 | Amani Toomer | .60 | .25 |
| 82 | Dorsey Levens | .60 | .25 |
| 83 | Brad Johnson | 1.00 | .40 |
| 84 | Ed McCaffrey | 1.00 | .40 |
| 85 | Charlie Garner | .60 | .25 |
| 86 | Brett Favre | 3.00 | 1.25 |
| 87 | J.J. Stokes | .60 | .25 |
| 88 | Steve Young | 1.25 | .50 |
| 89 | Jonathan Linton | .40 | .15 |
| 90 | Isaac Bruce | 1.00 | .40 |
| 91 | Shawn Jefferson | .40 | .15 |
| 92 | Rod Smith | .60 | .25 |
| 93 | Champ Bailey | .60 | .25 |
| 94 | Ricky Williams | 1.00 | .40 |
| 95 | Priest Holmes | 1.25 | .50 |
| 96 | Corey Bradford | .60 | .25 |
| 97 | Eric Moulds | 1.00 | .40 |
| 98 | Warrick Dunn | 1.00 | .40 |
| 99 | Jevon Kearse | 1.00 | .40 |
| 100 | Albert Connell | .40 | .15 |
| 101 | Az-Zahir Hakim | .40 | .15 |
| 102 | Marvin Harrison | 1.00 | .40 |
| 103 | Qadry Ismail | .60 | .25 |
| 104 | Oronde Gadsden | .60 | .25 |
| 105 | Rob Moore | .60 | .25 |
| 106 | Marshall Faulk | 1.50 | .60 |
| 107 | Steve Beuerlein | .60 | .25 |
| 108 | Torry Holt | 1.00 | .40 |
| 109 | Donovan McNabb | 1.50 | .60 |
| 110 | Rich Gannon | 1.00 | .40 |
| 111 | Jerome Bettis | 1.00 | .40 |
| 112 | Peyton Manning | 2.50 | 1.00 |
| 113 | Cris Carter | 1.00 | .40 |
| 114 | Jake Plummer | .60 | .25 |
| 115 | Kent Graham | .40 | .15 |
| 116 | Keenan McCardell | .60 | .25 |
| 117 | Tim Dwight | 1.00 | .40 |
| 118 | Fred Taylor | 1.00 | .40 |
| 119 | Jerry Rice | 2.00 | .75 |
| 120 | Michael Westbrook | .60 | .25 |
| 121 | Kurt Warner | 2.00 | .75 |
| 122 | Jimmy Smith | .60 | .25 |
| 123 | Emmitt Smith | 2.00 | .75 |
| 124 | Terrell Davis | 1.00 | .40 |
| 125 | Randy Moss | 2.00 | .75 |
| 126 | Akili Smith | .40 | .15 |
| 127 | Rocket Ismail | .60 | .25 |
| 128 | Jon Kitna | 1.00 | .40 |
| 129 | Elvis Grbac | .60 | .25 |
| 130 | Wesley Walls | .40 | .15 |
| 131 | Torrance Small | .40 | .15 |
| 132 | Tyrone Wheatley | .60 | .25 |
| 133 | Carl Pickens | .40 | .15 |
| 134 | Zach Thomas | 1.00 | .40 |
| 135 | Jacquez Green | .40 | .15 |
| 136 | Robert Smith | 1.00 | .40 |
| 137 | Keyshawn Johnson | 1.00 | .40 |
| 138 | Matthew Hatchette | .40 | .15 |
| 139 | Troy Aikman | 2.00 | .75 |
| 140 | Charles Johnson | .60 | .25 |
| 141 | Terry Battle EP | 1.00 | .40 |
| 142 | Pepe Pearson EP | 2.00 | .75 |
| 143 | Cory Sauter EP | 1.00 | .40 |
| 144 | Brian Shay EP | 1.00 | .40 |
| 145 | Marcus Crandell EP RC | 1.50 | .60 |
| 146 | Danny Wuerffel EP | 1.50 | .60 |
| 147 | L.C. Stevens EP | 1.00 | .40 |
| 148 | Ted White EP | 1.00 | .40 |
| 149 | Matt Lytle EP RC | 1.50 | .60 |
| 150 | Vershan Jackson EP RC | 1.00 | .40 |
| 151 | Mario Bailey EP | 1.00 | .40 |
| 152 | Darryl Daniel EP RC | 1.50 | .60 |
| 153 | Sean Morey EP RC | 1.50 | .60 |
| 154 | Jim Kubiak EP RC | 1.50 | .60 |
| 155 | Aaron Stecker EP RC | 2.00 | .75 |
| 156 | Damon Dunn EP RC | 1.50 | .60 |
| 157 | Kevin Daft EP | 1.00 | .40 |
| 158 | Corey Thomas EP | 1.00 | .40 |
| 159 | Deon Mitchell EP RC | 1.50 | .60 |
| 160 | Todd Floyd EP | 1.00 | .40 |
| 161 | Norman Miller EP RC | 1.00 | .40 |
| 162 | Jeremaine Copeland EP | 1.00 | .40 |
| 163 | Michael Blair EP | 1.00 | .40 |
| 164 | Ron Powlus EP RC | 2.00 | .75 |
| 165 | Pat Barnes EP | 1.50 | .60 |
| 166 | Dez White RC | 4.00 | 1.50 |
| 167 | Trung Canidate SP RC | 25.00 | 10.00 |
| 168 | Thomas Jones SP RC | 40.00 | 20.00 |
| 169 | Courtney Brown SP RC | 30.00 | 12.50 |
| 170 | Jamal Lewis SP RC | 50.00 | 20.00 |
| 171 | Chris Redman SP RC | 25.00 | 10.00 |
| 172 | Ron Dayne SP RC | 30.00 | 12.50 |
| 173 | Chad Pennington SP RC | 50.00 | 20.00 |
| 174 | Plaxico Burress SP RC | 50.00 | 20.00 |
| 175 | R.Jay Soward SP RC | 25.00 | 10.00 |
| 176 | Travis Taylor SP RC | 30.00 | 12.50 |
| 177 | Shaun Alexander SP RC | 40.00 | 15.00 |
| 178 | Brian Urlacher SP RC | 20.00 | 10.00 |
| 179 | Danny Farmer RC | 3.00 | 1.25 |
| 180 | Tee Martin SP RC | 30.00 | 12.50 |
| 181 | Sylvester Morris SP RC | 25.00 | 10.00 |
| 182 | Curtis Keaton RC | 3.00 | 1.25 |
| 183 | Peter Warrick SP RC | 30.00 | 12.50 |
| 184 | Anthony Becht RC | 4.00 | 1.50 |
| 185 | Travis Prentice SP RC | 25.00 | 10.00 |
| 186 | J.R. Redmond SP RC | 25.00 | 10.00 |
| 187 | Bubba Franks SP RC | 30.00 | 12.50 |
| 188 | Ron Dugans SP RC | 20.00 | 7.50 |
| 189 | Reuben Droughns RC | 5.00 | 2.00 |
| 190 | Corey Simon RC | 2.00 | .75 |
| 191 | Joe Hamilton RC | 3.00 | 1.25 |
| 192 | Laveranues Coles RC | 5.00 | 2.00 |
| 193 | Todd Pinkston SP RC | 30.00 | 12.50 |
| 194 | Jerry Porter SP RC | 50.00 | 20.00 |
| 195 | Dennis Northcutt RC | 4.00 | 1.50 |
| 196 | Tim Rattay RC | 4.00 | 1.50 |
| 197 | Giovanni Carmazzi RC | 2.00 | .75 |
| 198 | Mareno Philyaw RC | 2.00 | .75 |
| 199 | Avion Black RC | 3.00 | 1.25 |
| 200 | Chafie Fields RC | 2.00 | .75 |
| 201 | Rondell Mealey RC | 2.00 | .75 |
| 202 | Troy Walters RC | 4.00 | 1.50 |
| 203 | Frank Moreau RC | 2.00 | .75 |
| 204 | Vaughn Sanders RC | 2.00 | .75 |
| 205 | Sherrod Gideon RC | 2.00 | .75 |
| 206 | Doug Chapman RC | 3.00 | 1.25 |
| 207 | Marcus Knight RC | 3.00 | 1.25 |
| 208 | Jamel White RC | 3.00 | 1.25 |
| 209 | Windrell Hayes RC | 2.00 | .75 |
| 210 | Reggie Jones RC | 2.00 | .75 |
| 211 | Jarious Jackson RC | 3.00 | 1.25 |
| 212 | Ronney Jenkins RC | 3.00 | 1.25 |
| 213 | Quinton Spotwood RC | 3.00 | 1.25 |
| 214 | Rob Morris RC | 3.00 | 1.25 |
| 215 | Gari Scott RC | 2.00 | .75 |
| 216 | Kevin Thompson RC | 2.00 | .75 |
| 217 | Trevor Insley RC | 2.00 | .75 |
| 218 | Frank Murphy RC | 2.00 | .75 |
| 219 | Patrick Pass RC | 3.00 | 1.25 |
| 220 | Mike Anderson RC | 2.50 | 1.00 |
| 221 | Derrius Thompson RC | 4.00 | 1.50 |
| 222 | John Abraham RC | 6.00 | 2.50 |
| 223 | Dante Hall RC | 8.00 | 3.00 |
| 224 | Chad Morton RC | 4.00 | 1.50 |
| 225 | Ahmed Plummer RC | 4.00 | 1.50 |
| 226 | Julian Peterson RC | 4.00 | 1.50 |
| 227 | Mike Green RC | 3.00 | 1.25 |
| 228 | Michael Wiley RC | 3.00 | 1.25 |
| 229 | Spergon Wynn RC | 3.00 | 1.25 |
| 230 | Trevor Gaylor RC | 3.00 | 1.25 |
| 231 | Doug Johnson RC | 4.00 | 1.50 |
| 232 | Marc Bulger RC | 8.00 | 3.00 |
| 233 | Ron Dixon RC | 3.00 | 1.25 |
| 234 | Aaron Shea RC | 1.50 | .60 |
| 235 | Thomas Hamner RC | 2.00 | .75 |
| 236 | Tom Brady RC | 100.00 | 50.00 |
| 237 | Deltha O'Neal RC | 4.00 | 1.50 |
| 238 | Todd Husak RC | 4.00 | 1.50 |
| 239 | Erron Kinney RC | 4.00 | 1.50 |
| 240 | JaJuan Dawson RC | 2.00 | .75 |
| 241 | Nick Williams | 1.00 | .40 |
| 242 | Deon Grant RC | 3.00 | 1.25 |
| 243 | Brad Hoover RC | 3.00 | 1.25 |
| 244 | Kamil Loud | .40 | .15 |
| 245 | Rashard Anderson RC | 3.00 | 1.25 |
| 246 | Clint Stoerner RC | 1.50 | .60 |
| 247 | Antwan Harris RC | 2.00 | .75 |
| 248 | Jason Webster RC | 2.00 | .75 |
| 249 | Kevin McDougal RC | 3.00 | 1.25 |
| 250 | Tony Scott RC | 2.00 | .75 |
| 251 | Thabiti Davis RC | 2.00 | .75 |
| 252 | Ian Gold RC | 3.00 | 1.25 |
| 253 | Sammy Morris RC | 4.00 | 1.50 |
| 254 | Raynoch Thompson RC | 3.00 | 1.25 |
| 255 | Jeremy McDaniel | 1.00 | .40 |
| 256 | Terrelle Smith RC | 3.00 | 1.25 |
| 257 | Deon Dyer RC | 3.00 | 1.25 |
| 258 | Na'il Diggs RC | 3.00 | 1.25 |
| 259 | Brandon Short RC | 3.00 | 1.25 |
| 260 | Mike Brown RC | 8.00 | 3.00 |
| 261 | John Engelberger RC | 3.00 | 1.25 |
| 262 | Rogers Beckett RC | 3.00 | 1.25 |
| 263 | JaJuan Seider RC | 2.00 | .75 |
| 264 | Desmond Kitchings RC | 3.00 | 1.25 |
| 265 | Reggie Davis RC | 3.00 | 1.25 |
| 266 | Corey Moore RC | 2.00 | .75 |
| 267 | Cornelius Griffin RC | 3.00 | 1.25 |
| 268 | Stockar McDougle RC | 2.00 | .75 |
| 269 | James Williams RC | 3.00 | 1.25 |
| 270 | Darrell Harrison RC | 6.00 | 2.50 |

## 2001 Bowman Chrome

| | | | |
|---|---|---|---|
| | COMP.SET w/o SP's (110) | 25.00 | 10.00 |
| 1 | Emmitt Smith | 2.00 | .75 |
| 2 | James Stewart | .60 | .25 |
| 3 | Jeff Graham | .40 | .15 |
| 4 | Keyshawn Johnson | 1.00 | .40 |
| 5 | Stephen Davis | 1.00 | .40 |
| 6 | Chad Lewis | .40 | .15 |
| 7 | Drew Bledsoe | 1.25 | .50 |
| 8 | Fred Taylor | 1.00 | .40 |
| 9 | Mike Anderson | 1.00 | .40 |
| 10 | Tony Gonzalez | .60 | .25 |
| 11 | Aaron Brooks | 1.00 | .40 |
| 12 | Vinny Testaverde | .60 | .25 |
| 13 | Jerome Bettis | 1.00 | .40 |
| 14 | Marshall Faulk | 1.25 | .50 |
| 15 | Jeff Garcia | 1.00 | .40 |
| 16 | Terry Glenn | .60 | .25 |
| 17 | Jay Fiedler | 1.00 | .40 |
| 18 | Ahman Green | 1.00 | .40 |
| 19 | Cade McNown | .40 | .15 |
| 20 | Rob Johnson | .60 | .25 |
| 21 | Jamal Anderson | 1.00 | .40 |
| 22 | Corey Dillon | 1.00 | .40 |
| 23 | Jake Plummer | 1.00 | .40 |
| 24 | Rod Smith | .60 | .25 |
| 25 | Trent Green | 1.00 | .40 |
| 26 | Ricky Williams | 1.00 | .40 |
| 27 | Charlie Garner | .60 | .25 |
| 28 | Shaun Alexander | 3.00 | 1.25 |
| 29 | Jeff George | .60 | .25 |

| | | |
|---|---|---|
| ❏ 30 Torry Holt | 1.00 | .40 |
| ❏ 31 James Thrash | .60 | .25 |
| ❏ 32 Rich Gannon | 1.00 | .40 |
| ❏ 33 Ron Dayne | 1.00 | .40 |
| ❏ 34 Dedric Ward | .40 | .15 |
| ❏ 35 Edgerrin James | 1.25 | .50 |
| ❏ 36 Cris Carter | 1.00 | .40 |
| ❏ 37 Derrick Mason | .60 | .25 |
| ❏ 38 Brad Johnson | 1.00 | .40 |
| ❏ 39 Charlie Batch | 1.00 | .40 |
| ❏ 40 Joey Galloway | .60 | .25 |
| ❏ 41 James Allen | .60 | .25 |
| ❏ 42 Tim Biakabutuka | .60 | .25 |
| ❏ 43 Ray Lewis | 1.00 | .40 |
| ❏ 44 David Boston | .60 | .25 |
| ❏ 45 Kevin Johnson | .60 | .25 |
| ❏ 46 Jimmy Smith | .60 | .25 |
| ❏ 47 Joe Horn | .60 | .25 |
| ❏ 48 Terrell Owens | 1.00 | .40 |
| ❏ 49 Eddie George | 1.00 | .40 |
| ❏ 50 Brett Favre | 3.00 | 1.25 |
| ❏ 51 Wayne Chrebet | .60 | .25 |
| ❏ 52 Hines Ward | 1.00 | .40 |
| ❏ 53 Warrick Dunn | 1.00 | .40 |
| ❏ 54 Matt Hasselbeck | .60 | .25 |
| ❏ 55 Tiki Barber | 1.00 | .40 |
| ❏ 56 Lamar Smith | .60 | .25 |
| ❏ 57 Tim Couch | .60 | .25 |
| ❏ 58 Eric Moulds | .60 | .25 |
| ❏ 59 Shawn Jefferson | .40 | .15 |
| ❏ 60 Donald Hayes | .40 | .15 |
| ❏ 61 Brian Urlacher | 1.50 | .60 |
| ❏ 62 Steve McNair | 1.00 | .40 |
| ❏ 63 Kurt Warner | 2.00 | .75 |
| ❏ 64 Tim Brown | 1.00 | .40 |
| ❏ 65 Troy Brown | .60 | .25 |
| ❏ 66 Albert Connell | .40 | .15 |
| ❏ 67 Peyton Manning | 2.50 | 1.00 |
| ❏ 68 Peter Warrick | 1.00 | .40 |
| ❏ 69 Elvis Grbac | .60 | .25 |
| ❏ 70 Chris Chandler | .60 | .25 |
| ❏ 71 Akili Smith | .40 | .15 |
| ❏ 72 Keenan McCardell | .40 | .15 |
| ❏ 73 Kerry Collins | .60 | .25 |
| ❏ 74 Junior Seau | 1.00 | .40 |
| ❏ 75 Donovan McNabb | 1.25 | .50 |
| ❏ 76 Tony Banks | .60 | .25 |
| ❏ 77 Steve Beuerlein | .60 | .25 |
| ❏ 78 Daunte Culpepper | 1.00 | .40 |
| ❏ 79 Darrell Jackson | .60 | .25 |
| ❏ 80 Isaac Bruce | 1.00 | .40 |
| ❏ 81 Tyrone Wheatley | .60 | .25 |
| ❏ 82 Derrick Alexander | .60 | .25 |
| ❏ 83 Germane Crowell | .40 | .15 |
| ❏ 84 Jon Kitna | .60 | .25 |
| ❏ 85 Jamal Lewis | 1.50 | .60 |
| ❏ 86 Ed McCaffrey | 1.00 | .40 |
| ❏ 87 Mark Brunell | 1.00 | .40 |
| ❏ 88 Jeff Blake | .60 | .25 |
| ❏ 89 Duce Staley | 1.00 | .40 |
| ❏ 90 Doug Flutie | 1.00 | .40 |
| ❏ 91 Kordell Stewart | .60 | .25 |
| ❏ 92 Randy Moss | 2.00 | .75 |
| ❏ 93 Marvin Harrison | 1.00 | .40 |
| ❏ 94 Muhsin Muhammad | .60 | .25 |
| ❏ 95 Brian Griese | 1.00 | .40 |
| ❏ 96 Antonio Freeman | 1.00 | .40 |
| ❏ 97 Amani Toomer | .60 | .25 |
| ❏ 98 Oronde Gadsden | .60 | .25 |
| ❏ 99 Curtis Martin | 1.00 | .40 |
| ❏ 100 Jerry Rice | 2.00 | .75 |
| ❏ 101 Michael Pittman | .40 | .15 |
| ❏ 102 Shannon Sharpe | .60 | .25 |
| ❏ 103 Peerless Price | .60 | .25 |
| ❏ 104 Bill Schroeder | .60 | .25 |
| ❏ 105 Ike Hilliard | .40 | .15 |
| ❏ 106 Freddie Jones | .40 | .15 |
| ❏ 107 Tai Streets | .40 | .15 |
| ❏ 108 Ricky Watters | .60 | .25 |
| ❏ 109 Az-Zahir Hakim | .40 | .15 |
| ❏ 110 Jacquez Green | .40 | .15 |
| ❏ 111 George Layne RC | 5.00 | 2.00 |
| ❏ 112 Correll Buckhalter RC | 10.00 | 4.00 |
| ❏ 113 Tony Stewart RC | 8.00 | 3.00 |

| | | |
|---|---|---|
| ❏ 114 Chris Barnes RC | 5.00 | 2.00 |
| ❏ 115 A.J. Feeley RC | 8.00 | 3.00 |
| ❏ 116 Margin Hooks RC | 3.00 | 1.25 |
| ❏ 117 Anthony Henry RC | 8.00 | 3.00 |
| ❏ 118 Dwight Smith RC | 3.00 | 1.25 |
| ❏ 119 Torrance Marshall RC | 8.00 | 3.00 |
| ❏ 120 Gary Baxter RC | 5.00 | 2.00 |
| ❏ 121 Derek Combs RC | 5.00 | 2.00 |
| ❏ 122 Marcus Bell RC | 5.00 | 2.00 |
| ❏ 123 DeLawrence Grant RC | 3.00 | 1.25 |
| ❏ 124 Jameel Cook RC | 5.00 | 2.00 |
| ❏ 125 Eric Downing RC | 3.00 | 1.25 |
| ❏ 126 Marlon McCree RC | 5.00 | 2.00 |
| ❏ 127 Tay Cody RC | 3.00 | 1.25 |
| ❏ 128 Mario Monds RC | 3.00 | 1.25 |
| ❏ 129 Kenny Smith RC | 5.00 | 2.00 |
| ❏ 130 Sedrick Hodge RC | 3.00 | 1.25 |
| ❏ 131 Marcus Stroud RC | 8.00 | 3.00 |
| ❏ 132 Steve Smith RC | 30.00 | 15.00 |
| ❏ 133 Tyrone Robertson RC | 3.00 | 1.25 |
| ❏ 134 James Reed RC | 3.00 | 1.25 |
| ❏ 135 Kris Kocurek RC | 3.00 | 1.25 |
| ❏ 136 Dan O'Leary RC | 5.00 | 2.00 |
| ❏ 137 Harold Blackmon RC | 3.00 | 1.25 |
| ❏ 138 Fred Smoot RC | 8.00 | 3.00 |
| ❏ 139 Billy Baber RC | 3.00 | 1.25 |
| ❏ 140 Jarrod Cooper RC | 8.00 | 3.00 |
| ❏ 141 Travis Henry RC | 8.00 | 3.00 |
| ❏ 142 David Terrell RC | 8.00 | 3.00 |
| ❏ 143 Josh Heupel RC | 8.00 | 3.00 |
| ❏ 144 Drew Brees RC | 40.00 | 20.00 |
| ❏ 145 T.J. Houshmandzadeh RC | 10.00 | 4.00 |
| ❏ 146 Rod Gardner RC | 8.00 | 3.00 |
| ❏ 147 Richard Seymour RC | 5.00 | 2.00 |
| ❏ 148 Koren Robinson RC | 8.00 | 3.00 |
| ❏ 149 Scotty Anderson RC | 5.00 | 2.00 |
| ❏ 150 Marques Tuiasosopo RC | 8.00 | 3.00 |
| ❏ 151 John Capel RC | 5.00 | 2.00 |
| ❏ 152 LaMont Jordan RC | 15.00 | 6.00 |
| ❏ 153 James Jackson RC | 8.00 | 3.00 |
| ❏ 154 Bobby Newcombe RC | 5.00 | 2.00 |
| ❏ 155 Anthony Thomas RC | 8.00 | 3.00 |
| ❏ 156 Dan Alexander RC | 8.00 | 3.00 |
| ❏ 157 Quincy Carter RC | 8.00 | 3.00 |
| ❏ 158 Morlon Greenwood RC | 5.00 | 2.00 |
| ❏ 159 Robert Ferguson RC | 8.00 | 3.00 |
| ❏ 160 Sage Rosenfels RC | 8.00 | 3.00 |
| ❏ 161 Michael Stone RC | 3.00 | 1.25 |
| ❏ 162 Chris Weinke RC | 5.00 | 2.00 |
| ❏ 163 Travis Minor RC | 5.00 | 2.00 |
| ❏ 164 Gerard Warren RC | 8.00 | 3.00 |
| ❏ 165 Jamar Fletcher RC | 5.00 | 2.00 |
| ❏ 166 Andre Carter RC | 8.00 | 3.00 |
| ❏ 167 Deuce McAllister RC | 15.00 | 7.50 |
| ❏ 168 Dan Morgan RC | 8.00 | 3.00 |
| ❏ 169 Todd Heap RC | 8.00 | 3.00 |
| ❏ 170 Snoop Minnis RC | 5.00 | 2.00 |
| ❏ 171 Will Allen RC | 5.00 | 2.00 |
| ❏ 172 Freddie Mitchell RC | 8.00 | 3.00 |
| ❏ 173 Rudi Johnson RC | 15.00 | 6.00 |
| ❏ 174 Kevan Barlow RC | 8.00 | 3.00 |
| ❏ 175 Jamie Winborn RC | 5.00 | 2.00 |
| ❏ 176 Onome Ojo RC | 5.00 | 2.00 |
| ❏ 177 Leonard Davis RC | 5.00 | 2.00 |
| ❏ 178 Santana Moss RC | 12.00 | 5.00 |
| ❏ 179 Chris Chambers RC | 12.00 | 5.00 |
| ❏ 180 Michael Vick RC | 25.00 | 10.00 |
| ❏ 181 Michael Bennett RC | 8.00 | 3.00 |
| ❏ 182 Mike McMahon RC | 8.00 | 3.00 |
| ❏ 183 Jonathan Carter RC | 5.00 | 2.00 |
| ❏ 184 Jamal Reynolds RC | 8.00 | 3.00 |
| ❏ 185 Justin Smith RC | 8.00 | 3.00 |
| ❏ 186 Quincy Morgan RC | 8.00 | 3.00 |
| ❏ 187 Chad Johnson RC | 30.00 | 12.00 |
| ❏ 188 Jesse Palmer RC | 8.00 | 3.00 |
| ❏ 189 Reggie Wayne RC | 20.00 | 10.00 |
| ❏ 190 LaDainian Tomlinson RC | 120.00 | 60.00 |
| ❏ 191 Andre King RC | 5.00 | 2.00 |
| ❏ 192 Richmond Flowers RC | 5.00 | 2.00 |
| ❏ 193 Derrick Blaylock RC | 8.00 | 3.00 |
| ❏ 194 Cedrick Wilson RC | 8.00 | 3.00 |
| ❏ 195 Zeke Moreno RC | 8.00 | 3.00 |
| ❏ 196 Tommy Polley RC | 8.00 | 3.00 |
| ❏ 197 Damione Lewis RC | 5.00 | 2.00 |

| | | |
|---|---|---|
| ❏ 198 Aaron Schobel RC | 8.00 | 3.00 |
| ❏ 199 Alge Crumpler RC | 12.00 | 5.00 |
| ❏ 200 Nate Clements RC | 8.00 | 3.00 |
| ❏ 201 Quentin McCord RC | 5.00 | 2.00 |
| ❏ 202 Ken-Yon Rambo RC | 5.00 | 2.00 |
| ❏ 203 Milton Wynn RC | 5.00 | 2.00 |
| ❏ 204 Derrick Gibson RC | 5.00 | 2.00 |
| ❏ 205 Chris Taylor RC | 5.00 | 2.00 |
| ❏ 206 Corey Hall RC | 3.00 | 1.25 |
| ❏ 207 Vinny Sutherland RC | 5.00 | 2.00 |
| ❏ 208 Kendrell Bell RC | 12.00 | 5.00 |
| ❏ 209 Casey Hampton RC | 8.00 | 3.00 |
| ❏ 210 Demetric Evans RC | 3.00 | 1.25 |
| ❏ 211 Brian Allen RC | 3.00 | 1.25 |
| ❏ 212 Rodney Bailey RC | 3.00 | 1.25 |
| ❏ 213 Otis Leverette RC | 3.00 | 1.25 |
| ❏ 214 Ron Edwards RC | 3.00 | 1.25 |
| ❏ 215 Michael Jameson RC | 3.00 | 1.25 |
| ❏ 216 Markus Steele RC | 5.00 | 2.00 |
| ❏ 217 Jimmy Williams RC | 5.00 | 2.00 |
| ❏ 218 Roger Knight RC | 3.00 | 1.25 |
| ❏ 219 Randy Garner RC | 3.00 | 1.25 |
| ❏ 220 Raymond Perryman RC | 3.00 | 1.25 |
| ❏ 221 Karon Riley RC | 3.00 | 1.25 |
| ❏ 222 Adam Archuleta RC | 8.00 | 3.00 |
| ❏ 223 Arnold Jackson RC | 5.00 | 2.00 |
| ❏ 224 Ryan Pickett RC | 3.00 | 1.25 |
| ❏ 225 Shad Meier RC | 5.00 | 2.00 |
| ❏ 226 Reggie Germany RC | 5.00 | 2.00 |
| ❏ 227 Justin McCareins RC | 8.00 | 3.00 |
| ❏ 228 Idrees Bashir RC | 3.00 | 1.25 |
| ❏ 229 Josh Booty RC | 3.00 | 1.25 |
| ❏ 230 Eddie Berlin RC | 5.00 | 2.00 |
| ❏ 231 Heath Evans RC | 5.00 | 2.00 |
| ❏ 232 Alex Bannister RC | 5.00 | 2.00 |
| ❏ 233 Corey Alston RC | 3.00 | 1.25 |
| ❏ 234 Reggie White RC | 5.00 | 2.00 |
| ❏ 235 Orlando Huff RC | 3.00 | 1.25 |
| ❏ 236 Ken Lucas RC | 5.00 | 2.00 |
| ❏ 237 Matt Stewart RC | 3.00 | 1.25 |
| ❏ 238 Cedric Scott RC | 5.00 | 2.00 |
| ❏ 239 Ronney Daniels RC | 3.00 | 1.25 |
| ❏ 240 Kevin Kasper RC | 8.00 | 3.00 |
| ❏ 241 Tony Driver RC | 5.00 | 2.00 |
| ❏ 242 Kyle Vanden Bosch RC | 8.00 | 3.00 |
| ❏ 243 T.J. Turner RC | 3.00 | 1.25 |
| ❏ 244 Eric Westmoreland RC | 5.00 | 2.00 |
| ❏ 245 Ronald Flemons RC | 3.00 | 1.25 |
| ❏ 246 Eric Kelly RC | 3.00 | 1.25 |
| ❏ 247 Moran Norris RC | 3.00 | 1.25 |
| ❏ 248 Damerien McCants RC | 5.00 | 2.00 |
| ❏ 249 James Boyd RC | 3.00 | 1.25 |
| ❏ 250 Keith Adams RC | 3.00 | 1.25 |
| ❏ 251 Brandon Manumaleuna RC | 5.00 | 2.00 |
| ❏ 252 Dee Brown RC | 8.00 | 3.00 |
| ❏ 253 Ross Kolodziej RC | 3.00 | 1.25 |
| ❏ 254 Boo Williams RC | 5.00 | 2.00 |
| ❏ 255 Patrick Chukwurah RC | 3.00 | 1.25 |

## 2002 Bowman Chrome

| | | |
|---|---|---|
| ❏ COMP.SET w/o SP's (110) | 25.00 | 10.00 |
| ❏ 1 Emmitt Smith | 2.50 | 1.00 |
| ❏ 2 Drew Brees | .40 | .40 |
| ❏ 3 Duce Staley | 1.00 | .40 |
| ❏ 4 Curtis Martin | 1.00 | .40 |
| ❏ 5 Isaac Bruce | 1.00 | .40 |
| ❏ 6 Stephen Davis | .60 | .25 |
| ❏ 7 Darrell Jackson | .60 | .25 |

|  | | |
|---|---|---|
| ❏ 8 James Stewart | .60 | .25 |
| ❏ 9 Tim Couch | .60 | .25 |
| ❏ 10 Travis Henry | 1.00 | .40 |
| ❏ 11 Thomas Jones | .60 | .25 |
| ❏ 12 Jamal Lewis | 1.00 | .40 |
| ❏ 13 Chris Chambers | 1.00 | .40 |
| ❏ 14 Jeff Blake | .60 | .25 |
| ❏ 15 Plaxico Burress | .60 | .25 |
| ❏ 16 Michael Pittman | .40 | .15 |
| ❏ 17 Jeff Garcia | 1.00 | .40 |
| ❏ 18 Tim Brown | 1.00 | .40 |
| ❏ 19 Kent Graham | .40 | .15 |
| ❏ 20 Shannon Sharpe | .60 | .25 |
| ❏ 21 Corey Dillon | .60 | .25 |
| ❏ 22 Muhsin Muhammad | .60 | .25 |
| ❏ 23 Tony Gonzalez | .60 | .25 |
| ❏ 24 Qadry Ismail | .60 | .25 |
| ❏ 25 Mike McMahon | 1.00 | .40 |
| ❏ 26 Edgerrin James | 1.25 | .50 |
| ❏ 27 Daunte Culpepper | 1.00 | .40 |
| ❏ 28 Deuce McAllister | 1.25 | .50 |
| ❏ 29 Kerry Collins | .60 | .25 |
| ❏ 30 Eddie George | 1.00 | .40 |
| ❏ 31 Torry Holt | 1.00 | .40 |
| ❏ 32 Todd Pinkston | .60 | .25 |
| ❏ 33 Quincy Carter | .60 | .25 |
| ❏ 34 Rod Smith | .60 | .25 |
| ❏ 35 Michael Vick | 2.00 | .75 |
| ❏ 36 Jim Miller | .60 | .25 |
| ❏ 37 Troy Brown | .60 | .25 |
| ❏ 38 Wayne Chrebet | .60 | .25 |
| ❏ 39 Curtis Conway | .40 | .15 |
| ❏ 40 Reidel Anthony | .40 | .15 |
| ❏ 41 Mark Brunell | 1.00 | .40 |
| ❏ 42 Chris Weinke | .60 | .25 |
| ❏ 43 Eric Moulds | .60 | .25 |
| ❏ 44 Ike Hilliard | .60 | .25 |
| ❏ 45 Jay Fiedler | .60 | .25 |
| ❏ 46 Keyshawn Johnson | 1.00 | .40 |
| ❏ 47 Rod Gardner | .60 | .25 |
| ❏ 48 Chris Redman | .40 | .15 |
| ❏ 49 James Allen | .60 | .25 |
| ❏ 50 Kordell Stewart | .60 | .25 |
| ❏ 51 Priest Holmes | 1.25 | .50 |
| ❏ 52 Anthony Thomas | .60 | .25 |
| ❏ 53 Peter Warrick | .60 | .25 |
| ❏ 54 Jake Plummer | .60 | .25 |
| ❏ 55 Jerry Rice | 2.00 | .75 |
| ❏ 56 Joe Horn | .60 | .25 |
| ❏ 57 Derrick Mason | .60 | .25 |
| ❏ 58 Kurt Warner | 1.00 | .40 |
| ❏ 59 Antowain Smith | .60 | .25 |
| ❏ 60 Randy Moss | 2.00 | .75 |
| ❏ 61 Warrick Dunn | 1.00 | .40 |
| ❏ 62 Laveranues Coles | .60 | .25 |
| ❏ 63 LaDainian Tomlinson | 1.50 | .60 |
| ❏ 64 Michael Westbrook | .60 | .25 |
| ❏ 65 Travis Taylor | .60 | .25 |
| ❏ 66 Brian Griese | 1.00 | .40 |
| ❏ 67 Bill Schroeder | .60 | .25 |
| ❏ 68 Ahman Green | 1.00 | .40 |
| ❏ 69 Jimmy Smith | .60 | .25 |
| ❏ 70 Charlie Garner | .60 | .25 |
| ❏ 71 Terrell Owens | 1.00 | .40 |
| ❏ 72 Brad Johnson | .60 | .25 |
| ❏ 73 James Thrash | .60 | .25 |
| ❏ 74 Marvin Harrison | 1.00 | .40 |
| ❏ 75 Brett Favre | 2.50 | 1.00 |
| ❏ 76 Rocket Ismail | .60 | .25 |
| ❏ 77 David Boston | 1.00 | .40 |
| ❏ 78 Jermaine Lewis | .40 | .15 |
| ❏ 79 Aaron Brooks | 1.00 | .40 |
| ❏ 80 Shaun Alexander | 1.25 | .50 |
| ❏ 81 Steve McNair | 1.00 | .40 |
| ❏ 82 Marshall Faulk | 1.00 | .40 |
| ❏ 83 Terrell Davis | 1.00 | .40 |
| ❏ 84 Corey Bradford | .40 | .15 |
| ❏ 85 David Terrell | 1.00 | .40 |
| ❏ 86 Kevin Johnson | .60 | .25 |
| ❏ 87 Jon Kitna | .60 | .25 |
| ❏ 88 Az-Zahir Hakim | .40 | .15 |
| ❏ 89 Drew Bledsoe | 1.25 | .50 |
| ❏ 90 Garrison Hearst | .60 | .25 |
| ❏ 91 Doug Flutie | 1.00 | .40 |
| ❏ 92 Jerome Bettis | 1.00 | .40 |
| ❏ 93 Vinny Testaverde | .60 | .25 |
| ❏ 94 Tiki Barber | 1.00 | .40 |
| ❏ 95 Johnnie Morton | .60 | .25 |
| ❏ 96 Lamar Smith | .60 | .25 |
| ❏ 97 Marcus Robinson | .60 | .25 |
| ❏ 98 Fred Taylor | 1.00 | .40 |
| ❏ 99 Tom Brady | 2.50 | 1.00 |
| ❏ 100 Peyton Manning | 2.00 | .75 |
| ❏ 101 Donovan McNabb | 1.25 | .50 |
| ❏ 102 Rich Gannon | 1.00 | .40 |
| ❏ 103 Hines Ward | 1.00 | .40 |
| ❏ 104 Michael Bennett | .60 | .25 |
| ❏ 105 Ricky Williams | 1.00 | .40 |
| ❏ 106 Germane Crowell | .40 | .15 |
| ❏ 107 Joey Galloway | .60 | .25 |
| ❏ 108 Amani Toomer | .60 | .25 |
| ❏ 109 Trent Green | .60 | .25 |
| ❏ 110 Terry Glenn | .60 | .25 |
| ❏ 111 Donte Stallworth RC | 8.00 | 3.00 |
| ❏ 112 Mike Williams RC | 4.00 | 1.50 |
| ❏ 113 Kurt Kittner RC | 4.00 | 1.50 |
| ❏ 114 Josh Reed RC | 5.00 | 2.00 |
| ❏ 115 Raonall Smith RC | 4.00 | 1.50 |
| ❏ 116 David Garrard RC | 10.00 | 4.00 |
| ❏ 117 Eric Crouch RC | 5.00 | 2.00 |
| ❏ 118 Levi Jones RC | 4.00 | 1.50 |
| ❏ 119 Quentin Jammer RC | 5.00 | 2.00 |
| ❏ 120 Cliff Russell RC | 4.00 | 1.50 |
| ❏ 121 Jamin Elliott RC | 2.50 | 1.00 |
| ❏ 122 Roy Williams RC | 10.00 | 4.00 |
| ❏ 123 Marquise Walker RC | 4.00 | 1.50 |
| ❏ 124 Kalimba Edwards RC | 5.00 | 2.00 |
| ❏ 125 Daniel Graham RC | 5.00 | 2.00 |
| ❏ 126 Anthony Weaver RC | 4.00 | 1.50 |
| ❏ 127 Antonio Bryant RC | 5.00 | 2.00 |
| ❏ 128 DeShaun Foster RC | 5.00 | 2.00 |
| ❏ 129 Antwaan Randle El RC | 6.00 | 2.50 |
| ❏ 130 William Green RC | 5.00 | 2.00 |
| ❏ 131 Joey Harrington RC | 6.00 | 2.50 |
| ❏ 132 T.J. Duckett RC | 5.00 | 2.00 |
| ❏ 133 Javon Walker RC | 8.00 | 3.00 |
| ❏ 134 Albert Haynesworth RC | 5.00 | 2.00 |
| ❏ 135 Julius Peppers RC | 10.00 | 4.00 |
| ❏ 136 Clinton Portis RC | 15.00 | 6.00 |
| ❏ 137 Ashley Lelie RC | 10.00 | 4.00 |
| ❏ 138 Reche Caldwell RC | 5.00 | 2.00 |
| ❏ 139 Rohan Davey RC | 5.00 | 2.00 |
| ❏ 140 Patrick Ramsey RC | 5.00 | 2.00 |
| ❏ 141 Ron Johnson RC | 4.00 | 1.50 |
| ❏ 142 Jamar Martin RC | 4.00 | 1.50 |
| ❏ 143 Travis Stephens RC | 4.00 | 1.50 |
| ❏ 143AU Travis Stephens AU | 12.00 | 5.00 |
| ❏ 144 Darrell Hill RC | 4.00 | 1.50 |
| ❏ 145 Jon McGraw RC | 2.50 | 1.00 |
| ❏ 146 Javin Hunter RC | 2.50 | 1.00 |
| ❏ 146AU Javin Hunter AU | 10.00 | 4.00 |
| ❏ 147 Eddie Drummond RC | 4.00 | 1.50 |
| ❏ 148 Andre Lott RC | 5.00 | 2.00 |
| ❏ 149 Travis Fisher RC | 5.00 | 2.00 |
| ❏ 150 Lamont Brightful RC | 2.50 | 1.00 |
| ❏ 151 Rocky Calmus RC | 5.00 | 2.00 |
| ❏ 152 Wes Pate RC | 2.50 | 1.00 |
| ❏ 152AU Wes Pate AU | 10.00 | 4.00 |
| ❏ 153 Lamar Gordon RC | 5.00 | 2.00 |
| ❏ 154 Terry Jones RC | 4.00 | 1.50 |
| ❏ 155 Kyle Johnson RC | 2.50 | 1.00 |
| ❏ 155AU Kyle Johnson AU | 10.00 | 4.00 |
| ❏ 156 Daryl Jones RC | 4.00 | 1.50 |
| ❏ 157 Tellis Redmon RC | 4.00 | 1.50 |
| ❏ 158 Jarrod Baxter RC | 4.00 | 1.50 |
| ❏ 159 DeJuan Flowers RC | 4.00 | 1.50 |
| ❏ 160 Kelly Campbell RC | 4.00 | 1.50 |
| ❏ 161 Eddie Freeman RC | 2.50 | 1.00 |
| ❏ 162 Atrews Bell RC | 2.50 | 1.00 |
| ❏ 163 Omar Easy RC | 5.00 | 2.00 |
| ❏ 164 Jeremy Allen RC | 2.50 | 1.00 |
| ❏ 165 Andra Davis RC | 4.00 | 1.50 |
| ❏ 166 Mike Rumph RC | 5.00 | 2.00 |
| ❏ 167 Seth Burford RC | 4.00 | 1.50 |
| ❏ 168 Marquand Manuel RC | 2.50 | 1.00 |
| ❏ 169 Marques Anderson RC | 5.00 | 2.00 |
| ❏ 170 Ben Leber RC | 5.00 | 2.00 |
| ❏ 171 Ryan Denney RC | 4.00 | 1.50 |
| ❏ 172 Justin Peelle RC | 2.50 | 1.00 |
| ❏ 173 Lito Sheppard RC | 5.00 | 2.00 |
| ❏ 174 Damien Anderson RC | 4.00 | 1.50 |
| ❏ 175 Lamont Thompson RC | 4.00 | 1.50 |
| ❏ 176 David Priestley RC | 4.00 | 1.50 |
| ❏ 177 Michael Lewis RC | 5.00 | 2.00 |
| ❏ 178 Lee Mays RC | 4.00 | 1.50 |
| ❏ 179 Alan Harper RC | 2.50 | 1.00 |
| ❏ 180 Verron Haynes RC | 5.00 | 2.00 |
| ❏ 181 Chris Hope RC | 4.00 | 1.50 |
| ❏ 182 Derek Ross RC | 4.00 | 1.50 |
| ❏ 183 Joseph Jefferson RC | 4.00 | 1.50 |
| ❏ 184 Carlos Hall RC | 5.00 | 2.00 |
| ❏ 185 Robert Royal RC | 5.00 | 2.00 |
| ❏ 186 Sheldon Brown RC | 5.00 | 2.00 |
| ❏ 187 DeVeren Johnson RC | 4.00 | 1.50 |
| ❏ 188 Rock Cartwright RC | 6.00 | 2.50 |
| ❏ 189 Kendall Simmons RC | 4.00 | 1.50 |
| ❏ 190 Joe Burns RC | 4.00 | 1.50 |
| ❏ 191 David Givens RC | 12.00 | 5.00 |
| ❏ 192 John Owens RC | 4.00 | 1.50 |
| ❏ 193 Jarrett Ferguson RC | 4.00 | 1.50 |
| ❏ 194 Randy McMichael RC | 8.00 | 3.00 |
| ❏ 195 Chris Baker RC | 4.00 | 1.50 |
| ❏ 196 Rashad Bauman RC | 4.00 | 1.50 |
| ❏ 197 Matt Murphy RC | 4.00 | 1.50 |
| ❏ 198 Steve Bellisari RC | 4.00 | 1.50 |
| ❏ 199 Jeff Kelly RC | 4.00 | 1.50 |
| ❏ 200 Mark Anelli RC | 2.50 | 1.00 |
| ❏ 201 Darnell Sanders RC | 4.00 | 1.50 |
| ❏ 202 Coy Wire RC | 5.00 | 2.00 |
| ❏ 203 Ricky Williams RC | 4.00 | 1.50 |
| ❏ 204 Napoleon Harris RC | 5.00 | 2.00 |
| ❏ 205 Ennis Haywood RC | 4.00 | 1.50 |
| ❏ 206 Keyuo Craver RC | 4.00 | 1.50 |
| ❏ 207 Kahlil Hill RC | 4.00 | 1.50 |
| ❏ 208 J.T. O'Sullivan RC | 6.00 | 2.50 |
| ❏ 209 Woody Dantzler RC | 4.00 | 1.50 |
| ❏ 210 Phillip Buchanon RC | 5.00 | 2.00 |
| ❏ 211 Charles Grant RC | 5.00 | 2.00 |
| ❏ 212 Dusty Bonner RC | 2.50 | 1.00 |
| ❏ 213 James Allen RC | 2.50 | 1.00 |
| ❏ 214 Ronald Curry RC | 5.00 | 2.00 |
| ❏ 215 Deion Branch RC | 8.00 | 3.00 |
| ❏ 216 Larry Ned RC | 4.00 | 1.50 |
| ❏ 217 Kendall Newson RC | 2.50 | 1.00 |
| ❏ 218 Shaun Hill RC | 8.00 | 3.00 |
| ❏ 219 Akin Ayodele RC | 2.50 | 1.00 |
| ❏ 220 John Henderson RC | 5.00 | 2.00 |
| ❏ 221 Andre Davis AU RC | 12.00 | 5.00 |
| ❏ 222 Bryan Thomas AU A RC | 20.00 | 7.50 |
| ❏ 223 Brian Westbrook AU C RC | 100.00 | 50.00 |
| ❏ 224 Chad Hutchinson AU C RC | 12.00 | 5.00 |
| ❏ 225 Craig Nall AU D RC | 20.00 | 7.50 |
| ❏ 226 David Carr AU A RC | 40.00 | 15.00 |
| ❏ 227 Dwight Freeney AU D RC | 40.00 | 20.00 |
| ❏ 228 Adrian Peterson AU A RC | 30.00 | 12.00 |
| ❏ 229 Randy Fasani AU E RC | 12.00 | 5.00 |
| ❏ 230 Ed Reed AU A RC | 60.00 | 35.00 |
| ❏ 231 Freddie Milons AU B RC | 12.00 | 5.00 |
| ❏ 232 Herb Haygood AU E RC | 10.00 | 4.00 |
| ❏ 233 Jabar Gaffney AU A RC | 15.00 | 6.00 |
| ❏ 234 Josh McCown AU A RC | 30.00 | 12.00 |
| ❏ 235 Jeremy Shockey AU A RC | 60.00 | 25.00 |
| ❏ 236 Jake Schifino AU F RC | 12.00 | 5.00 |
| ❏ 237 Josh Scobey AU E RC | 20.00 | 7.50 |
| ❏ 238 Jonathan Wells AU D RC | 20.00 | 7.50 |
| ❏ 239 Ladell Betts AU A RC | 25.00 | 12.50 |
| ❏ 240 Luke Staley AU E RC | 12.00 | 5.00 |
| ❏ 241 Maurice Morris AU D RC | 20.00 | 7.50 |
| ❏ 242 Matt Schobel AU D RC | 12.00 | 5.00 |
| ❏ 243 Sam Simmons AU C RC | 10.00 | 4.00 |
| ❏ 244 Tim Carter AU A RC | 12.00 | 5.00 |
| ❏ 245 Tank Williams AU E RC | 12.00 | 5.00 |
| ❏ 246 Jerramy Stevens AU-A RC | 20.00 | 7.50 |
| ❏ 247 Jason McAddley AU C RC | 12.00 | 5.00 |
| ❏ 248 Ken Simonton AU D RC | 10.00 | 4.00 |
| ❏ 249 Chester Taylor AU F RC | 30.00 | 15.00 |
| ❏ 250 Brandon Doman AU C RC | 12.00 | 5.00 |

## 2003 Bowman Chrome

| | | |
|---|---|---|
| ❏ COMP.SET w/o SP's (110) | 25.00 | 10.00 |
| ❏ COMP.SET w/o AU's (220) | 100.00 | 50.00 |
| ❏ 1 Brett Favre | 2.50 | 1.00 |

| | | |
|---|---|---|
| ❏ 2 Jeremy Shockey | 1.00 | .40 |
| ❏ 3 Fred Taylor | 1.00 | .40 |
| ❏ 4 Rich Gannon | .75 | .30 |
| ❏ 5 Joey Galloway | .75 | .30 |
| ❏ 6 Ray Lewis | 1.00 | .40 |
| ❏ 7 Jeff Blake | .75 | .30 |
| ❏ 8 Stacey Mack | .60 | .25 |
| ❏ 9 Matt Hasselbeck | .75 | .30 |
| ❏ 10 Laveranues Coles | .75 | .30 |
| ❏ 11 Brad Johnson | .75 | .30 |
| ❏ 12 Tommy Maddox | .75 | .30 |
| ❏ 13 Curtis Martin | 1.00 | .40 |
| ❏ 14 Tom Brady | 2.50 | 1.00 |
| ❏ 15 Ricky Williams | .75 | .30 |
| ❏ 16 Stephen Davis | .75 | .30 |
| ❏ 17 Chad Johnson | 1.00 | .40 |
| ❏ 18 Joey Harrington | .75 | .30 |
| ❏ 19 Tony Gonzalez | .75 | .30 |
| ❏ 20 Peerless Price | .60 | .25 |
| ❏ 21 LaDainian Tomlinson | 1.50 | .60 |
| ❏ 22 James Thrash | .60 | .25 |
| ❏ 23 Charlie Garner | .75 | .30 |
| ❏ 24 Eddie George | .75 | .30 |
| ❏ 25 Terrell Owens | 1.00 | .40 |
| ❏ 26 Brian Urlacher | 1.50 | .60 |
| ❏ 27 Eric Moulds | .75 | .30 |
| ❏ 28 Emmitt Smith | 2.50 | 1.00 |
| ❏ 29 Tim Couch | .60 | .25 |
| ❏ 30 Jake Plummer | .75 | .30 |
| ❏ 31 Marvin Harrison | 1.00 | .40 |
| ❏ 32 Chris Chambers | .75 | .30 |
| ❏ 33 Tiki Barber | 1.00 | .40 |
| ❏ 34 Kurt Warner | 1.00 | .40 |
| ❏ 35 Michael Pittman | .60 | .25 |
| ❏ 36 Kevin Dyson | .75 | .30 |
| ❏ 37 Clinton Portis | 1.25 | .50 |
| ❏ 38 Peyton Manning | 2.00 | .75 |
| ❏ 39 Travis Taylor | .60 | .25 |
| ❏ 40 Jeff Garcia | 1.00 | .40 |
| ❏ 41 Patrick Ramsey | .75 | .30 |
| ❏ 42 Shaun Alexander | 1.00 | .40 |
| ❏ 43 Joe Horn | .75 | .30 |
| ❏ 44 Daunte Culpepper | .75 | .30 |
| ❏ 45 Travis Henry | .75 | .30 |
| ❏ 46 Brian Finneran | .60 | .25 |
| ❏ 47 William Green | .60 | .25 |
| ❏ 48 Kordell Stewart | .75 | .30 |
| ❏ 49 Reggie Wayne | .75 | .30 |
| ❏ 50 Priest Holmes | 1.00 | .40 |
| ❏ 51 Jay Fiedler | .75 | .30 |
| ❏ 52 Corey Dillon | .75 | .30 |
| ❏ 53 Jamal Lewis | 1.00 | .40 |
| ❏ 54 Mark Brunell | .75 | .30 |
| ❏ 55 Santana Moss | .75 | .30 |
| ❏ 56 Duce Staley | .75 | .30 |
| ❏ 57 Torry Holt | 1.00 | .40 |
| ❏ 58 Rod Gardner | .60 | .25 |
| ❏ 59 Kerry Collins | .75 | .30 |
| ❏ 60 Randy Moss | 1.25 | .50 |
| ❏ 61 Jerry Porter | .75 | .30 |
| ❏ 62 Plaxico Burress | .75 | .30 |
| ❏ 63 Steve McNair | 1.00 | .40 |
| ❏ 64 Muhsin Muhammad | .75 | .30 |
| ❏ 65 Drew Bledsoe | 1.00 | .40 |
| ❏ 66 T.J. Duckett | .75 | .30 |
| ❏ 67 Ahman Green | 1.00 | .40 |
| ❏ 68 Rod Smith | .75 | .30 |
| ❏ 69 Jimmy Smith | .75 | .30 |
| ❏ 70 Trent Green | .75 | .30 |
| ❏ 71 Tim Brown | 1.00 | .40 |
| ❏ 72 Jerome Bettis | 1.00 | .40 |
| ❏ 73 Isaac Bruce | 1.00 | .40 |
| ❏ 74 Derrick Mason | .75 | .30 |
| ❏ 75 Donovan McNabb | 1.25 | .50 |
| ❏ 76 Deuce McAllister | 1.00 | .40 |
| ❏ 77 Zach Thomas | 1.00 | .40 |
| ❏ 78 Garrison Hearst | .75 | .30 |
| ❏ 79 Koren Robinson | .75 | .30 |
| ❏ 80 Marshall Faulk | 1.00 | .40 |
| ❏ 81 Keyshawn Johnson | 1.00 | .40 |
| ❏ 82 Jake Delhomme | .75 | .30 |
| ❏ 83 Marty Booker | .75 | .30 |
| ❏ 84 James Stewart | .75 | .30 |
| ❏ 85 Corey Bradford | .60 | .25 |
| ❏ 86 Derrius-Thompson | .60 | .25 |
| ❏ 87 Edgerrin James | 1.00 | .40 |
| ❏ 88 Darrell Jackson | .75 | .30 |
| ❏ 89 Hines Ward | 1.00 | .40 |
| ❏ 90 David Boston | .60 | .25 |
| ❏ 91 Curtis Conway | .60 | .25 |
| ❏ 92 David Patten | .60 | .25 |
| ❏ 93 Michael Bennett | .75 | .30 |
| ❏ 94 Todd Heinrich | .60 | .25 |
| ❏ 95 Jerry Rice | 2.00 | .75 |
| ❏ 96 Jon Kitna | .75 | .30 |
| ❏ 97 Ed McCaffrey | .75 | .30 |
| ❏ 98 Donald Driver | .75 | .30 |
| ❏ 99 Anthony Thomas | .75 | .30 |
| ❏ 100 Michael Vick | .75 | .30 |
| ❏ 101 Terry Glenn | .75 | .30 |
| ❏ 102 Quincy Morgan | .60 | .25 |
| ❏ 103 David Carr | 1.00 | .40 |
| ❏ 104 Troy Brown | .75 | .30 |
| ❏ 105 Aaron Brooks | .75 | .30 |
| ❏ 106 Amani Toomer | .75 | .30 |
| ❏ 107 Drew Brees | 1.00 | .40 |
| ❏ 108 Chad Hutchinson | .60 | .25 |
| ❏ 109 Warrick Dunn | .75 | .30 |
| ❏ 110 Chad Pennington | 1.00 | .40 |
| ❏ 111 Brian St.Pierre RC | 5.00 | 2.00 |
| ❏ 112 Keenan Howry RC | 3.00 | 1.25 |
| ❏ 113 Sultan McCullough RC | 3.00 | 1.25 |
| ❏ 114 Terrence Newman RC | 6.00 | 2.50 |
| ❏ 115 Kelley Washington RC | 4.00 | 1.50 |
| ❏ 116 Musa Smith RC | 4.00 | 1.50 |
| ❏ 117 Victor Hobson RC | 3.00 | 1.25 |
| ❏ 118 Travis Anglin RC | 3.00 | 1.25 |
| ❏ 119 Artose Pinner RC | 3.00 | 1.25 |
| ❏ 120 Rashean Mathis RC | 4.00 | 1.50 |
| ❏ 121 DeWayne White RC | 3.00 | 1.25 |
| ❏ 122 Kevin Curtis RC | 6.00 | 2.50 |
| ❏ 123 Tyrone Calico RC | 4.00 | 1.50 |
| ❏ 124 Ricky Manning RC | 4.00 | 1.50 |
| ❏ 125 Cory Redding RC | 4.00 | 1.50 |
| ❏ 126 Dallas Clark RC | 5.00 | 2.00 |
| ❏ 127 Marcus Trufant RC | 5.00 | 2.00 |
| ❏ 128 Terrell Suggs RC | 6.00 | 2.50 |
| ❏ 129 Aaron Walker RC | 4.00 | 1.50 |
| ❏ 130 Calvin Pace RC | 4.00 | 1.50 |
| ❏ 131 Ken Dorsey RC | 5.00 | 2.00 |
| ❏ 132 Earnest Graham RC | 5.00 | 2.00 |
| ❏ 133 Cecil Sapp RC | 3.00 | 1.25 |
| ❏ 134 William Joseph RC | 3.00 | 1.25 |
| ❏ 135 Anquan Boldin RC | 12.00 | 5.00 |
| ❏ 136 Justin Griffith RC | 4.00 | 1.50 |
| ❏ 137 Teyo Johnson RC | 4.00 | 1.50 |
| ❏ 138 Chris Crocker RC | 4.00 | 1.50 |
| ❏ 139 Doug Gabriel RC | 4.00 | 1.50 |
| ❏ 140 Terry Pierce RC | 3.00 | 1.25 |
| ❏ 141 Bradie James RC | 5.00 | 2.00 |
| ❏ 142 Terrence Edwards RC | 3.00 | 1.25 |
| ❏ 143 E.J. Henderson RC | 4.00 | 1.50 |
| ❏ 144 Tony Romo RC | 60.00 | 30.00 |
| ❏ 145 DeWayne Robertson RC | 4.00 | 1.50 |
| ❏ 146 Dwone Hicks RC | 3.00 | 1.25 |
| ❏ 147 Carl Ford RC | 3.00 | 1.25 |
| ❏ 148 Ken Hamlin RC | 5.00 | 2.00 |
| ❏ 149 Adrian Madise RC | 3.00 | 1.25 |
| ❏ 150 Siddeeq Shabazz RC | 3.00 | 1.25 |
| ❏ 151 Dave Ragone RC | 4.00 | 1.50 |
| ❏ 152 Mike Seidman RC | 3.00 | 1.25 |
| ❏ 153 DeAndrew Rubin RC | 3.00 | 1.25 |
| ❏ 154 Mike Pinkard RC | 3.00 | 1.25 |
| ❏ 155 Nate Burleson RC | 4.00 | 1.50 |
| ❏ 156 Angelo Crowell RC | 4.00 | 1.50 |
| ❏ 157 J.R. Tolver RC | 4.00 | 1.50 |
| ❏ 158 Osi Umenyiora RC | 8.00 | 3.00 |
| ❏ 159 Nick Barnett RC | 4.00 | 1.50 |
| ❏ 160 Brandon Drumm RC | 3.00 | 1.25 |
| ❏ 161 Rien Long RC | 3.00 | 1.25 |
| ❏ 162 Zuriel Smith RC | 3.00 | 1.25 |
| ❏ 163 Onterrio Smith RC | 4.00 | 1.50 |
| ❏ 164 Kenny Peterson RC | 3.00 | 1.25 |
| ❏ 165 Chaun Thompson RC | 3.00 | 1.25 |
| ❏ 166 Terrence Holt RC | 4.00 | 1.50 |
| ❏ 167 Ovie Mughelli RC | 3.00 | 1.25 |
| ❏ 168 Bethel Johnson RC | 4.00 | 1.50 |
| ❏ 169 Avon Cobourne RC | 3.00 | 1.25 |
| ❏ 170 Andre Woolfolk RC | 4.00 | 1.50 |
| ❏ 171 George Wrighster RC | 3.00 | 1.25 |
| ❏ 172 Justin Fargas RC | 5.00 | 2.00 |
| ❏ 173 Marquel Blackwell RC | 3.00 | 1.25 |
| ❏ 174 Walter Young RC | 3.00 | 1.25 |
| ❏ 175 Kawika Mitchell RC | 5.00 | 2.00 |
| ❏ 176 Drayton Florence RC | 4.00 | 1.50 |
| ❏ 177 Jeremi Johnson RC | 3.00 | 1.25 |
| ❏ 178 Lee Suggs RC | 4.00 | 1.50 |
| ❏ 179 David Kircus RC | 5.00 | 2.00 |
| ❏ 180 Rex Grossman RC | 12.00 | 5.00 |
| ❏ 180AU Rex Grossman AU B | 60.00 | 25.00 |
| ❏ 181 Jon Olinger RC | 3.00 | 1.25 |
| ❏ 182 Dan Curley RC | 3.00 | 1.25 |
| ❏ 183 Andrew Pinnock RC | 4.00 | 1.50 |
| ❏ 184 Kirk Farmer RC | 3.00 | 1.25 |
| ❏ 185 Charles Rogers RC | 4.00 | 1.50 |
| ❏ 186 Alonzo Jackson RC | 3.00 | 1.25 |
| ❏ 187 Trent Smith RC | 4.00 | 1.50 |
| ❏ 188 Seneca Wallace RC | 5.00 | 2.00 |
| ❏ 189 Shane Walton RC | 3.00 | 1.25 |
| ❏ 190 Chris Brown RC | 5.00 | 2.00 |
| ❏ 191 Dahrran Diedrick RC | 3.00 | 1.25 |
| ❏ 192 Juston Wood RC | 3.00 | 1.25 |
| ❏ 193 Mike Doss RC | 5.00 | 2.00 |
| ❏ 194 Visanthe Shiancoe RC | 5.00 | 2.00 |
| ❏ 195 Andre Johnson RC | 10.00 | 4.00 |
| ❏ 196 Dennis Weathersby RC | 4.00 | 1.50 |
| ❏ 197 Chris Davis RC | 4.00 | 1.50 |
| ❏ 198 LaTarence Dunbar RC | 3.00 | 1.25 |
| ❏ 199 Eugene Wilson RC | 5.00 | 2.00 |
| ❏ 200 Ryan Hoag RC | 3.00 | 1.25 |
| ❏ 201 Chris Simms RC | 5.00 | 2.00 |
| ❏ 202 Curt Anes RC | 3.00 | 1.25 |
| ❏ 203 Taco Wallace RC | 3.00 | 1.25 |
| ❏ 204 David Tyree RC | 5.00 | 2.00 |
| ❏ 205 Nate Hybl RC | 4.00 | 1.50 |
| ❏ 206 Willis McGahee RC | 12.00 | 5.00 |
| ❏ 207 Casey Moore RC | 3.00 | 1.25 |
| ❏ 208 Piss Tinoisamoa RC | 5.00 | 2.00 |
| ❏ 209 Willie Ponder RC | 4.00 | 1.50 |
| ❏ 210 Donald Lee RC | 4.00 | 1.50 |
| ❏ 211 Nnamdi Asomugha RC | 4.00 | 1.50 |
| ❏ 212 Sammy Davis RC | 4.00 | 1.50 |
| ❏ 213 Joffrey Reynolds RC | 3.00 | 1.25 |
| ❏ 214 Eddie Moore RC | 3.00 | 1.25 |
| ❏ 215 Tony Hollings RC | 4.00 | 1.50 |
| ❏ 216 Nick Maddox RC | 3.00 | 1.25 |
| ❏ 217 Kevin Walter RC | 5.00 | 2.00 |
| ❏ 218 Dan Klecko RC | 4.00 | 1.50 |
| ❏ 219 Antwan Peek RC | 3.00 | 1.25 |
| ❏ 220 Tyler Brayton RC | 4.00 | 1.50 |
| ❏ 221 Byron Leftwich AU B RC | 30.00 | 12.00 |
| ❏ 222 Bobby Wade AU B RC | 10.00 | 4.00 |
| ❏ 223 Jerome McDougle AU C RC | 12.00 | 5.00 |
| ❏ 224 Michael Haynes AU B RC | 10.00 | 4.00 |
| ❏ 225 Taylor Jacobs AU D RC | 15.00 | 6.00 |
| ❏ 226 Shaun McDonald AU D RC | 15.00 | 6.00 |
| ❏ 227 Talman Gardner AU D RC | 10.00 | 4.00 |
| ❏ 228 Domanick Davis AU D RC | 15.00 | 6.00 |
| ❏ 229 Jason Witten AU D RC | 50.00 | 30.00 |
| ❏ 230 Jason Witten RC | 20.00 | 8.00 |
| ❏ 231 Kyle Boller AU B RC | 20.00 | 8.00 |
| ❏ 232 L.J. Smith AU C RC | 20.00 | 8.00 |
| ❏ 233 Boss Bailey AU C RC | 15.00 | 6.00 |
| ❏ 234 Billy McMullen AU D RC | 10.00 | 4.00 |
| ❏ 235 Larry Johnson AU B RC | 60.00 | 25.00 |
| ❏ 236 Kareem Kelly AU E RC | 10.00 | 4.00 |
| ❏ 237 Carson Palmer AU A RC | 300.00 | 150.00 |

| | | | |
|---|---|---|---|
| ❏ 238 Quentin Griffin AU D RC | 12.00 | 5.00 |
| ❏ 239 Kevin Garrett AU E RC | 10.00 | 4.00 |
| ❏ 240 Charles Tillman AU E RC | 20.00 | 8.00 |
| ❏ 241 Arnaz Battle AU D RC | 20.00 | 8.00 |
| ❏ 242 Brooks Bollinger AU E RC | 15.00 | 6.00 |
| ❏ 243 LaBrandon Toefield AU D RC | 12.00 | 5.00 |
| ❏ 244 Sam Aiken AU D RC | 12.00 | 5.00 |
| ❏ 245 Justin Gage AU D RC | 12.00 | 5.00 |
| ❏ 246 Gibran Hamdan AU D RC | 10.00 | 4.00 |

## 2004 Bowman Chrome

| | | | |
|---|---|---|---|
| ❏ COMP.SET w/o SP's (220) | 175.00 | 100.00 |
| ❏ COMP.SET w/o RC's (110) | 30.00 | 12.50 |
| ❏ ROOKIE AU/199 GROUP A ODDS 1:603 | | |
| ❏ ROOKIE AU/199 GROUP A ODDS 1:1293 | | |
| ❏ ROOKIE AU GROUP B ODDS 1:359 | | |
| ❏ ROOKIE AU GROUP D ODDS 1:21 | | |
| ❏ 1 Brett Favre | 2.50 | 1.00 |
| ❏ 2 Jay Fiedler | .60 | .25 |
| ❏ 3 Andre Davis | .60 | .25 |
| ❏ 4 Travis Henry | .75 | .30 |
| ❏ 5 Jimmy Smith | .75 | .30 |
| ❏ 6 Santana Moss | .75 | .30 |
| ❏ 7 Correll Buckhalter | .75 | .30 |
| ❏ 8 Randy Moss | 1.25 | .50 |
| ❏ 9 Edgerrin James | 1.00 | .40 |
| ❏ 10 Marc Bulger | .75 | .30 |
| ❏ 11 Derrick Mason | .75 | .30 |
| ❏ 12 Mark Brunell | .75 | .30 |
| ❏ 13 Donte Stallworth | .75 | .30 |
| ❏ 14 Deion Branch | .75 | .30 |
| ❏ 15 Jake Plummer | .75 | .30 |
| ❏ 16 Steve Smith | 1.00 | .40 |
| ❏ 17 Jon Kitna | .75 | .30 |
| ❏ 18 Andre Johnson | 1.00 | .40 |
| ❏ 19 A.J. Feeley | .75 | .30 |
| ❏ 20 Drew Bledsoe | 1.00 | .40 |
| ❏ 21 Antonio Bryant | .75 | .30 |
| ❏ 22 Reggie Wayne | .75 | .30 |
| ❏ 23 Thomas Jones | .75 | .30 |
| ❏ 24 Alge Crumpler | .75 | .30 |
| ❏ 25 Anquan Boldin | 1.00 | .40 |
| ❏ 26 Tim Rattay | .60 | .25 |
| ❏ 27 Charlie Garner | .75 | .30 |
| ❏ 28 James Thrash | .60 | .25 |
| ❏ 29 Koren Robinson | 1.00 | .40 |
| ❏ 30 Terrell Owens | 1.00 | .40 |
| ❏ 31 Amani Toomer | .75 | .30 |
| ❏ 32 Kelly Campbell | .60 | .25 |
| ❏ 33 Patrick Ramsey | .75 | .30 |
| ❏ 34 Plaxico Burress | .75 | .30 |
| ❏ 35 Chad Pennington | 1.00 | .40 |
| ❏ 36 Fred Taylor | .75 | .30 |
| ❏ 37 Domanick Davis | 1.00 | .40 |
| ❏ 38 DeShaun Foster | .75 | .30 |
| ❏ 39 T.J. Duckett | .75 | .30 |
| ❏ 40 Ahman Green | 1.00 | .40 |
| ❏ 41 Lee Suggs | 1.00 | .40 |
| ❏ 42 Tony Gonzalez | 1.00 | .40 |
| ❏ 43 Rich Gannon | .75 | .30 |
| ❏ 44 Kevan Barlow | .75 | .30 |
| ❏ 45 Torry Holt | 1.00 | .40 |
| ❏ 46 Aaron Brooks | .75 | .30 |
| ❏ 47 Tyrone Calico | .75 | .30 |
| ❏ 48 Keenan McCardell | .60 | .25 |
| ❏ 49 Hines Ward | 1.00 | .40 |
| ❏ 50 LaDainian Tomlinson | 1.50 | .60 |
| ❏ 51 Dante Hall | .75 | .30 |

| | | | |
|---|---|---|---|
| ❏ 52 Marcus Pollard | .60 | .25 |
| ❏ 53 Corey Dillon | .75 | .30 |
| ❏ 54 Justin McCareins | .60 | .25 |
| ❏ 55 Stephen Davis | .75 | .30 |
| ❏ 56 Jeff Garcia | 1.00 | .40 |
| ❏ 57 Ashley Lelie | .75 | .30 |
| ❏ 58 Javon Walker | .75 | .30 |
| ❏ 59 Kyle Boller | .75 | .30 |
| ❏ 60 Chad Johnson | .75 | .30 |
| ❏ 61 Anthony Thomas | .75 | .30 |
| ❏ 62 Byron Leftwich | .75 | .30 |
| ❏ 63 David Boston | .60 | .25 |
| ❏ 64 Onterrio Smith | .60 | .25 |
| ❏ 65 Deuce McAllister | 1.00 | .40 |
| ❏ 66 Antwaan Randle El | .75 | .30 |
| ❏ 67 Justin Fargas | .75 | .30 |
| ❏ 68 Laveranues Coles | .75 | .30 |
| ❏ 69 Quincy Morgan | .60 | .25 |
| ❏ 70 Priest Holmes | 1.00 | .40 |
| ❏ 71 Robert Ferguson | .60 | .25 |
| ❏ 72 Charles Rogers | .75 | .30 |
| ❏ 73 Drew Brees | 1.00 | .40 |
| ❏ 74 Matt Hasselbeck | 1.00 | .40 |
| ❏ 75 Peyton Manning | 2.00 | .75 |
| ❏ 76 Rudi Johnson | .75 | .30 |
| ❏ 77 Jake Delhomme | .75 | .30 |
| ❏ 78 Tiki Barber | 1.00 | .40 |
| ❏ 79 Brad Johnson | .75 | .30 |
| ❏ 80 Steve McNair | 1.00 | .40 |
| ❏ 81 Willis McGahee | 1.00 | .40 |
| ❏ 82 Josh McCown | .75 | .30 |
| ❏ 83 Garrison Hearst | .75 | .30 |
| ❏ 84 Quincy Carter | .60 | .25 |
| ❏ 85 Ricky Williams | 1.00 | .40 |
| ❏ 86 Trent Green | .75 | .30 |
| ❏ 87 Curtis Martin | 1.00 | .40 |
| ❏ 88 Jerry Porter | .75 | .30 |
| ❏ 89 Brian Westbrook | 1.00 | .40 |
| ❏ 90 Clinton Portis | 1.00 | .40 |
| ❏ 91 Eric Moulds | .75 | .30 |
| ❏ 92 Marcel Shipp | 1.00 | .40 |
| ❏ 93 Joey Harrington | .75 | .30 |
| ❏ 94 David Carr | .75 | .30 |
| ❏ 95 Marvin Harrison | 1.00 | .40 |
| ❏ 96 Joe Horn | .75 | .30 |
| ❏ 97 Chris Chambers | .75 | .30 |
| ❏ 98 Darrell Jackson | .75 | .30 |
| ❏ 99 Eddie George | .75 | .30 |
| ❏ 100 Donovan McNabb | 1.00 | .40 |
| ❏ 101 Marshall Faulk | 1.00 | .40 |
| ❏ 102 Rex Grossman | 1.00 | .40 |
| ❏ 103 Tai Streets | .60 | .25 |
| ❏ 104 Jeremy Shockey | .75 | .30 |
| ❏ 105 Jamal Lewis | .75 | .30 |
| ❏ 106 Tom Brady | 2.50 | 1.00 |
| ❏ 107 Shaun Alexander | 1.00 | .40 |
| ❏ 108 Carson Palmer | 1.25 | .50 |
| ❏ 109 Daunte Culpepper | 1.00 | .40 |
| ❏ 110 Michael Vick | 1.50 | .60 |
| ❏ 111 Roethlis AU/199 RC | 300.00 | 150.00 |
| ❏ 112 Tommie Harris RC | 4.00 | 1.50 |
| ❏ 113 Thomas Tapeh RC | 3.00 | 1.25 |
| ❏ 114 Matt Schaub RC | 12.00 | 5.00 |
| ❏ 115 Jonathan Smith RC | 2.50 | 1.00 |
| ❏ 116 Ricardo Colclough RC | 4.00 | 1.50 |
| ❏ 117 Jeff Dugan RC | 2.50 | 1.00 |
| ❏ 118 Larry Fitzgerald RC | 12.00 | 5.00 |
| ❏ 119 Gibril Wilson RC | 4.00 | 1.50 |
| ❏ 120 Sean Taylor RC | 4.00 | 1.50 |
| ❏ 121 Marquise Hill RC | 2.50 | 1.00 |
| ❏ 122 Cedric Cobbs RC | 3.00 | 1.25 |
| ❏ 123 Rich Gardner RC | 3.00 | 1.25 |
| ❏ 124 Chris Cooley RC | 4.00 | 1.50 |
| ❏ 125 Ben Troupe RC | 2.50 | 1.00 |
| ❏ 126 Antwan Odom RC | 3.00 | 1.25 |
| ❏ 127 Stuart Schweigert RC | 2.50 | 1.00 |
| ❏ 128 Derek Abney RC | 2.50 | 1.00 |
| ❏ 129 Keary Colbert RC | 4.00 | 1.50 |
| ❏ 130 Jeris McIntyre RC | 2.50 | 1.00 |
| ❏ 131 Matt Kranchick RC | 2.50 | 1.00 |
| ❏ 132 Rodney Leisle RC | 2.50 | 1.00 |
| ❏ 133 Vince Wilfork RC | 4.00 | 1.50 |
| ❏ 134 Darnell Dockett RC | 2.50 | 1.00 |
| ❏ 135 Jeremy LeSueur RC | 2.50 | 1.00 |

| | | | |
|---|---|---|---|
| ❏ 136 Gilbert Gardner RC | 2.50 | 1.00 |
| ❏ 137 Amon Gordon RC | 2.50 | 1.00 |
| ❏ 138 Darius Watts RC | 3.00 | 1.25 |
| ❏ 139 Junior Siavii RC | 2.50 | 1.00 |
| ❏ 140 Igor Olshansky RC | 4.00 | 1.50 |
| ❏ 141 Mewelde Moore RC | 4.00 | 1.50 |
| ❏ 142 Nathan Vasher RC | 4.00 | 1.50 |
| ❏ 143 Randy Starks RC | 2.50 | 1.00 |
| ❏ 144 Isaac Sopoaga RC | 2.50 | 1.00 |
| ❏ 145 Drew Henson RC | 2.50 | 1.00 |
| ❏ 146 Erik Coleman RC | 3.00 | 1.25 |
| ❏ 147 Robert Kent RC | 2.50 | 1.00 |
| ❏ 148 Jammal Lord RC | 2.50 | 1.00 |
| ❏ 149 Richard Seigler RC | 2.50 | 1.00 |
| ❏ 150 Niko Koutouvides RC | 2.50 | 1.00 |
| ❏ 151 Brandon Miree RC | 2.50 | 1.00 |
| ❏ 152 Dunta Robinson RC | 3.00 | 1.25 |
| ❏ 153 Courtney Anderson RC | 2.50 | 1.00 |
| ❏ 154 Bruce Perry RC | 2.50 | 1.00 |
| ❏ 155 Shaun Phillips RC | 2.50 | 1.00 |
| ❏ 156 Greg Jones RC | 4.00 | 1.50 |
| ❏ 157 Tank Johnson RC | 3.00 | 1.25 |
| ❏ 158 Dwan Edwards RC | 2.50 | 1.00 |
| ❏ 159 Julius Jones RC | 10.00 | 4.00 |
| ❏ 160 Chad Lavalais RC | 2.50 | 1.00 |
| ❏ 161 Tim Anderson RC | 3.00 | 1.25 |
| ❏ 162 Jarrett Payton RC | 3.00 | 1.25 |
| ❏ 163 Matt Ware RC | 4.00 | 1.50 |
| ❏ 164 DeAngelo Hall RC | 4.00 | 1.50 |
| ❏ 165 Ben Hartsock RC | 2.50 | 1.00 |
| ❏ 166 Keith Smith RC | 2.50 | 1.00 |
| ❏ 167 Michael Jenkins RC | 4.00 | 1.50 |
| ❏ 168 Quincy Wilson RC | 3.00 | 1.25 |
| ❏ 169 Dontarrious Thomas RC | 3.00 | 1.25 |
| ❏ 170 Tony Hargrove RC | 2.50 | 1.00 |
| ❏ 171 Ben Watson RC | 4.00 | 1.50 |
| ❏ 172 Triandos Luke RC | 2.50 | 1.00 |
| ❏ 173 Kellen Winslow RC | 8.00 | 3.00 |
| ❏ 174 Patrick Crayton RC | 5.00 | 2.00 |
| ❏ 175 Devard Darling RC | 2.50 | 1.00 |
| ❏ 176 Shawntae Spencer RC | 2.50 | 1.00 |
| ❏ 177 Will Smith RC | 3.00 | 1.25 |
| ❏ 178 Darrion Scott RC | 3.00 | 1.25 |
| ❏ 179 Wes Welker RC | 10.00 | 4.00 |
| ❏ 180 Ryan Dinwiddie RC | 2.50 | 1.00 |
| ❏ 181 Rod Davis RC | 2.50 | 1.00 |
| ❏ 182 Casey Clausen RC | 3.00 | 1.25 |
| ❏ 183 Clarence Moore RC | 2.50 | 1.00 |
| ❏ 184 D.J. Hackett RC | 4.00 | 1.50 |
| ❏ 185 Devery Henderson RC | 4.00 | 1.50 |
| ❏ 186 Sean Jones RC | 3.00 | 1.25 |
| ❏ 187 Bruce Thornton RC | 2.50 | 1.00 |
| ❏ 188 Tatum Bell RC | 4.00 | 1.50 |
| ❏ 189 Tim Euhus RC | 2.50 | 1.00 |
| ❏ 190 John Standeford RC | 2.50 | 1.00 |
| ❏ 191 Reggie Torbor RC | 2.50 | 1.00 |
| ❏ 192 Rashaun Woods RC | 2.50 | 1.00 |
| ❏ 193 Jason Shivers RC | 2.50 | 1.00 |
| ❏ 194 Ahmad Carroll RC | 4.00 | 1.50 |
| ❏ 195 Keyaron Fox RC | 3.00 | 1.25 |
| ❏ 196 Von Hutchins RC | 2.50 | 1.00 |
| ❏ 197 Marcus Tubbs RC | 2.50 | 1.00 |
| ❏ 198 Daryl Smith RC | 3.00 | 1.25 |
| ❏ 199 Robert Gallery RC | 4.00 | 1.50 |
| ❏ 200 Marquis Cooper RC | 4.00 | 1.50 |
| ❏ 201 Bernard Berrian RC | 4.00 | 1.50 |
| ❏ 202 Derrick Strait RC | 2.50 | 1.00 |
| ❏ 203 Travis LaBoy RC | 3.00 | 1.25 |
| ❏ 204 Caleb Miller RC | 2.50 | 1.00 |
| ❏ 205 Michael Clayton RC | 4.00 | 1.50 |
| ❏ 206 Will Poole RC | 2.50 | 1.00 |
| ❏ 207 Derrick Hamilton RC | 2.50 | 1.00 |
| ❏ 208 Glenn Earl RC | 2.50 | 1.00 |
| ❏ 209 Donnell Washington RC | 3.00 | 1.25 |
| ❏ 210 Nate Lawrie RC | 2.50 | 1.00 |
| ❏ 211 Keiwan Ratliff RC | 2.50 | 1.00 |
| ❏ 212 Luke McCown RC | 3.00 | 1.25 |
| ❏ 213 Joey Thomas RC | 2.50 | 1.00 |
| ❏ 214 Shawn Andrews RC | 3.00 | 1.25 |
| ❏ 215 Derrick Ward RC | 4.00 | 1.50 |
| ❏ 216 Reggie Williams RC | 4.00 | 1.50 |
| ❏ 217 Rod Rutherford RC | 2.50 | 1.00 |
| ❏ 218 Michael Gaines RC | 2.50 | 1.00 |
| ❏ 219 Will Allen RC | 3.00 | 1.25 |

| | | | |
|---|---|---|---|
| ❑ 220 J.P. Losman RC | 5.00 | 2.00 |
| ❑ 221 Roy Williams AU/199 RC | 80.00 | 40.00 |
| ❑ 222 Kevin Jones AU/199 RC | 50.00 | 20.00 |
| ❑ 223 Philip Rivers AU/199 RC | 200.00 | 100.00 |
| ❑ 224 Steven Jackson AU/199 RC | 200.00 | 100.00 |
| ❑ 225 Eli Manning AU/199 RC | 250.00 | 125.00 |
| ❑ 226 Cody Pickett AU D RC | 12.00 | 5.00 |
| ❑ 227 P.K. Sam AU D RC | 10.00 | 4.00 |
| ❑ 228 Maurice Mann AU D RC | 10.00 | 4.00 |
| ❑ 229 Andy Hall AU D RC | 12.00 | 5.00 |
| ❑ 230 Chris Perry AU D RC | 15.00 | 6.00 |
| ❑ 231 Ernest Wilford AU C RC | 15.00 | 6.00 |
| ❑ 232 Kenechi Udeze AU D RC | 15.00 | 6.00 |
| ❑ 233 Michael Boulware AU D RC | 15.00 | 6.00 |
| ❑ 234 B.J. Symons AU D RC | 10.00 | 4.00 |
| ❑ 235 Jared Lorenzen AU D RC | 12.00 | 5.00 |
| ❑ 236 Matt Mauck AU D RC | 12.00 | 5.00 |
| ❑ 237 Carlos Francis AU D RC | 10.00 | 4.00 |
| ❑ 238 Michael Turner AU D RC | 50.00 | 25.00 |
| ❑ 239 Lee Evans AU B RC | 40.00 | 20.00 |
| ❑ 240 Jerricho Cotchery AU D RC | 20.00 | 10.00 |
| ❑ 241 John Navarre AU D RC | 12.00 | 5.00 |
| ❑ 242 Jonathan Vilma AU D RC | 25.00 | 7.50 |
| ❑ 243 Josh Harris AU D RC | 10.00 | 4.00 |
| ❑ 244 Jeff Smoker AU C RC | 12.00 | 5.00 |
| ❑ 245 Jamaar Taylor AU D RC | 10.00 | 4.00 |

## 2005 Bowman Chrome

| | | |
|---|---|---|
| ❑ COMP.SET w/o AU's (220) | 100.00 | 40.00 |
| ❑ COMP.SET w/o RC's (170) | 30.00 | 12.50 |
| ❑ ROOK.AU GROUP A ODDS 1,381 H, 1:1011 R | | |
| ❑ ROOK.AU GROUP B ODDS 1:156 H, 1,449 R | | |
| ❑ ROOK.AU GROUP C ODDS 1,318 H, 1,899 R | | |
| ❑ ROOK.AU GROUP D ODDS 1,296 H, 1,899 R | | |
| ❑ ROOK.AU GROUP E ODDS 1,281 H, 1,809 R | | |
| ❑ ROOK.AU GROUP F ODDS 1,132 H, 404 R | | |
| ❑ ROOK.AU GROUP G ODDS 1:39 H, 1:108 R | | |
| ❑ ROOKIE AU/199 ODDS 1,685 H, 1:1348 R | | |
| ❑ UNPRICED PRINT.PLATE 1/1 ODDS 1,975 H | | |
| ❑ 1 Peyton Manning | 1.50 | .60 |
| ❑ 2 Priest Holmes | 1.00 | .40 |
| ❑ 3 Anquan Boldin | .75 | .30 |
| ❑ 4 Michael Vick | 1.00 | .40 |
| ❑ 5 Drew Brees | .75 | .30 |
| ❑ 6 Terrell Owens | 1.00 | .40 |
| ❑ 7 Curtis Martin | 1.00 | .40 |
| ❑ 8 Tom Brady | 2.00 | .75 |
| ❑ 9 Maurice Carthon CO | .60 | .25 |
| ❑ 10 Brett Favre | 2.50 | 1.00 |
| ❑ 11 Marshall Faulk | 1.00 | .40 |
| ❑ 12 Corey Dillon | .75 | .30 |
| ❑ 13 Julius Jones | 1.00 | .40 |
| ❑ 14 Jamal Lewis | .75 | .30 |
| ❑ 15 Keary Colbert | .60 | .25 |
| ❑ 16 Joey Harrington | 1.00 | .40 |
| ❑ 17 Domanick Davis | .60 | .25 |
| ❑ 18 Eli Manning | 2.00 | .75 |
| ❑ 19 Brad Childress CO | .75 | .30 |
| ❑ 20 Steve McNair | 1.00 | .40 |
| ❑ 21 Plaxico Burress | .75 | .30 |
| ❑ 22 Chad Pennington | 1.00 | .40 |
| ❑ 23 Patrick Ramsey | .75 | .30 |
| ❑ 24 Brian Griese | .75 | .30 |
| ❑ 25 Matt Hasselbeck | .75 | .30 |
| ❑ 26 Chris Chambers | .75 | .30 |
| ❑ 27 Marc Bulger | .75 | .30 |
| ❑ 28 Jake Delhomme | 1.00 | .40 |
| ❑ 29 Shaun Alexander | 1.00 | .40 |

| | | |
|---|---|---|
| ❑ 30 Laveranues Coles | .75 | .30 |
| ❑ 31 A.J. Feeley | .60 | .30 |
| ❑ 32 Ashley Lelie | .60 | .25 |
| ❑ 33 Deuce McAllister | 1.00 | .40 |
| ❑ 34 Chris Brown | .75 | .30 |
| ❑ 35 Nate Burleson | .75 | .30 |
| ❑ 36 Darrell Jackson | .75 | .30 |
| ❑ 37 Lee Evans | .75 | .30 |
| ❑ 38 Jeremy Shockey | 1.00 | .40 |
| ❑ 39 Muhsin Muhammad | .75 | .30 |
| ❑ 40 Deion Branch | .75 | .30 |
| ❑ 41 DeShaun Foster | .75 | .30 |
| ❑ 42 Reggie Wayne | .75 | .30 |
| ❑ 43 Michael Jenkins | .75 | .30 |
| ❑ 44 Andre Johnson | .75 | .30 |
| ❑ 45 Javon Walker | .75 | .30 |
| ❑ 46 Joe Horn | .75 | .30 |
| ❑ 47 Fred Taylor | 1.00 | .40 |
| ❑ 48 Tony Gonzalez | .75 | .30 |
| ❑ 49 J.P. Losman | 1.00 | .40 |
| ❑ 50 Clinton Portis | 1.00 | .40 |
| ❑ 51 Randy Moss | 1.00 | .40 |
| ❑ 52 Jake Plummer | .75 | .30 |
| ❑ 53 Tiki Barber | 1.00 | .40 |
| ❑ 54 Edgerrin James | .75 | .30 |
| ❑ 55 Jerome Bettis | 1.00 | .40 |
| ❑ 56 Brandon Lloyd | .60 | .25 |
| ❑ 57 Romeo Crennel CO | 1.00 | .40 |
| ❑ 58 Antonio Gates | 1.00 | .40 |
| ❑ 59 Donovan McNabb | 1.00 | .40 |
| ❑ 60 Drew Bennett | .75 | .30 |
| ❑ 61 David Carr | .75 | .30 |
| ❑ 62 Trent Green | .75 | .30 |
| ❑ 63 Drew Bledsoe | 1.00 | .40 |
| ❑ 64 Donte Stallworth | .75 | .30 |
| ❑ 65 Alge Crumpler | .75 | .30 |
| ❑ 66 Jason Witten | .75 | .30 |
| ❑ 67 Thomas Jones | .75 | .30 |
| ❑ 68 Rex Grossman | 1.00 | .40 |
| ❑ 69 LaMont Jordan | .75 | .30 |
| ❑ 70 Kurt Warner | 1.00 | .40 |
| ❑ 71 Ahman Green | 1.00 | .40 |
| ❑ 72 Ben Roethlisberger | 2.50 | 1.00 |
| ❑ 73 Mike Nolan CO | .75 | .30 |
| ❑ 74 Brian Westbrook | 1.00 | .40 |
| ❑ 75 Carson Palmer | 1.00 | .40 |
| ❑ 76 Stephen Davis | .75 | .30 |
| ❑ 77 Jonathan Vilma | .75 | .30 |
| ❑ 78 Willis McGahee | 1.00 | .40 |
| ❑ 79 Rudi Johnson | .75 | .30 |
| ❑ 80 Jerry Porter | .75 | .30 |
| ❑ 81 Charles Rogers | .60 | .25 |
| ❑ 82 Dwight Freeney | .75 | .30 |
| ❑ 83 Tim Lewis CO | .60 | .25 |
| ❑ 84 Aaron Brooks | .60 | .25 |
| ❑ 85 Kyle Boller | .75 | .30 |
| ❑ 86 Isaac Bruce | .75 | .30 |
| ❑ 87 Chad Johnson | 1.00 | .40 |
| ❑ 88 Kevin Jones | .75 | .30 |
| ❑ 89 Eric Moulds | .75 | .30 |
| ❑ 90 Sean Taylor | .75 | .30 |
| ❑ 91 Chris Perry | .60 | .25 |
| ❑ 92 Kerry Collins | .75 | .30 |
| ❑ 93 Steven Jackson | 1.25 | .50 |
| ❑ 94 LaDainian Tomlinson | 1.50 | .60 |
| ❑ 95 Torry Holt | .75 | .30 |
| ❑ 96 Lee Suggs | .75 | .30 |
| ❑ 97 Santana Moss | .75 | .30 |
| ❑ 98 Hines Ward | 1.00 | .40 |
| ❑ 99 Daunte Culpepper | 1.00 | .40 |
| ❑ 100 Travis Henry | .75 | .30 |
| ❑ 101 Ricky Williams | .75 | .30 |
| ❑ 102 Ricky Williams WR | 1.00 | .40 |
| ❑ 103 Tatum Bell | .75 | .30 |
| ❑ 104 Dante Hall | .75 | .30 |
| ❑ 105 Larry Fitzgerald | 1.00 | .40 |
| ❑ 106 Marvin Harrison | 1.00 | .40 |
| ❑ 107 Byron Leftwich | .75 | .30 |
| ❑ 108 T.J. Houshmandzadeh | .75 | .30 |
| ❑ 109 Michael Clayton | .75 | .30 |
| ❑ 110 Ted Cottrell CO | .60 | .25 |
| ❑ 111 Carlos Rogers RC | 3.00 | 1.25 |
| ❑ 112 Kyle Orton RC | 4.00 | 1.50 |
| ❑ 113 Marion Barber RC | 10.00 | 4.00 |

| | | |
|---|---|---|
| ❑ 114 Mark Bradley RC | 3.00 | 1.25 |
| ❑ 115 Travis Johnson RC | 2.00 | .75 |
| ❑ 116 Antrel Rolle RC | 3.00 | 1.25 |
| ❑ 117 Jason Campbell RC | 6.00 | 2.50 |
| ❑ 118 Justin Miller RC | 2.50 | 1.00 |
| ❑ 119 J.J. Arrington RC | 3.00 | 1.25 |
| ❑ 120 Marcus Spears RC | 3.00 | 1.25 |
| ❑ 121 Vincent Jackson RC | 2.50 | 1.00 |
| ❑ 122 Erasmus James RC | 2.50 | 1.00 |
| ❑ 123 Heath Miller RC | 6.00 | 2.50 |
| ❑ 124 Eric Shelton RC | 2.50 | 1.00 |
| ❑ 125 Cedric Benson RC | 3.00 | 1.25 |
| ❑ 126 Mark Clayton RC | 3.00 | 1.25 |
| ❑ 127 Anthony Davis RC | 2.50 | 1.00 |
| ❑ 128 Charlie Frye RC | 3.00 | 1.25 |
| ❑ 129 Fred Gibson RC | 2.50 | 1.00 |
| ❑ 130 Reggie Brown RC | 3.00 | 1.25 |
| ❑ 131 Andrew Walter RC | 3.00 | 1.25 |
| ❑ 132 Adam Jones RC | 3.00 | 1.25 |
| ❑ 133 David Greene RC | 2.50 | 1.00 |
| ❑ 134 Maurice Clarett RC | 2.50 | 1.00 |
| ❑ 135 Roscoe Parrish RC | 2.50 | 1.00 |
| ❑ 136 Chris Henry RC | 3.00 | 1.25 |
| ❑ 137 Mike Nugent RC | 2.50 | 1.00 |
| ❑ 138 Kevin Burnett RC | 2.50 | 1.00 |
| ❑ 139 Matt Roth RC | 2.50 | 1.00 |
| ❑ 140 Barrett Ruud RC | 3.00 | 1.25 |
| ❑ 141 Kirk Morrison RC | 2.50 | 1.00 |
| ❑ 142 Brock Berlin RC | 2.50 | 1.00 |
| ❑ 143 Bryant McFadden RC | 2.50 | 1.00 |
| ❑ 144 Scott Starks RC | 2.50 | 1.00 |
| ❑ 145 Stanford Routt RC | 2.50 | 1.00 |
| ❑ 146 Oshiomogho Atogwe RC | 2.00 | .75 |
| ❑ 147 Jovan Witherspoon RC | 2.00 | .75 |
| ❑ 148 Boomer Grigsby RC | 3.00 | 1.25 |
| ❑ 149 Lance Mitchell RC | 2.50 | 1.00 |
| ❑ 150 Darryl Blackstock RC | 2.00 | .75 |
| ❑ 151 Ellis Hobbs RC | 3.00 | 1.25 |
| ❑ 152 James Kilian RC | 2.00 | .75 |
| ❑ 153 Willie Parker RC | 3.00 | 1.25 |
| ❑ 154 Justin Tuck RC | 4.00 | 1.50 |
| ❑ 155 Luis Castillo RC | 3.00 | 1.25 |
| ❑ 156 Paris Warren RC | 2.50 | 1.00 |
| ❑ 157 Corey Webster RC | 3.00 | 1.25 |
| ❑ 158 Tab Perry RC | 2.50 | 1.00 |
| ❑ 159 Rian Wallace RC | 2.50 | 1.00 |
| ❑ 160 Joel Dreessen RC | 2.50 | 1.00 |
| ❑ 161 Khalif Barnes RC | 2.00 | .75 |
| ❑ 162 David Pollack RC | 2.50 | 1.00 |
| ❑ 163 Zach Tuiasosopo RC | 2.00 | .75 |
| ❑ 164 Ryan Riddle RC | 2.00 | .75 |
| ❑ 165 Travis Daniels RC | 2.50 | 1.00 |
| ❑ 166 Eric King RC | 2.00 | .75 |
| ❑ 167 Jason Brown RC | 3.00 | 1.25 |
| ❑ 168 Manuel White RC | 2.50 | 1.00 |
| ❑ 169 Jordan Beck RC | 2.50 | 1.00 |
| ❑ 170 Lofa Tatupu RC | 4.00 | 1.50 |
| ❑ 171 Will Peoples RC | 2.50 | 1.00 |
| ❑ 172 Chad Friehauf RC | 2.50 | 1.00 |
| ❑ 173 Brady Poppinga RC | 3.00 | 1.25 |
| ❑ 174 Anttaj Hawthorne RC | 2.50 | 1.00 |
| ❑ 175 Nick Collins RC | 3.00 | 1.25 |
| ❑ 176 Craig Ochs RC | 2.50 | 1.00 |
| ❑ 177 Billy Bajema RC | 2.00 | .75 |
| ❑ 178 Jon Goldsberry RC | 2.50 | 1.00 |
| ❑ 179 Jared Newberry RC | 2.50 | 1.00 |
| ❑ 180 Odell Thurman RC | 3.00 | 1.25 |
| ❑ 181 Kelvin Hayden RC | 2.50 | 1.00 |
| ❑ 182 Jamaal Brimmer RC | 2.00 | .75 |
| ❑ 183 Jonathan Babineaux RC | 2.50 | 1.00 |
| ❑ 184 Bo Scaife RC | 2.50 | 1.00 |
| ❑ 185 Bryan Randall RC | 2.50 | 1.00 |
| ❑ 186 James Butler RC | 2.50 | 1.00 |
| ❑ 187 Harry Williams RC | 2.50 | 1.00 |
| ❑ 188 Leroy Hill RC | 3.00 | 1.25 |
| ❑ 189 Josh Bullocks RC | 3.00 | 1.25 |
| ❑ 190 Alfred Fincher RC | 2.50 | 1.00 |
| ❑ 191 Antonio Perkins RC | 2.50 | 1.00 |
| ❑ 192 Bobby Purify RC | 2.50 | 1.00 |
| ❑ 193 Darrent Williams RC | 3.00 | 1.25 |
| ❑ 194 Darian Durant RC | 3.00 | 1.25 |
| ❑ 195 Fred Amey RC | 2.50 | 1.00 |
| ❑ 196 Ronald Bartell RC | 2.50 | 1.00 |
| ❑ 197 Kerry Rhodes RC | 2.50 | 1.25 |

| | | |
|---|---|---|
| ❑ 198 Jerome Carter RC | 2.00 | .75 |
| ❑ 199 Roddy White RC | 4.00 | 1.50 |
| ❑ 200 Nehemiah Broughton RC | 2.50 | 1.00 |
| ❑ 201 Keron Henry RC | 2.00 | .75 |
| ❑ 202 Jerome Collins RC | 2.50 | 1.00 |
| ❑ 203 Trent Cole RC | 3.00 | 1.25 |
| ❑ 204 Alphonso Hodge RC | 2.00 | .75 |
| ❑ 205 Marviel Underwood RC | 2.50 | 1.00 |
| ❑ 206 Marlin Jackson RC | 2.50 | 1.00 |
| ❑ 207 Madison Hedgecock RC | 3.00 | 1.25 |
| ❑ 208 Chris Spencer RC | 3.00 | 1.25 |
| ❑ 209 Vincent Fuller RC | 2.50 | 1.00 |
| ❑ 210 Marcus Maxwell RC | 2.00 | .75 |
| ❑ 211 Dustin Fox RC | 3.00 | 1.25 |
| ❑ 212 Timmy Chang RC | 2.50 | 1.00 |
| ❑ 213 Walter Reyes RC | 2.00 | .75 |
| ❑ 214 Donte Nicholson RC | 2.50 | 1.00 |
| ❑ 215 Stanley Wilson RC | 2.50 | 1.00 |
| ❑ 216 Dan Cody RC | 3.00 | 1.25 |
| ❑ 217 Alex Barron RC | 2.00 | .75 |
| ❑ 218 Taylor Stubblefield RC | 2.00 | .75 |
| ❑ 219 Shaun Cody RC | 2.50 | 1.00 |
| ❑ 220 Steve Savoy RC | 2.00 | .75 |
| ❑ 221 Aaron Rodgers AU/199 RC | 150.00 | 90.00 |
| ❑ 222 Alex Smith QB AU/199 RC | 120.00 | 60.00 |
| ❑ 223 Bray.Edwards AU/199 RC | 150.00 | 75.00 |
| ❑ 224 Cadill.Williams AU/199 RC | 80.00 | 40.00 |
| ❑ 225 Mike Williams AU/199 | 40.00 | 15.00 |
| ❑ 226 Ronnie Brown AU/199 RC | 120.00 | 50.00 |
| ❑ 227 T.Williamson AU/199 RC | 40.00 | 15.00 |
| ❑ 228 Dante Ridgeway AU B RC | 10.00 | 4.00 |
| ❑ 229 Channing Crowder AU G RC | 12.00 | 5.00 |
| ❑ 230 Chase Lyman AU E RC | 10.00 | 4.00 |
| ❑ 231 Courtney Roby AU F RC | 12.00 | 5.00 |
| ❑ 232 Damien Nash AU G RC | 12.00 | 5.00 |
| ❑ 233 Dan Orlovsky AU C RC | 15.00 | 6.00 |
| ❑ 234 Fabian Washington AU B RC | 15.00 | 6.00 |
| ❑ 235 Shawne Merriman AU B RC | 40.00 | 20.00 |
| ❑ 236 Cedric Houston AU G RC | 15.00 | 6.00 |
| ❑ 237 Alex Smith TE AU D RC | 15.00 | 6.00 |
| ❑ 238 Brandon Jones AU B RC | 15.00 | 6.00 |
| ❑ 239 Alvin Pearman AU G RC | 12.00 | 5.00 |
| ❑ 240 Derek Anderson AU C RC | 40.00 | 25.00 |
| ❑ 241 J.R. Russell AU G RC | 10.00 | 4.00 |
| ❑ 242 Jerome Mathis AU F RC | 15.00 | 6.00 |
| ❑ 243 Josh Davis AU A RC | 10.00 | 4.00 |
| ❑ 244 Kay-Jay Harris AU G RC | 12.00 | 5.00 |
| ❑ 245 Rasheed Marshall AU F RC | 12.00 | 5.00 |
| ❑ 246 Matt Jones AU/199 RC | 60.00 | 25.00 |
| ❑ 247 Chad Owens AU G RC | 15.00 | 6.00 |
| ❑ 248 Larry Brackins AU A RC | 10.00 | 4.00 |
| ❑ 249 Matt Cassel AU G RC | 50.00 | 25.00 |
| ❑ 250 Noah Herron AU G RC | 15.00 | 6.00 |
| ❑ 251 Roydell Williams AU G RC | 12.00 | 5.00 |
| ❑ 252 Ryan Fitzpatrick AU F RC | 15.00 | 6.00 |
| ❑ 253 Derrick Johnson AU E RC | 15.00 | 6.00 |
| ❑ 254 DeMarcus Ware AU D RC | 30.00 | 15.00 |
| ❑ 255 Brandon Jacobs AU A RC | 50.00 | 25.00 |
| ❑ 256 Craig Bragg AU G RC | 10.00 | 4.00 |
| ❑ 257 Ryan Moats AU G RC | 15.00 | 6.00 |
| ❑ 258 Stefan LeFors AU G RC | 12.00 | 5.00 |
| ❑ 259 Frank Gore AU B RC | 60.00 | 30.00 |
| ❑ DSB Bogut/A.Smith QB AU/100 | 120.00 | 60.00 |

## 2006 Bowman Chrome

| | | |
|---|---|---|
| ❑ 1 Devin Aromashodu RC | 1.50 | .60 |
| ❑ 2 Daniel Bullocks RC | 2.00 | .75 |
| ❑ 3 Winston Justice RC | 2.00 | .75 |
| ❑ 4 Lawrence Vickers RC | 1.50 | .60 |
| ❑ 5 Bernard Pollard RC | 1.50 | .60 |
| ❑ 6 Abdul Hodge RC | 2.00 | .75 |
| ❑ 7 Jovon Bouknight RC | 1.50 | .60 |
| ❑ 8 Wali Lundy RC | 2.00 | .75 |
| ❑ 9 Jonathan Orr RC | 1.50 | .60 |
| ❑ 10 Gerald Riggs RC | 2.00 | .75 |
| ❑ 11 Chris Gocong RC | 1.50 | .60 |
| ❑ 12 David Kirtman RC | 1.50 | .60 |
| ❑ 13 Quinn Sypniewski RC | 1.50 | .60 |
| ❑ 14 Richard Marshall RC | 1.50 | .60 |
| ❑ 15 Darryl Tapp RC | 1.50 | .60 |
| ❑ 16 Charles Davis RC | 1.50 | .60 |
| ❑ 17 Tim Massaquoi RC | 1.50 | .60 |
| ❑ 18 DeMario Minter RC | 1.50 | .60 |
| ❑ 19 Hank Baskett RC | 2.00 | .75 |
| ❑ 20 Andre Hall RC | 2.00 | .75 |
| ❑ 21 Cody Hodges RC | 1.50 | .60 |
| ❑ 22 Greg Lee RC | 1.50 | .60 |
| ❑ 23 Danieal Manning RC | 2.00 | .75 |
| ❑ 24 Jason Hatcher RC | 1.50 | .60 |
| ❑ 25 Ben Obomanu RC | 1.50 | .60 |
| ❑ 26 Dusty Dvoracek RC | 2.00 | .75 |
| ❑ 27 Domenik Hixon RC | 2.50 | 1.00 |
| ❑ 28 Josh Betts RC | 1.50 | .60 |
| ❑ 29 Marques Colston RC | 5.00 | 2.00 |
| ❑ 30 P.J. Pope RC | 2.00 | .75 |
| ❑ 31 Gabe Watson RC | 1.50 | .60 |
| ❑ 32 Alan Zemaitis RC | 2.00 | .75 |
| ❑ 33 Jeff King RC | 1.50 | .60 |
| ❑ 34 Damien Rhodes RC | 1.50 | .60 |
| ❑ 35 Orien Harris RC | 1.50 | .60 |
| ❑ 36 David Anderson RC | 1.50 | .60 |
| ❑ 37 Garrett Mills RC | 2.00 | .75 |
| ❑ 38 Anthony Schlegel RC | 1.50 | .60 |
| ❑ 39 Omar Gaither RC | 1.50 | .60 |
| ❑ 40 Freddie Keiaho RC | 1.50 | .60 |
| ❑ 41 J.J. Outlaw RC | 1.50 | .60 |
| ❑ 42 Tony Scheffler RC | 2.00 | .75 |
| ❑ 43 Dee Webb RC | 1.50 | .60 |
| ❑ 44 Drew Olson RC | 1.50 | .60 |
| ❑ 45 Martin Nance RC | 1.50 | .60 |
| ❑ 46 Ko Simpson RC | 1.50 | .60 |
| ❑ 47 Jesse Mahelona RC | 1.50 | .60 |
| ❑ 48 Owen Daniels RC | 2.00 | .75 |
| ❑ 49 Delanie Walker RC | 1.50 | .60 |
| ❑ 50 Eric Smith RC | 1.50 | .60 |
| ❑ 51 Darrell Hackney RC | 1.50 | .60 |
| ❑ 52 Freddie Roach RC | 1.50 | .60 |
| ❑ 53 James Anderson RC | 1.25 | .50 |
| ❑ 54 Anthony Smith RC | 2.00 | .75 |
| ❑ 55 Gerris Wilkinson RC | 1.25 | .50 |
| ❑ 56 Tamba Hali RC | 4.00 | 1.50 |
| ❑ 57 Jerome Harrison RC | 4.00 | 1.50 |
| ❑ 58 Jason Allen RC | 4.00 | 1.50 |
| ❑ 59 Brodrick Bunkley RC | 4.00 | 1.50 |
| ❑ 60 Bobby Carpenter RC | 4.00 | 1.50 |
| ❑ 61 Johnathan Joseph RC | 3.00 | 1.25 |
| ❑ 62 Travis Wilson RC | 4.00 | 1.50 |
| ❑ 63 Reggie McNeal RC | 3.00 | 1.25 |
| ❑ 64 Haloti Ngata RC | 4.00 | 1.50 |
| ❑ 65 Manny Lawson RC | 4.00 | 1.50 |
| ❑ 66 Donte Whitner RC | 4.00 | 1.50 |
| ❑ 67 Derek Hagan RC | 4.00 | 1.50 |
| ❑ 68 Devin Hester RC | 8.00 | 3.00 |
| ❑ 69 Jeremy Bloom RC | 3.00 | 1.25 |
| ❑ 70 Ashton Youboty RC | 4.00 | 1.50 |
| ❑ 71 Kamerion Wimbley RC | 4.00 | 1.50 |
| ❑ 72 Charlie Whitehurst RC | 4.00 | 1.50 |
| ❑ 73 Darnell Bing RC | 4.00 | 1.50 |
| ❑ 74 Adam Jennings RC | 3.00 | 1.25 |
| ❑ 75 Tim Day RC | 3.00 | 1.25 |
| ❑ 76 Jeff Webb RC | 3.00 | 1.25 |
| ❑ 77 D.J. Shockley RC | 4.00 | 1.50 |
| ❑ 78 Marcus Vick RC | 3.00 | 1.25 |
| ❑ 79 Thomas Howard RC | 4.00 | 1.50 |
| ❑ 80 Todd Watkins RC | 3.00 | 1.25 |
| ❑ 81 Davin Joseph RC | 3.00 | 1.25 |
| ❑ 82 Pat Watkins RC | 4.00 | 1.50 |
| ❑ 83 Jon Alston RC | 4.00 | 1.50 |
| ❑ 84 Ernie Sims RC | 4.00 | 1.50 |
| ❑ 85 D'Qwell Jackson RC | 3.00 | 1.25 |
| ❑ 86 Corey Bramlet RC | 3.00 | 1.25 |
| ❑ 87 Antonio Cromartie RC | 4.00 | 1.50 |
| ❑ 88 A.J. Nicholson RC | 2.50 | 1.00 |
| ❑ 89 Kevin McMahan RC | 3.00 | 1.25 |
| ❑ 90 J.D. Runnels RC | 3.00 | 1.25 |
| ❑ 91 Nate Salley RC | 3.00 | 1.25 |
| ❑ 92 Matt Shelton RC | 4.00 | 1.50 |
| ❑ 93 Brett Basanez RC | 4.00 | 1.50 |
| ❑ 94 Rocky McIntosh RC | 4.00 | 1.50 |
| ❑ 95 Anthony Mix RC | 3.00 | 1.25 |
| ❑ 96 Jimmy Williams RC | 4.00 | 1.50 |
| ❑ 97 Marcus McNeill RC | 3.00 | 1.25 |
| ❑ 98 DeMeco Ryans RC | 5.00 | 2.00 |
| ❑ 99 Dwayne Slay RC | 3.00 | 1.25 |
| ❑ 100 John David Washington RC | 3.00 | 1.25 |
| ❑ 101 P.J. Daniels RC | 3.00 | 1.25 |
| ❑ 102 Kelly Jennings RC | 4.00 | 1.50 |
| ❑ 103 John McCargo RC | 3.00 | 1.25 |
| ❑ 104 Paul Pinegar RC | 3.00 | 1.25 |
| ❑ 105 Ray Edwards RC | 3.00 | 1.25 |
| ❑ 106 Elvis Dumervil RC | 2.50 | 1.00 |
| ❑ 107 Travis Lulay RC | 3.00 | 1.25 |
| ❑ 108 Bennie Brazell RC | 3.00 | 1.25 |
| ❑ 109 Dominique Byrd RC | 3.00 | 1.25 |
| ❑ 110 Nick Mangold RC | 3.00 | 1.25 |
| ❑ 111 Plaxico Burress | .75 | .30 |
| ❑ 112 Shaun Alexander | 1.00 | .40 |
| ❑ 113 Muhsin Muhammad | .75 | .30 |
| ❑ 114 Jake Plummer | .75 | .30 |
| ❑ 115 Deuce McAllister | .75 | .30 |
| ❑ 116 T.J. Houshmandzadeh | .75 | .30 |
| ❑ 117 Carson Palmer | 1.00 | .40 |
| ❑ 118 Willis McGahee | 1.00 | .40 |
| ❑ 119 Terrell Owens | 1.00 | .40 |
| ❑ 120 Fred Taylor | .75 | .30 |
| ❑ 121 Dante Hall | .75 | .30 |
| ❑ 122 Brad Johnson | .75 | .30 |
| ❑ 123 Reggie Wayne | .75 | .30 |
| ❑ 124 DeShaun Foster | .75 | .30 |
| ❑ 125 Tony Gonzalez | .75 | .30 |
| ❑ 126 Javon Walker | .75 | .30 |
| ❑ 127 Marc Bulger | .75 | .30 |
| ❑ 128 LaDainian Tomlinson | 1.25 | .50 |
| ❑ 129 Byron Leftwich | .75 | .30 |
| ❑ 130 Dwight Freeney | .75 | .30 |
| ❑ 131 Kevin Jones | 1.00 | .40 |
| ❑ 132 Hines Ward | 1.00 | .40 |
| ❑ 133 Randy Moss | 1.00 | .40 |
| ❑ 134 Edgerrin James | .75 | .30 |
| ❑ 135 Ahman Green | .75 | .30 |
| ❑ 136 Steven Jackson | 1.00 | .40 |
| ❑ 137 Ben Roethlisberger | 1.50 | .60 |
| ❑ 138 Daunte Culpepper | 1.00 | .40 |
| ❑ 139 Santana Moss | .75 | .30 |
| ❑ 140 Jonathan Vilma | .75 | .30 |
| ❑ 141 Gary Kubiak CO | .60 | .25 |
| ❑ 142 Marvin Harrison | 1.00 | .40 |
| ❑ 143 Trent Green | .75 | .30 |
| ❑ 144 Chris Chambers | .75 | .30 |
| ❑ 145 Chris Brown | .75 | .30 |
| ❑ 146 Eli Manning | 1.25 | .50 |
| ❑ 147 Corey Dillon | .75 | .30 |
| ❑ 148 Anquan Boldin | .75 | .30 |
| ❑ 149 Donovan McNabb | 1.00 | .40 |
| ❑ 150 Drew Bennett | .75 | .30 |
| ❑ 151 Jason Witten | .75 | .30 |
| ❑ 152 Eric Moulds | .75 | .30 |
| ❑ 153 Billy Volek | .75 | .30 |
| ❑ 154 Chris Cooley | .75 | .30 |
| ❑ 155 Larry Johnson | .75 | .30 |
| ❑ 156 Willie Parker | 1.25 | .50 |
| ❑ 157 Cadillac Williams | 1.00 | .40 |
| ❑ 158 Philip Rivers | 1.00 | .40 |
| ❑ 159 Reuben Droughns | .75 | .30 |
| ❑ 160 Joey Galloway | .75 | .30 |
| ❑ 161 Lee Evans | .75 | .30 |
| ❑ 162 Jamal Lewis | .75 | .30 |
| ❑ 163 Brett Favre | 2.00 | .75 |
| ❑ 164 Clinton Portis | 1.00 | .40 |
| ❑ 165 Rod Marinelli CO | .60 | .25 |
| ❑ 166 Tom Brady | 1.50 | .60 |
| ❑ 167 Torry Holt | .75 | .30 |
| ❑ 168 Rudi Johnson | .75 | .30 |
| ❑ 169 Priest Holmes | .75 | .30 |
| ❑ 170 Tatum Bell | .75 | .30 |
| ❑ 171 Jeremy Shockey | 1.00 | .40 |

| | | |
|---|---|---|
| ❏ 172 Shawne Merriman | .75 | .30 |
| ❏ 173 Alge Crumpler | .75 | .30 |
| ❏ 174 Marion Barber | 1.00 | .40 |
| ❏ 175 Steve Smith | 1.00 | .40 |
| ❏ 176 Mike McCarthy CO | .60 | .25 |
| ❏ 177 David Carr | .75 | .30 |
| ❏ 178 Julius Jones | 1.00 | .40 |
| ❏ 179 Chad Johnson | .75 | .30 |
| ❏ 180 Curtis Martin | 1.00 | .40 |
| ❏ 181 Peyton Manning | 1.50 | .60 |
| ❏ 182 LaMont Jordan | .75 | .30 |
| ❏ 183 Tiki Barber | 1.00 | .40 |
| ❏ 184 Darrell Jackson | .75 | .30 |
| ❏ 185 J.P. Losman | .75 | .30 |
| ❏ 186 Drew Brees | 1.00 | .40 |
| ❏ 187 Isaac Bruce | .75 | .30 |
| ❏ 188 Drew Bledsoe | .75 | .30 |
| ❏ 189 Roy Williams WR | 1.00 | .40 |
| ❏ 190 Donte Stallworth | .60 | .25 |
| ❏ 191 Odell Thurman | .60 | .25 |
| ❏ 192 Chester Taylor | .75 | .30 |
| ❏ 193 Randy McMichael | .60 | .25 |
| ❏ 194 Larry Fitzgerald | 1.00 | .40 |
| ❏ 195 Charlie Frye | .75 | .30 |
| ❏ 196 Keary Colbert | .75 | .30 |
| ❏ 197 Patrick Ramsey | .75 | .30 |
| ❏ 198 Mark Clayton | .75 | .30 |
| ❏ 199 Michael Jenkins | .75 | .30 |
| ❏ 200 Jake Delhomme | .75 | .30 |
| ❏ 201 Aaron Rodgers | 1.00 | .40 |
| ❏ 202 Andre Johnson | .75 | .30 |
| ❏ 203 Matt Hasselbeck | .75 | .30 |
| ❏ 204 Reggie Brown | .75 | .30 |
| ❏ 205 Warrick Dunn | .75 | .30 |
| ❏ 206 Kurt Warner | .75 | .30 |
| ❏ 207 Antonio Gates | 1.00 | .40 |
| ❏ 208 Terry Glenn | .75 | .30 |
| ❏ 209 Steve McNair | .75 | .30 |
| ❏ 210 Alex Smith QB | 1.00 | .40 |
| ❏ 211 Joe Horn | .75 | .30 |
| ❏ 212 Domanick Davis | .75 | .30 |
| ❏ 213 Deion Branch | .75 | .30 |
| ❏ 214 Todd Heap | .75 | .30 |
| ❏ 215 Chad Pennington | .75 | .30 |
| ❏ 216 Brandon Lloyd | .75 | .30 |
| ❏ 217 Rod Smith | .75 | .30 |
| ❏ 218 Ronnie Brown | 1.00 | .40 |
| ❏ 219 Braylon Edwards | 1.00 | .40 |
| ❏ 220 Michael Vick | 1.00 | .40 |
| ❏ 221 Vince Young RC | 20.00 | 8.00 |
| ❏ 222 Jay Cutler RC | 15.00 | 6.00 |
| ❏ 223 Reggie Bush RC | 25.00 | 10.00 |
| ❏ 224 Matt Leinart RC | 12.00 | 5.00 |
| ❏ 225 Vernon Davis RC | 4.00 | 1.50 |
| ❏ 226 A.J. Hawk RC | 8.00 | 3.00 |
| ❏ 227 Santonio Holmes RC | 10.00 | 4.00 |
| ❏ 228 DeAngelo Williams RC | 6.00 | 2.50 |
| ❏ 229 LenDale White RC | 8.00 | 3.00 |
| ❏ 230 Sinorice Moss RC | 4.00 | 1.50 |
| ❏ 231 Joseph Addai RC | 12.00 | 5.00 |
| ❏ 232 Mike Bell RC | 4.00 | 1.50 |
| ❏ 233 Will Blackmon RC | 4.00 | 1.50 |
| ❏ 234 Brian Calhoun RC | 3.00 | 1.25 |
| ❏ 235 Kellen Clemens RC | 5.00 | 2.00 |
| ❏ 236 Brodie Croyle RC | 5.00 | 2.00 |
| ❏ 237 Maurice Drew RC | 8.00 | 3.00 |
| ❏ 238 Anthony Fasano RC | 4.00 | 1.50 |
| ❏ 239 D'Brickashaw Ferguson RC | 4.00 | 1.50 |
| ❏ 240 Quinton Ganther RC | 4.00 | 1.50 |
| ❏ 241 Bruce Gradkowski RC | 4.00 | 1.50 |
| ❏ 242 Skyler Green RC | 4.00 | 1.50 |
| ❏ 243 Chad Greenway RC | 4.00 | 1.50 |
| ❏ 244 Marques Hagans RC | 3.00 | 1.25 |
| ❏ 245 Michael Huff RC | 4.00 | 1.50 |
| ❏ 246 Cedric Humes RC | 4.00 | 1.50 |
| ❏ 247 Tarvaris Jackson RC | 4.00 | 1.50 |
| ❏ 248 Omar Jacobs RC | 3.00 | 1.25 |
| ❏ 249 Greg Jennings RC | 6.00 | 2.50 |
| ❏ 250 Mathias Kiwanuka RC | 5.00 | 2.00 |
| ❏ 251 Joe Klopfenstein RC | 3.00 | 1.25 |
| ❏ 252 Marcedes Lewis RC | 4.00 | 1.50 |
| ❏ 253 Brandon Marshall RC | 5.00 | 2.00 |
| ❏ 254 Ingle Martin RC | 4.00 | 1.50 |
| ❏ 255 Dontrell Moore RC | 3.00 | 1.25 |

| | | |
|---|---|---|
| ❏ 256 Jerious Norwood RC | 5.00 | 2.00 |
| ❏ 257 Leonard Pope RC | 4.00 | 1.50 |
| ❏ 258 Willie Reid RC | 4.00 | 1.50 |
| ❏ 259 Michael Robinson RC | 4.00 | 1.50 |
| ❏ 260 Brad Smith RC | 4.00 | 1.50 |
| ❏ 261 Maurice Stovall RC | 4.00 | 1.50 |
| ❏ 262 David Thomas RC | 4.00 | 1.50 |
| ❏ 263 Leon Washington RC | 4.00 | 1.50 |
| ❏ 264 Brandon Williams RC | 4.00 | 1.50 |
| ❏ 265 Demetrius Williams RC | 4.00 | 1.50 |
| ❏ 266 Tye Hill RC | 4.00 | 1.50 |
| ❏ 267 Mike Hass RC | 4.00 | 1.50 |
| ❏ 268 Jason Avant RC | 4.00 | 1.50 |
| ❏ 269 Chad Jackson RC | 3.00 | 1.25 |
| ❏ 270 Laurence Maroney RC | 10.00 | 4.00 |
| ❏ 271 Anwar Phillips RC | 3.00 | 1.25 |
| ❏ 272 David Kirtman RC | 3.00 | 1.25 |
| ❏ 273 Roman Harper RC | 3.00 | 1.25 |
| ❏ 274 Spencer Havner RC | 3.00 | 1.25 |
| ❏ 275 Erik Meyer RC | 3.00 | 1.25 |

## 2007 Bowman Chrome

| | | |
|---|---|---|
| ❏ COMPLETE SET (220) | 100.00 | 40.00 |
| ❏ COMP.SHORT SET (55) | 20.00 | 8.00 |
| ❏ COMP.VET SET (110) | 15.00 | 6.00 |
| ❏ 1-55 INSERTED IN BOWMAN PACKS | | |
| ❏ BC1 Kenny Irons RC | 1.50 | .60 |
| ❏ BC2 David Clowney RC | 1.25 | .60 |
| ❏ BC3 Courtney Taylor RC | 1.25 | .50 |
| ❏ BC4 Amobi Okoye RC | 1.50 | .60 |
| ❏ BC5 Jamaal Anderson RC | 1.25 | .50 |
| ❏ BC6 Adam Carriker RC | 1.25 | .50 |
| ❏ BC7 Jarvis Moss RC | 1.25 | .50 |
| ❏ BC8 Anthony Spencer RC | 1.50 | .60 |
| ❏ BC9 Jon Beason RC | 1.50 | .60 |
| ❏ BC10 Darrelle Revis RC | 1.25 | .50 |
| ❏ BC11 Aaron Ross RC | 1.50 | .60 |
| ❏ BC12 Reggie Nelson RC | 1.25 | .50 |
| ❏ BC13 Michael Griffin RC | 1.25 | .50 |
| ❏ BC14 Brandon Meriweather RC | 1.50 | .60 |
| ❏ BC15 Tyler Palko RC | 1.50 | .60 |
| ❏ BC16 Jared Zabransky RC | 1.50 | .60 |
| ❏ BC17 Lester Ricard RC | 3.00 | 1.25 |
| ❏ BC18 Darius Walker RC | 1.50 | .60 |
| ❏ BC19 Ahmad Bradshaw RC | 2.00 | .75 |
| ❏ BC20 Thomas Clayton RC | 1.25 | .50 |
| ❏ BC21 Rhema McKnight RC | 1.25 | .50 |
| ❏ BC22 Scott Chandler RC | 1.25 | .50 |
| ❏ BC23 Matt Spaeth RC | 1.25 | .50 |
| ❏ BC24 Ben Patrick RC | 1.25 | .50 |
| ❏ BC25 Clark Harris RC | 1.25 | .50 |
| ❏ BC26 Martrez Milner RC | 1.25 | .50 |
| ❏ BC27 Joe Newton RC | 1.25 | .50 |
| ❏ BC28 DeMarcus Tank Tyler RC | 1.25 | .50 |
| ❏ BC29 Justin Harrell RC | 1.50 | .60 |
| ❏ BC30 LaMarr Woodley RC | 1.25 | .50 |
| ❏ BC31 David Harris RC | 1.25 | .50 |
| ❏ BC32 Buster Davis RC | 1.25 | .50 |
| ❏ BC33 Rufus Alexander RC | 1.50 | .60 |
| ❏ BC34 Earl Everett RC | 1.25 | .50 |
| ❏ BC35 Stewart Bradley RC | 1.25 | .50 |
| ❏ BC36 Prescott Burgess RC | 1.25 | .50 |
| ❏ BC37 Daymeion Hughes RC | 1.25 | .50 |
| ❏ BC38 Marcus McCauley RC | 1.25 | .50 |
| ❏ BC39 Chris Houston RC | 1.25 | .50 |
| ❏ BC40 David Irons RC | 1.00 | .40 |
| ❏ BC41 Levi Brown RC | 1.25 | .50 |
| ❏ BC42 Joe Staley RC | 1.25 | .50 |

| | | |
|---|---|---|
| ❏ BC43 Steve Breaston RC | 1.50 | .60 |
| ❏ BC44 Le'Ron McClain RC | 2.50 | 1.00 |
| ❏ BC45 Joel Filani RC | 1.25 | .50 |
| ❏ BC46 Justise Hairston RC | 1.25 | .50 |
| ❏ BC47 Nate Ilaoa RC | 1.50 | .60 |
| ❏ BC48 Brett Ratliff RC | 1.50 | .60 |
| ❏ BC49 Roy Hall RC | 1.50 | .60 |
| ❏ BC50 Legedu Naanee RC | 1.50 | .60 |
| ❏ BC51 Jarrett Hicks RC | 1.25 | .50 |
| ❏ BC52 Sonny Shackelford RC | 1.25 | .50 |
| ❏ BC53 Jordan Kent RC | 1.25 | .50 |
| ❏ BC54 John Broussard RC | 1.25 | .50 |
| ❏ BC55 Chandler Williams RC | 1.25 | .50 |
| ❏ BC56 JaMarcus Russell RC | 10.00 | 4.00 |
| ❏ BC57 Brady Quinn RC | 12.00 | 5.00 |
| ❏ BC58 Drew Stanton RC | 4.00 | 1.50 |
| ❏ BC59 Troy Smith RC | 5.00 | 2.00 |
| ❏ BC60 Kevin Kolb RC | 6.00 | 2.50 |
| ❏ BC61 Trent Edwards RC | 10.00 | 4.00 |
| ❏ BC62 John Beck RC | 4.00 | 1.50 |
| ❏ BC63 Jordan Palmer RC | 4.00 | 1.50 |
| ❏ BC64 Chris Leak RC | 3.00 | 1.25 |
| ❏ BC65 Adrian Peterson RC | 30.00 | 12.00 |
| ❏ BC66 Marshawn Lynch RC | 8.00 | 3.00 |
| ❏ BC67 Brandon Jackson RC | 4.00 | 1.50 |
| ❏ BC68 Michael Bush RC | 4.00 | 1.50 |
| ❏ BC69 Antonio Pittman RC | 4.00 | 1.50 |
| ❏ BC70 Tony Hunt RC | 4.00 | 1.50 |
| ❏ BC71 Lorenzo Booker RC | 4.00 | 1.50 |
| ❏ BC72 Chris Henry RC | 4.00 | 1.50 |
| ❏ BC73 Brian Leonard RC | 4.00 | 1.50 |
| ❏ BC74 Garrett Wolfe RC | 4.00 | 1.50 |
| ❏ BC75 Calvin Johnson RC | 10.00 | 4.00 |
| ❏ BC76 Ted Ginn RC | 6.00 | 2.50 |
| ❏ BC77 Dwayne Jarrett RC | 6.00 | 2.50 |
| ❏ BC78 Dwayne Bowe RC | 8.00 | 3.00 |
| ❏ BC79 Sidney Rice RC | 4.00 | 1.50 |
| ❏ BC80 Robert Meachem RC | 4.00 | 1.50 |
| ❏ BC81 Anthony Gonzalez RC | 6.00 | 2.50 |
| ❏ BC82 Craig Buster Davis RC | 4.00 | 1.50 |
| ❏ BC83 Aundrae Allison RC | 3.00 | 1.25 |
| ❏ BC84 Chansi Stuckey RC | 3.00 | 1.25 |
| ❏ BC85 Alan Branch RC | 3.00 | 1.25 |
| ❏ BC86 Steve Smith USC RC | 5.00 | 2.00 |
| ❏ BC87 Paul Williams RC | 3.00 | 1.25 |
| ❏ BC88 Johnnie Lee Higgins RC | 3.00 | 1.25 |
| ❏ BC89 Jason Hill RC | 4.00 | 1.50 |
| ❏ BC90 Greg Olsen RC | 5.00 | 2.00 |
| ❏ BC91 Yamon Figurs RC | 3.00 | 1.25 |
| ❏ BC92 Gaines Adams RC | 4.00 | 1.50 |
| ❏ BC93 Patrick Willis RC | 8.00 | 3.00 |
| ❏ BC94 Joe Thomas RC | 4.00 | 1.50 |
| ❏ BC95 Isaiah Stanback RC | 4.00 | 1.50 |
| ❏ BC96 Paul Posluszny RC | 5.00 | 2.00 |
| ❏ BC97 Jeff Rowe RC | 3.00 | 1.25 |
| ❏ BC98 Zac Taylor RC | 4.00 | 1.50 |
| ❏ BC99 Dwayne Wright RC | 3.00 | 1.25 |
| ❏ BC100 Kenneth Darby RC | 4.00 | 1.50 |
| ❏ BC101 Selvin Young RC | 6.00 | 2.50 |
| ❏ BC102 Gary Russell RC | 4.00 | 1.50 |
| ❏ BC103 Kolby Smith RC | 4.00 | 1.50 |
| ❏ BC104 Dallas Baker RC | 3.00 | 1.25 |
| ❏ BC105 Jacoby Jones RC | 4.00 | 1.50 |
| ❏ BC106 Ryne Robinson RC | 3.00 | 1.25 |
| ❏ BC107 Chris Davis RC | 3.00 | 1.25 |
| ❏ BC108 Laron Landry RC | 5.00 | 2.00 |
| ❏ BC109 Leon Hall RC | 3.00 | 1.25 |
| ❏ BC110 Lawrence Timmons RC | 4.00 | 1.50 |
| ❏ BC111 Matt Leinart | 1.00 | .40 |
| ❏ BC112 Jason Campbell | .75 | .30 |
| ❏ BC113 J.P. Losman | .60 | .25 |
| ❏ BC114 Rex Grossman | .75 | .30 |
| ❏ BC115 Tony Romo | 2.00 | .75 |
| ❏ BC116 Brett Favre | 2.00 | .75 |
| ❏ BC117 Trent Green | .75 | .30 |
| ❏ BC118 Drew Brees | .75 | .30 |
| ❏ BC119 Chad Pennington | .75 | .30 |
| ❏ BC120 Ben Roethlisberger | 1.25 | .50 |
| ❏ BC121 Alex Smith QB | 1.00 | .40 |
| ❏ BC122 Marc Bulger | .75 | .30 |
| ❏ BC123 Edgerrin James | .75 | .30 |
| ❏ BC124 Jamal Lewis | .75 | .30 |
| ❏ BC125 DeShaun Foster | .75 | .30 |
| ❏ BC126 Cedric Benson | .75 | .30 |

| | | | |
|---|---|---|---|
| BC127 Rudi Johnson | .75 | .30 |
| BC128 Dominic Rhodes | .75 | .30 |
| BC129 Fred Taylor | .75 | .30 |
| BC130 Larry Johnson | .75 | .30 |
| BC131 Chester Taylor | .60 | .25 |
| BC132 Deuce McAllister | .75 | .30 |
| BC133 Brandon Jacobs | .75 | .30 |
| BC134 Willie Parker | 1.00 | .40 |
| BC135 Frank Gore | 1.00 | .40 |
| BC136 Steven Jackson | 1.00 | .40 |
| BC137 Clinton Portis | .75 | .30 |
| BC138 Anquan Boldin | .75 | .30 |
| BC139 Derrick Mason | .60 | .25 |
| BC140 Steve Smith | .75 | .30 |
| BC141 Chad Johnson | .75 | .30 |
| BC142 Braylon Edwards | .75 | .30 |
| BC143 Terry Glenn | .75 | .30 |
| BC144 Mike Furrey | .75 | .30 |
| BC145 Donald Driver | .75 | .30 |
| BC146 Andre Johnson | .75 | .30 |
| BC147 Marvin Harrison | 1.00 | .40 |
| BC148 Chris Chambers | .75 | .30 |
| BC149 Devery Henderson | .60 | .25 |
| BC150 Marques Colston | 1.00 | .40 |
| BC151 Amani Toomer | .75 | .30 |
| BC152 Laveranues Coles | .75 | .30 |
| BC153 Donte Stallworth | .75 | .30 |
| BC154 Hines Ward | 1.00 | .40 |
| BC155 Keenan McCardell | .60 | .25 |
| BC156 Arnaz Battle | .60 | .25 |
| BC157 Deion Branch | .75 | .30 |
| BC158 Kevin Curtis | .60 | .25 |
| BC159 Isaac Bruce | .75 | .30 |
| BC160 Santana Moss | .75 | .30 |
| BC161 Kellen Winslow | .75 | .30 |
| BC162 Jeremy Shockey | .75 | .30 |
| BC163 Vernon Davis | .75 | .30 |
| BC164 Travis Henry | .75 | .30 |
| BC165 Todd Heap | .60 | .25 |
| BC166 Matt Schaub | .75 | .30 |
| BC167 Steve McNair | .75 | .30 |
| BC168 Jake Delhomme | .75 | .30 |
| BC169 Carson Palmer | 1.00 | .40 |
| BC170 Jay Cutler | 1.00 | .40 |
| BC171 Peyton Manning | 1.50 | .60 |
| BC172 Tom Brady | 2.00 | .75 |
| BC173 Eli Manning | 1.00 | .40 |
| BC174 Donovan McnabB | 1.00 | .40 |
| BC175 Philip Rivers | 1.00 | .40 |
| BC176 Matt Hasselbeck | .75 | .30 |
| BC177 Vince Young | 1.00 | .40 |
| BC178 Warrick Dunn | .75 | .30 |
| BC179 Willis McGahee | .75 | .30 |
| BC180 DeAngelo Williams | 1.00 | .40 |
| BC181 Thomas Jones | .75 | .30 |
| BC182 Julius Jones | .75 | .30 |
| BC183 Joseph Addai | 1.00 | .40 |
| BC184 Maurice Jones-Drew | 1.00 | .40 |
| BC185 Ronnie Brown | .75 | .30 |
| BC186 Laurence Maroney | 1.00 | .40 |
| BC187 Reggie Bush | 1.25 | .50 |
| BC188 Brian Westbrook | .75 | .30 |
| BC189 LaDainian Tomlinson | 1.25 | .50 |
| BC190 Shaun Alexander | .75 | .30 |
| BC191 Cadillac Williams | .75 | .30 |
| BC192 Michael Turner | .75 | .30 |
| BC193 Larry Fitzgerald | 1.00 | .40 |
| BC194 Lee Evans | .75 | .30 |
| BC195 Muhsin Muhammad | .75 | .30 |
| BC196 T.J. Houshmandzadeh | .75 | .30 |
| BC197 Terrell Owens | 1.00 | .40 |
| BC198 Javon Walker | .75 | .30 |
| BC199 Roy Williams WR | .75 | .30 |
| BC200 Greg Jennings | .75 | .30 |
| BC201 Reggie Wayne | .75 | .30 |
| BC202 Matt Jones | .75 | .30 |
| BC203 Troy Williamson | .60 | .25 |
| BC204 Joe Horn | .75 | .30 |
| BC205 Plaxico Burress | .75 | .30 |
| BC206 Jerricho Cotchery | .60 | .25 |
| BC207 Randy Moss | 1.00 | .40 |
| BC208 Reggie Brown | .75 | .30 |
| BC209 Santonio Holmes | .75 | .30 |
| BC210 Eric Parker | .60 | .25 |
| BC211 Antonio Bryant | .75 | .30 |
| BC212 Darrell Jackson | .75 | .30 |
| BC213 Torry Holt | .75 | .30 |
| BC214 Antwaan Randle El | .60 | .25 |
| BC215 Alge Crumpler | .75 | .30 |
| BC216 Tony Gonzalez | .75 | .30 |
| BC217 Antonio Gates | .75 | .30 |
| BC218 Tarvaris Jackson | .75 | .30 |
| BC219 Drew Bennett | .60 | .25 |
| BC220 Byron Leftwich | .75 | .30 |

## 1995 Bowman's Best

| | | | |
|---|---|---|---|
| COMPLETE SET (180) | 100.00 | 40.00 |
| R1 Ki-Jana Carter RC | 1.50 | .60 |
| R2 Tony Boselli RC | 1.50 | .60 |
| R3 Steve McNair RC | 15.00 | 6.00 |
| R4 Michael Westbrook RC | 1.50 | .60 |
| R5 Kerry Collins RC | 6.00 | 2.50 |
| R6 Kevin Carter RC | 1.50 | .60 |
| R7 Mike Mamula RC | .40 | .15 |
| R8 Joey Galloway RC | 6.00 | 2.50 |
| R9 Kyle Brady RC | 1.50 | .60 |
| R10 Ray McElroy RC | .40 | .15 |
| R11 Derrick Alexander DE RC | .40 | .15 |
| R12 Warren Sapp RC | 6.00 | 2.50 |
| R13 Mark Fields RC | 1.50 | .60 |
| R14 Ruben Brown RC | 1.50 | .60 |
| R15 Ellis Johnson RC | .40 | .15 |
| R16 Hugh Douglas RC | 1.50 | .60 |
| R17 Alundis Brice RC | .40 | .15 |
| R18 Napoleon Kaufman RC | 5.00 | 2.00 |
| R19 James O. Stewart RC | 3.00 | 1.25 |
| R20 Luther Elliss RC | .40 | .15 |
| R21 Rashaan Salaam RC | .75 | .30 |
| R22 Tyrone Poole RC | 1.50 | .60 |
| R23 Ty Law RC | 4.00 | 1.50 |
| R24 Korey Stringer RC | .75 | .30 |
| R25 Billy Milner RC | .40 | .15 |
| R26 Roell Preston RC | .75 | .30 |
| R27 Mark Bruener RC | .75 | .30 |
| R28 Derrick Brooks RC | 6.00 | 2.50 |
| R29 Blake Brockermeyer RC | .40 | .15 |
| R30 Mike Frederick RC | .40 | .15 |
| R31 Trezelle Jenkins RC | .40 | .15 |
| R32 Craig Newsome RC | .40 | .15 |
| R33 Matt O'Dwyer RC | .40 | .15 |
| R34 Terrance Shaw RC | .40 | .15 |
| R35 Anthony Cook RC | .40 | .15 |
| R36 Darick Holmes RC | .75 | .30 |
| R37 Cory Raymer RC | .40 | .15 |
| R38 Zach Wiegert RC | .40 | .15 |
| R39 Sam Shade RC | .40 | .15 |
| R40 Brian DeMarco RC | .40 | .15 |
| R41 Ron Davis RC | .40 | .15 |
| R42 Orlando Thomas RC | .40 | .15 |
| R43 Derek West RC | .40 | .15 |
| R44 Ray Zellars RC | .75 | .30 |
| R45 Todd Collins RC | 5.00 | 2.00 |
| R46 Linc Harden RC | .40 | .15 |
| R47 Frank Sanders RC | 1.50 | .60 |
| R48 Ken Dilger RC | 1.50 | .60 |
| R49 Barrett Robbins RC | .40 | .15 |
| R50 Bobby Taylor RC | 2.50 | 1.00 |
| R51 Terrell Fletcher RC | .40 | .15 |
| R52 Jack Jackson RC | .40 | .15 |
| R53 Jeff Kopp RC | .40 | .15 |
| R54 Brendan Stai RC | .40 | .15 |
| R55 Corey Fuller RC | .40 | .15 |
| R56 Todd Sauerbrun RC | .40 | .15 |
| R57 Dameian Jeffries RC | .40 | .15 |
| R58 Troy Dumas RC | .40 | .15 |
| R59 Charlie Williams RC | .40 | .15 |
| R60 Kordell Stewart RC | 6.00 | 2.50 |
| R61 Jay Barker RC | .40 | .15 |
| R62 Jesse James RC | .40 | .15 |
| R63 Shane Hannah RC | .40 | .15 |
| R64 Rob Johnson RC | 4.00 | 1.50 |
| R65 Darius Holland RC | .40 | .15 |
| R66 William Henderson RC | 5.00 | 2.00 |
| R67 Chris Sanders RC | .75 | .30 |
| R68 Darryl Pounds RC | .40 | .15 |
| R69 Melvin Tuten RC | .40 | .15 |
| R70 David Sloan RC | .40 | .15 |
| R71 Chris Hudson RC | .40 | .15 |
| R72 William Strong RC | .40 | .15 |
| R73 Brian Williams LB RC | .40 | .15 |
| R74 Curtis Martin RC | 15.00 | 6.00 |
| R75 Mike Verstegen RC | .40 | .15 |
| R76 Justin Armour RC | .40 | .15 |
| R77 Lorenzo Styles RC | .40 | .15 |
| R78 Oliver Gibson RC | .40 | .15 |
| R79 Zack Crockett RC | .75 | .30 |
| R80 Tau Pupua RC | .40 | .15 |
| R81 Tamarick Vanover RC | 1.50 | .60 |
| R82 Steve McLaughlin RC | .40 | .15 |
| R83 Sean Harris RC | .40 | .15 |
| R84 Eric Zeier RC | 1.50 | .60 |
| R85 Rodney Young RC | .40 | .15 |
| R86 Chad May RC | .40 | .15 |
| R87 Evan Pilgrim RC | .40 | .15 |
| R88 James A. Stewart RC | .40 | .15 |
| R89 Torey Hunter RC | .40 | .15 |
| R90 Antonio Freeman RC | 4.00 | 1.50 |
| V1 Rob Moore | .60 | .25 |
| V2 Craig Heyward | .60 | .25 |
| V3 Jim Kelly | 1.25 | .50 |
| V4 John Kasay | .30 | .10 |
| V5 Jeff Graham | .30 | .10 |
| V6 Jeff Blake RC | 2.50 | 1.00 |
| V7 Antonio Langham | .30 | .10 |
| V8 Troy Aikman | 3.00 | 1.25 |
| V9 Simon Fletcher | .30 | .10 |
| V10 Barry Sanders | 5.00 | 2.00 |
| V11 Edgar Bennett | .60 | .25 |
| V12 Ray Childress | .30 | .10 |
| V13 Ray Buchanan | .30 | .10 |
| V14 Desmond Howard | .60 | .25 |
| V15 Dale Carter | .30 | .10 |
| V16 Troy Vincent | .30 | .10 |
| V17 David Palmer | .30 | .10 |
| V18 Ben Coates | .60 | .25 |
| V19 Derek Brown TE | .30 | .10 |
| V20 Dave Brown | .60 | .25 |
| V21 Mo Lewis | .30 | .10 |
| V22 Harvey Williams | .30 | .10 |
| V23 Randall Cunningham | 1.25 | .50 |
| V24 Kevin Greene | .60 | .25 |
| V25 Junior Seau | 1.25 | .50 |
| V26 Merton Hanks | .30 | .10 |
| V27 Cortez Kennedy | .60 | .25 |
| V28 Troy Drayton | .30 | .10 |
| V29 Hardy Nickerson | .30 | .10 |
| V30 Brian Mitchell | .30 | .10 |
| V31 Raymont Harris | .30 | .10 |
| V32 Keith Goganious | .30 | .10 |
| V33 Andre Reed | .60 | .25 |
| V34 Terance Mathis | .60 | .25 |
| V35 Garrison Hearst | 1.25 | .50 |
| V36 Glyn Milburn | .30 | .10 |
| V37 Emmitt Smith | 5.00 | 2.00 |
| V38 Vinny Testaverde | .60 | .25 |
| V39 Darnay Scott | .60 | .25 |
| V40 Mickey Washington | .30 | .10 |
| V41 Craig Erickson | .30 | .10 |
| V42 Chris Chandler | 1.25 | .50 |
| V43 Brett Favre | 6.00 | 2.50 |
| V44 Scott Mitchell | .60 | .25 |
| V45 Chris Slade | .30 | .10 |
| V46 Warren Moon | .60 | .25 |
| V47 Dan Marino | 6.00 | 2.50 |
| V48 Greg Hill | .60 | .25 |
| V49 Rocket Ismail | .60 | .25 |

| | | |
|---|---|---|
| V50 Bobby Houston | .30 | .10 |
| V51 Rodney Hampton | .60 | .25 |
| V52 Jim Everett | .30 | .10 |
| V53 Rick Mirer | .60 | .25 |
| V54 Steve Young | 2.50 | 1.00 |
| V55 Dennis Gibson | .30 | .10 |
| V56 Rod Woodson | .60 | .25 |
| V57 Calvin Williams | .60 | .25 |
| V58 Tom Carter | .30 | .10 |
| V59 Trent Dilfer | 1.25 | .50 |
| V60 Shane Conlan | .30 | .10 |
| V61 Cornelius Bennett | .60 | .25 |
| V62 Eric Metcalf | .60 | .25 |
| V63 Frank Reich | .30 | .10 |
| V64 Eric Hill | .30 | .10 |
| V65 Erik Kramer | .30 | .10 |
| V66 Michael Irvin | 1.25 | .50 |
| V67 Tony McGee | .30 | .10 |
| V68 Andre Rison | .60 | .25 |
| V69 Shannon Sharpe | .60 | .25 |
| V70 Quentin Coryatt | .60 | .25 |
| V71 Robert Brooks | 1.25 | .50 |
| V72 Steve Beuerlein | .60 | .25 |
| V73 Herman Moore | 1.25 | .50 |
| V74 Jack Del Rio | .30 | .10 |
| V75 Dave Meggett | .30 | .10 |
| V76 Pete Stoyanovich | .30 | .10 |
| V77 Neil Smith | .60 | .25 |
| V78 Corey Miller | .30 | .10 |
| V79 Tim Brown | 1.25 | .50 |
| V80 Tyrone Hughes | .60 | .25 |
| V81 Boomer Esiason | .60 | .25 |
| V82 Natrone Means | .60 | .25 |
| V83 Chris Warren | .60 | .25 |
| V84 Byron Bam Morris | .30 | .10 |
| V85 Jerry Rice | 3.00 | 1.25 |
| V86 Michael Zordich | .30 | .10 |
| V87 Errict Rhett | .60 | .25 |
| V88 Henry Ellard | .60 | .25 |
| V89 Chris Miller | .30 | .10 |
| V90 John Elway | 6.00 | 2.50 |

## 1996 Bowman's Best

| | | |
|---|---|---|
| COMPLETE SET (180) | 80.00 | 40.00 |
| 1 Emmitt Smith | 3.00 | 1.25 |
| 2 Kordell Stewart | .75 | .30 |
| 3 Mark Chmura | .40 | .15 |
| 4 Sean Dawkins | .20 | .07 |
| 5 Steve Young | 1.50 | .60 |
| 6 Tamarick Vanover | .40 | .15 |
| 7 Scott Mitchell | .40 | .15 |
| 8 Aaron Hayden | .20 | .07 |
| 9 William Thomas | .20 | .07 |
| 10 Dan Marino | 4.00 | 1.50 |
| 11 Curtis Conway | .75 | .30 |
| 12 Steve Atwater | .20 | .07 |
| 13 Derrick Brooks | .75 | .30 |
| 14 Rick Mirer | .40 | .15 |
| 15 Mark Brunell | 1.00 | .40 |
| 16 Garrison Hearst | .40 | .15 |
| 17 Eric Turner | .20 | .07 |
| 18 Mark Carrier WR | .20 | .07 |
| 19 Darnay Scott | .40 | .15 |
| 20 Steve McNair | 1.50 | .60 |
| 21 Jim Everett | .20 | .07 |
| 22 Wayne Chrebet | 1.00 | .40 |
| 23 Ben Coates | .40 | .15 |
| 24 Harvey Williams | .20 | .07 |
| 25 Michael Westbrook | .75 | .30 |
| 26 Kevin Carter | .20 | .07 |
| 27 Dave Brown | .20 | .07 |
| 28 Jake Reed | .40 | .15 |
| 29 Thurman Thomas | .75 | .30 |
| 30 Jeff George | .40 | .15 |
| 31 Carnell Lake | .20 | .07 |
| 32 J.J. Stokes | .75 | .30 |
| 33 Jay Novacek | .20 | .07 |
| 34 Brett Perriman | .20 | .07 |
| 35 Robert Brooks | .75 | .30 |
| 36 Neil Smith | .40 | .15 |
| 37 Chris Zorich | .20 | .07 |
| 38 Micheal Barrow | .20 | .07 |
| 39 Quentin Coryatt | .20 | .07 |
| 40 Kerry Collins | .75 | .30 |
| 41 Aeneas Williams | .20 | .07 |
| 42 James O.Stewart | .40 | .15 |
| 43 Warren Moon | .40 | .15 |
| 44 Willie McGinest | .20 | .07 |
| 45 Rodney Hampton | .40 | .15 |
| 46 Jeff Hostetler | .20 | .07 |
| 47 Darrell Green | .20 | .07 |
| 48 Warren Sapp | .20 | .07 |
| 49 Troy Drayton | .20 | .07 |
| 50 Junior Seau | .75 | .30 |
| 51 Mike Mamula | .20 | .07 |
| 52 Antonio Langham | .20 | .07 |
| 53 Eric Metcalf | .20 | .07 |
| 54 Adrian Murrell | .40 | .15 |
| 55 Joey Galloway | .75 | .30 |
| 56 Anthony Miller | .40 | .15 |
| 57 Carl Pickens | .40 | .15 |
| 58 Bruce Smith | .40 | .15 |
| 59 Merton Hanks | .20 | .07 |
| 60 Troy Aikman | 2.00 | .75 |
| 61 Erik Kramer | .20 | .07 |
| 62 Tyrone Poole | .20 | .07 |
| 63 Michael Jackson | .40 | .15 |
| 64 Rob Moore | .40 | .15 |
| 65 Marcus Allen | .75 | .30 |
| 66 Orlando Thomas | .20 | .07 |
| 67 Dave Meggett | .20 | .07 |
| 68 Trent Dilfer | .75 | .30 |
| 69 Herman Moore | .40 | .15 |
| 70 Brett Favre | 4.00 | 1.50 |
| 71 Blaine Bishop | .20 | .07 |
| 72 Eric Allen | .20 | .07 |
| 73 Bernie Parmalee | .20 | .07 |
| 74 Kyle Brady | .20 | .07 |
| 75 Terry McDaniel | .20 | .07 |
| 76 Rodney Peete | .20 | .07 |
| 77 Yancey Thigpen | .40 | .15 |
| 78 Stan Humphries | .40 | .15 |
| 79 Craig Heyward | .20 | .07 |
| 80 Rashaan Salaam | .40 | .15 |
| 81 Shannon Sharpe | .40 | .15 |
| 82 Jim Harbaugh | .40 | .15 |
| 83 Vinnie Clark | .20 | .07 |
| 84 Steve Bono | .20 | .07 |
| 85 Drew Bledsoe | 1.00 | .40 |
| 86 Ken Norton | .20 | .07 |
| 87 Brian Mitchell | .20 | .07 |
| 88 Hardy Nickerson | .20 | .07 |
| 89 Todd Lyght | .20 | .07 |
| 90 Barry Sanders | 3.00 | 1.25 |
| 91 Robert Blackmon | .20 | .07 |
| 92 Larry Centers | .40 | .15 |
| 93 Jim Kelly | .75 | .30 |
| 94 Laman Lester | .20 | .07 |
| 95 Cris Carter | .75 | .30 |
| 96 Hugh Douglas | .40 | .15 |
| 97 Michael Strahan | .40 | .15 |
| 98 Lee Woodall | .20 | .07 |
| 99 Michael Irvin | .75 | .30 |
| 100 Marshall Faulk | 1.00 | .40 |
| 101 Terance Mathis | .20 | .07 |
| 102 Eric Zeier | .20 | .07 |
| 103 Marty Carter | .20 | .07 |
| 104 Steve Tovar | .20 | .07 |
| 105 Isaac Bruce | .75 | .30 |
| 106 Tony Martin | .40 | .15 |
| 107 Dale Carter | .40 | .15 |
| 108 Terry Kirby | .40 | .15 |
| 109 Tyrone Hughes | .20 | .07 |
| 110 Bryce Paup | .20 | .07 |
| 111 Errict Rhett | .40 | .15 |
| 112 Ricky Watters | .40 | .15 |
| 113 Chris Chandler | .40 | .15 |
| 114 Edgar Bennett | .40 | .15 |
| 115 John Elway | 4.00 | 1.50 |
| 116 Sam Mills | .20 | .07 |
| 117 Seth Joyner | .20 | .07 |
| 118 Jeff Lageman | .20 | .07 |
| 119 Chris Calloway | .20 | .07 |
| 120 Curtis Martin | 1.50 | .60 |
| 121 Ken Harvey | .20 | .07 |
| 122 Eugene Daniel | .20 | .07 |
| 123 Tim Brown | .75 | .30 |
| 124 Mo Lewis | .20 | .07 |
| 125 Jeff Blake | .75 | .30 |
| 126 Jessie Tuggle | .20 | .07 |
| 127 Vinny Testaverde | .40 | .15 |
| 128 Chris Warren | .40 | .15 |
| 129 Terrell Davis | 1.50 | .60 |
| 130 Greg Lloyd | .40 | .15 |
| 131 Deion Sanders | 1.00 | .40 |
| 132 Derrick Thomas | .75 | .30 |
| 133 Darryll Lewis | .20 | .07 |
| 134 Reggie White | .75 | .30 |
| 135 Jerry Rice | 2.00 | .75 |
| 136 Tony Banks RC | 1.00 | .40 |
| 137 Derrick Mayes RC | 1.00 | .40 |
| 138 Leeland McElroy RC | .50 | .20 |
| 139 Bryan Still RC | .50 | .20 |
| 140 Tim Biakabutuka RC | 1.00 | .40 |
| 141 Rickey Dudley RC | 1.00 | .40 |
| 142 Tory James RC | .50 | .20 |
| 143 Lawyer Milloy RC | 1.25 | .50 |
| 144 Mike Ulufale RC | .25 | .08 |
| 145 Bobby Engram RC | 1.00 | .40 |
| 146 Willie Anderson RC | .25 | .08 |
| 147 Terrell Owens RC | 15.00 | 7.50 |
| 148 Jonathan Ogden RC | 1.00 | .40 |
| 149 Darrius Johnson RC | .25 | .08 |
| 150 Kevin Hardy RC | 1.00 | .40 |
| 151 Simeon Rice RC | 2.50 | 1.00 |
| 152 Alex Molden RC | .25 | .08 |
| 153 Cedric Jones RC | .25 | .08 |
| 154 Duane Clemons RC | .25 | .08 |
| 155 Karim Abdul-Jabbar RC | 1.00 | .40 |
| 156 Dedric Mathis RC | .25 | .08 |
| 157 John Michels RC | .25 | .08 |
| 158 Winslow Oliver RC | .25 | .08 |
| 159 Stepfret Williams RC | .25 | .08 |
| 160 Eddie Kennison RC | 1.00 | .40 |
| 161 Marcus Coleman RC | .25 | .08 |
| 162 Tedy Bruschi RC | 20.00 | 7.50 |
| 163 Detron Smith RC | .25 | .08 |
| 164 Ray Lewis RC | 25.00 | 12.50 |
| 165 Marvin Harrison RC | 15.00 | 7.50 |
| 166 Je'rod Cherry RC | .25 | .08 |
| 167 Jerris McPhail RC | .25 | .08 |
| 168 Eric Moulds RC | 8.00 | 3.00 |
| 169 Walt Harris RC | .25 | .08 |
| 170 Eddie George RC | 8.00 | 3.00 |
| 171 Jermaine Lewis RC | 1.00 | .40 |
| 172 Jeff Lewis RC | .50 | .20 |
| 173 Ray Mickens RC | .25 | .08 |
| 174 Amani Toomer RC | 5.00 | 2.00 |
| 175 Zach Thomas RC | 3.00 | 1.25 |
| 176 Lawrence Phillips RC | .50 | .20 |
| 177 John Mobley RC | .25 | .08 |
| 178 Anthony Dorsett RC | .25 | .08 |
| 179 DeRon Jenkins RC | .20 | .07 |
| 180 Keyshawn Johnson RC | 6.00 | 2.50 |

## 1997 Bowman's Best

| | | |
|---|---|---|
| COMPLETE SET (125) | 30.00 | 12.50 |
| 1 Brett Favre | 4.00 | 1.50 |
| 2 Larry Centers | .60 | .25 |
| 3 Trent Dilfer | 1.00 | .40 |
| 4 Rodney Hampton | .60 | .25 |
| 5 Wesley Walls | .60 | .25 |
| 6 Jerome Bettis | 1.00 | .40 |
| 7 Keyshawn Johnson | .40 | .15 |
| 8 Keenan McCardell | .60 | .25 |
| 9 Terry Allen | 1.00 | .40 |

| | | |
|---|---|---|
| ❑ 10 Troy Aikman | 2.00 | .75 |
| ❑ 11 Tony Banks | .60 | .25 |
| ❑ 12 Ty Detmer | .60 | .25 |
| ❑ 13 Chris Chandler | .60 | .25 |
| ❑ 14 Marshall Faulk | 1.25 | .50 |
| ❑ 15 Heath Shuler | .40 | .15 |
| ❑ 16 Stan Humphries | .60 | .25 |
| ❑ 17 Bryan Cox | .40 | .15 |
| ❑ 18 Chris Spielman | .40 | .15 |
| ❑ 19 Derrick Thomas | 1.00 | .40 |
| ❑ 20 Steve Young | 1.25 | .50 |
| ❑ 21 Desmond Howard | .60 | .25 |
| ❑ 22 Jeff Blake | .60 | .25 |
| ❑ 23 Michael Jackson | .60 | .25 |
| ❑ 24 Cris Carter | 1.00 | .40 |
| ❑ 25 Joey Galloway | .60 | .25 |
| ❑ 26 Simeon Rice | .60 | .25 |
| ❑ 27 Reggie White | 1.00 | .40 |
| ❑ 28 Dave Brown | .40 | .15 |
| ❑ 29 Mike Alstott | 1.00 | .40 |
| ❑ 30 Emmitt Smith | 3.00 | 1.25 |
| ❑ 31 Anthony Johnson | .40 | .15 |
| ❑ 32 Mark Brunell | 1.25 | .50 |
| ❑ 33 Ricky Watters | .60 | .25 |
| ❑ 34 Terrell Davis | 1.25 | .50 |
| ❑ 35 Ben Coates | .60 | .25 |
| ❑ 36 Gus Frerotte | .40 | .15 |
| ❑ 37 Andre Reed | .60 | .25 |
| ❑ 38 Isaac Bruce | 1.00 | .40 |
| ❑ 39 Junior Seau | 1.00 | .40 |
| ❑ 40 Eddie George | 1.00 | .40 |
| ❑ 41 Adrian Murrell | .60 | .25 |
| ❑ 42 Jake Reed | .60 | .25 |
| ❑ 43 Karim Abdul-Jabbar | .60 | .25 |
| ❑ 44 Scott Mitchell | .60 | .25 |
| ❑ 45 Ki-Jana Carter | .40 | .15 |
| ❑ 46 Curtis Conway | .60 | .25 |
| ❑ 47 Jim Harbaugh | .60 | .25 |
| ❑ 48 Tim Brown | 1.00 | .40 |
| ❑ 49 Mario Bates | .40 | .15 |
| ❑ 50 Jerry Rice | 2.00 | .75 |
| ❑ 51 Byron Bam Morris | .40 | .15 |
| ❑ 52 Marcus Allen | 1.00 | .40 |
| ❑ 53 Errict Rhett | .40 | .15 |
| ❑ 54 Steve McNair | 1.25 | .50 |
| ❑ 55 Kerry Collins | 1.00 | .40 |
| ❑ 56 Bert Emanuel | .60 | .25 |
| ❑ 57 Curtis Martin | 1.25 | .50 |
| ❑ 58 Bryce Paup | .40 | .15 |
| ❑ 59 Brad Johnson | 1.00 | .40 |
| ❑ 60 John Elway | 4.00 | 1.50 |
| ❑ 61 Natrone Means | .60 | .25 |
| ❑ 62 Deion Sanders | 1.00 | .40 |
| ❑ 63 Tony Martin | .60 | .25 |
| ❑ 64 Michael Westbrook | .60 | .25 |
| ❑ 65 Chris Calloway | .40 | .15 |
| ❑ 66 Antonio Freeman | 1.00 | .40 |
| ❑ 67 Rob Johnson | 1.00 | .40 |
| ❑ 68 Kent Graham | .40 | .15 |
| ❑ 69 O.J. McDuffie | .60 | .25 |
| ❑ 70 Barry Sanders | 3.00 | 1.25 |
| ❑ 71 Chris Warren | .60 | .25 |
| ❑ 72 Kordell Stewart | 1.00 | .40 |
| ❑ 73 Thurman Thomas | 1.00 | .40 |
| ❑ 74 Marvin Harrison | 1.00 | .40 |
| ❑ 75 Carl Pickens | .60 | .25 |
| ❑ 76 Brent Jones | .40 | .15 |
| ❑ 77 Irving Fryar | .60 | .25 |

| | | |
|---|---|---|
| ❑ 78 Neil O'Donnell | .60 | .25 |
| ❑ 79 Elvis Grbac | .60 | .25 |
| ❑ 80 Drew Bledsoe | 1.25 | .50 |
| ❑ 81 Shannon Sharpe | .60 | .25 |
| ❑ 82 Vinny Testaverde | .60 | .25 |
| ❑ 83 Chris Sanders | .40 | .15 |
| ❑ 84 Herman Moore | .60 | .25 |
| ❑ 85 Jeff George | .60 | .25 |
| ❑ 86 Bruce Smith | .60 | .25 |
| ❑ 87 Robert Smith | .60 | .25 |
| ❑ 88 Kevin Hardy | .40 | .15 |
| ❑ 89 Kevin Greene | .60 | .25 |
| ❑ 90 Dan Marino | 4.00 | 1.50 |
| ❑ 91 Michael Irvin | 1.00 | .40 |
| ❑ 92 Garrison Hearst | .60 | .25 |
| ❑ 93 Lake Dawson | .40 | .15 |
| ❑ 94 Lawrence Phillips | .40 | .15 |
| ❑ 95 Terry Glenn | 1.00 | .40 |
| ❑ 96 Jake Plummer RC | 6.00 | 2.50 |
| ❑ 97 Byron Hanspard RC | .60 | .25 |
| ❑ 98 Bryant Westbrook RC | .40 | .15 |
| ❑ 99 Troy Davis RC | .60 | .25 |
| ❑ 100 Danny Wuerffel RC | 1.00 | .40 |
| ❑ 101 Tony Gonzalez RC | 4.00 | 1.50 |
| ❑ 102 Jim Druckenmiller RC | .60 | .25 |
| ❑ 103 Kevin Lockett RC | .40 | .15 |
| ❑ 104 Renaldo Wynn RC | .40 | .15 |
| ❑ 105 James Farrior RC | 1.00 | .40 |
| ❑ 106 Rae Carruth RC | .40 | .15 |
| ❑ 107 Tom Knight RC | .40 | .15 |
| ❑ 108 Corey Dillon RC | 8.00 | 3.00 |
| ❑ 109 Kenny Holmes RC | 1.00 | .40 |
| ❑ 110 Orlando Pace RC | 1.00 | .40 |
| ❑ 111 Reidel Anthony RC | 1.00 | .40 |
| ❑ 112 Chad Scott RC | .60 | .25 |
| ❑ 113 Antowain Smith RC | 3.00 | 1.25 |
| ❑ 114 David LaFleur RC | .40 | .15 |
| ❑ 115 Yatil Green RC | .60 | .25 |
| ❑ 116 Darrell Russell RC | .40 | .15 |
| ❑ 117 Joey Kent RC | 1.00 | .40 |
| ❑ 118 Darnell Autry RC | .60 | .25 |
| ❑ 119 Peter Boulware RC | .60 | .25 |
| ❑ 120 Shawn Springs RC | .60 | .25 |
| ❑ 121 Ike Hilliard RC | 1.50 | .60 |
| ❑ 122 Dwayne Rudd RC | 1.00 | .40 |
| ❑ 123 Reinard Wilson RC | .60 | .25 |
| ❑ 124 Michael Booker RC | .40 | .15 |
| ❑ 125 Warrick Dunn RC | 4.00 | 1.50 |

## 1998 Bowman's Best

| | | |
|---|---|---|
| ❑ COMPLETE SET (125) | 80.00 | 30.00 |
| ❑ 1 Emmitt Smith | 3.00 | 1.25 |
| ❑ 2 Reggie White | 1.00 | .40 |
| ❑ 3 Jake Plummer | 1.00 | .40 |
| ❑ 4 Ike Hilliard | .40 | .15 |
| ❑ 5 Isaac Bruce | 1.00 | .40 |
| ❑ 6 Trent Dilfer | 1.00 | .40 |
| ❑ 7 Ricky Watters | .60 | .25 |
| ❑ 8 Jeff George | .60 | .25 |
| ❑ 9 Wayne Chrebet | 1.00 | .40 |
| ❑ 10 Brett Favre | 4.00 | 1.50 |
| ❑ 11 Terry Allen | 1.00 | .40 |
| ❑ 12 Bert Emanuel | .40 | .15 |
| ❑ 13 Andre Reed | .60 | .25 |
| ❑ 14 Andre Rison | .60 | .25 |
| ❑ 15 Jeff Blake | .60 | .25 |
| ❑ 16 Steve McNair | 1.00 | .40 |
| ❑ 17 Joey Galloway | .60 | .25 |

| | | |
|---|---|---|
| ❑ 18 Irving Fryar | .60 | .25 |
| ❑ 19 Dorsey Levens | 1.00 | .40 |
| ❑ 20 Jerry Rice | 2.00 | .75 |
| ❑ 21 Kerry Collins | .60 | .25 |
| ❑ 22 Michael Jackson | .40 | .15 |
| ❑ 23 Kordell Stewart | 1.00 | .40 |
| ❑ 24 Junior Seau | 1.00 | .40 |
| ❑ 25 Jimmy Smith | .60 | .25 |
| ❑ 26 Michael Westbrook | .60 | .25 |
| ❑ 27 Eddie George | 1.00 | .40 |
| ❑ 28 Cris Carter | 1.00 | .40 |
| ❑ 29 Jason Sehorn | .60 | .25 |
| ❑ 30 Warrick Dunn | 1.00 | .40 |
| ❑ 31 Garrison Hearst | 1.00 | .40 |
| ❑ 32 Erik Kramer | .40 | .15 |
| ❑ 33 Chris Chandler | .60 | .25 |
| ❑ 34 Michael Irvin | 1.00 | .40 |
| ❑ 35 Marshall Faulk | 1.25 | .50 |
| ❑ 36 Warren Moon | 1.00 | .40 |
| ❑ 37 Rickey Dudley | .40 | .15 |
| ❑ 38 Drew Bledsoe | 1.50 | .60 |
| ❑ 39 Antowain Smith | 1.00 | .40 |
| ❑ 40 Terrell Davis | 1.00 | .40 |
| ❑ 41 Gus Frerotte | .60 | .25 |
| ❑ 42 Robert Brooks | .60 | .25 |
| ❑ 43 Tony Banks | .60 | .25 |
| ❑ 44 Terrell Owens | 1.00 | .40 |
| ❑ 45 Edgar Bennett | .40 | .15 |
| ❑ 46 Rob Moore | .60 | .25 |
| ❑ 47 J.J. Stokes | .60 | .25 |
| ❑ 48 Yancey Thigpen | .40 | .15 |
| ❑ 49 Elvis Grbac | .60 | .25 |
| ❑ 50 John Elway | 4.00 | 1.50 |
| ❑ 51 Charles Johnson | .40 | .15 |
| ❑ 52 Karim Abdul-Jabbar | 1.00 | .40 |
| ❑ 53 Carl Pickens | .60 | .25 |
| ❑ 54 Peter Boulware | .40 | .15 |
| ❑ 55 Chris Warren | .60 | .25 |
| ❑ 56 Terance Mathis | .60 | .25 |
| ❑ 57 Andre Hastings | .40 | .15 |
| ❑ 58 Jake Reed | .60 | .25 |
| ❑ 59 Mike Alstott | .40 | .15 |
| ❑ 60 Mark Brunell | 1.00 | .40 |
| ❑ 61 Herman Moore | .60 | .25 |
| ❑ 62 Troy Aikman | 2.00 | .75 |
| ❑ 63 Fred Lane | .40 | .15 |
| ❑ 64 Rod Smith | .60 | .25 |
| ❑ 65 Terry Glenn | 1.00 | .40 |
| ❑ 66 Jerome Bettis | 1.00 | .40 |
| ❑ 67 Derrick Thomas | 1.00 | .40 |
| ❑ 68 Marvin Harrison | 1.00 | .40 |
| ❑ 69 Adrian Murrell | .40 | .15 |
| ❑ 70 Curtis Martin | 1.00 | .40 |
| ❑ 71 Bobby Hoying | .60 | .25 |
| ❑ 72 Darrell Green | .60 | .25 |
| ❑ 73 Sean Dawkins | .40 | .15 |
| ❑ 74 Robert Smith | 1.00 | .40 |
| ❑ 75 Antonio Freeman | 1.00 | .40 |
| ❑ 76 Scott Mitchell | .60 | .25 |
| ❑ 77 Curtis Conway | .60 | .25 |
| ❑ 78 Rae Carruth | .40 | .15 |
| ❑ 79 Jamal Anderson | 1.00 | .40 |
| ❑ 80 Dan Marino | 4.00 | 1.50 |
| ❑ 81 Brad Johnson | 1.00 | .40 |
| ❑ 82 Danny Kanell | .60 | .25 |
| ❑ 83 Charlie Garner | .60 | .25 |
| ❑ 84 Rob Johnson | .60 | .25 |
| ❑ 85 Natrone Means | .60 | .25 |
| ❑ 86 Tim Brown | 1.00 | .40 |
| ❑ 87 Keyshawn Johnson | 1.00 | .40 |
| ❑ 88 Ben Coates | .60 | .25 |
| ❑ 89 Derrick Alexander | .60 | .25 |
| ❑ 90 Steve Young | 1.25 | .50 |
| ❑ 91 Shannon Sharpe | .60 | .25 |
| ❑ 92 Corey Dillon | .60 | .25 |
| ❑ 93 Bruce Smith | .60 | .25 |
| ❑ 94 Errict Rhett | .60 | .25 |
| ❑ 95 Jim Harbaugh | .40 | .15 |
| ❑ 96 Napoleon Kaufman | 1.00 | .40 |
| ❑ 97 Glenn Foley | .60 | .25 |
| ❑ 98 Tony Gonzalez | 1.00 | .40 |
| ❑ 99 Keenan McCardell | .60 | .25 |
| ❑ 100 Barry Sanders | 3.00 | 1.25 |
| ❑ 101 Charles Woodson RC | 3.00 | 1.25 |

| | | |
|---|---|---|
| ❑ 102 Tim Dwight RC | 2.50 | 1.00 |
| ❑ 103 Marcus Nash RC | 1.25 | .50 |
| ❑ 104 Joe Jurevicius RC | 2.50 | 1.00 |
| ❑ 105 Jacquez Green RC | 2.00 | .75 |
| ❑ 106 Kevin Dyson RC | 2.50 | 1.00 |
| ❑ 107 Keith Brooking RC | 2.50 | 1.00 |
| ❑ 108 Andre Wadsworth RC | 2.00 | .75 |
| ❑ 109 Randy Moss RC | 15.00 | 6.00 |
| ❑ 110 Robert Edwards RC | 2.00 | .75 |
| ❑ 111 Pat Johnson RC | 2.00 | .75 |
| ❑ 112 Peyton Manning RC | 25.00 | 10.00 |
| ❑ 113 Duane Starks RC | 1.25 | .50 |
| ❑ 114 Grant Wistrom RC | 2.00 | .75 |
| ❑ 115 Anthony Simmons RC | 2.00 | .75 |
| ❑ 116 Takeo Spikes RC | 2.50 | 1.00 |
| ❑ 117 Tony Simmons RC | 2.00 | .75 |
| ❑ 118 Jerome Pathon RC | 2.50 | 1.00 |
| ❑ 119 Ryan Leaf RC | 2.50 | 1.00 |
| ❑ 120 Skip Hicks RC | 2.00 | .75 |
| ❑ 121 Curtis Enis RC | 1.25 | .50 |
| ❑ 122 Germane Crowell RC | 2.00 | .75 |
| ❑ 123 John Avery RC | 2.00 | .75 |
| ❑ 124 Hines Ward RC | 10.00 | 5.00 |
| ❑ 125 Fred Taylor RC | 4.00 | 1.50 |

## 1999 Bowman's Best

| | | |
|---|---|---|
| ❑ COMPLETE SET (133) | 80.00 | 30.00 |
| ❑ 1 Randy Moss | 2.50 | 1.00 |
| ❑ 2 Skip Hicks | .40 | .15 |
| ❑ 3 Robert Smith | 1.00 | .40 |
| ❑ 4 Drew Bledsoe | 1.25 | .50 |
| ❑ 5 Tim Brown | 1.00 | .40 |
| ❑ 6 Marshall Faulk | 1.25 | .50 |
| ❑ 7 Terance Mathis | .60 | .25 |
| ❑ 8 Sean Dawkins | .40 | .15 |
| ❑ 9 Ed McCaffrey | .60 | .25 |
| ❑ 10 Jamal Anderson | 1.00 | .40 |
| ❑ 11 Antonio Freeman | 1.00 | .40 |
| ❑ 12 Terry Kirby | .60 | .25 |
| ❑ 13 Vinny Testaverde | .60 | .25 |
| ❑ 14 Eddie George | 1.00 | .40 |
| ❑ 15 Ricky Watters | .60 | .25 |
| ❑ 16 Johnnie Morton | .60 | .25 |
| ❑ 17 Natrone Means | 1.00 | .40 |
| ❑ 18 Terry Glenn | 1.00 | .40 |
| ❑ 19 Michael Westbrook | .60 | .25 |
| ❑ 20 Doug Flutie | 1.00 | .40 |
| ❑ 21 Jake Plummer | .60 | .25 |
| ❑ 22 Damay Scott | .60 | .25 |
| ❑ 23 Andre Rison | .60 | .25 |
| ❑ 24 Jon Kitna | 1.00 | .40 |
| ❑ 25 Dan Marino | 3.00 | 1.25 |
| ❑ 26 Ike Hilliard | .60 | .25 |
| ❑ 27 Warrick Dunn | 1.00 | .40 |
| ❑ 28 Jerome Bettis | 1.00 | .40 |
| ❑ 29 Curtis Conway | .60 | .25 |
| ❑ 30 Emmitt Smith | 2.00 | .75 |
| ❑ 31 Jimmy Smith | .60 | .25 |
| ❑ 32 Isaac Bruce | 1.00 | .40 |
| ❑ 33 Jerry Rice | 2.00 | .75 |
| ❑ 34 Curtis Martin | 1.00 | .40 |
| ❑ 35 Steve McNair | 1.00 | .40 |
| ❑ 36 Jeff Blake | .60 | .25 |
| ❑ 37 Rob Moore | .60 | .25 |
| ❑ 38 Dorsey Levens | 1.00 | .40 |
| ❑ 39 Terrell Davis | 1.00 | .40 |
| ❑ 40 John Elway | 3.00 | 1.25 |
| ❑ 41 Trent Dilfer | .60 | .25 |

| | | |
|---|---|---|
| ❑ 42 Joey Galloway | .60 | .25 |
| ❑ 43 Keyshawn Johnson | 1.00 | .40 |
| ❑ 44 O.J. McDuffie | .60 | .25 |
| ❑ 45 Fred Taylor | 1.00 | .40 |
| ❑ 46 Andre Reed | .60 | .25 |
| ❑ 47 Frank Sanders | .60 | .25 |
| ❑ 48 Keenan McCardell | .60 | .25 |
| ❑ 49 Elvis Grbac | .60 | .25 |
| ❑ 50 Barry Sanders | 3.00 | 1.25 |
| ❑ 51 Terrell Owens | 1.00 | .40 |
| ❑ 52 Trent Green | 1.00 | .40 |
| ❑ 53 Brad Johnson | 1.00 | .40 |
| ❑ 54 Rich Gannon | 1.00 | .40 |
| ❑ 55 Randall Cunningham | 1.00 | .40 |
| ❑ 56 Tony Martin | .60 | .25 |
| ❑ 57 Rod Smith | .60 | .25 |
| ❑ 58 Eric Moulds | 1.00 | .40 |
| ❑ 59 Yancey Thigpen | .40 | .15 |
| ❑ 60 Brett Favre | 3.00 | 1.25 |
| ❑ 61 Cris Carter | 1.00 | .40 |
| ❑ 62 Marvin Harrison | 1.00 | .40 |
| ❑ 63 Chris Chandler | 1.00 | .40 |
| ❑ 64 Antowain Smith | 1.00 | .40 |
| ❑ 65 Carl Pickens | .60 | .25 |
| ❑ 66 Shannon Sharpe | .60 | .25 |
| ❑ 67 Mike Alstott | 1.00 | .40 |
| ❑ 68 J.J. Stokes | .60 | .25 |
| ❑ 69 Ben Coates | .60 | .25 |
| ❑ 70 Peyton Manning | 3.00 | 1.25 |
| ❑ 71 Duce Staley | 1.00 | .40 |
| ❑ 72 Michael Irvin | .60 | .25 |
| ❑ 73 Tim Biakabutaka | .60 | .25 |
| ❑ 74 Priest Holmes | 1.50 | .60 |
| ❑ 75 Steve Young | 1.25 | .50 |
| ❑ 76 Jerome Pathon | .60 | .25 |
| ❑ 77 Wayne Chrebet | 1.00 | .40 |
| ❑ 78 Bert Emanuel | .40 | .15 |
| ❑ 79 Curtis Enis | .60 | .25 |
| ❑ 80 Mark Brunell | 1.00 | .40 |
| ❑ 81 Herman Moore | .60 | .25 |
| ❑ 82 Corey Dillon | 1.00 | .40 |
| ❑ 83 Jim Harbaugh | .60 | .25 |
| ❑ 84 Gary Brown | .40 | .15 |
| ❑ 85 Kordell Stewart | 1.00 | .40 |
| ❑ 86 Garrison Hearst | .60 | .25 |
| ❑ 87 Rocket Ismail | .60 | .25 |
| ❑ 88 Charlie Batch | 1.00 | .40 |
| ❑ 89 Napoleon Kaufman | .60 | .25 |
| ❑ 90 Troy Aikman | 2.00 | .75 |
| ❑ 91 Brett Favre BP | 1.50 | .60 |
| ❑ 92 Randy Moss BP | 1.25 | .50 |
| ❑ 93 Terrell Davis BP | 1.00 | .40 |
| ❑ 94 Barry Sanders BP | 1.50 | .60 |
| ❑ 95 Peyton Manning BP | 1.50 | .60 |
| ❑ 96 Troy Edwards BP | .60 | .25 |
| ❑ 97 Cade McNown BP | .60 | .25 |
| ❑ 98 Edgerrin James BP | 2.50 | 1.00 |
| ❑ 99 Torry Holt BP | 1.00 | .40 |
| ❑ 100 Tim Couch RC | 4.00 | 1.50 |
| ❑ 101 Chris Claiborne RC | 1.00 | .40 |
| ❑ 102 Brock Huard RC | 2.00 | .75 |
| ❑ 103 Amos Zereoue RC | 1.00 | .40 |
| ❑ 104 Sedrick Irvin RC | 1.00 | .40 |
| ❑ 105 Kevin Faulk RC | 2.00 | .75 |
| ❑ 106 Ebenezer Ekuban RC | 1.00 | .40 |
| ❑ 107 Daunte Culpepper RC | 8.00 | 3.00 |
| ❑ 108 Rob Konrad RC | 1.50 | .60 |
| ❑ 109 James Johnson RC | 1.50 | .60 |
| ❑ 110 Kurt Warner RC | 10.00 | 4.00 |
| ❑ 111 Mike Cloud RC | 1.50 | .60 |
| ❑ 112 Andy Katzenmoyer RC | 1.50 | .60 |
| ❑ 113 Jevon Kearse RC | 3.00 | 1.25 |
| ❑ 114 Akili Smith RC | 1.50 | .60 |
| ❑ 115 Edgerrin James RC | 8.00 | 3.00 |
| ❑ 116 Cecil Collins RC | 1.50 | .60 |
| ❑ 117 Chris McAlister RC | 1.50 | .60 |
| ❑ 118 Donovan McNabb RC | 10.00 | 4.00 |
| ❑ 119 Kevin Johnson RC | 2.00 | .75 |
| ❑ 120 Torry Holt RC | 5.00 | 2.00 |
| ❑ 121 Antoine Winfield RC | 1.50 | .60 |
| ❑ 122 Michael Bishop RC | 1.50 | .60 |
| ❑ 123 Joe Germaine RC | 1.50 | .60 |
| ❑ 124 David Boston RC | 2.00 | .75 |
| ❑ 125 D'Wayne Bates RC | 1.50 | .60 |

| | | |
|---|---|---|
| ❑ 126 Champ Bailey RC | 2.50 | 1.00 |
| ❑ 127 Cade McNown RC | 1.50 | .60 |
| ❑ 128 Shaun King RC | 1.50 | .60 |
| ❑ 129 Peerless Price RC | 2.00 | .75 |
| ❑ 130 Troy Edwards RC | 1.50 | .60 |
| ❑ 131 Karsten Bailey RC | 1.50 | .60 |
| ❑ 132 Tim Couch RC | 2.00 | .75 |
| ❑ 133 Ricky Williams RC | 4.00 | 1.50 |
| ❑ C1 Rookie Class Photo | 8.00 | 3.00 |

## 2000 Bowman's Best

| | | |
|---|---|---|
| ❑ COMPLETE SET (150) | 500.00 | 250.00 |
| ❑ 1 Troy Edwards | .30 | .10 |
| ❑ 2 Kurt Warner | 1.50 | .60 |
| ❑ 3 Steve McNair | .75 | .30 |
| ❑ 4 Terry Glenn | .75 | .30 |
| ❑ 5 Charlie Batch | .75 | .30 |
| ❑ 6 Patrick Jeffers | .75 | .30 |
| ❑ 7 Jake Plummer | .75 | .30 |
| ❑ 8 Derrick Alexander | .50 | .20 |
| ❑ 9 Joey Galloway | .50 | .20 |
| ❑ 10 Tony Banks | .50 | .20 |
| ❑ 11 Robert Smith | .75 | .30 |
| ❑ 12 Jerry Rice | 1.50 | .60 |
| ❑ 13 Jeff Garcia | .75 | .30 |
| ❑ 14 Michael Westbrook | .50 | .20 |
| ❑ 15 Curtis Conway | .50 | .20 |
| ❑ 16 Brian Griese | .75 | .30 |
| ❑ 17 Peyton Manning | 2.00 | .75 |
| ❑ 18 Daunte Culpepper | 1.00 | .40 |
| ❑ 19 Frank Sanders | .50 | .20 |
| ❑ 20 Muhsin Muhammad | .50 | .20 |
| ❑ 21 Corey Dillon | .75 | .30 |
| ❑ 22 Brett Favre | 2.50 | 1.00 |
| ❑ 23 Warrick Dunn | .75 | .30 |
| ❑ 24 Tim Brown | .75 | .30 |
| ❑ 25 Kerry Collins | .50 | .20 |
| ❑ 26 Brad Johnson | .50 | .20 |
| ❑ 27 Rocket Ismail | .50 | .20 |
| ❑ 28 Jamal Anderson | .50 | .20 |
| ❑ 29 Jimmy Smith | .50 | .20 |
| ❑ 30 Torry Holt | .75 | .30 |
| ❑ 31 Duce Staley | .75 | .30 |
| ❑ 32 Drew Bledsoe | 1.00 | .40 |
| ❑ 33 Jerome Bettis | .75 | .30 |
| ❑ 34 Keyshawn Johnson | .75 | .30 |
| ❑ 35 Fred Taylor | .75 | .30 |
| ❑ 36 Akili Smith | .30 | .10 |
| ❑ 37 Rob Johnson | .50 | .20 |
| ❑ 38 Elvis Grbac | .30 | .10 |
| ❑ 39 Antonio Freeman | .75 | .30 |
| ❑ 40 Curtis Enis | .30 | .10 |
| ❑ 41 Terance Mathis | .50 | .20 |
| ❑ 42 Terrell Davis | .75 | .30 |
| ❑ 43 Randy Moss | 1.50 | .60 |
| ❑ 44 Jon Kitna | .75 | .30 |
| ❑ 45 Curtis Martin | .75 | .30 |
| ❑ 46 Terrell Owens | .75 | .30 |
| ❑ 47 Robert Smith | .75 | .30 |
| ❑ 48 Albert Connell | .30 | .10 |
| ❑ 49 Edgerrin James | 1.25 | .50 |
| ❑ 50 Tony Gonzalez | .50 | .20 |
| ❑ 51 Eric Moulds | .75 | .30 |
| ❑ 52 Natrone Means | .50 | .20 |
| ❑ 53 Carl Pickens | .50 | .20 |
| ❑ 54 Mark Brunell | .75 | .30 |
| ❑ 55 Rob Moore | .50 | .20 |
| ❑ 56 Marshall Faulk | 1.00 | .40 |

|  |  | | |
|---|---|---|---|
| 57 | Stephen Davis | .75 | .30 |
| 58 | Rich Gannon | .75 | .30 |
| 59 | Ricky Williams | .75 | .30 |
| 60 | Emmitt Smith | 1.50 | .60 |
| 61 | Germane Crowell | .30 | .10 |
| 62 | Doug Flutie | .50 | .20 |
| 63 | O.J. McDuffie | .50 | .20 |
| 64 | Chris Chandler | .50 | .20 |
| 65 | Qadry Ismail | .50 | .20 |
| 66 | Tim Couch | .50 | .20 |
| 67 | James Stewart | .50 | .20 |
| 68 | Marvin Harrison | .75 | .30 |
| 69 | Cris Carter | .75 | .30 |
| 70 | Cade McNown | .30 | .10 |
| 71 | Marcus Robinson | .75 | .30 |
| 72 | Steve Beuerlein | .50 | .20 |
| 73 | Jevon Kearse | .75 | .30 |
| 74 | Eddie George | .75 | .30 |
| 75 | Donovan McNabb | 1.25 | .50 |
| 76 | Jeff Blake | .50 | .20 |
| 77 | Wayne Chrebet | .50 | .20 |
| 78 | Kordell Stewart | .50 | .20 |
| 79 | Steve Young | 1.00 | .40 |
| 80 | Mike Alstott | .75 | .30 |
| 81 | Ricky Watters | .50 | .20 |
| 82 | Charlie Garner | .50 | .20 |
| 83 | Troy Aikman | 1.50 | .60 |
| 84 | Dorsey Levens | .50 | .20 |
| 85 | Ike Hilliard | .50 | .20 |
| 86 | Shaun King | .30 | .10 |
| 87 | Isaac Bruce | .75 | .30 |
| 88 | Tyrone Wheatley | .50 | .20 |
| 89 | Amani Toomer | .50 | .20 |
| 90 | Ed McCaffrey | .75 | .30 |
| 91 | E.James/M.Faulk BP | .75 | .30 |
| 92 | D.Bledsoe/B.Johnson BP | .75 | .30 |
| 93 | J.Smith/R.Moss BP | 1.00 | .40 |
| 94 | E.George/S.Davis BP | .50 | .20 |
| 95 | M.Brunell/T.Aikman BP | 1.00 | .40 |
| 96 | M.Harrison/C.Carter BP | .75 | .30 |
| 97 | C.Martin/E.Smith BP | 1.00 | .40 |
| 98 | T.Brown/I.Bruce BP | .50 | .20 |
| 99 | F.Taylor/R.Williams BP | .75 | .30 |
| 100 | K.Warner/P.Manning BP | 1.00 | .40 |
| 101 | Shaun Alexander RC | 20.00 | 10.00 |
| 102 | Thomas Jones RC | 12.00 | 5.00 |
| 103 | Courtney Brown RC | 6.00 | 2.50 |
| 104 | Curtis Keaton RC | 6.00 | 2.50 |
| 105 | Jerry Porter RC | 10.00 | 4.00 |
| 106 | Corey Simon RC | 8.00 | 3.00 |
| 107 | Dez White RC | 8.00 | 3.00 |
| 108 | Jamal Lewis RC | 15.00 | 6.00 |
| 109 | Ron Dayne RC | 8.00 | 3.00 |
| 110 | R.Jay Soward RC | 6.00 | 2.50 |
| 111 | Tee Martin RC | 8.00 | 3.00 |
| 112 | Brian Urlacher RC | 25.00 | 10.00 |
| 113 | Reuben Droughns RC | 8.00 | 3.00 |
| 114 | Travis Taylor RC | 10.00 | 4.00 |
| 115 | Plaxico Burress RC | 15.00 | 6.00 |
| 116 | Chad Pennington RC | 15.00 | 6.00 |
| 117 | Sylvester Morris RC | 6.00 | 2.50 |
| 118 | Ron Dugans RC | 4.00 | 1.50 |
| 119 | Joe Hamilton RC | 6.00 | 2.50 |
| 120 | Chris Redman RC | 6.00 | 2.50 |
| 121 | Trung Canidate RC | 6.00 | 2.50 |
| 122 | J.R. Redmond RC | 6.00 | 2.50 |
| 123 | Danny Farmer RC | 6.00 | 2.50 |
| 124 | Todd Pinkston RC | 8.00 | 3.00 |
| 125 | Dennis Northcutt RC | 8.00 | 3.00 |
| 126 | Laveranues Coles RC | 10.00 | 4.00 |
| 127 | Bubba Franks RC | 8.00 | 3.00 |
| 128 | Travis Prentice RC | 6.00 | 2.50 |
| 129 | Peter Warrick RC | 8.00 | 3.00 |
| 130 | Anthony Becht RC | 8.00 | 3.00 |
| 131 | Ike Charlton RC | 4.00 | 1.50 |
| 132 | Shaun Ellis RC | 8.00 | 3.00 |
| 133 | Sean Morey RC | 6.00 | 2.50 |
| 134 | Sebastian Janikowski RC | 8.00 | 3.00 |
| 135 | Aaron Stecker RC | 4.00 | 1.50 |
| 136 | Ronney Jenkins RC | 6.00 | 2.50 |
| 137 | Jamel White RC | 6.00 | 2.50 |
| 138 | Nick Williams RC | 4.00 | 1.50 |
| 139 | Andy McCullough RC | 4.00 | 1.50 |
| 140 | Kevin Daft RC | 4.00 | 1.50 |
| 141 | Thomas Hamner RC | 4.00 | 1.50 |
| 142 | Tim Rattay RC | 8.00 | 3.00 |
| 143 | Spergon Wynn RC | 6.00 | 2.50 |
| 144 | Brandon Short RC | 6.00 | 2.50 |
| 145 | Chad Morton RC | 8.00 | 3.00 |
| 146 | Gari Scott RC | 4.00 | 1.50 |
| 147 | Frank Murphy RC | 4.00 | 1.50 |
| 148 | James Williams RC | 6.00 | 2.50 |
| 149 | Windrell Hayes RC | 6.00 | 2.50 |
| 150 | Doug Johnson RC | 8.00 | 3.00 |

## 2001 Bowman's Best

MICHAEL VICK ATLANTA FALCONS

|  |  | | |
|---|---|---|---|
| | COMP.SET w/o SP's (100) | 20.00 | 7.50 |
| 1 | Jerry Rice | 1.50 | .60 |
| 2 | Doug Flutie | .75 | .30 |
| 3 | Drew Bledsoe | 1.00 | .40 |
| 4 | Edgerrin James | 1.00 | .40 |
| 5 | Muhsin Muhammad | .50 | .20 |
| 6 | Charlie Batch | .75 | .30 |
| 7 | Marshall Faulk | 1.00 | .40 |
| 8 | Trent Green | .75 | .30 |
| 9 | Rich Gannon | .75 | .30 |
| 10 | Emmitt Smith | 1.50 | .60 |
| 11 | Steve McNair | .75 | .30 |
| 12 | Darrell Jackson | .75 | .30 |
| 13 | Amani Toomer | .50 | .20 |
| 14 | Jimmy Smith | .50 | .20 |
| 15 | Kevin Johnson | .50 | .20 |
| 16 | Ray Lewis | .75 | .30 |
| 17 | Peter Warrick | .75 | .30 |
| 18 | Cris Carter | .75 | .30 |
| 19 | Jerome Bettis | .75 | .30 |
| 20 | Keyshawn Johnson | .75 | .30 |
| 21 | Joey Galloway | .50 | .20 |
| 22 | Chris Chandler | .50 | .20 |
| 23 | Brett Favre | 2.50 | 1.00 |
| 24 | Aaron Brooks | .75 | .30 |
| 25 | Kurt Warner | 1.50 | .60 |
| 26 | Jeff Graham | .30 | .10 |
| 27 | Curtis Martin | .75 | .30 |
| 28 | Mike Anderson | .75 | .30 |
| 29 | Eric Moulds | .75 | .30 |
| 30 | David Boston | .75 | .30 |
| 31 | Elvis Grbac | .50 | .20 |
| 32 | James Stewart | .50 | .20 |
| 33 | Randy Moss | 1.50 | .60 |
| 34 | Donovan McNabb | 1.00 | .40 |
| 35 | Matt Hasselbeck | .50 | .20 |
| 36 | Stephen Davis | .75 | .30 |
| 37 | Brad Johnson | .75 | .30 |
| 38 | Jamal Anderson | .75 | .30 |
| 39 | Tim Biakabutuka | .50 | .20 |
| 40 | Antonio Freeman | .75 | .30 |
| 41 | Mark Brunell | .75 | .30 |
| 42 | Tiki Barber | .75 | .30 |
| 43 | Charlie Garner | .50 | .20 |
| 44 | Eddie George | .75 | .30 |
| 45 | Ricky Williams | .75 | .30 |
| 46 | Rob Johnson | .50 | .20 |
| 47 | Jake Plummer | .50 | .20 |
| 48 | Peyton Manning | 2.00 | .75 |
| 49 | Lamar Smith | .50 | .20 |
| 50 | Corey Dillon | .75 | .30 |
| 51 | Derrick Alexander | .50 | .20 |
| 52 | Troy Brown | .50 | .20 |
| 53 | Wayne Chrebet | .50 | .20 |
| 54 | Shaun Alexander | 1.00 | .40 |
| 55 | Jeff George | .50 | .20 |
| 56 | Tim Brown | .75 | .30 |
| 57 | Brian Griese | .75 | .30 |
| 58 | Cade McNown | .30 | .10 |
| 59 | Jamal Lewis | 1.25 | .50 |
| 60 | Germane Crowell | .30 | .10 |
| 61 | Junior Seau | .75 | .30 |
| 62 | Warrick Dunn | .75 | .30 |
| 63 | Isaac Bruce | .75 | .30 |
| 64 | Terry Glenn | .50 | .20 |
| 65 | Fred Taylor | .75 | .30 |
| 66 | Tim Couch | .50 | .20 |
| 67 | Akili Smith | .30 | .10 |
| 68 | Tony Gonzalez | .50 | .20 |
| 69 | Kerry Collins | .50 | .20 |
| 70 | James Thrash | .50 | .20 |
| 71 | Terrell Owens | .75 | .30 |
| 72 | Derrick Mason | .50 | .20 |
| 73 | Tyrone Wheatley | .50 | .20 |
| 74 | Oronde Gadsden | .50 | .20 |
| 75 | Ahman Green | .75 | .30 |
| 76 | Jon Kitna | .50 | .20 |
| 77 | Tony Banks | .50 | .20 |
| 78 | Marvin Harrison | .75 | .30 |
| 79 | Daunte Culpepper | .75 | .30 |
| 80 | Vinny Testaverde | .50 | .20 |
| 81 | Chad Lewis | .30 | .10 |
| 82 | Torry Holt | .75 | .30 |
| 83 | Jeff Garcia | .75 | .30 |
| 84 | Rod Smith | .50 | .20 |
| 85 | Marcus Robinson | .75 | .30 |
| 86 | Keenan McCardell | .30 | .10 |
| 87 | Joe Horn | .50 | .20 |
| 88 | Kordell Stewart | .50 | .20 |
| 89 | Jay Fiedler | .75 | .30 |
| 90 | Ed McCaffrey | .75 | .30 |
| 91 | E.George/S.Davis | .50 | .20 |
| 92 | P.Manning/J.Garcia | 1.50 | .60 |
| 93 | R.Smith/T.Holt | .75 | .30 |
| 94 | E.James/M.Faulk | 1.50 | .60 |
| 95 | E.Grbac/D.Culpepper | .75 | .30 |
| 96 | M.Harrison/R.Moss | 1.25 | .50 |
| 97 | M.Anderson/E.Smith | .75 | .30 |
| 98 | B.Griese/K.Warner | 1.00 | .40 |
| 99 | M.Muhammad/E.McCaffrey | .75 | .30 |
| 100 | E.Moulds/T.Owens | .75 | .30 |
| 101 | David Terrell JSY RC | 8.00 | 3.00 |
| 102 | Kevan Barlow JSY RC | 8.00 | 3.00 |
| 103 | Quincy Morgan JSY RC | 8.00 | 3.00 |
| 104 | Chris Weinke JSY RC | 8.00 | 3.00 |
| 105 | Josh Heupel JSY RC | 8.00 | 3.00 |
| 106 | Chris Chambers JSY RC | 15.00 | 6.00 |
| 107 | Reggie Wayne JSY RC | 20.00 | 7.50 |
| 108 | Gerard Warren JSY RC | 8.00 | 3.00 |
| 109 | Freddie Mitchell JSY RC | 8.00 | 3.00 |
| 110 | Anthony Thomas JSY RC | 8.00 | 3.00 |
| 111 | Robert Ferguson JSY RC | 8.00 | 3.00 |
| 112 | Deuce McAllister JSY RC | 20.00 | 7.50 |
| 113 | Travis Henry JSY RC | 8.00 | 3.00 |
| 114 | Rod Gardner JSY RC | 8.00 | 3.00 |
| 115 | Michael Bennett JSY RC | 8.00 | 3.00 |
| 116 | Santana Moss JSY RC | 15.00 | 6.00 |
| 117 | Chad Johnson JSY RC | 25.00 | 10.00 |
| 118 | Jesse Palmer JSY RC | 8.00 | 3.00 |
| 119 | James Jackson JSY RC | 8.00 | 3.00 |
| 120 | Dan Morgan JSY RC | 8.00 | 3.00 |
| 121 | Drew Brees JSY RC | 20.00 | 10.00 |
| 122 | Travis Minor RC | 4.00 | 1.50 |
| 123 | Quincy Carter RC | 6.00 | 2.50 |
| 124 | LaDainian Tomlinson RC | 80.00 | 40.00 |
| 125 | Michael Vick RC | 12.00 | 5.00 |
| 126 | Ryan Pickett RC | 2.50 | 1.00 |
| 127 | Mike McMahon RC | 6.00 | 2.50 |
| 128 | Alex Bannister RC | 4.00 | 1.50 |
| 129 | A.J. Feeley RC | 6.00 | 2.50 |
| 130 | Shad Meier RC | 4.00 | 1.50 |
| 131 | Jamie Winborn RC | 4.00 | 1.50 |
| 132 | Fred Smoot RC | 6.00 | 2.50 |
| 133 | Milton Wynn RC | 4.00 | 1.50 |
| 134 | Onome Ojo RC | 4.00 | 1.50 |
| 135 | Jonathan Carter RC | 4.00 | 1.50 |
| 136 | Todd Heap RC | 6.00 | 2.50 |
| 137 | Bobby Newcombe RC | 4.00 | 1.50 |
| 138 | Tony Stewart RC | 6.00 | 2.50 |
| 139 | Torrance Marshall RC | 6.00 | 2.50 |

| | | |
|---|---|---|
| 140 Jamal Reynolds RC | 6.00 | 2.50 |
| 141 Jamar Fletcher RC | 4.00 | 1.50 |
| 142 Richard Seymour RC | 6.00 | 2.50 |
| 143 Tay Cody RC | 2.50 | 1.00 |
| 144 Koren Robinson RC | 6.00 | 2.50 |
| 145 Eddie Berlin RC | 4.00 | 1.50 |
| 146 Damione Lewis RC | 4.00 | 1.50 |
| 147 Marques Tuiasosopo RC | 8.00 | 3.00 |
| 148 Snoop Minnis RC | 4.00 | 1.50 |
| 149 Chris Barnes RC | 4.00 | 1.50 |
| 150 Leonard Davis RC | 4.00 | 1.50 |
| 151 Vinny Sutherland RC | 4.00 | 1.50 |
| 152 Rudi Johnson RC | 12.00 | 5.00 |
| 153 Derrick Gibson RC | 4.00 | 1.50 |
| 154 Dan Alexander RC | 6.00 | 2.50 |
| 155 Darnerien McCants RC | 4.00 | 1.50 |
| 156 Adam Archuleta RC | 6.00 | 2.50 |
| 157 Correll Buckhalter RC | 8.00 | 3.00 |
| 158 LaMont Jordan RC | 12.00 | 5.00 |
| 159 Quentin McCord RC | 4.00 | 1.50 |
| 160 Justin Smith RC | 6.00 | 2.50 |
| 161 Nate Clements RC | 6.00 | 2.50 |
| 162 Alge Crumpler RC | 8.00 | 4.00 |
| 163 Dan O'Leary RC | 4.00 | 1.50 |
| 164 Sage Rosenfels RC | 8.00 | 3.00 |
| 165 Andre Carter RC | 6.00 | 2.50 |
| 166 Marcus Stroud RC | 6.00 | 2.50 |
| 167 Will Allen RC | 4.00 | 1.50 |
| 168 Tommy Polley RC | 6.00 | 2.50 |
| 169 Justin McCareins RC | 6.00 | 2.50 |
| 170 Josh Booty RC | 6.00 | 2.50 |

## 2002 Bowman's Best

*Emmitt Smith*

| | | |
|---|---|---|
| COMP.SET w/o SP's (90) | 40.00 | 15.00 |
| 1 Peyton Manning | 3.00 | 1.25 |
| 2 Chris Weinke | 1.00 | .40 |
| 3 Daunte Culpepper | 1.50 | .60 |
| 4 Deuce McAllister | 2.00 | .75 |
| 5 Duce Staley | 1.50 | .60 |
| 6 Koren Robinson | 1.00 | .40 |
| 7 Emmitt Smith | 4.00 | 1.50 |
| 8 Jamal Lewis | 1.50 | .60 |
| 9 Jake Plummer | 1.00 | .40 |
| 10 Tim Brown | 1.50 | .60 |
| 11 LaDainian Tomlinson | 2.50 | 1.00 |
| 12 Derrick Mason | 1.00 | .40 |
| 13 Keyshawn Johnson | 1.50 | .60 |
| 14 Priest Holmes | 2.00 | .75 |
| 15 Marcus Robinson | 1.00 | .40 |
| 16 Drew Bledsoe | 2.00 | .75 |
| 17 Troy Brown | 1.00 | .40 |
| 18 Ahman Green | 1.50 | .60 |
| 19 Edgerrin James | 2.00 | .75 |
| 20 Hines Ward | 1.50 | .60 |
| 21 Marshall Faulk | 2.00 | .75 |
| 22 Rod Gardner | 1.00 | .40 |
| 23 Amani Toomer | 1.00 | .40 |
| 24 Ricky Williams | 1.50 | .60 |
| 25 Peter Warrick | 1.50 | .60 |
| 26 Ray Lewis | 1.50 | .60 |
| 27 Warrick Dunn | 1.00 | .40 |
| 28 Jermaine Lewis | 1.00 | .40 |
| 29 Mark Brunell | 1.50 | .60 |
| 30 Randy Moss | 3.00 | 1.25 |
| 31 Laveranues Coles | 1.00 | .40 |
| 32 Kordell Stewart | 1.00 | .40 |
| 33 Darrell Jackson | 1.00 | .40 |
| 34 Jeff Garcia | 1.50 | .60 |

| | | |
|---|---|---|
| 35 Eddie George | 1.50 | .60 |
| 36 Tim Dwight | 1.00 | .40 |
| 37 Trent Green | 1.00 | .40 |
| 38 Quincy Carter | 1.00 | .40 |
| 39 Mike McMahon | 1.50 | .60 |
| 40 Corey Dillon | 1.00 | .40 |
| 41 Corey Bradford | .60 | .25 |
| 42 Aaron Brooks | 1.50 | .60 |
| 43 Todd Pinkston | 1.00 | .40 |
| 44 Isaac Bruce | 1.50 | .60 |
| 45 Shane Matthews | 1.00 | .40 |
| 46 Eric Moulds | 1.00 | .40 |
| 47 Anthony Thomas | 1.50 | .60 |
| 48 David Boston | 1.50 | .60 |
| 49 Kevin Johnson | 1.00 | .40 |
| 50 Brett Favre | 4.00 | 1.50 |
| 51 Ron Dayne | 1.00 | .40 |
| 52 Donovan McNabb | 2.00 | .75 |
| 53 Brad Johnson | 1.00 | .40 |
| 54 Garrison Hearst | 1.00 | .40 |
| 55 Jimmy Smith | 1.00 | .40 |
| 56 Muhsin Muhammad | 1.00 | .40 |
| 57 Michael Vick | 3.00 | 1.25 |
| 58 Kerry Collins | 1.00 | .40 |
| 59 Jerome Bettis | 1.50 | .60 |
| 60 Trent Dilfer | 1.50 | .60 |
| 61 Torry Holt | 1.50 | .60 |
| 62 Stephen Davis | 1.50 | .60 |
| 63 Steve McNair | 1.50 | .60 |
| 64 Marvin Harrison | 1.50 | .60 |
| 65 Zach Thomas | 1.50 | .60 |
| 66 Antowain Smith | 1.00 | .40 |
| 67 Joe Horn | 1.00 | .40 |
| 68 Jim Miller | 1.00 | .40 |
| 69 Travis Taylor | 1.00 | .40 |
| 70 James Allen | 1.00 | .40 |
| 71 Tom Brady | 4.00 | 1.50 |
| 72 Tiki Barber | 1.50 | .60 |
| 73 Doug Flutie | 1.50 | .60 |
| 74 Rich Gannon | 1.50 | .60 |
| 75 Kurt Warner | 1.50 | .60 |
| 76 Michael Pittman | .60 | .25 |
| 77 Curtis Martin | 1.50 | .60 |
| 78 Plaxico Burress | 1.50 | .60 |
| 79 Terrell Owens | 1.50 | .60 |
| 80 Tony Gonzalez | 1.00 | .40 |
| 81 Michael Bennett | 1.50 | .60 |
| 82 Brian Griese | 1.50 | .60 |
| 83 Tim Couch | 1.00 | .40 |
| 84 Shaun Alexander | 2.00 | .75 |
| 85 Drew Brees | 1.50 | .60 |
| 86 Vinny Testaverde | 1.00 | .40 |
| 87 Chris Chambers | 1.50 | .60 |
| 88 David Terrell | 1.50 | .60 |
| 89 Rod Smith | 1.00 | .40 |
| 90 Jerry Rice | 3.00 | 1.25 |
| 91 David Carr JSY RC | 12.00 | 5.00 |
| 92 Joey Harrington JSY RC | 10.00 | 4.00 |
| 93 Marquise Walker JSY RC | 6.00 | 2.50 |
| 94 Ladell Betts JSY RC | 8.00 | 3.00 |
| 95 David Garrard JSY RC | 15.00 | 6.00 |
| 96 Antwaan Randle El JSY RC | 10.00 | 4.00 |
| 97 Antonio Bryant JSY RC | 8.00 | 3.00 |
| 98 Eric Crouch JSY RC | 8.00 | 3.00 |
| 99 Tim Carter JSY RC | 6.00 | 2.50 |
| 100 William Green JSY RC | 8.00 | 3.00 |
| 101 Rohan Davey JSY RC | 8.00 | 3.00 |
| 102 Julius Peppers JSY RC | 15.00 | 6.00 |
| 103 Donte Stallworth JSY RC | 12.00 | 5.00 |
| 104 Ashley Lelie JSY RC | 8.00 | 3.00 |
| 105 Jeremy Shockey JSY RC | 15.00 | 6.00 |
| 106 Javon Walker JSY RC | 12.00 | 5.00 |
| 107 Patrick Ramsey JSY RC | 10.00 | 4.00 |
| 108 Roy Williams JSY RC | 15.00 | 6.00 |
| 109 T.J. Duckett JSY RC | 10.00 | 4.00 |
| 110 Jabar Gaffney JSY RC | 8.00 | 3.00 |
| 111 Andre Davis JSY RC | 6.00 | 2.50 |
| 112 Reche Caldwell JSY RC | 8.00 | 3.00 |
| 113 Josh McCown JSY RC | 10.00 | 4.00 |
| 114 Maurice Morris JSY RC | 8.00 | 3.00 |
| 115 Ron Johnson JSY RC | 6.00 | 2.50 |
| 116 DeShaun Foster JSY RC | 10.00 | 4.00 |
| 117 Clinton Portis JSY RC | 25.00 | 10.00 |
| 118 Aaron Lockett AU RC | 6.00 | 2.50 |

| | | |
|---|---|---|
| 119 Robert Thomas AU RC | 12.00 | 5.00 |
| 121 Atrews Bell AU RC | 6.00 | 2.50 |
| 122 Brandon Doman AU RC | 10.00 | 4.00 |
| 124 Bryan Thomas AU RC | 10.00 | 4.00 |
| 125 Bryant McKinnie AU RC | 10.00 | 4.00 |
| 126 Chad Hutchinson AU RC | 10.00 | 4.00 |
| 127 Charles Grant AU RC | 12.00 | 5.00 |
| 128 Chester Taylor AU RC | 30.00 | 15.00 |
| 129 Craig Nall AU RC | 15.00 | 6.00 |
| 130 Deion Branch AU RC | 30.00 | 15.00 |
| 131 Doug Jolley AU RC | 12.00 | 5.00 |
| 132 Dwight Freeney AU RC | 40.00 | 20.00 |
| 133 Ed Reed AU RC | 50.00 | 25.00 |
| 134 Freddie Milons AU RC | 10.00 | 4.00 |
| 135 Herb Haygood AU RC | 6.00 | 2.50 |
| 136 J.T. O'Sullivan AU RC | 25.00 | 10.00 |
| 137 Jake Schifino AU RC | 10.00 | 4.00 |
| 138 Jason McAddley AU RC | 10.00 | 4.00 |
| 139 Jeff Kelly AU RC | 10.00 | 4.00 |
| 140 Jerramy Stevens AU RC | 12.00 | 5.00 |
| 141 John Henderson AU RC | 12.00 | 5.00 |
| 142 Jonathan Wells AU RC | 12.00 | 5.00 |
| 143 Josh Scobey AU RC | 12.00 | 5.00 |
| 144 Kelly Campbell AU RC | 10.00 | 4.00 |
| 145 Kahlil Hill AU RC | 10.00 | 4.00 |
| 146 Kalimba Edwards AU RC | 12.00 | 5.00 |
| 147 Ken Simonton AU RC | 6.00 | 2.50 |
| 148 Kurt Kittner AU RC | 10.00 | 4.00 |
| 149 Lamar Gordon AU RC | 12.00 | 5.00 |
| 150 Leonard Henry AU RC | 10.00 | 4.00 |
| 151 Lito Sheppard AU RC | 12.00 | 5.00 |
| 152 Luke Staley AU RC | 10.00 | 4.00 |
| 153 Matt Schobel AU RC | 10.00 | 4.00 |
| 154 Mike Rumph AU RC | 12.00 | 5.00 |
| 155 Najeh Davenport AU RC | 12.00 | 5.00 |
| 156 Napoleon Harris AU RC | 12.00 | 5.00 |
| 158 Quentin Jammer AU RC | 12.00 | 5.00 |
| 159 Randy Fasani AU RC | 10.00 | 4.00 |
| 160 Ronald Curry AU RC | 20.00 | 8.00 |
| 161 Ryan Sims AU RC | 12.00 | 5.00 |
| 162 Sam Simmons AU RC | 6.00 | 2.50 |
| 163 Seth Burford AU RC | 10.00 | 4.00 |
| 164 Tellis Redmon AU RC | 10.00 | 4.00 |
| 165 Terry Charles AU RC | 10.00 | 4.00 |
| 166 Tracey Wistrom AU RC | 10.00 | 4.00 |
| 167 Verron Haynes AU RC | 20.00 | 7.50 |
| 168 Wes Pate AU RC | 6.00 | 2.50 |
| 169 Wendell Bryant AU RC | 6.00 | 2.50 |
| 170 Damien Anderson AU RC | 10.00 | 4.00 |

## 2004 Bowman's Best

| | | |
|---|---|---|
| COMP.SET w/o SP's (100) | 50.00 | 25.00 |
| RC JSY GROUP A ODDS 1:130 | | |
| RC JSY GROUP B ODDS 1:236 | | |
| RC JSY GROUP C ODDS 1:86 | | |
| RC JSY GROUP D ODDS 1:38 | | |
| RC JSY GROUP E ODDS 1:31 | | |
| RC JSY GROUP F ODDS 1:27 | | |
| RC JSY GROUP G ODDS 1:50 | | |
| RC JSY GROUP H ODDS 1:89 | | |
| RC JSY GROUP I ODDS 1:29 | | |
| RC AU/199 STATED ODDS 1:311 | | |
| RC AU STATED ODDS 1:3 | | |
| 1 Brett Favre | 3.00 | 1.25 |
| 2 Chris Chambers | 1.00 | .40 |
| 3 Kyle Boller | 1.00 | .40 |
| 4 Brian Urlacher | 1.25 | .50 |
| 5 Marvin Harrison | 1.25 | .50 |

| | | |
|---|---|---|
| ❏ 6 Matt Hasselbeck | 1.00 | .50 |
| ❏ 7 Aaron Brooks | 1.00 | .40 |
| ❏ 8 Curtis Martin | 1.25 | .50 |
| ❏ 9 Keenan McCardell | .75 | .30 |
| ❏ 10 Terrell Owens | 1.25 | .50 |
| ❏ 11 Jimmy Smith | 1.00 | .40 |
| ❏ 12 Garrison Hearst | 1.00 | .40 |
| ❏ 13 Joe Horn | 1.00 | .40 |
| ❏ 14 David Carr | 1.00 | .40 |
| ❏ 15 Tom Brady | 3.00 | - 1.25 |
| ❏ 16 Shaun Alexander | 1.25 | .50 |
| ❏ 17 Tommy Maddox | 1.00 | .40 |
| ❏ 18 Tiki Barber | 1.25 | .50 |
| ❏ 19 Trent Green | 1.00 | .40 |
| ❏ 20 Anquan Boldin | 1.25 | .50 |
| ❏ 21 Peerless Price | 1.00 | .40 |
| ❏ 22 Jake Delhomme | 1.00 | .40 |
| ❏ 23 Eric Moulds | 1.00 | .40 |
| ❏ 24 Quincy Carter | .75 | .30 |
| ❏ 25 Steve McNair | 1.25 | .50 |
| ❏ 26 Tim Rattay | .75 | .30 |
| ❏ 27 Laveranues Coles | 1.00 | .40 |
| ❏ 28 Corey Dillon | 1.25 | .50 |
| ❏ 29 Byron Leftwich | 1.25 | .50 |
| ❏ 30 Chad Pennington | 1.25 | .50 |
| ❏ 31 Korren Robinson | 1.25 | .50 |
| ❏ 32 Plaxico Burress | 1.00 | .40 |
| ❏ 33 Steve Smith | 1.00 | .40 |
| ❏ 34 Warrick Dunn | 1.00 | .40 |
| ❏ 35 Jamal Lewis | 1.00 | .40 |
| ❏ 36 Charles Rogers | 1.00 | .40 |
| ❏ 37 Tony Gonzalez | 1.25 | .50 |
| ❏ 38 Jake Plummer | 1.00 | .40 |
| ❏ 39 Chad Johnson | 1.00 | .40 |
| ❏ 40 Peyton Manning | 2.50 | 1.00 |
| ❏ 41 Daunte Culpepper | 1.25 | .50 |
| ❏ 42 Fred Taylor | 1.25 | .50 |
| ❏ 43 Amani Toomer | 1.00 | .40 |
| ❏ 44 Santana Moss | 1.25 | .50 |
| ❏ 45 Deuce McAllister | 1.25 | .50 |
| ❏ 46 Rex Grossman | 1.25 | .50 |
| ❏ 47 Ray Lewis | 1.25 | .50 |
| ❏ 48 Hines Ward | 1.25 | .50 |
| ❏ 49 Darrell Jackson | 1.00 | .40 |
| ❏ 50 Randy Moss | 1.50 | .60 |
| ❏ 51 Carson Palmer | 1.50 | .60 |
| ❏ 52 Rod Smith | 1.00 | .40 |
| ❏ 53 Drew Bledsoe | 1.25 | .50 |
| ❏ 54 Brad Johnson | 1.00 | .40 |
| ❏ 55 Travis Henry | 1.00 | .40 |
| ❏ 56 Joey Harrington | 1.25 | .50 |
| ❏ 57 Edgerrin James | 1.25 | .50 |
| ❏ 58 Kurt Warner | 1.25 | .50 |
| ❏ 59 Josh McCown | 1.00 | .40 |
| ❏ 60 Clinton Portis | 1.25 | .50 |
| ❏ 61 Brian Westbrook | 1.25 | .50 |
| ❏ 62 Marc Bulger | 1.00 | .40 |
| ❏ 63 Charlie Garner | 1.00 | .40 |
| ❏ 64 Torry Holt | 1.25 | .50 |
| ❏ 65 LaDainian Tomlinson | 2.00 | .75 |
| ❏ 66 Mark Brunell | 1.00 | .40 |
| ❏ 67 Derrick Mason | 1.00 | .40 |
| ❏ 68 Andre Johnson | 1.00 | .40 |
| ❏ 69 Keyshawn Johnson | 1.00 | .40 |
| ❏ 70 Ahman Green | 1.00 | .40 |
| ❏ 71 Rudi Johnson | 1.00 | .40 |
| ❏ 72 Stephen Davis | 1.00 | .40 |
| ❏ 73 Jeff Garcia | 1.25 | .50 |
| ❏ 74 Michael Strahan | 1.00 | .40 |
| ❏ 75 Michael Vick | 1.25 | .50 |
| ❏ 76 Ricky Williams | 1.25 | .50 |
| ❏ 77 Domanick Davis | 1.25 | .50 |
| ❏ 78 Priest Holmes | 1.25 | .50 |
| ❏ 79 Marshall Faulk | 1.25 | .50 |
| ❏ 80 Donovan McNabb | 1.25 | .50 |
| ❏ 81 Dunta Robinson RC | 3.00 | 1.25 |
| ❏ 82 Robert Gallery RC | 1.50 | .60 |
| ❏ 83 Ben Troupe RC | 3.00 | 1.25 |
| ❏ 84 Antwan Odom RC | 1.50 | .60 |
| ❏ 85 Brandon Miree RC | 2.50 | 1.00 |
| ❏ 86 Darnell Dockett RC | 2.50 | 1.00 |
| ❏ 87 Vince Wilfork RC | 4.00 | 1.50 |
| ❏ 88 Randy Starks RC | 4.00 | 1.50 |
| ❏ 89 Chris Cooley RC | 4.00 | 1.50 |

| | | |
|---|---|---|
| ❏ 90 Dwan Edwards RC | 2.50 | 1.00 |
| ❏ 91 Patrick Crayton RC | 5.00 | 2.00 |
| ❏ 92 Sean Jones RC | 3.00 | 1.25 |
| ❏ 93 Sean Ryan RC | 2.50 | 1.00 |
| ❏ 94 Chris Gamble RC | 3.00 | 1.25 |
| ❏ 95 Will Smith RC | 3.00 | 1.25 |
| ❏ 96 Sloan Thomas RC | 3.00 | 1.25 |
| ❏ 97 Tim Euhus RC | 2.50 | 1.00 |
| ❏ 98 Tommie Harris RC | 4.00 | 1.50 |
| ❏ 99 Will Poole RC | 4.00 | 1.50 |
| ❏ 100 Karlos Dansby RC | 4.00 | 1.50 |
| ❏ 101 Bernard Berrian JSY RC D | 6.00 | 2.50 |
| ❏ 102 DeAngelo Hall JSY RC A | 6.00 | 2.50 |
| ❏ 103 Mewelde Moore JSY RC G | 6.00 | 2.50 |
| ❏ 104 Rashaun Woods JSY RC G | 4.00 | 1.50 |
| ❏ 105 Reggie Williams JSY RC | 6.00 | 2.50 |
| ❏ 106 Derrick Hamilton JSY RC F | 4.00 | 1.50 |
| ❏ 107 Kellen Winslow JSY RC C | 15.00 | 6.00 |
| ❏ 108 Devard Darling JSY RC D | 5.00 | 2.00 |
| ❏ 109 Michael Clayton JSY RC B | 6.00 | 2.50 |
| ❏ 110 Larry Fitzgerald JSY RC E | 15.00 | 6.00 |
| ❏ 111 Greg Jones JSY RC E | 6.00 | 2.50 |
| ❏ 112 Chris Perry JSY RC H | 6.00 | 2.50 |
| ❏ 113 Lee Evans JSY RC F | 8.00 | 3.00 |
| ❏ 114 Tatum Bell JSY RC I | 6.00 | 2.50 |
| ❏ 115 Steven Jackson JSY RC I | 15.00 | 6.00 |
| ❏ 116 Matt Schaub JSY RC A | 15.00 | 6.00 |
| ❏ 117 Ben Troupe JSY | 5.00 | 2.00 |
| ❏ 118 Devery Henderson JSY RC F | 6.00 | 2.50 |
| ❏ 119 Ben Watson JSY RC E | 6.00 | 2.50 |
| ❏ 120 J.P. Losman JSY RC I | 6.00 | 3.00 |
| ❏ 121 Keary Colbert JSY RC F | 6.00 | 2.50 |
| ❏ 122 Darius Watts JSY RC C | 5.00 | 2.00 |
| ❏ 123 Cedric Cobbs JSY RC E | 5.00 | 2.00 |
| ❏ 124 Luke McCown JSY RC A | 6.00 | 2.50 |
| ❏ 125 Michael Jenkins JSY RC A | 6.00 | 2.50 |
| ❏ 126 Eli Manning AU/ RC | 150.00 | 75.00 |
| ❏ 127 Roy Williams AU/199 RC | 80.00 | 40.00 |
| ❏ 128 Kevin Jones AU/199 RC | 40.00 | 15.00 |
| ❏ 129 Philip Rivers AU/199 RC | 100.00 | 50.00 |
| ❏ 130 Roethlis AU/199 RC | 200.00 | 125.00 |
| ❏ 131 Carlos Francis AU RC | 8.00 | 3.00 |
| ❏ 132 Bradlee Van Pelt AU RC | 10.00 | 4.00 |
| ❏ 133 Michael Turner AU RC | 40.00 | 20.00 |
| ❏ 134 Kenechi Udeze AU RC | 12.00 | 5.00 |
| ❏ 135 Jeff Smoker AU RC | 10.00 | 4.00 |
| ❏ 136 Josh Harris AU RC | 8.00 | 3.00 |
| ❏ 137 Derrick Strait AU RC | 10.00 | 4.00 |
| ❏ 138 Jonathan Vilma AU RC | 12.00 | 5.00 |
| ❏ 139 Triandos Luke AU RC | 8.00 | 3.00 |
| ❏ 140 Jim Sorgi AU RC | 12.00 | 5.00 |
| ❏ 141 Ryan Krause AU RC | 8.00 | 3.00 |
| ❏ 142 Julius Jones AU RC | 40.00 | 15.00 |
| ❏ 143 Mark Jones AU RC | 8.00 | 3.00 |
| ❏ 144 P.K. Sam AU RC | 8.00 | 3.00 |
| ❏ 145 B.J. Symons AU RC | 8.00 | 3.00 |
| ❏ 146 Admchinobe Echemandu AU RC | 10.00 | 4.00 |
| ❏ 147 Casey Bramlet AU RC | 8.00 | 3.00 |
| ❏ 148 Clarence Moore AU RC | 10.00 | 4.00 |
| ❏ 149 D.J. Williams AU RC | 12.00 | 5.00 |
| ❏ 150 Jeris McIntyre AU RC | 8.00 | 3.00 |
| ❏ 151 Jerricho Cotchery AU RC | 15.00 | 6.00 |
| ❏ 152 Andy Hall AU RC | 8.00 | 3.00 |
| ❏ 153 Samie Parker AU RC | 10.00 | 4.00 |
| ❏ 154 Maurice Mann AU RC | 8.00 | 3.00 |
| ❏ 155 Jonathan Smith AU RC | 8.00 | 3.00 |
| ❏ 156 Derrick Ward AU RC | 15.00 | 6.00 |
| ❏ 157 D.J. Hackett AU RC | 15.00 | 6.00 |
| ❏ 158 Craig Krenzel AU RC | 12.00 | 5.00 |
| ❏ 159 Jared Lorenzen AU RC | 10.00 | 4.00 |
| ❏ 160 Cody Pickett AU RC | 10.00 | 4.00 |
| ❏ 161 Jamaar Taylor AU RC | 8.00 | 3.00 |
| ❏ 162 Michael Boulware AU RC | 12.00 | 6.00 |
| ❏ 163 Matt Mauck AU RC | 10.00 | 4.00 |
| ❏ 164 John Navarre AU RC | 8.00 | 3.00 |
| ❏ 165 Ahmad Carroll AU RC | 10.00 | 4.00 |
| ❏ 166 Bruce Perry AU RC | 8.00 | 3.00 |
| ❏ 167 Erik Jensen AU RC | 8.00 | 3.00 |
| ❏ 168 Matt Kranchick AU RC | 12.00 | 5.00 |
| ❏ 169 Courtney Anderson AU RC | 8.00 | 3.00 |
| ❏ 170 Nate Lawrie AU RC | 8.00 | 3.00 |
| ❏ 171 Thomas Tapeh AU RC | 10.00 | 4.00 |
| ❏ 172 Courtney Watson AU RC | 10.00 | 4.00 |
| ❏ 173 Drew Carter AU RC | 12.00 | 5.00 |

| | | |
|---|---|---|
| ❏ 174 Ricardo Colclough AU RC | 12.00 | 5.00 |
| ❏ 175 Dontarrious Thomas AU RC | 10.00 | 4.00 |
| ❏ 176 Erndt Wilford AU RC | 12.00 | 5.00 |
| ❏ 177 Quincy Wilson AU RC | 10.00 | 4.00 |
| ❏ 178 Derek Abney AU RC | 8.00 | 3.00 |
| ❏ 179 Jeff Dugan AU RC | | |
| ❏ 180 Ben Hartsock AU RC | 10.00 | 4.00 |
| ❏ 181 Matt Kegel AU RC | 12.00 | 5.00 |
| ❏ 182 Derrick Knight AU RC | 8.00 | 3.00 |
| ❏ 183 Teddy Lehman AU RC | 10.00 | 4.00 |
| ❏ 184 Johnnie Morant AU RC | 10.00 | 4.00 |
| ❏ 185A B.Sanders AU RC Long AU | 150.00 | 100.00 |
| ❏ 185B B.Sanders AU RC Short AU | 100.00 | 50.00 |
| ❏ 186 Michael Gaines AU RC | 8.00 | 3.00 |
| ❏ 187 Daryl Smith AU RC | 10.00 | 4.00 |
| ❏ 188 Jason Babin AU RC | 10.00 | 4.00 |

## 2005 Bowman's Best

| | | |
|---|---|---|
| ❏ COMP.SET w/o SPs (100) | 40.00 | 15.00 |
| ❏ ROOKIE JSY STATED ODDS 1:14 | | |
| ❏ ROOKIE JSY PRINT RUN 799 SER.#d SETS | | |
| ❏ ROOKIE AU/999 STATED ODDS 1:8 | | |
| ❏ ROOKIE AU/999 STATED ODDS 1:296 | | |
| ❏ ROOKIE AU PRINT RUN 999 SER.#d SETS | | |
| ❏ UNPRICED GOLD PRINT RUN 1 SET | | |
| ❏ UNPRICED PRINT.PLATE PRINT RUN 1 SET | | |
| ❏ 1 Tiki Barber | 1.00 | .40 |
| ❏ 2 Peyton Manning | 1.50 | .60 |
| ❏ 3 Tony Gonzalez | .75 | .30 |
| ❏ 4 Terrell Owens | 1.00 | .40 |
| ❏ 5 Brett Favre | 2.50 | 1.00 |
| ❏ 6 Rudi Johnson | .75 | .30 |
| ❏ 7 Hines Ward | 1.00 | .40 |
| ❏ 8 Andre Johnson | .75 | .30 |
| ❏ 9 Tom Brady | 2.00 | .75 |
| ❏ 10 LaDainian Tomlinson | 1.50 | .60 |
| ❏ 11 Daunte Culpepper | 1.00 | .40 |
| ❏ 12 Muhsin Muhammad | .75 | .30 |
| ❏ 13 Dwight Freeney | .75 | .30 |
| ❏ 14 Curtis Martin | 1.00 | .40 |
| ❏ 15 Eli Manning | 2.00 | .75 |
| ❏ 16 Willis McGahee | 1.00 | .40 |
| ❏ 17 Steve McNair | 1.00 | .40 |
| ❏ 18 Jamal Lewis | .75 | .30 |
| ❏ 19 Reggie Wayne | .75 | .30 |
| ❏ 20 Trent Green | .75 | .30 |
| ❏ 21 Isaac Bruce | .75 | .30 |
| ❏ 22 Edgerrin James | .75 | .30 |
| ❏ 23 Marc Bulger | .75 | .30 |
| ❏ 24 Torry Holt | .75 | .30 |
| ❏ 25 Deuce McAllister | 1.00 | .40 |
| ❏ 26 Jake Plummer | .75 | .30 |
| ❏ 27 Randy Moss | 1.00 | .40 |
| ❏ 28 Drew Brees | 1.00 | .40 |
| ❏ 29 Ahman Green | 1.00 | .40 |
| ❏ 30 Marvin Harrison | 1.00 | .40 |
| ❏ 31 Michael Vick | 1.00 | .40 |
| ❏ 32 Julius Jones | 1.00 | .40 |
| ❏ 33 Matt Hasselbeck | .75 | .30 |
| ❏ 34 Priest Holmes | 1.00 | .40 |
| ❏ 35 Drew Bennett | .75 | .30 |
| ❏ 36 Donovan McNabb | 1.00 | .40 |
| ❏ 37 Chad Johnson | .75 | .30 |
| ❏ 38 Fred Taylor | 1.00 | .40 |
| ❏ 39 Chris Brown | .75 | .30 |
| ❏ 40 Jake Delhomme | 1.00 | .40 |
| ❏ 41 Joe Horn | .75 | .30 |
| ❏ 42 Chad Pennington | 1.00 | .40 |

|  |  | | |
|---|---|---|---|
| ❑ 43 | Corey Dillon | .75 | .30 |
| ❑ 44 | Byron Leftwich | .75 | .30 |
| ❑ 45 | Javon Walker | .75 | .30 |
| ❑ 46 | Ben Roethlisberger | 2.50 | 1.00 |
| ❑ 47 | Eric Moulds | .75 | .30 |
| ❑ 48 | Domanick Davis | .60 | .25 |
| ❑ 49 | Steven Jackson | 1.25 | .50 |
| ❑ 50 | Shaun Alexander | 1.00 | .40 |
| ❑ 51 | Stanford Routt RC | 3.00 | 1.25 |
| ❑ 52 | Marion Barber RC | 12.00 | 5.00 |
| ❑ 53 | Matt Roth RC | 4.00 | 1.50 |
| ❑ 54 | James Kilian RC | 2.50 | 1.00 |
| ❑ 55 | Alex Barron RC | 2.50 | 1.00 |
| ❑ 56 | Madison Hedgecock RC | 4.00 | 1.50 |
| ❑ 57 | Patrick Estes RC | 2.50 | 1.00 |
| ❑ 58 | Bryant McFadden RC | 3.00 | 1.25 |
| ❑ 59 | Dan Cody RC | 4.00 | 1.50 |
| ❑ 60 | Justin Miller RC | 3.00 | 1.25 |
| ❑ 61 | Paris Warren RC | 3.00 | 1.25 |
| ❑ 62 | Marcus Spears RC | 4.00 | 1.50 |
| ❑ 63 | Odell Thurman RC | 4.00 | 1.50 |
| ❑ 64 | Craphonso Thorpe RC | 3.00 | 1.25 |
| ❑ 65 | Dustin Fox RC | 4.00 | 1.50 |
| ❑ 66 | David Pollack RC | 3.00 | 1.25 |
| ❑ 67 | Anthony Davis RC | 3.00 | 1.25 |
| ❑ 68 | Mike Nugent RC | 3.00 | 1.25 |
| ❑ 69 | David Greene RC | 3.00 | 1.25 |
| ❑ 70 | Rick Razzano RC | 2.50 | 1.00 |
| ❑ 70AU | Rick Razzano AU | 8.00 | 3.00 |
| ❑ 71 | Mike Patterson RC | 3.00 | 1.25 |
| ❑ 72 | Derek Anderson RC | 6.00 | 2.50 |
| ❑ 72AU | Derek Anderson AU | 30.00 | 15.00 |
| ❑ 73 | Marlin Jackson RC | 3.00 | 1.25 |
| ❑ 73AU | Marlin Jackson AU | 10.00 | 4.00 |
| ❑ 74 | Roberger Grigsby RC | 4.00 | 1.50 |
| ❑ 75 | Kevin Burnett RC | 3.00 | 1.25 |
| ❑ 76 | Ryan Riddle RC | 2.50 | 1.00 |
| ❑ 77 | Brock Berlin RC | 3.00 | 1.25 |
| ❑ 78 | Khalif Barnes RC | 2.50 | 1.00 |
| ❑ 79 | Marcus Maxwell RC | 2.50 | 1.00 |
| ❑ 80 | Fred Gibson RC | 3.00 | 1.25 |
| ❑ 81 | T.A. McLendon RC | 2.50 | 1.00 |
| ❑ 82 | Kirk Morrison RC | 4.00 | 1.50 |
| ❑ 83 | Sean Considine RC | 2.50 | 1.00 |
| ❑ 84 | Luis Castillo RC | 4.00 | 1.50 |
| ❑ 85 | Darryl Blackstock RC | 2.50 | 1.00 |
| ❑ 86 | Airese Currie RC | 3.00 | 1.25 |
| ❑ 87 | Corey Webster RC | 4.00 | 1.25 |
| ❑ 88 | Kurt Campbell RC | 2.50 | 1.00 |
| ❑ 89 | Ellis Hobbs RC | 4.00 | 1.50 |
| ❑ 90 | Timmy Chang RC | 3.00 | 1.25 |
| ❑ 91 | Travis Johnson RC | 2.50 | 1.00 |
| ❑ 92 | Eric Moore RC | 2.50 | 1.00 |
| ❑ 93 | Barrett Ruud RC | 4.00 | 1.50 |
| ❑ 94 | Erasmus James RC | 3.00 | 1.25 |
| ❑ 95 | Anttaj Hawthorne RC | 3.00 | 1.25 |
| ❑ 96 | Manuel White RC | 3.00 | 1.25 |
| ❑ 97 | Rian Wallace RC | 3.00 | 1.25 |
| ❑ 98 | Justin Tuck RC | 5.00 | 2.00 |
| ❑ 99 | Travis Daniels RC | 3.00 | 1.25 |
| ❑ 100 | Donte Nicholson RC | 3.00 | 1.25 |
| ❑ 101 | Matt Jones RC | 10.00 | 4.00 |
| ❑ 102 | J.J. Arrington JSY RC | 6.00 | 2.50 |
| ❑ 103 | Mark Bradley JSY RC | 6.00 | 2.50 |
| ❑ 104 | Reggie Brown JSY RC | 6.00 | 2.50 |
| ❑ 105 | Jason Campbell JSY RC | 12.00 | 5.00 |
| ❑ 106 | Maurice Clarett JSY | 5.00 | 2.00 |
| ❑ 107 | Mark Clayton JSY RC | 6.00 | 2.50 |
| ❑ 108 | Braylon Edwards JSY RC | 20.00 | 8.00 |
| ❑ 109 | Ciatrick Fason JSY RC | 5.00 | 2.00 |
| ❑ 110 | Charlie Frye JSY RC | 6.00 | 2.50 |
| ❑ 111 | Frank Gore JSY RC | 15.00 | 6.00 |
| ❑ 112 | Vincent Jackson JSY RC | 6.00 | 2.50 |
| ❑ 113 | Adam Jones JSY RC | 6.00 | 2.50 |
| ❑ 114 | Stefan LeFors JSY | 5.00 | 2.00 |
| ❑ 114AU | Stefan LeFors AU RC | 10.00 | 4.00 |
| ❑ 115 | Ryan Moats JSY | 5.00 | 2.00 |
| ❑ 115AU | Ryan Moats AU RC | 12.00 | 5.00 |
| ❑ 116 | Vernand Morency JSY RC | 6.00 | 2.50 |
| ❑ 117 | Terrence Murphy JSY RC | 6.00 | 2.50 |
| ❑ 118 | Kyle Orton JSY RC | 8.00 | 3.00 |
| ❑ 119 | Roscoe Parrish JSY RC | 5.00 | 2.00 |
| ❑ 120 | Courtney Roby JSY RC | 5.00 | 2.00 |
| ❑ 121 | Carlos Rogers JSY RC | 6.00 | 2.50 |
| ❑ 122 | Antrel Rolle JSY RC | 6.00 | 2.50 |
| ❑ 123 | Eric Shelton JSY RC | 5.00 | 2.00 |
| ❑ 124 | Andrew Walter JSY RC | 6.00 | 2.50 |
| ❑ 125 | Roddy White JSY RC | 8.00 | 3.00 |
| ❑ 126 | Cadillac Williams JSY RC | 12.00 | 5.00 |
| ❑ 127 | Troy Williamson JSY RC | 6.00 | 2.50 |
| ❑ 128 | Cedric Benson AU/199 RC | 40.00 | 15.00 |
| ❑ 129 | Aaron Rodgers AU/199 RC | 120.00 | 60.00 |
| ❑ 130 | Alex Smith QB AU/199 RC | 120.00 | 60.00 |
| ❑ 131 | Mike Williams AU/199 | 20.00 | 8.00 |
| ❑ 132 | Ronnie Brown AU/199 RC | 120.00 | 50.00 |
| ❑ 133 | Adrian McPherson AU RC | 10.00 | 4.00 |
| ❑ 134 | Brandon Jacobs AU RC | 30.00 | 12.50 |
| ❑ 135 | Chad Owens AU RC | 12.00 | 5.00 |
| ❑ 136 | Chase Lyman AU RC | 8.00 | 3.00 |
| ❑ 137 | Chris Henry AU RC | 12.00 | 5.00 |
| ❑ 138 | Craig Bragg AU RC | 8.00 | 3.00 |
| ❑ 139 | Damien Nash AU RC | 10.00 | 4.00 |
| ❑ 140 | Dante Ridgeway AU RC | 8.00 | 3.00 |
| ❑ 141 | Darren Sproles AU RC | 20.00 | 10.00 |
| ❑ 142 | Deandra Cobb AU RC | 10.00 | 4.00 |
| ❑ 143 | Gino Guidugli AU RC | 8.00 | 3.00 |
| ❑ 144 | J.R. Russell AU RC | 8.00 | 3.00 |
| ❑ 145 | Jerome Mathis AU RC | 12.00 | 5.00 |
| ❑ 146 | Josh Davis AU RC | 8.00 | 3.00 |
| ❑ 147 | Kay-Jay Harris AU RC | 10.00 | 4.00 |
| ❑ 148 | Larry Brackins AU RC | 8.00 | 3.00 |
| ❑ 149 | Matt Cassel AU RC | 30.00 | 15.00 |
| ❑ 150 | Noah Herron AU RC | 12.00 | 5.00 |
| ❑ 151 | Rasheed Marshall AU RC | 10.00 | 4.00 |
| ❑ 152 | Roydell Williams AU RC | 10.00 | 4.00 |
| ❑ 153 | Ryan Fitzpatrick AU RC | 12.00 | 5.00 |
| ❑ 154 | Steve Savoy AU RC | 8.00 | 3.00 |
| ❑ 155 | Tab Perry AU RC | 10.00 | 4.00 |
| ❑ 156 | Shawne Merriman AU RC | 20.00 | 8.00 |
| ❑ 157 | Charles Frederick AU RC | 8.00 | 3.00 |
| ❑ 158 | Alvin Pearman AU RC | 10.00 | 4.00 |
| ❑ 159 | Channing Crowder AU RC | 10.00 | 4.00 |
| ❑ 160 | Fabian Washington AU RC | 12.00 | 5.00 |
| ❑ 161 | Dan Orlovsky AU RC | 12.00 | 5.00 |
| ❑ 162 | Derrick Johnson AU RC | 12.00 | 5.00 |
| ❑ 163 | Alex Smith TE AU RC | 8.00 | 3.00 |
| ❑ 164 | Cedric Houston AU RC | 12.00 | 5.00 |
| ❑ 165 | Brandon Jones AU RC | 12.00 | 5.00 |
| ❑ 166 | DeMarcus Ware AU RC | 20.00 | 8.00 |
| ❑ 167 | Lionel Gates AU RC | 8.00 | 3.00 |

## 1996 Donruss

|  |  | | |
|---|---|---|---|
| ❑ | COMPLETE SET (240) | 20.00 | 7.50 |
| ❑ 1 | Barry Sanders | 1.50 | .60 |
| ❑ 2 | Flipper Anderson | .10 | .02 |
| ❑ 3 | Ben Coates | .20 | .07 |
| ❑ 4 | Rob Johnson | .40 | .15 |
| ❑ 5 | Rodney Hampton | .20 | .07 |
| ❑ 6 | Desmond Howard | .20 | .07 |
| ❑ 7 | Craig Heyward | .10 | .02 |
| ❑ 8 | Alvin Harper | .10 | .02 |
| ❑ 9 | Todd Collins | .20 | .07 |
| ❑ 10 | Ken Norton Jr. | .10 | .02 |
| ❑ 11 | Stan Humphries | .20 | .07 |
| ❑ 12 | Aeneas Williams | .10 | .02 |
| ❑ 13 | Jeff Hostetler | .10 | .02 |
| ❑ 14 | Frank Sanders | .20 | .07 |
| ❑ 15 | J.J. Birden | .10 | .02 |
| ❑ 16 | Bryce Paup | .10 | .02 |
| ❑ 17 | Bill Brooks | .10 | .02 |
| ❑ 18 | Kevin Williams | .10 | .02 |
| ❑ 19 | Boomer Esiason | .20 | .07 |
| ❑ 20 | O.J. McDuffie | .20 | .07 |
| ❑ 21 | Eric Swann | .10 | .02 |
| ❑ 22 | Neil Smith | .20 | .07 |
| ❑ 23 | Charlie Garner | .20 | .07 |
| ❑ 24 | Greg Lloyd | .20 | .07 |
| ❑ 25 | Willie Jackson | .20 | .07 |
| ❑ 26 | Shawn Jefferson | .10 | .02 |
| ❑ 27 | Rodney Peete | .10 | .02 |
| ❑ 28 | Michael Westbrook | .40 | .15 |
| ❑ 29 | J.J. Stokes | .40 | .15 |
| ❑ 30 | Troy Aikman | 1.00 | .40 |
| ❑ 31 | Sean Dawkins | .10 | .02 |
| ❑ 32 | Larry Centers | .20 | .07 |
| ❑ 33 | Herschel Walker | .20 | .07 |
| ❑ 34 | Stoney Case | .10 | .02 |
| ❑ 35 | Kevin Greene | .20 | .07 |
| ❑ 36 | Quinn Early | .10 | .02 |
| ❑ 37 | Fred Barnett | .10 | .02 |
| ❑ 38 | Andre Coleman | .10 | .02 |
| ❑ 39 | Mark Chmura | .20 | .07 |
| ❑ 40 | Adrian Murrell | .20 | .07 |
| ❑ 41 | Roosevelt Potts | .10 | .02 |
| ❑ 42 | Jay Novacek | .10 | .02 |
| ❑ 43 | Derrick Alexander | .20 | .07 |
| ❑ 44 | Ken Dilger | .20 | .07 |
| ❑ 45 | Rob Moore | .20 | .07 |
| ❑ 46 | Cris Carter | .40 | .15 |
| ❑ 47 | Jeff Blake | .40 | .15 |
| ❑ 48 | Derek Loville | .10 | .02 |
| ❑ 49 | Tyrone Wheatley | .20 | .07 |
| ❑ 50 | Terrell Fletcher | .10 | .02 |
| ❑ 51 | Sherman Williams | .10 | .02 |
| ❑ 52 | Justin Armour | .10 | .02 |
| ❑ 53 | Kordell Stewart | .40 | .15 |
| ❑ 54 | Tim Brown | .40 | .15 |
| ❑ 55 | Kevin Carter | .10 | .02 |
| ❑ 56 | Andre Rison | .20 | .07 |
| ❑ 57 | James O.Stewart | .20 | .07 |
| ❑ 58 | Brent Jones | .10 | .02 |
| ❑ 59 | Erik Kramer | .10 | .02 |
| ❑ 60 | Floyd Turner | .10 | .02 |
| ❑ 61 | Ricky Watters | .20 | .07 |
| ❑ 62 | Hardy Nickerson | .10 | .02 |
| ❑ 63 | Aaron Craver | .10 | .02 |
| ❑ 64 | Dave Krieg | .20 | .07 |
| ❑ 65 | Warren Moon | .20 | .07 |
| ❑ 66 | Wayne Chrebet | .50 | .20 |
| ❑ 67 | Napoleon Kaufman | .40 | .15 |
| ❑ 68 | Terance Mathis | .10 | .02 |
| ❑ 69 | Chad May | .10 | .02 |
| ❑ 70 | Andre Reed | .20 | .07 |
| ❑ 71 | Reggie White | .40 | .15 |
| ❑ 72 | Brett Favre | 2.00 | .75 |
| ❑ 73 | Chris Zorich | .10 | .02 |
| ❑ 74 | Kerry Collins | .40 | .15 |
| ❑ 75 | Herman Moore | .20 | .07 |
| ❑ 76 | Yancey Thigpen | .20 | .07 |
| ❑ 77 | Glenn Foley | .20 | .07 |
| ❑ 78 | Quentin Coryatt | .10 | .02 |
| ❑ 79 | Terry Kirby | .20 | .07 |
| ❑ 80 | Edgar Bennett | .20 | .07 |
| ❑ 81 | Mark Brunell | .60 | .25 |
| ❑ 82 | Heath Shuler | .20 | .07 |
| ❑ 83 | Gus Frerotte | .20 | .07 |
| ❑ 84 | Deion Sanders | .60 | .25 |
| ❑ 85 | Calvin Williams | .10 | .02 |
| ❑ 86 | Junior Seau | .40 | .15 |
| ❑ 87 | Jim Kelly | .40 | .15 |
| ❑ 88 | Daryl Johnston | .20 | .07 |
| ❑ 89 | Irving Fryar | .20 | .07 |
| ❑ 90 | Brian Blades | .10 | .02 |
| ❑ 91 | Willie Davis | .10 | .02 |
| ❑ 92 | Jerome Bettis | .40 | .15 |
| ❑ 93 | Marcus Allen | .40 | .15 |
| ❑ 94 | Jeff Graham | .10 | .02 |
| ❑ 95 | Rick Mirer | .20 | .07 |
| ❑ 96 | Harvey Williams | .10 | .02 |
| ❑ 97 | Steve Atwater | .10 | .02 |
| ❑ 98 | Carl Pickens | .20 | .07 |
| ❑ 99 | Darick Holmes | .10 | .02 |
| ❑ 100 | Bruce Smith | .20 | .07 |
| ❑ 101 | Vinny Testaverde | .20 | .07 |
| ❑ 102 | Thurman Thomas | .40 | .15 |
| ❑ 103 | Drew Bledsoe | .60 | .25 |

|  |  | | |
|---|---|---|---|
| ❏ 104 | Bernie Parmalee | .10 | .02 |
| ❏ 105 | Greg Hill | .20 | .07 |
| ❏ 106 | Steve McNair | .75 | .30 |
| ❏ 107 | Andre Hastings | .10 | .02 |
| ❏ 108 | Eric Metcalf | .10 | .02 |
| ❏ 109 | Kimble Anders | .20 | .07 |
| ❏ 110 | Steve Tasker | .10 | .02 |
| ❏ 111 | Mark Carrier WR | .10 | .02 |
| ❏ 112 | Jerry Rice | 1.00 | .40 |
| ❏ 113 | Joey Galloway | .40 | .15 |
| ❏ 114 | Robert Smith | .20 | .07 |
| ❏ 115 | Hugh Douglas | .20 | .07 |
| ❏ 116 | Willie McGinest | .10 | .02 |
| ❏ 117 | Terrell Davis | .75 | .30 |
| ❏ 118 | Cortez Kennedy | .10 | .02 |
| ❏ 119 | Marshall Faulk | .50 | .20 |
| ❏ 120 | Michael Haynes | .10 | .02 |
| ❏ 121 | Isaac Bruce | .40 | .15 |
| ❏ 122 | Brian Mitchell | .10 | .02 |
| ❏ 123 | Bryan Cox | .10 | .02 |
| ❏ 124 | Tamarick Vanover | .20 | .07 |
| ❏ 125 | William Floyd | .20 | .07 |
| ❏ 126 | Chris Chandler | .20 | .07 |
| ❏ 127 | Carnell Lake | .10 | .02 |
| ❏ 128 | Aaron Bailey | .10 | .02 |
| ❏ 129 | Darnay Scott | .20 | .07 |
| ❏ 130 | Darren Woodson | .20 | .07 |
| ❏ 131 | Ernie Mills | .10 | .02 |
| ❏ 132 | Charles Haley | .10 | .02 |
| ❏ 133 | Rocket Ismail | .10 | .02 |
| ❏ 134 | Bert Emanuel | .10 | .02 |
| ❏ 135 | Lake Dawson | .10 | .02 |
| ❏ 136 | Jake Reed | .20 | .07 |
| ❏ 137 | Dave Brown | .10 | .02 |
| ❏ 138 | Steve Bono | .10 | .02 |
| ❏ 139 | Terry Allen | .20 | .07 |
| ❏ 140 | Errict Rhett | .20 | .07 |
| ❏ 141 | Rod Woodson | .20 | .07 |
| ❏ 142 | Charles Johnson | .10 | .02 |
| ❏ 143 | Emmitt Smith | 1.50 | .60 |
| ❏ 144 | Ki-Jana Carter | .20 | .07 |
| ❏ 145 | Garrison Hearst | .20 | .07 |
| ❏ 146 | Rashaan Salaam | .20 | .07 |
| ❏ 147 | Tony Boselli | .10 | .02 |
| ❏ 148 | Derrick Thomas | .40 | .15 |
| ❏ 149 | Mark Seay | .10 | .02 |
| ❏ 150 | Derrick Alexander | .10 | .02 |
| ❏ 151 | Christian Fauria | .10 | .02 |
| ❏ 152 | Aaron Hayden | .10 | .02 |
| ❏ 153 | Chris Warren | .20 | .07 |
| ❏ 154 | Dave Meggett | .10 | .02 |
| ❏ 155 | Jeff George | .20 | .07 |
| ❏ 156 | Jackie Harris | .10 | .02 |
| ❏ 157 | Michael Irvin | .40 | .15 |
| ❏ 158 | Scott Mitchell | .20 | .07 |
| ❏ 159 | Trent Dilfer | .40 | .15 |
| ❏ 160 | Kyle Brady | .10 | .02 |
| ❏ 161 | Dan Marino | 2.00 | .75 |
| ❏ 162 | Curtis Martin | .75 | .30 |
| ❏ 163 | Mario Bates | .20 | .07 |
| ❏ 164 | Erric Pegram | .10 | .02 |
| ❏ 165 | Eric Zeier | .10 | .02 |
| ❏ 166 | Rodney Thomas | .10 | .02 |
| ❏ 167 | Neil O'Donnell | .20 | .07 |
| ❏ 168 | Warren Sapp | .10 | .02 |
| ❏ 169 | Jim Harbaugh | .20 | .07 |
| ❏ 170 | Henry Ellard | .10 | .02 |
| ❏ 171 | Anthony Miller | .20 | .07 |
| ❏ 172 | Derrick Moore | .10 | .02 |
| ❏ 173 | John Elway | 2.00 | .75 |
| ❏ 174 | Vincent Brisby | .10 | .02 |
| ❏ 175 | Antonio Freeman | .40 | .15 |
| ❏ 176 | Chris Sanders | .20 | .07 |
| ❏ 177 | Steve Young | .75 | .30 |
| ❏ 178 | Shannon Sharpe | .20 | .07 |
| ❏ 179 | Brett Perriman | .10 | .02 |
| ❏ 180 | Orlando Thomas | .10 | .02 |
| ❏ 181 | Eric Bjornson | .10 | .02 |
| ❏ 182 | Natrone Means | .20 | .07 |
| ❏ 183 | Jim Everett | .10 | .02 |
| ❏ 184 | Curtis Conway | .40 | .15 |
| ❏ 185 | Robert Brooks | .40 | .15 |
| ❏ 186 | Tony Martin | .20 | .07 |
| ❏ 187 | Mark Carrier DB | .10 | .02 |

|  |  | | |
|---|---|---|---|
| ❏ 188 | LeShon Johnson | .10 | .02 |
| ❏ 189 | Bernie Kosar | .10 | .02 |
| ❏ 190 | Ray Zellars | .10 | .02 |
| ❏ 191 | Steve Walsh | .10 | .02 |
| ❏ 192 | Craig Erickson | .10 | .02 |
| ❏ 193 | Tommy Maddox | .40 | .15 |
| ❏ 194 | Leslie O'Neal | .10 | .02 |
| ❏ 195 | Harold Green | .10 | .02 |
| ❏ 196 | Steve Beuerlein | .20 | .07 |
| ❏ 197 | Ronald Moore | .10 | .02 |
| ❏ 198 | Leslie Shepherd | .10 | .02 |
| ❏ 199 | Leroy Hoard | .10 | .02 |
| ❏ 200 | Michael Jackson | .20 | .07 |
| ❏ 201 | Will Moore | .10 | .02 |
| ❏ 202 | Ricky Ervins | .10 | .02 |
| ❏ 203 | Keith Jennings | .10 | .02 |
| ❏ 204 | Eric Green | .10 | .02 |
| ❏ 205 | Mark Rypien | .10 | .02 |
| ❏ 206 | Torrance Small | .10 | .02 |
| ❏ 207 | Sean Gilbert | .10 | .02 |
| ❏ 208 | Mike Alstott RC | 1.00 | .40 |
| ❏ 209 | Willie Anderson RC | .10 | .02 |
| ❏ 210 | Alex Molden RC | .10 | .02 |
| ❏ 211 | Jonathan Ogden RC | .40 | .15 |
| ❏ 212 | Stepfret Williams RC | .20 | .07 |
| ❏ 213 | Jeff Lewis RC | .20 | .07 |
| ❏ 214 | Regan Upshaw RC | .10 | .02 |
| ❏ 215 | Daryl Gardener RC | .10 | .02 |
| ❏ 216 | Danny Kanell RC | .40 | .15 |
| ❏ 217 | John Mobley RC | .10 | .02 |
| ❏ 218 | Reggie Brown LB RC | .10 | .02 |
| ❏ 219 | Muhsin Muhammad RC | 1.00 | .40 |
| ❏ 220 | Kevin Hardy RC | .40 | .15 |
| ❏ 221 | Stanley Pritchett RC | .20 | .07 |
| ❏ 222 | Cedric Jones RC | .10 | .02 |
| ❏ 223 | Marco Battaglia RC | .10 | .02 |
| ❏ 224 | Duane Clemons RC | .10 | .02 |
| ❏ 225 | Jerald Moore RC | .20 | .07 |
| ❏ 226 | Simeon Rice RC | 1.00 | .40 |
| ❏ 227 | Chris Darkins RC | .10 | .02 |
| ❏ 228 | Bobby Hoying RC | .40 | .15 |
| ❏ 229 | Stephen Davis RC | 1.50 | .60 |
| ❏ 230 | Walt Harris RC | .10 | .02 |
| ❏ 231 | Jermane Mayberry RC | .10 | .02 |
| ❏ 232 | Tony Brackens RC | .40 | .15 |
| ❏ 233 | Eric Moulds RC | 1.25 | .50 |
| ❏ 234 | Alex Van Dyke RC | .20 | .07 |
| ❏ 235 | Marvin Harrison RC | 2.50 | 1.00 |
| ❏ 236 | Rickey Dudley RC | .40 | .15 |
| ❏ 237 | Terrell Owens RC | 2.50 | 1.00 |
| ❏ 238 | Jerry Rice CL | .40 | .15 |
| ❏ 239 | Dan Marino CL | .40 | .15 |
| ❏ 240 | Emmitt Smith CL | .40 | .15 |

## 1997 Donruss

EMMITT SMITH

|  |  | | |
|---|---|---|---|
| ❏ | COMPLETE SET (230) | 20.00 | 7.50 |
| ❏ 1 | Dan Marino | 2.00 | .75 |
| ❏ 2 | Brett Favre | 2.00 | .75 |
| ❏ 3 | Emmitt Smith | 1.50 | .60 |
| ❏ 4 | Eddie George | .50 | .20 |
| ❏ 5 | Karim Abdul-Jabbar | .30 | .10 |
| ❏ 6 | Terrell Davis | .60 | .25 |
| ❏ 7 | Curtis Martin | .60 | .25 |
| ❏ 8 | Drew Bledsoe | .60 | .25 |
| ❏ 9 | Jerry Rice | 1.00 | .40 |
| ❏ 10 | Troy Aikman | 1.00 | .40 |
| ❏ 11 | Barry Sanders | 1.50 | .60 |
| ❏ 12 | Mark Brunell | .60 | .25 |

|  |  | | |
|---|---|---|---|
| ❏ 13 | Kerry Collins | .50 | .20 |
| ❏ 14 | Steve Young | .60 | .25 |
| ❏ 15 | Kordell Stewart | .50 | .20 |
| ❏ 16 | Eddie Kennison | .30 | .10 |
| ❏ 17 | Terry Glenn | .50 | .20 |
| ❏ 18 | John Elway | 2.00 | .75 |
| ❏ 19 | Joey Galloway | .30 | .10 |
| ❏ 20 | Deion Sanders | .50 | .20 |
| ❏ 21 | Keyshawn Johnson | .50 | .20 |
| ❏ 22 | Lawrence Phillips | .20 | .07 |
| ❏ 23 | Ricky Watters | .30 | .10 |
| ❏ 24 | Marvin Harrison | .50 | .20 |
| ❏ 25 | Bobby Engram | .30 | .10 |
| ❏ 26 | Marshall Faulk | .60 | .25 |
| ❏ 27 | Carl Pickens | .30 | .10 |
| ❏ 28 | Isaac Bruce | .50 | .20 |
| ❏ 29 | Herman Moore | .50 | .20 |
| ❏ 30 | Jerome Bettis | .50 | .20 |
| ❏ 31 | Rashaan Salaam | .20 | .07 |
| ❏ 32 | Errict Rhett | .20 | .07 |
| ❏ 33 | Tim Biakabutuka | .30 | .10 |
| ❏ 34 | Robert Brooks | .30 | .10 |
| ❏ 35 | Antonio Freeman | .30 | .10 |
| ❏ 36 | Steve McNair | .60 | .25 |
| ❏ 37 | Jeff Blake | .30 | .10 |
| ❏ 38 | Tony Banks | .30 | .10 |
| ❏ 39 | Terrell Owens | .60 | .25 |
| ❏ 40 | Eric Moulds | .30 | .10 |
| ❏ 41 | Leeland McElroy | .20 | .07 |
| ❏ 42 | Chris Sanders | .20 | .07 |
| ❏ 43 | Thurman Thomas | .30 | .10 |
| ❏ 44 | Bruce Smith | .30 | .10 |
| ❏ 45 | Reggie White | .50 | .20 |
| ❏ 46 | Chris Warren | .30 | .10 |
| ❏ 47 | J.J. Stokes | .30 | .10 |
| ❏ 48 | Ben Coates | .30 | .10 |
| ❏ 49 | Tim Brown | .50 | .20 |
| ❏ 50 | Marcus Allen | .30 | .10 |
| ❏ 51 | Michael Irvin | .50 | .20 |
| ❏ 52 | William Floyd | .30 | .10 |
| ❏ 53 | Ken Dilger | .20 | .07 |
| ❏ 54 | Bobby Taylor | .20 | .07 |
| ❏ 55 | Keenan McCardell | .30 | .10 |
| ❏ 56 | Raymont Harris | .30 | .10 |
| ❏ 57 | Keith Byars | .20 | .07 |
| ❏ 58 | O.J. McDuffie | .30 | .10 |
| ❏ 59 | Robert Smith | .30 | .10 |
| ❏ 60 | Bert Emanuel | .20 | .07 |
| ❏ 61 | Rick Mirer | .20 | .07 |
| ❏ 62 | Vinny Testaverde | .20 | .07 |
| ❏ 63 | Kyle Brady | .20 | .07 |
| ❏ 64 | Mark Bruener | .20 | .07 |
| ❏ 65 | Neil O'Donnell | .30 | .10 |
| ❏ 66 | Anthony Johnson | .20 | .07 |
| ❏ 67 | Ken Norton | .20 | .07 |
| ❏ 68 | Warren Sapp | .30 | .10 |
| ❏ 69 | Amani Toomer | .30 | .10 |
| ❏ 70 | Simeon Rice | .30 | .10 |
| ❏ 71 | Kevin Hardy | .20 | .07 |
| ❏ 72 | Junior Seau | .50 | .20 |
| ❏ 73 | Neil Smith | .30 | .10 |
| ❏ 74 | LeShon Johnson | .20 | .07 |
| ❏ 75 | Quinn Early | .20 | .07 |
| ❏ 76 | Andre Reed | .30 | .10 |
| ❏ 77 | Jake Reed | .30 | .10 |
| ❏ 78 | Elvis Grbac | .30 | .10 |
| ❏ 79 | Tyrone Wheatley | .30 | .10 |
| ❏ 80 | Adrian Murrell | .30 | .10 |
| ❏ 81 | Fred Barnett | .20 | .07 |
| ❏ 82 | Darrell Green | .30 | .10 |
| ❏ 83 | Stan Humphries | .30 | .10 |
| ❏ 84 | Troy Drayton | .20 | .07 |
| ❏ 85 | Steve Atwater | .20 | .07 |
| ❏ 86 | Quentin Coryatt | .20 | .07 |
| ❏ 87 | Dan Wilkinson | .20 | .07 |
| ❏ 88 | Scott Mitchell | .30 | .10 |
| ❏ 89 | Willie McGinest | .20 | .07 |
| ❏ 90 | Kevin Smith | .20 | .07 |
| ❏ 91 | Gus Frerotte | .20 | .07 |
| ❏ 92 | Byron Bam Morris | .20 | .07 |
| ❏ 93 | Darick Holmes | .20 | .07 |
| ❏ 94 | Zach Thomas | .50 | .20 |
| ❏ 95 | Tom Carter | .20 | .07 |
| ❏ 96 | Cortez Kennedy | .20 | .07 |

| | | | | | | | | | |
|---|---|---|---|---|---|---|---|---|---|
| 97 Kevin Williams | .20 | .07 | 161 James Jett | .30 | .10 | 12 Errict Rhett | .40 | .15 |
| 98 Michael Haynes | .20 | .07 | 182 James O.Stewart | .30 | .10 | 13 Doug Flutie | .60 | .25 |
| 99 Lamont Warren | .20 | .07 | 183 Warren Moon | .50 | .20 | 14 Eric Moulds | .60 | .25 |
| 100 Jeff Graham | .20 | .07 | 184 Herschel Walker | .30 | .10 | 15 Antowain Smith | .60 | .25 |
| 101 Alex Van Dyke | .20 | .07 | 185 Ki-Jana Carter | .20 | .07 | 16 Thurman Thomas | .40 | .15 |
| 102 Jim Everett | .20 | .07 | 186 Leslie O'Neal | .20 | .07 | 17 Andre Reed | .40 | .15 |
| 103 Chris Chandler | .30 | .10 | 187 Danny Kanell | .20 | .07 | 18 Bruce Smith | .40 | .15 |
| 104 Qadry Ismail | .20 | .07 | 188 Eric Bjornson | .20 | .07 | 19 Tim Biakabutuka | .40 | .15 |
| 105 Ray Zellars | .20 | .07 | 189 Alex Molden | .20 | .07 | 20 Rae Carruth | .25 | .08 |
| 106 Chris T. Jones | .20 | .07 | 190 Bryant Young | .20 | .07 | 21 Muhsin Muhammad | .40 | .15 |
| 107 Charlie Garner | .20 | .10 | 191 Merton Hanks | .20 | .07 | 22 Curtis Enis | .25 | .08 |
| 108 Bobby Hoying | .30 | .10 | 192 Heath Shuler | .20 | .07 | 23 Curtis Conway | .40 | .15 |
| 109 Mark Chmura | .30 | .10 | 193 Brian Blades | .20 | .07 | 24 Bobby Engram | .40 | .15 |
| 110 Cris Carter | .50 | .20 | 194 Steve Bono | .30 | .10 | 25 Corey Dillon | .60 | .25 |
| 111 Darnay Scott | .20 | .07 | 195 Wayne Simmons | .20 | .07 | 26 Carl Pickens | .40 | .15 |
| 112 Anthony Miller | .20 | .07 | 196 Warrick Dunn RC | 1.50 | .60 | 27 Jeff Blake | .40 | .15 |
| 113 Desmond Howard | .20 | .07 | 197 Peter Boulware RC | .50 | .20 | 28 Darnay Scott | .40 | .15 |
| 114 Terance Mathis | .30 | .10 | 198 David LaFleur RC | .20 | .07 | 29 Ty Detmer | .40 | .15 |
| 115 Rodney Hampton | .30 | .10 | 199 Shawn Springs RC | .30 | .10 | 30 Leslie Shepherd | .25 | .08 |
| 116 Napoleon Kaufman | .50 | .20 | 200 Reidel Anthony RC | .50 | .20 | 31 Emmitt Smith | 1.25 | .50 |
| 117 Jim Harbaugh | .30 | .10 | 201 Jim Druckenmiller RC | .30 | .10 | 32 Troy Aikman | 1.25 | .50 |
| 118 Shannon Sharpe | .30 | .10 | 202 Orlando Pace RC | .50 | .20 | 33 Michael Irvin | .40 | .15 |
| 119 Irving Fryar | .20 | .07 | 203 Yatil Green RC | .30 | .10 | 34 Deion Sanders | .60 | .25 |
| 120 Garrison Hearst | .30 | .10 | 204 Bryant Westbrook RC | .20 | .07 | 35 Rocket Ismail | .40 | .15 |
| 121 Terry Allen | .50 | .20 | 205 Tiki Barber RC | 3.00 | 1.25 | 36 John Elway | 2.00 | .75 |
| 122 Larry Centers | .30 | .10 | 206 James Farrior RC | .50 | .20 | 37 Terrell Davis | .60 | .25 |
| 123 Sean Dawkins | .20 | .07 | 207 Rae Carruth RC | .20 | .07 | 38 Ed McCaffrey | .40 | .15 |
| 124 Jeff George | .30 | .10 | 208 Danny Wuerffel RC | .50 | .20 | 39 Shannon Sharpe | .40 | .15 |
| 125 Tony Martin | .30 | .10 | 209 Corey Dillon RC | 3.00 | 1.25 | 40 Rod Smith | .25 | .08 |
| 126 Mike Alstott | .50 | .20 | 210 Ike Hilliard RC | .75 | .30 | 41 Bubby Brister | .25 | .08 |
| 127 Rickey Dudley | .30 | .10 | 211 Tony Gonzalez RC | 1.50 | .60 | 42 Brian Griese | .40 | .15 |
| 128 Kevin Carter | .20 | .07 | 212 Antowain Smith RC | 1.25 | .50 | 43 Barry Sanders | 2.00 | .75 |
| 129 Derrick Alexander WR | .30 | .10 | 213 Pat Barnes RC | .50 | .20 | 44 Charlie Batch | .60 | .25 |
| 130 Greg Lloyd | .20 | .07 | 214 Troy Davis RC | .30 | .10 | 45 Herman Moore | .40 | .15 |
| 131 Bryce Paup | .20 | .07 | 215 Byron Hanspard RC | .30 | .10 | 46 Germane Crowell | .25 | .08 |
| 132 Derrick Thomas | .50 | .20 | 216 Joey Kent RC | .50 | .20 | 47 Johnnie Morton | .40 | .15 |
| 133 Greg Hill | .20 | .07 | 217 Jake Plummer RC | 2.50 | 1.00 | 48 Ron Rivers | .25 | .08 |
| 134 Jamal Anderson | .50 | .20 | 218 Kenny Holmes RC | .50 | .20 | 49 Brett Favre | 2.00 | .75 |
| 135 Curtis Conway | .30 | .10 | 219 Darnell Autry RC | .30 | .10 | 50 Antonio Freeman | .60 | .25 |
| 136 Frank Sanders | .30 | .10 | 220 Darrell Russell RC | .20 | .07 | 51 Dorsey Levens | .60 | .25 |
| 137 Brett Perriman | .20 | .07 | 221 Walter Jones RC | .50 | .20 | 52 Mark Chmura | .40 | .15 |
| 138 Edgar Bennett | .30 | .10 | 222 Dwayne Rudd RC | .50 | .20 | 53 Corey Bradford | .60 | .25 |
| 139 Wayne Chrebet | .50 | .20 | 223 Tom Knight RC | .20 | .07 | 54 Bill Schroeder | .25 | .08 |
| 140 Natrone Means | .30 | .10 | 224 Kevin Lockett RC | .30 | .10 | 55 Peyton Manning ERR | 2.00 | .75 |
| 141 Eric Metcalf | .30 | .10 | 225 Will Blackwell RC | .30 | .10 | 56 Marvin Harrison | .60 | .25 |
| 142 Trent Dilfer | .50 | .20 | 226 Dan Marino CL | .40 | .15 | 57 E.G. Green | .25 | .08 |
| 143 Terry Kirby | .30 | .10 | 227 Brett Favre CL | .40 | .15 | 58 Fred Taylor | .60 | .25 |
| 144 Johnnie Morton | .30 | .10 | 228 Emmitt Smith CL | .50 | .20 | 59 Mark Brunell | .60 | .25 |
| 145 Dale Carter | .20 | .07 | 229 Barry Sanders CL | .50 | .20 | 60 Tavian Banks | .25 | .08 |
| 146 Michael Westbrook | .30 | .10 | 230 Jerry Rice CL | .25 | .08 | 61 Jimmy Smith | .40 | .15 |
| 147 Stanley Pritchett | .20 | .07 | P1 Drew Bledsoe Promo | 1.00 | .40 | 62 Keenan McCardell | .40 | .15 |
| 148 Todd Collins | .20 | .07 | P2 Mark Brunell Promo | 1.00 | .40 | 63 Warren Moon | .60 | .25 |
| 149 Tamarick Vanover | .20 | .07 | P3 Barry Sanders Promo | 1.50 | .60 | 64 Derrick Alexander WR | .40 | .15 |
| 150 Kevin Greene | .30 | .10 | | | | 65 Byron Bam Morris | .25 | .08 |
| 151 Lamar Lathon | .20 | .07 | **1999 Donruss** | | | 66 Elvis Grbac | .40 | .15 |
| 152 Muhsin Muhammad | .30 | .10 | | | | 67 Andre Rison | .40 | .15 |
| 153 Dorsey Levens | .50 | .20 | | | | 68 Dan Marino | 2.00 | .75 |
| 154 Rod Woodson | .30 | .10 | | | | 69 Karim Abdul-Jabbar | .40 | .15 |
| 155 Brent Jones | .20 | .07 | | | | 70 O.J. McDuffie | .40 | .15 |
| 156 Michael Jackson | .20 | .07 | | | | 71 Tony Martin | .25 | .08 |
| 157 Shawn Jefferson | .20 | .07 | | | | 72 Randy Moss | 1.50 | .60 |
| 158 Kimble Anders | .20 | .07 | | | | 73 Cris Carter | .60 | .25 |
| 159 Sean Gilbert | .20 | .07 | | | | 74 Randall Cunningham | .60 | .25 |
| 160 Carnell Lake | .20 | .07 | | | | 75 Robert Smith | .60 | .25 |
| 161 Darren Woodson | .20 | .07 | | | | 76 Jeff George | .40 | .15 |
| 162 Dave Meggett | .20 | .07 | | | | 77 Jake Reed | .40 | .15 |
| 163 Henry Ellard | .20 | .07 | | | | 78 Terry Allen | .40 | .15 |
| 164 Eric Swann | .20 | .07 | COMPLETE SET (200) | 100.00 | 40.00 | 79 Drew Bledsoe | .75 | .30 |
| 165 Tony Boselli | .20 | .07 | COMP.SET w/o SP's (150) | 20.00 | 10.00 | 80 Terry Glenn | .60 | .25 |
| 166 Daryl Johnston | .30 | .10 | 1 Jake Plummer | .40 | .15 | 81 Ben Coates | .40 | .15 |
| 167 Willie Jackson | .20 | .07 | 2 Rob Moore | .40 | .15 | 82 Tony Simmons | .25 | .08 |
| 168 Wesley Walls | .30 | .10 | 3 Adrian Murrell | .40 | .15 | 83 Cam Cleeland | .25 | .08 |
| 169 Mario Bates | .20 | .07 | 4 Frank Sanders | .40 | .15 | 84 Eddie Kennison | .40 | .15 |
| 170 Lake Dawson | .20 | .07 | 5 Jamal Anderson | .60 | .25 | 85 Kerry Collins | .25 | .08 |
| 171 Mike Mamula | .20 | .07 | 6 Tim Dwight | .40 | .15 | 86 Ike Hilliard | .25 | .08 |
| 172 Ed McCaffrey | .30 | .10 | 7 Terance Mathis | .40 | .15 | 87 Gary Brown | .25 | .08 |
| 173 Tony Brackens | .20 | .07 | 8 Chris Chandler | .40 | .15 | 88 Joe Jurevicius | .40 | .15 |
| 174 Craig Heyward | .20 | .07 | 9 Byron Hanspard | .25 | .08 | 89 Kent Graham | .25 | .08 |
| 175 Harvey Williams | .20 | .07 | 10 Priest Holmes | 1.00 | .40 | 90 Wayne Chrebet | .40 | .15 |
| 176 Dave Brown | .20 | .07 | 11 Jermaine Lewis | .40 | .15 | 91 Keyshawn Johnson | .60 | .25 |
| 177 Aaron Glenn | .20 | .07 | | | | 92 Curtis Martin | .60 | .25 |
| 178 Jeff Hostetler | .20 | .07 | | | | 93 Vinny Testaverde | .40 | .15 |
| 179 Alvin Harper | .20 | .07 | | | | 94 Tim Brown | .60 | .25 |
| 180 Ty Detmer | .30 | .10 | | | | 95 Napoleon Kaufman | .60 | .25 |

**1999 Donruss**

|  |  | | |
|---|---|---|---|
| 96 | Charles Woodson | .60 | .25 |
| 97 | Tyrone Wheatley | .40 | .15 |
| 98 | Rich Gannon | .60 | .25 |
| 99 | Charles Johnson | .25 | .08 |
| 100 | Duce Staley | .60 | .25 |
| 101 | Kordell Stewart | .40 | .15 |
| 102 | Jerome Bettis | .60 | .25 |
| 103 | Hines Ward | .60 | .25 |
| 104 | Ryan Leaf | .40 | .15 |
| 105 | Natrone Means | .40 | .15 |
| 106 | Jim Harbaugh | .40 | .15 |
| 107 | Junior Seau | .60 | .25 |
| 108 | Michael Ricks | .25 | .08 |
| 109 | Jerry Rice | 1.25 | .50 |
| 110 | Steve Young | .75 | .30 |
| 111 | Garrison Hearst | .40 | .15 |
| 112 | Terrell Owens | .60 | .25 |
| 113 | Lawrence Phillips | .40 | .15 |
| 114 | J.J. Stokes | .40 | .15 |
| 115 | Sean Dawkins | .25 | .08 |
| 116 | Derrick Mayes | .25 | .08 |
| 117 | Joey Galloway | .40 | .15 |
| 118 | Jon Kitna | .60 | .25 |
| 119 | Ahman Green | .60 | .25 |
| 120 | Ricky Watters | .40 | .15 |
| 121 | Isaac Bruce | .60 | .25 |
| 122 | Marshall Faulk | .75 | .30 |
| 123 | Az-Zahir Hakim | .25 | .08 |
| 124 | Warrick Dunn | .60 | .25 |
| 125 | Mike Alstott | .60 | .25 |
| 126 | Trent Dilfer | .40 | .15 |
| 127 | Reidel Anthony | .40 | .15 |
| 128 | Jacquez Green | .25 | .08 |
| 129 | Warren Sapp | .40 | .15 |
| 130 | Eddie George | .60 | .25 |
| 131 | Steve McNair | .60 | .25 |
| 132 | Kevin Dyson | .40 | .15 |
| 133 | Yancey Thigpen | .25 | .08 |
| 134 | Frank Wycheck | .25 | .08 |
| 135 | Stephen Davis | .60 | .25 |
| 136 | Brad Johnson | .60 | .25 |
| 137 | Skip Hicks | .40 | .15 |
| 138 | Michael Westbrook | .40 | .15 |
| 139 | Darrell Green | .25 | .08 |
| 140 | Albert Connell | .25 | .08 |
| 141 | Tim Couch RC | 2.00 | .75 |
| 142 | Donovan McNabb RC | 8.00 | 3.00 |
| 143 | Akili Smith RC | 1.50 | .60 |
| 144 | Edgerrin James RC | 6.00 | 2.50 |
| 145 | Ricky Williams RC | 3.00 | 1.25 |
| 146 | Torry Holt RC | 4.00 | 1.50 |
| 147 | Champ Bailey RC | 2.50 | 1.00 |
| 148 | David Boston RC | 2.00 | .75 |
| 149 | Andy Katzenmoyer RC | 1.50 | .60 |
| 150 | Chris McAlister RC | 1.50 | .60 |
| 151 | Daunte Culpepper RC | 6.00 | 2.50 |
| 152 | Cade McNown RC | 1.50 | .60 |
| 153 | Troy Edwards RC | 1.50 | .60 |
| 154 | Kevin Johnson RC | 2.00 | .75 |
| 155 | James Johnson RC | 1.50 | .60 |
| 156 | Rob Konrad RC | 1.50 | .60 |
| 157 | Jim Kleinsasser RC | 2.00 | .75 |
| 158 | Kevin Faulk RC | 2.00 | .75 |
| 159 | Joe Montgomery RC | 1.50 | .60 |
| 160 | Shaun King RC | 1.50 | .60 |
| 161 | Peerless Price RC | 2.00 | .75 |
| 162 | Mike Cloud RC | 1.50 | .60 |
| 163 | Jermaine Fazande RC | 1.50 | .60 |
| 164 | D'Wayne Bates RC | 1.50 | .60 |
| 165 | Brock Huard RC | 2.00 | .75 |
| 166 | Marty Booker RC | 2.00 | .75 |
| 167 | Karsten Bailey RC | 1.50 | .60 |
| 168 | Shawn Bryson RC | 2.00 | .75 |
| 169 | Jeff Paulk RC | 1.00 | .40 |
| 170 | Travis McGriff RC | 1.00 | .40 |
| 171 | Amos Zereoue RC | 2.00 | .75 |
| 172 | Craig Yeast RC | 1.50 | .60 |
| 173 | Joe Germaine RC | 1.50 | .60 |
| 174 | Dameane Douglas RC | 1.50 | .60 |
| 175 | Brandon Stokley RC | 2.50 | 1.00 |
| 176 | Larry Parker RC | 2.00 | .75 |
| 177 | Joel Makovicka RC | 2.00 | .75 |
| 178 | Wane McGarity RC | 1.00 | .40 |
| 179 | Na Brown RC | 1.50 | .60 |
| 180 | Cecil Collins RC | 1.00 | .40 |
| 181 | Nick Williams RC | 1.50 | .60 |
| 182 | Charlie Rogers RC | 1.50 | .60 |
| 183 | Darrin Chiaverini RC | 1.50 | .60 |
| 184 | Terry Jackson RC | 1.50 | .60 |
| 185 | De'Mond Parker RC | 1.00 | .40 |
| 186 | Sedrick Irvin RC | 1.00 | .40 |
| 187 | MarTay Jenkins RC | 2.00 | .75 |
| 188 | Kurt Warner RC | 12.00 | 5.00 |
| 189 | Michael Bishop RC | 2.00 | .75 |
| 190 | Sean Bennett RC | 1.00 | .40 |
| 191 | Jamal Anderson CL | .25 | .08 |
| 192 | Eric Moulds CL | .25 | .08 |
| 193 | Terrell Davis CL | .60 | .25 |
| 194 | John Elway CL | .75 | .30 |
| 195 | Barry Sanders CL | .75 | .30 |
| 196 | Peyton Manning CL | .75 | .30 |
| 197 | Fred Taylor CL | .60 | .25 |
| 198 | Dan Marino CL | .75 | .30 |
| 199 | Randy Moss CL | .60 | .25 |
| 200 | Terrell Owens CL | .40 | .15 |

## 2000 Donruss

| | | | |
|---|---|---|---|
| COMPLETE SET (250) | | 400.00 | 150.00 |
| COMP.SET w/o SP's (150) | | 20.00 | 7.50 |
| 1 | Jake Plummer | .30 | .10 |
| 2 | Frank Sanders | .30 | .10 |
| 3 | Rob Moore | .30 | .10 |
| 4 | David Boston | .50 | .20 |
| 5 | Tim Dwight | .50 | .20 |
| 6 | Jamal Anderson | .50 | .20 |
| 7 | Chris Chandler | .30 | .10 |
| 8 | Terance Mathis | .30 | .10 |
| 9 | Tony Banks | .30 | .10 |
| 10 | Jermaine Lewis | .30 | .10 |
| 11 | Shannon Sharpe | .30 | .10 |
| 12 | Trent Dilfer | .30 | .10 |
| 13 | Qadry Ismail | .30 | .10 |
| 14 | Eric Moulds | .50 | .20 |
| 15 | Doug Flutie | .50 | .20 |
| 16 | Antowain Smith | .30 | .10 |
| 17 | Jonathan Linton | .20 | .07 |
| 18 | Peerless Price | .30 | .10 |
| 19 | Rob Johnson | .30 | .10 |
| 20 | Natrone Means | .30 | .10 |
| 21 | Muhsin Muhammad | .30 | .10 |
| 22 | Wesley Walls | .30 | .10 |
| 23 | Tim Biakabutuka | .30 | .10 |
| 24 | Steve Beuerlein | .30 | .10 |
| 25 | Patrick Jeffers | .30 | .10 |
| 26 | Curtis Enis | .20 | .07 |
| 27 | Cade McNown | .20 | .07 |
| 28 | Bobby Engram | .30 | .10 |
| 29 | Marcus Robinson | .50 | .20 |
| 30 | Marty Booker | .30 | .10 |
| 31 | Corey Dillon | .50 | .20 |
| 32 | Damay Scott | .30 | .10 |
| 33 | Carl Pickens | .30 | .10 |
| 34 | Akili Smith | .20 | .07 |
| 35 | Michael Basnight | .20 | .07 |
| 36 | Tim Couch | .30 | .10 |
| 37 | Kevin Johnson | .50 | .20 |
| 38 | Karim Abdul-Jabbar | .30 | .10 |
| 39 | Errict Rhett | .30 | .10 |
| 40 | Darrin Chiaverini | .20 | .07 |
| 41 | Emmitt Smith | 1.00 | .40 |
| 42 | Troy Aikman | 1.00 | .40 |
| 43 | Joey Galloway | .30 | .10 |
| 44 | Randall Cunningham | .50 | .20 |
| 45 | Michael Irvin | .30 | .10 |
| 46 | Rocket Ismail | .30 | .10 |
| 47 | Jason Tucker | .20 | .07 |
| 48 | Terrell Davis | .50 | .20 |
| 49 | John Elway | 1.50 | .60 |
| 50 | Olandis Gary | .30 | .10 |
| 51 | Ed McCaffrey | .30 | .10 |
| 52 | Rod Smith | .30 | .10 |
| 53 | Brian Griese | .50 | .20 |
| 54 | Charlie Batch | .50 | .20 |
| 55 | Barry Sanders | 1.25 | .50 |
| 56 | Herman Moore | .30 | .10 |
| 57 | Johnnie Morton | .30 | .10 |
| 58 | Germane Crowell | .20 | .07 |
| 59 | James Stewart | .30 | .10 |
| 60 | Brett Favre | 1.50 | .60 |
| 61 | Dorsey Levens | .30 | .10 |
| 62 | Antonio Freeman | .50 | .20 |
| 63 | Corey Bradford | .30 | .10 |
| 64 | Bill Schroeder | .30 | .10 |
| 65 | E.G. Green | .20 | .07 |
| 66 | Peyton Manning | 1.25 | .50 |
| 67 | Edgerrin James | .75 | .30 |
| 68 | Marvin Harrison | .50 | .20 |
| 69 | Terrence Wilkins | .20 | .07 |
| 70 | Mark Brunell | .50 | .20 |
| 71 | Fred Taylor | .50 | .20 |
| 72 | Keenan McCardell | .30 | .10 |
| 73 | Jimmy Smith | .30 | .10 |
| 74 | Warren Moon | .50 | .20 |
| 75 | Elvis Grbac | .30 | .10 |
| 76 | Tony Gonzalez | .30 | .10 |
| 77 | Dan Marino | 1.50 | .60 |
| 78 | O.J. McDuffie | .30 | .10 |
| 79 | Tony Martin | .30 | .10 |
| 80 | James Johnson | .20 | .07 |
| 81 | Thurman Thomas | .50 | .20 |
| 82 | Randy Moss | 1.00 | .40 |
| 83 | Daunte Culpepper | .60 | .25 |
| 84 | Cris Carter | .50 | .20 |
| 85 | Robert Smith | .30 | .10 |
| 86 | John Randle | .30 | .10 |
| 87 | Drew Bledsoe | .60 | .25 |
| 88 | Terry Glenn | .30 | .10 |
| 89 | Kevin Faulk | .30 | .10 |
| 90 | Ricky Williams | .50 | .20 |
| 91 | Jeff Blake | .30 | .10 |
| 92 | Jake Reed | .30 | .10 |
| 93 | Amani Toomer | .30 | .10 |
| 94 | Kerry Collins | .30 | .10 |
| 95 | Tiki Barber | .50 | .20 |
| 96 | Ike Hilliard | .30 | .10 |
| 97 | Curtis Martin | .50 | .20 |
| 98 | Vinny Testaverde | .30 | .10 |
| 99 | Wayne Chrebet | .30 | .10 |
| 100 | Ray Lucas | .30 | .10 |
| 101 | Charles Woodson | .50 | .20 |
| 102 | Napoleon Kaufman | .30 | .10 |
| 103 | Tim Brown | .50 | .20 |
| 104 | Tyrone Wheatley | .30 | .10 |
| 105 | Rich Gannon | .50 | .20 |
| 106 | Duce Staley | .50 | .20 |
| 107 | Donovan McNabb | .75 | .30 |
| 108 | Amos Zereoue | .50 | .20 |
| 109 | Kordell Stewart | .30 | .10 |
| 110 | Jerome Bettis | .50 | .20 |
| 111 | Troy Edwards | .20 | .07 |
| 112 | Ryan Leaf | .30 | .10 |
| 113 | Junior Seau | .50 | .20 |
| 114 | Jim Harbaugh | .30 | .10 |
| 115 | Jermaine Fazande | .20 | .07 |
| 116 | Curtis Conway | .30 | .10 |
| 117 | Steve Young | .60 | .25 |
| 118 | Jerry Rice | 1.00 | .40 |
| 119 | Terrell Owens | .50 | .20 |
| 120 | Charlie Garner | .30 | .10 |
| 121 | Jeff Garcia | .50 | .20 |
| 122 | Jon Kitna | .50 | .20 |
| 123 | Ricky Watters | .30 | .10 |
| 124 | Derrick Mayes | .30 | .10 |
| 125 | Kurt Warner | 1.00 | .40 |
| 126 | Marshall Faulk | .60 | .25 |
| 127 | Torry Holt | .50 | .20 |

|  |  | | |
|---|---|---|---|
| 128 | Az-Zahir Hakim | .30 | .10 |
| 129 | Isaac Bruce | .50 | .20 |
| 130 | Mike Alstott | .50 | .20 |
| 131 | Warrick Dunn | .50 | .20 |
| 132 | Shaun King | .20 | .07 |
| 133 | Keyshawn Johnson | .50 | .20 |
| 134 | Jacquez Green | .20 | .07 |
| 135 | Reidel Anthony | .30 | .10 |
| 136 | Warren Sapp | .30 | .10 |
| 137 | Eddie George | .50 | .20 |
| 138 | Steve McNair | .50 | .20 |
| 139 | Yancey Thigpen | .20 | .07 |
| 140 | Kevin Dyson | .30 | .10 |
| 141 | Frank Wycheck | .30 | .10 |
| 142 | Jevon Kearse | .50 | .20 |
| 143 | Stephen Davis | .50 | .20 |
| 144 | Skip Hicks | .20 | .07 |
| 145 | Brad Johnson | .50 | .20 |
| 146 | Bruce Smith | .30 | .10 |
| 147 | Michael Westbrook | .30 | .10 |
| 148 | Albert Connell | .20 | .07 |
| 149 | Jeff George | .30 | .10 |
| 150 | Deion Sanders | .50 | .20 |
| 151 | Courtney Brown RC | 6.00 | 2.50 |
| 152 | Corey Simon RC | 6.00 | 2.50 |
| 153 | Brian Urlacher RC | 25.00 | 10.00 |
| 154 | Shaun Ellis RC | 6.00 | 2.50 |
| 155 | John Abraham RC | 6.00 | 2.50 |
| 156 | Deltha O'Neal RC | 6.00 | 2.50 |
| 157 | Ahmed Plummer RC | 6.00 | 2.50 |
| 158 | Chris Hovan RC | 5.00 | 2.00 |
| 159 | Rob Morris RC | 5.00 | 2.00 |
| 160 | Keith Bulluck RC | 6.00 | 2.50 |
| 161 | Darren Howard RC | 5.00 | 2.00 |
| 162 | John Engelberger RC | 5.00 | 2.00 |
| 163 | Raynoch Thompson RC | 5.00 | 2.00 |
| 164 | Cornelius Griffin RC | 5.00 | 2.00 |
| 165 | William Bartee RC | 5.00 | 2.00 |
| 166 | Fred Robbins RC | 3.00 | 1.25 |
| 167 | Micheal Boireau RC | 3.00 | 1.25 |
| 168 | Brandon Short RC | 5.00 | 2.00 |
| 169 | Jacoby Shepherd RC | 3.00 | 1.25 |
| 170 | Peter Warrick RC | 6.00 | 2.50 |
| 171 | Jamal Lewis RC | 15.00 | 6.00 |
| 172 | Thomas Jones RC | 10.00 | 4.00 |
| 173 | Plaxico Burress RC | 12.00 | 5.00 |
| 174 | Travis Taylor RC | 6.00 | 2.50 |
| 175 | Ron Dayne RC | 6.00 | 2.50 |
| 176 | Bubba Franks RC | 6.00 | 2.50 |
| 177 | Sebastian Janikowski RC | 6.00 | 2.50 |
| 178 | Chad Pennington RC | 15.00 | 6.00 |
| 179 | Shaun Alexander RC | 20.00 | 8.00 |
| 180 | Sylvester Morris RC | 5.00 | 2.00 |
| 181 | Anthony Becht RC | 6.00 | 2.50 |
| 182 | R.Jay Soward RC | 5.00 | 2.00 |
| 183 | Trung Canidate RC | 5.00 | 2.00 |
| 184 | Dennis Northcutt RC | 6.00 | 2.50 |
| 185 | Todd Pinkston RC | 5.00 | 2.00 |
| 186 | Jerry Porter RC | 8.00 | 3.00 |
| 187 | Travis Prentice RC | 5.00 | 2.00 |
| 188 | Giovanni Carmazzi RC | 3.00 | 1.25 |
| 189 | Ron Dugans RC | 3.00 | 1.25 |
| 190 | Erron Kinney RC | 6.00 | 2.50 |
| 191 | Dez White RC | 6.00 | 2.50 |
| 192 | Chris Cole RC | 5.00 | 2.00 |
| 193 | Ron Dixon RC | 5.00 | 2.00 |
| 194 | Chris Redman RC | 5.00 | 2.00 |
| 195 | J.R. Redmond RC | 5.00 | 2.00 |
| 196 | Laveranues Coles RC | 8.00 | 3.00 |
| 197 | JaJuan Dawson RC | 3.00 | 1.25 |
| 198 | Darrell Jackson RC | 12.00 | 5.00 |
| 199 | Reuben Droughns RC | 8.00 | 3.00 |
| 200 | Doug Chapman RC | 5.00 | 2.00 |
| 201 | Terrelle Smith RC | 5.00 | 2.00 |
| 202 | Curtis Keaton RC | 5.00 | 2.00 |
| 203 | Gari Scott RC | 3.00 | 1.25 |
| 204 | Danny Farmer RC | 5.00 | 2.00 |
| 205 | Hank Poteat RC | 5.00 | 2.00 |
| 206 | Ben Kelly RC | 3.00 | 1.25 |
| 207 | Corey Moore RC | 5.00 | 2.00 |
| 208 | Na'il Diggs RC | 5.00 | 2.00 |
| 209 | Aaron Shea RC | 5.00 | 2.00 |
| 210 | Trevor Gaylor RC | 5.00 | 2.00 |
| 211 | Julian Peterson RC | 6.00 | 2.50 |
| 212 | Frank Moreau RC | 5.00 | 2.00 |
| 213 | Deon Dyer RC | 5.00 | 2.00 |
| 214 | Avion Black RC | 5.00 | 2.00 |
| 215 | Paul Smith RC | 5.00 | 2.00 |
| 216 | Michael Wiley RC | 5.00 | 2.00 |
| 217 | Dante Hall RC | 12.00 | 5.00 |
| 218 | Mike Brown RC | 10.00 | 4.00 |
| 219 | Sammy Morris RC | 6.00 | 2.50 |
| 220 | Billy Volek RC | 10.00 | 4.00 |
| 221 | Tee Martin RC | 6.00 | 2.50 |
| 222 | Troy Walters RC | 6.00 | 2.50 |
| 223 | Chad Morton RC | 6.00 | 2.50 |
| 224 | Erik Flowers RC | 5.00 | 2.00 |
| 225 | Ronney Jenkins RC | 5.00 | 2.00 |
| 226 | Thomas Hamner RC | 3.00 | 1.25 |
| 227 | Mareno Philyaw RC | 3.00 | 1.25 |
| 228 | James Williams RC | 5.00 | 2.00 |
| 229 | Mike Anderson RC | 8.00 | 3.00 |
| 230 | Tom Brady RC | 200.00 | 100.00 |
| 231 | Mike Green RC | 5.00 | 2.00 |
| 232 | Todd Husak RC | 6.00 | 2.50 |
| 233 | Tim Rattay RC | 6.00 | 2.50 |
| 234 | Jarious Jackson RC | 5.00 | 2.00 |
| 235 | Joe Hamilton RC | 5.00 | 2.00 |
| 236 | Shyrone Stith RC | 5.00 | 2.00 |
| 237 | Rondell Mealey RC | 3.00 | 1.25 |
| 238 | Demario Brown RC | 3.00 | 1.25 |
| 239 | Chris Coleman RC | 3.00 | 1.25 |
| 240 | Dwayne Goodrich RC | 3.00 | 1.25 |
| 241 | Drew Haddad RC | 3.00 | 1.25 |
| 242 | Doug Johnson RC | 6.00 | 2.50 |
| 243 | Windrell Hayes RC | 5.00 | 2.00 |
| 244 | Charles Lee RC | 3.00 | 1.25 |
| 245 | Kevin McDougal RC | 3.00 | 1.25 |
| 246 | Spergon Wynn RC | 5.00 | 2.00 |
| 247 | Shockmain Davis RC | 3.00 | 1.25 |
| 248 | Jamel White RC | 5.00 | 2.00 |
| 249 | Bashir Yamini RC | 3.00 | 1.25 |
| 250 | Kwame Cavil RC | 3.00 | 1.25 |

## 2002 Donruss

Randy Moss

|  |  | | |
|---|---|---|---|
| | COMPLETE SET (300) | 150.00 | 75.00 |
| | COMP.SET w/o SP's (100) | 20.00 | 7.50 |
| 1 | Jake Plummer | .30 | .10 |
| 2 | David Boston | .50 | .20 |
| 3 | MarTay Jenkins | .20 | .07 |
| 4 | Thomas Jones | .20 | .07 |
| 5 | Frank Sanders | .20 | .07 |
| 6 | Shawn Jefferson | .20 | .07 |
| 7 | Alge Crumpler | .20 | .07 |
| 8 | Michael Vick | 1.00 | .40 |
| 9 | Jamal Anderson | .30 | .10 |
| 10 | Warrick Dunn | .50 | .20 |
| 11 | Peter Boulware | .20 | .07 |
| 12 | Jamal Lewis | .50 | .20 |
| 13 | Jeff Blake | .20 | .07 |
| 14 | Travis Taylor | .30 | .10 |
| 15 | Ray Lewis | .50 | .20 |
| 16 | Todd Heap | .50 | .20 |
| 17 | Nate Clements | .20 | .07 |
| 18 | Alex Van Pelt | .20 | .07 |
| 19 | Reggie Germany | .20 | .07 |
| 20 | Larry Centers | .20 | .07 |
| 21 | Eric Moulds | .30 | .10 |
| 22 | Travis Henry | .50 | .20 |
| 23 | Wesley Walls | .20 | .07 |
| 24 | Steve Smith | .50 | .20 |
| 25 | Lamar Smith | .30 | .10 |
| 26 | Patrick Jeffers | .20 | .07 |
| 27 | Chris Weinke | .30 | .10 |
| 28 | Muhsin Muhammad | .30 | .10 |
| 29 | Marcus Robinson | .30 | .10 |
| 30 | Jim Miller | .20 | .07 |
| 31 | Anthony Thomas | .30 | .10 |
| 32 | David Terrell | .50 | .20 |
| 33 | Brian Urlacher | .75 | .30 |
| 34 | Marty Booker | .20 | .07 |
| 35 | Darnay Scott | .20 | .07 |
| 36 | Jon Kitna | .30 | .10 |
| 37 | Chad Johnson | .50 | .20 |
| 38 | T.J. Houshmandzadeh | .30 | .10 |
| 39 | Corey Dillon | .30 | .10 |
| 40 | Peter Warrick | .30 | .10 |
| 41 | Gerard Warren | .20 | .07 |
| 42 | Anthony Henry | .20 | .07 |
| 43 | Quincy Morgan | .20 | .07 |
| 44 | JaJuan Dawson | .20 | .07 |
| 45 | Tim Couch | .30 | .10 |
| 46 | Kevin Johnson | .30 | .10 |
| 47 | James Jackson | .20 | .07 |
| 48 | La'Roi Glover | .20 | .07 |
| 49 | Anthony Wright | .20 | .07 |
| 50 | Rocket Ismail | .30 | .10 |
| 51 | Troy Hambrick | .20 | .07 |
| 52 | Emmitt Smith | 1.25 | .50 |
| 53 | Quincy Carter | .30 | .10 |
| 54 | Joey Galloway | .30 | .10 |
| 55 | Shannon Sharpe | .30 | .10 |
| 56 | Kevin Kasper | .20 | .07 |
| 57 | Olandis Gary | .30+ | .10 |
| 58 | Brian Griese | .50 | .20 |
| 59 | Rod Smith | .30 | .10 |
| 60 | Terrell Davis | .50 | .20 |
| 61 | Ed McCaffrey | .50 | .20 |
| 62 | Mike Anderson | .30 | .10 |
| 63 | Bill Schroeder | .30 | .10 |
| 65 | Scotty Anderson | .20 | .07 |
| 66 | James Stewart | .20 | .07 |
| 67 | Az-Zahir Hakim | .20 | .07 |
| 68 | Germane Crowell | .20 | .07 |
| 69 | Kabeer Gbaja-Biamila | .30 | .10 |
| 70 | LeRoy Butler | .20 | .07 |
| 71 | Antonio Freeman | .50 | .20 |
| 72 | Bubba Franks | .30 | .10 |
| 73 | Brett Favre | 1.25 | .50 |
| 74 | Ahman Green | .50 | .20 |
| 75 | Terry Glenn | .30 | .10 |
| 76 | Jamie Sharper | .20 | .07 |
| 77 | Tony Simmons | .20 | .07 |
| 78 | James Allen | .20 | .07 |
| 79 | Terrence Wilkins | .20 | .07 |
| 80 | Dominic Rhodes | .30 | .10 |
| 81 | Qadry Ismail | .30 | .10 |
| 82 | Peyton Manning | 1.00 | .40 |
| 83 | Edgerrin James | .60 | .25 |
| 84 | Marvin Harrison | .50 | .20 |
| 85 | Reggie Wayne | .50 | .20 |
| 86 | Fred Taylor | .50 | .20 |
| 87 | Elvis Joseph | .20 | .07 |
| 88 | Mark Brunell | .30 | .10 |
| 89 | Keenan McCardell | .20 | .07 |
| 90 | Jimmy Smith | .30 | .10 |
| 91 | Kyle Brady | .20 | .07 |
| 92 | Derrick Alexander | .30 | .10 |
| 93 | Johnnie Morton | .30 | .10 |
| 94 | Trent Green | .30 | .10 |
| 95 | Priest Holmes | .60 | .25 |
| 96 | Tony Gonzalez | .50 | .20 |
| 97 | Snoop Minnis | .20 | .07 |
| 98 | Travis Minor | .30 | .10 |
| 99 | Oronde Gadsden | .30 | .10 |
| 100 | Jay Fiedler | .20 | .07 |
| 101 | Chris Chambers | .50 | .20 |
| 102 | Ricky Williams | .50 | .20 |
| 103 | Zach Thomas | .50 | .20 |
| 104 | Byron Chamberlain | .20 | .07 |
| 105 | Todd Bouman | .20 | .07 |
| 106 | Daunte Culpepper | .50 | .20 |
| 107 | Michael Bennett | .30 | .10 |
| 108 | Randy Moss | 1.00 | .40 |
| 109 | Cris Carter | .50 | .20 |

|  |  | | |
|---|---|---|---|
| ❑ 110 | David Patten | .20 | .07 |
| ❑ 111 | Donald Hayes | .20 | .07 |
| ❑ 112 | Tom Brady | 1.25 | .50 |
| ❑ 113 | Antowain Smith | .30 | .10 |
| ❑ 114 | Troy Brown | .30 | .10 |
| ❑ 115 | Drew Bledsoe | .60 | .25 |
| ❑ 116 | Bryan Cox | .20 | .07 |
| ❑ 117 | Boo Williams | .20 | .07 |
| ❑ 118 | Aaron Brooks | .50 | .20 |
| ❑ 119 | Deuce McAllister | .60 | .25 |
| ❑ 120 | Joe Horn | .30 | .10 |
| ❑ 121 | Amani Toomer | .30 | .10 |
| ❑ 122 | Ron Dayne | .30 | .10 |
| ❑ 123 | Kerry Collins | .30 | .10 |
| ❑ 124 | Ike Hilliard | .20 | .07 |
| ❑ 125 | Tiki Barber | .50 | .20 |
| ❑ 126 | Michael Strahan | .30 | .10 |
| ❑ 127 | Chad Pennington | .60 | .25 |
| ❑ 128 | Santana Moss | .50 | .20 |
| ❑ 129 | LaMont Jordan | .50 | .20 |
| ❑ 130 | Curtis Martin | .50 | .20 |
| ❑ 131 | Wayne Chrebet | .30 | .10 |
| ❑ 132 | Laveranues Coles | .30 | .10 |
| ❑ 133 | Vinny Testaverde | .30 | .10 |
| ❑ 134 | Charles Woodson | .30 | .10 |
| ❑ 135 | Tyrone Wheatley | .30 | .10 |
| ❑ 136 | Jerry Porter | .20 | .07 |
| ❑ 137 | Rich Gannon | .50 | .20 |
| ❑ 138 | Charlie Garner | .30 | .10 |
| ❑ 139 | Tim Brown | .50 | .20 |
| ❑ 140 | Jerry Rice | 1.00 | .40 |
| ❑ 141 | James Thrash | .30 | .10 |
| ❑ 142 | Todd Pinkston | .20 | .10 |
| ❑ 143 | A.J. Feeley | .50 | .20 |
| ❑ 144 | Donovan McNabb | .60 | .25 |
| ❑ 145 | Duce Staley | .30 | .10 |
| ❑ 146 | Freddie Mitchell | .30 | .10 |
| ❑ 147 | Correll Buckhalter | .20 | .07 |
| ❑ 148 | Casey Hampton | .20 | .07 |
| ❑ 149 | Hines Ward | .50 | .20 |
| ❑ 150 | Chris Fuamatu-Ma'afala | .20 | .07 |
| ❑ 151 | Jerome Bettis | .50 | .20 |
| ❑ 152 | Kordell Stewart | .30 | .10 |
| ❑ 153 | Plaxico Burress | .50 | .20 |
| ❑ 154 | Kendrell Bell | .50 | .20 |
| ❑ 155 | Trevor Gaylor | .20 | .07 |
| ❑ 156 | Curtis Conway | .20 | .07 |
| ❑ 157 | Doug Flutie | .50 | .20 |
| ❑ 158 | Drew Brees | .75 | .30 |
| ❑ 159 | LaDainian Tomlinson | .75 | .30 |
| ❑ 160 | Junior Seau | .30 | .10 |
| ❑ 161 | Bryant Young | .20 | .07 |
| ❑ 162 | Andre Carter | .30 | .10 |
| ❑ 163 | Eric Johnson | .20 | .07 |
| ❑ 164 | Jeff Garcia | .50 | .20 |
| ❑ 165 | Garrison Hearst | .30 | .10 |
| ❑ 166 | Terrell Owens | .50 | .20 |
| ❑ 167 | Kevan Barlow | .30 | .10 |
| ❑ 168 | Levon Kirkland | .20 | .07 |
| ❑ 169 | Ricky Watters | .20 | .07 |
| ❑ 170 | Trent Dilfer | .30 | .10 |
| ❑ 171 | Shaun Alexander | .60 | .25 |
| ❑ 172 | Koren Robinson | .30 | .10 |
| ❑ 173 | Darrell Jackson | .30 | .10 |
| ❑ 174 | Adam Archuleta | .20 | .07 |
| ❑ 175 | Aeneas Williams | .20 | .07 |
| ❑ 176 | Trung Canidate | .30 | .10 |
| ❑ 177 | Kurt Warner | .50 | .20 |
| ❑ 178 | Marshall Faulk | .50 | .20 |
| ❑ 179 | Torry Holt | .50 | .20 |
| ❑ 180 | Isaac Bruce | .30 | .10 |
| ❑ 181 | John Lynch | .30 | .10 |
| ❑ 182 | Joe Jurevicius | .20 | .07 |
| ❑ 183 | Brad Johnson | .30 | .10 |
| ❑ 184 | Rob Johnson | .20 | .10 |
| ❑ 185 | Keyshawn Johnson | .50 | .20 |
| ❑ 186 | Mike Alstott | .30 | .10 |
| ❑ 187 | Warren Sapp | .30 | .10 |
| ❑ 188 | Drew Bennett | .50 | .20 |
| ❑ 189 | Frank Wycheck | .20 | .07 |
| ❑ 190 | Kevin Dyson | .30 | .10 |
| ❑ 191 | Steve McNair | .50 | .20 |
| ❑ 192 | Eddie George | .50 | .20 |
| ❑ 193 | Jevon Kearse | .30 | .10 |
| ❑ 194 | Derrick Mason | .30 | .10 |
| ❑ 195 | Champ Bailey | .30 | .10 |
| ❑ 196 | Darrell Green | .20 | .07 |
| ❑ 197 | Bruce Smith | .20 | .07 |
| ❑ 198 | Jacquez Green | .20 | .07 |
| ❑ 199 | Stephen Davis | .30 | .10 |
| ❑ 200 | Rod Gardner | .30 | .10 |
| ❑ 201 | David Carr RC | 4.00 | 1.50 |
| ❑ 202 | Joey Harrington RC | 4.00 | 1.50 |
| ❑ 203 | Patrick Ramsey RC | 3.00 | 1.25 |
| ❑ 204 | Kurt Kittner RC | 2.50 | 1.00 |
| ❑ 205 | Rohan Davey RC | 3.00 | 1.25 |
| ❑ 206 | Josh McCown RC | 4.00 | 1.50 |
| ❑ 207 | David Garrard RC | 6.00 | 2.50 |
| ❑ 208 | Randy Fasani RC | 2.50 | 1.00 |
| ❑ 209 | Atrews Bell RC | 1.50 | .60 |
| ❑ 210 | Brandon Doman RC | 2.50 | 1.00 |
| ❑ 211 | Eric Crouch RC | 3.00 | 1.25 |
| ❑ 212 | Woody Dantzler RC | 2.50 | 1.00 |
| ❑ 213 | Chad Hutchinson RC | 2.50 | 1.00 |
| ❑ 214 | Zak Kustok RC | 3.00 | 1.25 |
| ❑ 215 | Ronald Curry RC | 3.00 | 1.25 |
| ❑ 216 | William Green RC | 3.00 | 1.25 |
| ❑ 217 | T.J. Duckett RC | 3.00 | 1.25 |
| ❑ 218 | Clinton Portis RC | 10.00 | 4.00 |
| ❑ 219 | DeShaun Foster RC | 3.00 | 1.25 |
| ❑ 220 | Lamar Gordon RC | 3.00 | 1.25 |
| ❑ 221 | Jonathan Wells RC | 3.00 | 1.25 |
| ❑ 222 | Adrian Peterson RC | 4.00 | 1.50 |
| ❑ 223 | Ladell Betts RC | 3.00 | 1.25 |
| ❑ 224 | Maurice Morris RC | 3.00 | 1.25 |
| ❑ 225 | Brian Westbrook RC | 8.00 | 3.00 |
| ❑ 226 | Luke Staley RC | 2.50 | 1.00 |
| ❑ 227 | Travis Stephens RC | 2.50 | 1.00 |
| ❑ 228 | Craig Nall RC | 3.00 | 1.25 |
| ❑ 229 | Chester Taylor RC | 6.00 | 2.50 |
| ❑ 230 | Ken Simonton RC | 1.50 | .60 |
| ❑ 231 | Verron Haynes RC | 3.00 | 1.25 |
| ❑ 232 | Tellis Redmon RC | 2.50 | 1.00 |
| ❑ 233 | J.T. O'Sullivan RC | 4.00 | 1.50 |
| ❑ 234 | Major Applewhite RC | 3.00 | 1.25 |
| ❑ 235 | Ricky Williams RC | 2.50 | 1.00 |
| ❑ 236 | James Mungro RC | 3.00 | 1.25 |
| ❑ 237 | Josh Scobey RC | 3.00 | 1.25 |
| ❑ 238 | Najeh Davenport RC | 3.00 | 1.25 |
| ❑ 239 | Dicenzo Miller RC | 1.50 | .60 |
| ❑ 240 | Ennis Haywood RC | 2.50 | 1.00 |
| ❑ 241 | Jabar Gaffney RC | 3.00 | 1.25 |
| ❑ 242 | Antonio Bryant RC | 3.00 | 1.25 |
| ❑ 243 | Donte Stallworth RC | 5.00 | 2.00 |
| ❑ 244 | Josh Reed RC | 3.00 | 1.25 |
| ❑ 245 | Ashley Lelie RC | 6.00 | 2.50 |
| ❑ 246 | Reche Caldwell RC | 3.00 | 1.25 |
| ❑ 247 | Marquise Walker RC | 2.50 | 1.00 |
| ❑ 248 | Javon Walker RC | 5.00 | 2.00 |
| ❑ 249 | Andre Davis RC | 2.50 | 1.00 |
| ❑ 250 | Antwaan Randle El RC | 4.00 | 1.50 |
| ❑ 251 | Kelly Campbell RC | 2.50 | 1.00 |
| ❑ 252 | Cliff Russell RC | 2.50 | 1.00 |
| ❑ 253 | Kahlil Hill RC | 2.50 | 1.00 |
| ❑ 254 | Ron Johnson RC | 2.50 | 1.00 |
| ❑ 255 | Deion Branch RC | 5.00 | 2.00 |
| ❑ 256 | Brian Poli-Dixon RC | 2.50 | 1.00 |
| ❑ 257 | Freddie Milons RC | 2.50 | 1.00 |
| ❑ 258 | Lee Mays RC | 2.50 | 1.00 |
| ❑ 259 | Tim Carter RC | 2.50 | 1.00 |
| ❑ 260 | Terry Charles RC | 2.50 | 1.00 |
| ❑ 261 | Jamar Martin RC | 2.50 | 1.00 |
| ❑ 262 | Jason McAddley RC | 2.50 | 1.00 |
| ❑ 263 | Chris Hope RC | 3.00 | 1.25 |
| ❑ 264 | Howard Green RC | 1.50 | .60 |
| ❑ 265 | Jeremy Shockey RC | 5.00 | 2.00 |
| ❑ 266 | Daniel Graham RC | 3.00 | 1.25 |
| ❑ 267 | Eddie Freeman RC | 1.50 | .60 |
| ❑ 268 | Julius Peppers RC | 6.00 | 2.50 |
| ❑ 269 | Kalimba Edwards RC | 3.00 | 1.25 |
| ❑ 270 | Dwight Freeney RC | 5.00 | 2.00 |
| ❑ 271 | Dennis Johnson RC | 1.50 | .60 |
| ❑ 272 | Alex Brown RC | 3.00 | 1.25 |
| ❑ 273 | Bryan Thomas RC | 2.50 | 1.00 |
| ❑ 274 | Bryan Fletcher RC | 1.50 | .60 |
| ❑ 275 | Will Overstreet RC | 1.50 | .60 |
| ❑ 276 | Ryan Denney RC | 2.50 | 1.00 |
| ❑ 277 | Charles Grant RC | 3.00 | 1.25 |
| ❑ 278 | John Henderson RC | 3.00 | 1.25 |
| ❑ 279 | Albert Haynesworth RC | 3.00 | 1.25 |
| ❑ 280 | Wendell Bryant RC | 1.50 | .60 |
| ❑ 281 | Ryan Sims RC | 3.00 | 1.25 |
| ❑ 282 | Anthony Weaver RC | 2.50 | 1.00 |
| ❑ 283 | Larry Tripplett RC | 1.50 | .60 |
| ❑ 284 | Alan Harper RC | 1.50 | .60 |
| ❑ 285 | Napoleon Harris RC | 3.00 | 1.25 |
| ❑ 286 | Robert Thomas RC | 3.00 | 1.25 |
| ❑ 287 | Levar Fisher RC | 1.50 | .60 |
| ❑ 288 | Andra Davis RC | 2.50 | 1.00 |
| ❑ 289 | Quentin Jammer RC | 3.00 | 1.25 |
| ❑ 290 | Phillip Buchanon RC | 3.00 | 1.25 |
| ❑ 291 | Keyuo Craver RC | 2.50 | 1.00 |
| ❑ 292 | Lito Sheppard RC | 3.00 | 1.25 |
| ❑ 293 | Rocky Calmus RC | 3.00 | 1.25 |
| ❑ 294 | Mike Rumph RC | 3.00 | 1.25 |
| ❑ 295 | Mike Echols RC | 1.50 | .60 |
| ❑ 296 | Joseph Jefferson RC | 2.50 | 1.00 |
| ❑ 297 | Roy Williams RC | 6.00 | 2.50 |
| ❑ 298 | Ed Reed RC | 8.00 | 3.00 |
| ❑ 299 | Michael Lewis RC | 3.00 | 1.25 |
| ❑ 300 | Eddie Drummond RC | 2.50 | 1.00 |

## 2001 Donruss Classics

|  |  | | |
|---|---|---|---|
| ❑ | COMP.SET w/ SPs (100) | 20.00 | 7.50 |
| ❑ 1 | David Boston | .75 | .30 |
| ❑ 2 | Jake Plummer | .50 | .20 |
| ❑ 3 | Thomas Jones | .50 | .20 |
| ❑ 4 | Jamal Anderson | .75 | .30 |
| ❑ 5 | Chris Redman | .30 | .10 |
| ❑ 6 | Elvis Grbac | .50 | .20 |
| ❑ 7 | Jamal Lewis | 1.25 | .50 |
| ❑ 8 | Qadry Ismail | .50 | .20 |
| ❑ 9 | Ray Lewis | .75 | .30 |
| ❑ 10 | Shannon Sharpe | .50 | .20 |
| ❑ 11 | Travis Taylor | .50 | .20 |
| ❑ 12 | Eric Moulds | .50 | .20 |
| ❑ 13 | Rob Johnson | .50 | .20 |
| ❑ 14 | Muhsin Muhammad | .50 | .20 |
| ❑ 15 | Brian Urlacher | 1.25 | .50 |
| ❑ 16 | Cade McNown | .30 | .10 |
| ❑ 17 | Marcus Robinson | .75 | .30 |
| ❑ 18 | Akili Smith | .30 | .10 |
| ❑ 19 | Corey Dillon | .75 | .30 |
| ❑ 20 | Peter Warrick | .75 | .30 |
| ❑ 21 | Courtney Brown | .50 | .20 |
| ❑ 22 | Tim Couch | .50 | .20 |
| ❑ 23 | Emmitt Smith | 1.50 | .60 |
| ❑ 24 | Brian Griese | .75 | .30 |
| ❑ 25 | Ed McCaffrey | .75 | .30 |
| ❑ 26 | Olandis Gary | .50 | .20 |
| ❑ 27 | Mike Anderson | .50 | .20 |
| ❑ 28 | Rod Smith | .50 | .20 |
| ❑ 29 | Terrell Davis | .75 | .30 |
| ❑ 30 | Charlie Batch | .50 | .20 |
| ❑ 31 | James Stewart | .50 | .20 |
| ❑ 32 | Ahman Green | .75 | .30 |
| ❑ 33 | Antonio Freeman | .75 | .30 |
| ❑ 34 | Brett Favre | 2.50 | 1.00 |
| ❑ 35 | Edgerrin James | 1.00 | .40 |
| ❑ 36 | Marvin Harrison | .75 | .30 |
| ❑ 37 | Peyton Manning | 2.00 | .75 |
| ❑ 38 | Fred Taylor | .75 | .30 |
| ❑ 39 | Jimmy Smith | .50 | .20 |
| ❑ 40 | Keenan McCardell | .30 | .10 |
| ❑ 41 | Mark Brunell | .75 | .30 |
| ❑ 42 | Sylvester Morris | .30 | .10 |

| # | Player | Hi | Lo |
|---|--------|------|------|
| 43 | Tony Gonzalez | .50 | .20 |
| 44 | Zach Thomas | .75 | .30 |
| 45 | Jay Fiedler | .75 | .30 |
| 46 | Lamar Smith | .50 | .20 |
| 47 | Cris Carter | .75 | .30 |
| 48 | Daunte Culpepper | .75 | .30 |
| 49 | Randy Moss | 1.50 | .60 |
| 50 | Drew Bledsoe | 1.00 | .40 |
| 51 | Terry Glenn | .50 | .20 |
| 52 | Aaron Brooks | .75 | .30 |
| 53 | Joe Horn | .50 | .20 |
| 54 | Ricky Williams | .75 | .30 |
| 55 | Amani Toomer | .50 | .20 |
| 56 | Ike Hilliard | .50 | .20 |
| 57 | Kerry Collins | .50 | .20 |
| 58 | Ron Dayne | .75 | .30 |
| 59 | Tiki Barber | .75 | .30 |
| 60 | Chad Pennington | 1.25 | .50 |
| 61 | Curtis Martin | .75 | .30 |
| 62 | Laveranues Coles | .75 | .30 |
| 63 | Vinny Testaverde | .50 | .20 |
| 64 | Wayne Chrebet | .50 | .20 |
| 65 | Charles Woodson | .50 | .20 |
| 66 | Rich Gannon | .75 | .30 |
| 67 | Tim Brown | .75 | .30 |
| 68 | Tyrone Wheatley | .50 | .20 |
| 69 | Corey Simon | .50 | .20 |
| 70 | Donovan McNabb | 1.00 | .40 |
| 71 | Duce Staley | .75 | .30 |
| 72 | Jerome Bettis | .75 | .30 |
| 73 | Plaxico Burress | .75 | .30 |
| 74 | Doug Flutie | .75 | .30 |
| 75 | Junior Seau | .75 | .30 |
| 76 | Jeff Garcia | .75 | .30 |
| 77 | Jerry Rice | 1.50 | .60 |
| 78 | Giovanni Carmazzi | .30 | .10 |
| 79 | Terrell Owens | .75 | .30 |
| 80 | Darrell Jackson | .75 | .30 |
| 81 | Ricky Watters | .50 | .20 |
| 82 | Shaun Alexander | 1.00 | .40 |
| 83 | Isaac Bruce | .75 | .30 |
| 84 | Kurt Warner | 2.50 | 1.00 |
| 85 | Marshall Faulk | 1.00 | .40 |
| 86 | Torry Holt | .75 | .30 |
| 87 | Brad Johnson | .75 | .30 |
| 88 | Keyshawn Johnson | .75 | .30 |
| 89 | Mike Alstott | .75 | .30 |
| 90 | Shaun King | .30 | .10 |
| 91 | Warren Sapp | .50 | .20 |
| 92 | Warrick Dunn | .75 | .30 |
| 93 | Eddie George | .75 | .30 |
| 94 | Jevon Kearse | .50 | .20 |
| 95 | Steve McNair | .75 | .30 |
| 96 | Jeff George | .50 | .20 |
| 97 | Stephen Davis | .75 | .30 |
| 98 | Charlie Garner | .50 | .20 |
| 99 | Trent Dilfer | .50 | .20 |
| 100 | Troy Aikman | 1.25 | .50 |
| 101 | Michael Vick RC | 15.00 | 15.00 |
| 102 | Drew Brees RC | 25.00 | 10.00 |
| 103 | Chris Weinke RC | 6.00 | 2.50 |
| 104 | Mike McMahon RC | 6.00 | 2.50 |
| 105 | Jesse Palmer RC | 6.00 | 2.50 |
| 106 | Quincy Carter RC | 6.00 | 2.50 |
| 107 | Josh Heupel RC | 6.00 | 2.50 |
| 108 | Tim Hasselbeck RC | 6.00 | 2.50 |
| 109 | LaDainian Tomlinson RC | 50.00 | 25.00 |
| 110 | Deuce McAllister RC | 12.00 | 5.00 |
| 111 | Michael Bennett RC | 6.00 | 2.50 |
| 112 | Anthony Thomas RC | 6.00 | 2.50 |
| 113 | LaMont Jordan RC | 12.00 | 5.00 |
| 114 | Travis Henry RC | 6.00 | 2.50 |
| 115 | Kevan Barlow RC | 6.00 | 2.50 |
| 116 | Travis Minor RC | 4.00 | 1.50 |
| 117 | Rudi Johnson RC | 12.00 | 5.00 |
| 118 | David Allen RC | 4.00 | 1.50 |
| 119 | Heath Evans RC | 4.00 | 1.50 |
| 120 | Moran Norris RC | 2.50 | 1.00 |
| 121 | David Terrell RC | 6.00 | 2.50 |
| 122 | Koren Robinson RC | 6.00 | 2.50 |
| 123 | Rod Gardner RC | 6.00 | 2.50 |
| 124 | Santana Moss RC | 10.00 | 4.00 |
| 125 | Freddie Mitchell RC | 6.00 | 2.50 |
| 126 | Reggie Wayne RC | 12.00 | 5.00 |
| 127 | Quincy Morgan RC | 6.00 | 2.50 |
| 128 | Chad Johnson RC | 20.00 | 7.50 |
| 129 | Robert Ferguson RC | 6.00 | 2.50 |
| 130 | Chris Chambers RC | 10.00 | 4.00 |
| 131 | Snoop Minnis RC | 4.00 | 1.50 |
| 132 | Eddie Berlin RC | 4.00 | 1.50 |
| 133 | Alex Bannister RC | 4.00 | 1.50 |
| 134 | Todd Heap RC | 6.00 | 2.50 |
| 135 | Alge Crumpler RC | 8.00 | 3.00 |
| 136 | Justin Smith RC | 6.00 | 2.50 |
| 137 | Andre Carter RC | 6.00 | 2.50 |
| 138 | Jamal Reynolds RC | 6.00 | 2.50 |
| 139 | Richard Seymour RC | 6.00 | 2.50 |
| 140 | Marcus Stroud RC | 6.00 | 2.50 |
| 141 | Casey Hampton RC | 6.00 | 2.50 |
| 142 | Gerard Warren RC | 6.00 | 2.50 |
| 143 | Torrance Marshall RC | 6.00 | 2.50 |
| 144 | Brian Allen RC | 2.50 | 1.00 |
| 145 | Morlon Greenwood RC | 4.00 | 1.50 |
| 146 | Keith Adams RC | 2.50 | 1.00 |
| 147 | Will Allen RC | 4.00 | 1.50 |
| 148 | Nate Clements RC | 6.00 | 2.50 |
| 149 | Adam Archuleta RC | 6.00 | 2.50 |
| 150 | Hakim Akbar RC | 2.50 | 1.00 |
| 151 | James Lofton | 1.00 | .40 |
| 152 | Jim Kelly | 2.50 | 1.00 |
| 153 | Gale Sayers | 2.50 | 1.00 |
| 154 | Mike Singletary | 2.00 | .75 |
| 155 | Boomer Esiason | 1.50 | .60 |
| 156 | Charlie Joiner | 1.00 | .40 |
| 157 | Ken Anderson | 1.50 | .60 |
| 158 | Y.A. Tittle | 2.00 | .75 |
| 159 | Jim Brown | 3.00 | 1.25 |
| 160 | Otto Graham | 1.50 | .60 |
| 161 | Ozzie Newsome | 1.00 | .40 |
| 162 | Drew Pearson | 1.50 | .60 |
| 163 | Lance Alworth | 1.50 | .60 |
| 164 | Roger Staubach | 4.00 | 1.50 |
| 165 | Tony Dorsett | 2.00 | .75 |
| 166 | John Elway | 5.00 | 2.00 |
| 167 | Barry Sanders | 3.00 | 1.25 |
| 168 | Bart Starr | 2.00 | .75 |
| 169 | Paul Hornung | 2.00 | .75 |
| 170 | Earl Campbell | 2.00 | .75 |
| 171 | Warren Moon | 2.00 | .75 |
| 172 | Johnny Unitas | 3.00 | 1.25 |
| 173 | Deacon Jones | 1.50 | .60 |
| 174 | Eric Dickerson | 1.50 | .60 |
| 175 | Bob Griese | 2.00 | .75 |
| 176 | Dan Marino | 5.00 | 2.00 |
| 177 | Larry Csonka | 2.00 | .75 |
| 178 | Paul Warfield | 2.00 | .75 |
| 179 | Fran Tarkenton | 2.50 | 1.00 |
| 180 | Archie Manning | 1.50 | .60 |
| 181 | Frank Gifford | 2.00 | .75 |
| 182 | Lawrence Taylor | 2.00 | .75 |
| 183 | Dan Fouts | 2.00 | .75 |
| 184 | Don Maynard | 1.50 | .60 |
| 185 | Joe Namath | 4.00 | 1.50 |
| 186 | Fred Biletnikoff | 2.00 | .75 |
| 187 | Marcus Allen | 2.50 | 1.00 |
| 188 | Jim Plunkett | 1.50 | .60 |
| 189 | Franco Harris | 2.50 | 1.00 |
| 190 | Terry Bradshaw | 4.00 | 1.50 |
| 191 | Joe Montana | 10.00 | 4.00 |
| 192 | Roger Craig | 1.50 | .60 |
| 193 | Steve Young | 2.50 | 1.00 |
| 194 | Dwight Clark | 1.50 | .60 |
| 195 | Steve Largent | 2.00 | .75 |
| 196 | Art Monk | 1.50 | .60 |
| 197 | Charley Taylor | 1.50 | .60 |
| 198 | Joe Theismann | 2.00 | .75 |
| 199 | Sammy Baugh | 2.00 | .75 |
| 200 | Sonny Jurgensen | 2.00 | .75 |

## 2002 Donruss Classics

| # | Player | Hi | Lo |
|---|--------|------|------|
| | COMP SET w/o SP's (100) | 20.00 | 7.50 |
| 1 | David Boston | .75 | .30 |
| 2 | Jake Plummer | .50 | .20 |
| 3 | Jamal Anderson | .50 | .20 |
| 4 | Michael Vick | 1.50 | .60 |
| 5 | Chris Weinke | .50 | .20 |
| 6 | Muhsin Muhammad | .50 | .20 |
| 7 | Steve Smith | .75 | .30 |
| 8 | Anthony Thomas | .50 | .20 |
| 9 | David Terrell | .75 | .30 |
| 10 | Brian Urlacher | 1.25 | .50 |
| 11 | Marty Booker | .50 | .20 |
| 12 | Quincy Carter | .50 | .20 |
| 13 | Emmitt Smith | 2.00 | .75 |
| 14 | Mike McMahon | .75 | .30 |
| 15 | James Stewart | .50 | .20 |
| 16 | Brett Favre | 2.00 | .75 |
| 17 | Ahman Green | .75 | .30 |
| 18 | Antonio Freeman | .75 | .30 |
| 19 | Michael Bennett | .50 | .20 |
| 20 | Randy Moss | 1.50 | .60 |
| 21 | Cris Carter | .75 | .30 |
| 22 | Daunte Culpepper | .75 | .30 |
| 23 | Aaron Brooks | .75 | .30 |
| 24 | Ricky Williams | .75 | .30 |
| 25 | Deuce McAllister | 1.00 | .40 |
| 26 | Kerry Collins | .50 | .20 |
| 27 | Michael Strahan | .50 | .20 |
| 28 | Donovan McNabb | 1.00 | .40 |
| 29 | Duce Staley | .75 | .30 |
| 30 | Freddie Mitchell | .50 | .20 |
| 31 | Correll Buckhalter | .50 | .20 |
| 32 | Jeff Garcia | .75 | .30 |
| 33 | Terrell Owens | .75 | .30 |
| 34 | Garrison Hearst | .50 | .20 |
| 35 | Marshall Faulk | .75 | .30 |
| 36 | Isaac Bruce | .75 | .30 |
| 37 | Kurt Warner | .75 | .30 |
| 38 | Torry Holt | .75 | .30 |
| 39 | Brad Johnson | .75 | .30 |
| 40 | Keyshawn Johnson | .75 | .30 |
| 41 | Mike Alstott | .75 | .30 |
| 42 | Warrick Dunn | .75 | .30 |
| 43 | Stephen Davis | .50 | .20 |
| 44 | Rod Gardner | .50 | .20 |
| 45 | Bruce Smith | .30 | .10 |
| 46 | Elvis Grbac | .50 | .20 |
| 47 | Ray Lewis | .75 | .30 |
| 48 | Jamal Lewis | .75 | .30 |
| 49 | Rob Johnson | .50 | .20 |
| 50 | Eric Moulds | .50 | .20 |
| 51 | Travis Henry | .75 | .30 |
| 52 | Corey Dillon | .75 | .30 |
| 53 | Peter Warrick | .50 | .20 |
| 54 | Tim Couch | .50 | .20 |
| 55 | James Jackson | .30 | .10 |
| 56 | Kevin Johnson | .50 | .20 |
| 57 | Brian Griese | .75 | .30 |
| 58 | Terrell Davis | .75 | .30 |
| 59 | Rod Smith | .75 | .30 |
| 60 | Mike Anderson | .75 | .30 |
| 61 | Peyton Manning | 1.50 | .60 |
| 62 | Marvin Harrison | .75 | .30 |
| 63 | Edgerrin James | 1.00 | .40 |
| 64 | Dominic Rhodes | .75 | .30 |
| 65 | Mark Brunell | .75 | .30 |
| 66 | Fred Taylor | .75 | .30 |
| 67 | Jimmy Smith | .50 | .20 |
| 68 | Tony Gonzalez | .50 | .20 |
| 69 | Trent Green | .50 | .20 |
| 70 | Priest Holmes | 1.00 | .40 |
| 71 | Snoop Minnis | .30 | .10 |
| 72 | Jay Fiedler | .50 | .20 |
| 73 | Lamar Smith | .50 | .20 |
| 74 | Chris Chambers | .75 | .30 |
| 75 | Tom Brady | 2.00 | .75 |

| | | |
|---|---|---|
| ❑ 76 Drew Bledsoe | 1.00 | .40 |
| ❑ 77 Antowain Smith | .50 | .20 |
| ❑ 78 Troy Brown | .50 | .20 |
| ❑ 79 Vinny Testaverde | .50 | .20 |
| ❑ 80 Curtis Martin | .75 | .30 |
| ❑ 81 Wayne Chrebet | .50 | .20 |
| ❑ 82 Laveranues Coles | .50 | .20 |
| ❑ 83 Tim Brown | .75 | .30 |
| ❑ 84 Jerry Rice | 1.50 | .60 |
| ❑ 85 Rich Gannon | .75 | .30 |
| ❑ 86 Charlie Garner | .50 | .20 |
| ❑ 87 Kordell Stewart | .50 | .20 |
| ❑ 88 Jerome Bettis | .75 | .30 |
| ❑ 89 Kendrell Bell | .75 | .30 |
| ❑ 90 Plaxico Burress | .50 | .20 |
| ❑ 91 Drew Brees | .75 | .30 |
| ❑ 92 LaDainian Tomlinson | 1.25 | .50 |
| ❑ 93 Doug Flutie | .75 | .30 |
| ❑ 94 Shaun Alexander | 1.00 | .40 |
| ❑ 95 Matt Hasselbeck | .50 | .20 |
| ❑ 96 Koren Robinson | .50 | .20 |
| ❑ 97 Steve McNair | .75 | .30 |
| ❑ 98 Eddie George | .75 | .30 |
| ❑ 99 Derrick Mason | .50 | .20 |
| ❑ 100 Jevon Kearse | .50 | .20 |
| ❑ 101 Joe Montana | 12.00 | 5.00 |
| ❑ 102 Joe Namath | 5.00 | 2.00 |
| ❑ 103 Warren Moon | 3.00 | 1.25 |
| ❑ 104 Dan Marino | 10.00 | 4.00 |
| ❑ 105 Steve Bartkowski | 2.50 | 1.00 |
| ❑ 106 John Elway | 10.00 | 4.00 |
| ❑ 107 Troy Aikman | 5.00 | 2.00 |
| ❑ 108 Steve Young | 3.00 | 1.25 |
| ❑ 109 Terry Bradshaw | 5.00 | 2.00 |
| ❑ 110 Bart Starr | 6.00 | 2.50 |
| ❑ 111 Bert Jones | 1.50 | .60 |
| ❑ 112 Craig Morton | 2.50 | 1.00 |
| ❑ 113 Bob Griese | 3.00 | 1.25 |
| ❑ 114 Dan Fouts | 3.00 | 1.25 |
| ❑ 115 Phil Simms | 2.50 | 1.00 |
| ❑ 116 Jim McMahon | 4.00 | 1.50 |
| ❑ 117 Joe Theismann | 3.00 | 1.25 |
| ❑ 118 Ken Stabler | 5.00 | 2.00 |
| ❑ 119 Johnny Unitas | 5.00 | 2.00 |
| ❑ 120 Roger Staubach | 5.00 | 2.00 |
| ❑ 121 Len Dawson | 3.00 | 1.25 |
| ❑ 122 Tony Dorsett | 4.00 | 1.50 |
| ❑ 123 Gale Sayers | 5.00 | 2.00 |
| ❑ 124 Jim Kelly | 4.00 | 1.50 |
| ❑ 125 Herschel Walker | 2.50 | 1.00 |
| ❑ 126 John Riggins | 4.00 | 1.50 |
| ❑ 127 Eric Dickerson | 2.50 | 1.00 |
| ❑ 128 Franco Harris | 4.00 | 1.50 |
| ❑ 129 Earl Campbell | 3.00 | 1.25 |
| ❑ 130 Thurman Thomas | 2.50 | 1.00 |
| ❑ 131 Barry Sanders | 5.00 | 2.00 |
| ❑ 132 Marcus Allen | 4.00 | 1.50 |
| ❑ 134 Natrone Means | 1.50 | .60 |
| ❑ 135 Steve Largent | 3.00 | 1.25 |
| ❑ 136 Don Maynard | 2.50 | 1.00 |
| ❑ 137 Henry Ellard | 2.50 | 1.00 |
| ❑ 138 Sterling Sharpe | 3.00 | 1.25 |
| ❑ 139 Art Monk | 2.50 | 1.00 |
| ❑ 140 Andre Reed | 2.50 | 1.00 |
| ❑ 141 Raymond Berry | 2.50 | 1.00 |
| ❑ 142 Ozzie Newsome | 2.50 | 1.00 |
| ❑ 143 William Perry | 2.50 | 1.00 |
| ❑ 144 Deacon Jones | 2.50 | 1.00 |
| ❑ 145 Howie Long | 4.00 | 1.50 |
| ❑ 146 L.C. Greenwood | 2.50 | 1.00 |
| ❑ 147 Ronnie Lott | 2.50 | 1.00 |
| ❑ 148 Dick Butkus | 5.00 | 2.00 |
| ❑ 149 Fran Tarkenton | 4.00 | 1.50 |
| ❑ 150 Mike Singletary | 3.00 | 1.25 |
| ❑ 151 David Carr RC | 8.00 | 3.00 |
| ❑ 152 Joey Harrington RC | 8.00 | 3.00 |
| ❑ 153 Patrick Ramsey RC | 6.00 | 2.50 |
| ❑ 154 Kurt Kittner RC | 5.00 | 2.00 |
| ❑ 155 DeShaun Foster RC | 6.00 | 2.50 |
| ❑ 156 William Green RC | 6.00 | 2.50 |
| ❑ 157 Clinton Portis RC | 20.00 | 7.50 |
| ❑ 158 T.J. Duckett RC | 6.00 | 2.50 |
| ❑ 159 Cliff Russell RC | 5.00 | 2.00 |
| ❑ 160 Antonio Bryant RC | 6.00 | 2.50 |

| | | |
|---|---|---|
| ❑ 161 Donte Stallworth RC | 10.00 | 4.00 |
| ❑ 162 Reche Caldwell RC | 6.00 | 2.50 |
| ❑ 163 Jabar Gaffney RC | 6.00 | 2.50 |
| ❑ 164 Ashley Lelie RC | 12.00 | 5.00 |
| ❑ 165 Andre Davis RC | 5.00 | 2.00 |
| ❑ 166 Josh Reed RC | 6.00 | 2.50 |
| ❑ 167 Ron Johnson RC | 5.00 | 2.00 |
| ❑ 168 Kelly Campbell RC | 5.00 | 2.00 |
| ❑ 169 Javon Walker RC | 10.00 | 4.00 |
| ❑ 170 Antwaan Randle El RC | 8.00 | 3.00 |
| ❑ 171 Marquise Walker RC | 5.00 | 2.00 |
| ❑ 172 Jeremy Shockey RC | 10.00 | 4.00 |
| ❑ 173 Jerramy Stevens RC | 6.00 | 2.50 |
| ❑ 174 Daniel Graham RC | 6.00 | 2.50 |
| ❑ 175 Julius Peppers RC | 12.00 | 5.00 |
| ❑ 176 Kalimba Edwards RC | 6.00 | 2.50 |
| ❑ 177 Alex Brown RC | 6.00 | 2.50 |
| ❑ 178 Will Overstreet RC | 5.00 | 2.00 |
| ❑ 179 Dwight Freeney RC | 10.00 | 4.00 |
| ❑ 180 John Henderson RC | 6.00 | 2.50 |
| ❑ 181 Ryan Sims RC | 6.00 | 2.50 |
| ❑ 182 Albert Haynesworth RC | 6.00 | 2.50 |
| ❑ 183 Wendell Bryant RC | 3.00 | 1.25 |
| ❑ 184 Anthony Weaver RC | 5.00 | 2.00 |
| ❑ 185 Napoleon Harris RC | 6.00 | 2.50 |
| ❑ 186 Robert Thomas RC | 6.00 | 2.50 |
| ❑ 187 Quentin Jammer RC | 6.00 | 2.50 |
| ❑ 188 Ed Reed RC | 15.00 | 6.00 |
| ❑ 189 Roy Williams RC | 12.00 | 5.00 |
| ❑ 190 Phillip Buchanon RC | 6.00 | 2.50 |
| ❑ 191 Lito Sheppard RC | 6.00 | 2.50 |
| ❑ 192 Mike Rumph RC | 5.00 | 2.00 |
| ❑ 193 Keyuo Craver RC | 5.00 | 2.00 |
| ❑ 194 Randy Fasani RC | 5.00 | 2.00 |
| ❑ 195 Rohan Davey RC | 6.00 | 2.50 |
| ❑ 196 Chad Hutchinson RC | 5.00 | 2.00 |
| ❑ 197 Eric Crouch RC | 6.00 | 2.50 |
| ❑ 198 Lamar Gordon RC | 6.00 | 2.50 |
| ❑ 199 Brian Westbrook RC | 15.00 | 6.00 |
| ❑ 200 Adrian Peterson RC | 8.00 | 3.00 |

**2004 Donruss Classics**

| | | |
|---|---|---|
| ❑ COMP.SET w/o SP's (100) | 20.00 | 7.50 |
| ❑ 1 Anquan Boldin | .75 | .30 |
| ❑ 2 Emmitt Smith | 1.50 | .60 |
| ❑ 3 Michael Vick | .75 | .30 |
| ❑ 4 Peerless Price | .60 | .25 |
| ❑ 5 Warrick Dunn | .60 | .25 |
| ❑ 6 Jamal Lewis | .60 | .25 |
| ❑ 7 Kyle Boller | .60 | .25 |
| ❑ 8 Terrell Suggs | .50 | .20 |
| ❑ 9 Todd Heap | .60 | .25 |
| ❑ 10 Drew Bledsoe | .75 | .30 |
| ❑ 11 Travis Henry | .60 | .25 |
| ❑ 12 DeShaun Foster | .60 | .25 |
| ❑ 13 Jake Delhomme | .60 | .25 |
| ❑ 14 Stephen Davis | .60 | .25 |
| ❑ 15 Steve Smith | .75 | .30 |
| ❑ 16 Anthony Thomas | .60 | .25 |
| ❑ 17 Brian Urlacher | .75 | .30 |
| ❑ 18 Rex Grossman | .75 | .30 |
| ❑ 19 Chad Johnson | .60 | .25 |
| ❑ 20 Carson Palmer | 1.00 | .40 |
| ❑ 21 Rudi Johnson | .60 | .25 |
| ❑ 22 Andre Davis | .50 | .20 |
| ❑ 23 Lee Suggs | .75 | .30 |
| ❑ 24 Quincy Carter | .50 | .20 |
| ❑ 25 Roy Williams S | .60 | .25 |

| | | |
|---|---|---|
| ❑ 26 Clinton Portis | .75 | .30 |
| ❑ 27 Jake Plummer | .60 | .25 |
| ❑ 28 Rod Smith | .60 | .25 |
| ❑ 29 Charles Rogers | .60 | .25 |
| ❑ 30 Joey Harrington | .60 | .25 |
| ❑ 31 Ahman Green | .75 | .30 |
| ❑ 32 Brett Favre | 2.00 | .75 |
| ❑ 33 Javon Walker | .60 | .25 |
| ❑ 34 Andre Johnson | .75 | .30 |
| ❑ 35 David Carr | .75 | .30 |
| ❑ 36 Domanick Davis | .75 | .30 |
| ❑ 37 Edgerrin James | .75 | .30 |
| ❑ 38 Marvin Harrison | .75 | .30 |
| ❑ 39 Peyton Manning | 1.50 | .60 |
| ❑ 40 Reggie Wayne | .60 | .25 |
| ❑ 41 Byron Leftwich | .75 | .30 |
| ❑ 42 Fred Taylor | .60 | .25 |
| ❑ 43 Jimmy Smith | .60 | .25 |
| ❑ 44 Priest Holmes | .75 | .30 |
| ❑ 45 Dante Hall | .60 | .25 |
| ❑ 46 Tony Gonzalez | .75 | .30 |
| ❑ 47 Trent Green | .60 | .25 |
| ❑ 48 Chris Chambers | .60 | .25 |
| ❑ 49 Ricky Williams | .75 | .30 |
| ❑ 50 Zach Thomas | .75 | .30 |
| ❑ 51 Daunte Culpepper | .75 | .30 |
| ❑ 52 Michael Bennett | .60 | .25 |
| ❑ 53 Randy Moss | 1.00 | .40 |
| ❑ 54 Deion Branch | .60 | .25 |
| ❑ 55 Adam Vinatieri | .75 | .30 |
| ❑ 56 Tedy Bruschi | .75 | .30 |
| ❑ 57 Tom Brady | 2.00 | .75 |
| ❑ 58 Aaron Brooks | .60 | .25 |
| ❑ 59 Deuce McAllister | .75 | .30 |
| ❑ 60 Donte' Stallworth | .60 | .25 |
| ❑ 61 Joe Horn | .60 | .25 |
| ❑ 62 Jeremy Shockey | .60 | .25 |
| ❑ 63 Kerry Collins | .60 | .25 |
| ❑ 64 Michael Strahan | .60 | .25 |
| ❑ 65 Tiki Barber | .75 | .30 |
| ❑ 66 Chad Pennington | .75 | .30 |
| ❑ 67 Curtis Martin | .75 | .30 |
| ❑ 68 Santana Moss | .60 | .25 |
| ❑ 69 Jerry Rice | 1.50 | .60 |
| ❑ 70 Charles Woodson | .75 | .30 |
| ❑ 71 Rod Woodson | .60 | .25 |
| ❑ 72 Tim Brown | .75 | .30 |
| ❑ 73 Brian Westbrook | .75 | .30 |
| ❑ 74 Correll Buckhalter | .60 | .25 |
| ❑ 75 Donovan McNabb | .75 | .30 |
| ❑ 76 Antwaan Randle El | .60 | .25 |
| ❑ 77 Hines Ward | .75 | .30 |
| ❑ 78 Kendrell Bell | .50 | .20 |
| ❑ 79 David Boston | .50 | .20 |
| ❑ 80 Drew Brees | .75 | .30 |
| ❑ 81 LaDainian Tomlinson | 1.25 | .50 |
| ❑ 82 Jeff Garcia | .75 | .30 |
| ❑ 83 Kevan Barlow | .60 | .25 |
| ❑ 84 Terrell Owens | .75 | .30 |
| ❑ 85 Koren Robinson | .75 | .30 |
| ❑ 86 Matt Hasselbeck | .75 | .30 |
| ❑ 87 Shaun Alexander | .75 | .30 |
| ❑ 88 Isaac Bruce | .60 | .25 |
| ❑ 89 Marc Bulger | .60 | .25 |
| ❑ 90 Marshall Faulk | .75 | .30 |
| ❑ 91 Torry Holt | .75 | .30 |
| ❑ 92 Brad Johnson | .60 | .25 |
| ❑ 93 Keenan McCardell | .50 | .20 |
| ❑ 94 Keyshawn Johnson | .60 | .25 |
| ❑ 95 Derrick Mason | .60 | .25 |
| ❑ 96 Eddie George | .60 | .25 |
| ❑ 97 Steve McNair | .60 | .25 |
| ❑ 98 LaVar Arrington | .60 | .25 |
| ❑ 99 Laveranues Coles | .60 | .25 |
| ❑ 100 Patrick Ramsey | .60 | .25 |
| ❑ 101 Archie Manning | 2.00 | .75 |
| ❑ 102 Bart Starr | 5.00 | 2.00 |
| ❑ 103 Bo Jackson | 3.00 | 1.25 |
| ❑ 104 Bob Griese | 2.00 | .75 |
| ❑ 105 Christian Okoye | 1.25 | .50 |
| ❑ 106 Daryl Johnston | 2.00 | .75 |
| ❑ 107 Deacon Jones | 1.50 | .60 |
| ❑ 108 Deion Sanders | 2.00 | .75 |
| ❑ 109 Dick Butkus | 3.00 | 1.25 |

|  |  | | |
|---|---|---|---|
| ❏ 110 | Lynn Swann | 2.50 | 1.00 |
| ❏ 111 | Don Maynard | 1.50 | .60 |
| ❏ 112 | Don Shula | 2.00 | .75 |
| ❏ 113 | Franco Harris | 2.50 | 1.00 |
| ❏ 114 | Fred Biletnikoff | 2.00 | .75 |
| ❏ 115 | Gale Sayers | 2.50 | 1.00 |
| ❏ 116 | George Blanda | 2.00 | .75 |
| ❏ 117 | Herman Edwards | 1.50 | .60 |
| ❏ 118 | Herschel Walker | 1.50 | .60 |
| ❏ 119 | Jack Lambert | 3.00 | 1.25 |
| ❏ 120 | James Lofton | 1.25 | .50 |
| ❏ 121 | Jim Plunkett | 1.50 | .60 |
| ❏ 122 | Jim Thorpe | 2.00 | .75 |
| ❏ 123 | Joe Greene | 2.00 | .75 |
| ❏ 124 | John Riggins | 2.50 | 1.00 |
| ❏ 125 | L.C. Greenwood | 1.50 | .60 |
| ❏ 126 | Larry Csonka | 2.00 | .75 |
| ❏ 127 | Leroy Kelly | 1.50 | .60 |
| ❏ 128 | Walter Payton | 8.00 | 3.00 |
| ❏ 129 | Marcus Allen | 2.00 | .75 |
| ❏ 130 | Mark Bavaro | 1.25 | .50 |
| ❏ 131 | Mel Blount | 1.50 | .60 |
| ❏ 132 | Michael Irvin | 2.00 | .75 |
| ❏ 133 | Mike Ditka | 2.00 | .75 |
| ❏ 134 | Mike Singletary | 2.00 | .75 |
| ❏ 135 | Ozzie Newsome | 1.50 | .60 |
| ❏ 136 | Paul Hornung | 2.00 | .75 |
| ❏ 137 | Paul Warfield | 1.50 | .60 |
| ❏ 138 | Randall Cunningham | 1.50 | .60 |
| ❏ 139 | Ray Nitschke | 2.00 | .75 |
| ❏ 140 | Reggie White | 2.00 | .75 |
| ❏ 141 | Richard Dent | 1.25 | .50 |
| ❏ 142 | Sammy Baugh | 2.00 | .75 |
| ❏ 143 | Sonny Jurgensen | 1.50 | .60 |
| ❏ 144 | Sterling Sharpe | 1.50 | .60 |
| ❏ 145 | Steve Largent | 2.00 | .75 |
| ❏ 146 | Terrell Davis | 2.00 | .75 |
| ❏ 147 | Terry Bradshaw | 4.00 | 1.50 |
| ❏ 148 | Thurman Thomas | 1.50 | .60 |
| ❏ 149 | Tony Dorsett | 2.00 | .75 |
| ❏ 150 | Warren Moon | 1.50 | .60 |
| ❏ 151 | John Navarre RC | 4.00 | 1.50 |
| ❏ 152 | Derek Abney RC | 3.00 | 1.25 |
| ❏ 153 | Ryan Dinwiddie RC | 3.00 | 1.25 |
| ❏ 154 | Bruce Perry/100 RC | 20.00 | 7.50 |
| ❏ 155 | Adimchinobe Echemandu RC | 4.00 | 1.50 |
| ❏ 156 | Troy Fleming RC | 3.00 | 1.25 |
| ❏ 157 | Brandon Miree RC | 3.00 | 1.25 |
| ❏ 158 | Jarrett Payton RC | 4.00 | 1.50 |
| ❏ 159 | Ben Hartsock RC | 4.00 | 1.50 |
| ❏ 160 | Chris Cooley RC | 5.00 | 2.00 |
| ❏ 161 | Derrick Ward RC | 5.00 | 2.00 |
| ❏ 162 | Triandos Luke RC | 3.00 | 1.25 |
| ❏ 163 | Clarence Moore RC | 4.00 | 1.50 |
| ❏ 164 | D.J. Hackett RC | 5.00 | 2.00 |
| ❏ 165 | Mark Jones RC | 3.00 | 1.25 |
| ❏ 166 | Sloan Thomas RC | 4.00 | 1.50 |
| ❏ 167 | Jamaar Taylor RC | 3.00 | 1.25 |
| ❏ 168 | Casey Bramlet RC | 3.00 | 1.25 |
| ❏ 169 | Drew Carter RC | 5.00 | 2.00 |
| ❏ 170 | Antwan Odom RC | 4.00 | 1.50 |
| ❏ 171 | Marquise Hill RC | 3.00 | 1.25 |
| ❏ 172 | Ricardo Colclough RC | 5.00 | 2.00 |
| ❏ 173 | Keith Smith RC | 3.00 | 1.25 |
| ❏ 174 | Joey Thomas RC | 3.00 | 1.25 |
| ❏ 175 | Stuart Schweigert RC | 4.00 | 1.50 |
| ❏ 176 | Cody Pickett RC | 5.00 | 2.00 |
| ❏ 177 | B.J. Symons RC | 4.00 | 1.50 |
| ❏ 178 | Matt Mauck RC | 5.00 | 2.00 |
| ❏ 179 | Bradlee Van Pelt RC | 5.00 | 2.00 |
| ❏ 180 | Jim Sorgi RC | 6.00 | 2.50 |
| ❏ 181 | Ernest Wilford RC | 6.00 | 2.50 |
| ❏ 182 | Bernard Berrian RC | 6.00 | 2.50 |
| ❏ 183 | Darius Watts RC | 5.00 | 2.00 |
| ❏ 184 | Derrick Hamilton RC | 4.00 | 1.50 |
| ❏ 185 | Jerricho Cotchery RC | 6.00 | 2.50 |
| ❏ 186 | Jerris McIntyre RC | 4.00 | 1.50 |
| ❏ 187 | Carlos Francis RC | 4.00 | 1.50 |
| ❏ 188 | Maurice Mann RC | 4.00 | 1.50 |
| ❏ 189 | Randy Starks RC | 4.00 | 1.50 |
| ❏ 190 | Darnell Dockett RC | 4.00 | 1.50 |
| ❏ 191 | Marcus Tubbs RC | 4.00 | 1.50 |
| ❏ 192 | Daryl Smith RC | 5.00 | 2.00 |
| ❏ 193 | Karlos Dansby RC | 6.00 | 2.50 |
| ❏ 194 | Michael Boulware RC | 6.00 | 2.50 |
| ❏ 195 | Teddy Lehman RC | 5.00 | 2.00 |
| ❏ 196 | Will Poole RC | 6.00 | 2.50 |
| ❏ 197 | Derrick Strait RC | 5.00 | 2.00 |
| ❏ 198 | Ahmad Carroll RC | 6.00 | 2.50 |
| ❏ 199 | Jeremy LeSueur RC | 4.00 | 1.50 |
| ❏ 200 | Bob Sanders RC | 15.00 | 6.00 |
| ❏ 201 | J.P. Losman RC | 8.00 | 3.00 |
| ❏ 202 | Matt Schaub RC | 20.00 | 8.00 |
| ❏ 203 | Josh Harris RC | 4.00 | 1.50 |
| ❏ 204 | Luke McCown RC | 6.00 | 2.50 |
| ❏ 205 | Quincy Wilson RC | 5.00 | 2.00 |
| ❏ 206 | Michael Turner RC | 12.00 | 5.00 |
| ❏ 207 | Mewelde Moore RC | 6.00 | 2.50 |
| ❏ 208 | Cedric Cobbs RC | 5.00 | 2.00 |
| ❏ 209 | Ben Watson RC | 6.00 | 2.50 |
| ❏ 210 | Michael Jenkins RC | 6.00 | 2.50 |
| ❏ 211 | Devery Henderson RC | 6.00 | 2.50 |
| ❏ 212 | Johnnie Morant RC | 5.00 | 2.00 |
| ❏ 213 | Keary Colbert RC | 6.00 | 2.50 |
| ❏ 214 | Devard Darling RC | 5.00 | 2.00 |
| ❏ 215 | P.K. Sam RC | 4.00 | 1.50 |
| ❏ 216 | Samie Parker RC | 5.00 | 2.00 |
| ❏ 217 | Jason Babin RC | 5.00 | 2.00 |
| ❏ 218 | Tommie Harris RC | 6.00 | 2.50 |
| ❏ 219 | Vince Wilfork RC | 6.00 | 2.50 |
| ❏ 220 | Jonathan Vilma RC | 6.00 | 2.50 |
| ❏ 221 | D.J. Williams RC | 6.00 | 2.50 |
| ❏ 222 | Chris Gamble RC | 5.00 | 2.00 |
| ❏ 223 | Matt Ware RC | 6.00 | 2.50 |
| ❏ 224 | Shawntae Spencer RC | 4.00 | 1.50 |
| ❏ 225 | Sean Jones RC | 5.00 | 2.00 |
| ❏ 226 | Drew Henson RC | 5.00 | 2.00 |
| ❏ 227 | Ben Roethlisberger RC | 60.00 | 25.00 |
| ❏ 228 | Eli Manning RC | 50.00 | 20.00 |
| ❏ 229 | Philip Rivers RC | 25.00 | 10.00 |
| ❏ 230 | Steven Jackson RC | 25.00 | 10.00 |
| ❏ 231 | Kevin Jones RC | 8.00 | 3.00 |
| ❏ 232 | Chris Perry RC | 8.00 | 3.00 |
| ❏ 233 | Greg Jones RC | 8.00 | 3.00 |
| ❏ 234 | Tatum Bell RC | 8.00 | 3.00 |
| ❏ 235 | Jeff Smoker RC | 6.00 | 2.50 |
| ❏ 236 | Julius Jones RC | 20.00 | 8.00 |
| ❏ 237 | Kellen Winslow RC | 15.00 | 6.00 |
| ❏ 238 | Ben Troupe RC | 6.00 | 2.50 |
| ❏ 239 | Larry Fitzgerald RC | 25.00 | 10.00 |
| ❏ 240 | Craig Krenzel RC | 8.00 | 3.00 |
| ❏ 241 | Roy Williams RC | 20.00 | 8.00 |
| ❏ 242 | Reggie Williams RC | 8.00 | 3.00 |
| ❏ 243 | Michael Clayton RC | 8.00 | 3.00 |
| ❏ 244 | Lee Evans RC | 10.00 | 4.00 |
| ❏ 245 | Rashaun Woods RC | 5.00 | 2.00 |
| ❏ 246 | Kenechi Udeze RC | 8.00 | 3.00 |
| ❏ 247 | Will Smith RC | 6.00 | 2.50 |
| ❏ 248 | DeAngelo Hall RC | 9.00 | 3.00 |
| ❏ 249 | Dunta Robinson RC | 6.00 | 2.50 |
| ❏ 250 | Sean Taylor RC | 8.00 | 3.00 |

## 2005 Donruss Classics

| | | | |
|---|---|---|---|
| ❏ COMP.SET w/o SP's (100) | 20.00 | 7.50 |
| ❏ 101-150 LEG PRINT RUN 1000 SER.#'d SETS | | |
| ❏ 151-175 PRINT RUN 1999 SER.#'d SETS | | |
| ❏ 176-200 PRINT RUN 999 SER.#'d SETS | | |
| ❏ 201-225 PRINT RUN 999 SER.#'d SETS | | |
| ❏ 226-250 AU PRINT RUN 499 SER.#'d SETS | | |
| ❏ 1 Kurt Warner | .75 | .30 |
| ❏ 2 Josh McCown | .60 | .25 |
| ❏ 3 Larry Fitzgerald | .75 | .30 |
| ❏ 4 Alge Crumpler | .60 | .25 |
| ❏ 5 Michael Vick | .75 | .30 |
| ❏ 6 Warrick Dunn | .60 | .25 |
| ❏ 7 Todd Heap | .60 | .25 |
| ❏ 8 Jamal Lewis | .60 | .25 |
| ❏ 9 Kyle Boller | .60 | .25 |
| ❏ 10 Drew Bledsoe | .75 | .30 |
| ❏ 11 Lee Evans | .60 | .25 |
| ❏ 12 Willis McGahee | .75 | .30 |
| ❏ 13 Steve Smith | .75 | .30 |
| ❏ 14 Jake Delhomme | .60 | .25 |
| ❏ 15 Muhsin Muhammad | .60 | .25 |
| ❏ 16 Brian Urlacher | .75 | .30 |
| ❏ 17 Rex Grossman | .75 | .30 |
| ❏ 18 Thomas Jones | .60 | .25 |
| ❏ 19 Carson Palmer | .75 | .30 |
| ❏ 20 Chad Johnson | .75 | .30 |
| ❏ 21 Rudi Johnson | .60 | .25 |
| ❏ 22 Antonio Bryant | .50 | .25 |
| ❏ 23 Kellen Winslow Jr. | .75 | .30 |
| ❏ 24 Lee Suggs | .60 | .25 |
| ❏ 25 Julius Jones | .75 | .30 |
| ❏ 26 Keyshawn Johnson | .60 | .25 |
| ❏ 27 Roy Williams S | .60 | .25 |
| ❏ 28 Jake Plummer | .60 | .25 |
| ❏ 29 Rod Smith | .60 | .25 |
| ❏ 30 Tatum Bell | .75 | .30 |
| ❏ 31 Joey Harrington | .75 | .30 |
| ❏ 32 Kevin Jones | .60 | .25 |
| ❏ 33 Roy Williams WR | .75 | .30 |
| ❏ 34 Ahman Green | .75 | .30 |
| ❏ 35 Brett Favre | 2.00 | .75 |
| ❏ 36 Javon Walker | .60 | .25 |
| ❏ 37 Andre Johnson | .60 | .25 |
| ❏ 38 David Carr | .60 | .25 |
| ❏ 39 Domanick Davis | .50 | .20 |
| ❏ 40 Edgerrin James | .75 | .30 |
| ❏ 41 Marvin Harrison | .75 | .30 |
| ❏ 42 Peyton Manning | 1.25 | .50 |
| ❏ 43 Reggie Wayne | .60 | .25 |
| ❏ 44 Byron Leftwich | .60 | .25 |
| ❏ 45 Fred Taylor | .75 | .30 |
| ❏ 46 Jimmy Smith | .60 | .25 |
| ❏ 47 Priest Holmes | .75 | .30 |
| ❏ 48 Tony Gonzalez | .60 | .25 |
| ❏ 49 Trent Green | .60 | .25 |
| ❏ 50 A.J. Feeley | .50 | .20 |
| ❏ 51 Chris Chambers | .60 | .25 |
| ❏ 52 Zach Thomas | .75 | .30 |
| ❏ 53 Daunte Culpepper | .75 | .30 |
| ❏ 54 Michael Bennett | .60 | .25 |
| ❏ 55 Randy Moss | .75 | .30 |
| ❏ 56 Corey Dillon | .60 | .25 |
| ❏ 57 David Givens | .60 | .25 |
| ❏ 58 Tom Brady | 1.50 | .60 |
| ❏ 59 Aaron Brooks | .50 | .20 |
| ❏ 60 Deuce McAllister | .75 | .30 |
| ❏ 61 Joe Horn | .60 | .25 |
| ❏ 62 Eli Manning | 1.50 | .60 |
| ❏ 63 Jeremy Shockey | .75 | .30 |
| ❏ 64 Tiki Barber | .75 | .30 |
| ❏ 65 Chad Pennington | .75 | .30 |
| ❏ 66 Curtis Martin | .75 | .30 |
| ❏ 67 Santana Moss | .60 | .25 |
| ❏ 68 Jerry Porter | .60 | .25 |
| ❏ 69 Kerry Collins | .60 | .25 |
| ❏ 70 J.P. Losman | .75 | .30 |
| ❏ 71 Brian Westbrook | .75 | .30 |
| ❏ 72 Donovan McNabb | .75 | .30 |
| ❏ 73 Terrell Owens | .75 | .30 |
| ❏ 74 Ben Roethlisberger | 2.00 | .75 |
| ❏ 75 Duce Staley | .60 | .25 |
| ❏ 76 Hines Ward | .75 | .30 |
| ❏ 77 Jerome Bettis | .75 | .30 |
| ❏ 78 Antonio Gates | .75 | .30 |
| ❏ 79 Drew Brees | .75 | .30 |
| ❏ 80 LaDainian Tomlinson | 1.25 | .50 |
| ❏ 81 Brandon Lloyd | .50 | .20 |
| ❏ 82 Kevan Barlow | .50 | .20 |
| ❏ 83 Laveranues Coles | .60 | .25 |
| ❏ 84 Darrell Jackson | .60 | .25 |
| ❏ 85 Jerry Rice | 1.50 | .60 |
| ❏ 86 Matt Hasselbeck | .60 | .25 |
| ❏ 87 Shaun Alexander | .75 | .30 |

| | | |
|---|---|---|
| ❑ 88 Isaac Bruce | .60 | .25 |
| ❑ 89 Marc Bulger | .60 | .25 |
| ❑ 90 Steven Jackson | 1.00 | .40 |
| ❑ 91 Torry Holt | .60 | .25 |
| ❑ 92 Brian Griese | .60 | .25 |
| ❑ 93 Michael Clayton | .60 | .25 |
| ❑ 94 Mike Alstott | .60 | .25 |
| ❑ 95 Chris Brown | .60 | .25 |
| ❑ 96 Drew Bennett | .60 | .25 |
| ❑ 97 Steve McNair | .75 | .30 |
| ❑ 98 Clinton Portis | .75 | .30 |
| ❑ 99 LaVar Arrington | .75 | .30 |
| ❑ 100 Patrick Ramsey | .60 | .25 |
| ❑ 101 Don Shula | 3.00 | 1.25 |
| ❑ 102 James Lofton | 2.50 | 1.00 |
| ❑ 103 Thurman Thomas | 4.00 | 1.50 |
| ❑ 104 Gale Sayers | 5.00 | 2.00 |
| ❑ 105 Mike Singletary | 4.00 | 1.50 |
| ❑ 106 Boomer Esiason | 3.00 | 1.25 |
| ❑ 107 Cris Collinsworth | 3.00 | 1.25 |
| ❑ 108 Ickey Woods | 2.50 | 1.00 |
| ❑ 109 Jim Brown | 5.00 | 2.00 |
| ❑ 110 Leroy Kelly | 3.00 | 1.25 |
| ❑ 111 Ozzie Newsome | 3.00 | 1.25 |
| ❑ 112 Paul Warfield | 3.00 | 1.25 |
| ❑ 113 Deion Sanders | 5.00 | 2.00 |
| ❑ 114 Herschel Walker | 3.00 | 1.25 |
| ❑ 115 Mike Ditka | 4.00 | 1.50 |
| ❑ 116 Michael Irvin | 4.00 | 1.50 |
| ❑ 117 Roger Staubach | 6.00 | 2.50 |
| ❑ 118 Tony Dorsett | 3.00 | 1.25 |
| ❑ 119 Troy Aikman | 5.00 | 2.00 |
| ❑ 120 John Elway | 8.00 | 3.00 |
| ❑ 121 Barry Sanders | 6.00 | 2.50 |
| ❑ 122 Bart Starr | 6.00 | 2.50 |
| ❑ 123 Paul Hornung | 4.00 | 1.50 |
| ❑ 124 Sterling Sharpe | 3.00 | 1.25 |
| ❑ 125 Warren Moon | 4.00 | 1.50 |
| ❑ 126 Christian Okoye | 2.50 | 1.00 |
| ❑ 127 Marcus Allen | 4.00 | 1.50 |
| ❑ 128 Deacon Jones | 3.00 | 1.25 |
| ❑ 129 Bob Griese | 4.00 | 1.50 |
| ❑ 130 Dan Marino | 10.00 | 4.00 |
| ❑ 131 Fran Tarkenton | 4.00 | 1.50 |
| ❑ 132 Y.A. Tittle | 4.00 | 1.50 |
| ❑ 133 Don Maynard | 3.00 | 1.25 |
| ❑ 134 Joe Namath | 6.00 | 2.50 |
| ❑ 135 Jim Plunkett | 3.00 | 1.25 |
| ❑ 136 Bo Jackson | 5.00 | 2.00 |
| ❑ 137 Herman Edwards | 2.50 | 1.00 |
| ❑ 138 Randall Cunningham | 3.00 | 1.25 |
| ❑ 139 Franco Harris | 4.00 | 1.50 |
| ❑ 140 Jack Lambert | 4.00 | 1.50 |
| ❑ 141 Joe Greene | 4.00 | 1.50 |
| ❑ 142 L.C. Greenwood | 3.00 | 1.25 |
| ❑ 143 Terry Bradshaw | 6.00 | 2.50 |
| ❑ 144 Dan Fouts | 4.00 | 1.50 |
| ❑ 145 Joe Montana | 10.00 | 4.00 |
| ❑ 146 John Taylor | 3.00 | 1.25 |
| ❑ 147 Roger Craig | 4.00 | 1.50 |
| ❑ 148 Steve Young | 5.00 | 2.00 |
| ❑ 149 Steve Largent | 4.00 | 1.50 |
| ❑ 150 Sonny Jurgensen | 3.00 | 1.25 |
| ❑ 151 Adam Jones RC | 5.00 | 2.00 |
| ❑ 152 Antrel Rolle RC | 5.00 | 2.00 |
| ❑ 153 Carlos Rogers RC | 5.00 | 2.00 |
| ❑ 154 DeMarcus Ware RC | 8.00 | 3.00 |
| ❑ 155 Shawne Merriman RC | 8.00 | 3.00 |
| ❑ 156 Thomas Davis RC | 4.00 | 1.50 |
| ❑ 157 Derrick Johnson RC | 5.00 | 2.00 |
| ❑ 158 Travis Johnson RC | 3.00 | 1.25 |
| ❑ 159 David Pollack RC | 4.00 | 1.50 |
| ❑ 160 Erasmus James RC | 4.00 | 1.50 |
| ❑ 161 Marcus Spears RC | 5.00 | 2.00 |
| ❑ 162 Fabian Washington RC | 5.00 | 2.00 |
| ❑ 163 Luis Castillo RC | 5.00 | 2.00 |
| ❑ 164 Marlin Jackson RC | 4.00 | 1.50 |
| ❑ 165 Mike Patterson RC | 4.00 | 1.50 |
| ❑ 166 Brodney Pool RC | 4.00 | 1.50 |
| ❑ 167 Barrett Ruud RC | 5.00 | 2.00 |
| ❑ 168 Shaun Cody RC | 4.00 | 1.50 |
| ❑ 169 Stanford Routt RC | 4.00 | 1.50 |
| ❑ 170 Josh Bullocks RC | 5.00 | 2.00 |
| ❑ 171 Kevin Burnett RC | 4.00 | 1.50 |

| | | |
|---|---|---|
| ❑ 172 Corey Webster RC | 5.00 | 2.00 |
| ❑ 173 Lofa Tatupu RC | 6.00 | 2.50 |
| ❑ 174 Justin Miller RC | 4.00 | 1.50 |
| ❑ 175 Odell Thurman RC | 5.00 | 2.00 |
| ❑ 176 Heath Miller RC | 12.00 | 5.00 |
| ❑ 177 Vernand Morency RC | 6.00 | 2.50 |
| ❑ 178 Ryan Moats RC | 6.00 | 2.50 |
| ❑ 179 Courtney Roby RC | 5.00 | 2.00 |
| ❑ 180 Alex Smith TE RC | 6.00 | 2.50 |
| ❑ 181 Kevin Everett RC | 6.00 | 2.50 |
| ❑ 182 Brandon Jones RC | 6.00 | 2.50 |
| ❑ 183 Maurice Clarett | 5.00 | 2.00 |
| ❑ 184 Marion Barber RC | 20.00 | 8.00 |
| ❑ 185 Brandon Jacobs RC | 8.00 | 3.00 |
| ❑ 186 Matt Cassel RC | 15.00 | 6.00 |
| ❑ 187 Stefan LeFors RC | 5.00 | 2.00 |
| ❑ 188 Alvin Pearman RC | 5.00 | 2.00 |
| ❑ 189 James Kilian RC | 4.00 | 1.50 |
| ❑ 190 Airese Currie RC | 5.00 | 2.00 |
| ❑ 191 Damien Nash RC | 5.00 | 2.00 |
| ❑ 192 Dan Orlovsky RC | 6.00 | 2.50 |
| ❑ 193 Larry Brackins RC | 4.00 | 1.50 |
| ❑ 194 Rasheed Marshall RC | 5.00 | 2.00 |
| ❑ 195 Marcus Maxwell RC | 4.00 | 1.50 |
| ❑ 196 LeRon McCoy RC | 4.00 | 1.50 |
| ❑ 197 Harry Williams RC | 5.00 | 2.00 |
| ❑ 198 Noah Herron RC | 6.00 | 2.50 |
| ❑ 199 Tab Perry RC | 6.00 | 2.50 |
| ❑ 200 Chad Owens RC | 6.00 | 2.50 |
| ❑ 201 Alex Smith QB RC | 10.00 | 4.00 |
| ❑ 202 Ronnie Brown RC | 20.00 | 8.00 |
| ❑ 203 Braylon Edwards RC | 20.00 | 8.00 |
| ❑ 204 Cedric Benson RC | 6.00 | 2.50 |
| ❑ 205 Cadillac Williams RC | 12.00 | 5.00 |
| ❑ 206 Troy Williamson RC | 6.00 | 2.50 |
| ❑ 207 Mike Williams | 6.00 | 2.50 |
| ❑ 208 Matt Jones RC | 10.00 | 4.00 |
| ❑ 209 Mark Clayton RC | 6.00 | 2.50 |
| ❑ 210 Aaron Rodgers RC | 20.00 | 8.00 |
| ❑ 211 Jason Campbell RC | 12.00 | 5.00 |
| ❑ 212 Roddy White RC | 8.00 | 3.00 |
| ❑ 213 Reggie Brown RC | 6.00 | 2.50 |
| ❑ 214 Mark Bradley RC | 6.00 | 2.50 |
| ❑ 215 J.J. Arrington RC | 6.00 | 2.50 |
| ❑ 216 Eric Shelton RC | 6.00 | 2.50 |
| ❑ 217 Roscoe Parrish RC | 5.00 | 2.00 |
| ❑ 218 Terrence Murphy RC | 4.00 | 1.50 |
| ❑ 219 Vincent Jackson RC | 6.00 | 2.50 |
| ❑ 220 Frank Gore RC | 15.00 | 6.00 |
| ❑ 221 Charlie Frye RC | 6.00 | 2.50 |
| ❑ 222 Andrew Walter RC | 6.00 | 2.50 |
| ❑ 223 David Greene RC | 5.00 | 2.00 |
| ❑ 224 Kyle Orton RC | 8.00 | 3.00 |
| ❑ 225 Carlos Fason RC | 5.00 | 2.00 |
| ❑ 226 Cedric Houston AU RC | 15.00 | 6.00 |
| ❑ 227 Dante Ridgeway AU RC | 10.00 | 4.00 |
| ❑ 228 Craig Bragg AU RC | 10.00 | 4.00 |
| ❑ 229 Deandra Cobb AU RC | 12.00 | 5.00 |
| ❑ 230 Derek Anderson AU RC | 40.00 | 20.00 |
| ❑ 231 Paris Warren AU RC | 12.00 | 5.00 |
| ❑ 232 Lionel Gates AU RC | 10.00 | 4.00 |
| ❑ 233 Anthony Davis AU RC | 12.00 | 5.00 |
| ❑ 234 Ryan Fitzpatrick AU RC | 10.00 | 4.00 |
| ❑ 235 J.R. Russell AU RC | 10.00 | 4.00 |
| ❑ 236 Dan Cody AU RC | 10.00 | 4.00 |
| ❑ 237 Bryant McFadden AU RC | 12.00 | 5.00 |
| ❑ 238 Adrian McPherson AU RC | 12.00 | 5.00 |
| ❑ 239 Chris Henry AU RC | 15.00 | 6.00 |
| ❑ 240 Craphonso Thorpe AU RC | 12.00 | 5.00 |
| ❑ 241 Darren Sproles AU RC | 25.00 | 15.00 |
| ❑ 242 Fred Gibson AU RC | 12.00 | 5.00 |
| ❑ 243 Jerome Mathis AU RC | 15.00 | 6.00 |
| ❑ 244 Josh Davis AU RC | 10.00 | 4.00 |
| ❑ 245 Kay-Jay Harris AU RC | 12.00 | 5.00 |
| ❑ 246 Matt Roth AU RC | 12.00 | 5.00 |
| ❑ 247 Roydell Williams AU RC | 12.00 | 5.00 |
| ❑ 248 Steve Savoy AU RC | 10.00 | 4.00 |
| ❑ 249 T.A. McLendon AU RC | 10.00 | 4.00 |
| ❑ 250 Taylor Stubblefield AU RC | 10.00 | 4.00 |

## 2006 Donruss Classics

| | | |
|---|---|---|
| ❑ COMP.SET w/o SP's (100) | 20.00 | 7.50 |
| ❑ LEGEND PRINT RUN 1000 SER. #'d SETS | | |
| ❑ 1 Anquan Boldin | .60 | .25 |

| | | |
|---|---|---|
| ❑ 2 Kurt Warner | .60 | .25 |
| ❑ 3 Larry Fitzgerald | .75 | .30 |
| ❑ 4 Marcel Shipp | .60 | .25 |
| ❑ 5 Alge Crumpler | .60 | .25 |
| ❑ 6 Michael Vick | .60 | .25 |
| ❑ 7 Warrick Dunn | .60 | .25 |
| ❑ 8 Jamal Lewis | .60 | .25 |
| ❑ 9 Kyle Boller | .60 | .25 |
| ❑ 10 Eric Moulds | .60 | .25 |
| ❑ 11 J.P. Losman | .60 | .25 |
| ❑ 12 Willis McGahee | .60 | .25 |
| ❑ 13 Jake Delhomme | .60 | .25 |
| ❑ 14 Stephen Davis | .60 | .25 |
| ❑ 15 Steve Smith | .75 | .30 |
| ❑ 16 Cedric Benson | .60 | .25 |
| ❑ 17 Kyle Orton | .50 | .20 |
| ❑ 18 Muhsin Muhammad | .60 | .25 |
| ❑ 19 Thomas Jones | .60 | .25 |
| ❑ 20 Carson Palmer | .60 | .25 |
| ❑ 21 Chad Johnson | .60 | .25 |
| ❑ 22 Rudi Johnson | .60 | .25 |
| ❑ 23 T.J. Houshmandzadeh | .60 | .25 |
| ❑ 24 Braylon Edwards | .60 | .25 |
| ❑ 25 Reuben Droughns | .60 | .25 |
| ❑ 26 Trent Dilfer | .60 | .25 |
| ❑ 27 Drew Bledsoe | .75 | .30 |
| ❑ 28 Julius Jones | .60 | .25 |
| ❑ 29 Keyshawn Johnson | .60 | .25 |
| ❑ 30 Terry Glenn | .60 | .25 |
| ❑ 31 Ashley Lelie | .60 | .25 |
| ❑ 32 Jake Plummer | .60 | .25 |
| ❑ 33 Tatum Bell | .60 | .25 |
| ❑ 34 Joey Harrington | .50 | .20 |
| ❑ 35 Kevin Jones | .75 | .30 |
| ❑ 36 Roy Williams WR | .75 | .30 |
| ❑ 37 Aaron Rodgers | .75 | .30 |
| ❑ 38 Brett Favre | 1.50 | .60 |
| ❑ 39 Samkon Gado | .75 | .30 |
| ❑ 40 Andre Johnson | .60 | .25 |
| ❑ 41 David Carr | .60 | .25 |
| ❑ 42 Domanick Davis | .60 | .25 |
| ❑ 43 Edgerrin James | .60 | .25 |
| ❑ 44 Marvin Harrison | .75 | .30 |
| ❑ 45 Peyton Manning | 1.25 | .50 |
| ❑ 46 Reggie Wayne | .60 | .25 |
| ❑ 47 Byron Leftwich | .60 | .25 |
| ❑ 48 Fred Taylor | .60 | .25 |
| ❑ 49 Jimmy Smith | .60 | .25 |
| ❑ 50 Matt Jones | .60 | .25 |
| ❑ 51 Larry Johnson | .60 | .25 |
| ❑ 52 Tony Gonzalez | .60 | .25 |
| ❑ 53 Trent Green | .60 | .25 |
| ❑ 54 Chris Chambers | .60 | .25 |
| ❑ 55 Ricky Williams | .60 | .25 |
| ❑ 56 Ronnie Brown | .75 | .30 |
| ❑ 57 Daunte Culpepper | .75 | .30 |
| ❑ 58 Mewelde Moore | .50 | .20 |
| ❑ 59 Nate Burleson | .60 | .25 |
| ❑ 60 Corey Dillon | .60 | .25 |
| ❑ 61 Deion Branch | .60 | .25 |
| ❑ 62 Tom Brady | 1.25 | .50 |
| ❑ 63 Aaron Brooks | .60 | .25 |
| ❑ 64 Deuce McAllister | .60 | .25 |
| ❑ 65 Donte Stallworth | .60 | .25 |
| ❑ 66 Eli Manning | 1.00 | .40 |
| ❑ 67 Plaxico Burress | .60 | .25 |
| ❑ 68 Tiki Barber | .75 | .30 |
| ❑ 69 Chad Pennington | .60 | .25 |

| | | |
|---|---|---|
| 70 Curtis Martin | .75 | .30 |
| 71 Laveranues Coles | .60 | .25 |
| 72 Kerry Collins | .60 | .25 |
| 73 LaMont Jordan | .60 | .25 |
| 74 Randy Moss | .75 | .30 |
| 75 Brian Westbrook | .60 | .25 |
| 76 Donovan McNabb | .75 | .30 |
| 77 Reggie Brown | .60 | .25 |
| 78 Ben Roethlisberger | 1.25 | .50 |
| 79 Hines Ward | .75 | .30 |
| 80 Willie Parker | 1.00 | .40 |
| 81 Antonio Gates | .75 | .30 |
| 82 Drew Brees | .75 | .30 |
| 83 LaDainian Tomlinson | 1.00 | .40 |
| 84 Alex Smith QB | .75 | .30 |
| 85 Frank Gore | .75 | .30 |
| 86 Darrell Jackson | .60 | .25 |
| 87 Matt Hasselbeck | .60 | .25 |
| 88 Shaun Alexander | .75 | .30 |
| 89 Marc Bulger | .60 | .25 |
| 90 Steven Jackson | .75 | .30 |
| 91 Torry Holt | .60 | .25 |
| 92 Cadillac Williams | .75 | .30 |
| 93 Joey Galloway | .60 | .25 |
| 94 Michael Clayton | .60 | .25 |
| 95 Chris Brown | .60 | .25 |
| 96 Steve McNair | .60 | .25 |
| 97 Drew Bennett | .60 | .25 |
| 98 Clinton Portis | .75 | .30 |
| 99 Mark Brunell | .60 | .25 |
| 100 Santana Moss | .60 | .25 |
| 101 Brodie Croyle/999 RC | 8.00 | 3.00 |
| 102 Omar Jacobs/1499 RC | 5.00 | 2.00 |
| 103 Charlie Whitehurst/999 RC | 6.00 | 2.50 |
| 104 Tarvaris Jackson/999 RC | 6.00 | 2.50 |
| 105 Kellen Clemens/999 RC | 8.00 | 3.00 |
| 106 Vince Young/599 RC | 25.00 | 10.00 |
| 107 Reggie McNeal/1499 RC | 5.00 | 2.00 |
| 108 Marcus Vick/1499 RC | 5.00 | 2.00 |
| 109 DonTrell Moore/1499 RC | 5.00 | 2.00 |
| 110 Willie Reid/1499 RC | 6.00 | 2.50 |
| 111 Matt Leinart/599 RC | 25.00 | 10.00 |
| 112 Jay Cutler/599 RC | 30.00 | 12.00 |
| 113 Brad Smith/1499 RC | 6.00 | 2.50 |
| 114 Joseph Addai/599 RC | 25.00 | 10.00 |
| 115 DeAngelo Williams/599 RC | 12.00 | 5.00 |
| 116 Laurence Maroney/999 RC | 20.00 | 8.00 |
| 117 Jerious Norwood/999 RC | 8.00 | 3.00 |
| 118 Claude Wroten/1499 RC | 4.00 | 1.50 |
| 119 Antonio Cromartie/1499 RC | 6.00 | 2.50 |
| 120 Maurice Drew/999 RC | 12.00 | 5.00 |
| 121 Anwar Phillips/1499 RC | 5.00 | 2.00 |
| 122 LenDale White/599 RC | 15.00 | 6.00 |
| 123 Reggie Bush/599 RC | 30.00 | 12.00 |
| 124 Cedric Humes/1499 RC | 6.00 | 2.50 |
| 125 Jerome Harrison/1499 RC | 6.00 | 2.50 |
| 126 Brian Calhoun/999 RC | 5.00 | 2.00 |
| 127 Joe Klopfenstein/999 RC | 5.00 | 2.00 |
| 128 Leonard Pope/1499 RC | 6.00 | 2.50 |
| 129 Vernon Davis/599 RC | 8.00 | 3.00 |
| 130 Anthony Fasano/999 RC | 6.00 | 2.50 |
| 131 Marcedes Lewis/999 RC | 6.00 | 2.50 |
| 132 Dominique Byrd/1499 RC | 5.00 | 2.00 |
| 133 Derek Hagan/1499 RC | 6.00 | 2.50 |
| 134 Pat Watkins/1499 RC | 6.00 | 2.50 |
| 135 Todd Watkins/1499 RC | 5.00 | 2.00 |
| 136 Jeremy Bloom/1499 RC | 5.00 | 2.00 |
| 137 Chad Jackson/599 RC | 6.00 | 2.50 |
| 138 Devin Hester/1499 RC | 12.00 | 5.00 |
| 139 Sinorice Moss/599 RC | 8.00 | 3.00 |
| 140 Jason Avant/1499 RC | 6.00 | 2.50 |
| 141 Maurice Stovall/1499 RC | 6.00 | 2.50 |
| 142 Santonio Holmes/599 RC | 20.00 | 8.00 |
| 143 Travis Wilson/999 RC | 6.00 | 2.50 |
| 144 Demetrius Williams/1499 RC | 6.00 | 2.50 |
| 145 Bernard Pollard/1499 RC | 5.00 | 2.00 |
| 146 Michael Robinson/1499 RC | 6.00 | 2.50 |
| 147 Brandon Marshall/1499 RC | 8.00 | 3.00 |
| 148 Greg Jennings/1499 RC | 10.00 | 4.00 |
| 149 Brandon Williams/1499 RC | 6.00 | 2.50 |
| 150 Jonathan Orr/1499 RC | 5.00 | 2.00 |
| 151 David Thomas/1499 RC | 6.00 | 2.50 |
| 152 Skyler Green/1499 RC | 5.00 | 2.00 |
| 153 Mario Williams/499 RC | 12.00 | 5.00 |
| 154 Ernie Sims/999 RC | 6.00 | 2.50 |
| 155 A.J. Hawk/599 RC | 15.00 | 6.00 |
| 156 Donte Whitner/1499 RC | 6.00 | 2.50 |
| 157 Michael Huff/999 RC | 6.00 | 2.50 |
| 158 Leon Washington/1499 RC | 6.00 | 2.50 |
| 159 P.J. Daniels/1499 RC | 5.00 | 2.00 |
| 160 Cory Rodgers/1499 RC | 5.00 | 2.00 |
| 161 Tony Scheffler AU/499 RC | 20.00 | 8.00 |
| 162 Paul Pinegar AU/999 RC | 10.00 | 4.00 |
| 163 D.J. Shockley AU/599 RC | 20.00 | 8.00 |
| 164 Ben Obomanu AU/899 RC | 10.00 | 4.00 |
| 165 Adam Jennings AU/999 RC | 12.00 | 5.00 |
| 166 Brandon Kirsch AU/999 RC | 12.00 | 5.00 |
| 167 Mike Bell AU/999 RC | 15.00 | 6.00 |
| 168 De'Arrius Howard AU/999 RC | 12.00 | 5.00 |
| 169 Martin Nance AU/999 RC | 10.00 | 4.00 |
| 170 Miles Austin AU/999 RC | 15.00 | 7.50 |
| 171 Wendell Mathis AU/999 RC | 10.00 | 4.00 |
| 172 Gerald Riggs AU/905 RC | 12.00 | 5.00 |
| 173 Hank Baskett AU/999 RC | 12.00 | 5.00 |
| 174 Greg Lee AU/999 RC | 10.00 | 4.00 |
| 175 Quinton Ganther AU/799 RC | 12.00 | 5.00 |
| 176 Garrett Mills/1499 RC | 6.00 | 2.50 |
| 177 Jeff Webb AU/599 RC | 12.00 | 5.00 |
| 178 Delanie Walker AU/599 RC | 12.00 | 5.00 |
| 179 D'Brick. Ferguson AU/599 RC | 15.00 | 6.00 |
| 180 Mathias Kiwanuka AU/499 RC | 20.00 | 8.00 |
| 181 Kamerion Wimbley AU/499 RC | 15.00 | 6.00 |
| 182 Tamba Hali AU/499 RC | 15.00 | 6.00 |
| 183 Brodrick Bunkley AU/499 RC | 15.00 | 6.00 |
| 184 Gabe Watson/1499 RC | 5.00 | 2.00 |
| 185 Haloti Ngata AU/499 RC | 15.00 | 6.00 |
| 186 DeMeco Ryans AU/599 RC | 20.00 | 8.00 |
| 187 A.J. Nicholson/1499 RC | 4.00 | 1.50 |
| 188 Abdul Hodge AU/999 RC | 12.00 | 5.00 |
| 189 Chad Greenway AU/499 RC | 15.00 | 6.00 |
| 190 D'Qwell Jackson AU/599 RC | 12.00 | 5.00 |
| 191 Manny Lawson AU/499 RC | 15.00 | 6.00 |
| 192 Bobby Carpenter AU/499 RC | 15.00 | 6.00 |
| 193 Jon Alston AU/999 RC | 12.00 | 5.00 |
| 194 Thomas Howard AU/599 RC | 15.00 | 6.00 |
| 195 Tye Hill AU/499 RC | 15.00 | 6.00 |
| 196 Kelly Jennings AU/499 RC | 15.00 | 6.00 |
| 197 Ashton Youboty AU/999 RC | 12.00 | 5.00 |
| 198 Alan Zemaitis AU/999 RC | 12.00 | 5.00 |
| 199 Johnathan Joseph AU/499 RC | 12.00 | 5.00 |
| 200 Jimmy Williams AU/599 RC | 15.00 | 6.00 |
| 201 Ko Simpson AU/999 RC | 10.00 | 4.00 |
| 202 Jason Allen AU/499 RC | 25.00 | 12.50 |
| 203 Darnell Bing AU/999 RC | 12.00 | 5.00 |
| 204 Erik Meyer AU/999 RC | 10.00 | 4.00 |
| 205 Bruce Gradkowski AU/499 RC | 15.00 | 6.00 |
| 206 Darrell Hackney AU/999 RC | 10.00 | 4.00 |
| 207 Derrick Ross AU/799 RC | 10.00 | 4.00 |
| 208 Drew Olson AU/999 RC | 10.00 | 4.00 |
| 209 Taurean Henderson AU/999 RC | 12.00 | 5.00 |
| 210 Andre Hall AU/999 RC | 12.00 | 5.00 |
| 211 Devin Aromashodu AU/899 RC | 10.00 | 4.00 |
| 212 Mike Hass AU/599 RC | 15.00 | 6.00 |
| 213 Ingle Martin AU/499 RC | 15.00 | 6.00 |
| 214 Marques Hagans AU/499 RC | 12.00 | 5.00 |
| 215 Wali Lundy AU/499 RC | 15.00 | 6.00 |
| 216 Domenik Hixon AU/499 RC | 20.00 | 8.00 |
| 217 Ethan Kilmer AU/899 RC | 12.00 | 5.00 |
| 218 Bennie Brazell/1499 RC | 5.00 | 2.00 |
| 219 David Anderson/1499 RC | 5.00 | 2.00 |
| 220 Marques Colston AU/770 RC | 50.00 | 20.00 |
| 221 Kevin McMahan AU/999 RC | 10.00 | 4.00 |
| 222 Anthony Mix/1499 RC | 5.00 | 2.00 |
| 223 John McCargo AU/499 RC | 12.00 | 5.00 |
| 224 Rocky McIntosh/1499 RC | 6.00 | 2.50 |
| 225 Cedric Griffin AU/599 RC | 6.00 | 2.50 |
| 226 Barry Sanders | 6.00 | 2.50 |
| 227 Bart Starr | 6.00 | 2.50 |
| 228 Bo Jackson | 5.00 | 2.00 |
| 229 Bob Griese | 4.00 | 1.50 |
| 230 Bobby Layne | 4.00 | 1.50 |
| 231 Boomer Esiason | 3.00 | 1.25 |
| 232 Bulldog Turner | 3.00 | 1.25 |
| 233 Dan Marino | 8.00 | 3.00 |
| 234 Deacon Jones | 3.00 | 1.25 |
| 235 Derrick Thomas | 4.00 | 1.50 |
| 236 Dick Butkus | 5.00 | 2.00 |
| 237 Don Meredith | 4.00 | 1.50 |
| 238 Eric Dickerson | 3.00 | 1.25 |
| 239 Fran Tarkenton | 5.00 | 2.00 |
| 240 Fred Biletnikoff | 4.00 | 1.50 |
| 241 Gale Sayers | 5.00 | 2.00 |
| 242 Harvey Martin | 2.50 | 1.00 |
| 243 Herman Edwards | 3.00 | 1.25 |
| 244 Jack Lambert | 4.00 | 1.50 |
| 245 Jim Brown | 5.00 | 2.00 |
| 246 Jim Kelly | 5.00 | 2.00 |
| 247 Jim Plunkett | 3.00 | 1.25 |
| 248 Jim Thorpe | 5.00 | 2.00 |
| 249 Joe Montana | 8.00 | 3.00 |
| 250 John Elway | 6.00 | 2.50 |
| 251 John Riggins | 4.00 | 1.50 |
| 252 Johnny Unitas | 6.00 | 2.50 |
| 253 Len Dawson | 4.00 | 1.50 |
| 254 Marcus Allen | 4.00 | 1.50 |
| 255 Mike Singletary | 4.00 | 1.50 |
| 256 Ozzie Newsome | 3.00 | 1.25 |
| 257 Phil Simms | 3.00 | 1.25 |
| 258 Ray Nitschke | 4.00 | 1.50 |
| 259 Red Grange | 5.00 | 2.00 |
| 260 Roger Staubach | 6.00 | 2.50 |
| 261 Ronnie Lott | 3.00 | 1.25 |
| 262 Steve Largent | 4.00 | 1.50 |
| 263 Terry Bradshaw | 6.00 | 2.50 |
| 264 Troy Aikman | 5.00 | 2.00 |
| 265 Walter Payton | 8.00 | 3.00 |
| 266 Bill Dudley | 3.00 | 1.25 |
| 267 Joe Perry | 3.00 | 1.25 |
| 268 Charley Trippi | 2.50 | 1.00 |
| 269 Paul Lowe | 2.50 | 1.00 |
| 270 Clem Daniels | 2.50 | 1.00 |
| 271 Ken Kavanaugh | 2.50 | 1.00 |
| 272 Andre Reed | 3.00 | 1.25 |
| 273 Steve Van Buren | 3.00 | 1.25 |
| 274 Jim Taylor | 4.00 | 1.50 |

# 2007 Donruss Classics

| | | |
|---|---|---|
| 1 Anquan Boldin | .60 | .25 |
| 2 Edgerrin James | .60 | .25 |
| 3 Larry Fitzgerald | .75 | .30 |
| 4 Matt Leinart | .75 | .30 |
| 5 Alge Crumpler | .60 | .25 |
| 6 Michael Vick | .75 | .30 |
| 7 Warrick Dunn | .60 | .25 |
| 8 Todd Heap | .50 | .20 |
| 9 Mark Clayton | .60 | .25 |
| 10 Steve McNair | .60 | .25 |
| 11 J.P. Losman | .50 | .20 |
| 12 Lee Evans | .60 | .25 |
| 13 Willis McGahee | .60 | .25 |
| 14 DeAngelo Williams | .75 | .30 |
| 15 Jake Delhomme | .60 | .25 |
| 16 Steve Smith | .60 | .25 |
| 17 Brian Urlacher | .75 | .30 |
| 18 Muhsin Muhammad | .60 | .25 |
| 19 Rex Grossman | .60 | .25 |
| 20 Thomas Jones | .60 | .25 |
| 21 Carson Palmer | .75 | .30 |
| 22 Chad Johnson | .60 | .25 |
| 23 Rudi Johnson | .60 | .25 |
| 24 T.J. Houshmandzadeh | .60 | .25 |
| 25 Braylon Edwards | .60 | .25 |
| 26 Charlie Frye | .60 | .25 |
| 27 Julius Jones | .60 | .25 |
| 28 Terrell Owens | .75 | .30 |
| 29 Tony Romo | 1.50 | .60 |

| | | | |
|---|---|---:|---:|
| ❏ 30 | Javon Walker | .60 | .25 |
| ❏ 31 | Jay Cutler | .75 | .30 |
| ❏ 32 | Mike Bell | .60 | .25 |
| ❏ 33 | Jon Kitna | .50 | .20 |
| ❏ 34 | Kevin Jones | .50 | .20 |
| ❏ 35 | Roy Williams WR | .60 | .25 |
| ❏ 36 | Brett Favre | 1.50 | .60 |
| ❏ 37 | Donald Driver | .60 | .25 |
| ❏ 38 | Ahman Green | .60 | .25 |
| ❏ 39 | Andre Johnson | .60 | .25 |
| ❏ 40 | Matt Schaub | .60 | .25 |
| ❏ 41 | Eric Moulds | .60 | .25 |
| ❏ 42 | Joseph Addai | .75 | .30 |
| ❏ 43 | Marvin Harrison | .75 | .30 |
| ❏ 44 | Peyton Manning | 1.25 | .50 |
| ❏ 45 | Reggie Wayne | .60 | .25 |
| ❏ 46 | Byron Leftwich | .60 | .25 |
| ❏ 47 | Fred Taylor | .60 | .25 |
| ❏ 48 | Maurice Jones-Drew | .75 | .30 |
| ❏ 49 | Larry Johnson | .60 | .25 |
| ❏ 50 | Tony Gonzalez | .60 | .25 |
| ❏ 51 | Trent Green | .60 | .25 |
| ❏ 52 | Chris Chambers | .60 | .25 |
| ❏ 53 | Daunte Culpepper | .60 | .25 |
| ❏ 54 | Ronnie Brown | .60 | .25 |
| ❏ 55 | Chester Taylor | .50 | .20 |
| ❏ 56 | Tarvaris Jackson | .60 | .25 |
| ❏ 57 | Travis Taylor | .50 | .20 |
| ❏ 58 | Tom Brady | 1.50 | .60 |
| ❏ 59 | Corey Dillon | .60 | .25 |
| ❏ 60 | Laurence Maroney | .75 | .30 |
| ❏ 61 | Deuce McAllister | .60 | .25 |
| ❏ 62 | Drew Brees | .60 | .25 |
| ❏ 63 | Marques Colston | .75 | .30 |
| ❏ 64 | Reggie Bush | 1.00 | .40 |
| ❏ 65 | Eli Manning | .75 | .30 |
| ❏ 66 | Jeremy Shockey | .60 | .25 |
| ❏ 67 | Plaxico Burress | .60 | .25 |
| ❏ 68 | Chad Pennington | .60 | .25 |
| ❏ 69 | Laveranues Coles | .60 | .25 |
| ❏ 70 | Leon Washington | .60 | .25 |
| ❏ 71 | LaMont Jordan | .60 | .25 |
| ❏ 72 | Michael Huff | .60 | .25 |
| ❏ 73 | Randy Moss | .75 | .30 |
| ❏ 74 | Brian Westbrook | .60 | .25 |
| ❏ 75 | Donovan McNabb | .75 | .30 |
| ❏ 76 | Reggie Brown | .60 | .25 |
| ❏ 77 | Ben Roethlisberger | 1.00 | .40 |
| ❏ 78 | Hines Ward | .75 | .30 |
| ❏ 79 | Willie Parker | .75 | .30 |
| ❏ 80 | Antonio Gates | .60 | .25 |
| ❏ 81 | LaDainian Tomlinson | 1.00 | .40 |
| ❏ 82 | Philip Rivers | .75 | .30 |
| ❏ 83 | Alex Smith QB | .75 | .30 |
| ❏ 84 | Frank Gore | .75 | .30 |
| ❏ 85 | Vernon Davis | .60 | .25 |
| ❏ 86 | Darrell Jackson | .60 | .25 |
| ❏ 87 | Matt Hasselbeck | .60 | .25 |
| ❏ 88 | Shaun Alexander | .60 | .25 |
| ❏ 89 | Marc Bulger | .60 | .25 |
| ❏ 90 | Steven Jackson | .60 | .25 |
| ❏ 91 | Torry Holt | .60 | .25 |
| ❏ 92 | Bruce Gradkowski | .50 | .20 |
| ❏ 93 | Cadillac Williams | .60 | .25 |
| ❏ 94 | Joey Galloway | .60 | .25 |
| ❏ 95 | Drew Bennett | .50 | .20 |
| ❏ 96 | Vince Young | .75 | .30 |
| ❏ 97 | Travis Henry | .60 | .25 |
| ❏ 98 | Clinton Portis | .60 | .25 |
| ❏ 99 | Jason Campbell | .60 | .25 |
| ❏ 100 | Santana Moss | .60 | .25 |
| ❏ 101 | Archie Manning | 5.00 | 2.00 |
| ❏ 103 | Bill Bates | 4.00 | 1.50 |
| ❏ 104 | Bob Hayes | 6.00 | 2.50 |
| ❏ 105 | Bob Lilly | 4.00 | 1.50 |
| ❏ 106 | Bobby Mitchell | 4.00 | 1.50 |
| ❏ 108 | Charley Taylor | 4.00 | 1.50 |
| ❏ 109 | Charlie Joiner | 4.00 | 1.50 |
| ❏ 110 | Cliff Harris | 3.00 | 1.25 |
| ❏ 111 | Cris Collinsworth | 4.00 | 1.50 |
| ❏ 112 | Dan Fouts | 5.00 | 2.00 |
| ❏ 113 | Darryle Lamonica | 3.00 | 1.25 |
| ❏ 114 | Dave Casper | 4.00 | 1.50 |
| ❏ 115 | Don Maynard | 4.00 | 1.50 |

| | | | |
|---|---|---:|---:|
| ❏ 116 | Earl Campbell | 5.00 | 2.00 |
| ❏ 117 | Forrest Gregg | 3.00 | 1.25 |
| ❏ 118 | Franco Harris | 5.00 | 2.00 |
| ❏ 120 | Gale Sayers | 6.00 | 2.50 |
| ❏ 121 | Gene Upshaw | 3.00 | 1.25 |
| ❏ 122 | George Blanda | 4.00 | 1.50 |
| ❏ 123 | Hugh McElhenny | 4.00 | 1.50 |
| ❏ 124 | Jack Youngblood | 4.00 | 1.50 |
| ❏ 125 | Boyd Dowler | 3.00 | 1.25 |
| ❏ 126 | Jan Stenerud | 3.00 | 1.25 |
| ❏ 127 | Jim McMahon | 6.00 | 2.50 |
| ❏ 128 | Harlon Hill | 4.00 | 1.50 |
| ❏ 129 | Joe Namath | 6.00 | 2.50 |
| ❏ 130 | Joe Theismann | 5.00 | 2.00 |
| ❏ 131 | John Mackey | 4.00 | 1.50 |
| ❏ 133 | Kellen Winslow | 4.00 | 1.50 |
| ❏ 134 | Ken Stabler | 6.00 | 2.50 |
| ❏ 135 | Lenny Moore | 4.00 | 1.50 |
| ❏ 136 | Lou Groza | 4.00 | 1.50 |
| ❏ 137 | Mark Duper | 3.00 | 1.25 |
| ❏ 138 | Michael Irvin | 4.00 | 1.50 |
| ❏ 139 | Paul Warfield | 4.00 | 1.50 |
| ❏ 140 | Randall Cunningham | 4.00 | 1.50 |
| ❏ 141 | Roger Craig | 4.00 | 1.50 |
| ❏ 142 | Ron Mix | 3.00 | 1.25 |
| ❏ 143 | Roosevelt Brown | 3.00 | 1.25 |
| ❏ 144 | Roosevelt Grier | 3.00 | 1.25 |
| ❏ 145 | Sam Huff | 4.00 | 1.50 |
| ❏ 146 | Sammy Baugh | 5.00 | 2.00 |
| ❏ 147 | Sterling Sharpe | 4.00 | 1.50 |
| ❏ 148 | Tim Brown | 5.00 | 2.00 |
| ❏ 149 | Y.A. Tittle | 5.00 | 2.00 |
| ❏ 150 | Yale Lary | 3.00 | 1.25 |
| ❏ 151 | JaMarcus Russell/599 RC | 25.00 | 10.00 |
| ❏ 152 | Brady Quinn/599 RC | 30.00 | 12.00 |
| ❏ 153 | Kevin Kolb/1499 RC | 6.00 | 2.50 |
| ❏ 154 | John Beck/1499 RC | 6.00 | 2.50 |
| ❏ 155 | Drew Stanton/1499 RC | 6.00 | 2.50 |
| ❏ 156 | Trent Edwards/1499 RC | 15.00 | 6.00 |
| ❏ 157 | Isaiah Stanback/1499 RC | 6.00 | 2.50 |
| ❏ 158 | Troy Smith/1499 RC | 8.00 | 3.00 |
| ❏ 159 | Adrian Peterson/599 RC | 80.00 | 30.00 |
| ❏ 160 | Marshawn Lynch/599 RC | 20.00 | 8.00 |
| ❏ 161 | Kenny Irons/599 RC | 10.00 | 4.00 |
| ❏ 162 | Chris Henry/599 RC | 10.00 | 4.00 |
| ❏ 163 | Brian Leonard/599 RC | 10.00 | 4.00 |
| ❏ 164 | Brandon Jackson/599 RC | 10.00 | 4.00 |
| ❏ 165 | Lorenzo Booker/599 RC | 10.00 | 4.00 |
| ❏ 166 | Tony Hunt/599 RC | 10.00 | 4.00 |
| ❏ 167 | Garrett Wolfe/599 RC | 10.00 | 4.00 |
| ❏ 168 | Michael Bush/599 RC | 10.00 | 4.00 |
| ❏ 169 | Antonio Pittman/1499 RC | 6.00 | 2.50 |
| ❏ 170 | Kolby Smith/1499 RC | 6.00 | 2.50 |
| ❏ 171 | DeShawn Wynn/1499 RC | 6.00 | 2.50 |
| ❏ 172 | Calvin Johnson/599 RC | 25.00 | 10.00 |
| ❏ 173 | Ted Ginn Jr.RC/599 RC | 15.00 | 6.00 |
| ❏ 174 | Dwayne Bowe/599 RC | 20.00 | 8.00 |
| ❏ 175 | Robert Meachem/599 RC | 10.00 | 4.00 |
| ❏ 176 | Craig Buster Davis/599 RC | 10.00 | 4.00 |
| ❏ 177 | Antonio Gonzalez/599 RC | 15.00 | 6.00 |
| ❏ 178 | Sidney Rice/1499 RC | 6.00 | 2.50 |
| ❏ 179 | Dwayne Jarrett/1499 RC | 6.00 | 2.50 |
| ❏ 180 | Steve Smith USC/1499 RC | 8.00 | 3.00 |
| ❏ 181 | Jacoby Jones/1499 RC | 6.00 | 2.50 |
| ❏ 182 | Yamon Figurs/1499 RC | 6.00 | 2.50 |
| ❏ 183 | Laurent Robinson/1499 RC | 5.00 | 2.00 |
| ❏ 184 | Jason Hill/1499 RC | 6.00 | 2.50 |
| ❏ 185 | James Jones/1499 RC | 6.00 | 2.50 |
| ❏ 186 | Mike Walker/1499 RC | 5.00 | 2.00 |
| ❏ 187 | Paul Williams/1499 RC | 5.00 | 2.00 |
| ❏ 188 | Johnnie Lee Higgins/1499 RC | 5.00 | 2.00 |
| ❏ 189 | Chris Davis/1499 RC | 5.00 | 2.00 |
| ❏ 190 | Aundrae Allison/1499 RC | 5.00 | 2.00 |
| ❏ 191 | David Clowney/1499 RC | 5.00 | 2.00 |
| ❏ 192 | Courtney Taylor/1499 RC | 5.00 | 2.00 |
| ❏ 193 | Dallas Baker/1499 RC | 5.00 | 2.00 |
| ❏ 194 | Greg Olsen/1499 RC | 8.00 | 3.00 |
| ❏ 195 | Zach Miller/1499 RC | 4.00 | 1.50 |
| ❏ 196 | Amobi Okoye/1499 RC | 6.00 | 2.50 |
| ❏ 197 | Alan Branch/1499 RC | 5.00 | 2.00 |
| ❏ 198 | Gaines Adams/1499 RC | 5.00 | 2.00 |
| ❏ 199 | Jamaal Anderson/1499 RC | 5.00 | 2.00 |
| ❏ 200 | Adam Carriker/1499 RC | 5.00 | 2.00 |
| ❏ 201 | Jarvis Moss/1499 RC | 6.00 | 2.50 |

| | | | |
|---|---|---:|---:|
| ❏ 202 | Anthony Spencer/1499 RC | 6.00 | 2.50 |
| ❏ 203 | LaMarr Woodley/1499 RC | 6.00 | 2.50 |
| ❏ 204 | Tim Crowder/1499 RC | 6.00 | 2.50 |
| ❏ 205 | Victor Abiamiri/1499 RC | 6.00 | 2.50 |
| ❏ 206 | Patrick Willis/1499 RC | 12.00 | 5.00 |
| ❏ 207 | David Harris/1499 RC | 5.00 | 2.00 |
| ❏ 208 | Lawrence Timmons/1499 RC | 6.00 | 2.50 |
| ❏ 209 | Jon Beason/1499 RC | 6.00 | 2.50 |
| ❏ 210 | Paul Posluszny/1499 RC | 8.00 | 3.00 |
| ❏ 211 | Leon Hall/1499 RC | 6.00 | 2.50 |
| ❏ 212 | Aaron Ross/1499 RC | 6.00 | 2.50 |
| ❏ 213 | Chris Houston/1499 RC | 5.00 | 2.00 |
| ❏ 214 | Eric Wright/1499 RC | 6.00 | 2.50 |
| ❏ 215 | Josh Wilson/1499 RC | 5.00 | 2.00 |
| ❏ 216 | LaRon Landry/1499 RC | 8.00 | 3.00 |
| ❏ 217 | Michael Griffin/1499 RC | 6.00 | 2.50 |
| ❏ 218 | Reggie Nelson/1499 RC | 6.00 | 2.50 |
| ❏ 219 | Brandon Meriweather/1499 RC | 6.00 | 2.50 |
| ❏ 220 | Sabby Piscitelli/1499 RC | 5.00 | 2.00 |
| ❏ 221 | Jordan Palmer AU/499 RC | 20.00 | 8.00 |
| ❏ 222 | Jon Cornish AU/999 RC | 10.00 | 4.00 |
| ❏ 223 | Jared Zabransky AU/499 RC | 20.00 | 8.00 |
| ❏ 224 | Jarrett Hicks AU/999 RC | 10.00 | 4.00 |
| ❏ 225 | Kenneth Darby AU/499 RC | 20.00 | 8.00 |
| ❏ 226 | Steve Breaston AU/499 RC | 20.00 | 8.00 |
| ❏ 227 | Matt Spaeth AU/999 RC | 20.00 | 8.00 |
| ❏ 228 | Stewart Bradley AU/499 RC | 8.00 | 3.00 |
| ❏ 229 | Tymere Zimmerman AU/999 RC | 10.00 | 4.00 |
| ❏ 230 | Kenny Scott AU/999 RC | 8.00 | 3.00 |
| ❏ 231 | Chris Leak AU/499 RC | 15.00 | 6.00 |
| ❏ 232 | Ronnie McGill AU/999 RC | 10.00 | 4.00 |
| ❏ 233 | D.Tyler AU/499 RC EXCH | 10.00 | 4.00 |
| ❏ 234 | Syndric Steptoe AU/499 RC | .15.00 | 6.00 |
| ❏ 235 | C.Johnson AU/499 RC EXCH | 12.00 | 5.00 |
| ❏ 236 | Chansi Stuckey AU/499 RC | 15.00 | 6.00 |
| ❏ 237 | Nate Ilaoa AU/499 RC | 20.00 | 8.00 |
| ❏ 238 | Buster Davis AU/499 RC EXCH | 15.00 | 6.00 |
| ❏ 239 | Aaron Fairooz AU/999 RC | 10.00 | 4.00 |
| ❏ 240 | Jeff Rowe AU/499 RC | 15.00 | 6.00 |
| ❏ 241 | Rhema McKnight AU/999 RC | 10.00 | 4.00 |
| ❏ 242 | Danny Ware AU/999 RC | 10.00 | 4.00 |
| ❏ 243 | Tyler Palko AU/999 RC | 12.00 | 5.00 |
| ❏ 244 | Syvelle Newton AU/999 RC | 10.00 | 4.00 |
| ❏ 245 | Michael Okwo AU/499 RC | 15.00 | 6.00 |
| ❏ 246 | Brandon Siler AU/999 RC | 10.00 | 4.00 |
| ❏ 247 | Ryan McBean AU/999 RC | 12.00 | 5.00 |
| ❏ 248 | Ray McDonald AU/499 RC | 15.00 | 6.00 |
| ❏ 249 | David Ball AU/999 RC | 8.00 | 3.00 |
| ❏ 250 | Alonzo Coleman AU/999 RC | 10.00 | 4.00 |
| ❏ 251 | H.B. Blades AU/999 RC | 10.00 | 4.00 |
| ❏ 252 | Thomas Clayton AU/499 RC | 8.00 | 3.00 |
| ❏ 253 | Darius Walker AU/499 RC | 20.00 | 8.00 |
| ❏ 254 | Jordan Kent AU/499 RC EXCH | 15.00 | 6.00 |
| ❏ 255 | Dwayne Wright AU/499 RC | 15.00 | 6.00 |
| ❏ 256 | Rufus Alexander AU/999 RC | 12.00 | 5.00 |
| ❏ 257 | Gary Russell AU/999 RC | 12.00 | 5.00 |
| ❏ 258 | Aaron Rouse AU/499 RC | 20.00 | 8.00 |
| ❏ 259 | Joel Filani AU/499 RC | 15.00 | 6.00 |
| ❏ 260 | Zak DeOssie AU/999 RC | 10.00 | 4.00 |
| ❏ 261 | Scott Chandler AU/499 RC | 15.00 | 6.00 |
| ❏ 262 | Jerard Rabb AU/999 RC EXCH | 10.00 | 4.00 |
| ❏ 263 | Tim Shaw AU/999 RC | 10.00 | 4.00 |
| ❏ 264 | Jemalle Cornelius AU/999 RC | 10.00 | 4.00 |
| ❏ 265 | Ahmad Bradshaw AU/499 RC | 40.00 | 15.00 |
| ❏ 266 | Earl Everett AU/999 RC | 10.00 | 4.00 |
| ❏ 267 | D'Juan Woods AU/999 RC | 10.00 | 4.00 |
| ❏ 268 | Toby Korrodi AU/999 RC | 10.00 | 4.00 |
| ❏ 269 | Ryne Robinson AU/499 RC | 15.00 | 6.00 |
| ❏ 270 | Selvin Young AU/999 RC | 25.00 | 10.00 |
| ❏ 271 | Marcus McCauley AU/499 RC | 15.00 | 6.00 |
| ❏ 272 | Daymeion Hughes AU/499 RC | 15.00 | 6.00 |
| ❏ 273 | A.J. Davis AU/999 RC | 8.00 | 3.00 |
| ❏ 274 | David Irons AU/999 RC | 8.00 | 3.00 |
| ❏ 275 | Josh Gattis AU/999 RC | 8.00 | 3.00 |

## 2008 Donruss Classics

| | | | |
|---|---|---:|---:|
| ❏ 1 | Edgerrin James | .60 | .25 |
| ❏ 2 | Larry Fitzgerald | .75 | .30 |
| ❏ 3 | Matt Leinart | .75 | .30 |
| ❏ 4 | Warrick Dunn | .60 | .25 |
| ❏ 5 | Roddy White | .60 | .25 |
| ❏ 6 | Alge Crumpler | .60 | .25 |
| ❏ 7 | Willis McGahee | .60 | .25 |
| ❏ 8 | Mark Clayton | .60 | .25 |

|  |  | | |
|---|---|---|---|
| 9 | Derrick Mason | .50 | .20 |
| 10 | Trent Edwards | .75 | .30 |
| 11 | Marshawn Lynch | .75 | .30 |
| 12 | Lee Evans | .60 | .25 |
| 13 | DeAngelo Williams | .60 | .25 |
| 14 | DeShaun Foster | .60 | .25 |
| 15 | Steve Smith | .60 | .25 |
| 16 | Cedric Benson | .50 | .20 |
| 17 | Bernard Berrian | .60 | .25 |
| 18 | Greg Olsen | .60 | .25 |
| 19 | Carson Palmer | .75 | .30 |
| 20 | Chad Johnson | .60 | .25 |
| 21 | T.J. Houshmandzadeh | .60 | .25 |
| 22 | Rudi Johnson | .60 | .25 |
| 23 | Brady Quinn | .75 | .30 |
| 24 | Jamal Lewis | .60 | .25 |
| 25 | Braylon Edwards | .60 | .25 |
| 26 | Tony Romo | 1.25 | .50 |
| 27 | Terrell Owens | .75 | .30 |
| 28 | Jason Witten | .60 | .25 |
| 29 | Marion Barber | .75 | .30 |
| 30 | Jay Cutler | .75 | .30 |
| 31 | Brandon Marshall | .60 | .25 |
| 32 | Brandon Stokley | .60 | .25 |
| 33 | Jon Kitna | .60 | .25 |
| 34 | Roy Williams WR | .60 | .25 |
| 35 | Shaun McDonald | .50 | .20 |
| 36 | Aaron Rodgers | .75 | .30 |
| 37 | Greg Jennings | .60 | .25 |
| 38 | Ryan Grant | .75 | .30 |
| 39 | Matt Schaub | .60 | .25 |
| 40 | Andre Johnson | .60 | .25 |
| 41 | Kevin Walter | .50 | .20 |
| 42 | Peyton Manning | 1.25 | .50 |
| 43 | Reggie Wayne | .60 | .25 |
| 44 | Joseph Addai | .75 | .30 |
| 45 | Dallas Clark | .60 | .25 |
| 46 | David Garrard | .60 | .25 |
| 47 | Fred Taylor | .60 | .25 |
| 48 | Maurice Jones-Drew | .60 | .25 |
| 49 | Larry Johnson | .60 | .25 |
| 50 | Tony Gonzalez | .60 | .25 |
| 51 | Dwayne Bowe | .60 | .25 |
| 52 | Ronnie Brown | .60 | .25 |
| 53 | Ted Ginn Jr. | .60 | .25 |
| 54 | John Beck | .50 | .20 |
| 55 | Tarvaris Jackson | .60 | .25 |
| 56 | Adrian Peterson | 1.50 | .60 |
| 57 | Chester Taylor | .60 | .25 |
| 58 | Tom Brady | 1.25 | .50 |
| 59 | Randy Moss | .75 | .30 |
| 60 | Wes Welker | .75 | .30 |
| 61 | Laurence Maroney | .60 | .25 |
| 62 | Drew Brees | .75 | .30 |
| 63 | Marques Colston | .75 | .30 |
| 64 | Reggie Bush | .75 | .30 |
| 65 | Eli Manning | .75 | .30 |
| 66 | Plaxico Burress | .60 | .25 |
| 67 | Brandon Jacobs | .60 | .25 |
| 68 | Kellen Clemens | .60 | .25 |
| 69 | Jerricho Cotchery | .50 | .20 |
| 70 | Thomas Jones | .60 | .25 |
| 71 | Justin Fargas | .50 | .20 |
| 72 | Jerry Porter | .60 | .25 |
| 73 | JaMarcus Russell | .75 | .30 |
| 74 | Donovan McNabb | .75 | .30 |
| 75 | Brian Westbrook | .60 | .25 |
| 76 | Kevin Curtis | .50 | .20 |
| 77 | Ben Roethlisberger | 1.00 | .40 |
| 78 | Willie Parker | .60 | .25 |
| 79 | Hines Ward | .75 | .30 |
| 80 | Philip Rivers | .75 | .30 |
| 81 | LaDainian Tomlinson | 1.00 | .40 |
| 82 | Antonio Gates | .60 | .25 |
| 83 | Frank Gore | .60 | .25 |
| 84 | Vernon Davis | .50 | .20 |
| 85 | Devin Hester | .75 | .30 |
| 86 | Matt Hasselbeck | .60 | .25 |
| 87 | Julius Jones | .60 | .25 |
| 88 | Deion Branch | .60 | .25 |
| 89 | Marc Bulger | .60 | .25 |
| 90 | Steven Jackson | .75 | .30 |
| 91 | Torry Holt | .60 | .25 |
| 92 | Jeff Garcia | .60 | .25 |
| 93 | Earnest Graham | .50 | .20 |
| 94 | Joey Galloway | .60 | .25 |
| 95 | Vince Young | .75 | .30 |
| 96 | LenDale White | .60 | .25 |
| 97 | Roydell Williams | .50 | .20 |
| 98 | Jason Campbell | .60 | .25 |
| 99 | Chris Cooley | .60 | .25 |
| 100 | Clinton Portis | .60 | .25 |
| 101 | Jay Novacek | 4.00 | 1.50 |
| 102 | Knute Rockne | 8.00 | 3.00 |
| 103 | Tom Landry | 6.00 | 2.50 |
| 104 | Sammy Baugh | 5.00 | 2.00 |
| 105 | Willie Lanier | 3.00 | 1.25 |
| 106 | Ken Strong | 3.00 | 1.25 |
| 107 | Marion Motley | 4.00 | 1.50 |
| 108 | Tom Fears | 3.00 | 1.25 |
| 109 | Bob Waterfield | 4.00 | 1.50 |
| 110 | Hank Stram | 4.00 | 1.50 |
| 111 | Elroy Hirsch | 4.00 | 1.50 |
| 112 | Dick Lane | 3.00 | 1.25 |
| 113 | Jim Parker | 3.00 | 1.25 |
| 114 | Red Grange | 6.00 | 2.50 |
| 115 | Bobby Layne | 5.00 | 2.00 |
| 116 | Norm Van Brocklin | 4.00 | 1.50 |
| 117 | Michael Irvin | 4.00 | 1.50 |
| 118 | Steve Largent | 5.00 | 2.00 |
| 119 | Dick Butkus | 6.00 | 2.50 |
| 120 | Ray Nitschke | 5.00 | 2.00 |
| 121 | Lawrence Taylor | 5.00 | 2.00 |
| 122 | Bob Lilly | 4.00 | 1.50 |
| 123 | Mike Singletary | 5.00 | 2.00 |
| 124 | Y.A. Tittle | 5.00 | 2.00 |
| 125 | Steve Young | 6.00 | 2.50 |
| 126 | Tim Brown | 5.00 | 2.00 |
| 127 | Joe Greene | 5.00 | 2.00 |
| 128 | Paul Krause | 3.00 | 1.25 |
| 129 | Troy Aikman | 6.00 | 2.50 |
| 130 | Bo Jackson | 6.00 | 2.50 |
| 131 | George Blanda | 5.00 | 2.00 |
| 132 | Charlie Joiner | 3.00 | 1.25 |
| 133 | Walter Payton | 10.00 | 4.00 |
| 134 | Jack Youngblood | 3.00 | 1.25 |
| 135 | Ozzie Newsome | 4.00 | 1.50 |
| 136 | Dan Marino | 10.00 | 4.00 |
| 137 | John Elway | 8.00 | 3.00 |
| 138 | Joe Montana | 10.00 | 4.00 |
| 139 | Barry Sanders | 8.00 | 3.00 |
| 140 | Doak Walker | 5.00 | 2.00 |
| 141 | Lem Barney | 3.00 | 1.25 |
| 142 | Bert Bell | 3.00 | 1.25 |
| 143 | Bulldog Turner | 4.00 | 1.50 |
| 144 | Greasy Neale | 3.00 | 1.25 |
| 145 | Ernie Stautner | 3.00 | 1.25 |
| 146 | Frank Gatski | 3.00 | 1.25 |
| 147 | Leo Nomellini | 3.00 | 1.25 |
| 150 | Otto Graham | 5.00 | 2.00 |
| 151 | Brandon Flowers AU/499 RC | 15.00 | 6.00 |
| 152 | Tracy Porter AU/499 RC | 12.00 | 5.00 |
| 153 | Terrell Thomas RC | 5.00 | 2.00 |
| 154 | Chevis Jackson AU/375 RC | 12.00 | 5.00 |
| 155 | Reggie Smith AU/499 RC | 12.00 | 5.00 |
| 156 | Phillip Merling RC | 5.00 | 2.00 |
| 157 | Calais Campbell RC | 5.00 | 2.00 |
| 158 | Quentin Groves RC | 5.00 | 2.00 |
| 159 | Pat Sims RC | 5.00 | 2.00 |
| 160 | Dan Connor RC | 6.00 | 2.50 |
| 161 | Shawn Crable AU/436 RC | 15.00 | 6.00 |
| 162 | Xavier Adibi RC | 5.00 | 2.00 |
| 163 | Jerod Mayo RC | 10.00 | 4.00 |
| 164 | Jordon Dizon RC | 6.00 | 2.50 |
| 165 | Jake Long RC | 8.00 | 3.00 |
| 166 | Matt Ryan RC | 25.00 | 10.00 |
| 167 | Brian Brohm RC | 8.00 | 3.00 |
| 168 | Chad Henne RC | 10.00 | 4.00 |
| 169 | Dennis Dixon RC | 6.00 | 2.50 |
| 170 | Erik Ainge RC | 6.00 | 2.50 |
| 171 | Colt Brennan RC | 15.00 | 6.00 |
| 172 | Andre Woodson RC | 6.00 | 2.50 |
| 173 | Marcus Thomas RC | 5.00 | 2.00 |
| 174 | Darren McFadden RC | 15.00 | 6.00 |
| 175 | Jonathan Stewart RC | 15.00 | 6.00 |
| 176 | Felix Jones RC | 15.00 | 6.00 |
| 177 | Rashard Mendenhall RC | 12.00 | 5.00 |
| 178 | Tashard Choice RC | 6.00 | 2.50 |
| 179 | Ryan Torain AU/499 RC | 30.00 | 15.00 |
| 180 | Tim Hightower RC | 12.00 | 5.00 |
| 181 | Craig Steltz AU/499 RC | 12.00 | 5.00 |
| 182 | Caleb Campbell RC | 6.00 | 2.50 |
| 183 | Dustin Keller RC | 6.00 | 2.50 |
| 184 | John Carlson RC | 6.00 | 2.50 |
| 185 | Fred Davis RC | 6.00 | 2.50 |
| 186 | Martellus Bennett AU/499 RC | 15.00 | 6.00 |
| 187 | Donnie Avery RC | 8.00 | 3.00 |
| 188 | Devin Thomas RC | 6.00 | 2.50 |
| 189 | Jordy Nelson RC | 8.00 | 3.00 |
| 190 | James Hardy RC | 6.00 | 2.50 |
| 191 | Eddie Royal RC | 12.00 | 5.00 |
| 192 | Jerome Simpson RC | 5.00 | 2.00 |
| 193 | DeSean Jackson RC | 12.00 | 5.00 |
| 194 | Malcolm Kelly RC | 6.00 | 2.50 |
| 195 | Limas Sweed RC | 8.00 | 3.00 |
| 196 | Earl Bennett RC | 6.00 | 2.50 |
| 197 | Early Doucet RC | 6.00 | 2.50 |
| 198 | Harry Douglas RC | 6.00 | 2.50 |
| 199 | Mario Manningham RC | 6.00 | 2.50 |
| 200 | Andre Caldwell RC | 5.00 | 2.00 |
| 201 | Leodis McKelvin AU/499 RC | 15.00 | 6.00 |
| 202 | Antoine Cason AU/499 RC | 15.00 | 6.00 |
| 203 | D.Rodgers-Crom AU/499 RC | 15.00 | 6.00 |
| 204 | Aqib Talib RC | 6.00 | 2.50 |
| 205 | Mike Jenkins RC | 6.00 | 2.50 |
| 206 | Vernon Gholston AU/499 RC | 15.00 | 6.00 |
| 207 | Derrick Harvey AU/499 RC | 12.00 | 5.00 |
| 208 | L.Jackson AU/499 RC | 12.00 | 5.00 |
| 209 | Chris Long AU/499 RC | 20.00 | 8.00 |
| 210 | Kentwan Balmer AU/499 RC | 12.00 | 5.00 |
| 211 | Glenn Dorsey RC | 8.00 | 3.00 |
| 212 | Sedrick Ellis RC | 6.00 | 2.50 |
| 213 | Jacob Hester AU/499 RC | 15.00 | 6.00 |
| 214 | Owen Schmitt AU/499 RC | 15.00 | 6.00 |
| 215 | Peyton Hillis AU/499 RC | 25.00 | 10.00 |
| 216 | Kenny Phillips RC | 6.00 | 2.50 |
| 217 | Curtis Lofton AU/499 RC | 15.00 | 6.00 |
| 218 | Keith Rivers AU/499 RC | 15.00 | 6.00 |
| 219 | Joe Flacco AU/399 RC | 60.00 | 30.00 |
| 220 | Matt Flynn AU/399 RC | 20.00 | 8.00 |
| 221 | Kevin O'Connell AU/499 RC | 20.00 | 8.00 |
| 222 | John D.Booty AU/349 RC | 20.00 | 8.00 |
| 223 | Josh Johnson AU/399 RC | 15.00 | 6.00 |
| 224 | Matt Forte AU/499 RC | 40.00 | 25.00 |
| 225 | Thomas Brown AU/499 RC | 15.00 | 6.00 |
| 226 | C.Washington AU/499 RC | 12.00 | 5.00 |
| 227 | Justin Forsett AU/499 RC | 15.00 | 6.00 |
| 228 | Cory Boyd AU/499 RC | 12.00 | 5.00 |
| 229 | Allen Patrick AU/499 RC | 12.00 | 5.00 |
| 230 | Chris Johnson AU/499 RC | 40.00 | 20.00 |
| 231 | Ray Rice AU/499 RC | 25.00 | 10.00 |
| 232 | K.Smith AU/99 RC EXCH | 60.00 | 30.00 |
| 233 | Mike Hart AU/499 RC | 20.00 | 8.00 |
| 234 | Jamaal Charles AU/499 RC | 20.00 | 8.00 |
| 235 | Steve Slaton AU/99 RC | 60.00 | 35.00 |
| 236 | Brad Cottam AU/499 RC | 15.00 | 6.00 |
| 237 | Jermichael Finley AU/499 RC | 15.00 | 6.00 |
| 238 | Martin Rucker AU/499 RC | 12.00 | 5.00 |
| 239 | Jacob Tamme AU/499 RC | 15.00 | 6.00 |
| 240 | Kellen Davis AU/499 RC | 10.00 | 4.00 |
| 241 | Will Franklin AU/499 RC | 15.00 | 6.00 |
| 242 | Marcus Smith AU/499RC | 12.00 | 5.00 |
| 243 | Keenan Burton RC | 5.00 | 2.00 |
| 244 | Josh Morgan AU/499 RC | 12.00 | 5.00 |
| 245 | Kevin Robinson RC | 5.00 | 2.00 |
| 246 | Paul Hubbard AU/499 RC | 12.00 | 5.00 |

| | | | |
|---|---|---|---|
| ❑ 247 Adrian Arrington RC | 5.00 | 2.00 |
| ❑ 248 Marcus Monk AU/499 RC | 15.00 | 6.00 |
| ❑ 249 Lavelle Hawkins AU/499 RC | 12.00 | 5.00 |
| ❑ 250 Dexter Jackson AU/499 RC | 15.00 | 6.00 |

## 1999 Donruss Elite

| | | |
|---|---|---|
| ❑ COMPLETE SET (200) | 100.00 | 40.00 |
| ❑ COMP.SET w/o SP's (160) | 30.00 | 15.00 |
| ❑ 1 Warren Moon | 1.25 | .50 |
| ❑ 2 Terry Allen UER | .75 | .30 |
| ❑ 3 Jeff George | .75 | .30 |
| ❑ 4 Brett Favre | 4.00 | 1.50 |
| ❑ 5 Rob Moore | .75 | .30 |
| ❑ 6 Bubby Brister | .50 | .20 |
| ❑ 7 John Elway | 4.00 | 1.50 |
| ❑ 8 Troy Aikman | 2.50 | 1.00 |
| ❑ 9 Steve McNair | 1.25 | .50 |
| ❑ 10 Charlie Batch | 1.25 | .50 |
| ❑ 11 Elvis Grbac | .75 | .30 |
| ❑ 12 Trent Dilfer | .75 | .30 |
| ❑ 13 Kerry Collins | .75 | .30 |
| ❑ 14 Neil O'Donnell | .50 | .20 |
| ❑ 15 Tony Simmons | .50 | .20 |
| ❑ 16 Ryan Leaf | 1.25 | .50 |
| ❑ 17 Bobby Hoying | .75 | .30 |
| ❑ 18 Marvin Harrison | 1.25 | .50 |
| ❑ 19 Keyshawn Johnson | 1.25 | .50 |
| ❑ 20 Cris Carter | 1.25 | .50 |
| ❑ 21 Deion Sanders | 1.25 | .50 |
| ❑ 22 Emmitt Smith UER | 2.50 | 1.00 |
| ❑ 23 Antowain Smith | 1.25 | .50 |
| ❑ 24 Terry Fair | .50 | .20 |
| ❑ 25 Robert Holcombe | .50 | .20 |
| ❑ 26 Napoleon Kaufman | 1.25 | .50 |
| ❑ 27 Eddie George | 1.25 | .50 |
| ❑ 28 Corey Dillon | 1.25 | .50 |
| ❑ 29 Adrian Murrell | .75 | .30 |
| ❑ 30 Charles Way | .50 | .20 |
| ❑ 31 Amp Lee | .50 | .20 |
| ❑ 32 Ricky Watters | .75 | .30 |
| ❑ 33 Gary Brown | .50 | .20 |
| ❑ 34 Thurman Thomas | .75 | .30 |
| ❑ 35 Pat Johnson | .50 | .20 |
| ❑ 36 Jerome Bettis | 1.25 | .50 |
| ❑ 37 Muhsin Muhammad | .75 | .30 |
| ❑ 38 Kimble Anders | .75 | .30 |
| ❑ 39 Curtis Enis | .50 | .20 |
| ❑ 40 Mike Alstott | 1.25 | .50 |
| ❑ 41 Charles Johnson | .50 | .20 |
| ❑ 42 Chris Warren | .50 | .20 |
| ❑ 43 Tony Banks | .75 | .30 |
| ❑ 44 Leroy Hoard | .50 | .20 |
| ❑ 45 Chris Fuamatu-Ma'afala | .50 | .20 |
| ❑ 46 Michael Irvin | 1.25 | .50 |
| ❑ 47 Robert Edwards | .50 | .20 |
| ❑ 48 Hines Ward | 1.25 | .50 |
| ❑ 49 Trent Green | 1.25 | .50 |
| ❑ 50 Eric Zeier | .50 | .20 |
| ❑ 51 Sean Dawkins | .50 | .20 |
| ❑ 52 Yancey Thigpen | .50 | .20 |
| ❑ 53 Jacquez Green | .50 | .20 |
| ❑ 54 Zach Thomas | 1.25 | .50 |
| ❑ 55 Junior Seau | 1.25 | .50 |
| ❑ 56 Darnay Scott | .50 | .20 |
| ❑ 57 Kent Graham | .50 | .20 |
| ❑ 58 O.J. Santiago | .50 | .20 |
| ❑ 59 Tony Gonzalez | 1.25 | .50 |
| ❑ 60 Ty Detmer | .50 | .20 |

| | | |
|---|---|---|
| ❑ 61 Albert Connell | .50 | .20 |
| ❑ 62 James Jett | .75 | .30 |
| ❑ 63 Bert Emanuel | .75 | .30 |
| ❑ 64 Derrick Alexander WR | .75 | .30 |
| ❑ 65 Wesley Walls | .75 | .30 |
| ❑ 66 Jake Reed | .75 | .30 |
| ❑ 67 Randall Cunningham | 1.25 | .50 |
| ❑ 68 Leslie Shepherd | .50 | .20 |
| ❑ 69 Mark Chmura | .50 | .20 |
| ❑ 70 Bobby Engram | .75 | .30 |
| ❑ 71 Rickey Dudley | .50 | .20 |
| ❑ 72 Darick Holmes | .50 | .20 |
| ❑ 73 Andre Reed | .75 | .30 |
| ❑ 74 Az-Zahir Hakim | .50 | .20 |
| ❑ 75 Cameron Cleeland | .50 | .20 |
| ❑ 76 Lamar Thomas | .50 | .20 |
| ❑ 77 Oronde Gadsden | .75 | .30 |
| ❑ 78 Ben Coates | .75 | .30 |
| ❑ 79 Bruce Smith | .75 | .30 |
| ❑ 80 Jerry Rice | 2.50 | 1.00 |
| ❑ 81 Tim Brown | 1.25 | .50 |
| ❑ 82 Michael Westbrook | .75 | .30 |
| ❑ 83 J.J. Stokes | .75 | .30 |
| ❑ 84 Shannon Sharpe | .75 | .30 |
| ❑ 85 Reidel Anthony | .75 | .30 |
| ❑ 86 Antonio Freeman | 1.25 | .50 |
| ❑ 87 Keenan McCardell | .75 | .30 |
| ❑ 88 Terry Glenn | 1.25 | .50 |
| ❑ 89 Andre Rison | .75 | .30 |
| ❑ 90 Neil Smith | .75 | .30 |
| ❑ 91 Terrance Mathis | .75 | .30 |
| ❑ 92 Rocket Ismail | .75 | .30 |
| ❑ 93 Byron Bam Morris | .50 | .20 |
| ❑ 94 Ike Hilliard | .50 | .20 |
| ❑ 95 Eddie Kennison | .75 | .30 |
| ❑ 96 Tavian Banks | .50 | .20 |
| ❑ 97 Yatil Green | .50 | .20 |
| ❑ 98 Frank Wycheck | .50 | .20 |
| ❑ 99 Warren Sapp UER | .50 | .20 |
| ❑ 100 Germane Crowell | .50 | .20 |
| ❑ 101 Curtis Martin | 2.50 | 1.00 |
| ❑ 102 John Avery | 1.00 | .40 |
| ❑ 103 Eric Moulds | 2.50 | 1.00 |
| ❑ 104 Randy Moss | 8.00 | 3.00 |
| ❑ 105 Terrell Owens | 2.50 | 1.00 |
| ❑ 106 Vinny Testaverde | 1.50 | .60 |
| ❑ 107 Doug Flutie | 1.25 | .50 |
| ❑ 108 Mark Brunell | 1.25 | .50 |
| ❑ 109 Isaac Bruce UER | 2.50 | 1.00 |
| ❑ 110 Kordell Stewart | 1.50 | .60 |
| ❑ 111 Drew Bledsoe | 3.00 | 1.25 |
| ❑ 112 Chris Chandler | 1.50 | .60 |
| ❑ 113 Dan Marino | 8.00 | 3.00 |
| ❑ 114 Brian Griese | 2.50 | 1.00 |
| ❑ 115 Carl Pickens | 1.50 | .60 |
| ❑ 116 Jake Plummer | 1.50 | .60 |
| ❑ 117 Natrone Means | 1.50 | .60 |
| ❑ 118 Peyton Manning | 10.00 | 4.00 |
| ❑ 119 Garrison Hearst | 2.50 | 1.00 |
| ❑ 120 Barry Sanders | 8.00 | 3.00 |
| ❑ 121 Steve Young | 3.00 | 1.25 |
| ❑ 122 Rashaan Shehee | 1.00 | .40 |
| ❑ 123 Ed McCaffrey | 1.50 | .60 |
| ❑ 124 Charles Woodson | 2.50 | 1.00 |
| ❑ 125 Dorsey Levens | 2.50 | 1.00 |
| ❑ 126 Robert Smith | 2.50 | 1.00 |
| ❑ 127 Greg Hill | 1.00 | .40 |
| ❑ 128 Fred Taylor | 2.50 | 1.00 |
| ❑ 129 Marcus Nash | 1.00 | .40 |
| ❑ 130 Terrell Davis | 2.50 | 1.00 |
| ❑ 131 Ahman Green | 2.50 | 1.00 |
| ❑ 132 Jamal Anderson | 2.50 | 1.00 |
| ❑ 133 Karim Abdul-Jabbar | 1.50 | .60 |
| ❑ 134 Jermaine Lewis | 1.50 | .60 |
| ❑ 135 Jerome Pathon | 1.50 | .60 |
| ❑ 136 Brad Johnson | 2.50 | 1.00 |
| ❑ 137 Herman Moore | 1.50 | .60 |
| ❑ 138 Tim Dwight | 2.50 | 1.00 |
| ❑ 139 Johnnie Morton | 1.00 | .40 |
| ❑ 140 Marshall Faulk | 3.00 | 1.25 |
| ❑ 141 Frank Sanders | 1.50 | .60 |
| ❑ 142 Kevin Dyson | 1.50 | .60 |
| ❑ 143 Curtis Conway | 1.50 | .60 |
| ❑ 144 Derrick Mayes | 1.00 | .40 |

| | | |
|---|---|---|
| ❑ 145 O.J. McDuffie | 1.50 | .60 |
| ❑ 146 Joe Jurevicius | 1.50 | .60 |
| ❑ 147 Jon Kitna | 2.50 | 1.00 |
| ❑ 148 Joey Galloway | 1.50 | .60 |
| ❑ 149 Jimmy Smith | 1.50 | .60 |
| ❑ 150 Skip Hicks | 1.00 | .40 |
| ❑ 151 Rod Smith | 1.50 | .60 |
| ❑ 152 Duce Staley | 2.50 | 1.00 |
| ❑ 153 James Stewart | 1.00 | .40 |
| ❑ 154 Rob Johnson | 1.50 | .60 |
| ❑ 155 Mikhael Ricks | 1.00 | .40 |
| ❑ 156 Wayne Chrebet | 1.50 | .60 |
| ❑ 157 Robert Brooks | 1.50 | .60 |
| ❑ 158 Tim Biakabutuka | 1.50 | .60 |
| ❑ 159 Priest Holmes | 4.00 | 1.25 |
| ❑ 160 Warrick Dunn | 2.50 | 1.00 |
| ❑ 161 Champ Bailey RC | 5.00 | 2.00 |
| ❑ 162 D'Wayne Bates RC | 2.50 | 1.00 |
| ❑ 163 Michael Bishop RC | 3.00 | 1.25 |
| ❑ 164 David Boston RC | 3.00 | 1.25 |
| ❑ 165 Na Brown RC | 2.50 | 1.00 |
| ❑ 166 Chris Claiborne RC | 1.50 | .60 |
| ❑ 167 Joe Montgomery RC | 2.50 | 1.00 |
| ❑ 168 Mike Cloud RC | 2.50 | 1.00 |
| ❑ 169 Travis McGriff RC | 1.50 | .60 |
| ❑ 170 Tim Couch RC | 3.00 | 1.25 |
| ❑ 171 Daunte Culpepper RC | 12.00 | 5.00 |
| ❑ 172 Autry Denson RC | 2.50 | 1.00 |
| ❑ 173 Jermaine Fazande RC | 2.50 | 1.00 |
| ❑ 174 Troy Edwards RC | 2.50 | 1.00 |
| ❑ 175 Kevin Faulk RC | 3.00 | 1.25 |
| ❑ 176 Dee Miller RC UER | 1.50 | .60 |
| ❑ 177 Brock Huard RC | 3.00 | 1.25 |
| ❑ 178 Torry Holt RC | 8.00 | 3.00 |
| ❑ 179 Sedrick Irvin RC | 1.50 | .60 |
| ❑ 180 Edgerrin James RC | 12.00 | 5.00 |
| ❑ 181 Joe Germaine RC | 2.50 | 1.00 |
| ❑ 182 James Johnson RC | 2.50 | 1.00 |
| ❑ 183 Kevin Johnson RC | 2.50 | 1.00 |
| ❑ 184 Andy Katzenmoyer RC | 2.50 | 1.00 |
| ❑ 185 Jevon Kearse RC | 6.00 | 2.50 |
| ❑ 186 Shaun King RC | 2.50 | 1.00 |
| ❑ 187 Rob Konrad RC | 3.00 | 1.25 |
| ❑ 188 Jim Kleinsasser RC | 3.00 | 1.25 |
| ❑ 189 Chris McAlister RC | 2.50 | 1.00 |
| ❑ 190 Donovan McNabb RC | 15.00 | 6.00 |
| ❑ 191 Cade McNown RC | 2.50 | 1.00 |
| ❑ 192 De'Mond Parker RC | 1.00 | .40 |
| ❑ 193 Craig Yeast RC | 2.50 | 1.00 |
| ❑ 194 Shawn Bryson RC | 3.00 | 1.25 |
| ❑ 195 Peerless Price RC | 3.00 | 1.25 |
| ❑ 196 Darnell McDonald RC | 2.50 | 1.00 |
| ❑ 197 Akili Smith RC | 1.50 | .60 |
| ❑ 198 Tai Streets RC | 3.00 | 1.25 |
| ❑ 199 Ricky Williams RC | 6.00 | 2.50 |
| ❑ 200 Amos Zereoue RC | 2.50 | 1.00 |

## 2000 Donruss Elite

| | | |
|---|---|---|
| ❑ COMPLETE SET (200) | 500.00 | 300.00 |
| ❑ 1 Jake Plummer | .50 | .20 |
| ❑ 2 David Boston | .75 | .30 |
| ❑ 3 Rob Moore | .50 | .20 |
| ❑ 4 Chris Chandler | .50 | .20 |
| ❑ 5 Tim Dwight | .75 | .30 |
| ❑ 6 Terance Mathis | .50 | .20 |
| ❑ 7 Jamal Anderson | .75 | .30 |
| ❑ 8 Priest Holmes | 1.00 | .40 |
| ❑ 9 Tony Banks | .50 | .20 |

|  |  | | |
|---|---|---|---|
| ❑ 10 | Shannon Sharpe | .50 | .20 |
| ❑ 11 | Qadry Ismail | .50 | .20 |
| ❑ 12 | Eric Moulds | .75 | .30 |
| ❑ 13 | Doug Flutie | .50 | .20 |
| ❑ 14 | Antowain Smith | .50 | .20 |
| ❑ 15 | Peerless Price | .50 | .20 |
| ❑ 16 | Muhsin Muhammad | .50 | .20 |
| ❑ 17 | Tim Biakabutuka | .50 | .20 |
| ❑ 18 | Patrick Jeffers | .75 | .30 |
| ❑ 19 | Steve Beuerlein | .50 | .20 |
| ❑ 20 | Wesley Walls | .50 | .10 |
| ❑ 21 | Curtis Enis | .30 | .10 |
| ❑ 22 | Marcus Robinson | .75 | .30 |
| ❑ 23 | Carl Pickens | .75 | .30 |
| ❑ 24 | Corey Dillon | .75 | .30 |
| ❑ 25 | Akili Smith | .30 | .10 |
| ❑ 26 | Damay Scott | .50 | .20 |
| ❑ 27 | Kevin Johnson | .75 | .30 |
| ❑ 28 | Errict Rhett | .50 | .20 |
| ❑ 29 | Emmitt Smith | 1.50 | .60 |
| ❑ 30 | Deion Sanders | .75 | .30 |
| ❑ 31 | Troy Aikman | 1.50 | .60 |
| ❑ 32 | Joey Galloway | .50 | .20 |
| ❑ 33 | Michael Irvin | .50 | .20 |
| ❑ 34 | Rocket Ismail | .50 | .20 |
| ❑ 35 | Jason Tucker | .30 | .10 |
| ❑ 36 | Ed McCaffrey | .75 | .30 |
| ❑ 37 | Rod Smith | .50 | .20 |
| ❑ 38 | Brian Griese | .75 | .30 |
| ❑ 39 | Terrell Davis | .75 | .30 |
| ❑ 40 | Olandis Gary | .75 | .30 |
| ❑ 41 | Charlie Batch | .50 | .20 |
| ❑ 42 | Johnnie Morton | .50 | .20 |
| ❑ 43 | Herman Moore | .50 | .20 |
| ❑ 44 | James Stewart | .50 | .20 |
| ❑ 45 | Dorsey Levens | .50 | .20 |
| ❑ 46 | Antonio Freeman | .75 | .30 |
| ❑ 47 | Brett Favre | 2.50 | 1.00 |
| ❑ 48 | Bill Schroeder | .50 | .20 |
| ❑ 49 | Peyton Manning | 2.00 | .75 |
| ❑ 50 | Keenan McCardell | .50 | .20 |
| ❑ 51 | Fred Taylor | .75 | .30 |
| ❑ 52 | Jimmy Smith | .50 | .20 |
| ❑ 53 | Elvis Grbac | .50 | .20 |
| ❑ 54 | Tony Gonzalez | .50 | .20 |
| ❑ 55 | Derrick Alexander | .50 | .20 |
| ❑ 56 | Dan Marino | 2.50 | 1.00 |
| ❑ 57 | Tony Martin | .50 | .20 |
| ❑ 58 | James Johnson | .30 | .10 |
| ❑ 59 | Damon Huard | .75 | .30 |
| ❑ 60 | Thurman Thomas | .75 | .30 |
| ❑ 61 | Robert Smith | .75 | .30 |
| ❑ 62 | Randall Cunningham | .75 | .30 |
| ❑ 63 | Jeff George | .50 | .20 |
| ❑ 64 | Terry Glenn | .50 | .20 |
| ❑ 65 | Drew Bledsoe | 1.00 | .40 |
| ❑ 66 | Jeff Blake | .50 | .20 |
| ❑ 67 | Amani Toomer | .50 | .20 |
| ❑ 68 | Kerry Collins | .50 | .20 |
| ❑ 69 | Joe Montgomery | .30 | .10 |
| ❑ 70 | Vinny Testaverde | .50 | .20 |
| ❑ 71 | Ray Lucas | .50 | .20 |
| ❑ 72 | Keyshawn Johnson | .75 | .30 |
| ❑ 73 | Wayne Chrebet | .50 | .20 |
| ❑ 74 | Napoleon Kaufman | .50 | .20 |
| ❑ 75 | Tim Brown | .75 | .30 |
| ❑ 76 | Rich Gannon | .75 | .30 |
| ❑ 77 | Duce Staley | .75 | .30 |
| ❑ 78 | Kordell Stewart | .50 | .20 |
| ❑ 79 | Jerome Bettis | .75 | .30 |
| ❑ 80 | Troy Edwards | .30 | .10 |
| ❑ 81 | Natrone Means | .50 | .10 |
| ❑ 82 | Curtis Conway | .50 | .20 |
| ❑ 83 | Jim Harbaugh | .50 | .20 |
| ❑ 84 | Junior Seau | .75 | .30 |
| ❑ 85 | Jermaine Fazande | .30 | .10 |
| ❑ 86 | Terrell Owens | .75 | .30 |
| ❑ 87 | Charlie Garner | .50 | .20 |
| ❑ 88 | Steve Young | 1.00 | .40 |
| ❑ 89 | Jeff Garcia | .75 | .30 |
| ❑ 90 | Derrick Mayes | .50 | .20 |
| ❑ 91 | Ricky Watters | .50 | .20 |
| ❑ 92 | Az-Zahir Hakim | .50 | .20 |
| ❑ 93 | Torry Holt | .75 | .30 |
| ❑ 94 | Warren Sapp | .50 | .20 |
| ❑ 95 | Mike Alstott | .75 | .30 |
| ❑ 96 | Warrick Dunn | .75 | .30 |
| ❑ 97 | Kevin Dyson | .50 | .20 |
| ❑ 98 | Bruce Smith | .50 | .20 |
| ❑ 99 | Albert Connell | .30 | .10 |
| ❑ 100 | Michael Westbrook | .50 | .20 |
| ❑ 101 | Cade McNown | .30 | .10 |
| ❑ 102 | Tim Couch | 2.00 | .75 |
| ❑ 103 | John Elway | 6.00 | 2.50 |
| ❑ 104 | Barry Sanders | 5.00 | 2.00 |
| ❑ 105 | Germane Crowell | 1.25 | .50 |
| ❑ 106 | Marvin Harrison | 2.00 | .75 |
| ❑ 107 | Edgerrin James | 3.00 | 1.25 |
| ❑ 108 | Mark Brunell | 2.00 | .75 |
| ❑ 109 | Randy Moss | 4.00 | 1.50 |
| ❑ 110 | Cris Carter | 2.00 | .75 |
| ❑ 111 | Daunte Culpepper | 2.50 | 1.00 |
| ❑ 112 | Ricky Williams | .75 | .30 |
| ❑ 113 | Curtis Martin | 2.00 | .75 |
| ❑ 114 | Donovan McNabb | 3.00 | 1.25 |
| ❑ 115 | Jerry Rice | 4.00 | 1.50 |
| ❑ 116 | Jon Kitna | 2.00 | .75 |
| ❑ 147 | Isaac Bruce | 2.00 | .75 |
| ❑ 118 | Marshall Faulk | 2.50 | 1.00 |
| ❑ 119 | Kurt Warner | 4.00 | 1.50 |
| ❑ 120 | Shaun King | .30 | .10 |
| ❑ 121 | Eddie George | 2.00 | .75 |
| ❑ 122 | Steve McNair | 2.00 | .75 |
| ❑ 123 | Jevon Kearse | 2.00 | .75 |
| ❑ 124 | Stephen Davis | 2.00 | .75 |
| ❑ 125 | Brad Johnson | 2.00 | .75 |
| ❑ 126 | Mike Anderson RC | 2.50 | 1.00 |
| ❑ 127 | Peter Warrick RC | 5.00 | 2.00 |
| ❑ 128 | Courtney Brown RC | 2.00 | .75 |
| ❑ 129 | Plaxico Burress RC | 10.00 | 4.00 |
| ❑ 130 | Corey Simon RC | 5.00 | 2.00 |
| ❑ 131 | Thomas Jones RC | 8.00 | 3.00 |
| ❑ 132 | Travis Taylor RC | 2.00 | .75 |
| ❑ 133 | Shaun Alexander RC | 20.00 | 8.00 |
| ❑ 134 | Deon Grant RC | 4.00 | 1.50 |
| ❑ 135 | Chris Redman RC | 4.00 | 1.50 |
| ❑ 136 | Chad Pennington RC | 12.00 | 5.00 |
| ❑ 137 | Jamal Lewis RC | 12.00 | 5.00 |
| ❑ 138 | Brian Urlacher RC | 25.00 | 10.00 |
| ❑ 139 | Keith Bulluck RC | 5.00 | 2.00 |
| ❑ 140 | Bubba Franks RC | 5.00 | 2.00 |
| ❑ 141 | Dez White RC | 5.00 | 2.00 |
| ❑ 142 | Na'il Diggs RC | 4.00 | 1.50 |
| ❑ 143 | Ahmed Plummer RC | 5.00 | 2.00 |
| ❑ 144 | Ron Dayne RC | 5.00 | 2.00 |
| ❑ 145 | Shaun Ellis RC | 5.00 | 2.00 |
| ❑ 146 | Sylvester Morris RC | 4.00 | 1.50 |
| ❑ 147 | Deltha O'Neal RC | 5.00 | 2.00 |
| ❑ 148 | Raynoch Thompson RC | 4.00 | 1.50 |
| ❑ 149 | R.Jay Soward RC | 4.00 | 1.50 |
| ❑ 150 | Mario Edwards RC | 4.00 | 1.50 |
| ❑ 151 | John Engelberger RC | 4.00 | 1.50 |
| ❑ 152 | Dwayne Goodrich RC | 5.00 | 2.00 |
| ❑ 153 | Sherrod Gideon RC | 2.50 | 1.00 |
| ❑ 154 | John Abraham RC | 5.00 | 2.00 |
| ❑ 155 | Ben Kelly RC | 5.00 | 2.00 |
| ❑ 156 | Travis Prentice RC | 4.00 | 1.50 |
| ❑ 157 | Darrell Jackson RC | 10.00 | 4.00 |
| ❑ 158 | Giovanni Carmazzi RC | 2.50 | 1.00 |
| ❑ 159 | Anthony Lucas RC | 2.50 | 1.00 |
| ❑ 160 | Danny Farmer RC | 4.00 | 1.50 |
| ❑ 161 | Dennis Northcutt RC | 5.00 | 2.00 |
| ❑ 162 | Troy Walters RC | 5.00 | 2.00 |
| ❑ 163 | Laverannes Coles RC | 6.00 | 2.50 |
| ❑ 164 | Tee Martin RC | 5.00 | 2.00 |
| ❑ 165 | J.R. Redmond RC | 4.00 | 1.50 |
| ❑ 166 | Tim Rattay RC | 5.00 | 2.00 |
| ❑ 167 | Jerry Porter RC | 6.00 | 2.50 |
| ❑ 168 | Sebastian Janikowski RC | 5.00 | 2.00 |
| ❑ 169 | Michael Wiley RC | 4.00 | 1.50 |
| ❑ 170 | Reuben Droughns RC | 6.00 | 2.50 |
| ❑ 171 | Trung Canidate RC | 4.00 | 1.50 |
| ❑ 172 | Shyrone Stith RC | 5.00 | 2.00 |
| ❑ 173 | Chris Hovan RC | 4.00 | 1.50 |
| ❑ 174 | Brandon Short RC | 5.00 | 2.00 |
| ❑ 175 | Mark Roman RC | 4.00 | 1.50 |
| ❑ 176 | Trevor Gaylor RC | 4.00 | 1.50 |
| ❑ 177 | Chris Cole RC | 4.00 | 1.50 |
| ❑ 178 | Hank Poteat RC | 4.00 | 1.50 |
| ❑ 179 | Darren Howard RC | 4.00 | 1.50 |
| ❑ 180 | Rob Morris RC | 5.00 | 2.00 |
| ❑ 181 | Spergon Wynn RC | 4.00 | 1.50 |
| ❑ 182 | Marc Bulger RC | 10.00 | 5.00 |
| ❑ 183 | Tom Brady RC | 150.00 | 75.00 |
| ❑ 184 | Todd Husak RC | 5.00 | 2.00 |
| ❑ 185 | Gari Scott RC | 2.50 | 1.00 |
| ❑ 186 | Erron Kinney RC | 4.00 | 1.50 |
| ❑ 187 | Julian Peterson RC | 5.00 | 2.00 |
| ❑ 188 | Sammy Morris RC | 5.00 | 2.00 |
| ❑ 189 | Rondell Mealey RC | 2.50 | 1.00 |
| ❑ 190 | Doug Chapman RC | 4.00 | 1.50 |
| ❑ 191 | Ron Dugans RC | 2.50 | 1.00 |
| ❑ 192 | Deon Dyer RC | 4.00 | 1.50 |
| ❑ 193 | Fred Robbins RC | 2.50 | 1.00 |
| ❑ 194 | Ike Charlton RC | 5.00 | 2.00 |
| ❑ 195 | Mareno Philyaw RC | 2.50 | 1.00 |
| ❑ 196 | Thomas Hamner RC | 2.50 | 1.00 |
| ❑ 197 | Jarious Jackson RC | 4.00 | 1.50 |
| ❑ 198 | Anthony Becht RC | 5.00 | 2.00 |
| ❑ 199 | Joe Hamilton RC | 4.00 | 1.50 |
| ❑ 200 | Todd Pinkston RC | 5.00 | 2.00 |

## 2001 Donruss Elite

|  |  | | |
|---|---|---|---|
| ❑ | COMP.SET w/o SP's (100) | 20.00 | 7.50 |
| ❑ 1 | David Boston | .60 | .25 |
| ❑ 2 | Jake Plummer | .40 | .15 |
| ❑ 3 | Thomas Jones | .40 | .15 |
| ❑ 4 | Jamal Anderson | .60 | .25 |
| ❑ 5 | Chris Redman | .25 | .08 |
| ❑ 6 | Jamal Lewis | 1.00 | .40 |
| ❑ 7 | Shannon Sharpe | .40 | .15 |
| ❑ 8 | Travis Taylor | .40 | .15 |
| ❑ 9 | Trent Dilfer | .40 | .15 |
| ❑ 10 | Doug Flutie | .60 | .25 |
| ❑ 11 | Eric Moulds | .40 | .15 |
| ❑ 12 | Rob Johnson | .40 | .15 |
| ❑ 13 | Muhsin Muhammad | .40 | .15 |
| ❑ 14 | Steve Beuerlein | .25 | .08 |
| ❑ 15 | Brian Urlacher | 1.00 | .40 |
| ❑ 16 | Cade McNown | .25 | .08 |
| ❑ 17 | Marcus Robinson | .60 | .25 |
| ❑ 18 | Akili Smith | .25 | .08 |
| ❑ 19 | Corey Dillon | .60 | .25 |
| ❑ 20 | Peter Warrick | .60 | .25 |
| ❑ 21 | Kevin Johnson | .40 | .15 |
| ❑ 22 | Tim Couch | .40 | .15 |
| ❑ 23 | Emmitt Smith | 1.25 | .50 |
| ❑ 24 | Troy Aikman | 1.00 | .40 |
| ❑ 25 | Brian Griese | .60 | .25 |
| ❑ 26 | John Elway | 2.00 | .75 |
| ❑ 27 | Mike Anderson | .60 | .25 |
| ❑ 28 | Rod Smith | .40 | .15 |
| ❑ 29 | Terrell Davis | .60 | .25 |
| ❑ 30 | Barry Sanders | 1.25 | .50 |
| ❑ 31 | Charlie Batch | .60 | .25 |
| ❑ 32 | James Stewart | .40 | .15 |
| ❑ 33 | Ahman Green | .60 | .25 |
| ❑ 34 | Antonio Freeman | .60 | .25 |
| ❑ 35 | Brett Favre | 2.00 | .75 |
| ❑ 36 | Edgerrin James | .75 | .30 |
| ❑ 37 | Marvin Harrison | .60 | .25 |
| ❑ 38 | Peyton Manning | 1.50 | .60 |
| ❑ 39 | Fred Taylor | .60 | .25 |
| ❑ 40 | Jimmy Smith | .40 | .15 |
| ❑ 41 | Keenan McCardell | .25 | .08 |
| ❑ 42 | Mark Brunell | .60 | .25 |

| | | |
|---|---|---|
| ❑ 43 Derrick Alexander | .40 | .15 |
| ❑ 44 Elvis Grbac | .40 | .15 |
| ❑ 45 Sylvester Morris | .25 | .08 |
| ❑ 46 Tony Gonzalez | .40 | .15 |
| ❑ 47 Dan Marino | 2.00 | .75 |
| ❑ 48 Jay Fiedler | .60 | .25 |
| ❑ 49 Lamar Smith | .40 | .15 |
| ❑ 50 Oronde Gadsden | .40 | .15 |
| ❑ 51 Cris Carter | .60 | .25 |
| ❑ 52 Daunte Culpepper | .60 | .25 |
| ❑ 53 Randy Moss | 1.25 | .50 |
| ❑ 54 Robert Smith | .40 | .15 |
| ❑ 55 Drew Bledsoe | .75 | .30 |
| ❑ 56 Terry Glenn | .25 | .08 |
| ❑ 57 Aaron Brooks | .60 | .25 |
| ❑ 58 Joe Horn | .40 | .15 |
| ❑ 59 Ricky Williams | .60 | .25 |
| ❑ 60 Amani Toomer | .25 | .08 |
| ❑ 61 Ike Hilliard | .40 | .15 |
| ❑ 62 Kerry Collins | .40 | .15 |
| ❑ 63 Ron Dayne | .60 | .25 |
| ❑ 64 Tiki Barber | .60 | .25 |
| ❑ 65 Chad Pennington | 1.00 | .40 |
| ❑ 66 Curtis Martin | .60 | .25 |
| ❑ 67 Vinny Testaverde | .40 | .15 |
| ❑ 68 Wayne Chrebet | .40 | .15 |
| ❑ 69 Rich Gannon | .60 | .25 |
| ❑ 70 Tim Brown | .60 | .25 |
| ❑ 71 Tyrone Wheatley | .40 | .15 |
| ❑ 72 Donovan McNabb | .75 | .30 |
| ❑ 73 Jerome Bettis | .60 | .25 |
| ❑ 74 Plaxico Burress | .60 | .25 |
| ❑ 75 Junior Seau | .60 | .25 |
| ❑ 76 Charlie Garner | .40 | .15 |
| ❑ 77 Jeff Garcia | .60 | .25 |
| ❑ 78 Jerry Rice | 1.25 | .50 |
| ❑ 79 Terrell Owens | .60 | .25 |
| ❑ 80 Darrell Jackson | .60 | .25 |
| ❑ 81 Ricky Watters | .40 | .15 |
| ❑ 82 Shaun Alexander | .75 | .30 |
| ❑ 83 Isaac Bruce | .60 | .25 |
| ❑ 84 Kurt Warner | 1.25 | .50 |
| ❑ 85 Marshall Faulk | .75 | .30 |
| ❑ 86 Torry Holt | .60 | .25 |
| ❑ 87 Trent Green | .60 | .25 |
| ❑ 88 Keyshawn Johnson | .60 | .25 |
| ❑ 89 Shaun King | .25 | .08 |
| ❑ 90 Warren Sapp | .40 | .15 |
| ❑ 91 Warrick Dunn | .60 | .25 |
| ❑ 92 Eddie George | .60 | .25 |
| ❑ 93 Jevon Kearse | .40 | .15 |
| ❑ 94 Steve McNair | .60 | .25 |
| ❑ 95 Albert Connell | .25 | .08 |
| ❑ 96 Jeff George | .25 | .08 |
| ❑ 97 Brad Johnson | .60 | .25 |
| ❑ 98 Bruce Smith | .25 | .08 |
| ❑ 99 Michael Westbrook | .40 | .15 |
| ❑ 100 Stephen Davis | .60 | .25 |
| ❑ 101 Michael Vick RC | 25.00 | 10.00 |
| ❑ 102 Drew Brees RC | 40.00 | 20.00 |
| ❑ 103 Chris Weinke RC | 10.00 | 4.00 |
| ❑ 104 Quincy Carter RC | 10.00 | 4.00 |
| ❑ 105 Sage Rosenfels RC | 10.00 | 4.00 |
| ❑ 106 Josh Heupel RC | 10.00 | 4.00 |
| ❑ 107 Tony Driver RC | 6.00 | 2.50 |
| ❑ 108 Ben Leard RC | 6.00 | 2.50 |
| ❑ 109 Marques Tuiasosopo RC | 10.00 | 4.00 |
| ❑ 110 Tim Hasselbeck RC | 10.00 | 4.00 |
| ❑ 111 Mike McMahon RC | 10.00 | 4.00 |
| ❑ 112 Deuce McAllister RC | 25.00 | 10.00 |
| ❑ 113 LaMont Jordan RC | 25.00 | 10.00 |
| ❑ 114 LaDainian Tomlinson RC | 80.00 | 40.00 |
| ❑ 115 James Jackson RC | 10.00 | 4.00 |
| ❑ 116 Anthony Thomas RC | 10.00 | 4.00 |
| ❑ 117 Travis Henry RC | 10.00 | 4.00 |
| ❑ 118 DeAngelo Evans RC | 6.00 | 2.50 |
| ❑ 119 Travis Minor RC | 6.00 | 2.50 |
| ❑ 120 Rudi Johnson RC | 25.00 | 12.50 |
| ❑ 121 Michael Bennett RC | 10.00 | 4.00 |
| ❑ 122 Kevan Barlow RC | 10.00 | 4.00 |
| ❑ 123 Dan Alexander RC | 10.00 | 4.00 |
| ❑ 124 David Allen RC | 6.00 | 2.50 |
| ❑ 125 Correll Buckhalter RC | 12.00 | 5.00 |
| ❑ 126 David Rivers RC | 6.00 | 2.50 |

| | | |
|---|---|---|
| ❑ 127 Reggie White RC | 6.00 | 2.50 |
| ❑ 128 Moran Norris RC | 4.00 | 1.50 |
| ❑ 129 Ja'Mar Toombs RC | 6.00 | 2.50 |
| ❑ 130 Jason McKinley RC | 6.00 | 2.50 |
| ❑ 131 Scotty Anderson RC | 6.00 | 2.50 |
| ❑ 132 Dustin McClintock RC | 10.00 | 4.00 |
| ❑ 133 Heath Evans RC | 6.00 | 2.50 |
| ❑ 134 David Terrell RC | 10.00 | 4.00 |
| ❑ 135 Santana Moss RC | 15.00 | 6.00 |
| ❑ 136 Rod Gardner RC | 10.00 | 4.00 |
| ❑ 137 Quincy Morgan RC | 10.00 | 4.00 |
| ❑ 138 Freddie Mitchell RC | 10.00 | 4.00 |
| ❑ 139 Boo Williams RC | 6.00 | 2.50 |
| ❑ 140 Reggie Wayne RC | 25.00 | 10.00 |
| ❑ 141 Ronney Daniels RC | 4.00 | 1.50 |
| ❑ 142 Bobby Newcombe RC | 6.00 | 2.50 |
| ❑ 143 Reggie Germany/250 RC | 12.00 | 5.00 |
| ❑ 144 Jesse Palmer RC | 10.00 | 4.00 |
| ❑ 145 Robert Ferguson RC | 10.00 | 4.00 |
| ❑ 146 Ken-Yon Rambo RC | 6.00 | 2.50 |
| ❑ 147 Alex Bannister RC | 6.00 | 2.50 |
| ❑ 148 Koren Robinson RC | 10.00 | 4.00 |
| ❑ 149 Chad Johnson RC | 30.00 | 12.50 |
| ❑ 150 Chris Chambers RC | 15.00 | 6.00 |
| ❑ 151 Javon Green RC | 6.00 | 2.50 |
| ❑ 152 Snoop Minnis RC | 6.00 | 2.50 |
| ❑ 153 Vinny Sutherland RC | 6.00 | 2.50 |
| ❑ 154 Cedrick Wilson RC | 10.00 | 4.00 |
| ❑ 155 John Capel/250 RC | 12.00 | 5.00 |
| ❑ 156 T.J. Houshmandzadeh RC | 12.00 | 5.00 |
| ❑ 157 Todd Heap RC | 10.00 | 4.00 |
| ❑ 158 Alge Crumpler RC | 15.00 | 6.00 |
| ❑ 159 Jabari Holloway RC | 6.00 | 2.50 |
| ❑ 160 Marcellus Rivers RC | 6.00 | 2.50 |
| ❑ 161 Rashon Burns RC | 4.00 | 1.50 |
| ❑ 162 Tony Stewart RC | 10.00 | 4.00 |
| ❑ 163 Jevaris Johnson RC | 6.00 | 2.50 |
| ❑ 164 Jamal Reynolds RC | 10.00 | 4.00 |
| ❑ 165 Andre Carter RC | 10.00 | 4.00 |
| ❑ 166 David Warren RC | 4.00 | 1.50 |
| ❑ 167 Justin Smith RC | 10.00 | 4.00 |
| ❑ 168 Josh Booty RC | 6.00 | 2.50 |
| ❑ 169 Karon Riley RC | 4.00 | 1.50 |
| ❑ 170 Cedric Scott RC | 4.00 | 1.50 |
| ❑ 171 Kenny Smith RC | 6.00 | 2.50 |
| ❑ 172 Richard Seymour RC | 10.00 | 4.00 |
| ❑ 173 Willie Howard RC | 6.00 | 2.50 |
| ❑ 174 Markus Steele RC | 6.00 | 2.50 |
| ❑ 175 Marcus Stroud RC | 10.00 | 4.00 |
| ❑ 176 Damione Lewis RC | 6.00 | 2.50 |
| ❑ 177 Casey Hampton RC | 10.00 | 4.00 |
| ❑ 178 Ennis Davis RC | 4.00 | 1.50 |
| ❑ 179 Gerard Warren RC | .60 | .25 |
| ❑ 180 Tommy Polley RC | 10.00 | 4.00 |
| ❑ 181 Kendrell Bell/250 RC | 40.00 | 15.00 |
| ❑ 182 Dan Morgan RC | 10.00 | 4.00 |
| ❑ 183 Morlon Greenwood RC | 6.00 | 2.50 |
| ❑ 184 Quinton Caver/250 RC | 10.00 | 4.00 |
| ❑ 185 Keith Adams RC | 4.00 | 1.50 |
| ❑ 186 Brian Allen RC | 4.00 | 1.50 |
| ❑ 187 Carlos Polk RC | 4.00 | 1.50 |
| ❑ 188 Torrance Marshall RC | 10.00 | 4.00 |
| ❑ 189 Jamie Winborn RC | 6.00 | 2.50 |
| ❑ 190 Jamar Fletcher RC | 6.00 | 2.50 |
| ❑ 191 Ken Lucas RC | 4.00 | 1.50 |
| ❑ 192 Fred Smoot RC | 10.00 | 4.00 |
| ❑ 193 Nate Clements RC | 10.00 | 4.00 |
| ❑ 194 Will Allen RC | 6.00 | 2.50 |
| ❑ 195 Willie Middlebrooks/250 RC | 10.00 | 4.00 |
| ❑ 196 Gary Baxter RC | 6.00 | 2.50 |
| ❑ 197 Derrick Gibson RC | 6.00 | 2.50 |
| ❑ 198 Robert Carswell/250 RC | 10.00 | 4.00 |
| ❑ 199 Hakim Akbar RC | 4.00 | 1.50 |
| ❑ 200 Adam Archuleta RC | 10.00 | 4.00 |

## 2002 Donruss Elite

| | | |
|---|---|---|
| COMP. SET w/o SP's (100) | 20.00 | 7.50 |
| ❑ 1 Elvis Grbac | .30 | .10 |
| ❑ 2 Jamal Lewis | .50 | .20 |
| ❑ 3 Ray Lewis | .50 | .20 |
| ❑ 4 Travis Henry | .50 | .20 |
| ❑ 5 Eric Moulds | .50 | .20 |
| ❑ 6 Corey Dillon | .30 | .10 |
| ❑ 7 Peter Warrick | .30 | .10 |

| | | |
|---|---|---|
| ❑ 8 Tim Couch | .30 | .10 |
| ❑ 9 James Jackson | .20 | .07 |
| ❑ 10 Kevin Johnson | .30 | .10 |
| ❑ 11 Mike Anderson | .50 | .20 |
| ❑ 12 Terrell Davis | .50 | .20 |
| ❑ 13 Brian Griese | .50 | .20 |
| ❑ 14 Rod Smith | .30 | .10 |
| ❑ 15 Marvin Harrison | .50 | .20 |
| ❑ 16 Reggie Wayne | .50 | .20 |
| ❑ 17 Dominic Rhodes | .50 | .20 |
| ❑ 18 Edgerrin James | .60 | .25 |
| ❑ 19 Mark Brunell | .50 | .20 |
| ❑ 20 Keenan McCardell | .20 | .07 |
| ❑ 21 Jimmy Smith | .30 | .10 |
| ❑ 22 Tony Gonzalez | .30 | .10 |
| ❑ 23 Trent Green | .30 | .10 |
| ❑ 24 Priest Holmes | .60 | .25 |
| ❑ 25 Snoop Minnis | .20 | .07 |
| ❑ 26 Chris Chambers | .50 | .20 |
| ❑ 27 Jay Fiedler | .30 | .10 |
| ❑ 28 Travis Minor | .20 | .07 |
| ❑ 29 Lamar Smith | .30 | .10 |
| ❑ 30 Tom Brady | 1.25 | .50 |
| ❑ 31 Troy Brown | .30 | .10 |
| ❑ 32 Antowain Smith | .30 | .10 |
| ❑ 33 Laveranues Coles | .50 | .20 |
| ❑ 34 Curtis Martin | .50 | .20 |
| ❑ 35 Vinny Testaverde | .30 | .10 |
| ❑ 36 Wayne Chrebet | .30 | .10 |
| ❑ 37 Tim Brown | .50 | .20 |
| ❑ 38 Rich Gannon | .50 | .20 |
| ❑ 39 Jerry Rice | 1.00 | .40 |
| ❑ 40 Charlie Garner | .30 | .10 |
| ❑ 41 Jerome Bettis | .50 | .20 |
| ❑ 42 Plaxico Burress | .30 | .10 |
| ❑ 43 Kordell Stewart | .50 | .20 |
| ❑ 44 Kendrell Bell | .50 | .20 |
| ❑ 45 Doug Flutie | .50 | .20 |
| ❑ 46 LaDainian Tomlinson | .75 | .30 |
| ❑ 47 Junior Seau | .50 | .20 |
| ❑ 48 Drew Brees | .50 | .20 |
| ❑ 49 Shaun Alexander | .60 | .25 |
| ❑ 50 Koren Robinson | .30 | .10 |
| ❑ 51 Ricky Watters | .30 | .10 |
| ❑ 52 Eddie George | .50 | .20 |
| ❑ 53 Derrick Mason | .30 | .10 |
| ❑ 54 Steve McNair | .50 | .20 |
| ❑ 55 David Boston | .30 | .10 |
| ❑ 56 Jake Plummer | .30 | .10 |
| ❑ 57 Chris Chandler | .30 | .10 |
| ❑ 58 Jamal Anderson | .30 | .10 |
| ❑ 59 Michael Vick | 1.00 | .40 |
| ❑ 60 Wesley Walls | .20 | .07 |
| ❑ 61 Chris Weinke | .30 | .10 |
| ❑ 62 David Terrell | .50 | .20 |
| ❑ 63 Anthony Thomas | .30 | .10 |
| ❑ 64 Brian Urlacher | .75 | .30 |
| ❑ 65 Quincy Carter | .30 | .10 |
| ❑ 66 Rocket Ismail | .30 | .10 |
| ❑ 67 Emmitt Smith | 1.25 | .50 |
| ❑ 68 James Stewart | .30 | .10 |
| ❑ 69 Germane Crowell | .20 | .07 |
| ❑ 70 Mike McMahon | .50 | .20 |
| ❑ 71 Brett Favre | 1.25 | .50 |
| ❑ 72 Ahman Green | .50 | .20 |
| ❑ 73 Antonio Freeman | .50 | .20 |
| ❑ 74 Marcus Robinson | .30 | .10 |
| ❑ 75 Cris Carter | .50 | .20 |

|  |  | | |
|---|--------|---|---|
| ❏ 76 | Daunte Culpepper | .50 | .20 |
| ❏ 77 | Randy Moss | 1.00 | .40 |
| ❏ 78 | Aaron Brooks | .50 | .20 |
| ❏ 79 | Deuce McAllister | .60 | .25 |
| ❏ 80 | Ricky Williams | .50 | .20 |
| ❏ 81 | Kerry Collins | .30 | .10 |
| ❏ 82 | Ron Dayne | .30 | .10 |
| ❏ 83 | Amani Toomer | .30 | .10 |
| ❏ 84 | Correll Buckhalter | .30 | .10 |
| ❏ 85 | James Thrash | .30 | .10 |
| ❏ 86 | Freddie Mitchell | .30 | .10 |
| ❏ 87 | Duce Staley | .50 | .20 |
| ❏ 88 | Jeff Garcia | .50 | .20 |
| ❏ 89 | Garrison Hearst | .50 | .20 |
| ❏ 90 | Terrell Owens | .50 | .20 |
| ❏ 91 | Isaac Bruce | .50 | .20 |
| ❏ 92 | Marshall Faulk | .50 | .20 |
| ❏ 93 | Torry Holt | .50 | .20 |
| ❏ 94 | Kurt Warner | .50 | .20 |
| ❏ 95 | Mike Alstott | .50 | .20 |
| ❏ 96 | Brad Johnson | .30 | .10 |
| ❏ 97 | Keyshawn Johnson | .50 | .20 |
| ❏ 98 | Stephen Davis | .30 | .10 |
| ❏ 99 | Rod Gardner | .30 | .10 |
| ❏ 100 | Tony Banks | .20 | .07 |
| ❏ 101 | David Carr RC | 15.00 | 6.00 |
| ❏ 102 | Joey Harrington RC | 20.00 | 7.50 |
| ❏ 103 | Rohan Davey RC | 15.00 | 6.00 |
| ❏ 104 | Chad Hutchinson RC | 12.00 | 5.00 |
| ❏ 105 | Patrick Ramsey RC | 12.00 | 5.00 |
| ❏ 106 | Kurt Kittner RC | 12.00 | 5.00 |
| ❏ 107 | Eric Crouch RC | 15.00 | 6.00 |
| ❏ 108 | David Garrard RC | 30.00 | 15.00 |
| ❏ 109 | Ronald Curry RC | 15.00 | 6.00 |
| ❏ 110 | Zak Kustok RC | 15.00 | 6.00 |
| ❏ 111 | Woody Dantzler RC | 12.00 | 5.00 |
| ❏ 112 | Wes Pate RC | 6.00 | 2.50 |
| ❏ 113 | Brian Westbrook RC | 30.00 | 12.50 |
| ❏ 114 | Josh McCown RC | 20.00 | 7.50 |
| ❏ 115 | Travis Stephens RC | 12.00 | 5.00 |
| ❏ 116 | Luke Staley RC | 12.00 | 5.00 |
| ❏ 117 | William Green RC | 15.00 | 6.00 |
| ❏ 118 | Clinton Portis RC | 50.00 | 20.00 |
| ❏ 119 | DeShaun Foster RC | 15.00 | 6.00 |
| ❏ 120 | Verron Haynes RC | 15.00 | 6.00 |
| ❏ 121 | T.J. Duckett RC | 15.00 | 6.00 |
| ❏ 122 | Antwoine Womack RC | 12.00 | 5.00 |
| ❏ 123 | Leonard Henry RC | 12.00 | 5.00 |
| ❏ 124 | Lamar Gordon RC | 15.00 | 6.00 |
| ❏ 125 | Adrian Peterson RC | 20.00 | 7.50 |
| ❏ 126 | Chester Taylor RC | 30.00 | 12.50 |
| ❏ 127 | Damien Anderson RC | 12.00 | 5.00 |
| ❏ 128 | Maurice Morris RC | 15.00 | 6.00 |
| ❏ 129 | Ricky Williams RC | 12.00 | 5.00 |
| ❏ 130 | Terry Charles RC | 12.00 | 5.00 |
| ❏ 131 | Demontray Carter RC | 6.00 | 2.50 |
| ❏ 132 | Jason McAddley RC | 12.00 | 5.00 |
| ❏ 133 | Ladell Betts RC | 15.00 | 6.00 |
| ❏ 134 | Cortlen Johnson RC | 6.00 | 2.50 |
| ❏ 135 | James Mungro RC | 15.00 | 6.00 |
| ❏ 136 | Atrews Bell RC | 6.00 | 2.50 |
| ❏ 137 | Josh Scobey RC | 15.00 | 6.00 |
| ❏ 138 | Justin Peelle RC | 6.00 | 2.50 |
| ❏ 139 | Najeh Davenport RC | 15.00 | 6.00 |
| ❏ 140 | Josh Reed RC | 15.00 | 6.00 |
| ❏ 141 | Marquise Walker RC | 12.00 | 5.00 |
| ❏ 142 | Jabar Gaffney RC | 15.00 | 6.00 |
| ❏ 143 | Antwaan Randle El RC | 20.00 | 7.50 |
| ❏ 144 | Ashley Lelie RC | 30.00 | 12.50 |
| ❏ 145 | Tavon Mason RC | 6.00 | 2.50 |
| ❏ 146 | Antonio Bryant RC | 15.00 | 6.00 |
| ❏ 147 | Javon Walker RC | 25.00 | 10.00 |
| ❏ 148 | Kelly Campbell RC | 12.00 | 5.00 |
| ❏ 149 | Ron Johnson RC | 12.00 | 5.00 |
| ❏ 150 | Andre Davis RC | 12.00 | 5.00 |
| ❏ 151 | Cliff Russell RC | 12.00 | 5.00 |
| ❏ 152 | Reche Caldwell RC | 15.00 | 6.00 |
| ❏ 153 | Kyle Johnson RC | 6.00 | 2.50 |
| ❏ 154 | Freddie Milons RC | 12.00 | 5.00 |
| ❏ 155 | Brian Poli-Dixon RC | 12.00 | 5.00 |
| ❏ 156 | David Thornton RC | 6.00 | 2.50 |
| ❏ 157 | Bryan Thomas RC | 12.00 | 5.00 |
| ❏ 158 | Kahlil Hill RC | 12.00 | 5.00 |
| ❏ 159 | Deion Branch RC | 25.00 | 10.00 |
| ❏ 160 | Akin Ayodele RC | 6.00 | 2.50 |
| ❏ 161 | Donte Stallworth RC | 25.00 | 10.00 |
| ❏ 162 | Tim Carter RC | 12.00 | 5.00 |
| ❏ 163 | Kenyon Coleman RC | 6.00 | 2.50 |
| ❏ 164 | Jeremy Shockey RC | 20.00 | 8.00 |
| ❏ 165 | Eddie Freeman RC | 6.00 | 2.50 |
| ❏ 166 | Tracey Wistrom RC | 12.00 | 5.00 |
| ❏ 167 | Daniel Graham RC | 15.00 | 6.00 |
| ❏ 168 | Julius Peppers RC | 30.00 | 12.50 |
| ❏ 169 | Alex Brown RC | 15.00 | 6.00 |
| ❏ 170 | Dwight Freeney RC | 25.00 | 10.00 |
| ❏ 171 | Kalimba Edwards RC | 15.00 | 6.00 |
| ❏ 172 | Dennis Johnson RC | 6.00 | 2.50 |
| ❏ 173 | Travis Fisher RC | 15.00 | 6.00 |
| ❏ 174 | John Henderson RC | 15.00 | 6.00 |
| ❏ 175 | Anthony Weaver RC | 12.00 | 5.00 |
| ❏ 176 | Ryan Sims RC | 15.00 | 6.00 |
| ❏ 177 | Alan Harper RC | 6.00 | 2.50 |
| ❏ 178 | Larry Tripplett RC | 6.00 | 2.50 |
| ❏ 179 | Wendell Bryant RC | 6.00 | 2.50 |
| ❏ 180 | Albert Haynesworth RC | 15.00 | 6.00 |
| ❏ 181 | Levar Fisher RC | 6.00 | 2.50 |
| ❏ 182 | Andra Davis RC | 12.00 | 5.00 |
| ❏ 183 | Joseph Jefferson RC | 12.00 | 5.00 |
| ❏ 184 | Lamont Thompson RC | 12.00 | 5.00 |
| ❏ 185 | Robert Thomas RC | 15.00 | 6.00 |
| ❏ 186 | Michael Lewis RC | 15.00 | 6.00 |
| ❏ 187 | Rocky Calmus RC | 15.00 | 6.00 |
| ❏ 188 | Napoleon Harris RC | 15.00 | 6.00 |
| ❏ 189 | Lito Sheppard RC | 15.00 | 6.00 |
| ❏ 190 | Quentin Jammer RC | 15.00 | 6.00 |
| ❏ 191 | Roy Williams RC | 30.00 | 12.50 |
| ❏ 192 | Marques Anderson RC | 15.00 | 6.00 |
| ❏ 193 | Chris Hope RC | 15.00 | 6.00 |
| ❏ 194 | Raonall Smith RC | 12.00 | 5.00 |
| ❏ 195 | Mike Rumph RC | 15.00 | 6.00 |
| ❏ 196 | James Allen RC | 6.00 | 2.50 |
| ❏ 197 | Ed Reed RC | 30.00 | 15.00 |
| ❏ 198 | Mike Williams RC | 15.00 | 6.00 |
| ❏ 199 | Phillip Buchanon RC | 15.00 | 6.00 |
| ❏ 200 | Bryant McKinnie RC | 12.00 | 5.00 |

## 2004 Donruss Elite

|  |  | | |
|---|--------|---|---|
| ❏ COMP.SET w/o SP's (100) | | 20.00 | 7.50 |
| ❏ ROOKIE PRINT RUN 500 SER.#'d SETS | | | |
| ❏ 1 | Emmitt Smith | 2.00 | .75 |
| ❏ 2 | Anquan Boldin | 1.00 | .40 |
| ❏ 3 | Michael Vick | 1.00 | .40 |
| ❏ 4 | Peerless Price | .75 | .30 |
| ❏ 5 | T.J. Duckett | .75 | .30 |
| ❏ 6 | Warrick Dunn | .75 | .30 |
| ❏ 7 | Jamal Lewis | .75 | .30 |
| ❏ 8 | Kyle Boller | .75 | .30 |
| ❏ 9 | Todd Heap | .75 | .30 |
| ❏ 10 | Ray Lewis | 1.00 | .40 |
| ❏ 11 | Drew Bledsoe | .75 | .40 |
| ❏ 12 | Eric Moulds | .75 | .30 |
| ❏ 13 | Travis Henry | .75 | .30 |
| ❏ 14 | Jake Delhomme | .75 | .30 |
| ❏ 15 | Stephen Davis | .75 | .30 |
| ❏ 16 | Steve Smith | 1.00 | .40 |
| ❏ 17 | Anthony Thomas | .75 | .30 |
| ❏ 18 | Brian Urlacher | 1.00 | .40 |
| ❏ 19 | Rex Grossman | .75 | .30 |
| ❏ 20 | Chad Johnson | .75 | .30 |
| ❏ 21 | Carson Palmer | 1.25 | .50 |
| ❏ 22 | Rudi Johnson | .75 | .30 |
| ❏ 23 | Peter Warrick | .75 | .30 |
| ❏ 24 | Andre Davis | .60 | .25 |
| ❏ 25 | Tim Couch | .75 | .30 |
| ❏ 26 | Quincy Carter | .60 | .25 |
| ❏ 27 | Roy Williams S | .75 | .30 |
| ❏ 28 | Terrence Newman | .75 | .30 |
| ❏ 29 | Clinton Portis | 1.00 | .40 |
| ❏ 30 | Jake Plummer | .75 | .30 |
| ❏ 31 | Rod Smith | .75 | .30 |
| ❏ 32 | Charles Rogers | .75 | .30 |
| ❏ 33 | Joey Harrington | .75 | .30 |
| ❏ 34 | Ahman Green | 1.00 | .40 |
| ❏ 35 | Brett Favre | 2.50 | 1.00 |
| ❏ 36 | Javon Walker | .75 | .30 |
| ❏ 37 | Andre Johnson | 1.00 | .40 |
| ❏ 38 | David Carr | .75 | .30 |
| ❏ 39 | Domanick Davis | 1.00 | .40 |
| ❏ 40 | Edgerrin James | 1.00 | .40 |
| ❏ 41 | Marvin Harrison | 1.00 | .40 |
| ❏ 42 | Peyton Manning | 2.00 | .75 |
| ❏ 43 | Reggie Wayne | .75 | .30 |
| ❏ 44 | Byron Leftwich | 1.00 | .40 |
| ❏ 45 | Fred Taylor | 1.00 | .40 |
| ❏ 46 | Jimmy Smith | .75 | .30 |
| ❏ 47 | Priest Holmes | 1.00 | .40 |
| ❏ 48 | Tony Gonzalez | 1.00 | .40 |
| ❏ 49 | Trent Green | .75 | .30 |
| ❏ 50 | Chris Chambers | .75 | .30 |
| ❏ 51 | Ricky Williams | 1.00 | .40 |
| ❏ 52 | Zach Thomas | 1.00 | .40 |
| ❏ 53 | Daunte Culpepper | 1.00 | .40 |
| ❏ 54 | Michael Bennett | .75 | .30 |
| ❏ 55 | Moe Williams | .60 | .25 |
| ❏ 56 | Randy Moss | 1.25 | .50 |
| ❏ 57 | Deion Branch | .75 | .30 |
| ❏ 58 | Tom Brady | 2.50 | 1.00 |
| ❏ 59 | Tedy Bruschi | 1.00 | .40 |
| ❏ 60 | Aaron Brooks | .75 | .30 |
| ❏ 61 | Deuce McAllister | .75 | .30 |
| ❏ 62 | Joe Horn | .75 | .30 |
| ❏ 63 | Jeremy Shockey | .75 | .30 |
| ❏ 64 | Kerry Collins | .75 | .30 |
| ❏ 65 | Michael Strahan | .75 | .30 |
| ❏ 66 | Tiki Barber | 1.00 | .40 |
| ❏ 67 | Chad Pennington | 1.00 | .40 |
| ❏ 68 | Curtis Martin | 1.00 | .40 |
| ❏ 69 | Santana Moss | .75 | .30 |
| ❏ 70 | Jerry Porter | .75 | .30 |
| ❏ 71 | Jerry Rice | 2.00 | .75 |
| ❏ 72 | Tim Brown | 1.00 | .40 |
| ❏ 73 | Brian Westbrook | 1.00 | .40 |
| ❏ 74 | Correll Buckhalter | .75 | .30 |
| ❏ 75 | Donovan McNabb | 1.25 | .50 |
| ❏ 76 | Hines Ward | 1.00 | .40 |
| ❏ 77 | Kendrell Bell | .60 | .25 |
| ❏ 78 | Plaxico Burress | .75 | .30 |
| ❏ 79 | David Boston | .60 | .25 |
| ❏ 80 | Drew Brees | 1.00 | .40 |
| ❏ 81 | LaDainian Tomlinson | 1.50 | .60 |
| ❏ 82 | Jeff Garcia | 1.00 | .40 |
| ❏ 83 | Kevan Barlow | .75 | .30 |
| ❏ 84 | Terrell Owens | 1.00 | .40 |
| ❏ 85 | Koren Robinson | 1.00 | .40 |
| ❏ 86 | Matt Hasselbeck | 1.00 | .40 |
| ❏ 87 | Shaun Alexander | 1.00 | .40 |
| ❏ 88 | Isaac Bruce | .75 | .30 |
| ❏ 89 | Marc Bulger | .75 | .30 |
| ❏ 90 | Marshall Faulk | 1.00 | .40 |
| ❏ 91 | Torry Holt | 1.00 | .40 |
| ❏ 92 | Brad Johnson | .75 | .30 |
| ❏ 93 | Derrick Brooks | .75 | .30 |
| ❏ 94 | Keenan McCardell | .60 | .25 |
| ❏ 95 | Derrick Mason | .75 | .30 |
| ❏ 96 | Eddie George | .75 | .30 |
| ❏ 97 | Steve McNair | 1.00 | .40 |
| ❏ 98 | Jevon Kearse | .75 | .30 |
| ❏ 99 | Laveranues Coles | .75 | .30 |
| ❏ 100 | Patrick Ramsey | .75 | .30 |
| ❏ 101 | Adimchinobe Echemandu RC | 6.00 | 2.50 |
| ❏ 102 | Ahmad Carroll RC | 8.00 | 3.00 |
| ❏ 103 | Antwan Odom RC | 6.00 | 2.50 |
| ❏ 104 | B.J. Johnson RC | 5.00 | 2.00 |
| ❏ 105 | Ben Roethlisberger RC | 60.00 | 25.00 |
| ❏ 106 | Ben Troupe RC | 6.00 | 2.50 |
| ❏ 107 | Ben Watson RC | 8.00 | 3.00 |

|  |  | | |
|---|---|---|---|
| ❑ 108 | Bernard Berrian RC | 8.00 | 3.00 |
| ❑ 109 | Bob Sanders RC | 20.00 | 8.00 |
| ❑ 110 | Brandon Everage RC | 5.00 | 2.00 |
| ❑ 111 | Brandon Miree RC | 5.00 | 2.00 |
| ❑ 112 | Carlos Francis RC | 5.00 | 2.00 |
| ❑ 113 | Cedric Cobbs RC | 6.00 | 2.50 |
| ❑ 114 | Chad Lavalais RC | 5.00 | 2.00 |
| ❑ 115 | Chris Collins RC | 5.00 | 2.00 |
| ❑ 116 | Chris Gamble RC | 6.00 | 2.50 |
| ❑ 117 | Chris Perry RC | 8.00 | 3.00 |
| ❑ 118 | Cody Pickett RC | 6.00 | 2.50 |
| ❑ 119 | Craig Krenzel RC | 8.00 | 3.00 |
| ❑ 120 | D.J. Hackett RC | 8.00 | 3.00 |
| ❑ 121 | D.J. Williams RC | 6.00 | 2.50 |
| ❑ 122 | Darius Watts RC | 6.00 | 2.50 |
| ❑ 123 | Darnell Dockett RC | 5.00 | 2.00 |
| ❑ 124 | DeAngelo Hall RC | 8.00 | 3.00 |
| ❑ 125 | Derek Abney RC | 5.00 | 2.00 |
| ❑ 126 | Derrick Hamilton RC | 5.00 | 2.00 |
| ❑ 127 | Derrick Strait RC | 6.00 | 2.50 |
| ❑ 128 | Devard Darling RC | 6.00 | 2.50 |
| ❑ 129 | Devery Henderson RC | 8.00 | 3.00 |
| ❑ 130 | Dontarrious Thomas RC | 6.00 | 2.50 |
| ❑ 131 | Drew Henson RC | 5.00 | 2.00 |
| ❑ 132 | Dunta Robinson RC | 6.00 | 2.50 |
| ❑ 133 | Dwan Edwards RC | 5.00 | 2.00 |
| ❑ 134 | Eli Manning RC | 50.00 | 20.00 |
| ❑ 135 | Ernest Wilford RC | 8.00 | 3.00 |
| ❑ 136 | Fred Russell RC | 6.00 | 2.50 |
| ❑ 137 | Greg Jones RC | 8.00 | 3.00 |
| ❑ 138 | Igor Olshansky RC | 8.00 | 3.00 |
| ❑ 139 | J.P. Losman RC | 10.00 | 4.00 |
| ❑ 140 | Jared Lorenzen RC | 6.00 | 2.50 |
| ❑ 141 | Jarrett Payton RC | 6.00 | 2.50 |
| ❑ 142 | Jason Babin RC | 6.00 | 2.50 |
| ❑ 143 | Jason Fife RC | 5.00 | 2.00 |
| ❑ 144 | Jeff Smoker RC | 6.00 | 2.50 |
| ❑ 145 | Jeremy LeSueur RC | 5.00 | 2.00 |
| ❑ 146 | Jerricho Cotchery RC | 8.00 | 3.00 |
| ❑ 147 | John Navarre RC | 6.00 | 2.50 |
| ❑ 148 | John Standeford RC | 5.00 | 2.00 |
| ❑ 149 | Johnnie Morant RC | 5.00 | 2.00 |
| ❑ 150 | Jonathan Vilma RC | 8.00 | 3.00 |
| ❑ 151 | Josh Davis RC | 6.00 | 2.50 |
| ❑ 152 | Josh Harris RC | 5.00 | 2.00 |
| ❑ 153 | Julius Jones RC | 20.00 | 8.00 |
| ❑ 154 | Justin Jenkins RC | 5.00 | 2.00 |
| ❑ 155 | Karlos Dansby RC | 5.00 | 2.00 |
| ❑ 156 | Keary Colbert RC | 8.00 | 3.00 |
| ❑ 157 | Keith Smith RC | 5.00 | 2.00 |
| ❑ 158 | Keiwan Ratliff RC | 5.00 | 2.00 |
| ❑ 159 | Kellen Winslow RC | 15.00 | 6.00 |
| ❑ 160 | Kendrick Starling RC | 5.00 | 2.00 |
| ❑ 161 | Kenechi Udeze RC | 8.00 | 3.00 |
| ❑ 162 | Kevin Jones RC | 8.00 | 3.00 |
| ❑ 163 | Larry Fitzgerald RC | 25.00 | 10.00 |
| ❑ 164 | Lee Evans RC | 10.00 | 4.00 |
| ❑ 165 | Luke McCown RC | 8.00 | 3.00 |
| ❑ 166 | Marquise Hill RC | 5.00 | 2.00 |
| ❑ 167 | Matt Schaub RC | 25.00 | 10.00 |
| ❑ 168 | Matt Ware RC | 8.00 | 3.00 |
| ❑ 169 | Matt Mauck RC | 6.00 | 2.50 |
| ❑ 170 | Maurice Mann RC | 5.00 | 2.00 |
| ❑ 171 | Mewelde Moore RC | 8.00 | 3.00 |
| ❑ 172 | Michael Boulware RC | 8.00 | 3.00 |
| ❑ 173 | Michael Clayton RC | 8.00 | 3.00 |
| ❑ 174 | Michael Jenkins RC | 8.00 | 3.00 |
| ❑ 175 | Michael Turner RC | 15.00 | 6.00 |
| ❑ 176 | B.J. Symons RC | 8.00 | 3.00 |
| ❑ 177 | Nathan Vasher RC | 8.00 | 3.00 |
| ❑ 178 | P.K. Sam RC | 5.00 | 2.00 |
| ❑ 179 | Philip Rivers RC | 25.00 | 10.00 |
| ❑ 180 | Quincy Wilson RC | 6.00 | 2.50 |
| ❑ 181 | Ran Carthon RC | 5.00 | 2.00 |
| ❑ 182 | Randy Starks RC | 5.00 | 2.00 |
| ❑ 183 | Rashaun Woods RC | 5.00 | 2.00 |
| ❑ 184 | Reggie Williams RC | 8.00 | 3.00 |
| ❑ 185 | Ricardo Colclough RC | 8.00 | 3.00 |
| ❑ 186 | Robert Kent RC | 5.00 | 2.00 |
| ❑ 187 | Roy Williams RC | 20.00 | 8.00 |
| ❑ 188 | Samie Parker RC | 5.00 | 2.00 |
| ❑ 189 | Scott Rislov RC | 5.00 | 2.00 |
| ❑ 190 | Sean Jones RC | 8.00 | 3.00 |
| ❑ 191 | Sean Taylor RC | 8.00 | 3.00 |
| ❑ 192 | Steven Jackson RC | 25.00 | 10.00 |
| ❑ 193 | Stuart Schweigert RC | 6.00 | 2.50 |
| ❑ 194 | Tatum Bell RC | 8.00 | 3.00 |
| ❑ 195 | Teddy Lehman RC | 6.00 | 2.50 |
| ❑ 196 | Tommie Harris RC | 8.00 | 3.00 |
| ❑ 197 | Troy Fleming RC | 5.00 | 2.00 |
| ❑ 198 | Vince Wilfork RC | 8.00 | 3.00 |
| ❑ 199 | Will Poole RC | 8.00 | 3.00 |
| ❑ 200 | Will Smith RC | 6.00 | 2.50 |

## 2005 Donruss Elite

|  |  | | |
|---|---|---|---|
| ❑ | COMP.SET w/o SP's (100) | 20.00 | 7.50 |
| ❑ | 101-200 PRINT RUN 499 SER.#d SETS | | |
| ❑ 1 | Kurt Warner | 1.00 | .40 |
| ❑ 2 | Larry Fitzgerald | 1.00 | .40 |
| ❑ 3 | Anquan Boldin | .75 | .30 |
| ❑ 4 | Emmitt Smith | 2.00 | .75 |
| ❑ 5 | Michael Vick | 1.00 | .40 |
| ❑ 6 | Warrick Dunn | .75 | .30 |
| ❑ 7 | Alge Crumpler | .75 | .30 |
| ❑ 8 | Jamal Lewis | .75 | .30 |
| ❑ 9 | Kyle Boller | .75 | .30 |
| ❑ 10 | Ray Lewis | 1.00 | .40 |
| ❑ 11 | Drew Bledsoe | 1.00 | .40 |
| ❑ 12 | Willis McGahee | 1.00 | .40 |
| ❑ 13 | Travis Henry | .75 | .30 |
| ❑ 14 | Eric Moulds | .75 | .30 |
| ❑ 15 | Rex Grossman | 1.00 | .40 |
| ❑ 16 | Brian Urlacher | 1.00 | .40 |
| ❑ 17 | Thomas Jones | 1.00 | .40 |
| ❑ 18 | Carson Palmer | 1.00 | .40 |
| ❑ 19 | Rudi Johnson | .75 | .30 |
| ❑ 20 | Chad Johnson | 1.00 | .40 |
| ❑ 21 | J.P. Losman | .75 | .30 |
| ❑ 22 | Lee Suggs | .75 | .30 |
| ❑ 23 | Antonio Bryant | .60 | .25 |
| ❑ 24 | Julius Jones | 1.00 | .40 |
| ❑ 25 | Roy Williams S | .75 | .30 |
| ❑ 26 | Keyshawn Johnson | .75 | .30 |
| ❑ 27 | Jake Plummer | .75 | .30 |
| ❑ 28 | Tatum Bell | .75 | .30 |
| ❑ 29 | Rod Smith | .75 | .30 |
| ❑ 30 | Joey Harrington | 1.00 | .40 |
| ❑ 31 | Kevin Jones | .75 | .30 |
| ❑ 32 | Roy Williams WR | 1.00 | .40 |
| ❑ 33 | Brett Favre | 2.50 | 1.00 |
| ❑ 34 | Ahman Green | 1.00 | .40 |
| ❑ 35 | Javon Walker | .75 | .30 |
| ❑ 36 | David Carr | .75 | .30 |
| ❑ 37 | Andre Johnson | .75 | .30 |
| ❑ 38 | Domanick Davis | .60 | .25 |
| ❑ 39 | Peyton Manning | 1.50 | .60 |
| ❑ 40 | Edgerrin James | .75 | .30 |
| ❑ 41 | Brandon Stokley | .60 | .25 |
| ❑ 42 | Reggie Wayne | .75 | .30 |
| ❑ 43 | Marvin Harrison | 1.00 | .40 |
| ❑ 44 | Byron Leftwich | .75 | .30 |
| ❑ 45 | Jimmy Smith | .75 | .30 |
| ❑ 46 | Fred Taylor | 1.00 | .40 |
| ❑ 47 | Trent Green | .75 | .30 |
| ❑ 48 | Priest Holmes | 1.00 | .40 |
| ❑ 49 | Tony Gonzalez | .75 | .30 |
| ❑ 50 | A.J. Feeley | .60 | .25 |
| ❑ 51 | Chris Chambers | .75 | .30 |
| ❑ 52 | Daunte Culpepper | 1.00 | .40 |
| ❑ 53 | Randy Moss | 1.00 | .40 |
| ❑ 54 | Onterrio Smith | .60 | .25 |
| ❑ 55 | Corey Dillon | .75 | .30 |
| ❑ 56 | Tom Brady | 2.00 | .75 |
| ❑ 57 | David Givens | .75 | .30 |
| ❑ 58 | Aaron Brooks | .60 | .25 |
| ❑ 59 | Deuce McAllister | 1.00 | .40 |
| ❑ 60 | Joe Horn | .75 | .30 |
| ❑ 61 | Eli Manning | 2.00 | .75 |
| ❑ 62 | Tiki Barber | 1.00 | .40 |
| ❑ 63 | Jeremy Shockey | 1.00 | .40 |
| ❑ 64 | Chad Pennington | 1.00 | .40 |
| ❑ 65 | Curtis Martin | 1.00 | .40 |
| ❑ 66 | Santana Moss | .75 | .30 |
| ❑ 67 | Kerry Collins | .75 | .30 |
| ❑ 68 | Jerry Porter | .75 | .30 |
| ❑ 69 | Donovan McNabb | 1.00 | .40 |
| ❑ 70 | Terrell Owens | 1.00 | .40 |
| ❑ 71 | Brian Westbrook | 1.00 | .40 |
| ❑ 72 | Ben Roethlisberger | 2.50 | 1.00 |
| ❑ 73 | Plaxico Burress | .75 | .30 |
| ❑ 74 | Hines Ward | 1.00 | .40 |
| ❑ 75 | Jerome Bettis | 1.00 | .40 |
| ❑ 76 | Duce Staley | .75 | .30 |
| ❑ 77 | Antonio Gates | 1.00 | .40 |
| ❑ 78 | Drew Brees | 1.00 | .40 |
| ❑ 79 | LaDainian Tomlinson | 1.50 | .60 |
| ❑ 80 | Brandon Lloyd | .60 | .25 |
| ❑ 81 | Kevan Barlow | .60 | .25 |
| ❑ 82 | Matt Hasselbeck | .75 | .30 |
| ❑ 83 | Shaun Alexander | 1.00 | .40 |
| ❑ 84 | Darrell Jackson | .75 | .30 |
| ❑ 85 | Jerry Rice | 2.00 | .75 |
| ❑ 86 | Marc Bulger | .75 | .30 |
| ❑ 87 | Marshall Faulk | 1.00 | .40 |
| ❑ 88 | Steven Jackson | 1.25 | .50 |
| ❑ 89 | Isaac Bruce | .75 | .30 |
| ❑ 90 | Torry Holt | .75 | .30 |
| ❑ 91 | Michael Clayton | .75 | .30 |
| ❑ 92 | Brian Griese | .75 | .30 |
| ❑ 93 | Mike Alstott | .75 | .30 |
| ❑ 94 | Steve McNair | 1.00 | .40 |
| ❑ 95 | Derrick Mason | .75 | .30 |
| ❑ 96 | Chris Brown | .75 | .30 |
| ❑ 97 | Drew Bennett | .75 | .30 |
| ❑ 98 | Patrick Ramsey | .75 | .30 |
| ❑ 99 | Clinton Portis | 1.00 | .40 |
| ❑ 100 | LaVar Arrington | .75 | .30 |
| ❑ 101 | Aaron Rodgers | 30.00 | 12.00 |
| ❑ 102 | Adam Jones RC | 10.00 | 4.00 |
| ❑ 103 | Adrian McPherson RC | 8.00 | 3.00 |
| ❑ 104A | Alex Smith TE ERR RC | 10.00 | 4.00 |
| ❑ 104B | Alex Smith TE COR RC | 10.00 | 4.00 |
| ❑ 105A | Alex Smith QB ERR RC | 15.00 | 6.00 |
| ❑ 105B | Alex Smith QB COR RC | 15.00 | 6.00 |
| ❑ 106 | Alvin Pearman RC | 8.00 | 3.00 |
| ❑ 107 | Andrew Walter RC | 10.00 | 4.00 |
| ❑ 108 | Anthony Davis RC | 8.00 | 3.00 |
| ❑ 109 | Antrel Rolle RC | 10.00 | 4.00 |
| ❑ 110 | Anttaj Hawthorne RC | 8.00 | 3.00 |
| ❑ 111 | Brandon Browner RC | 6.00 | 2.50 |
| ❑ 112 | Brandon Jacobs RC | 12.00 | 5.00 |
| ❑ 113 | Braylon Edwards RC | 30.00 | 12.00 |
| ❑ 114 | Brock Berlin RC | 8.00 | 3.00 |
| ❑ 115 | Brandon Jones RC | 8.00 | 3.00 |
| ❑ 116 | Bryant McFadden RC | 8.00 | 3.00 |
| ❑ 117 | Carlos Rogers RC | 10.00 | 4.00 |
| ❑ 118 | Cadillac Williams RC | 20.00 | 8.00 |
| ❑ 119 | Cedric Benson RC | 10.00 | 4.00 |
| ❑ 120 | Cedric Houston RC | 10.00 | 4.00 |
| ❑ 121 | Channing Crowder RC | 8.00 | 3.00 |
| ❑ 122 | Charles Frederick RC | 10.00 | 4.00 |
| ❑ 123 | Charlie Frye RC | 10.00 | 4.00 |
| ❑ 124 | Chase Lyman RC | 6.00 | 2.50 |
| ❑ 125 | Chris Henry RC | 10.00 | 4.00 |
| ❑ 126 | Chris Rix RC | 8.00 | 3.00 |
| ❑ 127 | Ciatrick Fason RC | 8.00 | 3.00 |
| ❑ 128 | Corey Webster RC | 10.00 | 4.00 |
| ❑ 129 | Courtney Roby RC | 8.00 | 3.00 |
| ❑ 130 | Craig Bragg RC | 6.00 | 2.50 |
| ❑ 131 | Craphonso Thorpe RC | 8.00 | 3.00 |
| ❑ 132 | Damien Nash RC | 8.00 | 3.00 |
| ❑ 133 | Dan Cody RC | 10.00 | 4.00 |
| ❑ 134 | Dan Orlovsky RC | 10.00 | 4.00 |
| ❑ 135 | Dante Ridgeway RC | 6.00 | 2.50 |
| ❑ 136 | Darian Durant RC | 10.00 | 4.00 |
| ❑ 137 | Darren Sproles RC | 12.00 | 5.00 |

|  |  | | |
|---|---|---|---|
| ❑ 138 | Darryl Blackstock RC | 6.00 | 2.50 |
| ❑ 139 | David Greene RC | 8.00 | 3.00 |
| ❑ 140 | David Pollack RC | 8.00 | 3.00 |
| ❑ 141 | DeMarcus Ware RC | 15.00 | 6.00 |
| ❑ 142 | Derek Anderson RC | 15.00 | 6.00 |
| ❑ 143 | Derrick Johnson RC | 10.00 | 4.00 |
| ❑ 144 | Erasmus James RC | 8.00 | 3.00 |
| ❑ 145 | Eric Shelton RC | 8.00 | 3.00 |
| ❑ 146 | Ernest Shazor RC | 8.00 | 3.00 |
| ❑ 147 | Fabian Washington RC | 10.00 | 4.00 |
| ❑ 148 | Frank Gore UER RC | 25.00 | 10.00 |
| ❑ 149 | Fred Amey RC | 8.00 | 3.00 |
| ❑ 150 | Fred Gibson RC | 8.00 | 3.00 |
| ❑ 151 | Maurice Clarett RC | 6.00 | 2.50 |
| ❑ 152 | Gino Guidugli RC | 6.00 | 2.50 |
| ❑ 153 | Heath Miller RC | 20.00 | 8.00 |
| ❑ 154 | J.J. Arrington RC | 10.00 | 4.00 |
| ❑ 155 | J.R. Russell RC | 6.00 | 2.50 |
| ❑ 156 | Jason Campbell RC | 20.00 | 8.00 |
| ❑ 157 | Jason White RC | 10.00 | 4.00 |
| ❑ 158 | Jerome Mathis RC | 10.00 | 4.00 |
| ❑ 159 | Josh Bullocks RC | 10.00 | 4.00 |
| ❑ 160 | Josh Davis RC | 6.00 | 2.50 |
| ❑ 161 | Justin Miller RC | 8.00 | 3.00 |
| ❑ 162 | Justin Tuck RC | 12.00 | 5.00 |
| ❑ 163 | Kay-Jay Harris RC | 8.00 | 3.00 |
| ❑ 164 | Kevin Burnett RC | 8.00 | 3.00 |
| ❑ 165 | Kyle Orton RC | 12.00 | 5.00 |
| ❑ 166 | Larry Brackins RC | 6.00 | 2.50 |
| ❑ 167 | Marcus Spears RC | 10.00 | 4.00 |
| ❑ 168 | Marion Barber RC | 30.00 | 12.00 |
| ❑ 169 | Mark Bradley RC | 10.00 | 4.00 |
| ❑ 170 | Mark Clayton RC | 10.00 | 4.00 |
| ❑ 171 | Marlin Jackson RC | 8.00 | 3.00 |
| ❑ 172 | Matt Jones RC | 15.00 | 6.00 |
| ❑ 173 | Matt Roth RC | 8.00 | 3.00 |
| ❑ 174 | Mike Patterson RC | 8.00 | 3.00 |
| ❑ 175 | Mike Williams RC | 10.00 | 4.00 |
| ❑ 176 | Airese Currie RC | 8.00 | 3.00 |
| ❑ 177 | Reggie Brown RC | 10.00 | 4.00 |
| ❑ 178 | Roddy White RC | 12.00 | 5.00 |
| ❑ 179 | Ronnie Brown RC | 30.00 | 12.00 |
| ❑ 180 | Roscoe Parrish RC | 8.00 | 3.00 |
| ❑ 181 | Roydell Williams RC | 8.00 | 3.00 |
| ❑ 182 | Ryan Fitzpatrick RC | 10.00 | 4.00 |
| ❑ 183 | Rasheed Marshall RC | 8.00 | 3.00 |
| ❑ 184 | Ryan Moats RC | 10.00 | 4.00 |
| ❑ 185 | Shaun Cody RC | 8.00 | 3.00 |
| ❑ 186 | Shawne Merriman RC | 15.00 | 6.00 |
| ❑ 187 | Chad Owens RC | 10.00 | 4.00 |
| ❑ 188 | Stefan LeFors RC | 8.00 | 3.00 |
| ❑ 189 | Steve Savoy RC | 6.00 | 2.50 |
| ❑ 190 | T.A. McLendon RC | 6.00 | 2.50 |
| ❑ 191 | Tab Perry RC | 10.00 | 4.00 |
| ❑ 192 | Taylor Stubblefield RC | 6.00 | 2.50 |
| ❑ 193 | Terrence Murphy RC | 6.00 | 2.50 |
| ❑ 194 | Thomas Davis RC | 8.00 | 3.00 |
| ❑ 195 | Timmy Chang RC | 8.00 | 3.00 |
| ❑ 196 | Travis Johnson RC | 6.00 | 2.50 |
| ❑ 197 | Troy Williamson RC | 10.00 | 4.00 |
| ❑ 198 | Vernand Morency RC | 10.00 | 4.00 |
| ❑ 199 | Vincent Jackson RC | 10.00 | 4.00 |
| ❑ 200 | Walter Reyes RC | 6.00 | 2.50 |

**2006 Donruss Elite**

| | | | |
|---|---|---|---|
| ❑ COMP.SET w/o RC's (100) | | 20.00 | 7.50 |
| ❑ ROOKIE PRINT RUN 599 SER.#'d SETS | | | |

|  |  | | |
|---|---|---|---|
| ❑ 1 | Anquan Boldin | .75 | .30 |
| ❑ 2 | Kurt Warner | .75 | .30 |
| ❑ 3 | Larry Fitzgerald | 1.00 | .40 |
| ❑ 4 | Marcel Shipp | .60 | .25 |
| ❑ 5 | Alge Crumpler | .75 | .30 |
| ❑ 6 | Michael Vick | 1.00 | .40 |
| ❑ 7 | Warrick Dunn | .75 | .30 |
| ❑ 8 | Derrick Mason | .75 | .30 |
| ❑ 9 | Jamal Lewis | .75 | .30 |
| ❑ 10 | Kyle Boller | .75 | .30 |
| ❑ 11 | J.P. Losman | .75 | .30 |
| ❑ 12 | Lee Evans | .75 | .30 |
| ❑ 13 | Willis McGahee | 1.00 | .40 |
| ❑ 14 | Jake Delhomme | .75 | .30 |
| ❑ 15 | Stephen Davis | .75 | .30 |
| ❑ 16 | Steve Smith | 1.00 | .40 |
| ❑ 17 | Cedric Benson | .75 | .30 |
| ❑ 18 | Kyle Orton | .60 | .25 |
| ❑ 19 | Thomas Jones | .75 | .30 |
| ❑ 20 | Carson Palmer | 1.00 | .40 |
| ❑ 21 | Chad Johnson | 1.00 | .40 |
| ❑ 22 | Rudi Johnson | .75 | .30 |
| ❑ 23 | Braylon Edwards | 1.00 | .40 |
| ❑ 24 | Reuben Droughns | .75 | .30 |
| ❑ 25 | Trent Dilfer | .75 | .30 |
| ❑ 26 | Drew Bledsoe | 1.00 | .40 |
| ❑ 27 | Julius Jones | .75 | .30 |
| ❑ 28 | Keyshawn Johnson | .75 | .30 |
| ❑ 29 | Jake Plummer | .75 | .30 |
| ❑ 30 | Rod Smith | .75 | .30 |
| ❑ 31 | Tatum Bell | .75 | .30 |
| ❑ 32 | Joey Harrington | .60 | .25 |
| ❑ 33 | Kevin Jones | 1.00 | .40 |
| ❑ 34 | Roy Williams WR | 1.00 | .40 |
| ❑ 35 | Aaron Rodgers | 1.00 | .40 |
| ❑ 36 | Brett Favre | 2.00 | .75 |
| ❑ 37 | Ahman Green | .75 | .30 |
| ❑ 38 | Andre Johnson | .75 | .30 |
| ❑ 39 | David Carr | .75 | .30 |
| ❑ 40 | Domanick Davis | .75 | .30 |
| ❑ 41 | Edgerrin James | .75 | .30 |
| ❑ 42 | Marvin Harrison | 1.00 | .40 |
| ❑ 43 | Peyton Manning | 1.50 | .60 |
| ❑ 44 | Byron Leftwich | .75 | .30 |
| ❑ 45 | Fred Taylor | .75 | .30 |
| ❑ 46 | Jimmy Smith | .75 | .30 |
| ❑ 47 | Matt Jones | .75 | .30 |
| ❑ 48 | Larry Johnson | .75 | .30 |
| ❑ 49 | Tony Gonzalez | .75 | .30 |
| ❑ 50 | Trent Green | .75 | .30 |
| ❑ 51 | Chris Chambers | .75 | .30 |
| ❑ 52 | Ricky Williams | .60 | .25 |
| ❑ 53 | Ronnie Brown | .75 | .30 |
| ❑ 54 | Randy McMichael | .60 | .25 |
| ❑ 55 | Daunte Culpepper | 1.00 | .40 |
| ❑ 56 | Mewelde Moore | .60 | .25 |
| ❑ 57 | Nate Burleson | .75 | .30 |
| ❑ 58 | Corey Dillon | .75 | .30 |
| ❑ 59 | Deion Branch | .75 | .30 |
| ❑ 60 | Tom Brady | 1.50 | .60 |
| ❑ 61 | Aaron Brooks | .75 | .30 |
| ❑ 62 | Deuce McAllister | .75 | .30 |
| ❑ 63 | Donte Stallworth | .75 | .30 |
| ❑ 64 | Eli Manning | 1.25 | .50 |
| ❑ 65 | Jeremy Shockey | .75 | .30 |
| ❑ 66 | Plaxico Burress | .75 | .30 |
| ❑ 67 | Tiki Barber | 1.00 | .40 |
| ❑ 68 | Chad Pennington | .75 | .30 |
| ❑ 69 | Curtis Martin | 1.00 | .40 |
| ❑ 70 | Laveranues Coles | .75 | .30 |
| ❑ 71 | Kerry Collins | .75 | .30 |
| ❑ 72 | LaMont Jordan | .75 | .30 |
| ❑ 73 | Randy Moss | 1.00 | .40 |
| ❑ 74 | Donovan McNabb | 1.00 | .40 |
| ❑ 75 | Reggie Brown | .75 | .30 |
| ❑ 76 | Brian Westbrook | .75 | .30 |
| ❑ 77 | Ben Roethlisberger | 1.50 | .60 |
| ❑ 78 | Duce Staley | .60 | .25 |
| ❑ 79 | Hines Ward | 1.00 | .40 |
| ❑ 80 | Antonio Gates | 1.00 | .40 |
| ❑ 81 | Drew Brees | 1.00 | .40 |
| ❑ 82 | LaDainian Tomlinson | 1.25 | .50 |
| ❑ 83 | Alex Smith QB | 1.00 | .40 |
| ❑ 84 | Kevan Barlow | .75 | .30 |

|  |  | | |
|---|---|---|---|
| ❑ 85 | Brandon Lloyd | .75 | .30 |
| ❑ 86 | Darrell Jackson | .75 | .30 |
| ❑ 87 | Matt Hasselbeck | .75 | .30 |
| ❑ 88 | Shaun Alexander | 1.00 | .40 |
| ❑ 89 | Marc Bulger | .75 | .30 |
| ❑ 90 | Steven Jackson | 1.00 | .40 |
| ❑ 91 | Torry Holt | .75 | .30 |
| ❑ 92 | Cadillac Williams | 1.00 | .40 |
| ❑ 93 | Joey Galloway | .75 | .30 |
| ❑ 94 | Michael Clayton | .75 | .30 |
| ❑ 95 | Chris Brown | .75 | .30 |
| ❑ 96 | Drew Bennett | .75 | .30 |
| ❑ 97 | Steve McNair | .75 | .30 |
| ❑ 98 | Clinton Portis | 1.00 | .40 |
| ❑ 99 | Mark Brunell | .75 | .30 |
| ❑ 100 | Santana Moss | .75 | .30 |
| ❑ 101 | A.J. Hawk RC | 25.00 | 10.00 |
| ❑ 102 | Abdul Hodge RC | 12.00 | 5.00 |
| ❑ 103 | Adam Jennings RC | 10.00 | 4.00 |
| ❑ 104 | Alan Zemaitis RC | 12.00 | 5.00 |
| ❑ 105 | Andre Hall RC | 12.00 | 5.00 |
| ❑ 106 | Anthony Fasano RC | 12.00 | 5.00 |
| ❑ 107 | Anthony Mix RC | 10.00 | 4.00 |
| ❑ 108 | Ashton Youboty RC | 12.00 | 5.00 |
| ❑ 109 | Miles Austin RC | 12.00 | 5.00 |
| ❑ 110 | Barrick Nealy RC | 10.00 | 4.00 |
| ❑ 111 | Ben Obomanu RC | 10.00 | 4.00 |
| ❑ 112 | Bobby Carpenter RC | 12.00 | 5.00 |
| ❑ 113 | Brad Smith RC | 12.00 | 5.00 |
| ❑ 114 | Brandon Kirsch RC | 10.00 | 4.00 |
| ❑ 115 | Brandon Marshall RC | 15.00 | 6.00 |
| ❑ 116 | Brandon Williams RC | 12.00 | 5.00 |
| ❑ 117 | Brett Elliott RC | 12.00 | 5.00 |
| ❑ 118 | Brian Calhoun RC | 10.00 | 4.00 |
| ❑ 119 | Brodie Croyle RC | 15.00 | 6.00 |
| ❑ 120 | Brodrick Bunkley RC | 12.00 | 5.00 |
| ❑ 121 | Bruce Gradkowski RC | 12.00 | 5.00 |
| ❑ 122 | Cedric Griffin RC | 10.00 | 4.00 |
| ❑ 123 | Cedric Humes RC | 12.00 | 5.00 |
| ❑ 124 | Chad Greenway RC | 12.00 | 5.00 |
| ❑ 125 | Chad Jackson RC | 10.00 | 4.00 |
| ❑ 126 | Charlie Whitehurst RC | 12.00 | 5.00 |
| ❑ 127 | Corey Rodgers RC | 12.00 | 5.00 |
| ❑ 128 | D.J. Shockley RC | 12.00 | 5.00 |
| ❑ 129 | Darnell Bing RC | 12.00 | 5.00 |
| ❑ 130 | Darrell Hackney RC | 10.00 | 4.00 |
| ❑ 131 | David Thomas RC | 12.00 | 5.00 |
| ❑ 132 | D'Brickashaw Ferguson RC | 12.00 | 5.00 |
| ❑ 133 | DeAngelo Williams RC | 20.00 | 8.00 |
| ❑ 134 | De'Arrius Howard RC | 12.00 | 5.00 |
| ❑ 135 | Dee Webb RC | 10.00 | 4.00 |
| ❑ 136 | Delanie Walker RC | 12.00 | 5.00 |
| ❑ 137 | DeMeco Ryans RC | 15.00 | 6.00 |
| ❑ 138 | Demetrius Williams RC | 12.00 | 5.00 |
| ❑ 139 | Derek Hagan RC | 12.00 | 5.00 |
| ❑ 140 | Derrick Ross RC | 10.00 | 4.00 |
| ❑ 141 | Devin Aromashodu RC | 10.00 | 4.00 |
| ❑ 142 | Devin Hester RC | 25.00 | 10.00 |
| ❑ 143 | Dominique Byrd RC | 10.00 | 4.00 |
| ❑ 144 | Donte Whitner RC | 12.00 | 5.00 |
| ❑ 145 | DonTrell Moore RC | 10.00 | 4.00 |
| ❑ 146 | D'Qwell Jackson RC | 10.00 | 4.00 |
| ❑ 147 | Drew Olson RC | 10.00 | 4.00 |
| ❑ 148 | Eric Winston RC | 6.00 | 2.50 |
| ❑ 149 | Erik Meyer RC | 10.00 | 4.00 |
| ❑ 150 | Ernie Sims RC | 12.00 | 5.00 |
| ❑ 151 | Gabe Watson RC | 10.00 | 4.00 |
| ❑ 152 | Gerald Riggs RC | 10.00 | 4.00 |
| ❑ 153 | Ryan Gilbert RC | 10.00 | 4.00 |
| ❑ 154 | Greg Jennings RC | 20.00 | 8.00 |
| ❑ 155 | Greg Lee RC | 10.00 | 4.00 |
| ❑ 156 | Haloti Ngata RC | 12.00 | 5.00 |
| ❑ 157 | Hank Baskett RC | 12.00 | 5.00 |
| ❑ 158 | Ingle Martin RC | 12.00 | 5.00 |
| ❑ 159 | Jason Allen RC | 12.00 | 5.00 |
| ❑ 160 | Jason Avant RC | 12.00 | 5.00 |
| ❑ 161 | Jason Carter RC | 10.00 | 4.00 |
| ❑ 162 | Jay Cutler RC | 50.00 | 20.00 |
| ❑ 163 | Jeff King RC | 10.00 | 4.00 |
| ❑ 164 | Jeff Webb RC | 10.00 | 4.00 |
| ❑ 165 | Jeremy Bloom RC | 10.00 | 4.00 |
| ❑ 166 | Jerious Norwood RC | 15.00 | 6.00 |
| ❑ 167 | Jerome Harrison RC | 12.00 | 5.00 |
| ❑ 168 | Jimmy Williams RC | 12.00 | 5.00 |

| | | |
|---|---|---|
| ☐ 169 Joe Klopfenstein RC | 10.00 | 4.00 |
| ☐ 170 Jon Alston RC | 12.00 | 5.00 |
| ☐ 171 Johnathan Joseph RC | 10.00 | 4.00 |
| ☐ 172 Jonathan Orr RC | 10.00 | 4.00 |
| ☐ 173 Joseph Addai RC | 40.00 | 15.00 |
| ☐ 174 Kai Parham RC | 12.00 | 5.00 |
| ☐ 175 Kamerion Wimbley RC | 12.00 | 5.00 |
| ☐ 176 Kellen Clemens RC | 15.00 | 6.00 |
| ☐ 177 Kelly Jennings RC | 12.00 | 5.00 |
| ☐ 178 Kent Smith RC | 12.00 | 5.00 |
| ☐ 179 Ko Simpson RC | 10.00 | 4.00 |
| ☐ 180 Laurence Maroney RC | 30.00 | 12.00 |
| ☐ 181 Lawrence Vickers RC | 10.00 | 4.00 |
| ☐ 182 LenDale White RC | 25.00 | 10.00 |
| ☐ 183 Leon Washington RC | 12.00 | 5.00 |
| ☐ 184 Leonard Pope RC | 12.00 | 5.00 |
| ☐ 185 Manny Lawson RC | 12.00 | 5.00 |
| ☐ 186 Marcedes Lewis RC | 12.00 | 5.00 |
| ☐ 187 Marcus Vick RC | 10.00 | 4.00 |
| ☐ 188 Mario Williams RC | 20.00 | 8.00 |
| ☐ 189 Marques Colston RC | 30.00 | 12.00 |
| ☐ 190 Martin Nance RC | 10.00 | 4.00 |
| ☐ 191 Mathias Kiwanuka RC | 15.00 | 6.00 |
| ☐ 192 Matt Leinart RC | 40.00 | 15.00 |
| ☐ 193 Maurice Drew RC | 25.00 | 10.00 |
| ☐ 194 Maurice Stovall RC | 12.00 | 5.00 |
| ☐ 195 Michael Huff RC | 12.00 | 5.00 |
| ☐ 196 Michael Robinson RC | 12.00 | 5.00 |
| ☐ 197 Mike Bell RC | 12.00 | 5.00 |
| ☐ 198 Mike Hass RC | 12.00 | 5.00 |
| ☐ 199 Omar Jacobs RC | 10.00 | 4.00 |
| ☐ 200 Owen Daniels RC | 12.00 | 5.00 |
| ☐ 201 P.J. Daniels RC | 10.00 | 4.00 |
| ☐ 202 Paul Pinegar RC | 10.00 | 4.00 |
| ☐ 203 Quinton Ganther RC | 12.00 | 5.00 |
| ☐ 204 Reggie Bush RC | 50.00 | 20.00 |
| ☐ 205 Reggie McNeal RC | 10.00 | 4.00 |
| ☐ 206 Rodrique Wright RC | 6.00 | 2.50 |
| ☐ 207 Santonio Holmes RC | 30.00 | 12.00 |
| ☐ 208 Sinorice Moss RC | 12.00 | 5.00 |
| ☐ 209 Skyler Green RC | 12.00 | 5.00 |
| ☐ 210 Tamba Hali RC | 12.00 | 5.00 |
| ☐ 211 Tarvaris Jackson RC | 12.00 | 5.00 |
| ☐ 212 Taurean Henderson RC | 10.00 | 4.00 |
| ☐ 213 Terrence Whitehead RC | 10.00 | 4.00 |
| ☐ 214 Tim Day RC | 10.00 | 4.00 |
| ☐ 215 Todd Watkins RC | 10.00 | 4.00 |
| ☐ 216 Tony Scheffler RC | 12.00 | 5.00 |
| ☐ 217 Travis Lulay RC | 10.00 | 4.00 |
| ☐ 218 Travis Wilson RC | 12.00 | 5.00 |
| ☐ 219 Tye Hill RC | 12.00 | 5.00 |
| ☐ 220 Vernon Davis RC | 12.00 | 5.00 |
| ☐ 221 Vince Young RC | 40.00 | 15.00 |
| ☐ 222 Wali Lundy RC | 10.00 | 4.00 |
| ☐ 223 Wendell Mathis RC | 10.00 | 4.00 |
| ☐ 224 Willie Reid RC | 12.00 | 5.00 |
| ☐ 225 Winston Justice RC | 12.00 | 5.00 |

## 2007 Donruss Elite

| | | |
|---|---|---|
| ☐ 1 Anquan Boldin | .75 | .30 |
| ☐ 2 Edgerrin James | .75 | .30 |
| ☐ 3 Matt Leinart | 1.00 | .40 |
| ☐ 4 Alge Crumpler | .75 | .30 |
| ☐ 5 Michael Vick | 1.00 | .40 |
| ☐ 6 Jerious Norwood | .75 | .30 |
| ☐ 7 Warrick Dunn | .75 | .30 |
| ☐ 8 Jamal Lewis | .75 | .30 |
| ☐ 9 Mark Clayton | .75 | .30 |

| | | |
|---|---|---|
| ☐ 10 Steve McNair | .75 | .30 |
| ☐ 11 J.P. Losman | .60 | .25 |
| ☐ 12 Lee Evans | .75 | .30 |
| ☐ 13 Willis McGahee | .75 | .30 |
| ☐ 14 DeAngelo Williams | 1.00 | .40 |
| ☐ 15 Jake Delhomme | .75 | .30 |
| ☐ 16 Steve Smith | .75 | .30 |
| ☐ 17 Bernard Berrian | .60 | .25 |
| ☐ 18 Rex Grossman | .75 | .30 |
| ☐ 19 Thomas Jones | .75 | .30 |
| ☐ 20 Carson Palmer | 1.00 | .40 |
| ☐ 21 Chad Johnson | .75 | .30 |
| ☐ 22 Rudi Johnson | .75 | .30 |
| ☐ 23 T.J. Houshmandzadeh | .75 | .30 |
| ☐ 24 Braylon Edwards | .75 | .30 |
| ☐ 25 Charlie Frye | .75 | .30 |
| ☐ 26 Reuben Droughns | .75 | .30 |
| ☐ 27 Julius Jones | .75 | .30 |
| ☐ 28 Terrell Owens | 1.00 | .40 |
| ☐ 29 Tony Romo | 2.00 | .75 |
| ☐ 30 Javon Walker | .75 | .30 |
| ☐ 31 Jay Cutler | 1.00 | .40 |
| ☐ 32 Mike Bell | .75 | .30 |
| ☐ 33 Jon Kitna | .60 | .25 |
| ☐ 34 Kevin Jones | .75 | .30 |
| ☐ 35 Roy Williams WR | .75 | .30 |
| ☐ 36 Brett Favre | 2.00 | .75 |
| ☐ 37 Donald Driver | .75 | .30 |
| ☐ 38 Ahman Green | .75 | .30 |
| ☐ 39 Andre Johnson | .75 | .30 |
| ☐ 40 Matt Schaub | .75 | .30 |
| ☐ 41 Wali Lundy | .60 | .25 |
| ☐ 42 Joseph Addai | 1.00 | .40 |
| ☐ 43 Marvin Harrison | 1.00 | .40 |
| ☐ 44 Peyton Manning | 1.50 | .60 |
| ☐ 45 Reggie Wayne | .75 | .30 |
| ☐ 46 Byron Leftwich | .75 | .30 |
| ☐ 47 Fred Taylor | .75 | .30 |
| ☐ 48 Maurice Jones-Drew | 1.00 | .40 |
| ☐ 49 Larry Johnson | .75 | .30 |
| ☐ 50 Tony Gonzalez | .75 | .30 |
| ☐ 51 Trent Green | .75 | .30 |
| ☐ 52 Chris Chambers | .75 | .30 |
| ☐ 53 Daunte Culpepper | .75 | .30 |
| ☐ 54 Ronnie Brown | .75 | .30 |
| ☐ 55 Chester Taylor | .60 | .25 |
| ☐ 56 Tarvaris Jackson | .75 | .30 |
| ☐ 57 Travis Taylor | .60 | .25 |
| ☐ 58 Tom Brady | 2.00 | .75 |
| ☐ 59 Corey Dillon | .75 | .30 |
| ☐ 60 Laurence Maroney | 1.00 | .40 |
| ☐ 61 Deuce McAllister | .75 | .30 |
| ☐ 62 Drew Brees | .75 | .30 |
| ☐ 63 Marques Colston | 1.00 | .40 |
| ☐ 64 Reggie Bush | 1.25 | .50 |
| ☐ 65 Brandon Jacobs | .75 | .30 |
| ☐ 66 Eli Manning | 1.00 | .40 |
| ☐ 67 Jeremy Shockey | .75 | .30 |
| ☐ 68 Chad Pennington | .75 | .30 |
| ☐ 69 Laveranues Coles | .75 | .30 |
| ☐ 70 Leon Washington | .75 | .30 |
| ☐ 71 Ronald Curry | .75 | .30 |
| ☐ 72 LaMont Jordan | .75 | .30 |
| ☐ 73 Randy Moss | 1.00 | .40 |
| ☐ 74 Brian Westbrook | .75 | .30 |
| ☐ 75 Donovan McNabb | 1.00 | .40 |
| ☐ 76 Reggie Brown | .75 | .30 |
| ☐ 77 Ben Roethlisberger | 1.25 | .50 |
| ☐ 78 Hines Ward | 1.00 | .40 |
| ☐ 79 Willie Parker | 1.00 | .40 |
| ☐ 80 Antonio Gates | .75 | .30 |
| ☐ 81 LaDainian Tomlinson | 1.25 | .50 |
| ☐ 82 Philip Rivers | 1.00 | .40 |
| ☐ 83 Alex Smith QB | 1.00 | .40 |
| ☐ 84 Frank Gore | 1.00 | .40 |
| ☐ 85 Vernon Davis | .75 | .30 |
| ☐ 86 Darrell Jackson | .75 | .30 |
| ☐ 87 Matt Hasselbeck | 1.00 | .40 |
| ☐ 88 Shaun Alexander | 1.00 | .40 |
| ☐ 89 Marc Bulger | .75 | .30 |
| ☐ 90 Steven Jackson | 1.00 | .40 |
| ☐ 91 Torry Holt | .75 | .30 |
| ☐ 92 Chris Simms | .60 | .25 |
| ☐ 93 Cadillac Williams | .75 | .30 |

| | | |
|---|---|---|
| ☐ 94 Joey Galloway | .75 | .30 |
| ☐ 95 Drew Bennett | .60 | .25 |
| ☐ 96 LenDale White | .75 | .30 |
| ☐ 97 Vince Young | 1.00 | .40 |
| ☐ 98 Clinton Portis | .75 | .30 |
| ☐ 99 Jason Campbell | .75 | .30 |
| ☐ 100 Santana Moss | .75 | .30 |
| ☐ 101 A.J. Davis RC | 8.00 | 3.00 |
| ☐ 102 Aaron Ross RC | 12.00 | 5.00 |
| ☐ 103 Aaron Rouse RC | 12.00 | 5.00 |
| ☐ 104 Adam Carriker RC | 10.00 | 4.00 |
| ☐ 105 Adrian Peterson RC | 60.00 | 25.00 |
| ☐ 106 Ahmad Bradshaw RC | 15.00 | 6.00 |
| ☐ 107 Alan Branch RC | 10.00 | 4.00 |
| ☐ 108 Amobi Okoye RC | 12.00 | 5.00 |
| ☐ 109 Anthony Gonzalez RC | 20.00 | 8.00 |
| ☐ 110 Anthony Spencer RC | 12.00 | 5.00 |
| ☐ 111 Antonio Pittman RC | 12.00 | 5.00 |
| ☐ 112 Aundrae Allison RC | 10.00 | 4.00 |
| ☐ 113 Brady Quinn RC | 40.00 | 15.00 |
| ☐ 114 Brandon Jackson RC | 12.00 | 5.00 |
| ☐ 115 Brandon Meriweather RC | 12.00 | 5.00 |
| ☐ 116 Brandon Siler RC | 10.00 | 4.00 |
| ☐ 117 Brian Leonard RC | 12.00 | 5.00 |
| ☐ 118 Calvin Johnson RC | 30.00 | 12.00 |
| ☐ 119 Chansi Stuckey RC | 10.00 | 4.00 |
| ☐ 120 Chris Davis RC | 10.00 | 4.00 |
| ☐ 121 Chris Henry RC | 12.00 | 5.00 |
| ☐ 122 Chris Houston RC | 10.00 | 4.00 |
| ☐ 123 Chris Leak RC | 12.00 | 5.00 |
| ☐ 124 Courtney Taylor RC | 10.00 | 4.00 |
| ☐ 125 Craig Buster Davis RC | 12.00 | 5.00 |
| ☐ 126 Dallas Baker RC | 10.00 | 4.00 |
| ☐ 127 Darius Walker RC | 12.00 | 5.00 |
| ☐ 128 Darrelle Revis RC | 12.00 | 5.00 |
| ☐ 129 David Ball RC | 8.00 | 3.00 |
| ☐ 130 David Clowney RC | 10.00 | 4.00 |
| ☐ 131 David Harris RC | 10.00 | 4.00 |
| ☐ 132 DeShawn Wynn RC | 12.00 | 5.00 |
| ☐ 133 D'Juan Woods RC | 10.00 | 4.00 |
| ☐ 134 Drew Stanton RC | 12.00 | 5.00 |
| ☐ 135 Dwayne Bowe RC | 25.00 | 10.00 |
| ☐ 136 Dwayne Jarrett RC | 12.00 | 5.00 |
| ☐ 137 Dwayne Wright RC | 10.00 | 4.00 |
| ☐ 138 Eric Weddle RC | 10.00 | 4.00 |
| ☐ 139 Gaines Adams RC | 12.00 | 5.00 |
| ☐ 140 Garrett Wolfe RC | 12.00 | 5.00 |
| ☐ 141 Gary Russell RC | 12.00 | 5.00 |
| ☐ 142 Greg Olsen RC | 15.00 | 6.00 |
| ☐ 143 H.B. Blades RC | 10.00 | 4.00 |
| ☐ 144 Isaiah Stanback RC | 12.00 | 5.00 |
| ☐ 145 Jacoby Jones RC | 12.00 | 5.00 |
| ☐ 146 Jamaal Anderson RC | 10.00 | 4.00 |
| ☐ 147 JaMarcus Russell RC | 40.00 | 20.00 |
| ☐ 148 James Jones RC | 12.00 | 5.00 |
| ☐ 149 Jared Zabransky RC | 12.00 | 5.00 |
| ☐ 150 Jarrett Hicks RC | 10.00 | 4.00 |
| ☐ 151 Jarvis Moss RC | 12.00 | 5.00 |
| ☐ 152 Jason Hill RC | 12.00 | 5.00 |
| ☐ 153 Jason Snelling RC | 10.00 | 4.00 |
| ☐ 154 Jeff Rowe RC | 10.00 | 4.00 |
| ☐ 155 Joel Filani RC | 10.00 | 4.00 |
| ☐ 156 John Beck RC | 12.00 | 5.00 |
| ☐ 157 Johnnie Lee Higgins RC | 12.00 | 5.00 |
| ☐ 158 Jon Beason RC | 12.00 | 5.00 |
| ☐ 159 Jon Cornish RC | 10.00 | 4.00 |
| ☐ 160 Jonathan Wade RC | 10.00 | 4.00 |
| ☐ 161 Jordan Kent RC | 12.00 | 5.00 |
| ☐ 162 Jordan Palmer RC | 12.00 | 5.00 |
| ☐ 163 Kenneth Darby RC | 12.00 | 5.00 |
| ☐ 164 Kenny Irons RC | 12.00 | 5.00 |
| ☐ 165 Kevin Kolb RC | 20.00 | 8.00 |
| ☐ 166 Kolby Smith RC | 12.00 | 5.00 |
| ☐ 167 LaRon Landry RC | 15.00 | 6.00 |
| ☐ 168 Laurent Robinson RC | 10.00 | 4.00 |
| ☐ 169 Lawrence Timmons RC | 12.00 | 5.00 |
| ☐ 170 Leon Hall RC | 10.00 | 4.00 |
| ☐ 171 Lorenzo Booker RC | 12.00 | 5.00 |
| ☐ 172 Marshawn Lynch RC | 25.00 | 10.00 |
| ☐ 173 Matt Trannon RC | 10.00 | 4.00 |
| ☐ 174 Michael Bush RC | 12.00 | 5.00 |
| ☐ 175 Michael Griffin RC | 12.00 | 5.00 |
| ☐ 176 Mike Walker RC | 10.00 | 4.00 |
| ☐ 177 Nate Ilaoa RC | 12.00 | 5.00 |

| | | |
|---|---|---|
| ☐ 178 Patrick Willis RC | 25.00 | 10.00 |
| ☐ 179 Paul Posluszny RC | 15.00 | 6.00 |
| ☐ 180 Paul Williams RC | 10.00 | 4.00 |
| ☐ 181 Reggie Nelson RC | 10.00 | 4.00 |
| ☐ 182 Rhema McKnight RC | 10.00 | 4.00 |
| ☐ 183 Robert Meachem RC | 12.00 | 5.00 |
| ☐ 184 Rufus Alexander RC | 12.00 | 5.00 |
| ☐ 185 Ryan Moore RC | 10.00 | 4.00 |
| ☐ 186 Selvin Young RC | 20.00 | 8.00 |
| ☐ 187 Sidney Rice RC | 12.00 | 5.00 |
| ☐ 188 Steve Breaston RC | 12.00 | 5.00 |
| ☐ 189 Steve Smith USC RC | 15.00 | 6.00 |
| ☐ 190 Syvelle Newton RC | 10.00 | 4.00 |
| ☐ 191 DeMarcus Tank Tyler RC | 10.00 | 4.00 |
| ☐ 192 Ted Ginn Jr. RC | 20.00 | 8.00 |
| ☐ 193 Tony Hunt RC | 12.00 | 5.00 |
| ☐ 194 Trent Edwards RC | 30.00 | 12.00 |
| ☐ 195 Troy Smith RC | 15.00 | 6.00 |
| ☐ 196 Tyler Palko RC | 12.00 | 5.00 |
| ☐ 197 Tymere Zimmerman RC | 10.00 | 4.00 |
| ☐ 198 Yamon Figurs RC | 12.00 | 5.00 |
| ☐ 199 Zac Taylor RC | 12.00 | 5.00 |
| ☐ 200 Zach Miller RC | 8.00 | 3.00 |

## 2008 Donruss Elite

| | | |
|---|---|---|
| ☐ 1 Anquan Boldin | .75 | .30 |
| ☐ 2 Edgerrin James | .75 | .30 |
| ☐ 3 Larry Fitzgerald | 1.00 | .40 |
| ☐ 4 Matt Leinart | 1.00 | .40 |
| ☐ 5 Alge Crumpler | .75 | .30 |
| ☐ 6 Warrick Dunn | .75 | .30 |
| ☐ 7 Roddy White | .75 | .30 |
| ☐ 8 Willis McGahee | .75 | .30 |
| ☐ 9 Todd Heap | .60 | .25 |
| ☐ 10 Derrick Mason | .60 | .25 |
| ☐ 11 Marshawn Lynch | 1.00 | .40 |
| ☐ 12 Trent Edwards | .75 | .30 |
| ☐ 13 Lee Evans | .75 | .30 |
| ☐ 14 Steve Smith | .75 | .30 |
| ☐ 15 DeShaun Foster | .75 | .30 |
| ☐ 16 DeAngelo Williams | .75 | .30 |
| ☐ 17 Cedric Benson | .60 | .25 |
| ☐ 18 Bernard Berrian | .75 | .30 |
| ☐ 19 Devin Hester | 1.00 | .40 |
| ☐ 20 Carson Palmer | 1.00 | .40 |
| ☐ 21 T.J. Houshmandzadeh | .75 | .30 |
| ☐ 22 Chad Johnson | .75 | .30 |
| ☐ 23 Jamal Lewis | .75 | .30 |
| ☐ 24 Braylon Edwards | .75 | .30 |
| ☐ 25 Kellen Winslow | .75 | .30 |
| ☐ 26 Tony Romo | 1.50 | .60 |
| ☐ 27 Terrell Owens | 1.00 | .40 |
| ☐ 28 Jason Witten | .75 | .30 |
| ☐ 29 Jay Cutler | 1.00 | .40 |
| ☐ 30 Travis Henry | .75 | .30 |
| ☐ 31 Brandon Marshall | .75 | .30 |
| ☐ 32 Jon Kitna | .75 | .30 |
| ☐ 33 Roy Williams WR | .75 | .30 |
| ☐ 34 Calvin Johnson | 1.00 | .40 |
| ☐ 35 Brett Favre | 2.50 | 1.00 |
| ☐ 36 Greg Jennings | .75 | .30 |
| ☐ 37 Ryan Grant | 1.00 | .40 |
| ☐ 38 Matt Schaub | .75 | .30 |
| ☐ 39 Ahman Green | .75 | .30 |
| ☐ 40 Andre Johnson | 1.00 | .40 |
| ☐ 41 Peyton Manning | 1.50 | .60 |
| ☐ 42 Reggie Wayne | .75 | .30 |
| ☐ 43 Marvin Harrison | 1.00 | .40 |

| | | |
|---|---|---|
| ☐ 44 Joseph Addai | 1.00 | .40 |
| ☐ 45 David Garrard | .75 | .30 |
| ☐ 46 Fred Taylor | .75 | .30 |
| ☐ 47 Reggie Williams | .75 | .30 |
| ☐ 48 Larry Johnson | .75 | .30 |
| ☐ 49 Tony Gonzalez | .75 | .30 |
| ☐ 50 Dwayne Bowe | .75 | .30 |
| ☐ 51 Derek Hagan | .60 | .25 |
| ☐ 52 Ronnie Brown | .75 | .30 |
| ☐ 53 Ted Ginn Jr. | .75 | .30 |
| ☐ 54 Tarvaris Jackson | .75 | .30 |
| ☐ 55 Chester Taylor | .60 | .25 |
| ☐ 56 Adrian Peterson | 2.00 | .75 |
| ☐ 57 Tom Brady | 1.50 | .60 |
| ☐ 58 Laurence Maroney | .75 | .30 |
| ☐ 59 Randy Moss | 1.00 | .40 |
| ☐ 60 Wes Welker | 1.00 | .40 |
| ☐ 61 Drew Brees | 1.00 | .40 |
| ☐ 62 Reggie Bush | 1.00 | .40 |
| ☐ 63 Marques Colston | .75 | .30 |
| ☐ 64 Eli Manning | 1.00 | .40 |
| ☐ 65 Brandon Jacobs | .75 | .30 |
| ☐ 66 Plaxico Burress | .75 | .30 |
| ☐ 67 Thomas Jones | .75 | .30 |
| ☐ 68 Jerricho Cotchery | .60 | .25 |
| ☐ 69 Laveranues Coles | .75 | .30 |
| ☐ 70 JaMarcus Russell | 1.00 | .40 |
| ☐ 71 Justin Fargas | .60 | .25 |
| ☐ 72 Jerry Porter | .75 | .30 |
| ☐ 73 Donovan McNabb | 1.00 | .40 |
| ☐ 74 Brian Westbrook | .75 | .30 |
| ☐ 75 Kevin Curtis | .60 | .25 |
| ☐ 76 Ben Roethlisberger | 1.25 | .50 |
| ☐ 77 Willie Parker | .75 | .30 |
| ☐ 78 Santonio Holmes | .75 | .30 |
| ☐ 79 Hines Ward | 1.00 | .40 |
| ☐ 80 Philip Rivers | 1.00 | .40 |
| ☐ 81 LaDainian Tomlinson | 1.25 | .50 |
| ☐ 82 Antonio Gates | .75 | .30 |
| ☐ 83 Frank Gore | .75 | .30 |
| ☐ 84 Arnaz Battle | .60 | .25 |
| ☐ 85 Vernon Davis | .60 | .25 |
| ☐ 86 Matt Hasselbeck | .75 | .30 |
| ☐ 87 Shaun Alexander | .75 | .30 |
| ☐ 88 Deion Branch | .75 | .30 |
| ☐ 89 Marc Bulger | .75 | .30 |
| ☐ 90 Torry Holt | .75 | .30 |
| ☐ 91 Steven Jackson | 1.00 | .40 |
| ☐ 92 Jeff Garcia | .75 | .30 |
| ☐ 93 Joey Galloway | .75 | .30 |
| ☐ 94 Earnest Graham | .60 | .25 |
| ☐ 95 Vince Young | 1.00 | .40 |
| ☐ 96 LenDale White | .75 | .30 |
| ☐ 97 Roydell Williams | .60 | .25 |
| ☐ 98 Clinton Portis | .75 | .30 |
| ☐ 99 Chris Cooley | .75 | .30 |
| ☐ 100 Santana Moss | .75 | .30 |
| ☐ 101 Matt Ryan AU/199 RC | 150.00 | 75.00 |
| ☐ 102 Brian Brohm AU/199 RC | 50.00 | 20.00 |
| ☐ 103 Chad Henne AU/199 RC | 50.00 | 20.00 |
| ☐ 104 Andre Woodson AU/249 RC | 20.00 | 8.00 |
| ☐ 105 Joe Flacco AU/299 RC | 80.00 | 50.00 |
| ☐ 106 John David Booty/999 RC | 8.00 | 3.00 |
| ☐ 107 Josh Johnson/999 RC | 6.00 | 2.50 |
| ☐ 108 Erik Ainge AU/299 RC | 20.00 | 8.00 |
| ☐ 109 Colt Brennan AU/249 RC | 80.00 | 40.00 |
| ☐ 110 Dennis Dixon AU/299 RC | 20.00 | 8.00 |
| ☐ 111 Kevin O'Connell/999 RC | 8.00 | 3.00 |
| ☐ 112 Matt Flynn/999 RC | 8.00 | 3.00 |
| ☐ 113 Bernard Morris/999 RC | 5.00 | 2.00 |
| ☐ 114 Sam Keller/999 RC | 6.00 | 2.50 |
| ☐ 115 Paul Smith/999 RC | 5.00 | 2.00 |
| ☐ 116 Darren McFadden AU/199 RC | 100.00 | 50.00 |
| ☐ 117 Jonathan Stewart AU/199 RC | 60.00 | 30.00 |
| ☐ 118 Rashard Mendenhall AU/199 RC | 100.00 | 50.00 |
| ☐ 119 Felix Jones AU/199 RC | 100.00 | 50.00 |
| ☐ 120 Chris Johnson/999 RC | 15.00 | 6.00 |
| ☐ 121 Jamaal Charles/999 RC | 8.00 | 3.00 |
| ☐ 122 Ray Rice AU/299 RC | 8.00 | 3.00 |
| ☐ 123 Steve Slaton/999 RC | 12.00 | 5.00 |
| ☐ 124 Mike Hart/999 RC | 8.00 | 3.00 |
| ☐ 125 Matt Forte AU/299 RC | 60.00 | 35.00 |
| ☐ 126 Tashard Choice AU/299 RC | 25.00 | 10.00 |

| | | |
|---|---|---|
| ☐ 127 Kevin Smith/999 RC | 10.00 | 4.00 |
| ☐ 128 Allen Patrick/999 RC | 5.00 | 2.00 |
| ☐ 129 Thomas Brown/999 RC | 6.00 | 2.50 |
| ☐ 130 Justin Forsett AU/299 RC | 20.00 | 8.00 |
| ☐ 131 Cory Boyd AU/299 RC | 15.00 | 6.00 |
| ☐ 132 Dantrell Savage/999 RC | 6.00 | 2.50 |
| ☐ 133 Kalvin McRae/999 RC | 5.00 | 2.00 |
| ☐ 134 Darrell Strong AU/299 RC | 15.00 | 6.00 |
| ☐ 135 Owen Schmidt AU/299 RC | 20.00 | 8.00 |
| ☐ 136 Peyton Hillis AU/299 RC | 30.00 | 15.00 |
| ☐ 137 Jacob Hester AU/299 RC | 20.00 | 8.00 |
| ☐ 138 Fred Davis/999 RC | 6.00 | 2.50 |
| ☐ 139 Martellus Bennett AU/299 RC | 20.00 | 8.00 |
| ☐ 140 John Carlson AU/299 RC | 20.00 | 8.00 |
| ☐ 141 Martin Rucker/999 RC | 5.00 | 2.00 |
| ☐ 142 Brad Cottam AU/299 RC | 20.00 | 8.00 |
| ☐ 143 Jermichael Finley/999 RC | 6.00 | 2.50 |
| ☐ 144 Jacob Tamme/999 RC | 6.00 | 2.50 |
| ☐ 145 Dustin Keller AU/299 RC | 25.00 | 10.00 |
| ☐ 146 Kellen Davis/999 RC | 4.00 | 1.50 |
| ☐ 147 DeSean Jackson AU/249 RC | 40.00 | 20.00 |
| ☐ 148 James Hardy AU/299 RC | 20.00 | 8.00 |
| ☐ 149 Malcolm Kelly AU/249 RC | 20.00 | 8.00 |
| ☐ 150 Early Doucet AU/199 RC | 20.00 | 8.00 |
| ☐ 151 Limas Sweed AU/249 RC | 40.00 | 20.00 |
| ☐ 152 Andre Caldwell AU/299 RC | 15.00 | 6.00 |
| ☐ 153 Mario Manningham AU/299 RC | 20.00 | 8.00 |
| ☐ 154 Devin Thomas AU/299 RC | 20.00 | 8.00 |
| ☐ 155 Donnie Avery AU/299 RC | 25.00 | 10.00 |
| ☐ 156 Earl Bennett AU/299 RC | 20.00 | 8.00 |
| ☐ 157 Eddie Royal AU/249 RC | 40.00 | 15.00 |
| ☐ 158 Lavelle Hawkins AU/299 RC | 15.00 | 6.00 |
| ☐ 159 DJ Hall/999 RC | 6.00 | 2.50 |
| ☐ 160 Adarius Bowman/999 RC | 5.00 | 2.00 |
| ☐ 161 Jordy Nelson AU/249 RC | 30.00 | 15.00 |
| ☐ 162 Harry Douglas/999 RC | 6.00 | 2.50 |
| ☐ 163 Jerome Simpson AU/299 RC | 15.00 | 6.00 |
| ☐ 164 Dorien Bryant/999 RC | 6.00 | 2.50 |
| ☐ 165 Will Franklin/999 RC | 6.00 | 2.50 |
| ☐ 166 Keenan Burton/999 RC | 6.00 | 2.50 |
| ☐ 167 Kevin Robinson/999 RC | 6.00 | 2.50 |
| ☐ 168 Paul Hubbard/999 RC | 15.00 | 6.00 |
| ☐ 169 Davone Bess/999 RC | 8.00 | 3.00 |
| ☐ 170 Adrian Arrington/999 RC | 6.00 | 2.50 |
| ☐ 171 Dexter Jackson AU/299 RC | 20.00 | 8.00 |
| ☐ 172 Ryan Grice-Mullen/999 RC | 6.00 | 2.50 |
| ☐ 173 Darius Reynaud/999 RC | 5.00 | 2.00 |
| ☐ 174 Josh Morgan AU/299 RC | 20.00 | 8.00 |
| ☐ 175 Anthony Alridge/999 RC | 5.00 | 2.00 |
| ☐ 176 Jason Rivers/999 RC | 6.00 | 2.50 |
| ☐ 177 Marcus Smith AU/299 RC | 15.00 | 6.00 |
| ☐ 178 Mark Bradford/999 RC | 5.00 | 2.00 |
| ☐ 179 Marcus Monk AU/299 RC | 20.00 | 8.00 |
| ☐ 180 Chris Long/999 RC | 8.00 | 3.00 |
| ☐ 181 Vernon Gholston/999 RC | 6.00 | 2.50 |
| ☐ 182 Derrick Harvey/999 RC | 6.00 | 2.50 |
| ☐ 183 Glenn Dorsey/999 RC | 8.00 | 3.00 |
| ☐ 184 Sedrick Ellis/999 RC | 6.00 | 2.50 |
| ☐ 185 Dan Connor AU/299 RC | 15.00 | 6.00 |
| ☐ 186 Curtis Lofton/999 RC | 6.00 | 2.50 |
| ☐ 187 Keith Rivers AU/299 RC | 20.00 | 8.00 |
| ☐ 188 Xavier Adibi/999 RC | 5.00 | 2.00 |
| ☐ 189 Ali Highsmith/999 RC | 4.00 | 1.50 |
| ☐ 190 Quentin Groves AU/299 RC | 15.00 | 6.00 |
| ☐ 191 Erin Henderson/999 RC | 5.00 | 2.00 |
| ☐ 192 Mike Jenkins/999 RC | 6.00 | 2.50 |
| ☐ 193 Antoine Cason AU/299 RC | 20.00 | 8.00 |
| ☐ 194 D.Rodgers-Cromartie/999 RC | 6.00 | 2.50 |
| ☐ 195 Leodis McKelvin/999 RC | 6.00 | 2.50 |
| ☐ 196 Aqib Talib/999 RC | 6.00 | 2.50 |
| ☐ 197 Reggie Smith/999 RC | 5.00 | 2.00 |
| ☐ 198 Tracy Porter AU/299 RC | 15.00 | 6.00 |
| ☐ 199 Terrell Thomas AU/299 RC | 15.00 | 6.00 |
| ☐ 200 Kenny Phillips/999 RC | 6.00 | 2.50 |

## 2006 Donruss Threads

| | | |
|---|---|---|
| ☐ 1 Braylon Edwards | 1.00 | .40 |
| ☐ 2 Jason Witten | .75 | .30 |
| ☐ 3 Julius Jones | 1.00 | .40 |
| ☐ 4 Roy Williams S | .75 | .30 |
| ☐ 5 Terry Glenn | .75 | .30 |
| ☐ 6 Ashley Lelie | .75 | .30 |
| ☐ 7 Kevin Jones | 1.00 | .40 |
| ☐ 8 Mike Williams | 1.00 | .40 |

|  |  | | |
|---|---|---|---|
| 9 | Roy Williams WR | 1.00 | .40 |
| 10 | Aaron Rodgers | 1.00 | .40 |
| 11 | Tatum Bell | .75 | .30 |
| 12 | Samkon Gado | 1.00 | .40 |
| 13 | Corey Bradford | .60 | .25 |
| 14 | Dallas Clark | .75 | .30 |
| 15 | Matt Jones | .75 | .30 |
| 16 | Larry Johnson | .75 | .30 |
| 17 | Byron Leftwich | .75 | .30 |
| 18 | Fred Taylor | .75 | .30 |
| 19 | Anquan Boldin | .75 | .30 |
| 20 | Kurt Warner | .75 | .30 |
| 21 | Larry Fitzgerald | 1.00 | .40 |
| 22 | Alge Crumpler | .75 | .30 |
| 23 | Michael Vick | 1.00 | .40 |
| 24 | Warrick Dunn | .75 | .30 |
| 25 | Jamal Lewis | .75 | .30 |
| 26 | Ray Lewis | 1.00 | .40 |
| 27 | Eric Moulds | .75 | .30 |
| 28 | Josh Reed | .60 | .25 |
| 29 | Lee Evans | .75 | .30 |
| 30 | Steve Smith | 1.00 | .40 |
| 31 | Brian Urlacher | 1.00 | .40 |
| 32 | Thomas Jones | .75 | .30 |
| 33 | Chad Johnson | .75 | .30 |
| 34 | Rudi Johnson | .75 | .30 |
| 35 | T.J. Houshmandzadeh | .75 | .30 |
| 36 | Reuben Droughns | .75 | .30 |
| 37 | Drew Bledsoe | 1.00 | .40 |
| 38 | Keyshawn Johnson | .75 | .30 |
| 39 | Jake Plummer | .75 | .30 |
| 40 | Rod Smith | .75 | .30 |
| 41 | Mike Anderson | .75 | .30 |
| 42 | Joey Harrington | .60 | .25 |
| 43 | Brett Favre | 2.00 | .75 |
| 44 | Donald Driver | .75 | .30 |
| 45 | Javon Walker | .75 | .30 |
| 46 | Andre Johnson | .75 | .30 |
| 47 | David Carr | .75 | .30 |
| 48 | Domanick Davis | .75 | .30 |
| 49 | Edgerrin James | .75 | .30 |
| 50 | Marvin Harrison | 1.00 | .40 |
| 51 | Peyton Manning | 1.50 | .60 |
| 52 | Reggie Wayne | .75 | .30 |
| 53 | Jimmy Smith | .75 | .30 |
| 54 | Tony Gonzalez | .75 | .30 |
| 55 | Trent Green | .75 | .30 |
| 56 | Eddie Kennison | .60 | .25 |
| 57 | Chris Chambers | .75 | .30 |
| 58 | Zach Thomas | .75 | .30 |
| 59 | Daunte Culpepper | 1.00 | .40 |
| 60 | Corey Dillon | .75 | .30 |
| 61 | Deion Branch | .75 | .30 |
| 62 | Tedy Bruschi | .75 | .30 |
| 63 | Tom Brady | 1.50 | .60 |
| 64 | Deuce McAllister | .75 | .30 |
| 65 | Donte Stallworth | .75 | .30 |
| 66 | Jeremy Shockey | 1.00 | .40 |
| 67 | Tiki Barber | 1.00 | .40 |
| 68 | Chad Pennington | .75 | .30 |
| 69 | Curtis Martin | 1.00 | .40 |
| 70 | Donovan McNabb | 1.00 | .40 |
| 71 | Antwaan Randle El | .75 | .30 |
| 72 | Hines Ward | 1.00 | .40 |
| 73 | Antonio Gates | 1.00 | .40 |
| 74 | Drew Brees | 1.00 | .40 |
| 75 | Keenan McCardell | .75 | .30 |
| 76 | LaDainian Tomlinson | 1.25 | .50 |
| 77 | Alex Smith QB | 1.00 | .40 |
| 78 | Brandon Lloyd | .75 | .30 |
| 79 | Frank Gore | 1.00 | .40 |
| 80 | Kevan Barlow | .75 | .30 |
| 81 | Darrell Jackson | .75 | .30 |
| 82 | Joe Jurevicius | .75 | .30 |
| 83 | Matt Hasselbeck | .75 | .30 |
| 84 | Shaun Alexander | 1.00 | .40 |
| 85 | Shaun McDonald | .60 | .25 |
| 86 | Marc Bulger | .75 | .30 |
| 87 | Steven Jackson | 1.00 | .40 |
| 88 | Torry Holt | .75 | .30 |
| 89 | Cadillac Williams | 1.00 | .40 |
| 90 | Chris Simms | .75 | .30 |
| 91 | Joey Galloway | .75 | .30 |
| 92 | Michael Clayton | .75 | .30 |
| 93 | Chris Brown | .75 | .30 |
| 94 | Drew Bennett | .75 | .30 |
| 95 | Steve McNair | .75 | .30 |
| 96 | Tyrone Calico | .60 | .25 |
| 97 | Clinton Portis | 1.00 | .40 |
| 98 | David Patten | .60 | .25 |
| 99 | Mark Brunell | .75 | .30 |
| 100 | Santana Moss | .75 | .30 |
| 101 | Randy McMichael | .75 | .30 |
| 102 | Ronnie Brown | 1.00 | .40 |
| 103 | Mewelde Moore | .60 | .25 |
| 104 | Nate Burleson | .75 | .30 |
| 105 | Troy Williamson | .75 | .30 |
| 106 | David Givens | .75 | .30 |
| 107 | Aaron Brooks | .75 | .30 |
| 108 | Laveranues Coles | .75 | .30 |
| 109 | Justin McCareins | .75 | .30 |
| 110 | Kerry Collins | .75 | .30 |
| 111 | LaMont Jordan | .75 | .30 |
| 112 | Randy Moss | 1.00 | .40 |
| 113 | Jerry Porter | .75 | .30 |
| 114 | Brian Westbrook | .75 | .30 |
| 115 | Plaxico Burress | .75 | .30 |
| 116 | Joe Horn | .75 | .30 |
| 117 | Eli Manning | 1.25 | .50 |
| 118 | Reggie Brown | .75 | .30 |
| 119 | Ryan Moats | .75 | .30 |
| 120 | Ben Roethlisberger | 1.50 | .60 |
| 121 | Willie Parker | 1.25 | .50 |
| 122 | Marcus Pollard | .60 | .25 |
| 123 | Bubba Franks | .75 | .30 |
| 124 | Jabar Gaffney | .60 | .25 |
| 125 | Brandon Stokley | .75 | .30 |
| 126 | Ernest Wilford | .75 | .30 |
| 127 | Dante Hall | .75 | .30 |
| 128 | Marty Booker | .60 | .25 |
| 129 | Samie Parker | .75 | .30 |
| 130 | J.J. Arrington | .75 | .30 |
| 131 | Marcel Shipp | .75 | .30 |
| 132 | Michael Jenkins | .75 | .30 |
| 133 | T.J. Duckett | .60 | .25 |
| 134 | Derrick Mason | .75 | .30 |
| 135 | Kyle Boller | .75 | .30 |
| 136 | Mark Clayton | .75 | .30 |
| 137 | Willis McGahee | 1.00 | .40 |
| 138 | DeShaun Foster | .75 | .30 |
| 139 | Jake Delhomme | .75 | .30 |
| 140 | Julius Peppers | .75 | .30 |
| 141 | Keary Colbert | .75 | .30 |
| 142 | Stephen Davis | .75 | .30 |
| 143 | Todd Heap | .75 | .30 |
| 144 | J.P. Losman | .75 | .30 |
| 145 | Muhsin Muhammad | .75 | .30 |
| 146 | Carson Palmer | 1.00 | .40 |
| 147 | Cedric Benson | .75 | .30 |
| 148 | Rex Grossman | 1.00 | .40 |
| 149 | Charlie Frye | .75 | .30 |
| 150 | Dennis Northcutt | .60 | .25 |
| 151 | Mathias Kiwanuka RC | 8.00 | 3.00 |
| 152 | Ingle Martin RC | 6.00 | 2.50 |
| 153 | Reggie McNeal RC | 5.00 | 2.00 |
| 154 | Bruce Gradkowski RC | 6.00 | 2.50 |
| 155 | D.J. Shockley RC | 6.00 | 2.50 |
| 156 | Paul Pinegar RC | 5.00 | 2.00 |
| 157 | Brandon Kirsch RC | 6.00 | 2.50 |
| 158 | P.J. Daniels RC | 5.00 | 2.00 |
| 159 | Marques Hagans RC | 5.00 | 2.00 |
| 160 | Jerome Harrison RC | 6.00 | 2.50 |
| 161 | Wali Lundy RC | 6.00 | 2.50 |
| 162 | Cedric Humes RC | 6.00 | 2.50 |
| 163 | Quinton Ganther RC | 6.00 | 2.50 |
| 164 | Mike Bell RC | 6.00 | 2.50 |
| 165 | John David Washington RC | 5.00 | 2.00 |
| 166 | Anthony Fasano RC | 6.00 | 2.50 |
| 167 | Tony Scheffler RC | 6.00 | 2.50 |
| 168 | Leonard Pope RC | 6.00 | 2.50 |
| 169 | David Thomas RC | 6.00 | 2.50 |
| 170 | Dominique Byrd RC | 5.00 | 2.00 |
| 171 | Devin Hester RC | 12.00 | 5.00 |
| 172 | Willie Reid RC | 6.00 | 2.50 |
| 173 | Brad Smith RC | 6.00 | 2.50 |
| 174 | Cory Rodgers RC | 6.00 | 2.50 |
| 175 | Domenik Hixon RC | 8.00 | 3.00 |
| 176 | Jeremy Bloom RC | 5.00 | 2.00 |
| 177 | Jonathan Orr RC | 5.00 | 2.00 |
| 178 | Jeff Webb RC | 5.00 | 2.00 |
| 179 | Ethan Kilmer RC | 5.00 | 2.00 |
| 180 | Bennie Brazell RC | 6.00 | 2.50 |
| 181 | David Anderson RC | 5.00 | 2.00 |
| 182 | Kevin McMahan RC | 5.00 | 2.00 |
| 183 | Anthony Mix RC | 5.00 | 2.00 |
| 184 | D'Brickashaw Ferguson RC | 6.00 | 2.50 |
| 185 | Kamerion Wimbley RC | 6.00 | 2.50 |
| 186 | Tamba Hali RC | 6.00 | 2.50 |
| 187 | Haloti Ngata RC | 6.00 | 2.50 |
| 188 | Brodrick Bunkley RC | 6.00 | 2.50 |
| 189 | John McCargo RC | 5.00 | 2.00 |
| 190 | Claude Wroten RC | 4.00 | 1.50 |
| 191 | Gabe Watson RC | 5.00 | 2.00 |
| 192 | D'Qwell Jackson RC | 5.00 | 2.00 |
| 193 | Abdul Hodge RC | 6.00 | 2.50 |
| 194 | Ernie Sims RC | 6.00 | 2.50 |
| 195 | Chad Greenway RC | 6.00 | 2.50 |
| 196 | Bobby Carpenter RC | 6.00 | 2.50 |
| 197 | Manny Lawson RC | 6.00 | 2.50 |
| 198 | DeMeco Ryans RC | 8.00 | 3.00 |
| 199 | Rocky McIntosh RC | 6.00 | 2.50 |
| 200 | Thomas Howard RC | 6.00 | 2.50 |
| 201 | Jon Alston RC | 5.00 | 2.00 |
| 202 | A.J. Nicholson RC | 4.00 | 1.50 |
| 203 | Tye Hill RC | 6.00 | 2.50 |
| 204 | Antonio Cromartie RC | 6.00 | 2.50 |
| 205 | Johnathan Joseph RC | 5.00 | 2.00 |
| 206 | Kelly Jennings RC | 5.00 | 2.00 |
| 207 | Ashton Youboty RC | 5.00 | 2.00 |
| 208 | Alan Zemaitis RC | 5.00 | 2.00 |
| 209 | Jason Allen RC | 5.00 | 2.00 |
| 210 | Cedric Griffin RC | 5.00 | 2.00 |
| 211 | Ko Simpson RC | 5.00 | 2.00 |
| 212 | Pat Watkins RC | 5.00 | 2.00 |
| 213 | Donte Whitner RC | 6.00 | 2.50 |
| 214 | Bernard Pollard RC | 5.00 | 2.00 |
| 215 | Darnell Bing RC | 5.00 | 2.00 |
| 216 | Marcus Vick RC | 6.00 | 2.50 |
| 217 | Roman Harper RC | 5.00 | 2.00 |
| 218 | Anthony Smith RC | 5.00 | 2.00 |
| 219 | Daniel Bullocks RC | 5.00 | 2.00 |
| 220 | Eric Smith RC | 5.00 | 2.00 |
| 221 | Danieal Manning RC | 6.00 | 2.50 |
| 222 | Anthony Schlegel RC | 5.00 | 2.00 |
| 223 | Dusty Dvoracek RC | 5.00 | 2.00 |
| 224 | Darryl Tapp RC | 5.00 | 2.00 |
| 225 | Chris Gocong RC | 5.00 | 2.00 |
| 226 | Brandon Williams AU/240 RC | 50.00 | 20.00 |
| 227 | Michael Robinson AU/240 RC | 50.00 | 20.00 |
| 228 | Vernon Davis AU/100 RC | 50.00 | 20.00 |
| 229 | Brandon Marshall AU/240 RC | 60.00 | 25.00 |
| 230 | Travis Wilson AU/180 RC | 50.00 | 20.00 |
| 231 | Maurice Stovall AU/140 RC | 50.00 | 20.00 |
| 232 | Matt Leinart AU/140 RC | 200.00 | 100.00 |
| 233 | Ch.Whitehurst AU/200 RC | 50.00 | 20.00 |
| 234 | Derek Hagan AU/100 RC | 50.00 | 20.00 |
| 235 | Jason Avant AU/150 RC | 50.00 | 20.00 |
| 236 | Jerious Norwood AU/210 RC | 60.00 | 25.00 |
| 237 | Sinorice Moss AU/100 RC | 50.00 | 20.00 |
| 238 | Marcedes Lewis AU/100 RC | 50.00 | 20.00 |
| 239 | Maurice Drew AU/100 RC | 100.00 | 40.00 |
| 240 | Kellen Clemens AU/210 RC | 60.00 | 25.00 |
| 241 | Leon Washington AU/200 RC | 50.00 | 20.00 |
| 242 | Brian Calhoun AU/140 RC | 40.00 | 15.00 |
| 243 | A.J. Hawk AU/100 RC | 100.00 | 40.00 |
| 244 | DeAn.Williams AU/160 RC | 80.00 | 40.00 |

|  | | |
|---|---|---|
| 245 Chad Jackson AU/140 RC | 40.00 | 15.00 |
| 246 L.Maroney AU/140 RC | 120.00 | 50.00 |
| 247 Michael Huff AU/100 RC | 50.00 | 20.00 |
| 248 Joe Klopfenstein AU/240 RC | 40.00 | 15.00 |
| 249 Dem.Williams AU/160 RC | 50.00 | 20.00 |
| 250 Reggie Bush AU/100 RC | 250.00 | 125.00 |
| 251 Omar Jacobs AU/120 RC | 40.00 | 15.00 |
| 252 Santonio Holmes AU/120 RC | 120.00 | 50.00 |
| 253 Mario Williams AU/100 RC | 80.00 | 30.00 |
| 254 LenDale White AU/100 RC | 100.00 | 40.00 |
| 255 Vince Young AU/120 RC | 200.00 | 100.00 |
| 256 Tarvaris Jackson AU/210 RC | 50.00 | 20.00 |
| 257 Jay Cutler AU/120 RC | 250.00 | 125.00 |
| 258 Joseph Addai AU/100 RC | 150.00 | 60.00 |
| 259 Brodie Croyle AU/120 RC | 60.00 | 25.00 |
| 260 Greg Jennings AU/240 RC | 80.00 | 40.00 |
| 261 Erik Meyer AU RC | 10.00 | 4.00 |
| 262 Drew Olson AU RC | 10.00 | 4.00 |
| 263 Darrell Hackney AU RC | 10.00 | 4.00 |
| 264 Andre Hall AU RC | 12.00 | 5.00 |
| 265 Taurean Henderson AU RC | 12.00 | 5.00 |
| 266 Derrick Ross AU RC | 10.00 | 4.00 |
| 267 De'Arrius Howard AU RC | 12.00 | 5.00 |
| 268 Wendell Mathis AU RC | 10.00 | 4.00 |
| 269 Gerald Riggs AU RC | 12.00 | 5.00 |
| 270 Garrett Mills AU RC | 12.00 | 5.00 |
| 271 Jai Lewis AU RC | 10.00 | 4.00 |
| 272 Skyler Green AU RC | 10.00 | 4.00 |
| 273 Mike Hass AU RC | 12.00 | 5.00 |
| 274 Delanie Walker AU RC | 10.00 | 4.00 |
| 275 Adam Jennings AU RC | 10.00 | 4.00 |
| 276 Todd Watkins AU RC | 10.00 | 4.00 |
| 277 Devin Aromashodu AU RC | 10.00 | 4.00 |
| 278 Ben Obomanu AU RC | 10.00 | 4.00 |
| 279 Marques Colston AU RC | 50.00 | 20.00 |
| 280 Miles Austin AU RC | 15.00 | 7.50 |
| 281 Martin Nance AU RC | 10.00 | 4.00 |
| 282 Greg Lee AU RC | 10.00 | 4.00 |
| 283 Hank Baskett AU RC | 12.00 | 5.00 |
| 284 Jimmy Williams AU RC | 12.00 | 5.00 |
| 285 Anwar Phillips AU RC | 10.00 | 4.00 |

## 2007 Donruss Threads

| | | |
|---|---|---|
| 1 Anquan Boldin | .75 | .30 |
| 2 Larry Fitzgerald | 1.00 | .40 |
| 3 Alge Crumpler | .75 | .30 |
| 4 Michael Vick | 1.00 | .40 |
| 5 Steve McNair | .75 | .30 |
| 6 Ray Lewis | 1.00 | .40 |
| 7 Keyshawn Johnson | .75 | .30 |
| 8 Steve Smith | .75 | .30 |
| 9 Brian Urlacher | 1.00 | .40 |
| 10 Muhsin Muhammad | .75 | .30 |
| 11 Chad Johnson | .75 | .30 |
| 12 Rudi Johnson | .75 | .30 |
| 13 T.J. Houshmandzadeh | .75 | .30 |
| 14 Terry Glenn | .75 | .30 |
| 15 Terrell Owens | 1.00 | .40 |
| 16 Jon Kitna | .60 | .25 |
| 17 Brett Favre | 2.00 | .75 |
| 18 Peyton Manning | 1.50 | .60 |
| 19 Fred Taylor | .75 | .30 |
| 20 Eddie Kennison | .60 | .25 |
| 21 Larry Johnson | .75 | .30 |
| 22 Tony Gonzalez | .75 | .30 |
| 23 Trent Green | .75 | .30 |
| 24 Chris Chambers | .75 | .30 |
| 25 Marty Booker | .60 | .25 |

|  | | |
|---|---|---|
| 26 Tom Brady | 2.00 | .75 |
| 27 Donte Stallworth | .75 | .30 |
| 28 Deuce McAllister | .75 | .30 |
| 29 Drew Brees | .75 | .30 |
| 30 Reuben Droughns | .75 | .30 |
| 31 Jeremy Shockey | .75 | .30 |
| 32 Plaxico Burress | .75 | .30 |
| 33 Chad Pennington | .75 | .30 |
| 34 Jerricho Cotchery | .60 | .25 |
| 35 Laveranues Coles | .75 | .30 |
| 36 LaMont Jordan | .75 | .30 |
| 37 Brian Westbrook UER | .75 | .30 |
| 38 Donovan McNabb | -1.00 | .40 |
| 39 Hines Ward | 1.00 | .40 |
| 40 Antonio Gates | .75 | .30 |
| 41 LaDainian Tomlinson | 1.25 | .50 |
| 42 Arnaz Battle | .60 | .25 |
| 43 Darrell Jackson | .75 | .30 |
| 44 Deion Branch | .75 | .30 |
| 45 Matt Hasselbeck | .75 | .30 |
| 46 Jerramy Stevens | .60 | .25 |
| 47 Shaun Alexander | .75 | .30 |
| 48 Isaac Bruce | .75 | .30 |
| 49 Marc Bulger | .75 | .30 |
| 50 Drew Bennett | .60 | .25 |
| 51 Torry Holt | .75 | .30 |
| 52 Joey Galloway | .75 | .30 |
| 53 Mike Alstott | .75 | .30 |
| 54 Travis Henry | .75 | .30 |
| 55 Clinton Portis | .75 | .30 |
| 56 Santana Moss | .75 | .30 |
| 57 Edgerrin James | .75 | .30 |
| 58 Matt Leinart | 1.00 | .40 |
| 59 Jerious Norwood | .75 | .30 |
| 60 Warrick Dunn | .75 | .30 |
| 61 Mark Clayton | .75 | .30 |
| 62 J.P. Losman | .75 | .30 |
| 63 Josh Reed | .60 | .25 |
| 64 Lee Evans | .75 | .30 |
| 65 DeAngelo Williams | 1.00 | .40 |
| 66 DeShaun Foster | .75 | .30 |
| 67 Jake Delhomme | .75 | .30 |
| 68 Bernard Berrian | .60 | .25 |
| 69 Cedric Benson | .75 | .30 |
| 70 Rex Grossman | .75 | .30 |
| 71 Carson Palmer | 1.00 | .40 |
| 72 Braylon Edwards | .75 | .30 |
| 73 Kellen Winslow | .75 | .30 |
| 74 Charlie Frye | .75 | .30 |
| 75 Julius Jones | .75 | .30 |
| 76 Marion Barber | 1.00 | .40 |
| 77 Javon Walker | .75 | .30 |
| 78 Jay Cutler | 1.00 | .40 |
| 79 Mike Bell | .75 | .30 |
| 80 Donald Driver | .75 | .30 |
| 81 Greg Jennings | .75 | .30 |
| 82 Andre Johnson | .75 | .30 |
| 83 Matt Schaub | .75 | .30 |
| 84 Wali Lundy | .60 | .25 |
| 85 Joseph Addai | 1.00 | .40 |
| 86 Marvin Harrison | 1.00 | .40 |
| 87 Kevin Jones | .60 | .25 |
| 88 Roy Williams WR | .75 | .30 |
| 89 Mike Furrey | .75 | .30 |
| 90 A.J. Hawk | 1.00 | .40 |
| 91 Reggie Wayne | .75 | .30 |
| 92 Dallas Clark | .60 | .25 |
| 93 Byron Leftwich | .75 | .30 |
| 94 Maurice Jones-Drew | 1.00 | .40 |
| 95 Reggie Williams | .75 | .30 |
| 96 Tony Romo | 2.00 | .75 |
| 97 Daunte Culpepper | .75 | .30 |
| 98 Ronnie Brown | .75 | .30 |
| 99 Chester Taylor | .75 | .30 |
| 100 Travis Taylor | .60 | .25 |
| 101 Ben Watson | .60 | .25 |
| 102 Laurence Maroney | 1.00 | .40 |
| 103 Bo Scaife | .60 | .25 |
| 104 Peerless Price | .60 | .25 |
| 105 Marques Colston | 1.00 | .40 |
| 106 Reggie Bush | 1.25 | .50 |
| 107 Brandon Jacobs | .75 | .30 |
| 108 Eli Manning | 1.00 | .40 |
| 109 Leon Washington | .75 | .30 |

|  | | |
|---|---|---|
| 110 Kevan Barlow | .75 | .30 |
| 111 Randy Moss | 1.00 | .40 |
| 112 Troy Polamalu | 1.00 | .40 |
| 113 Willie Parker | 1.00 | .40 |
| 114 Santonio Holmes | .75 | .30 |
| 115 Philip Rivers | 1.00 | .40 |
| 116 Shawne Merriman | .75 | .30 |
| 117 Alex Smith QB | 1.00 | .40 |
| 118 Frank Gore | 1.00 | .40 |
| 119 Vernon Davis | .75 | .30 |
| 120 Reggie Brown | .75 | .30 |
| 121 Ben Roethlisberger | 1.25 | .50 |
| 122 Steven Jackson | 1.00 | .40 |
| 123 Bruce Gradkowski | .60 | .25 |
| 124 Cadillac Williams | .75 | .30 |
| 125 Chris Cooley | .60 | .25 |
| 126 Michael Jenkins | .75 | .30 |
| 127 Demetrius Williams | .60 | .25 |
| 128 Roy Williams S | .75 | .30 |
| 129 Owen Daniels | .60 | .25 |
| 130 Hank Baskett | .75 | .30 |
| 131 Marcedes Lewis | .60 | .25 |
| 132 Brandon Marshall | .75 | .30 |
| 133 John Madsen | .60 | .25 |
| 134 Michael Huff | .75 | .30 |
| 135 Joe Klopfenstein | .60 | .25 |
| 136 Vincent Jackson | .75 | .30 |
| 137 Todd Heap | .60 | .25 |
| 138 Tarvaris Jackson | .75 | .30 |
| 139 Troy Williamson | .60 | .25 |
| 140 Ronald Curry | .75 | .30 |
| 141 Ahman Green | .75 | .30 |
| 142 LenDale White | .75 | .30 |
| 143 Vince Young | 1.00 | .40 |
| 144 Thomas Jones | .75 | .30 |
| 145 Jamal Lewis | .75 | .30 |
| 146 Joe Horn | .75 | .30 |
| 147 Tatum Bell | .60 | .25 |
| 148 Willis McGahee | .75 | .30 |
| 149 Jason Campbell | .75 | .30 |
| 150 Ladell Betts | .60 | .25 |
| 151 John Broussard RC | 5.00 | 2.00 |
| 152 Michael Allan RC | 4.00 | 1.50 |
| 153 Tyler Thigpen RC | 8.00 | 3.00 |
| 154 Chandler Williams RC | 5.00 | 2.00 |
| 155 Eric Weddle RC | 5.00 | 2.00 |
| 156 Derek Stanley RC | 5.00 | 2.00 |
| 157 Justise Hairston RC | 5.00 | 2.00 |
| 158 Johnathan Holland RC | 5.00 | 2.00 |
| 159 Legedu Naanee RC | 6.00 | 2.50 |
| 160 Courtney Taylor RC | 5.00 | 2.00 |
| 161 David Irons RC | 4.00 | 1.50 |
| 162 Joel Filani RC | 5.00 | 2.00 |
| 163 H.B. Blades RC | 5.00 | 2.00 |
| 164 Rufus Alexander RC | 6.00 | 2.50 |
| 165 Roy Hall RC | 6.00 | 2.50 |
| 166 Eric Frampton RC | 5.00 | 2.00 |
| 167 Tim Shaw RC | 5.00 | 2.00 |
| 168 Tymere Zimmerman RC | 5.00 | 2.00 |
| 169 Jeff Rowe RC | 5.00 | 2.00 |
| 170 Josh Gattis RC | 4.00 | 1.50 |
| 171 Brandon Myles RC | 5.00 | 2.00 |
| 172 Earl Everett RC | 5.00 | 2.00 |
| 173 Steve Breaston RC | 6.00 | 2.50 |
| 174 Ryan McBean RC | 5.00 | 2.00 |
| 175 Scott Chandler RC | 5.00 | 2.00 |
| 176 Chris Davis RC | 5.00 | 2.00 |
| 177 Fred Bennett RC | 4.00 | 1.50 |
| 178 Ryne Robinson RC | 5.00 | 2.00 |
| 179 Zak DeOssie RC | 5.00 | 2.00 |
| 180 Dwayne Wright RC | 5.00 | 2.00 |
| 181 A.J. Davis RC | 4.00 | 1.50 |
| 182 Ray McDonald RC | 5.00 | 2.00 |
| 183 Daymeion Hughes RC | 5.00 | 2.00 |
| 184 Michael Okwo RC | 5.00 | 2.00 |
| 185 Aaron Rouse RC | 6.00 | 2.50 |
| 186 Stewart Bradley RC | 5.00 | 2.50 |
| 187 Jonathan Wade RC | 5.00 | 2.00 |
| 188 Charles Johnson RC | 4.00 | 1.50 |
| 189 Demarcus Tank Tyler RC | 5.00 | 2.00 |
| 190 Mike Walker RC | 5.00 | 2.00 |
| 191 James Jones RC | 6.00 | 2.50 |
| 192 Matt Spaeth RC | 5.00 | 2.50 |
| 193 Laurent Robinson RC | 5.00 | 2.00 |

❏ 194 Jacoby Jones RC 6.00 2.50
❏ 195 Marcus McCauley RC 5.00 2.00
❏ 196 Buster Davis RC 5.00 2.00
❏ 197 Quentin Moses RC 5.00 2.00
❏ 198 Sabby Piscitelli RC 6.00 2.50
❏ 199 Dan Bazuin RC 5.00 2.00
❏ 200 Ikaika Alama-Francis RC 6.00 2.50
❏ 201 Victor Abiamiri RC 6.00 2.50
❏ 202 Tim Crowder RC 6.00 2.50
❏ 203 Josh Wilson RC 6.00 2.50
❏ 204 Eric Wright RC 6.00 2.50
❏ 205 David Harris RC 6.00 2.50
❏ 206 LaMarr Woodley RC 6.00 2.50
❏ 207 Chris Houston RC 6.00 2.50
❏ 208 Zach Miller RC 6.00 2.50
❏ 209 Aaron Fairooz RC 5.00 2.00
❏ 210 Alan Branch RC 5.00 2.00
❏ 211 Anthony Spencer RC 6.00 2.50
❏ 212 Jon Beason RC 6.00 2.50
❏ 213 Brandon Meriweather RC 5.00 2.00
❏ 214 Reggie Nelson RC 5.00 2.00
❏ 215 Aaron Ross RC 6.00 2.50
❏ 216 Michael Griffin RC 6.00 2.50
❏ 217 Ronnie McGill RC 5.00 2.00
❏ 218 Jarvis Moss RC 6.00 2.50
❏ 219 Darrelle Revis RC 6.00 2.50
❏ 220 Lawrence Timmons RC 6.00 2.50
❏ 221 Adam Carriker RC 5.00 2.00
❏ 222 Amobi Okoye RC 6.00 2.50
❏ 223 Jamaal Anderson RC 5.00 2.00
❏ 224 Sywelle Newton RC 5.00 2.00
❏ 225 Levi Brown RC 6.00 2.50
❏ 226 Chansi Stuckey AU/499 RC 12.00 5.00
❏ 227 Nate Ilaoa AU/999 RC 12.00 5.00
❏ 228 Brandon Siler AU/198 RC 12.00 5.00
❏ 229 J.Snelling AU/999 RC EXCH 10.00 4.00
❏ 230 Kenneth Darby AU/999 RC 12.00 5.00
❏ 231 Ahmad Bradshaw AU/999 RC 30.00 12.00
❏ 232 Thomas Clayton AU/763 RC 10.00 4.00
❏ 233 Dallas Baker AU/499 RC 12.00 5.00
❏ 234 Ben Patrick AU/849 RC EXCH 10.00 4.00
❏ 235 Jordan Kent AU/999 RC 10.00 4.00
❏ 236 Jordan Palmer AU/299 RC 15.00 6.00
❏ 237 Chris Leak AU/299 RC 12.00 5.00
❏ 238 Jon Cornish AU/876 RC 10.00 4.00
❏ 239 Jared Zabransky AU/299 RC 15.00 6.00
❏ 240 Rhema McKnight AU/999 RC 10.00 4.00
❏ 241 Selvin Young AU/999 RC 25.00 10.00
❏ 242 Gary Russell AU/981 RC 12.00 5.00
❏ 243 Jerard Rabb AU/999 RC EXCH 10.00 4.00
❏ 244 Jemalie Comelius AU/581 RC 12.00 5.00
❏ 245 Alonzo Coleman AU/781 RC 10.00 4.00
❏ 246 Danny Ware AU/999 RC 10.00 4.00
❏ 247 David Ball AU/999 RC 8.00 3.00
❏ 248 D'Juan Woods AU/456 RC 12.00 5.00
❏ 249 Syndric Steptoe AU/676 RC 10.00 4.00
❏ 250 Jarrett Hicks AU/999 RC 10.00 4.00
❏ 251 Trent Edwards/140 AU RC 80.00 40.00
❏ 252 Marshawn Lynch/100 AU RC 120.00 60.00
❏ 253 Chris Henry RB/105 AU RC 60.00 25.00
❏ 254 Paul Williams/200 AU RC 60.00 30.00
❏ 255 Sidney Rice/100 AU RC 60.00 25.00
❏ 256 Adrian Peterson/120 AU RC 350.00 175.00
❏ 257 Drew Stanton/140 AU RC 50.00 20.00
❏ 258 Calvin Johnson/105 AU RC 200.00 100.00
❏ 259 Yamon Figurs/150 AU RC 60.00 30.00
❏ 260 Troy Smith/100 AU RC 80.00 40.00
❏ 261 Brian Leonard/210 AU RC 60.00 25.00
❏ 262 Greg Olsen/125 AU RC 80.00 40.00
❏ 263 Kenny Irons/100 AU RC 60.00 30.00
❏ 264 Joe Thomas/120 AU RC 80.00 40.00
❏ 265 Brady Quinn/125 AU RC 200.00 100.00
❏ 266 Brandon Jackson/140 AU RC 60.00 25.00
❏ 267 Steve Smith/150 AU RC 100.00 50.00
❏ 268 Dwayne Jarrett/100 AU RC 50.00 20.00
❏ 269 Ted Ginn Jr./100 AU RC 100.00 50.00
❏ 270 John Beck/120 AU RC 50.00 20.00
❏ 271 Lorenzo Booker/150 AU RC 60.00 30.00
❏ 272 Antonio Pittman/100 AU RC 60.00 30.00
❏ 273 Robert Meachem/140 AU RC 60.00 30.00
❏ 274 Dwayne Bowe/100 AU RC 100.00 50.00
❏ 275 Anthony Gonzalez/160 AU RC 80.00 40.00
❏ 276 JaMarcus Russell/140 AU RC 150.00 75.00
❏ 277 Michael Bush/120 AU RC 80.00 30.00

❏ 278 J.Lee Higgins/175 AU RC 50.00 25.00
❏ 279 Kevin Kolb/100 AU RC 100.00 50.00
❏ 280 Gaines Adams/150 AU RC 80.00 30.00
❏ 281 Patrick Willis/150 AU RC 80.00 40.00
❏ 282 Jason Hill/120 AU RC 50.00 20.00
❏ 283 Isaiah Stanback/200 AU RC 60.00 30.00
❏ 284 Kolby Smith/125 AU RC 60.00 25.00
❏ 285 Leon Hall/120 AU RC 60.00 30.00
❏ 286 Darius Walker/180 AU RC 50.00 20.00
❏ 287 David Clowney/175 AU RC 50.00 25.00
❏ 288 LaRon Landry/150 AU RC 80.00 40.00
❏ 289 Paul Posluszny/180 AU RC 120.00 60.00
❏ 290 Garrett Wolfe/125 AU RC 50.00 20.00
❏ 291 Tony Hunt/120 AU RC EXCH 80.00 30.00
❏ 292 Craig Davis/150 AU RC EXCH 60.00 30.00
❏ 293 DeShaun Wynn/120 AU RC 60.00 30.00
❏ 294 Aundrae Allison/175 AU RC 40.00 15.00

## 2008 Donruss Threads

❏ 1 Anquan Boldin .60 .25
❏ 2 Larry Fitzgerald .75 .30
❏ 3 Warrick Dunn .60 .25
❏ 4 Derrick Mason .50 .20
❏ 5 Steve Smith .60 .25
❏ 6 Brian Urlacher .75 .30
❏ 7 Chad Johnson .60 .25
❏ 8 Terrell Owens .75 .30
❏ 9 Tony Gonzalez .60 .25
❏ 10 Rex Grossman .60 .25
❏ 11 Torry Holt .60 .25
❏ 12 Isaac Bruce .60 .25
❏ 13 Jeff Garcia .60 .25
❏ 14 Santana Moss .60 .25
❏ 15 LaDainian Tomlinson 1.00 .40
❏ 16 Matt Hasselbeck .60 .25
❏ 17 Julius Jones .50 .20
❏ 18 Earnest Graham .50 .20
❏ 19 Joey Galloway .60 .25
❏ 20 Ike Hilliard .50 .20
❏ 21 Vince Young .75 .30
❏ 22 Jason Taylor .60 .25
❏ 23 Tom Brady 1.25 .50
❏ 24 Randy Moss .75 .30
❏ 25 Donte Stallworth .60 .25
❏ 26 Deuce McAllister .60 .25
❏ 27 Eli Manning .75 .30
❏ 28 Michael Strahan .60 .25
❏ 29 Thomas Jones .60 .25
❏ 30 Laveranues Coles .60 .25
❏ 31 Jerry Porter .60 .25
❏ 32 Correll Buckhalter .60 .25
❏ 33 Donovan McNabb .75 .30
❏ 34 Hines Ward .75 .30
❏ 35 Troy Scheffler .60 .25
❏ 36 Jason Witten .60 .25
❏ 37 DeMarcus Ware .60 .25
❏ 38 Jay Cutler .75 .30
❏ 39 Brandon Marshall .60 .25
❏ 40 Brandon Stokley .50 .20
❏ 41 Selvin Young .60 .25
❏ 42 Jon Kitna .60 .25
❏ 43 Roy Williams WR .60 .25
❏ 44 Shaun McDonald .50 .20
❏ 45 Calvin Johnson .75 .30
❏ 46 Aaron Rodgers .75 .30
❏ 47 Ryan Grant .60 .25
❏ 48 Donald Driver .60 .25
❏ 49 Greg Jennings .60 .25

❏ 50 James Jones .50 .20
❏ 51 Matt Schaub .60 .25
❏ 52 Owen Daniels .50 .20
❏ 53 Andre Johnson .60 .25
❏ 54 Kevin Walter .50 .20
❏ 55 Ahman Green .60 .25
❏ 56 Peyton Manning 1.25 .50
❏ 57 Marvin Harrison .75 .30
❏ 58 Joseph Addai .75 .30
❏ 59 Reggie Wayne .60 .25
❏ 60 Dallas Clark .60 .25
❏ 61 David Garrard .60 .25
❏ 62 Fred Taylor .60 .25
❏ 63 Maurice Jones-Drew .60 .25
❏ 64 Reggie Williams .60 .25
❏ 65 Larry Johnson .60 .25
❏ 66 Kolby Smith .60 .25
❏ 67 Dwayne Bowe .60 .25
❏ 68 Ted Ginn Jr. .60 .25
❏ 69 Ronnie Brown .60 .25
❏ 70 John Beck .50 .20
❏ 71 Tarvaris Jackson .60 .25
❏ 72 Adrian Peterson 1.50 .60
❏ 73 Chester Taylor .50 .20
❏ 74 Sidney Rice .60 .25
❏ 75 Wes Welker .75 .30
❏ 76 Laurence Maroney .60 .25
❏ 77 Drew Brees .75 .30
❏ 78 Reggie Bush .75 .30
❏ 79 Marques Colston .60 .25
❏ 80 Brandon Jacobs .60 .25
❏ 81 Plaxico Burress .60 .25
❏ 82 Derrick Ward .50 .20
❏ 83 Kellen Clemens .60 .25
❏ 84 Leon Washington .60 .25
❏ 85 Jerricho Cotchery .60 .25
❏ 86 Matt Leinart .75 .30
❏ 87 Edgerrin James .60 .25
❏ 88 JaMarcus Russell .75 .30
❏ 89 Justin Fargas .50 .20
❏ 90 Alge Crumpler .60 .25
❏ 91 Jerious Norwood .60 .25
❏ 92 Roddy White .60 .25
❏ 93 Ronald Curry .60 .25
❏ 94 Willis McGahee .60 .25
❏ 95 Mark Clayton .60 .25
❏ 96 Brian Westbrook .60 .25
❏ 97 Kevin Curtis .50 .20
❏ 98 Ed Reed .60 .25
❏ 99 Ray Lewis .75 .30
❏ 100 Reggie Brown .60 .25
❏ 101 Trent Edwards .60 .25
❏ 102 Marshawn Lynch .75 .30
❏ 103 Ben Roethlisberger 1.00 .40
❏ 104 Willie Parker .60 .25
❏ 105 Lee Evans .60 .25
❏ 106 Josh Reed .50 .20
❏ 107 Santonio Holmes .60 .25
❏ 108 Jake Delhomme .60 .25
❏ 109 DeShaun Foster .60 .25
❏ 110 Heath Miller .60 .25
❏ 111 Philip Rivers .75 .30
❏ 112 DeAngelo Williams .60 .25
❏ 113 Drew Carter .50 .20
❏ 114 Adrian Peterson Bears .50 .20
❏ 115 Antonio Gates .60 .25
❏ 116 Shawne Merriman .60 .25
❏ 117 Bernard Berrian .60 .25
❏ 118 Cedric Benson .60 .25
❏ 119 Vincent Jackson .50 .20
❏ 120 Alex Smith QB .60 .25
❏ 121 Devin Hester .75 .30
❏ 122 Carson Palmer .75 .30
❏ 123 Frank Gore .60 .25
❏ 124 T.J. Houshmandzadeh .60 .25
❏ 125 Rudi Johnson .50 .20
❏ 126 Vernon Davis .60 .25
❏ 127 Patrick Willis .60 .25
❏ 128 Kenny Watson .50 .20
❏ 129 Derek Anderson .60 .25
❏ 130 Jamal Lewis .60 .25
❏ 131 Kellen Winslow .60 .25
❏ 132 Maurice Morris .50 .20
❏ 133 Nate Burleson .50 .20

| | | |
|---|---|---|
| ☐ 134 Braylon Edwards | .60 | .25 |
| ☐ 135 Josh Cribbs | .60 | .25 |
| ☐ 136 Deion Branch | .60 | .25 |
| ☐ 137 Marc Bulger | .60 | .25 |
| ☐ 138 Tony Romo | 1.25 | .50 |
| ☐ 139 Marion Barber | .75 | .30 |
| ☐ 140 Steven Jackson | .75 | .30 |
| ☐ 141 Randy McMichael | .50 | .20 |
| ☐ 142 Cadillac Williams | .60 | .25 |
| ☐ 143 LenDale White | .60 | .25 |
| ☐ 144 Chris Brown | .50 | .20 |
| ☐ 145 Roydell Williams | .50 | .20 |
| ☐ 146 Justin Gage | .50 | .20 |
| ☐ 147 Jason Campbell | .60 | .25 |
| ☐ 148 Clinton Portis | .60 | .25 |
| ☐ 149 Chris Cooley | .50 | .20 |
| ☐ 150 Ladell Betts | .50 | .20 |
| ☐ 151 Arron Arrington AU/299 RC | 10.00 | 4.00 |
| ☐ 152 Alex Brink/999 RC | 6.00 | 2.50 |
| ☐ 153 Ali Highsmith AU/999 RC | 8.00 | 3.00 |
| ☐ 154 Anthony Alridge AU/999 RC | 10.00 | 4.00 |
| ☐ 155 Antoine Cason/999 RC | 6.00 | 2.50 |
| ☐ 156 Antwaun Molden/999 RC | 5.00 | 2.00 |
| ☐ 157 Aqib Talib/999 RC | 6.00 | 2.50 |
| ☐ 158 Arman Shields/999 RC | 5.00 | 2.00 |
| ☐ 159 Brad Cottam AU/299 RC | 12.00 | 5.00 |
| ☐ 160 Brandon Flowers/999 RC | 6.00 | 2.50 |
| ☐ 161 Bruce Davis/999 RC | 6.00 | 2.50 |
| ☐ 162 Calais Campbell AU/299 RC | 10.00 | 4.00 |
| ☐ 163 Caleb Campbell AU/299 RC | 15.00 | 6.00 |
| ☐ 164 Charles Godfrey/999 RC | 6.00 | 2.50 |
| ☐ 165 Ch.Washington AU/299 RC | 10.00 | 4.00 |
| ☐ 166 Chevis Jackson AU/299 RC | 10.00 | 4.00 |
| ☐ 167 Cory Boyd AU/299 RC | 10.00 | |
| ☐ 168 Craig Steltz AU/299 RC | 10.00 | 4.00 |
| ☐ 169 Craig Stevens/999 RC | 5.00 | 2.00 |
| ☐ 170 Curtis Lofton AU/999 RC | 12.00 | 5.00 |
| ☐ 171 DaJuan Morgan/999 RC | 5.00 | 2.00 |
| ☐ 172 Dantrell Savage AU/999 RC | 12.00 | 5.00 |
| ☐ 173 Darius Reynaud AU/999 RC | 10.00 | 4.00 |
| ☐ 174 Darrell Strong AU/999 RC | 10.00 | 4.00 |
| ☐ 175 Davone Bess AU/999 RC | 15.00 | 6.00 |
| ☐ 176 Derek Fine/999 RC | 5.00 | 2.00 |
| ☐ 177 Derrick Harvey/999 RC | 6.00 | 2.50 |
| ☐ 178 DJ Hall AU/999 RC, | 12.00 | 5.00 |
| ☐ 179 D.Rodgers-Cromartie/999 RC | 6.00 | 2.50 |
| ☐ 180 Erin Henderson/999 RC | 5.00 | 2.00 |
| ☐ 181 Ernie Wheelwright AU/755 RC | 10.00 | 4.00 |
| ☐ 182 Fred Davis/999 RC | 6.00 | 2.50 |
| ☐ 183 Gary Barnidge/999 RC | 5.00 | 2.00 |
| ☐ 184 Joe Jon Finley/999 RC | 5.00 | 2.00 |
| ☐ 185 Jacob Hester AU/299 RC | 12.00 | 5.00 |
| ☐ 186 Jacob Tamme/999 RC | 6.00 | 2.50 |
| ☐ 187 Jalen Parmele/999 RC | 5.00 | 2.00 |
| ☐ 188 Jamar Adams AU/775 RC | 10.00 | 4.00 |
| ☐ 189 Jason Rivers AU/999 RC | 12.00 | 5.00 |
| ☐ 190 Jaymar Johnson/999 RC | 5.00 | 2.00 |
| ☐ 191 Jed Collins AU/999 RC | 10.00 | 4.00 |
| ☐ 192 Jermichael Finley/999 RC | 6.00 | 2.50 |
| ☐ 193 Jerod Mayo/999 RC | 10.00 | 4.00 |
| ☐ 194 John Carlson/999 RC | 6.00 | 2.50 |
| ☐ 195 Jonathan Hefney AU/928 RC | 10.00 | 4.00 |
| ☐ 196 Jordon Dizon AU/299 RC | 15.00 | 6.00 |
| ☐ 197 Josh Morgan AU/499 RC | 20.00 | 8.00 |
| ☐ 198 Justin Forsett AU/999 RC | 12.00 | 5.00 |
| ☐ 199 Justin Harper/999 RC | 5.00 | 2.00 |
| ☐ 200 Kalvin McRae AU/999 RC | 10.00 | 4.00 |
| ☐ 201 Keenan Burton/999 RC | 5.00 | 2.00 |
| ☐ 202 Kellen Davis AU/299 RC | 8.00 | 3.00 |
| ☐ 203 Kenneth Moore/999 RC | 5.00 | 2.00 |
| ☐ 204 Kentwan Balmer/999 RC | 5.00 | 2.00 |
| ☐ 205 Kevin Robinson AU/299 RC | 10.00 | 4.00 |
| ☐ 206 Lawrence Jackson/999 RC | 5.00 | 2.00 |
| ☐ 207 Leodis McKelvin/999 RC | 6.00 | 2.50 |
| ☐ 208 Marcus Henry/999 RC | 5.00 | 2.00 |
| ☐ 209 Marcus Monk AU/350 RC | 12.00 | 5.00 |
| ☐ 210 Marcus Smith AU/999 RC | 10.00 | 4.00 |
| ☐ 211 M.Thomas AU/299 RC EXCH | 10.00 | 4.00 |
| ☐ 212 Mario Urrutia/999 RC | 5.00 | 2.00 |
| ☐ 213 Mark Bradford AU/999 RC | 10.00 | 4.00 |
| ☐ 214 Martellus Bennett/999 RC | 6.00 | 2.50 |
| ☐ 215 Martin Rucker AU/299 RC | 10.00 | 4.00 |
| ☐ 216 Matt Sherry/999 RC | 5.00 | 2.00 |
| ☐ 217 Owen Schmitt AU/199 RC | 12.00 | 5.00 |

| | | |
|---|---|---|
| ☐ 218 Pat Sims/999 RC | 5.00 | 2.00 |
| ☐ 219 Patrick Lee/999 RC | 6.00 | 2.50 |
| ☐ 220 Paul Hubbard AU/699 RC | 10.00 | 4.00 |
| ☐ 221 Paul Smith AU/999 RC | 12.00 | 5.00 |
| ☐ 222 Peyton Hillis AU/299 RC | 25.00 | 12.50 |
| ☐ 223 Phillip Merling/999 RC | 5.00 | 2.00 |
| ☐ 224 Philip Wheeler/999 RC | 6.00 | 2.50 |
| ☐ 225 Pierre Garcon/999 RC | 6.00 | 2.50 |
| ☐ 226 Quentin Groves AU/299 RC | 10.00 | 4.00 |
| ☐ 227 Reggie Smith/999 RC | 5.00 | 2.00 |
| ☐ 228 Ryan Grice-Mullen AU/999 RC | 12.00 | 5.00 |
| ☐ 229 Ryan Torain AU/199 RC | 20.00 | 8.00 |
| ☐ 230 Sam Keller AU/999 RC | 12.00 | 5.00 |
| ☐ 231 Sedrick Ellis/999 RC | 6.00 | 2.50 |
| ☐ 232 Shawn Crable AU/299 RC | 15.00 | 6.00 |
| ☐ 233 Adarius Bowman AU/999 RC | 10.00 | 4.00 |
| ☐ 234 Simeon Castille AU/805 RC | 12.00 | 5.00 |
| ☐ 235 Steve Johnson/999 RC | 6.00 | 2.50 |
| ☐ 236 Tavares Gooden/999 RC | 5.00 | 2.00 |
| ☐ 237 Terrell Thomas/999 RC | 5.00 | 2.00 |
| ☐ 238 Terrence Wheatley/999 RC | 5.00 | 2.00 |
| ☐ 239 Robert Killebrew AU/830 RC | 10.00 | 4.00 |
| ☐ 240 Thomas Brown/999 RC | 6.00 | 2.50 |
| ☐ 241 Tim Hightower AU/299 RC | 35.00 | 20.00 |
| ☐ 242 Tom Zbikowski/999 RC | 8.00 | 3.00 |
| ☐ 243 Tom Santi/999 RC | 5.00 | 2.00 |
| ☐ 244 Bernard Morris AU/999 RC | 10.00 | 4.00 |
| ☐ 245 Tracy Porter AU/299 RC | 10.00 | 4.00 |
| ☐ 246 Vernon Gholston/999 RC | 6.00 | 2.50 |
| ☐ 247 Will Franklin AU/199 RC | 12.00 | 5.00 |
| ☐ 248 Xavier Adibi/999 RC | 5.00 | 2.00 |
| ☐ 249 Xavier Omon/999 RC | 6.00 | 2.50 |
| ☐ 250 Zackary Bowman/999 RC | 5.00 | 2.00 |
| ☐ 252 Chad Henne AU/100 RC | 80.00 | 40.00 |
| ☐ 253 Chris Long AU/100 | 60.00 | 30.00 |
| ☐ 254 Donnie Avery AU/100 RC | 40.00 | 20.00 |
| ☐ 255 Eddie Royal AU/100 RC | 80.00 | 40.00 |
| ☐ 256 Felix Jones AU/100 RC | 150.00 | 75.00 |
| ☐ 257 James Hardy AU/100 RC | 50.00 | 25.00 |
| ☐ 258 John David Booty AU/100 RC | 50.00 | 25.00 |
| ☐ 259 Kevin Smith AU/100 RC EXCH | 80.00 | 40.00 |
| ☐ 260 Malcolm Kelly AU/100 RC | 60.00 | 30.00 |
| ☐ 261 Matt Forte AU/100 RC | 120.00 | 60.00 |
| ☐ 262 Matt Ryan AU/100 RC | 250.00 | 125.00 |
| ☐ 263 Ray Rice AU/100 RC | 80.00 | 40.00 |
| ☐ 264 DeSean Jackson AU/105 RC | 80.00 | 40.00 |
| ☐ 265 Andre Caldwell AU/120 RC | 30.00 | 12.00 |
| ☐ 266 Darren McFadden AU/120 RC | 150.00 | 75.00 |
| ☐ 267 Dustin Keller AU/120 RC | 50.00 | 25.00 |
| ☐ 268 Early Doucet AU/120 RC | 50.00 | 25.00 |
| ☐ 269 Glenn Dorsey AU/120 RC | 80.00 | 40.00 |
| ☐ 270 Jake Long AU/120 RC | 60.00 | 30.00 |
| ☐ 271 Joe Flacco AU/120 RC | 175.00 | 100.00 |
| ☐ 272 Kevin O'Connell AU/120 RC | 50.00 | 25.00 |
| ☐ 273 Steve Slaton AU/120 RC | 80.00 | 40.00 |
| ☐ 274 Limas Sweed AU/125 RC EXCH | 100.00 | 50.00 |
| ☐ 275 Earl Bennett AU/140 RC | 50.00 | 20.00 |
| ☐ 276 Chris Johnson AU/140 RC | 100.00 | 50.00 |
| ☐ 277 Dexter Jackson AU/140 RC | 50.00 | 20.00 |
| ☐ 278 Harry Douglas AU/140 RC | 40.00 | 15.00 |
| ☐ 279 Jamaal Charles AU/140 RC | 60.00 | 30.00 |
| ☐ 280 Jerome Simpson AU/140 RC | 50.00 | 20.00 |
| ☐ 281 Jonathan Stewart AU/140 RC | 100.00 | 50.00 |
| ☐ 282 Devin Thomas AU/150 RC | 60.00 | 25.00 |
| ☐ 283 Jordy Nelson AU/150 RC | 80.00 | 30.00 |
| ☐ 284 Mario Manningham AU/150 RC | 50.00 | 20.00 |
| ☐ 285 Rashard Mendenhall AU/150 RC | 120.00 | 60.00 |
| ☐ 286 Dennis Dixon AU/100 RC | 50.00 | 25.00 |
| ☐ 287 Erik Ainge AU/100 RC EXCH | 50.00 | 25.00 |
| ☐ 288 Mike Hart AU/100 RC | 80.00 | 40.00 |
| ☐ 289 Mike Jenkins AU/105 RC EXCH | 50.00 | 25.00 |
| ☐ 290 Dan Connor AU/120 RC | 50.00 | 25.00 |
| ☐ 291 Dorien Bryant AU/120 RC | 40.00 | 15.00 |
| ☐ 292 Keith Rivers AU/120 RC | 40.00 | 15.00 |
| ☐ 293 Kenny Phillips AU/120 RC EXCH | 50.00 | 20.00 |
| ☐ 294 Matt Flynn AU/125 RC | 50.00 | 20.00 |
| ☐ 295 Lavelle Hawkins AU/140 RC | 40.00 | 15.00 |
| ☐ 296 Allen Patrick AU/140 RC | 30.00 | 12.00 |
| ☐ 297 Andre Woodson AU/140 RC | 40.00 | 15.00 |
| ☐ 298 Colt Brennan AU/140 RC | 120.00 | 60.00 |
| ☐ 299 Josh Johnson AU/140 RC | 40.00 | 15.00 |
| ☐ 300 Tashard Choice AU/150 RC | 50.00 | 25.00 |

## 1992 Finest

| | | |
|---|---|---|
| ☐ COMPLETE SET (45) | 20.00 | 7.50 |
| ☐ 1 Neal Anderson | .50 | .20 |
| ☐ 2 Cornelius Bennett | .50 | .20 |
| ☐ 3 Marion Butts | .30 | .10 |
| ☐ 4 Anthony Carter | .50 | .20 |
| ☐ 5 Mike Croel | .30 | .10 |
| ☐ 6 John Elway | 5.00 | 2.00 |
| ☐ 7 Jim Everett | .30 | .10 |
| ☐ 8 Ernest Givins | .30 | .10 |
| ☐ 9 Rodney Hampton | .50 | .20 |
| ☐ 10 Alvin Harper | .30 | .10 |
| ☐ 11 Michael Irvin | 1.00 | .40 |
| ☐ 12 Rickey Jackson | .30 | .10 |
| ☐ 13 Seth Joyner | .30 | .10 |
| ☐ 14 James Lofton | .50 | .20 |
| ☐ 15 Ronnie Lott | .50 | .20 |
| ☐ 16 Eric Metcalf | .50 | .20 |
| ☐ 17 Chris Miller | .30 | .10 |
| ☐ 18 Art Monk | .50 | .20 |
| ☐ 19 Warren Moon | 1.00 | .40 |
| ☐ 20 Rob Moore | .50 | .20 |
| ☐ 21 Anthony Munoz | .30 | .10 |
| ☐ 22 Christian Okoye | .30 | .10 |
| ☐ 23 Andre Rison | .50 | .20 |
| ☐ 24 Leonard Russell | .30 | .10 |
| ☐ 25 Mark Rypien | .50 | .20 |
| ☐ 26 Barry Sanders | 5.00 | 2.00 |
| ☐ 27 Emmitt Smith | 6.00 | 2.50 |
| ☐ 28 Pat Swilling | .30 | .10 |
| ☐ 29 John Taylor | .50 | .20 |
| ☐ 30 Derrick Thomas | 1.00 | .40 |
| ☐ 31 Thurman Thomas | 1.00 | .40 |
| ☐ 32 Reggie White | 1.00 | .40 |
| ☐ 33 Rod Woodson | 1.00 | .40 |
| ☐ 34 Edgar Bennett | .50 | .20 |
| ☐ 35 Terrell Buckley | .30 | .10 |
| ☐ 36 Keith Hamilton | .50 | .20 |
| ☐ 37 Amp Lee | .30 | .10 |
| ☐ 38 Ricardo McDonald | .30 | .10 |
| ☐ 39 Chris Mims | .30 | .10 |
| ☐ 40 Robert Porcher | 1.00 | .40 |
| ☐ 41 Leon Searcy | .30 | .10 |
| ☐ 42 Siran Stacy | .30 | .10 |
| ☐ 43 Tommy Vardell | .30 | .10 |
| ☐ 44 Bob Whitfield | .30 | .10 |
| ☐ NNO Checklist | .30 | .10 |

## 1994 Finest

| | | |
|---|---|---|
| ☐ COMPLETE SET (220) | 40.00 | 15.00 |
| ☐ 1 Emmitt Smith | 6.00 | 2.50 |

|  | | |
|---|---|---|
| ☐ 2 Calvin Williams | .60 | .25 |
| ☐ 3 Mark Collins | .30 | .10 |
| ☐ 4 Steve McMichael | .60 | .25 |
| ☐ 5 Jim Kelly | 1.25 | .50 |
| ☐ 6 Michael Dean Perry | .60 | .25 |
| ☐ 7 Wayne Simmons | .30 | .10 |
| ☐ 8 Rocket Ismail | .60 | .25 |
| ☐ 9 Mark Rypien | .30 | .10 |
| ☐ 10 Brian Blades | .60 | .25 |
| ☐ 11 Barry Word | .30 | .10 |
| ☐ 12 Jerry Rice | 4.00 | 1.50 |
| ☐ 13 Derrick Fenner | .30 | .10 |
| ☐ 14 Karl Mecklenburg | .30 | .10 |
| ☐ 15 Reggie Cobb | .30 | .10 |
| ☐ 16 Eric Swann | .60 | .25 |
| ☐ 17 Neil Smith | .60 | .25 |
| ☐ 18 Barry Foster | .30 | .10 |
| ☐ 19 Willie Roaf | .30 | .10 |
| ☐ 20 Troy Drayton | .30 | .10 |
| ☐ 21 Warren Moon | 1.25 | .50 |
| ☐ 22 Richmond Webb | .30 | .10 |
| ☐ 23 Anthony Miller | .60 | .25 |
| ☐ 24 Chris Slade | .30 | .10 |
| ☐ 25 Mel Gray | .30 | .10 |
| ☐ 26 Ronnie Lott | .60 | .25 |
| ☐ 27 Andre Rison | .60 | .25 |
| ☐ 28 Jeff George | 1.25 | .50 |
| ☐ 29 John Copeland | .30 | .10 |
| ☐ 30 Derrick Thomas | 1.25 | .50 |
| ☐ 31 Sterling Sharpe | .60 | .25 |
| ☐ 32 Chris Doleman | .30 | .10 |
| ☐ 33 Monte Coleman | .30 | .10 |
| ☐ 34 Mark Bavaro | .30 | .10 |
| ☐ 35 Kevin Williams WR | .60 | .25 |
| ☐ 36 Eric Metcalf | .60 | .25 |
| ☐ 37 Brent Jones | .60 | .25 |
| ☐ 38 Steve Tasker | .60 | .25 |
| ☐ 39 Dave Meggett | .30 | .10 |
| ☐ 40 Howie Long | 1.25 | .50 |
| ☐ 41 Rick Mirer | 1.25 | .50 |
| ☐ 42 Jerome Bettis | 4.00 | 1.50 |
| ☐ 43 Marion Butts | .30 | .10 |
| ☐ 44 Barry Sanders | 6.00 | 2.50 |
| ☐ 45 Jason Elam | .60 | .25 |
| ☐ 46 Broderick Thomas | .30 | .10 |
| ☐ 47 Derek Brown RBK | .30 | .10 |
| ☐ 48 Lorenzo White | .30 | .10 |
| ☐ 49 Neil O'Donnell | 1.25 | .50 |
| ☐ 50 Chris Burkett | .30 | .10 |
| ☐ 51 John Offerdahl | .30 | .10 |
| ☐ 52 Rohn Stark | .30 | .10 |
| ☐ 53 Neal Anderson | .30 | .10 |
| ☐ 54 Steve Beuerlein | .60 | .25 |
| ☐ 55 Bruce Armstrong | .30 | .10 |
| ☐ 56 Lincoln Kennedy | .30 | .10 |
| ☐ 57 Darrell Green | .30 | .10 |
| ☐ 58 Ricardo McDonald | .30 | .10 |
| ☐ 59 Chris Warren | .60 | .25 |
| ☐ 60 Mark Jackson | .30 | .10 |
| ☐ 61 Pepper Johnson | .30 | .10 |
| ☐ 62 Chris Spielman | .60 | .25 |
| ☐ 63 Marcus Allen | 1.25 | .50 |
| ☐ 64 Jim Everett | .60 | .25 |
| ☐ 65 Greg Townsend | .30 | .10 |
| ☐ 66 Cris Carter | 1.50 | .60 |
| ☐ 67 Don Beebe | .30 | .10 |
| ☐ 68 Reggie Langhorne | .30 | .10 |
| ☐ 69 Randall Cunningham | 1.25 | .50 |
| ☐ 70 Johnny Holland | .30 | .10 |
| ☐ 71 Morten Andersen | .30 | .10 |
| ☐ 72 Leonard Marshall | .30 | .10 |
| ☐ 73 Keith Jackson | .30 | .10 |
| ☐ 74 Leslie O'Neal | .30 | .10 |
| ☐ 75 Hardy Nickerson | .60 | .25 |
| ☐ 76 Dan Williams | .30 | .10 |
| ☐ 77 Steve Young | 3.00 | 1.25 |
| ☐ 78 Deon Figures | .30 | .10 |
| ☐ 79 Michael Irvin | 1.25 | .50 |
| ☐ 80 Luis Sharpe | .30 | .10 |
| ☐ 81 Andre Tippett | .30 | .10 |
| ☐ 82 Ricky Sanders | .30 | .10 |
| ☐ 83 Eric Pegram | .30 | .10 |
| ☐ 84 Albert Lewis | .30 | .10 |
| ☐ 85 Anthony Blaylock | .30 | .10 |
| ☐ 86 Pat Swilling | .30 | .10 |
| ☐ 87 Duane Bickett | .30 | .10 |
| ☐ 88 Myron Guyton | .30 | .10 |
| ☐ 89 Clay Matthews | .30 | .10 |
| ☐ 90 Jim McMahon | .60 | .25 |
| ☐ 91 Bruce Smith | 1.25 | .50 |
| ☐ 92 Reggie White | 1.25 | .50 |
| ☐ 93 Shannon Sharpe | .60 | .25 |
| ☐ 94 Rickey Jackson | .30 | .10 |
| ☐ 95 Ronnie Harmon | .30 | .10 |
| ☐ 96 Terry McDaniel | .30 | .10 |
| ☐ 97 Bryan Cox | .30 | .10 |
| ☐ 98 Webster Slaughter | .30 | .10 |
| ☐ 99 Boomer Esiason | .60 | .25 |
| ☐ 100 Tim Krumrie | .30 | .10 |
| ☐ 101 Cortez Kennedy | .60 | .25 |
| ☐ 102 Henry Ellard | .60 | .25 |
| ☐ 103 Clyde Simmons | .30 | .10 |
| ☐ 104 Craig Erickson | .30 | .10 |
| ☐ 105 Eric Green | .30 | .10 |
| ☐ 106 Gary Clark | .60 | .25 |
| ☐ 107 Jay Novacek | .60 | .25 |
| ☐ 108 Dana Stubblefield | .60 | .25 |
| ☐ 109 Mike Johnson | .30 | .10 |
| ☐ 110 Ray Crockett | .30 | .10 |
| ☐ 111 Leonard Russell | .30 | .10 |
| ☐ 112 Robert Smith | 1.25 | .50 |
| ☐ 113 Art Monk | .60 | .25 |
| ☐ 114 Ray Childress | .30 | .10 |
| ☐ 115 O.J. McDuffie | 1.25 | .50 |
| ☐ 116 Tim Brown | 1.25 | .50 |
| ☐ 117 Kevin Ross | .30 | .10 |
| ☐ 118 Richard Dent | .60 | .25 |
| ☐ 119 John Elway | 8.00 | 3.00 |
| ☐ 120 James Hasty | .30 | .10 |
| ☐ 121 Gary Plummer | .30 | .10 |
| ☐ 122 Pierce Holt | .30 | .10 |
| ☐ 123 Eric Martin | .30 | .10 |
| ☐ 124 Brett Favre | 8.00 | 3.00 |
| ☐ 125 Cornelius Bennett | .60 | .25 |
| ☐ 126 Jessie Hester | .30 | .10 |
| ☐ 127 Lewis Tillman | .30 | .10 |
| ☐ 128 Qadry Ismail | 1.25 | .50 |
| ☐ 129 Jay Schroeder | .30 | .10 |
| ☐ 130 Curtis Conway | 1.25 | .50 |
| ☐ 131 Santana Dotson | .30 | .10 |
| ☐ 132 Nick Lowery | .30 | .10 |
| ☐ 133 Lomas Brown | .30 | .10 |
| ☐ 134 Reggie Roby | .30 | .10 |
| ☐ 135 John L. Williams | .30 | .10 |
| ☐ 136 Vinny Testaverde | .60 | .25 |
| ☐ 137 Seth Joyner | .30 | .10 |
| ☐ 138 Ethan Horton | .30 | .10 |
| ☐ 139 Jackie Slater | .30 | .10 |
| ☐ 140 Rod Bernstine | .30 | .10 |
| ☐ 141 Rob Moore | .60 | .25 |
| ☐ 142 Dan Marino | 8.00 | 3.00 |
| ☐ 143 Ken Harvey | .30 | .10 |
| ☐ 144 Ernest Givins | .60 | .25 |
| ☐ 145 Russell Maryland | .30 | .10 |
| ☐ 146 Drew Bledsoe | 3.00 | 1.25 |
| ☐ 147 Kevin Greene | .60 | .25 |
| ☐ 148 Bobby Hebert | .30 | .10 |
| ☐ 149 Junior Seau | 1.25 | .50 |
| ☐ 150 Tim McDonald | .30 | .10 |
| ☐ 151 Thurman Thomas | 1.25 | .50 |
| ☐ 152 Phil Simms | .60 | .25 |
| ☐ 153 Terrell Buckley | .30 | .10 |
| ☐ 154 Sam Mills | .30 | .10 |
| ☐ 155 Anthony Carter | .60 | .25 |
| ☐ 156 Kelvin Martin | .30 | .10 |
| ☐ 157 Shane Conlan | .30 | .10 |
| ☐ 158 Irving Fryar | .60 | .25 |
| ☐ 159 Demetrius DuBose | .30 | .10 |
| ☐ 160 David Klingler | .30 | .10 |
| ☐ 161 Herman Moore | 1.25 | .50 |
| ☐ 162 Jeff Hostetler | .60 | .25 |
| ☐ 163 Tommy Vardell | .30 | .10 |
| ☐ 164 Craig Heyward | .60 | .25 |
| ☐ 165 Wilber Marshall | .30 | .10 |
| ☐ 166 Quentin Coryatt | .30 | .10 |
| ☐ 167 Glyn Milburn | .60 | .25 |
| ☐ 168 Fred Barnett | .60 | .25 |
| ☐ 169 Charles Haley | .60 | .25 |
| ☐ 170 Carl Banks | .30 | .10 |
| ☐ 171 Ricky Proehl | .30 | .10 |
| ☐ 172 Joe Montana | 8.00 | 3.00 |
| ☐ 173 Johnny Mitchell | .30 | .10 |
| ☐ 174 Andre Reed | .60 | .25 |
| ☐ 175 Marco Coleman | .30 | .10 |
| ☐ 176 Vaughan Johnson | .30 | .10 |
| ☐ 177 Carl Pickens | .60 | .25 |
| ☐ 178 Dwight Stone | .30 | .10 |
| ☐ 179 Ricky Watters | .60 | .25 |
| ☐ 180 Michael Haynes | .60 | .25 |
| ☐ 181 Roger Craig | .60 | .25 |
| ☐ 182 Cleveland Gary | .30 | .10 |
| ☐ 183 Steve Emtman | .30 | .10 |
| ☐ 184 Patrick Bates | .30 | .10 |
| ☐ 185 Mark Carrier WR | .60 | .25 |
| ☐ 186 Brad Hopkins | .30 | .10 |
| ☐ 187 Dennis Smith | .30 | .10 |
| ☐ 188 Natrone Means | 1.25 | .50 |
| ☐ 189 Michael Jackson | .60 | .25 |
| ☐ 190 Ken Norton Jr. | .60 | .25 |
| ☐ 191 Carlton Gray | .30 | .10 |
| ☐ 192 Edgar Bennett | 1.25 | .50 |
| ☐ 193 Lawrence Taylor | 1.25 | .50 |
| ☐ 194 Marv Cook | .30 | .10 |
| ☐ 195 Eric Curry | .30 | .10 |
| ☐ 196 Victor Bailey | .30 | .10 |
| ☐ 197 Ryan McNeil | .30 | .10 |
| ☐ 198 Rod Woodson | .60 | .25 |
| ☐ 199 Earnest Byner | .30 | .10 |
| ☐ 200 Marvin Jones | .30 | .10 |
| ☐ 201 Thomas Smith | .30 | .10 |
| ☐ 202 Troy Aikman | 4.00 | 1.50 |
| ☐ 203 Audray McMillian | .30 | .10 |
| ☐ 204 Wade Wilson | .30 | .10 |
| ☐ 205 George Teague | .30 | .10 |
| ☐ 206 Deion Sanders | 2.00 | .75 |
| ☐ 207 Will Shields | .60 | .25 |
| ☐ 208 John Taylor | .60 | .25 |
| ☐ 209 Jim Harbaugh | 1.25 | .50 |
| ☐ 210 Micheal Barrow | .30 | .10 |
| ☐ 211 Harold Green | .30 | .10 |
| ☐ 212 Steve Everitt | .30 | .10 |
| ☐ 213 Flipper Anderson | .30 | .10 |
| ☐ 214 Rodney Hampton | .60 | .25 |
| ☐ 215 Steve Atwater | .30 | .10 |
| ☐ 216 James Trapp | .30 | .10 |
| ☐ 217 Terry Kirby | 1.25 | .50 |
| ☐ 218 Garrison Hearst | 1.25 | .50 |
| ☐ 219 Jeff Bryant | .30 | .10 |
| ☐ 220 Roosevelt Potts | .30 | .10 |

## 1995 Finest

|  | | |
|---|---|---|
| ☐ COMPLETE SET (275) | 80.00 | 30.00 |
| ☐ COMP.SERIES 1 (165) | 20.00 | 10.00 |
| ☐ COMP.SERIES 2 (110) | 60.00 | 25.00 |
| ☐ 1 Natrone Means | .60 | .25 |
| ☐ 2 Dave Meggett | .25 | .08 |
| ☐ 3 Tim Bowens | .25 | .08 |
| ☐ 4 Jay Novacek | .60 | .25 |
| ☐ 5 Michael Jackson | .60 | .25 |
| ☐ 6 Calvin Williams | .60 | .25 |
| ☐ 7 Neil Smith | .60 | .25 |
| ☐ 8 Chris Gardocki | .25 | .08 |
| ☐ 9 Jeff Burris | .25 | .08 |
| ☐ 10 Warren Moon | .60 | .25 |
| ☐ 11 Gary Anderson K | .25 | .08 |
| ☐ 12 Bert Emanuel | 1.25 | .50 |

|  |  | | |
|---|---|---|---|
| 13 | Rick Tuten | .25 | .08 |
| 14 | Steve Wallace | .25 | .08 |
| 15 | Marion Butts | .25 | .08 |
| 16 | Johnnie Morton | .60 | .25 |
| 17 | Rob Moore | .60 | .25 |
| 18 | Wayne Gandy | .25 | .08 |
| 19 | Quentin Coryatt | .25 | .08 |
| 20 | Richmond Webb | .25 | .08 |
| 21 | Errict Rhett | .60 | .25 |
| 22 | Joe Johnson | .25 | .08 |
| 23 | Gary Brown | .25 | .08 |
| 24 | Jeff Hostetler | .60 | .25 |
| 25 | Larry Centers | .60 | .25 |
| 26 | Tom Carter | .25 | .08 |
| 27 | Steve Atwater | .25 | .08 |
| 28 | Doug Pelfrey | .25 | .08 |
| 29 | Bryce Paup | .60 | .25 |
| 30 | Erik Williams | .25 | .08 |
| 31 | Henry Jones | .25 | .08 |
| 32 | Stanley Richard | .25 | .08 |
| 33 | Marcus Allen | 1.25 | .50 |
| 34 | Antonio Langham | .25 | .08 |
| 35 | Lewis Tillman | .25 | .08 |
| 36 | Thomas Randolph | .25 | .08 |
| 37 | Byron Bam Morris | .60 | .25 |
| 38 | David Palmer | .60 | .25 |
| 39 | Ricky Watters | .60 | .25 |
| 40 | Brett Perriman | .60 | .25 |
| 41 | Will Wolford | .25 | .08 |
| 42 | Burt Grossman | .25 | .08 |
| 43 | Vincent Brisby | .25 | .08 |
| 44 | Ronnie Lott | .60 | .25 |
| 45 | Brian Blades | .25 | .08 |
| 46 | Brent Jones | .25 | .08 |
| 47 | Anthony Newman * | .25 | .08 |
| 48 | Willie Roaf | .25 | .08 |
| 49 | Paul Gruber | .25 | .08 |
| 50 | Jeff George | .60 | .25 |
| 51 | Jamir Miller | .25 | .08 |
| 52 | Anthony Miller | .60 | .25 |
| 53 | Darrell Green | .25 | .08 |
| 54 | Steve Wisniewski | .25 | .08 |
| 55 | Dan Wilkinson | .60 | .25 |
| 56 | Brett Favre | 5.00 | 2.00 |
| 57 | Leslie O'Neal | .60 | .25 |
| 58 | Keith Byars | .25 | .08 |
| 59 | James Washington | .25 | .08 |
| 60 | Andre Reed | .60 | .25 |
| 61 | Ken Norton Jr. | .60 | .25 |
| 62 | John Randle | .60 | .25 |
| 63 | Lake Dawson | .60 | .25 |
| 64 | Greg Montgomery | .25 | .08 |
| 65 | Erric Pegram | .60 | .25 |
| 66 | Steve Everitt | .25 | .08 |
| 67 | Chris Brantley | .25 | .08 |
| 68 | Rod Woodson | .60 | .25 |
| 69 | Eugene Robinson | .25 | .08 |
| 70 | Dave Brown | .60 | .25 |
| 71 | Ricky Reynolds | .25 | .08 |
| 72 | Rohn Stark | .25 | .08 |
| 73 | Randal Hill | .25 | .08 |
| 74 | Brian Washington | .25 | .08 |
| 75 | Heath Shuler | .60 | .25 |
| 76 | Darion Conner | .25 | .08 |
| 77 | Terry McDaniel | .25 | .08 |
| 78 | Al Del Greco | .25 | .08 |
| 79 | Allen Aldridge | .25 | .08 |
| 80 | Trace Armstrong | .25 | .08 |
| 81 | Darnay Scott | .60 | .25 |
| 82 | Charlie Garner | 1.25 | .50 |
| 83 | Harold Bishop | .25 | .08 |
| 84 | Reggie White | 1.25 | .50 |
| 85 | Shawn Jefferson | .25 | .08 |
| 86 | Irving Spikes | .60 | .25 |
| 87 | Mel Gray | .25 | .08 |
| 88 | D.J. Johnson | .25 | .08 |
| 89 | Daryl Johnston | .60 | .25 |
| 90 | Joe Montana | 5.00 | 2.00 |
| 91 | Michael Strahan | 1.25 | .50 |
| 92 | Robert Blackmon | .25 | .08 |
| 93 | Ryan Yarborough | .60 | .25 |
| 94 | Terry Allen | .60 | .25 |
| 95 | Michael Haynes | .60 | .25 |
| 96 | Jim Harbaugh | .60 | .25 |
| 97 | Micheal Barrow | .25 | .08 |
| 98 | John Thierry | .25 | .08 |
| 99 | Seth Joyner | .25 | .08 |
| 100 | Deion Sanders | 2.00 | .75 |
| 101 | Eric Turner | .25 | .08 |
| 102 | LeShon Johnson | .60 | .25 |
| 103 | John Copeland | .25 | .08 |
| 104 | Cornelius Bennett | .60 | .25 |
| 105 | Sean Gilbert | .60 | .25 |
| 106 | Herschel Walker | .60 | .25 |
| 107 | Henry Ellard | .60 | .25 |
| 108 | Neil O'Donnell | .60 | .25 |
| 109 | Charles Wilson | .25 | .08 |
| 110 | Willie McGinest | .60 | .25 |
| 111 | Tim Brown | 1.25 | .50 |
| 112 | Simon Fletcher | .25 | .08 |
| 113 | Broderick Thomas | .25 | .08 |
| 114 | Tom Waddle | .25 | .08 |
| 115 | Jessie Tuggle | .25 | .08 |
| 116 | Maurice Hurst | .25 | .08 |
| 117 | Aubrey Beavers | .25 | .08 |
| 118 | Donnell Bennett | .60 | .25 |
| 119 | Shante Carver | .25 | .08 |
| 120 | Eric Metcalf | .60 | .25 |
| 121 | John Carney | .25 | .08 |
| 122 | Thomas Lewis | .60 | .25 |
| 123 | Johnny Mitchell | .25 | .08 |
| 124 | Trent Dilfer | 1.25 | .50 |
| 125 | Marshall Faulk | 3.00 | 1.25 |
| 126 | Ernest Givins | .25 | .08 |
| 127 | Aeneas Williams | .25 | .08 |
| 128 | Bucky Brooks | .25 | .08 |
| 129 | Todd Steussie | .25 | .08 |
| 130 | Randall Cunningham | 1.25 | .50 |
| 131 | Reggie Brooks | .60 | .25 |
| 132 | Morten Andersen | .25 | .08 |
| 133 | James Jett | .60 | .25 |
| 134 | George Teague | .25 | .08 |
| 135 | John Taylor | .25 | .08 |
| 136 | Charles Johnson | .60 | .25 |
| 137 | Isaac Bruce | 2.50 | 1.00 |
| 138 | Jason Elam | .60 | .25 |
| 139 | Carl Pickens | .60 | .25 |
| 140 | Chris Warren | .60 | .25 |
| 141 | Bruce Armstrong | .25 | .08 |
| 142 | Mark Carrier DB | .25 | .08 |
| 143 | Irving Fryar | .60 | .25 |
| 144 | Van Malone | .25 | .08 |
| 145 | Charles Haley | .60 | .25 |
| 146 | Chris Calloway | .25 | .08 |
| 147 | J.J. Birden | .25 | .08 |
| 148 | Tony Bennett | .25 | .08 |
| 149 | Lincoln Kennedy | .25 | .08 |
| 150 | Stan Humphries | .60 | .25 |
| 151 | Hardy Nickerson | .25 | .08 |
| 152 | Randall McDaniel | .25 | .08 |
| 153 | Marcus Robertson | .25 | .08 |
| 154 | Ronald Moore | .25 | .08 |
| 155 | Thurman Thomas | 1.25 | .50 |
| 156 | Tommy Vardell | .25 | .08 |
| 157 | Ken Ruettgers | .25 | .08 |
| 158 | Rob Fredrickson | .25 | .08 |
| 159 | Johnny Bailey | .25 | .08 |
| 160 | Greg Lloyd | .60 | .25 |
| 161 | David Alexander | .25 | .08 |
| 162 | Kevin Mawae | .25 | .08 |
| 163 | Derek Brown RBK | .25 | .08 |
| 164 | William Floyd | .60 | .25 |
| 165 | Aaron Glenn | .25 | .08 |
| 166 | Joey Galloway RC | 8.00 | 3.00 |
| 167 | Troy Drayton | .25 | .08 |
| 168 | Derrmontti Dawson | .60 | .25 |
| 169 | Ronald Moore | .25 | .08 |
| 170 | Dan Marino | 5.00 | 2.00 |
| 171 | Dennis Gibson | .25 | .08 |
| 172 | Raymont Harris | .25 | .08 |
| 173 | Shannon Sharpe | .60 | .25 |
| 174 | Kevin Williams | .60 | .25 |
| 175 | Jim Everett | .25 | .08 |
| 176 | Rocket Ismail | .60 | .25 |
| 177 | Mark Fields RC | 1.25 | .50 |
| 178 | George Koonce | .25 | .08 |
| 179 | Chris Hudson | .25 | .08 |
| 180 | Jerry Rice | 2.50 | 1.00 |
| 181 | Dewayne Washington | .60 | .25 |
| 182 | Dale Carter | .60 | .25 |
| 183 | Pete Stoyanovich | .25 | .08 |
| 184 | Blake Brockermeyer | .25 | .08 |
| 185 | Troy Aikman | 2.50 | 1.00 |
| 186 | Jeff Blake RC | 2.50 | 1.00 |
| 187 | Troy Vincent | .25 | .08 |
| 188 | Lamar Lathon | .25 | .08 |
| 189 | Tony Boselli | 1.25 | .50 |
| 190 | Emmitt Smith | 4.00 | 1.50 |
| 191 | Bobby Houston | .25 | .08 |
| 192 | Edgar Bennett | .60 | .25 |
| 193 | Derrick Brooks RC | 8.00 | 3.00 |
| 194 | Ricky Proehl | .25 | .08 |
| 195 | Rodney Hampton | .60 | .25 |
| 196 | Dave Krieg | .25 | .08 |
| 197 | Vinny Testaverde | .60 | .25 |
| 198 | Erik Kramer | .25 | .08 |
| 199 | Ben Coates | .60 | .25 |
| 200 | Steve Young | 2.00 | .75 |
| 201 | Glyn Milburn | .25 | .08 |
| 202 | Bryan Cox | .25 | .08 |
| 203 | Luther Elliss | .25 | .08 |
| 204 | Mark McMillian | .25 | .08 |
| 205 | Jerome Bettis | 1.25 | .50 |
| 206 | Craig Heyward | .60 | .25 |
| 207 | Ray Buchanan | .25 | .08 |
| 208 | Kimble Anders | .60 | .25 |
| 209 | Kevin Greene | .60 | .25 |
| 210 | Eric Allen | .25 | .08 |
| 211 | Ricardo McDonald | .25 | .08 |
| 212 | Ruben Brown RC | 1.50 | .60 |
| 213 | Harvey Williams | .25 | .08 |
| 214 | Broderick Thomas | .25 | .08 |
| 215 | Frank Reich | .25 | .08 |
| 216 | Frank Sanders RC | 1.50 | .60 |
| 217 | Craig Newsome | .25 | .08 |
| 218 | Merton Hanks | .25 | .08 |
| 219 | Chris Miller | .25 | .08 |
| 220 | John Elway | 5.00 | 2.00 |
| 221 | Ernest Givins | .25 | .08 |
| 222 | Boomer Esiason | .60 | .25 |
| 223 | Reggie Roby | .25 | .08 |
| 224 | Qadry Ismail | .60 | .25 |
| 225 | Ki-Jana Carter RC | 1.50 | .60 |
| 226 | Leo Lett | .25 | .08 |
| 227 | Eric Hill | .25 | .08 |
| 228 | Scott Mitchell | .60 | .25 |
| 229 | Craig Erickson | .25 | .08 |
| 230 | Drew Bledsoe | 2.00 | .75 |
| 231 | Sean Landeta | .25 | .08 |
| 232 | Barrett Brooks | .25 | .08 |
| 233 | Brian Mitchell | .25 | .08 |
| 234 | Tyrone Poole | 1.25 | .50 |
| 235 | Desmond Howard | .60 | .25 |
| 236 | Wayne Simmons | .25 | .08 |
| 237 | Michael Westbrook RC | 1.50 | .60 |
| 238 | Quinn Early | .60 | .25 |
| 239 | Willie Davis | .60 | .25 |
| 240 | Rashaan Salaam RC | .75 | .30 |
| 241 | Devin Bush | .25 | .08 |
| 242 | Dana Stubblefield | .60 | .25 |
| 243 | Dexter Carter | .25 | .08 |
| 244 | Shane Conlan | .25 | .08 |
| 245 | Keith Elias RC | .25 | .08 |
| 246 | Robert Brooks | 1.25 | .50 |
| 247 | Garrison Hearst | 1.25 | .50 |
| 248 | Eric Zeier RC | 1.50 | .60 |
| 249 | Nate Newton | .60 | .25 |
| 250 | Barry Sanders | 4.00 | 1.50 |
| 251 | Dave Meggett | .25 | .08 |
| 252 | Courtney Hawkins | .25 | .08 |
| 253 | Cortez Kennedy | .60 | .25 |
| 254 | Mario Bates | .60 | .25 |
| 255 | Junior Seau | 1.25 | .50 |
| 256 | Brian Washington | .25 | .08 |
| 257 | Darius Holland | .25 | .08 |
| 258 | Jeff Graham | .25 | .08 |
| 259 | Rob Moore | .60 | .25 |
| 260 | Andre Rison | .60 | .25 |
| 261 | Kerry Collins RC | 8.00 | 4.00 |
| 262 | Roosevelt Potts | .25 | .08 |
| 263 | Cris Carter | 1.25 | .50 |
| 264 | Curtis Martin RC | 15.00 | 6.00 |

| | | |
|---|---|---|
| ☐ 265 Rick Mirer | .60 | .25 |
| ☐ 266 Mo Lewis | .25 | .08 |
| ☐ 267 Mike Sherrard | .25 | .08 |
| ☐ 268 Herman Moore | 1.25 | .50 |
| ☐ 269 Eric Metcalf | .25 | .08 |
| ☐ 270 Ray Childress | .25 | .08 |
| ☐ 271 Chris Slade | .25 | .08 |
| ☐ 272 Michael Irvin | 1.25 | .50 |
| ☐ 273 Jim Kelly | 1.25 | .50 |
| ☐ 274 Terance Mathis | .60 | .25 |
| ☐ 275 LeRoy Butler | .25 | .08 |

## 1996 Finest

| | | |
|---|---|---|
| ☐ COMPLETE SET (359) | 300.00 | 150.00 |
| ☐ COMP.SERIES 1 (191) | 200.00 | 100.00 |
| ☐ COMP.SERIES 2 (168) | 100.00 | 50.00 |
| ☐ COMP.BRONZE SER.1 (110) | 40.00 | 18.00 |
| ☐ COMP.BRONZE SER.2 (110) | 40.00 | 15.00 |
| ☐ B2 Jay Novacek B | .60 | .25 |
| ☐ B3 Ray Buchanan B | .30 | .10 |
| ☐ B5 Phil Hansen B | .30 | .10 |
| ☐ B6 Mike Mamula B | .30 | .10 |
| ☐ B9 Bernie Parmalee B | .30 | .10 |
| ☐ B10 Herman Moore B | .60 | .25 |
| ☐ B11 Shawn Jefferson B | .30 | .10 |
| ☐ B12 Chris Doleman B | .30 | .10 |
| ☐ B13 Erik Kramer B | .60 | .25 |
| ☐ B15 Orlando Thomas B | .30 | .10 |
| ☐ B16 Terrell Davis B | 4.00 | 1.50 |
| ☐ B18 Roman Phifer B | .30 | .10 |
| ☐ B19 Trent Dilfer B | .60 | .25 |
| ☐ B21 Darnay Scott B | .60 | .25 |
| ☐ B22 Steve McNair B | 4.00 | 1.50 |
| ☐ B23 Lamar Lathon B | .30 | .10 |
| ☐ B26 Thomas Randolph B | .30 | .10 |
| ☐ B27 Michael Jackson B | .60 | .25 |
| ☐ B28 Seth Joyner B | .30 | .10 |
| ☐ B29 Jeff Lageman B | .30 | .10 |
| ☐ B30 Darryl Williams B | .30 | .10 |
| ☐ B32 Erric Pegram B | .60 | .25 |
| ☐ B34 Sean Dawkins B | .60 | .25 |
| ☐ B38 Dan Saleaumua B UER 28 | .30 | .10 |
| ☐ B39 Henry Thomas B | .30 | .10 |
| ☐ B43 Pat Swilling B | .30 | .10 |
| ☐ B44 Marty Carter B | .30 | .10 |
| ☐ B45 Anthony Miller B | .60 | .25 |
| ☐ B48 Chris Warren B | .60 | .25 |
| ☐ B49 Derek Brown RBK B | .30 | .10 |
| ☐ B51 Blaine Bishop B | .30 | .10 |
| ☐ B52 Jake Reed B | .60 | .25 |
| ☐ B55 Vencie Glenn B | .30 | .10 |
| ☐ B58 Derrick Alexander WR B | .60 | .25 |
| ☐ B64 Jessie Tuggle B | .30 | .10 |
| ☐ B65 Terrance Shaw B | .30 | .10 |
| ☐ B66 David Sloan B | .60 | .25 |
| ☐ B68 Brent Jones B | .60 | .25 |
| ☐ B70 William Thomas B | .30 | .10 |
| ☐ B71 Robert Smith B | .60 | .25 |
| ☐ B72 Wayne Simmons B | .30 | .10 |
| ☐ B73 Jim Harbaugh B | .60 | .25 |
| ☐ B76 Wayne Chrebet B | 1.00 | .40 |
| ☐ B77 Chris Hudson B | .30 | .10 |
| ☐ B79 Stevon Moore B | .30 | .10 |
| ☐ B80 Chris Calloway B | .30 | .10 |
| ☐ B81 Tom Carter B | .30 | .10 |
| ☐ B82 Dave Meggett B | .30 | .10 |
| ☐ B83 Sam Mills B | .60 | .25 |
| ☐ B86 Renaldo Turnbull B | .30 | .10 |

| | | |
|---|---|---|
| ☐ B87 Derrick Brooks B | 1.00 | .40 |
| ☐ B89 Eugene Robinson B | .30 | .10 |
| ☐ B91 Rodney Thomas B | .30 | .10 |
| ☐ B92 Dan Wilkinson B | .30 | .10 |
| ☐ B93 Mark Fields B | .30 | .10 |
| ☐ B94 Warren Sapp B | .30 | .10 |
| ☐ B95 Curtis Martin B | 4.00 | 1.50 |
| ☐ B97 Ray Crockett B | .30 | .10 |
| ☐ B98 Ed McDaniel B | .30 | .10 |
| ☐ B101 Craig Heyward B | .30 | .10 |
| ☐ B102 Ellis Johnson B | .30 | .10 |
| ☐ B104 O.J. McDuffie B | .60 | .25 |
| ☐ B105 J.J. Stokes B | 1.00 | .40 |
| ☐ B106 Mo Lewis B | .30 | .10 |
| ☐ B108 Rob Moore B | .60 | .25 |
| ☐ B110 Tyrone Wheatley B | .60 | .25 |
| ☐ B111 Ken Harvey B | .30 | .10 |
| ☐ B113 Willie Green B | .30 | .10 |
| ☐ B114 Willie Davis B | .60 | .25 |
| ☐ B115 Andy Harmon B | .30 | .10 |
| ☐ B117 Bryan Cox B | .30 | .10 |
| ☐ B119 Bert Emanuel B | .60 | .25 |
| ☐ B120 Greg Lloyd B | .60 | .25 |
| ☐ B122 Willie Jackson B | .60 | .25 |
| ☐ B123 Lorenzo Lynch B | .30 | .10 |
| ☐ B124 Pepper Johnson B | .30 | .10 |
| ☐ B128 Tyrone Poole B | .30 | .10 |
| ☐ B129 Neil Smith B | .60 | .25 |
| ☐ B130 Eddie Robinson B | .30 | .10 |
| ☐ B131 Bryce Paup B | .60 | .25 |
| ☐ B134 Troy Aikman B | 5.00 | 2.00 |
| ☐ B136 Chris Sanders B | .60 | .25 |
| ☐ B138 Jim Everett B | .30 | .10 |
| ☐ B139 Frank Sanders B | .60 | .25 |
| ☐ B141 Cortez Kennedy B | .30 | .10 |
| ☐ B143 Derrick Alexander DE B | .30 | .10 |
| ☐ B144 Rob Fredrickson B | .30 | .10 |
| ☐ B145 Chris Zorich B | .30 | .10 |
| ☐ B146 Devin Bush B | .30 | .10 |
| ☐ B149 Troy Vincent B | .30 | .10 |
| ☐ B151 Deion Sanders B | 2.50 | 1.00 |
| ☐ B152 James O. Stewart B | .60 | .25 |
| ☐ B156 Lawrence Dawsey B | .30 | .10 |
| ☐ B157 Robert Brooks B | 1.00 | .40 |
| ☐ B158 Rashaan Salaam B | .60 | .25 |
| ☐ B161 Tim Brown B | .60 | .25 |
| ☐ B162 Brendan Stai B | .30 | .10 |
| ☐ B163 Sean Gilbert B | .30 | .10 |
| ☐ B169 Calvin Williams B | .30 | .10 |
| ☐ B171 Ruben Brown B | .30 | .10 |
| ☐ B172 Eric Green B | .30 | .10 |
| ☐ B175 Jerry Rice B | 5.00 | 2.00 |
| ☐ B176 Bruce Smith B | 1.00 | .40 |
| ☐ B177 Mark Bruener B | .30 | .10 |
| ☐ B179 Lamont Warren B | .30 | .10 |
| ☐ B180 Tamarick Vanover B | 1.00 | .40 |
| ☐ B182 Scott Mitchell B | .60 | .25 |
| ☐ B186 Terry Wooden B | .30 | .10 |
| ☐ B187 Ken Norton B | .60 | .25 |
| ☐ B188 Jeff Herrod B | .30 | .10 |
| ☐ B192 Gus Frerotte B | .60 | .25 |
| ☐ B194 Brett Maxie B | .30 | .10 |
| ☐ B198 Eddie Kennison B RC | 1.00 | .40 |
| ☐ B201 Marcus Jones B RC | .30 | .10 |
| ☐ B202 Terry Allen B | .60 | .25 |
| ☐ B203 Leroy Hoard B | .30 | .10 |
| ☐ B205 Reggie White B | 1.00 | .40 |
| ☐ B206 Larry Centers B | .60 | .25 |
| ☐ B208 Vincent Brisby B | .30 | .10 |
| ☐ B209 Michael Timpson B | .30 | .10 |
| ☐ B211 John Mobley B RC | .30 | .10 |
| ☐ B212 Clay Matthews B | .60 | .25 |
| ☐ B213 Shannon Sharpe B | .60 | .25 |
| ☐ B214 Tony Bennett B | .30 | .10 |
| ☐ B216 Mickey Washington B | .30 | .10 |
| ☐ B217 Fred Barnett B | .30 | .10 |
| ☐ B218 Michael Haynes B | .60 | .25 |
| ☐ B219 Stan Humphries B | .60 | .25 |
| ☐ B221 Winston Moss B | .30 | .10 |
| ☐ B222 Tim Biakabutuka B RC | 1.00 | .40 |
| ☐ B223 Leeland McElroy B RC | .60 | .25 |
| ☐ B224 Vinnie Clark B | .30 | .10 |
| ☐ B225 Keyshawn Johnson B RC | 5.00 | 2.00 |
| ☐ B228 Tony Woods B | .30 | .10 |

| | | |
|---|---|---|
| ☐ B231 Anthony Pleasant B | .30 | .10 |
| ☐ B232 Jeff George B | .60 | .25 |
| ☐ B233 Curtis Conway B | 1.00 | .40 |
| ☐ B235 Jeff Lewis B RC | .60 | .25 |
| ☐ B236 Edgar Bennett B | .60 | .25 |
| ☐ B237 Regan Upshaw B RC | .30 | .10 |
| ☐ B238 William Fuller B | .30 | .10 |
| ☐ B241 Willie Anderson B RC | .30 | .10 |
| ☐ B242 Derrick Thomas B | 1.00 | .40 |
| ☐ B243 Marvin Harrison B RC | 15.00 | 6.00 |
| ☐ B244 Darion Conner B | .30 | .10 |
| ☐ B245 Antonio Langham B | .30 | .10 |
| ☐ B246 Rodney Peete B | .30 | .10 |
| ☐ B247 Tim McDonald B | .30 | .10 |
| ☐ B248 Robert Jones B | .30 | .10 |
| ☐ B251 Mark Carrier DB B | .30 | .10 |
| ☐ B252 Stephen Grant B | .30 | .10 |
| ☐ B254 Jeff Hostetler B | .60 | .25 |
| ☐ B255 Darrell Green B | .30 | .10 |
| ☐ B261 Eric Swann B | .60 | .25 |
| ☐ B263 Irv Smith B | .30 | .10 |
| ☐ B264 Tim McKyer B | .30 | .10 |
| ☐ B266 Sean Jones B | .30 | .10 |
| ☐ B271 Yancey Thigpen B | .60 | .25 |
| ☐ B273 Quentin Coryatt B | .30 | .10 |
| ☐ B274 Hardy Nickerson B | .30 | .10 |
| ☐ B275 Ricardo McDonald B | .30 | .10 |
| ☐ B277 Robert Blackmon B | .30 | .10 |
| ☐ B279 Alonzo Spellman B | .30 | .10 |
| ☐ B281 Rickey Dudley B RC | 1.00 | .40 |
| ☐ B282 Joe Cain B | .30 | .10 |
| ☐ B284 John Randle B | .60 | .25 |
| ☐ B286 Vinny Testaverde B | .60 | .25 |
| ☐ B289 Henry Jones B | .30 | .10 |
| ☐ B290 Simeon Rice B RC | 2.50 | 1.00 |
| ☐ B295 Leslie O'Neal B | .30 | .10 |
| ☐ B297 Greg Hill B | .60 | .25 |
| ☐ B301 Eric Metcalf B | .60 | .25 |
| ☐ B303 Jerome Woods B RC | .30 | .10 |
| ☐ B306 Anthony Smith B | .30 | .10 |
| ☐ B307 Darren Perry B | .30 | .10 |
| ☐ B311 James Hasty B | .30 | .10 |
| ☐ B312 Cris Carter B | 1.00 | .40 |
| ☐ B314 Lawrence Phillips B RC | .60 | .25 |
| ☐ B317 Aeneas Williams B | .30 | .10 |
| ☐ B318 Eric Hill B | .30 | .10 |
| ☐ B319 Kevin Hardy B RC | 1.00 | .40 |
| ☐ B321 Chris Chandler B | .60 | .25 |
| ☐ B322 Rocket Ismail B | .60 | .25 |
| ☐ B323 Anthony Parker B | .30 | .10 |
| ☐ B324 John Thierry B | .30 | .10 |
| ☐ B325 Micheal Barrow B | .30 | .10 |
| ☐ B326 Henry Ford B | .30 | .10 |
| ☐ B327 Aaron Hayden B RC | .30 | .10 |
| ☐ B328 Terance Mathis B | .30 | .10 |
| ☐ B329 Kirk Pointer B RC | .30 | .10 |
| ☐ B330 Ray Mickens B RC | .30 | .10 |
| ☐ B331 Jermane Mayberry B RC | .30 | .10 |
| ☐ B332 Mario Bates B | .60 | .25 |
| ☐ B333 Carlton Gray B | .30 | .10 |
| ☐ B334 Derek Loville B | .30 | .10 |
| ☐ B335 Mike Alstott B RC | 5.00 | 2.00 |
| ☐ B336 Eric Guilford B | .30 | .10 |
| ☐ B337 Marvcus Patton B | .30 | .10 |
| ☐ B338 Terrell Owens B RC | 15.00 | 6.00 |
| ☐ B339 Lance Johnstone B RC | .60 | .25 |
| ☐ B340 Lake Dawson B | .60 | .25 |
| ☐ B341 Winslow Oliver B RC | .30 | .10 |
| ☐ B342 Adrian Murrell B | .60 | .25 |
| ☐ B343 Jason Belser B | .30 | .10 |
| ☐ B344 Brian Dawkins B RC | 6.00 | 2.50 |
| ☐ B345 Reggie Brown B RC | .30 | .10 |
| ☐ B346 Shaun Gayle B | .30 | .10 |
| ☐ B347 Tony Brackens B RC | 1.00 | .40 |
| ☐ B348 Thomas Lewis B | .30 | .10 |
| ☐ B349 Kelvin Pritchett B | .30 | .10 |
| ☐ B350 Bobby Engram B RC | 1.00 | .40 |
| ☐ B351 Moe Williams B RC | 2.50 | 1.00 |
| ☐ B352 Thomas Smith B | .30 | .10 |
| ☐ B353 Dexter Carter B | .30 | .10 |
| ☐ B354 Qadry Ismail B | .30 | .10 |
| ☐ B355 Marco Battaglia B RC | .30 | .10 |
| ☐ B356 Levon Kirkland B | .30 | .10 |
| ☐ B357 Eric Allen B | .30 | .10 |

| | | | |
|---|---|---|---|
| ❏ B358 Bobby Hoying B RC | 1.00 | .40 |
| ❏ B359 Checklist B | .30 | .10 |
| ❏ G1 Kordell Stewart G | 5.00 | 2.00 |
| ❏ G7 Kimble Anders G | 1.50 | .60 |
| ❏ G8 Merton Hanks G | 1.50 | .60 |
| ❏ G17 Rick Mirer G | 3.00 | 1.25 |
| ❏ G33 Craig Newsome G | 1.50 | .60 |
| ❏ G36 Bryce Paup G | 1.50 | .60 |
| ❏ G40 Dan Marino G | 25.00 | 10.00 |
| ❏ G42 Andre Coleman G | 1.50 | .60 |
| ❏ G47 Kevin Carter G | 1.50 | .60 |
| ❏ G60 Mark Brunell G | 5.00 | 2.00 |
| ❏ G61 David Palmer G | 3.00 | 1.25 |
| ❏ G75 Carnell Lake G | 1.50 | .60 |
| ❏ G96 Joey Galloway G | 5.00 | 2.00 |
| ❏ G112 Melvin Tuten G | 1.50 | .60 |
| ❏ G121 Aaron Glenn G | 1.50 | .60 |
| ❏ G132 Brett Favre G | 25.00 | 10.00 |
| ❏ G133 Ken Dilger G | 3.00 | 1.25 |
| ❏ G140 Barry Sanders G | 20.00 | 7.50 |
| ❏ G142 Glyn Milburn G | 1.50 | .60 |
| ❏ G148 Brett Perriman G | 3.00 | 1.25 |
| ❏ G160 Kerry Collins G | 5.00 | 2.00 |
| ❏ G164 Lee Woodall G | 1.50 | .60 |
| ❏ G173 Marshall Faulk G | 6.00 | 2.50 |
| ❏ G178 Troy Aikman G | 12.00 | 5.00 |
| ❏ G190 Drew Bledsoe G | 5.00 | 2.00 |
| ❏ G191 Checklist G | 1.50 | .60 |
| ❏ G193 Michael Irvin G | 5.00 | 2.00 |
| ❏ G196 Warren Moon G | 3.00 | 1.25 |
| ❏ G200 Steve Young G | 12.00 | 5.00 |
| ❏ G207 Alex Van Dyke G RC | 3.00 | 1.25 |
| ❏ G220 Cris Carter G | 5.00 | 2.00 |
| ❏ G230 John Elway G | 25.00 | 10.00 |
| ❏ G234 Charles Haley G | 1.50 | .60 |
| ❏ G240 Jim Kelly G | 5.00 | 2.00 |
| ❏ G250 Rodney Hampton G | 3.00 | 1.25 |
| ❏ G256 Errict Rhett G | 3.00 | 1.25 |
| ❏ G257 Alex Molden G | 1.50 | .60 |
| ❏ G260 Kevin Hardy G | 3.00 | 1.25 |
| ❏ G267 Bryant Young G | 3.00 | 1.25 |
| ❏ G268 Jeff Blake G | 3.00 | 1.25 |
| ❏ G270 Keyshawn Johnson G | 5.00 | 2.00 |
| ❏ G278 Junior Seau G | 5.00 | 2.00 |
| ❏ G285 Terry Kirby G | 3.00 | 1.25 |
| ❏ G293 Hugh Douglas G | 3.00 | 1.25 |
| ❏ G296 Reggie White G | 5.00 | 2.00 |
| ❏ G298 Elvis Grbac G | 3.00 | 1.25 |
| ❏ G300 Emmitt Smith G | 20.00 | 7.50 |
| ❏ G309 Ricky Watters G | 3.00 | 1.25 |
| ❏ S4 Brett Favre S | 15.00 | 6.00 |
| ❏ S14 Chester McGlockton S | .75 | .30 |
| ❏ S20 Tyrone Hughes S | .75 | .30 |
| ❏ S24 Ty Law S | 3.00 | 1.25 |
| ❏ S25 Brian Mitchell S | .75 | .30 |
| ❏ S31 Darren Woodson S | 1.50 | .60 |
| ❏ S35 Brian Mitchell S | .75 | .30 |
| ❏ S37 Dana Stubblefield S | 1.50 | .60 |
| ❏ S41 Kerry Collins S | 3.00 | 1.25 |
| ❏ S46 Orlando Thomas S | .75 | .30 |
| ❏ S50 Jerry Rice S | 8.00 | 3.00 |
| ❏ S53 Willie McGinest S | .75 | .30 |
| ❏ S54 Blake Brockermeyer S | .75 | .30 |
| ❏ S56 Michael Westbrook S | 3.00 | 1.25 |
| ❏ S57 Garrison Hearst S | 3.00 | 1.25 |
| ❏ S59 Kyle Brady S | 1.50 | .60 |
| ❏ S62 Tim Brown S | 1.50 | .60 |
| ❏ S63 Jeff Graham S | .75 | .30 |
| ❏ S67 Dan Marino S | 15.00 | 6.00 |
| ❏ S69 Tamarick Vanover S | 3.00 | 1.25 |
| ❏ S74 Daryl Johnston S | 1.50 | .60 |
| ❏ S78 Frank Sanders S | 1.50 | .60 |
| ❏ S84 Darryll Lewis S | .75 | .30 |
| ❏ S85 Carl Pickens S | 1.50 | .60 |
| ❏ S88 Jerome Bettis S | 3.00 | 1.25 |
| ❏ S90 Terrell Davis S | 6.00 | 2.50 |
| ❏ S99 Napoleon Kaufman S | 3.00 | 1.25 |
| ❏ S100 Rashaan Salaam S | 1.50 | .60 |
| ❏ S103 Barry Sanders S | 15.00 | 6.00 |
| ❏ S107 Tony Boselli S | 1.50 | .60 |
| ❏ S109 Eric Zeier S | 1.50 | .60 |
| ❏ S116 Bruce Smith S | 3.00 | 1.25 |
| ❏ S118 Zack Crockett S | .75 | .30 |
| ❏ S125 Joey Galloway S | 3.00 | 1.25 |
| ❏ S126 Heath Shuler S | 1.50 | .60 |
| ❏ S127 Curtis Martin S | 6.00 | 2.50 |
| ❏ S135 Greg Lloyd S | 1.50 | .60 |
| ❏ S137 Marshall Faulk S | 4.00 | 1.50 |
| ❏ S147 Tyrone Poole S | .75 | .30 |
| ❏ S150 J.J. Stokes S | 3.00 | 1.25 |
| ❏ S153 Drew Bledsoe S | 3.00 | 1.25 |
| ❏ S154 Terry McDaniel S | .75 | .30 |
| ❏ S155 Terrell Fletcher S | .75 | .30 |
| ❏ S159 Dave Brown S | .75 | .30 |
| ❏ S165 Jim Harbaugh S | 1.50 | .60 |
| ❏ S166 Larry Brown S | .75 | .30 |
| ❏ S167 Neil Smith S | 1.50 | .60 |
| ❏ S168 Herman Moore S | 1.50 | .60 |
| ❏ S170 Deion Sanders S | 5.00 | 2.00 |
| ❏ S174 Mark Chmura S | 1.50 | .60 |
| ❏ S181 Chris Warren S | 1.50 | .60 |
| ❏ S183 Robert Brooks S | 3.00 | 1.25 |
| ❏ S184 Steve McNair S | 6.00 | 2.50 |
| ❏ S185 Kordell Stewart S | 3.00 | 1.25 |
| ❏ S189 Charlie Garner S | 1.50 | .60 |
| ❏ S195 Harvey Williams S | .75 | .30 |
| ❏ S197 Jeff George S | 1.50 | .60 |
| ❏ S199 Ricky Watters S | 1.50 | .60 |
| ❏ S204 Steve Bono S | 1.50 | .60 |
| ❏ S210 Jeff Blake S | 3.00 | 1.25 |
| ❏ S215 Phillippi Sparks S | .75 | .30 |
| ❏ S226 William Floyd S | 1.50 | .60 |
| ❏ S227 Troy Drayton S | .75 | .30 |
| ❏ S229 Rodney Hampton S | 1.50 | .60 |
| ❏ S239 Duane Clemons S RC | .75 | .30 |
| ❏ S249 Curtis Conway S | 3.00 | 1.25 |
| ❏ S253 John Mobley S | .75 | .30 |
| ❏ S258 Chris Slade S | .75 | .30 |
| ❏ S262 Eric Metcalf S | 1.50 | .60 |
| ❏ S265 Emmitt Smith S | 12.00 | 5.00 |
| ❏ S269 Jeff Hostetler S | 1.50 | .60 |
| ❏ S272 Thurman Thomas S | 3.00 | 1.25 |
| ❏ S276 Steve Atwater S | .75 | .30 |
| ❏ S280 Isaac Bruce S | 3.00 | 1.25 |
| ❏ S283 Neil O'Donnell S | 1.50 | .60 |
| ❏ S287 Jim Kelly S | 3.00 | 1.25 |
| ❏ S288 Lawrence Phillips S | 3.00 | 1.25 |
| ❏ S291 Terance Mathis S | .75 | .30 |
| ❏ S292 Errict Rhett S | 1.50 | .60 |
| ❏ S294 Santo Stephens S | .75 | .30 |
| ❏ S299 Walt Harris S | .75 | .30 |
| ❏ S302 Jamir Miller S | .75 | .30 |
| ❏ S304 Ben Coates S | 1.50 | .60 |
| ❏ S305 Marcus Allen S | 3.00 | 1.25 |
| ❏ S308 Jonathan Ogden S RC | 3.00 | 1.25 |
| ❏ S310 John Elway S | 15.00 | 6.00 |
| ❏ S313 Irving Fryar S | 1.50 | .60 |
| ❏ S315 Junior Seau S | 3.00 | 1.25 |
| ❏ S316 Alex Molden S RC | .75 | .30 |
| ❏ S320 Steve Young S | 6.00 | 2.50 |

## 1997 Finest

| | | | |
|---|---|---|---|
| ❏ COMPLETE SET (350) | 500.00 | 250.00 |
| ❏ COMP SERIES 1 SET (175) | 250.00 | 125.00 |
| ❏ COMP SERIES 2 SET (175) | 250.00 | 125.00 |
| ❏ COMP BRONZE SER.1 (100) | 25.00 | 10.00 |
| ❏ COMP BRONZE SER.2 (100) | 40.00 | 15.00 |
| ❏ 1 Mark Brunell B | 2.00 | .75 |
| ❏ 2 Chris Slade B | .60 | .25 |
| ❏ 3 Chris Doleman B | .60 | .25 |
| ❏ 4 Chris Hudson B | .60 | .25 |

| | | | |
|---|---|---|---|
| ❏ 5 Karim Abdul-Jabbar B | 1.00 | .40 |
| ❏ 6 Darren Perry B | .60 | .25 |
| ❏ 7 Daryl Johnston B | 1.00 | .40 |
| ❏ 8 Rob Moore B UER | .60 | .25 |
| ❏ 9 Robert Smith B | 1.00 | .40 |
| ❏ 10 Terry Allen B | 1.50 | .60 |
| ❏ 11 Jason Dunn B | .60 | .25 |
| ❏ 12 Henry Thomas B | .60 | .25 |
| ❏ 13 Rod Stephens B | .60 | .25 |
| ❏ 14 Ray Mickens B | .60 | .25 |
| ❏ 15 Ty Detmer B | .60 | .25 |
| ❏ 16 Fred Barnett B | .60 | .25 |
| ❏ 17 Derrick Alexander WR B | 1.00 | .40 |
| ❏ 18 Marcus Robertson B | .60 | .25 |
| ❏ 19 Robert Blackmon B | .60 | .25 |
| ❏ 20 Isaac Bruce B | 1.50 | .60 |
| ❏ 21 Chester McGlockton B | .60 | .25 |
| ❏ 22 Stan Humphries B | 1.00 | .40 |
| ❏ 23 Lonnie Marts B | .60 | .25 |
| ❏ 24 Jason Sehorn B | 1.00 | .40 |
| ❏ 25 Bobby Engram B UER | 1.00 | .40 |
| ❏ 26 Brett Perriman B UER | .60 | .25 |
| ❏ 27 Stevon Moore B | .60 | .25 |
| ❏ 28 Jamal Anderson B | 1.50 | .60 |
| ❏ 29 Wayne Martin B | .60 | .25 |
| ❏ 30 Michael Irvin B UER | 1.50 | .60 |
| ❏ 31 Thomas Smith B | .60 | .25 |
| ❏ 32 Tony Brackens B | .60 | .25 |
| ❏ 33 Eric Davis B | .60 | .25 |
| ❏ 34 James O.Stewart B | 1.00 | .40 |
| ❏ 35 Ki-Jana Carter B | .60 | .25 |
| ❏ 36 Ken Norton B | .60 | .25 |
| ❏ 37 William Thomas B | .60 | .25 |
| ❏ 38 Tim Brown B | 1.50 | .60 |
| ❏ 39 Lawrence Phillips B | 1.00 | .40 |
| ❏ 40 Ricky Watters B | 1.00 | .40 |
| ❏ 41 Tony Bennett B | .60 | .25 |
| ❏ 42 Jessie Armstead B | .60 | .25 |
| ❏ 43 Trent Dilfer B | 1.50 | .60 |
| ❏ 44 Rodney Hampton B | 1.00 | .40 |
| ❏ 45 Sam Mills B | .60 | .25 |
| ❏ 46 Rodney Harrison B RC | 3.00 | 1.25 |
| ❏ 47 Rob Fredrickson B | .60 | .25 |
| ❏ 48 Eric Hill B | .60 | .25 |
| ❏ 49 Bennie Blades B | .60 | .25 |
| ❏ 50 Eddie George B | 1.50 | .60 |
| ❏ 51 Dave Brown B | .60 | .25 |
| ❏ 52 Raymont Harris B | .60 | .25 |
| ❏ 53 Steve Tovar B | .60 | .25 |
| ❏ 54 Thurman Thomas B | 1.50 | .60 |
| ❏ 55 Leeland McElroy B | .60 | .25 |
| ❏ 56 Brian Mitchell B UER | .60 | .25 |
| ❏ 57 Eric Allen B | .60 | .25 |
| ❏ 58 Vinny Testaverde B | 1.00 | .40 |
| ❏ 59 Marvin Washington B | .60 | .25 |
| ❏ 60 Junior Seau B | 1.50 | .60 |
| ❏ 61 Bert Emanuel B | 1.00 | .40 |
| ❏ 62 Kevin Carter B | .60 | .25 |
| ❏ 63 Mark Carrier DB B | .60 | .25 |
| ❏ 64 Andre Coleman B | .60 | .25 |
| ❏ 65 Chris Warren B | 1.00 | .40 |
| ❏ 66 Aeneas Williams B | .60 | .25 |
| ❏ 67 Eugene Robinson B | .60 | .25 |
| ❏ 68 Darren Woodson B | .60 | .25 |
| ❏ 69 Anthony Johnson B | .60 | .25 |
| ❏ 70 Terry Glenn B | 1.50 | .60 |
| ❏ 71 Troy Vincent B | .60 | .25 |
| ❏ 72 John Copeland B | .60 | .25 |
| ❏ 73 Warren Sapp B | 1.00 | .40 |
| ❏ 74 Bobby Hebert B | .60 | .25 |
| ❏ 75 Jeff Hostetler B | .60 | .25 |
| ❏ 76 Willie Davis B | .60 | .25 |
| ❏ 77 Mickey Washington B | .60 | .25 |
| ❏ 78 Cortez Kennedy B | .60 | .25 |
| ❏ 79 Michael Strahan B | 1.00 | .40 |
| ❏ 80 Jerome Bettis B | 1.50 | .60 |
| ❏ 81 Andre Hastings B UER | .60 | .25 |
| ❏ 82 Simeon Rice B | 1.00 | .40 |
| ❏ 83 Cornelius Bennett B | .60 | .25 |
| ❏ 84 Napoleon Kaufman B | 1.50 | .60 |
| ❏ 85 Jim Harbaugh B | 1.00 | .40 |
| ❏ 86 Aaron Hayden B | .60 | .25 |
| ❏ 87 Gus Frerotte B | .60 | .25 |
| ❏ 88 Jeff Blake B | 1.00 | .40 |

| # | Card | Price 1 | Price 2 |
|---|------|---------|---------|
| 89 | Anthony Miller B UER | .60 | .25 |
| 90 | Deion Sanders B | 1.50 | .60 |
| 91 | Curtis Conway B | 1.00 | .40 |
| 92 | William Floyd B | 1.00 | .40 |
| 93 | Eric Moulds B UER | 1.50 | .60 |
| 94 | Mel Gray B | .60 | .25 |
| 95 | Andre Rison B UER | 1.00 | .40 |
| 96 | Eugene Daniel B | .60 | .25 |
| 97 | Jason Belser B | .60 | .25 |
| 98 | Mike Mamula B | .60 | .25 |
| 99 | Jim Everett B | .60 | .25 |
| 100 | Checklist B | .60 | .25 |
| 101 | Drew Bledsoe S | 4.00 | 1.50 |
| 102 | Shannon Sharpe S | 2.00 | .75 |
| 103 | Ken Harvey S | 1.25 | .50 |
| 104 | Isaac Bruce S | 3.00 | 1.25 |
| 105 | Terry Allen S | 3.00 | 1.25 |
| 106 | Lawyer Milloy S | 2.00 | .75 |
| 107 | Ashley Ambrose S | 1.25 | .50 |
| 108 | Alfred Williams S | 1.25 | .50 |
| 109 | Hugh Douglas S | 1.25 | .50 |
| 110 | Junior Seau S | 3.00 | 1.25 |
| 111 | Kordell Stewart S | 3.00 | 1.25 |
| 112 | Adrian Murrell S | 2.00 | .75 |
| 113 | Byron Barn Morris S | 1.25 | .50 |
| 114 | Terrell Buckley S | 1.25 | .50 |
| 115 | Dan Marino S | 12.00 | 5.00 |
| 116 | Willie Clay S | 1.25 | .50 |
| 117 | Neil Smith S | 2.00 | .75 |
| 118 | Blaine Bishop S | 1.25 | .50 |
| 119 | John Mobley S | 1.25 | .50 |
| 120 | Herman Moore S | 2.00 | .75 |
| 121 | Keyshawn Johnson S | 3.00 | 1.25 |
| 122 | Boomer Esiason S | 2.00 | .75 |
| 123 | Marshall Faulk S | 4.00 | 1.50 |
| 124 | Keith Jackson S | 1.25 | .50 |
| 125 | Ricky Watters S | 2.00 | .75 |
| 126 | Carl Pickens S | 2.00 | .75 |
| 127 | Cris Carter S | 3.00 | 1.25 |
| 128 | Mike Alstott S | 3.00 | 1.25 |
| 129 | Simeon Rice S | 2.00 | .75 |
| 130 | Troy Aikman S | 6.00 | 2.50 |
| 131 | Tamarick Vanover S | 2.00 | .75 |
| 132 | Marquez Pope S | 1.25 | .50 |
| 133 | Winslow Oliver S | 1.25 | .50 |
| 134 | Edgar Bennett S | 2.00 | .75 |
| 135 | Dave Meggett S | 1.25 | .50 |
| 136 | Marcus Allen S | 3.00 | 1.25 |
| 137 | Jerry Rice S | 6.00 | 2.50 |
| 138 | Steve Atwater S | 1.25 | .50 |
| 139 | Tim McDonald S | 1.25 | .50 |
| 140 | Barry Sanders S | 10.00 | 4.00 |
| 141 | Eddie George S | 3.00 | 1.25 |
| 142 | Wesley Walls S | 1.25 | .50 |
| 143 | Jerome Bettis S | 3.00 | 1.25 |
| 144 | Kevin Greene S | 2.00 | .75 |
| 145 | Terrell Davis S | 4.00 | 1.50 |
| 146 | Gus Frerotte S | 2.00 | .75 |
| 147 | Joey Galloway S | 2.00 | .75 |
| 148 | Vinny Testaverde S | 2.00 | .75 |
| 149 | Hardy Nickerson S | 1.25 | .50 |
| 150 | Brett Favre S | 12.00 | 5.00 |
| 151 | Desmond Howard G | 1.50 | .60 |
| 152 | Keyshawn Johnson G | 5.00 | 2.00 |
| 153 | Tony Banks G | 5.00 | 2.00 |
| 154 | Chris Spielman G | 1.50 | .60 |
| 155 | Reggie White G | 5.00 | 2.00 |
| 156 | Zach Thomas G | 5.00 | 2.00 |
| 157 | Carl Pickens G | 3.00 | 1.25 |
| 158 | Karim Abdul-Jabbar G | 5.00 | 2.00 |
| 159 | Chad Brown G | 1.50 | .60 |
| 160 | Kerry Collins G | 5.00 | 2.00 |
| 161 | Marvin Harrison G | 5.00 | 2.00 |
| 162 | Steve Young G | 6.00 | 2.50 |
| 163 | Deion Sanders G | 5.00 | 2.00 |
| 164 | Trent Dilfer G | 5.00 | 2.00 |
| 165 | Barry Sanders G | 15.00 | 6.00 |
| 166 | Cris Carter G | 5.00 | 2.00 |
| 167 | Keenan McCardell G | 3.00 | 1.25 |
| 168 | Terry Glenn G | 5.00 | 2.00 |
| 169 | Emmitt Smith G | 15.00 | 6.00 |
| 170 | John Elway G | 20.00 | 7.50 |
| 171 | Jerry Rice G | 10.00 | 4.00 |
| 172 | Troy Aikman G | 10.00 | 4.00 |
| 173 | Curtis Martin G | 6.00 | 2.50 |
| 174 | Darrell Green G | 1.50 | .60 |
| 175 | Mark Brunell G | 6.00 | 2.50 |
| 176 | Corey Dillon B RC | 12.00 | 5.00 |
| 177 | Tyrone Poole B | .60 | .25 |
| 178 | Anthony Pleasant B | .60 | .25 |
| 179 | Frank Sanders B | 1.00 | .40 |
| 180 | Troy Aikman B | 3.00 | 1.50 |
| 181 | Bill Romanowski B | .60 | .25 |
| 182 | Ty Law B | 1.00 | .40 |
| 183 | Orlando Thomas B | .60 | .25 |
| 184 | Quentin Coryatt B | .60 | .25 |
| 185 | Kenny Holmes RC B | 1.25 | .50 |
| 186 | Bryant Young B | .60 | .25 |
| 187 | Michael Sinclair B | .60 | .25 |
| 188 | Mike Tomczak B | .60 | .25 |
| 189 | Bobby Taylor B | .60 | .25 |
| 190 | Brett Favre B | 6.00 | 3.00 |
| 191 | Kent Graham B | .60 | .25 |
| 192 | Jessie Tuggle B | .60 | .25 |
| 193 | Jimmy Smith B | 1.00 | .40 |
| 194 | Greg Hill B | .60 | .25 |
| 195 | Yatil Green B RC | .75 | .30 |
| 196 | Mark Fields B | .60 | .25 |
| 197 | Phillippi Sparks B | .60 | .25 |
| 198 | Aaron Glenn B | .60 | .25 |
| 199 | Pat Swilling B | .60 | .25 |
| 200 | Barry Sanders B | 5.00 | 2.00 |
| 201 | Mark Chmura B | 1.00 | .40 |
| 202 | Marco Coleman B | .60 | .25 |
| 203 | Merton Hanks B | .60 | .25 |
| 204 | Brian Blades B | .60 | .25 |
| 205 | Erict Rhett B | .60 | .25 |
| 206 | Henry Ellard B | .60 | .25 |
| 207 | Andre Reed B | 1.00 | .40 |
| 208 | Bryan Cox B | .60 | .25 |
| 209 | Darnay Scott B | 1.00 | .40 |
| 210 | John Elway B | 6.00 | 3.00 |
| 211 | Glyn Milburn B | .60 | .25 |
| 212 | Don Beebe B | .60 | .25 |
| 213 | Kevin Lockett B RC | .75 | .30 |
| 214 | Dorsey Levens B | 1.50 | .60 |
| 215 | Kordell Stewart B | 1.50 | .60 |
| 216 | Larry Centers B | 1.00 | .40 |
| 217 | Cris Carter B | 1.50 | .60 |
| 218 | Willie McGinest B | .60 | .25 |
| 219 | Renaldo Wynn RC B | .30 | .10 |
| 220 | Jerry Rice B | 3.00 | 1.50 |
| 221 | Reidel Anthony B RC | .75 | .30 |
| 222 | Mark Carrier WR B | .60 | .25 |
| 223 | Quinn Early B | .60 | .25 |
| 224 | Chris Sanders B | .60 | .25 |
| 225 | Shawn Springs B RC | .75 | .30 |
| 226 | Kevin Smith B | .60 | .25 |
| 227 | Ben Coates B | 1.00 | .40 |
| 228 | Tyrone Wheatley B | 1.00 | .40 |
| 229 | Antonio Freeman B | 1.50 | .60 |
| 230 | Dan Marino B | 6.00 | 3.00 |
| 231 | Dwayne Rudd RC B | .50 | .25 |
| 232 | Leslie O'Neal B | .60 | .25 |
| 233 | Brent Jones B | .60 | .25 |
| 234 | Jake Plummer B RC | 10.00 | 4.00 |
| 235 | Kerry Collins B | 1.50 | .60 |
| 236 | Rashaan Salaam B | .60 | .25 |
| 237 | Tyrone Braxton B | .60 | .25 |
| 238 | Herman Moore B | 1.00 | .40 |
| 239 | Keyshawn Johnson B | 1.50 | .60 |
| 240 | Drew Bledsoe B | 2.00 | .75 |
| 241 | Rickey Dudley B | 1.00 | .40 |
| 242 | Antowain Smith B RC | 5.00 | 2.00 |
| 243 | Jeff Lageman B | .60 | .25 |
| 244 | Chris T. Jones B | .60 | .25 |
| 245 | Steve Young B | 2.00 | .75 |
| 246 | Eddie Robinson B | .60 | .25 |
| 247 | Chad Cota B | .60 | .25 |
| 248 | Michael Jackson B | 1.00 | .40 |
| 249 | Robert Porcher B | .60 | .25 |
| 250 | Reggie White B | 1.50 | .60 |
| 251 | Carnell Lake B | .60 | .25 |
| 252 | Chris Calloway B | .60 | .25 |
| 253 | Terance Mathis B | 1.00 | .40 |
| 254 | Carl Pickens B | 1.00 | .40 |
| 255 | Curtis Martin B | 2.00 | .75 |
| 256 | Jeff Graham B | .60 | .25 |
| 257 | Regan Upshaw RC B | .30 | .10 |
| 258 | Sean Gilbert B | .60 | .25 |
| 259 | Will Blackwell B RC | .75 | .30 |
| 260 | Emmitt Smith B | 5.00 | 2.50 |
| 261 | Reinard Wilson RC B | .75 | .30 |
| 262 | Darrell Russell RC B | .30 | .10 |
| 263 | Wayne Chrebet B | 1.00 | .40 |
| 264 | Kevin Hardy B | .60 | .25 |
| 265 | Shannon Sharpe B | 1.00 | .40 |
| 266 | Harvey Williams B | .60 | .25 |
| 267 | John Randle B | 1.00 | .40 |
| 268 | Tim Bowens B | .60 | .25 |
| 269 | Tony Gonzalez B RC | 6.00 | 2.50 |
| 270 | Warrick Dunn B RC | 6.00 | 2.50 |
| 271 | Sean Dawkins B | .60 | .25 |
| 272 | Darryll Lewis B | .60 | .25 |
| 273 | Alonzo Spellman B | .60 | .25 |
| 274 | Mark Collins B | .60 | .25 |
| 275 | Checklist Card B | .60 | .25 |
| 276 | Pat Barnes S RC | 2.00 | .75 |
| 277 | Dana Stubblefield S | 2.00 | .75 |
| 278 | Dan Wilkinson S | 1.25 | .50 |
| 279 | Bryce Paup S | 1.25 | .50 |
| 280 | Kerry Collins S | 3.00 | 1.25 |
| 281 | Derrick Brooks S | 3.00 | 1.25 |
| 282 | Walter Jones S RC | 3.00 | 1.25 |
| 283 | Terry McDaniel S | 1.25 | .50 |
| 284 | James Farrior RC S | 3.00 | 1.25 |
| 285 | Curtis Martin S | 4.00 | 1.50 |
| 286 | O.J. McDuffie S | 2.00 | .75 |
| 287 | Natrone Means S | 2.00 | .75 |
| 288 | Bryant Westbrook RC S | 2.00 | .75 |
| 289 | Peter Boulware RC S | 3.00 | 1.25 |
| 290 | Emmitt Smith S | 10.00 | 4.00 |
| 291 | Joey Kent S RC | 3.00 | 1.25 |
| 292 | Eddie Kennison S | 2.00 | .75 |
| 293 | LeRoy Butler S | 1.25 | .50 |
| 294 | Dale Carter S | 1.25 | .50 |
| 295 | Jim Druckenmiller S RC | 4.00 | 1.50 |
| 296 | Byron Hanspard S RC | 2.00 | .75 |
| 297 | Jeff Blake S | 2.00 | .75 |
| 298 | Levon Kirkland S | 1.25 | .50 |
| 299 | Michael Westbrook S | 2.00 | .75 |
| 300 | John Elway S | 12.00 | 5.00 |
| 301 | Lamar Lathon S | 1.25 | .50 |
| 302 | Ray Lewis S | 5.00 | 2.00 |
| 303 | Steve McNair S | 4.00 | 1.50 |
| 304 | Shawn Springs S | 2.00 | .75 |
| 305 | Karim Abdul-Jabbar S | 2.00 | .75 |
| 306 | Orlando Pace S RC | 3.00 | 1.25 |
| 307 | Scott Mitchell S | 1.25 | .50 |
| 308 | Walt Harris S | 1.25 | .50 |
| 309 | Bruce Smith S | 2.00 | .75 |
| 310 | Reggie White S | 3.00 | 1.25 |
| 311 | Eric Swann S | 1.25 | .50 |
| 312 | Derrick Thomas S | 3.00 | 1.25 |
| 313 | Tony Martin S | 2.00 | .75 |
| 314 | Darrell Russell RC S | 2.00 | .75 |
| 315 | Mark Brunell S | 4.00 | 1.50 |
| 316 | Trent Dilfer S | 3.00 | 1.25 |
| 317 | Irving Fryar S | 1.25 | .50 |
| 318 | Amani Toomer S | 2.00 | .75 |
| 319 | Jake Reed S | 2.00 | .75 |
| 320 | Steve Young S | 4.00 | 1.50 |
| 321 | Troy Davis S RC | 2.00 | .75 |
| 322 | Jim Harbaugh S | 2.00 | .75 |
| 323 | Neil O'Donnell S | 1.25 | .50 |
| 324 | Terry Glenn S | 3.00 | 1.25 |
| 325 | Deion Sanders S | 3.00 | 1.25 |
| 326 | Gus Frerotte S | 2.00 | .75 |
| 327 | Tom Knight RC S | 2.00 | .75 |
| 328 | Peter Boulware S | 2.00 | .75 |
| 329 | Jerome Bettis S | 5.00 | 2.00 |
| 330 | Orlando Pace S | 5.00 | 2.00 |
| 331 | Darnell Autry G RC | 3.00 | 1.25 |
| 332 | Ike Hilliard G RC | 12.00 | 5.00 |
| 333 | David LaFleur G RC | 1.50 | .60 |
| 334 | Jim Harbaugh G | 3.00 | 1.25 |
| 335 | Eddie George G | 5.00 | 2.00 |
| 336 | Vinny Testaverde G | 3.00 | 1.25 |
| 337 | Terry Allen G | 3.00 | 1.25 |
| 338 | Jim Druckenmiller G | 5.00 | 2.00 |
| 339 | Ricky Watters G | 3.00 | 1.25 |
| 340 | Brett Favre G | 20.00 | 7.50 |

| | | |
|---|---|---|
| ☐ 341 Simeon Rice G | 3.00 | 1.25 |
| ☐ 342 Shannon Sharpe G | 3.00 | 1.25 |
| ☐ 343 Kordell Stewart G | 5.00 | 2.00 |
| ☐ 344 Isaac Bruce G | 5.00 | 2.00 |
| ☐ 345 Drew Bledsoe G | 6.00 | 2.50 |
| ☐ 346 Jeff Blake G | 3.00 | 1.25 |
| ☐ 347 Herman Moore G | 3.00 | 1.25 |
| ☐ 348 Junior Seau G | 5.00 | 2.00 |
| ☐ 349 Rae Carruth G RC | 1.50 | .60 |
| ☐ 350 Dan Marino G | 20.00 | 7.50 |
| ☐ P5 K.Abdul-Jabbar Promo | 1.50 | .60 |
| ☐ P32 Tony Brackens Promo | 1.50 | .60 |
| ☐ P45 Sam Mills Promo | 1.50 | .60 |
| ☐ P70 Terry Glenn Promo | 1.50 | .60 |
| ☐ P87 Gus Frerotte Promo | 1.50 | .60 |

## 1998 Finest

| | | |
|---|---|---|
| ☐ COMPLETE SET (270) | 80.00 | 30.00 |
| ☐ COMP.SERIES 1 (150) | 50.00 | 20.00 |
| ☐ COMP.SERIES 2 (120) | 30.00 | 12.50 |
| ☐ 1 John Elway | 4.00 | 1.50 |
| ☐ 2 Terance Mathis | .60 | .25 |
| ☐ 3 Jermaine Lewis | .60 | .25 |
| ☐ 4 Fred Lane | .40 | .15 |
| ☐ 5 Simeon Rice | .40 | .15 |
| ☐ 6 David Dunn | .40 | .15 |
| ☐ 7 Dexter Coakley | .40 | .15 |
| ☐ 8 Carl Pickens | .60 | .25 |
| ☐ 9 Antonio Freeman | 1.00 | .40 |
| ☐ 10 Herman Moore | .60 | .25 |
| ☐ 11 Kevin Hardy | .40 | .15 |
| ☐ 12 Tony Gonzalez | 1.00 | .40 |
| ☐ 13 O.J. McDuffie | .40 | .15 |
| ☐ 14 David Palmer | .40 | .15 |
| ☐ 15 Lawyer Milloy | .60 | .25 |
| ☐ 16 Danny Kanell | .60 | .25 |
| ☐ 17 Randal Hill | .40 | .15 |
| ☐ 18 Chris Slade | .40 | .15 |
| ☐ 19 Charlie Garner | .60 | .25 |
| ☐ 20 Mark Brunell | 1.00 | .40 |
| ☐ 21 Donnell Woolford | .40 | .15 |
| ☐ 22 Freddie Jones | .40 | .15 |
| ☐ 23 Ken Norton | .40 | .15 |
| ☐ 24 Tony Banks | .60 | .25 |
| ☐ 25 Isaac Bruce | 1.00 | .40 |
| ☐ 26 Willie Davis | .40 | .15 |
| ☐ 27 Cris Dishman | .40 | .15 |
| ☐ 28 Aeneas Williams | .40 | .15 |
| ☐ 29 Michael Booker | .40 | .15 |
| ☐ 30 Cris Carter | 1.00 | .40 |
| ☐ 31 Michael McCrary | .40 | .15 |
| ☐ 32 Eric Moulds | 1.00 | .40 |
| ☐ 33 Rae Carruth | .40 | .15 |
| ☐ 34 Bobby Engram | .60 | .25 |
| ☐ 35 Jeff Blake | .60 | .25 |
| ☐ 36 Deion Sanders | 1.00 | .40 |
| ☐ 37 Rod Smith | .60 | .25 |
| ☐ 38 Bryant Westbrook | .40 | .15 |
| ☐ 39 Mark Chmura | .60 | .25 |
| ☐ 40 Tim Brown | 1.00 | .40 |
| ☐ 41 Bobby Taylor | .40 | .15 |
| ☐ 42 James Stewart | .60 | .25 |
| ☐ 43 Kimble Anders | .40 | .15 |
| ☐ 44 Karim Abdul-Jabbar | 1.00 | .40 |
| ☐ 45 Willie McGinest | .40 | .15 |
| ☐ 46 Jessie Armstead | .40 | .15 |
| ☐ 47 Brad Johnson | 1.00 | .40 |
| ☐ 48 Greg Lloyd | .40 | .15 |

| | | |
|---|---|---|
| ☐ 49 Stephen Davis | .40 | .15 |
| ☐ 50 Jerome Bettis | 1.00 | .40 |
| ☐ 51 Warren Sapp | .60 | .25 |
| ☐ 52 Horace Copeland | .40 | .15 |
| ☐ 53 Chad Brown | .40 | .15 |
| ☐ 54 Chris Canty | .40 | .15 |
| ☐ 55 Robert Smith | 1.00 | .40 |
| ☐ 56 Pete Mitchell | .40 | .15 |
| ☐ 57 Aaron Bailey | .40 | .15 |
| ☐ 58 Robert Porcher | .40 | .15 |
| ☐ 59 John Mobley | .40 | .15 |
| ☐ 60 Tony Martin | .60 | .25 |
| ☐ 61 Michael Irvin | 1.00 | .40 |
| ☐ 62 Charles Way | .40 | .15 |
| ☐ 63 Raymont Harris | .40 | .15 |
| ☐ 64 Chuck Smith | .40 | .15 |
| ☐ 65 Larry Centers | .40 | .15 |
| ☐ 66 Greg Hill | .40 | .15 |
| ☐ 67 Kenny Holmes | .40 | .15 |
| ☐ 68 John Lynch | .60 | .25 |
| ☐ 69 Michael Sinclair | .40 | .15 |
| ☐ 70 Steve Young | 1.25 | .50 |
| ☐ 71 Michael Strahan | .60 | .25 |
| ☐ 72 Levon Kirkland | .40 | .15 |
| ☐ 73 Rickey Dudley | .40 | .15 |
| ☐ 74 Marcus Allen | 1.00 | .40 |
| ☐ 75 John Randle | .60 | .25 |
| ☐ 76 Erik Kramer | .40 | .15 |
| ☐ 77 Neil Smith | .60 | .25 |
| ☐ 78 Byron Hanspard | .40 | .15 |
| ☐ 79 Quinn Early | .40 | .15 |
| ☐ 80 Warren Moon | 1.00 | .40 |
| ☐ 81 William Thomas | .40 | .15 |
| ☐ 82 Ben Coates | .60 | .25 |
| ☐ 83 Lake Dawson | .40 | .15 |
| ☐ 84 Steve McNair | 1.00 | .40 |
| ☐ 85 Gus Frerotte | .40 | .15 |
| ☐ 86 Rodney Harrison | .60 | .25 |
| ☐ 87 Reggie White | 1.00 | .40 |
| ☐ 88 Derrick Thomas | 1.00 | .40 |
| ☐ 89 Dale Carter | .40 | .15 |
| ☐ 90 Warrick Dunn | 1.00 | .40 |
| ☐ 91 Will Blackwell | .40 | .15 |
| ☐ 92 Troy Vincent | .40 | .15 |
| ☐ 93 Johnnie Morton | .60 | .25 |
| ☐ 94 David LaFleur | .40 | .15 |
| ☐ 95 Tony McGee | .40 | .15 |
| ☐ 96 Lonnie Johnson | .40 | .15 |
| ☐ 97 Thurman Thomas | 1.00 | .40 |
| ☐ 98 Chris Chandler | .60 | .25 |
| ☐ 99 Jamal Anderson | 1.00 | .40 |
| ☐ 100 Checklist | .40 | .15 |
| ☐ 101 Marshall Faulk | 1.50 | .60 |
| ☐ 102 Chris Calloway | .40 | .15 |
| ☐ 103 Chris Spielman | .40 | .15 |
| ☐ 104 Zach Thomas | 1.00 | .40 |
| ☐ 105 Jeff George | .60 | .25 |
| ☐ 106 Darrell Russell | .40 | .15 |
| ☐ 107 Darryll Lewis | .40 | .15 |
| ☐ 108 Reidel Anthony | .60 | .25 |
| ☐ 109 Terrell Owens | 1.00 | .40 |
| ☐ 110 Rob Moore | .60 | .25 |
| ☐ 111 Darrell Green | .60 | .25 |
| ☐ 112 Merton Hanks | .40 | .15 |
| ☐ 113 Shawn Jefferson | .40 | .15 |
| ☐ 114 Chris Sanders | .40 | .15 |
| ☐ 115 Scott Mitchell | .60 | .25 |
| ☐ 116 Vaughn Hebron | .40 | .15 |
| ☐ 117 Ed McCaffrey | .60 | .25 |
| ☐ 118 Bruce Smith | .60 | .25 |
| ☐ 119 Peter Boulware | .40 | .15 |
| ☐ 120 Brett Favre | 4.00 | 1.50 |
| ☐ 121 Peyton Manning RC | 30.00 | 12.00 |
| ☐ 122 Brian Griese RC | 5.00 | 2.00 |
| ☐ 123 Tavian Banks RC | 1.50 | .60 |
| ☐ 124 Duane Starks RC | 1.00 | .40 |
| ☐ 125 Robert Holcombe RC | 1.50 | .60 |
| ☐ 126 Brian Simmons RC | 1.50 | .60 |
| ☐ 127 Skip Hicks RC | 1.50 | .60 |
| ☐ 128 Keith Brooking RC | 2.50 | 1.00 |
| ☐ 129 Ahman Green RC | 6.00 | 2.50 |
| ☐ 130 Jerome Pathon RC | 2.50 | 1.00 |
| ☐ 131 Curtis Enis RC | 1.00 | .40 |
| ☐ 132 Grant Wistrom RC | 1.50 | .60 |

| | | |
|---|---|---|
| ☐ 133 Germane Crowell RC | 1.50 | .60 |
| ☐ 134 Jacquez Green RC | 1.50 | .60 |
| ☐ 135 Randy Moss RC | 20.00 | 8.00 |
| ☐ 136 Jason Peter RC | 1.00 | .40 |
| ☐ 137 John Avery RC | 1.50 | .60 |
| ☐ 138 Takeo Spikes RC | 2.50 | 1.00 |
| ☐ 139 Pat Johnson RC | 1.50 | .60 |
| ☐ 140 Andre Wadsworth RC | 1.50 | .60 |
| ☐ 141 Fred Taylor RC | 4.00 | 1.50 |
| ☐ 142 Charles Woodson RC | 3.00 | 1.25 |
| ☐ 143 Marcus Nash RC | 1.00 | .40 |
| ☐ 144 Robert Edwards RC | 1.50 | .60 |
| ☐ 145 Kevin Dyson RC | 2.50 | 1.00 |
| ☐ 146 Joe Jurevicius RC | 2.50 | 1.00 |
| ☐ 147 Anthony Simmons RC | 1.50 | .60 |
| ☐ 148 Hines Ward RC | 10.00 | 5.00 |
| ☐ 149 Greg Ellis RC | 1.00 | .40 |
| ☐ 150 Ryan Leaf RC | 2.50 | 1.00 |
| ☐ 151 Jerry Rice | 2.00 | .75 |
| ☐ 152 Tony Martin | .60 | .25 |
| ☐ 153 Checklist | .40 | .15 |
| ☐ 154 Rob Johnson | .60 | .25 |
| ☐ 155 Shannon Sharpe | .60 | .25 |
| ☐ 156 Bert Emanuel | .60 | .25 |
| ☐ 157 Eric Metcalf | .40 | .15 |
| ☐ 158 Natrone Means | .60 | .25 |
| ☐ 159 Derrick Alexander | .60 | .25 |
| ☐ 160 Emmitt Smith | 3.00 | 1.25 |
| ☐ 161 Jeff Burris | .40 | .15 |
| ☐ 162 Chris Warren | .60 | .25 |
| ☐ 163 Corey Fuller | .40 | .15 |
| ☐ 164 Courtney Hawkins | .40 | .15 |
| ☐ 165 James McKnight | 1.00 | .40 |
| ☐ 166 Shawn Springs | .40 | .15 |
| ☐ 167 Wayne Martin | .40 | .15 |
| ☐ 168 Michael Westbrook | .60 | .25 |
| ☐ 169 Michael Jackson | .40 | .15 |
| ☐ 170 Dan Marino | 4.00 | 1.50 |
| ☐ 171 Amp Lee | .40 | .15 |
| ☐ 172 James Jett | .60 | .25 |
| ☐ 173 Ty Law | .60 | .25 |
| ☐ 174 Kerry Collins | .60 | .25 |
| ☐ 175 Robert Brooks | .60 | .25 |
| ☐ 176 Blaine Bishop | .40 | .15 |
| ☐ 177 Stephen Boyd | .40 | .15 |
| ☐ 178 Keyshawn Johnson | 1.00 | .40 |
| ☐ 179 Deon Figures | .40 | .15 |
| ☐ 180 Allen Aldridge | .40 | .15 |
| ☐ 181 Corey Miller | .40 | .15 |
| ☐ 182 Chad Lewis | .60 | .25 |
| ☐ 183 Derrick Rodgers | .40 | .15 |
| ☐ 184 Troy Drayton | .40 | .15 |
| ☐ 185 Darren Woodson | .40 | .15 |
| ☐ 186 Ken Dilger | .40 | .15 |
| ☐ 187 Elvis Grbac | .60 | .25 |
| ☐ 188 Terrell Fletcher | .40 | .15 |
| ☐ 189 Frank Sanders | .60 | .25 |
| ☐ 190 Curtis Martin | 1.00 | .40 |
| ☐ 191 Derrick Brooks | 1.00 | .40 |
| ☐ 192 Darrien Gordon | .40 | .15 |
| ☐ 193 Andre Reed | .60 | .25 |
| ☐ 194 Darnay Scott | .60 | .25 |
| ☐ 195 Curtis Conway | .60 | .25 |
| ☐ 196 Tim McDonald | .40 | .15 |
| ☐ 197 Sean Dawkins | .40 | .15 |
| ☐ 198 Napoleon Kaufman | 1.00 | .40 |
| ☐ 199 Willie Clay | .40 | .15 |
| ☐ 200 Terrell Davis | 1.00 | .40 |
| ☐ 201 Wesley Walls | .60 | .25 |
| ☐ 202 Santana Dotson | .40 | .15 |
| ☐ 203 Frank Wycheck | .40 | .15 |
| ☐ 204 Wayne Chrebet | 1.00 | .40 |
| ☐ 205 Andre Rison | .60 | .25 |
| ☐ 206 Jason Sehorn | .60 | .25 |
| ☐ 207 Jessie Tuggle | .40 | .15 |
| ☐ 208 Kevin Turner | .40 | .15 |
| ☐ 209 Jason Taylor | .60 | .25 |
| ☐ 210 Yancey Thigpen | .40 | .15 |
| ☐ 211 Jake Reed | .60 | .25 |
| ☐ 212 Carnell Lake | .40 | .15 |
| ☐ 213 Joey Galloway | 1.00 | .40 |
| ☐ 214 Andre Hastings | .40 | .15 |
| ☐ 215 Terry Allen | 1.00 | .40 |
| ☐ 216 Jim Harbaugh | .60 | .25 |

|  |  | | |
|---|---|---|---|
| ❑ 217 | Tony Banks | .60 | .25 |
| ❑ 218 | Greg Clark | .40 | .15 |
| ❑ 219 | Corey Dillon | 1.00 | .40 |
| ❑ 220 | Troy Aikman | 2.00 | .75 |
| ❑ 221 | Antowain Smith | 1.00 | .40 |
| ❑ 222 | Steve Atwater | .40 | .15 |
| ❑ 223 | Trent Dilfer | 1.00 | .40 |
| ❑ 224 | Junior Seau | 1.00 | .40 |
| ❑ 225 | Garrison Hearst | 1.00 | .40 |
| ❑ 226 | Eric Allen | .40 | .15 |
| ❑ 227 | Chad Cota | .40 | .15 |
| ❑ 228 | Vinny Testaverde | .60 | .25 |
| ❑ 229 | Duce Staley | 1.25 | .50 |
| ❑ 230 | Drew Bledsoe | 1.50 | .60 |
| ❑ 231 | Charles Johnson | .40 | .15 |
| ❑ 232 | Jake Plummer | 1.00 | .40 |
| ❑ 233 | Errict Rhett | .60 | .25 |
| ❑ 234 | Doug Evans | .40 | .15 |
| ❑ 235 | Phillippi Sparks | .40 | .15 |
| ❑ 236 | Ashley Ambrose | .40 | .15 |
| ❑ 237 | Bryan Cox | .40 | .15 |
| ❑ 238 | Kevin Smith | .40 | .15 |
| ❑ 239 | Hardy Nickerson | .40 | .15 |
| ❑ 240 | Terry Glenn | 1.00 | .40 |
| ❑ 241 | Lee Woodall | .40 | .15 |
| ❑ 242 | Andre Coleman | .40 | .15 |
| ❑ 243 | Michael Bates | .40 | .15 |
| ❑ 244 | Mark Fields | .40 | .15 |
| ❑ 245 | Eddie Kennison | .60 | .25 |
| ❑ 246 | Dana Stubblefield | .40 | .15 |
| ❑ 247 | Bobby Hoying | .60 | .25 |
| ❑ 248 | Mo Lewis | .40 | .15 |
| ❑ 249 | Derrick Mayes | .60 | .25 |
| ❑ 250 | Eddie George | 1.00 | .40 |
| ❑ 251 | Mike Alstott | 1.00 | .40 |
| ❑ 252 | J.J. Stokes | .60 | .25 |
| ❑ 253 | Adrian Murrell | .60 | .25 |
| ❑ 254 | Kevin Greene | .60 | .25 |
| ❑ 255 | LeRoy Butler | .40 | .15 |
| ❑ 256 | Glenn Foley | .60 | .25 |
| ❑ 257 | Jimmy Smith | .60 | .25 |
| ❑ 258 | Tiki Barber | 1.00 | .40 |
| ❑ 259 | Irving Fryar | .60 | .25 |
| ❑ 260 | Ricky Watters | .60 | .25 |
| ❑ 261 | Jeff Graham | .40 | .15 |
| ❑ 262 | Kordell Stewart | 1.00 | .40 |
| ❑ 263 | Rod Woodson | .60 | .25 |
| ❑ 264 | Leslie Shepherd | .40 | .15 |
| ❑ 265 | Ryan McNeil | .40 | .15 |
| ❑ 266 | Ike Hilliard | .60 | .25 |
| ❑ 267 | Keenan McCardell | .60 | .25 |
| ❑ 268 | Marvin Harrison | 1.00 | .40 |
| ❑ 269 | Dorsey Levens | 1.00 | .40 |
| ❑ 270 | Barry Sanders | 3.00 | 1.25 |

**1999 Finest**

| | | | |
|---|---|---|---|
| ❑ COMPLETE SET (175) | | 80.00 | 30.00 |
| ❑ COMP.SET w/o SPs (124) | | 30.00 | 15.00 |
| ❑ 1 | Peyton Manning | 3.00 | 1.25 |
| ❑ 2 | Priest Holmes | 1.50 | .60 |
| ❑ 3 | Kordell Stewart | .60 | .25 |
| ❑ 4 | Shannon Sharpe | .60 | .25 |
| ❑ 5 | Andre Rison | .60 | .25 |
| ❑ 6 | Rickey Dudley | .40 | .15 |
| ❑ 7 | Duce Staley | 1.00 | .40 |
| ❑ 8 | Randall Cunningham | 1.00 | .40 |
| ❑ 9 | Warrick Dunn | 1.00 | .40 |
| ❑ 10 | Dan Marino | 3.00 | 1.25 |

|  |  | | |
|---|---|---|---|
| ❑ 11 | Kevin Greene | .40 | .15 |
| ❑ 12 | Garrison Hearst | .60 | .25 |
| ❑ 13 | Eric Moulds | 1.00 | .40 |
| ❑ 14 | Marvin Harrison | 1.00 | .40 |
| ❑ 15 | Eddie George | 1.00 | .40 |
| ❑ 16 | Vinny Testaverde | .60 | .25 |
| ❑ 17 | Brad Johnson | 1.00 | .40 |
| ❑ 18 | Derrick Thomas | 1.00 | .40 |
| ❑ 19 | Chris Chandler | .60 | .25 |
| ❑ 20 | Troy Aikman | 2.00 | .75 |
| ❑ 21 | Terance Mathis | .60 | .25 |
| ❑ 22 | Terrell Owens | 1.00 | .40 |
| ❑ 23 | Junior Seau | 1.00 | .40 |
| ❑ 24 | Cris Carter | 1.00 | .40 |
| ❑ 25 | Fred Taylor | 1.00 | .40 |
| ❑ 26 | Adrian Murrell | .60 | .25 |
| ❑ 27 | Terry Glenn | 1.00 | .40 |
| ❑ 28 | Rod Smith | .60 | .25 |
| ❑ 29 | Darnay Scott | .60 | .25 |
| ❑ 30 | Brett Favre | 3.00 | 1.25 |
| ❑ 31 | Cam Cleeland | .40 | .15 |
| ❑ 32 | Ricky Watters | .60 | .25 |
| ❑ 33 | Derrick Alexander | .60 | .25 |
| ❑ 34 | Bruce Smith | .60 | .25 |
| ❑ 35 | Steve McNair | 1.00 | .40 |
| ❑ 36 | Wayne Chrebet | .60 | .25 |
| ❑ 37 | Herman Moore | .60 | .25 |
| ❑ 38 | Bert Emanuel | .60 | .25 |
| ❑ 39 | Michael Irvin | .60 | .25 |
| ❑ 40 | Steve Young | 1.25 | .50 |
| ❑ 41 | Napoleon Kaufman | 1.00 | .40 |
| ❑ 42 | Tim Biakabutuka | .60 | .25 |
| ❑ 43 | Isaac Bruce | 1.00 | .40 |
| ❑ 44 | J.J. Stokes | .60 | .25 |
| ❑ 45 | Antonio Freeman | 1.00 | .40 |
| ❑ 46 | John Randle | .60 | .25 |
| ❑ 47 | Frank Sanders | .60 | .25 |
| ❑ 48 | O.J. McDuffie | .60 | .25 |
| ❑ 49 | Keenan McCardell | .60 | .25 |
| ❑ 50 | Randy Moss | 2.50 | 1.00 |
| ❑ 51 | Ed McCaffrey | .60 | .25 |
| ❑ 52 | Yancey Thigpen | .40 | .15 |
| ❑ 53 | Curtis Conway | .60 | .25 |
| ❑ 54 | Mike Alstott | 1.00 | .40 |
| ❑ 55 | Deion Sanders | 1.00 | .40 |
| ❑ 56 | Dorsey Levens | 1.00 | .40 |
| ❑ 57 | Joey Galloway | .60 | .25 |
| ❑ 58 | Natrone Means | .60 | .25 |
| ❑ 59 | Tim Brown | 1.00 | .40 |
| ❑ 60 | Jerry Rice | 2.00 | .75 |
| ❑ 61 | Robert Smith | 1.00 | .40 |
| ❑ 62 | Carl Pickens | .60 | .25 |
| ❑ 63 | Ben Coates | .60 | .25 |
| ❑ 64 | Jerome Bettis | 1.00 | .40 |
| ❑ 65 | Corey Dillon | 1.00 | .40 |
| ❑ 66 | Curtis Martin | 1.00 | .40 |
| ❑ 67 | Jimmy Smith | .60 | .25 |
| ❑ 68 | Keyshawn Johnson | 1.00 | .40 |
| ❑ 69 | Charlie Batch | 1.00 | .40 |
| ❑ 70 | Jamal Anderson | 1.00 | .40 |
| ❑ 71 | Mark Brunell | 1.00 | .40 |
| ❑ 72 | Antowain Smith | 1.00 | .40 |
| ❑ 73 | Aeneas Williams | .40 | .15 |
| ❑ 74 | Wesley Walls | .60 | .25 |
| ❑ 75 | Jake Plummer | .60 | .25 |
| ❑ 76 | Oronde Gadsden | .60 | .25 |
| ❑ 77 | Gary Brown | .40 | .15 |
| ❑ 78 | Peter Boulware | .40 | .15 |
| ❑ 79 | Stephen Alexander | .40 | .15 |
| ❑ 80 | Barry Sanders | 3.00 | 1.25 |
| ❑ 81 | Warren Sapp | .60 | .25 |
| ❑ 82 | Michael Sinclair | .40 | .15 |
| ❑ 83 | Freddie Jones | .40 | .15 |
| ❑ 84 | Ike Hilliard | .60 | .25 |
| ❑ 85 | Jake Reed | .60 | .25 |
| ❑ 86 | Tim Dwight | 1.00 | .40 |
| ❑ 87 | Johnnie Morton | .60 | .25 |
| ❑ 88 | Robert Brooks | .60 | .25 |
| ❑ 89 | Rocket Ismail | .60 | .25 |
| ❑ 90 | Emmitt Smith | 2.00 | .75 |
| ❑ 91 | Ricky Proehl | .40 | .15 |
| ❑ 92 | James Jett | .40 | .15 |
| ❑ 93 | Karim Abdul-Jabbar | .60 | .25 |
| ❑ 94 | Mark Chmura | .40 | .15 |

|  |  | | |
|---|---|---|---|
| ❑ 95 | Andre Reed | .60 | .25 |
| ❑ 96 | Michael Westbrook | .60 | .25 |
| ❑ 97 | Michael Strahan | .60 | .25 |
| ❑ 98 | Chad Brown | .40 | .15 |
| ❑ 99 | Trent Dilfer | .60 | .25 |
| ❑ 100 | Terrell Davis | 1.00 | .40 |
| ❑ 101 | Aaron Glenn | .40 | .15 |
| ❑ 102 | Skip Hicks | .40 | .15 |
| ❑ 103 | Tony Gonzalez | 1.00 | .40 |
| ❑ 104 | Ty Law | .40 | .15 |
| ❑ 105 | Jermaine Lewis | .60 | .25 |
| ❑ 106 | Ray Lewis | 1.00 | .40 |
| ❑ 107 | Zach Thomas | 1.00 | .40 |
| ❑ 108 | Reidel Anthony | .60 | .25 |
| ❑ 109 | Levon Kirkland | .40 | .15 |
| ❑ 110 | Drew Bledsoe | 1.25 | .50 |
| ❑ 111 | Bobby Engram | .60 | .25 |
| ❑ 112 | Jerome Pathon | .40 | .15 |
| ❑ 113 | Muhsin Muhammad | .60 | .25 |
| ❑ 114 | Vonnie Holliday | .40 | .15 |
| ❑ 115 | Bill Romanowski | .40 | .15 |
| ❑ 116 | Marshall Faulk | 1.25 | .50 |
| ❑ 117 | Ty Detmer | .60 | .25 |
| ❑ 118 | Mo Lewis | .40 | .15 |
| ❑ 119 | Charles Woodson | 1.00 | .40 |
| ❑ 120 | Doug Flutie | 1.00 | .40 |
| ❑ 121 | Jon Kitna | 1.00 | .40 |
| ❑ 122 | Courtney Hawkins | .40 | .15 |
| ❑ 123 | Trent Green | 1.00 | .40 |
| ❑ 124 | John Elway | 3.00 | 1.25 |
| ❑ 125 | Barry Sanders GM | 5.00 | 2.00 |
| ❑ 126 | Brett Favre GM | 5.00 | 2.00 |
| ❑ 127 | Curtis Martin GM | 1.50 | .60 |
| ❑ 128 | Dan Marino GM | 5.00 | 2.00 |
| ❑ 129 | Eddie George GM | 1.00 | .40 |
| ❑ 130 | Emmitt Smith GM | 5.00 | 2.00 |
| ❑ 131 | Jamal Anderson GM | 1.50 | .60 |
| ❑ 132 | Jerry Rice GM | 3.00 | 1.25 |
| ❑ 133 | John Elway GM | 5.00 | 2.00 |
| ❑ 134 | Terrell Davis GM | 2.50 | 1.00 |
| ❑ 135 | Troy Aikman GM | 3.00 | 1.25 |
| ❑ 136 | Skip Hicks SN | .40 | .15 |
| ❑ 137 | Charles Woodson SN | 1.00 | .40 |
| ❑ 138 | Charlie Batch SN | 2.50 | 1.00 |
| ❑ 139 | Curtis Enis SN | 1.50 | .60 |
| ❑ 140 | Fred Taylor SN | 2.50 | 1.00 |
| ❑ 141 | Jake Plummer SN | 1.50 | .60 |
| ❑ 142 | Peyton Manning SN | 5.00 | 2.00 |
| ❑ 143 | Randy Moss SN | 4.00 | 1.50 |
| ❑ 144 | Corey Dillon SN | 1.50 | .60 |
| ❑ 145 | Priest Holmes SN | 1.50 | .60 |
| ❑ 146 | Warrick Dunn SN | 1.50 | .60 |
| ❑ 147 | Jevon Kearse RC | 4.00 | 1.50 |
| ❑ 148 | Chris Claiborne RC | 1.50 | .60 |
| ❑ 149 | Akili Smith RC | 1.50 | .60 |
| ❑ 150 | Brock Huard RC | 3.00 | 1.25 |
| ❑ 151 | Daunte Culpepper RC | 10.00 | 4.00 |
| ❑ 152 | Edgerrin James RC | 10.00 | 4.00 |
| ❑ 153 | Cecil Collins RC | 1.50 | .60 |
| ❑ 154 | Kevin Faulk RC | 3.00 | 1.25 |
| ❑ 155 | Amos Zereoue RC | 3.00 | 1.25 |
| ❑ 156 | James Johnson RC | 2.50 | 1.00 |
| ❑ 157 | Sedrick Irvin RC | 1.50 | .60 |
| ❑ 158 | Ricky Williams RC | 5.00 | 2.00 |
| ❑ 159 | Mike Cloud RC | 2.50 | 1.00 |
| ❑ 160 | Chris McAlister RC | 1.50 | .60 |
| ❑ 161 | Rob Konrad RC | 2.50 | 1.00 |
| ❑ 162 | Champ Bailey RC | 3.00 | 1.25 |
| ❑ 163 | Ebenezer Ekuban RC | 2.50 | 1.00 |
| ❑ 164 | Tim Couch RC | 3.00 | 1.25 |
| ❑ 165 | Cade McNown RC | 2.50 | 1.00 |
| ❑ 166 | Donovan McNabb RC | 12.00 | 5.00 |
| ❑ 167 | Joe Germaine RC | 2.50 | 1.00 |
| ❑ 168 | Shaun King RC | 2.50 | 1.00 |
| ❑ 169 | Peerless Price RC | 3.00 | 1.25 |
| ❑ 170 | Kevin Johnson RC | 2.50 | 1.00 |
| ❑ 171 | Troy Edwards RC | 2.50 | 1.00 |
| ❑ 172 | Karsten Bailey RC | 2.50 | 1.00 |
| ❑ 173 | David Boston RC | 3.00 | 1.25 |
| ❑ 174 | D'Wayne Bates RC | 2.50 | 1.00 |
| ❑ 175 | Torry Holt RC | 6.00 | 2.50 |

## 2000 Finest

| | | | |
|---|---|---|---|
| ☐ COMPLETE SET (205) | | 400.00 | 150.00 |
| ☐ 1 Tim Dwight | | .75 | .30 |
| ☐ 2 Cade McNown | | .30 | .10 |
| ☐ 3 Drew Bledsoe | | 1.00 | .40 |
| ☐ 4 Torry Holt | | .75 | .30 |
| ☐ 5 Derrick Mayes | | .50 | .20 |
| ☐ 6 Vinny Testaverde | | .75 | .30 |
| ☐ 7 Patrick Jeffers | | .75 | .30 |
| ☐ 8 Dorsey Levens | | .50 | .20 |
| ☐ 9 James Johnson | | .30 | .10 |
| ☐ 10 Champ Bailey | | .50 | .20 |
| ☐ 11 Jeff George | | .50 | .20 |
| ☐ 12 Shawn Jefferson | | .30 | .10 |
| ☐ 13 Terrence Wilkins | | .30 | .10 |
| ☐ 14 J.J. Stokes | | .50 | .20 |
| ☐ 15 Doug Flutie | | .75 | .30 |
| ☐ 16 Corey Dillon | | .75 | .30 |
| ☐ 17 Rod Smith | | .50 | .20 |
| ☐ 18 Jimmy Smith | | .50 | .20 |
| ☐ 19 Amani Toomer | | .50 | .20 |
| ☐ 20 Curtis Conway | | .50 | .20 |
| ☐ 21 Brad Johnson | | .75 | .30 |
| ☐ 22 Edgerrin James | | 1.25 | .50 |
| ☐ 23 Derrick Alexander | | .50 | .20 |
| ☐ 24 Terrell Owens | | .75 | .30 |
| ☐ 25 Kurt Warner | | 1.50 | .60 |
| ☐ 26 Frank Sanders | | .50 | .20 |
| ☐ 27 Tony Banks | | .50 | .20 |
| ☐ 28 Troy Aikman | | 1.50 | .60 |
| ☐ 29 Curtis Enis | | .30 | .10 |
| ☐ 30 Eddie George | | .75 | .30 |
| ☐ 31 Bill Schroeder | | .50 | .20 |
| ☐ 32 Kent Graham | | .30 | .10 |
| ☐ 33 Mike Alstott | | .75 | .30 |
| ☐ 34 Steve Young | | 1.00 | .40 |
| ☐ 35 Jacquez Green | | .30 | .10 |
| ☐ 36 Frank Wycheck | | .30 | .10 |
| ☐ 37 Kerry Collins | | .50 | .20 |
| ☐ 38 Stephen Davis | | .75 | .30 |
| ☐ 39 Tony Gonzalez | | .50 | .20 |
| ☐ 40 Tyrone Wheatley | | .50 | .20 |
| ☐ 41 Brett Favre | | 2.50 | 1.00 |
| ☐ 42 Joey Galloway | | .50 | .20 |
| ☐ 43 Terrell Davis | | .75 | .30 |
| ☐ 44 Marvin Harrison | | .75 | .30 |
| ☐ 45 Zach Thomas | | .50 | .20 |
| ☐ 46 Jerry Rice | | 1.50 | .60 |
| ☐ 47 Keyshawn Johnson | | .75 | .30 |
| ☐ 48 Rob Johnson | | .50 | .20 |
| ☐ 49 Rocket Ismail | | .50 | .20 |
| ☐ 50 Elvis Grbac | | .50 | .20 |
| ☐ 51 Warrick Dunn | | .75 | .30 |
| ☐ 52 Jevon Kearse | | .75 | .30 |
| ☐ 53 Albert Connell | | .30 | .10 |
| ☐ 54 Muhsin Muhammad | | .50 | .20 |
| ☐ 55 Carl Pickens | | .50 | .20 |
| ☐ 56 Peyton Manning | | 2.00 | .75 |
| ☐ 57 Daunte Culpepper | | 1.00 | .40 |
| ☐ 58 Ike Hilliard | | .50 | .20 |
| ☐ 59 Steve McNair | | .75 | .30 |
| ☐ 60 Sean Dawkins | | .30 | .10 |
| ☐ 61 Steve Beuerlein | | .50 | .20 |
| ☐ 62 Priest Holmes | | 1.00 | .40 |
| ☐ 63 Jim Harbaugh | | .50 | .20 |
| ☐ 64 Germane Crowell | | .30 | .10 |
| ☐ 65 Cris Carter | | .75 | .30 |
| ☐ 66 Jamal Anderson | | .75 | .30 |
| ☐ 67 Kevin Johnson | | .75 | .30 |
| ☐ 68 Herman Moore | | .50 | .20 |
| ☐ 69 Ricky Williams | | .75 | .30 |
| ☐ 70 Rich Gannon | | .75 | .30 |
| ☐ 71 Isaac Bruce | | .75 | .30 |
| ☐ 72 Peerless Price | | .50 | .20 |
| ☐ 73 Az-Zahir Hakim | | .50 | .20 |
| ☐ 74 Mark Brunell | | .75 | .30 |
| ☐ 75 Rob Moore | | .50 | .20 |
| ☐ 76 Antowain Smith | | .50 | .20 |
| ☐ 77 Tim Biakabutuka | | .50 | .20 |
| ☐ 78 Ed McCaffrey | | .75 | .30 |
| ☐ 79 Tony Martin | | .50 | .20 |
| ☐ 80 Marcus Robinson | | .75 | .30 |
| ☐ 81 Kevin Dyson | | .50 | .20 |
| ☐ 82 Wesley Walls | | .30 | .10 |
| ☐ 83 Chris Chandler | | .50 | .20 |
| ☐ 84 Keenan McCardell | | .50 | .20 |
| ☐ 85 Napoleon Kaufman | | .50 | .20 |
| ☐ 86 Emmitt Smith | | 1.50 | .60 |
| ☐ 87 James Stewart | | .50 | .20 |
| ☐ 88 Tim Brown | | .75 | .30 |
| ☐ 89 Ricky Watters | | .50 | .20 |
| ☐ 90 Johnnie Morton | | .50 | .20 |
| ☐ 91 Jake Plummer | | .50 | .20 |
| ☐ 92 Olandis Gary | | .75 | .30 |
| ☐ 93 Jerome Bettis | | .75 | .30 |
| ☐ 94 Terry Glenn | | .50 | .20 |
| ☐ 95 Kordell Stewart | | .50 | .20 |
| ☐ 96 Charlie Garner | | .50 | .20 |
| ☐ 97 Yancey Thigpen | | .30 | .10 |
| ☐ 98 Michael Westbrook | | .50 | .20 |
| ☐ 99 Bobby Engram | | .50 | .20 |
| ☐ 100 Eric Moulds | | .75 | .30 |
| ☐ 101 Darnay Scott | | .50 | .20 |
| ☐ 102 Antonio Freeman | | .75 | .30 |
| ☐ 103 Wayne Chrebet | | .50 | .20 |
| ☐ 104 Akili Smith | | .30 | .10 |
| ☐ 105 Jeff Blake | | .50 | .20 |
| ☐ 106 Curtis Martin | | .75 | .30 |
| ☐ 107 Errict Rhett | | .50 | .20 |
| ☐ 108 Damon Huard | | .75 | .30 |
| ☐ 109 Jeff Graham | | .30 | .10 |
| ☐ 110 Terance Mathis | | .50 | .20 |
| ☐ 111 Jon Kitna | | .75 | .30 |
| ☐ 112 Tim Couch | | .50 | .20 |
| ☐ 113 Fred Taylor | | .75 | .30 |
| ☐ 114 Qadry Ismail | | .50 | .20 |
| ☐ 115 Donovan McNabb | | 1.25 | .50 |
| ☐ 116 Charles Johnson | | .50 | .20 |
| ☐ 117 Troy Edwards | | .30 | .10 |
| ☐ 118 Shaun King | | .30 | .10 |
| ☐ 119 Charlie Batch | | .75 | .30 |
| ☐ 120 Robert Smith | | .75 | .30 |
| ☐ 121 Marshall Faulk | | 1.00 | .40 |
| ☐ 122 Brian Griese | | .75 | .30 |
| ☐ 123 O.J. McDuffie | | .50 | .20 |
| ☐ 124 Randy Moss | | 1.50 | .60 |
| ☐ 125 Duce Staley | | .75 | .30 |
| ☐ 126 Peter Warrick RC | | 8.00 | 3.00 |
| ☐ 127 Dez White RC | | 8.00 | 3.00 |
| ☐ 128 Ron Dayne RC | | 8.00 | 3.00 |
| ☐ 129 J.R. Redmond RC | | 6.00 | 2.50 |
| ☐ 130 Thomas Jones RC | | 12.00 | 5.00 |
| ☐ 131 Plaxico Burress RC | | 15.00 | 6.00 |
| ☐ 132 Reuben Droughns RC | | 10.00 | 4.00 |
| ☐ 133 Shaun Alexander RC | | 15.00 | 6.00 |
| ☐ 134 Ron Dugans RC | | 6.00 | 2.50 |
| ☐ 135 Travis Prentice RC | | 6.00 | 2.50 |
| ☐ 136 Joe Hamilton RC | | 6.00 | 2.50 |
| ☐ 137 Curtis Keaton RC | | 6.00 | 2.50 |
| ☐ 138 Chris Redman RC | | 6.00 | 2.50 |
| ☐ 139 Chad Pennington RC | | 20.00 | 7.50 |
| ☐ 140 Travis Taylor RC | | 8.00 | 3.00 |
| ☐ 141 Bubba Franks RC | | 8.00 | 3.00 |
| ☐ 142 Dennis Northcutt RC | | 8.00 | 3.00 |
| ☐ 143 Jerry Porter RC | | 10.00 | 4.00 |
| ☐ 144 Sylvester Morris RC | | 6.00 | 2.50 |
| ☐ 145 Anthony Becht RC | | 8.00 | 3.00 |
| ☐ 146 Trung Canidate RC | | 6.00 | 2.50 |
| ☐ 147 Jamal Lewis RC | | 20.00 | 7.50 |
| ☐ 148 R.Jay Soward RC | | 6.00 | 2.50 |
| ☐ 149 Tee Martin RC | | 8.00 | 3.00 |
| ☐ 150 Courtney Brown RC | | 8.00 | 3.00 |
| ☐ 151 Brian Urlacher RC | | 30.00 | 12.50 |
| ☐ 152 Danny Farmer RC | | 6.00 | 2.50 |
| ☐ 153 Laveranues Coles RC | | 10.00 | 4.00 |
| ☐ 154 Todd Pinkston RC | | 8.00 | 3.00 |
| ☐ 155 Corey Simon RC | | 8.00 | 3.00 |
| ☐ 156 Spergon Wynn RC | | 6.00 | 2.50 |
| ☐ 157 Tim Rattay RC | | 8.00 | 3.00 |
| ☐ 158 Todd Husak RC | | 8.00 | 3.00 |
| ☐ 159 Aaron Shea RC | | 6.00 | 2.50 |
| ☐ 160 Giovanni Carmazzi RC | | 6.00 | 2.50 |
| ☐ 161 Trevor Gaylor RC | | 6.00 | 2.50 |
| ☐ 162 JaJuan Dawson RC | | 6.00 | 2.50 |
| ☐ 163 Jarious Jackson RC | | 6.00 | 2.50 |
| ☐ 164 Chris Samuels RC | | 6.00 | 2.50 |
| ☐ 165 Rob Morris RC | | 6.00 | 2.50 |
| ☐ 166 P.Warrick/R.Moss IF | | 2.00 | .75 |
| ☐ 167 R.Moss/P.Warrick IF | | 2.00 | .75 |
| ☐ 168 T.Prentice/S.Davis IF | | 1.50 | .60 |
| ☐ 169 S.Davis/T.Prentice IF | | 1.50 | .60 |
| ☐ 170 C.Redman/K.Warner IF | | 1.50 | .60 |
| ☐ 171 K.Warner/C.Redman IF | | 1.50 | .60 |
| ☐ 172 Syl.Morris/J.Smith IF | | 1.50 | .60 |
| ☐ 173 J.Smith/Syl.Morris IF | | 1.50 | .60 |
| ☐ 174 C.Pennington/P.Manning IF | | 4.00 | 1.50 |
| ☐ 175 P.Manning/C.Pennington IF | | 4.00 | 1.50 |
| ☐ 176 R.Soward/M.Harrison IF | | 1.50 | .60 |
| ☐ 177 M.Harrison/R.Soward IF | | 1.50 | .60 |
| ☐ 178 R.Dayne/J.Anderson IF | | 1.50 | .60 |
| ☐ 179 J.Anderson/R.Dayne IF | | 1.50 | .60 |
| ☐ 180 S.Alexander/E.George IF | | 2.50 | 1.00 |
| ☐ 181 E.George/S.Alexander IF | | 2.00 | .75 |
| ☐ 182 C.Brown/B.Smith IF | | 1.50 | .60 |
| ☐ 183 B.Smith/C.Brown IF | | 1.50 | .60 |
| ☐ 184 J.Lewis/E.James IF | | 3.00 | 1.25 |
| ☐ 185 E.James/J.Lewis IF | | 3.00 | 1.25 |
| ☐ 186 T.Canidate/E.Smith IF | | 3.00 | 1.25 |
| ☐ 187 E.Smith/T.Canidate IF | | 3.00 | 1.25 |
| ☐ 188 T.Taylor/C.Carter IF | | 2.00 | .75 |
| ☐ 189 C.Carter/T.Taylor IF | | 2.00 | .75 |
| ☐ 190 C.Keaton/M.Faulk IF | | 2.00 | .75 |
| ☐ 191 M.Faulk/C.Keaton IF | | 2.00 | .75 |
| ☐ 192 P.Burress/J.Rice IF | | 3.00 | 1.25 |
| ☐ 193 J.Rice/P.Burress IF | | 3.00 | 1.25 |
| ☐ 194 T.Jones/T.Davis IF | | 2.00 | .75 |
| ☐ 195 T.Davis/T.Jones IF | | 2.00 | .75 |
| ☐ 196 Peyton Manning GM | | 5.00 | 2.00 |
| ☐ 197 Randy Moss GM | | 4.00 | 1.50 |
| ☐ 198 Terrell Davis GM | | 1.50 | .60 |
| ☐ 199 Marshall Faulk GM | | 2.50 | 1.00 |
| ☐ 200 Edgerrin James GM | | 4.00 | 1.50 |
| ☐ 201 Emmitt Smith GM | | 4.00 | 1.50 |
| ☐ 202 Ricky Williams GM | | 1.50 | .60 |
| ☐ 203 Kurt Warner GM | | 3.00 | 1.25 |
| ☐ 204 Eddie George GM | | 1.50 | .60 |
| ☐ 205 Brett Favre GM | | 6.00 | 2.50 |

## 2001 Finest

MIKE ANDERSON
RUNNING BACK

| | | | |
|---|---|---|---|
| ☐ COMP.SET w/o SP's (100) | | 40.00 | 20.00 |
| ☐ 1 Eddie George | | 1.25 | .50 |
| ☐ 2 Jay Fiedler | | 1.25 | .50 |
| ☐ 3 Peter Warrick | | 1.25 | .50 |
| ☐ 4 Vinny Testaverde | | .75 | .30 |
| ☐ 5 Charles Johnson | | .50 | .20 |
| ☐ 6 Ahman Green | | 1.25 | .50 |
| ☐ 7 Isaac Bruce | | 1.25 | .50 |
| ☐ 8 Junior Seau | | 1.25 | .50 |
| ☐ 9 Daunte Culpepper | | 1.25 | .50 |

|  |  | | |
|---|---|---|---|
| ❑ 10 | Ike Hilliard | .75 | .30 |
| ❑ 11 | Tony Banks | .75 | .30 |
| ❑ 12 | Steve Beuerlein | .75 | .30 |
| ❑ 13 | Jamal Anderson | 1.25 | .50 |
| ❑ 14 | Tyrone Wheatley | .75 | .30 |
| ❑ 15 | Sylvester Morris | .50 | .20 |
| ❑ 16 | Edgerrin James | 1.50 | .60 |
| ❑ 17 | Shaun King | .50 | .20 |
| ❑ 18 | Terrell Owens | 1.25 | .50 |
| ❑ 19 | Donovan Mcnabb | 1.50 | .60 |
| ❑ 20 | Cade Mcnown | .50 | .20 |
| ❑ 21 | Elvis Grbac | .75 | .30 |
| ❑ 22 | James Stewart | .75 | .30 |
| ❑ 23 | Joe Horn | .75 | .30 |
| ❑ 24 | Randy Moss | 2.50 | 1.00 |
| ❑ 25 | Matt Hasselbeck | .75 | .30 |
| ❑ 26 | Jerome Bettis | 1.25 | .50 |
| ❑ 27 | Bill Schroeder | .75 | .30 |
| ❑ 28 | Jake Plummer | .75 | .30 |
| ❑ 29 | Rod Smith | .75 | .30 |
| ❑ 30 | Akili Smith | .50 | .20 |
| ❑ 31 | Jimmy Smith | .75 | .30 |
| ❑ 32 | Oronde Gadsden | .75 | .30 |
| ❑ 33 | Kerry Collins | .75 | .30 |
| ❑ 34 | Warrick Dunn | 1.25 | .50 |
| ❑ 35 | Jeff Graham | .50 | .20 |
| ❑ 36 | Ray Lewis | 1.25 | .50 |
| ❑ 37 | Joey Galloway | .75 | .30 |
| ❑ 38 | Tim Brown | 1.25 | .50 |
| ❑ 39 | Derrick Alexander | .75 | .30 |
| ❑ 40 | Jerry Rice | 2.50 | 1.00 |
| ❑ 41 | Muhsin Muhammad | .75 | .30 |
| ❑ 42 | Shawn Jefferson | .50 | .20 |
| ❑ 43 | Curtis Martin | 1.25 | .50 |
| ❑ 44 | Terry Glenn | .75 | .30 |
| ❑ 45 | Marvin Harrison | 1.25 | .50 |
| ❑ 46 | Mike Anderson | 1.25 | .50 |
| ❑ 47 | Stephen Davis | 1.25 | .50 |
| ❑ 48 | Chad Lewis | .50 | .20 |
| ❑ 49 | Fred Taylor | 1.25 | .50 |
| ❑ 50 | Corey Dillon | 1.25 | .50 |
| ❑ 51 | Charlie Batch | 1.25 | .50 |
| ❑ 52 | Kevin Johnson | .75 | .30 |
| ❑ 53 | Brett Favre | 4.00 | 1.50 |
| ❑ 54 | Marshall Faulk | 1.50 | .60 |
| ❑ 55 | Kordell Stewart | .75 | .30 |
| ❑ 56 | Steve McNair | 1.25 | .50 |
| ❑ 57 | Jeff Blake | .75 | .30 |
| ❑ 58 | Eric Moulds | .75 | .30 |
| ❑ 59 | Emmitt Smith | 2.50 | 1.00 |
| ❑ 60 | David Boston | 1.25 | .50 |
| ❑ 61 | Cris Carter | 1.25 | .50 |
| ❑ 62 | Peyton Manning | 3.00 | 1.25 |
| ❑ 63 | Keyshawn Johnson | 1.25 | .50 |
| ❑ 64 | Doug Flutie | 1.25 | .50 |
| ❑ 65 | Drew Bledsoe | 1.50 | .60 |
| ❑ 66 | Ricky Williams | 1.25 | .50 |
| ❑ 67 | Keenan Mccardell | .50 | .20 |
| ❑ 68 | Brian Urlacher | 2.00 | .75 |
| ❑ 69 | Jamal Lewis | 2.00 | .75 |
| ❑ 70 | Ed McCaffrey | 1.25 | .50 |
| ❑ 71 | Antonio Freeman | 1.25 | .50 |
| ❑ 72 | Darrell Jackson | 1.25 | .50 |
| ❑ 73 | Jeff George | .75 | .30 |
| ❑ 74 | Chris Chandler | .75 | .30 |
| ❑ 75 | Germane Crowell | .50 | .20 |
| ❑ 76 | Tim Biakabutuka | .75 | .30 |
| ❑ 77 | Jon Kitna | .75 | .30 |
| ❑ 78 | Troy Brown | .75 | .30 |
| ❑ 79 | Lamar Smith | .75 | .30 |
| ❑ 80 | Derrick Mason | .75 | .30 |
| ❑ 81 | Hines Ward | 1.25 | .50 |
| ❑ 82 | Mark Brunell | 1.25 | .50 |
| ❑ 83 | Trent Dilfer | .75 | .30 |
| ❑ 84 | Tim Couch | .75 | .30 |
| ❑ 85 | Donald Hayes | .50 | .20 |
| ❑ 86 | Amani Toomer | .75 | .30 |
| ❑ 87 | Tony Gonzalez | .75 | .30 |
| ❑ 88 | Rich Gannon | 1.25 | .50 |
| ❑ 89 | Rob Johnson | .75 | .30 |
| ❑ 90 | Torry Holt | 1.25 | .50 |
| ❑ 91 | Jeff Garcia | 1.25 | .50 |
| ❑ 92 | Kurt Warner | 2.50 | 1.00 |
| ❑ 93 | Aaron Brooks | 1.25 | .50 |
| ❑ 94 | Brian Griese | 1.25 | .50 |
| ❑ 95 | James Allen | .75 | .30 |
| ❑ 96 | Wayne Chrebet | .75 | .30 |
| ❑ 97 | Tiki Barber | 1.25 | .50 |
| ❑ 98 | Brad Johnson | 1.25 | .50 |
| ❑ 99 | Ricky Watters | .75 | .30 |
| ❑ 100 | Charlie Garner | .75 | .30 |
| ❑ 101 | Andre Carter RC | 10.00 | 4.00 |
| ❑ 102 | Dan Morgan RC | 10.00 | 4.00 |
| ❑ 103 | Gerard Warren RC | 10.00 | 4.00 |
| ❑ 104 | Jesse Palmer RC | 10.00 | 4.00 |
| ❑ 105 | Josh Heupel RC | 10.00 | 4.00 |
| ❑ 106 | Justin Smith RC | 10.00 | 4.00 |
| ❑ 107 | LaMont Jordan RC | 20.00 | 10.00 |
| ❑ 108 | Leonard Davis RC | 6.00 | 2.50 |
| ❑ 109 | Marques Tuiasosopo RC | 10.00 | 4.00 |
| ❑ 110 | Snoop Minnis RC | 6.00 | 2.50 |
| ❑ 111 | Quincy Carter RC | 10.00 | 4.00 |
| ❑ 112 | Quincy Morgan RC | 10.00 | 4.00 |
| ❑ 113 | Richard Seymour RC | 10.00 | 4.00 |
| ❑ 114 | Rudi Johnson RC | 20.00 | 7.50 |
| ❑ 115 | Sage Rosenfels RC | 10.00 | 4.00 |
| ❑ 116 | Todd Heap RC | 10.00 | 4.00 |
| ❑ 117 | Travis Minor RC | 6.00 | 2.50 |
| ❑ 118 | Will Allen RC | 6.00 | 2.50 |
| ❑ 119 | Jamal Reynolds RC | 10.00 | 4.00 |
| ❑ 120 | Scotty Anderson RC | 6.00 | 2.50 |
| ❑ 121 | Anthony Thomas RC | 10.00 | 4.00 |
| ❑ 122 | Chad Johnson RC | 25.00 | 10.00 |
| ❑ 123 | Chris Chambers RC | 15.00 | 6.00 |
| ❑ 124 | Chris Weinke RC | 10.00 | 4.00 |
| ❑ 125 | David Terrell RC | 10.00 | 4.00 |
| ❑ 126 | Deuce McAllister RC | 20.00 | 7.50 |
| ❑ 127 | Drew Brees RC | 40.00 | 15.00 |
| ❑ 128 | Freddie Mitchell RC | 10.00 | 4.00 |
| ❑ 129 | James Jackson RC | 10.00 | 4.00 |
| ❑ 130 | Kevan Barlow RC | 10.00 | 4.00 |
| ❑ 131 | Koren Robinson RC | 10.00 | 4.00 |
| ❑ 132 | LaDainian Tomlinson RC | 120.00 | 60.00 |
| ❑ 133 | Michael Bennett RC | 10.00 | 4.00 |
| ❑ 134 | Michael Vick RC | 25.00 | 10.00 |
| ❑ 135 | Mike McMahon RC | 10.00 | 4.00 |
| ❑ 136 | Reggie Wayne RC | 20.00 | 7.50 |
| ❑ 137 | Robert Ferguson RC | 10.00 | 4.00 |
| ❑ 138 | Rod Gardner RC | 10.00 | 4.00 |
| ❑ 139 | Santana Moss RC | 15.00 | 6.00 |
| ❑ 140 | Travis Henry RC | 10.00 | 4.00 |

## 2002 Finest

|  |  | | |
|---|---|---|---|
| COMP.SET w/o SP's (62) | | 40.00 | 15.00 |
| ❑ 1 | Peyton Manning | 2.50 | 1.00 |
| ❑ 2 | Troy Brown | .75 | .30 |
| ❑ 3 | Curtis Martin | 1.25 | .50 |
| ❑ 4 | Kordell Stewart | .75 | .30 |
| ❑ 5 | Michael Pittman | .50 | .20 |
| ❑ 6 | Rod Gardner | .75 | .30 |
| ❑ 7 | Germane Crowell | .50 | .20 |
| ❑ 8 | Terrell Davis | 1.25 | .50 |
| ❑ 9 | Eric Moulds | .75 | .30 |
| ❑ 10 | Jake Plummer | .75 | .30 |
| ❑ 11 | Tony Gonzalez | .75 | .30 |
| ❑ 12 | Ricky Williams | 1.25 | .50 |
| ❑ 13 | Deuce McAllister | 1.50 | .60 |
| ❑ 14 | Jerry Rice | 2.50 | 1.00 |
| ❑ 15 | Torry Holt | 1.25 | .50 |
| ❑ 16 | Michael Vick | 2.50 | 1.00 |
| ❑ 17 | David Terrell | .75 | .30 |
| ❑ 18 | Terry Glenn | .75 | .30 |
| ❑ 19 | Mark Brunell | 1.25 | .50 |
| ❑ 20 | Vinny Testaverde | .75 | .30 |
| ❑ 21 | Jerome Bettis | 1.25 | .50 |
| ❑ 22 | Randy Moss | 2.50 | 1.00 |
| ❑ 23 | Marvin Harrison | 1.25 | .50 |
| ❑ 24 | Chris Weinke | .75 | .30 |
| ❑ 25 | Tiki Barber | 1.25 | .50 |
| ❑ 26 | Corey Bradford | .50 | .20 |
| ❑ 27 | David Boston | 1.25 | .50 |
| ❑ 28 | Emmitt Smith | 3.00 | 1.25 |
| ❑ 29 | Santana Moss | 1.25 | .50 |
| ❑ 30 | Brian Griese | 1.25 | .50 |
| ❑ 31 | Priest Holmes | 1.50 | .60 |
| ❑ 32 | Rich Gannon | 1.25 | .50 |
| ❑ 33 | Antowain Smith | .75 | .30 |
| ❑ 34 | Marcus Robinson | .75 | .30 |
| ❑ 35 | Warrick Dunn | 1.25 | .50 |
| ❑ 36 | Daunte Culpepper | 1.25 | .50 |
| ❑ 37 | Shaun Alexander | 1.50 | .60 |
| ❑ 38 | Kurt Warner | 1.25 | .50 |
| ❑ 39 | Quincy Carter | .75 | .30 |
| ❑ 40 | Ray Lewis | 1.25 | .50 |
| ❑ 41 | Aaron Brooks | 1.25 | .50 |
| ❑ 42 | Plaxico Burress | .75 | .30 |
| ❑ 43 | Jamal Lewis | 1.25 | .50 |
| ❑ 44 | Ahman Green | 1.25 | .50 |
| ❑ 45 | Rod Smith | .75 | .30 |
| ❑ 46 | Tim Couch | .75 | .30 |
| ❑ 47 | Muhsin Muhammad | .75 | .30 |
| ❑ 48 | Drew Bledsoe | 1.50 | .60 |
| ❑ 49 | Anthony Thomas | .75 | .30 |
| ❑ 50 | Tom Brady | 3.00 | 1.25 |
| ❑ 51 | Trent Green | .75 | .30 |
| ❑ 52 | Charlie Garner | .75 | .30 |
| ❑ 53 | Darrell Jackson | .75 | .30 |
| ❑ 54 | Mike McMahon | 1.25 | .50 |
| ❑ 55 | Donovan McNabb | 1.50 | .60 |
| ❑ 56 | Fred Taylor | 1.25 | .50 |
| ❑ 57 | Corey Dillon | .75 | .30 |
| ❑ 58 | Keyshawn Johnson | 1.25 | .50 |
| ❑ 59 | Drew Brees | 1.25 | .50 |
| ❑ 60 | Steve McNair | 1.25 | .50 |
| ❑ 61 | Jimmy Smith | .75 | .30 |
| ❑ 62 | Terrell Owens | 1.25 | .50 |
| ❑ 63 | Eddie George JSY/499 | 20.00 | 7.50 |
| ❑ 64 | Jeff Garcia JSY/999 | 15.00 | 6.00 |
| ❑ 65 | LaDain Tomlinson JSY/999 | 25.00 | 10.00 |
| ❑ 66 | Cris Carter JSY/999 | 20.00 | 7.50 |
| ❑ 67 | Chris Chambers JSY/999 | 20.00 | 7.50 |
| ❑ 68 | Brian Urlacher JSY/999 | 25.00 | 10.00 |
| ❑ 69 | Tim Brown JSY/999 | 15.00 | 6.00 |
| ❑ 70 | Marshall Faulk JSY/999 | 20.00 | 7.50 |
| ❑ 71 | Stephen Davis JSY/999 | 12.00 | 5.00 |
| ❑ 72 | Jevon Kearse JSY/999 | 12.00 | 5.00 |
| ❑ 73 | Edgerrin James JSY/999 | 15.00 | 6.00 |
| ❑ 74 | Mike Anderson JSY/999 | 15.00 | 6.00 |
| ❑ 75 | Warren Sapp JSY/499 | 20.00 | 7.50 |
| ❑ 76 | Brett Favre JSY/499 | 30.00 | 15.00 |
| ❑ 77 | Julius Peppers RC | 6.00 | 2.50 |
| ❑ 78 | Tim Carter RC | 3.00 | 1.25 |
| ❑ 79 | Travis Stephens RC | 3.00 | 1.25 |
| ❑ 80 | Jabar Gaffney RC | 4.00 | 1.50 |
| ❑ 81 | Cliff Russell RC | 3.00 | 1.25 |
| ❑ 82 | Reche Caldwell RC | 4.00 | 1.50 |
| ❑ 83 | Maurice Morris RC | 4.00 | 1.50 |
| ❑ 84 | Antwaan Randle El RC | 5.00 | 2.00 |
| ❑ 85 | Ladell Betts RC | 4.00 | 1.50 |
| ❑ 86 | Daniel Graham RC | 4.00 | 1.50 |
| ❑ 87 | Jeremy Shockey RC | 6.00 | 2.50 |
| ❑ 88 | Mike Williams RC | 3.00 | 1.25 |
| ❑ 89 | Josh McCown RC | 5.00 | 2.00 |
| ❑ 90 | Rohan Davey RC | 4.00 | 1.50 |
| ❑ 91 | David Garrard RC | 8.00 | 3.00 |
| ❑ 92 | Dwight Freeney RC | 6.00 | 2.50 |
| ❑ 93 | Leonard Henry RC | 3.00 | 1.25 |
| ❑ 94 | Albert Haynesworth RC | 4.00 | 1.50 |
| ❑ 95 | Herb Haygood RC | 2.00 | .75 |
| ❑ 96 | Kurt Kittner RC | 3.00 | 1.25 |
| ❑ 97 | Jason McAddley RC | 3.00 | 1.25 |
| ❑ 98 | Bryan Thomas RC | 3.00 | 1.25 |
| ❑ 99 | Wendell Bryant RC | 2.00 | .75 |
| ❑ 100 | Mike Rumph RC | 4.00 | 1.50 |
| ❑ 101 | Chad Hutchinson RC | 3.00 | 1.25 |
| ❑ 102 | Brian Westbrook RC | 10.00 | 4.00 |

| | | |
|---|---|---|
| ❑ 103 Deion Branch RC | 6.00 | 2.50 |
| ❑ 104 John Henderson RC | 4.00 | 1.50 |
| ❑ 105 Jerramy Stevens RC | 4.00 | 1.50 |
| ❑ 106 Tracey Wistrom RC | 3.00 | 1.25 |
| ❑ 107 Phillip Buchanon RC | 4.00 | 1.50 |
| ❑ 108 Matt Schobel RC | 3.00 | 1.25 |
| ❑ 109 Ed Reed RC | 10.00 | 4.00 |
| ❑ 110 Randy Fasani RC | 3.00 | 1.25 |
| ❑ 111 Josh Scobey RC | 4.00 | 1.50 |
| ❑ 112 Luke Staley RC | 3.00 | 1.25 |
| ❑ 113 Anthony Weaver RC | 3.00 | 1.25 |
| ❑ 114 Kyle Johnson RC | 2.00 | .75 |
| ❑ 115 David Carr RC | 25.00 | 12.50 |
| ❑ 116 Joey Harrington AU RC | 25.00 | 12.50 |
| ❑ 117 Donte Stallworth AU RC | 40.00 | 15.00 |
| ❑ 118 Ashley Lelie AU RC | 15.00 | 6.00 |
| ❑ 119 Patrick Ramsey AU RC | 20.00 | 7.50 |
| ❑ 120 William Green AU RC | 20.00 | 7.50 |
| ❑ 121 Josh Reed AU RC | 20.00 | 7.50 |
| ❑ 122 Clinton Portis AU RC | 60.00 | 30.00 |
| ❑ 123 Antonio Bryant AU RC | 15.00 | 6.00 |
| ❑ 124 Javon Walker AU RC | 30.00 | 12.00 |
| ❑ 125 Roy Williams AU RC | 40.00 | 15.00 |
| ❑ 126 Marquise Walker AU RC | 20.00 | 7.50 |
| ❑ 127 Quentin Jammer AU RC | 20.00 | 7.50 |
| ❑ 128 DeShaun Foster AU RC | 25.00 | 12.00 |
| ❑ 129 Andre Davis AU RC | 20.00 | 7.50 |
| ❑ 130 Ron Johnson AU RC | 20.00 | 7.50 |
| ❑ 131 Lamar Gordon AU RC | 20.00 | 7.50 |
| ❑ 132 T.J. Duckett AU/300 RC | 25.00 | 10.00 |
| ❑ 133 Freddie Milons AU RC | 20.00 | 7.50 |
| ❑ 134 Eric Crouch AU RC | 20.00 | 7.50 |
| ❑ 135 Adrian Peterson AU RC | 25.00 | 10.00 |
| ❑ 136 Damien Anderson AU RC | 20.00 | 7.50 |

## 2003 Finest

| | | |
|---|---|---|
| ❑ COMP.SET w/o SP's (100) | 50.00 | 20.00 |
| ❑ 1 Chad Pennington | 1.00 | .40 |
| ❑ 2 Tommy Maddox | .75 | .30 |
| ❑ 3 Brett Favre | 2.50 | 1.00 |
| ❑ 4 Eric Moulds | .75 | .30 |
| ❑ 5 Randy Moss | 1.25 | .50 |
| ❑ 6 Duce Staley | .75 | .30 |
| ❑ 7 Derrick Mason | .75 | .30 |
| ❑ 8 Shaun Alexander | 1.00 | .40 |
| ❑ 9 Peyton Manning | 2.00 | .75 |
| ❑ 10 Kerry Collins | .75 | .30 |
| ❑ 11 Joe Horn | .75 | .30 |
| ❑ 12 Laveranues Coles | .75 | .30 |
| ❑ 13 Marty Booker | .75 | .30 |
| ❑ 14 Emmitt Smith | 2.50 | 1.00 |
| ❑ 15 Edgerrin James | 1.00 | .40 |
| ❑ 16 Aaron Brooks | .75 | .40 |
| ❑ 17 Curtis Martin | 1.00 | .40 |
| ❑ 18 Hines Ward | 1.00 | .40 |
| ❑ 19 Rod Smith | .75 | .30 |
| ❑ 20 Priest Holmes | 1.00 | .40 |
| ❑ 21 Jerry Rice | 2.00 | .75 |
| ❑ 22 Peerless Price | .60 | .25 |
| ❑ 23 Mark Brunell | .75 | .30 |
| ❑ 24 Trent Green | .75 | .30 |
| ❑ 25 David Boston | .60 | .25 |
| ❑ 26 Chris Chambers | 1.00 | .40 |
| ❑ 27 Marshall Faulk | 1.00 | .40 |
| ❑ 28 Fred Taylor | 1.00 | .40 |
| ❑ 29 Tim Couch | .60 | .25 |
| ❑ 30 Amani Toomer | .75 | .30 |
| ❑ 31 Travis Henry | .75 | .30 |

| | | |
|---|---|---|
| ❑ 32 Jeff Blake | .75 | .30 |
| ❑ 33 Troy Brown | .75 | .30 |
| ❑ 34 Charlie Garner | .75 | .30 |
| ❑ 35 Tom Brady | 2.50 | 1.00 |
| ❑ 36 Warrick Dunn | .75 | .30 |
| ❑ 37 Plaxico Burress | 1.00 | .40 |
| ❑ 38 Marvin Harrison | 1.00 | .40 |
| ❑ 39 Clinton Portis | 1.25 | .50 |
| ❑ 40 Deuce McAllister | 1.00 | .40 |
| ❑ 41 Matt Hasselbeck | .75 | .30 |
| ❑ 42 Jeff Garcia | 1.00 | .40 |
| ❑ 43 David Carr | 1.00 | .40 |
| ❑ 44 Ahman Green | 1.00 | .40 |
| ❑ 45 Eddie George | .75 | .30 |
| ❑ 46 Drew Brees | 1.00 | .40 |
| ❑ 47 Tiki Barber | 1.00 | .40 |
| ❑ 48 Jay Fiedler | .75 | .30 |
| ❑ 49 Curtis Conway | .60 | .25 |
| ❑ 50 Steve McNair | 1.00 | .40 |
| ❑ 51 Donald Driver | 1.00 | .40 |
| ❑ 52 Jake Plummer | .75 | .30 |
| ❑ 53 Jamal Lewis | 1.00 | .40 |
| ❑ 54 Corey Dillon | .75 | .30 |
| ❑ 55 Stephen Davis | .75 | .30 |
| ❑ 56 Terrell Owens | 1.00 | .40 |
| ❑ 57 Torry Holt | 1.00 | .40 |
| ❑ 58 Chad Johnson | 1.00 | .40 |
| ❑ 59 Chad Hutchinson | .60 | .25 |
| ❑ 60 Kurt Warner | 1.00 | .40 |
| ❑ 61 Troy Polamalu RC | 20.00 | 8.00 |
| ❑ 62 Eugene Wilson RC | 3.00 | 1.25 |
| ❑ 63 Juston Wood RC | 2.00 | .75 |
| ❑ 64 Anquan Boldin RC | 8.00 | 3.00 |
| ❑ 65 Doug Gabriel RC | 2.50 | 1.00 |
| ❑ 66 Domanick Davis RC | 3.00 | 1.25 |
| ❑ 67 J.R. Tolver RC | 2.50 | 1.00 |
| ❑ 68 Jerome McDougle RC | 2.00 | .75 |
| ❑ 69 Keenan Howry RC | 2.00 | .75 |
| ❑ 70 Teyo Johnson RC | 2.50 | 1.00 |
| ❑ 71 Bethel Johnson RC | 2.50 | 1.00 |
| ❑ 72 Ken Hamlin RC | 3.00 | 1.25 |
| ❑ 73 L.J. Smith RC | 3.00 | 1.25 |
| ❑ 74 Rashean Mathis RC | 2.50 | 1.00 |
| ❑ 75 Arnaz Battle RC | 3.00 | 1.25 |
| ❑ 76 B.J. Askew RC | 2.50 | 1.00 |
| ❑ 77 Mike Doss RC | 3.00 | 1.25 |
| ❑ 78 Kevin Curtis RC | 4.00 | 1.50 |
| ❑ 79 Terence Newman RC | 4.00 | 1.50 |
| ❑ 80 Shaun McDonald RC | 3.00 | 1.25 |
| ❑ 81 Kevin Williams RC | 3.00 | 1.25 |
| ❑ 82 Nate Burleson RC | 2.50 | 1.00 |
| ❑ 83 Tyrone Calico RC | 2.50 | 1.00 |
| ❑ 84 DeWayne White RC | 2.00 | .75 |
| ❑ 85 Marcus Trufant RC | 3.00 | 1.25 |
| ❑ 86 Nick Barnett RC | 2.50 | 1.00 |
| ❑ 87 Bennie Joppru RC | 2.00 | .75 |
| ❑ 88 Andre Woolfolk RC | 2.50 | 1.00 |
| ❑ 89 Billy McMullen RC | 2.00 | .75 |
| ❑ 90 Boss Bailey RC | 2.50 | 1.00 |
| ❑ 91 William Joseph RC | 2.00 | .75 |
| ❑ 92 Michael Haynes RC | 2.50 | 1.00 |
| ❑ 93 DeWayne Robertson RC | 2.50 | 1.00 |
| ❑ 94 LaTarence Dunbar RC | 2.00 | .75 |
| ❑ 95 David Tyree RC | 3.00 | 1.25 |
| ❑ 96 Walter Young RC | 2.00 | .75 |
| ❑ 97 E.J. Henderson RC | 2.50 | 1.00 |
| ❑ 98 Ty Warren RC | 3.00 | 1.25 |
| ❑ 99 Zuriel Smith RC | 2.00 | .75 |
| ❑ 100 Brock Forsey RC | 2.50 | 1.00 |
| ❑ 101 Ricky Williams JSY RC | 10.00 | 4.00 |
| ❑ 102 Drew Bledsoe JSY C | 12.00 | 5.00 |
| ❑ 103 Joey Harrington JSY C | 12.00 | 5.00 |
| ❑ 104 Tim Brown JSY C | 12.00 | 5.00 |
| ❑ 105 Brian Urlacher JSY C | 20.00 | 8.00 |
| ❑ 106 Zach Thomas JSY C | 12.00 | 5.00 |
| ❑ 107 Jeremy Shockey JSY C | 12.00 | 5.00 |
| ❑ 108 Michael Strahan JSY A | 12.00 | 5.00 |
| ❑ 109 Jason Taylor JSY C | 10.00 | 4.00 |
| ❑ 110 Donovan McNabb JSY C | 15.00 | 6.00 |
| ❑ 111 LaDainian Tomlinson JSY B | 25.00 | 10.00 |
| ❑ 112 Rich Gannon JSY C | 10.00 | 4.00 |
| ❑ 113 Brad Johnson JSY C | 10.00 | 4.00 |
| ❑ 114 Daunte Culpepper JSY C | 12.00 | 5.00 |
| ❑ 115 Michael Vick JSY C | 12.00 | 5.00 |

| | | |
|---|---|---|
| ❑ 116 Jimmy Smith JSY B | 12.00 | 5.00 |
| ❑ 117 Keyshawn Johnson JSY C | 12.00 | 5.00 |
| ❑ 118 Keith Brooking JSY C | 10.00 | 4.00 |
| ❑ 119 Carson Palmer AU/399 RC | 100.00 | 50.00 |
| ❑ 120 Byron Leftwich AU/399 RC | 40.00 | 15.00 |
| ❑ 121 Chris Simms AU/399 RC | 25.00 | 10.00 |
| ❑ 122 Kyle Boller AU/399 RC | 25.00 | 10.00 |
| ❑ 123 Justin Fargas AU RC | 15.00 | 6.00 |
| ❑ 124 Seneca Wallace AU RC | 15.00 | 6.00 |
| ❑ 125 Larry Johnson AU RC | 40.00 | 15.00 |
| ❑ 126 Kareem Kelly AU RC | 10.00 | 4.00 |
| ❑ 127 Willis McGahee AU/399 RC | 50.00 | 20.00 |
| ❑ 128 Kelley Washington AU RC | 12.00 | 5.00 |
| ❑ 129 Brian St.Pierre AU RC | 15.00 | 6.00 |
| ❑ 130 Kliff Kingsbury AU RC | 12.00 | 5.00 |
| ❑ 131 Ken Dorsey AU RC | 12.00 | 5.00 |
| ❑ 132 Bryant Johnson AU RC | 15.00 | 6.00 |
| ❑ 133 Dallas Clark AU RC | 25.00 | 10.00 |
| ❑ 134 Chris Brown AU RC | 15.00 | 6.00 |
| ❑ 135 Taylor Jacobs AU RC | 12.00 | 5.00 |
| ❑ 136 Artose Pinner AU RC | 12.00 | 5.00 |
| ❑ 137 Lee Suggs AU RC | 12.00 | 5.00 |
| ❑ 138 LaBrandon Toefield AU RC | 12.00 | 5.00 |
| ❑ 139 Jason Witten AU RC | 40.00 | 25.00 |
| ❑ 140 Brad Banks AU RC | 12.00 | 5.00 |
| ❑ 141 Earnest Graham AU RC | 20.00 | 8.00 |
| ❑ 142 Bobby Wade AU RC | 12.00 | 5.00 |
| ❑ 143 Talman Gardner AU RC | 10.00 | 4.00 |
| ❑ 144 Justin Gage AU RC | 12.00 | 5.00 |
| ❑ 145 Sam Aiken AU RC | 12.00 | 5.00 |
| ❑ 146 Musa Smith AU RC | 12.00 | 5.00 |
| ❑ 147 Terrell Suggs AU RC | 20.00 | 8.00 |
| ❑ 148 Brandon Lloyd AU RC | 15.00 | 6.00 |
| ❑ 150 Rex Grossman AU RC | 40.00 | 15.00 |

## 2004 Finest

| | | |
|---|---|---|
| ❑ COMP.SET w/o SP's (100) | 40.00 | 15.00 |
| ❑ COMP.SET w/o RC's (60) | 12.00 | 5.00 |
| ❑ 108-134 AU/399 RC STATED ODDS 1:120 | | |
| ❑ 108-134 AU/999 RC STATED ODDS 1:12 | | |
| ❑ 1 Steve McNair | .75 | .30 |
| ❑ 2 Corey Dillon | .60 | .25 |
| ❑ 3 Joey Harrington | .60 | .25 |
| ❑ 4 Travis Henry | .60 | .25 |
| ❑ 5 Donovan McNabb | .75 | .30 |
| ❑ 6 Jamal Lewis | .60 | .25 |
| ❑ 7 Jeff Garcia | .75 | .30 |
| ❑ 8 Fred Taylor | .60 | .25 |
| ❑ 9 Aaron Brooks | .60 | .25 |
| ❑ 10 Marc Bulger | .75 | .30 |
| ❑ 11 Keenan McCardell | .50 | .25 |
| ❑ 12 David Carr | .60 | .25 |
| ❑ 13 Charles Rogers | .60 | .25 |
| ❑ 14 Ray Lewis | .75 | .30 |
| ❑ 15 Priest Holmes | .75 | .30 |
| ❑ 16 Curtis Martin | .75 | .30 |
| ❑ 17 Plaxico Burress | .60 | .25 |
| ❑ 18 Shaun Alexander | .75 | .30 |
| ❑ 19 Brad Johnson | .60 | .25 |
| ❑ 20 Marvin Harrison | .75 | .30 |
| ❑ 21 Rod Smith | .60 | .25 |
| ❑ 22 Jake Delhomme | .60 | .25 |
| ❑ 23 Santana Moss | .60 | .25 |
| ❑ 24 Trent Green | .60 | .25 |
| ❑ 25 Michael Vick | .75 | .30 |
| ❑ 26 Tim Rattay | .50 | .20 |
| ❑ 27 Chris Chambers | .60 | .25 |
| ❑ 28 Robert Ferguson | .50 | .20 |

|  |  | | |
|---|---|---|---|
| 29 | Tiki Barber | .75 | .30 |
| 30 | Terrell Owens | .75 | .30 |
| 31 | Marshall Faulk | .75 | .30 |
| 32 | Quincy Carter | .50 | .20 |
| 33 | Stephen Davis | .60 | .25 |
| 34 | Josh McCown | .60 | .25 |
| 35 | Jeremy Shockey | .60 | .25 |
| 36 | Tommy Maddox | .60 | .25 |
| 37 | Derrick Mason | .60 | .25 |
| 38 | Kerry Collins | .60 | .25 |
| 39 | Jimmy Smith | .60 | .25 |
| 40 | Chad Pennington | .75 | .30 |
| 41 | Domanick Davis | .75 | .30 |
| 42 | Darrell Jackson | .60 | .25 |
| 43 | Steve Smith | .75 | .30 |
| 44 | Drew Bledsoe | .75 | .30 |
| 45 | Deuce McAllister | .75 | .30 |
| 46 | Jerry Porter | .60 | .25 |
| 47 | Peerless Price | .60 | .25 |
| 48 | Eric Moulds | .60 | .25 |
| 49 | Garrison Hearst | .60 | .25 |
| 50 | Brett Favre | 2.00 | .75 |
| 51 | Amani Toomer | .60 | .25 |
| 52 | Andre Johnson | .75 | .30 |
| 53 | Edgerrin James | .75 | .30 |
| 54 | Rex Grossman | .75 | .30 |
| 55 | Daunte Culpepper | .75 | .30 |
| 56 | Tony Gonzalez | .75 | .30 |
| 57 | Byron Leftwich | .75 | .30 |
| 58 | Mark Brunell | .60 | .25 |
| 59 | Laveranues Coles | .60 | .25 |
| 60 | Matt Hasselbeck | .75 | .30 |
| 61 | Chris Gamble RC | 1.50 | .60 |
| 62 | Michael Turner RC | 4.00 | 1.50 |
| 63 | Julius Jones RC | 5.00 | 2.00 |
| 64 | Dunta Robinson RC | 1.50 | .60 |
| 65 | Sean Taylor RC | 2.00 | .75 |
| 66 | Ahmad Carroll RC | 2.00 | .75 |
| 67 | Derrick Strait RC | 1.50 | .60 |
| 68 | Dontarrious Thomas RC | 1.50 | .60 |
| 69 | Jason Babin RC | 1.50 | .60 |
| 70 | Reggie Williams RC | 2.00 | .75 |
| 71 | Dwan Edwards RC | 1.25 | .50 |
| 72 | Rashaun Woods RC | 1.25 | .50 |
| 73 | Ricardo Colclough RC | 2.00 | .75 |
| 74 | Will Smith RC | 1.50 | .60 |
| 75 | Kellen Winslow RC | 4.00 | 1.50 |
| 76 | Roy Williams RC | 5.00 | 2.00 |
| 77 | B.J. Symons RC | 1.25 | .50 |
| 78 | Carlos Francis RC | 1.25 | .50 |
| 79 | Triandos Luke RC | 1.25 | .50 |
| 80 | Drew Henson RC | 1.25 | .50 |
| 81 | Keiwan Ratliff RC | 1.25 | .50 |
| 82 | Will Poole RC | 2.00 | .75 |
| 83 | Tommie Harris RC | 2.00 | .75 |
| 84 | Steven Jackson RC | 6.00 | 2.50 |
| 85 | Greg Jones RC | 2.00 | .75 |
| 86 | Vince Wilfork RC | 2.00 | .75 |
| 87 | DeAngelo Hall RC | 2.00 | .75 |
| 88 | Daryl Smith RC | 1.50 | .60 |
| 89 | Teddy Lehman RC | 1.50 | .60 |
| 90 | Casey Bramlet RC | 1.25 | .50 |
| 91 | Marcus Tubbs RC | 1.25 | .50 |
| 92 | Andy Hall RC | 1.50 | .60 |
| 93 | Jim Sorgi RC | 2.00 | .75 |
| 94 | Kenechi Udeze RC | 2.00 | .75 |
| 95 | Darius Watts RC | 1.50 | .60 |
| 96 | Tank Johnson RC | 1.50 | .60 |
| 97 | Matt Mauck RC | 1.50 | .60 |
| 98 | Bradlee Van Pelt RC | 1.50 | .60 |
| 99 | D.J. Williams RC | 2.00 | .75 |
| 100 | Larry Fitzgerald RC | 6.00 | 2.50 |
| 101 | Peyton Manning JSY | 15.00 | 6.00 |
| 102 | Clinton Portis JSY | 8.00 | 3.00 |
| 103 | Chad Johnson JSY | 8.00 | 3.00 |
| 104 | Randy Moss JSY | 10.00 | 4.00 |
| 105 | Tom Brady JSY | 20.00 | 7.50 |
| 106 | LaDainian Tomlinson JSY | 10.00 | 4.00 |
| 107 | Ahman Green JSY | 8.00 | 3.00 |
| 108 | Roethlisberger AU/399 RC | 250.00 | 125.00 |
| 109 | Philip Rivers AU/399 RC | 100.00 | 50.00 |
| 110 | Eli Manning AU/399 RC | 200.00 | 100.00 |
| 111 | Kevin Jones AU/399 RC | 20.00 | 8.00 |
| 112 | Bernard Berrian AU RC | 15.00 | 6.00 |
| 113 | Jeff Smoker AU RC | 12.00 | 5.00 |
| 114 | Mewelde Moore AU RC | 15.00 | 6.00 |
| 115 | Michael Clayton AU RC | 15.00 | 6.00 |
| 116 | Jonathan Vilma AU RC | 15.00 | 6.00 |
| 117 | Johnnie Morant AU RC | 12.00 | 5.00 |
| 118 | Devard Darling AU RC | 12.00 | 5.00 |
| 119 | Cedric Cobbs AU RC | 12.00 | 5.00 |
| 120 | Chris Perry AU/399 RC | 20.00 | 8.00 |
| 121 | Ernest Wilford AU RC | 15.00 | 6.00 |
| 122 | Michael Jenkins AU RC | 20.00 | 8.00 |
| 123 | Jerricho Cotchery AU RC | 20.00 | 8.00 |
| 124 | P.K. Sam AU RC | 10.00 | 4.00 |
| 125 | Tatum Bell AU RC | 15.00 | 6.00 |
| 126 | Derrick Hamilton AU RC | 10.00 | 4.00 |
| 127 | Luke McCown AU RC | 15.00 | 6.00 |
| 128 | Devery Henderson AU RC | 15.00 | 6.00 |
| 129 | Craig Krenzel AU RC | 15.00 | 6.00 |
| 130 | J.P. Losman AU RC | 20.00 | 8.00 |
| 131 | Lee Evans AU RC | 15.00 | 6.00 |
| 132 | Matt Schaub AU RC | 50.00 | 20.00 |
| 133 | Robert Gallery AU RC | 15.00 | 6.00 |
| 134 | Keary Colbert AU RC | 15.00 | 6.00 |

## 2005 Finest

COMPLETE SET (183)
UNPRICED FRAMED REF. PRINT RUN 1 SET
UNPRICED FRAM.XFRAC. PRINT RUN 1 SET
UNPRICED GOLD XFRAC.PRINT RUN 10 SETS
UNPRICED PRINT.PLATE PRINT RUN 1 SET
UNPRICED SUPERFRACTORS #d TO 1

|  |  | | |
|---|---|---|---|
| 1 | Muhsin Muhammad | .60 | .25 |
| 2 | Kevin Jones | .60 | .25 |
| 3 | Eli Manning | 1.50 | .60 |
| 4 | Kevan Barlow | .50 | .20 |
| 5 | Randy Moss | .75 | .30 |
| 6 | Brian Griese | .60 | .25 |
| 7 | Dante Hall | .60 | .25 |
| 8 | Chris Brown | .60 | .25 |
| 9 | Antonio Gates | .75 | .30 |
| 10 | Champ Bailey | .60 | .25 |
| 11 | Eric Moulds | .60 | .25 |
| 12 | Ray Lewis | .75 | .30 |
| 13 | Larry Fitzgerald | .75 | .30 |
| 14 | Byron Leftwich | .75 | .30 |
| 15 | Marvin Harrison | .75 | .30 |
| 16 | Stephen Davis | .60 | .25 |
| 17 | Laveranues Coles | .60 | .25 |
| 18 | Shaun Alexander | .75 | .30 |
| 19 | Drew Bledsoe | .75 | .30 |
| 20 | Sean Taylor | .60 | .25 |
| 21 | Deuce McAllister | .75 | .30 |
| 22 | Nate Burleson | .60 | .25 |
| 23 | A.J. Feeley | .50 | .20 |
| 24 | Jerome Bettis | .75 | .30 |
| 25 | Torry Holt | .60 | .25 |
| 26 | LaDainian Tomlinson | 1.25 | .50 |
| 27 | Travis Henry | .60 | .25 |
| 28 | T.J. Houshmandzadeh | .60 | .25 |
| 29 | Fred Taylor | .75 | .30 |
| 30 | Michael Jenkins | .60 | .25 |
| 31 | Edgerrin James | .75 | .30 |
| 32 | Terrell Owens | .75 | .30 |
| 33 | Jason Witten | .75 | .30 |
| 34 | Clinton Portis | .75 | .30 |
| 35 | Deion Branch | .60 | .25 |
| 36 | Priest Holmes | .75 | .30 |
| 37 | Javon Walker | .60 | .25 |
| 38 | Rex Grossman | .75 | .30 |
| 39 | Domanick Davis | .50 | .20 |
| 40 | Allen Rossum | .50 | .20 |
| 41 | Dwight Freeney | .60 | .25 |
| 42 | Jimmy Smith | .60 | .25 |
| 43 | Tiki Barber | .75 | .30 |
| 44 | Steve McNair | .75 | .30 |
| 45 | Steven Jackson | 1.00 | .40 |
| 46 | Joe Horn | .60 | .25 |
| 47 | Randy McMichael | .50 | .20 |
| 48 | J.P. Losman | .75 | .30 |
| 49 | Warrick Dunn | .60 | .25 |
| 50 | Tatum Bell | .60 | .25 |
| 51 | Roy Williams WR | .75 | .30 |
| 52 | Curtis Martin | .75 | .30 |
| 53 | Donovan McNabb | .75 | .30 |
| 54 | LaMont Jordan | .60 | .25 |
| 55 | Marc Bulger | .60 | .25 |
| 56 | Drew Bennett | .50 | .20 |
| 57 | Julius Jones | .75 | .30 |
| 58 | Santana Moss | .75 | .30 |
| 59 | Michael Bennett | .50 | .20 |
| 60 | Tony Gonzalez | .60 | .25 |
| 61 | Jamal Lewis | .60 | .25 |
| 62 | Keary Colbert | .50 | .20 |
| 63 | Carson Palmer | .75 | .30 |
| 64 | Dunta Robinson | .50 | .20 |
| 65 | Brandon Stokley | .50 | .20 |
| 66 | Brett Favre | 2.00 | .75 |
| 67 | Jonathan Vilma | .60 | .25 |
| 68 | Darrell Jackson | .60 | .25 |
| 69 | Michael Pittman | .50 | .20 |
| 70 | Drew Brees | .75 | .30 |
| 71 | Amani Toomer | .60 | .25 |
| 72 | Corey Dillon | .60 | .25 |
| 73 | Willis McGahee | .75 | .30 |
| 74 | Michael Vick | .75 | .30 |
| 75 | Chad Johnson | .60 | .25 |
| 76 | Anquan Boldin | .60 | .25 |
| 77 | Kerry Collins | .60 | .25 |
| 78 | Marshall Faulk | .75 | .30 |
| 79 | Roy Williams S | .75 | .30 |
| 80 | Trent Green | .60 | .25 |
| 81 | Chris Gamble | .60 | .25 |
| 82 | Ahman Green | .75 | .30 |
| 83 | Todd Heap | .60 | .25 |
| 84 | Brandon Lloyd | .50 | .20 |
| 85 | Andre Johnson | .60 | .25 |
| 86 | Lee Suggs | .60 | .25 |
| 87 | Plaxico Burress | .60 | .25 |
| 88 | Hines Ward | .75 | .30 |
| 89 | Rod Smith | .60 | .25 |
| 90 | Joey Harrington | .75 | .30 |
| 91 | Derrick Mason | .60 | .25 |
| 92 | Rudi Johnson | .60 | .25 |
| 93 | Isaac Bruce | .60 | .25 |
| 94 | Chris Chambers | .60 | .25 |
| 95 | Matt Hasselbeck | .75 | .30 |
| 96 | Donte Stallworth | .60 | .25 |
| 97 | Philip Rivers | .75 | .30 |
| 98 | Michael Clayton | .60 | .25 |
| 99 | Alge Crumpler | .60 | .25 |
| 100 | Chad Pennington | .75 | .30 |
| 101 | Brian Westbrook | .75 | .30 |
| 102 | Daunte Culpepper | .75 | .30 |
| 103 | Jeremy Shockey | .75 | .30 |
| 104 | Jerry Porter | .60 | .25 |
| 105 | Tom Brady | 1.50 | .60 |
| 106 | Lee Evans | .60 | .25 |
| 107 | Jake Delhomme | .75 | .30 |
| 108 | Ben Roethlisberger | 2.00 | .75 |
| 109 | Jake Plummer | .60 | .25 |
| 110 | Charles Rogers | .50 | .20 |
| 111 | Patrick Ramsey | .60 | .25 |
| 112 | Reggie Wayne | .75 | .30 |
| 113 | Reuben Droughns | .50 | .20 |
| 114 | Aaron Brooks | .50 | .20 |
| 115 | David Carr | .60 | .25 |
| 116 | Thomas Jones | .60 | .25 |
| 117 | Ashley Lelie | .50 | .20 |
| 118 | Donald Driver | .75 | .30 |
| 119 | Billy Volek | .60 | .25 |
| 120 | Peyton Manning | 1.25 | .50 |
| 121 | Frank Gore RC | 6.00 | 2.50 |
| 122 | Adam Jones RC | 2.50 | 1.00 |

| | | | |
|---|---|---|---|
| ❑ 123 Antrel Rolle RC | 2.50 | 1.00 |
| ❑ 124 Roddy White RC | 3.00 | 1.25 |
| ❑ 125 Derrick Johnson RC | 2.50 | 1.00 |
| ❑ 126 Troy Williamson RC | 2.50 | 1.00 |
| ❑ 127 Maurice Clarett | 2.00 | .75 |
| ❑ 128 Dan Orlovsky RC | 2.50 | 1.00 |
| ❑ 129 Andrew Walter RC | 2.50 | 1.00 |
| ❑ 130 Reggie Brown RC | 2.50 | 1.00 |
| ❑ 131 Matt Jones RC | 4.00 | 1.50 |
| ❑ 132 David Greene RC | 2.00 | .75 |
| ❑ 133 Jerome Mathis RC | 2.50 | 1.00 |
| ❑ 134 Thomas Davis RC | 2.00 | .75 |
| ❑ 135 Roscoe Parrish RC | 2.00 | .75 |
| ❑ 136 Ciatrick Fason RC | 2.00 | .75 |
| ❑ 137 David Pollack RC | 2.00 | .75 |
| ❑ 138 Kyle Orton RC | 3.00 | 1.25 |
| ❑ 139 Heath Miller RC | 5.00 | 2.00 |
| ❑ 140 Courtney Roby RC | 2.00 | .75 |
| ❑ 141 Terrence Murphy RC | 1.50 | .60 |
| ❑ 142 DeMarcus Ware RC | 4.00 | 1.50 |
| ❑ 143 Fabian Washington RC | 2.50 | 1.00 |
| ❑ 144 J.J. Arrington RC | 2.50 | 1.00 |
| ❑ 145 Fred Gibson RC | 2.00 | .75 |
| ❑ 146 Carlos Rogers RC | 2.50 | 1.00 |
| ❑ 147 Eric Shelton RC | 2.00 | .75 |
| ❑ 148 Craphonso Thorpe RC | 2.00 | .75 |
| ❑ 149 Anthony Davis RC | 2.00 | .75 |
| ❑ 150 Marion Barber RC | 8.00 | 3.00 |
| ❑ 151 Aaron Rodgers AU/299 RC | 100.00 | 50.00 |
| ❑ 152 Alex Smith QB AU/299 RC | 60.00 | 30.00 |
| ❑ 153 Braylon Edwards AU/299 RC | 60.00 | 30.00 |
| ❑ 154 Cadillac Williams AU/299 RC | 60.00 | 30.00 |
| ❑ 155 Cedric Benson AU/299 RC | 40.00 | 15.00 |
| ❑ 156 Charlie Frye AU/299 RC | 30.00 | 12.00 |
| ❑ 157 Jason Campbell AU/299 RC | 60.00 | 25.00 |
| ❑ 158 Mark Clayton AU/299 RC | 40.00 | 15.00 |
| ❑ 159 Mike Williams AU/299 | 25.00 | 10.00 |
| ❑ 160 Ronnie Brown AU/299 RC | 80.00 | 40.00 |
| ❑ 161 Alex Smith TE AU RC | 12.00 | 5.00 |
| ❑ 162 Alvin Pearman AU RC | 10.00 | 4.00 |
| ❑ 163 Brandon Jacobs AU RC | 30.00 | 12.00 |
| ❑ 164 Channing Crowder AU RC | 10.00 | 4.00 |
| ❑ 165 Chris Henry AU RC | 12.00 | 5.00 |
| ❑ 166 Courtney Roby AU RC | 10.00 | 4.00 |
| ❑ 167 Derek Anderson AU RC | 30.00 | 15.00 |
| ❑ 168 Mark Bradley AU RC | 12.00 | 5.00 |
| ❑ 169 Ryan Fitzpatrick AU RC | 12.00 | 5.00 |
| ❑ 170 Ryan Moats AU RC | 12.00 | 5.00 |
| ❑ 171 Stefan LeFors AU RC | 10.00 | 4.00 |
| ❑ 172 Steve Savoy AU RC | 8.00 | 3.00 |
| ❑ 173 Tab Perry AU RC | 12.00 | 5.00 |
| ❑ 174 Timmy Chang AU RC | 10.00 | 4.00 |
| ❑ 175 Vincent Jackson AU RC | 12.00 | 5.00 |
| ❑ 176 Charles Frederick AU RC | 10.00 | 4.00 |
| ❑ 177 Kay-Jay Harris AU RC | 10.00 | 4.00 |
| ❑ 178 Darren Sproles AU RC | 20.00 | 10.00 |
| ❑ 179 Adrian McPherson AU RC | 10.00 | 4.00 |
| ❑ 180 Craig Bragg AU RC | 8.00 | 3.00 |
| ❑ 181 J.R. Russell AU RC | 8.00 | 3.00 |
| ❑ 182 Gino Guidugli AU RC | 8.00 | 3.00 |
| ❑ 183 Vernand Morency AU RC | 12.00 | 5.00 |

**2006 Finest**

| | | |
|---|---|---|
| ❑ COMP. SET w/o AU's (150) | 30.00 | 12.50 |
| ❑ 1 Muhsin Muhammad | .60 | .25 |
| ❑ 2 Kevin Jones | .75 | .30 |
| ❑ 3 Eli Manning | 1.00 | .40 |
| ❑ 4 Marion Barber | .75 | .30 |

| | | |
|---|---|---|
| ❑ 5 Randy Moss | .75 | .30 |
| ❑ 6 Odell Thurman | .50 | .20 |
| ❑ 7 Dante Hall | .60 | .25 |
| ❑ 8 Chris Brown | .60 | .25 |
| ❑ 9 Antonio Gates | .75 | .30 |
| ❑ 10 Champ Bailey | .60 | .25 |
| ❑ 11 Eric Moulds | .60 | .25 |
| ❑ 12 Ray Lewis | .75 | .30 |
| ❑ 13 Larry Fitzgerald | .75 | .30 |
| ❑ 14 Byron Leftwich | .60 | .25 |
| ❑ 15 Marvin Harrison | .75 | .30 |
| ❑ 16 Larry Johnson | .60 | .25 |
| ❑ 17 Steve Smith | .75 | .30 |
| ❑ 18 Shaun Alexander | .75 | .30 |
| ❑ 19 Drew Bledsoe | .75 | .30 |
| ❑ 20 Joey Galloway | .60 | .25 |
| ❑ 21 Deuce McAllister | .60 | .25 |
| ❑ 22 Ben Obomanu RC | 3.00 | 1.25 |
| ❑ 23 Chester Taylor | .60 | .25 |
| ❑ 24 Delanie Walker RC | 3.00 | 1.25 |
| ❑ 25 Torry Holt | .60 | .25 |
| ❑ 26 LaDainian Tomlinson | 1.00 | .40 |
| ❑ 27 Derrick Mason | .60 | .25 |
| ❑ 28 T.J. Houshmandzadeh | .60 | .25 |
| ❑ 29 Fred Taylor | .60 | .25 |
| ❑ 30 Michael Jenkins | .60 | .25 |
| ❑ 31 Edgerrin James | .60 | .25 |
| ❑ 32 Terrell Owens | .75 | .30 |
| ❑ 33 Jason Witten | .60 | .25 |
| ❑ 34 Clinton Portis | .60 | .25 |
| ❑ 35 Deion Branch | .60 | .25 |
| ❑ 36 Priest Holmes | .60 | .25 |
| ❑ 37 Quinton Ganther RC | 4.00 | 1.50 |
| ❑ 38 Kurt Warner | .75 | .30 |
| ❑ 39 Domanick Davis | .60 | .25 |
| ❑ 40 Chris Simms | .60 | .25 |
| ❑ 41 Dwight Freeney | .60 | .25 |
| ❑ 42 Daniel Bullocks RC | 4.00 | 1.50 |
| ❑ 43 Tiki Barber | .75 | .30 |
| ❑ 44 Steve McNair | .60 | .25 |
| ❑ 45 Steven Jackson | .75 | .30 |
| ❑ 46 Joe Horn | .60 | .25 |
| ❑ 47 Randy McMichael | .50 | .20 |
| ❑ 48 Cedric Humes RC | 4.00 | 1.50 |
| ❑ 49 Warrick Dunn | .60 | .25 |
| ❑ 50 Tatum Bell | .60 | .25 |
| ❑ 51 P.J. Pope RC | 4.00 | 1.50 |
| ❑ 52 Curtis Martin | .75 | .30 |
| ❑ 53 Donovan McNabb | .75 | .30 |
| ❑ 54 LaMont Jordan | .60 | .25 |
| ❑ 55 Marc Bulger | .60 | .25 |
| ❑ 56 Drew Bennett | .60 | .25 |
| ❑ 57 Julius Jones | .60 | .25 |
| ❑ 58 Santana Moss | .60 | .25 |
| ❑ 59 Ronnie Brown | .75 | .30 |
| ❑ 60 Tony Gonzalez | .60 | .25 |
| ❑ 61 Jamal Lewis | .60 | .25 |
| ❑ 62 D.J. Shockley RC | 4.00 | 1.50 |
| ❑ 63 Carson Palmer | .75 | .30 |
| ❑ 64 Jonathan Orr RC | 3.00 | 1.25 |
| ❑ 65 Brandon Stokley | .60 | .25 |
| ❑ 66 Brett Favre | 1.50 | .60 |
| ❑ 67 Jonathan Vilma | .60 | .25 |
| ❑ 68 Darrell Jackson | .60 | .25 |
| ❑ 69 Brian Urlacher | .75 | .30 |
| ❑ 70 Drew Brees | .75 | .30 |
| ❑ 71 Mike Williams | .75 | .30 |
| ❑ 72 Corey Dillon | .60 | .25 |
| ❑ 73 Willis McGahee | .60 | .25 |
| ❑ 74 Michael Vick | .75 | .30 |
| ❑ 75 Chad Johnson | .60 | .25 |
| ❑ 76 Anquan Boldin | .60 | .25 |
| ❑ 77 Shawne Merriman | .60 | .25 |
| ❑ 78 Willie Parker | 1.00 | .40 |
| ❑ 79 Roy Williams S | .60 | .25 |
| ❑ 80 Trent Green | .60 | .25 |
| ❑ 81 Chris Gamble | .50 | .20 |
| ❑ 82 Ahman Green | .60 | .25 |
| ❑ 83 Todd Heap | .60 | .25 |
| ❑ 84 Brett Basanez RC | 4.00 | 1.50 |
| ❑ 85 Andre Johnson | .60 | .25 |
| ❑ 86 Abdul Hodge RC | 4.00 | 1.50 |
| ❑ 87 Plaxico Burress | .60 | .25 |
| ❑ 88 Hines Ward | .75 | .30 |

| | | |
|---|---|---|
| ❑ 89 Rod Smith | .60 | .25 |
| ❑ 90 Cadillac Williams | .75 | .30 |
| ❑ 91 Braylon Edwards | .75 | .30 |
| ❑ 92 Rudi Johnson | .60 | .25 |
| ❑ 93 Isaac Bruce | .60 | .25 |
| ❑ 94 Chris Chambers | .60 | .25 |
| ❑ 95 Matt Hasselbeck | .60 | .25 |
| ❑ 96 Donte Stallworth | .60 | .25 |
| ❑ 97 Philip Rivers | .75 | .30 |
| ❑ 98 Will Blackmon RC | 4.00 | 1.50 |
| ❑ 99 Alge Crumpler | .60 | .25 |
| ❑ 100 Chad Pennington | .60 | .25 |
| ❑ 101 Darrell Bing RC | 4.00 | 1.50 |
| ❑ 102 Daunte Culpepper | .75 | .30 |
| ❑ 103 Jeremy Shockey | .60 | .25 |
| ❑ 104 Jerry Porter | .60 | .25 |
| ❑ 105 Tom Brady | 1.25 | .50 |
| ❑ 106 Jeff Webb RC | 3.00 | 1.25 |
| ❑ 107 Jake Delhomme | .60 | .25 |
| ❑ 108 Ben Roethlisberger | 1.25 | .50 |
| ❑ 109 Jake Plummer | .60 | .25 |
| ❑ 110 Paul Pinegar RC | 3.00 | 1.25 |
| ❑ 111 Kevin McMahan RC | 3.00 | 1.25 |
| ❑ 112 Reggie Wayne | .60 | .25 |
| ❑ 113 Bennie Brazell RC | 3.00 | 1.25 |
| ❑ 114 Todd Watkins RC | 3.00 | 1.25 |
| ❑ 115 David Carr | .60 | .25 |
| ❑ 116 Cory Rodgers RC | 4.00 | 1.50 |
| ❑ 117 Leon Washington RC | 4.00 | 1.50 |
| ❑ 118 Michael Strahan | .60 | .25 |
| ❑ 119 P.J. Daniels RC | 3.00 | 1.25 |
| ❑ 120 Peyton Manning | 1.25 | .50 |
| ❑ 121 Brandon Marshall RC | 5.00 | 2.00 |
| ❑ 122 Jerome Harrison RC | 4.00 | 1.50 |
| ❑ 123 Mario Williams RC | 6.00 | 2.50 |
| ❑ 124 Ernie Sims RC | 4.00 | 1.50 |
| ❑ 125 Devin Hester RC | 8.00 | 3.00 |
| ❑ 126 Jimmy Williams RC | 4.00 | 1.50 |
| ❑ 127 Charlie Whitehurst RC | 4.00 | 1.50 |
| ❑ 128 Jason Avant RC | 4.00 | 1.50 |
| ❑ 129 Marcus Vick RC | 3.00 | 1.25 |
| ❑ 130 Mathias Kiwanuka RC | 5.00 | 2.00 |
| ❑ 131 Brodrick Bunkley RC | 3.00 | 1.25 |
| ❑ 132 Reggie McNeal RC | 3.00 | 1.25 |
| ❑ 133 Dominique Byrd RC | 3.00 | 1.25 |
| ❑ 134 Jason Allen RC | 4.00 | 1.50 |
| ❑ 135 D'Qwell Jackson RC | 3.00 | 1.25 |
| ❑ 136 Donte Whitner RC | 4.00 | 1.50 |
| ❑ 137 Willie Reid RC | 4.00 | 1.50 |
| ❑ 138 Kamerion Wimbley RC | 4.00 | 1.50 |
| ❑ 139 Martin Nance RC | 3.00 | 1.25 |
| ❑ 140 Haloti Ngata RC | 3.00 | 1.25 |
| ❑ 141 Devin Aromashodu RC | 3.00 | 1.25 |
| ❑ 142 Jeremy Bloom RC | 3.00 | 1.25 |
| ❑ 143 Manny Lawson RC | 4.00 | 1.50 |
| ❑ 144 Johnathan Joseph RC | 3.00 | 1.25 |
| ❑ 145 Brad Smith RC | 4.00 | 1.50 |
| ❑ 146 Thomas Howard RC | 4.00 | 1.50 |
| ❑ 147 Demetrius Williams RC | 4.00 | 1.50 |
| ❑ 148 Antonio Cromartie RC | 4.00 | 1.50 |
| ❑ 149 Bobby Carpenter RC | 4.00 | 1.50 |
| ❑ 150 Tamba Hali RC | 4.00 | 1.50 |
| ❑ 151 Reggie Bush AU/199 RC | 150.00 | 75.00 |
| ❑ 152 Matt Leinart AU/199 RC | 120.00 | 60.00 |
| ❑ 153 Vince Young AU/199 RC | 120.00 | 60.00 |
| ❑ 154 Jay Cutler AU/199 RC | 150.00 | 75.00 |
| ❑ 155 S.Holmes AU/199 RC | 50.00 | 30.00 |
| ❑ 156 LenDale White AU/199 RC | 50.00 | 20.00 |
| ❑ 157 DeA.Williams AU/199 RC | 50.00 | 20.00 |
| ❑ 158 Sinorice Moss AU/199 RC | 20.00 | 8.00 |
| ❑ 159 Vernon Davis AU/199 RC | 25.00 | 10.00 |
| ❑ 160 Joseph Addai AU/199 RC | 100.00 | 50.00 |
| ❑ 161 Omar Jacobs AU/199 RC | 20.00 | 8.00 |
| ❑ 162 Chad Jackson AU/199 RC | 20.00 | 8.00 |
| ❑ 163 Chad Greenway AU/199 RC | 12.00 | 5.00 |
| ❑ 164 Maurice Drew AU/199 RC | 50.00 | 25.00 |
| ❑ 165 D.Ferguson AU/199 RC | 12.00 | 5.00 |
| ❑ 166 Anthony Fasano AU/199 RC | 12.00 | 5.00 |
| ❑ 167 Derek Hagan AU/199 RC | 20.00 | 8.00 |
| ❑ 168 A.J. Hawk AU/199 RC | 100.00 | 50.00 |
| ❑ 169 David Thomas AU RC | 20.00 | 8.00 |
| ❑ 170 Brian Calhoun AU RC | 20.00 | 8.00 |
| ❑ 171 Kellen Clemens AU RC | 20.00 | 10.00 |
| ❑ 172 Tarvaris Jackson AU RC | 20.00 | 8.00 |

| | | | |
|---|---|---|---|
| ☐ 173 M.Stovall AU RC EXCH | 12.00 | 5.00 |
| ☐ 174 Michael Huff AU/199 RC | 25.00 | 10.00 |
| ☐ 175 Greg Jennings AU RC | 30.00 | 15.00 |
| ☐ 176 Joe Klopfenstein AU RC | 10.00 | 4.00 |
| ☐ 177 Leonard Pope AU RC | 12.00 | 5.00 |
| ☐ 178 Michael Robinson AU RC | 12.00 | 5.00 |
| ☐ 179 Ingle Martin AU RC | 10.00 | 4.00 |
| ☐ 180 Wali Lundy AU RC | 12.00 | 5.00 |
| ☐ 181 Drew Olson AU RC | 10.00 | 4.00 |
| ☐ 182 Jerious Norwood AU RC | 30.00 | 12.00 |
| ☐ 183 Travis Wilson AU RC | 12.00 | 5.00 |
| ☐ 184 Tye Hill AU RC | 12.00 | 5.00 |
| ☐ 185 Brandon Williams AU RC | 12.00 | 5.00 |
| ☐ 186 Marques Hagans AU RC | 10.00 | 4.00 |

## 2007 Finest

| | | | |
|---|---|---|---|
| ☐ COMPLETE SET (150) | 60.00 | 30.00 |
| ☐ 1 Peyton Manning | 1.25 | .50 |
| ☐ 2 Drew Brees | .60 | .25 |
| ☐ 3 Donovan McNabb | .75 | .30 |
| ☐ 4 Tony Romo | 1.50 | .60 |
| ☐ 5 Carson Palmer | .75 | .30 |
| ☐ 6 Mark Bulger | .60 | .25 |
| ☐ 7 Philip Rivers | .75 | .30 |
| ☐ 8 Tom Brady | 1.50 | .60 |
| ☐ 9 J.P. Losman | .50 | .20 |
| ☐ 10 Steve McNair | .60 | .25 |
| ☐ 11 Eli Manning | .75 | .30 |
| ☐ 12 Matt Hasselbeck | .60 | .25 |
| ☐ 13 Alex Smith QB | .75 | .30 |
| ☐ 14 Ben Roethlisberger | 1.00 | .40 |
| ☐ 15 Matt Leinart | .75 | .30 |
| ☐ 16 Rex Grossman | .60 | .25 |
| ☐ 17 Brett Favre | 1.50 | .60 |
| ☐ 18 Vince Young | .75 | .30 |
| ☐ 19 Jay Cutler | .75 | .30 |
| ☐ 20 Chad Pennington | .60 | .25 |
| ☐ 21 LaDainian Tomlinson | 1.00 | .40 |
| ☐ 22 Larry Johnson | .60 | .25 |
| ☐ 23 Frank Gore | .60 | .25 |
| ☐ 24 Steven Jackson | .75 | .30 |
| ☐ 25 Willie Parker | .60 | .25 |
| ☐ 26 Rudi Johnson | .60 | .25 |
| ☐ 27 Brian Westbrook | .60 | .25 |
| ☐ 28 Chester Taylor | .50 | .20 |
| ☐ 29 Travis Henry | .60 | .25 |
| ☐ 30 Thomas Jones | .60 | .25 |
| ☐ 31 Edgerrin James | .60 | .25 |
| ☐ 32 Fred Taylor | .60 | .25 |
| ☐ 33 Warrick Dunn | .60 | .25 |
| ☐ 34 Jamal Lewis | .60 | .25 |
| ☐ 35 Julius Jones | .60 | .25 |
| ☐ 36 Joseph Addai | .75 | .30 |
| ☐ 37 Ahman Green | .60 | .25 |
| ☐ 38 Deuce McAllister | .60 | .25 |
| ☐ 39 Ronnie Brown | .60 | .25 |
| ☐ 40 Maurice Jones-Drew | .75 | .30 |
| ☐ 41 DeShaun Foster | .50 | .20 |
| ☐ 42 Shaun Alexander | .60 | .25 |
| ☐ 43 Cadillac Williams | .60 | .25 |
| ☐ 44 Laurence Maroney | .75 | .30 |
| ☐ 45 Cedric Benson | .60 | .25 |
| ☐ 46 Dominic Rhodes | .60 | .25 |
| ☐ 47 Jerious Norwood | .60 | .25 |
| ☐ 48 Brandon Jacobs | .60 | .25 |
| ☐ 49 DeAngelo Williams | .60 | .25 |
| ☐ 50 Willis McGahee | .60 | .25 |
| ☐ 51 Clinton Portis | .60 | .25 |

| | | | |
|---|---|---|---|
| ☐ 52 Chad Johnson | .60 | .25 |
| ☐ 53 Marvin Harrison | .75 | .30 |
| ☐ 54 Roy Williams WR | .60 | .25 |
| ☐ 55 Reggie Wayne | .60 | .25 |
| ☐ 56 Donald Driver | .60 | .25 |
| ☐ 57 Lee Evans | .60 | .25 |
| ☐ 58 Anquan Boldin | .60 | .25 |
| ☐ 59 Torry Holt | .60 | .25 |
| ☐ 60 Terrell Owens | .75 | .30 |
| ☐ 61 Steve Smith | .60 | .25 |
| ☐ 62 Andre Johnson | .60 | .25 |
| ☐ 63 Laveraneus Coles | .60 | .25 |
| ☐ 64 Javon Walker | .60 | .25 |
| ☐ 65 T.J. Houshmandzadeh | .60 | .25 |
| ☐ 66 Marques Colston | .75 | .30 |
| ☐ 67 Terry Glenn | .60 | .25 |
| ☐ 68 Plaxico Burress | .60 | .25 |
| ☐ 69 Hines Ward | .75 | .30 |
| ☐ 70 Jerricho Cotchery | .50 | .20 |
| ☐ 71 Larry Fitzgerald | .75 | .30 |
| ☐ 72 Braylon Edwards | .60 | .25 |
| ☐ 73 Santana Moss | .60 | .25 |
| ☐ 74 Santonio Holmes | .60 | .25 |
| ☐ 75 Mike Furrey | .60 | .25 |
| ☐ 76 Isaac Bruce | .60 | .25 |
| ☐ 77 Derrick Mason | .50 | .20 |
| ☐ 78 Randy Moss | .75 | .30 |
| ☐ 79 Greg Jennings | .60 | .25 |
| ☐ 80 Devin Hester | .75 | .30 |
| ☐ 81 Muhsin Muhammad | .60 | .25 |
| ☐ 82 Kellen Winslow | .60 | .25 |
| ☐ 83 Todd Heap | .50 | .20 |
| ☐ 84 Tony Gonzalez | .60 | .25 |
| ☐ 85 Antonio Gates | .60 | .25 |
| ☐ 86 Jeremy Shockey | .60 | .25 |
| ☐ 87 Jason Witten | .60 | .25 |
| ☐ 88 Randy McMichael | .50 | .20 |
| ☐ 89 Alge Crumpler | .60 | .25 |
| ☐ 90 L.J. Smith | .50 | .20 |
| ☐ 91 Champ Bailey | .60 | .25 |
| ☐ 92 DeAngelo Hall | .60 | .25 |
| ☐ 93 Asante Samuel | .50 | .20 |
| ☐ 94 Julius Peppers | .60 | .25 |
| ☐ 95 Jason Taylor | .50 | .20 |
| ☐ 96 Michael Strahan | .60 | .25 |
| ☐ 97 Shawne Merriman | .60 | .25 |
| ☐ 98 Brian Urlacher | .75 | .30 |
| ☐ 99 Troy Polamalu | .75 | .30 |
| ☐ 100 Ed Reed | .60 | .25 |
| ☐ 101 JaMarcus Russell RC | 10.00 | 4.00 |
| ☐ 102 Brady Quinn RC | 12.00 | 5.00 |
| ☐ 103 John Beck RC | 4.00 | 1.50 |
| ☐ 104 Kevin Kolb RC | 6.00 | 2.50 |
| ☐ 105 Trent Edwards RC | 10.00 | 4.00 |
| ☐ 106 Troy Smith RC | 5.00 | 2.00 |
| ☐ 107 Drew Stanton RC | 4.00 | 1.50 |
| ☐ 108 Chris Leak RC | 3.00 | 1.25 |
| ☐ 109 Jordan Palmer RC | 4.00 | 1.50 |
| ☐ 110 Drew Tate RC | 3.00 | 1.25 |
| ☐ 111 Isaiah Stanback RC | 4.00 | 1.50 |
| ☐ 112 Adrian Peterson RC | 30.00 | 12.00 |
| ☐ 113 Marshawn Lynch RC | 8.00 | 3.00 |
| ☐ 114 Brandon Jackson RC | 4.00 | 1.50 |
| ☐ 115 Kenny Irons RC | 4.00 | 1.50 |
| ☐ 116 Michael Bush RC | 3.00 | 1.25 |
| ☐ 117 Lorenzo Booker RC | 4.00 | 1.50 |
| ☐ 118 Brian Leonard RC | 4.00 | 1.50 |
| ☐ 119 Garrett Wolfe RC | 4.00 | 1.50 |
| ☐ 120 Antonio Pittman RC | 4.00 | 1.50 |
| ☐ 121 Selvin Young RC | 6.00 | 2.50 |
| ☐ 122 Chris Henry RB RC | 4.00 | 1.50 |
| ☐ 123 Tony Hunt RC | 4.00 | 1.50 |
| ☐ 124 Kenneth Darby RC | 4.00 | 1.50 |
| ☐ 125 Kolby Smith RC | 4.00 | 1.50 |
| ☐ 126 Darius Walker RC | 4.00 | 1.50 |
| ☐ 127 Greg Olsen RC | 5.00 | 2.00 |
| ☐ 128 Dwayne Bowe RC | 8.00 | 3.00 |
| ☐ 129 Craig Buster Davis RC | 4.00 | 1.50 |
| ☐ 130 Ted Ginn Jr. RC | 6.00 | 2.50 |
| ☐ 131 Anthony Gonzalez RC | 6.00 | 2.50 |
| ☐ 132 Yamon Figurs RC | 4.00 | 1.50 |
| ☐ 133 Jason Hill RC | 4.00 | 1.50 |
| ☐ 134 Dwayne Jarrett RC | 4.00 | 1.50 |
| ☐ 135 Calvin Johnson RC | 10.00 | 4.00 |

| | | | |
|---|---|---|---|
| ☐ 136 Robert Meachem RC | 4.00 | 1.50 |
| ☐ 137 Sidney Rice RC | 4.00 | 1.50 |
| ☐ 138 Steve Smith USC RC | 5.00 | 2.00 |
| ☐ 139 Paul Williams RC | 3.00 | 1.25 |
| ☐ 140 Steve Breaston RC | 4.00 | 1.50 |
| ☐ 141 David Clowney RC | 3.00 | 1.25 |
| ☐ 142 Aundrea Allison RC | 3.00 | 1.25 |
| ☐ 143 Ryne Robinson RC | 3.00 | 1.25 |
| ☐ 144 Joe Thomas RC | 4.00 | 1.50 |
| ☐ 145 Leon Hall RC | 3.00 | 1.25 |
| ☐ 146 Gaines Adams RC | 4.00 | 1.50 |
| ☐ 147 LaRon Landry RC | 5.00 | 2.00 |
| ☐ 148 Amobi Okoye RC | 4.00 | 1.50 |
| ☐ 149 Patrick Willis RC | 8.00 | 3.00 |
| ☐ 150 Lawrence Timmons RC | 4.00 | 1.50 |

## 2008 Finest

| | | | |
|---|---|---|---|
| ☐ 1 Drew Brees | .75 | .30 |
| ☐ 2 Tom Brady | 1.25 | .50 |
| ☐ 3 Peyton Manning | .75 | .30 |
| ☐ 4 Carson Palmer | .60 | .25 |
| ☐ 5 Ben Roethlisberger | 1.00 | .40 |
| ☐ 6 Tony Romo | 1.25 | .50 |
| ☐ 7 Vince Young | .75 | .30 |
| ☐ 8 David Garrard | .60 | .25 |
| ☐ 9 Jeff Garcia | .60 | .25 |
| ☐ 10 Derek Anderson | .60 | .25 |
| ☐ 11 Matt Hasselbeck | .60 | .25 |
| ☐ 12 Donovan McNabb | .75 | .30 |
| ☐ 13 Philip Rivers | .75 | .30 |
| ☐ 14 Jay Cutler | .75 | .30 |
| ☐ 15 Matt Leinart | .60 | .25 |
| ☐ 16 Jason Campbell | .60 | .25 |
| ☐ 17 Matt Schaub | .50 | .25 |
| ☐ 18 Jon Kitna | .60 | .25 |
| ☐ 19 Marc Bulger | .60 | .25 |
| ☐ 20 Eli Manning | .75 | .30 |
| ☐ 21 Willie Parker | .60 | .25 |
| ☐ 22 Clinton Portis | .60 | .25 |
| ☐ 23 Adrian Peterson | 1.50 | .60 |
| ☐ 24 LaDainian Tomlinson | 1.00 | .40 |
| ☐ 25 Marion Barber | .75 | .30 |
| ☐ 26 Brian Westbrook | .60 | .25 |
| ☐ 27 Fred Taylor | .60 | .25 |
| ☐ 28 Marshawn Lynch | .75 | .30 |
| ☐ 29 Joseph Addai | .60 | .25 |
| ☐ 30 Willis McGahee | .60 | .25 |
| ☐ 31 Frank Gore | .60 | .25 |
| ☐ 32 Larry Johnson | .60 | .25 |
| ☐ 33 Jamal Lewis | .60 | .25 |
| ☐ 34 Edgerrin James | .60 | .25 |
| ☐ 35 Thomas Jones | .60 | .25 |
| ☐ 36 Brandon Jacobs | .60 | .25 |
| ☐ 37 LenDale White | .75 | .30 |
| ☐ 38 Justin Fargas | .50 | .20 |
| ☐ 39 Ryan Grant | .75 | .30 |
| ☐ 40 Earnest Graham | .60 | .25 |
| ☐ 41 Laurence Maroney | .75 | .30 |
| ☐ 42 Steven Jackson | .75 | .30 |
| ☐ 43 DeAngelo Williams | .60 | .25 |
| ☐ 44 Shaun Alexander | .60 | .25 |
| ☐ 45 Maurice Jones-Drew | .75 | .30 |
| ☐ 46 Reggie Bush | .75 | .30 |
| ☐ 47 Chester Taylor | .50 | .20 |
| ☐ 48 Rudi Johnson | .60 | .25 |
| ☐ 49 Ronnie Brown | .60 | .25 |
| ☐ 50 Travis Henry | .60 | .25 |
| ☐ 51 Cedric Benson | .50 | .20 |

| | | |
|---|---|---|
| ❑ 52 Chad Johnson | .60 | .25 |
| ❑ 53 Reggie Wayne | .60 | .25 |
| ❑ 54 Anquan Boldin | .60 | .25 |
| ❑ 55 Randy Moss | .75 | .30 |
| ❑ 56 Plaxico Burress | .60 | .25 |
| ❑ 57 Terrell Owens | .75 | .30 |
| ❑ 58 Andre Johnson | .60 | .25 |
| ❑ 59 Larry Fitzgerald | .75 | .30 |
| ❑ 60 Braylon Edwards | .60 | .25 |
| ❑ 61 Steve Smith | .60 | .25 |
| ❑ 62 Wes Welker | .75 | .30 |
| ❑ 63 T.J. Houshmandzadeh | .60 | .25 |
| ❑ 64 Derrick Mason | .50 | .20 |
| ❑ 65 Brandon Marshall | .60 | .25 |
| ❑ 66 Marques Colston | .60 | .25 |
| ❑ 67 Bobby Engram | .50 | .20 |
| ❑ 68 Torry Holt | .60 | .25 |
| ❑ 69 Roddy White | .60 | .25 |
| ❑ 70 Jerricho Cotchery | .60 | .25 |
| ❑ 71 Donald Driver | .60 | .25 |
| ❑ 72 Roy Williams WR | .60 | .25 |
| ❑ 73 Hines Ward | .75 | .30 |
| ❑ 74 Santonio Holmes | .60 | .25 |
| ❑ 75 Joey Galloway | .60 | .25 |
| ❑ 76 Greg Jennings | .60 | .25 |
| ❑ 77 Dwayne Bowe | .60 | .25 |
| ❑ 78 Calvin Johnson | .75 | .30 |
| ❑ 79 Santana Moss | .60 | .25 |
| ❑ 80 Kevin Curtis | .60 | .25 |
| ❑ 81 Chris Chambers | .60 | .25 |
| ❑ 82 Kellen Winslow | .60 | .25 |
| ❑ 83 Tony Gonzalez | .60 | .25 |
| ❑ 84 Antonio Gates | .60 | .25 |
| ❑ 85 Jeremy Shockey | .60 | .25 |
| ❑ 86 Jason Witten | .60 | .25 |
| ❑ 87 Chris Cooley | .60 | .25 |
| ❑ 88 Owen Daniels | .50 | .20 |
| ❑ 89 Dallas Clark | .60 | .25 |
| ❑ 90 Vernon Davis | .50 | .20 |
| ❑ 91 Antonio Cromartie | .50 | .20 |
| ❑ 92 Marcus Trufant | .50 | .20 |
| ❑ 93 Terence Newman | .50 | .20 |
| ❑ 94 Osi Umenyiora | .50 | .20 |
| ❑ 95 Mario Williams | .60 | .25 |
| ❑ 96 Patrick Willis | .60 | .25 |
| ❑ 97 Shawne Merriman | .60 | .25 |
| ❑ 98 DeMarcus Ware | .60 | .25 |
| ❑ 99 Ed Reed | .60 | .25 |
| ❑ 100 Bob Sanders | .60 | .25 |
| ❑ 101 Erik Ainge RC | 5.00 | 2.00 |
| ❑ 102 John David Booty RC | 6.00 | 2.50 |
| ❑ 103 Colt Brennan RC | 12.00 | 5.00 |
| ❑ 104 Brian Brohm RC | 6.00 | 2.50 |
| ❑ 105 Joe Flacco RC | 15.00 | 6.00 |
| ❑ 106 Chad Henne RC | 8.00 | 3.00 |
| ❑ 107 Josh Johnson RC | 5.00 | 2.00 |
| ❑ 108 Anthony Morelli RC | 5.00 | 2.00 |
| ❑ 109 Matt Ryan RC | 20.00 | 8.00 |
| ❑ 110 Andre Woodson RC | 5.00 | 2.00 |
| ❑ 111 Kyle Wright RC | 4.00 | 1.50 |
| ❑ 112 Jamaal Charles RC | 6.00 | 2.50 |
| ❑ 113 Tashard Choice RC | 5.00 | 2.00 |
| ❑ 114 Matt Forte RC | 12.00 | 5.00 |
| ❑ 115 Mike Hart RC | 6.00 | 2.50 |
| ❑ 116 Chris Johnson RC | 12.00 | 5.00 |
| ❑ 117 Felix Jones RC | 12.00 | 5.00 |
| ❑ 118 Darren McFadden RC | 12.00 | 5.00 |
| ❑ 119 Rashard Mendenhall RC | 10.00 | 4.00 |
| ❑ 120 Allen Patrick RC | 4.00 | 1.50 |
| ❑ 121 Ray Rice RC | 6.00 | 2.50 |
| ❑ 122 Dustin Keller RC | 5.00 | 2.00 |
| ❑ 123 Steve Slaton RC | 10.00 | 4.00 |
| ❑ 124 Kevin Smith RC | 8.00 | 3.00 |
| ❑ 125 Jonathan Stewart RC | 12.00 | 5.00 |
| ❑ 126 Kevin O'Connell RC | 6.00 | 2.50 |
| ❑ 127 Adrian Arrington RC | 4.00 | 1.50 |
| ❑ 128 Donnie Avery RC | 6.00 | 2.50 |
| ❑ 129 Earl Bennett RC | 5.00 | 2.00 |
| ❑ 130 Dexter Jackson RC | 5.00 | 2.00 |
| ❑ 131 Jerome Simpson RC | 4.00 | 1.50 |
| ❑ 132 Keenan Burton RC | 4.00 | 1.50 |
| ❑ 133 Andre Caldwell RC | 4.00 | 1.50 |
| ❑ 134 Early Doucet RC | 5.00 | 2.00 |
| ❑ 135 Harry Douglas RC | 5.00 | 2.00 |

| | | |
|---|---|---|
| ❑ 136 James Hardy RC | 5.00 | 2.00 |
| ❑ 137 Jordy Nelson RC | 6.00 | 2.50 |
| ❑ 138 DeSean Jackson RC | 10.00 | 4.00 |
| ❑ 139 Malcolm Kelly RC | 5.00 | 2.00 |
| ❑ 140 Mario Manningham RC | 5.00 | 2.00 |
| ❑ 141 Limas Sweed RC | 6.00 | 2.50 |
| ❑ 142 Eddie Royal RC | 10.00 | 4.00 |
| ❑ 143 Devin Thomas RC | 5.00 | 2.00 |
| ❑ 144 John Carlson RC | 5.00 | 2.00 |
| ❑ 145 Chris Long RC | 6.00 | 2.50 |
| ❑ 146 Vernon Gholston RC | 5.00 | 2.00 |
| ❑ 147 Dominique Rodgers-Cromartie RC | 5.00 | 2.00 |
| ❑ 148 Keith Rivers RC | 5.00 | 2.00 |
| ❑ 149 Jake Long RC | 6.00 | 2.50 |
| ❑ 150 Glenn Dorsey RC | 6.00 | 2.50 |
| ❑ 151 Brett Favre | 30.00 | 12.50 |

## 1995 Flair

| | | |
|---|---|---|
| ❑ COMPLETE SET (220) | 30.00 | 12.50 |
| ❑ 1 Larry Centers | .40 | .15 |
| ❑ 2 Garrison Hearst | .75 | .30 |
| ❑ 3 Seth Joyner | .20 | .07 |
| ❑ 4 Dave Krieg | .20 | .07 |
| ❑ 5 Rob Moore | .40 | .15 |
| ❑ 6 Frank Sanders RC | .75 | .30 |
| ❑ 7 Eric Swann | .40 | .15 |
| ❑ 8 Devin Bush | .20 | .07 |
| ❑ 9 Chris Doleman | .20 | .07 |
| ❑ 10 Bert Emanuel | .75 | .30 |
| ❑ 11 Jeff George | .40 | .15 |
| ❑ 12 Craig Heyward | .40 | .15 |
| ❑ 13 Terance Mathis | .40 | .15 |
| ❑ 14 Eric Metcalf | .40 | .15 |
| ❑ 15 Cornelius Bennett | .40 | .15 |
| ❑ 16 Jeff Burris | .20 | .07 |
| ❑ 17 Todd Collins RC | 2.50 | 1.00 |
| ❑ 18 Russell Copeland | .20 | .07 |
| ❑ 19 Jim Kelly | .75 | .30 |
| ❑ 20 Andre Reed | .40 | .15 |
| ❑ 21 Bruce Smith | .75 | .30 |
| ❑ 22 Don Beebe | .20 | .07 |
| ❑ 23 Mark Carrier WR | .40 | .15 |
| ❑ 24 Kerry Collins RC | 2.50 | 1.00 |
| ❑ 25 Barry Foster | .40 | .15 |
| ❑ 26 Pete Metzelaars | .20 | .07 |
| ❑ 27 Tyrone Poole | .75 | .30 |
| ❑ 28 Frank Reich | .20 | .07 |
| ❑ 29 Curtis Conway | .75 | .30 |
| ❑ 30 Chris Gedney | .20 | .07 |
| ❑ 31 Jeff Graham | .20 | .07 |
| ❑ 32 Raymont Harris | .20 | .07 |
| ❑ 33 Erik Kramer | .20 | .07 |
| ❑ 34 Rashaan Salaam | .40 | .15 |
| ❑ 35 Lewis Tillman | .20 | .07 |
| ❑ 36 Michael Timpson | .20 | .07 |
| ❑ 37 Jeff Blake RC | 1.00 | .40 |
| ❑ 38 Ki-Jana Carter RC | .75 | .30 |
| ❑ 39 Tony Mcgee | .20 | .07 |
| ❑ 40 Carl Pickens | .40 | .15 |
| ❑ 41 Corey Sawyer | .20 | .07 |
| ❑ 42 Darnay Scott | .40 | .15 |
| ❑ 43 Dan Wilkinson | .40 | .15 |
| ❑ 44 Derrick Alexander WR | .75 | .30 |
| ❑ 45 Leroy Hoard | .20 | .07 |
| ❑ 46 Michael Jackson | .40 | .15 |
| ❑ 47 Antonio Langham | .20 | .07 |
| ❑ 48 Andre Rison | .40 | .15 |
| ❑ 49 Vinny Testaverde | .40 | .15 |

| | | |
|---|---|---|
| ❑ 50 Eric Turner | .20 | .07 |
| ❑ 51 Troy Aikman | 2.00 | .75 |
| ❑ 52 Charles Haley | .40 | .15 |
| ❑ 53 Michael Irvin | .75 | .30 |
| ❑ 54 Daryl Johnston | .40 | .15 |
| ❑ 55 Leon Lett | .20 | .07 |
| ❑ 56 Jay Novacek | .40 | .15 |
| ❑ 57 Emmitt Smith | 3.00 | 1.25 |
| ❑ 58 Kevin Williams WR | .40 | .15 |
| ❑ 59 Steve Atwater | .20 | .07 |
| ❑ 60 Rod Bernstine | .20 | .07 |
| ❑ 61 John Elway | 4.00 | 1.50 |
| ❑ 62 Glyn Milburn | .20 | .07 |
| ❑ 63 Anthony Miller | .40 | .15 |
| ❑ 64 Mike Pritchard | .20 | .07 |
| ❑ 65 Shannon Sharpe | .40 | .15 |
| ❑ 66 Scott Mitchell | .40 | .15 |
| ❑ 67 Herman Moore | .75 | .30 |
| ❑ 68 Johnnie Morton | .40 | .15 |
| ❑ 69 Brett Perriman | .40 | .15 |
| ❑ 70 Barry Sanders | 3.00 | 1.25 |
| ❑ 71 Chris Spielman | .40 | .15 |
| ❑ 72 Edgar Bennett | .40 | .15 |
| ❑ 73 Robert Brooks | .75 | .30 |
| ❑ 74 Brett Favre | 4.00 | 1.50 |
| ❑ 75 LeShon Johnson | .40 | .15 |
| ❑ 76 Sean Jones | .20 | .07 |
| ❑ 77 George Teague | .20 | .07 |
| ❑ 78 Reggie White | .75 | .30 |
| ❑ 79 Micheal Barrow | .20 | .07 |
| ❑ 80 Gary Brown | .20 | .07 |
| ❑ 81 Mel Gray | .20 | .07 |
| ❑ 82 Haywood Jeffires | .20 | .07 |
| ❑ 83 Steve McNair RC | 4.00 | 1.50 |
| ❑ 84 Rodney Thomas RC | .40 | .15 |
| ❑ 85 Trev Alberts | .20 | .07 |
| ❑ 86 Flipper Anderson | .20 | .07 |
| ❑ 87 Tony Bennett | .20 | .07 |
| ❑ 88 Quentin Coryatt | .40 | .15 |
| ❑ 89 Sean Dawkins | .40 | .15 |
| ❑ 90 Craig Erickson | .20 | .07 |
| ❑ 91 Marshall Faulk | 2.50 | 1.00 |
| ❑ 92 Steve Beuerlein | .40 | .15 |
| ❑ 93 Tony Boselli RC | .75 | .30 |
| ❑ 94 Reggie Cobb | .20 | .07 |
| ❑ 95 Ernest Givins | .40 | .15 |
| ❑ 96 Desmond Howard | .40 | .15 |
| ❑ 97 Jeff Lageman | .20 | .07 |
| ❑ 98 James O. Stewart RC | 1.50 | .60 |
| ❑ 99 Marcus Allen | .75 | .30 |
| ❑ 100 Steve Bono | .40 | .15 |
| ❑ 101 Dale Carter | .20 | .07 |
| ❑ 102 Willie Davis | .40 | .15 |
| ❑ 103 Lake Dawson | .40 | .15 |
| ❑ 104 Greg Hill | .40 | .15 |
| ❑ 105 Neil Smith | .40 | .15 |
| ❑ 106 Tim Bowens | .20 | .07 |
| ❑ 107 Bryan Cox | .20 | .07 |
| ❑ 108 Irving Fryar | .40 | .15 |
| ❑ 109 Eric Green | .20 | .07 |
| ❑ 110 Terry Kirby | .40 | .15 |
| ❑ 111 Dan Marino | 4.00 | 1.50 |
| ❑ 112 O.J. McDuffie | .75 | .30 |
| ❑ 113 Bernie Parmalee | .40 | .15 |
| ❑ 114 Derrick Alexander DE RC | .20 | .07 |
| ❑ 115 Cris Carter | .75 | .30 |
| ❑ 116 Qadry Ismail | .20 | .07 |
| ❑ 117 Warren Moon | .40 | .15 |
| ❑ 118 Jake Reed | .40 | .15 |
| ❑ 119 Robert Smith | .75 | .30 |
| ❑ 120 Dewayne Washington | .20 | .07 |
| ❑ 121 Drew Bledsoe | 1.25 | .50 |
| ❑ 122 Vincent Brisby | .20 | .07 |
| ❑ 123 Ben Coates | .40 | .15 |
| ❑ 124 Curtis Martin RC | 4.00 | 1.50 |
| ❑ 125 Willie McGinest | .40 | .15 |
| ❑ 126 Dave Meggett | .20 | .07 |
| ❑ 127 Chris Slade UER RC | .20 | .07 |
| ❑ 128 Eric Allen | .20 | .07 |
| ❑ 129 Mario Bates | .40 | .15 |
| ❑ 130 Jim Everett | .20 | .07 |
| ❑ 131 Michael Haynes | .40 | .15 |
| ❑ 132 Tyrone Hughes | .20 | .07 |
| ❑ 133 Renaldo Turnbull | .20 | .07 |

| □ | | | |
|---|---|---|---|
| □ 134 | Ray Zellars RC | .40 | .15 |
| □ 135 | Michael Brooks | .20 | .07 |
| □ 136 | Dave Brown | .40 | .15 |
| □ 137 | Rodney Hampton | .40 | .15 |
| □ 138 | Thomas Lewis | .20 | .15 |
| □ 139 | Mike Sherrard | .20 | .07 |
| □ 140 | Herschel Walker | .40 | .15 |
| □ 141 | Tyrone Wheatley RC | 1.50 | .60 |
| □ 142 | Kyle Brady RC | .75 | .30 |
| □ 143 | Boomer Esiason | .40 | .15 |
| □ 144 | Aaron Glenn | .20 | .07 |
| □ 145 | Mo Lewis | .20 | .07 |
| □ 146 | Johnny Mitchell | .20 | .07 |
| □ 147 | Ronald Moore | .20 | .07 |
| □ 148 | Joe Aska | .20 | .15 |
| □ 149 | Tim Brown | .75 | .30 |
| □ 150 | Jeff Hostetler | .40 | .15 |
| □ 151 | Rocket Ismail | .40 | .15 |
| □ 152 | Napoleon Kaufman RC | 1.50 | .60 |
| □ 153 | Chester McGlockton | .20 | .15 |
| □ 154 | Harvey Williams | .20 | .07 |
| □ 155 | Fred Barnett | .20 | .15 |
| □ 156 | Randall Cunningham | .75 | .30 |
| □ 157 | Charlie Garner | .75 | .30 |
| □ 158 | Mike Mamula RC | .20 | .07 |
| □ 159 | Kevin Turner | .20 | .07 |
| □ 160 | Ricky Watters | .40 | .15 |
| □ 161 | Calvin Williams | .40 | .15 |
| □ 162 | Mark Bruener RC | .40 | .15 |
| □ 163 | Kevin Greene | .40 | .15 |
| □ 164 | Charles Johnson | .40 | .15 |
| □ 165 | Greg Lloyd | .40 | .15 |
| □ 166 | Byron Bam Morris | .20 | .07 |
| □ 167 | Neil O'Donnell | .40 | .15 |
| □ 168 | Kordell Stewart RC | 2.00 | .75 |
| □ 169 | John L. Williams | .20 | .07 |
| □ 170 | Rod Woodson | .40 | .15 |
| □ 171 | Jerome Bettis | .75 | .30 |
| □ 172 | Isaac Bruce | 1.25 | .50 |
| □ 173 | Kevin Carter RC | .75 | .30 |
| □ 174 | Troy Drayton | .20 | .07 |
| □ 175 | Sean Gilbert | .20 | .07 |
| □ 176 | Carlos Jenkins | .20 | .07 |
| □ 177 | Todd Lyght | .20 | .07 |
| □ 178 | Chris Miller | .20 | .07 |
| □ 179 | Andre Coleman | .20 | .07 |
| □ 180 | Stan Humphries | .40 | .15 |
| □ 181 | Shawn Jefferson | .40 | .15 |
| □ 182 | Natrone Means | .40 | .15 |
| □ 183 | Leslie O'Neal | .40 | .15 |
| □ 184 | Junior Seau | .75 | .30 |
| □ 185 | Mark Seay | .20 | .07 |
| □ 186 | William Floyd | .40 | .15 |
| □ 187 | Merton Hanks | .20 | .07 |
| □ 188 | Brent Jones | .20 | .07 |
| □ 189 | Ken Norton | .40 | .15 |
| □ 190 | Jerry Rice | 2.00 | .75 |
| □ 191 | Deion Sanders | 1.00 | .40 |
| □ 192 | J.J. Stokes RC | .75 | .30 |
| □ 193 | Dana Stubblefield | .40 | .15 |
| □ 194 | Steve Young | 1.50 | .60 |
| □ 195 | Sam Adams | .20 | .07 |
| □ 196 | Brian Blades | .40 | .15 |
| □ 197 | Joey Galloway | 2.00 | .75 |
| □ 198 | Cortez Kennedy | .40 | .15 |
| □ 199 | Rick Mirer | .40 | .15 |
| □ 200 | Chris Warren | .40 | .15 |
| □ 201 | Derrick Brooks RC | 2.00 | .75 |
| □ 202 | Lawrence Dawsey | .20 | .07 |
| □ 203 | Trent Dilfer | .75 | .30 |
| □ 204 | Alvin Harper | .20 | .07 |
| □ 205 | Jackie Harris | .20 | .07 |
| □ 206 | Courtney Hawkins | .20 | .07 |
| □ 207 | Hardy Nickerson | .20 | .07 |
| □ 208 | Errict Rhett | .40 | .15 |
| □ 209 | Warren Sapp RC | 2.00 | .75 |
| □ 210 | Terry Allen | .40 | .15 |
| □ 211 | Tom Carter | .20 | .07 |
| □ 212 | Henry Ellard | .40 | .15 |
| □ 213 | Darrell Green | .40 | .15 |
| □ 214 | Brian Mitchell | .20 | .07 |
| □ 215 | Heath Shuler | .40 | .15 |
| □ 216 | Michael Westbrook RC | .75 | .30 |
| □ 217 | Tydus Winans | .20 | .07 |

| □ 218 | Checklist | .20 | .07 |
|---|---|---|---|
| □ 219 | Checklist | .20 | .07 |
| □ 220 | Checklist | .40 | .15 |
| □ S1 | Michael Irvin Sample | 1.25 | .50 |

## 2002 Flair

| □ COMP.SET w/o SP's (90) | 25.00 | 10.00 |
|---|---|---|
| □ 1 Jeff Garcia | 1.25 | .50 |
| □ 2 Jevon Kearse | .75 | .30 |
| □ 3 Chris Weinke | .75 | .30 |
| □ 4 Ray Lewis | 1.25 | .50 |
| □ 5 Donovan McNabb | 1.50 | .60 |
| □ 6 Tiki Barber | 1.25 | .50 |
| □ 7 Rich Gannon | 1.25 | .50 |
| □ 8 Jamal Anderson | .75 | .30 |
| □ 9 Curtis Martin | 1.25 | .50 |
| □ 10 Darrell Jackson | .75 | .30 |
| □ 11 Ricky Williams | 1.25 | .50 |
| □ 12 Drew Brees | 1.25 | .50 |
| □ 13 Mark Brunell | 1.25 | .50 |
| □ 14 Johnnie Morton | .75 | .30 |
| □ 15 Quincy Carter | .75 | .30 |
| □ 16 Brian Urlacher | 2.00 | .75 |
| □ 17 Peerless Price | .75 | .30 |
| □ 18 Drew Bledsoe | 1.50 | .60 |
| □ 19 Aaron Brooks | 1.25 | .50 |
| □ 20 Derrick Mason | .75 | .30 |
| □ 21 Charlie Garner | .75 | .30 |
| □ 22 Mike Alstott | 1.25 | .50 |
| □ 23 Freddie Mitchell | .75 | .30 |
| □ 24 Isaac Bruce | 1.25 | .50 |
| □ 25 Hines Ward | 1.25 | .50 |
| □ 26 Doug Flutie | 1.25 | .50 |
| □ 27 Terrell Owens | 1.25 | .50 |
| □ 28 Peyton Manning | 2.50 | 1.00 |
| □ 29 Ron Dayne | .75 | .30 |
| □ 30 Peter Warrick | .75 | .30 |
| □ 31 Randy Moss | 2.50 | 1.00 |
| □ 32 Priest Holmes | 1.50 | .60 |
| □ 33 Joey Galloway | .75 | .30 |
| □ 34 Jimmy Smith | .75 | .30 |
| □ 35 Marvin Harrison | 1.25 | .50 |
| □ 36 Junior Seau | 1.25 | .50 |
| □ 37 Zach Thomas | 1.25 | .50 |
| □ 38 Antowain Smith | .75 | .30 |
| □ 39 Marty Booker | .75 | .30 |
| □ 40 Deuce McAllister | 1.50 | .60 |
| □ 41 Rod Smith | .75 | .30 |
| □ 42 Michael Westbrook | .50 | .20 |
| □ 43 Antonio Freeman | 1.25 | .50 |
| □ 44 Kerry Collins | .75 | .30 |
| □ 45 Koren Robinson | .75 | .30 |
| □ 46 Jamal Lewis | 1.25 | .50 |
| □ 47 Duce Staley | 1.25 | .50 |
| □ 48 Jerome Bettis | 1.25 | .50 |
| □ 49 David Terrell | 1.25 | .50 |
| □ 50 Daunte Culpepper | 1.25 | .50 |
| □ 51 Tim Couch | .75 | .30 |
| □ 52 Brian Griese | 1.25 | .50 |
| □ 53 Marshall Faulk | 1.25 | .50 |
| □ 54 Brad Johnson | .75 | .30 |
| □ 55 Eddie George | 1.25 | .50 |
| □ 56 Kurt Warner | 1.25 | .50 |
| □ 57 Steve McNair | 1.25 | .50 |
| □ 58 Stephen Davis | .75 | .30 |
| □ 59 Corey Dillon | .75 | .30 |
| □ 60 Troy Brown | 1.25 | .50 |
| □ 61 Warrick Dunn | 1.25 | .50 |

| □ 62 Ed McCaffrey | 1.25 | .50 |
|---|---|---|
| □ 63 Amani Toomer | .75 | .30 |
| □ 64 Rod Gardner | .75 | .30 |
| □ 65 Mike McMahon | 1.25 | .50 |
| □ 66 Wayne Chrebet | .75 | .30 |
| □ 67 Jake Plummer | 1.25 | .50 |
| □ 68 Edgerrin James | 1.50 | .60 |
| □ 69 Eric Moulds | .75 | .30 |
| □ 70 Tony Gonzalez | .75 | .30 |
| □ 71 Marcus Robinson | .75 | .30 |
| □ 72 Muhsin Muhammad | .75 | .30 |
| □ 73 Trent Dilfer | .75 | .30 |
| □ 74 Kevin Johnson | .75 | .30 |
| □ 75 Fred Taylor | 1.25 | .50 |
| □ 76 Terrell Davis | 1.25 | .50 |
| □ 77 Emmitt Smith | 3.00 | 1.25 |
| □ 78 Az-Zahir Hakim | .50 | .20 |
| □ 79 Tim Brown | 1.25 | .50 |
| □ 80 Jerry Rice | 2.50 | 1.00 |
| □ 81 Warren Sapp | .75 | .30 |
| □ 82 Michael Strahan | .75 | .30 |
| □ 83 Garrison Hearst | .75 | .30 |
| □ 84 David Boston | 1.25 | .50 |
| □ 85 Michael Vick | 2.50 | 1.00 |
| □ 86 Anthony Thomas | .75 | .30 |
| □ 87 Ahman Green | 1.25 | .50 |
| □ 88 Chris Chambers | 1.25 | .50 |
| □ 89 Tom Brady | 3.00 | 1.25 |
| □ 90 Plaxico Burress | .75 | .30 |
| □ 91 LaDainian Tomlinson | 2.00 | .75 |
| □ 92 Shaun Alexander | 1.50 | .60 |
| □ 93 Torry Holt | 1.25 | .50 |
| □ 94 Kordell Stewart | .75 | .30 |
| □ 95 Chad Pennington | 1.50 | .60 |
| □ 96 Chris Redman | .50 | .20 |
| □ 97 Kendrell Bell | 1.25 | .50 |
| □ 98 Michael Bennett | .75 | .30 |
| □ 99 Joe Horn | .75 | .30 |
| □ 100 Brett Favre | 3.00 | 1.25 |
| □ 101 David Carr RC | 8.00 | 3.00 |
| □ 102 Joey Harrington RC | 8.00 | 3.00 |
| □ 103 Ashley Lelie RC | 12.00 | 5.00 |
| □ 104 Javon Walker RC | 10.00 | 4.00 |
| □ 105 Reche Caldwell RC | 5.00 | 2.00 |
| □ 106 Andre Davis RC | 5.00 | 2.00 |
| □ 107 William Green RC | 6.00 | 2.50 |
| □ 108 Antonio Bryant RC | 6.00 | 2.50 |
| □ 109 Clinton Portis RC | 20.00 | 7.50 |
| □ 110 Luke Staley RC | 5.00 | 2.00 |
| □ 111 Josh Reed RC | 6.00 | 2.50 |
| □ 112 Ron Johnson RC | 5.00 | 2.00 |
| □ 113 Lamar Gordon RC | 5.00 | 2.00 |
| □ 114 Cliff Russell RC | 5.00 | 2.00 |
| □ 115 Eric Crouch RC | 6.00 | 2.50 |
| □ 116 Ladell Betts RC | 6.00 | 2.50 |
| □ 117 Patrick Ramsey RC | 8.00 | 3.00 |
| □ 118 Adrian Peterson RC | 8.00 | 3.00 |
| □ 119 DeShaun Foster RC | 6.00 | 2.50 |
| □ 120 Tim Carter RC | 5.00 | 2.00 |
| □ 121 Jabar Gaffney RC | 6.00 | 2.50 |
| □ 122 T.J. Duckett RC | 6.00 | 2.50 |
| □ 123 Julius Peppers RC | 12.00 | 5.00 |
| □ 124 Rohan Davey RC | 6.00 | 2.50 |
| □ 125 Antwaan Randle El RC | 20.00 | 8.00 |
| □ 126 Jeremy Shockey RC | 10.00 | 4.00 |
| □ 127 Donte Stallworth RC | 10.00 | 4.00 |
| □ 128 Marquise Walker RC | 5.00 | 2.00 |
| □ 129 Brian Westbrook RC | 15.00 | 6.00 |
| □ 130 Randy Fasani RC | 6.00 | 2.50 |
| □ 131 Jonathan Wells RC | 6.00 | 2.50 |
| □ 132 Travis Stephens RC | 5.00 | 2.00 |
| □ 133 Daniel Graham RC | 6.00 | 2.50 |
| □ 134 Maurice Morris RC | 6.00 | 2.50 |
| □ 135 David Garrard RC | 12.00 | 5.00 |

## 2004 Flair

| □ COMP.SET w/o SP's (60) | 40.00 | 20.00 |
|---|---|---|
| □ ROOKIE STATED ODDS 1:100 RETAIL | | |
| □ ROOKIE PRINT RUN 799 SER.#'d SETS | | |
| □ 1 Clinton Portis | 1.50 | .60 |
| □ 2 Deuce McAllister | 1.50 | .60 |
| □ 3 Marshall Faulk | 1.50 | .60 |
| □ 4 Tom Brady | 4.00 | 1.50 |
| □ 5 Ahman Green | 1.50 | .60 |

| | | |
|---|---|---|
| ❏ 6 LaDainian Tomlinson | 2.50 | 1.00 |
| ❏ 7 Lee Suggs | 1.50 | .60 |
| ❏ 8 Amani Toomer | 1.25 | .50 |
| ❏ 9 Priest Holmes | 1.50 | .60 |
| ❏ 10 Peerless Price | 1.25 | .50 |
| ❏ 11 Warren Sapp | 1.25 | .50 |
| ❏ 12 Andre Davis | 1.00 | .40 |
| ❏ 13 Chad Pennington | 1.50 | .60 |
| ❏ 14 Quincy Carter | 1.00 | .40 |
| ❏ 15 Santana Moss | 1.25 | .50 |
| ❏ 16 Antonio Bryant | 1.25 | .50 |
| ❏ 17 Jerry Porter | 1.25 | .50 |
| ❏ 18 Laveranues Coles | 1.25 | .50 |
| ❏ 19 Daunte Culpepper | 1.50 | .60 |
| ❏ 20 Stephen Davis | 1.25 | .50 |
| ❏ 21 Rich Gannon | 1.25 | .50 |
| ❏ 22 Chad Johnson | 1.50 | .60 |
| ❏ 23 Ashley Lelie | 1.25 | .50 |
| ❏ 24 Ray Lewis | 1.50 | .60 |
| ❏ 25 Joey Harrington | 1.50 | .60 |
| ❏ 26 Brian Westbrook | 1.50 | .60 |
| ❏ 27 Marvin Harrison | 1.50 | .60 |
| ❏ 28 Torry Holt | 1.50 | .60 |
| ❏ 29 Kevan Barlow | 1.25 | .50 |
| ❏ 30 Peyton Manning | 3.00 | 1.25 |
| ❏ 31 Andre Johnson | 1.50 | .60 |
| ❏ 32 Steve Smith | 1.50 | .60 |
| ❏ 33 Troy Brown | 1.25 | .50 |
| ❏ 34 Brian Urlacher | 1.50 | .60 |
| ❏ 35 Anquan Boldin | 1.50 | .60 |
| ❏ 36 Matt Hasselbeck | 1.50 | .60 |
| ❏ 37 Edgerrin James | 1.50 | .60 |
| ❏ 38 Dante Hall | 1.25 | .50 |
| ❏ 39 Brad Johnson | 1.25 | .50 |
| ❏ 40 Jamal Lewis | 1.25 | .50 |
| ❏ 41 Rudi Johnson | 1.25 | .50 |
| ❏ 42 Michael Strahan | 1.25 | .50 |
| ❏ 43 Donovan McNabb | 1.50 | .60 |
| ❏ 44 Steve McNair | 1.50 | .60 |
| ❏ 45 Ricky Williams | 1.50 | .60 |
| ❏ 46 Jake Delhomme | 1.25 | .50 |
| ❏ 47 Patrick Ramsey | 1.25 | .50 |
| ❏ 48 Randy Moss | 2.00 | .75 |
| ❏ 49 David Carr | 1.25 | .50 |
| ❏ 50 Jeff Garcia | 1.50 | .60 |
| ❏ 51 Shaun Alexander | 1.50 | .60 |
| ❏ 52 Byron Leftwich | 1.50 | .60 |
| ❏ 53 Michael Vick | 1.50 | .60 |
| ❏ 54 Brett Favre | 4.00 | 1.50 |
| ❏ 55 Hines Ward | 1.50 | .60 |
| ❏ 56 Chris Chambers | 1.25 | .50 |
| ❏ 57 Eddie George | 1.25 | .50 |
| ❏ 58 Eric Moulds | 1.25 | .50 |
| ❏ 59 Plaxico Burress | 1.25 | .50 |
| ❏ 60 Charles Rogers | 1.25 | .50 |
| ❏ 61 Eli Manning RC | 25.00 | 10.00 |
| ❏ 62 Larry Fitzgerald RC | 12.00 | 5.00 |
| ❏ 63 Chris Perry RC | 4.00 | 1.50 |
| ❏ 64 Ben Roethlisberger RC | 30.00 | 12.00 |
| ❏ 65 Roy Williams RC | 10.00 | 4.00 |
| ❏ 66 Kellen Winslow RC | 8.00 | 3.00 |
| ❏ 67 Steven Jackson RC | 12.00 | 5.00 |
| ❏ 68 Kevin Jones RC | 4.00 | 1.50 |
| ❏ 69 Reggie Williams RC | 4.00 | 1.50 |
| ❏ 70 Michael Clayton RC | 4.00 | 1.50 |
| ❏ 71 Rashaun Woods RC | 2.50 | 1.00 |
| ❏ 72 Ben Troupe RC | 3.00 | 1.50 |
| ❏ 73 Greg Jones RC | 4.00 | 1.50 |

| | | |
|---|---|---|
| ❏ 74 J.P. Losman RC | 5.00 | 2.00 |
| ❏ 75 Philip Rivers RC | 12.00 | 5.00 |
| ❏ 76 Michael Jenkins RC | 4.00 | 1.50 |
| ❏ 77 Darius Watts RC | 3.00 | 1.25 |
| ❏ 78 Michael Turner RC | 8.00 | 3.00 |
| ❏ 79 Lee Evans RC | 5.00 | 2.00 |
| ❏ 80 Drew Henson RC | 2.50 | 1.00 |
| ❏ 81 Luke McCown RC | 4.00 | 1.50 |
| ❏ 82 Julius Jones RC | 10.00 | 4.00 |
| ❏ 83 Bernard Berrian RC | 4.00 | 1.50 |
| ❏ 84 Keary Colbert RC | 4.00 | 1.50 |
| ❏ 85 Tatum Bell RC | 4.00 | 1.50 |

## 1999 Flair Showcase

| | | |
|---|---|---|
| ❏ COMPLETE SET (192) | 600.00 | 300.00 |
| ❏ COMP.SET w/o SPs (160) | 50.00 | 20.00 |
| ❏ 1 Troy Aikman PW | 2.00 | .75 |
| ❏ 2 Jamal Anderson PW | .40 | .15 |
| ❏ 3 Charlie Batch PW | 1.00 | .40 |
| ❏ 4 Jerome Bettis PW | .40 | .15 |
| ❏ 5 Drew Bledsoe PW | 1.25 | .50 |
| ❏ 6 Mark Brunell PW | 1.00 | .40 |
| ❏ 7 Randall Cunningham PW | 1.00 | .40 |
| ❏ 8 Terrell Davis PW | 1.00 | .40 |
| ❏ 9 Corey Dillon PW | 1.00 | .40 |
| ❏ 10 Warrick Dunn PW | 1.00 | .40 |
| ❏ 11 Curtis Enis PW | .40 | .15 |
| ❏ 12 Marshall Faulk PW | 1.25 | .50 |
| ❏ 13 Brett Favre PW | 3.00 | 1.25 |
| ❏ 14 Doug Flutie PW | 1.00 | .40 |
| ❏ 15 Eddie George PW | 1.00 | .40 |
| ❏ 16 Brian Griese PW | 1.00 | .40 |
| ❏ 17 Keyshawn Johnson PW | 1.00 | .40 |
| ❏ 18 Peyton Manning PW | 3.00 | 1.25 |
| ❏ 19 Dan Marino PW | 3.00 | 1.25 |
| ❏ 20 Curtis Martin PW | 1.00 | .40 |
| ❏ 21 Steve McNair PW | 1.00 | .40 |
| ❏ 22 Randy Moss PW | 2.50 | 1.00 |
| ❏ 23 Terrell Owens PW | 1.00 | .40 |
| ❏ 24 Jake Plummer PW | .60 | .25 |
| ❏ 25 Jerry Rice PW | 2.00 | .75 |
| ❏ 26 Barry Sanders PW | 3.00 | 1.25 |
| ❏ 27 Antowain Smith PW | 1.00 | .40 |
| ❏ 28 Emmitt Smith PW | 2.00 | .75 |
| ❏ 29 Kordell Stewart PW | .60 | .25 |
| ❏ 30 J.J. Stokes PW | .60 | .25 |
| ❏ 31 Fred Taylor PW | 1.00 | .40 |
| ❏ 32 Steve Young PW | 1.25 | .50 |
| ❏ 33 Troy Aikman PN | 2.00 | .75 |
| ❏ 34 Mike Alstott PN | 1.00 | .40 |
| ❏ 35 Jamal Anderson PN | 1.00 | .40 |
| ❏ 36 Charlie Batch PN | 1.00 | .40 |
| ❏ 37 Jerome Bettis PN | 1.00 | .40 |
| ❏ 38 Drew Bledsoe PN | 1.25 | .50 |
| ❏ 39 Mark Brunell PN | 1.00 | .40 |
| ❏ 40 Cris Carter PN | 1.00 | .40 |
| ❏ 41 Mark Chmura PN | .40 | .15 |
| ❏ 42 Wayne Chrebet PN | .60 | .25 |
| ❏ 43 Kerry Collins PN | .40 | .15 |
| ❏ 44 Randall Cunningham PN | 1.00 | .40 |
| ❏ 45 Terrell Davis PN | 1.00 | .40 |
| ❏ 46 Trent Dilfer PN | .60 | .25 |
| ❏ 47 Corey Dillon PN | 1.00 | .40 |
| ❏ 48 Warrick Dunn PN | 1.00 | .40 |
| ❏ 49 Kevin Dyson PN | .60 | .25 |
| ❏ 50 Curtis Enis PN | .40 | .15 |
| ❏ 51 Marshall Faulk PN | 1.25 | .50 |
| ❏ 52 Brett Favre PN | 3.00 | 1.25 |

| | | |
|---|---|---|
| ❏ 53 Doug Flutie PN | 1.00 | .40 |
| ❏ 54 Antonio Freeman PN | 1.00 | .40 |
| ❏ 55 Eddie George PN | 1.00 | .40 |
| ❏ 56 Terry Glenn PN | 1.00 | .40 |
| ❏ 57 Tony Gonzalez PN | 1.00 | .40 |
| ❏ 58 Elvis Grbac PN | .60 | .25 |
| ❏ 59 Jacquez Green PN | .40 | .15 |
| ❏ 60 Brian Griese PN | 1.00 | .40 |
| ❏ 61 Marvin Harrison PN | 1.00 | .40 |
| ❏ 62 Garrison Hearst PN | .60 | .25 |
| ❏ 63 Skip Hicks PN | .40 | .15 |
| ❏ 64 Priest Holmes PN | 1.50 | .60 |
| ❏ 65 Michael Irvin PN | .60 | .25 |
| ❏ 66 Brad Johnson PN | .60 | .25 |
| ❏ 67 Keyshawn Johnson PN | 1.00 | .40 |
| ❏ 68 Napoleon Kaufman PN | 1.00 | .40 |
| ❏ 69 Dorsey Levens PN | 1.00 | .40 |
| ❏ 70 Peyton Manning PN | 3.00 | 1.25 |
| ❏ 71 Dan Marino PN | 3.00 | 1.25 |
| ❏ 72 Curtis Martin PN | 1.00 | .40 |
| ❏ 73 Ed McCaffrey PN | .60 | .25 |
| ❏ 74 Keenan McCardell PN | .60 | .25 |
| ❏ 75 O.J. McDuffie PN | .60 | .25 |
| ❏ 76 Steve McNair PN | 1.00 | .40 |
| ❏ 77 Scott Mitchell PN | .40 | .15 |
| ❏ 78 Randy Moss PN | 2.50 | 1.00 |
| ❏ 79 Eric Moulds PN | 1.00 | .40 |
| ❏ 80 Terrell Owens PN | 1.00 | .40 |
| ❏ 81 Lawrence Phillips PN | .60 | .25 |
| ❏ 82 Jake Plummer PN | .60 | .25 |
| ❏ 83 Jerry Rice PN | 2.00 | .75 |
| ❏ 84 Andre Rison PN | .60 | .25 |
| ❏ 85 Barry Sanders PN | 3.00 | 1.25 |
| ❏ 86 Shannon Sharpe PN | 1.00 | .40 |
| ❏ 87 Antowain Smith PN | 1.00 | .40 |
| ❏ 88 Emmitt Smith PN | 2.00 | .75 |
| ❏ 89 Rod Smith PN | .60 | .25 |
| ❏ 90 Duce Staley PN | 1.00 | .40 |
| ❏ 91 Kordell Stewart PN | .60 | .25 |
| ❏ 92 J.J. Stokes PN | .60 | .25 |
| ❏ 93 Fred Taylor PN | 1.00 | .40 |
| ❏ 94 Vinny Testaverde PN | .60 | .25 |
| ❏ 95 Ricky Watters PN | .60 | .25 |
| ❏ 96 Steve Young PN | 1.25 | .50 |
| ❏ 97 Mike Alstott | 1.00 | .40 |
| ❏ 98 Jamal Anderson | 1.00 | .40 |
| ❏ 99 Charlie Batch | 1.00 | .40 |
| ❏ 100 Jerome Bettis | 1.00 | .40 |
| ❏ 101 Tim Biakabutuka | .60 | .25 |
| ❏ 102 Drew Bledsoe | 1.25 | .50 |
| ❏ 103 Tim Brown | 1.00 | .40 |
| ❏ 104 Mark Brunell | 1.00 | .40 |
| ❏ 105 Cris Carter | 1.00 | .40 |
| ❏ 106 Chris Chandler | .40 | .15 |
| ❏ 107 Mark Chmura | .40 | .15 |
| ❏ 108 Wayne Chrebet | .60 | .25 |
| ❏ 109 Ben Coates | .60 | .25 |
| ❏ 110 Kerry Collins | .60 | .25 |
| ❏ 111 Randall Cunningham | 1.00 | .40 |
| ❏ 112 Trent Dilfer | .60 | .25 |
| ❏ 113 Corey Dillon | 1.00 | .40 |
| ❏ 114 Warrick Dunn | 1.00 | .40 |
| ❏ 115 Kevin Dyson | .60 | .25 |
| ❏ 116 Curtis Enis | .40 | .15 |
| ❏ 117 Marshall Faulk | 1.25 | .50 |
| ❏ 118 Doug Flutie | 1.00 | .40 |
| ❏ 119 Antonio Freeman | 1.00 | .40 |
| ❏ 120 Joey Galloway | 1.00 | .40 |
| ❏ 121 Rich Gannon | 1.00 | .40 |
| ❏ 122 Eddie George | 1.00 | .40 |
| ❏ 123 Terry Glenn | 1.00 | .40 |
| ❏ 124 Tony Gonzalez | 1.00 | .40 |
| ❏ 125 Elvis Grbac | .60 | .25 |
| ❏ 126 Jacquez Green | .40 | .15 |
| ❏ 127 Brian Griese | 1.00 | .40 |
| ❏ 128 Marvin Harrison | 1.00 | .40 |
| ❏ 129 Garrison Hearst | .60 | .25 |
| ❏ 130 Skip Hicks | .40 | .15 |
| ❏ 131 Priest Holmes | 1.50 | .60 |
| ❏ 132 Michael Irvin | .60 | .25 |
| ❏ 133 Brad Johnson | .60 | .25 |
| ❏ 134 Napoleon Kaufman | 1.00 | .40 |
| ❏ 135 Terry Kirby | .40 | .15 |
| ❏ 136 Dorsey Levens | 1.00 | .40 |

|  |  | | |
|---|---|---|---|
| 137 | Curtis Martin | 1.00 | .40 |
| 138 | Ed McCaffrey | .60 | .25 |
| 139 | Keenan McCardell | .60 | .25 |
| 140 | O.J. McDuffie | .60 | .25 |
| 141 | Steve McNair | 1.00 | .40 |
| 142 | Natrone Means | .60 | .25 |
| 143 | Scott Mitchell | .40 | .15 |
| 144 | Herman Moore | .60 | .25 |
| 145 | Eric Moulds | 1.00 | .40 |
| 146 | Terrell Owens | 1.00 | .40 |
| 147 | Lawrence Phillips | .60 | .25 |
| 148 | Jerry Rice | 2.00 | .75 |
| 149 | Andre Rison | .60 | .25 |
| 150 | Deion Sanders | 1.00 | .40 |
| 151 | Shannon Sharpe | .60 | .25 |
| 152 | Antowain Smith | 1.00 | .40 |
| 153 | Rod Smith | .60 | .25 |
| 154 | Duce Staley | 1.00 | .40 |
| 155 | Kordell Stewart | .60 | .25 |
| 156 | J.J. Stokes | .60 | .25 |
| 157 | Vinny Testaverde | .60 | .25 |
| 158 | Yancey Thigpen | .40 | .15 |
| 159 | Ricky Watters | .60 | .25 |
| 160 | Steve Young | 1.25 | .50 |
| 161 | Troy Aikman SP | 12.00 | 6.00 |
| 162 | Champ Bailey SP | 12.00 | 5.00 |
| 163 | Karsten Bailey RC | 8.00 | 3.00 |
| 164 | D'Wayne Bates RC | 8.00 | 3.00 |
| 165 | David Boston RC | 10.00 | 4.00 |
| 166 | Mike Cloud RC | 8.00 | 3.00 |
| 167 | Cecil Collins RC | 5.00 | 2.00 |
| 168 | Tim Couch RC | 10.00 | 4.00 |
| 169 | Daunte Culpepper RC | 40.00 | 15.00 |
| 170 | Terrell Davis SP | 6.00 | 2.50 |
| 171 | Troy Edwards RC | 8.00 | 3.00 |
| 172 | Kevin Faulk RC | 10.00 | 4.00 |
| 173 | Brett Favre SP | 20.00 | 10.00 |
| 174 | Torry Holt RC | 25.00 | 10.00 |
| 175 | Sedrick Irvin RC | 5.00 | 2.00 |
| 176 | Edgerrin James RC | 40.00 | 15.00 |
| 177 | James Johnson RC | 8.00 | 3.00 |
| 178 | Kevin Johnson RC | 10.00 | 4.00 |
| 179 | Keyshawn Johnson SP | 5.00 | 2.00 |
| 180 | Peyton Manning SP | 20.00 | 10.00 |
| 181 | Dan Marino SP | 20.00 | 10.00 |
| 182 | Donovan McNabb RC | 50.00 | 20.00 |
| 183 | Cade McNown RC | 8.00 | 3.00 |
| 184 | Joe Montgomery RC | 8.00 | 3.00 |
| 185 | Randy Moss SP | 15.00 | 6.00 |
| 186 | Jake Plummer SP | 6.00 | 2.50 |
| 187 | Peerless Price RC | 10.00 | 4.00 |
| 188 | Barry Sanders SP | 20.00 | 10.00 |
| 189 | Akili Smith RC | 8.00 | 3.00 |
| 190 | Emmitt Smith SP | 12.00 | 6.00 |
| 191 | Fred Taylor SP | 8.00 | 3.00 |
| 192 | Ricky Williams SP | 20.00 | 7.50 |
| P24 | Jake Plummer PW Promo | 1.00 | .40 |
| P82 | Jake Plummer PN Promo | 1.00 | .40 |
| P147 | Jake Plummer Promo | 1.00 | .40 |

## 2006 Flair Showcase

| | | |
|---|---|---|
| COMP.SET w/o SP's (100) | 20.00 | 8.00 |

101-142 PRINT RUN 699 SER.#'d SETS
143-184 PRINT RUN 499 SER.#'d SETS
185-226 PRINT RUN 299 SER.#'d SETS
227-236 PRINT RUN 199 SER.#'d SETS
237-268 PRINT RUN 999 SER.#'d SETS

|  |  | | |
|---|---|---|---|
| 1 | Edgerrin James | .60 | .25 |
| 2 | Larry Fitzgerald | .75 | .30 |
| 3 | Anquan Boldin | .60 | .25 |
| 4 | Michael Vick | .75 | .30 |
| 5 | Warrick Dunn | .60 | .25 |
| 6 | Roddy White | .50 | .20 |
| 7 | Steve McNair | .60 | .25 |
| 8 | Jamal Lewis | .60 | .25 |
| 9 | Derrick Mason | .60 | .25 |
| 10 | Willis McGahee | .75 | .30 |
| 11 | Lee Evans | .60 | .25 |
| 12 | J.P. Losman | .60 | .25 |
| 13 | Jake Delhomme | .60 | .25 |
| 14 | DeShaun Foster | .60 | .25 |
| 15 | Steve Smith | .75 | .30 |
| 16 | Rex Grossman | .75 | .30 |
| 17 | Thomas Jones | .60 | .25 |
| 18 | Muhsin Muhammad | .60 | .25 |
| 19 | Brian Urlacher | .75 | .30 |
| 20 | Carson Palmer | .75 | .30 |
| 21 | Rudi Johnson | .60 | .25 |
| 22 | Chad Johnson | .75 | .30 |
| 23 | Charlie Frye | .60 | .25 |
| 24 | Reuben Droughns | .60 | .25 |
| 25 | Braylon Edwards | .75 | .30 |
| 26 | Drew Bledsoe | .75 | .30 |
| 27 | Julius Jones | .75 | .30 |
| 28 | Terrell Owens | .75 | .30 |
| 29 | Jake Plummer | .60 | .25 |
| 30 | Tatum Bell | .60 | .25 |
| 31 | Javon Walker | .60 | .25 |
| 32 | Kevin Jones | .75 | .30 |
| 33 | Roy Williams WR | .75 | .30 |
| 34 | Mike Williams | .75 | .30 |
| 35 | Brett Favre | 1.50 | .60 |
| 36 | Ahman Green | .60 | .25 |
| 37 | Donald Driver | .60 | .25 |
| 38 | David Carr | .60 | .25 |
| 39 | Eric Moulds | .60 | .25 |
| 40 | Andre Johnson | .60 | .25 |
| 41 | Peyton Manning | 1.25 | .50 |
| 42 | Marvin Harrison | .75 | .30 |
| 43 | Reggie Wayne | .60 | .25 |
| 44 | Byron Leftwich | .60 | .25 |
| 45 | Fred Taylor | .60 | .25 |
| 46 | Ernest Wilford | .60 | .25 |
| 47 | Trent Green | .60 | .25 |
| 48 | Larry Johnson | .60 | .25 |
| 49 | Tony Gonzalez | .60 | .25 |
| 50 | Eddie Kennison | .50 | .20 |
| 51 | Daunte Culpepper | .75 | .30 |
| 52 | Ronnie Brown | .75 | .30 |
| 53 | Chris Chambers | .60 | .25 |
| 54 | Brad Johnson | .60 | .25 |
| 55 | Chester Taylor | .60 | .25 |
| 56 | Troy Williamson | .60 | .25 |
| 57 | Tom Brady | 1.25 | .50 |
| 58 | Corey Dillon | .60 | .25 |
| 59 | Troy Brown | .50 | .20 |
| 60 | Drew Brees | .75 | .30 |
| 61 | Deuce McAllister | .60 | .25 |
| 62 | Joe Horn | .60 | .25 |
| 63 | Eli Manning | 1.00 | .40 |
| 64 | Tiki Barber | .75 | .30 |
| 65 | Plaxico Burress | .60 | .25 |
| 66 | Jeremy Shockey | .75 | .30 |
| 67 | Chad Pennington | .60 | .25 |
| 68 | Curtis Martin | .75 | .30 |
| 69 | Laveranues Coles | .60 | .25 |
| 70 | Aaron Brooks | .60 | .25 |
| 71 | LaMont Jordan | .60 | .25 |
| 72 | Randy Moss | .75 | .30 |
| 73 | Jerry Porter | .60 | .25 |
| 74 | Donovan McNabb | .75 | .30 |
| 75 | Brian Westbrook | .60 | .25 |
| 76 | Reggie Brown | .60 | .25 |
| 77 | Ben Roethlisberger | 1.25 | .50 |
| 78 | Willie Parker | 1.00 | .40 |
| 79 | Hines Ward | .75 | .30 |
| 80 | Philip Rivers | .75 | .30 |
| 81 | LaDainian Tomlinson | 1.00 | .40 |
| 82 | Antonio Gates | .75 | .30 |
| 83 | Alex Smith QB | .75 | .30 |
| 84 | Frank Gore | .75 | .30 |
| 85 | Antonio Bryant | .60 | .25 |
| 86 | Matt Hasselbeck | .60 | .25 |
| 87 | Shaun Alexander | .75 | .30 |
| 88 | Nate Burleson | .60 | .25 |
| 89 | Marc Bulger | .60 | .25 |
| 90 | Steven Jackson | .75 | .30 |
| 91 | Torry Holt | .60 | .25 |
| 92 | Chris Simms | .60 | .25 |
| 93 | Cadillac Williams | .75 | .30 |
| 94 | Joey Galloway | .60 | .25 |
| 95 | Kerry Collins | .60 | .25 |
| 96 | David Givens | .60 | .25 |
| 97 | Drew Bennett | .60 | .25 |
| 98 | Mark Brunell | .75 | .30 |
| 99 | Clinton Portis | .75 | .30 |
| 100 | Santana Moss | .60 | .25 |
| 101 | Todd Watkins RC | 5.00 | 2.00 |
| 102 | Adam Jennings RC | 5.00 | 2.00 |
| 103 | David Pittman RC | 5.00 | 2.00 |
| 104 | Dawan Landry RC | 6.00 | 2.50 |
| 105 | Ko Simpson RC | 5.00 | 2.00 |
| 106 | James Anderson RC | 4.00 | 1.50 |
| 107 | Dusty Dvoracek RC | 6.00 | 2.50 |
| 108 | Jamar Williams RC | 5.00 | 2.00 |
| 109 | Bennie Brazell RC | 5.00 | 2.00 |
| 110 | Leon Williams RC | 5.00 | 2.00 |
| 111 | Lawrence Vickers RC | 5.00 | 2.00 |
| 112 | Elvis Dumervil RC | 4.00 | 1.50 |
| 113 | Domenik Hixon RC | 8.00 | 3.00 |
| 114 | Antoine Bethea RC | 6.00 | 2.50 |
| 115 | David Anderson RC | 5.00 | 2.00 |
| 116 | Freddie Keiaho RC | 5.00 | 2.00 |
| 117 | Clint Ingram RC | 5.00 | 2.00 |
| 118 | Jeff Webb RC | 5.00 | 2.00 |
| 119 | Devin Aromashodu RC | 5.00 | 2.00 |
| 120 | Mike Hass RC | 6.00 | 2.50 |
| 121 | Josh Lay RC | 3.00 | 1.25 |
| 122 | Marques Colston RC | 15.00 | 6.00 |
| 123 | Gerris Wilkinson RC | 4.00 | 1.50 |
| 124 | Barry Cofield RC | 5.00 | 2.00 |
| 125 | Guy Whimper RC | 4.00 | 1.50 |
| 126 | Nick Mangold RC | 3.00 | 1.25 |
| 127 | Anthony Schlegel RC | 5.00 | 2.00 |
| 128 | Eric Smith RC | 5.00 | 2.00 |
| 129 | Darnell Bing RC | 6.00 | 2.50 |
| 130 | Anthony Smith RC | 6.00 | 2.50 |
| 131 | Charlie Whitehurst RC | 6.00 | 2.50 |
| 132 | Delanie Walker RC | 5.00 | 2.00 |
| 133 | Marcus Hudson RC | 5.00 | 2.00 |
| 134 | David Kirtman RC | 5.00 | 2.00 |
| 135 | Victor Adeyanju RC | 5.00 | 2.00 |
| 136 | Davin Joseph RC | 5.00 | 2.00 |
| 137 | Marcus McNeill RC | 5.00 | 2.00 |
| 138 | Calvin Lowry RC | 6.00 | 2.50 |
| 139 | Stephen Tulloch RC | 5.00 | 2.00 |
| 140 | Tema Nande RC | 5.00 | 2.00 |
| 141 | Jonathan Orr RC | 5.00 | 2.00 |
| 142 | Jon Alston RC | 6.00 | 2.50 |
| 143 | Jimmy Williams RC | 8.00 | 3.00 |
| 144 | D.J. Shockley RC | 6.00 | 2.50 |
| 145 | Demetrius Williams RC | 6.00 | 2.50 |
| 146 | P.J. Daniels RC | 6.00 | 2.50 |
| 147 | Quinn Sypniewski RC | 6.00 | 2.50 |
| 148 | Ashton Youboty RC | 8.00 | 3.00 |
| 149 | Richard Marshall RC | 6.00 | 2.50 |
| 150 | Jeff King RC | 5.00 | 2.00 |
| 151 | Danieal Manning RC | 8.00 | 3.00 |
| 152 | Reggie McNeal RC | 8.00 | 3.00 |
| 153 | D'Qwell Jackson RC | 6.00 | 2.50 |
| 154 | Jerome Harrison RC | 8.00 | 3.00 |
| 155 | Skyler Green RC | 8.00 | 3.00 |
| 156 | Brandon Marshall RC | 10.00 | 4.00 |
| 157 | Daniel Bullocks RC | 8.00 | 3.00 |
| 158 | Abdul Hodge RC | 8.00 | 3.00 |
| 159 | Cory Rodgers RC | 8.00 | 3.00 |
| 160 | Ingle Martin RC | 8.00 | 3.00 |
| 161 | Stephen Gostkowski RC | 6.00 | 2.50 |
| 162 | Wali Lundy RC | 8.00 | 3.00 |
| 163 | Bernard Pollard RC | 5.00 | 2.00 |
| 164 | Marcus Vick RC | 6.00 | 2.50 |
| 165 | Cedric Griffin RC | 6.00 | 2.50 |
| 166 | Garrett Mills RC | 8.00 | 3.00 |
| 167 | Roman Harper RC | 6.00 | 2.50 |
| 168 | Brad Smith RC | 8.00 | 3.00 |
| 169 | Leon Washington RC | 8.00 | 3.00 |

| | | |
|---|---|---|
| ❏ 170 Ahmad Brooks RC | 6.00 | 2.50 |
| ❏ 171 Thomas Howard RC | 8.00 | 3.00 |
| ❏ 172 Jason Avant RC | 8.00 | 3.00 |
| ❏ 173 Jeremy Bloom RC | 6.00 | 2.50 |
| ❏ 174 Omar Jacobs RC | 6.00 | 2.50 |
| ❏ 175 Mike Bell RC | 8.00 | 3.00 |
| ❏ 176 Cedric Humes RC | 8.00 | 3.00 |
| ❏ 177 Michael Robinson RC | 8.00 | 3.00 |
| ❏ 178 Ben Obomanu RC | 6.00 | 2.50 |
| ❏ 179 Darryl Tapp RC | 6.00 | 2.50 |
| ❏ 180 Claude Wroten RC | 5.00 | 2.00 |
| ❏ 181 Dominique Byrd RC | 6.00 | 2.50 |
| ❏ 182 Marques Hagans RC | 6.00 | 2.50 |
| ❏ 183 Bruce Gradkowski RC | 8.00 | 3.00 |
| ❏ 184 Rocky McIntosh RC | 8.00 | 3.00 |
| ❏ 185 Leonard Pope RC | 8.00 | 3.00 |
| ❏ 186 Jerious Norwood RC | 10.00 | 4.00 |
| ❏ 187 Haloti Ngata RC | 8.00 | 3.00 |
| ❏ 188 Donte Whitner RC | 8.00 | 3.00 |
| ❏ 189 John McCargo RC | 6.00 | 2.50 |
| ❏ 190 Devin Hester RC | 15.00 | 6.00 |
| ❏ 191 Johnathan Joseph RC | 6.00 | 2.50 |
| ❏ 192 Kamerion Wimbley RC | 8.00 | 3.00 |
| ❏ 193 Travis Wilson RC | 8.00 | 3.00 |
| ❏ 194 Bobby Carpenter RC | 8.00 | 3.00 |
| ❏ 195 Anthony Fasano RC | 8.00 | 3.00 |
| ❏ 196 Tony Scheffler RC | 8.00 | 3.00 |
| ❏ 197 Ernie Sims RC | 8.00 | 3.00 |
| ❏ 198 Brian Calhoun RC | 6.00 | 2.50 |
| ❏ 199 A.J. Hawk RC | 15.00 | 6.00 |
| ❏ 200 Greg Jennings RC | 12.00 | 5.00 |
| ❏ 201 Mario Williams RC | 12.00 | 5.00 |
| ❏ 202 DeMeco Ryans RC | 10.00 | 4.00 |
| ❏ 203 Marcedes Lewis RC | 8.00 | 3.00 |
| ❏ 204 Maurice Drew RC | 15.00 | 6.00 |
| ❏ 205 Tamba Hali RC | 8.00 | 3.00 |
| ❏ 206 Brodie Croyle RC | 10.00 | 4.00 |
| ❏ 207 Jason Allen RC | 8.00 | 3.00 |
| ❏ 208 Derek Hagan RC | 8.00 | 3.00 |
| ❏ 209 Chad Greenway RC | 8.00 | 3.00 |
| ❏ 210 Tarvaris Jackson RC | 8.00 | 3.00 |
| ❏ 211 Chad Jackson RC | 6.00 | 2.50 |
| ❏ 212 David Thomas RC | 8.00 | 3.00 |
| ❏ 213 Mathias Kiwanuka RC | 10.00 | 4.00 |
| ❏ 214 Sinorice Moss RC | 8.00 | 3.00 |
| ❏ 215 D'Brickashaw Ferguson RC | 8.00 | 3.00 |
| ❏ 216 Kellen Clemens RC | 10.00 | 4.00 |
| ❏ 217 Michael Huff RC | 8.00 | 3.00 |
| ❏ 218 Brodrick Bunkley RC | 8.00 | 3.00 |
| ❏ 219 Willie Reid RC | 8.00 | 3.00 |
| ❏ 220 Antonio Cromartie RC | 8.00 | 3.00 |
| ❏ 221 Manny Lawson RC | 8.00 | 3.00 |
| ❏ 222 Brandon Williams RC | 8.00 | 3.00 |
| ❏ 223 Kelly Jennings RC | 8.00 | 3.00 |
| ❏ 224 Tye Hill RC | 8.00 | 3.00 |
| ❏ 225 Joe Klopfenstein RC | 6.00 | 2.50 |
| ❏ 226 Maurice Stovall RC | 8.00 | 3.00 |
| ❏ 227 Matt Leinart RC | 30.00 | 12.00 |
| ❏ 228 DeAngelo Williams RC | 15.00 | 6.00 |
| ❏ 229 Jay Cutler RC | 40.00 | 15.00 |
| ❏ 230 Joseph Addai RC | 30.00 | 12.00 |
| ❏ 231 Laurence Maroney RC | 25.00 | 10.00 |
| ❏ 232 Reggie Bush RC | 40.00 | 15.00 |
| ❏ 233 Santonio Holmes RC | 25.00 | 10.00 |
| ❏ 234 Vernon Davis RC | 10.00 | 4.00 |
| ❏ 235 Vince Young RC | 30.00 | 12.00 |
| ❏ 236 LenDale White RC | 20.00 | 8.00 |
| ❏ 237 Edgerrin James | 3.00 | 1.25 |
| ❏ 238 Michael Vick | 4.00 | 1.50 |
| ❏ 239 Jamal Lewis | 3.00 | 1.25 |
| ❏ 240 Willis McGahee | 4.00 | 1.50 |
| ❏ 241 Steve Smith | 4.00 | 1.50 |
| ❏ 242 Brian Urlacher | 4.00 | 1.50 |
| ❏ 243 Carson Palmer | 4.00 | 1.50 |
| ❏ 244 Charlie Frye | 3.00 | 1.25 |
| ❏ 245 Terrell Owens | 4.00 | 1.50 |
| ❏ 246 Jake Plummer | 3.00 | 1.25 |
| ❏ 247 Kevin Jones | 4.00 | 1.50 |
| ❏ 248 Brett Favre | 8.00 | 3.00 |
| ❏ 249 David Carr | 3.00 | 1.25 |
| ❏ 250 Peyton Manning | 6.00 | 2.50 |
| ❏ 251 Byron Leftwich | 3.00 | 1.25 |
| ❏ 252 Larry Johnson | 3.00 | 1.25 |
| ❏ 253 Daunte Culpepper | 4.00 | 1.50 |

| | | |
|---|---|---|
| ❏ 254 Brad Johnson | 3.00 | 1.25 |
| ❏ 255 Tom Brady | 6.00 | 2.50 |
| ❏ 256 Drew Brees | 4.00 | 1.50 |
| ❏ 257 Eli Manning | 5.00 | 2.00 |
| ❏ 258 Curtis Martin | 4.00 | 1.50 |
| ❏ 259 Randy Moss | 4.00 | 1.50 |
| ❏ 260 Donovan McNabb | 4.00 | 1.50 |
| ❏ 261 Ben Roethlisberger | 6.00 | 2.50 |
| ❏ 262 LaDainian Tomlinson | 5.00 | 2.00 |
| ❏ 263 Alex Smith QB | 4.00 | 1.50 |
| ❏ 264 Shaun Alexander | 4.00 | 1.50 |
| ❏ 265 Marc Bulger | 3.00 | 1.25 |
| ❏ 266 Cadillac Williams | 4.00 | 1.50 |
| ❏ 267 Drew Bennett | 3.00 | 1.25 |
| ❏ 268 Clinton Portis | 4.00 | 1.50 |

## 1960 Fleer

| | | |
|---|---|---|
| ❏ COMPLETE SET (132) | 750.00 | 500.00 |
| ❏ WRAPPER (5-CENT) | 25.00 | 20.00 |
| ❏ 1 Harvey White RC ! | 20.00 | 12.00 |
| ❏ 2 Tom Corky Tharp | 3.50 | 2.00 |
| ❏ 3 Dan McGrew | 3.50 | 2.00 |
| ❏ 4 Bob White | 3.50 | 2.00 |
| ❏ 5 Dick Jamieson | 3.50 | 2.00 |
| ❏ 6 Sam Salerno | 3.50 | 2.00 |
| ❏ 7 Sid Gillman RC CO ! | 20.00 | 12.00 |
| ❏ 8 Ben Preston | 3.50 | 2.00 |
| ❏ 9 George Blanch | 3.50 | 2.00 |
| ❏ 10 Bob Stransky | 3.50 | 2.00 |
| ❏ 11 Fran Curci | 3.50 | 2.00 |
| ❏ 12 George Shirkey | 3.50 | 2.00 |
| ❏ 13 Paul Larson | 3.50 | 2.00 |
| ❏ 14 John Stolte | 3.50 | 2.00 |
| ❏ 15 Serafino Fazio RC | 5.00 | 2.50 |
| ❏ 16 Tom Dimitroff | 3.50 | 2.00 |
| ❏ 17 Elbert Dubenion RC | 12.00 | 6.00 |
| ❏ 18 Hogan Wharton | 3.50 | 2.00 |
| ❏ 19 Tom O'Connell | 3.50 | 2.00 |
| ❏ 20 Sammy Baugh CO | 50.00 | 30.00 |
| ❏ 21 Tony Sardisco | 3.50 | 2.00 |
| ❏ 22 Alan Cann | 3.50 | 2.00 |
| ❏ 23 Mike Hudock | 3.50 | 2.00 |
| ❏ 24 Bill Atkins | 3.50 | 2.00 |
| ❏ 25 Charlie Jackson | 3.50 | 2.00 |
| ❏ 26 Frank Tripucka | 6.00 | 3.00 |
| ❏ 27 Tony Teresa | 3.50 | 2.00 |
| ❏ 28 Joe Amstutz | 3.50 | 2.00 |
| ❏ 29 Bob Fee RC | 3.50 | 2.00 |
| ❏ 30 Jim Baldwin | 3.50 | 2.00 |
| ❏ 31 Jim Yates | 3.50 | 2.00 |
| ❏ 32 Don Flynn | 3.50 | 2.00 |
| ❏ 33 Ken Adamson | 3.50 | 2.00 |
| ❏ 34 Ron Drzewiecki | 3.50 | 2.00 |
| ❏ 35 J.W. Slack | 3.50 | 2.00 |
| ❏ 36 Bob Yates | 3.50 | 2.00 |
| ❏ 37 Gary Cobb | 3.50 | 2.00 |
| ❏ 38 Jacky Lee RC | 5.00 | 2.50 |
| ❏ 39 Jack Spikes RC | 5.00 | 2.50 |
| ❏ 40 Jim Padgett | 3.50 | 2.00 |
| ❏ 41 Jack Larscheid UER RC | 3.50 | 2.00 |
| ❏ 42 Bob Reifsnyder RC | 3.50 | 2.00 |
| ❏ 43 Fran Rogel | 3.50 | 2.00 |
| ❏ 44 Ray Moss | 3.50 | 2.00 |
| ❏ 45 Tony Banfield RC | 5.00 | 2.50 |
| ❏ 46 George Herring | 3.50 | 2.00 |
| ❏ 47 Willie Smith RC | 3.50 | 2.00 |
| ❏ 48 Buddy Allen | 3.50 | 2.00 |
| ❏ 49 Bill Brown LB | 3.50 | 2.00 |

| | | |
|---|---|---|
| ❏ 50 Ken Ford RC | 3.50 | 2.00 |
| ❏ 51 Billy Kinard | 3.50 | 2.00 |
| ❏ 52 Buddy Mayfield | 3.50 | 2.00 |
| ❏ 53 Bill Krisher | 3.50 | 2.00 |
| ❏ 54 Frank Bernardi | 3.50 | 2.00 |
| ❏ 55 Lou Saban RC CO | 5.00 | 2.50 |
| ❏ 56 Gene Cockrell | 3.50 | 2.00 |
| ❏ 57 Sam Sanders | 3.50 | 2.00 |
| ❏ 58 George Blanda | 50.00 | 30.00 |
| ❏ 59 Sherrill Headrick RC | 5.00 | 2.50 |
| ❏ 60 Carl Larpenter | 3.50 | 2.00 |
| ❏ 61 Gene Prebola | 3.50 | 2.00 |
| ❏ 62 Dick Chorovich | 3.50 | 2.00 |
| ❏ 63 Bob McNamara | 3.50 | 2.00 |
| ❏ 64 Tom Saidock | 3.50 | 2.00 |
| ❏ 65 Willie Evans | 3.50 | 2.00 |
| ❏ 66 Billy Cannon RC UER | 18.00 | 10.00 |
| ❏ 67 Sam McCord | 3.50 | 2.00 |
| ❏ 68 Mike Simmons | 3.50 | 2.00 |
| ❏ 69 Jim Swink RC | 5.00 | 2.50 |
| ❏ 70 Don Hitt | 3.50 | 2.00 |
| ❏ 71 Gerhard Schwedes | 3.50 | 2.00 |
| ❏ 72 Thurlow Cooper | 3.50 | 2.00 |
| ❏ 73 Abner Haynes RC | 18.00 | 10.00 |
| ❏ 74 Billy Shoemake | 3.50 | 2.00 |
| ❏ 75 Marv Lasater | 3.50 | 2.00 |
| ❏ 76 Paul Lowe RC | 15.00 | 7.50 |
| ❏ 77 Bruce Hartman | 3.50 | 2.00 |
| ❏ 78 Blanche Martin | 3.50 | 2.00 |
| ❏ 79 Gene Grabosky | 3.50 | 2.00 |
| ❏ 80 Lou Rymkus CO | 5.00 | 2.50 |
| ❏ 81 Chris Burford RC | 8.00 | 4.00 |
| ❏ 82 Don Allen | 3.50 | 2.00 |
| ❏ 83 Bob Nelson C | 3.50 | 2.00 |
| ❏ 84 Jim Woodard | 3.50 | 2.00 |
| ❏ 85 Tom Rychlec | 3.50 | 2.00 |
| ❏ 86 Bob Cox | 3.50 | 2.00 |
| ❏ 87 Jerry Cornelison | 3.50 | 2.00 |
| ❏ 88 Jack Work | 3.50 | 2.00 |
| ❏ 89 Sam DeLuca | 3.50 | 2.00 |
| ❏ 90 Rommie Loudd | 3.50 | 2.00 |
| ❏ 91 Teddy Edmondson | 3.50 | 2.00 |
| ❏ 92 Buster Ramsey CO | 3.50 | 2.00 |
| ❏ 93 Doug Asad | 3.50 | 2.00 |
| ❏ 94 Jimmy Harris | 3.50 | 2.00 |
| ❏ 95 Larry Cundiff | 3.50 | 2.00 |
| ❏ 96 Richie Lucas RC | 6.00 | 3.00 |
| ❏ 97 Don Norwood | 3.50 | 2.00 |
| ❏ 98 Larry Grantham RC | 5.00 | 2.50 |
| ❏ 99 Bill Mathis RC | 6.00 | 3.00 |
| ❏ 100 Mel Branch RC | 5.00 | 2.50 |
| ❏ 101 Marvin Terrell | 3.50 | 2.00 |
| ❏ 102 Charlie Flowers | 3.50 | 2.00 |
| ❏ 103 John McMullan | 3.50 | 2.00 |
| ❏ 104 Charlie Kaaihue | 3.50 | 2.00 |
| ❏ 105 Joe Schaffer | 3.50 | 2.00 |
| ❏ 106 Al Day | 3.50 | 2.00 |
| ❏ 107 Johnny Carson | 3.50 | 2.00 |
| ❏ 108 Alan Goldstein | 3.50 | 2.00 |
| ❏ 109 Doug Cline | 3.50 | 2.00 |
| ❏ 110 Al Carmichael | 3.50 | 2.00 |
| ❏ 111 Bob Dee | 3.50 | 2.00 |
| ❏ 112 John Bredice | 3.50 | 2.00 |
| ❏ 113 Don Floyd | 3.50 | 2.00 |
| ❏ 114 Ronnie Cain | 3.50 | 2.00 |
| ❏ 115 Stan Flowers | 3.50 | 2.00 |
| ❏ 116 Hank Stram RC CO | 40.00 | 25.00 |
| ❏ 117 Bob Dougherty | 3.50 | 2.00 |
| ❏ 118 Ron Mix RC | 40.00 | 25.00 |
| ❏ 119 Roger Ellis | 3.50 | 2.00 |
| ❏ 120 Elvin Caldwell | 3.50 | 2.00 |
| ❏ 121 Bill Kimber | 3.50 | 2.00 |
| ❏ 122 Jim Matheny | 3.50 | 2.00 |
| ❏ 123 Curley Johnson RC | 3.50 | 2.00 |
| ❏ 124 Jack Kemp RC | 150.00 | 75.00 |
| ❏ 125 Ed Denk | 3.50 | 2.00 |
| ❏ 126 Jerry McFarland | 3.50 | 2.00 |
| ❏ 127 Dan Lanphear | 3.50 | 2.00 |
| ❏ 128 Paul Maguire RC | 18.00 | 10.00 |
| ❏ 129 Ray Collins | 3.50 | 2.00 |
| ❏ 130 Ron Burton RC | 6.00 | 3.00 |
| ❏ 131 Eddie Erdelatz CO | 3.50 | 2.00 |
| ❏ 132 Ron Beagle RC ! | 15.00 | 7.50 |

# 1961 Fleer

DON MAYNARD
END                    NEW YORK TITANS

| | | |
|---|---|---|
| ☐ COMPLETE SET (220) | 1600.00 | 1000.00 |
| ☐ COMMON CARD (1-132) | 4.00 | 2.50 |
| ☐ COMMON CARD (133-220) | 6.00 | 3.50 |
| ☐ WRAPPER (5-CENT, SER.1) | 25.00 | 20.00 |
| ☐ WRAPPER (5-CENT, SER.2) | 30.00 | 25.00 |
| ☐ 1 Ed Brown ! | 15.00 | 7.50 |
| ☐ 2 Rick Casares | 6.00 | 3.00 |
| ☐ 3 Willie Galimore | 6.00 | 3.00 |
| ☐ 4 Jim Dooley | 4.00 | 2.50 |
| ☐ 5 Harlon Hill | 4.00 | 2.50 |
| ☐ 6 Stan Jones | 7.00 | 3.50 |
| ☐ 7 J.C. Caroline | 4.00 | 2.50 |
| ☐ 8 Joe Fortunato | 4.00 | 2.50 |
| ☐ 9 Doug Atkins | 8.00 | 4.00 |
| ☐ 10 Milt Plum | 6.00 | 3.00 |
| ☐ 11 Jim Brown | 150.00 | 90.00 |
| ☐ 12 Bobby Mitchell | 10.00 | 5.00 |
| ☐ 13 Ray Renfro | 6.00 | 3.00 |
| ☐ 14 Gern Nagler | 4.00 | 2.50 |
| ☐ 15 Jim Shofner | 4.00 | 2.50 |
| ☐ 16 Vince Costello | 4.00 | 2.50 |
| ☐ 17 Galen Fiss | 4.00 | 2.50 |
| ☐ 18 Walt Michaels | 6.00 | 3.00 |
| ☐ 19 Bob Gain | 4.00 | 2.50 |
| ☐ 20 Mal Hammack | 4.00 | 2.50 |
| ☐ 21 Frank Mestnik RC | 4.00 | 2.50 |
| ☐ 22 Bobby Joe Conrad | 6.00 | 3.00 |
| ☐ 23 John David Crow | 6.00 | 3.00 |
| ☐ 24 Sonny Randle RC | 6.00 | 3.00 |
| ☐ 25 Don Gillis | 4.00 | 2.50 |
| ☐ 26 Jerry Norton | 4.00 | 2.50 |
| ☐ 27 Bill Stacy | 4.00 | 2.50 |
| ☐ 28 Leo Sugar | 4.00 | 2.50 |
| ☐ 29 Frank Fuller | 4.00 | 2.50 |
| ☐ 30 Johnny Unitas | 60.00 | 35.00 |
| ☐ 31 Alan Ameche | 7.00 | 3.50 |
| ☐ 32 Lenny Moore | 15.00 | 7.50 |
| ☐ 33 Raymond Berry | 15.00 | 7.50 |
| ☐ 34 Jim Mutscheller | 4.00 | 2.50 |
| ☐ 35 Jim Parker | 7.00 | 3.50 |
| ☐ 36 Bill Pellington | 4.00 | 2.50 |
| ☐ 37 Gino Marchetti | 10.00 | 5.00 |
| ☐ 38 Gene Lipscomb | 7.00 | 3.50 |
| ☐ 39 Art Donovan | 15.00 | 7.50 |
| ☐ 40 Eddie LeBaron | 6.00 | 3.00 |
| ☐ 41 Don Meredith RC | 150.00 | 90.00 |
| ☐ 42 Don McIlhenny | 4.00 | 2.50 |
| ☐ 43 L.G. Dupre | 4.00 | 2.50 |
| ☐ 44 Fred Dugan | 4.00 | 2.50 |
| ☐ 45 Billy Howton | 6.00 | 3.00 |
| ☐ 46 Duane Putnam | 4.00 | 2.50 |
| ☐ 47 Gene Cronin | 4.00 | 2.50 |
| ☐ 48 Jerry Tubbs | 4.00 | 2.50 |
| ☐ 49 Clarence Peaks | 4.00 | 2.50 |
| ☐ 50 Ted Dean RC | 4.00 | 2.50 |
| ☐ 51 Tommy McDonald | 8.00 | 4.00 |
| ☐ 52 Bill Barnes | 4.00 | 2.50 |
| ☐ 53 Pete Retzlaff | 6.00 | 3.00 |
| ☐ 54 Bobby Walston | 4.00 | 2.50 |
| ☐ 55 Chuck Bednarik | 12.00 | 6.00 |
| ☐ 56 Maxie Baughan RC | 6.00 | 3.00 |
| ☐ 57 Bob Pellegrini | 4.00 | 2.50 |
| ☐ 58 Jesse Richardson | 4.00 | 2.50 |
| ☐ 59 John Brodie RC | 50.00 | 30.00 |
| ☐ 60 J.D. Smith RB | 6.00 | 3.00 |
| ☐ 61 Ray Norton RC | 4.00 | 2.50 |

| | | |
|---|---|---|
| ☐ 62 Monty Stickles RC | 4.00 | 2.50 |
| ☐ 63 Bob St.Clair | 7.00 | 3.50 |
| ☐ 64 Dave Baker | 4.00 | 2.50 |
| ☐ 65 Abe Woodson | 4.00 | 2.50 |
| ☐ 66 Matt Hazeltine | 4.00 | 2.50 |
| ☐ 67 Leo Nomellini | 10.00 | 5.00 |
| ☐ 68 Charley Conerly | 10.00 | 5.00 |
| ☐ 69 Kyle Rote | 7.00 | 3.50 |
| ☐ 70 Jack Stroud | 4.00 | 2.50 |
| ☐ 71 Roosevelt Brown | 7.00 | 3.50 |
| ☐ 72 Jim Patton | 4.00 | 2.50 |
| ☐ 73 Erich Barnes | 4.00 | 2.50 |
| ☐ 74 Sam Huff | 15.00 | 7.50 |
| ☐ 75 Andy Robustelli | 10.00 | 5.00 |
| ☐ 76 Dick Modzelewski | 4.00 | 2.50 |
| ☐ 77 Roosevelt Grier | 7.00 | 3.50 |
| ☐ 78 Earl Morrall | 7.00 | 3.50 |
| ☐ 79 Jim Ninowski | 4.00 | 2.50 |
| ☐ 80 Nick Pietrosante RC | 6.00 | 3.00 |
| ☐ 81 Howard Cassady | 6.00 | 3.00 |
| ☐ 82 Jim Gibbons | 4.00 | 2.50 |
| ☐ 83 Gail Cogdill RC | 6.00 | 3.00 |
| ☐ 84 Dick Lane | 7.00 | 3.50 |
| ☐ 85 Yale Lary | 7.00 | 3.50 |
| ☐ 86 Joe Schmidt | 8.00 | 4.00 |
| ☐ 87 Darris McCord | 4.00 | 2.50 |
| ☐ 88 Bart Starr | 60.00 | 35.00 |
| ☐ 89 Jim Taylor | 50.00 | 30.00 |
| ☐ 90 Paul Hornung | 55.00 | 30.00 |
| ☐ 91 Tom Moore RC | 8.00 | 4.00 |
| ☐ 92 Boyd Dowler RC | 15.00 | 7.50 |
| ☐ 93 Max McGee | 7.00 | 3.50 |
| ☐ 94 Forrest Gregg | 8.00 | 4.00 |
| ☐ 95 Jerry Kramer | 10.00 | 5.00 |
| ☐ 96 Jim Ringo | 8.00 | 4.00 |
| ☐ 97 Bill Forester | 6.00 | 3.00 |
| ☐ 98 Frank Ryan | 6.00 | 3.00 |
| ☐ 99 Ollie Matson | 12.00 | 6.00 |
| ☐ 100 Jon Arnett | 6.00 | 3.00 |
| ☐ 101 Dick Bass RC | 6.00 | 3.00 |
| ☐ 102 Jim Phillips | 4.00 | 2.50 |
| ☐ 103 Del Shofner | 6.00 | 3.00 |
| ☐ 104 Art Hunter | 4.00 | 2.50 |
| ☐ 105 Lindon Crow | 4.00 | 2.50 |
| ☐ 106 Les Richter | 6.00 | 3.00 |
| ☐ 107 Lou Michaels | 6.00 | 3.00 |
| ☐ 108 Ralph Guglielmi | 4.00 | 2.50 |
| ☐ 109 Don Bosseler | 4.00 | 2.50 |
| ☐ 110 John Olszewski | 4.00 | 2.50 |
| ☐ 111 Bill Anderson | 4.00 | 2.50 |
| ☐ 112 Joe Walton | 4.00 | 2.50 |
| ☐ 113 Jim Schrader | 4.00 | 2.50 |
| ☐ 114 Gary Glick | 4.00 | 2.50 |
| ☐ 115 Ralph Felton | 4.00 | 2.50 |
| ☐ 116 Bob Toneff | 4.00 | 2.50 |
| ☐ 117 Bobby Layne | 40.00 | 25.00 |
| ☐ 118 John Henry Johnson | 7.00 | 3.50 |
| ☐ 119 Tom Tracy | 6.00 | 3.00 |
| ☐ 120 Jimmy Orr RC | 7.00 | 3.50 |
| ☐ 121 John Nisby | 4.00 | 2.50 |
| ☐ 122 Dean Derby | 4.00 | 2.50 |
| ☐ 123 John Reger | 4.00 | 2.50 |
| ☐ 124 George Tarasovic | 4.00 | 2.50 |
| ☐ 125 Ernie Stautner | 10.00 | 5.00 |
| ☐ 126 George Shaw | 4.00 | 2.50 |
| ☐ 127 Hugh McElhenny | 12.00 | 6.00 |
| ☐ 128 Dick Haley | 4.00 | 2.50 |
| ☐ 129 Dave Middleton | 4.00 | 2.50 |
| ☐ 130 Perry Richards | 4.00 | 2.50 |
| ☐ 131 Gene Johnson DB | 4.00 | 2.50 |
| ☐ 132 Don Joyce ! | 4.00 | 2.50 |
| ☐ 133 Johnny Green ! | 8.00 | 4.00 |
| ☐ 134 Wray Carlton RC | 8.00 | 4.00 |
| ☐ 135 Richie Lucas | 8.00 | 4.00 |
| ☐ 136 Elbert Dubenion ! | 8.00 | 4.00 |
| ☐ 137 Tom Rychlec | 6.00 | 3.50 |
| ☐ 138 Mack Yoho | 6.00 | 3.50 |
| ☐ 139 Phil Blazer | 6.00 | 3.50 |
| ☐ 140 Dan McGrew | 6.00 | 3.50 |
| ☐ 141 Bill Atkins | 6.00 | 3.50 |
| ☐ 142 Archie Matsos RC | 6.00 | 3.50 |
| ☐ 143 Gene Grabosky | 6.00 | 3.50 |
| ☐ 144 Frank Tripucka | 10.00 | 5.00 |
| ☐ 145 Al Carmichael | 6.00 | 3.50 |

| | | |
|---|---|---|
| ☐ 146 Bob McNamara | 6.00 | 3.50 |
| ☐ 147 Lionel Taylor RC | 15.00 | 7.50 |
| ☐ 148 Eldon Danenhauer | 6.00 | 3.50 |
| ☐ 149 Willie Smith | 6.00 | 3.50 |
| ☐ 150 Carl Larpenter | 6.00 | 3.50 |
| ☐ 151 Ken Adamson | 6.00 | 3.50 |
| ☐ 152 Goose Gonsoulin RC UER | 10.00 | 5.00 |
| ☐ 153 Joe Young | 6.00 | 3.50 |
| ☐ 154 Gordy Holz RC | 6.00 | 3.50 |
| ☐ 155 Jack Kemp | 120.00 | 60.00 |
| ☐ 156 Charlie Flowers | 6.00 | 3.50 |
| ☐ 157 Paul Lowe | 10.00 | 5.00 |
| ☐ 158 Don Norton | 6.00 | 3.50 |
| ☐ 159 Howard Clark | 6.00 | 3.50 |
| ☐ 160 Paul Maguire | 15.00 | 7.50 |
| ☐ 161 Ernie Wright RC | 8.00 | 4.00 |
| ☐ 162 Ron Mix | 15.00 | 7.50 |
| ☐ 163 Fred Cole | 6.00 | 3.50 |
| ☐ 164 Jim Sears | 6.00 | 3.50 |
| ☐ 165 Volney Peters | 6.00 | 3.50 |
| ☐ 166 George Blanda | 45.00 | 25.00 |
| ☐ 167 Jacky Lee | 8.00 | 4.00 |
| ☐ 168 Bob White | 6.00 | 3.50 |
| ☐ 169 Doug Cline | 6.00 | 3.50 |
| ☐ 170 Dave Smith RB | 6.00 | 3.50 |
| ☐ 171 Billy Cannon | 15.00 | 7.50 |
| ☐ 172 Bill Groman | 6.00 | 3.50 |
| ☐ 173 Al Jamison | 6.00 | 3.50 |
| ☐ 174 Jim Norton | 6.00 | 3.50 |
| ☐ 175 Dennit Morris | 6.00 | 3.50 |
| ☐ 176 Don Floyd | 6.00 | 3.50 |
| ☐ 177 Butch Songin | 6.00 | 3.50 |
| ☐ 178 Billy Lott | 6.00 | 3.50 |
| ☐ 179 Ron Burton | 10.00 | 5.00 |
| ☐ 180 Jim Colclough | 6.00 | 3.50 |
| ☐ 181 Charley Leo | 6.00 | 3.50 |
| ☐ 182 Walt Cudzik | 6.00 | 3.50 |
| ☐ 183 Fred Bruney | 6.00 | 3.50 |
| ☐ 184 Ross O'Hanley | 6.00 | 3.50 |
| ☐ 185 Tony Sardisco | 6.00 | 3.50 |
| ☐ 186 Harry Jacobs | 6.00 | 3.50 |
| ☐ 187 Bob Dee | 6.00 | 3.50 |
| ☐ 188 Tom Flores RC | 30.00 | 15.00 |
| ☐ 189 Jack Larscheid | 6.00 | 3.50 |
| ☐ 190 Dick Christy | 6.00 | 3.50 |
| ☐ 191 Alan Miller RC | 6.00 | 3.50 |
| ☐ 192 James Smith | 6.00 | 3.50 |
| ☐ 193 Gerald Burch | 6.00 | 3.50 |
| ☐ 194 Gene Prebola | 6.00 | 3.50 |
| ☐ 195 Alan Goldstein | 6.00 | 3.50 |
| ☐ 196 Don Manoukian | 6.00 | 3.50 |
| ☐ 197 Jim Otto RC | 75.00 | 40.00 |
| ☐ 198 Wayne Crow | 6.00 | 3.50 |
| ☐ 199 Cotton Davidson RC | 8.00 | 4.00 |
| ☐ 200 Randy Duncan RC | 8.00 | 4.00 |
| ☐ 201 Jack Spikes | 8.00 | 4.00 |
| ☐ 202 Johnny Robinson RC | 15.00 | 7.50 |
| ☐ 203 Abner Haynes | 15.00 | 7.50 |
| ☐ 204 Chris Burford | 8.00 | 4.00 |
| ☐ 205 Bill Krisher | 6.00 | 3.50 |
| ☐ 206 Marvin Terrell | 6.00 | 3.50 |
| ☐ 207 Jimmy Harris | 6.00 | 3.50 |
| ☐ 208 Mel Branch | 8.00 | 4.00 |
| ☐ 209 Paul Miller | 6.00 | 3.50 |
| ☐ 210 Al Dorow | 6.00 | 3.50 |
| ☐ 211 Dick Jamieson | 6.00 | 3.50 |
| ☐ 212 Pete Hart | 6.00 | 3.50 |
| ☐ 213 Bill Shockley | 6.00 | 3.50 |
| ☐ 214 Dewey Bohling | 6.00 | 3.50 |
| ☐ 215 Don Maynard RC | 80.00 | 40.00 |
| ☐ 216 Bob Mischak | 6.00 | 3.50 |
| ☐ 217 Mike Hudock | 6.00 | 3.50 |
| ☐ 218 Bob Reifsnyder | 6.00 | 3.50 |
| ☐ 219 Tom Saidock | 6.00 | 3.50 |
| ☐ 220 Sid Youngelman ! | 20.00 | 12.00 |

# 1962 Fleer

| | | |
|---|---|---|
| ☐ COMPLETE SET (88) | 900.00 | 500.00 |
| ☐ WRAPPER (5-CENT) | 200.00 | 100.00 |
| ☐ 1 Billy Lott ! | 16.00 | 8.00 |
| ☐ 2 Ron Burton | 10.00 | 5.00 |
| ☐ 3 Gino Cappelletti RC | 15.00 | 7.50 |
| ☐ 4 Babe Parilli | 10.00 | 5.00 |
| ☐ 5 Jim Colclough | 7.00 | 3.50 |

| | | |
|---|---|---|
| ❑ 6 Tony Sardisco | 7.00 | 3.50 |
| ❑ 7 Walt Cudzik | 7.00 | 3.50 |
| ❑ 8 Bob Dee | 7.00 | 3.50 |
| ❑ 9 Tommy Addison RC | 8.00 | 4.00 |
| ❑ 10 Harry Jacobs | 7.00 | 3.50 |
| ❑ 11 Ross O'Hanley | 7.00 | 3.50 |
| ❑ 12 Art Baker | 7.00 | 3.50 |
| ❑ 13 Johnny Green | 7.00 | 3.50 |
| ❑ 14 Elbert Dubenion | 10.00 | 5.00 |
| ❑ 15 Tom Rychlec | 7.00 | 3.50 |
| ❑ 16 Billy Shaw RC | 40.00 | 20.00 |
| ❑ 17 Ken Rice | 7.00 | 3.50 |
| ❑ 18 Bill Atkins | 7.00 | 3.50 |
| ❑ 19 Richie Lucas | 8.00 | 4.00 |
| ❑ 20 Archie Matsos | 7.00 | 3.50 |
| ❑ 21 Laverne Torczon | 7.00 | 3.50 |
| ❑ 22 Warren Rabb | 7.00 | 3.50 |
| ❑ 23 Jack Spikes | 8.00 | 4.00 |
| ❑ 24 Cotton Davidson | 8.00 | 4.00 |
| ❑ 25 Abner Haynes | 15.00 | 7.50 |
| ❑ 26 Jimmy Saxton | 7.00 | 3.50 |
| ❑ 27 Chris Burford | 8.00 | 4.00 |
| ❑ 28 Bill Miller | 7.00 | 3.50 |
| ❑ 29 Sherrill Headrick | 8.00 | 4.00 |
| ❑ 30 E.J.Holub RC | 8.00 | 4.00 |
| ❑ 31 Jerry Mays RC | 10.00 | 5.00 |
| ❑ 32 Mel Branch | 8.00 | 4.00 |
| ❑ 33 Paul Rochester RC | 7.00 | 3.50 |
| ❑ 34 Frank Tripucka | 10.00 | 5.00 |
| ❑ 35 Gene Mingo | 7.00 | 3.50 |
| ❑ 36 Lionel Taylor | 12.00 | 6.00 |
| ❑ 37 Ken Adamson | 7.00 | 3.50 |
| ❑ 38 Eldon Danenhauer | 7.00 | 3.50 |
| ❑ 39 Goose Gonsoulin | 10.00 | 5.00 |
| ❑ 40 Gordy Holz | 7.00 | 3.50 |
| ❑ 41 Bud McFadin | 8.00 | 4.00 |
| ❑ 42 Jim Stinnette | 7.00 | 3.50 |
| ❑ 43 Bob Hudson RC | 7.00 | 3.50 |
| ❑ 44 George Herring | 7.00 | 3.50 |
| ❑ 45 Charley Tolar RC | 7.00 | 3.50 |
| ❑ 46 George Blanda | 50.00 | 30.00 |
| ❑ 47 Billy Cannon | 15.00 | 7.50 |
| ❑ 48 Charlie Hennigan RC | 15.00 | 7.50 |
| ❑ 49 Bill Groman | 7.00 | 3.50 |
| ❑ 50 Al Jamison | 7.00 | 3.50 |
| ❑ 51 Tony Banfield | 7.00 | 3.50 |
| ❑ 52 Jim Norton | 7.00 | 3.50 |
| ❑ 53 Dennit Morris | 7.00 | 3.50 |
| ❑ 54 Don Floyd | 7.00 | 3.50 |
| ❑ 55 Ed Husmann UER | 7.00 | 3.50 |
| ❑ 56 Robert Brooks | 7.00 | 3.50 |
| ❑ 57 Al Dorow | 7.00 | 3.50 |
| ❑ 58 Dick Christy | 7.00 | 3.50 |
| ❑ 59 Don Maynard | 50.00 | 30.00 |
| ❑ 60 Art Powell | 10.00 | 5.00 |
| ❑ 61 Mike Hudock | 7.00 | 3.50 |
| ❑ 62 Bill Mathis | 8.00 | 4.00 |
| ❑ 63 Butch Songin | 7.00 | 3.50 |
| ❑ 64 Larry Grantham | 7.00 | 3.50 |
| ❑ 65 Nick Mumley | 7.00 | 3.50 |
| ❑ 66 Tom Saidock | 7.00 | 3.50 |
| ❑ 67 Alan Miller | 7.00 | 3.50 |
| ❑ 68 Tom Flores | 15.00 | 7.50 |
| ❑ 69 Bob Coolbaugh | 7.00 | 3.50 |
| ❑ 70 George Fleming | 7.00 | 3.50 |
| ❑ 71 Wayne Hawkins RC | 7.00 | 3.50 |
| ❑ 72 Jim Otto | 40.00 | 25.00 |
| ❑ 73 Wayne Crow | 7.00 | 3.50 |

| | | |
|---|---|---|
| ❑ 74 Fred Williamson RC | 30.00 | 18.00 |
| ❑ 75 Tom Louderback | 7.00 | 3.50 |
| ❑ 76 Volney Peters | 7.00 | 3.50 |
| ❑ 77 Charley Powell | 7.00 | 3.50 |
| ❑ 78 Don Norton | 7.00 | 3.50 |
| ❑ 79 Jack Kemp | 125.00 | 75.00 |
| ❑ 80 Paul Lowe | 10.00 | 5.00 |
| ❑ 81 Dave Kocourek | 7.00 | 3.50 |
| ❑ 82 Ron Mix | 15.00 | 7.50 |
| ❑ 83 Ernie Wright | 10.00 | 5.00 |
| ❑ 84 Dick Harris | 7.00 | 3.50 |
| ❑ 85 Bill Hudson | 7.00 | 3.50 |
| ❑ 86 Ernie Ladd RC | 25.00 | 15.00 |
| ❑ 87 Earl Faison RC | 8.00 | 4.00 |
| ❑ 88 Ron Nery ! | 18.00 | 9.00 |

## 1963 Fleer

| | | |
|---|---|---|
| ❑ COMPLETE SET (88) | 1800.00 | 1200.00 |
| ❑ WRAPPER (5-CENT) | 120.00 | 60.00 |
| ❑ 1 Larry Garron RC | 20.00 | 10.00 |
| ❑ 2 Babe Parilli | 10.00 | 5.00 |
| ❑ 3 Ron Burton | 12.00 | 6.00 |
| ❑ 4 Jim Colclough | 8.00 | 4.00 |
| ❑ 5 Gino Cappelletti | 12.00 | 6.00 |
| ❑ 6 Charles Long RC SP | 150.00 | 75.00 |
| ❑ 7 Billy Neighbors RC | 8.00 | 4.00 |
| ❑ 8 Dick Felt | 8.00 | 4.00 |
| ❑ 9 Tommy Addison | 8.00 | 4.00 |
| ❑ 10 Nick Buoniconti RC | 80.00 | 45.00 |
| ❑ 11 Larry Eisenhauer RC | 8.00 | 4.00 |
| ❑ 12 Bill Mathis | 8.00 | 4.00 |
| ❑ 13 Lee Grosscup RC | 10.00 | 5.00 |
| ❑ 14 Dick Christy | 8.00 | 4.00 |
| ❑ 15 Don Maynard | 50.00 | 30.00 |
| ❑ 16 Alex Kroll RC | 8.00 | 4.00 |
| ❑ 17 Bob Mischak | 8.00 | 4.00 |
| ❑ 18 Dainard Paulson | 8.00 | 4.00 |
| ❑ 19 Lee Riley | 8.00 | 4.00 |
| ❑ 20 Larry Grantham | 10.00 | 5.00 |
| ❑ 21 Hubert Bobo | 8.00 | 4.00 |
| ❑ 22 Nick Mumley | 8.00 | 4.00 |
| ❑ 23 Cookie Gilchrist RC | 50.00 | 30.00 |
| ❑ 24 Jack Kemp | 150.00 | 75.00 |
| ❑ 25 Wray Carlton | 8.00 | 4.00 |
| ❑ 26 Elbert Dubenion | 10.00 | 5.00 |
| ❑ 27 Ernie Warlick RC | 10.00 | 5.00 |
| ❑ 28 Billy Shaw | 15.00 | 7.50 |
| ❑ 29 Ken Rice | 8.00 | 4.00 |
| ❑ 30 Booker Edgerson | 8.00 | 4.00 |
| ❑ 31 Ray Abruzzese | 8.00 | 4.00 |
| ❑ 32 Mike Stratton RC | 15.00 | 7.50 |
| ❑ 33 Tom Sestak RC | 12.00 | 6.00 |
| ❑ 34 Charley Tolar | 8.00 | 4.00 |
| ❑ 35 Dave Smith RB | 8.00 | 4.00 |
| ❑ 36 George Blanda | 55.00 | 30.00 |
| ❑ 37 Billy Cannon | 15.00 | 7.50 |
| ❑ 38 Charlie Hennigan | 10.00 | 5.00 |
| ❑ 39 Bob Talamini RC | 8.00 | 4.00 |
| ❑ 40 Jim Norton | 8.00 | 4.00 |
| ❑ 41 Tony Banfield | 8.00 | 4.00 |
| ❑ 42 Doug Cline | 8.00 | 4.00 |
| ❑ 43 Don Floyd | 8.00 | 4.00 |
| ❑ 44 Ed Husmann | 8.00 | 4.00 |
| ❑ 45 Curtis McClinton RC | 15.00 | 7.50 |
| ❑ 46 Jack Spikes | 10.00 | 5.00 |
| ❑ 47 Len Dawson RC | 200.00 | 125.00 |
| ❑ 48 Abner Haynes | 15.00 | 7.50 |
| ❑ 49 Chris Burford | 10.00 | 5.00 |

| | | |
|---|---|---|
| ❑ 50 Fred Arbanas RC | 12.00 | 6.00 |
| ❑ 51 Johnny Robinson | 10.00 | 5.00 |
| ❑ 52 E.J. Holub | 10.00 | 5.00 |
| ❑ 53 Sherrill Headrick | 10.00 | 5.00 |
| ❑ 54 Mel Branch | 10.00 | 5.00 |
| ❑ 55 Jerry Mays | 10.00 | 5.00 |
| ❑ 56 Cotton Davidson | 10.00 | 5.00 |
| ❑ 57 Clem Daniels RC | 15.00 | 7.50 |
| ❑ 58 Bo Roberson RC | 10.00 | 5.00 |
| ❑ 59 Art Powell | 12.00 | 6.00 |
| ❑ 60 Bob Coolbaugh | 8.00 | 4.00 |
| ❑ 61 Wayne Hawkins | 8.00 | 4.00 |
| ❑ 62 Jim Otto | 30.00 | 18.00 |
| ❑ 63 Fred Williamson | 20.00 | 10.00 |
| ❑ 64 Bob Dougherty SP | 120.00 | 60.00 |
| ❑ 65 Dalva Allen | 8.00 | 4.00 |
| ❑ 66 Chuck McMurtry | 8.00 | 4.00 |
| ❑ 67 Gerry McDougall RC | 8.00 | 4.00 |
| ❑ 68 Tobin Rote | 10.00 | 5.00 |
| ❑ 69 Paul Lowe | 12.00 | 6.00 |
| ❑ 70 Keith Lincoln RC | 40.00 | 25.00 |
| ❑ 71 Dave Kocourek | 8.00 | 4.00 |
| ❑ 72 Lance Alworth RC | 250.00 | 125.00 |
| ❑ 73 Ron Mix | 25.00 | 15.00 |
| ❑ 74 Charley McNeil RC | 8.00 | 4.00 |
| ❑ 75 Emil Karas | 8.00 | 4.00 |
| ❑ 76 Ernie Ladd | 20.00 | 10.00 |
| ❑ 77 Earl Faison | 8.00 | 4.00 |
| ❑ 78 Jim Stinnette | 8.00 | 4.00 |
| ❑ 79 Frank Tripucka | 12.00 | 6.00 |
| ❑ 80 Don Stone | 8.00 | 4.00 |
| ❑ 81 Bob Scarpitto | 8.00 | 4.00 |
| ❑ 82 Lionel Taylor | 12.00 | 6.00 |
| ❑ 83 Jerry Tarr | 8.00 | 4.00 |
| ❑ 84 Eldon Danenhauer | 8.00 | 4.00 |
| ❑ 85 Goose Gonsoulin | 10.00 | 5.00 |
| ❑ 86 Jim Fraser | 8.00 | 4.00 |
| ❑ 87 Chuck Gavin | 8.00 | 4.00 |
| ❑ 88 Bud McFadin ! | 20.00 | 10.00 |
| ❑ NNO Checklist SP ! | 350.00 | 150.00 |

## 1990 Fleer

| | | |
|---|---|---|
| ❑ COMPLETE SET (400) | 10.00 | 4.00 |
| ❑ 1 Harris Barton | .04 | .01 |
| ❑ 2 Chet Brooks | .04 | .01 |
| ❑ 3 Michael Carter | .04 | .01 |
| ❑ 4 Mike Cofer UER | .04 | .01 |
| ❑ 5 Roger Craig | .10 | .02 |
| ❑ 6 Kevin Fagan RC | .04 | .01 |
| ❑ 7 Charles Haley UER | .10 | .02 |
| ❑ 8 Pierce Holt RC | .04 | .01 |
| ❑ 9 Ronnie Lott | .10 | .02 |
| ❑ 10A Joe Montana ERR | 1.25 | .50 |
| ❑ 10B Joe Montana COR | 1.25 | .50 |
| ❑ 11 Bubba Paris | .04 | .01 |
| ❑ 12 Tom Rathman | .04 | .01 |
| ❑ 13 Jerry Rice | .75 | .30 |
| ❑ 14 John Taylor | .25 | .08 |
| ❑ 15 Keena Turner | .04 | .01 |
| ❑ 16 Michael Walter | .04 | .01 |
| ❑ 17 Steve Young | .50 | .20 |
| ❑ 18 Steve Atwater | .10 | .02 |
| ❑ 19 Tyrone Braxton | .04 | .01 |
| ❑ 20 Michael Brooks RC | .04 | .01 |
| ❑ 21 John Elway | 1.25 | .50 |
| ❑ 22 Simon Fletcher | .04 | .01 |
| ❑ 23 Bobby Humphrey | .04 | .01 |
| ❑ 24 Mark Jackson | .04 | .01 |

| Card | .04 | .01 |
|---|---|---|
| ❏ 25 Vance Johnson | .04 | .01 |
| ❏ 26 Greg Kragen | .04 | .01 |
| ❏ 27 Ken Lanier RC | .04 | .01 |
| ❏ 28 Karl Mecklenburg | .04 | .01 |
| ❏ 29 Orson Mobley RC | .04 | .01 |
| ❏ 30 Steve Sewell | .04 | .01 |
| ❏ 31 Dennis Smith | .04 | .01 |
| ❏ 32 David Treadwell | .04 | .01 |
| ❏ 33 Flipper Anderson | .04 | .01 |
| ❏ 34 Greg Bell | .04 | .01 |
| ❏ 35 Henry Ellard | .10 | .02 |
| ❏ 36 Jim Everett | .10 | .02 |
| ❏ 37 Jerry Gray | .04 | .01 |
| ❏ 38 Kevin Greene | .10 | .02 |
| ❏ 39 Pete Holohan | .04 | .01 |
| ❏ 40 LeRoy Irvin | .04 | .01 |
| ❏ 41 Mike Lansford | .04 | .01 |
| ❏ 42 Buford McGee RC | .04 | .01 |
| ❏ 43 Tom Newberry | .04 | .01 |
| ❏ 44 Vince Newsome RC | .04 | .01 |
| ❏ 45 Jackie Slater | .04 | .01 |
| ❏ 46 Mike Wilcher | .04 | .01 |
| ❏ 47 Matt Bahr | .04 | .01 |
| ❏ 48 Brian Brennan | .04 | .01 |
| ❏ 49 Thane Gash RC | .04 | .01 |
| ❏ 50 Mike Johnson | .04 | .01 |
| ❏ 51 Bernie Kosar | .10 | .02 |
| ❏ 52 Reggie Langhorne | .04 | .01 |
| ❏ 53 Tim Manoa | .04 | .01 |
| ❏ 54 Clay Matthews | .10 | .02 |
| ❏ 55 Eric Metcalf | .25 | .08 |
| ❏ 56 Frank Minnifield | .04 | .01 |
| ❏ 57 Gregg Rakoczy RC UER | .04 | .01 |
| ❏ 58 Webster Slaughter | .10 | .02 |
| ❏ 59 Bryan Wagner | .04 | .01 |
| ❏ 60 Felix Wright | .04 | .01 |
| ❏ 61 Raul Allegre | .04 | .01 |
| ❏ 62 Ottis Anderson UER | .10 | .02 |
| ❏ 63 Carl Banks | .04 | .01 |
| ❏ 64 Mark Bavaro | .04 | .01 |
| ❏ 65 Maurice Carthon | .04 | .01 |
| ❏ 66 Mark Collins UER | .04 | .01 |
| ❏ 67 Jeff Hostetler RC | .25 | .08 |
| ❏ 68 Erik Howard | .04 | .01 |
| ❏ 69 Pepper Johnson | .04 | .01 |
| ❏ 70 Sean Landeta | .04 | .01 |
| ❏ 71 Lionel Manuel | .04 | .01 |
| ❏ 72 Leonard Marshall | .04 | .01 |
| ❏ 73 Dave Meggett | .10 | .02 |
| ❏ 74 Bart Oates | .04 | .01 |
| ❏ 75 Doug Riesenberg RC | .04 | .01 |
| ❏ 76 Phil Simms | .10 | .02 |
| ❏ 77 Lawrence Taylor | .25 | .08 |
| ❏ 78 Erik Allen | .04 | .01 |
| ❏ 79 Jerome Brown | .04 | .01 |
| ❏ 80 Keith Byars | .04 | .01 |
| ❏ 81 Cris Carter | .50 | .20 |
| ❏ 82A Byron Evans RC ERR | .15 | .05 |
| ❏ 82B Randall Cunningham | .15 | .05 |
| ❏ 83A Ron Heller RC OT ERR | .15 | .05 |
| ❏ 83B Byron Evans RC COR | .15 | .05 |
| ❏ 84 Ron Heller RC OT COR | .04 | .01 |
| ❏ 85 Terry Hoage RC | .04 | .01 |
| ❏ 86 Keith Jackson | .10 | .02 |
| ❏ 87 Seth Joyner | .10 | .02 |
| ❏ 88 Mike Quick | .04 | .01 |
| ❏ 89 Mike Schad | .04 | .01 |
| ❏ 90 Clyde Simmons | .04 | .01 |
| ❏ 91 John Teltschik | .04 | .01 |
| ❏ 92 Anthony Toney | .04 | .01 |
| ❏ 93 Reggie White | .25 | .08 |
| ❏ 94 Ray Berry | .04 | .01 |
| ❏ 95 Joey Browner | .04 | .01 |
| ❏ 96 Anthony Carter | .10 | .02 |
| ❏ 97 Chris Doleman | .04 | .01 |
| ❏ 98 Rick Fenney | .04 | .01 |
| ❏ 99 Rich Gannon RC | 1.50 | .60 |
| ❏ 100 Hassan Jones | .04 | .01 |
| ❏ 101 Steve Jordan | .04 | .01 |
| ❏ 102 Rich Karlis | .04 | .01 |
| ❏ 103 Andre Ware RC | .25 | .08 |
| ❏ 104 Kirk Lowdermilk | .04 | .01 |
| ❏ 105 Keith Millard | .04 | .01 |
| ❏ 106 Scott Studwell | .04 | .01 |
| ❏ 107 Herschel Walker | .10 | .02 |
| ❏ 108 Wade Wilson | .10 | .02 |
| ❏ 109 Gary Zimmerman | .10 | .02 |
| ❏ 110 Don Beebe | .10 | .02 |
| ❏ 111 Cornelius Bennett | .10 | .02 |
| ❏ 112 Shane Conlan | .04 | .01 |
| ❏ 113 Jim Kelly | .25 | .08 |
| ❏ 114 Scott Norwood UER | .04 | .01 |
| ❏ 115 Mark Kelso UER | .04 | .01 |
| ❏ 116 Larry Kinnebrew | .04 | .01 |
| ❏ 117 Pete Metzelaars | .04 | .01 |
| ❏ 118 Scott Radecic | .04 | .01 |
| ❏ 119 Andre Reed | .25 | .08 |
| ❏ 120 Jim Ritcher RC | .04 | .01 |
| ❏ 121 Bruce Smith | .25 | .08 |
| ❏ 122 Leonard Smith | .04 | .01 |
| ❏ 123 Art Still | .04 | .01 |
| ❏ 124 Thurman Thomas | .25 | .08 |
| ❏ 125 Steve Brown | .04 | .01 |
| ❏ 126 Ray Childress | .04 | .01 |
| ❏ 127 Ernest Givins | .10 | .02 |
| ❏ 128 John Grimsley | .04 | .01 |
| ❏ 129 Alonzo Highsmith | .04 | .01 |
| ❏ 130 Drew Hill | .04 | .01 |
| ❏ 131 Bruce Matthews | .10 | .02 |
| ❏ 132 Johnny Meads | .04 | .01 |
| ❏ 133 Warren Moon UER | .25 | .08 |
| ❏ 134 Mike Munchak | .10 | .02 |
| ❏ 135 Mike Rozier | .04 | .01 |
| ❏ 136 Dean Steinkuhler | .04 | .01 |
| ❏ 137 Lorenzo White | .04 | .01 |
| ❏ 138 Tony Zendejas | .04 | .01 |
| ❏ 139 Gary Anderson K | .04 | .01 |
| ❏ 140 Bubby Brister | .04 | .01 |
| ❏ 141 Thomas Everett | .04 | .01 |
| ❏ 142 Derek Hill | .04 | .01 |
| ❏ 143 Merril Hoge | .04 | .01 |
| ❏ 144 Tim Johnson | .04 | .01 |
| ❏ 145 Louis Lipps | .10 | .02 |
| ❏ 146 David Little | .04 | .01 |
| ❏ 147 Greg Lloyd | .25 | .08 |
| ❏ 148 Mike Mularkey | .04 | .01 |
| ❏ 149 John Rienstra RC | .04 | .01 |
| ❏ 150 Gerald Williams RC UER | .04 | .01 |
| ❏ 151 Keith Willis UER | .04 | .01 |
| ❏ 152 Rod Woodson | .25 | .08 |
| ❏ 153 Tim Worley | .04 | .01 |
| ❏ 154 Gary Clark | .25 | .08 |
| ❏ 155 Darryl Grant | .04 | .01 |
| ❏ 156 Darrell Green | .10 | .02 |
| ❏ 157 Joe Jacoby | .04 | .01 |
| ❏ 158 Jim Lachey | .04 | .01 |
| ❏ 159 Chip Lohmiller | .04 | .01 |
| ❏ 160 Charles Mann | .04 | .01 |
| ❏ 161 Wilber Marshall | .04 | .01 |
| ❏ 162 Mark May | .04 | .01 |
| ❏ 163 Ralf Mojsiejenko | .04 | .01 |
| ❏ 164 Art Monk UER | .10 | .02 |
| ❏ 165 Gerald Riggs | .10 | .02 |
| ❏ 166 Mark Rypien | .10 | .02 |
| ❏ 167 Ricky Sanders | .04 | .01 |
| ❏ 168 Don Warren | .04 | .01 |
| ❏ 169 Robert Brown RC | .04 | .01 |
| ❏ 170 Blair Bush | .04 | .01 |
| ❏ 171 Brent Fullwood | .04 | .01 |
| ❏ 172 Tim Harris | .04 | .01 |
| ❏ 173 Chris Jacke | .04 | .01 |
| ❏ 174 Perry Kemp | .04 | .01 |
| ❏ 175 Don Majkowski | .04 | .01 |
| ❏ 176 Tony Mandarich | .04 | .01 |
| ❏ 177 Mark Murphy | .04 | .01 |
| ❏ 178 Brian Noble | .04 | .01 |
| ❏ 179 Ken Ruettgers | .04 | .01 |
| ❏ 180 Sterling Sharpe | .25 | .08 |
| ❏ 181 Ed West RC | .04 | .01 |
| ❏ 182 Keith Woodside | .04 | .01 |
| ❏ 183 Morten Andersen | .04 | .01 |
| ❏ 184 Stan Brock | .04 | .01 |
| ❏ 185 Jim Dombrowski RC | .04 | .01 |
| ❏ 186 John Fourcade | .04 | .01 |
| ❏ 187 Bobby Hebert | .04 | .01 |
| ❏ 188 Craig Heyward | .10 | .02 |
| ❏ 189 Dalton Hilliard | .04 | .01 |
| ❏ 190 Rickey Jackson | .10 | .02 |
| ❏ 191 Buford Jordan | .04 | .01 |
| ❏ 192 Eric Martin | .04 | .01 |
| ❏ 193 Robert Massey | .04 | .01 |
| ❏ 194 Sam Mills | .10 | .02 |
| ❏ 195 Pat Swilling | .10 | .02 |
| ❏ 196 Jim Wilks | .04 | .01 |
| ❏ 197 John Alt RC | .04 | .01 |
| ❏ 198 Walker Lee Ashley | .04 | .01 |
| ❏ 199 Steve DeBerg | .04 | .01 |
| ❏ 200 Leonard Griffin | .04 | .01 |
| ❏ 201 Albert Lewis | .04 | .01 |
| ❏ 202 Nick Lowery | .04 | .01 |
| ❏ 203 Bill Maas | .04 | .01 |
| ❏ 204 Pete Mandley | .04 | .01 |
| ❏ 205 Chris Martin RC | .04 | .01 |
| ❏ 206 Christian Okoye | .04 | .01 |
| ❏ 207 Stephone Paige | .04 | .01 |
| ❏ 208 Kevin Porter RC | .04 | .01 |
| ❏ 209 Derrick Thomas | .25 | .08 |
| ❏ 210 Lewis Billups | .04 | .01 |
| ❏ 211 James Brooks | .10 | .02 |
| ❏ 212 Jason Buck | .04 | .01 |
| ❏ 213 Rickey Dixon RC | .04 | .01 |
| ❏ 214 Boomer Esiason | .10 | .02 |
| ❏ 215 David Fulcher | .04 | .01 |
| ❏ 216 Rodney Holman | .04 | .01 |
| ❏ 217 Lee Johnson | .04 | .01 |
| ❏ 218 Tim Krumrie | .04 | .01 |
| ❏ 219 Tim McGee | .04 | .01 |
| ❏ 220 Anthony Munoz | .10 | .02 |
| ❏ 221 Bruce Reimers RC | .04 | .01 |
| ❏ 222 Leon White | .04 | .01 |
| ❏ 223 Ickey Woods | .04 | .01 |
| ❏ 224 Harvey Armstrong RC | .04 | .01 |
| ❏ 225 Michael Ball RC | .04 | .01 |
| ❏ 226 Chip Banks | .04 | .01 |
| ❏ 227 Pat Beach | .04 | .01 |
| ❏ 228 Duane Bickett | .04 | .01 |
| ❏ 229 Bill Brooks | .04 | .01 |
| ❏ 230 Jon Hand | .04 | .01 |
| ❏ 231 Andre Rison | .25 | .08 |
| ❏ 232 Rohn Stark | .04 | .01 |
| ❏ 233 Donnell Thompson | .04 | .01 |
| ❏ 234 Jack Trudeau | .04 | .01 |
| ❏ 235 Clarence Verdin | .04 | .01 |
| ❏ 236 Mark Clayton | .10 | .02 |
| ❏ 237 Jeff Cross | .04 | .01 |
| ❏ 238 Jeff Dellenbach RC | .04 | .01 |
| ❏ 239 Mark Duper | .10 | .02 |
| ❏ 240 Ferrell Edmunds | .04 | .01 |
| ❏ 241 Hugh Green UER | .04 | .01 |
| ❏ 242 E.J. Junior | .04 | .01 |
| ❏ 243 Marc Logan | .04 | .01 |
| ❏ 244 Dan Marino | 1.25 | .50 |
| ❏ 245 John Offerdahl | .04 | .01 |
| ❏ 246 Reggie Roby | .04 | .01 |
| ❏ 247 Sammie Smith | .04 | .01 |
| ❏ 248 Pete Stoyanovich | .04 | .01 |
| ❏ 249 Marcus Allen | .25 | .08 |
| ❏ 250 Eddie Anderson RC | .04 | .01 |
| ❏ 251 Steve Beuerlein | .10 | .02 |
| ❏ 252 Mike Dyal | .04 | .01 |
| ❏ 253 Mervyn Fernandez | .04 | .01 |
| ❏ 254 Bob Golic | .04 | .01 |
| ❏ 255 Mike Harden | .04 | .01 |
| ❏ 256 Bo Jackson | .30 | .10 |
| ❏ 257 Howie Long UER | .25 | .08 |
| ❏ 258 Don Mosebar | .04 | .01 |
| ❏ 259 Jay Schroeder | .04 | .01 |
| ❏ 260 Steve Smith | .04 | .01 |
| ❏ 261 Greg Townsend | .04 | .01 |
| ❏ 262 Lionel Washington | .04 | .01 |
| ❏ 263 Brian Blades | .10 | .02 |
| ❏ 264 Jeff Bryant | .04 | .01 |
| ❏ 265 Grant Feasel RC | .04 | .01 |
| ❏ 266 Jacob Green | .04 | .01 |
| ❏ 267 James Jefferson | .04 | .01 |
| ❏ 268 Norm Johnson | .04 | .01 |
| ❏ 269 Dave Krieg UER | .10 | .02 |
| ❏ 270 Travis McNeal | .04 | .01 |
| ❏ 271 Joe Nash | .04 | .01 |
| ❏ 272 Rufus Porter | .04 | .01 |
| ❏ 273 Kelly Stouffer | .04 | .01 |
| ❏ 274 John L. Williams | .04 | .01 |

| | | |
|---|---|---|
| ❏ 275 Jim Arnold | .04 | .01 |
| ❏ 276 Jerry Ball | .04 | .01 |
| ❏ 277 Bennie Blades | .04 | .01 |
| ❏ 278 Lomas Brown | .04 | .01 |
| ❏ 279 Michael Cofer | .04 | .01 |
| ❏ 280 Bob Gagliano | .04 | .01 |
| ❏ 281 Richard Johnson | .04 | .01 |
| ❏ 282 Eddie Murray | .04 | .01 |
| ❏ 283 Rodney Peete | .10 | .02 |
| ❏ 284 Barry Sanders | 1.25 | .50 |
| ❏ 285 Eric Sanders | .04 | .01 |
| ❏ 286 Chris Spielman | .25 | .08 |
| ❏ 287 Eric Williams RC | .04 | .01 |
| ❏ 288 Neal Anderson | .10 | .02 |
| ❏ 289A Kevin Butler P/P | .25 | .08 |
| ❏ 289B Kevin Butler K/P | .25 | .08 |
| ❏ 289C Kevin Butler P/K | .25 | .08 |
| ❏ 289D Kevin Butler K/K | .04 | .01 |
| ❏ 290 Jim Covert | .04 | .01 |
| ❏ 291 Richard Dent | .10 | .02 |
| ❏ 292 Dennis Gentry | .04 | .01 |
| ❏ 293 Jim Harbaugh | .25 | .08 |
| ❏ 294 Jay Hilgenberg | .04 | .01 |
| ❏ 295 Vestee Jackson | .04 | .01 |
| ❏ 296 Steve McMichael | .10 | .02 |
| ❏ 297 Ron Morris | .04 | .01 |
| ❏ 298 Brad Muster | .04 | .01 |
| ❏ 299 Mike Singletary | .10 | .02 |
| ❏ 300 James Thornton UER | .04 | .01 |
| ❏ 301 Mike Tomczak | .10 | .02 |
| ❏ 302 Keith Van Horne | .04 | .01 |
| ❏ 303 Chris Bahr UER | .04 | .01 |
| ❏ 304 Martin Bayless RC | .04 | .01 |
| ❏ 305 Marion Butts | .10 | .02 |
| ❏ 306 Gill Byrd | .04 | .01 |
| ❏ 307 Arthur Cox | .04 | .01 |
| ❏ 308 Burt Grossman | .04 | .01 |
| ❏ 309 Jamie Holland | .04 | .01 |
| ❏ 310 Jim McMahon | .10 | .02 |
| ❏ 311 Anthony Miller | .25 | .08 |
| ❏ 312 Leslie O'Neal | .10 | .02 |
| ❏ 313 Billy Ray Smith | .04 | .01 |
| ❏ 314 Tim Spencer | .04 | .01 |
| ❏ 315 Broderick Thompson RC | .04 | .01 |
| ❏ 316 Lee Williams | .04 | .01 |
| ❏ 317 Bruce Armstrong | .04 | .01 |
| ❏ 318 Tim Goad RC | .04 | .01 |
| ❏ 319 Steve Grogan | .10 | .02 |
| ❏ 320 Roland James | .04 | .01 |
| ❏ 321 Cedric Jones | .04 | .01 |
| ❏ 322 Fred Marion | .04 | .01 |
| ❏ 323 Stanley Morgan | .04 | .01 |
| ❏ 324 Robert Perryman | .04 | .01 |
| ❏ 325 Johnny Rembert | .04 | .01 |
| ❏ 326 Ed Reynolds | .04 | .01 |
| ❏ 327 Kenneth Sims | .04 | .01 |
| ❏ 328 John Stephens | .10 | .02 |
| ❏ 329 Danny Villa RC | .04 | .01 |
| ❏ 330 Robert Awalt | .04 | .01 |
| ❏ 331 Anthony Bell | .04 | .01 |
| ❏ 332 Rich Camarillo | .04 | .01 |
| ❏ 333 Earl Ferrell | .04 | .01 |
| ❏ 334 Roy Green | .10 | .02 |
| ❏ 335 Gary Hogeboom | .04 | .01 |
| ❏ 336 Cedric Mack | .04 | .01 |
| ❏ 337 Freddie Joe Nunn | .04 | .01 |
| ❏ 338 Luis Sharpe | .04 | .01 |
| ❏ 339 Vai Sikahema | .04 | .01 |
| ❏ 340 J.T. Smith | .04 | .01 |
| ❏ 341 Tom Tupa RC | .04 | .01 |
| ❏ 342 Percy Snow RC | .04 | .01 |
| ❏ 343 Mark Carrier WR | .25 | .08 |
| ❏ 344 Randy Grimes | .04 | .01 |
| ❏ 345 Paul Gruber | .04 | .01 |
| ❏ 346 Ron Hall | .04 | .01 |
| ❏ 347 Jeff George RC | .50 | .20 |
| ❏ 348 Bruce Hill UER | .04 | .01 |
| ❏ 349 William Howard UER | .04 | .01 |
| ❏ 350 Donald Igwebuike | .04 | .01 |
| ❏ 351 Chris Mohr RC | .04 | .01 |
| ❏ 352 Winston Moss RC | .04 | .01 |
| ❏ 353 Ricky Reynolds | .04 | .01 |
| ❏ 354 Mark Robinson | .04 | .01 |
| ❏ 355 Lars Tate | .04 | .01 |

| | | |
|---|---|---|
| ❏ 356 Vinny Testaverde | .10 | .02 |
| ❏ 357 Broderick Thomas | .04 | .01 |
| ❏ 358 Troy Benson | .04 | .01 |
| ❏ 359 Jeff Criswell RC | .04 | .01 |
| ❏ 360 Tony Eason | .04 | .01 |
| ❏ 361 James Hasty | .04 | .01 |
| ❏ 362 Johnny Hector | .04 | .01 |
| ❏ 363 Bobby Humphery UER | .04 | .01 |
| ❏ 364 Pat Leahy | .04 | .01 |
| ❏ 365 Erik McMillan | .04 | .01 |
| ❏ 366 Freeman McNeil | .04 | .01 |
| ❏ 367 Ken O'Brien | .04 | .01 |
| ❏ 368 Ron Stallworth | .04 | .01 |
| ❏ 369 Al Toon | .10 | .02 |
| ❏ 370 Blair Thomas RC | .04 | .01 |
| ❏ 371 Aundray Bruce | .04 | .01 |
| ❏ 372 Tony Casillas | .04 | .01 |
| ❏ 373 Shawn Collins | .04 | .01 |
| ❏ 374 Evan Cooper | .04 | .01 |
| ❏ 375 Bill Fralic | .04 | .01 |
| ❏ 376 Scott Fulhage | .04 | .01 |
| ❏ 377 Mike Gann | .04 | .01 |
| ❏ 378 Ron Heller TE | .04 | .01 |
| ❏ 379 Keith Jones | .04 | .01 |
| ❏ 380 Mike Kenn | .04 | .01 |
| ❏ 381 Chris Miller | .25 | .08 |
| ❏ 382 Deion Sanders UER | .50 | .20 |
| ❏ 383 John Settle | .04 | .01 |
| ❏ 384 Troy Aikman | .75 | .30 |
| ❏ 385 Bill Bates | .10 | .02 |
| ❏ 386 Willie Broughton | .04 | .01 |
| ❏ 387 Steve Folsom | .04 | .01 |
| ❏ 388 Ray Horton UER | .04 | .01 |
| ❏ 389 Michael Irvin | .25 | .08 |
| ❏ 390 Jim Jeffcoat | .04 | .01 |
| ❏ 391 Eugene Lockhart | .04 | .01 |
| ❏ 392 Kelvin Martin RC | .04 | .01 |
| ❏ 393 Nate Newton | .10 | .02 |
| ❏ 394 Mike Saxon UER | .04 | .01 |
| ❏ 395 Derrick Shepard | .04 | .01 |
| ❏ 396 Steve Walsh | .10 | .02 |
| ❏ 397 Joe Montana/Rice MVP's | .75 | .30 |
| ❏ 398 Checklist Card UER | .04 | .01 |
| ❏ 399 Checklist Card UER | .04 | .01 |
| ❏ 400 Checklist Card | .04 | .01 |

## 1990 Fleer Update

EMMITT SMITH

| | | |
|---|---|---|
| ❏ COMP.FACT.SET (120) | 25.00 | 12.50 |
| ❏ U1 Albert Bentley | .08 | .02 |
| ❏ U2 Dean Biasucci | .08 | .02 |
| ❏ U3 Ray Donaldson | .08 | .02 |
| ❏ U4 Jeff George | 1.25 | .50 |
| ❏ U5 Ray Agnew RC | .08 | .02 |
| ❏ U6 Greg McMurtry RC | .08 | .02 |
| ❏ U7 Chris Singleton RC | .08 | .02 |
| ❏ U8 James Francis RC | .08 | .02 |
| ❏ U9 Harold Green RC | .30 | .10 |
| ❏ U10 John Elliott | .08 | .02 |
| ❏ U11 Rodney Hampton RC | .30 | .10 |
| ❏ U12 Gary Reasons | .08 | .02 |
| ❏ U13 Lewis Tillman | .08 | .02 |
| ❏ U14 Everson Walls | .08 | .02 |
| ❏ U15 David Alexander RC | .08 | .02 |
| ❏ U16 Jim McMahon | .15 | .05 |
| ❏ U17 Ben Smith RC | .08 | .02 |
| ❏ U18 Andre Waters | .08 | .02 |
| ❏ U19 Calvin Williams RC | .15 | .05 |
| ❏ U20 Earnest Byner | .08 | .02 |

| | | |
|---|---|---|
| ❏ U21 Andre Collins RC | .08 | .02 |
| ❏ U22 Russ Grimm | .08 | .02 |
| ❏ U23 Stan Humphries RC | .30 | .10 |
| ❏ U24 Martin Mayhew RC | .08 | .02 |
| ❏ U25 Barry Foster RC | .30 | .10 |
| ❏ U26 Eric Green RC | .15 | .05 |
| ❏ U27 Tunch Ilkin | .08 | .02 |
| ❏ U28 Hardy Nickerson | .15 | .05 |
| ❏ U29 Jerrol Williams | .08 | .02 |
| ❏ U30 Mike Baab | .08 | .02 |
| ❏ U31 Leroy Hoard RC | .50 | .20 |
| ❏ U32 Eddie Johnson RC | .08 | .02 |
| ❏ U33 William Fuller | .15 | .05 |
| ❏ U34 Haywood Jeffires RC | .30 | .10 |
| ❏ U35 Don Maggs RC | .08 | .02 |
| ❏ U36 Allen Pinkett | .08 | .02 |
| ❏ U37 Robert Awalt | .08 | .02 |
| ❏ U38 Dennis McKinnon | .08 | .02 |
| ❏ U39 Ken Norton Jr. RC | .30 | .10 |
| ❏ U40 Emmitt Smith RC | 20.00 | 7.50 |
| ❏ U41 Alexander Wright RC | .08 | .02 |
| ❏ U42 Eric Hill | .08 | .02 |
| ❏ U43 Johnny Johnson RC | .15 | .05 |
| ❏ U44 Timm Rosenbach | .08 | .02 |
| ❏ U45 Anthony Thompson RC | .08 | .02 |
| ❏ U46 Dexter Carter RC | .08 | .02 |
| ❏ U47 Eric Davis RC UER | .15 | .05 |
| ❏ U48 Keith DeLong | .08 | .02 |
| ❏ U49 Brent Jones RC | .30 | .10 |
| ❏ U50 Darryl Pollard RC | .08 | .02 |
| ❏ U51 Steve Wallace RC | .30 | .10 |
| ❏ U52 Bern Brostek RC | .08 | .02 |
| ❏ U53 Aaron Cox | .08 | .02 |
| ❏ U54 Cleveland Gary | .08 | .02 |
| ❏ U55 Fred Strickland RC | .08 | .02 |
| ❏ U56 Pat Terrell RC | .06 | .02 |
| ❏ U57 Steve Broussard RC | .08 | .02 |
| ❏ U58 Scott Case | .08 | .02 |
| ❏ U59 Brian Jordan RC | .15 | .05 |
| ❏ U60 Andre Rison | .30 | .10 |
| ❏ U61 Kevin Haverdink | .08 | .02 |
| ❏ U62 Rueben Mayes | .08 | .02 |
| ❏ U63 Steve Walsh | .15 | .05 |
| ❏ U64 Greg Bell | .08 | .02 |
| ❏ U65 Tim Brown | .30 | .10 |
| ❏ U66 Willie Gault | .15 | .05 |
| ❏ U67 Vance Mueller RC | .08 | .02 |
| ❏ U68 Bill Pickel | .08 | .02 |
| ❏ U69 Aaron Wallace RC | .08 | .02 |
| ❏ U70 Glenn Parker RC | .08 | .02 |
| ❏ U71 Frank Reich | .30 | .10 |
| ❏ U72 Leon Seals RC | .08 | .02 |
| ❏ U73 Darryl Talley | .08 | .02 |
| ❏ U74 Brad Baxter RC | .08 | .02 |
| ❏ U75 Jeff Criswell | .08 | .02 |
| ❏ U76 Jeff Lageman | .08 | .02 |
| ❏ U77 Rob Moore RC | 1.50 | .60 |
| ❏ U78 Blair Thomas | .15 | .05 |
| ❏ U79 Louis Oliver | .08 | .02 |
| ❏ U80 Tony Paige | .08 | .02 |
| ❏ U81 Richmond Webb RC | .30 | .10 |
| ❏ U82 Robert Blackmon RC | .08 | .02 |
| ❏ U83 Derrick Fenner RC | .08 | .02 |
| ❏ U84 Andy Heck | .08 | .02 |
| ❏ U85 Cortez Kennedy RC | .30 | .10 |
| ❏ U86 Terry Wooden RC | .08 | .02 |
| ❏ U87 Jeff Donaldson | .08 | .02 |
| ❏ U88 Tim Grunhard RC | .08 | .02 |
| ❏ U89 Emile Harry RC | .08 | .02 |
| ❏ U90 Dan Saleaumua | .08 | .02 |
| ❏ U91 Percy Snow | .08 | .02 |
| ❏ U92 Andre Ware | .30 | .10 |
| ❏ U93 Darrell Fullington RC | .08 | .02 |
| ❏ U94 Mike Merriweather | .08 | .02 |
| ❏ U95 Henry Thomas | .08 | .02 |
| ❏ U96 Robert Brown | .08 | .02 |
| ❏ U97 LeRoy Butler RC | .30 | .10 |
| ❏ U98 Anthony Dilweg | .08 | .02 |
| ❏ U99 Darrell Thompson RC | .08 | .02 |
| ❏ U100 Keith Woodside | .08 | .02 |
| ❏ U101 Gary Plummer | .08 | .02 |
| ❏ U102 Junior Seau RC | 5.00 | 2.00 |
| ❏ U103 Billy Joe Tolliver | .08 | .02 |
| ❏ U104 Mark Vlasic | .08 | .02 |

|  | | |
|---|---|---|
| ❏ U105 Gary Anderson RB | .08 | .02 |
| ❏ U106 Jan Beckles RC | .08 | .02 |
| ❏ U107 Reggie Cobb RC | .08 | .02 |
| ❏ U108 Keith McCants RC | .08 | .02 |
| ❏ U109 Mark Bortz RC | .08 | .02 |
| ❏ U110 Maury Buford | .08 | .02 |
| ❏ U111 Mark Carrier RC DB | .30 | .10 |
| ❏ U112 Dan Hampton | .15 | .05 |
| ❏ U113 William Perry | .15 | .05 |
| ❏ U114 Ron Rivera | .08 | .02 |
| ❏ U115 Lemuel Stinson | .08 | .02 |
| ❏ U116 Melvin Bratton RC | .08 | .02 |
| ❏ U117 Gary Kubiak RC | .30 | .10 |
| ❏ U118 Alton Montgomery RC | .08 | .02 |
| ❏ U119 Ricky Nattiel | .08 | .02 |
| ❏ U120 Checklist 1-132 | .08 | .02 |

## 1991 Fleer

Marcus Allen Raiders RB

|  | | |
|---|---|---|
| ❏ COMPLETE SET (432) | 8.00 | 4.00 |
| ❏ 1 Shane Conlan | .05 | .01 |
| ❏ 2 John Davis RC | .05 | .01 |
| ❏ 3 Kent Hull | .05 | .01 |
| ❏ 4 James Lofton | .10 | .02 |
| ❏ 5 Keith McKeller | .05 | .01 |
| ❏ 6 Scott Norwood | .05 | .01 |
| ❏ 7 Nate Odomes | .05 | .01 |
| ❏ 8 Andre Reed | .10 | .02 |
| ❏ 9 Jim Ritcher | .05 | .01 |
| ❏ 10 Leon Seals | .05 | .01 |
| ❏ 11 Bruce Smith | .25 | .08 |
| ❏ 12 Leonard Smith | .05 | .01 |
| ❏ 13 Steve Tasker | .10 | .02 |
| ❏ 14 Thurman Thomas | .25 | .08 |
| ❏ 15 Lewis Billups | .05 | .01 |
| ❏ 16 James Brooks | .10 | .02 |
| ❏ 17 Eddie Brown | .05 | .01 |
| ❏ 18 Carl Carter | .05 | .01 |
| ❏ 19 Boomer Esiason | .10 | .02 |
| ❏ 20 James Francis | .05 | .01 |
| ❏ 21 David Fulcher | .05 | .01 |
| ❏ 22 Harold Green | .10 | .02 |
| ❏ 23 Rodney Holman | .05 | .01 |
| ❏ 24 Bruce Kozerski | .05 | .01 |
| ❏ 25 Tim McGee | .05 | .01 |
| ❏ 26 Anthony Munoz | .10 | .02 |
| ❏ 27 Bruce Reimers | .05 | .01 |
| ❏ 28 Ickey Woods | .05 | .01 |
| ❏ 29 Carl Zander | .05 | .01 |
| ❏ 30 Mike Baab | .05 | .01 |
| ❏ 31 Brian Brennan | .05 | .01 |
| ❏ 32 Rob Burnett RC | .10 | .02 |
| ❏ 33 Paul Farren | .05 | .01 |
| ❏ 34 Thane Gash | .05 | .01 |
| ❏ 35 David Grayson | .05 | .01 |
| ❏ 36 Mike Johnson | .05 | .01 |
| ❏ 37 Reggie Langhorne | .05 | .01 |
| ❏ 38 Kevin Mack | .05 | .01 |
| ❏ 39 Eric Metcalf | .10 | .02 |
| ❏ 40 Frank Minnifield | .05 | .01 |
| ❏ 41 Gregg Rakoczy | .05 | .01 |
| ❏ 42 Felix Wright | .05 | .01 |
| ❏ 43 Steve Atwater | .05 | .01 |
| ❏ 44 Michael Brooks | .05 | .01 |
| ❏ 45 John Elway | 1.25 | .50 |
| ❏ 46 Simon Fletcher | .05 | .01 |
| ❏ 47 Bobby Humphrey | .05 | .01 |
| ❏ 48 Mark Jackson | .05 | .01 |
| ❏ 49 Keith Kartz | .05 | .01 |

|  | | |
|---|---|---|
| ❏ 50 Clarence Kay | .05 | .01 |
| ❏ 51 Greg Kragen | .05 | .01 |
| ❏ 52 Karl Mecklenburg | .05 | .01 |
| ❏ 53 Warren Powers | .05 | .01 |
| ❏ 54 Dennis Smith | .05 | .01 |
| ❏ 55 Jim Szymanski | .05 | .01 |
| ❏ 56 David Treadwell | .05 | .01 |
| ❏ 57 Michael Young | .05 | .01 |
| ❏ 58 Ray Childress | .05 | .01 |
| ❏ 59 Curtis Duncan | .05 | .01 |
| ❏ 60 William Fuller | .10 | .02 |
| ❏ 61 Ernest Givins | .10 | .02 |
| ❏ 62 Drew Hill | .05 | .01 |
| ❏ 63 Haywood Jeffires | .10 | .02 |
| ❏ 64 Richard Johnson DB | .05 | .01 |
| ❏ 65 Sean Jones | .10 | .02 |
| ❏ 66 Don Maggs | .05 | .01 |
| ❏ 67 Bruce Matthews | .10 | .02 |
| ❏ 68 Johnny Meads | .05 | .01 |
| ❏ 69 Greg Montgomery | .05 | .01 |
| ❏ 70 Warren Moon | .25 | .08 |
| ❏ 71 Mike Munchak | .10 | .02 |
| ❏ 72 Allen Pinkett | .05 | .01 |
| ❏ 73 Lorenzo White | .05 | .01 |
| ❏ 74 Pat Beach | .05 | .01 |
| ❏ 75 Albert Bentley | .05 | .01 |
| ❏ 76 Dean Biasucci | .05 | .01 |
| ❏ 77 Duane Bickett | .05 | .01 |
| ❏ 78 Bill Brooks | .05 | .01 |
| ❏ 79 Sam Clancy | .05 | .01 |
| ❏ 80 Ray Donaldson | .05 | .01 |
| ❏ 81 Jeff George | .25 | .08 |
| ❏ 82 Alan Grant | .05 | .01 |
| ❏ 83 Jessie Hester | .05 | .01 |
| ❏ 84 Jeff Herrod | .05 | .01 |
| ❏ 85 Rohn Stark | .05 | .01 |
| ❏ 86 Jack Trudeau | .05 | .01 |
| ❏ 87 Clarence Verdin | .05 | .01 |
| ❏ 88 John Alt | .05 | .01 |
| ❏ 89 Steve DeBerg | .05 | .01 |
| ❏ 90 Tim Grunhard | .05 | .01 |
| ❏ 91 Dino Hackett | .05 | .01 |
| ❏ 92 Jonathan Hayes | .05 | .01 |
| ❏ 93 Albert Lewis | .05 | .01 |
| ❏ 94 Nick Lowery | .05 | .01 |
| ❏ 95 Bill Maas UER | .05 | .01 |
| ❏ 96 Christian Okoye | .10 | .02 |
| ❏ 97 Stephone Paige | .05 | .01 |
| ❏ 98 Kevin Porter | .05 | .01 |
| ❏ 99 David Szott | .05 | .01 |
| ❏ 100 Derrick Thomas | .25 | .08 |
| ❏ 101 Barry Word FFC | .05 | .01 |
| ❏ 102 Marcus Allen | .25 | .08 |
| ❏ 103 Thomas Benson | .05 | .01 |
| ❏ 104 Tim Brown | .25 | .08 |
| ❏ 105 Riki Ellison | .05 | .01 |
| ❏ 106 Mervyn Fernandez | .05 | .01 |
| ❏ 107 Willie Gault | .10 | .02 |
| ❏ 108 Bob Golic | .05 | .01 |
| ❏ 109 Ethan Horton FFC | .05 | .01 |
| ❏ 110 Bo Jackson | .30 | .10 |
| ❏ 111 Howie Long | .25 | .08 |
| ❏ 112 Don Mosebar | .05 | .01 |
| ❏ 113 Jerry Robinson | .05 | .01 |
| ❏ 114 Jay Schroeder | .05 | .01 |
| ❏ 115 Steve Smith | .05 | .01 |
| ❏ 116 Greg Townsend | .05 | .01 |
| ❏ 117 Steve Wisniewski | .05 | .01 |
| ❏ 118 Mark Clayton | .10 | .02 |
| ❏ 119 Mark Duper | .10 | .02 |
| ❏ 120 Ferrell Edmunds | .05 | .01 |
| ❏ 121 Hugh Green | .05 | .01 |
| ❏ 122 David Griggs | .05 | .01 |
| ❏ 123 Jim C. Jensen | .05 | .01 |
| ❏ 124 Dan Marino | 1.25 | .50 |
| ❏ 125 Tim McKyer | .05 | .01 |
| ❏ 126 John Offerdahl | .05 | .01 |
| ❏ 127 Louis Oliver | .05 | .01 |
| ❏ 128 Tony Paige | .05 | .01 |
| ❏ 129 Reggie Roby | .05 | .01 |
| ❏ 130 Keith Sims | .05 | .01 |
| ❏ 131 Sammie Smith | .05 | .01 |
| ❏ 132 Pete Stoyanovich | .05 | .01 |
| ❏ 133 Richmond Webb | .05 | .01 |

|  | | |
|---|---|---|
| ❏ 134 Bruce Armstrong | .05 | .01 |
| ❏ 135 Vincent Brown | .05 | .01 |
| ❏ 136 Hart Lee Dykes | .05 | .01 |
| ❏ 137 Irving Fryar | .10 | .02 |
| ❏ 138 Tim Goad | .05 | .01 |
| ❏ 139 Tommy Hodson | .05 | .01 |
| ❏ 140 Maurice Hurst | .05 | .01 |
| ❏ 141 Ronnie Lippett | .05 | .01 |
| ❏ 142 Greg McMurtry | .05 | .01 |
| ❏ 143 Ed Reynolds | .05 | .01 |
| ❏ 144 John Stephens | .05 | .01 |
| ❏ 145 Andre Tippett | .05 | .01 |
| ❏ 146 Danny Villa | .05 | .01 |
| ❏ 147 Brad Baxter | .05 | .01 |
| ❏ 148 Kyle Clifton | .05 | .01 |
| ❏ 149 Jeff Criswell | .05 | .01 |
| ❏ 150 James Hasty | .05 | .01 |
| ❏ 151 Jeff Lageman | .05 | .01 |
| ❏ 152 Pat Leahy | .05 | .01 |
| ❏ 153 Rob Moore | .25 | .08 |
| ❏ 154 Al Toon | .10 | .02 |
| ❏ 155 Gary Anderson K | .05 | .01 |
| ❏ 156 Bubby Brister | .05 | .01 |
| ❏ 157 Chris Calloway | .05 | .01 |
| ❏ 158 Donald Evans | .05 | .01 |
| ❏ 159 Eric Green | .05 | .01 |
| ❏ 160 Bryan Hinkle | .05 | .01 |
| ❏ 161 Merril Hoge | .05 | .01 |
| ❏ 162 Tunch Ilkin | .05 | .01 |
| ❏ 163 Louis Lipps | .05 | .01 |
| ❏ 164 David Little | .05 | .01 |
| ❏ 165 Mike Mularkey | .05 | .01 |
| ❏ 166 Gerald Williams | .05 | .01 |
| ❏ 167 Warren Williams | .05 | .01 |
| ❏ 168 Rod Woodson | .25 | .08 |
| ❏ 169 Tim Worley | .05 | .01 |
| ❏ 170 Martin Bayless | .05 | .01 |
| ❏ 171 Marion Butts | .10 | .02 |
| ❏ 172 Gill Byrd | .05 | .01 |
| ❏ 173 Frank Cornish | .05 | .01 |
| ❏ 174 Arthur Cox | .05 | .01 |
| ❏ 175 Burt Grossman | .05 | .01 |
| ❏ 176 Anthony Miller | .10 | .02 |
| ❏ 177 Leslie O'Neal | .10 | .02 |
| ❏ 178 Gary Plummer | .05 | .01 |
| ❏ 179 Junior Seau | .25 | .08 |
| ❏ 180 Billy Joe Tolliver | .05 | .01 |
| ❏ 181 Derrick Walker RC | .05 | .01 |
| ❏ 182 Lee Williams | .05 | .01 |
| ❏ 183 Robert Blackmon | .05 | .01 |
| ❏ 184 Brian Blades | .10 | .02 |
| ❏ 185 Grant Feasel | .05 | .01 |
| ❏ 186 Derrick Fenner | .05 | .01 |
| ❏ 187 Andy Heck | .05 | .01 |
| ❏ 188 Norm Johnson | .05 | .01 |
| ❏ 189 Tommy Kane | .05 | .01 |
| ❏ 190 Cortez Kennedy | .25 | .08 |
| ❏ 191 Dave Krieg | .10 | .02 |
| ❏ 192 Travis McNeal | .05 | .01 |
| ❏ 193 Eugene Robinson | .05 | .01 |
| ❏ 194 Chris Warren FFC | .25 | .08 |
| ❏ 195 John L. Williams | .05 | .01 |
| ❏ 196 Steve Broussard | .05 | .01 |
| ❏ 197 Scott Case | .05 | .01 |
| ❏ 198 Shawn Collins | .05 | .01 |
| ❏ 199 Darion Conner UER | .05 | .01 |
| ❏ 200 Tory Epps | .05 | .01 |
| ❏ 201 Bill Fralic | .05 | .01 |
| ❏ 202 Michael Haynes FFC | .25 | .08 |
| ❏ 203 Chris Hinton | .05 | .01 |
| ❏ 204 Keith Jones | .05 | .01 |
| ❏ 205 Brian Jordan | .10 | .02 |
| ❏ 206 Mike Kenn | .05 | .01 |
| ❏ 207 Chris Miller | .10 | .02 |
| ❏ 208 Andre Rison | .10 | .02 |
| ❏ 209 Mike Rozier | .05 | .01 |
| ❏ 210 Deion Sanders | .40 | .15 |
| ❏ 211 Gary Wilkins | .05 | .01 |
| ❏ 212 Neal Anderson | .10 | .02 |
| ❏ 213 Trace Armstrong | .05 | .01 |
| ❏ 214 Mark Bortz | .05 | .01 |
| ❏ 215 Kevin Butler | .05 | .01 |
| ❏ 216 Mark Carrier DB | .10 | .02 |
| ❏ 217 Wendell Davis FFC | .05 | .01 |

| | | |
|---|---|---|
| ☐ 218 Richard Dent | .10 | .02 |
| ☐ 219 Dennis Gentry | .05 | .01 |
| ☐ 220 Jim Harbaugh | .25 | .08 |
| ☐ 221 Jay Hilgenberg | .05 | .01 |
| ☐ 222 Steve McMichael | .10 | .02 |
| ☐ 223 Ron Morris | .05 | .01 |
| ☐ 224 Brad Muster | .05 | .01 |
| ☐ 225 Mike Singletary | .10 | .02 |
| ☐ 226 James Thornton | .05 | .01 |
| ☐ 227 Tommie Agee | .05 | .01 |
| ☐ 228 Troy Aikman | .75 | .30 |
| ☐ 229 Jack Del Rio | .10 | .02 |
| ☐ 230 Issiac Holt | .05 | .01 |
| ☐ 231 Ray Horton | .05 | .01 |
| ☐ 232 Jim Jeffcoat | .05 | .01 |
| ☐ 233 Eugene Lockhart | .05 | .01 |
| ☐ 234 Kelvin Martin | .05 | .01 |
| ☐ 235 Nate Newton | .10 | .02 |
| ☐ 236 Mike Saxon | .05 | .01 |
| ☐ 237 Emmitt Smith | 2.50 | 1.00 |
| ☐ 238A Daniel Stubbs | .10 | .02 |
| ☐ 238B Daniel Stubbs | .10 | .02 |
| ☐ 239 Jim Arnold | .05 | .01 |
| ☐ 240 Jerry Ball | .05 | .01 |
| ☐ 241 Bennie Blades | .05 | .01 |
| ☐ 242 Lomas Brown | .05 | .01 |
| ☐ 243 Robert Clark | .05 | .01 |
| ☐ 244 Mike Cofer | .05 | .01 |
| ☐ 245 Mel Gray | .10 | .02 |
| ☐ 246 Rodney Peete | .10 | .02 |
| ☐ 247 Barry Sanders | 1.25 | .51 |
| ☐ 248 Andre Ware | .10 | .02 |
| ☐ 249 Matt Brock RC | .05 | .01 |
| ☐ 250 Robert Brown | .05 | .01 |
| ☐ 251 Anthony Dilweg | .05 | .01 |
| ☐ 252 Johnny Holland | .05 | .01 |
| ☐ 253 Tim Harris | .05 | .01 |
| ☐ 254 Chris Jacke | .05 | .01 |
| ☐ 255 Perry Kemp | .05 | .01 |
| ☐ 256 Don Majkowski UER | .05 | .01 |
| ☐ 257 Tony Mandarich | .05 | .01 |
| ☐ 258 Mark Murphy | .05 | .01 |
| ☐ 259 Brian Noble | .05 | .01 |
| ☐ 260 Jeff Query | .05 | .01 |
| ☐ 261 Sterling Sharpe | .25 | .08 |
| ☐ 262 Ed West | .05 | .01 |
| ☐ 263 Keith Woodside | .05 | .01 |
| ☐ 264 Flipper Anderson | .05 | .01 |
| ☐ 265 Aaron Cox | .05 | .01 |
| ☐ 266 Henry Ellard | .10 | .02 |
| ☐ 267 Jim Everett | .10 | .02 |
| ☐ 268 Cleveland Gary | .05 | .01 |
| ☐ 269 Kevin Greene | .10 | .02 |
| ☐ 270 Pete Holohan | .05 | .01 |
| ☐ 271 Mike Lansford | .05 | .01 |
| ☐ 272 Duval Love RC | .05 | .01 |
| ☐ 273 Buford McGee | .05 | .01 |
| ☐ 274 Tom Newberry | .05 | .01 |
| ☐ 275 Jackie Slater | .05 | .01 |
| ☐ 276 Frank Stams | .05 | .01 |
| ☐ 277 Alfred Anderson | .05 | .01 |
| ☐ 278 Joey Browner | .05 | .01 |
| ☐ 279 Anthony Carter | .10 | .02 |
| ☐ 280 Chris Doleman | .05 | .01 |
| ☐ 281 Rick Fenney | .05 | .01 |
| ☐ 282 Rich Gannon | .25 | .08 |
| ☐ 283 Hassan Jones | .05 | .01 |
| ☐ 284 Steve Jordan | .05 | .01 |
| ☐ 285 Carl Lee | .05 | .01 |
| ☐ 286 Randall McDaniel | .10 | .02 |
| ☐ 287 Keith Millard | .05 | .01 |
| ☐ 288 Herschel Walker | .10 | .02 |
| ☐ 289 Wade Wilson | .10 | .02 |
| ☐ 290 Gary Zimmerman | .10 | .02 |
| ☐ 291 Morten Andersen | .05 | .01 |
| ☐ 292 Jim Dombrowski | .05 | .01 |
| ☐ 293 Gill Fenerty | .05 | .01 |
| ☐ 294 Craig Heyward | .10 | .02 |
| ☐ 295 Dalton Hilliard | .05 | .01 |
| ☐ 296 Rickey Jackson | .05 | .01 |
| ☐ 297 Vaughan Johnson | .05 | .01 |
| ☐ 298 Eric Martin | .05 | .01 |
| ☐ 299 Robert Massey | .05 | .01 |
| ☐ 300 Rueben Mayes | .05 | .01 |

| | | |
|---|---|---|
| ☐ 301 Sam Mills | .05 | .01 |
| ☐ 302 Brett Perriman | .25 | .08 |
| ☐ 303 Pat Swilling | .10 | .02 |
| ☐ 304 Steve Walsh | .05 | .01 |
| ☐ 305 Ottis Anderson | .10 | .02 |
| ☐ 306 Matt Bahr | .05 | .01 |
| ☐ 307 Mark Bavaro | .05 | .01 |
| ☐ 308 Maurice Carthon | .05 | .01 |
| ☐ 309 Mark Collins | .05 | .01 |
| ☐ 310 John Elliott | .05 | .01 |
| ☐ 311 Rodney Hampton | .25 | .08 |
| ☐ 312 Jeff Hostetler | .10 | .02 |
| ☐ 313 Erik Howard | .05 | .01 |
| ☐ 314 Pepper Johnson | .05 | .01 |
| ☐ 315 Sean Landeta | .05 | .01 |
| ☐ 316 Dave Meggett | .10 | .02 |
| ☐ 317 Bart Oates | .05 | .01 |
| ☐ 318 Phil Simms | .10 | .02 |
| ☐ 319 Lawrence Taylor | .25 | .08 |
| ☐ 320 Reyna Thompson | .05 | .01 |
| ☐ 321 Everson Walls | .05 | .01 |
| ☐ 322 Eric Allen | .05 | .01 |
| ☐ 323 Fred Barnett FFC | .25 | .08 |
| ☐ 324 Jerome Brown | .05 | .01 |
| ☐ 325 Keith Byars | .05 | .01 |
| ☐ 326 Randall Cunningham | .25 | .08 |
| ☐ 327 Byron Evans | .05 | .01 |
| ☐ 328 Ron Heller | .05 | .01 |
| ☐ 329 Keith Jackson | .10 | .02 |
| ☐ 330 Seth Joyner | .10 | .02 |
| ☐ 331 Heath Sherman | .05 | .01 |
| ☐ 332 Clyde Simmons | .05 | .01 |
| ☐ 333 Ben Smith | .05 | .01 |
| ☐ 334 Anthony Toney | .05 | .01 |
| ☐ 335 Andre Waters | .05 | .01 |
| ☐ 336 Reggie White | .25 | .08 |
| ☐ 337 Calvin Williams | .10 | .02 |
| ☐ 338 Anthony Bell | .05 | .01 |
| ☐ 339 Rich Camarillo | .05 | .01 |
| ☐ 340 Roy Green | .05 | .01 |
| ☐ 341 Tim Jorden RC | .05 | .01 |
| ☐ 342 Cedric Mack | .05 | .01 |
| ☐ 343 Dexter Manley | .05 | .01 |
| ☐ 344 Freddie Joe Nunn | .05 | .01 |
| ☐ 345 Ricky Proehl | .05 | .01 |
| ☐ 346 Tootie Robbins | .05 | .01 |
| ☐ 347 Timm Rosenbach | .05 | .01 |
| ☐ 348 Luis Sharpe | .05 | .01 |
| ☐ 349 Vai Sikahema | .05 | .01 |
| ☐ 350 Anthony Thompson | .05 | .01 |
| ☐ 351 Lonnie Young | .05 | .01 |
| ☐ 352 Dexter Carter | .05 | .01 |
| ☐ 353 Mike Cofer | .05 | .01 |
| ☐ 354 Kevin Fagan | .05 | .01 |
| ☐ 355 Don Griffin | .05 | .01 |
| ☐ 356 Charles Haley UER | .10 | .02 |
| ☐ 357 Pierce Holt | .05 | .01 |
| ☐ 358 Brent Jones | .25 | .08 |
| ☐ 359 Guy McIntyre | .05 | .01 |
| ☐ 360 Joe Montana | 1.25 | .50 |
| ☐ 361 Darryl Pollard | .05 | .01 |
| ☐ 362 Tom Rathman | .05 | .01 |
| ☐ 363 Jerry Rice | .75 | .30 |
| ☐ 364 Bill Romanowski | .05 | .01 |
| ☐ 365 John Taylor | .10 | .02 |
| ☐ 366 Steve Wallace | .10 | .02 |
| ☐ 367 Steve Young | .75 | .30 |
| ☐ 368 Gary Anderson RB | .05 | .01 |
| ☐ 369 Ian Beckles | .05 | .01 |
| ☐ 370 Mark Carrier WR | .25 | .08 |
| ☐ 371 Reggie Cobb | .05 | .01 |
| ☐ 372 Reuben Davis | .05 | .01 |
| ☐ 373 Randy Grimes | .05 | .01 |
| ☐ 374 Wayne Haddix | .05 | .01 |
| ☐ 375 Ron Hall | .05 | .01 |
| ☐ 376 Harry Hamilton | .05 | .01 |
| ☐ 377 Bruce Hill | .05 | .01 |
| ☐ 378 Keith McCants | .05 | .01 |
| ☐ 379 Bruce Perkins | .05 | .01 |
| ☐ 380 Vinny Testaverde UER | .10 | .02 |
| ☐ 381 Broderick Thomas | .05 | .01 |
| ☐ 382 Jeff Bostic | .05 | .01 |
| ☐ 383 Earnest Byner | .05 | .01 |
| ☐ 384 Gary Clark | .25 | .08 |

| | | |
|---|---|---|
| ☐ 385 Darryl Grant | .05 | .01 |
| ☐ 386 Darrell Green | .05 | .01 |
| ☐ 387 Stan Humphries | .25 | .08 |
| ☐ 388 Jim Lachey | .05 | .01 |
| ☐ 389 Charles Mann | .05 | .01 |
| ☐ 390 Wilber Marshall | .05 | .01 |
| ☐ 391 Art Monk | .10 | .02 |
| ☐ 392 Gerald Riggs | .05 | .01 |
| ☐ 393 Mark Rypien | .10 | .02 |
| ☐ 394 Ricky Sanders | .05 | .01 |
| ☐ 395 Don Warren | .05 | .01 |
| ☐ 396 Bruce Smith HIT | .10 | .02 |
| ☐ 397 Reggie White HIT | .10 | .02 |
| ☐ 398 Lawrence Taylor HIT | .10 | .02 |
| ☐ 399 David Fulcher HIT | .05 | .01 |
| ☐ 400 Derrick Thomas HIT | .10 | .02 |
| ☐ 401 Mark Carrier DB HIT | .05 | .01 |
| ☐ 402 Mike Singletary HIT | .10 | .02 |
| ☐ 403 Charles Haley HIT | .05 | .01 |
| ☐ 404 Jeff Cross HIT | .05 | .01 |
| ☐ 405 Leslie O'Neal HIT | .10 | .02 |
| ☐ 406 Tim Harris HIT | .05 | .01 |
| ☐ 407 Steve Atwater HIT | .05 | .01 |
| ☐ 408 Joe Montana LL UER | .50 | .20 |
| ☐ 409 Randall Cunningham LL | .10 | .02 |
| ☐ 410 Warren Moon LL | .10 | .02 |
| ☐ 411 Andre Rison LL UER 412 | .10 | .02 |
| ☐ 412 Haywood Jeffires LL | .10 | .02 |
| ☐ 413 Stephone Paige LL | .05 | .01 |
| ☐ 414 Phil Simms LL | .10 | .02 |
| ☐ 415 Barry Sanders LL | .50 | .20 |
| ☐ 416 Bo Jackson LL | .10 | .02 |
| ☐ 417 Thurman Thomas LL | .10 | .02 |
| ☐ 418 Emmitt Smith LL | 1.25 | .50 |
| ☐ 419 John L. Williams LL | .05 | .01 |
| ☐ 420 Nick Bell RC | .05 | .01 |
| ☐ 421 Eric Bieniemy RC | .05 | .01 |
| ☐ 422 Mike Dumas RC UER | .05 | .01 |
| ☐ 423 Russell Maryland RC | .25 | .08 |
| ☐ 424 Derek Russell RC | .05 | .01 |
| ☐ 425 Chris Smith RC | .05 | .01 |
| ☐ 426 Mike Stonebreaker RP | .05 | .01 |
| ☐ 427 Pat Tyrance RP | .05 | .01 |
| ☐ 428 Kenny Walker RC | .05 | .01 |
| ☐ 429 Checklist 1-108 UER | .05 | .01 |
| ☐ 430 Checklist 109-216 | .05 | .01 |
| ☐ 431 Checklist 217-324 | .05 | .01 |
| ☐ 432 Checklist 325-432 | .05 | .01 |

## 1992 Fleer

| | | |
|---|---|---|
| ☐ COMPLETE SET (480) | 10.00 | 5.00 |
| ☐ 1 Steve Broussard | .05 | .01 |
| ☐ 2 Rick Bryan | .05 | .01 |
| ☐ 3 Scott Case | .05 | .01 |
| ☐ 4 Tory Epps | .05 | .01 |
| ☐ 5 Bill Fralic | .05 | .01 |
| ☐ 6 Moe Gardner | .05 | .01 |
| ☐ 7 Michael Haynes | .10 | .02 |
| ☐ 8 Chris Hinton | .10 | .02 |
| ☐ 9 Brian Jordan | .10 | .02 |
| ☐ 10 Mike Kenn | .10 | .02 |
| ☐ 11 Tim McKyer | .10 | .02 |
| ☐ 12 Chris Miller | .10 | .02 |
| ☐ 13 Erric Pegram | .10 | .02 |
| ☐ 14 Mike Pritchard | .10 | .02 |
| ☐ 15 Andre Rison | .10 | .02 |
| ☐ 16 Jessie Tuggle | .05 | .01 |
| ☐ 17 Carlton Bailey RC | .05 | .02 |

|  |  | | |
|---|---|---|---|
| 18 | Howard Ballard | .05 | .01 |
| 19 | Don Beebe | .05 | .01 |
| 20 | Cornelius Bennett | .10 | .02 |
| 21 | Shane Conlan | .05 | .01 |
| 22 | Kent Hull | .05 | .01 |
| 23 | Mark Kelso | .05 | .01 |
| 24 | James Lofton | .10 | .02 |
| 25 | Keith McKeller | .05 | .01 |
| 26 | Scott Norwood | .05 | .01 |
| 27 | Nate Odomes | .05 | .01 |
| 28 | Frank Reich | .10 | .02 |
| 29 | Jim Ritcher | .05 | .01 |
| 30 | Leon Seals | .05 | .01 |
| 31 | Darryl Talley | .05 | .01 |
| 32 | Steve Tasker | .10 | .02 |
| 33 | Thurman Thomas | .25 | .08 |
| 34 | Will Wolford | .05 | .01 |
| 35 | Neal Anderson | .05 | .01 |
| 36 | Trace Armstrong | .05 | .01 |
| 37 | Mark Carrier DB | .05 | .01 |
| 38 | Richard Dent | .10 | .02 |
| 39 | Shaun Gayle | .05 | .01 |
| 40 | Jim Harbaugh | .25 | .08 |
| 41 | Jay Hilgenberg | .05 | .01 |
| 42 | Darren Lewis | .05 | .01 |
| 43 | Steve McMichael | .10 | .02 |
| 44 | Brad Muster | .05 | .01 |
| 45 | William Perry | .10 | .02 |
| 46 | John Roper | .05 | .01 |
| 47 | Lemuel Stinson | .05 | .01 |
| 48 | Stan Thomas | .05 | .01 |
| 49 | Keith Van Horne | .05 | .01 |
| 50 | Tom Waddle | .05 | .01 |
| 51 | Donnell Woolford | .05 | .01 |
| 52 | Chris Zorich | .10 | .02 |
| 53 | Eddie Brown | .05 | .01 |
| 54 | James Francis | .05 | .01 |
| 55 | David Fulcher | .05 | .01 |
| 56 | David Grant | .05 | .01 |
| 57 | Harold Green | .05 | .01 |
| 58 | Rodney Holman | .05 | .01 |
| 59 | Lee Johnson | .05 | .01 |
| 60 | Tim Krumrie | .05 | .01 |
| 61 | Anthony Munoz | .10 | .02 |
| 62 | Joe Walter RC | .05 | .01 |
| 63 | Mike Baab | .05 | .01 |
| 64 | Stephen Braggs | .05 | .01 |
| 65 | Richard Brown RC | .05 | .01 |
| 66 | Dan Fike | .05 | .01 |
| 67 | Scott Galbraith RC | .05 | .01 |
| 68 | Randy Hilliard RC | .05 | .01 |
| 69 | Michael Jackson | .10 | .02 |
| 70 | Tony Jones T | .05 | .01 |
| 71 | Ed King | .05 | .01 |
| 72 | Kevin Mack | .05 | .01 |
| 73 | Clay Matthews | .10 | .02 |
| 74 | Eric Metcalf | .10 | .02 |
| 75 | Vince Newsome | .05 | .01 |
| 76 | John Rienstra | .05 | .01 |
| 77 | Steve Beuerlein | .10 | .02 |
| 78 | Larry Brown DB | .05 | .01 |
| 79 | Tony Casillas | .05 | .01 |
| 80 | Alvin Harper | .10 | .02 |
| 81 | Issiac Holt | .05 | .01 |
| 82 | Ray Horton | .05 | .01 |
| 83 | Michael Irvin | .25 | .08 |
| 84 | Daryl Johnston | .25 | .08 |
| 85 | Kelvin Martin | .05 | .01 |
| 86 | Nate Newton | .10 | .02 |
| 87 | Ken Norton | .10 | .02 |
| 88 | Jay Novacek | .10 | .02 |
| 89 | Emmitt Smith | 1.50 | .60 |
| 90 | Vinson Smith RC | .05 | .01 |
| 91 | Mark Stepnoski | .10 | .02 |
| 92 | Steve Atwater | .05 | .01 |
| 93 | Mike Croel | .05 | .01 |
| 94 | John Elway | 1.25 | .50 |
| 95 | Simon Fletcher | .05 | .01 |
| 96 | Gaston Green | .05 | .01 |
| 97 | Mark Jackson | .05 | .01 |
| 98 | Keith Kartz | .05 | .01 |
| 99 | Greg Kragen | .05 | .01 |
| 100 | Greg Lewis | .05 | .01 |
| 101 | Karl Mecklenburg | .05 | .01 |
| 102 | Derek Russell | .05 | .01 |
| 103 | Steve Sewell | .05 | .01 |
| 104 | Dennis Smith | .05 | .01 |
| 105 | David Treadwell | .05 | .01 |
| 106 | Kenny Walker | .05 | .01 |
| 107 | Doug Widell | .05 | .01 |
| 108 | Michael Young | .05 | .01 |
| 109 | Jerry Ball | .05 | .01 |
| 110 | Bennie Blades | .05 | .01 |
| 111 | Lomas Brown | .05 | .01 |
| 112 | Scott Conover RC | .05 | .01 |
| 113 | Ray Crockett | .05 | .01 |
| 114 | Mike Farr | .05 | .01 |
| 115 | Mel Gray | .10 | .02 |
| 116 | Willie Green | .05 | .01 |
| 117 | Tracy Hayworth RC | .05 | .01 |
| 118 | Erik Kramer | .10 | .02 |
| 119 | Herman Moore | .25 | .08 |
| 120 | Dan Owens | .05 | .01 |
| 121 | Rodney Peete | .10 | .02 |
| 122 | Brett Perriman | .05 | .01 |
| 123 | Barry Sanders | 1.25 | .50 |
| 124 | Chris Spielman | .10 | .02 |
| 125 | Marc Spindler | .05 | .01 |
| 126 | Tony Bennett | .05 | .01 |
| 127 | Matt Brock | .05 | .01 |
| 128 | LeRoy Butler | .05 | .01 |
| 129 | Johnny Holland | .05 | .01 |
| 130 | Perry Kemp | .05 | .01 |
| 131 | Don Majkowski | .05 | .01 |
| 132 | Mark Murphy | .05 | .01 |
| 133 | Brian Noble | .05 | .01 |
| 134 | Bryce Paup | .05 | .01 |
| 135 | Sterling Sharpe | .25 | .08 |
| 136 | Scott Stephen | .05 | .01 |
| 137 | Darrell Thompson | .05 | .01 |
| 138 | Mike Tomczak | .05 | .01 |
| 139 | Esera Tuaolo | .05 | .01 |
| 140 | Keith Woodside | .05 | .01 |
| 141 | Ray Childress | .05 | .01 |
| 142 | Cris Dishman | .05 | .01 |
| 143 | Curtis Duncan | .05 | .01 |
| 144 | John Flannery | .05 | .01 |
| 145 | William Fuller | .10 | .02 |
| 146 | Ernest Givins | .10 | .02 |
| 147 | Haywood Jeffires | .10 | .02 |
| 148 | Sean Jones | .10 | .02 |
| 149 | Lamar Lathon | .05 | .01 |
| 150 | Bruce Matthews | .05 | .01 |
| 151 | Bubba McDowell | .05 | .01 |
| 152 | Johnny Meads | .05 | .01 |
| 153 | Warren Moon | .25 | .08 |
| 154 | Mike Munchak | .10 | .02 |
| 155 | Al Smith | .05 | .01 |
| 156 | Doug Smith | .05 | .01 |
| 157 | Lorenzo White | .10 | .02 |
| 158 | Michael Ball | .05 | .01 |
| 159 | Chip Banks | .05 | .01 |
| 160 | Duane Bickett | .05 | .01 |
| 161 | Bill Brooks | .05 | .01 |
| 162 | Ken Clark | .05 | .01 |
| 163 | Jon Hand | .05 | .01 |
| 164 | Jeff Herrod | .05 | .01 |
| 165 | Jessie Hester | .05 | .01 |
| 166 | Scott Radecic | .05 | .01 |
| 167 | Rohn Stark | .05 | .01 |
| 168 | Clarence Verdin | .05 | .01 |
| 169 | John Alt | .05 | .01 |
| 170 | Tim Barnett | .05 | .01 |
| 171 | Tim Grunhard | .05 | .01 |
| 172 | Dino Hackett | .05 | .01 |
| 173 | Jonathan Hayes | .05 | .01 |
| 174 | Bill Maas | .05 | .01 |
| 175 | Chris Martin | .05 | .01 |
| 176 | Christian Okoye | .10 | .02 |
| 177 | Stephone Paige | .05 | .01 |
| 178 | Jayice Pearson RC | .05 | .01 |
| 179 | Kevin Porter | .05 | .01 |
| 180 | Kevin Ross | .05 | .01 |
| 181 | Dan Saleaumua | .05 | .01 |
| 182 | Tracy Simien RC | .05 | .01 |
| 183 | Neil Smith | .25 | .08 |
| 184 | Derrick Thomas | .25 | .08 |
| 185 | Robb Thomas | .05 | .01 |
| 186 | Mark Vlasic | .05 | .01 |
| 187 | Barry Word | .05 | .01 |
| 188 | Marcus Allen | .25 | .08 |
| 189 | Eddie Anderson | .05 | .01 |
| 190 | Nick Bell | .05 | .01 |
| 191 | Tim Brown | .25 | .08 |
| 192 | Scott Davis | .05 | .01 |
| 193 | Riki Ellison | .05 | .01 |
| 194 | Mervyn Fernandez | .05 | .01 |
| 195 | Willie Gault | .10 | .02 |
| 196 | Jeff Gossett | .05 | .01 |
| 197 | Ethan Horton | .05 | .01 |
| 198 | Jeff Jaeger | .05 | .01 |
| 199 | Howie Long | .25 | .08 |
| 200 | Ronnie Lott | .10 | .02 |
| 201 | Todd Marinovich | .05 | .01 |
| 202 | Don Mosebar | .05 | .01 |
| 203 | Jay Schroeder | .05 | .01 |
| 204 | Greg Townsend | .05 | .01 |
| 205 | Lionel Washington | .05 | .01 |
| 206 | Steve Wisniewski | .05 | .01 |
| 207 | Flipper Anderson | .05 | .01 |
| 208 | Bern Brostek | .05 | .01 |
| 209 | Robert Delpino | .05 | .01 |
| 210 | Henry Ellard | .10 | .02 |
| 211 | Jim Everett | .10 | .02 |
| 212 | Cleveland Gary | .05 | .01 |
| 213 | Kevin Greene | .10 | .02 |
| 214 | Darryl Henley | .05 | .01 |
| 215 | Damone Johnson | .05 | .01 |
| 216 | Larry Kelm | .05 | .01 |
| 217 | Todd Lyght | .05 | .01 |
| 218 | Jackie Slater | .05 | .01 |
| 219 | Michael Stewart | .05 | .01 |
| 220 | Pat Terrell UER | .05 | .01 |
| 221 | Robert Young | .05 | .01 |
| 222 | Mark Clayton | .10 | .02 |
| 223 | Bryan Cox | .10 | .02 |
| 224 | Aaron Craver | .05 | .01 |
| 225 | Jeff Cross | .05 | .01 |
| 226 | Mark Duper | .05 | .01 |
| 227 | Harry Galbreath | .05 | .01 |
| 228 | David Griggs | .05 | .01 |
| 229 | Mark Higgs | .05 | .01 |
| 230 | Vestee Jackson | .05 | .01 |
| 231 | John Offerdahl | .05 | .01 |
| 232 | Louis Oliver | .05 | .01 |
| 233 | Tony Paige | .05 | .01 |
| 234 | Reggie Roby | .05 | .01 |
| 235 | Sammie Smith | .05 | .01 |
| 236 | Pete Stoyanovich | .05 | .01 |
| 237 | Richmond Webb | .05 | .01 |
| 238 | Terry Allen | .25 | .08 |
| 239 | Ray Berry | .05 | .01 |
| 240 | Joey Browner | .05 | .01 |
| 241 | Anthony Carter | .10 | .02 |
| 242 | Cris Carter | .50 | .20 |
| 243 | Chris Doleman | .05 | .01 |
| 244 | Rich Gannon | .25 | .08 |
| 245 | Tim Irwin | .05 | .01 |
| 246 | Steve Jordan | .05 | .01 |
| 247 | Carl Lee | .05 | .01 |
| 248 | Randall McDaniel | .10 | .02 |
| 249 | Mike Merriweather | .05 | .01 |
| 250 | Harry Newsome | .05 | .01 |
| 251 | John Randle | .10 | .02 |
| 252 | Henry Thomas | .05 | .01 |
| 253 | Herschel Walker | .10 | .02 |
| 254 | Ray Agnew | .05 | .01 |
| 255 | Bruce Armstrong | .05 | .01 |
| 256 | Vincent Brown | .05 | .01 |
| 257 | Marv Cook | .05 | .01 |
| 258 | Irving Fryar | .10 | .02 |
| 259 | Pat Harlow | .05 | .01 |
| 260 | Tommy Hodson | .05 | .01 |
| 261 | Maurice Hurst | .05 | .01 |
| 262 | Ronnie Lippett | .05 | .01 |
| 263 | Eugene Lockhart | .05 | .01 |
| 264 | Greg McMurtry | .05 | .01 |
| 265 | Hugh Millen | .05 | .01 |
| 266 | Leonard Russell | .10 | .02 |
| 267 | Andre Tippett | .05 | .01 |
| 268 | Brent Williams | .05 | .01 |
| 269 | Morten Andersen | .05 | .01 |

| | | |
|---|---|---|
| ☐ 270 Gene Alkins | .05 | .01 |
| ☐ 271 Wesley Carroll | .05 | .01 |
| ☐ 272 Jim Dombrowski | .05 | .01 |
| ☐ 273 Quinn Early | .10 | .02 |
| ☐ 274 Gill Fenerty | .05 | .01 |
| ☐ 275 Bobby Hebert | .05 | .01 |
| ☐ 276 Joel Hilgenberg | .05 | .01 |
| ☐ 277 Rickey Jackson | .05 | .01 |
| ☐ 278 Vaughan Johnson | .05 | .01 |
| ☐ 279 Eric Martin | .05 | .01 |
| ☐ 280 Brett Maxie | .05 | .01 |
| ☐ 281 Fred McAfee RC | .05 | .01 |
| ☐ 282 Sam Mills | .05 | .01 |
| ☐ 283 Pat Swilling | .10 | .02 |
| ☐ 284 Floyd Turner | .05 | .01 |
| ☐ 285 Steve Walsh | .05 | .01 |
| ☐ 286 Frank Warren | .05 | .01 |
| ☐ 287 Stephen Baker | .05 | .01 |
| ☐ 288 Maurice Carthon | .05 | .01 |
| ☐ 289 Mark Collins | .05 | .01 |
| ☐ 290 John Elliott | .05 | .01 |
| ☐ 291 Myron Guyton | .05 | .01 |
| ☐ 292 Rodney Hampton | .10 | .02 |
| ☐ 293 Jeff Hostetler | .10 | .02 |
| ☐ 294 Mark Ingram | .05 | .01 |
| ☐ 295 Pepper Johnson | .05 | .01 |
| ☐ 296 Sean Landeta | .05 | .01 |
| ☐ 297 Leonard Marshall | .05 | .01 |
| ☐ 298 Dave Meggett | .10 | .02 |
| ☐ 299 Bart Oates | .05 | .01 |
| ☐ 300 Phil Simms | .10 | .02 |
| ☐ 301 Reyna Thompson | .05 | .01 |
| ☐ 302 Lewis Tillman | .05 | .01 |
| ☐ 303 Brad Baxter | .05 | .01 |
| ☐ 304 Kyle Clifton | .05 | .01 |
| ☐ 305 James Hasty | .05 | .01 |
| ☐ 306 Joe Kelly | .05 | .01 |
| ☐ 307 Jeff Lageman | .05 | .01 |
| ☐ 308 Mo Lewis | .05 | .01 |
| ☐ 309 Erik McMillan | .05 | .01 |
| ☐ 310 Rob Moore | .10 | .02 |
| ☐ 311 Tony Stargell | .05 | .01 |
| ☐ 312 Jim Sweeney | .05 | .01 |
| ☐ 313 Marvin Washington | .05 | .01 |
| ☐ 314 Lonnie Young | .05 | .01 |
| ☐ 315 Eric Allen | .05 | .01 |
| ☐ 316 Fred Barnett | .25 | .08 |
| ☐ 317 Jerome Brown | .05 | .01 |
| ☐ 318 Keith Byars | .05 | .01 |
| ☐ 319 Wes Hopkins | .05 | .01 |
| ☐ 320 Keith Jackson | .10 | .02 |
| ☐ 321 James Joseph | .05 | .01 |
| ☐ 322 Seth Joyner | .10 | .02 |
| ☐ 323 Jeff Kemp | .05 | .01 |
| ☐ 324 Roger Ruzek | .05 | .01 |
| ☐ 325 Clyde Simmons | .05 | .01 |
| ☐ 326 William Thomas | .05 | .01 |
| ☐ 327 Reggie White | .25 | .08 |
| ☐ 328 Calvin Williams | .10 | .02 |
| ☐ 329 Rich Camarillo | .05 | .01 |
| ☐ 330 Ken Harvey | .05 | .01 |
| ☐ 331 Eric Hill | .05 | .01 |
| ☐ 332 Johnny Johnson | .05 | .01 |
| ☐ 333 Ernie Jones | .05 | .01 |
| ☐ 334 Tim Jorden | .05 | .01 |
| ☐ 335 Tim McDonald | .05 | .01 |
| ☐ 336 Freddie Joe Nunn | .05 | .01 |
| ☐ 337 Luis Sharpe | .05 | .01 |
| ☐ 338 Eric Swann | .10 | .02 |
| ☐ 339 Aeneas Williams | .10 | .02 |
| ☐ 340 Gary Anderson K | .05 | .01 |
| ☐ 341 Bubby Brister | .05 | .01 |
| ☐ 342 Adrian Cooper | .05 | .01 |
| ☐ 343 Barry Foster | .10 | .02 |
| ☐ 344 Eric Green | .05 | .01 |
| ☐ 345 Bryan Hinkle | .05 | .01 |
| ☐ 346 Tunch Ilkin | .05 | .01 |
| ☐ 347 Carnell Lake | .05 | .01 |
| ☐ 348 Louis Lipps | .05 | .01 |
| ☐ 349 David Little | .05 | .01 |
| ☐ 350 Greg Lloyd | .10 | .02 |
| ☐ 351 Neil O'Donnell | .25 | .08 |
| ☐ 352 Dwight Stone | .05 | .01 |
| ☐ 353 Rod Woodson | .25 | .08 |

| | | |
|---|---|---|
| ☐ 354 Rod Bernstine | .05 | .01 |
| ☐ 355 Eric Bieniemy | .05 | .01 |
| ☐ 356 Marion Butts | .05 | .01 |
| ☐ 357 Gill Byrd | .05 | .01 |
| ☐ 358 John Friesz | .10 | .02 |
| ☐ 359 Burt Grossman | .05 | .01 |
| ☐ 360 Courtney Hall | .05 | .01 |
| ☐ 361 Ronnie Harmon | .05 | .01 |
| ☐ 362 Shawn Jefferson | .05 | .01 |
| ☐ 363 Nate Lewis | .05 | .01 |
| ☐ 364 Craig McEwen RC | .05 | .01 |
| ☐ 365 Eric Moten | .05 | .01 |
| ☐ 366 Joe Phillips | .05 | .01 |
| ☐ 367 Gary Plummer | .05 | .01 |
| ☐ 368 Henry Rolling | .05 | .01 |
| ☐ 369 Broderick Thompson | .05 | .01 |
| ☐ 370 Harris Barton | .05 | .01 |
| ☐ 371 Steve Bono RC | .25 | .08 |
| ☐ 372 Todd Bowles | .05 | .01 |
| ☐ 373 Dexter Carter | .05 | .01 |
| ☐ 374 Michael Carter | .05 | .01 |
| ☐ 375 Mike Cofer | .05 | .01 |
| ☐ 376 Keith DeLong | .05 | .01 |
| ☐ 377 Charles Haley | .10 | .02 |
| ☐ 378 Merton Hanks | .10 | .02 |
| ☐ 379 Tim Harris | .05 | .01 |
| ☐ 380 Brent Jones | .10 | .02 |
| ☐ 381 Guy McIntyre | .05 | .01 |
| ☐ 382 Tom Rathman | .05 | .01 |
| ☐ 383 Bill Romanowski | .05 | .01 |
| ☐ 384 Jesse Sapolu | .05 | .01 |
| ☐ 385 John Taylor | .10 | .02 |
| ☐ 386 Steve Young | .60 | .25 |
| ☐ 387 Robert Blackmon | .05 | .01 |
| ☐ 388 Brian Blades | .10 | .02 |
| ☐ 389 Jacob Green | .05 | .01 |
| ☐ 390 Dwayne Harper | .05 | .01 |
| ☐ 391 Andy Heck | .05 | .01 |
| ☐ 392 Tommy Kane | .05 | .01 |
| ☐ 393 John Kasay | .05 | .01 |
| ☐ 394 Cortez Kennedy | .10 | .02 |
| ☐ 395 Bryan Millard | .05 | .01 |
| ☐ 396 Rufus Porter | .05 | .01 |
| ☐ 397 Eugene Robinson | .05 | .01 |
| ☐ 398 John L. Williams | .05 | .01 |
| ☐ 399 Terry Wooden | .05 | .01 |
| ☐ 400 Gary Anderson RB | .05 | .01 |
| ☐ 401 Ian Beckles | .05 | .01 |
| ☐ 402 Mark Carrier WR | .10 | .02 |
| ☐ 403 Reggie Cobb | .05 | .01 |
| ☐ 404 Lawrence Dawsey | .10 | .02 |
| ☐ 405 Ron Hall | .05 | .01 |
| ☐ 406 Keith McCants | .05 | .01 |
| ☐ 407 Charles McRae | .05 | .01 |
| ☐ 408 Tim Newton | .05 | .01 |
| ☐ 409 Jesse Solomon | .05 | .01 |
| ☐ 410 Vinny Testaverde | .10 | .02 |
| ☐ 411 Broderick Thomas | .05 | .01 |
| ☐ 412 Robert Wilson | .05 | .01 |
| ☐ 413 Jeff Bostic | .05 | .01 |
| ☐ 414 Earnest Byner | .05 | .01 |
| ☐ 415 Gary Clark | .25 | .08 |
| ☐ 416 Andre Collins | .05 | .01 |
| ☐ 417 Brad Edwards | .05 | .01 |
| ☐ 418 Kurt Gouveia | .05 | .01 |
| ☐ 419 Darrell Green | .05 | .01 |
| ☐ 420 Joe Jacoby | .05 | .01 |
| ☐ 421 Jim Lachey | .05 | .01 |
| ☐ 422 Chip Lohmiller | .05 | .01 |
| ☐ 423 Charles Mann | .05 | .01 |
| ☐ 424 Wilber Marshall | .05 | .01 |
| ☐ 425 Ron Middleton RC | .05 | .01 |
| ☐ 426 Brian Mitchell | .10 | .02 |
| ☐ 427 Art Monk | .10 | .02 |
| ☐ 428 Mark Rypien | .05 | .01 |
| ☐ 429 Ricky Sanders | .05 | .01 |
| ☐ 430 Mark Schlereth RC | .05 | .01 |
| ☐ 431 Fred Stokes | .05 | .01 |
| ☐ 432 Edgar Bennett RC | .25 | .08 |
| ☐ 433 Brian Bollinger RC | .05 | .01 |
| ☐ 434 Joe Bowden RC | .05 | .01 |
| ☐ 435 Terrell Buckley RC | .05 | .01 |
| ☐ 436 Willie Clay RC | .05 | .01 |
| ☐ 437 Steve Gordon RC | .05 | .01 |

| | | |
|---|---|---|
| ☐ 438 Keith Hamilton RC | .10 | .02 |
| ☐ 439 Carlos Huerta | .05 | .01 |
| ☐ 440 Matt LaBounty RC | .05 | .01 |
| ☐ 441 Amp Lee RC | .05 | .01 |
| ☐ 442 Ricardo McDonald RC | .05 | .01 |
| ☐ 443 Chris Mims RC | .10 | .02 |
| ☐ 444 Michael Moody RC | .05 | .01 |
| ☐ 445 Patrick Rowe RC | .05 | .01 |
| ☐ 446 Leon Searcy RC | .10 | .02 |
| ☐ 447 Siran Stacy RC | .05 | .01 |
| ☐ 448 Kevin Turner RC | .05 | .01 |
| ☐ 449 Tommy Vardell RC | .10 | .02 |
| ☐ 450 Bob Whitfield RC | .05 | .01 |
| ☐ 451 Darryl Williams RC | .05 | .01 |
| ☐ 452 Thurman Thomas LL | .10 | .02 |
| ☐ 453 Emmitt Smith LL | .75 | .30 |
| ☐ 454 Haywood Jeffires LL | .05 | .01 |
| ☐ 455 Michael Irvin LL | .10 | .02 |
| ☐ 456 Mark Clayton LL | .05 | .01 |
| ☐ 457 Barry Sanders LL | .60 | .25 |
| ☐ 458 Pete Stoyanovich LL | .05 | .01 |
| ☐ 459 Chip Lohmiller LL | .05 | .01 |
| ☐ 460 William Fuller LL | .05 | .01 |
| ☐ 461 Pat Swilling LL | .05 | .01 |
| ☐ 462 Ronnie Lott LL | .05 | .01 |
| ☐ 463 Ray Crockett LL | .05 | .01 |
| ☐ 464 Tim McKyer LL | .05 | .01 |
| ☐ 465 Aeneas Williams LL | .05 | .01 |
| ☐ 466 Rod Woodson LL | .10 | .02 |
| ☐ 467 Mel Gray LL | .05 | .01 |
| ☐ 468 Nate Lewis LL | .05 | .01 |
| ☐ 469 Steve Young LL | .30 | .10 |
| ☐ 470 Reggie Roby LL | .05 | .01 |
| ☐ 471 John Elway PV | .60 | .25 |
| ☐ 472 Ronnie Lott PV | .05 | .01 |
| ☐ 473 Art Monk PV UER | .05 | .01 |
| ☐ 474 Warren Moon PV | .10 | .02 |
| ☐ 475 Emmitt Smith PV | .75 | .30 |
| ☐ 476 Thurman Thomas PV | .10 | .02 |
| ☐ 477 Checklist 1-120 | .05 | .01 |
| ☐ 478 Checklist 121-240 | .05 | .01 |
| ☐ 479 Checklist 241-360 | .05 | .01 |
| ☐ 480 Checklist 361-480 | .05 | .01 |

## 1993 Fleer

| | | |
|---|---|---|
| ☐ COMPLETE SET (500) | 20.00 | 10.00 |
| ☐ 1 Dan Saleaumua | .05 | .01 |
| ☐ 2 Bryan Cox | .05 | .01 |
| ☐ 3 Dermontti Dawson | .05 | .01 |
| ☐ 4 Michael Jackson | .10 | .02 |
| ☐ 5 Calvin Williams | .10 | .02 |
| ☐ 6 Terry McDaniel | .05 | .01 |
| ☐ 7 Jack Del Rio | .05 | .01 |
| ☐ 8 Steve Atwater | .05 | .01 |
| ☐ 9 Ernie Jones | .05 | .01 |
| ☐ 10 Brad Muster | .05 | .01 |
| ☐ 11 Harold Green | .05 | .01 |
| ☐ 12 Eric Bieniemy | .05 | .01 |
| ☐ 13 Eric Dorsey | .05 | .01 |
| ☐ 14 Fred Barnett | .10 | .02 |
| ☐ 15 Cleveland Gary | .05 | .01 |
| ☐ 16 Darion Conner | .05 | .01 |
| ☐ 17 Jerry Ball | .05 | .01 |
| ☐ 18 Tony Casillas | .05 | .01 |
| ☐ 19 Brian Blades | .10 | .02 |
| ☐ 20 Tony Bennett | .05 | .01 |
| ☐ 21 Reggie Cobb | .05 | .01 |
| ☐ 22 Kurt Gouveia | .05 | .01 |

|  |  | | |
|---|---|---|---|
| 23 | Greg McMurtry | .05 | .01 |
| 24 | Kyle Clifton | .05 | .01 |
| 25 | Trace Armstrong | .05 | .01 |
| 26 | Terry Allen | .25 | .08 |
| 27 | Steve Bono | .10 | .02 |
| 28 | Barry Word | .05 | .01 |
| 29 | Mark Duper | .05 | .01 |
| 30 | Nate Newton | .10 | .02 |
| 31 | Will Wolford | .05 | .01 |
| 32 | Curtis Duncan | .05 | .01 |
| 33 | Nick Bell | .05 | .01 |
| 34 | Don Beebe | .05 | .01 |
| 35 | Mike Croel | .05 | .01 |
| 36 | Rich Camarillo | .05 | .01 |
| 37 | Wade Wilson | .05 | .01 |
| 38 | John Taylor | .10 | .02 |
| 39 | Marion Butts | .05 | .01 |
| 40 | Rodney Hampton | .10 | .02 |
| 41 | Seth Joyner | .05 | .01 |
| 42 | Wilber Marshall | .05 | .01 |
| 43 | Bobby Hebert | .05 | .01 |
| 44 | Bennie Blades | .05 | .01 |
| 45 | Thomas Everett | .05 | .01 |
| 46 | Ricky Sanders | .05 | .01 |
| 47 | Matt Brock | .05 | .01 |
| 48 | Lawrence Dawsey | .05 | .01 |
| 49 | Brad Edwards | .05 | .01 |
| 50 | Vincent Brown | .05 | .01 |
| 51 | Jeff Lageman | .05 | .01 |
| 52 | Mark Carrier DB | .05 | .01 |
| 53 | Cris Carter | .25 | .08 |
| 54 | Brent Jones | .10 | .02 |
| 55 | Barry Foster | .10 | .02 |
| 56 | Derrick Thomas | .25 | .08 |
| 57 | Scott Zolak | .05 | .01 |
| 58 | Mark Stepnoski | .05 | .01 |
| 59 | Eric Metcalf | .10 | .02 |
| 60 | Al Smith | .05 | .01 |
| 61 | Ronnie Harmon | .05 | .01 |
| 62 | Cornelius Bennett | .10 | .02 |
| 63 | Karl Mecklenburg | .05 | .01 |
| 64 | Chris Chandler | .10 | .02 |
| 65 | Toi Cook | .05 | .01 |
| 66 | Tim Krumrie | .05 | .01 |
| 67 | Gill Byrd | .05 | .01 |
| 68 | Mark Jackson | .05 | .01 |
| 69 | Tim Harris | .05 | .01 |
| 70 | Shane Conlan | .05 | .01 |
| 71 | Moe Gardner | .05 | .01 |
| 72 | Lomas Brown | .05 | .01 |
| 73 | Charles Haley | .10 | .02 |
| 74 | Mark Rypien | .05 | .01 |
| 75 | LeRoy Butler | .05 | .01 |
| 76 | Steve DeBerg | .05 | .01 |
| 77 | Darrell Green | .05 | .01 |
| 78 | Marv Cook | .05 | .01 |
| 79 | Chris Burkett | .05 | .01 |
| 80 | Richard Dent | .10 | .02 |
| 81 | Roger Craig | .10 | .02 |
| 82 | Amp Lee | .05 | .01 |
| 83 | Eric Green | .05 | .01 |
| 84 | Willie Davis | .25 | .08 |
| 85 | Mark Higgs | .05 | .01 |
| 86 | Carlton Haselrig | .05 | .01 |
| 87 | Tommy Vardell | .05 | .01 |
| 88 | Haywood Jeffires | .10 | .02 |
| 89 | Tim Brown | .25 | .08 |
| 90 | Randall McDaniel | .10 | .02 |
| 91 | John Elway | 1.50 | .60 |
| 92 | Ken Harvey | .05 | .01 |
| 93 | Joel Hilgenberg | .05 | .01 |
| 94 | Steve Wallace | .05 | .01 |
| 95 | Stan Humphries | .10 | .02 |
| 96 | Greg Jackson | .05 | .01 |
| 97 | Clyde Simmons | .05 | .01 |
| 98 | Jim Everett | .10 | .02 |
| 99 | Michael Haynes | .10 | .02 |
| 100 | Mel Gray | .10 | .02 |
| 101 | Alvin Harper | .10 | .02 |
| 102 | Art Monk | .10 | .02 |
| 103 | Brett Favre | 2.00 | .75 |
| 104 | Keith McCants | .05 | .01 |
| 105 | Charles Mann | .05 | .01 |
| 106 | Leonard Russell | .10 | .02 |
| 107 | Mo Lewis | .05 | .01 |
| 108 | Shaun Gayle | .05 | .01 |
| 109 | Chris Doleman | .05 | .01 |
| 110 | Tim McDonald | .05 | .01 |
| 111 | Louis Oliver | .05 | .01 |
| 112 | Greg Lloyd | .10 | .02 |
| 113 | Chip Banks | .05 | .01 |
| 114 | Sean Jones | .05 | .01 |
| 115 | Ethan Horton | .05 | .01 |
| 116 | Kenneth Davis | .05 | .01 |
| 117 | Simon Fletcher | .05 | .01 |
| 118 | Johnny Johnson | .05 | .01 |
| 119 | Vaughan Johnson | .05 | .01 |
| 120 | Derrick Fenner | .05 | .01 |
| 121 | Nate Lewis | .05 | .01 |
| 122 | Pepper Johnson | .05 | .01 |
| 123 | Heath Sherman | .05 | .01 |
| 124 | Darryl Henley | .05 | .01 |
| 125 | Pierce Holt | .05 | .01 |
| 126 | Herman Moore | .25 | .08 |
| 127 | Michael Irvin | .25 | .08 |
| 128 | Tommy Kane | .05 | .01 |
| 129 | Jackie Harris | .05 | .01 |
| 130 | Hardy Nickerson | .10 | .02 |
| 131 | Chip Lohmiller | .05 | .01 |
| 132 | Andre Tippett | .05 | .01 |
| 133 | Leonard Marshall | .05 | .01 |
| 134 | Craig Heyward | .10 | .02 |
| 135 | Anthony Carter | .10 | .02 |
| 136 | Tom Rathman | .05 | .01 |
| 137 | Lorenzo White | .05 | .01 |
| 138 | Nick Lowery | .05 | .01 |
| 139 | John Offerdahl | .05 | .01 |
| 140 | Neil O'Donnell | .25 | .08 |
| 141 | Clarence Verdin | .05 | .01 |
| 142 | Ernest Givins | .10 | .02 |
| 143 | Jeff Wright | .05 | .01 |
| 144 | Michael Brooks | .05 | .01 |
| 145 | Freddie Joe Nunn | .05 | .01 |
| 146 | William Perry | .10 | .02 |
| 147 | Daniel Stubbs | .05 | .01 |
| 148 | Morten Andersen | .05 | .01 |
| 149 | Dave Meggett | .05 | .01 |
| 150 | Andre Waters | .05 | .01 |
| 151 | Todd Lyght | .05 | .01 |
| 152 | Chris Miller | .10 | .02 |
| 153 | Rodney Peete | .05 | .01 |
| 154 | Jim Jeffcoat | .05 | .01 |
| 155 | Cortez Kennedy | .10 | .02 |
| 156 | Johnny Holland | .05 | .01 |
| 157 | Ricky Reynolds | .05 | .01 |
| 158 | Kevin Greene | .10 | .02 |
| 159 | Jeff Herrod | .05 | .01 |
| 160 | Bruce Matthews | .05 | .01 |
| 161 | Anthony Smith | .05 | .01 |
| 162 | Henry Jones | .05 | .01 |
| 163 | Rob Burnett | .05 | .01 |
| 164 | Eric Swann | .10 | .02 |
| 165 | Tom Waddle | .05 | .01 |
| 166 | Alfred Williams | .05 | .01 |
| 167 | Darren Carrington RC | .05 | .01 |
| 168 | Mike Sherrard | .05 | .01 |
| 169 | Frank Reich | .10 | .02 |
| 170 | Anthony Newman RC | .05 | .01 |
| 171 | Mike Pritchard | .10 | .02 |
| 172 | Andre Ware | .05 | .01 |
| 173 | Daryl Johnston | .25 | .08 |
| 174 | Rufus Porter | .05 | .01 |
| 175 | Reggie White | .25 | .08 |
| 176 | Charles Mincy PC | .05 | .01 |
| 177 | Pete Stoyanovich | .05 | .01 |
| 178 | Rod Woodson | .25 | .08 |
| 179 | Anthony Johnson | .10 | .02 |
| 180 | Cody Carlson | .05 | .01 |
| 181 | Gaston Green | .05 | .01 |
| 182 | Audray McMillian | .05 | .01 |
| 183 | Aeneas Williams | .05 | .01 |
| 184 | Jarrod Bunch | .05 | .01 |
| 185 | Dennis Smith | .05 | .01 |
| 186 | Quinn Early | .10 | .02 |
| 187 | James Hasty | .05 | .01 |
| 190 | Darryl Talley | .05 | .01 |
| 191 | Jon Vaughn | .05 | .01 |
| 192 | Andre Rison | .10 | .02 |
| 193 | Kelvin Pritchett | .05 | .01 |
| 194 | Ken Norton Jr. | .10 | .02 |
| 195 | Chris Warren | .10 | .02 |
| 196 | Sterling Sharpe | .25 | .08 |
| 197 | Christian Okoye | .05 | .01 |
| 198 | Richmond Webb | .05 | .01 |
| 199 | James Francis | .05 | .01 |
| 200 | Reggie Langhorne | .05 | .01 |
| 201 | J.J. Birden | .05 | .01 |
| 202 | Aaron Wallace | .05 | .01 |
| 203 | Henry Thomas | .05 | .01 |
| 204 | Clay Matthews | .10 | .02 |
| 205 | Robert Massey | .05 | .01 |
| 206 | Donnel Woolford | .05 | .01 |
| 207 | Ricky Watters | .25 | .08 |
| 208 | Wayne Martin | .05 | .01 |
| 209 | Rob Moore | .10 | .02 |
| 210 | Steve Tasker | .10 | .02 |
| 211 | Jackie Slater | .05 | .01 |
| 212 | Steve Young | .75 | .30 |
| 213 | Barry Sanders | 1.25 | .50 |
| 214 | Jay Novacek | .10 | .02 |
| 215 | Eugene Robinson | .05 | .01 |
| 216 | Duane Bickett | .05 | .01 |
| 217 | Broderick Thomas | .05 | .01 |
| 218 | David Fulcher | .05 | .01 |
| 219 | Rohn Stark | .05 | .01 |
| 220 | Warren Moon | .25 | .08 |
| 221 | Steve Wisniewski | .05 | .01 |
| 222 | Nate Odomes | .05 | .01 |
| 223 | Shannon Sharpe | .25 | .08 |
| 224 | Byron Evans | .05 | .01 |
| 225 | Mark Collins | .05 | .01 |
| 226 | Rod Bernstine | .05 | .01 |
| 227 | Sam Mills | .05 | .01 |
| 228 | Marvin Washington | .05 | .01 |
| 229 | Thurman Thomas | .25 | .08 |
| 830 | Brent Williams | .05 | .01 |
| 231 | Jessie Tuggle | .05 | .01 |
| 232 | Chris Spielman | .10 | .02 |
| 233 | Emmitt Smith | 1.50 | .60 |
| 234 | John L. Williams | .05 | .01 |
| 235 | Jeff Cross | .05 | .01 |
| 236 | Chris Doleman AW | .05 | .01 |
| 237 | John Elway AW | .75 | .30 |
| 238 | Barry Foster AW | .05 | .01 |
| 239 | Cortez Kennedy AW | .05 | .01 |
| 240 | Steve Young AW | .40 | .15 |
| 241 | Barry Foster LL | .05 | .01 |
| 242 | Warren Moon LL | .05 | .01 |
| 243 | Sterling Sharpe LL | .05 | .01 |
| 244 | Emmitt Smith LL | .75 | .30 |
| 245 | Thurman Thomas LL | .10 | .02 |
| 246 | Michael Irvin PV | .10 | .02 |
| 247 | Steve Young PV | .40 | .15 |
| 248 | Barry Foster PV | .05 | .01 |
| 249 | Checklist | .05 | .01 |
| 250 | Checklist | .05 | .01 |
| 251 | Checklist | .05 | .01 |
| 252 | Checklist | .05 | .01 |
| 253 | Troy Aikman AW | .40 | .15 |
| 254 | Jason Hanson AW | .05 | .01 |
| 255 | Carl Pickens AW | .10 | .02 |
| 256 | Santana Dotson AW | .05 | .01 |
| 257 | Dale Carter AW | .05 | .01 |
| 258 | Clyde Simmons LL | .05 | .01 |
| 259 | Audray McMillian LL | .05 | .01 |
| 260 | Henry Jones LL | .05 | .01 |
| 261 | Deion Sanders LL | .25 | .08 |
| 262 | Haywood Jeffires LL | .05 | .01 |
| 263 | Deion Sanders PV | .25 | .08 |
| 264 | Andre Reed PV | .10 | .02 |
| 265 | Vince Workman | .05 | .01 |
| 266 | Robert Brown | .05 | .01 |
| 267 | Ray Agnew | .05 | .01 |
| 268 | Ronnie Lott | .10 | .02 |
| 269 | Wesley Carroll | .05 | .01 |
| 270 | John Randle | .10 | .02 |
| 271 | Rodney Culver | .05 | .01 |
| 272 | David Alexander | .05 | .01 |
| 273 | Troy Aikman | .75 | .30 |
| 274 | Bernie Kosar | .10 | .02 |

| | | |
|---|---|---|
| ☐ 275 Scott Case | .05 | .01 |
| ☐ 276 Dan McGwire | .05 | .01 |
| ☐ 277 John Alt | .05 | .01 |
| ☐ 278 Dan Marino | 1.50 | .60 |
| ☐ 279 Santana Dotson | .10 | .02 |
| ☐ 280 Johnny Mitchell | .05 | .01 |
| ☐ 281 Alonzo Spellman | .05 | .01 |
| ☐ 282 Adrian Cooper | .05 | .01 |
| ☐ 283 Gary Clark | .10 | .02 |
| ☐ 284 Vance Johnson | .05 | .01 |
| ☐ 285 Eric Martin | .05 | .01 |
| ☐ 286 Jesse Solomon | .05 | .01 |
| ☐ 287 Carl Banks | .05 | .01 |
| ☐ 288 Harris Barton | .05 | .01 |
| ☐ 289 Jim Harbaugh | .25 | .08 |
| ☐ 290 Bubba McDowell | .05 | .01 |
| ☐ 291 Anthony McDowell RC | .05 | .01 |
| ☐ 292 Terrell Buckley | .05 | .01 |
| ☐ 293 Bruce Armstrong | .05 | .01 |
| ☐ 294 Kurt Barber | .05 | .01 |
| ☐ 295 Reginald Jones | .05 | .01 |
| ☐ 296 Steve Jordan | .05 | .01 |
| ☐ 297 Kerry Cash | .05 | .01 |
| ☐ 298 Ray Crockett | .05 | .01 |
| ☐ 299 Keith Byars | .05 | .01 |
| ☐ 300 Russell Maryland | .05 | .01 |
| ☐ 301 Johnny Bailey | .05 | .01 |
| ☐ 302 Vinnie Clark | .05 | .01 |
| ☐ 303 Terry Wooden | .05 | .01 |
| ☐ 304 Harvey Williams | .10 | .02 |
| ☐ 305 Marco Coleman | .05 | .01 |
| ☐ 306 Mark Wheeler | .05 | .01 |
| ☐ 307 Greg Townsend | .05 | .01 |
| ☐ 308 Tim McGee | .05 | .01 |
| ☐ 309 Donald Evans | .05 | .01 |
| ☐ 310 Randal Hill | .05 | .01 |
| ☐ 311 Kenny Walker | .05 | .01 |
| ☐ 312 Dalton Hilliard | .05 | .01 |
| ☐ 313 Howard Ballard | .05 | .01 |
| ☐ 314 Phil Simms | .10 | .02 |
| ☐ 315 Jerry Rice | 1.00 | .40 |
| ☐ 316 Courtney Hall | .05 | .01 |
| ☐ 317 Darren Lewis | .05 | .01 |
| ☐ 318 Greg Montgomery | .05 | .01 |
| ☐ 319 Paul Gruber | .05 | .01 |
| ☐ 320 George Koonce RC | .05 | .01 |
| ☐ 321 Eugene Chung | .05 | .01 |
| ☐ 322 Mike Brim | .05 | .01 |
| ☐ 323 Patrick Hunter | .05 | .01 |
| ☐ 324 Todd Scott | .05 | .01 |
| ☐ 325 Steve Emtman | .05 | .01 |
| ☐ 326 Andy Harmon RC | .10 | .02 |
| ☐ 327 Larry Brown DB | .05 | .01 |
| ☐ 328 Chuck Cecil | .05 | .01 |
| ☐ 329 Tim McKyer | .05 | .01 |
| ☐ 330 Jeff Bryant | .05 | .01 |
| ☐ 331 Tim Barnett | .05 | .01 |
| ☐ 332 Irving Fryar | .10 | .02 |
| ☐ 333 Tyji Armstrong | .05 | .01 |
| ☐ 334 Brad Baxter | .05 | .01 |
| ☐ 335 Shane Collins | .05 | .01 |
| ☐ 336 Jeff Graham | .10 | .02 |
| ☐ 337 Ricky Proehl | .05 | .01 |
| ☐ 338 Tommy Maddox | .25 | .08 |
| ☐ 339 Jim Dombrowski | .05 | .01 |
| ☐ 340 Bill Brooks | .05 | .01 |
| ☐ 341 Dave Brown RC | .25 | .08 |
| ☐ 342 Eric Davis | .05 | .01 |
| ☐ 343 Leslie O'Neal | .10 | .02 |
| ☐ 344 Jim Morrissey | .05 | .01 |
| ☐ 345 Mike Munchak | .10 | .02 |
| ☐ 346 Ron Hall | .05 | .01 |
| ☐ 347 Brian Noble | .05 | .01 |
| ☐ 348 Chris Singleton | .05 | .01 |
| ☐ 349 Boomer Esiason | .10 | .02 |
| ☐ 350 Ray Roberts | .05 | .01 |
| ☐ 351 Gary Zimmerman | .05 | .01 |
| ☐ 352 Quentin Coryatt | .10 | .02 |
| ☐ 353 Willie Green | .05 | .01 |
| ☐ 354 Randall Cunningham | .25 | .08 |
| ☐ 355 Kevin Smith | .10 | .02 |
| ☐ 356 Michael Dean Perry | .10 | .02 |
| ☐ 357 Tim Green | .05 | .01 |
| ☐ 358 Dwayne Harper | .05 | .01 |

| | | |
|---|---|---|
| ☐ 359 Dale Carter | .05 | .01 |
| ☐ 360 Keith Jackson | .10 | .02 |
| ☐ 361 Martin Mayhew | .05 | .01 |
| ☐ 362 Brian Washington | .05 | .01 |
| ☐ 363 Earnest Byner | .05 | .01 |
| ☐ 364 D.J. Johnson | .05 | .01 |
| ☐ 365 Timm Rosenbach | .05 | .01 |
| ☐ 366 Doug Widell | .05 | .01 |
| ☐ 367 Vaughn Dunbar | .05 | .01 |
| ☐ 368 Phil Hansen | .05 | .01 |
| ☐ 369 Mike Fox | .05 | .01 |
| ☐ 370 Dana Hall | .05 | .01 |
| ☐ 371 Junior Seau | .25 | .08 |
| ☐ 372 Steve McMichael | .10 | .02 |
| ☐ 373 Eddie Robinson | .05 | .01 |
| ☐ 374 Milton Mack RC | .05 | .01 |
| ☐ 375 Mike Prior | .05 | .01 |
| ☐ 376 Jerome Henderson | .05 | .01 |
| ☐ 377 Scott Mersereau | .05 | .01 |
| ☐ 378 Neal Anderson | .05 | .01 |
| ☐ 379 Harry Newsome | .05 | .01 |
| ☐ 380 John Baylor | .05 | .01 |
| ☐ 381 Bill Fralic | .05 | .01 |
| ☐ 382 Mark Bavaro | .05 | .01 |
| ☐ 383 Robert Jones | .05 | .01 |
| ☐ 384 Tyronne Stowe | .05 | .01 |
| ☐ 385 Deion Sanders | .50 | .20 |
| ☐ 386 Robert Blackmon | .05 | .01 |
| ☐ 387 Neil Smith | .25 | .08 |
| ☐ 388 Mark Ingram | .05 | .01 |
| ☐ 389 Mark Carrier WR | .10 | .02 |
| ☐ 390 Browning Nagle | .05 | .01 |
| ☐ 391 Ricky Ervins | .05 | .01 |
| ☐ 392 Carnell Lake | .05 | .01 |
| ☐ 393 Luis Sharpe | .05 | .01 |
| ☐ 394 Greg Kragen | .05 | .01 |
| ☐ 395 Tommy Barnhardt | .05 | .01 |
| ☐ 396 Mark Kelso | .05 | .01 |
| ☐ 397 Kent Graham RC | .25 | .08 |
| ☐ 398 Bill Romanowski | .05 | .01 |
| ☐ 399 Anthony Miller | .10 | .02 |
| ☐ 400 John Roper | .05 | .01 |
| ☐ 401 Lamar Rogers | .05 | .01 |
| ☐ 402 Troy Auzenne | .05 | .01 |
| ☐ 403 Webster Slaughter | .05 | .01 |
| ☐ 404 David Brandon | .05 | .01 |
| ☐ 405 Chris Hinton | .05 | .01 |
| ☐ 406 Andy Heck | .05 | .01 |
| ☐ 407 Tracy Simien | .05 | .01 |
| ☐ 408 Troy Vincent | .05 | .01 |
| ☐ 409 Jason Hanson | .05 | .01 |
| ☐ 410 Rod Jones CB RC | .05 | .01 |
| ☐ 411 Al Noga | .05 | .01 |
| ☐ 412 Ernie Mills | .05 | .01 |
| ☐ 413 Willie Gault | .05 | .01 |
| ☐ 414 Henry Ellard | .10 | .02 |
| ☐ 415 Rickey Jackson | .05 | .01 |
| ☐ 416 Bruce Smith | .25 | .08 |
| ☐ 417 Derek Brown TE | .05 | .01 |
| ☐ 418 Kevin Fagan | .05 | .01 |
| ☐ 419 Gary Plummer | .05 | .01 |
| ☐ 420 Wendell Davis | .05 | .01 |
| ☐ 421 Craig Thompson | .05 | .01 |
| ☐ 422 Wes Hopkins | .05 | .01 |
| ☐ 423 Ray Childress | .05 | .01 |
| ☐ 424 Pat Harlow | .05 | .01 |
| ☐ 425 Howie Long | .25 | .08 |
| ☐ 426 Shane Dronett | .05 | .01 |
| ☐ 427 Sean Salisbury | .05 | .01 |
| ☐ 428 Dwight Hollier RC | .05 | .01 |
| ☐ 429 Brett Perriman | .25 | .08 |
| ☐ 430 Donald Hollas RC | .05 | .01 |
| ☐ 431 Jim Lachey | .05 | .01 |
| ☐ 432 Darren Perry | .05 | .01 |
| ☐ 433 Lionel Washington | .05 | .01 |
| ☐ 434 Sean Gilbert | .10 | .02 |
| ☐ 435 Gene Atkins | .05 | .01 |
| ☐ 436 Jim Kelly | .25 | .08 |
| ☐ 437 Neil Smith | .25 | .08 |
| ☐ 438 Don Griffin | .05 | .01 |
| ☐ 439 Jerrol Williams | .05 | .01 |
| ☐ 440 Bryce Paup | .10 | .02 |
| ☐ 441 Darryl Williams | .05 | .01 |
| ☐ 442 Vai Sikahema | .05 | .01 |

| | | |
|---|---|---|
| ☐ 443 Cris Dishman | .05 | .01 |
| ☐ 444 Kevin Mack | .05 | .01 |
| ☐ 445 Winston Moss | .05 | .01 |
| ☐ 446 Tyrone Braxton | .05 | .01 |
| ☐ 447 Mike Merriweather | .05 | .01 |
| ☐ 448 Tony Paige | .05 | .01 |
| ☐ 449 Robert Porcher | .05 | .01 |
| ☐ 450 Ricardo McDonald | .05 | .01 |
| ☐ 451 Danny Copeland | .05 | .01 |
| ☐ 452 Tony Tolbert | .05 | .01 |
| ☐ 453 Eric Dickerson | .10 | .02 |
| ☐ 454 Flipper Anderson | .05 | .01 |
| ☐ 455 Dave Krieg | .10 | .02 |
| ☐ 456 Brad Lamb RC | .05 | .01 |
| ☐ 457 Bart Oates | .05 | .01 |
| ☐ 458 Guy McIntyre | .05 | .01 |
| ☐ 459 Stanley Richard | .05 | .01 |
| ☐ 460 Edgar Bennett | .25 | .08 |
| ☐ 461 Pat Carter | .05 | .01 |
| ☐ 462 Eric Allen | .05 | .01 |
| ☐ 463 William Fuller | .05 | .01 |
| ☐ 464 James Jones DT | .05 | .01 |
| ☐ 465 Chester McGlockton | .10 | .02 |
| ☐ 466 Charles Dimry | .05 | .01 |
| ☐ 467 Tim Grunhard | .05 | .01 |
| ☐ 468 Jarvis Williams | .05 | .01 |
| ☐ 469 Tracy Scroggins | .05 | .01 |
| ☐ 470 David Klingler | .05 | .01 |
| ☐ 471 Andre Collins | .05 | .01 |
| ☐ 472 Erik Williams | .05 | .01 |
| ☐ 473 Eddie Anderson | .05 | .01 |
| ☐ 474 Marc Boutte | .05 | .01 |
| ☐ 475 Joe Montana | 1.50 | .60 |
| ☐ 476 Andre Reed | .10 | .02 |
| ☐ 477 Lawrence Taylor | .25 | .08 |
| ☐ 478 Jeff George | .25 | .08 |
| ☐ 479 Chris Mims | .05 | .01 |
| ☐ 480 Ken Ruettgers | .05 | .01 |
| ☐ 481 Roman Phifer | .05 | .01 |
| ☐ 482 William Thomas | .05 | .01 |
| ☐ 483 Lamar Lathon | .05 | .01 |
| ☐ 484 Vinny Testaverde | .10 | .02 |
| ☐ 485 Mike Kenn | .05 | .01 |
| ☐ 486 Greg Lewis | .05 | .01 |
| ☐ 487 Chris Martin | .05 | .01 |
| ☐ 488 Maurice Hurst | .05 | .01 |
| ☐ 489 Pat Swilling | .05 | .01 |
| ☐ 490 Carl Pickens | .10 | .02 |
| ☐ 491 Tony Smith RB | .05 | .01 |
| ☐ 492 James Washington | .05 | .01 |
| ☐ 493 Jeff Hostetler | .10 | .02 |
| ☐ 494 Jeff Chadwick | .05 | .01 |
| ☐ 495 Kevin Ross | .05 | .01 |
| ☐ 496 Jim Ritcher | .05 | .01 |
| ☐ 497 Jessie Hester | .05 | .01 |
| ☐ 498 Burt Grossman | .05 | .01 |
| ☐ 499 Keith Van Horne | .05 | .01 |
| ☐ 500 Gerald Robinson | .05 | .01 |
| ☐ P1 Promo Panel | 5.00 | 2.00 |

## 1994 Fleer

| | | |
|---|---|---|
| ☐ COMPLETE SET (480) | 20.00 | 10.00 |
| ☐ 1 Michael Bankston | .05 | .01 |
| ☐ 2 Steve Beuerlein | .10 | .02 |
| ☐ 3 John Booty | .05 | .01 |
| ☐ 4 Rich Camarillo | .05 | .01 |
| ☐ 5 Chuck Cecil | .05 | .01 |
| ☐ 6 Larry Centers | .25 | .08 |

|  |  | | |
|---|---|---|---|
| ❑ 7 | Gary Clark | .10 | .02 |
| ❑ 8 | Garrison Hearst | .25 | .08 |
| ❑ 9 | Eric Hill | .05 | .01 |
| ❑ 10 | Randal Hill | .05 | .01 |
| ❑ 11 | Ronald Moore | .05 | .01 |
| ❑ 12 | Ricky Proehl | .05 | .01 |
| ❑ 13 | Luis Sharpe | .05 | .01 |
| ❑ 14 | Clyde Simmons | .05 | .01 |
| ❑ 15 | Tyronne Stowe | .05 | .01 |
| ❑ 16 | Eric Swann | .10 | .02 |
| ❑ 17 | Aeneas Williams | .05 | .01 |
| ❑ 18 | Darion Conner | .05 | .01 |
| ❑ 19 | Moe Gardner | .05 | .01 |
| ❑ 20 | Jumpy Geathers | .05 | .01 |
| ❑ 21 | Jeff George | .25 | .08 |
| ❑ 22 | Roger Harper | .05 | .01 |
| ❑ 23 | Bobby Hebert | .05 | .01 |
| ❑ 24 | Pierce Holt | .05 | .01 |
| ❑ 25 | D.J. Johnson | .05 | .01 |
| ❑ 26 | Mike Kenn | .05 | .01 |
| ❑ 27 | Lincoln Kennedy | .05 | .01 |
| ❑ 28 | Erric Pegram | .05 | .01 |
| ❑ 29 | Mike Pritchard | .05 | .01 |
| ❑ 30 | Andre Rison | .10 | .02 |
| ❑ 31 | Deion Sanders | .50 | .20 |
| ❑ 32 | Tony Smith RB | .05 | .01 |
| ❑ 33 | Jesse Solomon | .05 | .01 |
| ❑ 34 | Jessie Tuggle | .05 | .01 |
| ❑ 35 | Don Beebe | .05 | .01 |
| ❑ 36 | Cornelius Bennett | .10 | .02 |
| ❑ 37 | Bill Brooks | .05 | .01 |
| ❑ 38 | Kenneth Davis | .05 | .01 |
| ❑ 39 | John Fina | .05 | .01 |
| ❑ 40 | Phil Hansen | .05 | .01 |
| ❑ 41 | Kent Hull | .05 | .01 |
| ❑ 42 | Henry Jones | .05 | .01 |
| ❑ 43 | Jim Kelly | .25 | .08 |
| ❑ 44 | Pete Metzelaars | .05 | .01 |
| ❑ 45 | Marvcus Patton | .05 | .01 |
| ❑ 46 | Andre Reed | .10 | .02 |
| ❑ 47 | Frank Reich | .10 | .02 |
| ❑ 48 | Bruce Smith | .25 | .08 |
| ❑ 49 | Thomas Smith | .05 | .01 |
| ❑ 50 | Darryl Talley | .05 | .01 |
| ❑ 51 | Steve Tasker | .10 | .02 |
| ❑ 52 | Thurman Thomas | .25 | .08 |
| ❑ 53 | Jeff Wright | .05 | .01 |
| ❑ 54 | Neal Anderson | .05 | .01 |
| ❑ 55 | Trace Armstrong | .05 | .01 |
| ❑ 56 | Troy Auzenne | .05 | .01 |
| ❑ 57 | Joe Cain RC | .05 | .01 |
| ❑ 58 | Mark Carrier DB | .25 | .08 |
| ❑ 59 | Curtis Conway | .25 | .08 |
| ❑ 60 | Richard Dent | .10 | .02 |
| ❑ 61 | Shaun Gayle | .05 | .01 |
| ❑ 62 | Andy Heck | .05 | .01 |
| ❑ 63 | Dante Jones | .05 | .01 |
| ❑ 64 | Erik Kramer | .10 | .02 |
| ❑ 65 | Steve McMichael | .10 | .02 |
| ❑ 66 | Terry Obee | .05 | .01 |
| ❑ 67 | Vinson Smith | .05 | .01 |
| ❑ 68 | Alonzo Spellman | .05 | .01 |
| ❑ 69 | Tom Waddle | .05 | .01 |
| ❑ 70 | Donnell Woolford | .05 | .01 |
| ❑ 71 | Tim Worley | .05 | .01 |
| ❑ 72 | Chris Zorich | .05 | .01 |
| ❑ 73 | Mike Brim | .05 | .01 |
| ❑ 74 | John Copeland | .05 | .01 |
| ❑ 75 | Derrick Fenner | .05 | .01 |
| ❑ 76 | James Francis | .05 | .01 |
| ❑ 77 | Harold Green | .05 | .01 |
| ❑ 78 | Rod Jones CB | .05 | .01 |
| ❑ 79 | David Klingler | .05 | .01 |
| ❑ 80 | Bruce Kozerski | .05 | .01 |
| ❑ 81 | Tim Krumrie | .05 | .01 |
| ❑ 82 | Ricardo McDonald | .05 | .01 |
| ❑ 83 | Tim McGee | .05 | .01 |
| ❑ 84 | Tony McGee | .05 | .01 |
| ❑ 85 | Louis Oliver | .05 | .01 |
| ❑ 86 | Carl Pickens | .10 | .02 |
| ❑ 87 | Jeff Query | .05 | .01 |
| ❑ 88 | Daniel Stubbs | .05 | .01 |
| ❑ 89 | Steve Tovar | .05 | .01 |
| ❑ 90 | Alfred Williams | .05 | .01 |
| ❑ 91 | Darryl Williams | .05 | .01 |
| ❑ 92 | Rob Burnett | .05 | .01 |
| ❑ 93 | Mark Carrier WR | .10 | .02 |
| ❑ 94 | Leroy Hoard | .05 | .01 |
| ❑ 95 | Michael Jackson | .10 | .02 |
| ❑ 96 | Mike Johnson | .05 | .01 |
| ❑ 97 | Pepper Johnson | .05 | .01 |
| ❑ 98 | Tony Jones T | .05 | .01 |
| ❑ 99 | Clay Matthews | .05 | .01 |
| ❑ 100 | Eric Metcalf | .10 | .02 |
| ❑ 101 | Stevon Moore | .05 | .01 |
| ❑ 102 | Michael Dean Perry | .10 | .02 |
| ❑ 103 | Anthony Pleasant | .05 | .01 |
| ❑ 104 | Vinny Testaverde | .10 | .02 |
| ❑ 105 | Eric Turner | .05 | .01 |
| ❑ 106 | Tommy Vardell | .05 | .01 |
| ❑ 107 | Troy Aikman | 1.00 | .40 |
| ❑ 108 | Larry Brown DB | .05 | .01 |
| ❑ 109 | Dixon Edwards | .05 | .01 |
| ❑ 110 | Charles Haley | .10 | .02 |
| ❑ 111 | Alvin Harper | .10 | .02 |
| ❑ 112 | Michael Irvin | .25 | .08 |
| ❑ 113 | Jim Jeffcoat | .05 | .01 |
| ❑ 114 | Daryl Johnston | .10 | .02 |
| ❑ 115 | Leon Lett | .05 | .01 |
| ❑ 116 | Russell Maryland | .05 | .01 |
| ❑ 117 | Nate Newton | .05 | .01 |
| ❑ 118 | Ken Norton Jr. | .10 | .02 |
| ❑ 119 | Jay Novacek | .10 | .02 |
| ❑ 120 | Darrin Smith | .05 | .01 |
| ❑ 121 | Emmitt Smith | 1.50 | .60 |
| ❑ 122 | Kevin Smith | .05 | .01 |
| ❑ 123 | Mark Stepnoski | .05 | .01 |
| ❑ 124 | Tony Tolbert | .05 | .01 |
| ❑ 125 | Erik Williams | .05 | .01 |
| ❑ 126 | Kevin Williams WR | .10 | .02 |
| ❑ 127 | Darren Woodson | .10 | .02 |
| ❑ 128 | Steve Atwater | .05 | .01 |
| ❑ 129 | Rod Bernstine | .05 | .01 |
| ❑ 130 | Ray Crockett | .05 | .01 |
| ❑ 131 | Mike Croel | .05 | .01 |
| ❑ 132 | Robert Delpino | .05 | .01 |
| ❑ 133 | Shane Dronett | .05 | .01 |
| ❑ 134 | Jason Elam | .10 | .02 |
| ❑ 135 | John Elway | 2.00 | .75 |
| ❑ 136 | Simon Fletcher | .05 | .01 |
| ❑ 137 | Greg Kragen | .05 | .01 |
| ❑ 138 | Karl Mecklenburg | .05 | .01 |
| ❑ 139 | Glyn Milburn | .10 | .02 |
| ❑ 140 | Anthony Miller | .10 | .02 |
| ❑ 141 | Derek Russell | .05 | .01 |
| ❑ 142 | Shannon Sharpe | .10 | .02 |
| ❑ 143 | Dennis Smith | .05 | .01 |
| ❑ 144 | Dan Williams | .05 | .01 |
| ❑ 145 | Gary Zimmerman | .05 | .01 |
| ❑ 146 | Bennie Blades | .05 | .01 |
| ❑ 147 | Lomas Brown | .05 | .01 |
| ❑ 148 | Bill Fralic | .05 | .01 |
| ❑ 149 | Mel Gray | .05 | .01 |
| ❑ 150 | Willie Green | .05 | .01 |
| ❑ 151 | Jason Hanson | .05 | .01 |
| ❑ 152 | Robert Massey | .05 | .01 |
| ❑ 153 | Ryan McNeil | .05 | .01 |
| ❑ 154 | Scott Mitchell | .10 | .02 |
| ❑ 155 | Derrick Moore | .05 | .01 |
| ❑ 156 | Herman Moore | .25 | .08 |
| ❑ 157 | Brett Perriman | .10 | .02 |
| ❑ 158 | Robert Porcher | .05 | .01 |
| ❑ 159 | Kelvin Pritchett | .05 | .01 |
| ❑ 160 | Barry Sanders | 1.50 | .60 |
| ❑ 161 | Tracy Scroggins | .05 | .01 |
| ❑ 162 | Chris Spielman | .10 | .02 |
| ❑ 163 | Pat Swilling | .05 | .01 |
| ❑ 164 | Edgar Bennett | .25 | .08 |
| ❑ 165 | Robert Brooks | .25 | .08 |
| ❑ 166 | Terrell Buckley | .05 | .01 |
| ❑ 167 | LeRoy Butler | .05 | .01 |
| ❑ 168 | Brett Favre | 2.00 | .75 |
| ❑ 169 | Harry Galbreath | .05 | .01 |
| ❑ 170 | Jackie Harris | .05 | .01 |
| ❑ 171 | Johnny Holland | .05 | .01 |
| ❑ 172 | Chris Jacke | .05 | .01 |
| ❑ 173 | George Koonce | .05 | .01 |
| ❑ 174 | Bryce Paup | .10 | .02 |
| ❑ 175 | Ken Ruettgers | .05 | .01 |
| ❑ 176 | Sterling Sharpe | .10 | .02 |
| ❑ 177 | Wayne Simmons | .05 | .01 |
| ❑ 178 | George Teague | .05 | .01 |
| ❑ 179 | Darrell Thompson | .05 | .01 |
| ❑ 180 | Reggie White | .25 | .08 |
| ❑ 181 | Gary Brown | .05 | .01 |
| ❑ 182 | Cody Carlson | .05 | .01 |
| ❑ 183 | Ray Childress | .05 | .01 |
| ❑ 184 | Cris Dishman | .05 | .01 |
| ❑ 185 | Ernest Givins | .10 | .02 |
| ❑ 186 | Haywood Jeffires | .10 | .02 |
| ❑ 187 | Sean Jones | .05 | .01 |
| ❑ 188 | Lamar Lathon | .05 | .01 |
| ❑ 189 | Bruce Matthews | .05 | .01 |
| ❑ 190 | Bubba McDowell | .05 | .01 |
| ❑ 191 | Glenn Montgomery | .05 | .01 |
| ❑ 192 | Greg Montgomery | .05 | .01 |
| ❑ 193 | Warren Moon | .25 | .08 |
| ❑ 194 | Bo Orlando | .05 | .01 |
| ❑ 195 | Marcus Robertson | .05 | .01 |
| ❑ 196 | Eddie Robinson | .05 | .01 |
| ❑ 197 | Webster Slaughter | .05 | .01 |
| ❑ 198 | Lorenzo White | .05 | .01 |
| ❑ 199 | John Baylor | .05 | .01 |
| ❑ 200 | Jason Belser | .05 | .01 |
| ❑ 201 | Tony Bennett | .05 | .01 |
| ❑ 202 | Dean Biasucci | .05 | .01 |
| ❑ 203 | Ray Buchanan | .05 | .01 |
| ❑ 204 | Kerry Cash | .05 | .01 |
| ❑ 205 | Quentin Coryatt | .05 | .01 |
| ❑ 206 | Eugene Daniel | .05 | .01 |
| ❑ 207 | Steve Emtman | .05 | .01 |
| ❑ 208 | Jon Hand | .05 | .01 |
| ❑ 209 | Jim Harbaugh | .25 | .08 |
| ❑ 210 | Jeff Herrod | .05 | .01 |
| ❑ 211 | Anthony Johnson | .10 | .02 |
| ❑ 212 | Roosevelt Potts | .05 | .01 |
| ❑ 213 | Rohn Stark | .05 | .01 |
| ❑ 214 | Will Wolford | .05 | .01 |
| ❑ 215 | Marcus Allen | .25 | .08 |
| ❑ 216 | John Alt | .05 | .01 |
| ❑ 217 | Kimble Anders | .05 | .01 |
| ❑ 218 | J.J. Birden | .05 | .01 |
| ❑ 219 | Dale Carter | .05 | .01 |
| ❑ 220 | Keith Cash | .05 | .01 |
| ❑ 221 | Tony Casillas | .05 | .01 |
| ❑ 222 | Willie Davis | .10 | .02 |
| ❑ 223 | Tim Grunhard | .05 | .01 |
| ❑ 224 | Nick Lowery | .05 | .01 |
| ❑ 225 | Charles Mincy | .05 | .01 |
| ❑ 226 | Joe Montana | 2.00 | .75 |
| ❑ 227 | Dan Saleaumua | .05 | .01 |
| ❑ 228 | Tracy Simien | .05 | .01 |
| ❑ 229 | Neil Smith | .10 | .02 |
| ❑ 230 | Derrick Thomas | .25 | .08 |
| ❑ 231 | Eddie Anderson | .05 | .01 |
| ❑ 232 | Tim Brown | .25 | .08 |
| ❑ 233 | Nolan Harrison | .05 | .01 |
| ❑ 234 | Jeff Hostetler | .10 | .02 |
| ❑ 235 | Rocket Ismail | .10 | .02 |
| ❑ 236 | Jeff Jaeger | .05 | .01 |
| ❑ 237 | James Jett | .05 | .01 |
| ❑ 238 | Joe Kelly | .05 | .01 |
| ❑ 239 | Albert Lewis | .05 | .01 |
| ❑ 240 | Terry McDaniel | .05 | .01 |
| ❑ 241 | Chester McGlockton | .05 | .01 |
| ❑ 242 | Winston Moss | .05 | .01 |
| ❑ 243 | Gerald Perry | .05 | .01 |
| ❑ 244 | Greg Robinson | .05 | .01 |
| ❑ 245 | Anthony Smith | .05 | .01 |
| ❑ 246 | Steve Smith | .05 | .01 |
| ❑ 247 | Greg Townsend | .05 | .01 |
| ❑ 248 | Lionel Washington | .05 | .01 |
| ❑ 249 | Steve Wisniewski | .05 | .01 |
| ❑ 250 | Alexander Wright | .05 | .01 |
| ❑ 251 | Flipper Anderson | .05 | .01 |
| ❑ 252 | Jerome Bettis | .50 | .20 |
| ❑ 253 | Marc Boutte | .05 | .01 |
| ❑ 254 | Shane Conlan | .05 | .01 |
| ❑ 255 | Troy Drayton | .05 | .01 |
| ❑ 256 | Henry Ellard | .10 | .02 |
| ❑ 257 | Sean Gilbert | .05 | .01 |
| ❑ 258 | Nate Lewis | .05 | .01 |

|  |  | | |
|---|---|---|---|
| 259 | Todd Lyght | .05 | .01 |
| 260 | Chris Miller | .05 | .01 |
| 261 | Anthony Newman | .05 | .01 |
| 262 | Roman Phifer | .05 | .01 |
| 263 | Henry Rolling | .05 | .01 |
| 264 | T.J. Rubley RC | .05 | .01 |
| 265 | Jackie Slater | .05 | .01 |
| 266 | Fred Stokes | .05 | .01 |
| 267 | Robert Young | .05 | .01 |
| 268 | Gene Atkins | .05 | .01 |
| 269 | J.B. Brown | .05 | .01 |
| 270 | Keith Byars | .05 | .01 |
| 271 | Marco Coleman | .05 | .01 |
| 272 | Bryan Cox | .05 | .01 |
| 273 | Jeff Cross | .05 | .01 |
| 274 | Irving Fryar | .10 | .02 |
| 275 | Mark Higgs | .05 | .01 |
| 276 | Dwight Hollier | .05 | .01 |
| 277 | Mark Ingram | .05 | .01 |
| 278 | Keith Jackson | .05 | .01 |
| 279 | Terry Kirby | .25 | .08 |
| 280 | Bernie Kosar | .10 | .02 |
| 281 | Dan Marino | 2.00 | .75 |
| 282 | O.J. McDuffie | .25 | .08 |
| 283 | Keith Sims | .05 | .01 |
| 284 | Pete Stoyanovich | .05 | .01 |
| 285 | Troy Vincent | .05 | .01 |
| 286 | Richmond Webb | .05 | .01 |
| 287 | Terry Allen | .10 | .02 |
| 288 | Anthony Carter | .10 | .02 |
| 289 | Cris Carter | .50 | .20 |
| 290 | Jack Del Rio | .05 | .01 |
| 291 | Chris Doleman | .05 | .01 |
| 292 | Vencie Glenn | .05 | .01 |
| 293 | Scottie Graham RC | .10 | .02 |
| 294 | Chris Hinton | .05 | .01 |
| 295 | Qadry Ismail | .25 | .08 |
| 296 | Carlos Jenkins | .05 | .01 |
| 297 | Steve Jordan | .05 | .01 |
| 298 | Carl Lee | .05 | .01 |
| 299 | Randall McDaniel | .10 | .02 |
| 300 | John Randle | .10 | .02 |
| 301 | Todd Scott | .05 | .01 |
| 302 | Robert Smith | .25 | .08 |
| 303 | Fred Strickland | .05 | .01 |
| 304 | Henry Thomas | .05 | .01 |
| 305 | Bruce Armstrong | .05 | .01 |
| 306 | Harlon Barnett | .05 | .01 |
| 307 | Drew Bledsoe | .75 | .30 |
| 308 | Vincent Brown | .05 | .01 |
| 309 | Ben Coates | .10 | .02 |
| 310 | Todd Collins | .05 | .01 |
| 311 | Myron Guyton | .05 | .01 |
| 312 | Pat Harlow | .05 | .01 |
| 313 | Maurice Hurst | .05 | .01 |
| 314 | Leonard Russell | .05 | .01 |
| 315 | Chris Slade | .05 | .01 |
| 316 | Michael Timpson | .05 | .01 |
| 317 | Andre Tippett | .05 | .01 |
| 318 | Morten Andersen | .05 | .01 |
| 319 | Derek Brown RBK | .05 | .01 |
| 320 | Vince Buck | .05 | .01 |
| 321 | Toi Cook | .05 | .01 |
| 322 | Quinn Early | .10 | .02 |
| 323 | Jim Everett | .10 | .02 |
| 324 | Michael Haynes | .10 | .02 |
| 325 | Tyrone Hughes | .10 | .02 |
| 326 | Rickey Jackson | .05 | .01 |
| 327 | Vaughan Johnson | .05 | .01 |
| 328 | Eric Martin | .05 | .01 |
| 329 | Wayne Martin | .05 | .01 |
| 330 | Sam Mills | .05 | .01 |
| 331 | Willie Roaf | .05 | .01 |
| 332 | Irv Smith | .05 | .01 |
| 333 | Keith Taylor | .05 | .01 |
| 334 | Renaldo Turnbull | .05 | .01 |
| 335 | Carlton Bailey | .05 | .01 |
| 336 | Michael Brooks | .05 | .01 |
| 337 | Jarrod Bunch | .05 | .01 |
| 338 | Chris Calloway | .05 | .01 |
| 339 | Mark Collins | .05 | .01 |
| 340 | Howard Cross | .05 | .01 |
| 341 | Stacey Dillard RC | .05 | .01 |
| 342 | John Elliott | .05 | .01 |
| 343 | Rodney Hampton | .10 | .02 |
| 344 | Greg Jackson | .05 | .01 |
| 345 | Mark Jackson | .05 | .01 |
| 346 | Dave Meggett | .05 | .01 |
| 347 | Corey Miller | .05 | .01 |
| 348 | Mike Sherrard | .05 | .01 |
| 349 | Phil Simms | .10 | .02 |
| 350 | Lewis Tillman | .05 | .01 |
| 351 | Brad Baxter | .05 | .01 |
| 352 | Kyle Clifton | .05 | .01 |
| 353 | Boomer Esiason | .10 | .02 |
| 354 | James Hasty | .05 | .01 |
| 355 | Bobby Houston | .05 | .01 |
| 356 | Johnny Johnson | .05 | .01 |
| 357 | Jeff Lageman | .05 | .01 |
| 358 | Mo Lewis | .05 | .01 |
| 359 | Ronnie Lott | .10 | .02 |
| 360 | Leonard Marshall | .05 | .01 |
| 361 | Johnny Mitchell | .05 | .01 |
| 362 | Rob Moore | .10 | .02 |
| 363 | Brian Washington | .05 | .01 |
| 364 | Marvin Washington | .05 | .01 |
| 365 | Eric Allen | .05 | .01 |
| 367 | Fred Barnett | .10 | .02 |
| 368 | Bubby Brister | .05 | .01 |
| 369 | Randall Cunningham | .25 | .08 |
| 370 | Byron Evans | .05 | .01 |
| 371 | William Fuller | .05 | .01 |
| 372 | Andy Harmon | .05 | .01 |
| 373 | Seth Joyner | .05 | .01 |
| 374 | William Perry | .10 | .02 |
| 375 | Leonard Renfro | .05 | .01 |
| 376 | Heath Sherman | .05 | .01 |
| 377 | Ben Smith | .05 | .01 |
| 378 | William Thomas | .05 | .01 |
| 379 | Herschel Walker | .10 | .02 |
| 380 | Calvin Williams | .10 | .02 |
| 381 | Chad Brown | .05 | .01 |
| 382 | Dermontti Dawson | .05 | .01 |
| 383 | Deon Figures | .05 | .01 |
| 384 | Barry Foster | .05 | .01 |
| 385 | Jeff Graham | .05 | .01 |
| 386 | Eric Green | .05 | .01 |
| 387 | Kevin Greene | .10 | .02 |
| 388 | Carlton Haselrig | .05 | .01 |
| 389 | Levon Kirkland | .05 | .01 |
| 390 | Carnell Lake | .05 | .01 |
| 391 | Greg Lloyd | .10 | .02 |
| 392 | Neil O'Donnell | .25 | .08 |
| 393 | Darren Perry | .05 | .01 |
| 394 | Dwight Stone | .05 | .01 |
| 395 | Leroy Thompson | .05 | .01 |
| 396 | Rod Woodson | .10 | .02 |
| 397 | Marion Butts | .05 | .01 |
| 398 | John Carney | .05 | .01 |
| 399 | Darren Carrington | .05 | .01 |
| 400 | Burt Grossman | .05 | .01 |
| 401 | Courtney Hall | .05 | .01 |
| 402 | Ronnie Harmon | .05* | .01 |
| 403 | Stan Humphries | .10 | .02 |
| 404 | Shawn Jefferson | .05 | .01 |
| 405 | Vance Johnson | .05 | .01 |
| 406 | Chris Mims | .05 | .01 |
| 407 | Leslie O'Neal | .05 | .01 |
| 408 | Stanley Richard | .05 | .01 |
| 409 | Junior Seau | .25 | .08 |
| 410 | Harris Barton | .05 | .01 |
| 411 | Dennis Brown | .05 | .01 |
| 412 | Eric Davis | .05 | .01 |
| 413 | Merton Hanks | .10 | .02 |
| 414 | John Johnson | .05 | .01 |
| 415 | Brent Jones | .10 | .02 |
| 416 | Marc Logan | .05 | .01 |
| 417 | Tim McDonald | .05 | .01 |
| 418 | Gary Plummer | .05 | .01 |
| 419 | Tom Rathman | .05 | .01 |
| 420 | Jerry Rice | 1.00 | .40 |
| 421 | Bill Romanowski | .05 | .01 |
| 422 | Jesse Sapolu | .05 | .01 |
| 423 | Dana Stubblefield | .10 | .02 |
| 424 | John Taylor | .10 | .02 |
| 425 | Steve Wallace | .05 | .01 |
| 426 | Ted Washington | .05 | .01 |
| 427 | Ricky Watters | .10 | .02 |
| 428 | Troy Wilson RC | .05 | .01 |
| 429 | Steve Young | .75 | .30 |
| 430 | Howard Ballard | .05 | .01 |
| 431 | Michael Bates | .05 | .01 |
| 432 | Robert Blackmon | .05 | .01 |
| 433 | Brian Blades | .10 | .02 |
| 434 | Ferrell Edmunds | .05 | .01 |
| 435 | Carlton Gray | .05 | .01 |
| 436 | Patrick Hunter | .05 | .01 |
| 437 | Cortez Kennedy | .10 | .02 |
| 438 | Kelvin Martin | .05 | .01 |
| 439 | Rick Mirer | .25 | .08 |
| 440 | Nate Odomes | .05 | .01 |
| 441 | Ray Roberts | .05 | .01 |
| 442 | Eugene Robinson | .05 | .01 |
| 443 | Rod Stephens | .05 | .01 |
| 444 | Chris Warren | .10 | .02 |
| 445 | John L. Williams | .05 | .01 |
| 446 | Terry Wooden | .05 | .01 |
| 447 | Marty Carter | .05 | .01 |
| 448 | Reggie Cobb | .05 | .01 |
| 449 | Lawrence Dawsey | .05 | .01 |
| 450 | Santana Dotson | .10 | .02 |
| 451 | Craig Erickson | .05 | .01 |
| 452 | Thomas Everett | .05 | .01 |
| 453 | Paul Gruber | .05 | .01 |
| 454 | Courtney Hawkins | .05 | .01 |
| 455 | Martin Mayhew | .05 | .01 |
| 456 | Hardy Nickerson | .10 | .02 |
| 457 | Ricky Reynolds | .05 | .01 |
| 458 | Vince Workman | .05 | .01 |
| 459 | Reggie Brooks | .10 | .02 |
| 460 | Earnest Byner | .05 | .01 |
| 461 | Andre Collins | .05 | .01 |
| 462 | Brad Edwards | .05 | .01 |
| 463 | Kurt Gouveia | .05 | .01 |
| 464 | Darrell Green | .05 | .01 |
| 465 | Ken Harvey | .05 | .01 |
| 466 | Ethan Horton | .05 | .01 |
| 467 | A.J. Johnson | .05 | .01 |
| 468 | Tim Johnson | .05 | .01 |
| 469 | Jim Lachey | .05 | .01 |
| 470 | Chip Lohmiller | .05 | .01 |
| 471 | Art Monk | .10 | .02 |
| 472 | Sterling Palmer RC | .05 | .01 |
| 473 | Mark Rypien | .05 | .01 |
| 474 | Ricky Sanders | .05 | .01 |
| 475 | Checklist 1-106 | .05 | .01 |
| 476 | Checklist 107-214 | .05 | .01 |
| 477 | Checklist 215-317 | .05 | .01 |
| 478 | Checklist 318-409 | .05 | .01 |
| 479 | Checklist 410-480/Inserts | .05 | .01 |
| 480 | Inserts Checklist | .05 | .01 |
| P244 | Jerome Bettis Promo | 1.00 | .40 |

## 1995 Fleer

|  |  | | |
|---|---|---|---|
| | COMPLETE SET (400) | 25.00 | 10.00 |
| 1 | Michael Bankston | .10 | .02 |
| 2 | Larry Centers | .20 | .07 |
| 3 | Gary Clark | .10 | .02 |
| 4 | Eric Hill | .10 | .02 |
| 5 | Seth Joyner | .10 | .02 |
| 6 | Dave Krieg | .10 | .02 |
| 7 | Lorenzo Lynch | .10 | .02 |
| 8 | Jamir Miller | .10 | .02 |
| 9 | Ronald Moore | .10 | .02 |
| 10 | Ricky Proehl | .10 | .02 |

|  |  | | |
|---|---|---|---|
| 11 | Clyde Simmons | .10 | .02 |
| 12 | Eric Swann | .20 | .07 |
| 13 | Aeneas Williams | .10 | .02 |
| 14 | J.J. Birden | .10 | .02 |
| 15 | Chris Doleman | .10 | .02 |
| 16 | Bert Emanuel | .30 | .10 |
| 17 | Jumpy Geathers | .10 | .02 |
| 18 | Jeff George | .20 | .07 |
| 19 | Roger Harper | .10 | .02 |
| 20 | Craig Heyward | .20 | .07 |
| 21 | Pierce Holt | .10 | .02 |
| 22 | D.J. Johnson | .10 | .02 |
| 23 | Terance Mathis | .20 | .07 |
| 24 | Clay Matthews | .20 | .07 |
| 25 | Andre Rison | .20 | .07 |
| 26 | Chuck Smith | .10 | .02 |
| 27 | Jessie Tuggle | .10 | .02 |
| 28 | Cornelius Bennett | .20 | .07 |
| 29 | Bryce Brooks | .10 | .02 |
| 30 | Jeff Burris | .10 | .02 |
| 31 | Russell Copeland | .10 | .02 |
| 32 | Matt Darby | .10 | .02 |
| 33 | Phil Hansen | .10 | .02 |
| 34 | Henry Jones | .10 | .02 |
| 35 | Jim Kelly | .30 | .10 |
| 36 | Mark Maddox RC | .10 | .02 |
| 37 | Bryce Paup | .20 | .07 |
| 38 | Andre Reed | .20 | .07 |
| 39 | Bruce Smith | .30 | .10 |
| 40 | Darryl Talley | .10 | .02 |
| 41 | Dewell Brewer RC | .10 | .02 |
| 42 | Mike Fox | .10 | .02 |
| 43 | Eric Guilford | .10 | .02 |
| 44 | Lamar Lathon | .10 | .02 |
| 45 | Pete Metzelaars | .10 | .02 |
| 46 | Sam Mills | .20 | .07 |
| 47 | Frank Reich | .10 | .02 |
| 48 | Rod Smith DB | .20 | .07 |
| 49 | Jack Trudeau | .10 | .02 |
| 50 | Trace Armstrong | .10 | .02 |
| 51 | Joe Cain | .10 | .02 |
| 52 | Mark Carrier DB | .10 | .02 |
| 53 | Curtis Conway | .30 | .10 |
| 54 | Shaun Gayle | .10 | .02 |
| 55 | Jeff Graham | .10 | .02 |
| 56 | Raymont Harris | .10 | .02 |
| 57 | Erik Kramer | .10 | .02 |
| 58 | Lewis Tillman | .10 | .02 |
| 59 | Tom Waddle | .10 | .02 |
| 60 | Steve Walsh | .10 | .02 |
| 61 | Donnell Woolford | .10 | .02 |
| 62 | Chris Zorich | .10 | .02 |
| 63 | Jeff Blake RC | .60 | .25 |
| 64 | Mike Brim | .10 | .02 |
| 65 | Steve Broussard | .10 | .02 |
| 66 | James Francis | .10 | .02 |
| 67 | Ricardo McDonald | .10 | .02 |
| 68 | Tony McGee | .10 | .02 |
| 69 | Carl Pickens | .20 | .07 |
| 70 | Darnay Scott | .20 | .07 |
| 71 | Steve Tovar | .10 | .02 |
| 72 | Dan Wilkinson | .20 | .07 |
| 73 | Alfred Williams | .10 | .02 |
| 74 | Darryl Williams | .10 | .02 |
| 75 | Derrick Alexander WR | .30 | .10 |
| 76 | Randy Baldwin | .10 | .02 |
| 77 | Carl Banks | .10 | .02 |
| 78 | Rob Burnett | .10 | .02 |
| 79 | Steve Everitt | .10 | .02 |
| 80 | Leroy Hoard | .10 | .02 |
| 81 | Michael Jackson | .20 | .07 |
| 82 | Pepper Johnson | .10 | .02 |
| 83 | Tony Jones T | .10 | .02 |
| 84 | Antonio Langham | .10 | .02 |
| 85 | Eric Metcalf | .20 | .07 |
| 86 | Stevon Moore | .10 | .02 |
| 87 | Anthony Pleasant | .10 | .02 |
| 88 | Vinny Testaverde | .20 | .07 |
| 89 | Eric Turner | .10 | .02 |
| 90 | Troy Aikman | 1.00 | .40 |
| 91 | Charles Haley | .20 | .07 |
| 92 | Michael Irvin | .30 | .10 |
| 93 | Daryl Johnston | .20 | .07 |
| 94 | Robert Jones | .10 | .02 |
| 95 | Leon Lett | .10 | .02 |
| 96 | Russell Maryland | .10 | .02 |
| 97 | Nate Newton | .20 | .07 |
| 98 | Jay Novacek | .20 | .07 |
| 99 | Darrin Smith | .10 | .02 |
| 100 | Emmitt Smith | 1.50 | .60 |
| 101 | Kevin Smith | .10 | .02 |
| 102 | Erik Williams | .10 | .02 |
| 103 | Kevin Williams WR | .20 | .07 |
| 104 | Darren Woodson | .20 | .07 |
| 105 | Elijah Alexander | .10 | .02 |
| 106 | Steve Atwater | .10 | .02 |
| 107 | Ray Crockett | .10 | .02 |
| 108 | Shane Dronett | .10 | .02 |
| 109 | Jason Elam | .20 | .07 |
| 110 | John Elway | 2.00 | .75 |
| 111 | Simon Fletcher | .10 | .02 |
| 112 | Glyn Milburn | .10 | .02 |
| 113 | Anthony Miller | .20 | .07 |
| 114 | Michael Dean Perry | .20 | .07 |
| 115 | Mike Pritchard | .10 | .02 |
| 116 | Derek Russell | .10 | .02 |
| 117 | Leonard Russell | .10 | .02 |
| 118 | Shannon Sharpe | .20 | .07 |
| 119 | Gary Zimmerman | .10 | .02 |
| 120 | Bennie Blades | .10 | .02 |
| 121 | Lomas Brown | .10 | .02 |
| 122 | Willie Clay | .10 | .02 |
| 123 | Mike Johnson | .10 | .02 |
| 124 | Robert Massey | .10 | .02 |
| 125 | Scott Mitchell | .20 | .07 |
| 126 | Herman Moore | .30 | .10 |
| 127 | Brett Perriman | .20 | .07 |
| 128 | Robert Porcher | .10 | .02 |
| 129 | Barry Sanders | 1.50 | .60 |
| 130 | Chris Spielman | .20 | .07 |
| 131 | Henry Thomas | .10 | .02 |
| 132 | Edgar Bennett | .20 | .07 |
| 133 | LeRoy Butler | .10 | .02 |
| 134 | Mark Chmura | .10 | .02 |
| 135 | Brett Favre | 2.00 | .75 |
| 136 | Sean Jones | .10 | .02 |
| 137 | John Jurkovic | .10 | .02 |
| 138 | George Koonce | .10 | .02 |
| 139 | Wayne Simmons | .10 | .02 |
| 140 | George Teague | .10 | .02 |
| 141 | Reggie White | .30 | .10 |
| 142 | Micheal Barrow | .10 | .02 |
| 143 | Gary Brown | .10 | .02 |
| 144 | Cody Carlson | .10 | .02 |
| 145 | Ray Childress | .10 | .02 |
| 146 | Cris Dishman | .10 | .02 |
| 147 | Ernest Givins | .20 | .07 |
| 148 | Mel Gray | .10 | .02 |
| 149 | Darryll Lewis | .10 | .02 |
| 150 | Bruce Matthews | .10 | .02 |
| 151 | Marcus Robertson | .10 | .02 |
| 152 | Webster Slaughter | .10 | .02 |
| 153 | Al Smith | .10 | .02 |
| 154 | Mark Stepnoski | .10 | .02 |
| 155 | Trev Alberts | .10 | .02 |
| 156 | Flipper Anderson | .10 | .02 |
| 157 | Jason Belser | .10 | .02 |
| 158 | Tony Bennett | .10 | .02 |
| 159 | Ray Buchanan | .10 | .02 |
| 160 | Quentin Coryatt | .20 | .07 |
| 161 | Sean Dawkins | .20 | .07 |
| 162 | Steve Emtman | .10 | .02 |
| 163 | Marshall Faulk | 1.25 | .50 |
| 164 | Stephen Grant RC | .10 | .02 |
| 165 | Jim Harbaugh | .20 | .07 |
| 166 | Jeff Herrod | .10 | .02 |
| 167 | Tony Siragusa | .10 | .02 |
| 168 | Steve Beuerlein | .20 | .07 |
| 169 | Darren Carrington | .10 | .02 |
| 170 | Reggie Cobb | .10 | .02 |
| 171 | Kelvin Martin | .10 | .02 |
| 172 | Kelvin Pritchett | .10 | .02 |
| 173 | Joel Smeenge | .10 | .02 |
| 174 | James Williams LB | .10 | .02 |
| 175 | Marcus Allen | .30 | .10 |
| 176 | Kimble Anders | .20 | .07 |
| 177 | Dale Carter | .10 | .02 |
| 178 | Mark Collins | .10 | .02 |
| 179 | Willie Davis | .20 | .07 |
| 180 | Lake Dawson | .10 | .02 |
| 181 | Greg Hill | .20 | .07 |
| 182 | Darren Mickell | .10 | .02 |
| 183 | Joe Montana | 2.00 | .75 |
| 184 | Tracy Simien | .10 | .02 |
| 185 | Neil Smith | .20 | .07 |
| 186 | William White | .10 | .02 |
| 187 | Greg Biekert | .10 | .02 |
| 188 | Tim Brown | .30 | .10 |
| 189 | Rob Fredrickson | .10 | .02 |
| 190 | Andrew Glover RC | .10 | .02 |
| 191 | Nolan Harrison | .10 | .02 |
| 192 | Jeff Hostetler | .20 | .07 |
| 193 | Rocket Ismail | .20 | .07 |
| 194 | Terry McDaniel | .10 | .02 |
| 195 | Chester McGlockton | .20 | .07 |
| 196 | Winston Moss | .10 | .02 |
| 197 | Anthony Smith | .10 | .02 |
| 198 | Harvey Williams | .20 | .07 |
| 199 | Steve Wisniewski | .10 | .02 |
| 200 | Johnny Bailey | .10 | .02 |
| 201 | Jerome Bettis | .30 | .10 |
| 202 | Isaac Bruce | .50 | .20 |
| 203 | Shane Conlan | .10 | .02 |
| 204 | Troy Drayton | .10 | .02 |
| 205 | Sean Gilbert | .20 | .07 |
| 206 | Jessie Hester | .10 | .02 |
| 207 | Jimmie Jones | .10 | .02 |
| 208 | Todd Lyght | .10 | .02 |
| 209 | Chris Miller | .10 | .02 |
| 210 | Roman Phifer | .10 | .02 |
| 211 | Marquez Pope | .10 | .02 |
| 212 | Robert Young | .10 | .02 |
| 213 | Gene Atkins | .10 | .02 |
| 214 | Aubrey Beavers | .10 | .02 |
| 215 | Tim Bowens | .10 | .02 |
| 216 | Bryan Cox | .10 | .02 |
| 217 | Jeff Cross | .10 | .02 |
| 218 | Irving Fryar | .20 | .07 |
| 219 | Eric Green | .10 | .02 |
| 220 | Mark Ingram | .10 | .02 |
| 221 | Terry Kirby | .20 | .07 |
| 222 | Dan Marino | 2.00 | .75 |
| 223 | O.J. McDuffie | .30 | .10 |
| 224 | Bernie Parmalee | .10 | .02 |
| 225 | Keith Sims | .10 | .02 |
| 226 | Irving Spikes | .10 | .02 |
| 227 | Michael Stewart | .10 | .02 |
| 228 | Troy Vincent | .10 | .02 |
| 229 | Richmond Webb | .10 | .02 |
| 230 | Terry Allen | .20 | .07 |
| 231 | Cris Carter | .30 | .10 |
| 232 | Jack Del Rio | .10 | .02 |
| 233 | Vencie Glenn | .10 | .02 |
| 234 | Qadry Ismail | .10 | .02 |
| 235 | Carlos Jenkins | .10 | .02 |
| 236 | Ed McDaniel | .10 | .02 |
| 237 | Randall McDaniel | .15 | .05 |
| 238 | Warren Moon | .20 | .07 |
| 239 | Anthony Parker | .10 | .02 |
| 240 | John Randle | .10 | .02 |
| 241 | Jake Reed | .20 | .07 |
| 242 | Fuad Reveiz | .10 | .02 |
| 243 | Broderick Thomas | .10 | .02 |
| 244 | Dewayne Washington | .10 | .02 |
| 245 | Bruce Armstrong | .10 | .02 |
| 246 | Drew Bledsoe | .60 | .25 |
| 247 | Vincent Brisby | .10 | .02 |
| 248 | Vincent Brown | .10 | .02 |
| 249 | Marion Butts | .10 | .02 |
| 250 | Ben Coates | .20 | .07 |
| 251 | Tim Goad | .10 | .02 |
| 252 | Myron Guyton | .10 | .02 |
| 253 | Maurice Hurst | .10 | .02 |
| 254 | Mike Jones | .10 | .02 |
| 255 | Willie McGinest | .20 | .07 |
| 256 | Dave Meggett | .20 | .07 |
| 257 | Ricky Reynolds | .10 | .02 |
| 258 | Chris Slade | .10 | .02 |
| 259 | Michael Timpson | .10 | .02 |
| 260 | Mario Bates | .20 | .07 |
| 261 | Derek Brown RBK | .10 | .02 |
| 262 | Darion Conner | .10 | .02 |
| 263 | Quinn Early | .20 | .07 |
| 264 | Jim Everett | .10 | .02 |

| | | |
|---|---|---|
| ☐ 265 Michael Haynes | .20 | .07 |
| ☐ 266 Tyrone Hughes | .20 | .07 |
| ☐ 267 Joe Johnson | .10 | .02 |
| ☐ 268 Wayne Martin | .10 | .02 |
| ☐ 269 Willie Roaf | .10 | .02 |
| ☐ 270 Irv Smith | .10 | .02 |
| ☐ 271 Jimmy Spencer | .10 | .02 |
| ☐ 272 Winfred Tubbs | .10 | .02 |
| ☐ 273 Renaldo Turnbull | .10 | .02 |
| ☐ 274 Michael Brooks | .10 | .02 |
| ☐ 275 Dave Brown | .20 | .07 |
| ☐ 276 Chris Calloway | .10 | .02 |
| ☐ 277 Jesse Campbell | .10 | .02 |
| ☐ 278 Howard Cross | .10 | .02 |
| ☐ 279 John Elliott | .10 | .02 |
| ☐ 280 Keith Hamilton | .10 | .02 |
| ☐ 281 Rodney Hampton | .20 | .07 |
| ☐ 282 Thomas Lewis | .10 | .02 |
| ☐ 283 Thomas Randolph | .10 | .02 |
| ☐ 284 Mike Sherrard | .10 | .02 |
| ☐ 285 Michael Strahan | .30 | .10 |
| ☐ 286 Brad Baxter | .10 | .02 |
| ☐ 287 Tony Casillas | .10 | .02 |
| ☐ 288 Kyle Clifton | .10 | .02 |
| ☐ 289 Boomer Esiason | .20 | .07 |
| ☐ 290 Aaron Glenn | .10 | .02 |
| ☐ 291 Bobby Houston | .10 | .02 |
| ☐ 292 Johnny Johnson | .10 | .02 |
| ☐ 293 Jeff Lageman | .10 | .02 |
| ☐ 294 Mo Lewis | .10 | .02 |
| ☐ 295 Johnny Mitchell | .10 | .02 |
| ☐ 296 Rob Moore | .20 | .07 |
| ☐ 297 Marcus Turner | .10 | .02 |
| ☐ 298 Marvin Washington | .10 | .02 |
| ☐ 299 Eric Allen | .10 | .02 |
| ☐ 300 Fred Barnett | .20 | .07 |
| ☐ 301 Randall Cunningham | .30 | .10 |
| ☐ 302 Byron Evans | .10 | .02 |
| ☐ 303 William Fuller | .10 | .02 |
| ☐ 304 Charlie Garner | .30 | .10 |
| ☐ 305 Andy Harmon | .10 | .02 |
| ☐ 306 Greg Jackson | .10 | .02 |
| ☐ 307 Bill Romanowski | .10 | .02 |
| ☐ 308 William Thomas | .10 | .02 |
| ☐ 309 Herschel Walker | .20 | .07 |
| ☐ 310 Calvin Williams | .10 | .02 |
| ☐ 311 Michael Zordich | .10 | .02 |
| ☐ 312 Chad Brown | .20 | .07 |
| ☐ 313 Dermontti Dawson | .10 | .02 |
| ☐ 314 Barry Foster | .20 | .07 |
| ☐ 315 Kevin Greene | .20 | .07 |
| ☐ 316 Charles Johnson | .20 | .07 |
| ☐ 317 Levon Kirkland | .10 | .02 |
| ☐ 318 Carnell Lake | .10 | .02 |
| ☐ 319 Greg Lloyd | .20 | .07 |
| ☐ 320 Byron Bam Morris | .10 | .02 |
| ☐ 321 Neil O'Donnell | .20 | .07 |
| ☐ 322 Darren Perry | .10 | .02 |
| ☐ 323 Ray Seals | .10 | .02 |
| ☐ 324 John L. Williams | .10 | .02 |
| ☐ 325 Rod Woodson | .20 | .07 |
| ☐ 326 John Carney | .10 | .02 |
| ☐ 327 Andre Coleman | .10 | .02 |
| ☐ 328 Courtney Hall | .10 | .02 |
| ☐ 329 Ronnie Harmon | .10 | .02 |
| ☐ 330 Dwayne Harper | .10 | .02 |
| ☐ 331 Stan Humphries | .20 | .07 |
| ☐ 332 Shawn Jefferson | .10 | .02 |
| ☐ 333 Tony Martin | .20 | .07 |
| ☐ 334 Natrone Means | .20 | .07 |
| ☐ 335 Chris Mims | .10 | .02 |
| ☐ 336 Leslie O'Neal | .20 | .07 |
| ☐ 337 Alfred Pupunu RC | .10 | .02 |
| ☐ 338 Junior Seau | .30 | .10 |
| ☐ 339 Mark Seay | .10 | .02 |
| ☐ 340 Eric Davis | .10 | .02 |
| ☐ 341 William Floyd | .20 | .07 |
| ☐ 342 Merton Hanks | .10 | .02 |
| ☐ 343 Rickey Jackson | .10 | .02 |
| ☐ 344 Brent Jones | .10 | .02 |
| ☐ 345 Tim McDonald | .10 | .02 |
| ☐ 346 Ken Norton Jr. | .10 | .02 |
| ☐ 347 Gary Plummer | .10 | .02 |
| ☐ 348 Jerry Rice | 1.00 | .40 |

| | | |
|---|---|---|
| ☐ 349 Deion Sanders | .40 | .15 |
| ☐ 350 Jesse Sapolu | .10 | .02 |
| ☐ 351 Dana Stubblefield | .20 | .07 |
| ☐ 352 John Taylor | .10 | .02 |
| ☐ 353 Steve Wallace | .10 | .02 |
| ☐ 354 Ricky Watters | .20 | .07 |
| ☐ 355 Lee Woodall | .10 | .02 |
| ☐ 356 Bryant Young | .20 | .07 |
| ☐ 357 Steve Young | .75 | .30 |
| ☐ 358 Sam Adams | .10 | .02 |
| ☐ 359 Howard Ballard | .10 | .02 |
| ☐ 360 Robert Blackmon | .10 | .02 |
| ☐ 361 Brian Blades | .20 | .07 |
| ☐ 362 Carlton Gray | .10 | .02 |
| ☐ 363 Cortez Kennedy | .20 | .07 |
| ☐ 364 Rick Mirer | .20 | .07 |
| ☐ 365 Eugene Robinson | .10 | .02 |
| ☐ 366 Chris Warren | .20 | .07 |
| ☐ 367 Terry Wooden | .10 | .02 |
| ☐ 368 Brad Culpepper | .10 | .02 |
| ☐ 369 Lawrence Dawsey | .10 | .02 |
| ☐ 370 Trent Dilfer | .30 | .10 |
| ☐ 371 Santana Dotson | .10 | .02 |
| ☐ 372 Craig Erickson | .10 | .02 |
| ☐ 373 Thomas Everett | .10 | .02 |
| ☐ 374 Paul Gruber | .10 | .02 |
| ☐ 375 Alvin Harper | .10 | .02 |
| ☐ 376 Jackie Harris | .10 | .02 |
| ☐ 377 Courtney Hawkins | .10 | .02 |
| ☐ 378 Martin Mayhew | .10 | .02 |
| ☐ 379 Hardy Nickerson | .10 | .02 |
| ☐ 380 Errict Rhett | .20 | .07 |
| ☐ 381 Charles Wilson | .10 | .02 |
| ☐ 382 Reggie Brooks | .20 | .07 |
| ☐ 383 Tom Carter | .10 | .02 |
| ☐ 384 Andre Collins | .10 | .02 |
| ☐ 385 Henry Ellard | .20 | .07 |
| ☐ 386 Ricky Ervins | .10 | .02 |
| ☐ 387 Darrell Green | .20 | .07 |
| ☐ 388 Ken Harvey | .10 | .02 |
| ☐ 389 Brian Mitchell | .10 | .02 |
| ☐ 390 Stanley Richard | .10 | .02 |
| ☐ 391 Heath Shuler | .20 | .07 |
| ☐ 392 Rod Stephens | .10 | .02 |
| ☐ 393 Tyrone Stowe | .10 | .02 |
| ☐ 394 Tydus Winans | .10 | .02 |
| ☐ 395 Tony Woods | .10 | .02 |
| ☐ 396 Checklist | .10 | .02 |
| ☐ 397 Checklist | .10 | .02 |
| ☐ 398 Checklist | .10 | .02 |
| ☐ 399 Checklist | .10 | .02 |
| ☐ 400 Checklist | .10 | .02 |

**1996 Fleer**

| | | |
|---|---|---|
| ☐ COMPLETE SET (200) | 20.00 | 7.50 |
| ☐ 1 Garrison Hearst | .20 | .07 |
| ☐ 2 Rob Moore | .20 | .07 |
| ☐ 3 Frank Sanders | .20 | .07 |
| ☐ 4 Eric Swann | .10 | .02 |
| ☐ 5 Aeneas Williams | .10 | .02 |
| ☐ 6 Jeff George | .20 | .07 |
| ☐ 7 Craig Heyward | .10 | .02 |
| ☐ 8 Terance Mathis | .10 | .02 |
| ☐ 9 Eric Metcalf | .10 | .02 |
| ☐ 10 Michael Jackson | .20 | .07 |
| ☐ 11 Andre Rison | .20 | .07 |
| ☐ 12 Vinny Testaverde | .20 | .07 |
| ☐ 13 Eric Turner | .10 | .02 |

| | | |
|---|---|---|
| ☐ 14 Darick Holmes | .10 | .02 |
| ☐ 15 Jim Kelly | .30 | .10 |
| ☐ 16 Bryce Paup | .10 | .02 |
| ☐ 17 Bruce Smith | .20 | .07 |
| ☐ 18 Thurman Thomas | .30 | .10 |
| ☐ 19 Kerry Collins | .30 | .10 |
| ☐ 20 Lamar Lathon | .10 | .02 |
| ☐ 21 Derrick Moore | .10 | .02 |
| ☐ 22 Tyrone Poole | .10 | .02 |
| ☐ 23 Curtis Conway | .30 | .10 |
| ☐ 24 Bryan Cox | .10 | .02 |
| ☐ 25 Erik Kramer | .10 | .02 |
| ☐ 26 Rashaan Salaam | .20 | .07 |
| ☐ 27 Jeff Blake | .30 | .10 |
| ☐ 28 Ki-Jana Carter | .20 | .07 |
| ☐ 29 Carl Pickens | .20 | .07 |
| ☐ 30 Darnay Scott | .20 | .07 |
| ☐ 31 Troy Aikman | .75 | .30 |
| ☐ 32 Charles Haley | .20 | .07 |
| ☐ 33 Michael Irvin | .30 | .10 |
| ☐ 34 Daryl Johnston | .20 | .07 |
| ☐ 35 Jay Novacek | .10 | .02 |
| ☐ 36 Deion Sanders | .40 | .15 |
| ☐ 37 Emmitt Smith | 1.25 | .50 |
| ☐ 38 Steve Atwater | .10 | .02 |
| ☐ 39 Terrell Davis | .60 | .25 |
| ☐ 40 John Elway | 1.50 | .60 |
| ☐ 41 Anthony Miller | .20 | .07 |
| ☐ 42 Shannon Sharpe | .20 | .07 |
| ☐ 43 Scott Mitchell | .20 | .07 |
| ☐ 44 Herman Moore | .20 | .07 |
| ☐ 45 Johnnie Morton | .20 | .07 |
| ☐ 46 Brett Perriman | .10 | .02 |
| ☐ 47 Barry Sanders | 1.25 | .50 |
| ☐ 48 Edgar Bennett | .20 | .07 |
| ☐ 49 Robert Brooks | .30 | .10 |
| ☐ 50 Mark Chmura | .20 | .07 |
| ☐ 51 Brett Favre | 1.50 | .60 |
| ☐ 52 Reggie White | .30 | .10 |
| ☐ 53 Mel Gray | .10 | .02 |
| ☐ 54 Steve McNair | .60 | .25 |
| ☐ 55 Chris Sanders | .20 | .07 |
| ☐ 56 Rodney Thomas | .10 | .02 |
| ☐ 57 Quentin Coryatt | .10 | .02 |
| ☐ 58 Sean Dawkins | .10 | .02 |
| ☐ 59 Ken Dilger | .20 | .07 |
| ☐ 60 Marshall Faulk | .40 | .15 |
| ☐ 61 Jim Harbaugh | .20 | .07 |
| ☐ 62 Tony Boselli | .10 | .02 |
| ☐ 63 Mark Brunell | .50 | .20 |
| ☐ 64 Natrone Means | .20 | .07 |
| ☐ 65 James O.Stewart | .20 | .07 |
| ☐ 66 Marcus Allen | .30 | .10 |
| ☐ 67 Steve Bono | .10 | .02 |
| ☐ 68 Neil Smith | .10 | .02 |
| ☐ 69 Derrick Thomas | .30 | .10 |
| ☐ 70 Tamarick Vanover | .20 | .07 |
| ☐ 71 Fred Barnett | .10 | .02 |
| ☐ 72 Eric Green | .10 | .02 |
| ☐ 73 Dan Marino | 1.50 | .60 |
| ☐ 74 O.J. McDuffie | .20 | .07 |
| ☐ 75 Bernie Parmalee | .10 | .02 |
| ☐ 76 Cris Carter | .30 | .10 |
| ☐ 77 Qadry Ismail | .20 | .07 |
| ☐ 78 Warren Moon | .20 | .07 |
| ☐ 79 Jake Reed | .20 | .07 |
| ☐ 80 Robert Smith | .20 | .07 |
| ☐ 81 Drew Bledsoe | .50 | .20 |
| ☐ 82 Vincent Brisby | .10 | .02 |
| ☐ 83 Ben Coates | .20 | .07 |
| ☐ 84 Curtis Martin | .60 | .25 |
| ☐ 85 Dave Meggett | .10 | .02 |
| ☐ 86 Mario Bates | .10 | .02 |
| ☐ 87 Jim Everett | .10 | .02 |
| ☐ 88 Michael Haynes | .10 | .02 |
| ☐ 89 Renaldo Turnbull | .10 | .02 |
| ☐ 90 Dave Brown | .10 | .02 |
| ☐ 91 Rodney Hampton | .20 | .07 |
| ☐ 92 Thomas Lewis | .10 | .02 |
| ☐ 93 Tyrone Wheatley | .20 | .07 |
| ☐ 94 Kyle Brady | .10 | .02 |
| ☐ 95 Hugh Douglas | .20 | .07 |
| ☐ 96 Aaron Glenn | .10 | .02 |
| ☐ 97 Jeff Graham | .10 | .02 |

|  |  | | |
|---|---|---|---|
| ❑ 98 | Adrian Murrell | .20 | .07 |
| ❑ 99 | Neil O'Donnell | .20 | .07 |
| ❑ 100 | Tim Brown | .30 | .10 |
| ❑ 101 | Jeff Hostetler | .10 | .02 |
| ❑ 102 | Napoleon Kaufman | .30 | .10 |
| ❑ 103 | Chester McGlockton | .10 | .02 |
| ❑ 104 | Harvey Williams | .10 | .02 |
| ❑ 105 | William Fuller | .10 | .02 |
| ❑ 106 | Charlie Garner | .20 | .07 |
| ❑ 107 | Ricky Watters | .20 | .07 |
| ❑ 108 | Calvin Williams | .10 | .02 |
| ❑ 109 | Jerome Bettis | .30 | .10 |
| ❑ 110 | Greg Lloyd | .20 | .07 |
| ❑ 111 | Byron Bam Morris | .10 | .02 |
| ❑ 112 | Kordell Stewart | .30 | .10 |
| ❑ 113 | Yancey Thigpen | .20 | .07 |
| ❑ 114 | Rod Woodson | .20 | .07 |
| ❑ 115 | Isaac Bruce | .10 | .02 |
| ❑ 116 | Troy Drayton | .10 | .02 |
| ❑ 117 | Leslie O'Neal | .10 | .02 |
| ❑ 118 | Steve Walsh | .10 | .02 |
| ❑ 119 | Marco Coleman | .10 | .02 |
| ❑ 120 | Aaron Hayden | .10 | .02 |
| ❑ 121 | Stan Humphries | .20 | .07 |
| ❑ 122 | Junior Seau | .30 | .10 |
| ❑ 123 | William Floyd | .20 | .07 |
| ❑ 124 | Brent Jones | .10 | .02 |
| ❑ 125 | Ken Norton | .10 | .02 |
| ❑ 126 | Jerry Rice | .75 | .30 |
| ❑ 127 | J.J. Stokes | .30 | .10 |
| ❑ 128 | Steve Young | .60 | .25 |
| ❑ 129 | Brian Blades | .10 | .02 |
| ❑ 130 | Joey Galloway | .30 | .10 |
| ❑ 131 | Rick Mirer | .20 | .07 |
| ❑ 132 | Chris Warren | .20 | .07 |
| ❑ 133 | Trent Dilfer | .30 | .10 |
| ❑ 134 | Alvin Harper | .10 | .02 |
| ❑ 135 | Hardy Nickerson | .10 | .02 |
| ❑ 136 | Errict Rhett | .20 | .07 |
| ❑ 137 | Terry Allen | .20 | .07 |
| ❑ 138 | Henry Ellard | .10 | .02 |
| ❑ 139 | Heath Shuler | .20 | .07 |
| ❑ 140 | Michael Westbrook | .30 | .10 |
| ❑ 141 | Karim Abdul-Jabbar RC | .30 | .10 |
| ❑ 142 | Mike Alstott RC | 1.00 | .40 |
| ❑ 143 | Marco Battaglia RC | .10 | .02 |
| ❑ 144 | Tim Biakabutuka RC | .30 | .10 |
| ❑ 145 | Tony Brackens RC | .10 | .02 |
| ❑ 146 | Duane Clemons RC | .10 | .02 |
| ❑ 147 | Ernie Conwell RC | .10 | .02 |
| ❑ 148 | Chris Darkins RC | .10 | .02 |
| ❑ 149 | Stephen Davis RC | 1.50 | .60 |
| ❑ 150 | Brian Dawkins RC | 1.25 | .50 |
| ❑ 151 | Rickey Dudley RC | .30 | .10 |
| ❑ 152 | Jason Dunn RC | .20 | .07 |
| ❑ 153 | Bobby Engram RC | .30 | .10 |
| ❑ 154 | Daryl Gardener RC | .10 | .02 |
| ❑ 155 | Eddie George RC | 1.25 | .50 |
| ❑ 156 | Terry Glenn RC | 1.00 | .40 |
| ❑ 157 | Kevin Hardy RC | .30 | .10 |
| ❑ 158 | Walt Harris RC | .10 | .02 |
| ❑ 159 | Marvin Harrison RC | 2.50 | 1.00 |
| ❑ 160 | Bobby Hoying RC | .30 | .10 |
| ❑ 161 | Keyshawn Johnson RC | 1.00 | .40 |
| ❑ 162 | Cedric Jones RC | .10 | .02 |
| ❑ 163 | Marcus Jones RC | .10 | .02 |
| ❑ 164 | Eddie Kennison RC | .30 | .10 |
| ❑ 165 | Ray Lewis RC | 2.50 | 1.00 |
| ❑ 166 | Derrick Mayes RC | .30 | .10 |
| ❑ 167 | Leeland McElroy RC | .20 | .07 |
| ❑ 168 | Johnny McWilliams RC | .20 | .07 |
| ❑ 169 | John Mobley RC | .10 | .02 |
| ❑ 170 | Alex Molden RC | .10 | .02 |
| ❑ 171 | Eric Moulds RC | 1.25 | .50 |
| ❑ 172 | Muhsin Muhammad RC | 1.00 | .40 |
| ❑ 173 | Jonathan Ogden RC | .30 | .10 |
| ❑ 174 | Lawrence Phillips RC | .30 | .10 |
| ❑ 175 | Stanley Pritchett RC | .20 | .07 |
| ❑ 176 | Simeon Rice RC | .75 | .30 |
| ❑ 177 | Bryan Still RC | .20 | .07 |
| ❑ 178 | Amani Toomer RC | 1.00 | .40 |
| ❑ 179 | Regan Upshaw RC | .10 | .02 |
| ❑ 180 | Alex Van Dyke RC | .20 | .07 |
| ❑ 181 | Barry Sanders PFW | .60 | .25 |

|  |  | | |
|---|---|---|---|
| ❑ 182 | Marcus Allen PFW | .30 | .10 |
| ❑ 183 | Bryce Paup PFW | .10 | .02 |
| ❑ 184 | Jerry Rice PFW | .40 | .15 |
| ❑ 185 | D.Howard/B.Christian PFW | .20 | .07 |
| ❑ 186 | Leon Lett PFW | .10 | .02 |
| ❑ 187 | Brett Favre PFW | .75 | .30 |
| ❑ 188 | G.Lloyd/D.Thomas PFW | .10 | .02 |
| ❑ 189 | Jeff Blake PFW | .20 | .07 |
| ❑ 190 | Emmitt Smith PFW | .60 | .25 |
| ❑ 191 | J.Elway/J.Hostetler PFW | .40 | .15 |
| ❑ 192 | Chiefs PFW | .10 | .02 |
| ❑ 193 | Marshall Faulk PFW | .30 | .10 |
| ❑ 194 | T.Aikman/S.Young PFW | .40 | .15 |
| ❑ 195 | Dan Marino PFW | .75 | .30 |
| ❑ 196 | Donta Jones PFW | .10 | .02 |
| ❑ 197 | Jim Kelly PFW | .30 | .10 |
| ❑ 198 | Checklist | .10 | .02 |
| ❑ 199 | Checklist | .10 | .02 |
| ❑ 200 | Checklist | .10 | .02 |
| ❑ P1 | Promo Sheet/WFloyd/TDil/Favre | 4.00 | 1.50 |

## 1997 Fleer

|  |  | | |
|---|---|---|---|
| ❑ COMPLETE SET (450) | | 40.00 | 15.00 |
| ❑ 1 | Mark Brunell | 1.00 | .40 |
| ❑ 2 | Andre Reed | .50 | .20 |
| ❑ 3 | Darrell Green | .50 | .20 |
| ❑ 4 | Mario Bates | .30 | .10 |
| ❑ 5 | Eddie George | .75 | .30 |
| ❑ 6 | Cris Carter | .75 | .30 |
| ❑ 7 | Terrell Owens | 1.00 | .40 |
| ❑ 8 | Bill Romanowski | .30 | .10 |
| ❑ 9 | Isaac Bruce | .75 | .30 |
| ❑ 10 | Eric Curry | .30 | .10 |
| ❑ 11 | Danny Kanell | .30 | .10 |
| ❑ 12 | Ki-Jana Carter | .30 | .10 |
| ❑ 13 | Antonio Freeman | .75 | .30 |
| ❑ 14 | Ricky Watters | .50 | .20 |
| ❑ 15 | Ty Law | .50 | .20 |
| ❑ 16 | Alonzo Spellman | .30 | .10 |
| ❑ 17 | Kordell Stewart | .75 | .30 |
| ❑ 18 | Jerry Rice | 1.50 | .60 |
| ❑ 19 | Derrick Alexander WR | .50 | .20 |
| ❑ 20 | Barry Sanders | 2.50 | 1.00 |
| ❑ 21 | Keyshawn Johnson | .75 | .30 |
| ❑ 22 | Emmitt Smith | 2.50 | 1.00 |
| ❑ 23 | Ricky Proehl | .30 | .10 |
| ❑ 24 | Daryl Gardener | .30 | .10 |
| ❑ 25 | Dan Saleaumua | .30 | .10 |
| ❑ 26 | Kevin Greene | .50 | .20 |
| ❑ 27 | Junior Seau | .75 | .30 |
| ❑ 28 | Randall McDaniel | .30 | .10 |
| ❑ 29 | Marshall Faulk | 1.00 | .40 |
| ❑ 30 | Lorenzo Lynch | .30 | .10 |
| ❑ 31 | Terance Mathis | .50 | .20 |
| ❑ 32 | Warren Sapp | .50 | .20 |
| ❑ 33 | Chris Sanders | .30 | .10 |
| ❑ 34 | Tom Carter | .30 | .10 |
| ❑ 35 | Aeneas Williams | .30 | .10 |
| ❑ 36 | Lawrence Phillips | .30 | .10 |
| ❑ 37 | John Elway | 3.00 | 1.25 |
| ❑ 38 | Stanley Richard | .30 | .10 |
| ❑ 39 | Darryl Williams | .30 | .10 |
| ❑ 40 | Phillippi Sparks | .30 | .10 |
| ❑ 41 | Tedy Bruschi | 1.50 | .60 |
| ❑ 42 | Merton Hanks | .30 | .10 |
| ❑ 43 | Ray Lewis | 1.25 | .50 |
| ❑ 44 | Erik Williams | .30 | .10 |
| ❑ 45 | Jason Gildon | .30 | .10 |

|  |  | | |
|---|---|---|---|
| ❑ 46 | George Koonce | .30 | .10 |
| ❑ 47 | Louis Oliver | .30 | .10 |
| ❑ 48 | Muhsin Muhammad | .50 | .20 |
| ❑ 49 | Daryl Hobbs | .30 | .10 |
| ❑ 50 | Terry Glenn | .75 | .30 |
| ❑ 51 | Marvin Harrison | .75 | .30 |
| ❑ 52 | Brian Dawkins | .30 | .10 |
| ❑ 53 | Dale Carter | .30 | .10 |
| ❑ 54 | Alex Molden | .30 | .10 |
| ❑ 55 | Raymont Harris | .30 | .10 |
| ❑ 56 | Jeff Burris | .30 | .10 |
| ❑ 57 | Don Beebe | .30 | .10 |
| ❑ 58 | Jamir Miller | .30 | .10 |
| ❑ 59 | Carl Pickens | .50 | .20 |
| ❑ 60 | Antonio London | .30 | .10 |
| ❑ 61 | Courtney Hall | .30 | .10 |
| ❑ 62 | Derrick Brooks | .75 | .30 |
| ❑ 63 | Chris Boniol | .30 | .10 |
| ❑ 64 | Jeff Lageman | .30 | .10 |
| ❑ 65 | Roy Barker | .30 | .10 |
| ❑ 66 | Devin Bush | .30 | .10 |
| ❑ 67 | Aaron Glenn | .30 | .10 |
| ❑ 68 | Wayne Simmons | .30 | .10 |
| ❑ 69 | Steve Atwater | .30 | .10 |
| ❑ 70 | Jimmie Jones | .30 | .10 |
| ❑ 71 | Mark Carrier WR | .30 | .10 |
| ❑ 72 | Chris Chandler | .50 | .20 |
| ❑ 73 | Andy Harmon | .30 | .10 |
| ❑ 74 | John Friesz | .30 | .10 |
| ❑ 75 | Karim Abdul-Jabbar | .50 | .20 |
| ❑ 76 | Levon Kirkland | .30 | .10 |
| ❑ 77 | Torrance Small | .30 | .10 |
| ❑ 78 | Harvey Williams | .30 | .10 |
| ❑ 79 | Chris Calloway | .30 | .10 |
| ❑ 80 | Vinny Testaverde | .50 | .20 |
| ❑ 81 | Bryant Young | .30 | .10 |
| ❑ 82 | Ray Buchanan | .30 | .10 |
| ❑ 83 | Robert Smith | .50 | .20 |
| ❑ 84 | Robert Brooks | .50 | .20 |
| ❑ 85 | Ray Crockett | .30 | .10 |
| ❑ 86 | Bennie Blades | .30 | .10 |
| ❑ 87 | Mark Carrier DB | .30 | .10 |
| ❑ 88 | Mike Tomczak | .30 | .10 |
| ❑ 89 | Derick Holmes | .30 | .10 |
| ❑ 90 | Drew Bledsoe | 1.00 | .40 |
| ❑ 91 | Darren Woodson | .30 | .10 |
| ❑ 92 | Dan Wilkinson | .30 | .10 |
| ❑ 93 | Charles Way | .30 | .10 |
| ❑ 94 | Ray Farmer | .30 | .10 |
| ❑ 95 | Marcus Allen | .75 | .30 |
| ❑ 96 | Marco Coleman | .30 | .10 |
| ❑ 97 | Zach Thomas | .75 | .30 |
| ❑ 98 | Wesley Walls | .50 | .20 |
| ❑ 99 | Frank Wycheck | .30 | .10 |
| ❑ 100 | Troy Aikman | 1.50 | .60 |
| ❑ 101 | Clyde Simmons | .30 | .10 |
| ❑ 102 | Courtney Hawkins | .30 | .10 |
| ❑ 103 | Chuck Smith | .30 | .10 |
| ❑ 104 | Neil O'Donnell | .50 | .20 |
| ❑ 105 | Kevin Carter | .30 | .10 |
| ❑ 106 | Chris Slade | .30 | .10 |
| ❑ 107 | Jessie Armstead | .30 | .10 |
| ❑ 108 | Sean Dawkins | .30 | .10 |
| ❑ 109 | Robert Blackmon | .30 | .10 |
| ❑ 110 | Kevin Smith | .30 | .10 |
| ❑ 111 | Lonnie Johnson | .30 | .10 |
| ❑ 112 | Craig Newsome | .30 | .10 |
| ❑ 113 | Jonathan Ogden | .30 | .10 |
| ❑ 114 | Chris Zorich | .30 | .10 |
| ❑ 115 | Tim Brown | .75 | .30 |
| ❑ 116 | Fred Barnett | .30 | .10 |
| ❑ 117 | Michael Haynes | .30 | .10 |
| ❑ 118 | Eric Hill | .30 | .10 |
| ❑ 119 | Ronnie Harmon | .30 | .10 |
| ❑ 120 | Sean Gilbert | .30 | .10 |
| ❑ 121 | Derrick Alexander DE | .30 | .10 |
| ❑ 122 | Derrick Thomas | .75 | .30 |
| ❑ 123 | Tyrone Wheatley | .30 | .10 |
| ❑ 124 | Cortez Kennedy | .50 | .20 |
| ❑ 125 | Jeff George | .50 | .20 |
| ❑ 126 | Chad Cota | .30 | .10 |
| ❑ 127 | Gary Zimmerman | .30 | .10 |
| ❑ 128 | Johnnie Morton | .50 | .20 |
| ❑ 129 | Chad Brown | .30 | .10 |

|  |  | | |
|---|---|---|---|
| 130 | Marvcus Patton | .30 | .10 |
| 131 | James O.Stewart | .50 | .20 |
| 132 | Terry Kirby | .50 | .20 |
| 133 | Chris Mims | .30 | .10 |
| 134 | William Thomas | .30 | .10 |
| 135 | Steve Tasker | .30 | .10 |
| 136 | Jason Belser | .30 | .10 |
| 137 | Bryan Cox | .30 | .10 |
| 138 | Jessie Tuggle | .30 | .10 |
| 139 | Ashley Ambrose | .30 | .10 |
| 140 | Mark Chmura | .50 | .20 |
| 141 | Jeff Hostetler | .30 | .10 |
| 142 | Rich Owens | .30 | .10 |
| 143 | Willie Davis | .30 | .10 |
| 144 | Hardy Nickerson | .30 | .10 |
| 145 | Curtis Martin | 1.00 | .40 |
| 146 | Ken Norton | .30 | .10 |
| 147 | Victor Green | .30 | .10 |
| 148 | Anthony Miller | .30 | .10 |
| 149 | John Kasay | .30 | .10 |
| 150 | O.J. McDuffie | .50 | .20 |
| 151 | Darren Perry | .30 | .10 |
| 152 | Luther Elliss | .30 | .10 |
| 153 | Greg Hill | .30 | .10 |
| 154 | John Randle | .50 | .20 |
| 155 | Stephen Grant | .30 | .10 |
| 156 | Leon Lett | .30 | .10 |
| 157 | Darrien Gordon | .30 | .10 |
| 158 | Ray Zellars | .30 | .10 |
| 159 | Michael Jackson | .50 | .20 |
| 160 | Leslie O'Neal | .30 | .10 |
| 161 | Bruce Smith | .50 | .20 |
| 162 | Santana Dotson | .30 | .10 |
| 163 | Bobby Hebert | .30 | .10 |
| 164 | Keith Hamilton | .30 | .10 |
| 165 | Tony Boselli | .30 | .10 |
| 166 | Alfred Williams | .30 | .10 |
| 167 | Ty Detmer | .50 | .20 |
| 168 | Chester McGlockton | .30 | .10 |
| 169 | William Floyd | .50 | .20 |
| 170 | Bruce Matthews | .30 | .10 |
| 171 | Simeon Rice | .50 | .20 |
| 172 | Scott Mitchell | .50 | .20 |
| 173 | Ricardo McDonald | .30 | .10 |
| 174 | Tyrone Poole | .30 | .10 |
| 175 | Greg Lloyd | .30 | .10 |
| 176 | Bruce Armstrong | .30 | .10 |
| 177 | Erik Kramer | .30 | .10 |
| 178 | Kimble Anders | .50 | .20 |
| 179 | Lamar Smith | .75 | .30 |
| 180 | Tony Tolbert | .30 | .10 |
| 181 | Joe Aska | .30 | .10 |
| 182 | Eric Allen | .30 | .10 |
| 183 | Eric Turner | .30 | .10 |
| 184 | Brad Johnson | .75 | .30 |
| 185 | Tony Martin | .50 | .20 |
| 186 | Mike Mamula | .30 | .10 |
| 187 | Irving Spikes | .30 | .10 |
| 188 | Keith Jackson | .30 | .10 |
| 189 | Carlton Bailey | .30 | .10 |
| 190 | Tyrone Braxton | .30 | .10 |
| 191 | Chad Bratzke | .30 | .10 |
| 192 | Adrian Murrell | .50 | .20 |
| 193 | Roman Phifer | .30 | .10 |
| 194 | Todd Collins | .30 | .10 |
| 195 | Chris Warren | .50 | .20 |
| 196 | Kevin Hardy | .30 | .10 |
| 197 | Rick Mirer | .30 | .10 |
| 198 | Cornelius Bennett | .30 | .10 |
| 199 | Jimmy Hitchcock | .30 | .10 |
| 200 | Michael Irvin | .75 | .30 |
| 201 | Quentin Coryatt | .30 | .10 |
| 202 | Reggie White | .75 | .30 |
| 203 | Larry Centers | .50 | .20 |
| 204 | Rodney Thomas | .30 | .10 |
| 205 | Dana Stubblefield | .30 | .10 |
| 206 | Rod Woodson | .50 | .20 |
| 207 | Rhett Hall | .30 | .10 |
| 208 | Steve Tovar | .30 | .10 |
| 209 | Michael Westbrook | .50 | .20 |
| 210 | Steve Wisniewski | .30 | .10 |
| 211 | Carlester Crumpler | .30 | .10 |
| 212 | Elvis Grbac | .50 | .20 |
| 213 | Tim Bowens | .30 | .10 |
| 214 | Robert Porcher | .30 | .10 |
| 215 | John Carney | .30 | .10 |
| 216 | Anthony Newman | .30 | .10 |
| 217 | Earnest Byner | .30 | .10 |
| 218 | Dewayne Washington | .30 | .10 |
| 219 | Willie Green | .30 | .10 |
| 220 | Terry Allen | .75 | .30 |
| 221 | William Fuller | .30 | .10 |
| 222 | Al Del Greco | .30 | .10 |
| 223 | Trent Dilfer | .75 | .30 |
| 224 | Michael Dean Perry | .30 | .10 |
| 225 | Larry Allen | .30 | .10 |
| 226 | Mark Brunner | .30 | .10 |
| 227 | Clay Matthews | .30 | .10 |
| 228 | Reuben Brown | .30 | .10 |
| 229 | Edgar Bennett | .50 | .20 |
| 230 | Neil Smith | .50 | .20 |
| 231 | Ken Harvey | .30 | .10 |
| 232 | Kyle Brady | .30 | .10 |
| 233 | Corey Miller | .30 | .10 |
| 234 | Tony Siragusa | .30 | .10 |
| 235 | Todd Sauerbrun | .30 | .10 |
| 236 | Daniel Stubbs | .30 | .10 |
| 237 | Robb Thomas | .30 | .10 |
| 238 | Jimmy Smith | .50 | .20 |
| 239 | Marquez Pope | .30 | .10 |
| 240 | Tim Biakabutaka | .50 | .20 |
| 241 | Jamie Asher | .30 | .10 |
| 242 | Steve McNair | 1.00 | .40 |
| 243 | Harold Green | .30 | .10 |
| 244 | Frank Sanders | .50 | .20 |
| 245 | Joe Johnson | .30 | .10 |
| 246 | Eric Bieniemy | .30 | .10 |
| 247 | Kevin Turner | .30 | .10 |
| 248 | Rickey Dudley | .50 | .20 |
| 249 | Orlando Thomas | .30 | .10 |
| 250 | Dan Marino | 3.00 | 1.25 |
| 251 | Deion Sanders | .75 | .30 |
| 252 | Dan Williams | .30 | .10 |
| 253 | Sam Gash | .30 | .10 |
| 254 | Lonnie Marts | .30 | .10 |
| 255 | Mo Lewis | .30 | .10 |
| 256 | Charles Johnson | .50 | .20 |
| 257 | Chris Jacke | .30 | .10 |
| 258 | Keenan McCardell | .50 | .20 |
| 259 | Donnell Woolford | .30 | .10 |
| 260 | Terrance Shaw | .30 | .10 |
| 261 | Jason Dunn | .30 | .10 |
| 262 | Willie McGinest | .30 | .10 |
| 263 | Ken Dilger | .30 | .10 |
| 264 | Keith Lyle | .30 | .10 |
| 265 | Antonio Langham | .30 | .10 |
| 266 | Carlton Gray | .30 | .10 |
| 267 | LeShon Johnson | .30 | .10 |
| 268 | Thurman Thomas | .75 | .30 |
| 269 | Jesse Campbell | .30 | .10 |
| 270 | Carnell Lake | .30 | .10 |
| 271 | Cris Dishman | .30 | .10 |
| 272 | Kevin Williams | .30 | .10 |
| 273 | Troy Brown | .30 | .10 |
| 274 | William Roaf | .30 | .10 |
| 275 | Terrell Davis | 1.00 | .40 |
| 276 | Herman Moore | .50 | .20 |
| 277 | Walt Harris | .30 | .10 |
| 278 | Mark Collins | .30 | .10 |
| 279 | Bert Emanuel | .50 | .20 |
| 280 | Qadry Ismail | .50 | .20 |
| 281 | Phil Hansen | .30 | .10 |
| 282 | Steve Young | 1.00 | .40 |
| 283 | Michael Sinclair | .30 | .10 |
| 284 | Jeff Graham | .30 | .10 |
| 285 | Sam Mills | .30 | .10 |
| 286 | Terry McDaniel | .30 | .10 |
| 287 | Eugene Robinson | .30 | .10 |
| 288 | Tony Bennett | .30 | .10 |
| 289 | Daryl Johnston | .50 | .20 |
| 290 | Eric Swann | .30 | .10 |
| 291 | Byron Bam Morris | .30 | .10 |
| 292 | Thomas Lewis | .30 | .10 |
| 293 | Terrell Fletcher | .30 | .10 |
| 294 | Gus Frerotte | .30 | .10 |
| 295 | Stanley Pritchett | .30 | .10 |
| 296 | Mike Alstott | .75 | .30 |
| 297 | Will Shields | .30 | .10 |
| 298 | Errict Rhett | .30 | .10 |
| 299 | Garrison Hearst | .50 | .20 |
| 300 | Kerry Collins | .75 | .30 |
| 301 | Darryll Lewis | .30 | .10 |
| 302 | Chris T. Jones | .30 | .10 |
| 303 | Yancey Thigpen | .50 | .20 |
| 304 | Jackie Harris | .30 | .10 |
| 305 | Steve Christie | .30 | .10 |
| 306 | Gilbert Brown | .50 | .20 |
| 307 | Terry Wooden | .30 | .10 |
| 308 | Pete Mitchell | .30 | .10 |
| 309 | Tim McDonald | .30 | .10 |
| 310 | Jake Reed | .50 | .20 |
| 311 | Ed McCaffrey | .50 | .20 |
| 312 | Chris Doleman | .30 | .10 |
| 313 | Eric Metcalf | .50 | .20 |
| 314 | Ricky Reynolds | .30 | .10 |
| 315 | David Sloan | .30 | .10 |
| 316 | Marvin Washington | .30 | .10 |
| 317 | Herschel Walker | .50 | .20 |
| 318 | Michael Timpson | .30 | .10 |
| 319 | Blaine Bishop | .30 | .10 |
| 320 | Irv Smith | .30 | .10 |
| 321 | Seth Joyner | .30 | .10 |
| 322 | Terrell Buckley | .30 | .10 |
| 323 | Michael Strahan | .50 | .20 |
| 324 | Sam Adams | .30 | .10 |
| 325 | Leslie Shepherd | .30 | .10 |
| 326 | James Jett | .50 | .20 |
| 327 | Anthony Pleasant | .30 | .10 |
| 328 | Lee Woodall | .30 | .10 |
| 329 | Shannon Sharpe | .50 | .20 |
| 330 | Jamal Anderson | .75 | .30 |
| 331 | Andre Hastings | .30 | .10 |
| 332 | Troy Vincent | .30 | .10 |
| 333 | Sean LaChapelle | .30 | .10 |
| 334 | Winslow Oliver | .30 | .10 |
| 335 | Sean Jones | .30 | .10 |
| 336 | Darnay Scott | .50 | .20 |
| 337 | Todd Lyght | .30 | .10 |
| 338 | Leonard Russell | .30 | .10 |
| 339 | Nate Newton | .30 | .10 |
| 340 | Zack Crockett | .30 | .10 |
| 341 | Amp Lee | .30 | .10 |
| 342 | Bobby Engram | .50 | .20 |
| 343 | Mike Hollis | .30 | .10 |
| 344 | Rodney Hampton | .50 | .20 |
| 345 | Mel Gray | .30 | .10 |
| 346 | Van Malone | .30 | .10 |
| 347 | Aaron Craver | .30 | .10 |
| 348 | Jim Everett | .30 | .10 |
| 349 | Trace Armstrong | .30 | .10 |
| 350 | Pat Swilling | .30 | .10 |
| 351 | Brent Jones | .50 | .20 |
| 352 | Chris Spielman | .30 | .10 |
| 353 | Brett Perriman | .30 | .10 |
| 354 | Brian Kinchen | .30 | .10 |
| 355 | Joey Galloway | .50 | .20 |
| 356 | Henry Ellard | .30 | .10 |
| 357 | Ben Coates | .50 | .20 |
| 358 | Dorsey Levens | .75 | .30 |
| 359 | Charlie Garner | .50 | .20 |
| 360 | Eric Pegram | .30 | .10 |
| 361 | Anthony Johnson | .30 | .10 |
| 362 | Rashaan Salaam | .30 | .10 |
| 363 | Jeff Blake | .50 | .20 |
| 364 | Kent Graham | .30 | .10 |
| 365 | Broderick Thomas | .30 | .10 |
| 366 | Richmond Webb | .30 | .10 |
| 367 | Alfred Pupunu | .30 | .10 |
| 368 | Mark Stepnoski | .30 | .10 |
| 369 | David Dunn | .30 | .10 |
| 370 | Bobby Houston | .30 | .10 |
| 371 | Andre Reed | .50 | .20 |
| 372 | Quinn Early | .30 | .10 |
| 373 | LeRoy Butler | .30 | .10 |
| 374 | Kurt Gouveia | .30 | .10 |
| 375 | Greg Biekert | .30 | .10 |
| 376 | Jim Harbaugh | .50 | .20 |
| 377 | Eric Bjornson | .30 | .10 |
| 378 | Craig Heyward | .30 | .10 |
| 379 | Steve Bono | .50 | .20 |
| 380 | Tony Banks | .75 | .30 |
| 381 | John Mobley | .30 | .10 |

| | | |
|---|---|---|
| ☐ 382 Irving Fryar | .50 | .20 |
| ☐ 383 Dermontti Dawson | .30 | .10 |
| ☐ 384 Eric Davis | .30 | .10 |
| ☐ 385 Natrone Means | .50 | .20 |
| ☐ 386 Jason Sehorn | .50 | .20 |
| ☐ 387 Michael McCrary | .30 | .10 |
| ☐ 388 Corwin Brown | .30 | .10 |
| ☐ 389 Kevin Glover | .30 | .10 |
| ☐ 390 Jerris McPhail | .30 | .10 |
| ☐ 391 Bobby Taylor | .30 | .10 |
| ☐ 392 Tony McGee | .30 | .10 |
| ☐ 393 Curtis Conway | .50 | .20 |
| ☐ 394 Napoleon Kaufman | .75 | .30 |
| ☐ 395 Brian Blades | .30 | .10 |
| ☐ 396 Richard Dent | .30 | .10 |
| ☐ 397 Dave Brown | .30 | .10 |
| ☐ 398 Stan Humphries | .50 | .20 |
| ☐ 399 Stevon Moore | .30 | .10 |
| ☐ 400 Brett Favre | 3.00 | 1.50 |
| ☐ 401 Jerome Bettis | .75 | .30 |
| ☐ 402 Darrin Smith | .30 | .10 |
| ☐ 403 Chris Penn | .30 | .10 |
| ☐ 404 Rob Moore | .50 | .20 |
| ☐ 405 Micheal Barrow | .30 | .10 |
| ☐ 406 Tony Brackens | .30 | .10 |
| ☐ 407 Wayne Martin | .30 | .10 |
| ☐ 408 Warren Moon | .75 | .30 |
| ☐ 409 Jason Elam | .50 | .20 |
| ☐ 410 J.J. Birden | .30 | .10 |
| ☐ 411 Hugh Douglas | .30 | .10 |
| ☐ 412 Lamar Lathon | .30 | .10 |
| ☐ 413 John Kidd | .30 | .10 |
| ☐ 414 Bryce Paup | .30 | .10 |
| ☐ 415 Shawn Jefferson | .30 | .10 |
| ☐ 416 Leeland McElroy SS | .30 | .10 |
| ☐ 417 Elbert Shelley SS | .30 | .10 |
| ☐ 418 Jermaine Lewis SS | .50 | .20 |
| ☐ 419 Eric Moulds SS | .75 | .30 |
| ☐ 420 Michael Bates SS | .30 | .10 |
| ☐ 421 John Mangum SS | .30 | .10 |
| ☐ 422 Corey Sawyer SS | .30 | .10 |
| ☐ 423 Jim Schwantz SS RC | .30 | .10 |
| ☐ 424 Rod Smith WR SS | .75 | .30 |
| ☐ 425 Glyn Milburn SS | .30 | .10 |
| ☐ 426 Desmond Howard SS | .50 | .20 |
| ☐ 427 John Henry Mills SS RC | .30 | .10 |
| ☐ 428 Cary Blanchard SS RC | .30 | .10 |
| ☐ 429 Chris Hudson SS | .30 | .10 |
| ☐ 430 Tamarick Vanover SS | .50 | .20 |
| ☐ 431 Kirby Dar Dar SS RC | .50 | .20 |
| ☐ 432 David Palmer SS | .50 | .20 |
| ☐ 433 Dave Meggett SS | .30 | .10 |
| ☐ 434 Tyrone Hughes SS | .30 | .10 |
| ☐ 435 Amani Toomer SS | .50 | .20 |
| ☐ 436 Wayne Chrebet SS | .50 | .20 |
| ☐ 437 Carl Kidd RC SS | .30 | .10 |
| ☐ 438 Derrick Witherspoon SS | .30 | .10 |
| ☐ 439 Jahine Arnold SS | .30 | .10 |
| ☐ 440 Andre Coleman SS | .30 | .10 |
| ☐ 441 Jeff Wilkins SS | .30 | .10 |
| ☐ 442 Jay Bellamy SS RC | .30 | .10 |
| ☐ 443 Eddie Kennison SS | .50 | .20 |
| ☐ 444 Nilo Silvan SS | .30 | .10 |
| ☐ 445 Brian Mitchell SS | .30 | .10 |
| ☐ 446 Garrison Hearst CL | .50 | .20 |
| ☐ 447 Napoleon Kaufman CL | .75 | .30 |
| ☐ 448 Brian Mitchell CL | .30 | .10 |
| ☐ 449 Rodney Hampton CL | .30 | .10 |
| ☐ 450 Edgar Bennett CL | .30 | .10 |
| ☐ S1 Mark Chmura Sample | 1.00 | .40 |
| ☐ AU1 Reggie White AUTO | 125.00 | 75.00 |

## 2006 Fleer

| | | |
|---|---|---|
| ☐ 1 Anquan Boldin | .40 | .15 |
| ☐ 2 Larry Fitzgerald | .50 | .20 |
| ☐ 3 J.J. Arrington | .40 | .15 |
| ☐ 4 Michael Vick | .50 | .20 |
| ☐ 5 Warrick Dunn | .40 | .15 |
| ☐ 6 Roddy White | .30 | .12 |
| ☐ 7 Jamal Lewis | .40 | .15 |
| ☐ 8 Kyle Boller | .40 | .15 |
| ☐ 9 Derrick Mason | .40 | .15 |
| ☐ 10 Willis McGahee | .40 | .15 |
| ☐ 11 J.P. Losman | .40 | .15 |

| | | |
|---|---|---|
| ☐ 12 Lee Evans | .40 | .15 |
| ☐ 13 Steve Smith | .50 | .20 |
| ☐ 14 Jake Delhomme | .40 | .15 |
| ☐ 15 DeShaun Foster | .40 | .15 |
| ☐ 16 Rex Grossman | .50 | .20 |
| ☐ 17 Brian Urlacher | .50 | .20 |
| ☐ 18 Thomas Jones | .40 | .15 |
| ☐ 19 Carson Palmer | .50 | .20 |
| ☐ 20 Chad Johnson | .40 | .15 |
| ☐ 21 Rudi Johnson | .40 | .15 |
| ☐ 22 Charlie Frye | .40 | .15 |
| ☐ 23 Braylon Edwards | .50 | .20 |
| ☐ 24 Reuben Droughns | .40 | .15 |
| ☐ 25 Julius Jones | .50 | .20 |
| ☐ 26 Drew Bledsoe | .50 | .20 |
| ☐ 27 Terry Glenn | .40 | .15 |
| ☐ 28 Jake Plummer | .40 | .15 |
| ☐ 29 Tatum Bell | .40 | .15 |
| ☐ 30 Champ Bailey | .40 | .15 |
| ☐ 31 Rod Smith | .40 | .15 |
| ☐ 32 Roy Williams WR | .50 | .20 |
| ☐ 33 Kevin Jones | .50 | .20 |
| ☐ 34 Mike Williams | .50 | .20 |
| ☐ 35 Brett Favre | 1.00 | .40 |
| ☐ 36 Ahman Green | .40 | .15 |
| ☐ 37 Javon Walker | .40 | .15 |
| ☐ 38 David Carr | .40 | .15 |
| ☐ 39 Andre Johnson | .40 | .15 |
| ☐ 40 Domanick Davis | .40 | .15 |
| ☐ 41 Peyton Manning | .75 | .30 |
| ☐ 42 Edgerrin James | .50 | .20 |
| ☐ 43 Marvin Harrison | .50 | .20 |
| ☐ 44 Reggie Wayne | .40 | .15 |
| ☐ 45 Byron Leftwich | .40 | .15 |
| ☐ 46 Fred Taylor | .40 | .15 |
| ☐ 47 Ernest Wilford | .40 | .15 |
| ☐ 48 Larry Johnson | .40 | .15 |
| ☐ 49 Trent Green | .40 | .15 |
| ☐ 50 Tony Gonzalez | .40 | .15 |
| ☐ 51 Ronnie Brown | .50 | .20 |
| ☐ 52 Ricky Williams | .30 | .10 |
| ☐ 53 Chris Chambers | .40 | .15 |
| ☐ 54 Daunte Culpepper | .50 | .20 |
| ☐ 55 Troy Williamson | .40 | .15 |
| ☐ 56 Brad Johnson | .40 | .15 |
| ☐ 57 Tom Brady | .75 | .30 |
| ☐ 58 Deion Branch | .40 | .15 |
| ☐ 59 Corey Dillon | .40 | .15 |
| ☐ 60 Deuce McAllister | .40 | .15 |
| ☐ 61 Donte Stallworth | .40 | .15 |
| ☐ 62 Joe Horn | .40 | .15 |
| ☐ 63 Eli Manning | .60 | .25 |
| ☐ 64 Tiki Barber | .50 | .20 |
| ☐ 65 Plaxico Burress | .40 | .15 |
| ☐ 66 Jeremy Shockey | .50 | .20 |
| ☐ 67 Chad Pennington | .40 | .15 |
| ☐ 68 Curtis Martin | .50 | .20 |
| ☐ 69 Laveranues Coles | .40 | .15 |
| ☐ 70 Randy Moss | .50 | .20 |
| ☐ 71 Aaron Brooks | .40 | .15 |
| ☐ 72 LaMont Jordan | .40 | .15 |
| ☐ 73 Donovan McNabb | .50 | .20 |
| ☐ 74 Brian Westbrook | .40 | .15 |
| ☐ 75 Terrell Owens | .50 | .20 |
| ☐ 76 Ben Roethlisberger | .75 | .30 |
| ☐ 77 Hines Ward | .50 | .20 |
| ☐ 78 Willie Parker | .60 | .25 |
| ☐ 79 Heath Miller | .40 | .15 |

| | | |
|---|---|---|
| ☐ 80 LaDainian Tomlinson | .60 | .25 |
| ☐ 81 Drew Brees | .50 | .20 |
| ☐ 82 Antonio Gates | .50 | .20 |
| ☐ 83 Alex Smith QB | .50 | .20 |
| ☐ 84 Antonio Bryant | .40 | .15 |
| ☐ 85 Frank Gore | .50 | .20 |
| ☐ 86 Shaun Alexander | .40 | .15 |
| ☐ 87 Matt Hasselbeck | .40 | .15 |
| ☐ 88 Darrell Jackson | .40 | .15 |
| ☐ 89 Marc Bulger | .40 | .15 |
| ☐ 90 Steven Jackson | .40 | .15 |
| ☐ 91 Torry Holt | .40 | .15 |
| ☐ 92 Cadillac Williams | .50 | .20 |
| ☐ 93 Chris Simms | .40 | .15 |
| ☐ 94 Joey Galloway | .40 | .15 |
| ☐ 95 Steve McNair | .40 | .15 |
| ☐ 96 Chris Brown | .40 | .15 |
| ☐ 97 Drew Bennett | .40 | .15 |
| ☐ 98 Clinton Portis | .50 | .20 |
| ☐ 99 Santana Moss | .40 | .15 |
| ☐ 100 Mark Brunell | .40 | .15 |
| ☐ 101 A.J. Hawk RC | 4.00 | 1.50 |
| ☐ 102 A.J. Nicholson RC | 1.25 | .50 |
| ☐ 103 Abdul Hodge RC | 2.00 | .75 |
| ☐ 104 Andre Hall RC | 2.00 | .75 |
| ☐ 105 Anthony Fasano RC | 2.00 | .75 |
| ☐ 106 Antonio Cromartie RC | 2.00 | .75 |
| ☐ 107 Ashton Youboty RC | 2.00 | .75 |
| ☐ 108 Bobby Carpenter RC | 2.00 | .75 |
| ☐ 109 Brad Smith RC | 2.00 | .75 |
| ☐ 110 Greg Jennings RC | 3.00 | 1.25 |
| ☐ 111 Brandon Williams RC | 1.50 | .60 |
| ☐ 112 Brian Calhoun RC | 1.50 | .60 |
| ☐ 113 Brodie Croyle RC | 2.50 | 1.00 |
| ☐ 114 Brodrick Bunkley RC | 2.00 | .75 |
| ☐ 115 Bruce Gradkowski RC | 2.00 | .75 |
| ☐ 116 Chad Greenway RC | 2.00 | .75 |
| ☐ 117 Chad Jackson RC | 1.50 | .60 |
| ☐ 118 Charles Davis RC | 1.50 | .60 |
| ☐ 119 Charles Gordon RC | 1.50 | .60 |
| ☐ 120 Charlie Whitehurst RC | 2.00 | .75 |
| ☐ 121 Claude Wroten RC | 1.25 | .50 |
| ☐ 122 Cory Rodgers RC | 2.00 | .75 |
| ☐ 123 D.J. Shockley RC | 2.00 | .75 |
| ☐ 124 Darnell Bing RC | 2.00 | .75 |
| ☐ 125 Darrell Hackney RC | 1.50 | .60 |
| ☐ 126 David Thomas RC | 1.50 | .60 |
| ☐ 127 D'Brickashaw Ferguson RC | 2.00 | .75 |
| ☐ 128 DeAngelo Williams RC | 3.00 | 1.25 |
| ☐ 129 DeMeco Ryans RC | 2.50 | 1.00 |
| ☐ 130 Demetrius Williams RC | 2.00 | .75 |
| ☐ 131 Derek Hagan RC | 2.00 | .75 |
| ☐ 132 Devin Hester RC | 4.00 | 1.50 |
| ☐ 133 Dominique Byrd RC | 1.50 | .60 |
| ☐ 134 DonTrell Moore RC | 1.50 | .60 |
| ☐ 135 D'Qwell Jackson RC | 1.50 | .60 |
| ☐ 136 Drew Olson RC | 1.50 | .60 |
| ☐ 137 Elvis Dumervil RC | 1.25 | .50 |
| ☐ 138 Ernie Sims RC | 2.00 | .75 |
| ☐ 139 Garrett Mills RC | 2.00 | .75 |
| ☐ 140 Gerald Riggs RC | 2.00 | .75 |
| ☐ 141 Greg Lee RC | 1.50 | .60 |
| ☐ 142 Haloti Ngata RC | 2.00 | .75 |
| ☐ 143 Hank Baskett RC | 2.00 | .75 |
| ☐ 144 Jason Allen RC | 2.00 | .75 |
| ☐ 145 Jason Avant RC | 2.00 | .75 |
| ☐ 146 Jay Cutler RC | 8.00 | 3.00 |
| ☐ 147 Jeff Webb RC | 1.50 | .60 |
| ☐ 148 Jeremy Bloom RC | 1.50 | .60 |
| ☐ 149 Jerome Harrison RC | 2.00 | .75 |
| ☐ 150 Jimmy Williams RC | 2.00 | .75 |
| ☐ 151 Joe Klopfenstein RC | 1.50 | .60 |
| ☐ 152 Johnathan Joseph RC | 1.50 | .60 |
| ☐ 153 Joseph Addai RC | 6.00 | 2.50 |
| ☐ 154 Jovon Bouknight RC | 1.50 | .60 |
| ☐ 155 Kai Parham RC | 2.00 | .75 |
| ☐ 156 Kamerion Wimbley RC | 2.00 | .75 |
| ☐ 157 Kellen Clemens RC | 2.50 | 1.00 |
| ☐ 158 Kelly Jennings RC | 2.00 | .75 |
| ☐ 159 Ko Simpson RC | 1.50 | .60 |
| ☐ 160 Laurence Maroney RC | 5.00 | 2.00 |
| ☐ 161 Lawrence Vickers RC | 1.50 | .60 |
| ☐ 162 LenDale White RC | 4.00 | 1.50 |
| ☐ 163 Leon Washington RC | 2.00 | .75 |

| | | | |
|---|---|---|---|
| ❏ 164 Leonard Pope RC | 2.00 | .75 |
| ❏ 165 Manny Lawson RC | 2.00 | .75 |
| ❏ 166 Marcedes Lewis RC | 2.00 | .75 |
| ❏ 167 Marcus McNeill RC | 1.50 | .60 |
| ❏ 168 Donte Whitner RC | 2.00 | .75 |
| ❏ 169 Mario Williams RC | 3.00 | 1.25 |
| ❏ 170 Martin Nance RC | 1.50 | .60 |
| ❏ 171 Mathias Kiwanuka RC | 2.50 | 1.00 |
| ❏ 172 Matt Bernstein RC | 1.00 | .40 |
| ❏ 173 Matt Leinart RC | 6.00 | 2.50 |
| ❏ 174 Maurice Drew RC | 4.00 | 1.50 |
| ❏ 175 Maurice Stovall RC | 2.00 | .75 |
| ❏ 176 Michael Huff RC | 2.00 | .75 |
| ❏ 177 Michael Robinson RC | 2.00 | .75 |
| ❏ 178 Mike Hass RC | 2.00 | .75 |
| ❏ 179 Omar Jacobs RC | 1.50 | .60 |
| ❏ 180 Orien Harris RC | 1.50 | .60 |
| ❏ 181 Owen Daniels RC | 2.00 | .75 |
| ❏ 182 Miles Austin RC | 2.00 | .75 |
| ❏ 183 Reggie Bush RC | 8.00 | 3.00 |
| ❏ 184 Reggie McNeal RC | 1.50 | .60 |
| ❏ 185 Santonio Holmes RC | 5.00 | 2.00 |
| ❏ 186 Sinorice Moss RC | 2.00 | .75 |
| ❏ 187 Skyler Green RC | 2.00 | .75 |
| ❏ 188 Tony Scheffler RC | 2.00 | .75 |
| ❏ 189 Tamba Hali RC | 2.00 | .75 |
| ❏ 190 Tarvaris Jackson RC | 2.00 | .75 |
| ❏ 191 Thomas Howard RC | 2.00 | .75 |
| ❏ 192 Tim Day RC | 1.50 | .60 |
| ❏ 193 Todd Watkins RC | 1.50 | .60 |
| ❏ 194 Travis Wilson RC | 2.00 | .75 |
| ❏ 195 Tye Hill RC | 2.00 | .75 |
| ❏ 196 Vernon Davis RC | 2.00 | .75 |
| ❏ 197 Vince Young RC | 6.00 | 2.50 |
| ❏ 198 Wali Lundy RC | 2.00 | .75 |
| ❏ 199 Will Blackmon RC | 2.00 | .75 |
| ❏ 200 Winston Justice RC | 2.00 | .75 |

## 1997 Fleer Goudey

FRANK H. FLEER

| | | | |
|---|---|---|---|
| ❏ COMPLETE SET (150) | 15.00 | 6.00 |
| ❏ 1 Michael Jackson | .30 | .10 |
| ❏ 2 Ray Lewis | .75 | .30 |
| ❏ 3 Vinny Testaverde | .30 | .10 |
| ❏ 4 Eric Turner | .20 | .07 |
| ❏ 5 Jim Kelly | .50 | .20 |
| ❏ 6 Bryce Paup | .20 | .07 |
| ❏ 7 Andre Reed | .30 | .10 |
| ❏ 8 Bruce Smith | .30 | .10 |
| ❏ 9 Thurman Thomas | .50 | .20 |
| ❏ 10 Jeff Blake | .30 | .10 |
| ❏ 11 Ki-Jana Carter | .20 | .07 |
| ❏ 12 Carl Pickens | .30 | .10 |
| ❏ 13 Darnay Scott | .30 | .10 |
| ❏ 14 Terrell Davis | .60 | .25 |
| ❏ 15 John Elway | 2.00 | .75 |
| ❏ 16 Anthony Miller | .20 | .07 |
| ❏ 17 John Mobley | .20 | .07 |
| ❏ 18 Shannon Sharpe | .30 | .10 |
| ❏ 19 Chris Chandler | .30 | .10 |
| ❏ 20 Eddie George | .50 | .20 |
| ❏ 21 Steve McNair | .60 | .25 |
| ❏ 22 Chris Sanders | .20 | .07 |
| ❏ 23 Quentin Coryatt | .20 | .07 |
| ❏ 24 Sean Dawkins | .20 | .07 |
| ❏ 25 Ken Dilger | .20 | .07 |
| ❏ 26 Marshall Faulk | .65 | .25 |
| ❏ 27 Jim Harbaugh | .30 | .10 |
| ❏ 28 Marvin Harrison | .50 | .20 |
| ❏ 29 Tony Brackens | .20 | .07 |
| ❏ 30 Mark Brunell | .60 | .25 |

| | | | |
|---|---|---|---|
| ❏ 31 Kevin Hardy | .20 | .07 |
| ❏ 32 Keenan McCardell | .30 | .10 |
| ❏ 33 James O.Stewart | .30 | .10 |
| ❏ 34 Marcus Allen | .50 | .20 |
| ❏ 35 Steve Bono | .30 | .10 |
| ❏ 36 Dale Carter | .20 | .07 |
| ❏ 37 Neil Smith | .30 | .10 |
| ❏ 38 Derrick Thomas | .50 | .20 |
| ❏ 39 Tamarick Vanover | .30 | .10 |
| ❏ 40 Karim Abdul-Jabbar | .30 | .10 |
| ❏ 41 Dan Marino | 2.00 | .75 |
| ❏ 42 O.J. McDuffie | .30 | .10 |
| ❏ 43 Stanley Pritchett | .20 | .07 |
| ❏ 44 Zach Thomas | .50 | .20 |
| ❏ 45 Drew Bledsoe | .60 | .25 |
| ❏ 46 Ben Coates | .30 | .10 |
| ❏ 47 Terry Glenn | .50 | .20 |
| ❏ 48 Shawn Jefferson | .20 | .07 |
| ❏ 49 Curtis Martin | .60 | .25 |
| ❏ 50 Dave Meggett | .20 | .07 |
| ❏ 51 Hugh Douglas | .20 | .07 |
| ❏ 52 Keyshawn Johnson | .50 | .20 |
| ❏ 53 Adrian Murrell | .30 | .10 |
| ❏ 54 Tim Brown | .50 | .20 |
| ❏ 55 Rickey Dudley | .30 | .10 |
| ❏ 56 Jeff Hostetler | .20 | .07 |
| ❏ 57 Napoleon Kaufman | .50 | .20 |
| ❏ 58 Chester McGlockton | .20 | .07 |
| ❏ 59 Jerome Bettis | .50 | .20 |
| ❏ 60 Andre Hastings | .20 | .07 |
| ❏ 61 Greg Lloyd | .20 | .07 |
| ❏ 62 Kordell Stewart | .50 | .20 |
| ❏ 63 Yancey Thigpen | .30 | .10 |
| ❏ 64 Rod Woodson | .30 | .10 |
| ❏ 65 Andre Coleman | .20 | .07 |
| ❏ 66 Stan Humphries | .30 | .10 |
| ❏ 67 Tony Martin | .30 | .10 |
| ❏ 68 Leonard Russell | .20 | .07 |
| ❏ 69 Junior Seau | .50 | .20 |
| ❏ 70 Brian Blades | .20 | .07 |
| ❏ 71 Joey Galloway | .30 | .10 |
| ❏ 72 Chris Warren | .30 | .10 |
| ❏ 73 Larry Centers | .20 | .07 |
| ❏ 74 Leeland McElroy | .30 | .10 |
| ❏ 75 Simeon Rice | .30 | .10 |
| ❏ 76 Frank Sanders | .30 | .10 |
| ❏ 77 Eric Swann | .20 | .07 |
| ❏ 78 Jamal Anderson | .50 | .20 |
| ❏ 79 Bert Emanuel | .30 | .10 |
| ❏ 80 Terance Mathis | .30 | .10 |
| ❏ 81 Eric Metcalf | .30 | .10 |
| ❏ 82 Tim Biakabutuka | .30 | .10 |
| ❏ 83 Kerry Collins | .50 | .20 |
| ❏ 84 Kevin Greene | .30 | .10 |
| ❏ 85 Muhsin Muhammad | .30 | .10 |
| ❏ 86 Wesley Walls | .30 | .10 |
| ❏ 87 Curtis Conway | .30 | .10 |
| ❏ 88 Bryan Cox | .20 | .07 |
| ❏ 89 Walt Harris | .20 | .07 |
| ❏ 90 Erik Kramer | .20 | .07 |
| ❏ 91 Rashaan Salaam | .20 | .07 |
| ❏ 92 Troy Aikman | 1.00 | .40 |
| ❏ 93 Michael Irvin | .50 | .20 |
| ❏ 94 Daryl Johnston | .30 | .10 |
| ❏ 95 Leon Lett | .20 | .07 |
| ❏ 96 Deion Sanders | .50 | .20 |
| ❏ 97 Emmitt Smith | 1.50 | .60 |
| ❏ 98 Scott Mitchell | .30 | .10 |
| ❏ 99 Herman Moore | .30 | .10 |
| ❏ 100 Johnnie Morton | .30 | .10 |
| ❏ 101 Brett Perriman | .20 | .07 |
| ❏ 102 Barry Sanders | 1.50 | .60 |
| ❏ 103 Edgar Bennett | .30 | .10 |
| ❏ 104 Robert Brooks | .30 | .10 |
| ❏ 105 Brett Favre | 2.00 | .75 |
| ❏ 106 Antonio Freeman | .50 | .20 |
| ❏ 107 Keith Jackson | .20 | .07 |
| ❏ 108 Reggie White | .50 | .20 |
| ❏ 109 Cris Carter | .50 | .20 |
| ❏ 110 Warren Moon | .50 | .20 |
| ❏ 111 John Randle | .30 | .10 |
| ❏ 112 Jake Reed | .30 | .10 |
| ❏ 113 Robert Smith | .30 | .10 |
| ❏ 114 Jim Everett | .20 | .07 |

| | | | |
|---|---|---|---|
| ❏ 115 Michael Haynes | .20 | .07 |
| ❏ 116 Alex Molden | .20 | .07 |
| ❏ 117 Ray Zellars | .20 | .07 |
| ❏ 118 Chris Calloway | .20 | .07 |
| ❏ 119 Rodney Hampton | .30 | .10 |
| ❏ 120 Phillippi Sparks | .20 | .07 |
| ❏ 121 Amani Toomer | .30 | .10 |
| ❏ 122 Ty Detmer | .30 | .10 |
| ❏ 123 Jason Dunn | .20 | .07 |
| ❏ 124 Irving Fryar | .30 | .10 |
| ❏ 125 Chris T. Jones | .20 | .07 |
| ❏ 126 Ricky Watters | .30 | .10 |
| ❏ 127 Tony Banks | .30 | .10 |
| ❏ 128 Isaac Bruce | .50 | .20 |
| ❏ 129 Eddie Kennison | .30 | .10 |
| ❏ 130 Lawrence Phillips | .20 | .07 |
| ❏ 131 Merton Hanks | .20 | .07 |
| ❏ 132 Terry Kirby | .20 | .07 |
| ❏ 133 Ken Norton | .20 | .07 |
| ❏ 134 Jerry Rice | 1.00 | .40 |
| ❏ 135 J.J. Stokes | .30 | .10 |
| ❏ 136 Steve Young | .60 | .25 |
| ❏ 137 Alvin Harper | .20 | .07 |
| ❏ 138 Jackie Harris | .20 | .07 |
| ❏ 139 Hardy Nickerson | .20 | .07 |
| ❏ 140 Errict Rhett | .30 | .10 |
| ❏ 141 Terry Allen | .50 | .20 |
| ❏ 142 Henry Ellard | .20 | .07 |
| ❏ 143 Gus Frerotte | .20 | .07 |
| ❏ 144 Brian Mitchell | .20 | .07 |
| ❏ 145 Michael Westbrook | .30 | .10 |
| ❏ 146 Chuck Bednarik | .30 | .10 |
| ❏ 146AU Chuck Bednarik AUTO | 50.00 | 20.00 |
| ❏ 147 Y.A. Tittle | .30 | .10 |
| ❏ 147AU Y.A. Tittle AUTO | 50.00 | 20.00 |
| ❏ 148 Checklist | .20 | .07 |
| ❏ 149 Checklist | .20 | .07 |
| ❏ 150 Checklist | .20 | .07 |
| ❏ P1 Brett Favre Promo | 2.00 | .75 |

## 1997 Fleer Goudey II

HENRY H FLEER

| | | | |
|---|---|---|---|
| ❏ COMPLETE SET (150) | 20.00 | 7.50 |
| ❏ 1 Gale Sayers SP | .50 | .20 |
| ❏ 1AU Gale Sayers AUTO | 100.00 | 40.00 |
| ❏ 1RT Gale Sayers Rare Trad. | 8.00 | 4.00 |
| ❏ 2 Vinny Testaverde | .30 | .10 |
| ❏ 3 Jeff George | .30 | .10 |
| ❏ 4 Brett Favre | 2.00 | .75 |
| ❏ 5 Eddie Kennison | .20 | .07 |
| ❏ 6 Ken Norton | .20 | .07 |
| ❏ 7 John Elway | 2.00 | .75 |
| ❏ 8 Troy Aikman | 1.00 | .40 |
| ❏ 9 Steve McNair | .60 | .25 |
| ❏ 10 Kordell Stewart | .50 | .20 |
| ❏ 11 Drew Bledsoe | .50 | .20 |
| ❏ 12 Kerry Collins | .50 | .20 |
| ❏ 13 Dan Marino | 2.00 | .75 |
| ❏ 14 Brad Johnson | .50 | .20 |
| ❏ 15 Todd Collins | .20 | .07 |
| ❏ 16 Ki-Jana Carter | .20 | .07 |
| ❏ 17 Pat Barnes RC | .50 | .20 |
| ❏ 18 Aeneas Williams | .20 | .07 |
| ❏ 19 Keyshawn Johnson | .50 | .20 |
| ❏ 20 Barry Sanders | 1.50 | .60 |
| ❏ 21 Tiki Barber RC | 3.00 | 1.25 |
| ❏ 22 Emmitt Smith | 1.50 | .60 |
| ❏ 23 Kevin Hardy | .20 | .07 |
| ❏ 24 Mario Bates | .20 | .07 |
| ❏ 25 Ricky Watters | .30 | .10 |
| ❏ 26 Chris Canty RC | .20 | .07 |

| | | |
|---|---|---|
| ☐ 27 Eddie George | .50 | .20 |
| ☐ 28 Curtis Martin | .60 | .25 |
| ☐ 29 Adrian Murrell | .30 | .10 |
| ☐ 30 Terrell Davis | .60 | .25 |
| ☐ 31 Rashaan Salaam | .20 | .07 |
| ☐ 32 Marcus Allen | .50 | .20 |
| ☐ 33 Karim Abdul-Jabbar | .50 | .20 |
| ☐ 34 Thurman Thomas | .50 | .20 |
| ☐ 35 Marvin Harrison | .50 | .20 |
| ☐ 36 Jerome Bettis | .50 | .20 |
| ☐ 37 Larry Centers | .30 | .10 |
| ☐ 38 Stan Humphries | .30 | .10 |
| ☐ 39 Lawrence Phillips | .20 | .07 |
| ☐ 40 Gale Sayers SP | .50 | .20 |
| ☐ 40AU Gale Sayers AUTO | 100.00 | 40.00 |
| ☐ 40RT Gale Sayers Rare Trad. | 8.00 | 4.00 |
| ☐ 41 Henry Ellard | .20 | .07 |
| ☐ 42 Chris Warren | .30 | .10 |
| ☐ 43 Robert Brooks | .30 | .10 |
| ☐ 44 Sedrick Shaw RC | .30 | .10 |
| ☐ 45 Muhsin Muhammad | .30 | .10 |
| ☐ 46 Napoleon Kaufman | .50 | .20 |
| ☐ 47 Reidel Anthony RC | .50 | .20 |
| ☐ 48 Jamal Anderson | .50 | .20 |
| ☐ 49 Scott Mitchell | .30 | .10 |
| ☐ 50 Mark Brunell | .60 | .25 |
| ☐ 51 William Thomas | .20 | .07 |
| ☐ 52 Bryan Cox | .20 | .07 |
| ☐ 53 Carl Pickens | .30 | .10 |
| ☐ 54 Chris Spielman | .20 | .07 |
| ☐ 55 Junior Seau | .50 | .20 |
| ☐ 56 Hardy Nickerson | .20 | .07 |
| ☐ 57 Dwayne Rudd RC | .50 | .20 |
| ☐ 58 Peter Boulware RC | .50 | .20 |
| ☐ 59 Jim Druckenmiller RC | .30 | .10 |
| ☐ 60 Michael Westbrook | .30 | .10 |
| ☐ 61 Shawn Springs RC | .30 | .10 |
| ☐ 62 Zach Thomas | .50 | .20 |
| ☐ 63 David LaFleur RC | .20 | .07 |
| ☐ 64 Darrell Russell RC | .20 | .07 |
| ☐ 65 Jake Plummer RC | 2.50 | 1.00 |
| ☐ 66 Tim Biakabutuka | .30 | .10 |
| ☐ 67 Tyrone Wheatley | .30 | .10 |
| ☐ 68 Elvis Grbac | .30 | .10 |
| ☐ 69 Antonio Freeman | .50 | .20 |
| ☐ 70 Wayne Chrebet | .50 | .20 |
| ☐ 71 Walter Jones RC | .20 | .07 |
| ☐ 72 Marshall Faulk | .60 | .25 |
| ☐ 73 Jason Dunn | .20 | .07 |
| ☐ 74 Darnay Scott | .30 | .10 |
| ☐ 75 Errict Rhett | .30 | .10 |
| ☐ 76 Orlando Pace RC | .50 | .20 |
| ☐ 77 Natrone Means | .30 | .10 |
| ☐ 78 Bruce Smith | .30 | .10 |
| ☐ 79 Jamie Sharper RC | .30 | .10 |
| ☐ 80 Jerry Rice | 1.00 | .40 |
| ☐ 81 Tim Brown | .50 | .20 |
| ☐ 82 Brian Mitchell | .20 | .07 |
| ☐ 83 Andre Reed | .30 | .10 |
| ☐ 84 Herman Moore | .30 | .10 |
| ☐ 85 Rob Moore | .30 | .10 |
| ☐ 86 Rae Carruth RC | .20 | .07 |
| ☐ 87 Bert Emanuel | .20 | .07 |
| ☐ 88 Michael Irvin | .50 | .20 |
| ☐ 89 Mark Chmura | .20 | .07 |
| ☐ 90 Tony Brackens | .20 | .07 |
| ☐ 91 Kevin Greene | .30 | .10 |
| ☐ 92 Reggie White | .50 | .20 |
| ☐ 93 Derrick Thomas | .50 | .20 |
| ☐ 94 Troy Davis RC | .30 | .10 |
| ☐ 95 Greg Lloyd | .20 | .07 |
| ☐ 96 Cortez Kennedy | .20 | .07 |
| ☐ 97 Simeon Rice | .30 | .10 |
| ☐ 98 Terrell Owens | .60 | .25 |
| ☐ 99 Hugh Douglas | .20 | .07 |
| ☐ 100 Terry Glenn | .50 | .20 |
| ☐ 101 Jim Harbaugh | .30 | .10 |
| ☐ 102 Shannon Sharpe | .30 | .10 |
| ☐ 103 Joey Kent RC | .50 | .20 |
| ☐ 104 Jeff Blake | .30 | .10 |
| ☐ 105 Terry Allen | .50 | .20 |
| ☐ 106 Cris Carter | .50 | .20 |
| ☐ 107 Amani Toomer | .30 | .10 |
| ☐ 108 Derrick Alexander WR | .30 | .10 |

| | | |
|---|---|---|
| ☐ 109 Darnell Autry RC | .30 | .10 |
| ☐ 110 Irving Fryar | .30 | .10 |
| ☐ 111 Bryant Westbrook RC | .20 | .07 |
| ☐ 112 Tony Banks | .30 | .10 |
| ☐ 113 Michael Booker RC | .20 | .07 |
| ☐ 114 Yatil Green RC | .30 | .10 |
| ☐ 115 James Farrior RC | .50 | .20 |
| ☐ 116 Warrick Dunn RC | 1.50 | .60 |
| ☐ 117 Greg Hill | .20 | .07 |
| ☐ 118 Tony Martin | .30 | .10 |
| ☐ 119 Chris Sanders | .20 | .07 |
| ☐ 120 Charles Johnson | .20 | .07 |
| ☐ 121 John Mobley | .20 | .07 |
| ☐ 122 Keenan McCardell | .30 | .10 |
| ☐ 123 Willie McGinest | .20 | .07 |
| ☐ 124 O.J. McDuffie | .30 | .10 |
| ☐ 125 Deion Sanders | .50 | .20 |
| ☐ 126 Curtis Conway | .30 | .10 |
| ☐ 127 Desmond Howard | .30 | .10 |
| ☐ 128 Johnnie Morton | .30 | .10 |
| ☐ 129 Ike Hilliard | .75 | .30 |
| ☐ 130 Gus Frerotte | .20 | .07 |
| ☐ 131 Tom Knight | .20 | .07 |
| ☐ 132 Sean Dawkins | .20 | .07 |
| ☐ 133 Isaac Bruce | .50 | .20 |
| ☐ 134 Wesley Walls | .30 | .10 |
| ☐ 135 Danny Wuerffel RC | .50 | .20 |
| ☐ 136 Tony Gonzalez RC | 1.50 | .60 |
| ☐ 137 Ben Coates | .30 | .10 |
| ☐ 138 Joey Galloway | .30 | .10 |
| ☐ 139 Michael Jackson | .30 | .10 |
| ☐ 140 Steve Young | .60 | .25 |
| ☐ 141 Corey Dillon RC | 3.00 | 1.25 |
| ☐ 142 Jake Reed | .30 | .10 |
| ☐ 143 Edgar Bennett | .30 | .10 |
| ☐ 144 Ty Detmer | .30 | .10 |
| ☐ 145 Darrell Green | .30 | .10 |
| ☐ 146 Antowain Smith RC | 1.25 | .50 |
| ☐ 147 Mike Alstott | .50 | .20 |
| ☐ 148 Checklist | .20 | .07 |
| ☐ 149 Checklist | .20 | .07 |
| ☐ 150 Gale Sayers SP | .50 | .20 |
| ☐ 150AU Gale Sayers AUTO | 100.00 | 40.00 |
| ☐ 150RT Gale Sayers Rare Trad. | 8.00 | 4.00 |
| ☐ P92 Reggie White Promo | .50 | .20 |

## 1998 Fleer Tradition

| | | |
|---|---|---|
| ☐ COMPLETE SET (250) | 40.00 | 20.00 |
| ☐ 1 Brett Favre | 2.00 | .75 |
| ☐ 2 Barry Sanders | 1.50 | .60 |
| ☐ 3 John Elway | 2.00 | .75 |
| ☐ 4 Emmitt Smith | 1.50 | .60 |
| ☐ 5 Dan Marino | 2.00 | .75 |
| ☐ 6 Eddie George | .50 | .20 |
| ☐ 7 Jerry Rice | 1.00 | .40 |
| ☐ 8 Jake Plummer | .50 | .20 |
| ☐ 9 Joey Galloway | .30 | .10 |
| ☐ 10 Mike Alstott | .50 | .20 |
| ☐ 11 Brian Mitchell | .20 | .07 |
| ☐ 12 Keyshawn Johnson | .50 | .20 |
| ☐ 13 Jerald Moore | .20 | .07 |
| ☐ 14 Randal Hill | .20 | .07 |
| ☐ 15 Byron Hanspard | .20 | .07 |
| ☐ 16 Jeff George | .30 | .10 |
| ☐ 17 Terry Glenn | .50 | .20 |
| ☐ 18 Jerome Bettis | .50 | .20 |
| ☐ 19 Curtis Conway | .30 | .10 |
| ☐ 20 Fred Lane | .20 | .07 |

| | | |
|---|---|---|
| ☐ 21 Isaac Bruce | .50 | .20 |
| ☐ 22 Tiki Barber | .50 | .20 |
| ☐ 23 Bobby Hoying | .30 | .10 |
| ☐ 24 Marcus Allen | .50 | .20 |
| ☐ 25 Dana Stubblefield | .20 | .07 |
| ☐ 26 Peter Boulware | .20 | .07 |
| ☐ 27 John Randle | .20 | .07 |
| ☐ 28 Jason Sehorn | .30 | .10 |
| ☐ 29 Rod Smith | .30 | .10 |
| ☐ 30 Michael Sinclair | .20 | .07 |
| ☐ 31 Marshall Faulk | .60 | .25 |
| ☐ 32 Karl Williams | .20 | .07 |
| ☐ 33 Kordell Stewart | .50 | .20 |
| ☐ 34 Corey Dillon | .50 | .20 |
| ☐ 35 Bryant Young | .20 | .07 |
| ☐ 36 Charlie Garner | .30 | .10 |
| ☐ 37 Andre Reed | .30 | .10 |
| ☐ 38 Ray Buchanan | .20 | .07 |
| ☐ 39 Brett Perriman | .20 | .07 |
| ☐ 40 Leon Lett | .20 | .07 |
| ☐ 41 Keenan McCardell | .20 | .07 |
| ☐ 42 Eric Swann | .20 | .07 |
| ☐ 43 Leslie Shepherd | .20 | .07 |
| ☐ 44 Curtis Martin | .50 | .20 |
| ☐ 45 Andre Rison | .30 | .10 |
| ☐ 46 Keith Lyle | .20 | .07 |
| ☐ 47 Rae Carruth | .20 | .07 |
| ☐ 48 William Henderson | .30 | .10 |
| ☐ 49 Sean Dawkins | .20 | .07 |
| ☐ 50 Terrell Davis | .50 | .20 |
| ☐ 51 Tim Brown | .30 | .10 |
| ☐ 52 Willie McGinest | .20 | .07 |
| ☐ 53 Jermaine Lewis | .30 | .10 |
| ☐ 54 Ricky Watters | .30 | .10 |
| ☐ 55 Freddie Jones | .20 | .07 |
| ☐ 56 Robert Smith | .50 | .20 |
| ☐ 57 Reidel Anthony | .30 | .10 |
| ☐ 58 James Stewart | .30 | .10 |
| ☐ 59 Earl Holmes RC | .30 | .10 |
| ☐ 60 Dale Carter | .20 | .07 |
| ☐ 61 Michael Irvin | .50 | .20 |
| ☐ 62 Jason Taylor | .30 | .10 |
| ☐ 63 Eric Metcalf | .20 | .07 |
| ☐ 64 LeRoy Butler | .20 | .07 |
| ☐ 65 Jamal Anderson | .50 | .20 |
| ☐ 66 Jamie Asher | .20 | .07 |
| ☐ 67 Chris Sanders | .20 | .07 |
| ☐ 68 Warren Sapp | .30 | .10 |
| ☐ 69 Ray Zellars | .20 | .07 |
| ☐ 70 Carl Pickens | .30 | .10 |
| ☐ 71 Garrison Hearst | .50 | .20 |
| ☐ 72 Eddie Kennison | .30 | .10 |
| ☐ 73 John Mobley | .20 | .07 |
| ☐ 74 Rob Johnson | .30 | .10 |
| ☐ 75 William Thomas | .20 | .07 |
| ☐ 76 Drew Bledsoe | .75 | .30 |
| ☐ 77 Micheal Barrow | .20 | .07 |
| ☐ 78 Jim Harbaugh | .30 | .10 |
| ☐ 79 Terry McDaniel | .20 | .07 |
| ☐ 80 Johnnie Morton | .30 | .10 |
| ☐ 81 Danny Kanell | .30 | .10 |
| ☐ 82 Larry Centers | .20 | .07 |
| ☐ 83 Courtney Hawkins | .20 | .07 |
| ☐ 84 Tony Brackens | .20 | .07 |
| ☐ 85 Tony Gonzalez | .50 | .20 |
| ☐ 86 Aaron Glenn | .20 | .07 |
| ☐ 87 Cris Carter | .50 | .20 |
| ☐ 88 Chuck Smith | .20 | .07 |
| ☐ 89 Tamarick Vanover | .20 | .07 |
| ☐ 90 Karim Abdul-Jabbar | .50 | .20 |
| ☐ 91 Bryant Westbrook | .20 | .07 |
| ☐ 92 Mike Pritchard | .20 | .07 |
| ☐ 93 Darren Woodson | .20 | .07 |
| ☐ 94 Wesley Walls | .30 | .10 |
| ☐ 95 Tony Banks | .30 | .10 |
| ☐ 96 Michael Westbrook | .30 | .10 |
| ☐ 97 Shannon Sharpe | .30 | .10 |
| ☐ 98 Jeff Blake | .30 | .10 |
| ☐ 99 Terrell Owens | .50 | .20 |
| ☐ 100 Warrick Dunn | .50 | .20 |
| ☐ 101 Levon Kirkland | .20 | .07 |
| ☐ 102 Frank Wycheck | .20 | .07 |
| ☐ 103 Gus Frerotte | .20 | .07 |
| ☐ 104 Simeon Rice | .30 | .10 |

|  |  | | |
|---|---|---|---|
| 105 | Shawn Jefferson | .20 | .07 |
| 106 | Irving Fryar | .30 | .10 |
| 107 | Michael McCrary | .20 | .07 |
| 108 | Robert Brooks | .30 | .10 |
| 109 | Chris Chandler | .30 | .10 |
| 110 | Junior Seau | .50 | .20 |
| 111 | O.J. McDuffie | .30 | .10 |
| 112 | Glenn Foley | .30 | .10 |
| 113 | Darryl Williams | .20 | .07 |
| 114 | Elvis Grbac | .30 | .10 |
| 115 | Napoleon Kaufman | .50 | .20 |
| 116 | Anthony Miller | .20 | .07 |
| 117 | Troy Davis | .20 | .07 |
| 118 | Charles Way | .20 | .07 |
| 119 | Scott Mitchell | .30 | .10 |
| 120 | Ken Harvey | .20 | .07 |
| 121 | Tyrone Hughes | .20 | .07 |
| 122 | Mark Brunell | .50 | .20 |
| 123 | David Palmer | .20 | .07 |
| 124 | Rob Moore | .30 | .10 |
| 125 | Kerry Collins | .30 | .10 |
| 126 | Will Blackwell | .20 | .07 |
| 127 | Ray Crockett | .20 | .07 |
| 128 | Leslie O'Neal | .20 | .07 |
| 129 | Antowain Smith | .50 | .20 |
| 130 | Carlester Crumpler | .20 | .07 |
| 131 | Michael Jackson | .20 | .07 |
| 132 | Trent Dilfer | .50 | .20 |
| 133 | Dan Williams | .20 | .07 |
| 134 | Dorsey Levens | .50 | .20 |
| 135 | Ty Law | .30 | .10 |
| 136 | Rickey Dudley | .20 | .07 |
| 137 | Jessie Tuggle | .20 | .07 |
| 138 | Darrien Gordon | .20 | .07 |
| 139 | Kevin Turner | .20 | .07 |
| 140 | Willie Davis | .20 | .07 |
| 141 | Zach Thomas | .50 | .20 |
| 142 | Tony McGee | .20 | .07 |
| 143 | Dexter Coakley | .20 | .07 |
| 144 | Troy Brown | .30 | .10 |
| 145 | Leeland McElroy | .20 | .07 |
| 146 | Michael Strahan | .30 | .10 |
| 147 | Ken Dilger | .20 | .07 |
| 148 | Bryce Paup | .20 | .07 |
| 149 | Herman Moore | .30 | .10 |
| 150 | Reggie White | .50 | .20 |
| 151 | Dewayne Washington | .20 | .07 |
| 152 | Natrone Means | .30 | .10 |
| 153 | Ben Coates | .30 | .10 |
| 154 | Bert Emanuel | .30 | .10 |
| 155 | Steve Young | .60 | .25 |
| 156 | Jimmy Smith | .30 | .10 |
| 157 | Darrell Green | .30 | .10 |
| 158 | Troy Aikman | 1.00 | .40 |
| 159 | Greg Hill | .20 | .07 |
| 160 | Raymont Harris | .20 | .07 |
| 161 | Troy Drayton | .20 | .07 |
| 162 | Stevon Moore | .20 | .07 |
| 163 | Warren Moon | .50 | .20 |
| 164 | Wayne Martin | .20 | .07 |
| 165 | Jason Gildon | .20 | .07 |
| 166 | Chris Calloway | .20 | .07 |
| 167 | Aeneas Williams | .20 | .07 |
| 168 | Michael Bates | .20 | .07 |
| 169 | Hugh Douglas | .20 | .07 |
| 170 | Brad Johnson | .50 | .20 |
| 171 | Bruce Smith | .30 | .10 |
| 172 | Neil Smith | .30 | .10 |
| 173 | James McKnight | .50 | .20 |
| 174 | Robert Porcher | .20 | .07 |
| 175 | Merton Hanks | .20 | .07 |
| 176 | Ki-Jana Carter | .20 | .07 |
| 177 | Mo Lewis | .20 | .07 |
| 178 | Chester McGlockton | .20 | .07 |
| 179 | Zack Crockett | .20 | .07 |
| 180 | Derrick Thomas | .50 | .20 |
| 181 | J.J. Stokes | .30 | .10 |
| 182 | Derrick Rodgers | .20 | .07 |
| 183 | Daryl Johnston | .30 | .10 |
| 184 | Chris Penn | .20 | .07 |
| 185 | Steve Atwater | .20 | .07 |
| 186 | Amp Lee | .20 | .07 |
| 187 | Frank Sanders | .30 | .10 |
| 188 | Chris Slade | .20 | .07 |
| 189 | Mark Chmura | .30 | .10 |
| 190 | Kimble Anders | .30 | .10 |
| 191 | Charles Johnson | .20 | .07 |
| 192 | William Floyd | .20 | .07 |
| 193 | Jay Graham | .20 | .07 |
| 194 | Hardy Nickerson | .20 | .07 |
| 195 | Terry Allen | .50 | .20 |
| 196 | James Jett | .30 | .10 |
| 197 | Jessie Armstead | .20 | .07 |
| 198 | Yancey Thigpen | .30 | .10 |
| 199 | Terance Mathis | .30 | .10 |
| 200 | Steve McNair | .50 | .20 |
| 201 | Wayne Chrebet | .50 | .20 |
| 202 | Jamir Miller | .20 | .07 |
| 203 | Duce Staley | .60 | .25 |
| 204 | Deion Sanders | .50 | .20 |
| 205 | Carnell Lake | .20 | .07 |
| 206 | Ed McCaffrey | .30 | .10 |
| 207 | Shawn Springs | .20 | .07 |
| 208 | Tony Martin | .30 | .10 |
| 209 | Jerris McPhail | .20 | .07 |
| 210 | Darnay Scott | .30 | .10 |
| 211 | Jake Reed | .30 | .10 |
| 212 | Adrian Murrell | .30 | .10 |
| 213 | Quinn Early | .20 | .07 |
| 214 | Marvin Harrison | .50 | .20 |
| 215 | Ryan McNeil | .20 | .07 |
| 216 | Derrick Alexander | .30 | .10 |
| 217 | Ray Lewis | .50 | .20 |
| 218 | Antonio Freeman | .50 | .20 |
| 219 | Dwayne Rudd | .20 | .07 |
| 220 | Muhsin Muhammad | .30 | .10 |
| 221 | Kevin Hardy | .20 | .07 |
| 222 | Andre Hastings | .20 | .07 |
| 223 | John Avery RC | .75 | .30 |
| 224 | Keith Brooking RC | 1.25 | .50 |
| 225 | Kevin Dyson RC | 1.25 | .50 |
| 226 | Robert Edwards RC | .75 | .30 |
| 227 | Greg Ellis RC | .50 | .20 |
| 228 | Curtis Enis RC | .50 | .20 |
| 229 | Terry Fair RC | .75 | .30 |
| 230 | Ahman Green RC | 4.00 | 1.50 |
| 231 | Jacquez Green RC | .75 | .30 |
| 232 | Brian Griese RC | 3.00 | 1.25 |
| 233 | Skip Hicks RC | .75 | .30 |
| 234 | Ryan Leaf RC | .75 | .30 |
| 235 | Peyton Manning RC | 15.00 | 6.00 |
| 236 | R.W. McQuarters RC | .75 | .30 |
| 237 | Randy Moss RC | 10.00 | 4.00 |
| 238 | Marcus Nash RC | .50 | .20 |
| 239 | Anthony Simmons RC | .75 | .30 |
| 240 | Brian Simmons RC | .75 | .30 |
| 241 | Takeo Spikes RC | 1.25 | .50 |
| 242 | Duane Starks RC | .50 | .20 |
| 243 | Fred Taylor RC | 2.00 | .75 |
| 244 | Andre Wadsworth RC | .75 | .30 |
| 245 | Shaun Williams RC | .75 | .30 |
| 246 | Grant Wistrom RC | .75 | .30 |
| 247 | Charles Woodson RC | 1.50 | .60 |
| 248 | Checklist | .20 | .07 |
| 249 | Checklist | .20 | .07 |
| 250 | Checklist | .20 | .07 |

## 1999 Fleer Tradition

|  |  | | |
|---|---|---|---|
| | COMPLETE SET (300) | 40.00 | 20.00 |
| 1 | Randy Moss | 1.25 | .50 |
| 2 | Peyton Manning | 1.50 | .60 |
| 3 | Barry Sanders | 1.50 | .60 |
| 4 | Terrell Davis | .50 | .20 |
| 5 | Brett Favre | 1.50 | .60 |
| 6 | Fred Taylor | .50 | .20 |
| 7 | Jake Plummer | .30 | .10 |
| 8 | John Elway | 1.50 | .60 |
| 9 | Emmitt Smith | 1.00 | .40 |
| 10 | Kerry Collins | .20 | .07 |
| 11 | Peter Boulware | .20 | .07 |
| 12 | Jamal Anderson | .50 | .20 |
| 13 | Doug Flutie | .50 | .20 |
| 14 | Michael Sinclair | .20 | .07 |
| 15 | Corey Dillon | .50 | .20 |
| 16 | Curtis Conway | .30 | .10 |
| 17 | Ty Detmer | .30 | .10 |
| 18 | Robert Brooks | .30 | .10 |
| 19 | Dale Carter | .20 | .07 |
| 20 | Charlie Batch | .50 | .20 |
| 21 | Ken Dilger | .20 | .07 |
| 22 | Troy Aikman | 1.00 | .40 |
| 23 | Tavian Banks | .20 | .07 |
| 24 | Cris Carter | .50 | .20 |
| 25 | Derrick Alexander WR | .30 | .10 |
| 26 | Chris Bordano RC | .20 | .07 |
| 27 | Karim Abdul-Jabbar | .30 | .10 |
| 28 | Jessie Armstead | .20 | .07 |
| 29 | Drew Bledsoe | .60 | .25 |
| 30 | Brian Dawkins | .50 | .20 |
| 31 | Wayne Chrebet | .30 | .10 |
| 32 | Garrison Hearst | .30 | .10 |
| 33 | Eric Allen | .20 | .07 |
| 34 | Tony Banks | .30 | .10 |
| 35 | Jerome Bettis | .50 | .20 |
| 36 | Stephen Alexander | .20 | .07 |
| 37 | Rodney Harrison | .20 | .07 |
| 38 | Mike Alstott | .50 | .20 |
| 39 | Chad Brown | .20 | .07 |
| 40 | Johnny McWilliams | .20 | .07 |
| 41 | Kevin Dyson | .30 | .10 |
| 42 | Keith Brooking | .30 | .10 |
| 43 | Jim Harbaugh | .30 | .10 |
| 44 | Bobby Engram | .30 | .10 |
| 45 | John Holecek | .20 | .07 |
| 46 | Steve Beuerlein | .20 | .07 |
| 47 | Tony McGee | .20 | .07 |
| 48 | Greg Ellis | .20 | .07 |
| 49 | Corey Fuller | .20 | .07 |
| 50 | Stephen Boyd | .20 | .07 |
| 51 | Marshall Faulk | .60 | .25 |
| 52 | LeRoy Butler | .20 | .07 |
| 53 | Reggie Barlow | .20 | .07 |
| 54 | Randall Cunningham | .50 | .20 |
| 55 | Aeneas Williams | .20 | .07 |
| 56 | Kimble Anders | .30 | .10 |
| 57 | Cam Cleeland | .20 | .07 |
| 58 | John Avery | .20 | .07 |
| 59 | Gary Brown | .20 | .07 |
| 60 | Ben Coates | .30 | .10 |
| 61 | Koy Detmer | .20 | .07 |
| 62 | Bryan Cox | .20 | .07 |
| 63 | Edgar Bennett | .20 | .07 |
| 64 | Tim Brown | .50 | .20 |
| 65 | Isaac Bruce | .50 | .20 |
| 66 | Eddie George | .50 | .20 |
| 67 | Reidel Anthony | .30 | .10 |
| 68 | Charlie Jones | .20 | .07 |
| 69 | Terry Allen | .30 | .10 |
| 70 | Joey Galloway | .30 | .10 |
| 71 | Jamir Miller | .20 | .07 |
| 72 | Will Blackwell | .20 | .07 |
| 73 | Ray Buchanan | .20 | .07 |
| 74 | Priest Holmes | .75 | .30 |
| 75 | Michael Irvin | .30 | .10 |
| 76 | Jonathan Linton | .20 | .07 |
| 77 | Curtis Enis | .30 | .10 |
| 78 | Neil O'Donnell | .30 | .10 |
| 79 | Tim Biakabutuka | .30 | .10 |
| 80 | Terry Kirby | .20 | .07 |
| 81 | Germane Crowell | .20 | .07 |
| 82 | Jason Elam | .20 | .07 |
| 83 | Mark Chmura | .20 | .07 |
| 84 | Marvin Harrison | .50 | .20 |
| 85 | Jimmy Hitchcock | .20 | .07 |
| 86 | Tony Brackens | .20 | .07 |
| 87 | Sean Dawkins | .20 | .07 |

| | | | |
|---|---|---:|---:|
| ☐ | 88 Tony Gonzalez | .50 | .20 |
| ☐ | 89 Kent Graham | .20 | .07 |
| ☐ | 90 Oronde Gadsden | .20 | .10 |
| ☐ | 91 Hugh Douglas | .20 | .07 |
| ☐ | 92 Robert Edwards | .20 | .07 |
| ☐ | 93 R.W. McQuarters | .20 | .07 |
| ☐ | 94 Aaron Glenn | .20 | .07 |
| ☐ | 95 Kevin Carter | .20 | .07 |
| ☐ | 96 Rickey Dudley | .20 | .07 |
| ☐ | 97 Derrick Brooks | .50 | .20 |
| ☐ | 98 Mark Bruener | .20 | .07 |
| ☐ | 99 Darrell Green | .20 | .10 |
| ☐ | 100 Jessie Tuggle | .20 | .07 |
| ☐ | 101 Freddie Jones | .20 | .07 |
| ☐ | 102 Rob Moore | .30 | .10 |
| ☐ | 103 Ahman Green | .50 | .20 |
| ☐ | 104 Chris Chandler | .30 | .10 |
| ☐ | 105 Steve McNair | .50 | .20 |
| ☐ | 106 Kevin Greene | .30 | .10 |
| ☐ | 107 Jermaine Lewis | .30 | .10 |
| ☐ | 108 Erik Kramer | .20 | .07 |
| ☐ | 109 Eric Moulds | .50 | .20 |
| ☐ | 110 Terry Fair | .20 | .07 |
| ☐ | 111 Carl Pickens | .30 | .10 |
| ☐ | 112 La'Roi Glover RC | 1.25 | .50 |
| ☐ | 113 Chris Spielman | .20 | .07 |
| ☐ | 114 Leroy Hoard | .20 | .07 |
| ☐ | 115 Mark Brunell | .50 | .20 |
| ☐ | 116 Patrick Jeffers RC | 3.00 | 1.50 |
| ☐ | 117 Elvis Grbac | .30 | .10 |
| ☐ | 118 Ike Hilliard | .20 | .07 |
| ☐ | 119 Sam Madison | .20 | .07 |
| ☐ | 120 Terrell Owens | .50 | .20 |
| ☐ | 121 Rich Gannon | .50 | .20 |
| ☐ | 122 Skip Hicks | .20 | .07 |
| ☐ | 123 Eric Green | .20 | .07 |
| ☐ | 124 Trent Dilfer | .30 | .10 |
| ☐ | 125 Terry Glenn | .50 | .20 |
| ☐ | 126 Trent Green | .50 | .20 |
| ☐ | 127 Charles Johnson | .20 | .07 |
| ☐ | 128 Adrian Murrell | .30 | .10 |
| ☐ | 129 Jason Gildon | .20 | .07 |
| ☐ | 130 Tim Dwight | .50 | .20 |
| ☐ | 131 Ryan Leaf | .50 | .20 |
| ☐ | 132 Rocket Ismail | .50 | .20 |
| ☐ | 133 Jon Kitna | .50 | .20 |
| ☐ | 134 Alonzo Mayes | .20 | .07 |
| ☐ | 135 Yancey Thigpen | .20 | .07 |
| ☐ | 136 David LaFleur | .20 | .07 |
| ☐ | 137 Ray Lewis | .50 | .20 |
| ☐ | 138 Herman Moore | .50 | .20 |
| ☐ | 139 Brian Griese | .50 | .20 |
| ☐ | 140 Antonio Freeman | .50 | .20 |
| ☐ | 141 Darnay Scott | .20 | .07 |
| ☐ | 142 Ed McDaniel | .20 | .07 |
| ☐ | 143 Andre Reed | .30 | .10 |
| ☐ | 144 Andre Hastings | .20 | .07 |
| ☐ | 145 Chris Warren | .20 | .07 |
| ☐ | 146 Kevin Hardy | .20 | .07 |
| ☐ | 147 Joe Jurevicius | .30 | .10 |
| ☐ | 148 Jerome Pathon | .20 | .07 |
| ☐ | 149 Duce Staley | .50 | .20 |
| ☐ | 150 Dan Marino | 1.50 | .60 |
| ☐ | 151 Jerry Rice | 1.00 | .40 |
| ☐ | 152 Byron Bam Morris | .20 | .07 |
| ☐ | 153 Az-Zahir Hakim | .20 | .07 |
| ☐ | 154 Ty Law | .30 | .10 |
| ☐ | 155 Warrick Dunn | .50 | .20 |
| ☐ | 156 Keyshawn Johnson | .50 | .20 |
| ☐ | 157 Brian Mitchell | .20 | .07 |
| ☐ | 158 James Jett | .30 | .10 |
| ☐ | 159 Fred Lane | .20 | .07 |
| ☐ | 160 Courtney Hawkins | .20 | .07 |
| ☐ | 161 Andre Wadsworth | .20 | .07 |
| ☐ | 162 Natrone Means | .20 | .07 |
| ☐ | 163 Andrew Glover | .20 | .07 |
| ☐ | 164 Anthony Simmons | .20 | .07 |
| ☐ | 165 Leon Lett | .20 | .07 |
| ☐ | 166 Frank Wycheck | .20 | .07 |
| ☐ | 167 Barry Minter | .20 | .07 |
| ☐ | 168 Michael McCrary | .20 | .07 |
| ☐ | 169 Johnnie Morton | .30 | .10 |
| ☐ | 170 Jay Riemersma | .20 | .07 |
| ☐ | 171 Vonnie Holliday | .20 | .07 |
| ☐ | 172 Brian Simmons | .20 | .07 |
| ☐ | 173 Joe Johnson | .20 | .07 |
| ☐ | 174 Ed McCaffrey | .30 | .10 |
| ☐ | 175 Jason Sehorn | .20 | .07 |
| ☐ | 176 Keenan McCardell | .30 | .10 |
| ☐ | 177 Bobby Taylor | .20 | .07 |
| ☐ | 178 Andre Rison | .30 | .10 |
| ☐ | 179 Greg Hill | .20 | .07 |
| ☐ | 180 O.J. McDuffie | .30 | .10 |
| ☐ | 181 Darren Woodson | .20 | .07 |
| ☐ | 182 Willie McGinest | .20 | .07 |
| ☐ | 183 J.J. Stokes | .30 | .10 |
| ☐ | 184 Leon Johnson | .20 | .07 |
| ☐ | 185 Bert Emanuel | .20 | .10 |
| ☐ | 186 Napoleon Kaufman | .50 | .20 |
| ☐ | 187 Leslie Shepherd | .20 | .07 |
| ☐ | 188 Levon Kirkland | .20 | .07 |
| ☐ | 189 Simeon Rice | .30 | .10 |
| ☐ | 190 Mikhael Ricks | .20 | .07 |
| ☐ | 191 Robert Smith | .50 | .20 |
| ☐ | 192 Michael Sinclair | .20 | .07 |
| ☐ | 193 Muhsin Muhammad | .30 | .10 |
| ☐ | 194 Duane Starks | .20 | .07 |
| ☐ | 195 Terance Mathis | .20 | .10 |
| ☐ | 196 Antowain Smith | .50 | .20 |
| ☐ | 197 Tony Parrish | .20 | .07 |
| ☐ | 198 Takeo Spikes | .20 | .07 |
| ☐ | 199 Ernie Mills | .20 | .07 |
| ☐ | 200 John Mobley | .20 | .07 |
| ☐ | 201 Pete Mitchell | .20 | .07 |
| ☐ | 202 Darick Holmes | .20 | .07 |
| ☐ | 203 Derrick Thomas | .50 | .20 |
| ☐ | 204 David Palmer | .20 | .07 |
| ☐ | 205 John Taylor | .20 | .07 |
| ☐ | 206 Sammy Knight | .20 | .07 |
| ☐ | 207 Dwayne Rudd | .20 | .07 |
| ☐ | 208 Lawyer Milloy | .30 | .10 |
| ☐ | 209 Michael Strahan | .30 | .10 |
| ☐ | 210 Mo Lewis | .20 | .07 |
| ☐ | 211 William Thomas | .20 | .07 |
| ☐ | 212 Darrell Russell | .20 | .07 |
| ☐ | 213 Brad Johnson | .50 | .20 |
| ☐ | 214 Kordell Stewart | .50 | .20 |
| ☐ | 215 Robert Holcombe | .20 | .07 |
| ☐ | 216 Junior Seau | .50 | .20 |
| ☐ | 217 Jacquez Green | .20 | .07 |
| ☐ | 218 Shawn Springs | .20 | .07 |
| ☐ | 219 Michael Westbrook | .20 | .10 |
| ☐ | 220 Rod Woodson | .30 | .10 |
| ☐ | 221 Frank Sanders | .30 | .10 |
| ☐ | 222 Bruce Smith | .30 | .10 |
| ☐ | 223 Eugene Robinson | .20 | .07 |
| ☐ | 224 Bill Romanowski | .20 | .07 |
| ☐ | 225 Wesley Walls | .20 | .07 |
| ☐ | 226 Jimmy Smith | .30 | .10 |
| ☐ | 227 Deion Sanders | .50 | .20 |
| ☐ | 228 Lamar Thomas | .20 | .07 |
| ☐ | 229 Dorsey Levens | .20 | .07 |
| ☐ | 230 Tony Simmons | .20 | .07 |
| ☐ | 231 John Randle | .20 | .10 |
| ☐ | 232 Curtis Martin | .50 | .20 |
| ☐ | 233 Bryant Young | .20 | .07 |
| ☐ | 234 Charles Woodson | .50 | .20 |
| ☐ | 235 Charles Way | .20 | .07 |
| ☐ | 236 Zach Thomas | .50 | .20 |
| ☐ | 237 Ricky Proehl | .20 | .07 |
| ☐ | 238 Ricky Watters | .30 | .10 |
| ☐ | 239 Hardy Nickerson | .20 | .07 |
| ☐ | 240 Shannon Sharpe | .30 | .10 |
| ☐ | 241 O.J. Santiago | .20 | .07 |
| ☐ | 242 Vinny Testaverde | .20 | .07 |
| ☐ | 243 Roell Preston | .20 | .07 |
| ☐ | 244 James Stewart | .20 | .07 |
| ☐ | 245 Jake Reed | .30 | .10 |
| ☐ | 246 Steve Young | .60 | .25 |
| ☐ | 247 Shaun Williams | .20 | .07 |
| ☐ | 248 Rod Smith | .30 | .10 |
| ☐ | 249 Warren Sapp | .30 | .10 |
| ☐ | 250 Champ Bailey RC | 1.50 | .60 |
| ☐ | 251 Karsten Bailey RC | .75 | .30 |
| ☐ | 252 D'Wayne Bates RC | .75 | .30 |
| ☐ | 253 Michael Bishop RC | 1.25 | .50 |
| ☐ | 254 David Boston RC | 1.25 | .50 |
| ☐ | 255 Na Brown RC | .75 | .30 |
| ☐ | 257 Fernando Bryant RC | .75 | .30 |
| ☐ | 258 Shawn Bryson RC | 1.25 | .50 |
| ☐ | 259 Darrin Chiaverini RC | .75 | .30 |
| ☐ | 260 Chris Claiborne RC | .40 | .15 |
| ☐ | 261 Mike Cloud RC | .75 | .30 |
| ☐ | 262 Cecil Collins RC | .40 | .15 |
| ☐ | 263 Tim Couch RC | 1.25 | .50 |
| ☐ | 264 Scott Covington RC | 1.25 | .50 |
| ☐ | 265 Daunte Culpepper RC | 5.00 | 2.00 |
| ☐ | 266 Antuan Edwards RC | .40 | .15 |
| ☐ | 267 Troy Edwards RC | .75 | .30 |
| ☐ | 268 Ebenezer Ekuban RC | .75 | .30 |
| ☐ | 269 Kevin Faulk RC | 1.25 | .50 |
| ☐ | 270 Jermaine Fazande RC | .75 | .30 |
| ☐ | 271 Joe Germaine RC | .75 | .30 |
| ☐ | 272 Martin Gramatica RC | .40 | .15 |
| ☐ | 273 Torry Holt RC | 3.00 | 1.25 |
| ☐ | 274 Brock Huard RC | 1.25 | .50 |
| ☐ | 275 Sedrick Irvin RC | .40 | .15 |
| ☐ | 276 Sheldon Jackson RC | .75 | .30 |
| ☐ | 277 Edgerrin James RC | 5.00 | 2.00 |
| ☐ | 278 James Johnson RC | .75 | .30 |
| ☐ | 279 Kevin Johnson RC | 1.25 | .50 |
| ☐ | 280 Malcolm Johnson RC | .40 | .15 |
| ☐ | 281 Andy Katzenmoyer RC | .75 | .30 |
| ☐ | 282 Jevon Kearse RC | 2.00 | .75 |
| ☐ | 283 Patrick Kerney RC | 1.25 | .50 |
| ☐ | 284 Shaun King RC | .75 | .30 |
| ☐ | 285 Jim Kleinsasser RC | 1.25 | .50 |
| ☐ | 286 Rob Konrad RC | 1.25 | .50 |
| ☐ | 287 Chris McAlister RC | .75 | .30 |
| ☐ | 288 Donovan McNabb RC | 6.00 | 2.50 |
| ☐ | 289 Cade McNown RC | .75 | .30 |
| ☐ | 290 Dee Miller RC | .40 | .15 |
| ☐ | 291 Joe Montgomery RC | .75 | .30 |
| ☐ | 292 De'Mond Parker RC | .40 | .15 |
| ☐ | 293 Peerless Price RC | 1.25 | .50 |
| ☐ | 294 Akili Smith RC | .75 | .30 |
| ☐ | 295 Justin Swift RC | .40 | .15 |
| ☐ | 296 Jerame Tuman RC | 1.25 | .50 |
| ☐ | 297 Ricky Williams RC | 2.50 | 1.00 |
| ☐ | 298 Antoine Winfield RC | .75 | .30 |
| ☐ | 299 Craig Yeast RC | .75 | .30 |
| ☐ | 300 Amos Zereoue RC | 1.25 | .50 |
| ☐ | P6 Fred Taylor Promo | 1.00 | .40 |

## 2000 Fleer Tradition

| | | | |
|---|---|---:|---:|
| ☐ | COMPLETE SET (400) | 60.00 | 25.00 |
| ☐ | 1 Kevin Johnson | .50 | .20 |
| ☐ | 2 Chris Chandler | .30 | .10 |
| ☐ | 3 Peerless Price | .30 | .10 |
| ☐ | 4 Andre Rison | .30 | .10 |
| ☐ | 5 Curtis Enis | .20 | .07 |
| ☐ | 6 Tim Couch | .50 | .20 |
| ☐ | 7 Brian Dawkins | .50 | .20 |
| ☐ | 8 Akili Smith | .20 | .07 |
| ☐ | 9 Kevin Faulk | .30 | .10 |
| ☐ | 10 Joey Galloway | .30 | .10 |
| ☐ | 11 Bill Romanowski | .20 | .07 |
| ☐ | 12 Charlie Batch | .50 | .20 |
| ☐ | 13 Terrence Wilkins | .20 | .07 |
| ☐ | 14 Kevin Hardy | .20 | .07 |
| ☐ | 15 Cade McNown | .20 | .07 |
| ☐ | 16 Elvis Grbac | .30 | .10 |
| ☐ | 17 Cris Carter | .50 | .20 |
| ☐ | 18 Willie McGinest | .20 | .07 |
| ☐ | 19 Michael Bishop | .20 | .07 |
| ☐ | 20 Lee Woodall | .20 | .07 |

|  |  | | |
|---|--------|-----|-----|
| 21 | Jake Reed | .30 | .10 |
| 22 | Bryan Cox | .20 | .07 |
| 23 | Chris Sanders | .20 | .07 |
| 24 | Tavian Banks | .20 | .07 |
| 25 | Levon Kirkland | .20 | .07 |
| 26 | James Hundon | .20 | .07 |
| 27 | Junior Seau | .50 | .20 |
| 28 | Darren Woodson | .20 | .07 |
| 29 | Kevin Carter | .20 | .07 |
| 30 | Joe Jurevicius | .20 | .07 |
| 31 | John Lynch | .30 | .10 |
| 32 | Steve McNair | .50 | .20 |
| 33 | Jake Plummer | .30 | .10 |
| 34 | Antonio Freeman | .50 | .20 |
| 35 | Peter Boulware | .20 | .07 |
| 36 | Brad Johnson | .50 | .20 |
| 37 | Bobby Engram | .30 | .10 |
| 38 | David Boston | .50 | .20 |
| 39 | Jason Tucker | .20 | .07 |
| 40 | Troy Brown | .30 | .10 |
| 41 | Brian Griese | .50 | .20 |
| 42 | Dorsey Levens | .30 | .10 |
| 43 | Cornelius Bennett | .20 | .07 |
| 44 | Donovan McNabb | .75 | .30 |
| 45 | Rob Johnson | .30 | .10 |
| 46 | Robert Smith | .50 | .20 |
| 47 | Stanley Pritchett | .20 | .07 |
| 48 | Tedy Bruschi | .50 | .20 |
| 49 | Dan Marino | 1.50 | .60 |
| 50 | Amani Toomer | .30 | .10 |
| 51 | Aaron Glenn | .20 | .07 |
| 52 | Rickey Dudley | .20 | .07 |
| 53 | Tim Brown | .50 | .20 |
| 54 | Jim Harbaugh | .30 | .10 |
| 55 | Terrell Owens | .50 | .20 |
| 56 | Jason Sehorn | .20 | .07 |
| 57 | Cortez Kennedy | .20 | .07 |
| 58 | London Fletcher RC | .30 | .10 |
| 59 | Simeon Rice | .30 | .10 |
| 60 | Shaun King | .50 | .20 |
| 61 | Stephen Davis | .50 | .20 |
| 62 | Andre Wadsworth | .20 | .07 |
| 63 | Kyle Brady | .20 | .07 |
| 64 | Priest Holmes | .60 | .25 |
| 65 | Patrick Jeffers | .50 | .20 |
| 66 | Barry Minter | .20 | .07 |
| 67 | Curtis Martin | .50 | .20 |
| 68 | Darrin Chiaverini | .20 | .07 |
| 69 | Robert Thomas | .20 | .07 |
| 70 | Samari Rolle | .20 | .07 |
| 71 | Robert Porcher | .20 | .07 |
| 72 | Jerry Rice | 1.00 | .40 |
| 73 | Bill Schroeder | .30 | .10 |
| 74 | Chad Bratzke | .20 | .07 |
| 75 | Tony Brackens | .20 | .07 |
| 76 | O.J. McDuffie | .30 | .10 |
| 77 | John Randle | .30 | .10 |
| 78 | Michael Pittman | .20 | .07 |
| 79 | Drew Bledsoe | .60 | .25 |
| 80 | Ike Hilliard | .20 | .07 |
| 81 | Victor Green | .20 | .07 |
| 82 | Duce Staley | .50 | .20 |
| 83 | Bruce Smith | .30 | .10 |
| 84 | Amos Zereoue | .30 | .10 |
| 85 | Charlie Garner | .30 | .10 |
| 86 | Shawn Springs | .20 | .07 |
| 87 | Kurt Warner | 1.00 | .40 |
| 88 | Eddie George | .50 | .20 |
| 89 | Michael Westbrook | .30 | .10 |
| 90 | Dexter Coakley | .20 | .07 |
| 91 | Rob Moore | .30 | .10 |
| 92 | Duane Starks | .20 | .07 |
| 93 | Steve Beuerlein | .30 | .10 |
| 94 | Marty Booker | .20 | .07 |
| 95 | Karim Abdul-Jabbar | .30 | .10 |
| 96 | Troy Aikman | 1.00 | .40 |
| 97 | Germane Crowell | .30 | .10 |
| 98 | Matt Hasselbeck | .30 | .10 |
| 99 | E.G. Green | .20 | .07 |
| 100 | Mark Brunell | .50 | .20 |
| 101 | Tony Martin | .20 | .07 |
| 102 | Darrell Green | .30 | .10 |
| 103 | Ricky Williams | .50 | .20 |
| 104 | Michael Strahan | .30 | .10 |
| 105 | Vinny Testaverde | .30 | .10 |
| 106 | Charles Johnson | .30 | .10 |
| 107 | Hines Ward | .50 | .20 |
| 108 | Bryant Young | .20 | .07 |
| 109 | Mo Lewis | .20 | .07 |
| 110 | Greg Clark | .20 | .07 |
| 111 | Jon Kitna | .50 | .20 |
| 112 | Jacquez Green | .30 | .10 |
| 113 | Kevin Dyson | .30 | .10 |
| 114 | Stephen Alexander | .20 | .07 |
| 115 | Cam Cleeland | .20 | .07 |
| 116 | Keith Poole | .20 | .07 |
| 117 | Az-Zahir Hakim | .30 | .10 |
| 118 | Tim Dwight | .50 | .20 |
| 119 | Corey Bradford | .20 | .07 |
| 120 | Carlos Emmons | .20 | .07 |
| 121 | Trent Dilfer | .30 | .10 |
| 122 | Lance Schulters | .20 | .07 |
| 123 | Byron Hanspard | .20 | .07 |
| 124 | Tim Biakabutuka | .30 | .10 |
| 125 | Eddie Kennison | .30 | .10 |
| 126 | Terry Kirby | .20 | .07 |
| 127 | Mike McKenzie | .20 | .07 |
| 128 | Fred Beasley | .20 | .07 |
| 129 | Chad Brown | .20 | .07 |
| 130 | Terrell Davis | .50 | .20 |
| 131 | Herman Moore | .30 | .10 |
| 132 | Vonnie Holliday | .20 | .07 |
| 133 | Jim Miller | .20 | .07 |
| 134 | Peyton Manning | 1.25 | .50 |
| 135 | Derrick Alexander | .30 | .10 |
| 136 | Oronde Gadsden | .30 | .10 |
| 137 | Robert Griffith | .20 | .07 |
| 138 | Troy Edwards | .20 | .07 |
| 139 | Damon Huard | .50 | .20 |
| 140 | Jessie Armstead | .20 | .07 |
| 141 | Charles Woodson | .30 | .10 |
| 142 | Troy Vincent | .20 | .07 |
| 143 | Natrone Means | .30 | .10 |
| 144 | Jeff Garcia | .50 | .20 |
| 145 | Terry Glenn | .30 | .10 |
| 146 | Marshall Faulk | .60 | .25 |
| 147 | Pat Johnson | .20 | .07 |
| 148 | Frank Wycheck | .20 | .07 |
| 149 | Champ Bailey | .30 | .10 |
| 150 | Jamal Anderson | .50 | .20 |
| 151 | Doug Flutie | .50 | .20 |
| 152 | Michael Bates | .20 | .07 |
| 153 | Corey Dillon | .50 | .20 |
| 154 | Keith McKenzie | .20 | .07 |
| 155 | Orpheus Roye | .20 | .07 |
| 156 | Olandis Gary | .50 | .20 |
| 157 | Johnnie Morton | .30 | .10 |
| 158 | Brett Favre | 1.50 | .60 |
| 159 | Adrian Murrell | .20 | .07 |
| 160 | Fred Taylor | .50 | .20 |
| 161 | Tony Gonzalez | .30 | .10 |
| 162 | Zach Thomas | .50 | .20 |
| 163 | Randy Moss | 1.00 | .40 |
| 164 | Marcus Robinson | .50 | .20 |
| 165 | Tiki Barber | .50 | .20 |
| 166 | Rich Gannon | .50 | .20 |
| 167 | Jeremiah Trotter RC | .50 | .20 |
| 168 | Jermaine Fazande | .20 | .07 |
| 169 | Steve Young | .60 | .25 |
| 170 | Isaac Bruce | .50 | .20 |
| 171 | Warrick Dunn | .50 | .20 |
| 172 | Yancey Thigpen | .20 | .07 |
| 173 | Rod Smith | .30 | .10 |
| 174 | Albert Connell | .20 | .07 |
| 175 | Freddie Jones | .20 | .07 |
| 176 | Terance Mathis | .30 | .10 |
| 177 | Eric Moulds | .50 | .20 |
| 178 | Brian Mitchell | .20 | .07 |
| 179 | Wesley Walls | .20 | .07 |
| 180 | Carl Pickens | .30 | .10 |
| 181 | Errict Rhett | .30 | .10 |
| 182 | Madre Hill | .20 | .07 |
| 183 | Jason Elam | .20 | .07 |
| 184 | Greg Ellis | .20 | .07 |
| 185 | David Sloan | .20 | .07 |
| 186 | Edgerrin James | .75 | .30 |
| 187 | Jimmy Smith | .30 | .10 |
| 188 | Tony Richardson RC | .20 | .07 |
| 189 | James Hasty | .20 | .07 |
| 190 | Sam Madison | .20 | .07 |
| 191 | Tony Simmons | .20 | .07 |
| 192 | Andre Hastings | .20 | .07 |
| 193 | Keyshawn Johnson | .50 | .20 |
| 194 | Na Brown | .20 | .07 |
| 195 | Napoleon Kaufman | .30 | .10 |
| 196 | Torrance Small | .20 | .07 |
| 197 | Curtis Conway | .30 | .10 |
| 198 | Jeff Graham | .20 | .07 |
| 199 | Jason Hanson | .20 | .07 |
| 200 | Torry Holt | .50 | .20 |
| 201 | Derrick Mayes | .30 | .10 |
| 202 | Warren Sapp | .30 | .10 |
| 203 | Kimble Anders | .20 | .07 |
| 204 | Blaine Bishop | .20 | .07 |
| 205 | Leroy Hoard | .20 | .07 |
| 206 | Larry Centers | .20 | .07 |
| 207 | O.J. Santiago | .20 | .07 |
| 208 | Antowain Smith | .30 | .10 |
| 209 | Chuck Smith | .20 | .07 |
| 210 | Takeo Spikes | .20 | .07 |
| 211 | Rocket Ismail | .30 | .10 |
| 212 | Ed McCaffrey | .50 | .20 |
| 213 | Karsten Bailey | .20 | .07 |
| 214 | Terry Fair | .20 | .07 |
| 215 | Ken Dilger | .20 | .07 |
| 216 | Jamie Martin | .30 | .10 |
| 217 | Cris Dishman | .20 | .07 |
| 218 | Jay Fiedler | .30 | .10 |
| 219 | Lawyer Milloy | .30 | .10 |
| 220 | Jake Delhomme RC | 3.00 | 1.25 |
| 221 | Wayne Chrebet | .30 | .10 |
| 222 | Darrell Russell | .20 | .07 |
| 223 | Christian Fauria | .20 | .07 |
| 224 | Jerome Bettis | .50 | .20 |
| 225 | Ryan Leaf | .30 | .10 |
| 226 | Ricky Watters | .30 | .10 |
| 227 | Keenan McCardell | .30 | .10 |
| 228 | Grant Wistrom | .20 | .07 |
| 229 | Jevon Kearse | .50 | .20 |
| 230 | Frank Sanders | .30 | .10 |
| 231 | Shannon Sharpe | .30 | .10 |
| 232 | Jonathan Linton | .20 | .07 |
| 233 | Alonzo Mayes | .20 | .07 |
| 234 | Jason Garrett | .20 | .07 |
| 235 | Kordell Stewart | .30 | .10 |
| 236 | David LaFleur | .20 | .07 |
| 237 | Kenny Bynum | .20 | .07 |
| 238 | Byron Chamberlain | .20 | .07 |
| 239 | Tyrone Davis | .20 | .07 |
| 240 | Jerome Pathon | .30 | .10 |
| 241 | Alvis Whitted | .20 | .07 |
| 242 | Kevin Lockett | .20 | .07 |
| 243 | Matthew Hatchette | .20 | .07 |
| 244 | Rod Woodson | .30 | .10 |
| 245 | Joe Horn | .30 | .10 |
| 246 | Ronnie Powell | .20 | .07 |
| 247 | Dedric Ward | .20 | .07 |
| 248 | James Johnson | .30 | .10 |
| 249 | James Jett | .20 | .07 |
| 250 | Bobby Shaw RC | .50 | .20 |
| 251 | J.J. Stokes | .30 | .10 |
| 252 | Paul Shields RC | .20 | .07 |
| 253 | Sean Dawkins | .20 | .07 |
| 254 | Hardy Nickerson | .20 | .07 |
| 255 | Stephen Boyd | .20 | .07 |
| 256 | Chris Warren | .20 | .07 |
| 257 | Kerry Collins | .30 | .10 |
| 258 | Isaac Byrd | .20 | .07 |
| 259 | Bobby Hoying | .20 | .07 |
| 260 | Daunte Culpepper | .60 | .25 |
| 261 | Moe Williams | .30 | .10 |
| 262 | Kamil Loud | .20 | .07 |
| 263 | Derrick Brooks | .50 | .20 |
| 264 | Jay Riemersma | .20 | .07 |
| 265 | Ray Lucas | .30 | .10 |
| 266 | Jason Gildon | .20 | .07 |
| 267 | James Stewart | .30 | .10 |
| 268 | Marcellus Wiley | .20 | .07 |
| 269 | Craig Yeast | .20 | .07 |
| 270 | Michael Bankston | .30 | .10 |
| 271 | Tyrone Wheatley | .30 | .10 |
| 272 | Martin Gramatica | .20 | .07 |

| | | | |
|---|---|---|---|
| 273 | Phillip Daniels RC | .30 | .10 |
| 274 | Richard Huntley | .20 | .07 |
| 275 | Muhsin Muhammad | .20 | .10 |
| 276 | Todd Lyght | .20 | .07 |
| 277 | Carlester Crumpler | .20 | .07 |
| 278 | Jeff Lewis | .20 | .07 |
| 279 | Jeff George | .30 | .10 |
| 280 | Jeff Blake | .30 | .10 |
| 281 | Michael McCrary | .20 | .07 |
| 282 | Shawn Jefferson | .20 | .07 |
| 283 | Mark Bruener | .20 | .07 |
| 284 | Donnie Abraham | .20 | .07 |
| 285 | Yatil Green | .20 | .07 |
| 286 | Jermaine Lewis | .20 | .07 |
| 287 | Rob Fredrickson | .20 | .07 |
| 288 | Thurman Thomas | .30 | .10 |
| 289 | Kent Graham | .20 | .07 |
| 290 | Damay Scott | .30 | .10 |
| 291 | Tony Graziani | .30 | .10 |
| 292 | Qadry Ismail | .30 | .10 |
| 293 | Aeneas Williams | .20 | .07 |
| 294 | Marvin Harrison | .50 | .20 |
| 295 | Jimmy Hitchcock | .20 | .07 |
| 296 | Bob Christian | .20 | .07 |
| 297 | Pete Mitchell | .20 | .07 |
| 298 | Mike Alstott | .50 | .20 |
| 299 | Emmitt Smith | 1.00 | .40 |
| 300 | Trevor Pryce | .20 | .07 |
| 301 | Tony Banks | .30 | .10 |
| 302 | Mikhael Ricks | .20 | .07 |
| 303 | Randall Cunningham | .50 | .20 |
| 304 | Thomas Jones RC | 1.25 | .50 |
| 305 | Mark Simoneau RC | .60 | .25 |
| 306 | Jamal Lewis RC | 2.00 | .75 |
| 307 | Kwame Cavil RC | .40 | .15 |
| 308 | Rashard Anderson RC | .60 | .25 |
| 309 | Brian Urlacher RC | 3.00 | 1.25 |
| 310 | Peter Warrick RC | .75 | .30 |
| 311 | Courtney Brown RC | .75 | .30 |
| 312 | Michael Wiley RC | .60 | .25 |
| 313 | Chris Cole RC | .60 | .25 |
| 314 | Reuben Droughns RC | .75 | .30 |
| 315 | Bubba Franks RC | .75 | .30 |
| 316 | Rob Morris RC | .60 | .25 |
| 317 | R.Jay Soward RC | .60 | .25 |
| 318 | Sylvester Morris RC | .60 | .25 |
| 319 | Ben Kelly RC | .30 | .15 |
| 320 | Doug Chapman RC | .60 | .25 |
| 321 | J.R. Redmond RC | .60 | .25 |
| 322 | Darren Howard RC | .60 | .25 |
| 323 | Ron Dayne RC | .75 | .30 |
| 324 | Chad Pennington RC | 2.00 | .75 |
| 325 | Jerry Porter RC | .75 | .30 |
| 326 | Corey Simon RC | .75 | .30 |
| 327 | Plaxico Burress RC | 1.50 | .60 |
| 328 | Trung Canidate RC | .60 | .25 |
| 329 | Rogers Beckett RC | .60 | .25 |
| 330 | Giovanni Carmazzi RC | .40 | .15 |
| 331 | Shaun Alexander RC | 2.50 | 1.00 |
| 332 | Joe Hamilton RC | .60 | .25 |
| 333 | Keith Bullock RC | .75 | .30 |
| 334 | Todd Husak RC | .75 | .30 |
| 335 | D.Walker RC/R.Thompson RC | .60 | .25 |
| 336 | M.Philyaw RC/A.Midget RC | .40 | .15 |
| 337 | C.Redman RC/T.Taylor RC | .75 | .30 |
| 338 | Sam Morris RC/A.Black RC | .75 | .30 |
| 339 | D.Grant RC/A.McKinley RC | .60 | .25 |
| 340 | D.White RC/F.Murphy RC | .75 | .30 |
| 341 | C.Keaton RC/R.Dugans RC | .75 | .30 |
| 342 | Prentice RC/Northcutt RC | .60 | .25 |
| 343 | D.Grant RC/D.Goodrich RC | .40 | .15 |
| 344 | D.O'Neal RC/I.Gold RC | .75 | .30 |
| 345 | S.McDougle RC/B.Green RC | .40 | .15 |
| 346 | A.Lucas RC/N.Diggs RC | .60 | .25 |
| 347 | M.Washington RC/D.Kendra RC | .60 | .25 |
| 348 | T.Slaughter RC/S.Stith RC | .60 | .25 |
| 349 | W.Bartee RC/F.Moreau RC | .60 | .25 |
| 350 | D.Dyer RC/T.Wade RC | .60 | .25 |
| 351 | C.Hovan RC/T.Walters | .75 | .30 |
| 352 | T.Brady RC/Stachelski RC | 30.00 | 12.50 |
| 353 | M.Bulger RC/T.Smith RC | 1.50 | .60 |
| 354 | C.Griffin RC/R.Dixon RC | .60 | .25 |
| 355 | L.Coles RC/A.Becht RC | .75 | .30 |
| 356 | Janikowski RC/Lechler RC | .75 | .30 |
| 357 | T.Pinkston RC/G.Scott RC | .75 | .30 |
| 358 | D.Farmer RC/T.Martin RC | .60 | .25 |
| 359 | B.Young RC/J.Shepherd RC | .60 | .25 |
| 360 | J.Seider RC/T.Gaylor RC | .60 | .25 |
| 361 | T.Rattay RC/C.Fields RC | .75 | .30 |
| 362 | D.Jackson RC/J.Williams RC | 1.25 | .50 |
| 363 | N.Webster RC/J.Whalen RC | .40 | .15 |
| 364 | E.Kinney RC/C.Coleman RC | .75 | .30 |
| 365 | C.Samuels RC/L.Murray RC | .60 | .25 |
| 366 | Cardinals IA/Plummer | .30 | .10 |
| 367 | Falcons IA/Chandlr/Andrson | .30 | .10 |
| 368 | Ravens IA/Boulware | .20 | .07 |
| 369 | Bills IA/Flutie | .30 | .10 |
| 370 | Panthers IA/Beuerlein | .30 | .10 |
| 371 | Bears IA/McNown | .20 | .07 |
| 372 | Bengals IA/Dillon | .30 | .10 |
| 373 | Browns IA/Couch | .30 | .10 |
| 374 | Cowboys IA/Smith | .50 | .20 |
| 375 | Broncos IA/Gary | .30 | .10 |
| 376 | Lions IA/Batch | .30 | .10 |
| 377 | Packers IA/Levens | .30 | .10 |
| 378 | Colts IA/James | .60 | .25 |
| 379 | Jaguars IA/Brackens | .20 | .07 |
| 380 | Chiefs IA/Grbac | .20 | .07 |
| 381 | Dolphins IA/Marino | .75 | .30 |
| 382 | Vikings IA/Rob.Smith | .30 | .10 |
| 383 | Patriots IA/Bledsoe | .30 | .10 |
| 384 | Saints IA/Williams | .50 | .20 |
| 385 | Giants IA/Armstead | .20 | .07 |
| 386 | Jets IA/Martin | .30 | .10 |
| 387 | Raiders IA/Kaufman | .30 | .10 |
| 388 | Eagles IA/McNabb | .30 | .10 |
| 389 | Steelers IA/Bettis | .30 | .10 |
| 390 | Rams IA/Faulk | .50 | .20 |
| 391 | Chargers IA/Fazande | .20 | .07 |
| 392 | 49ers IA/Garner | .30 | .10 |
| 393 | Seahawks IA/Kennedy | .20 | .07 |
| 394 | Buccaneers IA/Alstott | .30 | .10 |
| 395 | Titans IA/McNair | .30 | .10 |
| 396 | Redskins IA/S.Davis | .30 | .10 |
| 397 | Tim Couch CL | .30 | .10 |
| 398 | Peyton Manning CL | .60 | .25 |
| 399 | Kurt Warner CL | .50 | .20 |
| 400 | Randy Moss CL | .50 | .20 |

## 2001 Fleer Tradition

| | | | |
|---|---|---|---|
| | COMPLETE SET (450) | 40.00 | 20.00 |
| 1 | Thomas Jones | .40 | .15 |
| 2 | Bruce Smith | .25 | .08 |
| 3 | Marvin Harrison | .60 | .25 |
| 4 | Darrell Jackson | .60 | .25 |
| 5 | Trent Green | .60 | .25 |
| 6 | Wesley Walls | .25 | .08 |
| 7 | Jimmy Smith | .40 | .15 |
| 8 | Isaac Bruce | .25 | .08 |
| 9 | Jamal Anderson | .60 | .25 |
| 10 | Marty Booker | .25 | .08 |
| 11 | Elvis Grbac | .40 | .15 |
| 12 | Joe Jurevicius | .25 | .08 |
| 13 | Reidel Anthony | .25 | .08 |
| 14 | Damay Scott | .25 | .08 |
| 15 | Oronde Gadsden | .40 | .15 |
| 16 | Shawn Bryson | .25 | .08 |
| 17 | Jonathan Ogden | .25 | .08 |
| 18 | Aaron Shea | .25 | .08 |
| 19 | Randy Moss | 1.25 | .50 |
| 20 | Eddie George | .60 | .25 |
| 21 | Stephen Davis | .60 | .25 |
| 22 | Emmitt Smith | 1.25 | .50 |
| 23 | Willie McGinest | .25 | .08 |
| 24 | Trent Dilfer | .40 | .15 |
| 25 | Peter Boulware | .25 | .08 |
| 26 | Rod Smith | .40 | .15 |
| 27 | Ricky Williams | .60 | .25 |
| 28 | Albert Connell | .25 | .08 |
| 29 | Robert Porcher | .25 | .08 |
| 30 | Jessie Armstead | .25 | .08 |
| 31 | Shane Matthews | .25 | .08 |
| 32 | Eric Moulds | .40 | .15 |
| 33 | Kurt Schulz | .25 | .08 |
| 34 | Richie Anderson | .25 | .08 |
| 35 | Ron Dugans | .25 | .08 |
| 36 | Steve Beuerlein | .40 | .15 |
| 37 | Darren Sharper | .25 | .08 |
| 38 | Andre Rison | .40 | .15 |
| 39 | Courtney Brown | .40 | .15 |
| 40 | Eddie Kennison | .40 | .15 |
| 41 | Ken Dilger | .25 | .08 |
| 42 | Charles Johnson | .25 | .08 |
| 43 | Dexter Coakley | .25 | .08 |
| 44 | Akili Smith | .25 | .08 |
| 45 | R.Jay Soward | .25 | .08 |
| 46 | Danny Farmer | .25 | .08 |
| 47 | Dez White | .25 | .08 |
| 48 | Olandis Gary | .40 | .15 |
| 49 | Wali Rainer | .25 | .08 |
| 50 | Derrick Alexander | .40 | .15 |
| 51 | Donnie Abraham | .25 | .08 |
| 52 | David Sloan | .25 | .08 |
| 53 | Larry Allen | .25 | .08 |
| 54 | Sam Madison | .25 | .08 |
| 55 | Troy Edwards | .25 | .08 |
| 56 | Ryan Longwell | .25 | .08 |
| 57 | Brian Griese | .60 | .25 |
| 58 | Joe Johnson | .40 | .15 |
| 59 | Reggie Jones | .25 | .08 |
| 60 | Mike Peterson | .25 | .08 |
| 61 | Bill Romanowski | .25 | .08 |
| 62 | Kevin Faulk | .40 | .15 |
| 63 | Tai Streets | .25 | .08 |
| 64 | Tony Brackens | .25 | .08 |
| 65 | James Stewart | .40 | .15 |
| 66 | Joe Horn | .40 | .15 |
| 67 | Kurt Warner | 1.25 | .50 |
| 68 | Eric Hicks RC | .25 | .08 |
| 69 | Bryan Westbrook | .25 | .08 |
| 70 | Tiki Barber | .60 | .25 |
| 71 | Frank Sanders | .25 | .08 |
| 72 | Olindo Mare | .25 | .08 |
| 73 | Bill Schroeder | .40 | .15 |
| 74 | Anthony Becht | .25 | .08 |
| 75 | Rob Johnson | .40 | .15 |
| 76 | Troy Brown | .40 | .15 |
| 77 | Chad Bratzke | .25 | .08 |
| 78 | Rickey Dudley | .25 | .08 |
| 79 | Doug Johnson | .25 | .08 |
| 80 | Joe Johnson | .25 | .08 |
| 81 | Keenan McCardell | .25 | .08 |
| 82 | Tim Brown | .60 | .25 |
| 83 | Blaine Bishop | .25 | .08 |
| 84 | Ron Dixon | .25 | .08 |
| 85 | Michael Cloud | .25 | .08 |
| 86 | Todd Pinkston | .25 | .08 |
| 87 | Shannon Sharpe | .40 | .15 |
| 88 | Marvin Jones | .25 | .08 |
| 89 | Zach Thomas | .60 | .25 |
| 90 | Kordell Stewart | .40 | .15 |
| 91 | Champ Bailey | .40 | .15 |
| 92 | Jacquez Green | .25 | .08 |
| 93 | Daunte Culpepper | .60 | .25 |
| 94 | Freddie Jones | .25 | .08 |
| 95 | Donald Hayes | .25 | .08 |
| 96 | Rich Gannon | .60 | .25 |
| 97 | Ty Law | .40 | .15 |
| 98 | Grant Wistrom | .25 | .08 |
| 99 | James Allen | .25 | .08 |
| 100 | Corey Simon | .25 | .08 |
| 101 | Jeff Blake | .25 | .08 |
| 102 | Bryant Young | .25 | .08 |
| 103 | Craig Yeast | .25 | .08 |
| 104 | Bobby Shaw | .25 | .08 |
| 105 | Kerry Collins | .40 | .15 |

|  |  | | |
|---|---|---|---|
| ☐ 106 | Brock Huard | .25 | .08 |
| ☐ 107 | JaJuan Dawson | .25 | .08 |
| ☐ 108 | Jeff Graham | .25 | .08 |
| ☐ 109 | Chad Pennington | 1.00 | .40 |
| ☐ 110 | Jake Plummer | .40 | .15 |
| ☐ 111 | James McKnight | .40 | .15 |
| ☐ 112 | Terrell Owens | .60 | .25 |
| ☐ 113 | Mo Lewis | .25 | .08 |
| ☐ 114 | Jeremy McDaniel | .25 | .08 |
| ☐ 115 | Ed McCaffrey | .60 | .25 |
| ☐ 116 | Ricky Watters | .25 | .08 |
| ☐ 117 | Jerry Porter | .40 | .15 |
| ☐ 118 | Shawn Jefferson | .25 | .08 |
| ☐ 119 | Charlie Batch | .60 | .25 |
| ☐ 120 | Justin Watson | .25 | .08 |
| ☐ 121 | Donovan McNabb | .75 | .30 |
| ☐ 122 | Shaun King | .25 | .08 |
| ☐ 123 | Brett Favre | 2.00 | .75 |
| ☐ 124 | Ronald McKinnon | .25 | .08 |
| ☐ 125 | Richard Huntley | .25 | .08 |
| ☐ 126 | Ray Lewis | .60 | .25 |
| ☐ 127 | Jerome Pathon | .40 | .15 |
| ☐ 128 | Sam Cowart | .25 | .08 |
| ☐ 129 | Ryan Leaf | .40 | .15 |
| ☐ 130 | Greg Clark | .25 | .08 |
| ☐ 131 | Tony Boselli | .25 | .08 |
| ☐ 132 | Frank Wycheck | .25 | .08 |
| ☐ 133 | Charlie Garner | .40 | .15 |
| ☐ 134 | Tony Siragusa | .25 | .08 |
| ☐ 135 | Sylvester Morris | .25 | .08 |
| ☐ 136 | Qadry Ismail | .40 | .15 |
| ☐ 137 | Jon Kitna | .40 | .15 |
| ☐ 138 | James Thrash | .40 | .15 |
| ☐ 139 | Lamar Smith | .40 | .15 |
| ☐ 140 | Brad Johnson | .60 | .25 |
| ☐ 141 | London Fletcher | .25 | .08 |
| ☐ 142 | Tim Biakabutuka | .25 | .08 |
| ☐ 143 | Ed McDaniel | .25 | .08 |
| ☐ 144 | Tony Parrish | .25 | .08 |
| ☐ 145 | David Boston | .60 | .25 |
| ☐ 146 | Brian Urlacher | 1.00 | .40 |
| ☐ 147 | Drew Bledsoe | .75 | .30 |
| ☐ 148 | David Patten | .25 | .08 |
| ☐ 149 | Marcellus Wiley | .25 | .08 |
| ☐ 150 | Peter Warrick | .60 | .25 |
| ☐ 151 | La'Roi Glover | .25 | .08 |
| ☐ 152 | Troy Aikman | 1.00 | .40 |
| ☐ 153 | Chris Chandler | .40 | .15 |
| ☐ 154 | Travis Prentice | .25 | .08 |
| ☐ 155 | Ike Hilliard | .40 | .15 |
| ☐ 156 | John Mobley | .25 | .08 |
| ☐ 157 | Warren Sapp | .40 | .15 |
| ☐ 158 | Joey Galloway | .40 | .15 |
| ☐ 159 | Laveranues Coles | .60 | .25 |
| ☐ 160 | Germane Crowell | .25 | .08 |
| ☐ 161 | Jamal Lewis | 1.00 | .40 |
| ☐ 162 | Mike Anderson | .40 | .15 |
| ☐ 163 | Charles Woodson | .40 | .15 |
| ☐ 164 | Antonio Freeman | .60 | .25 |
| ☐ 165 | Derrick Mason | .40 | .15 |
| ☐ 166 | Chris Claiborne | .25 | .08 |
| ☐ 167 | Brian Mitchell | .25 | .08 |
| ☐ 168 | Mike Vanderjagt | .25 | .08 |
| ☐ 169 | Rod Woodson | .40 | .15 |
| ☐ 170 | Doug Chapman | .25 | .08 |
| ☐ 171 | John Lynch | .40 | .15 |
| ☐ 172 | Kevin Hardy | .25 | .08 |
| ☐ 173 | Sam Shade | .25 | .08 |
| ☐ 174 | Edgerrin James | .75 | .30 |
| ☐ 175 | Brian Dawkins | .40 | .15 |
| ☐ 176 | Donnie Edwards | .25 | .08 |
| ☐ 177 | Patrick Jeffers | .40 | .15 |
| ☐ 178 | Mark Brunell | .60 | .25 |
| ☐ 179 | Junior Seau | .60 | .25 |
| ☐ 180 | Trace Armstrong | .25 | .08 |
| ☐ 181 | Marcus Robinson | .40 | .15 |
| ☐ 182 | Tony Gonzalez | .40 | .15 |
| ☐ 183 | J.J. Stokes | .40 | .15 |
| ☐ 184 | Jake Reed | .40 | .15 |
| ☐ 185 | Corey Dillon | .60 | .25 |
| ☐ 186 | Jay Fiedler | .60 | .25 |
| ☐ 187 | Christian Fauria | .25 | .08 |
| ☐ 188 | Sammy Knight | .25 | .08 |
| ☐ 189 | Kevin Johnson | .40 | .15 |
| ☐ 190 | Matthew Hatchette | .25 | .08 |
| ☐ 191 | Az-Zahir Hakim | .40 | .15 |
| ☐ 192 | Keith Hamilton | .25 | .08 |
| ☐ 193 | Darren Woodson | .25 | .08 |
| ☐ 194 | Terry Glenn | .40 | .15 |
| ☐ 195 | Simeon Rice | .40 | .15 |
| ☐ 196 | Keyshawn Johnson | .60 | .25 |
| ☐ 197 | Terrell Davis | .60 | .25 |
| ☐ 198 | William Roaf | .25 | .08 |
| ☐ 199 | Doug Flutie | .60 | .25 |
| ☐ 200 | Kevin Carter | .25 | .08 |
| ☐ 201 | Stephen Boyd | .25 | .08 |
| ☐ 202 | Michael Strahan | .40 | .15 |
| ☐ 203 | Ray Buchanan | .25 | .08 |
| ☐ 204 | Tyrone Wheatley | .40 | .15 |
| ☐ 205 | Jason Hanson | .25 | .08 |
| ☐ 206 | Wayne Chrebet | .40 | .15 |
| ☐ 207 | Samari Rolle | .25 | .08 |
| ☐ 208 | Duce Staley | .60 | .25 |
| ☐ 209 | Dorsey Levens | .40 | .15 |
| ☐ 210 | Sebastian Janikowski | .25 | .08 |
| ☐ 211 | Duane Starks | .25 | .08 |
| ☐ 212 | Jason Gildon | .25 | .08 |
| ☐ 213 | Terrence Wilkins | .25 | .08 |
| ☐ 214 | Eric Allen | .25 | .08 |
| ☐ 215 | Deion Sanders | .60 | .25 |
| ☐ 216 | Curtis Conway | .40 | .15 |
| ☐ 217 | Fred Taylor | .60 | .25 |
| ☐ 218 | Troy Vincent | .25 | .08 |
| ☐ 219 | Mike Minter RC | .40 | .15 |
| ☐ 220 | Jeff Garcia | .60 | .25 |
| ☐ 221 | Tony Richardson | .25 | .08 |
| ☐ 222 | Jerome Bettis | .60 | .25 |
| ☐ 223 | Chad Morton | .25 | .08 |
| ☐ 224 | Tony Horne | .25 | .08 |
| ☐ 225 | Dave Moore | .25 | .08 |
| ☐ 226 | Victor Green | .25 | .08 |
| ☐ 227 | Chris Sanders | .25 | .08 |
| ☐ 228 | Marshall Faulk | .75 | .30 |
| ☐ 229 | Cris Carter | .60 | .25 |
| ☐ 230 | Rodney Harrison | .25 | .08 |
| ☐ 231 | Tim Couch | .40 | .15 |
| ☐ 232 | Antowain Smith | .40 | .15 |
| ☐ 233 | Lawyer Milloy | .25 | .08 |
| ☐ 234 | Lance Schulters | .25 | .08 |
| ☐ 235 | Michael Wiley | .25 | .08 |
| ☐ 236 | Steve McNair | .60 | .25 |
| ☐ 237 | Aaron Brooks | .60 | .25 |
| ☐ 238 | Anthony Simmons | .25 | .08 |
| ☐ 239 | Dwayne Carswell | .25 | .08 |
| ☐ 240 | Priest Holmes | .75 | .30 |
| ☐ 241 | Amani Toomer | .40 | .15 |
| ☐ 242 | Aeneas Williams | .25 | .08 |
| ☐ 243 | MarTay Jenkins | .25 | .08 |
| ☐ 244 | Jeff George | .40 | .15 |
| ☐ 245 | Vinny Testaverde | .40 | .15 |
| ☐ 246 | Peerless Price | .40 | .15 |
| ☐ 247 | Bubba Franks | .40 | .15 |
| ☐ 248 | Randall Cunningham | .60 | .25 |
| ☐ 249 | Aaron Brown | .25 | .08 |
| ☐ 250 | Terance Mathis | .40 | .15 |
| ☐ 251 | Peyton Manning | 1.50 | .60 |
| ☐ 252 | Terrell Buckley | .25 | .08 |
| ☐ 253 | Greg Biekert | .25 | .08 |
| ☐ 254 | Martin Gramatica | .25 | .08 |
| ☐ 255 | Kyle Brady | .25 | .08 |
| ☐ 256 | Johnnie Morton | .40 | .15 |
| ☐ 257 | Jeremiah Trotter | .40 | .15 |
| ☐ 258 | Travis Taylor | .40 | .15 |
| ☐ 259 | Frank Moreau | .25 | .08 |
| ☐ 260 | LeRoy Butler | .25 | .08 |
| ☐ 261 | Plaxico Burress | .60 | .25 |
| ☐ 262 | Randall Godfrey | .25 | .08 |
| ☐ 263 | Jason Taylor | .40 | .15 |
| ☐ 264 | Jeff Burris | .25 | .08 |
| ☐ 265 | Jim Harbaugh | .40 | .15 |
| ☐ 266 | Marco Coleman | .25 | .08 |
| ☐ 267 | Robert Smith | .40 | .15 |
| ☐ 268 | Mike Hollis | .25 | .08 |
| ☐ 269 | Jerry Rice | 1.25 | .50 |
| ☐ 270 | Muhsin Muhammad | .40 | .15 |
| ☐ 271 | J.R. Redmond | .25 | .08 |
| ☐ 272 | Brian Walker | .25 | .08 |
| ☐ 273 | Orlando Pace | .25 | .08 |
| ☐ 274 | Cade McNown | .25 | .08 |
| ☐ 275 | Darren Howard | .25 | .08 |
| ☐ 276 | Ron Dayne | .60 | .25 |
| ☐ 277 | Shaun Alexander | .75 | .30 |
| ☐ 278 | Brandon Bennett | .25 | .08 |
| ☐ 279 | Jason Sehorn | .25 | .08 |
| ☐ 280 | Matt Hasselbeck | .40 | .15 |
| ☐ 281 | Michael Pittman | .25 | .08 |
| ☐ 282 | Dennis Northcutt | .40 | .15 |
| ☐ 283 | Dedric Ward | .25 | .08 |
| ☐ 284 | Curtis Martin | .60 | .25 |
| ☐ 285 | Sammy Morris | .25 | .08 |
| ☐ 286 | Rocket Ismail | .40 | .15 |
| ☐ 287 | Jon Ritchie | .25 | .08 |
| ☐ 288 | Shaun Ellis | .25 | .08 |
| ☐ 289 | Tim Dwight | .60 | .25 |
| ☐ 290 | Trevor Pryce | .25 | .08 |
| ☐ 291 | Warrick Dunn | .60 | .25 |
| ☐ 292 | Napoleon Kaufman | .40 | .15 |
| ☐ 293 | Mike Alstott | .60 | .25 |
| ☐ 294 | Herman Moore | .40 | .15 |
| ☐ 295 | Chad Lewis | .25 | .08 |
| ☐ 296 | Hugh Douglas | .25 | .08 |
| ☐ 297 | Chris Redman | .40 | .15 |
| ☐ 298 | Ahman Green | .60 | .25 |
| ☐ 299 | Hines Ward | .60 | .25 |
| ☐ 300 | Mark Brunener | .25 | .08 |
| ☐ 301 | Jevon Kearse | .40 | .15 |
| ☐ 302 | Jermaine Fazande | .25 | .08 |
| ☐ 303 | Terrell Fletcher | .25 | .08 |
| ☐ 304 | Torry Holt | .60 | .25 |
| ☐ 305 | Chris McAlister | .25 | .08 |
| ☐ 306 | Jason Elam | .25 | .08 |
| ☐ 307 | Fred Beasley | .25 | .08 |
| ☐ 308 | Frank Wycheck UH | .25 | .08 |
| ☐ 309 | Michael McCrary UH | .25 | .08 |
| ☐ 310 | Mark Brunell UH | .60 | .25 |
| ☐ 311 | Tim Couch UH | .40 | .15 |
| ☐ 312 | Takeo Spikes UH | .25 | .08 |
| ☐ 313 | Jerome Bettis UH | .40 | .15 |
| ☐ 314 | Zach Thomas UH | .40 | .15 |
| ☐ 315 | Drew Bledsoe UH | .60 | .25 |
| ☐ 316 | Wayne Chrebet UH | .25 | .08 |
| ☐ 317 | Jay Riemersma UH | .25 | .08 |
| ☐ 318 | Marvin Harrison UH | .40 | .15 |
| ☐ 319 | Ed McCaffrey UH | .40 | .15 |
| ☐ 320 | Tony Gonzalez UH | .25 | .08 |
| ☐ 321 | Tim Brown UH | .40 | .15 |
| ☐ 322 | Junior Seau UH | .40 | .15 |
| ☐ 323 | Shawn Springs UH | .25 | .08 |
| ☐ 324 | Troy Aikman UH | .40 | .15 |
| ☐ 325 | Pat Tillman UH RC | 20.00 | 8.00 |
| ☐ 326 | David Akers UH RC | .40 | .15 |
| ☐ 327 | Michael Strahan UH | .40 | .15 |
| ☐ 328 | Darrell Green UH | .25 | .08 |
| ☐ 329 | Kurt Warner UH | .60 | .25 |
| ☐ 330 | Jeff Garcia UH | .40 | .15 |
| ☐ 331 | Aaron Brooks UH | .40 | .15 |
| ☐ 332 | Jamal Anderson UH | .40 | .15 |
| ☐ 333 | Brad Hoover UH | .25 | .08 |
| ☐ 334 | Cris Carter UH | .40 | .15 |
| ☐ 335 | Derrick Brooks UH | .25 | .08 |
| ☐ 336 | Antonio Freeman UH | .40 | .15 |
| ☐ 337 | Luther Elliss UH | .25 | .08 |
| ☐ 338 | James Allen UH | .25 | .08 |
| ☐ 339 | Arizona Cardinals TC | .40 | .15 |
| ☐ 340 | Atlanta Falcons TC | .40 | .15 |
| ☐ 341 | Baltimore Ravens TC | .60 | .25 |
| ☐ 342 | Buffalo Bills TC | .25 | .08 |
| ☐ 343 | Carolina Panthers TC | .25 | .08 |
| ☐ 344 | Chicago Bears TC | .60 | .25 |
| ☐ 345 | Cincinnati Bengals TC | .40 | .15 |
| ☐ 346 | Cleveland Browns TC | .25 | .08 |
| ☐ 347 | Cowboys TC/Emmitt | .60 | .25 |
| ☐ 348 | Denver Broncos TC | .40 | .15 |
| ☐ 349 | Detroit Lions TC | .25 | .08 |
| ☐ 350 | Packers TC/Favre | 1.00 | .40 |
| ☐ 351 | Colts TC/James | .60 | .25 |
| ☐ 352 | Jacksonville Jaguars TC | .60 | .25 |
| ☐ 353 | Kansas City Chiefs TC | .25 | .08 |
| ☐ 354 | Miami Dolphins TC | .40 | .15 |
| ☐ 355 | Minnesota Vikings TC | .60 | .25 |
| ☐ 356 | New England Patriots TC | .60 | .25 |
| ☐ 357 | New Orleans Saints TC | .40 | .15 |

|  |  | | |
|---|---|---|---|
| 358 | New York Giants TC | .40 | .15 |
| 359 | New York Jets TC | .40 | .15 |
| 360 | Oakland Raiders TC | .40 | .15 |
| 361 | Philadelphia Eagles TC | .60 | .25 |
| 362 | Pittsburgh Steelers TC | .40 | .15 |
| 363 | San Diego Chargers TC | .25 | .08 |
| 364 | San Francisco 49ers TC | .25 | .08 |
| 365 | Seattle Seahawks TC | .25 | .08 |
| 366 | Rams TC/Warner | .60 | .25 |
| 367 | Tampa Bay Buccaneers TC | .40 | .15 |
| 368 | Tennessee Titans TC | .40 | .15 |
| 369 | Washington Redskins TC | .40 | .15 |
| 370 | Buffalo Bills TL | .25 | .08 |
| 371 | Indianapolis Colts TL | .60 | .25 |
| 372 | Miami Dolphins TL | .25 | .08 |
| 373 | New England Patriots TL | .40 | .15 |
| 374 | New York Jets TL | .40 | .15 |
| 375 | Baltimore Ravens TL | .40 | .15 |
| 376 | Cincinnati Bengals TL | .25 | .08 |
| 377 | Cleveland Browns TL | .25 | .08 |
| 378 | Jacksonville Jaguars TL | .40 | .15 |
| 379 | Pittsburgh Steelers TL | .40 | .15 |
| 380 | Tennessee Titans TL | .40 | .15 |
| 381 | Denver Broncos TL | .40 | .15 |
| 382 | Kansas City Chiefs TL | .40 | .15 |
| 383 | Oakland Raiders TL | .40 | .15 |
| 384 | San Diego Chargers TL | .25 | .08 |
| 385 | Seattle Seahawks TL | .25 | .08 |
| 386 | Arizona Cardinals TL | .25 | .08 |
| 387 | Dallas Cowboys TL | .60 | .25 |
| 388 | New York Giants TL | .40 | .15 |
| 389 | Philadelphia Eagles TL | .40 | .15 |
| 390 | Washington Redskins TL | .40 | .15 |
| 391 | Chicago Bears TL | .25 | .08 |
| 392 | Detroit Lions TL | .25 | .08 |
| 393 | Green Bay Packers TL | .60 | .25 |
| 394 | Minnesota Vikings TL | .60 | .25 |
| 395 | Tampa Bay Buccaneers TL | .40 | .15 |
| 396 | Atlanta Falcons TL | .25 | .08 |
| 397 | Carolina Panthers TL | .25 | .08 |
| 398 | New Orleans Saints TL | .40 | .15 |
| 399 | San Francisco 49ers TL | .40 | .15 |
| 400 | St. Louis Rams TL | .60 | .25 |
| 401 | Michael Vick RC | 2.50 | 1.00 |
| 402 | Drew Brees RC | 4.00 | 1.50 |
| 403 | Michael Bennett RC | 1.25 | .50 |
| 404 | David Terrell RC | 1.25 | .50 |
| 405 | Deuce McAllister RC | 2.50 | 1.00 |
| 406 | Santana Moss RC | 2.00 | .75 |
| 407 | Koren Robinson RC | 1.25 | .50 |
| 408 | Chris Weinke RC | 1.25 | .50 |
| 409 | Reggie Wayne RC | 2.50 | 1.00 |
| 410 | Rod Gardner RC | 1.25 | .50 |
| 411 | James Jackson RC | 1.25 | .50 |
| 412 | Travis Henry RC | 1.25 | .50 |
| 413 | Josh Heupel RC | 1.25 | .50 |
| 414 | LaDainian Tomlinson RC | 15.00 | 7.50 |
| 415 | Chad Johnson RC | 3.00 | 1.25 |
| 416 | Sage Rosenfels RC | 1.25 | .50 |
| 417 | Quincy Morgan RC | 1.25 | .50 |
| 418 | Ken-Yon Rambo RC | .75 | .30 |
| 419 | LaMont Jordan RC | 2.50 | 1.00 |
| 420 | Anthony Thomas RC | 1.25 | .50 |
| 421 | Dave Dickenson RC | .75 | .30 |
| 422 | Travis Minor RC | .75 | .30 |
| 423 | Kevan Barlow RC | 1.25 | .50 |
| 424 | Chris Chambers RC | 2.00 | .75 |
| 425 | Richard Seymour RC | 1.25 | .50 |
| 426 | Gerard Warren RC | 1.25 | .50 |
| 427 | Jamar Fletcher RC | .75 | .30 |
| 428 | Freddie Mitchell RC | 1.25 | .50 |
| 429 | Jamal Reynolds RC | 1.25 | .50 |
| 430 | Marques Tuiasosopo RC | 1.25 | .50 |
| 431 | Snoop Minnis RC | .75 | .30 |
| 432 | Mike McMahon RC | 1.25 | .50 |
| 433 | Robert Ferguson RC | 1.25 | .50 |
| 434 | Rooney Daniels RC | .50 | .20 |
| 435 | Rudi Johnson RC | 2.50 | 1.00 |
| 436 | Vinny Sutherland RC | .75 | .30 |
| 437 | Josh Booty RC | 1.25 | .50 |
| 438 | Reggie White RC | .75 | .30 |
| 439 | Todd Heap RC | 1.25 | .50 |
| 440 | Justin Smith RC | 1.25 | .50 |
| 441 | Andre Carter RC | 1.25 | .50 |
| 442 | Bobby Newcombe RC | .75 | .30 |
| 443 | Alex Bannister RC | .75 | .30 |
| 444 | Correll Buckhalter RC | 1.50 | .60 |
| 445 | Quincy Carter RC | 1.25 | .50 |
| 446 | Jesse Palmer RC | 1.25 | .50 |
| 447 | Heath Evans RC | .75 | .30 |
| 448 | Dan Morgan RC | 1.25 | .50 |
| 449 | Justin McCareins RC | 1.25 | .50 |
| 450 | Alge Crumpler RC | 1.50 | .60 |

## 2001 Fleer Tradition Glossy

|  |  | | |
|---|---|---|---|
| | COMP.SET w/o SP's (400) | 40.00 | 20.00 |
| 1 | Thomas Jones | .50 | .20 |
| 2 | Bruce Smith | .50 | .10 |
| 3 | Marvin Harrison | .75 | .30 |
| 4 | Darrell Jackson | .75 | .30 |
| 5 | Trent Green | .75 | .30 |
| 6 | Wesley Walls | .30 | .10 |
| 7 | Jimmy Smith | .50 | .20 |
| 8 | Isaac Bruce | .75 | .30 |
| 9 | Jamal Anderson | .75 | .30 |
| 10 | Marty Booker | .30 | .10 |
| 11 | Elvis Grbac | .50 | .20 |
| 12 | Joe Jurevicius | .30 | .10 |
| 13 | Reidel Anthony | .30 | .10 |
| 14 | Damay Scott | .30 | .10 |
| 15 | Orrondo Gadsden | .50 | .20 |
| 16 | Shawn Bryson | .30 | .10 |
| 17 | Jonathan Ogden | .30 | .10 |
| 18 | Aaron Shea | .30 | .10 |
| 19 | Randy Moss | 1.50 | .60 |
| 20 | Eddie George | .75 | .30 |
| 21 | Stephen Davis | .75 | .30 |
| 22 | Emmitt Smith | 1.50 | .60 |
| 23 | Willie McGinest | .30 | .10 |
| 24 | Trent Dilfer | .50 | .20 |
| 25 | Peter Boulware | .30 | .10 |
| 26 | Rod Smith | .50 | .20 |
| 27 | Ricky Williams | .75 | .30 |
| 28 | Albert Connell | .30 | .10 |
| 29 | Robert Porcher | .30 | .10 |
| 30 | Jessie Armstead | .30 | .10 |
| 31 | Shane Matthews | .30 | .10 |
| 32 | Eric Moulds | .50 | .20 |
| 33 | Kurt Schulz | .30 | .10 |
| 34 | Richie Anderson | .30 | .10 |
| 35 | Ron Dugans | .30 | .10 |
| 36 | Steve Beuerlein | .50 | .20 |
| 37 | Darren Sharper | .30 | .10 |
| 38 | Andre Rison | .50 | .20 |
| 39 | Courtney Brown | .50 | .20 |
| 40 | Eddie Kennison | .30 | .10 |
| 41 | Ken Dilger | .30 | .10 |
| 42 | Charles Johnson | .30 | .10 |
| 43 | Dexter Coakley | .30 | .10 |
| 44 | Akili Smith | .50 | .20 |
| 45 | R.Jay Soward | .30 | .10 |
| 46 | Danny Farmer | .30 | .10 |
| 47 | Dez White | .30 | .10 |
| 48 | Olandis Gary | .50 | .20 |
| 49 | Wali Rainer | .30 | .10 |
| 50 | Derrick Alexander | .50 | .20 |
| 51 | Donnie Abraham | .30 | .10 |
| 52 | David Sloan | .30 | .10 |
| 53 | Larry Allen | .30 | .10 |
| 54 | Sam Madison | .30 | .10 |
| 55 | Troy Edwards | .30 | .10 |
| 56 | Ryan Longwell | .30 | .10 |
| 57 | Brian Griese | .75 | .30 |
| 58 | John Randle | .50 | .20 |
| 59 | Reggie Jones | .30 | .10 |
| 60 | Mike Peterson | .30 | .10 |
| 61 | Bill Romanowski | .30 | .10 |
| 62 | Kevin Faulk | .50 | .20 |
| 63 | Tai Streets | .30 | .10 |
| 64 | Tony Brackens | .30 | .10 |
| 65 | James Stewart | .50 | .20 |
| 66 | Joe Horn | .50 | .20 |
| 67 | Kurt Warner | 1.50 | .60 |
| 68 | Eric Hicks RC | .30 | .10 |
| 69 | Bryan Westbrook | .30 | .10 |
| 70 | Tiki Barber | .75 | .30 |
| 71 | Frank Sanders | .30 | .10 |
| 72 | Olindo Mare | .30 | .10 |
| 73 | Bill Schroeder | .50 | .20 |
| 74 | Anthony Becht | .30 | .10 |
| 75 | Rob Johnson | .50 | .20 |
| 76 | Troy Brown | .50 | .20 |
| 77 | Chad Bratzke | .30 | .10 |
| 78 | Rickey Dudley | .30 | .10 |
| 79 | Doug Johnson | .30 | .10 |
| 80 | Joe Johnson | .30 | .10 |
| 81 | Keenan McCardell | .30 | .10 |
| 82 | Tim Brown | .75 | .30 |
| 83 | Blaine Bishop | .30 | .10 |
| 84 | Ron Dixon | .30 | .10 |
| 85 | Michael Cloud | .30 | .10 |
| 86 | Todd Pinkston | .30 | .10 |
| 87 | Shannon Sharpe | .50 | .20 |
| 88 | Marvin Jones | .30 | .10 |
| 89 | Zach Thomas | .75 | .30 |
| 90 | Kordell Stewart | .50 | .20 |
| 91 | Champ Bailey | .50 | .20 |
| 92 | Jacquez Green | .30 | .10 |
| 93 | Daunte Culpepper | .75 | .30 |
| 94 | Freddie Jones | .30 | .10 |
| 95 | Donald Hayes | .30 | .10 |
| 96 | Rich Gannon | .75 | .30 |
| 97 | Ty Law | .50 | .20 |
| 98 | Grant Wistrom | .30 | .10 |
| 99 | James Allen | .50 | .20 |
| 100 | Corey Simon | .50 | .20 |
| 101 | Jeff Blake | .50 | .20 |
| 102 | Bryant Young | .30 | .10 |
| 103 | Craig Yeast | .30 | .10 |
| 104 | Bobby Shaw | .30 | .10 |
| 105 | Kerry Collins | .50 | .20 |
| 106 | Brock Huard | .30 | .10 |
| 107 | JaJuan Dawson | .30 | .10 |
| 108 | Jeff Graham | .30 | .10 |
| 109 | Chad Pennington | 1.25 | .50 |
| 110 | Jake Plummer | .50 | .20 |
| 111 | James McKnight | .30 | .10 |
| 112 | Terrell Owens | .75 | .30 |
| 113 | Mo Lewis | .30 | .10 |
| 114 | Jeremy McDaniel | .30 | .10 |
| 115 | Ed McCaffrey | .75 | .30 |
| 116 | Ricky Watters | .30 | .10 |
| 117 | Jerry Porter | .30 | .10 |
| 118 | Shawn Jefferson | .30 | .10 |
| 119 | Charlie Batch | .75 | .30 |
| 120 | Justin Watson | .30 | .10 |
| 121 | Donovan McNabb | 1.00 | .40 |
| 122 | Shaun King | .50 | .20 |
| 123 | Brett Favre | 2.50 | 1.00 |
| 124 | Ronald McKinnon | .30 | .10 |
| 125 | Richard Huntley | .30 | .10 |
| 126 | Ray Lewis | .75 | .30 |
| 127 | Jerome Pathon | .30 | .10 |
| 128 | Sam Cowart | .30 | .10 |
| 129 | Ryan Leaf | .50 | .20 |
| 130 | Greg Clark | .30 | .10 |
| 131 | Tony Boselli | .30 | .10 |
| 132 | Frank Wycheck | .30 | .10 |
| 133 | Charlie Garner | .50 | .20 |
| 134 | Tony Siragusa | .30 | .10 |
| 135 | Sylvester Morris | .50 | .20 |
| 136 | Qadry Ismail | .50 | .20 |
| 137 | Jon Kitna | .50 | .20 |
| 138 | James Thrash | .50 | .20 |

|  |  | | |
|---|---|---|---|
| 139 | Lamar Smith | .50 | .20 |
| 140 | Brad Johnson | .75 | .30 |
| 141 | London Fletcher | .30 | .10 |
| 142 | Tim Biakabutaka | .50 | .20 |
| 143 | Ed McDaniel | .30 | .10 |
| 144 | Tony Parrish | .30 | .10 |
| 145 | David Boston | .75 | .30 |
| 146 | Brian Urlacher | 1.25 | .50 |
| 147 | Drew Bledsoe | 1.00 | .40 |
| 148 | David Patten | .30 | .10 |
| 149 | Marcellus Wiley | .30 | .10 |
| 150 | Peter Warrick | .75 | .30 |
| 151 | La'Roi Glover | .30 | .10 |
| 152 | Troy Aikman | 1.25 | .50 |
| 153 | Chris Chandler | .50 | .20 |
| 154 | Travis Prentice | .50 | .20 |
| 155 | Ike Hilliard | .50 | .20 |
| 156 | John Mobley | .30 | .10 |
| 157 | Warren Sapp | .50 | .20 |
| 158 | Joey Galloway | .50 | .20 |
| 159 | Laveranues Coles | .75 | .30 |
| 160 | Germane Crowell | .30 | .10 |
| 161 | Jamal Lewis | 1.25 | .50 |
| 162 | Mike Anderson | .75 | .30 |
| 163 | Charles Woodson | .50 | .20 |
| 164 | Antonio Freeman | .75 | .30 |
| 165 | Derrick Mason | .50 | .20 |
| 166 | Chris Claiborne | .30 | .10 |
| 167 | Brian Mitchell | .30 | .10 |
| 168 | Mike Vanderjagt | .30 | .10 |
| 169 | Rod Woodson | .50 | .20 |
| 170 | Doug Chapman | .30 | .10 |
| 171 | John Lynch | .50 | .20 |
| 172 | Kevin Hardy | .30 | .10 |
| 173 | Sam Shade | .30 | .10 |
| 174 | Edgerrin James | 1.00 | .40 |
| 175 | Brian Dawkins | .50 | .20 |
| 176 | Donnie Edwards | .30 | .10 |
| 177 | Patrick Jeffers | .50 | .20 |
| 178 | Mark Brunell | .75 | .30 |
| 179 | Junior Seau | .75 | .30 |
| 180 | Trace Armstrong | .30 | .10 |
| 181 | Marcus Robinson | .75 | .30 |
| 182 | Tony Gonzalez | .50 | .20 |
| 183 | J.J. Stokes | .50 | .20 |
| 184 | Jake Reed | .50 | .20 |
| 185 | Corey Dillon | .75 | .30 |
| 186 | Jay Fiedler | .75 | .30 |
| 187 | Christian Fauria | .30 | .10 |
| 188 | Sammy Knight | .30 | .10 |
| 189 | Kevin Johnson | .50 | .20 |
| 190 | Matthew Hatchette | .30 | .10 |
| 191 | Az-Zahir Hakim | .30 | .10 |
| 192 | Keith Hamilton | .30 | .10 |
| 193 | Darren Woodson | .30 | .10 |
| 194 | Terry Glenn | .50 | .20 |
| 195 | Simeon Rice | .50 | .20 |
| 196 | Keyshawn Johnson | .75 | .30 |
| 197 | Terrell Davis | .75 | .30 |
| 198 | William Roaf | .30 | .10 |
| 199 | Doug Flutie | .75 | .30 |
| 200 | Kevin Carter | .30 | .10 |
| 201 | Stephen Boyd | .30 | .10 |
| 202 | Michael Strahan | .50 | .20 |
| 203 | Ray Buchanan | .30 | .10 |
| 204 | Tyrone Wheatley | .50 | .20 |
| 205 | Jason Hanson | .30 | .10 |
| 206 | Wayne Chrebet | .50 | .20 |
| 207 | Samari Rolle | .30 | .10 |
| 208 | Duce Staley | .75 | .30 |
| 209 | Dorsey Levens | .50 | .20 |
| 210 | Sebastian Janikowski | .30 | .10 |
| 211 | Duane Starks | .30 | .10 |
| 212 | Jason Gildon | .30 | .10 |
| 213 | Terrence Wilkins | .30 | .10 |
| 214 | Eric Allen | .30 | .10 |
| 215 | Deion Sanders | .75 | .30 |
| 216 | Curtis Conway | .50 | .20 |
| 217 | Fred Taylor | .75 | .30 |
| 218 | Troy Vincent | .30 | .10 |
| 219 | Mike Minter | .30 | .10 |
| 220 | Jeff Garcia | .75 | .30 |
| 221 | Tony Richardson | .30 | .10 |
| 222 | Jerome Bettis | .75 | .30 |
| 223 | Chad Morton | .30 | .10 |
| 224 | Tony Horne | .30 | .10 |
| 225 | Dave Moore | .30 | .10 |
| 226 | Victor Green | .30 | .10 |
| 227 | Chris Sanders | .30 | .10 |
| 228 | Marshall Faulk | 1.00 | .40 |
| 229 | Cris Carter | .75 | .30 |
| 230 | Rodney Harrison | .30 | .10 |
| 231 | Tim Couch | .50 | .20 |
| 232 | Antowain Smith | .50 | .20 |
| 233 | Lawyer Milloy | .50 | .20 |
| 234 | Lance Schulters | .30 | .10 |
| 235 | Michael Wiley | .30 | .10 |
| 236 | Steve McNair | .75 | .30 |
| 237 | Aaron Brooks | .75 | .30 |
| 238 | Anthony Simmons | .30 | .10 |
| 239 | Dwayne Carswell | .30 | .10 |
| 240 | Priest Holmes | 1.00 | .40 |
| 241 | Amani Toomer | .50 | .20 |
| 242 | Aeneas Williams | .30 | .10 |
| 243 | MarTay Jenkins | .30 | .10 |
| 244 | Jeff George | .50 | .20 |
| 245 | Vinny Testaverde | .50 | .20 |
| 246 | Peerless Price | .50 | .20 |
| 247 | Bubba Franks | .50 | .20 |
| 248 | Randall Cunningham | .75 | .30 |
| 249 | Aaron Glenn | .30 | .10 |
| 250 | Terance Mathis | .50 | .20 |
| 251 | Peyton Manning | 2.00 | .75 |
| 252 | Terrell Buckley | .30 | .10 |
| 253 | Greg Biekert | .30 | .10 |
| 254 | Martin Gramatica | .30 | .10 |
| 255 | Kyle Brady | .30 | .10 |
| 256 | Johnnie Morton | .50 | .20 |
| 257 | Jeremiah Trotter | .50 | .20 |
| 258 | Travis Taylor | .50 | .20 |
| 259 | Frank Moreau | .30 | .10 |
| 260 | LeRoy Butler | .30 | .10 |
| 261 | Plaxico Burress | .75 | .30 |
| 262 | Randall Godfrey | .30 | .10 |
| 263 | Jason Taylor | .30 | .10 |
| 264 | Jeff Burris | .30 | .10 |
| 265 | Jim Harbaugh | .50 | .20 |
| 266 | Marcoa Coleman | .30 | .10 |
| 267 | Robert Smith | .75 | .30 |
| 268 | Mike Hollis | .30 | .10 |
| 269 | Jerry Rice | 1.50 | .60 |
| 270 | Muhsin Muhammad | .50 | .20 |
| 271 | J.R. Redmond | .30 | .10 |
| 272 | Brian Walker | .30 | .10 |
| 273 | Orlando Pace | .30 | .10 |
| 274 | Cade McNown | .30 | .10 |
| 275 | Darren Howard | .30 | .10 |
| 276 | Ron Dayne | .75 | .30 |
| 277 | Shaun Alexander | 1.00 | .40 |
| 278 | Brandon Bennett | .30 | .10 |
| 279 | Jason Sehorn | .30 | .10 |
| 280 | Matt Hasselbeck | .50 | .20 |
| 281 | Michael Pittman | .30 | .10 |
| 282 | Dennis Northcutt | .50 | .20 |
| 283 | Dedric Ward | .30 | .10 |
| 284 | Curtis Martin | .75 | .30 |
| 285 | Sammy Morris | .30 | .10 |
| 286 | Rocket Ismail | .50 | .20 |
| 287 | Jon Ritchie | .30 | .10 |
| 288 | Shaun Ellis | .30 | .10 |
| 289 | Tim Dwight | .75 | .30 |
| 290 | Trevor Pryce | .30 | .10 |
| 291 | Warrick Dunn | .75 | .30 |
| 292 | Napoleon Kaufman | .50 | .20 |
| 293 | Mike Alstott | .75 | .30 |
| 294 | Herman Moore | .50 | .20 |
| 295 | Chad Lewis | .30 | .10 |
| 296 | Hugh Douglas | .30 | .10 |
| 297 | Chris Redman | .30 | .10 |
| 298 | Ahman Green | .75 | .30 |
| 299 | Hines Ward | .75 | .30 |
| 300 | Mark Bruener | .30 | .10 |
| 301 | Jevon Kearse | .50 | .20 |
| 302 | Jermaine Fazande | .30 | .10 |
| 303 | Terrell Fletcher | .30 | .10 |
| 304 | Torry Holt | .75 | .30 |
| 305 | Chris McAlister | .30 | .10 |
| 306 | Jason Elam | .30 | .10 |
| 307 | Fred Beasley | .30 | .10 |
| 308 | Frank Wycheck UH | .30 | .10 |
| 309 | Michael McCrary UH | .30 | .10 |
| 310 | Mark Brunell UH | .75 | .30 |
| 311 | Tim Couch UH | .50 | .20 |
| 312 | Takeo Spikes UH | .30 | .10 |
| 313 | Jerome Bettis UH | .50 | .20 |
| 314 | Zach Thomas UH | .75 | .30 |
| 315 | Drew Bledsoe UH | .75 | .30 |
| 316 | Wayne Chrebet UH | .30 | .10 |
| 317 | Jay Riemersma UH | .30 | .10 |
| 318 | Marvin Harrison UH | .50 | .20 |
| 319 | Ed McCaffrey UH | .50 | .20 |
| 320 | Tony Gonzalez UH | .30 | .10 |
| 321 | Tim Brown UH | .50 | .20 |
| 322 | Junior Seau UH | .50 | .20 |
| 323 | Shawn Springs UH | .30 | .10 |
| 324 | Troy Aikman UH | .75 | .30 |
| 325 | Pat Tillman UH RC | 20.00 | 8.00 |
| 326 | David Akers UH RC | .50 | .20 |
| 327 | Michael Strahan UH | .50 | .20 |
| 328 | Darrell Green UH | .30 | .10 |
| 329 | Kurt Warner UH | 1.00 | .40 |
| 330 | Jeff Garcia UH | .50 | .20 |
| 331 | Aaron Brooks UH | .50 | .20 |
| 332 | Jamal Anderson UH | .50 | .20 |
| 333 | Brad Hoover UH | .30 | .10 |
| 334 | Cris Carter UH | .50 | .20 |
| 335 | Derrick Brooks UH | .75 | .30 |
| 336 | Antonio Freeman UH | .50 | .20 |
| 337 | Luther Elliss UH | .30 | .10 |
| 338 | James Allen UH | .30 | .10 |
| 339 | Arizona Cardinals TC | .50 | .20 |
| 340 | Atlanta Falcons TC | .50 | .20 |
| 341 | Baltimore Ravens TC | .30 | .10 |
| 342 | Buffalo Bills TC | .30 | .10 |
| 343 | Carolina Panthers TC | .30 | .10 |
| 344 | Chicago Bears TC | .75 | .30 |
| 345 | Cincinnati Bengals TC | .50 | .20 |
| 346 | Cleveland Browns TC | .30 | .10 |
| 347 | Cowboys TC/Emmitt | .75 | .30 |
| 348 | Denver Broncos TC | .50 | .20 |
| 349 | Detroit Lions TC | .30 | .10 |
| 350 | Packers TC/Favre | 1.25 | .50 |
| 351 | Colts TC/James | .75 | .30 |
| 352 | Jacksonville Jaguars TC | .75 | .30 |
| 353 | Kansas City Chiefs TC | .30 | .10 |
| 354 | Miami Dolphins TC | .50 | .20 |
| 355 | Minnesota Vikings TC | .50 | .20 |
| 356 | New England Patriots TC | .75 | .30 |
| 357 | New Orleans Saints TC | .50 | .20 |
| 358 | New York Giants TC | .50 | .20 |
| 359 | New York Jets TC | .50 | .20 |
| 360 | Oakland Raiders TC | .50 | .20 |
| 361 | Philadelphia Eagles TC | .75 | .30 |
| 362 | Pittsburgh Steelers TC | .50 | .20 |
| 363 | San Diego Chargers TC | .30 | .10 |
| 364 | San Francisco 49ers TC | .30 | .10 |
| 365 | Seattle Seahawks TC | .30 | .10 |
| 366 | Rams TC/Warner | .75 | .30 |
| 367 | Tampa Bay Buccaneers TC | .50 | .20 |
| 368 | Tennessee Titans TC | .50 | .20 |
| 369 | Washington Redskins TC | .50 | .20 |
| 370 | Buffalo Bills TL | .50 | .20 |
| 371 | Indianapolis Colts TL | .75 | .30 |
| 372 | Miami Dolphins TL | .30 | .10 |
| 373 | New England Patriots TL | .50 | .20 |
| 374 | New York Jets TL | .30 | .10 |
| 375 | Baltimore Ravens TL | .50 | .20 |
| 376 | Cincinnati Bengals TL | .30 | .10 |
| 377 | Cleveland Browns TL | .30 | .10 |
| 378 | Jacksonville Jaguars TL | .50 | .20 |
| 379 | Pittsburgh Steelers TL | .50 | .20 |
| 380 | Tennessee Titans TL | .50 | .20 |
| 381 | Denver Broncos TL | .50 | .20 |
| 382 | Kansas City Chiefs TL | .50 | .20 |
| 383 | Oakland Raiders TL | .50 | .20 |
| 384 | San Diego Chargers TL | .50 | .20 |
| 385 | Seattle Seahawks TL | .50 | .20 |
| 386 | Arizona Cardinals TL | .30 | .10 |
| 387 | Dallas Cowboys TL | .75 | .30 |
| 388 | New York Giants TL | .50 | .20 |
| 389 | Philadelphia Eagles TL | .50 | .20 |
| 390 | Washington Redskins TL | .50 | .20 |

| | | |
|---|---|---|
| 391 Chicago Bears TL | .30 | .10 |
| 392 Detroit Lions TL | .30 | .10 |
| 393 Green Bay Packers TL | .75 | .30 |
| 394 Minnesota Vikings TL | .75 | .30 |
| 395 Tampa Bay Buccaneers TL | .50 | .20 |
| 396 Atlanta Falcons TL | .30 | .10 |
| 397 Carolina Panthers TL | .30 | .10 |
| 398 New Orleans Saints TL | .50 | .20 |
| 399 San Francisco 49ers TL | .50 | .20 |
| 400 St. Louis Rams TL | .75 | .30 |
| 401 Michael Vick RC | 10.00 | 4.00 |
| 402 Drew Brees RC | 15.00 | 6.00 |
| 403 Michael Bennett RC | 4.00 | 1.50 |
| 404 David Terrell RC | 4.00 | 1.50 |
| 405 Deuce McAllister RC | 10.00 | 4.00 |
| 406 Santana Moss RC | 8.00 | 3.00 |
| 407 Koren Robinson RC | 4.00 | 1.50 |
| 408 Chris Weinke RC | 4.00 | 1.50 |
| 409 Reggie Wayne RC | 10.00 | 4.00 |
| 410 Rod Gardner RC | 4.00 | 1.50 |
| 411 James Jackson RC | 4.00 | 1.50 |
| 412 Travis Henry RC | 4.00 | 1.50 |
| 413 Josh Heupel RC | 4.00 | 1.50 |
| 415 Chad Johnson RC | 12.00 | 5.00 |
| 416 Sage Rosenfels RC | 4.00 | 1.50 |
| 417 Quincy Morgan RC | 4.00 | 1.50 |
| 418 Ken-Yon Rambo RC | 3.00 | 1.25 |
| 419 LaMont Jordan RC | 10.00 | 4.00 |
| 420 Anthony Thomas RC | 4.00 | 1.50 |
| 421 Dave Dickenson RC | 3.00 | 1.25 |
| 422 Travis Minor RC | 3.00 | 1.25 |
| 423 Kevan Barlow RC | 4.00 | 1.50 |
| 424 Chris Chambers RC | 8.00 | 3.00 |
| 425 Richard Seymour RC | 4.00 | 1.50 |
| 426 Gerard Warren RC | 4.00 | 1.50 |
| 427 Jamar Fletcher RC | 3.00 | 1.25 |
| 428 Freddie Mitchell RC | 4.00 | 1.50 |
| 429 Jamal Reynolds RC | 4.00 | 1.50 |
| 430 Marques Tuiasosopo RC | 4.00 | 1.50 |
| 431 Snoop Minnis RC | 3.00 | 1.25 |
| 432 Mike McMahon RC | 4.00 | 1.50 |
| 433 Robert Ferguson RC | 4.00 | 1.50 |
| 434 Ronney Daniels RC | 3.00 | 1.25 |
| 435 Rudi Johnson RC | 10.00 | 4.00 |
| 436 Vinny Sutherland RC | 3.00 | 1.25 |
| 437 Josh Booty RC | 4.00 | 1.50 |
| 438 Reggie White RC | 3.00 | 1.25 |
| 439 Todd Heap RC | 4.00 | 1.50 |
| 440 Justin Smith RC | 4.00 | 1.50 |
| 441 Andre Carter RC | 4.00 | 1.50 |
| 442 Bobby Newcombe RC | 3.00 | 1.25 |
| 443 Alex Bannister RC | 3.00 | 1.25 |
| 444 Correll Buckhalter RC | 6.00 | 2.50 |
| 445 Quincy Carter RC | 4.00 | 1.50 |
| 446 Jesse Palmer RC | 4.00 | 1.50 |
| 447 Heath Evans RC | 3.00 | 1.25 |
| 448 Dan Morgan RC | 4.00 | 1.50 |
| 449 Justin McCareins RC | 4.00 | 1.50 |
| 450 Alge Crumpler RC | 5.00 | 2.00 |
| 414 LaDainian Tomlinson RC | 50.00 | 20.00 |

## 2002 Fleer Tradition

| | | |
|---|---|---|
| COMPLETE SET (300) | 80.00 | 30.00 |
| 1 Jeff Garcia | .60 | .25 |
| 2 Brian Simmons | .25 | .08 |
| 3 Kordell Stewart | .40 | .15 |
| 4 Chris Weinke | .40 | .15 |
| 5 Donovan McNabb | .75 | .30 |

| | | |
|---|---|---|
| 6 Antoine Winfield | .25 | .08 |
| 7 Ray Lewis | .60 | .25 |
| 8 Drew Brees | .60 | .25 |
| 9 Frank Sanders | .25 | .08 |
| 10 Rich Gannon | .60 | .25 |
| 11 Jamal Anderson | .40 | .15 |
| 12 Curtis Martin | .60 | .25 |
| 13 Darrell Jackson | .40 | .15 |
| 14 Micheal Barrow | .25 | .08 |
| 15 Jeff Wilkins | .25 | .08 |
| 16 Ricky Williams | .60 | .25 |
| 17 Brad Johnson | .40 | .15 |
| 18 Tedy Bruschi | .60 | .25 |
| 19 Frank Wycheck | .25 | .08 |
| 20 Byron Chamberlain | .25 | .08 |
| 21 Terry Glenn | .25 | .08 |
| 22 James McKnight | .25 | .08 |
| 23 Thomas Jones | .40 | .15 |
| 24 Jamie Sharper | .25 | .08 |
| 25 Trent Green | .40 | .15 |
| 26 Mike Rucker RC | 1.00 | .40 |
| 27 Mark Bruneli | .60 | .25 |
| 28 Takeo Spikes | .25 | .08 |
| 29 Dominic Rhodes | .60 | .25 |
| 30 Jim Miller | .25 | .08 |
| 31 Corey Bradford | .25 | .08 |
| 32 Jamir Miller | .25 | .08 |
| 33 Johnnie Morton | .40 | .15 |
| 34 Rocket Ismail | .40 | .15 |
| 35 Mike Anderson | .60 | .25 |
| 36 James Allen | .40 | .15 |
| 37 Quincy Carter | .40 | .15 |
| 38 Germane Crowell | .25 | .08 |
| 39 Quincy Morgan | .25 | .08 |
| 40 Kabeer Gbaja-Biamila | .40 | .15 |
| 41 Reggie Wayne | .60 | .25 |
| 42 Brian Urlacher | 1.00 | .40 |
| 43 Stacey Mack | .25 | .08 |
| 44 Justin Smith | .25 | .08 |
| 45 Snoop Minnis | .25 | .08 |
| 46 Donald Hayes | .25 | .08 |
| 47 Jay Fiedler | .40 | .15 |
| 48 Nate Clements | .25 | .08 |
| 49 Drew Bledsoe | .75 | .30 |
| 50 Peter Boulware | .25 | .08 |
| 51 Lawyer Milloy | .40 | .15 |
| 52 Michael Pittman | .25 | .08 |
| 53 Aaron Brooks | .60 | .25 |
| 54 Maurice Smith | .25 | .08 |
| 55 Ike Hilliard | .40 | .15 |
| 56 Derrick Mason | .40 | .15 |
| 57 LaMont Jordan | .60 | .25 |
| 58 Charlie Garner | .40 | .15 |
| 59 Mike Alstott | .60 | .25 |
| 60 Freddie Mitchell | .25 | .08 |
| 61 Isaac Bruce | .40 | .15 |
| 62 Hines Ward | .60 | .25 |
| 63 John Randle | .25 | .08 |
| 64 Doug Flutie | .60 | .25 |
| 65 Terrell Owens | .60 | .25 |
| 66 Garrison Hearst | .40 | .15 |
| 67 Rodney Harrison | .25 | .08 |
| 68 Koren Robinson | .40 | .15 |
| 69 Amos Zereoue | .60 | .25 |
| 70 Aeneas Williams | .25 | .08 |
| 71 Hugh Douglas | .25 | .08 |
| 72 Jacquez Green | .25 | .08 |
| 73 Sebastian Janikowski | .25 | .08 |
| 74 Kevin Dyson | .40 | .15 |
| 75 Terance Mathis | .25 | .08 |
| 76 Vinny Testaverde | .40 | .15 |
| 77 Kwamie Lassiter | .25 | .08 |
| 78 Ron Dayne | .40 | .15 |
| 79 Jonathan Ogden | .25 | .08 |
| 80 Charlie Clemons RC | .25 | .08 |
| 81 Peter Warrick | .40 | .15 |
| 82 Adam Vinatieri | .60 | .25 |
| 83 Ted Washington | .25 | .08 |
| 84 Randy Moss | 1.25 | .50 |
| 85 Rosevelt Colvin RC | 1.00 | .40 |
| 86 Oronde Gadsden | .40 | .15 |
| 87 Anthony Henry | .25 | .08 |
| 88 Priest Holmes | .75 | .30 |
| 89 Joey Galloway | .40 | .15 |

| | | |
|---|---|---|
| 90 Jimmy Smith | .40 | .15 |
| 91 Bill Romanowski | .25 | .08 |
| 92 Chris Claiborne | .40 | .15 |
| 93 Marvin Harrison | .60 | .25 |
| 94 Vonnie Holliday | .25 | .08 |
| 95 Darren Sharper | .25 | .08 |
| 96 Chad Bratzke | .25 | .08 |
| 97 James Stewart | .40 | .15 |
| 98 Fred Taylor | .60 | .25 |
| 99 Jason Elam | .25 | .08 |
| 100 Keyshawn Johnson | .60 | .25 |
| 101 Dexter Coakley | .25 | .08 |
| 102 Zach Thomas | .60 | .25 |
| 103 Jamel White | .25 | .08 |
| 104 Antowain Smith | .40 | .15 |
| 105 Marty Booker | .25 | .08 |
| 106 Deuce McAllister | .75 | .30 |
| 107 Adam Archuleta | .25 | .08 |
| 108 Rod Smith | .40 | .15 |
| 109 Tony Boselli | .25 | .08 |
| 110 Joe Johnson | .25 | .08 |
| 111 Simeon Rice | .25 | .08 |
| 112 Cory Schlesinger | .25 | .08 |
| 113 La'Roi Glover | .25 | .08 |
| 114 Tiki Barber | .60 | .25 |
| 115 Michael Westbrook | .25 | .08 |
| 116 Antonio Freeman | .60 | .25 |
| 117 Kerry Collins | .40 | .15 |
| 118 Laveranues Coles | .40 | .15 |
| 119 Jay Feely | .25 | .08 |
| 120 Champ Bailey | .40 | .15 |
| 121 Peyton Manning | 1.25 | .50 |
| 122 Chad Pennington | .75 | .30 |
| 123 Anthony Dorsett | .25 | .08 |
| 124 Jamal Lewis | .60 | .25 |
| 125 Marcus Pollard | .25 | .08 |
| 126 Charles Woodson | .40 | .15 |
| 127 Duce Staley | .60 | .25 |
| 128 Travis Henry | .60 | .25 |
| 129 Tony Brackens | .25 | .08 |
| 130 Jeremiah Trotter | .25 | .08 |
| 131 Jerome Bettis | .60 | .25 |
| 132 Chad Johnson | .60 | .25 |
| 133 Lamar Smith | .40 | .15 |
| 134 Joey Porter | .60 | .25 |
| 135 Curtis Conway | .25 | .08 |
| 136 David Terrell | .60 | .25 |
| 137 Daunte Culpepper | .60 | .25 |
| 138 Chris Fuamatu-Ma'afala | .25 | .08 |
| 139 J.J. Stokes | .25 | .08 |
| 140 Tim Couch | .40 | .15 |
| 141 Ty Law | .40 | .15 |
| 142 Vinny Sutherland | .25 | .08 |
| 143 Trung Canidate | .40 | .15 |
| 144 Larry Allen | .25 | .08 |
| 145 Darren Howard | .25 | .08 |
| 146 Ricky Watters | .40 | .15 |
| 147 Grant Wistrom | .25 | .08 |
| 148 Brian Griese | .60 | .25 |
| 149 Jason Sehorn | .25 | .08 |
| 150 Marshall Faulk | .60 | .25 |
| 151 Martin Gramatica | .25 | .08 |
| 152 Robert Porcher | .25 | .08 |
| 153 Richie Anderson | .25 | .08 |
| 154 Derrick Brooks | .60 | .25 |
| 155 Jevon Kearse | .40 | .15 |
| 156 Bill Schroeder | .25 | .08 |
| 157 Marvin Jones | .25 | .08 |
| 158 Eddie George | .60 | .25 |
| 159 Keith Brooking | .25 | .08 |
| 160 Ryan Longwell | .25 | .08 |
| 161 Brian Dawkins | .40 | .15 |
| 162 Chris Redman | .25 | .08 |
| 163 Az-Zahir Hakim | .25 | .08 |
| 164 James Thrash | .25 | .08 |
| 165 Rob Johnson | .40 | .15 |
| 166 Hardy Nickerson | .25 | .08 |
| 167 Chad Scott | .25 | .08 |
| 168 Jon Kitna | .40 | .15 |
| 169 Donnie Edwards | .25 | .08 |
| 170 Andre Carter | .25 | .08 |
| 171 Warrick Holdman | .25 | .08 |
| 172 Jason Taylor | .60 | .25 |
| 173 Levon Kirkland | .25 | .08 |

|  |  | | |
|---|---|---|---|
| ❏ 174 | Mike Brown | .60 | .25 |
| ❏ 175 | David Patten | .25 | .08 |
| ❏ 176 | Kurt Warner | .60 | .25 |
| ❏ 177 | Fred Smoot | .25 | .08 |
| ❏ 178 | Dat Nguyen | .25 | .08 |
| ❏ 179 | Joe Horn | .40 | .15 |
| ❏ 180 | John Lynch | .40 | .15 |
| ❏ 181 | Troy Hambrick | .25 | .08 |
| ❏ 182 | John Carney | .25 | .08 |
| ❏ 183 | Wesley Walls | .25 | .08 |
| ❏ 184 | Deltha O'Neal | .25 | .08 |
| ❏ 185 | Joe Jurevicius | .25 | .08 |
| ❏ 186 | Steve McNair | .60 | .25 |
| ❏ 187 | Scotty Anderson | .25 | .08 |
| ❏ 188 | John Abraham | .40 | .15 |
| ❏ 189 | Stephen Davis | .40 | .15 |
| ❏ 190 | Nate Wayne | .25 | .08 |
| ❏ 191 | Corey Simon | .25 | .08 |
| ❏ 192 | Joel Makovicka | .25 | .08 |
| ❏ 193 | Rob Morris | .25 | .08 |
| ❏ 194 | Cordell Buckhalter | .40 | .15 |
| ❏ 195 | Qadry Ismail | .25 | .08 |
| ❏ 196 | Keenan McCardell | .25 | .08 |
| ❏ 197 | Jason Gildon | .25 | .08 |
| ❏ 198 | Peerless Price | .25 | .08 |
| ❏ 199 | Tony Richardson | .25 | .08 |
| ❏ 200 | Kevan Barlow | .40 | .15 |
| ❏ 201 | Corey Dillon | .40 | .15 |
| ❏ 202 | Sam Madison | .25 | .08 |
| ❏ 203 | Chad Brown | .25 | .08 |
| ❏ 204 | Dez White | .25 | .08 |
| ❏ 205 | Troy Brown | .40 | .15 |
| ❏ 206 | Orlando Pace | .25 | .08 |
| ❏ 207 | Jermaine Lewis | .25 | .08 |
| ❏ 208 | Willie Jackson | .25 | .08 |
| ❏ 209 | Warrick Dunn | .60 | .25 |
| ❏ 210 | James Jackson | .25 | .08 |
| ❏ 211 | Sammy Knight | .25 | .08 |
| ❏ 212 | Ronde Barber | .25 | .08 |
| ❏ 213 | Ed McCaffrey | .25 | .08 |
| ❏ 214 | Amani Toomer | .40 | .15 |
| ❏ 215 | Rod Gardner | .40 | .15 |
| ❏ 216 | Mike McMahon | .60 | .25 |
| ❏ 217 | Wayne Chrebet | .40 | .15 |
| ❏ 218 | Jake Plummer | .40 | .15 |
| ❏ 219 | Bubba Franks | .40 | .15 |
| ❏ 220 | Shane Lechler | .40 | .15 |
| ❏ 221 | Travis Taylor | .40 | .15 |
| ❏ 222 | Edgerrin James | .75 | .30 |
| ❏ 223 | David Akers | .25 | .08 |
| ❏ 224 | Eric Moulds | .40 | .15 |
| ❏ 225 | Mike Vanderjagt | .25 | .08 |
| ❏ 226 | Kendrell Bell | .60 | .25 |
| ❏ 227 | Darnay Scott | .25 | .08 |
| ❏ 228 | Tony Gonzalez | .40 | .15 |
| ❏ 229 | Marcellus Wiley | .25 | .08 |
| ❏ 230 | Marcus Robinson | .25 | .08 |
| ❏ 231 | Muhsin Muhammad | .40 | .15 |
| ❏ 232 | Trent Dilfer | .40 | .15 |
| ❏ 233 | Kevin Johnson | .40 | .15 |
| ❏ 234 | Travis Minor | .25 | .08 |
| ❏ 235 | London Fletcher | .25 | .08 |
| ❏ 236 | Reggie Swinton | .25 | .08 |
| ❏ 237 | Michael Bennett | .40 | .15 |
| ❏ 238 | Brett Favre DD | 1.50 | .60 |
| ❏ 239 | Terrell Davis DD | .60 | .25 |
| ❏ 240 | Emmitt Smith DD | 1.50 | .60 |
| ❏ 241 | Shannon Sharpe DD | .40 | .15 |
| ❏ 242 | Cris Carter DD | .60 | .25 |
| ❏ 243 | Tim Brown DD | .60 | .25 |
| ❏ 244 | Jerry Rice DD | 1.25 | .50 |
| ❏ 245 | Bruce Smith DD | .40 | .15 |
| ❏ 246 | Warren Sapp DD | .40 | .15 |
| ❏ 247 | Michael Strahan DD | .40 | .15 |
| ❏ 248 | Junior Seau DD | .60 | .25 |
| ❏ 249 | Darrell Green DD | .25 | .08 |
| ❏ 250 | Rod Woodson DD | .40 | .15 |
| ❏ 251 | David Boston DD | .60 | .25 |
| ❏ 252 | Michael Vick BB | 1.25 | .50 |
| ❏ 253 | Anthony Thomas BB | .40 | .15 |
| ❏ 254 | Ahman Green BB | .60 | .25 |
| ❏ 255 | Chris Chambers BB | .60 | .25 |
| ❏ 256 | Tom Brady BB | 1.50 | .60 |
| ❏ 257 | Plaxico Burress BB | .40 | .15 |

|  |  | | |
|---|---|---|---|
| ❏ 258 | LaDainian Tomlinson BB | 1.00 | .40 |
| ❏ 259 | Shaun Alexander BB | .75 | .30 |
| ❏ 260 | Torry Holt BB | .60 | .25 |
| ❏ 261 | Julius Peppers RC | 4.00 | 1.50 |
| ❏ 262 | William Green RC | 2.00 | .75 |
| ❏ 263 | Joey Harrington RC | 2.50 | 1.00 |
| ❏ 264 | Jabar Gaffney RC | 2.00 | .75 |
| ❏ 265 | T.J. Duckett RC | 2.00 | .75 |
| ❏ 266 | Antwaan Randle El RC | 2.50 | 1.00 |
| ❏ 267 | Javon Walker RC | 3.00 | 1.25 |
| ❏ 268 | David Carr RC | 2.50 | 1.00 |
| ❏ 269 | DeShaun Foster RC | 3.00 | 1.25 |
| ❏ 270 | Donte Stallworth RC | 3.00 | 1.25 |
| ❏ 271 | Antonio Bryant RC | 2.00 | .75 |
| ❏ 272 | Clinton Portis RC | 6.00 | 2.50 |
| ❏ 273 | Josh Reed RC | 2.00 | .75 |
| ❏ 274 | Ashley Lelie RC | 4.00 | 1.50 |
| ❏ 275 | Patrick Ramsey RC | 2.00 | .75 |
| ❏ 276 | J.Wells RC/A.Peterson RC | 2.00 | .75 |
| ❏ 277 | Q.Jammer RC/R.Williams RC | 4.00 | 1.50 |
| ❏ 278 | J.Shockey RC/D.Graham RC | 3.00 | 1.25 |
| ❏ 279 | E.Crouch RC/Applewhite RC | 2.00 | .75 |
| ❏ 280 | Buchanon RC/Sheppard RC | 2.00 | .75 |
| ❏ 281 | K.Hill RC/D.Branch RC | 3.00 | 1.25 |
| ❏ 282 | R.Sirgs RC/W.Bryant RC | 2.00 | .75 |
| ❏ 283 | J.Scobey RC/Westbrook RC | 5.00 | 2.00 |
| ❏ 284 | L.Betts RC/O.Easy RC | 2.00 | .75 |
| ❏ 285 | A.Davis RC/D.Jones RC | 1.50 | .60 |
| ❏ 286 | C.Russell RC/C.Taylor RC | 3.00 | 1.25 |
| ❏ 287 | McAddley RC/J.McCown RC | 2.50 | 1.00 |
| ❏ 288 | D.Garrard RC/R.Davey RC | 4.00 | 1.50 |
| ❏ 289 | M.Walker RC/R.Johnson RC | 1.50 | .60 |
| ❏ 290 | L.Staley RC/L.Gordon RC | 2.00 | .75 |
| ❏ 291 | R.Caldwell RC/L.May RC | 2.00 | .75 |
| ❏ 292 | R.Thomas RC/N.Harris RC | 2.00 | .75 |
| ❏ 293 | M.Morris RC/J.Stevens RC | 2.00 | .75 |
| ❏ 294 | K.Kittner RC/R.Fasani RC | 1.50 | .60 |
| ❏ 295 | R.Calmus RC/J.Schifino RC | 2.00 | .75 |
| ❏ 296 | T.Carter RC/F.Milons RC | 1.50 | .60 |
| ❏ 297 | Wistrom RC/Stephens RC | 2.00 | .75 |
| ❏ 298 | M.Williams RC/D.Freeney RC | 3.00 | 1.25 |
| ❏ 299 | Hendersn RC/Haynesworth RC | 2.50 | 1.00 |
| ❏ 300 | N.Davenport RC/C.Nall RC | 2.00 | .75 |

## 2003 Fleer Tradition

CHARLIE GARNER — Running Back — RAIDERS

|  |  | | |
|---|---|---|---|
| ❏ | COMPLETE SET (300) | 40.00 | 15.00 |
| ❏ 1 | Aaron Glenn | .40 | .15 |
| ❏ 2 | Jerry Rice | 1.25 | .50 |
| ❏ 3 | Chad Hutchinson | .50 | .20 |
| ❏ 4 | Kris Jenkins | .40 | .15 |
| ❏ 5 | Ed Reed | .60 | .25 |
| ❏ 6 | Ed McCaffrey | .50 | .20 |
| ❏ 7 | Rod Gardner | .50 | .20 |
| ❏ 8 | Aaron Brooks | .50 | .20 |
| ❏ 9 | Chad Pennington | .60 | .25 |
| ❏ 10 | Jevon Kearse | .50 | .20 |
| ❏ 11 | Kurt Warner | .60 | .25 |
| ❏ 12 | Eddie George | .50 | .20 |
| ❏ 13 | Ron Dugans | .40 | .15 |
| ❏ 14 | Adam Vinatieri | .60 | .25 |
| ❏ 15 | Jimmy Smith | .50 | .20 |
| ❏ 16 | Chad Johnson | .60 | .25 |
| ❏ 17 | Kyle Brady | .40 | .15 |
| ❏ 18 | Eddie Kennison | .40 | .15 |
| ❏ 19 | Joe Jurevicius | .50 | .20 |
| ❏ 20 | Ronde Barber | .50 | .20 |
| ❏ 21 | Adam Archuleta | .40 | .15 |
| ❏ 22 | Champ Bailey | .50 | .20 |

|  |  | | |
|---|---|---|---|
| ❏ 23 | Joe Horn | .50 | .20 |
| ❏ 24 | Ladell Betts | .50 | .20 |
| ❏ 25 | Edgerrin James | .60 | .25 |
| ❏ 26 | Rosevelt Colvin | .50 | .20 |
| ❏ 27 | Ahman Green | .60 | .25 |
| ❏ 28 | Joey Porter | .60 | .25 |
| ❏ 29 | Charles Woodson | .50 | .20 |
| ❏ 30 | Lance Schulters | .40 | .15 |
| ❏ 31 | Edgerton Hartwell | .40 | .15 |
| ❏ 32 | Joey Galloway | .50 | .20 |
| ❏ 33 | Roy Williams | .60 | .25 |
| ❏ 34 | Al Wilson | .50 | .20 |
| ❏ 35 | Charlie Garner | .50 | .20 |
| ❏ 36 | John Lynch | .50 | .20 |
| ❏ 37 | La'Roi Glover | .40 | .15 |
| ❏ 38 | Emmitt Smith | 1.50 | .60 |
| ❏ 39 | Ryan Longwell | .50 | .20 |
| ❏ 40 | Alge Crumpler | .50 | .20 |
| ❏ 41 | John Abraham | .50 | .20 |
| ❏ 42 | Chris Hovan | .50 | .20 |
| ❏ 43 | Laveranues Coles | .50 | .20 |
| ❏ 44 | Eric Hicks | .40 | .15 |
| ❏ 45 | Johnnie Morton | .50 | .20 |
| ❏ 46 | Sam Madison | .50 | .20 |
| ❏ 47 | Amani Toomer | .50 | .20 |
| ❏ 48 | Chris Redman | .40 | .15 |
| ❏ 49 | Jon Kitna | .50 | .20 |
| ❏ 50 | Leonard Little | .40 | .15 |
| ❏ 51 | Eric Moulds | .50 | .20 |
| ❏ 52 | Santana Moss | .50 | .20 |
| ❏ 53 | Amos Zereoue | .40 | .15 |
| ❏ 54 | Jonathan Wells | .40 | .15 |
| ❏ 55 | Chris Chambers | .60 | .25 |
| ❏ 56 | London Fletcher | .40 | .15 |
| ❏ 57 | Frank Wycheck | .40 | .15 |
| ❏ 58 | Josh McCown | .50 | .20 |
| ❏ 59 | Shannon Sharpe | .50 | .20 |
| ❏ 60 | Andre Carter | .40 | .15 |
| ❏ 61 | Corey Dillon | .50 | .20 |
| ❏ 62 | Josh Reed | .40 | .15 |
| ❏ 63 | Marc Boerigter | .40 | .15 |
| ❏ 64 | Fred Smoot | .40 | .15 |
| ❏ 65 | Shaun Alexander | .60 | .25 |
| ❏ 66 | Andre Davis | .40 | .15 |
| ❏ 67 | Julian Peterson | .40 | .15 |
| ❏ 68 | Corey Bradford | .40 | .15 |
| ❏ 69 | Marc Bulger | .60 | .25 |
| ❏ 70 | Fred Taylor | .60 | .25 |
| ❏ 71 | Junior Seau | .50 | .20 |
| ❏ 72 | Simeon Rice | .50 | .20 |
| ❏ 73 | Anthony Thomas | .50 | .20 |
| ❏ 74 | Correll Buckhalter | .50 | .20 |
| ❏ 75 | Justin Smith | .50 | .20 |
| ❏ 76 | Marcel Shipp | .40 | .15 |
| ❏ 77 | Garrison Hearst | .50 | .20 |
| ❏ 78 | Stacey Mack | .40 | .15 |
| ❏ 79 | Antowain Smith | .50 | .20 |
| ❏ 80 | Kabeer Gbaja-Biamila | .50 | .20 |
| ❏ 81 | Curtis Martin | .60 | .25 |
| ❏ 82 | Marcellus Wiley | .40 | .15 |
| ❏ 83 | Gary Walker | .40 | .15 |
| ❏ 84 | Kalimba Edwards | .40 | .15 |
| ❏ 85 | Stephen Davis | .50 | .20 |
| ❏ 86 | Antwaan Randle El | .50 | .20 |
| ❏ 87 | Curtis Conway | .40 | .15 |
| ❏ 88 | Keith Brooking | .50 | .20 |
| ❏ 89 | Mark Word RC | .60 | .25 |
| ❏ 90 | Greg Ellis | .50 | .20 |
| ❏ 91 | Steve McNair | .60 | .25 |
| ❏ 92 | Ashley Lelie | .40 | .15 |
| ❏ 93 | Kelly Holcomb | .50 | .20 |
| ❏ 94 | Darrell Jackson | .50 | .20 |
| ❏ 95 | Mark Brunell | .50 | .20 |
| ❏ 96 | Hugh Douglas | .50 | .20 |
| ❏ 97 | Kendrell Bell | .50 | .20 |
| ❏ 98 | Steve Smith | .60 | .25 |
| ❏ 99 | Bill Schroeder | .40 | .15 |
| ❏ 100 | Darren Howard | .50 | .20 |
| ❏ 101 | Kevan Barlow | .50 | .20 |
| ❏ 102 | Marshall Faulk | .60 | .25 |
| ❏ 103 | Ike Hilliard | .50 | .20 |
| ❏ 104 | T.J. Duckett | .60 | .25 |
| ❏ 105 | Bobby Taylor | .40 | .15 |
| ❏ 106 | Kevin Carter | .50 | .20 |

|  |  | | |
|---|---|---|---|
| 107 | Darren Sharper | .50 | .20 |
| 108 | Marty Booker | .50 | .20 |
| 109 | Isaac Bruce | .60 | .25 |
| 110 | Kevin Hardy | .40 | .15 |
| 111 | Tai Streets | .40 | .15 |
| 112 | Brad Johnson | .50 | .20 |
| 113 | Daunte Culpepper | .60 | .25 |
| 114 | Kevin Johnson | .40 | .15 |
| 115 | Matt Hasselbeck | .50 | .20 |
| 116 | Jabar Gaffney | .40 | .15 |
| 117 | Takeo Spikes | .40 | .15 |
| 118 | Brett Favre | 1.50 | .60 |
| 119 | Keyshawn Johnson | .60 | .25 |
| 120 | David Akers | .40 | .15 |
| 121 | Maurice Morris | .40 | .15 |
| 122 | Jake Delhomme | .50 | .20 |
| 123 | Kordell Stewart | .50 | .20 |
| 124 | Terrell Davis | .60 | .25 |
| 125 | Brian Kelly | .40 | .15 |
| 126 | David Terrell | .40 | .15 |
| 127 | Koren Robinson | .50 | .20 |
| 128 | Michael Strahan | .50 | .20 |
| 129 | Jake Plummer | .50 | .20 |
| 130 | Terrell Owens | .60 | .25 |
| 131 | Brian Urlacher | 1.00 | .40 |
| 132 | David Patten | .40 | .15 |
| 133 | Michael Vick | .60 | .25 |
| 134 | Jamal Lewis | .60 | .25 |
| 135 | Terry Glenn | .50 | .20 |
| 136 | Brian Simmons | .40 | .15 |
| 137 | David Boston | .40 | .15 |
| 138 | Michael Bennett | .50 | .20 |
| 139 | James Stewart | .50 | .20 |
| 140 | Tiki Barber | .50 | .20 |
| 141 | Brian Griese | .50 | .20 |
| 142 | Deion Branch | .50 | .20 |
| 143 | Mike Peterson | .40 | .15 |
| 144 | James Mungro | .40 | .15 |
| 145 | Tim Couch | .40 | .15 |
| 146 | Brian Dawkins | .40 | .15 |
| 147 | Dennis Northcutt | .40 | .15 |
| 148 | Mike Alstott | .50 | .20 |
| 149 | James Thrash | .40 | .15 |
| 150 | Tim Brown | .60 | .25 |
| 151 | Brian Finneran | .40 | .15 |
| 152 | Derrick Brooks | .40 | .15 |
| 153 | Muhsin Muhammad | .50 | .20 |
| 154 | Jason Elam | .40 | .15 |
| 155 | Tim Dwight | .40 | .15 |
| 156 | Bruce Smith | .50 | .20 |
| 157 | Derrick Mason | .50 | .20 |
| 158 | Napoleon Harris | .40 | .15 |
| 159 | Jason Gildon | .40 | .15 |
| 160 | Todd Heap | .50 | .20 |
| 161 | Aaron Schobel | .40 | .15 |
| 162 | Derrius Thompson | .40 | .15 |
| 163 | Nate Clements | .50 | .20 |
| 164 | Jason McAddley | .40 | .15 |
| 165 | Todd Pinkston | .40 | .15 |
| 166 | Bubba Franks | .50 | .20 |
| 167 | Deuce McAllister | .60 | .25 |
| 168 | Patrick Surtain | .40 | .15 |
| 169 | Javon Walker | .50 | .20 |
| 170 | Tom Brady | 1.50 | .60 |
| 171 | Dexter Coakley | .50 | .20 |
| 172 | Patrick Kerney | .50 | .20 |
| 173 | Jay Fiedler | .50 | .20 |
| 174 | Tommy Maddox | .50 | .20 |
| 175 | Donald Driver | .60 | .25 |
| 176 | Patrick Ramsey | .50 | .20 |
| 177 | Olandis Gary | .40 | .15 |
| 178 | Tony Gonzalez | .50 | .20 |
| 179 | Donnie Edwards | .50 | .20 |
| 180 | Peter Boulware | .50 | .20 |
| 181 | Jeff Blake | .50 | .20 |
| 182 | Torry Holt | .60 | .25 |
| 183 | Donovan McNabb | .75 | .30 |
| 184 | Peter Warrick | .50 | .20 |
| 185 | Jeff Garcia | .50 | .20 |
| 186 | Travis Henry | .50 | .20 |
| 187 | Doug Jolley | .40 | .15 |
| 188 | Peyton Manning | 1.25 | .50 |
| 189 | Jerome Bettis | .60 | .25 |
| 190 | Travis Taylor | .40 | .15 |
| 191 | Drew Brees | .60 | .25 |
| 192 | Phillip Buchanon | .40 | .15 |
| 193 | Jerramy Stevens | .40 | .15 |
| 194 | Trent Green | .50 | .20 |
| 195 | Duce Staley | .50 | .20 |
| 196 | Plaxico Burress | .60 | .25 |
| 197 | Jerry Porter | .50 | .20 |
| 198 | Trevor Pryce | .50 | .20 |
| 199 | Dwight Freeney | .50 | .20 |
| 200 | Quincy Morgan | .40 | .15 |
| 201 | Troy Vincent | .50 | .20 |
| 202 | Randy McMichael | .40 | .15 |
| 203 | Troy Hambrick | .40 | .15 |
| 204 | Randy Moss | .75 | .30 |
| 205 | Troy Brown | .50 | .20 |
| 206 | Ray Lewis | .60 | .25 |
| 207 | Trung Canidate | .40 | .15 |
| 208 | Raynoch Thompson | .40 | .15 |
| 209 | Ty Law | .50 | .20 |
| 210 | Reggie Wayne | .50 | .20 |
| 211 | Warren Sapp | .50 | .20 |
| 212 | Richard Seymour | .50 | .20 |
| 213 | Warrick Dunn | .50 | .20 |
| 214 | Robert Ferguson | .40 | .15 |
| 215 | Wayne Chrebet | .50 | .20 |
| 216 | Rod Coleman RC | .40 | .15 |
| 217 | Will Allen | .40 | .15 |
| 218 | Rod Woodson | .60 | .25 |
| 219 | Zach Thomas | .50 | .20 |
| 220 | Rod Smith | .50 | .20 |
| 221 | Ricky Williams | .60 | .25 |
| 222 | LaDainian Tomlinson | 1.00 | .40 |
| 223 | Priest Holmes | .60 | .25 |
| 224 | Rich Gannon | .50 | .20 |
| 225 | Drew Bledsoe | .50 | .20 |
| 226 | Kerry Collins | .50 | .20 |
| 227 | Marvin Harrison | .60 | .25 |
| 228 | Hines Ward | .60 | .25 |
| 229 | Peerless Price | .40 | .15 |
| 230 | Jason Taylor | .50 | .20 |
| 231 | Jeremy Shockey | .60 | .25 |
| 232 | Clinton Portis | .75 | .30 |
| 233 | Antonio Bryant | .50 | .20 |
| 234 | Donte Stallworth | .50 | .20 |
| 235 | David Carr | .50 | .20 |
| 236 | Joey Harrington | .60 | .25 |
| 237 | William Green | .40 | .15 |
| 238 | Julius Peppers | .60 | .25 |
| 239 | Shipp/Thompson/Wilson | .30 | .12 |
| 240 | Vick/Dunn/Finner/Brooking | .40 | .15 |
| 241 | Lewis/Hartwell/Taylor/Reed | .50 | .20 |
| 242 | Bled/Henry/Mould/Fletch | .50 | .20 |
| 243 | Peppers/Smith/Muhammad | .50 | .20 |
| 244 | Booker/Urlacher/Thomas | .75 | .30 |
| 245 | Dillon/Smith/Johnson/Kitna | .50 | .20 |
| 246 | Couch/Green/Morgan/Word | .30 | .12 |
| 247 | Hutchinson/Galloway/Williams/Ellis | .50 | .20 |
| 248 | Portis/Smith/Wilson | .60 | .25 |
| 249 | Harring/Stew/Schr/Edwards | .50 | .20 |
| 250 | Favre/Green/Driver/KGB | .50 | .20 |
| 251 | Carr/Wells/Bradford/Glenn | .50 | .20 |
| 252 | Mann/James/Harr/Freen | 1.00 | .40 |
| 253 | Brunell/Taylor/Smith/McCree | .50 | .20 |
| 254 | Green/Holmes/Kenn/Hicks | .40 | .15 |
| 255 | Willms/Chamb/Thom/Tayl | .40 | .15 |
| 256 | Culp/Benn/Moss/Williams | .60 | .25 |
| 257 | Brady/Smith/Brown/Vina | 1.25 | .50 |
| 258 | Brooks/McAllister/Horn/Howard | .50 | .20 |
| 259 | Collins/Barber/Toomer/Strahan | .50 | .20 |
| 260 | Pennington/Martin/Chrebet /Abraham | .50 | .20 |
| 261 | Gannon/Garn/Rice/Woods | .50 | .20 |
| 262 | McNabb/Staley/Pinkston/Taylor | .50 | .20 |
| 263 | Maddox/Zereoue/Ward /Gildon/Porter | .50 | .20 |
| 264 | Brees/Tomlinson/Edwards | .75 | .30 |
| 265 | Garcia/Hearst/Owens/Carter | .50 | .20 |
| 266 | Hasselbeck/Alexander /Robin/Tongue | .50 | .20 |
| 267 | Bulger/Faulk/Holt/Little | .50 | .20 |
| 268 | B.John/Key.John/S.Rice/Kelly | .40 | .15 |
| 269 | McNair/George/Mason/Schulters | .50 | .20 |
| 270 | Ramsey/Gardner/Smoot | .40 | .15 |
| 271 | Carson Palmer RC | 5.00 | 2.00 |
| 272 | Kyle Boller RC | 1.25 | .50 |
| 273 | Byron Leftwich RC | 2.00 | .75 |
| 274 | Willis McGahee RC | 3.00 | 1.25 |
| 275 | Larry Johnson RC | 3.00 | 1.25 |
| 276 | Charles Rogers RC | 1.00 | .40 |
| 277 | Andre Johnson RC | 2.50 | 1.00 |
| 278 | Bryant Johnson RC | 1.25 | .50 |
| 279 | Rex Grossman RC | 3.00 | 1.25 |
| 280 | Taylor Jacobs RC | 1.00 | .40 |
| 281 | Rober.RC/Sull RC/Will RC | 1.25 | .50 |
| 282 | Jopp RC/Davis RC/Rag RC | 1.25 | .50 |
| 283 | Witt RC/Clark RC/Smith RC | 2.50 | 1.00 |
| 284 | Edwds RC/Smith RC/Bail RC | 1.00 | .40 |
| 285 | Suggs RC/Brown RC/Smith RC | 1.25 | .50 |
| 286 | Griff RC/Pinn RC/Askew RC | 1.00 | .40 |
| 287 | Fargi RC/Gabr RC/Johns RC | 1.25 | .50 |
| 288 | Kenn RC/Joseph RC/Warr RC | 1.25 | .50 |
| 289 | Sug RC/Haym RC/McDo RC | 1.50 | .60 |
| 290 | Wash RC/Curt RC/Burfes RC | 1.00 | .40 |
| 291 | Wall RC/Dors RC/Simms RC | 1.25 | .50 |
| 292 | Wade RC/Aik RC/Gage RC | 1.00 | .40 |
| 293 | McCull RC/Sapp RC/Grah RC | 1.25 | .50 |
| 294 | Kely RC/Gard RC/Tolv RC | 1.00 | .40 |
| 295 | Johns RC/Bold RC/Calic RC | 3.00 | 1.25 |
| 296 | Lloyd RC/McM RC/McD RC | 1.25 | .50 |
| 297 | Kels RC/White RC/Doss RC | .75 | .30 |
| 298 | Newm RC/Truf RC/Wool RC | 1.50 | .60 |
| 299 | Horno RC/King RC/St.P RC | 15.00 | 7.50 |
| 300 | Pinn RC/Toel RC/Cobou RC | 15.00 | 15.00 |

## 2004 Fleer Tradition

KEVIN JONES
RUNNING BACK
DETROIT LIONS

| | | | |
|---|---|---|---|
| COMPLETE SET (360) | | 100.00 | 50.00 |
| COMP.SET w/o SP's (330) | | 30.00 | 15.00 |
| 1 | Dolphins TL | .40 | .15 |
| 2 | Bills TL | .40 | .15 |
| 3 | Patriots TL | .75 | .30 |
| 4 | Jets TL | .40 | .15 |
| 5 | Colts TL | .75 | .30 |
| 6 | Jaguars TL | .40 | .15 |
| 7 | Titans TL | .25 | .08 |
| 8 | Texans TL | .40 | .15 |
| 9 | Raiders TL | .60 | .25 |
| 10 | Broncos TL | .40 | .15 |
| 11 | Chiefs TL | .40 | .15 |
| 12 | Chargers TL | .50 | .20 |
| 13 | Steelers TL | .60 | .25 |
| 14 | Browns TL | .25 | .08 |
| 15 | Bengals TL | .40 | .15 |
| 16 | Ravens TL | .40 | .15 |
| 17 | Eagles TL | .40 | .15 |
| 18 | Giants TL | .40 | .15 |
| 19 | Redskins TL | .40 | .15 |
| 20 | Cowboys TL | .50 | .20 |
| 21 | Vikings TL | .60 | .25 |
| 22 | Packers TL | .75 | .30 |
| 23 | Bears TL | .60 | .25 |
| 24 | Lions TL | .40 | .15 |
| 25 | 49ers TL | .40 | .15 |
| 26 | Rams TL | .40 | .15 |
| 27 | Seahawks TL | .40 | .15 |
| 28 | Cardinals TL | .25 | .08 |
| 29 | Panthers TL | .40 | .15 |
| 30 | Buccaneers TL | .25 | .08 |
| 31 | Falcons TL | .25 | .08 |
| 32 | Saints TL | .40 | .15 |
| 33 | Anquan Boldin | .50 | .20 |
| 34 | Michael Vick | .50 | .20 |

|  |  | | |  |  | | |  |  | | |
|---|---|---|---|---|---|---|---|---|---|---|---|
| 35 | Kyle Boller | .40 | .15 | 119 | Tedy Bruschi | .50 | .20 | 203 | Artose Pinner | .30 | .12 |
| 36 | Aeneas Williams | .30 | .12 | 120 | Chris Chambers | .40 | .15 | 204 | Kevin Johnson | .30 | .12 |
| 37 | Jake Delhomme | .40 | .15 | 121 | Freddie Mitchell | .30 | .12 | 205 | Kabeer Gbaja-Biamila | .40 | .15 |
| 38 | Rex Grossman | .50 | .20 | 122 | Amani Toomer | .40 | .15 | 206 | Marcus Coleman | .30 | .12 |
| 39 | Carson Palmer | .60 | .25 | 123 | Curtis Martin | .50 | .20 | 207 | Johnnie Morton | .40 | .15 |
| 40 | Quincy Morgan | .30 | .12 | 124 | Eric Moulds | .40 | .15 | 208 | Jason Taylor | .50 | .20 |
| 41 | Terry Glenn | .40 | .15 | 125 | Darrell Jackson | .40 | .15 | 209 | Kevin Williams | .30 | .12 |
| 42 | Jake Plummer | .40 | .15 | 126 | Clinton Portis | .50 | .20 | 210 | David Givens | .40 | .15 |
| 43 | Joey Harrington | .40 | .15 | 127 | Jay Fiedler | .30 | .12 | 211 | Charles Grant | .30 | .12 |
| 44 | Brett Favre | 1.25 | .50 | 128 | Todd Heap | .40 | .15 | 212 | Ike Hilliard | .40 | .15 |
| 45 | Jeff Garcia | .50 | .20 | 129 | Dexter Jackson | .30 | .12 | 213 | Wayne Chrebet | .40 | .15 |
| 46 | Peyton Manning | 1.00 | .40 | 130 | James Jackson | .30 | .12 | 214 | Teyo Johnson | .40 | .15 |
| 47 | Byron Leftwich | .50 | .20 | 131 | Shannon Sharpe | .40 | .15 | 215 | Brian Dawkins | .40 | .15 |
| 48 | Trent Green | .40 | .15 | 132 | Donald Driver | .50 | .20 | 216 | Antwaan Randle El | .40 | .15 |
| 49 | A.J. Feeley | .40 | .15 | 133 | Billy Miller | .30 | .12 | 217 | Eric Parker | .40 | .15 |
| 50 | Daunte Culpepper | .50 | .20 | 134 | Dante Hall | .40 | .15 | 218 | Josh McCown | .40 | .15 |
| 51 | Tom Brady | 1.25 | .50 | 135 | Onterrio Smith | .30 | .12 | 219 | Tim Rattay | .30 | .12 |
| 52 | Aaron Brooks | .40 | .15 | 136 | Joe Horn | .40 | .15 | 220 | Brian Finneran | .30 | .12 |
| 53 | Kerry Collins | .40 | .15 | 137 | Shaun Ellis | .30 | .12 | 221 | Chad Brown | .30 | .12 |
| 54 | Chad Pennington | .50 | .20 | 138 | L.J. Smith | .40 | .15 | 222 | Ed Reed | .40 | .15 |
| 55 | Rich Gannon | .40 | .15 | 139 | Jerry Porter | .40 | .15 | 223 | Dane Looker | .40 | .15 |
| 56 | Donovan McNabb | .50 | .20 | 140 | Reggie Wayne | .40 | .15 | 224 | Aaron Schobel | .30 | .12 |
| 57 | Tommy Maddox | .40 | .15 | 141 | Derrick Brooks | .30 | .12 | 225 | Joe Jurevicius | .30 | .12 |
| 58 | Drew Brees | .50 | .20 | 142 | Terrell Suggs | .30 | .12 | 226 | Ricky Manning | .30 | .12 |
| 59 | Terrell Owens | .50 | .20 | 143 | Randy McMichael | .30 | .12 | 227 | Jevon Kearse | .40 | .15 |
| 60 | Matt Hasselbeck | .50 | .20 | 144 | Mike Alstott | .40 | .15 | 228 | Laveranues Coles | .40 | .15 |
| 61 | Kurt Warner | .50 | .20 | 145 | Nate Poole RC | .50 | .20 | 229 | Kelley Washington | .30 | .12 |
| 62 | Brad Johnson | .40 | .15 | 146 | Chris Brown | .40 | .15 | 230 | William Green | .30 | .12 |
| 63 | Jerome Bettis | .50 | .20 | 147 | Torry Holt | .50 | .20 | 231 | Terence Newman | .40 | .15 |
| 64 | Keith Bulluck | .30 | .12 | 148 | Adewale Ogunleye | .40 | .15 | 232 | Bryant Johnson | .40 | .15 |
| 65 | Rod Gardner | .30 | .12 | 149 | Peter Warrick | .40 | .15 | 233 | Peerless Price | .40 | .15 |
| 66 | Eddie George | .40 | .15 | 150 | Alge Crumpler | .40 | .15 | 234 | Peter Boulware | .40 | .15 |
| 67 | Warren Sapp | .40 | .15 | 151 | Charlie Garner | .40 | .15 | 235 | Drew Bledsoe | .50 | .20 |
| 68 | Marc Bulger | .40 | .15 | 152 | Jeremy Shockey | .40 | .15 | 236 | Kris Jenkins | .40 | .15 |
| 69 | Shaun Alexander | .50 | .20 | 153 | Simeon Rice | .40 | .15 | 237 | Marty Booker | .40 | .15 |
| 70 | Tai Streets | .30 | .12 | 154 | Julian Peterson | .40 | .15 | 238 | Matt Schobel | .30 | .12 |
| 71 | LaDainian Tomlinson | .75 | .30 | 155 | Patrick Ramsey | .40 | .15 | 239 | Earl Little | .30 | .12 |
| 72 | Steve McNair | .50 | .20 | 156 | Shawn Springs | .30 | .12 | 240 | Antonio Bryant | .40 | .15 |
| 73 | Brian Westbrook | .50 | .20 | 157 | Marcus Stroud | .30 | .12 | 241 | Al Wilson | .30 | .12 |
| 74 | Jerry Rice | 1.00 | .40 | 158 | Keyshawn Johnson | .40 | .15 | 242 | Dre Bly | .30 | .12 |
| 75 | Santana Moss | .40 | .15 | 159 | Steve Smith | .50 | .20 | 243 | Javon Walker | .40 | .15 |
| 76 | Moe Williams | .30 | .12 | 160 | Ty Law | .40 | .15 | 244 | David Carr | .40 | .15 |
| 77 | Deuce McAllister | .50 | .20 | 161 | Derrick Mason | .40 | .15 | 245 | Mike Vanderjagt | .30 | .12 |
| 78 | Adam Vinatieri | .50 | .20 | 162 | Josh Reed | .50 | .20 | 246 | Fred Taylor | .40 | .15 |
| 79 | Randy Moss | .60 | .25 | 163 | Fred Smoot | .30 | .12 | 247 | Eddie Kennison | .30 | .12 |
| 80 | Ricky Williams | .50 | .20 | 164 | Muhsin Muhammad | .40 | .15 | 248 | Patrick Surtain | .30 | .12 |
| 81 | Priest Holmes | .50 | .20 | 165 | Justin Gage | .40 | .15 | 249 | Jim Kleinsasser | .30 | .12 |
| 82 | Jimmy Smith | .40 | .15 | 166 | Chad Johnson | .40 | .15 | 250 | Daniel Graham | .30 | .12 |
| 83 | Edgerrin James | .50 | .20 | 167 | Dennis Northcutt | .30 | .12 | 251 | Jerome Pathon | .30 | .12 |
| 84 | Andre Johnson | .50 | .20 | 168 | Joey Galloway | .40 | .15 | 252 | Tiki Barber | .50 | .20 |
| 85 | Ahman Green | .50 | .20 | 169 | Ashley Lelie | .40 | .15 | 253 | John Abraham | .40 | .15 |
| 86 | Charles Rogers | .40 | .15 | 170 | Casey Fitzsimmons | .30 | .12 | 254 | Justin Fargas | .40 | .15 |
| 87 | Champ Bailey | .40 | .15 | 171 | Dwight Freeney | .50 | .20 | 255 | Correll Buckhalter | .30 | .12 |
| 88 | Roy Williams S | .40 | .15 | 172 | Nick Barnett | .40 | .15 | 256 | Plaxico Burress | .40 | .15 |
| 89 | Tim Couch | .40 | .15 | 173 | LaBrandon Toefield | .30 | .12 | 257 | Quentin Jammer | .30 | .12 |
| 90 | Corey Dillon | .40 | .15 | 174 | Jabar Gaffney | .40 | .15 | 258 | Kevan Barlow | .40 | .15 |
| 91 | Thomas Jones | .40 | .15 | 175 | Tony Gonzalez | .50 | .20 | 259 | Koren Robinson | .50 | .20 |
| 92 | Stephen Davis | .40 | .15 | 176 | Zach Thomas | .50 | .20 | 260 | Leonard Little | .30 | .12 |
| 93 | Travis Henry | .40 | .15 | 177 | Nate Burleson | .40 | .15 | 261 | John Lynch | .40 | .15 |
| 94 | Jamal Lewis | .40 | .15 | 178 | Deion Branch | .40 | .15 | 262 | Tyrone Calico | .30 | .12 |
| 95 | Warrick Dunn | .40 | .15 | 179 | Boo Williams | .30 | .12 | 263 | Taylor Jacobs | .30 | .12 |
| 96 | Emmitt Smith | 1.00 | .40 | 180 | Michael Strahan | .40 | .15 | 264 | Joey Porter | .30 | .12 |
| 97 | Mark Brunell | .40 | .15 | 181 | Anthony Becht | .30 | .12 | 265 | Freddie Jones | .30 | .12 |
| 98 | Willis McGahee | .50 | .20 | 182 | Charles Woodson | .50 | .20 | 266 | Marcus Pollard | .30 | .12 |
| 99 | Duce Staley | .40 | .15 | 183 | Sheldon Brown | .30 | .12 | 267 | Mike Peterson | .30 | .12 |
| 100 | Lee Suggs | .50 | .20 | 184 | Kendrell Bell | .30 | .12 | 268 | Justin Griffith | .30 | .12 |
| 101 | Rod Smith | .40 | .15 | 185 | Kassim Osgood | .30 | .12 | 269 | Shawn Bryson | .30 | .12 |
| 102 | Marvin Harrison | .50 | .20 | 186 | Tony Parrish | .30 | .12 | 270 | Will Allen | .30 | .12 |
| 103 | Larry Johnson | .75 | .30 | 187 | Marcel Shipp | .50 | .20 | 271 | Antonio Gates | .50 | .20 |
| 104 | Michael Bennett | .40 | .15 | 188 | Bobby Engram | .40 | .15 | 272 | Chris McAlister | .30 | .12 |
| 105 | Donte Stallworth | .40 | .15 | 189 | Keith Brooking | .30 | .12 | 273 | Tony Hollings | .30 | .12 |
| 106 | DeShaun Foster | .40 | .15 | 190 | Isaac Bruce | .40 | .15 | 274 | Cedrick Wilson | .30 | .12 |
| 107 | Hines Ward | .50 | .20 | 191 | Travis Taylor | .30 | .12 | 275 | Adam Archuleta | .30 | .12 |
| 108 | T.J. Duckett | .40 | .15 | 192 | Charles Lee | .30 | .12 | 276 | London Fletcher | .30 | .12 |
| 109 | Brian Urlacher | .50 | .20 | 193 | Takeo Spikes | .30 | .12 | 277 | Drew Bennett | .40 | .15 |
| 110 | Boss Bailey | .30 | .12 | 194 | Justin McCareins | .30 | .12 | 278 | Rod Smart | .40 | .15 |
| 111 | Tim Brown | .50 | .20 | 195 | Julius Peppers | .40 | .15 | 279 | LaMont Jordan | .50 | .20 |
| 112 | David Boston | .30 | .12 | 196 | LaVar Arrington | .40 | .15 | 280 | Jerry Azumah | .30 | .12 |
| 113 | Marshall Faulk | .50 | .20 | 197 | Dez White | .30 | .12 | 281 | Bubba Franks | .40 | .15 |
| 114 | Jason Witten | .50 | .20 | 198 | Rudi Johnson | .40 | .15 | 282 | Troy Edwards | .30 | .12 |
| 115 | Richard Seymour | .30 | .12 | 199 | Andre Davis | .30 | .12 | 283 | Willie McGinest | .40 | .15 |
| 116 | Domanick Davis | .50 | .20 | 200 | Quincy Carter | .30 | .12 | 284 | Morten Andersen | .30 | .12 |
| 117 | Jon Kitna | .40 | .15 | 201 | Quentin Griffin | .40 | .15 | 285 | Dat Nguyen | .30 | .12 |
| 118 | Ray Lewis | .50 | .20 | 202 | Dallas Clark | .40 | .15 | 286 | Samari Rolle | .30 | .12 |

|  |  | | |
|---|---|---|---|
| ❏ 287 | Brian Simmons | .30 | .12 |
| ❏ 288 | Chike Okeafor | .30 | .15 |
| ❏ 289 | Rodney Harrison | .40 | .15 |
| ❏ 290 | Jason Elam | .30 | .15 |
| ❏ 291 | Tim Dwight | .40 | .15 |
| ❏ 292 | Corey Bradford | .40 | .15 |
| ❏ 293 | Charles Tillman | .40 | .15 |
| ❏ 294 | Tim Carter | .30 | .12 |
| ❏ 295 | Ahmed Plummer | .30 | .12 |
| ❏ 296 | Troy Walters | .40 | .15 |
| ❏ 297 | Michael Lewis | .40 | .15 |
| ❏ 298 | Tony James | .30 | .12 |
| ❏ 299 | Doug Flutie | .50 | .20 |
| ❏ 300 | Az-Zahir Hakim | .30 | .12 |
| ❏ 301 | Itula Mili | .30 | .12 |
| ❏ 302 | Jamie Sharper | .30 | .12 |
| ❏ 303 | Vonnie Holliday | .30 | .12 |
| ❏ 304 | Brian Russell RC | .50 | .20 |
| ❏ 305 | Bryan Gilmore | .30 | .12 |
| ❏ 306 | Darren Sharper | .30 | .12 |
| ❏ 307 | Kyle Brady | .40 | .15 |
| ❏ 308 | David Tyree | .50 | .20 |
| ❏ 309 | Andre Carter | .30 | .12 |
| ❏ 310 | Lawyer Milloy | .30 | .12 |
| ❏ 311 | David Terrell | .30 | .12 |
| ❏ 312 | Richie Anderson | .30 | .12 |
| ❏ 313 | Darren Howard | .30 | .12 |
| ❏ 314 | Sebastian Janikowski | .30 | .12 |
| ❏ 315 | Kimo von Oelhoffen | .30 | .12 |
| ❏ 316 | Donnie Edwards | .40 | .15 |
| ❏ 317 | Brandon Lloyd | .30 | .12 |
| ❏ 318 | Robert Ferguson | .30 | .12 |
| ❏ 319 | Derek Smith | .30 | .12 |
| ❏ 320 | Anthony Thomas | .30 | .10 |
| ❏ 321 | Ken Hamlin | .30 | .12 |
| ❏ 322 | Ronde Barber | .30 | .15 |
| ❏ 323 | Erron Kinney | .30 | .12 |
| ❏ 324 | Tom Brady AW | 1.00 | .40 |
| ❏ 325 | Peyton Manning AW | .75 | .30 |
| ❏ 326 | Steve McNair AW | .40 | .15 |
| ❏ 327 | Jamal Lewis AW | .30 | .12 |
| ❏ 328 | Ray Lewis AW | .40 | .15 |
| ❏ 329 | Anquan Boldin AW | .40 | .15 |
| ❏ 330 | Terrell Suggs AW | .25 | .10 |
| ❏ 331 | Eli Manning RC | 12.00 | 5.00 |
| ❏ 332 | Larry Fitzgerald RC | 6.00 | 2.50 |
| ❏ 333 | Ben Roethlisberger RC | 15.00 | 6.00 |
| ❏ 334 | Tatum Bell RC | 2.00 | .75 |
| ❏ 335 | Roy Williams RC | 5.00 | 2.00 |
| ❏ 336 | Drew Henson RC | 1.25 | .50 |
| ❏ 337 | Philip Rivers RC | 6.00 | 2.50 |
| ❏ 338 | Rashaun Woods RC | 1.25 | .50 |
| ❏ 339 | Kevin Jones RC | 2.00 | .75 |
| ❏ 340 | Sean Taylor RC | 2.00 | .75 |
| ❏ 341 | Steven Jackson RC | 6.00 | 2.50 |
| ❏ 342 | Kellen Winslow RC | 4.00 | 1.50 |
| ❏ 343 | Chris Perry RC | 2.00 | .75 |
| ❏ 344 | J.P. Losman RC | 2.50 | 1.00 |
| ❏ 345 | Greg Jones RC | 2.00 | .75 |
| ❏ 346 | Reggie Williams RC | 2.00 | .75 |
| ❏ 347 | Michael Clayton RC | 2.00 | .75 |
| ❏ 348 | Jonathan Vilma RC | 2.00 | .75 |
| ❏ 349 | Julius Jones RC | 5.00 | 2.00 |
| ❏ 350 | Michael Jenkins RC | 2.00 | .75 |
| ❏ 351 | E.Manning/Rivers/Roethlis. | 25.00 | 12.50 |
| ❏ 352 | Fitzgerald/Re.Will/Ro.Will. | 8.00 | 3.00 |
| ❏ 353 | Evans RC/Berr./RC/Ham.RC | 4.00 | 1.50 |
| ❏ 354 | Ude.RC/Poole RC/Colb.RC | 2.50 | 1.00 |
| ❏ 355 | Gamb.RC/Rob.RC/Hall RC | 2.00 | .75 |
| ❏ 356 | Trou.RC/Wats.RC/Harts.RC | 3.00 | 1.25 |
| ❏ 357 | Darl.RC/Morant RC/Wilf.RC | 2.50 | 1.00 |
| ❏ 358 | McCo.RC/Pick.RC/Sch.RC | 5.00 | 2.00 |
| ❏ 359 | Bell/Turn.RC/Cobbs RC | 5.00 | 2.00 |
| ❏ 360 | Moore RC/Wils.RC/Kni.RC | 3.00 | 1.25 |

## 1999 Leaf Certified

| | | | |
|---|---|---|---|
| ❏ | COMPLETE SET (225) | 200.00 | 100.00 |
| ❏ | COMP.SET w/o RCs 175) | 40.00 | 15.00 |
| ❏ 1 | Simeon Rice | .60 | .25 |
| ❏ 2 | Frank Sanders | .40 | .15 |
| ❏ 3 | Andre Wadsworth | .40 | .15 |
| ❏ 4 | Larry Centers | .40 | .15 |
| ❏ 5 | Byron Hanspard | .40 | .15 |
| ❏ 6 | Terance Mathis | .60 | .25 |

|  |  | | |
|---|---|---|---|
| ❏ 7 | O.J. Santiago | .40 | .15 |
| ❏ 8 | Chris Calloway | .40 | .15 |
| ❏ 9 | Michael Jackson | .40 | .15 |
| ❏ 10 | Rod Woodson | .60 | .25 |
| ❏ 11 | Pat Johnson | .40 | .15 |
| ❏ 12 | Rob Johnson | .60 | .25 |
| ❏ 13 | Andre Reed | .60 | .25 |
| ❏ 14 | Tim Biakabutuka | .40 | .15 |
| ❏ 15 | Rae Carruth | .40 | .15 |
| ❏ 16 | Fred Lane | .40 | .15 |
| ❏ 17 | Muhsin Muhammad | .60 | .25 |
| ❏ 18 | Wesley Walls | .60 | .25 |
| ❏ 19 | Edgar Bennett | .40 | .15 |
| ❏ 20 | Curtis Conway | .60 | .25 |
| ❏ 21 | Bobby Engram | .60 | .25 |
| ❏ 22 | Jeff Blake | .60 | .25 |
| ❏ 23 | Darnay Scott | .40 | .15 |
| ❏ 24 | Ty Detmer | .40 | .15 |
| ❏ 25 | Sedrick Shaw | .40 | .15 |
| ❏ 26 | Leslie Shepherd | .40 | .15 |
| ❏ 27 | Terry Kirby | .40 | .15 |
| ❏ 28 | Chris Warren | .40 | .15 |
| ❏ 29 | Rocket Ismail | .60 | .25 |
| ❏ 30 | Marcus Nash | .40 | .15 |
| ❏ 31 | Neil Smith | .60 | .25 |
| ❏ 32 | Bubby Brister | .40 | .15 |
| ❏ 33 | Brian Griese | 1.00 | .40 |
| ❏ 34 | Germane Crowell | .60 | .25 |
| ❏ 35 | Johnnie Morton | .60 | .25 |
| ❏ 36 | Gus Frerotte | .60 | .25 |
| ❏ 37 | Robert Brooks | .60 | .25 |
| ❏ 38 | Mark Chmura | .40 | .15 |
| ❏ 39 | Derrick Mayes | .40 | .15 |
| ❏ 40 | Jerome Pathon | .40 | .15 |
| ❏ 41 | Jimmy Smith | .60 | .25 |
| ❏ 42 | James Stewart | .40 | .15 |
| ❏ 43 | Tavian Banks | .40 | .15 |
| ❏ 44 | Derrick Alexander WR | .40 | .15 |
| ❏ 45 | Kimble Anders | .60 | .25 |
| ❏ 46 | Elvis Grbac | .60 | .25 |
| ❏ 47 | Derrick Thomas | 1.00 | .40 |
| ❏ 48 | Byron Bam Morris | .40 | .15 |
| ❏ 49 | Tony Gonzalez | 1.00 | .40 |
| ❏ 50 | John Avery | .40 | .15 |
| ❏ 51 | Tyrone Wheatley | .60 | .25 |
| ❏ 52 | Zach Thomas | 1.00 | .40 |
| ❏ 53 | Lamar Thomas | .40 | .15 |
| ❏ 54 | Jeff George | .60 | .25 |
| ❏ 55 | John Randle | .60 | .25 |
| ❏ 56 | Jake Reed | .40 | .15 |
| ❏ 57 | Leroy Hoard | .40 | .15 |
| ❏ 58 | Robert Edwards | .60 | .25 |
| ❏ 59 | Ben Coates | .60 | .25 |
| ❏ 60 | Tony Simmons | .40 | .15 |
| ❏ 61 | Shawn Jefferson | .40 | .15 |
| ❏ 62 | Eddie Kennison | .60 | .25 |
| ❏ 63 | Lamar Smith | .40 | .15 |
| ❏ 64 | Tiki Barber | 1.00 | .40 |
| ❏ 65 | Kerry Collins | .60 | .25 |
| ❏ 66 | Ike Hilliard | .40 | .15 |
| ❏ 67 | Gary Brown | .40 | .15 |
| ❏ 68 | Joe Jurevicius | .60 | .25 |
| ❏ 69 | Kent Graham | .40 | .15 |
| ❏ 70 | Dedric Ward | .40 | .15 |
| ❏ 71 | Terry Allen | .60 | .25 |
| ❏ 72 | Neil O'Donnell | .60 | .25 |
| ❏ 73 | Desmond Howard | .60 | .25 |
| ❏ 74 | James Jett | .60 | .25 |

|  |  | | |
|---|---|---|---|
| ❏ 75 | Jon Ritchie | .40 | .15 |
| ❏ 76 | Rickey Dudley | .40 | .15 |
| ❏ 77 | Charles Johnson | .40 | .15 |
| ❏ 78 | Chris Fuamatu-Ma'afala | .40 | .15 |
| ❏ 79 | Hines Ward | 1.00 | .40 |
| ❏ 80 | Ryan Leaf | 1.00 | .40 |
| ❏ 81 | Jim Harbaugh | .60 | .25 |
| ❏ 82 | Junior Seau | 1.00 | .40 |
| ❏ 83 | Mikhael Ricks | .40 | .15 |
| ❏ 84 | J.J. Stokes | .60 | .25 |
| ❏ 85 | Ahman Green | 1.00 | .40 |
| ❏ 86 | Tony Banks | .60 | .25 |
| ❏ 87 | Robert Holcombe | .40 | .15 |
| ❏ 88 | Az-Zahir Hakim | .40 | .15 |
| ❏ 89 | Greg Hill | .40 | .15 |
| ❏ 90 | Trent Green | 1.00 | .40 |
| ❏ 91 | Eric Zeier | .40 | .15 |
| ❏ 92 | Reidel Anthony | .60 | .25 |
| ❏ 93 | Bert Emanuel | .60 | .25 |
| ❏ 94 | Warren Sapp | .40 | .15 |
| ❏ 95 | Kevin Dyson | .60 | .25 |
| ❏ 96 | Yancey Thigpen | .40 | .15 |
| ❏ 97 | Frank Wycheck | .40 | .15 |
| ❏ 98 | Michael Westbrook | .60 | .25 |
| ❏ 99 | Albert Connell | .40 | .15 |
| ❏ 100 | Darrell Green | .60 | .25 |
| ❏ 101 | Rob Moore | .60 | .25 |
| ❏ 102 | Adrian Murrell | .60 | .25 |
| ❏ 103 | Jake Plummer | 1.00 | .40 |
| ❏ 104 | Chris Chandler | .60 | .25 |
| ❏ 105 | Jamal Anderson | 1.00 | .40 |
| ❏ 106 | Tim Dwight | 1.00 | .40 |
| ❏ 107 | Jermaine Lewis | .40 | .15 |
| ❏ 108 | Priest Holmes | 2.50 | 1.00 |
| ❏ 109 | Bruce Smith | 1.00 | .40 |
| ❏ 110 | Eric Moulds | 1.00 | .40 |
| ❏ 111 | Antowain Smith | 1.50 | .60 |
| ❏ 112 | Curtis Enis | 1.00 | .40 |
| ❏ 113 | Corey Dillon | 1.50 | .60 |
| ❏ 114 | Michael Irvin | 1.00 | .40 |
| ❏ 115 | Ed McCaffrey | 1.00 | .40 |
| ❏ 116 | Shannon Sharpe | 1.00 | .40 |
| ❏ 117 | Terrell Davis | 1.50 | .60 |
| ❏ 118 | Charlie Batch | 1.50 | .60 |
| ❏ 119 | Antonio Freeman | 1.00 | .40 |
| ❏ 120 | Dorsey Levens | 1.00 | .40 |
| ❏ 121 | Marvin Harrison | 1.50 | .60 |
| ❏ 122 | Peyton Manning | 5.00 | 2.00 |
| ❏ 123 | Keenan McCardell | 1.00 | .40 |
| ❏ 124 | Fred Taylor | 1.50 | .60 |
| ❏ 125 | Andre Rison | 1.00 | .40 |
| ❏ 126 | O.J. McDuffie | 1.00 | .40 |
| ❏ 127 | Karim Abdul-Jabbar | 1.00 | .40 |
| ❏ 128 | Randy Moss | 4.00 | 1.50 |
| ❏ 129 | Terry Glenn | 1.00 | .40 |
| ❏ 130 | Vinny Testaverde | 1.00 | .40 |
| ❏ 131 | Keyshawn Johnson | 1.00 | .40 |
| ❏ 132 | Curtis Martin | 1.00 | .40 |
| ❏ 133 | Wayne Chrebet | 1.00 | .40 |
| ❏ 134 | Napoleon Kaufman | 1.00 | .40 |
| ❏ 135 | Charles Woodson | 1.00 | .40 |
| ❏ 136 | Duce Staley | 1.50 | .60 |
| ❏ 137 | Kordell Stewart | 1.50 | .60 |
| ❏ 138 | Terrell Owens | 1.50 | .60 |
| ❏ 139 | Ricky Watters | 1.00 | .40 |
| ❏ 140 | Joey Galloway | 1.00 | .40 |
| ❏ 141 | Jon Kitna | 1.50 | .60 |
| ❏ 142 | Isaac Bruce | 1.50 | .60 |
| ❏ 143 | Jacquez Green | 1.00 | .40 |
| ❏ 144 | Warrick Dunn | 1.50 | .60 |
| ❏ 145 | Mike Alstott | 1.00 | .40 |
| ❏ 146 | Trent Dilfer | 1.00 | .40 |
| ❏ 147 | Steve McNair | 1.00 | .40 |
| ❏ 148 | Eddie George | 1.50 | .60 |
| ❏ 149 | Skip Hicks | 1.00 | .40 |
| ❏ 150 | Brad Johnson | 1.50 | .60 |
| ❏ 151 | Doug Flutie | 1.50 | .60 |
| ❏ 152 | Thurman Thomas | 1.00 | .40 |
| ❏ 153 | Carl Pickens | 1.00 | .40 |
| ❏ 154 | Emmitt Smith | 5.00 | 2.00 |
| ❏ 155 | Troy Aikman | 5.00 | 2.00 |
| ❏ 156 | Deion Sanders | 1.50 | .60 |
| ❏ 157 | John Elway | 8.00 | 3.00 |
| ❏ 158 | Rod Smith | 1.00 | .40 |

| | | |
|---|---|---|
| ❏ 159 Barry Sanders | 8.00 | 3.00 |
| ❏ 160 Herman Moore | 1.50 | .60 |
| ❏ 161 Brett Favre | 8.00 | 3.00 |
| ❏ 162 Mark Brunell | 1.50 | .60 |
| ❏ 163 Warren Moon | 1.50 | .60 |
| ❏ 164 Dan Marino | 8.00 | 3.00 |
| ❏ 165 Randall Cunningham | 1.50 | .60 |
| ❏ 166 Robert Smith | 1.50 | .60 |
| ❏ 167 Cris Carter | 1.50 | .60 |
| ❏ 168 Drew Bledsoe | 3.00 | 1.25 |
| ❏ 169 Tim Brown | 1.50 | .60 |
| ❏ 170 Jerome Bettis | 1.50 | .60 |
| ❏ 171 Natrone Means | 1.00 | .40 |
| ❏ 172 Jerry Rice | 5.00 | 2.00 |
| ❏ 173 Steve Young | 3.00 | 1.25 |
| ❏ 174 Garrison Hearst | 1.50 | .60 |
| ❏ 175 Marshall Faulk | 3.00 | 1.25 |
| ❏ 176 David Boston RC | 5.00 | 2.00 |
| ❏ 177 Jeff Paulk RC | 2.00 | .75 |
| ❏ 178 Reginald Kelly RC | 2.00 | .75 |
| ❏ 179 Scott Covington RC | 5.00 | 2.00 |
| ❏ 180 Chris McAlister RC | 3.00 | 1.25 |
| ❏ 181 Shawn Bryson RC | 5.00 | 2.00 |
| ❏ 182 Peerless Price RC | 5.00 | 2.00 |
| ❏ 183 Cade McNown RC | 3.00 | 1.25 |
| ❏ 184 Michael Bishop RC | 5.00 | 2.00 |
| ❏ 185 D'Wayne Bates RC | 3.00 | 1.25 |
| ❏ 186 Marty Booker RC | 5.00 | 2.00 |
| ❏ 187 Akili Smith RC | 2.00 | .75 |
| ❏ 188 Craig Yeast RC | 3.00 | 1.25 |
| ❏ 189 Tim Couch RC | 5.00 | 2.00 |
| ❏ 190 Kevin Johnson RC | 5.00 | 2.00 |
| ❏ 191 Wane McGarity RC | 2.00 | .75 |
| ❏ 192 Olandis Gary RC | 5.00 | 2.00 |
| ❏ 193 Travis McGriff RC | 2.00 | .75 |
| ❏ 194 Sedrick Irvin RC | 2.00 | .75 |
| ❏ 195 Chris Claiborne RC | 2.00 | .75 |
| ❏ 196 De'Mond Parker RC | 2.00 | .75 |
| ❏ 197 Dee Miller RC | 2.00 | .75 |
| ❏ 198 Edgerrin James RC | 15.00 | 6.00 |
| ❏ 199 Mike Cloud RC | 3.00 | 1.25 |
| ❏ 200 Larry Parker RC | 5.00 | 2.00 |
| ❏ 201 Cecil Collins RC | 2.00 | .75 |
| ❏ 202 James Johnson RC | 3.00 | 1.25 |
| ❏ 203 Rob Konrad RC | 5.00 | 2.00 |
| ❏ 204 Daunte Culpepper RC | 15.00 | 6.00 |
| ❏ 205 Jim Kleinsasser RC | 5.00 | 2.00 |
| ❏ 206 Kevin Faulk RC | 5.00 | 2.00 |
| ❏ 207 Andy Katzenmoyer RC | 3.00 | 1.25 |
| ❏ 208 Ricky Williams RC | 8.00 | 3.00 |
| ❏ 209 Joe Montgomery RC | 3.00 | 1.25 |
| ❏ 210 Sean Bennett RC | 2.00 | .75 |
| ❏ 211 Dameane Douglas RC | 5.00 | 2.00 |
| ❏ 212 Donovan McNabb RC | 20.00 | 7.50 |
| ❏ 213 Na Brown RC | 3.00 | 1.25 |
| ❏ 214 Amos Zereoue RC | 5.00 | 2.00 |
| ❏ 215 Troy Edwards RC | 3.00 | 1.25 |
| ❏ 216 Jermaine Fazande RC | 3.00 | 1.25 |
| ❏ 217 Tai Streets RC | 5.00 | 2.00 |
| ❏ 218 Brock Huard RC | 5.00 | 2.00 |
| ❏ 219 Charlie Rogers RC | 3.00 | 1.25 |
| ❏ 220 Karsten Bailey RC | 3.00 | 1.25 |
| ❏ 221 Joe Germaine RC | 3.00 | 1.25 |
| ❏ 222 Torry Holt RC | 10.00 | 4.00 |
| ❏ 223 Shaun King RC | 3.00 | 1.25 |
| ❏ 224 Jevon Kearse RC | 8.00 | 3.00 |
| ❏ 225 Champ Bailey RC | 6.00 | 2.50 |

## 2000 Leaf Certified

| | | |
|---|---|---|
| ❏ COMP.SET w/o RC's (150) | 40.00 | 15.00 |
| ❏ 1 Frank Sanders | .40 | .15 |
| ❏ 2 Rob Moore | .60 | .25 |
| ❏ 3 Simeon Rice | .40 | .15 |
| ❏ 4 David Boston | 1.00 | .40 |
| ❏ 5 Tim Dwight | 1.00 | .40 |
| ❏ 6 Jamal Anderson | 1.00 | .40 |
| ❏ 7 Chris Chandler | .40 | .15 |
| ❏ 8 Terance Mathis | .40 | .15 |
| ❏ 9 Priest Holmes | 1.25 | .50 |
| ❏ 10 Rod Woodson | .60 | .25 |
| ❏ 11 Tony Banks | .40 | .15 |
| ❏ 12 Jermaine Lewis | .40 | .15 |
| ❏ 13 Shannon Sharpe | .40 | .15 |
| ❏ 14 Qadry Ismail | .60 | .25 |

| | | |
|---|---|---|
| ❏ 15 Doug Flutie | 1.00 | .40 |
| ❏ 16 Antowain Smith | .60 | .25 |
| ❏ 17 Peerless Price | .60 | .25 |
| ❏ 18 Rob Johnson | .40 | .15 |
| ❏ 19 Muhsin Muhammad | .60 | .25 |
| ❏ 20 Wesley Walls | .40 | .15 |
| ❏ 21 Tim Biakabutuka | .40 | .15 |
| ❏ 22 Steve Beuerlein | .40 | .15 |
| ❏ 23 Patrick Jeffers | .40 | .15 |
| ❏ 24 Natrone Means | .40 | .15 |
| ❏ 25 Curtis Enis | .40 | .15 |
| ❏ 26 Bobby Engram | .40 | .15 |
| ❏ 27 Marcus Robinson | 1.00 | .40 |
| ❏ 28 Eddie Kennison | .40 | .15 |
| ❏ 29 Marty Booker | .60 | .25 |
| ❏ 30 Damay Scott | .40 | .15 |
| ❏ 31 Carl Pickens | .40 | .15 |
| ❏ 32 Karim Abdul-Jabbar | .40 | .15 |
| ❏ 33 Errict Rhett | .40 | .15 |
| ❏ 34 Darrin Chiaverini | .40 | .15 |
| ❏ 35 Randall Cunningham | .60 | .25 |
| ❏ 36 Michael Irvin | .40 | .15 |
| ❏ 37 Rocket Ismail | .40 | .15 |
| ❏ 38 Ed McCaffrey | 1.00 | .40 |
| ❏ 39 Rod Smith | .40 | .15 |
| ❏ 40 Herman Moore | .60 | .25 |
| ❏ 41 Johnnie Morton | .40 | .15 |
| ❏ 42 James Stewart | .40 | .15 |
| ❏ 43 Bill Schroeder | .60 | .25 |
| ❏ 44 Ahman Green | 1.00 | .40 |
| ❏ 45 Terrence Wilkins | .40 | .15 |
| ❏ 46 Keenan McCardell | .40 | .15 |
| ❏ 47 Derrick Alexander | .40 | .15 |
| ❏ 48 Elvis Grbac | .40 | .15 |
| ❏ 49 Tony Gonzalez | .40 | .15 |
| ❏ 50 O.J. McDuffie | .40 | .15 |
| ❏ 51 Tony Martin | .40 | .15 |
| ❏ 52 James Johnson | .40 | .15 |
| ❏ 53 Thurman Thomas | .40 | .15 |
| ❏ 54 Jay Fiedler | 1.00 | .40 |
| ❏ 55 Damon Huard | .40 | .15 |
| ❏ 56 Leroy Hoard | .40 | .15 |
| ❏ 57 Terry Glenn | .60 | .25 |
| ❏ 58 Kevin Faulk | .40 | .15 |
| ❏ 59 Jeff Blake | .40 | .15 |
| ❏ 60 Jake Reed | .40 | .15 |
| ❏ 61 Amani Toomer | .40 | .15 |
| ❏ 62 Kerry Collins | .40 | .15 |
| ❏ 63 Ike Hilliard | .40 | .15 |
| ❏ 64 Joe Montgomery | .40 | .15 |
| ❏ 65 Vinny Testaverde | .40 | .15 |
| ❏ 66 Wayne Chrebet | .40 | .15 |
| ❏ 67 Ray Lucas | .60 | .25 |
| ❏ 68 Napoleon Kaufman | .60 | .25 |
| ❏ 69 Charles Woodson | .40 | .15 |
| ❏ 70 Tyrone Wheatley | .40 | .15 |
| ❏ 71 Rich Gannon | 1.00 | .40 |
| ❏ 72 Duce Staley | 1.00 | .40 |
| ❏ 73 Kordell Stewart | .60 | .25 |
| ❏ 74 Jerome Bettis | 1.00 | .40 |
| ❏ 75 Troy Edwards | .40 | .15 |
| ❏ 76 Junior Seau | 1.00 | .40 |
| ❏ 77 Jim Harbaugh | .40 | .15 |
| ❏ 78 Curtis Conway | .60 | .25 |
| ❏ 79 Jermaine Fazande | .40 | .15 |
| ❏ 80 Terrell Owens | 1.00 | .40 |
| ❏ 81 Charlie Garner | .40 | .15 |
| ❏ 82 Garrison Hearst | .40 | .15 |

| | | |
|---|---|---|
| ❏ 83 Jeff Garcia | 1.00 | .40 |
| ❏ 84 Derrick Mayes | .40 | .15 |
| ❏ 85 Az-Zahir Hakim | .40 | .15 |
| ❏ 86 Mike Alstott | 1.00 | .40 |
| ❏ 87 Warrick Dunn | 1.00 | .40 |
| ❏ 88 Jacquez Green | .40 | .15 |
| ❏ 89 Warren Sapp | .40 | .15 |
| ❏ 90 Yancey Thigpen | .40 | .15 |
| ❏ 91 Kevin Dyson | .40 | .15 |
| ❏ 92 Frank Wycheck | .40 | .15 |
| ❏ 93 Jevon Kearse | 1.00 | .40 |
| ❏ 94 Adrian Murrell | .40 | .15 |
| ❏ 95 Bruce Smith | .40 | .15 |
| ❏ 96 Michael Westbrook | .40 | .15 |
| ❏ 97 Albert Connell | .40 | .15 |
| ❏ 98 Champ Bailey | .60 | .25 |
| ❏ 99 Jeff George | .40 | .15 |
| ❏ 100 Deion Sanders | 1.00 | .40 |
| ❏ 101 Jake Plummer | 1.00 | .40 |
| ❏ 102 Eric Moulds | 1.50 | .60 |
| ❏ 103 Cade McNown | .40 | .15 |
| ❏ 104 Corey Dillon | 1.50 | .60 |
| ❏ 105 Akili Smith | .60 | .25 |
| ❏ 106 Tim Couch | 1.00 | .40 |
| ❏ 107 Kevin Johnson | 1.50 | .60 |
| ❏ 108 Emmitt Smith | 3.00 | 1.25 |
| ❏ 109 Troy Aikman | 3.00 | 1.25 |
| ❏ 110 Joey Galloway | 1.00 | .40 |
| ❏ 111 John Elway | 5.00 | 2.00 |
| ❏ 112 Terrell Davis | 1.00 | .40 |
| ❏ 113 Olandis Gary | 1.50 | .60 |
| ❏ 114 Brian Griese | 1.50 | .60 |
| ❏ 115 Charlie Batch | 1.50 | .60 |
| ❏ 116 Barry Sanders | 4.00 | 1.50 |
| ❏ 117 Germane Crowell | .60 | .25 |
| ❏ 118 Brett Favre | 5.00 | 2.00 |
| ❏ 119 Dorsey Levens | .60 | .25 |
| ❏ 120 Antonio Freeman | 1.50 | .60 |
| ❏ 121 Peyton Manning | 4.00 | 1.50 |
| ❏ 122 Edgerrin James | 2.50 | 1.00 |
| ❏ 123 Marvin Harrison | 1.50 | .60 |
| ❏ 124 Mark Brunell | 1.00 | .40 |
| ❏ 125 Fred Taylor | 1.50 | .60 |
| ❏ 126 Jimmy Smith | 1.00 | .40 |
| ❏ 127 Dan Marino | 5.00 | 2.00 |
| ❏ 128 Randy Moss | 3.00 | 1.25 |
| ❏ 129 Daunte Culpepper | 2.00 | .75 |
| ❏ 130 Cris Carter | 1.50 | .60 |
| ❏ 131 Robert Smith | 1.50 | .60 |
| ❏ 132 Drew Bledsoe | 2.00 | .75 |
| ❏ 133 Ricky Williams | 1.50 | .60 |
| ❏ 134 Curtis Martin | 1.50 | .60 |
| ❏ 135 Tim Brown | 1.50 | .60 |
| ❏ 136 Donovan McNabb | 2.50 | 1.00 |
| ❏ 137 Jerry Rice | 3.00 | 1.25 |
| ❏ 138 Steve Young | 2.00 | .75 |
| ❏ 139 Jon Kitna | 1.50 | .60 |
| ❏ 140 Ricky Watters | .60 | .25 |
| ❏ 141 Kurt Warner | 3.00 | 1.25 |
| ❏ 142 Marshall Faulk | 2.00 | .75 |
| ❏ 143 Torry Holt | 1.50 | .60 |
| ❏ 144 Isaac Bruce | 1.50 | .60 |
| ❏ 145 Shaun King | .40 | .15 |
| ❏ 146 Keyshawn Johnson | 1.50 | .60 |
| ❏ 147 Eddie George | 1.00 | .40 |
| ❏ 148 Steve McNair | 1.50 | .60 |
| ❏ 149 Stephen Davis | 1.50 | .60 |
| ❏ 150 Brad Johnson | 1.50 | .60 |
| ❏ 151 Rogers Beckett RC | 4.00 | 1.50 |
| ❏ 152 Erik Flowers RC | 4.00 | 1.50 |
| ❏ 153 Demario Brown RC | 2.50 | 1.00 |
| ❏ 154 Doug Johnson RC | 5.00 | 2.00 |
| ❏ 155 Deon Grant RC | 4.00 | 1.50 |
| ❏ 156 Ian Gold RC | 4.00 | 1.50 |
| ❏ 157 Brian Urlacher RC | 20.00 | 7.50 |
| ❏ 158 Frank Murphy RC | 2.50 | 1.00 |
| ❏ 159 James Whalen RC | 2.50 | 1.00 |
| ❏ 160 JaJuan Dawson RC | 2.50 | 1.00 |
| ❏ 161 William Bartee RC | 4.00 | 1.50 |
| ❏ 162 Aaron Shea RC | 1.00 | .40 |
| ❏ 163 Deltha O'Neal RC | 5.00 | 2.00 |
| ❏ 164 Jarious Jackson RC | 4.00 | 1.50 |
| ❏ 165 Muneer Moore RC | 2.50 | 1.00 |
| ❏ 166 Hank Poteat RC | 4.00 | 1.50 |

## 2001 Leaf Certified Materials

| | | |
|---|---|---|
| 167 Jacoby Shepherd RC | 2.50 | 1.00 |
| 168 Ben Kelly RC | 2.50 | 1.00 |
| 169 Orantes Grant RC | 2.50 | 1.00 |
| 170 Chris Hovan RC | 4.00 | 1.50 |
| 171 Leon Murray RC | 2.50 | 1.00 |
| 172 Marc Bulger RC | 10.00 | 4.00 |
| 173 Chad Morton RC | 5.00 | 2.00 |
| 174 Na'il Diggs RC | 4.00 | 1.50 |
| 175 Shaun Ellis RC | 5.00 | 2.00 |
| 176 John Abraham RC | 5.00 | 2.00 |
| 177 Fred Robbins RC | 2.50 | 1.00 |
| 178 Marcus Knight RC | 4.00 | 1.50 |
| 179 Thomas Hamner RC | 2.50 | 1.00 |
| 180 Cornelius Griffin RC | 4.00 | 1.50 |
| 181 Raynoch Thompson RC | 4.00 | 1.50 |
| 182 Paul Smith RC | 4.00 | 1.50 |
| 183 Ahmed Plummer RC | 5.00 | 2.00 |
| 184 John Engelberger RC | 4.00 | 1.50 |
| 185 Darren Howard RC | 4.00 | 1.50 |
| 186 Corey Moore RC | 2.50 | 1.00 |
| 187 Joe Hamilton RC | 4.00 | 1.50 |
| 188 Rob Morris RC | 4.00 | 1.50 |
| 189 Keith Bulluck RC | 5.00 | 2.00 |
| 190 Todd Husak RC | 5.00 | 2.00 |
| 191 Mareno Philyaw RC | 3.00 | 1.25 |
| 192 Kwame Cavil RC | 3.00 | 1.25 |
| 193 Sammy Morris RC | 6.00 | 2.50 |
| 194 Avion Black RC | 5.00 | 2.00 |
| 195 Bashir Yamini RC | 3.00 | 1.25 |
| 196 Curtis Keaton RC | 5.00 | 2.00 |
| 197 Mike Anderson RC | 8.00 | 3.00 |
| 198 Bubba Franks RC | 6.00 | 2.50 |
| 199 Anthony Lucas RC | 3.00 | 1.25 |
| 200 Rondell Mealey RC | 3.00 | 1.25 |
| 201 Terrelle Smith RC | 5.00 | 2.00 |
| 202 Frank Moreau RC | 5.00 | 2.00 |
| 203 Deon Dyer RC | 5.00 | 2.00 |
| 204 Quinton Spotwood RC | 3.00 | 1.25 |
| 205 Troy Walters RC | 10.00 | 4.00 |
| 206 Doug Chapman RC | 5.00 | 2.00 |
| 207 Tom Brady RC | 200.00 | 100.00 |
| 208 Sherrod Gideon RC | 3.00 | 1.25 |
| 209 Ron Dixon RC | 5.00 | 2.00 |
| 210 Anthony Becht RC | 6.00 | 2.50 |
| 211 James Williams RC | 5.00 | 2.00 |
| 212 Sebastian Janikowski RC | 6.00 | 2.50 |
| 213 Corey Simon RC | 6.00 | 2.50 |
| 214 Gari Scott RC | 3.00 | 1.25 |
| 215 Dante Hall RC | 12.00 | 5.00 |
| 216 Tim Rattay RC | 6.00 | 2.50 |
| 217 Chafie Fields RC | 3.00 | 1.25 |
| 218 Trung Canidate RC | 5.00 | 2.00 |
| 219 Chris Coleman RC | 6.00 | 2.50 |
| 220 Erron Kinney RC | 6.00 | 2.50 |
| 221 Thomas Jones RC | 15.00 | 6.00 |
| 222 Travis Taylor RC | 10.00 | 4.00 |
| 223 Chris Redman RC | 8.00 | 3.00 |
| 224 Jamal Lewis RC | 25.00 | 10.00 |
| 225 Dez White RC | 10.00 | 4.00 |
| 226 Peter Warrick RC | 10.00 | 4.00 |
| 227 Ron Dugans RC | 8.00 | 3.00 |
| 228 Courtney Brown RC | 10.00 | 4.00 |
| 229 Travis Prentice RC | 8.00 | 3.00 |
| 230 Dennis Northcutt RC | 10.00 | 4.00 |
| 231 Michael Wiley RC | 8.00 | 3.00 |
| 232 Chris Cole RC | 8.00 | 3.00 |
| 233 Reuben Droughns RC | 10.00 | 4.00 |
| 234 R.Jay Soward RC | 8.00 | 3.00 |
| 235 Shyrone Stith RC | 8.00 | 3.00 |
| 236 Sylvester Morris RC | 8.00 | 3.00 |
| 237 J.R. Redmond RC | 8.00 | 3.00 |
| 238 Ron Dayne RC | 10.00 | 4.00 |
| 239 Chad Pennington RC | 25.00 | 10.00 |
| 240 Laveranues Coles RC | 12.00 | 5.00 |
| 241 Jerry Porter RC | 10.00 | 4.00 |
| 242 Todd Pinkston RC | 10.00 | 4.00 |
| 243 Plaxico Burress RC | 20.00 | 7.50 |
| 244 Danny Farmer RC | 8.00 | 3.00 |
| 245 Tee Martin RC | 10.00 | 4.00 |
| 246 Trevor Gaylor RC | 8.00 | 3.00 |
| 247 Giovanni Carmazzi RC | 8.00 | 3.00 |
| 248 Darrell Jackson RC | 12.00 | 5.00 |
| 249 Shaun Alexander RC | 25.00 | 10.00 |
| 250 Chris Samuels RC | 8.00 | 3.00 |
| COMP.SET w/o SPs (100) | 30.00 | 12.50 |
| 1 Aaron Brooks | 1.00 | .40 |
| 2 Ahman Green | 1.00 | .40 |
| 3 Akili Smith | .40 | .15 |
| 4 Amani Toomer | .60 | .25 |
| 5 Antonio Freeman | 1.00 | .40 |
| 6 Barry Sanders | 2.00 | .75 |
| 7 Brad Johnson | 1.00 | .40 |
| 8 Brett Favre | 3.00 | 1.25 |
| 9 Brian Griese | 1.00 | .40 |
| 10 Brian Urlacher | 1.50 | .60 |
| 11 Bruce Smith | .40 | .15 |
| 12 Cade McNown | .40 | .15 |
| 13 Chad Pennington | 1.50 | .60 |
| 14 Charlie Batch | 1.00 | .40 |
| 15 Charlie Garner | .60 | .25 |
| 16 Corey Dillon | 1.00 | .40 |
| 17 Cris Carter | 1.00 | .40 |
| 18 Curtis Martin | 1.00 | .40 |
| 19 Dan Marino | 3.00 | 1.25 |
| 20 Darrell Jackson | .40 | .15 |
| 21 Daunte Culpepper | 1.00 | .40 |
| 22 David Boston | 1.00 | .40 |
| 23 Derrick Alexander | .60 | .25 |
| 24 Donovan McNabb | 1.25 | .50 |
| 25 Dorsey Levens | .60 | .25 |
| 26 Doug Flutie | 1.00 | .40 |
| 27 Drew Bledsoe | 1.25 | .50 |
| 28 Ed McCaffrey | 1.00 | .40 |
| 29 Eddie George | 1.00 | .40 |
| 30 Edgerrin James | 1.25 | .50 |
| 31 Elvis Grbac | .60 | .25 |
| 32 Emmitt Smith | 2.00 | .75 |
| 33 Eric Moulds | 1.00 | .40 |
| 34 Frank Wycheck | .40 | .15 |
| 35 Fred Taylor | 1.00 | .40 |
| 36 Ike Hilliard | .60 | .25 |
| 37 Isaac Bruce | 1.00 | .40 |
| 38 Jacquez Green | .40 | .15 |
| 39 Jake Plummer | .60 | .25 |
| 40 Jamal Anderson | 1.00 | .40 |
| 41 Jamal Lewis | 1.50 | .60 |
| 42 James Stewart | .60 | .25 |
| 43 Jay Fiedler | 1.00 | .40 |
| 44 Jeff Garcia | 1.00 | .40 |
| 45 Jeff George | .60 | .25 |
| 46 Jerome Bettis | 1.00 | .40 |
| 47 Jerry Rice | 2.00 | .75 |
| 48 Jevon Kearse | .60 | .25 |
| 49 Jimmy Smith | .60 | .25 |
| 50 Joe Horn | .60 | .25 |
| 51 Joey Galloway | .60 | .25 |
| 52 John Elway | 3.00 | 1.25 |
| 53 Junior Seau | 1.00 | .40 |
| 54 Keenan McCardell | .40 | .15 |
| 55 Kerry Collins | 1.00 | .40 |
| 56 Keyshawn Johnson | 1.00 | .40 |
| 57 Kurt Warner | 2.00 | .75 |
| 58 Lamar Smith | .60 | .25 |
| 59 Laveranues Coles | 1.00 | .40 |
| 60 Marcus Robinson | 1.00 | .40 |
| 61 Mark Brunell | 1.00 | .40 |
| 62 Marshall Faulk | 1.25 | .50 |
| 63 Marvin Harrison | 1.00 | .40 |
| 64 Matt Hasselbeck | .60 | .25 |
| 65 Mike Alstott | 1.00 | .40 |
| 66 Mike Anderson | 1.00 | .40 |
| 67 Muhsin Muhammad | .60 | .25 |
| 68 Peter Warrick | 1.00 | .40 |
| 69 Peyton Manning | 2.50 | 1.00 |
| 70 Plaxico Burress | 2.00 | .75 |
| 71 Randy Moss | 2.00 | .75 |
| 72 Ray Lewis | 1.00 | .40 |
| 73 Rich Gannon | 1.00 | .40 |
| 74 Ricky Watters | .60 | .25 |
| 75 Ricky Williams | 1.00 | .40 |
| 76 Rob Johnson | 1.00 | .40 |
| 77 Rod Smith | .60 | .25 |
| 78 Ron Dayne | 1.00 | .40 |
| 79 Shannon Sharpe | .60 | .25 |
| 80 Shaun Alexander | 1.25 | .50 |
| 81 Stephen Davis | 1.00 | .40 |
| 82 Steve McNair | 1.00 | .40 |
| 83 Steve Young | 1.00 | .40 |
| 84 Sylvester Morris | .40 | .15 |
| 85 Terrell Davis | 1.00 | .40 |
| 86 Terrell Owens | 1.00 | .40 |
| 87 Terry Glenn | .60 | .25 |
| 88 Thomas Jones | .60 | .25 |
| 89 Tiki Barber | 1.00 | .40 |
| 90 Tim Brown | 1.00 | .40 |
| 91 Tim Couch | .60 | .25 |
| 92 Tony Gonzalez | .60 | .25 |
| 93 Torry Holt | 1.00 | .40 |
| 94 Travis Taylor | .60 | .25 |
| 95 Troy Aikman | 1.50 | .60 |
| 96 Tyrone Wheatley | .60 | .25 |
| 97 Vinny Testaverde | .60 | .25 |
| 98 Warren Sapp | .60 | .25 |
| 99 Warrick Dunn | 1.00 | .40 |
| 100 Wayne Chrebet | .60 | .25 |
| 101 Chris Taylor RC | 6.00 | 2.50 |
| 102 Ken-Yon Rambo RC | 6.00 | 2.50 |
| 103 Correll Buckhalter RC | 12.00 | 5.00 |
| 104 A.J. Feeley RC | 10.00 | 4.00 |
| 105 Josh Booty RC | 10.00 | 4.00 |
| 106 LaMont Jordan RC | 25.00 | 10.00 |
| 107 Alge Crumpler RC | 12.00 | 5.00 |
| 108 Jamal Reynolds RC | 10.00 | 4.00 |
| 109 Nate Clements RC | 10.00 | 4.00 |
| 110 Will Allen RC | 6.00 | 2.50 |
| 111 Santana Moss FF RC | 25.00 | 10.00 |
| 112 Chad Johnson FF RC | 50.00 | 25.00 |
| 113 Chris Chambers FF RC | 25.00 | 10.00 |
| 114 David Terrell FF RC | 15.00 | 6.00 |
| 115 Freddie Mitchell FF RC | 15.00 | 6.00 |
| 116 Koren Robinson FF RC | 15.00 | 6.00 |
| 117 Quincy Morgan FF RC | 15.00 | 6.00 |
| 118 Reggie Wayne FF RC | 30.00 | 12.50 |
| 119 Robert Ferguson FF RC | 15.00 | 6.00 |
| 120 Rod Gardner FF RC | 15.00 | 6.00 |
| 121 Snoop Minnis FF RC | 10.00 | 4.00 |
| 122 Josh Heupel FF RC | 15.00 | 6.00 |
| 123 Anthony Thomas FF RC | 15.00 | 6.00 |
| 124 Deuce McAllister FF RC | 30.00 | 12.50 |
| 125 James Jackson FF RC | 15.00 | 6.00 |
| 126 Travis Minor FF RC | 10.00 | 4.00 |
| 127 Kevan Barlow FF RC | 15.00 | 6.00 |
| 128 LaDainian Tomlinson FF RC | 100.00 | 60.00 |
| 129 Todd Heap FF RC | 15.00 | 6.00 |
| 130 Michael Bennett FF RC | 15.00 | 6.00 |
| 131 Rudi Johnson FF RC | 30.00 | 12.50 |
| 132 Travis Henry FF RC | 15.00 | 6.00 |
| 133 Michael Vick FF RC | 30.00 | 12.00 |
| 134 Drew Brees FF RC | 50.00 | 25.00 |
| 135 Chris Weinke FF RC | 15.00 | 6.00 |
| 136 Quincy Carter FF RC | 15.00 | 6.00 |
| 137 Mike McMahon FF RC | 15.00 | 6.00 |
| 138 Jesse Palmer FF RC | 15.00 | 6.00 |
| 139 Marq Tuiasosopo FF RC | 15.00 | 6.00 |
| 140 Dan Morgan FF RC | 15.00 | 6.00 |
| 141 Gerard Warren FF RC | 15.00 | 6.00 |
| 142 Leonard Davis FF RC | 10.00 | 4.00 |
| 143 Andre Carter FF RC | 15.00 | 6.00 |
| 144 Justin Smith FF RC | 15.00 | 6.00 |
| 145 Sage Rosenfels FF RC | 15.00 | 6.00 |

## 2002 Leaf Certified

| | | |
|---|---|---|
| ☐ COMP.SET w/o SP's (100) | 25.00 | 10.00 |
| ☐ 1 David Boston | 1.00 | .40 |
| ☐ 2 Jake Plummer | .60 | .25 |
| ☐ 3 Michael Vick | 2.00 | .75 |
| ☐ 4 Jamal Anderson | .60 | .25 |
| ☐ 5 Chris Redman | .40 | .15 |
| ☐ 6 Ray Lewis | 1.00 | .40 |
| ☐ 7 Eric Moulds | .60 | .25 |
| ☐ 8 Travis Henry | 1.00 | .40 |
| ☐ 9 Nate Clements | .40 | .15 |
| ☐ 10 Chris Weinke | .60 | .25 |
| ☐ 11 Muhsin Muhammad | .40 | .15 |
| ☐ 12 Wesley Walls | .40 | .15 |
| ☐ 13 Anthony Thomas | .60 | .25 |
| ☐ 14 Brian Urlacher | 1.50 | .60 |
| ☐ 15 Dez White | .40 | .15 |
| ☐ 16 Corey Dillon | .60 | .25 |
| ☐ 17 Peter Warrick | .60 | .25 |
| ☐ 18 Tim Couch | .60 | .25 |
| ☐ 19 Kevin Johnson | .60 | .25 |
| ☐ 20 James Jackson | .40 | .15 |
| ☐ 21 Emmitt Smith | 2.50 | 1.00 |
| ☐ 22 Quincy Carter | .60 | .25 |
| ☐ 23 Brian Griese | 1.00 | .40 |
| ☐ 24 Ed McCaffrey | 1.00 | .40 |
| ☐ 25 Rod Smith | .60 | .25 |
| ☐ 26 Terrell Davis | 1.00 | .40 |
| ☐ 27 Mike Anderson | 1.00 | .40 |
| ☐ 28 Germane Crowell | .40 | .15 |
| ☐ 29 James Stewart | .60 | .25 |
| ☐ 30 Charlie Batch | .60 | .25 |
| ☐ 31 Antonio Freeman | 1.00 | .40 |
| ☐ 32 Brett Favre | 2.50 | 1.00 |
| ☐ 33 Ahman Green | 1.00 | .40 |
| ☐ 34 LeRoy Butler | .40 | .15 |
| ☐ 35 Edgerrin James | 1.25 | .50 |
| ☐ 36 Marvin Harrison | 1.00 | .40 |
| ☐ 37 Peyton Manning | 2.00 | .75 |
| ☐ 38 Fred Taylor | 1.00 | .40 |
| ☐ 39 Jimmy Smith | .60 | .25 |
| ☐ 40 Mark Brunell | 1.00 | .40 |
| ☐ 41 Keenan McCardell | .40 | .15 |
| ☐ 42 Tony Gonzalez | .60 | .25 |
| ☐ 43 Priest Holmes | 1.25 | .50 |
| ☐ 44 Jay Fiedler | .60 | .25 |
| ☐ 45 Chris Chambers | 1.00 | .40 |
| ☐ 46 Zach Thomas | 1.00 | .40 |
| ☐ 47 Travis Minor | .40 | .15 |
| ☐ 48 Cris Carter | 1.00 | .40 |
| ☐ 49 Daunte Culpepper | 1.00 | .40 |
| ☐ 50 Randy Moss | 2.00 | .75 |
| ☐ 51 Drew Bledsoe | 1.25 | .50 |
| ☐ 52 Tom Brady | 2.50 | 1.00 |
| ☐ 53 Antowain Smith | .60 | .25 |
| ☐ 54 Troy Brown | .40 | .15 |
| ☐ 55 Aaron Brooks | 1.00 | .40 |
| ☐ 56 Ricky Williams | 1.00 | .40 |
| ☐ 57 Ron Dayne | .60 | .25 |
| ☐ 58 Kerry Collins | .60 | .25 |
| ☐ 59 Michael Strahan | .60 | .25 |
| ☐ 60 Amani Toomer | .60 | .25 |
| ☐ 61 Chad Pennington | 1.25 | .50 |
| ☐ 62 Curtis Martin | 1.00 | .40 |
| ☐ 63 Vinny Testaverde | .60 | .25 |
| ☐ 64 Wayne Chrebet | .60 | .25 |
| ☐ 65 Charles Woodson | .60 | .25 |

| | | |
|---|---|---|
| ☐ 66 Rich Gannon | 1.00 | .40 |
| ☐ 67 Tim Brown | 1.00 | .40 |
| ☐ 68 Jerry Rice | 2.00 | .75 |
| ☐ 69 Tyrone Wheatley | .60 | .25 |
| ☐ 70 Donovan McNabb | 1.25 | .50 |
| ☐ 71 Duce Staley | 1.00 | .40 |
| ☐ 72 Todd Pinkston | .60 | .25 |
| ☐ 73 Correll Buckhalter | .60 | .25 |
| ☐ 74 Jerome Bettis | 1.00 | .40 |
| ☐ 75 Kordell Stewart | .60 | .25 |
| ☐ 76 Plaxico Burress | .60 | .25 |
| ☐ 77 Hines Ward | 1.00 | .40 |
| ☐ 78 Junior Seau | 1.00 | .40 |
| ☐ 79 LaDainian Tomlinson | 1.50 | .60 |
| ☐ 80 Doug Flutie | 1.00 | .40 |
| ☐ 81 Terrell Owens | 1.00 | .40 |
| ☐ 82 Jeff Garcia | 1.00 | .40 |
| ☐ 83 Ricky Watters | .60 | .25 |
| ☐ 84 Shaun Alexander | 1.25 | .50 |
| ☐ 85 Koren Robinson | .60 | .25 |
| ☐ 86 Isaac Bruce | 1.00 | .40 |
| ☐ 87 Kurt Warner | 1.00 | .40 |
| ☐ 88 Marshall Faulk | 1.00 | .40 |
| ☐ 89 Torry Holt | 1.00 | .40 |
| ☐ 90 Keyshawn Johnson | .60 | .25 |
| ☐ 91 Mike Alstott | 1.00 | .40 |
| ☐ 92 Warren Sapp | .60 | .25 |
| ☐ 93 Brad Johnson | .60 | .25 |
| ☐ 94 Eddie George | 1.00 | .40 |
| ☐ 95 Jevon Kearse | .60 | .25 |
| ☐ 96 Steve McNair | 1.00 | .40 |
| ☐ 97 Derrick Mason | .60 | .25 |
| ☐ 98 Frank Wycheck | .40 | .15 |
| ☐ 99 Champ Bailey | .60 | .25 |
| ☐ 100 Stephen Davis | .60 | .25 |
| ☐ 101 Ladell Betts JSY RC | 8.00 | 3.00 |
| ☐ 102 Antonio Bryant JSY RC | 8.00 | 3.00 |
| ☐ 103 Reche Caldwell JSY RC | 8.00 | 3.00 |
| ☐ 104 David Carr JSY RC | 12.00 | 5.00 |
| ☐ 105 Tim Carter JSY RC | 5.00 | 2.00 |
| ☐ 106 Eric Crouch JSY RC | 8.00 | 3.00 |
| ☐ 107 Rohan Davey JSY RC | 8.00 | 3.00 |
| ☐ 108 Andre Davis JSY RC | 5.00 | 2.00 |
| ☐ 109 T.J. Duckett JSY RC | 8.00 | 3.00 |
| ☐ 110 DeShaun Foster JSY RC | 8.00 | 3.00 |
| ☐ 111 Jabar Gaffney JSY RC | 8.00 | 3.00 |
| ☐ 112 Daniel Graham JSY RC | 8.00 | 3.00 |
| ☐ 113 William Green FB RC | 8.00 | 3.00 |
| ☐ 114 Joey Harrington JSY RC | 10.00 | 4.00 |
| ☐ 115 David Garrard JSY RC | 15.00 | 6.00 |
| ☐ 116 Ron Johnson JSY RC | 5.00 | 2.00 |
| ☐ 117 Ashley Lelie JSY RC | 15.00 | 6.00 |
| ☐ 118 Josh McCown JSY RC | 10.00 | 4.00 |
| ☐ 119 Maurice Morris JSY RC | 8.00 | 3.00 |
| ☐ 120 Julius Peppers JSY RC | 15.00 | 6.00 |
| ☐ 121 Clinton Portis JSY RC | 25.00 | 10.00 |
| ☐ 122 Patrick Ramsey JSY RC | 8.00 | 3.00 |
| ☐ 123 Antwaan Randle El JSY RC | 10.00 | 4.00 |
| ☐ 124 Josh Reed JSY RC | 8.00 | 3.00 |
| ☐ 125 Cliff Russell JSY RC | 5.00 | 2.00 |
| ☐ 126 Jeremy Shockey JSY RC | 15.00 | 6.00 |
| ☐ 127 Donte Stallworth JSY RC | 12.00 | 5.00 |
| ☐ 128 Travis Stephens JSY RC | 5.00 | 2.00 |
| ☐ 129 Javon Walker JSY RC | 12.00 | 5.00 |
| ☐ 130 Marquise Walker JSY RC | 5.00 | 2.00 |
| ☐ 131 Roy Williams JSY RC | 15.00 | 6.00 |
| ☐ 132 Mike Williams JSY RC | 5.00 | 2.00 |

## 2004 Leaf Certified Materials

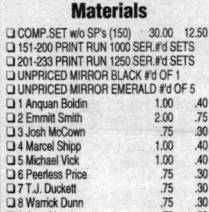

| | | |
|---|---|---|
| ☐ COMP.SET w/o SP's (150) | 30.00 | 12.50 |
| ☐ 151-200 PRINT RUN 1000 SER.#'d SETS | | |
| ☐ 201-233 PRINT RUN 1250 SER.#'d SETS | | |
| ☐ UNPRICED MIRROR BLACK #'d OF 1 | | |
| ☐ UNPRICED MIRROR EMERALD #'d OF 5 | | |
| ☐ 1 Anquan Boldin | 1.00 | .40 |
| ☐ 2 Emmitt Smith | 2.00 | .75 |
| ☐ 3 Josh McCown | .75 | .30 |
| ☐ 4 Marcel Shipp | 1.00 | .40 |
| ☐ 5 Michael Vick | 2.00 | .75 |
| ☐ 6 Peerless Price | .75 | .30 |
| ☐ 7 T.J. Duckett | .75 | .30 |
| ☐ 8 Warrick Dunn | .75 | .30 |
| ☐ 9 Jamal Lewis | .75 | .30 |

| | | |
|---|---|---|
| ☐ 10 Kyle Boller | .75 | .30 |
| ☐ 11 Ray Lewis | 1.00 | .40 |
| ☐ 12 Terrell Suggs | .60 | .25 |
| ☐ 13 Todd Heap | .75 | .30 |
| ☐ 14 Drew Bledsoe | 1.00 | .40 |
| ☐ 15 Eric Moulds | .75 | .30 |
| ☐ 16 Travis Henry | .75 | .30 |
| ☐ 17 Julius Peppers | .75 | .30 |
| ☐ 18 Muhsin Muhammad | .75 | .30 |
| ☐ 19 Stephen Davis | .75 | .30 |
| ☐ 20 Anthony Thomas | .75 | .30 |
| ☐ 21 Brian Urlacher | 1.00 | .40 |
| ☐ 22 Rex Grossman | 1.00 | .40 |
| ☐ 23 Chad Johnson | .75 | .30 |
| ☐ 24 Corey Dillon | .75 | .30 |
| ☐ 25 Peter Warrick | .75 | .30 |
| ☐ 26 Jeff Garcia | 1.00 | .40 |
| ☐ 27 Tim Couch | .75 | .30 |
| ☐ 28 William Green | .60 | .25 |
| ☐ 29 Antonio Bryant | .75 | .30 |
| ☐ 30 Keyshawn Johnson | .75 | .30 |
| ☐ 31 Quincy Carter | .60 | .25 |
| ☐ 32 Roy Williams S | .75 | .30 |
| ☐ 33 Terence Newman | .75 | .30 |
| ☐ 34 Ashley Lelie | .75 | .30 |
| ☐ 35 Ed McCaffrey | 1.00 | .40 |
| ☐ 36 Jake Plummer | .75 | .30 |
| ☐ 37 Mike Anderson | .75 | .30 |
| ☐ 38 Rod Smith | .75 | .30 |
| ☐ 39 Charles Rogers | .75 | .30 |
| ☐ 40 Joey Harrington | .75 | .30 |
| ☐ 41 Ahman Green | 1.00 | .40 |
| ☐ 42 Brett Favre | 2.50 | 1.00 |
| ☐ 43 Donald Driver | 1.00 | .40 |
| ☐ 44 Javon Walker | .75 | .30 |
| ☐ 45 Robert Ferguson | .60 | .25 |
| ☐ 46 Andre Johnson | 1.00 | .40 |
| ☐ 47 David Carr | .75 | .30 |
| ☐ 48 Edgerrin James | 1.00 | .40 |
| ☐ 49 Marvin Harrison | 1.00 | .40 |
| ☐ 50 Peyton Manning | 2.00 | .75 |
| ☐ 51 Reggie Wayne | .75 | .30 |
| ☐ 52 Byron Leftwich | 1.00 | .40 |
| ☐ 53 Fred Taylor | .75 | .30 |
| ☐ 54 Jimmy Smith | .75 | .30 |
| ☐ 55 Dante Hall | .75 | .30 |
| ☐ 56 Priest Holmes | 1.00 | .40 |
| ☐ 57 Tony Gonzalez | 1.00 | .40 |
| ☐ 58 Trent Green | .75 | .30 |
| ☐ 59 A.J. Feeley | .75 | .30 |
| ☐ 60 Chris Chambers | .75 | .30 |
| ☐ 61 David Boston | .60 | .25 |
| ☐ 62 Jason Taylor | 1.00 | .40 |
| ☐ 63 Jay Fiedler | .60 | .25 |
| ☐ 64 Junior Seau | 1.00 | .40 |
| ☐ 65 Randy McMillan | .60 | .25 |
| ☐ 66 Ricky Williams | 1.00 | .40 |
| ☐ 67 Zach Thomas | 1.00 | .40 |
| ☐ 68 Daunte Culpepper | .75 | .30 |
| ☐ 69 Michael Bennett | .75 | .30 |
| ☐ 70 Randy Moss | 1.25 | .50 |
| ☐ 71 Tom Brady | 2.50 | 1.00 |
| ☐ 72 Troy Brown | .75 | .30 |
| ☐ 73 Ty Law | .75 | .30 |
| ☐ 74 Aaron Brooks | .75 | .30 |
| ☐ 75 Deuce McAllister | 1.00 | .40 |
| ☐ 76 Donte Stallworth | .75 | .30 |
| ☐ 77 Amani Toomer | .75 | .30 |

| | | |
|---|---|---|
| ☐ 78 Jeremy Shockey | .75 | .30 |
| ☐ 79 Kerry Collins | .75 | .30 |
| ☐ 80 Michael Strahan | .75 | .30 |
| ☐ 81 Tiki Barber | 1.00 | .40 |
| ☐ 82 Chad Pennington | 1.00 | .40 |
| ☐ 83 Curtis Martin | 1.00 | .40 |
| ☐ 84 Justin McCareins | .60 | .25 |
| ☐ 85 Santana Moss | .75 | .30 |
| ☐ 86 Charles Woodson | 1.00 | .40 |
| ☐ 87 Jerry Rice | 2.00 | .75 |
| ☐ 88 Rich Gannon | .75 | .30 |
| ☐ 89 Tim Brown | 1.00 | .40 |
| ☐ 90 Warren Sapp | .75 | .30 |
| ☐ 91 Correll Buckhalter | .75 | .30 |
| ☐ 92 Donovan McNabb | 1.00 | .40 |
| ☐ 93 Freddie Mitchell | .60 | .25 |
| ☐ 94 Jevon Kearse | .75 | .30 |
| ☐ 95 Terrell Owens | 1.00 | .40 |
| ☐ 96 Antwaan Randle El | .75 | .30 |
| ☐ 97 Duce Staley | .75 | .30 |
| ☐ 98 Hines Ward | 1.00 | .40 |
| ☐ 99 Jerome Bettis | 1.00 | .40 |
| ☐ 100 Plaxico Burress | 1.00 | .40 |
| ☐ 101 Doug Flutie | 1.00 | .40 |
| ☐ 102 LaDainian Tomlinson | 1.50 | .60 |
| ☐ 103 Koren Robinson | 1.00 | .40 |
| ☐ 104 Matt Hasselbeck | 1.00 | .40 |
| ☐ 105 Shaun Alexander | 1.00 | .40 |
| ☐ 106 Isaac Bruce | .75 | .30 |
| ☐ 107 Kurt Warner | 1.00 | .40 |
| ☐ 108 Marc Bulger | .75 | .30 |
| ☐ 109 Marshall Faulk | 1.00 | .40 |
| ☐ 110 Torry Holt | .75 | .30 |
| ☐ 111 Brad Johnson | .75 | .30 |
| ☐ 112 Mike Alstott | .75 | .30 |
| ☐ 113 Derrick Mason | .75 | .30 |
| ☐ 114 Drew Bennett | .75 | .30 |
| ☐ 115 Eddie George | .75 | .30 |
| ☐ 116 Frank Wycheck | .75 | .30 |
| ☐ 117 Keith Bulluck | .60 | .25 |
| ☐ 118 Steve McNair | 1.00 | .40 |
| ☐ 119 Clinton Calico | .75 | .30 |
| ☐ 120 Clinton Portis | 1.00 | .40 |
| ☐ 121 LaVar Arrington | .75 | .30 |
| ☐ 122 Laveranues Coles | .75 | .30 |
| ☐ 123 Mark Brunell | .75 | .30 |
| ☐ 124 Patrick Ramsey | .75 | .30 |
| ☐ 125 Rod Gardner | .60 | .25 |
| ☐ 126 Jake Plummer FLB | .75 | .30 |
| ☐ 127 Thomas Jones FLB | .75 | .30 |
| ☐ 128 Priest Holmes FLB | 1.00 | .40 |
| ☐ 129 Jim Kelly FLB | 1.50 | .60 |
| ☐ 130 Doug Flutie FLB | 1.00 | .40 |
| ☐ 131 Walter Payton FLB | 6.00 | 2.50 |
| ☐ 132 Troy Aikman FLB | 2.50 | 1.00 |
| ☐ 133 John Elway FLB | 4.00 | 1.50 |
| ☐ 134 Barry Sanders FLB | 4.00 | 1.50 |
| ☐ 135 Mark Brunell FLB | .75 | .30 |
| ☐ 136 Earl Campbell FLB | 1.50 | .60 |
| ☐ 137 Joe Montana FLB | 5.00 | 2.00 |
| ☐ 138 Dan Marino FLB | 5.00 | 2.00 |
| ☐ 139 Curtis Martin FLB | 1.00 | .40 |
| ☐ 140 Drew Bledsoe FLB | 1.00 | .40 |
| ☐ 141 Ricky Williams FLB | 1.00 | .40 |
| ☐ 142 Junior Seau FLB | .75 | .30 |
| ☐ 143 Charlie Garner FLB | .75 | .30 |
| ☐ 144 Jerry Rice FLB | 2.00 | .75 |
| ☐ 145 Ahman Green FLB | 1.00 | .40 |
| ☐ 146 Jerome Bettis FLB | 1.00 | .40 |
| ☐ 147 Trent Green FLB | .75 | .30 |
| ☐ 148 Warrick Dunn FLB | .75 | .30 |
| ☐ 149 Deion Sanders FLB | 1.00 | .40 |
| ☐ 150 Stephen Davis FLB | .75 | .30 |
| ☐ 151 Admchinobe Echemandu AU RC | 10.00 | 4.00 |
| ☐ 152 Ahmad Carroll RC | 6.00 | 2.50 |
| ☐ 153 Andy Hall AU RC | 10.00 | 4.00 |
| ☐ 154 B.J. Johnson AU RC | 10.00 | 4.00 |
| ☐ 155 B.J. Symons AU RC | 15.00 | 6.00 |
| ☐ 156 Bradlee Van Pelt AU RC | 20.00 | 8.00 |
| ☐ 157 Brandon Miree AU RC | 10.00 | 4.00 |
| ☐ 158 Bruce Perry AU RC | 15.00 | 6.00 |
| ☐ 159 Carlos Francis AU RC | 10.00 | 4.00 |
| ☐ 160 Casey Bramlet AU RC | 10.00 | 4.00 |
| ☐ 161 Chris Gamble RC | 5.00 | 2.00 |

| | | |
|---|---|---|
| ☐ 162 Clarence Moore AU RC | 15.00 | 6.00 |
| ☐ 163 Cody Pickett AU RC | 15.00 | 6.00 |
| ☐ 164 Craig Krenzel AU RC | 15.00 | 6.00 |
| ☐ 165 D.J. Hackett RC | 6.00 | 2.50 |
| ☐ 166 D.J. Williams RC | 6.00 | 2.50 |
| ☐ 167 Derrick Ward AU RC | 15.00 | 6.00 |
| ☐ 168 Drew Carter AU RC | 15.00 | 6.00 |
| ☐ 169 Ernest Wilford RC | 6.00 | 2.50 |
| ☐ 170 Drew Henson RC | 4.00 | 1.50 |
| ☐ 171 Jamaar Taylor AU RC | 15.00 | 6.00 |
| ☐ 172 Jared Lorenzen AU RC | 10.00 | 4.00 |
| ☐ 173 Jarrett Payton AU RC | 15.00 | 6.00 |
| ☐ 174 Jason Babin AU RC EXCH | 15.00 | 6.00 |
| ☐ 175 Jeff Smoker AU RC | 15.00 | 6.00 |
| ☐ 176 Jeris McIntyre RC | 10.00 | 4.00 |
| ☐ 177 Jerricho Cotchery RC | 6.00 | 2.50 |
| ☐ 178 Jim Sorgi AU RC | 15.00 | 6.00 |
| ☐ 179 John Navarre AU RC | 15.00 | 6.00 |
| ☐ 180 Patrick Crayton AU RC | 20.00 | 10.00 |
| ☐ 181 Johnnie Morant RC | 5.00 | 2.00 |
| ☐ 182 Sean Taylor RC | 6.00 | 2.50 |
| ☐ 183 Jonathan Vilma RC | 6.00 | 2.50 |
| ☐ 184 Josh Harris RC | 4.00 | 1.50 |
| ☐ 185 Kenechi Udeze RC | 6.00 | 2.50 |
| ☐ 186 Mark Jones AU RC | 10.00 | 4.00 |
| ☐ 187 Matt Mauck AU RC | 15.00 | 6.00 |
| ☐ 188 Maurice Mann AU RC | 10.00 | 4.00 |
| ☐ 189 Michael Turner RC | 12.00 | 5.00 |
| ☐ 190 P.K. Sam RC | 4.00 | 1.50 |
| ☐ 191 Quincy Wilson RC | 5.00 | 2.00 |
| ☐ 192 Ran Carthon AU RC | 10.00 | 4.00 |
| ☐ 193 Ryan Krause AU RC | 10.00 | 4.00 |
| ☐ 194 Samie Parker RC | 5.00 | 2.00 |
| ☐ 195 Sloan Thomas AU RC | 10.00 | 4.00 |
| ☐ 196 Tommie Harris RC | 6.00 | 2.50 |
| ☐ 197 Triandos Luke AU RC | 15.00 | 6.00 |
| ☐ 198 Troy Fleming AU RC | 10.00 | 4.00 |
| ☐ 199 Vince Wilfork RC | 6.00 | 2.50 |
| ☐ 200 Will Smith RC | 5.00 | 2.00 |
| ☐ 201 Larry Fitzgerald JSY RC | 20.00 | 7.50 |
| ☐ 202 DeAngelo Hall JSY RC | 10.00 | 4.00 |
| ☐ 203 Matt Schaub JSY RC | 20.00 | 7.50 |
| ☐ 204 Michael Jenkins JSY RC | 8.00 | 3.00 |
| ☐ 205 Devard Darling JSY RC | 8.00 | 3.00 |
| ☐ 206 J.P. Losman JSY RC | 12.00 | 5.00 |
| ☐ 207 Lee Evans JSY RC | 10.00 | 4.00 |
| ☐ 208 Keary Colbert JSY RC | 8.00 | 3.00 |
| ☐ 209 Bernard Berrian JSY RC | 10.00 | 4.00 |
| ☐ 210 Chris Perry JSY RC | 10.00 | 4.00 |
| ☐ 211 Kellen Winslow JSY RC | 12.00 | 5.00 |
| ☐ 212 Luke McCown JSY RC | 8.00 | 3.00 |
| ☐ 213 Julius Jones JSY RC | 20.00 | 7.50 |
| ☐ 214 Darius Watts JSY RC | 8.00 | 3.00 |
| ☐ 215 Tatum Bell JSY RC | 12.00 | 5.00 |
| ☐ 216 Kevin Jones JSY RC | 12.00 | 5.00 |
| ☐ 217 Roy Williams JSY RC | 15.00 | 6.00 |
| ☐ 218 Dunta Robinson JSY RC | 8.00 | 3.00 |
| ☐ 219 Greg Jones JSY RC | 10.00 | 4.00 |
| ☐ 220 Reggie Williams JSY RC | 10.00 | 4.00 |
| ☐ 221 Mewelde Moore JSY RC | 8.00 | 3.00 |
| ☐ 222 Ben Watson JSY RC | 8.00 | 3.00 |
| ☐ 223 Cedric Cobbs JSY RC | 8.00 | 3.00 |
| ☐ 224 Devery Henderson JSY RC | 8.00 | 3.00 |
| ☐ 225 Eli Manning JSY RC | 30.00 | 15.00 |
| ☐ 226 Robert Gallery JSY RC | 8.00 | 3.00 |
| ☐ 227 Ben Roethlisberger JSY RC | 40.00 | 15.00 |
| ☐ 228 Philip Rivers JSY RC | 20.00 | 7.50 |
| ☐ 229 Derrick Hamilton JSY RC | 8.00 | 3.00 |
| ☐ 230 Rashaun Woods JSY RC | 8.00 | 3.00 |
| ☐ 231 Steven Jackson JSY RC | 20.00 | 7.50 |
| ☐ 232 Michael Clayton JSY RC | 10.00 | 4.00 |
| ☐ 233 Ben Troupe JSY RC | 8.00 | 3.00 |

## 2005 Leaf Certified Materials

| | | |
|---|---|---|
| ☐ COMP.SET w/o RCs (150) | 40.00 | 15.00 |
| ☐ 151-200 PRINT RUN 1000 SER.#'d SETS | | |
| ☐ 1 Anquan Boldin | .75 | .30 |
| ☐ 2 Josh McCown | .60 | .25 |
| ☐ 3 Larry Fitzgerald | 1.00 | .40 |
| ☐ 4 Michael Vick | 1.00 | .40 |
| ☐ 5 Peerless Price | .60 | .25 |
| ☐ 6 T.J. Duckett | .60 | .25 |
| ☐ 7 Warrick Dunn | .75 | .30 |

| | | |
|---|---|---|
| ☐ 8 Jamal Lewis | .75 | .30 |
| ☐ 9 Kyle Boller | .75 | .30 |
| ☐ 10 Todd Heap | .75 | .30 |
| ☐ 11 Ray Lewis | 1.00 | .40 |
| ☐ 12 Terrell Suggs | .75 | .30 |
| ☐ 13 Drew Bledsoe | 1.00 | .40 |
| ☐ 14 Eric Moulds | .75 | .30 |
| ☐ 15 J.P. Losman | .75 | .30 |
| ☐ 16 Lee Evans | .75 | .30 |
| ☐ 17 Willis McGahee | 1.00 | .40 |
| ☐ 18 DeShaun Foster | .75 | .30 |
| ☐ 19 Jake Delhomme | 1.00 | .40 |
| ☐ 20 Steve Smith | 1.00 | .40 |
| ☐ 21 Brian Urlacher | 1.00 | .40 |
| ☐ 22 Rex Grossman | 1.00 | .40 |
| ☐ 23 Carson Palmer | 1.00 | .40 |
| ☐ 24 Chad Johnson | .75 | .30 |
| ☐ 25 Rudi Johnson | .75 | .30 |
| ☐ 26 Kellen Winslow Jr. | 1.00 | .40 |
| ☐ 27 Kelly Holcomb | .75 | .25 |
| ☐ 28 Lee Suggs | .75 | .25 |
| ☐ 29 William Green | .75 | .25 |
| ☐ 30 Julius Jones | 1.00 | .40 |
| ☐ 31 Keyshawn Johnson | .75 | .30 |
| ☐ 32 Roy Williams S | .75 | .30 |
| ☐ 33 Terence Newman | .60 | .25 |
| ☐ 34 Ashley Lelie | .60 | .25 |
| ☐ 35 Champ Bailey | .75 | .30 |
| ☐ 36 Darius Watts | .60 | .25 |
| ☐ 37 Jake Plummer | .75 | .30 |
| ☐ 38 Tatum Bell | .75 | .30 |
| ☐ 39 Charles Rogers | .60 | .25 |
| ☐ 40 Joey Harrington | .75 | .30 |
| ☐ 41 Kevin Jones | .75 | .30 |
| ☐ 42 Roy Williams WR | 1.00 | .40 |
| ☐ 43 Ahman Green | 1.00 | .40 |
| ☐ 44 Brett Favre | 2.50 | 1.00 |
| ☐ 45 Javon Walker | .75 | .30 |
| ☐ 46 Robert Ferguson | .75 | .30 |
| ☐ 47 Andre Johnson | .75 | .30 |
| ☐ 48 David Carr | .75 | .30 |
| ☐ 49 Domanick Davis | .60 | .25 |
| ☐ 50 Dallas Clark | .75 | .30 |
| ☐ 51 Edgerrin James | 1.00 | .40 |
| ☐ 52 Marvin Harrison | 1.00 | .40 |
| ☐ 53 Peyton Manning | 1.50 | .60 |
| ☐ 54 Reggie Wayne | .75 | .30 |
| ☐ 55 Byron Leftwich | .75 | .30 |
| ☐ 56 Fred Taylor | 1.00 | .40 |
| ☐ 57 Jimmy Smith | .75 | .30 |
| ☐ 58 Reggie Williams | .75 | .30 |
| ☐ 59 Priest Holmes | 1.00 | .40 |
| ☐ 60 Tony Gonzalez | .75 | .30 |
| ☐ 61 Trent Green | .75 | .30 |
| ☐ 62 Chris Chambers | .75 | .30 |
| ☐ 63 Jason Taylor | .75 | .30 |
| ☐ 64 Junior Seau | 1.00 | .40 |
| ☐ 65 Zach Thomas | 1.00 | .40 |
| ☐ 66 Daunte Culpepper | 1.00 | .40 |
| ☐ 67 Michael Bennett | .75 | .30 |
| ☐ 68 Randy Moss | 1.50 | .60 |
| ☐ 69 Corey Dillon | .75 | .30 |
| ☐ 70 Tom Brady | 2.00 | .75 |
| ☐ 71 Deion Branch | .75 | .30 |
| ☐ 72 Aaron Brooks | .60 | .25 |
| ☐ 73 Deuce McAllister | 1.00 | .40 |
| ☐ 74 Donte Stallworth | .75 | .30 |
| ☐ 75 Joe Horn | .75 | .30 |

| | | |
|---|---|---|
| ❑ 76 Eli Manning | 2.00 | .75 |
| ❑ 77 Jeremy Shockey | 1.00 | .40 |
| ❑ 78 Michael Strahan | .75 | .30 |
| ❑ 79 Tiki Barber | 1.00 | .40 |
| ❑ 80 Anthony Becht | .60 | .25 |
| ❑ 81 Chad Pennington | 1.00 | .40 |
| ❑ 82 Curtis Martin | 1.00 | .40 |
| ❑ 83 Justin McCareins | .60 | .25 |
| ❑ 84 Laveranues Coles | .75 | .30 |
| ❑ 85 Santana Moss | .75 | .30 |
| ❑ 86 Shaun Ellis | .60 | .25 |
| ❑ 87 Jerry Porter | .75 | .30 |
| ❑ 88 Brian Westbrook | 1.00 | .40 |
| ❑ 89 Chad Lewis | .60 | .25 |
| ❑ 90 Donovan McNabb | 1.00 | .40 |
| ❑ 91 Freddie Mitchell | .60 | .25 |
| ❑ 92 Hugh Douglas | .60 | .25 |
| ❑ 93 Jevon Kearse | .75 | .30 |
| ❑ 94 Terrell Owens | 1.00 | .40 |
| ❑ 95 Todd Pinkston | .60 | .25 |
| ❑ 96 Antwaan Randle El | .75 | .30 |
| ❑ 97 Ben Roethlisberger | 2.50 | 1.00 |
| ❑ 98 Duce Staley | .75 | .30 |
| ❑ 99 Hines Ward | 1.00 | .40 |
| ❑ 100 Jerome Bettis | 1.00 | .40 |
| ❑ 101 Antonio Gates | 1.00 | .40 |
| ❑ 102 Drew Brees | 1.00 | .40 |
| ❑ 103 LaDainian Tomlinson | 1.50 | .60 |
| ❑ 104 Kevan Barlow | .60 | .25 |
| ❑ 105 Darrell Jackson | .75 | .30 |
| ❑ 106 Koren Robinson | .75 | .30 |
| ❑ 107 Matt Hasselbeck | .75 | .30 |
| ❑ 108 Shaun Alexander | .75 | .30 |
| ❑ 109 Marc Bulger | .75 | .30 |
| ❑ 110 Steven Jackson | 1.25 | .50 |
| ❑ 111 Torry Holt | .75 | .30 |
| ❑ 112 Michael Clayton | .75 | .30 |
| ❑ 113 Chris Brown | .75 | .30 |
| ❑ 114 Drew Bennett | .75 | .30 |
| ❑ 115 Keith Bulluck | .60 | .25 |
| ❑ 116 Steve McNair | 1.00 | .40 |
| ❑ 117 Clinton Portis | 1.00 | .40 |
| ❑ 118 LaVar Arrington | 1.25 | .50 |
| ❑ 119 John Riggins | 1.25 | .50 |
| ❑ 120 Sean Taylor | .75 | .30 |
| ❑ 121 Jake Plummer | .75 | .30 |
| ❑ 122 Thomas Jones | .75 | .30 |
| ❑ 123 Doug Flutie | 1.00 | .40 |
| ❑ 124 Walter Payton | 3.00 | 1.25 |
| ❑ 125 Corey Dillon | .75 | .30 |
| ❑ 126 Troy Aikman | 1.50 | .60 |
| ❑ 127 Terrell Davis | 1.00 | .40 |
| ❑ 128 Marshall Faulk | 1.00 | .40 |
| ❑ 129 Dan Marino | 3.00 | 1.25 |
| ❑ 130 Thurman Thomas | 1.25 | .50 |
| ❑ 131 Warren Moon | 1.25 | .50 |
| ❑ 132 Curtis Martin | 1.00 | .40 |
| ❑ 133 Drew Bledsoe | 1.00 | .40 |
| ❑ 134 Kerry Collins | .75 | .30 |
| ❑ 135 Keyshawn Johnson | .75 | .30 |
| ❑ 136 A.J. Feeley | .60 | .25 |
| ❑ 137 Duce Staley | .75 | .30 |
| ❑ 138 Junior Seau | 1.00 | .40 |
| ❑ 139 Jerry Rice | 2.00 | .75 |
| ❑ 140 Steve Young | 1.50 | .60 |
| ❑ 141 Jerome Bettis | 1.00 | .40 |
| ❑ 142 Kurt Warner | 1.00 | .40 |
| ❑ 143 Trent Green | .75 | .30 |
| ❑ 144 Keyshawn Johnson | .75 | .30 |
| ❑ 145 Warren Sapp | .75 | .30 |
| ❑ 146 Warrick Dunn | .75 | .30 |
| ❑ 147 Jevon Kearse | .75 | .30 |
| ❑ 148 Deion Sanders | 1.50 | .60 |
| ❑ 149 Laveranues Coles | .75 | .30 |
| ❑ 150 Stephen Davis | .75 | .30 |
| ❑ 151 Cedric Benson RC | 5.00 | 2.00 |
| ❑ 152 Mike Williams | 5.00 | 2.00 |
| ❑ 153 DeMarcus Ware RC | 8.00 | 3.00 |
| ❑ 154 Shawne Merriman RC | 8.00 | 3.00 |
| ❑ 155 Thomas Davis RC | 4.00 | 1.50 |
| ❑ 156 Derrick Johnson RC | 5.00 | 2.00 |
| ❑ 157 Travis Johnson RC | 3.00 | 1.25 |
| ❑ 158 David Pollack RC | 4.00 | 1.50 |
| ❑ 159 Erasmus James RC | 4.00 | 1.50 |

| | | |
|---|---|---|
| ❑ 160 Marcus Spears RC | 5.00 | 2.00 |
| ❑ 161 Fabian Washington RC | 5.00 | 2.00 |
| ❑ 162 Aaron Rodgers RC | 15.00 | 6.00 |
| ❑ 163 Marlin Jackson RC | 4.00 | 1.50 |
| ❑ 164 Heath Miller RC | 10.00 | 4.00 |
| ❑ 165 Matt Roth RC | 5.00 | 2.00 |
| ❑ 166 Dan Cody RC | 5.00 | 2.00 |
| ❑ 167 Bryant McFadden RC | 4.00 | 1.50 |
| ❑ 168 Chris Henry RC | 5.00 | 2.00 |
| ❑ 169 David Greene RC | 4.00 | 1.50 |
| ❑ 170 Brandon Jones RC | 5.00 | 2.00 |
| ❑ 171 Marion Barber RC | 15.00 | 6.00 |
| ❑ 172 Brandon Jacobs RC | 6.00 | 2.50 |
| ❑ 173 Jerome Mathis RC | 5.00 | 2.00 |
| ❑ 174 Craphonso Thorpe RC | 4.00 | 1.50 |
| ❑ 175 Alvin Pearman RC | 4.00 | 1.50 |
| ❑ 176 Darren Sproles RC | 6.00 | 2.50 |
| ❑ 177 Fred Gibson RC | 4.00 | 1.50 |
| ❑ 178 Roydell Williams RC | 4.00 | 1.50 |
| ❑ 179 Airese Currie RC | 4.00 | 1.50 |
| ❑ 180 Damien Nash RC | 4.00 | 1.50 |
| ❑ 181 Dan Orlovsky RC | 5.00 | 2.00 |
| ❑ 182 Adrian McPherson RC | 4.00 | 1.50 |
| ❑ 183 Larry Brackins RC | 3.00 | 1.25 |
| ❑ 184 Rasheed Marshall RC | 4.00 | 1.50 |
| ❑ 185 Cedric Houston RC | 5.00 | 2.00 |
| ❑ 186 Chad Owens RC | 5.00 | 2.00 |
| ❑ 187 Tab Perry RC | 5.00 | 2.00 |
| ❑ 188 Dante Ridgeway RC | 3.00 | 1.25 |
| ❑ 189 Craig Bragg RC | 3.00 | 1.25 |
| ❑ 190 Deandra Cobb RC | 4.00 | 1.50 |
| ❑ 191 Derek Anderson RC | 8.00 | 3.00 |
| ❑ 192 Paris Warren RC | 4.00 | 1.50 |
| ❑ 193 Lionel Gates RC | 3.00 | 1.25 |
| ❑ 194 Anthony Davis RC | 4.00 | 1.50 |
| ❑ 195 Ryan Fitzpatrick RC | 5.00 | 2.00 |
| ❑ 196 J.R. Russell RC | 3.00 | 1.25 |
| ❑ 197 Jason White RC | 5.00 | 2.00 |
| ❑ 198 Kay-Jay Harris RC | 4.00 | 1.50 |
| ❑ 199 T.A. McLendon RC | 3.00 | 1.25 |
| ❑ 200 Taylor Stubblefield RC | 3.00 | 1.25 |
| ❑ 201 Adam Jones JSY/1499 RC | 8.00 | 3.00 |
| ❑ 202 Alex Smith QB JSY/499 RC | 30.00 | 12.50 |
| ❑ 203 Andrew Walter JSY/1249 RC | 8.00 | 3.00 |
| ❑ 204 Antrel Rolle JSY/999 RC | 8.00 | 3.00 |
| ❑ 205 Braylon Edwards JSY/499 RC | 25.00 | 10.00 |
| ❑ 206 Cadillac Williams JSY/499 RC | 30.00 | 12.50 |
| ❑ 207 Carlos Rogers JSY/1499 RC | 5.00 | 2.00 |
| ❑ 208 Charlie Frye JSY/1499 RC | 5.00 | 2.00 |
| ❑ 209 Ciatrick Fason JSY/1499 RC | 6.00 | 2.50 |
| ❑ 210 Courtney Roby JSY/1249 RC | 6.00 | 2.50 |
| ❑ 211 Eric Shelton JSY/999 RC | 6.00 | 2.50 |
| ❑ 212 Frank Gore JSY/999 RC | 12.00 | 5.00 |
| ❑ 213 J.J. Arrington JSY/499 RC | 10.00 | 4.00 |
| ❑ 214 Kyle Orton JSY/1499 RC | 10.00 | 4.00 |
| ❑ 215 Jason Campbell JSY/749 RC | 12.00 | 5.00 |
| ❑ 216 Mark Bradley JSY/999 RC | 8.00 | 3.00 |
| ❑ 217 Mark Clayton JSY/499 RC | 10.00 | 4.00 |
| ❑ 218 Matt Jones JSY/749 RC | 12.00 | 5.00 |
| ❑ 219 Maurice Clarett JSY/999 RC | 6.00 | 2.50 |
| ❑ 220 Reggie Brown JSY/999 RC | 8.00 | 3.00 |
| ❑ 221 Roddy White JSY/749 RC | 10.00 | 4.00 |
| ❑ 222 Ronnie Brown JSY/499 RC | 30.00 | 12.50 |
| ❑ 223 Roscoe Parrish JSY/999 RC | 6.00 | 2.50 |
| ❑ 224 Ryan Moats JSY/999 RC | 8.00 | 3.00 |
| ❑ 225 Stefan LeFors JSY/1499 RC | 6.00 | 2.50 |
| ❑ 226 Terrence Murphy JSY/1499 RC | 5.00 | 2.00 |
| ❑ 227 Troy Williamson JSY/749 RC | 10.00 | 4.00 |
| ❑ 228 Vernand Morency JSY/1499 RC | 8.00 | 3.00 |
| ❑ 229 Vincent Jackson JSY/1499 RC | 8.00 | 3.00 |

## 2006 Leaf Certified Materials

| | | |
|---|---|---|
| ❑ COMP.SET w/o SP's (150) | 40.00 | 15.00 |
| ❑ 1 Anquan Boldin | .75 | .30 |
| ❑ 2 Edgerrin James | .75 | .30 |
| ❑ 3 Kurt Warner | .75 | .30 |
| ❑ 4 Larry Fitzgerald | 1.00 | .40 |
| ❑ 5 Alge Crumpler | .75 | .30 |
| ❑ 6 Brian Finneran | .60 | .25 |
| ❑ 7 Michael Jenkins | .75 | .30 |
| ❑ 8 Michael Vick | 1.00 | .40 |
| ❑ 9 Warrick Dunn | .75 | .30 |
| ❑ 10 Derrick Mason | .75 | .30 |

STEVEN JACKSON
St. LOUIS RAMS

| | | |
|---|---|---|
| ❑ 11 Jamal Lewis | .75 | .30 |
| ❑ 12 Kyle Boller | .75 | .30 |
| ❑ 13 Todd Heap | .75 | .30 |
| ❑ 14 Mark Clayton | .75 | .30 |
| ❑ 15 Eric Moulds | .75 | .30 |
| ❑ 16 J.P. Losman | .75 | .30 |
| ❑ 17 Josh Reed | .60 | .25 |
| ❑ 18 Lee Evans | .75 | .30 |
| ❑ 19 Willis McGahee | 1.00 | .40 |
| ❑ 20 DeShaun Foster | .75 | .30 |
| ❑ 21 Jake Delhomme | .75 | .30 |
| ❑ 22 Stephen Davis | .75 | .30 |
| ❑ 23 Keary Colbert | .75 | .30 |
| ❑ 24 Steve Smith | 1.00 | .40 |
| ❑ 25 Brian Urlacher | 1.00 | .40 |
| ❑ 26 Cedric Benson | .75 | .30 |
| ❑ 27 Muhsin Muhammad | .75 | .30 |
| ❑ 28 Rex Grossman | 1.00 | .40 |
| ❑ 29 Thomas Jones | .75 | .30 |
| ❑ 30 Carson Palmer | 1.00 | .40 |
| ❑ 31 Chad Johnson | .75 | .30 |
| ❑ 32 Rudi Johnson | .75 | .30 |
| ❑ 33 T.J. Houshmandzadeh | .75 | .30 |
| ❑ 34 Charlie Frye | .75 | .30 |
| ❑ 35 Dennis Northcutt | .60 | .25 |
| ❑ 36 Braylon Edwards | 1.00 | .40 |
| ❑ 37 Reuben Droughns | .75 | .30 |
| ❑ 38 Drew Bledsoe | 1.00 | .40 |
| ❑ 39 Julius Jones | .75 | .30 |
| ❑ 40 Terrell Owens | 1.00 | .40 |
| ❑ 41 Jason Witten | .75 | .30 |
| ❑ 42 Terry Glenn | .75 | .30 |
| ❑ 43 Roy Williams S | .75 | .30 |
| ❑ 44 Jake Plummer | .75 | .30 |
| ❑ 45 Rod Smith | .75 | .30 |
| ❑ 46 Tatum Bell | .75 | .30 |
| ❑ 47 Ashley Lelie | .75 | .30 |
| ❑ 48 Josh McCown | .75 | .30 |
| ❑ 49 Kevin Jones | 1.00 | .40 |
| ❑ 50 Mike Williams | 1.00 | .40 |
| ❑ 51 Roy Williams WR | .75 | .30 |
| ❑ 52 Ahman Green | .75 | .30 |
| ❑ 53 Brett Favre | 2.00 | .75 |
| ❑ 54 Aaron Rodgers | 1.00 | .40 |
| ❑ 55 Samkon Gado | 1.00 | .40 |
| ❑ 56 Donald Driver | .75 | .30 |
| ❑ 57 Robert Ferguson | .60 | .25 |
| ❑ 58 Andre Johnson | .75 | .30 |
| ❑ 59 David Carr | .75 | .30 |
| ❑ 60 Domanick Davis | .75 | .30 |
| ❑ 61 Dallas Clark | .75 | .30 |
| ❑ 62 Marvin Harrison | 1.00 | .40 |
| ❑ 63 Peyton Manning | 1.50 | .60 |
| ❑ 64 Reggie Wayne | .75 | .30 |
| ❑ 65 Brandon Stokley | .75 | .30 |
| ❑ 66 Byron Leftwich | .75 | .30 |
| ❑ 67 Fred Taylor | .75 | .30 |
| ❑ 68 Jimmy Smith | .75 | .30 |
| ❑ 69 Matt Jones | .75 | .30 |
| ❑ 70 Larry Johnson | .75 | .30 |
| ❑ 71 Tony Gonzalez | .75 | .30 |
| ❑ 72 Trent Green | .75 | .30 |
| ❑ 73 Eddie Kennison | .60 | .25 |
| ❑ 74 Samie Parker | .60 | .25 |
| ❑ 75 Chris Chambers | .75 | .30 |
| ❑ 76 Daunte Culpepper | 1.00 | .40 |
| ❑ 77 Randy McMichael | .60 | .25 |
| ❑ 78 Ronnie Brown | 1.00 | .40 |

|  |  | | |
|---|---|---|---|
| 79 | Marty Booker | .60 | .25 |
| 80 | Zach Thomas | 1.00 | .40 |
| 81 | Brad Johnson | .75 | .30 |
| 82 | Mewelde Moore | .60 | .25 |
| 83 | Nate Burleson | .75 | .30 |
| 84 | Troy Williamson | .75 | .30 |
| 85 | Deion Branch | .75 | .30 |
| 86 | Tom Brady | 1.50 | .60 |
| 87 | Corey Dillon | .75 | .30 |
| 88 | Daniel Graham | .60 | .25 |
| 89 | Troy Brown | .60 | .25 |
| 90 | Deuce McAllister | .75 | .30 |
| 91 | Donte Stallworth | .75 | .30 |
| 92 | Drew Brees | 1.00 | .40 |
| 93 | Joe Horn | .75 | .30 |
| 94 | Devery Henderson | .60 | .25 |
| 95 | Eli Manning | 1.25 | .50 |
| 96 | Jeremy Shockey | 1.00 | .40 |
| 97 | Plaxico Burress | .75 | .30 |
| 98 | Amani Toomer | .75 | .30 |
| 99 | Tiki Barber | 1.00 | .40 |
| 100 | Chad Pennington | .75 | .30 |
| 101 | Curtis Martin | 1.00 | .40 |
| 102 | Laveranues Coles | .75 | .30 |
| 103 | Justin McCareins | .60 | .25 |
| 104 | Jerry Porter | .75 | .30 |
| 105 | LaMont Jordan | .75 | .30 |
| 106 | Doug Gabriel | .60 | .25 |
| 107 | Randy Moss | 1.00 | .40 |
| 108 | Brian Westbrook | .75 | .30 |
| 109 | Donovan McNabb | 1.00 | .40 |
| 110 | Reggie Brown | .75 | .30 |
| 111 | Chad Lewis | .50 | .20 |
| 112 | Ryan Moats | .75 | .30 |
| 113 | Jevon Kearse | .75 | .30 |
| 114 | Ben Roethlisberger | 1.50 | .60 |
| 115 | Heath Miller | .75 | .30 |
| 116 | Hines Ward | 1.00 | .40 |
| 117 | Willie Parker | 1.25 | .50 |
| 118 | Troy Polamalu | 1.25 | .50 |
| 119 | Antonio Gates | 1.00 | .40 |
| 120 | Eric Parker | .60 | .25 |
| 121 | Keenan McCardell | .75 | .30 |
| 122 | LaDainian Tomlinson | 1.25 | .50 |
| 123 | Philip Rivers | 1.00 | .40 |
| 124 | Alex Smith QB | 1.00 | .40 |
| 125 | Antonio Bryant | .75 | .30 |
| 126 | Frank Gore | 1.00 | .40 |
| 127 | Kevan Barlow | .75 | .30 |
| 128 | Darrell Jackson | .75 | .30 |
| 129 | Jerramy Stevens | .75 | .30 |
| 130 | Matt Hasselbeck | .75 | .30 |
| 131 | Shaun Alexander | 1.00 | .40 |
| 132 | Isaac Bruce | .75 | .30 |
| 133 | Marc Bulger | .75 | .30 |
| 134 | Marshall Faulk | .75 | .30 |
| 135 | Steven Jackson | 1.00 | .40 |
| 136 | Torry Holt | .75 | .30 |
| 137 | Cadillac Williams | 1.00 | .40 |
| 138 | Chris Simms | .75 | .30 |
| 139 | Joey Galloway | .75 | .30 |
| 140 | Michael Clayton | .75 | .30 |
| 141 | Brandon Jones | .60 | .25 |
| 142 | Chris Brown | .75 | .30 |
| 143 | Drew Bennett | .75 | .30 |
| 144 | Tyrone Calico | .60 | .25 |
| 145 | Steve McNair | .75 | .30 |
| 146 | Antwaan Randle El | .75 | .30 |
| 147 | Clinton Portis | 1.00 | .40 |
| 148 | Mark Brunell | .75 | .30 |
| 149 | Santana Moss | .75 | .30 |
| 150 | Jason Campbell | .75 | .30 |
| 151 | Brodie Croyle/500 RC | 10.00 | 4.00 |
| 152 | Greg Jennings/500 RC | 12.00 | 5.00 |
| 153 | Joseph Addai/500 RC | 25.00 | 10.00 |
| 154 | Bennie Brazell/1000 RC | 4.00 | 1.50 |
| 155 | David Thomas/500 RC | 8.00 | 3.00 |
| 156 | Marques Colston/1000 RC | 12.00 | 5.00 |
| 157 | Reggie McNeal/500 RC | 6.00 | 2.50 |
| 158 | D.J. Shockley/1000 RC | 5.00 | 2.00 |
| 159 | Dominique Byrd/500 RC | 6.00 | 2.50 |
| 160 | Antonio Cromartie/1000 RC | 5.00 | 2.00 |
| 161 | Donte Whitner/1000 RC | 5.00 | 2.00 |
| 162 | Anwar Phillips/1000 RC | 4.00 | 1.50 |
| 163 | A.J. Nicholson/1000 RC | 3.00 | 1.25 |
| 164 | De'Arrius Howard/500 RC | 8.00 | 3.00 |
| 165 | Erik Meyer/500 RC | 6.00 | 2.50 |
| 166 | Darrell Hackney/1000 RC | 4.00 | 1.50 |
| 167 | Paul Pinegar/500 RC | 8.00 | 3.00 |
| 168 | Brandon Kirsch/500 RC | 8.00 | 3.00 |
| 169 | Quinton Ganther/1000 RC | 5.00 | 2.00 |
| 170 | Andre Hall/1000 RC | 5.00 | 2.00 |
| 171 | Derrick Ross/1000 RC | 4.00 | 1.50 |
| 172 | Mike Bell/1000 RC | 5.00 | 2.00 |
| 173 | Wendell Mathis/500 RC | 6.00 | 2.50 |
| 174 | Garrett Mills/500 RC | 8.00 | 3.00 |
| 175 | David Anderson/1000 RC | 4.00 | 1.50 |
| 176 | Kevin McMahan/1000 RC | 4.00 | 1.50 |
| 177 | Martin Nance/1000 RC | 4.00 | 1.50 |
| 178 | Greg Lee/500 RC | 6.00 | 2.50 |
| 179 | Anthony Mix/500 RC | 6.00 | 2.50 |
| 180 | D.Ferguson/500 RC | 8.00 | 3.00 |
| 181 | Tamba Hali/500 RC | 8.00 | 3.00 |
| 182 | Haloti Ngata/1000 RC | 5.00 | 2.00 |
| 183 | Claude Wroten/1000 RC | 3.00 | 1.25 |
| 184 | Gabe Watson/1000 RC | 4.00 | 1.50 |
| 185 | D'Qwell Jackson/1000 RC | 4.00 | 1.50 |
| 186 | Abdul Hodge/500 RC | 8.00 | 3.00 |
| 187 | Chad Greenway/500 RC | 8.00 | 3.00 |
| 188 | Bobby Carpenter/1000 RC | 5.00 | 2.00 |
| 189 | DeMeco Ryans/500 RC | 10.00 | 4.00 |
| 190 | Rocky McIntosh/500 RC | 8.00 | 3.00 |
| 191 | Thomas Howard/1000 RC | 5.00 | 2.00 |
| 192 | Jon Alston/500 RC | 8.00 | 3.00 |
| 193 | Jimmy Williams/1000 RC | 5.00 | 2.00 |
| 194 | Ashton Youboty/500 RC | 6.00 | 2.50 |
| 195 | Alan Zemaitis/1000 RC | 5.00 | 2.00 |
| 196 | Cedric Griffin/500 RC | 6.00 | 2.50 |
| 197 | Ko Simpson/1000 RC | 5.00 | 2.00 |
| 198 | Pat Watkins/500 RC | 6.00 | 2.50 |
| 199 | Bernard Pollard/1000 RC | 5.00 | 2.00 |
| 200 | Jay Cutler/500 RC | 20.00 | 8.00 |
| 201 | Chad Jackson JSY/1400 RC | 8.00 | 3.00 |
| 202 | L.Maroney JSY/550 RC | 20.00 | 8.00 |
| 203 | Tar.Jackson JSY/1400 RC | 6.00 | 2.50 |
| 204 | Michael Huff JSY/1400 RC | 6.00 | 2.50 |
| 205 | Mario Williams JSY/1400 RC | 10.00 | 4.00 |
| 206 | Mar.Lewis JSY/1400 RC | 8.00 | 3.00 |
| 207 | Maurice Drew JSY/1400 RC | 12.00 | 5.00 |
| 208 | Vince Young JSY/550 RC | 25.00 | 10.00 |
| 209 | LenDale White JSY/550 RC | 12.00 | 5.00 |
| 210 | Reggie Bush JSY/550 RC | 40.00 | 15.00 |
| 211 | Matt Leinart JSY/550 RC | 25.00 | 10.00 |
| 212 | M.Robinson JSY/1400 RC | 8.00 | 3.00 |
| 213 | Vernon Davis JSY/550 RC | 12.00 | 5.00 |
| 214 | Br.Williams JSY/1400 RC | 8.00 | 3.00 |
| 215 | Derek Hagan JSY/1400 RC | 8.00 | 3.00 |
| 216 | Jason Avant JSY/1400 RC | 6.00 | 2.50 |
| 217 | B.Marshall JSY/1400 RC | 8.00 | 3.00 |
| 218 | Omar Jacobs JSY/1400 RC | 8.00 | 3.00 |
| 219 | Santonio Holmes JSY/550 RC | 15.00 | 6.00 |
| 220 | J.Norwood JSY/1400 RC | 8.00 | 3.00 |
| 221 | Dem.Williams JSY/1400 RC | 8.00 | 3.00 |
| 222 | Sinorice Moss JSY/1400 RC | 8.00 | 3.00 |
| 223 | L.Washington JSY/1400 RC | 6.00 | 2.50 |
| 224 | Kellen Clemens JSY/900 RC | 8.00 | 3.00 |
| 225 | A.J. Hawk JSY/550 RC | 20.00 | 8.00 |
| 226 | Maurice Stovall JSY/1400 RC | 8.00 | 3.00 |
| 227 | DeA.Williams JSY/550 RC | 12.00 | 5.00 |
| 228 | C.Whitehurst JSY/1400 RC | 6.00 | 2.50 |
| 229 | Travis Wilson JSY/1400 RC | 8.00 | 3.00 |
| 230 | J.Klopfenstein JSY/1400 RC | 8.00 | 3.00 |
| 231 | Brian Calhoun JSY/1400 RC | 8.00 | 3.00 |
| 232 | Barry Sanders JSY/150 | 25.00 | 10.00 |
| 233 | Jerry Rice JSY/150 | 20.00 | 8.00 |
| 234 | Dan Marino JSY/150 | 30.00 | 12.00 |
| 235 | Earl Campbell JSY/150 | 15.00 | 6.00 |
| 236 | Jim Brown JSY/100 | 25.00 | 10.00 |
| 237 | Joe Montana JSY/125 | 25.00 | 10.00 |
| 238 | Troy Aikman JSY/150 | 25.00 | 10.00 |
| 239 | Walter Payton JSY/100 | 40.00 | 15.00 |
| 240 | Terry Bradshaw JSY/150 | 25.00 | 10.00 |
| 241 | John Elway JSY/150 | 25.00 | 10.00 |
| 242 | Fred Biletnikoff JSY/100 | 15.00 | 6.00 |
| 243 | Lance Alworth JSY/125 | 15.00 | 6.00 |
| 244 | Ronnie Lott JSY/150 | 15.00 | 6.00 |
| 245 | Yale Lary JSY/125 | 15.00 | 6.00 |
| 246 | Bart Starr JSY/80 | 30.00 | 12.00 |
| 247 | Doak Walker JSY/75 | 25.00 | 10.00 |
| 248 | Gale Sayers JSY/100 | 20.00 | 8.00 |
| 249 | Bo Jackson JSY/150 | 15.00 | 6.00 |
| 250 | Roger Staubach JSY/125 | 25.00 | 10.00 |
| 251 | Dick Butkus JSY/150 | 20.00 | 8.00 |

## 2007 Leaf Certified Materials

|  |  | | |
|---|---|---|---|
| 1 | Tony Romo | 2.00 | .75 |
| 2 | Julius Jones | .75 | .30 |
| 3 | Terry Glenn | .75 | .30 |
| 4 | Terrell Owens | 1.00 | .40 |
| 5 | Jason Witten | .75 | .30 |
| 6 | Patrick Crayton | .60 | .25 |
| 7 | Eli Manning | .75 | .40 |
| 8 | Plaxico Burress | .75 | .30 |
| 9 | Jeremy Shockey | .75 | .30 |
| 10 | Brandon Jacobs | .75 | .30 |
| 11 | Sinorice Moss | .75 | .30 |
| 12 | Donovan McNabb | 1.00 | .40 |
| 13 | Brian Westbrook | .75 | .30 |
| 14 | Reggie Brown | .75 | .30 |
| 15 | Hank Baskett | .75 | .30 |
| 16 | Jason Campbell | .75 | .30 |
| 17 | Clinton Portis | .75 | .30 |
| 18 | Santana Moss | .75 | .30 |
| 19 | Chris Cooley | .60 | .25 |
| 20 | Ladell Betts | .60 | .25 |
| 21 | Rex Grossman | .75 | .30 |
| 22 | Cedric Benson | .75 | .30 |
| 23 | Bernard Berrian | .60 | .25 |
| 24 | Devin Hester | 1.00 | .40 |
| 25 | Brian Urlacher | 1.00 | .40 |
| 26 | Jon Kitna | .60 | .25 |
| 27 | Roy Williams WR | .75 | .30 |
| 28 | Mike Furrey | .60 | .25 |
| 29 | Tatum Bell | .60 | .25 |
| 30 | Brett Favre | 2.00 | .75 |
| 31 | Donald Driver | .75 | .30 |
| 32 | Greg Jennings | .75 | .30 |
| 33 | Nick Barnett | .60 | .25 |
| 34 | Tarvaris Jackson | .75 | .30 |
| 35 | Chester Taylor | .60 | .25 |
| 36 | Troy Williamson | .60 | .25 |
| 37 | Michael Vick | 1.00 | .40 |
| 38 | Warrick Dunn | .75 | .30 |
| 39 | Joe Horn | .75 | .30 |
| 40 | Michael Jenkins | .75 | .30 |
| 41 | Alge Crumpler | .75 | .30 |
| 42 | Jerious Norwood | .75 | .30 |
| 43 | Jake Delhomme | .75 | .30 |
| 44 | DeShaun Foster | .75 | .30 |
| 45 | Steve Smith | .75 | .30 |
| 46 | DeAngelo Williams | 1.00 | .40 |
| 47 | Drew Brees | 1.00 | .40 |
| 48 | Deuce McAllister | .75 | .30 |
| 49 | Marques Colston | 1.00 | .40 |
| 50 | Devery Henderson | .60 | .25 |
| 51 | Reggie Bush | 1.25 | .50 |
| 52 | Cadillac Williams | .75 | .30 |
| 53 | Joey Galloway | .75 | .30 |
| 54 | Michael Clayton | .75 | .30 |
| 55 | Derrick Brooks | .75 | .30 |
| 56 | Matt Leinart | 1.00 | .40 |
| 57 | Edgerrin James | .75 | .30 |
| 58 | Anquan Boldin | .75 | .30 |
| 59 | Larry Fitzgerald | 1.00 | .40 |

|  |  | | |
|---|---|---|---|
| 60 | Marc Bulger | .75 | .30 |
| 61 | Steven Jackson | 1.00 | .40 |
| 62 | Torry Holt | .75 | .30 |
| 63 | Isaac Bruce | .75 | .30 |
| 64 | Randy McMichael | .60 | .25 |
| 65 | Drew Bennett | .60 | .25 |
| 66 | Alex Smith QB | 1.00 | .40 |
| 67 | Frank Gore | 1.00 | .40 |
| 68 | Vernon Davis | .75 | .30 |
| 69 | Darrell Jackson | .75 | .30 |
| 70 | Matt Hasselbeck | .75 | .30 |
| 71 | Shaun Alexander | .75 | .30 |
| 72 | Deion Branch | .75 | .30 |
| 73 | Nate Burleson | .60 | .25 |
| 74 | J.P. Losman | .60 | .25 |
| 75 | Anthony Thomas | .60 | .25 |
| 76 | Lee Evans | .75 | .30 |
| 77 | Josh Reed | .60 | .25 |
| 78 | Daunte Culpepper | .75 | .30 |
| 79 | Ronnie Brown | .75 | .30 |
| 80 | Chris Chambers | .75 | .30 |
| 81 | Marty Booker | .60 | .25 |
| 82 | Jason Taylor | .60 | .25 |
| 83 | Zach Thomas | .75 | .30 |
| 84 | Tom Brady | 2.00 | .75 |
| 85 | Laurence Maroney | 1.00 | .40 |
| 86 | Randy Moss | 1.00 | .40 |
| 87 | Ben Watson | .60 | .25 |
| 88 | Donte Stallworth | .75 | .30 |
| 89 | Tedy Bruschi | 1.00 | .40 |
| 90 | Chad Pennington | .75 | .30 |
| 91 | Thomas Jones | .75 | .30 |
| 92 | Laveranues Coles | .75 | .30 |
| 93 | Jerricho Cotchery | .60 | .25 |
| 94 | Leon Washington | .75 | .30 |
| 95 | Steve McNair | .75 | .30 |
| 96 | Willis McGahee | .75 | .30 |
| 97 | Demetrius Williams | .60 | .25 |
| 98 | Todd Heap | .60 | .25 |
| 99 | Ray Lewis | 1.00 | .40 |
| 100 | Mark Clayton | .75 | .30 |
| 101 | Carson Palmer | 1.00 | .40 |
| 102 | Rudi Johnson | .75 | .30 |
| 103 | Chad Johnson | .75 | .30 |
| 104 | T.J. Houshmandzadeh | .75 | .30 |
| 105 | Charlie Frye | .75 | .30 |
| 106 | Braylon Edwards | .75 | .30 |
| 107 | Kellen Winslow | .75 | .30 |
| 108 | Jamal Lewis | .75 | .30 |
| 109 | Ben Roethlisberger | 1.25 | .50 |
| 110 | Willie Parker | 1.00 | .40 |
| 111 | Hines Ward | 1.00 | .40 |
| 112 | Heath Miller | .60 | .25 |
| 113 | Troy Polamalu | 1.00 | .40 |
| 114 | Ahman Green | .75 | .30 |
| 115 | Andre Johnson | .75 | .30 |
| 116 | Matt Schaub | .75 | .30 |
| 117 | DeMeco Ryans | .75 | .30 |
| 118 | Peyton Manning | 1.50 | .60 |
| 119 | Joseph Addai | 1.00 | .40 |
| 120 | Marvin Harrison | 1.00 | .40 |
| 121 | Reggie Wayne | .75 | .30 |
| 122 | Dallas Clark | .60 | .25 |
| 123 | Byron Leftwich | .75 | .30 |
| 124 | Fred Taylor | .75 | .30 |
| 125 | Matt Jones | .75 | .30 |
| 126 | Reggie Williams | .75 | .30 |
| 127 | Marcedes Lewis | .60 | .25 |
| 128 | Maurice Jones-Drew | 1.00 | .40 |
| 129 | Ernest Wilford | .60 | .25 |
| 130 | Vince Young | 1.00 | .40 |
| 131 | LenDale White | .75 | .30 |
| 132 | Brandon Jones | .60 | .25 |
| 133 | Jay Cutler | 1.00 | .40 |
| 134 | Travis Henry | .75 | .30 |
| 135 | Javon Walker | .75 | .30 |
| 136 | Rod Smith | .75 | .30 |
| 137 | Champ Bailey | .75 | .30 |
| 138 | Mike Bell | .75 | .30 |
| 139 | Brandon Marshall | .75 | .30 |
| 140 | Larry Johnson | 1.00 | .40 |
| 141 | Eddie Kennison | .60 | .25 |
| 142 | Tony Gonzalez | .75 | .30 |
| 143 | Brodie Croyle | .75 | .30 |
| 144 | LaMont Jordan | .75 | .30 |
| 145 | Ronald Curry | .75 | .30 |
| 146 | Philip Rivers | 1.00 | .40 |
| 147 | LaDainian Tomlinson | 1.25 | .50 |
| 148 | Michael Turner | .75 | .30 |
| 149 | Antonio Gates | .75 | .30 |
| 150 | Shawne Merriman | .75 | .30 |
| 151 | Aaron Ross RC | 5.00 | 2.00 |
| 152 | Adam Carriker RC | 4.00 | 1.50 |
| 153 | Ahmad Bradshaw RC | 6.00 | 2.50 |
| 154 | Alan Branch RC | 4.00 | 1.50 |
| 155 | Chansi Stuckey RC | 4.00 | 1.50 |
| 156 | Charles Johnson RC | 3.00 | 1.25 |
| 157 | Chris Leak RC | 5.00 | 2.00 |
| 158 | Jarvis Moss RC | 5.00 | 2.00 |
| 159 | Dan Bazuin RC | 4.00 | 1.50 |
| 160 | David Harris RC | 4.00 | 1.50 |
| 161 | Dwayne Wright RC | 4.00 | 1.50 |
| 162 | Eric Frampton RC | 4.00 | 1.50 |
| 163 | Eric Wright RC | 4.00 | 1.50 |
| 164 | Jared Zabransky RC | 5.00 | 2.00 |
| 165 | Jason Snelling RC | 4.00 | 1.50 |
| 166 | Jordan Palmer RC | 5.00 | 2.00 |
| 167 | Kenneth Darby RC | 5.00 | 2.00 |
| 168 | LaMarr Woodley RC | 5.00 | 2.00 |
| 169 | LaRon Landry RC | 6.00 | 2.50 |
| 170 | Lawrence Timmons RC | 5.00 | 2.00 |
| 171 | Leon Hall RC | 4.00 | 1.50 |
| 172 | Michael Griffin RC | 5.00 | 2.00 |
| 173 | Mike Walker RC | 4.00 | 1.50 |
| 174 | Paul Posluszny RC | 6.00 | 2.50 |
| 175 | Thomas Clayton RC | 4.00 | 1.50 |
| 176 | Amobi Okoye AU RC | 12.00 | 5.00 |
| 177 | Anthony Spencer AU RC | 12.00 | 5.00 |
| 178 | Aundrae Allison AU RC | 10.00 | 4.00 |
| 179 | Ben Patrick AU RC | 10.00 | 4.00 |
| 180 | Brandon Meriweather AU RC | 12.00 | 5.00 |
| 181 | Chris Davis AU RC | 10.00 | 4.00 |
| 182 | Chris Houston AU RC | 10.00 | 4.00 |
| 183 | Craig Buster Davis AU RC EXCH | 12.00 | 5.00 |
| 184 | Dallas Baker AU RC | 10.00 | 4.00 |
| 185 | Darius Walker AU RC | 12.00 – | 5.00 |
| 186 | Darrelle Revis AU RC | 12.00 | 5.00 |
| 187 | David Clowney AU RC | 12.00 | 5.00 |
| 188 | DeShawn Wynn AU RC | 12.00 | 5.00 |
| 189 | Ikaika Alama-Francis AU RC | 12.00 | 5.00 |
| 190 | Isaiah Stanback AU RC | 12.00 | 5.00 |
| 191 | Jacoby Jones AU RC | 12.00 | 5.00 |
| 192 | Jamaal Anderson AU RC | 10.00 | 4.00 |
| 193 | James Jones AU RC | 12.00 | 5.00 |
| 194 | Courtney Taylor AU RC | 10.00 | 4.00 |
| 195 | Jon Beason AU RC | 12.00 | 5.00 |
| 196 | Jonathan Wade AU RC | 10.00 | 4.00 |
| 197 | Josh Wilson AU RC | 10.00 | 4.00 |
| 198 | Kolby Smith AU RC | 12.00 | 5.00 |
| 199 | Laurent Robinson AU RC | 10.00 | 4.00 |
| 200 | Reggie Nelson AU RC | 10.00 | 4.00 |
| 201 | Dwayne Jarrett JSY RC | 8.00 | 3.00 |
| 202 | Johnnie Lee Higgins JSY RC | 6.00 | 2.50 |
| 203 | Michael Bush JSY RC | 8.00 | 3.00 |
| 204 | Antonio Pittman JSY RC | 8.00 | 3.00 |
| 205 | Patrick Willis JSY RC | 15.00 | 6.00 |
| 206 | Gaines Adams JSY RC | 8.00 | 3.00 |
| 207 | Tony Hunt JSY RC | 8.00 | 3.00 |
| 208 | Chris Henry RB JSY RC | 8.00 | 3.00 |
| 209 | John Beck JSY RC | 8.00 | 3.00 |
| 210 | Dwayne Bowe JSY RC | 15.00 | 6.00 |
| 211 | Brian Leonard JSY RC | 8.00 | 3.00 |
| 212 | Anthony Gonzalez JSY RC | 12.00 | 5.00 |
| 213 | Trent Edwards JSY RC | 20.00 | 8.00 |
| 214 | Jason Hill JSY RC | 8.00 | 3.00 |
| 215 | JaMarcus Russell JSY/849 RC | 20.00 | 8.00 |
| 216 | Ted Ginn Jr. JSY RC | 12.00 | 5.00 |
| 217 | Paul Williams JSY RC | 6.00 | 2.50 |
| 218 | Garrett Wolfe JSY RC | 8.00 | 3.00 |
| 219 | Adrian Peterson JSY/849 RC | 30.00 | 12.00 |
| 220 | Kevin Kolb JSY RC | 8.00 | 3.00 |
| 221 | Marshawn Lynch JSY RC | 15.00 | 6.00 |
| 222 | Steve Smith USC JSY RC | 10.00 | 4.00 |
| 223 | Greg Olsen JSY RC | 10.00 | 4.00 |
| 224 | Kenny Irons JSY RC | 8.00 | 3.00 |
| 225 | Brandon Jackson JSY RC | 8.00 | 3.00 |
| 226 | Yamon Figurs JSY RC | 8.00 | 3.00 |
| 227 | Lorenzo Booker JSY RC | 8.00 | 3.00 |
| 228 | Drew Stanton JSY RC | 8.00 | 3.00 |
| 229 | Brady Quinn JSY/849 RC | 25.00 | 10.00 |
| 230 | Joe Thomas JSY RC | 8.00 | 3.00 |
| 231 | Robert Meachem JSY RC | 8.00 | 3.00 |
| 232 | Troy Smith JSY RC | 10.00 | 4.00 |
| 233 | Sidney Rice JSY RC | 10.00 | 4.00 |
| 234 | Calvin Johnson JSY/849 RC | 25.00 | 10.00 |
| 235 | Bart Starr JSY | 30.00 | 12.00 |
| 236 | Bob Griese JSY | 20.00 | 8.00 |
| 237 | Bobby Layne/50 JSY | 25.00 | 10.00 |
| 238 | Bulldog Turner JSY | 20.00 | 8.00 |
| 239 | Earl Campbell JKT | 20.00 | 8.00 |
| 240 | Franco Harris JSY | 20.00 | 8.00 |
| 241 | James Lofton JSY | 12.00 | 5.00 |
| 242 | Jim McMahon JSY | 25.00 | 10.00 |
| 243 | Jim Thorpe JSY | 100.00 | 60.00 |
| 244 | Joe Namath JSY | 25.00 | 10.00 |
| 246 | Lou Groza JSY | 15.00 | 6.00 |
| 247 | Ray Nitschke JSY | 25.00 | 10.00 |
| 248 | Ron Mix JSY | 12.00 | 5.00 |
| 249 | Roosevelt Brown JSY | 12.00 | 5.00 |
| 250 | Sam Huff JSY | 15.00 | 6.00 |
| 251 | Sammy Baugh JSY | 40.00 | 20.00 |
| 252 | Sid Luckman JSY | 30.00 | 15.00 |
| 253 | Otto Graham JSY | 30.00 | 15.00 |
| 254 | Y.A. Tittle JSY | 20.00 | 8.00 |

## 2008 Leaf Certified Materials

|  |  | | |
|---|---|---|---|
| 1 | Matt Leinart | 1.00 | .40 |
| 2 | Larry Fitzgerald | 1.00 | .40 |
| 3 | Anquan Boldin | .75 | .30 |
| 4 | Edgerrin James | .75 | .30 |
| 5 | Jerious Norwood | .75 | .30 |
| 6 | Roddy White | .75 | .30 |
| 7 | Joe Horn | .75 | .30 |
| 8 | Michael Turner | .75 | .30 |
| 9 | Willis McGahee | .75 | .30 |
| 10 | Derrick Mason | .60 | .25 |
| 11 | Mark Clayton | .75 | .30 |
| 12 | Demetrius Williams | .60 | .25 |
| 13 | Trent Edwards | 1.00 | .40 |
| 14 | Marshawn Lynch | 1.00 | .40 |
| 15 | Lee Evans | .75 | .30 |
| 16 | Steve Smith | .75 | .30 |
| 17 | DeAngelo Williams | .75 | .30 |
| 18 | Julius Peppers | .75 | .30 |
| 19 | Jake Delhomme | .75 | .30 |
| 20 | Adrian Peterson | .60 | .25 |
| 21 | Greg Olsen | .75 | .30 |
| 22 | Devin Hester | 1.00 | .40 |
| 23 | Brian Urlacher | 1.00 | .40 |
| 24 | Rex Grossman | .75 | .30 |
| 25 | Carson Palmer | 1.00 | .40 |
| 26 | Chad Johnson | .75 | .30 |
| 27 | T.J. Houshmandzadeh | .75 | .30 |
| 28 | Rudi Johnson | .75 | .30 |
| 29 | Derek Anderson | .75 | .30 |
| 30 | Jamal Lewis | .75 | .30 |
| 31 | Kellen Winslow | .75 | .30 |
| 32 | Braylon Edwards | .75 | .30 |
| 33 | Tony Romo | 1.50 | .60 |
| 34 | Terrell Owens | 1.00 | .40 |
| 35 | Marion Barber | 1.00 | .40 |
| 36 | Jason Witten | .75 | .30 |
| 37 | Jay Cutler | 1.00 | .40 |
| 38 | Selvin Young | .75 | .30 |

| | | |
|---|---|---|
| ❏ 39 Brandon Marshall | .75 | .30 |
| ❏ 40 Brandon Stokley | .75 | .30 |
| ❏ 41 Jon Kitna | .75 | .30 |
| ❏ 42 Roy Williams WR | .75 | .30 |
| ❏ 43 Calvin Johnson | 1.00 | .40 |
| ❏ 44 Mike Furrey | .75 | .30 |
| ❏ 45 Aaron Rodgers | 1.00 | .40 |
| ❏ 46 Ryan Grant | 1.00 | .40 |
| ❏ 47 Greg Jennings | .75 | .30 |
| ❏ 48 Donald Driver | .75 | .30 |
| ❏ 49 Matt Schaub | .75 | .30 |
| ❏ 50 Ahman Green | .75 | .30 |
| ❏ 51 Andre Johnson | .75 | .30 |
| ❏ 52 Kevin Walter | .60 | .25 |
| ❏ 53 DeMeco Ryans | .75 | .30 |
| ❏ 54 Peyton Manning | 1.50 | .60 |
| ❏ 55 Joseph Addai | 1.00 | .40 |
| ❏ 56 Marvin Harrison | 1.00 | .40 |
| ❏ 57 Reggie Wayne | .75 | .30 |
| ❏ 58 Dallas Clark | .75 | .30 |
| ❏ 59 Anthony Gonzalez | .75 | .30 |
| ❏ 60 David Garrard | .75 | .30 |
| ❏ 61 Fred Taylor | .75 | .30 |
| ❏ 62 Maurice Jones-Drew | .75 | .30 |
| ❏ 63 Reggie Williams | .75 | .30 |
| ❏ 64 Marcedes Lewis | .60 | .25 |
| ❏ 65 Matt Jones | .75 | .30 |
| ❏ 66 Jerry Porter | .75 | .30 |
| ❏ 67 Brodie Croyle | 1.00 | .40 |
| ❏ 68 Larry Johnson | .75 | .30 |
| ❏ 69 Kolby Smith | .60 | .25 |
| ❏ 70 Tony Gonzalez | .75 | .30 |
| ❏ 71 Dwayne Bowe | .75 | .30 |
| ❏ 72 John Beck | .60 | .25 |
| ❏ 73 Ronnie Brown | .75 | .30 |
| ❏ 74 Ted Ginn Jr. | .75 | .30 |
| ❏ 75 Derek Hagan | .60 | .25 |
| ❏ 76 Jason Taylor | .75 | .30 |
| ❏ 77 Bernard Berrian | .75 | .30 |
| ❏ 78 Tarvaris Jackson | .75 | .30 |
| ❏ 79 Adrian Peterson | 2.00 | .75 |
| ❏ 80 Chester Taylor | .60 | .25 |
| ❏ 81 Sidney Rice | .75 | .30 |
| ❏ 82 Tom Brady | 1.50 | .60 |
| ❏ 83 Randy Moss | 1.00 | .40 |
| ❏ 84 Laurence Maroney | .75 | .30 |
| ❏ 85 Wes Welker | 1.00 | .40 |
| ❏ 86 Drew Brees | 1.00 | .40 |
| ❏ 87 Reggie Bush | 1.00 | .40 |
| ❏ 88 Deuce McAllister | .75 | .30 |
| ❏ 89 Marques Colston | .75 | .30 |
| ❏ 90 Eli Manning | 1.00 | .40 |
| ❏ 91 Plaxico Burress | .75 | .30 |
| ❏ 92 Brandon Jacobs | .75 | .30 |
| ❏ 93 Amani Toomer | .75 | .30 |
| ❏ 94 Jeremy Shockey | .75 | .30 |
| ❏ 95 Steve Smith USC | .75 | .30 |
| ❏ 96 Michael Strahan | .75 | .30 |
| ❏ 97 Kellen Clemens | .75 | .30 |
| ❏ 98 Leon Washington | .60 | .25 |
| ❏ 99 Jerricho Cotchery | .60 | .25 |
| ❏ 100 Laveranues Coles | .75 | .30 |
| ❏ 101 Thomas Jones | .75 | .30 |
| ❏ 102 Javon Walker | .75 | .30 |
| ❏ 103 JaMarcus Russell | 1.00 | .40 |
| ❏ 104 Justin Fargas | .60 | .25 |
| ❏ 105 Michael Bush | .75 | .30 |
| ❏ 106 Zach Miller | .75 | .30 |
| ❏ 107 Donovan McNabb | 1.00 | .40 |
| ❏ 108 Brian Westbrook | .75 | .30 |
| ❏ 109 Kevin Curtis | .60 | .25 |
| ❏ 110 Reggie Brown | .75 | .30 |
| ❏ 111 Greg Lewis | .60 | .25 |
| ❏ 112 Ben Roethlisberger | 1.25 | .50 |
| ❏ 113 Willie Parker | .75 | .30 |
| ❏ 114 Hines Ward | 1.00 | .40 |
| ❏ 115 Santonio Holmes | .75 | .30 |
| ❏ 116 Philip Rivers | 1.00 | .40 |
| ❏ 117 LaDainian Tomlinson | 1.25 | .50 |
| ❏ 118 Vincent Jackson | .60 | .25 |
| ❏ 119 Antonio Gates | .75 | .30 |
| ❏ 120 Brett Favre | 6.00 | 2.50 |
| ❏ 121 Alex Smith QB | .75 | .30 |
| ❏ 122 Frank Gore | .75 | .30 |

| | | |
|---|---|---|
| ❏ 123 Michael Robinson | .60 | .25 |
| ❏ 124 Vernon Davis | .60 | .25 |
| ❏ 125 Isaac Bruce | .75 | .30 |
| ❏ 126 Patrick Willis | .75 | .30 |
| ❏ 127 Matt Hasselbeck | .75 | .30 |
| ❏ 128 Nate Burleson | .60 | .25 |
| ❏ 129 Deion Branch | .75 | .30 |
| ❏ 130 Julius Jones | .75 | .30 |
| ❏ 131 Marc Bulger | .75 | .30 |
| ❏ 132 Steven Jackson | 1.00 | .40 |
| ❏ 133 Torry Holt | .75 | .30 |
| ❏ 134 Warrick Dunn | .75 | .30 |
| ❏ 135 Jeff Garcia | .75 | .30 |
| ❏ 136 Cadillac Williams | .75 | .30 |
| ❏ 137 Earnest Graham | .60 | .25 |
| ❏ 138 Joey Galloway | .75 | .30 |
| ❏ 139 Michael Clayton | .75 | .30 |
| ❏ 140 Vince Young | 1.00 | .40 |
| ❏ 141 LenDale White | .75 | .30 |
| ❏ 142 Justin Gage | .60 | .25 |
| ❏ 143 Roydell Williams | .60 | .25 |
| ❏ 144 Alge Crumpler | .75 | .30 |
| ❏ 145 Brandon Jones | .60 | .25 |
| ❏ 146 Jason Campbell | .75 | .30 |
| ❏ 147 Clinton Portis | .75 | .30 |
| ❏ 148 Ladell Betts | .60 | .25 |
| ❏ 149 Santana Moss | .75 | .30 |
| ❏ 150 Chris Cooley | .75 | .30 |
| ❏ 151 Adrian Arrington AU/999 | 8.00 | 3.00 |
| ❏ 152 Andre Woodson AU | 4.00 | 1.50 |
| ❏ 153 Antoine Cason AU/749 | 4.00 | 1.50 |
| ❏ 154 Aqib Talib AU/999 | 10.00 | 4.00 |
| ❏ 155 Brad Cottam AU/999 RC | 4.00 | 1.50 |
| ❏ 156 Brandon Flowers AU/899 | 10.00 | 4.00 |
| ❏ 157 Chauncey Washington AU/799 RC | 8.00 | 3.00 |
| ❏ 158 Chevis Jackson RC | 3.00 | 1.25 |
| ❏ 159 Colt Brennan RC | 10.00 | 4.00 |
| ❏ 160 Curtis Lofton AU/999 RC | 10.00 | 4.00 |
| ❏ 161 Dan Connor RC | 4.00 | 1.50 |
| ❏ 162 Dennis Dixon RC | 4.00 | 1.50 |
| ❏ 163 Derrick Harvey RC | 3.00 | 1.25 |
| ❏ 164 Dominique Rodgers-Cromartie RC | 4.00 | 1.50 |
| ❏ 165 Erik Ainge AU/699 RC | 10.00 | 4.00 |
| ❏ 166 Fred Davis AU/999 RC | 4.00 | 1.50 |
| ❏ 167 Jacob Hester AU/399 RC | 12.00 | 5.00 |
| ❏ 168 Jermichael Finley RC | 4.00 | 1.50 |
| ❏ 169 Jerod Mayo RC | 6.00 | 2.50 |
| ❏ 170 John Carlson RC | 4.00 | 1.50 |
| ❏ 171 Josh Johnson RC | 4.00 | 1.50 |
| ❏ 172 Jordon Dizon AU/299 RC | 12.00 | 5.00 |
| ❏ 173 Josh Morgan RC | 4.00 | 1.50 |
| ❏ 174 Justin Forsett AU/649 RC | 10.00 | 4.00 |
| ❏ 175 Keenan Burton RC | 3.00 | 1.25 |
| ❏ 176 Keith Rivers RC | 4.00 | 1.50 |
| ❏ 177 Kenny Phillips RC | 4.00 | 1.50 |
| ❏ 178 Kevin Robinson AU/999 RC | 8.00 | 3.00 |
| ❏ 179 Lavelle Hawkins RC | 3.00 | 1.25 |
| ❏ 180 Leodis McKelvin AU/999 RC | 10.00 | 4.00 |
| ❏ 181 Marcus Smith RC | 3.00 | 1.25 |
| ❏ 182 Marcus Thomas AU/499 RC | 10.00 | 4.00 |
| ❏ 183 Martellus Bennett RC | 4.00 | 1.50 |
| ❏ 184 Matt Flynn RC | 5.00 | 2.00 |
| ❏ 185 Mike Jenkins RC | 4.00 | 1.50 |
| ❏ 186 Mike Hart RC | 5.00 | 2.00 |
| ❏ 187 Paul Hubbard RC | 3.00 | 1.25 |
| ❏ 188 Peyton Hillis AU/499 RC | 20.00 | 8.00 |
| ❏ 189 Quentin Groves AU/275 RC | 12.00 | 5.00 |
| ❏ 190 Reggie Smith RC | 3.00 | 1.25 |
| ❏ 191 Ryan Torain AU/299 RC | 12.00 | 5.00 |
| ❏ 192 Sedrick Ellis RC | 4.00 | 1.50 |
| ❏ 193 Shawn Crable RC | 4.00 | 1.50 |
| ❏ 194 Tashard Choice AU/999 RC | 15.00 | 6.00 |
| ❏ 195 Terrell Thomas AU/999 RC | 8.00 | 3.00 |
| ❏ 196 Thomas Brown AU/999 RC | 10.00 | 4.00 |
| ❏ 197 Tim Hightower AU/499 RC | 25.00 | 10.00 |
| ❏ 198 Tracy Porter AU/999 RC | 8.00 | 3.00 |
| ❏ 199 Vernon Gholston AU/999 RC | 10.00 | 4.00 |
| ❏ 200 Will Franklin AU/249 RC | 12.00 | 5.00 |
| ❏ 201 Andre Caldwell JSY RC | 5.00 | 2.00 |
| ❏ 202 Dustin Keller JSY RC | 6.00 | 2.50 |
| ❏ 203 Earl Bennett JSY RC | 6.00 | 2.50 |
| ❏ 204 Early Doucet JSY RC | 6.00 | 2.50 |
| ❏ 205 Glenn Dorsey JSY RC | 8.00 | 3.00 |
| ❏ 206 Harry Douglas JSY RC | 6.00 | 2.50 |

| | | |
|---|---|---|
| ❏ 207 John David Booty JSY RC | 8.00 | 3.00 |
| ❏ 208 Kevin O'Connell JSY RC | 8.00 | 3.00 |
| ❏ 209 Darren McFadden JSY RC | 25.00 | 10.00 |
| ❏ 210 Jonathan Stewart JSY RC | 15.00 | 6.00 |
| ❏ 211 Felix Jones JSY RC | 20.00 | 8.00 |
| ❏ 212 Rashard Mendenhall JSY RC | 12.00 | 5.00 |
| ❏ 213 Chris Johnson JSY RC | 15.00 | 6.00 |
| ❏ 214 Matt Forte JSY RC | 15.00 | 6.00 |
| ❏ 215 Ray Rice JSY RC | 8.00 | 3.00 |
| ❏ 216 Kevin Smith JSY RC | 10.00 | 4.00 |
| ❏ 217 Jamaal Charles JSY RC | 8.00 | 3.00 |
| ❏ 218 Steve Slaton JSY RC | 12.00 | 5.00 |
| ❏ 219 Matt Ryan JSY RC | 20.00 | 8.00 |
| ❏ 220 Joe Flacco JSY RC | 20.00 | 8.00 |
| ❏ 221 Brian Brohm JSY RC | 8.00 | 3.00 |
| ❏ 222 Chad Henne JSY RC | 10.00 | 4.00 |
| ❏ 223 Donnie Avery JSY RC | 8.00 | 3.00 |
| ❏ 224 Devin Thomas JSY RC | 6.00 | 2.50 |
| ❏ 225 Jordy Nelson JSY RC | 8.00 | 3.00 |
| ❏ 226 James Hardy JSY RC | 6.00 | 2.50 |
| ❏ 227 Eddie Royal JSY RC | 12.00 | 5.00 |
| ❏ 228 DeSean Jackson JSY RC | 12.00 | 5.00 |
| ❏ 229 Malcolm Kelly JSY RC | 6.00 | 2.50 |
| ❏ 230 Limas Sweed JSY RC | 8.00 | 3.00 |
| ❏ 231 Mario Manningham JSY RC | 6.00 | 2.50 |
| ❏ 232 Jerome Simpson JSY RC | 5.00 | 2.00 |
| ❏ 233 Dexter Jackson JSY RC | 6.00 | 2.50 |
| ❏ 234 Jake Long JSY RC | 8.00 | 3.00 |
| ❏ 235 Bart Starr JSY | 25.00 | 10.00 |
| ❏ 236 Johnny Unitas JSY/75 | 30.00 | 12.00 |
| ❏ 237 Brett Favre JSY | 30.00 | 12.00 |
| ❏ 238 Tom Landry JSY | 30.00 | 12.00 |
| ❏ 239 Hank Stram JSY | 15.00 | 6.00 |
| ❏ 240 Chuck Foreman JSY | 10.00 | 4.00 |
| ❏ 241 Dan Marino JSY | 30.00 | 12.00 |
| ❏ 242 Andre Reed JSY | 12.00 | 5.00 |
| ❏ 243 Frank Gifford JSY/50 | 15.00 | 6.00 |
| ❏ 244 John Riggins JSY | 12.00 | 5.00 |
| ❏ 245 John Stallworth JSY | 12.00 | 5.00 |
| ❏ 246 John Elway JSY | 25.00 | 10.00 |
| ❏ 247 Emmitt Smith JSY | 30.00 | 12.00 |
| ❏ 248 Randall Cunningham JSY | 15.00 | 6.00 |
| ❏ 249 Reggie White JSY | 15.00 | 6.00 |
| ❏ 250 John Matuszak JSY | 15.00 | 6.00 |
| ❏ 251 Troy Aikman JSY | 20.00 | 8.00 |
| ❏ 252 Billy Sims JSY | 12.00 | 5.00 |
| ❏ 253 Willie Brown JSY | 10.00 | 4.00 |
| ❏ 254 Barry Sanders JSY | 25.00 | 10.00 |
| ❏ 255 Walter Payton JSY | 30.00 | 12.00 |

## 2000 Leaf Limited

| | | |
|---|---|---|
| ❏ COMP.SET w/o SPs (200) | 120.00 | 60.00 |
| ❏ 1 Ben Coates | .50 | .20 |
| ❏ 2 Joe Horn | .75 | .30 |
| ❏ 3 Jonathan Linton | .50 | .20 |
| ❏ 4 Derrick Mason | .75 | .30 |
| ❏ 5 Ray Lucas | .75 | .30 |
| ❏ 6 Brock Huard | .75 | .30 |
| ❏ 7 Frank Wycheck | .50 | .20 |
| ❏ 8 Michael Strahan | .75 | .30 |
| ❏ 9 Jessie Armstead | .50 | .20 |
| ❏ 10 Stephen Alexander | .50 | .20 |
| ❏ 11 Larry Centers | .50 | .20 |
| ❏ 12 Michael Pittman | .50 | .20 |
| ❏ 13 Priest Holmes | 1.50 | .60 |
| ❏ 14 Jermaine Lewis | .75 | .30 |
| ❏ 15 Jay Riemersma | .50 | .20 |
| ❏ 16 Wesley Walls | .50 | .20 |

|  |  | | |
|---|--------|------|-----|
| ❑ 17 | Curtis Enis | .50 | .20 |
| ❑ 18 | Bobby Engram | .75 | .30 |
| ❑ 19 | Jim Miller | .50 | .20 |
| ❑ 20 | Eddie Kennison | .75 | .30 |
| ❑ 21 | Errict Rhett | .50 | .20 |
| ❑ 22 | Chris Warren | .50 | .20 |
| ❑ 23 | Byron Chamberlain | .50 | .20 |
| ❑ 24 | Desmond Howard | .75 | .30 |
| ❑ 25 | Lamar Smith | .50 | .20 |
| ❑ 26 | Robert Porcher | .50 | .20 |
| ❑ 27 | Corey Bradford | .75 | .30 |
| ❑ 28 | Donald Driver | 1.25 | .50 |
| ❑ 29 | Ahman Green | 1.25 | .50 |
| ❑ 30 | Ken Dilger | .50 | .20 |
| ❑ 31 | James McKnight | .75 | .30 |
| ❑ 32 | Kimble Anders | .50 | .20 |
| ❑ 33 | Zach Thomas | 1.25 | .50 |
| ❑ 34 | James Johnson | .50 | .20 |
| ❑ 35 | Lawyer Milloy | .75 | .30 |
| ❑ 36 | Ty Law | .75 | .30 |
| ❑ 37 | Willie McGinest | .50 | .20 |
| ❑ 38 | Jason Sehorn | .75 | .30 |
| ❑ 39 | Andre Rison | .75 | .30 |
| ❑ 40 | Rickey Dudley | .50 | .20 |
| ❑ 41 | Patrick Jeffers | 1.25 | .50 |
| ❑ 42 | Darrell Russell | .50 | .20 |
| ❑ 43 | Charles Johnson | .75 | .30 |
| ❑ 44 | Michael Westbrook | .75 | .30 |
| ❑ 45 | Levron Kirkland | .50 | .20 |
| ❑ 46 | Ryan Leaf | .75 | .30 |
| ❑ 47 | Sean Dawkins | .50 | .20 |
| ❑ 48 | Todd Lyght | .50 | .20 |
| ❑ 49 | Kevin Carter | .50 | .20 |
| ❑ 50 | Neil O'Donnell | .50 | .20 |
| ❑ 51 | Randall Cunningham | 1.50 | .60 |
| ❑ 52 | Oronde Gadsden | 1.00 | .40 |
| ❑ 53 | O.J. McDuffie | 1.00 | .40 |
| ❑ 54 | Jake Reed | 1.00 | .40 |
| ❑ 55 | Brian Milne | .60 | .25 |
| ❑ 56 | Kordell Stewart | 1.00 | .40 |
| ❑ 57 | Derrick Mayes | 1.00 | .40 |
| ❑ 58 | Az-Zahir Hakim | .60 | .25 |
| ❑ 59 | Jacquez Green | .60 | .25 |
| ❑ 60 | Andre Reed | 1.00 | .40 |
| ❑ 61 | Deion Sanders | 1.50 | .60 |
| ❑ 62 | Frank Sanders | 1.00 | .40 |
| ❑ 63 | Rob Moore | 1.00 | .40 |
| ❑ 64 | Shawn Jefferson | .60 | .25 |
| ❑ 65 | Pat Johnson | .60 | .25 |
| ❑ 66 | Peter Boulware | .60 | .25 |
| ❑ 67 | Donald Hayes | .60 | .25 |
| ❑ 68 | Marty Booker | 1.00 | .40 |
| ❑ 69 | Leslie Shepherd | .60 | .25 |
| ❑ 70 | Jason Tucker | .60 | .25 |
| ❑ 71 | Johnnie Morton | 1.00 | .40 |
| ❑ 72 | Germane Crowell | .60 | .25 |
| ❑ 73 | Herman Moore | 1.00 | .40 |
| ❑ 74 | Bill Schroeder | 1.00 | .40 |
| ❑ 75 | E.G. Green | .60 | .25 |
| ❑ 76 | Jerome Pathon | 1.00 | .40 |
| ❑ 77 | Tony Brackens | .60 | .25 |
| ❑ 78 | Tony Richardson RC | .60 | .25 |
| ❑ 79 | Sam Madison | .60 | .25 |
| ❑ 80 | Jeff George | 1.00 | .40 |
| ❑ 81 | Matthew Hatchette | .60 | .25 |
| ❑ 82 | Kevin Faulk | 1.00 | .40 |
| ❑ 83 | Jeff Blake | 1.00 | .40 |
| ❑ 84 | Ike Hilliard | 1.00 | .40 |
| ❑ 85 | Napoleon Kaufman | 1.00 | .40 |
| ❑ 86 | Charles Woodson | 1.00 | .40 |
| ❑ 87 | Na Brown | .60 | .25 |
| ❑ 88 | Hines Ward | 1.50 | .60 |
| ❑ 89 | Troy Edwards | .60 | .25 |
| ❑ 90 | Curtis Conway | 1.00 | .40 |
| ❑ 91 | Junior Seau | 1.50 | .60 |
| ❑ 92 | Jim Harbaugh | 1.00 | .40 |
| ❑ 93 | J.J. Stokes | 1.50 | .60 |
| ❑ 94 | Jon Kitna | 1.50 | .60 |
| ❑ 95 | Reidel Anthony | .60 | .25 |
| ❑ 96 | Warrick Dunn | 1.50 | .60 |
| ❑ 97 | Carl Pickens | 1.00 | .40 |
| ❑ 98 | Yancey Thigpen | .60 | .25 |
| ❑ 99 | Albert Connell | .60 | .25 |
| ❑ 100 | Irving Fryar | 1.00 | .40 |
| ❑ 101 | Qadry Ismail | 1.25 | .50 |
| ❑ 102 | Shannon Sharpe | 1.25 | .50 |
| ❑ 103 | Joey Galloway | 1.25 | .50 |
| ❑ 104 | Ed McCaffrey | 2.00 | .75 |
| ❑ 105 | Rod Smith | 1.25 | .50 |
| ❑ 106 | Terrell Owens | 2.00 | .75 |
| ❑ 107 | Warren Sapp | 1.25 | .50 |
| ❑ 108 | Jevon Kearse | 2.00 | .75 |
| ❑ 109 | Bruce Smith | 1.25 | .50 |
| ❑ 110 | Champ Bailey | 1.25 | .50 |
| ❑ 111 | David Boston | 2.00 | .75 |
| ❑ 112 | Tim Dwight | 2.00 | .75 |
| ❑ 113 | Terance Mathis | 1.25 | .50 |
| ❑ 114 | Tony Banks | 1.25 | .50 |
| ❑ 115 | Shawn Bryson | .75 | .30 |
| ❑ 116 | Peerless Price | 1.25 | .50 |
| ❑ 117 | Muhsin Muhammad | 1.25 | .50 |
| ❑ 118 | Tim Biakabutuka | 1.25 | .50 |
| ❑ 119 | Steve Beuerlein | 1.25 | .50 |
| ❑ 120 | Corey Dillon | 2.00 | .75 |
| ❑ 121 | Kevin Johnson | 2.00 | .75 |
| ❑ 122 | Rocket Ismail | 1.25 | .50 |
| ❑ 123 | Charlie Batch | 2.00 | .75 |
| ❑ 124 | James Stewart | 1.25 | .50 |
| ❑ 125 | Terrence Wilkins | .75 | .30 |
| ❑ 126 | Keenan McCardell | 1.25 | .50 |
| ❑ 127 | Mark Brunell | 2.00 | .75 |
| ❑ 128 | Fred Taylor | 2.00 | .75 |
| ❑ 129 | Derrick Alexander | 1.25 | .50 |
| ❑ 130 | Tony Gonzalez | 1.25 | .50 |
| ❑ 131 | Warren Moon | 2.00 | .75 |
| ❑ 132 | Thurman Thomas | 2.00 | .75 |
| ❑ 133 | Tony Martin | 1.25 | .50 |
| ❑ 134 | Jay Fiedler | 1.25 | .50 |
| ❑ 135 | John Randle | 1.25 | .50 |
| ❑ 136 | Troy Brown | 1.25 | .50 |
| ❑ 137 | Amani Toomer | 1.25 | .50 |
| ❑ 138 | Kerry Collins | 1.25 | .50 |
| ❑ 139 | Tiki Barber | 2.00 | .75 |
| ❑ 140 | Wayne Chrebet | 1.25 | .50 |
| ❑ 141 | Tyrone Wheatley | 1.25 | .50 |
| ❑ 142 | Duce Staley | 2.00 | .75 |
| ❑ 143 | Jermaine Fazande | .75 | .30 |
| ❑ 144 | Charlie Garner | 1.25 | .50 |
| ❑ 145 | Tony Holt | .75 | .30 |
| ❑ 146 | Mike Alstott | 2.00 | .75 |
| ❑ 147 | Shaun King | .50 | .20 |
| ❑ 148 | Darrell Green | .75 | .30 |
| ❑ 149 | Brad Johnson | 2.00 | .75 |
| ❑ 150 | Olandis Gary | 2.00 | .75 |
| ❑ 151 | Jake Plummer | 1.25 | .50 |
| ❑ 152 | Chris Chandler | 1.50 | .60 |
| ❑ 153 | Jamal Anderson | 2.50 | 1.00 |
| ❑ 154 | Eric Moulds | 2.50 | 1.00 |
| ❑ 155 | Doug Flutie | 2.50 | 1.00 |
| ❑ 156 | Rob Johnson | 1.50 | .50 |
| ❑ 157 | Marcus Robinson | 2.50 | 1.00 |
| ❑ 158 | Cade McNown | 1.00 | .40 |
| ❑ 159 | Akili Smith | 1.00 | .40 |
| ❑ 160 | Tim Couch | 1.50 | .60 |
| ❑ 161 | Emmitt Smith | 5.00 | 2.00 |
| ❑ 162 | Troy Aikman | 5.00 | 2.00 |
| ❑ 163 | Brian Griese | 2.50 | 1.00 |
| ❑ 164 | John Elway | 8.00 | 3.00 |
| ❑ 165 | Terrell Davis | 2.50 | 1.00 |
| ❑ 166 | Dorsey Levens | 1.50 | .60 |
| ❑ 167 | Antonio Freeman | 2.50 | 1.00 |
| ❑ 168 | Brett Favre | 8.00 | 3.00 |
| ❑ 169 | Marvin Harrison | 2.50 | 1.00 |
| ❑ 170 | Peyton Manning | 6.00 | 2.50 |
| ❑ 171 | Edgerrin James | 4.00 | 1.50 |
| ❑ 172 | Jimmy Smith | 1.50 | .60 |
| ❑ 173 | Elvis Grbac | 1.50 | .60 |
| ❑ 174 | Dan Marino | 8.00 | 3.00 |
| ❑ 175 | Randy Moss | 5.00 | 2.00 |
| ❑ 176 | Cris Carter | 2.50 | 1.00 |
| ❑ 177 | Robert Smith | 2.50 | 1.00 |
| ❑ 178 | Daunte Culpepper | 3.00 | 1.25 |
| ❑ 179 | Terry Glenn | 1.50 | .60 |
| ❑ 180 | Drew Bledsoe | 3.00 | 1.25 |
| ❑ 181 | Ricky Williams | 1.25 | .50 |
| ❑ 182 | Jake Delhomme RC | 8.00 | 3.00 |
| ❑ 183 | Curtis Martin | 2.50 | 1.00 |
| ❑ 184 | Vinny Testaverde | 1.50 | .60 |
| ❑ 185 | Tim Brown | 2.50 | 1.00 |
| ❑ 186 | Rich Gannon | 2.50 | 1.00 |
| ❑ 187 | Donovan McNabb | 3.00 | 1.25 |
| ❑ 188 | Jerome Bettis | 2.50 | 1.00 |
| ❑ 189 | Bobby Shaw RC | 2.50 | 1.00 |
| ❑ 190 | Jerry Rice | 5.00 | 2.00 |
| ❑ 191 | Steve Young | 3.00 | 1.25 |
| ❑ 192 | Jeff Garcia | 2.50 | 1.00 |
| ❑ 193 | Ricky Watters | 1.00 | .40 |
| ❑ 194 | Isaac Bruce | 2.50 | 1.00 |
| ❑ 195 | Marshall Faulk | 3.00 | 1.25 |
| ❑ 196 | Kurt Warner | 5.00 | 2.00 |
| ❑ 197 | Keyshawn Johnson | 2.50 | 1.00 |
| ❑ 198 | Eddie George | 2.50 | 1.00 |
| ❑ 199 | Steve McNair | 2.50 | 1.00 |
| ❑ 200 | Stephen Davis | 2.50 | 1.00 |
| ❑ 201 | Bobby Brooks RC | 3.00 | 1.25 |
| ❑ 202 | Cornelius Griffin RC | 4.00 | 1.50 |
| ❑ 203 | Danny Clark RC | 4.00 | 1.50 |
| ❑ 204 | Pat Dennis RC | 3.00 | 1.25 |
| ❑ 205 | Tommy Hendricks RC | 5.00 | 2.00 |
| ❑ 206 | Fred Jones RC | 3.00 | 1.25 |
| ❑ 207 | Isaiah Kacyvenski RC | 3.00 | 1.25 |
| ❑ 208 | Keith Miller RC | 3.00 | 1.25 |
| ❑ 209 | Andre O'Neal RC | 3.00 | 1.25 |
| ❑ 210 | Justin Snow RC | 3.00 | 1.25 |
| ❑ 211 | Armegis Spearman RC | 4.00 | 1.50 |
| ❑ 212 | Lester Towns RC | 3.00 | 1.25 |
| ❑ 213 | Antonio Wilson RC | 3.00 | 1.25 |
| ❑ 214 | Greg Wesley RC | 5.00 | 2.00 |
| ❑ 215 | Jabari Issa RC | 3.00 | 1.25 |
| ❑ 216 | Darwin Walker RC | 3.00 | 1.25 |
| ❑ 217 | Reggie Grimes RC | 3.00 | 1.25 |
| ❑ 218 | Rian Lindell RC | 3.00 | 1.25 |
| ❑ 219 | Chris Combs RC | 3.00 | 1.25 |
| ❑ 220 | Rashard Anderson RC | 4.00 | 1.50 |
| ❑ 221 | Erik Flowers RC | 3.00 | 1.25 |
| ❑ 222 | Corey Moore RC | 3.00 | 1.25 |
| ❑ 223 | Rob Meier RC | 3.00 | 1.25 |
| ❑ 224 | John Milem RC | 3.00 | 1.25 |
| ❑ 225 | Jeremiah Parker RC | 3.00 | 1.25 |
| ❑ 226 | Neil Rackers RC | 5.00 | 2.00 |
| ❑ 227 | Josh Taves RC | 4.00 | 1.50 |
| ❑ 228 | Mao Tosi RC | 3.00 | 1.25 |
| ❑ 229 | Gary Berry RC | 3.00 | 1.25 |
| ❑ 230 | Matt Bowen RC | 3.00 | 1.25 |
| ❑ 231 | Ralph Brown RC | 3.00 | 1.25 |
| ❑ 232 | Tony Darden RC | 3.00 | 1.25 |
| ❑ 233 | Arturo Freeman RC | 3.00 | 1.25 |
| ❑ 234 | David Gibson RC | 3.00 | 1.25 |
| ❑ 235 | Demario Brown RC | 3.00 | 1.25 |
| ❑ 236 | Deveron Harper RC | 3.00 | 1.25 |
| ❑ 237 | Johnnie Harris RC | 3.00 | 1.25 |
| ❑ 238 | Marcus Knight RC | 4.00 | 1.50 |
| ❑ 239 | Ronnie Heard RC | 4.00 | 1.50 |
| ❑ 240 | Eric Johnson RC | 4.00 | 1.50 |
| ❑ 241 | John Keith RC | 3.00 | 1.25 |
| ❑ 242 | Anthony Malbrough RC | 3.00 | 1.25 |
| ❑ 243 | Anthony Mitchell RC | 3.00 | 1.25 |
| ❑ 244 | Aric Morris RC | 3.00 | 1.25 |
| ❑ 245 | Bobby Myers RC | 3.00 | 1.25 |
| ❑ 246 | Erik Olson RC | 3.00 | 1.25 |
| ❑ 247 | Lewis Sanders RC | 3.00 | 1.25 |
| ❑ 248 | Tony Scott RC | 3.00 | 1.25 |
| ❑ 249 | David Terrell RC | 5.00 | 2.00 |
| ❑ 250 | Travares Tillman RC | 3.00 | 1.25 |
| ❑ 251 | David Stachelski RC | 4.00 | 1.50 |
| ❑ 252 | Darren Howard RC | 5.00 | 2.00 |
| ❑ 253 | Frank Chamberlin RC | 3.00 | 1.25 |
| ❑ 254 | Na'il Diggs RC | 5.00 | 2.00 |
| ❑ 255 | Orantes Grant RC | 4.00 | 1.50 |
| ❑ 256 | Barrett Green RC | 4.00 | 1.50 |
| ❑ 257 | Kory Minor RC | 4.00 | 1.50 |
| ❑ 258 | Deon Grant RC | 5.00 | 2.00 |
| ❑ 259 | Mark Simoneau RC | 5.00 | 2.00 |
| ❑ 260 | Raynoch Thompson RC | 5.00 | 2.00 |
| ❑ 261 | Kenyatta Wright RC | 4.00 | 1.50 |
| ❑ 262 | Marcus Bell LB RC | 4.00 | 1.50 |
| ❑ 263 | Jack Golden RC | 4.00 | 1.50 |
| ❑ 264 | Thomas Hamner RC | 4.00 | 1.50 |
| ❑ 265 | Sekou Sanyika RC | 4.00 | 1.50 |
| ❑ 266 | Marcus Washington RC | 5.00 | 2.00 |
| ❑ 267 | Tim Seder RC | 5.00 | 2.00 |
| ❑ 268 | Paul Edinger RC | 6.00 | 2.50 |

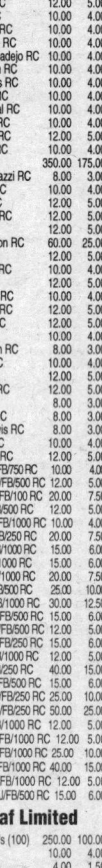

|  |  | | |
|---|---|---|---|
| ❑ 269 | Michael Boireau RC | 4.00 | 1.50 |
| ❑ 270 | Byron Frisch RC | 4.00 | 1.50 |
| ❑ 271 | Ketric Sanford RC | 4.00 | 1.50 |
| ❑ 272 | Frank Murphy RC | 4.00 | 1.50 |
| ❑ 273 | Robaire Smith RC | 4.00 | 1.50 |
| ❑ 274 | Adalius Thomas RC | 15.00 | 6.00 |
| ❑ 275 | William Bartee RC | 5.00 | 2.00 |
| ❑ 276 | Robert Bean RC | 5.00 | 2.00 |
| ❑ 277 | Tyrone Carter RC | 6.00 | 2.50 |
| ❑ 278 | Ike Charlton RC | 4.00 | 1.50 |
| ❑ 279 | Mario Edwards RC | 5.00 | 2.00 |
| ❑ 280 | Dwayne Goodrich RC | 4.00 | 1.50 |
| ❑ 281 | Michael Hawthorne RC | 4.00 | 1.50 |
| ❑ 282 | Kareem Larrimore RC | 4.00 | 1.50 |
| ❑ 283 | Mark Roman RC | 5.00 | 2.00 |
| ❑ 284 | Jacoby Shepherd RC | 4.00 | 1.50 |
| ❑ 285 | Jason Webster RC | 4.00 | 1.50 |
| ❑ 286 | Jimmy Wyrick RC | 4.00 | 1.50 |
| ❑ 287 | Rashidi Barnes RC | 4.00 | 1.50 |
| ❑ 288 | David Barrett RC | 4.00 | 1.50 |
| ❑ 289 | Ainsley Battles RC | 4.00 | 1.50 |
| ❑ 290 | Lamar Chapman RC | 4.00 | 1.50 |
| ❑ 291 | Todd Franz RC | 4.00 | 1.50 |
| ❑ 292 | Michael Green RC | 4.00 | 1.50 |
| ❑ 293 | Antwan Harris RC | 4.00 | 1.50 |
| ❑ 294 | Brandon Jennings RC | 4.00 | 1.50 |
| ❑ 295 | Darrick Vaughn RC | 4.00 | 1.50 |
| ❑ 296 | David Macklin RC | 4.00 | 1.50 |
| ❑ 297 | Bobby Brown RC | 4.00 | 1.50 |
| ❑ 298 | Reggie Stephens RC | 4.00 | 1.50 |
| ❑ 299 | Kevin Kennedy RC | 4.00 | 1.50 |
| ❑ 300 | Raion Hill RC | 4.00 | 1.50 |
| ❑ 301 | Windrell Hayes RC | 8.00 | 3.00 |
| ❑ 302 | DaShon Polk RC | 8.00 | 3.00 |
| ❑ 303 | Tywan Mitchell RC | 8.00 | 3.00 |
| ❑ 304 | Casey Crawford RC | 6.00 | 2.50 |
| ❑ 305 | Hank Poteat RC | 8.00 | 3.00 |
| ❑ 306 | Mondriel Fulcher RC | 6.00 | 2.50 |
| ❑ 307 | Cory Geason RC | 6.00 | 2.50 |
| ❑ 308 | James Hill RC | 6.00 | 2.50 |
| ❑ 309 | Brian Jennings RC | 6.00 | 2.50 |
| ❑ 310 | John Jones RC | 8.00 | 3.00 |
| ❑ 311 | Anthony Lucas RC | 6.00 | 2.50 |
| ❑ 312 | Mike Leach RC | 6.00 | 2.50 |
| ❑ 313 | Dustin Lyman RC | 6.00 | 2.50 |
| ❑ 314 | Derek Rackley RC | 6.00 | 2.50 |
| ❑ 315 | Sebastian Janikowski RC | 10.00 | 4.00 |
| ❑ 316 | Brad St.Louis RC | 6.00 | 2.50 |
| ❑ 317 | Jay Tant RC | 6.00 | 2.50 |
| ❑ 318 | Austin Wheatley RC | 6.00 | 2.50 |
| ❑ 319 | Jermaine Wiggins RC | 10.00 | 4.00 |
| ❑ 320 | Todd Yoder RC | 8.00 | 3.00 |
| ❑ 321 | Deon Dyer RC | 8.00 | 3.00 |
| ❑ 322 | Jim Finn RC | 8.00 | 3.00 |
| ❑ 323 | Herbert Goodman RC | 8.00 | 3.00 |
| ❑ 324 | Mike Green RC | 8.00 | 3.00 |
| ❑ 325 | Dante Hall RC | 15.00 | 6.00 |
| ❑ 326 | Thabiti Davis RC | 6.00 | 2.50 |
| ❑ 327 | Kevin Houser RC | 8.00 | 3.00 |
| ❑ 328 | Jonas Lewis RC | 6.00 | 2.50 |
| ❑ 329 | Chad Morton RC | 10.00 | 4.00 |
| ❑ 330 | Patrick Pass RC | 8.00 | 3.00 |
| ❑ 331 | Maurice Smith RC | 10.00 | 4.00 |
| ❑ 332 | Paul Smith RC | 8.00 | 3.00 |
| ❑ 333 | Terrelle Smith RC | 8.00 | 3.00 |
| ❑ 334 | Craig Walendy RC | 6.00 | 2.50 |
| ❑ 335 | Jamel White RC | 8.00 | 3.00 |
| ❑ 336 | Jarious Jackson RC | 8.00 | 3.00 |
| ❑ 337 | Matt Lytle RC | 8.00 | 3.00 |
| ❑ 338 | Ron Powlus RC | 10.00 | 4.00 |
| ❑ 339 | Ian Gold RC | 8.00 | 3.00 |
| ❑ 340 | Brandon Short RC | 8.00 | 3.00 |
| ❑ 341 | T.J. Slaughter RC | 6.00 | 2.50 |
| ❑ 342 | Nate Webster RC | 6.00 | 2.50 |
| ❑ 343 | John Engelberger RC | 8.00 | 3.00 |
| ❑ 344 | Rogers Beckett RC | 8.00 | 3.00 |
| ❑ 345 | Mike Brown RC | 15.00 | 6.00 |
| ❑ 346 | Anthony Wright RC | 10.00 | 4.00 |
| ❑ 347 | Danny Farmer RC | 8.00 | 3.00 |
| ❑ 348 | Clint Stoerner RC | 8.00 | 3.00 |
| ❑ 349 | Julian Peterson RC | 10.00 | 4.00 |
| ❑ 350 | Ahmed Plummer RC | 8.00 | 3.00 |
| ❑ 351 | Avion Black RC | 10.00 | 4.00 |
| ❑ 352 | Kwame Cavil RC | 8.00 | 3.00 |
| ❑ 353 | Chris Cole RC | 10.00 | 4.00 |
| ❑ 354 | Chris Coleman RC | 8.00 | 3.00 |
| ❑ 355 | Trevor Gaylor RC | 10.00 | 4.00 |
| ❑ 356 | Damon Hodge RC | 10.00 | 4.00 |
| ❑ 357 | Darrell Jackson RC | 25.00 | 10.00 |
| ❑ 358 | Reggie Jones RC | 8.00 | 3.00 |
| ❑ 359 | Charles Lee RC | 8.00 | 3.00 |
| ❑ 360 | Jerry Porter RC | 12.00 | 5.00 |
| ❑ 361 | Bobby Shaw | 10.00 | 4.00 |
| ❑ 362 | Ron Dugans RC | 8.00 | 3.00 |
| ❑ 363 | James Williams RC | 10.00 | 4.00 |
| ❑ 364 | Bashir Yamini RC | 8.00 | 3.00 |
| ❑ 365 | Anthony Becht RC | 12.00 | 5.00 |
| ❑ 366 | Erron Kinney RC | 12.00 | 5.00 |
| ❑ 367 | Aaron Shea RC | 10.00 | 4.00 |
| ❑ 368 | Chris Samuels RC | 10.00 | 4.00 |
| ❑ 369 | Trung Canidate RC | 10.00 | 4.00 |
| ❑ 370 | Obafemi Ayanbadejo RC | 10.00 | 4.00 |
| ❑ 371 | Doug Chapman RC | 10.00 | 4.00 |
| ❑ 372 | Ronney Jenkins RC | 10.00 | 4.00 |
| ❑ 373 | Curtis Keaton RC | 10.00 | 4.00 |
| ❑ 374 | Kevin McDougal RC | 10.00 | 4.00 |
| ❑ 375 | Frank Moreau RC | 10.00 | 4.00 |
| ❑ 376 | Aaron Stecker RC | 12.00 | 5.00 |
| ❑ 377 | Shyrone Stith RC | 10.00 | 4.00 |
| ❑ 378 | Tom Brady RC | 350.00 | 175.00 |
| ❑ 379 | Giovanni Carmazzi RC | 8.00 | 3.00 |
| ❑ 380 | Joe Hamilton RC | 10.00 | 4.00 |
| ❑ 381 | Todd Husak RC | 12.00 | 5.00 |
| ❑ 382 | Doug Johnson RC | 12.00 | 5.00 |
| ❑ 383 | Tee Martin RC | 12.00 | 5.00 |
| ❑ 384 | Chad Pennington RC | 60.00 | 25.00 |
| ❑ 385 | Tim Rattay RC | 12.00 | 5.00 |
| ❑ 386 | Chris Redman RC | 10.00 | 4.00 |
| ❑ 387 | Billy Volek RC | 12.00 | 5.00 |
| ❑ 388 | Spergon Wynn RC | 10.00 | 4.00 |
| ❑ 389 | John Abraham RC | 12.00 | 5.00 |
| ❑ 390 | Keith Bulluck RC | 12.00 | 5.00 |
| ❑ 391 | Rob Morris RC | 10.00 | 4.00 |
| ❑ 392 | JaJuan Dawson RC | 8.00 | 3.00 |
| ❑ 393 | Chris Hovan RC | 10.00 | 4.00 |
| ❑ 394 | Shaun Ellis RC | 12.00 | 5.00 |
| ❑ 395 | Deltha O'Neal RC | 12.00 | 5.00 |
| ❑ 396 | Gari Scott RC | 8.00 | 3.00 |
| ❑ 397 | Dialleo Burks RC | 8.00 | 3.00 |
| ❑ 398 | Shockmain Davis RC | 8.00 | 3.00 |
| ❑ 399 | Brad Hoover RC | 10.00 | 4.00 |
| ❑ 400 | Brian Finneran RC | 12.00 | 5.00 |
| ❑ 401 | Sylvester Morris J/FB/750 RC | 10.00 | 4.00 |
| ❑ 402 | Denn Northcutt J/FB/500 RC | 12.00 | 5.00 |
| ❑ 403 | Todd Pinkston J/FB/100 RC | 20.00 | 7.50 |
| ❑ 404 | Larry Foster J/FB/500 RC | 12.00 | 5.00 |
| ❑ 405 | R.Jay Soward J/FB/1000 RC | 12.00 | 5.00 |
| ❑ 406 | Travis Taylor J/FB/250 RC | 20.00 | 7.50 |
| ❑ 407 | Peter Warrick J/FB/1000 RC | 15.00 | 6.00 |
| ❑ 408 | Dez White J/FB/1000 RC | 15.00 | 6.00 |
| ❑ 409 | Ron Dayne J/FB/1000 RC | 20.00 | 7.50 |
| ❑ 410 | Thomas Jones J/FB/500 RC | 25.00 | 10.00 |
| ❑ 411 | Jamal Lewis J/FB/1000 RC | 30.00 | 12.50 |
| ❑ 412 | Sammy Morris J/FB/500 RC | 15.00 | 6.00 |
| ❑ 413 | Travis Prentice J/FB/500 RC | 12.00 | 5.00 |
| ❑ 414 | J.R. Redmond J/FB/250 RC | 15.00 | 6.00 |
| ❑ 415 | Michael Wiley FB/1000 RC | 12.00 | 5.00 |
| ❑ 416 | Laver Coles J/FB/250 RC | 40.00 | 15.00 |
| ❑ 417 | Bubba Franks J/FB/500 RC | 15.00 | 6.00 |
| ❑ 418 | Mike Anderson J/FB/250 RC | 25.00 | 10.00 |
| ❑ 419 | Plaxico Burress J/FB/250 RC | 50.00 | 25.00 |
| ❑ 420 | Ron Dixon J/FB/1000 RC | 15.00 | 6.00 |
| ❑ 421 | Troy Walters J/FB/1000 RC | 12.00 | 5.00 |
| ❑ 422 | Sha Alexander J/FB/1000 RC | 25.00 | 10.00 |
| ❑ 423 | Brian Urlacher J/FB/1000 RC | 40.00 | 15.00 |
| ❑ 424 | Corey Simon J/FB/1000 RC | 12.00 | 5.00 |
| ❑ 425 | Courtney Brown J/FB/500 RC | 15.00 | 6.00 |

## 2003 Leaf Limited

|  |  | | |
|---|---|---|---|
| ❑ | COMP.SET w/o SP's (100) | 250.00 | 100.00 |
| ❑ 1 | Emmitt Smith | 10.00 | 4.00 |
| ❑ 2 | Michael Vick | 4.00 | 1.50 |
| ❑ 3 | Peerless Price | 2.50 | 1.00 |
| ❑ 4 | T.J. Duckett | 3.00 | 1.25 |
| ❑ 5 | Jamal Lewis | 4.00 | 1.50 |
| ❑ 6 | Drew Bledsoe | 4.00 | 1.50 |
| ❑ 7 | Eric Moulds | 3.00 | 1.25 |
| ❑ 8 | Travis Henry | 4.00 | 1.50 |
| ❑ 9 | Jim Kelly | 5.00 | 2.00 |
| ❑ 10 | Julius Peppers | 4.00 | 1.50 |
| ❑ 11 | Dick Butkus | 6.00 | 2.50 |
| ❑ 12 | Mike Singletary | 4.00 | 1.50 |
| ❑ 13 | Walter Payton | 12.00 | 5.00 |
| ❑ 14 | Anthony Thomas | 3.00 | 1.25 |
| ❑ 15 | Brian Urlacher | 6.00 | 2.50 |
| ❑ 16 | Marty Booker | 3.00 | 1.25 |
| ❑ 17 | Corey Dillon | 3.00 | 1.25 |
| ❑ 18 | Jim Thorpe | 5.00 | 2.00 |
| ❑ 19 | Jim Brown | 6.00 | 2.50 |
| ❑ 20 | Tim Couch | 2.50 | 1.00 |
| ❑ 21 | William Green | 2.50 | 1.00 |
| ❑ 22 | Deion Sanders | 4.00 | 1.50 |
| ❑ 23 | Michael Irvin | 4.00 | 1.50 |
| ❑ 24 | Roger Staubach | 6.00 | 2.50 |
| ❑ 25 | Troy Aikman | 5.00 | 2.00 |
| ❑ 26 | Tony Dorsett | 4.00 | 1.50 |
| ❑ 27 | Antonio Bryant | 4.00 | 1.50 |
| ❑ 28 | Clinton Portis | 5.00 | 2.00 |
| ❑ 29 | Jake Plummer | 3.00 | 1.25 |
| ❑ 30 | Rod Smith | 3.00 | 1.25 |
| ❑ 31 | Barry Sanders | 10.00 | 4.00 |
| ❑ 32 | Doak Walker | 4.00 | 1.50 |
| ❑ 33 | Joey Harrington | 4.00 | 1.50 |
| ❑ 34 | Bart Starr | 6.00 | 2.50 |
| ❑ 35 | Ahman Green | 4.00 | 1.50 |
| ❑ 36 | Brett Favre | 10.00 | 4.00 |
| ❑ 37 | Donald Driver | 4.00 | 1.50 |
| ❑ 38 | David Carr | 4.00 | 1.50 |
| ❑ 39 | Don Shula | 4.00 | 1.50 |
| ❑ 40 | Johnny Unitas | 8.00 | 3.00 |
| ❑ 41 | Edgerrin James | 4.00 | 1.50 |
| ❑ 42 | Marvin Harrison | 4.00 | 1.50 |
| ❑ 43 | Peyton Manning | 8.00 | 3.00 |
| ❑ 44 | Fred Taylor | 4.00 | 1.50 |
| ❑ 45 | Jimmy Smith | 3.00 | 1.25 |
| ❑ 46 | Mark Brunell | 3.00 | 1.25 |
| ❑ 47 | Marcus Allen | 4.00 | 1.50 |
| ❑ 48 | Priest Holmes | 4.00 | 1.50 |
| ❑ 49 | Tony Gonzalez | 3.00 | 1.25 |
| ❑ 50 | Trent Green | 3.00 | 1.25 |
| ❑ 51 | Dan Marino | 12.00 | 5.00 |
| ❑ 52 | Bob Griese | 4.00 | 1.50 |
| ❑ 53 | Chris Chambers | 3.00 | 1.25 |
| ❑ 54 | Ricky Williams | 3.00 | 1.25 |
| ❑ 55 | Fran Tarkenton | 4.00 | 1.50 |
| ❑ 56 | Daunte Culpepper | 4.00 | 1.50 |
| ❑ 57 | Michael Bennett | 3.00 | 1.25 |
| ❑ 58 | Randy Moss | 5.00 | 2.00 |
| ❑ 59 | Tom Brady | 10.00 | 4.00 |
| ❑ 60 | Aaron Brooks | 3.00 | 1.25 |
| ❑ 61 | Deuce McAllister | 4.00 | 1.50 |
| ❑ 62 | Donte Stallworth | 3.00 | 1.25 |
| ❑ 63 | Mark Bavaro | 3.00 | 1.25 |
| ❑ 64 | Jeremy Shockey | 4.00 | 1.50 |
| ❑ 65 | Kerry Collins | 3.00 | 1.25 |
| ❑ 66 | Tiki Barber | 4.00 | 1.50 |
| ❑ 67 | Joe Namath | 6.00 | 2.50 |
| ❑ 68 | Chad Pennington | 4.00 | 1.50 |
| ❑ 69 | Curtis Martin | 4.00 | 1.50 |
| ❑ 70 | Jerry Porter | 3.00 | 1.25 |
| ❑ 71 | Jerry Rice | 8.00 | 3.00 |
| ❑ 72 | Rich Gannon | 3.00 | 1.25 |
| ❑ 73 | Tim Brown | 4.00 | 1.50 |
| ❑ 74 | Donovan McNabb | 5.00 | 2.00 |
| ❑ 75 | Terry Bradshaw | 6.00 | 2.50 |
| ❑ 76 | Antwaan Randle El | 3.00 | 1.25 |
| ❑ 77 | Plaxico Burress | 3.00 | 1.25 |
| ❑ 78 | Tommy Maddox | 3.00 | 1.25 |
| ❑ 79 | David Boston | 2.50 | 1.00 |
| ❑ 80 | Drew Brees | 4.00 | 1.50 |
| ❑ 81 | LaDainian Tomlinson | 6.00 | 2.50 |
| ❑ 82 | Joe Montana | 12.00 | 5.00 |
| ❑ 83 | Steve Young | 5.00 | 2.00 |
| ❑ 84 | Jeff Garcia | 4.00 | 1.50 |
| ❑ 85 | Terrell Owens | 4.00 | 1.50 |
| ❑ 86 | Koren Robinson | 3.00 | 1.25 |

|  |  | | |
|---|---|---|---|
| 87 | Matt Hasselbeck | 3.00 | 1.25 |
| 88 | Shaun Alexander | 4.00 | 1.50 |
| 89 | Isaac Bruce | 4.00 | 1.50 |
| 90 | Kurt Warner | 4.00 | 1.50 |
| 91 | Marshall Faulk | 4.00 | 1.50 |
| 92 | Torry Holt | 4.00 | 1.50 |
| 93 | Brad Johnson | 3.00 | 1.25 |
| 94 | Keyshawn Johnson | 4.00 | 1.50 |
| 95 | Earl Campbell | 4.00 | 1.50 |
| 96 | Eddie George | 3.00 | 1.25 |
| 97 | Steve McNair | 4.00 | 1.50 |
| 98 | John Riggins | 4.00 | 1.50 |
| 99 | Laveranues Coles | 3.00 | 1.25 |
| 100 | Patrick Ramsey | 3.00 | 1.25 |
| 101 | LaTarce Dunbar RC | 4.00 | 1.50 |
| 102 | Sam Aiken RC | 5.00 | 2.00 |
| 103 | Bobby Wade RC | 5.00 | 2.00 |
| 104 | Justin Gage RC | 5.00 | 2.00 |
| 105 | Lee Suggs RC | 5.00 | 2.00 |
| 106 | Jason Witten RC | 12.00 | 5.00 |
| 107 | Quentin Griffin RC | 5.00 | 2.00 |
| 108 | Domanick Davis RC | 6.00 | 2.50 |
| 109 | LaBrandon Toefield RC | 5.00 | 2.00 |
| 110 | J.R. Tolver RC | 5.00 | 2.00 |
| 111 | Kliff Kingsbury RC | 5.00 | 2.00 |
| 112 | Talman Gardner RC | 4.00 | 1.50 |
| 113 | Teyo Johnson RC | 5.00 | 2.00 |
| 114 | Billy McMullen RC | 4.00 | 1.50 |
| 115 | L.J. Smith RC | 6.00 | 2.50 |
| 116 | Brian St-Pierre RC | 6.00 | 2.50 |
| 117 | Brandon Lloyd RC | 6.00 | 2.50 |
| 118 | Seneca Wallace RC | 6.00 | 2.50 |
| 119 | Kevin Curtis RC | 8.00 | 3.00 |
| 120 | Shaun McDonald RC | 6.00 | 2.50 |
| 121 | Terrell Suggs RC | 8.00 | 3.00 |
| 122 | Terence Newman RC | 8.00 | 3.00 |
| 123 | Tony Romo RC | 50.00 | 25.00 |
| 124 | DeWayne Robertson RC | 5.00 | 2.00 |
| 125 | Marcus Trufant RC | 6.00 | 2.50 |
| 126 | Artose Pinner RC | 15.00 | 6.00 |
| 127 | Bryant Johnson AU RC | 25.00 | 10.00 |
| 128 | Kelley Washington AU RC | 20.00 | 8.00 |
| 129 | Dallas Clark AU RC | 30.00 | 12.00 |
| 130 | Onterrio Smith AU RC | 20.00 | 8.00 |
| 131 | Tony Hollings AU RC | 20.00 | 8.00 |
| 132 | Tyrone Calico AU RC | 20.00 | 8.00 |
| 133 | Carson Palmer AU RC | 120.00 | 60.00 |
| 134 | Byron Leftwich AU RC | 40.00 | 15.00 |
| 135 | Rex Grossman AU RC | 60.00 | 25.00 |
| 136 | Kyle Boller AU RC | 25.00 | 10.00 |
| 137 | Chris Simms AU RC | 25.00 | 10.00 |
| 138 | Dave Ragone AU RC | 15.00 | 6.00 |
| 139 | Ken Dorsey AU RC | 20.00 | 8.00 |
| 140 | Willis McGahee AU RC | 60.00 | 25.00 |
| 141 | Larry Johnson AU RC | 60.00 | 25.00 |
| 142 | Musa Smith AU RC | 20.00 | 8.00 |
| 143 | Chris Brown AU RC | 25.00 | 10.00 |
| 144 | Charles Rogers AU RC | 20.00 | 8.00 |
| 145 | Andre Johnson AU RC | 60.00 | 30.00 |
| 146 | Taylor Jacobs AU RC | 20.00 | 8.00 |
| 147 | Anquan Boldin AU RC | 80.00 | 40.00 |
| 148 | Bethel Johnson AU RC | 20.00 | 8.00 |
| 149 | Justin Fargas AU RC | 25.00 | 10.00 |
| 150 | Nate Burleson AU RC | 20.00 | 8.00 |

## 2004 Leaf Limited

201-233 JSY AU PRINT RUN 150 SETS

|  |  | | |
|---|---|---|---|
| 1 | A.J. Feeley | 3.00 | 1.25 |
| 2 | Aaron Brooks | 3.00 | 1.25 |
| 3 | Ahman Green | 4.00 | 1.50 |
| 4 | Andre Johnson | 4.00 | 1.50 |
| 5 | Anquan Boldin | 4.00 | 1.50 |
| 6 | Antwaan Randle El | 3.00 | 1.25 |
| 7 | Ashley Lelie | 3.00 | 1.25 |
| 8 | Brad Johnson | 3.00 | 1.25 |
| 9 | Brett Favre | 10.00 | 4.00 |
| 10 | Brian Urlacher | 4.00 | 1.50 |
| 11 | Brian Westbrook | 4.00 | 1.50 |
| 12 | Byron Leftwich | 4.00 | 1.50 |
| 13 | Carson Palmer | 5.00 | 2.00 |
| 14 | Chad Johnson | 4.00 | 1.50 |
| 15 | Chad Pennington | 4.00 | 1.50 |
| 16 | Charlie Garner | 3.00 | 1.25 |
| 17 | Charles Rogers | 3.00 | 1.25 |
| 18 | Chris Brown | 4.00 | 1.50 |
| 19 | Chris Chambers | 3.00 | 1.25 |
| 20 | Clinton Portis | 4.00 | 1.50 |
| 21 | Corey Dillon | 4.00 | 1.50 |
| 22 | Deion Sanders | 4.00 | 1.50 |
| 23 | Curtis Martin | 4.00 | 1.50 |
| 24 | Daunte Culpepper | 4.00 | 1.50 |
| 25 | David Terrell | 2.50 | 1.00 |
| 26 | David Carr | 4.00 | 1.50 |
| 27 | Deion Branch | 3.00 | 1.25 |
| 28 | Derrick Mason | 3.00 | 1.25 |
| 29 | DeShaun Foster | 4.00 | 1.50 |
| 30 | Deuce McAllister | 4.00 | 1.50 |
| 31 | Domanick Davis | 4.00 | 1.50 |
| 32 | Donovan McNabb | 4.00 | 1.50 |
| 33 | Donte Stallworth | 3.00 | 1.25 |
| 34 | Drew Bledsoe | 4.00 | 1.50 |
| 35 | Duce Staley | 4.00 | 1.50 |
| 36 | Eddie George | 4.00 | 1.50 |
| 37 | Edgerrin James | 4.00 | 1.50 |
| 38 | Emmitt Smith | 10.00 | 4.00 |
| 39 | Eric Moulds | 3.00 | 1.25 |
| 40 | Fred Taylor | 4.00 | 1.50 |
| 41 | Hines Ward | 4.00 | 1.50 |
| 42 | Isaac Bruce | 3.00 | 1.25 |
| 43 | Jake Delhomme | 3.00 | 1.25 |
| 44 | Jake Plummer | 4.00 | 1.50 |
| 45 | Javon Walker | 3.00 | 1.25 |
| 46 | Jeff Garcia | 4.00 | 1.50 |
| 47 | Jeremy Shockey | 3.00 | 1.25 |
| 48 | Jerome Bettis | 4.00 | 1.50 |
| 49 | Jerry Porter | 3.00 | 1.25 |
| 50 | Jerry Rice | 8.00 | 3.00 |
| 51 | Jevon Kearse | 3.00 | 1.25 |
| 52 | Jimmy Smith | 3.00 | 1.25 |
| 53 | Joe Horn | 3.00 | 1.25 |
| 54 | Joey Harrington | 4.00 | 1.50 |
| 55 | Josh McCown | 3.00 | 1.25 |
| 56 | Kevan Barlow | 3.00 | 1.25 |
| 57 | Koren Robinson | 4.00 | 1.50 |
| 58 | Kyle Boller | 4.00 | 1.50 |
| 59 | LaDainian Tomlinson | 6.00 | 2.50 |
| 60 | LaVar Arrington | 3.00 | 1.25 |
| 61 | Laveranues Coles | 4.00 | 1.50 |
| 62 | Lee Suggs | 4.00 | 1.50 |
| 63 | Marc Bulger | 3.00 | 1.25 |
| 64 | Mark Brunell | 4.00 | 1.50 |
| 65 | Marshall Faulk | 4.00 | 1.50 |
| 66 | Marvin Harrison | 4.00 | 1.50 |
| 67 | Matt Hasselbeck | 3.00 | 1.25 |
| 68 | Michael Bennett | 3.00 | 1.25 |
| 69 | Michael Strahan | 3.00 | 1.25 |
| 70 | Michael Vick | 4.00 | 1.50 |
| 71 | Peerless Price | 3.00 | 1.25 |
| 72 | Peter Warrick | 3.00 | 1.25 |
| 73 | Peyton Manning | 8.00 | 3.00 |
| 74 | Priest Holmes | 4.00 | 1.50 |
| 75 | Quentin Griffin | 5.00 | 2.00 |
| 76 | Randy Moss | 4.00 | 1.50 |
| 77 | Ray Lewis | 4.00 | 1.50 |
| 78 | Rex Grossman | 2.50 | 1.00 |
| 79 | Lamar Gordon | 3.00 | 1.25 |
| 80 | Rod Smith | 3.00 | 1.25 |
| 81 | Roy Williams S | 3.00 | 1.25 |
| 82 | Rudi Johnson | 4.00 | 1.50 |
| 83 | Santana Moss | 3.00 | 1.25 |
| 84 | Shaun Alexander | 4.00 | 1.50 |
| 85 | Stephen Davis | 3.00 | 1.25 |
| 86 | Steve McNair | 4.00 | 1.50 |
| 87 | Steve Smith | 4.00 | 1.50 |
| 88 | T.J. Duckett | 3.00 | 1.25 |
| 89 | Terrell Owens | 4.00 | 1.50 |
| 90 | Thomas Jones | 3.00 | 1.25 |
| 91 | Tiki Barber | 4.00 | 1.50 |
| 92 | Tim Brown | 4.00 | 1.50 |
| 93 | Tom Brady | 10.00 | 4.00 |
| 94 | Tony Gonzalez | 4.00 | 1.50 |
| 95 | Torry Holt | 4.00 | 1.50 |
| 96 | Travis Henry | 3.00 | 1.25 |
| 97 | Trent Green | 3.00 | 1.25 |
| 98 | Warren Sapp | 3.00 | 1.25 |
| 99 | William Green | 2.50 | 1.00 |
| 100 | Willis McGahee | 4.00 | 1.50 |
| 101 | Barry Sanders | 12.00 | 5.00 |
| 102 | Bart Starr | 12.00 | 5.00 |
| 103 | Bo Jackson | 8.00 | 3.00 |
| 104 | Bob Griese | 5.00 | 2.00 |
| 105 | Bronko Nagurski | 5.00 | 2.00 |
| 106 | Dan Marino | 15.00 | 6.00 |
| 107 | Deion Sanders | 5.00 | 2.00 |
| 108 | Dick Butkus | 8.00 | 3.00 |
| 109 | Doak Walker | 5.00 | 2.00 |
| 110 | Don Maynard | 4.00 | 1.50 |
| 111 | Don Shula | 5.00 | 2.00 |
| 112 | Earl Campbell | 5.00 | 2.00 |
| 113 | Fran Tarkenton | 5.00 | 2.00 |
| 114 | Franco Harris | 6.00 | 2.50 |
| 115 | Fred Biletnikoff | 5.00 | 2.00 |
| 116 | Gale Sayers | 6.00 | 2.50 |
| 117 | Herman Edwards | 4.00 | 1.50 |
| 118 | Jim Brown | 8.00 | 3.00 |
| 119 | Jim Kelly | 5.00 | 2.00 |
| 120 | Jim Thorpe | 5.00 | 2.00 |
| 121 | Jimmy Johnson | 4.00 | 1.50 |
| 122 | Joe Greene | 5.00 | 2.00 |
| 123 | Joe Montana | 15.00 | 6.00 |
| 124 | Joe Namath | 10.00 | 4.00 |
| 125 | John Elway | 12.00 | 5.00 |
| 126 | John Riggins | 6.00 | 2.50 |
| 127 | Johnny Unitas | 12.00 | 5.00 |
| 128 | Larry Csonka | 5.00 | 2.00 |
| 129 | Lawrence Taylor | 6.00 | 2.50 |
| 130 | Marcus Allen | 5.00 | 2.00 |
| 131 | Mark Bavaro | 3.00 | 1.25 |
| 132 | Michael Irvin | 5.00 | 2.00 |
| 133 | Mike Ditka | 5.00 | 2.00 |
| 134 | Mike Singletary | 5.00 | 2.00 |
| 135 | Ozzie Newsome | 4.00 | 1.50 |
| 136 | Paul Warfield | 4.00 | 1.50 |
| 137 | Randall Cunningham | 4.00 | 1.50 |
| 138 | Ray Nitschke | 5.00 | 2.00 |
| 139 | Reggie White | 5.00 | 2.00 |
| 140 | Reggie White | 5.00 | 2.00 |
| 141 | Roger Staubach | 8.00 | 3.00 |
| 142 | Sterling Sharpe | 4.00 | 1.50 |
| 143 | Steve Largent | 5.00 | 2.00 |
| 144 | Terrell Davis | 5.00 | 2.00 |
| 145 | Terry Bradshaw | 10.00 | 4.00 |
| 146 | Thurman Thomas | 4.00 | 1.50 |
| 147 | Tony Dorsett | 5.00 | 2.00 |
| 148 | Troy Aikman | 8.00 | 3.00 |
| 149 | Walter Payton | 20.00 | 8.00 |
| 150 | Warren Moon | 4.00 | 1.50 |
| 151 | Ahmad Carroll RC | 10.00 | 4.00 |
| 152 | Andy Hall RC | 8.00 | 3.00 |
| 153 | Antwan Odom RC | 8.00 | 3.00 |
| 154 | B.J. Symons RC | 6.00 | 2.50 |
| 155 | Carlos Francis RC | 6.00 | 2.50 |
| 156 | Casey Bramlet RC | 6.00 | 2.50 |
| 157 | Chris Cooley RC | 10.00 | 4.00 |
| 158 | Chris Gamble RC | 8.00 | 3.00 |
| 159 | Clarence Moore RC | 8.00 | 3.00 |
| 160 | Cody Pickett RC | 8.00 | 3.00 |
| 161 | Courtney Watson RC | 8.00 | 3.00 |
| 162 | Craig Krenzel RC | 10.00 | 4.00 |
| 163 | D.J. Hackett RC | 10.00 | 4.00 |
| 164 | D.J. Williams RC | 10.00 | 4.00 |
| 165 | Derrick Strait RC | 8.00 | 3.00 |
| 166 | Dontarrious Thomas RC | 8.00 | 3.00 |
| 167 | Drew Henson RC | 6.00 | 2.50 |
| 168 | Ernest Wilford RC | 10.00 | 4.00 |
| 169 | Jamaar Taylor RC | 6.00 | 2.50 |
| 170 | Jason Babin RC | 8.00 | 3.00 |
| 171 | Jeff Smoker RC | 8.00 | 3.00 |
| 172 | Jerricho Cotchery RC | 10.00 | 4.00 |
| 173 | Jim Sorgi RC | 10.00 | 4.00 |
| 174 | Joey Thomas RC | 6.00 | 2.50 |
| 175 | John Navarre RC | 8.00 | 3.00 |
| 176 | Johnnie Morant RC | 8.00 | 3.00 |
| 177 | Jonathan Vilma RC | 10.00 | 4.00 |
| 178 | Josh Harris RC | 6.00 | 2.50 |
| 179 | Keiwan Ratliff RC | 6.00 | 2.50 |
| 180 | Kenechi Udeze RC | 10.00 | 4.00 |
| 181 | Kris Wilson RC | 8.00 | 3.00 |
| 182 | Marcus Tubbs RC | 6.00 | 2.50 |
| 183 | Marquise Hill RC | 6.00 | 2.50 |

| | | |
|---|---|---|
| ❏ 184 Matt Mauck RC | 8.00 | 3.00 |
| ❏ 185 Maurice Mann RC | 6.00 | 2.50 |
| ❏ 186 Michael Boulware RC | 10.00 | 4.00 |
| ❏ 187 Michael Turner RC | 20.00 | 8.00 |
| ❏ 188 P.K. Sam RC | 6.00 | 2.50 |
| ❏ 189 Patrick Crayton RC | 12.00 | 5.00 |
| ❏ 190 Ricardo Colclough RC | 10.00 | 4.00 |
| ❏ 191 Richard Smith RC | 6.00 | 2.50 |
| ❏ 192 Samie Parker RC | 10.00 | 4.00 |
| ❏ 193 Sean Taylor RC | 10.00 | 4.00 |
| ❏ 194 Teddy Lehman RC | 6.00 | 2.50 |
| ❏ 195 Thomas Tapeh RC | 8.00 | 3.00 |
| ❏ 196 Tommie Harris RC | 10.00 | 4.00 |
| ❏ 197 Triandos Luke RC | 6.00 | 2.50 |
| ❏ 198 Troy Fleming RC | 6.00 | 2.50 |
| ❏ 199 Vince Wilfork RC | 10.00 | 4.00 |
| ❏ 200 Will Smith RC | 8.00 | 3.00 |
| ❏ 201 Larry Fitzgerald JSY AU RC | 100.00 | 60.00 |
| ❏ 203 Matt Schaub JSY AU RC | 100.00 | 40.00 |
| ❏ 204 Michael Jenkins JSY AU RC | 30.00 | 12.50 |
| ❏ 205 Devard Darling JSY AU RC | 30.00 | 12.50 |
| ❏ 206 J.P. Losman JSY AU RC | 50.00 | 25.00 |
| ❏ 207 Lee Evans JSY AU RC | 40.00 | 20.00 |
| ❏ 208 Keary Colbert JSY AU RC | 30.00 | 12.50 |
| ❏ 209 Bernard Berrian JSY AU RC | 30.00 | 20.00 |
| ❏ 211 K.Winslow JSY AU RC | 60.00 | 30.00 |
| ❏ 212 Luke McCown JSY AU RC | 30.00 | 12.50 |
| ❏ 213 Julius Jones JSY AU RC | 100.00 | 40.00 |
| ❏ 214 Darius Watts JSY AU RC | 30.00 | 12.50 |
| ❏ 215 Tatum Bell JSY AU RC | 30.00 | 12.50 |
| ❏ 216 Kevin Jones JSY AU RC | 40.00 | 15.00 |
| ❏ 217 Roy Will.WR JSY AU RC | 100.00 | 50.00 |
| ❏ 218 Dunta Robinson JSY AU RC | 30.00 | 12.50 |
| ❏ 219 Greg Jones JSY AU RC | 30.00 | 12.50 |
| ❏ 220 Reggie Williams JSY AU RC | 30.00 | 12.00 |
| ❏ 221 Mewelde Moore JSY AU RC | 30.00 | 12.50 |
| ❏ 222 Ben Watson JSY AU RC | 30.00 | 12.50 |
| ❏ 223 Cedric Cobbs JSY AU RC | 30.00 | 12.50 |
| ❏ 224 Devery Henderson JSY AU RC | 30.00 | 12.50 |
| ❏ 225 Eli Manning JSY AU RC | 175.00 | 100.00 |
| ❏ 226 Robert Gallery JSY AU RC | 30.00 | 12.50 |
| ❏ 227 Roethlisberger JSY AU RC | 200.00 | 125.00 |
| ❏ 228 Philip Rivers JSY AU RC | 120.00 | 60.00 |
| ❏ 229 Derrick Hamilton JSY AU RC | 30.00 | 12.50 |
| ❏ 230 Rashaun Woods JSY AU RC | 30.00 | 12.50 |
| ❏ 231 Stev.Jackson JSY AU RC | 100.00 | 50.00 |
| ❏ 233 Ben Troupe JSY AU RC | 30.00 | 12.50 |

## 2005 Leaf Limited

❏ 1-150 PRINT RUN 599 SER.#'d SETS
❏ 151-200 ROOKIE PRINT RUN 250
❏ 201-229 JSY AU PRINT RUN 100 SETS
❏ UNPRICED PLATINUM SER.#'d TO 1

| | | |
|---|---|---|
| ❏ 1 Anquan Boldin | 3.00 | 1.25 |
| ❏ 2 Kurt Warner | 4.00 | 1.50 |
| ❏ 3 Larry Fitzgerald | 4.00 | 1.50 |
| ❏ 4 Alge Crumpler | 3.00 | 1.25 |
| ❏ 5 Michael Vick | 4.00 | 1.50 |
| ❏ 6 Warrick Dunn | 3.00 | 1.25 |
| ❏ 7 Jamal Lewis | 3.00 | 1.25 |
| ❏ 8 Kyle Boller | 3.00 | 1.25 |
| ❏ 9 Ray Lewis | 4.00 | 1.50 |
| ❏ 10 Derrick Mason | 3.00 | 1.25 |
| ❏ 11 J.P. Losman | 4.00 | 1.50 |
| ❏ 12 Lee Evans | 4.00 | 1.50 |
| ❏ 13 Willis McGahee | 4.00 | 1.50 |
| ❏ 14 DeShaun Foster | 3.00 | 1.25 |
| ❏ 15 Jake Delhomme | 4.00 | 1.50 |
| ❏ 16 Steve Smith | 4.00 | 1.50 |
| ❏ 17 Brian Urlacher | 4.00 | 1.50 |
| ❏ 18 Rex Grossman | 4.00 | 1.50 |
| ❏ 19 Muhsin Muhammad | 3.00 | 1.25 |
| ❏ 20 Carson Palmer | 4.00 | 1.50 |
| ❏ 21 Chad Johnson | 3.00 | 1.25 |
| ❏ 22 Rudi Johnson | 3.00 | 1.25 |
| ❏ 23 Antonio Bryant | 2.50 | 1.00 |
| ❏ 24 Lee Suggs | 3.00 | 1.25 |
| ❏ 25 Trent Dilfer | 3.00 | 1.25 |
| ❏ 26 Drew Bledsoe | 4.00 | 1.50 |
| ❏ 27 Julius Jones | 4.00 | 1.50 |
| ❏ 28 Keyshawn Johnson | 3.00 | 1.25 |
| ❏ 29 Roy Williams S | 3.00 | 1.25 |
| ❏ 30 Ashley Lelie | 2.50 | 1.00 |
| ❏ 31 Jake Plummer | 3.00 | 1.25 |
| ❏ 32 Tatum Bell | 3.00 | 1.25 |
| ❏ 33 Rod Smith | 3.00 | 1.25 |
| ❏ 34 Joey Harrington | 4.00 | 1.50 |
| ❏ 35 Kevin Jones | 3.00 | 1.25 |
| ❏ 36 Roy Williams WR | 4.00 | 1.50 |
| ❏ 37 Ahman Green | 4.00 | 1.50 |
| ❏ 38 Brett Favre | 10.00 | 4.00 |
| ❏ 39 Javon Walker | 3.00 | 1.25 |
| ❏ 40 Andre Johnson | 3.00 | 1.25 |
| ❏ 41 David Carr | 3.00 | 1.25 |
| ❏ 42 Domanick Davis | 2.50 | 1.00 |
| ❏ 43 Edgerrin James | 3.00 | 1.25 |
| ❏ 44 Marvin Harrison | 4.00 | 1.50 |
| ❏ 45 Peyton Manning | 6.00 | 2.50 |
| ❏ 46 Reggie Wayne | 3.00 | 1.25 |
| ❏ 47 Byron Leftwich | 3.00 | 1.25 |
| ❏ 48 Fred Taylor | 4.00 | 1.50 |
| ❏ 49 Jimmy Smith | 3.00 | 1.25 |
| ❏ 50 Priest Holmes | 4.00 | 1.50 |
| ❏ 51 Tony Gonzalez | 3.00 | 1.25 |
| ❏ 52 Trent Green | 3.00 | 1.25 |
| ❏ 53 Chris Chambers | 3.00 | 1.25 |
| ❏ 54 Ricky Williams | 3.00 | 1.25 |
| ❏ 55 Daunte Culpepper | 4.00 | 1.50 |
| ❏ 56 Nate Burleson | 3.00 | 1.25 |
| ❏ 57 Michael Bennett | 3.00 | 1.25 |
| ❏ 58 Corey Dillon | 3.00 | 1.25 |
| ❏ 59 Deion Branch | 3.00 | 1.25 |
| ❏ 60 Tom Brady | 8.00 | 3.00 |
| ❏ 61 Aaron Brooks | 2.50 | 1.00 |
| ❏ 62 Deuce McAllister | 3.00 | 1.25 |
| ❏ 63 Joe Horn | 3.00 | 1.25 |
| ❏ 64 Eli Manning | 8.00 | 3.00 |
| ❏ 65 Jeremy Shockey | 3.00 | 1.25 |
| ❏ 66 Plaxico Burress | 3.00 | 1.25 |
| ❏ 67 Tiki Barber | 4.00 | 1.50 |
| ❏ 68 Chad Pennington | 4.00 | 1.50 |
| ❏ 69 Curtis Martin | 4.00 | 1.50 |
| ❏ 70 Laveranues Coles | 3.00 | 1.25 |
| ❏ 71 Kerry Collins | 3.00 | 1.25 |
| ❏ 72 LaMont Jordan | 3.00 | 1.25 |
| ❏ 73 Randy Moss | 4.00 | 1.50 |
| ❏ 74 Brian Westbrook | 4.00 | 1.50 |
| ❏ 75 Donovan McNabb | 4.00 | 1.50 |
| ❏ 76 Terrell Owens | 4.00 | 1.50 |
| ❏ 77 Ben Roethlisberger | 10.00 | 4.00 |
| ❏ 78 Duce Staley | 3.00 | 1.25 |
| ❏ 79 Hines Ward | 4.00 | 1.50 |
| ❏ 80 Jerome Bettis | 4.00 | 1.50 |
| ❏ 81 Antonio Gates | 4.00 | 1.50 |
| ❏ 82 Drew Brees | 4.00 | 1.50 |
| ❏ 83 LaDainian Tomlinson | 6.00 | 2.50 |
| ❏ 84 Brandon Lloyd | 2.50 | 1.00 |
| ❏ 85 Kevan Barlow | 2.50 | 1.00 |
| ❏ 86 Darrell Jackson | 3.00 | 1.25 |
| ❏ 87 Matt Hasselbeck | 3.00 | 1.25 |
| ❏ 88 Shaun Alexander | 4.00 | 1.50 |
| ❏ 89 Marc Bulger | 3.00 | 1.25 |
| ❏ 90 Steven Jackson | 5.00 | 2.00 |
| ❏ 91 Torry Holt | 4.00 | 1.50 |
| ❏ 92 Brian Griese | 3.00 | 1.25 |
| ❏ 93 Michael Clayton | 3.00 | 1.25 |
| ❏ 94 Chris Brown | 3.00 | 1.25 |
| ❏ 95 Drew Bennett | 3.00 | 1.25 |
| ❏ 96 Steve McNair | 4.00 | 1.50 |
| ❏ 97 Clinton Portis | 4.00 | 1.50 |
| ❏ 98 LaVar Arrington | 3.00 | 1.25 |
| ❏ 99 Patrick Ramsey | 3.00 | 1.25 |
| ❏ 100 Santana Moss | 3.00 | 1.25 |
| ❏ 101 Barry Sanders | 8.00 | 3.00 |
| ❏ 102 Bart Starr | 8.00 | 3.00 |
| ❏ 103 Bo Jackson | 6.00 | 2.50 |
| ❏ 104 Brian Piccolo | 8.00 | 3.00 |
| ❏ 105 Bob Griese | 5.00 | 2.00 |
| ❏ 106 Dan Fouts | 5.00 | 2.00 |
| ❏ 107 Dan Marino | 12.00 | 5.00 |
| ❏ 108 Deacon Jones | 4.00 | 1.50 |
| ❏ 109 Doak Walker | 5.00 | 2.00 |
| ❏ 110 Don Maynard | 4.00 | 1.50 |
| ❏ 111 Don Meredith | 5.00 | 2.00 |
| ❏ 112 Don Shula | 4.00 | 1.50 |
| ❏ 113 Earl Campbell | 5.00 | 2.00 |
| ❏ 114 Eric Dickerson | 4.00 | 1.50 |
| ❏ 115 Fran Tarkenton | 5.00 | 2.00 |
| ❏ 116 Franco Harris | 5.00 | 2.00 |
| ❏ 117 Gale Sayers | 6.00 | 2.50 |
| ❏ 118 Jack Lambert | 5.00 | 2.00 |
| ❏ 119 James Lofton | 3.00 | 1.25 |
| ❏ 120 Jim Brown | 6.00 | 2.50 |
| ❏ 121 Jim Kelly | 6.00 | 2.50 |
| ❏ 122 Jim Thorpe | 6.00 | 2.50 |
| ❏ 123 Joe Greene | 5.00 | 2.00 |
| ❏ 124 Joe Montana | 12.00 | 5.00 |
| ❏ 125 Joe Namath | 8.00 | 3.00 |
| ❏ 126 John Elway | 10.00 | 4.00 |
| ❏ 127 John Riggins | 5.00 | 2.00 |
| ❏ 128 Johnny Unitas | 8.00 | 3.00 |
| ❏ 129 Lawrence Taylor | 5.00 | 2.00 |
| ❏ 130 Leroy Kelly | 4.00 | 1.50 |
| ❏ 131 Marcus Allen | 5.00 | 2.00 |
| ❏ 132 Michael Irvin | 5.00 | 2.00 |
| ❏ 133 Mike Ditka | 5.00 | 2.00 |
| ❏ 134 Mike Singletary | 5.00 | 2.00 |
| ❏ 135 Ozzie Newsome | 4.00 | 1.50 |
| ❏ 136 Paul Hornung | 5.00 | 2.00 |
| ❏ 137 Paul Warfield | 4.00 | 1.50 |
| ❏ 138 Randall Cunningham | 4.00 | 1.50 |
| ❏ 139 Red Grange | 6.00 | 2.50 |
| ❏ 140 Roger Staubach | 8.00 | 3.00 |
| ❏ 141 Sammy Baugh | 5.00 | 2.00 |
| ❏ 142 Sonny Jurgensen | 4.00 | 1.50 |
| ❏ 143 Steve Largent | 5.00 | 2.00 |
| ❏ 144 Steve Young | 6.00 | 2.50 |
| ❏ 145 Terrell Davis | 5.00 | 2.00 |
| ❏ 146 Terry Bradshaw | 8.00 | 3.00 |
| ❏ 147 Tony Dorsett | 4.00 | 1.50 |
| ❏ 148 Troy Aikman | 6.00 | 2.50 |
| ❏ 149 Walter Payton | 12.00 | 5.00 |
| ❏ 150 Warren Moon | 5.00 | 2.00 |
| ❏ 151 Aaron Rodgers RC | 25.00 | 10.00 |
| ❏ 152 Adrian McPherson RC | 6.00 | 2.50 |
| ❏ 153 Airese Currie RC | 6.00 | 2.50 |
| ❏ 154 Alvin Pearman RC | 6.00 | 2.50 |
| ❏ 155 Anthony Davis RC | 6.00 | 2.50 |
| ❏ 156 Brandon Jacobs RC | 10.00 | 4.00 |
| ❏ 157 Brandon Jones RC | 8.00 | 3.00 |
| ❏ 158 Cedric Benson RC | 8.00 | 3.00 |
| ❏ 159 Cedric Houston RC | 8.00 | 3.00 |
| ❏ 160 Chad Owens RC | 8.00 | 3.00 |
| ❏ 161 Chris Henry RC | 8.00 | 3.00 |
| ❏ 162 Nate Washington RC | 8.00 | 3.00 |
| ❏ 163 Craig Bragg RC | 8.00 | 3.00 |
| ❏ 164 Craphonso Thorpe RC | 6.00 | 2.50 |
| ❏ 165 Damien Nash RC | 6.00 | 2.50 |
| ❏ 166 Dan Orlovsky RC | 8.00 | 3.00 |
| ❏ 167 Dante Ridgeway RC | 6.00 | 2.50 |
| ❏ 168 Darren Sproles RC | 10.00 | 4.00 |
| ❏ 169 David Greene RC | 6.00 | 2.50 |
| ❏ 170 David Pollack RC | 6.00 | 2.50 |
| ❏ 171 Deandra Cobb RC | 6.00 | 2.50 |
| ❏ 172 DeMarcus Ware RC | 12.00 | 5.00 |
| ❏ 173 Derek Anderson RC | 12.00 | 5.00 |
| ❏ 174 Derrick Johnson RC | 8.00 | 3.00 |
| ❏ 175 Erasmus James RC | 6.00 | 2.50 |
| ❏ 176 Fabian Washington RC | 8.00 | 3.00 |
| ❏ 177 Fred Gibson RC | 8.00 | 3.00 |
| ❏ 178 Harry Williams RC | 6.00 | 2.50 |
| ❏ 179 Heath Miller RC | 15.00 | 6.00 |
| ❏ 180 J.R. Russell RC | 5.00 | 2.00 |
| ❏ 181 James Kilian RC | 5.00 | 2.00 |
| ❏ 182 Jerome Mathis RC | 8.00 | 3.00 |
| ❏ 183 Larry Brackins RC | 5.00 | 2.00 |
| ❏ 184 LeRon McCoy RC | 5.00 | 2.00 |
| ❏ 185 Lionel Gates RC | 5.00 | 2.00 |
| ❏ 186 Marcus Spears RC | 6.00 | 2.50 |
| ❏ 187 Marion Barber RC | 25.00 | 10.00 |
| ❏ 188 Marlin Jackson RC | 6.00 | 2.50 |
| ❏ 189 Matt Cassel RC | 20.00 | 8.00 |
| ❏ 190 Mike Williams RC | 8.00 | 3.00 |
| ❏ 191 Noah Herron RC | 8.00 | 3.00 |
| ❏ 192 Paris Warren RC | 6.00 | 2.50 |
| ❏ 193 Reshard Marshall RC | 5.00 | 2.00 |
| ❏ 194 Roscoe Crosby RC | 5.00 | 2.00 |
| ❏ 195 Roydell Williams RC | 6.00 | 2.50 |
| ❏ 196 Ryan Fitzpatrick RC | 12.00 | 5.00 |
| ❏ 197 Shawne Merriman RC | 12.00 | 5.00 |

| | | |
|---|---|---|
| ☐ 198 Tab Perry RC | 8.00 | 3.00 |
| ☐ 199 Thomas Davis RC | 6.00 | 2.50 |
| ☐ 200 Travis Johnson RC | 5.00 | 2.00 |
| ☐ 201 Adam Jones JSY AU RC | 25.00 | 10.00 |
| ☐ 202 Alex Smith QB JSY AU RC | 40.00 | 15.00 |
| ☐ 203 Andrew Walter JSY AU RC | 25.00 | 10.00 |
| ☐ 204 Antrel Rolle JSY AU RC | 25.00 | 10.00 |
| ☐ 205 Braylon Edwards JSY AU RC | 80.00 | 30.00 |
| ☐ 206 Cadillac Williams JSY AU RC | 50.00 | 20.00 |
| ☐ 207 Carlos Rogers JSY AU RC | 25.00 | 10.00 |
| ☐ 208 Charlie Frye JSY AU RC | 25.00 | 10.00 |
| ☐ 209 Ciatrick Fason JSY AU RC | 20.00 | 8.00 |
| ☐ 210 Courtney Roby JSY AU RC | 20.00 | 8.00 |
| ☐ 211 Eric Shelton JSY AU RC | 20.00 | 8.00 |
| ☐ 212 Frank Gore JSY AU RC | 60.00 | 25.00 |
| ☐ 213 J.J. Arrington JSY AU RC | 25.00 | 10.00 |
| ☐ 214 Kyle Orton JSY AU RC | 30.00 | 15.00 |
| ☐ 215 Jason Campbell JSY AU RC | 50.00 | 20.00 |
| ☐ 216 Mark Bradley JSY AU RC | 20.00 | 8.00 |
| ☐ 217 Mark Clayton JSY AU RC | 25.00 | 10.00 |
| ☐ 218 Matt Jones JSY AU RC | 40.00 | 15.00 |
| ☐ 219 Maurice Clarett JSY AU RC | 20.00 | 8.00 |
| ☐ 220 Reggie Brown JSY AU RC | 25.00 | 10.00 |
| ☐ 221 Ronnie Brown JSY AU RC | 80.00 | 30.00 |
| ☐ 222 Roddy White JSY AU RC | 35.00 | 20.00 |
| ☐ 223 Ryan Moats JSY AU RC | 20.00 | 8.00 |
| ☐ 224 Roscoe Parrish JSY AU RC | 20.00 | 8.00 |
| ☐ 225 Terrell LeFors JSY AU RC | 20.00 | 8.00 |
| ☐ 226 Terrence Murphy JSY AU RC | 15.00 | 6.00 |
| ☐ 227 Troy Williamson JSY AU RC | 25.00 | 10.00 |
| ☐ 228 Vernand Morency JSY AU RC | 25.00 | 10.00 |
| ☐ 229 Vincent Jackson JSY AU RC | 25.00 | 10.00 |

## 2006 Leaf Limited

WALTER PAYTON

| | | |
|---|---|---|
| ☐ 1 Alex Smith QB | 4.00 | 1.50 |
| ☐ 2 Antonio Bryant | 3.00 | 1.25 |
| ☐ 3 Frank Gore | 4.00 | 1.50 |
| ☐ 4 Rex Grossman | 4.00 | 1.50 |
| ☐ 5 Thomas Jones | 3.00 | 1.25 |
| ☐ 6 Cedric Benson | 3.00 | 1.25 |
| ☐ 7 Carson Palmer | 4.00 | 1.50 |
| ☐ 8 Chad Johnson | 4.00 | 1.50 |
| ☐ 9 Rudi Johnson | 3.00 | 1.25 |
| ☐ 10 T.J. Houshmandzadeh | 3.00 | 1.25 |
| ☐ 11 J.P. Losman | 3.00 | 1.25 |
| ☐ 12 Lee Evans | 3.00 | 1.25 |
| ☐ 13 Willis McGahee | 4.00 | 1.50 |
| ☐ 14 Jake Plummer | 3.00 | 1.25 |
| ☐ 15 Javon Walker | 3.00 | 1.25 |
| ☐ 16 Rod Smith | 3.00 | 1.25 |
| ☐ 17 Tatum Bell | 3.00 | 1.25 |
| ☐ 18 Braylon Edwards | 4.00 | 1.50 |
| ☐ 19 Charlie Frye | 3.00 | 1.25 |
| ☐ 20 Reuben Droughns | 3.00 | 1.25 |
| ☐ 21 Cadillac Williams | 4.00 | 1.50 |
| ☐ 22 Chris Simms | 3.00 | 1.25 |
| ☐ 23 Joey Galloway | 3.00 | 1.25 |
| ☐ 24 Anquan Boldin | 3.00 | 1.25 |
| ☐ 25 Edgerrin James | 3.00 | 1.25 |
| ☐ 26 Kurt Warner | 4.00 | 1.50 |
| ☐ 27 Larry Fitzgerald | 4.00 | 1.50 |
| ☐ 28 Antonio Gates | 4.00 | 1.50 |
| ☐ 29 Keenan McCardell | 3.00 | 1.25 |
| ☐ 30 LaDainian Tomlinson | 5.00 | 2.00 |
| ☐ 31 Philip Rivers | 4.00 | 1.50 |
| ☐ 32 Eddie Kennison | 2.50 | 1.00 |
| ☐ 33 Larry Johnson | 3.00 | 1.25 |
| ☐ 34 Priest Holmes | 3.00 | 1.25 |
| ☐ 35 Trent Green | 3.00 | 1.25 |
| ☐ 36 Tony Gonzalez | 3.00 | 1.25 |
| ☐ 37 Dallas Clark | 3.00 | 1.25 |
| ☐ 38 Marvin Harrison | 4.00 | 1.50 |

| | | |
|---|---|---|
| ☐ 39 Peyton Manning | 6.00 | 2.50 |
| ☐ 40 Reggie Wayne | 3.00 | 1.25 |
| ☐ 41 Drew Bledsoe | 4.00 | 1.50 |
| ☐ 42 Julius Jones | 4.00 | 1.50 |
| ☐ 43 Roy Williams S | 3.00 | 1.25 |
| ☐ 44 Terrell Owens | 4.00 | 1.50 |
| ☐ 45 Terry Glenn | 3.00 | 1.25 |
| ☐ 46 Chris Chambers | 3.00 | 1.25 |
| ☐ 47 Daunte Culpepper | 4.00 | 1.50 |
| ☐ 48 Marty Booker | 2.50 | 1.00 |
| ☐ 49 Ronnie Brown | 4.00 | 1.50 |
| ☐ 50 Brian Westbrook | 4.00 | 1.50 |
| ☐ 51 Donovan McNabb | 4.00 | 1.50 |
| ☐ 52 Jevon Kearse | 3.00 | 1.25 |
| ☐ 53 Reggie Brown | 3.00 | 1.25 |
| ☐ 54 Alge Crumpler | 3.00 | 1.25 |
| ☐ 55 Michael Vick | 4.00 | 1.50 |
| ☐ 56 Warrick Dunn | 3.00 | 1.25 |
| ☐ 57 Eli Manning | 5.00 | 2.00 |
| ☐ 58 Jeremy Shockey | 4.00 | 1.50 |
| ☐ 59 Plaxico Burress | 4.00 | 1.50 |
| ☐ 60 Tiki Barber | 4.00 | 1.50 |
| ☐ 61 Byron Leftwich | 3.00 | 1.25 |
| ☐ 62 Fred Taylor | 3.00 | 1.25 |
| ☐ 63 Jimmy Smith | 3.00 | 1.25 |
| ☐ 64 Matt Jones | 3.00 | 1.25 |
| ☐ 65 Josh McCown | 3.00 | 1.25 |
| ☐ 66 Roy Williams WR | 4.00 | 1.50 |
| ☐ 67 Kevin Jones | 4.00 | 1.50 |
| ☐ 68 Aaron Rodgers | 4.00 | 1.50 |
| ☐ 69 Brett Favre | 8.00 | 3.00 |
| ☐ 70 Robert Ferguson | 2.50 | 1.00 |
| ☐ 71 Samkon Gado | 4.00 | 1.50 |
| ☐ 72 Ahman Green | 3.00 | 1.25 |
| ☐ 73 DeShaun Foster | 3.00 | 1.25 |
| ☐ 74 Jake Delhomme | 4.00 | 1.50 |
| ☐ 75 Keary Colbert | 3.00 | 1.25 |
| ☐ 76 Steve Smith | 4.00 | 1.50 |
| ☐ 77 Corey Dillon | 3.00 | 1.25 |
| ☐ 78 Deion Branch | 3.00 | 1.25 |
| ☐ 79 Tedy Bruschi | 3.00 | 1.25 |
| ☐ 80 Tom Brady | 6.00 | 2.50 |
| ☐ 81 Jerry Porter | 3.00 | 1.25 |
| ☐ 82 Randy Moss | 4.00 | 1.50 |
| ☐ 83 LaMont Jordan | 3.00 | 1.25 |
| ☐ 84 Isaac Bruce | 3.00 | 1.25 |
| ☐ 85 Marc Bulger | 4.00 | 1.50 |
| ☐ 86 Steven Jackson | 4.00 | 1.50 |
| ☐ 87 Torry Holt | 4.00 | 1.50 |
| ☐ 88 Derrick Mason | 3.00 | 1.25 |
| ☐ 89 Mark Clayton | 3.00 | 1.25 |
| ☐ 90 Steve McNair | 3.00 | 1.25 |
| ☐ 91 Jamal Lewis | 3.00 | 1.25 |
| ☐ 92 Antwaan Randle El | 3.00 | 1.25 |
| ☐ 93 Clinton Portis | 4.00 | 1.50 |
| ☐ 94 Santana Moss | 3.00 | 1.25 |
| ☐ 95 Chad Pennington | 4.00 | 1.50 |
| ☐ 96 Laveranues Coles | 3.00 | 1.25 |
| ☐ 97 Curtis Martin | 4.00 | 1.50 |
| ☐ 98 Mewelde Moore | 2.50 | 1.00 |
| ☐ 99 Troy Williamson | 3.00 | 1.25 |
| ☐ 100 Brad Johnson | 3.00 | 1.25 |
| ☐ 101 Darrell Jackson | 3.00 | 1.25 |
| ☐ 102 Matt Hasselbeck | 3.00 | 1.25 |
| ☐ 103 Nate Burleson | 3.00 | 1.25 |
| ☐ 104 Shaun Alexander | 4.00 | 1.50 |
| ☐ 105 Ben Roethlisberger | 6.00 | 2.50 |
| ☐ 106 Hines Ward | 3.00 | 1.25 |
| ☐ 107 Willie Parker | 5.00 | 2.00 |
| ☐ 108 Donte Stallworth | 3.00 | 1.25 |
| ☐ 109 Drew Brees | 4.00 | 1.50 |
| ☐ 110 Deuce McAllister | 3.00 | 1.25 |
| ☐ 111 Andre Johnson | 4.00 | 1.50 |
| ☐ 112 David Carr | 3.00 | 1.25 |
| ☐ 113 Domanick Davis | 3.00 | 1.25 |
| ☐ 114 Eric Moulds | 3.00 | 1.25 |
| ☐ 115 David Givens | 3.00 | 1.25 |
| ☐ 116 Drew Bennett | 3.00 | 1.25 |
| ☐ 117 Chris Brown | 3.00 | 1.25 |
| ☐ 118 Bob Griese | 5.00 | 2.00 |
| ☐ 119 Daryle Lamonica | 3.00 | 1.25 |
| ☐ 120 Dave Casper | 3.00 | 1.25 |
| ☐ 121 Don Meredith | 5.00 | 2.00 |
| ☐ 122 Herschel Walker | 4.00 | 1.50 |
| ☐ 123 Jack Lambert | 5.00 | 2.00 |
| ☐ 124 Jackie Smith | 3.00 | 1.25 |
| ☐ 125 Jim Otto | 3.00 | 1.25 |
| ☐ 126 John Riggins | 5.00 | 2.00 |
| ☐ 127 John Stallworth | 4.00 | 1.50 |

| | | |
|---|---|---|
| ☐ 128 Lawrence Taylor | 5.00 | 2.00 |
| ☐ 129 Lester Hayes | 3.00 | 1.25 |
| ☐ 130 L.C. Greenwood | 4.00 | 1.50 |
| ☐ 131 Paul Warfield | 4.00 | 1.50 |
| ☐ 132 Barry Sanders | 8.00 | 3.00 |
| ☐ 133 Bart Starr | 8.00 | 3.00 |
| ☐ 134 Billy Sims | 4.00 | 1.50 |
| ☐ 135 Bulldog Turner | 6.00 | 2.50 |
| ☐ 136 Deion Sanders | 6.00 | 2.50 |
| ☐ 137 Dutch Clark | 4.00 | 1.50 |
| ☐ 138 Forrest Gregg | 3.00 | 1.25 |
| ☐ 139 Gale Sayers | 6.00 | 2.50 |
| ☐ 140 Jim Brown | 6.00 | 2.50 |
| ☐ 141 Jim Thorpe | 6.00 | 2.50 |
| ☐ 142 Joe Montana | 10.00 | 4.00 |
| ☐ 143 John Elway | 8.00 | 3.00 |
| ☐ 144 Johnny Unitas | 8.00 | 3.00 |
| ☐ 145 Lance Alworth | 4.00 | 1.50 |
| ☐ 146 Raymond Berry | 4.00 | 1.50 |
| ☐ 147 Doak Walker | 5.00 | 2.00 |
| ☐ 148 Red Grange | 6.00 | 2.50 |
| ☐ 149 Walter Payton | 10.00 | 4.00 |
| ☐ 150 Yale Lary | 3.00 | 1.25 |
| ☐ 151 Adam Jennings RC | 6.00 | 2.50 |
| ☐ 152 Alan Zemaitis RC | 8.00 | 3.00 |
| ☐ 153 Patrick Cobbs RC | 6.00 | 2.50 |
| ☐ 154 Anthony Schlegel RC | 6.00 | 2.50 |
| ☐ 155 Anthony Smith RC | 8.00 | 3.00 |
| ☐ 156 Antonio Cromartie RC | 8.00 | 3.00 |
| ☐ 157 Ashton Youboty RC | 8.00 | 3.00 |
| ☐ 158 Bernie Brazell RC | 6.00 | 2.50 |
| ☐ 159 Bernard Pollard RC | 6.00 | 2.50 |
| ☐ 160 Brodrick Bunkley RC | 8.00 | 3.00 |
| ☐ 161 Calvin Lowry RC | 8.00 | 3.00 |
| ☐ 162 Cedric Griffin RC | 8.00 | 3.00 |
| ☐ 163 Cedric Humes RC | 6.00 | 2.50 |
| ☐ 164 Charles Davis RC | 6.00 | 2.50 |
| ☐ 165 Chris Gocong RC | 6.00 | 2.50 |
| ☐ 166 Claude Wroten RC | 5.00 | 2.00 |
| ☐ 167 Clint Ingram RC | 8.00 | 3.00 |
| ☐ 168 D.J. Shockley RC | 8.00 | 3.00 |
| ☐ 169 Danieal Manning RC | 6.00 | 2.50 |
| ☐ 170 Daniel Bullocks RC | 8.00 | 3.00 |
| ☐ 171 Darnell Bing RC | 6.00 | 2.50 |
| ☐ 172 Chris Hannon RC | 6.00 | 2.50 |
| ☐ 173 Darryl Tapp RC | 6.00 | 2.50 |
| ☐ 174 David Anderson RC | 6.00 | 2.50 |
| ☐ 175 David Kirtman RC | 6.00 | 2.50 |
| ☐ 176 David Pittman RC | 6.00 | 2.50 |
| ☐ 177 Davin Joseph RC | 6.00 | 2.50 |
| ☐ 178 Sam Hurd RC | 12.00 | 5.00 |
| ☐ 179 Delanie Walker RC | 6.00 | 2.50 |
| ☐ 180 DeMeco Ryans RC | 10.00 | 4.00 |
| ☐ 181 Derrick Ross RC | 6.00 | 2.50 |
| ☐ 182 Devin Hester RC | 15.00 | 6.00 |
| ☐ 183 Domenik Hixon RC | 10.00 | 4.00 |
| ☐ 184 Dominique Byrd RC | 6.00 | 2.50 |
| ☐ 185 Donte Whitner RC | 8.00 | 3.00 |
| ☐ 186 D'Qwell Jackson RC | 6.00 | 2.50 |
| ☐ 187 Dusty Dvoracek RC | 8.00 | 3.00 |
| ☐ 188 Eric Smith RC | 6.00 | 2.50 |
| ☐ 189 Fred Evans RC | 6.00 | 2.50 |
| ☐ 190 Ernie Sims RC | 8.00 | 3.00 |
| ☐ 191 Ethan Kilmer RC | 6.00 | 2.50 |
| ☐ 192 Freddie Keiaho RC | 6.00 | 2.50 |
| ☐ 193 Frostee Rucker RC | 6.00 | 2.50 |
| ☐ 194 Gabe Watson RC | 6.00 | 2.50 |
| ☐ 195 Garrett Mills RC | 8.00 | 3.00 |
| ☐ 196 Dawan Landry RC | 6.00 | 2.50 |
| ☐ 197 Gerris Wilkinson RC | 5.00 | 2.00 |
| ☐ 198 Jarrad Page RC | 6.00 | 2.50 |
| ☐ 199 Haloti Ngata RC | 8.00 | 3.00 |
| ☐ 200 Hank Baskett RC | 6.00 | 2.50 |
| ☐ 201 Jai Lewis RC | 6.00 | 2.50 |
| ☐ 202 Jamar Williams RC | 6.00 | 2.50 |
| ☐ 203 James Anderson RC | 5.00 | 2.00 |
| ☐ 204 Jason Allen RC | 6.00 | 2.50 |
| ☐ 205 Jason Hatcher RC | 6.00 | 2.50 |
| ☐ 206 Chris Barclay RC | 6.00 | 2.50 |
| ☐ 207 J.D. Runnels RC | 6.00 | 2.50 |
| ☐ 208 Jeff King RC | 6.00 | 2.50 |
| ☐ 209 Jeffrey Webb RC | 6.00 | 2.50 |
| ☐ 210 Jerome Harrison RC | 8.00 | 3.00 |
| ☐ 211 Jimmy Williams RC | 8.00 | 3.00 |
| ☐ 212 John David Washington RC | 6.00 | 2.50 |
| ☐ 213 Jon Alston RC | 6.00 | 2.50 |
| ☐ 214 Johnathan Joseph RC | 6.00 | 2.50 |
| ☐ 215 Kamerion Wimbley RC | 8.00 | 3.00 |
| ☐ 216 Kelly Jennings RC | 8.00 | 3.00 |

| | | | |
|---|---|---|---|
| ☐ 217 Charles Sharon RC | 6.00 | 2.50 |
| ☐ 218 Ko Simpson RC | 6.00 | 2.50 |
| ☐ 219 Lawrence Vickers RC | 6.00 | 2.50 |
| ☐ 220 Leon Williams RC | 6.00 | 2.50 |
| ☐ 221 Leonard Pope RC | 8.00 | 3.00 |
| ☐ 222 Marques Colston RC | 25.00 | 10.00 |
| ☐ 223 Martin Nance RC | 6.00 | 2.50 |
| ☐ 224 Mathias Kiwanuka RC | 10.00 | 4.00 |
| ☐ 225 Mike Bell RC | 8.00 | 3.00 |
| ☐ 226 Mike Hass RC | 8.00 | 3.00 |
| ☐ 227 Miles Austin RC | 8.00 | 3.00 |
| ☐ 228 Nate Salley RC | 6.00 | 2.50 |
| ☐ 229 Nick Mangold RC | 6.00 | 2.50 |
| ☐ 230 Owen Daniels RC | 8.00 | 3.00 |
| ☐ 231 Shaun Bodiford RC | 6.00 | 2.50 |
| ☐ 232 Quinn Sypniewski RC | 6.00 | 2.50 |
| ☐ 233 Quinton Ganther RC | 8.00 | 3.00 |
| ☐ 234 Richard Marshall RC | 6.00 | 2.50 |
| ☐ 235 Rocky McIntosh RC | 8.00 | 3.00 |
| ☐ 236 Roman Harper RC | 6.00 | 2.50 |
| ☐ 237 Stephen Tulloch RC | 6.00 | 2.50 |
| ☐ 238 Brett Basanez RC | 8.00 | 3.00 |
| ☐ 239 Tamba Hali RC | 8.00 | 3.00 |
| ☐ 240 Brett Elliott RC | 8.00 | 3.00 |
| ☐ 241 Thomas Howard RC | 6.00 | 2.50 |
| ☐ 242 Tim Jennings RC | 6.00 | 2.50 |
| ☐ 243 Jason Carter RC | 6.00 | 2.50 |
| ☐ 244 Todd Watkins RC | 6.00 | 2.50 |
| ☐ 245 Tony Scheffler RC | 8.00 | 3.00 |
| ☐ 246 Tye Hill RC | 8.00 | 3.00 |
| ☐ 247 Victor Adeyanju RC | 6.00 | 2.50 |
| ☐ 248 Wendell Mathis RC | 6.00 | 2.50 |
| ☐ 249 Will Blackmon RC | 8.00 | 3.00 |
| ☐ 250 Willie Reid RC | 8.00 | 3.00 |
| ☐ 251 Mario Williams JSY AU RC | 30.00 | 12.00 |
| ☐ 252 Reggie Bush JSY AU RC | 150.00 | 75.00 |
| ☐ 253 Vince Young JSY AU RC | 120.00 | 60.00 |
| ☐ 254 A.J. Hawk JSY AU RC | 60.00 | 25.00 |
| ☐ 255 Vernon Davis JSY AU RC | 20.00 | 8.00 |
| ☐ 256 Michael Huff JSY AU RC | 20.00 | 8.00 |
| ☐ 257 Matt Leinart JSY AU RC | 120.00 | 60.00 |
| ☐ 258 Jay Cutler JSY AU RC | 125.00 | 75.00 |
| ☐ 259 L.Maroney JSY AU RC | 100.00 | 50.00 |
| ☐ 260 Santonio Holmes JSY AU RC | 50.00 | 25.00 |
| ☐ 261 DeA.Williams JSY AU RC | 60.00 | 25.00 |
| ☐ 262 Marcedes Lewis JSY AU RC | 20.00 | 8.00 |
| ☐ 263 Joseph Addai JSY AU RC | 100.00 | 50.00 |
| ☐ 264 Chad Jackson JSY AU RC | 15.00 | 6.00 |
| ☐ 265 Sinorice Moss JSY AU RC | 20.00 | 8.00 |
| ☐ 266 LenDale White JSY AU RC | 40.00 | 20.00 |
| ☐ 267 Kellen Clemens JSY AU RC | 40.00 | 20.00 |
| ☐ 268 Greg Jennings AU RC | 40.00 | 20.00 |
| ☐ 269 Joe Klopfenstein JSY AU RC | 15.00 | 6.00 |
| ☐ 270 Maurice Drew JSY AU RC | 80.00 | 30.00 |
| ☐ 271 Tarvaris Jackson JSY AU RC | 20.00 | 8.00 |
| ☐ 272 Brian Calhoun JSY AU RC | 15.00 | 6.00 |
| ☐ 273 Travis Wilson JSY AU RC | 20.00 | 8.00 |
| ☐ 274 Jerious Norwood JSY AU RC | 50.00 | 25.00 |
| ☐ 275 C.Whitehurst JSY AU RC | 20.00 | 8.00 |
| ☐ 276 Derek Hagan JSY AU RC | 20.00 | 8.00 |
| ☐ 277 Brandon Williams JSY AU RC | 20.00 | 8.00 |
| ☐ 278 Brodie Croyle AU RC | 50.00 | 25.00 |
| ☐ 279 Maurice Stovall JSY AU RC | 20.00 | 8.00 |
| ☐ 280 Michael Robinson JSY AU RC | 20.00 | 8.00 |
| ☐ 281 Jason Avant JSY AU RC | 20.00 | 8.00 |
| ☐ 282 Dem.Williams JSY AU RC | 20.00 | 8.00 |
| ☐ 283 Leon Washington JSY AU RC | 30.00 | 12.00 |
| ☐ 284 Brandon Marshall JSY AU RC | 30.00 | 15.00 |
| ☐ 285 Omar Jacobs JSY AU RC | 15.00 | 6.00 |
| ☐ 286 Anthony Fasano AU RC | 25.00 | 12.50 |
| ☐ 287 Ingle Martin AU RC | 20.00 | 8.00 |
| ☐ 288 Reggie McNeal AU RC | 15.00 | 6.00 |
| ☐ 289 Brad Smith AU RC | 20.00 | 8.00 |
| ☐ 290 Jeremy Bloom AU RC | 15.00 | 6.00 |
| ☐ 291 Bruce Gradkowski AU RC | 20.00 | 8.00 |
| ☐ 292 P.J. Daniels AU RC | 15.00 | 6.00 |
| ☐ 293 Cory Rodgers AU RC | 20.00 | 8.00 |
| ☐ 294 Skyler Green AU RC | 20.00 | 8.00 |
| ☐ 295 Bobby Carpenter AU RC | 20.00 | 8.00 |
| ☐ 296 Arom/Obom/Mix AU/100 | 25.00 | 12.50 |
| ☐ 297 Hodge/Greenway AU/100 | 40.00 | 20.00 |
| ☐ 298 M.Hill/McCar/Lwsn AU/100 | 50.00 | 20.00 |
| ☐ 299 Fasano/Stovall AU/50 | 40.00 | 20.00 |
| ☐ 300 Hawk/Carpenter AU/50 | 50.00 | 20.00 |
| ☐ 301 Leinart/Bush/Wht AU/25 | 300.00 | 150.00 |
| ☐ 302 Young/Thomas AU/50 | 50.00 | 20.00 |
| ☐ 303 Olson/Drew/Lewis AU/100 | 60.00 | 35.00 |
| ☐ 304 Hagans/Lundy/Ferg AU/100 | 40.00 | 20.00 |
| ☐ 305 Cafn/Willms/Orr AU/100 | 20.00 | 8.00 |

| | | |
|---|---|---|
| ☐ TC Steve Smith TC/500 | 6.00 | 2.50 |
| ☐ TCA Steve Smith TC AU/50 | 40.00 | 20.00 |

**2007 Leaf Limited**

| | | |
|---|---|---|
| ☐ 1 Anquan Boldin | 3.00 | 1.25 |
| ☐ 2 Edgerrin James | 3.00 | 1.25 |
| ☐ 3 Larry Fitzgerald | 4.00 | 1.50 |
| ☐ 4 Matt Leinart | 4.00 | 1.50 |
| ☐ 5 Alge Crumpler | 3.00 | 1.25 |
| ☐ 6 Warrick Dunn | 3.00 | 1.25 |
| ☐ 7 Jerious Norwood | 3.00 | 1.25 |
| ☐ 8 Willis McGahee | 3.00 | 1.25 |
| ☐ 9 Steve McNair | 3.00 | 1.25 |
| ☐ 10 Mark Clayton | 3.00 | 1.25 |
| ☐ 11 Anthony Thomas | 2.50 | 1.00 |
| ☐ 12 J.P. Losman | 2.50 | 1.00 |
| ☐ 13 Lee Evans | 3.00 | 1.25 |
| ☐ 14 Jake Delhomme | 3.00 | 1.25 |
| ☐ 15 Steve Smith | 3.00 | 1.25 |
| ☐ 16 DeAngelo Williams | 4.00 | 1.50 |
| ☐ 17 Rex Grossman | 3.00 | 1.25 |
| ☐ 18 Cedric Benson | 3.00 | 1.25 |
| ☐ 19 Bernard Berrian | 3.00 | 1.25 |
| ☐ 20 Carson Palmer | 4.00 | 1.50 |
| ☐ 21 Chad Johnson | 3.00 | 1.25 |
| ☐ 22 Rudi Johnson | 3.00 | 1.25 |
| ☐ 23 T.J. Houshmandzadeh | 3.00 | 1.25 |
| ☐ 24 Kellen Winslow | 3.00 | 1.25 |
| ☐ 25 Braylon Edwards | 3.00 | 1.25 |
| ☐ 26 Jamal Lewis | 3.00 | 1.25 |
| ☐ 27 Julius Jones | 3.00 | 1.25 |
| ☐ 28 Terrell Owens | 4.00 | 1.50 |
| ☐ 29 Tony Romo | 8.00 | 3.00 |
| ☐ 30 Jay Cutler | 4.00 | 1.50 |
| ☐ 31 Javon Walker | 3.00 | 1.25 |
| ☐ 32 Travis Henry | 3.00 | 1.25 |
| ☐ 33 Tatum Bell | 2.50 | 1.00 |
| ☐ 34 Roy Williams WR | 3.00 | 1.25 |
| ☐ 35 Jon Kitna | 2.50 | 1.00 |
| ☐ 36 Brett Favre | 8.00 | 3.00 |
| ☐ 37 Donald Driver | 3.00 | 1.25 |
| ☐ 38 Greg Jennings | 3.00 | 1.25 |
| ☐ 39 Matt Schaub | 3.00 | 1.25 |
| ☐ 40 Andre Johnson | 3.00 | 1.25 |
| ☐ 41 Ahman Green | 3.00 | 1.25 |
| ☐ 42 Peyton Manning | 6.00 | 2.50 |
| ☐ 43 Marvin Harrison | 4.00 | 1.50 |
| ☐ 44 Reggie Wayne | 4.00 | 1.50 |
| ☐ 45 Joseph Addai | 4.00 | 1.50 |
| ☐ 46 David Garrard | 3.00 | 1.25 |
| ☐ 47 Fred Taylor | 3.00 | 1.25 |
| ☐ 48 Maurice Jones-Drew | 4.00 | 1.50 |
| ☐ 49 Brodie Croyle | 3.00 | 1.25 |
| ☐ 50 Larry Johnson | 3.00 | 1.25 |
| ☐ 51 Tony Gonzalez | 3.00 | 1.25 |
| ☐ 52 Trent Green | 3.00 | 1.25 |
| ☐ 53 Ronnie Brown | 3.00 | 1.25 |
| ☐ 54 Chris Chambers | 3.00 | 1.25 |
| ☐ 55 Tarvaris Jackson | 3.00 | 1.25 |
| ☐ 56 Troy Williamson | 2.50 | 1.00 |
| ☐ 57 Chester Taylor | 2.50 | 1.00 |
| ☐ 58 Tom Brady | 8.00 | 3.00 |
| ☐ 59 Randy Moss | 4.00 | 1.50 |
| ☐ 60 Laurence Maroney | 4.00 | 1.50 |
| ☐ 61 Donte Stallworth | 3.00 | 1.25 |
| ☐ 62 Drew Brees | 3.00 | 1.25 |
| ☐ 63 Deuce McAllister | 3.00 | 1.25 |
| ☐ 64 Reggie Bush | 5.00 | 2.00 |
| ☐ 65 Marques Colston | 4.00 | 1.50 |
| ☐ 66 Eli Manning | 4.00 | 1.50 |
| ☐ 67 Jeremy Shockey | 3.00 | 1.25 |
| ☐ 68 Brandon Jacobs | 3.00 | 1.25 |

| | | |
|---|---|---|
| ☐ 69 Chad Pennington | 3.00 | 1.25 |
| ☐ 70 Thomas Jones | 3.00 | 1.25 |
| ☐ 71 Laveranues Coles | 3.00 | 1.25 |
| ☐ 72 Jerry Porter | 3.00 | 1.25 |
| ☐ 73 LaMont Jordan | 3.00 | 1.25 |
| ☐ 74 Donovan McNabb | 4.00 | 1.50 |
| ☐ 75 Brian Westbrook | 3.00 | 1.25 |
| ☐ 76 Reggie Brown | 3.00 | 1.25 |
| ☐ 77 Ben Roethlisberger | 5.00 | 2.00 |
| ☐ 78 Hines Ward | 4.00 | 1.50 |
| ☐ 79 Willie Parker | 4.00 | 1.50 |
| ☐ 80 Philip Rivers | 4.00 | 1.50 |
| ☐ 81 Antonio Gates | 3.00 | 1.25 |
| ☐ 82 LaDainian Tomlinson | 5.00 | 2.00 |
| ☐ 83 Alex Smith QB | 4.00 | 1.50 |
| ☐ 84 Darrell Jackson | 3.00 | 1.25 |
| ☐ 85 Frank Gore | 4.00 | 1.50 |
| ☐ 86 Matt Hasselbeck | 3.00 | 1.25 |
| ☐ 87 Shaun Alexander | 4.00 | 1.50 |
| ☐ 88 Deion Branch | 3.00 | 1.25 |
| ☐ 89 Marc Bulger | 3.00 | 1.25 |
| ☐ 90 Steven Jackson | 4.00 | 1.50 |
| ☐ 91 Torry Holt | 3.00 | 1.25 |
| ☐ 92 Jeff Garcia | 3.00 | 1.25 |
| ☐ 93 Cadillac Williams | 3.00 | 1.25 |
| ☐ 94 Joey Galloway | 3.00 | 1.25 |
| ☐ 95 Vince Young | 4.00 | 1.50 |
| ☐ 96 Brandon Jones | 2.50 | 1.00 |
| ☐ 97 LenDale White | 3.00 | 1.25 |
| ☐ 98 Jason Campbell | 3.00 | 1.25 |
| ☐ 99 Clinton Portis | 3.00 | 1.25 |
| ☐ 100 Santana Moss | 3.00 | 1.25 |
| ☐ 101 Alan Page | 5.00 | 2.00 |
| ☐ 102 Barry Sanders | 12.00 | 5.00 |
| ☐ 103 Bart Starr | 12.00 | 5.00 |
| ☐ 104 Bill Dudley | 6.00 | 2.50 |
| ☐ 105 Billy Howton | 5.00 | 2.00 |
| ☐ 106 Bob Griese | 8.00 | 3.00 |
| ☐ 107 Bobby Layne | 8.00 | 3.00 |
| ☐ 108 Boyd Dowler | 5.00 | 2.00 |
| ☐ 109 Charley Taylor | 6.00 | 2.50 |
| ☐ 110 Charley Trippi | 6.00 | 2.50 |
| ☐ 111 Charlie Joiner | 6.00 | 2.50 |
| ☐ 112 Chuck Bednarik | 6.00 | 2.50 |
| ☐ 113 Cris Collinsworth | 6.00 | 2.50 |
| ☐ 114 Dan Fouts | 8.00 | 3.00 |
| ☐ 115 Dan Hampton | 6.00 | 2.50 |
| ☐ 116 Dan Marino | 15.00 | 6.00 |
| ☐ 117 Dante Lavelli | 5.00 | 2.00 |
| ☐ 118 Darrell Green | 6.00 | 2.50 |
| ☐ 119 Daryle Lamonica | 5.00 | 2.00 |
| ☐ 120 Deacon Jones | 6.00 | 2.50 |
| ☐ 121 Dick Butkus | 10.00 | 4.00 |
| ☐ 122 Doak Walker | 6.00 | 2.50 |
| ☐ 123 Don Maynard | 6.00 | 2.50 |
| ☐ 124 Don Perkins | 5.00 | 2.00 |
| ☐ 125 Dutch Clark | 6.00 | 2.50 |
| ☐ 126 Earl Campbell | 8.00 | 3.00 |
| ☐ 127 Forrest Gregg | 5.00 | 2.00 |
| ☐ 128 Fran Tarkenton | 10.00 | 4.00 |
| ☐ 129 Franco Harris | 8.00 | 3.00 |
| ☐ 130 Fred Biletnikoff | 8.00 | 3.00 |
| ☐ 131 Gale Sayers | 10.00 | 4.00 |
| ☐ 132 Gene Upshaw | 5.00 | 2.00 |
| ☐ 133 George Blanda | 6.00 | 2.50 |
| ☐ 134 Harlon Hill | 5.00 | 2.00 |
| ☐ 135 Jack Lambert | 8.00 | 3.00 |
| ☐ 136 Jack Youngblood | 6.00 | 2.50 |
| ☐ 137 James Lofton | 6.00 | 2.50 |
| ☐ 138 Jan Stenerud | 5.00 | 2.00 |
| ☐ 139 Jethro Pugh | 5.00 | 2.00 |
| ☐ 140 Jim Brown | 10.00 | 4.00 |
| ☐ 141 Jim Kelly | 10.00 | 4.00 |
| ☐ 142 Jim McMahon | 5.00 | 2.00 |
| ☐ 143 Jim Otto | 5.00 | 2.00 |
| ☐ 144 Jim Thorpe | 10.00 | 4.00 |
| ☐ 145 Jimmy Orr | 5.00 | 2.00 |
| ☐ 146 Joe Greene | 8.00 | 3.00 |
| ☐ 147 Joe Montana | 15.00 | 6.00 |
| ☐ 148 Joe Namath | 10.00 | 4.00 |
| ☐ 149 Joe Theismann | 8.00 | 3.00 |
| ☐ 150 John Elway | 12.00 | 5.00 |
| ☐ 151 John Mackey | 6.00 | 2.50 |
| ☐ 152 John Riggins | 6.00 | 2.50 |
| ☐ 153 John Stallworth | 6.00 | 2.50 |
| ☐ 154 Johnny Morris | 5.00 | 2.00 |
| ☐ 155 Johnny Unitas | 12.00 | 5.00 |
| ☐ 156 Kellen Winslow Sr. | 6.00 | 2.50 |
| ☐ 157 Ken Stabler | 10.00 | 4.00 |

| | | |
|---|---|---|
| 158 Lance Alworth | 6.00 | 2.50 |
| 159 Larry Csonka | 5.00 | 2.00 |
| 160 Larry Little | 5.00 | 2.00 |
| 161 Lee Roy Selmon | 6.00 | 2.50 |
| 162 Len Dawson | 8.00 | 3.00 |
| 163 Lou Groza | 6.00 | 2.50 |
| 164 Lydell Mitchell | 5.00 | 2.00 |
| 165 Marcus Allen | 8.00 | 3.00 |
| 166 Mark Duper | 5.00 | 2.00 |
| 167 Merlin Olsen | 8.00 | 3.00 |
| 168 Mike Singletary | 8.00 | 3.00 |
| 169 Ollie Matson | 6.00 | 2.50 |
| 170 Otto Graham | 8.00 | 3.00 |
| 171 Ozzie Newsome | 6.00 | 2.50 |
| 172 Paul Hornung | 8.00 | 3.00 |
| 173 Paul Warfield | 6.00 | 2.50 |
| 174 Phil Simms | 6.00 | 2.50 |
| 175 Randall Cunningham | 6.00 | 2.50 |
| 176 Ray Nitschke | 8.00 | 3.00 |
| 177 Raymond Berry | 6.00 | 2.50 |
| 178 Red Grange | 10.00 | 4.00 |
| 179 Rick Casares | 5.00 | 2.00 |
| 180 Ron Mix | 5.00 | 2.00 |
| 181 Roger Craig | 6.00 | 2.50 |
| 182 Roger Staubach | 12.00 | 5.00 |
| 183 Rosey Brown | 5.00 | 2.00 |
| 184 Rosey Grier | 5.00 | 2.00 |
| 185 Ronnie Lott | 6.00 | 2.50 |
| 186 Sam Huff | 6.00 | 2.50 |
| 187 Sammy Baugh | 8.00 | 3.00 |
| 188 Sid Luckman | 8.00 | 3.00 |
| 189 Sonny Jurgensen | 6.00 | 2.50 |
| 190 Sterling Sharpe | 6.00 | 2.50 |
| 191 Steve Largent | 8.00 | 3.00 |
| 192 Steve Young | 10.00 | 4.00 |
| 193 Ted Hendricks | 6.00 | 2.50 |
| 194 Thurman Thomas | 6.00 | 2.50 |
| 195 Tim Brown | 8.00 | 3.00 |
| 196 Tiki Barber | 8.00 | 3.00 |
| 197 Troy Aikman | 10.00 | 4.00 |
| 198 Walter Payton | 15.00 | 6.00 |
| 199 Willie Brown | 6.00 | 2.50 |
| 200 Elroy Hirsch | 6.00 | 2.50 |
| 201 Brandon McDonald RC | 6.00 | 2.50 |
| 202 David Irons RC | 6.00 | 2.50 |
| 203 Fred Bennett RC | 6.00 | 2.50 |
| 204 Nick Graham RC | 8.00 | 3.00 |
| 205 Rashad Barksdale RC | 6.00 | 2.50 |
| 206 Tanard Jackson RC | 6.00 | 2.50 |
| 207 Tarell Brown RC | 6.00 | 2.50 |
| 208 Usama Young RC | 8.00 | 3.00 |
| 209 William Gay RC | 6.00 | 2.50 |
| 210 Jarvis Moss RC | 10.00 | 4.00 |
| 211 Le'Ron McClain RC | 15.00 | 6.00 |
| 212 Kevin Payne RC | 6.00 | 2.50 |
| 213 Adam Hayward RC | 8.00 | 3.00 |
| 214 Brandon Siler RC | 8.00 | 3.00 |
| 215 Chad Nkang RC | 8.00 | 3.00 |
| 216 Clint Session RC | 8.00 | 3.00 |
| 217 Desmond Bishop RC | 6.00 | 2.50 |
| 218 Edmond Miles RC | 8.00 | 3.00 |
| 219 H.B. Blades RC | 8.00 | 3.00 |
| 220 Justin Durant RC | 8.00 | 3.00 |
| 221 Justin Rogers RC | 10.00 | 4.00 |
| 222 Nate Harris RC | 6.00 | 2.50 |
| 223 Quincy Black RC | 8.00 | 3.00 |
| 224 Quinton Culberson RC | 6.00 | 2.50 |
| 225 Ramon Guzman RC | 6.00 | 2.50 |
| 226 Stephen Nicholas RC | 8.00 | 3.00 |
| 227 Tim Shaw RC | 8.00 | 3.00 |
| 228 Tony Taylor RC | 8.00 | 3.00 |
| 229 Zak DeOssie RC | 10.00 | 4.00 |
| 230 Mason Crosby RC | 10.00 | 4.00 |
| 231 Nick Folk RC | 10.00 | 4.00 |
| 232 Matt Gutierrez RC | 10.00 | 4.00 |
| 233 Matt Moore RC | 10.00 | 4.00 |
| 234 Tyler Thigpen RC | 12.00 | 5.00 |
| 235 Clifton Dawson RC | 10.00 | 4.00 |
| 236 Gary Russell RC | 10.00 | 4.00 |
| 237 Kenton Keith RC | 10.00 | 4.00 |
| 238 Pierre Thomas RC | 15.00 | 6.00 |
| 239 Gerald Alexander RC | 6.00 | 2.50 |
| 240 John Wendling RC | 8.00 | 3.00 |
| 241 Eric Frampton RC | 8.00 | 3.00 |
| 242 Eric Weddle RC | 8.00 | 3.00 |
| 243 Daniel Coats RC | 8.00 | 3.00 |
| 244 Michael Matthews RC | 8.00 | 3.00 |
| 245 Biren Ealy RC | 8.00 | 3.00 |
| 246 Bobby Sippio RC | 8.00 | 3.00 |
| 247 Glenn Holt RC | 8.00 | 3.00 |
| 248 John Broussard RC | 8.00 | 3.00 |
| 249 Legedu Naanee RC | 10.00 | 4.00 |
| 250 Syndric Steptoe RC | 8.00 | 3.00 |
| 251 Levi Brown AU RC | 12.00 | 5.00 |
| 252 Jamaal Anderson AU RC | 10.00 | 4.00 |
| 253 Amobi Okoye AU RC | 10.00 | 4.00 |
| 254 Adam Carriker AU RC | 10.00 | 4.00 |
| 255 Darrelle Revis AU RC | 12.00 | 5.00 |
| 256 Michael Griffin AU RC | 12.00 | 5.00 |
| 257 Aaron Ross AU RC | 12.00 | 5.00 |
| 258 Brandon Meriweather AU RC EXCH | 12.00 | 5.00 |
| 259 Jon Beason AU RC | 12.00 | 5.00 |
| 260 Anthony Spencer AU RC | 10.00 | 4.00 |
| 261 Alan Branch AU RC EXCH | 10.00 | 4.00 |
| 262 Chris Houston AU RC | 10.00 | 4.00 |
| 263 LaMarr Woodley AU RC | 20.00 | 10.00 |
| 264 David Harris AU RC | 10.00 | 4.00 |
| 265 Eric Wright AU RC EXCH | 12.00 | 5.00 |
| 266 Josh Wilson AU RC | 10.00 | 4.00 |
| 267 Tim Crowder AU RC | 10.00 | 4.00 |
| 268 Victor Abiamiri AU RC | 12.00 | 5.00 |
| 269 Ikaika Alama-Francis AU RC | 12.00 | 5.00 |
| 270 Dan Bazuin AU RC | 10.00 | 4.00 |
| 271 Sabby Piscitelli AU RC | 10.00 | 4.00 |
| 272 Quentin Moses AU RC | 10.00 | 4.00 |
| 273 Buster Davis AU RC EXCH | 10.00 | 4.00 |
| 274 Marcus McCauley AU RC | 10.00 | 4.00 |
| 275 Matt Spaeth AU RC | 12.00 | 5.00 |
| 276 Demarcus Tate Tyler AU RC EXCH | 12.00 | 5.00 |
| 277 Charles Johnson AU RC EXCH | 8.00 | 3.00 |
| 278 Jonathan Wade AU RC | 10.00 | 4.00 |
| 279 Stewart Bradley AU RC | 12.00 | 5.00 |
| 280 Aaron Rouse AU RC | 12.00 | 5.00 |
| 281 Michael Okwo AU RC | 10.00 | 4.00 |
| 282 Daymeion Hughes AU RC | 10.00 | 4.00 |
| 283 Ray McDonald AU RC | 10.00 | 4.00 |
| 284 Thomas Clayton AU RC EXCH | 10.00 | 4.00 |
| 285 DeShawn Wynn AU RC | 12.00 | 5.00 |
| 286 Jason Snelling AU RC EXCH | 10.00 | 4.00 |
| 287 Kenneth Darby AU RC | 12.00 | 5.00 |
| 288 Ahmad Bradshaw AU291 RC | 40.00 | 15.00 |
| 289 Nate Ilaoa AU/203 RC | 12.00 | 5.00 |
| 290 Joel Filani AU RC | 10.00 | 4.00 |
| 291 Courtney Taylor AU RC | 10.00 | 4.00 |
| 292 Jordan Kent AU/245 RC | 10.00 | 4.00 |
| 293 Dallas Baker AU RC | 10.00 | 4.00 |
| 294 Roy Hall AU RC | 12.00 | 5.00 |
| 295 Chansi Stuckey AU RC EXCH | 10.00 | 4.00 |
| 296 Scott Chandler AU RC | 12.00 | 5.00 |
| 297 Ben Patrick AU RC | 10.00 | 4.00 |
| 298 Chris Leak AU RC | 10.00 | 4.00 |
| 299 Jared Zabransky AU RC EXCH | 12.00 | 5.00 |
| 300 Selvin Young AU/194 RC | 40.00 | 20.00 |
| 301 Adrian Peterson JSY AU RC | 300.00 | 175.00 |
| 302 Anthony Gonzalez JSY AU RC | 50.00 | 25.00 |
| 303 Antonio Pittman JSY AU RC EXCH | 20.00 | 8.00 |
| 304 Aundrae Allison AU RC | 20.00 | 8.00 |
| 305 Brady Quinn JSY AU RC | 150.00 | 75.00 |
| 306 Br.Jackson JSY AU RC EXCH | 20.00 | 8.00 |
| 307 Brian Leonard JSY AU RC | 20.00 | 8.00 |
| 308 Calvin Johnson JSY AU RC | 100.00 | 40.00 |
| 309 Chris Davis AU RC | 15.00 | 6.00 |
| 310 Chris Henry RB JSY AU RC EXCH | 20.00 | 8.00 |
| 311 Craig Davis JSY AU RC | 20.00 | 8.00 |
| 312 David Clowney AU RC | 20.00 | 8.00 |
| 313 Drew Stanton JSY AU RC | 20.00 | 8.00 |
| 314 Dwayne Bowe JSY AU RC | 50.00 | 25.00 |
| 315 Dwayne Jarrett JSY AU RC | 20.00 | 8.00 |
| 316 Dwayne Wright AU RC | 15.00 | 6.00 |
| 317 Gaines Adams JSY AU RC | 20.00 | 8.00 |
| 318 Garrett Wolfe JSY AU RC | 20.00 | 8.00 |
| 319 Greg Olsen JSY AU RC | 30.00 | 12.00 |
| 320 Isaiah Stanback AU RC | 20.00 | 8.00 |
| 321 Jacoby Jones AU RC | 20.00 | 8.00 |
| 322 JaMarcus Russell JSY AU RC | 80.00 | 40.00 |
| 323 James Jones AU RC | 20.00 | 8.00 |
| 324 Jason Hill JSY AU RC | 20.00 | 8.00 |
| 325 Jeff Rowe AU RC | 15.00 | 6.00 |
| 326 Joe Thomas JSY AU RC EXCH | 20.00 | 8.00 |
| 327 John Beck JSY AU RC | 20.00 | 8.00 |
| 328 J.Lee Higgins JSY AU RC | 15.00 | 6.00 |
| 329 Jordan Palmer AU RC | 20.00 | 8.00 |
| 330 Kenny Irons JSY AU RC EXCH | 20.00 | 8.00 |
| 331 Kevin Kolb JSY AU RC | 60.00 | 30.00 |
| 332 Kolby Smith AU RC | 20.00 | 8.00 |
| 333 LaRon Landry AU RC | 25.00 | 10.00 |
| 334 Laurent Robinson AU RC | 15.00 | 6.00 |
| 335 Lawrence Timmons AU RC | 20.00 | 8.00 |
| 336 Leon Hall AU RC | 15.00 | 6.00 |
| 337 Lorenzo Booker JSY AU RC | 20.00 | 8.00 |
| 338 Marshawn Lynch JSY AU RC | 80.00 | 40.00 |
| 339 Michael Bush JSY AU RC | 25.00 | 10.00 |
| 340 Mike Walker AU RC | 15.00 | 6.00 |
| 341 Patrick Willis JSY AU RC | 50.00 | 20.00 |
| 342 Paul Posluszny AU RC | 25.00 | 10.00 |
| 343 Paul Williams JSY AU RC | 15.00 | 6.00 |
| 344 Reggie Nelson AU RC | 15.00 | 6.00 |
| 345 Robert Meachem JSY AU RC | 20.00 | 8.00 |
| 346 Ryne Robinson AU RC | 15.00 | 6.00 |
| 347 Sidney Rice JSY AU RC | 20.00 | 8.00 |
| 348 Steve Breaston AU RC | 20.00 | 8.00 |
| 349 Steve Smith USC JSY AU RC | 40.00 | 15.00 |
| 350 Ted Ginn Jr. JSY AU RC | 40.00 | 15.00 |
| 351 Tony Hunt JSY AU RC | 20.00 | 8.00 |
| 352 Trent Edwards JSY AU RC | 60.00 | 30.00 |
| 353 T. Smith JSY AU RC EXCH | 30.00 | 12.00 |
| 354 Yamon Figurs JSY AU RC | 20.00 | 8.00 |
| 355 Zach Miller AU RC | 12.00 | 5.00 |

## 1998 Leaf Rookies and Stars

| | | |
|---|---|---|
| COMPLETE SET (300) | 250.00 | 125.00 |
| 1 Keyshawn Johnson | .60 | .25 |
| 2 Marvin Harrison | .60 | .25 |
| 3 Eddie Kennison | .40 | .15 |
| 4 Bryant Young | .25 | .08 |
| 5 Darren Woodson | .25 | .08 |
| 6 Tyrone Wheatley | .40 | .15 |
| 7 Michael Westbrook | .40 | .15 |
| 8 Charles Way | .25 | .08 |
| 9 Ricky Watters | .40 | .15 |
| 10 Chris Warren | .40 | .15 |
| 11 Wesley Walls | .40 | .15 |
| 12 Tamarick Vanover | .25 | .08 |
| 13 Zach Thomas | .60 | .25 |
| 14 Derrick Thomas | .60 | .25 |
| 15 Yancey Thigpen | .25 | .08 |
| 16 Vinny Testaverde | .40 | .15 |
| 17 Dana Stubblefield | .25 | .08 |
| 18 J.J. Stokes | .40 | .15 |
| 19 James Stewart | .40 | .15 |
| 20 Jeff George | .40 | .15 |
| 21 John Randle | .40 | .15 |
| 22 Gary Brown | .25 | .08 |
| 23 Ed McCaffrey | .40 | .15 |
| 24 James Jett | .40 | .15 |
| 25 Rob Johnson | .40 | .15 |
| 26 Daryl Johnston | .40 | .15 |
| 27 Jermaine Lewis | .40 | .15 |
| 28 Tony Martin | .40 | .15 |
| 29 Derrick Mayes | .40 | .15 |
| 30 Keenan McCardell | .40 | .15 |
| 31 O.J. McDuffie | .40 | .15 |
| 32 Chris Chandler | .40 | .15 |
| 33 Doug Flutie | .60 | .25 |
| 34 Scott Mitchell | .40 | .15 |
| 35 Warren Moon | .60 | .25 |
| 36 Rob Moore | .40 | .15 |
| 37 Johnnie Morton | .40 | .15 |
| 38 Neil O'Donnell | .40 | .15 |
| 39 Rich Gannon | .60 | .25 |
| 40 Andre Reed | .40 | .15 |
| 41 Jake Reed | .40 | .15 |
| 42 Errict Rhett | .40 | .15 |
| 43 Simeon Rice | .40 | .15 |

|  | | |
|---|---|---|
| ❑ 44 Andre Rison | .40 | .15 |
| ❑ 45 Eric Moulds | .60 | .25 |
| ❑ 46 Frank Sanders | .40 | .15 |
| ❑ 47 Damay Scott | .40 | .15 |
| ❑ 48 Junior Seau | .60 | .25 |
| ❑ 49 Shannon Sharpe | .40 | .15 |
| ❑ 50 Bruce Smith | .40 | .15 |
| ❑ 51 Jimmy Smith | .40 | .15 |
| ❑ 52 Robert Smith | .60 | .25 |
| ❑ 53 Derrick Alexander | .40 | .15 |
| ❑ 54 Kimble Anders | .40 | .15 |
| ❑ 55 Jamal Anderson | .60 | .25 |
| ❑ 56 Mario Bates | .40 | .15 |
| ❑ 57 Edgar Bennett | .25 | .08 |
| ❑ 58 Tim Biakabutuka | .40 | .15 |
| ❑ 59 Ki-Jana Carter | .25 | .08 |
| ❑ 60 Larry Centers | .25 | .08 |
| ❑ 61 Mark Chmura | .40 | .15 |
| ❑ 62 Wayne Chrebet | .60 | .25 |
| ❑ 63 Ben Coates | .40 | .15 |
| ❑ 64 Curtis Conway | .40 | .15 |
| ❑ 65 Randall Cunningham | .60 | .25 |
| ❑ 66 Ricky Dudley | .25 | .08 |
| ❑ 67 Bert Emanuel | .40 | .15 |
| ❑ 68 Bobby Engram | .40 | .15 |
| ❑ 69 William Floyd | .25 | .08 |
| ❑ 70 Irving Fryar | .40 | .15 |
| ❑ 71 Elvis Grbac | .40 | .15 |
| ❑ 72 Kevin Greene | .40 | .15 |
| ❑ 73 Jim Harbaugh | .40 | .15 |
| ❑ 74 Raymont Harris | .25 | .08 |
| ❑ 75 Garrison Hearst | .40 | .15 |
| ❑ 76 Greg Hill | .25 | .08 |
| ❑ 77 Desmond Howard | .40 | .15 |
| ❑ 78 Bobby Hoying | .40 | .15 |
| ❑ 79 Michael Jackson | .25 | .08 |
| ❑ 80 Terry Allen | .60 | .25 |
| ❑ 81 Jerome Bettis | .60 | .25 |
| ❑ 82 Jeff Blake | .40 | .15 |
| ❑ 83 Robert Brooks | .40 | .15 |
| ❑ 84 Tim Brown | .60 | .25 |
| ❑ 85 Isaac Bruce | .60 | .25 |
| ❑ 86 Cris Carter | .60 | .25 |
| ❑ 87 Ty Detmer | .40 | .15 |
| ❑ 88 Trent Dilfer | .40 | .15 |
| ❑ 89 Marshall Faulk | .75 | .30 |
| ❑ 90 Antonio Freeman | .60 | .25 |
| ❑ 91 Gus Frerotte | .25 | .08 |
| ❑ 92 Joey Galloway | .40 | .15 |
| ❑ 93 Michael Irvin | .40 | .15 |
| ❑ 94 Brad Johnson | .60 | .25 |
| ❑ 95 Danny Kanell | .40 | .15 |
| ❑ 96 Napoleon Kaufman | .60 | .25 |
| ❑ 97 Dorsey Levens | .60 | .25 |
| ❑ 98 Natrone Means | .40 | .15 |
| ❑ 99 Herman Moore | .40 | .15 |
| ❑ 100 Adrian Murrell | .40 | .15 |
| ❑ 101 Carl Pickens | .40 | .15 |
| ❑ 102 Rod Smith | .40 | .15 |
| ❑ 103 Thurman Thomas | .40 | .15 |
| ❑ 104 Reggie White | .60 | .25 |
| ❑ 105 Jim Druckenmiller | .25 | .08 |
| ❑ 106 Antowain Smith | .60 | .25 |
| ❑ 107 Reidel Anthony | .40 | .15 |
| ❑ 108 Ike Hilliard | .40 | .15 |
| ❑ 109 Rae Carruth | .25 | .08 |
| ❑ 110 Troy Davis | .25 | .08 |
| ❑ 111 Terance Mathis | .40 | .15 |
| ❑ 112 Brett Favre | 2.50 | 1.00 |
| ❑ 113 Dan Marino | 2.50 | 1.00 |
| ❑ 114 Emmitt Smith | 2.00 | .75 |
| ❑ 115 Barry Sanders | 2.00 | .75 |
| ❑ 116 Eddie George | .60 | .25 |
| ❑ 117 Drew Bledsoe | 1.00 | .40 |
| ❑ 118 Troy Aikman | 1.25 | .50 |
| ❑ 119 Terrell Davis | .60 | .25 |
| ❑ 120 John Elway | 2.50 | 1.00 |
| ❑ 121 Mark Brunell | .60 | .25 |
| ❑ 122 Jerry Rice | 1.25 | .50 |
| ❑ 123 Kordell Stewart | .60 | .25 |
| ❑ 124 Steve McNair | .60 | .25 |
| ❑ 125 Curtis Martin | .60 | .25 |
| ❑ 126 Steve Young | .75 | .30 |
| ❑ 127 Kerry Collins | .40 | .15 |
| ❑ 128 Terry Glenn | .40 | .15 |
| ❑ 129 Deion Sanders | .60 | .25 |
| ❑ 130 Mike Alstott | .60 | .25 |
| ❑ 131 Tony Banks | .40 | .15 |
| ❑ 132 Karim Abdul-Jabbar | .60 | .25 |
| ❑ 133 Terrell Owens | .60 | .25 |
| ❑ 134 Yatil Green | .25 | .08 |
| ❑ 135 Tony Gonzalez | .60 | .25 |
| ❑ 136 Byron Hanspard | .25 | .08 |
| ❑ 137 David LaFleur | .25 | .06 |
| ❑ 138 Danny Wuerffel | .25 | .08 |
| ❑ 139 Tiki Barber | .60 | .25 |
| ❑ 140 Peter Boulware | .25 | .08 |
| ❑ 141 Will Blackwell | .25 | .08 |
| ❑ 142 Warrick Dunn | .60 | .25 |
| ❑ 143 Corey Dillon | .60 | .25 |
| ❑ 144 Jake Plummer | .60 | .25 |
| ❑ 145 Neil Smith | .40 | .15 |
| ❑ 146 Charles Johnson | .25 | .08 |
| ❑ 147 Fred Lane | .25 | .08 |
| ❑ 148 Dan Wilkinson | .25 | .08 |
| ❑ 149 Ken Norton Jr. | .25 | .08 |
| ❑ 150 Stephen Davis | .25 | .08 |
| ❑ 151 Gilbert Brown | .25 | .08 |
| ❑ 152 Kenny Bynum SP | .25 | .08 |
| ❑ 153 Derrick Cullors | .25 | .08 |
| ❑ 154 Charlie Garner | .40 | .15 |
| ❑ 155 Jeff Graham | .25 | .08 |
| ❑ 156 Warren Sapp | .40 | .15 |
| ❑ 157 Jerald Moore | .25 | .08 |
| ❑ 158 Sean Dawkins | .25 | .08 |
| ❑ 159 Charlie Jones | .25 | .08 |
| ❑ 160 Kevin Lockett | .25 | .08 |
| ❑ 161 James McKnight | .60 | .25 |
| ❑ 162 Chris Penn | .25 | .08 |
| ❑ 163 Leslie Shepherd | .25 | .08 |
| ❑ 164 Karl Williams | .25 | .08 |
| ❑ 165 Mark Bruener | .25 | .08 |
| ❑ 166 Ernie Conwell | .25 | .08 |
| ❑ 167 Ken Dilger | .25 | .08 |
| ❑ 168 Troy Drayton | .25 | .08 |
| ❑ 169 Freddie Jones | .25 | .08 |
| ❑ 170 Dale Carter | .25 | .08 |
| ❑ 171 Charles Woodson RC | 8.00 | 3.00 |
| ❑ 172 Alonzo Mayes RC | 2.50 | 1.00 |
| ❑ 173 Andre Wadsworth RC | 4.00 | 1.50 |
| ❑ 174 Grant Wistrom RC | 4.00 | 1.50 |
| ❑ 175 Greg Ellis RC | 2.50 | 1.00 |
| ❑ 176 Chris Howard RC | 2.50 | 1.00 |
| ❑ 177 Keith Brooking RC | 6.00 | 2.50 |
| ❑ 178 Takeo Spikes RC | 6.00 | 2.50 |
| ❑ 179 Anthony Simmons RC | 4.00 | 1.50 |
| ❑ 180 Brian Simmons RC | 4.00 | 1.50 |
| ❑ 181 Sam Cowart RC | 4.00 | 1.50 |
| ❑ 182 Ken Oxendine RC | 2.50 | 1.00 |
| ❑ 183 Vonnie Holliday RC | 4.00 | 1.50 |
| ❑ 184 Terry Fair RC | 4.00 | 1.50 |
| ❑ 185 Shaun Williams RC | 4.00 | 1.50 |
| ❑ 186 Tremayne Stephens RC | 2.50 | 1.00 |
| ❑ 187 Duane Starks RC | 2.50 | 1.00 |
| ❑ 188 Jason Peter RC | 2.50 | 1.00 |
| ❑ 189 Tebucky Jones RC | 2.50 | 1.00 |
| ❑ 190 Donovin Darius RC | 4.00 | 1.50 |
| ❑ 191 R.W. McQuarters RC | 4.00 | 1.50 |
| ❑ 192 Corey Chavous RC | 6.00 | 2.50 |
| ❑ 193 Cameron Cleeland RC | 2.50 | 1.00 |
| ❑ 194 Stephen Alexander RC | 4.00 | 1.50 |
| ❑ 195 Rod Rutledge RC | 2.50 | 1.00 |
| ❑ 196 Scott Frost RC | 2.50 | 1.00 |
| ❑ 197 Fred Beasley RC | 2.50 | 1.00 |
| ❑ 198 Dorian Boose RC | 2.50 | 1.00 |
| ❑ 199 Randy Moss RC | 30.00 | 12.00 |
| ❑ 200 Jacquez Green RC | 4.00 | 1.50 |
| ❑ 201 Marcus Nash RC | 2.50 | 1.00 |
| ❑ 202 Hines Ward RC | 25.00 | 12.50 |
| ❑ 203 Kevin Dyson RC | 6.00 | 2.50 |
| ❑ 204 E.G. Green RC | 4.00 | 1.50 |
| ❑ 205 Germane Crowell RC | 6.00 | 2.50 |
| ❑ 206 Joe Jurevicius RC | 6.00 | 2.50 |
| ❑ 207 Tony Simmons RC | 4.00 | 1.50 |
| ❑ 208 Tim Dwight RC | 6.00 | 2.50 |
| ❑ 209 Az-Zahir Hakim RC | 6.00 | 2.50 |
| ❑ 210 Jerome Pathon RC | 6.00 | 2.50 |
| ❑ 211 Pat Johnson RC | 4.00 | 1.50 |
| ❑ 212 Michael Ricks RC | 4.00 | 1.50 |
| ❑ 213 Donald Hayes RC | 4.00 | 1.50 |
| ❑ 214 Jammi German RC | 2.50 | 1.00 |
| ❑ 215 Larry Shannon RC | 2.50 | 1.00 |
| ❑ 216 Brian Alford RC | 2.50 | 1.00 |
| ❑ 217 Curtis Enis RC | 2.50 | 1.00 |
| ❑ 218 Fred Taylor RC | 10.00 | 4.00 |
| ❑ 219 Robert Edwards RC | 4.00 | 1.50 |
| ❑ 220 Ahman Green RC | 15.00 | 6.00 |
| ❑ 221 Tavian Banks RC | 4.00 | 1.50 |
| ❑ 222 Skip Hicks RC | 4.00 | 1.50 |
| ❑ 223 Robert Holcombe RC | 4.00 | 1.50 |
| ❑ 224 John Avery RC | 4.00 | 1.50 |
| ❑ 225 Chris Fuamatu-Ma'afala RC | 4.00 | 1.50 |
| ❑ 226 Michael Pittman RC | 8.00 | 4.00 |
| ❑ 227 Rashaan Shehee RC | 4.00 | 1.50 |
| ❑ 228 Jonathan Linton RC | 4.00 | 1.50 |
| ❑ 229 Jon Ritchie RC | 4.00 | 1.50 |
| ❑ 230 Chris Floyd RC | 2.50 | 1.00 |
| ❑ 231 Wilmont Perry RC | 2.50 | 1.00 |
| ❑ 232 Raymond Priester RC | 2.50 | 1.00 |
| ❑ 233 Peyton Manning RC | 50.00 | 20.00 |
| ❑ 234 Ryan Leaf RC | 6.00 | 2.50 |
| ❑ 235 Brian Griese RC | 12.00 | 5.00 |
| ❑ 236 Jeff Ogden RC | 6.00 | 2.50 |
| ❑ 237 Charlie Batch RC | 6.00 | 2.50 |
| ❑ 238 Moses Moreno RC | 2.50 | 1.00 |
| ❑ 239 Jonathan Quinn RC | 6.00 | 2.50 |
| ❑ 240 Flozell Adams RC | 2.50 | 1.00 |
| ❑ 241 Brett Favre PT | 12.00 | 5.00 |
| ❑ 242 Dan Marino PT | 12.00 | 5.00 |
| ❑ 243 Emmitt Smith PT | 10.00 | 4.00 |
| ❑ 244 Barry Sanders PT | 10.00 | 4.00 |
| ❑ 245 Eddie George PT | 2.50 | 1.00 |
| ❑ 246 Drew Bledsoe PT | 5.00 | 2.00 |
| ❑ 247 Troy Aikman PT | 6.00 | 2.50 |
| ❑ 248 Terrell Davis PT | 2.50 | 1.00 |
| ❑ 249 John Elway PT | 12.00 | 5.00 |
| ❑ 250 Carl Pickens PT | 2.50 | 1.00 |
| ❑ 251 Jerry Rice PT | 6.00 | 2.50 |
| ❑ 252 Kordell Stewart PT | 2.50 | 1.00 |
| ❑ 253 Steve McNair PT | 2.50 | 1.00 |
| ❑ 254 Curtis Martin PT | 2.50 | 1.00 |
| ❑ 255 Steve Young PT | 4.00 | 1.50 |
| ❑ 256 Herman Moore PT | 2.50 | 1.00 |
| ❑ 257 Dorsey Levens PT | 2.50 | 1.00 |
| ❑ 258 Deion Sanders PT | 2.50 | 1.00 |
| ❑ 259 Napoleon Kaufman PT | 2.50 | 1.00 |
| ❑ 260 Warrick Dunn PT | 2.50 | 1.00 |
| ❑ 261 Corey Dillon PT | 2.50 | 1.00 |
| ❑ 262 Jerome Bettis PT | 2.50 | 1.00 |
| ❑ 263 Tim Brown PT | 2.50 | 1.00 |
| ❑ 264 Cris Carter PT | 2.50 | 1.00 |
| ❑ 265 Antonio Freeman PT | 2.50 | 1.00 |
| ❑ 266 Randy Moss PT | 15.00 | 6.00 |
| ❑ 267 Curtis Enis PT | 2.50 | 1.00 |
| ❑ 268 Fred Taylor PT | 4.00 | 1.50 |
| ❑ 269 Robert Edwards PT | 2.50 | 1.00 |
| ❑ 270 Peyton Manning PT | 25.00 | 10.00 |
| ❑ 271 Barry Sanders TL | 1.00 | .40 |
| ❑ 272 Eddie George TL | .40 | .15 |
| ❑ 273 Troy Aikman TL | .60 | .25 |
| ❑ 274 Mark Brunell TL | .25 | .08 |
| ❑ 275 Kordell Stewart TL | .60 | .25 |
| ❑ 276 Tim Biakabutuka TL | .25 | .08 |
| ❑ 277 Terry Glenn TL | .25 | .08 |
| ❑ 278 Mike Alstott TL | .25 | .08 |
| ❑ 279 Tony Banks TL | .25 | .08 |
| ❑ 280 Karim Abdul-Jabbar TL | .25 | .08 |
| ❑ 281 Terrell Owens TL | .40 | .15 |
| ❑ 282 Byron Hanspard TL | .25 | .08 |
| ❑ 283 Jake Plummer TL | .40 | .15 |
| ❑ 284 Terry Allen TL | .25 | .08 |
| ❑ 285 Jeff Blake TL | .25 | .08 |
| ❑ 286 Brad Johnson TL | .25 | .08 |
| ❑ 287 Danny Kanell TL | .25 | .08 |
| ❑ 288 Natrone Means TL | .25 | .08 |
| ❑ 289 Rod Smith TL | .25 | .08 |
| ❑ 290 Thurman Thomas TL | .25 | .08 |
| ❑ 291 Reggie White TL | .25 | .08 |
| ❑ 292 Troy Davis TL | .25 | .08 |
| ❑ 293 Curtis Conway TL | .25 | .08 |
| ❑ 294 Irving Fryar TL | .25 | .08 |
| ❑ 295 Jim Harbaugh TL | .25 | .08 |
| ❑ 296 Andre Rison TL | .25 | .08 |
| ❑ 297 Ricky Watters TL | .25 | .08 |
| ❑ 298 Keyshawn Johnson TL | .25 | .08 |
| ❑ 299 Jeff George TL | .25 | .08 |
| ❑ 300 Marshall Faulk TL | .60 | .25 |

## 1999 Leaf Rookies and Stars

| | | |
|---|---|---|
| ❑ COMPLETE SET (300) | 150.00 | 75.00 |
| ❑ COMP.SET w/o SP's (200) | 30.00 | 15.00 |
| ❑ 1 Frank Sanders | .40 | .15 |
| ❑ 2 Adrian Murrell | .40 | .15 |
| ❑ 3 Rob Moore | .40 | .15 |
| ❑ 4 Simeon Rice | .40 | .15 |
| ❑ 5 Michael Pittman | .25 | .08 |

| ❏ | | | |
|---|---|---|---|
| ❏ 6 | Jake Plummer | .40 | .15 |
| ❏ 7 | Chris Chandler | .40 | .15 |
| ❏ 8 | Tim Dwight | .40 | .15 |
| ❏ 9 | Chris Calloway | .25 | .08 |
| ❏ 10 | Terance Mathis | .40 | .15 |
| ❏ 11 | Jamal Anderson | .60 | .25 |
| ❏ 12 | Byron Hanspard | .25 | .08 |
| ❏ 13 | O.J. Santiago | .25 | .08 |
| ❏ 14 | Ken Oxendine | .25 | .08 |
| ❏ 15 | Priest Holmes | 1.00 | .40 |
| ❏ 16 | Scott Mitchell | .40 | .15 |
| ❏ 17 | Tony Banks | .40 | .15 |
| ❏ 18 | Patrick Johnson | .25 | .08 |
| ❏ 19 | Rod Woodson | .40 | .15 |
| ❏ 20 | Jermaine Lewis | .40 | .15 |
| ❏ 21 | Errict Rhett | .40 | .15 |
| ❏ 22 | Stoney Case | .25 | .08 |
| ❏ 23 | Andre Reed | .40 | .15 |
| ❏ 24 | Eric Moulds | .60 | .25 |
| ❏ 25 | Rob Johnson | .40 | .15 |
| ❏ 26 | Doug Flutie | .60 | .25 |
| ❏ 27 | Bruce Smith | .40 | .15 |
| ❏ 28 | Jay Riemersma | .25 | .08 |
| ❏ 29 | Antowain Smith | .40 | .15 |
| ❏ 30 | Thurman Thomas | .40 | .15 |
| ❏ 31 | Jonathan Linton | .25 | .08 |
| ❏ 32 | Muhsin Muhammad | .40 | .15 |
| ❏ 33 | Rae Carruth | .25 | .08 |
| ❏ 34 | Wesley Walls | .40 | .15 |
| ❏ 35 | Fred Lane | .40 | .15 |
| ❏ 36 | Kevin Greene | .25 | .08 |
| ❏ 37 | Tim Biakabutuka | .40 | .15 |
| ❏ 38 | Curtis Enis | .25 | .08 |
| ❏ 39 | Shane Matthews | .40 | .15 |
| ❏ 40 | Bobby Engram | .40 | .15 |
| ❏ 41 | Curtis Conway | .40 | .15 |
| ❏ 42 | Marcus Robinson | 1.25 | .50 |
| ❏ 43 | Dhanny Scott | .25 | .08 |
| ❏ 44 | Carl Pickens | .40 | .15 |
| ❏ 45 | Corey Dillon | .60 | .25 |
| ❏ 46 | Jeff Blake | .40 | .15 |
| ❏ 47 | Tony Kirby | .25 | .08 |
| ❏ 48 | Ty Detmer | .25 | .08 |
| ❏ 49 | Leslie Shepherd | .25 | .08 |
| ❏ 50 | Karim Abdul-Jabbar | .40 | .15 |
| ❏ 51 | Emmitt Smith | 1.25 | .50 |
| ❏ 52 | Deion Sanders | .60 | .25 |
| ❏ 53 | Michael Irvin | .40 | .15 |
| ❏ 54 | Rocket Ismail | .40 | .15 |
| ❏ 55 | David LaFleur | .25 | .08 |
| ❏ 56 | Troy Aikman | 1.25 | .50 |
| ❏ 57 | Ed McCaffrey | .40 | .15 |
| ❏ 58 | Rod Smith | .40 | .15 |
| ❏ 59 | Shannon Sharpe | .40 | .15 |
| ❏ 60 | Brian Griese | .60 | .25 |
| ❏ 61 | John Elway | 2.00 | .75 |
| ❏ 62 | Bubby Brister | .25 | .08 |
| ❏ 63 | Neil Smith | .40 | .15 |
| ❏ 64 | Terrell Davis | .60 | .25 |
| ❏ 65 | John Avery | .25 | .08 |
| ❏ 66 | Derek Loville | .25 | .08 |
| ❏ 67 | Ron Rivers | .25 | .08 |
| ❏ 68 | Herman Moore | .40 | .15 |
| ❏ 69 | Johnnie Morton | .40 | .15 |
| ❏ 70 | Charlie Batch | .60 | .25 |
| ❏ 71 | Barry Sanders | 2.00 | .75 |
| ❏ 72 | Germane Crowell | .25 | .08 |
| ❏ 73 | Greg Hill | .25 | .08 |
| ❏ 74 | Gus Frerotte | .25 | .08 |
| ❏ 75 | Corey Bradford | .25 | .08 |
| ❏ 76 | Dorsey Levens | .60 | .25 |
| ❏ 77 | Antonio Freeman | .60 | .25 |
| ❏ 78 | Mark Chmura | .25 | .08 |
| ❏ 79 | Brett Favre | 2.00 | .75 |
| ❏ 80 | Bill Schroeder | .40 | .15 |
| ❏ 81 | Matt Hasselbeck | .60 | .25 |
| ❏ 82 | E.G. Green | .25 | .08 |
| ❏ 83 | Ken Dilger | .25 | .08 |
| ❏ 84 | Jerome Pathon | .25 | .08 |
| ❏ 85 | Marvin Harrison | .60 | .25 |
| ❏ 86 | Peyton Manning | 2.00 | .75 |
| ❏ 87 | Tavian Banks | .25 | .08 |
| ❏ 88 | Keenan McCardell | .40 | .15 |
| ❏ 89 | Mark Brunell | .60 | .25 |
| ❏ 90 | Fred Taylor | .60 | .25 |
| ❏ 91 | Jimmy Smith | .40 | .15 |
| ❏ 92 | James Stewart | .40 | .15 |
| ❏ 93 | Kyle Brady | .25 | .08 |
| ❏ 94 | Derrick Thomas | .60 | .25 |
| ❏ 95 | Rashaan Shehee | .25 | .08 |
| ❏ 96 | Derrick Alexander WR | .40 | .15 |
| ❏ 97 | Byron Bam Morris | .25 | .08 |
| ❏ 98 | Andre Rison | .40 | .15 |
| ❏ 99 | Elvis Grbac | .40 | .15 |
| ❏ 100 | Tony Gonzalez | .60 | .25 |
| ❏ 101 | Donnell Bennett | .25 | .08 |
| ❏ 102 | Warren Moon | .60 | .25 |
| ❏ 103 | Zach Thomas | .60 | .25 |
| ❏ 104 | Oronde Gadsden | .40 | .15 |
| ❏ 105 | Dan Marino | 2.00 | .75 |
| ❏ 106 | O.J. McDuffie | .40 | .15 |
| ❏ 107 | Tony Martin | .40 | .15 |
| ❏ 108 | Randy Moss | 1.50 | .60 |
| ❏ 109 | Cris Carter | .60 | .25 |
| ❏ 110 | Robert Smith | .60 | .25 |
| ❏ 111 | Randall Cunningham | .60 | .25 |
| ❏ 112 | Jake Reed | .40 | .15 |
| ❏ 113 | John Randle | .40 | .15 |
| ❏ 114 | Leroy Hoard | .40 | .15 |
| ❏ 115 | Jeff George | .40 | .15 |
| ❏ 116 | Ty Law | .40 | .15 |
| ❏ 117 | Shawn Jefferson | .25 | .08 |
| ❏ 118 | Troy Brown | .40 | .15 |
| ❏ 119 | Robert Edwards | .40 | .15 |
| ❏ 120 | Tony Simmons | .25 | .08 |
| ❏ 121 | Terry Glenn | .60 | .25 |
| ❏ 122 | Ben Coates | .40 | .15 |
| ❏ 123 | Drew Bledsoe | .75 | .30 |
| ❏ 124 | Terry Allen | .40 | .15 |
| ❏ 125 | Cameron Cleeland | .25 | .08 |
| ❏ 126 | Eddie Kennison | .40 | .15 |
| ❏ 127 | Amani Toomer | .25 | .08 |
| ❏ 128 | Kerry Collins | .40 | .15 |
| ❏ 129 | Joe Jurevicius | .25 | .08 |
| ❏ 130 | Tiki Barber | .60 | .25 |
| ❏ 131 | Ike Hilliard | .25 | .08 |
| ❏ 132 | Michael Strahan | .40 | .15 |
| ❏ 133 | Gary Brown | .25 | .08 |
| ❏ 134 | Jason Sehorn | .25 | .08 |
| ❏ 135 | Curtis Martin | .60 | .25 |
| ❏ 136 | Vinny Testaverde | .40 | .15 |
| ❏ 137 | Dedric Ward | .25 | .08 |
| ❏ 138 | Keyshawn Johnson | .60 | .25 |
| ❏ 139 | Wayne Chrebet | .40 | .15 |
| ❏ 140 | Tyrone Wheatley | .40 | .15 |
| ❏ 141 | Napoleon Kaufman | .60 | .25 |
| ❏ 142 | Tim Brown | .60 | .25 |
| ❏ 143 | Rickey Dudley | .25 | .08 |
| ❏ 144 | Jon Ritchie | .25 | .08 |
| ❏ 145 | James Jett | .25 | .08 |
| ❏ 146 | Rich Gannon | .60 | .25 |
| ❏ 147 | Charles Woodson | .60 | .25 |
| ❏ 148 | Charles Johnson | .25 | .08 |
| ❏ 149 | Duce Staley | .60 | .25 |
| ❏ 150 | Will Blackwell | .25 | .08 |
| ❏ 151 | Kordell Stewart | .40 | .15 |
| ❏ 152 | Jerome Bettis | .60 | .25 |
| ❏ 153 | Hines Ward | .60 | .25 |
| ❏ 154 | Richard Huntley | .40 | .15 |
| ❏ 155 | Natrone Means | .40 | .15 |
| ❏ 156 | Mikhael Ricks | .25 | .08 |
| ❏ 157 | Junior Seau | .40 | .15 |
| ❏ 158 | Jim Harbaugh | .40 | .15 |
| ❏ 159 | Ryan Leaf | .60 | .25 |
| ❏ 160 | Erik Kramer | .25 | .08 |
| ❏ 161 | Terrell Owens | .60 | .25 |
| ❏ 162 | J.J. Stokes | .40 | .15 |
| ❏ 163 | Lawrence Phillips | .25 | .08 |
| ❏ 164 | Charlie Garner | .25 | .08 |
| ❏ 165 | Jerry Rice | 1.25 | .50 |
| ❏ 166 | Garrison Hearst | .40 | .15 |
| ❏ 167 | Steve Young | .75 | .30 |
| ❏ 168 | Derrick Mayes | .40 | .15 |
| ❏ 169 | Ahman Green | .60 | .25 |
| ❏ 170 | Joey Galloway | .60 | .25 |
| ❏ 171 | Ricky Watters | .40 | .15 |
| ❏ 172 | Jon Kitna | .60 | .25 |
| ❏ 173 | Sean Dawkins | .25 | .08 |
| ❏ 174 | Az-Zahir Hakim | .25 | .08 |
| ❏ 175 | Robert Holcombe | .25 | .08 |
| ❏ 176 | Isaac Bruce | .60 | .25 |
| ❏ 177 | Amp Lee | .25 | .08 |
| ❏ 178 | Marshall Faulk | .75 | .30 |
| ❏ 179 | Trent Green | .60 | .25 |
| ❏ 180 | Eric Zeier | .40 | .15 |
| ❏ 181 | Bert Emanuel | .40 | .15 |
| ❏ 182 | Jacquez Green | .25 | .08 |
| ❏ 183 | Reidel Anthony | .40 | .15 |
| ❏ 184 | Warren Sapp | .25 | .08 |
| ❏ 185 | Mike Alstott | .60 | .25 |
| ❏ 186 | Warrick Dunn | .60 | .25 |
| ❏ 187 | Trent Dilfer | .40 | .15 |
| ❏ 188 | Neil O'Donnell | .40 | .15 |
| ❏ 189 | Eddie George | .60 | .25 |
| ❏ 190 | Yancey Thigpen | .25 | .08 |
| ❏ 191 | Steve McNair | .60 | .25 |
| ❏ 192 | Kevin Dyson | .40 | .15 |
| ❏ 193 | Frank Wycheck | .25 | .08 |
| ❏ 194 | Stephen Davis | .60 | .25 |
| ❏ 195 | Stephen Alexander | .25 | .08 |
| ❏ 196 | Darrell Green | .25 | .08 |
| ❏ 197 | Skip Hicks | .40 | .15 |
| ❏ 198 | Brad Johnson | .60 | .25 |
| ❏ 199 | Michael Westbrook | .40 | .15 |
| ❏ 200 | Albert Connell | .25 | .08 |
| ❏ 201 | David Boston RC | 3.00 | 1.50 |
| ❏ 202 | Joel Makovicka RC | 2.50 | 1.25 |
| ❏ 203 | Chris Greisen RC | 2.50 | 1.25 |
| ❏ 204 | Jeff Paulk RC | 1.50 | .75 |
| ❏ 205 | Reginald Kelly RC | 2.50 | 1.25 |
| ❏ 206 | Chris McAlister RC | 2.50 | 1.25 |
| ❏ 207 | Brandon Stokley RC | 4.00 | 1.50 |
| ❏ 208 | Antoine Winfield RC | 2.50 | 1.25 |
| ❏ 209 | Bobby Collins RC | 1.50 | .75 |
| ❏ 210 | Peerless Price RC | 3.00 | 1.50 |
| ❏ 211 | Shawn Bryson RC | 3.00 | 1.50 |
| ❏ 212 | Sheldon Jackson RC | 2.50 | 1.25 |
| ❏ 213 | Kamil Loud RC | 1.50 | .75 |
| ❏ 214 | D'Wayne Bates RC | 2.50 | 1.25 |
| ❏ 215 | Jerry Azumah RC | 2.50 | 1.25 |
| ❏ 216 | Marty Booker RC | 3.00 | 1.50 |
| ❏ 217 | Cade McNown RC | 2.50 | 1.25 |
| ❏ 218 | James Allen RC | 3.00 | 1.50 |
| ❏ 219 | Nick Williams RC | 2.50 | 1.25 |
| ❏ 220 | Akili Smith RC | 2.50 | 1.25 |
| ❏ 221 | Craig Yeast RC | 2.50 | 1.25 |
| ❏ 222 | Damon Griffen RC | 2.50 | 1.25 |
| ❏ 223 | Scott Covington RC | 1.50 | .75 |
| ❏ 224 | Michael Basnight RC | 1.50 | .75 |
| ❏ 225 | Ronnie Powell RC | 1.50 | .75 |
| ❏ 226 | Rahim Abdullah RC | 2.50 | 1.25 |
| ❏ 227 | Tim Couch RC | 3.00 | 1.50 |
| ❏ 228 | Kevin Johnson RC | 3.00 | 1.50 |
| ❏ 229 | Darrin Chiaverini RC | 2.50 | 1.25 |
| ❏ 230 | Mark Campbell RC | 2.50 | 1.25 |
| ❏ 231 | Mike Lucky RC | 2.50 | 1.25 |
| ❏ 232 | Robert Thomas RC | 2.50 | 1.25 |
| ❏ 233 | Ebenezer Ekuban RC | 2.50 | 1.25 |
| ❏ 234 | Dat Nguyen RC | 3.00 | 1.50 |
| ❏ 235 | Wane McGarity RC | 1.50 | .75 |
| ❏ 236 | Jason Tucker RC | 2.50 | 1.25 |
| ❏ 237 | Olandis Gary RC | 3.00 | 1.50 |
| ❏ 238 | Al Wilson RC | 3.00 | 1.50 |
| ❏ 239 | Travis McGriff RC | 1.50 | .75 |
| ❏ 240 | Desmond Clark RC | 3.00 | 1.50 |
| ❏ 241 | Andre Cooper RC | 1.50 | .75 |
| ❏ 242 | Chris Watson RC | 1.50 | .75 |
| ❏ 243 | Sedrick Irvin RC | 1.50 | .75 |
| ❏ 244 | Chris Claiborne RC | 1.50 | .75 |
| ❏ 245 | Cory Sauter RC | 1.50 | .75 |
| ❏ 246 | Brock Olivo RC | 1.50 | .75 |
| ❏ 247 | De'Mond Parker RC | 1.50 | .75 |
| ❏ 248 | Aaron Brooks RC | 6.00 | 2.50 |
| ❏ 249 | Antuan Edwards RC | 2.50 | 1.25 |
| ❏ 250 | Basil Mitchell RC | 1.50 | .75 |
| ❏ 251 | Terrence Wilkins RC | 2.50 | 1.25 |
| ❏ 252 | Edgerrin James RC | 15.00 | 6.00 |
| ❏ 253 | Fernando Bryant RC | 2.50 | 1.25 |
| ❏ 254 | Mike Cloud RC | 2.50 | 1.25 |
| ❏ 255 | Larry Parker RC | 3.00 | 1.50 |

| | | | |
|---|---|---|---|
| 256 | Rob Konrad RC | 3.00 | 1.50 |
| 257 | Cecil Collins RC | 1.50 | .75 |
| 258 | James Johnson RC | 2.50 | 1.25 |
| 259 | Jim Kleinsasser RC | 3.00 | 1.50 |
| 260 | Daunte Culpepper RC | 15.00 | 6.00 |
| 261 | Michael Bishop RC | 3.00 | 1.50 |
| 262 | Andy Katzenmoyer RC | 2.50 | 1.25 |
| 263 | Kevin Faulk RC | 2.50 | 1.25 |
| 264 | Brett Bech RC | 1.50 | .75 |
| 265 | Ricky Williams RC | 8.00 | 3.00 |
| 266 | Sean Bennett RC | 1.50 | .75 |
| 267 | Joe Montgomery RC | 2.50 | 1.25 |
| 268 | Dan Campbell RC | 1.50 | .75 |
| 269 | Ray Lucas RC | 2.50 | 1.25 |
| 270 | Scott Dreisbach RC | 2.50 | 1.25 |
| 271 | Jed Weaver RC | 1.50 | .75 |
| 272 | Dameane Douglas RC | 2.50 | 1.25 |
| 273 | Cecil Martin RC | 2.50 | 1.25 |
| 274 | Donovan McNabb RC | 20.00 | 7.50 |
| 275 | Na Brown RC | 2.50 | 1.25 |
| 276 | Jerame Tuman RC | 2.50 | 1.25 |
| 277 | Amos Zereoue RC | 3.00 | 1.50 |
| 278 | Troy Edwards RC | 2.50 | 1.25 |
| 279 | Jermaine Fazande RC | 2.50 | 1.25 |
| 280 | Steve Heiden RC | 3.00 | 1.50 |
| 281 | Jeff Garcia RC | 20.00 | 7.50 |
| 282 | Terry Jackson RC | 2.50 | 1.25 |
| 283 | Charlie Rogers RC | 2.50 | 1.25 |
| 284 | Brock Huard RC | 2.50 | 1.25 |
| 285 | Karsten Bailey RC | 2.50 | 1.25 |
| 286 | Lamar Bailey RC | 1.50 | .75 |
| 287 | Justin Watson RC | 1.50 | .75 |
| 288 | Kurt Warner RC | 20.00 | 7.50 |
| 289 | Torry Holt RC | 12.00 | 5.00 |
| 290 | Joe Germaine RC | 2.50 | 1.25 |
| 291 | Dre' Bly RC | 3.00 | 1.50 |
| 292 | Martin Gramatica RC | 1.50 | .75 |
| 293 | Rabih Abdullah RC | 2.50 | 1.25 |
| 294 | Shaun King RC | 2.50 | 1.25 |
| 295 | Anthony McFarland RC | 2.50 | 1.25 |
| 296 | Darnell McDonald RC | 2.50 | 1.25 |
| 297 | Kevin Daft RC | 2.50 | 1.25 |
| 298 | Jevon Kearse RC | 8.00 | 3.00 |
| 299 | Mike Sellers | .25 | .08 |
| 300 | Champ Bailey RC | 6.00 | 2.50 |

## 2000 Leaf Rookies and Stars

| | | | |
|---|---|---|---|
| | COMP.SET w/SP's (100) | 15.00 | 6.00 |
| 1 | Jake Plummer | .40 | .15 |
| 2 | David Boston | .60 | .25 |
| 3 | Tim Dwight | .60 | .25 |
| 4 | Jamal Anderson | .60 | .25 |
| 5 | Chris Chandler | .40 | .15 |
| 6 | Tony Banks | .40 | .15 |
| 7 | Qadry Ismail | .40 | .15 |
| 8 | Eric Moulds | .60 | .25 |
| 9 | Doug Flutie | .60 | .25 |
| 10 | Lamar Smith | .40 | .15 |
| 11 | Peerless Price | .40 | .15 |
| 12 | Rob Johnson | .40 | .15 |
| 13 | Reggie White | .60 | .25 |
| 14 | Muhsin Muhammad | .40 | .15 |
| 15 | Steve Beuerlein | .40 | .15 |
| 16 | Cade McNown | .25 | .08 |
| 17 | Derrick Alexander | .40 | .15 |
| 18 | Marcus Robinson | .60 | .25 |
| 19 | Corey Dillon | .60 | .25 |
| 20 | Akili Smith | .25 | .08 |
| 21 | Tim Couch | .40 | .15 |
| 22 | Kevin Johnson | .60 | .25 |

| | | | |
|---|---|---|---|
| 23 | Emmitt Smith | 1.25 | .50 |
| 24 | Troy Aikman | 1.25 | .50 |
| 25 | Joey Galloway | .40 | .15 |
| 26 | Rocket Ismail | .40 | .15 |
| 27 | John Elway | 2.00 | .75 |
| 28 | Terrell Davis | .60 | .25 |
| 29 | Brian Griese | .40 | .15 |
| 30 | Olandis Gary | .60 | .25 |
| 31 | Ed McCaffrey | .60 | .25 |
| 32 | Rod Smith | .40 | .15 |
| 33 | Barry Sanders | 1.50 | .60 |
| 34 | Charlie Batch | .60 | .25 |
| 35 | Germane Crowell | .25 | .08 |
| 36 | James Stewart | .40 | .15 |
| 37 | Brett Favre | 2.00 | .75 |
| 38 | Dorsey Levens | .40 | .15 |
| 39 | Antonio Freeman | .60 | .25 |
| 40 | Peyton Manning | 1.50 | .60 |
| 41 | Edgerrin James | 1.00 | .40 |
| 42 | Marvin Harrison | .60 | .25 |
| 43 | Fred Taylor | .60 | .25 |
| 44 | Mark Brunell | .60 | .25 |
| 45 | Jimmy Smith | .40 | .15 |
| 46 | Elvis Grbac | .40 | .15 |
| 47 | Tony Gonzalez | .40 | .15 |
| 48 | Dan Marino | 2.00 | .75 |
| 49 | Joe Horn | .40 | .15 |
| 50 | Jay Fiedler | .40 | .15 |
| 51 | James Allen | .40 | .15 |
| 52 | Randy Moss | 1.25 | .50 |
| 53 | Daunte Culpepper | .75 | .30 |
| 54 | Cris Carter | .60 | .25 |
| 55 | Robert Smith | .60 | .25 |
| 56 | Drew Bledsoe | .75 | .30 |
| 57 | Terry Glenn | .60 | .25 |
| 58 | Ricky Williams | .60 | .25 |
| 59 | Amani Toomer | .40 | .15 |
| 60 | Kerry Collins | .40 | .15 |
| 61 | Curtis Martin | .60 | .25 |
| 62 | Vinny Testaverde | .40 | .15 |
| 63 | Wayne Chrebet | .60 | .25 |
| 64 | Tim Brown | .60 | .25 |
| 65 | Tyrone Wheatley | .40 | .15 |
| 66 | Rich Gannon | .60 | .25 |
| 67 | Donovan McNabb | 1.00 | .40 |
| 68 | Duce Staley | .60 | .25 |
| 69 | Jerome Bettis | .60 | .25 |
| 70 | Donald Hayes | .25 | .08 |
| 71 | Junior Seau | .60 | .25 |
| 72 | Jermaine Fazande | .25 | .08 |
| 73 | Jerry Rice | 1.25 | .50 |
| 74 | Steve Young | .75 | .30 |
| 75 | Terrell Owens | .60 | .25 |
| 76 | Charlie Garner | .40 | .15 |
| 77 | Jeff Garcia | .60 | .25 |
| 78 | Tim Biakabutuka | .40 | .15 |
| 79 | Tiki Barber | .60 | .25 |
| 80 | Ricky Watters | .40 | .15 |
| 81 | Kurt Warner | 1.25 | .50 |
| 82 | Marshall Faulk | .75 | .30 |
| 83 | Isaac Bruce | .60 | .25 |
| 84 | Torry Holt | .60 | .25 |
| 85 | Mike Alstott | .60 | .25 |
| 86 | Warrick Dunn | .60 | .25 |
| 87 | Shaun King | .60 | .25 |
| 88 | Keyshawn Johnson | .60 | .25 |
| 89 | Warren Sapp | .40 | .15 |
| 90 | Eddie George | .60 | .25 |
| 91 | Jevon Kearse | .60 | .25 |
| 92 | Steve McNair | .60 | .25 |
| 93 | Carl Pickens | .40 | .15 |
| 94 | Deion Sanders | .60 | .25 |
| 95 | Stephen Davis | .60 | .25 |
| 96 | Brad Johnson | .60 | .25 |
| 97 | Bruce Smith | .40 | .15 |
| 98 | Michael Westbrook | .40 | .15 |
| 99 | Albert Connell | .25 | .08 |
| 100 | Jeff George | .40 | .15 |
| 101 | Thomas Jones RC | 12.00 | 5.00 |
| 102 | Bashir Yamini RC | 5.00 | 2.00 |
| 103 | Jamal Lewis RC | 20.00 | 8.00 |
| 104 | Travis Taylor RC | 8.00 | 3.00 |
| 105 | Chris Redman RC | 6.00 | 2.50 |
| 106 | Avion Black RC | 6.00 | 2.50 |
| 107 | Sammy Morris RC | 8.00 | 3.00 |
| 108 | Dez White RC | 8.00 | 3.00 |
| 109 | Peter Warrick RC | 8.00 | 3.00 |
| 110 | Ron Dugans RC | 5.00 | 2.00 |
| 111 | Curtis Keaton RC | 6.00 | 2.50 |

| | | | |
|---|---|---|---|
| 112 | Danny Farmer RC | 6.00 | 2.50 |
| 113 | Courtney Brown RC | 8.00 | 3.00 |
| 114 | Dennis Northcutt RC | 8.00 | 3.00 |
| 115 | Travis Prentice RC | 6.00 | 2.50 |
| 116 | JaJuan Dawson RC | 5.00 | 2.00 |
| 117 | Spergon Wynn RC | 6.00 | 2.50 |
| 118 | Michael Wiley RC | 6.00 | 2.50 |
| 119 | Chris Cole RC | 6.00 | 2.50 |
| 120 | Mike Anderson RC | 12.00 | 5.00 |
| 121 | Muneer Moore RC | 5.00 | 2.00 |
| 122 | Reuben Droughns RC | 8.00 | 3.00 |
| 123 | Bubba Franks RC | 8.00 | 3.00 |
| 124 | Anthony Lucas RC | 5.00 | 2.00 |
| 125 | Charles Lee RC | 5.00 | 2.00 |
| 126 | R.Jay Soward RC | 6.00 | 2.50 |
| 127 | Shyrone Stith RC | 6.00 | 2.50 |
| 128 | Sylvester Morris RC | 6.00 | 2.50 |
| 129 | Frank Moreau RC | 6.00 | 2.50 |
| 130 | Dante Hall RC | 10.00 | 4.00 |
| 131 | Doug Chapman RC | 6.00 | 2.50 |
| 132 | Troy Walters RC | 8.00 | 3.00 |
| 133 | J.R. Redmond RC | 6.00 | 2.50 |
| 134 | Tom Brady RC | 200.00 | 100.00 |
| 135 | Terrelle Smith RC | 6.00 | 2.50 |
| 136 | Chad Morton RC | 8.00 | 3.00 |
| 137 | Ron Dayne RC | 8.00 | 3.00 |
| 138 | Ron Dixon RC | 6.00 | 2.50 |
| 139 | Chad Pennington RC | 20.00 | 8.00 |
| 140 | Anthony Becht RC | 8.00 | 3.00 |
| 141 | Laveranues Coles RC | 10.00 | 4.00 |
| 142 | Windrell Hayes RC | 6.00 | 2.50 |
| 143 | Sebastian Janikowski RC | 8.00 | 3.00 |
| 144 | Jerry Porter RC | 8.00 | 3.00 |
| 145 | Corey Simon RC | 6.00 | 2.50 |
| 146 | Todd Pinkston RC | 6.00 | 2.50 |
| 147 | Gari Scott RC | 5.00 | 2.00 |
| 148 | Plaxico Burress RC | 15.00 | 6.00 |
| 149 | Tee Martin RC | 8.00 | 3.00 |
| 150 | Trevor Gaylor RC | 6.00 | 2.50 |
| 151 | Ronney Jenkins RC | 6.00 | 2.50 |
| 152 | Giovanni Carmazzi RC | 5.00 | 2.00 |
| 153 | Tim Rattay RC | 8.00 | 3.00 |
| 154 | Shaun Alexander RC | 20.00 | 8.00 |
| 155 | Darrell Jackson RC | 10.00 | 4.00 |
| 156 | James Williams RC | 6.00 | 2.50 |
| 157 | Trung Canidate RC | 6.00 | 2.50 |
| 158 | Joe Hamilton RC | 6.00 | 2.50 |
| 159 | Erron Kinney RC | 8.00 | 3.00 |
| 160 | Todd Husak RC | 8.00 | 3.00 |
| 161 | Raynoch Thompson RC | 6.00 | 2.50 |
| 162 | Darwin Walker RC | 5.00 | 2.00 |
| 163 | Jay Tant RC | 6.00 | 2.50 |
| 164 | Doug Johnson RC | 8.00 | 3.00 |
| 165 | Robert Bean RC | 6.00 | 2.50 |
| 166 | Mark Simoneau RC | 6.00 | 2.50 |
| 167 | John Jones RC | 6.00 | 2.50 |
| 168 | Obafemi Ayanbadejo RC | 6.00 | 2.50 |
| 169 | Mike Brown RC | 10.00 | 4.00 |
| 170 | Shockmain Davis RC | 5.00 | 2.00 |
| 171 | Erik Flowers RC | 6.00 | 2.50 |
| 172 | Corey Moore RC | 5.00 | 2.00 |
| 173 | Drew Haddad RC | 5.00 | 2.00 |
| 174 | Kwame Cavil RC | 5.00 | 2.00 |
| 175 | Pat Dennis RC | 5.00 | 2.00 |
| 176 | Rashard Anderson RC | 6.00 | 2.50 |
| 177 | Brian Finneran RC | 8.00 | 3.00 |
| 178 | Na'il Diggs RC | 6.00 | 2.50 |
| 179 | Marc Bulger RC | 15.00 | 6.00 |
| 180 | Mondriel Fulcher RC | 5.00 | 2.00 |
| 181 | Dwayne Carswell RC | 5.00 | 2.00 |
| 182 | Brian Urlacher RC | 25.00 | 10.00 |
| 183 | Paul Edinger RC | 8.00 | 3.00 |
| 184 | Karon Coleman RC | 6.00 | 2.50 |
| 185 | Aaron Shea RC | 6.00 | 2.50 |
| 186 | Fabien Bownes RC | 5.00 | 2.00 |
| 187 | Damon Hodge RC | 6.00 | 2.50 |
| 188 | Dwayne Goodrich RC | 6.00 | 2.50 |
| 189 | Clint Stoerner RC | 6.00 | 2.50 |
| 190 | James Whalen RC | 5.00 | 2.00 |
| 191 | Deltha O'Neal RC | 8.00 | 3.00 |
| 192 | Ian Gold RC | 6.00 | 2.50 |
| 193 | Kenoy Kennedy RC | 5.00 | 2.00 |
| 194 | Jarious Jackson RC | 6.00 | 2.50 |
| 195 | Leroy Fields RC | 5.00 | 2.00 |
| 196 | Bearrett Green RC | 5.00 | 2.00 |
| 197 | Joey Jamison RC | 5.00 | 2.00 |
| 198 | Rondell Mealey RC | 5.00 | 2.00 |
| 199 | Rob Morris RC | 6.00 | 2.50 |
| 200 | Marcus Washington RC | 6.00 | 2.50 |

| | | | |
|---|---|---|---|
| ❏ 201 Trevor Insley RC | 5.00 | 2.00 |
| ❏ 202 Jamel White RC | 6.00 | 2.50 |
| ❏ 203 Kevin McDougal RC | 6.00 | 2.50 |
| ❏ 204 Ibn Green RC | 5.00 | 2.00 |
| ❏ 205 T.J. Slaughter RC | 5.00 | 2.00 |
| ❏ 206 Emanuel Smith RC | 5.00 | 2.00 |
| ❏ 207 Herbert Goodman RC | 6.00 | 2.50 |
| ❏ 208 William Bartee RC | 5.00 | 2.00 |
| ❏ 209 Orantes Grant RC | 5.00 | 2.00 |
| ❏ 210 Brad Hoover RC | 6.00 | 2.50 |
| ❏ 211 Deon Dyer RC | 6.00 | 2.50 |
| ❏ 212 Jonas Lewis RC | 5.00 | 2.00 |
| ❏ 213 Chris Hovan RC | 6.00 | 2.50 |
| ❏ 214 Fred Robbins RC | 5.00 | 2.00 |
| ❏ 215 Michael Boireau RC | 5.00 | 2.00 |
| ❏ 216 Giles Cole RC | 5.00 | 2.00 |
| ❏ 217 Dave Stachelski RC | 5.00 | 2.00 |
| ❏ 218 Patrick Pass RC | 6.00 | 2.50 |
| ❏ 219 Darren Howard RC | 6.00 | 2.50 |
| ❏ 220 Austin Wheatley RC | 5.00 | 2.00 |
| ❏ 221 Kevin Houser RC | 6.00 | 2.50 |
| ❏ 222 Rian Lindell RC | 5.00 | 2.00 |
| ❏ 223 Jake Delhomme RC | 50.00 | 25.00 |
| ❏ 224 Cornelius Griffin RC | 6.00 | 2.50 |
| ❏ 225 Shaun Ellis RC | 8.00 | 3.00 |
| ❏ 226 John Abraham RC | 8.00 | 3.00 |
| ❏ 227 Travares Tillman RC | 5.00 | 2.00 |
| ❏ 228 Julian Peterson RC | 8.00 | 3.00 |
| ❏ 229 Marcus Knight RC | 6.00 | 2.50 |
| ❏ 230 Thomas Hamner RC | 5.00 | 2.00 |
| ❏ 231 Hank Poteat RC | 6.00 | 2.50 |
| ❏ 232 Neil Rackers RC | 8.00 | 3.00 |
| ❏ 233 Bobby Shaw RC | 5.00 | 2.00 |
| ❏ 234 Rogers Beckett RC | 6.00 | 2.50 |
| ❏ 235 Reggie Jones RC | 5.00 | 2.00 |
| ❏ 236 Tim Seder RC | 6.00 | 2.50 |
| ❏ 237 Durell Price RC | 5.00 | 2.00 |
| ❏ 238 Ahmed Plummer RC | 8.00 | 3.00 |
| ❏ 239 John Engelberger RC | 6.00 | 2.50 |
| ❏ 240 Paul Smith RC | 6.00 | 2.50 |
| ❏ 241 Chafie Fields RC | 5.00 | 2.00 |
| ❏ 242 Kevin Feterik RC | 5.00 | 2.00 |
| ❏ 243 Jacoby Shepherd RC | 5.00 | 2.00 |
| ❏ 244 Nate Webster RC | 5.00 | 2.00 |
| ❏ 245 Ketric Sanford RC | 5.00 | 2.00 |
| ❏ 246 Tavarus Hogans RC | 5.00 | 2.00 |
| ❏ 247 Keith Bulluck RC | 8.00 | 3.00 |
| ❏ 248 Mike Green RC | 6.00 | 2.50 |
| ❏ 249 Chris Coleman RC | 8.00 | 3.00 |
| ❏ 250 Demario Brown RC | 5.00 | 2.00 |
| ❏ 251 Billy Volek RC | 10.00 | 4.00 |
| ❏ 252 Mareno Philyaw RC | 5.00 | 2.00 |
| ❏ 253 Ethan Howell RC | 5.00 | 2.00 |
| ❏ 254 Chris Samuels RC | 2.00 | *2.50 |
| ❏ 255 Brandon Short RC | 5.00 | 2.00 |
| ❏ 256 Maurice Smith RC | 6.00 | 2.50 |
| ❏ 257 Frank Murphy RC | 5.00 | 2.00 |
| ❏ 258 Darrick Vaughn RC | 5.00 | 2.00 |
| ❏ 259 Payton Williams RC | 5.00 | 2.00 |
| ❏ 260 JaJuan Seider RC | 5.00 | 2.00 |
| ❏ 261 Antonio Banks EP RC | 2.00 | .75 |
| ❏ 262 Jonathan Brown EP RC | 2.00 | .75 |
| ❏ 263 Ontiwaun Carter EP RC | 2.00 | .75 |
| ❏ 264 Jeremaine Copeland EP | 2.00 | .75 |
| ❏ 265 Ralph Dawkins EP RC | 3.00 | 1.25 |
| ❏ 266 Marques Douglas EP RC | 2.00 | .75 |
| ❏ 267 Kevin Drake EP RC | 2.00 | .75 |
| ❏ 268 Damon Dunn EP RC | 3.00 | 1.25 |
| ❏ 269 Todd Floyd EP RC | 2.00 | .75 |
| ❏ 270 Tony Graziani EP | 3.00 | 1.25 |
| ❏ 271 Derrick Ham EP RC | 3.00 | 1.25 |
| ❏ 272 Duane Hawthome EP RC | 3.00 | 1.25 |
| ❏ 273 Alonzo Johnson EP RC | 2.00 | .75 |
| ❏ 274 Mark Kacmarynski EP RC | 2.00 | .75 |
| ❏ 275 Eric Kresser EP | 2.00 | .75 |
| ❏ 276 Jim Kubiak EP RC | 3.00 | 1.25 |
| ❏ 277 Blaine McEimurry EP RC | 2.00 | .75 |
| ❏ 278 Scott Milanovich EP | 3.00 | 1.25 |
| ❏ 279 Norman Miller EP RC | 2.00 | .75 |
| ❏ 280 Sean Morey EP RC | 3.00 | 1.25 |
| ❏ 281 Jeff Ogden EP RC | 3.00 | 1.25 |
| ❏ 282 Pepe Pearson EP RC | 2.00 | .75 |
| ❏ 283 Ron Powlus EP RC | 4.00 | 1.50 |
| ❏ 284 Jason Shelley EP RC | 2.00 | .75 |
| ❏ 285 Ben Snell EP RC | 2.00 | .75 |
| ❏ 286 Aaron Stecker EP RC | 4.00 | 1.50 |
| ❏ 287 L.C. Stevens EP | 2.00 | .75 |
| ❏ 288 Mike Sutton EP RC | 2.00 | .75 |
| ❏ 289 Damian Vaughn EP RC | 2.00 | .75 |

| | | | |
|---|---|---|---|
| ❏ 290 Ted White EP | 2.00 | .75 |
| ❏ 291 Marcus Crandell EP RC | 3.00 | 1.25 |
| ❏ 292 Darryl Daniel EP RC | 3.00 | 1.25 |
| ❏ 293 Jesse Haynes EP | 2.00 | .75 |
| ❏ 294 Matt Lytle EP RC | 3.00 | 1.25 |
| ❏ 295 Deon Mitchell EP RC | 3.00 | 1.25 |
| ❏ 296 Kendrick Nord EP RC | 2.00 | .75 |
| ❏ 297 Ronnie Powell EP | 2.00 | .75 |
| ❏ 298 Selucio Sanford EP RC | 3.00 | 1.25 |
| ❏ 299 Corey Thomas EP | 2.00 | .75 |
| ❏ 300 Vershan Jackson EP RC | 2.00 | .75 |
| ❏ 301 Michael Vick XRC | 25.00 | 10.00 |
| ❏ 302 Drew Brees XRC | 15.00 | 6.00 |
| ❏ 303 Quincy Carter XRC | 10.00 | 4.00 |
| ❏ 304 Marques Tuiasosopa XRC | 12.00 | 5.00 |
| ❏ 305 Chris Weinke XRC | 10.00 | 4.00 |
| ❏ 306 LaDainian Tomlinson XRC | 80.00 | 30.00 |
| ❏ 307 Deuce McAllister XRC | 25.00 | 10.00 |
| ❏ 308 Michael Bennett XRC | 10.00 | 4.00 |
| ❏ 309 Anthony Thomas XRC | 10.00 | 4.00 |
| ❏ 310 LaMont Jordan XRC | 20.00 | 8.00 |
| ❏ 311 David Terrell XRC | 10.00 | 4.00 |
| ❏ 312 Koren Robinson XRC | 10.00 | 4.00 |
| ❏ 313 Rod Gardner XRC | 10.00 | 4.00 |
| ❏ 314 Santana Moss XRC | 20.00 | 8.00 |
| ❏ 315 Freddie Mitchell XRC | 8.00 | 3.00 |
| ❏ 316 Gerard Warren XRC | 8.00 | 3.00 |
| ❏ 317 Justin Smith XRC | 10.00 | 4.00 |
| ❏ 318 Richard Seymour XRC | 20.00 | 8.00 |
| ❏ 319 Andre Carter XRC | 8.00 | 3.00 |
| ❏ 320 Jamal Reynolds XRC | 8.00 | 3.00 |

## 2001 Leaf Rookies and Stars

| | | | |
|---|---|---|---|
| ❏ COMP. SET w/o SP's (100) | 20.00 | 7.50 |
| ❏ 1 Aaron Brooks | .60 | .25 |
| ❏ 2 Ahman Green | .60 | .25 |
| ❏ 3 Antonio Freeman | .60 | .25 |
| ❏ 4 Brad Johnson | .60 | .25 |
| ❏ 5 Brett Favre | 2.00 | .75 |
| ❏ 6 Brian Griese | .60 | .25 |
| ❏ 7 Brian Urlacher | 1.00 | .40 |
| ❏ 8 Bruce Smith | .25 | .08 |
| ❏ 9 Cade McNown | .25 | .08 |
| ❏ 10 Chad Pennington | 1.00 | .40 |
| ❏ 11 Champ Bailey | .40 | .15 |
| ❏ 12 Charles Woodson | .40 | .15 |
| ❏ 13 Charlie Batch | .60 | .25 |
| ❏ 14 Charlie Garner | .40 | .15 |
| ❏ 15 Corey Dillon | .60 | .25 |
| ❏ 16 Cris Carter | .60 | .25 |
| ❏ 17 Curtis Martin | .60 | .25 |
| ❏ 18 Dan Marino | 2.50 | 1.00 |
| ❏ 19 Daunte Culpepper | .60 | .25 |
| ❏ 20 David Boston | .60 | .25 |
| ❏ 21 Deion Sanders | .60 | .25 |
| ❏ 22 Donovan McNabb | .75 | .30 |
| ❏ 23 Doug Flutie | .60 | .25 |
| ❏ 24 Drew Bledsoe | .75 | .30 |
| ❏ 25 Duce Staley | .40 | .15 |
| ❏ 26 Ed McCaffrey | .60 | .25 |
| ❏ 27 Eddie Goerge | .60 | .25 |
| ❏ 28 Edgerrin James | .75 | .30 |
| ❏ 29 Elvis Grbac | .40 | .15 |
| ❏ 30 Emmitt Smith | 1.25 | .50 |
| ❏ 31 Eric Moulds | .40 | .15 |
| ❏ 32 Fred Taylor | .60 | .25 |
| ❏ 33 Germane Crowell | .25 | .08 |
| ❏ 34 Ike Hilliard | .40 | .15 |
| ❏ 35 Isaac Bruce | .60 | .25 |
| ❏ 36 Jake Plummer | .40 | .15 |

| | | | |
|---|---|---|---|
| ❏ 37 Jamal Anderson | .60 | .25 |
| ❏ 38 Jamal Lewis | 1.00 | .40 |
| ❏ 39 James Allen | .40 | .15 |
| ❏ 40 James Stewart | .40 | .15 |
| ❏ 41 Jay Fiedler | .60 | .25 |
| ❏ 42 Jeff Garcia | .60 | .25 |
| ❏ 43 Jeff George | .40 | .15 |
| ❏ 44 Jeff Lewis | .25 | .08 |
| ❏ 45 Jerome Bettis | .60 | .25 |
| ❏ 46 Jerry Rice | 1.25 | .50 |
| ❏ 47 Jevon Kearse | .40 | .15 |
| ❏ 48 Jimmy Smith | .40 | .15 |
| ❏ 49 Joey Galloway | .40 | .15 |
| ❏ 50 John Elway | 2.50 | 1.00 |
| ❏ 51 Junior Seau | .60 | .25 |
| ❏ 52 Keenan McCardell | .25 | .08 |
| ❏ 53 Kerry Collins | .40 | .15 |
| ❏ 54 Kevin Johnson | .40 | .15 |
| ❏ 55 Keyshawn Johnson | .60 | .25 |
| ❏ 56 Kordell Stewart | .40 | .15 |
| ❏ 57 Kurt Warner | 1.25 | .50 |
| ❏ 58 Lamar Smith | .40 | .15 |
| ❏ 59 Marcus Robinson | .60 | .25 |
| ❏ 60 Mark Brunell | .60 | .25 |
| ❏ 61 Marshall Faulk | .75 | .30 |
| ❏ 62 Marvin Harrison | .60 | .25 |
| ❏ 63 Matt Hasselbeck | .40 | .15 |
| ❏ 64 Mike Alstott | .60 | .25 |
| ❏ 65 Mike Anderson | .60 | .25 |
| ❏ 66 Muhsin Muhammad | .40 | .15 |
| ❏ 67 Peter Warrick | .60 | .25 |
| ❏ 68 Peyton Manning | 1.50 | .60 |
| ❏ 69 Priest Holmes | .75 | .30 |
| ❏ 70 Randy Moss | 1.25 | .50 |
| ❏ 71 Ray Lewis | .60 | .25 |
| ❏ 72 Rich Gannon | .60 | .25 |
| ❏ 73 Ricky Watters | .40 | .15 |
| ❏ 74 Ricky Williams | .60 | .25 |
| ❏ 75 Rob Johnson | .40 | .15 |
| ❏ 76 Rod Smith | .40 | .15 |
| ❏ 77 Ron Dayne | .60 | .25 |
| ❏ 78 Shannon Sharpe | .40 | .15 |
| ❏ 79 Shaun Alexander | .75 | .30 |
| ❏ 80 Stephen Davis | .60 | .25 |
| ❏ 81 Steve McNair | .60 | .25 |
| ❏ 82 Steve Young | .75 | .30 |
| ❏ 83 Sylvester Morris | .25 | .08 |
| ❏ 84 Terrell Davis | .60 | .25 |
| ❏ 85 Terrell Owens | .60 | .25 |
| ❏ 86 Thomas Jones | .40 | .15 |
| ❏ 87 Tim Brown | .60 | .25 |
| ❏ 88 Tim Couch | .40 | .15 |
| ❏ 89 Tony Banks | .40 | .15 |
| ❏ 90 Tony Gonzalez | .40 | .15 |
| ❏ 91 Torry Holt | .60 | .25 |
| ❏ 92 Travis Taylor | .40 | .15 |
| ❏ 93 Trent Green | .60 | .25 |
| ❏ 94 Troy Aikman | 1.00 | .40 |
| ❏ 95 Tyrone Wheatley | .40 | .15 |
| ❏ 96 Vinny Testaverde | .40 | .15 |
| ❏ 97 Warren Sapp | .40 | .15 |
| ❏ 98 Warrick Dunn | .60 | .25 |
| ❏ 99 Wayne Chrebet | .40 | .15 |
| ❏ 100 Zach Thomas | .60 | .25 |
| ❏ 101 A.J. Feeley RC | 6.00 | 2.50 |
| ❏ 102 Josh Booty RC | 6.00 | 2.50 |
| ❏ 103 Roderick Robinson RC | 4.00 | 1.50 |
| ❏ 104 Renaldo Hill RC | 4.00 | 1.50 |
| ❏ 105 Harold Blackmon RC | 2.50 | 1.00 |
| ❏ 106 Rudi Johnson RC | 10.00 | 4.00 |
| ❏ 107 Curtis Fuller RC | 2.50 | 1.00 |
| ❏ 108 Dan Alexander RC | 6.00 | 2.50 |
| ❏ 109 Anthony Thomas RPS | 6.00 | 2.50 |
| ❏ 110 Travis Minor RPS | 3.00 | 1.25 |
| ❏ 111 Heath Evans RC | 4.00 | 1.50 |
| ❏ 112 Joe Walker RC | 2.50 | 1.00 |
| ❏ 113 Moran Norris RC | 2.50 | 1.00 |
| ❏ 114 Quincy Carter RPS | 4.00 | 1.50 |
| ❏ 115 Michael Vick RPS | 8.00 | 3.00 |
| ❏ 116 Vinny Sutherland RC | 4.00 | 1.50 |
| ❏ 117 Scotty Anderson RC | 4.00 | 1.50 |
| ❏ 118 Eddie Berlin RC | 4.00 | 1.50 |
| ❏ 119 Jonathan Carter RC | 4.00 | 1.50 |
| ❏ 120 Monty Beisel RC | 6.00 | 2.50 |
| ❏ 121 T.J. Houshmandzadeh RC | 8.00 | 3.00 |
| ❏ 122 Rodney Bailey RC | 2.50 | 1.00 |
| ❏ 123 Reggie Germany RC | 4.00 | 1.50 |
| ❏ 124 Ellis Wyms RC | 2.50 | 1.00 |
| ❏ 125 Koren Robinson RPS | 6.00 | 2.50 |

| | | |
|---|---|---|
| ❑ 126 Antonio Pierce RC | 12.00 | 5.00 |
| ❑ 127 Arnold Jackson RC | 4.00 | 1.50 |
| ❑ 128 Andre Rone RC | 2.50 | 1.00 |
| ❑ 129 Richard Newsome RC | 2.50 | 1.00 |
| ❑ 130 Ifeanyi Ohalete RC | 2.50 | 1.00 |
| ❑ 131 Dan O'Leary RC | 4.00 | 1.50 |
| ❑ 132 Shad Meier RC | 4.00 | 1.50 |
| ❑ 133 Jay Feely RC | 2.50 | 1.00 |
| ❑ 134 Brandon Manumaleuna RC | 4.00 | 1.50 |
| ❑ 135 Riall Johnson RC | 2.50 | 1.00 |
| ❑ 136 Snoop Minnis RPS | 4.00 | 1.50 |
| ❑ 137 Jermaine Hampton RC | 2.50 | 1.00 |
| ❑ 138 Johnny Huggins RC | 2.50 | 1.00 |
| ❑ 139 Marcellus Rivers RC | 4.00 | 1.50 |
| ❑ 140 Andre Carter RC | 6.00 | 2.50 |
| ❑ 141 Michael Stone RC | 2.50 | 1.00 |
| ❑ 142 Tony Dixon RC | 4.00 | 1.50 |
| ❑ 143 Bhawoh Jue RC | 6.00 | 2.50 |
| ❑ 144 Will Peterson RC | 4.00 | 1.50 |
| ❑ 145 Anthony Henry RC | 6.00 | 2.50 |
| ❑ 146 Marques Tuiasosopo RPS | 4.00 | 1.50 |
| ❑ 147 Reggie Swinton RC | 4.00 | 1.50 |
| ❑ 148 Robert Carswell RC | 2.50 | 1.00 |
| ❑ 149 Freddie Mitchell RPS | 3.00 | 1.25 |
| ❑ 150 Idrees Bashir RC | 2.50 | 1.00 |
| ❑ 151 James Boyd RC | 2.50 | 1.00 |
| ❑ 152 Chris Chambers RPS | 6.00 | 2.50 |
| ❑ 153 Aaron Schobel RC | 6.00 | 2.50 |
| ❑ 154 Dominic Raiola RC | 2.50 | 1.00 |
| ❑ 155 Derrick Burgess RC | 6.00 | 2.50 |
| ❑ 156 DeLawrence Grant RC | 2.50 | 1.00 |
| ❑ 157 Karon Riley RC | 2.50 | 1.00 |
| ❑ 158 Cedric Scott RC | 4.00 | 1.50 |
| ❑ 159 Patrick Washington RC | 4.00 | 1.50 |
| ❑ 160 Eric Johnson RC | 10.00 | 4.00 |
| ❑ 161 Tevita Ofahengaue RC | 2.50 | 1.00 |
| ❑ 162 Chris Cooper RC | 4.00 | 1.50 |
| ❑ 163 Fred Wakefield RC | 4.00 | 1.50 |
| ❑ 164 Kenny Smith RC | 4.00 | 1.50 |
| ❑ 165 Marcus Bell RC | 4.00 | 1.50 |
| ❑ 166 Mario Fatafehi RC | 4.00 | 1.50 |
| ❑ 167 Anthony Herron RC | 2.50 | 1.00 |
| ❑ 168 Joe Tafoya RC | 2.50 | 1.00 |
| ❑ 169 Morlon Greenwood RC | 4.00 | 1.50 |
| ❑ 170 Orlando Huff RC | 2.50 | 1.00 |
| ❑ 171 Carlos Polk RC | 2.50 | 1.00 |
| ❑ 172 Edgerton Hartwell RC | 2.50 | 1.00 |
| ❑ 173 Zeke Moreno RC | 6.00 | 2.50 |
| ❑ 174 Alex Lincoln RC | 4.00 | 1.50 |
| ❑ 175 Quinton Caver RC | 4.00 | 1.50 |
| ❑ 176 Matt Stewart RC | 2.50 | 1.00 |
| ❑ 177 Markus Steele RC | 2.50 | 1.00 |
| ❑ 178 Dwight Smith RC | 2.50 | 1.00 |
| ❑ 179 Reggie Wayne RPS | 8.00 | 3.00 |
| ❑ 180 Jerametrius Butler RC | 4.00 | 1.50 |
| ❑ 181 Jason Doering RC | 2.50 | 1.00 |
| ❑ 182 John Howell RC | 2.50 | 1.00 |
| ❑ 183 Alvin Porter RC | 2.50 | 1.00 |
| ❑ 184 Eric Downing RC | 2.50 | 1.00 |
| ❑ 185 John Nix RC | 2.50 | 1.00 |
| ❑ 186 Tim Baker RC | 2.50 | 1.00 |
| ❑ 187 Robert Garza RC | 2.50 | 1.00 |
| ❑ 188 Randy Chevrier RC | 2.50 | 1.00 |
| ❑ 189 Drew Brees RPS | 12.00 | 5.00 |
| ❑ 190 Shawn Worthen RC | 2.50 | 1.00 |
| ❑ 191 Drew Bennett RC | 20.00 | 8.00 |
| ❑ 192 Marlon McCree RC | 4.00 | 1.50 |
| ❑ 193 David Terrell RPS | 4.00 | 1.50 |
| ❑ 194 Jeff Backus RC | 4.00 | 1.50 |
| ❑ 195 Otis Leverette RC | 2.50 | 1.00 |
| ❑ 196 Jason Glenn RC | 6.00 | 2.50 |
| ❑ 197 Rashad Holman RC | 2.50 | 1.00 |
| ❑ 198 T.J. Turner RC | 2.50 | 1.00 |
| ❑ 199 Lynn Scott RC | 6.00 | 2.50 |
| ❑ 200 Bill Gramatica RC | 2.50 | 1.00 |
| ❑ 201 Michael Vick RC | 20.00 | 8.00 |
| ❑ 202 Drew Brees RC | 30.00 | 12.00 |
| ❑ 203 Quincy Carter RC | 8.00 | 3.00 |
| ❑ 204 Jesse Palmer RC | 8.00 | 3.00 |
| ❑ 205 Mike McMahon RC | 8.00 | 3.00 |
| ❑ 206 Dave Dickenson RC | 4.00 | 1.50 |
| ❑ 207 Jameel Cook RC | 5.00 | 2.00 |
| ❑ 208 Marques Tuiasosopo RC | 8.00 | 3.00 |
| ❑ 209 Chris Weinke RC | 6.00 | 2.50 |
| ❑ 210 Sage Rosenfels RC | 6.00 | 2.50 |
| ❑ 211 Josh Heupel RC | 8.00 | 3.00 |
| ❑ 212 LaDainian Tomlinson RC | 80.00 | 40.00 |
| ❑ 213 Michael Bennett RC | 8.00 | 3.00 |
| ❑ 214 Anthony Thomas RC | 8.00 | 3.00 |

| | | |
|---|---|---|
| ❑ 215 Travis Henry RC | 8.00 | 3.00 |
| ❑ 216 James Jackson RC | 6.00 | 2.50 |
| ❑ 217 Correll Buckhalter RC | 10.00 | 4.00 |
| ❑ 218 Derrick Blaylock RC | 8.00 | 3.00 |
| ❑ 219 Dee Brown RC | 8.00 | 3.00 |
| ❑ 220 LeVar Woods RC | 5.00 | 2.00 |
| ❑ 221 Deuce McAllister RC | 15.00 | 6.00 |
| ❑ 222 LaMont Jordan RC | 15.00 | 6.00 |
| ❑ 223 Kevan Barlow RC | 8.00 | 3.00 |
| ❑ 224 Travis Minor RC | 5.00 | 2.00 |
| ❑ 225 David Terrell RC | 8.00 | 3.00 |
| ❑ 226 Koren Robinson RC | 8.00 | 3.00 |
| ❑ 227 Rod Gardner RC | 8.00 | 3.00 |
| ❑ 228 Santana Moss RC | 12.00 | 5.00 |
| ❑ 229 Freddie Mitchell RC | 8.00 | 3.00 |
| ❑ 230 Reggie Wayne RC | 15.00 | 6.00 |
| ❑ 231 Quincy Morgan RC | 8.00 | 3.00 |
| ❑ 232 Chris Chambers RC | 12.00 | 5.00 |
| ❑ 233 Steve Smith RC | 20.00 | 10.00 |
| ❑ 234 Snoop Minnis RC | 5.00 | 2.00 |
| ❑ 235 Justin McCareins RC | 8.00 | 3.00 |
| ❑ 236 Onome Ojo RC | 5.00 | 2.00 |
| ❑ 237 Damerien McCants RC | 5.00 | 2.00 |
| ❑ 238 Mike McMahon RPS | 3.00 | 1.25 |
| ❑ 239 Cedrick Wilson RC | 8.00 | 3.00 |
| ❑ 240 Kevin Kasper RC | 6.00 | 2.50 |
| ❑ 241 Chris Taylor RC | 5.00 | 2.00 |
| ❑ 242 Ken-Yon Rambo RC | 8.00 | 3.00 |
| ❑ 243 Richmond Flowers RC | 5.00 | 2.00 |
| ❑ 244 Andre King RC | 5.00 | 2.00 |
| ❑ 245 Boo Williams RC | 5.00 | 2.00 |
| ❑ 246 Adrian Wilson RC | 10.00 | 4.00 |
| ❑ 247 Cory Bird RC | 5.00 | 2.00 |
| ❑ 248 Alex Bannister RC | 5.00 | 2.00 |
| ❑ 249 Elvis Joseph RC | 5.00 | 2.00 |
| ❑ 250 Chad Johnson RC | 20.00 | 7.50 |
| ❑ 251 Robert Ferguson RC | 8.00 | 3.00 |
| ❑ 252 David Martin RC | 5.00 | 2.00 |
| ❑ 253 Quentin McCord RC | 5.00 | 2.00 |
| ❑ 254 Todd Heap RC | 8.00 | 3.00 |
| ❑ 255 Alge Crumpler RC | 10.00 | 5.00 |
| ❑ 256 Nate Clements RC | 8.00 | 3.00 |
| ❑ 257 Will Allen RC | 5.00 | 2.00 |
| ❑ 258 Willie Middlebrooks RC | 5.00 | 2.00 |
| ❑ 259 Fred Smoot RC | 8.00 | 3.00 |
| ❑ 260 Andre Dyson RC | 3.00 | 1.25 |
| ❑ 261 Gary Baxter RC | 5.00 | 2.00 |
| ❑ 262 Jamar Fletcher RC | 5.00 | 2.00 |
| ❑ 263 Ken Lucas RC | 5.00 | 2.00 |
| ❑ 264 Tay Cody RC | 3.00 | 1.25 |
| ❑ 265 Eric Kelly RC | 3.00 | 1.25 |
| ❑ 266 Adam Archuleta RC | 8.00 | 3.00 |
| ❑ 267 Derrick Gibson RC | 5.00 | 2.00 |
| ❑ 268 Jarrod Cooper RC | 8.00 | 3.00 |
| ❑ 269 Hakim Akbar RC | 3.00 | 1.25 |
| ❑ 270 Tony Driver RC | 5.00 | 2.00 |
| ❑ 271 Justin Smith RC | 8.00 | 3.00 |
| ❑ 272 Andre Carter RC | 8.00 | 3.00 |
| ❑ 273 Jamal Reynolds RC | 8.00 | 3.00 |
| ❑ 274 Gerard Warren RC | 8.00 | 3.00 |
| ❑ 275 Richard Seymour RC | 8.00 | 3.00 |
| ❑ 276 Damione Lewis RC | 5.00 | 2.00 |
| ❑ 277 Casey Hampton RC | 5.00 | 2.00 |
| ❑ 278 Marcus Stroud RC | 8.00 | 3.00 |
| ❑ 279 Benjamin Gay RC | 6.00 | 2.50 |
| ❑ 280 Shaun Rogers RC | 8.00 | 3.00 |
| ❑ 281 Dan Morgan RC | 8.00 | 3.00 |
| ❑ 282 Kendrell Bell RC | 12.00 | 5.00 |
| ❑ 283 Tommy Polley RC | 8.00 | 3.00 |
| ❑ 284 Jamie Winborn RC | 5.00 | 2.00 |
| ❑ 285 Sedrick Hodge RC | 3.00 | 1.25 |
| ❑ 286 Torrance Marshall RC | 5.00 | 2.00 |
| ❑ 287 Eric Westmoreland RC | 5.00 | 2.00 |
| ❑ 288 Brian Allen RC | 3.00 | 1.25 |
| ❑ 289 Brandon Spoon RC | 8.00 | 3.00 |
| ❑ 290 Henry Burris RC | 5.00 | 2.00 |
| ❑ 291 Leonard Davis RC | 5.00 | 2.00 |
| ❑ 292 Kenyatta Walker RC | 3.00 | 1.25 |
| ❑ 293 Cedric James RC | 5.00 | 2.00 |
| ❑ 294 Sean Brewer RC | 3.00 | 1.25 |
| ❑ 295 Jason Brookins RC | 6.00 | 2.50 |
| ❑ 296 Kyle Vanden Bosch RC | 8.00 | 3.00 |
| ❑ 297 Nick Goings RC | 8.00 | 3.00 |
| ❑ 298 Kris Jenkins RC | 8.00 | 3.00 |
| ❑ 299 Dominic Rhodes RC | 12.00 | 6.00 |
| ❑ 300 Leonard Myers RC | 3.00 | 1.25 |

## 2002 Leaf Rookies and Stars

| | | |
|---|---|---|
| ❑ COMPLETE SET (300) | 250.00 | 100.00 |
| ❑ COMP. SET w/o SP's (100) | 25.00 | 10.00 |
| ❑ 1 Jake Plummer | .75 | .30 |
| ❑ 2 David Boston | .75 | .30 |
| ❑ 3 Thomas Jones | .50 | .20 |
| ❑ 4 Michael Vick | 1.50 | .60 |
| ❑ 5 Warrick Dunn | .75 | .30 |
| ❑ 6 Jamal Lewis | .75 | .30 |
| ❑ 7 Chris Redman | .30 | .10 |
| ❑ 8 Ray Lewis | .75 | .30 |
| ❑ 9 Drew Bledsoe | 1.00 | .40 |
| ❑ 10 Travis Henry | .75 | .30 |
| ❑ 11 Eric Moulds | .50 | .20 |
| ❑ 12 Steve Smith | .75 | .30 |
| ❑ 13 Chris Weinke | .50 | .20 |
| ❑ 14 Lamar Smith | .50 | .20 |
| ❑ 15 Anthony Thomas | .50 | .20 |
| ❑ 16 David Terrell | .75 | .30 |
| ❑ 17 Brian Urlacher | 1.25 | .50 |
| ❑ 18 Corey Dillon | .75 | .30 |
| ❑ 19 Michael Westbrook | .50 | .20 |
| ❑ 20 Peter Warrick | .50 | .20 |
| ❑ 21 Tim Couch | .50 | .20 |
| ❑ 22 James Jackson | .50 | .20 |
| ❑ 23 Kevin Johnson | .50 | .20 |
| ❑ 24 Quincy Carter | .50 | .20 |
| ❑ 25 Joey Galloway | .50 | .20 |
| ❑ 26 Emmitt Smith | 2.00 | .75 |
| ❑ 27 Terrell Davis | .75 | .30 |
| ❑ 28 Brian Griese | .75 | .30 |
| ❑ 29 Ed McCaffrey | .50 | .20 |
| ❑ 30 Rod Smith | .50 | .20 |
| ❑ 31 Mike McMahon | .75 | .30 |
| ❑ 32 Germane Crowell | .30 | .10 |
| ❑ 33 Az-Zahir Hakim | .30 | .10 |
| ❑ 34 Terry Glenn | .50 | .20 |
| ❑ 35 Brett Favre | 2.00 | .75 |
| ❑ 36 Ahman Green | .75 | .30 |
| ❑ 37 James Allen | .50 | .20 |
| ❑ 38 Corey Bradford | .30 | .10 |
| ❑ 39 Peyton Manning | 1.50 | .60 |
| ❑ 40 Edgerrin James | 1.00 | .40 |
| ❑ 41 Marvin Harrison | .75 | .30 |
| ❑ 42 Qadry Ismail | .50 | .20 |
| ❑ 43 Fred Taylor | .75 | .30 |
| ❑ 44 Mark Brunell | .75 | .30 |
| ❑ 45 Jimmy Smith | .50 | .20 |
| ❑ 46 Priest Holmes | 1.00 | .40 |
| ❑ 47 Tony Gonzalez | .50 | .20 |
| ❑ 48 Trent Green | .50 | .20 |
| ❑ 49 Johnnie Morton | .50 | .20 |
| ❑ 50 Chris Chambers | .75 | .30 |
| ❑ 51 Ricky Williams | .75 | .30 |
| ❑ 52 Zach Thomas | .75 | .30 |
| ❑ 53 Randy Moss | 1.50 | .60 |
| ❑ 54 Michael Bennett | .50 | .20 |
| ❑ 55 Derrick Alexander | .50 | .20 |
| ❑ 56 Daunte Culpepper | .75 | .30 |
| ❑ 57 Tom Brady | 2.00 | .75 |
| ❑ 58 Troy Brown | .50 | .20 |
| ❑ 59 Antowain Smith | .50 | .20 |
| ❑ 60 Joe Horn | .50 | .20 |
| ❑ 61 Aaron Brooks | .75 | .30 |
| ❑ 62 Deuce McAllister | 1.00 | .40 |
| ❑ 63 Kerry Collins | .50 | .20 |
| ❑ 64 Amani Toomer | .50 | .20 |
| ❑ 65 Michael Strahan | .50 | .20 |
| ❑ 66 Laveranues Coles | .50 | .20 |
| ❑ 67 Vinny Testaverde | .50 | .20 |

| | | |
|---|---|---|
| ❏ 68 Curtis Martin | .75 | .30 |
| ❏ 69 Rich Gannon | .75 | .30 |
| ❏ 70 Tim Brown | .75 | .30 |
| ❏ 71 Jerry Rice | 1.50 | .60 |
| ❏ 72 Donovan McNabb | 1.00 | .40 |
| ❏ 73 Freddie Mitchell | .50 | .20 |
| ❏ 74 Duce Staley | .75 | .30 |
| ❏ 75 Kordell Stewart | .50 | .20 |
| ❏ 76 Jerome Bettis | .75 | .30 |
| ❏ 77 Plaxico Burress | .50 | .20 |
| ❏ 78 Drew Bress | .75 | .30 |
| ❏ 79 LaDainian Tomlinson | 1.25 | .50 |
| ❏ 80 Junior Seau | .75 | .30 |
| ❏ 81 Jeff Garcia | .75 | .30 |
| ❏ 82 Garrison Hearst | .50 | .20 |
| ❏ 83 Terrell Owens | .75 | .30 |
| ❏ 84 Shaun Alexander | 1.00 | .40 |
| ❏ 85 Koren Robinson | .50 | .20 |
| ❏ 86 Kurt Warner | .75 | .30 |
| ❏ 87 Marshall Faulk | .75 | .30 |
| ❏ 88 Isaac Bruce | .75 | .30 |
| ❏ 89 Torry Holt | .75 | .30 |
| ❏ 90 Rob Johnson | .50 | .20 |
| ❏ 91 Brad Johnson | .50 | .20 |
| ❏ 92 Keyshawn Johnson | .75 | .30 |
| ❏ 93 Mike Alstott | .75 | .30 |
| ❏ 94 Eddie George | .75 | .30 |
| ❏ 95 Steve McNair | .75 | .30 |
| ❏ 96 Derrick Mason | .50 | .20 |
| ❏ 97 Jevon Kearse | .50 | .20 |
| ❏ 98 Stephen Davis | .50 | .20 |
| ❏ 99 Sage Rosenfels | .30 | .10 |
| ❏ 100 Rod Gardner | .50 | .20 |
| ❏ 101 Adrian Peterson RC | 6.00 | 2.50 |
| ❏ 102 Nick Rolovich RC | 4.00 | 1.50 |
| ❏ 103 Lew Thomas RC | 2.50 | 1.00 |
| ❏ 104 David Carr RC | 6.00 | 2.50 |
| ❏ 105 Daryl Jones RC | 4.00 | 1.50 |
| ❏ 106 Brandon Doman RC | 4.00 | 1.50 |
| ❏ 107 Ed Reed RC | 12.00 | 5.00 |
| ❏ 108 Tellis Redmon RC | 4.00 | 1.50 |
| ❏ 109 Andra Davis RC | 4.00 | 1.50 |
| ❏ 110 Kendall Newson RC | 2.50 | 1.00 |
| ❏ 111 Joe Burns RC | 4.00 | 1.50 |
| ❏ 112 Maurice Morris RC | 5.00 | 2.00 |
| ❏ 113 Craig Nall RC | 5.00 | 2.00 |
| ❏ 114 Phillip Buchanon RC | 5.00 | 2.00 |
| ❏ 115 Mike Echols RC | 2.50 | 1.00 |
| ❏ 116 Terry Jones Jr. RC | 4.00 | 1.50 |
| ❏ 117 Anthony Weaver RC | 4.00 | 1.50 |
| ❏ 118 Jeb Putzier RC | 5.00 | 2.00 |
| ❏ 119 Tony Fisher RC | 5.00 | 2.00 |
| ❏ 120 Joey Harrington RC | 6.00 | 2.50 |
| ❏ 121 Lamar Gordon RC | 5.00 | 2.00 |
| ❏ 122 Tracey Wistrom RC | 4.00 | 1.50 |
| ❏ 123 Ashley Lelie RC | 10.00 | 4.00 |
| ❏ 124 Will Witherspoon RC | 5.00 | 2.00 |
| ❏ 125 Travis Stephens RC | 4.00 | 1.50 |
| ❏ 126 J.T. O'Sullivan RC | 6.00 | 2.50 |
| ❏ 127 Brian Westbrook RC | 12.00 | 5.00 |
| ❏ 128 James Mungro RC | 5.00 | 2.00 |
| ❏ 129 Lamont Thompson RC | 4.00 | 1.50 |
| ❏ 130 Jarrod Baxter RC | 4.00 | 1.50 |
| ❏ 131 Andre Lott RC | 5.00 | 2.00 |
| ❏ 132 Steve Bellisari RC | 4.00 | 1.50 |
| ❏ 133 David Garrard RC | 10.00 | 4.00 |
| ❏ 134 Michael Lewis RC | 5.00 | 2.00 |
| ❏ 135 James Allen RC | 2.50 | 1.00 |
| ❏ 136 Bryant McKinnie RC | 4.00 | 1.50 |
| ❏ 137 Marques Anderson RC | 4.00 | 1.50 |
| ❏ 138 Rohan Davey RC | 5.00 | 2.00 |
| ❏ 139 Kyle Johnson RC | 2.50 | 1.00 |
| ❏ 140 Dusty Bonner RC | 2.50 | 1.00 |
| ❏ 141 DeShaun Foster RC | 5.00 | 2.00 |
| ❏ 142 Chad Hutchinson RC | 4.00 | 1.50 |
| ❏ 143 Jack Brewer RC | 4.00 | 1.50 |
| ❏ 144 Eddie Freeman RC | 2.50 | 1.00 |
| ❏ 145 Seth Burford RC | 4.00 | 1.50 |
| ❏ 146 Roosevelt Williams RC | 2.50 | 1.00 |
| ❏ 147 Jamin Elliott RC | 2.50 | 1.00 |
| ❏ 148 Charles Grant RC | 5.00 | 2.00 |
| ❏ 149 Jeff Kelly RC | 4.00 | 1.50 |
| ❏ 150 Cliff Russell RC | 4.00 | 1.50 |
| ❏ 151 Josh Scobey RC | 5.00 | 2.00 |
| ❏ 152 Tank Williams RC | 4.00 | 1.50 |
| ❏ 153 Larry Tripplett RC | 2.50 | 1.00 |
| ❏ 154 Clinton Portis RC | 15.00 | 6.00 |
| ❏ 155 Javin Hunter RC | 2.50 | 1.00 |
| ❏ 156 Deveren Johnson RC | 4.00 | 1.50 |

| | | |
|---|---|---|
| ❏ 157 Reche Caldwell RC | 5.00 | 2.00 |
| ❏ 158 Ronald Curry RC | 5.00 | 2.00 |
| ❏ 159 Chris Hope RC | 5.00 | 2.00 |
| ❏ 160 Damien Anderson RC | 4.00 | 1.50 |
| ❏ 161 Saleem Rasheed RC | 5.00 | 2.00 |
| ❏ 162 Albert Haynesworth RC | 5.00 | 2.00 |
| ❏ 163 Bryan Gilmore RC | 4.00 | 1.50 |
| ❏ 164 Wes Pate RC | 2.50 | 1.00 |
| ❏ 165 Deion Branch RC | 8.00 | 3.00 |
| ❏ 166 Ben Leber RC | 5.00 | 2.00 |
| ❏ 167 Andre Davis RC | 4.00 | 1.50 |
| ❏ 168 Darrell Hill RC | 4.00 | 1.50 |
| ❏ 169 Rodney Wright RC | 2.50 | 1.00 |
| ❏ 170 Demontray Carter RC | 2.50 | 1.00 |
| ❏ 171 Zak Kustok RC | 5.00 | 2.00 |
| ❏ 172 James Wofford RC | 4.00 | 1.50 |
| ❏ 173 David Priestley RC | 4.00 | 1.50 |
| ❏ 174 Donte Stallworth RC | 8.00 | 3.00 |
| ❏ 175 Marc Boerigter RC | 8.00 | 3.00 |
| ❏ 176 Freddie Milons RC | 4.00 | 1.50 |
| ❏ 177 John Simon RC | 4.00 | 1.50 |
| ❏ 178 Josh Norman RC | 5.00 | 2.00 |
| ❏ 179 Jabar Gaffney RC | 5.00 | 2.00 |
| ❏ 180 Doug Jolley RC | 5.00 | 2.00 |
| ❏ 181 Preston Parsons RC | 2.50 | 1.00 |
| ❏ 182 Chris Baker RC | 4.00 | 1.50 |
| ❏ 183 Javon Walker RC | 8.00 | 3.00 |
| ❏ 184 Justin Peelle RC | 2.50 | 1.00 |
| ❏ 185 Josh Reed RC | 5.00 | 2.00 |
| ❏ 186 Omar Easy RC | 5.00 | 2.00 |
| ❏ 187 Jerramy Stevens RC | 5.00 | 2.00 |
| ❏ 188 Shaun Hill RC | 6.00 | 2.50 |
| ❏ 189 David Thornton RC | 2.50 | 1.00 |
| ❏ 190 John Henderson RC | 5.00 | 2.00 |
| ❏ 191 Verron Haynes RC | 5.00 | 2.00 |
| ❏ 192 Dennis Johnson RC | 2.50 | 1.00 |
| ❏ 193 Napoleon Harris RC | 5.00 | 2.00 |
| ❏ 194 Jonathan Wells RC | 5.00 | 2.00 |
| ❏ 195 Howard Green RC | 2.50 | 1.00 |
| ❏ 196 Travis Fisher RC | 5.00 | 2.00 |
| ❏ 197 Anton Palepoi RC | 5.00 | 2.00 |
| ❏ 198 Ed Stansbury RC | 2.50 | 1.00 |
| ❏ 199 Josh McCown RC | 6.00 | 2.50 |
| ❏ 200 Alex Brown RC | 5.00 | 2.00 |
| ❏ 201 Joseph Jefferson RC | 4.00 | 1.50 |
| ❏ 202 Julius Peppers RC | 10.00 | 4.00 |
| ❏ 203 Larry Ned RC | 4.00 | 1.50 |
| ❏ 204 Rock Cartwright RC | 6.00 | 2.50 |
| ❏ 205 Kalimba Edwards RC | 5.00 | 2.00 |
| ❏ 206 Matt Schobel RC | 4.00 | 1.50 |
| ❏ 207 Maurice Jackson RC | 4.00 | 1.50 |
| ❏ 208 Kelly Campbell RC | 4.00 | 1.50 |
| ❏ 209 Mel Mitchell RC | 5.00 | 2.00 |
| ❏ 210 Ken Simonton RC | 2.50 | 1.00 |
| ❏ 211 Brian Allen RC | 4.00 | 1.50 |
| ❏ 212 Darnell Sanders RC | 4.00 | 1.50 |
| ❏ 213 Jesse Chatman RC | 5.00 | 2.00 |
| ❏ 214 Keyuo Craver RC | 4.00 | 1.50 |
| ❏ 215 Chester Taylor RC | 10.00 | 4.00 |
| ❏ 216 Kurt Kittner RC | 4.00 | 1.50 |
| ❏ 217 Derek Ross RC | 4.00 | 1.50 |
| ❏ 218 Charles Hill RC | 2.50 | 1.00 |
| ❏ 219 Jarvis Green RC | 4.00 | 1.50 |
| ❏ 220 Mike Jenkins RC | 2.50 | 1.00 |
| ❏ 221 Robert Royal RC | 5.00 | 2.00 |
| ❏ 222 Ladell Betts RC | 5.00 | 2.00 |
| ❏ 223 Antwoine Womack RC | 5.00 | 2.00 |
| ❏ 224 Raonall Smith RC | 4.00 | 1.50 |
| ❏ 225 Charles Stackhouse RC | 4.00 | 1.50 |
| ❏ 226 Quinn Gray RC | 5.00 | 2.00 |
| ❏ 227 Litt Lito Sheppard RC | 5.00 | 2.00 |
| ❏ 228 Ryan Van Dyke RC | 2.50 | 1.00 |
| ❏ 229 Will Overstreet RC | 2.50 | 1.00 |
| ❏ 230 Leonard Henry RC | 4.00 | 1.50 |
| ❏ 231 Dorsett Davis RC | 2.50 | 1.00 |
| ❏ 232 Marquand Manuel RC | 2.50 | 1.00 |
| ❏ 233 Luke Staley RC | 4.00 | 1.50 |
| ❏ 234 Carlos Hall RC | 5.00 | 2.00 |
| ❏ 235 Marcus Brady RC | 4.00 | 1.50 |
| ❏ 236 Ryan Denney RC | 4.00 | 1.50 |
| ❏ 237 Eric McCoo RC | 2.50 | 1.00 |
| ❏ 238 Major Applewhite RC | 5.00 | 2.00 |
| ❏ 239 Adam Tate RC | 2.50 | 1.00 |
| ❏ 240 Marquise Walker RC | 4.00 | 1.50 |
| ❏ 241 John Flowers RC | 2.50 | 1.00 |
| ❏ 242 Levar Fisher RC | 5.00 | 2.00 |
| ❏ 243 Ricky Williams RC | 4.00 | 1.50 |
| ❏ 244 Mike Rumph RC | 5.00 | 2.00 |
| ❏ 245 Delvin Joyce RC | 4.00 | 1.50 |

| | | |
|---|---|---|
| ❏ 246 Bryan Thomas RC | 4.00 | 1.50 |
| ❏ 247 Mike Williams RC | 4.00 | 1.50 |
| ❏ 248 Sam Brandon RC | 4.00 | 1.50 |
| ❏ 249 Eddie Drummond RC | 4.00 | 1.50 |
| ❏ 250 Najeh Davenport RC | 5.00 | 2.00 |
| ❏ 251 Brian Williams RC | 2.50 | 1.00 |
| ❏ 252 Scott Fujita RC | 5.00 | 2.00 |
| ❏ 253 Dwight Freeney RC | 8.00 | 3.00 |
| ❏ 254 Herb Haygood RC | 2.50 | 1.00 |
| ❏ 255 Patrick Ramsey RC | 5.00 | 2.00 |
| ❏ 256 Atnaf Harris RC | 2.50 | 1.00 |
| ❏ 257 Jason McAddley RC | 4.00 | 1.50 |
| ❏ 258 Pete Rebstock RC | 2.50 | 1.00 |
| ❏ 259 Quentin Jammer RC | 5.00 | 2.00 |
| ❏ 260 Luke Butkus RC | 2.50 | 1.00 |
| ❏ 261 Jeremy Allen RC | 2.50 | 1.00 |
| ❏ 262 Jake Schifino RC | 4.00 | 1.50 |
| ❏ 263 Randy Fasani RC | 4.00 | 1.50 |
| ❏ 264 Bryan Fletcher RC | 2.50 | 1.00 |
| ❏ 265 Jeremy Shockey RC | 8.00 | 3.00 |
| ❏ 266 Kevin Bentley RC | 2.50 | 1.00 |
| ❏ 267 Jon McGraw RC | 2.50 | 1.00 |
| ❏ 268 Robert Thomas RC | 5.00 | 2.00 |
| ❏ 269 Coy Wire RC | 5.00 | 2.00 |
| ❏ 270 Brian Poli-Dixon RC | 4.00 | 1.50 |
| ❏ 271 Willie Offord RC | 4.00 | 1.50 |
| ❏ 272 Rocky Calmus RC | 5.00 | 2.00 |
| ❏ 273 Sheldon Brown RC | 5.00 | 2.00 |
| ❏ 274 Terry Charles RC | 4.00 | 1.50 |
| ❏ 275 Ron Johnson RC | 4.00 | 1.50 |
| ❏ 276 Roy Williams RC | 10.00 | 4.00 |
| ❏ 277 Sam Simmons RC | 2.50 | 1.00 |
| ❏ 278 Andre Goodman RC | 5.00 | 2.00 |
| ❏ 279 Ryan Sims RC | 5.00 | 2.00 |
| ❏ 280 Antwaan Randle El RC | 6.00 | 2.50 |
| ❏ 281 Alan Harper RC | 2.50 | 1.00 |
| ❏ 282 Tavon Mason RC | 2.50 | 1.00 |
| ❏ 283 Katch Hill RC | 4.00 | 1.50 |
| ❏ 284 Antonio Bryant RC | 5.00 | 2.00 |
| ❏ 285 Akin Ayodele RC | 2.50 | 1.00 |
| ❏ 286 T.J. Duckett RC | 5.00 | 2.00 |
| ❏ 287 Kenyon Coleman RC | 2.50 | 1.00 |
| ❏ 288 Tim Carter RC | 4.00 | 1.50 |
| ❏ 289 Lamont Brightful RC | 2.50 | 1.00 |
| ❏ 290 Trev Faulk RC | 2.50 | 1.00 |
| ❏ 291 Randy McMichael RC | 8.00 | 3.00 |
| ❏ 292 Daniel Graham RC | 5.00 | 2.00 |
| ❏ 293 Wendell Bryant RC | 2.50 | 1.00 |
| ❏ 294 Jamar Martin RC | 4.00 | 1.50 |
| ❏ 295 Chris Luzar RC | 4.00 | 1.50 |
| ❏ 296 William Green RC | 5.00 | 2.00 |
| ❏ 297 Lee Mays RC | 4.00 | 1.50 |
| ❏ 298 Eric Crouch RC | 5.00 | 2.00 |
| ❏ 299 Steve Smith RC | 2.50 | 1.00 |
| ❏ 300 Woody Dantzler RC | 4.00 | 1.50 |

## 2003 Leaf Rookies and Stars

| | | |
|---|---|---|
| ❏ COMP.SET w/o SP's (100) | 20.00 | 7.50 |
| ❏ 1 Emmitt Smith | 2.00 | .75 |
| ❏ 2 Michael Vick | .75 | .30 |
| ❏ 3 Peerless Price | .50 | .20 |
| ❏ 4 T.J. Duckett | .60 | .25 |
| ❏ 5 Warrick Dunn | .60 | .25 |
| ❏ 6 Jamal Lewis | .75 | .30 |
| ❏ 7 Ray Lewis | .75 | .30 |
| ❏ 8 Drew Bledsoe | .75 | .30 |
| ❏ 9 Eric Moulds | .60 | .25 |
| ❏ 10 Josh Reed | .50 | .20 |
| ❏ 11 Travis Henry | .60 | .25 |
| ❏ 12 Julius Peppers | .75 | .30 |

| | | |
|---|---|---|
| ❑ 13 Anthony Thomas | .60 | .25 |
| ❑ 14 Brian Urlacher | 1.25 | .50 |
| ❑ 15 Marty Booker | .60 | .25 |
| ❑ 16 Kordell Stewart | .60 | .25 |
| ❑ 17 Corey Dillon | .60 | .25 |
| ❑ 18 Chad Johnson | .75 | .30 |
| ❑ 19 Tim Couch | .50 | .20 |
| ❑ 20 William Green | .50 | .20 |
| ❑ 21 Antonio Bryant | .75 | .30 |
| ❑ 22 Roy Williams | .75 | .30 |
| ❑ 23 Ashley Lelie | .50 | .20 |
| ❑ 24 Clinton Portis | 1.00 | .40 |
| ❑ 25 Ed McCaffrey | .60 | .25 |
| ❑ 26 Jake Plummer | .60 | .25 |
| ❑ 27 Rod Smith | .60 | .25 |
| ❑ 28 Joey Harrington | .75 | .30 |
| ❑ 29 Ahman Green | .75 | .30 |
| ❑ 30 Brett Favre | 2.00* | .75 |
| ❑ 31 Donald Driver | .75 | .30 |
| ❑ 32 Javon Walker | .60 | .25 |
| ❑ 33 David Carr | .75 | .30 |
| ❑ 34 Edgerrin James | .75 | .30 |
| ❑ 35 Marvin Harrison | .75 | .30 |
| ❑ 36 Peyton Manning | 1.50 | .60 |
| ❑ 37 Fred Taylor | .75 | .30 |
| ❑ 38 Jimmy Smith | .60 | .25 |
| ❑ 39 Mark Brunell | .60 | .25 |
| ❑ 40 Priest Holmes | .75 | .30 |
| ❑ 41 Tony Gonzalez | .60 | .25 |
| ❑ 42 Trent Green | .60 | .25 |
| ❑ 43 Chris Chambers | .60 | .25 |
| ❑ 44 Jay Fiedler | .60 | .25 |
| ❑ 45 Junior Seau | .75 | .30 |
| ❑ 46 Ricky Williams | .60 | .25 |
| ❑ 47 Zach Thomas | .60 | .25 |
| ❑ 48 Daunte Culpepper | .75 | .30 |
| ❑ 49 Michael Bennett | .60 | .25 |
| ❑ 50 Randy Moss | 1.00 | .40 |
| ❑ 51 Tom Brady | 2.00 | .75 |
| ❑ 52 Troy Brown | .60 | .25 |
| ❑ 53 Aaron Brooks | .60 | .25 |
| ❑ 54 Deuce McAllister | .75 | .30 |
| ❑ 55 Donte Stallworth | .60 | .25 |
| ❑ 56 Joe Horn | .60 | .25 |
| ❑ 57 Jeremy Shockey | .75 | .30 |
| ❑ 58 Kerry Collins | .60 | .25 |
| ❑ 59 Michael Strahan | .60 | .25 |
| ❑ 60 Tiki Barber | .75 | .30 |
| ❑ 61 Chad Pennington | .75 | .30 |
| ❑ 62 Curtis Martin | .75 | .30 |
| ❑ 63 Santana Moss | .60 | .25 |
| ❑ 64 Charles Woodson | .60 | .25 |
| ❑ 65 Jerry Rice | 1.50 | .60 |
| ❑ 66 Rich Gannon | .60 | .25 |
| ❑ 67 Tim Brown | .75 | .30 |
| ❑ 68 Donovan McNabb | 1.00 | .40 |
| ❑ 69 Antwaan Randle El | .60 | .25 |
| ❑ 70 Tommy Maddox | .60 | .25 |
| ❑ 71 Jerome Bettis | .75 | .30 |
| ❑ 72 Kendrell Bell | .50 | .20 |
| ❑ 73 Plaxico Burress | .75 | .30 |
| ❑ 74 David Boston | .50 | .20 |
| ❑ 75 Drew Brees | .75 | .30 |
| ❑ 76 LaDainian Tomlinson | 1.25 | .50 |
| ❑ 77 Kevan Barlow | .50 | .20 |
| ❑ 78 Jeff Garcia | .60 | .25 |
| ❑ 79 Terrell Owens | .75 | .30 |
| ❑ 80 Matt Hasselbeck | .60 | .25 |
| ❑ 81 Koren Robinson | .60 | .25 |
| ❑ 82 Shaun Alexander | .75 | .30 |
| ❑ 83 Isaac Bruce | .75 | .30 |
| ❑ 84 Kurt Warner | .75 | .30 |
| ❑ 85 Marshall Faulk | .75 | .30 |
| ❑ 86 Torry Holt | .75 | .30 |
| ❑ 87 Brad Johnson | .60 | .25 |
| ❑ 88 Keyshawn Johnson | .75 | .30 |
| ❑ 89 Mike Alstott | .75 | .30 |
| ❑ 90 Warren Sapp | .60 | .25 |
| ❑ 91 Eddie George | .75 | .30 |
| ❑ 92 Jevon Kearse | .60 | .25 |
| ❑ 93 Steve McNair | .75 | .30 |
| ❑ 94 Laveranues Coles | .60 | .25 |
| ❑ 95 Rod Gardner | .50 | .20 |
| ❑ 96 Patrick Ramsey | .60 | .25 |
| ❑ 97 Boller/Suggs/Smith CL | .75 | .30 |
| ❑ 98 R.Grossman/T.Jacobs CL | .60 | .25 |
| ❑ 99 A.Boldin/B.Johnson CL | .60 | .25 |
| ❑ 100 T.Calico/C.Brown CL | .50 | .20 |
| ❑ 101 Charles Tillman RC | 5.00 | 2.00 |

| | | |
|---|---|---|
| ❑ 102 Justin Griffith RC | 3.00 | 1.25 |
| ❑ 103 Ovie Mughelli RC | 2.50 | 1.00 |
| ❑ 104 Chris Edmonds RC | 2.50 | 1.00 |
| ❑ 105 Jeremi Johnson RC | 2.50 | 1.00 |
| ❑ 106 Malaefou MacKenzie RC | 2.50 | 1.00 |
| ❑ 107 James Lynch RC | 2.50 | 1.00 |
| ❑ 108 B.J. Askew RC | 3.00 | 1.25 |
| ❑ 109 Andrew Pinnock RC | 3.00 | 1.25 |
| ❑ 110 Chris Davis RC | 3.00 | 1.25 |
| ❑ 111 Dan Curley RC | 2.50 | 1.00 |
| ❑ 112 Lenny Walls RC | 2.50 | 1.00 |
| ❑ 113 Travis Fisher RC | 3.00 | 1.25 |
| ❑ 114 Ahmaad Galloway RC | 3.00 | 1.25 |
| ❑ 115 Joe Smith RC | 3.00 | 1.25 |
| ❑ 116 Reno Mahe RC | 3.00 | 1.25 |
| ❑ 117 Torrie Cox RC | 2.50 | 1.00 |
| ❑ 118 Kerry Carter RC | 2.50 | 1.00 |
| ❑ 119 Dwone Hicks RC | 2.50 | 1.00 |
| ❑ 120 Cato June RC | 5.00 | 2.00 |
| ❑ 121 Terry Pierce RC | 2.50 | 1.00 |
| ❑ 122 Eddie Moore RC | 2.50 | 1.00 |
| ❑ 123 Mike Seidman RC | 2.50 | 1.00 |
| ❑ 124 Michael Nattiel RC | 2.50 | 1.00 |
| ❑ 125 Casey Fitzsimmons RC | 3.00 | 1.25 |
| ❑ 126 George Wrighster RC | 2.50 | 1.00 |
| ❑ 127 Mike Pinkard RC | 2.50 | 1.00 |
| ❑ 128 Donald Lee RC | 3.00 | 1.25 |
| ❑ 129 Sean Berton RC | 2.50 | 1.00 |
| ❑ 130 Soloman Bates RC | 2.50 | 1.00 |
| ❑ 131 Zach Hilton RC | 2.50 | 1.00 |
| ❑ 132 Antonio Gates RC | 30.00 | 15.00 |
| ❑ 133 Aaron Walker RC | 3.00 | 1.25 |
| ❑ 134 Richard Angulo RC | 2.50 | 1.00 |
| ❑ 135 Will Heller RC | 3.00 | 1.25 |
| ❑ 136 Theo Sanders RC | 2.50 | 1.00 |
| ❑ 137 Jimmy Farris RC | 2.50 | 1.00 |
| ❑ 138 Ryan Nece RC | 3.00 | 1.25 |
| ❑ 139 Antonio Brown RC | 2.50 | 1.00 |
| ❑ 140 Clarence Coleman RC | 2.50 | 1.00 |
| ❑ 141 Lawrence Hamilton RC | 2.50 | 1.00 |
| ❑ 142 C.J. Jones RC | 2.50 | 1.00 |
| ❑ 143 Frisman Jackson RC | 3.00 | 1.25 |
| ❑ 144 Antonio Chatman RC | 4.00 | 1.50 |
| ❑ 145 Rocky Boiman RC | 3.00 | 1.25 |
| ❑ 146 Tron LaFavor RC | 2.50 | 1.00 |
| ❑ 147 Derick Armstrong RC | 3.00 | 1.25 |
| ❑ 148 J.J. Moses RC | 2.50 | 1.00 |
| ❑ 149 Aaron Moorehead RC | 3.00 | 1.25 |
| ❑ 150 Brad Pyatt RC | 2.50 | 1.00 |
| ❑ 151 Arland Bruce RC | 2.50 | 1.00 |
| ❑ 152 Chris Horn RC | 3.00 | 1.25 |
| ❑ 153 Kareem Kelly RC | 2.50 | 1.00 |
| ❑ 154 Talman Gardner RC | 2.50 | 1.00 |
| ❑ 155 David Tyree RC | 4.00 | 1.50 |
| ❑ 156 Willie Ponder RC | 2.50 | 1.00 |
| ❑ 157 Greg Lewis RC | 8.00 | 3.00 |
| ❑ 158 Eric Parker RC | 4.00 | 1.50 |
| ❑ 159 Kassim Osgood RC | 4.00 | 1.50 |
| ❑ 160 Jason Willis RC | 2.50 | 1.00 |
| ❑ 161 Akbar Gbaja-Biamila RC | 3.00 | 1.25 |
| ❑ 162 Mike Furrey RC | 10.00 | 4.00 |
| ❑ 163 Chris Kelsay RC | 3.00 | 1.25 |
| ❑ 164 Cory Redding RC | 3.00 | 1.25 |
| ❑ 165 Kenny Peterson RC | 3.00 | 1.25 |
| ❑ 166 Osi Umenyiora RC | 6.00 | 2.50 |
| ❑ 167 Tyler Brayton RC | 3.00 | 1.25 |
| ❑ 168 DeWayne White RC | 2.50 | 1.00 |
| ❑ 169 Kevin Williams RC | 4.00 | 1.50 |
| ❑ 170 Dan Klecko RC | 3.00 | 1.25 |
| ❑ 171 Johnathan Sullivan RC | 2.50 | 1.00 |
| ❑ 172 William Joseph RC | 2.50 | 1.00 |
| ❑ 173 Rien Long RC | 2.50 | 1.00 |
| ❑ 174 Angelo Crowell RC | 3.00 | 1.25 |
| ❑ 175 Chaun Thompson RC | 2.50 | 1.00 |
| ❑ 176 Bradie James RC | 4.00 | 1.50 |
| ❑ 177 Antwan Peek RC | 3.00 | 1.25 |
| ❑ 178 Kawika Mitchell RC | 4.00 | 1.50 |
| ❑ 179 Cie Grant RC | 3.00 | 1.25 |
| ❑ 180 E.J. Henderson RC | 3.00 | 1.25 |
| ❑ 181 Victor Hobson RC | 2.50 | 1.00 |
| ❑ 182 Alonzo Jackson RC | 2.50 | 1.00 |
| ❑ 183 Matt Wilhelm RC | 3.00 | 1.25 |
| ❑ 184 Pisa Tinoisamoa RC | 4.00 | 1.50 |
| ❑ 185 Ricky Manning RC | 3.00 | 1.25 |
| ❑ 186 Dennis Weathersby RC | 2.50 | 1.00 |
| ❑ 187 Donald Strickland RC | 2.50 | 1.00 |
| ❑ 188 Asante Samuel RC | 8.00 | 3.00 |
| ❑ 189 Eugene Wilson RC | 4.00 | 1.50 |
| ❑ 190 Nnamdi Asomugha RC | 4.00 | 1.50 |

| | | |
|---|---|---|
| ❑ 191 Ike Taylor RC | 8.00 | 3.00 |
| ❑ 192 Drayton Florence RC | 3.00 | 1.25 |
| ❑ 193 DeJuan Groce RC | 4.00 | 1.50 |
| ❑ 194 Shane Walton RC | 2.50 | 1.00 |
| ❑ 195 Terrence Holt RC | 3.00 | 1.25 |
| ❑ 196 Rashean Mathis RC | 3.00 | 1.25 |
| ❑ 197 Julian Battle RC | 3.00 | 1.25 |
| ❑ 198 Hanik Milligan RC | 2.50 | 1.00 |
| ❑ 199 Terrence Kiel RC | 3.00 | 1.25 |
| ❑ 200 David Kircus RC | 4.00 | 1.50 |
| ❑ 201 Lee Suggs RC | 4.00 | 1.50 |
| ❑ 202 Charles Rogers RC | 4.00 | 1.50 |
| ❑ 203 Brandon Lloyd RC | 5.00 | 2.00 |
| ❑ 204 Terrence Edwards RC | 3.00 | 1.25 |
| ❑ 205 Tony Romo RC | 80.00 | 40.00 |
| ❑ 206 Brooks Bollinger RC | 5.00 | 2.00 |
| ❑ 207 Jerome McDougle RC | 3.00 | 1.25 |
| ❑ 208 Jimmy Kennedy RC | 2.50 | 1.00 |
| ❑ 209 Ken Dorsey RC | 4.00 | 1.50 |
| ❑ 210 Kirk Farmer RC | 4.00 | 1.50 |
| ❑ 211 Mike Doss RC | 5.00 | 2.00 |
| ❑ 212 Chris Simms RC | 5.00 | 2.00 |
| ❑ 213 Cecil Sapp RC | 3.00 | 1.25 |
| ❑ 214 Justin Gage RC | 4.00 | 1.50 |
| ❑ 215 Sam Aiken RC | 4.00 | 1.50 |
| ❑ 216 Doug Gabriel RC | 4.00 | 1.50 |
| ❑ 217 Jason Witten RC | 10.00 | 4.00 |
| ❑ 218 Bennie Joppru RC | 3.00 | 1.25 |
| ❑ 219 Jason Gesser RC | 4.00 | 1.50 |
| ❑ 220 Brock Forsey RC | 4.00 | 1.50 |
| ❑ 221 Quentin Griffin RC | 4.00 | 1.50 |
| ❑ 222 Avon Cobourne RC | 4.00 | 1.50 |
| ❑ 223 Domanick Davis RC | 5.00 | 2.00 |
| ❑ 224 Boss Bailey RC | 4.00 | 1.50 |
| ❑ 225 Tony Hollings RC | 4.00 | 1.50 |
| ❑ 226 LaBrandon Toefield RC | 4.00 | 1.50 |
| ❑ 227 Arlen Harris RC | 3.00 | 1.25 |
| ❑ 228 Sultan McCullough RC | 3.00 | 1.25 |
| ❑ 229 Visanthe Shiancoe RC | 5.00 | 2.00 |
| ❑ 230 L.J. Smith RC | 5.00 | 2.00 |
| ❑ 231 LaTarence Dunbar RC | 3.00 | 1.25 |
| ❑ 232 Walter Young RC | 3.00 | 1.25 |
| ❑ 233 Bobby Wade RC | 4.00 | 1.50 |
| ❑ 234 Zuriel Smith RC | 3.00 | 1.25 |
| ❑ 235 Adrian Madise RC | 3.00 | 1.25 |
| ❑ 236 Ken Hamlin RC | 4.00 | 1.50 |
| ❑ 237 Carl Ford RC | 3.00 | 1.25 |
| ❑ 238 Cortez Hankton RC | 4.00 | 1.50 |
| ❑ 239 J.R. Tolver RC | 4.00 | 1.50 |
| ❑ 240 Keenan Howry RC | 3.00 | 1.25 |
| ❑ 241 Billy McMullen RC | 3.00 | 1.25 |
| ❑ 242 Arnaz Battle RC | 5.00 | 2.00 |
| ❑ 243 Shaun McDonald RC | 5.00 | 2.00 |
| ❑ 244 Andre Woolfolk RC | 4.00 | 1.50 |
| ❑ 245 Sammy Davis RC | 4.00 | 1.50 |
| ❑ 246 Calvin Pace RC | 4.00 | 1.50 |
| ❑ 247 Michael Haynes RC | 3.00 | 1.25 |
| ❑ 248 Ty Warren RC | 5.00 | 2.00 |
| ❑ 249 Nick Barnett RC | 4.00 | 1.50 |
| ❑ 250 Troy Polamalu RC | 30.00 | 15.00 |
| ❑ 251 Carson Palmer JSY RC | 30.00 | 12.00 |
| ❑ 252 Byron Leftwich JSY RC | 12.00 | 5.00 |
| ❑ 253 Kyle Boller JSY RC | 8.00 | 3.00 |
| ❑ 254 Rex Grossman JSY RC | 20.00 | 8.00 |
| ❑ 255 Dave Ragone JSY RC | 5.00 | 2.00 |
| ❑ 256 Brian St.Pierre JSY RC | 5.00 | 2.00 |
| ❑ 257 Kliff Kingsbury JSY RC | 6.00 | 2.50 |
| ❑ 258 Seneca Wallace JSY RC | 6.00 | 2.50 |
| ❑ 259 Larry Johnson JSY RC | 20.00 | 8.00 |
| ❑ 260 Willis McGahee JSY RC | 20.00 | 8.00 |
| ❑ 261 Justin Fargas JSY RC | 8.00 | 3.00 |
| ❑ 262 Onterrio Smith JSY RC | 6.00 | 2.50 |
| ❑ 263 Chris Brown JSY RC | 8.00 | 3.00 |
| ❑ 264 Musa Smith JSY RC | 6.00 | 2.50 |
| ❑ 265 Artose Pinner JSY RC | 5.00 | 2.50 |
| ❑ 266 Andre Johnson JSY RC | 15.00 | 6.00 |
| ❑ 267 Kelley Washington JSY RC | 6.00 | 2.50 |
| ❑ 268 Taylor Jacobs JSY RC | 6.00 | 2.50 |
| ❑ 269 Bryant Johnson JSY RC | 8.00 | 3.00 |
| ❑ 270 Tyrone Calico JSY RC | 6.00 | 2.50 |
| ❑ 271 Anquan Boldin JSY RC | 20.00 | 8.00 |
| ❑ 272 Bethel Johnson JSY RC | 6.00 | 2.50 |
| ❑ 273 Nate Burleson JSY RC | 6.00 | 2.50 |
| ❑ 274 Kevin Curtis JSY RC | 10.00 | 4.00 |
| ❑ 275 Dallas Clark JSY RC | 8.00 | 3.00 |
| ❑ 276 Teyo Johnson JSY RC | 6.00 | 2.50 |
| ❑ 277 Terrell Suggs JSY RC | 10.00 | 4.00 |
| ❑ 278 DeWayne Robertson JSY RC | 6.00 | 2.50 |
| ❑ 279 Terence Newman JSY RC | 10.00 | 4.00 |

| | | |
|---|---|---|
| ☐ 280 Marcus Trufant JSY RC | 8.00 | 3.00 |
| ☐ 281 C.Palmer/B.Leftwich JSY | 30.00 | 12.00 |
| ☐ 282 R.Grossman/B.St.Pierre JSY | 20.00 | 8.00 |
| ☐ 283 K.Boiler/D.Ragone JSY | 8.00 | 3.00 |
| ☐ 284 K.Kingsbury/S.Wallace JSY | 8.00 | 3.00 |
| ☐ 285 L.Johnson/W.McGahee JSY | 20.00 | 8.00 |
| ☐ 286 J.Fargas/O.Smith JSY | 8.00 | 3.00 |
| ☐ 287 C.Brown/M.Smith JSY | 8.00 | 3.00 |
| ☐ 288 A.Pinner/A.Johnson JSY | 8.00 | 3.00 |
| ☐ 289 K.Washington/T.Jacobs JSY | 6.00 | 2.50 |
| ☐ 290 B.Johnson/T.Calico JSY | 8.00 | 3.00 |
| ☐ 291 A.Boldin/B.Johnson JSY | 20.00 | 8.00 |
| ☐ 292 N.Burleson/K.Curtis JSY | 6.00 | 2.50 |
| ☐ 293 D.Clark/T.Johnson JSY | 8.00 | 3.00 |
| ☐ 294 T.Suggs/D.Robertson JSY | 10.00 | 4.00 |
| ☐ 295 T.Newman/M.Trufant JSY | 10.00 | 4.00 |

## 2004 Leaf Rookies and Stars

| | | |
|---|---|---|
| ☐ COMP.SET w/o SP's (200) | 60.00 | 30.00 |
| ☐ COMP.SET w/o RC's (100) | 20.00 | 7.50 |
| ☐ 251-283 JSY PRINT RUN 750 SER.#'d SETS | | |
| ☐ 284-299 PRINT RUN 500 SER.#'d SETS | | |
| ☐ 1 Anquan Boldin | .75 | .30 |
| ☐ 2 Emmitt Smith | 2.00 | .75 |
| ☐ 3 Josh McCown | .60 | .25 |
| ☐ 4 Michael Vick | .75 | .30 |
| ☐ 5 Peerless Price | .60 | .25 |
| ☐ 6 T.J. Duckett | .60 | .25 |
| ☐ 7 Warrick Dunn | .60 | .25 |
| ☐ 8 Jamal Lewis | .60 | .25 |
| ☐ 9 Kyle Boller | .60 | .25 |
| ☐ 10 Ray Lewis | .75 | .30 |
| ☐ 11 Drew Bledsoe | .75 | .30 |
| ☐ 12 Eric Moulds | .60 | .25 |
| ☐ 13 Travis Henry | .60 | .25 |
| ☐ 14 Jake Delhomme | .60 | .25 |
| ☐ 15 Stephen Davis | .60 | .25 |
| ☐ 16 Steve Smith | .75 | .30 |
| ☐ 17 Brian Urlacher | .75 | .30 |
| ☐ 18 Rex Grossman | .75 | .30 |
| ☐ 19 Thomas Jones | .60 | .25 |
| ☐ 20 Carson Palmer | 1.00 | .40 |
| ☐ 21 Chad Johnson | .60 | .25 |
| ☐ 22 Rudi Johnson | .60 | .25 |
| ☐ 23 Jeff Garcia | .75 | .30 |
| ☐ 24 William Green | .50 | .20 |
| ☐ 25 Keyshawn Johnson | .60 | .25 |
| ☐ 26 Terence Newman | .60 | .25 |
| ☐ 27 Roy Williams S | .60 | .25 |
| ☐ 28 Jake Plummer | .60 | .25 |
| ☐ 29 Quentin Griffin | .60 | .25 |
| ☐ 30 Rod Smith | .60 | .25 |
| ☐ 31 Charles Rogers | .60 | .25 |
| ☐ 32 Joey Harrington | .60 | .25 |
| ☐ 33 Ahman Green | .75 | .30 |
| ☐ 34 Brett Favre | 2.00 | .75 |
| ☐ 35 Javon Walker | .60 | .25 |
| ☐ 36 Andre Johnson | .75 | .30 |
| ☐ 37 David Carr | .60 | .25 |
| ☐ 38 Domanick Davis | .75 | .30 |
| ☐ 39 Edgerrin James | .75 | .30 |
| ☐ 40 Marvin Harrison | .75 | .30 |
| ☐ 41 Peyton Manning | 1.50 | .60 |
| ☐ 42 Byron Leftwich | .75 | .30 |
| ☐ 43 Fred Taylor | .60 | .25 |
| ☐ 44 Jimmy Smith | .60 | .25 |
| ☐ 45 Priest Holmes | .75 | .30 |
| ☐ 46 Tony Gonzalez | .75 | .30 |
| ☐ 47 Trent Green | .60 | .25 |
| ☐ 48 A.J. Feeley | .60 | .25 |

| | | |
|---|---|---|
| ☐ 49 Chris Chambers | .60 | .25 |
| ☐ 50 Deion Sanders | .75 | .30 |
| ☐ 51 Daunte Culpepper | .75 | .30 |
| ☐ 52 Michael Bennett | .60 | .25 |
| ☐ 53 Randy Moss | 1.00 | .40 |
| ☐ 54 Corey Dillon | .60 | .25 |
| ☐ 55 Deion Branch | .60 | .25 |
| ☐ 56 Tom Brady | 2.00 | .75 |
| ☐ 57 Aaron Brooks | .60 | .25 |
| ☐ 58 Deuce McAllister | .75 | .30 |
| ☐ 59 Joe Horn | .60 | .25 |
| ☐ 60 Jeremy Shockey | .75 | .30 |
| ☐ 61 Michael Strahan | .60 | .25 |
| ☐ 62 Tiki Barber | .75 | .30 |
| ☐ 63 Chad Pennington | .75 | .30 |
| ☐ 64 Curtis Martin | .60 | .25 |
| ☐ 65 Santana Moss | .60 | .25 |
| ☐ 66 Jerry Porter | .60 | .25 |
| ☐ 67 Jerry Rice | 1.50 | .60 |
| ☐ 68 Warren Sapp | .60 | .25 |
| ☐ 69 Donovan McNabb | .75 | .30 |
| ☐ 70 Jevon Kearse | .60 | .25 |
| ☐ 71 Terrell Owens | .75 | .30 |
| ☐ 72 Duce Staley | .60 | .25 |
| ☐ 73 Hines Ward | .75 | .30 |
| ☐ 74 Jerome Bettis | .75 | .30 |
| ☐ 75 LaDainian Tomlinson | 1.25 | .50 |
| ☐ 76 Kevan Barlow | .60 | .25 |
| ☐ 77 Tim Rattay | .50 | .20 |
| ☐ 78 Koren Robinson | .60 | .25 |
| ☐ 79 Matt Hasselbeck | .75 | .30 |
| ☐ 80 Shaun Alexander | .75 | .30 |
| ☐ 81 Isaac Bruce | .60 | .25 |
| ☐ 82 Marc Bulger | .60 | .25 |
| ☐ 83 Marshall Faulk | .75 | .30 |
| ☐ 84 Torry Holt | .75 | .30 |
| ☐ 85 Brad Johnson | .60 | .25 |
| ☐ 86 Derrick Brooks | .60 | .25 |
| ☐ 87 Chris Brown | .60 | .25 |
| ☐ 88 Derrick Mason | .60 | .25 |
| ☐ 89 Eddie George | .75 | .30 |
| ☐ 90 Steve McNair | .75 | .30 |
| ☐ 91 Clinton Portis | .75 | .30 |
| ☐ 92 LaVar Arrington | .60 | .25 |
| ☐ 93 Laveranues Coles | .60 | .25 |
| ☐ 94 Mark Brunell | .60 | .25 |
| ☐ 95 Hall/Schaub/Jenkins CL | 1.50 | .60 |
| ☐ 96 Losman/L.Evans CL | .60 | .25 |
| ☐ 97 Winslow Jr./L.McCown CL | 1.00 | .40 |
| ☐ 98 D.Watts/T.Bell CL | .50 | .20 |
| ☐ 99 K.Jones/Ro.Will. CL | 1.25 | .50 |
| ☐ 100 G.Jones/Re.Will. CL | .60 | .25 |
| ☐ 101 Darnell Dockett RC | 2.50 | 1.00 |
| ☐ 102 Karlos Dansby RC | 4.00 | 1.50 |
| ☐ 103 Larry Croom RC | 2.50 | 1.00 |
| ☐ 104 Chad Lavalais RC | 2.50 | 1.00 |
| ☐ 105 Demorrio Williams RC | 4.00 | 1.50 |
| ☐ 106 B.J. Sams RC | 3.00 | 1.25 |
| ☐ 107 Dwan Edwards RC | 2.50 | 1.00 |
| ☐ 108 Jason Peters RC | 2.50 | 1.00 |
| ☐ 109 Shaud Williams RC | 3.00 | 1.25 |
| ☐ 110 Tim Anderson RC | 3.00 | 1.25 |
| ☐ 111 Tim Euhus RC | 2.50 | 1.00 |
| ☐ 112 Michael Gaines RC | 2.50 | 1.00 |
| ☐ 113 Rod Rutherford RC | 2.50 | 1.00 |
| ☐ 114 Leon Joe RC | 2.50 | 1.00 |
| ☐ 115 Nathan Vasher RC | 4.00 | 1.50 |
| ☐ 116 Caleb Miller RC | 2.50 | 1.00 |
| ☐ 117 Jamall Broussard RC | 2.50 | 1.00 |
| ☐ 118 Keiwan Ratliff RC | 2.50 | 1.00 |
| ☐ 119 Landon Johnson RC | 2.50 | 1.00 |
| ☐ 120 Madieu Williams RC | 2.50 | 1.00 |
| ☐ 121 Matthias Askew RC | 2.50 | 1.00 |
| ☐ 122 Robert Geathers RC | 2.50 | 1.00 |
| ☐ 123 Richard Alston RC | 2.50 | 1.00 |
| ☐ 124 Bruce Thornton RC | 2.50 | 1.00 |
| ☐ 125 Patrick Crayton RC | 5.00 | 2.00 |
| ☐ 126 Bradlee Van Pelt RC | 3.00 | 1.25 |
| ☐ 127 Charlie Adams RC | 2.50 | 1.00 |
| ☐ 128 Nate Jackson RC | 2.50 | 1.00 |
| ☐ 129 Roc Alexander RC | 2.50 | 1.00 |
| ☐ 130 Romar Crenshaw RC | 2.50 | 1.00 |
| ☐ 131 Keith Smith RC | 2.50 | 1.00 |
| ☐ 132 Joey Thomas RC | 2.50 | 1.00 |
| ☐ 133 Kelvin Kight RC | 2.50 | 1.00 |
| ☐ 134 Scott McBrien RC | 3.00 | 1.25 |
| ☐ 135 Andrae Thurman RC | 2.50 | 1.00 |
| ☐ 136 Derick Armstrong RC | 2.50 | 1.00 |
| ☐ 137 Glenn Earl RC | 2.50 | 1.00 |

| | | |
|---|---|---|
| ☐ 138 Kendrick Starling RC | 2.50 | 1.00 |
| ☐ 139 Ben Hartsock RC | 3.00 | 1.25 |
| ☐ 140 Gilbert Gardner RC | 2.50 | 1.00 |
| ☐ 141 Jason David RC | 2.50 | 1.00 |
| ☐ 142 Daryl Smith RC | 3.00 | 1.25 |
| ☐ 143 Jared Allen RC | 5.00 | 2.00 |
| ☐ 144 Jeris McIntyre RC | 2.50 | 1.00 |
| ☐ 145 John Booth RC | 2.50 | 1.00 |
| ☐ 146 Jonathan Smith RC | 2.50 | 1.00 |
| ☐ 147 Junior Siavii RC | 2.50 | 1.00 |
| ☐ 148 Keyaron Fox RC | 3.00 | 1.25 |
| ☐ 149 Kris Wilson RC | 3.00 | 1.25 |
| ☐ 150 Doug Easlick RC | 2.50 | 1.00 |
| ☐ 151 Fred Russell RC | 3.00 | 1.25 |
| ☐ 152 Tony Bua RC | 2.50 | 1.00 |
| ☐ 153 Will Poole RC | 4.00 | 1.50 |
| ☐ 154 Ben Nelson RC | 2.50 | 1.00 |
| ☐ 155 Brock Lesnar RC | 10.00 | 4.00 |
| ☐ 156 Butchie Wallace RC | 2.50 | 1.00 |
| ☐ 157 Darrion Scott RC | 3.00 | 1.25 |
| ☐ 158 Dontarrious Thomas RC | 3.00 | 1.25 |
| ☐ 159 Richard Owens RC | 2.50 | 1.00 |
| ☐ 160 Rod Davis RC | 2.50 | 1.00 |
| ☐ 161 Dexter Reid RC | 2.50 | 1.00 |
| ☐ 162 Kory Chapman RC | 2.50 | 1.00 |
| ☐ 163 Marquise Hill RC | 2.50 | 1.00 |
| ☐ 164 Courtney Watson RC | 3.00 | 1.25 |
| ☐ 165 Mike Karney RC | 3.00 | 1.25 |
| ☐ 166 Gibril Wilson RC | 4.00 | 1.50 |
| ☐ 167 Reggie Torbor RC | 2.50 | 1.00 |
| ☐ 168 Darrell McClover RC | 2.50 | 1.00 |
| ☐ 169 Derrick Strait RC | 3.00 | 1.25 |
| ☐ 170 Erik Coleman RC | 3.00 | 1.25 |
| ☐ 171 Johnathan Reese RC | 2.50 | 1.00 |
| ☐ 172 Rashad Washington RC | 2.50 | 1.00 |
| ☐ 173 Courtney Anderson RC | 2.50 | 1.00 |
| ☐ 174 Stuart Schweigert RC | 3.00 | 1.25 |
| ☐ 175 J.R. Reed RC | 2.50 | 1.00 |
| ☐ 176 Justin Jenkins RC | 2.50 | 1.00 |
| ☐ 177 Matt Ware RC | 4.00 | 1.50 |
| ☐ 178 Nate Lawrie RC | 2.50 | 1.00 |
| ☐ 179 Thomas Tapeh RC | 3.00 | 1.25 |
| ☐ 180 Matt Kranchick RC | 2.50 | 1.00 |
| ☐ 181 Willie Parker RC | 25.00 | 10.00 |
| ☐ 182 Igor Olshansky RC | 4.00 | 1.50 |
| ☐ 183 Ryan Krause RC | 2.50 | 1.00 |
| ☐ 184 Shaun Phillips RC | 2.50 | 1.00 |
| ☐ 185 Wes Welker RC | 12.00 | 5.00 |
| ☐ 186 Richard Seigler RC | 2.50 | 1.00 |
| ☐ 187 Shawntae Spencer RC | 2.50 | 1.00 |
| ☐ 188 Marcus Tubbs RC | 2.50 | 1.00 |
| ☐ 189 Niko Koutouvides RC | 2.50 | 1.00 |
| ☐ 190 Brandon Chillar RC | 3.00 | 1.25 |
| ☐ 191 Tony Hargrove RC | 2.50 | 1.00 |
| ☐ 192 Mark Jones RC | 2.50 | 1.00 |
| ☐ 193 Marquis Cooper RC | 4.00 | 1.50 |
| ☐ 194 Antwan Odom RC | 2.50 | 1.00 |
| ☐ 195 Michael Waddell RC | 2.50 | 1.00 |
| ☐ 196 Randy Starks RC | 2.50 | 1.00 |
| ☐ 197 Rich Gardner RC | 3.00 | 1.25 |
| ☐ 198 Travis Laboy RC | 2.50 | 1.00 |
| ☐ 199 Vick King RC | 2.50 | 1.00 |
| ☐ 200 Chris Cooley RC | 4.00 | 1.50 |
| ☐ 201 Adimchinobe Echemandu RC | 5.00 | 2.00 |
| ☐ 202 Ahmad Carroll RC | 6.00 | 2.50 |
| ☐ 203 Andy Hall RC | 5.00 | 2.00 |
| ☐ 204 B.J. Johnson RC | 4.00 | 1.50 |
| ☐ 205 B.J. Symons RC | 4.00 | 1.50 |
| ☐ 206 Brandon Miree RC | 4.00 | 1.50 |
| ☐ 207 Bruce Perry RC | 4.00 | 1.50 |
| ☐ 208 Carlos Francis RC | 4.00 | 1.50 |
| ☐ 209 Casey Bramlet RC | 4.00 | 1.50 |
| ☐ 210 Chris Gamble RC | 5.00 | 2.00 |
| ☐ 211 Clarence Moore RC | 5.00 | 2.00 |
| ☐ 212 Cody Pickett RC | 5.00 | 2.00 |
| ☐ 213 Craig Krenzel RC | 6.00 | 2.50 |
| ☐ 214 D.J. Hackett RC | 6.00 | 2.50 |
| ☐ 215 D.J. Williams RC | 6.00 | 2.50 |
| ☐ 216 Derrick Ward RC | 6.00 | 2.50 |
| ☐ 217 Drew Carter RC | 6.00 | 2.50 |
| ☐ 218 Drew Henson RC | 4.00 | 1.50 |
| ☐ 219 Ernest Wilford RC | 6.00 | 2.50 |
| ☐ 220 Jamaar Taylor RC | 4.00 | 1.50 |
| ☐ 221 Jared Lorenzen RC | 5.00 | 2.00 |
| ☐ 222 Jarrett Payton RC | 5.00 | 2.00 |
| ☐ 223 Jason Babin RC | 5.00 | 2.00 |
| ☐ 224 Jeff Smoker RC | 5.00 | 2.00 |
| ☐ 225 Jerricho Cotchery RC | 6.00 | 2.50 |
| ☐ 226 Jim Sorgi RC | 2.50 | 2.50 |

| | | |
|---|---|---|
| ❑ 227 John Navarre RC | 5.00 | 2.00 |
| ❑ 228 Johnnie Morant RC | 5.00 | 2.00 |
| ❑ 229 Jonathan Vilma RC | 6.00 | 2.50 |
| ❑ 230 Josh Harris RC | 4.00 | 1.50 |
| ❑ 231 Kenechi Udeze RC | 6.00 | 2.50 |
| ❑ 232 Matt Mauck RC | 5.00 | 2.00 |
| ❑ 233 Maurice Mann RC | 4.00 | 1.50 |
| ❑ 234 Michael Turner RC | 12.00 | 5.00 |
| ❑ 235 P.K. Sam RC | 4.00 | 1.50 |
| ❑ 236 Quincy Wilson RC | 5.00 | 2.00 |
| ❑ 237 Ran Carthon RC | 4.00 | 1.50 |
| ❑ 238 Ricardo Colclough RC | 6.00 | 2.50 |
| ❑ 239 Samie Parker RC | 5.00 | 2.00 |
| ❑ 240 Sean Jones RC | 5.00 | 2.00 |
| ❑ 241 Sean Taylor RC | 6.00 | 2.50 |
| ❑ 242 Sloan Thomas RC | 5.00 | 2.00 |
| ❑ 243 Tommie Harris RC | 6.00 | 2.50 |
| ❑ 244 Triandos Luke RC | 4.00 | 1.50 |
| ❑ 245 Troy Fleming RC | 4.00 | 1.50 |
| ❑ 246 Vince Wilfork RC | 6.00 | 2.50 |
| ❑ 247 Will Smith RC | 5.00 | 2.00 |
| ❑ 248 Michael Boulware RC | 6.00 | 2.50 |
| ❑ 249 Richard Smith RC | 4.00 | 1.50 |
| ❑ 250 Teddy Lehman RC | 5.00 | 2.00 |
| ❑ 251 Larry Fitzgerald JSY RC | 20.00 | 7.50 |
| ❑ 252 DeAngelo Hall JSY RC | 10.00 | 4.00 |
| ❑ 253 Matt Schaub JSY RC | 20.00 | 7.50 |
| ❑ 254 Michael Jenkins JSY RC | 8.00 | 3.00 |
| ❑ 255 Devard Darling JSY RC | 8.00 | 3.00 |
| ❑ 256 J.P. Losman JSY RC | 12.00 | 5.00 |
| ❑ 257 Lee Evans JSY RC | 10.00 | 4.00 |
| ❑ 258 Keary Colbert JSY RC | 8.00 | 3.00 |
| ❑ 259 Bernard Berrian JSY RC | 8.00 | 3.00 |
| ❑ 260 Chris Perry JSY RC | 10.00 | 4.00 |
| ❑ 261 Kellen Winslow Jr. JSY RC | 12.00 | 5.00 |
| ❑ 262 Luke McCown JSY RC | 8.00 | 3.00 |
| ❑ 263 Julius Jones JSY RC | 20.00 | 7.50 |
| ❑ 264 Darius Watts JSY RC | 8.00 | 3.00 |
| ❑ 265 Tatum Bell JSY RC | 10.00 | 4.00 |
| ❑ 266 Kevin Jones JSY RC | 12.00 | 5.00 |
| ❑ 267 Roy Williams JSY RC | 15.00 | 6.00 |
| ❑ 268 Dunta Robinson JSY RC | 8.00 | 3.00 |
| ❑ 269 Greg Jones JSY RC | 8.00 | 3.00 |
| ❑ 270 Reggie Williams JSY RC | 8.00 | 3.00 |
| ❑ 271 Mewelde Moore JSY RC | 8.00 | 3.00 |
| ❑ 272 Ben Watson JSY RC | 8.00 | 3.00 |
| ❑ 273 Cedric Cobbs JSY RC | 8.00 | 3.00 |
| ❑ 274 Devery Henderson JSY RC | 8.00 | 3.00 |
| ❑ 275 Eli Manning JSY RC | 30.00 | 15.00 |
| ❑ 276 Robert Gallery JSY RC | 8.00 | 3.00 |
| ❑ 277 Ben Roethlisberger JSY RC | 40.00 | 15.00 |
| ❑ 278 Philip Rivers JSY RC | 20.00 | 7.50 |
| ❑ 279 Derrick Hamilton JSY RC | 6.00 | 2.50 |
| ❑ 280 Rashaun Woods JSY RC | 8.00 | 3.00 |
| ❑ 281 Steven Jackson JSY RC | 20.00 | 7.50 |
| ❑ 282 Michael Clayton JSY RC | 10.00 | 4.00 |
| ❑ 283 Ben Troupe JSY RC | 8.00 | 3.00 |
| ❑ 284 E.Manning/Rivers JSY | 30.00 | 15.00 |
| ❑ 285 Fitzgerald/Ro.Williams JSY | 20.00 | 7.50 |
| ❑ 286 Winslow Jr./G.Jones JSY | 12.00 | 5.00 |
| ❑ 288 Re.Williams/Darling JSY | 8.00 | 3.00 |
| ❑ 289 Roethlisberger/Losman JSY | 40.00 | 15.00 |
| ❑ 292 L.Evans/M.Jenkins JSY | 12.00 | 5.00 |
| ❑ 293 R.Woods/T.Bell JSY | 10.00 | 4.00 |
| ❑ 294 K.Jones/Berrian JSY | 15.00 | 6.00 |
| ❑ 295 Watson/Troupe JSY | 8.00 | 3.00 |
| ❑ 297 M.Schaub/Hamilton JSY | 20.00 | 7.50 |
| ❑ 298 L.McCown/Watts JSY | 8.00 | 3.00 |
| ❑ 299 Colbert/Cobbs JSY | 8.00 | 3.00 |

## 2005 Leaf Rookies and Stars

| | | |
|---|---|---|
| ❑ COMP.SET w/o RC's (100) | 20.00 | 7.50 |
| ❑ 1-250 RC PRINT RUN 799 SER.#'d SETS | | |
| ❑ 251-279 JSY PRINT RUN 750 SER.#'d SETS | | |
| ❑ 280-293 JSY DUAL PRINT RUN 500 SER.#'d SETS | | |
| ❑ 1 Anquan Boldin | .60 | .25 |
| ❑ 2 Kurt Warner | .75 | .30 |
| ❑ 3 Larry Fitzgerald | .75 | .30 |
| ❑ 4 Michael Vick | .75 | .30 |
| ❑ 5 T.J. Duckett | .50 | .20 |
| ❑ 6 Warrick Dunn | .60 | .25 |
| ❑ 7 Jamal Lewis | .60 | .25 |
| ❑ 8 Kyle Boller | .60 | .25 |
| ❑ 9 Ray Lewis | .75 | .30 |
| ❑ 10 Derrick Mason | .60 | .25 |
| ❑ 11 J.P. Losman | .75 | .30 |
| ❑ 12 Lee Evans | .60 | .25 |

| | | |
|---|---|---|
| ❑ 13 Willis McGahee | .75 | .30 |
| ❑ 14 DeShaun Foster | .60 | .25 |
| ❑ 15 Jake Delhomme | .75 | .30 |
| ❑ 16 Steve Smith | .75 | .30 |
| ❑ 17 Brian Urlacher | .75 | .30 |
| ❑ 18 Rex Grossman | .75 | .30 |
| ❑ 19 Muhsin Muhammad | .60 | .25 |
| ❑ 20 Carson Palmer | .75 | .30 |
| ❑ 21 Chad Johnson | .60 | .25 |
| ❑ 22 Rudi Johnson | .60 | .25 |
| ❑ 23 Lee Suggs | .60 | .25 |
| ❑ 24 Drew Bledsoe | .75 | .30 |
| ❑ 25 Julius Jones | .75 | .30 |
| ❑ 26 Keyshawn Johnson | .60 | .25 |
| ❑ 27 Roy Williams S | .60 | .25 |
| ❑ 28 Ashley Lelie | .50 | .20 |
| ❑ 29 Jake Plummer | .60 | .25 |
| ❑ 30 Rod Smith | .60 | .25 |
| ❑ 31 Tatum Bell | .60 | .25 |
| ❑ 32 Joey Harrington | .75 | .30 |
| ❑ 33 Kevin Jones | .60 | .25 |
| ❑ 34 Roy Williams WR | .75 | .30 |
| ❑ 35 Ahman Green | .75 | .30 |
| ❑ 36 Brett Favre | 2.00 | .75 |
| ❑ 37 Javon Walker | .60 | .25 |
| ❑ 38 Andre Johnson | .60 | .25 |
| ❑ 39 David Carr | .60 | .25 |
| ❑ 40 Domanick Davis | .50 | .20 |
| ❑ 41 Edgerrin James | .60 | .25 |
| ❑ 42 Marvin Harrison | .75 | .30 |
| ❑ 43 Peyton Manning | 1.25 | .50 |
| ❑ 44 Reggie Wayne | .60 | .25 |
| ❑ 45 Byron Leftwich | .60 | .25 |
| ❑ 46 Fred Taylor | .75 | .30 |
| ❑ 47 Jimmy Smith | .60 | .25 |
| ❑ 48 Priest Holmes | .75 | .30 |
| ❑ 49 Tony Gonzalez | .60 | .25 |
| ❑ 50 Trent Green | .60 | .25 |
| ❑ 51 Chris Chambers | .60 | .25 |
| ❑ 52 Daunte Culpepper | .75 | .30 |
| ❑ 53 Michael Bennett | .60 | .25 |
| ❑ 54 Nate Burleson | .60 | .25 |
| ❑ 55 Corey Dillon | .60 | .25 |
| ❑ 56 Deion Branch | .60 | .25 |
| ❑ 57 Tom Brady | 1.50 | .60 |
| ❑ 58 Aaron Brooks | .50 | .20 |
| ❑ 59 Deuce McAllister | .75 | .30 |
| ❑ 60 Joe Horn | .60 | .25 |
| ❑ 61 Eli Manning | 1.50 | .60 |
| ❑ 62 Jeremy Shockey | .75 | .30 |
| ❑ 63 Tiki Barber | .75 | .30 |
| ❑ 64 Plaxico Burress | .60 | .25 |
| ❑ 65 Chad Pennington | .60 | .25 |
| ❑ 66 Curtis Martin | .75 | .30 |
| ❑ 67 Laveranues Coles | .60 | .25 |
| ❑ 68 Jerry Porter | .60 | .25 |
| ❑ 69 Kerry Collins | .60 | .25 |
| ❑ 70 LaMont Jordan | .60 | .25 |
| ❑ 71 Randy Moss | .75 | .30 |
| ❑ 72 Brian Westbrook | .75 | .30 |
| ❑ 73 Donovan McNabb | .75 | .30 |
| ❑ 74 Terrell Owens | .75 | .30 |
| ❑ 75 Ben Roethlisberger | 2.00 | .75 |
| ❑ 76 Duce Staley | .60 | .25 |
| ❑ 77 Hines Ward | .75 | .30 |
| ❑ 78 Jerome Bettis | .75 | .30 |
| ❑ 79 Antonio Gates | .75 | .30 |
| ❑ 80 Drew Brees | .75 | .30 |
| ❑ 81 LaDainian Tomlinson | 1.25 | .50 |
| ❑ 82 Kevan Barlow | .60 | .25 |
| ❑ 83 Darrell Jackson | .60 | .25 |
| ❑ 84 Matt Hasselbeck | .75 | .30 |

| | | |
|---|---|---|
| ❑ 85 Shaun Alexander | .75 | .30 |
| ❑ 86 Marc Bulger | .60 | .25 |
| ❑ 87 Steven Jackson | 1.00 | .40 |
| ❑ 88 Torry Holt | .60 | .25 |
| ❑ 89 Brian Griese | .60 | .25 |
| ❑ 90 Michael Clayton | .60 | .25 |
| ❑ 91 Chris Simms | .60 | .25 |
| ❑ 92 Drew Bennett | .60 | .25 |
| ❑ 93 Steve McNair | .75 | .30 |
| ❑ 94 Clinton Portis | .75 | .30 |
| ❑ 95 LaVar Arrington | .75 | .30 |
| ❑ 96 Santana Moss | .60 | .25 |
| ❑ 97 A.Smith QB CL/F.Gore | 1.25 | .50 |
| ❑ 98 B.Edwards CL/C.Frye | 2.50 | 1.00 |
| ❑ 99 C.Fason CL/T.Williamson | .60 | .25 |
| ❑ 100 C.Rogers CL/J.Campbell | 1.50 | .60 |
| ❑ 101 Travis Johnson RC | 2.50 | 1.00 |
| ❑ 102 Alex Smith TE RC | 4.00 | 1.50 |
| ❑ 103 Channing Crowder RC | 3.00 | 1.25 |
| ❑ 104 Craig Bragg RC | 2.50 | 1.00 |
| ❑ 105 Darrent Williams RC | 4.00 | 1.50 |
| ❑ 106 Derrick Wimbush RC | 3.00 | 1.25 |
| ❑ 107 Josh Cribbs RC | 12.00 | 5.00 |
| ❑ 108 Luis Castillo RC | 4.00 | 1.50 |
| ❑ 109 Matt Roth RC | 4.00 | 1.50 |
| ❑ 110 Mike Patterson RC | 3.00 | 1.25 |
| ❑ 111 Fred Gibson RC | 3.00 | 1.25 |
| ❑ 112 Marcus Spears RC | 4.00 | 1.50 |
| ❑ 113 Brodney Pool RC | 3.00 | 1.25 |
| ❑ 114 Barrett Ruud RC | 4.00 | 1.50 |
| ❑ 115 Stanford Routt RC | 3.00 | 1.25 |
| ❑ 116 Josh Bullocks RC | 3.00 | 1.25 |
| ❑ 117 Kevin Burnett RC | 3.00 | 1.25 |
| ❑ 118 Corey Webster RC | 4.00 | 1.50 |
| ❑ 119 Lofa Tatupu RC | 5.00 | 2.00 |
| ❑ 120 Mike Nugent RC | 3.00 | 1.25 |
| ❑ 121 Jim Leonhard RC | 3.00 | 1.25 |
| ❑ 122 Ronald Bartell RC | 3.00 | 1.25 |
| ❑ 123 Nick Collins RC | 4.00 | 1.50 |
| ❑ 124 Justin Miller RC | 3.00 | 1.25 |
| ❑ 125 Jonathan Babineaux RC | 3.00 | 1.25 |
| ❑ 126 Kelvin Hayden RC | 3.00 | 1.25 |
| ❑ 127 Matt McCoy RC | 3.00 | 1.25 |
| ❑ 128 Oshiomogho Atogwe RC | 2.50 | 1.00 |
| ❑ 129 Stanley Wilson RC | 3.00 | 1.25 |
| ❑ 130 Justin Tuck RC | 5.00 | 2.00 |
| ❑ 131 Eric Green RC | 3.00 | 1.25 |
| ❑ 132 Karl Paymah RC | 3.00 | 1.25 |
| ❑ 133 Kirk Morrison RC | 4.00 | 1.50 |
| ❑ 134 Dustin Fox RC | 4.00 | 1.50 |
| ❑ 135 Alfred Fincher RC | 3.00 | 1.25 |
| ❑ 136 Chris Henry RC | 4.00 | 1.50 |
| ❑ 137 Ellis Hobbs RC | 4.00 | 1.50 |
| ❑ 138 Scott Starks RC | 3.00 | 1.25 |
| ❑ 139 Jordan Beck RC | 3.00 | 1.25 |
| ❑ 140 Vincent Burns RC | 2.50 | 1.00 |
| ❑ 141 Darryl Blackstock RC | 2.50 | 1.00 |
| ❑ 142 Domonique Foxworth RC | 3.00 | 1.25 |
| ❑ 143 Leroy Hill RC | 4.00 | 1.50 |
| ❑ 144 Cedric Killings RC | 2.50 | 1.00 |
| ❑ 145 Leonard Weaver RC | 2.50 | 1.00 |
| ❑ 146 Sean Considine RC | 2.50 | 1.00 |
| ❑ 147 Antonio Perkins RC | 3.00 | 1.25 |
| ❑ 148 Travis Daniels RC | 3.00 | 1.25 |
| ❑ 149 Vincent Fuller RC | 3.00 | 1.25 |
| ❑ 150 Manuel White RC | 3.00 | 1.25 |
| ❑ 151 Kerry Rhodes RC | 4.00 | 1.50 |
| ❑ 152 Brady Poppinga RC | 4.00 | 1.50 |
| ❑ 153 Chris Canty RC | 4.00 | 1.50 |
| ❑ 154 James Sanders RC | 3.00 | 1.25 |
| ❑ 155 Matt Giordano RC | 3.00 | 1.25 |
| ❑ 156 Boomer Grigsby RC | 3.00 | 1.25 |
| ❑ 157 Donte Nicholson RC | 3.00 | 1.25 |
| ❑ 158 Jerome Collins RC | 3.00 | 1.25 |
| ❑ 159 Trent Cole RC | 4.00 | 1.50 |
| ❑ 160 Alphonso Hodge RC | 2.50 | 1.00 |
| ❑ 161 Jonathan Welsh RC | 2.50 | 1.00 |
| ❑ 162 Adam Seward RC | 3.00 | 1.25 |
| ❑ 163 Robert McCune RC | 3.00 | 1.25 |
| ❑ 164 Eric King RC | 2.50 | 1.00 |
| ❑ 165 Gerald Sensabaugh RC | 3.00 | 1.25 |
| ❑ 166 Justin Green RC | 4.00 | 1.50 |
| ❑ 167 Jeb Huckeba RC | 2.50 | 1.00 |
| ❑ 168 Michael Boley RC | 2.50 | 1.00 |
| ❑ 169 Andre Maddox RC | 2.50 | 1.00 |
| ❑ 170 Rian Wallace RC | 3.00 | 1.25 |
| ❑ 171 Michael Hawkins RC | 2.50 | 1.00 |
| ❑ 172 Lance Mitchell RC | 3.00 | 1.25 |
| ❑ 173 Ryan Claridge RC | 2.50 | 1.00 |

|  |  | | |
|---|------|------|------|
| 174 | James Butler RC | 3.00 | 1.25 |
| 175 | Ryan Riddle RC | 2.50 | 1.00 |
| 176 | Bo Scaife RC | 3.00 | 1.25 |
| 177 | Chris Harris RC | 3.00 | 1.25 |
| 178 | C.C. Brown RC | 2.50 | 1.00 |
| 179 | Pat Thomas RC | 2.50 | 1.00 |
| 180 | Derrick Johnson CB RC | 2.50 | 1.00 |
| 181 | Joel Dreessen RC | 3.00 | 1.25 |
| 182 | Rick Razzano RC | 2.50 | 1.00 |
| 183 | Nehemiah Broughton RC | 3.00 | 1.25 |
| 184 | Marcus Maxwell RC | 2.50 | 1.00 |
| 185 | Harry Williams RC | 2.50 | 1.00 |
| 186 | Patrick Estes RC | 2.50 | 1.00 |
| 187 | Billy Bajema RC | 2.50 | 1.00 |
| 188 | Madison Hedgecock RC | 4.00 | 1.50 |
| 189 | Manuel Wright RC | 3.00 | 1.25 |
| 190 | Roscoe Crosby RC | 2.50 | 1.00 |
| 191 | Wesley Duke RC | 3.00 | 1.25 |
| 192 | Ronnie Cruz RC | 2.50 | 1.00 |
| 193 | Adam Bergen RC | 2.50 | 1.00 |
| 194 | B.J. Ward RC | 2.50 | 1.00 |
| 195 | Stephen Spach RC | 2.50 | 1.00 |
| 196 | Marviel Underwood RC | 3.00 | 1.25 |
| 197 | John Bronson RC | 2.50 | 1.00 |
| 198 | Zak Keasey RC | 3.00 | 1.25 |
| 199 | Gregg Guenther RC | 2.50 | 1.00 |
| 200 | Jerome Carter RC | 2.50 | 1.00 |
| 201 | Aaron Rodgers RC | 15.00 | 6.00 |
| 202 | Adrian McPherson RC | 4.00 | 1.50 |
| 203 | Alvin Pearman RC | 4.00 | 1.50 |
| 204 | Airese Currie RC | 4.00 | 1.50 |
| 205 | Anthony Davis RC | 4.00 | 1.50 |
| 206 | Brandon Jacobs RC | 6.00 | 2.50 |
| 207 | Brandon Jones RC | 5.00 | 2.00 |
| 208 | Bryant McFadden RC | 4.00 | 1.50 |
| 209 | Cedric Benson RC | 5.00 | 2.00 |
| 210 | Cedric Houston RC | 5.00 | 2.00 |
| 211 | Chad Owens RC | 5.00 | 2.00 |
| 212 | Chris Henry RC | 5.00 | 2.00 |
| 213 | Graphonso Thorpe RC | 4.00 | 1.50 |
| 214 | Damien Nash RC | 4.00 | 1.50 |
| 215 | Dan Cody RC | 5.00 | 2.00 |
| 216 | Dan Orlovsky RC | 5.00 | 2.00 |
| 217 | Dante Ridgeway RC | 3.00 | 1.25 |
| 218 | Darren Sproles RC | 6.00 | 2.50 |
| 219 | David Greene RC | 4.00 | 1.50 |
| 220 | David Pollack RC | 4.00 | 1.50 |
| 221 | Deandra Cobb RC | 4.00 | 1.50 |
| 222 | DeMarcus Ware RC | 8.00 | 3.00 |
| 223 | Derek Anderson RC | 8.00 | 3.00 |
| 224 | Derrick Johnson RC | 5.00 | 2.00 |
| 225 | Fabian Washington RC | 5.00 | 2.00 |
| 226 | Roydell Williams RC | 4.00 | 1.50 |
| 227 | Heath Miller RC | 10.00 | 4.00 |
| 228 | J.R. Russell RC | 3.00 | 1.25 |
| 229 | James Kilian RC | 3.00 | 1.25 |
| 230 | Jerome Mathis RC | 5.00 | 2.00 |
| 231 | Larry Brackins RC | 3.00 | 1.25 |
| 232 | LeHon McCoy RC | 3.00 | 1.25 |
| 233 | Lionel Gates RC | 3.00 | 1.25 |
| 234 | Marion Barber RC | 15.00 | 6.00 |
| 235 | Marlin Jackson RC | 4.00 | 1.50 |
| 236 | Matt Cassel RC | 12.00 | 5.00 |
| 237 | Mike Williams RC | 5.00 | 2.00 |
| 238 | Nate Washington RC | 5.00 | 2.00 |
| 239 | Noah Herron RC | 5.00 | 2.00 |
| 240 | Fred Amey RC | 4.00 | 1.50 |
| 241 | Paris Warren RC | 4.00 | 1.50 |
| 242 | Rasheed Marshall RC | 4.00 | 1.50 |
| 243 | Ryan Fitzpatrick RC | 5.00 | 2.00 |
| 244 | Shaun Cody RC | 4.00 | 1.50 |
| 245 | Shawne Merriman RC | 8.00 | 3.00 |
| 246 | Tab Perry RC | 5.00 | 2.00 |
| 247 | Thomas Davis RC | 4.00 | 1.50 |
| 248 | Tyson Thompson RC | 5.00 | 2.00 |
| 249 | Chris Carr RC | 4.00 | 1.50 |
| 250 | Odell Thurman RC | 5.00 | 2.00 |
| 251 | Adam Jones JSY RC | 6.00 | 2.50 |
| 252 | Alex Smith QB JSY RC | 10.00 | 4.00 |
| 253 | Andrew Walter JSY RC | 6.00 | 2.50 |
| 254 | Antrel Rolle JSY RC | 6.00 | 2.50 |
| 255 | Braylon Edwards JSY RC | 20.00 | 8.00 |
| 256 | Carlos Rogers JSY RC | 6.00 | 2.50 |
| 257 | Cadillac Williams JSY RC | 12.00 | 5.00 |
| 258 | Charlie Frye JSY RC | 6.00 | 2.50 |
| 259 | Ciatrick Fason JSY RC | 5.00 | 2.00 |
| 260 | Courtney Roby JSY RC | 5.00 | 2.00 |
| 261 | Eric Shelton JSY RC | 6.00 | 2.50 |
| 262 | Frank Gore JSY RC | 15.00 | 6.00 |
| 263 | J.J. Arrington JSY RC | 6.00 | 2.50 |
| 264 | Jason Campbell JSY RC | 12.00 | 5.00 |
| 265 | Kyle Orton JSY RC | 8.00 | 3.00 |
| 266 | Mark Clayton JSY RC | 6.00 | 2.50 |
| 267 | Mark Bradley JSY RC | 6.00 | 2.50 |
| 268 | Matt Jones JSY RC | 10.00 | 4.00 |
| 269 | Maurice Clarett JSY | 5.00 | 2.00 |
| 270 | Reggie Brown JSY RC | 6.00 | 2.50 |
| 271 | Roddy White JSY RC | 8.00 | 3.00 |
| 272 | Ronnie Brown JSY RC | 20.00 | 8.00 |
| 273 | Roscoe Parrish JSY RC | 5.00 | 2.00 |
| 274 | Ryan Moats JSY RC | 6.00 | 2.50 |
| 275 | Stefan LeFors JSY RC | 5.00 | 2.00 |
| 276 | Terrence Murphy JSY RC | 5.00 | 2.00 |
| 277 | Troy Williamson JSY RC | 6.00 | 2.50 |
| 278 | Vernand Morency JSY RC | 6.00 | 2.50 |
| 279 | Vincent Jackson JSY RC | 6.00 | 2.50 |
| 280 | A.Smith QB J/J.Campbell J | 12.00 | 5.00 |
| 281 | R.Brown J/C.Williams J | 20.00 | 8.00 |
| 282 | B.Edwards J/T.Williamson J | 20.00 | 8.00 |
| 283 | A.Jones J/A.Rolle J | 6.00 | 2.50 |
| 284 | R.Parrish J/F.Gore J | 15.00 | 6.00 |
| 285 | C.Frye J/A.Walter J | 6.00 | 2.50 |
| 286 | J.Arrington J/E.Shelton J | 5.00 | 2.00 |
| 287 | C.Rogers J/K.Orton J | 8.00 | 3.00 |
| 288 | M.Clayton J/M.Bradley J | 6.00 | 2.50 |
| 289 | R.White J/Re.Brown J | 8.00 | 3.00 |
| 290 | T.Murphy J/C.Roby J | 5.00 | 2.00 |
| 291 | M.Clarett J/C.Fason J | 5.00 | 2.00 |
| 292 | R.Moats J/S.LeFors J | 5.00 | 2.00 |
| 293 | M.Jones J/V.Jackson J | 10.00 | 4.00 |

## 2006 Leaf Rookies and Stars

|  |  | | |
|---|------|------|------|
| 1 | Anquan Boldin | .50 | .20 |
| 2 | Edgerrin James | .50 | .20 |
| 3 | Kurt Warner | .50 | .20 |
| 4 | Larry Fitzgerald | .50 | .25 |
| 5 | Alge Crumpler | .50 | .20 |
| 6 | Michael Vick | .60 | .25 |
| 7 | Warrick Dunn | .50 | .20 |
| 8 | Derrick Mason | .50 | .20 |
| 9 | Jamal Lewis | .50 | .20 |
| 10 | Mike Anderson | .50 | .20 |
| 11 | Josh Reed | .40 | .15 |
| 12 | Lee Evans | .50 | .20 |
| 13 | Willis McGahee | .60 | .25 |
| 14 | DeShaun Foster | .50 | .20 |
| 15 | Jake Delhomme | .50 | .20 |
| 16 | Keyshawn Johnson | .50 | .20 |
| 17 | Steve Smith | .60 | .25 |
| 18 | Cedric Benson | .50 | .20 |
| 19 | Muhsin Muhammad | .50 | .20 |
| 20 | Rex Grossman | .60 | .25 |
| 21 | Carson Palmer | .60 | .25 |
| 22 | Chad Johnson | .60 | .25 |
| 23 | Rudi Johnson | .50 | .20 |
| 24 | T.J. Houshmandzadeh | .50 | .20 |
| 25 | Charlie Frye | .50 | .20 |
| 26 | Joe Jurevicius | .50 | .20 |
| 27 | Reuben Droughns | .50 | .20 |
| 28 | Drew Bledsoe | .60 | .25 |
| 29 | Terrell Owens | .60 | .25 |
| 30 | Terrell Owens | .60 | .25 |
| 31 | Jake Plummer | .50 | .20 |
| 32 | Jake Plummer | .50 | .20 |
| 33 | Rod Smith | .50 | .20 |
| 34 | Tatum Bell | .50 | .20 |
| 35 | Josh McCown | .50 | .20 |
| 36 | Kevin Jones | .60 | .25 |
| 37 | Roy Williams WR | .60 | .25 |
| 38 | Ahman Green | .50 | .20 |
| 39 | Brett Favre | 1.25 | .50 |
| 40 | Donald Driver | .50 | .20 |
| 41 | Robert Ferguson | .40 | .15 |
| 42 | Samkon Gado | .60 | .25 |
| 43 | Andre Johnson | .50 | .20 |
| 44 | David Carr | .50 | .20 |
| 45 | Domanick Davis | .50 | .20 |
| 46 | Eric Moulds | .50 | .20 |
| 47 | Marvin Harrison | .60 | .25 |
| 48 | Peyton Manning | 1.00 | .40 |
| 49 | Reggie Wayne | .50 | .20 |
| 50 | Dallas Clark | .50 | .20 |
| 51 | Fred Taylor | .50 | .20 |
| 52 | Byron Leftwich | .50 | .20 |
| 53 | Jimmy Smith | .50 | .20 |
| 54 | Larry Johnson | .50 | .20 |
| 55 | Tony Gonzalez | .50 | .20 |
| 56 | Trent Green | .50 | .20 |
| 57 | Eddie Kennison | .40 | .15 |
| 58 | Chris Chambers | .50 | .20 |
| 59 | Daunte Culpepper | .60 | .25 |
| 60 | Ronnie Brown | .60 | .25 |
| 61 | Chester Taylor | .50 | .20 |
| 62 | Brad Johnson | .50 | .20 |
| 63 | Deion Branch | .50 | .20 |
| 64 | Corey Dillon | .50 | .20 |
| 65 | Tom Brady | 1.00 | .40 |
| 66 | Deuce McAllister | .50 | .20 |
| 67 | Donte Stallworth | .50 | .20 |
| 68 | Drew Brees | .60 | .25 |
| 69 | Eli Manning | .75 | .30 |
| 70 | Plaxico Burress | .50 | .20 |
| 71 | Tiki Barber | .60 | .25 |
| 72 | Chad Pennington | .50 | .20 |
| 73 | Curtis Martin | .50 | .20 |
| 74 | Laveranues Coles | .50 | .20 |
| 75 | Aaron Brooks | .50 | .20 |
| 76 | LaMont Jordan | .50 | .20 |
| 77 | Randy Moss | .60 | .25 |
| 78 | Brian Westbrook | .50 | .20 |
| 79 | Donovan McNabb | .60 | .25 |
| 80 | Jabar Gaffney | .40 | .15 |
| 81 | Hines Ward | .60 | .25 |
| 82 | Ben Roethlisberger | 1.00 | .40 |
| 83 | Willie Parker | .75 | .30 |
| 84 | Antonio Gates | .60 | .25 |
| 85 | LaDainian Tomlinson | .75 | .30 |
| 86 | Philip Rivers | .60 | .25 |
| 87 | Alex Smith QB | .50 | .20 |
| 88 | Antonio Bryant | .50 | .20 |
| 89 | Kevan Barlow | .50 | .20 |
| 90 | Darrell Jackson | .50 | .20 |
| 91 | Matt Hasselbeck | .50 | .25 |
| 92 | Shaun Alexander | .60 | .25 |
| 93 | Torry Holt | .50 | .25 |
| 94 | Steven Jackson | .60 | .25 |
| 95 | Cadillac Williams | .60 | .25 |
| 96 | Joey Galloway | .50 | .20 |
| 97 | David Givens | .50 | .20 |
| 98 | Drew Bennett | .50 | .20 |
| 99 | Antwaan Randle El | .50 | .20 |
| 100 | Clinton Portis | .60 | .25 |
| 101 | Kamerion Wimbley RC | 4.00 | 1.50 |
| 102 | Mathias Kiwanuka RC | 5.00 | 2.00 |
| 103 | Reggie McNeal RC | 3.00 | 1.25 |
| 104 | Claude Wroten RC | 2.50 | 1.00 |
| 105 | Gabe Watson RC | 3.00 | 1.25 |
| 106 | D'Qwell Jackson RC | 3.00 | 1.25 |
| 107 | Todd Watkins RC | 3.00 | 1.25 |
| 108 | Bennie Brazell RC | 3.00 | 1.25 |
| 109 | David Anderson RC | 3.00 | 1.25 |
| 110 | John David Washington RC | 3.00 | 1.25 |
| 111 | Marques Hagans RC | 3.00 | 1.25 |
| 112 | Kevin Youngblood RC | 3.00 | 1.25 |
| 113 | Ben Obomanu RC | 3.00 | 1.25 |
| 114 | Jamal Jones RC | 3.00 | 1.25 |
| 115 | Nick Mangold RC | 3.00 | 1.25 |
| 116 | Devin Joseph RC | 3.00 | 1.25 |
| 117 | Erik Meyer RC | 3.00 | 1.25 |
| 118 | Tarvaun Henderson RC | 4.00 | 1.50 |
| 119 | A.J. Nicholson RC | 2.50 | 1.00 |
| 120 | Thomas Howard RC | 4.00 | 1.50 |
| 121 | Jon Alston RC | 3.00 | 1.25 |
| 122 | Ashton Youboty RC | 4.00 | 1.50 |
| 123 | Alan Zemaitis RC | 3.00 | 1.25 |
| 124 | Lawrence Vickers RC | 3.00 | 1.25 |
| 125 | J.D. Runnels RC | 3.00 | 1.25 |
| 126 | Ray Perkins RC | 3.00 | 1.25 |

|  |  | | |
|---|------|-----|-----|
| 127 | Jeff King RC | 3.00 | 1.25 |
| 128 | Quinn Sypniewski RC | 3.00 | 1.25 |
| 129 | Jason Carter RC | 3.00 | 1.25 |
| 130 | Malcolm Floyd RC | 4.00 | 1.50 |
| 131 | Mike Jennings RC | 3.00 | 1.25 |
| 132 | Chris Gocong RC | 3.00 | 1.25 |
| 133 | Frostee Rucker RC | 3.00 | 1.25 |
| 134 | Jason Hatcher RC | 3.00 | 1.25 |
| 135 | Victor Adeyanju RC | 3.00 | 1.25 |
| 136 | Elvis Dumervil RC | 2.50 | 1.00 |
| 137 | Ray Edwards RC | 3.00 | 1.25 |
| 138 | Anthony Schlegel RC | 3.00 | 1.25 |
| 139 | Freddie Keiaho RC | 3.00 | 1.25 |
| 140 | Gerris Wilkinson RC | 2.50 | 1.00 |
| 141 | Leon Williams RC | 3.00 | 1.25 |
| 142 | Stephen Tulloch RC | 3.00 | 1.25 |
| 143 | Jamar Williams RC | 3.00 | 1.25 |
| 144 | Clint Ingram RC | 4.00 | 1.50 |
| 145 | James Anderson RC | 2.50 | 1.00 |
| 146 | Darrell Hackney RC | 3.00 | 1.25 |
| 147 | Paul Pinegar RC | 3.00 | 1.25 |
| 148 | Brandon Kirsch RC | 4.00 | 1.50 |
| 149 | Andre Hall RC | 4.00 | 1.50 |
| 150 | De'Arrius Howard RC | 4.00 | 1.50 |
| 151 | Cedric Humes RC | 4.00 | 1.50 |
| 152 | Wendell Mathis RC | 3.00 | 1.25 |
| 153 | Gerald Riggs RC | 4.00 | 1.50 |
| 154 | Quinton Ganther RC | 4.00 | 1.50 |
| 155 | Martin Nance RC | 3.00 | 1.25 |
| 156 | Greg Lee RC | 3.00 | 1.25 |
| 157 | Jai Lewis RC | 3.00 | 1.25 |
| 158 | Cory Rodgers RC | 4.00 | 1.50 |
| 159 | Mike Espy RC | 4.00 | 1.50 |
| 160 | Chris Barclay RC | 3.00 | 1.25 |
| 161 | DeMeco Ryans RC | 5.00 | 2.00 |
| 162 | Rocky McIntosh RC | 4.00 | 1.50 |
| 163 | David Kirtman RC | 3.00 | 1.25 |
| 164 | Skyler Green RC | 3.00 | 1.25 |
| 165 | Will Blackmon RC | 4.00 | 1.50 |
| 166 | Darryl Tapp RC | 3.00 | 1.25 |
| 167 | Dusty Dvoracek RC | 4.00 | 1.50 |
| 168 | Richard Marshall RC | 3.00 | 1.25 |
| 169 | Tim Jennings RC | 3.00 | 1.25 |
| 170 | David Pittman RC | 3.00 | 1.25 |
| 171 | DeMario Minter RC | 3.00 | 1.25 |
| 172 | Marcus Maxey RC | 3.00 | 1.25 |
| 173 | Roman Harper RC | 3.00 | 1.25 |
| 174 | Anthony Smith RC | 4.00 | 1.50 |
| 175 | Nate Salley RC | 3.00 | 1.25 |
| 176 | Mike Hass RC | 4.00 | 1.50 |
| 177 | Greg Blue RC | 3.00 | 1.25 |
| 178 | Daniel Bullocks RC | 4.00 | 1.50 |
| 179 | Danieal Manning RC | 4.00 | 1.50 |
| 180 | Calvin Lowry RC | 4.00 | 1.50 |
| 181 | Eric Smith RC | 3.00 | 1.25 |
| 182 | Jimmy Williams RC | 4.00 | 1.50 |
| 183 | Cedric Griffin RC | 4.00 | 1.50 |
| 184 | Ko Simpson RC | 3.00 | 1.25 |
| 185 | Pat Watkins RC | 4.00 | 1.50 |
| 186 | Marcus Vick RC | 3.00 | 1.25 |
| 187 | Bernard Pollard RC | 4.00 | 1.50 |
| 188 | Daniel Bing RC | 4.00 | 1.50 |
| 189 | Cory Ross RC | 3.00 | 1.25 |
| 190 | Patrick Cobbs RC | 3.00 | 1.25 |
| 191 | Montell Owens RC | 3.00 | 1.25 |
| 192 | Chris Hannon RC | 3.00 | 1.25 |
| 193 | John Madsen RC | 4.00 | 1.50 |
| 194 | Shaun Bodiford RC | 3.00 | 1.25 |
| 195 | Fred Evans RC | 3.00 | 1.25 |
| 196 | Cletis Gordon RC | 2.00 | .75 |
| 197 | Jarrad Page RC | 4.00 | 1.50 |
| 198 | Brett Elliott RC | 4.00 | 1.50 |
| 199 | Brett Basanez RC | 4.00 | 1.50 |
| 200 | Drew Olson RC | 3.00 | 1.25 |
| 201 | Jay Cutler RC | 20.00 | 8.00 |
| 202 | Brodie Croyle RC | 6.00 | 2.50 |
| 203 | Ingle Martin RC | 5.00 | 2.00 |
| 204 | Derrick Ross RC | 4.00 | 1.50 |
| 205 | Bruce Gradkowski RC | 5.00 | 2.00 |
| 206 | D.J. Shockley RC | 5.00 | 2.00 |
| 207 | Joseph Addai RC | 15.00 | 6.00 |
| 208 | P.J. Daniels RC | 4.00 | 1.50 |
| 209 | Marques Colston RC | 12.00 | 5.00 |
| 210 | Jerome Harrison RC | 5.00 | 2.00 |
| 211 | Wali Lundy RC | 5.00 | 2.00 |
| 212 | Mike Bell RC | 5.00 | 2.00 |
| 213 | Miles Austin RC | 5.00 | 2.00 |
| 214 | Anthony Fasano RC | 5.00 | 2.00 |
| 215 | Tony Scheffler RC | 5.00 | 2.00 |
| 216 | Leonard Pope RC | 5.00 | 2.00 |
| 217 | David Thomas RC | 5.00 | 2.00 |
| 218 | Dominique Byrd RC | 4.00 | 1.50 |
| 219 | Garrett Mills RC | 5.00 | 2.00 |
| 220 | Hank Baskett RC | 5.00 | 2.00 |
| 221 | Greg Jennings RC | 8.00 | 3.00 |
| 222 | Devin Hester RC | 10.00 | 4.00 |
| 223 | Willie Reid RC | 5.00 | 2.00 |
| 224 | Brad Smith RC | 5.00 | 2.00 |
| 225 | Sam Hurd RC | 8.00 | 3.00 |
| 226 | Owen Daniels RC | 5.00 | 2.00 |
| 227 | Domenik Hixon RC | 6.00 | 2.50 |
| 228 | Jeremy Bloom RC | 4.00 | 1.50 |
| 229 | Dawan Landry RC | 5.00 | 2.00 |
| 230 | Jonathan Orr RC | 4.00 | 1.50 |
| 231 | Delanie Walker RC | 4.00 | 1.50 |
| 232 | Adam Jennings RC | 4.00 | 1.50 |
| 233 | Jeffrey Webb RC | 4.00 | 1.50 |
| 234 | Ethan Kilmer RC | 5.00 | 2.00 |
| 235 | Tye Hill RC | 5.00 | 2.00 |
| 236 | Jason Allen RC | 5.00 | 2.00 |
| 237 | Antonio Cromartie RC | 5.00 | 2.00 |
| 238 | D'Brickashaw Ferguson RC | 5.00 | 2.00 |
| 239 | Tamba Hali RC | 5.00 | 2.00 |
| 240 | Haloti Ngata RC | 5.00 | 2.00 |
| 241 | Broderick Bunkley RC | 5.00 | 2.00 |
| 242 | John McCargo RC | 4.00 | 1.50 |
| 244 | Kelly Jennings RC | 5.00 | 2.00 |
| 245 | Donte Whitner RC | 5.00 | 2.00 |
| 246 | Abdul Hodge RC | 5.00 | 2.00 |
| 247 | Ernie Sims RC | 5.00 | 2.00 |
| 248 | Chad Greenway RC | 5.00 | 2.00 |
| 249 | Bobby Carpenter RC | 5.00 | 2.00 |
| 250 | Manny Lawson RC | 5.00 | 2.00 |
| 251 | Matt Leinart JSY/599 RC | 20.00 | 8.00 |
| 252 | Kellen Clemens JSY RC | 6.00 | 2.50 |
| 253 | Tarvaris Jackson JSY RC | 6.00 | 2.50 |
| 254 | Charlie Whitehurst JSY RC | 6.00 | 2.50 |
| 255 | DeAn.Williams JSY/599 RC | 12.00 | 5.00 |
| 256 | Maurice Drew JSY RC | 10.00 | 4.00 |
| 257 | Brian Calhoun JSY RC | 6.00 | 2.50 |
| 258 | Jerious Norwood JSY RC | 10.00 | 4.00 |
| 259 | Vernon Davis JSY RC | 6.00 | 2.50 |
| 260 | Joe Klopfenstein JSY RC | 6.00 | 2.50 |
| 261 | Sinorice Moss JSY RC | 6.00 | 2.50 |
| 262 | Derek Hagan JSY RC | 6.00 | 2.50 |
| 263 | Brandon Williams JSY RC | 6.00 | 2.50 |
| 264 | Michael Robinson JSY RC | 6.00 | 2.50 |
| 265 | Jason Avant JSY RC | 5.00 | 2.00 |
| 266 | Brandon Marshall JSY RC | 6.00 | 2.50 |
| 267 | Demetrius Williams JSY RC | 6.00 | 2.50 |
| 268 | Mario Williams JSY RC | 8.00 | 3.00 |
| 269 | Michael Huff JSY.RC | 5.00 | 2.00 |
| 270 | Chad Jackson JSY RC | 6.00 | 2.50 |
| 271 | Vince Young JSY AU/249 RC | 120.00 | 60.00 |
| 272 | Omar Jacobs JSY AU/449 RC | 15.00 | 6.00 |
| 273 | Reggie Bush JSY AU/99 RC | 200.00 | 100.00 |
| 274 | L.Maroney JSY AU/99 RC | 100.00 | 50.00 |
| 275 | LenDale White JSY AU/249 RC | 40.00 | 15.00 |
| 276 | L.Washington JSY AU/199 RC | 25.00 | 12.50 |
| 277 | M.Lewis JSY AU/449 RC | 15.00 | 6.00 |
| 278 | S.Holmes JSY AU/449 RC | 40.00 | 25.00 |
| 279 | Travis Wilson JSY AU/449 RC | 12.00 | 5.00 |
| 280 | Maurice Stovall JSY AU/99 RC | 20.00 | 8.00 |
| 281 | A.J. Hawk JSY AU/99 RC | 60.00 | 30.00 |

### 2007 Leaf Rookies and Stars

|  |  | | |
|---|------|-----|-----|
| 1 | Tony Romo | 1.50 | .60 |
| 2 | Julius Jones | .60 | .25 |
| 3 | Terrell Owens | .75 | .30 |
| 4 | Eli Manning | .75 | .30 |
| 5 | Plaxico Burress | .60 | .25 |
| 6 | Jeremy Shockey | .60 | .25 |
| 7 | Brandon Jacobs | .60 | .25 |
| 8 | Donovan McNabb | .75 | .30 |
| 9 | Brian Westbrook | .60 | .25 |
| 10 | Reggie Brown | .60 | .25 |
| 11 | Jason Campbell | .60 | .25 |
| 12 | Clinton Portis | .60 | .25 |
| 13 | Santana Moss | .60 | .25 |
| 14 | Rex Grossman | .60 | .25 |
| 15 | Cedric Benson | .60 | .25 |
| 16 | Muhsin Muhammad | .50 | .20 |
| 17 | Jon Kitna | .50 | .20 |
| 18 | Roy Williams WR | .60 | .25 |
| 19 | Tatum Bell | .50 | .20 |
| 20 | Brett Favre | 1.50 | .60 |
| 21 | Vernand Morency | .60 | .25 |
| 22 | Donald Driver | .60 | .25 |
| 23 | Tarvaris Jackson | .60 | .25 |
| 24 | Chester Taylor | .50 | .20 |
| 25 | Troy Williamson | .50 | .20 |
| 26 | Jerious Norwood | .60 | .25 |
| 27 | Warrick Dunn | .60 | .25 |
| 28 | Alge Crumpler | .60 | .25 |
| 29 | Jake Delhomme | .60 | .25 |
| 30 | DeShaun Foster | .60 | .25 |
| 31 | Steve Smith | .60 | .25 |
| 32 | Drew Brees | .75 | .30 |
| 33 | Deuce McAllister | .60 | .25 |
| 34 | Marques Colston | .75 | .30 |
| 35 | Reggie Bush | 1.00 | .40 |
| 36 | Jeff Garcia | .60 | .25 |
| 37 | Cadillac Williams | .60 | .25 |
| 38 | Joey Galloway | .60 | .25 |
| 39 | Matt Leinart | .75 | .30 |
| 40 | Edgerrin James | .60 | .25 |
| 41 | Anquan Boldin | .60 | .25 |
| 42 | Larry Fitzgerald | .75 | .30 |
| 43 | Marc Bulger | .60 | .25 |
| 44 | Steven Jackson | .75 | .30 |
| 45 | Torry Holt | .60 | .25 |
| 46 | Alex Smith QB | .75 | .30 |
| 47 | Frank Gore | .75 | .30 |
| 48 | Vernon Davis | .60 | .25 |
| 49 | Matt Hasselbeck | .60 | .25 |
| 50 | Shaun Alexander | .60 | .25 |
| 51 | Deion Branch | .60 | .25 |
| 52 | J.P. Losman | .50 | .20 |
| 53 | Anthony Thomas | .50 | .20 |
| 54 | Lee Evans | .60 | .25 |
| 55 | Trent Green | .50 | .20 |
| 56 | Ronnie Brown | .60 | .25 |
| 57 | Chris Chambers | .50 | .25 |
| 58 | Tom Brady | 1.50 | .60 |
| 59 | Laurence Maroney | .75 | .30 |
| 60 | Randy Moss | .75 | .30 |
| 61 | Chad Pennington | .60 | .25 |
| 62 | Jerricho Cotchery | .50 | .20 |
| 63 | Leon Washington | .50 | .20 |
| 64 | Steve McNair | .60 | .25 |
| 65 | Willis McGahee | .60 | .25 |
| 66 | Mark Clayton | .50 | .20 |
| 67 | Carson Palmer | .75 | .30 |
| 68 | Rudi Johnson | .60 | .25 |
| 69 | Chad Johnson | .75 | .30 |
| 70 | T.J. Houshmandzadeh | .60 | .25 |
| 71 | Charlie Frye | .60 | .25 |
| 72 | Braylon Edwards | .60 | .25 |
| 73 | Jamal Lewis | .60 | .25 |
| 74 | Ben Roethlisberger | 1.00 | .40 |
| 75 | Willie Parker | .75 | .30 |
| 76 | Hines Ward | .75 | .30 |
| 77 | Ahman Green | .60 | .25 |
| 78 | Andre Johnson | .60 | .25 |
| 79 | Matt Schaub | .50 | .20 |
| 80 | Peyton Manning | 1.25 | .50 |
| 81 | Joseph Addai | .75 | .30 |
| 82 | Marvin Harrison | .75 | .30 |
| 83 | Reggie Wayne | .60 | .25 |
| 84 | Byron Leftwich | .60 | .25 |
| 85 | Fred Taylor | .60 | .25 |
| 86 | Maurice Jones-Drew | .75 | .30 |
| 87 | Vince Young | .75 | .30 |
| 88 | LenDale White | .60 | .25 |
| 89 | Brandon Jones | .60 | .25 |
| 90 | Jay Cutler | .75 | .30 |
| 91 | Javon Walker | .60 | .25 |

| | | |
|---|---|---|
| 92 Mike Bell | .60 | .25 |
| 93 Larry Johnson | .60 | .25 |
| 94 Tony Gonzalez | .60 | .25 |
| 95 Brodie Croyle | .75 | .30 |
| 96 LaMont Jordan | .60 | .25 |
| 97 Dominic Rhodes | .60 | .25 |
| 98 Philip Rivers | .75 | .30 |
| 99 LaDainian Tomlinson | 1.00 | .40 |
| 100 Antonio Gates | .60 | .25 |
| 101 Drew Brees ELE | 3.00 | 1.25 |
| 102 Reggie Bush ELE | 5.00 | 2.00 |
| 103 Brett Favre ELE | 8.00 | 3.00 |
| 104 Marvin Harrison ELE | 4.00 | 1.50 |
| 105 Eli Manning ELE | 4.00 | 1.50 |
| 106 Willie Parker ELE | 4.00 | 1.50 |
| 107 Brian Westbrook ELE | 3.00 | 1.25 |
| 108 Tom Brady ELE | 8.00 | 3.00 |
| 109 Jay Cutler ELE | 4.00 | 1.50 |
| 110 Rudi Johnson ELE | 3.00 | 1.25 |
| 111 J.P. Losman ELE | 2.50 | 1.00 |
| 112 Laurence Maroney ELE | 4.00 | 1.50 |
| 113 Carson Palmer ELE | 4.00 | 1.50 |
| 114 Ben Roethlisberger ELE | 5.00 | 2.00 |
| 115 Brian Urlacher ELE | 4.00 | 1.50 |
| 116 A.J. Davis RC | 3.00 | 1.25 |
| 117 Usama Young RC | 4.00 | 1.50 |
| 118 Aaron Rouse RC | 5.00 | 2.00 |
| 119 Ahmad Bradshaw RC | 6.00 | 2.50 |
| 120 Alan Branch RC | 4.00 | 1.50 |
| 121 Alonzo Coleman RC | 4.00 | 1.50 |
| 122 Amobi Okoye RC | 5.00 | 2.00 |
| 123 Anthony Spencer RC | 5.00 | 2.00 |
| 124 Deon Anderson RC | 4.00 | 1.50 |
| 125 Justin Durant RC | 4.00 | 1.50 |
| 126 Brandon Siler RC | 4.00 | 1.50 |
| 127 Buster Davis RC | 4.00 | 1.50 |
| 128 Charles Johnson RC | 3.00 | 1.25 |
| 129 Courtney Taylor RC | 4.00 | 1.50 |
| 130 Dallas Baker RC | 4.00 | 1.50 |
| 131 Dan Bazuin RC | 4.00 | 1.50 |
| 132 Danny Ware RC | 4.00 | 1.50 |
| 133 Darius Walker RC | 5.00 | 2.00 |
| 134 David Ball RC | 3.00 | 1.25 |
| 135 David Harris RC | 4.00 | 1.50 |
| 136 David Irons RC | 3.00 | 1.25 |
| 137 Daymeion Hughes RC | 4.00 | 1.50 |
| 138 Anthony Waters RC | 4.00 | 1.50 |
| 139 Antwan Barnes RC | 4.00 | 1.50 |
| 140 Eric Frampton RC | 4.00 | 1.50 |
| 141 Eric Weddle RC | 4.00 | 1.50 |
| 142 Eric Wright RC | 4.00 | 1.50 |
| 143 Fred Bennett RC | 3.00 | 1.25 |
| 144 Gary Russell RC | 5.00 | 2.00 |
| 145 H.B. Blades RC | 4.00 | 1.50 |
| 146 Jacoby Jones RC | 5.00 | 2.00 |
| 147 Clifton Dawson RC | 5.00 | 2.00 |
| 148 Kevin Boss RC | 8.00 | 3.00 |
| 149 Jarvis Moss RC | 5.00 | 2.00 |
| 150 Gerald Alexander RC | 3.00 | 1.25 |
| 151 Jeff Rowe RC | 4.00 | 1.50 |
| 152 Tanard Jackson RC | 3.00 | 1.25 |
| 153 Joel Filani RC | 4.00 | 1.50 |
| 154 Jon Abbate RC | 3.00 | 1.25 |
| 155 Jon Beason RC | 5.00 | 2.00 |
| 156 Marcus Mason RC | 5.00 | 2.00 |
| 157 Jonathan Wade RC | 4.00 | 1.50 |
| 158 Dante Rosario RC | 5.00 | 2.00 |
| 159 Josh Wilson RC | 4.00 | 1.50 |
| 160 Kenneth Darby RC | 5.00 | 2.00 |
| 161 Biren Ealy RC | 4.00 | 1.50 |
| 162 LaMarr Woodley RC | 5.00 | 2.00 |
| 163 Levi Brown RC | 5.00 | 2.00 |
| 164 Marcus McCauley RC | 4.00 | 1.50 |
| 165 Matt Spaeth RC | 5.00 | 2.00 |
| 166 Michael Okwo RC | 4.00 | 1.50 |
| 167 Mike Walker RC | 4.00 | 1.50 |
| 168 Quentin Moses RC | 4.00 | 1.50 |
| 169 Ray McDonald RC | 5.00 | 2.00 |
| 170 Reggie Ball RC | 4.00 | 1.50 |
| 171 Justin Harrell RC | 5.00 | 2.00 |
| 172 Ed Johnson RC | 5.00 | 2.00 |
| 173 Rufus Alexander RC | 5.00 | 2.00 |
| 174 Ryan McBean RC | 4.00 | 1.50 |
| 175 Ryne Robinson RC | 4.00 | 1.50 |
| 176 Sabby Piscitelli RC | 5.00 | 2.00 |
| 177 Scott Chandler RC | 4.00 | 1.50 |
| 178 Selvin Young RC | 8.00 | 3.00 |
| 179 Steve Breaston RC | 5.00 | 2.00 |
| 180 Stewart Bradley RC | 5.00 | 2.00 |
| 181 Turk McBride RC | 4.00 | 1.50 |
| 182 Demarcus Tank Tyler RC | 4.00 | 1.50 |
| 183 Tim Crowder RC | 5.00 | 2.00 |
| 184 Tim Shaw RC | 4.00 | 1.50 |
| 185 Kenton Keith RC | 5.00 | 2.00 |
| 186 Tyler Palko RC | 5.00 | 2.00 |
| 187 Mason Crosby RC | 5.00 | 2.00 |
| 188 Pierre Thomas RC | 10.00 | 4.00 |
| 189 Victor Abiamiri RC | 5.00 | 2.00 |
| 190 Zak DeOssie RC | 4.00 | 1.50 |
| 191 Tyler Thigpen RC | 6.00 | 2.50 |
| 192 Tony Ugoh RC | 4.00 | 1.50 |
| 193 Michael Allan RC | 3.00 | 1.25 |
| 194 Martrez Milner RC | 4.00 | 1.50 |
| 195 John Broussard RC | 4.00 | 1.50 |
| 196 Roy Hall RC | 5.00 | 2.00 |
| 197 Matt Gutierrez RC | 5.00 | 2.00 |
| 198 Legedu Naanee RC | 5.00 | 2.00 |
| 199 Derek Stanley RC | 4.00 | 1.50 |
| 200 Quincy Black RC | 4.00 | 1.50 |
| 201 Trent Edwards/99 AU RC | 80.00 | 30.00 |
| 202 Marshawn Lynch/99 AU RC | 60.00 | 30.00 |
| 203 Chris Henry/99 AU RC | 30.00 | 12.00 |
| 204 Paul Williams/299 AU RC | 15.00 | 6.00 |
| 205 Sidney Rice/99 AU RC EXCH | 30.00 | 12.00 |
| 206 Adrian Peterson/99 AU RC | 350.00 | 200.00 |
| 207 Drew Stanton/99 AU RC | 30.00 | 12.00 |
| 208 Calvin Johnson/99 AU RC | 120.00 | 60.00 |
| 209 Yamon Figurs/99 AU RC | 30.00 | 12.00 |
| 210 Troy Smith/99 AU RC EXCH | 40.00 | 15.00 |
| 211 Garrett Wolfe/249 AU RC | 20.00 | 8.00 |
| 212 Greg Olsen/99 AU RC | 40.00 | 15.00 |
| 213 Joe Thomas/99 AU RC. | 30.00 | 12.00 |
| 214 Brady Quinn/99 AU RC | 120.00 | 60.00 |
| 215 Ted Ginn Jr./99 AU RC EXCH | 50.00 | 20.00 |
| 216 John Beck/99 AU RC | 30.00 | 12.00 |
| 217 Antonio Pittman/99 AU RC EXCH | 30.00 | 12.00 |
| 218 Robert Meachem/99 AU RC | 30.00 | 12.00 |
| 219 J.J.Russell/99 AU RC | 100.00 | 50.00 |
| 220 M.Bush/99 AU RC EXCH | 30.00 | 12.00 |
| 221 Kevin Kolb/99 AU RC | 50.00 | 20.00 |
| 222 Tony Hunt/99 AU RC EXCH | 30.00 | 12.00 |
| 223 Patrick Willis/99 AU RC | 50.00 | 25.00 |
| 224 Jason Hill/249 AU RC | 20.00 | 8.00 |
| 225 Brandon Jackson/99 AU RC | 30.00 | 12.00 |
| 226 David Clowney/299 AU RC | 20.00 | 8.00 |
| 227 Kenny Irons/99 AU RC EXCH | 30.00 | 12.00 |
| 228 Leon Hall/99 AU RC EXCH | 25.00 | 10.00 |
| 229 Dwayne Bowe/99 AU RC | 60.00 | 30.00 |
| 230 Kolby Smith/299 AU RC | 25.00 | 10.00 |
| 231 Steve Smith/99 AU RC EXCH | 40.00 | 20.00 |
| 232 Dwayne Jarrett/99 AU RC | 30.00 | 12.00 |
| 233 Lorenzo Booker/99 AU RC | 30.00 | 12.00 |
| 234 Anthony Gonzalez/99 AU RC | 50.00 | 25.00 |
| 235 J.L.Higgins/99 AU RC | 25.00 | 10.00 |
| 236 Isaiah Stanback/299 AU RC | 20.00 | 8.00 |
| 237 L.Landry/249 AU RC EXCH | 25.00 | 10.00 |
| 238 Paul Posluszny/99 AU RC | 40.00 | 15.00 |
| 239 Brian Leonard/99 AU RC | 30.00 | 12.00 |
| 240 G.Adams/99 AU RC EXCH | 20.00 | 8.00 |
| 241 Cra.Davis/249 AU RC EXCH | 20.00 | 8.00 |
| 242 Aundrae Allison/249 AU RC | 15.00 | 6.00 |
| 243 D.Wynn/299 AU RC | 30.00 | 12.00 |
| 244 J.Anderson/249 AU RC | 15.00 | 6.00 |
| 245 Adam Carriker/99 AU RC | 25.00 | 10.00 |
| 246 Darrelle Revis/99 AU RC | 30.00 | 12.00 |
| 247 Lawrence Timmons/99 AU RC | 30.00 | 12.00 |
| 248 Michael Griffin/299 AU RC | 20.00 | 8.00 |
| 249 Aaron Ross/299 AU RC EXCH | 20.00 | 8.00 |
| 250 Reggie Nelson/99 AU RC | 25.00 | 10.00 |
| 251 B.Merriweather/299 AU RC EXCH | 20.00 | 8.00 |
| 252 Zach Miller/99 AU RC | 20.00 | 8.00 |
| 253 Chris Houston/299 AU RC | 15.00 | 6.00 |
| 254 I.Alama-Francis/299 AU RC EXCH | 20.00 | 8.00 |
| 255 Laurent Robinson/299 AU RC | 15.00 | 6.00 |
| 256 James Jones/246 AU RC | 20.00 | 8.00 |
| 257 D.Wright/299 AU RC | 15.00 | 6.00 |
| 258 Chris Davis/249 AU RC | 15.00 | 6.00 |
| 259 Thomas Clayton/299 AU RC | 15.00 | 6.00 |
| 260 Jordan Palmer/99 AU RC | 30.00 | 12.00 |
| 261 Jordan Kent/299 AU RC | 15.00 | 6.00 |
| 262 Charisi Stuckey/299 AU RC | 15.00 | 6.00 |
| 263 Nate Ilaoa/299 AU RC | 20.00 | 8.00 |
| 264 Chris Leak/99 AU RC | 25.00 | 10.00 |
| 265 J.Zabransky/99 AU RC | 30.00 | 12.00 |
| 266 Syndric Steptoe/299 AU RC | 15.00 | 6.00 |

# 2008 Leaf Rookies and Stars

| | | |
|---|---|---|
| 1 Matt Leinart | .75 | .30 |
| 2 Larry Fitzgerald | .75 | .30 |
| 3 Anquan Boldin | .60 | .25 |
| 4 Edgerrin James | .60 | .25 |
| 5 Roddy White | .60 | .25 |
| 6 Michael Turner | .60 | .25 |
| 7 Willis McGahee | .60 | .25 |
| 8 Derrick Mason | .50 | .20 |
| 9 Demetrius Williams | .50 | .20 |
| 10 Trent Edwards | .75 | .30 |
| 11 Marshawn Lynch | .75 | .30 |
| 12 Lee Evans | .60 | .25 |
| 13 Steve Smith | .60 | .25 |
| 14 DeAngelo Williams | .60 | .25 |
| 15 Julius Peppers | .60 | .25 |
| 16 Greg Olsen | .60 | .25 |
| 17 Devin Hester | .75 | .30 |
| 18 Rex Grossman | .60 | .25 |
| 19 Carson Palmer | .75 | .30 |
| 20 Chad Johnson | .60 | .25 |
| 21 T.J. Houshmandzadeh | .60 | .25 |
| 22 Chris Perry | .50 | .20 |
| 23 Derek Anderson | .60 | .25 |
| 24 Kellen Winslow | .60 | .25 |
| 25 Braylon Edwards | .60 | .25 |
| 26 Tony Romo | 1.25 | .50 |
| 27 Terrell Owens | .75 | .30 |
| 28 Marion Barber | .60 | .25 |
| 29 Jay Cutler | .75 | .30 |
| 30 Brandon Stokley | .60 | .25 |
| 31 Jon Kitna | .60 | .25 |
| 32 Roy Williams WR | .75 | .30 |
| 33 Calvin Johnson | .75 | .30 |
| 34 Aaron Rodgers | .75 | .30 |
| 35 Ryan Grant | .75 | .30 |
| 36 Donald Driver | .60 | .25 |
| 37 Matt Schaub | .60 | .25 |
| 38 Andre Johnson | .60 | .25 |
| 39 Kevin Walter | .50 | .20 |
| 40 Peyton Manning | 1.25 | .50 |
| 41 Joseph Addai | .75 | .30 |
| 42 Reggie Wayne | .60 | .25 |
| 43 Dallas Clark | .60 | .25 |
| 44 David Garrard | .60 | .25 |
| 45 Fred Taylor | .60 | .25 |
| 46 Maurice Jones-Drew | .60 | .25 |
| 47 Reggie Williams | .60 | .25 |
| 48 Brodie Croyle | .75 | .30 |
| 49 Larry Johnson | .60 | .25 |
| 50 Tony Gonzalez | .60 | .25 |
| 51 Chad Pennington | .60 | .25 |
| 52 Ronnie Brown | .60 | .25 |
| 53 Ted Ginn Jr. | .60 | .25 |
| 54 Tarvaris Jackson | .60 | .25 |
| 55 Adrian Peterson | 1.50 | .60 |
| 56 Sidney Rice | .60 | .25 |
| 57 Tom Brady | 1.25 | .50 |
| 58 Randy Moss | .75 | .30 |
| 59 Laurence Maroney | .60 | .25 |
| 60 Drew Brees | .75 | .30 |
| 61 Reggie Bush | .75 | .30 |
| 62 Deuce McAllister | .60 | .25 |
| 63 Eli Manning | .75 | .30 |
| 64 Plaxico Burress | .60 | .25 |
| 65 Brandon Jacobs | .60 | .25 |
| 66 Brett Favre | 5.00 | 2.00 |
| 67 Leon Washington | .50 | .20 |
| 68 Laveranues Coles | .60 | .25 |
| 69 JaMarcus Russell | .75 | .30 |

| | | |
|---|---|---|
| ❑ 70 Justin Fargas | .50 | .20 |
| ❑ 71 Zach Miller | .60 | .25 |
| ❑ 72 Donovan McNabb | .75 | .30 |
| ❑ 73 Brian Westbrook | .60 | .25 |
| ❑ 74 Reggie Brown | .60 | .25 |
| ❑ 75 Ben Roethlisberger | 1.00 | .40 |
| ❑ 76 Willie Parker | .60 | .25 |
| ❑ 77 Santonio Holmes | .60 | .25 |
| ❑ 78 Philip Rivers | .75 | .30 |
| ❑ 79 LaDainian Tomlinson | 1.00 | .40 |
| ❑ 80 Vincent Jackson | .60 | .25 |
| ❑ 81 Antonio Gates | .60 | .25 |
| ❑ 82 J.T. O'Sullivan | .60 | .25 |
| ❑ 83 Frank Gore | .60 | .25 |
| ❑ 84 Vernon Davis | .50 | .20 |
| ❑ 85 Matt Hasselbeck | .60 | .25 |
| ❑ 86 Deion Branch | .60 | .25 |
| ❑ 87 Julius Jones | .60 | .25 |
| ❑ 88 Marc Bulger | .60 | .25 |
| ❑ 89 Shawn Jackson | .75 | .30 |
| ❑ 90 Torry Holt | .60 | .25 |
| ❑ 91 Warrick Dunn | .60 | .25 |
| ❑ 92 Jeff Garcia | .60 | .25 |
| ❑ 93 Joey Galloway | .60 | .25 |
| ❑ 94 Vince Young | .75 | .30 |
| ❑ 95 LenDale White | .60 | .25 |
| ❑ 96 Roydell Williams | .50 | .20 |
| ❑ 97 Jason Campbell | .60 | .25 |
| ❑ 98 Clinton Portis | .60 | .25 |
| ❑ 99 Santana Moss | .60 | .25 |
| ❑ 100 Ladell Betts | .60 | .20 |
| ❑ 101 Trent Edwards ELE | 4.00 | 1.50 |
| ❑ 102 Marshawn Lynch ELE | 4.00 | 1.50 |
| ❑ 103 Braylon Edwards ELE | 4.00 | 1.50 |
| ❑ 104 Carson Palmer ELE | 4.00 | 1.50 |
| ❑ 105 Tom Brady ELE | 6.00 | 2.50 |
| ❑ 106 Matt Hasselbeck ELE | 3.00 | 1.25 |
| ❑ 107 Nate Burleson ELE | 2.50 | 1.00 |
| ❑ 108 Fred Taylor ELE | 3.00 | 1.25 |
| ❑ 109 David Garrard ELE | 3.00 | 1.25 |
| ❑ 110 Maurice Jones-Drew ELE | 3.00 | 1.25 |
| ❑ 111 Devin Hester ELE | 3.00 | 1.25 |
| ❑ 112 Willie Parker ELE | 3.00 | 1.25 |
| ❑ 113 Ben Roethlisberger ELE | 5.00 | 2.00 |
| ❑ 114 Ryan Grant ELE | 4.00 | 1.50 |
| ❑ 115 Eli Manning ELE | 4.00 | 1.50 |
| ❑ 116 Adrian Arrington RC | 4.00 | 1.50 |
| ❑ 117 Ali Highsmith RC | 3.00 | 1.25 |
| ❑ 118 Anthony Alridge RC | 4.00 | 1.50 |
| ❑ 119 Antoine Cason RC | 5.00 | 2.00 |
| ❑ 120 Aqib Talib RC | 5.00 | 2.00 |
| ❑ 121 Brad Cottam RC | 5.00 | 2.00 |
| ❑ 122 Brandon Flowers RC | 5.00 | 2.00 |
| ❑ 123 Calais Campbell RC | 5.00 | 2.00 |
| ❑ 124 Chauncey Washington RC | 4.00 | 1.50 |
| ❑ 125 Chevis Jackson RC | 4.00 | 1.50 |
| ❑ 126 Cory Boyd RC | 5.00 | 2.00 |
| ❑ 127 Craig Steltz RC | 4.00 | 1.50 |
| ❑ 128 Curtis Lofton RC | 5.00 | 2.00 |
| ❑ 129 DJ Hall RC | 5.00 | 2.00 |
| ❑ 130 Dantrell Savage RC | 5.00 | 2.00 |
| ❑ 131 Darius Reynaud RC | 4.00 | 1.50 |
| ❑ 132 Darrell Strong RC | 4.00 | 1.50 |
| ❑ 133 Davone Bess RC | 6.00 | 2.50 |
| ❑ 134 Derrick Harvey RC | 4.00 | 1.50 |
| ❑ 135 Dominique Rodgers-Cromartie | 5.00 | 2.00 |
| ❑ 136 Erin Henderson RC | 4.00 | 1.50 |
| ❑ 137 Ernie Wheelwright RC | 4.00 | 1.50 |
| ❑ 138 Fred Davis RC | 5.00 | 2.00 |
| ❑ 139 Joe Jon Finley RC | 4.00 | 1.50 |
| ❑ 140 Jacob Hester RC | 5.00 | 2.00 |
| ❑ 141 Jacob Tamme RC | 5.00 | 2.00 |
| ❑ 142 Jamar Adams RC | 4.00 | 1.50 |
| ❑ 143 Jason Rivers RC | 5.00 | 2.00 |
| ❑ 144 Jed Collins RC | 4.00 | 1.50 |
| ❑ 145 Jermichael Finley RC | 5.00 | 2.00 |
| ❑ 146 John Carlson RC | 5.00 | 2.00 |
| ❑ 147 Jonathan Hefney RC | 4.00 | 1.50 |
| ❑ 148 Jordon Dizon RC | 5.00 | 2.00 |
| ❑ 149 Josh Morgan RC | 5.00 | 2.00 |
| ❑ 150 Justin Forsett RC | 5.00 | 2.00 |
| ❑ 151 Kalvin McRae RC | 4.00 | 1.50 |
| ❑ 152 Keenan Burton RC | 4.00 | 1.50 |
| ❑ 153 Keilen Davis RC | 3.00 | 1.25 |
| ❑ 154 Kentwan Balmer RC | 4.00 | 1.50 |
| ❑ 155 Kevin Robinson RC | 4.00 | 1.50 |
| ❑ 156 Lawrence Jackson RC | 4.00 | 1.50 |
| ❑ 157 Leodis McKelvin RC | 5.00 | 2.00 |

| | | |
|---|---|---|
| ❑ 158 Marcus Monk RC | 5.00 | 2.00 |
| ❑ 159 Marcus Smith RC | 4.00 | 1.50 |
| ❑ 160 Marcus Thomas RC | 4.00 | 1.50 |
| ❑ 161 Mark Bradford RC | 4.00 | 1.50 |
| ❑ 162 Martellus Bennett RC | 5.00 | 2.00 |
| ❑ 163 Martin Rucker RC | 4.00 | 1.50 |
| ❑ 164 Mike Jenkins RC | 5.00 | 2.00 |
| ❑ 165 Owen Schmitt RC | 5.00 | 2.00 |
| ❑ 166 Pat Sims RC | 4.00 | 1.50 |
| ❑ 167 Paul Hubbard RC | 4.00 | 1.50 |
| ❑ 168 Paul Smith RC | 5.00 | 2.00 |
| ❑ 169 Peyton Hillis RC | 6.00 | 2.50 |
| ❑ 170 Phillip Merling RC | 4.00 | 1.50 |
| ❑ 171 Quentin Groves RC | 4.00 | 1.50 |
| ❑ 172 Reggie Smith RC | 4.00 | 1.50 |
| ❑ 173 Ryan Grice-Mullen RC | 4.00 | 1.50 |
| ❑ 174 Ryan Torain RC | 5.00 | 2.00 |
| ❑ 175 Sam Keller RC | 5.00 | 2.00 |
| ❑ 176 Sedrick Ellis RC | 5.00 | 2.00 |
| ❑ 177 Shawn Crable RC | 5.00 | 2.00 |
| ❑ 178 Simeon Castille RC | 5.00 | 2.00 |
| ❑ 179 Terrell Thomas RC | 4.00 | 1.50 |
| ❑ 180 Thomas Brown RC | 5.00 | 2.00 |
| ❑ 181 Tim Hightower RC | 10.00 | 4.00 |
| ❑ 182 Tracy Porter RC | 4.00 | 1.50 |
| ❑ 183 Vernon Gholston RC | 5.00 | 2.00 |
| ❑ 184 Will Franklin RC | 4.00 | 1.50 |
| ❑ 185 Xavier Adibi RC | 4.00 | 1.50 |
| ❑ 186 Alex Brink RC | 4.00 | 1.50 |
| ❑ 187 Jalen Parmele RC | 4.00 | 1.50 |
| ❑ 188 Xavier Omon RC | 5.00 | 2.00 |
| ❑ 189 Craig Stevens RC | 4.00 | 1.50 |
| ❑ 190 Derek Fine RC | 4.00 | 1.50 |
| ❑ 191 Gary Barnidge RC | 4.00 | 1.50 |
| ❑ 192 Arman Shields RC | 4.00 | 1.50 |
| ❑ 193 Kenneth Moore RC | 4.00 | 1.50 |
| ❑ 194 Marcus Henry RC | 4.00 | 1.50 |
| ❑ 195 Jaymar Johnson RC | 4.00 | 1.50 |
| ❑ 196 Pierre Garcon RC | 5.00 | 2.00 |
| ❑ 197 Patrick Lee RC | 5.00 | 2.00 |
| ❑ 198 Terrence Wheatley RC | 4.00 | 1.50 |
| ❑ 199 Tavares Gooden RC | 4.00 | 1.50 |
| ❑ 200 Bruce Davis RC | 4.00 | 1.50 |
| ❑ 201 Allen Patrick AU/268 RC | 15.00 | 6.00 |
| ❑ 202 Andre Caldwell AU/116 RC | 20.00 | 8.00 |
| ❑ 203 Andre Woodson AU/219 RC | 20.00 | 8.00 |
| ❑ 204 Brian Brohm AU/99 RC | 40.00 | 15.00 |
| ❑ 206 Chad Henne AU/99 RC EXCH | 50.00 | 20.00 |
| ❑ 207 Chris Johnson AU/166 RC | 100.00 | 50.00 |
| ❑ 208 Chris Long AU/99 RC EXCH | 30.00 | 12.00 |
| ❑ 209 Colt Brennan AU/213 RC | 60.00 | 30.00 |
| ❑ 210 Dan Connor AU/270 RC | 20.00 | 8.00 |
| ❑ 211 Darren McFadden AU/99 RC | 100.00 | 50.00 |
| ❑ 212 Dennis Dixon AU/218 RC | 20.00 | 8.00 |
| ❑ 213 DeSean Jackson AU/119 RC | 80.00 | 20.00 |
| ❑ 214 Devin Thomas AU/118 RC | 25.00 | 10.00 |
| ❑ 215 Dexter Jackson AU/132 RC | 25.00 | 10.00 |
| ❑ 216 Donnie Avery AU/129 RC | 30.00 | 12.00 |
| ❑ 217 Dustin Keller AU/115 RC | 25.00 | 10.00 |
| ❑ 218 Earl Bennett AU/118 RC | 25.00 | 10.00 |
| ❑ 219 Early Doucet AU/106 RC | 25.00 | 10.00 |
| ❑ 220 Eddie Royal AU/126 RC | 50.00 | 25.00 |
| ❑ 221 Erik Ainge AU/271 RC | 20.00 | 8.00 |
| ❑ 222 Felix Jones AU/99 RC | 100.00 | 50.00 |
| ❑ 223 Glenn Dorsey AU/99 RC | 40.00 | 15.00 |
| ❑ 224 Harry Douglas AU/99 RC | 30.00 | 12.00 |
| ❑ 225 Jake Long AU/99 RC | 40.00 | 15.00 |
| ❑ 226 Jamaal Charles AU/118 RC | 30.00 | 12.00 |
| ❑ 227 James Hardy AU/118 RC | 25.00 | 10.00 |
| ❑ 228 Jerod Mayo AU/52 RC | 60.00 | 30.00 |
| ❑ 229 Jerome Simpson AU/117 RC | 20.00 | 8.00 |
| ❑ 230 Joe Flacco AU/99 RC | 120.00 | 60.00 |
| ❑ 231 John David Booty AU/118 RC | 30.00 | 12.00 |
| ❑ 232 Jonathan Stewart AU/99 RC | 60.00 | 30.00 |
| ❑ 233 Jordy Nelson AU/99 RC | 40.00 | 15.00 |
| ❑ 234 Josh Johnson AU/268 RC | 20.00 | 8.00 |
| ❑ 235 Keith Rivers AU/263 RC | 15.00 | 6.00 |
| ❑ 236 Kenny Phillips AU/99 RC EXCH | 25.00 | 10.00 |
| ❑ 237 Kevin O'Connell AU/142 RC | 30.00 | 12.00 |
| ❑ 238 Kevin Smith AU/117 RC | 40.00 | 15.00 |
| ❑ 239 Lavelle Hawkins AU/273 RC | 15.00 | 6.00 |
| ❑ 240 Limas Sweed AU/103 RC | 30.00 | 12.00 |
| ❑ 241 Malcolm Kelly AU/108 RC | 25.00 | 10.00 |
| ❑ 242 Mario Manningham AU/118 RC | 25.00 | 10.00 |
| ❑ 243 Matt Flynn AU/263 RC | 25.00 | 10.00 |
| ❑ 244 Matt Forte AU/107 RC | 80.00 | 50.00 |
| ❑ 245 Matt Ryan AU/99 RC | 150.00 | 75.00 |
| ❑ 246 Mike Hart AU/263 RC EXCH | 15.00 | 6.00 |
| ❑ 247 Rashard Mendenhall AU/99 RC | 50.00 | 25.00 |

| | | |
|---|---|---|
| ❑ 248 Ray Rice AU/105 RC | 30.00 | 12.00 |
| ❑ 249 Steve Slaton AU/118 RC | 50.00 | 25.00 |
| ❑ 250 Tashard Choice AU/270 RC | 25.00 | 10.00 |

### 1991 Pacific

| | | |
|---|---|---|
| ❑ COMPLETE SET (660) | 15.00 | 7.50 |
| ❑ COMP.SERIES 1 (550) | 8.00 | 4.00 |
| ❑ COMP.FACT.SER.1 (550) | 10.00 | 5.00 |
| ❑ COMP.SERIES 2 (110) | 8.00 | 4.00 |
| ❑ COMP.FACT.SER.2 (110) | 12.00 | 6.00 |
| ❑ COMP.CHECKLIST SET (5) | 15.00 | 7.50 |
| ❑ 1 Deion Sanders | .40 | .15 |
| ❑ 2 Steve Broussard | .05 | .01 |
| ❑ 3 Aundray Bruce | .05 | .01 |
| ❑ 4 Rick Bryan | .05 | .01 |
| ❑ 5 John Rade | .05 | .01 |
| ❑ 6 Scott Case | .05 | .01 |
| ❑ 7 Tony Casillas | .05 | .01 |
| ❑ 8 Shawn Collins | .05 | .01 |
| ❑ 9 Darion Conner | .05 | .01 |
| ❑ 10 Tory Epps | .05 | .01 |
| ❑ 11 Bill Fralic | .05 | .01 |
| ❑ 12 Mike Gann | .05 | .01 |
| ❑ 13 Tim Green UER | .05 | .01 |
| ❑ 14 Chris Hinton | .05 | .01 |
| ❑ 15 Houston Hoover UER | .05 | .01 |
| ❑ 16 Chris Miller | .10 | .02 |
| ❑ 17 Andre Rison | .10 | .02 |
| ❑ 18 Mike Rozier | .05 | .01 |
| ❑ 19 Jessie Tuggle | .05 | .01 |
| ❑ 20 Don Beebe | .05 | .01 |
| ❑ 21 Ray Bentley | .05 | .01 |
| ❑ 22 Shane Conlan | .05 | .01 |
| ❑ 23 Kent Hull | .05 | .01 |
| ❑ 24 Mark Kelso | .05 | .01 |
| ❑ 25 James Lofton UER | .10 | .02 |
| ❑ 26 Scott Norwood | .05 | .01 |
| ❑ 27 Andre Reed | .10 | .02 |
| ❑ 28 Leonard Smith | .05 | .01 |
| ❑ 29 Bruce Smith | .25 | .08 |
| ❑ 30 Leon Seals | .05 | .01 |
| ❑ 31 Darryl Talley | .05 | .01 |
| ❑ 32 Steve Tasker | .10 | .02 |
| ❑ 33 Thurman Thomas | .25 | .08 |
| ❑ 34 James Williams | .05 | .01 |
| ❑ 35 Will Wolford | .05 | .01 |
| ❑ 36 Frank Reich | .10 | .02 |
| ❑ 37 Jeff Wright RC | .05 | .01 |
| ❑ 38 Neal Anderson | .10 | .02 |
| ❑ 39 Trace Armstrong | .05 | .01 |
| ❑ 40 Johnny Bailey UER | .05 | .01 |
| ❑ 41 Mark Bortz UER | .05 | .01 |
| ❑ 42 Cap Boso RC | .05 | .01 |
| ❑ 43 Kevin Butler | .05 | .01 |
| ❑ 44 Mark Carrier DB | .10 | .02 |
| ❑ 45 Jim Covert | .05 | .01 |
| ❑ 46 Wendell Davis | .05 | .01 |
| ❑ 47 Richard Dent | .10 | .02 |
| ❑ 48 Shaun Gayle | .05 | .01 |
| ❑ 49 Jim Harbaugh | .25 | .08 |
| ❑ 50 Jay Hilgenberg | .05 | .01 |
| ❑ 51 Brad Muster | .05 | .01 |
| ❑ 52 William Perry | .10 | .02 |
| ❑ 53 Mike Singletary UER | .10 | .02 |
| ❑ 54 Peter Tom Willis | .05 | .01 |
| ❑ 55 Donnell Woolford | .05 | .01 |
| ❑ 56 Steve McMichael | .10 | .02 |
| ❑ 57 Eric Ball | .05 | .01 |
| ❑ 58 Lewis Billups | .05 | .01 |
| ❑ 59 Jim Breech | .05 | .01 |
| ❑ 60 James Brooks | .10 | .02 |
| ❑ 61 Eddie Brown | .05 | .01 |

|  |  | | |
|---|---|---|---|
| 62 | Rickey Dixon | .05 | .01 |
| 63 | Boomer Esiason | .10 | .02 |
| 64 | James Francis | .05 | .01 |
| 65 | David Fulcher | .05 | .01 |
| 66 | David Grant | .05 | .01 |
| 67 | Harold Green UER | .05 | .01 |
| 68 | Rodney Holman | .05 | .01 |
| 69 | Stanford Jennings | .05 | .01 |
| 70A | Tim Krumrie ERR | .50 | .20 |
| 70B | Tim Krumrie COR | .30 | .10 |
| 71 | Tim McGee | .05 | .01 |
| 72 | Anthony Munoz | .10 | .02 |
| 73 | Mitchell Price RC | .05 | .01 |
| 74 | Eric Thomas | .05 | .01 |
| 75 | Ickey Woods | .05 | .01 |
| 76 | Mike Baab | .05 | .01 |
| 77 | Thane Gash | .05 | .01 |
| 78 | David Grayson | .05 | .01 |
| 79 | Mike Johnson | .05 | .01 |
| 80 | Reggie Langhorne | .05 | .01 |
| 81 | Kevin Mack | .05 | .01 |
| 82 | Clay Matthews | .10 | .02 |
| 83A | Eric Metcalf ERR | .50 | .20 |
| 83B | Eric Metcalf COR | .30 | .10 |
| 84 | Frank Minnifield | .05 | .01 |
| 85 | Mike Oliphant | .05 | .01 |
| 86 | Mike Pagel | .05 | .01 |
| 87 | John Talley | .05 | .01 |
| 88 | Lawyer Tillman | .05 | .01 |
| 89 | Gregg Rakoczy UER | .05 | .01 |
| 90 | Bryan Wagner | .05 | .01 |
| 91 | Rob Burnett RC | .10 | .02 |
| 92 | Tommie Agee | .05 | .01 |
| 93 | Troy Aikman UER | .75 | .30 |
| 94A | Bill Bates ERR | .50 | .20 |
| 94B | Bill Bates COR | .30 | .10 |
| 95 | Jack Del Rio | .10 | .02 |
| 96 | Issiac Holt UER | .05 | .01 |
| 97 | Michael Irvin | .25 | .08 |
| 98 | Jim Jeffcoat UER | .05 | .01 |
| 99 | Jimmie Jones | .05 | .01 |
| 100 | Kelvin Martin | .05 | .01 |
| 101 | Nate Newton | .10 | .02 |
| 102 | Danny Noonan | .05 | .01 |
| 103 | Ken Norton Jr. | .10 | .02 |
| 104 | Jay Novacek | .25 | .08 |
| 105 | Mike Saxon | .05 | .01 |
| 106 | Derrick Shepard | .05 | .01 |
| 107 | Emmitt Smith | 2.50 | 1.00 |
| 108 | Daniel Stubbs | .05 | .01 |
| 109 | Tony Tolbert | .05 | .01 |
| 110 | Alexander Wright | .05 | .01 |
| 111 | Steve Atwater | .05 | .01 |
| 112 | Melvin Bratton | .05 | .01 |
| 113 | Tyrone Braxton UER | .05 | .01 |
| 114 | Alphonso Carreker | .05 | .01 |
| 115 | John Elway | 1.25 | .50 |
| 116 | Simon Fletcher | .05 | .01 |
| 117 | Bobby Humphrey | .05 | .01 |
| 118 | Mark Jackson | .05 | .01 |
| 119 | Vance Johnson | .05 | .01 |
| 120 | Greg Kragen UER | .05 | .01 |
| 121 | Karl Mecklenburg UER | .05 | .01 |
| 122A | Orsen Mobley ERR | .50 | .20 |
| 122B | Orson Mobley COR | .10 | .02 |
| 123 | Alton Montgomery | .05 | .01 |
| 124 | Ricky Nattiel | .05 | .01 |
| 125 | Steve Sewell | .05 | .01 |
| 126 | Shannon Sharpe | .50 | .20 |
| 127 | Dennis Smith | .05 | .01 |
| 128A | Andre Townsend RC ERR | .50 | .20 |
| 128B | Andre Townsend RC COR | .10 | .02 |
| 129 | Mike Horan | .05 | .01 |
| 130 | Jerry Ball | .05 | .01 |
| 131 | Bennie Blades | .05 | .01 |
| 132 | Lomas Brown | .05 | .01 |
| 133 | Jeff Campbell UER | .05 | .01 |
| 134 | Robert Clark | .05 | .01 |
| 135 | Michael Cofer | .05 | .01 |
| 136 | Dennis Gibson | .05 | .01 |
| 137 | Mel Gray | .10 | .02 |
| 138 | LeRoy Irvin UER | .05 | .01 |
| 139 | George Jamison RC | .05 | .01 |
| 140 | Richard Johnson | .05 | .01 |
| 141 | Eddie Murray | .05 | .01 |
| 142 | Dan Owens | .05 | .01 |
| 143 | Rodney Peete | .10 | .02 |
| 144 | Barry Sanders | 1.25 | .50 |
| 145 | Chris Spielman | .10 | .02 |
| 146 | Marc Spindler | .05 | .01 |
| 147 | Andre Ware | .10 | .02 |
| 148 | William White | .05 | .01 |
| 149 | Tony Bennett | .10 | .02 |
| 150 | Robert Brown | .05 | .01 |
| 151 | LeRoy Butler | .10 | .02 |
| 152 | Anthony Dilweg | .05 | .01 |
| 153 | Michael Haddix | .05 | .01 |
| 154 | Ron Hallstrom | .05 | .01 |
| 155 | Tim Harris | .05 | .01 |
| 156 | Johnny Holland | .05 | .01 |
| 157 | Chris Jacke | .05 | .01 |
| 158 | Perry Kemp | .05 | .01 |
| 159 | Mark Lee | .05 | .01 |
| 160 | Don Majkowski | .05 | .01 |
| 161 | Tony Mandarich UER | .05 | .01 |
| 162 | Mark Murphy | .05 | .01 |
| 163 | Brian Noble | .05 | .01 |
| 164 | Shawn Patterson | .05 | .01 |
| 165 | Jeff Query | .05 | .01 |
| 166 | Sterling Sharpe | .25 | .08 |
| 167 | Darrell Thompson | .05 | .01 |
| 168 | Ed West | .05 | .01 |
| 169 | Ray Childress UER | .05 | .01 |
| 170A | Cris Dishman RC ERR Chris | .10 | |
| 170B | Cris Dishman RC ERR/COR | .10 | .02 |
| 170C | Cris Dishman RC COR | .10 | .02 |
| 171 | Curtis Duncan | .05 | .01 |
| 172 | William Fuller | .10 | .02 |
| 173 | Ernest Givins UER | .10 | .02 |
| 174 | Drew Hill | .05 | .01 |
| 175A | Haywood Jeffires ERR | .25 | .08 |
| 175B | Haywood Jeffires COR | .25 | .08 |
| 176 | Sean Jones | .10 | .02 |
| 177 | Lamar Lathon | .05 | .01 |
| 178 | Bruce Matthews | .10 | .02 |
| 179 | Bubba McDowell | .05 | .01 |
| 180 | Johnny Meads | .05 | .01 |
| 181 | Warren Moon UER | .25 | .08 |
| 182 | Mike Munchak | .10 | .02 |
| 183 | Allen Pinkett | .05 | .01 |
| 184 | Dean Steinkuhler UER | .05 | .01 |
| 185 | Lorenzo White UER | .05 | .01 |
| 186A | John Grimsley ERR | .50 | .20 |
| 186B | John Grimsley COR | .10 | .02 |
| 187 | Pat Beach | .05 | .01 |
| 188 | Albert Bentley | .05 | .01 |
| 189 | Dean Biasucci | .05 | .01 |
| 190 | Duane Bickett | .05 | .01 |
| 191 | Bill Brooks | .05 | .01 |
| 192 | Eugene Daniel | .05 | .01 |
| 193 | Jeff George | .25 | .08 |
| 194 | Jon Hand | .05 | .01 |
| 195 | Jeff Herrod | .05 | .01 |
| 196A | Jessie Hester ERR Jesse | .30 | .10 |
| 196B | Jessie Hester ERR | .10 | .02 |
| 197 | Mike Prior | .05 | .01 |
| 198 | Stacey Simmons | .05 | .01 |
| 199 | Rohn Stark | .05 | .01 |
| 200 | Pat Tomberlin | .05 | .01 |
| 201 | Clarence Verdin | .05 | .01 |
| 202 | Keith Taylor | .05 | .01 |
| 203 | Jack Trudeau | .05 | .01 |
| 204 | Chip Banks | .05 | .01 |
| 205 | John Alt | .05 | .01 |
| 206 | Deron Cherry | .05 | .01 |
| 207 | Steve DeBerg | .10 | .02 |
| 208 | Tim Grunhard | .05 | .01 |
| 209 | Albert Lewis | .05 | .01 |
| 210 | Nick Lowery UER | .05 | .01 |
| 211 | Bill Maas | .05 | .01 |
| 212 | Chris Martin | .05 | .01 |
| 213 | Todd McNair | .05 | .01 |
| 214 | Christian Okoye | .05 | .01 |
| 215 | Stephone Paige | .05 | .01 |
| 216 | Steve Pelluer | .05 | .01 |
| 217 | Kevin Porter | .05 | .01 |
| 218 | Kevin Ross | .05 | .01 |
| 219 | Dan Saleaumua | .05 | .01 |
| 220 | Neil Smith | .25 | .08 |
| 221 | David Scott UER | .05 | .01 |
| 222 | Derrick Thomas | .25 | .08 |
| 223 | Barry Word | .05 | .01 |
| 224 | Percy Snow | .05 | .01 |
| 225 | Marcus Allen | .25 | .08 |
| 226 | Eddie Anderson UER | .05 | .01 |
| 227 | Steve Beuerlein UER | .05 | .01 |
| 228A | Tim Brown ERR NPO | .25 | .08 |
| 228B | Tim Brown COR | .25 | .08 |
| 229 | Scott Davis | .05 | .01 |
| 230 | Mike Dyal | .05 | .01 |
| 231 | Mervyn Fernandez UER | .05 | .01 |
| 232 | Willie Gault UER | .05 | .01 |
| 233 | Ethan Horton UER | .05 | .01 |
| 234 | Bo Jackson UER | .30 | .10 |
| 235 | Howie Long | .25 | .08 |
| 236 | Terry McDaniel | .05 | .01 |
| 237 | Max Montoya | .05 | .01 |
| 238 | Don Mosebar | .05 | .01 |
| 239 | Jay Schroeder | .05 | .01 |
| 240 | Steve Smith | .05 | .01 |
| 241 | Greg Townsend | .05 | .01 |
| 242 | Aaron Wallace | .05 | .01 |
| 243 | Lionel Washington | .05 | .01 |
| 244A | Steve Wisniewski ERR | .10 | .02 |
| 244B | Steve Wisniewski ERR/COR | .75 | .30 |
| 244C | Steve Wisniewski COR | .10 | .02 |
| 245 | Flipper Anderson | .05 | .01 |
| 246 | Latin Berry RC | .05 | .01 |
| 247 | Robert Delpino | .05 | .01 |
| 248 | Marcus Dupree | .05 | .01 |
| 249 | Henry Ellard | .10 | .02 |
| 250 | Jim Everett | .10 | .02 |
| 251 | Cleveland Gary | .05 | .01 |
| 252 | Jerry Gray | .05 | .01 |
| 253 | Kevin Greene | .10 | .02 |
| 254 | Pete Holohan UER | .05 | .01 |
| 255 | Buford McGee | .05 | .01 |
| 256 | Tom Newberry | .05 | .01 |
| 257A | Irv Pankey ERR | .50 | .20 |
| 257B | Irv Pankey COR | .10 | .02 |
| 258 | Jackie Slater | .05 | .01 |
| 259 | Doug Smith | .05 | .01 |
| 260 | Frank Stams | .05 | .01 |
| 261 | Michael Stewart | .05 | .01 |
| 262 | Fred Strickland | .05 | .01 |
| 263 | J.B. Brown UER | .05 | .01 |
| 264 | Mark Clayton | .10 | .02 |
| 265 | Jeff Cross | .05 | .01 |
| 266 | Mark Dennis UER | .05 | .01 |
| 267 | Mark Duper | .10 | .02 |
| 268 | Ferrell Edmunds | .05 | .01 |
| 269 | Dan Marino | 1.25 | .50 |
| 270 | John Offerdahl | .05 | .01 |
| 271 | Louis Oliver | .05 | .01 |
| 272 | Tony Paige | .05 | .01 |
| 273 | Reggie Roby | .05 | .01 |
| 274 | Sammie Smith | .05 | .01 |
| 275 | Keith Sims | .05 | .01 |
| 276 | Brian Sochia | .05 | .01 |
| 277 | Pete Stoyanovich | .05 | .01 |
| 278 | Richmond Webb | .05 | .01 |
| 279 | Jarvis Williams | .05 | .01 |
| 280 | Tim McKyer | .05 | .01 |
| 281A | Jim C. Jensen ERR | .50 | .20 |
| 281B | Jim C. Jensen COR | .10 | .02 |
| 282 | Scott Secules RC | .05 | .01 |
| 283 | Ray Berry | .05 | .01 |
| 284 | Joey Browner UER | .05 | .01 |
| 285 | Anthony Carter | .10 | .02 |
| 286A | Cris Carter ERR Chris | .50 | .20 |
| 286B | Cris Carter ERR/COR Chris | 1.50 | .60 |
| 286C | Cris Carter COR | .50 | .20 |
| 287 | Chris Doleman | .05 | .01 |
| 288 | Mark Dusbabek UER | .05 | .01 |
| 289 | Hassan Jones | .05 | .01 |
| 290 | Steve Jordan | .05 | .01 |
| 291 | Carl Lee | .05 | .01 |
| 292 | Kirk Lowdermilk | .05 | .01 |
| 293 | Randall McDaniel | .10 | .02 |
| 294 | Mike Merriweather | .05 | .01 |
| 295A | Keith Millard UER | .20 | .07 |
| 295B | Keith Millard COR | 2.50 | 1.00 |
| 296 | Al Noga UER | .05 | .01 |
| 297 | Scott Studwell UER | .05 | .01 |
| 298 | Henry Thomas | .05 | .01 |
| 299 | Herschel Walker | .10 | .02 |
| 300 | Gary Zimmerman | .10 | .02 |
| 301 | Rich Gannon | .25 | .08 |
| 302 | Wade Wilson UER | .10 | .02 |
| 303 | Vincent Brown | .05 | .01 |
| 304 | Marv Cook | .05 | .01 |
| 305 | Hart Lee Dykes | .05 | .01 |
| 306 | Irving Fryar | .10 | .02 |
| 307 | Tommy Hodson UER | .05 | .01 |
| 308 | Maurice Hurst | .05 | .01 |
| 309 | Ronnie Lippett UER | .05 | .01 |
| 310 | Fred Marion | .05 | .01 |

| Card | Price 1 | Price 2 |
|---|---|---|
| ❑ 311 Greg McMurtry | .05 | .01 |
| ❑ 312 Johnny Rembert | .05 | .01 |
| ❑ 313 Chris Singleton | .05 | .01 |
| ❑ 314 Ed Reynolds | .05 | .01 |
| ❑ 315 Andre Tippett | .05 | .01 |
| ❑ 316 Garin Veris | .05 | .01 |
| ❑ 317 Brent Williams | .05 | .01 |
| ❑ 318A John Stephens ERR | .10 | .02 |
| ❑ 318B John Stephens ERR/COR | .75 | .30 |
| ❑ 318C John Stephens COR | .10 | .02 |
| ❑ 319 Sammy Martin | .05 | .01 |
| ❑ 320 Bruce Armstrong | .05 | .01 |
| ❑ 321A Morten Andersen ERR | .30 | .10 |
| ❑ 321B Morten Andersen ERR/COR | .75 | .30 |
| ❑ 321C Morten Andersen COR | .10 | .02 |
| ❑ 322 Gene Atkins UER | .05 | .01 |
| ❑ 323 Vince Buck | .05 | .01 |
| ❑ 324 John Fourcade | .05 | .01 |
| ❑ 325 Kevin Haverdink | .05 | .01 |
| ❑ 326 Bobby Hebert | .05 | .01 |
| ❑ 327 Craig Heyward | .10 | .02 |
| ❑ 328 Dalton Hilliard | .05 | .01 |
| ❑ 329 Rickey Jackson | .05 | .01 |
| ❑ 330A Vaughan Johnson ERR | .20 | .07 |
| ❑ 330B Vaughan Johnson COR | 2.50 | 1.00 |
| ❑ 331 Eric Martin | .05 | .01 |
| ❑ 332 Wayne Martin | .05 | .01 |
| ❑ 333 Rueben Mayes UER | .05 | .01 |
| ❑ 334 Sam Mills | .05 | .01 |
| ❑ 335 Brett Perriman | .25 | .08 |
| ❑ 336 Pat Swilling | .10 | .02 |
| ❑ 337 Renaldo Turnbull | .05 | .01 |
| ❑ 338 Lonzell Hill | .05 | .01 |
| ❑ 339 Steve Walsh | .05 | .01 |
| ❑ 340 Carl Banks UER | .05 | .01 |
| ❑ 341 Mark Bavaro UER | .05 | .01 |
| ❑ 342 Maurice Carthon | .05 | .01 |
| ❑ 343 Pat Harlow RC | .05 | .01 |
| ❑ 344 Eric Dorsey | .05 | .01 |
| ❑ 345 John Elliott | .05 | .01 |
| ❑ 346 Rodney Hampton | .25 | .08 |
| ❑ 347 Jeff Hostetler | .10 | .02 |
| ❑ 348 Erik Howard UER | .05 | .01 |
| ❑ 349 Pepper Johnson | .05 | .01 |
| ❑ 350A Sean Landeta ERR | .10 | .02 |
| ❑ 350B Sean Landeta COR | .50 | .20 |
| ❑ 351 Leonard Marshall | .05 | .01 |
| ❑ 352 Dave Meggett | .10 | .02 |
| ❑ 353A Bart Oates ERR | .10 | .02 |
| ❑ 353B Bart Oates ERR/COR | .75 | .30 |
| ❑ 353C Bart Oates COR | .10 | .02 |
| ❑ 354 Gary Reasons | .05 | .01 |
| ❑ 355 Phil Simms | .10 | .02 |
| ❑ 356 Lawrence Taylor | .25 | .08 |
| ❑ 357 Reyna Thompson | .05 | .01 |
| ❑ 358 Brian Williams OL UER | .05 | .01 |
| ❑ 359 Matt Bahr | .05 | .01 |
| ❑ 360 Mark Ingram | .10 | .02 |
| ❑ 361 Brad Baxter | .05 | .01 |
| ❑ 362 Mark Boyer | .05 | .01 |
| ❑ 363 Dennis Byrd | .05 | .01 |
| ❑ 364 Dave Cadigan UER | .05 | .01 |
| ❑ 365 Kyle Clifton | .05 | .01 |
| ❑ 366 James Hasty | .05 | .01 |
| ❑ 367 Joe Kelly UER | .05 | .01 |
| ❑ 368 Jeff Lageman | .05 | .01 |
| ❑ 369 Pat Leahy UER | .05 | .01 |
| ❑ 370 Terance Mathis | .10 | .02 |
| ❑ 371 Erik McMillan | .05 | .01 |
| ❑ 372 Rob Moore | .25 | .08 |
| ❑ 373 Ken O'Brien | .05 | .01 |
| ❑ 374 Tony Stargell | .05 | .01 |
| ❑ 375 Jim Sweeney UER | .05 | .01 |
| ❑ 376 Al Toon | .10 | .02 |
| ❑ 377 Johnny Hector | .05 | .01 |
| ❑ 378 Jeff Criswell | .05 | .01 |
| ❑ 379 Mike Haight RC | .05 | .01 |
| ❑ 380 Troy Benson | .05 | .01 |
| ❑ 381 Eric Allen | .05 | .01 |
| ❑ 382 Fred Barnett | .25 | .08 |
| ❑ 383 Jerome Brown | .05 | .01 |
| ❑ 384 Keith Byars | .05 | .01 |
| ❑ 385 Randall Cunningham | .25 | .08 |
| ❑ 386 Byron Evans | .05 | .01 |
| ❑ 387 Wes Hopkins | .05 | .01 |
| ❑ 388 Keith Jackson | .10 | .02 |
| ❑ 389 Seth Joyner UER | .10 | .02 |
| ❑ 390 Bobby Wilson RC | .05 | .01 |
| ❑ 391 Heath Sherman | .05 | .01 |
| ❑ 392 Clyde Simmons UER | .05 | .01 |
| ❑ 393 Ben Smith | .05 | .01 |
| ❑ 394 Andre Waters | .05 | .01 |
| ❑ 395 Reggie White UER | .25 | .08 |
| ❑ 396 Calvin Williams | .10 | .02 |
| ❑ 397 Al Harris | .05 | .01 |
| ❑ 398 Anthony Toney | .05 | .01 |
| ❑ 399 Mike Quick | .05 | .01 |
| ❑ 400 Anthony Bell | .05 | .01 |
| ❑ 401 Rich Camarillo | .05 | .01 |
| ❑ 402 Roy Green | .05 | .01 |
| ❑ 403 Ken Harvey | .10 | .02 |
| ❑ 404 Eric Hill | .05 | .01 |
| ❑ 405 Garth Jax RC UER | .05 | .01 |
| ❑ 406 Ernie Jones | .05 | .01 |
| ❑ 407A Cedric Mack ERR | .20 | .07 |
| ❑ 407B Cedric Mack COR | 2.50 | 1.00 |
| ❑ 408 Dexter Manley | .05 | .01 |
| ❑ 409 Tim McDonald | .05 | .01 |
| ❑ 410 Freddie Joe Nunn | .05 | .01 |
| ❑ 411 Ricky Proehl | .05 | .01 |
| ❑ 412 Moe Gardner RC | .05 | .01 |
| ❑ 413 Timm Rosenbach | .05 | .01 |
| ❑ 414 Luis Sharpe UER | .05 | .01 |
| ❑ 415 Vai Sikahema UER | .05 | .01 |
| ❑ 416 Anthony Thompson | .05 | .01 |
| ❑ 417 Ron Wolfley UER | .05 | .01 |
| ❑ 418 Lonnie Young | .05 | .01 |
| ❑ 419 Gary Anderson K | .05 | .01 |
| ❑ 420 Bubby Brister | .05 | .01 |
| ❑ 421 Thomas Everett | .05 | .01 |
| ❑ 422 Eric Green | .05 | .01 |
| ❑ 423 Delton Hall | .05 | .01 |
| ❑ 424 Bryan Hinkle | .05 | .01 |
| ❑ 425 Merril Hoge | .05 | .01 |
| ❑ 426 Carnell Lake | .05 | .01 |
| ❑ 427 Louis Lipps | .05 | .01 |
| ❑ 428 David Little | .05 | .01 |
| ❑ 429 Greg Lloyd | .25 | .08 |
| ❑ 430 Mike Mularkey | .05 | .01 |
| ❑ 431 Keith Willis UER | .05 | .01 |
| ❑ 432 Dwayne Woodruff | .05 | .01 |
| ❑ 433 Rod Woodson | .25 | .08 |
| ❑ 434 Tim Worley | .05 | .01 |
| ❑ 435 Warren Williams | .05 | .01 |
| ❑ 436 Terry Long UER | .05 | .01 |
| ❑ 437 Martin Bayless | .05 | .01 |
| ❑ 438 Jarrod Bunch RC | .05 | .01 |
| ❑ 439 Marion Butts | .10 | .02 |
| ❑ 440 Gill Byrd UER | .05 | .01 |
| ❑ 441 Arthur Cox | .05 | .01 |
| ❑ 442 John Friesz | .25 | .08 |
| ❑ 443 Leo Goeas | .05 | .01 |
| ❑ 444 Burt Grossman | .05 | .01 |
| ❑ 445 Courtney Hall UER | .05 | .01 |
| ❑ 446 Ronnie Harmon | .05 | .01 |
| ❑ 447 Nate Lewis RC | .05 | .01 |
| ❑ 448 Anthony Miller | .10 | .02 |
| ❑ 449 Leslie O'Neal | .10 | .02 |
| ❑ 450 Gary Plummer | .05 | .01 |
| ❑ 451 Junior Seau | .25 | .08 |
| ❑ 452 Billy Ray Smith | .05 | .01 |
| ❑ 453 Billy Joe Tolliver | .05 | .01 |
| ❑ 454 Broderick Thompson | .05 | .01 |
| ❑ 455 Lee Williams | .05 | .01 |
| ❑ 456 Michael Carter | .05 | .01 |
| ❑ 457 Mike Cofer | .05 | .01 |
| ❑ 458 Kevin Fagan | .05 | .01 |
| ❑ 459 Charles Haley | .10 | .02 |
| ❑ 460 Pierce Holt | .05 | .01 |
| ❑ 461 Johnnie Jackson UER RC | .05 | .01 |
| ❑ 462 Brent Jones | .25 | .08 |
| ❑ 463 Guy McIntyre | .05 | .01 |
| ❑ 464 Joe Montana | 1.25 | .50 |
| ❑ 465A Bubba Paris ERR | .10 | .02 |
| ❑ 465B Bubba Paris ERR/COR | .50 | .20 |
| ❑ 465C Bubba Paris COR | .10 | .02 |
| ❑ 466 Tom Rathman UER | .05 | .01 |
| ❑ 467 Jerry Rice UER | .75 | .30 |
| ❑ 468 Mike Sherrard | .05 | .01 |
| ❑ 469 John Taylor UER | .10 | .02 |
| ❑ 470 Steve Young | .75 | .30 |
| ❑ 471 Dennis Brown | .05 | .01 |
| ❑ 472 Dexter Carter | .05 | .01 |
| ❑ 473 Bill Romanowski | .05 | .01 |
| ❑ 474 Dave Waymer | .05 | .01 |
| ❑ 475 Robert Blackmon | .05 | .01 |
| ❑ 476 Derrick Fenner | .05 | .01 |
| ❑ 477 Nesby Glasgow UER | .05 | .01 |
| ❑ 478 Jacob Green | .05 | .01 |
| ❑ 479 Andy Heck | .05 | .01 |
| ❑ 480 Norm Johnson UER | .05 | .01 |
| ❑ 481 Tommy Kane | .05 | .01 |
| ❑ 482 Cortez Kennedy | .25 | .08 |
| ❑ 483A Dave Krieg ERR | .20 | .07 |
| ❑ 483B Dave Krieg COR | 2.50 | 1.00 |
| ❑ 484 Bryan Millard | .05 | .01 |
| ❑ 485 Joe Nash | .05 | .01 |
| ❑ 486 Rufus Porter | .05 | .01 |
| ❑ 487 Eugene Robinson | .05 | .01 |
| ❑ 488 Mike Tice RC | .05 | .01 |
| ❑ 489 Chris Warren | .25 | .08 |
| ❑ 490 John L. Williams UER | .05 | .01 |
| ❑ 491 Terry Wooden | .05 | .01 |
| ❑ 492 Tony Woods | .05 | .01 |
| ❑ 493 Brian Blades | .10 | .02 |
| ❑ 494 Paul Skansi | .05 | .01 |
| ❑ 495 Gary Anderson RB | .05 | .01 |
| ❑ 496 Mark Carrier WR | .25 | .08 |
| ❑ 497 Chris Chandler | .25 | .08 |
| ❑ 498 Steve Christie | .05 | .01 |
| ❑ 499 Reggie Cobb | .10 | .02 |
| ❑ 500 Reuben Davis | .05 | .01 |
| ❑ 501 Willie Drewrey UER | .05 | .01 |
| ❑ 502 Randy Grimes | .05 | .01 |
| ❑ 503 Paul Gruber | .05 | .01 |
| ❑ 504 Wayne Haddix | .05 | .01 |
| ❑ 505 Ron Hall | .05 | .01 |
| ❑ 506 Harry Hamilton | .05 | .01 |
| ❑ 507 Bruce Hill | .05 | .01 |
| ❑ 508 Eugene Marve | .05 | .01 |
| ❑ 509 Keith McCants | .05 | .01 |
| ❑ 510 Winston Moss | .05 | .01 |
| ❑ 511 Kevin Murphy | .05 | .01 |
| ❑ 512 Mark Robinson | .05 | .01 |
| ❑ 513 Vinny Testaverde | .10 | .02 |
| ❑ 514 Broderick Thomas | .05 | .01 |
| ❑ 515A Jeff Bostic UER | .10 | .02 |
| ❑ 515B Jeff Bostic COR | .10 | .02 |
| ❑ 516 Todd Bowles | .05 | .01 |
| ❑ 517 Earnest Byner | .05 | .01 |
| ❑ 518 Gary Clark | .25 | .08 |
| ❑ 519 Craig Erickson RC | .25 | .08 |
| ❑ 520 Darryl Grant | .05 | .01 |
| ❑ 521 Darrell Green | .05 | .01 |
| ❑ 522 Russ Grimm | .05 | .01 |
| ❑ 523 Stan Humphries | .25 | .08 |
| ❑ 524 Joe Jacoby UER | .05 | .01 |
| ❑ 525 Jim Lachey | .05 | .01 |
| ❑ 526 Chip Lohmiller | .05 | .01 |
| ❑ 527 Charles Mann | .05 | .01 |
| ❑ 528 Wilber Marshall | .05 | .01 |
| ❑ 529A Art Monk | .10 | .02 |
| ❑ 529B Art Monk | .10 | .02 |
| ❑ 530 Tracy Rocker | .05 | .01 |
| ❑ 531 Mark Rypien | .10 | .02 |
| ❑ 532 Ricky Sanders UER | .05 | .01 |
| ❑ 533 Alvin Walton UER | .05 | .01 |
| ❑ 534 Todd Marinovich RC UER | .05 | .01 |
| ❑ 535 Mike Dumas RC | .05 | .01 |
| ❑ 536A Russell Maryland RC ERR | .25 | .08 |
| ❑ 536B Russell Maryland RC COR | .25 | .08 |
| ❑ 537 Eric Turner RC UER | .10 | .02 |
| ❑ 538 Ernie Mills RC | .10 | .02 |
| ❑ 539 Ed King RC | .05 | .01 |
| ❑ 540 Mike Stonebreaker | .05 | .01 |
| ❑ 541 Chris Zorich RC | .25 | .08 |
| ❑ 542A Mike Croel RC ERR | .05 | .01 |
| ❑ 542B Mike Croel RC COR | .05 | .01 |
| ❑ 543 Eric Moten RC | .05 | .01 |
| ❑ 544 Dan McGwire RC | .05 | .01 |
| ❑ 545 Keith Cash RC | .05 | .01 |
| ❑ 546 Kenny Walker RC UER | .05 | .01 |
| ❑ 547 Leroy Hoard UER | .10 | .02 |
| ❑ 548 Luis Cristobal UER | .05 | .01 |
| ❑ 549 Stacy Danley | .05 | .01 |
| ❑ 550 Todd Lyght RC | .05 | .01 |
| ❑ 551 Brett Favre RC | 8.00 | 3.00 |
| ❑ 552 Mike Pritchard RC | .25 | .08 |
| ❑ 553 Moe Gardner | .05 | .01 |
| ❑ 554 Tim McKyer | .05 | .01 |
| ❑ 555 Erric Pegram RC | .25 | .08 |
| ❑ 556 Norm Johnson | .05 | .01 |
| ❑ 557 Bruce Pickens RC | .05 | .01 |
| ❑ 558 Henry Jones RC | .10 | .02 |
| ❑ 559 Phil Hansen RC | .05 | .01 |
| ❑ 560 Cornelius Bennett | .10 | .02 |
| ❑ 561 Stan Thomas | .05 | .01 |

| | | |
|---|---|---|
| ☐ 562 Chris Zorich | .10 | .02 |
| ☐ 563 Anthony Morgan RC | .05 | .01 |
| ☐ 564 Darren Lewis RC | .05 | .01 |
| ☐ 565 Mike Stonebreaker RC | .05 | .01 |
| ☐ 566 Alfred Williams RC | .05 | .01 |
| ☐ 567 Lamar Rogers RC | .05 | .01 |
| ☐ 568 Erik Wilhelm RC UER | .05 | .01 |
| ☐ 569 Ed King | .05 | .01 |
| ☐ 570 Michael Jackson RC WR | .25 | .08 |
| ☐ 571 James Jones RC DT | .05 | .01 |
| ☐ 572 Russell Maryland | .25 | .08 |
| ☐ 573 Dixon Edwards RC | .05 | .01 |
| ☐ 574 Darrick Brownlow RC | .05 | .01 |
| ☐ 575 Larry Brown RC DB | .10 | .02 |
| ☐ 576 Mike Croel | .05 | .01 |
| ☐ 577 Keith Traylor RC | .05 | .01 |
| ☐ 578 Kenny Walker RC | .05 | .01 |
| ☐ 579 Reggie Johnson RC | .05 | .01 |
| ☐ 580 Herman Moore RC | .25 | .08 |
| ☐ 581 Kelvin Pritchett RC | .10 | .02 |
| ☐ 582 Kevin Scott RC | .05 | .01 |
| ☐ 583 Vinnie Clark RC | .05 | .01 |
| ☐ 584 Esera Tuaolo RC | .05 | .01 |
| ☐ 585 Don Davey | .05 | .01 |
| ☐ 586 Blair Kiel RC | .05 | .01 |
| ☐ 587 Mike Dumas | .05 | .01 |
| ☐ 588 Darryl Lewis RC | .10 | .02 |
| ☐ 589 John Flannery RC | .05 | .01 |
| ☐ 590 Kevin Donnalley RC | .05 | .01 |
| ☐ 591 Shane Curry | .05 | .01 |
| ☐ 592 Mark Vander Poel RC | .05 | .01 |
| ☐ 593 Dave McCloughan | .05 | .01 |
| ☐ 594 Mel Agee RC | .05 | .01 |
| ☐ 595 Kerry Cash RC | .05 | .01 |
| ☐ 596 Harvey Williams RC | .25 | .08 |
| ☐ 597 Joe Valerio | .05 | .01 |
| ☐ 598 Tim Barnett RC UER | .05 | .01 |
| ☐ 599 Todd Marinovich | .05 | .02 |
| ☐ 600 Nick Bell RC | .05 | .02 |
| ☐ 601 Roger Craig | .10 | .02 |
| ☐ 602 Ronnie Lott | .10 | .02 |
| ☐ 603 Mike Jones RC LB | .05 | .01 |
| ☐ 604 Todd Lyght | .05 | .01 |
| ☐ 605 Roman Phifer RC | .05 | .01 |
| ☐ 606 David Lang RC | .05 | .01 |
| ☐ 607 Aaron Craver RC | .05 | .01 |
| ☐ 608 Mark Higgs RC | .05 | .01 |
| ☐ 609 Chris Green | .05 | .01 |
| ☐ 610 Randy Baldwin RC | .05 | .01 |
| ☐ 611 Pat Harlow | .05 | .01 |
| ☐ 612 Leonard Russell RC | .25 | .08 |
| ☐ 613 Jerome Henderson RC | .05 | .01 |
| ☐ 614 Scott Zolak RC | .05 | .01 |
| ☐ 615 Jon Vaughn RC | .05 | .01 |
| ☐ 616 Harry Colon RC | .05 | .01 |
| ☐ 617 Wesley Carroll RC | .05 | .01 |
| ☐ 618 Quinn Early | .10 | .02 |
| ☐ 619 Reginald Jones RC | .05 | .01 |
| ☐ 620 Jarrod Bunch | .05 | .01 |
| ☐ 621 Kanavis McGhee RC | .05 | .01 |
| ☐ 622 Ed McCaffrey RC | 2.00 | .75 |
| ☐ 623 Browning Nagle RC | .05 | .01 |
| ☐ 624 Mo Lewis RC | .10 | .02 |
| ☐ 625 Blair Thomas | .05 | .01 |
| ☐ 626 Antone Davis RC | .05 | .01 |
| ☐ 627 Jim McMahon | .10 | .02 |
| ☐ 628 Scott Kowalkowski RC | .05 | .01 |
| ☐ 629 Brad Goebel RC | .05 | .01 |
| ☐ 630 William Thomas RC | .05 | .01 |
| ☐ 631 Eric Swann RC | .25 | .08 |
| ☐ 632 Mike Jones DE RC | .05 | .01 |
| ☐ 633 Aeneas Williams RC | .25 | .08 |
| ☐ 634 Dexter Davis RC | .05 | .01 |
| ☐ 635 Tom Tupa UER | .05 | .01 |
| ☐ 636 Johnny Johnson | .05 | .01 |
| ☐ 637 Randal Hill RC | .10 | .02 |
| ☐ 638 Jeff Graham RC WR | .25 | .08 |
| ☐ 639 Ernie Mills | .05 | .01 |
| ☐ 640 Adrian Cooper RC | .05 | .01 |
| ☐ 641 Stanley Richard RC | .05 | .01 |
| ☐ 642 Eric Bieniemy RC | .05 | .01 |
| ☐ 643 Eric Moten | .05 | .01 |
| ☐ 644 Shawn Jefferson RC | .10 | .02 |
| ☐ 645 Ted Washington RC | .05 | .01 |
| ☐ 646 John Johnson RC | .05 | .01 |
| ☐ 647 Dan McGwire | .05 | .01 |
| ☐ 648 Doug Thomas RC | .05 | .01 |
| ☐ 649 David Daniels RC | .05 | .01 |
| ☐ 650 John Kasay RC | .10 | .02 |

| | | |
|---|---|---|
| ☐ 651 Jeff Kemp | .05 | .01 |
| ☐ 652 Charles McRae RC | .05 | .01 |
| ☐ 653 Lawrence Dawsey RC | .10 | .02 |
| ☐ 654 Robert Wilson RC | .05 | .01 |
| ☐ 655 Dexter Manley | .05 | .01 |
| ☐ 656 Chuck Weatherspoon RC | .05 | .01 |
| ☐ 657 Tim Ryan G RC | .05 | .01 |
| ☐ 658 Bobby Wilson | .05 | .01 |
| ☐ 659 Ricky Ervins RC | .10 | .02 |
| ☐ 660 Matt Millen | .10 | .02 |

### 1992 Pacific

| | | |
|---|---|---|
| ☐ COMPLETE SET (660) | 15.00 | 6.00 |
| ☐ COMP.FACT.SET (690) | 25.00 | 10.00 |
| ☐ COMP.SERIES 1 (330) | 8.00 | 3.00 |
| ☐ COMP.SERIES 2 (330) | 8.00 | 3.00 |
| ☐ COMP.CHECKLIST SET (5) | 3.00 | 1.50 |
| ☐ 1 Steve Broussard | .05 | .01 |
| ☐ 2 Darion Conner | .05 | .01 |
| ☐ 3 Tory Epps | .05 | .01 |
| ☐ 4 Michael Haynes | .10 | .02 |
| ☐ 5 Chris Hinton | .05 | .01 |
| ☐ 6 Mike Kenn | .05 | .01 |
| ☐ 7 Tim McKyer | .05 | .01 |
| ☐ 8 Chris Miller | .10 | .02 |
| ☐ 9 Erric Pegram | .10 | .02 |
| ☐ 10 Mike Pritchard | .10 | .02 |
| ☐ 11 Moe Gardner | .05 | .01 |
| ☐ 12 Tim Green | .05 | .01 |
| ☐ 13 Norm Johnson | .05 | .01 |
| ☐ 14 Don Beebe | .05 | .01 |
| ☐ 15 Cornelius Bennett | .10 | .02 |
| ☐ 16 Al Edwards | .05 | .01 |
| ☐ 17 Mark Kelso | .05 | .01 |
| ☐ 18 James Lofton | .10 | .02 |
| ☐ 19 Frank Reich | .10 | .02 |
| ☐ 20 Leon Seals | .05 | .01 |
| ☐ 21 Darryl Talley | .05 | .01 |
| ☐ 22 Thurman Thomas | .25 | .08 |
| ☐ 23 Kent Hull | .05 | .01 |
| ☐ 24 Jeff Wright | .05 | .01 |
| ☐ 25 Nate Odomes | .05 | .01 |
| ☐ 26 Carwell Gardner | .05 | .01 |
| ☐ 27 Neal Anderson | .05 | .01 |
| ☐ 28 Mark Carrier DB | .05 | .01 |
| ☐ 29 Johnny Bailey | .05 | .01 |
| ☐ 30 Jim Harbaugh | .25 | .08 |
| ☐ 31 Jay Hilgenberg | .05 | .01 |
| ☐ 32 William Perry | .10 | .02 |
| ☐ 33 Wendell Davis | .05 | .01 |
| ☐ 34 Donnell Woolford | .05 | .01 |
| ☐ 35 Keith Van Horne | .05 | .01 |
| ☐ 36 Shaun Gayle | .05 | .01 |
| ☐ 37 Tom Waddle | .05 | .01 |
| ☐ 38 Chris Zorich | .10 | .02 |
| ☐ 39 Tom Thayer | .05 | .01 |
| ☐ 40 Rickey Dixon | .05 | .01 |
| ☐ 41 James Francis | .05 | .01 |
| ☐ 42 David Fulcher | .05 | .01 |
| ☐ 43 Reggie Rembert | .05 | .01 |
| ☐ 44 Anthony Munoz | .10 | .02 |
| ☐ 45 Harold Green | .05 | .01 |
| ☐ 46 Mitchell Price | .05 | .01 |
| ☐ 47 Rodney Holman | .05 | .01 |
| ☐ 48 Bruce Kozerski | .05 | .01 |
| ☐ 49 Bruce Reimers | .05 | .01 |
| ☐ 50 Erik Wilhelm | .05 | .01 |
| ☐ 51 Harlon Barnett | .05 | .01 |
| ☐ 52 Mike Johnson | .05 | .01 |
| ☐ 53 Brian Brennan | .05 | .01 |
| ☐ 54 Ed King | .05 | .01 |
| ☐ 55 Reggie Langhorne | .05 | .01 |

| | | |
|---|---|---|
| ☐ 56 James Jones DT | .05 | .01 |
| ☐ 57 Mike Baab | .05 | .01 |
| ☐ 58 Dan Fike | .05 | .01 |
| ☐ 59 Frank Minnifield | .05 | .01 |
| ☐ 60 Clay Matthews | .10 | .02 |
| ☐ 61 Kevin Mack | .05 | .01 |
| ☐ 62 Tony Casillas | .05 | .01 |
| ☐ 63 Jay Novacek | .10 | .02 |
| ☐ 64 Larry Brown DB | .05 | .01 |
| ☐ 65 Michael Irvin | .25 | .08 |
| ☐ 66 Jack Del Rio | .05 | .01 |
| ☐ 67 Ken Willis | .05 | .01 |
| ☐ 68 Emmitt Smith | 1.50 | .60 |
| ☐ 69 Alan Veingrad | .05 | .01 |
| ☐ 70 John Gesek | .05 | .01 |
| ☐ 71 Steve Beuerlein | .10 | .02 |
| ☐ 72 Vinson Smith RC | .05 | .01 |
| ☐ 73 Steve Atwater | .05 | .01 |
| ☐ 74 Mike Croel | .05 | .01 |
| ☐ 75 John Elway | 1.25 | .50 |
| ☐ 76 Gaston Green | .05 | .01 |
| ☐ 77 Mike Horan | .05 | .01 |
| ☐ 78 Vance Johnson | .05 | .01 |
| ☐ 79 Karl Mecklenburg | .05 | .01 |
| ☐ 80 Shannon Sharpe | .25 | .08 |
| ☐ 81 David Treadwell | .05 | .01 |
| ☐ 82 Kenny Walker | .05 | .01 |
| ☐ 83 Greg Lewis | .05 | .01 |
| ☐ 84 Shawn Moore | .05 | .01 |
| ☐ 85 Alton Montgomery | .05 | .01 |
| ☐ 86 Michael Young | .05 | .01 |
| ☐ 87 Jerry Ball | .05 | .01 |
| ☐ 88 Bennie Blades | .05 | .01 |
| ☐ 89 Mel Gray | .10 | .02 |
| ☐ 90 Herman Moore | .25 | .08 |
| ☐ 91 Erik Kramer | .10 | .02 |
| ☐ 92 Willie Green | .05 | .01 |
| ☐ 93 George Jamison | .05 | .01 |
| ☐ 94 Chris Spielman | .10 | .02 |
| ☐ 95 Kelvin Pritchett | .05 | .01 |
| ☐ 96 William White | .05 | .01 |
| ☐ 97 Mike Utley | .10 | .02 |
| ☐ 98 Tony Bennett | .05 | .01 |
| ☐ 99 LeRoy Butler | .05 | .01 |
| ☐ 100 Vinnie Clark | .05 | .01 |
| ☐ 101 Ron Hallstrom | .05 | .01 |
| ☐ 102 Chris Jacke | .05 | .01 |
| ☐ 103 Tony Mandarich | .05 | .01 |
| ☐ 104 Sterling Sharpe | .25 | .08 |
| ☐ 105 Don Majkowski | .05 | .01 |
| ☐ 106 Johnny Holland | .05 | .01 |
| ☐ 107 Esera Tuaolo | .05 | .01 |
| ☐ 108 Darrell Thompson | .05 | .01 |
| ☐ 109 Bubba McDowell | .05 | .01 |
| ☐ 110 Curtis Duncan | .05 | .01 |
| ☐ 111 Lamar Lathon | .05 | .01 |
| ☐ 112 Drew Hill | .05 | .01 |
| ☐ 113 Bruce Matthews | .05 | .01 |
| ☐ 114 Bo Orlando RC | .05 | .01 |
| ☐ 115 Don Maggs | .05 | .01 |
| ☐ 116 Lorenzo White | .05 | .01 |
| ☐ 117 Ernest Givins | .10 | .02 |
| ☐ 118 Tony Jones WR | .05 | .01 |
| ☐ 119 Dean Steinkuhler | .05 | .01 |
| ☐ 120 Dean Biasucci | .05 | .01 |
| ☐ 121 Duane Bickett | .05 | .01 |
| ☐ 122 Bill Brooks | .05 | .01 |
| ☐ 123 Ken Clark | .05 | .01 |
| ☐ 124 Jessie Hester | .05 | .01 |
| ☐ 125 Anthony Johnson | .10 | .02 |
| ☐ 126 Chip Banks | .05 | .01 |
| ☐ 127 Mike Prior | .05 | .01 |
| ☐ 128 Rohn Stark | .05 | .01 |
| ☐ 129 Jeff Herrod | .05 | .01 |
| ☐ 130 Clarence Verdin | .05 | .01 |
| ☐ 131 Tim Manoa | .05 | .01 |
| ☐ 132 Brian Baldinger RC | .05 | .01 |
| ☐ 133 Tim Barnett | .05 | .01 |
| ☐ 134 J.J. Birden | .05 | .01 |
| ☐ 135 Deron Cherry | .05 | .01 |
| ☐ 136 Steve DeBerg | .05 | .01 |
| ☐ 137 Nick Lowery | .05 | .01 |
| ☐ 138 Todd McNair | .05 | .01 |
| ☐ 139 Christian Okoye | .05 | .01 |
| ☐ 140 Mark Vlasic | .05 | .01 |
| ☐ 141 Dan Saleaumua | .05 | .01 |
| ☐ 142 Neil Smith | .25 | .08 |
| ☐ 143 Robb Thomas | .05 | .01 |
| ☐ 144 Eddie Anderson | .05 | .01 |

| | | |
|---|---|---|
| ☐ 145 Nick Bell | .05 | .01 |
| ☐ 146 Tim Brown | .25 | .08 |
| ☐ 147 Roger Craig | .10 | .02 |
| ☐ 148 Jeff Gossett | .05 | .01 |
| ☐ 149 Ethan Horton | .05 | .01 |
| ☐ 150 Jamie Holland | .05 | .01 |
| ☐ 151 Jeff Jaeger | .05 | .01 |
| ☐ 152 Todd Marinovich | .05 | .01 |
| ☐ 153 Marcus Allen | .25 | .08 |
| ☐ 154 Steve Smith | .05 | .01 |
| ☐ 155 Flipper Anderson | .05 | .01 |
| ☐ 156 Robert Delpino | .05 | .01 |
| ☐ 157 Cleveland Gary | .05 | .01 |
| ☐ 158 Kevin Greene | .10 | .02 |
| ☐ 159 Dale Hatcher | .05 | .01 |
| ☐ 160 Duval Love | .05 | .01 |
| ☐ 161 Ron Brown | .05 | .01 |
| ☐ 162 Jackie Slater | .05 | .01 |
| ☐ 163 Doug Smith | .05 | .01 |
| ☐ 164 Aaron Cox | .05 | .01 |
| ☐ 165 Larry Kelm | .05 | .01 |
| ☐ 166 Mark Clayton | .10 | .02 |
| ☐ 167 Louis Oliver | .05 | .01 |
| ☐ 168 Mark Higgs | .05 | .01 |
| ☐ 169 Aaron Craver | .05 | .01 |
| ☐ 170 Sammie Smith | .05 | .01 |
| ☐ 171 Tony Paige | .05 | .01 |
| ☐ 172 Jeff Cross | .05 | .01 |
| ☐ 173 David Griggs | .05 | .01 |
| ☐ 174 Richmond Webb | .05 | .01 |
| ☐ 175 Vestee Jackson | .05 | .01 |
| ☐ 176 Jim C. Jensen | .05 | .01 |
| ☐ 177 Anthony Carter | .10 | .02 |
| ☐ 178 Cris Carter | .50 | .20 |
| ☐ 179 Chris Doleman | .05 | .01 |
| ☐ 180 Rich Gannon | .25 | .08 |
| ☐ 181 Al Noga | .05 | .01 |
| ☐ 182 Randall McDaniel | .10 | .02 |
| ☐ 183 Todd Scott | .05 | .01 |
| ☐ 184 Henry Thomas | .05 | .01 |
| ☐ 185 Felix Wright | .05 | .01 |
| ☐ 186 Gary Zimmerman | .05 | .01 |
| ☐ 187 Herschel Walker | .10 | .02 |
| ☐ 188 Vincent Brown | .05 | .01 |
| ☐ 189 Harry Colon | .05 | .01 |
| ☐ 190 Irving Fryar | .10 | .02 |
| ☐ 191 Marv Cook | .05 | .01 |
| ☐ 192 Leonard Russell | .10 | .02 |
| ☐ 193 Hugh Millen | .05 | .01 |
| ☐ 194 Pat Harlow | .05 | .01 |
| ☐ 195 Jon Vaughn | .05 | .01 |
| ☐ 196 Ben Coates RC | .75 | .30 |
| ☐ 197 Johnny Rembert | .05 | .01 |
| ☐ 198 Greg McMurtry | .05 | .01 |
| ☐ 199 Morten Andersen | .05 | .01 |
| ☐ 200 Tommy Barnhardt | .05 | .01 |
| ☐ 201 Bobby Hebert | .05 | .01 |
| ☐ 202 Dalton Hilliard | .05 | .01 |
| ☐ 203 Sam Mills | .05 | .01 |
| ☐ 204 Pat Swilling | .05 | .01 |
| ☐ 205 Rickey Jackson | .05 | .01 |
| ☐ 206 Stan Brock | .05 | .01 |
| ☐ 207 Reginald Jones | .05 | .01 |
| ☐ 208 Gill Fenerty | .05 | .01 |
| ☐ 209 Eric Martin | .05 | .01 |
| ☐ 210 Matt Bahr | .05 | .01 |
| ☐ 211 Rodney Hampton | .10 | .02 |
| ☐ 212 Jeff Hostetler | .10 | .02 |
| ☐ 213 Pepper Johnson | .05 | .01 |
| ☐ 214 Leonard Marshall | .05 | .01 |
| ☐ 215 Doug Riesenberg | .05 | .01 |
| ☐ 216 Stephen Baker | .05 | .01 |
| ☐ 217 Mike Fox | .05 | .01 |
| ☐ 218 Bart Oates | .05 | .01 |
| ☐ 219 Everson Walls | .05 | .01 |
| ☐ 220 Gary Reasons | .05 | .01 |
| ☐ 221 Jeff Lageman | .05 | .01 |
| ☐ 222 Joe Kelly | .05 | .01 |
| ☐ 223 Mo Lewis | .05 | .01 |
| ☐ 224 Tony Stargell | .05 | .01 |
| ☐ 225 Jim Sweeney | .05 | .01 |
| ☐ 226 Freeman McNeil | .10 | .02 |
| ☐ 227 Brian Washington | .05 | .01 |
| ☐ 228 Johnny Hector | .05 | .01 |
| ☐ 229 Terance Mathis | .10 | .02 |
| ☐ 230 Rob Moore | .10 | .02 |
| ☐ 231 Brad Baxter | .05 | .01 |
| ☐ 232 Eric Allen | .05 | .01 |
| ☐ 233 Fred Barnett | .10 | .02 |

| | | |
|---|---|---|
| ☐ 234 Jerome Brown | .05 | .01 |
| ☐ 235 Keith Byars | .05 | .01 |
| ☐ 236 William Thomas | .05 | .01 |
| ☐ 237 Jessie Small | .05 | .01 |
| ☐ 238 Robert Drummond | .05 | .01 |
| ☐ 239 Reggie White | .25 | .08 |
| ☐ 240 James Joseph | .05 | .01 |
| ☐ 241 Brad Goebel | .05 | .01 |
| ☐ 242 Clyde Simmons | .05 | .01 |
| ☐ 243 Rich Camarillo | .05 | .01 |
| ☐ 244 Ken Harvey | .05 | .01 |
| ☐ 245 Garth Jax | .05 | .01 |
| ☐ 246 Johnny Johnson | .05 | .01 |
| ☐ 247 Mike Jones | .05 | .01 |
| ☐ 248 Ernie Jones | .05 | .01 |
| ☐ 249 Tom Tupa | .05 | .01 |
| ☐ 250 Ron Wolfley | .05 | .01 |
| ☐ 251 Luis Sharpe | .05 | .01 |
| ☐ 252 Eric Swann | .10 | .02 |
| ☐ 253 Anthony Thompson | .05 | .01 |
| ☐ 254 Gary Anderson K | .05 | .01 |
| ☐ 255 Dermontti Dawson | .05 | .01 |
| ☐ 256 Jeff Graham | .25 | .08 |
| ☐ 257 Eric Green | .05 | .01 |
| ☐ 258 Louis Lipps | .05 | .01 |
| ☐ 259 Neil O'Donnell | .10 | .02 |
| ☐ 260 Rod Woodson | .25 | .08 |
| ☐ 261 Dwight Stone | .05 | .01 |
| ☐ 262 Aaron Jones | .05 | .01 |
| ☐ 263 Keith Willis | .05 | .01 |
| ☐ 264 Ernie Mills | .05 | .01 |
| ☐ 265 Martin Bayless | .05 | .01 |
| ☐ 266 Rod Bernstine | .05 | .01 |
| ☐ 267 John Carney | .05 | .01 |
| ☐ 268 John Friesz | .10 | .02 |
| ☐ 269 Nate Lewis | .05 | .01 |
| ☐ 270 Shawn Jefferson | .05 | .01 |
| ☐ 271 Burt Grossman | .05 | .01 |
| ☐ 272 Eric Moten | .05 | .01 |
| ☐ 273 Gary Plummer | .05 | .01 |
| ☐ 274 Henry Rolling | .05 | .01 |
| ☐ 275 Steve Hendrickson RC | .05 | .01 |
| ☐ 276 Michael Carter | .05 | .01 |
| ☐ 277 Steve Bono RC | .25 | .08 |
| ☐ 278 Dexter Carter | .05 | .01 |
| ☐ 279 Mike Cofer | .05 | .01 |
| ☐ 280 Charles Haley | .10 | .02 |
| ☐ 281 Tom Rathman | .05 | .01 |
| ☐ 282 Guy McIntyre | .05 | .01 |
| ☐ 283 John Taylor | .10 | .02 |
| ☐ 284 Dave Waymer | .05 | .01 |
| ☐ 285 Steve Wallace | .05 | .01 |
| ☐ 286 Jamie Williams | .05 | .01 |
| ☐ 287 Brian Blades | .10 | .02 |
| ☐ 288 Jeff Bryant | .05 | .01 |
| ☐ 289 Grant Feasel | .05 | .01 |
| ☐ 290 Jacob Green | .05 | .01 |
| ☐ 291 Andy Heck | .05 | .01 |
| ☐ 292 Kelly Stouffer | .05 | .01 |
| ☐ 293 John Kasay | .05 | .01 |
| ☐ 294 Cortez Kennedy | .10 | .02 |
| ☐ 295 Bryan Millard | .05 | .01 |
| ☐ 296 Eugene Robinson | .05 | .01 |
| ☐ 297 Tony Woods | .05 | .01 |
| ☐ 298 Jesse Anderson UER | .05 | .01 |
| ☐ 299 Gary Anderson RB | .05 | .01 |
| ☐ 300 Mark Carrier WR | .10 | .02 |
| ☐ 301 Reggie Cobb | .05 | .01 |
| ☐ 302 Robert Wilson | .05 | .01 |
| ☐ 303 Jesse Solomon | .05 | .01 |
| ☐ 304 Broderick Thomas | .05 | .01 |
| ☐ 305 Lawrence Dawsey | .10 | .02 |
| ☐ 306 Charles McRae | .05 | .01 |
| ☐ 307 Paul Gruber | .05 | .01 |
| ☐ 308 Vinny Testaverde | .10 | .02 |
| ☐ 309 Brian Mitchell | .10 | .02 |
| ☐ 310 Darrell Green | .10 | .02 |
| ☐ 311 Art Monk | .10 | .02 |
| ☐ 312 Russ Grimm | .05 | .01 |
| ☐ 313 Mark Rypien | .05 | .01 |
| ☐ 314 Bobby Wilson | .05 | .01 |
| ☐ 315 Wilber Marshall | .05 | .01 |
| ☐ 316 Gerald Riggs | .05 | .01 |
| ☐ 317 Chip Lohmiller | .05 | .01 |
| ☐ 318 Joe Jacoby | .05 | .01 |
| ☐ 319 Martin Mayhew | .05 | .01 |
| ☐ 320 Amp Lee RC | .05 | .01 |
| ☐ 321 Terrell Buckley RC | .05 | .01 |
| ☐ 322 Tommy Vardell RC | .05 | .01 |

| | | |
|---|---|---|
| ☐ 323 Ricardo McDonald RC | .05 | .01 |
| ☐ 324 Joe Bowden RC | .05 | .01 |
| ☐ 325 Darryl Williams RC | .05 | .01 |
| ☐ 326 Carlos Huerta | .05 | .01 |
| ☐ 327 Patrick Rowe RC | .05 | .01 |
| ☐ 328 Siran Stacy RC | .05 | .01 |
| ☐ 329 Dexter McNabb RC | .05 | .01 |
| ☐ 330 Willie Clay RC | .05 | .01 |
| ☐ 331 Oliver Barnett | .05 | .01 |
| ☐ 332 Aundray Bruce | .05 | .01 |
| ☐ 333 Ken Tippins RC | .05 | .01 |
| ☐ 334 Jessie Tuggle | .05 | .01 |
| ☐ 335 Brian Jordan | .10 | .02 |
| ☐ 336 Andre Rison | .10 | .02 |
| ☐ 337 Houston Hoover | .05 | .01 |
| ☐ 338 Bill Fralic | .05 | .01 |
| ☐ 339 Pat Chaffey RC | .05 | .01 |
| ☐ 340 Keith Jones | .05 | .01 |
| ☐ 341 Jaime Dukes RC | .05 | .01 |
| ☐ 342 Chris Mohr | .05 | .01 |
| ☐ 343 John Davis | .05 | .01 |
| ☐ 344 Ray Bentley | .05 | .01 |
| ☐ 345 Scott Norwood | .05 | .01 |
| ☐ 346 Shane Conlan | .05 | .01 |
| ☐ 347 Steve Tasker | .10 | .02 |
| ☐ 348 Will Wolford | .05 | .01 |
| ☐ 349 Gary Baldinger RC | .05 | .01 |
| ☐ 350 Kirby Jackson | .05 | .01 |
| ☐ 351 Jamie Mueller | .05 | .01 |
| ☐ 352 Pete Metzelaars | .05 | .01 |
| ☐ 353 Richard Dent | .10 | .02 |
| ☐ 354 Ron Rivera | .05 | .01 |
| ☐ 355 Jim Morrissey | .05 | .01 |
| ☐ 356 John Roper | .05 | .01 |
| ☐ 357 Steve McMichael | .10 | .02 |
| ☐ 358 Ron Morris | .05 | .01 |
| ☐ 359 Darren Lewis | .05 | .01 |
| ☐ 360 Anthony Morgan | .05 | .01 |
| ☐ 361 Stan Thomas | .05 | .01 |
| ☐ 362 James Thornton | .05 | .01 |
| ☐ 363 Brad Muster | .05 | .01 |
| ☐ 364 Tim Krumrie | .05 | .01 |
| ☐ 365 Lee Johnson | .05 | .01 |
| ☐ 366 Eric Ball | .05 | .01 |
| ☐ 367 Alonzo Mitz RC | .05 | .01 |
| ☐ 368 David Grant | .05 | .01 |
| ☐ 369 Lynn James | .05 | .01 |
| ☐ 370 Lewis Billups | .05 | .01 |
| ☐ 371 Jim Breech | .05 | .01 |
| ☐ 372 Alfred Williams | .05 | .01 |
| ☐ 373 Wayne Haddix | .05 | .01 |
| ☐ 374 Tim McGee | .05 | .01 |
| ☐ 375 Michael Jackson | .10 | .02 |
| ☐ 376 Leroy Hoard | .10 | .02 |
| ☐ 377 Tony Jones T | .05 | .01 |
| ☐ 378 Vince Newsome | .05 | .01 |
| ☐ 379 Todd Philcox RC | .05 | .01 |
| ☐ 380 Eric Metcalf | .10 | .02 |
| ☐ 381 John Rienstra | .05 | .01 |
| ☐ 382 Matt Stover | .05 | .01 |
| ☐ 383 Brian Hansen | .05 | .01 |
| ☐ 384 Joe Morris | .05 | .01 |
| ☐ 385 Anthony Pleasant | .05 | .01 |
| ☐ 386 Mark Stepnoski | .05 | .01 |
| ☐ 387 Erik Williams | .05 | .01 |
| ☐ 388 Jimmie Jones | .05 | .01 |
| ☐ 389 Kevin Gogan | .05 | .01 |
| ☐ 390 Manny Hendrix RC | .05 | .01 |
| ☐ 391 Issiac Holt | .05 | .01 |
| ☐ 392 Ken Norton | .10 | .02 |
| ☐ 393 Tommie Agee | .05 | .01 |
| ☐ 394 Alvin Harper | .10 | .02 |
| ☐ 395 Alexander Wright | .05 | .01 |
| ☐ 396 Mike Saxon | .05 | .01 |
| ☐ 397 Michael Brooks | .05 | .01 |
| ☐ 398 Bobby Humphrey | .05 | .01 |
| ☐ 399 Ken Lanier | .05 | .01 |
| ☐ 400 Steve Sewell | .05 | .01 |
| ☐ 401 Robert Perryman | .05 | .01 |
| ☐ 402 Wymon Henderson | .05 | .01 |
| ☐ 403 Keith Kartz | .05 | .01 |
| ☐ 404 Clarence Kay | .05 | .01 |
| ☐ 405 Keith Traylor | .05 | .01 |
| ☐ 406 Doug Widell | .05 | .01 |
| ☐ 407 Dennis Smith | .05 | .01 |
| ☐ 408 Marc Spindler | .05 | .01 |
| ☐ 409 Lomas Brown | .05 | .01 |
| ☐ 410 Robert Clark | .05 | .01 |
| ☐ 411 Eric Andolsek | .05 | .01 |

| | | |
|---|---|---|
| ☐ 412 Mike Farr | .05 | .01 |
| ☐ 413 Ray Crockett | .05 | .01 |
| ☐ 414 Jeff Campbell | .05 | .01 |
| ☐ 415 Dan Owens | .05 | .01 |
| ☐ 416 Jim Arnold | .05 | .01 |
| ☐ 417 Barry Sanders | 1.25 | .50 |
| ☐ 418 Eddie Murray | .05 | .01 |
| ☐ 419 Vince Workman | .05 | .01 |
| ☐ 420 Ed West | .05 | .01 |
| ☐ 421 Charles Wilson | .05 | .01 |
| ☐ 422 Perry Kemp | .05 | .01 |
| ☐ 423 Chuck Cecil | .05 | .01 |
| ☐ 424 James Campen | .05 | .01 |
| ☐ 425 Robert Brown | .05 | .01 |
| ☐ 426 Brian Noble | .05 | .01 |
| ☐ 427 Rich Moran | .05 | .01 |
| ☐ 428 Vai Sikahema | .05 | .01 |
| ☐ 429 Allen Rice | .05 | .01 |
| ☐ 430 Haywood Jeffires | .10 | .02 |
| ☐ 431 Warren Moon | .25 | .08 |
| ☐ 432 Greg Montgomery | .05 | .01 |
| ☐ 433 Sean Jones | .05 | .01 |
| ☐ 434 Richard Johnson CB | .05 | .01 |
| ☐ 435 Al Smith | .05 | .01 |
| ☐ 436 Johnny Meads | .05 | .01 |
| ☐ 437 William Fuller | .05 | .01 |
| ☐ 438 Mike Munchak | .10 | .02 |
| ☐ 439 Ray Childress | .05 | .01 |
| ☐ 440 Cody Carlson | .05 | .01 |
| ☐ 441 Scott Radecic | .05 | .01 |
| ☐ 442 Quintus McDonald RC | .05 | .01 |
| ☐ 443 Eugene Daniel | .05 | .01 |
| ☐ 444 Mark Herrmann RC | .05 | .01 |
| ☐ 445 John Baylor RC | .05 | .01 |
| ☐ 446 Dave McCloughan | .05 | .01 |
| ☐ 447 Mark Vander Poel | .05 | .01 |
| ☐ 448 Randy Dixon | .05 | .01 |
| ☐ 449 Keith Taylor | .05 | .01 |
| ☐ 450 Alan Grant | .05 | .01 |
| ☐ 451 Tony Siragusa | .05 | .01 |
| ☐ 452 Rich Baldinger | .05 | .01 |
| ☐ 453 Derrick Thomas | .25 | .08 |
| ☐ 454 Bill Jones RC | .05 | .01 |
| ☐ 455 Troy Stradford | .05 | .01 |
| ☐ 456 Barry Word | .05 | .01 |
| ☐ 457 Tim Grunhard | .05 | .01 |
| ☐ 458 Chris Martin | .05 | .01 |
| ☐ 459 Jayice Pearson RC | .05 | .01 |
| ☐ 460 Dino Hackett | .05 | .01 |
| ☐ 461 David Lutz | .05 | .01 |
| ☐ 462 Albert Lewis | .05 | .01 |
| ☐ 463 Fred Jones RC | .05 | .01 |
| ☐ 464 Winston Moss | .05 | .01 |
| ☐ 465 Sam Graddy RC | .05 | .01 |
| ☐ 466 Steve Wisniewski | .05 | .01 |
| ☐ 467 Jay Schroeder | .05 | .01 |
| ☐ 468 Ronnie Lott | .10 | .02 |
| ☐ 469 Willie Gault | .10 | .02 |
| ☐ 470 Greg Townsend | .05 | .01 |
| ☐ 471 Max Montoya | .05 | .01 |
| ☐ 472 Howie Long | .25 | .08 |
| ☐ 473 Lionel Washington | .05 | .01 |
| ☐ 474 Riki Ellison | .05 | .01 |
| ☐ 475 Tom Newberry | .05 | .01 |
| ☐ 476 Damone Johnson | .05 | .01 |
| ☐ 477 Pat Terrell | .05 | .01 |
| ☐ 478 Marcus Dupree | .05 | .01 |
| ☐ 479 Todd Lyght | .05 | .01 |
| ☐ 480 Buford McGee | .05 | .01 |
| ☐ 481 Bern Brostek | .05 | .01 |
| ☐ 482 Jim Price | .05 | .01 |
| ☐ 483 Robert Young | .05 | .01 |
| ☐ 484 Tony Zendejas | .05 | .01 |
| ☐ 485 Robert Bailey RC | .05 | .01 |
| ☐ 486 Alvin Wright | .05 | .01 |
| ☐ 487 Pat Carter | .05 | .01 |
| ☐ 488 Pete Stoyanovich | .05 | .01 |
| ☐ 489 Reggie Roby | .05 | .01 |
| ☐ 490 Harry Galbreath | .05 | .01 |
| ☐ 491 Mike McGruder RC | .05 | .01 |
| ☐ 492 J.B. Brown | .05 | .01 |
| ☐ 493 E.J. Junior | .05 | .01 |
| ☐ 494 Ferrell Edmunds | .05 | .01 |
| ☐ 495 Scott Secules | .05 | .01 |
| ☐ 496 Greg Baty RC | .05 | .01 |
| ☐ 497 Mike Iaquaniello | .05 | .01 |
| ☐ 498 Keith Sims | .05 | .01 |
| ☐ 499 John Randle | .10 | .02 |
| ☐ 500 Joey Browner | .05 | .01 |
| ☐ 501 Steve Jordan | .05 | .01 |
| ☐ 502 Darrin Nelson | .05 | .01 |
| ☐ 503 Audray McMillian | .05 | .01 |
| ☐ 504 Harry Newsome | .05 | .01 |
| ☐ 505 Hassan Jones | .05 | .01 |
| ☐ 506 Ray Berry | .05 | .01 |
| ☐ 507 Mike Merriweather | .05 | .01 |
| ☐ 508 Leo Lewis | .05 | .01 |
| ☐ 509 Tim Irwin | .05 | .01 |
| ☐ 510 Kirk Lowdermilk | .05 | .01 |
| ☐ 511 Alfred Anderson | .05 | .01 |
| ☐ 512 Michael Timpson RC | .05 | .01 |
| ☐ 513 Jerome Henderson | .05 | .01 |
| ☐ 514 Andre Tippett | .05 | .01 |
| ☐ 515 Chris Singleton | .05 | .01 |
| ☐ 516 John Stephens | .05 | .01 |
| ☐ 517 Ronnie Lippett | .05 | .01 |
| ☐ 518 Bruce Armstrong | .05 | .01 |
| ☐ 519 Marion Hobby RC | .05 | .01 |
| ☐ 520 Tim Goad | .05 | .01 |
| ☐ 521 Mickey Washington RC | .05 | .01 |
| ☐ 522 Fred Smerlas | .05 | .01 |
| ☐ 523 Wayne Martin | .05 | .01 |
| ☐ 524 Frank Warren | .05 | .01 |
| ☐ 525 Floyd Turner | .05 | .01 |
| ☐ 526 Wesley Carroll | .05 | .01 |
| ☐ 527 Gene Atkins | .05 | .01 |
| ☐ 528 Vaughan Johnson | .05 | .01 |
| ☐ 529 Hoby Brenner | .05 | .01 |
| ☐ 530 Renaldo Turnbull | .05 | .01 |
| ☐ 531 Joel Hilgenberg | .05 | .01 |
| ☐ 532 Craig Heyward | .10 | .02 |
| ☐ 533 Vince Buck | .05 | .01 |
| ☐ 534 Jim Dombrowski | .05 | .01 |
| ☐ 535 Fred McAfee RC | .05 | .01 |
| ☐ 536 Phil Simms | .10 | .02 |
| ☐ 537 Lewis Tillman | .05 | .01 |
| ☐ 538 John Elliott | .05 | .01 |
| ☐ 539 Dave Meggett | .10 | .02 |
| ☐ 540 Mark Collins | .05 | .01 |
| ☐ 541 Ottis Anderson | .10 | .02 |
| ☐ 542 Bobby Abrams | .05 | .01 |
| ☐ 543 Sean Landeta | .05 | .01 |
| ☐ 544 Brian Williams OL | .05 | .01 |
| ☐ 545 Erik Howard | .05 | .01 |
| ☐ 546 Mark Ingram | .05 | .01 |
| ☐ 547 Kanavis McGhee | .05 | .01 |
| ☐ 548 Kyle Clifton | .05 | .01 |
| ☐ 549 Marvin Washington | .05 | .01 |
| ☐ 550 Jeff Criswell | .05 | .01 |
| ☐ 551 Dave Cadigan | .05 | .01 |
| ☐ 552 Chris Burkett | .05 | .01 |
| ☐ 553 Erik McMillan | .05 | .01 |
| ☐ 554 James Hasty | .05 | .01 |
| ☐ 555 Louie Aguiar RC | .05 | .01 |
| ☐ 556 Troy Johnson RC | .05 | .01 |
| ☐ 557 Troy Taylor RC | .05 | .01 |
| ☐ 558 Pat Kelly RC | .05 | .01 |
| ☐ 559 Heath Sherman | .05 | .01 |
| ☐ 560 Roger Ruzek | .05 | .01 |
| ☐ 561 Andre Waters | .05 | .01 |
| ☐ 562 Izel Jenkins | .05 | .01 |
| ☐ 563 Keith Jackson | .10 | .02 |
| ☐ 564 Byron Evans | .05 | .01 |
| ☐ 565 Wes Hopkins | .05 | .01 |
| ☐ 566 Rich Miano | .05 | .01 |
| ☐ 567 Seth Joyner | .05 | .01 |
| ☐ 568 Thomas Sanders | .05 | .01 |
| ☐ 569 David Alexander | .05 | .01 |
| ☐ 570 Jeff Kemp | .05 | .01 |
| ☐ 571 Jock Jones RC | .05 | .01 |
| ☐ 572 Craig Patterson RC | .05 | .01 |
| ☐ 573 Robert Massey | .05 | .01 |
| ☐ 574 Bill Lewis | .05 | .01 |
| ☐ 575 Freddie Joe Nunn | .05 | .01 |
| ☐ 576 Aeneas Williams | .10 | .02 |
| ☐ 577 John Jackson WR | .05 | .01 |
| ☐ 578 Tim McDonald | .05 | .01 |
| ☐ 579 Michael Zordich RC | .05 | .01 |
| ☐ 580 Eric Hill | .05 | .01 |
| ☐ 581 Lorenzo Lynch | .05 | .01 |
| ☐ 582 Vernice Smith RC | .05 | .01 |
| ☐ 583 Greg Lloyd | .10 | .02 |
| ☐ 584 Carnell Lake | .05 | .01 |
| ☐ 585 Hardy Nickerson | .10 | .02 |
| ☐ 586 Delton Hall | .05 | .01 |
| ☐ 587 Gerald Williams | .05 | .01 |
| ☐ 588 Bryan Hinkle | .05 | .01 |
| ☐ 589 Barry Foster | .10 | .02 |
| ☐ 590 Bubby Brister | .10 | .02 |
| ☐ 591 Rick Strom RC | .05 | .01 |
| ☐ 592 David Little | .05 | .01 |
| ☐ 593 Leroy Thompson RC | .05 | .01 |
| ☐ 594 Eric Bieniemy | .05 | .01 |
| ☐ 595 Courtney Hall | .05 | .01 |
| ☐ 596 George Thornton | .05 | .01 |
| ☐ 597 Donnie Elder | .05 | .01 |
| ☐ 598 Billy Ray Smith | .05 | .01 |
| ☐ 599 Gill Byrd | .05 | .01 |
| ☐ 600 Marion Butts | .05 | .01 |
| ☐ 601 Ronnie Harmon | .05 | .01 |
| ☐ 602 Anthony Shelton | .05 | .01 |
| ☐ 603 Mark May | .05 | .01 |
| ☐ 604 Craig McEwen RC | .05 | .01 |
| ☐ 605 Steve Young | .60 | .25 |
| ☐ 606 Keith Henderson | .05 | .01 |
| ☐ 607 Pierce Holt | .05 | .01 |
| ☐ 608 Roy Foster | .05 | .01 |
| ☐ 609 Don Griffin | .05 | .01 |
| ☐ 610 Harry Sydney | .05 | .01 |
| ☐ 611 Todd Bowles | .05 | .01 |
| ☐ 612 Ted Washington | .05 | .01 |
| ☐ 613 Johnnie Jackson | .05 | .01 |
| ☐ 614 Jesse Sapolu | .05 | .01 |
| ☐ 615 Brent Jones | .10 | .02 |
| ☐ 616 Travis McNeal | .05 | .01 |
| ☐ 617 Darrick Brilz RC | .05 | .01 |
| ☐ 618 Terry Wooden | .05 | .01 |
| ☐ 619 Tommy Kane | .05 | .01 |
| ☐ 620 Nesby Glasgow | .05 | .01 |
| ☐ 621 Dwayne Harper | .05 | .01 |
| ☐ 622 Rick Tuten | .05 | .01 |
| ☐ 623 Chris Warren | .10 | .02 |
| ☐ 624 John L. Williams | .05 | .01 |
| ☐ 625 Rufus Porter | .05 | .01 |
| ☐ 626 David Daniels | .05 | .01 |
| ☐ 627 Keith McCants | .05 | .01 |
| ☐ 628 Reuben Davis | .05 | .01 |
| ☐ 629 Mark Royals | .05 | .01 |
| ☐ 630 Marty Carter RC | .05 | .01 |
| ☐ 631 Ian Beckles | .05 | .01 |
| ☐ 632 Ron Hall | .05 | .01 |
| ☐ 633 Eugene Marve | .05 | .01 |
| ☐ 634 Willie Drewrey | .05 | .01 |
| ☐ 635 Tom McHale RC | .05 | .01 |
| ☐ 636 Kevin Murphy | .05 | .01 |
| ☐ 637 Robert Hardy RC | .05 | .01 |
| ☐ 638 Ricky Sanders | .05 | .01 |
| ☐ 639 Gary Clark | .10 | .02 |
| ☐ 640 Andre Collins | .05 | .01 |
| ☐ 641 Brad Edwards | .05 | .01 |
| ☐ 642 Monte Coleman | .05 | .01 |
| ☐ 643 Clarence Vaughn RC | .05 | .01 |
| ☐ 644 Fred Stokes | .05 | .01 |
| ☐ 645 Charles Mann | .05 | .01 |
| ☐ 646 Earnest Byner | .05 | .01 |
| ☐ 647 Jim Lachey | .05 | .01 |
| ☐ 648 Jeff Bostic | .05 | .01 |
| ☐ 649 Chris Mims RC | .05 | .01 |
| ☐ 650 George Williams RC | .05 | .01 |
| ☐ 651 Ed Cunningham RC | .05 | .01 |
| ☐ 652 Tony Smith RC WR | .05 | .01 |
| ☐ 653 Will Furrer RC | .05 | .01 |
| ☐ 654 Matt Elliott RC | .05 | .01 |
| ☐ 655 Mike Mooney RC | .05 | .01 |
| ☐ 656 Eddie Blake RC | .05 | .01 |
| ☐ 657 Leon Searcy RC | .05 | .01 |
| ☐ 658 Kevin Turner RC | .05 | .01 |
| ☐ 659 Keith Hamilton RC | .10 | .02 |
| ☐ 660 Alan Haller RC | .05 | .01 |

## 1993 Pacific

| | | |
|---|---|---|
| ☐ COMPLETE SET (440) | 20.00 | 10.00 |
| ☐ 1 Emmitt Smith | 1.50 | .60 |
| ☐ 2 Troy Aikman | .75 | .30 |
| ☐ 3 Larry Brown DB | .05 | .01 |
| ☐ 4 Tony Casillas | .05 | .01 |
| ☐ 5 Thomas Everett | .05 | .01 |
| ☐ 6 Alvin Harper | .10 | .02 |
| ☐ 7 Michael Irvin | .25 | .08 |
| ☐ 8 Charles Haley | .10 | .02 |
| ☐ 9 Leon Lett RC | .10 | .02 |
| ☐ 10 Kevin Smith | .10 | .02 |
| ☐ 11 Robert Jones | .05 | .01 |
| ☐ 12 Jimmy Smith | .25 | .08 |
| ☐ 13 Derrick Gainer RC | .05 | .01 |
| ☐ 14 Lin Elliott | .05 | .01 |
| ☐ 15 William Thomas | .05 | .01 |

| | | |
|---|---|---|
| ❏ 16 Clyde Simmons | .05 | .01 |
| ❏ 17 Seth Joyner | .05 | .01 |
| ❏ 18 Randall Cunningham | .25 | .08 |
| ❏ 19 Byron Evans | .05 | .01 |
| ❏ 20 Fred Barnett | .10 | .02 |
| ❏ 21 Calvin Williams | .10 | .02 |
| ❏ 22 James Joseph | .05 | .01 |
| ❏ 23 Heath Sherman | .05 | .01 |
| ❏ 24 Siran Stacy | .05 | .01 |
| ❏ 25 Andy Harmon | .10 | .02 |
| ❏ 26 Eric Allen | .05 | .01 |
| ❏ 27 Herschel Walker | .10 | .02 |
| ❏ 28 Vai Sikahema | .05 | .01 |
| ❏ 29 Earnest Byner | .05 | .01 |
| ❏ 30 Jeff Bostic | .05 | .01 |
| ❏ 31 Monte Coleman | .05 | .01 |
| ❏ 32 Ricky Ervins | .05 | .01 |
| ❏ 33 Darrell Green | .05 | .01 |
| ❏ 34 Mark Schlereth | .05 | .01 |
| ❏ 35 Mark Rypien | .10 | .02 |
| ❏ 36 Art Monk | .10 | .02 |
| ❏ 37 Brian Mitchell | .10 | .02 |
| ❏ 38 Clip Lohmiller | .05 | .01 |
| ❏ 39 Charles Mann | .05 | .01 |
| ❏ 40 Shane Collins | .05 | .01 |
| ❏ 41 Jim Lachey | .05 | .01 |
| ❏ 42 Desmond Howard | .10 | .02 |
| ❏ 43 Rodney Hampton | .10 | .02 |
| ❏ 44 Dave Brown RC | .25 | .08 |
| ❏ 45 Mark Collins | .05 | .01 |
| ❏ 46 Jarrod Bunch | .05 | .01 |
| ❏ 47 William Roberts | .05 | .01 |
| ❏ 48 Sean Landeta | .05 | .01 |
| ❏ 49 Lawrence Taylor | .25 | .08 |
| ❏ 50 Ed McCaffrey | .25 | .08 |
| ❏ 51 Bart Oates | .05 | .01 |
| ❏ 52 Pepper Johnson | .05 | .01 |
| ❏ 53 Eric Dorsey | .05 | .01 |
| ❏ 54 Erik Howard | .05 | .01 |
| ❏ 55 Phil Simms | .10 | .02 |
| ❏ 56 Derek Brown TE | .05 | .01 |
| ❏ 57 Johnny Bailey | .05 | .01 |
| ❏ 58 Rich Camarillo | .05 | .01 |
| ❏ 59 Larry Centers RC | .25 | .08 |
| ❏ 60 Chris Chandler | .05 | .01 |
| ❏ 61 Randal Hill | .05 | .01 |
| ❏ 62 Ricky Proehl | .05 | .01 |
| ❏ 63 Freddie Joe Nunn | .05 | .01 |
| ❏ 64 Robert Massey | .05 | .01 |
| ❏ 65 Aeneas Williams | .05 | .01 |
| ❏ 66 Luis Sharpe | .05 | .01 |
| ❏ 67 Eric Swann | .10 | .02 |
| ❏ 68 Timm Rosenbach | .05 | .01 |
| ❏ 69 Anthony Edwards RC | .05 | .01 |
| ❏ 70 Greg Davis | .05 | .01 |
| ❏ 71 Terry Allen | .25 | .08 |
| ❏ 72 Anthony Carter | .10 | .02 |
| ❏ 73 Cris Carter | .25 | .08 |
| ❏ 74 Roger Craig | .10 | .02 |
| ❏ 75 Jack Del Rio | .05 | .01 |
| ❏ 76 Chris Doleman | .05 | .01 |
| ❏ 77 Rich Gannon | .25 | .08 |
| ❏ 78 Hassan Jones | .05 | .01 |
| ❏ 79 Steve Jordan | .05 | .01 |
| ❏ 80 Randall McDaniel | .10 | .02 |
| ❏ 81 Sean Salisbury | .05 | .01 |
| ❏ 82 Harry Newsome | .05 | .01 |
| ❏ 83 Carlos Jenkins | .05 | .01 |
| ❏ 84 Jake Reed | .25 | .08 |
| ❏ 85 Edgar Bennett | .25 | .08 |
| ❏ 86 Tony Bennett | .05 | .01 |
| ❏ 87 Terrell Buckley | .05 | .01 |

| | | |
|---|---|---|
| ❏ 88 Ty Detmer | .25 | .08 |
| ❏ 89 Brett Favre | 2.00 | .75 |
| ❏ 90 Chris Jacke | .05 | .01 |
| ❏ 91 Sterling Sharpe | .25 | .08 |
| ❏ 92 James Campen | .05 | .01 |
| ❏ 93 Brian Noble | .05 | .01 |
| ❏ 94 Lester Archambeau RC | .05 | .01 |
| ❏ 95 Harry Sydney | .05 | .01 |
| ❏ 96 Corey Harris | .05 | .01 |
| ❏ 97 Don Majkowski | .05 | .01 |
| ❏ 98 Ken Ruettgers | .05 | .01 |
| ❏ 99 Lomas Brown | .05 | .01 |
| ❏ 100 Jason Hanson | .05 | .01 |
| ❏ 101 Robert Porcher | .05 | .01 |
| ❏ 102 Chris Spielman | .10 | .02 |
| ❏ 103 Erik Kramer | .10 | .02 |
| ❏ 104 Tracy Scroggins | .05 | .01 |
| ❏ 105 Rodney Peete | .05 | .01 |
| ❏ 106 Barry Sanders | 1.25 | .50 |
| ❏ 107 Herman Moore | .25 | .08 |
| ❏ 108 Brett Perriman | .25 | .08 |
| ❏ 109 Mel Gray | .10 | .02 |
| ❏ 110 Dennis Gibson | .05 | .01 |
| ❏ 111 Bennie Blades | .05 | .01 |
| ❏ 112 Andre Ware | .05 | .01 |
| ❏ 113 Gary Anderson RB | .05 | .01 |
| ❏ 114 Tyji Armstrong | .05 | .01 |
| ❏ 115 Reggie Cobb | .05 | .01 |
| ❏ 116 Marty Carter | .05 | .01 |
| ❏ 117 Lawrence Dawsey | .05 | .01 |
| ❏ 118 Steve DeBerg | .05 | .01 |
| ❏ 119 Ron Hall | .05 | .01 |
| ❏ 120 Courtney Hawkins | .05 | .01 |
| ❏ 121 Broderick Thomas | .05 | .01 |
| ❏ 122 Keith McCants | .05 | .01 |
| ❏ 123 Bruce Reimers | .05 | .01 |
| ❏ 124 Darrick Brownlow | .05 | .01 |
| ❏ 125 Mark Wheeler | .05 | .01 |
| ❏ 126 Ricky Reynolds | .05 | .01 |
| ❏ 127 Neal Anderson | .05 | .01 |
| ❏ 128 Trace Armstrong | .05 | .01 |
| ❏ 129 Mark Carrier DB | .05 | .01 |
| ❏ 130 Richard Dent | .10 | .02 |
| ❏ 131 Wendell Davis | .05 | .01 |
| ❏ 132 Darren Lewis | .05 | .01 |
| ❏ 133 Tom Waddle | .05 | .01 |
| ❏ 134 Jim Harbaugh | .25 | .08 |
| ❏ 135 Steve McMichael | .10 | .02 |
| ❏ 136 William Perry | .10 | .02 |
| ❏ 137 Alonzo Spellman | .05 | .01 |
| ❏ 138 John Roper | .05 | .01 |
| ❏ 139 Peter Tom Willis | .05 | .01 |
| ❏ 140 Dante Jones | .05 | .01 |
| ❏ 141 Harris Barton | .05 | .01 |
| ❏ 142 Michael Carter | .05 | .01 |
| ❏ 143 Eric Davis | .05 | .01 |
| ❏ 144 Dana Hall | .05 | .01 |
| ❏ 145 Amp Lee | .05 | .01 |
| ❏ 146 Don Griffin | .05 | .01 |
| ❏ 147 Jerry Rice | 1.00 | .40 |
| ❏ 148 Ricky Watters | .25 | .08 |
| ❏ 149 Steve Young | .75 | .30 |
| ❏ 150 Bill Romanowski | .05 | .01 |
| ❏ 151 Klaus Wilmsmeyer | .05 | .01 |
| ❏ 152 Steve Bono | .10 | .02 |
| ❏ 153 Tom Rathman | .05 | .01 |
| ❏ 154 Odessa Turner | .05 | .01 |
| ❏ 155 Morten Andersen | .05 | .01 |
| ❏ 156 Richard Cooper | .05 | .01 |
| ❏ 157 Toi Cook | .05 | .01 |
| ❏ 158 Quinn Early | .10 | .02 |
| ❏ 159 Vaughn Dunbar | .05 | .01 |
| ❏ 160 Rickey Jackson | .05 | .01 |
| ❏ 161 Wayne Martin | .05 | .01 |
| ❏ 162 Hoby Brenner | .05 | .01 |
| ❏ 163 Joel Hilgenberg | .05 | .01 |
| ❏ 164 Mike Buck | .05 | .01 |
| ❏ 165 Torrance Small | .05 | .01 |
| ❏ 166 Eric Martin | .05 | .01 |
| ❏ 167 Vaughan Johnson | .05 | .01 |
| ❏ 168 Sam Mills | .05 | .01 |
| ❏ 169 Steve Broussard | .05 | .01 |
| ❏ 170 Darion Conner | .05 | .01 |
| ❏ 171 Drew Hill | .05 | .01 |
| ❏ 172 Chris Hinton | .05 | .01 |
| ❏ 173 Chris Miller | .10 | .02 |
| ❏ 174 Tim McKyer | .05 | .01 |
| ❏ 175 Norm Johnson | .05 | .01 |
| ❏ 176 Mike Pritchard | .10 | .02 |

| | | |
|---|---|---|
| ❏ 177 Andre Rison | .10 | .02 |
| ❏ 178 Deion Sanders | .50 | .20 |
| ❏ 179 Tony Smith RB | .05 | .01 |
| ❏ 180 Bruce Pickens | .05 | .01 |
| ❏ 181 Michael Haynes | .10 | .02 |
| ❏ 182 Jessie Tuggle | .05 | .01 |
| ❏ 183 Marc Boutte | .05 | .01 |
| ❏ 184 Don Bracken | .05 | .01 |
| ❏ 185 Bern Brostek | .05 | .01 |
| ❏ 186 Henry Ellard | .10 | .02 |
| ❏ 187 Jim Everett | .10 | .02 |
| ❏ 188 Sean Gilbert | .10 | .02 |
| ❏ 189 Cleveland Gary | .05 | .01 |
| ❏ 190 Todd Kinchen | .05 | .01 |
| ❏ 191 Pat Terrell | .05 | .01 |
| ❏ 192 Jackie Slater | .05 | .01 |
| ❏ 193 David Lang | .05 | .01 |
| ❏ 194 Flipper Anderson | .05 | .01 |
| ❏ 195 Tony Zendejas | .05 | .01 |
| ❏ 196 Roman Phifer | .05 | .01 |
| ❏ 197 Steve Christie | .05 | .01 |
| ❏ 198 Cornelius Bennett | .10 | .02 |
| ❏ 199 Phil Hansen | .05 | .01 |
| ❏ 200 Don Beebe | .05 | .01 |
| ❏ 201 Mark Kelso | .05 | .01 |
| ❏ 202 Bruce Smith | .25 | .08 |
| ❏ 203 Darryl Talley | .05 | .01 |
| ❏ 204 Andre Reed | .10 | .02 |
| ❏ 205 Mike Lodish | .05 | .01 |
| ❏ 206 Jim Kelly | .25 | .08 |
| ❏ 207 Thurman Thomas | .25 | .08 |
| ❏ 208 Kenneth Davis | .05 | .01 |
| ❏ 209 Frank Reich | .10 | .02 |
| ❏ 210 Kent Hull | .05 | .01 |
| ❏ 211 Marco Coleman | .05 | .01 |
| ❏ 212 Bryan Cox | .05 | .01 |
| ❏ 213 Jeff Cross | .05 | .01 |
| ❏ 214 Mark Higgs | .05 | .01 |
| ❏ 215 Keith Jackson | .10 | .02 |
| ❏ 216 Scott Miller | .05 | .01 |
| ❏ 217 John Offerdahl | .05 | .01 |
| ❏ 218 Dan Marino | 1.50 | .60 |
| ❏ 219 Keith Sims | .05 | .01 |
| ❏ 220 Chuck Klingbeil | .05 | .01 |
| ❏ 221 Troy Vincent | .05 | .01 |
| ❏ 222 Mike Williams RC WR | .05 | .01 |
| ❏ 223 Pete Stoyanovich | .05 | .01 |
| ❏ 224 J.B. Brown | .05 | .01 |
| ❏ 225 Ashley Ambrose | .05 | .01 |
| ❏ 226 Jason Belser RC | .05 | .01 |
| ❏ 227 Jeff George | .25 | .08 |
| ❏ 228 Quentin Coryatt | .10 | .02 |
| ❏ 229 Duane Bickett | .05 | .01 |
| ❏ 230 Steve Emtman | .05 | .01 |
| ❏ 231 Anthony Johnson | .10 | .02 |
| ❏ 232 Rohn Stark | .05 | .01 |
| ❏ 233 Jessie Hester | .05 | .01 |
| ❏ 234 Reggie Langhorne | .05 | .01 |
| ❏ 235 Clarence Verdin | .05 | .01 |
| ❏ 236 Dean Biasucci | .05 | .01 |
| ❏ 237 Jack Trudeau | .05 | .01 |
| ❏ 238 Tony Siragusa | .05 | .01 |
| ❏ 239 Chris Burkett | .05 | .01 |
| ❏ 240 Brad Baxter | .05 | .01 |
| ❏ 241 Rob Moore | .10 | .02 |
| ❏ 242 Browning Nagle | .05 | .01 |
| ❏ 243 Jim Sweeney | .05 | .01 |
| ❏ 244 Kurt Barber | .05 | .01 |
| ❏ 245 Siupeli Malamala RC | .05 | .01 |
| ❏ 246 Mike Brim | .05 | .01 |
| ❏ 247 Mo Lewis | .05 | .01 |
| ❏ 248 Johnny Mitchell | .05 | .01 |
| ❏ 249 Ken Whisenhunt RC | .30 | .10 |
| ❏ 250 James Hasty | .05 | .01 |
| ❏ 251 Kyle Clifton | .05 | .01 |
| ❏ 252 Terance Mathis | .10 | .02 |
| ❏ 253 Ray Agnew | .05 | .01 |
| ❏ 254 Eugene Chung | .05 | .01 |
| ❏ 255 Marv Cook | .05 | .01 |
| ❏ 256 Johnny Rembert | .05 | .01 |
| ❏ 257 Maurice Hurst | .05 | .01 |
| ❏ 258 Jon Vaughn | .05 | .01 |
| ❏ 259 Leonard Russell | .10 | .02 |
| ❏ 260 Pat Harlow | .05 | .01 |
| ❏ 261 Andre Tippett | .05 | .01 |
| ❏ 262 Michael Timpson | .05 | .01 |
| ❏ 263 Greg McMurtry | .05 | .01 |
| ❏ 264 Chris Singleton | .05 | .01 |
| ❏ 265 Reggie Redding RC | .05 | .01 |

| | | | | | | |
|---|---|---|---|---|---|---|
| ❑ 266 Walter Stanley | .05 | .01 | ❑ 355 Tommy Maddox | .25 | .08 | |
| ❑ 267 Gary Anderson K | .05 | .01 | ❑ 356 Karl Mecklenburg | .05 | .01 | |
| ❑ 268 Merril Hoge | .05 | .01 | ❑ 357 Shane Dronett | .05 | .01 | |
| ❑ 269 Barry Foster | .10 | .02 | ❑ 358 Kenny Walker | .05 | .01 | |
| ❑ 270 Charles Davenport | .05 | .01 | ❑ 359 Reggie Rivers RC | .05 | .01 | |
| ❑ 271 Jeff Graham | .10 | .02 | ❑ 360 Cedric Tillman RC | .05 | .01 | |
| ❑ 272 Adrian Cooper | .05 | .01 | ❑ 361 Arthur Marshall RC | .05 | .01 | |
| ❑ 273 David Little | .05 | .01 | ❑ 362 Greg Lewis | .05 | .01 | |
| ❑ 274 Neil O'Donnell | .25 | .09 | ❑ 363 Shannon Sharpe | .25 | .08 | |
| ❑ 275 Rod Woodson | .25 | .08 | ❑ 364 Doug Widell | .05 | .01 | |
| ❑ 276 Ernie Mills | .05 | .01 | ❑ 365 Todd Marinovich | .05 | .01 | |
| ❑ 277 Dwight Stone | .05 | .01 | ❑ 366 Nick Bell | .05 | .01 | |
| ❑ 278 Darren Perry | .05 | .01 | ❑ 367 Eric Dickerson | .10 | .02 | |
| ❑ 279 Dermontti Dawson | .05 | .01 | ❑ 368 Max Montoya | .05 | .01 | |
| ❑ 280 Carlton Haselrig | .05 | .01 | ❑ 369 Winston Moss | .05 | .01 | |
| ❑ 281 Pat Coleman | .05 | .01 | ❑ 370 Howie Long | .25 | .08 | |
| ❑ 282 Ernest Givins | .10 | .02 | ❑ 371 Willie Gault | .05 | .01 | |
| ❑ 283 Warren Moon | .25 | .08 | ❑ 372 Tim Brown | .25 | .08 | |
| ❑ 284 Haywood Jeffires | .10 | .02 | ❑ 373 Steve Smith | .05 | .01 | |
| ❑ 285 Cody Carlson | .05 | .01 | ❑ 374 Steve Wisniewski | .05 | .01 | |
| ❑ 286 Ray Childress | .05 | .01 | ❑ 375 Alexander Wright | .05 | .01 | |
| ❑ 287 Bruce Matthews | .05 | .01 | ❑ 376 Ethan Horton | .05 | .01 | |
| ❑ 288 Webster Slaughter | .05 | .01 | ❑ 377 Napoleon McCallum | .05 | .01 | |
| ❑ 289 Bo Orlando | .05 | .01 | ❑ 378 Terry McDaniel | .05 | .01 | |
| ❑ 290 Lorenzo White | .05 | .01 | ❑ 379 Patrick Hunter | .05 | .01 | |
| ❑ 291 Eddie Robinson | .05 | .01 | ❑ 380 Robert Blackmon | .05 | .01 | |
| ❑ 292 Bubba McDowell | .05 | .01 | ❑ 381 John Kasay | .05 | .01 | |
| ❑ 293 Bucky Richardson | .05 | .01 | ❑ 382 Cortez Kennedy | .10 | .02 | |
| ❑ 294 Sean Jones | .05 | .01 | ❑ 383 Andy Heck | .05 | .01 | |
| ❑ 295 David Brandon | .05 | .01 | ❑ 384 Bill Hitchcock RC | .05 | .01 | |
| ❑ 296 Shawn Collins | .05 | .01 | ❑ 385 Rick Mirer RC | .25 | .08 | |
| ❑ 297 Lawyer Tillman | .05 | .01 | ❑ 386 Jeff Bryant | .05 | .01 | |
| ❑ 298 Bob Dahl | .05 | .01 | ❑ 387 Eugene Robinson | .05 | .01 | |
| ❑ 299 Kevin Mack | .05 | .01 | ❑ 388 John L. Williams | .05 | .01 | |
| ❑ 300 Bernie Kosar | .10 | .02 | ❑ 389 Chris Warren | .10 | .02 | |
| ❑ 301 Tommy Vardell | .05 | .01 | ❑ 390 Rufus Porter | .05 | .01 | |
| ❑ 302 Jay Hilgenberg | .05 | .01 | ❑ 391 Joe Tofflemire RC | .05 | .01 | |
| ❑ 303 Michael Dean Perry | .10 | .02 | ❑ 392 Dan McGwire | .05 | .01 | |
| ❑ 304 Michael Jackson | .10 | .02 | ❑ 393 Boomer Esiason | .10 | .02 | |
| ❑ 305 Eric Metcalf | .10 | .02 | ❑ 394 Brad Muster | .05 | .01 | |
| ❑ 306 Rico Smith RC | .05 | .01 | ❑ 395 James Lofton | .10 | .02 | |
| ❑ 307 Stevon Moore RC | .05 | .01 | ❑ 396 Tim McGee | .05 | .01 | |
| ❑ 308 Leroy Hoard | .10 | .02 | ❑ 397 Steve Beuerlein | .10 | .02 | |
| ❑ 309 Eric Ball | .05 | .01 | ❑ 398 Gaston Green | .05 | .01 | |
| ❑ 310 Derrick Fenner | .05 | .01 | ❑ 399 Bill Brooks | .05 | .01 | |
| ❑ 311 James Francis | .05 | .01 | ❑ 400 Ronnie Lott | .10 | .02 | |
| ❑ 312 Ricardo McDonald | .05 | .01 | ❑ 401 Jay Schroeder | .05 | .01 | |
| ❑ 313 Tim Krumrie | .05 | .01 | ❑ 402 Marcus Allen | .25 | .08 | |
| ❑ 314 Carl Pickens | .10 | .02 | ❑ 403 Kevin Greene | .10 | .02 | |
| ❑ 315 David Klingler | .05 | .01 | ❑ 404 Kirk Lowdermilk | .05 | .01 | |
| ❑ 316 Donald Hollas RC | .05 | .01 | ❑ 405 Hugh Millen | .05 | .01 | |
| ❑ 317 Harold Green | .05 | .01 | ❑ 406 Pat Swilling | .05 | .01 | |
| ❑ 318 Daniel Stubbs | .05 | .01 | ❑ 407 Bobby Hebert | .05 | .01 | |
| ❑ 319 Alfred Williams | .05 | .01 | ❑ 408 Carl Banks | .05 | .01 | |
| ❑ 320 Darryl Williams | .05 | .01 | ❑ 409 Jeff Hostetler | .10 | .02 | |
| ❑ 321 Mike Arthur RC | .05 | .01 | ❑ 410 Leonard Marshall | .05 | .01 | |
| ❑ 322 Leonard Wheeler | .05 | .01 | ❑ 411 Ken O'Brien | .05 | .01 | |
| ❑ 323 Gill Byrd | .05 | .01 | ❑ 412 Joe Montana | 1.50 | .60 | |
| ❑ 324 Eric Bieniemy | .05 | .01 | ❑ 413 Reggie White | .25 | .08 | |
| ❑ 325 Marion Butts | .05 | .01 | ❑ 414 Gary Clark | .10 | .02 | |
| ❑ 326 John Carney | .05 | .01 | ❑ 415 Johnny Johnson | .05 | .01 | |
| ❑ 327 Stan Humphries | .10 | .02 | ❑ 416 Tim McDonald | .05 | .01 | |
| ❑ 328 Ronnie Harmon | .05 | .01 | ❑ 417 Pierce Holt | .05 | .01 | |
| ❑ 329 Junior Seau | .25 | .08 | ❑ 418 Gino Torretta RC | .10 | .02 | |
| ❑ 330 Nate Lewis | .05 | .01 | ❑ 419 Glyn Milburn RC | .25 | .08 | |
| ❑ 331 Harry Swayne | .05 | .01 | ❑ 420 O.J.McDuffie RC | .25 | .08 | |
| ❑ 332 Leslie O'Neal | .10 | .02 | ❑ 421 Coleman Rudolph RC | .05 | .01 | |
| ❑ 333 Eric Moten | .05 | .01 | ❑ 422 Reggie Brooks RC | .10 | .02 | |
| ❑ 334 Blaise Winter RC | .05 | .01 | ❑ 423 Garrison Hearst RC | .60 | .25 | |
| ❑ 335 Anthony Miller | .10 | .02 | ❑ 424 Leonard Renfro RC | .05 | .01 | |
| ❑ 336 Gary Plummer | .05 | .01 | ❑ 425 Kevin Williams RC WR | .25 | .08 | |
| ❑ 337 Willie Davis | .25 | .08 | ❑ 426 Demetrius DuBose RC | .05 | .01 | |
| ❑ 338 J.J. Birden | .05 | .01 | ❑ 427 Elvis Grbac RC | 1.25 | .50 | |
| ❑ 339 Tim Barnett | .05 | .01 | ❑ 428 Lincoln Kennedy RC | .05 | .01 | |
| ❑ 340 Dave Krieg | .10 | .02 | ❑ 429 Carlton Gray RC | .05 | .01 | |
| ❑ 341 Barry Word | .05 | .01 | ❑ 430 Micheal Barrow RC | .25 | .08 | |
| ❑ 342 Tracy Simien | .05 | .01 | ❑ 431 George Teague RC | .10 | .02 | |
| ❑ 343 Christian Okoye | .05 | .01 | ❑ 432 Curtis Conway RC | .40 | .15 | |
| ❑ 344 Todd McNair | .05 | .01 | ❑ 433 Natrone Means RC | .25 | .08 | |
| ❑ 345 Dan Saleaumua | .05 | .01 | ❑ 434 Jerome Bettis RC | 5.00 | 2.00 | |
| ❑ 346 Derrick Thomas | .25 | .08 | ❑ 435 Drew Bledsoe RC | 2.00 | .75 | |
| ❑ 347 Harvey Williams | .10 | .02 | ❑ 436 Robert Smith RC | 1.00 | .40 | |
| ❑ 348 Kimble Anders RC | .25 | .08 | ❑ 437 Deon Figures RC | .05 | .01 | |
| ❑ 349 Tim Grunhard | .05 | .01 | ❑ 438 Qadry Ismail RC | .25 | .08 | |
| ❑ 350 Tony Hargain RC UER | .05 | .01 | ❑ 439 Chris Slade RC | .10 | .02 | |
| ❑ 351 Simon Fletcher | .05 | .01 | ❑ 440 Dana Stubblefield RC | .05 | .01 | |
| ❑ 352 John Elway | 1.50 | .60 | | | | |
| ❑ 353 Mike Croel | .05 | .01 | | | | |
| ❑ 354 Steve Atwater | .05 | .01 | | | | |

## 1994 Pacific

| | | |
|---|---|---|
| ❑ COMPLETE SET (450) | 30.00 | 15.00 |
| ❑ 1 Troy Aikman | 1.00 | .40 |
| ❑ 2 Charles Haley | .10 | .02 |
| ❑ 3 Alvin Harper | .10 | .02 |
| ❑ 4 Michael Irvin | .25 | .08 |
| ❑ 5 Jim Jeffcoat | .05 | .01 |
| ❑ 6 Daryl Johnston | .10 | .02 |
| ❑ 7 Robert Jones | .05 | .01 |
| ❑ 8 Brock Marion RC | .25 | .08 |
| ❑ 9 Russell Maryland | .05 | .01 |
| ❑ 10 Ken Norton | .10 | .02 |
| ❑ 11 Jay Novacek | .10 | .02 |
| ❑ 12 Emmitt Smith | 1.50 | .60 |
| ❑ 13 Kevin Smith | .05 | .01 |
| ❑ 14 Tony Tolbert | .05 | .01 |
| ❑ 15 Kevin Williams WR | .10 | .02 |
| ❑ 16 Don Beebe | .05 | .01 |
| ❑ 17 Cornelius Bennett | .10 | .02 |
| ❑ 18 Bill Brooks | .05 | .01 |
| ❑ 19 Steve Christie | .05 | .01 |
| ❑ 20 Russell Copeland | .05 | .01 |
| ❑ 21 Kenneth Davis | .05 | .01 |
| ❑ 22 Kent Hull | .05 | .01 |
| ❑ 23 Jim Kelly | .25 | .08 |
| ❑ 24 Pete Metzelaars | .05 | .01 |
| ❑ 25 Andre Reed | .10 | .02 |
| ❑ 26 Frank Reich | .10 | .02 |
| ❑ 27 Bruce Smith | .25 | .08 |
| ❑ 28 Darryl Talley | .05 | .01 |
| ❑ 29 Steve Tasker | .10 | .02 |
| ❑ 30 Thurman Thomas | .25 | .08 |
| ❑ 31 Steve Bono | .10 | .02 |
| ❑ 32 Dexter Carter | .05 | .01 |
| ❑ 33 Kevin Fagan | .05 | .01 |
| ❑ 34 Dana Hall | .05 | .01 |
| ❑ 35 Brent Jones | .10 | .02 |
| ❑ 36 Amp Lee | .05 | .01 |
| ❑ 37 Marc Logan | .05 | .01 |
| ❑ 38 Tim McDonald | .05 | .01 |
| ❑ 39 Guy McIntyre | .05 | .01 |
| ❑ 40 Tom Rathman | .05 | .01 |
| ❑ 41 Jerry Rice | 1.00 | .40 |
| ❑ 42 Dana Stubblefield | .10 | .02 |
| ❑ 43 Steve Wallace | .05 | .01 |
| ❑ 44 Ricky Watters | .10 | .02 |
| ❑ 45 Steve Young | .75 | .30 |
| ❑ 46 Marcus Allen | .25 | .08 |
| ❑ 47 Kimble Anders | .10 | .02 |
| ❑ 48 Tim Barnett | .05 | .01 |
| ❑ 49 J.J. Birden | .05 | .01 |
| ❑ 50 Dale Carter | .05 | .01 |
| ❑ 51 Jonathan Hayes | .05 | .01 |
| ❑ 52 Dave Krieg | .10 | .02 |
| ❑ 53 Albert Lewis | .05 | .01 |
| ❑ 54 Nick Lowery | .05 | .01 |
| ❑ 55 Joe Montana | 2.00 | .75 |
| ❑ 56 Neil Smith | .10 | .02 |
| ❑ 57 John Stephens | .05 | .01 |
| ❑ 58 Derrick Thomas | .25 | .08 |
| ❑ 59 Harvey Williams | .10 | .02 |
| ❑ 60 Gary Brown | .05 | .01 |
| ❑ 61 Gary Brown | .05 | .01 |
| ❑ 62 Cody Carlson | .05 | .01 |
| ❑ 63 Ray Childress | .05 | .01 |
| ❑ 64 Curtis Duncan | .05 | .01 |
| ❑ 65 Ernest Givins | .10 | .02 |
| ❑ 66 Haywood Jeffires | .10 | .02 |
| ❑ 67 Wilber Marshall | .05 | .01 |
| ❑ 68 Bubba McDowell | .05 | .01 |
| ❑ 69 Warren Moon | .25 | .08 |

|  |  | | |
|---|--------|------|------|
| 70 | Mike Munchak | .10 | .02 |
| 71 | Marcus Robertson | .05 | .01 |
| 72 | Webster Slaughter | .05 | .01 |
| 73 | Gary Wellman RC | .05 | .01 |
| 74 | Lorenzo White | .05 | .01 |
| 75 | Ray Crockett | .05 | .01 |
| 76 | Jason Hanson | .05 | .01 |
| 77 | Rodney Holman | .05 | .01 |
| 78 | George Jamison | .05 | .01 |
| 79 | Erik Kramer | .10 | .02 |
| 80 | Ryan McNeil | .05 | .01 |
| 81 | Derrick Moore | .05 | .01 |
| 82 | Andre Ware | .25 | .08 |
| 83 | Rodney Peete | .05 | .01 |
| 84 | Brett Perriman | .10 | .02 |
| 85 | Barry Sanders | 1.50 | .60 |
| 86 | Chris Spielman | .10 | .02 |
| 87 | Pat Swilling | .05 | .01 |
| 88 | Vernon Turner | .05 | .01 |
| 89 | Andre Ware | .05 | .01 |
| 90 | Michael Brooks | .05 | .01 |
| 91 | Dave Brown | .10 | .02 |
| 92 | Derek Brown TE | .05 | .01 |
| 93 | Jarrod Bunch | .05 | .01 |
| 94 | Chris Calloway | .05 | .01 |
| 95 | Kent Graham | .10 | .02 |
| 96 | Rodney Hampton | .10 | .02 |
| 97 | Mark Jackson | .05 | .01 |
| 98 | Ed McCaffrey | .25 | .08 |
| 99 | Dave Meggett | .05 | .01 |
| 100 | Aaron Pierce | .05 | .01 |
| 101 | Mike Sherrard | .05 | .01 |
| 102 | Phil Simms | .10 | .02 |
| 103 | Lewis Tillman | .05 | .01 |
| 104 | Eddie Anderson | .05 | .01 |
| 105 | Patrick Bates | .05 | .01 |
| 106 | Nick Bell | .05 | .01 |
| 107 | Tim Brown | .25 | .08 |
| 108 | Willie Gault | .05 | .01 |
| 109 | Jeff Gossett | .05 | .01 |
| 110 | Ethan Horton | .05 | .01 |
| 111 | Jeff Hostetler | .10 | .02 |
| 112 | Rocket Ismail | .10 | .02 |
| 113 | Chester McGlockton | .05 | .01 |
| 114 | Anthony Smith | .05 | .01 |
| 115 | Steve Smith | .05 | .01 |
| 116 | Greg Townsend | .05 | .01 |
| 117 | Steve Wisniewski | .05 | .01 |
| 118 | Alexander Wright | .05 | .01 |
| 119 | Steve Atwater | .05 | .01 |
| 120 | Rod Bernstine | .05 | .01 |
| 121 | Mike Croel | .05 | .01 |
| 122 | Shane Dronett | .05 | .01 |
| 123 | Jason Elam | .10 | .02 |
| 124 | John Elway | 2.00 | .75 |
| 125 | Brian Habib | .05 | .01 |
| 126 | Rondell Jones | .05 | .01 |
| 127 | Tommy Maddox | .25 | .08 |
| 128 | Karl Mecklenburg | .05 | .01 |
| 129 | Glyn Milburn | .10 | .02 |
| 130 | Derek Russell | .05 | .01 |
| 131 | Shannon Sharpe | .10 | .02 |
| 132 | Dennis Smith | .05 | .01 |
| 133 | Edgar Bennett | .25 | .08 |
| 134 | Tony Bennett | .05 | .01 |
| 135 | Robert Brooks | .25 | .08 |
| 136 | Terrell Buckley | .05 | .01 |
| 137 | LeRoy Butler | .05 | .01 |
| 138 | Mark Clayton | .05 | .01 |
| 139 | Ty Detmer | .10 | .02 |
| 140 | Brett Favre | 2.00 | .75 |
| 141 | John Jurkovic RC | .05 | .01 |
| 142 | Bryce Paup | .10 | .02 |
| 143 | Sterling Sharpe | .10 | .02 |
| 144 | George Teague | .05 | .01 |
| 145 | Darrell Thompson | .05 | .01 |
| 146 | Ed West | .05 | .01 |
| 147 | Reggie White | .25 | .08 |
| 148 | Terry Allen | .10 | .02 |
| 149 | Anthony Carter | .10 | .02 |
| 150 | Cris Carter | .50 | .20 |
| 151 | Roger Craig | .10 | .02 |
| 152 | Jack Del Rio | .05 | .01 |
| 153 | Chris Doleman | .05 | .01 |
| 154 | Scottie Graham RC | .10 | .02 |
| 155 | Eric Guilford RC | .05 | .01 |
| 156 | Qadry Ismail | .25 | .08 |
| 157 | Steve Jordan | .05 | .01 |
| 158 | Randall McDaniel | .10 | .02 |
| 159 | Jim McMahon | .10 | .02 |
| 160 | Audray McMillian | .05 | .01 |
| 161 | Sean Salisbury | .05 | .01 |
| 162 | Robert Smith | .25 | .08 |
| 163 | Henry Thomas | .05 | .01 |
| 164 | Gary Anderson K | .05 | .01 |
| 165 | Deon Figures | .05 | .01 |
| 166 | Barry Foster | .05 | .01 |
| 167 | Jeff Graham | .05 | .01 |
| 168 | Kevin Greene | .10 | .02 |
| 169 | Dave Hoffman | .05 | .01 |
| 170 | Merril Hoge | .05 | .01 |
| 171 | Gary Jones | .05 | .01 |
| 172 | Greg Lloyd | .10 | .02 |
| 173 | Ernie Mills | .05 | .01 |
| 174 | Neil O'Donnell | .25 | .08 |
| 175 | Darren Perry | .05 | .01 |
| 176 | Leon Searcy | .05 | .01 |
| 177 | Leroy Thompson | .05 | .01 |
| 178 | Willie Williams RC | .05 | .01 |
| 179 | Rod Woodson | .10 | .02 |
| 180 | Keith Byars | .05 | .01 |
| 181 | Marco Coleman | .05 | .01 |
| 182 | Bryan Cox | .05 | .01 |
| 183 | Irving Fryar | .10 | .02 |
| 184 | John Grimsley | .05 | .01 |
| 185 | Mark Higgs | .05 | .01 |
| 186 | Mark Ingram | .05 | .01 |
| 187 | Keith Jackson | .05 | .01 |
| 188 | Terry Kirby | .25 | .08 |
| 189 | Dan Marino | 2.00 | .75 |
| 190 | O.J. McDuffie | .25 | .08 |
| 191 | Scott Mitchell | .10 | .02 |
| 192 | Pete Stoyanovich | .05 | .01 |
| 193 | Troy Vincent | .05 | .01 |
| 194 | Richmond Webb | .05 | .01 |
| 195 | Brad Baxter | .05 | .01 |
| 196 | Chris Burkett | .05 | .01 |
| 197 | Rob Carpenter WR | .05 | .01 |
| 198 | Boomer Esiason | .10 | .02 |
| 199 | Johnny Johnson | .05 | .01 |
| 200 | Jeff Lageman | .05 | .01 |
| 201 | Mo Lewis | .05 | .01 |
| 202 | Ronnie Lott | .10 | .02 |
| 203 | Leonard Marshall | .05 | .01 |
| 204 | Terance Mathis | .10 | .02 |
| 205 | Johnny Mitchell | .05 | .01 |
| 206 | Rob Moore | .10 | .02 |
| 207 | Anthony Prior | .05 | .01 |
| 208 | Blair Thomas | .05 | .01 |
| 209 | Brian Washington | .05 | .01 |
| 210 | Eric Bieniemy | .05 | .01 |
| 211 | Marion Butts | .05 | .01 |
| 212 | Gill Byrd | .05 | .01 |
| 213 | John Carney | .05 | .01 |
| 214 | Darren Carrington | .05 | .01 |
| 215 | John Friesz | .10 | .02 |
| 216 | Ronnie Harmon | .05 | .01 |
| 217 | Stan Humphries | .10 | .02 |
| 218 | Nate Lewis | .05 | .01 |
| 219 | Natrone Means | .25 | .08 |
| 220 | Anthony Miller | .10 | .02 |
| 221 | Chris Mims | .05 | .01 |
| 222 | Eric Moten | .05 | .01 |
| 223 | Leslie O'Neal | .05 | .01 |
| 224 | Junior Seau | .25 | .08 |
| 225 | Morten Andersen | .05 | .01 |
| 226 | Gene Atkins | .05 | .01 |
| 227 | Derek Brown RBK | .05 | .01 |
| 228 | Toi Cook | .05 | .01 |
| 229 | Vaughn Dunbar | .05 | .01 |
| 230 | Quinn Early | .10 | .02 |
| 231 | Reggie Freeman | .05 | .01 |
| 232 | Tyrone Hughes | .10 | .02 |
| 233 | Rickey Jackson | .05 | .01 |
| 234 | Eric Martin | .05 | .01 |
| 235 | Sam Mills | .05 | .01 |
| 236 | Brad Muster | .05 | .01 |
| 237 | Torrance Small | .05 | .01 |
| 238 | Irv Smith | .05 | .01 |
| 239 | Wade Wilson | .05 | .01 |
| 240 | Eric Allen | .05 | .01 |
| 241 | Victor Bailey | .05 | .01 |
| 242 | Fred Barnett | .10 | .02 |
| 243 | Mark Bavaro | .05 | .01 |
| 244 | Bubby Brister | .10 | .02 |
| 245 | Randall Cunningham | .25 | .08 |
| 246 | Antone Davis | .05 | .01 |
| 247 | Britt Hager RC | .05 | .01 |
| 248 | Vaughn Hebron | .05 | .01 |
| 249 | James Joseph | .05 | .01 |
| 250 | Seth Joyner | .05 | .01 |
| 251 | Rich Miano | .05 | .01 |
| 252 | Heath Sherman | .05 | .01 |
| 253 | Clyde Simmons | .05 | .01 |
| 254 | Herschel Walker | .10 | .02 |
| 255 | Calvin Williams | .10 | .02 |
| 256 | Jerry Ball | .05 | .01 |
| 257 | Mark Carrier WR | .10 | .02 |
| 258 | Michael Jackson | .10 | .02 |
| 259 | Mike Johnson | .05 | .01 |
| 260 | James Jones DT | .05 | .01 |
| 261 | Brian Kinchen | .05 | .01 |
| 262 | Clay Matthews | .05 | .01 |
| 263 | Eric Metcalf | .10 | .02 |
| 264 | Stevon Moore | .05 | .01 |
| 265 | Michael Dean Perry | .10 | .02 |
| 266 | Todd Philcox | .05 | .01 |
| 267 | Anthony Pleasant | .05 | .01 |
| 268 | Vinny Testaverde | .10 | .02 |
| 269 | Eric Turner | .05 | .01 |
| 270 | Tommy Vardell | .05 | .01 |
| 271 | Neal Anderson | .05 | .01 |
| 272 | Trace Armstrong | .05 | .01 |
| 273 | Mark Carrier DB | .05 | .01 |
| 274 | Bob Christian | .05 | .01 |
| 275 | Curtis Conway | .25 | .08 |
| 276 | Richard Dent | .10 | .02 |
| 277 | Robert Green | .05 | .01 |
| 278 | Jim Harbaugh | .25 | .08 |
| 279 | Craig Heyward | .10 | .02 |
| 280 | Terry Obee | .05 | .01 |
| 281 | Alonzo Spellman | .05 | .01 |
| 282 | Tom Waddle | .05 | .01 |
| 283 | Peter Tom Willis | .05 | .01 |
| 284 | Donnell Woolford | .05 | .01 |
| 285 | Tim Worley | .05 | .01 |
| 286 | Chris Zorich | .05 | .01 |
| 287 | Steve Broussard | .05 | .01 |
| 288 | Darion Conner | .05 | .01 |
| 289 | Jumpy Geathers | .05 | .01 |
| 290 | Michael Haynes | .10 | .02 |
| 291 | Bobby Hebert | .05 | .01 |
| 292 | Lincoln Kennedy | .05 | .01 |
| 293 | Chris Miller | .05 | .01 |
| 294 | David Mims RC | .05 | .01 |
| 295 | Erric Pegram | .05 | .01 |
| 296 | Mike Pritchard | .05 | .01 |
| 297 | Andre Rison | .10 | .02 |
| 298 | Deion Sanders | .50 | .20 |
| 299 | Chuck Smith | .05 | .01 |
| 300 | Tony Smith RB | .05 | .01 |
| 301 | Johnny Bailey | .05 | .01 |
| 302 | Steve Beuerlein | .10 | .02 |
| 303 | Chuck Cecil | .05 | .01 |
| 304 | Chris Chandler | .10 | .02 |
| 305 | Gary Clark | .10 | .02 |
| 306 | Rick Cunningham RC | .05 | .01 |
| 307 | Ken Harvey | .05 | .01 |
| 308 | Garrison Hearst | .25 | .08 |
| 309 | Randal Hill | .05 | .01 |
| 310 | Robert Massey | .05 | .01 |
| 311 | Ronald Moore | .05 | .01 |
| 312 | Ricky Proehl | .05 | .01 |
| 313 | Eric Swann | .10 | .02 |
| 314 | Aeneas Williams | .05 | .01 |
| 315 | Michael Bates | .05 | .01 |
| 316 | Brian Blades | .10 | .02 |
| 317 | Carlton Gray | .05 | .01 |
| 318 | Paul Green RC | .05 | .01 |
| 319 | Patrick Hunter | .05 | .01 |
| 320 | John Kasay | .05 | .01 |
| 321 | Cortez Kennedy | .10 | .02 |
| 322 | Kelvin Martin | .05 | .01 |
| 323 | Dan McGwire | .05 | .01 |
| 324 | Rick Mirer | .25 | .08 |
| 325 | Eugene Robinson | .05 | .01 |
| 326 | Rick Tuten | .05 | .01 |
| 327 | Chris Warren | .10 | .02 |
| 328 | John L. Williams | .05 | .01 |
| 329 | Reggie Cobb | .05 | .01 |
| 330 | Horace Copeland | .05 | .01 |
| 331 | Lawrence Dawsey | .05 | .01 |
| 332 | Santana Dotson | .10 | .02 |
| 333 | Courtney Hawkins | .05 | .01 |
| 334 | Ron Hall | .05 | .01 |
| 335 | Courtney Hawkins | .05 | .01 |
| 336 | Keith McCants | .05 | .01 |

| | | |
|---|---|---|
| 337 Hardy Nickerson | .10 | .02 |
| 338 Mazio Royster RC | .05 | .01 |
| 339 Broderick Thomas | .05 | .01 |
| 340 Casey Weldon RC | .25 | .08 |
| 341 Mark Wheeler | .05 | .01 |
| 342 Vince Workman | .05 | .01 |
| 343 Flipper Anderson | .05 | .01 |
| 344 Jerome Bettis | .50 | .20 |
| 345 Richard Buchanan | .05 | .01 |
| 346 Shane Conlan | .05 | .01 |
| 347 Troy Drayton | .05 | .01 |
| 348 Henry Ellard | .10 | .02 |
| 349 Jim Everett | .10 | .02 |
| 350 Cleveland Gary | .05 | .01 |
| 351 Sean Gilbert | .05 | .01 |
| 352 David Lang | .05 | .01 |
| 353 Todd Lyght | .05 | .01 |
| 354 T.J. Rubley | .05 | .01 |
| 355 Jackie Slater | .05 | .01 |
| 356 Russell White | .10 | .02 |
| 357 Bruce Armstrong | .05 | .01 |
| 358 Drew Bledsoe | .75 | .30 |
| 359 Vincent Brisby | .10 | .02 |
| 360 Vincent Brown | .05 | .01 |
| 361 Ben Coates | .10 | .02 |
| 362 Marv Cook | .05 | .01 |
| 363 Ray Crittenden RC | .05 | .01 |
| 364 Corey Croom RC | .05 | .01 |
| 365 Pat Harlow | .05 | .01 |
| 366 Dion Lambert | .05 | .01 |
| 367 Greg McMurtry | .05 | .01 |
| 368 Leonard Russell | .05 | .01 |
| 369 Scott Secules | .05 | .01 |
| 370 Chris Slade | .05 | .01 |
| 371 Michael Timpson | .05 | .01 |
| 372 Kevin Turner | .05 | .01 |
| 373 Ashley Ambrose | .05 | .01 |
| 374 Dean Biasucci | .05 | .01 |
| 375 Duane Bickett | .05 | .01 |
| 376 Quentin Coryatt | .05 | .01 |
| 377 Rodney Culver | .05 | .01 |
| 378 Sean Dawkins RC | .25 | .08 |
| 379 Jeff George | .25 | .08 |
| 380 Jeff Herrod | .05 | .01 |
| 381 Jessie Hester | .05 | .01 |
| 382 Anthony Johnson | .10 | .02 |
| 383 Reggie Langhorne | .05 | .01 |
| 384 Roosevelt Potts | .05 | .01 |
| 385 William Schultz RC | .05 | .01 |
| 386 Rohn Stark | .05 | .01 |
| 387 Clarence Verdin | .05 | .01 |
| 388 Carl Banks | .05 | .01 |
| 389 Reggie Brooks | .10 | .02 |
| 390 Earnest Byner | .05 | .01 |
| 391 Tom McGee | .05 | .01 |
| 392 Cary Conklin | .05 | .01 |
| 393 Pat Eilers RC | .05 | .01 |
| 394 Ricky Ervins | .05 | .01 |
| 395 Rich Gannon | .05 | .08 |
| 396 Darrell Green | .05 | .01 |
| 397 Desmond Howard | .10 | .02 |
| 398 Chip Lohmiller | .05 | .01 |
| 399 Sterling Palmer RC | .05 | .01 |
| 400 Mark Rypien | .05 | .01 |
| 401 Ricky Sanders | .05 | .01 |
| 402 Johnny Thomas CB | .05 | .01 |
| 403 John Copeland | .05 | .01 |
| 404 Derrick Fenner | .05 | .01 |
| 405 Alex Gordon | .05 | .01 |
| 406 Harold Green | .05 | .01 |
| 407 Lance Gunn | .05 | .01 |
| 408 David Klingler | .05 | .01 |
| 409 Ricardo McDonald | .05 | .01 |
| 410 Tim McGee | .05 | .01 |
| 411 Reggie Rembert | .05 | .01 |
| 412 Patrick Robinson | .05 | .01 |
| 413 Jay Schroeder | .05 | .01 |
| 414 Erik Wilhelm | .05 | .01 |
| 415 Alfred Williams | .05 | .01 |
| 416 Darryl Williams | .05 | .01 |
| 417 Sam Adams RC | .10 | .02 |
| 418 Mario Bates RC | .25 | .08 |
| 419 James Bostic RC | .05 | .01 |
| 420 Bucky Brooks RC | .05 | .01 |
| 421 Jeff Burris RC | .10 | .02 |
| 422 Shante Carver RC | .05 | .01 |
| 423 Jeff Cothran RC | .05 | .01 |
| 424 Lake Dawson RC | .10 | .02 |
| 425 Trent Dilfer RC | 1.25 | .50 |

| | | |
|---|---|---|
| 426 Marshall Faulk RC | 5.00 | 2.00 |
| 427 Cory Fleming RC | .05 | .01 |
| 428 William Floyd RC | .25 | .08 |
| 429 Glenn Foley RC | .25 | .08 |
| 430 Rob Fredrickson RC | .10 | .02 |
| 431 Charlie Garner RC | 1.25 | .50 |
| 432 Greg Hill RC | .25 | .08 |
| 433 Charles Johnson RC | .25 | .08 |
| 434 Calvin Jones RC | .05 | .01 |
| 435 Jimmy Klingler RC | .05 | .01 |
| 436 Antonio Langham RC | .10 | .02 |
| 437 Kevin Lee RC | .05 | .01 |
| 438 Chuck Levy RC | .05 | .01 |
| 439 Willie McGinest RC | .25 | .08 |
| 440 Jamir Miller RC | .10 | .02 |
| 441 Johnnie Morton RC | .50 | .20 |
| 442 David Palmer RC | .25 | .08 |
| 443 Errict Rhett RC | .25 | .08 |
| 444 Corey Sawyer RC | .10 | .02 |
| 445 Darnay Scott RC | .50 | .20 |
| 446 Heath Shuler RC | .25 | .08 |
| 447 Lamar Smith RC | 1.25 | .50 |
| 448 Dan Wilkinson RC | .10 | .02 |
| 449 Bernard Williams RC | .05 | .01 |
| 450 Bryant Young RC | .40 | .15 |
| P1 Sterling Sharpe Promo | .75 | .30 |

## 1995 Pacific

| | | |
|---|---|---|
| COMPLETE SET (450) | 25.00 | 10.00 |
| 1 Randy Baldwin | .10 | .02 |
| 2 Tommy Barnhardt | .10 | .02 |
| 3 Tim McKyer | .10 | .02 |
| 4 Sam Mills | .20 | .07 |
| 5 Brian O'Neal | .10 | .02 |
| 6 Frank Reich | .10 | .02 |
| 7 Jack Trudeau | .10 | .02 |
| 8 Vernon Turner | .10 | .02 |
| 9 Kerry Collins RC | 2.00 | .75 |
| 10 Shawn King | .10 | .02 |
| 11 Steve Beuerlein | .20 | .07 |
| 12 Derek Brown TE | .10 | .02 |
| 13 Reggie Clark | .10 | .02 |
| 14 Reggie Cobb | .10 | .02 |
| 15 Desmond Howard | .20 | .07 |
| 16 Jeff Lageman | .10 | .02 |
| 17 Kelvin Pritchett | .10 | .02 |
| 18 Cedric Tillman | .10 | .02 |
| 19 Tony Boselli RC | .30 | .10 |
| 20 James O. Stewart RC | 1.25 | .50 |
| 21 Eric Davis | .10 | .02 |
| 22 William Floyd | .20 | .07 |
| 23 Elvis Grbac | .30 | .10 |
| 24 Brent Jones | .20 | .07 |
| 25 Ken Norton, Jr. | .20 | .07 |
| 26 Bart Oates | .10 | .02 |
| 27 Jerry Rice | 1.00 | .40 |
| 28 Deion Sanders | .40 | .15 |
| 29 John Taylor | .20 | .07 |
| 30 Adam Walker RC | .10 | .02 |
| 31 Steve Wallace | .10 | .02 |
| 32 Ricky Watters | .20 | .07 |
| 33 Lee Woodall | .10 | .02 |
| 34 Bryant Young | .20 | .07 |
| 35 Steve Young | .75 | .30 |
| 36 J.J. Stokes RC | .30 | .10 |
| 37 Troy Aikman | 1.00 | .40 |
| 38 Larry Allen | .20 | .07 |
| 39 Chris Boniol RC | .20 | .07 |
| 40 Lincoln Coleman | .10 | .02 |
| 41 Charles Haley | .20 | .07 |
| 42 Alvin Harper | .10 | .02 |
| 43 Chad Hennings | .10 | .02 |

| | | |
|---|---|---|
| 44 Michael Irvin | .30 | .10 |
| 45 Daryl Johnston | .20 | .07 |
| 46 Leon Lett | .10 | .02 |
| 47 Nate Newton | .20 | .07 |
| 48 Jay Novacek | .20 | .07 |
| 49 Emmitt Smith | 1.50 | .60 |
| 50 James Washington | .10 | .02 |
| 51 Kevin Williams | .20 | .07 |
| 52 Sherman Williams RC | .10 | .02 |
| 53 Barry Foster | .20 | .07 |
| 54 Eric Green | .10 | .02 |
| 55 Kevin Greene | .20 | .07 |
| 56 Andre Hastings | .20 | .07 |
| 57 Charles Johnson | .20 | .07 |
| 58 Greg Lloyd | .20 | .07 |
| 59 Ernie Mills | .10 | .02 |
| 60 Byron Bam Morris | .20 | .07 |
| 61 Neil O'Donnell | .20 | .07 |
| 62 Darren Perry | .10 | .02 |
| 63 Yancey Thigpen RC | .20 | .07 |
| 64 Mike Tomczak | .10 | .02 |
| 65 John L. Williams | .10 | .02 |
| 66 Rod Woodson | .20 | .07 |
| 67 Mark Bruener RC | .20 | .07 |
| 68 Kordell Stewart RC | 1.50 | .60 |
| 69 Jeff Brohm RC | .10 | .02 |
| 70 Andre Coleman | .10 | .02 |
| 71 Reuben Davis | .10 | .02 |
| 72 Dennis Gibson | .10 | .02 |
| 73 Darrien Gordon | .10 | .02 |
| 74 Stan Humphries | .20 | .07 |
| 75 Shawn Jefferson | .10 | .02 |
| 76 Tony Martin | .20 | .07 |
| 77 Natrone Means | .20 | .07 |
| 78 Shannon Mitchell RC | .10 | .02 |
| 79 Leslie O'Neal | .20 | .07 |
| 80 Alfred Pupunu | .10 | .02 |
| 81 Stanley Richard | .10 | .02 |
| 82 Junior Seau | .30 | .10 |
| 83 Mark Seay | .10 | .02 |
| 84 Derrick Alexander WR | .30 | .10 |
| 85 Carl Banks | .10 | .02 |
| 86 Isaac Booth | .10 | .02 |
| 87 Rob Burnett | .10 | .02 |
| 88 Earnest Byner | .10 | .02 |
| 89 Steve Everitt | .10 | .02 |
| 90 Leroy Hoard | .10 | .02 |
| 91 Pepper Johnson | .10 | .02 |
| 92 Antonio Langham | .10 | .02 |
| 93 Eric Metcalf | .20 | .07 |
| 94 Anthony Pleasant | .10 | .02 |
| 95 Frank Stams | .10 | .02 |
| 96 Vinny Testaverde | .20 | .07 |
| 97 Eric Turner | .20 | .07 |
| 98 Mike Miller RC | .10 | .02 |
| 99 Craig Powell RC | .10 | .02 |
| 100 Gene Atkins | .10 | .02 |
| 101 Aubrey Beavers | .10 | .02 |
| 102 Tim Bowens | .20 | .07 |
| 103 Keith Byars | .10 | .02 |
| 104 Bryan Cox | .10 | .02 |
| 105 Aaron Craver | .10 | .02 |
| 106 Jeff Cross | .10 | .02 |
| 107 Irving Fryar | .20 | .07 |
| 108 Dan Marino | 2.00 | .75 |
| 109 O.J. McDuffie | .30 | .10 |
| 110 Bernie Parmalee | .20 | .07 |
| 111 James Saxon | .10 | .02 |
| 112 Keith Sims | .10 | .02 |
| 113 Irving Spikes | .20 | .07 |
| 114 Pete Mitchell RC | .20 | .07 |
| 115 Terry Allen | .20 | .07 |
| 116 Cris Carter | .30 | .10 |
| 117 Adrian Cooper | .10 | .02 |
| 118 Bernard Dalney | .10 | .02 |
| 119 Jack Del Rio | .20 | .07 |
| 120 Vencie Glenn | .10 | .02 |
| 121 Qadry Ismail | .20 | .07 |
| 122 Carlos Jenkins | .10 | .02 |
| 123 Andrew Jordan | .10 | .02 |
| 124 Ed McDaniel | .10 | .02 |
| 125 Warren Moon | .30 | .10 |
| 126 David Palmer | .20 | .07 |
| 127 John Randle | .20 | .07 |
| 128 Jake Reed | .20 | .07 |
| 129 Derrick Alexander DE RC | .10 | .02 |
| 130 Chad May RC | .10 | .02 |
| 131 Korey Stringer RC | .20 | .07 |
| 132 Bruce Armstrong | .10 | .02 |

|  |  | | |
|---|---|---|---|
| 133 | Drew Bledsoe | .60 | .25 |
| 134 | Vincent Brisby | .10 | .02 |
| 135 | Troy Brown | .30 | .10 |
| 136 | Vincent Brown | .10 | .02 |
| 137 | Marion Butts | .10 | .02 |
| 138 | Ben Coates | .20 | .07 |
| 139 | Ray Crittenden | .10 | .02 |
| 140 | Maurice Hurst | .10 | .02 |
| 141 | Aaron Jones | .10 | .02 |
| 142 | Willie McGinest | .20 | .07 |
| 143 | Marty Moore RC | .30 | .10 |
| 144 | Mike Pitts | .10 | .02 |
| 145 | Leroy Thompson | .10 | .02 |
| 146 | Michael Timpson | .10 | .02 |
| 147 | Bennie Blades | .10 | .02 |
| 148 | Jocelyn Borgella | .10 | .02 |
| 149 | Anthony Carter | .20 | .07 |
| 150 | Willie Clay | .10 | .02 |
| 151 | Mel Gray | .10 | .02 |
| 152 | Mike Johnson | .10 | .02 |
| 153 | Dave Krieg | .10 | .02 |
| 154 | Robert Massey | .10 | .02 |
| 155 | Scott Mitchell | .20 | .07 |
| 156 | Herman Moore | .30 | .10 |
| 157 | Johnnie Morton | .20 | .07 |
| 158 | Barry Sanders | 1.50 | .60 |
| 159 | Chris Spielman | .20 | .07 |
| 160 | Broderick Thomas | .10 | .02 |
| 161 | Cory Schlesinger RC | .20 | .07 |
| 162 | Marcus Allen | .30 | .10 |
| 163 | Donnell Bennett | .20 | .07 |
| 164 | J.J. Birden | .10 | .02 |
| 165 | Matt Blundin RC | .10 | .02 |
| 166 | Steve Bono | .20 | .07 |
| 167 | Dale Carter | .20 | .07 |
| 168 | Lake Lawson | .20 | .07 |
| 169 | Ron Dickerson | .10 | .02 |
| 170 | Lin Elliott | .10 | .02 |
| 171 | Jaime Fields | .10 | .02 |
| 172 | Greg Hill | .20 | .07 |
| 173 | Danan Hughes | .10 | .02 |
| 174 | Neil Smith | .20 | .07 |
| 175 | Steve Stenstrom RC | .10 | .02 |
| 176 | Edgar Bennett | .20 | .07 |
| 177 | Robert Brooks | .20 | .07 |
| 178 | Mark Brunell | .60 | .25 |
| 179 | Doug Evans RC | .30 | .10 |
| 180 | Brett Favre | 2.00 | .75 |
| 181 | Corey Harris | .10 | .02 |
| 182 | LeShon Johnson | .20 | .07 |
| 183 | Sean Jones | .10 | .02 |
| 184 | Lenny McGill RC | .10 | .02 |
| 185 | Terry Mickens | .10 | .02 |
| 186 | Sterling Sharpe | .20 | .07 |
| 187 | Joe Sims | .10 | .02 |
| 188 | Darrell Thompson | .10 | .02 |
| 189 | Reggie White | .30 | .10 |
| 190 | Craig Newsome RC | .10 | .02 |
| 191 | Tim Brown | .30 | .10 |
| 192 | Vince Evans | .10 | .02 |
| 193 | Rob Fredrickson | .10 | .02 |
| 194 | Andrew Glover RC | .10 | .02 |
| 195 | Jeff Hostetler | .20 | .07 |
| 196 | Rocket Ismail | .20 | .07 |
| 197 | Jeff Jaeger | .10 | .02 |
| 198 | James Jett | .20 | .07 |
| 199 | Chester McGlockton | .20 | .07 |
| 200 | Don Mosebar | .10 | .02 |
| 201 | Tom Rathman | .10 | .02 |
| 202 | Harvey Williams | .10 | .02 |
| 203 | Steve Wisniewski | .10 | .02 |
| 204 | Alexander Wright | .10 | .02 |
| 205 | Napoleon Kaufman RC | 1.25 | .50 |
| 206 | Trace Armstrong | .10 | .02 |
| 207 | Curtis Conway | .30 | .10 |
| 208 | Raymont Harris | .10 | .02 |
| 209 | Erik Kramer | .10 | .02 |
| 210 | Nate Lewis | .10 | .02 |
| 211 | Shane Matthews RC | .30 | .10 |
| 212 | John Thierry | .10 | .02 |
| 213 | Lewis Tillman | .10 | .02 |
| 214 | Tom Waddle | .10 | .02 |
| 215 | Steve Walsh | .10 | .02 |
| 216 | James Williams T RC | .10 | .02 |
| 217 | Donnell Woolford | .10 | .02 |
| 218 | Chris Zorich | .10 | .02 |
| 219 | Rashaan Salaam RC | .20 | .07 |
| 220 | John Booty | .10 | .02 |
| 221 | Michael Brooks | .10 | .02 |
| 222 | Dave Brown | .20 | .07 |
| 223 | Chris Calloway | .10 | .02 |
| 224 | Gary Downs | .10 | .02 |
| 225 | Kent Graham | .20 | .07 |
| 226 | Keith Hamilton | .10 | .02 |
| 227 | Rodney Hampton | .20 | .07 |
| 228 | Brian Kozlowski | .10 | .02 |
| 229 | Thomas Lewis | .20 | .07 |
| 230 | Dave Meggett | .10 | .02 |
| 231 | Aaron Pierce | .10 | .02 |
| 232 | Mike Sherrard | .10 | .02 |
| 233 | Phillippi Sparks | .10 | .02 |
| 234 | Tyrone Wheatley RC | 1.25 | .50 |
| 235 | Trev Alberts | .10 | .02 |
| 236 | Aaron Bailey RC | .10 | .02 |
| 237 | Jason Belser | .10 | .02 |
| 238 | Tony Bennett | .10 | .02 |
| 239 | Kerry Cash | .10 | .02 |
| 240 | Marshall Faulk | 1.25 | .50 |
| 241 | Stephen Grant | .10 | .02 |
| 242 | Jeff Herrod | .10 | .02 |
| 243 | Ronald Humphrey | .10 | .02 |
| 244 | Kirk Lowdermilk | .10 | .02 |
| 245 | Don Majkowski | .10 | .02 |
| 246 | Tony McCoy | .10 | .02 |
| 247 | Floyd Turner | .10 | .02 |
| 248 | Lamont Warren | .10 | .02 |
| 249 | Zack Crockett RC | .20 | .07 |
| 250 | Michael Bankston | .10 | .02 |
| 251 | Larry Centers | .20 | .07 |
| 252 | Gary Clark | .10 | .02 |
| 253 | Ed Cunningham | .10 | .02 |
| 254 | Garrison Hearst | .30 | .10 |
| 255 | Eric Hill | .10 | .02 |
| 256 | Terry Irving | .10 | .02 |
| 257 | Lorenzo Lynch | .10 | .02 |
| 258 | Jamir Miller | .10 | .02 |
| 259 | Ronald Moore | .10 | .02 |
| 260 | Terry Samuels | .10 | .02 |
| 261 | Jay Schroeder | .10 | .02 |
| 262 | Eric Swann | .20 | .07 |
| 263 | Aeneas Williams | .10 | .02 |
| 264 | Frank Sanders RC | .30 | .10 |
| 265 | Morten Andersen | .10 | .02 |
| 266 | Mario Bates | .20 | .07 |
| 267 | Derek Brown RBK | .10 | .02 |
| 268 | Darion Conner | .10 | .02 |
| 269 | Quinn Early | .10 | .02 |
| 270 | Jim Everett | .10 | .02 |
| 271 | Michael Haynes | .20 | .07 |
| 272 | Wayne Martin | .10 | .02 |
| 273 | Derrell Mitchell RC | .10 | .02 |
| 274 | Lorenzo Neal | .10 | .02 |
| 275 | Jimmy Spencer | .10 | .02 |
| 276 | Winfred Tubbs | .10 | .02 |
| 277 | Renaldo Turnbull | .10 | .02 |
| 278 | Jeff Uhlenhake | .10 | .02 |
| 279 | Steve Atwater | .10 | .02 |
| 280 | Keith Burns RC | .10 | .02 |
| 281 | Butler By'Not'e RC | .20 | .07 |
| 282 | Jeff Campbell | .10 | .02 |
| 283 | Derrick Clark RC | .10 | .02 |
| 284 | Shane Dronett | .10 | .02 |
| 285 | Jason Elam | .20 | .07 |
| 286 | John Elway | 2.00 | .75 |
| 287 | Jerry Evans | .10 | .02 |
| 288 | Karl Mecklenburg | .10 | .02 |
| 289 | Glyn Milburn | .10 | .02 |
| 290 | Anthony Miller | .20 | .07 |
| 291 | Tom Rouen | .10 | .02 |
| 292 | Leonard Russell | .10 | .02 |
| 293 | Shannon Sharpe | .20 | .07 |
| 294 | Steve Russ RC | .10 | .02 |
| 295 | Mel Agee | .10 | .02 |
| 296 | Lester Archambeau | .10 | .02 |
| 297 | Bert Emanuel | .30 | .10 |
| 298 | Jeff George | .20 | .07 |
| 299 | Craig Heyward | .20 | .07 |
| 300 | Bobby Hebert | .10 | .02 |
| 301 | D.J. Johnson | .10 | .02 |
| 302 | Mike Kenn | .10 | .02 |
| 303 | Terance Mathis | .20 | .07 |
| 304 | Clay Matthews | .10 | .02 |
| 305 | Eric Pegram | .20 | .07 |
| 306 | Andre Rison | .20 | .07 |
| 307 | Chuck Smith | .10 | .02 |
| 308 | Jessie Tuggle | .10 | .02 |
| 309 | Lorenzo Styles RC | .10 | .02 |
| 310 | Cornelius Bennett | .20 | .07 |
| 311 | Bill Brooks | .10 | .02 |
| 312 | Jeff Burris | .10 | .02 |
| 313 | Carwell Gardner | .10 | .02 |
| 314 | Kent Hull | .10 | .02 |
| 315 | Yonel Jourdain | .10 | .02 |
| 316 | Jim Kelly | .30 | .10 |
| 317 | Vince Marrow | .10 | .02 |
| 318 | Pete Metzelaars | .10 | .02 |
| 319 | Andre Reed | .20 | .07 |
| 320 | Kurt Schulz RC | .10 | .02 |
| 321 | Bruce Smith | .30 | .10 |
| 322 | Darryl Talley | .10 | .02 |
| 323 | Matt Darby | .10 | .02 |
| 324 | Justin Armour RC | .10 | .02 |
| 325 | Todd Collins RC | 1.25 | .50 |
| 326 | David Alexander DE | .10 | .02 |
| 327 | Eric Allen | .10 | .02 |
| 328 | Fred Barnett | .20 | .07 |
| 329 | Randall Cunningham | .30 | .10 |
| 330 | William Fuller | .10 | .02 |
| 331 | Charlie Garner | .30 | .10 |
| 332 | Vaughn Hebron | .10 | .02 |
| 333 | James Joseph | .10 | .02 |
| 334 | Bill Romanowski | .10 | .02 |
| 335 | Ken Rose | .10 | .02 |
| 336 | Jeff Snyder | .10 | .02 |
| 337 | William Thomas | .10 | .02 |
| 338 | Herschel Walker | .20 | .07 |
| 339 | Calvin Williams | .10 | .02 |
| 340 | Dave Barr RC | .10 | .02 |
| 341 | Chidi Ahanotu | .10 | .02 |
| 342 | Barney Bussey | .10 | .02 |
| 343 | Horace Copeland | .10 | .02 |
| 344 | Trent Dilfer | .30 | .10 |
| 345 | Craig Erickson | .10 | .02 |
| 346 | Paul Gruber | .10 | .02 |
| 347 | Courtney Hawkins | .10 | .02 |
| 348 | Lonnie Marts | .10 | .02 |
| 349 | Martin Mayhew | .10 | .02 |
| 350 | Hardy Nickerson | .10 | .02 |
| 351 | Errict Rhett | .20 | .07 |
| 352 | Lamar Thomas | .10 | .02 |
| 353 | Charles Wilson | .10 | .02 |
| 354 | Vince Workman | .10 | .02 |
| 355 | Derrick Brooks RC | 1.50 | .60 |
| 356 | Warren Sapp RC | 1.50 | .60 |
| 357 | Sam Adams | .10 | .02 |
| 358 | Michael Bates | .10 | .02 |
| 359 | Brian Blades | .20 | .07 |
| 360 | Carlton Gray | .10 | .02 |
| 361 | Bill Hitchcock | .10 | .02 |
| 362 | Cortez Kennedy | .20 | .07 |
| 363 | Rick Mirer | .20 | .07 |
| 364 | Eugene Robinson | .10 | .02 |
| 365 | Michael Sinclair | .10 | .02 |
| 366 | Steve Smith | .10 | .02 |
| 367 | Bob Spitulski | .10 | .02 |
| 368 | Rick Tuten | .10 | .02 |
| 369 | Chris Warren | .20 | .07 |
| 370 | Terrence Warren | .10 | .02 |
| 371 | Christian Fauria RC | .20 | .07 |
| 372 | Joey Galloway RC | 1.50 | .60 |
| 373 | Boomer Esiason | .20 | .07 |
| 374 | Aaron Glenn | .10 | .02 |
| 375 | Victor Green RC | .10 | .02 |
| 376 | Johnny Johnson | .10 | .02 |
| 377 | Mo Lewis | .10 | .02 |
| 378 | Ronnie Lott | .20 | .07 |
| 379 | Nick Lowery | .10 | .02 |
| 380 | Johnny Mitchell | .10 | .02 |
| 381 | Rob Moore | .20 | .07 |
| 382 | Adrian Murrell | .20 | .07 |
| 383 | Anthony Prior | .10 | .02 |
| 384 | Brian Washington | .10 | .02 |
| 385 | Matt Willig RC | .10 | .02 |
| 386 | Kyle Brady RC | .30 | .10 |
| 387 | Flipper Anderson | .10 | .02 |
| 388 | Johnny Bailey | .10 | .02 |
| 389 | Jerome Bettis | .30 | .10 |
| 390 | Isaac Bruce | .50 | .20 |
| 391 | Shane Conlan | .10 | .02 |
| 392 | Troy Drayton | .10 | .02 |
| 393 | D'Marco Farr | .10 | .02 |
| 394 | Jessie Hester | .10 | .02 |
| 395 | Todd Kinchen | .10 | .02 |
| 396 | Ron Middleton | .10 | .02 |
| 397 | Chris Miller | .10 | .02 |
| 398 | Marquez Pope | .10 | .02 |
| 399 | Robert Young | .10 | .02 |

| | | |
|---|---|---|
| 400 Tony Zendejas | .10 | .02 |
| 401 Kevin Carter RC | .30 | .10 |
| 402 Reggie Brooks | .20 | .07 |
| 403 Tom Carter | .10 | .02 |
| 404 Andre Collins | .10 | .02 |
| 405 Pat Eilers | .10 | .02 |
| 406 Henry Ellard | .20 | .07 |
| 407 Ricky Ervins | .10 | .02 |
| 408 Gus Frerotte | .20 | .07 |
| 409 Ken Harvey | .10 | .02 |
| 410 Jim Lachey | .10 | .02 |
| 411 Brian Mitchell | .10 | .02 |
| 412 Reggie Roby | .10 | .02 |
| 413 Heath Shuler | .20 | .07 |
| 414 Tyrone Stowe | .10 | .02 |
| 415 Tydus Winans | .10 | .02 |
| 416 Cory Raymer RC | .10 | .02 |
| 417 Michael Westbrook RC | .30 | .10 |
| 418 Jeff Blake RC | .75 | .30 |
| 419 Steve Broussard | .10 | .02 |
| 420 Dave Cadigan | .10 | .02 |
| 421 Jeff Cothran | .10 | .02 |
| 422 Derrick Fenner | .10 | .02 |
| 423 James Francis | .10 | .02 |
| 424 Lee Johnson | .10 | .02 |
| 425 Louis Oliver | .10 | .02 |
| 426 Carl Pickens | .20 | .07 |
| 427 Jeff Query | .10 | .02 |
| 428 Corey Sawyer | .10 | .02 |
| 429 Damay Scott | .20 | .07 |
| 430 Dan Wilkinson | .10 | .02 |
| 431 Alfred Williams | .10 | .02 |
| 432 Ki-Jana Carter RC | .30 | .10 |
| 433 David Dunn RC | .10 | .02 |
| 434 John Walsh RC | .10 | .02 |
| 435 Gary Brown | .10 | .02 |
| 436 Pat Carter | .10 | .02 |
| 437 Ray Childress | .10 | .02 |
| 438 Ernest Givins | .10 | .02 |
| 439 Haywood Jeffires | .10 | .02 |
| 440 Lamar Lathon | .10 | .02 |
| 441 Bruce Matthews | .10 | .02 |
| 442 Marcus Robertson | .10 | .02 |
| 443 Eddie Robinson | .10 | .02 |
| 444 Malcolm Seabron RC | .10 | .02 |
| 445 Webster Slaughter | .10 | .02 |
| 446 Al Smith | .10 | .02 |
| 447 Billy Joe Tolliver | .10 | .02 |
| 448 Lorenzo White | .10 | .02 |
| 449 Steve McNair RC | 3.00 | 1.25 |
| 450 Rodney Thomas RC | .20 | .07 |
| P1 Natrone Means Promo | 1.00 | .40 |
| P1J Natrone Means Promo | 1.00 | .40 |

## 1996 Pacific

| | | |
|---|---|---|
| COMPLETE SET (450) | 40.00 | 20.00 |
| 1 Jeff Feagles | .10 | .02 |
| 2 Rob Moore | .20 | .07 |
| 3 Clyde Simmons | .10 | .02 |
| 4 Mike Buck | .10 | .02 |
| 5 Aeneas Williams | .10 | .02 |
| 6 Simeon Rice RC | 1.00 | .40 |
| 7 Garrison Hearst | .20 | .07 |
| 8 Eric Swann | .10 | .02 |
| 9 Dave Krieg | .10 | .02 |
| 10 Leeland McElroy RC | .20 | .07 |
| 11 Oscar McBride | .10 | .02 |
| 12 Frank Sanders | .20 | .07 |
| 13 Larry Centers | .10 | .02 |
| 14 Seth Joyner | .10 | .02 |
| 15 Stevie Anderson | .10 | .02 |
| 16 Craig Heyward | .10 | .02 |

| | | |
|---|---|---|
| 17 Devin Bush | .10 | .02 |
| 18 Eric Metcalf | .10 | .02 |
| 19 Jeff George | .20 | .07 |
| 20 Richard Huntley RC | .20 | .07 |
| 21 Jamal Anderson RC | .50 | .20 |
| 22 Bert Emanuel | .20 | .07 |
| 23 Terance Mathis | .10 | .02 |
| 24 Roman Fortin | .10 | .02 |
| 25 Jessie Tuggle | .10 | .02 |
| 26 Morten Andersen | .10 | .02 |
| 27 Chris Doleman | .10 | .02 |
| 28 D.J. Johnson | .10 | .02 |
| 29 Kevin Ross | .10 | .02 |
| 30 Michael Jackson | .10 | .02 |
| 31 Eric Zeier | .10 | .02 |
| 32 Jonathan Ogden RC | .40 | .15 |
| 33 Eric Turner | .10 | .02 |
| 34 Andre Rison | .20 | .07 |
| 35 Lorenzo White | .10 | .02 |
| 36 Earnest Byner | .10 | .02 |
| 37 Derrick Alexander WR | .20 | .07 |
| 38 Brian Kinchen | .10 | .02 |
| 39 Anthony Pleasant | .10 | .02 |
| 40 Vinny Testaverde | .20 | .07 |
| 41 Pepper Johnson | .10 | .02 |
| 42 Frank Hartley | .10 | .02 |
| 43 Craig Powell | .10 | .02 |
| 44 Leroy Hoard | .10 | .02 |
| 45 Kent Hull | .10 | .02 |
| 46 Bryce Paup | .20 | .07 |
| 47 Andre Reed | .20 | .07 |
| 48 Darick Holmes | .10 | .02 |
| 49 Russell Copeland | .10 | .02 |
| 50 Jerry Ostroski | .10 | .02 |
| 51 Chris Green | .10 | .02 |
| 52 Eric Moulds RC | 1.25 | .50 |
| 53 Justin Armour | .10 | .02 |
| 54 Jim Kelly | .40 | .15 |
| 55 Cornelius Bennett | .10 | .02 |
| 56 Steve Tasker | .10 | .02 |
| 57 Thurman Thomas | .40 | .15 |
| 58 Bruce Smith | .20 | .07 |
| 59 Todd Collins | .10 | .02 |
| 60 Shawn King | .10 | .02 |
| 61 Don Beebe | .10 | .02 |
| 62 John Kasay | .10 | .02 |
| 63 Tim McKyer | .10 | .02 |
| 64 Darion Conner | .10 | .02 |
| 65 Pete Metzelaars | .10 | .02 |
| 66 Derrick Moore | .10 | .02 |
| 67 Blake Brockermeyer | .10 | .02 |
| 68 Tim Biakabutuka RC | .40 | .15 |
| 69 Sam Mills | .10 | .02 |
| 70 Vince Workman | .10 | .02 |
| 71 Kerry Collins | .40 | .15 |
| 72 Carlton Bailey | .10 | .02 |
| 73 Mark Carrier WR | .10 | .02 |
| 74 Donnell Woolford | .10 | .02 |
| 75 Walt Harris RC | .10 | .02 |
| 76 John Thierry | .10 | .02 |
| 77 Al Fontenot RC | .10 | .02 |
| 78 Lewis Tillman | .10 | .02 |
| 79 Curtis Conway | .40 | .15 |
| 80 Chris Zorich | .10 | .02 |
| 81 Mark Carrier DB | .10 | .02 |
| 82 Bobby Engram RC | .40 | .15 |
| 83 Alonzo Spellman | .10 | .02 |
| 84 Rashaan Salaam | .20 | .07 |
| 85 Michael Timpson | .10 | .02 |
| 86 Nate Lewis | .10 | .02 |
| 87 James Williams T | .10 | .02 |
| 88 Jeff Graham | .10 | .02 |
| 89 Erik Kramer | .10 | .02 |
| 90 Willie Anderson | .10 | .02 |
| 91 Tony McGee | .10 | .02 |
| 92 Marco Battaglia | .10 | .02 |
| 93 Dan Wilkinson | .10 | .02 |
| 94 John Walsh | .10 | .02 |
| 95 Eric Bieniemy | .10 | .02 |
| 96 Ricardo McDonald | .10 | .02 |
| 97 Carl Pickens | .20 | .07 |
| 98 Kevin Sargent | .10 | .02 |
| 99 David Dunn | .10 | .02 |
| 100 Jeff Blake | .40 | .15 |
| 101 Harold Green | .10 | .02 |
| 102 James Francis | .10 | .02 |
| 103 John Copeland | .10 | .02 |
| 104 Damay Scott | .20 | .07 |
| 105 Darren Woodson | .20 | .07 |

| | | |
|---|---|---|
| 106 Jay Novacek | .10 | .02 |
| 107 Charles Haley | .20 | .07 |
| 108 Mark Tuinei | .10 | .02 |
| 109 Michael Irvin | .40 | .15 |
| 110 Troy Aikman | 1.00 | .40 |
| 111 Chris Boniol | .10 | .02 |
| 112 Sherman Williams | .10 | .02 |
| 113 Deion Sanders | .60 | .25 |
| 114 Emmitt Smith | 1.50 | .60 |
| 115 Eric Bjornson | .10 | .02 |
| 116 Nate Newton | .10 | .02 |
| 117 Larry Allen | .10 | .02 |
| 118 Kevin Williams | .10 | .02 |
| 119 Leon Lett | .10 | .02 |
| 120 John Mobley | .10 | .02 |
| 121 Anthony Miller | .20 | .07 |
| 122 Brian Habib | .10 | .02 |
| 123 Aaron Craver | .10 | .02 |
| 124 Glyn Milburn | .10 | .02 |
| 125 Shannon Sharpe | .20 | .07 |
| 126 Steve Atwater | .10 | .02 |
| 127 Jason Elam | .20 | .07 |
| 128 John Elway | 2.00 | .75 |
| 129 Reggie Rivers | .10 | .02 |
| 130 Mike Pritchard | .10 | .02 |
| 131 Vance Johnson | .10 | .02 |
| 132 Terrell Davis | .75 | .30 |
| 133 Tyrone Braxton | .10 | .02 |
| 134 Ed McCaffrey | .20 | .07 |
| 135 Brett Perriman | .10 | .02 |
| 136 Chris Spielman | .10 | .02 |
| 137 Luther Elliss | .10 | .02 |
| 138 Johnnie Morton | .20 | .07 |
| 139 Zefross Moss | .10 | .02 |
| 140 Barry Sanders | 1.50 | .60 |
| 141 Lomas Brown | .10 | .02 |
| 142 Cory Schlesinger | .10 | .02 |
| 143 Jason Hanson | .10 | .02 |
| 144 Kevin Johnson | .10 | .02 |
| 145 Ron Rivers RC | .20 | .07 |
| 146 Aubrey Matthews | .10 | .02 |
| 147 Reggie Brown LB RC | .40 | .15 |
| 148 Herman Moore | .20 | .07 |
| 149 Scott Mitchell | .20 | .07 |
| 150 Brett Favre | 2.00 | .75 |
| 151 Sean Jones | .10 | .02 |
| 152 LeRoy Butler | .10 | .02 |
| 153 Mark Chmura | .20 | .07 |
| 154 Derrick Mayes RC | .40 | .15 |
| 155 Mark Ingram | .10 | .02 |
| 156 Antonio Freeman | .40 | .15 |
| 157 Chris Darkins RC | .10 | .02 |
| 158 Robert Brooks | .40 | .15 |
| 159 William Henderson | .40 | .15 |
| 160 George Koonce | .10 | .02 |
| 161 Craig Newsome | .10 | .02 |
| 162 Darius Holland | .10 | .02 |
| 163 George Teague | .10 | .02 |
| 164 Edgar Bennett | .20 | .07 |
| 165 Reggie White | .40 | .15 |
| 166 Micheal Barrow | .10 | .02 |
| 167 Mel Gray | .10 | .02 |
| 168 Anthony Dorsett | .10 | .02 |
| 169 Roderick Lewis | .10 | .02 |
| 170 Henry Ford | .10 | .02 |
| 171 Mark Stepnoski | .10 | .02 |
| 172 Chris Sanders | .20 | .07 |
| 173 Anthony Cook | .10 | .02 |
| 174 Eddie Robinson | .10 | .02 |
| 175 Steve McNair | .75 | .30 |
| 176 Haywood Jeffires | .10 | .02 |
| 177 Eddie George RC | 1.25 | .50 |
| 178 Marion Butts | .10 | .02 |
| 179 Malcolm Seabron | .10 | .02 |
| 180 Rodney Thomas | .10 | .02 |
| 181 Ken Dilger | .20 | .07 |
| 182 Zack Crockett | .10 | .02 |
| 183 Tony Bennett | .10 | .02 |
| 184 Quentin Coryatt | .10 | .02 |
| 185 Marshall Faulk | .50 | .20 |
| 186 Sean Dawkins | .10 | .02 |
| 187 Jim Harbaugh | .20 | .07 |
| 188 Eugene Daniel | .10 | .02 |
| 189 Roosevelt Potts | .10 | .02 |
| 190 Lamont Warren | .10 | .02 |
| 191 Will Wolford | .10 | .02 |
| 192 Tony Siragusa | .10 | .02 |
| 193 Aaron Bailey | .10 | .02 |
| 194 Trev Alberts | .10 | .02 |

| | | |
|---|---|---|
| ❑ 195 Kevin Hardy | .20 | .07 |
| ❑ 196 Greg Spann | .10 | .02 |
| ❑ 197 Steve Beuerlein | .20 | .07 |
| ❑ 198 Steve Taneyhill | .10 | .02 |
| ❑ 199 Vaughn Dunbar | .10 | .02 |
| ❑ 200 Mark Brunell | .60 | .25 |
| ❑ 201 Bernard Carter | .10 | .02 |
| ❑ 202 James O. Stewart | .20 | .07 |
| ❑ 203 Tony Boselli | .10 | .02 |
| ❑ 204 Chris Doering | .10 | .02 |
| ❑ 205 Willie Jackson | .20 | .07 |
| ❑ 206 Tony Brackens RC | .40 | .15 |
| ❑ 207 Ernest Givins | .10 | .02 |
| ❑ 208 Le'Shai Maston | .10 | .02 |
| ❑ 209 Pete Mitchell | .20 | .07 |
| ❑ 210 Desmond Howard | .20 | .07 |
| ❑ 211 Vinnie Clark | .10 | .02 |
| ❑ 212 Jeff Lageman | .10 | .02 |
| ❑ 213 Derrick Walker | .10 | .02 |
| ❑ 214 Dan Saleaumua | .10 | .02 |
| ❑ 215 Derrick Thomas | .40 | .15 |
| ❑ 216 Neil Smith | .20 | .07 |
| ❑ 217 Willie Davis | .10 | .02 |
| ❑ 218 Mark Collins | .10 | .02 |
| ❑ 219 Lake Dawson | .10 | .02 |
| ❑ 220 Greg Hill | .20 | .07 |
| ❑ 221 Anthony Davis | .10 | .02 |
| ❑ 222 Kimble Anders | .20 | .07 |
| ❑ 223 Webster Slaughter | .10 | .02 |
| ❑ 224 Tamarick Vanover | .20 | .07 |
| ❑ 225 Marcus Allen | .40 | .15 |
| ❑ 226 Steve Bono | .10 | .02 |
| ❑ 227 Will Shields | .10 | .02 |
| ❑ 228 Karim Abdul-Jabbar RC | .40 | .15 |
| ❑ 229 Tim Bowens | .10 | .02 |
| ❑ 230 Keith Sims | .10 | .02 |
| ❑ 231 Terry Kirby | .20 | .07 |
| ❑ 232 Gene Atkins | .10 | .02 |
| ❑ 233 Dan Marino | 2.00 | .75 |
| ❑ 234 Richmond Webb | .10 | .02 |
| ❑ 235 Gary Clark | .10 | .02 |
| ❑ 236 O.J. McDuffie | .20 | .07 |
| ❑ 237 Marco Coleman | .10 | .02 |
| ❑ 238 Bernie Parmalee | .10 | .02 |
| ❑ 239 Randal Hill | .10 | .02 |
| ❑ 240 Bryan Cox | .10 | .02 |
| ❑ 241 Irving Fryar | .20 | .07 |
| ❑ 242 Derrick Alexander DE | .10 | .02 |
| ❑ 243 Qadry Ismail | .20 | .07 |
| ❑ 244 Warren Moon | .20 | .07 |
| ❑ 245 Cris Carter | .40 | .15 |
| ❑ 246 Chad May | .10 | .02 |
| ❑ 247 Robert Smith | .20 | .07 |
| ❑ 248 Fuad Reveiz | .10 | .02 |
| ❑ 249 Orlando Thomas | .10 | .02 |
| ❑ 250 Chris Hinton | .10 | .02 |
| ❑ 251 Jack Del Rio | .10 | .02 |
| ❑ 252 Moe Williams RB RC | 1.00 | .40 |
| ❑ 253 Roy Barker | .10 | .02 |
| ❑ 254 Jake Reed | .20 | .07 |
| ❑ 255 Adrian Cooper | .10 | .02 |
| ❑ 256 Curtis Martin | .75 | .30 |
| ❑ 257 Ben Coates | .20 | .07 |
| ❑ 258 Drew Bledsoe | .60 | .25 |
| ❑ 259 Maurice Hurst | .10 | .02 |
| ❑ 260 Troy Brown | .40 | .15 |
| ❑ 261 Bruce Armstrong | .10 | .02 |
| ❑ 262 Myron Guyton | .10 | .02 |
| ❑ 263 Dave Meggett | .10 | .02 |
| ❑ 264 Terry Glenn RC | 1.00 | .40 |
| ❑ 265 Chris Slade | .10 | .02 |
| ❑ 266 Vincent Brisby | .10 | .02 |
| ❑ 267 Willie McGinest | .10 | .02 |
| ❑ 268 Vincent Brown | .10 | .02 |
| ❑ 269 Will Moore | .10 | .02 |
| ❑ 270 Jay Barker | .10 | .02 |
| ❑ 271 Ray Zellars | .10 | .02 |
| ❑ 272 Derek Brown RBK | .20 | .07 |
| ❑ 273 William Roaf | .10 | .02 |
| ❑ 274 Quinn Early | .10 | .02 |
| ❑ 275 Michael Haynes | .10 | .02 |
| ❑ 276 Rufus Porter | .10 | .02 |
| ❑ 277 Renaldo Turnbull | .10 | .02 |
| ❑ 278 Wayne Martin | .10 | .02 |
| ❑ 279 Tyrone Hughes | .10 | .02 |
| ❑ 280 Irv Smith | .10 | .02 |
| ❑ 281 Eric Allen | .10 | .02 |
| ❑ 282 Mark Fields | .10 | .02 |
| ❑ 283 Mario Bates | .20 | .07 |

| | | |
|---|---|---|
| ❑ 284 Jim Everett | .10 | .02 |
| ❑ 285 Vince Buck | .10 | .02 |
| ❑ 286 Alex Molden RC | .10 | .02 |
| ❑ 287 Tyrone Wheatley | .20 | .07 |
| ❑ 288 Chris Calloway | .10 | .02 |
| ❑ 289 Jessie Armstead | .10 | .02 |
| ❑ 290 Arthur Marshall | .10 | .02 |
| ❑ 291 Aaron Pierce | .10 | .02 |
| ❑ 292 Dave Brown | .10 | .02 |
| ❑ 293 Rodney Hampton | .20 | .07 |
| ❑ 294 Jumbo Elliott | .10 | .02 |
| ❑ 295 Mike Sherrard | .10 | .02 |
| ❑ 296 Howard Cross | .10 | .02 |
| ❑ 297 Michael Brooks | .10 | .02 |
| ❑ 298 Herschel Walker | .20 | .07 |
| ❑ 299 Danny Kanell RC | .40 | .15 |
| ❑ 300 Keith Elias | .10 | .02 |
| ❑ 301 Bobby Houston | .10 | .02 |
| ❑ 302 Dexter Carter | .10 | .02 |
| ❑ 303 Tony Casillas | .10 | .02 |
| ❑ 304 Kyle Brady | .10 | .02 |
| ❑ 305 Glenn Foley | .20 | .07 |
| ❑ 306 Ronald Moore | .10 | .02 |
| ❑ 307 Ryan Yarborough | .10 | .02 |
| ❑ 308 Aaron Glenn | .10 | .02 |
| ❑ 309 Adrian Murrell | .20 | .07 |
| ❑ 310 Boomer Esiason | .20 | .07 |
| ❑ 311 Kyle Clifton | .10 | .02 |
| ❑ 312 Wayne Chrebet | .60 | .25 |
| ❑ 313 Erik Howard | .10 | .02 |
| ❑ 314 Keyshawn Johnson RC | 1.00 | .40 |
| ❑ 315 Marvin Washington | .10 | .02 |
| ❑ 316 Johnny Mitchell | .10 | .02 |
| ❑ 317 Alex Van Dyke RC | .20 | .07 |
| ❑ 318 Billy Joe Hobert | .10 | .02 |
| ❑ 319 Andrew Glover | .10 | .02 |
| ❑ 320 Vince Evans | .10 | .02 |
| ❑ 321 Chester McGlockton | .10 | .02 |
| ❑ 322 Pat Swilling | .10 | .02 |
| ❑ 323 Rocket Ismail | .10 | .02 |
| ❑ 324 Eddie Anderson | .10 | .02 |
| ❑ 325 Rickey Dudley RC | .40 | .15 |
| ❑ 326 Steve Wisniewski | .10 | .02 |
| ❑ 327 Harvey Williams | .10 | .02 |
| ❑ 328 Napoleon Kaufman | .40 | .15 |
| ❑ 329 Tim Brown | .40 | .15 |
| ❑ 330 Jeff Hostetler | .10 | .02 |
| ❑ 331 Anthony Smith | .10 | .02 |
| ❑ 332 Terry McDaniel | .10 | .02 |
| ❑ 333 Charlie Garner | .20 | .07 |
| ❑ 334 Ricky Watters | .20 | .07 |
| ❑ 335 Brian Dawkins RC | 1.25 | .50 |
| ❑ 336 Randall Cunningham | .40 | .15 |
| ❑ 337 Gary Anderson | .10 | .02 |
| ❑ 338 Calvin Williams | .10 | .02 |
| ❑ 339 Chris T. Jones | .20 | .07 |
| ❑ 340 Bobby Hoying RC | .40 | .15 |
| ❑ 341 William Fuller | .10 | .02 |
| ❑ 342 William Thomas | .10 | .02 |
| ❑ 343 Mike Mamula | .10 | .02 |
| ❑ 344 Fred Barnett | .10 | .02 |
| ❑ 345 Rodney Peete | .10 | .02 |
| ❑ 346 Mark McMillian | .10 | .02 |
| ❑ 347 Bobby Taylor | .10 | .02 |
| ❑ 348 Yancey Thigpen | .20 | .07 |
| ❑ 349 Neil O'Donnell | .20 | .07 |
| ❑ 350 Rod Woodson | .20 | .07 |
| ❑ 351 Kordell Stewart | .40 | .15 |
| ❑ 352 Dermontti Dawson | .10 | .02 |
| ❑ 353 Norm Johnson | .10 | .02 |
| ❑ 354 Ernie Mills | .10 | .02 |
| ❑ 355 Byron Bam Morris | .10 | .02 |
| ❑ 356 Mark Bruener | .10 | .02 |
| ❑ 357 Kevin Greene | .20 | .07 |
| ❑ 358 Greg Lloyd | .10 | .02 |
| ❑ 359 Andre Hastings | .10 | .02 |
| ❑ 360 Erric Pegram | .10 | .02 |
| ❑ 361 Carnell Lake | .10 | .02 |
| ❑ 362 Dwayne Harper | .10 | .02 |
| ❑ 363 Ronnie Harmon | .10 | .02 |
| ❑ 364 Leslie O'Neal | .10 | .02 |
| ❑ 365 John Carney | .10 | .02 |
| ❑ 366 Stan Humphries | .20 | .07 |
| ❑ 367 Brian Roche RC | .10 | .02 |
| ❑ 368 Terrell Fletcher | .10 | .02 |
| ❑ 369 Shaun Gayle | .10 | .02 |
| ❑ 370 Alfred Pupunu | .10 | .02 |
| ❑ 371 Shawn Jefferson | .10 | .02 |
| ❑ 372 Junior Seau | .40 | .15 |

| | | |
|---|---|---|
| ❑ 373 Mark Seay | .10 | .02 |
| ❑ 374 Aaron Hayden | .10 | .02 |
| ❑ 375 Tony Martin | .20 | .07 |
| ❑ 376 Steve Young | .75 | .30 |
| ❑ 377 J.J. Stokes | .40 | .15 |
| ❑ 378 Jerry Rice | 1.00 | .40 |
| ❑ 379 Derek Loville | .10 | .02 |
| ❑ 380 Lee Woodall | .10 | .02 |
| ❑ 381 Terrell Owens RC | 2.50 | 1.00 |
| ❑ 382 Elvis Grbac | .20 | .07 |
| ❑ 383 Ricky Ervins | .10 | .02 |
| ❑ 384 Eric Davis | .10 | .02 |
| ❑ 385 Dana Stubblefield | .10 | .02 |
| ❑ 386 Gary Plummer | .10 | .02 |
| ❑ 387 Tim McDonald | .10 | .02 |
| ❑ 388 William Floyd | .20 | .07 |
| ❑ 389 Ken Norton Jr. | .10 | .02 |
| ❑ 390 Merton Hanks | .10 | .02 |
| ❑ 391 Bart Oates | .10 | .02 |
| ❑ 392 Brent Jones | .10 | .02 |
| ❑ 393 Steve Broussard | .10 | .02 |
| ❑ 394 Robert Blackmon | .10 | .02 |
| ❑ 395 Rick Tuten | .10 | .02 |
| ❑ 396 Pete Kendall | .10 | .02 |
| ❑ 397 John Friesz | .10 | .02 |
| ❑ 398 Terry Wooden | .10 | .02 |
| ❑ 399 Rick Mirer | .20 | .07 |
| ❑ 400 Chris Warren | .20 | .07 |
| ❑ 401 Joey Galloway | .40 | .15 |
| ❑ 402 Howard Ballard | .10 | .02 |
| ❑ 403 Jason Kyle | .10 | .02 |
| ❑ 404 Kevin Mawae | .10 | .02 |
| ❑ 405 Mack Strong | .40 | .15 |
| ❑ 406 Reggie Brown RBK RC | .10 | .02 |
| ❑ 407 Cortez Kennedy | .10 | .02 |
| ❑ 408 Sean Gilbert | .10 | .02 |
| ❑ 409 J.T. Thomas | .10 | .02 |
| ❑ 410 Shane Conlan | .10 | .02 |
| ❑ 411 Johnny Bailey | .10 | .02 |
| ❑ 412 Mark Rypien | .10 | .02 |
| ❑ 413 Leonard Russell | .10 | .02 |
| ❑ 414 Troy Drayton | .10 | .02 |
| ❑ 415 Jerome Bettis | .40 | .15 |
| ❑ 416 Jessie Hester | .10 | .02 |
| ❑ 417 Isaac Bruce | .40 | .15 |
| ❑ 418 Roman Phifer | .10 | .02 |
| ❑ 419 Todd Kinchen | .10 | .02 |
| ❑ 420 Alexander Wright | .10 | .02 |
| ❑ 421 Marcus Jones RC | .10 | .02 |
| ❑ 422 Horace Copeland | .10 | .02 |
| ❑ 423 Eric Curry | .10 | .02 |
| ❑ 424 Courtney Hawkins | .10 | .02 |
| ❑ 425 Alvin Harper | .10 | .02 |
| ❑ 426 Derrick Brooks | .40 | .15 |
| ❑ 427 Errict Rhett | .20 | .07 |
| ❑ 428 Trent Dilfer | .40 | .15 |
| ❑ 429 Hardy Nickerson | .10 | .02 |
| ❑ 430 Brad Culpepper | .10 | .02 |
| ❑ 431 Warren Sapp | .10 | .02 |
| ❑ 432 Reggie Roby | .10 | .02 |
| ❑ 433 Santana Dotson | .10 | .02 |
| ❑ 434 Jerry Ellison | .10 | .02 |
| ❑ 435 Lawrence Dawsey | .10 | .02 |
| ❑ 436 Heath Shuler | .20 | .07 |
| ❑ 437 Stanley Richard | .20 | .07 |
| ❑ 438 Rod Stephens | .10 | .02 |
| ❑ 439 Stephen Davis RC | 1.50 | .60 |
| ❑ 440 Terry Allen | .20 | .07 |
| ❑ 441 Michael Westbrook | .40 | .15 |
| ❑ 442 Ken Harvey | .10 | .02 |
| ❑ 443 Coleman Bell | .10 | .02 |
| ❑ 444 Marvcus Patton | .10 | .02 |
| ❑ 445 Gus Frerotte | .20 | .07 |
| ❑ 446 Leslie Shepherd | .10 | .02 |
| ❑ 447 Tom Carter | .10 | .02 |
| ❑ 448 Brian Mitchell | .10 | .02 |
| ❑ 449 Darrell Green | .10 | .02 |
| ❑ 450A Tony Woods | .10 | .02 |
| ❑ 450B Chris Warren Promo | .50 | .20 |
| ❑ CW1 Chris Warren Promo | 1.00 | .40 |

## 1997 Pacific

| | | |
|---|---|---|
| ❑ COMPLETE SET (450) | 30.00 | 15.00 |
| ❑ 1 Lomas Brown | .20 | .07 |
| ❑ 2 Pat Carter | .20 | .07 |
| ❑ 3 Larry Centers | .30 | .10 |
| ❑ 4 Matt Darby | .20 | .07 |
| ❑ 5 Marcus Dowdell | .20 | .07 |
| ❑ 6 Aaron Graham | .20 | .07 |

|  |  | | |
|---|---|---|---|
| ❏ 7 | Kent Graham | .20 | .07 |
| ❏ 8 | LeShon Johnson | .20 | .07 |
| ❏ 9 | Seth Joyner | .20 | .07 |
| ❏ 10 | Leeland McElroy | .20 | .07 |
| ❏ 11 | Rob Moore | .30 | .10 |
| ❏ 12 | Simeon Rice | .30 | .10 |
| ❏ 13 | Eric Swann | .20 | .07 |
| ❏ 14 | Aeneas Williams | .20 | .07 |
| ❏ 15 | Morten Andersen | .20 | .07 |
| ❏ 16 | Jamal Anderson | .50 | .20 |
| ❏ 17 | Lester Archambeau | .20 | .07 |
| ❏ 18 | Cornelius Bennett | .20 | .07 |
| ❏ 19 | J.J. Birden | .20 | .07 |
| ❏ 20 | Antone Davis | .20 | .07 |
| ❏ 21 | Bert Emanuel | .30 | .10 |
| ❏ 22 | Travis Hall RC | .20 | .07 |
| ❏ 23 | Bobby Hebert | .20 | .07 |
| ❏ 24 | Craig Heyward | .20 | .07 |
| ❏ 25 | Terance Mathis | .30 | .10 |
| ❏ 26 | Tim McKyer | .20 | .07 |
| ❏ 27 | Eric Metcalf | .30 | .10 |
| ❏ 28 | Jessie Tuggle | .20 | .07 |
| ❏ 29 | Derrick Alexander WR | .30 | .10 |
| ❏ 30 | Orlando Brown | .20 | .07 |
| ❏ 31 | Rob Burnett | .20 | .07 |
| ❏ 32 | Earnest Byner | .20 | .07 |
| ❏ 33 | Ray Ethridge | .20 | .07 |
| ❏ 34 | Steve Everitt | .20 | .07 |
| ❏ 35 | Carwell Gardner | .20 | .07 |
| ❏ 36 | Michael Jackson | .30 | .10 |
| ❏ 37 | Jermaine Lewis | .50 | .20 |
| ❏ 38 | Stevon Moore | .20 | .07 |
| ❏ 39 | Byron Bam Morris | .20 | .07 |
| ❏ 40 | Jonathan Ogden | .20 | .07 |
| ❏ 41 | Vinny Testaverde | .30 | .10 |
| ❏ 42 | Todd Collins | .20 | .07 |
| ❏ 43 | Russell Copeland | .20 | .07 |
| ❏ 44 | Quinn Early | .20 | .07 |
| ❏ 45 | John Fina | .20 | .07 |
| ❏ 46 | Phil Hansen | .20 | .07 |
| ❏ 47 | Eric Moulds | .50 | .20 |
| ❏ 48 | Bryce Paup | .20 | .07 |
| ❏ 49 | Andre Reed | .30 | .10 |
| ❏ 50 | Kurt Schulz | .20 | .07 |
| ❏ 51 | Bruce Smith | .30 | .10 |
| ❏ 52 | Chris Spielman | .20 | .07 |
| ❏ 53 | Steve Tasker | .20 | .07 |
| ❏ 54 | Thurman Thomas | .50 | .20 |
| ❏ 55 | Carlton Bailey | .20 | .07 |
| ❏ 56 | Michael Bates | .20 | .07 |
| ❏ 57 | Blake Brockermeyer | .20 | .07 |
| ❏ 58 | Mark Carrier WR | .20 | .07 |
| ❏ 59 | Kerry Collins | .50 | .20 |
| ❏ 60 | Eric Davis | .20 | .07 |
| ❏ 61 | Kevin Greene | .30 | .10 |
| ❏ 62 | Rocket Ismail | .20 | .07 |
| ❏ 63 | Anthony Johnson | .20 | .07 |
| ❏ 64 | Shawn King | .20 | .07 |
| ❏ 65 | Greg Kragen | .20 | .07 |
| ❏ 66 | Sam Mills | .20 | .07 |
| ❏ 67 | Tyrone Poole | .20 | .07 |
| ❏ 68 | Wesley Walls | .30 | .10 |
| ❏ 69 | Mark Carrier DB | .20 | .07 |
| ❏ 70 | Curtis Conway | .30 | .10 |
| ❏ 71 | Bobby Engram | .30 | .10 |
| ❏ 72 | Jim Flanigan | .20 | .07 |
| ❏ 73 | Al Fontenot | .20 | .07 |
| ❏ 74 | Raymont Harris | .20 | .07 |
| ❏ 75 | Walt Harris | .20 | .07 |
| ❏ 76 | Andy Heck | .20 | .07 |
| ❏ 77 | Dave Krieg | .20 | .07 |
| ❏ 78 | Rashaan Salaam | .20 | .07 |
| ❏ 79 | Vinson Smith | .20 | .07 |
| ❏ 80 | Alonzo Spellman | .20 | .07 |
| ❏ 81 | Michael Timpson | .20 | .07 |
| ❏ 82 | James Williams | .20 | .07 |
| ❏ 83 | Ashley Ambrose | .20 | .07 |
| ❏ 84 | Eric Bieniemy | .20 | .07 |
| ❏ 85 | Jeff Blake | .30 | .10 |
| ❏ 86 | Ki-Jana Carter | .20 | .07 |
| ❏ 87 | John Copeland | .20 | .07 |
| ❏ 88 | David Dunn | .20 | .07 |
| ❏ 89 | Jeff Mill | .20 | .07 |
| ❏ 90 | Ricardo McDonald | .20 | .07 |
| ❏ 91 | Tony McGee | .20 | .07 |
| ❏ 92 | Greg Myers | .20 | .07 |
| ❏ 93 | Carl Pickens | .30 | .10 |
| ❏ 94 | Corey Sawyer | .20 | .07 |
| ❏ 95 | Darnay Scott | .30 | .10 |
| ❏ 96 | Dan Wilkinson | .20 | .07 |
| ❏ 97 | Troy Aikman | 1.00 | .40 |
| ❏ 98 | Larry Allen | .20 | .07 |
| ❏ 99 | Eric Bjornson | .20 | .07 |
| ❏ 100 | Ray Donaldson | .20 | .07 |
| ❏ 101 | Michael Irvin | .50 | .20 |
| ❏ 102 | Daryl Johnston | .30 | .10 |
| ❏ 103 | Nate Newton | .20 | .07 |
| ❏ 104 | Deion Sanders | .50 | .20 |
| ❏ 105 | Jim Schwantz RC | .20 | .07 |
| ❏ 106 | Emmitt Smith | 1.50 | .60 |
| ❏ 107 | Broderick Thomas | .20 | .07 |
| ❏ 108 | Tony Tolbert | .20 | .07 |
| ❏ 109 | Erik Williams | .20 | .07 |
| ❏ 110 | Sherman Williams | .20 | .07 |
| ❏ 111 | Darren Woodson | .20 | .07 |
| ❏ 112 | Steve Atwater | .20 | .07 |
| ❏ 113 | Aaron Craver | .20 | .07 |
| ❏ 114 | Ray Crockett | .20 | .07 |
| ❏ 115 | Terrell Davis | .60 | .25 |
| ❏ 116 | Jason Elam | .30 | .10 |
| ❏ 117 | John Elway | 2.00 | .75 |
| ❏ 118 | Todd Kinchen | .20 | .07 |
| ❏ 119 | Ed McCaffrey | .30 | .10 |
| ❏ 120 | Anthony Miller | .20 | .07 |
| ❏ 121 | John Mobley | .20 | .07 |
| ❏ 122 | Michael Dean Perry | .20 | .07 |
| ❏ 123 | Reggie Rivers | .20 | .07 |
| ❏ 124 | Shannon Sharpe | .30 | .10 |
| ❏ 125 | Alfred Williams | .20 | .07 |
| ❏ 126 | Reggie Brown LB | .30 | .10 |
| ❏ 127 | Luther Elliss | .20 | .07 |
| ❏ 128 | Kevin Glover | .20 | .07 |
| ❏ 129 | Jason Hanson | .20 | .07 |
| ❏ 130 | Pepper Johnson | .20 | .07 |
| ❏ 131 | Glyn Milburn | .20 | .07 |
| ❏ 132 | Scott Mitchell | .30 | .10 |
| ❏ 133 | Herman Moore | .30 | .10 |
| ❏ 134 | Johnnie Morton | .30 | .10 |
| ❏ 135 | Brett Perriman | .20 | .07 |
| ❏ 136 | Robert Porcher | .20 | .07 |
| ❏ 137 | Ron Rivers | .20 | .07 |
| ❏ 138 | Barry Sanders | 1.50 | .60 |
| ❏ 139 | Henry Thomas | .20 | .07 |
| ❏ 140 | Don Beebe | .20 | .07 |
| ❏ 141 | Edgar Bennett | .30 | .10 |
| ❏ 142 | Robert Brooks | .30 | .10 |
| ❏ 143 | LeRoy Butler | .20 | .07 |
| ❏ 144 | Mark Chmura | .30 | .10 |
| ❏ 145 | Brett Favre | 2.00 | .75 |
| ❏ 146 | Antonio Freeman | .50 | .20 |
| ❏ 147 | Chris Jacke | .20 | .07 |
| ❏ 148 | Travis Jervey | .30 | .10 |
| ❏ 149 | Sean Jones | .20 | .07 |
| ❏ 150 | Dorsey Levens | .50 | .20 |
| ❏ 151 | John Michels | .20 | .07 |
| ❏ 152 | Craig Newsome | .20 | .07 |
| ❏ 153 | Eugene Robinson | .20 | .07 |
| ❏ 154 | Reggie White | .50 | .20 |
| ❏ 155 | Micheal Barrow | .20 | .07 |
| ❏ 156 | Blaine Bishop | .20 | .07 |
| ❏ 157 | Chris Chandler | .30 | .10 |
| ❏ 158 | Anthony Cook | .20 | .07 |
| ❏ 159 | Malcolm Floyd | .20 | .07 |
| ❏ 160 | Eddie George | .50 | .20 |
| ❏ 161 | Roderick Lewis | .20 | .07 |
| ❏ 162 | Steve McNair | .60 | .25 |
| ❏ 163 | John Henry Mills RC | .20 | .07 |
| ❏ 164 | Derek Russell | .20 | .07 |
| ❏ 165 | Chris Sanders | .20 | .07 |
| ❏ 166 | Mark Stepnoski | .20 | .07 |
| ❏ 167 | Frank Wycheck | .20 | .07 |
| ❏ 168 | Robert Young | .20 | .07 |
| ❏ 169 | Trev Alberts | .20 | .07 |
| ❏ 170 | Aaron Bailey | .20 | .07 |
| ❏ 171 | Tony Bennett | .20 | .07 |
| ❏ 172 | Ray Buchanan | .20 | .07 |
| ❏ 173 | Quentin Coryatt | .20 | .07 |
| ❏ 174 | Eugene Daniel | .20 | .07 |
| ❏ 175 | Sean Dawkins | .20 | .07 |
| ❏ 176 | Ken Dilger | .20 | .07 |
| ❏ 177 | Marshall Faulk | .60 | .25 |
| ❏ 178 | Jim Harbaugh | .30 | .10 |
| ❏ 179 | Marvin Harrison | .50 | .20 |
| ❏ 180 | Paul Justin | .20 | .07 |
| ❏ 181 | Lamont Warren | .20 | .07 |
| ❏ 182 | Bernard Whittington | .20 | .07 |
| ❏ 183 | Tony Boselli | .20 | .07 |
| ❏ 184 | Tony Brackens | .20 | .07 |
| ❏ 185 | Mark Brunell | .60 | .25 |
| ❏ 186 | Brian DeMarco | .20 | .07 |
| ❏ 187 | Rich Griffith | .20 | .07 |
| ❏ 188 | Kevin Hardy | .20 | .07 |
| ❏ 189 | Willie Jackson | .20 | .07 |
| ❏ 190 | Jeff Lageman | .20 | .07 |
| ❏ 191 | Keenan McCardell | .30 | .10 |
| ❏ 192 | Natrone Means | .30 | .10 |
| ❏ 193 | Pete Mitchell | .20 | .07 |
| ❏ 194 | Joel Smeenge | .20 | .07 |
| ❏ 195 | Jimmy Smith | .30 | .10 |
| ❏ 196 | James O.Stewart | .30 | .10 |
| ❏ 197 | Marcus Allen | .50 | .20 |
| ❏ 198 | John Alt | .20 | .07 |
| ❏ 199 | Kimble Anders | .30 | .10 |
| ❏ 200 | Steve Bono | .30 | .10 |
| ❏ 201 | Vaughn Booker | .20 | .07 |
| ❏ 202 | Dale Carter | .20 | .07 |
| ❏ 203 | Mark Collins | .20 | .07 |
| ❏ 204 | Greg Hill | .20 | .07 |
| ❏ 205 | Joe Horn | .50 | .20 |
| ❏ 206 | Dan Saleaumua | .20 | .07 |
| ❏ 207 | Will Shields | .20 | .07 |
| ❏ 208 | Neil Smith | .30 | .10 |
| ❏ 209 | Derrick Thomas | .50 | .20 |
| ❏ 210 | Tamarick Vanover | .30 | .10 |
| ❏ 211 | Karim Abdul-Jabbar | .50 | .20 |
| ❏ 212 | Fred Barnett | .20 | .07 |
| ❏ 213 | Tim Bowens | .20 | .07 |
| ❏ 214 | Kirby Dar Dar RC | .30 | .10 |
| ❏ 215 | Troy Drayton | .20 | .07 |
| ❏ 216 | Craig Erickson | .20 | .07 |
| ❏ 217 | Daryl Gardener | .20 | .07 |
| ❏ 218 | Randal Hill | .20 | .07 |
| ❏ 219 | Dan Marino | 2.00 | .75 |
| ❏ 220 | O.J. McDuffie | .30 | .10 |
| ❏ 221 | Bernie Parmalee | .20 | .07 |
| ❏ 222 | Stanley Pritchett | .20 | .07 |
| ❏ 223 | Daniel Stubbs | .20 | .07 |
| ❏ 224 | Zach Thomas | .50 | .20 |
| ❏ 225 | Derrick Alexander DE | .20 | .07 |
| ❏ 226 | Cris Carter | .50 | .20 |
| ❏ 227 | Jeff Christy | .20 | .07 |
| ❏ 228 | Qadry Ismail | .30 | .10 |
| ❏ 229 | Brad Johnson | .50 | .20 |
| ❏ 230 | Andrew Jordan | .20 | .07 |
| ❏ 231 | Randall McDaniel | .20 | .07 |
| ❏ 232 | David Palmer | .20 | .07 |
| ❏ 233 | John Randle | .30 | .10 |
| ❏ 234 | Jake Reed | .30 | .10 |
| ❏ 235 | Scott Sisson | .20 | .07 |
| ❏ 236 | Korey Stringer | .20 | .07 |
| ❏ 237 | Darryl Talley | .20 | .07 |
| ❏ 238 | Orlando Thomas | .20 | .07 |
| ❏ 239 | Bruce Armstrong | .20 | .07 |
| ❏ 240 | Drew Bledsoe | .60 | .25 |
| ❏ 241 | Willie Clay | .20 | .07 |
| ❏ 242 | Ben Coates | .30 | .10 |
| ❏ 243 | Ferric Collons RC | .20 | .07 |
| ❏ 244 | Terry Glenn | .50 | .20 |
| ❏ 245 | Jerome Henderson | .20 | .07 |
| ❏ 246 | Shawn Jefferson | .20 | .07 |
| ❏ 247 | Dietrich Jells | .20 | .07 |
| ❏ 248 | Ty Law | .30 | .10 |
| ❏ 249 | Curtis Martin | .60 | .25 |
| ❏ 250 | Willie McGinest | .20 | .07 |
| ❏ 251 | Dave Meggett | .20 | .07 |
| ❏ 252 | Lawyer Milloy | .30 | .10 |
| ❏ 253 | Chris Slade | .20 | .07 |
| ❏ 254 | Je'rod Cherry | .20 | .07 |
| ❏ 255 | Jim Everett | .20 | .07 |
| ❏ 256 | Mark Fields | .20 | .07 |

| | | |
|---|---|---|
| 257 Michael Haynes | .20 | .07 |
| 258 Tyrone Hughes | .20 | .07 |
| 259 Haywood Jeffires | .20 | .07 |
| 260 Wayne Martin | .20 | .07 |
| 261 Mark McMillian | .20 | .07 |
| 262 Rufus Porter | .20 | .07 |
| 263 William Roaf | .20 | .07 |
| 264 Torrance Small | .20 | .07 |
| 265 Renaldo Turnbull | .20 | .07 |
| 266 Ray Zellars | .20 | .07 |
| 267 Jessie Armstead | .20 | .07 |
| 268 Chad Bratzke | .20 | .07 |
| 269 Dave Brown | .20 | .07 |
| 270 Chris Calloway | .20 | .07 |
| 271 Howard Cross | .20 | .07 |
| 272 Lawrence Dawsey | .20 | .07 |
| 273 Rodney Hampton | .30 | .10 |
| 274 Danny Kanell | .20 | .07 |
| 275 Arthur Marshall | .20 | .07 |
| 276 Aaron Pierce | .20 | .07 |
| 277 Phillippi Sparks | .20 | .07 |
| 278 Amani Toomer | .30 | .10 |
| 279 Charles Way | .20 | .07 |
| 280 Richie Anderson | .30 | .10 |
| 281 Fred Baxter | .20 | .07 |
| 282 Wayne Chrebet | .50 | .20 |
| 283 Kyle Clifton | .20 | .07 |
| 284 Jumbo Elliott | .20 | .07 |
| 285 Aaron Glenn | .20 | .07 |
| 286 Jeff Graham | .20 | .07 |
| 287 Bobby Hamilton RC | .20 | .07 |
| 288 Keyshawn Johnson | .50 | .20 |
| 289 Adrian Murrell | .30 | .10 |
| 290 Neil O'Donnell | .30 | .10 |
| 291 Webster Slaughter | .20 | .07 |
| 292 Alex Van Dyke | .20 | .07 |
| 293 Marvin Washington | .20 | .07 |
| 294 Joe Aska | .20 | .07 |
| 295 Jerry Ball | .20 | .07 |
| 296 Tim Brown | .50 | .20 |
| 297 Rickey Dudley | .30 | .10 |
| 298 Pat Harlow | .20 | .07 |
| 299 Nolan Harrison | .20 | .07 |
| 300 Billy Joe Hobert | .30 | .10 |
| 301 James Jett | .30 | .10 |
| 302 Napoleon Kaufman | .50 | .20 |
| 303 Lincoln Kennedy | .20 | .07 |
| 304 Albert Lewis | .20 | .07 |
| 305 Chester McGlockton | .20 | .07 |
| 306 Pat Swilling | .20 | .07 |
| 307 Steve Wisniewski | .20 | .07 |
| 308 Darion Conner | .20 | .07 |
| 309 Ty Detmer | .30 | .10 |
| 310 Jason Dunn | .20 | .07 |
| 311 Irving Fryar | .30 | .10 |
| 312 James Fuller | .20 | .07 |
| 313 William Fuller | .20 | .07 |
| 314 Charlie Garner | .30 | .10 |
| 315 Bobby Hoying | .30 | .10 |
| 316 Tom Hutton | .20 | .07 |
| 317 Chris T. Jones | .20 | .07 |
| 318 Mike Mamula | .20 | .07 |
| 319 Mark Seay | .20 | .07 |
| 320 Bobby Taylor | .20 | .07 |
| 321 Ricky Watters | .30 | .10 |
| 322 Jahine Arnold | .20 | .07 |
| 323 Jerome Bettis | .50 | .20 |
| 324 Chad Brown | .20 | .07 |
| 325 Mark Bruener | .20 | .07 |
| 326 Andre Hastings | .20 | .07 |
| 327 Norm Johnson | .20 | .07 |
| 328 Levon Kirkland | .20 | .07 |
| 329 Carnell Lake | .20 | .07 |
| 330 Greg Lloyd | .20 | .07 |
| 331 Ernie Mills | .20 | .07 |
| 332 Orpheus Roye RC | .20 | .07 |
| 333 Kordell Stewart | .50 | .20 |
| 334 Yancey Thigpen | .30 | .10 |
| 335 Mike Tomczak | .20 | .07 |
| 336 Rod Woodson | .30 | .10 |
| 337 Tony Banks | .30 | .10 |
| 338 Bern Brostek | .20 | .07 |
| 339 Isaac Bruce | .50 | .20 |
| 340 Ernie Conwell | .20 | .07 |
| 341 Keith Crawford | .20 | .07 |
| 342 Wayne Gandy | .20 | .07 |
| 343 Harold Green | .20 | .07 |
| 344 Carlos Jenkins | .20 | .07 |
| 345 Jimmie Jones | .20 | .07 |
| 346 Eddie Kennison | .30 | .10 |
| 347 Todd Lyght | .20 | .07 |
| 348 Leslie O'Neal | .20 | .07 |
| 349 Lawrence Phillips | .20 | .07 |
| 350 Greg Robinson | .20 | .07 |
| 351 Darren Bennett | .20 | .07 |
| 352 Lewis Bush | .20 | .07 |
| 353 Eric Castle | .20 | .07 |
| 354 Terrell Fletcher | .20 | .07 |
| 355 Darrien Gordon | .20 | .07 |
| 356 Kurt Gouveia | .20 | .07 |
| 357 Aaron Hayden | .20 | .07 |
| 358 Stan Humphries | .30 | .10 |
| 359 Tony Martin | .30 | .10 |
| 360 Vaughn Parker RC | .20 | .07 |
| 361 Brian Roche | .20 | .07 |
| 362 Leonard Russell | .20 | .07 |
| 363 Junior Seau | .50 | .20 |
| 364 Roy Barker | .20 | .07 |
| 365 Harris Barton | .20 | .07 |
| 366 Dexter Carter | .20 | .07 |
| 367 Chris Doleman | .20 | .07 |
| 368 Tyronne Drakeford | .20 | .07 |
| 369 Elvis Grbac | .30 | .10 |
| 370 Derek Loville | .20 | .07 |
| 371 Tim McDonald | .20 | .07 |
| 372 Ken Norton | .20 | .07 |
| 373 Terrell Owens | .60 | .25 |
| 374 Gary Plummer | .20 | .07 |
| 375 Jerry Rice | 1.00 | .40 |
| 376 Dana Stubblefield | .20 | .07 |
| 377 Lee Woodall | .20 | .07 |
| 378 Steve Young | .60 | .25 |
| 379 Robert Blackmon | .20 | .07 |
| 380 Brian Blades | .20 | .07 |
| 381 Carlester Crumpler | .20 | .07 |
| 382 Christian Fauria | .20 | .07 |
| 383 John Friesz | .20 | .07 |
| 384 Joey Galloway | .30 | .10 |
| 385 Derrick Graham | .20 | .07 |
| 386 Cortez Kennedy | .20 | .07 |
| 387 Warren Moon | .50 | .20 |
| 388 Winston Moss | .20 | .07 |
| 389 Mike Pritchard | .20 | .07 |
| 390 Michael Sinclair | .20 | .07 |
| 391 Lamar Smith | .50 | .20 |
| 392 Chris Warren | .30 | .10 |
| 393 Chidi Ahanotu | .20 | .07 |
| 394 Mike Alstott | .50 | .20 |
| 395 Reggie Brooks | .20 | .07 |
| 396 Trent Dilfer | .50 | .20 |
| 397 Jerry Ellison | .20 | .07 |
| 398 Paul Gruber | .20 | .07 |
| 399 Alvin Harper | .20 | .07 |
| 400 Courtney Hawkins | .20 | .07 |
| 401 Dave Moore | .20 | .07 |
| 402 Errict Rhett | .20 | .07 |
| 403 Warren Sapp | .30 | .10 |
| 404 Nilo Silvan | .20 | .07 |
| 405 Regan Upshaw | .20 | .07 |
| 406 Casey Weldon | .20 | .07 |
| 407 Terry Allen | .50 | .20 |
| 408 Jamie Asher | .20 | .07 |
| 409 Bill Brooks | .20 | .07 |
| 410 Tom Carter | .20 | .07 |
| 411 Henry Ellard | .20 | .07 |
| 412 Gus Frerotte | .20 | .07 |
| 413 Darrell Green | .30 | .10 |
| 414 Ken Harvey | .20 | .07 |
| 415 Tre Johnson | .20 | .07 |
| 416 Brian Mitchell | .20 | .07 |
| 417 Rich Owens | .20 | .07 |
| 418 Heath Shuler | .30 | .10 |
| 419 Michael Westbrook | .30 | .10 |
| 420 Tony Woods | .20 | .07 |
| 421 Reidel Anthony RC | .50 | .20 |
| 422 Darnell Autry RC | .50 | .20 |
| 423 Tiki Barber RC | 3.00 | 1.25 |
| 424 Pat Barnes RC | .50 | .20 |
| 425 Terry Battle RC | .20 | .07 |
| 426 Will Blackwell RC | .30 | .10 |
| 427 Peter Boulware RC | .50 | .20 |
| 428 Rae Carruth RC | .20 | .07 |
| 429 Troy Davis RC | .30 | .10 |
| 430 Jim Druckenmiller RC | .30 | .10 |
| 431 Warrick Dunn RC | 1.50 | .60 |
| 432 Marc Edwards RC | .20 | .07 |
| 433 James Farrior RC | .20 | .07 |
| 434 Yatil Green RC | .30 | .10 |
| 435 Byron Hanspard RC | .30 | .10 |
| 436 Ike Hilliard RC | .75 | .30 |
| 437 David LaFleur RC | .20 | .07 |
| 438 Kevin Lockett RC | .30 | .10 |
| 439 Sam Madison RC | .50 | .20 |
| 440 Brian Manning RC | .30 | .10 |
| 441 Orlando Pace RC | .50 | .20 |
| 442 Jake Plummer RC | 2.50 | 1.00 |
| 443 Chad Scott RC | .30 | .10 |
| 444 Sedrick Shaw RC | .30 | .10 |
| 445 Antowain Smith RC | 1.25 | .50 |
| 446 Shawn Springs RC | .30 | .10 |
| 447 Ross Verba RC | .20 | .07 |
| 448 Bryant Westbrook RC | .20 | .07 |
| 449 Renaldo Wynn RC | .20 | .07 |
| 450 Jimmy Johnson CO | .30 | .10 |
| S1 Mark Brunell Sample | 1.00 | .40 |

## 1998 Pacific

| | | |
|---|---|---|
| COMPLETE SET (450) | 60.00 | 25.00 |
| 1 Mario Bates | .25 | .15 |
| 2 Lomas Brown | .25 | .08 |
| 3 Larry Centers | .25 | .08 |
| 4 Chris Gedney | .25 | .08 |
| 5 Terry Irving | .25 | .08 |
| 6 Tom Knight | .25 | .08 |
| 7 Eric Metcalf | .25 | .08 |
| 8 Jamir Miller | .25 | .08 |
| 9 Rob Moore | .40 | .15 |
| 10 Joe Nedney | .25 | .08 |
| 11 Jake Plummer | .60 | .25 |
| 12 Simeon Rice | .25 | .08 |
| 13 Frank Sanders | .40 | .15 |
| 14 Eric Swann | .25 | .08 |
| 15 Aeneas Williams | .25 | .08 |
| 16 Morten Andersen | .25 | .08 |
| 17 Jamal Anderson | .60 | .25 |
| 18 Michael Booker | .25 | .08 |
| 19 Keith Brooking RC | 1.50 | .60 |
| 20 Ray Buchanan | .25 | .08 |
| 21 Devin Bush | .25 | .08 |
| 22 Chris Chandler | .40 | .15 |
| 23 Tony Graziani | .25 | .08 |
| 24 Harold Green | .25 | .08 |
| 25 Byron Hanspard | .25 | .08 |
| 26 Todd Kinchen | .25 | .08 |
| 27 Tony Martin | .40 | .15 |
| 28 Terance Mathis | .40 | .15 |
| 29 Eugene Robinson | .25 | .08 |
| 30 O.J. Santiago | .25 | .08 |
| 31 Chuck Smith | .25 | .08 |
| 32 Jessie Tuggle | .25 | .08 |
| 33 Bob Whitfield | .25 | .08 |
| 34 Peter Boulware | .25 | .08 |
| 35 Jay Graham | .25 | .08 |
| 36 Eric Green | .25 | .08 |
| 37 Jim Harbaugh | .40 | .15 |
| 38 Michael Jackson | .25 | .08 |
| 39 Jermaine Lewis | .40 | .15 |
| 40 Ray Lewis | .60 | .25 |
| 41 Michael McCrary | .25 | .08 |
| 42 Stevon Moore | .25 | .08 |
| 43 Jonathan Ogden | .25 | .08 |
| 44 Errict Rhett | .40 | .15 |
| 45 Matt Stover | .25 | .08 |
| 46 Rod Woodson | .40 | .15 |
| 47 Eric Zeier | .40 | .15 |
| 48 Ruben Brown | .25 | .08 |
| 49 Steve Christie | .25 | .08 |
| 50 Quinn Early | .25 | .08 |
| 51 John Fina | .25 | .08 |
| 52 Doug Flutie | .60 | .25 |

|  |  | | |
|---|---|---|---|
| ☐ 53 | Phil Hansen | .25 | .08 |
| ☐ 54 | Lonnie Johnson | .25 | .08 |
| ☐ 55 | Rob Johnson | .40 | .15 |
| ☐ 56 | Henry Jones | .25 | .08 |
| ☐ 57 | Eric Moulds | .60 | .25 |
| ☐ 58 | Andre Reed | .40 | .15 |
| ☐ 59 | Antowain Smith | .60 | .25 |
| ☐ 60 | Bruce Smith | .25 | .08 |
| ☐ 61 | Thurman Thomas | .60 | .25 |
| ☐ 62 | Ted Washington | .25 | .08 |
| ☐ 63 | Michael Bates | .25 | .08 |
| ☐ 64 | Tim Biakabutuka | .40 | .15 |
| ☐ 65 | Blake Brockermeyer | .25 | .08 |
| ☐ 66 | Mark Carrier | .25 | .08 |
| ☐ 67 | Rae Carruth | .40 | .15 |
| ☐ 68 | Kerry Collins | .40 | .15 |
| ☐ 69 | Doug Evans | .25 | .08 |
| ☐ 70 | William Floyd | .25 | .08 |
| ☐ 71 | Sean Gilbert | .25 | .08 |
| ☐ 72 | Rocket Ismail | .25 | .08 |
| ☐ 73 | John Kasay | .25 | .08 |
| ☐ 74 | Fred Lane | .25 | .08 |
| ☐ 75 | Lamar Lathon | .25 | .08 |
| ☐ 76 | Muhsin Muhammad | .40 | .15 |
| ☐ 77 | Wesley Walls | .40 | .15 |
| ☐ 78 | Edgar Bennett | .25 | .08 |
| ☐ 79 | Tom Carter | .25 | .08 |
| ☐ 80 | Curtis Conway | .40 | .15 |
| ☐ 81 | Bobby Engram | .40 | .15 |
| ☐ 82 | Curtis Enis RC | .75 | .30 |
| ☐ 83 | Jim Flanigan | .25 | .08 |
| ☐ 84 | Walt Harris | .25 | .08 |
| ☐ 85 | Jeff Jaeger | .25 | .08 |
| ☐ 86 | Erik Kramer | .25 | .08 |
| ☐ 87 | John Mangum | .25 | .08 |
| ☐ 88 | Glyn Milburn | .25 | .08 |
| ☐ 89 | Barry Minter | .25 | .08 |
| ☐ 90 | Chris Penn | .25 | .08 |
| ☐ 91 | Todd Sauerbrun | .25 | .08 |
| ☐ 92 | James Williams | .25 | .08 |
| ☐ 93 | Ashley Ambrose | .25 | .08 |
| ☐ 94 | Willie Anderson | .25 | .08 |
| ☐ 95 | Eric Bieniemy | .25 | .08 |
| ☐ 96 | Jeff Blake | .40 | .15 |
| ☐ 97 | Ki-Jana Carter | .25 | .08 |
| ☐ 98 | John Copeland | .25 | .08 |
| ☐ 99 | Corey Dillon | .60 | .25 |
| ☐ 100 | Tony McGee | .25 | .08 |
| ☐ 101 | Neil O'Donnell | .40 | .15 |
| ☐ 102 | Carl Pickens | .25 | .08 |
| ☐ 103 | Kevin Sargent | .25 | .08 |
| ☐ 104 | Damay Scott | .40 | .15 |
| ☐ 105 | Takeo Spikes RC | 1.50 | .60 |
| ☐ 106 | Troy Aikman | 1.25 | .50 |
| ☐ 107 | Larry Allen | .25 | .08 |
| ☐ 108 | Eric Bjornson | .25 | .08 |
| ☐ 109 | Billy Davis | .25 | .08 |
| ☐ 110 | Jason Garrett RC | 1.25 | .50 |
| ☐ 111 | Michael Irvin | .60 | .25 |
| ☐ 112 | Daryl Johnston | .40 | .15 |
| ☐ 113 | David LaFleur | .25 | .08 |
| ☐ 114 | Everett McIver | .25 | .08 |
| ☐ 115 | Ernie Mills | .25 | .08 |
| ☐ 116 | Nate Newton | .25 | .08 |
| ☐ 117 | Deion Sanders | .60 | .25 |
| ☐ 118 | Emmitt Smith | 2.00 | .75 |
| ☐ 119 | Kevin Smith | .25 | .08 |
| ☐ 120 | Erik Williams | .25 | .08 |
| ☐ 121 | Steve Atwater | .25 | .08 |
| ☐ 122 | Tyrone Braxton | .25 | .08 |
| ☐ 123 | Ray Crockett | .25 | .08 |
| ☐ 124 | Terrell Davis | .60 | .25 |
| ☐ 125 | Jason Elam | .25 | .08 |
| ☐ 126 | John Elway | 2.50 | 1.00 |
| ☐ 127 | Willie Green | .25 | .08 |
| ☐ 128 | Brian Griese RC | 3.00 | 1.25 |
| ☐ 129 | Tony Jones | .25 | .08 |
| ☐ 130 | Ed McCaffrey | .40 | .15 |
| ☐ 131 | John Mobley | .25 | .08 |
| ☐ 132 | Tom Nalen | .25 | .08 |
| ☐ 133 | Marcus Nash RC | .75 | .30 |
| ☐ 134 | Bill Romanowski | .25 | .08 |
| ☐ 135 | Shannon Sharpe | .40 | .15 |
| ☐ 136 | Neil Smith | .40 | .15 |
| ☐ 137 | Rod Smith | .25 | .08 |
| ☐ 138 | Keith Traylor | .25 | .08 |
| ☐ 139 | Stephen Boyd | .25 | .08 |
| ☐ 140 | Mark Carrier DB | .25 | .08 |
| ☐ 141 | Charlie Batch RC | 1.50 | .60 |
| ☐ 142 | Jason Hanson | .25 | .08 |
| ☐ 143 | Scott Mitchell | .40 | .15 |
| ☐ 144 | Herman Moore | .40 | .15 |
| ☐ 145 | Johnnie Morton | .40 | .15 |
| ☐ 146 | Robert Porcher | .25 | .08 |
| ☐ 147 | Ron Rivers | .25 | .08 |
| ☐ 148 | Barry Sanders | 2.00 | .75 |
| ☐ 149 | Tracy Scroggins | .25 | .08 |
| ☐ 150 | David Sloan | .25 | .08 |
| ☐ 151 | Tommy Vardell | .25 | .08 |
| ☐ 152 | Kerwin Waldroup | .25 | .08 |
| ☐ 153 | Bryant Westbrook | .25 | .08 |
| ☐ 154 | Robert Brooks | .40 | .15 |
| ☐ 155 | Gilbert Brown | .25 | .08 |
| ☐ 156 | LeRoy Butler | .25 | .08 |
| ☐ 157 | Mark Chmura | .40 | .15 |
| ☐ 158 | Earl Dotson | .25 | .08 |
| ☐ 159 | Santana Dotson | .25 | .08 |
| ☐ 160 | Brett Favre | 2.50 | 1.00 |
| ☐ 161 | Antonio Freeman | .60 | .25 |
| ☐ 162 | Raymont Harris | .25 | .08 |
| ☐ 163 | William Henderson | .40 | .15 |
| ☐ 164 | Vonnie Holliday RC | 1.25 | .50 |
| ☐ 165 | George Koonce | .25 | .08 |
| ☐ 166 | Dorsey Levens | .60 | .25 |
| ☐ 167 | Derrick Mayes | .40 | .15 |
| ☐ 168 | Craig Newsome | .25 | .08 |
| ☐ 169 | Ross Verba | .25 | .08 |
| ☐ 170 | Reggie White | .60 | .25 |
| ☐ 171 | Elijah Alexander | .25 | .08 |
| ☐ 172 | Aaron Bailey | .25 | .08 |
| ☐ 173 | Jason Belser | .25 | .08 |
| ☐ 174 | Robert Blackmon | .25 | .08 |
| ☐ 175 | Zack Crockett | .25 | .08 |
| ☐ 176 | Ken Dilger | .25 | .08 |
| ☐ 177 | Marshall Faulk | .75 | .30 |
| ☐ 178 | Tarik Glenn | .25 | .08 |
| ☐ 179 | Marvin Harrison | .60 | .25 |
| ☐ 180 | Tony Mandarich | .25 | .08 |
| ☐ 181 | Peyton Manning RC | 15.00 | 6.00 |
| ☐ 182 | Marcus Pollard | .25 | .08 |
| ☐ 183 | Lamont Warren | .25 | .08 |
| ☐ 184 | Tavian Banks RC | 1.25 | .50 |
| ☐ 185 | Reggie Barlow | .25 | .08 |
| ☐ 186 | Tony Boselli | .25 | .08 |
| ☐ 187 | Tony Brackens | .25 | .08 |
| ☐ 188 | Mark Brunell | .60 | .25 |
| ☐ 189 | Kevin Hardy | .25 | .08 |
| ☐ 190 | Mike Hollis | .25 | .08 |
| ☐ 191 | Jeff Lageman | .25 | .08 |
| ☐ 192 | Keenan McCardell | .40 | .15 |
| ☐ 193 | Pete Mitchell | .25 | .08 |
| ☐ 194 | Bryce Paup | .25 | .08 |
| ☐ 195 | Leon Searcy | .25 | .08 |
| ☐ 196 | Jimmy Smith | .40 | .15 |
| ☐ 197 | James Stewart | .40 | .15 |
| ☐ 198 | Fred Taylor RC | 2.50 | 1.00 |
| ☐ 199 | Renaldo Wynn | .25 | .08 |
| ☐ 200 | Derrick Alexander WR | .40 | .15 |
| ☐ 201 | Kimble Anders | .25 | .08 |
| ☐ 202 | Donnell Bennett | .25 | .08 |
| ☐ 203 | Dale Carter | .25 | .08 |
| ☐ 204 | Anthony Davis | .25 | .08 |
| ☐ 205 | Rich Gannon | .60 | .25 |
| ☐ 206 | Tony Gonzalez | .60 | .25 |
| ☐ 207 | Elvis Grbac | .25 | .08 |
| ☐ 208 | James Hasty | .25 | .08 |
| ☐ 209 | Leslie O'Neal | .25 | .08 |
| ☐ 210 | Andre Rison | .40 | .15 |
| ☐ 211 | Rashaan Shehee RC | 1.25 | .50 |
| ☐ 212 | Will Shields | .25 | .08 |
| ☐ 213 | Pete Stoyanovich | .25 | .08 |
| ☐ 214 | Derrick Thomas | .60 | .25 |
| ☐ 215 | Tamarick Vanover | .25 | .08 |
| ☐ 216 | Karim Abdul-Jabbar | .60 | .25 |
| ☐ 217 | Trace Armstrong | .25 | .08 |
| ☐ 218 | John Avery RC | 1.25 | .50 |
| ☐ 219 | Tim Bowens | .25 | .08 |
| ☐ 220 | Terrell Buckley | .25 | .08 |
| ☐ 221 | Troy Drayton | .25 | .08 |
| ☐ 222 | Daryl Gardener | .25 | .08 |
| ☐ 223 | Damon Huard RC | 8.00 | 3.00 |
| ☐ 224 | Charles Jordan | .25 | .08 |
| ☐ 225 | Dan Marino | 2.50 | 1.00 |
| ☐ 226 | O.J. McDuffie | .40 | .15 |
| ☐ 227 | Bernie Parmalee | .25 | .08 |
| ☐ 228 | Stanley Pritchett | .25 | .08 |
| ☐ 229 | Derrick Rodgers | .25 | .08 |
| ☐ 230 | Lamar Thomas | .25 | .08 |
| ☐ 231 | Zach Thomas | .60 | .25 |
| ☐ 232 | Richmond Webb | .25 | .08 |
| ☐ 233 | Derrick Alexander DE | .25 | .08 |
| ☐ 234 | Jerry Ball | .25 | .08 |
| ☐ 235 | Cris Carter | .60 | .25 |
| ☐ 236 | Randall Cunningham | .60 | .25 |
| ☐ 237 | Charles Evans | .25 | .08 |
| ☐ 238 | Corey Fuller | .25 | .08 |

## 1998 Pacific

|  |  | | |
|---|---|---|---|
| ☐ 239 | Andrew Glover | .25 | .08 |
| ☐ 240 | Leroy Hoard | .25 | .08 |
| ☐ 241 | Brad Johnson | .60 | .25 |
| ☐ 242 | Ed McDaniel | .25 | .08 |
| ☐ 243 | Randall McDaniel | .25 | .08 |
| ☐ 244 | Randy Moss RC | 10.00 | 4.00 |
| ☐ 245 | John Randle | .40 | .15 |
| ☐ 246 | Jake Reed | .40 | .15 |
| ☐ 247 | Dwayne Rudd | .25 | .08 |
| ☐ 248 | Robert Smith | .60 | .25 |
| ☐ 249 | Bruce Armstrong | .25 | .08 |
| ☐ 250 | Drew Bledsoe | 1.00 | .40 |
| ☐ 251 | Vincent Brisby | .25 | .08 |
| ☐ 252 | Tedy Bruschi | 1.25 | .50 |
| ☐ 253 | Ben Coates | .40 | .15 |
| ☐ 254 | Derrick Cullors | .25 | .08 |
| ☐ 255 | Terry Glenn | .60 | .25 |
| ☐ 256 | Shawn Jefferson | .25 | .08 |
| ☐ 257 | Ted Johnson | .25 | .08 |
| ☐ 258 | Ty Law | .40 | .15 |
| ☐ 259 | Willie McGinest | .25 | .08 |
| ☐ 260 | Lawyer Milloy | .40 | .15 |
| ☐ 261 | Sedrick Shaw | .25 | .08 |
| ☐ 262 | Chris Slade | .25 | .08 |
| ☐ 263 | Troy Davis | .25 | .08 |
| ☐ 264 | Mark Fields | .25 | .08 |
| ☐ 265 | Andre Hastings | .25 | .08 |
| ☐ 266 | Billy Joe Hobert | .25 | .08 |
| ☐ 267 | Qadry Ismail | .40 | .15 |
| ☐ 268 | Tony Johnson | .25 | .08 |
| ☐ 269 | Sammy Knight RC | .60 | .25 |
| ☐ 270 | Wayne Martin | .25 | .08 |
| ☐ 271 | Chris Naeole | .25 | .08 |
| ☐ 272 | Keith Poole | .25 | .08 |
| ☐ 273 | William Roaf | .25 | .08 |
| ☐ 274 | Pio Sagapolutele | .25 | .08 |
| ☐ 275 | Danny Wuerffel | .40 | .15 |
| ☐ 276 | Ray Zellars | .25 | .08 |
| ☐ 277 | Jessie Armstead | .25 | .08 |
| ☐ 278 | Tiki Barber | .60 | .25 |
| ☐ 279 | Chris Calloway | .25 | .08 |
| ☐ 280 | Percy Ellsworth | .25 | .08 |
| ☐ 281 | Sam Garnes RC | .75 | .30 |
| ☐ 282 | Kent Graham | .25 | .08 |
| ☐ 283 | Ike Hilliard | .40 | .15 |
| ☐ 284 | Danny Kanell | .40 | .15 |
| ☐ 285 | Corey Miller | .25 | .08 |
| ☐ 286 | Phillippi Sparks | .25 | .08 |
| ☐ 287 | Michael Strahan | .40 | .15 |
| ☐ 288 | Amani Toomer | .40 | .15 |

| | | |
|---|---|---|
| ❏ 289 Charles Way | .25 | .08 |
| ❏ 290 Tyrone Wheatley | .40 | .15 |
| ❏ 291 Tito Wooten | .25 | .08 |
| ❏ 292 Kyle Brady | .25 | .08 |
| ❏ 293 Keith Byars | .25 | .08 |
| ❏ 294 Wayne Chrebet | .60 | .25 |
| ❏ 295 John Elliott | .25 | .08 |
| ❏ 296 Glenn Foley | .40 | .15 |
| ❏ 297 Aaron Glenn | .25 | .08 |
| ❏ 298 Keyshawn Johnson | .60 | .25 |
| ❏ 299 Curtis Martin | .60 | .25 |
| ❏ 300 Otis Smith | .25 | .08 |
| ❏ 301 Vinny Testaverde | .40 | .15 |
| ❏ 302 Alex Van Dyke | .25 | .08 |
| ❏ 303 Dedric Ward | .25 | .08 |
| ❏ 304 Greg Biekert | .25 | .08 |
| ❏ 305 Tim Brown | .60 | .25 |
| ❏ 306 Rickey Dudley | .25 | .08 |
| ❏ 307 Jeff George | .40 | .15 |
| ❏ 308 Pat Harlow | .25 | .08 |
| ❏ 309 Desmond Howard | .40 | .15 |
| ❏ 310 James Jett | .40 | .15 |
| ❏ 311 Napoleon Kaufman | .60 | .25 |
| ❏ 312 Lincoln Kennedy | .25 | .08 |
| ❏ 313 Russell Maryland | .25 | .08 |
| ❏ 314 Darrell Russell | .25 | .08 |
| ❏ 315 Eric Turner | .25 | .08 |
| ❏ 316 Steve Wisniewski | .25 | .08 |
| ❏ 317 Charles Woodson RC | 2.00 | .75 |
| ❏ 318 James Darling | .75 | .30 |
| ❏ 319 Jason Dunn | .25 | .08 |
| ❏ 320 Irving Fryar | .40 | .15 |
| ❏ 321 Charlie Garner | .40 | .15 |
| ❏ 322 Jeff Graham | .25 | .08 |
| ❏ 323 Bobby Hoying | .40 | .15 |
| ❏ 324 Chad Lewis | .40 | .15 |
| ❏ 325 Rodney Peete | .25 | .08 |
| ❏ 326 Freddie Solomon | .25 | .08 |
| ❏ 327 Duce Staley | .75 | .30 |
| ❏ 328 Bobby Taylor | .25 | .08 |
| ❏ 329 William Thomas | .25 | .08 |
| ❏ 330 Kevin Turner | .25 | .08 |
| ❏ 331 Troy Vincent | .25 | .08 |
| ❏ 332 Jerome Bettis | .60 | .25 |
| ❏ 333 Will Blackwell | .25 | .08 |
| ❏ 334 Mark Bruener | .25 | .08 |
| ❏ 335 Andre Coleman | .25 | .08 |
| ❏ 336 Dermontti Dawson | .25 | .08 |
| ❏ 337 Jason Gildon | .25 | .08 |
| ❏ 338 Courtney Hawkins | .25 | .08 |
| ❏ 339 Charles Johnson | .25 | .08 |
| ❏ 340 Levon Kirkland | .25 | .08 |
| ❏ 341 Carnell Lake | .25 | .08 |
| ❏ 342 Tim Lester | .25 | .08 |
| ❏ 343 Joel Steed | .25 | .08 |
| ❏ 344 Kordell Stewart | .60 | .25 |
| ❏ 345 Will Wolford | .25 | .08 |
| ❏ 346 Tony Banks | .40 | .15 |
| ❏ 347 Isaac Bruce | .60 | .25 |
| ❏ 348 Ernie Conwell | .25 | .08 |
| ❏ 349 D'Marco Farr | .25 | .08 |
| ❏ 350 Wayne Gandy | .25 | .08 |
| ❏ 351 Jerome Pathon RC | 1.50 | .60 |
| ❏ 352 Eddie Kennison | .40 | .15 |
| ❏ 353 Amp Lee | .25 | .08 |
| ❏ 354 Keith Lyle | .25 | .08 |
| ❏ 355 Ryan McNeil | .25 | .08 |
| ❏ 356 Jerald Moore | .25 | .08 |
| ❏ 357 Orlando Pace | .25 | .08 |
| ❏ 358 Roman Phifer | .25 | .08 |
| ❏ 359 David Thompson RC | .75 | .30 |
| ❏ 360 Darren Bennett | .25 | .08 |
| ❏ 361 John Carney | .25 | .08 |
| ❏ 362 Marco Coleman | .25 | .08 |
| ❏ 363 Terrell Fletcher | .25 | .08 |
| ❏ 364 William Fuller | .25 | .08 |
| ❏ 365 Charlie Jones | .25 | .08 |
| ❏ 366 Freddie Jones | .25 | .08 |
| ❏ 367 Ryan Leaf RC | 1.50 | .60 |
| ❏ 368 Natrone Means | .40 | .15 |
| ❏ 369 Junior Seau | .60 | .25 |
| ❏ 370 Terrance Shaw | .25 | .08 |
| ❏ 371 Tremayne Stephens RC | .75 | .30 |
| ❏ 372 Bryan Still | .25 | .08 |
| ❏ 373 Aaron Taylor | .25 | .08 |

| | | |
|---|---|---|
| ❏ 374 Greg Clark | .25 | .08 |
| ❏ 375 Ty Detmer | .40 | .15 |
| ❏ 376 Jim Druckenmiller | .25 | .08 |
| ❏ 377 Marc Edwards | .25 | .08 |
| ❏ 378 Merton Hanks | .25 | .08 |
| ❏ 379 Garrison Hearst | .60 | .25 |
| ❏ 380 Chuck Levy | .25 | .08 |
| ❏ 381 Ken Norton | .25 | .08 |
| ❏ 382 Terrell Owens | .60 | .25 |
| ❏ 383 Marquez Pope | .25 | .08 |
| ❏ 384 Jerry Rice | 1.25 | .50 |
| ❏ 385 Irv Smith | .25 | .08 |
| ❏ 386 J.J. Stokes | .40 | .15 |
| ❏ 387 Iheanyi Uwaezuoke | .25 | .08 |
| ❏ 388 Bryant Young | .25 | .08 |
| ❏ 389 Steve Young | .75 | .30 |
| ❏ 390 Sam Adams | .25 | .08 |
| ❏ 391 Chad Brown | .25 | .08 |
| ❏ 392 Christian Fauria | .25 | .08 |
| ❏ 393 Joey Galloway | .40 | .15 |
| ❏ 394 Ahman Green RC | 4.00 | 1.50 |
| ❏ 395 Walter Jones | .25 | .08 |
| ❏ 396 Cortez Kennedy | .25 | .08 |
| ❏ 397 Jon Kitna | .60 | .25 |
| ❏ 398 James McKnight | .60 | .25 |
| ❏ 399 Warren Moon | .60 | .25 |
| ❏ 400 Mike Pritchard | .25 | .08 |
| ❏ 401 Michael Sinclair | .25 | .08 |
| ❏ 402 Shawn Springs | .25 | .08 |
| ❏ 403 Ricky Watters | .40 | .15 |
| ❏ 404 Darryl Williams | .25 | .08 |
| ❏ 405 Mike Alstott | .60 | .25 |
| ❏ 406 Reidel Anthony | .40 | .15 |
| ❏ 407 Derrick Brooks | .25 | .08 |
| ❏ 408 Brad Culpepper | .25 | .08 |
| ❏ 409 Trent Dilfer | .60 | .25 |
| ❏ 410 Warrick Dunn | .60 | .25 |
| ❏ 411 Bert Emanuel | .40 | .15 |
| ❏ 412 Jacquez Green RC | 1.25 | .50 |
| ❏ 413 Paul Gruber | .25 | .08 |
| ❏ 414 Patrick Hape RC | 1.25 | .50 |
| ❏ 415 Dave Moore | .25 | .08 |
| ❏ 416 Hardy Nickerson | .25 | .08 |
| ❏ 417 Warren Sapp | .25 | .08 |
| ❏ 418 Robb Thomas | .25 | .08 |
| ❏ 419 Regan Upshaw | .25 | .08 |
| ❏ 420 Karl Williams | .25 | .08 |
| ❏ 421 Blaine Bishop | .25 | .08 |
| ❏ 422 Anthony Cook | .25 | .08 |
| ❏ 423 Willie Davis | .25 | .08 |
| ❏ 424 Al Del Greco | .25 | .08 |
| ❏ 425 Kevin Dyson | .60 | .25 |
| ❏ 426 Henry Ford | .25 | .08 |
| ❏ 427 Eddie George | .60 | .25 |
| ❏ 428 Jackie Harris | .25 | .08 |
| ❏ 429 Steve McNair | .60 | .25 |
| ❏ 430 Chris Sanders | .25 | .08 |
| ❏ 431 Mark Stepnoski | .25 | .08 |
| ❏ 432 Yancey Thigpen | .25 | .08 |
| ❏ 433 Barron Wortham | .25 | .08 |
| ❏ 434 Frank Wycheck | .25 | .08 |
| ❏ 435 Stephen Alexander RC | 1.25 | .50 |
| ❏ 436 Terry Allen | .60 | .25 |
| ❏ 437 Jamie Asher | .25 | .08 |
| ❏ 438 Bob Dahl | .25 | .08 |
| ❏ 439 Stephen Davis | .40 | .15 |
| ❏ 440 Cris Dishman | .25 | .08 |
| ❏ 441 Gus Frerotte | .25 | .08 |
| ❏ 442 Darrell Green | .40 | .15 |
| ❏ 443 Trent Green | .75 | .30 |
| ❏ 444 Ken Harvey | .25 | .08 |
| ❏ 445 Skip Hicks RC | 1.25 | .50 |
| ❏ 446 Jeff Hostetler | .25 | .08 |
| ❏ 447 Brian Mitchell | .25 | .08 |
| ❏ 448 Leslie Shepherd | .25 | .08 |
| ❏ 449 Michael Westbrook | .40 | .15 |
| ❏ 450 Dan Wilkinson | .25 | .08 |
| ❏ S1 Warrick Dunn Sample | .25 | .08 |

**1999 Pacific**

| | | |
|---|---|---|
| ❏ COMPLETE SET (450) | 80.00 | 30.00 |
| ❏ 1 Mario Bates | .25 | .08 |
| ❏ 2 Larry Centers | .25 | .08 |
| ❏ 3 Chris Gedney | .25 | .08 |
| ❏ 4 Kwamie Lassiter RC | .60 | .25 |

| | | |
|---|---|---|
| ❏ 5 Johnny McWilliams | .25 | .08 |
| ❏ 6 Eric Metcalf | .25 | .08 |
| ❏ 7 Rob Moore | .40 | .15 |
| ❏ 8 Adrian Murrell | .40 | .15 |
| ❏ 9 Jake Plummer | .40 | .15 |
| ❏ 10 Simeon Rice | .25 | .08 |
| ❏ 11 Frank Sanders | .40 | .15 |
| ❏ 12 Andre Wadsworth | .25 | .08 |
| ❏ 13 Aeneas Williams | .25 | .08 |
| ❏ 14 M.Pittman/R.Anderson RC | 1.25 | .50 |
| ❏ 15 Morten Andersen | .25 | .08 |
| ❏ 16 Jamal Anderson | .60 | .25 |
| ❏ 17 Lester Archambeau | .25 | .08 |
| ❏ 18 Chris Chandler | .40 | .15 |
| ❏ 19 Bob Christian | .25 | .08 |
| ❏ 20 Steve DeBerg | .25 | .08 |
| ❏ 21 Tim Dwight | .60 | .25 |
| ❏ 22 Tony Martin | .40 | .15 |
| ❏ 23 Terance Mathis | .40 | .15 |
| ❏ 24 Eugene Robinson | .25 | .08 |
| ❏ 25 O.J. Santiago | .25 | .08 |
| ❏ 26 Chuck Smith | .25 | .08 |
| ❏ 27 Jessie Tuggle | .25 | .08 |
| ❏ 28 Jammi German/Ken Oxendine | .25 | .08 |
| ❏ 29 Peter Boulware | .25 | .08 |
| ❏ 30 Jay Graham | .25 | .08 |
| ❏ 31 Jim Harbaugh | .40 | .15 |
| ❏ 32 Priest Holmes | 1.00 | .40 |
| ❏ 33 Michael Jackson | .25 | .08 |
| ❏ 34 Jermaine Lewis | .40 | .15 |
| ❏ 35 Ray Lewis | .60 | .25 |
| ❏ 36 Michael McCrary | .25 | .08 |
| ❏ 37 Jonathan Ogden | .25 | .08 |
| ❏ 38 Errict Rhett | .25 | .08 |
| ❏ 39 James Roe RC | 1.00 | .40 |
| ❏ 40 Floyd Turner | .25 | .08 |
| ❏ 41 Rod Woodson | .40 | .15 |
| ❏ 42 Eric Zeier | .25 | .08 |
| ❏ 43 Wally Richardson/Patrick Johnson | .25 | .08 |
| ❏ 44 Ruben Brown | .25 | .08 |
| ❏ 45 Quinn Early | .25 | .08 |
| ❏ 46 Doug Flutie | .60 | .25 |
| ❏ 47 Sam Gash | .25 | .08 |
| ❏ 48 Phil Hansen | .25 | .08 |
| ❏ 49 Lonnie Johnson | .25 | .08 |
| ❏ 50 Rob Johnson | .40 | .15 |
| ❏ 51 Eric Moulds | .60 | .25 |
| ❏ 52 Andre Reed | .40 | .15 |
| ❏ 53 Jay Riemersma | .25 | .08 |
| ❏ 54 Antowain Smith | .60 | .25 |
| ❏ 55 Bruce Smith | .40 | .15 |
| ❏ 56 Thurman Thomas | .40 | .15 |
| ❏ 57 Ted Washington | .25 | .08 |
| ❏ 58 J.Linton/Kamil Loud RC | 1.00 | .40 |
| ❏ 59 Michael Bates | .25 | .08 |
| ❏ 60 Steve Beuerlein | .25 | .08 |
| ❏ 61 Tim Biakabutuka | .40 | .15 |
| ❏ 62 Mark Carrier WR | .25 | .08 |
| ❏ 63 Eric Davis | .25 | .08 |
| ❏ 64 William Floyd | .25 | .08 |
| ❏ 65 Sean Gilbert | .25 | .08 |
| ❏ 66 Kevin Greene | .25 | .08 |
| ❏ 67 Rocket Ismail | .40 | .15 |
| ❏ 68 Anthony Johnson | .25 | .08 |
| ❏ 69 Fred Lane | .25 | .08 |
| ❏ 70 Muhsin Muhammad | .40 | .15 |
| ❏ 71 Winslow Oliver | .25 | .08 |
| ❏ 72 Wesley Walls | .40 | .15 |

|  |  | | |
|---|------|---|---|
| 73 | D.Craig RC/S.Matthews | 1.50 | .60 |
| 74 | Edgar Bennett | .25 | .08 |
| 75 | Curtis Conway | .40 | .15 |
| 76 | Bobby Engram | .25 | .08 |
| 77 | Curtis Enis | .25 | .08 |
| 78 | Ty Hallock RC | 1.00 | .40 |
| 79 | Walt Harris | .25 | .08 |
| 80 | Jeff Jaeger | .25 | .08 |
| 81 | Erik Kramer | .25 | .08 |
| 82 | Glyn Milburn | .25 | .08 |
| 83 | Chris Penn | .25 | .08 |
| 84 | Steve Stenstrom | .25 | .08 |
| 85 | Ryan Wetnight | .25 | .08 |
| 86 | James Allen RC/Moreno | 1.50 | .60 |
| 87 | Ashley Ambrose | .25 | .08 |
| 88 | Brandon Bennett RC | 1.00 | .40 |
| 89 | Eric Bieniemy | .25 | .08 |
| 90 | Jeff Blake | .40 | .15 |
| 91 | Corey Dillon | .60 | .25 |
| 92 | Paul Justin | .25 | .08 |
| 93 | Eric Kresser RC | 1.00 | .40 |
| 94 | Tremain Mack | .25 | .08 |
| 95 | Tony McGee | .25 | .08 |
| 96 | Neil O'Donnell | .40 | .15 |
| 97 | Carl Pickens | .40 | .15 |
| 98 | Damay Scott | .25 | .08 |
| 99 | Takeo Spikes | .25 | .08 |
| 100 | Ty Detmer | .25 | .08 |
| 101 | Chris Gardocki | .25 | .08 |
| 102 | Damon Gibson | .25 | .08 |
| 103 | Antonio Langham | .25 | .08 |
| 104 | Jerris McPhail | .25 | .08 |
| 105 | Irv Smith | .25 | .08 |
| 106 | Freddie Solomon | .25 | .08 |
| 107 | S.Milanovich/Fred Brock RC | 1.00 | .40 |
| 108 | Troy Aikman | 1.25 | .50 |
| 109 | Larry Allen | .25 | .08 |
| 110 | Eric Bjornson | .25 | .08 |
| 111 | Billy Davis | .25 | .08 |
| 112 | Michael Irvin | .40 | .15 |
| 113 | David LaFleur | .25 | .08 |
| 114 | Ernie Mills | .25 | .08 |
| 115 | Nate Newton | .25 | .08 |
| 116 | Deion Sanders | .60 | .25 |
| 117 | Emmitt Smith | 1.25 | .50 |
| 118 | Chris Warren | .40 | .15 |
| 119 | Bubby Brister | .25 | .08 |
| 120 | Terrell Davis | .60 | .25 |
| 121 | Jason Elam | .25 | .08 |
| 122 | John Elway | 2.00 | .75 |
| 123 | Willie Green | .25 | .08 |
| 124 | Howard Griffith | .25 | .08 |
| 125 | Vaughn Hebron | .25 | .08 |
| 126 | Ed McCaffrey | .40 | .15 |
| 127 | John Mobley | .25 | .08 |
| 128 | Bill Romanowski | .25 | .08 |
| 129 | Shannon Sharpe | .40 | .15 |
| 130 | Neil Smith | .40 | .15 |
| 131 | Rod Smith | .40 | .15 |
| 132 | Brian Griese/M.Nash | .60 | .25 |
| 133 | Charlie Batch | .60 | .25 |
| 134 | Stephen Boyd | .25 | .08 |
| 135 | Mark Carrier DB | .25 | .08 |
| 136 | Germane Crowell | .25 | .08 |
| 137 | Terry Fair | .25 | .08 |
| 138 | Jason Hanson | .25 | .08 |
| 139 | Greg Jeffries RC | 1.00 | .40 |
| 140 | Herman Moore | .40 | .15 |
| 141 | Johnnie Morton | .25 | .08 |
| 142 | Robert Porcher | .25 | .08 |
| 143 | Ron Rivers | .25 | .08 |
| 144 | Barry Sanders | 2.00 | .75 |
| 145 | Tommy Vardell | .25 | .08 |
| 146 | Bryant Westbrook | .25 | .08 |
| 147 | Robert Brooks | .40 | .15 |
| 148 | LeRoy Butler | .25 | .08 |
| 149 | Mark Chmura | .25 | .08 |
| 150 | Tyrone Davis | .25 | .08 |
| 151 | Brett Favre | 2.00 | .75 |
| 152 | Antonio Freeman | .60 | .25 |
| 153 | Raymont Harris | .25 | .08 |
| 154 | Vonnie Holliday | .40 | .15 |
| 155 | Darick Holmes | .25 | .08 |
| 156 | Dorsey Levens | .60 | .25 |
| 157 | Brian Manning | .25 | .08 |
| 158 | Derrick Mayes | .25 | .08 |
| 159 | Roell Preston | .25 | .08 |
| 160 | Jeff Thomason | .25 | .08 |
| 161 | Tyrone Williams | .25 | .08 |
| 162 | C.Bradford/Michael Blair RC | 1.50 | .60 |
| 163 | Aaron Bailey | .25 | .08 |
| 164 | Ken Dilger | .25 | .08 |
| 165 | Marshall Faulk | .75 | .30 |
| 166 | E.G. Green | .25 | .08 |
| 167 | Marvin Harrison | .60 | .25 |
| 168 | Craig Heyward | .25 | .08 |
| 169 | Peyton Manning | 2.00 | .75 |
| 170 | Jerome Pathon | .40 | .15 |
| 171 | Marcus Pollard | .25 | .08 |
| 172 | Torrance Small | .25 | .08 |
| 173 | Mike Vanderjagt | .25 | .08 |
| 174 | Lamont Warren | .25 | .08 |
| 175 | Tavian Banks | .25 | .08 |
| 176 | Reggie Barlow | .25 | .08 |
| 177 | Tony Boselli | .25 | .08 |
| 178 | Tony Brackens | .25 | .08 |
| 179 | Mark Brunell | .60 | .25 |
| 180 | Kevin Hardy | .25 | .08 |
| 181 | Damon Jones | .25 | .08 |
| 182 | Jamie Martin | .60 | .25 |
| 183 | Keenan McCardell | .40 | .15 |
| 184 | Pete Mitchell | .25 | .08 |
| 185 | Bryce Paup | .25 | .08 |
| 186 | Jimmy Smith | .40 | .15 |
| 187 | Fred Taylor | .60 | .25 |
| 188 | Alvis Whitted/Chris Howard | .25 | .08 |
| 189 | Derrick Alexander WR | .40 | .15 |
| 190 | Kimble Anders | .40 | .15 |
| 191 | Donnell Bennett | .25 | .08 |
| 192 | Dale Carter | .25 | .08 |
| 193 | Rich Gannon | .60 | .25 |
| 194 | Tony Gonzalez | .60 | .25 |
| 195 | Elvis Grbac | .40 | .15 |
| 196 | Joe Horn | .25 | .08 |
| 197 | Kevin Lockett | .25 | .08 |
| 198 | Byron Bam Morris | .25 | .08 |
| 199 | Andre Rison | .40 | .15 |
| 200 | Derrick Thomas | .40 | .15 |
| 201 | Tamarick Vanover | .25 | .08 |
| 202 | Gregory Favors/Rashaan Shehee | .25 | .08 |
| 203 | Karim Abdul-Jabbar | .40 | .15 |
| 204 | Trace Armstrong | .25 | .08 |
| 205 | John Avery | .25 | .08 |
| 206 | Lorenzo Bromell RC | .60 | .25 |
| 207 | Terrell Buckley | .25 | .08 |
| 208 | Oronde Gadsden | .40 | .15 |
| 209 | Sam Madison | .25 | .08 |
| 210 | Dan Marino | 2.00 | .75 |
| 211 | O.J. McDuffie | .40 | .15 |
| 212 | Ed Perry RC | .60 | .25 |
| 213 | Jason Taylor | .25 | .08 |
| 214 | Lamar Thomas | .25 | .08 |
| 215 | Zach Thomas | .40 | .15 |
| 216 | H.Lusk/Nate Jacquet RC | 1.00 | .40 |
| 217 | T.Doxzon RC/D.Huard | 1.50 | .60 |
| 218 | Gary Anderson | .25 | .08 |
| 219 | Cris Carter | .60 | .25 |
| 220 | Randall Cunningham | .60 | .25 |
| 221 | Andrew Glover | .25 | .08 |
| 222 | Matthew Hatchette | .25 | .08 |
| 223 | Brad Johnson | .60 | .25 |
| 224 | Ed McDaniel | .25 | .08 |
| 225 | Randall McDaniel | .25 | .08 |
| 226 | Randy Moss | 1.50 | .60 |
| 227 | David Palmer | .25 | .08 |
| 228 | John Randle | .40 | .15 |
| 229 | Jake Reed | .40 | .15 |
| 230 | Robert Smith | .60 | .25 |
| 231 | Todd Steussie | .25 | .08 |
| 232 | S.Colinet RC/K.Mays | .25 | .08 |
| 233 | Jay Fiedler RC/T.Bouman RC | 6.00 | 2.50 |
| 234 | Drew Bledsoe | .75 | .30 |
| 235 | Troy Brown | .40 | .15 |
| 236 | Ben Coates | .40 | .15 |
| 237 | Derrick Cullors | .25 | .08 |
| 238 | Robert Edwards | .25 | .08 |
| 239 | Terry Glenn | .60 | .25 |
| 240 | Shawn Jefferson | .25 | .08 |
| 241 | Ty Law | .40 | .15 |
| 242 | Lawyer Milloy | .40 | .15 |
| 243 | Lovett Purnell RC | 1.00 | .40 |
| 244 | Sedrick Shaw | .25 | .08 |
| 245 | Tony Simmons | .25 | .08 |
| 246 | Chris Slade | .25 | .08 |
| 247 | R.Rutledge/Anth.Ladd RC | 1.00 | .40 |
| 248 | Chris Floyd/Harold Shaw | .25 | .08 |
| 249 | Ink Aleaga RC | 1.00 | .40 |
| 250 | Cameron Cleeland | .25 | .08 |
| 251 | Kerry Collins | .40 | .15 |
| 252 | Troy Davis | .25 | .08 |
| 253 | Sean Dawkins | .25 | .08 |
| 254 | Mark Fields | .25 | .08 |
| 255 | Andre Hastings | .25 | .08 |
| 256 | Sammy Knight | .25 | .08 |
| 257 | Keith Poole | .25 | .08 |
| 258 | William Roaf | .25 | .08 |
| 259 | Lamar Smith | .40 | .15 |
| 260 | Danny Wuerffel | .25 | .08 |
| 261 | Joan Wilcox RC/Brett Bech RC | 1.00 | .40 |
| 262 | Chris Bordano RC/W.Perry | 1.00 | .40 |
| 263 | Jessie Armstead | .25 | .08 |
| 264 | Tiki Barber | .60 | .25 |
| 265 | Chad Bratzke | .25 | .08 |
| 266 | Gary Brown | .25 | .08 |
| 267 | Chris Calloway | .25 | .08 |
| 268 | Howard Cross | .25 | .08 |
| 269 | Kent Graham | .25 | .08 |
| 270 | Ike Hilliard | .25 | .08 |
| 271 | Danny Kanell | .40 | .15 |
| 272 | Michael Strahan | .40 | .15 |
| 273 | Amani Toomer | .25 | .08 |
| 274 | Charles Way | .25 | .08 |
| 275 | Greg Comella RC/M.Cherry | 1.50 | .60 |
| 276 | Kyle Brady | .25 | .08 |
| 277 | Keith Byars | .25 | .08 |
| 278 | Chad Cascadden | .25 | .08 |
| 279 | Wayne Chrebet | .40 | .15 |
| 280 | Bryan Cox | .25 | .08 |
| 281 | Glenn Foley | .40 | .15 |
| 282 | Aaron Glenn | .25 | .08 |
| 283 | Keyshawn Johnson | .60 | .25 |
| 284 | Leon Johnson | .25 | .08 |
| 285 | Mo Lewis | .25 | .08 |
| 286 | Curtis Martin | .60 | .25 |
| 287 | Otis Smith | .25 | .08 |
| 288 | Vinny Testaverde | .40 | .15 |
| 289 | Dedric Ward | .25 | .08 |
| 290 | Tim Brown | .60 | .25 |
| 291 | Rickey Dudley | .25 | .08 |
| 292 | Jeff George | .40 | .15 |
| 293 | Desmond Howard | .40 | .15 |
| 294 | James Jett | .40 | .15 |
| 295 | Lance Johnstone | .25 | .08 |
| 296 | Randy Jordan | .25 | .08 |
| 297 | Napoleon Kaufman | .60 | .25 |
| 298 | Lincoln Kennedy | .25 | .08 |
| 299 | Terry Mickens | .25 | .08 |
| 300 | Darrell Russell | .25 | .08 |
| 301 | Harvey Williams | .25 | .08 |
| 302 | Ch.Woodson/Ritchie | .60 | .25 |
| 303 | Rodney Williams/Jermaine Williams | .25 | .08 |
| 304 | Koy Detmer | .25 | .08 |
| 305 | Hugh Douglas | .25 | .08 |
| 306 | Jason Dunn | .25 | .08 |
| 307 | Irving Fryar | .40 | .15 |
| 308 | Charlie Garner | .40 | .15 |
| 309 | Jeff Graham | .25 | .08 |
| 310 | Bobby Hoying | .40 | .15 |
| 311 | Rodney Peete | .25 | .08 |
| 312 | Allen Rossum | .25 | .08 |
| 313 | Duce Staley | .60 | .25 |
| 314 | William Thomas | .25 | .08 |
| 315 | Kevin Turner | .25 | .08 |
| 316 | K.Sinceno RC/C.Walker RC | 1.00 | .40 |
| 317 | Jahine Arnold | .25 | .08 |
| 318 | Jerome Bettis | .60 | .25 |
| 319 | Will Blackwell | .25 | .08 |
| 320 | Mark Bruener | .25 | .08 |
| 321 | Dermontti Dawson | .25 | .08 |
| 322 | Chris Fuamatu-Ma'afala | .25 | .08 |
| 323 | Courtney Hawkins | .25 | .08 |
| 324 | Richard Huntley | .40 | .15 |
| 325 | Charles Johnson | .25 | .08 |
| 326 | Levon Kirkland | .25 | .08 |
| 327 | Kordell Stewart | .40 | .15 |

| | | |
|---|---|---|
| ☐ 328 Hines Ward | .60 | .25 |
| ☐ 329 Dewayne Washington | .25 | .08 |
| ☐ 330 Tony Banks | .40 | .15 |
| ☐ 331 Steve Bono | .25 | .08 |
| ☐ 332 Isaac Bruce | .60 | .25 |
| ☐ 333 June Henley RC | 1.25 | .50 |
| ☐ 334 Robert Holcombe | .25 | .08 |
| ☐ 335 Mike Jones LB | .25 | .08 |
| ☐ 336 Eddie Kennison | .40 | .15 |
| ☐ 337 Amp Lee | .25 | .08 |
| ☐ 338 Jerald Moore | .25 | .08 |
| ☐ 339 Ricky Proehl | .25 | .08 |
| ☐ 340 J.T. Thomas | .25 | .08 |
| ☐ 341 Derrick Harris/Az-Zahir Hakim | .40 | .15 |
| ☐ 342 Roland Williams/Grant Wistrom | .25 | .08 |
| ☐ 343 Kurt Warner RC/T.Home ! | 12.00 | 5.00 |
| ☐ 344 Terrell Fletcher | .25 | .08 |
| ☐ 345 Greg Jackson | .25 | .08 |
| ☐ 346 Charlie Jones | .25 | .08 |
| ☐ 347 Freddie Jones | .25 | .08 |
| ☐ 348 Ryan Leaf | .60 | .25 |
| ☐ 349 Natrone Means | .40 | .15 |
| ☐ 350 Mikhael Ricks | .25 | .08 |
| ☐ 351 Junior Seau | .60 | .25 |
| ☐ 352 Bryan Still | .25 | .08 |
| ☐ 353 T.Stephens/P.Thelwell RC | 1.25 | .50 |
| ☐ 354 Greg Clark | .25 | .08 |
| ☐ 355 Marc Edwards | .25 | .08 |
| ☐ 356 Merton Hanks | .25 | .08 |
| ☐ 357 Garrison Hearst | .40 | .15 |
| ☐ 358 R.W. McQuarters | .25 | .08 |
| ☐ 359 Ken Norton Jr. | .25 | .08 |
| ☐ 360 Terrell Owens | .60 | .25 |
| ☐ 361 Jerry Rice | 1.25 | .50 |
| ☐ 362 J.J. Stokes | .40 | .15 |
| ☐ 363 Bryant Young | .25 | .08 |
| ☐ 364 Steve Young | .75 | .30 |
| ☐ 365 Chad Brown | .25 | .08 |
| ☐ 366 Christian Fauria | .25 | .08 |
| ☐ 367 Joey Galloway | .40 | .15 |
| ☐ 368 Ahman Green | .25 | .08 |
| ☐ 369 Cortez Kennedy | .25 | .08 |
| ☐ 370 Jon Kitna | .60 | .25 |
| ☐ 371 James McKnight | .40 | .15 |
| ☐ 372 Mike Pritchard | .25 | .08 |
| ☐ 373 Michael Sinclair | .25 | .08 |
| ☐ 374 Shawn Springs | .25 | .08 |
| ☐ 375 Ricky Watters | .40 | .15 |
| ☐ 376 Darryl Williams | .25 | .08 |
| ☐ 377 R.Wilson/K.Joseph RC | 1.50 | .60 |
| ☐ 378 Mike Alstott | .60 | .25 |
| ☐ 379 Reidel Anthony | .40 | .15 |
| ☐ 380 Derrick Brooks | .25 | .08 |
| ☐ 381 Trent Dilfer | .60 | .25 |
| ☐ 382 Warrick Dunn | .60 | .25 |
| ☐ 383 Bert Emanuel | .40 | .15 |
| ☐ 384 Jacquez Green | .25 | .08 |
| ☐ 385 Patrick Hape | .25 | .08 |
| ☐ 386 John Lynch | .40 | .15 |
| ☐ 387 Dave Moore | .25 | .08 |
| ☐ 388 Hardy Nickerson | .25 | .08 |
| ☐ 389 Warren Sapp | .40 | .15 |
| ☐ 390 Karl Williams | .25 | .08 |
| ☐ 391 Blaine Bishop | .25 | .08 |
| ☐ 392 Joe Bowden | .25 | .08 |
| ☐ 393 Isaac Byrd RC | 1.00 | .40 |
| ☐ 394 Willie Davis | .25 | .08 |
| ☐ 395 Al Del Greco | .25 | .08 |
| ☐ 396 Kevin Dyson | .40 | .15 |
| ☐ 397 Eddie George | .60 | .25 |
| ☐ 398 Jackie Harris | .25 | .08 |
| ☐ 399 Dave Krieg | .25 | .08 |
| ☐ 400 Steve McNair | .60 | .25 |
| ☐ 401 Michael Roan | .25 | .08 |
| ☐ 402 Yancey Thigpen | .25 | .08 |
| ☐ 403 Frank Wycheck | .25 | .08 |
| ☐ 404 Derrick Mason/Steve Matthews | .40 | .15 |
| ☐ 405 Stephen Alexander | .25 | .08 |
| ☐ 406 Terry Allen | .40 | .15 |
| ☐ 407 Jamie Asher | .25 | .08 |
| ☐ 408 Stephen Davis | .60 | .25 |
| ☐ 409 Darrell Green | .25 | .08 |
| ☐ 410 Trent Green | .60 | .25 |
| ☐ 411 Skip Hicks | .25 | .08 |
| ☐ 412 Brian Mitchell | .25 | .08 |

| | | |
|---|---|---|
| ☐ 413 Leslie Shepherd | .25 | .08 |
| ☐ 414 Michael Westbrook | .40 | .15 |
| ☐ 415 T.Hardy/Rabih Abdullah RC | 1.00 | .40 |
| ☐ 416 C.Thomas RC/M.Quinn RC | 1.00 | .40 |
| ☐ 417 J.Quinn/Kelly Holcomb RC | 8.00 | 3.00 |
| ☐ 418 Brian Alford/Blake Spence | 1.00 | .40 |
| ☐ 419 Andy Haase RC/Carlos King | 1.00 | .40 |
| ☐ 420 James Thrash RC/K.Hankton | 1.50 | .60 |
| ☐ 421 F.Beasley/Itula Mili RC | 1.25 | .50 |
| ☐ 422 Champ Bailey RC | 2.00 | .75 |
| ☐ 423 D'Wayne Bates RC | 1.25 | .50 |
| ☐ 424 Michael Bishop RC | 1.50 | .60 |
| ☐ 425 David Boston RC | 1.50 | .60 |
| ☐ 426 Shawn Bryson RC | 1.50 | .60 |
| ☐ 427 Tim Couch RC | 1.50 | .60 |
| ☐ 428 Scott Covington RC | 1.50 | .60 |
| ☐ 429 Daunte Culpepper RC | 6.00 | 2.50 |
| ☐ 430 Autry Denson RC | 1.25 | .50 |
| ☐ 431 Troy Edwards RC | 1.50 | .60 |
| ☐ 432 Kevin Faulk RC | 1.50 | .60 |
| ☐ 433 Joe Germaine RC | 1.25 | .50 |
| ☐ 434 Torry Holt RC | 4.00 | 1.50 |
| ☐ 435 Brock Huard RC | 1.50 | .60 |
| ☐ 436 Sedrick Irvin RC | 1.00 | .40 |
| ☐ 437 Edgerrin James RC | 6.00 | 2.50 |
| ☐ 438 Andy Katzenmoyer RC | 1.25 | .50 |
| ☐ 439 Shaun King RC | 1.25 | .50 |
| ☐ 440 Rob Konrad RC | 1.25 | .50 |
| ☐ 441 Donovan McNabb RC | 8.00 | 3.00 |
| ☐ 442 Cade McNown RC | 1.25 | .50 |
| ☐ 443 Billy Miller RC | 1.00 | .40 |
| ☐ 444 Dee Miller RC | 1.00 | .40 |
| ☐ 445 Sirr Parker RC | 1.00 | .40 |
| ☐ 446 Peerless Price RC | 1.50 | .60 |
| ☐ 447 Akili Smith RC | 1.25 | .50 |
| ☐ 448 Tai Streets RC | 1.50 | .60 |
| ☐ 449 Ricky Williams RC | 3.00 | 1.25 |
| ☐ 450 Amos Zereoue RC | 1.50 | .60 |
| ☐ S1 Warrick Dunn Sample | .60 | .25 |

## 2000 Pacific

| | | |
|---|---|---|
| ☐ COMPLETE SET (450) | 60.00 | 25.00 |
| ☐ 1 Mario Bates | .25 | .08 |
| ☐ 2 David Boston | .60 | .25 |
| ☐ 3 Rob Fredrickson | .25 | .08 |
| ☐ 4 Terry Hardy | .25 | .08 |
| ☐ 5 Rob Moore | .40 | .15 |
| ☐ 6 Adrian Murrell | .40 | .15 |
| ☐ 7 Michael Pittman | .25 | .08 |
| ☐ 8 Jake Plummer | .40 | .15 |
| ☐ 9 Simeon Rice | .40 | .15 |
| ☐ 10 Frank Sanders | .40 | .15 |
| ☐ 11 Aeneas Williams | .25 | .08 |
| ☐ 12 M.Cody/A.McCullough | .25 | .08 |
| ☐ 13 D.McKinley RC/J.Makovicka | .25 | .08 |
| ☐ 14 Jamal Anderson | .60 | .25 |
| ☐ 15 Chris Calloway | .25 | .08 |
| ☐ 16 Chris Chandler | .40 | .15 |
| ☐ 17 Bob Christian | .25 | .08 |
| ☐ 18 Tim Dwight | .60 | .25 |
| ☐ 19 Jammi German | .25 | .08 |
| ☐ 20 Ronnie Harris | .25 | .08 |
| ☐ 21 Terance Mathis | .40 | .15 |
| ☐ 22 Ken Oxendine | .25 | .08 |
| ☐ 23 O.J. Santiago | .25 | .08 |
| ☐ 24 Bob Whitfield | .25 | .08 |
| ☐ 25 E.Baker/R.Kelly | .25 | .08 |
| ☐ 26 Justin Armour | .25 | .08 |

| | | |
|---|---|---|
| ☐ 27 Tony Banks | .40 | .15 |
| ☐ 28 Peter Boulware | .25 | .08 |
| ☐ 29 Stoney Case | .25 | .08 |
| ☐ 30 Priest Holmes | .75 | .30 |
| ☐ 31 Qadry Ismail | .25 | .08 |
| ☐ 32 Patrick Johnson | .25 | .08 |
| ☐ 33 Michael McCrary | .25 | .08 |
| ☐ 34 Jonathan Ogden | .25 | .08 |
| ☐ 35 Errict Rhett | .40 | .15 |
| ☐ 36 Duane Starks | .25 | .08 |
| ☐ 37 Doug Flutie | .60 | .25 |
| ☐ 38 Rob Johnson | .40 | .15 |
| ☐ 39 Jonathan Linton | .25 | .08 |
| ☐ 40 Eric Moulds | .60 | .25 |
| ☐ 41 Peerless Price | .40 | .15 |
| ☐ 42 Andre Reed | .40 | .15 |
| ☐ 43 Jay Riemersma | .25 | .08 |
| ☐ 44 Antowain Smith | .40 | .15 |
| ☐ 45 Bruce Smith | .40 | .15 |
| ☐ 46 Thurman Thomas | .40 | .15 |
| ☐ 47 Kevin Williams | .25 | .08 |
| ☐ 48 B.Collins/S.Jackson | .25 | .08 |
| ☐ 49 Michael Bates | .25 | .08 |
| ☐ 50 Steve Beuerlein | .40 | .15 |
| ☐ 51 Tim Biakabutuka | .40 | .15 |
| ☐ 52 Antonio Edwards | .25 | .08 |
| ☐ 53 Donald Hayes | .25 | .08 |
| ☐ 54 Patrick Jeffers | .60 | .25 |
| ☐ 55 Anthony Johnson | .25 | .08 |
| ☐ 56 Jeff Lewis | .25 | .08 |
| ☐ 57 Eric Metcalf | .40 | .15 |
| ☐ 58 Muhsin Muhammad | .40 | .15 |
| ☐ 59 Jason Peter | .25 | .08 |
| ☐ 60 Wesley Walls | .40 | .15 |
| ☐ 61 John Allred | .25 | .08 |
| ☐ 62 Marty Booker | .40 | .15 |
| ☐ 63 Curtis Conway | .40 | .15 |
| ☐ 64 Bobby Engram | .25 | .08 |
| ☐ 65 Curtis Enis | .40 | .15 |
| ☐ 66 Shane Matthews | .25 | .08 |
| ☐ 67 Cade McNown | .25 | .08 |
| ☐ 68 Glyn Milburn | .25 | .08 |
| ☐ 69 Jim Miller | .25 | .08 |
| ☐ 70 Marcus Robinson | .60 | .25 |
| ☐ 71 Ryan Wetnight | .25 | .08 |
| ☐ 72 J.Allen/M.Brooks | .40 | .15 |
| ☐ 73 Jeff Blake | .40 | .15 |
| ☐ 74 Corey Dillon | .60 | .25 |
| ☐ 75 Rodney Heath RC | .25 | .08 |
| ☐ 76 Willie Jackson | .25 | .08 |
| ☐ 77 Tremain Mack | .25 | .08 |
| ☐ 78 Tony McGee | .25 | .08 |
| ☐ 79 Carl Pickens | .40 | .15 |
| ☐ 80 Darnay Scott | .40 | .15 |
| ☐ 81 Akili Smith | .40 | .15 |
| ☐ 82 Takeo Spikes | .25 | .08 |
| ☐ 83 Craig Yeast | .25 | .08 |
| ☐ 84 M.Basnight/N.Williams | .25 | .08 |
| ☐ 85 Karim Abdul-Jabbar | .40 | .15 |
| ☐ 86 Darrin Chiaverini | .25 | .08 |
| ☐ 87 Tim Couch | .40 | .15 |
| ☐ 88 Marc Edwards | .25 | .08 |
| ☐ 89 Kevin Johnson | .60 | .25 |
| ☐ 90 Terry Kirby | .25 | .08 |
| ☐ 91 Daylon McCutcheon | .25 | .08 |
| ☐ 92 Jamir Miller | .25 | .08 |
| ☐ 93 Leslie Shepherd | .25 | .08 |
| ☐ 94 Irv Smith | .25 | .08 |
| ☐ 95 M.Campbell/J.Dearth | .25 | .08 |
| ☐ 96 Z.Davis RC/D.Dunn RC | .40 | .15 |
| ☐ 97 M.Hill/T.Saleh RC | .25 | .08 |
| ☐ 98 Troy Aikman | 1.25 | .50 |
| ☐ 99 Eric Bjornson | .25 | .08 |
| ☐ 100 Dexter Coakley | .25 | .08 |
| ☐ 101 Greg Ellis | .25 | .08 |
| ☐ 102 Rocket Ismail | .40 | .15 |
| ☐ 103 David LaFleur | .25 | .08 |
| ☐ 104 Ernie Mills | .25 | .08 |
| ☐ 105 Jeff Ogden | .40 | .15 |
| ☐ 106 R.Neufeld RC/R.Thomas | .40 | .15 |
| ☐ 107 Deion Sanders | .60 | .25 |
| ☐ 108 Emmitt Smith | 1.25 | .50 |
| ☐ 109 Chris Warren | .25 | .08 |
| ☐ 110 M.Lucky/J.Tucker | .25 | .08 |
| ☐ 111 Byron Chamberlain | .25 | .08 |

| # | Player | Price 1 | Price 2 |
|---|--------|---------|---------|
| 112 | Terrell Davis | .60 | .25 |
| 113 | Jason Elam | .25 | .08 |
| 114 | Olandis Gary | .60 | .25 |
| 115 | Brian Griese | .60 | .25 |
| 116 | Ed McCaffrey | .25 | .08 |
| 117 | Trevor Pryce | .25 | .08 |
| 118 | Bill Romanowski | .25 | .08 |
| 119 | Shannon Sharpe | .40 | .15 |
| 120 | Rod Smith | .40 | .15 |
| 121 | Al Wilson | .25 | .08 |
| 122 | A.Cooper/C.Watson | .25 | .08 |
| 123 | Charlie Batch | .60 | .25 |
| 124 | Stephen Boyd | .25 | .08 |
| 125 | Chris Claiborne | .25 | .08 |
| 126 | Germane Crowell | .25 | .08 |
| 127 | Terry Fair | .25 | .08 |
| 128 | Gus Frerotte | .25 | .08 |
| 129 | Jason Hanson | .25 | .08 |
| 130 | Greg Hill | .25 | .08 |
| 131 | Herman Moore | .40 | .15 |
| 132 | Johnnie Morton | .40 | .15 |
| 133 | Barry Sanders | 1.50 | .60 |
| 134 | David Sloan | .25 | .08 |
| 135 | B.Olivo/C.Sauter | .25 | .08 |
| 136 | Corey Bradford | .40 | .15 |
| 137 | Tyrone Davis | .25 | .08 |
| 138 | Brett Favre | 2.00 | .75 |
| 139 | Antonio Freeman | .60 | .25 |
| 140 | Vonnie Holliday | .25 | .08 |
| 141 | Dorsey Levens | .40 | .15 |
| 142 | Keith McKenzie | .25 | .08 |
| 143 | Mike McKenzie | .25 | .08 |
| 144 | Bill Schroeder | .40 | .15 |
| 145 | Jeff Thomason | .25 | .08 |
| 146 | Frank Winters | .25 | .08 |
| 147 | Cornelius Bennett | .25 | .08 |
| 148 | Tony Blevins RC | .40 | .15 |
| 149 | Chad Bratzke | .25 | .08 |
| 150 | Ken Dilger | .25 | .08 |
| 151 | Tarik Glenn | .25 | .08 |
| 152 | E.G. Green | .25 | .08 |
| 153 | Marvin Harrison | .60 | .25 |
| 154 | Edgerrin James | 1.00 | .40 |
| 155 | Peyton Manning | 1.50 | .60 |
| 156 | Jerome Pathon | .40 | .15 |
| 157 | Marcus Pollard | .25 | .08 |
| 158 | Terrence Wilkins | .25 | .08 |
| 159 | I.Jones RC/P.Shields RC | .60 | .25 |
| 160 | Reggie Barlow | .25 | .08 |
| 161 | Aaron Beasley | .25 | .08 |
| 162 | Tony Boselli | .25 | .08 |
| 163 | Tony Brackens | .25 | .08 |
| 164 | Kyle Brady | .25 | .08 |
| 165 | Mark Brunell | .60 | .25 |
| 166 | Jay Fiedler | .60 | .25 |
| 167 | Kevin Hardy | .25 | .08 |
| 168 | Carnell Lake | .25 | .08 |
| 169 | Keenan McCardell | .40 | .15 |
| 170 | Jonathan Quinn | .25 | .08 |
| 171 | Jimmy Smith | .40 | .15 |
| 172 | James Hasty | .25 | .08 |
| 173 | Fred Taylor | .60 | .25 |
| 174 | L.Jackson RC/S.Mack | .60 | .25 |
| 175 | Derrick Alexander | .25 | .08 |
| 176 | Donnell Bennett | .25 | .08 |
| 177 | Donnie Edwards | .25 | .08 |
| 178 | Tony Gonzalez | .40 | .15 |
| 179 | Elvis Grbac | .40 | .15 |
| 180 | James Hasty | .25 | .08 |
| 181 | Joe Horn | .40 | .15 |
| 182 | Lonnie Johnson | .25 | .08 |
| 183 | Kevin Lockett | .25 | .08 |
| 184 | Larry Parker | .25 | .08 |
| 185 | Tony Richardson RC | .40 | .15 |
| 186 | Rashaan Shehee | .25 | .08 |
| 187 | Tamarick Vanover | .25 | .08 |
| 188 | Trace Armstrong | .25 | .08 |
| 189 | Oronde Gadsden | .40 | .15 |
| 190 | Damon Huard | .60 | .25 |
| 191 | Nate Jacquet | .25 | .08 |
| 192 | James Johnson | .25 | .08 |
| 193 | Rob Konrad | .25 | .08 |
| 194 | Sam Madison | .25 | .08 |
| 195 | Dan Marino | 2.00 | .75 |
| 196 | Tony Martin | .40 | .15 |
| 197 | O.J. McDuffie | .40 | .15 |
| 198 | Stanley Pritchett | .25 | .08 |
| 199 | Tim Ruddy | .25 | .08 |
| 200 | Patrick Surtain | .25 | .08 |
| 201 | Zach Thomas | .60 | .25 |
| 202 | Cris Carter | .60 | .25 |
| 203 | Duane Clemons | .25 | .08 |
| 204 | Carlester Crumpler | .25 | .08 |
| 205 | Daunte Culpepper | .75 | .30 |
| 206 | Jeff George | .40 | .15 |
| 207 | Matthew Hatchette | .25 | .08 |
| 208 | Leroy Hoard | .25 | .08 |
| 209 | Randy Moss | 1.25 | .50 |
| 210 | John Randle | .40 | .15 |
| 211 | Jake Reed | .40 | .15 |
| 212 | Robert Smith | .40 | .15 |
| 213 | Robert Tate | .25 | .08 |
| 214 | Terry Allen | .40 | .15 |
| 215 | Bruce Armstrong | .25 | .08 |
| 216 | Drew Bledsoe | .75 | .30 |
| 217 | Ben Coates | .25 | .08 |
| 218 | Kevin Faulk | .40 | .15 |
| 219 | Terry Glenn | .40 | .15 |
| 220 | Shawn Jefferson | .25 | .08 |
| 221 | Andy Katzenmoyer | .25 | .08 |
| 222 | Ty Law | .40 | .15 |
| 223 | Willie McGinest | .25 | .08 |
| 224 | Lawyer Milloy | .25 | .08 |
| 225 | Tony Simmons | .25 | .08 |
| 226 | M.Bishop/S.Morey RC | .25 | .08 |
| 227 | Cameron Cleeland | .25 | .08 |
| 228 | Troy Davis | .25 | .08 |
| 229 | Jake Delhomme RC | 3.00 | 1.25 |
| 230 | Andre Hastings | .25 | .08 |
| 231 | Eddie Kennison | .40 | .15 |
| 232 | Wilmont Perry | .25 | .08 |
| 233 | Dino Philyaw | .25 | .08 |
| 234 | Keith Poole | .25 | .08 |
| 235 | William Roaf | .25 | .08 |
| 236 | Billy Joe Tolliver | .25 | .08 |
| 237 | Fred Weary | .25 | .08 |
| 238 | Ricky Williams | .60 | .25 |
| 239 | Franklin RC/M.Powell RC | .25 | .08 |
| 240 | Jessie Armstead | .25 | .08 |
| 241 | Tiki Barber | .25 | .08 |
| 242 | Daniel Campbell | .25 | .08 |
| 243 | Kerry Collins | .40 | .15 |
| 244 | Percy Ellsworth | .25 | .08 |
| 245 | Kent Graham | .25 | .08 |
| 246 | Ike Hilliard | .40 | .15 |
| 247 | Cedric Jones | .25 | .08 |
| 248 | Bashir Levingston RC | .60 | .25 |
| 249 | Pete Mitchell | .25 | .08 |
| 250 | Michael Strahan | .40 | .15 |
| 251 | Amani Toomer | .25 | .08 |
| 252 | Charles Way | .25 | .08 |
| 253 | Andre Weathers RC | .40 | .15 |
| 254 | Richie Anderson | .40 | .15 |
| 255 | Wayne Chrebet | .40 | .15 |
| 256 | Marcus Coleman | .25 | .08 |
| 257 | Bryan Cox | .25 | .08 |
| 258 | Jason Fabini RC | .40 | .15 |
| 259 | Robert Farmer RC | .60 | .25 |
| 260 | Keyshawn Johnson | .60 | .25 |
| 261 | Ray Lucas | .25 | .08 |
| 262 | Curtis Martin | .60 | .25 |
| 263 | Kevin Mawae | .25 | .08 |
| 264 | Eric Ogbogu | .25 | .08 |
| 265 | Bernie Parmalee | .25 | .08 |
| 266 | Vinny Testaverde | .40 | .15 |
| 267 | Dedric Ward | .25 | .08 |
| 268 | Eric Barton RC | .25 | .08 |
| 269 | Tim Brown | .60 | .25 |
| 270 | Tony Bryant | .25 | .08 |
| 271 | Rickey Dudley | .25 | .08 |
| 272 | Rich Gannon | .40 | .15 |
| 273 | Bobby Hoying | .40 | .15 |
| 274 | James Jett | .25 | .08 |
| 275 | Napoleon Kaufman | .40 | .15 |
| 276 | Jon Ritchie | .25 | .08 |
| 277 | Darrell Russell | .25 | .08 |
| 278 | Kenny Shedd | .25 | .08 |
| 279 | Marquis Walker RC | .40 | .15 |
| 280 | Tyrone Wheatley | .40 | .15 |
| 281 | Charles Woodson | .40 | .15 |
| 282 | Luther Broughton RC | .40 | .15 |
| 283 | Al Harris RC | .25 | .08 |
| 284 | Greg Jefferson | .25 | .08 |
| 285 | Dietrich Jelis | .25 | .08 |
| 286 | Charles Johnson | .40 | .15 |
| 287 | Chad Lewis | .25 | .08 |
| 288 | Mike Mamula | .25 | .08 |
| 289 | Donovan McNabb | 1.00 | .40 |
| 290 | Doug Pederson | .25 | .08 |
| 291 | Allen Rossum | .25 | .08 |
| 292 | Torrance Small | .25 | .08 |
| 293 | Duce Staley | .60 | .25 |
| 294 | Jerome Bettis | .60 | .25 |
| 295 | Kris Brown | .25 | .08 |
| 296 | Mark Bruener | .25 | .08 |
| 297 | Troy Edwards | .40 | .15 |
| 298 | Jason Gildon | .25 | .08 |
| 299 | Richard Huntley | .25 | .08 |
| 300 | Bobby Shaw RC | .60 | .25 |
| 301 | Scott Shields RC | .40 | .15 |
| 302 | Kordell Stewart | .40 | .15 |
| 303 | Hines Ward | .60 | .25 |
| 304 | Amos Zereoue | .60 | .25 |
| 305 | M.Cushing RC/J.Tuman | .40 | .15 |
| 306 | P.Gonzalez/A.Wright RC | 1.50 | .60 |
| 307 | Isaac Bruce | .60 | .25 |
| 308 | Kevin Carter | .25 | .08 |
| 309 | Marshall Faulk | .75 | .30 |
| 310 | London Fletcher RC | .40 | .15 |
| 311 | Joe Germaine | .25 | .08 |
| 312 | Az-Zahir Hakim | .40 | .15 |
| 313 | Torry Holt | .60 | .25 |
| 314 | Tony Horne | .25 | .08 |
| 315 | Mike Jones LB | .25 | .08 |
| 316 | Dexter McCleon RC | .60 | .25 |
| 317 | Orlando Pace | .25 | .08 |
| 318 | Ricky Proehl | .25 | .08 |
| 319 | Kurt Warner | 1.25 | .50 |
| 320 | Roland Williams | .25 | .08 |
| 321 | Grant Wistrom | .25 | .08 |
| 322 | J.Hodgins RC/J.Watson | .25 | .08 |
| 323 | Jermaine Fazande | .25 | .08 |
| 324 | Jeff Graham | .25 | .08 |
| 325 | Jim Harbaugh | .40 | .15 |
| 326 | Raylee Johnson | .25 | .08 |
| 327 | Charlie Jones | .25 | .08 |
| 328 | Freddie Jones | .25 | .08 |
| 329 | Natrone Means | .25 | .08 |
| 330 | Chris Penn | .25 | .08 |
| 331 | Mikhail Ricks | .25 | .08 |
| 332 | Junior Seau | .60 | .25 |
| 333 | R.Davis RC/R.Reed RC | .40 | .15 |
| 334 | Fred Beasley | .25 | .08 |
| 335 | Brentson Buckner | .25 | .08 |
| 336 | Greg Clark | .25 | .08 |
| 337 | Dave Fiore RC | .25 | .08 |
| 338 | Charlie Garner | .40 | .15 |
| 339 | Mark Harris RC | .60 | .25 |
| 340 | Ramos McDonald RC | .40 | .15 |
| 341 | Terrell Owens | .60 | .25 |
| 342 | Jerry Rice | 1.25 | .50 |
| 343 | Lance Schulters | .25 | .08 |
| 344 | J.J. Stokes | .40 | .15 |
| 345 | Bryant Young | .25 | .08 |
| 346 | Steve Young | .75 | .30 |
| 347 | Jeff Garcia | .60 | .25 |
| 348 | Fabien Bownes RC | .25 | .08 |
| 349 | Chad Brown | .25 | .08 |
| 350 | Reggie Brown | .25 | .08 |
| 351 | Sean Dawkins | .25 | .08 |
| 352 | Christian Fauria | .25 | .08 |
| 353 | Ahman Green | .60 | .25 |
| 354 | Walter Jones | .25 | .08 |
| 355 | Cortez Kennedy | .25 | .08 |
| 356 | Jon Kitna | .60 | .25 |
| 357 | Derrick Mayes | .40 | .15 |
| 358 | Charlie Rogers | .25 | .08 |
| 359 | Shawn Springs | .25 | .08 |
| 360 | Ricky Watters | .40 | .15 |
| 361 | Donne Abraham | .25 | .08 |
| 362 | Mike Alstott | .60 | .25 |
| 363 | Reidel Anthony | .25 | .08 |
| 364 | Ronde Barber | .25 | .08 |
| 365 | Derrick Brooks | .60 | .25 |
| 366 | Warrick Dunn | .60 | .25 |

**2001 Pacific**

|  |  | | |
|---|---|---|---|
| 367 | Jacquez Green | .25 | .08 |
| 368 | Marcus Jones | .25 | .08 |
| 369 | Shaun King | .25 | .08 |
| 370 | John Lynch | .40 | .15 |
| 371 | Warren Sapp | .40 | .15 |
| 372 | Steve White RC | .25 | .08 |
| 373 | M.Gramatica/K.McLeod RC | .40 | .15 |
| 374 | Blaine Bishop | .25 | .08 |
| 375 | Al Del Greco | .25 | .08 |
| 376 | Kevin Dyson | .40 | .15 |
| 377 | Eddie George | .60 | .25 |
| 378 | Jevon Kearse | .60 | .25 |
| 379 | Derrick Mason | .40 | .15 |
| 380 | Bruce Matthews | .25 | .08 |
| 381 | Steve McNair | .60 | .25 |
| 382 | Neil O'Donnell | .25 | .08 |
| 383 | Yancey Thigpen | .25 | .08 |
| 384 | Frank Wycheck | .25 | .08 |
| 385 | K.Daft/L.Brown | .25 | .08 |
| 386 | Stephen Alexander | .25 | .08 |
| 387 | Champ Bailey | .40 | .15 |
| 388 | Larry Centers | .25 | .08 |
| 389 | Marco Coleman | .25 | .08 |
| 390 | Albert Connell | .25 | .08 |
| 391 | Stephen Davis | .60 | .25 |
| 392 | Irving Fryar | .40 | .15 |
| 393 | Skip Hicks | .25 | .08 |
| 394 | Brad Johnson | .60 | .25 |
| 395 | Michael Westbrook | .40 | .15 |
| 396 | O.Ayanbadejo RC/L.Gordon RC | .40 | .15 |
| 397 | D.Driver/R.Powell | .60 | .25 |
| 398 | T.Bouman/J.Brigham RC | .60 | .25 |
| 399 | B.Huard/S.Bonner | .25 | .08 |
| 400 | M.Sellers/S.George RC | .40 | .15 |
| 401 | Shaun Alexander RC | 4.00 | 1.50 |
| 402 | LaVar Arrington RC | 2.50 | 1.00 |
| 403 | Tom Brady RC | 40.00 | 20.00 |
| 404 | Demario Brown RC | .60 | .25 |
| 405 | Plaxico Burress RC | 2.50 | 1.00 |
| 406 | Trung Canidate RC | 1.00 | .40 |
| 407 | Giovanni Carmazzi RC | .60 | .25 |
| 408 | Kwame Cavil RC | .60 | .25 |
| 409 | Chrys Chukwuma RC | 1.25 | .50 |
| 410 | Ron Dayne RC | 1.25 | .50 |
| 411 | Reuben Droughns RC | 1.50 | .60 |
| 412 | Ron Dugans RC | .60 | .25 |
| 413 | Deon Dyer RC | 1.00 | .40 |
| 414 | Danny Farmer RC | 1.00 | .40 |
| 415 | Chafie Fields RC | .60 | .25 |
| 416 | Trevor Gaylor RC | 1.00 | .40 |
| 417 | Sherrod Gideon RC | .60 | .25 |
| 418 | Joey Goodspeed RC | .60 | .25 |
| 419 | Joe Hamilton RC | 1.00 | .40 |
| 420 | Tony Hartley RC | .60 | .25 |
| 421 | Todd Husak RC | 1.25 | .50 |
| 422 | Trevor Insley RC | .60 | .25 |
| 423 | Thomas Jones RC | 2.00 | .75 |
| 424 | Marcus Knight RC | 1.00 | .40 |
| 425 | Jamal Lewis RC | 3.00 | 1.25 |
| 426 | Anthony Lucas RC | 1.50 | .60 |
| 427 | Tee Martin RC | 1.25 | .50 |
| 428 | Rondell Mealey RC | .60 | .25 |
| 429 | Sylvester Morris RC | 1.00 | .40 |
| 430 | Chad Morton RC | 1.25 | .50 |
| 431 | Dennis Northcutt RC | 1.25 | .50 |
| 432 | Chad Pennington RC | 3.00 | 1.25 |
| 433 | Rodnick Phillips RC | .60 | .25 |
| 434 | Mareno Philyaw RC | .60 | .25 |
| 435 | Jerry Porter RC | 1.50 | .60 |
| 436 | Travis Prentice RC | 1.00 | .40 |
| 437 | Tim Rattay RC | 1.25 | .50 |
| 438 | Chris Redman RC | 1.00 | .40 |
| 439 | J.R. Redmond RC | 1.00 | .40 |
| 440 | Gari Scott RC | .60 | .25 |
| 441 | Keith Smith RC | .60 | .25 |
| 442 | Terrelle Smith RC | 1.00 | .40 |
| 443 | R.Jay Soward RC | 1.00 | .40 |
| 444 | Quinton Spotwood RC | .60 | .25 |
| 445 | Shyrone Stith RC | .60 | .25 |
| 446 | Travis Taylor RC | 1.25 | .50 |
| 447 | Troy Walters RC | 1.25 | .50 |
| 448 | Peter Warrick RC | 1.25 | .50 |
| 449 | Dez White RC | 1.25 | .50 |
| 450 | Michael Wiley RC | 1.00 | .40 |
| | COMP.SET w/o SP's (450) | 50.00 | 25.00 |
| 1 | David Boston | .60 | .25 |
| 2 | Mac Cody | .25 | .08 |
| 3 | Chris Gedney | .25 | .08 |
| 4 | Chris Greisen | .25 | .08 |
| 5 | Terry Hardy | .25 | .08 |
| 6 | MarTay Jenkins | .25 | .08 |
| 7 | Thomas Jones | .60 | .25 |
| 8 | Joel Makovicka | .25 | .08 |
| 9 | Tywan Mitchell | .25 | .08 |
| 10 | Rob Moore | .40 | .15 |
| 11 | Michael Pittman | .25 | .08 |
| 12 | Jake Plummer | .40 | .15 |
| 13 | Frank Sanders | .25 | .08 |
| 14 | Aeneas Williams | .25 | .08 |
| 15 | Jamal Anderson | .60 | .25 |
| 16 | Eugene Baker | .25 | .08 |
| 17 | Chris Chandler | .40 | .15 |
| 18 | Tim Dwight | .60 | .25 |
| 19 | Brian Finneran | .25 | .08 |
| 20 | Jammi German | .25 | .08 |
| 21 | Shawn Jefferson | .25 | .08 |
| 22 | Doug Johnson | .25 | .08 |
| 23 | Danny Kanell | .25 | .08 |
| 24 | Reggie Kelly | .25 | .08 |
| 25 | Terance Mathis | .40 | .15 |
| 26 | Derek Rackley | .25 | .08 |
| 27 | Ron Rivers | .25 | .08 |
| 28 | Maurice Smith | .40 | .15 |
| 29 | Sam Adams | .25 | .08 |
| 30 | Obafemi Ayanbadejo | .25 | .08 |
| 31 | Tony Banks | .40 | .15 |
| 32 | Trent Dilfer | .40 | .15 |
| 33 | Sam Gash | .25 | .08 |
| 34 | Priest Holmes | .75 | .30 |
| 35 | Qadry Ismail | .40 | .15 |
| 36 | Pat Johnson | .25 | .08 |
| 37 | Jamal Lewis | 1.00 | .40 |
| 38 | Jermaine Lewis | .25 | .08 |
| 39 | Ray Lewis | .60 | .25 |
| 40 | Chris Redman | .25 | .08 |
| 41 | Shannon Sharpe | .40 | .15 |
| 42 | Brandon Stokley | .40 | .15 |
| 43 | Travis Taylor | .40 | .15 |
| 44 | Shawn Bryson | .25 | .08 |
| 45 | Kwame Cavil | .25 | .08 |
| 46 | Sam Cowart | .25 | .08 |
| 47 | Doug Flutie | .60 | .25 |
| 48 | Rob Johnson | .40 | .15 |
| 49 | Jonathan Linton | .25 | .08 |
| 50 | Jeremy McDaniel | .25 | .08 |
| 51 | Sammy Morris | .25 | .08 |
| 52 | Eric Moulds | .40 | .15 |
| 53 | Peerless Price | .40 | .15 |
| 54 | Jay Riemersma | .25 | .08 |
| 55 | Antowain Smith | .25 | .08 |
| 56 | Chris Watson | .25 | .08 |
| 57 | Marcellus Wiley | .25 | .08 |
| 58 | Michael Bates | .25 | .08 |
| 59 | Steve Beuerlein | .40 | .15 |
| 60 | Tim Biakabutuka | .25 | .08 |
| 61 | Isaac Byrd | .25 | .08 |
| 62 | Dameyune Craig | .25 | .08 |
| 63 | William Floyd | .25 | .08 |
| 64 | Karl Hankton | .25 | .08 |
| 65 | Donald Hayes | .25 | .08 |
| 66 | Chris Hetherington RC | .40 | .15 |
| 67 | Brad Hoover | .25 | .08 |
| 68 | Patrick Jeffers | .60 | .25 |
| 69 | Muhsin Muhammad | .40 | .15 |
| 70 | Iheanyi Uwaezuoke | .25 | .08 |
| 71 | Wesley Walls | .40 | .15 |
| 72 | James Allen | .40 | .15 |
| 73 | Marlon Barnes | .25 | .08 |
| 74 | D'Wayne Bates | .25 | .08 |
| 75 | Marty Booker | .25 | .08 |
| 76 | Macey Brooks | .25 | .08 |
| 77 | Bobby Engram | .40 | .15 |
| 78 | Curtis Enis | .25 | .08 |
| 79 | Mark Hartsell RC | .40 | .15 |
| 80 | Eddie Kennison | .25 | .08 |
| 81 | Shane Matthews | .25 | .08 |
| 82 | Cade McNown | .40 | .15 |
| 83 | Jim Miller | .25 | .08 |
| 84 | Marcus Robinson | .40 | .15 |
| 85 | Brian Urlacher | 1.00 | .40 |
| 86 | Dez White | .25 | .08 |
| 87 | Brandon Bennett | .25 | .08 |
| 88 | Steve Bush RC | .40 | .15 |
| 89 | Corey Dillon | .60 | .25 |
| 90 | Ron Dugans | .25 | .08 |
| 91 | Danny Farmer | .25 | .08 |
| 92 | Damon Griffin | .25 | .08 |
| 93 | Cliff Groce | .40 | .15 |
| 94 | Curtis Keaton | .25 | .08 |
| 95 | Scott Mitchell | .25 | .08 |
| 96 | Darnay Scott | .40 | .15 |
| 97 | Akili Smith | .25 | .08 |
| 98 | Peter Warrick | .60 | .25 |
| 99 | Nick Williams | .25 | .08 |
| 100 | Craig Yeast | .25 | .08 |
| 101 | Bobby Brown | .25 | .08 |
| 102 | Darrin Chiaverini | .25 | .08 |
| 103 | Tim Couch | .40 | .15 |
| 104 | JaJuan Dawson | .25 | .08 |
| 105 | Marc Edwards | .25 | .08 |
| 106 | Kevin Johnson | .40 | .15 |
| 107 | Dennis Northcutt | .25 | .08 |
| 108 | David Patten | .25 | .08 |
| 109 | Doug Pederson | .25 | .08 |
| 110 | Travis Prentice | .25 | .08 |
| 111 | Errict Rhett | .25 | .08 |
| 112 | Aaron Shea | .25 | .08 |
| 113 | Kevin Thompson | .25 | .08 |
| 114 | Jamel White | .25 | .08 |
| 115 | Spergon Wynn | .25 | .08 |
| 116 | Troy Aikman | 1.00 | .40 |
| 117 | Chris Brazzell | .25 | .08 |
| 118 | Randall Cunningham | .60 | .25 |
| 119 | Jackie Harris | .25 | .08 |
| 120 | Damon Hodge | .25 | .08 |
| 121 | Rocket Ismail | .40 | .15 |
| 122 | David LaFleur | .25 | .08 |
| 123 | Wane McGarity | .25 | .08 |
| 124 | James McKnight | .40 | .15 |
| 125 | Emmitt Smith | 1.25 | .50 |
| 126 | Clint Stoerner | .25 | .08 |
| 127 | Jason Tucker | .25 | .08 |
| 128 | Michael Wiley | .25 | .08 |
| 129 | Anthony Wright | .25 | .08 |
| 130 | Mike Anderson | .60 | .25 |
| 131 | Dwayne Carswell | .25 | .08 |
| 132 | Byron Chamberlain | .25 | .08 |
| 133 | Desmond Clark | .25 | .08 |
| 134 | Chris Cole | .25 | .08 |
| 135 | KaRon Coleman | .25 | .08 |
| 136 | Terrell Davis | .60 | .25 |
| 137 | Gus Frerotte | .40 | .15 |
| 138 | Olandis Gary | .40 | .15 |
| 139 | Brian Griese | .60 | .25 |
| 140 | Howard Griffith | .25 | .08 |
| 141 | Jarious Jackson | .40 | .15 |
| 142 | Ed McCaffrey | .60 | .25 |
| 143 | Scottie Montgomery RC | .40 | .15 |
| 144 | Rod Smith | .40 | .15 |
| 145 | Charlie Batch | .60 | .25 |
| 146 | Stoney Case | .25 | .08 |
| 147 | Germane Crowell | .25 | .08 |
| 148 | Larry Foster | .25 | .08 |
| 149 | Desmond Howard | .25 | .08 |
| 150 | Sedrick Irvin | .40 | .15 |
| 151 | Herman Moore | .40 | .15 |

|  |  | | |
|---|---|---|---|
| 152 | Johnnie Morton | .40 | .15 |
| 153 | Robert Porcher | .25 | .08 |
| 154 | Cory Sauter | .25 | .08 |
| 155 | Cory Schlesinger | .25 | .08 |
| 156 | David Sloan | .25 | .08 |
| 157 | Brian Stablein | .25 | .08 |
| 158 | James Stewart | .40 | .15 |
| 159 | Corey Bradford | .25 | .08 |
| 160 | Tyrone Davis | .25 | .08 |
| 161 | Donald Driver | .40 | .15 |
| 162 | Brett Favre | 2.00 | .75 |
| 163 | Bubba Franks | .40 | .15 |
| 164 | Antonio Freeman | .60 | .25 |
| 165 | Herbert Goodman | .25 | .08 |
| 166 | Ahman Green | .60 | .25 |
| 167 | Matt Hasselbeck | .40 | .15 |
| 168 | William Henderson | .25 | .08 |
| 169 | Charles Lee | .25 | .08 |
| 170 | Dorsey Levens | .40 | .15 |
| 171 | Bill Schroeder | .40 | .15 |
| 172 | Darren Sharper | .25 | .08 |
| 173 | Matt Snider | .25 | .08 |
| 174 | Danny Wuerffel | .25 | .08 |
| 175 | Ken Dilger | .25 | .08 |
| 176 | Jim Finn | .25 | .08 |
| 177 | Lennox Gordon | .25 | .08 |
| 178 | E.G. Green | .25 | .08 |
| 179 | Marvin Harrison | .60 | .25 |
| 180 | Kelly Holcomb | .60 | .25 |
| 181 | Trevor Insley | .25 | .08 |
| 182 | Edgerrin James | .75 | .30 |
| 183 | Peyton Manning | 1.50 | .60 |
| 184 | Kevin McDougal | .25 | .08 |
| 185 | Jerome Pathon | .40 | .15 |
| 186 | Marcus Pollard | .25 | .08 |
| 187 | Justin Snow | .25 | .08 |
| 188 | Terrence Wilkins | .25 | .08 |
| 189 | Reggie Barlow | .25 | .08 |
| 190 | Kyle Brady | .25 | .08 |
| 191 | Mark Brunell | .60 | .25 |
| 192 | Kevin Hardy | .25 | .08 |
| 193 | Anthony Johnson | .25 | .08 |
| 194 | Stacey Mack | .25 | .08 |
| 195 | Jamie Martin | .40 | .15 |
| 196 | Keenan McCardell | .25 | .08 |
| 197 | Daimon Shelton | .25 | .08 |
| 198 | Jimmy Smith | .40 | .15 |
| 199 | R.Jay Soward | .25 | .08 |
| 200 | Shyrone Stith | .25 | .08 |
| 201 | Fred Taylor | .60 | .25 |
| 202 | Alvis Whitted | .25 | .08 |
| 203 | Jermaine Williams | .25 | .08 |
| 204 | Derrick Alexander | .40 | .15 |
| 205 | Kimble Anders | .25 | .08 |
| 206 | Donnell Bennett | .25 | .08 |
| 207 | Mike Cloud | .25 | .08 |
| 208 | Todd Collins | .25 | .08 |
| 209 | Tony Gonzalez | .40 | .15 |
| 210 | Elvis Grbac | .40 | .15 |
| 211 | Dante Hall | .60 | .25 |
| 212 | Kevin Lockett | .25 | .08 |
| 213 | Warren Moon | .40 | .15 |
| 214 | Frank Moreau | .25 | .08 |
| 215 | Sylvester Morris | .25 | .08 |
| 216 | Larry Parker | .25 | .08 |
| 217 | Tony Richardson | .25 | .08 |
| 218 | Trace Armstrong | .25 | .08 |
| 219 | Autry Denson | .25 | .08 |
| 220 | Bert Emanuel | .25 | .08 |
| 221 | Jay Fiedler | .60 | .25 |
| 222 | Oronde Gadsden | .40 | .15 |
| 223 | Damon Huard | .60 | .25 |
| 224 | James Johnson | .25 | .08 |
| 225 | Rob Konrad | .25 | .08 |
| 226 | Tony Martin | .25 | .08 |
| 227 | O.J. McDuffie | .25 | .08 |
| 228 | Mike Quinn | .25 | .08 |
| 229 | Lamar Smith | .25 | .08 |
| 230 | Jason Taylor | .25 | .08 |
| 231 | Thurman Thomas | .40 | .15 |
| 232 | Zach Thomas | .60 | .25 |
| 233 | Todd Bouman | .40 | .15 |
| 234 | Bubby Brister | .25 | .08 |
| 235 | Cris Carter | .60 | .25 |
| 236 | Daunte Culpepper | .60 | .25 |
| 237 | John Davis RC | .40 | .15 |
| 238 | Robert Griffith | .25 | .08 |
| 239 | Matthew Hatchette | .25 | .08 |
| 240 | Jim Kleinsasser | .25 | .08 |
| 241 | Randy Moss | 1.25 | .50 |
| 242 | John Randle | .25 | .08 |
| 243 | Robert Smith | .60 | .25 |
| 244 | Chris Walsh RC | .25 | .08 |
| 245 | Troy Walters | .25 | .08 |
| 246 | Moe Williams | .40 | .15 |
| 247 | Michael Bishop | .25 | .08 |
| 248 | Drew Bledsoe | .75 | .30 |
| 249 | Troy Brown | .40 | .15 |
| 250 | Tedy Bruschi | .50 | .20 |
| 251 | Tony Carter | .25 | .08 |
| 252 | Shockmain Davis | .25 | .08 |
| 253 | Kevin Faulk | .40 | .15 |
| 254 | Terry Glenn | .40 | .15 |
| 255 | Ty Law | .40 | .15 |
| 256 | Lawyer Milloy | .40 | .15 |
| 257 | J.R. Redmond | .25 | .08 |
| 258 | Harold Shaw | .25 | .08 |
| 259 | Tony Simmons | .25 | .08 |
| 260 | Jermaine Wiggins | .40 | .15 |
| 261 | Jeff Blake | .25 | .08 |
| 262 | Aaron Brooks | .60 | .25 |
| 263 | Cam Cleeland | .25 | .08 |
| 264 | Andrew Glover | .25 | .08 |
| 265 | La'Roi Glover | .25 | .08 |
| 266 | Joe Horn | .40 | .15 |
| 267 | Kevin Houser | .25 | .08 |
| 268 | Willie Jackson | .25 | .08 |
| 269 | Jerald Moore | .25 | .08 |
| 270 | Chad Morton | .25 | .08 |
| 271 | Keith Poole | .25 | .08 |
| 272 | Terrelle Smith | .25 | .08 |
| 273 | Ricky Williams | .60 | .25 |
| 274 | Robert Wilson | .25 | .08 |
| 275 | Jessie Armstead | .25 | .08 |
| 276 | Tiki Barber | .60 | .25 |
| 277 | Mike Cherry | .25 | .08 |
| 278 | Kerry Collins | .40 | .15 |
| 279 | Greg Comella | .25 | .08 |
| 280 | Thabiti Davis | .25 | .08 |
| 281 | Ron Dayne | .60 | .25 |
| 282 | Ron Dixon | .25 | .08 |
| 283 | Ike Hilliard | .25 | .08 |
| 284 | Joe Jurevicius | .25 | .08 |
| 285 | Jason Sehorn | .25 | .08 |
| 286 | Michael Strahan | .40 | .15 |
| 287 | Amani Toomer | .25 | .08 |
| 288 | Craig Walendy | .25 | .08 |
| 289 | Damon Washington RC | .40 | .15 |
| 290 | Richie Anderson | .25 | .08 |
| 291 | Anthony Becht | .25 | .08 |
| 292 | Wayne Chrebet | .40 | .15 |
| 293 | Laveranues Coles | .60 | .25 |
| 294 | Bryan Cox | .25 | .08 |
| 295 | Marvin Jones | .25 | .08 |
| 296 | Mo Lewis | .25 | .08 |
| 297 | Ray Lucas | .25 | .08 |
| 298 | Curtis Martin | .60 | .25 |
| 299 | Bernie Parmalee | .25 | .08 |
| 300 | Chad Pennington | 1.00 | .40 |
| 301 | Jerald Sowell | .25 | .08 |
| 302 | Dwight Stone | .25 | .08 |
| 303 | Vinny Testaverde | .40 | .15 |
| 304 | Dedric Ward | .25 | .08 |
| 305 | Tim Brown | .60 | .25 |
| 306 | Zack Crockett | .25 | .08 |
| 307 | Scott Dreisbach | .25 | .08 |
| 308 | Rickey Dudley | .25 | .08 |
| 309 | David Dunn | .25 | .08 |
| 310 | Mondriel Fulcher | .25 | .08 |
| 311 | Rich Gannon | .60 | .25 |
| 312 | James Jett | .25 | .08 |
| 313 | Randy Jordan | .25 | .08 |
| 314 | Napoleon Kaufman | .40 | .15 |
| 315 | Rodney Peete | .25 | .08 |
| 316 | Jerry Porter | .40 | .15 |
| 317 | Andre Rison | .40 | .15 |
| 318 | Tyrone Wheatley | .25 | .08 |
| 319 | Charles Woodson | .40 | .15 |
| 320 | Darnell Autry | .25 | .08 |
| 321 | Na Brown | .25 | .08 |
| 322 | Hugh Douglas | .25 | .08 |
| 323 | Charles Johnson | .25 | .08 |
| 324 | Chad Lewis | .25 | .08 |
| 325 | Cecil Martin | .25 | .08 |
| 326 | Donovan McNabb | .75 | .30 |
| 327 | Brian Mitchell | .25 | .08 |
| 328 | Todd Pinkston | .25 | .08 |
| 329 | Ron Powlus | .25 | .08 |
| 330 | Stanley Pritchett | .25 | .08 |
| 331 | Torrance Small | .25 | .08 |
| 332 | Duce Staley | .60 | .25 |
| 333 | Troy Vincent | .25 | .08 |
| 334 | Chris Warren | .25 | .08 |
| 335 | Jerome Bettis | .60 | .25 |
| 336 | Plaxico Burress | .60 | .25 |
| 337 | Troy Edwards | .25 | .08 |
| 338 | Chris Fuamatu-Ma'afala | .25 | .08 |
| 339 | Cory Geason | .25 | .08 |
| 340 | Kent Graham | .25 | .08 |
| 341 | Courtney Hawkins | .25 | .08 |
| 342 | Richard Huntley | .25 | .08 |
| 343 | Tee Martin | .40 | .15 |
| 344 | Bobby Shaw | .25 | .08 |
| 345 | Kordell Stewart | .40 | .15 |
| 346 | Hines Ward | .60 | .25 |
| 347 | Destiny Wright RC | .40 | .15 |
| 348 | Amos Zereoue | .60 | .25 |
| 349 | Isaac Bruce | .60 | .25 |
| 350 | Trung Canidate | .40 | .15 |
| 351 | Marshall Faulk | .75 | .30 |
| 352 | London Fletcher | .25 | .08 |
| 353 | Joe Germaine | .25 | .08 |
| 354 | Trent Green | .60 | .25 |
| 355 | Az-Zahir Hakim | .25 | .08 |
| 356 | James Hodgins | .25 | .08 |
| 357 | Robert Holcombe | .25 | .08 |
| 358 | Torry Holt | .60 | .25 |
| 359 | Tony Horne | .25 | .08 |
| 360 | Ricky Proehl | .25 | .08 |
| 361 | Chris Thomas RC | .40 | .15 |
| 362 | Kurt Warner | 1.25 | .50 |
| 363 | Justin Watson | .25 | .08 |
| 364 | Kenny Bynum | .25 | .08 |
| 365 | Robert Chancey | .25 | .08 |
| 366 | Curtis Conway | .40 | .15 |
| 367 | Jermaine Fazande | .25 | .08 |
| 368 | Terrell Fletcher | .25 | .08 |
| 369 | Trevor Gaylor | .25 | .08 |
| 370 | Jeff Graham | .25 | .08 |
| 371 | Jim Harbaugh | .40 | .15 |
| 372 | Rodney Harrison | .25 | .08 |
| 373 | Ronney Jenkins | .25 | .08 |
| 374 | Freddie Jones | .25 | .08 |
| 375 | Reggie Jones | .25 | .08 |
| 376 | Ryan Leaf | .40 | .15 |
| 377 | Junior Seau | .60 | .25 |
| 378 | Fred Beasley | .25 | .08 |
| 379 | Greg Clark | .25 | .08 |
| 380 | Jeff Garcia | .60 | .25 |
| 381 | Charlie Garner | .40 | .15 |
| 382 | Terry Jackson | .25 | .08 |
| 383 | Brian Jennings | .25 | .08 |
| 384 | Travis Jervey | .25 | .08 |
| 385 | Jonas Lewis | .25 | .08 |
| 386 | Terrell Owens | .60 | .25 |
| 387 | Jerry Rice | 1.25 | .50 |
| 388 | Paul Smith | .25 | .08 |
| 389 | J.J. Stokes | .40 | .15 |
| 390 | Tai Streets | .25 | .08 |
| 391 | Justin Swift | .25 | .08 |
| 392 | Shaun Alexander | .75 | .30 |
| 393 | Karsten Bailey | .25 | .08 |
| 394 | Chad Brown | .25 | .08 |
| 395 | Sean Dawkins | .25 | .08 |
| 396 | Christian Fauria | .25 | .08 |
| 397 | Brock Huard | .25 | .08 |
| 398 | Darrell Jackson | .25 | .08 |
| 399 | Jon Kitna | .60 | .25 |
| 400 | Derrick Mayes | .25 | .08 |
| 401 | Itula Mili | .25 | .08 |
| 402 | Charlie Rogers | .25 | .08 |
| 403 | Mack Strong | .40 | .15 |
| 404 | Ricky Watters | .25 | .08 |
| 405 | James Williams WR | .25 | .08 |
| 406 | Rabih Abdullah | .25 | .08 |

| | | |
|---|---|---|
| ❏ 407 Mike Alstott | .60 | .25 |
| ❏ 408 Reidel Anthony | .25 | .08 |
| ❏ 409 Derrick Brooks | .25 | .08 |
| ❏ 410 Warrick Dunn | .60 | .25 |
| ❏ 411 Jacquez Green | .25 | .08 |
| ❏ 412 Joe Hamilton | .25 | .08 |
| ❏ 413 Keyshawn Johnson | .25 | .08 |
| ❏ 414 Shaun King | .25 | .08 |
| ❏ 415 Charles Kirby RC | .60 | .25 |
| ❏ 416 Warren Sapp | .40 | .15 |
| ❏ 417 Aaron Stecker | .25 | .08 |
| ❏ 418 Todd Yoder | .25 | .08 |
| ❏ 419 Eric Zeier | .25 | .08 |
| ❏ 420 Chris Coleman | .25 | .08 |
| ❏ 421 Kevin Dyson | .40 | .15 |
| ❏ 422 Eddie George | .60 | .25 |
| ❏ 423 Jevon Kearse | .25 | .08 |
| ❏ 424 Erron Kinney | .25 | .08 |
| ❏ 425 Mike Leach | .25 | .08 |
| ❏ 426 Derrick Mason | .40 | .15 |
| ❏ 427 Steve McNair | .60 | .25 |
| ❏ 428 Lorenzo Neal | .25 | .08 |
| ❏ 429 Carl Pickens | .40 | .15 |
| ❏ 430 Chris Sanders | .25 | .08 |
| ❏ 431 Yancey Thigpen | .25 | .08 |
| ❏ 432 Rodney Thomas | .25 | .08 |
| ❏ 433 Frank Wycheck | .25 | .08 |
| ❏ 434 Stephen Alexander | .25 | .08 |
| ❏ 435 Champ Bailey | .40 | .15 |
| ❏ 436 Larry Centers | .25 | .08 |
| ❏ 437 Albert Connell | .25 | .08 |
| ❏ 438 Stephen Davis | .60 | .25 |
| ❏ 439 Zeron Flemister RC | .25 | .08 |
| ❏ 440 Irving Fryar | .40 | .15 |
| ❏ 441 Jeff George | .40 | .15 |
| ❏ 442 Skip Hicks | .25 | .08 |
| ❏ 443 Torid Husak | .25 | .08 |
| ❏ 444 Brad Johnson | .40 | .15 |
| ❏ 445 Adrian Murrell | .25 | .08 |
| ❏ 446 Deion Sanders | .60 | .25 |
| ❏ 447 Mike Sellers | .25 | .08 |
| ❏ 448 Derrius Thompson | .25 | .08 |
| ❏ 449 James Thrash | .40 | .15 |
| ❏ 450 Michael Westbrook | .25 | .08 |
| ❏ 451 Alex Bannister AU/1750 RC | 8.00 | 3.00 |
| ❏ 452 Kevan Barlow AU/1500 RC | 15.00 | 6.00 |
| ❏ 453 Drew Brees AU/1000 RC | 50.00 | 25.00 |
| ❏ 454 Travis Henry AU/1500 RC | 15.00 | 6.00 |
| ❏ 455 Chad Johnson AU/1750 RC | 30.00 | 12.50 |
| ❏ 456 M.McMahon AU/1000 RC | 10.00 | 4.00 |
| ❏ 457 B.Newcombe AU/1750 RC | 10.00 | 4.00 |
| ❏ 458 Sage Rosenfels AU/1000 RC | 20.00 | 7.50 |
| ❏ 459 L.Tomlinson AU/1500 RC | 120.00 | 60.00 |
| ❏ 460 Chris Weinke AU/1000 RC | 12.00 | 5.00 |
| ❏ 461 Tay Cody RC | 2.00 | .75 |
| ❏ 462 Adam Archuleta RC | 5.00 | 2.00 |
| ❏ 463 Will Allen RC | 2.50 | 1.00 |
| ❏ 464 Moran Norris RC | 2.00 | .75 |
| ❏ 465 Tommy Polley RC | 5.00 | 2.00 |
| ❏ 466 Ennis Davis RC | 2.00 | .75 |
| ❏ 467 Jamar Fletcher RC | 2.50 | 1.00 |
| ❏ 468 Derrick Gibson RC | 2.50 | 1.00 |
| ❏ 469 Sedrick Hodge RC | 2.00 | .75 |
| ❏ 470 Willie Howard RC | 2.50 | 1.00 |
| ❏ 471 Steve Hutchinson RC | 2.50 | 1.00 |
| ❏ 472 Michael Stone RC | 2.00 | .75 |
| ❏ 473 Vinny Sutherland/1750 RC | 3.00 | 1.25 |
| ❏ 474 Joe Tafoya RC | 2.00 | .75 |
| ❏ 475 Maurice Williams RC | 2.00 | .75 |
| ❏ 476 Pork Chop Womack RC | 2.00 | .75 |
| ❏ 477 Chad Ward RC | 2.00 | .75 |
| ❏ 478 Scotty Anderson/1750 RC | 3.00 | 1.25 |
| ❏ 479 Gary Baxter RC | 2.50 | 1.00 |
| ❏ 480 M.Tuiasosopo/1000 RC | 6.00 | 2.50 |
| ❏ 481 Tim Hasselbeck/1000 RC | 6.00 | 2.50 |
| ❏ 482 Clevan Thomas RC | 2.00 | .75 |
| ❏ 483 Marcus Stroud RC | 5.00 | 2.00 |
| ❏ 484 John Schlecht RC | 2.00 | .75 |
| ❏ 485 Brandon Spoon RC | 5.00 | 2.00 |
| ❏ 486 Alex Lincoln RC | 2.50 | 1.00 |
| ❏ 487 Anthony Thomas/1750 RC | 4.00 | 1.50 |
| ❏ 488 Freddie Mitchell/1750 RC | 4.00 | 1.50 |
| ❏ 489 Brian Allen RC | 2.50 | 1.00 |
| ❏ 490 Zeke Moreno RC | 5.00 | 2.00 |
| ❏ 491 Tony Driver RC | 5.00 | 2.00 |

| | | |
|---|---|---|
| ❏ 492 Kynan Forney RC | 2.00 | .75 |
| ❏ 493 Reggie Wayne/1750 RC | 10.00 | 4.00 |
| ❏ 494 Larry Casher RC | 2.50 | 1.00 |
| ❏ 495 Fred Wakefield RC | 2.50 | 1.00 |
| ❏ 496 Jeff Backus RC | 2.50 | 1.00 |
| ❏ 497 Jarrod Cooper RC | 5.00 | 2.00 |
| ❏ 498 Heath Evans RC | 5.00 | 2.00 |
| ❏ 499 James Jackson/1500 RC | 3.00 | 1.25 |
| ❏ 500 Jabari Holloway RC | 5.00 | 2.00 |
| ❏ 501 Quincy Morgan/1750 RC | 4.00 | 1.50 |
| ❏ 502 Josh Booty/1000 RC | 6.00 | 2.50 |
| ❏ 503 Ja'Mar Toombs RC | 2.50 | 1.00 |
| ❏ 504 Jason McKinley/1000 RC | 4.00 | 1.50 |
| ❏ 505 Reggie White/1500 RC | 3.00 | 1.25 |
| ❏ 506 Todd Heap/1750 RC | 4.00 | 1.50 |
| ❏ 507 Rudi Johnson/1500 RC | 10.00 | 4.00 |
| ❏ 508 Snoop Minnis/1750 RC | 3.00 | 1.25 |
| ❏ 509 David Terrell/1750 RC | 4.00 | 1.50 |
| ❏ 510 Torrance Marshall RC | 5.00 | 2.00 |
| ❏ 511 Michael Bennett/1500 RC | 5.00 | 2.00 |
| ❏ 512 Chris Chambers/1750 RC | 8.00 | 3.00 |
| ❏ 513 Ben Leard/1000 RC | 4.00 | 1.50 |
| ❏ 514 Rod Gardner/1750 RC | 4.00 | 1.50 |
| ❏ 515 Michael Vick/1000 RC | 25.00 | 10.00 |
| ❏ 516 Josh Heupel/1000 RC | 6.00 | 2.50 |
| ❏ 517 Jesse Palmer/1000 RC | 6.00 | 2.50 |
| ❏ 518 Quincy Carter/1000 RC | 6.00 | 2.50 |
| ❏ 519 A.J. Feeley/1500 RC | 6.00 | 2.50 |
| ❏ 520 David Rivers/1000 RC | 6.00 | 2.50 |
| ❏ 521 Deuce McAllister/1500 RC | 12.00 | 5.00 |
| ❏ 522 LaMont Jordan/1500 RC | 10.00 | 4.00 |
| ❏ 523 David Allen/1500 RC | 8.00 | 3.00 |
| ❏ 524 Correll Buckhalter/1500 RC | 12.00 | 5.00 |
| ❏ 525 Travis Minor/1500 | 6.00 | 2.50 |
| ❏ 526 Koren Robinson/1750 RC | 4.00 | 1.50 |
| ❏ 527 Santana Moss/1750 RC | 8.00 | 3.00 |
| ❏ 528 Robert Ferguson/1750 RC | 4.00 | 1.50 |
| ❏ 529 T.J.Houshmndzdh/1750 RC | 5.00 | 2.00 |
| ❏ 530 Cedrick Wilson/1750 RC | 4.00 | 1.50 |

**2002 Pacific**

| | | |
|---|---|---|
| ❏ COMPLETE SET (500) | 100.00 | 50.00 |
| ❏ 1 David Boston | .60 | .25 |
| ❏ 2 Arnold Jackson | .25 | .08 |
| ❏ 3 MarTay Jenkins | .25 | .08 |
| ❏ 4 Thomas Jones | .40 | .15 |
| ❏ 5 Kwamie Lassiter | .25 | .08 |
| ❏ 6 Joel Makovicka | .25 | .08 |
| ❏ 7 Ronald McKinnon | .25 | .08 |
| ❏ 8 Tywan Mitchell | .25 | .08 |
| ❏ 9 Michael Pittman | .25 | .08 |
| ❏ 10 Jake Plummer | .40 | .15 |
| ❏ 11 Frank Sanders | .25 | .08 |
| ❏ 12 Kyle Vanden Bosch | .25 | .08 |
| ❏ 13 Jamal Anderson | .40 | .15 |
| ❏ 14 Keith Brooking | .40 | .15 |
| ❏ 15 Chris Chandler | .40 | .15 |
| ❏ 16 Bob Christian | .25 | .08 |
| ❏ 17 Alge Crumpler | .40 | .15 |
| ❏ 18 Brian Finneran | .25 | .08 |
| ❏ 19 Shawn Jefferson | .25 | .08 |
| ❏ 20 Patrick Kerney | .25 | .08 |
| ❏ 21 Terance Mathis | .25 | .08 |
| ❏ 22 Maurice Smith | .40 | .15 |
| ❏ 23 Rodney Thomas | .25 | .08 |
| ❏ 24 Darrick Vaughn | .25 | .08 |
| ❏ 25 Michael Vick | 1.25 | .50 |
| ❏ 26 Sam Adams | .25 | .08 |

| | | |
|---|---|---|
| ❏ 27 Terry Allen | .25 | .08 |
| ❏ 28 Obafemi Ayanbadejo | .25 | .08 |
| ❏ 29 Peter Boulware | .25 | .08 |
| ❏ 30 Jason Brookins | .25 | .08 |
| ❏ 31 Randall Cunningham | .60 | .25 |
| ❏ 32 Elvis Grbac | .40 | .15 |
| ❏ 33 Todd Heap | .25 | .08 |
| ❏ 34 Qadry Ismail | .40 | .15 |
| ❏ 35 Jamal Lewis | .60 | .25 |
| ❏ 36 Ray Lewis | .60 | .25 |
| ❏ 37 Chris Redman | .25 | .08 |
| ❏ 38 Shannon Sharpe | .40 | .15 |
| ❏ 39 Brandon Stokley | .40 | .15 |
| ❏ 40 Travis Taylor | .40 | .15 |
| ❏ 41 Moe Williams | .25 | .08 |
| ❏ 42 Rod Woodson | .40 | .15 |
| ❏ 43 Shawn Bryson | .25 | .08 |
| ❏ 44 Larry Centers | .25 | .08 |
| ❏ 45 Nate Clements | .25 | .08 |
| ❏ 46 London Fletcher | .25 | .08 |
| ❏ 47 Reggie Germany | .25 | .08 |
| ❏ 48 Travis Henry | .60 | .25 |
| ❏ 49 Jeremy McDaniel | .25 | .08 |
| ❏ 50 Sammy Morris | .25 | .08 |
| ❏ 51 Eric Moulds | .40 | .15 |
| ❏ 52 Peerless Price | .40 | .15 |
| ❏ 53 Jay Riemersma | .25 | .08 |
| ❏ 54 Alex Van Pelt | .25 | .08 |
| ❏ 55 Tim Biakabutuka | .25 | .08 |
| ❏ 56 Isaac Byrd | .25 | .08 |
| ❏ 57 Doug Evans | .25 | .08 |
| ❏ 58 Donald Hayes | .25 | .08 |
| ❏ 59 Chris Hetherington | .25 | .08 |
| ❏ 60 Brad Hoover | .25 | .08 |
| ❏ 61 Richard Huntley | .25 | .08 |
| ❏ 62 Patrick Jeffers | .25 | .08 |
| ❏ 63 Matt Lytle | .25 | .08 |
| ❏ 64 Dan Morgan | .25 | .08 |
| ❏ 65 Muhsin Muhammad | .40 | .15 |
| ❏ 66 Mike Rucker RC | 1.00 | .40 |
| ❏ 67 Steve Smith | .60 | .25 |
| ❏ 68 Wesley Walls | .25 | .08 |
| ❏ 69 Chris Weinke | .40 | .15 |
| ❏ 70 James Allen | .40 | .15 |
| ❏ 71 Fred Baxter | .25 | .08 |
| ❏ 72 Marty Booker | .25 | .08 |
| ❏ 73 Mike Brown | .60 | .25 |
| ❏ 74 Rosevelt Colvin RC | 1.00 | .40 |
| ❏ 75 Phillip Daniels | .25 | .08 |
| ❏ 76 Leon Johnson | .25 | .08 |
| ❏ 77 Shane Matthews | .25 | .08 |
| ❏ 78 Jim Miller | .25 | .08 |
| ❏ 79 Tony Parrish | .25 | .08 |
| ❏ 80 Marcus Robinson | .40 | .15 |
| ❏ 81 David Terrell | .60 | .25 |
| ❏ 82 Anthony Thomas | .40 | .15 |
| ❏ 83 Brian Urlacher | 1.00 | .40 |
| ❏ 84 Ted Washington | .25 | .08 |
| ❏ 85 Dez White | .25 | .08 |
| ❏ 86 Brandon Bennett | .25 | .08 |
| ❏ 87 Corey Dillon | .40 | .15 |
| ❏ 88 Ron Dugans | .25 | .08 |
| ❏ 89 Danny Farmer | .25 | .08 |
| ❏ 90 T.J. Houshmandzadeh | .40 | .15 |
| ❏ 91 Chad Johnson | .60 | .25 |
| ❏ 92 Curtis Keaton | .25 | .08 |
| ❏ 93 Jon Kitna | .40 | .15 |
| ❏ 94 Tony McGee | .25 | .08 |
| ❏ 95 Lorenzo Neal | .25 | .08 |
| ❏ 96 Darnay Scott | .25 | .08 |
| ❏ 97 Akili Smith | .25 | .08 |
| ❏ 98 Justin Smith | .25 | .08 |
| ❏ 99 Takeo Spikes | .25 | .08 |
| ❏ 100 Peter Warrick | .40 | .15 |
| ❏ 101 Tim Couch | .40 | .15 |
| ❏ 102 JaJuan Dawson | .25 | .08 |
| ❏ 103 Benjamin Gay | .40 | .15 |
| ❏ 104 Anthony Henry | .25 | .08 |
| ❏ 105 James Jackson | .25 | .08 |
| ❏ 106 Kevin Johnson | .40 | .15 |
| ❏ 107 Andre King | .25 | .08 |
| ❏ 108 Jamir Miller | .25 | .08 |
| ❏ 109 Quincy Morgan | .25 | .08 |
| ❏ 110 Dennis Northcutt | .25 | .08 |
| ❏ 111 O.J. Santiago | .25 | .08 |

|  |  | | |
|---|---|---|---|
| 112 | Jamel White | .25 | .08 |
| 113 | Quincy Carter | .40 | .15 |
| 114 | Darrin Chiaverini | .60 | .25 |
| 115 | Dexter Coakley | .25 | .08 |
| 116 | Joey Galloway | .40 | .15 |
| 117 | Troy Hambrick | .25 | .08 |
| 118 | Rocket Ismail | .40 | .15 |
| 119 | Dat Nguyen | .25 | .08 |
| 120 | Ken-Yon Rambo | .25 | .08 |
| 121 | Emmitt Smith | 1.50 | .60 |
| 122 | Reggie Swinton | .25 | .08 |
| 123 | Robert Thomas | .25 | .08 |
| 124 | Michael Wiley | .25 | .08 |
| 125 | Anthony Wright | .25 | .08 |
| 126 | Mike Anderson | .60 | .25 |
| 127 | Dwayne Carswell | .25 | .08 |
| 128 | Desmond Clark | .25 | .08 |
| 129 | Chris Cole | .25 | .08 |
| 130 | Terrell Davis | .60 | .25 |
| 131 | Gus Frerotte | .25 | .08 |
| 132 | Olandis Gary | .40 | .15 |
| 133 | Brian Griese | .60 | .25 |
| 134 | Kevin Kasper | .25 | .08 |
| 135 | Ed McCaffrey | .40 | .15 |
| 136 | Phil McGeoghan RC | .40 | .15 |
| 137 | John Mobley | .25 | .08 |
| 138 | Scottie Montgomery | .25 | .08 |
| 139 | Deltha O'Neal | .25 | .08 |
| 140 | Trevor Pryce | .25 | .08 |
| 141 | Rod Smith | .40 | .15 |
| 142 | Al Wilson | .25 | .08 |
| 143 | Scotty Anderson | .25 | .08 |
| 144 | Charlie Batch | .40 | .15 |
| 145 | Aveion Cason | .60 | .25 |
| 146 | Germane Crowell | .60 | .25 |
| 147 | Reuben Droughns | .60 | .25 |
| 148 | Bert Emanuel | .25 | .08 |
| 149 | Larry Foster | .25 | .08 |
| 150 | Az-Zahir Hakim | .25 | .08 |
| 151 | Desmond Howard | .25 | .08 |
| 152 | Mike McMahon | .60 | .25 |
| 153 | Herman Moore | .40 | .15 |
| 154 | Johnnie Morton | .40 | .15 |
| 155 | Robert Porcher | .25 | .08 |
| 156 | Cory Schlesinger | .25 | .08 |
| 157 | David Sloan | .25 | .08 |
| 158 | James Stewart | .40 | .15 |
| 159 | Lamont Warren | .25 | .08 |
| 160 | Donald Driver | .40 | .15 |
| 161 | Brett Favre | 1.50 | .60 |
| 162 | Bubba Franks | .25 | .08 |
| 163 | Antonio Freeman | .60 | .25 |
| 164 | Kabeer Gbaja-Biamila | .40 | .15 |
| 165 | Terry Glenn | .40 | .15 |
| 166 | Ahman Green | .60 | .25 |
| 167 | William Henderson | .25 | .08 |
| 168 | Dorsey Levens | .40 | .15 |
| 169 | David Martin | .25 | .08 |
| 170 | Rondell Mealey | .25 | .08 |
| 171 | Bill Schroeder | .40 | .15 |
| 172 | Darren Sharper | .25 | .08 |
| 173 | Avion Black | .25 | .08 |
| 174 | Tony Boselli | .25 | .08 |
| 175 | Corey Bradford | .25 | .08 |
| 176 | Marcus Coleman | .25 | .08 |
| 177 | Leomont Evans | .25 | .08 |
| 178 | Aaron Glenn | .25 | .08 |
| 179 | Trevor Insley | .25 | .08 |
| 180 | Jermaine Lewis | .25 | .08 |
| 181 | Anthony Malbrough | .25 | .08 |
| 182 | Frank Moreau | .25 | .08 |
| 183 | Mike Quinn | .25 | .08 |
| 184 | Charlie Rogers | .25 | .08 |
| 185 | Jamie Sharper | .25 | .08 |
| 186 | Matt Snider | .25 | .08 |
| 187 | Gary Walker | .25 | .08 |
| 188 | Kevin Williams RC | .40 | .15 |
| 189 | Kailee Wong | .25 | .08 |
| 190 | Chad Bratzke | .25 | .08 |
| 191 | Ken Dilger | .25 | .08 |
| 192 | Marvin Harrison | .60 | .25 |
| 193 | Edgerrin James | .75 | .30 |
| 194 | Kevin McDougal | .25 | .08 |
| 195 | Rob Morris | .25 | .08 |
| 196 | Jerome Pathon | .25 | .08 |
| 197 | Marcus Pollard | .25 | .08 |
| 198 | Dominic Rhodes | .40 | .15 |
| 199 | Marcus Washington | .25 | .08 |
| 200 | Reggie Wayne | .60 | .25 |
| 201 | Terrence Wilkins | .25 | .08 |
| 202 | Tony Brackens | .25 | .08 |
| 203 | Kyle Brady | .25 | .08 |
| 204 | Mark Brunell | .60 | .25 |
| 205 | Donovin Darius | .25 | .08 |
| 206 | Sean Dawkins | .25 | .08 |
| 207 | Damon Gibson | .25 | .08 |
| 208 | Elvis Joseph | .25 | .08 |
| 209 | Stacey Mack | .25 | .08 |
| 210 | Keenan McCardell | .25 | .08 |
| 211 | Hardy Nickerson | .25 | .08 |
| 212 | Jonathan Quinn | .25 | .08 |
| 213 | Micah Ross RC | .25 | .08 |
| 214 | Jimmy Smith | .40 | .15 |
| 215 | Fred Taylor | .60 | .25 |
| 216 | Patrick Washington | .25 | .08 |
| 217 | Derrick Alexander | .40 | .15 |
| 218 | Mike Cloud | .25 | .08 |
| 219 | Donnie Edwards | .25 | .08 |
| 220 | Tony Gonzalez | .40 | .15 |
| 221 | Trent Green | .40 | .15 |
| 222 | Dante Hall | .60 | .25 |
| 223 | Priest Holmes | .75 | .30 |
| 224 | Eddie Kennison | .25 | .08 |
| 225 | Snoop Minnis | .25 | .08 |
| 226 | Larry Parker | .25 | .08 |
| 227 | Marcus Patton | .25 | .08 |
| 228 | Tony Richardson | .25 | .08 |
| 229 | Mikhael Ricks | .25 | .08 |
| 230 | Chris Chambers | .60 | .25 |
| 231 | Jay Fiedler | .40 | .15 |
| 232 | Oronde Gadsden | .25 | .08 |
| 233 | Rob Konrad | .25 | .08 |
| 234 | Sam Madison | .25 | .08 |
| 235 | Brock Marion | .25 | .08 |
| 236 | James McKnight | .25 | .08 |
| 237 | Travis Minor | .25 | .08 |
| 238 | Jeff Ogden | .25 | .08 |
| 239 | Lamar Smith | .40 | .15 |
| 240 | Jason Taylor | .25 | .08 |
| 241 | Zach Thomas | .60 | .25 |
| 242 | Dedric Ward | .25 | .08 |
| 243 | Ricky Williams | .60 | .25 |
| 244 | Michael Bennett | .40 | .15 |
| 245 | Todd Bouman | .25 | .08 |
| 246 | Cris Carter | .60 | .25 |
| 247 | Byron Chamberlain | .25 | .08 |
| 248 | Doug Chapman | .25 | .08 |
| 249 | Kenny Clark RC | .40 | .15 |
| 250 | Daunte Culpepper | .60 | .25 |
| 251 | Nate Jacquet | .25 | .08 |
| 252 | Jim Kleinsasser | .25 | .08 |
| 253 | Harold Morrow | .25 | .08 |
| 254 | Randy Moss | 1.25 | .50 |
| 255 | Jake Reed | .25 | .08 |
| 256 | Spergon Wynn | .25 | .08 |
| 257 | Drew Bledsoe | .75 | .30 |
| 258 | Tom Brady | 1.50 | .60 |
| 259 | Troy Brown | .40 | .15 |
| 260 | Fred Coleman | .25 | .08 |
| 261 | Marc Edwards | .25 | .08 |
| 262 | Kevin Faulk | .40 | .15 |
| 263 | Bobby Hamilton | .25 | .08 |
| 264 | Ty Law | .40 | .15 |
| 265 | Lawyer Milloy | .40 | .15 |
| 266 | David Patten | .25 | .08 |
| 267 | J.R. Redmond | .25 | .08 |
| 268 | Antowain Smith | .40 | .15 |
| 269 | Adam Vinatieri | .60 | .25 |
| 270 | Jermaine Wiggins | .25 | .08 |
| 271 | Aaron Brooks | .60 | .25 |
| 272 | Cam Cleeland | .25 | .08 |
| 273 | Charlie Clemons RC | .25 | .08 |
| 274 | James Fenderson RC | .40 | .15 |
| 275 | La'Roi Glover | .25 | .08 |
| 276 | Joe Horn | .40 | .15 |
| 277 | Willie Jackson | .25 | .08 |
| 278 | Sammy Knight | .25 | .08 |
| 279 | Michael Lewis | .25 | .08 |
| 280 | Deuce McAllister | .75 | .30 |
| 281 | Terrelle Smith | .25 | .08 |
| 282 | Boo Williams | .25 | .08 |
| 283 | Robert Wilson | .25 | .08 |
| 284 | Tiki Barber | .60 | .25 |
| 285 | Micheal Barrow | .25 | .08 |
| 286 | Kerry Collins | .40 | .15 |
| 287 | Greg Comella | .25 | .08 |
| 288 | Thabiti Davis | .25 | .08 |
| 289 | Ron Dayne | .40 | .15 |
| 290 | Ron Dixon | .25 | .08 |
| 291 | Ike Hilliard | .40 | .15 |
| 292 | Joe Jurevicius | .25 | .08 |
| 293 | Michael Strahan | .40 | .15 |
| 294 | Amani Toomer | .40 | .15 |
| 295 | Damon Washington | .25 | .08 |
| 296 | John Abraham | .40 | .15 |
| 297 | Richie Anderson | .25 | .08 |
| 298 | Anthony Becht | .25 | .08 |
| 299 | Wayne Chrebet | .40 | .15 |
| 300 | Laveranues Coles | .75 | .30 |
| 301 | James Farrior | .25 | .08 |
| 302 | Marvin Jones | .25 | .08 |
| 303 | LaMont Jordan | .60 | .25 |
| 304 | Curtis Martin | .60 | .25 |
| 305 | Santana Moss | .60 | .25 |
| 306 | Chad Pennington | .75 | .30 |
| 307 | Kevin Swayne | .25 | .08 |
| 308 | Vinny Testaverde | .40 | .15 |
| 309 | Craig Yeast | .25 | .08 |
| 310 | Greg Biekert | .25 | .08 |
| 311 | Tim Brown | .60 | .25 |
| 312 | Zack Crockett | .25 | .08 |
| 313 | Rich Gannon | .60 | .25 |
| 314 | Charlie Garner | .40 | .15 |
| 315 | Sebastian Janikowski | .25 | .08 |
| 316 | Randy Jordan | .25 | .08 |
| 317 | Terry Kirby | .25 | .08 |
| 318 | Jerry Porter | .25 | .08 |
| 319 | Jerry Rice | 1.25 | .50 |
| 320 | Jon Ritchie | .25 | .08 |
| 321 | Tyrone Wheatley | .25 | .08 |
| 322 | Roland Williams | .25 | .08 |
| 323 | Charles Woodson | .40 | .15 |
| 324 | Correll Buckhalter | .40 | .15 |
| 325 | Brian Dawkins | .40 | .15 |
| 326 | Hugh Douglas | .25 | .08 |
| 327 | A.J. Feeley | .60 | .25 |
| 328 | Duce Staley | .25 | .08 |
| 329 | Cecil Martin | .25 | .08 |
| 330 | Brian Mitchell | .25 | .08 |
| 331 | Freddie Mitchell | .40 | .15 |
| 332 | Todd Pinkston | .25 | .08 |
| 333 | Rod Smart RC | .60 | .25 |
| 334 | Duce Staley | .60 | .25 |
| 335 | James Thrash | .25 | .08 |
| 336 | Jeremiah Trotter | .25 | .08 |
| 337 | Troy Vincent | .25 | .08 |
| 338 | Kendrell Bell | .60 | .25 |
| 339 | Jerome Bettis | .60 | .25 |
| 340 | Demetrius Brown RC | .40 | .15 |
| 341 | Plaxico Burress | .60 | .25 |
| 342 | Troy Edwards | .25 | .08 |
| 343 | Chris Fuamatu-Ma'afala | .25 | .08 |
| 344 | Jason Gildon | .25 | .08 |
| 345 | Earl Holmes | .25 | .08 |
| 346 | Joey Porter | .25 | .08 |
| 347 | Chad Scott | .25 | .08 |
| 348 | Bobby Shaw | .25 | .08 |
| 349 | Kordell Stewart | .40 | .15 |
| 350 | Hines Ward | .60 | .25 |
| 351 | Amos Zereoue | .40 | .15 |
| 352 | Adam Archuleta | .25 | .08 |
| 353 | Dre' Bly | .25 | .08 |
| 354 | Isaac Bruce | .60 | .25 |
| 355 | Trung Canidate | .40 | .15 |
| 356 | Ernie Conwell | .25 | .08 |
| 357 | Marshall Faulk | .60 | .25 |
| 358 | Torry Holt | .60 | .25 |
| 359 | Leonard Little | .25 | .08 |
| 360 | Yo Murphy | .25 | .08 |
| 361 | Ricky Proehl | .25 | .08 |
| 362 | Kurt Warner | .60 | .25 |
| 363 | Aeneas Williams | .25 | .08 |
| 364 | Drew Brees | .60 | .25 |
| 365 | Curtis Conway | .40 | .15 |
| 366 | Tim Dwight | .40 | .15 |

| | | |
|---|---|---|
| ❑ 367 Terrell Fletcher | .25 | .08 |
| ❑ 368 Doug Flutie | .60 | .25 |
| ❑ 369 Jeff Graham | .25 | .08 |
| ❑ 370 Rodney Harrison | .25 | .08 |
| ❑ 371 Ronney Jenkins | .25 | .08 |
| ❑ 372 Raylee Johnson | .25 | .08 |
| ❑ 373 Freddie Jones | .25 | .08 |
| ❑ 374 Ryan McNeil | .25 | .08 |
| ❑ 375 Junior Seau | .60 | .25 |
| ❑ 376 LaDainian Tomlinson | 1.00 | .40 |
| ❑ 377 Marcellus Wiley | .25 | .08 |
| ❑ 378 Raven Barlow | .40 | .15 |
| ❑ 379 Fred Beasley | .25 | .08 |
| ❑ 380 Zack Bronson RC | .40 | .15 |
| ❑ 381 Andre Carter | .25 | .08 |
| ❑ 382 Jeff Garcia | .60 | .25 |
| ❑ 383 Garrison Hearst | .40 | .15 |
| ❑ 384 Terry Jackson | .25 | .08 |
| ❑ 385 Eric Johnson | .40 | .15 |
| ❑ 386 Saladin McCullough RC | .25 | .08 |
| ❑ 387 Terrell Owens | .60 | .25 |
| ❑ 388 Ahmed Plummer | .25 | .08 |
| ❑ 389 J.J. Stokes | .25 | .08 |
| ❑ 390 Tai Streets | .25 | .08 |
| ❑ 391 Vinny Sutherland | .25 | .08 |
| ❑ 392 Bryant Young | .25 | .08 |
| ❑ 393 Shaun Alexander | .75 | .30 |
| ❑ 394 Chad Brown | .25 | .08 |
| ❑ 395 Kerwin Cook RC | .40 | .15 |
| ❑ 396 Trent Dilfer | .40 | .15 |
| ❑ 397 Bobby Engram | .25 | .08 |
| ❑ 398 Christian Fauria | .25 | .08 |
| ❑ 399 Matt Hasselbeck | .40 | .15 |
| ❑ 400 Darrell Jackson | .40 | .15 |
| ❑ 401 John Randle | .40 | .15 |
| ❑ 402 Koren Robinson | .40 | .15 |
| ❑ 403 Anthony Simmons | .40 | .15 |
| ❑ 404 Mack Strong | .40 | .15 |
| ❑ 405 Ricky Watters | .25 | .08 |
| ❑ 406 James Williams WR | .25 | .08 |
| ❑ 407 Mike Alstott | .60 | .25 |
| ❑ 408 Ronde Barber | .25 | .08 |
| ❑ 409 Derrick Brooks | .25 | .08 |
| ❑ 410 Jameel Cook | .25 | .08 |
| ❑ 411 Warrick Dunn | .60 | .25 |
| ❑ 412 Jacquez Green | .25 | .08 |
| ❑ 413 Brad Johnson | .40 | .15 |
| ❑ 414 Keyshawn Johnson | .60 | .25 |
| ❑ 415 Rob Johnson | .40 | .15 |
| ❑ 416 John Lynch | .40 | .15 |
| ❑ 417 Dave Moore | .25 | .08 |
| ❑ 418 Warren Sapp | .40 | .15 |
| ❑ 419 Aaron Stecker | .25 | .08 |
| ❑ 420 Karl Williams | .25 | .08 |
| ❑ 421 Drew Bennett | .60 | .25 |
| ❑ 422 Eddie Berlin | .25 | .08 |
| ❑ 423 Rafael Cooper RC | .40 | .15 |
| ❑ 424 Kevin Dyson | .25 | .08 |
| ❑ 425 Eddie George | .60 | .25 |
| ❑ 426 Mike Green | .25 | .08 |
| ❑ 427 Skip Hicks | .25 | .08 |
| ❑ 428 Jevon Kearse | .40 | .15 |
| ❑ 429 Erron Kinney | .25 | .08 |
| ❑ 430 Derrick Mason | .40 | .15 |
| ❑ 431 Justin McCareins | .40 | .15 |
| ❑ 432 Steve McNair | .60 | .25 |
| ❑ 433 Neil O'Donnell | .25 | .08 |
| ❑ 434 Frank Wycheck | .25 | .08 |
| ❑ 435 Riedel Anthony | .25 | .08 |
| ❑ 436 Jessie Armstead | .25 | .08 |
| ❑ 437 Champ Bailey | .40 | .15 |
| ❑ 438 Tony Banks | .25 | .08 |
| ❑ 439 Michael Bates | .25 | .08 |
| ❑ 440 Donnell Bennett | .25 | .08 |
| ❑ 441 Ki-Jana Carter | .25 | .08 |
| ❑ 442 Stephen Davis | .40 | .15 |
| ❑ 443 Zeron Flemister | .25 | .08 |
| ❑ 444 Rod Gardner | .40 | .15 |
| ❑ 445 Kevin Lockett | .25 | .08 |
| ❑ 446 Eric Metcalf | .25 | .08 |
| ❑ 447 Sage Rosenfels | .25 | .08 |
| ❑ 448 Fred Smoot | .25 | .08 |
| ❑ 449 Michael Westbrook | .25 | .08 |
| ❑ 450 Danny Wuerffel | .25 | .08 |
| ❑ 451 Jason McAddley RC | 1.50 | .60 |

| | | |
|---|---|---|
| ❑ 452 Freddie Milons RC | 1.50 | .60 |
| ❑ 453 Bryan Thomas RC | 1.50 | .60 |
| ❑ 454 Levi Jones RC | 1.50 | .60 |
| ❑ 455 William Green RC | 2.00 | .75 |
| ❑ 456 Luke Staley RC | 1.50 | .60 |
| ❑ 457 Daniel Graham RC | 2.00 | .75 |
| ❑ 458 David Garrard RC | 4.00 | 1.50 |
| ❑ 459 Reche Caldwell RC | 2.00 | .75 |
| ❑ 460 Andra Davis RC | 1.50 | .60 |
| ❑ 461 Lito Sheppard RC | 2.00 | .75 |
| ❑ 462 Chris Hope RC | 2.00 | .75 |
| ❑ 463 Javon Walker RC | 3.00 | 1.25 |
| ❑ 464 David Carr RC | 2.50 | 1.00 |
| ❑ 465 Alan Harper RC | 1.00 | .40 |
| ❑ 466 Adrian Peterson RC | 2.50 | 1.00 |
| ❑ 467 Kelly Campbell RC | 1.50 | .60 |
| ❑ 468 Ashley Lelie RC | 4.00 | 1.50 |
| ❑ 469 Kurt Kittner RC | 1.50 | .60 |
| ❑ 470 Antwaan Randle El RC | 2.50 | 1.00 |
| ❑ 471 Ladell Betts RC | 2.00 | .75 |
| ❑ 472 Josh Reed RC | 2.00 | .75 |
| ❑ 473 Clinton Portis RC | 6.00 | 2.50 |
| ❑ 474 Ron Johnson RC | 1.50 | .60 |
| ❑ 475 Eric Crouch RC | 2.00 | .75 |
| ❑ 476 Tracey Wistrom RC | 1.50 | .60 |
| ❑ 477 David Neill RC | 1.50 | .60 |
| ❑ 478 Ronald Curry RC | 2.00 | .75 |
| ❑ 479 Lamar Gordon RC | 2.00 | .75 |
| ❑ 480 Damien Anderson RC | 1.50 | .60 |
| ❑ 481 Napoleon Harris RC | 2.00 | .75 |
| ❑ 482 Zak Kustok RC | 2.00 | .75 |
| ❑ 483 Rocky Calmus RC | 2.00 | .75 |
| ❑ 484 Roy Williams RC | 4.00 | 1.50 |
| ❑ 485 Joey Harrington RC | 2.50 | 1.00 |
| ❑ 486 Maurice Morris RC | 2.00 | .75 |
| ❑ 487 Antonio Bryant RC | 2.00 | .75 |
| ❑ 488 Josh McCown RC | 2.50 | 1.00 |
| ❑ 489 John Henderson RC | 2.00 | .75 |
| ❑ 490 Quentin Jammer RC | 2.00 | .75 |
| ❑ 491 Mike Williams RC | 1.50 | .60 |
| ❑ 492 Patrick Ramsey RC | 2.00 | .75 |
| ❑ 493 Kenyon Coleman RC | 1.00 | .40 |
| ❑ 494 DeShaun Foster RC | 2.00 | .75 |
| ❑ 495 Brian Poli-Dixon RC | 1.50 | .60 |
| ❑ 496 Cliff Russell RC | 1.50 | .60 |
| ❑ 497 Brian Westbrook RC | 5.00 | 2.00 |
| ❑ 498 Andre Davis RC | 1.50 | .60 |
| ❑ 499 Larry Tripplett RC | 1.00 | .40 |
| ❑ 500 Lamont Thompson RC | 1.50 | .60 |
| ❑ 501 T.J. Duckett RC | 2.00 | .75 |
| ❑ 502 Dameon Hunter RC | 1.00 | .40 |
| ❑ 503 Javin Hunter RC | 1.00 | .40 |
| ❑ 504 Tellis Redmon RC | 1.50 | .60 |
| ❑ 505 Chester Taylor RC | 4.00 | 1.50 |
| ❑ 506 Randy Fasani RC | 1.50 | .60 |
| ❑ 507 Julius Peppers RC | 4.00 | 1.50 |
| ❑ 508 Jamin Elliott RC | 1.00 | .40 |
| ❑ 509 Chad Hutchinson RC | 1.50 | .60 |
| ❑ 510 Eddie Drummond RC | 1.50 | .60 |
| ❑ 511 Craig Nall RC | 2.00 | .75 |
| ❑ 512 Jabar Gaffney RC | 2.00 | .75 |
| ❑ 513 Jonathan Wells RC | 2.00 | .75 |
| ❑ 514 Shaun Hill RC | 2.50 | 1.00 |
| ❑ 515 Deion Branch RC | 3.00 | 1.25 |
| ❑ 516 Rohan Davey RC | 2.00 | .75 |
| ❑ 517 J.T. O'Sullivan RC | 2.50 | 1.00 |
| ❑ 518 Tim Carter RC | 1.50 | .60 |
| ❑ 519 Daryl Jones RC | 1.50 | .60 |
| ❑ 520 Jeremy Shockey RC | 3.00 | 1.25 |
| ❑ 521 Seth Burford RC | 1.50 | .60 |
| ❑ 522 Brandon Doman RC | 1.50 | .60 |
| ❑ 523 Jerramy Stevens RC | 2.00 | .75 |
| ❑ 524 Travis Stephens RC | 1.50 | .60 |
| ❑ 525 Marquise Walker RC | 1.50 | .60 |

## 1964 Philadelphia

| | | |
|---|---|---|
| ❑ COMPLETE SET (198) | 900.00 | 600.00 |
| ❑ WRAPPER (1-CENT) | 40.00 | 18.00 |
| ❑ WRAPPER (5-CENT) | 20.00 | 10.00 |
| ❑ 1 Raymond Berry ! | 20.00 | 10.00 |
| ❑ 2 Tom Gilburg | 2.50 | 1.25 |
| ❑ 3 John Mackey RC | 30.00 | 18.00 |
| ❑ 4 Gino Marchetti | 5.00 | 2.50 |
| ❑ 5 Jim Martin | 2.50 | 1.25 |
| ❑ 6 Tom Matte RC | 6.00 | 3.00 |

JIM BROWN

| | | |
|---|---|---|
| ❑ 7 Jimmy Orr | 3.00 | 1.50 |
| ❑ 8 Jim Parker | 4.00 | 2.00 |
| ❑ 9 Bill Pellington | 2.50 | 1.25 |
| ❑ 10 Alex Sandusky | 2.50 | 1.25 |
| ❑ 11 Dick Szymanski | 2.50 | 1.25 |
| ❑ 12 Johnny Unitas | 45.00 | 25.00 |
| ❑ 13 Baltimore Colts | 3.00 | 1.50 |
| ❑ 14 Colts Play/Don Shula | 35.00 | 20.00 |
| ❑ 15 Doug Atkins | 5.00 | 2.50 |
| ❑ 16 Ronnie Bull | 2.50 | 1.25 |
| ❑ 17 Mike Ditka | 40.00 | 25.00 |
| ❑ 18 Joe Fortunato | 2.50 | 1.25 |
| ❑ 19 Willie Galimore | 3.00 | 1.50 |
| ❑ 20 Joe Marconi | 2.50 | 1.25 |
| ❑ 21 Bennie McRae RC | 2.50 | 1.25 |
| ❑ 22 Johnny Morris | 2.50 | 1.25 |
| ❑ 23 Richie Petitbon | 2.50 | 1.25 |
| ❑ 24 Mike Pyle | 2.50 | 1.25 |
| ❑ 25 Roosevelt Taylor RC | 4.00 | 2.00 |
| ❑ 26 Bill Wade | 3.00 | 1.50 |
| ❑ 27 Chicago Bears | 3.00 | 1.50 |
| ❑ 28 Bears Play/George Halas | 12.00 | 6.00 |
| ❑ 29 Johnny Brewer | 2.50 | 1.25 |
| ❑ 30 Jim Brown | 90.00 | 50.00 |
| ❑ 31 Gary Collins RC | 8.00 | 4.00 |
| ❑ 32 Vince Costello | 2.50 | 1.25 |
| ❑ 33 Galen Fiss | 2.50 | 1.25 |
| ❑ 34 Bill Glass | 2.50 | 1.25 |
| ❑ 35 Ernie Green RC | 3.00 | 1.50 |
| ❑ 36 Rich Kreitling | 2.50 | 1.25 |
| ❑ 37 John Morrow | 2.50 | 1.25 |
| ❑ 38 Frank Ryan | 3.00 | 1.50 |
| ❑ 39 Charlie Scales RC | 2.50 | 1.25 |
| ❑ 40 Dick Schafrath RC | 2.50 | 1.25 |
| ❑ 41 Cleveland Browns | 3.00 | 1.50 |
| ❑ 42 Cleveland Browns Play | 2.50 | 1.25 |
| ❑ 43 Don Bishop | 2.50 | 1.25 |
| ❑ 44 Frank Clarke RC | 3.00 | 1.50 |
| ❑ 45 Mike Connelly | 2.50 | 1.25 |
| ❑ 46 Lee Folkins | 2.50 | 1.25 |
| ❑ 47 Cornell Green RC | 8.00 | 4.00 |
| ❑ 48 Bob Lilly | 40.00 | 25.00 |
| ❑ 49 Amos Marsh | 2.50 | 1.25 |
| ❑ 50 Tommy McDonald | 5.00 | 2.50 |
| ❑ 51 Don Meredith | 35.00 | 20.00 |
| ❑ 52 Pettis Norman RC | 3.00 | 1.50 |
| ❑ 53 Don Perkins | 4.00 | 2.00 |
| ❑ 54 Guy Reese | 2.50 | 1.25 |
| ❑ 55 Dallas Cowboys | 4.00 | 2.00 |
| ❑ 56 Cowboys Play/T.Landry | 20.00 | 12.00 |
| ❑ 57 Terry Barr | 2.50 | 1.25 |
| ❑ 58 Roger Brown | 3.00 | 1.50 |
| ❑ 59 Gail Cogdill | 2.50 | 1.25 |
| ❑ 60 John Gordy | 2.50 | 1.25 |
| ❑ 61 Dick Lane | 4.00 | 2.00 |
| ❑ 62 Yale Lary | 4.00 | 2.00 |
| ❑ 63 Dan Lewis | 2.50 | 1.25 |
| ❑ 64 Darris McCord | 2.50 | 1.25 |
| ❑ 65 Earl Morrall | 3.00 | 1.50 |
| ❑ 66 Joe Schmidt | 5.00 | 2.50 |
| ❑ 67 Pat Studstill RC | 3.00 | 1.50 |
| ❑ 68 Wayne Walker RC | 3.00 | 1.50 |
| ❑ 69 Detroit Lions | 3.00 | 1.50 |
| ❑ 70 Detroit Lions | 2.50 | 1.25 |
| ❑ 71 Herb Adderley RC | 35.00 | 20.00 |
| ❑ 72 Willie Davis DE RC | 30.00 | 18.00 |
| ❑ 73 Forrest Gregg | 5.00 | 2.50 |
| ❑ 74 Paul Hornung | 35.00 | 20.00 |

|  |  | | |
|---|---|---|---|
| 75 | Hank Jordan | 5.00 | 2.50 |
| 76 | Jerry Kramer | 6.00 | 3.00 |
| 77 | Tom Moore | 3.00 | 1.50 |
| 78 | Jim Ringo | 5.00 | 2.50 |
| 79 | Bart Starr | 60.00 | 35.00 |
| 80 | Jim Taylor | 25.00 | 15.00 |
| 81 | Jesse Whittenton RC | 3.00 | 1.50 |
| 82 | Willie Wood | 8.00 | 4.00 |
| 83 | Green Bay Packers | 6.00 | 3.00 |
| 84 | Packers Play/Lombardi | 35.00 | 20.00 |
| 85 | Jon Arnett | 2.50 | 1.25 |
| 86 | Pervis Atkins RC | 2.50 | 1.25 |
| 87 | Dick Bass | 3.00 | 1.50 |
| 88 | Carroll Dale | 4.00 | 2.00 |
| 89 | Roman Gabriel | 6.00 | 3.00 |
| 90 | Ed Meador | 2.50 | 1.25 |
| 91 | Merlin Olsen RC | 50.00 | 30.00 |
| 92 | Jack Pardee RC | 4.00 | 2.00 |
| 93 | Jim Phillips | 2.50 | 1.25 |
| 94 | Carver Shannon | 2.50 | 1.25 |
| 95 | Frank Varrichione | 2.50 | 1.25 |
| 96 | Danny Villanueva | 2.50 | 1.25 |
| 97 | Los Angeles Rams | 3.00 | 1.50 |
| 98 | Los Angeles Rams Play | 2.50 | 1.25 |
| 99 | Grady Alderman RC | 2.50 | 1.25 |
| 100 | Larry Bowie | 2.50 | 1.25 |
| 101 | Bill Brown | 6.00 | 3.00 |
| 102 | Paul Flatley RC | 2.50 | 1.25 |
| 103 | Rip Hawkins | 2.50 | 1.25 |
| 104 | Jim Marshall | 8.00 | 4.00 |
| 105 | Tommy Mason | 3.00 | 1.50 |
| 106 | Jim Prestel | 2.50 | 1.25 |
| 107 | Jerry Reichow | 2.50 | 1.25 |
| 108 | Ed Sharockman | 2.50 | 1.25 |
| 109 | Fran Tarkenton | 35.00 | 20.00 |
| 110 | Mick Tingelhoff RC | 6.00 | 3.00 |
| 111 | Minnesota Vikings | 4.00 | 2.00 |
| 112 | Vikings Play/Van Brock. | 4.00 | 2.00 |
| 113 | Erich Barnes | 4.00 | 2.00 |
| 114 | Roosevelt Brown | 4.00 | 2.00 |
| 115 | Don Chandler | 2.50 | 1.25 |
| 116 | Darrell Dess | 2.50 | 1.25 |
| 117 | Frank Gifford | 35.00 | 20.00 |
| 118 | Dick James | 2.50 | 1.25 |
| 119 | Jim Katcavage | 2.50 | 1.25 |
| 120 | John Lovetere | 2.50 | 1.25 |
| 121 | Dick Lynch RC | 3.00 | 1.50 |
| 122 | Jim Patton | 2.50 | 1.25 |
| 123 | Del Shofner | 2.50 | 1.25 |
| 124 | Y.A.Tittle | 20.00 | 10.00 |
| 125 | New York Giants | 3.00 | 1.50 |
| 126 | New York Giants Play | 2.50 | 1.25 |
| 127 | Sam Baker | 2.50 | 1.25 |
| 128 | Maxie Baughan | 2.50 | 1.25 |
| 129 | Timmy Brown | 3.00 | 1.50 |
| 130 | Mike Clark | 2.50 | 1.25 |
| 131 | Irv Cross RC | 3.00 | 1.50 |
| 132 | Ted Dean | 2.50 | 1.25 |
| 133 | Ron Goodwin | 2.50 | 1.25 |
| 134 | King Hill | 2.50 | 1.25 |
| 135 | Clarence Peaks | 2.50 | 1.25 |
| 136 | Pete Retzlaff | 3.00 | 1.50 |
| 137 | Jim Schrader | 2.50 | 1.25 |
| 138 | Norm Snead | 3.00 | 1.50 |
| 139 | Philadelphia Eagles | 3.00 | 1.50 |
| 140 | Philadelphia Eagles Play | 2.50 | 1.25 |
| 141 | Gary Ballman RC | 2.50 | 1.25 |
| 142 | Charley Bradshaw RC | 2.50 | 1.25 |
| 143 | Ed Brown | 3.00 | 1.50 |
| 144 | John Henry Johnson | 4.00 | 2.00 |
| 145 | Joe Krupa | 2.50 | 1.25 |
| 146 | Bill Mack | 2.50 | 1.25 |
| 147 | Lou Michaels | 2.50 | 1.25 |
| 148 | Buzz Nutter | 2.50 | 1.25 |
| 149 | Myron Pottios | 2.50 | 1.25 |
| 150 | John Reger | 2.50 | 1.25 |
| 151 | Mike Sandusky | 2.50 | 1.25 |
| 152 | Clendon Thomas | 2.50 | 1.25 |
| 153 | Pittsburgh Steelers | 3.00 | 1.50 |
| 154 | Pittsburgh Steelers Play | 2.50 | 1.25 |
| 155 | Kermit Alexander RC | 3.00 | 1.50 |
| 156 | Bernie Casey | 2.50 | 1.25 |
| 157 | Dan Colchico | 2.50 | 1.25 |
| 158 | Clyde Conner | 2.50 | 1.25 |
| 159 | Tommy Davis | 2.50 | 1.25 |
| 160 | Matt Hazeltine | 2.50 | 1.25 |
| 161 | Jim Johnson RC | 20.00 | 10.00 |
| 162 | Don Lisbon RC | 2.50 | 1.25 |
| 163 | Lamar McHan | 2.50 | 1.25 |
| 164 | Bob St.Clair | 4.00 | 2.00 |
| 165 | J.D. Smith | 2.50 | 1.25 |
| 166 | Abe Woodson | 2.50 | 1.25 |
| 167 | San Francisco 49ers | 3.00 | 1.50 |
| 168 | San Francisco 49ers Play | 2.50 | 1.25 |
| 169 | Garland Boyette UER | 2.50 | 1.25 |
| 170 | Bobby Joe Conrad | 3.00 | 1.50 |
| 171 | Bob DeMarco RC | 2.50 | 1.25 |
| 172 | Ken Gray RC | 2.50 | 1.25 |
| 173 | Jimmy Hill | 2.50 | 1.25 |
| 174 | Charlie Johnson | 3.00 | 1.50 |
| 175 | Ernie McMillan | 2.50 | 1.25 |
| 176 | Dale Meinert | 2.50 | 1.25 |
| 177 | Luke Owens | 2.50 | 1.25 |
| 178 | Sonny Randle | 2.50 | 1.25 |
| 179 | Joe Robb | 2.50 | 1.25 |
| 180 | Bill Stacy | 2.50 | 1.25 |
| 181 | St. Louis Cardinals | 3.00 | 1.50 |
| 182 | St. Louis Cardinals Play | 2.50 | 1.25 |
| 183 | Bill Barnes | 2.50 | 1.25 |
| 184 | Don Bosseler | 2.50 | 1.25 |
| 185 | Sam Huff | 6.00 | 3.00 |
| 186 | Sonny Jurgensen | 20.00 | 10.00 |
| 187 | Bob Khayat | 2.50 | 1.25 |
| 188 | Riley Mattson | 2.50 | 1.25 |
| 189 | Bobby Mitchell | 6.00 | 3.00 |
| 190 | John Nisby | 2.50 | 1.25 |
| 191 | Vince Promuto | 2.50 | 1.25 |
| 192 | Joe Rutgens | 2.50 | 1.25 |
| 193 | Lonnie Sanders | 2.50 | 1.25 |
| 194 | Jim Steffen | 2.50 | 1.25 |
| 195 | Washington Redskins | 3.00 | 1.50 |
| 196 | Washington Redskins Play | 2.50 | 1.25 |
| 197 | Checklist 1 UER | 30.00 | 18.00 |
| 198 | Checklist 2 UER | 55.00 | 30.00 |

## 1965 Philadelphia

BART STARR

| | | | |
|---|---|---|---|
| COMPLETE SET (198) | | 800.00 | 500.00 |
| WRAPPER (5-CENT) | | 20.00 | 10.00 |
| 1 | Colts Team! | 15.00 | 7.50 |
| 2 | Raymond Berry | 10.00 | 5.00 |
| 3 | Bob Boyd DB | 2.00 | 1.00 |
| 4 | Wendell Harris | 2.00 | 1.00 |
| 5 | Jerry Logan | 2.00 | 1.00 |
| 6 | Tony Lorick | 2.00 | 1.00 |
| 7 | Lou Michaels | 2.00 | 1.00 |
| 8 | Lenny Moore | 8.00 | 4.00 |
| 9 | Jimmy Orr | 3.00 | 1.50 |
| 10 | Jim Parker | 4.00 | 2.00 |
| 11 | Dick Szymanski | 2.00 | 1.00 |
| 12 | Johnny Unitas | 40.00 | 25.00 |
| 13 | Bob Vogel RC | 2.00 | 1.00 |
| 14 | Colts Play/Don Shula | 20.00 | 12.00 |
| 15 | Chicago Bears | 3.00 | 1.50 |
| 16 | Jon Arnett | 2.00 | 1.00 |
| 17 | Doug Atkins | 5.00 | 2.50 |
| 18 | Rudy Bukich RC | 3.00 | 1.50 |
| 19 | Mike Ditka | 40.00 | 25.00 |
| 20 | Dick Evey | 2.00 | 1.00 |
| 21 | Joe Fortunato | 2.00 | 1.00 |
| 22 | Bobby Joe Green RC | 2.00 | 1.00 |
| 23 | Johnny Morris | 2.00 | 1.00 |
| 24 | Mike Pyle | 2.00 | 1.00 |
| 25 | Roosevelt Taylor | 3.00 | 1.50 |
| 26 | Bill Wade | 3.00 | 1.50 |
| 27 | Bob Wetoska | 2.00 | 1.00 |
| 28 | Bears Play/George Halas | 8.00 | 4.00 |
| 29 | Cleveland Browns | 3.00 | 1.50 |
| 30 | Walter Beach | 2.00 | 1.00 |
| 31 | Jim Brown | 80.00 | 50.00 |
| 32 | Gary Collins | 3.00 | 1.50 |
| 33 | Bill Glass | 2.00 | 1.00 |
| 34 | Ernie Green | 2.00 | 1.00 |
| 35 | Jim Houston RC | 2.00 | 1.00 |
| 36 | Dick Modzelewski | 2.00 | 1.00 |
| 37 | Bernie Parrish | 2.00 | 1.00 |
| 38 | Walter Roberts | 2.00 | 1.00 |
| 39 | Frank Ryan | 3.00 | 1.50 |
| 40 | Dick Schafrath | 2.00 | 1.00 |
| 41 | Paul Warfield RC | 90.00 | 50.00 |
| 42 | Cleveland Browns | 2.00 | 1.00 |
| 43 | Dallas Cowboys | 3.00 | 1.50 |
| 44 | Frank Clarke | 3.00 | 1.50 |
| 45 | Mike Connelly | 2.00 | 1.00 |
| 46 | Buddy Dial | 2.00 | 1.00 |
| 47 | Bob Lilly | 35.00 | 20.00 |
| 48 | Tony Liscio RC | 2.00 | 1.00 |
| 49 | Tommy McDonald | 5.00 | 2.50 |
| 50 | Don Meredith | 25.00 | 15.00 |
| 51 | Pettis Norman | 2.00 | 1.00 |
| 52 | Don Perkins | 4.00 | 2.00 |
| 53 | Mel Renfro RC | 40.00 | 25.00 |
| 54 | Jim Ridlon | 2.00 | 1.00 |
| 55 | Jerry Tubbs | 2.00 | 1.00 |
| 56 | Cowboys Play/T.Landry | 15.00 | 7.50 |
| 57 | Detroit Lions | 3.00 | 1.50 |
| 58 | Terry Barr | 2.00 | 1.00 |
| 59 | Roger Brown | 2.00 | 1.00 |
| 60 | Gail Cogdill | 2.00 | 1.00 |
| 61 | Jim Gibbons | 2.00 | 1.00 |
| 62 | John Gordy | 2.00 | 1.00 |
| 63 | Yale Lary | 4.00 | 2.00 |
| 64 | Dick LeBeau RC | 3.00 | 1.50 |
| 65 | Earl Morrall | 3.00 | 1.50 |
| 66 | Nick Pietrosante | 2.00 | 1.00 |
| 67 | Pat Studstill | 2.00 | 1.00 |
| 68 | Wayne Walker | 3.00 | 1.50 |
| 69 | Tom Watkins | 2.00 | 1.00 |
| 70 | Detroit Lions | 3.00 | 1.50 |
| 71 | Green Bay Packers | 6.00 | 3.00 |
| 72 | Herb Adderley | 8.00 | 4.00 |
| 73 | Willie Davis DE | 8.00 | 4.00 |
| 74 | Boyd Dowler | 4.00 | 2.00 |
| 75 | Forrest Gregg | 5.00 | 2.50 |
| 76 | Paul Hornung | 35.00 | 20.00 |
| 77 | Hank Jordan | 5.00 | 2.50 |
| 78 | Tom Moore | 3.00 | 1.50 |
| 79 | Ray Nitschke | 20.00 | 12.00 |
| 80 | Elijah Pitts RC | 8.00 | 4.00 |
| 81 | Bart Starr | 50.00 | 30.00 |
| 82 | Jim Taylor | 20.00 | 12.00 |
| 83 | Willie Wood | 6.00 | 3.00 |
| 84 | Packers Play/Lombardi | 20.00 | 12.00 |
| 85 | Los Angeles Rams | 3.00 | 1.50 |
| 86 | Dick Bass | 3.00 | 1.50 |
| 87 | Roman Gabriel | 5.00 | 2.50 |
| 88 | Roosevelt Grier | 4.00 | 2.00 |
| 89 | Deacon Jones | 10.00 | 5.00 |
| 90 | Lamar Lundy RC | 4.00 | 2.00 |
| 91 | Marlin McKeever | 2.00 | 1.00 |
| 92 | Ed Meador | 2.00 | 1.00 |
| 93 | Bill Munson RC | 4.00 | 2.00 |
| 94 | Merlin Olsen | 15.00 | 7.50 |
| 95 | Bobby Smith | 2.00 | 1.00 |
| 96 | Frank Varrichione | 2.00 | 1.00 |
| 97 | Ben Wilson | 2.00 | 1.00 |
| 98 | Los Angeles Rams | 2.00 | 1.00 |
| 99 | Minnesota Vikings | 3.00 | 1.50 |
| 100 | Grady Alderman | 2.00 | 1.00 |
| 101 | Hal Bedsole RC | 2.00 | 1.00 |
| 102 | Bill Brown | 3.00 | 1.50 |
| 103 | Bill Butler | 2.00 | 1.00 |
| 104 | Fred Cox RC | 3.00 | 1.50 |
| 105 | Carl Eller RC | 30.00 | 18.00 |
| 106 | Paul Flatley | 2.00 | 1.00 |
| 107 | Jim Marshall | 6.00 | 3.00 |
| 108 | Tommy Mason | 2.00 | 1.00 |
| 109 | George Rose | 2.00 | 1.00 |
| 110 | Fran Tarkenton | 25.00 | 15.00 |

| | | | | | | | | | | |
|---|---|---|---|---|---|---|---|---|---|---|
| 111 Mick Tingelhoff | 3.00 | 1.50 | 196 Washington Redskins | 2.00 | 1.00 | 62 Don Perkins | 3.00 | 1.50 |
| 112 Vikings Play/Van Brock. | 4.00 | 2.00 | 197 Checklist 1 ! | 30.00 | 15.00 | 63 Mel Renfro | 15.00 | 7.50 |
| 113 New York Giants | 3.00 | 1.50 | 198 Checklist 2 UER ! | 50.00 | 25.00 | 64 Danny Villanueva | 2.00 | 1.00 |
| 114 Erich Barnes | 2.00 | 1.00 | | | | 65 Dallas Cowboys | 2.00 | 1.00 |
| 115 Roosevelt Brown | 4.00 | 2.00 | **1966 Philadelphia** | | | 66 Detroit Lions | 3.00 | 1.50 |
| 116 Clarence Childs | 2.00 | 1.00 | | | | 67 Roger Brown | 2.00 | 1.00 |
| 117 Jerry Hillebrand | 2.00 | 1.00 | | | | 68 John Gordy | 2.00 | 1.00 |
| 118 Greg Larson RC | 3.00 | 1.50 | | | | 69 Alex Karras | 10.00 | 5.00 |
| 119 Dick Lynch | 2.00 | 1.00 | | | | 70 Dick LeBeau | 2.00 | 1.00 |
| 120 Joe Morrison RC | 4.00 | 2.00 | | | | 71 Amos Marsh | 2.00 | 1.00 |
| 121 Lou Slaby | 2.00 | 1.00 | | | | 72 Milt Plum | 3.00 | 1.50 |
| 122 Aaron Thomas RC | 2.00 | 1.00 | | | | 73 Bobby Smith | 2.00 | 1.00 |
| 123 Steve Thurlow | 2.00 | 1.00 | | | | 74 Wayne Rasmussen | 2.00 | 1.00 |
| 124 Ernie Wheelwright RC | 2.00 | 1.00 | | | | 75 Pat Studstill | 2.00 | 1.00 |
| 125 Gary Wood RC | 3.00 | 1.50 | | | | 76 Wayne Walker | 2.00 | 1.00 |
| 126 New York Giants | 2.00 | 1.00 | | | | 77 Tom Watkins | 2.00 | 1.00 |
| 127 Philadelphia Eagles | 3.00 | 1.50 | | | | 78 Detroit Lions | 2.00 | 1.00 |
| 128 Sam Baker | 2.00 | 1.00 | | | | 79 Green Bay Packers | 6.00 | 3.00 |
| 129 Maxie Baughan | 2.00 | 1.00 | | | | 80 Herb Adderley | 6.00 | 3.00 |
| 130 Timmy Brown | 3.00 | 1.50 | | | | 81 Lee Roy Caffey RC | 4.00 | 2.00 |
| 131 Jack Concannon RC | 2.00 | 1.00 | | | | 82 Don Chandler | 3.00 | 1.50 |
| 132 Irv Cross | 3.00 | 1.50 | | | | 83 Willie Davis DE | 6.00 | 3.00 |
| 133 Earl Gros | 2.00 | 1.00 | COMPLETE SET (198) | 900.00 | 600.00 | 84 Boyd Dowler | 4.00 | 2.00 |
| 134 Dave Lloyd | 2.00 | 1.00 | WRAPPER (5-CENT) | 20.00 | 10.00 | 85 Forrest Gregg | 4.00 | 2.00 |
| 135 Floyd Peters RC | 2.00 | 1.00 | 1 Falcons Insignia ! | 12.00 | 6.00 | 86 Tom Moore | 3.00 | 1.50 |
| 136 Nate Ramsey | 2.00 | 1.00 | 2 Larry Benz | 2.00 | 1.00 | 87 Ray Nitschke | 15.00 | 7.50 |
| 137 Pete Retzlaff | 3.00 | 1.50 | 3 Dennis Claridge | 2.00 | 1.00 | 88 Bart Starr | 50.00 | 30.00 |
| 138 Jim Ringo | 4.00 | 2.00 | 4 Perry Lee Dunn | 2.00 | 1.00 | 89 Jim Taylor | 20.00 | 12.00 |
| 139 Norm Snead | 4.00 | 2.00 | 5 Dan Grimm | 2.00 | 1.00 | 90 Willie Wood | 6.00 | 3.00 |
| 140 Philadelphia Eagles | 2.00 | 1.00 | 6 Alex Hawkins | 2.00 | 1.00 | 91 Green Bay Packers | 2.00 | 1.00 |
| 141 Pittsburgh Steelers | 3.00 | 1.50 | 7 Ralph Heck | 2.00 | 1.00 | 92 Los Angeles Rams | 3.00 | 1.50 |
| 142 John Baker | 2.00 | 1.00 | 8 Frank Lasky | 2.00 | 1.00 | 93 Willie Brown WR | 2.00 | 1.00 |
| 143 Gary Ballman | 2.00 | 1.00 | 9 Guy Reese | 2.00 | 1.00 | 94 Roman Gabriel/D.Bass | 4.00 | 2.00 |
| 144 Charley Bradshaw | 2.00 | 1.00 | 10 Bob Richards | 2.00 | 1.00 | 95 Bruce Gossett RC | 3.00 | 1.50 |
| 145 Ed Brown | 2.00 | 1.00 | 11 Ron Smith RC | 3.00 | 1.50 | 96 Deacon Jones | 6.00 | 3.00 |
| 146 Dick Haley | 2.00 | 1.00 | 12 Ernie Wheelwright | 2.00 | 1.00 | 97 Tommy McDonald | 5.00 | 2.50 |
| 147 John Henry Johnson | 4.00 | 2.00 | 13 Falcons Roster | 3.00 | 1.50 | 98 Marlin McKeever | 2.00 | 1.00 |
| 148 Brady Keys | 2.00 | 1.00 | 14 Baltimore Colts | 3.00 | 1.50 | 99 Aaron Martin | 2.00 | 1.00 |
| 149 Ray Lemek | 2.00 | 1.00 | 15 Raymond Berry | 8.00 | 4.00 | 100 Ed Meador | 2.00 | 1.00 |
| 150 Ben McGee | 2.00 | 1.00 | 16 Bob Boyd DB | 2.00 | 1.00 | 101 Bill Munson | 3.00 | 1.50 |
| 151 Clarence Peaks | 2.00 | 1.00 | 17 Jerry Logan | 2.00 | 1.00 | 102 Merlin Olsen | 8.00 | 4.00 |
| 152 Myron Pottios | 2.00 | 1.00 | 18 John Mackey | 6.00 | 3.00 | 103 Jim Stiger | 2.00 | 1.00 |
| 153 Clendon Thomas | 2.00 | 1.00 | 19 Tom Matte | 4.00 | 2.00 | 104 Rams Play/W.Brown | 3.00 | 1.50 |
| 154 Pittsburgh Steelers | 2.00 | 1.00 | 20 Lou Michaels | 2.00 | 1.00 | 105 Minnesota Vikings | 3.00 | 1.50 |
| 155 St. Louis Cardinals | 3.00 | 1.50 | 21 Lenny Moore | 8.00 | 4.00 | 106 Grady Alderman | 2.00 | 1.00 |
| 156 Jim Bakken RC | 3.00 | 1.50 | 22 Jimmy Orr | 3.00 | 1.50 | 107 Bill Brown | 3.00 | 1.50 |
| 157 Joe Childress | 2.00 | 1.00 | 23 Jim Parker | 4.00 | 2.00 | 108 Fred Cox | 2.00 | 1.00 |
| 158 Bobby Joe Conrad | 3.00 | 1.50 | 24 Johnny Unitas | 50.00 | 30.00 | 109 Paul Flatley | 2.00 | 1.00 |
| 159 Bob DeMarco | 2.00 | 1.00 | 25 Bob Vogel | 2.00 | 1.00 | 110 Rip Hawkins | 2.00 | 1.00 |
| 160 Pat Fischer RC | 4.00 | 2.00 | 26 Colts Play/Moore/Parker | 4.00 | 2.00 | 111 Tommy Mason | 2.00 | 1.00 |
| 161 Irv Goode | 2.00 | 1.00 | 27 Chicago Bears | 3.00 | 1.50 | 112 Ed Sharockman | 2.00 | 1.00 |
| 162 Ken Gray | 2.00 | 1.00 | 28 Doug Atkins | 4.00 | 2.00 | 113 Gordon Smith | 2.00 | 1.00 |
| 163 Charlie Johnson | 3.00 | 1.50 | 29 Rudy Bukich | 2.00 | 1.00 | 114 Fran Tarkenton | 30.00 | 15.00 |
| 164 Bill Koman | 2.00 | 1.00 | 30 Ronnie Bull | 2.00 | 1.00 | 115 Mick Tingelhoff | 3.00 | 1.50 |
| 165 Dale Meinert | 2.00 | 1.00 | 31 Dick Butkus RC ! | 250.00 | 150.00 | 116 Bobby Walden RC**/C | 2.00 | 1.00 |
| 166 Jerry Stovall RC | 3.00 | 1.50 | 32 Mike Ditka | 35.00 | 20.00 | 117 Minnesota Vikings | 2.00 | 1.00 |
| 167 Abe Woodson | 2.00 | 1.00 | 33 Joe Fortunato | 2.00 | 1.00 | 118 New York Giants | 3.00 | 1.50 |
| 168 St. Louis Cardinals | 2.00 | 1.00 | 34 Bobby Joe Green | 2.00 | 1.00 | 119 Roosevelt Brown | 4.00 | 2.00 |
| 169 San Francisco 49ers | 3.00 | 1.50 | 35 Roger LeClerc | 2.00 | 1.00 | 120 Henry Carr RC | 3.00 | 1.50 |
| 170 Kermit Alexander | 2.00 | 1.00 | 36 Johnny Morris | 2.00 | 1.00 | 121 Clarence Childs | 2.00 | 1.00 |
| 171 John Brodie | 10.00 | 5.00 | 37 Mike Pyle | 2.00 | 1.00 | 122 Tucker Frederickson RC | 3.00 | 1.50 |
| 172 Bernie Casey | 3.00 | 1.50 | 38 Gale Sayers RC ! | 225.00 | 125.00 | 123 Jerry Hillebrand | 2.00 | 1.00 |
| 173 John David Crow | 3.00 | 1.50 | 39 Bears Play/G.Sayers | 35.00 | 20.00 | 124 Greg Larson | 3.00 | 1.50 |
| 174 Tommy Davis | 2.00 | 1.00 | 40 Cleveland Browns | 3.00 | 1.50 | 125 Spider Lockhart RC | 3.00 | 1.50 |
| 175 Matt Hazeltine | 2.00 | 1.00 | 41 Jim Brown | 80.00 | 50.00 | 126 Dick Lynch | 2.00 | 1.00 |
| 176 Jim Johnson | 4.00 | 2.00 | 42 Gary Collins | 2.00 | 1.00 | 127 Earl Morrall/Scholtz | 3.00 | 1.50 |
| 177 Charlie Krueger RC | 2.00 | 1.00 | 43 Ross Fichtner | 2.00 | 1.00 | 128 Joe Morrison | 2.00 | 1.00 |
| 178 Roland Lakes | 2.00 | 1.00 | 44 Ernie Green | 2.00 | 1.00 | 129 Steve Thurlow | 2.00 | 1.00 |
| 179 George Mira RC | 3.00 | 1.50 | 45 Gene Hickerson RC | 25.00 | 15.00 | 130 New York Giants | 3.00 | 1.50 |
| 180 Dave Parks RC | 3.00 | 1.50 | 46 Jim Houston | 2.00 | 1.00 | 131 Philadelphia Eagles | 3.00 | 1.50 |
| 181 John Thomas RC | 2.00 | 1.00 | 47 John Morrow | 2.00 | 1.00 | 132 Sam Baker | 2.00 | 1.00 |
| 182 49ers Play/Christiansen | 2.00 | 1.00 | 48 Walter Roberts | 2.00 | 1.00 | 133 Maxie Baughan | 2.00 | 1.00 |
| 183 Washington Redskins | 3.00 | 1.50 | 49 Frank Ryan | 3.00 | 1.50 | 134 Bob Brown OT RC | 15.00 | 7.50 |
| 184 Pervis Atkins | 2.00 | 1.00 | 50 Dick Schafrath | 2.00 | 1.00 | 135 Timmy Brown | 3.00 | 1.50 |
| 185 Preston Carpenter | 2.00 | 1.00 | 51 Paul Wiggin RC | 2.00 | 1.00 | 136 Irv Cross | 3.00 | 1.50 |
| 186 Angelo Coia | 2.00 | 1.00 | 52 Cleveland Browns | 2.00 | 1.00 | 137 Earl Gros | 2.00 | 1.00 |
| 187 Sam Huff | 6.00 | 3.00 | 53 Dallas Cowboys | 3.00 | 1.50 | 138 Ray Poage | 2.00 | 1.00 |
| 188 Sonny Jurgensen | 15.00 | 7.50 | 54 George Andrie RC UER | 3.00 | 1.50 | 139 Nate Ramsey | 3.00 | 1.50 |
| 189 Paul Krause RC | 25.00 | 15.00 | 55 Frank Clarke | 3.00 | 1.50 | 140 Pete Retzlaff | 3.00 | 1.50 |
| 190 Jim Martin | 2.00 | 1.00 | 56 Mike Connelly | 2.00 | 1.00 | 141 Jim Ringo | 4.00 | 2.00 |
| 191 Bobby Mitchell | 5.00 | 2.50 | 57 Cornell Green | 4.00 | 2.00 | 142 Norm Snead | 4.00 | 2.00 |
| 192 John Nisby | 2.00 | 1.00 | 58 Bob Hayes RC | 60.00 | 35.00 | 143 Philadelphia Eagles | 3.00 | 1.50 |
| 193 John Paluck | 2.00 | 1.00 | 59 Chuck Howley RC | 18.00 | 10.00 | 144 Pittsburgh Steelers | 3.00 | 1.50 |
| 194 Vince Promuto | 2.00 | 1.00 | 60 Bob Lilly | 20.00 | 12.00 | 145 Gary Ballman | 2.00 | 1.00 |
| 195 Charley Taylor RC | 50.00 | 30.00 | 61 Don Meredith | 25.00 | 15.00 | 146 Charley Bradshaw | 2.00 | 1.00 |

|  | | |
|---|---|---|
| ☐ 147 Jim Butler | 2.00 | 1.00 |
| ☐ 148 Mike Clark | 2.00 | 1.00 |
| ☐ 149 Dick Hoak RC | 2.00 | 1.00 |
| ☐ 150 Roy Jefferson RC | 3.00 | 1.50 |
| ☐ 151 Frank Lambert | 2.00 | 1.00 |
| ☐ 152 Mike Lind | 2.00 | 1.00 |
| ☐ 153 Bill Nelsen RC | 4.00 | 2.00 |
| ☐ 154 Clarence Peaks | 2.00 | 1.00 |
| ☐ 155 Clendon Thomas | 2.00 | 1.00 |
| ☐ 156 Pittsburgh Steelers | 2.00 | 1.00 |
| ☐ 157 St. Louis Cardinals | 3.00 | 1.50 |
| ☐ 158 Jim Bakken | 3.00 | 1.00 |
| ☐ 159 Bobby Joe Conrad | 3.00 | 1.50 |
| ☐ 160 Willis Crenshaw RC | 2.00 | 1.00 |
| ☐ 161 Bob DeMarco | 2.00 | 1.00 |
| ☐ 162 Pat Fischer | 3.00 | 1.50 |
| ☐ 163 Charlie Johnson | 3.00 | 1.50 |
| ☐ 164 Dale Meinert | 2.00 | 1.00 |
| ☐ 165 Sonny Randle | 2.00 | 1.00 |
| ☐ 166 Sam Silas RC | 2.00 | 1.00 |
| ☐ 167 Bill Triplett | 2.00 | 1.00 |
| ☐ 168 Larry Wilson | 4.00 | 2.00 |
| ☐ 169 St. Louis Cardinals | 2.00 | 1.00 |
| ☐ 170 San Francisco 49ers | 3.00 | 1.50 |
| ☐ 171 Kermit Alexander | 2.00 | 1.00 |
| ☐ 172 Bruce Bosley | 2.00 | 1.00 |
| ☐ 173 John Brodie | 6.00 | 3.00 |
| ☐ 174 Bernie Casey | 3.00 | 1.50 |
| ☐ 175 John David Crow | 4.00 | 2.00 |
| ☐ 176 Tommy Davis | 2.00 | 1.00 |
| ☐ 177 Jim Johnson | 4.00 | 2.00 |
| ☐ 178 Gary Lewis RC | 2.00 | 1.00 |
| ☐ 179 Dave Parks | 2.00 | 1.00 |
| ☐ 180 Walter Rock RC | 3.00 | 1.50 |
| ☐ 181 Ken Willard RC | 4.00 | 2.00 |
| ☐ 182 San Francisco 49ers | 2.00 | 1.00 |
| ☐ 183 Washington Redskins | 2.00 | 1.00 |
| ☐ 184 Rickie Harris | 2.00 | 1.00 |
| ☐ 185 Sonny Jurgensen | 8.00 | 4.00 |
| ☐ 186 Paul Krause | 6.00 | 3.00 |
| ☐ 187 Bobby Mitchell | 6.00 | 3.00 |
| ☐ 188 Vince Promuto | 2.00 | 1.00 |
| ☐ 189 Pat Richter RC | 2.00 | 1.00 |
| ☐ 190 Joe Rutgens | 2.00 | 1.00 |
| ☐ 191 Johnny Sample | 2.00 | 1.00 |
| ☐ 192 Lonnie Sanders | 2.00 | 1.00 |
| ☐ 193 Tom Steffen | 2.00 | 1.00 |
| ☐ 194 Charley Taylor | 15.00 | 7.50 |
| ☐ 195 Washington Redskins | 2.00 | 1.00 |
| ☐ 196 Referee Signals | 3.00 | 1.50 |
| ☐ 197 Checklist 1 ! | 25.00 | 12.50 |
| ☐ 198 Checklist 2 UER ! | 50.00 | 25.00 |

## 1967 Philadelphia

JOHNNY UNITAS
BALTIMORE COLTS

| | | |
|---|---|---|
| ☐ COMPLETE SET (198) | 650.00 | 425.00 |
| ☐ WRAPPER (5-CENT) | 20.00 | 10.00 |
| ☐ 1 Falcons Team ! | 10.00 | 5.00 |
| ☐ 2 Junior Coffey RC | 3.00 | 1.50 |
| ☐ 3 Alex Hawkins | 2.00 | 1.00 |
| ☐ 4 Randy Johnson RC | 3.00 | 1.50 |
| ☐ 5 Lou Kirouac | 2.00 | 1.00 |
| ☐ 6 Billy Martin RC | 2.00 | 1.00 |
| ☐ 7 Tommy Nobis RC | 20.00 | 10.00 |
| ☐ 8 Jerry Richardson RC | 4.00 | 2.00 |
| ☐ 9 Marion Rushing | 2.00 | 1.00 |
| ☐ 10 Ron Smith | 2.00 | 1.00 |
| ☐ 11 Ernie Wheelwright UER | 2.00 | 1.00 |
| ☐ 12 Atlanta Falcons | 2.00 | 1.00 |

|  | | |
|---|---|---|
| ☐ 13 Baltimore Colts | 3.00 | 1.50 |
| ☐ 14 Raymond Berry UER | 7.00 | 3.50 |
| ☐ 15 Bob Boyd DB | 2.00 | 1.00 |
| ☐ 16 Ordell Braase RC | 2.00 | 1.00 |
| ☐ 17 Alvin Haymond RC | 2.00 | 1.00 |
| ☐ 18 Tony Lorick | 2.00 | 1.00 |
| ☐ 19 Lenny Lyles | 2.00 | 1.00 |
| ☐ 20 John Mackey | 5.00 | 2.50 |
| ☐ 21 Tom Matte | 3.00 | 1.50 |
| ☐ 22 Lou Michaels | 2.00 | 1.00 |
| ☐ 23 Johnny Unitas | 40.00 | 25.00 |
| ☐ 24 Baltimore Colts | 2.00 | 1.00 |
| ☐ 25 Chicago Bears | 3.00 | 1.50 |
| ☐ 26 Rudy Bukich UER | 2.00 | 1.00 |
| ☐ 27 Ronnie Bull | 2.00 | 1.00 |
| ☐ 28 Dick Butkus | 75.00 | 45.00 |
| ☐ 29 Mike Ditka | 30.00 | 18.00 |
| ☐ 30 Dick Gordon RC | 3.00 | 1.50 |
| ☐ 31 Roger LeClerc | 2.00 | 1.00 |
| ☐ 32 Bennie McRae | 2.00 | 1.00 |
| ☐ 33 Richie Petitbon | 2.00 | 1.00 |
| ☐ 34 Mike Pyle | 2.00 | 1.00 |
| ☐ 35 Gale Sayers | 75.00 | 45.00 |
| ☐ 36 Chicago Bears | 3.00 | 1.50 |
| ☐ 37 Cleveland Browns | 3.00 | 1.50 |
| ☐ 38 Johnny Brewer | 2.00 | 1.00 |
| ☐ 39 Gary Collins | 3.00 | 1.50 |
| ☐ 40 Ross Fichtner | 2.00 | 1.00 |
| ☐ 41 Ernie Green | 2.00 | 1.00 |
| ☐ 42 Gene Hickerson | 5.00 | 2.50 |
| ☐ 43 Leroy Kelly RC | 40.00 | 25.00 |
| ☐ 44 Frank Ryan | 3.00 | 1.50 |
| ☐ 45 Dick Schafrath | 2.00 | 1.00 |
| ☐ 46 Paul Warfield | 18.00 | 10.00 |
| ☐ 47 John Wooten | 2.00 | 1.00 |
| ☐ 48 Cleveland Browns | 2.00 | 1.00 |
| ☐ 49 Dallas Cowboys | 3.00 | 1.50 |
| ☐ 50 George Andrie | 2.00 | 1.00 |
| ☐ 51 Cornell Green | 3.00 | 1.50 |
| ☐ 52 Bob Hayes | 20.00 | 10.00 |
| ☐ 53 Chuck Howley | 4.00 | 2.00 |
| ☐ 54 Lee Roy Jordan RC | 20.00 | 12.00 |
| ☐ 55 Bob Lilly | 15.00 | 7.50 |
| ☐ 56 Dave Manders RC | 2.00 | 1.00 |
| ☐ 57 Don Meredith | 25.00 | 15.00 |
| ☐ 58 Dan Reeves RC | 30.00 | 18.00 |
| ☐ 59 Mel Renfro | 6.00 | 3.00 |
| ☐ 60 Dallas Cowboys | 3.00 | 1.50 |
| ☐ 61 Detroit Lions | 3.00 | 1.50 |
| ☐ 62 Roger Brown | 3.00 | 1.50 |
| ☐ 63 Gail Cogdill | 2.00 | 1.00 |
| ☐ 64 John Gordy | 2.00 | 1.00 |
| ☐ 65 Ron Kramer | 2.00 | 1.00 |
| ☐ 66 Dick LeBeau | 2.00 | 1.00 |
| ☐ 67 Mike Lucci RC | 4.00 | 2.00 |
| ☐ 68 Amos Marsh | 2.00 | 1.00 |
| ☐ 69 Tom Nowatzke | 2.00 | 1.00 |
| ☐ 70 Pat Studstill | 2.00 | 1.00 |
| ☐ 71 Karl Sweetan | 2.00 | 1.00 |
| ☐ 72 Detroit Lions | 2.00 | 1.00 |
| ☐ 73 Green Bay Packers | 5.00 | 2.50 |
| ☐ 74 Herb Adderley UER | 6.00 | 3.00 |
| ☐ 75 Lee Roy Caffey | 3.00 | 1.50 |
| ☐ 76 Willie Davis DE | 5.00 | 2.50 |
| ☐ 77 Forrest Gregg | 4.00 | 2.00 |
| ☐ 78 Hank Jordan | 4.00 | 2.00 |
| ☐ 79 Ray Nitschke | 12.00 | 6.00 |
| ☐ 80 Dave Robinson RC | 6.00 | 3.00 |
| ☐ 81 Bob Skoronski | 3.00 | 1.50 |
| ☐ 82 Bart Starr | 50.00 | 30.00 |
| ☐ 83 Willie Wood | 5.00 | 2.50 |
| ☐ 84 Green Bay Packers | 3.00 | 1.50 |
| ☐ 85 Los Angeles Rams | 3.00 | 1.50 |
| ☐ 86 Dick Bass | 3.00 | 1.50 |
| ☐ 87 Maxie Baughan | 2.00 | 1.00 |
| ☐ 88 Roman Gabriel | 4.00 | 2.00 |
| ☐ 89 Bruce Gossett | 2.00 | 1.00 |
| ☐ 90 Deacon Jones | 5.00 | 2.50 |
| ☐ 91 Tommy McDonald | 5.00 | 2.50 |
| ☐ 92 Marlin McKeever | 2.00 | 1.00 |
| ☐ 93 Tom Moore | 2.00 | 1.00 |
| ☐ 94 Merlin Olsen | 6.00 | 3.00 |
| ☐ 95 Clancy Williams | 2.00 | 1.00 |
| ☐ 96 Los Angeles Rams | 2.00 | 1.00 |
| ☐ 97 Minnesota Vikings | 3.00 | 1.50 |

|  | | |
|---|---|---|
| ☐ 98 Grady Alderman | 2.00 | 1.00 |
| ☐ 99 Bill Brown | 3.00 | 1.50 |
| ☐ 100 Fred Cox | 2.00 | 1.00 |
| ☐ 101 Paul Flatley | 2.00 | 1.00 |
| ☐ 102 Dale Hackbart RC | 2.00 | 1.00 |
| ☐ 103 Jim Marshall | 4.00 | 2.00 |
| ☐ 104 Tommy Mason | 2.00 | 1.00 |
| ☐ 105 Milt Sunde RC | 2.00 | 1.00 |
| ☐ 106 Fran Tarkenton | 20.00 | 10.00 |
| ☐ 107 Mick Tingelhoff | 3.00 | 1.50 |
| ☐ 108 Minnesota Vikings | 2.00 | 1.00 |
| ☐ 109 New York Giants | 3.00 | 1.50 |
| ☐ 110 Henry Carr | 2.00 | 1.00 |
| ☐ 111 Clarence Childs | 2.00 | 1.00 |
| ☐ 112 Allen Jacobs | 2.00 | 1.00 |
| ☐ 113 Homer Jones RC | 3.00 | 1.50 |
| ☐ 114 Tom Kennedy | 2.00 | 1.00 |
| ☐ 115 Spider Lockhart | 2.00 | 1.00 |
| ☐ 116 Joe Morrison | 2.00 | 1.00 |
| ☐ 117 Francis Peay | 2.00 | 1.00 |
| ☐ 118 Jeff Smith LB | 2.00 | 1.00 |
| ☐ 119 Aaron Thomas | 2.00 | 1.00 |
| ☐ 120 New York Giants | 2.00 | 1.00 |
| ☐ 121 Saints Insignia | 3.00 | 1.50 |
| ☐ 122 Charley Bradshaw | 2.00 | 1.00 |
| ☐ 123 Paul Hornung | 25.00 | 12.50 |
| ☐ 124 Elbert Kimbrough | 2.00 | 1.00 |
| ☐ 125 Earl Leggett RC | 2.00 | 1.00 |
| ☐ 126 Obert Logan | 2.00 | 1.00 |
| ☐ 127 Riley Mattson | 2.00 | 1.00 |
| ☐ 128 John Morrow | 2.00 | 1.00 |
| ☐ 129 Bob Scholtz | 2.00 | 1.00 |
| ☐ 130 Dave Whitsell RC | 2.00 | 1.00 |
| ☐ 131 Gary Wood | 2.00 | 1.00 |
| ☐ 132 Saints Roster UER 121 | 3.00 | 1.50 |
| ☐ 133 Philadelphia Eagles | 3.00 | 1.50 |
| ☐ 134 Sam Baker | 2.00 | 1.00 |
| ☐ 135 Bob Brown OT | 5.00 | 2.00 |
| ☐ 136 Timmy Brown | 3.00 | 1.50 |
| ☐ 137 Earl Gros | 2.00 | 1.00 |
| ☐ 138 Dave Lloyd | 2.00 | 1.00 |
| ☐ 139 Floyd Peters | 2.00 | 1.00 |
| ☐ 140 Pete Retzlaff | 3.00 | 1.50 |
| ☐ 141 Joe Scarpati | 2.00 | 1.00 |
| ☐ 142 Norm Snead | 3.00 | 1.50 |
| ☐ 143 Jim Skaggs | 2.00 | 1.00 |
| ☐ 144 Philadelphia Eagles | 2.00 | 1.00 |
| ☐ 145 Pittsburgh Steelers | 3.00 | 1.50 |
| ☐ 146 Bill Asbury | 3.00 | 1.00 |
| ☐ 147 John Baker | 2.00 | 1.00 |
| ☐ 148 Gary Ballman | 2.00 | 1.00 |
| ☐ 149 Mike Clark | 2.00 | 1.00 |
| ☐ 150 Riley Gunnels | 2.00 | 1.00 |
| ☐ 151 John Hilton | 2.00 | 1.00 |
| ☐ 152 Roy Jefferson | 3.00 | 1.50 |
| ☐ 153 Brady Keys | 2.00 | 1.00 |
| ☐ 154 Ben McGee | 2.00 | 1.00 |
| ☐ 155 Bill Nelsen | 3.00 | 1.50 |
| ☐ 156 Pittsburgh Steelers | 2.00 | 1.00 |
| ☐ 157 St. Louis Cardinals | 3.00 | 1.50 |
| ☐ 158 Jim Bakken | 2.00 | 1.00 |
| ☐ 159 Bobby Joe Conrad | 3.00 | 1.50 |
| ☐ 160 Ken Gray | 2.00 | 1.00 |
| ☐ 161 Charlie Johnson | 3.00 | 1.50 |
| ☐ 162 Joe Robb | 2.00 | 1.00 |
| ☐ 163 Johnny Roland RC | 3.00 | 1.50 |
| ☐ 164 Roy Shivers | 2.00 | 1.00 |
| ☐ 165 Jackie Smith RC | 15.00 | 7.50 |
| ☐ 166 Jerry Stovall | 2.00 | 1.00 |
| ☐ 167 Larry Wilson | 4.00 | 2.00 |
| ☐ 168 St. Louis Cardinals | 2.00 | 1.00 |
| ☐ 169 San Francisco 49ers | 3.00 | 1.50 |
| ☐ 170 Kermit Alexander | 2.00 | 1.00 |
| ☐ 171 Bruce Bosley | 2.00 | 1.00 |
| ☐ 172 John Brodie | 6.00 | 3.00 |
| ☐ 173 Bernie Casey | 3.00 | 1.50 |
| ☐ 174 Tommy Davis | 2.00 | 1.00 |
| ☐ 175 Howard Mudd | 2.00 | 1.00 |
| ☐ 176 Dave Parks | 2.00 | 1.00 |
| ☐ 177 John Thomas | 2.00 | 1.00 |
| ☐ 178 Dave Wilcox RC | 25.00 | 12.50 |
| ☐ 179 Ken Willard | 3.00 | 1.50 |
| ☐ 180 San Francisco 49ers | 2.00 | 1.00 |
| ☐ 181 Washington Redskins | 3.00 | 1.50 |
| ☐ 182 Charlie Gogolak RC | 2.00 | 1.00 |

| | | | |
|---|---|---|---|
| ❑ 183 Chris Hanburger RC | 5.00 | 2.50 |
| ❑ 184 Len Hauss RC | 3.00 | 1.50 |
| ❑ 185 Sonny Jurgensen | 7.00 | 3.50 |
| ❑ 186 Bobby Mitchell | 5.00 | 2.50 |
| ❑ 187 Brig Owens | 2.00 | 1.00 |
| ❑ 188 Jim Shorter | 2.00 | 1.00 |
| ❑ 189 Jerry Smith RC | 3.00 | 1.50 |
| ❑ 190 Charley Taylor | 8.00 | 4.00 |
| ❑ 191 A.D. Whitfield | 2.00 | 1.00 |
| ❑ 192 Washington Redskins | 2.00 | 1.00 |
| ❑ 193 Browns Play/Leroy Kelly | 6.00 | 3.00 |
| ❑ 194 New York Giants PC | 2.00 | 1.00 |
| ❑ 195 Atlanta Falcons PC | 2.00 | 1.00 |
| ❑ 196 Referee Signals | 3.00 | 1.50 |
| ❑ 197 Checklist 1 ! | 20.00 | 12.00 |
| ❑ 198 Checklist 2 UER ! | 40.00 | 20.00 |

## 1991 Pinnacle

| | | | |
|---|---|---|---|
| ❑ COMPLETE SET (415) | 20.00 | 7.50 |
| ❑ 1 Warren Moon | .40 | .15 |
| ❑ 2 Morten Andersen | .10 | .02 |
| ❑ 3 Rohn Stark | .10 | .02 |
| ❑ 4 Mark Bortz | .10 | .02 |
| ❑ 5 Mark Higgs RC | .10 | .02 |
| ❑ 6 Troy Aikman | 2.00 | .75 |
| ❑ 7 John Elway | 3.00 | 1.25 |
| ❑ 8 Neal Anderson | .20 | .07 |
| ❑ 9 Chris Doleman | .10 | .02 |
| ❑ 10 Jay Schroeder | .10 | .02 |
| ❑ 11 Sterling Sharpe | .40 | .15 |
| ❑ 12 Steve DeBerg | .10 | .02 |
| ❑ 13 Ronnie Lott | .20 | .07 |
| ❑ 14 Sean Landeta | .10 | .02 |
| ❑ 15 Jim Everett | .20 | .07 |
| ❑ 16 Jim Breech | .10 | .02 |
| ❑ 17 Barry Foster | .20 | .07 |
| ❑ 18 Mike Merriweather | .10 | .02 |
| ❑ 19 Eric Metcalf | .20 | .07 |
| ❑ 20 Mark Carrier DB | .20 | .07 |
| ❑ 21 James Brooks | .20 | .07 |
| ❑ 22 Nate Odomes | .10 | .02 |
| ❑ 23 Rodney Hampton | .40 | .15 |
| ❑ 24 Chris Miller | .20 | .07 |
| ❑ 25 Roger Craig | .20 | .07 |
| ❑ 26 Louis Oliver | .10 | .02 |
| ❑ 27 Allen Pinkett | .10 | .02 |
| ❑ 28 Bubby Brister | .10 | .02 |
| ❑ 29 Reyna Thompson | .10 | .02 |
| ❑ 30 Issiac Holt | .10 | .02 |
| ❑ 31 Steve Broussard | .10 | .02 |
| ❑ 32 Christian Okoye | .10 | .02 |
| ❑ 33 Dave Meggett | .20 | .07 |
| ❑ 34 Andre Reed | .20 | .07 |
| ❑ 35 Shane Conlan | .10 | .02 |
| ❑ 36 Eric Ball | .10 | .02 |
| ❑ 37 Johnny Bailey | .10 | .02 |
| ❑ 38 Don Majkowski | .10 | .02 |
| ❑ 39 Gerald Williams | .10 | .02 |
| ❑ 40 Kevin Mack | .10 | .02 |
| ❑ 41 Jeff Herrod | .10 | .02 |
| ❑ 42 Emmitt Smith | 6.00 | 2.50 |
| ❑ 43 Wendell Davis | .10 | .02 |
| ❑ 44 Lorenzo White | .10 | .02 |
| ❑ 45 Andre Rison | .20 | .07 |
| ❑ 46 Jerry Gray | .10 | .02 |
| ❑ 47 Dennis Smith | .10 | .02 |
| ❑ 48 Gaston Green | .10 | .02 |
| ❑ 49 Dermontti Dawson | .10 | .02 |

| | | | |
|---|---|---|---|
| ❑ 50 Jeff Hostetler | .20 | .07 |
| ❑ 51 Nick Lowery | .10 | .02 |
| ❑ 52 Merril Hoge | .10 | .02 |
| ❑ 53 Bobby Hebert | .10 | .02 |
| ❑ 54 Scott Case | .10 | .02 |
| ❑ 55 Jack Del Rio | .20 | .07 |
| ❑ 56 Cornelius Bennett | .20 | .07 |
| ❑ 57 Tony Mandarich | .10 | .02 |
| ❑ 58 Bill Brooks | .10 | .02 |
| ❑ 59 Jessie Tuggle | .10 | .02 |
| ❑ 60 Hugh Millen RC | .10 | .02 |
| ❑ 61 Tony Bennett | .20 | .07 |
| ❑ 62 Cris Dishman RC | .10 | .02 |
| ❑ 63 Darryl Henley RC | .10 | .02 |
| ❑ 64 Duane Bickett | .10 | .02 |
| ❑ 65 Jay Hilgenberg | .10 | .02 |
| ❑ 66 Joe Montana | 3.00 | 1.25 |
| ❑ 67 Bill Fralic | .10 | .02 |
| ❑ 68 Sam Mills | .10 | .02 |
| ❑ 69 Bruce Armstrong | .10 | .02 |
| ❑ 70 Dan Marino | 3.00 | 1.25 |
| ❑ 71 Jim Lachey | .10 | .02 |
| ❑ 72 Rod Woodson | .40 | .15 |
| ❑ 73 Simon Fletcher | .10 | .02 |
| ❑ 74 Bruce Matthews | .20 | .07 |
| ❑ 75 Howie Long | .40 | .15 |
| ❑ 76 John Friesz | .40 | .15 |
| ❑ 77 Karl Mecklenburg | .10 | .02 |
| ❑ 78 John L. Williams UER | .10 | .02 |
| ❑ 79 Rob Burnett RC | .20 | .07 |
| ❑ 80 Anthony Carter | .20 | .07 |
| ❑ 81 Henry Ellard | .20 | .07 |
| ❑ 82 Don Beebe | .10 | .02 |
| ❑ 83 Louis Lipps | .10 | .02 |
| ❑ 84 Greg McMurtry | .10 | .02 |
| ❑ 85 Will Wolford | .10 | .02 |
| ❑ 86 Eric Green | .10 | .02 |
| ❑ 87 Irving Fryar | .20 | .07 |
| ❑ 88 John Offerdahl | .10 | .02 |
| ❑ 89 John Alt | .10 | .02 |
| ❑ 90 Tom Tupa | .10 | .02 |
| ❑ 91 Don Mosebar | .10 | .02 |
| ❑ 92 Jeff George | .50 | .20 |
| ❑ 93 Vinny Testaverde | .20 | .07 |
| ❑ 94 Greg Townsend | .10 | .02 |
| ❑ 95 Derrick Fenner | .10 | .02 |
| ❑ 96 Brian Mitchell | .20 | .07 |
| ❑ 97 Herschel Walker | .20 | .07 |
| ❑ 98 Ricky Proehl | .10 | .02 |
| ❑ 99 Mark Clayton | .20 | .07 |
| ❑ 100 Derrick Thomas | .40 | .15 |
| ❑ 101 Jim Harbaugh | .40 | .15 |
| ❑ 102 Barry Word | .10 | .02 |
| ❑ 103 Jerry Rice | 2.00 | .75 |
| ❑ 104 Keith Byars | .10 | .02 |
| ❑ 105 Marion Butts | .20 | .07 |
| ❑ 106 Rich Moran | .10 | .02 |
| ❑ 107 Thurman Thomas | .40 | .15 |
| ❑ 108 Stephone Paige | .10 | .02 |
| ❑ 109 D.J. Johnson | .10 | .02 |
| ❑ 110 William Perry | .20 | .07 |
| ❑ 111 Haywood Jeffires | .20 | .07 |
| ❑ 112 Rodney Peete | .20 | .07 |
| ❑ 113 Andy Heck | .10 | .02 |
| ❑ 114 Kevin Ross | .10 | .02 |
| ❑ 115 Michael Carter | .10 | .02 |
| ❑ 116 Tim McKyer | .10 | .02 |
| ❑ 117 Kenneth Davis | .10 | .02 |
| ❑ 118 Richmond Webb | .10 | .02 |
| ❑ 119 Rich Camarillo | .10 | .02 |
| ❑ 120 James Francis | .10 | .02 |
| ❑ 121 Craig Heyward | .20 | .07 |
| ❑ 122 Hardy Nickerson | .20 | .07 |
| ❑ 123 Michael Brooks | .10 | .02 |
| ❑ 124 Fred Barnett | .40 | .15 |
| ❑ 125 Cris Carter | 1.00 | .40 |
| ❑ 126 Brian Jordan | .20 | .07 |
| ❑ 127 Pat Leahy | .10 | .02 |
| ❑ 128 Kevin Greene | .20 | .07 |
| ❑ 129 Trace Armstrong | .10 | .02 |
| ❑ 130 Eugene Lockhart | .10 | .02 |
| ❑ 131 Albert Lewis | .10 | .02 |
| ❑ 132 Ernie Jones | .10 | .02 |
| ❑ 133 Eric Martin | .10 | .02 |
| ❑ 134 Anthony Thompson | .10 | .02 |

| | | | |
|---|---|---|---|
| ❑ 135 Tim Krumrie | .10 | .02 |
| ❑ 136 James Lofton | .20 | .07 |
| ❑ 137 John Taylor | .20 | .07 |
| ❑ 138 Jeff Cross | .10 | .02 |
| ❑ 139 Tommy Kane | .10 | .02 |
| ❑ 140 Robb Thomas | .10 | .02 |
| ❑ 141 Gary Anderson K | .10 | .02 |
| ❑ 142 Mark Murphy | .10 | .02 |
| ❑ 143 Rickey Jackson | .10 | .02 |
| ❑ 144 Ken O'Brien | .10 | .02 |
| ❑ 145 Ernest Givins | .20 | .07 |
| ❑ 146 Jessie Hester | .10 | .02 |
| ❑ 147 Deion Sanders | .75 | .30 |
| ❑ 148 Keith Henderson RC | .10 | .02 |
| ❑ 149 Chris Singleton | .10 | .02 |
| ❑ 150 Rod Bernstine | .10 | .02 |
| ❑ 151 Quinn Early | .20 | .07 |
| ❑ 152 Boomer Esiason | .20 | .07 |
| ❑ 153 Mike Gann | .10 | .02 |
| ❑ 154 Dino Hackett | .10 | .02 |
| ❑ 155 Perry Kemp | .10 | .02 |
| ❑ 156 Mark Ingram | .10 | .02 |
| ❑ 157 Daryl Johnston | .75 | .30 |
| ❑ 158 Eugene Daniel | .10 | .02 |
| ❑ 159 Dalton Hilliard | .10 | .02 |
| ❑ 160 Rufus Porter | .10 | .02 |
| ❑ 161 Tunch Ilkin | .10 | .02 |
| ❑ 162 James Hasty | .10 | .02 |
| ❑ 163 Keith McKeller | .10 | .02 |
| ❑ 164 Heath Sherman | .10 | .02 |
| ❑ 165 Vai Sikahema | .10 | .02 |
| ❑ 166 Pat Terrell | .10 | .02 |
| ❑ 167 Anthony Munoz | .20 | .07 |
| ❑ 168 Brad Edwards RC | .10 | .02 |
| ❑ 169 Tom Rathman | .10 | .02 |
| ❑ 170 Steve McMichael | .20 | .07 |
| ❑ 171 Vaughan Johnson | .10 | .02 |
| ❑ 172 Nate Lewis RC | .10 | .02 |
| ❑ 173 Mark Rypien | .20 | .07 |
| ❑ 174 Rob Moore | .50 | .20 |
| ❑ 175 Tim Green | .10 | .02 |
| ❑ 176 Tony Casillas | .10 | .02 |
| ❑ 177 Jon Hand | .10 | .02 |
| ❑ 178 Todd McNair | .10 | .02 |
| ❑ 179 Toi Cook RC | .10 | .02 |
| ❑ 180 Eddie Brown | .10 | .02 |
| ❑ 181 Mark Jackson | .10 | .02 |
| ❑ 182 Pete Stoyanovich | .10 | .02 |
| ❑ 183 Bryce Paup RC | .40 | .15 |
| ❑ 184 Anthony Miller | .20 | .07 |
| ❑ 185 Guy McIntyre | .10 | .02 |
| ❑ 186 Broderick Thomas | .10 | .02 |
| ❑ 187 Frank Warren | .10 | .02 |
| ❑ 188 Drew Hill | .10 | .02 |
| ❑ 189 Chris Hinton | .10 | .02 |
| ❑ 190 Reggie White | .40 | .15 |
| ❑ 191 David Little | .10 | .02 |
| ❑ 192 David Fulcher | .10 | .02 |
| ❑ 193 Clarence Verdin | .10 | .02 |
| ❑ 194 Junior Seau | .60 | .25 |
| ❑ 195 Blair Thomas | .20 | .07 |
| ❑ 196 Stan Brock | .10 | .02 |
| ❑ 197 Gary Clark | .40 | .15 |
| ❑ 198 Michael Irvin | .40 | .15 |
| ❑ 199 Ronnie Harmon | .10 | .02 |
| ❑ 200 Steve Young | 2.00 | .75 |
| ❑ 201 Brian Noble | .10 | .02 |
| ❑ 202 Dan Stryzinski | .10 | .02 |
| ❑ 203 Darryl Talley | .10 | .02 |
| ❑ 204 David Alexander | .10 | .02 |
| ❑ 205 Pat Swilling | .20 | .07 |
| ❑ 206 Gary Plummer | .10 | .02 |
| ❑ 207 Robert Delpino | .10 | .02 |
| ❑ 208 Norm Johnson | .10 | .02 |
| ❑ 209 Mike Singletary | .20 | .07 |
| ❑ 210 Anthony Johnson | .40 | .15 |
| ❑ 211 Eric Allen | .10 | .02 |
| ❑ 212 Gill Fenerty | .10 | .02 |
| ❑ 213 Neil Smith | .40 | .15 |
| ❑ 214 Joe Phillips | .10 | .02 |
| ❑ 215 Ottis Anderson | .20 | .07 |
| ❑ 216 LeRoy Butler | .10 | .02 |
| ❑ 217 Ray Childress | .10 | .02 |
| ❑ 218 Rodney Holman | .10 | .02 |

| | | | |
|---|---|---|---|
| 220 Kevin Fagan | .10 | .02 |
| 221 Bruce Smith | .40 | .15 |
| 222 Brad Muster | .10 | .02 |
| 223 Mike Horan | .10 | .02 |
| 224 Steve Atwater | .10 | .02 |
| 225 Rich Gannon | .50 | .20 |
| 226 Anthony Pleasant | .10 | .02 |
| 227 Steve Jordan | .10 | .02 |
| 228 Lomas Brown | .10 | .02 |
| 229 Jackie Slater | .10 | .02 |
| 230 Brad Baxter | .10 | .02 |
| 231 Joe Morris | .10 | .02 |
| 232 Marcus Allen | .40 | .15 |
| 233 Chris Warren | .40 | .15 |
| 234 Johnny Johnson | .10 | .02 |
| 235 Phil Simms | .20 | .07 |
| 236 Dave Krieg | .20 | .07 |
| 237 Jim McMahon | .20 | .07 |
| 238 Richard Dent | .20 | .07 |
| 239 John Washington RC | .10 | .02 |
| 240 Sammie Smith | .10 | .02 |
| 241 Brian Brennan | .10 | .02 |
| 242 Cortez Kennedy | .40 | .15 |
| 243 Tim McDonald | .20 | .07 |
| 244 Charles Haley | .20 | .07 |
| 245 Joey Browner | .10 | .02 |
| 246 Eddie Murray | .10 | .02 |
| 247 Bob Golic | .10 | .02 |
| 248 Myron Guyton | .10 | .02 |
| 249 Dennis Byrd | .10 | .02 |
| 250 Barry Sanders | 3.00 | 1.25 |
| 251 Clay Matthews | .10 | .02 |
| 252 Pepper Johnson | .10 | .02 |
| 253 Eric Swann | .40 | .15 |
| 254 Lamar Lathon | .10 | .02 |
| 255 Andre Tippett | .10 | .02 |
| 256 Tom Newberry | .10 | .02 |
| 257 Kyle Clifton | .10 | .02 |
| 258 Leslie O'Neal | .20 | .07 |
| 259 Bubba McDowell | .10 | .02 |
| 260 Scott Davis | .10 | .02 |
| 261 Wilber Marshall | .10 | .02 |
| 262 Marv Cook | .10 | .02 |
| 263 Jeff Lageman | .10 | .02 |
| 264 Michael Young | .10 | .02 |
| 265 Gary Zimmerman | .10 | .02 |
| 266 Mike Munchak | .20 | .07 |
| 267 David Treadwell | .10 | .02 |
| 268 Steve Wisniewski | .10 | .02 |
| 269 Mark Duper | .20 | .07 |
| 270 Chris Spielman | .10 | .02 |
| 271 Brett Perriman | .40 | .15 |
| 272 Lionel Washington | .10 | .02 |
| 273 Lawrence Taylor | .40 | .15 |
| 274 Mark Collins | .10 | .02 |
| 275 Mark Carrier WR | .40 | .15 |
| 276 Paul Gruber | .10 | .02 |
| 277 Earnest Byner | .10 | .02 |
| 278 Andre Collins | .10 | .02 |
| 279 Reggie Cobb | .10 | .02 |
| 280 Art Monk | .20 | .07 |
| 281 Henry Jones RC | .20 | .07 |
| 282 Mike Pritchard RC | .40 | .15 |
| 283 Moe Gardner RC | .10 | .02 |
| 284 Chris Zorich RC | .40 | .15 |
| 285 Keith Traylor RC | .10 | .02 |
| 286 Mike Dumas RC | .10 | .02 |
| 287 Ed King RC | .10 | .02 |
| 288 Russell Maryland RC | .40 | .15 |
| 289 Alfred Williams RC | .10 | .02 |
| 290 Derek Russell RC | .10 | .02 |
| 291 Vinnie Clark RC | .10 | .02 |
| 292 Mike Croel RC | .10 | .02 |
| 293 Todd Marinovich RC | .10 | .02 |
| 294 Phil Hansen RC | .10 | .02 |
| 295 Aaron Craver RC | .10 | .02 |
| 296 Nick Bell RC | .10 | .02 |
| 297 Kenny Walker RC | .10 | .02 |
| 298 Roman Phifer RC | .10 | .02 |
| 299 Kanavis McGhee RC | .10 | .02 |
| 300 Ricky Ervins RC | .20 | .07 |
| 301 Jim Price RC | .10 | .02 |
| 302 John Johnson RC | .10 | .02 |
| 303 George Thornton RC | .10 | .02 |
| 304 Huey Richardson RC | .10 | .02 |
| 305 Harry Colon RC | .10 | .02 |
| 306 Antone Davis RC | .10 | .02 |
| 307 Todd Lyght RC | .10 | .02 |
| 308 Bryan Cox RC | .40 | .15 |
| 309 Brad Goebel RC | .10 | .02 |
| 310 Eric Moten RC | .10 | .02 |
| 311 John Kasay RC | .20 | .07 |
| 312 Esera Tuaolo RC | .10 | .02 |
| 313 Bobby Wilson RC | .10 | .02 |
| 314 Mo Lewis RC | .20 | .07 |
| 315 Harvey Williams RC | .40 | .15 |
| 316 Mike Stonebreaker RC | .10 | .02 |
| 317 Charles McRae RC | .10 | .02 |
| 318 John Flannery RC | .10 | .02 |
| 319 Ted Washington RC | .10 | .02 |
| 320 Stanley Richard RC | .10 | .02 |
| 321 Browning Nagle RC | .10 | .02 |
| 322 Ed McCaffrey RC | 5.00 | 2.00 |
| 323 Jeff Graham RC WR | .40 | .15 |
| 324 Stan Thomas | .10 | .02 |
| 325 Lawrence Dawsey RC | .20 | .07 |
| 326 Eric Bieniemy RC | .10 | .02 |
| 327 Tim Barnett RC | .10 | .02 |
| 328 Eric Pegram RC | .40 | .15 |
| 329 Lamar Rogers RC | .10 | .02 |
| 330 Ernie Mills RC | .20 | .07 |
| 331 Pat Harlow RC | .10 | .02 |
| 332 Greg Lewis RC | .10 | .02 |
| 333 Jarrod Bunch RC | .10 | .02 |
| 334 Dan McGwire RC | .10 | .02 |
| 335 Randal Hill RC | .20 | .07 |
| 336 Leonard Russell RC | .40 | .15 |
| 337 Carnell Lake | .10 | .02 |
| 338 Brian Blades | .20 | .07 |
| 339 Darrell Green | .10 | .02 |
| 340 Bobby Humphrey | .10 | .02 |
| 341 Mervyn Fernandez | .10 | .02 |
| 342 Ricky Sanders | .10 | .02 |
| 343 Keith Jackson | .20 | .07 |
| 344 Carl Banks | .10 | .02 |
| 345 Gill Byrd | .10 | .02 |
| 346 Al Toon | .20 | .07 |
| 347 Stephen Baker | .10 | .02 |
| 348 Randall Cunningham | .40 | .15 |
| 349 Flipper Anderson | .10 | .02 |
| 350 Jay Novacek | .40 | .15 |
| 351 Steve Young/B.Smith HH | .40 | .15 |
| 352 Barry Sanders/Browner HH | .75 | .30 |
| 353 Joe Montana/M.Carrier HH | .75 | .30 |
| 354 Thurman Thomas/L.Taylor | .20 | .07 |
| 355 Jerry Rice/Darr.Green HH | .50 | .20 |
| 356 Warren Moon Tech | .20 | .07 |
| 357 Anthony Munoz TECH | .10 | .02 |
| 358 Barry Sanders Tech | 1.25 | .50 |
| 359 Jerry Rice Tech | 1.25 | .50 |
| 360 Joey Browner TECH | .10 | .02 |
| 361 Morten Andersen TECH | .10 | .02 |
| 362 Sean Landeta TECH | .10 | .02 |
| 363 Thurman Thomas GW | .40 | .15 |
| 364 Emmitt Smith GW | 3.00 | 1.25 |
| 365 Gaston Green GW | .10 | .02 |
| 366 Barry Sanders GW | 1.25 | .50 |
| 367 Christian Okoye GW | .10 | .02 |
| 368 Earnest Byner GW | .10 | .02 |
| 369 Neal Anderson GW | .10 | .02 |
| 370 Herschel Walker GW | .10 | .02 |
| 371 Rodney Hampton GW | .40 | .15 |
| 372 Darryl Talley IDOL | .10 | .02 |
| 373 Mark Carrier IDOL | .10 | .02 |
| 374 Jim Breech IDOL | .10 | .02 |
| 375 R.Hampton/O.Anderson ID | .10 | .02 |
| 376 Kevin Mack IDOL | .10 | .02 |
| 377 S.Jordan/O.Robertson ID | .10 | .02 |
| 378 B.Esiason/B.Jones ID | .10 | .02 |
| 379 Steve DeBerg IDOL | .20 | .07 |
| 380 Al Toon IDOL | .10 | .02 |
| 381 Ronnie Lott/C.Taylor ID | .20 | .07 |
| 382 Henry Ellard IDOL | .10 | .02 |
| 383 Troy Aikman/Staubach ID | 1.25 | .50 |
| 384 T.Thomas/E.Campbell ID | .40 | .15 |
| 385 Dan Marino/Bradshaw ID | 1.50 | .60 |
| 386 Howie Long/Joe Greene ID | .20 | .07 |
| 387 Franco Harris IR | .20 | .07 |
| 388 Esera Tuaolo | .10 | .02 |
| 389 Super Bowl XXVI | .10 | .02 |

| | | | |
|---|---|---|---|
| 390 Charles Mann | .10 | .02 |
| 391 Kenny Walker Succeed | .10 | .02 |
| 392 Reggie Roby | .10 | .02 |
| 393 Bruce Pickens RC | .10 | .02 |
| 394 Ray Childress SIDE | .10 | .02 |
| 395 Karl Mecklenburg SIDE | .10 | .02 |
| 396 Dean Biasucci SIDE | .10 | .02 |
| 397 John Alt SIDE | .10 | .02 |
| 398 Marcus Allen SL | .20 | .07 |
| 399 John Offerdahl SIDE | .10 | .02 |
| 400 Richard Tardits RC SIDE | .10 | .02 |
| 401 Al Toon SIDE | .10 | .02 |
| 402 Joey Browner SIDE | .10 | .02 |
| 403 Spencer Tillman RC SIDE | .10 | .02 |
| 404 Jay Novacek SIDE | .20 | .07 |
| 405 Stephen Braggs SIDE | .10 | .02 |
| 406 Mike Tice RC SIDE | .10 | .02 |
| 407 Kevin Greene SIDE | .20 | .07 |
| 408 Reggie White SIDE | .20 | .07 |
| 409 Brian Noble SIDE | .10 | .02 |
| 410 Bart Oates SIDE | .10 | .02 |
| 411 Art Monk SIDE | .20 | .07 |
| 412 Ron Wolfley SIDE | .10 | .02 |
| 413 Louis Lipps SIDE | .10 | .02 |
| 414 Dante Jones RC SIDE | .20 | .07 |
| 415 Kenneth Davis SIDE | .10 | .02 |
| P1 Emmitt Smith Promo | 25.00 | 12.50 |

## 1992 Pinnacle

| | | | |
|---|---|---|---|
| COMPLETE SET (360) | 25.00 | 12.50 |
| 1 Reggie White | .50 | .20 |
| 2 Eric Green | .15 | .05 |
| 3 Craig Heyward | .30 | .10 |
| 4 Phil Simms | .30 | .10 |
| 5 Pepper Johnson | .15 | .05 |
| 6 Sean Landeta | .15 | .05 |
| 7 Dino Hackett | .15 | .05 |
| 8 Andre Ware | .15 | .05 |
| 9 Ricky Nattiel | .15 | .05 |
| 10 Jim Price | .15 | .05 |
| 11 Jim Ritcher | .15 | .05 |
| 12 Kelly Stouffer | .15 | .05 |
| 13 Ray Crockett | .15 | .05 |
| 14 Steve Tasker | .30 | .10 |
| 15 Barry Sanders | 3.00 | 1.25 |
| 16 Pat Swilling | .15 | .05 |
| 17 Moe Gardner | .15 | .05 |
| 18 Steve Young | 2.00 | .75 |
| 19 Chris Spielman | .30 | .10 |
| 20 Richard Dent | .30 | .10 |
| 21 Anthony Munoz | .30 | .10 |
| 22 Thurman Thomas | .50 | .20 |
| 23 Ricky Sanders | .15 | .05 |
| 24 Steve Atwater | .15 | .05 |
| 25 Tony Tolbert | .15 | .05 |
| 26 Haywood Jeffires | .30 | .10 |
| 27 Duane Bickett | .15 | .05 |
| 28 Tim McDonald | .15 | .05 |
| 29 Cris Carter | .75 | .30 |
| 30 Derrick Thomas | .50 | .20 |
| 31 Hugh Millen | .15 | .05 |
| 32 Bart Oates | .15 | .05 |
| 33 Darryl Talley | .15 | .05 |
| 34 Marion Butts | .15 | .05 |
| 35 Pete Stoyanovich | .15 | .05 |
| 36 Ronnie Lott | .30 | .10 |
| 37 Simon Fletcher | .15 | .05 |
| 38 Morten Andersen | .15 | .05 |

|  |  | | |
|---|---|---|---|
| 39 | Clyde Simmons | .15 | .05 |
| 40 | Mark Rypien | .15 | .05 |
| 41 | Henry Ellard | .30 | .10 |
| 42 | Michael Irvin | .50 | .20 |
| 43 | Louis Lipps | .15 | .05 |
| 44 | John L. Williams | .15 | .05 |
| 45 | Broderick Thomas | .15 | .05 |
| 46 | Don Majkowski | .15 | .05 |
| 47 | William Perry | .30 | .10 |
| 48 | David Fulcher | .15 | .05 |
| 49 | Tony Bennett | .15 | .05 |
| 50 | Clay Matthews | .30 | .10 |
| 51 | Warren Moon | .50 | .20 |
| 52 | Bruce Armstrong | .15 | .05 |
| 53 | Bill Brooks | .15 | .05 |
| 54 | Greg Townsend | .15 | .05 |
| 55 | Steve Broussard | .15 | .05 |
| 56 | Mel Gray | .30 | .10 |
| 57 | Kevin Mack | .15 | .05 |
| 58 | Emmitt Smith | 4.00 | 2.00 |
| 59 | Mike Croel | .15 | .05 |
| 60 | Brian Mitchell | .30 | .10 |
| 61 | Bennie Blades | .15 | .05 |
| 62 | Carnell Lake | .15 | .05 |
| 63 | Cornelius Bennett | .30 | .10 |
| 64 | Darrell Thompson | .15 | .05 |
| 65 | Jessie Hester | .15 | .05 |
| 66 | Marv Cook | .15 | .05 |
| 67 | Tim Brown | .50 | .20 |
| 68 | Mark Duper | .15 | .05 |
| 69 | Robert Delpino | .15 | .05 |
| 70 | Eric Martin | .15 | .05 |
| 71 | Wendell Davis | .15 | .05 |
| 72 | Vaughan Johnson | .15 | .05 |
| 73 | Brian Blades | .30 | .10 |
| 74 | Ed King | .15 | .05 |
| 75 | Gaston Green | .15 | .05 |
| 76 | Christian Okoye | .15 | .05 |
| 77 | Rohn Stark | .15 | .05 |
| 78 | Kevin Greene | .30 | .10 |
| 79 | Jay Novacek | .30 | .10 |
| 80 | Chip Lohmiller | .15 | .05 |
| 81 | Cris Dishman | .15 | .05 |
| 82 | Ethan Horton | .15 | .05 |
| 83 | Pat Harlow | .15 | .05 |
| 84 | Mark Ingram | .15 | .05 |
| 85 | Mark Carrier DB | .15 | .05 |
| 86 | Sam Mills | .15 | .05 |
| 87 | Mark Higgs | .15 | .05 |
| 88 | Keith Jackson | .30 | .10 |
| 89 | Gary Anderson K | .15 | .05 |
| 90 | Ken Harvey | .15 | .05 |
| 91 | Anthony Carter | .30 | .10 |
| 92 | Randall McDaniel | .15 | .05 |
| 93 | Johnny Johnson | .15 | .05 |
| 94 | Shane Conlan | .15 | .05 |
| 95 | Sterling Sharpe | .50 | .20 |
| 96 | Guy McIntyre | .15 | .05 |
| 97 | Albert Lewis | .15 | .05 |
| 98 | Chris Doleman | .15 | .05 |
| 99 | Andre Rison | .30 | .10 |
| 100 | Bobby Hebert | .15 | .05 |
| 101 | Dan Owens | .15 | .05 |
| 102 | Rodney Hampton | .30 | .10 |
| 103 | Ernie Jones | .15 | .05 |
| 104 | Reggie Cobb | .15 | .05 |
| 105 | Wilber Marshall | .15 | .05 |
| 106 | Mike Munchak | .30 | .10 |
| 107 | Cortez Kennedy | .15 | .05 |
| 108 | Todd Lyght | .15 | .05 |
| 109 | Burt Grossman | .15 | .05 |
| 110 | Ferrell Edmunds | .15 | .05 |
| 111 | Jim Everett | .30 | .10 |
| 112 | Hardy Nickerson | .30 | .10 |
| 113 | Andre Tippett | .15 | .05 |
| 114 | Ronnie Harmon | .15 | .05 |
| 115 | Andre Waters | .15 | .05 |
| 116 | Ernest Givins | .30 | .10 |
| 117 | Eric Hill | .15 | .05 |
| 118 | Eric Pegram | .30 | .10 |
| 119 | Jarrod Bunch | .15 | .05 |
| 120 | Marcus Allen | .50 | .20 |
| 121 | Barry Foster | .30 | .10 |
| 122 | Kent Hull | .15 | .05 |
| 123 | Neal Anderson | .15 | .05 |
| 124 | Stephen Braggs | .15 | .05 |
| 125 | Nick Lowery | .15 | .05 |
| 126 | Jeff Hostetler | .30 | .10 |
| 127 | Michael Carter | .15 | .05 |
| 128 | Don Warren | .15 | .05 |
| 129 | Brad Baxter | .15 | .05 |
| 130 | John Taylor | .30 | .10 |
| 131 | Harold Green | .15 | .05 |
| 132 | Mike Merriweather | .15 | .05 |
| 133 | Gary Clark | .50 | .20 |
| 134 | Vince Buck | .15 | .05 |
| 135 | Dan Saleaumua | .15 | .05 |
| 136 | Gary Zimmerman | .15 | .05 |
| 137 | Richmond Webb | .15 | .05 |
| 138 | Art Monk | .30 | .10 |
| 139 | Mervyn Fernandez | .15 | .05 |
| 140 | Mark Jackson | .15 | .05 |
| 141 | Freddie Joe Nunn | .15 | .05 |
| 142 | Jeff Lageman | .15 | .05 |
| 143 | Kenny Walker | .15 | .05 |
| 144 | Mark Carrier WR | .30 | .10 |
| 145 | Jon Vaughn | .15 | .05 |
| 146 | Greg Davis | .15 | .05 |
| 147 | Bubby Brister | .15 | .05 |
| 148 | Mo Lewis | .15 | .05 |
| 149 | Howie Long | .50 | .20 |
| 150 | Rod Bernstine | .15 | .05 |
| 151 | Nick Bell | .15 | .05 |
| 152 | Terry Allen | .50 | .20 |
| 153 | William Fuller | .15 | .05 |
| 154 | Dexter Carter | .15 | .05 |
| 155 | Gene Atkins | .15 | .05 |
| 156 | Don Beebe | .15 | .05 |
| 157 | Mark Collins | .15 | .05 |
| 158 | Jerry Ball | .15 | .05 |
| 159 | Fred Barnett | .50 | .20 |
| 160 | Rodney Holman | .15 | .05 |
| 161 | Stephen Baker | .15 | .05 |
| 162 | Jeff Graham | .50 | .20 |
| 163 | Leonard Russell | .30 | .10 |
| 164 | Jeff Gossett | .15 | .05 |
| 165 | Vinny Testaverde | .30 | .10 |
| 166 | Maurice Hurst | .15 | .05 |
| 167 | Louis Oliver | .15 | .05 |
| 168 | Jim Morrissey | .15 | .05 |
| 169 | Greg Kragen | .15 | .05 |
| 170 | Andre Collins | .15 | .05 |
| 171 | Dave Meggett | .30 | .10 |
| 172 | Keith Henderson | .15 | .05 |
| 173 | Vince Newsome | .15 | .05 |
| 174 | Chris Hinton | .15 | .05 |
| 175 | James Hasty | .15 | .05 |
| 176 | John Offerdahl | .15 | .05 |
| 177 | Lomas Brown | .15 | .05 |
| 178 | Neil O'Donnell | .30 | .10 |
| 179 | Leonard Marshall | .15 | .05 |
| 180 | Bubba McDowell | .15 | .05 |
| 181 | Herman Moore | .50 | .20 |
| 182 | Rob Moore | .30 | .10 |
| 183 | Earnest Byner | .15 | .05 |
| 184 | Keith McCants | .15 | .05 |
| 185 | Floyd Turner | .15 | .05 |
| 186 | Steve Jordan | .15 | .05 |
| 187 | Nate Odomes | .15 | .05 |
| 188 | Jeff Herrod | .15 | .05 |
| 189 | Jim Harbaugh | .50 | .20 |
| 190 | Jessie Tuggle | .15 | .05 |
| 191 | Al Smith | .15 | .05 |
| 192 | Lawrence Dawsey | .30 | .10 |
| 193 | Steve Bono RC | .50 | .20 |
| 194 | Greg Lloyd | .30 | .10 |
| 195 | Steve Wisniewski | .15 | .05 |
| 196 | Larry Kelm | .15 | .05 |
| 197 | Tommy Kane | .15 | .05 |
| 198 | Mark Schlereth RC | .15 | .05 |
| 199 | Ray Childress | .15 | .05 |
| 200 | Vincent Brown | .15 | .05 |
| 201 | Rodney Peete | .30 | .10 |
| 202 | Dennis Smith | .15 | .05 |
| 203 | Bruce Matthews | .15 | .05 |
| 204 | Rickey Jackson | .15 | .05 |
| 205 | Eric Allen | .15 | .05 |
| 206 | Rich Camarillo | .15 | .05 |
| 207 | Jim Lachey | .15 | .05 |
| 208 | Kevin Ross | .15 | .05 |
| 209 | Irving Fryar | .30 | .10 |
| 210 | Mark Clayton | .30 | .10 |
| 211 | Keith Byars | .15 | .05 |
| 212 | John Elway | 3.00 | 1.25 |
| 213 | Harris Barton | .15 | .05 |
| 214 | Aeneas Williams | .30 | .10 |
| 215 | Rich Gannon | .50 | .20 |
| 216 | Toi Cook | .15 | .05 |
| 217 | Rod Woodson | .50 | .20 |
| 218 | Gary Anderson RB | .15 | .05 |
| 219 | Reggie Roby | .15 | .05 |
| 220 | Karl Mecklenburg | .15 | .05 |
| 221 | Rufus Porter | .15 | .05 |
| 222 | Jon Hand | .15 | .05 |
| 223 | Tim Barnett | .15 | .05 |
| 224 | Eric Swann | .30 | .10 |
| 225 | Eugene Robinson | .15 | .05 |
| 226 | Michael Young | .15 | .05 |
| 227 | Frank Warren | .15 | .05 |
| 228 | Mike Kenn | .15 | .05 |
| 229 | Tim Green | .15 | .05 |
| 230 | Barry Word | .15 | .05 |
| 231 | Mike Pritchard | .30 | .10 |
| 232 | John Kasay | .15 | .05 |
| 233 | Derek Russell | .15 | .05 |
| 234 | Jim Breech | .15 | .05 |
| 235 | Pierce Holt | .15 | .05 |
| 236 | Tim Krumrie | .15 | .05 |
| 237 | William Roberts | .15 | .05 |
| 238 | Erik Kramer | .30 | .10 |
| 239 | Brett Perriman | .50 | .20 |
| 240 | Reyna Thompson | .15 | .05 |
| 241 | Chris Miller | .30 | .10 |
| 242 | Drew Hill | .15 | .05 |
| 243 | Curtis Duncan | .15 | .05 |
| 244 | Seth Joyner | .15 | .05 |
| 245 | Ken Norton Jr. | .30 | .10 |
| 246 | Calvin Williams | .30 | .10 |
| 247 | James Joseph | .15 | .05 |
| 248 | Bennie Thompson RC | .15 | .05 |
| 249 | Tunch Ilkin | .15 | .05 |
| 250 | Brad Edwards | .15 | .05 |
| 251 | Jeff Jaeger | .15 | .05 |
| 252 | Gill Byrd | .15 | .05 |
| 253 | Jeff Feagles | .15 | .05 |
| 254 | Jamie Dukes RC | .15 | .05 |
| 255 | Greg McMurtry | .15 | .05 |
| 256 | Anthony Johnson | .30 | .10 |
| 257 | Lamar Lathon | .15 | .05 |
| 258 | John Roper | .15 | .05 |
| 259 | Lorenzo White | .15 | .05 |
| 260 | Brian Noble | .15 | .05 |
| 261 | Chris Singleton | .15 | .05 |
| 262 | Todd Marinovich | .15 | .05 |
| 263 | Jay Hilgenberg | .15 | .05 |
| 264 | Kyle Clifton | .15 | .05 |
| 265 | Tony Casillas | .15 | .05 |
| 266 | James Francis | .15 | .05 |
| 267 | Eddie Anderson | .15 | .05 |
| 268 | Tim Harris | .15 | .05 |
| 269 | James Lofton | .30 | .10 |
| 270 | Jay Schroeder | .15 | .05 |
| 271 | Ed West | .15 | .05 |
| 272 | Don Mosebar | .15 | .05 |
| 273 | Jackie Slater | .15 | .05 |
| 274 | Fred McAfee RC | .15 | .05 |
| 275 | Steve Sewell | .15 | .05 |
| 276 | Charles Mann | .15 | .05 |
| 277 | Ron Hall | .15 | .05 |
| 278 | Darrell Green | .30 | .10 |
| 279 | Jeff Cross | .15 | .05 |
| 280 | Jeff Wright | .15 | .05 |
| 281 | Issiac Holt | .15 | .05 |
| 282 | Dermontti Dawson | .15 | .05 |
| 283 | Michael Haynes | .30 | .10 |
| 284 | Tony Mandarich | .15 | .05 |
| 285 | Leroy Hoard | .30 | .10 |
| 286 | Darryl Henley | .15 | .05 |
| 287 | Tim McGee | .15 | .05 |
| 288 | Willie Gault | .30 | .10 |
| 289 | Dalton Hilliard | .15 | .05 |
| 290 | Tim McKyer | .15 | .05 |
| 291 | Tom Waddle | .15 | .05 |
| 292 | Eric Thomas | .15 | .05 |
| 293 | Herschel Walker | .30 | .10 |

| | | |
|---|---|---|
| 294 Donnell Woolford | .15 | .05 |
| 295 James Brooks | .30 | .05 |
| 296 Brad Muster | .15 | .05 |
| 297 Brent Jones | .30 | .10 |
| 298 Erik Howard | .15 | .05 |
| 299 Alvin Harper | .30 | .10 |
| 300 Joey Browner | .15 | .05 |
| 301 Jack Del Rio | .15 | .05 |
| 302 Cleveland Gary | .15 | .05 |
| 303 Brett Favre | 6.00 | 3.00 |
| 304 Freeman McNeil | .15 | .05 |
| 305 Willie Green | .15 | .05 |
| 306 Percy Snow | .15 | .05 |
| 307 Neil Smith | .50 | .20 |
| 308 Eric Bieniemy | .15 | .05 |
| 309 Keith Traylor | .15 | .05 |
| 310 Ernie Mills | .15 | .05 |
| 311 Will Wolford | .15 | .05 |
| 312 Robert Young | .15 | .05 |
| 313 Anthony Smith | .15 | .05 |
| 314 Robert Porcher RC | .50 | .20 |
| 315 Leon Searcy RC | .15 | .05 |
| 316 Amp Lee RC | .15 | .05 |
| 317 Siran Stacy RC | .15 | .05 |
| 318 Patrick Rowe RC | .15 | .05 |
| 319 Chris Mims RC | .15 | .05 |
| 320 Matt Elliott RC | .15 | .05 |
| 321 Ricardo McDonald RC | .15 | .05 |
| 322 Keith Hamilton RC | .30 | .15 |
| 323 Edgar Bennett RC | .50 | .20 |
| 324 Chris Hakel RC | .15 | .05 |
| 325 Dexter McNabb RC | .15 | .05 |
| 326 Rod Milstead RC | .15 | .05 |
| 327 Joe Bowden RC | .15 | .05 |
| 328 Brian Bollinger RC | .15 | .05 |
| 329 Darryl Williams RC | .15 | .05 |
| 330 Tommy Vardell RC | .15 | .05 |
| 331 Glenn Parker SIDE | .15 | .05 |
| 332 Herschel Walker SIDE | .15 | .05 |
| 333 Mike Cofer SIDE | .15 | .05 |
| 334 Mark Rypien SIDE | .15 | .05 |
| 335 Andre Rison GW | .30 | .10 |
| 336 Henry Ellard GW | .15 | .05 |
| 337 Rob Moore GW | .15 | .05 |
| 338 Fred Barnett GW | .15 | .05 |
| 339 Mark Clayton GW | .15 | .05 |
| 340 Eric Martin GW | .15 | .05 |
| 341 Irving Fryar GW | .15 | .05 |
| 342 Tim Brown GW | .30 | .10 |
| 343 Sterling Sharpe GW | .30 | .10 |
| 344 Gary Clark GW | .15 | .05 |
| 345 John Mackey HOF | .15 | .05 |
| 346 Lem Barney HOF | .15 | .05 |
| 347 John Riggins HOF | .30 | .10 |
| 348 Marion Butts IDOL | .15 | .05 |
| 349 Jeff Lageman IDOL | .15 | .05 |
| 350 Eric Green IDOL | .15 | .05 |
| 351 Reggie White/Bob.Jones I | .30 | .10 |
| 352 Marv Cook IDOL | .15 | .05 |
| 353 John Elway/Staubach ID | 1.25 | .50 |
| 354 Steve Tasker IDOL | .15 | .05 |
| 355 Nick Lowery IDOL | .15 | .05 |
| 356 Mark Clayton/Warfield ID | .15 | .05 |
| 357 Warren Moon/R.Gabriel ID | .30 | .10 |
| 358 Eric Metcalf | .30 | .10 |
| 359 Charles Haley | .30 | .10 |
| 360 Terrell Buckley RC | .15 | .05 |
| P1 Promo Panel | 5.00 | 2.00 |

## 1993 Pinnacle

| | | |
|---|---|---|
| COMPLETE SET (360) | 20.00 | 7.50 |
| 1 Brett Favre | 3.00 | 1.25 |
| 2 Tommy Vardell | .10 | .02 |
| 3 Jarrod Bunch | .10 | .02 |
| 4 Mike Croel | .10 | .02 |
| 5 Morten Andersen | .10 | .02 |
| 6 Barry Foster | .20 | .07 |
| 7 Chris Spielman | .20 | .07 |
| 8 Jim Jeffcoat | .10 | .02 |
| 9 Ken Ruettgers | .10 | .02 |
| 10 Cris Dishman | .10 | .02 |
| 11 Ricky Watters | .40 | .15 |
| 12 Alfred Williams | .10 | .02 |
| 13 Mark Kelso | .10 | .02 |
| 14 Moe Gardner | .10 | .02 |

KANSAS CITY CHIEFS

Joe Montana

| | | |
|---|---|---|
| 15 Terry Allen | .40 | .15 |
| 16 Willie Gault | .10 | .02 |
| 17 Bubba McDowell | .10 | .02 |
| 18 Brian Mitchell | .20 | .07 |
| 19 Karl Mecklenburg | .10 | .02 |
| 20 Jim Everett | .20 | .07 |
| 21 Bobby Humphrey | .10 | .02 |
| 22 Tim Krumrie | .10 | .02 |
| 23 Ken Norton Jr. | .20 | .07 |
| 24 Wendell Davis | .10 | .02 |
| 25 Brad Baxter | .10 | .02 |
| 26 Mel Gray | .20 | .07 |
| 27 Jon Vaughn | .10 | .02 |
| 28 James Hasty | .10 | .02 |
| 29 Chris Warren | .20 | .07 |
| 30 Tim Harris | .10 | .02 |
| 31 Eric Metcalf | .20 | .07 |
| 32 Rob Moore | .20 | .07 |
| 33 Charles Haley | .20 | .07 |
| 34 Leonard Marshall | .10 | .02 |
| 35 Jeff Graham | .20 | .07 |
| 36 Eugene Robinson | .10 | .02 |
| 37 Darryl Talley | .10 | .02 |
| 38 Brent Jones | .20 | .07 |
| 39 Reggie Roby | .10 | .02 |
| 40 Bruce Armstrong | .10 | .02 |
| 41 Audray McMillian | .10 | .02 |
| 42 Bern Brostek | .10 | .02 |
| 43 Tony Bennett | .10 | .02 |
| 44 Albert Lewis | .10 | .02 |
| 45 Derrick Thomas | .40 | .15 |
| 46 Cris Carter | .40 | .15 |
| 47 Richmond Webb | .10 | .02 |
| 48 Sean Landeta | .10 | .02 |
| 49 Cleveland Gary | .10 | .02 |
| 50 Mark Carrier DB | .10 | .02 |
| 51 Lawrence Dawsey | .10 | .02 |
| 52 Lamar Lathon | .10 | .02 |
| 53 Nick Bell | .10 | .02 |
| 54 Curtis Duncan | .10 | .02 |
| 55 Irving Fryar | .20 | .07 |
| 56 Seth Joyner | .10 | .02 |
| 57 Jay Novacek | .20 | .07 |
| 58 John L. Williams | .10 | .02 |
| 59 Amp Lee | .10 | .02 |
| 60 Marion Butts | .10 | .02 |
| 61 Clyde Simmons | .10 | .02 |
| 62 Rich Gannon | .40 | .15 |
| 63 Anthony Johnson | .20 | .07 |
| 64 Dave Meggett | .10 | .02 |
| 65 James Francis | .10 | .02 |
| 66 Trace Armstrong | .10 | .02 |
| 67 Mo Lewis | .10 | .02 |
| 68 Cornelius Bennett | .20 | .07 |
| 69 Mark Duper | .20 | .07 |
| 70 Frank Reich | .20 | .07 |
| 71 Eric Green | .10 | .02 |
| 72 Bruce Matthews | .10 | .02 |
| 73 Steve Broussard | .10 | .02 |
| 74 Anthony Carter | .20 | .07 |
| 75 Sterling Sharpe | .40 | .15 |
| 76 Mike Kenn | .10 | .02 |
| 77 Andre Rison | .20 | .07 |
| 78 Todd Marinovich | .10 | .02 |
| 79 Vincent Brown | .10 | .02 |
| 80 Daryl Johnston | .20 | .07 |
| 81 Art Monk | .20 | .07 |
| 82 Reggie Cobb | .10 | .02 |

| | | |
|---|---|---|
| 83 Johnny Johnson | .10 | .02 |
| 84 Tommy Kane | .10 | .02 |
| 85 Rohn Stark | .10 | .02 |
| 86 Steve Tasker | .20 | .07 |
| 87 Ronnie Harmon | .10 | .02 |
| 88 Pepper Johnson | .10 | .02 |
| 89 Hardy Nickerson | .20 | .07 |
| 90 Alvin Harper | .20 | .07 |
| 91 Louis Oliver | .10 | .02 |
| 92 Rod Woodson | .40 | .15 |
| 93 Sam Mills | .10 | .02 |
| 94 Randall McDaniel | .15 | .05 |
| 95 Johnny Holland | .10 | .02 |
| 96 Jackie Slater | .10 | .02 |
| 97 Don Mosebar | .10 | .02 |
| 98 Andre Ware | .10 | .02 |
| 99 Kelvin Martin | .10 | .02 |
| 100 Emmitt Smith | 2.50 | 1.00 |
| 101 Michael Brooks | .10 | .02 |
| 102 Dan Saleaumua | .10 | .02 |
| 103 John Elway | 2.50 | 1.00 |
| 104 Henry Jones | .10 | .02 |
| 105 William Perry | .20 | .07 |
| 106 James Lofton | .20 | .07 |
| 107 Carnell Lake | .10 | .02 |
| 108 Chip Lohmiller | .10 | .02 |
| 109 Andre Tippett | .10 | .02 |
| 110 Barry Word | .10 | .02 |
| 111 Haywood Jeffires | .20 | .07 |
| 112 Kenny Walker | .10 | .02 |
| 113 John Randle | .10 | .02 |
| 114 Donnell Woolford | .10 | .02 |
| 115 Johnny Bailey | .10 | .02 |
| 116 Marcus Allen | .40 | .15 |
| 117 Mark Jackson | .10 | .02 |
| 118 Ray Agnew | .10 | .02 |
| 119 Gill Byrd | .10 | .02 |
| 120 Kyle Clifton | .10 | .02 |
| 121 Marv Cook | .10 | .02 |
| 122 Jerry Ball | .10 | .02 |
| 123 Steve Jordan | .10 | .02 |
| 124 Shannon Sharpe | .40 | .15 |
| 125 Brian Blades | .20 | .07 |
| 126 Rodney Hampton | .20 | .07 |
| 127 Bobby Hebert | .10 | .02 |
| 128 Jessie Tuggle | .10 | .02 |
| 129 Tom Newberry | .10 | .02 |
| 130 Keith McCants | .10 | .02 |
| 131 Richard Dent | .20 | .07 |
| 132 Herman Moore | .40 | .15 |
| 133 Michael Irvin | .40 | .15 |
| 134 Ernest Givins | .20 | .07 |
| 135 Mark Rypien | .10 | .02 |
| 136 Leonard Russell | .20 | .07 |
| 137 Reggie White | .40 | .15 |
| 138 Thurman Thomas | .40 | .15 |
| 139 Nick Lowery | .10 | .02 |
| 140 Al Smith | .10 | .02 |
| 141 Jackie Harris | .10 | .02 |
| 142 Duane Bickett | .10 | .02 |
| 143 Lawyer Tillman | .10 | .02 |
| 144 Steve Wisniewski | .10 | .02 |
| 145 Derrick Fenner | .10 | .02 |
| 146 Harris Barton | .10 | .02 |
| 147 Rich Camarillo | .10 | .02 |
| 148 John Offerdahl | .10 | .02 |
| 149 Mike Johnson | .10 | .02 |
| 150 Ricky Reynolds | .10 | .02 |
| 151 Fred Barnett | .20 | .07 |
| 152 Nate Newton | .20 | .07 |
| 153 Chris Doleman | .10 | .02 |
| 154 Todd Scott | .10 | .02 |
| 155 Tim McKyer | .10 | .02 |
| 156 Ken Harvey | .10 | .02 |
| 157 Jeff Feagles | .10 | .02 |
| 158 Vince Workman | .10 | .02 |
| 159 Bart Oates | .10 | .02 |
| 160 Chris Miller | .20 | .07 |
| 161 Pete Stoyanovich | .10 | .02 |
| 162 Steve Wallace | .10 | .02 |
| 163 Dermontti Dawson | .10 | .02 |
| 164 Kenneth Davis | .10 | .02 |
| 165 Mike Munchak | .20 | .07 |
| 166 George Jamison | .10 | .02 |
| 167 Christian Okoye | .10 | .02 |

|  |  | | |
|---|---|---|---|
| 168 | Chris Hinton | .10 | .02 |
| 169 | Vaughan Johnson | .10 | .02 |
| 170 | Gaston Green | .10 | .02 |
| 171 | Kevin Greene | .20 | .07 |
| 172 | Rob Burnett | .10 | .02 |
| 173 | Norm Johnson | .10 | .02 |
| 174 | Eric Hill | .10 | .02 |
| 175 | Lomas Brown | .10 | .02 |
| 176 | Chip Banks | .10 | .02 |
| 177 | Greg Townsend | .10 | .02 |
| 178 | David Fulcher | .10 | .02 |
| 179 | Gary Anderson RB | .10 | .02 |
| 180 | Brian Washington | .10 | .02 |
| 181 | Brett Perriman | .40 | .15 |
| 182 | Chris Chandler | .20 | .07 |
| 183 | Phil Hansen | .10 | .02 |
| 184 | Mark Clayton | .10 | .02 |
| 185 | Frank Warren | .10 | .02 |
| 186 | Tim Brown | .40 | .15 |
| 187 | Mark Stepnoski | .10 | .02 |
| 188 | Bryan Cox | .10 | .02 |
| 189 | Gary Zimmerman | .10 | .02 |
| 190 | Neil O'Donnell | .40 | .15 |
| 191 | Anthony Smith | .10 | .02 |
| 192 | Craig Heyward | .20 | .07 |
| 193 | Keith Byars | .10 | .02 |
| 194 | Sean Salisbury | .10 | .02 |
| 195 | Todd Lyght | .10 | .02 |
| 196 | Jessie Hester | .10 | .02 |
| 197 | Rufus Porter | .10 | .02 |
| 198 | Steve Christie | .10 | .02 |
| 199 | Nate Lewis | .10 | .02 |
| 200 | Barry Sanders | 2.00 | .75 |
| 201 | Michael Haynes | .20 | .07 |
| 202 | John Taylor | .20 | .07 |
| 203 | John Friesz | .20 | .07 |
| 204 | William Fuller | .10 | .02 |
| 205 | Dennis Smith | .10 | .02 |
| 206 | Adrian Cooper | .10 | .02 |
| 207 | Henry Thomas | .10 | .02 |
| 208 | Gerald Williams | .10 | .02 |
| 209 | Chris Burkett | .10 | .02 |
| 210 | Broderick Thomas | .10 | .02 |
| 211 | Marvin Washington | .10 | .02 |
| 212 | Bennie Blades | .10 | .02 |
| 213 | Tony Casillas | .10 | .02 |
| 214 | Bubby Brister | .10 | .02 |
| 215 | Don Griffin | .10 | .02 |
| 216 | Jeff Cross | .10 | .02 |
| 217 | Derrick Walker | .10 | .02 |
| 218 | Lorenzo White | .10 | .02 |
| 219 | Ricky Sanders | .10 | .02 |
| 220 | Rickey Jackson | .10 | .02 |
| 221 | Simon Fletcher | .10 | .02 |
| 222 | Troy Vincent | .10 | .02 |
| 223 | Gary Clark | .20 | .07 |
| 224 | Stanley Richard | .10 | .02 |
| 225 | Dave Krieg | .20 | .07 |
| 226 | Warren Moon | .40 | .15 |
| 227 | Reggie Langhorne | .10 | .02 |
| 228 | Kent Hull | .10 | .02 |
| 229 | Ferrell Edmunds | .10 | .02 |
| 230 | Cortez Kennedy | .20 | .07 |
| 231 | Hugh Millen | .10 | .02 |
| 232 | Eugene Chung | .10 | .02 |
| 233 | Rodney Peete | .10 | .02 |
| 234 | Tom Waddle | .10 | .02 |
| 235 | David Klingler | .10 | .02 |
| 236 | Mark Carrier WR | .20 | .07 |
| 237 | Jay Schroeder | .10 | .02 |
| 238 | James Jones DT | .10 | .02 |
| 239 | Phil Simms | .20 | .07 |
| 240 | Steve Atwater | .10 | .02 |
| 241 | Jeff Herrod | .10 | .02 |
| 242 | Dale Carter | .10 | .02 |
| 243 | Glenn Cadrez RC | .10 | .02 |
| 244 | Wayne Martin | .10 | .02 |
| 245 | Willie Davis | .40 | .15 |
| 246 | Lawrence Taylor | .40 | .15 |
| 247 | Stan Humphries | .20 | .07 |
| 248 | Byron Evans | .10 | .02 |
| 249 | Wilber Marshall | .10 | .02 |
| 250 | Michael Bankston RC | .10 | .02 |
| 251 | Steve McMichael | .20 | .07 |
| 252 | Brad Edwards | .10 | .02 |
| 253 | Will Wolford | .10 | .02 |
| 254 | Paul Gruber | .10 | .02 |
| 255 | Steve Young | 1.25 | .50 |
| 256 | Chuck Cecil | .10 | .02 |
| 257 | Pierce Holt | .10 | .02 |
| 258 | Anthony Miller | .20 | .07 |
| 259 | Carl Banks | .10 | .02 |
| 260 | Brad Muster | .10 | .02 |
| 261 | Clay Matthews | .20 | .07 |
| 262 | Rod Bernstine | .10 | .02 |
| 263 | Tim Barnett | .10 | .02 |
| 264 | Greg Lloyd | .20 | .07 |
| 265 | Sean Jones | .10 | .02 |
| 266 | J.J. Birden | .10 | .02 |
| 267 | Tim McDonald | .10 | .02 |
| 268 | Charles Mann | .10 | .02 |
| 269 | Bruce Smith | .40 | .15 |
| 270 | Sean Gilbert | .20 | .07 |
| 271 | Ricardo McDonald | .10 | .02 |
| 272 | Jeff Hostetler | .20 | .07 |
| 273 | Russell Maryland | .10 | .02 |
| 274 | Dave Brown RC | .40 | .15 |
| 275 | Ronnie Lott | .20 | .07 |
| 276 | Jim Kelly | .40 | .15 |
| 277 | Joe Montana | 2.50 | 1.00 |
| 278 | Eric Allen | .10 | .02 |
| 279 | Browning Nagle | .10 | .02 |
| 280 | Neal Anderson | .10 | .02 |
| 281 | Troy Aikman | 1.25 | .50 |
| 282 | Ed McCaffrey | .40 | .15 |
| 283 | Robert Jones | .10 | .02 |
| 284 | Dalton Hilliard | .10 | .02 |
| 285 | Johnny Mitchell | .10 | .02 |
| 286 | Jay Hilgenberg | .10 | .02 |
| 287 | Eric Martin | .10 | .02 |
| 288 | Steve Emtman | .10 | .02 |
| 289 | Vaughn Dunbar | .10 | .02 |
| 290 | Mark Wheeler | .10 | .02 |
| 291 | Leslie O'Neal | .20 | .07 |
| 292 | Jerry Rice | 1.50 | .60 |
| 293 | Neil Smith | .40 | .15 |
| 294 | Kerry Cash | .10 | .02 |
| 295 | Dan McGwire | .10 | .02 |
| 296 | Carl Pickens | .20 | .07 |
| 297 | Terrell Buckley | .10 | .02 |
| 298 | Randall Cunningham | .40 | .15 |
| 299 | Santana Dotson | .20 | .07 |
| 300 | Keith Jackson | .20 | .07 |
| 301 | Jim Lachey | .10 | .02 |
| 302 | Dan Marino | 2.50 | 1.00 |
| 303 | Lee Williams | .10 | .02 |
| 304 | Burt Grossman | .10 | .02 |
| 305 | Kevin Mack | .10 | .02 |
| 306 | Pat Swilling | .10 | .02 |
| 307 | Arthur Marshall RC | .10 | .02 |
| 308 | Jim Harbaugh | .40 | .15 |
| 309 | Kurt Barber | .10 | .02 |
| 310 | Harvey Williams | .20 | .07 |
| 311 | Ricky Ervins | .10 | .02 |
| 312 | Flipper Anderson | .10 | .02 |
| 313 | Bernie Kosar | .20 | .07 |
| 314 | Boomer Esiason | .20 | .07 |
| 315 | Deion Sanders | .75 | .30 |
| 316 | Ray Childress | .10 | .02 |
| 317 | Howie Long | .40 | .15 |
| 318 | Henry Ellard | .20 | .07 |
| 319 | Marco Coleman | .10 | .02 |
| 320 | Chris Mims | .10 | .02 |
| 321 | Quentin Coryatt | .20 | .07 |
| 322 | Jason Hanson | .10 | .02 |
| 323 | Ricky Proehl | .10 | .02 |
| 324 | Randal Hill | .10 | .02 |
| 325 | Vinny Testaverde | .20 | .07 |
| 326 | Jeff George | .40 | .15 |
| 327 | Junior Seau | .40 | .15 |
| 328 | Earnest Byner | .10 | .02 |
| 329 | Andre Reed | .20 | .07 |
| 330 | Phillippi Sparks | .10 | .02 |
| 331 | Kevin Ross | .10 | .02 |
| 332 | Clarence Verdin | .10 | .02 |
| 333 | Darryl Henley | .10 | .02 |
| 334 | Dana Hall | .10 | .02 |
| 335 | Greg McMurtry | .10 | .02 |
| 336 | Ron Hall | .10 | .02 |
| 337 | Darrell Green | .10 | .02 |
| 338 | Carlton Bailey | .10 | .02 |
| 339 | Irv Eatman | .10 | .02 |
| 340 | Greg Kragen | .10 | .02 |
| 341 | Wade Wilson | .10 | .02 |
| 342 | Klaus Wilmsmeyer | .10 | .02 |
| 343 | Derek Brown TE | .10 | .02 |
| 344 | Erik Williams | .10 | .02 |
| 345 | Jim McMahon | .20 | .07 |
| 346 | Mike Sherrard | .10 | .02 |
| 347 | Mark Bavaro | .10 | .02 |
| 348 | Anthony Munoz | .20 | .07 |
| 349 | Eric Dickerson | .20 | .07 |
| 350 | Steve Beuerlein | .20 | .07 |
| 351 | Tim McGee | .10 | .02 |
| 352 | Terry McDaniel | .10 | .02 |
| 353 | Dan Fouts HOF | .10 | .02 |
| 354 | Chuck Noll HOF | .20 | .07 |
| 355 | Bill Walsh RC HOF | .20 | .07 |
| 356 | Larry Little HOF | .10 | .02 |
| 357 | Todd Marinovich HH | .10 | .02 |
| 358 | Jeff George HH | .40 | .15 |
| 359 | Bernie Kosar HH | .20 | .07 |
| 360 | Rob Moore HH | .20 | .07 |
| NNO | Franco Harris AU/3000 | 25.00 | 12.50 |

## 1994 Pinnacle

|  |  | | |
|---|---|---|---|
| | COMPLETE SET (270) | 20.00 | 8.00 |
| 1 | Deion Sanders | .50 | .20 |
| 2 | Eric Metcalf | .20 | .07 |
| 3 | Barry Sanders | 2.00 | .75 |
| 4 | Ernest Givins | .20 | .07 |
| 5 | Phil Simms | .20 | .07 |
| 6 | Rod Woodson | .20 | .07 |
| 7 | Michael Irvin | .40 | .15 |
| 8 | Cortez Kennedy | .20 | .07 |
| 9 | Eric Martin | .10 | .02 |
| 10 | Jeff Hostetler | .20 | .07 |
| 11 | Sterling Sharpe | .20 | .07 |
| 12 | John Elway | 2.50 | 1.00 |
| 13 | Neal Anderson | .10 | .02 |
| 14 | Terry Kirby | .40 | .15 |
| 15 | Jim Everett | .10 | .02 |
| 16 | Lawrence Dawsey | .10 | .02 |
| 17 | Kelvin Martin | .10 | .02 |
| 18 | Tim McGee | .10 | .02 |
| 19 | Cris Carter | .50 | .20 |
| 20 | Ronnie Harmon | .10 | .02 |
| 21 | Jim Kelly | .40 | .15 |
| 22 | Steve Young | 1.00 | .40 |
| 23 | Johnny Johnson | .10 | .02 |
| 24 | Sean Gilbert | .10 | .02 |
| 25 | Brian Mitchell | .10 | .02 |
| 26 | Carl Pickens | .20 | .07 |
| 27 | Tim Brown | .40 | .15 |
| 28 | Reggie Langhorne | .10 | .02 |
| 29 | Webster Slaughter | .10 | .02 |
| 30 | Alvin Harper | .20 | .07 |
| 31 | Andre Rison | .20 | .07 |
| 32 | Derrick Thomas | .40 | .15 |
| 33 | Irving Fryar | .20 | .07 |
| 34 | Vinny Testaverde | .20 | .07 |
| 35 | Steve Beuerlein | .20 | .07 |
| 36 | Brett Favre | 2.50 | 1.00 |
| 37 | Barry Foster | .10 | .02 |
| 38 | Vaughan Johnson | .10 | .02 |
| 39 | Carlton Bailey | .10 | .02 |
| 40 | Steve Emtman | .10 | .02 |
| 41 | Anthony Miller | .20 | .07 |

| | | |
|---|---|---|
| ❑ 42 Jeff Cross | .10 | .02 |
| ❑ 43 Trace Armstrong | .10 | .02 |
| ❑ 44 Derek Russell | .10 | .02 |
| ❑ 45 Vincent Brisby | .20 | .07 |
| ❑ 46 Mark Jackson | .10 | .02 |
| ❑ 47 Eugene Robinson | .10 | .02 |
| ❑ 48 John Friesz | .20 | .07 |
| ❑ 49 Scott Mitchell | .20 | .07 |
| ❑ 50 Steve Atwater | .10 | .02 |
| ❑ 51 Ken Norton | .20 | .07 |
| ❑ 52 Vincent Brown | .10 | .02 |
| ❑ 53 Morten Andersen | .10 | .02 |
| ❑ 54 Gary Anderson K | .10 | .02 |
| ❑ 55 Eric Curry | .10 | .02 |
| ❑ 56 Henry Jones | .10 | .02 |
| ❑ 57 Flipper Anderson | .10 | .02 |
| ❑ 58 Pat Swilling | .10 | .02 |
| ❑ 59 Erric Pegram | .10 | .02 |
| ❑ 60 Bruce Matthews | .10 | .02 |
| ❑ 61 Willie Davis | .20 | .07 |
| ❑ 62 O.J. McDuffie | .40 | .15 |
| ❑ 63 Qadry Ismail | .40 | .15 |
| ❑ 64 Anthony Smith | .10 | .02 |
| ❑ 65 Eric Allen | .10 | .02 |
| ❑ 66 Marion Butts | .10 | .02 |
| ❑ 67 Chris Miller | .10 | .02 |
| ❑ 68 Terrell Buckley | .10 | .02 |
| ❑ 69 Thurman Thomas | .40 | .15 |
| ❑ 70 Roosevelt Potts | .10 | .02 |
| ❑ 71 Tony McGee | .10 | .02 |
| ❑ 72 Jason Hanson | .10 | .02 |
| ❑ 73 Victor Bailey | .10 | .02 |
| ❑ 74 Albert Lewis | .10 | .02 |
| ❑ 75 Nate Odomes | .10 | .02 |
| ❑ 76 Ben Coates | .20 | .07 |
| ❑ 77 Warren Moon | .40 | .15 |
| ❑ 78 Derek Brown RBK | .10 | .02 |
| ❑ 79 David Klingler | .10 | .02 |
| ❑ 80 Cleveland Gary | .10 | .02 |
| ❑ 81 Emmitt Smith | 2.00 | .75 |
| ❑ 82 Jay Novacek | .20 | .07 |
| ❑ 83 Dana Stubblefield | .20 | .07 |
| ❑ 84 Michael Brooks | .10 | .02 |
| ❑ 85 James Jett | .10 | .02 |
| ❑ 86 J.J. Birden | .10 | .02 |
| ❑ 87 William Fuller | .10 | .02 |
| ❑ 88 Glyn Milburn | .20 | .07 |
| ❑ 89 Tim Worley | .10 | .02 |
| ❑ 90 Brett Perriman | .20 | .07 |
| ❑ 91 Randall Cunningham | .40 | .15 |
| ❑ 92 Drew Bledsoe | 1.00 | .40 |
| ❑ 93 Jerome Bettis | .60 | .25 |
| ❑ 94 Boomer Esiason | .20 | .07 |
| ❑ 95 Garrison Hearst | .40 | .15 |
| ❑ 96 Bruce Smith | .40 | .15 |
| ❑ 97 Jackie Harris | .10 | .02 |
| ❑ 98 Jeff George | .40 | .15 |
| ❑ 99 Tom Waddle | .10 | .02 |
| ❑ 100 John Copeland | .10 | .02 |
| ❑ 101 Bobby Hebert | .10 | .02 |
| ❑ 102 Joe Montana | 2.50 | 1.00 |
| ❑ 103 Herman Moore | .40 | .15 |
| ❑ 104 Rick Mirer | .40 | .15 |
| ❑ 105 Ricky Watters | .20 | .07 |
| ❑ 106 Neil O'Donnell | .40 | .15 |
| ❑ 107 Herschel Walker | .20 | .07 |
| ❑ 108 Rob Moore | .20 | .07 |
| ❑ 109 Reggie Brooks | .20 | .07 |
| ❑ 110 Tommy Vardell | .10 | .02 |
| ❑ 111 Eric Green | .10 | .02 |
| ❑ 112 Stan Humphries | .20 | .07 |
| ❑ 113 Greg Robinson | .10 | .02 |
| ❑ 114 Eric Swann | .20 | .07 |
| ❑ 115 Courtney Hawkins | .10 | .02 |
| ❑ 116 Andre Reed | .20 | .07 |
| ❑ 117 Steve McMichael | .20 | .07 |
| ❑ 118 Gary Brown | .10 | .02 |
| ❑ 119 Terry Allen | .20 | .07 |
| ❑ 120 Dan Marino | 2.50 | 1.00 |
| ❑ 121 Gary Clark | .20 | .07 |
| ❑ 122 Chris Warren | .20 | .07 |
| ❑ 123 Pierce Holt | .10 | .02 |
| ❑ 124 Anthony Carter | .20 | .07 |
| ❑ 125 Quentin Coryatt | .10 | .02 |
| ❑ 126 Harold Green | .10 | .02 |
| ❑ 127 Leonard Russell | .10 | .02 |
| ❑ 128 Tim McDonald | .10 | .02 |
| ❑ 129 Chris Spielman | .20 | .07 |
| ❑ 130 Cody Carlson | .10 | .02 |
| ❑ 131 Ronald Moore | .10 | .02 |
| ❑ 132 Renaldo Turnbull | .10 | .02 |
| ❑ 133 Ronnie Lott | .20 | .07 |
| ❑ 134 Natrone Means | .40 | .15 |
| ❑ 135 Keith Byars | .10 | .02 |
| ❑ 136 Henry Ellard | .20 | .07 |
| ❑ 137 Steve Jordan | .10 | .02 |
| ❑ 138 Calvin Williams | .10 | .02 |
| ❑ 139 Brian Blades | .20 | .07 |
| ❑ 140 Michael Jackson | .20 | .07 |
| ❑ 141 Charles Haley | .20 | .07 |
| ❑ 142 Curtis Conway | .40 | .15 |
| ❑ 143 Nick Lowery | .10 | .02 |
| ❑ 144 Bill Brooks | .10 | .02 |
| ❑ 145 Michael Haynes | .20 | .07 |
| ❑ 146 Willie Green | .10 | .02 |
| ❑ 147 Duane Bickett | .10 | .02 |
| ❑ 148 Shannon Sharpe | .20 | .07 |
| ❑ 149 Ricky Proehl | .10 | .02 |
| ❑ 150 Troy Aikman | 1.25 | .50 |
| ❑ 151 Mike Sherrard | .10 | .02 |
| ❑ 152 Reggie Cobb | .10 | .02 |
| ❑ 153 Norm Johnson | .10 | .02 |
| ❑ 154 Neil Smith | .20 | .07 |
| ❑ 155 James Francis | .10 | .02 |
| ❑ 156 Greg McMurtry | .10 | .02 |
| ❑ 157 Greg Townsend | .10 | .02 |
| ❑ 158 Mel Gray | .10 | .02 |
| ❑ 159 Rocket Ismail | .20 | .07 |
| ❑ 160 Leslie O'Neal | .10 | .02 |
| ❑ 161 Johnny Mitchell | .10 | .02 |
| ❑ 162 Brent Jones | .20 | .07 |
| ❑ 163 Chris Doleman | .10 | .02 |
| ❑ 164 Seth Joyner | .10 | .02 |
| ❑ 165 Marco Coleman | .10 | .02 |
| ❑ 166 Mark Higgs | .10 | .02 |
| ❑ 167 John L. Williams | .10 | .02 |
| ❑ 168 Darrell Green | .10 | .02 |
| ❑ 169 Mark Carrier WR | .20 | .07 |
| ❑ 170 Reggie White | .40 | .15 |
| ❑ 171 Darryl Talley | .10 | .02 |
| ❑ 172 Russell Maryland | .10 | .02 |
| ❑ 173 Mark Collins | .10 | .02 |
| ❑ 174 Chris Jacke | .10 | .02 |
| ❑ 175 Richard Dent | .20 | .07 |
| ❑ 176 John Taylor | .20 | .07 |
| ❑ 177 Rodney Hampton | .20 | .07 |
| ❑ 178 Dwight Stone | .10 | .02 |
| ❑ 179 Cornelius Bennett | .20 | .07 |
| ❑ 180 Anthony Miller | .20 | .07 |
| ❑ 181 Jerry Rice | 1.25 | .50 |
| ❑ 182 Rod Bernstine | .10 | .02 |
| ❑ 183 Keith Hamilton | .10 | .02 |
| ❑ 184 Keith Jackson | .10 | .02 |
| ❑ 185 Craig Erickson | .10 | .02 |
| ❑ 186 Marcus Allen | .40 | .15 |
| ❑ 187 Marcus Robertson | .10 | .02 |
| ❑ 188 Junior Seau | .40 | .15 |
| ❑ 189 LeShon Johnson RC | .20 | .07 |
| ❑ 190 Perry Klein RC | .10 | .02 |
| ❑ 191 Bryant Young RC | .60 | .25 |
| ❑ 192 Byron Bam Morris RC | .20 | .07 |
| ❑ 193 Jeff Cothran RC | .10 | .02 |
| ❑ 194 Lamar Smith RC | 1.50 | .60 |
| ❑ 195 Calvin Jones RC | .10 | .02 |
| ❑ 196 James Bostic RC | .40 | .15 |
| ❑ 197 Dan Wilkinson RC | .20 | .07 |
| ❑ 198 Marshall Faulk RC | 6.00 | 2.50 |
| ❑ 199 Heath Shuler RC | .40 | .15 |
| ❑ 200 Willie McGinest RC | .40 | .15 |
| ❑ 201 Trev Alberts RC | .20 | .07 |
| ❑ 202 Trent Dilfer RC | 1.50 | .60 |
| ❑ 203 Sam Adams RC | .20 | .07 |
| ❑ 204 Charles Johnson RC | .40 | .15 |
| ❑ 205 Johnnie Morton RC | 1.50 | .60 |
| ❑ 206 Thomas Lewis RC | .20 | .07 |
| ❑ 207 Greg Hill RC | .40 | .15 |
| ❑ 208 William Floyd RC | .40 | .15 |
| ❑ 209 Derrick Alexander WR RC | .40 | .15 |
| ❑ 210 Darnay Scott RC | .75 | .30 |
| ❑ 211 Lake Dawson RC | .20 | .07 |
| ❑ 212 Errict Rhett RC | .40 | .15 |
| ❑ 213 Kevin Lee RC | .10 | .02 |
| ❑ 214 Chuck Levy RC | .10 | .02 |
| ❑ 215 David Palmer RC | .40 | .15 |
| ❑ 216 Ryan Yarborough RC | .10 | .02 |
| ❑ 217 Charlie Garner RC | 1.50 | .60 |
| ❑ 218 Mario Bates RC | .40 | .15 |
| ❑ 219 Jamir Miller RC | .20 | .07 |
| ❑ 220 Bucky Brooks RC | .10 | .02 |
| ❑ 221 Donnell Bennett RC | .40 | .15 |
| ❑ 222 Kevin Greene | .20 | .07 |
| ❑ 223 LeRoy Butler | .10 | .02 |
| ❑ 224 Anthony Pleasant | .10 | .02 |
| ❑ 225 Steve Christie | .10 | .02 |
| ❑ 226 Bill Romanowski | .10 | .02 |
| ❑ 227 Darren Carrington | .10 | .02 |
| ❑ 228 Chester McGlockton | .10 | .02 |
| ❑ 229 Jack Del Rio | .10 | .02 |
| ❑ 230 Kevin Smith | .10 | .02 |
| ❑ 231 Chris Zorich | .10 | .02 |
| ❑ 232 Donnell Woolford | .10 | .02 |
| ❑ 233 Tony Casillas | .10 | .02 |
| ❑ 234 Terry McDaniel | .10 | .02 |
| ❑ 235 Ray Childress | .10 | .02 |
| ❑ 236 John Randle | .20 | .07 |
| ❑ 237 Clyde Simmons | .10 | .02 |
| ❑ 238 Dante Jones | .10 | .02 |
| ❑ 239 Karl Mecklenburg | .10 | .02 |
| ❑ 240 Daryl Johnston | .20 | .07 |
| ❑ 241 Hardy Nickerson | .20 | .07 |
| ❑ 242 Jeff Lageman | .10 | .02 |
| ❑ 243 Lewis Tillman | .10 | .02 |
| ❑ 244 Jim McMahon | .20 | .07 |
| ❑ 245 Mike Pritchard | .10 | .02 |
| ❑ 246 Harvey Williams | .20 | .07 |
| ❑ 247 Sean Jones | .10 | .02 |
| ❑ 248 Stevon Moore | .10 | .02 |
| ❑ 249 Pete Metzelaars | .10 | .02 |
| ❑ 250 Mike Johnson | .10 | .02 |
| ❑ 251 Chris Slade | .10 | .02 |
| ❑ 252 Jessie Hester | .10 | .02 |
| ❑ 253 Louis Oliver | .10 | .02 |
| ❑ 254 Ken Harvey | .10 | .02 |
| ❑ 255 Bryan Cox | .10 | .02 |
| ❑ 256 Erik Kramer | .20 | .07 |
| ❑ 257 Andy Harmon | .10 | .02 |
| ❑ 258 Rickey Jackson | .10 | .02 |
| ❑ 259 Mark Carrier DB | .10 | .02 |
| ❑ 260 Greg Lloyd | .20 | .07 |
| ❑ 261 Robert Brooks | .20 | .07 |
| ❑ 262 Dave Brown | .20 | .07 |
| ❑ 263 Dennis Smith | .10 | .02 |
| ❑ 264 Michael Dean Perry | .20 | .07 |
| ❑ 265 Dan Saleaumua | .10 | .02 |
| ❑ 266 Mo Lewis | .10 | .02 |
| ❑ 267 AFC Checklist | .10 | .02 |
| ❑ 268 AFC Checklist | .10 | .02 |
| ❑ 269 NFC Checklist | .10 | .02 |
| ❑ 270 NFC Checklist | .10 | .02 |
| ❑ 271SP Jerry Rice TD King SP | 8.00 | 4.00 |
| ❑ NNO Drew Bledsoe Pin.Passer | 40.00 | 15.00 |

## 1995 Pinnacle

| | | |
|---|---|---|
| ❑ COMPLETE SET (250) | 20.00 | 8.00 |
| ❑ 1 Reggie White | .40 | .15 |
| ❑ 2 Troy Aikman | 1.00 | .40 |
| ❑ 3 Willie Davis | .20 | .07 |
| ❑ 4 Jerry Rice | 1.00 | .40 |

| | | |
|---|---|---|
| ☐ 5 Bruce Smith | .40 | .15 |
| ☐ 6 Keith Byars | .10 | .02 |
| ☐ 7 Chris Warren | .20 | .07 |
| ☐ 8 Erik Kramer | .10 | .02 |
| ☐ 9 Leon Lett | .10 | .02 |
| ☐ 10 Greg Lloyd | .20 | .07 |
| ☐ 11 Jackie Harris | .10 | .02 |
| ☐ 12 Irving Fryar | .20 | .07 |
| ☐ 13 Rodney Hampton | .20 | .07 |
| ☐ 14 Michael Irvin | .40 | .15 |
| ☐ 15 Michael Haynes | .20 | .07 |
| ☐ 16 Irving Spikes | .20 | .07 |
| ☐ 17 Calvin Williams | .20 | .07 |
| ☐ 18 Ken Norton Jr. | .20 | .07 |
| ☐ 19 Herman Moore | .40 | .15 |
| ☐ 20 Lewis Tillman | .10 | .02 |
| ☐ 21 Cortez Kennedy | .20 | .07 |
| ☐ 22 Dan Marino | 2.00 | .75 |
| ☐ 23 Eric Pegram | .20 | .07 |
| ☐ 24 Tim Brown | .40 | .15 |
| ☐ 25 Jeff Blake RC | .75 | .30 |
| ☐ 26 Brett Favre | 2.00 | .75 |
| ☐ 27 Garrison Hearst | .40 | .15 |
| ☐ 28 Ronnie Harmon | .10 | .02 |
| ☐ 29 Qadry Ismail | .20 | .07 |
| ☐ 30 Ben Coates | .20 | .07 |
| ☐ 31 Deion Sanders | .60 | .25 |
| ☐ 32 John Elway | 2.00 | .75 |
| ☐ 33 Natrone Means | .40 | .15 |
| ☐ 34 Derrick Alexander WR | .40 | .15 |
| ☐ 35 Craig Heyward | .20 | .07 |
| ☐ 36 Jake Reed | .20 | .07 |
| ☐ 37 Steve Walsh | .10 | .02 |
| ☐ 38 John Randle | .20 | .07 |
| ☐ 39 Barry Sanders | 1.50 | .60 |
| ☐ 40 Tydus Winans | .10 | .02 |
| ☐ 41 Thomas Lewis | .20 | .07 |
| ☐ 42 Jim Kelly | .40 | .15 |
| ☐ 43 Gus Frerotte | .20 | .07 |
| ☐ 44 Cris Carter | .40 | .15 |
| ☐ 45 Kevin Williams WR | .20 | .07 |
| ☐ 46 Dave Meggett | .10 | .02 |
| ☐ 47 Pat Swilling | .10 | .02 |
| ☐ 48 Neil O'Donnell | .20 | .07 |
| ☐ 49 Terance Mathis | .20 | .07 |
| ☐ 50 Desmond Howard | .20 | .07 |
| ☐ 51 Bryant Young | .20 | .07 |
| ☐ 52 Stan Humphries | .20 | .07 |
| ☐ 53 Alvin Harper | .20 | .07 |
| ☐ 54 Henry Ellard | .20 | .07 |
| ☐ 55 Jessie Hester | .10 | .02 |
| ☐ 56 Lorenzo White | .10 | .02 |
| ☐ 57 John Friesz | .20 | .07 |
| ☐ 58 Anthony Smith | .10 | .02 |
| ☐ 59 Bert Emanuel | .40 | .15 |
| ☐ 60 Gary Clark | .20 | .07 |
| ☐ 61 Bill Brooks | .10 | .02 |
| ☐ 62 Steve Young | .75 | .30 |
| ☐ 63 Jerome Bettis | .40 | .15 |
| ☐ 64 John Taylor | .10 | .02 |
| ☐ 65 Ricky Proehl | .10 | .02 |
| ☐ 66 Junior Seau | .40 | .15 |
| ☐ 67 Bubby Brister | .10 | .02 |
| ☐ 68 Neil Smith | .20 | .07 |
| ☐ 69 Dan McGwire | .10 | .02 |
| ☐ 70 Brett Perriman | .20 | .07 |
| ☐ 71 Chris Spielman | .20 | .07 |
| ☐ 72 Jeff George | .20 | .07 |
| ☐ 73 Emmitt Smith | 1.00 | .40 |
| ☐ 74 Chris Penn | .10 | .02 |
| ☐ 75 Derrick Fenner | .10 | .02 |
| ☐ 76 Reggie Brooks | .20 | .07 |
| ☐ 77 Chris Chandler | .20 | .07 |
| ☐ 78 Rod Woodson | .20 | .07 |
| ☐ 79 Isaac Bruce | .60 | .25 |
| ☐ 80 Reggie Cobb | .10 | .02 |
| ☐ 81 Bryce Paup | .20 | .07 |
| ☐ 82 Warren Moon | .20 | .07 |
| ☐ 83 Bryan Reeves | .10 | .02 |
| ☐ 84 Lake Dawson | .20 | .07 |
| ☐ 85 Larry Centers | .20 | .07 |
| ☐ 86 Marshall Faulk | 1.25 | .50 |
| ☐ 87 Jim Harbaugh | .20 | .07 |
| ☐ 88 Ray Childress | .10 | .02 |
| ☐ 89 Eric Metcalf | .20 | .07 |

| | | |
|---|---|---|
| ☐ 90 Ernie Mills | .10 | .02 |
| ☐ 91 Lamar Lathon | .10 | .02 |
| ☐ 92 Errict Rhett | .20 | .07 |
| ☐ 93 David Klingler | .20 | .07 |
| ☐ 94 Vincent Brown | .10 | .02 |
| ☐ 95 Andre Rison | .20 | .07 |
| ☐ 96 Brian Mitchell | .10 | .02 |
| ☐ 97 Mark Rypien | .10 | .02 |
| ☐ 98 Eugene Robinson | .10 | .02 |
| ☐ 99 Eric Green | .10 | .02 |
| ☐ 100 Rocket Ismail | .20 | .07 |
| ☐ 101 Flipper Anderson | .10 | .02 |
| ☐ 102 Randall Cunningham | .40 | .15 |
| ☐ 103 Ricky Watters | .20 | .07 |
| ☐ 104 Amp Lee | .10 | .02 |
| ☐ 105 Ernest Givins | .10 | .02 |
| ☐ 106 Daryl Johnston | .20 | .07 |
| ☐ 107 Dave Krieg | .10 | .02 |
| ☐ 108 Dana Stubblefield | .20 | .07 |
| ☐ 109 Torrance Small | .10 | .02 |
| ☐ 110 Yancey Thigpen RC | .20 | .07 |
| ☐ 111 Chester McGlockton | .20 | .07 |
| ☐ 112 Craig Erickson | .10 | .02 |
| ☐ 113 Herschel Walker | .20 | .07 |
| ☐ 114 Mike Sherrard | .10 | .02 |
| ☐ 115 Tony McGee | .10 | .02 |
| ☐ 116 Adrian Murrell | .20 | .07 |
| ☐ 117 Frank Reich | .10 | .02 |
| ☐ 118 Hardy Nickerson | .10 | .02 |
| ☐ 119 Andre Reed | .20 | .07 |
| ☐ 120 Leonard Russell | .10 | .02 |
| ☐ 121 Eric Allen | .10 | .02 |
| ☐ 122 Jeff Hostetler | .20 | .07 |
| ☐ 123 Barry Foster | .20 | .07 |
| ☐ 124 Anthony Miller | .20 | .07 |
| ☐ 125 Shawn Jefferson | .10 | .02 |
| ☐ 126 Richie Anderson RC | .50 | .20 |
| ☐ 127 Steve Bono | .20 | .07 |
| ☐ 128 Seth Joyner | .10 | .02 |
| ☐ 129 Darnay Scott | .20 | .07 |
| ☐ 130 Johnny Mitchell | .10 | .02 |
| ☐ 131 Eric Swann | .20 | .07 |
| ☐ 132 Drew Bledsoe | .60 | .25 |
| ☐ 133 Marcus Allen | .40 | .15 |
| ☐ 134 Carl Pickens | .20 | .07 |
| ☐ 135 Michael Brooks | .10 | .02 |
| ☐ 136 John L. Williams | .10 | .02 |
| ☐ 137 Steve Beuerlein | .20 | .07 |
| ☐ 138 Robert Smith | .40 | .15 |
| ☐ 139 O.J. McDuffie | .40 | .15 |
| ☐ 140 Haywood Jeffires | .10 | .02 |
| ☐ 141 Aeneas Williams | .10 | .02 |
| ☐ 142 Rick Mirer | .20 | .07 |
| ☐ 143 William Floyd | .20 | .07 |
| ☐ 144 Fred Barnett | .20 | .07 |
| ☐ 145 Leroy Hoard | .10 | .02 |
| ☐ 146 Terry Kirby | .20 | .07 |
| ☐ 147 Boomer Esiason | .20 | .07 |
| ☐ 148 Ken Harvey | .10 | .02 |
| ☐ 149 Cleveland Gary | .10 | .02 |
| ☐ 150 Brian Blades | .20 | .07 |
| ☐ 151 Eric Turner | .10 | .02 |
| ☐ 152 Vinny Testaverde | .20 | .07 |
| ☐ 153 Ronald Moore UER | .10 | .02 |
| ☐ 154 Curtis Conway | .40 | .15 |
| ☐ 155 Johnnie Morton | .20 | .07 |
| ☐ 156 Kenneth Davis | .10 | .02 |
| ☐ 157 Scott Mitchell | .20 | .07 |
| ☐ 158 Sean Gilbert | .20 | .07 |
| ☐ 159 Shannon Sharpe | .20 | .07 |
| ☐ 160 Mark Seay | .10 | .02 |
| ☐ 161 Cornelius Bennett | .20 | .07 |
| ☐ 162 Heath Shuler | .20 | .07 |
| ☐ 163 Byron Bam Morris | .10 | .02 |
| ☐ 164 Robert Brooks | .40 | .15 |
| ☐ 165 Glyn Milburn | .10 | .02 |
| ☐ 166 Gary Brown | .10 | .02 |
| ☐ 167 Jim Everett | .20 | .07 |
| ☐ 168 Steve Atwater | .10 | .02 |
| ☐ 169 Darren Woodson | .20 | .07 |
| ☐ 170 Mark Ingram | .10 | .02 |
| ☐ 171 Donnell Woolford | .10 | .02 |
| ☐ 172 Trent Dilfer | .40 | .15 |
| ☐ 173 Charlie Garner | .40 | .15 |
| ☐ 174 Charles Johnson | .20 | .07 |

| | | |
|---|---|---|
| ☐ 175 Mike Pritchard | .10 | .02 |
| ☐ 176 Derek Brown RBK | .10 | .02 |
| ☐ 177 Chris Miller | .10 | .02 |
| ☐ 178 Charles Haley | .20 | .07 |
| ☐ 179 J.J. Birden | .10 | .02 |
| ☐ 180 Jeff Graham | .10 | .02 |
| ☐ 181 Bernie Parmalee | .20 | .07 |
| ☐ 182 Mark Brunell | .60 | .25 |
| ☐ 183 Greg Hill | .20 | .07 |
| ☐ 184 Michael Timpson | .10 | .02 |
| ☐ 185 Terry Allen | .20 | .07 |
| ☐ 186 Ricky Ervins | .10 | .02 |
| ☐ 187 Dave Brown | .20 | .07 |
| ☐ 188 Dan Wilkinson | .20 | .07 |
| ☐ 189 Jay Novacek | .20 | .07 |
| ☐ 190 Harvey Williams | .10 | .02 |
| ☐ 191 Mario Bates | .20 | .07 |
| ☐ 192 Steve Young LAW | .50 | .20 |
| ☐ 193 Joe Montana | 2.00 | .75 |
| ☐ 194 Steve Young CW | .50 | .20 |
| ☐ 195 Troy Aikman PP | .60 | .25 |
| ☐ 196 Drew Bledsoe | .40 | .15 |
| ☐ 197 Dan Marino PP | 1.00 | .40 |
| ☐ 198 John Elway PP | 1.00 | .40 |
| ☐ 199 Brett Favre PP | 1.00 | .40 |
| ☐ 200 Heath Shuler | .20 | .07 |
| ☐ 201 Warren Moon PP | .10 | .02 |
| ☐ 202 Jim Kelly PP | .40 | .15 |
| ☐ 203 Jeff Hostetler PP | .20 | .07 |
| ☐ 204 Rick Mirer PP | .20 | .07 |
| ☐ 205 Dave Brown PP | .20 | .07 |
| ☐ 206 Randall Cunningham PP | .20 | .07 |
| ☐ 207 Neil O'Donnell PP | .20 | .07 |
| ☐ 208 Jim Everett PP | .10 | .02 |
| ☐ 209 Ki-Jana Carter RC | .40 | .15 |
| ☐ 210 Steve McNair RC | 3.00 | 1.25 |
| ☐ 211 Michael Westbrook RC | .40 | .15 |
| ☐ 212 Kerry Collins RC | 2.00 | .75 |
| ☐ 213 Joey Galloway RC | 1.50 | .60 |
| ☐ 214 Kyle Brady RC | .40 | .15 |
| ☐ 215 J.J. Stokes RC | .40 | .15 |
| ☐ 216 Tyrone Wheatley RC | 1.25 | .50 |
| ☐ 217 Rashaan Salaam RC | .20 | .07 |
| ☐ 218 Napoleon Kaufman RC | 1.25 | .50 |
| ☐ 219 Frank Sanders RC | .40 | .15 |
| ☐ 220 Stoney Case RC | .10 | .02 |
| ☐ 221 Todd Collins RC | 1.25 | .50 |
| ☐ 222 Warren Sapp RC | 1.50 | .60 |
| ☐ 223 Sherman Williams RC | .10 | .02 |
| ☐ 224 Rob Johnson RC | 1.00 | .40 |
| ☐ 225 Mark Bruener RC | .20 | .07 |
| ☐ 226 Derrick Brooks RC | 1.50 | .60 |
| ☐ 227 Chad May RC | .10 | .02 |
| ☐ 228 James A.Stewart RC | .10 | .02 |
| ☐ 229 Ray Zellars RC | .20 | .07 |
| ☐ 230 Dave Barr RC | .10 | .02 |
| ☐ 231 Kordell Stewart RC | 1.50 | .60 |
| ☐ 232 Jimmy Oliver RC | .10 | .02 |
| ☐ 233 Tony Boselli RC | .40 | .15 |
| ☐ 234 James O. Stewart RC | 1.25 | .50 |
| ☐ 235 Derrick Alexander DE RC | .10 | .02 |
| ☐ 236 Loveli Pinkney RC | .10 | .02 |
| ☐ 237 John Walsh RC | .10 | .02 |
| ☐ 238 Tyrone Davis RC | .10 | .02 |
| ☐ 239 Joe Aska RC | .10 | .02 |
| ☐ 240 Korey Stringer RC | .20 | .07 |
| ☐ 241 Hugh Douglas RC | .40 | .15 |
| ☐ 242 Christian Fauria RC | .20 | .07 |
| ☐ 243 Terrell Fletcher RC | .10 | .02 |
| ☐ 244 Dan Marino CL | .60 | .25 |
| ☐ 245 Drew Bledsoe CL | .40 | .15 |
| ☐ 246 John Elway CL | .40 | .15 |
| ☐ 247 Emmitt Smith CL | .50 | .20 |
| ☐ 248 Steve Young CL | .40 | .15 |
| ☐ 249 Barry Sanders CL | .60 | .25 |
| ☐ 250 Jerry Rice/Seau CL | .40 | .15 |
| ☐ 251SP Deion Sanders SP | 4.00 | 1.50 |

## 1996 Pinnacle

| | | |
|---|---|---|
| ☐ COMPLETE SET (200) | 20.00 | 8.00 |
| ☐ 1 Emmitt Smith | 1.50 | .60 |
| ☐ 2 Robert Brooks | .40 | .15 |
| ☐ 3 Joey Galloway | .40 | .15 |
| ☐ 4 Dan Marino | 2.00 | .75 |
| ☐ 5 Frank Sanders | .20 | .07 |

BRETT FAVRE

|  |  | | |
|---|---|---|---|
| ❏ 6 | Cris Carter | .40 | .15 |
| ❏ 7 | Jeff Blake | .40 | .15 |
| ❏ 8 | Steve McNair | .75 | .30 |
| ❏ 9 | Tamarick Vanover | .20 | .07 |
| ❏ 10 | Andre Reed | .20 | .07 |
| ❏ 11 | Junior Seau | .40 | .15 |
| ❏ 12 | Alvin Harper | .10 | .02 |
| ❏ 13 | Trent Dilfer | .40 | .15 |
| ❏ 14 | Kordell Stewart | .40 | .15 |
| ❏ 15 | Kyle Brady | .10 | .02 |
| ❏ 16 | Charles Haley | .20 | .07 |
| ❏ 17 | Greg Lloyd | .20 | .07 |
| ❏ 18 | Mario Bates | .20 | .07 |
| ❏ 19 | Shannon Sharpe | .20 | .07 |
| ❏ 20 | Scott Mitchell | .20 | .07 |
| ❏ 21 | Craig Heyward | .10 | .02 |
| ❏ 22 | Marcus Allen | .40 | .15 |
| ❏ 23 | Curtis Martin | .75 | .30 |
| ❏ 24 | Drew Bledsoe | .60 | .25 |
| ❏ 25 | Jerry Rice | 1.00 | .40 |
| ❏ 26 | Charlie Garner | .20 | .07 |
| ❏ 27 | Michael Irvin | .40 | .15 |
| ❏ 28 | Curtis Conway | .40 | .15 |
| ❏ 29 | Terrell Davis | .75 | .30 |
| ❏ 30 | Jeff Hostetler | .10 | .02 |
| ❏ 31 | Neil O'Donnell | .20 | .07 |
| ❏ 32 | Errict Rhett | .20 | .07 |
| ❏ 33 | Stan Humphries | .20 | .07 |
| ❏ 34 | Jeff Graham | .10 | .02 |
| ❏ 35 | Floyd Turner | .10 | .02 |
| ❏ 36 | Vincent Brisby | .10 | .02 |
| ❏ 37 | Steve Young | .75 | .30 |
| ❏ 38 | Carl Pickens | .20 | .07 |
| ❏ 39 | Terance Mathis | .10 | .02 |
| ❏ 40 | Brett Favre | 2.00 | .75 |
| ❏ 41 | Ki-Jana Carter | .20 | .07 |
| ❏ 42 | Jim Everett | .10 | .02 |
| ❏ 43 | Marshall Faulk | .50 | .20 |
| ❏ 44 | William Floyd | .20 | .07 |
| ❏ 45 | Deion Sanders | .60 | .25 |
| ❏ 46 | Garrison Hearst | .20 | .07 |
| ❏ 47 | Chris Sanders | .40 | .15 |
| ❏ 48 | Isaac Bruce | .20 | .07 |
| ❏ 49 | Natrone Means | .20 | .07 |
| ❏ 50 | Troy Aikman | 1.00 | .40 |
| ❏ 51 | Ben Coates | .20 | .07 |
| ❏ 52 | Tony Martin | .20 | .07 |
| ❏ 53 | Rod Woodson | .20 | .07 |
| ❏ 54 | Edgar Bennett | .20 | .07 |
| ❏ 55 | Eric Zeier | .10 | .02 |
| ❏ 56 | Steve Bono | .10 | .02 |
| ❏ 57 | Tim Brown | .40 | .15 |
| ❏ 58 | Kevin Williams | .10 | .02 |
| ❏ 59 | Erik Kramer | .10 | .02 |
| ❏ 60 | Jim Kelly | .40 | .15 |
| ❏ 61 | Larry Centers | .20 | .07 |
| ❏ 62 | Terrell Fletcher | .10 | .02 |
| ❏ 63 | Michael Westbrook | .40 | .15 |
| ❏ 64 | Kerry Collins | .40 | .15 |
| ❏ 65 | Jay Novacek | .10 | .02 |
| ❏ 66 | J.J. Stokes | .40 | .15 |
| ❏ 67 | John Elway | 2.00 | .75 |
| ❏ 68 | Jim Harbaugh | .20 | .07 |
| ❏ 69 | Aeneas Williams | .10 | .02 |
| ❏ 70 | Tyrone Wheatley | .20 | .07 |
| ❏ 71 | Chris Warren | .20 | .07 |
| ❏ 72 | Rodney Thomas | .10 | .02 |
| ❏ 73 | Jeff George | .20 | .07 |
| ❏ 74 | Rick Mirer | .20 | .07 |
| ❏ 75 | Yancey Thigpen | .20 | .07 |
| ❏ 76 | Herman Moore | .20 | .07 |
| ❏ 77 | Gus Frerotte | .20 | .07 |
| ❏ 78 | Anthony Miller | .20 | .07 |
| ❏ 79 | Ricky Watters | .20 | .07 |
| ❏ 80 | Sherman Williams | .10 | .02 |
| ❏ 81 | Hardy Nickerson | .10 | .02 |
| ❏ 82 | Henry Ellard | .10 | .02 |
| ❏ 83 | Aaron Craver | .10 | .02 |
| ❏ 84 | Rodney Peete | .10 | .02 |
| ❏ 85 | Eric Metcalf | .10 | .02 |
| ❏ 86 | Brian Blades | .10 | .02 |
| ❏ 87 | Rob Moore | .20 | .07 |
| ❏ 88 | Kimble Anders | .20 | .07 |
| ❏ 89 | Harvey Williams | .10 | .02 |
| ❏ 90 | Thurman Thomas | .40 | .15 |
| ❏ 91 | Dave Brown | .10 | .02 |
| ❏ 92 | Terry Allen | .20 | .07 |
| ❏ 93 | Ken Norton Jr. | .10 | .02 |
| ❏ 94 | Reggie White | .40 | .15 |
| ❏ 95 | Mark Chmura | .20 | .07 |
| ❏ 96 | Bert Emanuel | .20 | .07 |
| ❏ 97 | Brett Perriman | .10 | .02 |
| ❏ 98 | Antonio Freeman | .40 | .15 |
| ❏ 99 | Brian Mitchell | .10 | .02 |
| ❏ 100 | Orlando Thomas | .10 | .02 |
| ❏ 101 | Aaron Hayden | .10 | .02 |
| ❏ 102 | Quinn Early | .10 | .02 |
| ❏ 103 | Lovell Pinkney | .10 | .02 |
| ❏ 104 | Napoleon Kaufman | .40 | .15 |
| ❏ 105 | Daryl Johnston | .20 | .07 |
| ❏ 106 | Steve Tasker | .10 | .02 |
| ❏ 107 | Brent Jones | .10 | .02 |
| ❏ 108 | Mark Brunell | .60 | .25 |
| ❏ 109 | Leslie O'Neal | .10 | .02 |
| ❏ 110 | Irving Fryar | .20 | .07 |
| ❏ 111 | Jim Miller | .40 | .15 |
| ❏ 112 | Sean Dawkins | .10 | .02 |
| ❏ 113 | Boomer Esiason | .20 | .07 |
| ❏ 114 | Heath Shuler | .20 | .07 |
| ❏ 115 | Bruce Smith | .20 | .07 |
| ❏ 116 | Russell Maryland | .10 | .02 |
| ❏ 117 | Jake Reed | .20 | .07 |
| ❏ 118 | O.J. McDuffie | .20 | .07 |
| ❏ 119 | Erik Williams | .10 | .02 |
| ❏ 120 | Willie McGinest | .10 | .02 |
| ❏ 121 | Terry Kirby | .20 | .07 |
| ❏ 122 | Fred Barnett | .10 | .02 |
| ❏ 123 | Andre Hastings | .10 | .02 |
| ❏ 124 | Dale Hellestrae | .10 | .02 |
| ❏ 125 | Darren Woodson | .20 | .07 |
| ❏ 126 | Steve Atwater | .10 | .02 |
| ❏ 127 | Quentin Coryatt | .10 | .02 |
| ❏ 128 | Derrick Thomas | .40 | .15 |
| ❏ 129 | Nate Newton | .10 | .02 |
| ❏ 130 | Kevin Greene | .20 | .07 |
| ❏ 131 | Barry Sanders | 1.50 | .60 |
| ❏ 132 | Warren Moon | .20 | .07 |
| ❏ 133 | Rashaan Salaam | .20 | .07 |
| ❏ 134 | Rodney Hampton | .20 | .07 |
| ❏ 135 | James O.Stewart | .20 | .07 |
| ❏ 136 | Erric Pegram | .10 | .02 |
| ❏ 137 | Bryan Cox | .10 | .02 |
| ❏ 138 | Adrian Murrell | .20 | .07 |
| ❏ 139 | Robert Smith | .20 | .07 |
| ❏ 140 | Bernie Parmalee | .10 | .02 |
| ❏ 141 | Bryce Paup | .10 | .02 |
| ❏ 142 | Darick Holmes | .10 | .02 |
| ❏ 143 | Hugh Douglas | .20 | .07 |
| ❏ 144 | Ken Dilger | .10 | .02 |
| ❏ 145 | Derek Loville | .10 | .02 |
| ❏ 146 | Horace Copeland | .10 | .02 |
| ❏ 147 | Wayne Chrebet | .60 | .25 |
| ❏ 148 | Andre Coleman | .10 | .02 |
| ❏ 149 | Greg Hill | .20 | .07 |
| ❏ 150 | Eric Swann | .10 | .02 |
| ❏ 151 | Tyrone Hughes | .10 | .02 |
| ❏ 152 | Ernie Mills | .10 | .02 |
| ❏ 153 | Terry Glenn RC | 1.25 | .50 |
| ❏ 154 | Cedric Jones RC | .10 | .02 |
| ❏ 155 | Leeland McElroy RC | .20 | .07 |
| ❏ 156 | Bobby Engram RC | .40 | .15 |
| ❏ 157 | Willie Anderson RC | .10 | .02 |
| ❏ 158 | Mike Alstott RC | 1.25 | .50 |
| ❏ 159 | Alex Van Dyke RC | .20 | .07 |
| ❏ 160 | Jeff Lewis RC | .20 | .07 |
| ❏ 161 | Keyshawn Johnson RC | 1.25 | .50 |
| ❏ 162 | Regan Upshaw RC | .10 | .02 |
| ❏ 163 | Eric Moulds RC | 1.50 | .60 |
| ❏ 164 | Tim Biakabutuka RC | .40 | .15 |
| ❏ 165 | Kevin Hardy RC | .40 | .15 |
| ❏ 166 | Marvin Harrison RC | 3.00 | 1.25 |
| ❏ 167 | Karim Abdul-Jabbar RC | .40 | .15 |
| ❏ 168 | Tony Brackens RC | .40 | .15 |
| ❏ 169 | Stepfret Williams RC | .20 | .07 |
| ❏ 170 | Eddie George RC | 1.50 | .60 |
| ❏ 171 | Lawrence Phillips RC | .40 | .15 |
| ❏ 172 | Danny Kanell RC | .40 | .15 |
| ❏ 173 | Derrick Mayes RC | .40 | .15 |
| ❏ 174 | Daryl Gardener RC | .10 | .02 |
| ❏ 175 | Jonathan Ogden RC | .40 | .15 |
| ❏ 176 | Alex Molden RC | .10 | .02 |
| ❏ 177 | Chris Darkins RC | .10 | .02 |
| ❏ 178 | Stephen Davis RC | 2.00 | .75 |
| ❏ 179 | Rickey Dudley RC | .40 | .15 |
| ❏ 180 | Eddie Kennison RC | .40 | .15 |
| ❏ 181 | Simeon Rice RC | 1.00 | .40 |
| ❏ 182 | Bobby Hoying RC | .40 | .15 |
| ❏ 183 | Troy Aikman BF6 | .50 | .20 |
| ❏ 184 | Emmitt Smith BF6 | 1.00 | .40 |
| ❏ 185 | Michael Irvin BF6 | .20 | .07 |
| ❏ 186 | Deion Sanders BF6 | .40 | .15 |
| ❏ 187 | Daryl Johnston BF6 | .20 | .07 |
| ❏ 188 | Jay Novacek BF6 | .10 | .02 |
| ❏ 189 | Steve Young BF6 | .40 | .15 |
| ❏ 190 | Jerry Rice BF6 | .50 | .20 |
| ❏ 191 | J.J. Stokes BF6 | .40 | .15 |
| ❏ 192 | Ken Norton BF6 | .10 | .02 |
| ❏ 193 | William Floyd BF6 | .20 | .07 |
| ❏ 194 | Brent Jones BF6 | .10 | .02 |
| ❏ 195 | Dan Marino CL | .40 | .15 |
| ❏ 196 | Brett Favre CL | .40 | .15 |
| ❏ 197 | Emmitt Smith CL | .40 | .15 |
| ❏ 198 | Barry Sanders CL | .40 | .15 |
| ❏ 199 | ESmith/Mar/Faw/BSand CL | .40 | .15 |
| ❏ 200 | Brett Favre PackBack | 2.00 | .75 |

## 1997 Pinnacle

|  |  | | |
|---|---|---|---|
| ❏ | COMPLETE SET (200) | 20.00 | 7.50 |
| ❏ 1 | Brett Favre | 2.00 | .75 |
| ❏ 2 | Dan Marino | 2.00 | .75 |
| ❏ 3 | Emmitt Smith | 1.50 | .60 |
| ❏ 4 | Steve Young | .60 | .25 |
| ❏ 5 | Drew Bledsoe | .60 | .25 |
| ❏ 6 | Eddie George | .50 | .20 |
| ❏ 7 | Barry Sanders | 1.50 | .60 |
| ❏ 8 | Jerry Rice | 1.00 | .40 |
| ❏ 9 | John Elway | 2.00 | .75 |
| ❏ 10 | Troy Aikman | 1.00 | .40 |
| ❏ 11 | Kerry Collins | .50 | .20 |
| ❏ 12 | Rick Mirer | .20 | .07 |
| ❏ 13 | Jim Harbaugh | .30 | .10 |
| ❏ 14 | Elvis Grbac | .30 | .10 |
| ❏ 15 | Gus Frerotte | .20 | .07 |
| ❏ 16 | Neil O'Donnell | .30 | .10 |
| ❏ 17 | Jeff George | .30 | .10 |
| ❏ 18 | Kordell Stewart | .50 | .20 |
| ❏ 19 | Junior Seau | .30 | .10 |
| ❏ 20 | Vinny Testaverde | .30 | .10 |
| ❏ 21 | Terry Glenn | .50 | .20 |
| ❏ 22 | Anthony Johnson | .20 | .07 |
| ❏ 23 | Boomer Esiason | .30 | .10 |

| | | | | | | | | | |
|---|---|---|---|---|---|---|---|---|---|
| ❑ 24 Terrell Owens | .60 | .25 | ❑ 109 Terrell Buckley | .20 | .07 | ❑ 194 Barry Sanders I | .75 | .30 |
| ❑ 25 Natrone Means | .30 | .10 | ❑ 110 Deion Sanders | .50 | .20 | ❑ 195 Kerry Collins I | .30 | .10 |
| ❑ 26 Marcus Allen | .50 | .20 | ❑ 111 Carl Pickens | .30 | .10 | ❑ 196 Curtis Martin I | .50 | .20 |
| ❑ 27 James Jett | .30 | .10 | ❑ 112 Bobby Engram | .30 | .10 | ❑ 197 Terrell Davis I | .50 | .20 |
| ❑ 28 Chris T. Jones | .30 | .10 | ❑ 113 Andre Reed | .30 | .10 | ❑ 198 Bledsoe/KCollins/Marino CL | .50 | .20 |
| ❑ 29 Stan Humphries | .30 | .10 | ❑ 114 Terance Mathis | .30 | .10 | ❑ 199 SYoung/Brunell/JGeorge CL | .20 | .07 |
| ❑ 30 Keith Byars | .30 | .10 | ❑ 115 Herman Moore | .30 | .10 | ❑ 200 Aikman/Elway/Mirer CL | .20 | .07 |
| ❑ 31 John Friesz | .30 | .10 | ❑ 116 Robert Brooks | .30 | .10 | | | |
| ❑ 32 Mike Alstott | .50 | .20 | ❑ 117 Ken Dilger | .20 | .07 | | | |
| ❑ 33 Eddie Kennison | .30 | .10 | ❑ 118 Keenan McCardell | .30 | .10 | **1992 Playoff** | | |
| ❑ 34 Eric Moulds | .50 | .20 | ❑ 119 Andre Hastings | .20 | .07 | | | |
| ❑ 35 Frank Sanders | .30 | .10 | ❑ 120 Willie Davis | .20 | .07 | | | |
| ❑ 36 Daryl Johnston | .30 | .10 | ❑ 121 Bruce Smith | .30 | .10 | | | |
| ❑ 37 Cris Carter | .50 | .20 | ❑ 122 Rob Moore | .30 | .10 | | | |
| ❑ 38 Errict Rhett | .20 | .07 | ❑ 123 Johnnie Morton | .20 | .07 | | | |
| ❑ 39 Ben Coates | .30 | .10 | ❑ 124 Sean Dawkins | .20 | .07 | | | |
| ❑ 40 Shannon Sharpe | .30 | .10 | ❑ 125 Mario Bates | .20 | .07 | | | |
| ❑ 41 Jamal Anderson | .50 | .20 | ❑ 126 Henry Ellard | .20 | .07 | | | |
| ❑ 42 Tim Biakabutaka | .30 | .10 | ❑ 127 Derrick Alexander WR | .30 | .10 | | | |
| ❑ 43 Jeff Blake | .30 | .10 | ❑ 128 Kevin Greene | .30 | .10 | | | |
| ❑ 44 Michael Irvin | .50 | .20 | ❑ 129 Derrick Thomas | .30 | .10 | | | |
| ❑ 45 Terrell Davis | .60 | .25 | ❑ 130 Rod Woodson | .30 | .10 | | | |
| ❑ 46 Byron Bam Morris | .20 | .07 | ❑ 131 Rodney Hampton | .30 | .10 | | | |
| ❑ 47 Rashaan Salaam | .20 | .07 | ❑ 132 Marshall Faulk | .60 | .25 | | | |
| ❑ 48 Adrian Murrell | .30 | .10 | ❑ 133 Michael Westbrook | .30 | .10 | | | |
| ❑ 49 Ty Detmer | .20 | .07 | ❑ 134 Erik Kramer | .20 | .07 | | | |
| ❑ 50 Terry Allen | .50 | .20 | ❑ 135 Todd Collins | .20 | .07 | ❑ COMPLETE SET (150) | 25.00 | 10.00 |
| ❑ 51 Mark Brunell | .60 | .25 | ❑ 136 Bill Romanowski | .20 | .07 | ❑ 1 Emmitt Smith | 8.00 | 4.00 |
| ❑ 52 O.J. McDuffie | .30 | .10 | ❑ 137 Jake Reed | .30 | .10 | ❑ 2 Steve Young | 3.00 | 1.50 |
| ❑ 53 Willie McGinest | .30 | .10 | ❑ 138 Heath Shuler | .20 | .07 | ❑ 3 Jack Del Rio | .25 | .08 |
| ❑ 54 Chris Warren | .30 | .10 | ❑ 139 Keyshawn Johnson | .50 | .20 | ❑ 4 Bobby Hebert | .25 | .08 |
| ❑ 55 Trent Dilfer | .50 | .20 | ❑ 140 Marvin Harrison | .50 | .20 | ❑ 5 Shannon Sharpe | .75 | .30 |
| ❑ 56 Jerome Bettis | .50 | .20 | ❑ 141 Andre Rison | .30 | .10 | ❑ 6 Gary Clark | .75 | .30 |
| ❑ 57 Tamarick Vanover | .30 | .10 | ❑ 142 Zach Thomas | .50 | .20 | ❑ 7 Christian Okoye | .25 | .08 |
| ❑ 58 Ki-Jana Carter | .20 | .07 | ❑ 143 Eric Metcalf | .30 | .10 | ❑ 8 Ernest Givins | .40 | .15 |
| ❑ 59 Ray Zellars | .20 | .07 | ❑ 144 Amani Toomer | .30 | .10 | ❑ 9 Mike Horan | .25 | .08 |
| ❑ 60 J.J. Stokes | .30 | .10 | ❑ 145 Desmond Howard | .30 | .10 | ❑ 10 Dennis Gentry | .25 | .08 |
| ❑ 61 Cornelius Bennett | .20 | .07 | ❑ 146 Jimmy Smith | .30 | .10 | ❑ 11 Michael Irvin | .75 | .30 |
| ❑ 62 Scott Mitchell | .30 | .10 | ❑ 147 Brad Johnson | .50 | .20 | ❑ 12 Eric Floyd | .25 | .08 |
| ❑ 63 Tyrone Wheatley | .30 | .10 | ❑ 148 Troy Vincent | .20 | .07 | ❑ 13 Brent Jones | .40 | .15 |
| ❑ 64 Steve McNair | .60 | .25 | ❑ 149 Bryce Paup | .20 | .07 | ❑ 14 Anthony Carter | .40 | .15 |
| ❑ 65 Tony Banks | .30 | .10 | ❑ 150 Reggie White | .50 | .20 | ❑ 15 Tony Martin | .40 | .15 |
| ❑ 66 James O.Stewart | .30 | .10 | ❑ 151 Jake Plummer RC | 2.50 | 1.00 | ❑ 16 Greg Lewis UER | .25 | .08 |
| ❑ 67 Robert Smith | .30 | .10 | ❑ 152 Darnell Autry RC | .30 | .10 | ❑ 17 Todd McNair | .25 | .08 |
| ❑ 68 Thurman Thomas | .50 | .20 | ❑ 153 Tiki Barber RC | 3.00 | 1.25 | ❑ 18 Earnest Byner | .25 | .08 |
| ❑ 69 Mark Chmura | .30 | .10 | ❑ 154 Pat Barnes RC | .50 | .20 | ❑ 19 Steve Beuerlein | .40 | .15 |
| ❑ 70 Napoleon Kaufman | .50 | .20 | ❑ 155 Orlando Pace RC | .50 | .20 | ❑ 20 Roger Craig | .40 | .15 |
| ❑ 71 Ken Norton | .20 | .07 | ❑ 156 Peter Boulware RC | .50 | .20 | ❑ 21 Mark Higgs | .25 | .08 |
| ❑ 72 Herschel Walker | .30 | .10 | ❑ 157 Shawn Springs RC | .30 | .10 | ❑ 22 Guy McIntyre | .25 | .08 |
| ❑ 73 Joey Galloway | .30 | .10 | ❑ 158 Troy Davis RC | .30 | .10 | ❑ 23 Don Warren | .25 | .08 |
| ❑ 74 Neil Smith | .30 | .10 | ❑ 159 Ike Hilliard RC | .75 | .30 | ❑ 24 Alvin Harper | .40 | .15 |
| ❑ 75 Simeon Rice | .20 | .07 | ❑ 160 Jim Druckenmiller RC | .30 | .10 | ❑ 25 Mark Jackson | .25 | .08 |
| ❑ 76 Michael Jackson | .30 | .10 | ❑ 161 Warrick Dunn RC | 1.50 | .50 | ❑ 26 Chris Doleman | .25 | .08 |
| ❑ 77 Muhsin Muhammad | .30 | .10 | ❑ 162 James Farrior RC | .50 | .20 | ❑ 27 Jesse Sapolu | .25 | .08 |
| ❑ 78 Kevin Hardy | .20 | .07 | ❑ 163 Tony Gonzalez RC | 1.50 | .60 | ❑ 28 Tony Tolbert | .25 | .08 |
| ❑ 79 Irving Fryar | .20 | .07 | ❑ 164 Darrell Russell RC | .20 | .07 | ❑ 29 Wendell Davis | .25 | .08 |
| ❑ 80 Jeff Hostetler | .20 | .07 | ❑ 165 Byron Hanspard RC | .30 | .10 | ❑ 30 Dan Saleaumua | .25 | .08 |
| ❑ 81 Eric Swann | .20 | .07 | ❑ 166 Corey Dillon RC | 3.00 | 1.25 | ❑ 31 Jeff Bostic | .25 | .08 |
| ❑ 82 Jim Everett | .20 | .07 | ❑ 167 Kenny Holmes RC | .50 | .20 | ❑ 32 Jay Novacek | .40 | .15 |
| ❑ 83 Karim Abdul-Jabbar | .50 | .20 | ❑ 168 Walter Jones RC | .50 | .20 | ❑ 33 Cris Carter | 1.00 | .40 |
| ❑ 84 Garrison Hearst | .20 | .07 | ❑ 169 Danny Wuerffel RC | .50 | .20 | ❑ 34 Tony Paige | .25 | .08 |
| ❑ 85 Lawrence Phillips | .20 | .07 | ❑ 170 Tom Knight RC | .20 | .07 | ❑ 35 Greg Kragen | .25 | .08 |
| ❑ 86 Bryan Cox | .20 | .07 | ❑ 171 David LaFleur RC | .20 | .07 | ❑ 36 Jeff Dellenbach | .25 | .08 |
| ❑ 87 Larry Centers | .20 | .07 | ❑ 172 Kevin Lockett RC | .30 | .10 | ❑ 37 Keith DeLong | .25 | .08 |
| ❑ 88 Wesley Walls | .30 | .10 | ❑ 173 Will Blackwell RC | .30 | .10 | ❑ 38 Todd Scott | .25 | .08 |
| ❑ 89 Curtis Conway | .30 | .10 | ❑ 174 Reidel Anthony RC | .50 | .20 | ❑ 39 Jeff Feagles | .25 | .08 |
| ❑ 90 Darnay Scott | .30 | .10 | ❑ 175 Dwayne Rudd RC | .20 | .07 | ❑ 40 Mike Saxon | .25 | .08 |
| ❑ 91 Anthony Miller | .20 | .07 | ❑ 176 Yatil Green RC | .30 | .10 | ❑ 41 Martin Mayhew | .25 | .08 |
| ❑ 92 Edgar Bennett | .30 | .10 | ❑ 177 Antowain Smith RC | 1.25 | .50 | ❑ 42 Steve Bono RC | .75 | .30 |
| ❑ 93 Willie Green | .20 | .07 | ❑ 178 Rae Carruth RC | .20 | .07 | ❑ 43 Willie Davis WR RC | .40 | .15 |
| ❑ 94 Kent Graham | .20 | .07 | ❑ 179 Bryant Westbrook RC | .20 | .07 | ❑ 44 Mark Stepnoski | .40 | .15 |
| ❑ 95 Dave Brown | .20 | .07 | ❑ 180 Reinard Wilson RC | .30 | .10 | ❑ 45 Harry Newsome | .25 | .08 |
| ❑ 96 Wayne Chrebet | .50 | .20 | ❑ 181 Joey Kent RC | .50 | .20 | ❑ 46 Thane Gash | .25 | .08 |
| ❑ 97 Ricky Watters | .30 | .10 | ❑ 182 Renaldo Wynn RC | .20 | .07 | ❑ 47 Gaston Green | .25 | .08 |
| ❑ 98 Tony Martin | .30 | .10 | ❑ 183 Brett Favre I | 1.00 | .40 | ❑ 48 James Washington | .25 | .08 |
| ❑ 99 Warren Moon | .50 | .20 | ❑ 184 Emmitt Smith I | .75 | .30 | ❑ 49 Kenny Walker | .25 | .08 |
| ❑ 100 Curtis Martin | .60 | .25 | ❑ 185 Dan Marino I | 1.00 | .40 | ❑ 50 Jeff Davidson RC | .25 | .08 |
| ❑ 101 Dorsey Levens | .50 | .20 | ❑ 186 Troy Aikman I | .50 | .20 | ❑ 51 Shane Conlan | .25 | .08 |
| ❑ 102 Jim Pyne | .20 | .07 | ❑ 187 Jerry Rice I | 1.00 | .40 | ❑ 52 Richard Dent | .40 | .15 |
| ❑ 103 Antonio Freeman | .50 | .20 | ❑ 188 Drew Bledsoe I | .30 | .10 | ❑ 53 Haywood Jeffires | .40 | .15 |
| ❑ 104 Leeland McElroy | .20 | .07 | ❑ 189 Eddie George I | .50 | .20 | ❑ 54 Harry Galbreath | .25 | .08 |
| ❑ 105 Isaac Bruce | .50 | .20 | ❑ 190 Terry Glenn I | .30 | .10 | ❑ 55 Terry Allen | .75 | .30 |
| ❑ 106 Chris Sanders | .20 | .07 | ❑ 191 John Elway I | 1.00 | .40 | ❑ 56 Tommy Barnhardt | .25 | .08 |
| ❑ 107 Tim Brown | .50 | .20 | ❑ 192 Steve Young I | .30 | .10 | ❑ 57 Mike Golic | .25 | .08 |
| ❑ 108 Greg Lloyd | .20 | .07 | ❑ 193 Mark Brunell I | .50 | .20 | ❑ 58 Dalton Hilliard | .25 | .08 |

| | | |
|---|---|---|
| ❏ 59 Danny Copeland | .25 | .08 |
| ❏ 60 Jerry Fontenot RC | .25 | .08 |
| ❏ 61 Kelvin Martin | .25 | .08 |
| ❏ 62 Mark Kelso | .25 | .08 |
| ❏ 63 Wymon Henderson | .25 | .08 |
| ❏ 64 Mark Rypien | .25 | .08 |
| ❏ 65 Bobby Humphrey | .25 | .08 |
| ❏ 66 Rich Gannon UER | .75 | .30 |
| ❏ 67 Darren Lewis | .25 | .08 |
| ❏ 68 Barry Foster | .40 | .15 |
| ❏ 69 Ken Norton Jr. | .40 | .15 |
| ❏ 70 James Lofton | .40 | .15 |
| ❏ 71 Trace Armstrong | .25 | .08 |
| ❏ 72 Vestee Jackson | .25 | .08 |
| ❏ 73 Clyde Simmons | .25 | .08 |
| ❏ 74 Brad Muster | .25 | .08 |
| ❏ 75 Cornelius Bennett | .40 | .15 |
| ❏ 76 Mike Merriweather | .25 | .08 |
| ❏ 77 John Elway | 4.00 | 1.50 |
| ❏ 78 Herschel Walker | .40 | .15 |
| ❏ 79 Hassan Jones UER | .25 | .08 |
| ❏ 80 Jim Harbaugh | .75 | .30 |
| ❏ 81 Issiac Holt | .25 | .08 |
| ❏ 82 David Alexander | .25 | .08 |
| ❏ 83 Brian Mitchell | .40 | .15 |
| ❏ 84 Mark Tuinei | .25 | .08 |
| ❏ 85 Tom Rathman | .25 | .08 |
| ❏ 86 Reggie White | .75 | .30 |
| ❏ 87 William Perry | .40 | .15 |
| ❏ 88 Jeff Wright | .25 | .08 |
| ❏ 89 Keith Kartz | .25 | .08 |
| ❏ 90 Andre Waters | .25 | .08 |
| ❏ 91 Darryl Talley | .25 | .08 |
| ❏ 92 Morten Andersen | .25 | .08 |
| ❏ 93 Tom Waddle | .40 | .15 |
| ❏ 94 Felix Wright UER | .25 | .08 |
| ❏ 95 Keith Jackson | .40 | .15 |
| ❏ 96 Art Monk | .40 | .15 |
| ❏ 97 Seth Joyner | .25 | .08 |
| ❏ 98 Steve McMichael | .40 | .15 |
| ❏ 99 Thurman Thomas | .75 | .30 |
| ❏ 100 Warren Moon | .75 | .30 |
| ❏ 101 Tony Casillas | .25 | .08 |
| ❏ 102 Vance Johnson | .25 | .08 |
| ❏ 103 Doug Dawson RC | .25 | .08 |
| ❏ 104 Bill Maas | .25 | .08 |
| ❏ 105 Mark Clayton | .40 | .15 |
| ❏ 106 Hoby Brenner | .25 | .08 |
| ❏ 107 Gary Anderson K | .25 | .08 |
| ❏ 108 Marc Logan | .25 | .08 |
| ❏ 109 Ricky Sanders | .25 | .08 |
| ❏ 110 Vai Sikahema | .25 | .08 |
| ❏ 111 Neil Smith | .75 | .30 |
| ❏ 112 Cody Carlson | .40 | .15 |
| ❏ 113 Jimmie Jones | .25 | .08 |
| ❏ 114 Pat Swilling | .40 | .15 |
| ❏ 115 Neil O'Donnell | .40 | .15 |
| ❏ 116 Chip Lohmiller | .25 | .08 |
| ❏ 117 Mike Croel | .25 | .08 |
| ❏ 118 Pete Metzelaars | .25 | .08 |
| ❏ 119 Ray Childress | .25 | .08 |
| ❏ 120 Fred Banks | .25 | .08 |
| ❏ 121 Derek Kennard | .25 | .08 |
| ❏ 122 Daryl Johnston | .75 | .30 |
| ❏ 123 Lorenzo White UER | .25 | .08 |
| ❏ 124 Hardy Nickerson | .40 | .15 |
| ❏ 125 Derrick Thomas | .75 | .30 |
| ❏ 126 Steve Walsh | .25 | .08 |
| ❏ 127 Doug Widell | .25 | .08 |
| ❏ 128 Calvin Williams | .40 | .15 |
| ❏ 129 Tim Harris | .25 | .08 |
| ❏ 130 Rod Woodson | .75 | .30 |
| ❏ 131 Craig Heyward | .40 | .15 |
| ❏ 132 Barry Word | .25 | .08 |
| ❏ 133 Mark Duper | .25 | .08 |
| ❏ 134 Tim Johnson | .25 | .08 |
| ❏ 135 John Gesek | .25 | .08 |
| ❏ 136 Steve Jackson | .25 | .08 |
| ❏ 137 Dave Krieg | .40 | .15 |
| ❏ 138 Barry Sanders | 4.00 | 1.50 |
| ❏ 139 Michael Haynes | .40 | .15 |
| ❏ 140 Eric Metcalf | .40 | .15 |
| ❏ 141 Stan Humphries | .75 | .30 |
| ❏ 142 Sterling Sharpe | .75 | .30 |
| ❏ 143 Todd Marinovich | .25 | .08 |

| | | |
|---|---|---|
| ❏ 144 Rodney Hampton | .40 | .15 |
| ❏ 145 Rodney Peete | .40 | .15 |
| ❏ 146 Darryl Williams RC | .25 | .08 |
| ❏ 147 Darren Perry RC | .25 | .08 |
| ❏ 148 Terrell Buckley RC | .25 | .08 |
| ❏ 149 Amp Lee RC | .25 | .08 |
| ❏ 150 Ricky Watters | .75 | .30 |

## 1993 Playoff

| | | |
|---|---|---|
| ❏ COMPLETE SET (315) | 25.00 | 10.00 |
| ❏ 1 Troy Aikman | 1.50 | .60 |
| ❏ 2 Jerry Rice | 2.00 | .75 |
| ❏ 3 Keith Jackson | .20 | .07 |
| ❏ 4 Sean Gilbert | .20 | .07 |
| ❏ 5 Jim Kelly | .40 | .15 |
| ❏ 6 Junior Seau | .40 | .15 |
| ❏ 7 Deion Sanders | 1.00 | .40 |
| ❏ 8 Joe Montana | 3.00 | 1.25 |
| ❏ 9 Terrell Buckley | .10 | .02 |
| ❏ 10 Emmitt Smith | 3.00 | 1.25 |
| ❏ 11 Pete Stoyanovich | .10 | .02 |
| ❏ 12 Randall Cunningham | .40 | .15 |
| ❏ 13 Boomer Esiason | .20 | .07 |
| ❏ 14 Mike Saxon | .10 | .02 |
| ❏ 15 Chuck Cecil | .10 | .02 |
| ❏ 16 Vinny Testaverde | .20 | .07 |
| ❏ 17 Jeff Hostetler | .20 | .07 |
| ❏ 18 Mark Clayton | .10 | .02 |
| ❏ 19 Nick Bell | .10 | .02 |
| ❏ 20 Frank Reich | .20 | .07 |
| ❏ 21 Henry Ellard | .20 | .07 |
| ❏ 22 Andre Reed | .20 | .07 |
| ❏ 23 Mark Ingram | .10 | .02 |
| ❏ 24 Mike Brim | .10 | .02 |
| ❏ 25A Bernie Kosar ERR Kozar | .20 | .07 |
| ❏ 25B Bernie Kosar COR | .20 | .07 |
| ❏ 26 Jeff George | .40 | .15 |
| ❏ 27 Tommy Maddox | .40 | .15 |
| ❏ 28 Kent Graham RC | .40 | .15 |
| ❏ 29 David Klingler | .10 | .02 |
| ❏ 30 Robert Delpino | .10 | .02 |
| ❏ 31 Kevin Fagan | .10 | .02 |
| ❏ 32 Mark Bavaro | .10 | .02 |
| ❏ 33 Harold Green | .10 | .02 |
| ❏ 34 Shawn McCarthy | .10 | .02 |
| ❏ 35 Ricky Proehl | .10 | .02 |
| ❏ 36 Eugene Robinson | .10 | .02 |
| ❏ 37 Phil Simms | .20 | .07 |
| ❏ 38 David Lang | .10 | .02 |
| ❏ 39 Santana Dotson | .20 | .07 |
| ❏ 40 Brett Perriman | .40 | .15 |
| ❏ 41 Jim Harbaugh | .40 | .15 |
| ❏ 42 Keith Byars | .10 | .02 |
| ❏ 43 Quentin Coryatt | .20 | .07 |
| ❏ 44 Louis Oliver | .10 | .02 |
| ❏ 45 Howie Long | .40 | .15 |
| ❏ 46 Mike Sherrard | .10 | .02 |
| ❏ 47 Earnest Byner | .10 | .02 |
| ❏ 48 Neil Smith | .40 | .15 |
| ❏ 49 Audray McMillian | .10 | .02 |
| ❏ 50 Vaughn Dunbar | .10 | .02 |
| ❏ 51 Ronnie Lott | .20 | .07 |
| ❏ 52 Clyde Simmons | .10 | .02 |
| ❏ 53 Kevin Scott | .10 | .02 |
| ❏ 54 Bubby Brister | .10 | .02 |
| ❏ 55 Randal Hill | .10 | .02 |
| ❏ 56 Pat Swilling | .10 | .02 |
| ❏ 57 Steve Beuerlein | .20 | .07 |

| | | |
|---|---|---|
| ❏ 58 Gary Clark | .20 | .07 |
| ❏ 59 Brian Noble | .10 | .02 |
| ❏ 60 Leslie O'Neal | .10 | .02 |
| ❏ 61 Vincent Brown | .10 | .02 |
| ❏ 62 Edgar Bennett | .40 | .15 |
| ❏ 63 Anthony Carter | .20 | .07 |
| ❏ 64 Glenn Cadrez RC UER | .10 | .02 |
| ❏ 65 Dalton Hilliard | .10 | .02 |
| ❏ 66 James Lofton | .20 | .07 |
| ❏ 67 Walter Stanley | .10 | .02 |
| ❏ 68 Tim Harris | .10 | .02 |
| ❏ 69 Carl Banks | .10 | .02 |
| ❏ 70 Andre Ware | .10 | .02 |
| ❏ 71 Karl Mecklenburg | .10 | .02 |
| ❏ 72 Russell Maryland | .10 | .02 |
| ❏ 73 Leroy Thompson | .10 | .02 |
| ❏ 74 Tommy Kane | .10 | .02 |
| ❏ 75 Dan Marino | 3.00 | 1.25 |
| ❏ 76 Darrell Fullington | .10 | .02 |
| ❏ 77 Jessie Tuggle | .10 | .02 |
| ❏ 78 Bruce Smith | .40 | .15 |
| ❏ 79 Neal Anderson | .10 | .02 |
| ❏ 80 Kevin Mack | .10 | .02 |
| ❏ 81 Shane Dronett | .10 | .02 |
| ❏ 82 Nick Lowery | .10 | .02 |
| ❏ 83 Sheldon White | .10 | .02 |
| ❏ 84 Flipper Anderson | .10 | .02 |
| ❏ 85 Jeff Herrod | .10 | .02 |
| ❏ 86 Dwight Stone | .10 | .02 |
| ❏ 87 Dave Krieg | .20 | .07 |
| ❏ 88 Bryan Cox | .10 | .02 |
| ❏ 89 Greg McMurtry | .10 | .02 |
| ❏ 90 Rickey Jackson | .10 | .02 |
| ❏ 91 Ernie Mills | .10 | .02 |
| ❏ 92 Browning Nagle | .10 | .02 |
| ❏ 93 John Taylor | .20 | .07 |
| ❏ 94 Eric Dickerson | .20 | .07 |
| ❏ 95 Johnny Holland | .10 | .02 |
| ❏ 96 Anthony Miller | .20 | .07 |
| ❏ 97 Fred Barnett | .20 | .07 |
| ❏ 98 Ricky Ervins UER | .10 | .02 |
| ❏ 99 Leonard Russell | .20 | .07 |
| ❏ 100 Lawrence Taylor | .40 | .15 |
| ❏ 101 Tony Casillas | .10 | .02 |
| ❏ 102 John Elway | 3.00 | 1.25 |
| ❏ 103 Bernie Blades | .10 | .02 |
| ❏ 104 Harry Sydney | .10 | .02 |
| ❏ 105 Bubba McDowell | .10 | .02 |
| ❏ 106 Todd McNair | .10 | .02 |
| ❏ 107 Steve Smith | .10 | .02 |
| ❏ 108 Jim Everett | .20 | .07 |
| ❏ 109 Bobby Humphrey | .10 | .02 |
| ❏ 110 Rich Gannon | .40 | .15 |
| ❏ 111 Marv Cook | .10 | .02 |
| ❏ 112 Wayne Martin | .10 | .02 |
| ❏ 113 Sean Landeta | .10 | .02 |
| ❏ 114 Brad Baxter UER | .10 | .02 |
| ❏ 115 Reggie White | .40 | .15 |
| ❏ 116 Johnny Johnson | .10 | .02 |
| ❏ 117 Jeff Graham | .20 | .07 |
| ❏ 118 Darren Carrington RC | .10 | .02 |
| ❏ 119 Ricky Watters | .40 | .15 |
| ❏ 120 Art Monk | .20 | .07 |
| ❏ 121 Cornelius Bennett | .20 | .07 |
| ❏ 122 Wade Wilson | .10 | .02 |
| ❏ 123 Daniel Stubbs | .10 | .02 |
| ❏ 124 Brad Muster | .10 | .02 |
| ❏ 125 Mike Tomczak | .10 | .02 |
| ❏ 126 Jay Novacek | .20 | .07 |
| ❏ 127 Shannon Sharpe | .40 | .15 |
| ❏ 128 Rodney Peete | .10 | .02 |
| ❏ 129 Daryl Johnson | .40 | .15 |
| ❏ 130 Warren Moon | .40 | .15 |
| ❏ 131 Willie Gault | .10 | .02 |
| ❏ 132 Tony Martin | .40 | .15 |
| ❏ 133 Terry Allen | .20 | .07 |
| ❏ 134 Hugh Millen | .10 | .02 |
| ❏ 135 Rob Moore | .20 | .07 |
| ❏ 136 Andy Harmon RC | .20 | .07 |
| ❏ 137 Kelvin Martin | .10 | .02 |
| ❏ 138 Rod Woodson | .40 | .15 |
| ❏ 139 Nate Lewis | .10 | .02 |
| ❏ 140 Darryl Talley | .10 | .02 |
| ❏ 141 Guy McIntyre | .10 | .02 |
| ❏ 142 John L. Williams | .10 | .02 |

| | | |
|---|---|---|
| 143 Brad Edwards | .10 | .02 |
| 144 Trace Armstrong | .10 | .02 |
| 145 Kenneth Davis | .10 | .02 |
| 146 Clay Matthews | .20 | .07 |
| 147 Gaston Green | .10 | .02 |
| 148 Chris Spielman | .20 | .07 |
| 149 Cody Carlson | .10 | .02 |
| 150 Derrick Thomas | .40 | .15 |
| 151 Terry McDaniel | .10 | .02 |
| 152 Kevin Greene | .20 | .07 |
| 153 Roger Craig | .20 | .07 |
| 154 Craig Heyward | .20 | .07 |
| 155 Rodney Hampton | .20 | .07 |
| 156 Heath Sherman | .10 | .02 |
| 157 Mark Stepnoski | .10 | .02 |
| 158 Chris Chandler | .20 | .07 |
| 159 Rod Bernstine | .10 | .02 |
| 160 Pierce Holt | .10 | .02 |
| 161 Wilber Marshall | .10 | .02 |
| 162 Reggie Cobb | .10 | .02 |
| 163 Tom Rathman | .10 | .02 |
| 164 Michael Haynes | .20 | .07 |
| 165 Nate Odomes | .10 | .02 |
| 166 Tom Waddle | .10 | .02 |
| 167 Eric Ball | .10 | .02 |
| 168 Brett Favre | 4.00 | 1.50 |
| 169 Michael Jackson | .20 | .07 |
| 170 Lorenzo White | .10 | .02 |
| 171 Cleveland Gary | .10 | .02 |
| 172 Jay Schroeder | .10 | .02 |
| 173 Tony Paige | .10 | .02 |
| 174 Jack Del Rio | .10 | .02 |
| 175 Jon Vaughn | .10 | .02 |
| 176 Morten Andersen UER | .10 | .02 |
| 177 Chris Burkett | .10 | .02 |
| 178 Vai Sikahema | .10 | .02 |
| 179 Ronnie Harmon | .10 | .02 |
| 180 Amp Lee | .10 | .02 |
| 181 Chip Lohmiller | .10 | .02 |
| 182 Steve Broussard | .10 | .02 |
| 183 Don Beebe | .10 | .02 |
| 184 Tommy Vardell | .10 | .02 |
| 185 Keith Jennings | .10 | .02 |
| 186 Simon Fletcher | .10 | .02 |
| 187 Mel Gray | .20 | .07 |
| 188 Vince Workman | .10 | .02 |
| 189 Haywood Jeffires | .20 | .07 |
| 190 Barry Word | .10 | .02 |
| 191 Ethan Horton | .10 | .02 |
| 192 Mark Higgs | .10 | .02 |
| 193 Irving Fryar | .20 | .07 |
| 194 Charles Haley | .20 | .07 |
| 195 Steve Bono | .20 | .07 |
| 196 Mike Golic | .10 | .02 |
| 197 Gary Anderson K | .10 | .02 |
| 198 Sterling Sharpe | .40 | .15 |
| 199 Andre Tippett | .10 | .02 |
| 200 Thurman Thomas | .40 | .15 |
| 201 Chris Miller | .20 | .07 |
| 202 Henry Jones | .10 | .02 |
| 203 Mo Lewis | .10 | .02 |
| 204 Marion Butts | .10 | .02 |
| 205 Mike Johnson | .10 | .02 |
| 206 Alvin Harper | .20 | .07 |
| 207 Ray Childress | .10 | .02 |
| 208 Anthony Johnson | .20 | .07 |
| 209 Tony Bennett | .10 | .02 |
| 210 Anthony Newman K | .10 | .02 |
| 211 Christian Okoye | .10 | .02 |
| 212 Marcus Allen | .40 | .15 |
| 213 Jackie Harris | .10 | .02 |
| 214 Mark Duper | .10 | .02 |
| 215 Cris Carter | .40 | .15 |
| 216 John Stephens | .10 | .02 |
| 217 Barry Sanders | 2.50 | 1.00 |
| 218A H.Moore ERR Sherman | 1.25 | .50 |
| 218B Herman Moore COR | 2.50 | 1.00 |
| 219 Marvin Washington | .10 | .02 |
| 220 Calvin Williams | .20 | .07 |
| 221 John Randle | .10 | .02 |
| 222 Marco Coleman | .10 | .02 |
| 223 Eric Martin | .10 | .02 |
| 224 Dave Meggett | .10 | .02 |
| 225 Brian Washington | .10 | .02 |
| 226 Barry Foster | .20 | .07 |
| 227 Michael Zordich | .10 | .02 |
| 228 Stan Humphries | .20 | .07 |
| 229 Mike Cofer | .10 | .02 |
| 230 Chris Warren | .20 | .07 |
| 231 Keith McCants | .10 | .02 |
| 232 Mark Rypien | .10 | .02 |
| 233 James Francis | .10 | .02 |
| 234 Andre Rison | .20 | .07 |
| 235 William Perry | .20 | .07 |
| 236 Chip Banks | .10 | .02 |
| 237 Willie Davis | .40 | .15 |
| 238 Chris Doleman | .10 | .02 |
| 239 Tim Brown | .40 | .15 |
| 240 Darren Perry | .10 | .02 |
| 241 Johnny Bailey | .10 | .02 |
| 242 Ernest Givins | .20 | .07 |
| 243 John Carney | .10 | .02 |
| 244 Cortez Kennedy | .20 | .07 |
| 245 Lawrence Dawsey | .10 | .02 |
| 246 Martin Mayhew | .10 | .02 |
| 247 Shane Conlan | .10 | .02 |
| 248 J.J. Birden | .10 | .02 |
| 249 Quinn Early | .20 | .07 |
| 250 Michael Irvin | .40 | .15 |
| 251 Neil O'Donnell | .40 | .15 |
| 252 Stan Gelbaugh | .10 | .02 |
| 253 Drew Hill | .10 | .02 |
| 254 Wendell Davis | .10 | .02 |
| 255 Tim Johnson | .19 | .02 |
| 256 Seth Joyner | .10 | .02 |
| 257 Derrick Fenner | .10 | .02 |
| 258 Steve Young | 1.50 | .60 |
| 259 Jackie Slater | .10 | .02 |
| 260 Eric Metcalf | .20 | .07 |
| 261 Rufus Porter | .10 | .02 |
| 262 Ken Norton Jr. | .20 | .07 |
| 263 Tim McDonald | .10 | .02 |
| 264 Mark Jackson | .10 | .02 |
| 265 Hardy Nickerson | .20 | .07 |
| 266 Anthony Munoz | .20 | .07 |
| 267 Mark Carrier WR | .20 | .07 |
| 268 Mike Pritchard | .20 | .07 |
| 269 Steve Emtman | .10 | .02 |
| 270 Ricky Sanders | .10 | .02 |
| 271 Robert Massey | .10 | .02 |
| 272 Pete Metzelaars | .10 | .02 |
| 273 Reggie Langhorne | .10 | .02 |
| 274 Tim McGee | .10 | .02 |
| 275 Reggie Rivers RC | .10 | .02 |
| 276 Jimmie Jones | .10 | .02 |
| 277 Lorenzo White TB | .10 | .02 |
| 278 Emmitt Smith TB | 2.00 | .75 |
| 279 Thurman Thomas TB | .40 | .15 |
| 280 Barry Sanders TB | 1.50 | .60 |
| 281 Rodney Hampton TB | .20 | .07 |
| 282 Barry Foster TB | .20 | .07 |
| 283 Troy Aikman PC | 1.00 | .40 |
| 284 Michael Irvin PC | .20 | .07 |
| 285 Brett Favre PC | 2.50 | 1.00 |
| 286 Sterling Sharpe PC | .20 | .07 |
| 287 Steve Young PC | 1.00 | .40 |
| 288 Jerry Rice PC | 1.25 | .50 |
| 289 Stan Humphries PC | .20 | .07 |
| 290 Anthony Miller PC | .20 | .07 |
| 291 Dan Marino PC | 2.00 | .75 |
| 292 Keith Jackson RC | .10 | .02 |
| 293 Patrick Bates RC | .10 | .02 |
| 294 Jerome Bettis RC | 10.00 | 4.00 |
| 295 Drew Bledsoe RC | 6.00 | 2.50 |
| 296 Tom Carter RC | .20 | .07 |
| 297 Curtis Conway RC | 1.00 | .40 |
| 298 John Copeland RC | .20 | .07 |
| 299 Eric Curry RC | .10 | .02 |
| 300 Reggie Brooks RC | .20 | .07 |
| 301 Steve Everitt RC | .10 | .02 |
| 302 Deon Figures RC | .10 | .02 |
| 303 Garrison Hearst RC | 2.00 | .75 |
| 304 Qadry Ismail RC UER | .40 | .15 |
| 305 Marvin Jones RC | .10 | .02 |
| 306 Lincoln Kennedy RC | .10 | .02 |
| 307 O.J.McDuffie RC | .40 | .15 |
| 308 Rick Mirer RC | .40 | .15 |
| 309 Wayne Simmons RC | .10 | .02 |
| 310 Irv Smith RC | .10 | .02 |
| 311 Robert Smith RC | 3.00 | 1.25 |
| 312 Dana Stubblefield RC | .40 | .15 |
| 313 George Teague RC | .20 | .07 |
| 314 Dan Williams RC | .10 | .02 |
| 315 Kevin Williams RC WR | .40 | .15 |
| NNO Santa Claus | 2.00 | .75 |

## 1994 Playoff

| | | |
|---|---|---|
| COMPLETE SET (336) | 30.00 | 12.50 |
| 1 Joe Montana | 4.00 | 1.50 |
| 2 Derrick Thomas | .50 | .20 |
| 3 Dan Marino | 4.00 | 1.50 |
| 4 Cris Carter | .75 | .30 |
| 5 Boomer Esiason | .30 | .10 |
| 6 Bruce Smith | .50 | .20 |
| 7 Andre Rison | .30 | .10 |
| 8 Curtis Conway | .50 | .20 |
| 9 Michael Irvin | .50 | .20 |
| 10 Shannon Sharpe | .30 | .10 |
| 11 Pat Swilling | .15 | .05 |
| 12 John Parrella | .15 | .05 |
| 13 Mel Gray | .15 | .05 |
| 14 Ray Childress | .15 | .05 |
| 15 Willie Davis | .30 | .10 |
| 16 Rocket Ismail | .30 | .10 |
| 17 Jim Everett | .30 | .10 |
| 18 Mark Higgs | .15 | .05 |
| 19 Trace Armstrong | .15 | .05 |
| 20 Jim Kelly | .50 | .20 |
| 21 Rob Burnett | .15 | .05 |
| 22 Jay Novacek | .30 | .10 |
| 23 Robert Delpino | .15 | .05 |
| 24 Brett Perriman | .30 | .10 |
| 25 Troy Aikman | 2.00 | .75 |
| 26 Reggie White | .50 | .20 |
| 27 Lorenzo White | .15 | .05 |
| 28 Bubba McDowell | .15 | .05 |
| 29 Steve Emtman | .15 | .05 |
| 30 Brett Favre | 4.00 | 1.50 |
| 31 Derek Russell | .15 | .05 |
| 32 Jeff Hostetler | .30 | .10 |
| 33 Henry Ellard | .30 | .10 |
| 34 Jack Del Rio | .15 | .05 |
| 35 Mike Saxon | .15 | .05 |
| 36 Rickey Jackson | .15 | .05 |
| 37 Phil Simms | .30 | .10 |
| 38 Quinn Early | .30 | .10 |
| 39 Russell Copeland | .15 | .05 |
| 40 Carl Pickens | .30 | .10 |
| 41 Lance Gunn | .15 | .05 |
| 42 Bernie Kosar | .30 | .10 |
| 43 John Elway | 4.00 | 1.50 |
| 44 George Teague | .15 | .05 |
| 45 Nick Lowery | .15 | .05 |
| 46 Haywood Jeffires | .30 | .10 |
| 47 Will Shields | .15 | .05 |
| 48 Daryl Johnston | .30 | .10 |
| 49 Pete Metzelaars | .15 | .05 |
| 50 Warren Moon | .50 | .20 |
| 51 Cornelius Bennett | .30 | .10 |
| 52 Vinny Testaverde | .30 | .10 |
| 53 John Mangum RC | .15 | .05 |
| 54 Tommy Vardell | .15 | .05 |
| 55 Lincoln Coleman RC | .15 | .05 |
| 56 Karl Mecklenburg | .15 | .05 |
| 57 Jackie Harris | .15 | .05 |
| 58 Curtis Duncan | .15 | .05 |
| 59 Quentin Coryatt | .15 | .05 |
| 60 Tim Brown | .50 | .20 |

|  |  | | |
|---|---|---|---|
| ❏ 61 | Irving Fryar | .30 | .10 |
| ❏ 62 | Sean Gilbert | .15 | .05 |
| ❏ 63 | Qadry Ismail | .50 | .20 |
| ❏ 64 | Irv Smith | .15 | .05 |
| ❏ 65 | Mark Jackson | .15 | .05 |
| ❏ 66 | Ronnie Lott | .30 | .10 |
| ❏ 67 | Henry Jones | .15 | .05 |
| ❏ 68 | Horace Copeland | .15 | .05 |
| ❏ 69 | John Copeland | .15 | .05 |
| ❏ 70 | Mark Carrier WR | .30 | .10 |
| ❏ 71 | Michael Jackson | .30 | .10 |
| ❏ 72 | Jason Elam | .30 | .10 |
| ❏ 73 | Rod Bernstine | .15 | .05 |
| ❏ 74 | Wayne Simmons | .15 | .05 |
| ❏ 75 | Cody Carlson | .15 | .05 |
| ❏ 76 | Alexander Wright | .15 | .05 |
| ❏ 77 | Shane Conlan | .15 | .05 |
| ❏ 78 | Keith Jackson | .15 | .05 |
| ❏ 79 | Sean Salisbury | .15 | .05 |
| ❏ 80 | Vaughan Johnson | .15 | .05 |
| ❏ 81 | Rob Moore | .30 | .10 |
| ❏ 82 | Andre Reed | .30 | .10 |
| ❏ 83 | David Klingler | .15 | .05 |
| ❏ 84 | Jim Harbaugh | .50 | .20 |
| ❏ 85 | John Jett RC | .15 | .05 |
| ❏ 86 | Sterling Sharpe | .30 | .10 |
| ❏ 87 | Webster Slaughter | .15 | .05 |
| ❏ 88 | J.J. Birden | .15 | .05 |
| ❏ 89 | O.J.McDuffie | .50 | .20 |
| ❏ 90 | Andre Tippett | .15 | .05 |
| ❏ 91 | Don Beebe | .15 | .05 |
| ❏ 92 | Mark Stepnoski | .15 | .05 |
| ❏ 93 | Neil Smith | .30 | .10 |
| ❏ 94 | Terry Kirby | .50 | .20 |
| ❏ 95 | Wade Wilson | .15 | .05 |
| ❏ 96 | Darryl Talley | .15 | .05 |
| ❏ 97 | Anthony Smith | .15 | .05 |
| ❏ 98 | Willie Roaf | .15 | .05 |
| ❏ 99 | Mo Lewis | .15 | .05 |
| ❏ 100 | James Washington | .15 | .05 |
| ❏ 101 | Nate Odomes | .15 | .05 |
| ❏ 102 | Chris Gedney | .15 | .05 |
| ❏ 103 | Joe Walter | .15 | .05 |
| ❏ 104 | Alvin Harper | .30 | .10 |
| ❏ 105 | Simon Fletcher | .15 | .05 |
| ❏ 106 | Rodney Peete | .15 | .05 |
| ❏ 107 | Terrell Buckley | .15 | .05 |
| ❏ 108 | Jeff George | .50 | .20 |
| ❏ 109 | James Jett | .15 | .05 |
| ❏ 110 | Tony Casillas | .15 | .05 |
| ❏ 111 | Marco Coleman | .15 | .05 |
| ❏ 112 | Anthony Carter | .30 | .10 |
| ❏ 113 | Lincoln Kennedy | .15 | .05 |
| ❏ 114 | Chris Calloway | .15 | .05 |
| ❏ 115 | Randall Cunningham | .50 | .20 |
| ❏ 116 | Steve Beuerlein | .30 | .10 |
| ❏ 117 | Neil O'Donnell | .50 | .20 |
| ❏ 118 | Stan Humphries | .30 | .10 |
| ❏ 119 | John Taylor | .30 | .10 |
| ❏ 120 | Cortez Kennedy | .30 | .10 |
| ❏ 121 | Santana Dotson | .30 | .10 |
| ❏ 122 | Thomas Smith | .15 | .05 |
| ❏ 123 | Kevin Williams WR | .30 | .10 |
| ❏ 124 | Andre Ware | .15 | .05 |
| ❏ 125 | Ethan Horton | .15 | .05 |
| ❏ 126 | Mike Sherrard | .15 | .05 |
| ❏ 127 | Fred Barnett | .30 | .10 |
| ❏ 128 | Ricky Proehl | .15 | .05 |
| ❏ 129 | Kevin Greene | .30 | .10 |
| ❏ 130 | John Carney | .15 | .05 |
| ❏ 131 | Tim McDonald | .15 | .05 |
| ❏ 132 | Rick Mirer | .50 | .20 |
| ❏ 133 | Blair Thomas | .15 | .05 |
| ❏ 134 | Hardy Nickerson | .15 | .05 |
| ❏ 135 | Heath Sherman | .15 | .05 |
| ❏ 136 | Andre Hastings | .15 | .05 |
| ❏ 137 | Randal Hill | .15 | .05 |
| ❏ 138 | Mike Cofer | .15 | .05 |
| ❏ 139 | Brian Blades | .30 | .10 |
| ❏ 140 | Earnest Byner | .15 | .05 |
| ❏ 141 | Bill Bates | .30 | .10 |
| ❏ 142 | Junior Seau | .50 | .20 |
| ❏ 143 | Johnny Bailey | .15 | .05 |
| ❏ 144 | Dwight Stone | .15 | .05 |
| ❏ 145 | Todd Kelly | .15 | .05 |
| ❏ 146 | Tyrone Montgomery | .15 | .05 |
| ❏ 147 | Herschel Walker | .30 | .10 |
| ❏ 148 | Gary Clark | .30 | .10 |
| ❏ 149 | Eric Green | .15 | .05 |
| ❏ 150 | Steve Young | 1.50 | .60 |
| ❏ 151 | Anthony Miller | .30 | .10 |
| ❏ 152 | Dana Stubblefield | .30 | .10 |
| ❏ 153 | Dean Wells RC | .15 | .05 |
| ❏ 154 | Vincent Brisby | .30 | .10 |
| ❏ 155 | Chris Chandler | .30 | .10 |
| ❏ 156 | Clyde Simmons | .15 | .05 |
| ❏ 157 | Rod Woodson | .30 | .10 |
| ❏ 158 | Nate Lewis | .15 | .05 |
| ❏ 159 | Martin Harrison | .15 | .05 |
| ❏ 160 | Kelvin Martin | .15 | .05 |
| ❏ 161 | Craig Erickson | .15 | .05 |
| ❏ 162 | Johnny Mitchell | .15 | .05 |
| ❏ 163 | Calvin Williams | .30 | .10 |
| ❏ 164 | Deon Figures | .15 | .05 |
| ❏ 165 | Tom Rathman | .15 | .05 |
| ❏ 166 | Rick Hamilton | .15 | .05 |
| ❏ 167 | John L. Williams | .15 | .05 |
| ❏ 168 | Demetrius DuBose | .15 | .05 |
| ❏ 169 | Michael Brooks | .15 | .05 |
| ❏ 170 | Marion Butts | .15 | .05 |
| ❏ 171 | Brent Jones | .30 | .10 |
| ❏ 172 | Bobby Hebert | .15 | .05 |
| ❏ 173 | Brad Edwards | .15 | .05 |
| ❏ 174 | David Wyman | .15 | .05 |
| ❏ 175 | Herman Moore | .50 | .20 |
| ❏ 176 | LeRoy Butler | .15 | .05 |
| ❏ 177 | Reggie Langhorne | .15 | .05 |
| ❏ 178 | Dave Krieg | .30 | .10 |
| ❏ 179 | Patrick Bates | .15 | .05 |
| ❏ 180 | Erik Kramer | .15 | .05 |
| ❏ 181 | Troy Drayton | .15 | .05 |
| ❏ 182 | Dave Meggett | .15 | .05 |
| ❏ 183 | Eric Allen | .15 | .05 |
| ❏ 184 | Mark Bavaro | .15 | .05 |
| ❏ 185 | Leslie O'Neal | .15 | .05 |
| ❏ 186 | Jerry Rice | 2.00 | .75 |
| ❏ 187 | Desmond Howard | .30 | .10 |
| ❏ 188 | Deion Sanders | .75 | .30 |
| ❏ 189 | Bill Maas | .15 | .05 |
| ❏ 190 | Frank Wycheck RC | 2.00 | .75 |
| ❏ 191 | Ernest Givins | .30 | .10 |
| ❏ 192 | Terry McDaniel | .15 | .05 |
| ❏ 193 | Bryan Cox | .15 | .05 |
| ❏ 194 | Guy McIntyre | .15 | .05 |
| ❏ 195 | Pierce Holt | .15 | .05 |
| ❏ 196 | Fred Stokes | .15 | .05 |
| ❏ 197 | Mike Pritchard | .15 | .05 |
| ❏ 198 | Terry Obee | .15 | .05 |
| ❏ 199 | Mark Collins | .15 | .05 |
| ❏ 200 | Drew Bledsoe | 1.25 | .50 |
| ❏ 201 | Barry Word | .15 | .05 |
| ❏ 202 | Derrick Lassic | .15 | .05 |
| ❏ 203 | Chris Spielman | .30 | .10 |
| ❏ 204 | John Jurkovic RC | .30 | .10 |
| ❏ 205 | Ken Norton Jr. | .30 | .10 |
| ❏ 206 | Dale Carter | .15 | .05 |
| ❏ 207 | Chris Doleman | .15 | .05 |
| ❏ 208 | Keith Hamilton | .15 | .05 |
| ❏ 209 | Andy Harmon | .15 | .05 |
| ❏ 210 | John Friesz | .30 | .10 |
| ❏ 211 | Steve Bono | .30 | .10 |
| ❏ 212 | Mark Rypien | .15 | .05 |
| ❏ 213 | Ricky Sanders | .15 | .05 |
| ❏ 214 | Michael Haynes | .30 | .10 |
| ❏ 215 | Todd McNair | .15 | .05 |
| ❏ 216 | Leon Lett | .15 | .05 |
| ❏ 217 | Scott Mitchell | .30 | .10 |
| ❏ 218 | Mike Morris RC | .15 | .05 |
| ❏ 219 | Darrin Smith | .15 | .05 |
| ❏ 220 | Jim McMahon | .30 | .10 |
| ❏ 221 | Garrison Hearst | .50 | .20 |
| ❏ 222 | Leroy Thompson | .15 | .05 |
| ❏ 223 | Darren Carrington | .15 | .05 |
| ❏ 224 | Pete Stoyanovich | .15 | .05 |
| ❏ 225 | Chris Miller | .30 | .10 |
| ❏ 226 | Bruce Smith SP | .15 | .10 |
| ❏ 227 | Simon Fletcher SP | .15 | .05 |
| ❏ 228 | Reggie White SP | .50 | .20 |
| ❏ 229 | Neil Smith SP | .30 | .10 |
| ❏ 230 | Chris Doleman SP | .15 | .05 |
| ❏ 231 | Keith Hamilton SP | .15 | .05 |
| ❏ 232 | Dana Stubblefield SP | .15 | .05 |
| ❏ 233 | Erric Pegram GA | .15 | .05 |
| ❏ 234 | Thurman Thomas GA | .50 | .20 |
| ❏ 235 | Lewis Tillman GA | .15 | .05 |
| ❏ 236 | Harold Green GA | .15 | .05 |
| ❏ 237 | Eric Metcalf GA | .30 | .10 |
| ❏ 238 | Emmitt Smith GA | 3.00 | 1.25 |
| ❏ 239 | Glyn Milburn GA | .30 | .10 |
| ❏ 240 | Barry Sanders GA | 3.00 | 1.25 |
| ❏ 241 | Edgar Bennett GA | .30 | .10 |
| ❏ 242 | Gary Brown GA | .15 | .05 |
| ❏ 243 | Roosevelt Potts GA | .15 | .05 |
| ❏ 244 | Marcus Allen GA | .50 | .20 |
| ❏ 245 | Greg Robinson GA | .15 | .05 |
| ❏ 246 | Jerome Bettis GA | .75 | .30 |
| ❏ 247 | Keith Byars GA | .15 | .05 |
| ❏ 248 | Robert Smith GA | .50 | .20 |
| ❏ 249 | Leonard Russell GA | .15 | .05 |
| ❏ 250 | Derek Brown RBK GA | .15 | .05 |
| ❏ 251 | Rodney Hampton GA | .30 | .10 |
| ❏ 252 | Johnny Johnson GA | .15 | .05 |
| ❏ 253 | Vaughn Hebron GA | .15 | .05 |
| ❏ 254 | Ronald Moore GA | .15 | .05 |
| ❏ 255 | Barry Foster GA | .15 | .05 |
| ❏ 256 | Natrone Means GA | .50 | .20 |
| ❏ 257 | Ricky Watters GA | .30 | .10 |
| ❏ 258 | Chris Warren GA | .50 | .20 |
| ❏ 259 | Vince Workman GA | .15 | .05 |
| ❏ 260 | Reggie Brooks GA | .15 | .05 |
| ❏ 261 | Carolina Panthers | .40 | .15 |
| ❏ 262 | Jacksonville Jaguars | .40 | .15 |
| ❏ 263 | Troy Aikman SB | 1.00 | .40 |
| ❏ 264 | Barry Sanders SB | 1.50 | .60 |
| ❏ 265 | Emmitt Smith SB | 1.50 | .60 |
| ❏ 266 | Michael Irvin SB | .50 | .20 |
| ❏ 267 | Jerry Rice SB | 1.00 | .40 |
| ❏ 268 | Shannon Sharpe SB | .30 | .10 |
| ❏ 269 | Bob Kratch SB | .15 | .05 |
| ❏ 270 | Howard Ballard SB | .15 | .05 |
| ❏ 271 | Erik Williams SB | .15 | .05 |
| ❏ 272 | Guy McIntyre SB | .15 | .05 |
| ❏ 273 | Kevin Williams WR SB | .30 | .10 |
| ❏ 274 | Mel Gray SB | .15 | .05 |
| ❏ 275 | Eddie Murray SB | .15 | .05 |
| ❏ 276 | Mark Stepnoski SB | .15 | .05 |
| ❏ 277 | Tommy Barnhardt SB | .15 | .05 |
| ❏ 278 | Derrick Thomas SB | .30 | .10 |
| ❏ 279 | Ken Norton Jr. SB | .30 | .10 |
| ❏ 280 | Chris Spielman SB | .15 | .05 |
| ❏ 281 | Deion Sanders SB | .50 | .20 |
| ❏ 282 | Mark Collins SB | .15 | .05 |
| ❏ 283 | Bruce Smith SB | .30 | .10 |
| ❏ 284 | Reggie White SB | .50 | .20 |
| ❏ 285 | Sean Gilbert SB | .15 | .05 |
| ❏ 286 | Cortez Kennedy SB | .30 | .10 |
| ❏ 287 | Steve Atwater SB | .15 | .05 |
| ❏ 288 | Tim McDonald SB | .15 | .05 |
| ❏ 289 | Jerome Bettis SB | .75 | .30 |
| ❏ 290 | Dana Stubblefield SB | .30 | .10 |
| ❏ 291 | Bert Emanuel RC | .50 | .20 |
| ❏ 292 | Jeff Burris RC | .30 | .10 |
| ❏ 293 | Bucky Brooks RC | .15 | .05 |
| ❏ 294 | Dan Wilkinson RC | .30 | .10 |
| ❏ 295 | Darnay Scott RC | 1.00 | .40 |
| ❏ 296 | Derrick Alexander WR RC | .50 | .20 |
| ❏ 297 | Antonio Langham RC | .30 | .10 |
| ❏ 298 | Shante Carver RC | .15 | .05 |
| ❏ 299 | Shelby Hill RC | .15 | .05 |
| ❏ 300 | Larry Allen RC | .50 | .20 |
| ❏ 301 | Johnnie Morton RC | 2.00 | .75 |
| ❏ 302 | Van Malone RC | .15 | .05 |
| ❏ 303 | Aaron Taylor RC | .15 | .05 |
| ❏ 304 | Marshall Faulk RC | 6.00 | 2.50 |
| ❏ 305 | Eric Mahlum RC | .15 | .05 |
| ❏ 306 | Trev Alberts RC | .30 | .10 |
| ❏ 307 | Greg Hill RC | .50 | .20 |
| ❏ 308 | Donnell Bennett RC | .30 | .10 |
| ❏ 309 | Rob Fredrickson RC | .30 | .10 |
| ❏ 310 | James Folston RC | .15 | .05 |
| ❏ 311 | Isaac Bruce RC | 5.00 | 2.00 |
| ❏ 312 | Tim Ruddy RC | .15 | .05 |
| ❏ 313 | Aubrey Beavers RC | .15 | .05 |
| ❏ 314 | David Palmer RC | .50 | .20 |
| ❏ 315 | Dewayne Washington RC | .30 | .10 |

|  | | |
|---|---|---|
| ☐ 316 Willie McGinest RC | .50 | .20 |
| ☐ 317 Mario Bates RC | .50 | .20 |
| ☐ 318 Kevin Lee RC | .15 | .05 |
| ☐ 319 Jason Sehorn RC | .75 | .30 |
| ☐ 320 Thomas Randolph RC | .15 | .05 |
| ☐ 321 Ryan Yarborough RC | .15 | .05 |
| ☐ 322 Bernard Williams RC | .15 | .05 |
| ☐ 323 Chuck Levy RC | .15 | .05 |
| ☐ 324 Jamir Miller RC | .30 | .10 |
| ☐ 325 Charles Johnson RC | .50 | .20 |
| ☐ 326 Bryant Young RC | .75 | .30 |
| ☐ 327 William Floyd RC | .50 | .20 |
| ☐ 328 Kevin Mitchell RC | .15 | .05 |
| ☐ 329 Sam Adams RC | .30 | .10 |
| ☐ 330 Kevin Mawae RC | .50 | .20 |
| ☐ 331 Errict Rhett RC | .50 | .20 |
| ☐ 332 Trent Dilfer RC | 1.50 | .60 |
| ☐ 333 Heath Shuler RC | .50 | .20 |
| ☐ 334 Aaron Glenn RC | .50 | .20 |
| ☐ 335 Todd Steussie RC | .30 | .10 |
| ☐ 336 Toby Wright RC | .15 | .05 |
| ☐ NNO Gale Sayers Play.Club | 4.00 | 1.50 |
| ☐ NNO Gale Sayers AUTO | 60.00 | 25.00 |

## 1993 Playoff Contenders

|  | | |
|---|---|---|
| ☐ COMPLETE SET (150) | 20.00 | 7.50 |
| ☐ 1 Brett Favre | 3.00 | 1.50 |
| ☐ 2 Thurman Thomas | .40 | .15 |
| ☐ 3 Barry Word | .10 | .02 |
| ☐ 4 Herman Moore | .40 | .15 |
| ☐ 5 Reggie Langhorne | .10 | .02 |
| ☐ 6 Wilber Marshall | .10 | .02 |
| ☐ 7 Ricky Watters | .40 | .15 |
| ☐ 8 Marcus Allen | .40 | .15 |
| ☐ 9 Jeff Hostetler | .20 | .07 |
| ☐ 10 Steve Young | 1.00 | .40 |
| ☐ 11 Bobby Hebert | .10 | .02 |
| ☐ 12 David Klingler | .20 | .07 |
| ☐ 13 Craig Heyward | .20 | .07 |
| ☐ 14 Andre Reed | .20 | .07 |
| ☐ 15 Tommy Vardell | .10 | .02 |
| ☐ 16 Anthony Carter | .20 | .07 |
| ☐ 17 Mel Gray | .20 | .07 |
| ☐ 18 Dan Marino | 2.50 | 1.00 |
| ☐ 19 Haywood Jeffires | .20 | .07 |
| ☐ 20 Joe Montana | 2.50 | 1.00 |
| ☐ 21 Tim Brown | .40 | .15 |
| ☐ 22 Jim McMahon | .20 | .07 |
| ☐ 23 Scott Mitchell | .40 | .15 |
| ☐ 24 Rickey Jackson | .10 | .02 |
| ☐ 25 Troy Aikman | 1.50 | .60 |
| ☐ 26 Rodney Hampton | .20 | .07 |
| ☐ 27 Fred Barnett | .20 | .07 |
| ☐ 28 Gary Clark | .20 | .07 |
| ☐ 29 Barry Foster | .20 | .07 |
| ☐ 30 Brian Blades | .20 | .07 |
| ☐ 31 Tim McDonald | .10 | .02 |
| ☐ 32 Kelvin Martin | .10 | .02 |
| ☐ 33 Henry Jones | .10 | .02 |
| ☐ 34 Erric Pegram | .20 | .07 |
| ☐ 35 Don Beebe | .10 | .02 |
| ☐ 36 Eric Metcalf | .20 | .07 |
| ☐ 37 Charles Haley | .20 | .07 |
| ☐ 38 Robert Delpino | .10 | .02 |
| ☐ 39 Leonard Russell UER | .10 | .02 |
| ☐ 40 Jackie Harris | .10 | .02 |
| ☐ 41 Ernest Givins | .20 | .07 |
| ☐ 42 Willie Davis | .40 | .15 |

|  | | |
|---|---|---|
| ☐ 43 Alexander Wright | .10 | .02 |
| ☐ 44 Keith Byars | .10 | .02 |
| ☐ 45 Dave Meggett | .10 | .02 |
| ☐ 46 Johnny Johnson | .10 | .02 |
| ☐ 47 Mark Bavaro | .10 | .02 |
| ☐ 48 Seth Joyner | .10 | .02 |
| ☐ 49 Junior Seau | .40 | .15 |
| ☐ 50 Emmitt Smith | 2.50 | 1.25 |
| ☐ 51 Shannon Sharpe | .40 | .15 |
| ☐ 52 Rodney Peete | .10 | .02 |
| ☐ 53 Andre Rison | .20 | .07 |
| ☐ 54 Cornelius Bennett | .20 | .07 |
| ☐ 55 Mark Carrier WR | .20 | .07 |
| ☐ 56 Mark Clayton | .10 | .02 |
| ☐ 57 Warren Moon | .40 | .15 |
| ☐ 58 J.J. Birden | .10 | .02 |
| ☐ 59 Howie Long | .40 | .15 |
| ☐ 60 Irving Fryar | .20 | .07 |
| ☐ 61 Mark Jackson | .10 | .02 |
| ☐ 62 Eric Martin | .10 | .02 |
| ☐ 63 Herschel Walker | .20 | .07 |
| ☐ 64 Cortez Kennedy | .20 | .07 |
| ☐ 65 Steve Beuerlein | .20 | .07 |
| ☐ 66 Jim Kelly | .40 | .15 |
| ☐ 67 Bernie Kosar Cowboys | .20 | .07 |
| ☐ 68 Pat Swilling | .10 | .02 |
| ☐ 69 Michael Irvin | .40 | .15 |
| ☐ 70 Harvey Williams | .20 | .07 |
| ☐ 71 Steve Smith | .10 | .02 |
| ☐ 72 Wade Wilson | .10 | .02 |
| ☐ 73 Phil Simms | .20 | .07 |
| ☐ 74 Vinny Testaverde | .20 | .07 |
| ☐ 75 Barry Sanders | 2.50 | 1.00 |
| ☐ 76 Ken Norton Jr. | .20 | .07 |
| ☐ 77 Rod Woodson | .40 | .15 |
| ☐ 78 Webster Slaughter | .10 | .02 |
| ☐ 79 Derrick Thomas | .40 | .15 |
| ☐ 80 Mike Sherrard | .10 | .02 |
| ☐ 81 Calvin Williams | .20 | .07 |
| ☐ 82 Jay Novacek | .20 | .07 |
| ☐ 83 Michael Brooks | .10 | .02 |
| ☐ 84 Randall Cunningham | .40 | .15 |
| ☐ 85 Chris Warren | .20 | .07 |
| ☐ 86 Johnny Mitchell | .10 | .02 |
| ☐ 87 Jim Harbaugh | .40 | .15 |
| ☐ 88 Rod Bernstine | .10 | .02 |
| ☐ 89 John Elway | 2.50 | 1.00 |
| ☐ 90 Jerry Rice | 1.50 | .60 |
| ☐ 91 Brent Jones | .20 | .07 |
| ☐ 92 Cris Carter | .40 | .15 |
| ☐ 93 Alvin Harper | .20 | .07 |
| ☐ 94 Horace Copeland RC | .20 | .07 |
| ☐ 95 Rocket Ismail | .20 | .07 |
| ☐ 96 Darrin Smith RC | .20 | .07 |
| ☐ 97 Reggie Brooks RC | .20 | .07 |
| ☐ 98 Demetrius DuBose RC | .10 | .02 |
| ☐ 99 Eric Curry RC | .10 | .02 |
| ☐ 100 Rick Mirer RC | .40 | .15 |
| ☐ 101 Carlton Gray RC UER | .10 | .02 |
| ☐ 102 Dana Stubblefield RC | .40 | .15 |
| ☐ 103 Todd Kelly RC | .10 | .02 |
| ☐ 104 Natrone Means RC | .40 | .15 |
| ☐ 105 Darrien Gordon RC | .10 | .02 |
| ☐ 106 Deon Figures RC | .10 | .02 |
| ☐ 107 Garrison Hearst RC | 1.25 | .50 |
| ☐ 108 Ronald Moore RC | .20 | .07 |
| ☐ 109 Leonard Renfro RC | .10 | .02 |
| ☐ 110 Lester Holmes RC | .10 | .02 |
| ☐ 111 Vaughn Hebron RC | .10 | .02 |
| ☐ 112 Marvin Jones RC | .10 | .02 |
| ☐ 113 Irv Smith RC | .20 | .07 |
| ☐ 114 Willie Roaf RC | .20 | .07 |
| ☐ 115 Derek Brown RC RBK | .20 | .07 |
| ☐ 116 Vincent Brisby RC | .40 | .15 |
| ☐ 117 Drew Bledsoe RC | 4.00 | 1.50 |
| ☐ 118 Gino Torretta RC | .20 | .07 |
| ☐ 119 Robert Smith RC | 2.00 | .75 |
| ☐ 120 Qadry Ismail RC | .40 | .15 |
| ☐ 121 O.J. McDuffie RC | .40 | .15 |
| ☐ 122 Terry Kirby RC | .40 | .15 |
| ☐ 123 Troy Drayton RC | .20 | .07 |
| ☐ 124 Jerome Bettis RC | 6.00 | 2.50 |
| ☐ 125 Patrick Bates RC | .10 | .02 |
| ☐ 126 Roosevelt Potts RC | .10 | .02 |
| ☐ 127 Tom Carter RC | .20 | .07 |

|  | | |
|---|---|---|
| ☐ 128 Patrick Robinson RC | .10 | .02 |
| ☐ 129 Brad Hopkins RC | .10 | .02 |
| ☐ 130 George Teague RC | .20 | .07 |
| ☐ 131 Wayne Simmons RC | .10 | .02 |
| ☐ 132 Mark Brunell RC | 2.50 | 1.00 |
| ☐ 133 Ryan McNeil RC | .40 | .15 |
| ☐ 134 Dan Williams RC | .10 | .02 |
| ☐ 135 Glyn Milburn RC | .40 | .15 |
| ☐ 136 Kevin Williams RC WR | .40 | .15 |
| ☐ 137 Derrick Lassic RC | .10 | .02 |
| ☐ 138 Steve Everitt RC | .10 | .02 |
| ☐ 139 Lance Gunn RC | .10 | .02 |
| ☐ 140 John Copeland RC | .20 | .07 |
| ☐ 141 Curtis Conway RC | 1.00 | .40 |
| ☐ 142 Thomas Smith RC | .10 | .02 |
| ☐ 143 Russell Copeland RC | .20 | .07 |
| ☐ 144 Lincoln Kennedy RC | .10 | .02 |
| ☐ 145 Boomer Esiason CL | .10 | .02 |
| ☐ 146 Neil Smith CL | .10 | .02 |
| ☐ 147 Jack Del Rio CL | .10 | .02 |
| ☐ 148 Morten Andersen CL | .10 | .02 |
| ☐ 149 Sterling Sharpe CL | .20 | .07 |
| ☐ 150 Reggie White CL | .20 | .07 |

## 1994 Playoff Contenders

|  | | |
|---|---|---|
| ☐ COMPLETE SET (120) | 20.00 | 7.50 |
| ☐ 1 Drew Bledsoe | 1.00 | .40 |
| ☐ 2 Barry Sanders | 2.50 | 1.00 |
| ☐ 3 Jerry Rice | 1.50 | .60 |
| ☐ 4 Rod Woodson | .20 | .07 |
| ☐ 5 Irving Fryar | .20 | .07 |
| ☐ 6 Charles Haley | .20 | .07 |
| ☐ 7 Chris Warren | .20 | .07 |
| ☐ 8 Craig Erickson | .10 | .02 |
| ☐ 9 Eric Metcalf | .20 | .07 |
| ☐ 10 Marcus Allen | .40 | .15 |
| ☐ 11 Chris Miller | .20 | .07 |
| ☐ 12 Andre Rison | .20 | .07 |
| ☐ 13 Art Monk | .20 | .07 |
| ☐ 14 Calvin Williams | .20 | .07 |
| ☐ 15 Shannon Sharpe | .20 | .07 |
| ☐ 16 Rodney Hampton | .20 | .07 |
| ☐ 17 Marion Butts | .10 | .02 |
| ☐ 18 John Jurkovic RC | .20 | .07 |
| ☐ 19 Jim Kelly | .40 | .15 |
| ☐ 20 Emmitt Smith | 2.50 | 1.00 |
| ☐ 21 Jeff Hostetler | .20 | .07 |
| ☐ 22 Barry Foster | .10 | .02 |
| ☐ 23 Boomer Esiason | .20 | .07 |
| ☐ 24 Jim Harbaugh | .40 | .15 |
| ☐ 25 Joe Montana | 3.00 | 1.25 |
| ☐ 26 Jeff George | .20 | .07 |
| ☐ 27 Warren Moon | .40 | .15 |
| ☐ 28 Steve Young | 1.25 | .50 |
| ☐ 29 Randall Cunningham | .40 | .15 |
| ☐ 30 Shawn Jefferson | .10 | .02 |
| ☐ 31 Cortez Kennedy | .20 | .07 |
| ☐ 32 Reggie Brooks | .20 | .07 |
| ☐ 33 Alvin Harper | .20 | .07 |
| ☐ 34 Brent Jones | .20 | .07 |
| ☐ 35 O.J. McDuffie | .40 | .15 |
| ☐ 36 Jerome Bettis | .60 | .25 |
| ☐ 37 Daryl Johnston | .20 | .07 |
| ☐ 38 Herman Moore | .40 | .15 |
| ☐ 39 Reggie White | .40 | .15 |
| ☐ 40 Reggie White | .40 | .15 |
| ☐ 41 Junior Seau | .40 | .15 |
| ☐ 42 Dan Marino | 3.00 | 1.25 |

| | | |
|---|---|---|
| ❏ 43 Scott Mitchell | .20 | .07 |
| ❏ 44 John Elway | 3.00 | 1.25 |
| ❏ 45 Troy Aikman | 1.50 | .60 |
| ❏ 46 Terry Allen | .20 | .07 |
| ❏ 47 David Klingler | .10 | .02 |
| ❏ 48 Stan Humphries | .20 | .07 |
| ❏ 49 Rick Mirer | .40 | .15 |
| ❏ 50 Neil O'Donnell | .40 | .15 |
| ❏ 51 Keith Jackson | .10 | .02 |
| ❏ 52 Ricky Watters | .20 | .07 |
| ❏ 53 Dave Brown | .20 | .07 |
| ❏ 54 Neil Smith | .20 | .07 |
| ❏ 55 Johnny Mitchell | .10 | .02 |
| ❏ 56 Jackie Harris | .10 | .02 |
| ❏ 57 Terry Kirby | .40 | .15 |
| ❏ 58 Willie Davis | .20 | .07 |
| ❏ 59 Rob Moore | .20 | .07 |
| ❏ 60 Nate Newton | .10 | .02 |
| ❏ 61 Deion Sanders | .75 | .30 |
| ❏ 62 John Taylor | .20 | .07 |
| ❏ 63 Sterling Sharpe | .20 | .07 |
| ❏ 64 Natrone Means | .40 | .15 |
| ❏ 65 Steve Beuerlein | .20 | .07 |
| ❏ 66 Erik Kramer | .20 | .07 |
| ❏ 67 Qadry Ismail | .40 | .15 |
| ❏ 68 Johnny Johnson | .10 | .02 |
| ❏ 69 Herschel Walker | .20 | .07 |
| ❏ 70 Mark Stepnoski | .10 | .02 |
| ❏ 71 Brett Favre | 3.00 | 1.25 |
| ❏ 72 Dana Stubblefield | .20 | .07 |
| ❏ 73 Bruce Smith | .40 | .15 |
| ❏ 74 Leroy Hoard | .10 | .02 |
| ❏ 75 Steve Walsh | .10 | .02 |
| ❏ 76 Jay Novacek | .20 | .07 |
| ❏ 77 Derrick Thomas | .40 | .15 |
| ❏ 78 Keith Byars | .10 | .02 |
| ❏ 79 Ben Coates | .20 | .07 |
| ❏ 80 Lorenzo Neal | .10 | .02 |
| ❏ 81 Ronnie Lott | .20 | .07 |
| ❏ 82 Tim Brown | .40 | .15 |
| ❏ 83 Michael Irvin | .40 | .15 |
| ❏ 84 Ronald Moore | .10 | .02 |
| ❏ 85 Andre Reed | .20 | .07 |
| ❏ 86 James Jett | .10 | .02 |
| ❏ 87 Curtis Conway | .40 | .15 |
| ❏ 88 Bernie Parmalee RC | .40 | .15 |
| ❏ 89 Keith Cash | .10 | .02 |
| ❏ 90 Russell Copeland | .10 | .02 |
| ❏ 91 Kevin Williams WR | .20 | .07 |
| ❏ 92 Gary Brown | .10 | .02 |
| ❏ 93 Thurman Thomas | .40 | .15 |
| ❏ 94 Jamir Miller RC | .20 | .07 |
| ❏ 95 Bert Emanuel RC | .40 | .15 |
| ❏ 96 Bucky Brooks RC | .10 | .02 |
| ❏ 97 Jeff Burris RC | .20 | .07 |
| ❏ 98 Antonio Langham RC | .20 | .07 |
| ❏ 99 Derrick Alexander WR RC | .40 | .15 |
| ❏ 100 Dan Wilkinson RC | .20 | .07 |
| ❏ 101 Shante Carver RC | .10 | .02 |
| ❏ 102 Johnnie Morton RC | 2.00 | .75 |
| ❏ 103 LeShon Johnson RC | .20 | .07 |
| ❏ 104 Marshall Faulk RC | 6.00 | 2.50 |
| ❏ 105 Greg Hill RC | .40 | .15 |
| ❏ 106 Lake Dawson RC | .20 | .07 |
| ❏ 107 Irving Spikes RC | .20 | .07 |
| ❏ 108 David Palmer RC | .40 | .15 |
| ❏ 109 Willie McGinest RC | .40 | .15 |
| ❏ 110 Joe Johnson RC | .10 | .02 |
| ❏ 111 Aaron Glenn RC | .40 | .15 |
| ❏ 112 Charlie Garner RC | 1.50 | .60 |
| ❏ 113 Charles Johnson RC | .40 | .15 |
| ❏ 114 Byron Bam Morris RC | .20 | .07 |
| ❏ 115 Bryant Young RC | .60 | .25 |
| ❏ 116 William Floyd RC | .40 | .15 |
| ❏ 117 Trent Dilfer RC | 1.50 | .60 |
| ❏ 118 Errict Rhett RC | .40 | .15 |
| ❏ 119 Heath Shuler RC | .40 | .15 |
| ❏ 120 Gus Frerotte RC | 2.00 | .75 |

## 1995 Playoff Contenders

| | | |
|---|---|---|
| ❏ COMPLETE SET (150) | 25.00 | 10.00 |
| ❏ 1 Steve Young | 1.00 | .40 |
| ❏ 2 Jeff Blake RC | .75 | .30 |
| ❏ 3 Rick Mirer | .20 | .07 |
| ❏ 4 Brett Favre | 2.50 | 1.25 |

| | | |
|---|---|---|
| ❏ 5 Heath Shuler | .20 | .07 |
| ❏ 6 Steve Bono | .20 | .07 |
| ❏ 7 John Elway | 2.50 | 1.00 |
| ❏ 8 Troy Aikman | 1.25 | .50 |
| ❏ 9 Rodney Peete | .10 | .02 |
| ❏ 10 Gus Frerotte | .20 | .07 |
| ❏ 11 Drew Bledsoe | .75 | .30 |
| ❏ 12 Jim Kelly | .40 | .15 |
| ❏ 13 Dan Marino | 2.50 | 1.00 |
| ❏ 14 Errict Rhett | .20 | .07 |
| ❏ 15 Jeff Hostetler | .20 | .07 |
| ❏ 16 Erik Kramer | .10 | .02 |
| ❏ 17 Jim Everett | .10 | .02 |
| ❏ 18 Elvis Grbac | .40 | .15 |
| ❏ 19 Scott Mitchell | .20 | .07 |
| ❏ 20 Barry Sanders | 2.00 | .75 |
| ❏ 21 Deion Sanders | .75 | .30 |
| ❏ 22 Emmitt Smith | 2.00 | .75 |
| ❏ 23 Garrison Hearst | .40 | .15 |
| ❏ 24 Mario Bates | .20 | .07 |
| ❏ 25 Mark Brunell | .75 | .30 |
| ❏ 26 Robert Smith | .40 | .15 |
| ❏ 27 Rodney Hampton | .20 | .07 |
| ❏ 28 Marshall Faulk | 1.50 | .60 |
| ❏ 29 Greg Hill | .20 | .07 |
| ❏ 30 Bernie Parmalee | .20 | .07 |
| ❏ 31 Natrone Means | .20 | .07 |
| ❏ 32 Marcus Allen | .40 | .15 |
| ❏ 33 Byron Bam Morris | .10 | .02 |
| ❏ 34 Edgar Bennett | .20 | .07 |
| ❏ 35 Vincent Brisby | .10 | .02 |
| ❏ 36 Jerome Bettis | .40 | .15 |
| ❏ 37 Craig Heyward | .20 | .07 |
| ❏ 38 Anthony Miller | .20 | .07 |
| ❏ 39 Curtis Conway | .40 | .15 |
| ❏ 40 William Floyd | .20 | .07 |
| ❏ 41 Chris Warren | .20 | .07 |
| ❏ 42 Terry Kirby | .20 | .07 |
| ❏ 43 Herschel Walker | .20 | .07 |
| ❏ 44 Eric Metcalf | .20 | .07 |
| ❏ 45 Darnay Scott | .40 | .15 |
| ❏ 46 Jackie Harris | .10 | .02 |
| ❏ 47 Dana Stubblefield | .20 | .07 |
| ❏ 48 Daryl Johnston | .20 | .07 |
| ❏ 49 Dave Meggett | .10 | .02 |
| ❏ 50 Ricky Watters | .20 | .07 |
| ❏ 51 Ken Norton | .20 | .07 |
| ❏ 52 Boomer Esiason | .20 | .07 |
| ❏ 53 Lake Dawson | .20 | .07 |
| ❏ 54 Eric Green | .10 | .02 |
| ❏ 55 Junior Seau | .40 | .15 |
| ❏ 56 Yancey Thigpen RC | .40 | .15 |
| ❏ 57 James Jett | .20 | .07 |
| ❏ 58 Leonard Russell | .10 | .02 |
| ❏ 59 Brent Jones | .10 | .02 |
| ❏ 60 Trent Dilfer | .40 | .15 |
| ❏ 61 Terance Mathis | .20 | .07 |
| ❏ 62 Jeff George | .20 | .07 |
| ❏ 63 Alvin Harper | .10 | .02 |
| ❏ 64 Terry Allen | .20 | .07 |
| ❏ 65 Stan Humphries | .20 | .07 |
| ❏ 66 Robert Green | .10 | .02 |
| ❏ 67 Bryce Paup | .20 | .07 |
| ❏ 68 Tamarick Vanover RC | .40 | .15 |
| ❏ 69 Desmond Howard | .20 | .07 |
| ❏ 70 Derek Loville | .10 | .02 |
| ❏ 71 Dave Brown | .20 | .07 |
| ❏ 72 Carl Pickens | .20 | .07 |

| | | |
|---|---|---|
| ❏ 73 Gary Clark | .10 | .02 |
| ❏ 74 Gary Brown | .10 | .02 |
| ❏ 75 Brett Perriman | .20 | .07 |
| ❏ 76 Charlie Garner | .40 | .15 |
| ❏ 77 Ben Coates | .20 | .07 |
| ❏ 78 Bruce Smith | .40 | .15 |
| ❏ 79 Erric Pegram | .20 | .07 |
| ❏ 80 Jerry Rice | 1.25 | .50 |
| ❏ 81 Tim Brown | .40 | .15 |
| ❏ 82 John Taylor | .10 | .02 |
| ❏ 83 Will Moore | .10 | .02 |
| ❏ 84 Jay Novacek | .20 | .07 |
| ❏ 85 Kevin Williams | .20 | .07 |
| ❏ 86 Rocket Ismail | .20 | .07 |
| ❏ 87 Robert Brooks | .40 | .15 |
| ❏ 88 Michael Irvin | .40 | .15 |
| ❏ 89 Mark Chmura | .40 | .15 |
| ❏ 90 Shannon Sharpe | .20 | .07 |
| ❏ 91 Henry Ellard | .20 | .07 |
| ❏ 92 Reggie White | .40 | .15 |
| ❏ 93 Isaac Bruce | .75 | .30 |
| ❏ 94 Charles Haley | .20 | .07 |
| ❏ 95 Jake Reed | .20 | .07 |
| ❏ 96 Pete Metzelaars | .10 | .02 |
| ❏ 97 Dave Krieg | .10 | .02 |
| ❏ 98 Tony Martin | .20 | .07 |
| ❏ 99 Charles Jordan RC | .20 | .07 |
| ❏ 100 Bert Emanuel | .40 | .15 |
| ❏ 101 Andre Rison | .20 | .07 |
| ❏ 102 Jeff Graham | .10 | .02 |
| ❏ 103 O.J. McDuffie | .40 | .15 |
| ❏ 104 Randall Cunningham | .40 | .15 |
| ❏ 105 Harvey Williams | .10 | .02 |
| ❏ 106 Cris Carter | .40 | .15 |
| ❏ 107 Irving Fryar | .20 | .07 |
| ❏ 108 Jim Harbaugh | .20 | .07 |
| ❏ 109 Bernie Kosar | .10 | .02 |
| ❏ 110 Charles Johnson | .20 | .07 |
| ❏ 111 Warren Moon | .20 | .07 |
| ❏ 112 Neil O'Donnell | .20 | .07 |
| ❏ 113 Fred Barnett | .20 | .07 |
| ❏ 114 Herman Moore | .40 | .15 |
| ❏ 115 Chris Miller | .10 | .02 |
| ❏ 116 Vinny Testaverde | .20 | .07 |
| ❏ 117 Craig Erickson | .10 | .02 |
| ❏ 118 Qadry Ismail | .20 | .07 |
| ❏ 119 Willie Davis | .20 | .07 |
| ❏ 120 Michael Jackson | .20 | .07 |
| ❏ 121 Stoney Case RC | .40 | .15 |
| ❏ 122 Frank Sanders | .40 | .15 |
| ❏ 123 Todd Collins RC | 2.50 | 1.00 |
| ❏ 124 Kerry Collins RC | 2.00 | .75 |
| ❏ 125 Sherman Williams RC | .10 | .02 |
| ❏ 126 Terrell Davis RC | 2.50 | 1.00 |
| ❏ 127 Luther Elliss RC | .10 | .02 |
| ❏ 128 Steve McNair RC | 3.00 | 1.25 |
| ❏ 129 Chris Sanders RC | .40 | .15 |
| ❏ 130 Ki-Jana Carter RC | .40 | .15 |
| ❏ 131 Rodney Thomas RC | .40 | .15 |
| ❏ 132 Tony Boselli RC | .40 | .15 |
| ❏ 133 Rob Johnson RC | 1.00 | .40 |
| ❏ 134 James O. Stewart RC | 1.25 | .50 |
| ❏ 135 Chad May RC | .10 | .02 |
| ❏ 136 Eric Bjornson RC | .20 | .07 |
| ❏ 137 Tyrone Wheatley RC | 1.25 | .50 |
| ❏ 138 Kyle Brady RC | .40 | .15 |
| ❏ 139 Curtis Martin RC | 3.00 | 1.25 |
| ❏ 140 Eric Zeier RC | .40 | .15 |
| ❏ 141 Ray Zellars RC | .20 | .07 |
| ❏ 142 Napoleon Kaufman RC | 1.25 | .50 |
| ❏ 143 Mike Mamula RC | .20 | .07 |
| ❏ 144 Mark Bruener RC | .20 | .07 |
| ❏ 145 Kordell Stewart RC | 1.50 | .60 |
| ❏ 146 J.J. Stokes RC | .40 | .15 |
| ❏ 147 Joey Galloway RC | 1.50 | .60 |
| ❏ 148 Warren Sapp RC | 1.50 | .60 |
| ❏ 149 Michael Westbrook RC | .40 | .15 |
| ❏ 150 Rashaan Salaam RC | .40 | .15 |

## 1997 Playoff Contenders

| | | |
|---|---|---|
| ❏ COMPLETE SET (150) | 40.00 | 15.00 |
| ❏ 1 Kent Graham | .40 | .15 |
| ❏ 2 Leeland McElroy | .20 | .07 |
| ❏ 3 Rob Moore | .60 | .25 |
| ❏ 4 Frank Sanders | .60 | .25 |

|  |  | | |
|---|--------|------|------|
| 5 | Jake Plummer RC | 5.00 | 2.00 |
| 6 | Chris Chandler | .60 | .25 |
| 7 | Bert Emanuel | .60 | .25 |
| 8 | O.J. Santiago RC | .60 | .25 |
| 9 | Byron Hanspard RC | .60 | .25 |
| 10 | Vinny Testaverde | .60 | .25 |
| 11 | Michael Jackson | .60 | .25 |
| 12 | Earnest Byner | .40 | .15 |
| 13 | Jermaine Lewis | 1.00 | .40 |
| 14 | Derrick Alexander WR | .60 | .25 |
| 15 | Jay Graham RC | .60 | .25 |
| 16 | Todd Collins | .40 | .15 |
| 17 | Thurman Thomas | 1.00 | .40 |
| 18 | Bruce Smith | .60 | .25 |
| 19 | Andre Reed | .60 | .25 |
| 20 | Quinn Early | .40 | .15 |
| 21 | Antowain Smith RC | 2.50 | 1.00 |
| 22 | Kerry Collins | 1.00 | .40 |
| 23 | Tim Biakabutuka | .60 | .25 |
| 24 | Anthony Johnson | .40 | .15 |
| 25 | Wesley Walls | .60 | .25 |
| 26 | Fred Lane RC | .60 | .25 |
| 27 | Rae Carruth RC | .40 | .15 |
| 28 | Raymont Harris | .40 | .15 |
| 29 | Rick Mirer | .40 | .15 |
| 30 | Darnell Autry RC | .60 | .25 |
| 31 | Jeff Blake | .60 | .25 |
| 32 | Ki-Jana Carter | .40 | .15 |
| 33 | Carl Pickens | .60 | .25 |
| 34 | Darnay Scott | .60 | .25 |
| 35 | Corey Dillon RC | 6.00 | 2.50 |
| 36 | Troy Aikman | 2.00 | .75 |
| 37 | Emmitt Smith | 3.00 | 1.25 |
| 38 | Michael Irvin | 1.00 | .40 |
| 39 | Deion Sanders | 1.00 | .40 |
| 40 | Anthony Miller | .40 | .15 |
| 41 | Eric Bjornson | .40 | .15 |
| 42 | David LaFleur RC | .40 | .15 |
| 43 | John Elway | 4.00 | 1.50 |
| 44 | Terrell Davis | 1.25 | .50 |
| 45 | Shannon Sharpe | .60 | .25 |
| 46 | Ed McCaffrey | .60 | .25 |
| 47 | Rod Smith WR | 1.00 | .40 |
| 48 | Scott Mitchell | .60 | .25 |
| 49 | Barry Sanders | 3.00 | 1.25 |
| 50 | Herman Moore | .60 | .25 |
| 51 | Brett Favre | 4.00 | 1.50 |
| 52 | Dorsey Levens | 1.00 | .40 |
| 53 | William Henderson | .60 | .25 |
| 54 | Derrick Mayes | .60 | .25 |
| 55 | Antonio Freeman | 1.00 | .40 |
| 56 | Robert Brooks | .60 | .25 |
| 57 | Mark Chmura | .60 | .25 |
| 58 | Reggie White | 1.00 | .40 |
| 59 | Darren Sharper RC | 1.00 | .40 |
| 60 | Jim Harbaugh | .60 | .25 |
| 61 | Marshall Faulk | 1.25 | .50 |
| 62 | Marvin Harrison | 1.00 | .40 |
| 63 | Mark Brunell | 1.25 | .50 |
| 64 | Natrone Means | .60 | .25 |
| 65 | Jimmy Smith | .60 | .25 |
| 66 | Keenan McCardell | .60 | .25 |
| 67 | Elvis Grbac | .60 | .25 |
| 68 | Greg Hill | .40 | .15 |
| 69 | Marcus Allen | 1.00 | .40 |
| 70 | Andre Rison | .60 | .25 |
| 71 | Kimble Anders | .60 | .25 |
| 72 | Tony Gonzalez RC | 3.00 | 1.25 |
| 73 | Pat Barnes RC | 1.00 | .40 |
| 74 | Dan Marino | 4.00 | 1.50 |
| 75 | Karim Abdul-Jabbar | .60 | .25 |
| 76 | Zach Thomas | 1.00 | .40 |
| 77 | O.J. McDuffie | .60 | .25 |
| 78 | Brian Manning RC | .40 | .15 |
| 79 | Brad Johnson | 1.00 | .40 |
| 80 | Cris Carter | 1.00 | .40 |
| 81 | Jake Reed | .60 | .25 |
| 82 | Robert Smith | .60 | .25 |
| 83 | Drew Bledsoe | 1.25 | .50 |
| 84 | Curtis Martin | 1.25 | .50 |
| 85 | Ben Coates | .60 | .25 |
| 86 | Terry Glenn | 1.00 | .40 |
| 87 | Shawn Jefferson | .40 | .15 |
| 88 | Heath Shuler | .40 | .15 |
| 89 | Mario Bates | .40 | .15 |
| 90 | Andre Hastings | .40 | .15 |
| 91 | Troy Davis RC | .60 | .25 |
| 92 | Danny Wuerffel RC | .60 | .25 |
| 93 | Dave Brown | .40 | .15 |
| 94 | Chris Calloway | .40 | .15 |
| 95 | Tiki Barber RC | 6.00 | 2.50 |
| 96 | Mike Cherry RC | .40 | .15 |
| 97 | Neil O'Donnell | .60 | .25 |
| 98 | Keyshawn Johnson | 1.00 | .40 |
| 99 | Adrian Murrell | .60 | .25 |
| 100 | Wayne Chrebet | 1.00 | .40 |
| 101 | Dedric Ward RC | .60 | .25 |
| 102 | Leon Johnson RC | .60 | .25 |
| 103 | Jeff George | .60 | .25 |
| 104 | Napoleon Kaufman | 1.00 | .40 |
| 105 | Tim Brown | 1.00 | .40 |
| 106 | James Jett | .60 | .25 |
| 107 | Ty Detmer | .60 | .25 |
| 108 | Ricky Watters | .60 | .25 |
| 109 | Irving Fryar | .60 | .25 |
| 110 | Michael Timpson | .40 | .15 |
| 111 | Chad Lewis RC | 2.00 | .75 |
| 112 | Kordell Stewart | 1.00 | .40 |
| 113 | Jerome Bettis | 1.00 | .40 |
| 114 | Charles Johnson | .60 | .25 |
| 115 | George Jones RC | .60 | .25 |
| 116 | Will Blackwell RC | .60 | .25 |
| 117 | Stan Humphries | .60 | .25 |
| 118 | Junior Seau | 1.00 | .40 |
| 119 | Freddie Jones RC | .60 | .25 |
| 120 | Steve Young | 1.25 | .50 |
| 121 | Jerry Rice | 2.00 | .75 |
| 122 | Garrison Hearst | .60 | .25 |
| 123 | William Floyd | .60 | .25 |
| 124 | Terrell Owens | 1.25 | .50 |
| 125 | J.J. Stokes | .60 | .25 |
| 126 | Marc Edwards RC | .40 | .15 |
| 127 | Jim Druckenmiller RC | .60 | .25 |
| 128 | Warren Moon | 1.00 | .40 |
| 129 | Chris Warren | .60 | .25 |
| 130 | Joey Galloway | .60 | .25 |
| 131 | Shawn Springs RC | .60 | .25 |
| 132 | Tony Banks | .60 | .25 |
| 133 | Lawrence Phillips | .40 | .15 |
| 134 | Isaac Bruce | 1.00 | .40 |
| 135 | Eddie Kennison | .60 | .25 |
| 136 | Orlando Pace RC | 1.00 | .40 |
| 137 | Trent Dilfer | 1.00 | .40 |
| 138 | Mike Alstott | 1.00 | .40 |
| 139 | Horace Copeland | .40 | .15 |
| 140 | Jackie Harris | .40 | .15 |
| 141 | Warrick Dunn RC | 3.00 | 1.25 |
| 142 | Reidel Anthony RC | 1.00 | .40 |
| 143 | Steve McNair | 1.25 | .50 |
| 144 | Eddie George | 1.00 | .40 |
| 145 | Chris Sanders | .40 | .15 |
| 146 | Gus Frerotte | .40 | .15 |
| 147 | Terry Allen | 1.00 | .40 |
| 148 | Henry Ellard | .40 | .15 |
| 149 | Leslie Shepherd | .40 | .15 |
| 150 | Michael Westbrook | .60 | .25 |
| S1 | Terrell Davis Sample | 2.00 | .75 |

## 1998 Playoff Contenders Ticket

|  |  | | |
|---|--------|------|------|
| | COMP.SET w/o SPs (80) | 60.00 | 25.00 |
| 1 | Rob Moore | 1.25 | .50 |
| 2 | Jake Plummer | 2.00 | .75 |
| 3 | Jamal Anderson | 2.00 | .75 |
| 4 | Terance Mathis | 1.25 | .50 |
| 5 | Priest Holmes RC | 40.00 | 15.00 |
| 6 | Michael Jackson | .75 | .30 |
| 7 | Eric Zeier | 1.25 | .50 |
| 8 | Andre Reed | 1.25 | .50 |
| 9 | Antowain Smith | 2.00 | .75 |
| 10 | Bruce Smith | 1.25 | .50 |
| 11 | Thurman Thomas | 2.00 | .75 |
| 12 | Rocket Ismail | .75 | .30 |
| 13 | Wesley Walls | 1.25 | .50 |
| 14 | Curtis Conway | 1.25 | .50 |
| 15 | Jeff Blake | 1.25 | .50 |
| 16 | Corey Dillon | 2.00 | .75 |
| 17 | Carl Pickens | 1.25 | .50 |
| 18 | Troy Aikman | 4.00 | 1.50 |
| 19 | Michael Irvin | 2.00 | .75 |
| 20 | Ernie Mills | .75 | .30 |
| 21 | Deion Sanders | 2.00 | .75 |
| 22 | Emmitt Smith | 6.00 | 2.50 |
| 23 | Terrell Davis | 2.00 | .75 |
| 24 | John Elway | 8.00 | 3.00 |
| 25 | Neil Smith | 1.25 | .50 |
| 26 | Rod Smith WR | 1.25 | .50 |
| 27 | Herman Moore | 1.25 | .50 |
| 28 | Johnnie Morton | 1.25 | .50 |
| 29 | Barry Sanders | 6.00 | 2.50 |
| 30 | Robert Brooks | 1.25 | .50 |
| 31 | Brett Favre | 8.00 | 3.00 |
| 32 | Antonio Freeman | 2.00 | .75 |
| 33 | Dorsey Levens | 2.00 | .75 |
| 34 | Reggie White | 2.00 | .75 |
| 35 | Marshall Faulk | 2.50 | 1.00 |
| 36 | Mark Brunell | 2.00 | .75 |
| 37 | Jimmy Smith | 1.25 | .50 |
| 38 | James Stewart | 1.25 | .50 |
| 39 | Donnell Bennett | .75 | .30 |
| 40 | Andre Rison | 1.25 | .50 |
| 41 | Derrick Thomas | 2.00 | .75 |
| 42 | Karim Abdul-Jabbar | 2.00 | .75 |
| 43 | Dan Marino | 8.00 | 3.00 |
| 44 | Cris Carter | 2.00 | .75 |
| 45 | Brad Johnson | 2.00 | .75 |
| 46 | Robert Smith | 2.00 | .75 |
| 47 | Drew Bledsoe | 3.00 | 1.25 |
| 48 | Terry Glenn | 2.00 | .75 |
| 49 | Lamar Smith | 1.25 | .50 |
| 50 | Ike Hilliard | 1.25 | .50 |
| 51 | Danny Kanell | 1.25 | .50 |
| 52 | Wayne Chrebet | 2.00 | .75 |
| 53 | Keyshawn Johnson | 2.00 | .75 |
| 54 | Curtis Martin | 2.00 | .75 |
| 55 | Tim Brown | 2.00 | .75 |
| 56 | Rickey Dudley | .75 | .30 |
| 57 | Jeff George | 1.25 | .50 |
| 58 | Napoleon Kaufman | 2.00 | .75 |
| 59 | Irving Fryar | 1.25 | .50 |
| 60 | Jerome Bettis | 2.00 | .75 |
| 61 | Charles Johnson | .75 | .30 |
| 62 | Kordell Stewart | 2.00 | .75 |
| 63 | Natrone Means | 1.25 | .50 |
| 64 | Bryan Still | .75 | .30 |
| 65 | Garrison Hearst | 2.00 | .75 |
| 66 | Jerry Rice | 4.00 | 1.50 |
| 67 | Steve Young | 2.50 | 1.00 |
| 68 | Joey Galloway | 2.00 | .75 |
| 69 | Warren Moon | 2.00 | .75 |
| 70 | Ricky Watters | 1.25 | .50 |

|  |  | | |
|---|--------|--|--|
| ❑ 71 | Isaac Bruce | 2.00 | .75 |
| ❑ 72 | Mike Alstott | 2.00 | .75 |
| ❑ 73 | Reidel Anthony | 1.25 | .50 |
| ❑ 74 | Trent Dilfer | 2.00 | .75 |
| ❑ 75 | Warrick Dunn | 2.00 | .75 |
| ❑ 76 | Warren Sapp | 1.25 | .50 |
| ❑ 77 | Eddie George | 2.00 | .75 |
| ❑ 78 | Steve McNair | 2.00 | .75 |
| ❑ 79 | Terry Allen | 2.00 | .75 |
| ❑ 80 | Gus Frerotte | .75 | .30 |
| ❑ 81 | Andre Wadsworth AU/500* | 25.00 | 10.00 |
| ❑ 82 | Tim Dwight AU/500* | 40.00 | 15.00 |
| ❑ 83 | Curtis Enis AU/400* | 40.00 | 15.00 |
| ❑ 85 | Charlie Batch AU/500* | 40.00 | 15.00 |
| ❑ 86 | Germane Crowell AU/500* | 25.00 | 10.00 |
| ❑ 87 | Pey.Manning AU/200* | 3000.00 | 2000.00 |
| ❑ 88 | Jerome Pathon AU/500* | 40.00 | 15.00 |
| ❑ 89 | Fred Taylor AU/500* | 120.00 | 60.00 |
| ❑ 90 | Tavian Banks AU/500* | 25.00 | 10.00 |
| ❑ 92 | Randy Moss AU/300* | 500.00 | 250.00 |
| ❑ 93 | Robert Edwards AU/500* | 25.00 | 10.00 |
| ❑ 94 | Hines Ward AU/500* | 250.00 | 150.00 |
| ❑ 95 | Ryan Leaf AU/200* | 50.00 | 25.00 |
| ❑ 96 | Mikhael Ricks AU/500* | 25.00 | 10.00 |
| ❑ 97 | Ahman Green AU/500* | 60.00 | 25.00 |
| ❑ 98 | Jacquez Green AU/500* | 25.00 | 10.00 |
| ❑ 99 | Kevin Dyson AU/500* | 40.00 | 15.00 |
| ❑ 100 | Skip Hicks AU/500* | 25.00 | 10.00 |
| ❑ 103 | C.Fuamatu-Ma'afala AU/500* | 25.00 | 10.00 |

## 1999 Playoff Contenders SSD

| | | |
|--|--|--|
| ❑ COMPLETE SET (200) | 2000.00 | 1000.00 |
| ❑ COMP.SET w/o SP's (141) | 60.00 | 25.00 |
| ❑ 1 Randy Moss | 5.00 | 2.00 |
| ❑ 2 Randall Cunningham | 2.00 | .75 |
| ❑ 3 Cris Carter | 2.00 | .75 |
| ❑ 4 Robert Smith | .75 | .30 |
| ❑ 5 Jake Reed | 1.25 | .50 |
| ❑ 6 Albert Connell | .75 | .30 |
| ❑ 7 Jeff George | 1.25 | .50 |
| ❑ 8 Brett Favre | 6.00 | 2.50 |
| ❑ 9 Antonio Freeman | 2.00 | .75 |
| ❑ 10 Dorsey Levens | 2.00 | .75 |
| ❑ 11 Mark Chmura | 1.25 | .50 |
| ❑ 12 Mike Alstott | 2.00 | .75 |
| ❑ 13 Warrick Dunn | 2.00 | .75 |
| ❑ 14 Trent Dilfer | 1.25 | .50 |
| ❑ 15 Jacquez Green | .75 | .30 |
| ❑ 16 Reidel Anthony | .75 | .30 |
| ❑ 17 Warren Sapp | 1.25 | .50 |
| ❑ 18 Amani Toomer | .75 | .30 |
| ❑ 19 Curtis Enis | .75 | .30 |
| ❑ 20 Curtis Conway | 1.25 | .50 |
| ❑ 21 Bobby Engram | .75 | .30 |
| ❑ 22 Barry Sanders | 6.00 | 2.50 |
| ❑ 23 Charlie Batch | 2.00 | .75 |
| ❑ 24 Herman Moore | 1.25 | .50 |
| ❑ 25 Johnnie Morton | 1.25 | .50 |
| ❑ 26 Greg Hill | .75 | .30 |
| ❑ 27 Germane Crowell | 1.25 | .50 |
| ❑ 28 Kerry Collins | 1.25 | .50 |
| ❑ 29 Ike Hilliard | .75 | .30 |
| ❑ 30 Joe Jurevicius | 1.25 | .50 |
| ❑ 31 Stephen Davis | 2.00 | .75 |
| ❑ 32 Brad Johnson | 2.00 | .75 |
| ❑ 33 Skip Hicks | .75 | .30 |
| ❑ 34 Michael Westbrook | 1.25 | .50 |

| | | |
|--|--|--|
| ❑ 35 Jake Plummer | 1.25 | .50 |
| ❑ 36 Adrian Murrell | .75 | .30 |
| ❑ 37 Frank Sanders | 1.25 | .50 |
| ❑ 38 Rob Moore | 1.25 | .50 |
| ❑ 39 Gary Brown | .75 | .30 |
| ❑ 40 Duce Staley | 2.00 | .75 |
| ❑ 41 Charles Johnson | 1.25 | .50 |
| ❑ 42 Emmitt Smith | 4.00 | 1.50 |
| ❑ 43 Troy Aikman | 4.00 | 1.50 |
| ❑ 44 Michael Irvin | 1.25 | .50 |
| ❑ 45 Deion Sanders | 2.00 | .75 |
| ❑ 46 Rocket Ismail | 1.25 | .50 |
| ❑ 47 Jerry Rice | 4.00 | 1.50 |
| ❑ 48 Terrell Owens | 2.00 | .75 |
| ❑ 49 Steve Young | 2.50 | 1.00 |
| ❑ 50 Garrison Hearst | 1.25 | .50 |
| ❑ 51 J.J. Stokes | 1.25 | .50 |
| ❑ 52 Lawrence Phillips | 1.25 | .50 |
| ❑ 53 Jamal Anderson | 2.00 | .75 |
| ❑ 54 Chris Chandler | 1.25 | .50 |
| ❑ 55 Terance Mathis | 1.25 | .50 |
| ❑ 56 Tim Dwight | 2.00 | .75 |
| ❑ 57 Charlie Garner | 1.25 | .50 |
| ❑ 58 Chris Calloway | 1.25 | .50 |
| ❑ 59 Eddie Kennison | 1.25 | .50 |
| ❑ 60 Billy Joe Hobert | .75 | .30 |
| ❑ 61 Tim Biakabutuka | 1.25 | .50 |
| ❑ 62 Muhsin Muhammad | 1.25 | .50 |
| ❑ 63 Olandis Gary AU/1825 RC | 15.00 | 6.00 |
| ❑ 64 Wesley Walls | 1.25 | .50 |
| ❑ 65 Isaac Bruce | 2.00 | .75 |
| ❑ 66 Marshall Faulk | 2.50 | 1.00 |
| ❑ 67 Kordell Stewart | 1.25 | .50 |
| ❑ 68 Jerome Bettis | 2.00 | .75 |
| ❑ 69 Hines Ward | 2.00 | .75 |
| ❑ 70 Corey Dillon | 2.00 | .75 |
| ❑ 71 Carl Pickens | 1.25 | .50 |
| ❑ 72 Darnay Scott | 1.25 | .50 |
| ❑ 73 Steve McNair | 2.00 | .75 |
| ❑ 74 Eddie George | 2.00 | .75 |
| ❑ 75 Yancey Thigpen | .75 | .30 |
| ❑ 76 Kevin Dyson | 1.25 | .50 |
| ❑ 77 Fred Taylor | 2.00 | .75 |
| ❑ 78 Mark Brunell | 2.00 | .75 |
| ❑ 79 Jimmy Smith | 1.25 | .50 |
| ❑ 80 Keenan McCardell | 1.25 | .50 |
| ❑ 81 James Stewart | 1.25 | .50 |
| ❑ 82 Jermaine Lewis | 1.25 | .50 |
| ❑ 83 Priest Holmes | 3.00 | 1.25 |
| ❑ 84 Stoney Case | .75 | .30 |
| ❑ 85 Errict Rhett | 1.25 | .50 |
| ❑ 86 Bill Schroeder | .75 | .30 |
| ❑ 87 Terry Kirby | .75 | .30 |
| ❑ 88 Leslie Shepherd | .75 | .30 |
| ❑ 89 Terrence Wilkins/825 RC | 12.00 | 5.00 |
| ❑ 90 Dan Marino | 6.00 | 2.50 |
| ❑ 91 O.J. McDuffie | 1.25 | .50 |
| ❑ 92 Karim Abdul-Jabbar | 1.25 | .50 |
| ❑ 93 Zach Thomas | 2.00 | .75 |
| ❑ 94 Terry Allen | 1.25 | .50 |
| ❑ 95 Tony Martin | 1.25 | .50 |
| ❑ 96 Drew Bledsoe | 2.50 | 1.00 |
| ❑ 97 Terry Glenn | 2.00 | .75 |
| ❑ 98 Ben Coates | 1.25 | .50 |
| ❑ 99 Tony Simmons | .75 | .30 |
| ❑ 100 Curtis Martin | 2.00 | .75 |
| ❑ 101 Keyshawn Johnson | 2.00 | .75 |
| ❑ 102 Vinny Testaverde | 1.25 | .50 |
| ❑ 103 Wayne Chrebet | 2.00 | .75 |
| ❑ 104 Peyton Manning | 6.00 | 2.50 |
| ❑ 105 Marvin Harrison | 2.00 | .75 |
| ❑ 106 E.G. Green | .75 | .30 |
| ❑ 107 Doug Flutie | 2.00 | .75 |
| ❑ 108 Thurman Thomas | 2.00 | .75 |
| ❑ 109 Andre Reed | 1.25 | .50 |
| ❑ 110 Eric Moulds | 2.00 | .75 |
| ❑ 111 Antowain Smith | 2.00 | .75 |
| ❑ 112 Bruce Smith | 1.25 | .50 |
| ❑ 113 Terrell Davis | 2.00 | .75 |
| ❑ 114 John Elway | 6.00 | 2.50 |
| ❑ 115 Ed McCaffrey | 1.25 | .50 |
| ❑ 116 Rod Smith | 1.25 | .50 |
| ❑ 117 Shannon Sharpe | 1.25 | .50 |
| ❑ 118 Jeff Garcia AU/325 RC | 100.00 | 50.00 |
| ❑ 119 Brian Griese | 2.00 | .75 |
| ❑ 120 Justin Watson/325 RC | 25.00 | 10.00 |

| | | |
|--|--|--|
| ❑ 121 Bubby Brister | 1.25 | .50 |
| ❑ 122 Ryan Leaf | 2.00 | .75 |
| ❑ 123 Natrone Means | 1.25 | .50 |
| ❑ 124 Mikhael Ricks | .75 | .30 |
| ❑ 125 Junior Seau | 2.00 | .75 |
| ❑ 126 Jim Harbaugh | 1.25 | .50 |
| ❑ 127 Andre Rison | 1.25 | .50 |
| ❑ 128 Elvis Grbac | 1.25 | .50 |
| ❑ 129 Bam Morris | .75 | .30 |
| ❑ 130 Rashaan Shehee | .75 | .30 |
| ❑ 131 Warren Moon | 2.00 | .75 |
| ❑ 132 Tony Gonzalez | 2.00 | .75 |
| ❑ 133 Derrick Alexander | 1.25 | .50 |
| ❑ 134 Jon Kitna | 2.00 | .75 |
| ❑ 135 Ricky Watters | 1.25 | .50 |
| ❑ 136 Joey Galloway | 1.25 | .50 |
| ❑ 137 Ahman Green | 1.25 | .50 |
| ❑ 138 Derrick Mayes | 1.25 | .50 |
| ❑ 139 Tyrone Wheatley | 1.25 | .50 |
| ❑ 140 Napoleon Kaufman | 2.00 | .75 |
| ❑ 141 Tim Brown | 2.00 | .75 |
| ❑ 142 Charles Woodson | 2.00 | .75 |
| ❑ 143 Rich Gannon | 2.00 | .75 |
| ❑ 144 Rickey Dudley | .75 | .30 |
| ❑ 145 Az-Zahir Hakim | .75 | .30 |
| ❑ 146 Kurt Warner AU/1825 RC | 175.00 | 90.00 |
| ❑ 147 Sean Bennett AU/1325 RC | 10.00 | 4.00 |
| ❑ 148 Bran.Stokley AU/1325 RC | 25.00 | 10.00 |
| ❑ 149 Amos Zereoue AU/1325 RC | 12.00 | 5.00 |
| ❑ 150 Brock Huard AU/1375 RC | 15.00 | 6.00 |
| ❑ 151 Tim Couch AU/1025 RC | 25.00 | 10.00 |
| ❑ 152 Ricky Williams AU/725 RC | 50.00 | 25.00 |
| ❑ 153 Donov.McNabb AU/925 RC | 135.00 | 75.00 |
| ❑ 154 Edgerrin James AU/525 RC | 80.00 | 40.00 |
| ❑ 155 Torry Holt AU/1025 RC | 80.00 | 40.00 |
| ❑ 156 D.Culpepper AU/1025 RC | 60.00 | 30.00 |
| ❑ 157 Akili Smith AU/1025 RC | 12.00 | 5.00 |
| ❑ 158 Champ Bailey AU/1725 RC | 30.00 | 12.50 |
| ❑ 159 Chris Claiborne AU/1825 RC | 12.00 | 5.00 |
| ❑ 160A C.McAlister AU/1825 RC | 15.00 | 6.00 |
| ❑ 160B Jason Tucker AU/1825 | 10.00 | 4.00 |
| ❑ 161 Troy Edwards AU/1225 RC | 12.00 | 5.00 |
| ❑ 162 Jevon Kearse AU/325 RC | 60.00 | 30.00 |
| ❑ 163 Darnell McDonald AU/1825 RC | 10.00 | 4.00 |
| ❑ 164 David Boston AU/1025 RC | 12.00 | 5.00 |
| ❑ 165 Peerless Price AU/1325 RC | 15.00 | 6.00 |
| ❑ 166 E.Collins AU/1025 RC | 10.00 | 4.00 |
| ❑ 167 Rob Konrad AU/1325 RC | 10.00 | 4.00 |
| ❑ 168 Cade McNown AU/1025 RC | 12.00 | 5.00 |
| ❑ 169 Shawn Bryson AU/1825 RC | 10.00 | 4.00 |
| ❑ 170 Kevin Faulk AU/1325 RC | 25.00 | 10.00 |
| ❑ 171 Corby Jones AU/1825 RC | 10.00 | 4.00 |
| ❑ 172A Jam.Johnson No AU/1325 RC | 10.00 | 4.00 |
| ❑ 172B Patrick Jeffers AU/1325 | 12.00 | 5.00 |
| ❑ 173 Autry Denson AU/1825 RC | 10.00 | 4.00 |
| ❑ 174 Sedrick Irvin AU/1825 RC | 10.00 | 4.00 |
| ❑ 175 Michael Bishop AU/1825 RC | 12.00 | 5.00 |
| ❑ 176 Joe Germaine AU/825 RC | 12.00 | 5.00 |
| ❑ 177 DeMond Parker AU/1825 RC | 10.00 | 4.00 |
| ❑ 178A Shaun King No AU/1825 RC | 12.00 | 5.00 |
| ❑ 178B Ray Lucas AU/1825 | 15.00 | 6.00 |
| ❑ 179 D'Wayne Bates AU/1825 RC | 12.00 | 5.00 |
| ❑ 180 Tai Streets AU/1825 RC | 12.00 | 5.00 |
| ❑ 181 Na Brown AU/1825 RC | 10.00 | 4.00 |
| ❑ 182 Desmond Clark AU/1825 RC | 15.00 | 6.00 |
| ❑ 183 Jim Kleinsasser AU/1825 RC | 12.00 | 5.00 |
| ❑ 184 Kevin Johnson AU/1325 RC | 15.00 | 6.00 |
| ❑ 185 Joe Montgomery AU/1325 RC | 10.00 | 4.00 |
| ❑ 186 John Elway PT | 10.00 | 4.00 |
| ❑ 187 Dan Marino PT | 10.00 | 4.00 |
| ❑ 188 Jerry Rice PT | 6.00 | 2.50 |
| ❑ 189 Barry Sanders PT | 10.00 | 4.00 |
| ❑ 190 Steve Young PT | 4.00 | 1.50 |
| ❑ 191 Doug Flutie PT | 2.50 | 1.00 |
| ❑ 192 Troy Aikman PT | 6.00 | 2.50 |
| ❑ 193 Drew Bledsoe PT | 4.00 | 1.50 |
| ❑ 194 Brett Favre PT | 10.00 | 4.00 |
| ❑ 195 Randall Cunningham PT | 2.50 | 1.00 |
| ❑ 196 Terrell Davis PT | 2.50 | 1.00 |
| ❑ 197 Kordell Stewart PT | 2.50 | 1.00 |
| ❑ 198 Keyshawn Johnson PT | 2.50 | 1.00 |
| ❑ 199 Jake Plummer PT | 2.50 | 1.00 |
| ❑ 200 Peyton Manning PT | 10.00 | 4.00 |
| ❑ 201 Jay Fiedler/1825 AU | 15.00 | 6.00 |
| ❑ 202 Kevin Daft/325 AU | 30.00 | 12.00 |

## 2000 Playoff Contenders

| | | |
|---|---|---|
| ☐ COMP.SET w/o SP's (100) | 20.00 | 7.50 |
| ☐ 1 David Boston | .75 | .30 |
| ☐ 2 Jake Plummer | .50 | .20 |
| ☐ 3 Chris Chandler | .50 | .20 |
| ☐ 4 Jamal Anderson | .75 | .30 |
| ☐ 5 Tim Dwight | .75 | .30 |
| ☐ 6 Qadry Ismail | .50 | .20 |
| ☐ 7 Tony Banks | .50 | .20 |
| ☐ 8 Lamar Smith | .50 | .20 |
| ☐ 9 Doug Flutie | .75 | .30 |
| ☐ 10 Eric Moulds | .75 | .30 |
| ☐ 11 Peerless Price | .50 | .20 |
| ☐ 12 Rob Johnson | .50 | .20 |
| ☐ 13 Muhsin Muhammad | .50 | .20 |
| ☐ 14 Reggie White | .75 | .30 |
| ☐ 15 Steve Beuerlein | .50 | .20 |
| ☐ 16 Cade McNown | .30 | .10 |
| ☐ 17 Derrick Alexander | .50 | .20 |
| ☐ 18 Marcus Robinson | .50 | .20 |
| ☐ 19 Akili Smith | .30 | .10 |
| ☐ 20 Corey Dillon | .75 | .30 |
| ☐ 21 Kevin Johnson | .75 | .30 |
| ☐ 22 Tim Couch | .50 | .20 |
| ☐ 23 Emmitt Smith | 1.50 | .60 |
| ☐ 24 Joey Galloway | .50 | .20 |
| ☐ 25 Rocket Ismail | .50 | .20 |
| ☐ 26 Troy Aikman | 1.50 | .60 |
| ☐ 27 Brian Griese | .75 | .30 |
| ☐ 28 Ed McCaffrey | .75 | .30 |
| ☐ 29 John Elway | 2.50 | 1.00 |
| ☐ 30 Olandis Gary | .75 | .30 |
| ☐ 31 Rod Smith | .50 | .20 |
| ☐ 32 Terrell Davis | .75 | .30 |
| ☐ 33 Charlie Batch | .75 | .30 |
| ☐ 34 Germane Crowell | .30 | .10 |
| ☐ 35 James Stewart | .50 | .20 |
| ☐ 36 Barry Sanders | 2.00 | .75 |
| ☐ 37 Antonio Freeman | .50 | .20 |
| ☐ 38 Brett Favre | 2.50 | 1.00 |
| ☐ 39 Dorsey Levens | .50 | .20 |
| ☐ 40 Edgerrin James | 1.25 | .50 |
| ☐ 41 Marvin Harrison | .75 | .30 |
| ☐ 42 Peyton Manning | 2.00 | .75 |
| ☐ 43 Fred Taylor | .75 | .30 |
| ☐ 44 Jimmy Smith | .50 | .20 |
| ☐ 45 Mark Brunell | .75 | .30 |
| ☐ 46 Elvis Grbac | .50 | .20 |
| ☐ 47 Tony Gonzalez | .50 | .20 |
| ☐ 48 Dan Marino | 2.50 | 1.00 |
| ☐ 49 Joe Horn | .50 | .20 |
| ☐ 50 Jay Fiedler | .50 | .20 |
| ☐ 51 Thurman Thomas | .50 | .20 |
| ☐ 52 Cris Carter | .75 | .30 |
| ☐ 53 Daunte Culpepper | 1.00 | .40 |
| ☐ 54 Randy Moss | 1.50 | .60 |
| ☐ 55 Robert Smith | .75 | .30 |
| ☐ 56 Drew Bledsoe | 1.00 | .40 |
| ☐ 57 Terry Glenn | .50 | .20 |
| ☐ 58 Ricky Williams | .75 | .30 |
| ☐ 59 Amani Toomer | .30 | .10 |
| ☐ 60 Kerry Collins | .50 | .20 |
| ☐ 61 Curtis Martin | .75 | .30 |
| ☐ 62 Vinny Testaverde | .50 | .20 |
| ☐ 63 Wayne Chrebet | .50 | .20 |
| ☐ 64 Rich Gannon | .75 | .30 |
| ☐ 65 Tim Brown | .75 | .30 |
| ☐ 66 Tyrone Wheatley | .50 | .20 |
| ☐ 67 Donovan McNabb | 1.25 | .50 |
| ☐ 68 Duce Staley | .75 | .30 |
| ☐ 69 Jerome Bettis | .75 | .30 |
| ☐ 70 Jermaine Fazande | .30 | .10 |
| ☐ 71 Junior Seau | .75 | .30 |
| ☐ 72 Donald Hayes | .30 | .10 |
| ☐ 73 Charlie Garner | .50 | .20 |
| ☐ 74 Jeff Garcia | .75 | .30 |
| ☐ 75 Jerry Rice | 1.50 | .60 |
| ☐ 76 Steve Young | 1.00 | .40 |
| ☐ 77 Terrell Owens | .75 | .30 |
| ☐ 78 Tiki Barber | .75 | .30 |
| ☐ 79 Tim Biakabutuka | .50 | .20 |
| ☐ 80 Ricky Watters | .50 | .20 |
| ☐ 81 Isaac Bruce | .75 | .30 |
| ☐ 82 Kurt Warner | 1.50 | .60 |
| ☐ 83 Marshall Faulk | 1.00 | .40 |
| ☐ 84 Torry Holt | .75 | .30 |
| ☐ 85 Keyshawn Johnson | .75 | .30 |
| ☐ 86 Mike Alstott | .75 | .30 |
| ☐ 87 Shaun King | .30 | .10 |
| ☐ 88 Warren Sapp | .50 | .20 |
| ☐ 89 Warrick Dunn | .50 | .20 |
| ☐ 90 Eddie George | .75 | .30 |
| ☐ 91 Jevon Kearse | .75 | .30 |
| ☐ 92 Steve McNair | .75 | .30 |
| ☐ 93 Carl Pickens | .50 | .20 |
| ☐ 94 Albert Connell | .30 | .10 |
| ☐ 95 Brad Johnson | .75 | .30 |
| ☐ 96 Bruce Smith | .50 | .20 |
| ☐ 97 Deion Sanders | .75 | .30 |
| ☐ 98 Jeff George | .50 | .20 |
| ☐ 99 Michael Westbrook | .50 | .20 |
| ☐ 100 Stephen Davis | .75 | .30 |
| ☐ 101 Courtney Brown AU RC | 30.00 | 12.50 |
| ☐ 102 Corey Simon AU RC | 15.00 | 6.00 |
| ☐ 103 Brian Urlacher AU RC | 80.00 | 40.00 |
| ☐ 104 Deon Grant AU RC | 12.00 | 5.00 |
| ☐ 105 Peter Warrick AU RC | 15.00 | 6.00 |
| ☐ 106 Jamal Lewis AU RC | 50.00 | 25.00 |
| ☐ 108 Plaxico Burress AU RC | 50.00 | 25.00 |
| ☐ 109 Travis Taylor AU RC | 15.00 | 6.00 |
| ☐ 110 Ron Dayne AU RC | 25.00 | 10.00 |
| ☐ 111 Bubba Franks AU RC | 15.00 | 6.00 |
| ☐ 112 Chad Pennington AU RC | 50.00 | 25.00 |
| ☐ 113 Shaun Alexander AU RC | 40.00 | 15.00 |
| ☐ 114 Sylvester Morris AU RC | 12.00 | 5.00 |
| ☐ 115 Mike Anderson AU RC | 15.00 | 6.00 |
| ☐ 116 R.Jay Soward AU RC | 10.00 | 4.00 |
| ☐ 117 Trung Canidate AU RC | 12.00 | 5.00 |
| ☐ 118 Dennis Northcutt AU RC | 12.00 | 5.00 |
| ☐ 119 Todd Pinkston AU RC | 12.00 | 5.00 |
| ☐ 120 Jerry Porter AU RC | 25.00 | 10.00 |
| ☐ 121 Travis Prentice AU RC | 12.00 | 5.00 |
| ☐ 122 Giovanni Carmazzi AU RC | 10.00 | 4.00 |
| ☐ 123 Ron Dugans AU RC | 10.00 | 4.00 |
| ☐ 124 Dez White AU RC | 15.00 | 6.00 |
| ☐ 125 Chris Cole AU RC | 10.00 | 4.00 |
| ☐ 126 Ron Dixon AU RC | 12.00 | 5.00 |
| ☐ 127 Chris Redman AU RC | 15.00 | 6.00 |
| ☐ 128 J.R. Redmond AU RC | 12.00 | 5.00 |
| ☐ 129 Laveranues Coles AU RC | 30.00 | 12.50 |
| ☐ 130 JaJuan Dawson AU RC | 10.00 | 4.00 |
| ☐ 131 Darrell Jackson AU RC | 25.00 | 10.00 |
| ☐ 132 Reuben Droughns AU RC | 25.00 | 10.00 |
| ☐ 133 Doug Chapman AU RC | 12.00 | 5.00 |
| ☐ 134 Curtis Keaton AU RC | 12.00 | 5.00 |
| ☐ 135 Gari Scott AU RC | 10.00 | 4.00 |
| ☐ 136 Danny Farmer AU RC | 12.00 | 5.00 |
| ☐ 137 Trevor Gaylor AU RC | 12.00 | 5.00 |
| ☐ 138 Avion Black AU RC | 10.00 | 4.00 |
| ☐ 139 Michael Wiley AU RC | 12.00 | 5.00 |
| ☐ 140 Sammy Morris AU RC | 15.00 | 6.00 |
| ☐ 141 Tee Martin AU RC | 15.00 | 6.00 |
| ☐ 142 Troy Walters AU RC | 15.00 | 6.00 |
| ☐ 143 Marc Bulger AU RC | 40.00 | 15.00 |
| ☐ 144 Tom Brady AU RC | 1200.00 | 600.00 |
| ☐ 145 Todd Husak AU RC | 12.00 | 5.00 |
| ☐ 146 Tim Rattay AU RC | 15.00 | 6.00 |
| ☐ 147 Jarious Jackson AU RC | 12.00 | 5.00 |
| ☐ 148 Joe Hamilton AU RC | 12.00 | 5.00 |
| ☐ 149 Shyrone Stith AU RC | 12.00 | 5.00 |
| ☐ 150 Kwame Cavil AU RC | 10.00 | 4.00 |
| ☐ 151 Antonio Banks ET AU RC | 6.00 | 2.50 |
| ☐ 152 Jonathan Brown ET AU RC | 6.00 | 2.50 |
| ☐ 153 Ontiwaun Carter ET AU RC | 6.00 | 2.50 |
| ☐ 154 Jeremaine Copeland ET | 6.00 | 2.50 |
| ☐ 155 Ralph Dawkins ET AU RC | 8.00 | 3.00 |
| ☐ 156 Marques Douglas ET AU RC | 6.00 | 2.50 |
| ☐ 157 Kevin Drake ET AU RC | 6.00 | 2.50 |
| ☐ 158 Damon Dunn ET AU RC | 8.00 | 3.00 |
| ☐ 159 Todd Floyd ET AU RC | 6.00 | 2.50 |
| ☐ 160 Tony Graziani ET AU | 8.00 | 3.00 |
| ☐ 162 Duane Hawthorne ET AU RC | 8.00 | 3.00 |
| ☐ 163 Alonzo Johnson ET AU RC | 6.00 | 2.50 |
| ☐ 164 Mark Kacmarynski ET AU RC | 6.00 | 2.50 |
| ☐ 165 Eric Kresser ET AU | 6.00 | 2.50 |
| ☐ 166 Jim Kubiak ET AU RC | 8.00 | 3.00 |
| ☐ 167 Blaine McElmurry ET AU RC | 6.00 | 2.50 |
| ☐ 168 Scott Milanovich ET AU | 8.00 | 3.00 |
| ☐ 169 Norman Miller ET AU RC | 6.00 | 2.50 |
| ☐ 170 Sean Morey ET AU RC | 8.00 | 3.00 |
| ☐ 171 Jeff Ogden ET AU | 8.00 | 3.00 |
| ☐ 172 Pepe Pearson ET AU RC | 8.00 | 3.00 |
| ☐ 173 Ron Powlus ET AU | 8.00 | 3.00 |
| ☐ 174 Jason Shelley ET AU RC | 8.00 | 3.00 |
| ☐ 175 Ben Snell ET AU RC | 8.00 | 3.00 |
| ☐ 176 Aaron Stecker ET AU RC | 8.00 | 3.00 |
| ☐ 177 L.C. Stevens ET AU | 6.00 | 2.50 |
| ☐ 178 Mike Sutton ET AU RC | 6.00 | 2.50 |
| ☐ 179 Damian Vaughn ET AU RC | 6.00 | 2.50 |
| ☐ 180 Ted White ET AU | 8.00 | 2.50 |
| ☐ 181 Marcus Crandell ET AU RC | 8.00 | 3.00 |
| ☐ 182 Darryl Daniel ET AU RC | 8.00 | 3.00 |
| ☐ 183 Jesse Haynes ET AU | 6.00 | 2.50 |
| ☐ 184 Matt Lytle ET AU RC | 8.00 | 3.00 |
| ☐ 185 Deon Mitchell ET AU RC | 6.00 | 2.50 |
| ☐ 186 Kendrick Nord ET AU RC | 6.00 | 2.50 |
| ☐ 188 Selucio Sanford ET AU RC | 8.00 | 3.00 |
| ☐ 189 Corey Thomas ET AU | 6.00 | 2.50 |
| ☐ 190 Vershan Jackson ET AU RC | 6.00 | 2.50 |
| ☐ 191 Jake Plummer PT AU | 20.00 | 8.00 |
| ☐ 192 Jim Kelly PT AU | 30.00 | 12.50 |
| ☐ 193 Bernie Kosar PT AU | 30.00 | 12.50 |
| ☐ 194 Marvin Harrison PT AU | 30.00 | 12.50 |
| ☐ 196 Kerry Collins PT AU | 20.00 | 8.00 |
| ☐ 197 Kurt Warner PT AU | 40.00 | 20.00 |
| ☐ 198 Jevon Kearse PT AU | 20.00 | 8.00 |
| ☐ 199 Brad Johnson PT AU | 15.00 | 6.00 |
| ☐ 200 Jeff George PT AU | 15.00 | 6.00 |

## 2001 Playoff Contenders

| | | |
|---|---|---|
| ☐ COMP.SET w/o SP's (100) | 25.00 | 10.00 |
| ☐ 1 David Boston | 1.00 | .40 |
| ☐ 2 Jake Plummer | .60 | .25 |
| ☐ 3 Jamal Anderson | 1.00 | .40 |
| ☐ 4 Chris Chandler | .60 | .25 |
| ☐ 5 Elvis Grbac | .60 | .25 |
| ☐ 6 Brandon Stokley | .60 | .25 |
| ☐ 7 Travis Taylor | .60 | .25 |
| ☐ 8 Ray Lewis | 1.00 | .40 |
| ☐ 9 Rob Johnson | .60 | .25 |
| ☐ 10 Eric Moulds | .60 | .25 |
| ☐ 11 Tim Biakabutuka | .60 | .25 |
| ☐ 12 Muhsin Muhammad | .60 | .25 |
| ☐ 13 James Allen | .60 | .25 |
| ☐ 14 Brian Urlacher | 1.50 | .60 |
| ☐ 15 Peter Warrick | 1.00 | .40 |
| ☐ 16 Corey Dillon | 1.00 | .40 |
| ☐ 17 Tim Couch | .60 | .25 |
| ☐ 18 Kevin Johnson | .60 | .25 |
| ☐ 19 Rickey Dudley | .40 | .10 |
| ☐ 20 Emmitt Smith | 2.00 | .75 |

☐ 21 Joey Galloway .60 .25
☐ 22 Brian Griese 1.00 .40
☐ 23 Terrell Davis 1.00 .40
☐ 24 Mike Anderson 1.00 .40
☐ 25 Ed McCaffrey 1.00 .40
☐ 26 Rod Smith .60 .25
☐ 27 Charlie Batch 1.00 .40
☐ 28 James Stewart .60 .25
☐ 29 Germane Crowell .40 .10
☐ 30 Johnnie Morton .60 .25
☐ 31 Brett Favre 3.00 1.25
☐ 32 Ahman Green 1.00 .40
☐ 33 Antonio Freeman 1.00 .40
☐ 34 Peyton Manning 2.50 1.00
☐ 35 Edgerrin James 1.25 .50
☐ 36 Marvin Harrison 1.00 .40
☐ 37 Jerome Pathon .60 .25
☐ 38 Mark Brunell 1.00 .40
☐ 39 Fred Taylor 1.00 .40
☐ 40 Keenan McCardell .40 .10
☐ 41 Jimmy Smith .60 .25
☐ 42 Trent Green 1.00 .40
☐ 43 Priest Holmes 1.25 .50
☐ 44 Tony Gonzalez .60 .25
☐ 45 Derrick Alexander .60 .25
☐ 46 Jay Fiedler 1.00 .40
☐ 47 Lamar Smith .60 .25
☐ 48 Zach Thomas 1.00 .40
☐ 49 Oronde Gadsden .60 .25
☐ 50 Daunte Culpepper 1.00 .40
☐ 51 Randy Moss 2.00 .75
☐ 52 Cris Carter 1.00 .40
☐ 53 Drew Bledsoe 1.25 .50
☐ 54 J.R. Redmond .40 .10
☐ 55 Troy Brown .60 .25
☐ 56 Aaron Brooks 1.00 .40
☐ 57 Ricky Williams 1.00 .40
☐ 58 Joe Horn .60 .25
☐ 59 Kerry Collins .60 .25
☐ 60 Tiki Barber 1.00 .40
☐ 61 Ron Dayne 1.00 .40
☐ 62 Ike Hilliard .60 .25
☐ 63 Vinny Testaverde .60 .25
☐ 64 Curtis Martin 1.00 .40
☐ 65 Wayne Chrebet .60 .25
☐ 66 Laveranues Coles 1.00 .40
☐ 67 Rich Gannon 1.00 .40
☐ 68 Tyrone Wheatley .60 .25
☐ 69 Tim Brown 1.00 .40
☐ 70 Jerry Rice 2.00 .75
☐ 71 Donovan McNabb 1.25 .50
☐ 72 Duce Staley 1.00 .40
☐ 73 Todd Pinkston .60 .25
☐ 74 Kordell Stewart .60 .25
☐ 75 Jerome Bettis 1.00 .40
☐ 76 Plaxico Burress 1.00 .40
☐ 77 Doug Flutie 1.00 .40
☐ 78 Junior Seau 1.00 .40
☐ 79 Jeff Garcia 1.00 .40
☐ 80 Garrison Hearst .60 .25
☐ 81 Terrell Owens 1.00 .40
☐ 82 Matt Hasselbeck .60 .25
☐ 83 Ricky Watters .60 .25
☐ 84 Shaun Alexander 1.25 .50
☐ 85 Darrell Jackson 1.00 .40
☐ 86 Kurt Warner 2.00 .75
☐ 87 Marshall Faulk 1.25 .50
☐ 88 Isaac Bruce 1.00 .40
☐ 89 Torry Holt 1.00 .40
☐ 90 Brad Johnson 1.00 .40
☐ 91 Keyshawn Johnson 1.00 .40
☐ 92 Warrick Dunn 1.00 .40
☐ 93 Warren Sapp .60 .25
☐ 94 Steve McNair 1.00 .40
☐ 95 Eddie George 1.00 .40
☐ 96 Derrick Mason .60 .25
☐ 97 Jevon Kearse .60 .25
☐ 98 Stephen Davis 1.00 .40
☐ 99 Bruce Smith .60 .25
☐ 100 Michael Westbrook .60 .25
☐ 101 Adam Archuleta/50* RC 80.00 40.00
☐ 102 Alex Bannister AU RC 12.00 5.00
☐ 103 Alge Crumpler AU RC 20.00 8.00
☐ 104 Andre Carter AU/100* RC 50.00 20.00
☐ 105 Anthony Thomas AU/600* RC 15.00 6.00

☐ 106 Ben Leard AU RC 10.00 4.00
☐ 107 Bobby Newcombe AU RC 12.00 5.00
☐ 108 Brian Allen AU RC 10.00 4.00
☐ 109 Carlos Polk AU RC 10.00 4.00
☐ 110 Casey Hampton No Auto RC 15.00 6.00
☐ 111 Cedric Scott AU RC 10.00 4.00
☐ 112 Cedrick Wilson AU RC 25.00 10.00
☐ 113 Chad Johnson AU RC 100.00 50.00
☐ 114 C.Chambers AU/170* RC 150.00 75.00
☐ 115 Chris Weinke AU/300* RC 25.00 10.00
☐ 116 Correll Buckhalter AU/590* RC 30.00 12.50
☐ 117 Damione Lewis AU RC 15.00 6.00
☐ 118 Dan Morgan AU RC 20.00 8.00
☐ 119 Daniel Guy AU RC 10.00 4.00
☐ 120 David Allen AU RC 10.00 4.00
☐ 121 David Terrell AU/500* RC 15.00 6.00
☐ 122 Ken Lucas AU/276* RC 15.00 6.00
☐ 123 D.McAllister AU/500* RC 80.00 40.00
☐ 124 Drew Brees AU/300* RC 200.00 125.00
☐ 125 Eddie Berlin AU RC 10.00 4.00
☐ 126 Boo Williams AU/50* RC 60.00 30.00
☐ 127 Ennis Davis AU RC 10.00 4.00
☐ 128 Freddie Mitchell AU RC 15.00 6.00
☐ 129 Gary Baxter AU RC 12.00 5.00
☐ 130 Gerard Warren AU/200* RC 25.00 10.00
☐ 131 Hakim Akbar AU RC 10.00 4.00
☐ 132 Heath Evans AU RC 10.00 4.00
☐ 133 Jabari Holloway AU RC 10.00 4.00
☐ 134 Jamal Reynolds AU/500* RC 10.00 4.00
☐ 135 James Jackson AU RC 12.00 5.00
☐ 136 Jamie Winborn AU RC 10.00 4.00
☐ 137 Javon Green AU RC 10.00 4.00
☐ 138 Jesse Palmer AU RC 12.00 5.00
☐ 139 Dominic Rhodes AU/300* RC 40.00 15.00
☐ 140 Josh Heupel AU/150* RC 50.00 20.00
☐ 141 Justin Smith AU RC 15.00 6.00
☐ 142 Karon Riley AU RC 10.00 4.00
☐ 143 Keith Adams/50* RC 80.00 40.00
☐ 144 Kendrell Bell AU RC 20.00 8.00
☐ 145 Kenny Smith AU RC 12.00 5.00
☐ 146 Ken.Walker AU/50* RC 80.00 40.00
☐ 147 Ken-Yon Rambo AU RC 10.00 4.00
☐ 148 Kevan Barlow AU RC 20.00 8.00
☐ 149 Koren Robinson AU/400* RC 25.00 10.00
☐ 150 L.Tomlinson AU/600 RC 600.00 300.00
☐ 151 LaMont Jordan AU/50* RC 300.00 150.00
☐ 152 Leonard Davis/50* RC 80.00 40.00
☐ 153 Marcus Stroud AU RC 15.00 6.00
☐ 154 Marques Tuiasosopo AU RC 15.00 6.00
☐ 155 Snoop Minnis AU/295* RC 12.00 5.00
☐ 156 Michael Bennett AU/600* RC 25.00 10.00
☐ 157 Michael Vick AU/327* RC 100.00 50.00
☐ 158 Mike McMahon AU/529* RC 15.00 6.00
☐ 159 Moran Norris AU RC 10.00 4.00
☐ 160 Morlon Greenwood AU RC 10.00 4.00
☐ 161 Nate Clements/50* RC 80.00 40.00
☐ 162 Quincy Carter AU SP RC 60.00 25.00
☐ 163 Quincy Morgan AU RC 15.00 6.00
☐ 164 Jamar Fletcher/50* RC 80.00 40.00
☐ 165 Reggie Germany AU RC 10.00 4.00
☐ 166 Reggie Wayne AU/400* RC 135.00 75.00
☐ 167 Reggie White AU RC 10.00 4.00
☐ 168 Richard Seymour/50* RC 100.00 50.00
☐ 169 Robert Carswell/50* RC 60.00 30.00
☐ 170 Robert Ferguson AU RC 20.00 8.00
☐ 171 Rod Gardner AU/75* RC 80.00 40.00
☐ 172 Ronney Daniels AU RC 10.00 4.00
☐ 173 Rudi Johnson AU RC 80.00 40.00
☐ 174 Sage Rosenfels AU/400* RC 25.00 10.00
☐ 175 Santana Moss AU/500* RC 50.00 25.00
☐ 176 Shaun Rogers AU RC 15.00 6.00
☐ 177 Houshmandzadeh AU RC 50.00 30.00
☐ 178 Tim Hasselbeck AU RC 15.00 6.00
☐ 179 Todd Heap AU/169* RC 80.00 40.00
☐ 180 Tony Stewart AU RC 12.00 5.00
☐ 181 Torrance Marshall AU RC 12.00 5.00
☐ 182 Travis Henry AU/369* RC 40.00 15.00
☐ 183 Travis Minor AU RC 15.00 6.00
☐ 184 Vinny Sutherland AU RC 12.00 5.00
☐ 185 Will Allen AU RC 15.00 6.00
☐ 186 Willie Howard AU RC 10.00 4.00
☐ 187 W.Middlebrooks/50* RC 60.00 30.00
☐ 188 Derrick Blaylock AU/200* RC 30.00 12.50
☐ 189 A.J. Feeley AU/200* RC 50.00 20.00
☐ 190 Steve Smith AU/300* RC 200.00 100.00

☐ 191 Onome Ojo AU/200* RC 15.00 6.00
☐ 192 Dee Brown AU/300* RC 15.00 6.00
☐ 193 Kevin Kasper AU/200* RC 20.00 8.00
☐ 194 Dave Dickenson AU/300* RC 15.00 6.00
☐ 195 Chris Barnes AU/200* RC 15.00 6.00
☐ 196 Scotty Anderson AU/300* RC 15.00 6.00
☐ 197 Chris Taylor AU/300* RC 12.00 5.00
☐ 198 Cedric James AU/300* RC 15.00 6.00
☐ 199 Justin McCareins AU/200* RC 50.00 20.00
☐ 200 Tommy Polley AU/300* RC 15.00 6.00

## 2002 Playoff Contenders

☐ COMP.SET w/o SP's (100) 25.00 10.00
☐ 1 Drew Bledsoe 1.25 .50
☐ 2 Travis Henry 1.00 .40
☐ 3 Eric Moulds .60 .25
☐ 4 Chris Chambers 1.00 .40
☐ 5 Ricky Williams 1.00 .40
☐ 6 Zach Thomas 1.00 .40
☐ 7 Tom Brady 2.50 1.00
☐ 8 Antowain Smith .60 .25
☐ 9 Troy Brown .60 .25
☐ 10 Curtis Martin 1.00 .40
☐ 11 Vinny Testaverde .60 .25
☐ 12 Chad Pennington 1.25 .50
☐ 13 Jeff Blake .40 .15
☐ 14 Jamal Lewis 1.00 .40
☐ 15 Ray Lewis 1.00 .40
☐ 16 Michael Westbrook .40 .15
☐ 17 Corey Dillon .60 .25
☐ 18 Peter Warrick .60 .25
☐ 19 Tim Couch .60 .25
☐ 20 Quincy Morgan .60 .25
☐ 21 Kevin Johnson .60 .25
☐ 22 Kordell Stewart .60 .25
☐ 23 Plaxico Burress 1.00 .40
☐ 24 Jerome Bettis 1.00 .40
☐ 25 James Allen .60 .25
☐ 26 Corey Bradford .40 .15
☐ 27 Mark Brunell .60 .25
☐ 28 Fred Taylor .60 .25
☐ 29 Jimmy Smith .60 .25
☐ 30 Peyton Manning 2.00 .75
☐ 31 Reggie Wayne 1.00 .40
☐ 32 Marvin Harrison 1.00 .40
☐ 33 Edgerrin James 1.25 .50
☐ 34 Steve McNair .60 .25
☐ 35 Eddie George 1.00 .40
☐ 36 Jevon Kearse .60 .25
☐ 37 Derrick Mason .60 .25
☐ 38 Brian Griese 1.00 .40
☐ 39 Terrell Davis 1.00 .40
☐ 40 Ed McCaffrey .60 .25
☐ 41 Rod Smith .60 .25
☐ 42 Trent Green .60 .25
☐ 43 Priest Holmes 1.25 .50
☐ 44 Johnnie Morton .60 .25
☐ 45 Tony Gonzalez .60 .25
☐ 46 Rich Gannon 1.00 .40
☐ 47 Tim Brown 1.00 .40
☐ 48 Jerry Rice 2.00 .75
☐ 49 Charlie Garner .60 .25
☐ 50 Drew Brees 1.00 .40
☐ 51 LaDainian Tomlinson 1.50 .60
☐ 52 Junior Seau 1.00 .40
☐ 53 Quincy Carter .60 .25
☐ 54 Emmitt Smith 2.50 1.00
☐ 55 Joey Galloway .60 .25

|  |  | | |
|---|--------|------|------|
| 56 | Kerry Collins | .60 | .25 |
| 57 | Tiki Barber | 1.00 | .40 |
| 58 | Michael Strahan | .60 | .25 |
| 59 | Donovan McNabb | 1.25 | .50 |
| 60 | Duce Staley | 1.00 | .40 |
| 61 | Antonio Freeman | 1.00 | .40 |
| 62 | Derrius Thompson | .40 | .15 |
| 63 | Stephen Davis | .60 | .25 |
| 64 | Rod Gardner | .60 | .25 |
| 65 | Anthony Thomas | .60 | .25 |
| 66 | Marty Booker | .60 | .25 |
| 67 | Brian Urlacher | 1.50 | .60 |
| 68 | James Stewart | .60 | .25 |
| 69 | Az-Zahir Hakim | .40 | .15 |
| 70 | Brett Favre | 2.50 | 1.00 |
| 71 | Ahman Green | .60 | .40 |
| 72 | Donald Driver | .60 | .25 |
| 73 | Daunte Culpepper | 1.00 | .40 |
| 74 | Michael Bennett | .60 | .25 |
| 75 | Randy Moss | 2.00 | .75 |
| 76 | Michael Vick | 1.00 | .40 |
| 77 | Warrick Dunn | 1.00 | .40 |
| 78 | Chris Weinke | .60 | .25 |
| 79 | Lamar Smith | .60 | .25 |
| 80 | Steve Smith | 1.00 | .40 |
| 81 | Aaron Brooks | 1.00 | .40 |
| 82 | Deuce McAllister | 1.25 | .50 |
| 83 | Joe Horn | .60 | .25 |
| 84 | Brad Johnson | .60 | .25 |
| 85 | Keyshawn Johnson | 1.00 | .40 |
| 86 | Mike Alstott | 1.00 | .40 |
| 87 | Warren Sapp | .60 | .25 |
| 88 | Jake Plummer | .60 | .25 |
| 89 | Thomas Jones | .60 | .25 |
| 90 | David Boston | 1.00 | .40 |
| 91 | Kurt Warner | 1.00 | .40 |
| 92 | Marshall Faulk | 1.00 | .40 |
| 93 | Isaac Bruce | 1.00 | .40 |
| 94 | Torry Holt | 1.00 | .40 |
| 95 | Jeff Garcia | 1.00 | .40 |
| 96 | Garrison Hearst | .60 | .25 |
| 97 | Kevan Barlow | .60 | .25 |
| 98 | Terrell Owens | 1.00 | .40 |
| 99 | Trent Dilfer | .60 | .25 |
| 100 | Shaun Alexander | 1.25 | .50 |
| 101 | Adrian Peterson AU/360 RC | 40.00 | 20.00 |
| 102 | A.Haynesworth No Auto RC | 20.00 | 8.00 |
| 103 | Alex Brown AU/410 RC | 30.00 | 12.00 |
| 104 | Andra Davis AU/510 RC | 10.00 | 4.00 |
| 105 | Andre Davis AU/360 RC | 20.00 | 7.50 |
| 106 | Andre Lott AU/750 RC | 10.00 | 4.00 |
| 107 | Anthony Weaver AU/450 RC | 10.00 | 4.00 |
| 108 | Antonio Bryant AU/165 RC | 40.00 | 25.00 |
| 109 | Antw Randle El AU/135 RC | 60.00 | 30.00 |
| 110 | Ashley Lelie AU/360 RC | 20.00 | 7.50 |
| 111 | Brian Poli-Dixon AU/460 RC | 10.00 | 4.00 |
| 112 | Brian Westbrook AU/600 RC | 150.00 | 90.00 |
| 113 | Bryant McKinnie AU/600 RC | 15.00 | 6.00 |
| 114 | C Hutchinson AU/450 RC | 12.00 | 5.00 |
| 115 | Charles Grant AU/450 RC | 15.00 | 6.00 |
| 116 | Chester Taylor AU/345 RC | 10.00 | 15.00 |
| 117 | Cliff Russell AU/545 RC | 12.00 | 5.00 |
| 118 | Clinton Portis AU/360 RC | 120.00 | 70.00 |
| 119 | R.McMichael AU/400 RC | 20.00 | 7.50 |
| 120 | Damien Anderson AU/460 RC | 10.00 | 4.00 |
| 121 | Daniel Graham AU/185 RC | 40.00 | 15.00 |
| 122 | David Carr AU/250 RC | 30.00 | 15.00 |
| 123 | David Garrard AU/310 RC | 175.00 | 100.00 |
| 124 | Deion Branch AU/650 RC | 30.00 | 12.00 |
| 125 | John Simon AU/400 RC | 10.00 | 4.00 |
| 126 | DeShaun Foster AU/400 RC | 40.00 | 15.00 |
| 127 | Donte Stallworth AU/302 RC | 50.00 | 20.00 |
| 128 | Dwight Freeney AU/410 RC | 50.00 | 25.00 |
| 129 | Ed Reed AU/550 RC | 75.00 | 40.00 |
| 130 | Eric Crouch AU/280 RC | 25.00 | 10.00 |
| 131 | Freddie Milons AU/380 RC | 12.00 | 5.00 |
| 132 | Jabar Gaffney AU/315 RC | 20.00 | 7.50 |
| 133 | Javon Walker AU/435 RC | 40.00 | 15.00 |
| 134 | Jeremy Shockey AU/160 RC | 120.00 | 60.00 |
| 135 | Jeremy Stevens AU/250 RC | 30.00 | 12.50 |
| 136 | Joey Harrington AU/250 RC | 50.00 | 20.00 |
| 137 | John Henderson AU/360 RC | 20.00 | 7.50 |
| 138 | Jonathan Wells AU/485 RC | 25.00 | 10.00 |
| 139 | Josh McCown AU/595 RC | 40.00 | 20.00 |
| 140 | Josh Reed AU/290 RC | 40.00 | 15.00 |
| 141 | Josh Scobey AU/615 RC | 10.00 | 4.00 |
| 142 | Julius Peppers AU/40 RC | 600.00 | 350.00 |
| 143 | Kalimba Edwards AU/510 RC | 12.00 | 5.00 |
| 144 | Kelly Campbell AU/360 RC | 20.00 | 7.50 |
| 145 | Ken Simonton AU/650 RC | 10.00 | 4.00 |
| 146 | Keyuo Craver AU/850 RC | 10.00 | 4.00 |
| 147 | Kahlil AU/850 RC | 12.00 | 5.00 |
| 148 | Kurt Kittner AU/235 RC | 20.00 | 7.50 |
| 149 | Ladell Betts AU/600 RC | 40.00 | 20.00 |
| 150 | Lamar Gordon AU/600 RC | 15.00 | 6.00 |
| 151 | Levar Fisher AU/760 RC | 10.00 | 4.00 |
| 152 | Lito Sheppard AU/410 RC | 30.00 | 12.50 |
| 153 | Luke Staley AU/360 RC | 12.00 | 5.00 |
| 154 | Marquise Walker AU/330 RC | 20.00 | 7.50 |
| 155 | Maurice Morris AU/153 RC | 60.00 | 30.00 |
| 156 | Mike Rumph AU/510 RC | 15.00 | 6.00 |
| 157 | Mike Williams AU/500 RC | 12.00 | 5.00 |
| 158 | Najeh Davenport AU/460 RC | 30.00 | 12.50 |
| 159 | Napoleon Harris AU/900 RC | 12.00 | 5.00 |
| 160 | Patrick Ramsey AU/575 RC | 30.00 | 12.00 |
| 161 | Buchanon No AU/310 RC | 40.00 | 20.00 |
| 162 | Quentin Jammer AU/300 RC | 20.00 | 7.50 |
| 163 | Randy Fasani AU/500 RC | 15.00 | 6.00 |
| 164 | Reche Caldwell AU/360 RC | 15.00 | 6.00 |
| 165 | Robert Thomas AU/460 RC | 15.00 | 6.00 |
| 166 | Rocky Calmus AU/385 RC | 15.00 | 6.00 |
| 167 | Rohan Davey AU/295 RC | 30.00 | 12.00 |
| 168 | Ron Johnson AU/385 RC | 15.00 | 6.00 |
| 169 | Roy Williams AU/250 RC | 60.00 | 30.00 |
| 170 | Ryan Sims No AU/360 RC | 20.00 | 7.50 |
| 171 | Tavon Mason AU/690 RC | 10.00 | 4.00 |
| 172 | Terry Charles AU/750 RC | 10.00 | 4.00 |
| 173 | T.J. Duckett AU/335 RC | 30.00 | 12.00 |
| 174 | Tim Carter AU/600 RC | 12.00 | 5.00 |
| 175 | Travis Stephens AU/170 RC | 40.00 | 15.00 |
| 176 | Trev Faulk AU/600 RC | 10.00 | 4.00 |
| 177 | Wendell Bryant AU/560 RC | 10.00 | 4.00 |
| 178 | William Green AU/317 RC | 20.00 | 7.50 |
| 179 | Woody Dantzler AU/185 RC | 25.00 | 10.00 |
| 180 | Tony Fisher AU/340 RC | 20.00 | 7.50 |
| 181 | Javin Hunter AU/400 RC | 10.00 | 4.00 |
| 182 | Daryl Jones AU/400 RC | 10.00 | 4.00 |
| 183 | Jesse Chatman AU/400 RC | 15.00 | 6.00 |
| 184 | J.T. O'Sullivan AU/340 RC | 60.00 | 30.00 |
| 185 | Josh Norman AU/340 RC | 20.00 | 7.50 |
| 186 | James Mungro AU/100 RC | 60.00 | 30.00 |

## 2003 Playoff Contenders

|  |  | | |
|---|--------|------|------|
| | COMP.SET w/o SP's (100) | 20.00 | 7.50 |
| 1 | Roy Williams | .75 | .30 |
| 2 | Antonio Bryant | .75 | .30 |
| 3 | Jeremy Shockey | .75 | .30 |
| 4 | Kerry Collins | .60 | .25 |
| 5 | Tiki Barber | .75 | .30 |
| 6 | Michael Strahan | .60 | .25 |
| 7 | Donovan McNabb | 1.00 | .40 |
| 8 | Duce Staley | .60 | .25 |
| 9 | Todd Pinkston | .50 | .20 |
| 10 | Patrick Ramsey | .60 | .25 |
| 11 | Laveranues Coles | .60 | .25 |
| 12 | Rod Gardner | .50 | .20 |
| 13 | Drew Bledsoe | .75 | .30 |
| 14 | Travis Henry | .60 | .25 |
| 15 | Eric Moulds | .60 | .25 |
| 16 | Josh Reed | .50 | .20 |
| 17 | Ricky Williams | .60 | .25 |
| 18 | Jay Fiedler | .60 | .25 |
| 19 | Chris Chambers | .60 | .25 |
| 20 | Zach Thomas | .75 | .30 |
| 21 | Junior Seau | .75 | .30 |
| 22 | Tom Brady | 2.00 | .75 |
| 23 | Troy Brown | .60 | .25 |
| 24 | Chad Pennington | .75 | .30 |
| 25 | Curtis Martin | .75 | .30 |
| 26 | Santana Moss | .60 | .25 |
| 27 | Emmitt Smith | 2.00 | .75 |
| 28 | Jeff Garcia | .75 | .30 |
| 29 | Terrell Owens | .75 | .30 |
| 30 | Kevan Barlow | .50 | .20 |
| 31 | Shaun Alexander | .75 | .30 |
| 32 | Matt Hasselbeck | .60 | .25 |
| 33 | Koren Robinson | .60 | .25 |
| 34 | Kurt Warner | .75 | .30 |
| 35 | Marshall Faulk | .75 | .30 |
| 36 | Torry Holt | .75 | .30 |
| 37 | Isaac Bruce | .75 | .30 |
| 38 | Clinton Portis | 1.00 | .40 |
| 39 | Jake Plummer | .60 | .25 |
| 40 | Rod Smith | .60 | .25 |
| 41 | Ed McCaffrey | .60 | .25 |
| 42 | Ashley Lelie | .50 | .20 |
| 43 | Priest Holmes | .75 | .30 |
| 44 | Trent Green | .60 | .25 |
| 45 | Tony Gonzalez | .60 | .25 |
| 46 | Jerry Rice | 1.50 | .60 |
| 47 | Rich Gannon | .60 | .25 |
| 48 | Tim Brown | .75 | .30 |
| 49 | Jerry Porter | .60 | .25 |
| 50 | Charles Woodson | .60 | .25 |
| 51 | LaDainian Tomlinson | 1.25 | .50 |
| 52 | Drew Brees | .75 | .30 |
| 53 | David Boston | .50 | .20 |
| 54 | Brian Urlacher | 1.25 | .50 |
| 55 | Kordell Stewart | .60 | .25 |
| 56 | Marty Booker | .60 | .25 |
| 57 | Joey Harrington | .75 | .30 |
| 58 | Brett Favre | 2.00 | .75 |
| 59 | Ahman Green | .75 | .30 |
| 60 | Donald Driver | .75 | .30 |
| 61 | Javon Walker | .60 | .25 |
| 62 | Randy Moss | 1.00 | .40 |
| 63 | Daunte Culpepper | .75 | .30 |
| 64 | Michael Bennett | .60 | .25 |
| 65 | Jamal Lewis | .75 | .30 |
| 66 | Ray Lewis | .75 | .30 |
| 67 | Corey Dillon | .75 | .30 |
| 68 | Chad Johnson | .75 | .30 |
| 69 | William Green | .50 | .20 |
| 70 | Tim Couch | .50 | .20 |
| 71 | Quincy Morgan | .50 | .20 |
| 72 | Plaxico Burress | .75 | .30 |
| 73 | Tommy Maddox | .75 | .30 |
| 74 | Hines Ward | .75 | .30 |
| 75 | Antwaan Randle El | .75 | .30 |
| 76 | Michael Vick | .75 | .30 |
| 77 | Peerless Price | .50 | .20 |
| 78 | Warrick Dunn | .60 | .25 |
| 79 | T.J. Duckett | .75 | .30 |
| 80 | Julius Peppers | .75 | .30 |
| 81 | Stephen Davis | .60 | .25 |
| 82 | Deuce McAllister | .75 | .30 |
| 83 | Aaron Brooks | .60 | .25 |
| 84 | Joe Horn | .60 | .25 |
| 85 | Donte Stallworth | .60 | .20 |
| 86 | Mike Alstott | .75 | .30 |
| 87 | Brad Johnson | .75 | .30 |
| 88 | Keyshawn Johnson | .75 | .30 |
| 89 | Warren Sapp | .60 | .25 |
| 90 | David Carr | .75 | .30 |
| 91 | Jabar Gaffney | .50 | .20 |
| 92 | Peyton Manning | 1.50 | .60 |
| 93 | Edgerrin James | .75 | .30 |
| 94 | Marvin Harrison | .75 | .30 |
| 95 | Mark Brunell | .75 | .30 |
| 96 | Fred Taylor | .75 | .30 |
| 97 | Jimmy Smith | .60 | .25 |
| 98 | Steve McNair | .75 | .30 |
| 99 | Eddie George | .60 | .25 |
| 100 | Jevon Kearse | .60 | .25 |
| 101 | Lee Suggs AU/499 RC | 12.00 | 5.00 |
| 102 | Charles Rogers AU/500 RC | 50.00 | 20.00 |
| 103 | Brandon Lloyd AU/589 RC | 15.00 | 6.00 |
| 104 | Terrence Edwards AU/399 RC | 10.00 | 4.00 |

| | | |
|---|---|---|
| ❑ 105 Mike Pinkard AU/849 RC | 10.00 | 4.00 |
| ❑ 106 DeWayne White AU/524 RC | 10.00 | 4.00 |
| ❑ 107 Jero McDougle AU/339 RC | 10.00 | 4.00 |
| ❑ 108 Jimmy Kennedy AU/514 RC | 12.00 | 5.00 |
| ❑ 109 William Joseph AU/764 RC | 12.00 | 5.00 |
| ❑ 110 E.J. Henderson AU/774 RC | 12.00 | 5.00 |
| ❑ 111 Mike Doss AU/574 RC | 15.00 | 6.00 |
| ❑ 112A C.Simms Blk AU/31 RC | 50.00 | 20.00 |
| ❑ 112B C.Simms Blk AU/79 RC | 80.00 | 40.00 |
| ❑ 113 Cecil Sapp AU/474 RC | 10.00 | 4.00 |
| ❑ 114 Justin Gage AU/579 RC | 12.00 | 5.00 |
| ❑ 115 Sam Aiken AU/864 RC | 12.00 | 5.00 |
| ❑ 116 Doug Gabriel AU/389 RC | 12.00 | 5.00 |
| ❑ 117 Jason Witten AU/599 RC | 125.00 | 75.00 |
| ❑ 118 Bennie Joppru AU/449 RC | 10.00 | 4.00 |
| ❑ 119 Chris Kelsay AU/864 RC | 12.00 | 5.00 |
| ❑ 120 John Sullivan/924 RC | 6.00 | 2.50 |
| ❑ 121 Kevin Williams AU/764 RC | 20.00 | 7.50 |
| ❑ 122 Rien Long AU/849 RC | 10.00 | 4.00 |
| ❑ 123 Kenny Peterson/674 RC | 8.00 | 3.00 |
| ❑ 124 Boss Bailey AU/564 RC | 12.00 | 5.00 |
| ❑ 125 Denn Weathersby AU/774 RC | 10.00 | 4.00 |
| ❑ 126A Car.Palmer Blk AU/36 RC | 600.00 | 300.00 |
| ❑ 126B Car.Palmer Blu AU/158 RC | 400.00 | 200.00 |
| ❑ 127 Byron Leftwich AU/199 RC | 50.00 | 20.00 |
| ❑ 128 Kyle Boller AU/39 RC | 25.00 | 10.00 |
| ❑ 129 Rex Grossman AU/494 RC | 80.00 | 40.00 |
| ❑ 130 Dave Ragone AU/564 RC | 10.00 | 4.00 |
| ❑ 131 Brian St.Pierre AU/554 RC | 15.00 | 6.00 |
| ❑ 132 Kliff Kingsbury AU/879 RC | 12.00 | 5.00 |
| ❑ 133 Seneca Wallace AU/364 RC | 30.00 | 15.00 |
| ❑ 134 Larry Johnson AU/344 RC | 100.00 | 50.00 |
| ❑ 135 Will McGahee AU/369 RC | 80.00 | 40.00 |
| ❑ 136 Justin Fargas AU/354 RC | 40.00 | 15.00 |
| ❑ 137 Onterrio Smith AU/414 RC | 12.00 | 5.00 |
| ❑ 138 Chris Brown AU/279 RC | 40.00 | 15.00 |
| ❑ 139 Musa Smith AU/379 RC | 12.00 | 5.00 |
| ❑ 140 Artose Pinner AU/364 RC | 10.00 | 4.00 |
| ❑ 141 Andre Johnson AU/199 RC | 175.00 | 100.00 |
| ❑ 142 Kell Washington AU/472 RC | 25.00 | 10.00 |
| ❑ 143 Taylor Jacobs AU/349 RC | 12.00 | 5.00 |
| ❑ 144 Bryant Johnson AU/389 RC | 20.00 | 7.50 |
| ❑ 145 Tyrone Calico AU/499 RC | 12.00 | 5.00 |
| ❑ 146 Anquan Boldin AU/524 RC | 80.00 | 40.00 |
| ❑ 147 Bethel Johnson AU/484 RC | 12.00 | 5.00 |
| ❑ 148 Nate Burleson AU/549 RC | 20.00 | 8.00 |
| ❑ 149 Kevin Curtis AU/455 RC | 30.00 | 12.00 |
| ❑ 150 Dallas Clark AU/539 RC | 50.00 | 25.00 |
| ❑ 151 Teyo Johnson AU/389 RC | 12.00 | 5.00 |
| ❑ 152 Terrell Suggs AU/564 RC | 30.00 | 12.00 |
| ❑ 153 DeWayne Robertson/689 RC | 8.00 | 3.00 |
| ❑ 154 Terence Newman AU/364 RC | 40.00 | 20.00 |
| ❑ 155 Marcus Trufant AU/739 RC | 15.00 | 6.00 |
| ❑ 156 Tony Romo AU/999 RC | 500.00 | 250.00 |
| ❑ 157 Brooks Bollinger AU/974 RC | 15.00 | 6.00 |
| ❑ 158 Ken Dorsey AU/774 RC | 12.00 | 5.00 |
| ❑ 159 Kirk Farmer AU/999 RC | 12.00 | 5.00 |
| ❑ 160 Jason Gesser AU/999 RC | 12.00 | 5.00 |
| ❑ 161 Brock Forsey AU/999 RC | 12.00 | 5.00 |
| ❑ 162 Quentin Griffin AU/999 RC | 12.00 | 5.00 |
| ❑ 163 Avon Cobourne AU/974 RC | 10.00 | 4.00 |
| ❑ 164 Domanick Davis AU/999 RC | 15.00 | 6.00 |
| ❑ 165 Tony Hollings AU/974 RC | 12.00 | 5.00 |
| ❑ 166 LaBran.Toefield AU/799 RC | 12.00 | 5.00 |
| ❑ 167 Arlen Harris AU/974 RC | 10.00 | 4.00 |
| ❑ 168 Sult McCullough AU/999 RC | 10.00 | 4.00 |
| ❑ 169 Visant Shiancoe AU/999 RC | 15.00 | 6.00 |
| ❑ 170 L.J. Smith AU/974 RC | 15.00 | 6.00 |
| ❑ 171 LaTaren Dunbar AU/999 RC | 10.00 | 4.00 |
| ❑ 172 Walter Young AU/889 RC | 10.00 | 4.00 |
| ❑ 173 Bobby Wade AU/889 RC | 12.00 | 5.00 |
| ❑ 174 Zuriel Smith AU/989 RC | 10.00 | 4.00 |
| ❑ 175 Adrian Madise AU/999 RC | 10.00 | 4.00 |
| ❑ 176 Ken Hamlin AU/989 RC | 15.00 | 6.00 |
| ❑ 177 Carl Ford AU/999 RC | 10.00 | 4.00 |
| ❑ 178 Cortez Hankton AU/989 RC | 12.00 | 5.00 |
| ❑ 179 J.R. Tolver AU/889 RC | 12.00 | 5.00 |
| ❑ 180 Keenan Howry AU/999 RC | 10.00 | 4.00 |
| ❑ 181 Billy McMullen AU/899 RC | 10.00 | 4.00 |
| ❑ 182 Amaz Battle AU/989 RC | 25.00 | 10.00 |
| ❑ 183 Shaun McDonald AU/999 RC | 15.00 | 6.00 |
| ❑ 184 Andre Woolfolk AU/889 RC | 10.00 | 5.00 |
| ❑ 185 Sammy Davis AU/999 RC | 12.00 | 5.00 |
| ❑ 186 Calvin Pace AU/999 RC | 12.00 | 5.00 |
| ❑ 187 Michael Haynes AU/999 RC | 10.00 | 4.00 |

| | | |
|---|---|---|
| ❑ 188 Ty Warren AU/999 RC | 15.00 | 6.00 |
| ❑ 189 Nick Barnett AU/999 RC | 12.00 | 5.00 |
| ❑ 190 Troy Polamalu AU/989 RC | 175.00 | 90.00 |
| ❑ 191 Eric Parker AU/589 RC | 20.00 | 7.50 |
| ❑ 192 Justin Griffith AU/589 RC | 12.00 | 5.00 |
| ❑ 193 David Tyree AU/599 RC | 40.00 | 15.00 |
| ❑ 194 Pisa Tinoisamoa/599 RC | 10.00 | 4.00 |
| ❑ 195 Rashean Mathis AU/589 RC | 12.00 | 5.00 |
| ❑ 196 Mike Sherman AU/574 RC | 30.00 | 12.00 |
| ❑ 197 Dave Wannstedt AU/574 RC | 20.00 | 7.50 |
| ❑ 198 Dick Vermeil AU/574 RC | 30.00 | 12.00 |
| ❑ 199 Tony Dungy AU/574 RC | 80.00 | 40.00 |
| ❑ 200 Mike Martz AU/574 RC | 20.00 | 7.50 |

## 2004 Playoff Contenders

| | | |
|---|---|---|
| ❑ COMP.SET w/o SP's (100) | 20.00 | 7.50 |
| ❑ 1 Anquan Boldin | .75 | .30 |
| ❑ 2 Emmitt Smith | 2.00 | .75 |
| ❑ 3 Josh McCown | .60 | .25 |
| ❑ 4 Michael Vick | .75 | .30 |
| ❑ 5 Peerless Price | .60 | .25 |
| ❑ 6 T.J. Duckett | .60 | .25 |
| ❑ 7 Warrick Dunn | .60 | .25 |
| ❑ 8 Jamal Lewis | .60 | .25 |
| ❑ 9 Kyle Boller | .60 | .25 |
| ❑ 10 Ray Lewis | .75 | .30 |
| ❑ 11 Drew Bledsoe | .75 | .30 |
| ❑ 12 Eric Moulds | .60 | .25 |
| ❑ 13 Travis Henry | .60 | .25 |
| ❑ 14 Willis McGahee | .75 | .30 |
| ❑ 15 DeShaun Foster | .60 | .25 |
| ❑ 16 Jake Delhomme | .60 | .25 |
| ❑ 17 Stephen Davis | .60 | .25 |
| ❑ 18 Steve Smith | .75 | .30 |
| ❑ 19 Brian Urlacher | .75 | .30 |
| ❑ 20 Rex Grossman | .75 | .30 |
| ❑ 21 Thomas Jones | .60 | .25 |
| ❑ 22 Carson Palmer | 1.00 | .40 |
| ❑ 23 Chad Johnson | .60 | .25 |
| ❑ 24 Rudi Johnson | .60 | .25 |
| ❑ 25 Jeff Garcia | .60 | .25 |
| ❑ 26 Lee Suggs | .75 | .30 |
| ❑ 27 William Green | .60 | .25 |
| ❑ 28 Keyshawn Johnson | .60 | .25 |
| ❑ 29 Roy Williams S | .60 | .25 |
| ❑ 30 Eddie George | .60 | .25 |
| ❑ 31 Ashley Lelie | .60 | .25 |
| ❑ 32 Jake Plummer | .60 | .25 |
| ❑ 33 Quentin Griffin | .60 | .25 |
| ❑ 34 Rod Smith | .60 | .25 |
| ❑ 35 Charles Rogers | .60 | .25 |
| ❑ 36 Joey Harrington | .60 | .25 |
| ❑ 37 Ahman Green | .75 | .30 |
| ❑ 38 Brett Favre | 2.00 | .75 |
| ❑ 39 Javon Walker | .60 | .25 |
| ❑ 40 Andre Johnson | .75 | .30 |
| ❑ 41 David Carr | .60 | .25 |
| ❑ 42 Dumanick Davis | .75 | .30 |
| ❑ 43 Edgerrin James | .75 | .30 |
| ❑ 44 Marvin Harrison | .75 | .30 |
| ❑ 45 Peyton Manning | 1.50 | .60 |
| ❑ 46 Byron Leftwich | .75 | .30 |
| ❑ 47 Fred Taylor | .60 | .25 |
| ❑ 48 Jimmy Smith | .75 | .30 |
| ❑ 49 Priest Holmes | .75 | .30 |
| ❑ 50 Tony Gonzalez | .60 | .25 |
| ❑ 51 Trent Green | .60 | .25 |
| ❑ 52 A.J. Feeley | .60 | .25 |
| ❑ 53 Chris Chambers | .60 | .25 |

| | | |
|---|---|---|
| ❑ 54 Deion Sanders | .75 | .30 |
| ❑ 55 Daunte Culpepper | .75 | .30 |
| ❑ 56 Michael Bennett | .60 | .25 |
| ❑ 57 Randy Moss | 1.00 | .40 |
| ❑ 58 Corey Dillon | .60 | .25 |
| ❑ 59 Deion Branch | .60 | .25 |
| ❑ 60 Tom Brady | 2.00 | .75 |
| ❑ 61 Aaron Brooks | .60 | .25 |
| ❑ 62 Deuce McAllister | .75 | .30 |
| ❑ 63 Donte Stallworth | .60 | .25 |
| ❑ 64 Joe Horn | .60 | .25 |
| ❑ 65 Amani Toomer | .60 | .25 |
| ❑ 66 Jeremy Shockey | .60 | .25 |
| ❑ 67 Michael Strahan | .60 | .25 |
| ❑ 68 Tiki Barber | .75 | .30 |
| ❑ 69 Chad Pennington | .75 | .30 |
| ❑ 70 Curtis Martin | .75 | .30 |
| ❑ 71 Santana Moss | .60 | .25 |
| ❑ 72 Jerry Porter | .60 | .25 |
| ❑ 73 Jerry Rice | 1.50 | .60 |
| ❑ 74 Warren Sapp | .60 | .25 |
| ❑ 75 Brian Westbrook | .75 | .30 |
| ❑ 76 Donovan McNabb | .75 | .30 |
| ❑ 77 Jevon Kearse | .60 | .25 |
| ❑ 78 Terrell Owens | .60 | .25 |
| ❑ 79 Antwaan Randle El | .60 | .25 |
| ❑ 80 Hines Ward | .75 | .30 |
| ❑ 81 Jerome Bettis | .75 | .30 |
| ❑ 82 LaDainian Tomlinson | 1.25 | .50 |
| ❑ 83 Kevan Barlow | .60 | .25 |
| ❑ 84 Tim Rattay | .50 | .20 |
| ❑ 85 Koren Robinson | .75 | .30 |
| ❑ 86 Matt Hasselbeck | .75 | .30 |
| ❑ 87 Shaun Alexander | .75 | .30 |
| ❑ 88 Isaac Bruce | .60 | .25 |
| ❑ 89 Marc Bulger | .60 | .25 |
| ❑ 90 Marshall Faulk | .75 | .30 |
| ❑ 91 Torry Holt | .75 | .30 |
| ❑ 92 Brad Johnson | .60 | .25 |
| ❑ 93 Mike Alstott | .60 | .25 |
| ❑ 94 Chris Brown | .60 | .25 |
| ❑ 95 Derrick Mason | .60 | .25 |
| ❑ 96 Steve McNair | .75 | .30 |
| ❑ 97 Clinton Portis | .75 | .30 |
| ❑ 98 LaVar Arrington | .60 | .25 |
| ❑ 99 Laveranues Coles | .60 | .25 |
| ❑ 100 Mark Brunell | .60 | .25 |
| ❑ 101 Admchmide Echemandu AU RC | 12.00 | 5.00 |
| ❑ 102 Ahmad Carroll AU/574* RC | 15.00 | 6.00 |
| ❑ 103 Andy Hall AU RC | 12.00 | 5.00 |
| ❑ 104 B.J. Johnson AU RC | 10.00 | 4.00 |
| ❑ 105 B.J. Symons AU RC | 10.00 | 4.00 |
| ❑ 106 Roethlisberger AU/541* RC | 300.00 | 200.00 |
| ❑ 107 Ben Troupe AU/540* RC | 12.00 | 5.00 |
| ❑ 108 Ben Watson AU/660* RC | 15.00 | 6.00 |
| ❑ 109 Bernard Berrian AU/653* RC | 30.00 | 12.00 |
| ❑ 110 Brandon Miree AU RC | 10.00 | 4.00 |
| ❑ 111 Bruce Perry AU RC | 10.00 | 4.00 |
| ❑ 112 Carlos Francis AU RC | 10.00 | 4.00 |
| ❑ 113 Casey Bramlet AU RC | 10.00 | 4.00 |
| ❑ 114 Cedric Cobbs AU/630* RC | 12.00 | 5.00 |
| ❑ 115 Chris Gamble AU/490* RC | 12.00 | 5.00 |
| ❑ 116 Chris Perry AU/478* RC | 30.00 | 12.50 |
| ❑ 117 Clarence Moore AU RC | 12.00 | 5.00 |
| ❑ 118 Cody Pickett AU RC | 12.00 | 5.00 |
| ❑ 119 Craig Krenzel AU RC | 15.00 | 6.00 |
| ❑ 120 D.J. Hackett AU/325* RC | 35.00 | 20.00 |
| ❑ 121 D.J. Williams AU/490* RC | 15.00 | 6.00 |
| ❑ 122 Darius Watts AU RC | 12.00 | 5.00 |
| ❑ 123 DeAngelo Hall AU RC | 25.00 | 10.00 |
| ❑ 124 Derrick Hamilton AU/373* RC | 12.00 | 5.00 |
| ❑ 125 Derrick Ward AU RC | 40.00 | 15.00 |
| ❑ 126 Devard Darling AU/325* RC | 15.00 | 6.00 |
| ❑ 127 D.Henderson AU/475* RC | 25.00 | 10.00 |
| ❑ 128 Drew Carter AU RC | 15.00 | 6.00 |
| ❑ 129 Drew Henson AU/415* RC | 10.00 | 4.00 |
| ❑ 130 D.Robinson AU/660* RC | 12.00 | 5.00 |
| ❑ 131 Eli Manning AU/372* RC | 250.00 | 125.00 |
| ❑ 132 Ernest Wilford AU/365* RC | 30.00 | 12.00 |
| ❑ 133 Greg Jones AU/553* RC | 20.00 | 8.00 |
| ❑ 134 J.P. Losman AU/358* RC | 60.00 | 25.00 |
| ❑ 135 Jamaar Taylor AU RC | 10.00 | 4.00 |
| ❑ 136 Jared Lorenzen AU RC | 12.00 | 5.00 |
| ❑ 137 Jarrett Payton AU RC | 12.00 | 5.00 |
| ❑ 138 Jason Babin AU RC | 12.00 | 5.00 |

| | | | |
|---|---|---|---|
| ☐ 139 Jeff Smoker AU RC | 12.00 | 5.00 |
| ☐ 140 J.Cotchery AU325* RC | 50.00 | 20.00 |
| ☐ 141 Jim Sorgi AU RC | 15.00 | 6.00 |
| ☐ 142 John Navarre AU RC | 12.00 | 5.00 |
| ☐ 143 Johnnie Morant AU/325* RC | 15.00 | 6.00 |
| ☐ 144 Jonathan Vilma AU SP RC | 10.00 | 6.00 |
| ☐ 145 Josh Harris AU/555* RC | 10.00 | 4.00 |
| ☐ 146 Julius Jones AU/252* RC | 80.00 | 40.00 |
| ☐ 147 Keary Colbert AU/495* RC | 15.00 | 6.00 |
| ☐ 148 Kel.Winslow AU/135* RC | 200.00 | 100.00 |
| ☐ 149 Kenechi Udeze AU/475* RC | 15.00 | 6.00 |
| ☐ 150 Kevin Jones AU/327* RC | 40.00 | 20.00 |
| ☐ 151 L.Fitzgerald AU/50* RC | 750.00 | 450.00 |
| ☐ 152 Lee Evans AU/375* RC | 40.00 | 15.00 |
| ☐ 153 Luke McCown AU/543* RC | 15.00 | 6.00 |
| ☐ 154 Matt Mauck AU RC | 12.00 | 5.00 |
| ☐ 155 Matt Schaub AU/367* RC | 100.00 | 50.00 |
| ☐ 156 Maurice Mann AU RC | 10.00 | 4.00 |
| ☐ 157 Mewelde Moore AU/435* RC | 20.00 | 8.00 |
| ☐ 158 Michael Clayton AU/325* RC | 40.00 | 15.00 |
| ☐ 159 Michael Jenkins AU/412* RC | 30.00 | 12.00 |
| ☐ 160 M.Turner AU/535* RC | 100.00 | 60.00 |
| ☐ 161 P.K.Sam AU/300* RC | 12.00 | 5.00 |
| ☐ 162 Philip Rivers AU/556* RC | 120.00 | 60.00 |
| ☐ 163 Quincy Wilson AU/350* RC | 15.00 | 6.00 |
| ☐ 164 Ran Carthon AU RC | 10.00 | 4.00 |
| ☐ 165 Rashaun Woods AU RC | 10.00 | 4.00 |
| ☐ 166 Re.Williams AU/336* RC | 30.00 | 12.00 |
| ☐ 167 R.Colclough AU/640* RC | 15.00 | 6.00 |
| ☐ 168 Robert Gallery AU/310* RC | 30.00 | 12.00 |
| ☐ 169 Roy Williams AU/564* RC | 80.00 | 30.00 |
| ☐ 170 Samie Parker AU/356* RC | 15.00 | 6.00 |
| ☐ 171 Sean Jones AU RC | 12.00 | 5.00 |
| ☐ 172 S.Taylor/575* RC No Auto | 30.00 | 12.50 |
| ☐ 173 Sloan Thomas AU RC | 12.00 | 5.00 |
| ☐ 174 Steven Jackson AU/333* RC | 120.00 | 50.00 |
| ☐ 175 Tatum Bell AU/539* RC | 20.00 | 8.00 |
| ☐ 176 Tommie Harris AU/365* RC | 40.00 | 15.00 |
| ☐ 177 Triandos Luke AU RC | 10.00 | 4.00 |
| ☐ 178 Troy Fleming AU RC | 10.00 | 4.00 |
| ☐ 179 Vince Wilfork AU/315* RC | 20.00 | 8.00 |
| ☐ 180 Will Smith AU/565* RC | 12.00 | 5.00 |
| ☐ 181 Marcus Tubbs AU RC | 10.00 | 4.00 |
| ☐ 182 Michael Boulware AU RC | 15.00 | 6.00 |
| ☐ 183 Kris Wilson AU RC | 12.00 | 5.00 |
| ☐ 184 Richard Smith AU RC | 10.00 | 4.00 |
| ☐ 185 Teddy Lehman AU RC | 12.00 | 5.00 |
| ☐ 186 Chris Cooley AU RC | 60.00 | 35.00 |
| ☐ 187 Thomas Tapeh AU RC | 12.00 | 5.00 |
| ☐ 188A Willie Parker Blk AU RC | 120.00 | 60.00 |
| ☐ 188B Willie Parker Blu AU RC | 250.00 | 125.00 |
| ☐ 189 Patrick Crayton AU RC | 30.00 | 12.00 |
| ☐ 190 Kendrick Starling AU RC | 10.00 | 4.00 |
| ☐ 191 B.J. Sams AU RC | 12.00 | 5.00 |
| ☐ 192 Derick Armstrong AU RC | 10.00 | 4.00 |
| ☐ 193 Wes Welker AU RC | 80.00 | 40.00 |
| ☐ 194 Erik Coleman AU RC | 12.00 | 5.00 |
| ☐ 195 Gibril Wilson AU RC | 15.00 | 6.00 |
| ☐ 196 Andy Reid AU/335* RC | 30.00 | 12.00 |
| ☐ 197 Brian Billick AU/585* RC | 20.00 | 8.00 |
| ☐ 198 Jeff Fisher AU/585* RC | 30.00 | 12.00 |
| ☐ 199 Jon Gruden AU/585* RC | 20.00 | 8.00 |
| ☐ 200 Marvin Lewis AU/585* RC | 20.00 | 8.00 |

## 2005 Playoff Contenders

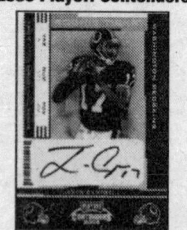

☐ COMP.SET w/o RC's (100) 20.00 7.50
☐ AU PRINT RUNS ANNOUNCED BY PLAYOFF
☐ UNPRICED CHAMPION.PRINT RUN 1 SET

| | | |
|---|---|---|
| ☐ 1 Anquan Boldin | .60 | .25 |
| ☐ 2 Kurt Warner | .75 | .30 |
| ☐ 3 Larry Fitzgerald | .75 | .30 |
| ☐ 4 Michael Vick | .75 | .30 |
| ☐ 5 T.J. Duckett | .50 | .20 |
| ☐ 6 Warrick Dunn | .60 | .25 |
| ☐ 7 Derrick Mason | .60 | .25 |
| ☐ 8 Jamal Lewis | .60 | .25 |
| ☐ 9 Kyle Boller | .60 | .25 |
| ☐ 10 Ray Lewis | .60 | .25 |
| ☐ 11 J.P. Losman | .75 | .30 |
| ☐ 12 Lee Evans | .60 | .25 |
| ☐ 13 Willis McGahee | .75 | .30 |
| ☐ 14 DeShaun Foster | .60 | .25 |
| ☐ 15 Jake Delhomme | .75 | .30 |
| ☐ 16 Steve Smith | .75 | .30 |
| ☐ 17 Brian Urlacher | .75 | .30 |
| ☐ 18 Muhsin Muhammad | .60 | .25 |
| ☐ 19 Rex Grossman | .75 | .30 |
| ☐ 20 Carson Palmer | .75 | .30 |
| ☐ 21 Chad Johnson | .75 | .30 |
| ☐ 22 Rudi Johnson | .60 | .25 |
| ☐ 23 Lee Suggs | .60 | .25 |
| ☐ 24 Trent Dilfer | .60 | .25 |
| ☐ 25 Drew Bledsoe | .75 | .30 |
| ☐ 26 Jason Witten | .60 | .25 |
| ☐ 27 Julius Jones | .75 | .30 |
| ☐ 28 Keyshawn Johnson | .60 | .25 |
| ☐ 29 Ashley Lelie | .50 | .20 |
| ☐ 30 Jake Plummer | .60 | .25 |
| ☐ 31 Rod Smith | .60 | .25 |
| ☐ 32 Tatum Bell | .60 | .25 |
| ☐ 33 Joey Harrington | .60 | .25 |
| ☐ 34 Kevin Jones | .75 | .30 |
| ☐ 35 Roy Williams WR | .75 | .30 |
| ☐ 36 Ahman Green | .75 | .30 |
| ☐ 37 Brett Favre | 2.00 | .75 |
| ☐ 38 Javon Walker | .60 | .25 |
| ☐ 39 Andre Johnson | .60 | .25 |
| ☐ 40 David Carr | .60 | .25 |
| ☐ 41 Domanick Davis | .50 | .20 |
| ☐ 42 Edgerrin James | .60 | .25 |
| ☐ 43 Marvin Harrison | .75 | .30 |
| ☐ 44 Peyton Manning | 1.25 | .50 |
| ☐ 45 Reggie Wayne | .60 | .25 |
| ☐ 46 Byron Leftwich | .60 | .25 |
| ☐ 47 Fred Taylor | .75 | .30 |
| ☐ 48 Jimmy Smith | .60 | .25 |
| ☐ 49 Priest Holmes | .75 | .30 |
| ☐ 50 Tony Gonzalez | .60 | .25 |
| ☐ 51 Trent Green | .60 | .25 |
| ☐ 52 Chris Chambers | .60 | .25 |
| ☐ 53 Ricky Williams | .75 | .30 |
| ☐ 54 Daunte Culpepper | .75 | .30 |
| ☐ 55 Michael Bennett | .60 | .25 |
| ☐ 56 Nate Burleson | .60 | .25 |
| ☐ 57 Corey Dillon | .60 | .25 |
| ☐ 58 Deion Branch | .60 | .25 |
| ☐ 59 Tom Brady | 1.50 | .60 |
| ☐ 60 Aaron Brooks | .60 | .25 |
| ☐ 61 Deuce McAllister | .75 | .30 |
| ☐ 62 Joe Horn | .60 | .25 |
| ☐ 63 Eli Manning | 1.50 | .60 |
| ☐ 64 Jeremy Shockey | .75 | .30 |
| ☐ 65 Plaxico Burress | .60 | .25 |
| ☐ 66 Tiki Barber | .75 | .30 |
| ☐ 67 Chad Pennington | .75 | .30 |
| ☐ 68 Curtis Martin | .75 | .30 |
| ☐ 69 Laveranues Coles | .60 | .25 |
| ☐ 70 Kerry Collins | .60 | .25 |
| ☐ 71 LaMont Jordan | .60 | .25 |
| ☐ 72 Randy Moss | .75 | .30 |
| ☐ 73 Brian Westbrook | .75 | .30 |
| ☐ 74 Donovan McNabb | .75 | .30 |
| ☐ 75 Terrell Owens | .75 | .30 |
| ☐ 76 Ben Roethlisberger | 2.00 | .75 |
| ☐ 77 Duce Staley | .60 | .25 |
| ☐ 78 Hines Ward | .75 | .30 |
| ☐ 79 Jerome Bettis | .75 | .30 |
| ☐ 80 Antonio Gates | .75 | .30 |
| ☐ 81 Drew Brees | .75 | .30 |
| ☐ 82 LaDainian Tomlinson | 1.25 | .50 |
| ☐ 83 Brandon Lloyd | .50 | .20 |
| ☐ 84 Kevan Barlow | .50 | .20 |
| ☐ 85 Darrell Jackson | .60 | .25 |

| | | |
|---|---|---|
| ☐ 86 Matt Hasselbeck | .60 | .25 |
| ☐ 87 Shaun Alexander | .75 | .30 |
| ☐ 88 Isaac Bruce | .60 | .25 |
| ☐ 89 Marc Bulger | .60 | .25 |
| ☐ 90 Steven Jackson | 1.00 | .40 |
| ☐ 91 Torry Holt | .60 | .25 |
| ☐ 92 Brian Griese | .60 | .25 |
| ☐ 93 Derrick Brooks | .60 | .25 |
| ☐ 94 Chris Brown | .60 | .25 |
| ☐ 95 Drew Bennett | .60 | .25 |
| ☐ 96 Steve McNair | .75 | .30 |
| ☐ 97 Travis Henry | .60 | .25 |
| ☐ 98 Clinton Portis | .75 | .30 |
| ☐ 99 LaVar Arrington | .75 | .30 |
| ☐ 100 Santana Moss | .60 | .25 |
| ☐ 101 Aaron Rodgers AU/530* RC | 175.00 | 100.00 |
| ☐ 102 Adam Jones AU RC | 25.00 | 10.00 |
| ☐ 103 A.McPherson AU/365* RC | 40.00 | 20.00 |
| ☐ 104 Alvin Pearman AU RC | 12.00 | 5.00 |
| ☐ 105 Airese Currie AU RC | 12.00 | 5.00 |
| ☐ 106 Alex Smith QB AU/401* RC | 60.00 | 30.00 |
| ☐ 107 Andrew Walter AU/99* RC | 200.00 | 100.00 |
| ☐ 108 Anthony Davis AU/366* RC | 20.00 | 8.00 |
| ☐ 109 Antrel Rolle AU RC | 15.00 | 6.00 |
| ☐ 110 Brandon Jacobs AU RC | 50.00 | 25.00 |
| ☐ 111 Brandon Jones AU RC | 15.00 | 6.00 |
| ☐ 112 Braylon Edwards AU RC | 100.00 | 50.00 |
| ☐ 113 Bryant McFadden AU/315* RC | 20.00 | 8.00 |
| ☐ 114 Carlos Rogers AU RC | 25.00 | 10.00 |
| ☐ 115 Cad.Williams AU/380* RC | 80.00 | 40.00 |
| ☐ 116 Cedric Benson AU/289* RC | 50.00 | 25.00 |
| ☐ 117 C.Houston AU/116* RC | 250.00 | 150.00 |
| ☐ 118 Chad Owens AU RC | 15.00 | 6.00 |
| ☐ 119 Charlie Frye AU RC | 15.00 | 6.00 |
| ☐ 120 Chris Henry AU RC | 15.00 | 6.00 |
| ☐ 121 Ciatrick Fason AU RC | 12.00 | 5.00 |
| ☐ 122 Courtney Roby AU RC | 12.00 | 5.00 |
| ☐ 123 Craig Bragg AU/425* RC | 20.00 | 8.00 |
| ☐ 124 C.Thorpe AU/416* RC | 12.00 | 5.00 |
| ☐ 125 Damien Nash AU RC | 12.00 | 5.00 |
| ☐ 126 Dan Cody AU/315* RC | 20.00 | 8.00 |
| ☐ 127 Dan Orlovsky AU RC | 15.00 | 6.00 |
| ☐ 128 Dante Ridgeway AU/373* RC | 10.00 | 4.00 |
| ☐ 129 Darren Sproles AU/454* RC | 75.00 | 40.00 |
| ☐ 130 David Greene AU RC | 12.00 | 5.00 |
| ☐ 131 David Pollack AU RC | 12.00 | 5.00 |
| ☐ 132 Deandra Cobb AU/440* RC | 12.00 | 5.00 |
| ☐ 133 DeMarcus Ware AU RC | 40.00 | 20.00 |
| ☐ 134 Derek Anderson AU/450* RC | 100.00 | 50.00 |
| ☐ 135 Derrick Johnson AU RC | 25.00 | 10.00 |
| ☐ 136 Erasmus James AU RC | 12.00 | 5.00 |
| ☐ 137 Eric Shelton AU RC | 12.00 | 5.00 |
| ☐ 138 Fabian Washington AU RC | 15.00 | 6.00 |
| ☐ 139 Frank Gore AU RC | 100.00 | 40.00 |
| ☐ 140 Fred Gibson AU/476* RC | 12.00 | 5.00 |
| ☐ 141 Heath Miller AU/510* RC | 50.00 | 25.00 |
| ☐ 142 J.J. Arrington AU/465* RC | 20.00 | 8.00 |
| ☐ 143 J.R. Russell AU/489* RC | 10.00 | 4.00 |
| ☐ 144 Jason Campbell AU RC | 80.00 | 50.00 |
| ☐ 145 Jason White AU RC | 15.00 | 6.00 |
| ☐ 146 Jerome Mathis AU/416* RC | 15.00 | 6.00 |
| ☐ 147 Josh Davis AU RC | 10.00 | 4.00 |
| ☐ 148 Kay-Jay Harris AU RC | 12.00 | 5.00 |
| ☐ 149 Kyle Orton AU RC | 40.00 | 20.00 |
| ☐ 150 Larry Brackins AU RC | 10.00 | 4.00 |
| ☐ 151 Lionel Gates AU/241* RC | 20.00 | 8.00 |
| ☐ 152 Marion Barber AU RC | 150.00 | 75.00 |
| ☐ 153 Mark Bradley AU RC | 15.00 | 6.00 |
| ☐ 154 Mark Clayton AU/494* RC | 25.00 | 10.00 |
| ☐ 155 Marlin Jackson AU RC | 12.00 | 5.00 |
| ☐ 156 Matt Jones AU/165* RC | 80.00 | 40.00 |
| ☐ 157 Matt Roth AU RC | 15.00 | 6.00 |
| ☐ 158 Maurice Clarett AU/89* RC | 135.00 | 75.00 |
| ☐ 159 Mike Williams AU/73* RC | 12.00 | 5.00 |
| ☐ 160 Paris Warren AU/241* RC | 25.00 | 10.00 |
| ☐ 161 Rasheed Marshall AU RC | 15.00 | 6.00 |
| ☐ 162 Reggie Brown AU/528* RC | 15.00 | 6.00 |
| ☐ 163 Roddy White AU RC | 30.00 | 15.00 |
| ☐ 164 Ronnie Brown AU/550* RC | 100.00 | 50.00 |
| ☐ 165 Roscoe Parrish AU RC | 12.00 | 5.00 |
| ☐ 166 Royd.Williams AU/491* RC | 12.00 | 5.00 |
| ☐ 167 R.Fitzpatrick AU/284* RC | 25.00 | 10.00 |
| ☐ 168 Ryan Moats AU RC | 15.00 | 6.00 |
| ☐ 169 Shaun Cody AU RC | 12.00 | 5.00 |
| ☐ 170 Shawne Merriman AU RC | 50.00 | 25.00 |

|  | | | |
|---|---|---|---|
| 171 | Stefan LeFors AU RC | 12.00 | 5.00 |
| 172 | Steve Savoy AU RC | 10.00 | 4.00 |
| 173 | T.A. McLendon AU RC | 10.00 | 4.00 |
| 174 | Tab Perry AU RC | 15.00 | 6.00 |
| 175 | Taylor Stubblefield AU RC | 10.00 | 4.00 |
| 176 | Terrence Murphy AU RC | 10.00 | 4.00 |
| 177 | Thomas Davis AU RC | 12.00 | 5.00 |
| 178 | Travis Johnson AU RC | 10.00 | 4.00 |
| 179 | T.Williamson AU/402* RC | 25.00 | 10.00 |
| 180 | Vernand Morency AU RC | 15.00 | 6.00 |
| 181 | Vincent Jackson AU RC | 15.00 | 6.00 |
| 182 | Alex Smith TE AU RC | 15.00 | 6.00 |
| 183 | Channing Crowder AU RC | 12.00 | 5.00 |
| 184 | Darrent Williams AU RC | 40.00 | 15.00 |
| 185 | Derrick Wimbush AU RC | 12.00 | 5.00 |
| 186 | James Kilian AU RC | 10.00 | 4.00 |
| 187 | Josh Cribbs AU RC | 50.00 | 30.00 |
| 188 | LeRon McCoy AU RC | 10.00 | 4.00 |
| 189 | Luis Castillo AU RC | 15.00 | 6.00 |
| 190 | Matt Cassel AU RC | 80.00 | 40.00 |
| 191 | Mike Patterson AU RC | 12.00 | 5.00 |
| 192 | Nate Washington AU RC | 20.00 | 10.00 |
| 193 | Noah Herron AU RC | 15.00 | 6.00 |
| 194 | Fred Amey AU RC | 12.00 | 5.00 |
| 195 | Tyson Thompson AU RC | 15.00 | 6.00 |
| 196 | Mike Nugent AU RC | 12.00 | 5.00 |
| 197 | Odell Thurman AU RC | 20.00 | 8.00 |
| 198 | Chris Carr AU RC | 12.00 | 5.00 |
| 199 | Bo Scaife AU RC | 10.00 | 5.00 |
| 200 | Billy Bajema AU RC | 10.00 | 4.00 |

## 2006 Playoff Contenders

| # | | | |
|---|---|---|---|
| | COMP.SET w/o RC's (100) | 20.00 | 8.00 |
| 1 | Anquan Boldin | .60 | .25 |
| 2 | Edgerrin James | .60 | .25 |
| 3 | Larry Fitzgerald | .75 | .30 |
| 4 | Alge Crumpler | .60 | .25 |
| 5 | Michael Vick | .75 | .30 |
| 6 | Warrick Dunn | .60 | .25 |
| 7 | Steve McNair | .60 | .25 |
| 8 | Mark Clayton | .60 | .25 |
| 9 | Derrick Mason | .60 | .25 |
| 10 | Lee Evans | .60 | .25 |
| 11 | Willis McGahee | .60 | .25 |
| 12 | Jake Delhomme | .60 | .25 |
| 13 | Keyshawn Johnson | .60 | .25 |
| 14 | Steve Smith | .75 | .30 |
| 15 | Cedric Benson | .60 | .25 |
| 16 | Brian Urlacher | .75 | .30 |
| 17 | Thomas Jones | .60 | .25 |
| 18 | Carson Palmer | .75 | .30 |
| 19 | Chad Johnson | .60 | .25 |
| 20 | Rudi Johnson | .60 | .25 |
| 21 | T.J. Houshmandzadeh | .60 | .25 |
| 22 | Charlie Frye | .60 | .25 |
| 23 | Braylon Edwards | .75 | .30 |
| 24 | Reuben Droughns | .60 | .25 |
| 25 | Tony Romo | 5.00 | 2.00 |
| 26 | Julius Jones | .75 | .30 |
| 27 | Roy Williams S | .60 | .25 |
| 28 | Terrell Owens | .75 | .30 |
| 29 | Javon Walker | .60 | .25 |
| 30 | Rod Smith | .60 | .25 |
| 31 | Tatum Bell | .60 | .25 |
| 32 | Roy Williams WR | .75 | .30 |
| 33 | Kevin Jones | .75 | .30 |
| 34 | Brett Favre | 1.50 | .60 |
| 35 | Robert Ferguson | .50 | .20 |

|  | | | |
|---|---|---|---|
| 36 | Samkon Gado | .75 | .30 |
| 37 | Andre Johnson | .60 | .25 |
| 38 | David Carr | .60 | .25 |
| 39 | Domanick Davis | .60 | .25 |
| 40 | Eric Moulds | .60 | .25 |
| 41 | Dallas Clark | .60 | .25 |
| 42 | Marvin Harrison | .75 | .30 |
| 43 | Peyton Manning | 1.25 | .50 |
| 44 | Reggie Wayne | .60 | .25 |
| 45 | Matt Jones | .60 | .25 |
| 46 | Byron Leftwich | .60 | .25 |
| 47 | Fred Taylor | .60 | .25 |
| 48 | Larry Johnson | .60 | .25 |
| 49 | Priest Holmes | .60 | .25 |
| 50 | Tony Gonzalez | .60 | .25 |
| 51 | Trent Green | .60 | .25 |
| 52 | Chris Chambers | .60 | .25 |
| 53 | Daunte Culpepper | .75 | .30 |
| 54 | Ronnie Brown | .75 | .30 |
| 55 | Chester Taylor | .60 | .25 |
| 56 | Brad Johnson | .60 | .25 |
| 57 | Corey Dillon | .60 | .25 |
| 58 | Deion Branch | .60 | .25 |
| 59 | Tom Brady | 1.25 | .50 |
| 60 | Tedy Bruschi | .60 | .25 |
| 61 | Deuce McAllister | .60 | .25 |
| 62 | Donte Stallworth | .60 | .25 |
| 63 | Drew Brees | .75 | .30 |
| 64 | Eli Manning | 1.00 | .40 |
| 65 | Jeremy Shockey | .75 | .30 |
| 66 | Tiki Barber | .75 | .30 |
| 67 | Chad Pennington | .60 | .25 |
| 68 | Curtis Martin | .60 | .25 |
| 69 | Laveranues Coles | .60 | .25 |
| 70 | Randy Moss | .60 | .25 |
| 71 | LaMont Jordan | .60 | .25 |
| 72 | Jerry Porter | .60 | .25 |
| 73 | Donovan McNabb | .75 | .30 |
| 74 | Reggie Brown | .60 | .25 |
| 75 | Ben Roethlisberger | 1.25 | .50 |
| 76 | Hines Ward | .75 | .30 |
| 77 | Willie Parker | 1.00 | .40 |
| 78 | Antonio Gates | .75 | .30 |
| 79 | Philip Rivers | .75 | .30 |
| 80 | LaDainian Tomlinson | 1.00 | .40 |
| 81 | Alex Smith QB | .75 | .30 |
| 82 | Antonio Bryant | .60 | .25 |
| 83 | Kevan Barlow | .60 | .25 |
| 84 | Darrell Jackson | .60 | .25 |
| 85 | Matt Hasselbeck | .60 | .25 |
| 86 | Nate Burleson | .60 | .25 |
| 87 | Shaun Alexander | .75 | .30 |
| 88 | Marc Bulger | .60+ | .25 |
| 89 | Steven Jackson | .75 | .30 |
| 90 | Isaac Bruce | .60 | .25 |
| 91 | Torry Holt | .75 | .30 |
| 92 | Cadillac Williams | .75 | .30 |
| 93 | Chris Simms | .60 | .25 |
| 94 | Joey Galloway | .60 | .25 |
| 95 | Chris Brown | .60 | .25 |
| 96 | David Givens | .60 | .25 |
| 97 | Drew Bennett | .60 | .25 |
| 98 | Clinton Portis | .75 | .30 |
| 99 | Santana Moss | .60 | .25 |
| 100 | Mark Brunell | .60 | .25 |
| 101 | Malcolm Floyd AU RC | 20.00 | 8.00 |
| 102 | Bart Scott AU RC | 40.00 | 20.00 |
| 103 | Reggie McNeal AU/457* RC | 20.00 | 8.00 |
| 104 | Domenik Hixon AU/349* RC | 30.00 | 15.00 |
| 105 | Vince Young AU/487* RC | 150.00 | 75.00 |
| 106 | Marcedes Lewis AU RC | 20.00 | 8.00 |
| 107 | Wali Lundy AU/400* RC EXCH | 40.00 | 20.00 |
| 108 | Tarvaris Jackson AU RC | 30.00 | 15.00 |
| 109 | Ko Simpson AU RC | 15.00 | 6.00 |
| 110 | Jason Allen AU RC | 20.00 | 8.00 |
| 111 | Anthony Fasano AU RC | 20.00 | 8.00 |
| 112 | Joe Klopfenstein AU RC | 15.00 | 6.00 |
| 113 | Marques Hagans AU RC | 12.00 | 5.00 |
| 114 | Jason Avant AU RC | 20.00 | 8.00 |
| 115 | Santonio Holmes AU RC | 60.00 | 35.00 |
| 116 | Marcus Vick AU/149* RC | 150.00 | 75.00 |
| 117 | Antonio Cromartie AU/322* RC | 30.00 | 15.00 |
| 118 | DeAngelo Williams AU RC | 50.00 | 25.00 |
| 119 | Laurence Maroney AU RC | 120.00 | 60.00 |
| 120 | Daniel Bullocks AU RC | 20.00 | 8.00 |

|  | | | |
|---|---|---|---|
| 121 | Jonathan Orr AU RC | 15.00 | 6.00 |
| 122 | Mike Bell AU RC | 25.00 | 10.00 |
| 123 | Kellen Clemens AU RC | 60.00 | 30.00 |
| 124 | Tim Jennings AU RC | 15.00 | 6.00 |
| 125 | Cory Rodgers AU RC | 20.00 | 8.00 |
| 126 | Jerome Harrison AU RC | 20.00 | 8.00 |
| 127 | Brad Smith AU/570* RC | 25.00 | 10.00 |
| 128 | Jeff Webb AU/250* RC EXCH | 40.00 | 20.00 |
| 129 | Will Blackmon AU RC | 15.00 | 6.00 |
| 130 | Quinton Ganther AU RC | 15.00 | 6.00 |
| 131 | Drew Olson AU RC | 15.00 | 6.00 |
| 132 | Omar Jacobs AU RC | 15.00 | 6.00 |
| 133 | Adam Jennings AU RC | 15.00 | 6.00 |
| 134 | Cedric Humes AU RC | 20.00 | 8.00 |
| 135 | Derrick Ross AU/250* RC | 80.00 | 40.00 |
| 136 | Charlie Whitehurst AU RC | 30.00 | 12.50 |
| 137 | Bobby Carpenter AU RC | 20.00 | 8.00 |
| 138 | Darryl Tapp AU RC | 15.00 | 6.00 |
| 139 | A.J. Hawk AU/399* RC | 80.00 | 40.00 |
| 140 | Bruce Gradkowski AU RC | 20.00 | 8.00 |
| 141 | Chad Greenway AU RC | 20.00 | 8.00 |
| 142 | John David Washington AU RC | 15.00 | 6.00 |
| 143 | Kamerion Wimbley AU RC | 20.00 | 8.00 |
| 144 | LenDale White AU/549* RC | 60.00 | 30.00 |
| 145 | Johnathan Joseph AU/549* RC | 20.00 | 8.00 |
| 146 | Maurice Drew AU RC | 85.00 | 10.00 |
| 147 | Brandon Marshall AU/608* RC | 80.00 | 50.00 |
| 148 | Vernon Davis AU/537* RC | 50.00 | 25.00 |
| 149 | Joseph Addai AU RC | 120.00 | 60.00 |
| 150 | Bennie Brazell AU RC | 12.00 | 5.00 |
| 151 | D.J. Shockley AU RC | 20.00 | 8.00 |
| 152 | Jay Cutler AU/501* RC | 250.00 | 125.00 |
| 153 | Wendell Mathis AU RC | 15.00 | 6.00 |
| 154 | Demetrius Williams AU RC | 20.00 | 8.00 |
| 155 | Dusty Dvoracek AU RC | 20.00 | 8.00 |
| 156 | DeMario Minter AU RC | 15.00 | 6.00 |
| 157 | Marcus Maxey AU RC | 15.00 | 6.00 |
| 158 | Brodie Croyle AU RC | 60.00 | 30.00 |
| 159 | Jeremy Bloom AU/473* RC | 40.00 | 15.00 |
| 160 | Todd Watkins AU RC | 12.00 | 5.00 |
| 161 | Cory Ross AU RC | 20.00 | 8.00 |
| 162 | Tamba Hali AU/500* RC | 25.00 | 10.00 |
| 163 | P.J. Daniels AU/555* RC | 20.00 | 8.00 |
| 164 | Brandon Williams AU RC | 20.00 | 8.00 |
| 165 | Devin Hester AU RC | 80.00 | 50.00 |
| 166 | Kelly Jennings AU/393* RC | 20.00 | 8.00 |
| 167 | Dawan Landry AU RC | 20.00 | 8.00 |
| 168 | Greg Jennings AU RC | 40.00 | 25.00 |
| 169 | Mathias Kiwanuka AU RC | 25.00 | 10.00 |
| 170 | Leon Washington AU RC | 40.00 | 15.00 |
| 171 | Richard Marshall AU RC | 15.00 | 6.00 |
| 172 | Haloti Ngata AU RC | 20.00 | 8.00 |
| 173 | Vernice Moss AU RC | 25.00 | 10.00 |
| 174 | Greg Blue AU RC | 15.00 | 6.00 |
| 175 | Chris Barclay AU RC | 15.00 | 6.00 |
| 176 | D'Qwell Jackson AU RC | 20.00 | 8.00 |
| 177 | Eric Smith AU RC | 12.00 | 5.00 |
| 178 | Ethan Kilmer AU RC | 20.00 | 8.00 |
| 179 | Mike Hass AU RC | 20.00 | 8.00 |
| 180 | Derek Hagan AU RC | 20.00 | 8.00 |
| 181 | Travis Wilson AU RC | 20.00 | 8.00 |
| 182 | Reggie Bush AU/645* RC | 200.00 | 100.00 |
| 183 | Maurice Stovall AU/579* RC | 40.00 | 20.00 |
| 184 | Skyler Green AU RC | 15.00 | 6.00 |
| 185 | Calvin Lowry AU RC | 15.00 | 6.00 |
| 186 | Jerious Norwood AU RC | 60.00 | 35.00 |
| 187 | Brodrick Bunkley AU/518* RC | 20.00 | 8.00 |
| 188 | Ernie Sims AU/611* RC | 20.00 | 8.00 |
| 189 | Ingle Martin AU RC | 20.00 | 8.00 |
| 190 | Anthony Mix AU RC | 15.00 | 6.00 |
| 191 | Patrick Cobbs AU RC | 15.00 | 6.00 |
| 192 | Delanie Walker AU/212* RC | 80.00 | 40.00 |
| 193 | Gabe Watson AU RC | 15.00 | 6.00 |
| 194 | Willie Reid AU/515* RC | 20.00 | 8.00 |
| 195 | Michael Huff AU RC | 30.00 | 15.00 |
| 196 | Mario Williams AU/395* RC | 40.00 | 20.00 |
| 197 | Chad Jackson AU RC | 25.00 | 10.00 |
| 198 | David Kirtman AU RC | 15.00 | 6.00 |
| 199 | B.Calhoun AU/407* RC EXCH | 40.00 | 16.00 |
| 200 | M.Robinson AU/512* RC EXCH | 30.00 | 12.00 |
| 201 | D.Ferguson AU/386* RC | 30.00 | 12.00 |
| 202 | Donte Whitner AU/518* RC | 25.00 | 10.00 |
| 203 | Roman Harper AU RC | 15.00 | 6.00 |
| 204 | Manny Lawson AU RC | 15.00 | 6.00 |
| 205 | DeMeco Ryans AU RC | 30.00 | 15.00 |

| | | | |
|---|---|---|---|
| ❑ 206 Anthony Smith AU RC | 30.00 | 15.00 |
| ❑ 207 Thomas Howard AU RC | 20.00 | 8.00 |
| ❑ 208 John McCargo AU RC | 12.00 | 5.00 |
| ❑ 209 David Pittman AU RC | 15.00 | 6.00 |
| ❑ 210 Danieal Manning AU RC | 15.00 | 6.00 |
| ❑ 211 Nate Salley AU RC | 12.00 | 5.00 |
| ❑ 212 Jimmy Williams AU/524* RC | 20.00 | 8.00 |
| ❑ 213 Rocky McIntosh AU RC | 20.00 | 8.00 |
| ❑ 214 Montell Owens AU RC | 12.00 | 5.00 |
| ❑ 215 Devin Aromashodu AU RC | 12.00 | 5.00 |
| ❑ 216 Ben Obomanu AU RC | 12.00 | 5.00 |
| ❑ 217 David Anderson AU RC | 15.00 | 6.00 |
| ❑ 218 Marques Colston AU RC | 60.00 | 30.00 |
| ❑ 219 Miles Austin AU RC | 25.00 | 12.50 |
| ❑ 220 Tony Scheffler AU/526* RC | 40.00 | 20.00 |
| ❑ 221 Leonard Pope AU/495* RC | 20.00 | 8.00 |
| ❑ 222 David Thomas AU RC | 20.00 | 8.00 |
| ❑ 223 Dominique Byrd AU RC | 15.00 | 6.00 |
| ❑ 224 Owen Daniels AU RC | 20.00 | 8.00 |
| ❑ 225 Garrett Mills AU RC | 15.00 | 6.00 |
| ❑ 226 Hank Baskett AU RC | 25.00 | 12.50 |
| ❑ 227 Jason Carter AU RC | 15.00 | 6.00 |
| ❑ 228 Sam Hurd AU RC | 20.00 | 8.00 |
| ❑ 229 Charles Sharon AU/250* RC | 100.00 | 50.00 |
| ❑ 230 Chris Hannon AU RC | 12.00 | 5.00 |
| ❑ 231 John Madsen AU RC | 20.00 | 8.00 |
| ❑ 232 Shaun Bodiford AU RC | 12.00 | 5.00 |
| ❑ 233 Mike Espy AU RC | 20.00 | 8.00 |
| ❑ 234 Abdul Hodge AU RC | 20.00 | 8.00 |
| ❑ 235 Anthony Montgomery AU RC | 15.00 | 6.00 |
| ❑ 236 Matt Leinart AU/567* RC | 120.00 | 60.00 |
| ❑ 237 Bernard Pollard AU/307* RC | 30.00 | 15.00 |
| ❑ 238 Pat Watkins AU/343* RC | 50.00 | 20.00 |
| ❑ 239 Cedric Griffin AU/357* RC | 30.00 | 15.00 |
| ❑ 240 A.J. Nicholson AU RC | 12.00 | 5.00 |
| ❑ 241 Claude Wroten AU/306* RC | 60.00 | 30.00 |
| ❑ 242 Tye Hill AU/368* RC | 30.00 | 12.50 |

## 2007 Playoff Contenders

| | | | |
|---|---|---|---|
| ❑ 1 Edgerrin James | .60 | .25 |
| ❑ 2 Larry Fitzgerald | .75 | .30 |
| ❑ 3 Anquan Boldin | .60 | .25 |
| ❑ 4 Matt Leinart | .75 | .30 |
| ❑ 5 Joey Harrington | .60 | .25 |
| ❑ 6 Warrick Dunn | .60 | .25 |
| ❑ 7 Joe Horn | .60 | .25 |
| ❑ 8 Steve McNair | .60 | .25 |
| ❑ 9 Willis McGahee | .60 | .25 |
| ❑ 10 Derrick Mason | .50 | .20 |
| ❑ 11 J.P. Losman | .50 | .20 |
| ❑ 12 Lee Evans | .60 | .25 |
| ❑ 13 Josh Reed | .50 | .20 |
| ❑ 14 Jake Delhomme | .60 | .25 |
| ❑ 15 DeShaun Foster | .60 | .25 |
| ❑ 16 Steve Smith | .60 | .25 |
| ❑ 17 Rex Grossman | .60 | .25 |
| ❑ 18 Bernard Berrian | .50 | .20 |
| ❑ 19 Cedric Benson | .60 | .25 |
| ❑ 20 Carson Palmer | .75 | .30 |
| ❑ 21 Chad Johnson | .60 | .25 |
| ❑ 22 T.J. Houshmandzadeh | .60 | .25 |
| ❑ 23 Rudi Johnson | .60 | .25 |
| ❑ 24 Braylon Edwards | .60 | .25 |
| ❑ 25 Kellen Winslow | .60 | .25 |
| ❑ 26 Jamal Lewis | .60 | .25 |
| ❑ 27 Tony Romo | 1.50 | .60 |
| ❑ 28 Terrell Owens | .75 | .30 |
| ❑ 29 Jason Witten | .60 | .25 |

| | | | |
|---|---|---|---|
| ❑ 30 Julius Jones | .60 | .25 |
| ❑ 31 Jay Cutler | .75 | .30 |
| ❑ 32 Javon Walker | .60 | .25 |
| ❑ 33 Travis Henry | .60 | .25 |
| ❑ 34 Jon Kitna | .50 | .20 |
| ❑ 35 Roy Williams WR | .60 | .25 |
| ❑ 36 Tatum Bell | .50 | .20 |
| ❑ 37 Brett Favre | 1.50 | .60 |
| ❑ 38 Donald Driver | .60 | .25 |
| ❑ 39 Greg Jennings | .60 | .25 |
| ❑ 40 Matt Schaub | .60 | .25 |
| ❑ 41 Ahman Green | .60 | .25 |
| ❑ 42 Andre Johnson | .60 | .25 |
| ❑ 43 Peyton Manning | 1.25 | .50 |
| ❑ 44 Joseph Addai | .75 | .30 |
| ❑ 45 Marvin Harrison | .60 | .25 |
| ❑ 46 Reggie Wayne | .60 | .25 |
| ❑ 47 David Garrard | .60 | .25 |
| ❑ 48 Fred Taylor | .60 | .25 |
| ❑ 49 Maurice Jones-Drew | .75 | .30 |
| ❑ 50 Larry Johnson | .60 | .25 |
| ❑ 51 Damon Huard | .60 | .25 |
| ❑ 52 Tony Gonzalez | .60 | .25 |
| ❑ 53 Trent Green | .60 | .25 |
| ❑ 54 Ronnie Brown | .60 | .25 |
| ❑ 55 Chris Chambers | .60 | .25 |
| ❑ 56 Troy Williamson | .50 | .20 |
| ❑ 57 Tarvaris Jackson | .60 | .25 |
| ❑ 58 Chester Taylor | .50 | .20 |
| ❑ 59 Tom Brady | 1.50 | .60 |
| ❑ 60 Randy Moss | .75 | .30 |
| ❑ 61 Laurence Maroney | .75 | .30 |
| ❑ 62 Drew Brees | .60 | .25 |
| ❑ 63 Deuce McAllister | .60 | .25 |
| ❑ 64 Reggie Bush | 1.00 | .40 |
| ❑ 65 Eli Manning | .75 | .30 |
| ❑ 66 Brandon Jacobs | .60 | .25 |
| ❑ 67 Plaxico Burress | .60 | .25 |
| ❑ 68 Chad Pennington | .60 | .25 |
| ❑ 69 Laveranues Coles | .60 | .25 |
| ❑ 70 Thomas Jones | .60 | .25 |
| ❑ 71 Ronald Curry | .50 | .20 |
| ❑ 72 LaMont Jordan | .60 | .25 |
| ❑ 73 Jerry Porter | .60 | .25 |
| ❑ 74 Donovan McNabb | .75 | .30 |
| ❑ 75 Brian Westbrook | .60 | .25 |
| ❑ 76 Ben Roethlisberger | 1.00 | .40 |
| ❑ 77 Willie Parker | .75 | .30 |
| ❑ 78 Hines Ward | .75 | .30 |
| ❑ 79 LaDainian Tomlinson | 1.00 | .40 |
| ❑ 80 Philip Rivers | .75 | .30 |
| ❑ 81 Antonio Gates | .60 | .25 |
| ❑ 82 Alex Smith QB | .60 | .25 |
| ❑ 83 Frank Gore | .75 | .30 |
| ❑ 84 Darrell Jackson | .60 | .25 |
| ❑ 85 Vernon Davis | .60 | .25 |
| ❑ 86 Deion Branch | .60 | .25 |
| ❑ 87 Matt Hasselbeck | .60 | .25 |
| ❑ 88 Shaun Alexander | .60 | .25 |
| ❑ 89 Marc Bulger | .60 | .25 |
| ❑ 90 Steven Jackson | .75 | .30 |
| ❑ 91 Torry Holt | .60 | .25 |
| ❑ 92 Jeff Garcia | .60 | .25 |
| ❑ 93 Cadillac Williams | .60 | .25 |
| ❑ 94 Joey Galloway | .60 | .25 |
| ❑ 95 Vince Young | .75 | .30 |
| ❑ 96 Chris Brown | .50 | .20 |
| ❑ 97 Brandon Jones | .50 | .20 |
| ❑ 98 Jason Campbell | .60 | .25 |
| ❑ 99 Clinton Portis | .60 | .25 |
| ❑ 100 Santana Moss | .60 | .25 |
| ❑ 101 Aaron Ross AU RC | 30.00 | 15.00 |
| ❑ 102 Aaron Rouse AU RC | 20.00 | 8.00 |
| ❑ 103 Adam Carriker AU/333* RC | 40.00 | 20.00 |
| ❑ 104 Adrian Peterson AU/555* RC | 250.00 | 125.00 |
| ❑ 105 A.Bradshaw AU RC EXCH | 60.00 | 30.00 |
| ❑ 106 Alan Branch AU/326* RC EXCH | 25.00 | 10.00 |
| ❑ 107 Amobi Okoye AU RC EXCH | 20.00 | 8.00 |
| ❑ 108 Anthony Gonzalez AU RC | 60.00 | 30.00 |
| ❑ 109 Anthony Spencer AU RC | 20.00 | 8.00 |
| ❑ 110 Antonio Pittman AU/533* RC EXCH | 25.00 | 10.00 |
| ❑ 111 Aundrae Allison AU RC | 20.00 | 8.00 |
| ❑ 112 Ben Patrick AU RC | 20.00 | 8.00 |
| ❑ 113 Biren Ealy AU RC EXCH | 20.00 | 8.00 |
| ❑ 114 Bobby Sippio AU RC | 15.00 | 6.00 |

| | | | |
|---|---|---|---|
| ❑ 115 Brady Quinn AU/534* RC | 150.00 | 75.00 |
| ❑ 116 Brandon Jackson AU RC | 25.00 | 10.00 |
| ❑ 117 Brandon Mebane AU RC | 15.00 | 6.00 |
| ❑ 118 Brandon Meriweather AU RC | 20.00 | 8.00 |
| ❑ 119 Brandon Siler AU RC | 15.00 | 6.00 |
| ❑ 120 Brian Leonard AU RC | 20.00 | 8.00 |
| ❑ 121 Brian Robison AU RC | 15.00 | 6.00 |
| ❑ 122 Buster Davis AU/246* RC EXCH | 40.00 | 20.00 |
| ❑ 123 Calvin Johnson AU/525* RC | 120.00 | 60.00 |
| ❑ 124 Chansi Stuckey AU/502* RC | 20.00 | 8.00 |
| ❑ 125 Ch.John AU/303* RC EXCH | 80.00 | 40.00 |
| ❑ 126 Chris Davis AU RC | 15.00 | 6.00 |
| ❑ 127 Chris Henry RB AU RC | 20.00 | 8.00 |
| ❑ 128 Chris Houston AU RC EXCH | 15.00 | 6.00 |
| ❑ 129 Clifton Ryan AU RC | 15.00 | 6.00 |
| ❑ 130 Clifton Dawson AU RC | 15.00 | 6.00 |
| ❑ 131 Courtney Taylor AU RC | 15.00 | 6.00 |
| ❑ 132 C.Davis AU RC EXCH | 25.00 | 10.00 |
| ❑ 133 Dallas Baker AU RC | 15.00 | 6.00 |
| ❑ 134 Dan Bazuin AU/198* RC | 50.00 | 25.00 |
| ❑ 135 Daymeion Hughes AU/383* RC | 25.00 | 10.00 |
| ❑ 136 Dante Rosario AU RC EXCH | 25.00 | 12.50 |
| ❑ 137 David Irons AU/198* RC | 40.00 | 20.00 |
| ❑ 138 Darrelle Revis AU/533* RC | 20.00 | 8.00 |
| ❑ 139 David Clowney AU/410* RC | 25.00 | 10.00 |
| ❑ 140 David Harris AU RC | 15.00 | 6.00 |
| ❑ 141 DeShawn Wynn AU/429* RC | 40.00 | 20.00 |
| ❑ 142 Drew Stanton AU RC | 40.00 | 15.00 |
| ❑ 143 Dwayne Bowe AU RC | 60.00 | 30.00 |
| ❑ 144 Dwayne Jarrett AU/484* RC | 40.00 | 15.00 |
| ❑ 145 Dwayne Wright AU/410* RC | 20.00 | 8.00 |
| ❑ 146 Ed Johnson AU RC | 12.00 | 5.00 |
| ❑ 147 Eric Frampton AU/452* RC | 20.00 | 8.00 |
| ❑ 148 Eric Weddle AU RC | 15.00 | 6.00 |
| ❑ 149 Eric Wright AU/273* RC EXCH | 50.00 | 25.00 |
| ❑ 150 Fred Bennett AU RC | 12.00 | 5.00 |
| ❑ 151 Gaines Adams AU RC | 20.00 | 8.00 |
| ❑ 152 Garrett Wolfe AU RC | 40.00 | 15.00 |
| ❑ 153 Glenn Holt AU RC | 15.00 | 6.00 |
| ❑ 154 Glenn Martinez AU RC | 20.00 | 8.00 |
| ❑ 155 Greg Olsen AU RC | 30.00 | 12.00 |
| ❑ 156 Greg Peterson AU RC | 15.00 | 6.00 |
| ❑ 157 H.B. Blades AU/383* RC | 20.00 | 8.00 |
| ❑ 158 I.Alama-Francis AU/222* RC | 40.00 | 20.00 |
| ❑ 159 Isaiah Stanback AU/510* RC | 25.00 | 10.00 |
| ❑ 160 Jacoby Jones AU/435* RC | 30.00 | 12.00 |
| ❑ 161 J.Anderson AU/123* RC SP | 120.00 | 60.00 |
| ❑ 162 JaMarcus Russell AU RC | 80.00 | 30.00 |
| ❑ 163 James Jones AU RC | 40.00 | 15.00 |
| ❑ 164 J.Zbransky AU/347* RC | 50.00 | 25.00 |
| ❑ 165 Jarvis Moss AU/227* RC | 60.00 | 30.00 |
| ❑ 166 Jason Hill AU RC SP | | |
| ❑ 167 Jeff Rowe AU/362* RC | 25.00 | 10.00 |
| ❑ 168 Joe Thomas AU/129* RC | 100.00 | 60.00 |
| ❑ 169 Joel Filani AU/483* RC | 20.00 | 8.00 |
| ❑ 170 John Beck AU RC | 40.00 | 15.00 |
| ❑ 171 John Broussard AU RC | 15.00 | 6.00 |
| ❑ 172 Johnnie Lee Higgins AU RC | 15.00 | 6.00 |
| ❑ 173 Jon Beason AU RC | 20.00 | 8.00 |
| ❑ 174 Jonathan Wade AU/365* RC AU RC | 20.00 | 8.00 |
| ❑ 175 Jordan Kent AU RC | 12.00 | 5.00 |
| ❑ 176 Josh Wilson AU/501* RC | 30.00 | 15.00 |
| ❑ 177 Justin Durant AU RC | 12.00 | 5.00 |
| ❑ 178 Kenneth Darby AU RC | 15.00 | 6.00 |
| ❑ 179 Kenny Irons AU/50* RC | 450.00 | 300.00 |
| ❑ 180 Kenton Keith AU RC | 25.00 | 10.00 |
| ❑ 181 Kevin Kolb AU RC | 50.00 | 25.00 |
| ❑ 182 Keyunta Dawson AU RC | 12.00 | 5.00 |
| ❑ 183 Kolby Smith AU/444* RC | 30.00 | 12.00 |
| ❑ 184 LaMarr Woodley AU RC | 25.00 | 10.00 |
| ❑ 185 LaRon Landry AU RC | 15.00 | 6.00 |
| ❑ 186 Laurent Robinson AU RC | 20.00 | 8.00 |
| ❑ 187 Lawrence Timmons AU RC | 20.00 | 8.00 |
| ❑ 188 Legedu Naanee AU RC | 15.00 | 6.00 |
| ❑ 189 Leon Hall AU RC | 15.00 | 6.00 |
| ❑ 190 Levi Brown AU/369* RC | 20.00 | 8.00 |
| ❑ 191 Lorenzo Booker AU RC | 25.00 | 10.00 |
| ❑ 192 Marcus McCauley AU/386* RC | 40.00 | 20.00 |
| ❑ 193 Marcus Thomas AU RC | 15.00 | 6.00 |
| ❑ 194 Marshawn Lynch AU/533* RC | 100.00 | 50.00 |
| ❑ 195 Martrez Milner AU RC EXCH | 20.00 | 8.00 |
| ❑ 196 Mason Crosby AU RC | 20.00 | 8.00 |
| ❑ 197 Matt Gutierrez AU RC EXCH | 25.00 | 10.00 |
| ❑ 198 Matt Moore AU RC | 25.00 | 10.00 |

| | | |
|---|---|---|
| 199 Matt Spaeth AU/237* RC | 50.00 | 25.00 |
| 200 Michael Bush AU RC | 30.00 | 12.00 |
| 201 Michael Griffin AU RC | 15.00 | 6.00 |
| 202 Michael Okwo AU/261* RC | 25.00 | 10.00 |
| 203 Mike Walker AU/248* RC | 50.00 | 25.00 |
| 204 Nick Folk AU RC | 30.00 | 12.00 |
| 205 Patrick Willis AU/239* RC | 100.00 | 50.00 |
| 206 Paul Posluszny AU RC | 30.00 | 12.00 |
| 207 Paul Williams AU RC | 20.00 | 8.00 |
| 208 Pierre Thomas AU RC | 30.00 | 15.00 |
| 209 Quentin Moses AU/498* RC | 20.00 | 8.00 |
| 210 Ray McDonald AU/519* RC | 20.00 | 8.00 |
| 211 Reggie Ball AU RC | 15.00 | 6.00 |
| 212 Reggie Nelson AU RC | 20.00 | 8.00 |
| 213 Robert Meachem AU RC | 40.00 | 20.00 |
| 214 Roy Hall AU RC | 20.00 | 8.00 |
| 215 Rufus Alexander AU RC | 15.00 | 6.00 |
| 216 Ryne Robinson AU/430* RC | 25.00 | 10.00 |
| 217 Sabby Piscitelli AU/337* RC | 30.00 | 12.00 |
| 218 Scott Chandler AU RC | 15.00 | 6.00 |
| 219 Selvin Young AU RC EXCH | 60.00 | 35.00 |
| 220 Sidney Rice AU/529* RC | 25.00 | 10.00 |
| 221 Stephen Nicholas AU RC | 12.00 | 5.00 |
| 222 Steve Breaston AU/274* RC | 40.00 | 25.00 |
| 223 Steve Smith AU/541 RC | 40.00 | 20.00 |
| 224 Stewart Bradley AU RC | 15.00 | 6.00 |
| 225 Syndric Steptoe AU/149* RC | 80.00 | 40.00 |
| 226 Tan.Jackson AU RC EXCH | 15.00 | 6.00 |
| 227 Ted Ginn AU/519 RC | 60.00 | 30.00 |
| 228 Thomas Clayton AU RC | 12.00 | 5.00 |
| 229 Tim Crowder AU/454* RC | 20.00 | 8.00 |
| 230 Tim Shaw AU/408* RC | 20.00 | 8.00 |
| 231 Tony Hunt AU RC | 20.00 | 8.00 |
| 232 Trent Edwards AU RC | 100.00 | 50.00 |
| 233 Troy Smith AU RC | 50.00 | 25.00 |
| 234 Turk McBride AU RC | 12.00 | 5.00 |
| 235 Tyler Palko AU RC | 25.00 | 10.00 |
| 236 Tyler Thigpen AU RC | 35.00 | 20.00 |
| 237 Victor Abiamiri AU/449* RC | 20.00 | 8.00 |
| 238 Yamon Figurs AU RC | 20.00 | 8.00 |
| 239 Zak DeOssie AU RC EXCH | 15.00 | 6.00 |
| 240 Zach Miller AU RC | 20.00 | 8.00 |

## 2008 Playoff Contenders

| | | |
|---|---|---|
| 1 Kurt Warner | .75 | .30 |
| 2 Larry Fitzgerald | .75 | .30 |
| 3 Anquan Boldin | .60 | .25 |
| 4 Edgerrin James | .60 | .25 |
| 5 Jerious Norwood | .60 | .25 |
| 6 Roddy White | .60 | .25 |
| 7 Michael Turner | .60 | .25 |
| 8 Willis McGahee | .60 | .25 |
| 9 Derrick Mason | .50 | .20 |
| 10 Le'Ron McClain | .75 | .30 |
| 11 Trent Edwards | .75 | .30 |
| 12 Marshawn Lynch | .75 | .30 |
| 13 Lee Evans | .60 | .25 |
| 14 Steve Smith | .60 | .25 |
| 15 DeAngelo Williams | .60 | .25 |
| 16 Jake Delhomme | .60 | .25 |
| 17 Greg Olsen | .60 | .25 |
| 18 Devin Hester | .75 | .30 |
| 19 Kyle Orton | .50 | .20 |
| 20 Carson Palmer | .75 | .30 |
| 21 Chad Johnson | .60 | .25 |
| 22 T.J. Houshmandzadeh | .60 | .25 |
| 23 Chris Perry | .50 | .20 |
| 24 Derek Anderson | .60 | .25 |

| | | |
|---|---|---|
| 25 Jamal Lewis | .60 | .25 |
| 26 Braylon Edwards | .60 | .25 |
| 27 Tony Romo | 1.25 | .50 |
| 28 Terrell Owens | .75 | .30 |
| 29 Marion Barber | .75 | .30 |
| 30 Jason Witten | .60 | .25 |
| 31 Jay Cutler | .75 | .30 |
| 32 Selvin Young | .60 | .25 |
| 33 Brandon Marshall | .60 | .25 |
| 34 Jon Kitna | .60 | .25 |
| 35 Roy Williams WR | .60 | .25 |
| 36 Calvin Johnson | .75 | .30 |
| 37 Aaron Rodgers | .75 | .30 |
| 38 Ryan Grant | .75 | .30 |
| 39 Greg Jennings | .60 | .25 |
| 40 Matt Schaub | .60 | .25 |
| 41 Ahman Green | .60 | .25 |
| 42 Andre Johnson | .60 | .25 |
| 43 Peyton Manning | 1.25 | .50 |
| 44 Joseph Addai | .75 | .30 |
| 45 Reggie Wayne | .60 | .25 |
| 46 David Garrard | .60 | .25 |
| 47 Fred Taylor | .60 | .25 |
| 48 Maurice Jones-Drew | .60 | .25 |
| 49 Brodie Croyle | .75 | .30 |
| 50 Larry Johnson | .60 | .25 |
| 51 Tony Gonzalez | .60 | .25 |
| 52 Chad Pennington | .60 | .25 |
| 53 Ronnie Brown | .60 | .25 |
| 54 Ted Ginn Jr. | .60 | .25 |
| 55 Tarvaris Jackson | .60 | .25 |
| 56 Adrian Peterson | 1.50 | .60 |
| 57 Chester Taylor | .50 | .20 |
| 58 Tom Brady | 1.25 | .50 |
| 59 Randy Moss | .75 | .30 |
| 60 Laurence Maroney | .60 | .25 |
| 61 Drew Brees | .75 | .30 |
| 62 Reggie Bush | .75 | .30 |
| 63 Marques Colston | .60 | .25 |
| 64 Eli Manning | .75 | .30 |
| 65 Plaxico Burress | .60 | .25 |
| 66 Brandon Jacobs | .60 | .25 |
| 67 Brett Favre | 4.00 | 1.50 |
| 68 Leon Washington | .50 | .20 |
| 69 Laveranues Coles | .50 | .20 |
| 70 Javon Walker | .60 | .25 |
| 71 JaMarcus Russell | .75 | .30 |
| 72 Justin Fargas | .50 | .20 |
| 73 Donovan McNabb | .75 | .30 |
| 74 Brian Westbrook | .60 | .25 |
| 75 Kevin Curtis | .50 | .20 |
| 76 Ben Roethlisberger | 1.00 | .40 |
| 77 Willie Parker | .60 | .25 |
| 78 Santonio Holmes | .60 | .25 |
| 79 Philip Rivers | .60 | .25 |
| 80 LaDainian Tomlinson | 1.00 | .40 |
| 81 Vincent Jackson | .50 | .20 |
| 82 Antonio Gates | .60 | .25 |
| 83 J.T. O'Sullivan | .60 | .25 |
| 84 Frank Gore | .60 | .25 |
| 85 Isaac Bruce | .60 | .25 |
| 86 Matt Hasselbeck | .60 | .25 |
| 87 Deion Branch | .60 | .25 |
| 88 Julius Jones | .60 | .25 |
| 89 Marc Bulger | .60 | .25 |
| 90 Steven Jackson | .75 | .30 |
| 91 Torry Holt | .60 | .25 |
| 92 Warrick Dunn | .60 | .25 |
| 93 Jeff Garcia | .60 | .25 |
| 94 Joey Galloway | .60 | .25 |
| 95 Vince Young | .75 | .30 |
| 96 LenDale White | .60 | .25 |
| 97 Justin Gage | .50 | .20 |
| 98 Jason Campbell | .60 | .25 |
| 99 Clinton Portis | .60 | .25 |
| 100 Chris Cooley | .60 | .25 |
| 101 Adrian Arrington AU RC | 15.00 | 6.00 |
| 102 Ali Highsmith AU/214* RC | 40.00 | 15.00 |
| 103 Allen Patrick AU RC | 20.00 | 8.00 |
| 104 Andre Caldwell AU RC | 20.00 | 8.00 |
| 105 Andre Woodson AU/250* RC | 40.00 | 15.00 |
| 106 Antoine Cason AU RC | 20.00 | 8.00 |
| 107 Aqib Talib AU RC | 20.00 | 8.00 |
| 108 Brad Cottam AU/132* RC | 60.00 | 30.00 |
| 109 Brandon Flowers AU/192* RC | 60.00 | 30.00 |

| | | |
|---|---|---|
| 110 Brian Brohm AU RC | 40.00 | 15.00 |
| 111 Calais Campbell AU RC | 15.00 | 6.00 |
| 112 Chad Henne AU RC | 60.00 | 30.00 |
| 113 C.Washington AU/114* RC | 120.00 | 60.00 |
| 114 Chevis Jackson AU RC | 15.00 | 6.00 |
| 115 Chris Johnson AU RC EXCH | 100.00 | 50.00 |
| 116 Chris Long AU RC | 30.00 | 15.00 |
| 117 Colt Brennan AU RC | 80.00 | 40.00 |
| 118 Craig Steltz AU RC | 15.00 | 6.00 |
| 119 Curtis Lofton AU RC | 20.00 | 8.00 |
| 120 Dan Connor AU RC | 20.00 | 8.00 |
| 121 Dantrell Savage AU/76* RC | 150.00 | 75.00 |
| 122 Darius Reynaud AU RC | 15.00 | 6.00 |
| 123 Darren McFadden AU RC | 150.00 | 90.00 |
| 124 Davone Bess AU RC | 25.00 | 10.00 |
| 125 Dennis Dixon AU RC | 40.00 | 20.00 |
| 126 Derrick Harvey AU RC | 15.00 | 6.00 |
| 127 DeSean Jackson AU RC | 60.00 | 30.00 |
| 128 Devin Thomas AU RC EXCH | 25.00 | 10.00 |
| 129 Dexter Jackson AU RC | 20.00 | 8.00 |
| 130 Dominique Rodgers-Cromartie AU RC | 20.00 | 8.00 |
| 131 Donnie Avery AU RC | 40.00 | 15.00 |
| 132 Dustin Keller AU RC | 30.00 | 12.00 |
| 133 Earl Bennett AU RC | 25.00 | 10.00 |
| 134 E.Doucet AU/113* RC EXCH | 100.00 | 50.00 |
| 135 Eddie Royal AU RC | 60.00 | 30.00 |
| 136 Erik Ainge AU/107* RC | 120.00 | 60.00 |
| 137 Erin Henderson AU/158* RC | 60.00 | 25.00 |
| 138 Felix Jones AU RC | 100.00 | 60.00 |
| 139 Fred Davis AU RC | 20.00 | 8.00 |
| 140 Glenn Dorsey AU RC | 25.00 | 10.00 |
| 141 Harry Douglas AU RC EXCH | 25.00 | 10.00 |
| 142 Jacob Hester AU RC | 20.00 | 8.00 |
| 143 Jacob Tamme AU RC | 30.00 | 12.00 |
| 144 Jake Long AU/163* RC | 40.00 | 15.00 |
| 145 Jamaal Charles AU RC | 40.00 | 15.00 |
| 146 James Hardy AU RC | 20.00 | 8.00 |
| 147 Jed Collins AU/30* RC | 400.00 | 250.00 |
| 148 Jermichael Finley AU/231* RC | 40.00 | 20.00 |
| 149 Jerod Mayo AU RC | 40.00 | 15.00 |
| 150 Jerome Simpson AU RC | 15.00 | 6.00 |
| 151 Joe Flacco AU/220* RC | 300.00 | 150.00 |
| 152 John Carlson AU RC | 20.00 | 8.00 |
| 153 John David Booty AU RC | 50.00 | 25.00 |
| 154A J.Stewart AU Blk RC | 80.00 | 40.00 |
| 154B J.Stewart AU Blk RC | 135.00 | 75.00 |
| 155 Jordon Dizon AU/188* RC | 40.00 | 20.00 |
| 156 Jordy Nelson AU RC | 30.00 | 12.00 |
| 157 Josh Johnson AU RC | 25.00 | 10.00 |
| 158 Josh Morgan AU RC | 25.00 | 10.00 |
| 159 Justin Forsett AU RC | 25.00 | 10.00 |
| 160 Keenan Burton AU RC | 25.00 | 10.00 |
| 161 Keith Rivers AU RC | 30.00 | 12.00 |
| 162 Kellen Davis AU RC | 20.00 | 8.00 |
| 163 Kenny Phillips AU RC | 20.00 | 8.00 |
| 164 Kentwan Balmer AU RC | 15.00 | 6.00 |
| 165 Kevin O'Connell AU RC | 50.00 | 25.00 |
| 166 Kevin Smith AU RC | 50.00 | 25.00 |
| 167 Lavelle Hawkins AU RC | 25.00 | 10.00 |
| 168 Lawrence Jackson AU RC | 15.00 | 6.00 |
| 169 Leodis McKelvin AU RC | 20.00 | 8.00 |
| 170 Limas Sweed AU RC | 40.00 | 15.00 |
| 171 M.Kelly AU/141* RC EXCH | 80.00 | 40.00 |
| 172 Marcus Smith AU RC | 15.00 | 6.00 |
| 173 Marcus Thomas AU/165* RC | 40.00 | 15.00 |
| 174 Mario Manningham AU RC | 20.00 | 8.00 |
| 175 Martellus Bennett AU RC | 20.00 | 8.00 |
| 176 Martin Rucker AU RC | 15.00 | 6.00 |
| 177 Matt Flynn AU RC | 30.00 | 12.00 |
| 178 Matt Forte AU RC | 100.00 | 60.00 |
| 179 Matt Ryan AU/246* RC | 350.00 | 200.00 |
| 180 Mike Hart AU RC | 30.00 | 15.00 |
| 181 Mike Jenkins AU RC | 20.00 | 8.00 |
| 182 Owen Schmitt AU RC | 20.00 | 8.00 |
| 183 Pat Sims AU RC | 15.00 | 6.00 |
| 184 Peyton Hillis AU/113* RC | 125.00 | 75.00 |
| 185 Philip Merling AU/100* RC | 80.00 | 40.00 |
| 186 Quentin Groves AU RC | 15.00 | 6.00 |
| 187 Rashard Mendenhall AU RC | 60.00 | 30.00 |
| 188 Ray Rice AU RC | 30.00 | 15.00 |
| 189 Reggie Smith AU/196* RC | 40.00 | 20.00 |
| 190 Ryan Torain AU/70* RC | 150.00 | 75.00 |
| 191 Sedrick Ellis AU RC | 20.00 | 8.00 |
| 192 Steve Slaton AU RC | 100.00 | 60.00 |

|  |  | | |
|---|---|---|---|
| 193 | Tashard Choice AU RC | 40.00 | 15.00 |
| 194 | Terrell Thomas AU RC | 20.00 | 8.00 |
| 195 | Thomas Brown AU/151* RC | 40.00 | 20.00 |
| 196 | Tim Hightower AU RC | 40.00 | 15.00 |
| 197 | Vernon Gholston AU RC | 20.00 | 8.00 |
| 198 | Will Franklin AU RC | 25.00 | 10.00 |
| 199 | Xavier Adibi AU RC | 25.00 | 10.00 |
| 200 | Witherspoon AU/150* RC EXCH | 60.00 | 30.00 |
| 201 | Caleb Hanie AU RC | 40.00 | 15.00 |
| 202 | Charles Godfrey AU RC | 15.00 | 6.00 |
| 203 | Chaz Schilens AU RC | 20.00 | 8.00 |
| 204 | Chris Horton AU RC | 30.00 | 15.00 |
| 205 | Derek Fine AU RC | 15.00 | 6.00 |
| 206 | Zackary Bowman AU RC | 15.00 | 6.00 |
| 207 | Dwight Lowery AU RC | 12.00 | 5.00 |
| 208 | Jalen Parmele AU RC | 15.00 | 6.00 |
| 209 | Jerome Felton AU RC | 12.00 | 5.00 |
| 210 | Kendall Langford AU RC | 20.00 | 8.00 |
| 211 | Kregg Lumpkin AU RC | 15.00 | 6.00 |
| 212 | Marcus Henry AU RC | 15.00 | 6.00 |
| 213 | Matthew Slater AU RC | 20.00 | 8.00 |
| 214 | Mike Cox AU RC | 15.00 | 6.00 |
| 215 | M.Tolbert AU/199* RC EXCH | 40.00 | 20.00 |
| 216 | Pierre Garcon AU RC | 20.00 | 8.00 |
| 217 | Quintin Demps AU RC | 15.00 | 6.00 |
| 218 | Sam Baker AU RC | 12.00 | 5.00 |
| 219 | Steve Johnson AU RC | 20.00 | 8.00 |
| 220 | Tavares Gooden AU RC | 15.00 | 6.00 |
| 221 | Terrence Wheatley AU RC | 15.00 | 6.00 |
| 222 | Tom Santi AU RC | 15.00 | 6.00 |
| 223 | Zbikowski AU/149* RC EXCH | 100.00 | 50.00 |
| 224 | Tyvon Branch AU RC | 15.00 | 6.00 |
| 225 | X.Omon AU/124* RC EXCH | 60.00 | 30.00 |

## 1998 Playoff Prestige Hobby

|  |  | | |
|---|---|---|---|
| | COMP.HOBBY SET (200) | 100.00 | 40.00 |
| 1 | John Elway | 8.00 | 3.00 |
| 2 | Steve Atwater | .75 | .30 |
| 3 | Terrell Davis | 2.00 | .75 |
| 4 | Bill Romanowski | .75 | .30 |
| 5 | Rod Smith | 1.25 | .50 |
| 6 | Shannon Sharpe | 1.25 | .50 |
| 7 | Ed McCaffrey | 1.25 | .50 |
| 8 | Neil Smith | 1.25 | .50 |
| 9 | Brett Favre | 8.00 | 3.00 |
| 10 | Dorsey Levens | 2.00 | .75 |
| 11 | LeRoy Butler | .75 | .30 |
| 12 | Antonio Freeman | 2.00 | .75 |
| 13 | Robert Brooks | 1.25 | .50 |
| 14 | Mark Chmura | .75 | .30 |
| 15 | Gilbert Brown | .75 | .30 |
| 16 | Kordell Stewart | 2.00 | .75 |
| 17 | Jerome Bettis | 2.00 | .75 |
| 18 | Levon Kirkland | .75 | .30 |
| 19 | Dermontti Dawson | .75 | .30 |
| 20 | Charles Johnson | .75 | .30 |
| 21 | Greg Lloyd | .75 | .30 |
| 22 | Levon Kirkland | .75 | .30 |
| 23 | Steve Young | 2.50 | 1.00 |
| 24 | Jim Druckenmiller | .75 | .30 |
| 25 | Garrison Hearst | 2.00 | .75 |
| 26 | Merton Hanks | .75 | .30 |
| 27 | Ken Norton | .75 | .30 |
| 28 | Jerry Rice | 4.00 | 1.50 |
| 29 | Terrell Owens | 2.00 | .75 |
| 30 | J.J. Stokes | 1.25 | .50 |
| 31 | Trent Dilfer | 2.00 | .75 |
| 32 | Warrick Dunn | 2.00 | .75 |
| 33 | Mike Alstott | 2.00 | .75 |
| 34 | Reidel Anthony | 1.25 | .50 |
| 35 | Warren Sapp | 1.25 | .50 |
| 36 | Elvis Grbac | 1.25 | .50 |
| 37 | Kimble Anders | 1.25 | .50 |
| 38 | Ted Popson | .75 | .30 |
| 39 | Derrick Thomas | 2.00 | .75 |
| 40 | Tony Gonzalez | 2.00 | .75 |
| 41 | Andre Rison | 1.25 | .50 |
| 42 | Derrick Alexander | 1.25 | .50 |
| 43 | Brad Johnson | 2.00 | .75 |
| 44 | Robert Smith | 2.00 | .75 |
| 45 | Randall McDaniel | .75 | .30 |
| 46 | Cris Carter | 2.00 | .75 |
| 47 | Jake Reed | 1.25 | .50 |
| 48 | John Randle | 1.25 | .50 |
| 49 | Drew Bledsoe | 3.00 | 1.25 |
| 50 | Willie Clay | .75 | .30 |
| 51 | Chris Slade | .75 | .30 |
| 52 | Willie McGinest | .75 | .30 |
| 53 | Shawn Jefferson | .75 | .30 |
| 54 | Ben Coates | 1.25 | .50 |
| 55 | Terry Glenn | 2.00 | .75 |
| 56 | Dan Hanson | .75 | .30 |
| 57 | Scott Mitchell | 1.25 | .50 |
| 58 | Barry Sanders | 6.00 | 2.50 |
| 59 | Herman Moore | 1.25 | .50 |
| 60 | Johnnie Morton | 1.25 | .50 |
| 61 | Mark Brunell | 2.00 | .75 |
| 62 | James Stewart | 1.25 | .50 |
| 63 | Tony Boselli | .75 | .30 |
| 64 | Jimmy Smith | 1.25 | .50 |
| 65 | Keenan McCardell | 1.25 | .50 |
| 66 | Dan Marino | 8.00 | 3.00 |
| 67 | Troy Drayton | .75 | .30 |
| 68 | Bernie Parmalee | .75 | .30 |
| 69 | Karim Abdul-Jabbar | 2.00 | .75 |
| 70 | Zach Thomas | 2.00 | .75 |
| 71 | O.J. McDuffie | 1.25 | .50 |
| 72 | Tim Bowens | .75 | .30 |
| 73 | Danny Kanell | 1.25 | .50 |
| 74 | Tiki Barber | 2.00 | .75 |
| 75 | Tyrone Wheatley | 1.25 | .50 |
| 76 | Charles Way | .75 | .30 |
| 77 | Jason Sehorn | 1.25 | .50 |
| 78 | Ike Hilliard | 1.25 | .50 |
| 79 | Michael Strahan | 1.25 | .50 |
| 80 | Troy Aikman | 4.00 | 1.50 |
| 81 | Deion Sanders | 2.00 | .75 |
| 82 | Emmitt Smith | 6.00 | 2.50 |
| 83 | Darren Woodson | .75 | .30 |
| 84 | Daryl Johnston | 1.25 | .50 |
| 85 | Michael Irvin | 2.00 | .75 |
| 86 | David LaFleur | .75 | .30 |
| 87 | Glenn Foley | 1.25 | .50 |
| 88 | Neil O'Donnell | 1.25 | .50 |
| 89 | Keyshawn Johnson | 2.00 | .75 |
| 90 | Aaron Glenn | .75 | .30 |
| 91 | Wayne Chrebet | 2.00 | .75 |
| 92 | Curtis Martin | 2.00 | .75 |
| 93 | Steve McNair | 2.00 | .75 |
| 94 | Eddie George | 2.00 | .75 |
| 95 | Bruce Matthews | .75 | .30 |
| 96 | Frank Wycheck | .75 | .30 |
| 97 | Yancey Thigpen | .75 | .30 |
| 98 | Gus Frerotte | .75 | .30 |
| 99 | Terry Allen | 2.00 | .75 |
| 100 | Michael Westbrook | 1.25 | .50 |
| 101 | Jamie Asher | .75 | .30 |
| 102 | Marshall Faulk | 2.50 | 1.00 |
| 103 | Zack Crockett | .75 | .30 |
| 104 | Ken Dilger | .75 | .30 |
| 105 | Marvin Harrison | 2.00 | .75 |
| 106 | Chris Chandler | 1.25 | .50 |
| 107 | Byron Hanspard | .75 | .30 |
| 108 | Jamal Anderson | 2.00 | .75 |
| 109 | Terance Mathis | 1.25 | .50 |
| 110 | Peter Boulware | .75 | .30 |
| 111 | Michael Jackson | .75 | .30 |
| 112 | Jim Harbaugh | 1.25 | .50 |
| 113 | Errict Rhett | 1.25 | .50 |
| 114 | Antowain Smith | 2.00 | .75 |
| 115 | Thurman Thomas | 2.00 | .75 |
| 116 | Bruce Smith | 1.25 | .50 |
| 117 | Doug Flutie | 2.00 | .75 |
| 118 | Rob Johnson | 1.25 | .50 |
| 119 | Kerry Collins | 1.25 | .50 |
| 120 | Fred Lane | .75 | .30 |
| 121 | Wesley Walls | 1.25 | .50 |
| 122 | William Floyd | .75 | .30 |
| 123 | Kevin Greene | 1.25 | .50 |
| 124 | Erik Kramer | .75 | .30 |
| 125 | Darnell Autry | .75 | .30 |
| 126 | Curtis Conway | 1.25 | .50 |
| 127 | Edgar Bennett | .75 | .30 |
| 128 | Jeff Blake | 1.25 | .50 |
| 129 | Corey Dillon | 2.00 | .75 |
| 130 | Carl Pickens | 1.25 | .50 |
| 131 | Damay Scott | 1.25 | .50 |
| 132 | Jake Plummer | 2.00 | .75 |
| 133 | Larry Centers | .75 | .30 |
| 134 | Frank Sanders | .75 | .30 |
| 135 | Rob Moore | 1.25 | .50 |
| 136 | Adrian Murrell | 1.25 | .50 |
| 137 | Troy Davis | .75 | .30 |
| 138 | Ray Zellars | .75 | .30 |
| 139 | Willie Roaf | .75 | .30 |
| 140 | Andre Hastings | .75 | .30 |
| 141 | Jeff George | 1.25 | .50 |
| 142 | Napoleon Kaufman | 2.00 | .75 |
| 143 | Desmond Howard | 1.25 | .50 |
| 144 | Tim Brown | 2.00 | .75 |
| 145 | James Jett | 1.25 | .50 |
| 146 | Rickey Dudley | .75 | .30 |
| 147 | Bobby Hoying | 1.25 | .50 |
| 148 | Duce Staley | 2.50 | 1.00 |
| 149 | Charlie Garner | 1.25 | .50 |
| 150 | Irving Fryar | 1.25 | .50 |
| 151 | Chris T. Jones | .75 | .30 |
| 152 | Tony Banks | 1.25 | .50 |
| 153 | Craig Heyward | .75 | .30 |
| 154 | Isaac Bruce | 2.00 | .75 |
| 155 | Eddie Kennison | 1.25 | .50 |
| 156 | Junior Seau | 2.00 | .75 |
| 157 | Tony Martin | 1.25 | .50 |
| 158 | Freddie Jones | .75 | .30 |
| 159 | Natrone Means | 1.25 | .50 |
| 160 | Warren Moon | 2.00 | .75 |
| 161 | Steve Broussard | .75 | .30 |
| 162 | Joey Galloway | 1.25 | .50 |
| 163 | Brian Blades | .75 | .30 |
| 164 | Ricky Watters | 1.25 | .50 |
| 165 | Peyton Manning RC | 25.00 | 10.00 |
| 166 | Ryan Leaf RC | 3.00 | 1.00 |
| 167 | Andre Wadsworth RC | 2.50 | 1.00 |
| 168 | Charles Woodson RC | 4.00 | 1.50 |
| 169 | Curtis Enis RC | 1.50 | .60 |
| 170 | Fred Taylor RC | 5.00 | 2.00 |
| 171 | Kevin Dyson RC | 3.00 | 1.25 |
| 172 | Robert Edwards RC | 2.50 | 1.00 |
| 173 | Randy Moss RC | 15.00 | 6.00 |
| 174 | R.W. McQuarters RC | 2.50 | 1.00 |
| 175 | John Avery RC | 2.50 | 1.00 |
| 176 | Marcus Nash RC | 1.50 | .60 |
| 177 | Jerome Pathon RC | 3.00 | 1.25 |
| 178 | Jacquez Green RC | 2.50 | 1.00 |
| 179 | Robert Holcombe RC | 2.50 | 1.00 |
| 180 | Pat Johnson RC | 2.50 | 1.00 |
| 181 | Germane Crowell RC | 2.50 | 1.00 |
| 182 | Tony Simmons RC | 2.50 | 1.00 |
| 183 | Joe Jurevicius RC | 3.00 | 1.25 |
| 184 | Mikhael Ricks RC | 2.50 | 1.00 |
| 185 | Charlie Batch RC | 3.00 | 1.25 |
| 186 | Jon Ritchie RC | 2.50 | 1.00 |
| 187 | Scott Frost RC | 1.50 | .60 |
| 188 | Skip Hicks RC | 2.50 | 1.00 |
| 189 | Brian Alford RC | 1.50 | .60 |
| 190 | E.G. Green RC | 2.50 | 1.00 |
| 191 | Jammi German RC | 1.50 | .60 |
| 192 | Ahman Green RC | 6.00 | 2.50 |
| 193 | Chris Floyd RC | 1.50 | .60 |
| 194 | Larry Shannon RC | 1.50 | .60 |
| 195 | Jonathan Quinn RC | 3.00 | 1.25 |
| 196 | Rashaan Shehee RC | 2.50 | 1.00 |
| 197 | Brian Griese RC | 6.00 | 2.50 |
| 198 | Hines Ward RC | 10.00 | 5.00 |
| 199 | Michael Pittman RC | 4.00 | 2.00 |
| 200 | Az-Zahir Hakim RC | 3.00 | 1.25 |

## 1999 Playoff Prestige EXP

| | | |
|---|---|---|
| ❑ COMPLETE SET (200) | 50.00 | 25.00 |
| ❑ 1 Anthony McFarland RC | 1.50 | .60 |
| ❑ 2 Al Wilson RC | 1.00 | .40 |
| ❑ 3 Jevon Kearse RC | 2.50 | 1.00 |
| ❑ 4 Aaron Brooks RC | 3.00 | 1.25 |
| ❑ 5 Travis McGriff RC | .75 | .30 |
| ❑ 6 Jeff Paulk RC | .75 | .30 |
| ❑ 7 Shawn Bryson RC | 1.50 | .60 |
| ❑ 8 Karsten Bailey RC | 1.00 | .40 |
| ❑ 9 Mike Cloud RC | 1.00 | .40 |
| ❑ 10 James Johnson RC | 1.00 | .40 |
| ❑ 11 Tai Streets RC | 1.50 | .60 |
| ❑ 12 Jermaine Fazande RC | 1.00 | .40 |
| ❑ 13 Ebenezer Ekuban RC | 1.00 | .40 |
| ❑ 14 Joe Montgomery RC | 1.00 | .40 |
| ❑ 15 Craig Yeast RC | 1.00 | .40 |
| ❑ 16 Joe Germaine RC | 1.00 | .40 |
| ❑ 17 Andy Katzenmoyer RC | 1.00 | .40 |
| ❑ 18 Kevin Faulk RC | 1.50 | .60 |
| ❑ 19 Chris McAlister RC | 1.00 | .40 |
| ❑ 20 Sedrick Irvin RC | .75 | .30 |
| ❑ 21 Brock Huard RC | 1.50 | .60 |
| ❑ 22 Cade McNown RC | 1.50 | .60 |
| ❑ 23 Shaun King RC | 1.00 | .40 |
| ❑ 24 Amos Zereoue RC | 1.50 | .60 |
| ❑ 25 Dameane Douglas RC | 1.00 | .40 |
| ❑ 26 D'Wayne Bates RC | 1.00 | .40 |
| ❑ 27 Kevin Johnson RC | 1.50 | .60 |
| ❑ 28 Rob Konrad RC | 1.50 | .60 |
| ❑ 29 Troy Edwards RC | 1.00 | .40 |
| ❑ 30 Peerless Price RC | 1.50 | .60 |
| ❑ 31 Daunte Culpepper RC | 6.00 | 2.50 |
| ❑ 32 Akili Smith RC | 1.00 | .40 |
| ❑ 33 David Boston RC | 1.50 | .60 |
| ❑ 34 Chris Claiborne RC | .75 | .30 |
| ❑ 35 Torry Holt RC | 4.00 | 1.50 |
| ❑ 36 Champ Bailey RC | 2.00 | .75 |
| ❑ 37 Edgerrin James RC | 6.00 | 2.50 |
| ❑ 38 Donovan McNabb RC | 8.00 | 3.00 |
| ❑ 39 Ricky Williams RC | 3.00 | 1.25 |
| ❑ 40 Tim Couch RC | 1.50 | .60 |
| ❑ 41 Charles Woodson RP | 1.00 | .40 |
| ❑ 42 Skip Hicks RP | .40 | .15 |
| ❑ 43 Brian Griese RP | 1.00 | .40 |
| ❑ 44 Tim Dwight RP | 1.00 | .40 |
| ❑ 45 Ryan Leaf RP | .60 | .25 |
| ❑ 46 Curtis Enis RP | .40 | .15 |
| ❑ 47 Charlie Batch RP | 1.00 | .40 |
| ❑ 48 Fred Taylor RP | 1.00 | .40 |
| ❑ 49 Peyton Manning RP | 1.50 | .60 |
| ❑ 50 Randy Moss RP | 1.25 | .50 |
| ❑ 51 Jim Harbaugh | .60 | .25 |
| ❑ 52 Warren Moon | 1.00 | .40 |
| ❑ 53 Jeff George | .60 | .25 |
| ❑ 54 Rich Gannon | 1.00 | .40 |
| ❑ 55 Scott Mitchell | .40 | .15 |
| ❑ 56 Kerry Collins | .60 | .25 |
| ❑ 57 Brad Johnson | 1.00 | .40 |
| ❑ 58 Charles Johnson | .40 | .15 |
| ❑ 59 Chris Calloway | .40 | .15 |
| ❑ 60 Tyrone Wheatley | .60 | .25 |
| ❑ 61 Michael Westbrook | .60 | .25 |
| ❑ 62 Skip Hicks | .40 | .15 |
| ❑ 63 Terry Allen | .60 | .25 |
| ❑ 64 Albert Connell | .40 | .15 |
| ❑ 65 Kevin Dyson | .60 | .25 |
| ❑ 66 Frank Wycheck | .40 | .15 |
| ❑ 67 Yancey Thigpen | .40 | .15 |
| ❑ 68 Steve McNair | 1.00 | .40 |
| ❑ 69 Eddie George | 1.00 | .40 |
| ❑ 70 Eric Zeier | .40 | .15 |
| ❑ 71 Jacquez Green | .40 | .15 |
| ❑ 72 Reidel Anthony | .60 | .25 |
| ❑ 73 Warren Sapp | .60 | .25 |
| ❑ 74 Mike Alstott | 1.00 | .40 |
| ❑ 75 Warrick Dunn | 1.00 | .40 |
| ❑ 76 Trent Dilfer | .60 | .25 |
| ❑ 77 Ahman Green | 1.00 | .40 |
| ❑ 78 Joey Galloway | .60 | .25 |
| ❑ 79 Ricky Watters | .60 | .25 |
| ❑ 80 Jon Kitna | .60 | .25 |
| ❑ 81 Amp Lee | .40 | .15 |
| ❑ 82 Isaac Bruce | 1.00 | .40 |
| ❑ 83 Robert Holcombe | .40 | .15 |
| ❑ 84 Greg Hill | .40 | .15 |
| ❑ 85 Marshall Faulk | 1.25 | .50 |
| ❑ 86 Trent Green | 1.00 | .40 |
| ❑ 87 J.J. Stokes | .60 | .25 |
| ❑ 88 Terrell Owens | 1.00 | .40 |
| ❑ 89 Jerry Rice | 2.00 | .75 |
| ❑ 90 Garrison Hearst | .60 | .25 |
| ❑ 91 Steve Young | 1.25 | .50 |
| ❑ 92 Junior Seau | 1.00 | .40 |
| ❑ 93 Mikhael Ricks | .40 | .15 |
| ❑ 94 Natrone Means | .60 | .25 |
| ❑ 95 Ryan Leaf | 1.00 | .40 |
| ❑ 96 Courtney Hawkins | .40 | .15 |
| ❑ 97 Chris Fuamatu-Ma'afala UER | .40 | .15 |
| ❑ 98 Jerome Bettis | 1.00 | .40 |
| ❑ 99 Kordell Stewart | .60 | .25 |
| ❑ 100 Bobby Hoying | .60 | .25 |
| ❑ 101 Charlie Garner | .60 | .25 |
| ❑ 102 Duce Staley | .60 | .25 |
| ❑ 103 Charles Woodson | 1.00 | .40 |
| ❑ 104 James Jett | .60 | .25 |
| ❑ 105 Rickey Dudley | .40 | .15 |
| ❑ 106 Tim Brown | 1.00 | .40 |
| ❑ 107 Napoleon Kaufman | 1.00 | .40 |
| ❑ 108 Wayne Chrebet | .60 | .25 |
| ❑ 109 Keyshawn Johnson | 1.00 | .40 |
| ❑ 110 Vinny Testaverde | .60 | .25 |
| ❑ 111 Curtis Martin | 1.00 | .40 |
| ❑ 112 Joe Jurevicius | .60 | .25 |
| ❑ 113 Tiki Barber | 1.00 | .40 |
| ❑ 114 Ike Hilliard | .40 | .15 |
| ❑ 115 Kent Graham | .40 | .15 |
| ❑ 116 Gary Brown | .40 | .15 |
| ❑ 117 Lamar Smith | .60 | .25 |
| ❑ 118 Eddie Kennison | .60 | .25 |
| ❑ 119 Cam Cleeland | .40 | .15 |
| ❑ 120 Tony Simmons | .40 | .15 |
| ❑ 121 Ben Coates | .60 | .25 |
| ❑ 122 Darick Holmes | .40 | .15 |
| ❑ 123 Terry Glenn | 1.00 | .40 |
| ❑ 124 Drew Bledsoe | 1.25 | .50 |
| ❑ 125 Leroy Hoard | .40 | .15 |
| ❑ 126 Jake Reed | .60 | .25 |
| ❑ 127 Randy Moss | 2.50 | 1.00 |
| ❑ 128 Cris Carter | 1.00 | .40 |
| ❑ 129 Robert Smith | .60 | .25 |
| ❑ 130 Randall Cunningham | 1.00 | .40 |
| ❑ 131 Lamar Thomas | .40 | .15 |
| ❑ 132 John Avery | .40 | .15 |
| ❑ 133 O.J. McDuffie | .60 | .25 |
| ❑ 134 Dan Marino | 3.00 | 1.25 |
| ❑ 135 Karim Abdul-Jabbar | .60 | .25 |
| ❑ 136 Rashaan Shehee | .40 | .15 |
| ❑ 137 Derrick Alexander WR | .60 | .25 |
| ❑ 138 Byron Bam Morris | .40 | .15 |
| ❑ 139 Andre Rison | .60 | .25 |
| ❑ 140 Elvis Grbac | .60 | .25 |
| ❑ 141 Tavian Banks | .40 | .15 |
| ❑ 142 Keenan McCardell | .60 | .25 |
| ❑ 143 Jimmy Smith | .60 | .25 |
| ❑ 144 Fred Taylor | 1.00 | .40 |
| ❑ 145 Mark Brunell | 1.00 | .40 |
| ❑ 146 Jerome Pathon | .40 | .15 |
| ❑ 147 Marvin Harrison | .60 | .25 |
| ❑ 148 Peyton Manning | 3.00 | 1.25 |
| ❑ 149 Robert Brooks | .40 | .15 |
| ❑ 150 Mark Chmura | .40 | .15 |
| ❑ 151 Antonio Freeman | 1.00 | .40 |
| ❑ 152 Dorsey Levens | 1.00 | .40 |
| ❑ 153 Brett Favre | 3.00 | 1.25 |
| ❑ 154 Johnnie Morton | .60 | .25 |
| ❑ 155 Germane Crowell | .40 | .15 |
| ❑ 156 Barry Sanders | 3.00 | 1.25 |
| ❑ 157 Herman Moore | .60 | .25 |
| ❑ 158 Charlie Batch | 1.00 | .40 |
| ❑ 159 Marcus Nash | .40 | .15 |
| ❑ 160 Shannon Sharpe | .60 | .25 |
| ❑ 161 Rod Smith | .60 | .25 |
| ❑ 162 Ed McCaffrey | .60 | .25 |
| ❑ 163 Terrell Davis | 1.00 | .40 |
| ❑ 164 John Elway | 3.00 | 1.25 |
| ❑ 165 Ernie Mills | .40 | .15 |
| ❑ 166 Michael Irvin | .60 | .25 |
| ❑ 167 Deion Sanders | 1.00 | .40 |
| ❑ 168 Emmitt Smith | 2.00 | .75 |
| ❑ 169 Troy Aikman | 2.00 | .75 |
| ❑ 170 Chris Spielman | .40 | .15 |
| ❑ 171 Terry Kirby | .40 | .15 |
| ❑ 172 Ty Detmer | .60 | .25 |
| ❑ 173 Leslie Shepherd | .40 | .15 |
| ❑ 174 Damay Scott | .40 | .15 |
| ❑ 175 Jeff Blake | .60 | .25 |
| ❑ 176 Carl Pickens | .60 | .25 |
| ❑ 177 Corey Dillon | 1.00 | .40 |
| ❑ 178 Bobby Engram | .40 | .15 |
| ❑ 179 Curtis Conway | .60 | .25 |
| ❑ 180 Curtis Enis | .60 | .25 |
| ❑ 181 Muhsin Muhammad | .60 | .25 |
| ❑ 182 Steve Beuerlein | .40 | .15 |
| ❑ 183 Tim Biakabutuka | .60 | .25 |
| ❑ 184 Bruce Smith | .60 | .25 |
| ❑ 185 Andre Reed | .60 | .25 |
| ❑ 186 Thurman Thomas | .60 | .25 |
| ❑ 187 Eric Moulds | 1.00 | .40 |
| ❑ 188 Antowain Smith | 1.00 | .40 |
| ❑ 189 Doug Flutie | 1.00 | .40 |
| ❑ 190 Jermaine Lewis | .60 | .25 |
| ❑ 191 Priest Holmes | 1.50 | .60 |
| ❑ 192 O.J. Santiago | .40 | .15 |
| ❑ 193 Tim Dwight | 1.00 | .40 |
| ❑ 194 Terance Mathis | .40 | .15 |
| ❑ 195 Chris Chandler | .60 | .25 |
| ❑ 196 Jamal Anderson | 1.00 | .40 |
| ❑ 197 Rob Moore | .60 | .25 |
| ❑ 198 Frank Sanders | .60 | .25 |
| ❑ 199 Adrian Murrell | .60 | .25 |
| ❑ 200 Jake Plummer | .60 | .25 |
| ❑ RR1 Barry Sanders RFR | 20.00 | 7.50 |

## 1999 Playoff Prestige SSD

| | | |
|---|---|---|
| ❑ COMPLETE SET (200) | 150.00 | 75.00 |
| ❑ COMP.SET w/o SP's (150) | 50.00 | 25.00 |
| ❑ 1 Jake Plummer | .75 | .30 |
| ❑ 2 Adrian Murrell | .75 | .30 |
| ❑ 3 Frank Sanders | .75 | .30 |
| ❑ 4 Rob Moore | .75 | .30 |
| ❑ 5 Jamal Anderson | 1.25 | .50 |
| ❑ 6 Chris Chandler | .75 | .30 |
| ❑ 7 Terance Mathis | .75 | .30 |
| ❑ 8 Tim Dwight | 1.25 | .50 |
| ❑ 9 O.J. Santiago | .50 | .20 |
| ❑ 10 Priest Holmes | 2.00 | .75 |
| ❑ 11 Jermaine Lewis | .75 | .30 |

| | | | |
|---|---|---|---|
| ☐ 12 Doug Flutie | 1.25 | .50 |
| ☐ 13 Antowain Smith | 1.25 | .50 |
| ☐ 14 Eric Moulds | 1.25 | .50 |
| ☐ 15 Thurman Thomas | .75 | .30 |
| ☐ 16 Andre Reed | .75 | .30 |
| ☐ 17 Bruce Smith | .75 | .30 |
| ☐ 18 Tim Biakabutuka | .75 | .30 |
| ☐ 19 Steve Beuerlein | .75 | .20 |
| ☐ 20 Muhsin Muhammad | .75 | .30 |
| ☐ 21 Curtis Enis | .75 | .20 |
| ☐ 22 Curtis Conway | .75 | .30 |
| ☐ 23 Bobby Engram | .50 | .20 |
| ☐ 24 Corey Dillon | 1.25 | .50 |
| ☐ 25 Carl Pickens | .75 | .30 |
| ☐ 26 Jeff Blake | .75 | .30 |
| ☐ 27 Darnay Scott | .50 | .20 |
| ☐ 28 Leslie Shepherd | .50 | .20 |
| ☐ 29 Ty Detmer | .50 | .20 |
| ☐ 30 Terry Kirby | .50 | .20 |
| ☐ 31 Chris Spielman | .50 | .20 |
| ☐ 32 Troy Aikman | 3.00 | 1.25 |
| ☐ 33 Emmitt Smith | 3.00 | 1.25 |
| ☐ 34 Deion Sanders | 1.25 | .50 |
| ☐ 35 Michael Irvin | .75 | .30 |
| ☐ 36 Ernie Mills | .50 | .20 |
| ☐ 37 John Elway | 5.00 | 2.00 |
| ☐ 38 Terrell Davis | 1.25 | .50 |
| ☐ 39 Ed McCaffrey | .75 | .30 |
| ☐ 40 Rod Smith | .75 | .30 |
| ☐ 41 Shannon Sharpe | .75 | .30 |
| ☐ 42 Marcus Nash | .50 | .20 |
| ☐ 43 Charlie Batch | 1.25 | .50 |
| ☐ 44 Herman Moore | .75 | .30 |
| ☐ 45 Barry Sanders | 5.00 | 2.00 |
| ☐ 46 Germane Crowell | .50 | .20 |
| ☐ 47 Johnnie Morton | .50 | .20 |
| ☐ 48 Brett Favre | 5.00 | 2.00 |
| ☐ 49 Dorsey Levens | 1.25 | .50 |
| ☐ 50 Antonio Freeman | 1.25 | .50 |
| ☐ 51 Mark Chmura | .50 | .20 |
| ☐ 52 Robert Brooks | .75 | .30 |
| ☐ 53 Peyton Manning | 5.00 | 2.00 |
| ☐ 54 Marvin Harrison | 1.25 | .50 |
| ☐ 55 Jerome Pathon | .50 | .20 |
| ☐ 56 Mark Brunell | 1.25 | .50 |
| ☐ 57 Fred Taylor | 1.25 | .50 |
| ☐ 58 Jimmy Smith | .75 | .30 |
| ☐ 59 Keenan McCardell | .75 | .30 |
| ☐ 60 Tavian Banks | .50 | .20 |
| ☐ 61 Elvis Grbac | .75 | .30 |
| ☐ 62 Andre Rison | .75 | .30 |
| ☐ 63 Byron Bam Morris | .50 | .20 |
| ☐ 64 Derrick Alexander WR | .75 | .30 |
| ☐ 65 Rashaan Shehee | .50 | .20 |
| ☐ 66 Karim Abdul-Jabbar | .75 | .30 |
| ☐ 67 Dan Marino | 5.00 | 2.00 |
| ☐ 68 O.J. McDuffie | .50 | .20 |
| ☐ 69 John Avery | .50 | .20 |
| ☐ 70 Lamar Thomas | .50 | .20 |
| ☐ 71 Randall Cunningham | 1.25 | .50 |
| ☐ 72 Robert Smith | 1.25 | .50 |
| ☐ 73 Cris Carter | 1.25 | .50 |
| ☐ 74 Randy Moss | 4.00 | 1.50 |
| ☐ 75 Jake Reed | .75 | .30 |
| ☐ 76 Leroy Hoard | .50 | .20 |
| ☐ 77 Drew Bledsoe | 2.00 | .75 |
| ☐ 78 Terry Glenn | 1.25 | .50 |
| ☐ 79 Darick Holmes | .50 | .20 |
| ☐ 80 Ben Coates | .75 | .30 |
| ☐ 81 Tony Simmons | .50 | .20 |
| ☐ 82 Cam Cleeland | .50 | .20 |
| ☐ 83 Eddie Kennison | .50 | .20 |
| ☐ 84 Lamar Smith | .50 | .20 |
| ☐ 85 Gary Brown | .50 | .20 |
| ☐ 86 Kent Graham | .50 | .20 |
| ☐ 87 Ike Hilliard | .50 | .20 |
| ☐ 88 Tiki Barber | 1.25 | .50 |
| ☐ 89 Joe Jurevicius | .75 | .30 |
| ☐ 90 Curtis Martin | 1.25 | .50 |
| ☐ 91 Vinny Testaverde | .75 | .30 |
| ☐ 92 Keyshawn Johnson | .75 | .30 |
| ☐ 93 Wayne Chrebet | .75 | .30 |
| ☐ 94 Napoleon Kaufman | .75 | .30 |
| ☐ 95 Tim Brown | 1.25 | .50 |
| ☐ 96 Rickey Dudley | .50 | .20 |

| | | | |
|---|---|---|---|
| ☐ 97 James Jett | .75 | .30 |
| ☐ 98 Charles Woodson | 1.25 | .50 |
| ☐ 99 Duce Staley | 1.25 | .50 |
| ☐ 100 Charlie Garner | .75 | .30 |
| ☐ 101 Bobby Hoying | .75 | .30 |
| ☐ 102 Kordell Stewart | 1.25 | .50 |
| ☐ 103 Jerome Bettis | 1.25 | .50 |
| ☐ 104 Chris Fuamatu-Ma'afala | .50 | .20 |
| ☐ 105 Courtney Hawkins | .50 | .20 |
| ☐ 106 Ryan Leaf | 1.25 | .50 |
| ☐ 107 Natrone Means | .75 | .30 |
| ☐ 108 Mikhael Ricks | .50 | .20 |
| ☐ 109 Junior Seau | 1.25 | .50 |
| ☐ 110 Steve Young | 2.00 | .75 |
| ☐ 111 Garrison Hearst | .75 | .30 |
| ☐ 112 Jerry Rice | 3.00 | 1.25 |
| ☐ 113 Terrell Owens | 1.25 | .50 |
| ☐ 114 J.J. Stokes | .75 | .30 |
| ☐ 115 Trent Green | 1.25 | .50 |
| ☐ 116 Marshall Faulk | 1.50 | .60 |
| ☐ 117 Greg Hill | .50 | .20 |
| ☐ 118 Robert Holcombe | .50 | .20 |
| ☐ 119 Isaac Bruce | 1.25 | .50 |
| ☐ 120 Amp Lee | .50 | .20 |
| ☐ 121 Jon Kitna | 1.25 | .50 |
| ☐ 122 Ricky Watters | .75 | .30 |
| ☐ 123 Joey Galloway | .75 | .30 |
| ☐ 124 Ahman Green | 1.25 | .50 |
| ☐ 125 Trent Dilfer | .75 | .30 |
| ☐ 126 Warrick Dunn | 1.25 | .50 |
| ☐ 127 Mike Alstott | 1.25 | .50 |
| ☐ 128 Warren Sapp | .75 | .30 |
| ☐ 129 Reidel Anthony | .75 | .30 |
| ☐ 130 Jacquez Green | .50 | .20 |
| ☐ 131 Eric Zeier | .50 | .20 |
| ☐ 132 Eddie George | 1.25 | .50 |
| ☐ 133 Steve McNair | 1.25 | .50 |
| ☐ 134 Yancey Thigpen | .50 | .20 |
| ☐ 135 Frank Wycheck | .50 | .20 |
| ☐ 136 Kevin Dyson | .75 | .30 |
| ☐ 137 Albert Connell | .50 | .20 |
| ☐ 138 Terry Allen | .75 | .30 |
| ☐ 139 Skip Hicks | .50 | .20 |
| ☐ 140 Michael Westbrook | .75 | .30 |
| ☐ 141 Tyrone Wheatley | .75 | .30 |
| ☐ 142 Chris Calloway | .50 | .20 |
| ☐ 143 Charles Johnson | .50 | .20 |
| ☐ 144 Brad Johnson | 1.25 | .50 |
| ☐ 145 Kerry Collins | .75 | .30 |
| ☐ 146 Scott Mitchell | .50 | .20 |
| ☐ 147 Rich Gannon | 1.25 | .50 |
| ☐ 148 Jeff George | .75 | .30 |
| ☐ 149 Warren Moon | 1.25 | .50 |
| ☐ 150 Jim Harbaugh | .75 | .30 |
| ☐ 151 Randy Moss RP | 6.00 | 2.50 |
| ☐ 152 Peyton Manning RP | 8.00 | 3.00 |
| ☐ 153 Fred Taylor RP | 2.50 | 1.00 |
| ☐ 154 Charlie Batch RP | 2.50 | 1.00 |
| ☐ 155 Curtis Enis RP | 1.50 | .60 |
| ☐ 156 Ryan Leaf RP | 1.50 | .60 |
| ☐ 157 Tim Dwight RP | 1.50 | .60 |
| ☐ 158 Brian Griese RP | 2.50 | 1.00 |
| ☐ 159 Skip Hicks RP | 1.50 | .60 |
| ☐ 160 Charles Woodson RP | 2.50 | 1.00 |
| ☐ 161 Tim Couch RC | 4.00 | 1.50 |
| ☐ 162 Ricky Williams RC | 6.00 | 2.50 |
| ☐ 163 Donovan McNabb RC | 15.00 | 6.00 |
| ☐ 164 Edgerrin James RC | 12.00 | 5.00 |
| ☐ 165 Champ Bailey RC | 5.00 | 2.00 |
| ☐ 166 Torry Holt RC | 8.00 | 3.00 |
| ☐ 167 Chris Claiborne RC | 2.00 | .75 |
| ☐ 168 David Boston RC | 4.00 | 1.50 |
| ☐ 169 Akili Smith RC | 1.50 | .60 |
| ☐ 170 Daunte Culpepper RC | 12.00 | 5.00 |
| ☐ 171 Peerless Price RC | 4.00 | 1.50 |
| ☐ 172 Troy Edwards RC | 3.00 | 1.25 |
| ☐ 173 Rob Konrad RC | 4.00 | 1.50 |
| ☐ 174 Kevin Johnson RC | 4.00 | 1.50 |
| ☐ 175 D'Wayne Bates RC | 3.00 | 1.25 |
| ☐ 176 Dameane Douglas RC | 3.00 | 1.25 |
| ☐ 177 Amos Zereoue RC | 4.00 | 1.50 |
| ☐ 178 Shaun King RC | 3.00 | 1.25 |
| ☐ 179 Cade McNown RC | 3.00 | 1.25 |
| ☐ 180 Brock Huard RC | 4.00 | 1.50 |
| ☐ 181 Sedrick Irvin RC | 2.00 | .75 |

| | | | |
|---|---|---|---|
| ☐ 182 Chris McAlister RC | 3.00 | 1.25 |
| ☐ 183 Kevin Faulk RC | 4.00 | 1.50 |
| ☐ 184 Andy Katzenmoyer RC | 3.00 | 1.25 |
| ☐ 185 Joe Germaine RC | 3.00 | 1.25 |
| ☐ 186 Craig Yeast RC | 3.00 | 1.25 |
| ☐ 187 Joe Montgomery RC | 3.00 | 1.25 |
| ☐ 188 Ebenezer Ekuban RC | 3.00 | 1.25 |
| ☐ 189 Jermaine Fazande RC | 3.00 | 1.25 |
| ☐ 190 Tai Streets RC | 4.00 | 1.50 |
| ☐ 191 James Johnson RC | 3.00 | 1.25 |
| ☐ 192 Mike Cloud RC | 3.00 | 1.25 |
| ☐ 193 Karsten Bailey RC | 3.00 | 1.25 |
| ☐ 194 Shawn Bryson RC | 4.00 | 1.50 |
| ☐ 195 Jeff Paulk RC | 2.00 | .75 |
| ☐ 196 Travis McGriff RC | 2.00 | .75 |
| ☐ 197 Aaron Brooks RC | 6.00 | 2.50 |
| ☐ 198 Jevon Kearse RC | 6.00 | 2.50 |
| ☐ 199 Al Wilson RC | 3.00 | 1.25 |
| ☐ 200 Anthony McFarland RC | 4.00 | 1.50 |

## 2000 Playoff Prestige

| | | | |
|---|---|---|---|
| ☐ COMPLETE SET (300) | 350.00 | 175.00 |
| ☐ COMP.SET w/o SP's (200) | 25.00 | 10.00 |
| ☐ 1 Frank Sanders | .40 | .15 |
| ☐ 2 Rob Moore | .40 | .15 |
| ☐ 3 Michael Pittman | .20 | .08 |
| ☐ 4 Jake Plummer | .40 | .15 |
| ☐ 5 David Boston | .60 | .25 |
| ☐ 6 Chris Chandler | .40 | .15 |
| ☐ 7 Tim Dwight | .60 | .25 |
| ☐ 8 Shawn Jefferson | .25 | .08 |
| ☐ 9 Terance Mathis | .40 | .15 |
| ☐ 10 Jamal Anderson | .60 | .25 |
| ☐ 11 Byron Hanspard | .25 | .08 |
| ☐ 12 Ken Oxendine | .25 | .08 |
| ☐ 13 Priest Holmes | .75 | .30 |
| ☐ 14 Tony Banks | .40 | .15 |
| ☐ 15 Shannon Sharpe | .40 | .15 |
| ☐ 16 Rod Woodson | .40 | .15 |
| ☐ 17 Jermaine Lewis | .40 | .15 |
| ☐ 18 Qadry Ismail | .40 | .15 |
| ☐ 19 Eric Moulds | .60 | .25 |
| ☐ 20 Doug Flutie | .60 | .25 |
| ☐ 21 Jay Riemersma | .25 | .08 |
| ☐ 22 Antowain Smith | .40 | .15 |
| ☐ 23 Jonathan Linton | .25 | .08 |
| ☐ 24 Peerless Price | .40 | .15 |
| ☐ 25 Rob Johnson | .40 | .15 |
| ☐ 26 Muhsin Muhammad | .40 | .15 |
| ☐ 27 Wesley Walls | .25 | .08 |
| ☐ 28 Tim Biakabutuka | .40 | .15 |
| ☐ 29 Steve Beuerlein | .40 | .15 |
| ☐ 30 Patrick Jeffers | .60 | .25 |
| ☐ 31 Natrone Means | .25 | .08 |
| ☐ 32 Curtis Enis | .25 | .08 |
| ☐ 33 Bobby Engram | .40 | .15 |
| ☐ 34 Marcus Robinson | .60 | .25 |
| ☐ 35 Marty Booker | .40 | .15 |
| ☐ 36 Cade McNown | .40 | .15 |
| ☐ 37 Darnay Scott | .40 | .15 |
| ☐ 38 Carl Pickens | .25 | .08 |
| ☐ 39 Corey Dillon | .60 | .25 |
| ☐ 40 Akili Smith | .40 | .15 |
| ☐ 41 Michael Basnight | .25 | .08 |
| ☐ 42 Karim Abdul-Jabbar | .25 | .08 |
| ☐ 43 Tim Couch | .40 | .15 |
| ☐ 44 Kevin Johnson | .60 | .25 |
| ☐ 45 Darrin Chiaverini | .25 | .08 |

|  |  | | |
|---|---|---|---|
| 46 | Errict Rhett | .40 | .15 |
| 47 | Emmitt Smith | 1.25 | .50 |
| 48 | Deion Sanders | .60 | .25 |
| 49 | Michael Irvin | .40 | .15 |
| 50 | Rocket Ismail | .40 | .15 |
| 51 | Troy Aikman | 1.25 | .50 |
| 52 | Jason Tucker | .25 | .08 |
| 53 | Joey Galloway | .40 | .15 |
| 54 | David LaFleur | .25 | .08 |
| 55 | Wane McGarity | .25 | .08 |
| 56 | Ed McCaffrey | .60 | .25 |
| 57 | Rod Smith | .40 | .15 |
| 58 | Brian Griese | .60 | .25 |
| 59 | John Elway | 2.00 | .75 |
| 60 | Gus Frerotte | .25 | .08 |
| 61 | Neil Smith | .25 | .08 |
| 62 | Terrell Davis | .60 | .25 |
| 63 | Olandis Gary | .60 | .25 |
| 64 | Johnnie Morton | .40 | .15 |
| 65 | Charlie Batch | .60 | .25 |
| 66 | Barry Sanders | 1.50 | .60 |
| 67 | James Stewart | .40 | .15 |
| 68 | Germane Crowell | .25 | .08 |
| 69 | Sedrick Irvin | .25 | .08 |
| 70 | Herman Moore | .40 | .15 |
| 71 | Corey Bradford | .40 | .15 |
| 72 | Dorsey Levens | .40 | .15 |
| 73 | Antonio Freeman | .60 | .25 |
| 74 | Brett Favre | 2.00 | .75 |
| 75 | De'Mond Parker | .25 | .08 |
| 76 | Bill Schroeder | .40 | .15 |
| 77 | Donald Driver | .60 | .25 |
| 78 | E.G. Green | .25 | .08 |
| 79 | Marvin Harrison | .60 | .25 |
| 80 | Peyton Manning | 1.50 | .60 |
| 81 | Terrence Wilkins | .25 | .08 |
| 82 | Edgerrin James | 1.00 | .40 |
| 83 | Keenan McCardell | .40 | .15 |
| 84 | Mark Brunell | .60 | .25 |
| 85 | Fred Taylor | .60 | .25 |
| 86 | Jimmy Smith | .40 | .15 |
| 87 | Derrick Alexander | .40 | .15 |
| 88 | Andre Rison | .40 | .15 |
| 89 | Elvis Grbac | .25 | .08 |
| 90 | Tony Gonzalez | .40 | .15 |
| 91 | Donnell Bennett | .25 | .08 |
| 92 | Warren Moon | .60 | .25 |
| 93 | Kimble Anders | .25 | .08 |
| 94 | Tony Richardson RC | .40 | .15 |
| 95 | Jay Fiedler | .60 | .25 |
| 96 | Zach Thomas | .60 | .25 |
| 97 | Oronde Gadsden | .40 | .15 |
| 98 | Dan Marino | 2.00 | .75 |
| 99 | O.J. McDuffie | .40 | .15 |
| 100 | Tony Martin | .40 | .15 |
| 101 | James Johnson | .25 | .08 |
| 102 | Rob Konrad | .25 | .08 |
| 103 | Damon Huard | .60 | .25 |
| 104 | Thurman Thomas | .40 | .15 |
| 105 | Randy Moss | 1.25 | .50 |
| 106 | Cris Carter | .60 | .25 |
| 107 | Robert Smith | .60 | .25 |
| 108 | Randall Cunningham | .60 | .25 |
| 109 | John Randle | .40 | .15 |
| 110 | Leroy Hoard | .25 | .08 |
| 111 | Daunte Culpepper | .75 | .30 |
| 112 | Matthew Hatchette | .25 | .08 |
| 113 | Troy Brown | .40 | .15 |
| 114 | Tony Simmons | .25 | .08 |
| 115 | Terry Glenn | .40 | .15 |
| 116 | Ben Coates | .25 | .08 |
| 117 | Drew Bledsoe | .75 | .30 |
| 118 | Terry Allen | .40 | .15 |
| 119 | Kevin Faulk | .25 | .08 |
| 120 | Ricky Williams | .60 | .25 |
| 121 | Jake Delhomme RC | 3.00 | 1.25 |
| 122 | Jake Reed | .40 | .15 |
| 123 | Jeff Blake | .40 | .15 |
| 124 | Amani Toomer | .40 | .15 |
| 125 | Kerry Collins | .40 | .15 |
| 126 | Tiki Barber | .60 | .25 |
| 127 | Ike Hilliard | .40 | .15 |
| 128 | Joe Montgomery | .25 | .08 |
| 129 | Sean Bennett | .25 | .08 |
| 130 | Curtis Martin | .60 | .25 |
| 131 | Vinny Testaverde | .40 | .15 |
| 132 | Wayne Chrebet | .40 | .15 |
| 133 | Ray Lucas | .40 | .15 |
| 134 | Tyrone Wheatley | .40 | .15 |
| 135 | Napoleon Kaufman | .40 | .15 |
| 136 | Tim Brown | .60 | .25 |
| 137 | Rickey Dudley | .25 | .08 |
| 138 | James Jett | .25 | .08 |
| 139 | Rich Gannon | .60 | .25 |
| 140 | Charles Woodson | .40 | .15 |
| 141 | Duce Staley | .60 | .25 |
| 142 | Donovan McNabb | 1.00 | .40 |
| 143 | Na Brown | .25 | .08 |
| 144 | Kordell Stewart | .60 | .25 |
| 145 | Jerome Bettis | .60 | .25 |
| 146 | Hines Ward | .60 | .25 |
| 147 | Troy Edwards | .25 | .08 |
| 148 | Curtis Conway | .40 | .15 |
| 149 | Junior Seau | .40 | .15 |
| 150 | Jim Harbaugh | .40 | .15 |
| 151 | Jermaine Fazande | .25 | .08 |
| 152 | Terrell Owens | .60 | .25 |
| 153 | J.J. Stokes | .40 | .15 |
| 154 | Charlie Garner | .40 | .15 |
| 155 | Jerry Rice | 1.25 | .50 |
| 156 | Garrison Hearst | .40 | .15 |
| 157 | Steve Young | .75 | .30 |
| 158 | Jeff Garcia | .60 | .25 |
| 159 | Derrick Mayes | .40 | .15 |
| 160 | Ahman Green | .40 | .15 |
| 161 | Ricky Watters | .40 | .15 |
| 162 | Jon Kitna | .60 | .25 |
| 163 | Karsten Bailey | .25 | .08 |
| 164 | Sean Dawkins | .25 | .08 |
| 165 | Az-Zahir Hakim | .40 | .15 |
| 166 | Isaac Bruce | .60 | .25 |
| 167 | Marshall Faulk | .75 | .30 |
| 168 | Trent Green | .40 | .15 |
| 169 | Kurt Warner | 1.25 | .50 |
| 170 | Torry Holt | .60 | .25 |
| 171 | Robert Holcombe | .25 | .08 |
| 172 | Kevin Carter | .25 | .08 |
| 173 | Keyshawn Johnson | .60 | .25 |
| 174 | Jacquez Green | .25 | .08 |
| 175 | Reidel Anthony | .25 | .08 |
| 176 | Warren Sapp | .40 | .15 |
| 177 | Mike Alstott | .60 | .25 |
| 178 | Warrick Dunn | .60 | .25 |
| 179 | Trent Dilfer | .40 | .15 |
| 180 | Shaun King | .25 | .08 |
| 181 | Neil O'Donnell | .25 | .08 |
| 182 | Darrell Green | .60 | .25 |
| 183 | Yancey Thigpen | .25 | .08 |
| 184 | Steve McNair | .60 | .25 |
| 185 | Kevin Dyson | .40 | .15 |
| 186 | Frank Wycheck | .25 | .08 |
| 187 | Jevon Kearse | .60 | .25 |
| 188 | Adrian Murrell | .25 | .08 |
| 189 | Jeff George | .40 | .15 |
| 190 | Stephen Davis | .60 | .25 |
| 191 | Stephen Alexander | .25 | .08 |
| 192 | Darrell Green | .25 | .08 |
| 193 | Skip Hicks | .25 | .08 |
| 194 | Brad Johnson | .60 | .25 |
| 195 | Michael Westbrook | .40 | .15 |
| 196 | Albert Connell | .25 | .08 |
| 197 | Irving Fryar | .40 | .15 |
| 198 | Brian Mitchell | .40 | .15 |
| 199 | Champ Bailey | .40 | .15 |
| 200 | Larry Centers | .25 | .08 |
| 201 | Jake Plummer PP | 1.25 | .50 |
| 202 | Doug Flutie PP | 1.25 | .50 |
| 203 | Eric Moulds PP | 1.25 | .50 |
| 204 | Muhsin Muhammad PP | 1.25 | .50 |
| 205 | Marcus Robinson PP | 1.25 | .50 |
| 206 | Cade McNown PP | 1.25 | .50 |
| 207 | Corey Dillon PP | 1.25 | .50 |
| 208 | Tim Couch PP | 1.25 | .50 |
| 209 | Kevin Johnson PP | 1.25 | .50 |
| 210 | Emmitt Smith PP | 3.00 | 1.25 |
| 211 | Troy Aikman PP | 3.00 | 1.25 |
| 212 | Brian Griese PP | 1.25 | .50 |
| 213 | Olandis Gary PP | 1.25 | .50 |
| 214 | Germane Crowell PP | 1.25 | .50 |
| 215 | Brett Favre PP | 5.00 | 2.00 |
| 216 | Charlie Batch PP | 1.25 | .50 |
| 217 | Antonio Freeman PP | 1.25 | .50 |
| 218 | Dorsey Levens PP | 1.25 | .50 |
| 219 | Peyton Manning PP | 4.00 | 1.50 |
| 220 | Edgerrin James PP | 2.50 | 1.00 |
| 221 | Marvin Harrison PP | 1.25 | .50 |
| 222 | Fred Taylor PP | 1.25 | .50 |
| 223 | Mark Brunell PP | 1.25 | .50 |
| 224 | Jimmy Smith PP | 1.25 | .50 |
| 225 | Dan Marino PP | 5.00 | 2.00 |
| 226 | Randy Moss PP | 3.00 | 1.25 |
| 227 | Cris Carter PP | 1.25 | .50 |
| 228 | Robert Smith PP | 1.25 | .50 |
| 229 | Drew Bledsoe PP | 2.00 | .75 |
| 230 | Terry Glenn PP | 1.25 | .50 |
| 231 | Ricky Williams PP | 1.25 | .50 |
| 232 | Amani Toomer PP | 1.25 | .50 |
| 233 | Keyshawn Johnson PP | 1.25 | .50 |
| 234 | Curtis Martin PP | 1.25 | .50 |
| 235 | Ray Lucas PP | 1.25 | .50 |
| 236 | Tim Brown PP | 1.25 | .50 |
| 237 | Duce Staley PP | 1.25 | .50 |
| 238 | Donovan McNabb PP | 2.50 | 1.00 |
| 239 | Jerry Rice PP | 3.00 | 1.25 |
| 240 | Jon Kitna PP | 1.25 | .50 |
| 241 | Isaac Bruce PP | 1.25 | .50 |
| 242 | Kurt Warner PP | 3.00 | 1.25 |
| 243 | Torry Holt PP | 1.25 | .50 |
| 244 | Mike Alstott PP | 1.25 | .50 |
| 245 | Marshall Faulk PP | 2.00 | .75 |
| 246 | Shaun King PP | .25 | .08 |
| 247 | Eddie George PP | 1.25 | .50 |
| 248 | Steve McNair PP | 1.25 | .50 |
| 249 | Stephen Davis PP | 1.25 | .50 |
| 250 | Brad Johnson PP | 1.25 | .50 |
| 251 | Rondell Mealey RC | 2.50 | 1.00 |
| 252 | Peter Warrick RC | 4.00 | 1.50 |
| 253 | Courtney Brown RC | 1.25 | .50 |
| 254 | Plaxico Burress RC | 8.00 | 3.00 |
| 255 | Corey Simon RC | 1.25 | .50 |
| 256 | Thomas Jones RC | 6.00 | 2.50 |
| 257 | Travis Taylor RC | 1.25 | .50 |
| 258 | Shaun Alexander RC | 12.00 | 5.00 |
| 259 | Chris Redman RC | 1.25 | .50 |
| 260 | Chad Pennington RC | 10.00 | 4.00 |
| 261 | Jamal Lewis RC | 10.00 | 4.00 |
| 262 | Bubba Franks RC | 4.00 | 1.50 |
| 263 | Dez White RC | 4.00 | 1.50 |
| 264 | Ron Dayne RC | 4.00 | 1.50 |
| 265 | Sylvester Morris RC | 3.00 | 1.25 |
| 266 | R.Jay Soward RC | 3.00 | 1.25 |
| 267 | Sherrod Gideon RC | 2.50 | 1.00 |
| 268 | Travis Prentice RC | 3.00 | 1.25 |
| 269 | Darrell Jackson RC | 8.00 | 3.00 |
| 270 | Giovanni Carmazzi RC | 2.50 | 1.00 |
| 271 | Anthony Lucas RC | 2.50 | 1.00 |
| 272 | Danny Farmer RC | 3.00 | 1.25 |
| 273 | Dennis Northcutt RC | 4.00 | 1.50 |
| 274 | Troy Walters RC | 4.00 | 1.50 |
| 275 | Laveranues Coles RC | 5.00 | 2.00 |
| 276 | Tee Martin RC | 4.00 | 1.50 |
| 277 | J.R. Redmond RC | 3.00 | 1.25 |
| 278 | Jerry Porter RC | 5.00 | 2.00 |
| 279 | Sebastian Janikowski RC | 4.00 | 1.50 |
| 280 | Michael Wiley RC | 3.00 | 1.25 |
| 281 | Reuben Droughns RC | 5.00 | 2.00 |
| 282 | Trung Canidate RC | 3.00 | 1.25 |
| 283 | Shyrone Stith RC | 3.00 | 1.25 |
| 284 | Trevor Gaylor RC | 3.00 | 1.25 |
| 285 | Marc Bulger RC | 8.00 | 3.00 |
| 286 | Tom Brady RC | 100.00 | 50.00 |
| 287 | Todd Husak RC | 4.00 | 1.50 |
| 288 | Jarious Jackson RC | 3.00 | 1.25 |
| 289 | Terrelle Smith RC | 3.00 | 1.25 |
| 290 | Chad Morton RC | 4.00 | 1.50 |
| 291 | Chris Cole RC | 4.00 | 1.50 |
| 292 | Kwame Cavil RC | 2.50 | 1.00 |
| 293 | JaJuan Dawson RC | 2.50 | 1.00 |
| 294 | Curtis Keaton RC | 3.00 | 1.25 |
| 295 | Tim Rattay RC | 4.00 | 1.50 |
| 296 | Joe Hamilton RC | 3.00 | 1.25 |
| 297 | Gari Scott RC | 2.50 | 1.00 |
| 298 | Mike Anderson RC | 5.00 | 2.00 |
| 299 | Ron Dugans RC | 2.50 | 1.00 |
| 300 | Todd Pinkston RC | 4.00 | 1.50 |

## 2002 Playoff Prestige

| | | |
|---|---|---|
| COMP. SET w/o SP's (150) | 40.00 | 15.00 |
| 1 David Boston | 1.25 | .50 |
| 2 MarTay Jenkins | .50 | .20 |
| 3 Jake Plummer | .75 | .30 |
| 4 Chris Chandler | .75 | .30 |
| 5 Jamal Anderson | .75 | .30 |
| 6 Michael Vick | 2.50 | 1.00 |
| 7 Maurice Smith | .75 | .30 |
| 8 Elvis Grbac | .75 | .30 |
| 9 Jamal Lewis | 1.25 | .50 |
| 10 Todd Heap | .50 | .20 |
| 11 Qadry Ismail | .75 | .30 |
| 12 Shannon Sharpe | .75 | .30 |
| 13 Ray Lewis | 1.25 | .50 |
| 14 Rod Woodson | .75 | .30 |
| 15 Travis Henry | .75 | .30 |
| 16 Rob Johnson | .75 | .30 |
| 17 Eric Moulds | .75 | .30 |
| 18 Nate Clements | .50 | .20 |
| 19 Donald Hayes | .50 | .20 |
| 20 Muhsin Muhammad | .75 | .30 |
| 21 Steve Smith | 1.25 | .50 |
| 22 Wesley Walls | .50 | .20 |
| 23 Chris Weinke | .75 | .30 |
| 24 James Allen | .75 | .30 |
| 25 David Terrell | 1.25 | .50 |
| 26 Anthony Thomas | .75 | .30 |
| 27 Dez White | .75 | .30 |
| 28 Brian Urlacher | 2.00 | .75 |
| 29 Mike Brown | 1.25 | .50 |
| 30 Corey Dillon | .75 | .30 |
| 31 Chad Johnson | 1.25 | .50 |
| 32 Peter Warrick | .75 | .30 |
| 33 Justin Smith | .50 | .20 |
| 34 Tim Couch | .75 | .30 |
| 35 James Jackson | .50 | .20 |
| 36 Quincy Morgan | .50 | .20 |
| 37 Kevin Johnson | .75 | .30 |
| 38 Gerard Warren | .50 | .20 |
| 39 Anthony Henry | .50 | .20 |
| 40 Quincy Carter | .75 | .30 |
| 41 Joey Galloway | .75 | .30 |
| 42 Rocket Ismail | .75 | .30 |
| 43 Ryan Leaf | .75 | .30 |
| 44 Emmitt Smith | 3.00 | 1.25 |
| 45 Troy Hambrick | .50 | .20 |
| 46 Mike Anderson | 1.25 | .50 |
| 47 Terrell Davis | 1.25 | .50 |
| 48 Brian Griese | 1.25 | .50 |
| 49 Rod Smith | .75 | .30 |
| 50 Ed McCaffrey | .75 | .30 |
| 51 Charlie Batch | .75 | .30 |
| 52 Johnnie Morton | .75 | .30 |
| 53 Germane Crowell | .50 | .20 |
| 54 James Stewart | .75 | .30 |
| 55 Shaun Rogers | .50 | .20 |
| 56 Brett Favre | 3.00 | 1.25 |
| 57 Antonio Freeman | 1.25 | .50 |
| 58 Ahman Green | 1.25 | .50 |
| 59 Bill Schroeder | .75 | .30 |
| 60 Kabeer Gbaja-Biamila | .75 | .30 |
| 61 Marvin Harrison | 1.25 | .50 |
| 62 Terrence Wilkins | .75 | .30 |
| 63 Dominic Rhodes | .75 | .30 |
| 64 Reggie Wayne | 1.25 | .50 |
| 65 Edgerrin James | 1.50 | .60 |
| 66 Mark Brunell | 1.25 | .50 |
| 67 Keenan McCardell | .50 | .20 |
| 68 Jimmy Smith | .75 | .30 |
| 69 Fred Taylor | 1.25 | .50 |
| 70 Derrick Alexander | .75 | .30 |
| 71 Tony Gonzalez | .75 | .30 |
| 72 Trent Green | .75 | .30 |
| 73 Priest Holmes | 1.50 | .60 |
| 74 Snoop Minnis | .50 | .20 |
| 75 Chris Chambers | 1.25 | .50 |
| 76 Jay Fiedler | .75 | .30 |
| 77 Travis Minor | .50 | .20 |
| 78 Lamar Smith | .75 | .30 |
| 79 Zach Thomas | 1.25 | .50 |
| 80 Michael Bennett | .75 | .30 |
| 81 Cris Carter | 1.25 | .50 |
| 82 Daunte Culpepper | 1.25 | .50 |
| 83 Randy Moss | 2.50 | 1.00 |
| 84 Drew Bledsoe | 1.50 | .60 |
| 85 Tom Brady | 3.00 | 1.25 |
| 86 Troy Brown | .75 | .30 |
| 87 Antowain Smith | .75 | .30 |
| 88 Aaron Brooks | 1.25 | .50 |
| 89 Joe Horn | .75 | .30 |
| 90 Deuce McAllister | 1.50 | .60 |
| 91 Ricky Williams | 1.25 | .50 |
| 92 Kerry Collins | .75 | .30 |
| 93 Ron Dayne | .75 | .30 |
| 94 Michael Strahan | .75 | .30 |
| 95 Jason Sehorn | .50 | .20 |
| 96 Wayne Chrebet | .75 | .30 |
| 97 Laveranues Coles | .75 | .30 |
| 98 LaMont Jordan | 1.25 | .50 |
| 99 Curtis Martin | 1.25 | .50 |
| 100 Santana Moss | 1.25 | .50 |
| 101 Vinny Testaverde | .75 | .30 |
| 102 Tim Brown | 1.25 | .50 |
| 103 Jerry Porter | .50 | .20 |
| 104 Jerry Rice | 2.50 | 1.00 |
| 105 Charlie Garner | .75 | .30 |
| 106 Tyrone Wheatley | .75 | .30 |
| 107 Charles Woodson | .75 | .30 |
| 108 Correll Buckhalter | .75 | .30 |
| 109 Todd Pinkston | .75 | .30 |
| 110 Freddie Mitchell | .75 | .30 |
| 111 James Thrash | .75 | .30 |
| 112 Duce Staley | 1.25 | .50 |
| 113 Jerome Bettis | 1.25 | .50 |
| 114 Plaxico Burress | .75 | .30 |
| 115 Kordell Stewart | .75 | .30 |
| 116 Hines Ward | 1.25 | .50 |
| 117 Kendrell Bell | 1.25 | .50 |
| 118 Drew Brees | 1.25 | .50 |
| 119 Curtis Conway | .50 | .20 |
| 120 Doug Flutie | 1.25 | .50 |
| 121 LaDainian Tomlinson | 2.00 | .75 |
| 122 Junior Seau | 1.25 | .50 |
| 123 Kevan Barlow | .75 | .30 |
| 124 Jeff Garcia | 1.25 | .50 |
| 125 Garrison Hearst | .75 | .30 |
| 126 Terrell Owens | 1.25 | .50 |
| 127 Andre Carter | .50 | .20 |
| 128 Shaun Alexander | 1.50 | .60 |
| 129 Matt Hasselbeck | .75 | .30 |
| 130 Koren Robinson | .75 | .30 |
| 131 Ricky Watters | .75 | .30 |
| 132 Isaac Bruce | 1.25 | .50 |
| 133 Trung Canidate | .75 | .30 |
| 134 Marshall Faulk | 1.25 | .50 |
| 135 Torry Holt | 1.25 | .50 |
| 136 Kurt Warner | 1.25 | .50 |
| 137 Mike Alstott | 1.25 | .50 |
| 138 Warrick Dunn | 1.25 | .50 |
| 139 Brad Johnson | .75 | .30 |
| 140 Keyshawn Johnson | 1.25 | .50 |
| 141 Warren Sapp | .75 | .30 |
| 142 Eddie George | 1.25 | .50 |
| 143 Derrick Mason | .75 | .30 |
| 144 Steve McNair | 1.25 | .50 |
| 145 Jevon Kearse | .75 | .30 |
| 146 Stephen Davis | .75 | .30 |
| 147 Rod Gardner | .75 | .30 |
| 148 Champ Bailey | .75 | .30 |
| 149 Bruce Smith | .50 | .20 |
| 150 Houston Texans | 1.50 | .60 |
| 151 David Carr RC | 5.00 | 2.00 |
| 152 Julius Peppers RC | 8.00 | 3.00 |
| 153 Joey Harrington RC | 5.00 | 2.00 |
| 154 Quentin Jammer RC | 4.00 | 1.50 |
| 155 Ryan Sims RC | 4.00 | 1.50 |
| 156 Bryant McKinnie RC | 3.00 | 1.25 |
| 157 Roy Williams RC | 8.00 | 3.00 |
| 158 John Henderson RC | 4.00 | 1.50 |
| 159 Dwight Freeney RC | 6.00 | 2.50 |
| 160 Wendell Bryant RC | 2.00 | .75 |
| 161 Donte Stallworth RC | 6.00 | 2.50 |
| 162 Jeremy Shockey RC | 6.00 | 2.50 |
| 163 Albert Haynesworth RC | 4.00 | 1.50 |
| 164 William Green RC | 4.00 | 1.50 |
| 165 Phillip Buchanon RC | 4.00 | 1.50 |
| 166 T.J. Duckett RC | 4.00 | 1.50 |
| 167 Ashley Lelie RC | 8.00 | 3.00 |
| 168 Javon Walker RC | 6.00 | 2.50 |
| 169 Daniel Graham RC | 4.00 | 1.50 |
| 170 Napoleon Harris RC | 4.00 | 1.50 |
| 171 Lito Sheppard RC | 4.00 | 1.50 |
| 172 Robert Thomas RC | 4.00 | 1.50 |
| 173 Patrick Ramsey RC | 4.00 | 1.50 |
| 174 Jabar Gaffney RC | 4.00 | 1.50 |
| 175 DeShaun Foster RC | 4.00 | 1.50 |
| 176 Kalimba Edwards RC | 4.00 | 1.50 |
| 177 Josh Reed RC | 4.00 | 1.50 |
| 178 Larry Tripplett RC | 2.00 | .75 |
| 179 Andre Davis RC | 3.00 | 1.25 |
| 180 Reche Caldwell RC | 4.00 | 1.50 |
| 181 Levar Fisher RC | 2.00 | .75 |
| 182 Clinton Portis RC | 12.00 | 5.00 |
| 183 Anthony Weaver RC | 3.00 | 1.25 |
| 184 Maurice Morris RC | 4.00 | 1.50 |
| 185 Ladell Betts RC | 4.00 | 1.50 |
| 186 Antwaan Randle El RC | 5.00 | 2.00 |
| 187 Antonio Bryant RC | 4.00 | 1.50 |
| 188 Rocky Calmus RC | 4.00 | 1.50 |
| 189 Josh McCown RC | 5.00 | 2.00 |
| 190 Lamar Gordon RC | 4.00 | 1.50 |
| 191 Marquise Walker RC | 3.00 | 1.25 |
| 192 Cliff Russell RC | 3.00 | 1.25 |
| 193 Eric Crouch RC | 4.00 | 1.50 |
| 194 Dennis Johnson RC | 2.00 | .75 |
| 195 Alex Brown RC | 4.00 | 1.50 |
| 196 David Garrard RC | 8.00 | 3.00 |
| 197 Rohan Davey RC | 4.00 | 1.50 |
| 198 Alan Harper RC | 2.00 | .75 |
| 199 Ron Johnson RC | 3.00 | 1.25 |
| 200 Andra Davis RC | 3.00 | 1.25 |
| 201 Kurt Kittner RC | 3.00 | 1.25 |
| 202 Freddie Milons RC | 3.00 | 1.25 |
| 203 Adrian Peterson RC | 5.00 | 2.00 |
| 204 Luke Staley RC | 3.00 | 1.25 |
| 205 Tracey Wistrom RC | 3.00 | 1.25 |
| 206 Woody Dantzler RC | 3.00 | 1.25 |
| 207 Chad Hutchinson RC | 4.00 | 1.50 |
| 208 Zak Kustok RC | 4.00 | 1.50 |
| 209 Damien Anderson RC | 4.00 | 1.50 |
| 210 James Mungro RC | 4.00 | 1.50 |
| 211 Cortlen Johnson RC | 2.00 | .75 |
| 212 Demontray Carter RC | 2.00 | .75 |
| 213 Kelly Campbell RC | 3.00 | 1.25 |
| 214 Brian Poli-Dixon RC | 3.00 | 1.25 |
| 215 Mike Rumph RC | 4.00 | 1.50 |
| 216 Najeh Davenport RC | 4.00 | 1.50 |

## 2003 Playoff Prestige

|  |  | | |
|---|---|---|---|
| | COMP.SET w/o RC's (150) | 30.00 | 12.50 |
| 1 | David Boston | .60 | .25 |
| 2 | Thomas Jones | .75 | .30 |
| 3 | Jake Plummer | .75 | .30 |
| 4 | Marcel Shipp | .60 | .25 |
| 5 | T.J. Duckett | .75 | .30 |
| 6 | Warrick Dunn | .75 | .30 |
| 7 | Michael Vick | 1.00 | .40 |
| 8 | Jeff Blake | .75 | .30 |
| 9 | Todd Heap | .75 | .30 |
| 10 | Jamal Lewis | 1.00 | .40 |
| 11 | Ray Lewis | 1.00 | .40 |
| 12 | Drew Bledsoe | 1.00 | .40 |
| 13 | Travis Henry | .75 | .30 |
| 14 | Eric Moulds | .75 | .30 |
| 15 | Peerless Price | .60 | .25 |
| 16 | Josh Reed | .60 | .25 |
| 17 | DeShaun Foster | .75 | .30 |
| 18 | Muhsin Muhammad | .75 | .30 |
| 19 | Steve Smith | 1.00 | .40 |
| 20 | Julius Peppers | 1.00 | .40 |
| 21 | Marty Booker | .75 | .30 |
| 22 | David Terrell | .60 | .25 |
| 23 | Anthony Thomas | .75 | .30 |
| 24 | Brian Urlacher | 1.50 | .60 |
| 25 | Corey Dillon | .75 | .30 |
| 26 | Chad Johnson | 1.00 | .40 |
| 27 | Jon Kitna | .75 | .30 |
| 28 | Peter Warrick | .75 | .30 |
| 29 | Tim Couch | .60 | .25 |
| 30 | Andre Davis | .60 | .25 |
| 31 | William Green | .60 | .25 |
| 32 | Quincy Morgan | .60 | .25 |
| 33 | Dennis Northcutt | .60 | .25 |
| 34 | Antonio Bryant | 1.00 | .40 |
| 35 | Quincy Carter | .60 | .25 |
| 36 | Troy Hambrick | .60 | .25 |
| 37 | Chad Hutchinson | .60 | .25 |
| 38 | Emmitt Smith | 2.50 | 1.00 |
| 39 | Roy Williams | .75 | .30 |
| 40 | Brian Griese | .75 | .30 |
| 41 | Ashley Lelie | .60 | .25 |
| 42 | Ed McCaffrey | .75 | .30 |
| 43 | Clinton Portis | 1.25 | .50 |
| 44 | Rod Smith | .75 | .30 |
| 45 | Germane Crowell | .60 | .25 |
| 46 | Az-Zahir Hakim | .60 | .25 |
| 47 | Joey Harrington | 1.00 | .40 |
| 48 | James Stewart | .75 | .30 |
| 49 | Donald Driver | 1.00 | .40 |
| 50 | Brett Favre | 2.50 | 1.00 |
| 51 | Terry Glenn | .75 | .30 |
| 52 | Ahman Green | 1.00 | .40 |
| 53 | Javon Walker | .75 | .30 |
| 54 | Corey Bradford | .60 | .25 |
| 55 | David Carr | .75 | .30 |
| 56 | Jabar Gaffney | .60 | .25 |
| 57 | Jonathan Wells | .60 | .25 |
| 58 | Marvin Harrison | 1.00 | .40 |
| 59 | Edgerrin James | 1.00 | .40 |
| 60 | Peyton Manning | 2.00 | .75 |
| 61 | James Mungro | .60 | .25 |
| 62 | Reggie Wayne | .75 | .30 |
| 63 | Mark Brunell | .75 | .30 |
| 64 | David Garrard | 1.00 | .40 |
| 65 | Stacey Mack | .60 | .25 |
| 66 | Jimmy Smith | .75 | .30 |
| 67 | Fred Taylor | 1.00 | .40 |
| 68 | Marc Boerigter | .60 | .25 |
| 69 | Tony Gonzalez | .75 | .30 |
| 70 | Trent Green | .75 | .30 |
| 71 | Priest Holmes | 1.00 | .40 |
| 72 | Eddie Kennison | .60 | .25 |
| 73 | Cris Carter | 1.00 | .40 |
| 74 | Chris Chambers | .75 | .30 |
| 75 | Jay Fiedler | .75 | .30 |
| 76 | Randy McMichael | .60 | .25 |
| 77 | Zach Thomas | .75 | .30 |
| 78 | Ricky Williams | .75 | .30 |
| 79 | Michael Bennett | .75 | .30 |
| 80 | Todd Bouman | .60 | .25 |
| 81 | Daunte Culpepper | 1.00 | .40 |
| 82 | Randy Moss | 1.25 | .50 |
| 83 | Tom Brady | 2.50 | 1.00 |
| 84 | Deion Branch | .75 | .30 |
| 85 | Troy Brown | .75 | .30 |
| 86 | Kevin Faulk | .75 | .30 |
| 87 | Antowain Smith | .75 | .30 |
| 88 | Aaron Brooks | .75 | .30 |
| 89 | Joe Horn | .75 | .30 |
| 90 | Deuce McAllister | 1.00 | .40 |
| 91 | Donte Stallworth | .75 | .30 |
| 92 | Tiki Barber | 1.00 | .40 |
| 93 | Kerry Collins | .75 | .30 |
| 94 | Jeremy Shockey | 1.00 | .40 |
| 95 | Michael Strahan | .75 | .30 |
| 96 | Amani Toomer | .75 | .30 |
| 97 | Laveranues Coles | .75 | .30 |
| 98 | LaMont Jordan | .75 | .30 |
| 99 | Curtis Martin | 1.00 | .40 |
| 100 | Santana Moss | .75 | .30 |
| 101 | Chad Pennington | 1.00 | .40 |
| 102 | Tim Brown | 1.00 | .40 |
| 103 | Rich Gannon | .75 | .30 |
| 104 | Charlie Garner | .75 | .30 |
| 105 | Jerry Rice | 2.00 | .75 |
| 106 | Charles Woodson | .75 | .30 |
| 107 | Antonio Freeman | .75 | .30 |
| 108 | Dorsey Levens | .75 | .30 |
| 109 | Donovan McNabb | 1.25 | .50 |
| 110 | Duce Staley | .75 | .30 |
| 111 | James Thrash | .60 | .25 |
| 112 | Jerome Bettis | 1.00 | .40 |
| 113 | Plaxico Burress | 1.00 | .40 |
| 114 | Tommy Maddox | .75 | .30 |
| 115 | Antwaan Randle El | .75 | .30 |
| 116 | Kordell Stewart | .75 | .30 |
| 117 | Hines Ward | 1.00 | .40 |
| 118 | Drew Brees | 1.00 | .40 |
| 119 | Curtis Conway | .60 | .25 |
| 120 | Junior Seau | 1.00 | .40 |
| 121 | LaDainian Tomlinson | 1.50 | .60 |
| 122 | Kevan Barlow | .60 | .25 |
| 123 | Jeff Garcia | 1.00 | .40 |
| 124 | Garrison Hearst | .75 | .30 |
| 125 | Terrell Owens | 1.00 | .40 |
| 126 | Shaun Alexander | 1.00 | .40 |
| 127 | Trent Dilfer | .75 | .30 |
| 128 | Darrell Jackson | .75 | .30 |
| 129 | Maurice Morris | .60 | .25 |
| 130 | Koren Robinson | .75 | .30 |
| 131 | Isaac Bruce | 1.00 | .40 |
| 132 | Marc Bulger | 1.00 | .40 |
| 133 | Marshall Faulk | 1.00 | .40 |
| 134 | Torry Holt | 1.00 | .40 |
| 135 | Kurt Warner | 1.00 | .40 |
| 136 | Mike Alstott | 1.00 | .40 |
| 137 | Brad Johnson | .75 | .30 |
| 138 | Keyshawn Johnson | 1.00 | .40 |
| 139 | Dexter Jackson | 1.25 | .50 |
| 140 | Warren Sapp | .75 | .30 |
| 141 | Kevin Dyson | .75 | .30 |
| 142 | Eddie George | .75 | .30 |
| 143 | Jevon Kearse | .75 | .30 |
| 144 | Derrick Mason | .75 | .30 |
| 145 | Steve McNair | 1.00 | .40 |
| 146 | Stephen Davis | .75 | .30 |
| 147 | Rod Gardner | .60 | .25 |
| 148 | Shane Matthews | .60 | .25 |
| 149 | Patrick Ramsey | .75 | .30 |
| 150 | Derrius Thompson | .60 | .25 |
| 151 | Byron Leftwich RC | 5.00 | 2.00 |
| 152 | Carson Palmer RC | 12.00 | 5.00 |
| 153 | Chris Simms RC | 3.00 | 1.25 |
| 154 | Kliff Kingsbury RC | 2.50 | 1.00 |
| 155 | Dave Ragone RC | 2.00 | .75 |
| 156 | Jason Gesser RC | 2.50 | 1.00 |
| 157 | Ken Dorsey RC | 2.50 | 1.00 |
| 158 | Kyle Boller RC | 3.00 | 1.25 |
| 159 | Brad Banks RC | 2.50 | 1.00 |
| 160 | Rex Grossman RC | 8.00 | 3.00 |
| 161 | Seneca Wallace RC | 3.00 | 1.25 |
| 162 | Brian St.Pierre RC | 3.00 | 1.25 |
| 163 | Larry Johnson RC | 8.00 | 3.00 |
| 164 | Earnest Graham RC | 3.00 | 1.25 |
| 165 | Musa Smith RC | 2.50 | 1.00 |
| 166 | Lee Suggs RC | 2.50 | 1.00 |
| 167 | Willis McGahee RC | 8.00 | 3.00 |
| 168 | Onterrio Smith RC | 2.50 | 1.00 |
| 170 | Sultan McCullough RC | 2.00 | .75 |
| 171 | Chris Brown RC | 3.00 | 1.25 |
| 172 | Justin Fargas RC | 2.00 | .75 |
| 173 | Avon Cobourne RC | 2.00 | .75 |
| 174 | Dahrran Diedrick RC | 2.00 | .75 |
| 175 | LaBrandon Toefield RC | 2.50 | 1.00 |
| 176 | Artose Pinner RC | 2.00 | .75 |
| 177 | Quentin Griffin RC | 2.50 | 1.00 |
| 178 | ReShard Lee RC | 3.00 | 1.25 |
| 179 | Andrew Pinnock RC | 2.50 | 1.00 |
| 180 | B.J. Askew RC | 2.50 | 1.00 |
| 181 | Andre Johnson RC | 6.00 | 2.50 |
| 182 | Brandon Lloyd RC | 3.00 | 1.25 |
| 183 | Bryant Johnson RC | 3.00 | 1.25 |
| 184 | Charles Rogers RC | 2.50 | 1.00 |
| 185 | Doug Gabriel RC | 2.50 | 1.00 |
| 186 | Justin Gage RC | 2.50 | 1.00 |
| 187 | Kareem Kelly RC | 2.00 | .75 |
| 188 | Kelley Washington RC | 2.50 | 1.00 |
| 189 | Taylor Jacobs RC | 2.50 | 1.00 |
| 190 | Terrence Edwards RC | 2.00 | .75 |
| 191 | Anquan Boldin RC | 8.00 | 3.00 |
| 192 | Billy McMullen RC | 2.00 | .75 |
| 193 | Tamar Gardner RC | 2.00 | .75 |
| 194 | Arnaz Battle RC | 3.00 | 1.25 |
| 195 | Sam Aiken RC | 2.50 | 1.00 |
| 196 | Bobby Wade RC | 2.50 | 1.00 |
| 197 | Jason Witten RC | 6.00 | 2.50 |
| 198 | Mike Bush RC | 2.00 | .75 |
| 199 | Keenan Howry RC | 2.00 | .75 |
| 200 | Jerel Myers RC | 2.00 | .75 |
| 200 | Dallas Clark RC | 3.00 | 1.25 |
| 201 | Mike Pinkard RC | 2.00 | .75 |
| 202 | Teyo Johnson RC | 2.50 | 1.00 |
| 203 | Trent Smith RC | 2.50 | 1.00 |
| 204 | George Wrighster RC | 2.00 | .75 |
| 205 | Jason Witten RC | 6.00 | 2.50 |
| 206 | Cory Redding RC | 2.00 | .75 |
| 207 | DeWayne White RC | 2.00 | .75 |
| 208 | Jerome McDougle RC | 2.00 | .75 |
| 209 | Michael Haynes RC | 2.00 | .75 |
| 210 | Chris Kelsay RC | 2.50 | 1.00 |
| 211 | Calvin Pace RC | 2.50 | 1.00 |
| 212 | Kenny King RC | 2.50 | 1.00 |
| 213 | Jimmy Kennedy RC | 2.50 | 1.00 |
| 214 | William Joseph RC | 2.00 | .75 |
| 215 | DeWayne Robertson RC | 2.50 | 1.00 |
| 216 | Jarret Johnson RC | 2.00 | .75 |
| 217 | Rien Long RC | 2.00 | .75 |
| 218 | Boss Bailey RC | 2.50 | 1.00 |
| 219 | Terrell Suggs RC | 4.00 | 1.50 |
| 220 | Terry Pierce RC | 2.00 | .75 |
| 221 | Bradie James RC | 3.00 | 1.25 |
| 222 | Angelo Crowell RC | 2.50 | 1.00 |
| 223 | Andre Woolfolk RC | 2.50 | 1.00 |
| 224 | Dennis Weathersby RC | 2.00 | .75 |
| 225 | Marcus Trufant RC | 3.00 | 1.25 |
| 226 | Terence Newman RC | 4.00 | 1.50 |
| 227 | Ricky Manning RC | 2.50 | 1.00 |
| 228 | Mike Doss RC | 3.00 | 1.25 |
| 229 | Julian Battle RC | 2.50 | 1.00 |
| 230 | Rashean Mathis RC | 2.50 | 1.00 |

## 2004 Playoff Prestige

|  |  | | |
|---|---|---|---|
| | COMP.SET w/ RC's (150) | 25.00 | 10.00 |
| 1 | Anquan Boldin | 1.00 | .40 |
| 2 | Emmitt Smith | 2.50 | 1.00 |
| 3 | Jeff Blake | .75 | .30 |
| 4 | Marcel Shipp | 1.00 | .40 |
| 5 | Michael Vick | 1.00 | .40 |

|  |  | | |
|---|---|---|---|
| 6 | Peerless Price | .75 | .30 |
| 7 | T.J. Duckett | .75 | .30 |
| 8 | Warrick Dunn | .75 | .30 |
| 9 | Ed Reed | .75 | .30 |
| 10 | Jamal Lewis | .75 | .30 |
| 11 | Kyle Boller | .75 | .30 |
| 12 | Ray Lewis | 1.00 | .40 |
| 13 | Todd Heap | .75 | .30 |
| 14 | Drew Bledsoe | 1.00 | .40 |
| 15 | Eric Moulds | .75 | .30 |
| 16 | Josh Reed | 1.00 | .40 |
| 17 | Travis Henry | .75 | .30 |
| 18 | DeShaun Foster | .75 | .30 |
| 19 | Stephen Davis | .75 | .30 |
| 20 | Jake Delhomme | .75 | .30 |
| 21 | Julius Peppers | .75 | .30 |
| 22 | Steve Smith | 1.00 | .40 |
| 23 | Anthony Thomas | .75 | .30 |
| 24 | Brian Urlacher | 1.00 | .40 |
| 25 | Marty Booker | .75 | .30 |
| 26 | Rex Grossman | 1.00 | .40 |
| 27 | Chad Johnson | .75 | .30 |
| 28 | Corey Dillon | .75 | .30 |
| 29 | Carson Palmer | 1.25 | .50 |
| 30 | Peter Warrick | .75 | .30 |
| 31 | Rudi Johnson | .75 | .30 |
| 32 | Andre Davis | .60 | .25 |
| 33 | Quincy Morgan | .60 | .25 |
| 34 | William Green | .60 | .25 |
| 35 | Kelly Holcomb | .75 | .30 |
| 36 | Antonio Bryant | .60 | .25 |
| 37 | Quincy Carter | .60 | .25 |
| 38 | Roy Williams S | .75 | .30 |
| 39 | Terence Newman | .75 | .30 |
| 40 | Terry Glenn | .75 | .30 |
| 41 | Troy Hambrick | .60 | .25 |
| 42 | Ashley Lelie | .75 | .30 |
| 43 | Clinton Portis | 1.00 | .40 |
| 44 | Rod Smith | .75 | .30 |
| 45 | Shannon Sharpe | .75 | .30 |
| 46 | Mike Anderson | .75 | .30 |
| 47 | Jake Plummer | .75 | .30 |
| 48 | Charles Rogers | .75 | .30 |
| 49 | Joey Harrington | .75 | .30 |
| 50 | Ahman Green | 1.00 | .40 |
| 51 | Brett Favre | 2.50 | 1.00 |
| 52 | Donald Driver | 1.00 | .40 |
| 53 | Javon Walker | .75 | .30 |
| 54 | Robert Ferguson | .60 | .25 |
| 55 | Andre Johnson | 1.00 | .40 |
| 56 | David Carr | .75 | .30 |
| 57 | Domanick Davis | 1.00 | .40 |
| 58 | Jabar Gaffney | .75 | .30 |
| 59 | Dwight Freeney | 1.00 | .40 |
| 60 | Dallas Clark | .75 | .30 |
| 61 | Edgerrin James | 1.00 | .40 |
| 62 | Marvin Harrison | 1.00 | .40 |
| 63 | Peyton Manning | 2.00 | .75 |
| 64 | Reggie Wayne | .75 | .30 |
| 65 | Byron Leftwich | 1.00 | .40 |
| 66 | Fred Taylor | .75 | .30 |
| 67 | Jimmy Smith | .75 | .30 |
| 68 | Johnnie Morton | .75 | .30 |
| 69 | Priest Holmes | 1.00 | .40 |
| 70 | Tony Gonzalez | 1.00 | .40 |
| 71 | Trent Green | .75 | .30 |
| 72 | Chris Chambers | .75 | .30 |
| 73 | Jay Fiedler | .60 | .25 |
| 74 | Randy McMichael | .60 | .25 |
| 75 | Ricky Williams | 1.00 | .40 |
| 76 | Zach Thomas | .75 | .30 |
| 77 | Daunte Culpepper | 1.00 | .40 |
| 78 | Kelly Campbell | .60 | .25 |
| 79 | Michael Bennett | .75 | .30 |
| 80 | Moe Williams | .60 | .25 |
| 81 | Nate Burleson | .75 | .30 |
| 82 | Randy Moss | 1.25 | .50 |
| 83 | Deion Branch | .75 | .30 |
| 84 | Kevin Faulk | .75 | .30 |
| 85 | Tom Brady | 2.50 | 1.00 |
| 86 | Troy Brown | .75 | .30 |
| 87 | Tedy Bruschi | 1.00 | .40 |
| 88 | Aaron Brooks | .75 | .30 |
| 89 | Deuce McAllister | 1.00 | .40 |
| 90 | Donte Stallworth | .75 | .30 |
| 91 | Joe Horn | .75 | .30 |
| 92 | Amani Toomer | .75 | .30 |
| 93 | Ike Hilliard | .75 | .30 |
| 94 | Jeremy Shockey | .75 | .30 |
| 95 | Kerry Collins | .75 | .30 |
| 96 | Michael Strahan | .75 | .30 |
| 97 | Tiki Barber | 1.00 | .40 |
| 98 | Chad Pennington | 1.00 | .40 |
| 99 | Curtis Martin | 1.00 | .40 |
| 100 | LaMont Jordan | 1.00 | .40 |
| 101 | Santana Moss | .75 | .30 |
| 102 | Charlie Garner | .75 | .30 |
| 103 | Jerry Porter | .75 | .30 |
| 104 | Jerry Rice | 2.00 | .75 |
| 105 | Justin Fargas | .75 | .30 |
| 106 | Rich Gannon | .75 | .30 |
| 107 | Rod Woodson | .75 | .30 |
| 108 | Tim Brown | 1.00 | .40 |
| 109 | Brian Westbrook | 1.00 | .40 |
| 110 | Correll Buckhalter | .75 | .30 |
| 111 | Donovan McNabb | 1.00 | .40 |
| 112 | Freddie Mitchell | .60 | .25 |
| 113 | James Thrash | .75 | .30 |
| 114 | Amos Zereoue | .60 | .25 |
| 115 | Antwaan Randle El | .75 | .30 |
| 116 | Hines Ward | 1.00 | .40 |
| 117 | Joey Porter | .75 | .30 |
| 118 | Kendrell Bell | .60 | .25 |
| 119 | Plaxico Burress | .75 | .30 |
| 120 | David Boston | .60 | .25 |
| 121 | Drew Brees | 1.00 | .40 |
| 122 | LaDainian Tomlinson | 1.50 | .60 |
| 123 | Jeff Garcia | 1.00 | .40 |
| 124 | Kevan Barlow | .75 | .30 |
| 125 | Tai Streets | .60 | .25 |
| 126 | Terrell Owens | 1.00 | .40 |
| 127 | Tim Rattay | .60 | .25 |
| 128 | Darrell Jackson | .75 | .30 |
| 129 | Koren Robinson | 1.00 | .40 |
| 130 | Matt Hasselbeck | 1.00 | .40 |
| 131 | Shaun Alexander | 1.00 | .40 |
| 132 | Isaac Bruce | .75 | .30 |
| 133 | Marc Bulger | .75 | .30 |
| 134 | Marshall Faulk | 1.00 | .40 |
| 135 | Torry Holt | 1.00 | .40 |
| 136 | Brad Johnson | .75 | .30 |
| 137 | Derrick Brooks | .75 | .30 |
| 138 | Keenan McCardell | .60 | .25 |
| 139 | Keyshawn Johnson | .75 | .30 |
| 140 | Mike Alstott | .75 | .30 |
| 141 | Derrick Mason | .75 | .30 |
| 142 | Drew Bennett | .75 | .30 |
| 143 | Jevon Kearse | .75 | .30 |
| 144 | Justin McCareins | .60 | .25 |
| 145 | Steve McNair | 1.00 | .40 |
| 146 | Tyrone Calico | .75 | .30 |
| 147 | Bruce Smith | 1.00 | .40 |
| 148 | Laveranues Coles | .75 | .30 |
| 149 | Patrick Ramsey | .75 | .30 |
| 150 | LaVar Arrington | .75 | .30 |
| 151 | Eli Manning RC | 15.00 | 6.00 |
| 152 | Larry Fitzgerald RC | 8.00 | 3.00 |
| 153 | Philip Rivers RC | 8.00 | 3.00 |
| 154 | Sean Taylor RC | 2.50 | 1.00 |
| 155 | Kellen Winslow RC | 5.00 | 2.00 |
| 156 | Roy Williams RC | 6.00 | 2.50 |
| 157 | DeAngelo Hall RC | 2.50 | 1.00 |
| 158 | Reggie Williams RC | 2.50 | 1.00 |
| 159 | Ben Roethlisberger RC | 20.00 | 8.00 |
| 160 | Jonathan Vilma RC | 2.50 | 1.00 |
| 161 | Lee Evans RC | 3.00 | 1.25 |
| 162 | Tommie Harris RC | 2.50 | 1.00 |
| 163 | Michael Clayton RC | 2.50 | 1.00 |
| 164 | D.J. Williams SP RC | 25.00 | 10.00 |
| 165 | Will Smith RC | 2.00 | .75 |
| 166 | Kenechi Udeze RC | 2.50 | 1.00 |
| 167 | Vince Wilfork SP RC | 25.00 | 10.00 |
| 168 | J.P. Losman RC | 3.00 | 1.25 |
| 169 | Steven Jackson SP RC | 50.00 | 20.00 |
| 170 | Ahmad Carroll RC | 2.50 | 1.00 |
| 171 | Chris Perry RC | 2.50 | 1.00 |
| 172 | Jason Babin RC | 20.00 | 8.00 |
| 173 | Chris Gamble RC | 2.00 | .75 |
| 174 | Michael Jenkins RC | 2.50 | 1.00 |
| 175 | Kevin Jones RC | 2.50 | 1.00 |
| 176 | Rashaun Woods RC | 1.50 | .60 |
| 177 | Ben Watson RC | 2.50 | 1.00 |
| 178 | Karlos Dansby RC | 2.50 | 1.00 |
| 179 | Teddy Lehman RC | 1.50 | .60 |
| 180 | Ricardo Colclough SP RC | 25.00 | 10.00 |
| 181 | Daryl Smith RC | 2.00 | .75 |
| 182 | Ben Troupe RC | 2.00 | .75 |
| 183 | Tatum Bell RC | 2.50 | 1.00 |
| 184 | Julius Jones RC | 6.00 | 2.50 |
| 185 | Bob Sanders RC | 6.00 | 2.50 |
| 186 | Devery Henderson RC | 2.50 | 1.00 |
| 187 | Dwan Edwards RC | 1.50 | .60 |
| 188 | Michael Boulware RC | 2.50 | 1.00 |
| 189 | Darius Watts RC | 2.00 | .75 |
| 190 | Greg Jones RC | 2.50 | 1.00 |
| 191 | Antwan Odom RC | 2.00 | .75 |
| 192 | Sean Jones RC | 20.00 | 8.00 |
| 193 | Courtney Watson RC | 2.50 | 1.00 |
| 194 | Keary Colbert RC | 2.50 | 1.00 |
| 195 | Keith Smith RC | 1.50 | .60 |
| 196 | Derrick Strait RC | 2.00 | .75 |
| 197 | Bernard Berrian RC | 25.00 | 10.00 |
| 198 | Devard Darling RC | 2.00 | .75 |
| 199 | Matt Schaub RC | 8.00 | 3.00 |
| 200 | Will Poole RC | 2.50 | 1.00 |
| 201 | Samie Parker RC | 2.00 | .75 |
| 202 | Luke McCown SP RC | 25.00 | 10.00 |
| 203 | Jerricho Cotchery RC | 2.50 | 1.00 |
| 204 | Mewelde Moore RC | 2.50 | 1.00 |
| 205 | Ernest Wilford RC | 2.50 | 1.00 |
| 206 | Cedric Cobbs SP RC | 20.00 | 8.00 |
| 207 | Johnnie Morant RC | 2.00 | .75 |
| 208 | Craig Krenzel RC | 2.50 | 1.00 |
| 209 | Michael Turner RC | 5.00 | 2.00 |
| 210 | D.J. Hackett RC | 2.50 | 1.00 |
| 211 | P.K. Sam RC | 1.50 | .60 |
| 212 | Josh Harris RC | 1.50 | .60 |
| 213 | Drew Henson RC | 1.50 | .60 |
| 214 | Jeff Smoker RC | 2.00 | .75 |
| 215 | John Navarre RC | 2.00 | .75 |
| 216 | Cody Pickett RC | 2.00 | .75 |
| 217 | Quincy Wilson RC | 2.00 | .75 |
| 218 | Derek Abney RC | 1.50 | .60 |
| 219 | Maurice Clarett SP RC | 20.00 | 8.00 |
| 220 | Mike Williams SP RC | 20.00 | 8.00 |
| 221 | B.J. Johnson RC | 1.50 | .60 |
| 222 | Brandon Everage RC | 1.50 | .60 |
| 223 | Derek McCoy RC | 1.50 | .60 |
| 224 | Jared Lorenzen RC | 2.00 | .75 |
| 225 | Jarrett Payton RC | 2.00 | .75 |
| 226 | Jason Fife RC | 1.50 | .60 |
| 227 | Robert Kent RC | 1.50 | .60 |

## 2005 Playoff Prestige

| | | |
|---|---|---|
| COMP.SET w/o SP's (234) | 100.00 | 50.00 |
| COMP.SET w/o RC's (150) | 25.00 | 10.00 |
| ONE 151-244 DRAFT PICK PER PACK | | |
| 1 Anquan Boldin | .75 | .30 |
| 2 Emmitt Smith | 2.00 | .75 |
| 3 Josh McCown | .75 | .30 |
| 4 Larry Fitzgerald | 1.00 | .40 |
| 5 Michael Vick | 1.00 | .40 |
| 6 Peerless Price | .60 | .25 |
| 7 Alge Crumpler | .75 | .30 |
| 8 T.J. Duckett | .60 | .25 |
| 9 Warrick Dunn | .75 | .30 |
| 10 Ed Reed | .75 | .30 |
| 11 Jamal Lewis | .75 | .30 |

| # | Player | Price | Price2 |
|---|--------|-------|--------|
| ☐ 12 | Kyle Boller | .75 | .30 |
| ☐ 13 | Ray Lewis | 1.00 | .40 |
| ☐ 14 | Todd Heap | .75 | .30 |
| ☐ 15 | Drew Bledsoe | 1.00 | .40 |
| ☐ 16 | Eric Moulds | .75 | .30 |
| ☐ 17 | Lee Evans | .75 | .30 |
| ☐ 18 | Travis Henry | .75 | .30 |
| ☐ 19 | Willis McGahee | 1.00 | .40 |
| ☐ 20 | Anthony Thomas | .60 | .25 |
| ☐ 21 | Brian Urlacher | 1.00 | .40 |
| ☐ 22 | Rex Grossman | 1.00 | .40 |
| ☐ 23 | David Terrell | .60 | .25 |
| ☐ 24 | Thomas Jones | .75 | .30 |
| ☐ 25 | Carson Palmer | 1.00 | .40 |
| ☐ 26 | Chad Johnson | .75 | .30 |
| ☐ 27 | Peter Warrick | .60 | .25 |
| ☐ 28 | Rudi Johnson | .75 | .30 |
| ☐ 29 | Antonio Bryant | .60 | .25 |
| ☐ 30 | William Green | .60 | .25 |
| ☐ 31 | Jeff Garcia | .75 | .30 |
| ☐ 32 | Kellen Winslow | 1.00 | .40 |
| ☐ 33 | Lee Suggs | .75 | .30 |
| ☐ 34 | Drew Henson | .60 | .25 |
| ☐ 35 | Julius Jones | 1.00 | .40 |
| ☐ 36 | Jason Witten | .75 | .30 |
| ☐ 37 | Keyshawn Johnson | .75 | .30 |
| ☐ 38 | Roy Williams S | .75 | .30 |
| ☐ 39 | Ashley Lelie | .60 | .25 |
| ☐ 40 | Champ Bailey | .75 | .30 |
| ☐ 41 | Jake Plummer | .75 | .30 |
| ☐ 42 | Reuben Droughns | .60 | .25 |
| ☐ 43 | Rod Smith | .75 | .30 |
| ☐ 44 | Charles Rogers | .60 | .25 |
| ☐ 45 | Joey Harrington | 1.00 | .40 |
| ☐ 46 | Kevin Jones | .75 | .30 |
| ☐ 47 | Roy Williams WR | 1.00 | .40 |
| ☐ 48 | Ahman Green | 1.00 | .40 |
| ☐ 49 | Donald Driver | 1.00 | .40 |
| ☐ 50 | Javon Walker | .75 | .30 |
| ☐ 51 | Brett Favre | 2.50 | 1.00 |
| ☐ 52 | Andre Johnson | .75 | .30 |
| ☐ 53 | David Carr | .75 | .30 |
| ☐ 54 | Domanick Davis | .60 | .25 |
| ☐ 55 | Jabar Gaffney | .60 | .25 |
| ☐ 56 | Edgerrin James | .75 | .30 |
| ☐ 57 | Marvin Harrison | 1.00 | .40 |
| ☐ 58 | Brandon Stokley | .60 | .25 |
| ☐ 59 | Peyton Manning | 1.50 | .60 |
| ☐ 60 | Reggie Wayne | .75 | .30 |
| ☐ 61 | Byron Leftwich | .75 | .30 |
| ☐ 62 | Fred Taylor | 1.00 | .40 |
| ☐ 63 | Jimmy Smith | .75 | .30 |
| ☐ 64 | Priest Holmes | 1.00 | .40 |
| ☐ 65 | Tony Gonzalez | .75 | .30 |
| ☐ 66 | Johnnie Morton | .75 | .30 |
| ☐ 67 | Trent Green | .75 | .30 |
| ☐ 68 | Chris Chambers | .75 | .30 |
| ☐ 69 | Randy McMichael | .60 | .25 |
| ☐ 70 | A.J. Feeley | .60 | .25 |
| ☐ 71 | Zach Thomas | 1.00 | .40 |
| ☐ 72 | Daunte Culpepper | 1.00 | .40 |
| ☐ 73 | Marcus Robinson | .75 | .30 |
| ☐ 74 | Mewelde Moore | .60 | .25 |
| ☐ 75 | Nate Burleson | .75 | .30 |
| ☐ 76 | Onterrio Smith | .60 | .25 |
| ☐ 77 | Randy Moss | 1.00 | .40 |
| ☐ 78 | Corey Dillon | .75 | .30 |
| ☐ 79 | Tom Brady | 2.00 | .75 |
| ☐ 80 | Deion Branch | .75 | .30 |
| ☐ 81 | Tedy Bruschi | 1.00 | .40 |
| ☐ 82 | David Givens | .75 | .30 |
| ☐ 83 | David Patten | .60 | .25 |
| ☐ 84 | Aaron Brooks | .60 | .25 |
| ☐ 85 | Deuce McAllister | 1.00 | .40 |
| ☐ 86 | Donte Stallworth | .75 | .30 |
| ☐ 87 | Joe Horn | .75 | .30 |
| ☐ 88 | Eli Manning | 2.00 | .75 |
| ☐ 89 | Jeremy Shockey | 1.00 | .40 |
| ☐ 90 | Kurt Warner | 1.00 | .40 |
| ☐ 91 | Michael Strahan | .75 | .30 |
| ☐ 92 | Tiki Barber | 1.00 | .40 |
| ☐ 93 | Amani Toomer | .75 | .30 |
| ☐ 94 | Chad Pennington | 1.00 | .40 |
| ☐ 95 | Curtis Martin | 1.00 | .40 |
| ☐ 96 | Santana Moss | .75 | .30 |
| ☐ 97 | Justin McCareins | .60 | .25 |
| ☐ 98 | Charles Woodson | .75 | .30 |
| ☐ 99 | Kerry Collins | .75 | .30 |
| ☐ 100 | Warren Sapp | .75 | .30 |
| ☐ 101 | Jerry Porter | .75 | .30 |
| ☐ 102 | Donovan McNabb | 1.00 | .40 |
| ☐ 103 | Jevon Kearse | .75 | .30 |
| ☐ 104 | Terrell Owens | 1.00 | .40 |
| ☐ 105 | Brian Westbrook | 1.00 | .40 |
| ☐ 106 | Todd Pinkston | .60 | .25 |
| ☐ 107 | Duce Staley | .75 | .30 |
| ☐ 108 | Hines Ward | 1.00 | .40 |
| ☐ 109 | Jerome Bettis | 1.00 | .40 |
| ☐ 110 | Joey Porter | .60 | .25 |
| ☐ 111 | Plaxico Burress | .75 | .30 |
| ☐ 112 | Ben Roethlisberger | 2.50 | 1.00 |
| ☐ 113 | Drew Brees | 1.00 | .40 |
| ☐ 114 | LaDainian Tomlinson | 1.50 | .60 |
| ☐ 115 | Keenan McCardell | .75 | .30 |
| ☐ 116 | Philip Rivers | 1.00 | .40 |
| ☐ 117 | Antonio Gates | 1.00 | .40 |
| ☐ 118 | Eric Johnson | .60 | .25 |
| ☐ 119 | Kevan Barlow | .60 | .25 |
| ☐ 120 | Brandon Lloyd | .60 | .25 |
| ☐ 121 | Tim Rattay | .60 | .25 |
| ☐ 122 | Darrell Jackson | .75 | .30 |
| ☐ 123 | Koren Robinson | .75 | .30 |
| ☐ 124 | Jerry Rice | 2.00 | .75 |
| ☐ 125 | Matt Hasselbeck | .75 | .30 |
| ☐ 126 | Shaun Alexander | 1.00 | .40 |
| ☐ 127 | Isaac Bruce | .75 | .30 |
| ☐ 128 | Marc Bulger | .75 | .30 |
| ☐ 129 | Marshall Faulk | 1.00 | .40 |
| ☐ 130 | Steven Jackson | 1.25 | .50 |
| ☐ 131 | Torry Holt | .75 | .30 |
| ☐ 132 | Derrick Brooks | .75 | .30 |
| ☐ 133 | Michael Clayton | .75 | .30 |
| ☐ 134 | Michael Pittman | .60 | .25 |
| ☐ 135 | Chris Simms | .75 | .30 |
| ☐ 136 | Chris Brown | .75 | .30 |
| ☐ 137 | Derrick Mason | .75 | .30 |
| ☐ 138 | Drew Bennett | .75 | .30 |
| ☐ 139 | Steve McNair | 1.00 | .40 |
| ☐ 140 | Clinton Portis | .75 | .30 |
| ☐ 141 | LaVar Arrington | 1.00 | .40 |
| ☐ 142 | Laveranues Coles | .75 | .30 |
| ☐ 143 | Patrick Ramsey | .75 | .30 |
| ☐ 144 | Rod Gardner | .60 | .25 |
| ☐ 145 | DeShaun Foster | .75 | .30 |
| ☐ 146 | Stephen Davis | .75 | .30 |
| ☐ 147 | Jake Delhomme | 1.00 | .40 |
| ☐ 148 | Muhsin Muhammad | .75 | .30 |
| ☐ 149 | Steve Smith | 1.00 | .40 |
| ☐ 150 | Keary Colbert | .60 | .25 |
| ☐ 151 | Aaron Rodgers SP RC | 50.00 | 20.00 |
| ☐ 152 | Adrian McPherson SP RC | 20.00 | 8.00 |
| ☐ 153 | Alex Smith QB RC | 4.00 | 1.50 |
| ☐ 154 | Andrew Walter RC | 2.50 | 1.00 |
| ☐ 155 | Brock Berlin RC | 2.00 | .75 |
| ☐ 156 | Charlie Frye SP RC | 25.00 | 10.00 |
| ☐ 157 | Chris Rix RC | 2.00 | .75 |
| ☐ 158 | Dan Orlovsky RC | 2.50 | 1.00 |
| ☐ 159 | Darian Durant RC | 2.50 | 1.00 |
| ☐ 160 | David Greene RC | 2.00 | .75 |
| ☐ 161 | Derek Anderson RC | 4.00 | 1.50 |
| ☐ 162 | Gino Guidugli RC | 1.50 | .60 |
| ☐ 163 | Jason Campbell RC | 5.00 | 2.00 |
| ☐ 164 | Jason White RC | 2.50 | 1.00 |
| ☐ 165 | Kyle Orton RC | 3.00 | 1.25 |
| ☐ 166 | Matt Jones SP RC | 30.00 | 12.00 |
| ☐ 167 | Ryan Fitzpatrick RC | 2.50 | 1.00 |
| ☐ 168 | Stefan LeFors RC | 2.00 | .75 |
| ☐ 169 | Timmy Chang RC | 2.00 | .75 |
| ☐ 170 | Alvin Pearman RC | 2.00 | .75 |
| ☐ 171 | Anthony Davis RC | 2.00 | .75 |
| ☐ 172 | Brandon Jacobs RC | 3.00 | 1.25 |
| ☐ 173 | Cadillac Williams RC | 5.00 | 2.00 |
| ☐ 174 | Cedric Benson RC | 2.50 | 1.00 |
| ☐ 175 | Cedric Houston RC | 2.50 | 1.00 |
| ☐ 176 | Ciatrick Fason RC | 2.00 | .75 |
| ☐ 177 | Damien Nash RC | 2.00 | .75 |
| ☐ 178 | Darren Sproles RC | 3.00 | 1.25 |
| ☐ 179 | Eric Shelton SP RC | 20.00 | 8.00 |
| ☐ 180 | Frank Gore SP RC | 40.00 | 15.00 |
| ☐ 181 | J.J. Arrington SP RC | 25.00 | 10.00 |
| ☐ 182 | Kay-Jay Harris RC | 2.00 | .75 |
| ☐ 183 | Marion Barber RC | 8.00 | 3.00 |
| ☐ 184 | Ronnie Brown RC | 8.00 | 3.00 |
| ☐ 185 | Ryan Moats RC | 2.50 | 1.00 |
| ☐ 186 | T.A. McLendon RC | 1.50 | .60 |
| ☐ 187 | Vernand Morency RC | 2.50 | 1.00 |
| ☐ 188 | Walter Reyes RC | 1.50 | .60 |
| ☐ 189 | Braylon Edwards RC | 8.00 | 3.00 |
| ☐ 190 | Charles Frederick RC | 2.00 | .75 |
| ☐ 191 | Chris Henry RC | 2.50 | 1.00 |
| ☐ 192 | Courtney Roby RC | 2.00 | .75 |
| ☐ 193 | Craig Bragg RC | 1.50 | .60 |
| ☐ 194 | Craphonso Thorpe SP RC | 20.00 | 8.00 |
| ☐ 195 | Dante Ridgeway RC | 1.50 | .60 |
| ☐ 196 | Fred Amey RC | 2.00 | .75 |
| ☐ 197 | Fred Gibson RC | 2.00 | .75 |
| ☐ 198 | J.R. Russell RC | 1.50 | .60 |
| ☐ 199 | Jerome Mathis RC | 25.00 | 10.00 |
| ☐ 200 | Josh Davis RC | 1.50 | .60 |
| ☐ 201 | Larry Brackins RC | 1.50 | .60 |
| ☐ 202 | Mark Bradley RC | 2.50 | 1.00 |
| ☐ 203 | Mark Clayton SP RC | 25.00 | 10.00 |
| ☐ 204 | Mike Williams RC | 2.50 | 1.00 |
| ☐ 205 | Reggie Brown RC | 2.50 | 1.00 |
| ☐ 206 | Roddy White RC | 3.00 | 1.25 |
| ☐ 207 | Roscoe Parrish RC | 2.00 | .75 |
| ☐ 208 | Roydell Williams RC | 2.00 | .75 |
| ☐ 209 | Steve Savoy RC | 1.50 | .60 |
| ☐ 210 | Tab Perry RC | 1.50 | .60 |
| ☐ 211 | Taylor Stubblefield RC | 1.50 | .60 |
| ☐ 212 | Terrence Murphy RC | 1.50 | .60 |
| ☐ 213 | Troy Williamson RC | 2.50 | 1.00 |
| ☐ 214 | Vincent Jackson RC | 2.50 | 1.00 |
| ☐ 215 | Alex Smith TE RC | 2.50 | 1.00 |
| ☐ 216 | Heath Miller RC | 5.00 | 2.00 |
| ☐ 217 | Dan Cody RC | 2.50 | 1.00 |
| ☐ 218 | David Pollack RC | 2.00 | .75 |
| ☐ 219 | Erasmus James RC | 2.00 | .75 |
| ☐ 220 | Justin Tuck RC | 3.00 | 1.25 |
| ☐ 221 | Marcus Spears RC | 2.50 | 1.00 |
| ☐ 222 | Matt Roth RC | 2.50 | 1.00 |
| ☐ 223 | Anttaj Hawthorne RC | 2.00 | .75 |
| ☐ 224 | Mike Patterson RC | 2.00 | .75 |
| ☐ 225 | Shaun Cody RC | 2.00 | .75 |
| ☐ 226 | Travis Johnson RC | 1.50 | .60 |
| ☐ 227 | Channing Crowder RC | 2.00 | .75 |
| ☐ 228 | Darryl Blackstock RC | 1.50 | .60 |
| ☐ 229 | DeMarcus Ware RC | 4.00 | 1.50 |
| ☐ 230 | Derrick Johnson RC | 2.50 | 1.00 |
| ☐ 231 | Kevin Burnett RC | 2.00 | .75 |
| ☐ 232 | Shawne Merriman RC | 4.00 | 1.50 |
| ☐ 233 | Adam Jones RC | 2.50 | 1.00 |
| ☐ 234 | Antrel Rolle RC | 2.50 | 1.00 |
| ☐ 235 | Brandon Browner RC | 1.50 | .60 |
| ☐ 236 | Bryant McFadden RC | 2.00 | .75 |
| ☐ 237 | Carlos Rogers RC | 2.50 | 1.00 |
| ☐ 238 | Corey Webster RC | 2.50 | 1.00 |
| ☐ 239 | Fabian Washington RC | 2.50 | 1.00 |
| ☐ 240 | Justin Miller RC | 2.00 | .75 |
| ☐ 241 | Marlin Jackson RC | 2.00 | .75 |
| ☐ 242 | Ernest Shazor RC | 2.00 | .75 |
| ☐ 243 | Josh Bullocks RC | 2.00 | .75 |
| ☐ 244 | Thomas Davis RC | 2.00 | .75 |

## 2006 Playoff Prestige

ROOKIE NEW YORK GIANTS

| | | |
|---|---|---|
| ☐ COMP.SET w/o SP's (239) | 100.00 | 50.00 |
| ☐ COMP.SET w/o RC's (150) | 25.00 | 10.00 |
| ☐ ONE ROOKIE PER HOBBY PACK | | |

|  |  | | |
|---|---|---|---|
| ☐ 1 | Anquan Boldin | .75 | .30 |
| ☐ 2 | J.J. Arrington | .75 | .30 |
| ☐ 3 | Josh McCown | .75 | .30 |
| ☐ 4 | Larry Fitzgerald | 1.00 | .40 |
| ☐ 5 | Marcel Shipp | .75 | .30 |
| ☐ 6 | Alge Crumpler | .75 | .30 |
| ☐ 7 | Michael Vick | 1.00 | .40 |
| ☐ 8 | T.J. Duckett | .60 | .25 |
| ☐ 9 | Warrick Dunn | .75 | .30 |
| ☐ 10 | Michael Jenkins | .75 | .30 |
| ☐ 11 | Derrick Mason | .75 | .30 |
| ☐ 12 | Jamal Lewis | .75 | .30 |
| ☐ 13 | Kyle Boller | .75 | .30 |
| ☐ 14 | Mark Clayton | .75 | .30 |
| ☐ 15 | Ray Lewis | .75 | .40 |
| ☐ 16 | Eric Moulds | .75 | .30 |
| ☐ 17 | J.P. Losman | .75 | .30 |
| ☐ 18 | Lee Evans | .75 | .30 |
| ☐ 19 | Willis McGahee | 1.00 | .40 |
| ☐ 20 | Jake Delhomme | .75 | .30 |
| ☐ 21 | Julius Peppers | .75 | .30 |
| ☐ 22 | Keary Colbert | .75 | .30 |
| ☐ 23 | Stephen Davis | .75 | .30 |
| ☐ 24 | Steve Smith | 1.00 | .40 |
| ☐ 25 | Brian Urlacher | 1.00 | .40 |
| ☐ 26 | Cedric Benson | .75 | .30 |
| ☐ 27 | Kyle Orton | .75 | .25 |
| ☐ 28 | Mark Bradley | .60 | .25 |
| ☐ 29 | Muhsin Muhammad | .75 | .30 |
| ☐ 30 | Thomas Jones | .75 | .30 |
| ☐ 31 | Carson Palmer | 1.00 | .40 |
| ☐ 32 | Chad Johnson | 1.00 | .40 |
| ☐ 33 | Rudi Johnson | .75 | .30 |
| ☐ 34 | T.J. Houshmandzadeh | .75 | .30 |
| ☐ 35 | Braylon Edwards | 1.00 | .40 |
| ☐ 36 | Dennis Northcutt | .60 | .25 |
| ☐ 37 | Antonio Bryant | .75 | .30 |
| ☐ 38 | Reuben Droughns | .75 | .30 |
| ☐ 39 | Trent Dilfer | .75 | .30 |
| ☐ 40 | Drew Bledsoe | 1.00 | .40 |
| ☐ 41 | Jason Witten | .75 | .30 |
| ☐ 42 | Julius Jones | 1.00 | .40 |
| ☐ 43 | Keyshawn Johnson | .75 | .30 |
| ☐ 44 | Roy Williams S | .75 | .30 |
| ☐ 45 | Terry Glenn | .75 | .30 |
| ☐ 46 | Kelley Lelie | .75 | .30 |
| ☐ 47 | Jake Plummer | .75 | .30 |
| ☐ 48 | Mike Anderson | .75 | .30 |
| ☐ 49 | Rod Smith | .75 | .30 |
| ☐ 50 | Tatum Bell | .75 | .30 |
| ☐ 51 | Joey Harrington | .60 | .25 |
| ☐ 52 | Kevin Jones | 1.00 | .40 |
| ☐ 53 | Mike Williams | 1.00 | .40 |
| ☐ 54 | Roy Williams WR | 1.00 | .40 |
| ☐ 55 | Aaron Rodgers | 1.00 | .40 |
| ☐ 56 | Brett Favre | 2.00 | .75 |
| ☐ 57 | Donald Driver | .75 | .30 |
| ☐ 58 | Javon Walker | .75 | .30 |
| ☐ 59 | Ahman Green | .75 | .30 |
| ☐ 60 | Andre Johnson | .75 | .30 |
| ☐ 61 | Corey Bradford | .60 | .25 |
| ☐ 62 | David Carr | .75 | .30 |
| ☐ 63 | Domanick Davis | .75 | .30 |
| ☐ 64 | Jabar Gaffney | .75 | .30 |
| ☐ 65 | Brandon Stokley | .75 | .30 |
| ☐ 66 | Dallas Clark | .75 | .30 |
| ☐ 67 | Edgerrin James | .75 | .30 |
| ☐ 68 | Marvin Harrison | 1.00 | .40 |
| ☐ 69 | Peyton Manning | 1.50 | .60 |
| ☐ 70 | Reggie Wayne | .75 | .30 |
| ☐ 71 | Byron Leftwich | .75 | .30 |
| ☐ 72 | Fred Taylor | .75 | .30 |
| ☐ 73 | Jimmy Smith | .75 | .30 |
| ☐ 74 | Matt Jones | .75 | .30 |
| ☐ 75 | Reggie Williams | .75 | .30 |
| ☐ 76 | Eddie Kennison | .75 | .25 |
| ☐ 77 | Larry Johnson | .75 | .30 |
| ☐ 78 | Priest Holmes | .75 | .30 |
| ☐ 79 | Tony Gonzalez | .75 | .30 |
| ☐ 80 | Trent Green | .75 | .30 |
| ☐ 81 | Chris Chambers | .75 | .30 |
| ☐ 82 | Marty Booker | .60 | .25 |
| ☐ 83 | Randy McMichael | .60 | .25 |
| ☐ 84 | Ricky Williams | .75 | .30 |
| ☐ 85 | Ronnie Brown | 1.00 | .40 |
| ☐ 86 | Zach Thomas | 1.00 | .40 |
| ☐ 87 | Daunte Culpepper | 1.00 | .40 |
| ☐ 88 | Mewelde Moore | .60 | .25 |
| ☐ 89 | Nate Burleson | .75 | .30 |
| ☐ 90 | Jim Kleinsasser | .60 | .25 |
| ☐ 91 | Corey Dillon | .75 | .30 |
| ☐ 92 | David Givens | .75 | .30 |
| ☐ 93 | Deion Branch | .75 | .30 |
| ☐ 94 | Tedy Bruschi | 1.00 | .40 |
| ☐ 95 | Tom Brady | 1.50 | .60 |
| ☐ 96 | Aaron Brooks | .75 | .30 |
| ☐ 97 | Deuce McAllister | .75 | .30 |
| ☐ 98 | Donte Stallworth | .75 | .30 |
| ☐ 99 | Joe Horn | .75 | .30 |
| ☐ 100 | Amani Toomer | .75 | .30 |
| ☐ 101 | Eli Manning | 1.25 | .50 |
| ☐ 102 | Jeremy Shockey | 1.00 | .40 |
| ☐ 103 | Plaxico Burress | .75 | .30 |
| ☐ 104 | Tiki Barber | 1.00 | .40 |
| ☐ 105 | Chad Pennington | .75 | .30 |
| ☐ 106 | Curtis Martin | 1.00 | .40 |
| ☐ 107 | Justin McCareins | .60 | .25 |
| ☐ 108 | Laveranues Coles | .75 | .30 |
| ☐ 109 | Jerry Porter | .75 | .30 |
| ☐ 110 | Kerry Collins | .75 | .30 |
| ☐ 111 | LaMont Jordan | .75 | .30 |
| ☐ 112 | Randy Moss | 1.00 | .40 |
| ☐ 113 | Brian Westbrook | .75 | .30 |
| ☐ 114 | Donovan McNabb | 1.00 | .40 |
| ☐ 115 | Terrell Owens | 1.00 | .40 |
| ☐ 116 | L.J. Smith | .60 | .25 |
| ☐ 117 | Ben Roethlisberger | 1.50 | .60 |
| ☐ 118 | Hines Ward | 1.00 | .40 |
| ☐ 119 | Heath Miller | .75 | .30 |
| ☐ 120 | Willie Parker | 1.25 | .50 |
| ☐ 121 | Jerome Bettis | 1.00 | .40 |
| ☐ 122 | Antonio Gates | 1.00 | .40 |
| ☐ 123 | Drew Brees | 1.00 | .40 |
| ☐ 124 | Keenan McCardell | .75 | .30 |
| ☐ 125 | LaDainian Tomlinson | 1.25 | .50 |
| ☐ 126 | Alex Smith QB | 1.00 | .40 |
| ☐ 127 | Brandon Lloyd | .75 | .30 |
| ☐ 128 | Frank Gore | 1.00 | .40 |
| ☐ 129 | Kevan Barlow | .75 | .30 |
| ☐ 130 | Darrell Jackson | .75 | .30 |
| ☐ 131 | Joe Jurevicius | .75 | .30 |
| ☐ 132 | Matt Hasselbeck | .75 | .30 |
| ☐ 133 | Shaun Alexander | 1.00 | .40 |
| ☐ 134 | Isaac Bruce | .75 | .30 |
| ☐ 135 | Marc Bulger | .75 | .30 |
| ☐ 136 | Marshall Faulk | .75 | .30 |
| ☐ 137 | Steven Jackson | 1.00 | .40 |
| ☐ 138 | Torry Holt | .75 | .30 |
| ☐ 139 | Cadillac Williams | 1.00 | .40 |
| ☐ 140 | Derrick Brooks | .75 | .30 |
| ☐ 141 | Joey Galloway | .75 | .30 |
| ☐ 142 | Michael Clayton | .75 | .30 |
| ☐ 143 | Brandon Jones | .60 | .25 |
| ☐ 144 | Chris Brown | .75 | .30 |
| ☐ 145 | Steve McNair | .75 | .30 |
| ☐ 146 | Tyrone Calico | .60 | .25 |
| ☐ 147 | Clinton Portis | 1.00 | .40 |
| ☐ 148 | Mark Brunell | .75 | .30 |
| ☐ 149 | Santana Moss | .75 | .30 |
| ☐ 150 | David Patten | .60 | .25 |
| ☐ 151 | A.J. Hawk SP RC | 40.00 | 15.00 |
| ☐ 152 | Abdul Hodge RC | 3.00 | 1.25 |
| ☐ 153 | Alan Zemaitis RC | 3.00 | 1.25 |
| ☐ 154 | Andre Hall RC | 3.00 | 1.25 |
| ☐ 155 | Anthony Fasano RC | 3.00 | 1.25 |
| ☐ 156 | Ashton Youboty RC | 3.00 | 1.25 |
| ☐ 157 | Erik Meyer RC | 2.50 | 1.00 |
| ☐ 158 | Bobby Carpenter RC | 3.00 | 1.25 |
| ☐ 159 | Brad Smith RC | 3.00 | 1.25 |
| ☐ 160 | Brandon Kirsch RC | 3.00 | 1.25 |
| ☐ 161 | Brandon Marshall SP RC | 20.00 | 8.00 |
| ☐ 162 | Brandon Williams RC | 3.00 | 1.25 |
| ☐ 163 | Brian Calhoun SP RC | 15.00 | 6.00 |
| ☐ 164 | Brodie Croyle SP RC | 25.00 | 12.50 |
| ☐ 165 | Brodrick Bunkley RC | 3.00 | 1.25 |
| ☐ 166 | Bruce Gradkowski RC | 3.00 | 1.25 |
| ☐ 167 | Cedric Griffin RC | 2.50 | 1.00 |
| ☐ 168 | Cedric Humes RC | 3.00 | 1.25 |
| ☐ 169 | Chad Greenway RC | 3.00 | 1.25 |
| ☐ 170 | Chad Jackson RC | 2.50 | 1.00 |
| ☐ 171 | Charlie Whitehurst RC | 3.00 | 1.25 |
| ☐ 172 | Cory Rodgers RC | 3.00 | 1.25 |
| ☐ 173 | D.J. Shockley RC | 3.00 | 1.25 |
| ☐ 174 | Darnell Bing RC | 3.00 | 1.25 |
| ☐ 175 | Darrell Hackney RC | 2.50 | 1.00 |
| ☐ 176 | David Thomas SP RC | 15.00 | 6.00 |
| ☐ 177 | D'Brickashaw Ferguson RC | 3.00 | 1.25 |
| ☐ 178 | DeAngelo Williams RC | 5.00 | 2.00 |
| ☐ 179 | Dee Webb RC | 2.50 | 1.00 |
| ☐ 180 | Delanie Walker RC | 2.50 | 1.00 |
| ☐ 181 | DeMeco Ryans RC | 4.00 | 1.50 |
| ☐ 182 | Demetrius Williams RC | 3.00 | 1.25 |
| ☐ 183 | Derek Hagan RC | 3.00 | 1.25 |
| ☐ 184 | Devin Aromashodu RC | 2.50 | 1.00 |
| ☐ 185 | Dominique Byrd RC | 2.50 | 1.00 |
| ☐ 186 | DonTrell Moore RC | 2.50 | 1.00 |
| ☐ 187 | D'Qwell Jackson RC | 2.50 | 1.00 |
| ☐ 188 | Drew Olson RC | 2.50 | 1.00 |
| ☐ 189 | Eric Winston RC | 1.50 | .60 |
| ☐ 190 | Ernie Sims RC | 3.00 | 1.25 |
| ☐ 191 | Gerald Riggs RC | 3.00 | 1.25 |
| ☐ 192 | Greg Jennings RC | 5.00 | 2.00 |
| ☐ 193 | Greg Lee RC | 2.50 | 1.00 |
| ☐ 194 | Haloti Ngata RC | 3.00 | 1.25 |
| ☐ 195 | Hank Baskett RC | 3.00 | 1.25 |
| ☐ 196 | Jason Avant RC | 3.00 | 1.25 |
| ☐ 197 | Jason Carter RC | 2.50 | 1.00 |
| ☐ 198 | Jay Cutler RC | 12.00 | 5.00 |
| ☐ 199 | Jeff Webb RC | 2.50 | 1.00 |
| ☐ 200 | Jeremy Bloom RC | 2.50 | 1.00 |
| ☐ 201 | Jerious Norwood RC | 4.00 | 1.50 |
| ☐ 202 | Jerome Harrison RC | 3.00 | 1.25 |
| ☐ 203 | Jimmy Williams RC | 3.00 | 1.25 |
| ☐ 204 | Joe Klopfenstein RC | 2.50 | 1.00 |
| ☐ 205 | Johnathan Joseph RC | 2.50 | 1.00 |
| ☐ 206 | Jonathan Orr RC | 2.50 | 1.00 |
| ☐ 207 | Joseph Addai RC | 10.00 | 4.00 |
| ☐ 208 | Kai Parham RC | 3.00 | 1.25 |
| ☐ 209 | Kamerion Wimbley RC | 3.00 | 1.25 |
| ☐ 210 | Kellen Clemens RC | 4.00 | 1.50 |
| ☐ 211 | Kelly Jennings RC | 3.00 | 1.25 |
| ☐ 212 | KJ Simpson RC | 2.50 | 1.00 |
| ☐ 213 | Laurence Maroney RC | 8.00 | 3.00 |
| ☐ 214 | Lawrence Vickers RC | 2.50 | 1.00 |
| ☐ 215 | LenDale White RC | 6.00 | 2.50 |
| ☐ 216 | Leon Washington RC | 3.00 | 1.25 |
| ☐ 217 | Leonard Pope RC | 3.00 | 1.25 |
| ☐ 218 | Marcedes Lewis RC | 3.00 | 1.25 |
| ☐ 219 | Marcus Vick SP RC | 20.00 | 8.00 |
| ☐ 220 | Mario Williams RC | 5.00 | 2.00 |
| ☐ 221 | Martin Nance RC | 2.50 | 1.00 |
| ☐ 222 | Mathias Kiwanuka RC | 4.00 | 1.50 |
| ☐ 223 | Matt Leinart RC | 10.00 | 4.00 |
| ☐ 224 | Maurice Drew SP RC | 30.00 | 15.00 |
| ☐ 225 | Maurice Stovall SP RC | 15.00 | 6.00 |
| ☐ 226 | Michael Huff RC | 3.00 | 1.25 |
| ☐ 227 | Michael Robinson SP RC | 15.00 | 6.00 |
| ☐ 228 | Mike Hass RC | 3.00 | 1.25 |
| ☐ 229 | Omar Jacobs RC | 2.50 | 1.00 |
| ☐ 230 | Paul Pinegar RC | 2.50 | 1.00 |
| ☐ 231 | Reggie Bush RC | 12.00 | 5.00 |
| ☐ 232 | Reggie McNeal RC | 2.50 | 1.00 |
| ☐ 233 | Rodrique Wright RC | 1.50 | .60 |
| ☐ 234 | Santonio Holmes RC | 8.00 | 3.00 |
| ☐ 235 | Sinorice Moss RC | 3.00 | 1.25 |
| ☐ 236 | Skyler Green RC | 3.00 | 1.25 |
| ☐ 237 | Tamba Hali RC | 3.00 | 1.25 |
| ☐ 238 | Tarvaris Jackson RC | 5.00 | 2.00 |
| ☐ 239 | Taurean Henderson RC | 2.50 | 1.00 |
| ☐ 240 | Terrence Whitehead RC | 2.50 | 1.00 |
| ☐ 241 | Tim Day SP RC | 15.00 | 6.00 |
| ☐ 242 | Todd Watkins RC | 2.50 | 1.00 |
| ☐ 243 | Travis Wilson RC | 3.00 | 1.25 |
| ☐ 244 | Tye Hill RC | 3.00 | 1.25 |
| ☐ 245 | Vernon Davis RC | 3.00 | 1.25 |
| ☐ 246 | Vince Young RC | 10.00 | 4.00 |
| ☐ 247 | Wali Lundy RC | 2.50 | 1.00 |
| ☐ 248 | Wendell Mathis RC | 2.50 | 1.00 |
| ☐ 249 | Willie Reid SP RC | 15.00 | 6.00 |
| ☐ 250 | Winston Justice RC | 3.00 | 1.25 |

**2007 Playoff Prestige**

| | | | |
|---|---|---|---|
| ☐ COMP.SET with SP's (240) | | 150.00 | 75.00 |
| ☐ COMP.SET w/o RC's (150) | | 25.00 | 10.00 |
| ☐ 1 Anquan Boldin | | .75 | .30 |

| | | |
|---|---|---|
| ❑ 2 Edgerrin James | .75 | .30 |
| ❑ 3 Larry Fitzgerald | 1.00 | .40 |
| ❑ 4 Matt Leinart | 1.00 | .40 |
| ❑ 5 Alge Crumpler | .75 | .30 |
| ❑ 6 Michael Vick | 1.00 | .40 |
| ❑ 7 Jerious Norwood | .75 | .30 |
| ❑ 8 Michael Jenkins | .75 | .30 |
| ❑ 9 Warrick Dunn | .75 | .30 |
| ❑ 10 Todd Heap | .60 | .25 |
| ❑ 11 Jamal Lewis | .75 | .30 |
| ❑ 12 Mark Clayton | .60 | .25 |
| ❑ 13 Demetrius Williams | .75 | .30 |
| ❑ 14 Steve McNair | .75 | .30 |
| ❑ 15 Ray Lewis | 1.00 | .40 |
| ❑ 16 J.P. Losman | .60 | .25 |
| ❑ 17 Josh Reed | .60 | .25 |
| ❑ 18 Lee Evans | .75 | .30 |
| ❑ 19 Willis McGahee | .75 | .30 |
| ❑ 20 DeAngelo Williams | 1.00 | .40 |
| ❑ 21 DeShaun Foster | .75 | .30 |
| ❑ 22 Jake Delhomme | .75 | .30 |
| ❑ 23 Keyshawn Johnson | .75 | .30 |
| ❑ 24 Steve Smith | .75 | .30 |
| ❑ 25 Bernard Berrian | .60 | .25 |
| ❑ 26 Brian Urlacher | 1.00 | .40 |
| ❑ 27 Cedric Benson | .75 | .30 |
| ❑ 28 Muhsin Muhammad | .75 | .30 |
| ❑ 29 Rex Grossman | .75 | .30 |
| ❑ 30 Thomas Jones | .75 | .30 |
| ❑ 31 Carson Palmer | 1.00 | .40 |
| ❑ 32 Chad Johnson | .75 | .30 |
| ❑ 33 Rudi Johnson | .75 | .30 |
| ❑ 34 T.J. Houshmandzadeh | .75 | .30 |
| ❑ 35 Braylon Edwards | .75 | .30 |
| ❑ 36 Kellen Winslow | .75 | .30 |
| ❑ 37 Charlie Frye | .75 | .30 |
| ❑ 38 Reuben Droughns | .75 | .30 |
| ❑ 39 Terry Glenn | .75 | .30 |
| ❑ 40 Julius Jones | .75 | .30 |
| ❑ 41 Roy Williams S | .75 | .30 |
| ❑ 42 Marion Barber | 1.00 | .40 |
| ❑ 43 Terrell Owens | 1.00 | .40 |
| ❑ 44 Tony Romo | 2.00 | .75 |
| ❑ 45 Javon Walker | .75 | .30 |
| ❑ 46 Jay Cutler | 1.00 | .40 |
| ❑ 47 Mike Bell | .75 | .30 |
| ❑ 48 Brandon Marshall | .75 | .30 |
| ❑ 49 Tatum Bell | .60 | .25 |
| ❑ 50 Jon Kitna | .60 | .25 |
| ❑ 51 Kevin Jones | .60 | .25 |
| ❑ 52 Roy Williams WR | .75 | .30 |
| ❑ 53 Mike Furrey | .75 | .30 |
| ❑ 54 A.J. Hawk | 1.00 | .40 |
| ❑ 55 Brett Favre | 2.00 | .75 |
| ❑ 56 Donald Driver | .75 | .30 |
| ❑ 57 Greg Jennings | .75 | .30 |
| ❑ 58 Ahman Green | .75 | .30 |
| ❑ 59 Andre Johnson | .75 | .30 |
| ❑ 60 David Carr | .75 | .30 |
| ❑ 61 Eric Moulds | .75 | .30 |
| ❑ 62 Owen Daniels | .60 | .25 |
| ❑ 63 Wali Lundy | .60 | .25 |
| ❑ 64 Joseph Addai | 1.00 | .40 |
| ❑ 65 Marvin Harrison | 1.00 | .40 |
| ❑ 66 Peyton Manning | 1.50 | .60 |
| ❑ 67 Reggie Wayne | .75 | .30 |
| ❑ 68 Dallas Clark | .60 | .25 |
| ❑ 69 Byron Leftwich | .75 | .30 |

| | | |
|---|---|---|
| ❑ 70 Fred Taylor | .75 | .30 |
| ❑ 71 Marcedes Lewis | .60 | .25 |
| ❑ 72 Maurice Jones-Drew | 1.00 | .40 |
| ❑ 73 Reggie Williams | .75 | .30 |
| ❑ 74 Eddie Kennison | .60 | .25 |
| ❑ 75 Larry Johnson | .75 | .30 |
| ❑ 76 Tony Gonzalez | .75 | .30 |
| ❑ 77 Trent Green | .75 | .30 |
| ❑ 78 Chris Chambers | .75 | .30 |
| ❑ 79 Daunte Culpepper | .75 | .30 |
| ❑ 80 Marty Booker | .60 | .25 |
| ❑ 81 Ronnie Brown | .75 | .30 |
| ❑ 82 Chester Taylor | .60 | .25 |
| ❑ 83 Tarvaris Jackson | .75 | .30 |
| ❑ 84 Troy Williamson | .60 | .25 |
| ❑ 85 Travis Taylor | .60 | .25 |
| ❑ 86 Ben Watson | .60 | .25 |
| ❑ 87 Tom Brady | 2.00 | .75 |
| ❑ 88 Corey Dillon | .75 | .30 |
| ❑ 89 Laurence Maroney | 1.00 | .40 |
| ❑ 90 Deuce McAllister | .75 | .30 |
| ❑ 91 Drew Brees | .75 | .30 |
| ❑ 92 Marques Colston | 1.00 | .40 |
| ❑ 93 Reggie Bush | 1.25 | .50 |
| ❑ 94 Joe Horn | .75 | .30 |
| ❑ 95 Brandon Jacobs | .75 | .30 |
| ❑ 96 Eli Manning | 1.00 | .40 |
| ❑ 97 Jeremy Shockey | .75 | .30 |
| ❑ 98 Plaxico Burress | .75 | .30 |
| ❑ 99 Chad Pennington | .75 | .30 |
| ❑ 100 Jerricho Cotchery | .60 | .25 |
| ❑ 101 Laveranues Coles | .75 | .30 |
| ❑ 102 Leon Washington | .75 | .30 |
| ❑ 103 Kevan Barlow | .75 | .30 |
| ❑ 104 Ronald Curry | .75 | .30 |
| ❑ 105 LaMont Jordan | .75 | .30 |
| ❑ 106 John Madsen | .60 | .25 |
| ❑ 107 Michael Huff | .75 | .30 |
| ❑ 108 Randy Moss | 1.00 | .40 |
| ❑ 109 Brian Westbrook | .75 | .30 |
| ❑ 110 Donovan McNabb | 1.00 | .40 |
| ❑ 111 Hank Baskett | .75 | .30 |
| ❑ 112 Donte Stallworth | .75 | .30 |
| ❑ 113 Reggie Brown | .75 | .30 |
| ❑ 114 Ben Roethlisberger | 1.25 | .50 |
| ❑ 115 Hines Ward | 1.00 | .40 |
| ❑ 116 Troy Polamalu | 1.00 | .40 |
| ❑ 117 Willie Parker | 1.00 | .40 |
| ❑ 118 Santonio Holmes | .75 | .30 |
| ❑ 119 Antonio Gates | .75 | .30 |
| ❑ 120 LaDainian Tomlinson | 1.25 | .50 |
| ❑ 121 Vincent Jackson | .60 | .25 |
| ❑ 122 Philip Rivers | 1.00 | .40 |
| ❑ 123 Shawne Merriman | .75 | .30 |
| ❑ 124 Alex Smith QB | 1.00 | .40 |
| ❑ 125 Antonio Bryant | .75 | .30 |
| ❑ 126 Frank Gore | 1.00 | .40 |
| ❑ 127 Vernon Davis | .75 | .30 |
| ❑ 128 Darrell Jackson | .75 | .30 |
| ❑ 129 Deion Branch | .75 | .30 |
| ❑ 130 Matt Hasselbeck | .75 | .30 |
| ❑ 131 Shaun Alexander | .75 | .30 |
| ❑ 132 Isaac Bruce | .75 | .30 |
| ❑ 133 Marc Bulger | .75 | .30 |
| ❑ 134 Steven Jackson | 1.00 | .40 |
| ❑ 135 Joe Klopfenstein | .60 | .25 |
| ❑ 136 Torry Holt | .75 | .30 |
| ❑ 137 Bruce Gradkowski | .60 | .25 |
| ❑ 138 Cadillac Williams | .75 | .30 |
| ❑ 139 Joey Galloway | .75 | .30 |
| ❑ 140 Mike Alstott | .75 | .30 |
| ❑ 141 Adam Jones | .60 | .25 |
| ❑ 142 Drew Bennett | .60 | .25 |
| ❑ 143 LenDale White | .75 | .30 |
| ❑ 144 Vince Young | 1.00 | .40 |
| ❑ 145 Travis Henry | .75 | .30 |
| ❑ 146 Clinton Portis | .75 | .30 |
| ❑ 147 Jason Campbell | .75 | .30 |
| ❑ 148 Ladell Betts | .60 | .25 |
| ❑ 149 Santana Moss | .75 | .30 |
| ❑ 150 Chris Cooley | .60 | .25 |
| ❑ 151 Brady Quinn RC | 10.00 | 4.00 |
| ❑ 152 JaMarcus Russell RC | 8.00 | 3.00 |
| ❑ 153 Troy Smith RC | 4.00 | 1.50 |
| ❑ 154 Drew Stanton RC | 3.00 | 1.25 |

| | | |
|---|---|---|
| ❑ 155 Adrian Peterson RC | 25.00 | 10.00 |
| ❑ 156 Marshawn Lynch RC | 6.00 | 2.50 |
| ❑ 157 Michael Bush RC | 3.00 | 1.25 |
| ❑ 158 Kenny Irons SP RC | 30.00 | 12.00 |
| ❑ 159 Antonio Pittman RC | 3.00 | 1.25 |
| ❑ 160 Tony Hunt RC | 3.00 | 1.25 |
| ❑ 161 Darius Walker SP RC | 30.00 | 12.00 |
| ❑ 162 DeShawn Wynn RC | 3.00 | 1.25 |
| ❑ 163 Calvin Johnson RC | 8.00 | 3.00 |
| ❑ 164 Ted Ginn Jr. RC | 5.00 | 2.00 |
| ❑ 165 Dwayne Jarrett RC | 3.00 | 1.25 |
| ❑ 166 Dwayne Bowe RC | 6.00 | 2.50 |
| ❑ 167 Robert Meachem RC | 3.00 | 1.25 |
| ❑ 169 Anthony Gonzalez SP RC | 50.00 | 20.00 |
| ❑ 170 Craig Buster Davis RC | 3.00 | 1.25 |
| ❑ 171 Johnnie Lee Higgins RC | 2.50 | 1.00 |
| ❑ 172 Steve Smith USC RC | 4.00 | 1.50 |
| ❑ 173 Chansi Stuckey RC | 2.50 | 1.00 |
| ❑ 174 David Clowney RC | 2.50 | 1.00 |
| ❑ 175 Aundrae Allison RC | 2.50 | 1.00 |
| ❑ 176 Jason Hill SP RC | 30.00 | 12.00 |
| ❑ 177 Zach Miller RC | 2.00 | .75 |
| ❑ 178 Greg Olsen RC | 4.00 | 1.50 |
| ❑ 179 Gaines Adams RC | 3.00 | 1.25 |
| ❑ 180 Jamaal Anderson RC | 2.50 | 1.00 |
| ❑ 181 Victor Abiamiri RC | 3.00 | 1.25 |
| ❑ 182 Adam Carriker RC | 2.50 | 1.00 |
| ❑ 183 LaMarr Woodley RC | 3.00 | 1.25 |
| ❑ 184 Quentin Moses RC | 2.50 | 1.00 |
| ❑ 185 Charles Johnson RC | 2.00 | .75 |
| ❑ 186 Alan Branch RC | 2.50 | 1.00 |
| ❑ 187 Amobi Okoye RC | 3.00 | 1.25 |
| ❑ 188 DeMarcus Tank Tyler RC | 2.50 | 1.00 |
| ❑ 189 Patrick Willis RC | 60.00 | 25.00 |
| ❑ 190 Paul Posluszny RC | 4.00 | 1.50 |
| ❑ 191 Lawrence Timmons RC | 3.00 | 1.25 |
| ❑ 192 Darrelle Revis RC | 3.00 | 1.25 |
| ❑ 193 Leon Hall RC | 2.50 | 1.00 |
| ❑ 194 Daymeion Hughes RC | 2.50 | 1.00 |
| ❑ 195 Chris Houston RC | 2.50 | 1.00 |
| ❑ 196 A.J. Davis RC | 2.00 | .75 |
| ❑ 197 Aaron Ross RC | 3.00 | 1.25 |
| ❑ 198 LaRon Landry RC | 4.00 | 1.50 |
| ❑ 199 Reggie Nelson RC | 2.50 | 1.00 |
| ❑ 200 Michael Griffin RC | 3.00 | 1.25 |
| ❑ 201 Trent Edwards RC | 6.00 | 3.00 |
| ❑ 202 Kevin Kolb RC | 5.00 | 2.00 |
| ❑ 203 John Beck RC | 3.00 | 1.25 |
| ❑ 204 Kenneth Darby RC | 3.00 | 1.25 |
| ❑ 205 Lorenzo Booker RC | 3.00 | 1.25 |
| ❑ 206 Jason Snelling RC | 2.50 | 1.00 |
| ❑ 207 Selvin Young RC | 5.00 | 2.00 |
| ❑ 208 Ahmad Bradshaw RC | 4.00 | 1.50 |
| ❑ 210 Courtney Taylor RC | 2.50 | 1.00 |
| ❑ 211 Paul Williams SP RC | 25.00 | 10.00 |
| ❑ 212 Rhema McKnight RC | 2.50 | 1.00 |
| ❑ 213 David Ball RC | 2.00 | .72 |
| ❑ 214 Syvelle Newton RC | 2.50 | 1.00 |
| ❑ 215 Joel Filani RC | 2.50 | 1.00 |
| ❑ 216 Chris Davis RC | 2.50 | 1.00 |
| ❑ 217 Laurent Robinson RC | 2.50 | 1.00 |
| ❑ 218 Jarrett Hicks RC | 2.50 | 1.00 |
| ❑ 219 Dallas Baker RC | 2.50 | 1.00 |
| ❑ 220 Matt Trannon RC | 2.50 | 1.00 |
| ❑ 221 Mike Walker RC | 2.50 | 1.00 |
| ❑ 222 Anthony Spencer RC | 3.00 | 1.25 |
| ❑ 223 Jarvis Moss RC | 3.00 | 1.25 |
| ❑ 224 Tim Crowder RC | 2.50 | 1.00 |
| ❑ 225 Brandon Siler RC | 2.50 | 1.00 |
| ❑ 226 David Harris RC | 2.50 | 1.00 |
| ❑ 227 Buster Davis RC | 2.50 | 1.00 |
| ❑ 228 Jon Abbate RC | 2.00 | .75 |
| ❑ 229 Rufus Alexander RC | 3.00 | 1.25 |
| ❑ 230 Jon Beason RC | 3.00 | 1.25 |
| ❑ 231 Jonathan Wade RC | 2.50 | 1.00 |
| ❑ 232 Marcus McCauley RC | 2.50 | 1.00 |
| ❑ 233 Tanard Jackson RC | 2.00 | .75 |
| ❑ 234 Kenny Scott RC | 2.00 | .75 |
| ❑ 235 Brandon Meriweather RC | 3.00 | 1.25 |
| ❑ 236 Aaron Rouse RC | 2.50 | 1.00 |
| ❑ 237 Eric Weddle RC | 2.50 | 1.00 |
| ❑ 238 Brian Leonard RC | 3.00 | 1.25 |
| ❑ 239 Jared Zabransky SP RC | 30.00 | 12.00 |
| ❑ 240 Chris Leak SP RC | 25.00 | 10.00 |
| ❑ 241 Jordan Palmer SP RC | 30.00 | 12.00 |

| | | | |
|---|---|---|---|
| ❏ 242 Garrett Wolfe SP RC | 30.00 | 12.00 |
| ❏ 243 Gary Russell RC | 3.00 | 1.25 |
| ❏ 244 Isaiah Stanback RC | 3.00 | 1.25 |
| ❏ 245 Tyler Palko RC | 3.00 | 1.25 |
| ❏ 246 Jeff Rowe RC | 2.50 | 1.00 |
| ❏ 248 Dwayne Wright RC | 2.50 | 1.00 |
| ❏ 249 Nate Ilaoa RC | 3.00 | 1.25 |
| ❏ 250 Steve Breaston RC | 3.00 | 1.25 |

## 2008 Playoff Prestige

| | | |
|---|---|---|
| ❏ 1 Anquan Boldin | .60 | .25 |
| ❏ 2 Larry Fitzgerald | .75 | .30 |
| ❏ 3 Edgerrin James | .60 | .25 |
| ❏ 4 Matt Leinart | .75 | .30 |
| ❏ 5 Warrick Dunn | .60 | .25 |
| ❏ 6 Roddy White | .50 | .20 |
| ❏ 7 Derrick Mason | .50 | .20 |
| ❏ 8 Todd Heap | .50 | .20 |
| ❏ 9 Willis McGahee | .60 | .25 |
| ❏ 10 J.P. Losman | .60 | .25 |
| ❏ 11 Lee Evans | .60 | .25 |
| ❏ 12 Marshawn Lynch | .75 | .30 |
| ❏ 13 Steve Smith | .60 | .25 |
| ❏ 14 Keary Colbert | .50 | .20 |
| ❏ 15 DeShaun Foster | .50 | .20 |
| ❏ 16 Bernard Berrian | .50 | .20 |
| ❏ 17 Cedric Benson | .50 | .20 |
| ❏ 18 Devin Hester | .75 | .30 |
| ❏ 19 Carson Palmer | .75 | .30 |
| ❏ 20 Rudi Johnson | .60 | .25 |
| ❏ 21 T.J. Houshmandzadeh | .60 | .25 |
| ❏ 22 Chad Johnson | .60 | .25 |
| ❏ 23 Derek Anderson | .60 | .25 |
| ❏ 24 Kellen Winslow | .60 | .25 |
| ❏ 25 Braylon Edwards | .60 | .25 |
| ❏ 26 Tony Romo | 1.25 | .50 |
| ❏ 27 Terrell Owens | .75 | .30 |
| ❏ 28 Marion Barber | .75 | .30 |
| ❏ 29 Jay Cutler | .75 | .30 |
| ❏ 30 Javon Walker | .60 | .25 |
| ❏ 31 Brandon Marshall | .60 | .25 |
| ❏ 32 Jon Kitna | .60 | .25 |
| ❏ 33 Calvin Johnson | .75 | .30 |
| ❏ 34 Roy Williams WR | .60 | .25 |
| ❏ 35 Brett Favre | 2.00 | .75 |
| ❏ 36 Donald Driver | .60 | .25 |
| ❏ 37 Greg Jennings | .60 | .25 |
| ❏ 38 Matt Schaub | .60 | .25 |
| ❏ 39 Andre Johnson | .60 | .25 |
| ❏ 40 Ahman Green | .60 | .25 |
| ❏ 41 Peyton Manning | 1.25 | .50 |
| ❏ 42 Joseph Addai | .75 | .30 |
| ❏ 43 Reggie Wayne | .75 | .30 |
| ❏ 44 Marvin Harrison | .75 | .30 |
| ❏ 45 David Garrard | .60 | .25 |
| ❏ 46 Fred Taylor | .60 | .25 |
| ❏ 47 Maurice Jones-Drew | .75 | .30 |
| ❏ 48 Tony Gonzalez | .60 | .25 |
| ❏ 49 Dwayne Bowe | .60 | .25 |
| ❏ 50 Larry Johnson | .60 | .25 |
| ❏ 51 Ted Ginn Jr. | .60 | .25 |
| ❏ 52 Ronnie Brown | .60 | .25 |
| ❏ 53 Tarvaris Jackson | .60 | .25 |
| ❏ 54 Adrian Peterson | 1.50 | .60 |
| ❏ 55 Chester Taylor | .50 | .20 |
| ❏ 56 Tom Brady | 1.25 | .50 |
| ❏ 57 Randy Moss | .75 | .30 |
| ❏ 58 Wes Welker | .75 | .30 |

| | | |
|---|---|---|
| ❏ 59 Laurence Maroney | .60 | .25 |
| ❏ 60 Drew Brees | .75 | .30 |
| ❏ 61 Reggie Bush | .75 | .30 |
| ❏ 62 Deuce McAllister | .60 | .25 |
| ❏ 63 Marques Colston | .60 | .25 |
| ❏ 64 Eli Manning | .75 | .30 |
| ❏ 65 Brandon Jacobs | .60 | .25 |
| ❏ 66 Plaxico Burress | .60 | .25 |
| ❏ 67 Jeremy Shockey | .60 | .25 |
| ❏ 68 Jerricho Cotchery | .50 | .20 |
| ❏ 69 Laveranues Coles | .60 | .25 |
| ❏ 70 Thomas Jones | .60 | .25 |
| ❏ 71 JaMarcus Russell | .75 | .30 |
| ❏ 72 Jerry Porter | .60 | .25 |
| ❏ 73 Ronald Curry | .60 | .25 |
| ❏ 74 Donovan McNabb | .75 | .30 |
| ❏ 75 Brian Westbrook | .60 | .25 |
| ❏ 76 Kevin Curtis | .50 | .20 |
| ❏ 77 Ben Roethlisberger | 1.00 | .40 |
| ❏ 78 Willie Parker | .60 | .25 |
| ❏ 79 Hines Ward | .75 | .30 |
| ❏ 80 Philip Rivers | .75 | .30 |
| ❏ 81 Antonio Gates | .60 | .25 |
| ❏ 82 LaDainian Tomlinson | 1.00 | .40 |
| ❏ 83 Alex Smith QB | .60 | .25 |
| ❏ 84 Frank Gore | .60 | .25 |
| ❏ 85 Vernon Davis | .50 | .20 |
| ❏ 86 Matt Hasselbeck | .60 | .25 |
| ❏ 87 Shaun Alexander | .60 | .25 |
| ❏ 88 Deion Branch | .60 | .25 |
| ❏ 89 Marc Bulger | .60 | .25 |
| ❏ 90 Steven Jackson | .75 | .30 |
| ❏ 91 Torry Holt | .60 | .25 |
| ❏ 92 Jeff Garcia | .60 | .25 |
| ❏ 93 Joey Galloway | .60 | .25 |
| ❏ 94 Cadillac Williams | .60 | .25 |
| ❏ 95 Vince Young | .75 | .30 |
| ❏ 96 LenDale White | .60 | .25 |
| ❏ 97 Brandon Jones | .50 | .20 |
| ❏ 98 Jason Campbell | .60 | .25 |
| ❏ 99 Clinton Portis | .60 | .25 |
| ❏ 100 Chris Cooley | .60 | .25 |
| ❏ 101 Adarius Bowman RC | 2.00 | .75 |
| ❏ 102 Adrian Arrington RC | 2.00 | .75 |
| ❏ 103 Ali Highsmith RC | 1.50 | .60 |
| ❏ 104 Allen Patrick RC | 2.00 | .75 |
| ❏ 105 Andre Caldwell RC | 2.00 | .75 |
| ❏ 106 Andre Woodson RC | 2.50 | 1.00 |
| ❏ 107 Anthony Alridge RC | 2.00 | .75 |
| ❏ 108 Antoine Cason RC | 2.50 | 1.00 |
| ❏ 109 Aqib Talib RC | 2.50 | 1.00 |
| ❏ 110 Chauncey Washington SP RC | 25.00 | 10.00 |
| ❏ 111 Bernard Morris RC | 2.50 | 1.00 |
| ❏ 112 Brad Cottam RC | 2.50 | 1.00 |
| ❏ 113 Brian Brohm RC | 3.00 | 1.25 |
| ❏ 114 Chad Henne RC | 4.00 | 1.50 |
| ❏ 115 Chris Johnson RC | 6.00 | 2.50 |
| ❏ 116 Chris Long SP RC | 40.00 | 15.00 |
| ❏ 117 Colt Brennan RC | 6.00 | 2.50 |
| ❏ 118 Cory Boyd RC | 2.00 | .75 |
| ❏ 119 Curtis Lofton RC | 2.50 | 1.00 |
| ❏ 120 DJ Hall RC | 2.50 | 1.00 |
| ❏ 121 Dan Connor SP RC | 30.00 | 12.00 |
| ❏ 122 Dantrell Savage RC | 2.00 | .75 |
| ❏ 123 Darius Reynaud RC | 2.00 | .75 |
| ❏ 124A Darren McFadden Red RC | 6.00 | 2.50 |
| ❏ 124B Darren McFadden Wht RC | 12.00 | 5.00 |
| ❏ 125 Davone Bess RC | 3.00 | 1.25 |
| ❏ 127 Derrick Harvey RC | 2.00 | .75 |
| ❏ 128 DeSean Jackson RC | 5.00 | 2.00 |
| ❏ 130 Dexter Jackson RC | 2.00 | .75 |
| ❏ 131 Dominique Rodgers-Cromartie RC | 2.50 | 1.00 |
| ❏ 132 Donnie Avery RC | 3.00 | 1.25 |
| ❏ 133 Dorien Bryant RC | 2.50 | 1.00 |
| ❏ 134 Earl Bennett RC | 2.50 | 1.00 |
| ❏ 135 Early Doucet RC | 2.50 | 1.00 |
| ❏ 136 Eddie Royal RC | 5.00 | 2.00 |
| ❏ 137 Erin Henderson RC | 2.00 | .75 |
| ❏ 139 Felix Jones SP RC | 50.00 | 20.00 |
| ❏ 140 Fred Davis RC | 2.50 | 1.00 |
| ❏ 141 Glenn Dorsey RC | 3.00 | 1.25 |
| ❏ 142 Harry Douglas SP RC | 20.00 | 8.00 |
| ❏ 143 Jacob Hester RC | 2.50 | 1.00 |
| ❏ 144 Jacob Tamme RC | 2.50 | 1.00 |
| ❏ 145 Jamaal Charles RC | 3.00 | 1.25 |

| | | |
|---|---|---|
| ❏ 147 Jason Rivers RC | 2.50 | 1.00 |
| ❏ 148 Jed Collins SP RC | 20.00 | 8.00 |
| ❏ 149 Jermichael Finley RC | 2.50 | 1.00 |
| ❏ 150 Jerome Simpson RC | 2.00 | .75 |
| ❏ 151 Joe Flacco RC | 8.00 | 3.00 |
| ❏ 152 John Carlson RC | 2.50 | 1.00 |
| ❏ 153 John David Booty RC | 3.00 | 1.25 |
| ❏ 154 Jonathan Stewart RC | 6.00 | 2.50 |
| ❏ 155 Jordy Nelson SP RC | 40.00 | 15.00 |
| ❏ 156 Josh Johnson RC | 2.50 | 1.00 |
| ❏ 158 Justin Forsett RC | 2.50 | 1.00 |
| ❏ 159 Kalvin McRae RC | 2.00 | .75 |
| ❏ 160 Keenan Burton RC | 2.00 | .75 |
| ❏ 161 Keith Rivers RC | 2.50 | 1.00 |
| ❏ 162 Kellen Davis RC | 1.50 | .60 |
| ❏ 163 Kenny Phillips RC | 2.50 | 1.00 |
| ❏ 164 Kevin O'Connell RC | 3.00 | 1.25 |
| ❏ 165 Kevin Robinson RC | 2.00 | .75 |
| ❏ 166 Kevin Smith SP RC | 40.00 | 15.00 |
| ❏ 167 Lavelle Hawkins RC | 2.00 | .75 |
| ❏ 168 Leodis McKelvin RC | 2.50 | 1.00 |
| ❏ 169 Limas Sweed RC | 3.00 | 1.25 |
| ❏ 171 Marcus Monk RC | 2.50 | 1.00 |
| ❏ 172 Marcus Smith RC | 2.00 | .75 |
| ❏ 173 Mario Manningham RC | 2.50 | 1.00 |
| ❏ 174 Mark Bradford RC | 2.00 | .75 |
| ❏ 175 Martellus Bennett RC | 2.50 | 1.00 |
| ❏ 176 Martin Rucker RC | 2.00 | .75 |
| ❏ 177 Matt Flynn SP RC | 30.00 | 12.00 |
| ❏ 178 Matt Forte RC | 6.00 | 2.50 |
| ❏ 179 Matt Ryan RC | 10.00 | 4.00 |
| ❏ 180 Mike Hart RC | 3.00 | 1.25 |
| ❏ 182 Owen Schmitt RC | 2.50 | 1.00 |
| ❏ 183 Paul Hubbard RC | 2.00 | .75 |
| ❏ 184 Paul Smith RC | 2.50 | 1.00 |
| ❏ 185 Peyton Hillis RC | 3.00 | 1.25 |
| ❏ 186 Quentin Groves RC | 2.00 | .75 |
| ❏ 187 Rashard Mendenhall RC | 5.00 | 2.00 |
| ❏ 188 Ray Rice RC | 3.00 | 1.25 |
| ❏ 189 Reggie Smith SP RC | 20.00 | 8.00 |
| ❏ 190 Ryan Grice-Mullen RC | 2.50 | 1.00 |
| ❏ 191 Sam Keller RC | 2.50 | 1.00 |
| ❏ 192 Sedrick Ellis RC | 2.50 | 1.00 |
| ❏ 193 Steve Slaton RC | 5.00 | 2.00 |
| ❏ 194 Tashard Choice RC | 2.50 | 1.00 |
| ❏ 195 Terrell Thomas RC | 2.00 | .75 |
| ❏ 196 Thomas Brown RC | 2.50 | 1.00 |
| ❏ 197 Tracy Porter RC | 2.00 | .75 |
| ❏ 198 Vernon Gholston RC | 2.50 | 1.00 |
| ❏ 199 Will Franklin RC | 2.50 | 1.00 |
| ❏ 200 Xavier Adibi RC | 2.00 | .75 |
| ❏ 201 Jake Long SP RC | 200.00 | 100.00 |

## 1989 Pro Set

| | | |
|---|---|---|
| ❏ COMPLETE SET (561) | 25.00 | 10.00 |
| ❏ COMP.SERIES 1 (440) | 6.00 | 3.00 |
| ❏ COMP.SERIES 2 (100) | 20.00 | 10.00 |
| ❏ COMP.FINAL FACT.SET (21) | 2.00 | .75 |
| ❏ 1 Stacey Bailey | .10 | .02 |
| ❏ 2 Aundray Bruce RC | .15 | .05 |
| ❏ 3 Rick Bryan | .10 | .02 |
| ❏ 4 Bobby Butler | .10 | .02 |
| ❏ 5 Scott Case RC | .10 | .02 |
| ❏ 6 Tony Casillas | .15 | .05 |
| ❏ 7 Floyd Dixon | .10 | .02 |
| ❏ 8 Rick Donnelly | .10 | .02 |
| ❏ 9 Bill Fralic | .15 | .05 |
| ❏ 10 Mike Gann | .10 | .02 |

|  |  | | |
|---|---|---|---|
| ☐ 11 | Mike Kenn | .10 | .02 |
| ☐ 12 | Chris Miller RC | .25 | .08 |
| ☐ 13 | John Rade | .10 | .02 |
| ☐ 14 | Gerald Riggs UER | .15 | .05 |
| ☐ 15 | John Settle RC | .10 | .02 |
| ☐ 16 | Marion Campbell CO | .10 | .02 |
| ☐ 17 | Cornelius Bennett | .15 | .05 |
| ☐ 18 | Derrick Burroughs | .10 | .02 |
| ☐ 19 | Shane Conlan | .15 | .05 |
| ☐ 20 | Ronnie Harmon | .15 | .05 |
| ☐ 21 | Kent Hull RC | .15 | .05 |
| ☐ 22 | Jim Kelly | .50 | .20 |
| ☐ 23 | Mark Kelso | .15 | .05 |
| ☐ 24 | Pete Metzelaars | .15 | .05 |
| ☐ 25 | Scott Norwood RC | .15 | .05 |
| ☐ 26 | Andre Reed | .25 | .08 |
| ☐ 27 | Fred Smerlas | .10 | .02 |
| ☐ 28 | Bruce Smith | .25 | .08 |
| ☐ 29 | Leonard Smith | .10 | .02 |
| ☐ 30 | Art Still | .10 | .02 |
| ☐ 31 | Darryl Talley | .15 | .05 |
| ☐ 32 | Thurman Thomas RC | 1.25 | .50 |
| ☐ 33 | Will Wolford RC | .10 | .02 |
| ☐ 34 | Marv Levy CO | .15 | .05 |
| ☐ 35 | Neal Anderson | .15 | .05 |
| ☐ 36 | Kevin Butler | .10 | .02 |
| ☐ 37 | Jim Covert | .15 | .05 |
| ☐ 38 | Richard Dent | .15 | .05 |
| ☐ 39 | Dave Duerson | .10 | .02 |
| ☐ 40 | Dennis Gentry | .10 | .02 |
| ☐ 41 | Dan Hampton | .15 | .05 |
| ☐ 42 | Jay Hilgenberg | .10 | .02 |
| ☐ 43 | Dennis McKinnon UER | .10 | .02 |
| ☐ 44 | Jim McMahon | .15 | .05 |
| ☐ 45 | Steve McMichael | .15 | .05 |
| ☐ 46 | Brad Muster RC | .15 | .05 |
| ☐ 47A | William Perry SP | 6.00 | 2.50 |
| ☐ 47B | Ron Morris RC | .10 | .02 |
| ☐ 48 | Ron Rivera | .10 | .02 |
| ☐ 49 | Vestee Jackson RC | .10 | .02 |
| ☐ 50 | Mike Singletary | .15 | .05 |
| ☐ 51 | Mike Tomczak | .15 | .05 |
| ☐ 52 | Keith Van Horne RC | .10 | .02 |
| ☐ 53A | Mike Ditka CO | .25 | .08 |
| ☐ 53B | Mike Ditka CO HOF | .25 | .08 |
| ☐ 54 | Lewis Billups | .10 | .02 |
| ☐ 55 | James Brooks | .15 | .05 |
| ☐ 56 | Eddie Brown | .10 | .02 |
| ☐ 57 | Jason Buck RC | .10 | .02 |
| ☐ 58 | Boomer Esiason | .15 | .05 |
| ☐ 59 | David Fulcher | .10 | .02 |
| ☐ 60A | Rodney Holman RC ERR | .15 | .05 |
| ☐ 60B | Rodney Holman RC COR | .25 | .08 |
| ☐ 61 | Reggie Williams | .15 | .05 |
| ☐ 62 | Joe Kelly RC | .10 | .02 |
| ☐ 63 | Tim Krumrie | .10 | .02 |
| ☐ 64 | Tim McGee | .15 | .05 |
| ☐ 65 | Max Montoya | .15 | .05 |
| ☐ 66 | Anthony Munoz | .15 | .05 |
| ☐ 67 | Jim Skow | .10 | .02 |
| ☐ 68 | Eric Thomas RC | .10 | .02 |
| ☐ 69 | Leon White | .10 | .02 |
| ☐ 70 | Ickey Woods RC | .15 | .05 |
| ☐ 71 | Carl Zander | .10 | .02 |
| ☐ 72 | Sam Wyche CO | .10 | .02 |
| ☐ 73 | Brian Brennan | .10 | .02 |
| ☐ 74 | Earnest Byner | .15 | .05 |
| ☐ 75 | Hanford Dixon | .10 | .02 |
| ☐ 76 | Mike Pagel | .10 | .02 |
| ☐ 77 | Bernie Kosar | .15 | .05 |
| ☐ 78 | Reggie Langhorne RC | .15 | .05 |
| ☐ 79 | Kevin Mack | .15 | .05 |
| ☐ 80 | Clay Matthews | .15 | .05 |
| ☐ 81 | Gerald McNeil | .10 | .02 |
| ☐ 82 | Frank Minnifield | .10 | .02 |
| ☐ 83 | Cody Risien | .10 | .02 |
| ☐ 84 | Webster Slaughter | .15 | .05 |
| ☐ 85 | Felix Wright | .10 | .02 |
| ☐ 86 | Bud Carson CO UER | .10 | .02 |
| ☐ 87 | Bill Bates | .15 | .05 |
| ☐ 88 | Kevin Brooks | .10 | .02 |
| ☐ 89 | Michael Irvin RC | 1.50 | .60 |
| ☐ 90 | Jim Jeffcoat | .10 | .02 |
| ☐ 91 | Ed Too Tall Jones | .15 | .05 |
| ☐ 92 | Eugene Lockhart RC | .10 | .02 |
| ☐ 93 | Nate Newton RC | .15 | .05 |
| ☐ 94 | Danny Noonan | .10 | .02 |
| ☐ 95 | Steve Pelluer | .10 | .02 |
| ☐ 96 | Herschel Walker | .15 | .05 |
| ☐ 97 | Everson Walls | .10 | .02 |
| ☐ 98 | Jimmy Johnson CO RC | .25 | .08 |
| ☐ 99 | Keith Bishop | .10 | .02 |
| ☐ 100A | John Elway DRAFT | 6.00 | 2.50 |
| ☐ 100B | John Elway TRADE | 2.00 | .75 |
| ☐ 101 | Simon Fletcher RC | .15 | .05 |
| ☐ 102 | Mike Harden | .10 | .02 |
| ☐ 103 | Mike Horan | .10 | .02 |
| ☐ 104 | Mark Jackson | .15 | .05 |
| ☐ 105 | Vance Johnson | .15 | .05 |
| ☐ 106 | Rulon Jones | .10 | .02 |
| ☐ 107 | Clarence Kay | .10 | .02 |
| ☐ 108 | Karl Mecklenburg | .15 | .05 |
| ☐ 109 | Ricky Nattiel | .10 | .02 |
| ☐ 110 | Steve Sewell RC | .10 | .02 |
| ☐ 111 | Dennis Smith | .15 | .05 |
| ☐ 112 | Gerald Willhite | .10 | .02 |
| ☐ 113 | Sammy Winder | .10 | .02 |
| ☐ 114 | Dan Reeves CO | .15 | .05 |
| ☐ 115 | Jim Arnold | .10 | .02 |
| ☐ 116 | Jerry Ball RC | .15 | .05 |
| ☐ 117 | Bennie Blades RC | .15 | .05 |
| ☐ 118 | Lomas Brown | .15 | .05 |
| ☐ 119 | Mike Cofer | .10 | .02 |
| ☐ 120 | Garry James | .10 | .02 |
| ☐ 121 | James Jones FB | .10 | .02 |
| ☐ 122 | Chuck Long | .10 | .02 |
| ☐ 123 | Pete Mandley | .10 | .02 |
| ☐ 124 | Eddie Murray | .10 | .02 |
| ☐ 125 | Chris Spielman RC | .25 | .08 |
| ☐ 126 | Dennis Gibson | .10 | .02 |
| ☐ 127 | Wayne Fontes CO | .10 | .02 |
| ☐ 128 | John Anderson | .10 | .02 |
| ☐ 129 | Brent Fullwood RC | .10 | .02 |
| ☐ 130 | Mark Cannon | .10 | .02 |
| ☐ 131 | Tim Harris | .10 | .02 |
| ☐ 132 | Mark Lee | .10 | .02 |
| ☐ 133 | Don Majkowski RC | .15 | .05 |
| ☐ 134 | Mark Murphy | .10 | .02 |
| ☐ 135 | Brian Noble | .10 | .02 |
| ☐ 136 | Ken Ruettgers RC | .10 | .02 |
| ☐ 137 | Johnny Holland | .10 | .02 |
| ☐ 138 | Randy Wright | .10 | .02 |
| ☐ 139 | Lindy Infante CO | .10 | .02 |
| ☐ 140 | Steve Brown | .10 | .02 |
| ☐ 141 | Ray Childress | .15 | .05 |
| ☐ 142 | Jeff Donaldson | .10 | .02 |
| ☐ 143 | Ernest Givins | .15 | .05 |
| ☐ 144 | John Grimsley | .10 | .02 |
| ☐ 145 | Alonzo Highsmith | .15 | .05 |
| ☐ 146 | Drew Hill | .15 | .05 |
| ☐ 147 | Robert Lyles | .10 | .02 |
| ☐ 148 | Bruce Matthews RC | .75 | .30 |
| ☐ 149 | Warren Moon | .25 | .08 |
| ☐ 150 | Mike Munchak | .15 | .05 |
| ☐ 151 | Allen Pinkett RC | .15 | .05 |
| ☐ 152 | Mike Rozier | .15 | .05 |
| ☐ 153 | Tony Zendejas | .10 | .02 |
| ☐ 154 | Jerry Glanville CO | .15 | .05 |
| ☐ 155 | Albert Bentley | .10 | .02 |
| ☐ 156 | Dean Biasucci | .10 | .02 |
| ☐ 157 | Duane Bickett | .10 | .02 |
| ☐ 158 | Bill Brooks | .15 | .05 |
| ☐ 159 | Chris Chandler RC | 1.00 | .40 |
| ☐ 160 | Pat Beach | .10 | .02 |
| ☐ 161 | Ray Donaldson | .10 | .02 |
| ☐ 162 | Jon Hand | .10 | .02 |
| ☐ 163 | Chris Hinton | .10 | .02 |
| ☐ 164 | Rohn Stark | .10 | .02 |
| ☐ 165 | Fredd Young | .10 | .02 |
| ☐ 166 | Ron Meyer CO | .10 | .02 |
| ☐ 167 | Lloyd Burruss | .10 | .02 |
| ☐ 168 | Carlos Carson | .10 | .02 |
| ☐ 169 | Deron Cherry | .15 | .05 |
| ☐ 170 | Irv Eatman | .10 | .02 |
| ☐ 171 | Dino Hackett | .10 | .02 |
| ☐ 172 | Steve DeBerg | .15 | .05 |
| ☐ 173 | Albert Lewis | .10 | .02 |
| ☐ 174 | Nick Lowery | .10 | .02 |
| ☐ 175 | Bill Maas | .10 | .02 |
| ☐ 176 | Christian Okoye | .15 | .05 |
| ☐ 177 | Stephone Paige | .15 | .05 |
| ☐ 178 | Mark Adickes | .10 | .02 |
| ☐ 179 | Kevin Ross RC | .15 | .05 |
| ☐ 180 | Neil Smith RC | .50 | .20 |
| ☐ 181 | M. Schottenheimer CO | .10 | .02 |
| ☐ 182 | Marcus Allen | .25 | .08 |
| ☐ 183 | Tim Brown RC | 1.50 | .60 |
| ☐ 184 | Willie Gault | .15 | .05 |
| ☐ 185 | Bo Jackson | .30 | .10 |
| ☐ 186 | Howie Long | .25 | .08 |
| ☐ 187 | Vann McElroy | .10 | .02 |
| ☐ 188 | Matt Millen | .15 | .05 |
| ☐ 189 | Don Mosebar RC | .10 | .02 |
| ☐ 190 | Bill Pickel | .10 | .02 |
| ☐ 191 | Jerry Robinson UER | .10 | .02 |
| ☐ 192 | Jay Schroeder | .10 | .02 |
| ☐ 193A | Stacey Toran | .10 | .02 |
| ☐ 193B | Stacey Toran | .50 | .20 |
| ☐ 194 | Mike Shanahan CO RC | .15 | .05 |
| ☐ 195 | Greg Bell | .10 | .02 |
| ☐ 196 | Ron Brown | .10 | .02 |
| ☐ 197 | Aaron Cox RC | .10 | .02 |
| ☐ 198 | Henry Ellard | .25 | .08 |
| ☐ 199 | Jim Everett | .15 | .05 |
| ☐ 200 | Jerry Gray | .10 | .02 |
| ☐ 201 | Kevin Greene | .25 | .08 |
| ☐ 202 | Pete Holohan | .10 | .02 |
| ☐ 203 | LeRoy Irvin | .15 | .05 |
| ☐ 204 | Mike Lansford | .10 | .02 |
| ☐ 205 | Tom Newberry RC | .10 | .02 |
| ☐ 206 | Mel Owens | .10 | .02 |
| ☐ 207 | Jackie Slater | .15 | .05 |
| ☐ 208 | Doug Smith | .10 | .02 |
| ☐ 209 | Mike Wilcher | .10 | .02 |
| ☐ 210 | John Robinson CO | .10 | .02 |
| ☐ 211 | John Bosa | .10 | .02 |
| ☐ 212 | Mark Brown | .10 | .02 |
| ☐ 213 | Mark Clayton | .15 | .05 |
| ☐ 214A | Ferrell Edmonds RC ERR | .50 | .20 |
| ☐ 214B | Ferrell Edmonds RC COR | .10 | .02 |
| ☐ 215 | Roy Foster | .10 | .02 |
| ☐ 216 | Lorenzo Hampton | .10 | .02 |
| ☐ 217 | Jim C.Jensen RC UER | .10 | .02 |
| ☐ 218 | William Judson | .10 | .02 |
| ☐ 219 | Eric Kumerow RC | .10 | .02 |
| ☐ 220 | Dan Marino | 2.00 | .75 |
| ☐ 221 | John Offerdahl | .15 | .05 |
| ☐ 222 | Fuad Reveiz | .10 | .02 |
| ☐ 223 | Reggie Roby | .10 | .02 |
| ☐ 224 | Brian Sochia | .10 | .02 |
| ☐ 225 | Don Shula CO RC | .25 | .08 |
| ☐ 226 | Alfred Anderson | .10 | .02 |
| ☐ 227 | Joey Browner | .10 | .02 |
| ☐ 228 | Anthony Carter | .15 | .05 |
| ☐ 229 | Chris Doleman | .15 | .05 |
| ☐ 230 | Hassan Jones RC | .10 | .02 |
| ☐ 231 | Steve Jordan | .15 | .05 |
| ☐ 232 | Tommy Kramer | .15 | .05 |
| ☐ 233 | Carl Lee RC | .10 | .02 |
| ☐ 234 | Kirk Lowdermilk RC | .10 | .02 |
| ☐ 235 | Randall McDaniel RC | 1.25 | .50 |
| ☐ 236 | Doug Martin | .10 | .02 |
| ☐ 237 | Keith Millard | .10 | .02 |
| ☐ 238 | Darrin Nelson | .10 | .02 |
| ☐ 239 | Jesse Solomon | .10 | .02 |
| ☐ 240 | Scott Studwell | .10 | .02 |
| ☐ 241 | Wade Wilson | .15 | .05 |
| ☐ 242 | Gary Zimmerman | .25 | .08 |
| ☐ 243 | Jerry Burns CO | .10 | .02 |
| ☐ 244 | Bruce Armstrong RC | .15 | .05 |
| ☐ 245 | Raymond Clayborn | .10 | .02 |
| ☐ 246 | Reggie Dupard | .10 | .02 |
| ☐ 247 | Tony Eason | .10 | .02 |
| ☐ 248 | Sean Farrell | .10 | .02 |
| ☐ 249 | Doug Flutie | .75 | .30 |
| ☐ 250 | Brent Williams RC | .10 | .02 |
| ☐ 251 | Roland James | .10 | .02 |
| ☐ 252 | Ronnie Lippett | .10 | .02 |
| ☐ 253 | Fred Marion | .10 | .02 |
| ☐ 254 | Larry McGrew | .10 | .02 |
| ☐ 255 | Stanley Morgan | .15 | .05 |
| ☐ 256 | Johnny Rembert RC | .10 | .02 |
| ☐ 257 | John Stephens RC | .15 | .05 |
| ☐ 258 | Andre Tippett | .25 | .08 |
| ☐ 259 | Garin Veris | .10 | .02 |

|  | | |
|---|---|---|
| 260A Raymond Berry CO | .15 | .05 |
| 260B Raymond Berry CO HOF | .15 | .05 |
| 261 Morten Andersen | .15 | .05 |
| 262 Hoby Brenner | .10 | .02 |
| 263 Stan Brock | .10 | .02 |
| 264 Brad Edelman | .10 | .02 |
| 265 Jumpy Geathers | .10 | .02 |
| 266A Bobby Hebert Passers | .50 | .20 |
| 266B Bobby Hebert Passes | .15 | .05 |
| 267 Craig Heyward RC | .25 | .08 |
| 268 Lonzell Hill | .10 | .02 |
| 269 Dalton Hilliard | .10 | .02 |
| 270 Rickey Jackson | .15 | .05 |
| 271 Steve Korte | .10 | .02 |
| 272 Eric Martin | .15 | .05 |
| 273 Rueben Mayes | .15 | .05 |
| 274 Sam Mills | .15 | .05 |
| 275 Brett Perriman RC | .25 | .08 |
| 276 Pat Swilling | .15 | .05 |
| 277 John Tice | .10 | .02 |
| 278 Jim Mora CO | .10 | .02 |
| 279 Eric Moore RC | .10 | .02 |
| 280 Carl Banks | .15 | .05 |
| 281 Mark Bavaro | .15 | .05 |
| 282 Maurice Carthon | .10 | .02 |
| 283 Mark Collins RC | .15 | .05 |
| 284 Erik Howard | .10 | .02 |
| 285 Terry Kinard | .10 | .02 |
| 286 Sean Landeta | .10 | .02 |
| 287 Lionel Manuel | .10 | .02 |
| 288 Leonard Marshall | .15 | .05 |
| 289 Joe Morris | .15 | .05 |
| 290 Bart Oates | .10 | .02 |
| 291 Phil Simms | .15 | .05 |
| 292 Lawrence Taylor | .25 | .08 |
| 293 Bill Parcells RC CO | .15 | .05 |
| 294 Dave Cadigan | .10 | .02 |
| 295 Kyle Clifton RC | .10 | .02 |
| 296 Alex Gordon | .10 | .02 |
| 297 James Hasty RC | .10 | .02 |
| 298 Johnny Hector | .10 | .02 |
| 299 Bobby Humphery | .15 | .05 |
| 300 Pat Leahy | .10 | .02 |
| 301 Marty Lyons | .10 | .02 |
| 302 Reggie McElroy RC | .15 | .05 |
| 303 Erik McMillan RC | .15 | .05 |
| 304 Freeman McNeil | .15 | .05 |
| 305 Ken O'Brien | .15 | .05 |
| 306 Pat Ryan | .10 | .02 |
| 307 Mickey Shuler | .10 | .02 |
| 308 Al Toon | .15 | .05 |
| 309 Jo Jo Townsell | .10 | .02 |
| 310 Roger Vick | .10 | .02 |
| 311 Joe Walton CO | .10 | .02 |
| 312 Jerome Brown | .15 | .05 |
| 313 Keith Byars | .15 | .05 |
| 314 Cris Carter RC | 1.50 | .60 |
| 315 Randall Cunningham | .40 | .15 |
| 316 Terry Hoage | .10 | .02 |
| 317 Wes Hopkins | .10 | .02 |
| 318 Keith Jackson RC | .25 | .08 |
| 319 Mike Quick | .15 | .05 |
| 320 Mike Reichenbach | .10 | .02 |
| 321 Dave Rimington | .10 | .02 |
| 322 John Teltschik | .10 | .02 |
| 323 Anthony Toney | .10 | .02 |
| 324 Andre Waters | .15 | .05 |
| 325 Reggie White | .25 | .08 |
| 326 Luis Zendejas | .10 | .02 |
| 327 Buddy Ryan CO | .15 | .05 |
| 328 Robert Awalt | .10 | .02 |
| 329 Tim McDonald RC | .15 | .05 |
| 330 Roy Green | .15 | .05 |
| 331 Neil Lomax | .15 | .05 |
| 332 Cedric Mack | .10 | .02 |
| 333 Stump Mitchell | .10 | .02 |
| 334 Niko Noga RC | .10 | .02 |
| 335 Jay Novacek RC | .25 | .08 |
| 336 Freddie Joe Nunn | .10 | .02 |
| 337 Luis Sharpe | .10 | .02 |
| 338 Vai Sikahema | .10 | .02 |
| 339 J.T. Smith | .10 | .02 |
| 340 Ron Wolfley | .10 | .02 |
| 341 Gene Stallings RC CO | .15 | .05 |
| 342 Gary Anderson K | .10 | .02 |
| 343 Bubby Brister RC | .25 | .08 |
| 344 Dermontti Dawson RC | .15 | .05 |
| 345 Thomas Everett RC | .10 | .02 |
| 346 Delton Hall RC | .10 | .02 |
| 347 Bryan Hinkle RC | .10 | .02 |
| 348 Merril Hoge RC | .15 | .05 |
| 349 Tunch Ilkin RC | .10 | .02 |
| 350 Aaron Jones RC | .10 | .02 |
| 351 Louis Lipps | .15 | .05 |
| 352 David Little | .10 | .02 |
| 353 Hardy Nickerson RC | .25 | .08 |
| 354 Rod Woodson RC | 1.00 | .40 |
| 355A Chuck Noll RC CO 1/3 | .15 | .05 |
| 355B Chuck Noll RC CO 1/2 | .15 | .05 |
| 356 Gary Anderson RB | .15 | .05 |
| 357 Rod Bernstine RC | .15 | .05 |
| 358 Gill Byrd | .10 | .02 |
| 359 Vencie Glenn | .10 | .02 |
| 360 Dennis McKnight | .10 | .02 |
| 361 Lionel James | .10 | .02 |
| 362 Mark Malone | .10 | .02 |
| 363A Anthony Miller RC 14.8 | .25 | .08 |
| 363B Anthony Miller RC 3 | .25 | .08 |
| 364 Ralf Mojsiejenko | .10 | .02 |
| 365 Leslie O'Neal | .15 | .05 |
| 366 Jamie Holland RC | .10 | .02 |
| 367 Lee Williams | .10 | .02 |
| 368 Dan Henning CO | .10 | .02 |
| 369 Harris Barton RC | .10 | .02 |
| 370 Michael Carter | .10 | .02 |
| 371 Mike Coler RC K | .10 | .02 |
| 372 Roger Craig | .25 | .08 |
| 373 Riki Ellison RC | .10 | .02 |
| 374 Jim Fahnhorst | .10 | .02 |
| 375 John Frank | .10 | .02 |
| 376 Jeff Fuller | .10 | .02 |
| 377 Don Griffin | .10 | .02 |
| 378 Charles Haley | .25 | |
| 379 Ronnie Lott | .15 | .05 |
| 380 Tim McKyer | .10 | .02 |
| 381 Joe Montana | 2.00 | .75 |
| 382 Tom Rathman | .15 | .05 |
| 383 Jerry Rice | 1.50 | .60 |
| 384 John Taylor RC | .50 | .20 |
| 385 Keena Turner | .10 | .02 |
| 386 Michael Walter | .10 | .02 |
| 387 Bubba Paris | .10 | .02 |
| 388 Steve Young | 1.00 | .40 |
| 389 George Seifert RC CO | .15 | .05 |
| 390 Brian Blades RC | .25 | .08 |
| 391A B.Bosworth Seattle | .30 | .10 |
| 391B B.Bosworth Seahawks | .30 | .10 |
| 392 Jeff Bryant | .10 | .02 |
| 393 Jacob Green | .15 | .05 |
| 394 Norm Johnson | .10 | .02 |
| 395 Dave Krieg | .15 | .05 |
| 396 Steve Largent | .25 | .08 |
| 397 Bryan Millard RC | .10 | .02 |
| 398 Paul Moyer | .10 | .02 |
| 399 Joe Nash | .10 | .02 |
| 400 Rufus Porter RC | .10 | .02 |
| 401 Eugene Robinson RC | .25 | .08 |
| 402 Bruce Scholtz | .10 | .02 |
| 403 Kelly Stouffer RC | .10 | .02 |
| 404A Curt Warner 1455 | 1.25 | .50 |
| 404B Curt Warner 6074 | .15 | .05 |
| 405 John L.Williams | .15 | .05 |
| 406 Tony Woods RC | .15 | .05 |
| 407 David Wyman | .10 | .02 |
| 408 Chuck Knox CO | .15 | .05 |
| 409 Mark Carrier RC WR | .25 | .08 |
| 410 Randy Grimes | .10 | .02 |
| 411 Paul Gruber RC | .15 | .05 |
| 412 Harry Hamilton | .10 | .02 |
| 413 Ron Holmes | .10 | .02 |
| 414 Donald Igwebuike | .10 | .02 |
| 415 Dan Turk | .10 | .02 |
| 416 Ricky Reynolds | .10 | .02 |
| 417 Bruce Hill RC | .10 | .02 |
| 418 Lars Tate | .10 | .02 |
| 419 Vinny Testaverde | .30 | .10 |
| 420 James Wilder | .10 | .02 |
| 421 Ray Perkins CO | .10 | .02 |
| 422 Jeff Bostic | .10 | .02 |
| 423 Kelvin Bryant | .10 | .02 |
| 424 Gary Clark | .25 | .08 |
| 425 Monte Coleman | .10 | .02 |
| 426 Darrell Green | .15 | .05 |
| 427 Joe Jacoby | .15 | .05 |
| 428 Jim Lachey | .15 | .05 |
| 429 Charles Mann | .10 | .02 |
| 430 Dexter Manley | .15 | .05 |
| 431 Darryl Grant | .10 | .02 |
| 432 Mark May RC | .15 | .05 |
| 433 Art Monk | .15 | .05 |
| 434 Mark Rypien RC | .25 | .08 |
| 435 Ricky Sanders | .15 | .05 |
| 436 Alvin Walton RC | .10 | .02 |
| 437 Don Warren | .10 | .02 |
| 438 Jamie Morris | .10 | .02 |
| 439 Doug Williams | .15 | .05 |
| 440 Joe Gibbs RC CO | .25 | .08 |
| 441 Marcus Cotton | .10 | .02 |
| 442 Joel Williams | .10 | .02 |
| 443 Joe Devlin | .10 | .02 |
| 444 Robb Riddick | .10 | .02 |
| 445 William Perry | .15 | .05 |
| 446 Thomas Sanders RC | .10 | .02 |
| 447 Brian Blados | .10 | .02 |
| 448 Cris Collinsworth | .15 | .05 |
| 449 Stanford Jennings | .10 | .02 |
| 450 Barry Krauss UER | .10 | .02 |
| 451 Ozzie Newsome | .15 | .05 |
| 452 Mike Oliphant RC | .10 | .02 |
| 453 Tony Dorsett | .25 | .08 |
| 454 Bruce McNorton | .10 | .02 |
| 455 Eric Dickerson | .15 | .05 |
| 456 Keith Bostic | .10 | .02 |
| 457 Sam Clancy RC | .10 | .02 |
| 458 Jack Del Rio RC | .25 | .08 |
| 459 Mike Webster | .15 | .05 |
| 460 Bob Golic | .10 | .02 |
| 461 Otis Wilson | .10 | .02 |
| 462 Mike Haynes | .15 | .05 |
| 463 Greg Townsend | .15 | .05 |
| 464 Mark Duper | .15 | .05 |
| 465 E.J. Junior | .15 | .05 |
| 466 Troy Stradford | .10 | .02 |
| 467 Mike Merriweather | .15 | .05 |
| 468 Irving Fryar | .25 | .08 |
| 469 Vaughan Johnson RC | .15 | .05 |
| 470 Pepper Johnson | .15 | .05 |
| 471 Gary Reasons RC | .10 | .02 |
| 472 Mark Haynes | .10 | .02 |
| 473 Wesley Walker | .15 | .05 |
| 474 Anthony Bell RC | .15 | .05 |
| 475 Earl Ferrell | .10 | .02 |
| 476 Craig Wolfley | .10 | .02 |
| 477 Billy Ray Smith | .10 | .02 |
| 478A Jim McMahon NOTR | .30 | .10 |
| 478B Jim McMahon TR | .15 | .05 |
| 478C Jim McMahon | 40.00 | 15.00 |
| 479 Eric Wright | .10 | .02 |
| 480A Earnest Byner NOTR | .15 | .05 |
| 480B Earnest Byner TR | .30 | .10 |
| 480C Earnest Byner | 40.00 | 15.00 |
| 481 Russ Grimm | .15 | .05 |
| 482 Wilber Marshall | .15 | .05 |
| 483A Gerald Riggs NOTR | .15 | .05 |
| 483B Gerald Riggs TR | .30 | .10 |
| 483C Gerald Riggs TR | 40.00 | 15.00 |
| 484 Brian Davis RC | .10 | .02 |
| 485 Shawn Collins RC | .10 | .02 |
| 486 Deion Sanders RC | 1.50 | .60 |
| 487 Trace Armstrong RC | .15 | .05 |
| 488 Donnell Woolford RC | .15 | .05 |
| 489 Eric Metcalf RC | .25 | .08 |
| 490 Troy Aikman RC | 6.00 | 2.50 |
| 491 Steve Walsh RC | .15 | .05 |
| 492 Steve Atwater RC | .25 | .08 |
| 493 Bobby Humphrey RC | .15 | .05 |
| 494 Barry Sanders RC | 6.00 | 2.50 |
| 495 Tony Mandarich RC | .15 | .05 |
| 496 David Williams RC | .10 | .02 |
| 497 Andre Rison RC UER | 1.00 | .40 |
| 498 Derrick Thomas RC | 1.50 | .60 |
| 499 Cleveland Gary RC | .10 | .02 |
| 500 Bill Hawkins RC | .10 | .02 |
| 501 Louis Oliver RC | .10 | .02 |
| 502 Sammie Smith RC | .10 | .02 |

| Card | .  | .  |
|---|---|---|
| 503 Hart Lee Dykes RC | .10 | .02 |
| 504 Wayne Martin RC | .10 | .02 |
| 505 Brian Williams OL RC | .10 | .02 |
| 506 Jeff Lageman RC | .15 | .05 |
| 507 Eric Hill RC | .10 | .05 |
| 508 Joe Wolf RC | .10 | .02 |
| 509 Timm Rosenbach RC | .15 | .05 |
| 510 Tom Ricketts RC | .10 | .02 |
| 511 Tim Worley RC | .10 | .02 |
| 512 Burt Grossman RC | .15 | .05 |
| 513 Keith DeLong RC | .10 | .02 |
| 514 Andy Heck RC | .10 | .02 |
| 515 Broderick Thomas RC | .25 | .08 |
| 516 Don Beebe RC | .25 | .08 |
| 517 James Thornton RC | .10 | .02 |
| 518 Eric Kattus | .10 | .02 |
| 519 Bruce Kozerski RC | .10 | .02 |
| 520 Brian Washington RC | .10 | .02 |
| 521 Rodney Peete RC | .50 | .20 |
| 522 Erik Affholter RC | .10 | .02 |
| 523 Anthony Dilweg RC | .10 | .02 |
| 524 O'Brien Alston | .10 | .02 |
| 525 Mike Elkins | .10 | .02 |
| 526 Jonathan Hayes RC | .10 | .02 |
| 527 Terry McDaniel RC | .10 | .02 |
| 528 Frank Stams RC | .10 | .02 |
| 529 Darryl Ingram RC | .10 | .02 |
| 530 Henry Thomas | .10 | .02 |
| 531 Eric Coleman DB | .10 | .02 |
| 532 Sheldon White RC | .10 | .02 |
| 533 Eric Allen RC | .25 | .08 |
| 534 Robert Drummond | .10 | .02 |
| 535A G.Williams RC bal | 10.00 | 5.00 |
| 535B G.Williams RC w/o scout | .25 | .08 |
| 535C G.Williams RC w/scout | .15 | .05 |
| 536 Billy Joe Tolliver RC | .15 | .05 |
| 537 Daniel Stubbs RC | .10 | .02 |
| 538 Wesley Walls RC | .40 | .15 |
| 539A James Jefferson RC*ERR | .30 | .10 |
| 539B James Jefferson RC COR | .10 | .02 |
| 540 Tracy Rocker | .10 | .02 |
| 541 Art Shell CO | .15 | .05 |
| 542 Lemuel Stinson RC | .10 | .02 |
| 543 Tyrone Braxton RC UER | .10 | .02 |
| 544 David Treadwell RC | .10 | .02 |
| 545 Flipper Anderson RC | .25 | .08 |
| 546 Dave Meggett RC | .25 | .08 |
| 547 Lewis Tillman RC | .15 | .05 |
| 548 Carnell Lake RC | .25 | .08 |
| 549 Marion Butts RC | .15 | .05 |
| 550 Sterling Sharpe RC | 1.00 | .40 |
| 551 Ezra Johnson | .10 | .02 |
| 552 Clarence Verdin RC** | .10 | .02 |
| 553 Mervyn Fernandez RC | .10 | .02 |
| 554 Ottis Anderson | .15 | .05 |
| 555 Gary Hogeboom | .10 | .02 |
| 556 Paul Palmer TR | .10 | .02 |
| 557 Jesse Solomon TR | .10 | .02 |
| 558 Chip Banks TR | .15 | .05 |
| 559 Steve Pelluer TR | .10 | .02 |
| 560 Darrin Nelson TR | .10 | .02 |
| 561 Herschel Walker TR | .15 | .05 |
| CC1 Pete Rozelle | .50 | .20 |

**1990 Pro Set**

JIM EVERETT QB-RAMS

| | | |
|---|---|---|
| COMPLETE SET (801) | 35.00 | 15.00 |
| COMP SERIES 1 (377) | 15.00 | 6.00 |
| COMP SERIES 2 (392) | 15.00 | 6.00 |

| Card | . | . |
|---|---|---|
| COMP.FINAL SERIES (32) | 5.00 | 2.00 |
| COMP.FINAL FACT. (32) | 5.00 | 2.00 |
| 1A Ba.Sanders ROY Hawaii | 80.00 | 30.00 |
| 1B Barry Sanders ROY | .60 | .25 |
| 2A Joe Montana POY 3521 ERR | .50 | .20 |
| 2B Joe Montana POY 3130 COR | .50 | .20 |
| 3 Lindy Infante RC | .04 | .01 |
| 4 Warren Moon MOY UER | .25 | .08 |
| 5 Keith Millard | .04 | .01 |
| 6 Derrick Thomas D.ROY | .25 | .08 |
| 7 Ottis Anderson | .10 | .02 |
| 8 Joe Montana LL UER | .50 | .20 |
| 9 Christian Okoye | .04 | .01 |
| 10 Thurman Thomas LL | .25 | .08 |
| 11 Mike Cofer | .04 | .01 |
| 12 Dalton Hilliard UER | .04 | .01 |
| 13 Sterling Sharpe LL | .25 | .08 |
| 14 Rich Camarillo | .04 | .01 |
| 15A Walter Stanley LL 87/8 | .50 | .20 |
| 15B Walter Stanley COR | .04 | .01 |
| 16 Rod Woodson | .25 | .08 |
| 17 Felix Wright | .04 | .01 |
| 18A Chris Doleman ERR | .50 | .20 |
| 18B Chris Doleman COR | .04 | .01 |
| 19A Andre Ware RC w/o strip | .10 | .02 |
| 19B Andre Ware RC w/stripe | .10 | .02 |
| 20A Mo Elewonibi RC | .04 | .01 |
| 20B Mo Elewonibi RC | .04 | .01 |
| 21A Percy Snow | .50 | .20 |
| 21B Percy Snow | .04 | .01 |
| 22A Anthony Thompson RC w/o | .04 | .01 |
| 22B Anthony Thompson RC w/ | .04 | .01 |
| 23 Buck Buchanan | .04 | .01 |
| 24 Bob Griese | .10 | .02 |
| 25A Franco Harris ERR | .50 | .20 |
| 25B Franco Harris COR | .10 | .02 |
| 26 Ted Hendricks | .04 | .01 |
| 27A Jack Lambert ERR | .50 | .20 |
| 27B Jack Lambert COR | .50 | .20 |
| 28 Tom Landry HOF | .10 | .02 |
| 29 Bob St.Clair | .04 | .01 |
| 30 Aundray Bruce UER | .04 | .01 |
| 31 Tony Casillas UER | .04 | .01 |
| 32 Shawn Collins | .04 | .01 |
| 33 Marcus Cotton | .04 | .01 |
| 34 Bill Fralic | .04 | .01 |
| 35 Chris Miller | .10 | .02 |
| 36 Deion Sanders UER | .50 | .20 |
| 37 John Settle | .04 | .01 |
| 38 Jerry Glanville CO | .04 | .01 |
| 39 Cornelius Bennett | .10 | .02 |
| 40 Jim Kelly | .25 | .08 |
| 41 Mark Kelso UER | .04 | .01 |
| 42 Scott Norwood | .04 | .01 |
| 43 Nate Odomes RC | .10 | .02 |
| 44 Scott Radecic | .04 | .01 |
| 45 Jim Ritcher RC | .04 | .01 |
| 46 Leonard Smith | .04 | .01 |
| 47 Darryl Talley | .04 | .01 |
| 48 Marv Levy CO | .10 | .02 |
| 49 Neal Anderson | .10 | .02 |
| 50 Kevin Butler | .04 | .01 |
| 51 Jim Covert | .04 | .01 |
| 52 Richard Dent | .10 | .02 |
| 53 Jay Hilgenberg | .04 | .01 |
| 54 Steve McMichael | .10 | .02 |
| 55 Ron Morris | .04 | .01 |
| 56 John Roper | .04 | .01 |
| 57 Mike Singletary | .10 | .02 |
| 58 Keith Van Horne | .04 | .01 |
| 59A Mike Ditka CO | .25 | .08 |
| 59B Mike Ditka CO | 5.00 | 2.00 |
| 60 Lewis Billups | .04 | .01 |
| 61 Eddie Brown | .04 | .01 |
| 62 Jason Buck | .04 | .01 |
| 63A Rickey Dixon RC ERR | .50 | .20 |
| 63B Rickey Dixon RC COR | .50 | .20 |
| 64 Tim McGee | .04 | .01 |
| 65 Eric Thomas | .04 | .01 |
| 66 Ickey Woods | .04 | .01 |
| 67 Carl Zander | .04 | .01 |
| 68A Sam Wyche CO ERR | .50 | .20 |
| 68B Sam Wyche CO COR | .50 | .20 |
| 69 Paul Farren RC | .04 | .01 |
| 70 Thane Gash RC | .04 | .01 |

| Card | . | . |
|---|---|---|
| 71 David Grayson | .04 | .01 |
| 72 Bernie Kosar | .10 | .02 |
| 73 Reggie Langhorne | .04 | .01 |
| 74 Eric Metcalf | .25 | .08 |
| 75A Ozzie Newsome ERR | .50 | .20 |
| 75B Ozzie Newsome COR | .50 | .20 |
| 75C Cody Risien SP | .50 | .20 |
| 76 Felix Wright | .04 | .01 |
| 77 Bud Carson CO | .04 | .01 |
| 78 Troy Aikman | .75 | .30 |
| 79 Michael Irvin | .25 | .08 |
| 80 Jim Jeffcoat | .04 | .01 |
| 81 Crawford Ker | .04 | .01 |
| 82 Eugene Lockhart | .04 | .01 |
| 83 Kelvin Martin RC | .04 | .01 |
| 84 Ken Norton Jr. RC | .25 | .08 |
| 85 Jimmy Johnson CO | .10 | .02 |
| 86 Steve Walker | .04 | .01 |
| 87 Tyrone Braxton | .04 | .01 |
| 88 John Elway | 1.25 | .50 |
| 89 Simon Fletcher | .04 | .01 |
| 90 Ron Holmes | .04 | .01 |
| 91 Bobby Humphrey | .04 | .01 |
| 92 Vance Johnson | .04 | .01 |
| 93 Ricky Nattiel | .04 | .01 |
| 94 Dan Reeves CO | .04 | .01 |
| 95 Jim Arnold | .04 | .01 |
| 96 Jerry Ball | .04 | .01 |
| 97 Bennie Blades | .04 | .01 |
| 98 Lomas Brown | .04 | .01 |
| 99 Michael Cofer | .04 | .01 |
| 100 Richard Johnson | .04 | .01 |
| 101 Eddie Murray | .04 | .01 |
| 102 Barry Sanders | 1.25 | .50 |
| 103 Chris Spielman | .25 | .08 |
| 104 William White RC | .04 | .01 |
| 105 Eric Williams RC | .04 | .01 |
| 106 Wayne Fontes CO UER | .04 | .01 |
| 107 Brent Fullwood | .04 | .01 |
| 108 Ron Hallstrom RC | .04 | .01 |
| 109 Tim Harris | .04 | .01 |
| 110A Johnny Holland ERR | .50 | .20 |
| 110B Johnny Holland COR | .50 | .20 |
| 111A Perry Kemp ERR | .50 | .20 |
| 111B Perry Kemp COR | .50 | .20 |
| 112 Don Majkowski | .04 | .01 |
| 113 Mark Murphy | .04 | .01 |
| 114A Sterling Sharpe ERR Gle | .25 | .08 |
| 114B Sterling Sharpe COR Chi | .50 | .20 |
| 115 Ed West RC | .04 | .01 |
| 116 Lindy Infante CO | .04 | .01 |
| 117 Steve Brown | .04 | .01 |
| 118 Ray Childress | .04 | .01 |
| 119 Ernest Givins | .10 | .02 |
| 120 John Grimsley | .04 | .01 |
| 121 Alonzo Highsmith | .04 | .01 |
| 122 Drew Hill | .04 | .01 |
| 123 Bubba McDowell | .04 | .01 |
| 124 Dean Steinkuhler | .04 | .01 |
| 125 Lorenzo White FPSC | .10 | .02 |
| 126 Tony Zendejas | .04 | .01 |
| 127 Jack Pardee CO | .04 | .01 |
| 128 Albert Bentley | .04 | .01 |
| 129 Dean Biasucci | .04 | .01 |
| 130 Duane Bickett | .04 | .01 |
| 131 Bill Brooks | .04 | .01 |
| 132 Jon Hand | .04 | .01 |
| 133 Mike Prior | .04 | .01 |
| 134A Andre Rison NOTR | .25 | .08 |
| 134B Andre Rison TR | .25 | .08 |
| 134C Andre Rison TR Lud/back | .25 | .08 |
| 135 Rohn Stark | .04 | .01 |
| 136 Donnell Thompson | .04 | .01 |
| 137 Clarence Verdin | .04 | .01 |
| 138 Fredd Young | .04 | .01 |
| 139 Ron Meyer CO | .04 | .01 |
| 140 John Alt RC | .04 | .01 |
| 141 Steve DeBerg | .04 | .01 |
| 142 Irv Eatman | .04 | .01 |
| 143 Dino Hackett | .04 | .01 |
| 144 Nick Lowery | .04 | .01 |
| 145 Bill Maas | .04 | .01 |
| 146 Stephone Paige | .04 | .01 |
| 147 Neil Smith | .25 | .08 |
| 148 M. Schottenheimer CO | .04 | .01 |

| # | Card | | |
|---|---|---|---|
| 149 | Steve Beuerlein FPSC | .10 | .02 |
| 150 | Tim Brown | .25 | .08 |
| 151 | Mike Dyal | .04 | .01 |
| 152A | Mervyn Fernandez ERR | .75 | .30 |
| 152B | Mervyn Fernandez COR | .75 | .30 |
| 153 | Willie Gault | .10 | .02 |
| 154 | Bob Golic | .04 | .01 |
| 155 | Bo Jackson | .30 | .10 |
| 156 | Don Mosebar | .04 | .01 |
| 157 | Steve Smith | .04 | .01 |
| 158 | Greg Townsend | .04 | .01 |
| 159 | Bruce Wilkerson RC | .04 | *.01 |
| 160 | Steve Wisniewski | .10 | .02 |
| 161A | Art Shell CO ERR | .50 | .20 |
| 161B | Art Shell CO COR | 8.00 | 3.00 |
| 161C | Art Shell CO COR | 10.00 | 4.00 |
| 162 | Flipper Anderson | .04 | .01 |
| 163 | Greg Bell UER | .04 | .01 |
| 164 | Henry Ellard | .10 | .02 |
| 165 | Jim Everett | .10 | .02 |
| 166 | Jerry Gray | .04 | .01 |
| 167 | Kevin Greene | .10 | .02 |
| 168 | Pete Holohan | .04 | .01 |
| 169 | Larry Kelm RC | .04 | .01 |
| 170 | Tom Newberry | .04 | .01 |
| 171 | Vince Newsome RC | .04 | .01 |
| 172 | Irv Pankey | .04 | .01 |
| 173 | Jackie Slater | .04 | .01 |
| 174 | Fred Strickland RC | .04 | .01 |
| 175 | Mike Wilcher UER | .04 | .01 |
| 176 | John Robinson CO UER | .04 | .01 |
| 177 | Mark Clayton | .10 | .02 |
| 178 | Roy Foster | .04 | .01 |
| 179 | Harry Galbreath RC | .04 | .01 |
| 180 | Jim C. Jensen | .04 | .01 |
| 181 | Dan Marino | 1.25 | .50 |
| 182 | Louis Oliver | .04 | .01 |
| 183 | Sammie Smith | .04 | .01 |
| 184 | Brian Sochia | .04 | .01 |
| 185 | Don Shula CO | .10 | .02 |
| 186 | Joey Browner | .10 | .02 |
| 187 | Anthony Carter | .10 | .02 |
| 188 | Chris Doleman | .04 | .01 |
| 189 | Steve Jordan | .04 | .01 |
| 190 | Carl Lee | .04 | .01 |
| 191 | Randall McDaniel | .15 | .05 |
| 192 | Mike Merriweather | .04 | .01 |
| 193 | Keith Millard | .04 | .01 |
| 194 | Al Noga | .04 | .01 |
| 195 | Scott Studwell | .04 | .01 |
| 196 | Henry Thomas | .04 | .01 |
| 197 | Herschel Walker | .10 | .02 |
| 198 | Wade Wilson | .10 | .02 |
| 199 | Gary Zimmerman | .10 | .02 |
| 200 | Jerry Burns CO | .04 | .01 |
| 201 | Vincent Brown RC | .04 | .01 |
| 202 | Hart Lee Dykes | .04 | .01 |
| 203 | Sean Farrell | .04 | .01 |
| 204A | Fred Marion belt | 250.00 | 100.00 |
| 204B | Fred Marion no belt | .04 | .01 |
| 205 | Stanley Morgan UER | .04 | .01 |
| 206 | Eric Sievers RC | .04 | .01 |
| 207 | John Stephens | .04 | .01 |
| 208 | Andre Tippett | .10 | .02 |
| 209 | Rod Rust CO | .04 | .01 |
| 210A | Morten Andersen ERR | .50 | .20 |
| 210B | Morten Andersen COR | .50 | .20 |
| 211 | Brad Edelman | .04 | .01 |
| 212 | John Fourcade | .04 | .01 |
| 213 | Dalton Hilliard | .10 | .02 |
| 214 | Rickey Jackson | .10 | .02 |
| 215 | Vaughan Johnson | .04 | .01 |
| 216A | Eric Martin ERR | .50 | .20 |
| 216B | Eric Martin COR | .50 | .20 |
| 217 | Sam Mills | .10 | .02 |
| 218 | Pat Swilling UER | .10 | .02 |
| 219 | Frank Warren RC | .04 | .01 |
| 220 | Jim Wilks | .04 | .01 |
| 221A | Jim Mora CO ERR | .50 | .20 |
| 221B | Jim Mora CO COR | .50 | .20 |
| 222 | Raul Allegre | .04 | .01 |
| 223 | Carl Banks | .04 | .01 |
| 224 | John Elliott | .04 | .01 |
| 225 | Erik Howard | .04 | .01 |
| 226 | Pepper Johnson | .04 | .01 |
| 227 | Leonard Marshall UER | .04 | .01 |
| 228 | Dave Meggett | .10 | .02 |
| 229 | Bart Oates | .04 | .01 |
| 230 | Phil Simms | .10 | .02 |
| 231 | Lawrence Taylor | .25 | .08 |
| 232 | Bill Parcells CO | .10 | .02 |
| 233 | Troy Benson | .04 | .01 |
| 234 | Kyle Clifton UER | .04 | .01 |
| 235 | Johnny Hector | .04 | .01 |
| 236 | Jeff Lageman | .04 | .01 |
| 237 | Pat Leahy | .04 | .01 |
| 238 | Freeman McNeil | .04 | .01 |
| 239 | Ken O'Brien | .04 | .01 |
| 240 | Al Toon | .10 | .02 |
| 241 | Jo Jo Townsell | .04 | .01 |
| 242 | Bruce Coslet CO | .04 | .01 |
| 243 | Eric Allen | .04 | .01 |
| 244 | Jerome Brown | .04 | .01 |
| 245 | Keith Byars | .04 | .01 |
| 246 | Cris Carter | .50 | .20 |
| 247 | Randall Cunningham | .25 | .08 |
| 248 | Keith Jackson | .10 | .02 |
| 249 | Mike Quick | .04 | .01 |
| 250 | Clyde Simmons | .04 | .01 |
| 251 | Andre Waters | .04 | .01 |
| 252 | Reggie White | .25 | .08 |
| 253 | Buddy Ryan CO | .04 | .01 |
| 254 | Rich Camarillo | .04 | .01 |
| 255 | Earl Ferrell | .04 | .01 |
| 256 | Roy Green | .10 | .02 |
| 257 | Ken Harvey RC | .25 | .08 |
| 258 | Ernie Jones RC | .04 | .01 |
| 259 | Tim McDonald | .04 | .01 |
| 260 | Timm Rosenbach UER | .04 | .01 |
| 261 | Luis Sharpe | .04 | .01 |
| 262 | Vai Sikahema | .04 | .01 |
| 263 | J.T. Smith | .04 | .01 |
| 264 | Ron Wolfley UER | .04 | .01 |
| 265 | Joe Bugel CO | .04 | .01 |
| 266 | Gary Anderson K | .04 | .01 |
| 267 | Bubby Brister | .10 | .02 |
| 268 | Merril Hoge | .04 | .01 |
| 269 | Carnell Lake | .04 | .01 |
| 270 | Louis Lipps | .10 | .02 |
| 271 | David Little | .04 | .01 |
| 272 | Greg Lloyd | .25 | .08 |
| 273 | Keith Willis | .04 | .01 |
| 274 | Tim Worley | .04 | .01 |
| 275 | Chuck Noll CO | .10 | .02 |
| 276 | Marion Butts | .10 | .02 |
| 277 | Gill Byrd | .04 | .01 |
| 278 | Vencie Glenn UER | .04 | .01 |
| 279 | Burt Grossman | .04 | .01 |
| 280 | Gary Plummer | .04 | .01 |
| 281 | Billy Ray Smith | .04 | .01 |
| 282 | Billy Joe Tolliver | .10 | .02 |
| 283 | Dan Henning CO | .04 | .01 |
| 284 | Harris Barton | .04 | .01 |
| 285 | Michael Carter | .04 | .01 |
| 286 | Mike Cofer | .04 | .01 |
| 287 | Roger Craig | .10 | .02 |
| 288 | Don Griffin | .04 | .01 |
| 289A | Charles Haley ERR | 10.00 | 4.00 |
| 289B | Charles Haley CO 5 fum | .75 | .30 |
| 290 | Pierce Holt RC | .04 | .01 |
| 291 | Ronnie Lott | .10 | .02 |
| 292 | Guy McIntyre | .04 | .01 |
| 293 | Joe Montana | 1.25 | .50 |
| 294 | Tom Rathman | .04 | .01 |
| 295 | Jerry Rice | .75 | .30 |
| 296 | Jesse Sapolu RC | .04 | .01 |
| 297 | John Taylor | .10 | .02 |
| 298 | Michael Walter | .04 | .01 |
| 299 | George Seifert CO | .10 | .02 |
| 300 | Jeff Bryant | .04 | .01 |
| 301 | Jacob Green | .04 | .01 |
| 302 | Norm Johnson UER | .04 | .01 |
| 303 | Bryan Millard | .04 | .01 |
| 304 | Joe Nash | .04 | .01 |
| 305 | Eugene Robinson | .04 | .01 |
| 306 | John L. Williams | .04 | .01 |
| 307 | David Wyman | .04 | .01 |
| 308 | Chuck Knox CO | .04 | .01 |
| 309 | Mark Carrier WR | .25 | .08 |
| 310 | Paul Gruber | .04 | .01 |
| 311 | Harry Hamilton | .04 | .01 |
| 312 | Bruce Hill | .04 | .01 |
| 313 | Donald Igwebuike | .04 | .01 |
| 314 | Kevin Murphy | .04 | .01 |
| 315 | Ervin Randle | .04 | .01 |
| 316 | Mark Robinson | .04 | .01 |
| 317 | Lars Tate | .04 | .01 |
| 318 | Vinny Testaverde | .10 | .02 |
| 319A | Ray Perkins CO ERR | .75 | .30 |
| 319B | Ray Perkins CO COR | .04 | .01 |
| 320 | Earnest Byner | .04 | .01 |
| 321 | Gary Clark | .25 | .08 |
| 322 | Darryl Grant | .04 | .01 |
| 323 | Darrell Green | .10 | .02 |
| 324 | Jim Lachey | .04 | .01 |
| 325 | Charles Mann | .04 | .01 |
| 326 | Wilber Marshall | .04 | .01 |
| 327 | Ralf Mojsiejenko | .04 | .01 |
| 328 | Art Monk | .10 | .02 |
| 329 | Gerald Riggs | .10 | .02 |
| 330 | Mark Rypien | .10 | .02 |
| 331 | Ricky Sanders | .10 | .02 |
| 332 | Alvin Walton | .04 | .01 |
| 333 | Joe Gibbs CO | .10 | .02 |
| 334 | Aloha Stadium | .04 | .01 |
| 335 | Brian Blades PB | .04 | .01 |
| 336 | James Brooks PB | .04 | .01 |
| 337 | Shane Conlan PB | .04 | .01 |
| 338A | Eric Dickerson PB SP | 3.00 | 1.25 |
| 338B | Lud Denny Promo | 200.00 | 75.00 |
| 339 | Ray Donaldson PB | .04 | .01 |
| 340 | Ferrell Edmunds PB | .04 | .01 |
| 341 | Boomer Esiason PB | .10 | .02 |
| 342 | David Fulcher PB | .04 | .01 |
| 343A | Chris Hinton PB | 8.00 | 3.00 |
| 343B | Chris Hinton PB | .04 | .01 |
| 344 | Rodney Holman PB | .04 | .01 |
| 345 | Kent Hull PB | .04 | .01 |
| 346 | Tunch Ilkin PB | .04 | .01 |
| 347 | Mike Johnson PB | .04 | .01 |
| 348 | Greg Kragen PB | .04 | .01 |
| 349 | Dave Krieg PB | .10 | .02 |
| 350 | Albert Lewis PB | .04 | .01 |
| 351 | Howie Long PB | .10 | .02 |
| 352 | Bruce Matthews PB | .04 | .01 |
| 353 | Clay Matthews PB | .04 | .01 |
| 354 | Erik McMillan PB | .04 | .01 |
| 355 | Karl Mecklenburg PB | .04 | .01 |
| 356 | Anthony Miller PB | .04 | .01 |
| 357 | Frank Minnifield PB | .04 | .01 |
| 358 | Max Montoya PB | .04 | .01 |
| 359 | Warren Moon PB | .25 | .08 |
| 360 | Mike Munchak PB | .04 | .01 |
| 361 | Anthony Munoz PB | .04 | .01 |
| 362 | John Offerdahl PB | .04 | .01 |
| 363 | Christian Okoye PB | .04 | .01 |
| 364 | Leslie O'Neal PB | .04 | .01 |
| 365 | Rufus Porter PB UER | .04 | .01 |
| 366 | Andre Reed PB | .10 | .02 |
| 367 | Johnny Rembert PB | .04 | .01 |
| 368 | Reggie Roby PB | .04 | .01 |
| 369 | Kevin Ross PB | .04 | .01 |
| 370 | Webster Slaughter PB | .04 | .01 |
| 371 | Bruce Smith PB | .10 | .02 |
| 372 | Dennis Smith PB | .04 | .01 |
| 373 | Derrick Thomas PB | .10 | .02 |
| 374 | Thurman Thomas PB | .25 | .08 |
| 375 | David Treadwell PB | .04 | .01 |
| 376 | Lee Williams PB | .04 | .01 |
| 377 | Rod Woodson PB | .10 | .02 |
| 378 | Bud Carson CO PB | .04 | .01 |
| 379 | Eric Allen PB | .04 | .01 |
| 380 | Neal Anderson PB | .04 | .01 |
| 381 | Jerry Ball PB | .04 | .01 |
| 382 | Joey Browner PB | .04 | .01 |
| 383 | Rich Camarillo PB | .04 | .01 |
| 384 | Mark Carrier WR PB | .04 | .01 |
| 385 | Roger Craig PB | .10 | .02 |
| 386A | Randall Cunningham PB | .50 | .20 |
| 386B | Randall Cunningham PB | .50 | .20 |
| 387 | Chris Doleman PB | .04 | .01 |
| 388 | Henry Ellard PB | .04 | .01 |
| 389 | Bill Fralic PB | .04 | .01 |
| 390 | Brent Fullwood PB | .04 | .01 |
| 391 | Jerry Gray PB | .04 | .01 |

| # | Card | | |
|---|---|---|---|
| ☐ 392 | Kevin Greene PB | .10 | .02 |
| ☐ 393 | Tim Harris PB | .04 | .01 |
| ☐ 394 | Jay Hilgenberg PB | .04 | .01 |
| ☐ 395 | Dalton Hilliard PB | .04 | .01 |
| ☐ 396 | Keith Jackson PB | .10 | .02 |
| ☐ 397 | Vaughan Johnson PB | .04 | .01 |
| ☐ 398 | Steve Jordan PB | .04 | .01 |
| ☐ 399 | Carl Lee PB | .04 | .01 |
| ☐ 400 | Ronnie Lott PB | .10 | .02 |
| ☐ 401 | Don Majkowski PB | .04 | .01 |
| ☐ 402 | Charles Mann PB | .04 | .01 |
| ☐ 403 | Randall McDaniel PB | .10 | .02 |
| ☐ 404 | Tim McDonald PB | .04 | .01 |
| ☐ 405 | Guy McIntyre PB | .04 | .01 |
| ☐ 406 | Dave Meggett PB | .04 | .01 |
| ☐ 407 | Keith Millard PB | .04 | .01 |
| ☐ 408 | Joe Montana PB | .50 | .20 |
| ☐ 409 | Eddie Murray PB | .04 | .01 |
| ☐ 410 | Tom Newberry PB | .04 | .01 |
| ☐ 411 | Jerry Rice PB | .50 | .20 |
| ☐ 412 | Mark Rypien PB | .04 | .01 |
| ☐ 413 | Barry Sanders PB | .60 | .25 |
| ☐ 414 | Luis Sharpe PB | .04 | .01 |
| ☐ 415 | Sterling Sharpe PB | .04 | .01 |
| ☐ 416 | Mike Singletary PB | .10 | .02 |
| ☐ 417 | Jackie Slater PB | .04 | .01 |
| ☐ 418 | Doug Smith PB | .04 | .01 |
| ☐ 419 | Chris Spielman PB | .04 | .01 |
| ☐ 420 | Pat Swilling PB | .04 | .01 |
| ☐ 421 | John Taylor PB | .10 | .02 |
| ☐ 422 | Lawrence Taylor PB | .10 | .02 |
| ☐ 423 | Reggie White PB | .10 | .02 |
| ☐ 424 | Ron Wolfley PB | .04 | .01 |
| ☐ 425 | Gary Zimmerman PB | .10 | .02 |
| ☐ 426 | John Robinson CO PB | .04 | .01 |
| ☐ 427 | Scott Case UER | .04 | .01 |
| ☐ 428 | Mike Kenn | .04 | .01 |
| ☐ 429 | Mike Gann | .04 | .01 |
| ☐ 430 | Tim Green RC | .04 | .01 |
| ☐ 431 | Michael Haynes RC | .25 | .08 |
| ☐ 432 | Jessie Tuggle RC UER | .04 | .01 |
| ☐ 433 | John Rade | .04 | .01 |
| ☐ 434 | Andre Rison | .25 | .08 |
| ☐ 435 | Don Beebe | .10 | .02 |
| ☐ 436 | Ray Bentley | .04 | .01 |
| ☐ 437 | Shane Conlan | .04 | .01 |
| ☐ 438 | Kent Hull | .04 | .01 |
| ☐ 439 | Pete Metzelaars | .04 | .01 |
| ☐ 440 | Andre Reed UER | .25 | .08 |
| ☐ 441 | Frank Reich FPSC | .25 | .08 |
| ☐ 442 | Leon Seals RC | .04 | .01 |
| ☐ 443 | Bruce Smith | .25 | .08 |
| ☐ 444 | Thurman Thomas | .25 | .08 |
| ☐ 445 | Will Wolford | .04 | .01 |
| ☐ 446 | Trace Armstrong | .04 | .01 |
| ☐ 447 | Mark Bortz RC | .04 | .01 |
| ☐ 448 | Tom Thayer RC | .04 | .01 |
| ☐ 449A | Dan Hampton ERR | .50 | .20 |
| ☐ 449B | Dan Hampton COR | 10.00 | 4.00 |
| ☐ 450 | Shaun Gayle RC | .04 | .01 |
| ☐ 451 | Dennis Gentry | .04 | .01 |
| ☐ 452 | Jim Harbaugh | .25 | .08 |
| ☐ 453 | Vestee Jackson | .04 | .01 |
| ☐ 454 | Brad Muster | .04 | .01 |
| ☐ 455 | William Perry | .10 | .02 |
| ☐ 456 | Ron Rivera | .04 | .01 |
| ☐ 457 | James Thornton | .04 | .01 |
| ☐ 458 | Mike Tomczak | .10 | .02 |
| ☐ 459 | Donnell Woolford | .04 | .01 |
| ☐ 460 | Eric Ball | .04 | .01 |
| ☐ 461 | James Brooks | .10 | .02 |
| ☐ 462 | David Fulcher | .04 | .01 |
| ☐ 463 | Boomer Esiason | .10 | .02 |
| ☐ 464 | Rodney Holman | .04 | .01 |
| ☐ 465 | Bruce Kozerski | .04 | .01 |
| ☐ 466 | Tim Krumrie | .04 | .01 |
| ☐ 467 | Anthony Munoz | .10 | .02 |
| ☐ 468 | Brian Blados | .04 | .01 |
| ☐ 469 | Mike Baab | .04 | .01 |
| ☐ 470 | Brian Brennan | .04 | .01 |
| ☐ 471 | Raymond Clayborn | .04 | .01 |
| ☐ 472 | Mike Johnson | .04 | .01 |
| ☐ 473 | Kevin Mack | .04 | .01 |
| ☐ 474 | Clay Matthews | .10 | .02 |
| ☐ 475 | Frank Minnifield | .04 | .01 |
| ☐ 476 | Gregg Rakoczy RC | .04 | .01 |
| ☐ 477 | Webster Slaughter | .10 | .02 |
| ☐ 478 | James Dixon | .04 | .01 |
| ☐ 479 | Robert Awalt UER | .04 | .01 |
| ☐ 480 | Dennis McKinnon UER | .04 | .01 |
| ☐ 481 | Danny Noonan | .04 | .01 |
| ☐ 482 | Jesse Solomon | .04 | .01 |
| ☐ 483 | Daniel Stubbs UER | .04 | .01 |
| ☐ 484 | Steve Walsh | .10 | .02 |
| ☐ 485 | Michael Brooks RC | .04 | .01 |
| ☐ 486 | Mark Jackson | .04 | .01 |
| ☐ 487 | Greg Kragen | .04 | .01 |
| ☐ 488 | Ken Lanier RC | .04 | .01 |
| ☐ 489 | Karl Mecklenburg | .04 | .01 |
| ☐ 490 | Steve Sewell | .04 | .01 |
| ☐ 491 | Dennis Smith | .04 | .01 |
| ☐ 492 | David Treadwell | .04 | .01 |
| ☐ 493 | Michael Young RC | .04 | .01 |
| ☐ 494 | Robert Clark RC | .04 | .01 |
| ☐ 495 | Dennis Gibson | .04 | .01 |
| ☐ 496A | Kevin Glover RC C/G | .50 | .20 |
| ☐ 496B | Kevin Glover RC C | .04 | .01 |
| ☐ 497 | Mel Gray | .10 | .02 |
| ☐ 498 | Rodney Peete | .10 | .02 |
| ☐ 499 | Dave Brown DB | .04 | .01 |
| ☐ 500 | Jerry Holmes | .04 | .01 |
| ☐ 501 | Chris Jacke | .04 | .01 |
| ☐ 502 | Alan Veingrad | .04 | .01 |
| ☐ 503 | Mark Lee | .04 | .01 |
| ☐ 504 | Tony Mandarich | .04 | .01 |
| ☐ 505 | Brian Noble | .04 | .01 |
| ☐ 506 | Jeff Query | .04 | .01 |
| ☐ 507 | Ken Ruettgers | .04 | .01 |
| ☐ 508 | Patrick Allen | .04 | .01 |
| ☐ 509 | Curtis Duncan | .04 | .01 |
| ☐ 510 | William Fuller | .10 | .02 |
| ☐ 511 | Haywood Jeffires RC | .25 | .08 |
| ☐ 512 | Sean Jones | .10 | .02 |
| ☐ 513 | Terry Kinard | .04 | .01 |
| ☐ 514 | Bruce Matthews | .10 | .02 |
| ☐ 515 | Gerald McNeil | .04 | .01 |
| ☐ 516 | Greg Montgomery RC | .04 | .01 |
| ☐ 517 | Warren Moon | .25 | .08 |
| ☐ 518 | Mike Munchak | .10 | .02 |
| ☐ 519 | Allen Pinkett | .04 | .01 |
| ☐ 520 | Pat Beach | .04 | .01 |
| ☐ 521 | Eugene Daniel | .04 | .01 |
| ☐ 522 | Kevin Call | .04 | .01 |
| ☐ 523 | Ray Donaldson | .04 | .01 |
| ☐ 524 | Jeff Herrod RC | .04 | .01 |
| ☐ 525 | Keith Taylor | .04 | .01 |
| ☐ 526 | Jack Trudeau | .04 | .01 |
| ☐ 527 | Deron Cherry | .04 | .01 |
| ☐ 528 | Jeff Donaldson | .04 | .01 |
| ☐ 529 | Albert Lewis | .04 | .01 |
| ☐ 530 | Pete Mandley | .04 | .01 |
| ☐ 531 | Chris Martin RC | .04 | .01 |
| ☐ 532 | Christian Okoye | .04 | .01 |
| ☐ 533 | Steve Pelluer | .04 | .01 |
| ☐ 534 | Kevin Ross | .04 | .01 |
| ☐ 535 | Dan Saleaumua | .04 | .01 |
| ☐ 536 | Derrick Thomas | .25 | .08 |
| ☐ 537 | Mike Webster | .10 | .02 |
| ☐ 538 | Marcus Allen | .25 | .08 |
| ☐ 539 | Greg Bell | .04 | .01 |
| ☐ 540 | Thomas Benson | .04 | .01 |
| ☐ 541 | Ron Brown | .04 | .01 |
| ☐ 542 | Scott Davis | .04 | .01 |
| ☐ 543 | Riki Ellison | .04 | .01 |
| ☐ 544 | Jamie Holland | .04 | .01 |
| ☐ 545 | Howie Long | .25 | .08 |
| ☐ 546 | Terry Mcdaniel | .04 | .01 |
| ☐ 547 | Max Montoya | .04 | .01 |
| ☐ 548 | Jay Schroeder | .04 | .01 |
| ☐ 549 | Lionel Washington | .04 | .01 |
| ☐ 550 | Robert Delpino FPSC | .04 | .01 |
| ☐ 551 | Bobby Humphery | .04 | .01 |
| ☐ 552 | Mike Lansford | .04 | .01 |
| ☐ 553 | Michael Stewart RC | .04 | .01 |
| ☐ 554 | Doug Smith | .04 | .01 |
| ☐ 555 | Curt Warner | .04 | .01 |
| ☐ 556 | Alvin Wright RC | .04 | .01 |
| ☐ 557 | Jeff Cross | .04 | .01 |
| ☐ 558 | Jeff Dellenbach RC | .04 | .01 |
| ☐ 559 | Mark Duper | .10 | .02 |
| ☐ 560 | Ferrell Edmunds | .04 | .01 |
| ☐ 561 | Tim McKyer | .04 | .01 |
| ☐ 562 | John Offerdahl | .04 | .01 |
| ☐ 563 | Reggie Roby | .04 | .01 |
| ☐ 564 | Pete Stoyanovich | .04 | .01 |
| ☐ 565 | Alfred Anderson | .04 | .01 |
| ☐ 566 | Ray Berry | .04 | .01 |
| ☐ 567 | Rick Fenney | .04 | .01 |
| ☐ 568 | Rich Gannon RC | 1.50 | .60 |
| ☐ 569 | Tim Irwin | .04 | .01 |
| ☐ 570 | Hassan Jones | .04 | .01 |
| ☐ 571 | Cris Carter | .50 | .20 |
| ☐ 572 | Kirk Lowdermilk | .04 | .01 |
| ☐ 573 | Reggie Rutland RC | .04 | .01 |
| ☐ 574 | Ken Stills | .04 | .01 |
| ☐ 575 | Bruce Armstrong | .04 | .01 |
| ☐ 576 | Irving Fryar | .10 | .02 |
| ☐ 577 | Roland James | .04 | .01 |
| ☐ 578 | Robert Perryman | .04 | .01 |
| ☐ 579 | Cedric Jones | .04 | .01 |
| ☐ 580 | Steve Grogan | .10 | .02 |
| ☐ 581 | Johnny Rembert | .04 | .01 |
| ☐ 582 | Ed Reynolds | .04 | .01 |
| ☐ 583 | Brent Williams | .04 | .01 |
| ☐ 584 | Marc Wilson | .04 | .01 |
| ☐ 585 | Hoby Brenner | .04 | .01 |
| ☐ 586 | Stan Brock | .04 | .01 |
| ☐ 587 | Jim Dombrowski RC | .04 | .01 |
| ☐ 588 | Joel Hilgenberg RC | .04 | .01 |
| ☐ 589 | Robert Massey | .04 | .01 |
| ☐ 590 | Floyd Turner FPSC | .04 | .01 |
| ☐ 591 | Ottis Anderson | .10 | .02 |
| ☐ 592 | Mark Bavaro | .04 | .01 |
| ☐ 593 | Maurice Carthon | .04 | .01 |
| ☐ 594 | Eric Dorsey RC | .04 | .01 |
| ☐ 595 | Myron Guyton | .04 | .01 |
| ☐ 596 | Jeff Hostetler RC | .25 | .08 |
| ☐ 597 | Sean Landeta | .04 | .01 |
| ☐ 598 | Lionel Manuel | .04 | .01 |
| ☐ 599 | Odessa Turner RC | .04 | .01 |
| ☐ 600 | Perry Williams | .04 | .01 |
| ☐ 601 | James Hasty | .04 | .01 |
| ☐ 602 | Erik McMillan | .04 | .01 |
| ☐ 603 | Alex Gordon UER | .04 | .01 |
| ☐ 604 | Ron Stallworth | .04 | .01 |
| ☐ 605 | Byron Evans RC | .04 | .01 |
| ☐ 606 | Ron Heller RC OT | .04 | .01 |
| ☐ 607 | Wes Hopkins | .04 | .01 |
| ☐ 608 | Mickey Shuler UER | .04 | .01 |
| ☐ 609 | Seth Joyner | .10 | .02 |
| ☐ 610 | Jim McMahon | .10 | .02 |
| ☐ 611 | Mike Pitts | .04 | .01 |
| ☐ 612 | Izel Jenkins RC | .04 | .01 |
| ☐ 613 | Anthony Bell | .04 | .01 |
| ☐ 614 | David Galloway | .04 | .01 |
| ☐ 615 | Eric Hill | .04 | .01 |
| ☐ 616 | Cedric Mack | .04 | .01 |
| ☐ 617 | Freddie Joe Nunn | .04 | .01 |
| ☐ 618 | Tootie Robbins | .04 | .01 |
| ☐ 619 | Tom Tupa RC | .04 | .01 |
| ☐ 620 | Joe Wolf | .04 | .01 |
| ☐ 621 | Dermontti Dawson | .10 | .02 |
| ☐ 622 | Thomas Everett | .04 | .01 |
| ☐ 623 | Tunch Ilkin | .04 | .01 |
| ☐ 624 | Hardy Nickerson | .10 | .02 |
| ☐ 625 | Gerald Williams RC | .04 | .01 |
| ☐ 626 | Rod Woodson | .25 | .08 |
| ☐ 627A | Rod Bernstine TE | .50 | .20 |
| ☐ 627B | Rod Bernstine RB | .04 | .01 |
| ☐ 628 | Courtney Hall | .04 | .01 |
| ☐ 629 | Ronnie Harmon | .10 | .02 |
| ☐ 630A | Anthony Miller WR | .25 | .08 |
| ☐ 630B | Anthony Miller WR-KR | .10 | .02 |
| ☐ 631 | Joe Phillips | .04 | .01 |
| ☐ 632A | Leslie O'Neal LB | .15 | .05 |
| ☐ 632B | Leslie O'Neal COR | .04 | .01 |
| ☐ 633A | David Richards RC G-T | .15 | .05 |
| ☐ 633B | David Richards RC G | .15 | .05 |
| ☐ 634 | Mark Vlasic FPSC | .04 | .01 |
| ☐ 635 | Lee Williams | .04 | .01 |
| ☐ 636 | Chet Brooks | .04 | .01 |
| ☐ 637 | Keena Turner | .04 | .01 |
| ☐ 638 | Kevin Fagan RC | .04 | .01 |
| ☐ 639 | Brent Jones RC | .25 | .08 |
| ☐ 640 | Matt Millen | .10 | .02 |

| | | |
|---|---|---|
| ❑ 641 Bubba Paris | .04 | .01 |
| ❑ 642 Bill Romanowski RC | 1.00 | .40 |
| ❑ 643 Fred Smerlas UER | .04 | .01 |
| ❑ 644 Dave Waymer | .04 | .01 |
| ❑ 645 Steve Young | .50 | .20 |
| ❑ 646 Brian Blades | .10 | .02 |
| ❑ 647 Andy Heck | .04 | .01 |
| ❑ 648 Dave Krieg | .10 | .02 |
| ❑ 649 Rufus Porter | .04 | .01 |
| ❑ 650 Kelly Stouffer | .04 | .01 |
| ❑ 651 Tony Woods | .04 | .01 |
| ❑ 652 Gary Anderson RB | .04 | .01 |
| ❑ 653 Reuben Davis | .04 | .01 |
| ❑ 654 Randy Grimes | .04 | .01 |
| ❑ 655 Ron Hall | .04 | .01 |
| ❑ 656 Eugene Marve | .04 | .01 |
| ❑ 657A Curt Jarvis ERR | .50 | .20 |
| ❑ 657B Curt Jarvis COR | 10.00 | 4.00 |
| ❑ 658 Ricky Reynolds | .04 | .01 |
| ❑ 659 Broderick Thomas | .04 | .01 |
| ❑ 660 Jeff Bostic | .04 | .01 |
| ❑ 661 Todd Bowles RC | .04 | .01 |
| ❑ 662 Ravin Caldwell | .04 | .01 |
| ❑ 663 Russ Grimm UER | .04 | .01 |
| ❑ 664 Joe Jacoby | .04 | .01 |
| ❑ 665 Mark May | .04 | .01 |
| ❑ 666 Walter Stanley | .04 | .01 |
| ❑ 667 Don Warren | .04 | .01 |
| ❑ 668 Stan Humphries RC | .25 | .08 |
| ❑ 669A Jeff George Illinois SP | 1.00 | .40 |
| ❑ 669B Jeff George RC | .50 | .20 |
| ❑ 670 Blair Thomas RC | .10 | .02 |
| ❑ 671 Cortez Kennedy RC UER | .25 | .08 |
| ❑ 672 Keith McCants RC | .04 | .01 |
| ❑ 673 Junior Seau RC | 1.25 | .50 |
| ❑ 674 Mark Carrier RC DB | .25 | .08 |
| ❑ 675 Andre Ware | .10 | .02 |
| ❑ 676 Chris Singleton RC UER | .04 | .01 |
| ❑ 677 Richmond Webb RC | .04 | .01 |
| ❑ 678 Ray Agnew RC | .04 | .01 |
| ❑ 679 Anthony Smith RC | .04 | .01 |
| ❑ 680 James Francis RC | .04 | .01 |
| ❑ 681 Percy Snow | .04 | .01 |
| ❑ 682 Renaldo Turnbull RC | .04 | .01 |
| ❑ 683 Lamar Lathon RC | .10 | .02 |
| ❑ 684 James Williams DB RC | .04 | .01 |
| ❑ 685 Emmitt Smith RC | 5.00 | 2.00 |
| ❑ 686 Tony Bennett RC | .25 | .08 |
| ❑ 687 Darrell Thompson RC | .04 | .01 |
| ❑ 688 Steve Broussard RC | .04 | .01 |
| ❑ 689 Eric Green RC | .10 | .02 |
| ❑ 690 Ben Smith RC | .04 | .01 |
| ❑ 691 Bern Brostek RC UER | .04 | .01 |
| ❑ 692 Rodney Hampton RC | .25 | .08 |
| ❑ 693 Dexter Carter RC | .04 | .01 |
| ❑ 694 Rob Moore RC | .50 | .20 |
| ❑ 695 Alexander Wright RC | .04 | .01 |
| ❑ 696 Darion Conner RC | .10 | .02 |
| ❑ 697 Reggie Rembert RC UER | .04 | .01 |
| ❑ 698A Terry Wooden RC 90 | .50 | .20 |
| ❑ 698B Terry Wooden RC 51 | .20 | .07 |
| ❑ 699 Reggie Cobb RC | .10 | .02 |
| ❑ 700 Anthony Thompson | .04 | .01 |
| ❑ 701 Fred Washington RC | .04 | .01 |
| ❑ 702 Ron Cox RC | .04 | .01 |
| ❑ 703 Robert Blackmon RC | .04 | .01 |
| ❑ 704 Dan Owens RC | .04 | .01 |
| ❑ 705 Anthony Johnson RC | .25 | .08 |
| ❑ 706 Aaron Wallace RC | .04 | .01 |
| ❑ 707 Harold Green RC | .25 | .08 |
| ❑ 708 Keith Sims RC | .04 | .01 |
| ❑ 709 Tim Grunhard RC | .04 | .01 |
| ❑ 710 Jeff Alm RC | .04 | .01 |
| ❑ 711 Carwell Gardner RC | .04 | .01 |
| ❑ 712 Kenny Davidson RC | .04 | .01 |
| ❑ 713 Vince Buck RC | .04 | .01 |
| ❑ 714 Leroy Hoard RC | .25 | .08 |
| ❑ 715 Andre Collins RC | .10 | .02 |
| ❑ 716 Dennis Brown RC | .04 | .01 |
| ❑ 717 LeRoy Butler RC | .25 | .08 |
| ❑ 718A Pat Terrell RC 41 | .50 | .20 |
| ❑ 718B Pat Terrell RC 37 | .20 | .07 |
| ❑ 719 Mike Bellamy RC | .04 | .01 |
| ❑ 720 Mike Fox RC | .04 | .01 |
| ❑ 721 Alton Montgomery RC | .04 | .01 |

| | | |
|---|---|---|
| ❑ 722 Eric Davis RC | .10 | .02 |
| ❑ 723A Oliver Barnett RC DT | .50 | .20 |
| ❑ 723B Oliver Barnett RC NT | .04 | .01 |
| ❑ 724 Houston Hoover RC | .04 | .01 |
| ❑ 725 Howard Ballard RC | .04 | .01 |
| ❑ 726 Keith McKeller RC | .04 | .01 |
| ❑ 727 Wendell Davis RC | .04 | .01 |
| ❑ 728 Peter Tom Willis RC | .04 | .01 |
| ❑ 729 Brent Clark RC | .04 | .01 |
| ❑ 730 Doug Widell RC | .04 | .01 |
| ❑ 731 Eric Andolsek | .04 | .01 |
| ❑ 732 Jeff Campbell RC | .04 | .01 |
| ❑ 733 Marc Spindler RC | .04 | .01 |
| ❑ 734 Keith Woodside | .04 | .01 |
| ❑ 735 Willis Peguese RC | .04 | .01 |
| ❑ 736 Frank Stams | .04 | .01 |
| ❑ 737 Jeff Uhlenhake | .04 | .01 |
| ❑ 738 Todd Kalis | .04 | .01 |
| ❑ 739 Tommy Hodson RC UER | .04 | .01 |
| ❑ 740 Greg McMurtry RC | .04 | .01 |
| ❑ 741 Mike Buck RC | .04 | .01 |
| ❑ 742 Mark Hawerdink UER | .04 | .01 |
| ❑ 743A Johnny Bailey RC 46 | .10 | .02 |
| ❑ 743B Johnny Bailey RC 22 | .10 | .02 |
| ❑ 744A Eric Moore | .15 | .05 |
| ❑ 744B Eric Moore | 10.00 | 4.00 |
| ❑ 745 Tony Stargell RC | .04 | .01 |
| ❑ 746 Fred Barnett RC | .25 | .08 |
| ❑ 747 Walter Reeves | .04 | .01 |
| ❑ 748 Derek Hill | .04 | .01 |
| ❑ 749 Quinn Early | .25 | .08 |
| ❑ 750 Ronald Lewis | .04 | .01 |
| ❑ 751 Ken Clark RC | .04 | .01 |
| ❑ 752 Garry Lewis RC | .04 | .01 |
| ❑ 753 James Lofton | .10 | .02 |
| ❑ 754 Steve Tasker UER | .25 | .08 |
| ❑ 755 Jim Shofner CO | .04 | .01 |
| ❑ 756 Jimmie Jones RC | .04 | .01 |
| ❑ 757 Jay Novacek | .25 | .08 |
| ❑ 758 Jessie Hester RC | .04 | .01 |
| ❑ 759 Barry Word RC | .04 | .01 |
| ❑ 760 Eddie Anderson RC | .04 | .01 |
| ❑ 761 Cleveland Gary | .04 | .01 |
| ❑ 762 Maurice Dupree RC | .04 | .01 |
| ❑ 763 David Griggs RC | .04 | .01 |
| ❑ 764 Rueben Mayes | .04 | .01 |
| ❑ 765 Stephen Baker FPSC | .04 | .01 |
| ❑ 766 Reyna Thompson RC UER | .04 | .01 |
| ❑ 767 Everson Walls | .04 | .01 |
| ❑ 768 Brad Baxter RC | .04 | .01 |
| ❑ 769 Steve Walsh | .10 | .02 |
| ❑ 770 Heath Sherman RC | .04 | .01 |
| ❑ 771 Johnny Johnson RC | .10 | .02 |
| ❑ 772A Dexter Manley ERR | 300.00 | 150.00 |
| ❑ 772B Dexter Manley RC | .25 | .08 |
| ❑ 773 Ricky Proehl RC | .25 | .08 |
| ❑ 774 Frank Cornish | .04 | .01 |
| ❑ 775 Tommy Kane RC | .04 | .01 |
| ❑ 776 Derrick Fenner RC | .04 | .01 |
| ❑ 777 Steve Christie RC | .04 | .01 |
| ❑ 778 Wayne Haddix RC | .04 | .01 |
| ❑ 779 Richard Williamson UER | .04 | .01 |
| ❑ 780 Brian Mitchell RC | .25 | .08 |
| ❑ 781 American Bowl/London | .04 | .01 |
| ❑ 782 American Bowl/Berlin | .04 | .01 |
| ❑ 783 American Bowl/Tokyo | .04 | .01 |
| ❑ 784 American Bowl/Montreal | .04 | .01 |
| ❑ 785A Berlin Wall | .75 | .30 |
| ❑ 785B Berlin Wall | .75 | .30 |
| ❑ 786 Al Davis NEWS | .04 | .01 |
| ❑ 787 Falcons Back in Black | .04 | .01 |
| ❑ 788 NFL Goes International | .04 | .01 |
| ❑ 789 Overseas Appeal | .04 | .01 |
| ❑ 790 Photo Contest | .04 | .01 |
| ❑ 791 Photo Contest | .04 | .01 |
| ❑ 792 Photo Contest | .04 | .01 |
| ❑ 793 Photo Contest | .04 | .01 |
| ❑ 794 Barry Sanders PHOTO | .50 | .20 |
| ❑ 795 Photo Contest | .04 | .01 |
| ❑ 796 Photo Contest | .04 | .01 |
| ❑ 797 Photo Contest | .04 | .01 |
| ❑ 798 Cris Carter PC | .04 | .01 |
| ❑ 799 Ronnie Lott School | .10 | .02 |
| ❑ 800D Mark Carrier DB D-ROY | .04 | .01 |
| ❑ 800O Emmitt Smith O-ROY | 1.50 | .60 |

| | | |
|---|---|---|
| ❑ 1990 Santa Claus SP | .50 | .20 |
| ❑ CC2 Paul Tagliabue SP | .40 | .15 |
| ❑ CC3 Joe Robbie Mem SP | .50 | .20 |
| ❑ SC Super Pro SP | .50 | .20 |
| ❑ SC4 Fred Washington UER | .04 | .01 |
| ❑ SP1 Payne Stewart SP | 1.00 | .40 |
| ❑ NNO Lombardi HOLO/10000* | 60.00 | 25.00 |
| ❑ NNO Super Bowl XXIV Logo | | .04 | .01 |

# 1991 Pro Set

MICHAEL IRVIN • WIDE RECEIVER
DALLAS COWBOYS

| | | |
|---|---|---|
| ❑ COMPLETE SET (850) | 35.00 | 15.00 |
| ❑ COMP.SERIES 1 (405) | 15.00 | 6.00 |
| ❑ COMP.SERIES 2 (407) | 15.00 | 6.00 |
| ❑ COMP.FINAL FACT. (38) | 5.00 | 2.00 |
| ❑ 1 D Mark Carrier DB D-ROY | .10 | .02 |
| ❑ 1 O Emmitt Smith O-ROY | 1.25 | .50 |
| ❑ 3 Joe Montana POY | .50 | .20 |
| ❑ 4 Art Shell | .10 | .02 |
| ❑ 5 Mike Singletary | .10 | .02 |
| ❑ 6 Bruce Smith | .10 | .02 |
| ❑ 7 Barry Word Comeback | .05 | .01 |
| ❑ 8A Jim Kelly LL w/LOGO | .25 | .08 |
| ❑ 8B Jim Kelly LL NO LOGO | .25 | .08 |
| ❑ 8C Jim Kelly LL Reg NO LOGO | 6.00 | 3.00 |
| ❑ 9 Warren Moon LL | .10 | .02 |
| ❑ 10 Barry Sanders LL | .50 | .20 |
| ❑ 11 Jerry Rice LL | .40 | .15 |
| ❑ 12 Jay Novacek LL | .10 | .02 |
| ❑ 13 Thurman Thomas LL | .10 | .02 |
| ❑ 14 Nick Lowery LL | .05 | .01 |
| ❑ 15 Mike Horan | .05 | .01 |
| ❑ 16 Clarence Verdin | .05 | .01 |
| ❑ 17 Kevin Clark LL RC | .05 | .01 |
| ❑ 18 Mark Carrier DB LL | .10 | .02 |
| ❑ 19A Derrick Thomas LL Bills | 20.00 | 7.50 |
| ❑ 19B Derrick Thomas LL COR | .10 | .02 |
| ❑ 20 Ottis Anderson ML | .10 | .02 |
| ❑ 21 Roger Craig ML | .10 | .02 |
| ❑ 22 Art Monk ML | .10 | .02 |
| ❑ 23 Chuck Noll ML | .10 | .02 |
| ❑ 24 Randall Cunningham ML | .10 | .02 |
| ❑ 25 Dan Marino ML | .50 | .20 |
| ❑ 26 49ers Road Record ML | .05 | .01 |
| ❑ 27 Earl Campbell HOF | .05 | .01 |
| ❑ 28 John Hannah HOF | .05 | .01 |
| ❑ 29 Stan Jones HOF | .05 | .01 |
| ❑ 30 Tex Schramm HOF | .05 | .01 |
| ❑ 31 Jan Stenerud HOF | .05 | .01 |
| ❑ 32 Russell Maryland RC TW | .10 | .02 |
| ❑ 33 Chris Zorich RC TW | .10 | .02 |
| ❑ 34 Darryll Lewis RC Thorpe | .10 | .02 |
| ❑ 35 Alfred Williams RC TW | .10 | .02 |
| ❑ 36 Rocket Ismail RC TW | 1.00 | .40 |
| ❑ 37 Ty Detmer RC HH | .40 | .15 |
| ❑ 38 Andre Ware Heisman | .10 | .02 |
| ❑ 39 Barry Sanders HH | .50 | .20 |
| ❑ 40 Tim Brown HH | .10 | .02 |
| ❑ 41 Vinny Testaverde HH | .10 | .02 |
| ❑ 42 Bo Jackson HH | .30 | .10 |
| ❑ 43 Mike Rozier HH | .05 | .01 |
| ❑ 44 Herschel Walker HH | .10 | .02 |
| ❑ 45 Marcus Allen HH | .10 | .02 |
| ❑ 46A James Lofton SB | .10 | .02 |
| ❑ 46B James Lofton SB | .10 | .02 |
| ❑ 47A Bruce Smith SB black ink | .10 | .02 |
| ❑ 47B Bruce Smith SB white ink | .10 | .02 |
| ❑ 48 Myron Guyton SB | .05 | .01 |
| ❑ 49 Stephen Baker SB | .05 | .01 |

| Card | Price | Price |
|---|---|---|
| ☐ 50 Mark Ingram SB UER | .05 | .01 |
| ☐ 51 Ottis Anderson SB | .10 | .02 |
| ☐ 52 Thurman Thomas SB | .25 | .08 |
| ☐ 53 Matt Bahr SB | .05 | .01 |
| ☐ 54 Scott Norwood SB | .05 | .01 |
| ☐ 55 Stephen Baker | .05 | .01 |
| ☐ 56 Carl Banks | .05 | .01 |
| ☐ 57 Mark Collins | .05 | .01 |
| ☐ 58 Steve DeOssie | .05 | .01 |
| ☐ 59 Eric Dorsey | .05 | .01 |
| ☐ 60 John Elliott | .05 | .01 |
| ☐ 61 Myron Guyton | .05 | .01 |
| ☐ 62 Rodney Hampton | .25 | .08 |
| ☐ 63 Jeff Hostetler | .10 | .02 |
| ☐ 64 Erik Howard | .05 | .01 |
| ☐ 65 Mark Ingram | .10 | .02 |
| ☐ 66 Greg Jackson RC | .05 | .01 |
| ☐ 67 Leonard Marshall | .05 | .01 |
| ☐ 68 Dave Meggett | .10 | .02 |
| ☐ 69 Eric Moore | .05 | .01 |
| ☐ 70 Bart Oates | .05 | .01 |
| ☐ 71 Gary Reasons | .05 | .01 |
| ☐ 72 Bill Parcells CO | .10 | .02 |
| ☐ 73 Howard Ballard | .05 | .01 |
| ☐ 74A Corn.Bennett w/LOGO | .25 | .08 |
| ☐ 74B Corn.Bennett NO LOGO | .05 | .01 |
| ☐ 75 Shane Conlan | .05 | .01 |
| ☐ 76 Kent Hull | .05 | .01 |
| ☐ 77 Kirby Jackson RC | .05 | .01 |
| ☐ 78A Jim Kelly w/LOGO | .60 | .25 |
| ☐ 78B Jim Kelly NO LOGO | .25 | .08 |
| ☐ 79 Mark Kelso | .05 | .01 |
| ☐ 80 Nate Odomes | .05 | .01 |
| ☐ 81 Andre Reed | .10 | .02 |
| ☐ 82 Jim Ritcher | .05 | .01 |
| ☐ 83 Bruce Smith | .25 | .08 |
| ☐ 84 Darryl Talley | .05 | .01 |
| ☐ 85 Steve Tasker | .10 | .02 |
| ☐ 86 Thurman Thomas | .25 | .08 |
| ☐ 87 James Williams | .05 | .01 |
| ☐ 88 Will Wolford | .05 | .01 |
| ☐ 89 Jeff Wright RC UER | .05 | .01 |
| ☐ 90 Marv Levy CO | .05 | .01 |
| ☐ 91 Steve Broussard | .05 | .01 |
| ☐ 92A Darion Conner ERR '99 | 10.00 | 4.00 |
| ☐ 92B Darion Conner COR | .25 | .08 |
| ☐ 93 Bill Fralic | .05 | .01 |
| ☐ 94 Tim Green | .05 | .01 |
| ☐ 95 Michael Haynes | .25 | .08 |
| ☐ 96 Chris Hinton | .05 | .01 |
| ☐ 97 Chris Miller UER | .10 | .02 |
| ☐ 98 Deion Sanders UER | .40 | .15 |
| ☐ 99 Jerry Glanville CO | .05 | .01 |
| ☐ 100 Kevin Butler | .05 | .01 |
| ☐ 101 Mark Carrier DB | .10 | .02 |
| ☐ 102 Jim Covert | .05 | .01 |
| ☐ 103 Richard Dent | .10 | .02 |
| ☐ 104 Jim Harbaugh | .25 | .08 |
| ☐ 105 Brad Muster | .05 | .01 |
| ☐ 106 Lemuel Stinson | .05 | .01 |
| ☐ 107 Keith Van Horne | .05 | .01 |
| ☐ 108 Mike Ditka CO UER | .25 | .08 |
| ☐ 109 Lewis Billups | .05 | .01 |
| ☐ 110 James Brooks | .10 | .02 |
| ☐ 111 Boomer Esiason | .10 | .02 |
| ☐ 112 James Francis | .05 | .01 |
| ☐ 113 David Fulcher | .05 | .01 |
| ☐ 114 Rodney Holman | .05 | .01 |
| ☐ 115 Tim McGee | .05 | .01 |
| ☐ 116 Anthony Munoz | .10 | .02 |
| ☐ 117 Sam Wyche | .05 | .01 |
| ☐ 118 Paul Farren | .05 | .01 |
| ☐ 119 Thane Gash | .05 | .01 |
| ☐ 120 Mike Johnson | .05 | .01 |
| ☐ 121A Bernie Kosar w/LOGO | .10 | .02 |
| ☐ 121B Bernie Kosar NO LOGO | .10 | .02 |
| ☐ 122 Clay Matthews | .05 | .01 |
| ☐ 123 Eric Metcalf | .10 | .02 |
| ☐ 124 Frank Minnifield | .05 | .01 |
| ☐ 125A Webster Slaughter | .10 | .02 |
| ☐ 125B Webster Slaughter | .10 | .02 |
| ☐ 126 Bill Belichick CO RC | 1.50 | .60 |
| ☐ 127 Tommie Agee | .05 | .01 |
| ☐ 128 Troy Aikman | .75 | .30 |
| ☐ 129 Jack Del Rio | .10 | .02 |
| ☐ 130 John Gesek RC | .05 | .01 |
| ☐ 131 Issiac Holt | .05 | .01 |
| ☐ 132 Michael Irvin | .25 | .08 |
| ☐ 133 Ken Norton | .10 | .02 |
| ☐ 134 Daniel Stubbs | .05 | .01 |
| ☐ 135 Jimmy Johnson CO | .10 | .02 |
| ☐ 136 Steve Atwater | .05 | .01 |
| ☐ 137 Michael Brooks | .05 | .01 |
| ☐ 138 John Elway | 1.25 | .50 |
| ☐ 139 Wymon Henderson | .05 | .01 |
| ☐ 140 Bobby Humphrey | .05 | .01 |
| ☐ 141 Mark Jackson | .05 | .01 |
| ☐ 142 Karl Mecklenburg | .05 | .01 |
| ☐ 143 Doug Widell | .05 | .01 |
| ☐ 144 Dan Reeves CO | .05 | .01 |
| ☐ 145 Eric Andolsek | .05 | .01 |
| ☐ 146 Jerry Ball | .05 | .01 |
| ☐ 147 Bennie Blades | .05 | .01 |
| ☐ 148 Lomas Brown | .05 | .01 |
| ☐ 149 Robert Clark | .05 | .01 |
| ☐ 150 Michael Cofer | .05 | .01 |
| ☐ 151 Dan Owens | .05 | .01 |
| ☐ 152 Rodney Peete | .05 | .02 |
| ☐ 153 Wayne Fontes CO | .05 | .01 |
| ☐ 154 Tim Harris | .05 | .01 |
| ☐ 155 Johnny Holland | .05 | .01 |
| ☐ 156 Don Majkowski | .05 | .01 |
| ☐ 157 Tony Mandarich | .05 | .01 |
| ☐ 158 Mark Murphy | .05 | .01 |
| ☐ 159 Brian Noble | .05 | .01 |
| ☐ 160 Jeff Query | .05 | .01 |
| ☐ 161 Sterling Sharpe | .25 | .08 |
| ☐ 162 Lindy Infante CO | .05 | .01 |
| ☐ 163 Ray Childress | .05 | .01 |
| ☐ 164 Ernest Givins | .10 | .02 |
| ☐ 165 Richard Johnson CB | .05 | .01 |
| ☐ 166 Bruce Matthews | .10 | .02 |
| ☐ 167 Warren Moon | .25 | .08 |
| ☐ 168 Mike Munchak | .05 | .01 |
| ☐ 169 Al Smith | .05 | .01 |
| ☐ 170 Lorenzo White | .05 | .01 |
| ☐ 171 Jack Pardee CO | .05 | .01 |
| ☐ 172 Albert Bentley | .05 | .01 |
| ☐ 173 Duane Bickett | .05 | .01 |
| ☐ 174 Bill Brooks | .05 | .01 |
| ☐ 175A E.Dickerson w/LOGO | .40 | .15 |
| ☐ 175B E.Dickerson NO LOGO 667 | 1.25 | .50 |
| ☐ 175C E.Dickerson NO LOGO 677 | .25 | .08 |
| ☐ 176 Ray Donaldson | .05 | .01 |
| ☐ 177 Jeff George | .25 | .08 |
| ☐ 178 Jeff Herrod | .05 | .01 |
| ☐ 179 Clarence Verdin | .05 | .01 |
| ☐ 180 Ron Meyer CO | .05 | .01 |
| ☐ 181 John Alt | .05 | .01 |
| ☐ 182 Steve DeBerg | .05 | .01 |
| ☐ 183 Albert Lewis | .05 | .01 |
| ☐ 184 Nick Lowery UER | .05 | .01 |
| ☐ 185 Christian Okoye | .05 | .01 |
| ☐ 186 Stephone Paige | .05 | .01 |
| ☐ 187 Kevin Porter | .05 | .01 |
| ☐ 188 Derrick Thomas | .25 | .08 |
| ☐ 189 Marty Schottenheimer CO | .05 | .01 |
| ☐ 190 Willie Gault | .10 | .02 |
| ☐ 191 Howie Long | .25 | .08 |
| ☐ 192 Terry McDaniel | .05 | .01 |
| ☐ 193 Jay Schroeder UER | .05 | .01 |
| ☐ 194 Steve Smith | .05 | .01 |
| ☐ 195 Greg Townsend | .05 | .01 |
| ☐ 196 Lionel Washington | .05 | .01 |
| ☐ 197 Steve Wisniewski UER | .05 | .01 |
| ☐ 198 Art Shell CO | .10 | .02 |
| ☐ 199 Henry Ellard | .10 | .02 |
| ☐ 200 Jim Everett | .10 | .02 |
| ☐ 201 Jerry Gray | .05 | .01 |
| ☐ 202 Kevin Greene | .10 | .02 |
| ☐ 203 Buford McGee | .05 | .01 |
| ☐ 204 Tom Newberry | .05 | .01 |
| ☐ 205 Frank Stams | .05 | .01 |
| ☐ 206 Alvin Wright | .05 | .01 |
| ☐ 207 John Robinson CO | .05 | .01 |
| ☐ 208 Jeff Cross | .05 | .01 |
| ☐ 209 Mark Duper | .10 | .02 |
| ☐ 210 Dan Marino | 1.25 | .50 |
| ☐ 211A Tim McKyer | .10 | .02 |
| ☐ 211B Tim McKyer TR | .25 | .08 |
| ☐ 212 John Offerdahl | .05 | .01 |
| ☐ 213 Sammie Smith | .05 | .01 |
| ☐ 214 Richmond Webb | .05 | .01 |
| ☐ 215 Jarvis Williams | .05 | .01 |
| ☐ 216 Don Shula CO | .10 | .02 |
| ☐ 217A D.Fulington ERR | .10 | .02 |
| ☐ 217B D.Fulington COR | .10 | .02 |
| ☐ 218 Tim Irwin | .05 | .01 |
| ☐ 219 Mike Merriweather | .05 | .01 |
| ☐ 220 Keith Millard | .05 | .01 |
| ☐ 221 Al Noga | .05 | .01 |
| ☐ 222 Henry Thomas | .05 | .01 |
| ☐ 223 Wade Wilson | .10 | .02 |
| ☐ 224 Gary Zimmerman | .10 | .02 |
| ☐ 225 Jerry Burns CO | .05 | .01 |
| ☐ 226 Bruce Armstrong | .05 | .01 |
| ☐ 227 Marv Cook FPSC | .05 | .01 |
| ☐ 228 Hart Lee Dykes | .05 | .01 |
| ☐ 229 Tommy Hodson | .05 | .01 |
| ☐ 230 Ronnie Lippett | .05 | .01 |
| ☐ 231 Ed Reynolds | .05 | .01 |
| ☐ 232 Chris Singleton | .05 | .01 |
| ☐ 233 John Stephens | .05 | .01 |
| ☐ 234 Dick MacPherson CO | .05 | .01 |
| ☐ 235 Stan Brock | .05 | .01 |
| ☐ 236 Craig Heyward | .10 | .02 |
| ☐ 237 Vaughan Johnson | .05 | .01 |
| ☐ 238 Robert Massey | .05 | .01 |
| ☐ 239 Brett Maxie | .05 | .01 |
| ☐ 240 Rueben Mayes | .05 | .01 |
| ☐ 241 Pat Swilling | .10 | .02 |
| ☐ 242 Renaldo Turnbull | .05 | .01 |
| ☐ 243 Jim Mora CO | .05 | .01 |
| ☐ 244 Kyle Clifton | .05 | .01 |
| ☐ 245 Jeff Criswell | .05 | .01 |
| ☐ 246 James Hasty | .05 | .01 |
| ☐ 247 Erik McMillan | .05 | .01 |
| ☐ 248 Scott Mersereau RC | .05 | .01 |
| ☐ 249 Ken O'Brien | .05 | .01 |
| ☐ 250A Blair Thomas w/LOGO | .25 | .08 |
| ☐ 250B Blair Thomas NO LOGO | .10 | .02 |
| ☐ 251 Al Toon | .10 | .02 |
| ☐ 252 Bruce Coslet CO | .05 | .01 |
| ☐ 253 Eric Allen | .05 | .01 |
| ☐ 254 Fred Barnett | .25 | .08 |
| ☐ 255 Keith Byars | .05 | .01 |
| ☐ 256 Randall Cunningham | .25 | .08 |
| ☐ 257 Seth Joyner | .10 | .02 |
| ☐ 258 Clyde Simmons | .05 | .01 |
| ☐ 259 Jessie Small | .05 | .01 |
| ☐ 260 Andre Waters | .05 | .01 |
| ☐ 261 Rich Kotite CO | .05 | .01 |
| ☐ 262 Roy Green | .05 | .01 |
| ☐ 263 Ernie Jones | .05 | .01 |
| ☐ 264 Tim McDonald | .05 | .01 |
| ☐ 265 Timm Rosenbach | .05 | .01 |
| ☐ 266 Rod Saddler | .05 | .01 |
| ☐ 267 Luis Sharpe | .05 | .01 |
| ☐ 268 Anthony Thompson UER | .05 | .01 |
| ☐ 269 Marcus Turner RC | .05 | .01 |
| ☐ 270 Joe Bugel CO | .05 | .01 |
| ☐ 271 Gary Anderson K | .05 | .01 |
| ☐ 272 Dermontti Dawson | .05 | .01 |
| ☐ 273 Eric Green | .05 | .01 |
| ☐ 274 Merril Hoge | .05 | .01 |
| ☐ 275 Tunch Ilkin | .05 | .01 |
| ☐ 276 D.J. Johnson | .05 | .01 |
| ☐ 277 Louis Lipps | .05 | .01 |
| ☐ 278 Rod Woodson | .25 | .08 |
| ☐ 279 Chuck Noll CO | .10 | .02 |
| ☐ 280 Martin Bayless | .05 | .01 |
| ☐ 281 Marion Butts UER | .10 | .02 |
| ☐ 282 Gill Byrd | .05 | .01 |
| ☐ 283 Burt Grossman | .05 | .01 |
| ☐ 284 Courtney Hall | .05 | .01 |
| ☐ 285 Anthony Miller | .10 | .02 |
| ☐ 286 Leslie O'Neal | .05 | .01 |
| ☐ 287 Billy Joe Tolliver | .05 | .01 |
| ☐ 288 Dan Henning CO | .05 | .01 |
| ☐ 289 Dexter Carter | .05 | .01 |
| ☐ 290 Michael Carter | .05 | .01 |
| ☐ 291 Kevin Fagan | .05 | .01 |
| ☐ 292 Pierce Holt | .05 | .01 |
| ☐ 293 Guy McIntyre | .05 | .01 |
| ☐ 294 Tom Rathman | .05 | .01 |

|  | | |  | | |  | | |
|---|---|---|---|---|---|---|---|---|
| ❑ 295 John Taylor | .10 | .02 | ❑ 371A Boomer Esiason | .50 | .20 | ❑ 446 Jamie Mueller | .05 | .01 |
| ❑ 296 Steve Young | .75 | .30 | ❑ 371B Boomer Esiason | .10 | .02 | ❑ 447 Scott Norwood | .05 | .01 |
| ❑ 297 George Seifert CO | .10 | .02 | ❑ 372A Troy Aikman Str.ST | .40 | .15 | ❑ 448 Frank Reich | .10 | .02 |
| ❑ 298 Brian Blades | .10 | .02 | ❑ 372B Troy Aikman Str.LT | .40 | .15 | ❑ 449 Leon Seals | .05 | .01 |
| ❑ 299 Jeff Bryant | .05 | .01 | ❑ 373A Carl Banks | .50 | .20 | ❑ 450 Leonard Smith | .05 | .01 |
| ❑ 300 Norm Johnson | .05 | .01 | ❑ 373B Carl Banks | .05 | .01 | ❑ 451 Neal Anderson | .10 | .02 |
| ❑ 301 Tommy Kane | .05 | .01 | ❑ 374A Jim Everett | .50 | .20 | ❑ 452 Trace Armstrong | .05 | .01 |
| ❑ 302 Cortez Kennedy UER | .25 | .08 | ❑ 374B Jim Everett | .10 | .02 | ❑ 453 Mark Bortz | .05 | .01 |
| ❑ 303 Bryan Millard | .05 | .01 | ❑ 375A Anth.Munoz dificul | .10 | .02 | ❑ 454 Wendell Davis | .05 | .01 |
| ❑ 304 John L. Williams | .05 | .01 | ❑ 375B Anth.Munoz dificil | .10 | .02 | ❑ 455 Shaun Gayle | .05 | .01 |
| ❑ 305 David Wyman | .05 | .01 | ❑ 375C Anth.Munoz large type | .10 | .02 | ❑ 456 Jay Hilgenberg | .05 | .01 |
| ❑ 306A Chuck Knox CO w/LOGO | .05 | .01 | ❑ 375D Anth.Munoz Quedate | .10 | .02 | ❑ 457 Steve McMichael | .10 | .02 |
| ❑ 306B Chuck Knox CO NO LOGO | .50 | .20 | ❑ 376A Ray Childress | 1.25 | .50 | ❑ 458 Mike Singletary | .10 | .02 |
| ❑ 307 Gary Anderson RB | .05 | .01 | ❑ 376B Ray Childress | .05 | .01 | ❑ 459 Donnell Woolford | .05 | .01 |
| ❑ 308 Reggie Cobb | .05 | .01 | ❑ 377A Charles Mann | 1.25 | .50 | ❑ 460 Jim Breech | .05 | .01 |
| ❑ 309 Randy Grimes | .05 | .01 | ❑ 377B Charles Mann | .05 | .01 | ❑ 461 Eddie Brown | .05 | .01 |
| ❑ 310 Harry Hamilton | .05 | .01 | ❑ 378A Jackie Slater | 1.25 | .50 | ❑ 462 Barney Bussey RC | .05 | .01 |
| ❑ 311 Bruce Hill | .05 | .01 | ❑ 378B Jackie Slater | .05 | .01 | ❑ 463 Bruce Kozerski | .05 | .01 |
| ❑ 312 Eugene Marve | .05 | .01 | ❑ 379 Jerry Rice PB | .40 | .15 | ❑ 464 Tim Krumrie | .05 | .01 |
| ❑ 313 Ervin Randle | .05 | .01 | ❑ 380 Andre Rison PB | .10 | .02 | ❑ 465 Bruce Reimers | .05 | .01 |
| ❑ 314 Vinny Testaverde | .10 | .02 | ❑ 381 Jim Lachey NFC | .05 | .01 | ❑ 466 Kevin Walker RC | .05 | .01 |
| ❑ 315 Richard Williamson CO | .05 | .01 | ❑ 382 Jackie Slater NFC | .05 | .01 | ❑ 467 Ickey Woods | .05 | .01 |
| ❑ 316 Earnest Byner | .05 | .01 | ❑ 383 Randall McDaniel NFC | .10 | .02 | ❑ 468 Carl Zander UER | .05 | .01 |
| ❑ 317 Gary Clark | .25 | .08 | ❑ 384 Mark Bortz NFC | .05 | .01 | ❑ 469 Mike Baab | .05 | .01 |
| ❑ 318A Andre Collins | .10 | .02 | ❑ 385 Jay Hilgenberg NFC | .05 | .01 | ❑ 470 Brian Brennan | .05 | .01 |
| ❑ 318B Andre Collins | .10 | .02 | ❑ 386 Keith Jackson NFC | .05 | .01 | ❑ 471 Rob Burnett RC | .10 | .02 |
| ❑ 319 Darryl Grant | .05 | .01 | ❑ 387 Joe Montana PB | .50 | .20 | ❑ 472 Raymond Clayborn | .05 | .01 |
| ❑ 320 Chip Lohmiller | .05 | .01 | ❑ 388 Barry Sanders PB | .50 | .20 | ❑ 473 Reggie Langhorne | .05 | .01 |
| ❑ 321 Martin Mayhew | .05 | .01 | ❑ 389 Neal Anderson NFC | .10 | .02 | ❑ 474 Kevin Mack | .05 | .01 |
| ❑ 322 Mark Rypien | .10 | .02 | ❑ 390 Reggie White NFC | .25 | .08 | ❑ 475 Anthony Pleasant | .05 | .01 |
| ❑ 323 Alvin Walton | .05 | .01 | ❑ 391 Chris Doleman NFC | .05 | .01 | ❑ 476 Joe Morris | .05 | .01 |
| ❑ 324 Joe Gibbs CO UER | .10 | .02 | ❑ 392 Jerome Brown NFC | .05 | .01 | ❑ 477 Dan Fike | .05 | .01 |
| ❑ 325 Jerry Glanville REP | .05 | .01 | ❑ 393 Charles Haley NFC | .05 | .01 | ❑ 478 Ray Horton | .05 | .01 |
| ❑ 326A J.Elway REP LOGO | 4.00 | 2.00 | ❑ 394 Lawrence Taylor PB | .25 | .08 | ❑ 479 Jim Jeffcoat | .05 | .01 |
| ❑ 326B J.Elway REP NO LOGO | 2.00 | .75 | ❑ 395 Pepper Johnson NFC | .05 | .01 | ❑ 480 Jimmie Jones | .05 | .01 |
| ❑ 327 Boomer Esiason REP | .05 | .01 | ❑ 396 Mike Singletary NFC | .10 | .02 | ❑ 481 Kelvin Martin | .05 | .01 |
| ❑ 328A Steve Tasker REP | 4.00 | 2.00 | ❑ 397 Darrell Green NFC | .05 | .01 | ❑ 482 Nate Newton | .10 | .02 |
| ❑ 328B Steve Tasker REP | 2.00 | .75 | ❑ 398 Carl Lee NFC | .05 | .01 | ❑ 483 Danny Noonan | .05 | .01 |
| ❑ 329 Jerry Rice REP | .40 | .15 | ❑ 399 Joey Browner NFC | .05 | .01 | ❑ 484 Jay Novacek | .25 | .08 |
| ❑ 330 Jeff Rutledge REP | .05 | .01 | ❑ 400 Ronnie Lott NFC | .10 | .02 | ❑ 485 Emmitt Smith | 2.50 | 1.00 |
| ❑ 331 K.C. Defense REP | .05 | .01 | ❑ 401 Sean Landeta NFC | .05 | .01 | ❑ 486 James Washington RC | .05 | .01 |
| ❑ 332 49ers Streak REP | .05 | .01 | ❑ 402 Morten Andersen NFC | .05 | .01 | ❑ 487 Simon Fletcher | .05 | .01 |
| ❑ 333 Monday Meeting REP | .05 | .01 | ❑ 403 Mel Gray NFC | .05 | .01 | ❑ 488 Ron Holmes | .05 | .01 |
| ❑ 334A R.Cunningham w/LOGO | .05 | .01 | ❑ 404 Reyna Thompson NFC | .05 | .01 | ❑ 489 Mike Horan | .05 | .01 |
| ❑ 334B R.Cunningham NO LOGO | .05 | .01 | ❑ 405 Jimmy Johnson CO NFC | .10 | .02 | ❑ 490 Vance Johnson | .05 | .01 |
| ❑ 335A Bo/Barry REP w/LOGO | .50 | .20 | ❑ 406 Andre Reed AFC | .10 | .02 | ❑ 491 Keith Kartz | .05 | .01 |
| ❑ 335B Bo/Barry REP NO LOGO | .50 | .20 | ❑ 407 Anthony Miller AFC | .10 | .02 | ❑ 492 Greg Kragen | .05 | .01 |
| ❑ 336 Lawrence Taylor REP | .25 | .08 | ❑ 408 Anthony Munoz AFC | .10 | .02 | ❑ 493 Ken Lanier | .05 | .01 |
| ❑ 337 Warren Moon REP | .25 | .08 | ❑ 409 Bruce Armstrong AFC | .05 | .01 | ❑ 494 Warren Powers | .05 | .01 |
| ❑ 338 Alan Grant REP | .05 | .01 | ❑ 410 Bruce Matthews AFC | .05 | .01 | ❑ 495 Dennis Smith | .05 | .01 |
| ❑ 339 Todd McNair REP | .05 | .01 | ❑ 411 Mike Munchak AFC | .05 | .01 | ❑ 496 Jeff Campbell | .05 | .01 |
| ❑ 340A Miami Dolphins REP | .05 | .01 | ❑ 412 Kent Hull AFC | .05 | .01 | ❑ 497 Ken Dallafior | .05 | .01 |
| ❑ 340B Miami Dolphins REP | .05 | .01 | ❑ 413 Rodney Holman AFC | .05 | .01 | ❑ 498 Dennis Gibson | .05 | .01 |
| ❑ 341A Highest Scoring REP | 4.00 | 2.00 | ❑ 414 Warren Moon Thomas PB | .25 | .08 | ❑ 499 Kevin Glover | .05 | .01 |
| ❑ 341B Highest Scoring REP | 2.00 | .75 | ❑ 415 Thurman Thomas PB | .25 | .08 | ❑ 500 Mel Gray | .10 | .02 |
| ❑ 342 Matt Bahr REP | .05 | .01 | ❑ 416 Marion Butts AFC | .10 | .02 | ❑ 501 Eddie Murray | .05 | .01 |
| ❑ 343 Robert Tisch NEW | .05 | .01 | ❑ 417 Bruce Smith AFC | .10 | .02 | ❑ 502 Barry Sanders | 1.25 | .50 |
| ❑ 344 Sam Jankovich NEW | .05 | .01 | ❑ 418 Greg Townsend AFC | .05 | .01 | ❑ 503 Chris Spielman | .10 | .02 |
| ❑ 345 In-the-Grasp NEW | .05 | .01 | ❑ 419 Ray Childress AFC | .05 | .01 | ❑ 504 William White | .05 | .01 |
| ❑ 346 Bo Jackson NEW | .10 | .02 | ❑ 420 Derrick Thomas PB | .25 | .08 | ❑ 505 Matt Brock RC | .05 | .01 |
| ❑ 347 NFL T.eacher of the | .05 | .01 | ❑ 421 Leslie O'Neal AFC | .10 | .02 | ❑ 506 Robert Brown | .05 | .01 |
| ❑ 348 Ronnie Lott NEW | .10 | .02 | ❑ 422 John Offerdahl AFC | .05 | .01 | ❑ 507 LeRoy Butler | .10 | .02 |
| ❑ 349 Super Bowl XXV | .10 | .02 | ❑ 423 Shane Conlan AFC | .05 | .01 | ❑ 508 James Campen RC | .05 | .01 |
| ❑ 350 Whitney Houston RC NEW | .10 | .02 | ❑ 424 Rod Woodson PB | .25 | .08 | ❑ 509 Jerry Holmes | .05 | .01 |
| ❑ 351 U.S. Troops in | .05 | .01 | ❑ 425 Albert Lewis AFC | .05 | .01 | ❑ 510 Perry Kemp | .05 | .01 |
| ❑ 352 Art McNally OFF | .05 | .01 | ❑ 426 Steve Atwater AFC | .05 | .01 | ❑ 511 Ken Ruettgers | .05 | .01 |
| ❑ 353 Dick Jorgensen OFF | .05 | .01 | ❑ 427 David Fulcher AFC | .05 | .01 | ❑ 512 Scott Stephen RC | .05 | .01 |
| ❑ 354 Jerry Seeman OFF | .05 | .01 | ❑ 428 Rohn Stark AFC | .05 | .01 | ❑ 513 Ed West | .05 | .01 |
| ❑ 355 Jim Tunney OFF | .05 | .01 | ❑ 429 Nick Lowery AFC | .05 | .01 | ❑ 514 Cris Dishman RC | .05 | .01 |
| ❑ 356 Gerry Austin OFF | .05 | .01 | ❑ 430 Clarence Verdin AFC | .05 | .01 | ❑ 515 Curtis Duncan | .05 | .01 |
| ❑ 357 Gene Barth OFF | .05 | .01 | ❑ 431 Steve Tasker AFC | .05 | .01 | ❑ 516 Drew Hill UER | .05 | .01 |
| ❑ 358 Red Cashion OFF | .05 | .01 | ❑ 432 Art Shell CO AFC | .10 | .02 | ❑ 517 Haywood Jeffires | .10 | .02 |
| ❑ 359 Tom Dooley OFF | .05 | .01 | ❑ 433 Scott Case | .05 | .01 | ❑ 518 Sean Jones | .10 | .02 |
| ❑ 360 Johnny Grier OFF | .05 | .01 | ❑ 434 Tory Epps UER | .05 | .01 | ❑ 519 Lamar Lathon | .05 | .01 |
| ❑ 361 Pat Haggerty OFF | .05 | .01 | ❑ 435 Mike Gann UER | .05 | .01 | ❑ 520 Don Maggs | .05 | .01 |
| ❑ 362 Dale Hamer OFF | .05 | .01 | ❑ 436 Brian Jordan FPSC UER | .10 | .02 | ❑ 521 Bubba McDowell | .05 | .01 |
| ❑ 363 Dick Hantak OFF | .05 | .01 | ❑ 437 Mike Kenn | .05 | .01 | ❑ 522 Johnny Meads | .05 | .01 |
| ❑ 364 Jerry Markbreit OFF | .05 | .01 | ❑ 438 John Rade | .05 | .01 | ❑ 523A Chip Banks ERR No Text | .50 | .20 |
| ❑ 365 Gordon McCarter OFF | .05 | .01 | ❑ 439 Andre Rison | .10 | .02 | ❑ 523B Chip Banks COR | .05 | .01 |
| ❑ 366 Bob McElwee OFF | .05 | .01 | ❑ 440 Mike Rozier | .05 | .01 | ❑ 524 Pat Beach | .05 | .01 |
| ❑ 367 Howard Roe OFF | .05 | .01 | ❑ 441 Jessie Tuggle | .05 | .01 | ❑ 525 Sam Clancy | .05 | .01 |
| ❑ 368 Tom White OFF | .05 | .01 | ❑ 442 Don Beebe | .05 | .01 | ❑ 526 Eugene Daniel | .05 | .01 |
| ❑ 369 Norm Schachter OFF | .05 | .01 | ❑ 443 John Davis RC | .05 | .01 | ❑ 527 Jon Hand | .05 | .01 |
| ❑ 370A Warren Moon Crack | .25 | .08 | ❑ 444 James Lofton | .10 | .02 | ❑ 528 Jessie Hester | .05 | .01 |
| ❑ 370B Warren Moon Crack | .25 | .08 | ❑ 445 Keith McKeller | .05 | .01 | ❑ 529A Mike Prior ERR No Text | .50 | .20 |

|  |  | | |
|---|---|---|---|
| ❏ 529B | Mike Prior COR | .05 | .01 |
| ❏ 530 | Keith Taylor | .05 | .01 |
| ❏ 531 | Donnell Thompson | .05 | .01 |
| ❏ 532 | Dino Hackett | .05 | .01 |
| ❏ 533 | David Lutz RC | .05 | .01 |
| ❏ 534 | Chris Martin | .05 | .01 |
| ❏ 535 | Kevin Ross | .05 | .01 |
| ❏ 536 | Dan Saleaumua | .05 | .01 |
| ❏ 537 | Neil Smith | .25 | .08 |
| ❏ 538 | Percy Snow | .05 | .01 |
| ❏ 539 | Robb Thomas | .05 | .01 |
| ❏ 540 | Barry Word | .05 | .01 |
| ❏ 541 | Marcus Allen | .25 | .08 |
| ❏ 542 | Eddie Anderson | .05 | .01 |
| ❏ 543 | Scott Davis | .05 | .01 |
| ❏ 544 | Mervyn Fernandez | .05 | .01 |
| ❏ 545 | Ethan Horton | .05 | .01 |
| ❏ 546 | Ronnie Lott | .10 | .02 |
| ❏ 547 | Don Mosebar | .05 | .01 |
| ❏ 548 | Jerry Robinson | .05 | .01 |
| ❏ 549 | Aaron Wallace | .05 | .01 |
| ❏ 550 | Flipper Anderson | .05 | .01 |
| ❏ 551 | Cleveland Gary | .05 | .01 |
| ❏ 552 | Damone Johnson RC | .05 | .01 |
| ❏ 553 | Duval Love RC | .05 | .01 |
| ❏ 554 | Irv Pankey | .05 | .01 |
| ❏ 555 | Mike Piel | .05 | .01 |
| ❏ 556 | Jackie Slater | .05 | .01 |
| ❏ 557 | Michael Stewart | .05 | .01 |
| ❏ 558 | Pat Terrell | .05 | .01 |
| ❏ 559 | J.B. Brown | .05 | .01 |
| ❏ 560 | Mark Clayton | .10 | .02 |
| ❏ 561 | Ferrell Edmunds | .05 | .01 |
| ❏ 562 | Harry Galbreath | .05 | .01 |
| ❏ 563 | David Griggs | .05 | .01 |
| ❏ 564 | Jim C. Jensen | .05 | .01 |
| ❏ 565 | Louis Oliver | .05 | .01 |
| ❏ 566 | Tony Paige | .05 | .01 |
| ❏ 567 | Keith Sims | .05 | .01 |
| ❏ 568 | Joey Browner | .05 | .01 |
| ❏ 569 | Anthony Carter | .10 | .02 |
| ❏ 570 | Chris Doleman | .05 | .01 |
| ❏ 571 | Rich Gannon UER | .25 | .08 |
| ❏ 572 | Hassan Jones | .05 | .01 |
| ❏ 573 | Steve Jordan | .05 | .01 |
| ❏ 574 | Carl Lee | .05 | .01 |
| ❏ 575 | Randall McDaniel | .05 | .02 |
| ❏ 576 | Herschel Walker | .10 | .02 |
| ❏ 577 | Ray Agnew | .05 | .01 |
| ❏ 578 | Vincent Brown | .05 | .01 |
| ❏ 579 | Irving Fryar | .10 | .02 |
| ❏ 580 | Tim Goad | .05 | .01 |
| ❏ 581 | Maurice Hurst | .05 | .01 |
| ❏ 582 | Fred Marion | .05 | .01 |
| ❏ 583 | Johnny Rembert | .05 | .01 |
| ❏ 584 | Andre Tippett | .05 | .01 |
| ❏ 585 | Brent Williams | .05 | .01 |
| ❏ 586 | Morten Andersen | .05 | .01 |
| ❏ 587 | Toi Cook RC | .05 | .01 |
| ❏ 588 | Jim Dombrowski | .05 | .01 |
| ❏ 589 | Dalton Hilliard | .05 | .01 |
| ❏ 590 | Rickey Jackson | .05 | .01 |
| ❏ 591 | Eric Martin | .05 | .01 |
| ❏ 592 | Sam Mills | .05 | .01 |
| ❏ 593 | Bobby Hebert | .05 | .01 |
| ❏ 594 | Steve Walsh | .05 | .01 |
| ❏ 595 | Ottis Anderson | .10 | .02 |
| ❏ 596 | Pepper Johnson | .05 | .01 |
| ❏ 597 | Bob Kratch RC | .05 | .01 |
| ❏ 598 | Sean Landeta | .05 | .01 |
| ❏ 599 | Doug Riesenberg | .05 | .01 |
| ❏ 600 | William Roberts | .05 | .01 |
| ❏ 601 | Phil Simms | .10 | .02 |
| ❏ 602 | Lawrence Taylor | .25 | .08 |
| ❏ 603 | Everson Walls | .05 | .01 |
| ❏ 604 | Brad Baxter | .05 | .01 |
| ❏ 605 | Dennis Byrd | .05 | .01 |
| ❏ 606 | Jeff Lageman | .05 | .01 |
| ❏ 607 | Pat Leahy | .05 | .01 |
| ❏ 608 | Rob Moore | .25 | .08 |
| ❏ 609 | Joe Mott | .05 | .01 |
| ❏ 610 | Tony Stargell | .05 | .01 |
| ❏ 611 | Brian Washington | .05 | .01 |
| ❏ 612 | Marvin Washington RC | .05 | .01 |
| ❏ 613 | David Alexander | .05 | .01 |
| ❏ 614 | Jerome Brown | .05 | .01 |
| ❏ 615 | Byron Evans | .05 | .01 |
| ❏ 616 | Ron Heller | .05 | .01 |
| ❏ 617 | Wes Hopkins | .05 | .01 |
| ❏ 618 | Keith Jackson | .10 | .02 |
| ❏ 619 | Heath Sherman | .05 | .01 |
| ❏ 620 | Reggie White | .25 | .08 |
| ❏ 621 | Calvin Williams | .05 | .01 |
| ❏ 622 | Ken Harvey | .10 | .02 |
| ❏ 623 | Eric Hill | .05 | .01 |
| ❏ 624 | Johnny Johnson | .05 | .01 |
| ❏ 625 | Freddie Joe Nunn | .05 | .01 |
| ❏ 626 | Ricky Proehl | .05 | .01 |
| ❏ 627 | Tootie Robbins | .05 | .01 |
| ❏ 628 | Jay Taylor | .05 | .01 |
| ❏ 629 | Tom Tupa | .05 | .01 |
| ❏ 630 | Jim Wahler RC | .05 | .01 |
| ❏ 631 | Bubby Brister | .05 | .01 |
| ❏ 632 | Thomas Everett | .05 | .01 |
| ❏ 633 | Bryan Hinkle | .05 | .01 |
| ❏ 634 | Carnell Lake | .05 | .01 |
| ❏ 635 | David Little | .05 | .01 |
| ❏ 636 | Hardy Nickerson | .10 | .02 |
| ❏ 637 | Gerald Williams | .05 | .01 |
| ❏ 638 | Keith Willis | .05 | .01 |
| ❏ 639 | Tim Worley | .05 | .01 |
| ❏ 640 | Rod Bernstine | .05 | .01 |
| ❏ 641 | Frank Cornish | .05 | .01 |
| ❏ 642 | Gary Plummer | .05 | .01 |
| ❏ 643 | Henry Rolling RC | .05 | .01 |
| ❏ 644 | Sam Seale | .05 | .01 |
| ❏ 645 | Junior Seau | .25 | .08 |
| ❏ 646 | Billy Ray Smith | .05 | .01 |
| ❏ 647 | Broderick Thompson | .05 | .01 |
| ❏ 648 | Derrick Walker RC | .05 | .01 |
| ❏ 649 | Todd Bowles | .05 | .01 |
| ❏ 650 | Don Griffin | .05 | .01 |
| ❏ 651 | Charles Haley | .10 | .02 |
| ❏ 652 | Brent Jones UER | .10 | .02 |
| ❏ 653 | Joe Montana | 1.25 | .50 |
| ❏ 654 | Jerry Rice | .75 | .30 |
| ❏ 655 | Bill Romanowski | .05 | .01 |
| ❏ 656 | Michael Walter | .05 | .01 |
| ❏ 657 | Dave Waymer | .05 | .01 |
| ❏ 658 | Jeff Chadwick | .05 | .01 |
| ❏ 659 | Derrick Fenner | .05 | .01 |
| ❏ 660 | Nesby Glasgow | .05 | .01 |
| ❏ 661 | Jacob Green | .05 | .01 |
| ❏ 662 | Dwayne Harper RC | .05 | .01 |
| ❏ 663 | Andy Heck | .05 | .01 |
| ❏ 664 | Dave Krieg | .10 | .02 |
| ❏ 665 | Rufus Porter | .05 | .01 |
| ❏ 666 | Eugene Robinson | .05 | .01 |
| ❏ 667 | Mark Carrier WR | .25 | .08 |
| ❏ 668 | Steve Christie | .05 | .01 |
| ❏ 669 | Reuben Davis | .05 | .01 |
| ❏ 670 | Paul Gruber | .05 | .01 |
| ❏ 671 | Wayne Haddix | .05 | .01 |
| ❏ 672 | Ron Hall | .05 | .01 |
| ❏ 673 | Keith McCants UER | .05 | .01 |
| ❏ 674 | Ricky Reynolds | .05 | .01 |
| ❏ 675 | Mark Robinson | .05 | .01 |
| ❏ 676 | Jeff Bostic | .05 | .01 |
| ❏ 677 | Darrell Green | .05 | .01 |
| ❏ 678 | Markus Koch | .05 | .01 |
| ❏ 679 | Jim Lachey | .05 | .01 |
| ❏ 680 | Charles Mann | .05 | .01 |
| ❏ 681 | Wilber Marshall | .05 | .01 |
| ❏ 682 | Art Monk | .10 | .02 |
| ❏ 683 | Gerald Riggs | .05 | .01 |
| ❏ 684 | Ricky Sanders | .05 | .01 |
| ❏ 685 | Ray Hamilton NEW | .05 | .01 |
| ❏ 686 | NFL announces NEW | .05 | .01 |
| ❏ 687 | Miami gets NEW | .05 | .01 |
| ❏ 688 | Giants' George Young NEW | .05 | .01 |
| ❏ 689 | Five-millionth fan NEW | .05 | .01 |
| ❏ 690 | Sports Illustrated NEW | .05 | .01 |
| ❏ 691 | American Bowl NEW | .05 | .01 |
| ❏ 692 | American Bowl NEW | .05 | .01 |
| ❏ 693 | American Bowl NEW | .05 | .01 |
| ❏ 694A | Russell Maryland | .25 | .08 |
| ❏ 694B | Joe Ferguson LEG | .05 | .01 |
| ❏ 695 | Carl Hairston LEG | .10 | .02 |
| ❏ 696 | Dan Hampton LEG | .10 | .02 |
| ❏ 697 | Mike Haynes LEG | .05 | .01 |
| ❏ 698 | Marty Lyons LEG | .05 | .01 |
| ❏ 699 | Ozzie Newsome LEGEND | .10 | .02 |
| ❏ 700 | Scott Studwell LEG | .05 | .01 |
| ❏ 701 | Mike Webster LEG | .05 | .01 |
| ❏ 702 | Dwayne Woodruff LEG | .05 | .01 |
| ❏ 703 | Larry Kennan CO | .05 | .01 |
| ❏ 704 | Stan Gelbaugh RC LL | .10 | .02 |
| ❏ 705 | John Brantley LL | .05 | .01 |
| ❏ 706 | Danny Lockett LL | .05 | .01 |
| ❏ 707 | Anthony Parker RC LL | .10 | .02 |
| ❏ 708 | Dan Crossman LL | .05 | .01 |
| ❏ 709 | Eric Wilkerson LL | .05 | .01 |
| ❏ 710 | Judd Garrett RC LL | .05 | .01 |
| ❏ 711 | Tony Baker LL | .05 | .01 |
| ❏ 712 | Ran.Cunningham PHOTO | .05 | .01 |
| ❏ 713 | 2nd Place BW PHOTO | .05 | .01 |
| ❏ 714 | 3rd Place BW PHOTO | .05 | .01 |
| ❏ 715 | 1st Place Color PHOTO | .05 | .01 |
| ❏ 716 | 2nd Place Color PHOTO | .05 | .01 |
| ❏ 717 | 3rd Place Color PHOTO | .05 | .01 |
| ❏ 718 | 1st Place Color PHOTO | .05 | .01 |
| ❏ 719 | 2nd Place Color PHOTO | .05 | .01 |
| ❏ 720 | 3rd Place Color PHOTO | .05 | .01 |
| ❏ 721 | Ray Bentley | .05 | .01 |
| ❏ 722 | Earnest Byner | .05 | .01 |
| ❏ 723 | Bill Fralic | .05 | .01 |
| ❏ 724 | Joe Jacoby | .05 | .01 |
| ❏ 725 | Howie Long | .25 | .08 |
| ❏ 726 | Dan Marino THINK | .50 | .20 |
| ❏ 727 | Ron Rivera | .05 | .01 |
| ❏ 728 | Mike Singletary | .10 | .02 |
| ❏ 729 | Cornelius Bennett | .10 | .02 |
| ❏ 730 | Russell Maryland | .25 | .08 |
| ❏ 731 | Eric Turner RC | .10 | .02 |
| ❏ 732 | Bruce Pickens RC UER | .05 | .01 |
| ❏ 733 | Mike Croel RC | .05 | .01 |
| ❏ 734 | Todd Lyght RC | .05 | .01 |
| ❏ 735 | Eric Swann RC | .25 | .08 |
| ❏ 736 | Charles McRae RC | .05 | .01 |
| ❏ 737 | Antone Davis RC | .05 | .01 |
| ❏ 738 | Stanley Richard RC | .05 | .01 |
| ❏ 739 | Herman Moore RC | .25 | .08 |
| ❏ 740 | Pat Harlow RC | .05 | .01 |
| ❏ 741 | Alvin Harper RC | .25 | .08 |
| ❏ 742 | Mike Pritchard RC | .25 | .08 |
| ❏ 743 | Leonard Russell RC | .05 | .01 |
| ❏ 744 | Huey Richardson RC | .05 | .01 |
| ❏ 745 | Dan McGwire RC | .05 | .01 |
| ❏ 746 | Bobby Wilson RC | .05 | .01 |
| ❏ 747 | Alfred Williams | .05 | .01 |
| ❏ 748 | Vinnie Clark RC | .05 | .01 |
| ❏ 749 | Kelvin Pritchett RC | .05 | .01 |
| ❏ 750 | Harvey Williams RC | .25 | .08 |
| ❏ 751 | Stan Thomas | .05 | .01 |
| ❏ 752 | Randal Hill RC | .10 | .02 |
| ❏ 753 | Todd Marinovich RC | .05 | .01 |
| ❏ 754 | Ted Washington RC | .05 | .01 |
| ❏ 755 | Henry Jones RC | .10 | .02 |
| ❏ 756 | Jarrod Bunch RC | .05 | .01 |
| ❏ 757 | Mike Dumas RC | .05 | .01 |
| ❏ 758 | Ed King RC | .05 | .01 |
| ❏ 759 | Reggie Johnson RC | .05 | .01 |
| ❏ 760 | Roman Phifer RC | .05 | .01 |
| ❏ 761 | Mike Jones DE RC | .05 | .01 |
| ❏ 762 | Brett Favre RC | 8.00 | 3.00 |
| ❏ 763 | Browning Nagle RC | .05 | .01 |
| ❏ 764 | Esera Tuaolo RC | .05 | .01 |
| ❏ 765 | George Thornton RC | .05 | .01 |
| ❏ 766 | Dixon Edwards RC | .05 | .01 |
| ❏ 767 | Darryll Lewis | .10 | .02 |
| ❏ 768 | Eric Bieniemy RC | .05 | .01 |
| ❏ 769 | Shane Curry | .05 | .01 |
| ❏ 770 | Jerome Henderson RC | .05 | .01 |
| ❏ 771 | Wesley Carroll RC | .05 | .01 |
| ❏ 772 | Nick Bell RC | .05 | .01 |
| ❏ 773 | John Flannery RC | .05 | .01 |
| ❏ 774 | Ricky Watters RC | 1.50 | .60 |
| ❏ 775 | Graham Armstrong RC WR | .25 | .08 |
| ❏ 776 | Eric Moten RC | .05 | .01 |
| ❏ 777 | Jesse Campbell RC | .05 | .01 |
| ❏ 778 | Chris Zorich | .10 | .02 |
| ❏ 779 | Joe Valerio | .05 | .01 |
| ❏ 780 | Doug Thomas RC | .05 | .01 |
| ❏ 781 | Lamar Rogers RC UER | .05 | .01 |
| ❏ 782 | John Johnson RC | .05 | .01 |

**1992 Pro Set**

| | | |
|---|---|---|
| 783 Phil Hansen RC | .05 | .01 |
| 784 Kanavis McGhee RC | .05 | .01 |
| 785 Calvin Stephens RC UER | .05 | .01 |
| 786 James Jones RC DT | .05 | .01 |
| 787 Reggie Barrett RC | .05 | .01 |
| 788 Aeneas Williams RC | .25 | .08 |
| 789 Aaron Craver RC | .05 | .01 |
| 790 Keith Traylor RC | .05 | .01 |
| 791 Godfrey Myles RC | .05 | .01 |
| 792 Mo Lewis RC | .10 | .02 |
| 793 James Richard RC | .05 | .01 |
| 794 Carlos Jenkins RC | .05 | .01 |
| 795 Lawrence Dawsey RC | .10 | .02 |
| 796 Don Davey RC | .05 | .01 |
| 797 Jake Reed RC | .50 | .20 |
| 798 Dave McCloughan RC | .05 | .01 |
| 799 Erik Williams RC | .10 | .02 |
| 800 Steve Jackson RC | .05 | .01 |
| 801 Bob Dahl RC | .05 | .01 |
| 802 Ernie Mills RC | .10 | .02 |
| 803 David Daniels RC | .05 | .01 |
| 804 Rob Selby RC | .05 | .01 |
| 805 Ricky Ervins RC | .10 | .02 |
| 806 Tim Barnett RC | .05 | .01 |
| 807 Chris Gardocki RC | .25 | .08 |
| 808 Kevin Donnalley RC | .05 | .01 |
| 809 Robert Wilson RC | .05 | .01 |
| 810 Chuck Webb RC | .05 | .01 |
| 811 Darryl Wren RC | .05 | .01 |
| 812 Ed McCaffrey RC | 2.00 | .75 |
| 813 Shula's 300th Victory | .05 | .01 |
| 814 Raiders-49ers sell | .05 | .01 |
| 815 NFL International NEWS | .05 | .01 |
| 816 Moe Gardner RC | .05 | .01 |
| 817 Tim McKyer | .05 | .01 |
| 818 Tom Waddle RC | .05 | .01 |
| 819 Michael Jackson RC WR | .25 | .08 |
| 820 Tony Casillas RC | .05 | .01 |
| 821 Gaston Green | .05 | .01 |
| 822 Kenny Walker RC | .05 | .01 |
| 823 Willie Green RC | .05 | .01 |
| 824 Erik Kramer RC | .25 | .08 |
| 825 William Fuller | .10 | .02 |
| 826 Allen Pinkett | .05 | .01 |
| 827 Rick Venturi CO | .05 | .01 |
| 828 Bill Maas | .05 | .01 |
| 829 Jeff Jaeger | .05 | .01 |
| 830 Robert Delpino | .05 | .01 |
| 831 Mark Higgs RC | .05 | .01 |
| 832 Reggie Roby | .05 | .01 |
| 833 Terry Allen RC | 1.50 | .60 |
| 834 Cris Carter | .50 | .20 |
| 835 John Randle RC | .60 | .25 |
| 836 Hugh Millen RC | .05 | .01 |
| 837 Jon Vaughn RC | .05 | .01 |
| 838 Gill Fenerty | .05 | .01 |
| 839 Floyd Turner | .05 | .01 |
| 840 Irv Eatman | .05 | .01 |
| 841 Lonnie Young | .05 | .01 |
| 842 Jim McMahon | .10 | .02 |
| 843 Randal Hill | .05 | .01 |
| 844 Barry Foster FPSC | .10 | .02 |
| 845 Neil O'Donnell RC | .25 | .08 |
| 846 John Friesz FPSC | .25 | .08 |
| 847 Broderick Thomas | .05 | .01 |
| 848 Brian Mitchell | .10 | .02 |
| 849 Mike Utley RC | .10 | .02 |
| 850 Mike Croel ROY | .05 | .01 |
| SC1 SB XXVI Theme Art | .05 | .01 |
| SC3 Jim Thorpe Pioneer | .75 | .30 |
| SC4 Otto Graham Pioneer | .75 | .30 |
| SC5 Paul Brown Pioneer | .75 | .30 |
| PSS1 Walter Payton | .50 | .20 |
| PSS2 Red Grange | .50 | .20 |
| MVPC25 Ottis Anderson | .25 | .08 |
| AU336 L.Taylor REP AU/500 | 175.00 | 100.00 |
| AU394 L.Taylor PB AU/500 | 175.00 | 100.00 |
| AU699 O.Newsome AU/500 | 50.00 | 25.00 |
| AU824 Erik Kramer AU | 50.00 | 25.00 |
| NNO Mini Pro Set Gazette | .25 | .08 |
| NNO Pro Set Gazette | .25 | .08 |
| NNO Santa Claus | .50 | .20 |
| NNO Super Bowl XXV Art | .25 | .08 |
| NNO Super Bowl XXV Logo | .25 | .08 |

| | | |
|---|---|---|
| COMPLETE SET (700) | 20.00 | 8.00 |
| COMP.SERIES 1 (400) | 10.00 | 4.00 |
| COMP.SERIES 2 (300) | 10.00 | 4.00 |
| 1 Mike Croel LL | .05 | .01 |
| 2 Thurman Thomas LL | .25 | .08 |
| 3 Wayne Fontes CO LL | .05 | .01 |
| 4 Anthony Munoz LL | .10 | .02 |
| 5 Steve Young LL | .30 | .10 |
| 6 Warren Moon LL | .10 | .02 |
| 7 Emmitt Smith LL | .60 | .25 |
| 8 Haywood Jeffires LL | .05 | .01 |
| 9 Marv Cook LL | .05 | .01 |
| 10 Michael Irvin LL | .25 | .08 |
| 11 Thurman Thomas LL | .25 | .08 |
| 12 Chip Lohmiller LL UER | .05 | .01 |
| 13 Barry Sanders LL | .50 | .20 |
| 14 Reggie Roby LL | .05 | .01 |
| 15 Mel Gray LL | .05 | .01 |
| 16 Ronnie Lott LL | .10 | .02 |
| 17 Pat Swilling LL | .05 | .01 |
| 18 Reggie White LL | .10 | .02 |
| 19 Haywood Jefires ML | .05 | .01 |
| 20 Pat Leahy MILE | .05 | .01 |
| 21 James Lofton MILE | .10 | .02 |
| 22 Art Monk MILE | .10 | .02 |
| 23 Don Shula MILE | .10 | .02 |
| 24A Nick Lowery MILE ERR | .05 | .01 |
| 24B Nick Lowery MILE COR | .05 | .01 |
| 25 John Elway ML | .50 | .20 |
| 26 Chicago Bears MILE | .05 | .01 |
| 27 Marcus Allen MILE | .10 | .02 |
| 28 Terrell Buckley RC | .05 | .01 |
| 29 Amp Lee RC | .05 | .01 |
| 30 Chris Mims RC | .05 | .01 |
| 31 Leon Searcy RC | .05 | .01 |
| 32 Jimmy Smith RC | 3.00 | 1.25 |
| 33 Siran Stacy RC | .05 | .01 |
| 34 Pete Gogolak INN | .05 | .01 |
| 35 Cheerleaders INN | .05 | .01 |
| 36 Houston Astrodome INN | .05 | .01 |
| 37 Week 1 REPLAY | .05 | .01 |
| 38 Week 2 REPLAY | .05 | .01 |
| 39 Week 3 REPLAY | .05 | .01 |
| 40 Week 4 REPLAY | .05 | .01 |
| 41 Week 5 REPLAY | .05 | .01 |
| 42 Week 6 REPLAY | .05 | .01 |
| 43 Thurman Thomas REP | .10 | .02 |
| 44 Week 8 REPLAY | .05 | .01 |
| 45 Week 9 REPLAY UER | .05 | .01 |
| 46 Week 10 REPLAY | .05 | .01 |
| 47 Week 11 REPLAY | .05 | .01 |
| 48 Week 12 REPLAY | .05 | .01 |
| 49 M.Irvin/S.Beuerlein REP | .10 | .02 |
| 50 Week 14 REPLAY | .05 | .01 |
| 51 Week 15 REPLAY | .05 | .01 |
| 52 Week 16 REPLAY | .05 | .01 |
| 53 Week 17 REPLAY | .05 | .01 |
| 54 AFC Wild Card REPLAY | .05 | .01 |
| 55 AFC Wild Card REPLAY | .05 | .01 |
| 56 NFC Wild Card REPLAY | .05 | .01 |
| 57 NFC Wild Card REPLAY | .05 | .01 |
| 58 AFC Divis. Playoff REPLAY | .05 | .01 |
| 59 Thurman Thomas REP | .10 | .02 |
| 60 Erik Kramer REP | .05 | .01 |
| 61 NFC Divis. Playoff REPLAY | .05 | .01 |
| 62 AFC Championship REPLAY | .05 | .01 |
| 63 NFC Championship REPLAY | .05 | .01 |

| | | |
|---|---|---|
| 64 Super Bowl XXVI REPLAY | .05 | .01 |
| 65 Super Bowl XXVI REPLAY | .05 | .01 |
| 66 Super Bowl XXVI REPLAY | .05 | .01 |
| 67 Super Bowl XXVI REPLAY | .05 | .01 |
| 68 Super Bowl XXVI REPLAY | .05 | .01 |
| 69 Thurman Thomas REP | .10 | .02 |
| 70 Super Bowl XXVI REP | .05 | .01 |
| 71 Super Bowl XXVI REPLAY | .05 | .01 |
| 72 Super Bowl XXVI REPLAY | .05 | .01 |
| 73 Jeff Bostic | .05 | .01 |
| 74 Earnest Byner | .05 | .01 |
| 75 Gary Clark | .25 | .08 |
| 76 Andre Collins | .05 | .01 |
| 77 Darrell Green | .05 | .01 |
| 78 Joe Jacoby | .05 | .01 |
| 79 Jim Lachey | .05 | .01 |
| 80 Chip Lohmiller | .05 | .01 |
| 81 Charles Mann | .05 | .01 |
| 82 Martin Mayhew | .05 | .01 |
| 83 Matt Millen | .10 | .02 |
| 84 Brian Mitchell | .10 | .02 |
| 85 Art Monk | .10 | .02 |
| 86 Gerald Riggs | .05 | .01 |
| 87 Mark Rypien | .05 | .01 |
| 88 Fred Stokes | .05 | .01 |
| 89 Bobby Wilson | .05 | .01 |
| 90 Joe Gibbs CO | .10 | .02 |
| 91 Howard Ballard | .05 | .01 |
| 92 Cornelius Bennett UER | .10 | .02 |
| 93 Kenneth Davis | .05 | .01 |
| 94 Al Edwards | .05 | .01 |
| 95 Kent Hull | .05 | .01 |
| 96 Kirby Jackson | .05 | .01 |
| 97 Mark Kelso | .05 | .01 |
| 98 James Lofton | .10 | .02 |
| 99 Keith McKeller | .05 | .01 |
| 100 Nate Odomes | .05 | .01 |
| 101 Jim Ritcher | .05 | .01 |
| 102 Leon Seals | .05 | .01 |
| 103 Steve Tasker | .10 | .02 |
| 104 Darryl Talley | .05 | .01 |
| 105 Thurman Thomas | .25 | .08 |
| 106 Will Wolford | .05 | .01 |
| 107 Jeff Wright | .05 | .01 |
| 108 Marv Levy CO | .05 | .01 |
| 109 Darion Conner | .05 | .01 |
| 110 Bill Fralic | .05 | .01 |
| 111 Moe Gardner | .05 | .01 |
| 112 Michael Haynes | .10 | .02 |
| 113 Chris Miller | .10 | .02 |
| 114 Eric Pegram | .10 | .02 |
| 115 Bruce Pickens | .05 | .01 |
| 116 Andre Rison | .10 | .02 |
| 117 Jerry Glanville CO | .05 | .01 |
| 118 Neal Anderson | .10 | .02 |
| 119 Trace Armstrong | .05 | .01 |
| 120 Wendell Davis | .05 | .01 |
| 121 Richard Dent | .10 | .02 |
| 122 Jay Hilgenberg | .05 | .01 |
| 123 Lemuel Stinson | .05 | .01 |
| 124 Stan Thomas | .05 | .01 |
| 125 Tom Waddle | .05 | .01 |
| 126 Mike Ditka CO | .25 | .08 |
| 127 James Brooks | .05 | .01 |
| 128 Eddie Brown | .05 | .01 |
| 129 David Fulcher | .05 | .01 |
| 130 Harold Green | .05 | .01 |
| 131 Tim Krumrie UER | .05 | .01 |
| 132 Anthony Munoz | .10 | .02 |
| 133 Craig Taylor | .05 | .01 |
| 134 Eric Thomas | .05 | .01 |
| 135 David Shula RC CO | .05 | .01 |
| 136 Mike Baab | .05 | .01 |
| 137 Brian Brennan | .05 | .01 |
| 138 Michael Jackson | .10 | .02 |
| 139 James Jones DT UER | .05 | .01 |
| 140 Ed King | .05 | .01 |
| 141 Clay Matthews | .10 | .02 |
| 142 Eric Metcalf | .10 | .02 |
| 143 Joe Morris | .05 | .01 |
| 144A Bill Belichick CO NPO | .25 | .08 |
| 144B Bill Belichick CO | .05 | .01 |
| 145 Steve Beuerlein | .10 | .02 |
| 146 Larry Brown DB | .05 | .01 |
| 147 Ray Horton | .05 | .01 |

| No. | Card | Val1 | Val2 |
|---|---|---|---|
| ❏ 148 | Ken Norton | .10 | .02 |
| ❏ 149 | Mike Saxon | .05 | .01 |
| ❏ 150 | Emmitt Smith | 1.50 | .60 |
| ❏ 151 | Mark Stepnoski | .10 | .02 |
| ❏ 152 | Alexander Wright | .05 | .01 |
| ❏ 153 | Jimmy Johnson CO | .10 | .02 |
| ❏ 154 | Mike Croel | .05 | .01 |
| ❏ 155 | John Elway | 1.25 | .50 |
| ❏ 156 | Gaston Green | .05 | .01 |
| ❏ 157 | Wymon Henderson | .05 | .01 |
| ❏ 158 | Karl Mecklenburg UER | .05 | .01 |
| ❏ 159 | Warren Powers | .05 | .01 |
| ❏ 160 | Steve Sewell UER | .05 | .01 |
| ❏ 161 | Doug Widell | .05 | .01 |
| ❏ 162 | Dan Reeves CO | .05 | .01 |
| ❏ 163 | Eric Andolsek | .05 | .01 |
| ❏ 164 | Jerry Ball | .05 | .01 |
| ❏ 165 | Bennie Blades | .05 | .01 |
| ❏ 166 | Ray Crockett | .05 | .01 |
| ❏ 167 | Willie Green | .05 | .01 |
| ❏ 168 | Erik Kramer | .10 | .02 |
| ❏ 169 | Barry Sanders | 1.25 | .50 |
| ❏ 170 | Chris Spielman UER | .05 | .01 |
| ❏ 171 | Wayne Fontes CO | .05 | .01 |
| ❏ 172 | Vinnie Clark | .05 | .01 |
| ❏ 173 | Tony Mandarich | .05 | .01 |
| ❏ 174 | Brian Noble | .05 | .01 |
| ❏ 175 | Bryce Paup | .25 | .08 |
| ❏ 176 | Sterling Sharpe | .25 | .08 |
| ❏ 177 | Darrell Thompson | .05 | .01 |
| ❏ 178 | Esera Tuaolo UER | .05 | .01 |
| ❏ 179 | Ed West | .05 | .01 |
| ❏ 180 | Mike Holmgren RC CO | .25 | .08 |
| ❏ 181 | Ray Childress | .05 | .01 |
| ❏ 182 | Cris Dishman | .05 | .01 |
| ❏ 183 | Curtis Duncan | .05 | .01 |
| ❏ 184 | William Fuller | .05 | .01 |
| ❏ 185 | Lamar Lathon | .05 | .01 |
| ❏ 186 | Warren Moon | .25 | .08 |
| ❏ 187 | Bo Orlando RC | .05 | .01 |
| ❏ 188 | Lorenzo White | .05 | .01 |
| ❏ 189 | Jack Pardee CO | .05 | .01 |
| ❏ 190 | Chip Banks | .05 | .01 |
| ❏ 191 | Dean Biasucci UER | .05 | .01 |
| ❏ 192 | Bill Brooks | .05 | .01 |
| ❏ 193 | Ray Donaldson | .05 | .01 |
| ❏ 194 | Jeff Herrod | .05 | .01 |
| ❏ 195 | Mike Prior | .05 | .01 |
| ❏ 196 | Mark Vander Poel | .05 | .01 |
| ❏ 197 | Clarence Verdin | .05 | .01 |
| ❏ 198 | Ted Marchibroda CO | .05 | .01 |
| ❏ 199 | John Alt | .05 | .01 |
| ❏ 200 | Deron Cherry | .05 | .01 |
| ❏ 201 | Steve DeBerg | .05 | .01 |
| ❏ 202 | Nick Lowery | .05 | .01 |
| ❏ 203 | Neil Smith | .25 | .08 |
| ❏ 204 | Derrick Thomas | .25 | .08 |
| ❏ 205 | Joe Valerio | .05 | .01 |
| ❏ 206 | Barry Word | .05 | .01 |
| ❏ 207 | M. Schottenheimer CO | .05 | .01 |
| ❏ 208 | Marcus Allen | .25 | .08 |
| ❏ 209 | Nick Bell | .05 | .01 |
| ❏ 210 | Tim Brown | .25 | .08 |
| ❏ 211 | Howie Long | .25 | .08 |
| ❏ 212 | Ronnie Lott | .10 | .02 |
| ❏ 213 | Todd Marinovich | .05 | .01 |
| ❏ 214 | Greg Townsend | .05 | .01 |
| ❏ 215 | Steve Wright | .05 | .01 |
| ❏ 216 | Art Shell CO | .10 | .02 |
| ❏ 217 | Flipper Anderson | .05 | .01 |
| ❏ 218 | Robert Delpino | .05 | .01 |
| ❏ 219 | Henry Ellard | .10 | .02 |
| ❏ 220 | Kevin Greene | .10 | .02 |
| ❏ 221 | Todd Lyght | .05 | .01 |
| ❏ 222 | Tom Newberry | .05 | .01 |
| ❏ 223 | Roman Phifer | .05 | .01 |
| ❏ 224 | Michael Stewart | .05 | .01 |
| ❏ 225 | Chuck Knox CO | .05 | .01 |
| ❏ 226 | Aaron Craver | .05 | .01 |
| ❏ 227 | Jeff Cross | .05 | .01 |
| ❏ 228 | Mark Duper | .05 | .01 |
| ❏ 229 | Ferrell Edmunds | .05 | .01 |
| ❏ 230 | Jim C. Jensen | .05 | .01 |
| ❏ 231 | Louis Oliver UER | .05 | .01 |
| ❏ 232 | Reggie Roby | .05 | .01 |
| ❏ 233 | Sammie Smith | .05 | .01 |
| ❏ 234 | Don Shula CO | .10 | .02 |
| ❏ 235 | Joey Browner | .05 | .01 |
| ❏ 236 | Anthony Carter | .10 | .02 |
| ❏ 237 | Chris Doleman | .05 | .01 |
| ❏ 238 | Steve Jordan | .05 | .01 |
| ❏ 239 | Kirk Lowdermilk | .05 | .01 |
| ❏ 240 | Henry Thomas | .05 | .01 |
| ❏ 241 | Herschel Walker | .10 | .02 |
| ❏ 242 | Felix Wright | .05 | .01 |
| ❏ 243 | Dennis Green CO RC | .10 | .02 |
| ❏ 244 | Ray Agnew | .05 | .01 |
| ❏ 245 | Marv Cook | .05 | .01 |
| ❏ 246 | Irving Fryar UER | .10 | .02 |
| ❏ 247 | Pat Harlow | .05 | .01 |
| ❏ 248 | Hugh Millen | .05 | .01 |
| ❏ 249 | Leonard Russell | .10 | .02 |
| ❏ 250 | Andre Tippett | .05 | .01 |
| ❏ 251 | Jon Vaughn | .05 | .01 |
| ❏ 252 | Dick MacPherson CO | .05 | .01 |
| ❏ 253 | Morten Andersen | .05 | .01 |
| ❏ 254 | Bobby Hebert | .05 | .01 |
| ❏ 255 | Joel Hilgenberg | .05 | .01 |
| ❏ 256 | Vaughan Johnson | .05 | .01 |
| ❏ 257 | Sam Mills | .05 | .01 |
| ❏ 258 | Pat Swilling | .05 | .01 |
| ❏ 259 | Floyd Turner | .05 | .01 |
| ❏ 260 | Steve Walsh | .05 | .01 |
| ❏ 261 | Jim Mora CO UER | .05 | .01 |
| ❏ 262 | Stephen Baker | .05 | .01 |
| ❏ 263 | Mark Collins | .05 | .01 |
| ❏ 264 | Rodney Hampton | .10 | .02 |
| ❏ 265 | Jeff Hostetler | .10 | .02 |
| ❏ 266 | Erik Howard | .05 | .01 |
| ❏ 267 | Sean Landeta | .05 | .01 |
| ❏ 268 | Gary Reasons UER | .05 | .01 |
| ❏ 269 | Everson Walls | .05 | .01 |
| ❏ 270 | Ray Handley CO | .05 | .01 |
| ❏ 271 | Louie Aguiar RC | .05 | .01 |
| ❏ 272 | Brad Baxter | .05 | .01 |
| ❏ 273 | Chris Burkett | .05 | .01 |
| ❏ 274 | Irv Eatman | .05 | .01 |
| ❏ 275 | Jeff Lageman | .05 | .01 |
| ❏ 276 | Freeman McNeil | .05 | .01 |
| ❏ 277 | Rob Moore | .10 | .02 |
| ❏ 278 | Lonnie Young | .05 | .01 |
| ❏ 279 | Bruce Coslet CO | .05 | .01 |
| ❏ 280 | Jerome Brown | .05 | .01 |
| ❏ 281 | Keith Byars | .05 | .01 |
| ❏ 282 | Bruce Collie UER | .05 | .01 |
| ❏ 283 | Keith Jackson | .10 | .02 |
| ❏ 284 | James Joseph | .05 | .01 |
| ❏ 285 | Seth Joyner | .05 | .01 |
| ❏ 286 | Andre Waters | .05 | .01 |
| ❏ 287 | Reggie White | .25 | .08 |
| ❏ 288 | Rich Kotite CO | .05 | .01 |
| ❏ 289 | Rich Camarillo | .05 | .01 |
| ❏ 290 | Garth Jax | .05 | .01 |
| ❏ 291 | Ernie Jones | .05 | .01 |
| ❏ 292 | Tim McDonald | .05 | .01 |
| ❏ 293 | Rod Saddler | .05 | .01 |
| ❏ 294 | Anthony Thompson UER | .05 | .01 |
| ❏ 295 | Tom Tupa UER | .05 | .01 |
| ❏ 296 | Ron Wolfley | .05 | .01 |
| ❏ 297 | Joe Bugel CO | .05 | .01 |
| ❏ 298 | Gary Anderson K | .05 | .01 |
| ❏ 299 | Jeff Graham | .25 | .08 |
| ❏ 300 | Eric Green | .05 | .01 |
| ❏ 301 | Bryan Hinkle | .05 | .01 |
| ❏ 302 | Tunch Ilkin | .05 | .01 |
| ❏ 303 | Louis Lipps | .05 | .01 |
| ❏ 304 | Neil O'Donnell | .10 | .02 |
| ❏ 305 | Rod Woodson | .25 | .08 |
| ❏ 306 | Bill Cowher CO RC | .75 | .30 |
| ❏ 307 | Eric Bieniemy | .05 | .01 |
| ❏ 308 | Marion Butts | .05 | .01 |
| ❏ 309 | John Friesz | .10 | .02 |
| ❏ 310 | Courtney Hall | .05 | .01 |
| ❏ 311 | Ronnie Harmon | .05 | .01 |
| ❏ 312 | Henry Rolling | .05 | .01 |
| ❏ 313 | Billy Ray Smith | .05 | .01 |
| ❏ 314 | George Thornton | .05 | .01 |
| ❏ 315 | Bobby Ross CO RC | .05 | .01 |
| ❏ 316 | Todd Bowles | .05 | .01 |
| ❏ 317 | Michael Carter | .05 | .01 |
| ❏ 318 | Don Griffin | .05 | .01 |
| ❏ 319 | Charles Haley | .10 | .02 |
| ❏ 320 | Brent Jones | .10 | .02 |
| ❏ 321 | John Taylor | .10 | .02 |
| ❏ 322 | Ted Washington | .05 | .01 |
| ❏ 323 | Steve Young | .60 | .25 |
| ❏ 324 | George Seifert CO | .10 | .02 |
| ❏ 325 | Brian Blades | .10 | .02 |
| ❏ 326 | Jacob Green | .05 | .01 |
| ❏ 327 | Patrick Hunter | .05 | .01 |
| ❏ 328 | Tommy Kane | .05 | .01 |
| ❏ 329 | Cortez Kennedy | .10 | .02 |
| ❏ 330 | Dave Krieg | .10 | .02 |
| ❏ 331 | Rufus Porter | .05 | .01 |
| ❏ 332 | John L. Williams | .05 | .01 |
| ❏ 333 | Tom Flores CO | .05 | .01 |
| ❏ 334 | Gary Anderson RB | .05 | .01 |
| ❏ 335 | Mark Carrier WR | .10 | .02 |
| ❏ 336 | Reuben Davis | .05 | .01 |
| ❏ 337 | Lawrence Dawsey | .05 | .01 |
| ❏ 338 | Keith McCants UER | .05 | .01 |
| ❏ 339 | Vinny Testaverde | .10 | .02 |
| ❏ 340 | Broderick Thomas | .05 | .01 |
| ❏ 341 | Robert Wilson | .05 | .01 |
| ❏ 342 | Sam Wyche CO | .05 | .01 |
| ❏ 343 | 1991 Teacher of | .05 | .01 |
| ❏ 344 | Owners Reject Instant | .05 | .01 |
| ❏ 345 | NFL Experience | .05 | .01 |
| ❏ 346 | Chuck Noll Retires | .10 | .02 |
| ❏ 347 | Isaac Curtis | .05 | .01 |
| ❏ 348 | Michael Irvin/D.Pearson | .10 | .02 |
| ❏ 349 | Barry Sanders/B.Sims | .50 | .20 |
| ❏ 350 | Todd Marinovich/K.Stable | .05 | .01 |
| ❏ 351 | Leonard Russell/C.James | .10 | .02 |
| ❏ 352 | Bob Golic | .05 | .01 |
| ❏ 353 | Pat Harlow | .05 | .01 |
| ❏ 354 | Esera Tuaolo | .05 | .01 |
| ❏ 355 | Mark Schlereth RC Envir. | .05 | .01 |
| ❏ 356 | Trace Armstrong | .05 | .01 |
| ❏ 357 | Eric Bieniemy | .05 | .01 |
| ❏ 358 | Bill Romanowski | .05 | .01 |
| ❏ 359 | Irv Eatman | .05 | .01 |
| ❏ 360 | Jonathan Hayes | .05 | .01 |
| ❏ 361 | Atlanta Falcons | .05 | .01 |
| ❏ 362 | Chicago Bears | .05 | .01 |
| ❏ 363 | Dallas Cowboys | .05 | .01 |
| ❏ 364 | Detroit Lions | .05 | .01 |
| ❏ 365 | Green Bay Packers | .05 | .01 |
| ❏ 366 | Los Angeles Rams | .05 | .01 |
| ❏ 367 | Minnesota Vikings | .05 | .01 |
| ❏ 368 | New Orleans Saints UER | .05 | .01 |
| ❏ 369 | New York Giants | .05 | .01 |
| ❏ 370 | Philadelphia Eagles | .05 | .01 |
| ❏ 371 | Phoenix Cardinals | .05 | .01 |
| ❏ 372 | San Francisco 49ers | .05 | .01 |
| ❏ 373 | Tampa Bay Buccaneers | .05 | .01 |
| ❏ 374 | Washington Redskins | .05 | .01 |
| ❏ 375 | Steve Atwater PB UER | .05 | .01 |
| ❏ 376 | Cornelius Bennett PB | .10 | .02 |
| ❏ 377 | Tim Brown PB | .10 | .02 |
| ❏ 378 | Marion Butts PB | .05 | .01 |
| ❏ 379 | Ray Childress PB | .05 | .01 |
| ❏ 380 | Mark Clayton PB | .05 | .01 |
| ❏ 381 | Marv Cook PB | .05 | .01 |
| ❏ 382 | Cris Dishman PB | .05 | .01 |
| ❏ 383 | William Fuller PB | .05 | .01 |
| ❏ 384 | Gaston Green PB | .05 | .01 |
| ❏ 385 | Jeff Jaeger PB | .05 | .01 |
| ❏ 386 | Haywood Jeffires PB | .10 | .02 |
| ❏ 387 | James Lofton PB | .10 | .02 |
| ❏ 388 | Ronnie Lott PB | .10 | .02 |
| ❏ 389 | Karl Mecklenburg PB UER | .05 | .01 |
| ❏ 390 | Warren Moon PB | .10 | .02 |
| ❏ 391 | Anthony Munoz PB | .05 | .01 |
| ❏ 392 | Dennis Smith PB | .05 | .01 |
| ❏ 393 | Neil Smith PB | .10 | .02 |
| ❏ 394 | Darryl Talley PB | .05 | .01 |
| ❏ 395 | Derrick Thomas PB | .10 | .02 |
| ❏ 396 | Thurman Thomas PB | .10 | .02 |
| ❏ 397 | Greg Townsend PB | .05 | .01 |
| ❏ 398 | Richmond Webb PB | .05 | .01 |
| ❏ 399 | Rod Woodson PB | .10 | .02 |
| ❏ 400 | Dan Reeves CO PB | .05 | .01 |
| ❏ 401 | Troy Aikman PB | .40 | .15 |
| ❏ 402 | Eric Allen PB | .05 | .01 |

|  |  | | |
|---|---|---|---|
| 403 | Bennie Blades PB | .05 | .01 |
| 404 | Lomas Brown PB | .05 | .01 |
| 405 | Mark Carrier DB PB | .05 | .01 |
| 406 | Gary Clark PB | .10 | .02 |
| 407 | Mel Gray PB | .05 | .01 |
| 408 | Darrell Green PB | .05 | .01 |
| 409 | Michael Irvin PB | .25 | .08 |
| 410 | Vaughan Johnson PB | .05 | .01 |
| 411 | Seth Joyner PB | .05 | .01 |
| 412 | Jim Lachey PB | .05 | .01 |
| 413 | Chip Lohmiller PB | .05 | .01 |
| 414 | Charles Mann PB | .05 | .01 |
| 415 | Chris Miller PB | .10 | .02 |
| 416 | Sam Mills PB | .05 | .01 |
| 417 | Bart Oates PB | .05 | .01 |
| 418 | Jerry Rice PB | .40 | .15 |
| 419 | Andre Rison PB | .25 | .08 |
| 420 | Mark Rypien PB | .05 | .01 |
| 421 | Barry Sanders PB | .50 | .20 |
| 422 | Deion Sanders PB | .25 | .08 |
| 423 | Mark Schlereth PB | .05 | .01 |
| 424 | Mike Singletary PB | .05 | .01 |
| 425 | Emmitt Smith PB | .60 | .25 |
| 426 | Pat Swilling PB | .05 | .01 |
| 427 | Reggie White PB | .10 | .02 |
| 428 | Rick Bryan | .05 | .01 |
| 429 | Tim Green | .05 | .01 |
| 430 | Drew Hill | .05 | .01 |
| 431 | Norm Johnson | .05 | .01 |
| 432 | Keith Jones | .05 | .01 |
| 433 | Mike Pritchard | .10 | .02 |
| 434 | Deion Sanders | .50 | .20 |
| 435 | Tony Smith RC RB | .05 | .01 |
| 436 | Jessie Tuggle | .05 | .01 |
| 437 | Steve Christie | .05 | .01 |
| 438 | Shane Conlan | .05 | .01 |
| 439 | Matt Darby RC | .05 | .01 |
| 440 | John Fina RC | .05 | .01 |
| 441 | Henry Jones | .05 | .01 |
| 442 | Jim Kelly | .25 | .08 |
| 443 | Pete Metzelaars | .05 | .01 |
| 444 | Andre Reed | .10 | .02 |
| 445 | Bruce Smith | .25 | .08 |
| 446 | Troy Auzenne RC | .05 | .01 |
| 447 | Mark Carrier RC | .05 | .01 |
| 448 | Will Furrer RC | .05 | .01 |
| 449 | Jim Harbaugh | .25 | .08 |
| 450 | Brad Muster | .05 | .01 |
| 451 | Darren Lewis | .05 | .01 |
| 452 | Mike Singletary | .10 | .02 |
| 453 | Alonzo Spellman RC | .10 | .02 |
| 454 | Chris Zorich | .10 | .02 |
| 455 | Jim Breech | .05 | .01 |
| 456 | Boomer Esiason | .10 | .02 |
| 457 | Derrick Fenner | .05 | .01 |
| 458 | James Francis | .05 | .01 |
| 459 | David Klingler RC | .05 | .01 |
| 460 | Tim McGee | .05 | .01 |
| 461 | Carl Pickens RC | .25 | .08 |
| 462 | Alfred Williams | .05 | .01 |
| 463 | Darryl Williams RC | .05 | .01 |
| 464 | Mark Bavaro | .05 | .01 |
| 465 | Jay Hilgenberg | .05 | .01 |
| 466 | Leroy Hoard | .10 | .02 |
| 467 | Bernie Kosar | .10 | .02 |
| 468 | Michael Dean Perry | .10 | .02 |
| 469 | Todd Philcox RC | .05 | .01 |
| 470 | Patrick Rowe RC | .05 | .01 |
| 471 | Tommy Vardell RC | .05 | .01 |
| 472 | Everson Walls | .05 | .01 |
| 473 | Troy Aikman | .75 | .30 |
| 474 | Kenneth Gant RC | .05 | .01 |
| 475 | Charles Haley | .10 | .02 |
| 476 | Michael Irvin | .25 | .08 |
| 477 | Robert Jones RC | .05 | .01 |
| 478 | Russell Maryland | .05 | .01 |
| 479 | Jay Novacek | .10 | .02 |
| 480 | Kevin Smith RC DB | .05 | .01 |
| 481 | Tony Tolbert | .05 | .01 |
| 482 | Steve Atwater | .05 | .01 |
| 483 | Shane Dronett RC | .05 | .01 |
| 484 | Simon Fletcher | .05 | .01 |
| 485 | Greg Lewis | .05 | .01 |
| 486 | Tommy Maddox RC | 2.00 | .75 |
| 487 | Shannon Sharpe | .25 | .08 |
| 488 | Dennis Smith | .05 | .01 |
| 489 | Sammie Smith | .05 | .01 |
| 490 | Kenny Walker | .05 | .01 |
| 491 | Lomas Brown | .05 | .01 |
| 492 | Mike Farr | .05 | .01 |
| 493 | Mel Gray | .10 | .02 |
| 494 | Jason Hanson RC | .10 | .02 |
| 495 | Herman Moore | .25 | .08 |
| 496 | Rodney Peete | .05 | .01 |
| 497 | Robert Porcher RC | .25 | .08 |
| 498 | Kelvin Pritchett | .05 | .01 |
| 499 | Andre Ware | .05 | .01 |
| 500 | Sanjay Beach RC | .05 | .01 |
| 501 | Edgar Bennett RC | .25 | .08 |
| 502 | Lewis Billups | .05 | .01 |
| 503 | Terrell Buckley | .05 | .01 |
| 504 | Ty Detmer | .25 | .08 |
| 505 | Brett Favre | 2.50 | 1.25 |
| 506 | Johnny Holland | .05 | .01 |
| 507 | Dexter McNabb RC | .05 | .01 |
| 508 | Vince Workman | .05 | .01 |
| 509 | Cody Carlson | .05 | .01 |
| 510 | Ernest Givins | .10 | .02 |
| 511 | Jerry Gray | .05 | .01 |
| 512 | Haywood Jeffires | .10 | .02 |
| 513 | Bruce Matthews | .05 | .01 |
| 514 | Bubba McDowell | .05 | .01 |
| 515 | Bucky Richardson RC | .05 | .01 |
| 516 | Webster Slaughter | .05 | .01 |
| 517 | Al Smith | .05 | .01 |
| 518 | Mel Agee | .05 | .01 |
| 519 | Ashley Ambrose RC | .25 | .08 |
| 520 | Kevin Call | .05 | .01 |
| 521 | Ken Clark | .05 | .01 |
| 522 | Quentin Coryatt RC | .05 | .01 |
| 523 | Steve Emtman RC | .05 | .01 |
| 524 | Jeff George | .25 | .08 |
| 525 | Jessie Hester | .05 | .01 |
| 526 | Anthony Johnson | .10 | .02 |
| 527 | Tim Barnett | .05 | .01 |
| 528 | Martin Bayless | .05 | .01 |
| 529 | J.J. Birden | .05 | .01 |
| 530 | Dale Carter RC | .10 | .02 |
| 531 | Dave Krieg | .05 | .01 |
| 532 | Albert Lewis | .05 | .01 |
| 533 | Nick Lowery | .05 | .01 |
| 534 | Christian Okoye | .05 | .01 |
| 535 | Harvey Williams | .25 | .08 |
| 536 | Aundray Bruce | .05 | .01 |
| 537 | Eric Dickerson | .10 | .02 |
| 538 | Willie Gault | .10 | .02 |
| 539 | Ethan Horton | .05 | .01 |
| 540 | Jeff Jaeger | .05 | .01 |
| 541 | Napoleon McCallum | .05 | .01 |
| 542 | Chester McGlockton RC | .10 | .02 |
| 543 | Steve Smith | .05 | .01 |
| 544 | Steve Wisniewski | .05 | .01 |
| 545 | Marc Boutte RC | .05 | .01 |
| 546 | Pat Carter | .05 | .01 |
| 547 | Jim Everett | .10 | .02 |
| 548 | Cleveland Gary | .05 | .01 |
| 549 | Sean Gilbert RC | .10 | .02 |
| 550 | Steve Israel RC | .05 | .01 |
| 551 | Todd Kinchen RC | .05 | .01 |
| 552 | Jackie Slater | .05 | .01 |
| 553 | Tony Zendejas | .05 | .01 |
| 554 | Robert Clark | .05 | .01 |
| 555 | Mark Clayton | .10 | .02 |
| 556 | Marco Coleman RC | .10 | .02 |
| 557 | Bryan Cox | .10 | .02 |
| 558 | Keith Jackson | .10 | .02 |
| 559 | Dan Marino | 1.25 | .50 |
| 560 | John Offerdahl | .05 | .01 |
| 561 | Troy Vincent RC | .05 | .01 |
| 562 | Richmond Webb | .05 | .01 |
| 563 | Terry Allen | .25 | .08 |
| 564 | Cris Carter | .50 | .20 |
| 565 | Roger Craig | .10 | .02 |
| 566 | Rich Gannon | .25 | .08 |
| 567 | Hassan Jones | .05 | .01 |
| 568 | Randall McDaniel | .05 | .01 |
| 569 | Al Noga | .05 | .01 |
| 570 | Todd Scott | .05 | .01 |
| 571 | Van Waiters RC | .05 | .01 |
| 572 | Bruce Armstrong | .05 | .01 |
| 573 | Gene Chilton RC | .05 | .01 |
| 574 | Eugene Chung RC | .05 | .01 |
| 575 | Todd Collins RC | .05 | .01 |
| 576 | Harl Lee Dykes | .05 | .01 |
| 577 | David Howard RC | .05 | .01 |
| 578 | Eugene Lockhart | .05 | .01 |
| 579 | Greg McMurtry | .05 | .01 |
| 580 | Rod Smith DB RC | .05 | .01 |
| 581 | Gene Atkins | .05 | .01 |
| 582 | Vince Buck | .05 | .01 |
| 583 | Wesley Carroll | .05 | .01 |
| 584 | Jim Dombrowski | .05 | .01 |
| 585 | Vaughn Dunbar RC | .05 | .01 |
| 586 | Craig Heyward | .10 | .02 |
| 587 | Dalton Hilliard | .05 | .01 |
| 588 | Wayne Martin | .05 | .01 |
| 589 | Renaldo Turnbull | .05 | .01 |
| 590 | Carl Banks | .05 | .01 |
| 591 | Derek Brown RC TE | .05 | .01 |
| 592 | Jarrod Bunch | .05 | .01 |
| 593 | Mark Ingram | .05 | .01 |
| 594 | Ed McCaffrey | .30 | .10 |
| 595 | Phil Simms | .10 | .02 |
| 596 | Phillippi Sparks RC | .05 | .01 |
| 597 | Lawrence Taylor | .25 | .08 |
| 598 | Lewis Tillman | .05 | .01 |
| 599 | Kyle Clifton | .05 | .01 |
| 600 | Mo Lewis | .05 | .01 |
| 601 | Terance Mathis | .10 | .02 |
| 602 | Scott Mersereau | .05 | .01 |
| 603 | Johnny Mitchell RC | .25 | .08 |
| 604 | Browning Nagle | .05 | .01 |
| 605 | Ken O'Brien | .05 | .01 |
| 606 | Al Toon | .10 | .02 |
| 607 | Marvin Washington | .05 | .01 |
| 608 | Eric Allen | .05 | .01 |
| 609 | Fred Barnett | .25 | .08 |
| 610 | John Booty | .05 | .01 |
| 611 | Randall Cunningham | .25 | .08 |
| 612 | Rich Miano | .05 | .01 |
| 613 | Clyde Simmons | .05 | .01 |
| 614 | Siran Stacy | .05 | .01 |
| 615 | Herschel Walker | .10 | .02 |
| 616 | Calvin Williams | .10 | .02 |
| 617 | Chris Chandler | .25 | .08 |
| 618 | Randal Hill | .05 | .01 |
| 619 | Johnny Johnson | .05 | .01 |
| 620 | Lorenzo Lynch | .05 | .01 |
| 621 | Robert Massey | .05 | .01 |
| 622 | Ricky Proehl | .05 | .01 |
| 623 | Timm Rosenbach | .05 | .01 |
| 624 | Tony Sacca RC | .05 | .01 |
| 625 | Aeneas Williams UER | .10 | .02 |
| 626 | Bubby Brister | .05 | .01 |
| 627 | Barry Foster | .10 | .02 |
| 628 | Merril Hoge | .05 | .01 |
| 629 | D.J. Johnson | .05 | .01 |
| 630 | David Little | .05 | .01 |
| 631 | Greg Lloyd | .10 | .02 |
| 632 | Ernie Mills | .05 | .01 |
| 633 | Leon Searcy RC | .05 | .01 |
| 634 | Dwight Stone | .05 | .01 |
| 635 | Sam Anno RC | .05 | .01 |
| 636 | Burt Grossman | .05 | .01 |
| 637 | Stan Humphries | .25 | .08 |
| 638 | Nate Lewis | .05 | .01 |
| 639 | Anthony Miller | .10 | .02 |
| 640 | Chris Mims | .25 | .08 |
| 641 | Marquez Pope RC | .05 | .01 |
| 642 | Stanley Richard | .05 | .01 |
| 643 | Junior Seau | .25 | .08 |
| 644 | Brian Bollinger RC | .05 | .01 |
| 645 | Steve Bono RC | .25 | .08 |
| 646 | Dexter Carter | .05 | .01 |
| 647 | Dana Hall RC | .05 | .01 |
| 648 | Amp Lee | .05 | .01 |
| 649 | Joe Montana | 1.25 | .50 |
| 650 | Tom Rathman | .05 | .01 |
| 651 | Jerry Rice | .75 | .30 |
| 652 | Ricky Watters | .25 | .08 |
| 653 | Robert Blackmon | .05 | .01 |
| 654 | John Kasay | .05 | .01 |
| 655 | Ronnie Lee RC | .05 | .01 |
| 656 | Dan McGwire | .05 | .01 |
| 657 | Ray Roberts RC | .05 | .01 |

| | | |
|---|---|---|
| ❏ 658 Kelly Stoufler | .05 | .01 |
| ❏ 659 Chris Warren | .25 | .08 |
| ❏ 660 Tony Woods | .05 | .01 |
| ❏ 661 David Wyman | .05 | .01 |
| ❏ 662 Reggie Cobb | .05 | .01 |
| ❏ 663A Steve DeBerg ERR | .10 | .02 |
| ❏ 663B Steve DeBerg COR | .10 | .02 |
| ❏ 664 Santana Dotson RC | .10 | .02 |
| ❏ 665 Willie Drewery | .05 | .01 |
| ❏ 666 Paul Gruber | .05 | .01 |
| ❏ 667 Ron Hall | .05 | .01 |
| ❏ 668 Courtney Hawkins RC | .10 | .02 |
| ❏ 669 Charles McRae | .05 | .01 |
| ❏ 670 Ricky Reynolds | .05 | .01 |
| ❏ 671 Monte Coleman | .05 | .01 |
| ❏ 672 Brad Edwards | .05 | .01 |
| ❏ 673 Jumpy Geathers UER | .05 | .01 |
| ❏ 674 Kelly Goodburn | .05 | .01 |
| ❏ 675 Kurt Gouveia | .05 | .01 |
| ❏ 676 Chris Hakel RC | .05 | .01 |
| ❏ 677 Wilber Marshall | .05 | .01 |
| ❏ 678 Ricky Sanders | .05 | .01 |
| ❏ 679 Mark Schlereth | .05 | .01 |
| ❏ 680 Buffalo Bills | .05 | .01 |
| ❏ 681 Cincinnati Bengals | .05 | .01 |
| ❏ 682 Cleveland Browns | .05 | .01 |
| ❏ 683 Denver Broncos | .05 | .01 |
| ❏ 684 Houston Oilers | .05 | .01 |
| ❏ 685 Indianapolis Colts | .05 | .01 |
| ❏ 686 Tracy Simien SG | .05 | .01 |
| ❏ 687 Los Angeles Raiders | .05 | .01 |
| ❏ 688 Miami Dolphins | .05 | .01 |
| ❏ 689 New England Patriots | .05 | .01 |
| ❏ 690 New York Jets | .05 | .01 |
| ❏ 691 Pittsburgh Steelers | .05 | .01 |
| ❏ 692 San Diego Chargers | .05 | .01 |
| ❏ 693 Seattle Seahawks | .05 | .01 |
| ❏ 694 Play Smart | .05 | .01 |
| ❏ 695 Hank Williams Jr. NEW | .75 | .30 |
| ❏ 696 3 Brothers in NFL NEWS | .05 | .01 |
| ❏ 697 Japan Bowl NEWS | .05 | .01 |
| ❏ 698 Georgia Dome NEWS | .05 | .01 |
| ❏ 699 Theme Art NEWS | .05 | .01 |
| ❏ 700 Mark Rypien SB MVP NEW | .05 | .01 |
| ❏ AU150 Emmitt Smith AU/1000 | 120.00 | 60.00 |
| ❏ AU168 Erik Kramer AU/1000 | 30.00 | 12.50 |
| ❏ NNO C.Smith Power Preview | .75 | .30 |
| ❏ NNO Santa Claus | .50 | .20 |
| ❏ SC5 Super Bowl XXVI Logo | .30 | .10 |
| ❏ P1 Cover Card Promo | 1.00 | .40 |

**1993 Pro Set**

| | | |
|---|---|---|
| ❏ COMPLETE SET (449) | 20.00 | 8.00 |
| ❏ 1 Marco Coleman | .05 | .01 |
| ❏ 2 Steve Young LL | .30 | .10 |
| ❏ 3 Mike Holmgren | .10 | .02 |
| ❏ 4 John Elway LL | .75 | .30 |
| ❏ 5 Steve Young LL | .30 | .10 |
| ❏ 6 Dan Marino LL | .75 | .30 |
| ❏ 7 Emmitt Smith LL | .75 | .30 |
| ❏ 8 Sterling Sharpe LL | .10 | .02 |
| ❏ 9 Jay Novacek | .05 | .01 |
| ❏ 10 Sterling Sharpe LL | .10 | .02 |
| ❏ 11 Thurman Thomas LL | .10 | .02 |
| ❏ 12 Pete Stoyanovich | .05 | .01 |
| ❏ 13 Greg Montgomery | .05 | .01 |
| ❏ 14 Johnny Bailey | .05 | .01 |
| ❏ 15 Jon Vaughn | .05 | .01 |

| | | |
|---|---|---|
| ❏ 16 Audray McMillian | .05 | .01 |
| ❏ 17 Clyde Simmons | .05 | .01 |
| ❏ 18 Cortez Kennedy | .05 | .01 |
| ❏ 19 AFC Wildcard | .05 | .01 |
| ❏ 20 AFC Wildcard | .05 | .05 |
| ❏ 21 AFC Wildcard | .05 | .01 |
| ❏ 22 NFC Wildcard | .05 | .01 |
| ❏ 23 AFC Divisional | .05 | .01 |
| ❏ 24 Dan Marino REP | .75 | .30 |
| ❏ 25 Troy Aikman REP | .50 | .20 |
| ❏ 26 Ricky Watters REP | .10 | .02 |
| ❏ 27 AFC Championship | .05 | .01 |
| ❏ 28 NFC Championship | .05 | .01 |
| ❏ 29 Super Bowl XXVIII Logo | .05 | .01 |
| ❏ 30 Troy Aikman | .75 | .30 |
| ❏ 31 Thomas Everett | .05 | .01 |
| ❏ 32 Charles Haley | .10 | .02 |
| ❏ 33 Alvin Harper | .10 | .02 |
| ❏ 34 Michael Irvin | .25 | .08 |
| ❏ 35 Robert Jones | .05 | .01 |
| ❏ 36 Russell Maryland | .05 | .01 |
| ❏ 37 Ken Norton | .10 | .02 |
| ❏ 38 Jay Novacek | .10 | .02 |
| ❏ 39 Emmitt Smith | 1.50 | .50 |
| ❏ 40 Darrin Smith RC | .10 | .02 |
| ❏ 41 Mark Stepnoski | .05 | .01 |
| ❏ 42 Kevin Williams RC WR | .25 | .08 |
| ❏ 43 Daryl Johnston | .25 | .08 |
| ❏ 44 Derrick Lassic RC | .05 | .01 |
| ❏ 45 Don Beebe | .05 | .01 |
| ❏ 46 Cornelius Bennett | .10 | .02 |
| ❏ 47 Bill Brooks | .05 | .01 |
| ❏ 48 Kenneth Davis | .05 | .01 |
| ❏ 49 Jim Kelly | .25 | .08 |
| ❏ 50 Andre Reed | .10 | .02 |
| ❏ 51 Bruce Smith | .25 | .08 |
| ❏ 52 Thomas Smith RC | .10 | .02 |
| ❏ 53 Darryl Talley | .05 | .01 |
| ❏ 54 Thurman Thomas | .25 | .08 |
| ❏ 55 Russell Copeland RC | .10 | .02 |
| ❏ 56 Steve Christie | .05 | .01 |
| ❏ 57 Pete Metzelaars | .05 | .01 |
| ❏ 58 Frank Reich | .10 | .02 |
| ❏ 59 Henry Jones | .05 | .01 |
| ❏ 60 Vinnie Clark | .05 | .01 |
| ❏ 61 Eric Dickerson | .10 | .02 |
| ❏ 62 Jumpy Geathers | .05 | .01 |
| ❏ 63 Roger Harper RC | .05 | .01 |
| ❏ 64 Michael Haynes | .10 | .02 |
| ❏ 65 Bobby Hebert | .05 | .01 |
| ❏ 66 Lincoln Kennedy RC | .05 | .01 |
| ❏ 67 Chris Miller | .10 | .02 |
| ❏ 68 Andre Rison | .10 | .02 |
| ❏ 69 Deion Sanders | .50 | .20 |
| ❏ 70 Jessie Tuggle | .05 | .01 |
| ❏ 71 Ron George | .05 | .01 |
| ❏ 72 Erric Pegram | .10 | .02 |
| ❏ 73 Melvin Jenkins | .05 | .01 |
| ❏ 74 Pierce Holt | .05 | .01 |
| ❏ 75 Neal Anderson | .05 | .01 |
| ❏ 76 Mark Carrier DB | .05 | .01 |
| ❏ 77 Curtis Conway RC | .40 | .15 |
| ❏ 78 Richard Dent | .10 | .02 |
| ❏ 79 Jim Harbaugh | .25 | .08 |
| ❏ 80 Craig Heyward | .10 | .02 |
| ❏ 81 Darren Lewis | .05 | .01 |
| ❏ 82 Alonzo Spellman | .05 | .01 |
| ❏ 83 Tom Waddle | .05 | .01 |
| ❏ 84 Wendell Davis | .05 | .01 |
| ❏ 85 Chris Zorich | .05 | .01 |
| ❏ 86 Carl Simpson RC | .05 | .01 |
| ❏ 87 Chris Gedney RC | .05 | .01 |
| ❏ 88 Trace Armstrong | .05 | .01 |
| ❏ 89 Peter Tom Willis | .05 | .01 |
| ❏ 90 John Copeland RC | .10 | .02 |
| ❏ 91 Derrick Fenner | .05 | .01 |
| ❏ 92 James Francis | .05 | .01 |
| ❏ 93 Harold Green | .10 | .02 |
| ❏ 94 David Klingler | .10 | .02 |
| ❏ 95 Tim Krumrie | .05 | .01 |
| ❏ 96 Tony McGee RC | .10 | .02 |
| ❏ 97 Carl Pickens | .25 | .08 |
| ❏ 98 Alfred Williams | .05 | .01 |
| ❏ 99 Doug Pelfrey RC | .05 | .01 |
| ❏ 100 Lance Gunn RC | .05 | .01 |

| | | |
|---|---|---|
| ❏ 101 Jay Schroeder | .05 | .01 |
| ❏ 102 Steve Tovar RC | .05 | .01 |
| ❏ 103 Jeff Query | .05 | .01 |
| ❏ 104 Ty Parten RC | .05 | .01 |
| ❏ 105 Jerry Ball | .05 | .01 |
| ❏ 106 Mark Carrier WR | .10 | .02 |
| ❏ 107 Rob Burnett | .05 | .01 |
| ❏ 108 Michael Jackson | .10 | .02 |
| ❏ 109 Mike Johnson | .05 | .01 |
| ❏ 110 Bernie Kosar | .10 | .02 |
| ❏ 111 Clay Matthews | .10 | .02 |
| ❏ 112 Eric Metcalf | .10 | .02 |
| ❏ 113 Michael Dean Perry | .10 | .02 |
| ❏ 114 Vinny Testaverde | .10 | .02 |
| ❏ 115 Eric Turner | .05 | .01 |
| ❏ 116 Tommy Vardell | .05 | .01 |
| ❏ 117 Leroy Hoard | .10 | .02 |
| ❏ 118 Steve Everitt RC | .05 | .01 |
| ❏ 119 Everson Walls | .05 | .01 |
| ❏ 120 Steve Atwater | .05 | .01 |
| ❏ 121 Rod Bernstine | .05 | .01 |
| ❏ 122 Mike Croel | .05 | .01 |
| ❏ 123 John Elway | 1.50 | .60 |
| ❏ 124 Simon Fletcher | .05 | .01 |
| ❏ 125 Glyn Milburn RC | .25 | .08 |
| ❏ 126 Reggie Rivers RC | .05 | .01 |
| ❏ 127 Shannon Sharpe | .25 | .08 |
| ❏ 128 Dennis Smith | .05 | .01 |
| ❏ 129 Dan Williams RC | .05 | .01 |
| ❏ 130 Rondell Jones RC | .05 | .01 |
| ❏ 131 Jason Elam RC | .25 | .08 |
| ❏ 132 Arthur Marshall RC | .05 | .01 |
| ❏ 133 Gary Zimmerman | .05 | .01 |
| ❏ 134 Karl Mecklenburg | .05 | .01 |
| ❏ 135 Bennie Blades | .05 | .01 |
| ❏ 136 Lomas Brown | .05 | .01 |
| ❏ 137 Bill Fralic | .05 | .01 |
| ❏ 138 Mel Gray | .10 | .02 |
| ❏ 139 Willie Green | .05 | .01 |
| ❏ 140 Ryan McNeil RC | .25 | .08 |
| ❏ 141 Rodney Peete | .05 | .01 |
| ❏ 142 Barry Sanders | 1.25 | .50 |
| ❏ 143 Chris Spielman | .10 | .02 |
| ❏ 144 Pat Swilling | .05 | .01 |
| ❏ 145 Andre Ware | .05 | .01 |
| ❏ 146 Herman Moore | .25 | .08 |
| ❏ 147 Tim McKyer | .05 | .01 |
| ❏ 148 Brett Perriman | .25 | .08 |
| ❏ 149 Antonio London RC | .05 | .01 |
| ❏ 150 Edgar Bennett | .25 | .08 |
| ❏ 151 Terrell Buckley | .05 | .01 |
| ❏ 152 Brett Favre | 2.00 | .75 |
| ❏ 153 Jackie Harris | .05 | .01 |
| ❏ 154 Johnny Holland | .05 | .01 |
| ❏ 155 Sterling Sharpe | .25 | .08 |
| ❏ 156 Tim Hauck | .05 | .01 |
| ❏ 157 George Teague RC | .10 | .02 |
| ❏ 158 Reggie White | .25 | .08 |
| ❏ 159 Mark Clayton | .05 | .01 |
| ❏ 160 Ty Detmer | .25 | .08 |
| ❏ 161 Wayne Simmons RC | .05 | .01 |
| ❏ 162 Mark Brunell RC | 1.50 | .60 |
| ❏ 163 Tony Bennett | .05 | .01 |
| ❏ 164 Brian Noble | .05 | .01 |
| ❏ 165 Cody Carlson | .05 | .01 |
| ❏ 166 Ray Childress | .05 | .01 |
| ❏ 167 Cris Dishman | .05 | .01 |
| ❏ 168 Curtis Duncan | .05 | .01 |
| ❏ 169 Brad Hopkins RC | .05 | .01 |
| ❏ 170 Haywood Jeffires | .10 | .02 |
| ❏ 171 Wilber Marshall | .05 | .01 |
| ❏ 172 Micheal Barrow RC UER | .25 | .08 |
| ❏ 173 Bubba McDowell | .05 | .01 |
| ❏ 174 Warren Moon | .25 | .08 |
| ❏ 175 Webster Slaughter | .05 | .01 |
| ❏ 176 Travis Hannah RC | .05 | .01 |
| ❏ 177 Lorenzo White | .10 | .02 |
| ❏ 178 Ernest Givins UER | .10 | .02 |
| ❏ 179 Keith McCants | .05 | .01 |
| ❏ 180 Kerry Cash | .05 | .01 |
| ❏ 181 Quentin Coryatt | .10 | .02 |
| ❏ 182 Kirk Lowdermilk | .05 | .01 |
| ❏ 183 Rodney Culver | .05 | .01 |
| ❏ 184 Rohn Stark | .05 | .01 |
| ❏ 185 Steve Emtman | .05 | .01 |

|  |  | | |
|---|---|---|---|
| 186 | Jeff George | .25 | .08 |
| 187 | Jeff Herrod | .05 | .01 |
| 188 | Reggie Langhorne | .05 | .01 |
| 189 | Roosevelt Potts RC | .05 | .01 |
| 190 | Jack Trudeau | .05 | .01 |
| 191 | Will Wolford | .05 | .01 |
| 192 | Jessie Hester | .05 | .01 |
| 193 | Anthony Johnson | .10 | .02 |
| 194 | Ray Buchanan RC | .25 | .08 |
| 195 | Dale Carter | .25 | .08 |
| 196 | Willie Davis | .25 | .08 |
| 197 | John Alt | .05 | .01 |
| 198 | Joe Montana | 1.50 | .60 |
| 199 | Will Shields RC | .25 | .08 |
| 200 | Neil Smith | .25 | .08 |
| 201 | Derrick Thomas | .25 | .08 |
| 202 | Harvey Williams | .10 | .02 |
| 203 | Marcus Allen | .25 | .08 |
| 204 | J.J. Birden | .05 | .01 |
| 205 | Tim Barnett | .05 | .01 |
| 206 | Albert Lewis | .05 | .01 |
| 207 | Nick Lowery | .05 | .01 |
| 208 | Dave Krieg | .10 | .02 |
| 209 | Keith Cash | .05 | .01 |
| 210 | Patrick Bates RC | .05 | .01 |
| 211 | Nick Bell | .05 | .01 |
| 212 | Tim Brown | .25 | .08 |
| 213 | Willie Gault | .05 | .01 |
| 214 | Ethan Horton | .05 | .01 |
| 215 | Jeff Hostetler | .10 | .02 |
| 216 | Howie Long | .25 | .08 |
| 217 | Greg Townsend | .05 | .01 |
| 218 | Rocket Ismail | .10 | .02 |
| 219 | Alexander Wright | .05 | .01 |
| 220 | Greg Robinson RC | .05 | .01 |
| 221 | Billy Joe Hobert RC | .25 | .08 |
| 222 | Steve Wisniewski | .05 | .01 |
| 223 | Steve Smith | .05 | .01 |
| 224 | Vince Evans | .05 | .01 |
| 225 | Flipper Anderson | .05 | .01 |
| 226 | Jerome Bettis RC | 4.00 | 1.50 |
| 227 | Troy Drayton RC | .10 | .02 |
| 228 | Henry Ellard | .10 | .02 |
| 229 | Jim Everett | .05 | .01 |
| 230 | Tony Zendejas | .05 | .01 |
| 231 | Todd Lyght | .05 | .01 |
| 232 | Todd Kinchen | .05 | .01 |
| 233 | Jackie Slater | .05 | .01 |
| 234 | Fred Stokes | .05 | .01 |
| 235 | Russell White RC | .10 | .02 |
| 236 | Cleveland Gary | .05 | .01 |
| 237 | Sean LaChapelle RC | .05 | .01 |
| 238 | Steve Israel | .05 | .01 |
| 239 | Shane Conlan | .05 | .01 |
| 240 | Keith Byars | .05 | .01 |
| 241 | Marco Coleman | .05 | .01 |
| 242 | Bryan Cox | .05 | .01 |
| 243 | Irving Fryar | .10 | .02 |
| 244 | Richmond Webb | .05 | .01 |
| 245 | Mark Higgs | .05 | .01 |
| 246 | Terry Kirby RC | .25 | .08 |
| 247 | Mark Ingram | .05 | .01 |
| 248 | John Offerdahl | .05 | .01 |
| 249 | Keith Jackson | .10 | .02 |
| 250 | Dan Marino | 1.50 | .60 |
| 251 | O.J. McDuffie RC | .25 | .08 |
| 252 | Louis Oliver | .05 | .01 |
| 253 | Pete Stoyanovich | .05 | .01 |
| 254 | Troy Vincent | .05 | .01 |
| 255 | Anthony Carter | .10 | .02 |
| 256 | Cris Carter | .25 | .08 |
| 257 | Roger Craig | .10 | .02 |
| 258 | Jack Del Rio | .05 | .01 |
| 259 | Chris Doleman | .05 | .01 |
| 260 | Barry Word | .05 | .01 |
| 261 | Qadry Ismail RC | .25 | .08 |
| 262 | Jim McMahon | .05 | .01 |
| 263 | Robert Smith RC | 1.25 | .50 |
| 264 | Fred Strickland | .05 | .01 |
| 265 | Randall McDaniel | .10 | .02 |
| 266 | Carl Lee | .05 | .01 |
| 267 | Olanda Truitt RC UER | .05 | .01 |
| 268 | Terry Allen | .25 | .08 |
| 269 | Audray McMillian | .05 | .01 |
| 270 | Drew Bledsoe RC | 2.50 | 1.00 |

|  |  | | |
|---|---|---|---|
| 271 | Eugene Chung | .05 | .01 |
| 272 | Marv Cook | .05 | .01 |
| 273 | Pat Harlow | .05 | .01 |
| 274 | Greg McMurtry | .05 | .01 |
| 275 | Leonard Russell | .10 | .02 |
| 276 | Chris Slade RC | .10 | .02 |
| 277 | Andre Tippett | .05 | .01 |
| 278 | Vincent Brisby RC | .25 | .08 |
| 279 | Ben Coates | .50 | .20 |
| 280 | Sam Gash RC | .25 | .08 |
| 281 | Bruce Armstrong | .05 | .01 |
| 282 | Rod Smith DB | .05 | .01 |
| 283 | Michael Timpson | .05 | .01 |
| 284 | Scott Sisson RC | .05 | .01 |
| 285 | Morten Andersen | .05 | .01 |
| 286 | Reggie Freeman RC | .05 | .01 |
| 287 | Dalton Hilliard | .05 | .01 |
| 288 | Rickey Jackson | .05 | .01 |
| 289 | Vaughan Johnson | .05 | .01 |
| 290 | Eric Martin | .05 | .01 |
| 291 | Sam Mills | .05 | .01 |
| 292 | Brad Muster | .05 | .01 |
| 293 | Willie Roaf RC | .10 | .02 |
| 294 | Irv Smith RC | .05 | .01 |
| 295 | Wade Wilson | .05 | .01 |
| 296 | Derek Brown RC RBK | .10 | .02 |
| 297 | Quinn Early | .10 | .02 |
| 298 | Steve Walsh | .05 | .01 |
| 299 | Renaldo Turnbull | .05 | .01 |
| 300 | Jessie Armstead RC | .10 | .02 |
| 301 | Carlton Bailey | .05 | .01 |
| 302 | Michael Brooks | .05 | .01 |
| 303 | Rodney Hampton | .10 | .02 |
| 304 | Ed McCaffrey | .25 | .08 |
| 305 | Dave Meggett | .05 | .01 |
| 306 | Bart Oates | .05 | .01 |
| 307 | Mike Sherrard | .05 | .01 |
| 308 | Phil Simms | .10 | .02 |
| 309 | Lawrence Taylor | .25 | .08 |
| 310 | Mark Jackson | .05 | .01 |
| 311 | Jarrod Bunch | .05 | .01 |
| 312 | Howard Cross | .05 | .01 |
| 313 | Michael Strahan RC | 1.50 | .60 |
| 314 | Marcus Buckley RC | .05 | .01 |
| 315 | Brad Baxter | .05 | .01 |
| 316 | Adrian Murrell RC | .25 | .08 |
| 317 | Boomer Esiason | .10 | .02 |
| 318 | Johnny Johnson | .05 | .01 |
| 319 | Marvin Jones RC | .05 | .01 |
| 320 | Jeff Lageman | .05 | .01 |
| 321 | Ronnie Lott | .10 | .02 |
| 322 | Leonard Marshall | .05 | .01 |
| 323 | Johnny Mitchell | .05 | .01 |
| 324 | Rob Moore | .10 | .02 |
| 325 | Browning Nagle | .05 | .01 |
| 326 | Blair Thomas | .05 | .01 |
| 327 | Brian Washington | .05 | .01 |
| 328 | Terance Mathis | .10 | .02 |
| 329 | Kyle Clifton | .05 | .01 |
| 330 | Eric Allen | .05 | .01 |
| 331 | Victor Bailey RC | .05 | .01 |
| 332 | Fred Barnett | .10 | .02 |
| 333 | Mark Bavaro | .05 | .01 |
| 334 | Randall Cunningham | .25 | .08 |
| 335 | Ken O'Brien | .05 | .01 |
| 336 | Seth Joyner | .10 | .02 |
| 337 | Leonard Renfro RC | .05 | .01 |
| 338 | Heath Sherman | .05 | .01 |
| 339 | Clyde Simmons | .05 | .01 |
| 340 | Herschel Walker | .10 | .02 |
| 341 | Calvin Williams | .10 | .02 |
| 342 | Bubby Brister | .05 | .01 |
| 343 | Vaughn Hebron RC | .05 | .01 |
| 344 | Keith Millard | .05 | .01 |
| 345 | Johnny Bailey | .05 | .01 |
| 346 | Steve Beuerlein | .10 | .02 |
| 347 | Chuck Cecil | .05 | .01 |
| 348 | Larry Centers RC | .25 | .08 |
| 349 | Chris Chandler | .10 | .02 |
| 350 | Ernest Dye RC | .05 | .01 |
| 351 | Garrison Hearst RC | .75 | .30 |
| 352 | Randal Hill | .05 | .01 |
| 353 | John Booty | .05 | .01 |
| 354 | Gary Clark | .10 | .02 |
| 355 | Ronald Moore RC | .10 | .02 |

|  |  | | |
|---|---|---|---|
| 356 | Ricky Proehl | .05 | .01 |
| 357 | Eric Swann | .10 | .02 |
| 358 | Ken Harvey | .05 | .01 |
| 359 | Ben Coleman RC | .05 | .01 |
| 360 | Deon Figures RC | .05 | .01 |
| 361 | Barry Foster | .10 | .02 |
| 362 | Jeff Graham | .10 | .02 |
| 363 | Eric Green | .05 | .01 |
| 364 | Kevin Greene | .10 | .02 |
| 365 | Andre Hastings RC | .10 | .02 |
| 366 | Greg Lloyd | .10 | .02 |
| 367 | Neil O'Donnell | .25 | .08 |
| 368 | Dermontti Dawson | .05 | .01 |
| 369 | Mike Tomczak | .05 | .01 |
| 370 | Rod Woodson | .25 | .08 |
| 371 | Chad Brown RC LB | .10 | .02 |
| 372 | Ernie Mills | .05 | .01 |
| 373 | Darren Perry | .05 | .01 |
| 374 | Leon Searcy | .05 | .01 |
| 375 | Marion Butts | .05 | .01 |
| 376 | John Carney | .05 | .01 |
| 377 | Ronnie Harmon | .05 | .01 |
| 378 | Stan Humphries | .10 | .02 |
| 379 | Nate Lewis | .05 | .01 |
| 380 | Natrone Means RC | .25 | .08 |
| 381 | Anthony Miller | .10 | .02 |
| 382 | Chris Mims | .05 | .01 |
| 383 | Leslie O'Neal | .10 | .02 |
| 384 | Joe Cocozzo RC | .05 | .01 |
| 385 | Junior Seau | .25 | .08 |
| 386 | Jerrol Williams | .05 | .01 |
| 387 | John Friesz | .10 | .02 |
| 388 | Darrien Gordon RC | .05 | .01 |
| 389 | Derrick Walker | .05 | .01 |
| 390 | Dana Hall | .05 | .01 |
| 391 | Brent Jones | .10 | .02 |
| 392 | Todd Kelly RC | .05 | .01 |
| 393 | Amp Lee | .05 | .01 |
| 394 | Tim McDonald | .05 | .01 |
| 395 | Jerry Rice | 1.00 | .40 |
| 396 | Dana Stubblefield RC | .25 | .08 |
| 397 | John Taylor | .10 | .02 |
| 398 | Ricky Watters | .25 | .08 |
| 399 | Steve Young | .75 | .30 |
| 400 | Steve Bono | .10 | .02 |
| 401 | Adrian Hardy | .05 | .01 |
| 402 | Tom Rathman | .05 | .01 |
| 403 | Elvis Grbac RC UER | 1.50 | .60 |
| 404 | Bill Romanowski | .05 | .01 |
| 405 | Brian Blades | .10 | .02 |
| 406 | Ferrell Edmunds | .05 | .01 |
| 407 | Carlton Gray RC | .05 | .01 |
| 408 | Cortez Kennedy | .10 | .02 |
| 409 | Kelvin Martin | .05 | .01 |
| 410 | Dan McGwire | .05 | .01 |
| 411 | Rick Mirer RC | .25 | .08 |
| 412 | Rufus Porter | .05 | .01 |
| 413 | Chris Warren | .10 | .02 |
| 414 | Jon Vaughn | .05 | .01 |
| 415 | John L. Williams | .05 | .01 |
| 416 | Eugene Robinson | .05 | .01 |
| 417 | Michael McCrary RC | .10 | .02 |
| 418 | Michael Bates RC | .05 | .01 |
| 419 | Stan Gelbaugh | .05 | .01 |
| 420 | Reggie Cobb | .05 | .01 |
| 421 | Eric Curry RC | .05 | .01 |
| 422 | Lawrence Dawsey | .05 | .01 |
| 423 | Santana Dotson | .10 | .02 |
| 424 | Craig Erickson | .10 | .02 |
| 425 | Ron Hall | .05 | .01 |
| 426 | Courtney Hawkins | .05 | .01 |
| 427 | Broderick Thomas | .05 | .01 |
| 428 | Vince Workman | .05 | .01 |
| 429 | Demetrius DuBose RC | .05 | .01 |
| 430 | Lamar Thomas RC | .05 | .01 |
| 431 | John Lynch RC | .60 | .25 |
| 432 | Hardy Nickerson | .10 | .02 |
| 433 | Horace Copeland RC | .10 | .02 |
| 434 | Steve DeBerg | .05 | .01 |
| 435 | Joe Jacoby | .05 | .01 |
| 436 | Tom Carter RC | .05 | .01 |
| 437 | Andre Collins | .05 | .01 |
| 438 | Darrell Green | .10 | .02 |
| 439 | Desmond Howard | .10 | .02 |
| 440 | Chip Lohmiller | .05 | .01 |

| | | |
|---|---|---|
| ☐ 441 Charles Mann | .05 | .01 |
| ☐ 442 Tim McGee | .05 | .01 |
| ☐ 443 Art Monk | .10 | .02 |
| ☐ 444 Mark Rypien | .05 | .01 |
| ☐ 445 Ricky Sanders | .05 | .01 |
| ☐ 446 Brian Mitchell | .10 | .02 |
| ☐ 447 Reggie Brooks RC | .10 | .02 |
| ☐ 448 Carl Banks | .05 | .01 |
| ☐ 449 Cary Conklin | .05 | .01 |
| ☐ NNO Santa Claus | 1.50 | .60 |

## 1989 Score

| | | |
|---|---|---|
| ☐ COMPLETE SET (330) | 80.00 | 40.00 |
| ☐ COMP.FACT.SET (330) | 80.00 | 40.00 |
| ☐ 1 Joe Montana | 4.00 | 1.50 |
| ☐ 2 Bo Jackson | .60 | .25 |
| ☐ 3 Boomer Esiason | .20 | .07 |
| ☐ 4 Roger Craig | .50 | .20 |
| ☐ 5 Ed Too Tall Jones | .20 | .07 |
| ☐ 6 Phil Simms | .20 | .07 |
| ☐ 7 Dan Hampton | .20 | .07 |
| ☐ 8 John Settle RC | .10 | .02 |
| ☐ 9 Bernie Kosar | .20 | .07 |
| ☐ 10 Al Toon | .20 | .07 |
| ☐ 11 Bubby Brister RC | 1.00 | .40 |
| ☐ 12 Mark Clayton | .20 | .07 |
| ☐ 13 Dan Marino | 4.00 | 1.50 |
| ☐ 14 Joe Morris | .10 | .02 |
| ☐ 15 Warren Moon | .50 | .20 |
| ☐ 16 Chuck Long | .10 | .02 |
| ☐ 17 Mark Jackson | .10 | .02 |
| ☐ 18 Michael Irvin RC | 10.00 | 4.00 |
| ☐ 19 Bruce Smith | .50 | .20 |
| ☐ 20 Anthony Carter | .20 | .07 |
| ☐ 21 Charles Haley | .50 | .20 |
| ☐ 22 Dave Duerson | .10 | .02 |
| ☐ 23 Troy Stradford | .10 | .02 |
| ☐ 24 Freeman McNeil | .10 | .02 |
| ☐ 25 Jerry Gray | .10 | .02 |
| ☐ 26 Bill Maas | .10 | .02 |
| ☐ 27 Chris Chandler RC | 4.00 | 1.50 |
| ☐ 28 Tom Newberry RC | .10 | .02 |
| ☐ 29 Albert Lewis | .10 | .02 |
| ☐ 30 Jay Schroeder | .10 | .02 |
| ☐ 31 Dalton Hilliard | .10 | .02 |
| ☐ 32 Tony Eason | .10 | .02 |
| ☐ 33 Rick Donnelly UER | .10 | .02 |
| ☐ 34 Herschel Walker | .20 | .07 |
| ☐ 35 Wesley Walker | .10 | .02 |
| ☐ 36 Chris Doleman | .20 | .07 |
| ☐ 37 Pat Swilling | .20 | .07 |
| ☐ 38 Joey Browner | .10 | .02 |
| ☐ 39 Shane Conlan | .20 | .07 |
| ☐ 40 Mike Tomczak | .20 | .07 |
| ☐ 41 Webster Slaughter | .10 | .02 |
| ☐ 42 Ray Donaldson | .10 | .02 |
| ☐ 43 Christian Okoye | .10 | .02 |
| ☐ 44 John Bosa | .10 | .02 |
| ☐ 45 Aaron Cox RC | .10 | .02 |
| ☐ 46 Bobby Hebert | .20 | .07 |
| ☐ 47 Carl Banks | .10 | .02 |
| ☐ 48 Jeff Fuller | .10 | .02 |
| ☐ 49 Gerald Willhite | .10 | .02 |
| ☐ 50 Mike Singletary | .20 | .07 |
| ☐ 51 Stanley Morgan | .20 | .07 |
| ☐ 52 Mark Bavaro | .20 | .07 |
| ☐ 53 Mickey Shuler | .10 | .02 |
| ☐ 54 Keith Millard | .10 | .02 |
| ☐ 55 Andre Tippett | .10 | .02 |
| ☐ 56 Vance Johnson | .20 | .07 |
| ☐ 57 Bennie Blades RC | .20 | .07 |
| ☐ 58 Tim Harris | .10 | .02 |
| ☐ 59 Hanford Dixon | .10 | .02 |
| ☐ 60 Chris Miller RC | 1.00 | .40 |
| ☐ 61 Cornelius Bennett | .50 | .20 |
| ☐ 62 Neal Anderson | .20 | .07 |
| ☐ 63 Ickey Woods RC UER | .50 | .20 |
| ☐ 64 Gary Anderson RB | .10 | .02 |
| ☐ 65 Vaughan Johnson RC | .10 | .02 |
| ☐ 66 Ronnie Lippett | .10 | .02 |
| ☐ 67 Mike Quick | .10 | .02 |
| ☐ 68 Roy Green | .20 | .07 |
| ☐ 69 Tim Krumrie | .10 | .02 |
| ☐ 70 Mark Malone | .10 | .02 |
| ☐ 71 James Jones FB | .10 | .02 |
| ☐ 72 Cris Carter RC | 10.00 | 4.00 |
| ☐ 73 Ricky Nattiel | .10 | .02 |
| ☐ 74 Jim Arnold UER | .10 | .02 |
| ☐ 75 Randall Cunningham | 1.00 | .40 |
| ☐ 76 John L.Williams | .20 | .07 |
| ☐ 77 Paul Gruber RC | .10 | .02 |
| ☐ 78 Rod Woodson RC | 3.00 | 1.25 |
| ☐ 79 Ray Childress | .10 | .02 |
| ☐ 80 Doug Williams | .20 | .07 |
| ☐ 81 Deron Cherry | .20 | .07 |
| ☐ 82 John Offerdahl | .10 | .02 |
| ☐ 83 Louis Lipps | .20 | .07 |
| ☐ 84 Neil Lomax | .10 | .02 |
| ☐ 85 Wade Wilson | .20 | .07 |
| ☐ 86 Tim Brown RC | 10.00 | 4.00 |
| ☐ 87 Chris Hinton | .10 | .02 |
| ☐ 88 Stump Mitchell | .10 | .02 |
| ☐ 89 Tunch Ilkin RC | .10 | .02 |
| ☐ 90 Steve Pelluer | .10 | .02 |
| ☐ 91 Brian Noble | .10 | .02 |
| ☐ 92 Reggie White | .50 | .20 |
| ☐ 93 Aundray Bruce RC | .10 | .02 |
| ☐ 94 Garry James | .10 | .02 |
| ☐ 95 Drew Hill | .10 | .02 |
| ☐ 96 Anthony Munoz | .20 | .07 |
| ☐ 97 James Wilder | .10 | .02 |
| ☐ 98 Dexter Manley | .10 | .02 |
| ☐ 99 Lee Williams | .10 | .02 |
| ☐ 100 Dave Krieg | .20 | .07 |
| ☐ 101A Keith Jackson RC 84 | .50 | .20 |
| ☐ 101B Keith Jackson RC 88 | .50 | .20 |
| ☐ 102 Luis Sharpe | .10 | .02 |
| ☐ 103 Kevin Greene | .50 | .20 |
| ☐ 104 Duane Bickett | .10 | .02 |
| ☐ 105 Mark Rypien RC | .50 | .20 |
| ☐ 106 Curt Warner | .10 | .02 |
| ☐ 107 Jacob Green | .10 | .02 |
| ☐ 108 Gary Clark | .50 | .20 |
| ☐ 109 Bruce Matthews RC | 3.00 | 1.25 |
| ☐ 110 Bill Fralic | .10 | .02 |
| ☐ 111 Bill Bates | .20 | .07 |
| ☐ 112 Jeff Bryant | .10 | .02 |
| ☐ 113 Charles Mann | .10 | .02 |
| ☐ 114 Richard Dent | .20 | .07 |
| ☐ 115 Bruce Hill RC | .10 | .02 |
| ☐ 116 Mark May RC | .10 | .02 |
| ☐ 117 Mark Collins RC | .10 | .02 |
| ☐ 118 Ron Holmes | .10 | .02 |
| ☐ 119 Scott Case RC | .10 | .02 |
| ☐ 120 Tom Rathman | .20 | .07 |
| ☐ 121 Dennis McKinnon | .10 | .02 |
| ☐ 122A Ricky Sanders ERR 46 | .25 | .08 |
| ☐ 122B Ricky Sanders COR 83 | .50 | .20 |
| ☐ 123 Michael Carter | .10 | .02 |
| ☐ 124 Ozzie Newsome | .20 | .07 |
| ☐ 125 Irving Fryar UER | .20 | .07 |
| ☐ 126A Ron Hall RC ERR | .25 | .08 |
| ☐ 126B Ron Hall RC COR | .25 | .08 |
| ☐ 127 Clay Matthews | .20 | .07 |
| ☐ 128 Leonard Marshall | .10 | .02 |
| ☐ 129 Kevin Mack | .10 | .02 |
| ☐ 130 Art Monk | .20 | .07 |
| ☐ 131 Garin Veris | .10 | .02 |
| ☐ 132 Steve Jordan | .10 | .02 |
| ☐ 133 Frank Minnifield | .10 | .02 |
| ☐ 134 Eddie Brown | .10 | .02 |
| ☐ 135 Stacey Bailey | .10 | .02 |
| ☐ 136 Rickey Jackson | .20 | .07 |
| ☐ 137 Henry Ellard | .20 | .07 |
| ☐ 138 Jim Burt | .10 | .02 |
| ☐ 139 Jerome Brown | .20 | .07 |
| ☐ 140 Rodney Holman RC | .10 | .02 |
| ☐ 141 Sammy Winder | .10 | .02 |
| ☐ 142 Marcus Cotton | .10 | .02 |
| ☐ 143 Jim Jeffcoat | .10 | .02 |
| ☐ 144 Rueben Mayes | .10 | .02 |
| ☐ 145 Jim McMahon | .20 | .07 |
| ☐ 146 Reggie Williams | .10 | .02 |
| ☐ 147 John Anderson | .10 | .02 |
| ☐ 148 Harris Barton RC | .10 | .02 |
| ☐ 149 Phillip Epps | .10 | .02 |
| ☐ 150 Jay Hilgenberg | .10 | .02 |
| ☐ 151 Earl Ferrell | .10 | .02 |
| ☐ 152 Andre Reed | .50 | .20 |
| ☐ 153 Dennis Gentry | .10 | .02 |
| ☐ 154 Max Montoya | .10 | .02 |
| ☐ 155 Darrin Nelson | .10 | .02 |
| ☐ 156 Jeff Chadwick | .10 | .02 |
| ☐ 157 James Brooks | .20 | .07 |
| ☐ 158 Keith Bishop | .10 | .02 |
| ☐ 159 Robert Awalt | .10 | .02 |
| ☐ 160 Marty Lyons | .10 | .02 |
| ☐ 161 Johnny Hector | .10 | .02 |
| ☐ 162 Tony Casillas | .10 | .02 |
| ☐ 163 Kyle Clifton RC | .10 | .02 |
| ☐ 164 Cody Risien | .10 | .02 |
| ☐ 165 Jamie Holland RC | .10 | .02 |
| ☐ 166 Merril Hoge RC | .20 | .07 |
| ☐ 167 Chris Spielman RC | 1.00 | .40 |
| ☐ 168 Carlos Carson | .10 | .02 |
| ☐ 169 Jerry Ball RC | .10 | .02 |
| ☐ 170 Don Majkowski RC | .50 | .20 |
| ☐ 171 Everson Walls | .10 | .02 |
| ☐ 172 Mike Rozier | .10 | .02 |
| ☐ 173 Matt Millen | .20 | .07 |
| ☐ 174 Karl Mecklenburg | .10 | .02 |
| ☐ 175 Paul Palmer | .10 | .02 |
| ☐ 176 Brian Blades RC UER | .50 | .20 |
| ☐ 177 Brent Fullwood RC | .10 | .02 |
| ☐ 178 Anthony Miller RC | .50 | .20 |
| ☐ 179 Brian Sochia | .10 | .02 |
| ☐ 180 Stephen Baker RC | .10 | .02 |
| ☐ 181 Jesse Solomon | .10 | .02 |
| ☐ 182 John Grimsley | .10 | .02 |
| ☐ 183 Timmy Newsome | .10 | .02 |
| ☐ 184 Steve Sewell RC | .10 | .02 |
| ☐ 185 Dean Biasucci | .10 | .02 |
| ☐ 186 Alonzo Highsmith | .10 | .02 |
| ☐ 187 Randy Grimes | .10 | .02 |
| ☐ 188A Mark Carrier RC WR ERR | 1.00 | .40 |
| ☐ 188B Mark Carrier RC WR COR | 1.00 | .40 |
| ☐ 189 Vann McElroy | .10 | .02 |
| ☐ 190 Greg Bell | .10 | .02 |
| ☐ 191 Quinn Early RC | 1.00 | .40 |
| ☐ 192 Lawrence Taylor | .50 | .20 |
| ☐ 193 Albert Bentley | .10 | .02 |
| ☐ 194 Ernest Givins | .20 | .07 |
| ☐ 195 Jackie Slater | .10 | .02 |
| ☐ 196 Jim Sweeney | .10 | .02 |
| ☐ 197 Freddie Joe Nunn | .10 | .02 |
| ☐ 198 Keith Byars | .20 | .07 |
| ☐ 199 Hardy Nickerson RC | .50 | .20 |
| ☐ 200 Steve Beuerlein RC | 4.00 | 1.50 |
| ☐ 201 Bruce Armstrong RC | .50 | .20 |
| ☐ 202 Lionel Manuel | .10 | .02 |
| ☐ 203 J.T. Smith | .10 | .02 |
| ☐ 204 Mark Ingram RC | .50 | .20 |
| ☐ 205 Fred Smerlas | .10 | .02 |
| ☐ 206 Bryan Hinkle RC | .10 | .02 |
| ☐ 207 Steve McMichael | .20 | .07 |
| ☐ 208 Nick Lowery | .10 | .02 |
| ☐ 209 Jack Trudeau | .10 | .02 |
| ☐ 210 Lorenzo Hampton | .10 | .02 |
| ☐ 211 Thurman Thomas RC | 8.00 | 3.00 |
| ☐ 212 Steve Young | 1.50 | .60 |
| ☐ 213 James Lofton | .50 | .20 |
| ☐ 214 Jim Covert | .10 | .02 |
| ☐ 215 Ronnie Lott | .20 | .07 |
| ☐ 216 Stephone Paige | .10 | .02 |
| ☐ 217 Mark Duper | .20 | .07 |
| ☐ 218A Willie Gault ERR 93 | .25 | .08 |
| ☐ 218B Willie Gault COR 83 | .50 | .20 |
| ☐ 219 Ken Ruettgers RC | .10 | .02 |

| | | |
|---|---|---|
| ❏ 220 Kevin Ross RC | .10 | .02 |
| ❏ 221 Jerry Rice | 3.00 | 1.50 |
| ❏ 222 Billy Ray Smith | .10 | .02 |
| ❏ 223 Jim Kelly | 1.00 | .40 |
| ❏ 224 Vinny Testaverde | 1.00 | .40 |
| ❏ 225 Steve Largent | .50 | .20 |
| ❏ 226 Warren Williams RC | .10 | .02 |
| ❏ 227 Morten Andersen | .10 | .02 |
| ❏ 228 Bill Brooks | .20 | .07 |
| ❏ 229 Reggie Langhorne RC | .10 | .02 |
| ❏ 230 Pepper Johnson | .10 | .02 |
| ❏ 231 Pat Leahy | .10 | .02 |
| ❏ 232 Fred Marion | .10 | .02 |
| ❏ 233 Gary Zimmerman | .20 | .07 |
| ❏ 234 Marcus Allen | .50 | .20 |
| ❏ 235 Gaston Green RC | .10 | .02 |
| ❏ 236 John Stephens RC | .10 | .02 |
| ❏ 237 Terry Kinard | .10 | .02 |
| ❏ 238 John Taylor RC | .50 | .20 |
| ❏ 239 Brian Bosworth | .20 | .07 |
| ❏ 240 Anthony Toney | .10 | .02 |
| ❏ 241 Ken O'Brien | .10 | .02 |
| ❏ 242 Howie Long | .50 | .20 |
| ❏ 243 Doug Flutie | 2.50 | 1.00 |
| ❏ 244 Jim Everett | .50 | .20 |
| ❏ 245 Broderick Thomas RC | .10 | .02 |
| ❏ 246 Deion Sanders RC | 10.00 | 4.00 |
| ❏ 247 Donnell Woolford RC | .10 | .02 |
| ❏ 248 Wayne Martin RC | .10 | .02 |
| ❏ 249 David Williams RC | .10 | .02 |
| ❏ 250 Bill Hawkins RC | .10 | .02 |
| ❏ 251 Eric Hill RC | .10 | .02 |
| ❏ 252 Burt Grossman RC | .10 | .02 |
| ❏ 253 Tracy Rocker | .10 | .02 |
| ❏ 254 Steve Wisniewski RC | .50 | .20 |
| ❏ 255 Jessie Small RC | .10 | .02 |
| ❏ 256 David Braxton | .10 | .02 |
| ❏ 257 Barry Sanders RC | 30.00 | 15.00 |
| ❏ 258 Derrick Thomas RC | 8.00 | 3.00 |
| ❏ 259 Eric Metcalf RC | 1.00 | .40 |
| ❏ 260 Keith DeLong RC | .10 | .02 |
| ❏ 261 Hart Lee Dykes RC | .10 | .02 |
| ❏ 262 Sammie Smith RC | .10 | .02 |
| ❏ 263 Steve Atwater RC | .50 | .20 |
| ❏ 264 Eric Ball RC | .10 | .02 |
| ❏ 265 Don Beebe RC | .50 | .20 |
| ❏ 266 Brian Williams OL RC | .10 | .02 |
| ❏ 267 Jeff Lageman RC | .10 | .02 |
| ❏ 268 Tim Worley RC | .10 | .02 |
| ❏ 269 Tony Mandarich RC | .10 | .02 |
| ❏ 270 Troy Aikman RC | 30.00 | 12.50 |
| ❏ 271 Andy Heck RC | .10 | .02 |
| ❏ 272 Andre Rison RC | 5.00 | 2.50 |
| ❏ 273 AFC Champ/Woods/Esiason | .10 | .02 |
| ❏ 274 NFC Champ/Joe Montana | 1.00 | .40 |
| ❏ 275 Joe Montana/Jerry Rice | 2.00 | .75 |
| ❏ 276 Rodney Carter | .10 | .02 |
| ❏ 277 Mark Jackson/V.Johnson/Nattiel | .10 | .02 |
| ❏ 278 John L. Williams | .10 | .02 |
| ❏ 279 Joe Montana/Jerry Rice | 2.00 | .75 |
| ❏ 280 Roy Green/Lomax | .10 | .02 |
| ❏ 281 Ran.Cunningham/K.Jackson | .10 | .02 |
| ❏ 282 Chris Doleman and | .10 | .02 |
| ❏ 283 Mark Duper and | .10 | .02 |
| ❏ 284 Bo Jackson/Marcus Allen | .60 | .25 |
| ❏ 285 Frank Minnifield AP | .10 | .02 |
| ❏ 286 Bruce Matthews AP | .40 | .15 |
| ❏ 287 Joey Browner AP | .10 | .02 |
| ❏ 288 Jay Hilgenberg AP | .10 | .02 |
| ❏ 289 Carl Lee RC AP | .10 | .02 |
| ❏ 290 Scott Norwood AP RC | .10 | .02 |
| ❏ 291 John Taylor AP | .50 | .20 |
| ❏ 292 Jerry Rice AP | 1.50 | .60 |
| ❏ 293A Keith Jackson AP 84 | .10 | .02 |
| ❏ 293B Keith Jackson AP 88 | .20 | .07 |
| ❏ 294 Gary Zimmerman AP | .20 | .07 |
| ❏ 295 Lawrence Taylor AP | .50 | .20 |
| ❏ 296 Reggie White AP | .50 | .20 |
| ❏ 297 Roger Craig AP | .20 | .07 |
| ❏ 298 Boomer Esiason AP | .20 | .07 |
| ❏ 299 Cornelius Bennett AP | .20 | .07 |
| ❏ 300 Mike Horan AP | .10 | .02 |
| ❏ 301 Deron Cherry AP | .10 | .02 |
| ❏ 302 Tom Newberry AP | .10 | .02 |
| ❏ 303 Mike Singletary AP | .20 | .07 |

| | | |
|---|---|---|
| ❏ 304 Shane Conlan AP | .10 | .02 |
| ❏ 305A Tim Brown AP ERR 80 | 2.00 | .75 |
| ❏ 305B Tim Brown AP COR 81 | 2.00 | .75 |
| ❏ 306 Henry Ellard AP | .20 | .07 |
| ❏ 307 Bruce Smith AP | .20 | .07 |
| ❏ 308 Tim Krumrie AP | .10 | .02 |
| ❏ 309 Anthony Munoz AP | .20 | .07 |
| ❏ 310 Darrell Green SPD | .10 | .02 |
| ❏ 311 Anthony Miller SPD | .50 | .20 |
| ❏ 312 Wesley Walker SPEED | .10 | .02 |
| ❏ 313 Ron Brown SPEED | .10 | .02 |
| ❏ 314 Bo Jackson SPD | .60 | .25 |
| ❏ 315 Phillip Epps SPEED | .10 | .02 |
| ❏ 316A Eric Thomas RC SPD 31 | .25 | .08 |
| ❏ 316B Eric Thomas RC SPD 22 | .50 | .20 |
| ❏ 317 Herschel Walker SPD | .20 | .07 |
| ❏ 318 Jacob Green PRED | .10 | .02 |
| ❏ 319 Andre Tippett PRED | .10 | .02 |
| ❏ 320 Freddie Joe Nunn PRED | .10 | .02 |
| ❏ 321 Reggie White PRED | .50 | .20 |
| ❏ 322 Lawrence Taylor PRED | .50 | .20 |
| ❏ 323 Greg Townsend PRED | .10 | .02 |
| ❏ 324 Tim Harris PRED | .10 | .02 |
| ❏ 325 Bruce Smith PRED | .20 | .07 |
| ❏ 326 Tony Dorsett RB | .50 | .20 |
| ❏ 327 Steve Largent RB | .50 | .20 |
| ❏ 328 Tim Brown RB | 2.00 | .75 |
| ❏ 329 Joe Montana RB | 1.50 | .60 |
| ❏ 330 Tom Landry Tribute | 1.00 | .40 |

**1990 Score**

| | | |
|---|---|---|
| ❏ COMPLETE SET (660) | 15.00 | 6.00 |
| ❏ COMP.FACT.SET (665) | 20.00 | 7.50 |
| ❏ 1 Joe Montana | 1.25 | .50 |
| ❏ 2 Christian Okoye | .04 | .01 |
| ❏ 3 Mike Singletary UER | .10 | .02 |
| ❏ 4 Jim Everett UER | .10 | .02 |
| ❏ 5 Phil Simms | .10 | .02 |
| ❏ 6 Brent Fullwood | .04 | .01 |
| ❏ 7 Bill Fralic | .04 | .01 |
| ❏ 8 Leslie O'Neal | .10 | .02 |
| ❏ 9 John Taylor | .25 | .08 |
| ❏ 10 Bo Jackson | .30 | .10 |
| ❏ 11 John Stephens | .04 | .01 |
| ❏ 12 Art Monk | .10 | .02 |
| ❏ 13 Dan Marino | 1.25 | .50 |
| ❏ 14 John Settle | .04 | .01 |
| ❏ 15 Don Majkowski | .04 | .01 |
| ❏ 16 Bruce Smith | .25 | .08 |
| ❏ 17 Brad Muster | .04 | .01 |
| ❏ 18 Jason Buck | .04 | .01 |
| ❏ 19 James Brooks | .10 | .02 |
| ❏ 20 Barry Sanders | 1.25 | .50 |
| ❏ 21 Troy Aikman | .75 | .30 |
| ❏ 22 Allen Pinkett | .04 | .01 |
| ❏ 23 Duane Bickett | .04 | .01 |
| ❏ 24 Kevin Ross | .04 | .01 |
| ❏ 25 John Elway | 1.25 | .50 |
| ❏ 26 Jeff Query | .04 | .01 |
| ❏ 27 Eddie Murray | .04 | .01 |
| ❏ 28 Richard Dent | .10 | .02 |
| ❏ 29 Lorenzo White | .04 | .01 |
| ❏ 30 Eric Metcalf | .25 | .08 |
| ❏ 31 Jeff Dellenbach RC | .04 | .01 |
| ❏ 32 Leon White | .04 | .01 |
| ❏ 33 Jim Jeffcoat | .04 | .01 |
| ❏ 34 Herschel Walker | .10 | .02 |
| ❏ 35 Mike Johnson UER | .04 | .01 |

| | | |
|---|---|---|
| ❏ 36 Joe Phillips | .04 | .01 |
| ❏ 37 Willie Gault | .10 | .02 |
| ❏ 38 Keith Millard | .04 | .01 |
| ❏ 39 Fred Marion | .04 | .01 |
| ❏ 40 Boomer Esiason | .10 | .02 |
| ❏ 41 Dermontti Dawson | .10 | .02 |
| ❏ 42 Dino Hackett | .04 | .01 |
| ❏ 43 Reggie Roby | .04 | .01 |
| ❏ 44 Roger Vick | .04 | .01 |
| ❏ 45 Bobby Hebert | .04 | .01 |
| ❏ 46 Don Beebe | .10 | .02 |
| ❏ 47 Neal Anderson | .10 | .02 |
| ❏ 48 Johnny Holland | .04 | .01 |
| ❏ 49 Bobby Humphrey | .04 | .01 |
| ❏ 50 Lawrence Taylor | .25 | .08 |
| ❏ 51 Billy Ray Smith | .04 | .01 |
| ❏ 52 Robert Perryman | .04 | .01 |
| ❏ 53 Gary Anderson K | .04 | .01 |
| ❏ 54 Raul Allegre | .04 | .01 |
| ❏ 55 Pat Swilling | .10 | .02 |
| ❏ 56 Chris Doleman | .04 | .01 |
| ❏ 57 Andre Reed | .25 | .08 |
| ❏ 58 Seth Joyner | .10 | .02 |
| ❏ 59 Bart Oates | .04 | .01 |
| ❏ 60 Bernie Kosar | .10 | .02 |
| ❏ 61 Dave Krieg | .10 | .02 |
| ❏ 62 Lars Tate | .04 | .01 |
| ❏ 63 Scott Norwood | .04 | .01 |
| ❏ 64 Kyle Clifton | .04 | .01 |
| ❏ 65 Alan Veingrad | .04 | .01 |
| ❏ 66 Gerald Riggs UER | .10 | .02 |
| ❏ 67 Tim Worley | .04 | .01 |
| ❏ 68 Rodney Holman | .04 | .01 |
| ❏ 69 Tony Zendejas | .04 | .01 |
| ❏ 70 Chris Miller | .25 | .08 |
| ❏ 71 Wilber Marshall | .04 | .01 |
| ❏ 72 Skip McClendon RC | .04 | .01 |
| ❏ 73 Jim Covert | .04 | .01 |
| ❏ 74 Sam Mills | .10 | .02 |
| ❏ 75 Chris Hinton | .04 | .01 |
| ❏ 76 Irv Eatman | .04 | .01 |
| ❏ 77 Bubba Paris UER | .04 | .01 |
| ❏ 78 John Elliott UER | .04 | .01 |
| ❏ 79 Thomas Everett | .04 | .01 |
| ❏ 80 Steve Smith | .04 | .01 |
| ❏ 81 Jackie Slater | .04 | .01 |
| ❏ 82 Kelvin Martin RC | .04 | .01 |
| ❏ 83 Jo Jo Townsell | .04 | .01 |
| ❏ 84 Jim C. Jensen | .04 | .01 |
| ❏ 85 Bobby Humphrey | .04 | .01 |
| ❏ 86 Mike Dyal | .04 | .01 |
| ❏ 87 Andre Rison UER | .25 | .08 |
| ❏ 88 Brian Sochia | .04 | .01 |
| ❏ 89 Greg Bell | .04 | .01 |
| ❏ 90 Dalton Hilliard | .04 | .01 |
| ❏ 91 Carl Banks | .04 | .01 |
| ❏ 92 Dennis Smith | .04 | .01 |
| ❏ 93 Bruce Matthews | .10 | .02 |
| ❏ 94 Charles Haley | .10 | .02 |
| ❏ 95 Deion Sanders | .50 | .20 |
| ❏ 96 Stephone Paige | .04 | .01 |
| ❏ 97 Marion Butts FSC | .10 | .02 |
| ❏ 98 Howie Long | .25 | .08 |
| ❏ 99 Donald Igwebuike | .04 | .01 |
| ❏ 100 Roger Craig UER | .10 | .02 |
| ❏ 101 Charles Mann | .04 | .01 |
| ❏ 102 Fredd Young | .04 | .01 |
| ❏ 103 Chris Jacke | .04 | .01 |
| ❏ 104 Scott Case | .04 | .01 |
| ❏ 105 Warren Moon | .25 | .08 |
| ❏ 106 Clyde Simmons | .04 | .01 |
| ❏ 107 Steve Atwater | .04 | .01 |
| ❏ 108 Morten Andersen | .04 | .01 |
| ❏ 109 Eugene Marve | .04 | .01 |
| ❏ 110 Thurman Thomas | .25 | .08 |
| ❏ 111 Carnell Lake | .04 | .01 |
| ❏ 112 Jim Kelly | .25 | .08 |
| ❏ 113 Stanford Jennings | .04 | .01 |
| ❏ 114 Jacob Green | .04 | .01 |
| ❏ 115 Karl Mecklenburg | .04 | .01 |
| ❏ 116 Ray Childress | .04 | .01 |
| ❏ 117 Erik McMillan | .04 | .01 |
| ❏ 118 Harry Newsome | .04 | .01 |
| ❏ 119 James Dixon | .04 | .01 |
| ❏ 120 Hassan Jones | .04 | .01 |

| | | |
|---|---|---|
| ❏ 121 Eric Allen | .04 | .01 |
| ❏ 122 Felix Wright | .04 | .01 |
| ❏ 123 Merril Hoge | .04 | .01 |
| ❏ 124 Eric Ball | .04 | .01 |
| ❏ 125 Flipper Anderson FSC | .04 | .01 |
| ❏ 126 James Jefferson | .04 | .01 |
| ❏ 127 Tim McDonald | .04 | .01 |
| ❏ 128 Larry Kinnebrew | .04 | .01 |
| ❏ 129 Mark Collins | .04 | .01 |
| ❏ 130 Ickey Woods | .04 | .01 |
| ❏ 131 Jeff Donaldson UER | .04 | .01 |
| ❏ 132 Rich Camarillo | .04 | .01 |
| ❏ 133 Melvin Bratton RC | .04 | .01 |
| ❏ 134A Kevin Butler | .35 | .12 |
| ❏ 134B Kevin Butler | .50 | .20 |
| ❏ 135 Albort Bentley | .04 | .01 |
| ❏ 136A Vai Sikahema | .35 | .12 |
| ❏ 136B Vai Sikahema | .50 | .20 |
| ❏ 137 Todd McNair RC | .04 | .01 |
| ❏ 138 Alonzo Highsmith | .04 | .01 |
| ❏ 139 Brian Blades | .10 | .02 |
| ❏ 140 Jeff Lageman | .04 | .01 |
| ❏ 141 Eric Thomas | .04 | .01 |
| ❏ 142 Derek Hill | .04 | .01 |
| ❏ 143 Rick Fenney | .04 | .01 |
| ❏ 144 Herman Heard | .04 | .01 |
| ❏ 145 Steve Young | .50 | .20 |
| ❏ 146 Kent Hull | .04 | .01 |
| ❏ 147A Joey Browner face left | .35 | .12 |
| ❏ 147B Joey Browner straight | .50 | .20 |
| ❏ 148 Frank Minnifield | .04 | .01 |
| ❏ 149 Robert Massey | .04 | .01 |
| ❏ 150 Dave Meggett | .10 | .02 |
| ❏ 151 Bubba McDowell | .04 | .01 |
| ❏ 152 Rickey Dixon RC | .04 | .01 |
| ❏ 153 Ray Donaldson | .04 | .01 |
| ❏ 154 Alvin Walton | .04 | .01 |
| ❏ 155 Mike Cofer | .04 | .01 |
| ❏ 156 Darryl Talley | .04 | .01 |
| ❏ 157 A.J. Johnson | .04 | .01 |
| ❏ 158 Jerry Gray | .04 | .01 |
| ❏ 159 Keith Byars | .04 | .01 |
| ❏ 160 Andy Heck | .04 | .01 |
| ❏ 161 Mike Munchak | .10 | .02 |
| ❏ 162 Dennis Gentry | .04 | .01 |
| ❏ 163 Timm Rosenbach UER | .04 | .01 |
| ❏ 164 Randall McDaniel | .15 | .05 |
| ❏ 165 Pat Leahy | .04 | .01 |
| ❏ 166 Bubby Brister | .10 | .02 |
| ❏ 167 Aundray Bruce | .04 | .01 |
| ❏ 168 Bill Brooks | .04 | .01 |
| ❏ 169 Eddie Anderson RC | .04 | .01 |
| ❏ 170 Ronnie Lott | .10 | .02 |
| ❏ 171 Jay Hilgenberg | .04 | .01 |
| ❏ 172 Joe Nash | .04 | .01 |
| ❏ 173 Simon Fletcher | .04 | .01 |
| ❏ 174 Shane Conlan | .04 | .01 |
| ❏ 175 Sean Landeta | .04 | .01 |
| ❏ 176 John Alt RC | .04 | .01 |
| ❏ 177 Clay Matthews | .10 | .02 |
| ❏ 178 Antnino Munoz | .10 | .02 |
| ❏ 179 Pete Holohan | .04 | .01 |
| ❏ 180 Robert Awalt | .04 | .01 |
| ❏ 181 Rohn Stark | .04 | .01 |
| ❏ 182 Vance Johnson | .04 | .01 |
| ❏ 183 David Fulcher | .04 | .01 |
| ❏ 184 Robert Delpino FSC | .04 | .01 |
| ❏ 185 Drew Hill | .04 | .01 |
| ❏ 186 Reggie Langhorne UER | .04 | .01 |
| ❏ 187 Lonzell Hill | .04 | .01 |
| ❏ 188 Tom Rathman UER | .04 | .01 |
| ❏ 189 Greg Montgomery RC | .04 | .01 |
| ❏ 190 Leonard Smith | .04 | .01 |
| ❏ 191 Chris Spielman | .25 | .08 |
| ❏ 192 Tom Newberry | .04 | .01 |
| ❏ 193 Cris Carter | .50 | .20 |
| ❏ 194 Kevin Porter RC | .04 | .01 |
| ❏ 195 Donnell Thompson | .04 | .01 |
| ❏ 196 Vaughan Johnson | .04 | .01 |
| ❏ 197 Steve McMichael | .10 | .02 |
| ❏ 198 Jim Sweeney | .04 | .01 |
| ❏ 199 Rich Karlis UER | .04 | .01 |
| ❏ 200 Jerry Rice | .75 | .30 |
| ❏ 201 Dan Hampton UER | .10 | .02 |
| ❏ 202 Jim Lachey | .04 | .01 |
| ❏ 203 Reggie White | .25 | .08 |
| ❏ 204 Jerry Ball | .04 | .01 |
| ❏ 205 Russ Grimm | .04 | .01 |
| ❏ 206 Tim Green RC | .04 | .01 |
| ❏ 207 Shawn Collins | .04 | .01 |
| ❏ 208A R.Mojsiejenko Chargers | .15 | .05 |
| ❏ 208B R.Mojsiejenko Redskins | .50 | .20 |
| ❏ 209 Trace Armstrong | .04 | .01 |
| ❏ 210 Keith Jackson | .10 | .02 |
| ❏ 211 Jamie Holland | .04 | .01 |
| ❏ 212 Mark Clayton | .10 | .02 |
| ❏ 213 Jeff Cross | .04 | .01 |
| ❏ 214 Bob Gagliano | .04 | .01 |
| ❏ 215 Louis Oliver UER | .04 | .01 |
| ❏ 216 Jim Arnold | .04 | .01 |
| ❏ 217 Robert Clark RC | .04 | .01 |
| ❏ 218 Gill Byrd | .04 | .01 |
| ❏ 219 Rodney Peete | .10 | .02 |
| ❏ 220 Anthony Miller | .25 | .08 |
| ❏ 221 Steve Grogan | .10 | .02 |
| ❏ 222 Vince Newsome RC | .04 | .01 |
| ❏ 223 Thomas Benson | .04 | .01 |
| ❏ 224 Kevin Murphy | .04 | .01 |
| ❏ 225 Henry Ellard | .10 | .02 |
| ❏ 226 Richard Johnson | .04 | .01 |
| ❏ 227 Jim Skow | .04 | .01 |
| ❏ 228 Keith Jones | .04 | .01 |
| ❏ 229 Dave Brown DB | .04 | .01 |
| ❏ 230 Marcus Allen | .25 | .08 |
| ❏ 231 Steve Walsh | .10 | .02 |
| ❏ 232 Jim Harbaugh | .25 | .08 |
| ❏ 233 Mel Gray | .10 | .02 |
| ❏ 234 David Treadwell | .04 | .01 |
| ❏ 235 John Offerdahl | .04 | .01 |
| ❏ 236 Gary Reasons | .04 | .01 |
| ❏ 237 Tim Krumrie | .04 | .01 |
| ❏ 238 Dave Duerson | .04 | .01 |
| ❏ 239 Gary Clark UER | .25 | .08 |
| ❏ 240 Mark Jackson | .04 | .01 |
| ❏ 241 Mark Murphy | .04 | .01 |
| ❏ 242 Jerry Holmes | .04 | .01 |
| ❏ 243 Tim McGee | .04 | .01 |
| ❏ 244 Mike Tomczak | .10 | .02 |
| ❏ 245 Sterling Sharpe UER | .25 | .08 |
| ❏ 246 Bennie Blades | .04 | .01 |
| ❏ 247 Ken Harvey RC UER | .25 | .08 |
| ❏ 248 Ron Heller | .04 | .01 |
| ❏ 249 Louis Lipps | .10 | .02 |
| ❏ 250 Wade Wilson | .10 | .02 |
| ❏ 251 Freddie Joe Nunn | .04 | .01 |
| ❏ 252 Jerome Brown UER | .04 | .01 |
| ❏ 253 Myron Guyton | .04 | .01 |
| ❏ 254 Nate Odomes RC | .10 | .02 |
| ❏ 255 Rod Woodson | .25 | .08 |
| ❏ 256 Cornelius Bennett | .10 | .02 |
| ❏ 257 Keith Woodside | .04 | .01 |
| ❏ 258 Jeff Uhlenhake UER | .04 | .01 |
| ❏ 259 Harry Hamilton | .04 | .01 |
| ❏ 260 Mark Bavaro | .04 | .01 |
| ❏ 261 Vinny Testaverde | .10 | .02 |
| ❏ 262 Steve DeBerg | .10 | .02 |
| ❏ 263 Steve Wisniewski UER | .10 | .02 |
| ❏ 264 Pete Mandley | .04 | .01 |
| ❏ 265 Tim Harris | .04 | .01 |
| ❏ 266 Jack Trudeau | .04 | .01 |
| ❏ 267 Mark Kelso | .04 | .01 |
| ❏ 268 Brian Noble | .04 | .01 |
| ❏ 269 Jesse Tuggle RC | .04 | .01 |
| ❏ 270 Ken O'Brien | .04 | .01 |
| ❏ 271 David Little | .04 | .01 |
| ❏ 272 Pete Stoyanovich | .04 | .01 |
| ❏ 273 Odessa Turner RC | .04 | .01 |
| ❏ 274 Anthony Toney | .04 | .01 |
| ❏ 275 Tunch Ilkin | .04 | .01 |
| ❏ 276 Carl Lee | .04 | .01 |
| ❏ 277 Hart Lee Dykes | .04 | .01 |
| ❏ 278 Al Noga | .04 | .01 |
| ❏ 279 Greg Lloyd | .25 | .08 |
| ❏ 280 Billy Joe Tolliver | .04 | .01 |
| ❏ 281 Kirk Lowdermilk | .04 | .01 |
| ❏ 282 Earl Ferrell | .04 | .01 |
| ❏ 283 Eric Sievers RC | .04 | .01 |
| ❏ 284 Steve Jordan | .04 | .01 |
| ❏ 285 Burt Grossman | .04 | .01 |
| ❏ 286 Johnny Rembert | .04 | .01 |
| ❏ 287 Jeff Jaeger RC | .04 | .01 |
| ❏ 288 James Hasty | .04 | .01 |
| ❏ 289 Tony Mandarich DP | .04 | .01 |
| ❏ 290 Chris Singleton RC | .04 | .01 |
| ❏ 291 Lynn James RC | .04 | .01 |
| ❏ 292 Andre Ware RC | .25 | .08 |
| ❏ 293 Ray Agnew RC | .04 | .01 |
| ❏ 294 Joel Smeenge RC | .04 | .01 |
| ❏ 295 Marc Spindler RC | .04 | .01 |
| ❏ 296 Renaldo Turnbull RC | .04 | .01 |
| ❏ 297 Reggie Rembert RC | .04 | .01 |
| ❏ 298 Jeff Alm RC | .04 | .01 |
| ❏ 299 Cortez Kennedy RC | .25 | .08 |
| ❏ 300 Blair Thomas RC | .10 | .02 |
| ❏ 301 Pat Terrell RC | .04 | .01 |
| ❏ 302 Junior Seau RC | 1.25 | .50 |
| ❏ 303 Mo Elewonibi RC | .04 | .01 |
| ❏ 304 Tony Bennett RC | .25 | .08 |
| ❏ 305 Percy Snow RC | .04 | .01 |
| ❏ 306 Richmond Webb RC | .04 | .01 |
| ❏ 307 Rodney Hampton RC | .25 | .08 |
| ❏ 308 Barry Foster RC | .25 | .08 |
| ❏ 309 John Friesz RC | .25 | .08 |
| ❏ 310 Ben Smith RC | .04 | .01 |
| ❏ 311 Joe Montana HG | .50 | .20 |
| ❏ 312 Jim Everett HG | .10 | .02 |
| ❏ 313 Mark Rypien HG | .10 | .02 |
| ❏ 314 Phil Simms HG UER | .10 | .02 |
| ❏ 315 Don Majkowski HG | .04 | .01 |
| ❏ 316 Boomer Esiason HG | .04 | .01 |
| ❏ 317 Warren Moon HG Moon | .25 | .08 |
| ❏ 318 Jim Kelly HG | .25 | .08 |
| ❏ 319 Bernie Kosar HG | .10 | .02 |
| ❏ 320 Dan Marino HG UER | .50 | .20 |
| ❏ 321 Christian Okoye GF | .04 | .01 |
| ❏ 322 Thurman Thomas GF | .25 | .08 |
| ❏ 323 James Brooks GF | .10 | .02 |
| ❏ 324 Bobby Humphrey GF | .04 | .01 |
| ❏ 325 Barry Sanders GF | .60 | .25 |
| ❏ 326 Neal Anderson GF | .04 | .01 |
| ❏ 327 Dalton Hilliard GF | .04 | .01 |
| ❏ 328 Greg Bell GF | .04 | .01 |
| ❏ 329 Roger Craig GF UER | .10 | .02 |
| ❏ 330 Bo Jackson GF | .30 | .10 |
| ❏ 331 Don Warren | .04 | .01 |
| ❏ 332 Rufus Porter | .04 | .01 |
| ❏ 333 Sammie Smith | .04 | .01 |
| ❏ 334 Lewis Tillman | .04 | .01 |
| ❏ 335 Michael Walter | .04 | .01 |
| ❏ 336 Marc Logan | .04 | .01 |
| ❏ 337 Ron Hallstrom RC | .04 | .01 |
| ❏ 338 Stanley Morgan | .04 | .01 |
| ❏ 339 Mark Robinson | .04 | .01 |
| ❏ 340 Frank Reich | .25 | .08 |
| ❏ 341 Chip Lohmiller FSC | .04 | .01 |
| ❏ 342 Steve Beuerlein | .10 | .02 |
| ❏ 343 John L. Williams | .04 | .01 |
| ❏ 344 Irving Fryar | .25 | .08 |
| ❏ 345 Anthony Carter | .10 | .02 |
| ❏ 346 Al Toon | .10 | .02 |
| ❏ 347 J.T. Smith | .04 | .01 |
| ❏ 348 Pierce Holt RC | .04 | .01 |
| ❏ 349 Ferrell Edmunds | .04 | .01 |
| ❏ 350 Mark Rypien | .10 | .02 |
| ❏ 351 Paul Gruber | .04 | .01 |
| ❏ 352 Ernest Givins | .10 | .02 |
| ❏ 353 Ervin Randle | .04 | .01 |
| ❏ 354 Guy McIntyre | .04 | .01 |
| ❏ 355 Webster Slaughter | .10 | .02 |
| ❏ 356 Reuben Davis | .04 | .01 |
| ❏ 357 Rickey Jackson | .10 | .02 |
| ❏ 358 Earnest Byner | .04 | .01 |
| ❏ 359 Eddie Brown | .04 | .01 |
| ❏ 360 Troy Stradford | .04 | .01 |
| ❏ 361 Pepper Johnson | .04 | .01 |
| ❏ 362 Ravin Caldwell | .04 | .01 |
| ❏ 363 Chris Mohr RC | .04 | .01 |
| ❏ 364 Jeff Bryant | .04 | .01 |
| ❏ 365 Bruce Collie | .04 | .01 |
| ❏ 366 Courtney Hall | .04 | .01 |
| ❏ 367 Jerry Olsavsky | .04 | .01 |
| ❏ 368 David Galloway | .04 | .01 |
| ❏ 369 Wes Hopkins | .04 | .01 |
| ❏ 370 Johnny Hector | .04 | .01 |
| ❏ 371 Clarence Verdin | .04 | .01 |

|  |  | | |  |  | | |  |  | | |
|---|--------|---|---|---|--------|---|---|---|--------|---|---|
| 372 | Nick Lowery | .04 | .01 | 457 | Lawyer Tillman | .04 | .01 | 542 | Doug Riesenberg RC | .04 | .01 |
| 373 | Tim Brown | .25 | .08 | 458 | Andre Tippett | .04 | .01 | 543 | Dan Fike | .04 | .01 |
| 374 | Kevin Greene | .10 | .02 | 459 | James Thornton | .04 | .01 | 544 | Clarence Kay | .04 | .01 |
| 375 | Leonard Marshall | .04 | .01 | 460 | Randy Grimes | .04 | .01 | 545 | Jim Burt | .04 | .01 |
| 376 | Roland James | .04 | .01 | 461 | Larry Roberts | .04 | .01 | 546 | Mike Horan | .04 | .01 |
| 377 | Scott Studwell | .04 | .01 | 462 | Ron Holmes | .04 | .01 | 547 | Al Harris | .04 | .01 |
| 378 | Jarvis Williams | .04 | .01 | 463 | Mike Wise DE | .04 | .01 | 548 | Maury Buford | .04 | .01 |
| 379 | Mike Saxon | .04 | .01 | 464 | Danny Copeland RC | .04 | .01 | 549 | Jerry Robinson | .04 | .01 |
| 380 | Kevin Mack | .04 | .01 | 465 | Bruce Wilkerson RC | .04 | .01 | 550 | Tracy Rocker | .04 | .01 |
| 381 | Joe Kelly | .04 | .01 | 466 | Mike Quick | .04 | .01 | 551 | Karl Mecklenburg CC | .04 | .01 |
| 382 | Tom Thayer RC | .04 | .01 | 467 | Mickey Shuler | .04 | .01 | 552 | Lawrence Taylor CC | .25 | .08 |
| 383 | Roy Green | .10 | .02 | 468 | Mike Prior | .04 | .01 | 553 | Derrick Thomas CC | .25 | .08 |
| 384 | Michael Brooks RC | .04 | .01 | 469 | Ron Rivera | .04 | .01 | 554 | Mike Singletary CC | .10 | .02 |
| 385 | Michael Cofer | .04 | .01 | 470 | Dean Biasucci | .04 | .01 | 555 | Tim Harris CC | .04 | .01 |
| 386 | Ken Ruettgers | .04 | .01 | 471 | Perry Williams | .04 | .01 | 556 | Jerry Rice RM | .50 | .20 |
| 387 | Dean Steinkuhler | .04 | .01 | 472 | Darren Comeaux UER | .04 | .01 | 557 | Art Monk RM | .10 | .02 |
| 388 | Maurice Carthon | .04 | .01 | 473 | Freeman McNeil | .04 | .01 | 558 | Mark Carrier WR RM | .10 | .02 |
| 389 | Ricky Sanders | .04 | .01 | 474 | Tyrone Braxton | .04 | .01 | 559 | Andre Reed RM | .10 | .02 |
| 390 | Winston Moss RC | .04 | .01 | 475 | Jay Schroeder | .04 | .01 | 560 | Sterling Sharpe RM | .25 | .08 |
| 391 | Tony Woods | .04 | .01 | 476 | Naz Worthen | .04 | .01 | 561 | Herschel Walker RM | .10 | .02 |
| 392 | Keith DeLong | .04 | .01 | 477 | Lionel Washington | .04 | .01 | 562 | Ottis Anderson GF | .10 | .02 |
| 393 | David Wyman | .04 | .01 | 478 | Carl Zander | .04 | .01 | 563 | Randall Cunningham HG | .10 | .02 |
| 394 | Vencie Glenn | .04 | .01 | 479 | Al(Bubba) Baker | .10 | .02 | 564 | John Elway HG | .50 | .20 |
| 395 | Harris Barton | .04 | .01 | 480 | Mike Merriweather | .04 | .01 | 565 | David Fulcher AP | .04 | .01 |
| 396 | Bryan Hinkle | .04 | .01 | 481 | Mike Gann | .04 | .01 | 566 | Ronnie Lott AP | .10 | .02 |
| 397 | Derek Kennard | .04 | .01 | 482 | Brent Williams | .04 | .01 | 567 | Jerry Gray AP | .04 | .01 |
| 398 | Heath Sherman RC | .04 | .01 | 483 | Eugene Robinson | .04 | .01 | 568 | Albert Lewis AP | .04 | .01 |
| 399 | Troy Benson | .04 | .01 | 484 | Ray Horton | .04 | .01 | 569 | Karl Mecklenburg AP | .04 | .01 |
| 400 | Gary Zimmerman | .10 | .02 | 485 | Bruce Armstrong | .04 | .01 | 570 | Mike Singletary AP | .10 | .02 |
| 401 | Norm Johnson | .10 | .02 | 486 | John Fourcade | .04 | .01 | 571 | Lawrence Taylor AP | .25 | .08 |
| 402 | Eugene Lockhart | .04 | .01 | 487 | Lewis Billups | .04 | .01 | 572 | Tim Harris AP | .04 | .01 |
| 403 | Tim Manoa | .04 | .01 | 488 | Scott Davis | .04 | .01 | 573 | Keith Millard AP | .04 | .01 |
| 404 | Reggie Williams | .04 | .01 | 489 | Kenneth Sims | .04 | .01 | 574 | Reggie White AP | .25 | .08 |
| 405 | Mark Bortz RC | .04 | .01 | 490 | Chris Chandler | .25 | .08 | 575 | Chris Doleman AP | .04 | .01 |
| 406 | Mike Kenn | .04 | .01 | 491 | Mark Lee | .04 | .01 | 576 | Dave Meggett AP | .10 | .02 |
| 407 | John Grimsley | .04 | .01 | 492 | Johnny Meads | .04 | .01 | 577 | Rod Woodson AP | .25 | .08 |
| 408 | Bill Romanowski RC | 1.00 | .40 | 493 | Tim Irwin | .04 | .01 | 578 | Sean Landeta AP | .04 | .01 |
| 409 | Perry Kemp | .04 | .01 | 494 | E.J. Junior | .04 | .01 | 579 | Eddie Murray AP | .04 | .01 |
| 410 | Norm Johnson | .04 | .01 | 495 | Hardy Nickerson | .10 | .02 | 580 | Barry Sanders AP | .60 | .25 |
| 411 | Broderick Thomas | .04 | .01 | 496 | Rob McGovern | .04 | .01 | 581 | Christian Okoye AP | .04 | .01 |
| 412 | Joe Wolf | .04 | .01 | 497 | Fred Strickland RC | .04 | .01 | 582 | Joe Montana AP | .50 | .20 |
| 413 | Andre Waters | .04 | .01 | 498 | Reggie Rutland RC | .04 | .01 | 583 | Jay Hilgenberg AP | .04 | .01 |
| 414 | Jason Staurovsky | .04 | .01 | 499 | Mel Owens | .04 | .01 | 584 | Bruce Matthews AP | .10 | .02 |
| 415 | Eric Martin | .04 | .01 | 500 | Derrick Thomas | .25 | .08 | 585 | Tom Newberry AP | .04 | .01 |
| 416 | Joe Prokop | .04 | .01 | 501 | Jerrol Williams | .04 | .01 | 586 | Gary Zimmerman AP | .10 | .02 |
| 417 | Steve Sewell | .04 | .01 | 502 | Maurice Hurst RC | .04 | .01 | 587 | Anthony Munoz AP | .10 | .02 |
| 418 | Cedric Jones | .04 | .01 | 503 | Larry Kelm RC | .04 | .01 | 588 | Keith Jackson AP | .10 | .02 |
| 419 | Alphonso Carreker | .04 | .01 | 504 | Herman Fontenot | .04 | .01 | 589 | Sterling Sharpe AP | .25 | .08 |
| 420 | Keith Willis | .04 | .01 | 505 | Pat Beach | .04 | .01 | 590 | Jerry Rice AP | .50 | .20 |
| 421 | Bobby Butler | .04 | .01 | 506 | Haywood Jeffires RC | .25 | .08 | 591 | Bo Jackson RB | .30 | .10 |
| 422 | John Roper | .04 | .01 | 507 | Neil Smith | .25 | .08 | 592 | Steve Largent RB | .25 | .08 |
| 423 | Tim Spencer | .04 | .01 | 508 | Cleveland Gary FSC | .04 | .01 | 593 | Flipper Anderson RB | .04 | .01 |
| 424 | Jesse Sapolu RC | .04 | .01 | 509 | William Perry | .10 | .02 | 594 | Joe Montana RB | .50 | .20 |
| 425 | Ron Wolfley | .04 | .01 | 510 | Michael Carter | .04 | .01 | 595 | Franco Harris HOF | .10 | .02 |
| 426 | Doug Smith | .04 | .01 | 511 | Walker Lee Ashley | .04 | .01 | 596 | Bob St. Clair HOF | .04 | .01 |
| 427 | William Howard | .04 | .01 | 512 | Bob Golic | .04 | .01 | 597 | Tom Landry HOF | .10 | .02 |
| 428 | Keith Van Horne | .04 | .01 | 513 | Danny Villa RC | .04 | .01 | 598 | Jack Lambert HOF | .10 | .02 |
| 429 | Tony Jordan | .04 | .01 | 514 | Matt Millen | .10 | .02 | 599 | Ted Hendricks HOF | .04 | .01 |
| 430 | Mervyn Fernandez | .04 | .01 | 515 | Don Griffin | .04 | .01 | 600A | Buck Buchanan HOF ERR 83 | .10 | .02 |
| 431 | Shaun Gayle RC | .04 | .01 | 516 | Jonathan Hayes | .04 | .01 | 600B | Buck Buchanan HOF COR 63 | .10 | .02 |
| 432 | Ricky Nattiel | .04 | .01 | 517 | Gerald Williams RC | .04 | .01 | 601 | Bob Griese HOF | .10 | .02 |
| 433 | Albert Lewis | .04 | .01 | 518 | Scott Fulhage | .04 | .01 | 602 | Super Bowl Wrap | .04 | .01 |
| 434 | Fred Banks RC | .04 | .01 | 519 | Irv Pankey | .04 | .01 | 603A | Vince Lombardi w/o logo | .20 | .07 |
| 435 | Henry Thomas | .04 | .01 | 520 | Randy Dixon RC | .04 | .01 | 603B | Vince Lombardi Curt.logo | .20 | .07 |
| 436 | Chet Brooks | .04 | .01 | 521 | Terry McDaniel | .04 | .01 | 604 | Mark Carrier WR UER | .10 | .02 |
| 437 | Mark Ingram | .10 | .02 | 522 | Dan Saleaumua | .04 | .01 | 605 | Randall Cunningham | .25 | .08 |
| 438 | Jeff Gossett | .04 | .01 | 523 | Darrin Nelson | .04 | .01 | 606 | Percy Snow C90 | .04 | .01 |
| 439 | Mike Wilcher | .04 | .01 | 524 | Leonard Griffin | .04 | .01 | 607 | Andre Ware C90 | .25 | .08 |
| 440 | Deron Cherry UER | .04 | .01 | 525 | Michael Ball RC | .04 | .01 | 608 | Blair Thomas C90 | .10 | .02 |
| 441 | Mike Rozier | .04 | .01 | 526 | Ernie Jones RC | .04 | .01 | 609 | Eric Green C90 | .04 | .01 |
| 442 | Jon Hand | .04 | .01 | 527 | Tony Eason UER | .04 | .01 | 610 | Reggie Rembert C90 | .04 | .01 |
| 443 | Ozzie Newsome | .10 | .02 | 528 | Ed Reynolds | .04 | .01 | 611 | Richmond Webb C90 | .04 | .01 |
| 444 | Sammy Martin | .04 | .01 | 529 | Gary Higgebottom | .04 | .01 | 612 | Bern Brostek C90 | .04 | .01 |
| 445 | Luis Sharpe | .04 | .01 | 530 | Don Mosebar | .04 | .01 | 613 | James Williams C90 | .04 | .01 |
| 446 | Lee Williams | .04 | .01 | 531 | Ottis Anderson | .10 | .02 | 614 | Mark Carrier DB C90 | .10 | .02 |
| 447 | Chris Martin RC | .04 | .01 | 532 | Bucky Scribner | .04 | .01 | 615 | Renaldo Turnbull C90 | .04 | .01 |
| 448 | Kevin Fagan RC | .04 | .01 | 533 | Aaron Cox | .04 | .01 | 616 | Cortez Kennedy C90 | .10 | .02 |
| 449 | Gene Lang | .04 | .01 | 534 | Sean Jones | .10 | .02 | 617 | Keith McCants C90 | .04 | .01 |
| 450 | Greg Townsend | .04 | .01 | 535 | Doug Flutie | .50 | .20 | 618 | Anthony Thompson RC | .04 | .01 |
| 451 | Robert Lyles | .04 | .01 | 536 | Leo Lewis | .04 | .01 | 619 | LeRoy Butler RC | .25 | .08 |
| 452 | Eric Hill | .04 | .01 | 537 | Art Still | .04 | .01 | 620 | Aaron Wallace RC | .04 | .01 |
| 453 | John Teltschik | .04 | .01 | 538 | Matt Bahr | .04 | .01 | 621 | Alexander Wright RC | .04 | .01 |
| 454 | Vestee Jackson | .04 | .01 | 539 | Keena Turner | .04 | .01 | 622 | Keith McCants RC | .04 | .01 |
| 455 | Bruce Reimers | .04 | .01 | 540 | Sammy Winder | .04 | .01 | 623 | Jimmie Jones RC | .04 | .01 |
| 456 | Butch Rolle RC | .04 | .01 | 541 | Mike Webster | .10 | .02 | 624 | Anthony Johnson RC | .25 | .08 |

| | | |
|---|---|---|
| ❑ 625 Fred Washington RC | .04 | .01 |
| ❑ 626 Mike Bellamy RC | .04 | .01 |
| ❑ 627 Mark Carrier DB RC | .25 | .08 |
| ❑ 628 Harold Green RC | .25 | .08 |
| ❑ 629 Eric Green RC | .10 | .02 |
| ❑ 630 Andre Collins RC | .04 | .01 |
| ❑ 631 Lamar Lathon RC | .10 | .02 |
| ❑ 632 Terry Wooden RC | .04 | .01 |
| ❑ 633 Jesse Anderson RC | .04 | .01 |
| ❑ 634 Jeff George RC | .50 | .20 |
| ❑ 635 Carwell Gardner RC | .04 | .01 |
| ❑ 636 Darrell Thompson RC | .04 | .01 |
| ❑ 637 Vince Buck RC | .04 | .01 |
| ❑ 638 Mike Jones TE RC | .04 | .01 |
| ❑ 639 Charles Arbuckle RC | .04 | .01 |
| ❑ 640 Dennis Brown RC | .04 | .01 |
| ❑ 641 James Williams DB RC | .04 | .01 |
| ❑ 642 Bern Brostek RC | .04 | .01 |
| ❑ 643 Darion Conner RC | .10 | .02 |
| ❑ 644 Mike Fox RC | .04 | .01 |
| ❑ 645 Cary Conklin RC | .04 | .01 |
| ❑ 646 Tim Grunhard RC | .04 | .01 |
| ❑ 647 Ron Cox RC | .04 | .01 |
| ❑ 648 Keith Sims RC | .04 | .01 |
| ❑ 649 Alton Montgomery RC | .04 | .01 |
| ❑ 650 Greg McMurtry RC | .04 | .01 |
| ❑ 651 Scott Mitchell RC | .25 | .08 |
| ❑ 652 Tim Ryan DE RC | .04 | .01 |
| ❑ 653 Jeff Mills RC | .04 | .01 |
| ❑ 654 Ricky Proehl RC | .25 | .08 |
| ❑ 655 Steve Broussard RC | .04 | .01 |
| ❑ 656 Peter Tom Willis RC | .04 | .01 |
| ❑ 657 Dexter Carter RC | .04 | .01 |
| ❑ 658 Tony Casillas RC | .04 | .01 |
| ❑ 659 Joe Morris RC | .04 | .01 |
| ❑ 660 Greg Kragen RC | .04 | .01 |
| ❑ B1 Matt Stover FF | .25 | .08 |
| ❑ B2 Demetrius Davis | .04 | .01 |
| ❑ B3 Ken McMichel | .04 | .01 |
| ❑ B4 Judd Garrett FF | .04 | .01 |
| ❑ B5 Elliott Searcy | .04 | .01 |

## 1990 Score Supplemental

| | | |
|---|---|---|
| ❑ COMP.FACT.SET (110) | 80.00 | 30.00 |
| ❑ 1T Marcus Dupree RC** | .15 | .05 |
| ❑ 2T Gary Kauric | .15 | .05 |
| ❑ 3T Everson Walls | .15 | .05 |
| ❑ 4T Elliott Smith | .15 | .05 |
| ❑ 5T Donald Evans RC UER | .30 | .10 |
| ❑ 6T Jerry Holmes | .15 | .05 |
| ❑ 7T Dan Stryzinski RC | .15 | .05 |
| ❑ 8T Gerald McNeil | .15 | .05 |
| ❑ 9T Rick Tuten RC | .15 | .05 |
| ❑ 10T Mickey Shuler | .15 | .05 |
| ❑ 11T Jay Novacek | .60 | .25 |
| ❑ 12T Eric Williams RC | .15 | .05 |
| ❑ 13T Stanley Morgan | .15 | .05 |
| ❑ 14T Wayne Haddix RC | .15 | .05 |
| ❑ 15T Gary Anderson RB | .15 | .05 |
| ❑ 16T Stan Humphries RC | .60 | .25 |
| ❑ 17T Raymond Clayborn | .15 | .05 |
| ❑ 18T Mark Boyer RC | .15 | .05 |
| ❑ 19T Dave Waymer | .15 | .05 |
| ❑ 20T Andre Rison | .60 | .25 |
| ❑ 21T Daniel Stubbs | .15 | .05 |
| ❑ 22T Mike Rozier | .15 | .05 |
| ❑ 23T Damian Johnson | .15 | .05 |
| ❑ 24T Don Smith RBK RC * | .15 | .05 |

| | | |
|---|---|---|
| ❑ 25T Max Montoya | .15 | .05 |
| ❑ 26T Terry Kinard | .15 | .05 |
| ❑ 27T Herb Welch | .15 | .05 |
| ❑ 28T Cliff Odom | .15 | .05 |
| ❑ 29T John Kidd | .15 | .05 |
| ❑ 30T Barry Word RC | .15 | .05 |
| ❑ 31T Rich Davis RC | .15 | .05 |
| ❑ 32T Mike Baab | .15 | .05 |
| ❑ 33T Ronnie Harmon | .30 | .10 |
| ❑ 34T Jeff Donaldson | .15 | .05 |
| ❑ 35T Riki Ellison | .15 | .05 |
| ❑ 36T Steve Walsh | .30 | .10 |
| ❑ 37T Bill Lewis RC | .15 | .05 |
| ❑ 38T Tim McKyer | .15 | .05 |
| ❑ 39T James Wilder | .15 | .05 |
| ❑ 40T Tony Paige | .15 | .05 |
| ❑ 41T Derrick Fenner RC | .15 | .05 |
| ❑ 42T Thane Gash RC | .15 | .05 |
| ❑ 43T Dave Duerson | .15 | .05 |
| ❑ 44T Clarence Weathers | .15 | .05 |
| ❑ 45T Matt Bahr | .15 | .05 |
| ❑ 46T Alonzo Highsmith | .15 | .05 |
| ❑ 47T Joe Kelly | .15 | .05 |
| ❑ 48T Chris Hinton | .15 | .05 |
| ❑ 49T Bobby Humphery | .15 | .05 |
| ❑ 50T Greg Bell | .15 | .05 |
| ❑ 51T Fred Smerlas | .15 | .05 |
| ❑ 52T Walter Stanley | .15 | .05 |
| ❑ 53T Jim Skow | .15 | .05 |
| ❑ 54T Renaldo Turnbull | .15 | .05 |
| ❑ 55T Bern Brostek | .15 | .05 |
| ❑ 56T Charles Wilson RC | .15 | .05 |
| ❑ 57T Keith McCants | .15 | .05 |
| ❑ 58T Alexander Wright | .30 | .10 |
| ❑ 59T Ian Beckles RC | .15 | .05 |
| ❑ 60T Eric Davis | .30 | .10 |
| ❑ 61T Chris Singleton | .15 | .05 |
| ❑ 62T Rob Moore RC | 2.50 | 1.00 |
| ❑ 63T Darion Conner | .30 | .10 |
| ❑ 64T Tim Grunhard | .15 | .05 |
| ❑ 65T Junior Seau | 6.00 | 2.50 |
| ❑ 66T Tony Stargell RC | .15 | .05 |
| ❑ 67T Anthony Thompson RC | .15 | .05 |
| ❑ 68T Cortez Kennedy | .60 | .25 |
| ❑ 69T Darrell Thompson | .15 | .05 |
| ❑ 70T Calvin Williams RC | .60 | .25 |
| ❑ 71T Rodney Hampton RC | .60 | .25 |
| ❑ 72T Terry Wooden | .15 | .05 |
| ❑ 73T Leo Goeas RC | .15 | .05 |
| ❑ 74T Ken Willis | .15 | .05 |
| ❑ 75T Ricky Proehl | .60 | .25 |
| ❑ 76T Steve Christie RC | .15 | .05 |
| ❑ 77T Andre Ware | .60 | .25 |
| ❑ 78T Jeff George | 2.50 | 1.00 |
| ❑ 79T Walter Wilson | .15 | .05 |
| ❑ 80T Johnny Bailey RC | .15 | .05 |
| ❑ 81T Harold Green | .30 | .10 |
| ❑ 82T Mark Carrier DB | .60 | .25 |
| ❑ 83T Frank Cornish | .15 | .05 |
| ❑ 84T James Williams | .15 | .05 |
| ❑ 85T James Francis RC | .15 | .05 |
| ❑ 86T Percy Snow | .15 | .05 |
| ❑ 87T Anthony Johnson | .60 | .25 |
| ❑ 88T Tim Ryan DE | .15 | .05 |
| ❑ 89T Dan Owens RC | .15 | .05 |
| ❑ 90T Aaron Wallace RC | .15 | .05 |
| ❑ 91T Steve Broussard | .15 | .05 |
| ❑ 92T Eric Green | .30 | .10 |
| ❑ 93T Blair Thomas | .30 | .10 |
| ❑ 94T Robert Blackmon RC | .15 | .05 |
| ❑ 95T Alan Grant RC | .15 | .05 |
| ❑ 96T Andre Collins | .15 | .05 |
| ❑ 97T Dexter Carter | .15 | .05 |
| ❑ 98T Reggie Cobb RC | .15 | .05 |
| ❑ 99T Dennis Brown | .15 | .05 |
| ❑ 100T Kenny Davidson RC | .15 | .05 |
| ❑ 101T Emmitt Smith RC | 60.00 | 25.00 |
| ❑ 102T Jeff Alm | .15 | .05 |
| ❑ 103T Alton Montgomery | .15 | .05 |
| ❑ 104T Tony Bennett | .30 | .10 |
| ❑ 105T Johnny Johnson RC | .30 | .10 |
| ❑ 106T Leroy Hoard RC | .60 | .25 |
| ❑ 107T Ray Agnew | .15 | .05 |
| ❑ 108T Richmond Webb | .15 | .05 |
| ❑ 109T Keith Sims | .15 | .05 |
| ❑ 110T Barry Foster | .60 | .25 |

## 1991 Score

| | | |
|---|---|---|
| ❑ COMPLETE SET (686) | 20.00 | 7.50 |
| ❑ COMP.FACT.SET (690) | 25.00 | 12.50 |
| ❑ 1 Joe Montana | 1.25 | .50 |
| ❑ 2 Eric Allen | .05 | .01 |
| ❑ 3 Rohn Stark | .05 | .01 |
| ❑ 4 Frank Reich | .10 | .02 |
| ❑ 5 Derrick Thomas | .25 | .08 |
| ❑ 6 Mike Singletary | .10 | .02 |
| ❑ 7 Boomer Esiason | .10 | .02 |
| ❑ 8 Matt Millen | .05 | .01 |
| ❑ 9 Chris Spielman | .10 | .02 |
| ❑ 10 Gerald McNeil | .05 | .01 |
| ❑ 11 Nick Lowery | .05 | .01 |
| ❑ 12 Randall Cunningham | .25 | .08 |
| ❑ 13 Marion Butts | .10 | .02 |
| ❑ 14 Tim Brown | .25 | .08 |
| ❑ 15 Emmitt Smith | 2.50 | 1.00 |
| ❑ 16 Rich Camarillo | .05 | .01 |
| ❑ 17 Mike Merriweather | .05 | .01 |
| ❑ 18 Derrick Fenner | .05 | .01 |
| ❑ 19 Clay Matthews | .10 | .02 |
| ❑ 20 Barry Sanders | 1.25 | .50 |
| ❑ 21 James Brooks | .10 | .02 |
| ❑ 22 Alton Montgomery | .05 | .01 |
| ❑ 23 Steve Atwater | .05 | .01 |
| ❑ 24 Ron Morris | .05 | .01 |
| ❑ 25 Brad Muster | .05 | .01 |
| ❑ 26 Andre Rison | .10 | .02 |
| ❑ 27 Brian Brennan | .05 | .01 |
| ❑ 28 Leonard Smith | .05 | .01 |
| ❑ 29 Kevin Butler | .05 | .01 |
| ❑ 30 Tim Harris | .05 | .01 |
| ❑ 31 Jay Novacek | .25 | .08 |
| ❑ 32 Eddie Murray | .05 | .01 |
| ❑ 33 Keith Woodside | .05 | .01 |
| ❑ 34 Ray Crockett RC | .05 | .01 |
| ❑ 35 Eugene Lockhart | .05 | .01 |
| ❑ 36 Bill Romanowski | .05 | .01 |
| ❑ 37 Eddie Brown | .05 | .01 |
| ❑ 38 Eugene Daniel | .05 | .01 |
| ❑ 39 Scott Fulhage | .05 | .01 |
| ❑ 40 Harold Green | .10 | .02 |
| ❑ 41 Mark Jackson | .05 | .01 |
| ❑ 42 Sterling Sharpe | .25 | .08 |
| ❑ 43 Mel Gray | .10 | .02 |
| ❑ 44 Jerry Holmes | .05 | .01 |
| ❑ 45 Allen Pinkett | .05 | .01 |
| ❑ 46 Warren Powers | .05 | .01 |
| ❑ 47 Rodney Peete | .10 | .02 |
| ❑ 48 Lorenzo White | .05 | .01 |
| ❑ 49 Dan Owens | .05 | .01 |
| ❑ 50 James Francis | .05 | .01 |
| ❑ 51 Ken Norton | .10 | .02 |
| ❑ 52 Ed West | .05 | .01 |
| ❑ 53 Andre Reed | .10 | .02 |
| ❑ 54 John Grimsley | .05 | .01 |
| ❑ 55 Michael Cofer | .05 | .01 |
| ❑ 56 Chris Doleman | .05 | .01 |
| ❑ 57 Pat Swilling | .10 | .02 |
| ❑ 58 Jessie Tuggle | .05 | .01 |
| ❑ 59 Mike Johnson | .05 | .01 |
| ❑ 60 Steve Walsh | .05 | .01 |
| ❑ 61 Sam Mills | .05 | .01 |
| ❑ 62 Don Mosebar | .05 | .01 |
| ❑ 63 Jay Hilgenberg | .05 | .01 |
| ❑ 64 Cleveland Gary | .05 | .01 |
| ❑ 65 Andre Tippett | .05 | .01 |

|  |  | | |
|---|---|---|---|
| 66 | Tom Newberry | .05 | .01 |
| 67 | Maurice Hurst | .05 | .01 |
| 68 | Louis Oliver | .05 | .01 |
| 69 | Fred Marion | .05 | .01 |
| 70 | Christian Okoye | .05 | .01 |
| 71 | Marv Cook FSC | .05 | .01 |
| 72 | Darryl Talley | .05 | .01 |
| 73 | Rick Fenney | .05 | .01 |
| 74 | Kelvin Martin | .05 | .01 |
| 75 | Howie Long | .25 | .08 |
| 76 | Steve Wisniewski | .05 | .01 |
| 77 | Karl Mecklenburg | .05 | .01 |
| 78 | Dan Saleaumua | .05 | .01 |
| 79 | Ray Childress | .05 | .01 |
| 80 | Henry Ellard | .10 | .02 |
| 81 | Ernest Givins UER | .10 | .02 |
| 82 | Ferrell Edmunds | .05 | .01 |
| 83 | Steve Jordan | .05 | .01 |
| 84 | Tony Mandarich | .05 | .01 |
| 85 | Eric Martin | .05 | .01 |
| 86 | Rich Gannon FSC | .25 | .08 |
| 87 | Irving Fryar | .10 | .02 |
| 88 | Tom Rathman | .05 | .01 |
| 89 | Dan Hampton | .10 | .02 |
| 90 | Barry Word | .05 | .01 |
| 91 | Kevin Greene | .10 | .02 |
| 92 | Sean Landeta | .05 | .01 |
| 93 | Trace Armstrong | .05 | .01 |
| 94 | Dennis Byrd | .05 | .01 |
| 95 | Timm Rosenbach | .05 | .01 |
| 96 | Anthony Toney | .05 | .01 |
| 97 | Tim Krumrie | .05 | .01 |
| 98 | Jerry Ball | .05 | .01 |
| 99 | Tim Green | .05 | .01 |
| 100 | Bo Jackson | .30 | .10 |
| 101 | Myron Guyton | .05 | .01 |
| 102 | Mike Mularkey | .05 | .01 |
| 103 | Jerry Gray | .05 | .01 |
| 104 | Scott Stephen RC | .05 | .01 |
| 105 | Anthony Bell | .05 | .01 |
| 106 | Lomas Brown | .05 | .01 |
| 107 | David Little | .05 | .01 |
| 108 | Brad Baxter FSC | .05 | .01 |
| 109 | Freddie Joe Nunn | .05 | .01 |
| 110 | Dave Meggett | .10 | .02 |
| 111 | Mark Rypien | .10 | .02 |
| 112 | Warren Williams | .05 | .01 |
| 113 | Ron Rivera | .05 | .01 |
| 114 | Terance Mathis | .10 | .02 |
| 115 | Anthony Munoz | .10 | .02 |
| 116 | Jeff Bryant | .05 | .01 |
| 117 | Issiac Holt | .05 | .01 |
| 118 | Steve Sewell | .05 | .01 |
| 119 | Tim Newton | .05 | .01 |
| 120 | Emile Harry | .05 | .01 |
| 121 | Gary Anderson K | .05 | .01 |
| 122 | Mark Lee | .05 | .01 |
| 123 | Alfred Anderson | .05 | .01 |
| 124 | Anthony Blaylock | .05 | .01 |
| 125 | Earnest Byner | .05 | .01 |
| 126 | Bill Maas | .05 | .01 |
| 127 | Keith Taylor | .05 | .01 |
| 128 | Cliff Odom | .05 | .01 |
| 129 | Bob Golic | .05 | .01 |
| 130 | Bart Oates | .05 | .01 |
| 131 | Jim Arnold | .05 | .01 |
| 132 | Jeff Herrod | .05 | .01 |
| 133 | Bruce Armstrong | .05 | .01 |
| 134 | Craig Heyward | .10 | .02 |
| 135 | Joey Browner | .05 | .01 |
| 136 | Darren Comeaux | .05 | .01 |
| 137 | Pat Beach | .05 | .01 |
| 138 | Dalton Hilliard | .05 | .01 |
| 139 | David Treadwell | .05 | .01 |
| 140 | Gary Anderson RB | .05 | .01 |
| 141 | Eugene Robinson | .05 | .01 |
| 142 | Scott Case | .05 | .01 |
| 143 | Paul Farren | .05 | .01 |
| 144 | Gill Fenerty | .05 | .01 |
| 145 | Tim Irwin | .05 | .01 |
| 146 | Norm Johnson | .05 | .01 |
| 147 | Willie Gault | .10 | .02 |
| 148 | Clarence Verdin | .05 | .01 |
| 149 | Jeff Uhlenhake | .05 | .01 |
| 150 | Erik McMillan | .05 | .01 |
| 151 | Kevin Ross | .05 | .01 |
| 152 | Pepper Johnson | .05 | .01 |
| 153 | Bryan Hinkle | .05 | .01 |
| 154 | Gary Clark | .25 | .08 |
| 155 | Robert Delpino | .05 | .01 |
| 156 | Doug Smith | .05 | .01 |
| 157 | Chris Martin | .05 | .01 |
| 158 | Ray Berry | .05 | .01 |
| 159 | Steve Christie | .05 | .01 |
| 160 | Don Smith RB | .05 | .01 |
| 161 | Greg McMurtry | .05 | .01 |
| 162 | Jack Del Rio | .10 | .02 |
| 163 | Floyd Dixon | .05 | .01 |
| 164 | Buford McGee | .05 | .01 |
| 165 | Brett Maxie | .05 | .01 |
| 166 | Morten Andersen | .05 | .01 |
| 167 | Kent Hull | .05 | .01 |
| 168 | Skip McClendon | .05 | .01 |
| 169 | Keith Sims | .05 | .01 |
| 170 | Leonard Marshall | .05 | .01 |
| 171 | Tony Woods | .05 | .01 |
| 172 | Byron Evans | .05 | .01 |
| 173 | Rob Burnett RC | .10 | .02 |
| 174 | Tory Epps | .05 | .01 |
| 175 | Toi Cook RC | .05 | .01 |
| 176 | John Elliott | .05 | .01 |
| 177 | Tommie Agee | .05 | .01 |
| 178 | Keith Van Horne | .05 | .01 |
| 179 | Dennis Smith | .05 | .01 |
| 180 | James Lofton | .10 | .02 |
| 181 | Art Monk | .10 | .02 |
| 182 | Anthony Carter | .10 | .02 |
| 183 | Louis Lipps | .05 | .01 |
| 184 | Bruce Hill | .05 | .01 |
| 185 | Michael Young | .05 | .01 |
| 186 | Eric Green | .05 | .01 |
| 187 | Barney Bussey RC | .05 | .01 |
| 188 | Curtis Duncan | .05 | .01 |
| 189 | Robert Awalt | .05 | .01 |
| 190 | Johnny Johnson | .05 | .01 |
| 191 | Jeff Cross | .05 | .01 |
| 192 | Keith McKeller | .05 | .01 |
| 193 | Robert Brown | .05 | .01 |
| 194 | Vincent Brown | .05 | .01 |
| 195 | Calvin Williams | .10 | .02 |
| 196 | Sean Jones | .10 | .02 |
| 197 | Willie Drewrey | .05 | .01 |
| 198 | Bubba McDowell | .05 | .01 |
| 199 | Al Noga | .05 | .01 |
| 200 | Ronnie Lott | .10 | .02 |
| 201 | Warren Moon | .25 | .08 |
| 202 | Chris Hinton | .05 | .01 |
| 203 | Jim Sweeney | .05 | .01 |
| 204 | Wayne Haddix | .05 | .01 |
| 205 | Tim Jorden RC | .05 | .01 |
| 206 | Marvin Allen | .05 | .01 |
| 207 | Jim Morrissey RC | .05 | .01 |
| 208 | Ben Smith | .05 | .01 |
| 209 | William White | .05 | .01 |
| 210 | Jim C. Jensen | .05 | .01 |
| 211 | Doug Reed | .05 | .01 |
| 212 | Ethan Horton | .05 | .01 |
| 213 | Chris Jacke | .05 | .01 |
| 214 | Johnny Hector | .05 | .01 |
| 215 | Drew Hill UER | .05 | .01 |
| 216 | Roy Green | .05 | .01 |
| 217 | Dean Steinkuhler | .05 | .01 |
| 218 | Cedric Mack | .05 | .01 |
| 219 | Chris Miller | .10 | .02 |
| 220 | Keith Byars | .05 | .01 |
| 221 | Lewis Billups | .05 | .01 |
| 222 | Roger Craig | .10 | .02 |
| 223 | Shaun Gayle | .05 | .01 |
| 224 | Mike Rozier | .05 | .01 |
| 225 | Troy Aikman | .75 | .30 |
| 226 | Bobby Humphrey | .05 | .01 |
| 227 | Eugene Marve | .05 | .01 |
| 228 | Michael Carter | .05 | .01 |
| 229 | Richard Johnson CB RC | .05 | .01 |
| 230 | Billy Joe Tolliver | .05 | .01 |
| 231 | Mark Murphy | .05 | .01 |
| 232 | John L. Williams | .05 | .01 |
| 233 | Ronnie Harmon | .05 | .01 |
| 234 | Thurman Thomas | .25 | .08 |
| 235 | Martin Mayhew | .05 | .01 |
| 236 | Richmond Webb | .05 | .01 |
| 237 | Gerald Riggs UER | .10 | .02 |
| 238 | Mike Prior | .05 | .01 |
| 239 | Mike Gann | .05 | .01 |
| 240 | Alvin Walton | .05 | .01 |
| 241 | Tim McGee | .05 | .01 |
| 242 | Bruce Matthews | .10 | .02 |
| 243 | Johnny Holland | .05 | .01 |
| 244 | Martin Bayless | .05 | .01 |
| 245 | Eric Metcalf | .10 | .02 |
| 246 | John Alt | .05 | .01 |
| 247 | Max Montoya | .05 | .01 |
| 248 | Rod Bernstine | .05 | .01 |
| 249 | Paul Gruber | .05 | .01 |
| 250 | Charles Haley | .10 | .02 |
| 251 | Scott Norwood | .05 | .01 |
| 252 | Michael Haddix | .05 | .01 |
| 253 | Ricky Sanders | .05 | .01 |
| 254 | Ervin Randle | .05 | .01 |
| 255 | Duane Bickett | .05 | .01 |
| 256 | Mike Munchak | .10 | .02 |
| 257 | Keith Jones | .05 | .01 |
| 258 | Riki Ellison | .05 | .01 |
| 259 | Vince Newsome | .05 | .01 |
| 260 | Lee Williams | .05 | .01 |
| 261 | Steve Smith | .05 | .01 |
| 262 | Sam Clancy | .05 | .01 |
| 263 | Pierce Holt | .05 | .01 |
| 264 | Jim Harbaugh | .25 | .08 |
| 265 | Dino Hackett | .05 | .01 |
| 266 | Andy Heck | .05 | .01 |
| 267 | Leo Goeas | .05 | .01 |
| 268 | Russ Grimm | .05 | .01 |
| 269 | Gill Byrd | .05 | .01 |
| 270 | Neal Anderson | .10 | .02 |
| 271 | Jackie Slater | .05 | .01 |
| 272 | Joe Nash | .05 | .01 |
| 273 | Todd Bowles | .05 | .01 |
| 274 | D.J. Dozier | .05 | .01 |
| 275 | Kevin Fagan | .05 | .01 |
| 276 | Don Warren | .05 | .01 |
| 277 | Jim Jeffcoat | .05 | .01 |
| 278 | Bruce Smith | .25 | .08 |
| 279 | Cortez Kennedy | .25 | .08 |
| 280 | Thane Gash | .05 | .01 |
| 281 | Perry Kemp | .05 | .01 |
| 282 | John Taylor | .10 | .02 |
| 283 | Stephone Paige | .05 | .01 |
| 284 | Paul Skansi | .05 | .01 |
| 285 | Shawn Collins | .05 | .01 |
| 286 | Mervyn Fernandez | .05 | .01 |
| 287 | Daniel Stubbs | .05 | .01 |
| 288 | Chip Lohmiller | .05 | .01 |
| 289 | Brian Blades | .10 | .02 |
| 290 | Mark Carrier WR | .25 | .08 |
| 291 | Carl Zander | .05 | .01 |
| 292 | David Wyman | .05 | .01 |
| 293 | Jeff Bostic | .05 | .01 |
| 294 | Irv Pankey | .05 | .01 |
| 295 | Keith Millard | .05 | .01 |
| 296 | Jamie Mueller | .05 | .01 |
| 297 | Bill Fralic | .05 | .01 |
| 298 | Wendell Davis FSC | .05 | .01 |
| 299 | Ken Clarke | .05 | .01 |
| 300 | Wymon Henderson UER | .05 | .01 |
| 301 | Jeff Campbell | .05 | .01 |
| 302 | Cody Carlson RC | .05 | .01 |
| 303 | Matt Brock RC | .05 | .01 |
| 304 | Maurice Carthon | .05 | .01 |
| 305 | Scott Mersereau RC | .05 | .01 |
| 306 | Steve Wright RC | .05 | .01 |
| 307 | J.B. Brown | .05 | .01 |
| 308 | Ricky Reynolds | .05 | .01 |
| 309 | Darryl Pollard | .05 | .01 |
| 310 | Donald Evans | .05 | .01 |
| 311 | Nick Bell RC | .10 | .02 |
| 312 | Pat Harlow RC | .05 | .01 |
| 313 | Dan McGwire RC | .10 | .02 |
| 314 | Mike Dumas RC | .05 | .01 |
| 315 | Mike Croel RC | .05 | .01 |
| 316 | Chris Smith RC | .05 | .01 |
| 317 | Kenny Walker RC | .05 | .01 |
| 318 | Todd Lyght RC | .05 | .01 |
| 319 | Mike Stonebreaker | .05 | .01 |
| 320 | Randall Cunningham 90 | .10 | .02 |

|  |  | | |
|---|--------|------|------|
| □ 321 | Terance Mathis 90 | .25 | .08 |
| □ 322 | Gaston Green 90 | .05 | .01 |
| □ 323 | Johnny Bailey 90 | .05 | .01 |
| □ 324 | Donnie Elder 90 | .05 | .01 |
| □ 325 | Dwight Stone 90 UER | .05 | .01 |
| □ 326 | J.J. Birden RC 90 | .10 | .02 |
| □ 327 | Alexander Wright 90 | .05 | .01 |
| □ 328 | Eric Metcalf 90 | .10 | .02 |
| □ 329 | Andre Rison TL | .10 | .02 |
| □ 330 | Warren Moon TL UER | .10 | .02 |
| □ 331 | Steve Tasker DT | .05 | .01 |
| □ 332 | Mel Gray DT | .10 | .02 |
| □ 333 | Nick Lowery DT | .05 | .01 |
| □ 334 | Sean Landeta DT | .05 | .01 |
| □ 335 | David Fulcher DT | .05 | .01 |
| □ 336 | Joey Browner DT | .05 | .01 |
| □ 337 | Albert Lewis DT | .05 | .01 |
| □ 338 | Rod Woodson DT | .10 | .02 |
| □ 339 | Shane Conlan DT | .05 | .01 |
| □ 340 | Pepper Johnson DT | .05 | .01 |
| □ 341 | Chris Spielman DT | .05 | .01 |
| □ 342 | Derrick Thomas DT | .10 | .02 |
| □ 343 | Ray Childress DT | .05 | .01 |
| □ 344 | Reggie White DT | .10 | .02 |
| □ 345 | Bruce Smith DT | .10 | .02 |
| □ 346 | Darrell Green | .05 | .01 |
| □ 347 | Ray Bentley | .05 | .01 |
| □ 348 | Herschel Walker | .10 | .02 |
| □ 349 | Rodney Holman | .05 | .01 |
| □ 350 | Al Toon | .05 | .01 |
| □ 351 | Harry Hamilton | .05 | .01 |
| □ 352 | Albert Lewis | .05 | .01 |
| □ 353 | Renaldo Turnbull | .05 | .01 |
| □ 354 | Junior Seau | .25 | .08 |
| □ 355 | Merril Hoge | .05 | .01 |
| □ 356 | Shane Conlan | .05 | .01 |
| □ 357 | Jay Schroeder | .05 | .01 |
| □ 358 | Steve Broussard | .05 | .01 |
| □ 359 | Mark Bavaro | .05 | .01 |
| □ 360 | Jim Lachey | .05 | .01 |
| □ 361 | Greg Townsend | .05 | .01 |
| □ 362 | Dave Krieg | .10 | .02 |
| □ 363 | Jessie Hester | .05 | .01 |
| □ 364 | Steve Tasker | .10 | .02 |
| □ 365 | Ron Hall | .05 | .01 |
| □ 366 | Pat Leahy | .05 | .01 |
| □ 367 | Jim Everett | .10 | .02 |
| □ 368 | Felix Wright | .05 | .01 |
| □ 369 | Ricky Proehl | .05 | .01 |
| □ 370 | Anthony Miller | .10 | .02 |
| □ 371 | Keith Jackson | .10 | .02 |
| □ 372 | Pete Stoyanovich | .05 | .01 |
| □ 373 | Tommy Kane | .05 | .01 |
| □ 374 | Richard Johnson | .05 | .01 |
| □ 375 | Randall McDaniel | .10 | .02 |
| □ 376 | John Stephens | .05 | .01 |
| □ 377 | Haywood Jeffires | .10 | .02 |
| □ 378 | Rodney Hampton | .25 | .08 |
| □ 379 | Tim Grunhard | .05 | .01 |
| □ 380 | Jerry Rice | .75 | .30 |
| □ 381 | Ken Harvey | .10 | .02 |
| □ 382 | Vaughan Johnson | .05 | .01 |
| □ 383 | J.T. Smith | .05 | .01 |
| □ 384 | Carnell Lake | .05 | .01 |
| □ 385 | Dan Marino | 1.25 | .50 |
| □ 386 | Kyle Clifton | .05 | .01 |
| □ 387 | Wilber Marshall | .05 | .01 |
| □ 388 | Pete Holohan | .05 | .01 |
| □ 389 | Gary Plummer | .05 | .01 |
| □ 390 | William Perry | .10 | .02 |
| □ 391 | Mark Robinson | .05 | .01 |
| □ 392 | Nate Odomes | .05 | .01 |
| □ 393 | Ickey Woods | .05 | .01 |
| □ 394 | Reyna Thompson | .05 | .01 |
| □ 395 | Deion Sanders | .40 | .15 |
| □ 396 | Harris Barton | .05 | .01 |
| □ 397 | Sammie Smith | .05 | .01 |
| □ 398 | Vinny Testaverde | .10 | .02 |
| □ 399 | Ray Donaldson | .05 | .01 |
| □ 400 | Tim McKyer | .05 | .01 |
| □ 401 | Nesby Glasgow | .05 | .01 |
| □ 402 | Brent Williams | .05 | .01 |
| □ 403 | Rob Moore | .25 | .08 |
| □ 404 | Bubby Brister | .05 | .01 |
| □ 405 | David Fulcher | .05 | .01 |
| □ 406 | Reggie Cobb | .05 | .01 |
| □ 407 | Jerome Brown | .05 | .01 |
| □ 408 | Erik Howard | .05 | .01 |
| □ 409 | Tony Paige | .05 | .01 |
| □ 410 | John Elway | 1.25 | .50 |
| □ 411 | Charles Mann | .05 | .01 |
| □ 412 | Luis Sharpe | .05 | .01 |
| □ 413 | Hassan Jones | .05 | .01 |
| □ 414 | Frank Minnifield | .05 | .01 |
| □ 415 | Steve DeBerg | .05 | .01 |
| □ 416 | Mark Carrier DB | .10 | .02 |
| □ 417 | Brian Jordan FSC | .10 | .02 |
| □ 418 | Reggie Langhorne | .05 | .01 |
| □ 419 | Don Majkowski | .05 | .01 |
| □ 420 | Marcus Allen | .25 | .08 |
| □ 421 | Michael Brooks | .05 | .01 |
| □ 422 | Vai Sikahema | .05 | .01 |
| □ 423 | Dermontti Dawson | .05 | .01 |
| □ 424 | Jacob Green | .05 | .01 |
| □ 425 | Flipper Anderson | .05 | .01 |
| □ 426 | Bill Brooks | .05 | .01 |
| □ 427 | Keith McCants | .05 | .01 |
| □ 428 | Ken O'Brien | .05 | .01 |
| □ 429 | Fred Barnett FSC | .25 | .08 |
| □ 430 | Mark Kelso | .10 | .02 |
| □ 431 | Mark Kelso | .05 | .01 |
| □ 432 | Leslie O'Neal | .10 | .02 |
| □ 433 | Ottis Anderson | .10 | .02 |
| □ 434 | Jesse Sapolu | .05 | .01 |
| □ 435 | Gary Zimmerman | .10 | .02 |
| □ 436 | Kevin Porter | .05 | .01 |
| □ 437 | Anthony Thompson | .05 | .01 |
| □ 438 | Robert Clark | .05 | .01 |
| □ 439 | Chris Warren | .25 | .08 |
| □ 440 | Gerald Williams | .05 | .01 |
| □ 441 | Jim Skow | .05 | .01 |
| □ 442 | Rick Donnelly | .05 | .01 |
| □ 443 | Guy McIntyre | .05 | .01 |
| □ 444 | Jeff Lageman | .05 | .01 |
| □ 445 | John Offerdahl | .05 | .01 |
| □ 446 | Clyde Simmons | .05 | .01 |
| □ 447 | John Kidd | .05 | .01 |
| □ 448 | Chip Banks | .05 | .01 |
| □ 449 | Johnny Meads | .05 | .01 |
| □ 450 | Rickey Jackson | .05 | .01 |
| □ 451 | Lee Johnson | .05 | .01 |
| □ 452 | Michael Irvin | .25 | .08 |
| □ 453 | Leon Seals | .05 | .01 |
| □ 454 | Darrell Thompson | .05 | .01 |
| □ 455 | Everson Walls | .05 | .01 |
| □ 456 | LeRoy Butler | .10 | .02 |
| □ 457 | Marcus Dupree | .05 | .01 |
| □ 458 | Kirk Lowdermilk | .05 | .01 |
| □ 459 | Chris Singleton | .05 | .01 |
| □ 460 | Seth Joyner | .10 | .02 |
| □ 461 | Rueben Mayes UER | .05 | .01 |
| □ 462 | Ernie Jones | .05 | .01 |
| □ 463 | Greg Kragen | .05 | .01 |
| □ 464 | Bennie Blades | .05 | .01 |
| □ 465 | Mark Bortz | .05 | .01 |
| □ 466 | Tony Stargell | .05 | .01 |
| □ 467 | Mike Cofer | .05 | .01 |
| □ 468 | Randy Grimes | .05 | .01 |
| □ 469 | Tim Worley | .05 | .01 |
| □ 470 | Kevin Mack | .05 | .01 |
| □ 471 | Wes Hopkins | .05 | .01 |
| □ 472 | Will Wolford | .05 | .01 |
| □ 473 | Sam Seale | .05 | .01 |
| □ 474 | Jim Ritcher | .05 | .01 |
| □ 475 | Jeff Hostetler FSC | .25 | .08 |
| □ 476 | Mitchell Price RC | .05 | .01 |
| □ 477 | Ken Lanier | .05 | .01 |
| □ 478 | Naz Worthen | .05 | .01 |
| □ 479 | Ed Reynolds | .05 | .01 |
| □ 480 | Mark Clayton | .10 | .02 |
| □ 481 | Matt Bahr | .05 | .01 |
| □ 482 | Gary Reasons | .05 | .01 |
| □ 483 | David Szott | .05 | .01 |
| □ 484 | Barry Foster | .10 | .02 |
| □ 485 | Bruce Reimers | .05 | .01 |
| □ 486 | Dean Biasucci | .05 | .01 |
| □ 487 | Cris Carter | .50 | .20 |
| □ 488 | Albert Bentley | .05 | .01 |
| □ 489 | Robert Massey | .05 | .01 |
| □ 490 | Al Smith | .05 | .01 |
| □ 491 | Greg Lloyd | .25 | .08 |
| □ 492 | Steve McMichael UER | .10 | .02 |
| □ 493 | Jeff Wright RC | .05 | .01 |
| □ 494 | Scott Davis | .05 | .01 |
| □ 495 | Freeman McNeil | .05 | .01 |
| □ 496 | Simon Fletcher | .05 | .01 |
| □ 497 | Terry McDaniel | .05 | .01 |
| □ 498 | Heath Sherman | .05 | .01 |
| □ 499 | Jeff Jaeger | .05 | .01 |
| □ 500 | Mark Collins | .05 | .01 |
| □ 501 | Tim Goad | .05 | .01 |
| □ 502 | Jeff George | .25 | .08 |
| □ 503 | Jimmie Jones | .05 | .01 |
| □ 504 | Henry Thomas | .05 | .01 |
| □ 505 | Steve Young | .75 | .30 |
| □ 506 | William Roberts | .05 | .01 |
| □ 507 | Neil Smith | .25 | .08 |
| □ 508 | Mike Saxon | .05 | .01 |
| □ 509 | Johnny Bailey | .05 | .01 |
| □ 510 | Broderick Thomas | .05 | .01 |
| □ 511 | Wade Wilson | .10 | .02 |
| □ 512 | Hart Lee Dykes | .05 | .01 |
| □ 513 | Hardy Nickerson | .10 | .02 |
| □ 514 | Tim McDonald | .05 | .01 |
| □ 515 | Frank Cornish | .05 | .01 |
| □ 516 | Jarvis Williams | .05 | .01 |
| □ 517 | Carl Lee | .05 | .01 |
| □ 518 | Carl Banks | .05 | .01 |
| □ 519 | Mike Golic | .05 | .01 |
| □ 520 | Brian Noble | .05 | .01 |
| □ 521 | James Hasty | .05 | .01 |
| □ 522 | Bubba Paris | .05 | .01 |
| □ 523 | Kevin Walker RC | .05 | .01 |
| □ 524 | William Fuller | .10 | .02 |
| □ 525 | Eddie Anderson | .05 | .01 |
| □ 526 | Roger Ruzek | .05 | .01 |
| □ 527 | Robert Blackmon | .05 | .01 |
| □ 528 | Vince Buck | .05 | .01 |
| □ 529 | Lawrence Taylor | .25 | .08 |
| □ 530 | Reggie Roby | .05 | .01 |
| □ 531 | Doug Riesenberg | .05 | .01 |
| □ 532 | Joe Jacoby | .05 | .01 |
| □ 533 | Kirby Jackson RC | .05 | .01 |
| □ 534 | Robb Thomas | .05 | .01 |
| □ 535 | Don Griffin | .05 | .01 |
| □ 536 | Andre Waters | .05 | .01 |
| □ 537 | Marc Logan | .05 | .01 |
| □ 538 | James Thornton | .05 | .01 |
| □ 539 | Ray Agnew | .05 | .01 |
| □ 540 | Frank Stams | .05 | .01 |
| □ 541 | Brett Perriman | .25 | .08 |
| □ 542 | Andre Ware | .10 | .02 |
| □ 543 | Kevin Haverdink | .05 | .01 |
| □ 544 | Greg Jackson RC | .05 | .01 |
| □ 545 | Tunch Ilkin | .05 | .01 |
| □ 546 | Dexter Carter | .05 | .01 |
| □ 547 | Rod Woodson | .25 | .08 |
| □ 548 | Donnell Woolford | .05 | .01 |
| □ 549 | Mark Boyer | .05 | .01 |
| □ 550 | Jeff Query | .05 | .01 |
| □ 551 | Burt Grossman | .05 | .01 |
| □ 552 | Mike Kenn | .05 | .01 |
| □ 553 | Richard Dent | .10 | .02 |
| □ 554 | Gaston Green | .05 | .01 |
| □ 555 | Phil Simms | .10 | .02 |
| □ 556 | Brent Jones | .25 | .08 |
| □ 557 | Ronnie Lippett | .05 | .01 |
| □ 558 | Mike Horan | .05 | .01 |
| □ 559 | Danny Noonan | .05 | .01 |
| □ 560 | Reggie White | .25 | .08 |
| □ 561 | Rufus Porter | .05 | .01 |
| □ 562 | Aaron Wallace | .05 | .01 |
| □ 563 | Walter Dean | .05 | .01 |
| □ 564A | Aaron Craver RC ERR | .05 | .01 |
| □ 564B | Aaron Craver RC COR | .05 | .01 |
| □ 565A | Russell Maryland RC ERR | .25 | .08 |
| □ 565B | Russell Maryland RC COR | .25 | .08 |
| □ 566 | Paul Justin RC | .05 | .01 |
| □ 567 | Walter Dean | .05 | .01 |
| □ 568 | Herman Moore RC | .25 | .08 |
| □ 569 | Bill Musgrave RC | .05 | .01 |
| □ 570 | Rob Carpenter RC WR | .05 | .01 |
| □ 571 | Greg Lewis RC | .05 | .01 |
| □ 572 | Ed King RC | .05 | .01 |
| □ 573 | Ernie Mills RC | .10 | .02 |

| | | |
|---|---|---|
| ☐ 574 Jake Reed RC | .50 | .20 |
| ☐ 575 Ricky Watters RC | 1.50 | .60 |
| ☐ 576 Derek Russell RC | .05 | .01 |
| ☐ 577 Shawn Moore RC | .05 | .01 |
| ☐ 578 Eric Bieniemy RC | .05 | .01 |
| ☐ 579 Chris Zorich RC | .25 | .08 |
| ☐ 580 Scott Miller | .05 | .01 |
| ☐ 581 Jarrod Bunch RC | .05 | .01 |
| ☐ 582 Ricky Ervins RC | .10 | .02 |
| ☐ 583 Browning Nagle RC | .05 | .01 |
| ☐ 584 Eric Turner RC | .10 | .02 |
| ☐ 585 William Thomas RC | .05 | .01 |
| ☐ 586 Stanley Richard RC | .05 | .01 |
| ☐ 587 Adrian Cooper RC | .05 | .01 |
| ☐ 588 Harvey Williams RC | .25 | .08 |
| ☐ 589 Alvin Harper RC | .25 | .08 |
| ☐ 590 John Carney | .05 | .01 |
| ☐ 591 Mark Vander Poel RC | .05 | .01 |
| ☐ 592 Mike Pritchard RC | .25 | .08 |
| ☐ 593 Eric Moten RC | .05 | .01 |
| ☐ 594 Moe Gardner RC | .05 | .01 |
| ☐ 595 Wesley Carroll RC | .05 | .01 |
| ☐ 596 Eric Swann RC | .25 | .08 |
| ☐ 597 Joe Kelly | .05 | .01 |
| ☐ 598 Steve Jackson RC | .05 | .01 |
| ☐ 599 Kelvin Pritchett RC | .10 | .02 |
| ☐ 600 Jesse Campbell RC | .05 | .01 |
| ☐ 601 Darryll Lewis RC UER | .10 | .02 |
| ☐ 602 Howard Griffith | .05 | .01 |
| ☐ 603 Blaise Bryant | .05 | .01 |
| ☐ 604 Vinnie Clark RC | .05 | .01 |
| ☐ 605 Mel Agee RC | .05 | .01 |
| ☐ 606 Bobby Wilson RC | .05 | .01 |
| ☐ 607 Kevin Donnalley RC | .05 | .01 |
| ☐ 608 Randal Hill RC | .10 | .02 |
| ☐ 609 Stan Thomas | .05 | .01 |
| ☐ 610 Mike Heldt | .05 | .01 |
| ☐ 611 Brett Favre RC | 8.00 | 3.00 |
| ☐ 612 Lawrence Dawsey RC UER | .10 | .02 |
| ☐ 613 Dennis Gibson | .05 | .01 |
| ☐ 614 Dean Dingman | .05 | .01 |
| ☐ 615 Bruce Pickens RC | .05 | .01 |
| ☐ 616 Todd Marinovich RC | .05 | .01 |
| ☐ 617 Gene Atkins | .05 | .01 |
| ☐ 618 Marcus Dupree | .05 | .01 |
| ☐ 619 Warren Moon Man of Year | .10 | .02 |
| ☐ 620 Joe Montana TM | .50 | .20 |
| ☐ 621 Neal Anderson MVP | .05 | .01 |
| ☐ 622 James Brooks MVP | .10 | .02 |
| ☐ 623 Thurman Thomas TM | .10 | .02 |
| ☐ 624 Bobby Humphrey MVP | .05 | .01 |
| ☐ 625 Kevin Mack MVP | .05 | .01 |
| ☐ 626 Mark Carrier WR MVP | .05 | .01 |
| ☐ 627 Johnny Johnson TM | .05 | .01 |
| ☐ 628 Marion Butts MVP | .10 | .02 |
| ☐ 629 Steve DeBerg MVP | .05 | .01 |
| ☐ 630 Jeff George TM | .10 | .02 |
| ☐ 631 Troy Aikman TM | .40 | .15 |
| ☐ 632 Dan Marino TM | .50 | .20 |
| ☐ 633 Randall Cunningham TM | .10 | .02 |
| ☐ 634 Andre Rison TM | .10 | .02 |
| ☐ 635 Pepper Johnson MVP | .05 | .01 |
| ☐ 636 Pat Leahy RC | .05 | .01 |
| ☐ 637 Barry Sanders TM | .50 | .20 |
| ☐ 638 Warren Moon TM | .10 | .02 |
| ☐ 639 Sterling Sharpe TM | .05 | .01 |
| ☐ 640 Bruce Armstrong MVP | .05 | .01 |
| ☐ 641 Bo Jackson TM | .10 | .02 |
| ☐ 642 Henry Ellard MVP | .10 | .02 |
| ☐ 643 Earnest Byner MVP | .05 | .01 |
| ☐ 644 Pat Swilling MVP | .05 | .01 |
| ☐ 645 John L. Williams MVP | .05 | .01 |
| ☐ 646 Rod Woodson TM | .10 | .02 |
| ☐ 647 Chris Doleman MVP | .05 | .01 |
| ☐ 648 Joey Browner CC | .05 | .01 |
| ☐ 649 Erik McMillan CC | .05 | .01 |
| ☐ 650 David Fulcher CC | .05 | .01 |
| ☐ 651A Ronnie Lott CC ERR | .10 | .02 |
| ☐ 651B Ronnie Lott CC COR | .05 | .01 |
| ☐ 652 Louis Oliver CC | .05 | .01 |
| ☐ 653 Mark Robinson CC | .05 | .01 |
| ☐ 654 Dennis Smith CC | .05 | .01 |
| ☐ 655 Reggie White SA ERR | .05 | .01 |
| ☐ 656 Charles Haley SA | .05 | .01 |
| ☐ 657 Leslie O'Neal SA | .10 | .02 |

| | | |
|---|---|---|
| ☐ 658 Kevin Greene SA | .10 | .02 |
| ☐ 659 Dennis Byrd SA | .05 | .01 |
| ☐ 660 Bruce Smith SA | .10 | .02 |
| ☐ 661 Derrick Thomas SACK | .10 | .02 |
| ☐ 662 Steve DeBerg TL | .05 | .01 |
| ☐ 663 Barry Sanders TL | .50 | .20 |
| ☐ 664 Thurman Thomas TL | .10 | .02 |
| ☐ 665 Jerry Rice TL | .40 | .15 |
| ☐ 666 Derrick Thomas TL | .10 | .02 |
| ☐ 667 Bruce Smith TL | .10 | .02 |
| ☐ 668 Mark Carrier DB TL | .05 | .01 |
| ☐ 669 Richard Johnson CB TL | .05 | .01 |
| ☐ 670 Jan Stenerud HOF | .05 | .01 |
| ☐ 671 Stan Jones HOF | .05 | .01 |
| ☐ 672 John Hannah HOF | .05 | .01 |
| ☐ 673 Tex Schramm HOF | .05 | .01 |
| ☐ 674 Earl Campbell HOF | .25 | .08 |
| ☐ 675 Emmitt Smith/Carrier ROY | .75 | .30 |
| ☐ 676 Warren Moon DT | .10 | .02 |
| ☐ 677 Barry Sanders DT | .50 | .20 |
| ☐ 678 Thurman Thomas DT | .25 | .08 |
| ☐ 679 Andre Reed DT | .10 | .02 |
| ☐ 680 Andre Rison DT | .10 | .02 |
| ☐ 681 Keith Jackson DT | .05 | .01 |
| ☐ 682 Bruce Armstrong DT | .05 | .01 |
| ☐ 683 Jim Lachey DT | .05 | .01 |
| ☐ 684 Bruce Matthews DT | .05 | .01 |
| ☐ 685 Mike Munchak DT | .05 | .01 |
| ☐ 686 Don Mosebar DT | .05 | .01 |
| ☐ B1 Jeff Hostetler BONUS SB | .25 | .08 |
| ☐ B2 Matt Bahr SB | .05 | .01 |
| ☐ B3 Ottis Anderson SB | .10 | .02 |
| ☐ B4 Ottis Anderson SB | .10 | .02 |

### 1992 Score

| | | |
|---|---|---|
| ☐ COMPLETE SET (550) | 25.00 | 12.50 |
| ☐ 1 Barry Sanders | 2.00 | .75 |
| ☐ 2 Pat Swilling | .05 | .01 |
| ☐ 3 Moe Gardner | .05 | .01 |
| ☐ 4 Steve Young | 1.00 | .40 |
| ☐ 5 Chris Spielman | .05 | .01 |
| ☐ 6 Richard Dent | .10 | .02 |
| ☐ 7 Anthony Munoz | .10 | .02 |
| ☐ 8 Martin Mayhew | .05 | .01 |
| ☐ 9 Terry McDaniel | .05 | .01 |
| ☐ 10 Thurman Thomas | .25 | .08 |
| ☐ 11 Ricky Sanders | .05 | .01 |
| ☐ 12 Steve Atwater | .05 | .01 |
| ☐ 13 Tony Tolbert | .05 | .01 |
| ☐ 14 Vince Workman | .05 | .01 |
| ☐ 15 Haywood Jeffires | .10 | .02 |
| ☐ 16 Duane Bickett | .05 | .01 |
| ☐ 17 Jeff Uhlenhake | .05 | .01 |
| ☐ 18 Tim McDonald | .05 | .01 |
| ☐ 19 Cris Carter | .50 | .20 |
| ☐ 20 Derrick Thomas | .25 | .08 |
| ☐ 21 Hugh Millen | .05 | .01 |
| ☐ 22 Bart Oates | .05 | .01 |
| ☐ 23 Eugene Robinson | .05 | .01 |
| ☐ 24 Jerrol Williams | .05 | .01 |
| ☐ 25 Reggie White | .25 | .08 |
| ☐ 26 Marion Butts | .05 | .01 |
| ☐ 27 Jim Sweeney | .05 | .01 |
| ☐ 28 Tom Newberry | .05 | .01 |
| ☐ 29 Pete Stoyanovich | .05 | .01 |
| ☐ 30 Ronnie Lott | .10 | .02 |
| ☐ 31 Simon Fletcher | .05 | .01 |
| ☐ 32 Dino Hackett | .05 | .01 |

| | | |
|---|---|---|
| ☐ 33 Morten Andersen | .05 | .01 |
| ☐ 34 Clyde Simmons | .05 | .01 |
| ☐ 35 Mark Rypien | .05 | .01 |
| ☐ 36 Greg Montgomery | .05 | .01 |
| ☐ 37 Nate Lewis | .05 | .01 |
| ☐ 38 Henry Ellard | .10 | .02 |
| ☐ 39 Luis Sharpe | .05 | .01 |
| ☐ 40 Michael Irvin | .25 | .08 |
| ☐ 41 Louis Lipps | .05 | .01 |
| ☐ 42 John L. Williams | .05 | .01 |
| ☐ 43 Broderick Thomas | .05 | .01 |
| ☐ 44 Michael Haynes | .10 | .02 |
| ☐ 45 Don Majkowski | .05 | .01 |
| ☐ 46 William Perry | .10 | .02 |
| ☐ 47 David Fulcher | .05 | .01 |
| ☐ 48 Tony Bennett | .05 | .01 |
| ☐ 49 Clay Matthews | .10 | .02 |
| ☐ 50 Warren Moon | .25 | .08 |
| ☐ 51 Bruce Armstrong | .05 | .01 |
| ☐ 52 Harry Newsome | .05 | .01 |
| ☐ 53 Bill Brooks | .05 | .01 |
| ☐ 54 Greg Townsend | .05 | .01 |
| ☐ 55 Tom Rathman | .05 | .01 |
| ☐ 56 Sean Landeta | .05 | .01 |
| ☐ 57 Kyle Clifton | .05 | .01 |
| ☐ 58 Steve Broussard | .05 | .01 |
| ☐ 59 Mark Carrier WR | .10 | .02 |
| ☐ 60 Mel Gray | .10 | .02 |
| ☐ 61 Tim Krumrie | .05 | .01 |
| ☐ 62 Rufus Porter | .05 | .01 |
| ☐ 63 Kevin Mack | .05 | .01 |
| ☐ 64 Todd Bowles | .05 | .01 |
| ☐ 65 Emmitt Smith | 2.50 | 1.25 |
| ☐ 66 Mike Croel | .05 | .01 |
| ☐ 67 Brian Mitchell | .10 | .02 |
| ☐ 68 Bernie Blades | .05 | .01 |
| ☐ 69 Carnell Lake | .05 | .01 |
| ☐ 70 Cornelius Bennett | .10 | .02 |
| ☐ 71 Darrell Thompson | .05 | .01 |
| ☐ 72 Wes Hopkins | .05 | .01 |
| ☐ 73 Jessie Hester | .05 | .01 |
| ☐ 74 Irv Eatman | .05 | .01 |
| ☐ 75 Marv Cook | .05 | .01 |
| ☐ 76 Tim Brown | .25 | .08 |
| ☐ 77 Pepper Johnson | .05 | .01 |
| ☐ 78 Mark Duper | .05 | .01 |
| ☐ 79 Robert Delpino | .05 | .01 |
| ☐ 80 Charles Mann | .05 | .01 |
| ☐ 81 Brian Jordan | .10 | .02 |
| ☐ 82 Wendell Davis | .05 | .01 |
| ☐ 83 Lee Johnson | .05 | .01 |
| ☐ 84 Ricky Reynolds | .05 | .01 |
| ☐ 85 Vaughan Johnson | .05 | .01 |
| ☐ 86 Brian Blades | .10 | .02 |
| ☐ 87 Sam Seale | .05 | .01 |
| ☐ 88 Ed King | .05 | .01 |
| ☐ 89 Gaston Green | .05 | .01 |
| ☐ 90 Christian Okoye | .05 | .01 |
| ☐ 91 Chris Jacke | .05 | .01 |
| ☐ 92 Rohn Stark | .05 | .01 |
| ☐ 93 Kevin Greene | .10 | .02 |
| ☐ 94 Jay Novacek | .10 | .02 |
| ☐ 95 Chip Lohmiller | .05 | .01 |
| ☐ 96 Cris Dishman | .05 | .01 |
| ☐ 97 Ethan Horton | .05 | .01 |
| ☐ 98 Pat Harlow | .05 | .01 |
| ☐ 99 Mark Ingram | .05 | .01 |
| ☐ 100 Mark Carrier DB | .05 | .01 |
| ☐ 101 Deron Cherry | .05 | .01 |
| ☐ 102 Sam Mills | .05 | .01 |
| ☐ 103 Mark Higgs | .05 | .01 |
| ☐ 104 Keith Jackson | .10 | .02 |
| ☐ 105 Steve Tasker | .10 | .02 |
| ☐ 106 Ken Harvey | .05 | .01 |
| ☐ 107 Bryan Hinkle | .05 | .01 |
| ☐ 108 Anthony Carter | .10 | .02 |
| ☐ 109 Johnny Hector | .05 | .01 |
| ☐ 110 Randall McDaniel | .10 | .02 |
| ☐ 111 Johnny Johnson | .05 | .01 |
| ☐ 112 Shane Conlan | .05 | .01 |
| ☐ 113 Ray Horton | .05 | .01 |
| ☐ 114 Sterling Sharpe | .25 | .08 |
| ☐ 115 Guy McIntyre | .05 | .01 |
| ☐ 116 Tom Waddle | .05 | .01 |
| ☐ 117 Albert Lewis | .05 | .01 |

| | | |
|---|---|---|
| ❏ 118 Riki Ellison | .05 | .01 |
| ❏ 119 Chris Doleman | .05 | .01 |
| ❏ 120 Andre Rison | .10 | .02 |
| ❏ 121 Bobby Hebert | .05 | .01 |
| ❏ 122 Dan Owens | .05 | .01 |
| ❏ 123 Rodney Hampton | .10 | .02 |
| ❏ 124 Ron Holmes | .05 | .01 |
| ❏ 125 Ernie Jones | .05 | .01 |
| ❏ 126 Michael Carter | .05 | .01 |
| ❏ 127 Reggie Cobb | .05 | .01 |
| ❏ 128 Esera Tuaolo | .05 | .01 |
| ❏ 129 Wilber Marshall | .05 | .01 |
| ❏ 130 Mike Munchak | .10 | .02 |
| ❏ 131 Cortez Kennedy | .10 | .02 |
| ❏ 132 Lamar Lathon | .05 | .01 |
| ❏ 133 Todd Lyght | .05 | .01 |
| ❏ 134 Jeff Feagles | .05 | .01 |
| ❏ 135 Burt Grossman | .05 | .01 |
| ❏ 136 Mike Cofer | .05 | .01 |
| ❏ 137 Frank Warren | .05 | .01 |
| ❏ 138 Jarvis Williams | .05 | .01 |
| ❏ 139 Eddie Brown | .05 | .01 |
| ❏ 140 John Elliott | .05 | .01 |
| ❏ 141 Jim Everett | .10 | .02 |
| ❏ 142 Hardy Nickerson | .10 | .02 |
| ❏ 143 Eddie Murray | .05 | .01 |
| ❏ 144 Andre Tippett | .05 | .01 |
| ❏ 145 Heath Sherman | .05 | .01 |
| ❏ 146 Ronnie Harmon | .05 | .01 |
| ❏ 147 Eric Metcalf | .10 | .02 |
| ❏ 148 Tony Martin | .10 | .02 |
| ❏ 149 Chris Burkett | .05 | .01 |
| ❏ 150 Andre Waters | .05 | .01 |
| ❏ 151 Ray Donaldson | .05 | .01 |
| ❏ 152 Paul Gruber | .05 | .01 |
| ❏ 153 Chris Singleton | .05 | .01 |
| ❏ 154 Clarence Kay | .05 | .01 |
| ❏ 155 Ernest Givins | .10 | .02 |
| ❏ 156 Eric Hill | .05 | .01 |
| ❏ 157 Jesse Sapolu | .05 | .01 |
| ❏ 158 Jack Del Rio | .05 | .01 |
| ❏ 159 Erric Pegram | .10 | .02 |
| ❏ 160 Joey Browner | .05 | .01 |
| ❏ 161 Marcus Allen | .25 | .08 |
| ❏ 162 Eric Moten | .05 | .01 |
| ❏ 163 Donnell Thompson | .05 | .01 |
| ❏ 164 Chuck Cecil | .05 | .01 |
| ❏ 165 Matt Millen | .10 | .02 |
| ❏ 166 Barry Foster | .10 | .02 |
| ❏ 167 Kent Hull | .05 | .01 |
| ❏ 168 Tony Jones WR | .05 | .01 |
| ❏ 169 Mike Prior | .05 | .01 |
| ❏ 170 Neal Anderson | .05 | .01 |
| ❏ 171 Roger Craig | .10 | .02 |
| ❏ 172 Felix Wright | .05 | .01 |
| ❏ 173 James Francis | .05 | .01 |
| ❏ 174 Eugene Lockhart | .05 | .01 |
| ❏ 175 Dalton Hilliard | .05 | .01 |
| ❏ 176 Nick Lowery | .05 | .01 |
| ❏ 177 Tim McKyer | .05 | .01 |
| ❏ 178 Lorenzo White | .05 | .01 |
| ❏ 179 Jeff Hostetler | .10 | .02 |
| ❏ 180 Jackie Harris RC | .25 | .08 |
| ❏ 181 Ken Norton | .10 | .02 |
| ❏ 182 Flipper Anderson | .05 | .01 |
| ❏ 183 Don Warren | .05 | .01 |
| ❏ 184 Brad Baxter | .05 | .01 |
| ❏ 185 John Taylor | .10 | .02 |
| ❏ 186 Harold Green | .05 | .01 |
| ❏ 187 James Washington | .05 | .01 |
| ❏ 188 Aaron Craver | .05 | .01 |
| ❏ 189 Mike Merriweather | .05 | .01 |
| ❏ 190 Gary Clark | .25 | .08 |
| ❏ 191 Vince Buck | .05 | .01 |
| ❏ 192 Cleveland Gary | .05 | .01 |
| ❏ 193 Dan Saleaumua | .05 | .01 |
| ❏ 194 Gary Zimmerman | .05 | .01 |
| ❏ 195 Richmond Webb | .05 | .01 |
| ❏ 196 Gary Plummer | .05 | .01 |
| ❏ 197 Willie Jones | .05 | .01 |
| ❏ 198 Chris Warren | .25 | .08 |
| ❏ 199 Mike Pritchard | .10 | .02 |
| ❏ 200 Art Monk | .10 | .02 |
| ❏ 201 Matt Stover | .05 | .01 |
| ❏ 202 Tim Grunhard | .05 | .01 |
| ❏ 203 Mervyn Fernandez | .05 | .01 |
| ❏ 204 Mark Jackson | .05 | .01 |
| ❏ 205 Freddie Joe Nunn | .05 | .01 |
| ❏ 206 Stan Thomas | .05 | .01 |
| ❏ 207 Keith McKeller | .05 | .01 |
| ❏ 208 Jeff Lageman | .05 | .01 |
| ❏ 209 Kenny Walker | .05 | .01 |
| ❏ 210 Dave Krieg | .10 | .02 |
| ❏ 211 Dean Biasucci | .05 | .01 |
| ❏ 212 Herman Moore | .25 | .08 |
| ❏ 213 Jon Vaughn | .05 | .01 |
| ❏ 214 Howard Cross | .05 | .01 |
| ❏ 215 Greg Davis | .05 | .01 |
| ❏ 216 Bubby Brister | .05 | .01 |
| ❏ 217 John Kasay | .05 | .01 |
| ❏ 218 Ron Hall | .05 | .01 |
| ❏ 219 Mo Lewis | .05 | .01 |
| ❏ 220 Eric Green | .05 | .01 |
| ❏ 221 Scott Case | .05 | .01 |
| ❏ 222 Sean Jones | .05 | .01 |
| ❏ 223 Winston Moss | .05 | .01 |
| ❏ 224 Reggie Langhorne | .05 | .01 |
| ❏ 225 Greg Lewis | .05 | .01 |
| ❏ 226 Todd McNair | .05 | .01 |
| ❏ 227 Rod Bernstine | .05 | .01 |
| ❏ 228 Joe Jacoby | .05 | .01 |
| ❏ 229 Brad Muster | .05 | .01 |
| ❏ 230 Nick Bell | .05 | .01 |
| ❏ 231 Terry Allen | .25 | .08 |
| ❏ 232 Cliff Odom | .05 | .01 |
| ❏ 233 Brian Hansen | .05 | .01 |
| ❏ 234 William Fuller | .05 | .01 |
| ❏ 235 Issiac Holt | .05 | .01 |
| ❏ 236 Dexter Carter | .05 | .01 |
| ❏ 237 Gene Atkins | .05 | .01 |
| ❏ 238 Pat Beach | .05 | .01 |
| ❏ 239 Tim McGee | .05 | .01 |
| ❏ 240 Dermontti Dawson | .05 | .01 |
| ❏ 241 Dan Fike | .05 | .01 |
| ❏ 242 Don Beebe | .05 | .01 |
| ❏ 243 Jeff Bostic | .05 | .01 |
| ❏ 244 Mark Collins | .05 | .01 |
| ❏ 245 Steve Sewell | .05 | .01 |
| ❏ 246 Steve Walsh | .05 | .01 |
| ❏ 247 Erik Kramer | .10 | .02 |
| ❏ 248 Scott Norwood | .05 | .01 |
| ❏ 249 Jesse Solomon | .05 | .01 |
| ❏ 250 Jerry Ball | .05 | .01 |
| ❏ 251 Eugene Daniel | .05 | .01 |
| ❏ 252 Michael Stewart | .05 | .01 |
| ❏ 253 Fred Barnett | .25 | .08 |
| ❏ 254 Rodney Holman | .05 | .01 |
| ❏ 255 Stephen Baker | .05 | .01 |
| ❏ 256 Don Griffin | .05 | .01 |
| ❏ 257 Will Wolford | .05 | .01 |
| ❏ 258 Perry Kemp | .05 | .01 |
| ❏ 259 Leonard Russell | .10 | .02 |
| ❏ 260 Jeff Gossett | .05 | .01 |
| ❏ 261 Dwayne Harper | .05 | .01 |
| ❏ 262 Vinny Testaverde | .10 | .02 |
| ❏ 263 Maurice Hurst | .05 | .01 |
| ❏ 264 Tony Casillas | .05 | .01 |
| ❏ 265 Louis Oliver | .05 | .01 |
| ❏ 266 Jim Morrissey | .05 | .01 |
| ❏ 267 Kenneth Davis | .05 | .01 |
| ❏ 268 John Alt | .05 | .01 |
| ❏ 269 Michael Zordich RC | .05 | .01 |
| ❏ 270 Brian Brennan | .05 | .01 |
| ❏ 271 Greg Kragen | .05 | .01 |
| ❏ 272 Andre Collins | .05 | .01 |
| ❏ 273 Dave Meggett | .10 | .02 |
| ❏ 274 Scott Fulhage | .05 | .01 |
| ❏ 275 Tony Zendejas | .05 | .01 |
| ❏ 276 Herschel Walker | .10 | .02 |
| ❏ 277 Keith Henderson | .05 | .01 |
| ❏ 278 Johnny Bailey | .05 | .01 |
| ❏ 279 Vince Newsome | .05 | .01 |
| ❏ 280 Chris Hinton | .05 | .01 |
| ❏ 281 Robert Blackmon | .05 | .01 |
| ❏ 282 James Hasty | .05 | .01 |
| ❏ 283 John Offerdahl | .05 | .01 |
| ❏ 284 Wesley Carroll | .05 | .01 |
| ❏ 285 Lomas Brown | .05 | .01 |
| ❏ 286 Neil O'Donnell | .10 | .02 |
| ❏ 287 Kevin Porter | .05 | .01 |
| ❏ 288 Lionel Washington | .05 | .01 |
| ❏ 289 Carlton Bailey RC | .05 | .01 |
| ❏ 290 Leonard Marshall | .05 | .01 |
| ❏ 291 John Carney | .05 | .01 |
| ❏ 292 Bubba McDowell | .05 | .01 |
| ❏ 293 Nate Newton | .05 | .01 |
| ❏ 294 Dave Waymer | .05 | .01 |
| ❏ 295 Rob Moore | .10 | .02 |
| ❏ 296 Earnest Byner | .05 | .01 |
| ❏ 297 Jason Staurovsky | .05 | .01 |
| ❏ 298 Keith McCants | .05 | .01 |
| ❏ 299 Floyd Turner | .05 | .01 |
| ❏ 300 Steve Jordan | .05 | .01 |
| ❏ 301 Nate Odomes | .05 | .01 |
| ❏ 302 Gerald Riggs | .05 | .01 |
| ❏ 303 Marvin Washington | .05 | .01 |
| ❏ 304 Anthony Thompson | .05 | .01 |
| ❏ 305 Steve DeBerg | .05 | .01 |
| ❏ 306 Jim Harbaugh | .25 | .08 |
| ❏ 307 Larry Brown DB | .05 | .01 |
| ❏ 308 Roger Ruzek | .05 | .01 |
| ❏ 309 Jessie Tuggle | .05 | .01 |
| ❏ 310 Al Smith | .05 | .01 |
| ❏ 311 Mark Kelso | .05 | .01 |
| ❏ 312 Lawrence Dawsey | .10 | .02 |
| ❏ 313 Steve Bono RC | .25 | .08 |
| ❏ 314 Greg Lloyd | .10 | .02 |
| ❏ 315 Steve Wisniewski | .05 | .01 |
| ❏ 316 Gill Fenerty | .05 | .01 |
| ❏ 317 Mark Stepnoski | .10 | .02 |
| ❏ 318 Derek Russell | .05 | .01 |
| ❏ 319 Chris Martin | .05 | .01 |
| ❏ 320 Shaun Gayle | .05 | .01 |
| ❏ 321 Bob Golic | .05 | .01 |
| ❏ 322 Larry Kelm | .05 | .01 |
| ❏ 323 Mike Brim RC | .05 | .01 |
| ❏ 324 Tommy Kane | .05 | .01 |
| ❏ 325 Mark Schlereth RC | .05 | .01 |
| ❏ 326 Ray Childress | .05 | .01 |
| ❏ 327 Richard Brown RC | .05 | .01 |
| ❏ 328 Vincent Brown | .05 | .01 |
| ❏ 329 Mike Farr UER | .05 | .01 |
| ❏ 330 Eric Swann | .10 | .02 |
| ❏ 331 Bill Fralic | .05 | .01 |
| ❏ 332 Rodney Peete | .10 | .02 |
| ❏ 333 Jerry Gray | .05 | .01 |
| ❏ 334 Ray Berry | .05 | .01 |
| ❏ 335 Dennis Smith | .05 | .01 |
| ❏ 336 Jeff Herrod | .05 | .01 |
| ❏ 337 Tony Mandarich | .05 | .01 |
| ❏ 338 Matt Bahr | .05 | .01 |
| ❏ 339 Mike Saxon | .05 | .01 |
| ❏ 340 Bruce Matthews | .05 | .01 |
| ❏ 341 Rickey Jackson | .05 | .01 |
| ❏ 342 Eric Allen | .05 | .01 |
| ❏ 343 Lonnie Young | .05 | .01 |
| ❏ 344 Steve McMichael | .10 | .02 |
| ❏ 345 Willie Gault | .10 | .02 |
| ❏ 346 Barry Word | .05 | .01 |
| ❏ 347 Rich Camarillo | .05 | .01 |
| ❏ 348 Bill Romanowski | .05 | .01 |
| ❏ 349 Jim Lachey | .05 | .01 |
| ❏ 350 Jim Ritcher | .05 | .01 |
| ❏ 351 Irving Fryar | .10 | .02 |
| ❏ 352 Gary Anderson K | .05 | .01 |
| ❏ 353 Henry Rolling | .05 | .01 |
| ❏ 354 Mark Bortz | .05 | .01 |
| ❏ 355 Mark Clayton | .10 | .02 |
| ❏ 356 Keith Woodside | .05 | .01 |
| ❏ 357 Jonathan Hayes | .05 | .01 |
| ❏ 358 Derrick Fenner | .05 | .01 |
| ❏ 359 Keith Byars | .05 | .01 |
| ❏ 360 Drew Hill | .05 | .01 |
| ❏ 361 Harris Barton | .05 | .01 |
| ❏ 362 John Kidd | .05 | .01 |
| ❏ 363 Aeneas Williams | .10 | .02 |
| ❏ 364 Brian Washington | .05 | .01 |
| ❏ 365 John Stephens | .05 | .01 |
| ❏ 366 Norm Johnson | .05 | .01 |
| ❏ 367 Darryl Henley | .05 | .01 |
| ❏ 368 William White | .05 | .01 |
| ❏ 369 Mark Murphy | .05 | .01 |
| ❏ 370 Myron Guyton | .05 | .01 |
| ❏ 371 Leon Seals | .05 | .01 |
| ❏ 372 Rich Gannon | .25 | .08 |

| | | |
|---|---|---|
| ❑ 373 Toi Cook | .05 | .01 |
| ❑ 374 Anthony Johnson | .10 | .01 |
| ❑ 375 Rod Woodson | .25 | .08 |
| ❑ 376 Alexander Wright | .05 | .01 |
| ❑ 377 Kevin Butler | .05 | .01 |
| ❑ 378 Neil Smith | .25 | .08 |
| ❑ 379 Gary Anderson RB | .05 | .01 |
| ❑ 380 Reggie Roby | .05 | .01 |
| ❑ 381 Jeff Bryant | .05 | .01 |
| ❑ 382 Ray Crockett | .05 | .01 |
| ❑ 383 Richard Johnson CB | .05 | .01 |
| ❑ 384 Hassan Jones | .05 | .01 |
| ❑ 385 Karl Mecklenburg | .05 | .01 |
| ❑ 386 Jeff Jaeger | .05 | .01 |
| ❑ 387 Keith Willis | .05 | .01 |
| ❑ 388 Phil Simms | .10 | .02 |
| ❑ 389 Kevin Ross | .05 | .01 |
| ❑ 390 Chris Miller | .10 | .02 |
| ❑ 391 Brian Noble | .05 | .01 |
| ❑ 392 Jamie Dukes RC | .05 | .01 |
| ❑ 393 George Jamison | .05 | .01 |
| ❑ 394 Rickey Dixon | .05 | .01 |
| ❑ 395 Carl Lee | .05 | .01 |
| ❑ 396 Jon Hand | .05 | .01 |
| ❑ 397 Kirby Jackson | .05 | .01 |
| ❑ 398 Pat Terrell | .05 | .01 |
| ❑ 399 Howie Long | .25 | .08 |
| ❑ 400 Michael Young | .05 | .01 |
| ❑ 401 Keith Sims | .05 | .01 |
| ❑ 402 Tommy Barnhardt | .05 | .01 |
| ❑ 403 Greg McMurtry | .05 | .01 |
| ❑ 404 Keith Van Horne | .05 | .01 |
| ❑ 405 Seth Joyner | .05 | .01 |
| ❑ 406 Jim Jeffcoat | .05 | .01 |
| ❑ 407 Courtney Hall | .05 | .01 |
| ❑ 408 Tony Covington | .05 | .01 |
| ❑ 409 Jacob Green | .05 | .01 |
| ❑ 410 Charles Haley | .10 | .02 |
| ❑ 411 Darryl Talley | .05 | .01 |
| ❑ 412 Jeff Cross | .05 | .01 |
| ❑ 413 John Elway | 2.00 | .75 |
| ❑ 414 Donald Evans | .05 | .01 |
| ❑ 415 Jackie Slater | .05 | .01 |
| ❑ 416 John Friesz | .10 | .02 |
| ❑ 417 Anthony Smith | .05 | .01 |
| ❑ 418 Gill Byrd | .05 | .01 |
| ❑ 419 Willie Drewrey | .05 | .01 |
| ❑ 420 Jay Hilgenberg | .05 | .01 |
| ❑ 421 David Treadwell | .05 | .01 |
| ❑ 422 Curtis Duncan | .05 | .01 |
| ❑ 423 Sammie Smith | .05 | .01 |
| ❑ 424 Henry Thomas | .05 | .01 |
| ❑ 425 James Lofton | .10 | .02 |
| ❑ 426 Fred Marion | .05 | .01 |
| ❑ 427 Bryce Paup | .25 | .08 |
| ❑ 428 Michael Timpson RC | .05 | .01 |
| ❑ 429 Reyna Thompson | .05 | .01 |
| ❑ 430 Mike Kenn | .05 | .01 |
| ❑ 431 Bill Maas | .05 | .01 |
| ❑ 432 Quinn Early | .10 | .02 |
| ❑ 433 Everson Walls | .05 | .01 |
| ❑ 434 Jimmie Jones | .05 | .01 |
| ❑ 435 Dwight Stone | .05 | .01 |
| ❑ 436 Harry Colon | .05 | .01 |
| ❑ 437 Don Mosebar | .05 | .01 |
| ❑ 438 Calvin Williams | .10 | .02 |
| ❑ 439 Tom Tupa | .05 | .01 |
| ❑ 440 Darrell Green | .05 | .01 |
| ❑ 441 Eric Thomas | .05 | .01 |
| ❑ 442 Terry Wooden | .05 | .01 |
| ❑ 443 Brett Perriman | .25 | .08 |
| ❑ 444 Todd Marinovich | .05 | .01 |
| ❑ 445 Jim Breech | .05 | .01 |
| ❑ 446 Eddie Anderson | .05 | .01 |
| ❑ 447 Jay Schroeder | .05 | .01 |
| ❑ 448 William Roberts | .05 | .01 |
| ❑ 449 Brad Edwards | .05 | .01 |
| ❑ 450 Tunch Ilkin | .05 | .01 |
| ❑ 451 Ivy Joe Hunter RC | .05 | .01 |
| ❑ 452 Robert Clark | .05 | .01 |
| ❑ 453 Tim Barnett | .05 | .01 |
| ❑ 454 Jarrod Bunch | .05 | .01 |
| ❑ 455 Tim Harris | .05 | .01 |
| ❑ 456 James Brooks | .10 | .02 |
| ❑ 457 Trace Armstrong | .05 | .01 |
| ❑ 458 Michael Brooks | .05 | .01 |
| ❑ 459 Andy Heck | .05 | .01 |
| ❑ 460 Greg Jackson | .05 | .01 |
| ❑ 461 Vance Johnson | .05 | .01 |
| ❑ 462 Kirk Lowdermilk | .05 | .01 |
| ❑ 463 Erik McMillan | .05 | .01 |
| ❑ 464 Scott Mersereau | .05 | .01 |
| ❑ 465 Jeff Wright | .05 | .01 |
| ❑ 466 Mike Tomczak | .05 | .01 |
| ❑ 467 David Alexander | .05 | .01 |
| ❑ 468 Bryan Millard | .05 | .01 |
| ❑ 469 John Randle | .10 | .02 |
| ❑ 470 Joel Hilgenberg | .05 | .01 |
| ❑ 471 Bennie Thompson RC | .05 | .01 |
| ❑ 472 Freeman McNeil | .05 | .01 |
| ❑ 473 Terry Orr RC | .05 | .01 |
| ❑ 474 Mike Horan | .05 | .01 |
| ❑ 475 Leroy Hoard | .10 | .02 |
| ❑ 476 Patrick Rowe RC | .05 | .01 |
| ❑ 477 Siran Stacy RC | .05 | .01 |
| ❑ 478 Amp Lee RC | .05 | .01 |
| ❑ 479 Eddie Blake RC | .05 | .01 |
| ❑ 480 Joe Bowden RC | .05 | .01 |
| ❑ 481 Rod Milstead RC | .05 | .01 |
| ❑ 482 Keith Hamilton RC | .10 | .02 |
| ❑ 483 Darryl Williams RC | .05 | .01 |
| ❑ 484 Robert Porcher RC | .25 | .08 |
| ❑ 485 Ed Cunningham RC | .05 | .01 |
| ❑ 486 Chris Mims RC | .05 | .01 |
| ❑ 487 Chris Hakel RC | .05 | .01 |
| ❑ 488 Jimmy Smith RC | 4.00 | 1.50 |
| ❑ 489 Todd Harrison RC | .05 | .01 |
| ❑ 490 Edgar Bennett RC | .25 | .08 |
| ❑ 491 Dexter McNabb RC | .05 | .01 |
| ❑ 492 Leon Searcy RC | .05 | .01 |
| ❑ 493 Tommy Vardell RC | .05 | .01 |
| ❑ 494 Terrell Buckley RC | .05 | .01 |
| ❑ 495 Kevin Turner RC | .05 | .01 |
| ❑ 496 Russ Campbell RC | .05 | .01 |
| ❑ 497 Torrance Small RC | .10 | .02 |
| ❑ 498 Nate Turner RC | .05 | .01 |
| ❑ 499 Cornelius Benton RC | .05 | .01 |
| ❑ 500 Matt Elliott RC | .05 | .01 |
| ❑ 501 Robert Stewart RC | .05 | .01 |
| ❑ 502 Muhammad Shamsid-Deen RC | .05 | .01 |
| ❑ 503 George Williams RC | .05 | .01 |
| ❑ 504 Pumpy Tudors RC | .05 | .01 |
| ❑ 505 Matt LaBounty RC | .05 | .01 |
| ❑ 506 Darryl Hardy RC | .05 | .01 |
| ❑ 507 Derrick Moore RC | .10 | .02 |
| ❑ 508 Willie Clay RC | .05 | .01 |
| ❑ 509 Bob Whitfield RC | .05 | .01 |
| ❑ 510 Ricardo McDonald RC | .05 | .01 |
| ❑ 511 Carlos Huerta RC | .05 | .01 |
| ❑ 512 Selwyn Jones RC | .05 | .01 |
| ❑ 513 Steve Gordon RC | .05 | .01 |
| ❑ 514 Bob Meeks RC | .05 | .01 |
| ❑ 515 Bennie Blades CC | .05 | .01 |
| ❑ 516 Andre Waters CC | .05 | .01 |
| ❑ 517 Bubba McDowell CC | .05 | .01 |
| ❑ 518 Kevin Porter CC | .05 | .01 |
| ❑ 519 Carnell Lake CC | .05 | .01 |
| ❑ 520 Leonard Russell ROY | .10 | .02 |
| ❑ 521 Mike Croel ROY | .05 | .01 |
| ❑ 522 Lawrence Dawsey ROY | .05 | .01 |
| ❑ 523 Moe Gardner ROY | .05 | .01 |
| ❑ 524 Steve Broussard LBM | .05 | .01 |
| ❑ 525 Dave Meggett LBM | .05 | .01 |
| ❑ 526 Darrell Green LBM | .05 | .01 |
| ❑ 527 Tony Jones WR LBM | .05 | .01 |
| ❑ 528 Barry Sanders LBM | 1.00 | .40 |
| ❑ 529 Pat Swilling SA | .05 | .01 |
| ❑ 530 Reggie White SA | .10 | .02 |
| ❑ 531 William Fuller SA | .05 | .01 |
| ❑ 532 Simon Fletcher SA | .05 | .01 |
| ❑ 533 Derrick Thomas SA | .10 | .02 |
| ❑ 534 Mark Rypien MOY | .05 | .01 |
| ❑ 535 John Mackey HOF | .05 | .01 |
| ❑ 536 John Riggins HOF | .10 | .02 |
| ❑ 537 Lem Barney HOF | .05 | .01 |
| ❑ 538 Shawn McCarthy RC 90 | .05 | .01 |
| ❑ 539 Al Edwards 90 | .05 | .01 |
| ❑ 540 Alexander Wright 90 | .05 | .01 |
| ❑ 541 Ray Crockett 90 | .05 | .01 |
| ❑ 542 Steve Young/J.Taylor 90 | .25 | .08 |

| | | |
|---|---|---|
| ❑ 543 Nate Lewis 90 | .05 | .01 |
| ❑ 544 Dexter Carter 90 | .05 | .01 |
| ❑ 545 Reggie Rutland 90 | .05 | .01 |
| ❑ 546 Jon Vaughn 90 | .05 | .01 |
| ❑ 547 Chris Martin 90 | .05 | .01 |
| ❑ 548 Warren Moon HL | .10 | .02 |
| ❑ 549 Super Bowl Highlights | .05 | .01 |
| ❑ 550 Robb Thomas | .05 | .01 |
| ❑ NNO Dick Butkus Promo | 8.00 | 4.00 |

## 1993 Score

| | | |
|---|---|---|
| ❑ COMPLETE SET (440) | 15.00 | 6.00 |
| ❑ 1 Barry Sanders | 1.25 | .50 |
| ❑ 2 Moe Gardner | .05 | .01 |
| ❑ 3 Ricky Watters | .25 | .08 |
| ❑ 4 Todd Lyght | .05 | .01 |
| ❑ 5 Rodney Hampton | .10 | .02 |
| ❑ 6 Curtis Duncan | .05 | .01 |
| ❑ 7 Barry Word | .05 | .01 |
| ❑ 8 Reggie Cobb | .05 | .01 |
| ❑ 9 Mike Kenn | .05 | .01 |
| ❑ 10 Michael Irvin | .25 | .08 |
| ❑ 11 Bryan Cox | .05 | .01 |
| ❑ 12 Chris Doleman | .05 | .01 |
| ❑ 13 Rod Woodson | .25 | .08 |
| ❑ 14 Emmitt Smith | 1.50 | .60 |
| ❑ 15 Pete Stoyanovich | .05 | .01 |
| ❑ 16 Steve Young | .75 | .30 |
| ❑ 17 Randall McDaniel | .10 | .02 |
| ❑ 18 Cortez Kennedy | .10 | .02 |
| ❑ 19 Mel Gray | .10 | .02 |
| ❑ 20 Barry Foster | .10 | .02 |
| ❑ 21 Tim Brown | .25 | .08 |
| ❑ 22 Todd McNair | .05 | .01 |
| ❑ 23 Anthony Johnson | .10 | .02 |
| ❑ 24 Nate Odomes | .05 | .01 |
| ❑ 25 Brett Favre | 2.00 | .75 |
| ❑ 26 Jack Del Rio | .05 | .01 |
| ❑ 27 Terry McDaniel | .05 | .01 |
| ❑ 28 Haywood Jeffires | .10 | .02 |
| ❑ 29 Jay Novacek | .10 | .02 |
| ❑ 30 Wilber Marshall | .05 | .01 |
| ❑ 31 Richmond Webb | .05 | .01 |
| ❑ 32 Steve Atwater | .05 | .01 |
| ❑ 33 James Lofton | .10 | .02 |
| ❑ 34 Harold Green | .05 | .01 |
| ❑ 35 Eric Metcalf | .10 | .02 |
| ❑ 36 Bruce Matthews | .05 | .01 |
| ❑ 37 Albert Lewis | .05 | .01 |
| ❑ 38 Jeff Herrod | .05 | .01 |
| ❑ 39 Vince Workman | .05 | .01 |
| ❑ 40 John Elway | 1.50 | .60 |
| ❑ 41 Brett Perriman | .25 | .08 |
| ❑ 42 Jon Vaughn | .05 | .01 |
| ❑ 43 Terry Allen | .25 | .08 |
| ❑ 44 Clyde Simmons | .05 | .01 |
| ❑ 45 Bennie Thompson | .05 | .01 |
| ❑ 46 Wendell Davis | .05 | .01 |
| ❑ 47 Bobby Hebert | .05 | .01 |
| ❑ 48 John Offerdahl | .05 | .01 |
| ❑ 49 Jeff Graham | .10 | .02 |
| ❑ 50 Steve Wisniewski | .05 | .01 |
| ❑ 51 Louis Oliver | .05 | .01 |
| ❑ 52 Rohn Stark | .05 | .01 |
| ❑ 53 Cleveland Gary | .05 | .01 |
| ❑ 54 John Randle | .10 | .02 |
| ❑ 55 Jim Everett | .10 | .02 |
| ❑ 56 Donnell Woolford | .05 | .01 |

|  |  | | |
|---|--------|---|---|
| 57 | Pepper Johnson | .05 | .01 |
| 58 | Irving Fryar | .10 | .02 |
| 59 | Greg Townsend | .05 | .01 |
| 60 | Chris Burkett | .05 | .01 |
| 61 | Johnny Johnson | .05 | .01 |
| 62 | Ronnie Harmon | .05 | .01 |
| 63 | Don Griffin | .05 | .01 |
| 64 | Wayne Martin | .05 | .01 |
| 65 | John L. Williams | .05 | .01 |
| 66 | Brad Edwards | .05 | .01 |
| 67 | Toi Cook | .05 | .01 |
| 68 | Lawrence Dawsey | .05 | .01 |
| 69 | Johnny Bailey | .05 | .01 |
| 70 | Mike Brim | .05 | .01 |
| 71 | Andre Rison | .10 | .02 |
| 72 | Cornelius Bennett | .10 | .02 |
| 73 | Brad Muster | .05 | .01 |
| 74 | Broderick Thomas | .05 | .01 |
| 75 | Tom Waddle | .05 | .01 |
| 76 | Paul Gruber | .05 | .01 |
| 77 | Jackie Harris | .05 | .01 |
| 78 | Kenneth Davis | .05 | .01 |
| 79 | Norm Johnson | .05 | .01 |
| 80 | Jim Jeffcoat | .05 | .01 |
| 81 | Chris Warren | .10 | .02 |
| 82 | Greg Kragen | .05 | .01 |
| 83 | Ricky Reynolds | .05 | .01 |
| 84 | Hardy Nickerson | .10 | .02 |
| 85 | Brian Mitchell | .10 | .02 |
| 86 | Rufus Porter | .05 | .01 |
| 87 | Greg Jackson | .05 | .01 |
| 88 | Seth Joyner | .05 | .01 |
| 89 | Tim Grunhard | .05 | .01 |
| 90 | Tim Harris | .05 | .01 |
| 91 | Sterling Sharpe | .25 | .08 |
| 92 | Daniel Stubbs | .05 | .01 |
| 93 | Rob Burnett | .05 | .01 |
| 94 | Rich Camarillo | .05 | .01 |
| 95 | Al Smith | .05 | .01 |
| 96 | Thurman Thomas | .25 | .08 |
| 97 | Morten Andersen | .05 | .01 |
| 98 | Reggie White | .25 | .08 |
| 99 | Gill Byrd | .05 | .01 |
| 100 | Pierce Holt | .05 | .01 |
| 101 | Tim McGee | .05 | .01 |
| 102 | Rickey Jackson | .05 | .01 |
| 103 | Vince Newsome | .05 | .01 |
| 104 | Chris Spielman | .10 | .02 |
| 105 | Tim McDonald | .05 | .01 |
| 106 | James Francis | .05 | .01 |
| 107 | Andre Tippett | .05 | .01 |
| 108 | Sam Mills | .05 | .01 |
| 109 | Hugh Millen | .05 | .01 |
| 110 | Brad Baxter | .05 | .01 |
| 111 | Ricky Sanders | .05 | .01 |
| 112 | Marion Butts | .10 | .02 |
| 113 | Fred Barnett | .10 | .02 |
| 114 | Wade Wilson | .05 | .01 |
| 115 | Dave Meggett | .05 | .01 |
| 116 | Kevin Greene | .10 | .02 |
| 117 | Reggie Langhorne | .05 | .01 |
| 118 | Simon Fletcher | .05 | .01 |
| 119 | Tommy Vardell | .05 | .01 |
| 120 | Darion Conner | .05 | .01 |
| 121 | Darren Lewis | .05 | .01 |
| 122 | Charles Mann | .05 | .01 |
| 123 | David Fulcher | .05 | .01 |
| 124 | Tommy Kane | .05 | .01 |
| 125 | Richard Brown | .05 | .01 |
| 126 | Nate Lewis | .05 | .01 |
| 127 | Tony Tolbert | .05 | .01 |
| 128 | Greg Lloyd | .10 | .02 |
| 129 | Herman Moore | .25 | .08 |
| 130 | Robert Massey | .05 | .01 |
| 131 | Chris Jacke | .05 | .01 |
| 132 | Keith Byars | .05 | .01 |
| 133 | William Fuller | .05 | .01 |
| 134 | Rob Moore | .10 | .02 |
| 135 | Duane Bickett | .05 | .01 |
| 136 | Jarrod Bunch | .05 | .01 |
| 137 | Ethan Horton | .05 | .01 |
| 138 | Leonard Russell | .10 | .02 |
| 139 | Darryl Henley | .05 | .01 |
| 140 | Tony Bennett | .05 | .01 |
| 141 | Harry Newsome | .05 | .01 |
| 142 | Kelvin Martin | .05 | .01 |
| 143 | Audray McMillian | .05 | .01 |
| 144 | Chip Lohmiller | .05 | .01 |
| 145 | Henry Jones | .05 | .01 |
| 146 | Rod Bernstine | .05 | .01 |
| 147 | Darryl Talley | .05 | .01 |
| 148 | Clarence Verdin | .05 | .01 |
| 149 | Derrick Thomas | .25 | .08 |
| 150 | Raleigh McKenzie | .05 | .01 |
| 151 | Phil Hansen | .05 | .01 |
| 152 | Lin Elliott RC | .05 | .01 |
| 153 | Chip Banks | .05 | .01 |
| 154 | Shannon Sharpe | .25 | .08 |
| 155 | David Williams | .05 | .01 |
| 156 | Gaston Green | .05 | .01 |
| 157 | Trace Armstrong | .05 | .01 |
| 158 | Todd Scott | .05 | .01 |
| 159 | Stan Humphries | .10 | .02 |
| 160 | Christian Okoye | .05 | .01 |
| 161 | Dennis Smith | .05 | .01 |
| 162 | Derek Kennard | .05 | .01 |
| 163 | Melvin Jenkins | .05 | .01 |
| 164 | Tommy Barnhardt | .05 | .01 |
| 165 | Eugene Robinson | .05 | .01 |
| 166 | Tom Rathman | .05 | .01 |
| 167 | Chris Chandler | .10 | .02 |
| 168 | Steve Broussard | .05 | .01 |
| 169 | Wymon Henderson | .05 | .01 |
| 170 | Bryce Paup | .10 | .02 |
| 171 | Kent Hull | .05 | .01 |
| 172 | Willie Davis | .25 | .08 |
| 173 | Richard Dent | .10 | .02 |
| 174 | Rodney Peete | .05 | .01 |
| 175 | Clay Matthews | .10 | .02 |
| 176 | Erik Williams | .05 | .01 |
| 177 | Mike Cofer | .05 | .01 |
| 178 | Mark Kelso | .05 | .01 |
| 179 | Kurt Gouveia | .05 | .01 |
| 180 | Keith McCants | .05 | .01 |
| 181 | Jim Arnold | .05 | .01 |
| 182 | Sean Jones | .05 | .01 |
| 183 | Chuck Cecil | .05 | .01 |
| 184 | Mark Rypien | .05 | .01 |
| 185 | William Perry | .10 | .02 |
| 186 | Mark Jackson | .05 | .01 |
| 187 | Jim Dombrowski | .05 | .01 |
| 188 | Heath Sherman | .05 | .01 |
| 189 | Bubba McDowell | .05 | .01 |
| 190 | Fuad Reveiz | .05 | .01 |
| 191 | Darren Perry | .05 | .01 |
| 192 | Karl Mecklenburg | .05 | .01 |
| 193 | Frank Reich | .10 | .02 |
| 194 | Tony Casillas | .05 | .01 |
| 195 | Jerry Ball | .05 | .01 |
| 196 | Jessie Hester | .05 | .01 |
| 197 | David Lang | .05 | .01 |
| 198 | Sean Landeta | .05 | .01 |
| 199 | Jerry Gray | .05 | .01 |
| 200 | Mark Higgs | .05 | .01 |
| 201 | Bruce Armstrong | .05 | .01 |
| 202 | Vaughan Johnson | .05 | .01 |
| 203 | Calvin Williams | .10 | .02 |
| 204 | Leonard Marshall | .05 | .01 |
| 205 | Mike Munchak | .10 | .02 |
| 206 | Kevin Ross | .05 | .01 |
| 207 | Daryl Johnston | .25 | .08 |
| 208 | Jay Schroeder | .05 | .01 |
| 209 | Mo Lewis | .05 | .01 |
| 210 | Carlton Haselrig | .05 | .01 |
| 211 | Cris Carter | .25 | .08 |
| 212 | Marv Cook | .05 | .01 |
| 213 | Mark Duper | .05 | .01 |
| 214 | Jackie Slater | .05 | .01 |
| 215 | Mike Prior | .05 | .01 |
| 216 | Warren Moon | .25 | .08 |
| 217 | Mike Saxon | .05 | .01 |
| 218 | Derrick Fenner | .05 | .01 |
| 219 | Brian Washington | .05 | .01 |
| 220 | Jessie Tuggle | .05 | .01 |
| 221 | Jeff Hostetler | .10 | .02 |
| 222 | Deion Sanders | .50 | .20 |
| 223 | Neal Anderson | .05 | .01 |
| 224 | Kevin Mack | .05 | .01 |
| 225 | Tommy Maddox | .25 | .08 |
| 226 | Neil Smith | .25 | .08 |
| 227 | Ronnie Lott | .10 | .02 |
| 228 | Flipper Anderson | .05 | .01 |
| 229 | Keith Jackson | .10 | .02 |
| 230 | Pat Swilling | .05 | .01 |
| 231 | Carl Banks | .05 | .01 |
| 232 | Eric Allen | .05 | .01 |
| 233 | Randal Hill | .05 | .01 |
| 234 | Burt Grossman | .05 | .01 |
| 235 | Jerry Rice | 1.00 | .40 |
| 236 | Santana Dotson | .10 | .02 |
| 237 | Andre Reed | .10 | .02 |
| 238 | Troy Aikman | .75 | .30 |
| 239 | Ray Childress | .05 | .01 |
| 240 | Phil Simms | .10 | .02 |
| 241 | Steve McMichael | .10 | .02 |
| 242 | Browning Nagle | .05 | .01 |
| 243 | Anthony Miller | .10 | .02 |
| 244 | Earnest Byner | .05 | .01 |
| 245 | Jay Hilgenberg | .05 | .01 |
| 246 | Jeff George | .25 | .08 |
| 247 | Marco Coleman | .05 | .01 |
| 248 | Mark Carrier DB | .05 | .01 |
| 249 | Howie Long | .25 | .08 |
| 250 | Ed McCaffrey | .25 | .08 |
| 251 | Jim Kelly | .25 | .08 |
| 252 | Henry Ellard | .10 | .02 |
| 253 | Joe Montana | 1.50 | .60 |
| 254 | Dale Carter | .05 | .01 |
| 255 | Boomer Esiason | .10 | .02 |
| 256 | Gary Clark | .10 | .02 |
| 257 | Carl Pickens | .10 | .02 |
| 258 | Dave Krieg | .05 | .01 |
| 259 | Russell Maryland | .05 | .01 |
| 260 | Randall Cunningham | .25 | .08 |
| 261 | Leslie O'Neal | .10 | .02 |
| 262 | Vinny Testaverde | .10 | .02 |
| 263 | Ricky Ervins | .05 | .01 |
| 264 | Chris Mims | .05 | .01 |
| 265 | Dan Marino | 1.50 | .60 |
| 266 | Eric Martin | .05 | .01 |
| 267 | Bruce Smith | .25 | .08 |
| 268 | Jim Harbaugh | .25 | .08 |
| 269 | Steve Emtman | .05 | .01 |
| 270 | Ricky Proehl | .05 | .01 |
| 271 | Vaughn Dunbar | .05 | .01 |
| 272 | Junior Seau | .25 | .08 |
| 273 | Sean Gilbert | .10 | .02 |
| 274 | Jim Lachey | .05 | .01 |
| 275 | Dalton Hilliard | .05 | .01 |
| 276 | David Klingler | .05 | .01 |
| 277 | Robert Jones | .05 | .01 |
| 278 | David Treadwell | .05 | .01 |
| 279 | Tracy Scroggins | .05 | .01 |
| 280 | Terrell Buckley | .05 | .01 |
| 281 | Quentin Coryatt | .10 | .02 |
| 282 | Jason Hanson | .05 | .01 |
| 283 | Shane Conlan | .05 | .01 |
| 284 | Guy McIntyre | .05 | .01 |
| 285 | Gary Zimmerman | .05 | .01 |
| 286 | Marty Carter | .05 | .01 |
| 287 | Jim Sweeney | .05 | .01 |
| 288 | Arthur Marshall RC | .05 | .01 |
| 289 | Eugene Chung | .05 | .01 |
| 290 | Mike Pritchard | .10 | .02 |
| 291 | Jim Ritcher | .05 | .01 |
| 292 | Todd Marinovich | .05 | .01 |
| 293 | Courtney Hall | .05 | .01 |
| 294 | Mark Collins | .05 | .01 |
| 295 | Troy Auzenne | .05 | .01 |
| 296 | Aeneas Williams | .05 | .01 |
| 297 | Andy Heck | .05 | .01 |
| 298 | Shaun Gayle | .05 | .01 |
| 299 | Kevin Fagan | .05 | .01 |
| 300 | Carnell Lake | .05 | .01 |
| 301 | Bernie Kosar | .10 | .02 |
| 302 | Maurice Hurst | .05 | .01 |
| 303 | Mike Merriweather | .05 | .01 |
| 304 | Reggie Roby | .05 | .01 |
| 305 | Darryl Williams | .05 | .01 |
| 306 | Jerome Bettis RC | 5.00 | 2.50 |
| 307 | Curtis Conway RC | .40 | .15 |
| 308 | Drew Bledsoe RC | 2.50 | 1.00 |
| 309 | John Copeland RC | .10 | .02 |
| 310 | Eric Curry RC | .05 | .01 |
| 311 | Lincoln Kennedy RC | .05 | .01 |

|  |  | | |
|---|---|---|---|
| 312 | Dan Williams RC | .05 | .01 |
| 313 | Patrick Bates RC | .05 | .01 |
| 314 | Tom Carter RC | .10 | .02 |
| 315 | Garrison Hearst RC | .75 | .30 |
| 316 | Joel Hilgenberg | .05 | .01 |
| 317 | Harris Barton | .05 | .01 |
| 318 | Jeff Lageman | .05 | .01 |
| 319 | Charles Mincy RC | .05 | .01 |
| 320 | Ricardo McDonald | .05 | .01 |
| 321 | Lorenzo White | .05 | .01 |
| 322 | Troy Vincent | .05 | .01 |
| 323 | Bennie Blades | .05 | .01 |
| 324 | Dana Hall | .05 | .01 |
| 325 | Ken Norton Jr. | .10 | .02 |
| 326 | Will Wolford | .05 | .01 |
| 327 | Neil O'Donnell | .25 | .08 |
| 328 | Tracy Simien | .05 | .01 |
| 329 | Darrell Green | .05 | .01 |
| 330 | Kyle Clifton | .05 | .01 |
| 331 | Elbert Shelley RC | .05 | .01 |
| 332 | Jeff Wright | .05 | .01 |
| 333 | Mike Johnson | .05 | .01 |
| 334 | John Gesek | .05 | .01 |
| 335 | Michael Brooks | .05 | .01 |
| 336 | George Jamison | .05 | .01 |
| 337 | Johnny Holland | .05 | .01 |
| 338 | Lamar Lathon | .05 | .01 |
| 339 | Rem Brostek | .05 | .01 |
| 340 | Steve Jordan | .05 | .01 |
| 341 | Gene Atkins | .05 | .01 |
| 342 | Aaron Wallace | .05 | .01 |
| 343 | Adrian Cooper | .05 | .01 |
| 344 | Amp Lee | .05 | .01 |
| 345 | Vincent Brown | .05 | .01 |
| 346 | James Hasty | .05 | .01 |
| 347 | Ron Hall | .05 | .01 |
| 348 | Matt Elliott | .05 | .01 |
| 349 | Tim Krumrie | .05 | .01 |
| 350 | Mark Stepnoski | .05 | .01 |
| 351 | Matt Stover | .05 | .01 |
| 352 | James Washington | .05 | .01 |
| 353 | Marc Spindler | .05 | .01 |
| 354 | Frank Warren | .05 | .01 |
| 355 | Vai Sikahema | .05 | .01 |
| 356 | Dan Saleaumua | .05 | .01 |
| 357 | Mark Clayton | .05 | .01 |
| 358 | Brent Jones | .10 | .02 |
| 359 | Andy Harmon RC | .10 | .02 |
| 360 | Anthony Parker | .05 | .01 |
| 361 | Chris Hinton | .05 | .01 |
| 362 | Greg Montgomery | .05 | .01 |
| 363 | Greg McMurtry | .05 | .01 |
| 364 | Craig Heyward | .10 | .02 |
| 365 | D.J. Johnson | .05 | .01 |
| 366 | Bill Romanowski | .05 | .01 |
| 367 | Steve Christie | .05 | .01 |
| 368 | Art Monk | .10 | .02 |
| 369 | Howard Ballard | .05 | .01 |
| 370 | Andre Collins | .05 | .01 |
| 371 | Alvin Harper | .10 | .02 |
| 372 | Blaise Winter RC | .05 | .01 |
| 373 | Ai Del Greco | .05 | .01 |
| 374 | Eric Green | .05 | .01 |
| 375 | Chris Mohr | .05 | .01 |
| 376 | Tom Newberry | .05 | .01 |
| 377 | Cris Dishman | .05 | .01 |
| 378 | Jumpy Geathers | .05 | .01 |
| 379 | Don Mosebar | .05 | .01 |
| 380 | Andre Ware | .05 | .01 |
| 381 | Marvin Washington | .05 | .01 |
| 382 | Bobby Humphrey | .05 | .01 |
| 383 | Marc Logan | .05 | .01 |
| 384 | Lomas Brown | .05 | .01 |
| 385 | Steve Tasker | .10 | .02 |
| 386 | Chris Miller | .10 | .02 |
| 387 | Tony Paige | .05 | .01 |
| 388 | Charles Haley | .10 | .02 |
| 389 | Rich Moran | .05 | .01 |
| 390 | Mike Sherrard | .05 | .01 |
| 391 | Nick Lowery | .05 | .01 |
| 392 | Henry Thomas | .05 | .01 |
| 393 | Keith Sims | .05 | .01 |
| 394 | Thomas Everett | .05 | .01 |
| 395 | Steve Wallace | .05 | .01 |
| 396 | John Carney | .05 | .01 |
| 397 | Tim Johnson | .05 | .01 |
| 398 | Jeff Gossett | .05 | .01 |
| 399 | Anthony Smith | .05 | .01 |
| 400 | Kelvin Pritchett | .05 | .01 |
| 401 | Dermontti Dawson | .05 | .01 |
| 402 | Alfred Williams | .05 | .01 |
| 403 | Michael Haynes | .10 | .02 |
| 404 | Bart Oates | .05 | .01 |
| 405 | Ken Lanier | .05 | .01 |
| 406 | Vencie Glenn | .05 | .01 |
| 407 | John Taylor | .10 | .02 |
| 408 | Nate Newton | .10 | .02 |
| 409 | Mark Carrier WR | .10 | .02 |
| 410 | Ken Harvey | .05 | .01 |
| 411 | Troy Aikman SB | .40 | .15 |
| 412 | Charles Haley SB | .05 | .01 |
| 413 | Warren Moon/Jeffires DT | .10 | .02 |
| 414 | Henry Jones DT | .05 | .01 |
| 415 | Rickey Jackson DT | .05 | .01 |
| 416 | Clyde Simmons DT | .05 | .01 |
| 417 | Dale Carter ROY | .05 | .01 |
| 418 | Carl Pickens ROY | .10 | .02 |
| 419 | Vaughn Dunbar ROY | .05 | .01 |
| 420 | Santana Dotson ROY | .05 | .01 |
| 421 | Steve Emtman 90 | .05 | .01 |
| 422 | Louis Oliver 90 | .05 | .01 |
| 423 | Carl Pickens 90 | .10 | .02 |
| 424 | Eddie Anderson 90 | .05 | .01 |
| 425 | Deion Sanders 90 | .25 | .08 |
| 426 | Jon Vaughn 90 | .05 | .01 |
| 427 | Darren Lewis 90 | .05 | .01 |
| 428 | Kevin Ross 90 | .05 | .01 |
| 429 | David Brandon 90 | .05 | .01 |
| 430 | Dave Meggett 90 | .05 | .01 |
| 431 | Jerry Rice HL | .50 | .20 |
| 432 | Sterling Sharpe HL | .10 | .02 |
| 433 | Art Monk HL | .05 | .01 |
| 434 | James Lofton HL | .05 | .01 |
| 435 | Lawrence Taylor | .10 | .02 |
| 436 | Bill Walsh RC HOF | .10 | .02 |
| 437 | Chuck Noll HOF | .10 | .02 |
| 438 | Dan Fouts HOF | .05 | .01 |
| 439 | Larry Little HOF | .05 | .01 |
| 440 | Steve Young MOY | .40 | .15 |
| NNO | Dick Butkus AU/3000 | 40.00 | 25.00 |

## 1994 Score

CRIS CARTER

|  |  | | |
|---|---|---|---|
| COMPLETE SET (330) | | 12.00 | 5.00 |
| 1 | Barry Sanders | 1.25 | .50 |
| 2 | Troy Aikman | .75 | .30 |
| 3 | Sterling Sharpe | .10 | .02 |
| 4 | Deion Sanders | .50 | .20 |
| 5 | Bruce Smith | .25 | .08 |
| 6 | Eric Metcalf | .10 | .02 |
| 7 | John Elway | 1.50 | .60 |
| 8 | Bruce Matthews | .05 | .01 |
| 9 | Rickey Jackson | .05 | .01 |
| 10 | Cortez Kennedy | .10 | .02 |
| 11 | Jerry Rice | .75 | .30 |
| 12 | Stanley Richard | .05 | .01 |
| 13 | Rod Woodson | .10 | .02 |
| 14 | Eric Swann | .05 | .01 |
| 15 | Eric Allen | .05 | .01 |
| 16 | Richard Dent | .10 | .02 |
| 17 | Carl Pickens | .10 | .02 |
| 18 | Rohn Stark | .05 | .01 |
| 19 | Marcus Allen | .25 | .08 |
| 20 | Steve Wisniewski | .05 | .01 |
| 21 | Jerome Bettis | .50 | .20 |
| 22 | Darrell Green | .05 | .01 |
| 23 | Lawrence Dawsey | .05 | .01 |
| 24 | Larry Centers | .25 | .08 |
| 25 | Steve Jordan | .05 | .01 |
| 26 | Johnny Johnson | .05 | .01 |
| 27 | Phil Simms | .10 | .02 |
| 28 | Bruce Armstrong | .05 | .01 |
| 29 | Willie Roaf | .05 | .01 |
| 30 | Andre Rison | .10 | .02 |
| 31 | Henry Jones | .05 | .01 |
| 32 | Warren Moon | .25 | .08 |
| 33 | Sean Gilbert | .05 | .01 |
| 34 | Ben Coates | .10 | .02 |
| 35 | Seth Joyner | .05 | .01 |
| 36 | Ronnie Harmon | .05 | .01 |
| 37 | Quentin Coryatt | .05 | .01 |
| 38 | Ricky Sanders | .05 | .01 |
| 39 | Gerald Williams | .05 | .01 |
| 40 | Emmitt Smith | 1.00 | .40 |
| 41 | Jason Hanson | .05 | .01 |
| 42 | Kevin Smith | .05 | .01 |
| 43 | Irving Fryar | .10 | .02 |
| 44 | Boomer Esiason | .10 | .02 |
| 45 | Darryl Talley | .05 | .01 |
| 46 | Paul Gruber | .05 | .01 |
| 47 | Anthony Smith | .05 | .01 |
| 48 | John Copeland | .05 | .01 |
| 49 | Michael Jackson | .10 | .02 |
| 50 | Shannon Sharpe | .10 | .02 |
| 51 | Reggie White | .25 | .08 |
| 52 | Andre Collins | .05 | .01 |
| 53 | Jack Del Rio | .05 | .01 |
| 54 | John Elliott | .05 | .01 |
| 55 | Kevin Greene | .10 | .02 |
| 56 | Steve Young | .60 | .25 |
| 57 | Eric Pegram | .05 | .01 |
| 58 | Donnell Woolford | .05 | .01 |
| 59 | Darryl Williams | .05 | .01 |
| 60 | Michael Irvin | .25 | .08 |
| 61 | Mel Gray | .05 | .01 |
| 62 | Greg Montgomery | .05 | .01 |
| 63 | Neil Smith | .10 | .02 |
| 64 | Andy Harmon | .05 | .01 |
| 65 | Dan Marino | 1.50 | .60 |
| 66 | Leonard Russell | .05 | .01 |
| 67 | Joe Montana | 1.50 | .60 |
| 68 | John Taylor | .10 | .02 |
| 69 | Cris Dishman | .05 | .01 |
| 70 | Cornelius Bennett | .10 | .02 |
| 71 | Harold Green | .05 | .01 |
| 72 | Anthony Pleasant | .05 | .01 |
| 73 | Dennis Smith | .05 | .01 |
| 74 | Bryce Paup | .10 | .02 |
| 75 | Jeff George | .25 | .08 |
| 76 | Henry Ellard | .10 | .02 |
| 77 | Randall McDaniel | .05 | .01 |
| 78 | Derek Brown RBK | .05 | .01 |
| 79 | Johnny Mitchell | .05 | .01 |
| 80 | Leroy Thompson | .05 | .01 |
| 81 | Junior Seau | .25 | .08 |
| 82 | Kelvin Martin | .05 | .01 |
| 83 | Guy McIntyre | .05 | .01 |
| 84 | Elbert Shelley | .05 | .01 |
| 85 | Louis Oliver | .05 | .01 |
| 86 | Tommy Vardell | .05 | .01 |
| 87 | Jeff Herrod | .05 | .01 |
| 88 | Edgar Bennett | .25 | .08 |
| 89 | Reggie Langhorne | .05 | .01 |
| 90 | Terry Kirby | .10 | .02 |
| 91 | Marcus Robertson | .05 | .01 |
| 92 | Mark Collins | .05 | .01 |
| 93 | Calvin Williams | .10 | .02 |
| 94 | Barry Foster | .10 | .02 |
| 95 | Brent Jones | .10 | .02 |
| 96 | Reggie Cobb | .10 | .02 |
| 97 | Ray Childress | .05 | .01 |
| 98 | Chris Miller | .05 | .01 |
| 99 | John Carney | .05 | .01 |
| 100 | Ricky Proehl | .05 | .01 |
| 101 | Renaldo Turnbull | .05 | .01 |
| 102 | John Randle | .10 | .02 |
| 103 | Flipper Anderson | .05 | .01 |
| 104 | Scottie Graham RC | .10 | .02 |
| 105 | Webster Slaughter | .05 | .01 |

| | | |
|---|---|---|
| ❑ 106 Tyrone Hughes | .10 | .02 |
| ❑ 107 Ken Norton Jr. | .10 | .02 |
| ❑ 108 Jim Kelly | .25 | .08 |
| ❑ 109 Michael Haynes | .10 | .02 |
| ❑ 110 Mark Carrier DB | .05 | .01 |
| ❑ 111 Eddie Murray | .10 | .02 |
| ❑ 112 Glyn Milburn | .10 | .02 |
| ❑ 113 Jackie Harris | .05 | .01 |
| ❑ 114 Dean Biasucci | .05 | .01 |
| ❑ 115 Tim Brown | .25 | .08 |
| ❑ 116 Mark Higgs | .05 | .01 |
| ❑ 117 Steve Emtman | .05 | .01 |
| ❑ 118 Clay Matthews | .05 | .01 |
| ❑ 119 Clyde Simmons | .05 | .01 |
| ❑ 120 Howard Ballard | .05 | .01 |
| ❑ 121 Ricky Watters | .10 | .02 |
| ❑ 122 William Fuller | .05 | .01 |
| ❑ 123 Robert Brooks | .25 | .08 |
| ❑ 124 Brian Blades | .10 | .02 |
| ❑ 125 Leslie O'Neal | .05 | .01 |
| ❑ 126 Gary Clark | .10 | .02 |
| ❑ 127 Jim Sweeney | .05 | .01 |
| ❑ 128 Vaughan Johnson | .05 | .01 |
| ❑ 129 Gary Brown | .05 | .01 |
| ❑ 130 Todd Lyght | .05 | .01 |
| ❑ 131 Nick Lowery | .05 | .01 |
| ❑ 132 Ernest Givins | .10 | .02 |
| ❑ 133 Lomas Brown | .05 | .01 |
| ❑ 134 Craig Erickson | .05 | .01 |
| ❑ 135 James Francis | .05 | .01 |
| ❑ 136 Andre Reed | .10 | .02 |
| ❑ 137 Jim Everett | .10 | .02 |
| ❑ 138 Nate Odomes | .05 | .01 |
| ❑ 139 Tom Waddle | .05 | .01 |
| ❑ 140 Stevon Moore | .05 | .01 |
| ❑ 141 Rod Bernstine | .05 | .01 |
| ❑ 142 Brett Favre | 1.50 | .60 |
| ❑ 143 Roosevelt Potts | .05 | .01 |
| ❑ 144 Chester McGlockton | .05 | .01 |
| ❑ 145 LeRoy Butler | .05 | .01 |
| ❑ 146 Charles Haley | .10 | .02 |
| ❑ 147 Rodney Hampton | .10 | .02 |
| ❑ 148 George Teague | .05 | .01 |
| ❑ 149 Gary Anderson K | .05 | .01 |
| ❑ 150 Mark Stepnoski | .05 | .01 |
| ❑ 151 Courtney Hawkins | .05 | .01 |
| ❑ 152 Tim Grunhard | .05 | .01 |
| ❑ 153 David Klingler | .05 | .01 |
| ❑ 154 Erik Williams | .05 | .01 |
| ❑ 155 Herman Moore | .25 | .08 |
| ❑ 156 Daryl Johnston | .10 | .02 |
| ❑ 157 Chris Zorich | .05 | .01 |
| ❑ 158 Shane Conlan | .05 | .01 |
| ❑ 159 Santana Dotson | .10 | .02 |
| ❑ 160 Sam Mills | .05 | .01 |
| ❑ 161 Ronnie Lott | .10 | .02 |
| ❑ 162 Jesse Sapolu | .05 | .01 |
| ❑ 163 Marion Butts | .05 | .01 |
| ❑ 164 Eugene Robinson | .05 | .01 |
| ❑ 165 Mark Schlereth | .05 | .01 |
| ❑ 166 John L. Williams | .05 | .01 |
| ❑ 167 Anthony Miller | .10 | .02 |
| ❑ 168 Rich Camarillo | .05 | .01 |
| ❑ 169 Jeff Lageman | .05 | .01 |
| ❑ 170 Michael Brooks | .05 | .01 |
| ❑ 171 Scott Mitchell | .10 | .02 |
| ❑ 172 Duane Bickett | .05 | .01 |
| ❑ 173 Willie Davis | .10 | .02 |
| ❑ 174 Maurice Hurst | .05 | .01 |
| ❑ 175 Brett Perriman | .10 | .02 |
| ❑ 176 Jay Novacek | .10 | .02 |
| ❑ 177 Terry Allen | .05 | .01 |
| ❑ 178 Pete Metzelaars | .05 | .01 |
| ❑ 179 Erik Kramer | .10 | .02 |
| ❑ 180 Neal Anderson | .05 | .01 |
| ❑ 181 Ethan Horton | .05 | .01 |
| ❑ 182 Tony Bennett | .05 | .01 |
| ❑ 183 Gary Zimmerman | .05 | .01 |
| ❑ 184 Jeff Hostetler | .10 | .02 |
| ❑ 185 Jeff Cross | .05 | .01 |
| ❑ 186 Vincent Brown | .05 | .01 |
| ❑ 187 Herschel Walker | .10 | .02 |
| ❑ 188 Courtney Hall | .05 | .01 |
| ❑ 189 Norm Johnson | .05 | .01 |
| ❑ 190 Hardy Nickerson | .10 | .02 |

| | | |
|---|---|---|
| ❑ 191 Greg Townsend | .05 | .01 |
| ❑ 192 Mike Munchak | .10 | .02 |
| ❑ 193 Dante Jones | .05 | .01 |
| ❑ 194 Vinny Testaverde | .10 | .02 |
| ❑ 195 Vance Johnson | .05 | .01 |
| ❑ 196 Chris Jacke | .05 | .01 |
| ❑ 197 Will Wolford | .05 | .01 |
| ❑ 198 Terry McDaniel | .05 | .01 |
| ❑ 199 Bryan Cox | .05 | .01 |
| ❑ 200 Nate Newton | .05 | .01 |
| ❑ 201 Keith Byars | .05 | .01 |
| ❑ 202 Neil O'Donnell | .25 | .08 |
| ❑ 203 Harris Barton | .05 | .01 |
| ❑ 204 Thurman Thomas | .25 | .08 |
| ❑ 205 Jeff Query | .05 | .01 |
| ❑ 206 Russell Maryland | .05 | .01 |
| ❑ 207 Pat Swilling | .05 | .01 |
| ❑ 208 Haywood Jeffires | .10 | .02 |
| ❑ 209 John Alt | .05 | .01 |
| ❑ 210 O.J. McDuffie | .25 | .08 |
| ❑ 211 Keith Sims | .05 | .01 |
| ❑ 212 Eric Martin | .05 | .01 |
| ❑ 213 Kyle Clifton | .05 | .01 |
| ❑ 214 Luis Sharpe | .05 | .01 |
| ❑ 215 Thomas Everett | .05 | .01 |
| ❑ 216 Chris Warren | .10 | .02 |
| ❑ 217 Chris Doleman | .05 | .01 |
| ❑ 218 Tony Jones T | .05 | .01 |
| ❑ 219 Karl Mecklenburg | .05 | .01 |
| ❑ 220 Rob Moore | .10 | .02 |
| ❑ 221 Jessie Hester | .05 | .01 |
| ❑ 222 Jeff Jaeger | .05 | .01 |
| ❑ 223 Keith Jackson | .05 | .01 |
| ❑ 224 Mo Lewis | .05 | .01 |
| ❑ 225 Mike Horan | .05 | .01 |
| ❑ 226 Eric Green | .05 | .01 |
| ❑ 227 Jim Ritcher | .05 | .01 |
| ❑ 228 Eric Curry | .05 | .01 |
| ❑ 229 Stan Humphries | .10 | .02 |
| ❑ 230 Mike Johnson | .05 | .01 |
| ❑ 231 Alvin Harper | .10 | .02 |
| ❑ 232 Bennie Blades | .05 | .01 |
| ❑ 233 Cris Carter | .50 | .20 |
| ❑ 234 Morten Andersen | .05 | .01 |
| ❑ 235 Brian Washington | .05 | .01 |
| ❑ 236 Eric Hill | .05 | .01 |
| ❑ 237 Natrone Means | .25 | .08 |
| ❑ 238 Carlton Bailey | .05 | .01 |
| ❑ 239 Anthony Carter | .10 | .02 |
| ❑ 240 Jessie Tuggle | .05 | .01 |
| ❑ 241 Tim Irwin | .05 | .01 |
| ❑ 242 Mark Carrier WR | .10 | .02 |
| ❑ 243 Steve Atwater | .05 | .01 |
| ❑ 244 Sean Jones | .05 | .01 |
| ❑ 245 Bernie Kosar | .10 | .02 |
| ❑ 246 Richmond Webb | .05 | .01 |
| ❑ 247 Dave Meggett | .05 | .01 |
| ❑ 248 Vincent Brisby | .10 | .02 |
| ❑ 249 Fred Barnett | .10 | .02 |
| ❑ 250 Greg Lloyd | .10 | .02 |
| ❑ 251 Tim McDonald | .05 | .01 |
| ❑ 252 Mike Pritchard | .05 | .01 |
| ❑ 253 Greg Robinson | .05 | .01 |
| ❑ 254 Tony McGee | .05 | .01 |
| ❑ 255 Chris Spielman | .10 | .02 |
| ❑ 256 Keith Loneker RC | .05 | .01 |
| ❑ 257 Derrick Thomas | .25 | .08 |
| ❑ 258 Wayne Martin | .05 | .01 |
| ❑ 259 Art Monk | .10 | .02 |
| ❑ 260 Andy Heck | .05 | .01 |
| ❑ 261 Chip Lohmiller | .05 | .01 |
| ❑ 262 Simon Fletcher | .05 | .01 |
| ❑ 263 Ricky Reynolds | .05 | .01 |
| ❑ 264 Chris Hinton | .05 | .01 |
| ❑ 265 Ronald Moore | .05 | .01 |
| ❑ 266 Rocket Ismail | .10 | .02 |
| ❑ 267 Pete Stoyanovich | .05 | .01 |
| ❑ 268 Mark Jackson | .05 | .01 |
| ❑ 269 Randall Cunningham | .25 | .08 |
| ❑ 270 Dermontti Dawson | .05 | .01 |
| ❑ 271 Bill Romanowski | .05 | .01 |
| ❑ 272 Tim Johnson | .05 | .01 |
| ❑ 273 Steve Tasker | .10 | .02 |
| ❑ 274 Keith Hamilton | .05 | .01 |
| ❑ 275 Pierce Holt | .05 | .01 |

| | | |
|---|---|---|
| ❑ 276 Heath Shuler RC | .25 | .08 |
| ❑ 277 Marshall Faulk RC | 5.00 | 2.00 |
| ❑ 278 Charles Johnson RC | .25 | .08 |
| ❑ 279 Sam Adams RC | .10 | .02 |
| ❑ 280 Trev Alberts RC | .10 | .02 |
| ❑ 281 Derrick Alexander WR RC | .25 | .08 |
| ❑ 282 Bryant Young RC | .40 | .15 |
| ❑ 283 Greg Hill RC | .25 | .08 |
| ❑ 284 Darnay Scott RC | .50 | .20 |
| ❑ 285 Willie McGinest RC | .25 | .08 |
| ❑ 286 Thomas Randolph RC | .05 | .01 |
| ❑ 287 Errict Rhett RC | .25 | .08 |
| ❑ 288 Lamar Smith RC | 1.25 | .50 |
| ❑ 289 William Floyd RC | .25 | .08 |
| ❑ 290 Johnnie Morton RC | .50 | .20 |
| ❑ 291 Jamir Miller RC | .10 | .02 |
| ❑ 292 David Palmer RC | .25 | .08 |
| ❑ 293 Dan Wilkinson RC | .10 | .02 |
| ❑ 294 Trent Dilfer RC | 1.25 | .50 |
| ❑ 295 Antonio Langham RC | .10 | .02 |
| ❑ 296 Chuck Levy RC | .05 | .01 |
| ❑ 297 John Thierry RC | .05 | .01 |
| ❑ 298 Kevin Lee RC | .05 | .01 |
| ❑ 299 Aaron Glenn RC | .25 | .08 |
| ❑ 300 Charlie Garner RC | 1.25 | .50 |
| ❑ 301 Lonnie Johnson RC | .05 | .01 |
| ❑ 302 LeShon Johnson RC | .10 | .02 |
| ❑ 303 Thomas Lewis RC | .10 | .02 |
| ❑ 304 Ryan Yarborough RC | .05 | .01 |
| ❑ 305 Mario Bates RC | .25 | .08 |
| ❑ 306 Buffalo Bills TC | .05 | .01 |
| ❑ 307 Cincinnati Bengals TC | .05 | .01 |
| ❑ 308 Cleveland Browns TC | .05 | .01 |
| ❑ 309 Denver Broncos TC | .05 | .01 |
| ❑ 310 Houston Oilers TC | .05 | .01 |
| ❑ 311 Indianapolis Colts TC | .05 | .01 |
| ❑ 312 Kansas City Chiefs TC | .05 | .01 |
| ❑ 313 Los Angeles Raiders TC | .05 | .01 |
| ❑ 314 Miami Dolphins TC | .05 | .01 |
| ❑ 315 New England Patriots TC | .05 | .01 |
| ❑ 316 New York Jets TC | .05 | .01 |
| ❑ 317 Pittsburgh Steelers TC | .05 | .01 |
| ❑ 318 San Diego Chargers TC | .05 | .01 |
| ❑ 319 Seattle Seahawks TC | .05 | .01 |
| ❑ 320 Garrison Hearst FF | .25 | .08 |
| ❑ 321 Drew Bledsoe FF | .75 | .30 |
| ❑ 322 Tyrone Hughes FF | .10 | .02 |
| ❑ 323 James Jett FF | .05 | .01 |
| ❑ 324 Tom Carter FF | .05 | .01 |
| ❑ 325 Reggie Brooks FF | .05 | .01 |
| ❑ 326 Dana Stubblefield FF | .10 | .02 |
| ❑ 327 Jerome Bettis FF | .25 | .08 |
| ❑ 328 Chris Slade FF | .05 | .01 |
| ❑ 329 Rick Mirer FF | .25 | .08 |
| ❑ 330 Emmitt Smith MVP | .50 | .20 |

## 1995 Score

HERSCHEL WALKER RB

GIANTS

| | | |
|---|---|---|
| ❑ COMPLETE SET (275) | 15.00 | 6.00 |
| ❑ 1 Steve Young | .60 | .25 |
| ❑ 2 Barry Sanders | 1.25 | .50 |
| ❑ 3 Jerry Rice | .75 | .30 |
| ❑ 4 Marshall Faulk | 1.00 | .40 |
| ❑ 5 Terance Mathis | .10 | .02 |
| ❑ 6 Rod Woodson | .10 | .02 |
| ❑ 7 Seth Joyner | .05 | .01 |
| ❑ 8 Michael Timpson | .05 | .01 |
| ❑ 9 Deion Sanders | .50 | .20 |
| ❑ 10 Emmitt Smith | 1.25 | .50 |

|  |  | | |
|---|--------|---|---|
| 11 | Cris Carter | .25 | .08 |
| 12 | Jake Reed | .10 | .02 |
| 13 | Reggie White | .25 | .08 |
| 14 | Shannon Sharpe | .10 | .02 |
| 15 | Troy Aikman | .75 | .30 |
| 16 | Andre Reed | .10 | .02 |
| 17 | Tyrone Hughes | .10 | .02 |
| 18 | Sterling Sharpe | .25 | .08 |
| 19 | Jerome Bettis | .25 | .08 |
| 20 | Irving Fryar | .10 | .02 |
| 21 | Warren Moon | .10 | .02 |
| 22 | Ben Coates | .10 | .02 |
| 23 | Frank Reich | .05 | .01 |
| 24 | Henry Ellard | .10 | .02 |
| 25 | Steve Atwater | .05 | .01 |
| 26 | Willie Davis | .10 | .02 |
| 27 | Michael Irvin | .25 | .08 |
| 28 | Harvey Williams | .05 | .01 |
| 29 | Aeneas Williams | .05 | .01 |
| 30 | Errict Rhett | .10 | .02 |
| 31 | Lorenzo White | .05 | .01 |
| 32 | John Elway | 1.50 | .60 |
| 33 | Rodney Hampton | .10 | .02 |
| 34 | Webster Slaughter | .05 | .01 |
| 35 | Eric Turner | .05 | .01 |
| 36 | Dan Marino | 1.50 | .60 |
| 37 | Daryl Johnston | .10 | .02 |
| 38 | Bruce Smith | .25 | .08 |
| 39 | Ronald Moore | .05 | .01 |
| 40 | Larry Centers | .10 | .02 |
| 41 | Curtis Conway | .25 | .08 |
| 42 | Drew Bledsoe | .50 | .20 |
| 43 | Quinn Early | .05 | .01 |
| 44 | Marcus Allen | .25 | .08 |
| 45 | Andre Rison | .10 | .02 |
| 46 | Jeff Blake RC | .50 | .20 |
| 47 | Barry Foster | .10 | .02 |
| 48 | Antonio Langham | .05 | .01 |
| 49 | Herman Moore | .25 | .08 |
| 50 | Flipper Anderson | .05 | .01 |
| 51 | Rick Mirer | .10 | .02 |
| 52 | Jay Novacek | .05 | .01 |
| 53 | Tim Bowens | .05 | .01 |
| 54 | Carl Pickens | .10 | .02 |
| 55 | Lewis Tillman | .05 | .01 |
| 56 | Lawrence Dawsey | .05 | .01 |
| 57 | Leroy Hoard | .05 | .01 |
| 58 | Steve Broussard | .05 | .01 |
| 59 | Dave Krieg | .05 | .01 |
| 60 | John Taylor | .05 | .01 |
| 61 | Johnny Mitchell | .05 | .01 |
| 62 | Jessie Hester | .05 | .01 |
| 63 | Johnny Bailey | .05 | .01 |
| 64 | Brett Favre | 1.50 | .60 |
| 65 | Bryce Paup | .10 | .02 |
| 66 | J.J. Birden | .05 | .01 |
| 67 | Steve Tasker | .05 | .01 |
| 68 | Edgar Bennett | .10 | .02 |
| 69 | Ray Buchanan | .05 | .01 |
| 70 | Brent Jones | .05 | .01 |
| 71 | Dave Meggett | .05 | .01 |
| 72 | Jeff Graham | .05 | .01 |
| 73 | Michael Brooks | .05 | .01 |
| 74 | Ricky Ervins | .05 | .01 |
| 75 | Chris Warren | .10 | .02 |
| 76 | Natrone Means | .10 | .02 |
| 77 | Tim Brown | .25 | .08 |
| 78 | Jim Everett | .05 | .01 |
| 79 | Chris Calloway | .05 | .01 |
| 80 | John L. Williams | .05 | .01 |
| 81 | Chris Chandler | .10 | .02 |
| 82 | Tim McDonald | .05 | .01 |
| 83 | Calvin Williams | .05 | .01 |
| 84 | Tony McGee | .05 | .01 |
| 85 | Erik Kramer | .05 | .01 |
| 86 | Eric Green | .05 | .01 |
| 87 | Nate Newton | .10 | .02 |
| 88 | Leonard Russell | .05 | .01 |
| 89 | Jeff George | .25 | .08 |
| 90 | Raymont Harris | .05 | .01 |
| 91 | Darnay Scott | .10 | .02 |
| 92 | Brian Mitchell | .05 | .01 |
| 93 | Craig Erickson | .05 | .01 |
| 94 | Cortez Kennedy | .10 | .02 |
| 95 | Derrick Alexander WR | .25 | .06 |
| 96 | Charles Haley | .10 | .02 |
| 97 | Randall Cunningham | .25 | .08 |
| 98 | Haywood Jeffires | .05 | .01 |
| 99 | Ronnie Harmon | .05 | .01 |
| 100 | Dale Carter | .10 | .02 |
| 101 | Dave Brown | .10 | .02 |
| 102 | Michael Haynes | .10 | .02 |
| 103 | Johnny Johnson | .05 | .01 |
| 104 | William Floyd | .10 | .02 |
| 105 | Jeff Hostetler | .10 | .02 |
| 106 | Bernie Parmalee | .10 | .02 |
| 107 | Mo Lewis | .05 | .01 |
| 108 | Byron Bam Morris | .05 | .01 |
| 109 | Vincent Brisby | .05 | .01 |
| 110 | John Randle | .10 | .02 |
| 111 | Steve Walsh | .05 | .01 |
| 112 | Terry Allen | .10 | .02 |
| 113 | Greg Lloyd | .10 | .02 |
| 114 | Marion Hanks | .05 | .01 |
| 115 | Mel Gray | .05 | .01 |
| 116 | Jim Kelly | .25 | .08 |
| 117 | Don Beebe | .05 | .01 |
| 118 | Floyd Turner | .05 | .01 |
| 119 | Neil Smith | .10 | .02 |
| 120 | Keith Byars | .05 | .01 |
| 121 | Rocket Ismail | .10 | .02 |
| 122 | Leslie O'Neal | .10 | .02 |
| 123 | Mike Sherrard | .05 | .01 |
| 124 | Marion Butts | .05 | .01 |
| 125 | Andre Coleman | .05 | .01 |
| 126 | Charles Johnson | .10 | .02 |
| 127 | Derrick Fenner | .05 | .01 |
| 128 | Vinny Testaverde | .10 | .02 |
| 129 | Chris Spielman | .10 | .02 |
| 130 | Bert Emanuel | .25 | .08 |
| 131 | Craig Heyward | .10 | .02 |
| 132 | Anthony Miller | .10 | .02 |
| 133 | Rob Moore | .10 | .02 |
| 134 | Gary Brown | .10 | .02 |
| 135 | David Klingler | .10 | .02 |
| 136 | Sean Dawkins | .10 | .02 |
| 137 | Terry McDaniel | .05 | .01 |
| 138 | Fred Barnett | .10 | .02 |
| 139 | Bryan Cox | .05 | .01 |
| 140 | Andrew Jordan | .05 | .01 |
| 141 | Leroy Thompson | .05 | .01 |
| 142 | Richmond Webb | .05 | .01 |
| 143 | Kimble Anders | .10 | .02 |
| 144 | Mario Bates | .10 | .02 |
| 145 | Irv Smith | .05 | .01 |
| 146 | Carnell Lake | .05 | .01 |
| 147 | Mark Seay | .05 | .01 |
| 148 | Dana Stubblefield | .10 | .02 |
| 149 | Kelvin Martin | .05 | .01 |
| 150 | Pete Metzelaars | .05 | .01 |
| 151 | Roosevelt Potts | .05 | .01 |
| 152 | Bubby Brister | .05 | .01 |
| 153 | Trent Dilfer | .25 | .08 |
| 154 | Ricky Proehl | .05 | .01 |
| 155 | Aaron Glenn | .05 | .01 |
| 156 | Eric Metcalf | .10 | .02 |
| 157 | Kevin Williams WR | .10 | .02 |
| 158 | Charlie Garner | .25 | .08 |
| 159 | Glyn Milburn | .10 | .02 |
| 160 | Fuad Reveiz | .05 | .01 |
| 161 | Brett Perriman | .10 | .02 |
| 162 | Neil O'Donnell | .10 | .02 |
| 163 | Tony Martin | .10 | .02 |
| 164 | Sam Adams | .05 | .01 |
| 165 | John Friesz | .05 | .01 |
| 166 | Bryant Young | .10 | .02 |
| 167 | Junior Seau | .25 | .08 |
| 168 | Ken Harvey | .05 | .01 |
| 169 | Bill Brooks | .05 | .01 |
| 170 | Eugene Robinson | .05 | .01 |
| 171 | Ricky Sanders | .05 | .01 |
| 172 | Rodney Peete | .05 | .01 |
| 173 | Boomer Esiason | .10 | .02 |
| 174 | Reggie Roby | .05 | .01 |
| 175 | Michael Jackson | .10 | .02 |
| 176 | Gus Frerotte | .10 | .02 |
| 177 | Terry Kirby | .10 | .02 |
| 178 | Jessie Tuggle | .05 | .01 |
| 179 | Courtney Hawkins | .05 | .01 |
| 180 | Heath Shuler | .25 | .08 |
| 181 | Jack Del Rio | .05 | .01 |
| 182 | O.J. McDuffie | .25 | .08 |
| 183 | Ricky Watters | .10 | .02 |
| 184 | Willie Roaf | .05 | .01 |
| 186 | Glenn Foley | .05 | .01 |
| 186 | Blair Thomas | .05 | .01 |
| 187 | Darren Woodson | .10 | .02 |
| 188 | Kevin Greene | .10 | .02 |
| 189 | Jeff Burris | .05 | .01 |
| 190 | Jay Schroeder | .05 | .01 |
| 191 | Stan Humphries | .10 | .02 |
| 192 | Irving Spikes | .10 | .02 |
| 193 | Jim Harbaugh | .10 | .02 |
| 194 | Robert Brooks | .25 | .08 |
| 195 | Greg Hill | .10 | .02 |
| 196 | Herschel Walker | .10 | .02 |
| 197 | Brian Blades | .10 | .02 |
| 198 | Mark Ingram | .05 | .01 |
| 199 | Kevin Turner | .05 | .01 |
| 200 | Lake Dawson | .10 | .02 |
| 201 | Alvin Harper | .05 | .01 |
| 202 | Derek Brown RBK | .05 | .01 |
| 203 | Qadry Ismail | .10 | .02 |
| 204 | Reggie Brooks | .10 | .02 |
| 205 | Steve Young SS | .30 | .10 |
| 206 | Emmitt Smith SS | .60 | .25 |
| 207 | Stan Humphries SS | .05 | .01 |
| 208 | Barry Sanders SS | .60 | .25 |
| 209 | Marshall Faulk SS | .40 | .15 |
| 210 | Drew Bledsoe SS | .25 | .08 |
| 211 | Jerry Rice SS | .40 | .15 |
| 212 | Tim Brown SS | .10 | .02 |
| 213 | Cris Carter SS | .25 | .08 |
| 214 | Dan Marino SS | .75 | .30 |
| 215 | Troy Aikman SS | .40 | .15 |
| 216 | Jerome Bettis SS | .10 | .02 |
| 217 | Deion Sanders SS | .25 | .08 |
| 218 | Junior Seau SS | .10 | .02 |
| 219 | John Elway SS | .75 | .30 |
| 220 | Warren Moon SS | .05 | .01 |
| 221 | Sterling Sharpe SS | .10 | .02 |
| 222 | Marcus Allen SS | .25 | .08 |
| 223 | Michael Irvin SS | .10 | .02 |
| 224 | Brett Favre SS | .75 | .30 |
| 225 | Rodney Hampton SS | .05 | .01 |
| 226 | Dave Brown SS | .10 | .02 |
| 227 | Ben Coates SS | .10 | .02 |
| 228 | Jim Kelly SS | .25 | .08 |
| 229 | Heath Shuler SS | .10 | .02 |
| 230 | Herman Moore SS | .25 | .08 |
| 231 | Jeff Hostetler SS | .10 | .02 |
| 232 | Rick Mirer SS | .10 | .02 |
| 233 | Byron Bam Morris SS | .05 | .01 |
| 234 | Terance Mathis SS | .05 | .01 |
| 235 | John Elway/B.Sanders CL | .40 | .15 |
| 236 | Troy Aikman CL | .25 | .08 |
| 237 | Jerry Rice CL | .25 | .08 |
| 238 | Emmitt Smith CL | .50 | .20 |
| 239 | Steve Young CL | .25 | .08 |
| 240 | Drew Bledsoe CL | .25 | .08 |
| 241 | Marshall Faulk CL | .25 | .08 |
| 242 | Dan Marino CL | .40 | .15 |
| 243 | Junior Seau CL | .10 | .02 |
| 244 | Ray Zellars RC | .10 | .02 |
| 245 | Rob Johnson RC | .75 | .30 |
| 246 | Tony Boselli RC | .25 | .08 |
| 247 | Kevin Carter RC | .25 | .08 |
| 248 | Steve McNair RC | 2.50 | 1.00 |
| 249 | Tyrone Wheatley RC | .75 | .30 |
| 250 | Steve Stenstrom RC | .05 | .01 |
| 251 | Stoney Case RC | .05 | .01 |
| 252 | Rodney Thomas RC | .10 | .02 |
| 253 | Michael Westbrook RC | .25 | .08 |
| 254 | Derrick Alexander DE RC | .05 | .01 |
| 255 | Kyle Brady RC | .25 | .08 |
| 256 | Kerry Collins RC | 2.00 | .75 |
| 257 | Rashaan Salaam RC | .10 | .02 |
| 258 | Frank Sanders RC | .25 | .08 |
| 259 | John Walsh RC | .05 | .01 |
| 260 | Sherman Williams RC | .10 | .02 |
| 261 | Ki-Jana Carter RC | .25 | .08 |
| 262 | Jack Jackson RC | .05 | .01 |
| 263 | J.J. Stokes RC | .25 | .08 |
| 264 | Kordell Stewart RC | 1.25 | .50 |
| 265 | Dave Barr RC | .05 | .01 |

|  |  | | |
|---|---|---|---|
| ☐ 266 | Eddie Goines RC | .05 | .01 |
| ☐ 267 | Warren Sapp RC | 1.25 | .50 |
| ☐ 268 | James O. Stewart RC | .75 | .30 |
| ☐ 269 | Joey Galloway RC | 1.25 | .50 |
| ☐ 270 | Tyrone Davis RC | .05 | .01 |
| ☐ 271 | Napoleon Kaufman RC | 1.00 | .40 |
| ☐ 272 | Mark Bruener RC | .10 | .02 |
| ☐ 273 | Todd Collins RC | .75 | .30 |
| ☐ 274 | Billy Williams RC | .05 | .01 |
| ☐ 275 | James A.Stewart RC | .05 | .05 |
| ☐ P264 | Kordell Stewart PROMO | 2.50 | 1.00 |
| ☐ AD3 | Steve Young | 3.00 | 1.25 |

**1996 Score**

|  |  | | |
|---|---|---|---|
| ☐ | COMPLETE SET (275) | 20.00 | 7.50 |
| ☐ 1 | Emmitt Smith | 1.25 | .50 |
| ☐ 2 | Flipper Anderson | .10 | .02 |
| ☐ 3 | Kordell Stewart | .40 | .15 |
| ☐ 4 | Bruce Smith | .20 | .07 |
| ☐ 5 | Marshall Faulk | .50 | .20 |
| ☐ 6 | William Floyd | .20 | .07 |
| ☐ 7 | Darren Woodson | .20 | .07 |
| ☐ 8 | Lake Dawson | .10 | .02 |
| ☐ 9 | Terry Allen | .20 | .07 |
| ☐ 10 | Ki-Jana Carter | .20 | .07 |
| ☐ 11 | Tony Boselli | .10 | .02 |
| ☐ 12 | Christian Fauria | .10 | .02 |
| ☐ 13 | Jeff George | .20 | .07 |
| ☐ 14 | Dan Marino | 1.50 | .60 |
| ☐ 15 | Rodney Thomas | .10 | .02 |
| ☐ 16 | Anthony Miller | .20 | .07 |
| ☐ 17 | Chris Sanders | .20 | .07 |
| ☐ 18 | Natrone Means | .20 | .07 |
| ☐ 19 | Curtis Conway | .40 | .15 |
| ☐ 20 | Ben Coates | .20 | .07 |
| ☐ 21 | Alvin Harper | .10 | .02 |
| ☐ 22 | Frank Sanders | .20 | .07 |
| ☐ 23 | Boomer Esiason | .10 | .02 |
| ☐ 24 | Lovell Pinkney | .10 | .02 |
| ☐ 25 | Troy Aikman | .75 | .30 |
| ☐ 26 | Quinn Early | .10 | .02 |
| ☐ 27 | Adrian Murrell | .20 | .07 |
| ☐ 28 | Chris Spielman | .10 | .02 |
| ☐ 29 | Tyrone Wheatley | .20 | .07 |
| ☐ 30 | Tim Brown | .40 | .15 |
| ☐ 31 | Erik Kramer | .10 | .02 |
| ☐ 32 | Warren Moon | .20 | .07 |
| ☐ 33 | Jimmy Oliver | .10 | .02 |
| ☐ 34 | Herman Moore | .20 | .07 |
| ☐ 35 | Quentin Coryatt | .10 | .02 |
| ☐ 36 | Heath Shuler | .20 | .07 |
| ☐ 37 | Jim Kelly | .40 | .15 |
| ☐ 38 | Mike Morris | .10 | .02 |
| ☐ 39 | Harvey Williams | .10 | .02 |
| ☐ 40 | Vinny Testaverde | .20 | .07 |
| ☐ 41 | Steve McNair | .60 | .25 |
| ☐ 42 | Jerry Rice | .75 | .30 |
| ☐ 43 | Darick Holmes | .10 | .02 |
| ☐ 44 | Kyle Brady | .10 | .02 |
| ☐ 45 | Greg Lloyd | .20 | .07 |
| ☐ 46 | Kerry Collins | .40 | .15 |
| ☐ 47 | Willie McGinest | .10 | .02 |
| ☐ 48 | Isaac Bruce | .40 | .15 |
| ☐ 49 | Carnell Lake | .10 | .02 |
| ☐ 50 | Charles Haley | .20 | .07 |
| ☐ 51 | Troy Vincent | .10 | .02 |
| ☐ 52 | Randall Cunningham | .40 | .15 |
| ☐ 53 | Rashaan Salaam | .20 | .07 |
| ☐ 54 | Willie Jackson | .20 | .07 |
| ☐ 55 | Chris Warren | .20 | .07 |
| ☐ 56 | Michael Irvin | .40 | .15 |
| ☐ 57 | Mario Bates | .20 | .07 |
| ☐ 58 | Warren Sapp | .10 | .02 |
| ☐ 59 | John Elway | 1.50 | .60 |
| ☐ 60 | Shannon Sharpe | .20 | .07 |
| ☐ 61 | Cornelius Bennett | .10 | .02 |
| ☐ 62 | Robert Brooks | .40 | .15 |
| ☐ 63 | Rodney Hampton | .20 | .07 |
| ☐ 64 | Ken Norton Jr. | .10 | .02 |
| ☐ 65 | Bryce Paup | .10 | .02 |
| ☐ 66 | Eric Swann | .10 | .02 |
| ☐ 67 | Rodney Peete | .10 | .02 |
| ☐ 68 | Larry Centers | .20 | .07 |
| ☐ 69 | Lamont Warren | .10 | .02 |
| ☐ 70 | Jay Novacek | .10 | .02 |
| ☐ 71 | Cris Carter | .40 | .15 |
| ☐ 72 | Terrell Fletcher | .10 | .02 |
| ☐ 73 | Andre Rison | .20 | .07 |
| ☐ 74 | Ricky Watters | .20 | .07 |
| ☐ 75 | Napoleon Kaufman | .40 | .15 |
| ☐ 76 | Reggie White | .40 | .15 |
| ☐ 77 | Yancey Thigpen | .20 | .07 |
| ☐ 78 | Terry Kirby | .20 | .07 |
| ☐ 79 | Deion Sanders | .40 | .15 |
| ☐ 80 | Irving Fryar | .20 | .07 |
| ☐ 81 | Marcus Allen | .40 | .15 |
| ☐ 82 | Carl Pickens | .20 | .07 |
| ☐ 83 | Drew Bledsoe | .50 | .20 |
| ☐ 84 | Eric Metcalf | .10 | .02 |
| ☐ 85 | Robert Smith | .20 | .07 |
| ☐ 86 | Tamarick Vanover | .20 | .07 |
| ☐ 87 | Henry Ellard | .10 | .02 |
| ☐ 88 | Kevin Greene | .20 | .07 |
| ☐ 89 | Mark Brunell | .50 | .20 |
| ☐ 90 | Terrell Davis | .60 | .25 |
| ☐ 91 | Brian Mitchell | .10 | .02 |
| ☐ 92 | Aaron Bailey | .10 | .02 |
| ☐ 93 | Rocket Ismail | .10 | .02 |
| ☐ 94 | Dave Brown | .10 | .02 |
| ☐ 95 | Rod Woodson | .20 | .07 |
| ☐ 96 | Sean Gilbert | .10 | .02 |
| ☐ 97 | Mark Seay | .10 | .02 |
| ☐ 98 | Zack Crockett | .10 | .02 |
| ☐ 99 | Scott Mitchell | .20 | .07 |
| ☐ 100 | Erric Pegram | .10 | .02 |
| ☐ 101 | David Palmer | .10 | .02 |
| ☐ 102 | Vincent Brisby | .10 | .02 |
| ☐ 103 | Brett Perriman | .10 | .02 |
| ☐ 104 | Jim Everett | .10 | .02 |
| ☐ 105 | Tony Martin | .20 | .07 |
| ☐ 106 | Desmond Howard | .20 | .07 |
| ☐ 107 | Stan Humphries | .20 | .07 |
| ☐ 108 | Bill Brooks | .10 | .02 |
| ☐ 109 | Neil Smith | .20 | .07 |
| ☐ 110 | Michael Westbrook | .40 | .15 |
| ☐ 111 | Herschel Walker | .20 | .07 |
| ☐ 112 | Andre Coleman | .10 | .02 |
| ☐ 113 | Derrick Alexander WR | .20 | .07 |
| ☐ 114 | Jeff Blake | .40 | .15 |
| ☐ 115 | Sherman Williams | .10 | .02 |
| ☐ 116 | James O.Stewart | .20 | .07 |
| ☐ 117 | Hardy Nickerson | .10 | .02 |
| ☐ 118 | Elvis Grbac | .20 | .07 |
| ☐ 119 | Brett Favre | 1.50 | .60 |
| ☐ 120 | Mike Sherrard | .10 | .02 |
| ☐ 121 | Edgar Bennett | .20 | .07 |
| ☐ 122 | Calvin Williams | .10 | .02 |
| ☐ 123 | Brian Blades | .10 | .02 |
| ☐ 124 | Jeff Graham | .10 | .02 |
| ☐ 125 | Gary Brown | .10 | .02 |
| ☐ 126 | Bernie Parmalee | .10 | .02 |
| ☐ 127 | Kimble Anders | .20 | .07 |
| ☐ 128 | Hugh Douglas | .20 | .07 |
| ☐ 129 | James A.Stewart | .10 | .02 |
| ☐ 130 | Eric Bjornson | .10 | .02 |
| ☐ 131 | Ken Dilger | .20 | .07 |
| ☐ 132 | Jerome Bettis | .40 | .15 |
| ☐ 133 | Cortez Kennedy | .20 | .07 |
| ☐ 134 | Bryan Cox | .10 | .02 |
| ☐ 135 | Darnay Scott | .20 | .07 |
| ☐ 136 | Bert Emanuel | .20 | .07 |
| ☐ 137 | Steve Bono | .20 | .07 |
| ☐ 138 | Charles Johnson | .10 | .02 |
| ☐ 139 | Glyn Milburn | .10 | .02 |
| ☐ 140 | Derrick Alexander DE | .10 | .02 |
| ☐ 141 | Dave Meggett | .10 | .02 |
| ☐ 142 | Trent Dilfer | .40 | .15 |
| ☐ 143 | Eric Zeier | .10 | .02 |
| ☐ 144 | Jim Harbaugh | .20 | .07 |
| ☐ 145 | Antonio Freeman | .40 | .15 |
| ☐ 146 | Orlando Thomas | .10 | .02 |
| ☐ 147 | Russell Maryland | .10 | .02 |
| ☐ 148 | Chad May | .10 | .02 |
| ☐ 149 | Craig Heyward | .10 | .02 |
| ☐ 150 | Aeneas Williams | .10 | .02 |
| ☐ 151 | Kevin Williams WR. | .10 | .02 |
| ☐ 152 | Charlie Garner | .20 | .07 |
| ☐ 153 | J.J. Stokes | .40 | .15 |
| ☐ 154 | Stoney Case | .10 | .02 |
| ☐ 155 | Mark Chmura | .20 | .07 |
| ☐ 156 | Mark Bruener | .10 | .02 |
| ☐ 157 | Derek Loville | .10 | .02 |
| ☐ 158 | Justin Armour | .10 | .02 |
| ☐ 159 | Brent Jones | .10 | .02 |
| ☐ 160 | Aaron Craver | .10 | .02 |
| ☐ 161 | Terance Mathis | .10 | .02 |
| ☐ 162 | Chris Zorich | .10 | .02 |
| ☐ 163 | Glenn Foley | .20 | .07 |
| ☐ 164 | Johnny Mitchell | .10 | .02 |
| ☐ 165 | Junior Seau | .40 | .15 |
| ☐ 166 | Willie Davis | .10 | .02 |
| ☐ 167 | Rick Mirer | .20 | .07 |
| ☐ 168 | Mark Jones LB | .10 | .02 |
| ☐ 169 | Greg Hill | .20 | .07 |
| ☐ 170 | Steve Tasker | .10 | .02 |
| ☐ 171 | Tony Bennett | .10 | .02 |
| ☐ 172 | Jeff Hostetler | .10 | .02 |
| ☐ 173 | Dave Krieg | .10 | .02 |
| ☐ 174 | Mark Carrier WR | .10 | .02 |
| ☐ 175 | Michael Haynes | .10 | .02 |
| ☐ 176 | Chris Chandler | .20 | .07 |
| ☐ 177 | Ernie Mills | .10 | .02 |
| ☐ 178 | Jake Reed | .20 | .07 |
| ☐ 179 | Errict Rhett | .20 | .07 |
| ☐ 180 | Garrison Hearst | .20 | .07 |
| ☐ 181 | Derrick Thomas | .40 | .15 |
| ☐ 182 | Aaron Hayden RC | .10 | .02 |
| ☐ 183 | Jackie Harris | .10 | .02 |
| ☐ 184 | Curtis Martin | .60 | .25 |
| ☐ 185 | Neil O'Donnell | .20 | .07 |
| ☐ 186 | Derrick Moore | .10 | .02 |
| ☐ 187 | Steve Young | .60 | .25 |
| ☐ 188 | Pat Swilling | .10 | .02 |
| ☐ 189 | Amp Lee | .10 | .02 |
| ☐ 190 | Rob Johnson | .40 | .15 |
| ☐ 191 | Todd Collins | .20 | .07 |
| ☐ 192 | J.J. Birden | .10 | .02 |
| ☐ 193 | O.J. McDuffie | .20 | .07 |
| ☐ 194 | Shawn Jefferson | .10 | .02 |
| ☐ 195 | Sean Dawkins | .10 | .02 |
| ☐ 196 | Fred Barnett | .10 | .02 |
| ☐ 197 | Roosevelt Potts | .10 | .02 |
| ☐ 198 | Rob Moore | .20 | .07 |
| ☐ 199 | Kevin Miniefield | .10 | .02 |
| ☐ 200 | Barry Sanders | 1.25 | .50 |
| ☐ 201 | Floyd Turner | .10 | .02 |
| ☐ 202 | Wayne Chrebet | .60 | .25 |
| ☐ 203 | Andre Reed | .20 | .07 |
| ☐ 204 | Tyrone Hughes | .10 | .02 |
| ☐ 205 | Keenan McCardell | .40 | .15 |
| ☐ 206 | Gus Frerotte | .20 | .07 |
| ☐ 207 | Daryl Johnston | .20 | .07 |
| ☐ 208 | Steve Broussard | .10 | .02 |
| ☐ 209 | Steve Atwater | .10 | .02 |
| ☐ 210 | Thurman Thomas | .40 | .15 |
| ☐ 211 | Andre Hastings | .10 | .02 |
| ☐ 212 | Joey Galloway | .40 | .15 |
| ☐ 213 | Kevin Carter | .10 | .02 |
| ☐ 214 | Keyshawn Johnson RC | 1.00 | .40 |
| ☐ 215 | Tony Brackens RC | .40 | .15 |
| ☐ 216 | Siegfried Williams RC | .20 | .07 |
| ☐ 217 | Mike Alstott RC | 1.00 | .40 |
| ☐ 218 | Terry Glenn RC | 1.00 | .40 |
| ☐ 219 | Tim Biakabutuka RC | .40 | .15 |
| ☐ 220 | Eric Moulds RC | 1.25 | .50 |
| ☐ 221 | Jeff Lewis RC | .20 | .07 |
| ☐ 222 | Bobby Engram RC | .40 | .15 |
| ☐ 223 | Cedric Jones RC | .10 | .02 |

| | | |
|---|---|---|
| ❏ 224 Stanley Pritchett RC | .20 | .07 |
| ❏ 225 Kevin Hardy RC | .40 | .15 |
| ❏ 226 Alex Van Dyke RC | .20 | .07 |
| ❏ 227 Willie Anderson RC | .10 | .02 |
| ❏ 228 Regan Upshaw RC | .10 | .02 |
| ❏ 229 Leeland McElroy RC | .20 | .07 |
| ❏ 230 Marvin Harrison RC | 2.50 | 1.00 |
| ❏ 231 Eddie George RC | 1.25 | .50 |
| ❏ 232 Lawrence Phillips RC | .40 | .15 |
| ❏ 233 Daryl Gardener RC | .10 | .02 |
| ❏ 234 Alex Molden RC | .10 | .02 |
| ❏ 235 Derrick Mayes RC | .40 | .15 |
| ❏ 236 John Mobley RC | .10 | .02 |
| ❏ 237 Israel Ifeanyi RC | .10 | .02 |
| ❏ 238 Pete Kendall RC | .10 | .02 |
| ❏ 239 Danny Kanell RC | .40 | .15 |
| ❏ 240 Jonathan Ogden RC | .40 | .15 |
| ❏ 241 Reggie Brown LB RC | .10 | .02 |
| ❏ 242 Marcus Jones RC | .10 | .02 |
| ❏ 243 Jon Stark RC | .10 | .02 |
| ❏ 244 Barry Sanders SE | .60 | .25 |
| ❏ 245 Brett Favre SE | .75 | .30 |
| ❏ 246 John Elway SE | .75 | .30 |
| ❏ 247 Dan Marino SE | .75 | .30 |
| ❏ 248 Drew Bledsoe SE | .40 | .15 |
| ❏ 249 Michael Irvin SE | .20 | .07 |
| ❏ 250 Troy Aikman SE | .40 | .15 |
| ❏ 251 Emmitt Smith SE | .50 | .20 |
| ❏ 252 Steve Young SE | .40 | .15 |
| ❏ 253 Jerry Rice SE | .40 | .15 |
| ❏ 254 Jeff Blake SE | .20 | .07 |
| ❏ 255 Tim Brown SE | .20 | .07 |
| ❏ 256 Eric Metcalf SE | .10 | .02 |
| ❏ 257 Rodney Hampton SE | .10 | .02 |
| ❏ 258 Scott Mitchell SE | .10 | .02 |
| ❏ 259 Garrison Hearst SE | .20 | .07 |
| ❏ 260 Larry Centers SE | .20 | .07 |
| ❏ 261 Neil O'Donnell SE | .20 | .07 |
| ❏ 262 Orlando Thomas SE | .10 | .02 |
| ❏ 263 Hugh Douglas SE | .10 | .02 |
| ❏ 264 Bill Brooks SE | .10 | .02 |
| ❏ 265 Harvey Williams SE | .10 | .02 |
| ❏ 266 Charles Haley SE | .20 | .07 |
| ❏ 267 Greg Lloyd SE | .20 | .07 |
| ❏ 268 Daryl Johnston SE | .20 | .07 |
| ❏ 269 Dan Marino CL | .40 | .15 |
| ❏ 270 Jeff Blake CL | .20 | .07 |
| ❏ 271 John Elway CL | .40 | .15 |
| ❏ 272 Emmitt Smith CL | .40 | .15 |
| ❏ 273 Brett Favre CL | .40 | .15 |
| ❏ 274 Jerry Rice CL | .40 | .15 |
| ❏ 275 Five Star Players CL | .40 | .15 |
| ❏ P1 Barry Sanders Promo | 2.00 | .75 |

### 1997 Score

| | | |
|---|---|---|
| ❏ COMPLETE SET (330) | 25.00 | 10.00 |
| ❏ 1 John Elway | 2.00 | .75 |
| ❏ 2 Drew Bledsoe | .60 | .25 |
| ❏ 3 Brett Favre | 2.00 | .75 |
| ❏ 4 Emmitt Smith | 1.50 | .60 |
| ❏ 5 Kerry Collins | .50 | .20 |
| ❏ 6 Jerry Rice | 1.00 | .40 |
| ❏ 7 Kordell Stewart | .50 | .20 |
| ❏ 8 Barry Sanders | 1.50 | .60 |
| ❏ 9 Dan Marino | 2.00 | .75 |
| ❏ 10 Steve Young | .60 | .25 |
| ❏ 11 Erik Kramer | .20 | .07 |
| ❏ 12 Warren Moon | .50 | .20 |

| | | |
|---|---|---|
| ❏ 13 Chris Calloway | .20 | .07 |
| ❏ 14 Doug Evans | .20 | .07 |
| ❏ 15 Darren Woodson | .20 | .07 |
| ❏ 16 Alonzo Spellman | .20 | .07 |
| ❏ 17 Greg Hill | .20 | .07 |
| ❏ 18 Aaron Craver | .20 | .07 |
| ❏ 19 Jeff Hostetler | .20 | .07 |
| ❏ 20 William Thomas | .20 | .07 |
| ❏ 21 Marco Coleman | .20 | .07 |
| ❏ 22 Wayne Simmons | .20 | .07 |
| ❏ 23 Donnell Woolford | .20 | .07 |
| ❏ 24 Vinny Testaverde | .30 | .10 |
| ❏ 25 Ed McCaffrey | .30 | .10 |
| ❏ 26 Jim Everett | .20 | .07 |
| ❏ 27 Gilbert Brown | .30 | .10 |
| ❏ 28 Jason Dunn | .20 | .07 |
| ❏ 29 Stanley Pritchett | .20 | .07 |
| ❏ 30 Joey Galloway | .30 | .10 |
| ❏ 31 Amani Toomer | .30 | .10 |
| ❏ 32 Chris Penn | .20 | .07 |
| ❏ 33 Aeneas Williams | .20 | .07 |
| ❏ 34 Bobby Taylor | .20 | .07 |
| ❏ 35 Bryan Still | .20 | .07 |
| ❏ 36 Ty Law | .30 | .10 |
| ❏ 37 Shannon Sharpe | .30 | .10 |
| ❏ 38 Marty Carter | .20 | .07 |
| ❏ 39 Sam Mills | .20 | .07 |
| ❏ 40 William Floyd | .30 | .10 |
| ❏ 41 Brad Johnson | .50 | .20 |
| ❏ 42 Sean Dawkins | .20 | .07 |
| ❏ 43 Michael Irvin | .50 | .20 |
| ❏ 44 Jeff George | .30 | .10 |
| ❏ 45 Brent Jones | .30 | .10 |
| ❏ 46 Mark Brunell | .60 | .25 |
| ❏ 47 Rob Moore | .30 | .10 |
| ❏ 48 Hardy Nickerson | .20 | .07 |
| ❏ 49 Chris Chandler | .30 | .10 |
| ❏ 50 Willie Anderson | .20 | .07 |
| ❏ 51 Isaac Bruce | .50 | .20 |
| ❏ 52 Natrone Means | .30 | .10 |
| ❏ 53 Tony Banks | .30 | .10 |
| ❏ 54 Marshall Faulk | .60 | .25 |
| ❏ 55 Michael Westbrook | .30 | .10 |
| ❏ 56 Bruce Smith | .30 | .10 |
| ❏ 57 Jamal Anderson | .50 | .20 |
| ❏ 58 Jackie Harris | .20 | .07 |
| ❏ 59 Sean Gilbert | .20 | .07 |
| ❏ 60 Ki-Jana Carter | .20 | .07 |
| ❏ 61 Eric Moulds | .50 | .20 |
| ❏ 62 James O Stewart | .30 | .10 |
| ❏ 63 Jeff Blake | .30 | .10 |
| ❏ 64 O.J. McDuffie | .30 | .10 |
| ❏ 65 Neil Smith | .30 | .10 |
| ❏ 66 Kevin Smith | .20 | .07 |
| ❏ 67 Terry Allen | .50 | .20 |
| ❏ 68 Sean LaChapelle | .20 | .07 |
| ❏ 69 Rashaan Salaam | .30 | .10 |
| ❏ 70 Jeff Graham | .20 | .07 |
| ❏ 71 Mark Carrier WR | .20 | .07 |
| ❏ 72 Allen Aldridge | .20 | .07 |
| ❏ 73 Keenan McCardell | .30 | .10 |
| ❏ 74 Willie McGinest | .20 | .07 |
| ❏ 75 Napoleon Kaufman | .50 | .20 |
| ❏ 76 Jerris McPhail | .20 | .07 |
| ❏ 77 Eric Swann | .20 | .07 |
| ❏ 78 Kimble Anders | .30 | .10 |
| ❏ 79 Charles Johnson | .30 | .10 |
| ❏ 80 Bryan Cox | .20 | .07 |
| ❏ 81 Johnnie Morton | .30 | .10 |
| ❏ 82 Andre Rison | .30 | .10 |
| ❏ 83 Corey Miller | .20 | .07 |
| ❏ 84 Troy Drayton | .20 | .07 |
| ❏ 85 Jim Harbaugh | .30 | .10 |
| ❏ 86 Wesley Walls | .30 | .10 |
| ❏ 87 Bryce Paup | .20 | .07 |
| ❏ 88 Curtis Martin | .60 | .25 |
| ❏ 89 Michael Sinclair | .20 | .07 |
| ❏ 90 Chris T. Jones | .20 | .07 |
| ❏ 91 Jake Reed | .30 | .10 |
| ❏ 92 LeRoy Butler | .20 | .07 |
| ❏ 93 Reggie Tongue | .20 | .07 |
| ❏ 94 Bert Emanuel | .30 | .10 |
| ❏ 95 Stan Humphries | .30 | .10 |
| ❏ 96 Neil O'Donnell | .30 | .10 |
| ❏ 97 Troy Vincent | .20 | .07 |

| | | |
|---|---|---|
| ❏ 98 Mike Alstott | .50 | .20 |
| ❏ 99 Chad Cota | .20 | .07 |
| ❏ 100 Marvin Harrison | .50 | .20 |
| ❏ 101 Terrell Owens | .60 | .25 |
| ❏ 102 Dave Brown | .20 | .07 |
| ❏ 103 Harvey Williams | .20 | .07 |
| ❏ 104 Desmond Howard | .30 | .10 |
| ❏ 105 Carl Pickens | .30 | .10 |
| ❏ 106 Kent Graham | .20 | .07 |
| ❏ 107 Michael Bates | .20 | .07 |
| ❏ 108 Terrell Davis | .60 | .25 |
| ❏ 109 Marcus Allen | .50 | .20 |
| ❏ 110 Ray Zellars | .20 | .07 |
| ❏ 111 Chris Warren | .30 | .10 |
| ❏ 112 Philippi Sparks | .20 | .07 |
| ❏ 113 Craig Erickson | .20 | .07 |
| ❏ 114 Eddie George | .50 | .20 |
| ❏ 115 Daryl Johnston | .30 | .10 |
| ❏ 116 Ricky Watters | .30 | .10 |
| ❏ 117 Tedy Bruschi | 1.00 | .40 |
| ❏ 118 Mike Mamula | .20 | .07 |
| ❏ 119 Ken Harvey | .20 | .07 |
| ❏ 120 John Randle | .30 | .10 |
| ❏ 121 Mark Chmura | .30 | .10 |
| ❏ 122 Sam Gash | .20 | .07 |
| ❏ 123 John Kasay | .20 | .07 |
| ❏ 124 Barry Minter | .20 | .07 |
| ❏ 125 Raymont Harris | .20 | .07 |
| ❏ 126 Derrick Thomas | .50 | .20 |
| ❏ 127 Trent Dilfer | .50 | .20 |
| ❏ 128 Carnell Lake | .20 | .07 |
| ❏ 129 Brian Dawkins | .50 | .20 |
| ❏ 130 Tyronne Drakeford | .20 | .07 |
| ❏ 131 Daryl Gardener | .20 | .07 |
| ❏ 132 Fred Strickland | .20 | .07 |
| ❏ 133 Kevin Hardy | .20 | .07 |
| ❏ 134 Winslow Oliver | .20 | .07 |
| ❏ 135 Herman Moore | .30 | .10 |
| ❏ 136 Keith Byars | .20 | .07 |
| ❏ 137 Harold Green | .20 | .07 |
| ❏ 138 Ty Detmer | .30 | .10 |
| ❏ 139 Lamar Thomas | .20 | .07 |
| ❏ 140 Elvis Grbac | .30 | .10 |
| ❏ 141 Edgar Bennett | .30 | .10 |
| ❏ 142 Cornelius Bennett | .20 | .07 |
| ❏ 143 Tony Tolbert | .20 | .07 |
| ❏ 144 James Hasty | .20 | .07 |
| ❏ 145 Ben Coates | .30 | .10 |
| ❏ 146 Errict Rhett | .20 | .07 |
| ❏ 147 Jason Sehorn | .30 | .10 |
| ❏ 148 Michael Jackson | .20 | .07 |
| ❏ 149 John Mobley | .20 | .07 |
| ❏ 150 Walt Harris | .20 | .07 |
| ❏ 151 Terry Kirby | .30 | .10 |
| ❏ 152 Devin Wyman | .20 | .07 |
| ❏ 153 Ray Crockett | .20 | .07 |
| ❏ 154 Quinn Early | .20 | .07 |
| ❏ 155 Rodney Thomas | .20 | .07 |
| ❏ 156 Mark Seay | .20 | .07 |
| ❏ 157 Derrick Alexander WR | .30 | .10 |
| ❏ 158 Lamar Lathon | .20 | .07 |
| ❏ 159 Anthony Miller | .20 | .07 |
| ❏ 160 Shawn Wooden RC | .20 | .07 |
| ❏ 161 Antonio Freeman | .50 | .20 |
| ❏ 162 Cortez Kennedy | .20 | .07 |
| ❏ 163 Rickey Dudley | .30 | .10 |
| ❏ 164 Tony Carter | .20 | .07 |
| ❏ 165 Kevin Williams | .20 | .07 |
| ❏ 166 Reggie White | .50 | .20 |
| ❏ 167 Tim Bowens | .20 | .07 |
| ❏ 168 Roy Barker | .20 | .07 |
| ❏ 169 Adrian Murrell | .30 | .10 |
| ❏ 170 Anthony Johnson | .20 | .07 |
| ❏ 171 Terry Glenn | .50 | .20 |
| ❏ 172 Jeff Lewis | .20 | .07 |
| ❏ 173 Dorsey Levens | .50 | .20 |
| ❏ 174 Willie Jackson | .20 | .07 |
| ❏ 175 Willie Clay | .20 | .07 |
| ❏ 176 Richmond Webb | .20 | .07 |
| ❏ 177 Shawn Lee | .20 | .07 |
| ❏ 178 Joe Aska | .20 | .07 |
| ❏ 179 Rod Woodson | .30 | .10 |
| ❏ 180 Jim Schwantz RC | .20 | .07 |
| ❏ 181 Alfred Williams | .20 | .07 |
| ❏ 182 Ferric Collons | .20 | .07 |

| | | |
|---|---|---|
| 183 Ken Norton Jr. | .20 | .07 |
| 184 Rick Mirer | .20 | .07 |
| 185 Leeland McElroy | .20 | .07 |
| 186 Rodney Hampton | .30 | .10 |
| 187 Ted Popson | .20 | .07 |
| 188 Fred Barnett | .20 | .07 |
| 189 Junior Seau | .50 | .20 |
| 190 Micheal Barrow | .20 | .07 |
| 191 Corey Widmer | .20 | .07 |
| 192 Rodney Peete | .20 | .07 |
| 193 Rod Smith WR | .50 | .20 |
| 194 Muhsin Muhammad | .30 | .10 |
| 195 Keith Jackson | .30 | .10 |
| 196 Jimmy Smith | .30 | .10 |
| 197 Dave Meggett | .20 | .07 |
| 198 Lawrence Phillips | .20 | .07 |
| 199 Chad Brown | .20 | .07 |
| 200 Darrin Smith | .20 | .07 |
| 201 Larry Centers | .30 | .10 |
| 202 Kevin Greene | .30 | .10 |
| 203 Sherman Williams | .20 | .07 |
| 204 Chris Sanders | .20 | .07 |
| 205 Shawn Jefferson | .20 | .07 |
| 206 Thurman Thomas | .50 | .20 |
| 207 Keyshawn Johnson | .50 | .20 |
| 208 Bryant Young | .20 | .07 |
| 209 Tim Biakabutuka | .30 | .10 |
| 210 Troy Aikman | 1.00 | .40 |
| 211 Quentin Coryatt | .20 | .07 |
| 212 Karim Abdul-Jabbar | .50 | .20 |
| 213 Brian Blades | .20 | .07 |
| 214 Ray Farmer | .20 | .07 |
| 215 Simeon Rice | .30 | .10 |
| 216 Tyrone Braxton | .20 | .07 |
| 217 Jerome Woods | .20 | .07 |
| 218 Charles Way | .30 | .10 |
| 219 Garrison Hearst | .30 | .10 |
| 220 Bobby Engram | .30 | .10 |
| 221 Billy Davis RC | .20 | .07 |
| 222 Ken Dilger | .20 | .07 |
| 223 Robert Smith | .30 | .10 |
| 224 John Friesz | .20 | .07 |
| 225 Charlie Garner | .30 | .10 |
| 226 Jerome Bettis | .50 | .20 |
| 227 Damay Scott | .30 | .10 |
| 228 Terance Mathis | .30 | .10 |
| 229 Brian Williams LB | .20 | .07 |
| 230 Cris Carter | .50 | .20 |
| 231 Michael Haynes | .20 | .07 |
| 232 Cedric Jones | .20 | .07 |
| 233 Danny Kanell | .30 | .10 |
| 234 Deion Sanders | .50 | .20 |
| 235 Steve Atwater | .20 | .07 |
| 236 Jonathan Ogden | .20 | .07 |
| 237 Lake Dawson | .20 | .07 |
| 238 Eric Allen | .20 | .07 |
| 239 Eddie Kennison | .30 | .10 |
| 240 Irving Fryar | .30 | .10 |
| 241 Michael Strahan | .30 | .10 |
| 242 Steve McNair | .60 | .25 |
| 243 Terrell Buckley | .20 | .07 |
| 244 Merton Hanks | .20 | .07 |
| 245 Jessie Armstead | .20 | .07 |
| 246 Dana Stubblefield | .20 | .07 |
| 247 Brett Perriman | .20 | .07 |
| 248 Mark Collins | .20 | .07 |
| 249 Willie Roaf | .20 | .07 |
| 250 Gus Frerotte | .20 | .07 |
| 251 William Fuller | .20 | .07 |
| 252 Tamarick Vanover | .30 | .10 |
| 253 Scott Mitchell | .30 | .10 |
| 254 Eric Metcalf | .30 | .10 |
| 255 Herschel Walker | .30 | .10 |
| 256 Robert Brooks | .30 | .10 |
| 257 Zach Thomas | .50 | .20 |
| 258 Alvin Harper | .20 | .07 |
| 259 Wayne Chrebet | .50 | .20 |
| 260 Bill Romanowski | .20 | .07 |
| 261 Willie Green | .20 | .07 |
| 262 Dale Carter | .20 | .07 |
| 263 Chris Slade | .20 | .07 |
| 264 J.J. Stokes | .30 | .10 |
| 265 Tim Brown | .50 | .20 |
| 266 Eric Davis | .20 | .07 |
| 267 Mark Carrier DB | .20 | .07 |

| | | |
|---|---|---|
| 268 Tony Martin | .30 | .10 |
| 269 Tyrone Wheatley | .30 | .10 |
| 270 Eugene Robinson | .20 | .07 |
| 271 Curtis Conway | .30 | .10 |
| 272 Michael Timpson | .20 | .07 |
| 273 Orlando Pace RC | .50 | .20 |
| 274 Tiki Barber RC | 3.00 | 1.25 |
| 275 Byron Hanspard RC | .30 | .10 |
| 276 Warrick Dunn RC | 1.50 | .60 |
| 277 Rae Carruth RC | .20 | .07 |
| 278 Bryant Westbrook RC | .20 | .07 |
| 279 Antowain Smith RC | 1.25 | .50 |
| 280 Peter Boulware RC | .50 | .20 |
| 281 Reidel Anthony RC | .50 | .20 |
| 282 Troy Davis RC | .30 | .10 |
| 283 Jake Plummer RC | 2.50 | 1.00 |
| 284 Chris Canty RC | .20 | .07 |
| 285 Dwayne Rudd RC | .50 | .20 |
| 286 Ike Hilliard RC | .75 | .30 |
| 287 Reinard Wilson RC | .20 | .07 |
| 288 Corey Dillon RC | 3.00 | 1.25 |
| 289 Tony Gonzalez RC | 1.50 | .60 |
| 290 Darnell Autry RC | .30 | .10 |
| 291 Kevin Lockett RC | .20 | .07 |
| 292 Darnell Russell RC | .20 | .07 |
| 293 Jim Druckenmiller RC | .30 | .10 |
| 294 Shon Mitchell RC | .20 | .07 |
| 295 Joey Kent RC | .50 | .20 |
| 296 Shawn Springs RC | .30 | .10 |
| 297 James Farrior RC | .30 | .10 |
| 298 Sedrick Shaw RC | .30 | .10 |
| 299 Marcus Harris RC | .20 | .07 |
| 300 Danny Wuerffel RC | .50 | .20 |
| 301 Marc Edwards RC | .20 | .07 |
| 302 Michael Booker RC | .20 | .07 |
| 303 David LaFleur RC | .20 | .07 |
| 304 Mike Adams WR RC | .20 | .07 |
| 305 Pat Barnes RC | .50 | .20 |
| 306 George Jones RC | .30 | .10 |
| 307 Yatil Green RC | .50 | .20 |
| 308 Drew Bledsoe TBP | .50 | .20 |
| 309 Troy Aikman TBP | .50 | .20 |
| 310 Terrell Davis TBP | .50 | .20 |
| 311 Jim Everett TBP | .20 | .07 |
| 312 John Elway TBP | 1.00 | .40 |
| 313 Barry Sanders TBP | .75 | .30 |
| 314 Jim Harbaugh TBP | .30 | .10 |
| 315 Steve Young TBP | .50 | .20 |
| 316 Dan Marino TBP | 1.00 | .40 |
| 317 Michael Irvin TBP | .50 | .20 |
| 318 Emmitt Smith TBP | .75 | .30 |
| 319 Jeff Hostetler TBP | .20 | .07 |
| 320 Mark Brunell TBP | .50 | .20 |
| 321 Jeff Blake TBP | .50 | .20 |
| 322 Scott Mitchell TBP | .20 | .07 |
| 323 Boomer Esiason TBP | .30 | .10 |
| 324 Jerome Bettis TBP | .50 | .20 |
| 325 Warren Moon TBP | .30 | .10 |
| 326 Neil O'Donnell TBP | .30 | .10 |
| 327 Jim Kelly TBP | .50 | .20 |
| 328 Dan Marino CL | .50 | .20 |
| 329 John Elway CL | .50 | .20 |
| 330 Drew Bledsoe CL | .30 | .10 |
| P1 Troy Aikman Promo | 1.00 | .40 |
| P2 Brett Favre Promo | 2.00 | .75 |
| P3 Dan Marino Promo | 2.00 | .75 |
| P4 Barry Sanders Promo | 1.50 | .60 |

## 1998 Score

| | | |
|---|---|---|
| COMPLETE SET (270) | 40.00 | 15.00 |
| 1 John Elway | 2.00 | .75 |
| 2 Kordell Stewart | .50 | .20 |
| 3 Warrick Dunn | .50 | .20 |
| 4 Brad Johnson | .50 | .20 |
| 5 Kerry Collins | .30 | .10 |
| 6 Danny Kanell | .20 | .07 |
| 7 Emmitt Smith | 1.50 | .60 |
| 8 Jamal Anderson | .50 | .20 |
| 9 Jim Harbaugh | .30 | .10 |
| 10 Tony Martin | .30 | .10 |
| 11 Rod Smith | .30 | .10 |
| 12 Dorsey Levens | .50 | .20 |
| 13 Steve McNair | .50 | .20 |
| 14 Derrick Thomas | .50 | .20 |
| 15 Rob Moore | .30 | .10 |

| | | |
|---|---|---|
| 16 Peter Boulware | .20 | .07 |
| 17 Terry Allen | .50 | .20 |
| 18 Joey Galloway | .30 | .10 |
| 19 Jerome Bettis | .50 | .20 |
| 20 Carl Pickens | .30 | .10 |
| 21 Napoleon Kaufman | .50 | .20 |
| 22 Troy Aikman | 1.00 | .40 |
| 23 Curtis Conway | .30 | .10 |
| 24 Adrian Murrell | .30 | .10 |
| 25 Elvis Grbac | .20 | .07 |
| 26 Garrison Hearst | .50 | .20 |
| 27 Chris Sanders | .20 | .07 |
| 28 Scott Mitchell | .30 | .10 |
| 29 Junior Seau | .50 | .20 |
| 30 Chris Chandler | .30 | .10 |
| 31 Kevin Hardy | .20 | .07 |
| 32 Terrell Davis | .50 | .20 |
| 33 Keyshawn Johnson | .50 | .20 |
| 34 Natrone Means | .30 | .10 |
| 35 Antowain Smith | .50 | .20 |
| 36 Jake Plummer | .50 | .20 |
| 37 Isaac Bruce | .50 | .20 |
| 38 Tony Banks | .30 | .10 |
| 39 Reidel Anthony | .20 | .07 |
| 40 Darren Woodson | .20 | .07 |
| 41 Corey Dillon | .50 | .20 |
| 42 Antonio Freeman | .50 | .20 |
| 43 Eddie George | .50 | .20 |
| 44 Yancey Thigpen | .20 | .07 |
| 45 Tim Brown | .50 | .20 |
| 46 Wayne Chrebet | .50 | .20 |
| 47 Andre Rison | .30 | .10 |
| 48 Michael Strahan | .30 | .10 |
| 49 Deion Sanders | .50 | .20 |
| 50 Eric Moulds | .50 | .20 |
| 51 Mark Brunell | .50 | .20 |
| 52 Rae Carruth | .20 | .07 |
| 53 Warren Sapp | .30 | .10 |
| 54 Mark Chmura | .30 | .10 |
| 55 Darrell Green | .30 | .10 |
| 56 Quinn Early | .20 | .07 |
| 57 Barry Sanders | 1.50 | .60 |
| 58 Neil O'Donnell | .30 | .10 |
| 59 Tony Brackens | .20 | .07 |
| 60 Willie Davis | .20 | .07 |
| 61 Shannon Sharpe | .30 | .10 |
| 62 Shawn Springs | .20 | .07 |
| 63 Tony Gonzalez | .50 | .20 |
| 64 Rodney Thomas | .20 | .07 |
| 65 Terance Mathis | .30 | .10 |
| 66 Brett Favre | 2.00 | .75 |
| 67 Eric Swann | .20 | .07 |
| 68 Kevin Turner | .20 | .07 |
| 69 Tyrone Wheatley | .30 | .10 |
| 70 Trent Dilfer | .20 | .07 |
| 71 Bryan Cox | .20 | .07 |
| 72 Lake Dawson | .20 | .07 |
| 73 Will Blackwell | .20 | .07 |
| 74 Fred Lane | .30 | .10 |
| 75 Ty Detmer | .30 | .10 |
| 76 Eddie Kennison | .30 | .10 |
| 77 Jimmy Smith | .30 | .10 |
| 78 Chris Calloway | .20 | .07 |
| 79 Shawn Jefferson | .20 | .07 |
| 80 Dan Marino | 2.00 | .75 |
| 81 LeRoy Butler | .20 | .07 |
| 82 William Roaf | .20 | .07 |
| 83 Rick Mirer | .20 | .07 |

| | | |
|---|---|---|
| 84 Dermontti Dawson | .20 | .07 |
| 85 Errict Rhett | .30 | .10 |
| 86 Lamar Thomas | .20 | .07 |
| 87 Lamar Lathon | .20 | .07 |
| 88 John Randle | .20 | .07 |
| 89 Darryl Williams | .20 | .07 |
| 90 Keenan McCardell | .30 | .10 |
| 91 Erik Kramer | .20 | .07 |
| 92 Ken Dilger | .20 | .07 |
| 93 Dave Meggett | .20 | .07 |
| 94 Jeff Blake | .30 | .10 |
| 95 Ed McCaffrey | .30 | .10 |
| 96 Charles Johnson | .20 | .07 |
| 97 Irving Spikes | .20 | .07 |
| 98 Mike Alstott | .50 | .20 |
| 99 Vincent Brisby | .20 | .07 |
| 100 Michael Westbrook | .30 | .10 |
| 101 Rickey Dudley | .20 | .07 |
| 102 Bert Emanuel | .30 | .10 |
| 103 Daryl Johnston | .30 | .10 |
| 104 Lawrence Phillips | .20 | .07 |
| 105 Eric Bieniemy | .20 | .07 |
| 106 Bryant Westbrook | .20 | .07 |
| 107 Rob Johnson | .30 | .10 |
| 108 Ray Zellars | .20 | .07 |
| 109 Anthony Johnson | .20 | .07 |
| 110 Reggie White | .50 | .20 |
| 111 Wesley Walls | .30 | .10 |
| 112 Amani Toomer | .30 | .10 |
| 113 Gary Brown | .20 | .07 |
| 114 Brian Blades | .20 | .07 |
| 115 Alex Van Dyke | .20 | .07 |
| 116 Michael Haynes | .20 | .07 |
| 117 Jessie Armstead | .20 | .07 |
| 118 James Jett | .30 | .10 |
| 119 Troy Drayton | .20 | .07 |
| 120 Craig Heyward | .20 | .07 |
| 121 Steve Atwater | .20 | .07 |
| 122 Tiki Barber | .50 | .20 |
| 123 Karim Abdul-Jabbar | .50 | .20 |
| 124 Kimble Anders | .30 | .10 |
| 125 Frank Sanders | .30 | .10 |
| 126 David Sloan | .20 | .07 |
| 127 Andre Hastings | .20 | .07 |
| 128 Vinny Testaverde | .30 | .10 |
| 129 Robert Smith | .50 | .20 |
| 130 Horace Copeland | .20 | .07 |
| 131 Larry Centers | .20 | .07 |
| 132 J.J. Stokes | .30 | .10 |
| 133 Ike Hilliard | .30 | .10 |
| 134 Muhsin Muhammad | .20 | .07 |
| 135 Sean Dawkins | .20 | .07 |
| 136 Raymont Harris | .20 | .07 |
| 137 Lamar Smith | .30 | .10 |
| 138 David Palmer | .20 | .07 |
| 139 Steve Young | .60 | .25 |
| 140 Bryan Still | .20 | .07 |
| 141 Keith Byars | .20 | .07 |
| 142 Cris Carter | .50 | .20 |
| 143 Charlie Garner | .30 | .10 |
| 144 Drew Bledsoe | .75 | .30 |
| 145 Simeon Rice | .30 | .10 |
| 146 Merton Hanks | .20 | .07 |
| 147 Aeneas Williams | .20 | .07 |
| 148 Rodney Hampton | .30 | .10 |
| 149 Zach Thomas | .50 | .20 |
| 150 Mark Bruener | .20 | .07 |
| 151 Jason Dunn | .20 | .07 |
| 152 Danny Wuerffel | .30 | .10 |
| 153 Jim Druckenmiller | .30 | .10 |
| 154 Greg Hill | .20 | .07 |
| 155 Earnest Byner | .20 | .07 |
| 156 Greg Lloyd | .20 | .07 |
| 157 John Mobley | .20 | .07 |
| 158 Tim Biakabutuka | .30 | .10 |
| 159 Terrell Owens | .50 | .20 |
| 160 O.J. McDuffie | .30 | .10 |
| 161 Glenn Foley | .30 | .10 |
| 162 Derrick Brooks | .50 | .20 |
| 163 Dave Brown | .20 | .07 |
| 164 Ki-Jana Carter | .30 | .10 |
| 165 Bobby Hoying | .30 | .10 |
| 166 Randal Hill | .20 | .07 |
| 167 Michael Irvin | .50 | .20 |
| 168 Bruce Smith | .30 | .10 |
| 169 Troy Davis | .20 | .07 |
| 170 Derrick Mayes | .30 | .10 |
| 171 Henry Ellard | .30 | .10 |
| 172 Dana Stubblefield | .20 | .07 |
| 173 Willie McGinest | .20 | .07 |
| 174 Leeland McElroy | .20 | .07 |
| 175 Edgar Bennett | .20 | .07 |
| 176 Robert Porcher | .20 | .07 |
| 177 Randall Cunningham | .50 | .20 |
| 178 Jim Everett | .20 | .07 |
| 179 Jake Reed | .30 | .10 |
| 180 Quentin Coryatt | .20 | .07 |
| 181 William Floyd | .20 | .07 |
| 182 Jason Sehorn | .30 | .10 |
| 183 Carnell Lake | .20 | .07 |
| 184 Dexter Coakley | .20 | .07 |
| 185 Derrick Alexander WR | .30 | .10 |
| 186 Johnnie Morton | .30 | .10 |
| 187 Irving Fryar | .30 | .10 |
| 188 Warren Moon | .50 | .20 |
| 189 Todd Collins | .20 | .07 |
| 190 Ken Norton Jr. | .20 | .07 |
| 191 Terry Glenn | .50 | .20 |
| 192 Rashaan Salaam | .20 | .07 |
| 193 Jerry Rice | 1.00 | .40 |
| 194 James O.Stewart | .20 | .07 |
| 195 David LaFleur | .20 | .07 |
| 196 Eric Green | .20 | .07 |
| 197 Gus Frerotte | .20 | .07 |
| 198 Willie Green | .20 | .07 |
| 199 Marshall Faulk | .60 | .25 |
| 200 Brett Perriman | .20 | .07 |
| 201 Darnay Scott | .30 | .10 |
| 202 Marvin Harrison | .50 | .20 |
| 203 Joe Aska | .20 | .07 |
| 204 Darrien Gordon | .20 | .07 |
| 205 Herman Moore | .30 | .10 |
| 206 Curtis Martin | .50 | .20 |
| 207 Derek Loville | .20 | .07 |
| 208 Dale Carter | .20 | .07 |
| 209 Heath Shuler | .20 | .07 |
| 210 Jonathan Ogden | .20 | .07 |
| 211 Leslie Shepherd | .20 | .07 |
| 212 Tony Boselli | .20 | .07 |
| 213 Eric Metcalf | .20 | .07 |
| 214 Neil Smith | .30 | .10 |
| 215 Anthony Miller | .20 | .07 |
| 216 Jeff George | .30 | .10 |
| 217 Charles Way | .20 | .07 |
| 218 Mario Bates | .30 | .10 |
| 219 Ben Coates | .30 | .10 |
| 220 Michael Jackson | .20 | .07 |
| 221 Thurman Thomas | .50 | .20 |
| 222 Kyle Brady | .20 | .07 |
| 223 Marcus Allen | .50 | .20 |
| 224 Robert Brooks | .30 | .10 |
| 225 Yatil Green | .20 | .07 |
| 226 Byron Hanspard | .20 | .07 |
| 227 Andre Reed | .30 | .10 |
| 228 Chris Warren | .20 | .07 |
| 229 Jackie Harris | .20 | .07 |
| 230 Ricky Watters | .30 | .10 |
| 231 Bobby Engram | .30 | .10 |
| 232 Tamarick Vanover | .20 | .07 |
| 233 Peyton Manning RC | 15.00 | 6.00 |
| 234 Curtis Enis RC | .75 | .30 |
| 235 Randy Moss RC | 10.00 | 4.00 |
| 236 Charles Woodson RC | 1.50 | .60 |
| 237 Robert Edwards RC | 1.00 | .40 |
| 238 Jacquez Green RC | 1.00 | .40 |
| 239 Keith Brooking RC | 1.50 | .60 |
| 240 Jerome Pathon RC | 1.50 | .60 |
| 241 Kevin Dyson RC | 1.50 | .60 |
| 242 Fred Taylor RC | 2.00 | .75 |
| 243 Tavian Banks RC | 1.00 | .40 |
| 244 Marcus Nash RC | .75 | .30 |
| 245 Brian Griese RC | 2.50 | 1.00 |
| 246 Andre Wadsworth RC | 1.00 | .40 |
| 247 Ahman Green RC | 4.00 | 1.50 |
| 248 Joe Jurevicius RC | 1.50 | .60 |
| 249 Germane Crowell RC | 1.00 | .40 |
| 250 Skip Hicks RC | 1.00 | .40 |
| 251 Ryan Leaf RC | 1.50 | .60 |
| 252 Hines Ward RC | 6.00 | 2.50 |
| 253 John Elway OS | 1.00 | .40 |
| 254 Mark Brunell OS | .50 | .20 |
| 255 Brett Favre OS | 1.00 | .40 |
| 256 Troy Aikman OS | .50 | .20 |
| 257 Warrick Dunn OS | .30 | .10 |
| 258 Barry Sanders OS | .75 | .30 |
| 259 Eddie George OS | .50 | .20 |
| 260 Kordell Stewart OS | .50 | .20 |
| 261 Emmitt Smith OS | .75 | .30 |
| 262 Steve Young OS | .50 | .20 |
| 263 Terrell Davis OS | .50 | .20 |
| 264 Dorsey Levens OS | .30 | .10 |
| 265 Dan Marino OS | 1.00 | .40 |
| 266 Jerry Rice OS | .50 | .20 |
| 267 Drew Bledsoe OS | .50 | .20 |
| 268 Brett Favre CL | .60 | .25 |
| 269 Barry Sanders CL | .50 | .20 |
| 270 Terrell Davis CL | .50 | .20 |
| 251AU Ryan Leaf AUTO | 40.00 | 15.00 |

## 1999 Score

| | | |
|---|---|---|
| COMPLETE SET (275) | 60.00 | 25.00 |
| COMP.SET w/o SP's (220) | 15.00 | 6.00 |
| 1 Randy Moss | 1.50 | .60 |
| 2 Randall Cunningham | .60 | .25 |
| 3 Cris Carter | .60 | .25 |
| 4 Robert Smith | .60 | .25 |
| 5 Jake Reed | .40 | .15 |
| 6 Leroy Hoard | .25 | .08 |
| 7 John Randle | .40 | .15 |
| 8 Brett Favre | 2.00 | .75 |
| 9 Antonio Freeman | .60 | .25 |
| 10 Dorsey Levens | .60 | .25 |
| 11 Robert Brooks | .40 | .15 |
| 12 Derrick Mayes | .40 | .15 |
| 13 Mark Chmura | .40 | .15 |
| 14 Darick Holmes | .25 | .08 |
| 15 Vonnie Holliday | .40 | .15 |
| 16 Mike Alstott | .60 | .25 |
| 17 Warrick Dunn | .60 | .25 |
| 18 Trent Dilfer | .40 | .15 |
| 19 Jacquez Green | .25 | .08 |
| 20 Reidel Anthony | .40 | .15 |
| 21 Warren Sapp | .40 | .15 |
| 22 Bert Emanuel | .40 | .15 |
| 23 Curtis Enis | .25 | .08 |
| 24 Curtis Conway | .40 | .15 |
| 25 Bobby Engram | .40 | .15 |
| 26 Erik Kramer | .40 | .15 |
| 27 Moses Moreno | .25 | .08 |
| 28 Edgar Bennett | .25 | .08 |
| 29 Barry Sanders | 2.00 | .75 |
| 30 Charlie Batch | .60 | .25 |
| 31 Herman Moore | .40 | .15 |
| 32 Johnnie Morton | .40 | .15 |
| 33 Germane Crowell | .25 | .08 |
| 34 Terry Fair | .25 | .08 |
| 35 Gary Brown | .25 | .08 |
| 36 Kent Graham | .25 | .08 |
| 37 Kerry Collins | .40 | .15 |
| 38 Charles Way | .25 | .08 |
| 39 Tiki Barber | .60 | .25 |
| 40 Ike Hilliard | .25 | .08 |
| 41 Joe Jurevicius | .40 | .15 |
| 42 Michael Strahan | .40 | .15 |
| 43 Jason Sehorn | .25 | .08 |
| 44 Brad Johnson | .60 | .25 |
| 45 Terry Allen | .40 | .15 |
| 46 Skip Hicks | .25 | .08 |

| | | | | | | | | | |
|---|---|---|---|---|---|---|---|---|---|
| ❏ 47 Michael Westbrook | .40 | .15 | ❏ 132 Kyle Brady | .25 | .08 | ❏ 217 Jon Ritchie | .25 | .08 |
| ❏ 48 Leslie Shepherd | .25 | .08 | ❏ 133 Tavian Banks | .25 | .08 | ❏ 218 Rich Gannon | .60 | .25 |
| ❏ 49 Stephen Alexander | .25 | .08 | ❏ 134 James Stewart | .40 | .15 | ❏ 219 Rickey Dudley | .25 | .08 |
| ❏ 50 Albert Connell | .25 | .08 | ❏ 135 Kevin Hardy | .25 | .08 | ❏ 220 James Jett | .40 | .15 |
| ❏ 51 Darrell Green | .40 | .15 | ❏ 136 Jonathan Quinn | .25 | .08 | ❏ 221 Tim Couch RC | 3.00 | 1.25 |
| ❏ 52 Jake Plummer | .40 | .15 | ❏ 137 Jermaine Lewis | .40 | .15 | ❏ 222 Ricky Williams RC | 4.00 | 1.50 |
| ❏ 53 Adrian Murrell | .25 | .08 | ❏ 138 Priest Holmes | 1.00 | .40 | ❏ 223 Donovan McNabb RC | 10.00 | 4.00 |
| ❏ 54 Frank Sanders | .40 | .15 | ❏ 139 Scott Mitchell | .40 | .15 | ❏ 224 Edgerrin James RC | 8.00 | 3.00 |
| ❏ 55 Rob Moore | .40 | .15 | ❏ 140 Eric Zeier | .40 | .15 | ❏ 225 Torry Holt RC | 6.00 | 2.50 |
| ❏ 56 Larry Centers | .25 | .08 | ❏ 141 Patrick Johnson | .25 | .08 | ❏ 226 Daunte Culpepper RC | 8.00 | 3.00 |
| ❏ 57 Simeon Rice | .40 | .15 | ❏ 142 Ray Lewis | .60 | .25 | ❏ 227 Akili Smith RC | 2.00 | .75 |
| ❏ 58 Andre Wadsworth | .25 | .08 | ❏ 143 Terry Kirby | .25 | .08 | ❏ 228 Champ Bailey RC | 4.00 | 1.50 |
| ❏ 59 Duce Staley | .60 | .25 | ❏ 144 Ty Detmer | .25 | .08 | ❏ 229 Chris Claiborne RC | 1.25 | .50 |
| ❏ 60 Charlie Johnson | .25 | .08 | ❏ 145 Irv Smith | .25 | .08 | ❏ 230 Chris McAlister RC | 2.00 | .75 |
| ❏ 61 Charlie Garner | .40 | .15 | ❏ 146 Chris Spielman | .25 | .08 | ❏ 231 Troy Edwards RC | 2.00 | .75 |
| ❏ 62 Bobby Hoying | .40 | .15 | ❏ 147 Antonio Langham | .25 | .08 | ❏ 232 Jevon Kearse RC | 5.00 | 2.00 |
| ❏ 63 Daryl Johnston | .40 | .15 | ❏ 148 Dan Marino | 2.00 | .75 | ❏ 233 Shaun King RC | 2.00 | .75 |
| ❏ 64 Emmitt Smith | 1.25 | .50 | ❏ 149 O.J. McDuffie | .40 | .15 | ❏ 234 David Boston RC | 3.00 | 1.25 |
| ❏ 65 Troy Aikman | 1.25 | .50 | ❏ 150 Oronde Gadsden | .40 | .15 | ❏ 235 Peerless Price RC | 3.00 | 1.25 |
| ❏ 66 Michael Irvin | .40 | .15 | ❏ 151 Karim Abdul-Jabbar | .40 | .15 | ❏ 236 Cecil Collins RC | 1.25 | .50 |
| ❏ 67 Deion Sanders | .60 | .25 | ❏ 152 Yatil Green | .25 | .08 | ❏ 237 Rob Konrad RC | 2.00 | .75 |
| ❏ 68 Chris Warren | .25 | .08 | ❏ 153 Zach Thomas | .60 | .25 | ❏ 238 Cade McNown UER RC | 2.00 | .75 |
| ❏ 69 Darren Woodson | .25 | .08 | ❏ 154 John Avery | .25 | .08 | ❏ 239 Shawn Bryson RC | 3.00 | 1.25 |
| ❏ 70 Rod Woodson | .40 | .15 | ❏ 155 Lamar Thomas | .25 | .08 | ❏ 240 Kevin Faulk RC | 3.00 | 1.25 |
| ❏ 71 Travis Jervey | .25 | .08 | ❏ 156 Drew Bledsoe | .75 | .30 | ❏ 241 Scott Covington RC | 2.00 | .75 |
| ❏ 72 Jerry Rice | 1.25 | .50 | ❏ 157 Terry Glenn | .60 | .25 | ❏ 242 James Johnson RC | 2.00 | .75 |
| ❏ 73 Terrell Owens | .60 | .25 | ❏ 158 Ben Coates | .40 | .15 | ❏ 243 Mike Cloud RC | 2.00 | .75 |
| ❏ 74 Steve Young | .75 | .30 | ❏ 159 Shawn Jefferson | .25 | .08 | ❏ 244 Aaron Brooks RC | 4.00 | 1.50 |
| ❏ 75 Garrison Hearst | .40 | .15 | ❏ 160 Sedrick Shaw | .25 | .08 | ❏ 245 Sedrick Irvin RC | 1.25 | .50 |
| ❏ 76 J.J. Stokes | .40 | .15 | ❏ 161 Tony Simmons | .25 | .08 | ❏ 246 Amos Zereoue RC | 3.00 | 1.25 |
| ❏ 77 Ken Norton | .25 | .08 | ❏ 162 Ty Law | .40 | .15 | ❏ 247 Jermaine Fazande RC | 2.00 | .75 |
| ❏ 78 R.W. McQuarters | .25 | .08 | ❏ 163 Robert Edwards | .25 | .08 | ❏ 248 Joe Germaine RC | 2.00 | .75 |
| ❏ 79 Bryant Young | .25 | .08 | ❏ 164 Curtis Martin | .60 | .25 | ❏ 249 Brock Huard RC | 3.00 | 1.25 |
| ❏ 80 Jamal Anderson | .60 | .25 | ❏ 165 Keyshawn Johnson | .60 | .25 | ❏ 250 Craig Yeast RC | 2.00 | .75 |
| ❏ 81 Chris Chandler | .40 | .15 | ❏ 166 Vinny Testaverde | .40 | .15 | ❏ 251 Travis McGriff RC | 1.25 | .50 |
| ❏ 82 Terance Mathis | .40 | .15 | ❏ 167 Aaron Glenn | .25 | .08 | ❏ 252 D'Wayne Bates RC | 2.00 | .75 |
| ❏ 83 Tim Dwight | .40 | .15 | ❏ 168 Wayne Chrebet | .40 | .15 | ❏ 253 Na Brown RC | 2.00 | .75 |
| ❏ 84 O.J. Santiago | .25 | .08 | ❏ 169 Dedric Ward | .25 | .08 | ❏ 254 Tai Streets RC | 3.00 | 1.25 |
| ❏ 85 Chris Calloway | .25 | .08 | ❏ 170 Peyton Manning | 2.00 | .75 | ❏ 255 Andy Katzenmoyer RC | 2.00 | .75 |
| ❏ 86 Keith Brooking | .25 | .08 | ❏ 171 Marshall Faulk | .75 | .30 | ❏ 256 Kevin Johnson RC | 3.00 | 1.25 |
| ❏ 87 Eddie Kennison | .40 | .15 | ❏ 172 Marvin Harrison | .60 | .25 | ❏ 257 Joe Montgomery RC | 2.00 | .75 |
| ❏ 88 Willie Roaf | .25 | .08 | ❏ 173 Jerome Pathon | .25 | .08 | ❏ 258 Karsten Bailey RC | 2.00 | .75 |
| ❏ 89 Cam Cleeland | .40 | .15 | ❏ 174 Ken Dilger | .25 | .08 | ❏ 259 De'Mond Parker RC | 1.25 | .50 |
| ❏ 90 Lamar Smith | .40 | .15 | ❏ 175 E.G. Green | .25 | .08 | ❏ 260 Reginald Kelly RC | 1.25 | .50 |
| ❏ 91 Sean Dawkins | .25 | .08 | ❏ 176 Doug Flutie | .60 | .25 | ❏ 261 Eddie George AP | 1.50 | .60 |
| ❏ 92 Tim Biakabutaka | .40 | .15 | ❏ 177 Thurman Thomas | .40 | .15 | ❏ 262 Jamal Anderson AP | 1.50 | .60 |
| ❏ 93 Muhsin Muhammad | .40 | .15 | ❏ 178 Andre Reed | .40 | .15 | ❏ 263 Barry Sanders AP | 6.00 | 2.50 |
| ❏ 94 Steve Beuerlein | .40 | .15 | ❏ 179 Eric Moulds | .60 | .25 | ❏ 264 Fred Taylor AP | 1.50 | .60 |
| ❏ 95 Rae Carruth | .25 | .08 | ❏ 180 Antowain Smith | .60 | .25 | ❏ 265 Keyshawn Johnson AP | 1.50 | .60 |
| ❏ 96 Wesley Walls | .40 | .15 | ❏ 181 Bruce Smith | .40 | .15 | ❏ 266 Jerry Rice AP | 4.00 | 1.50 |
| ❏ 97 Kevin Greene | .40 | .15 | ❏ 182 Rob Johnson | .40 | .15 | ❏ 267 Doug Flutie AP | 1.50 | .60 |
| ❏ 98 Trent Green | .25 | .08 | ❏ 183 Terrell Davis | .60 | .25 | ❏ 268 Deion Sanders AP | 1.50 | .60 |
| ❏ 99 Tony Banks | .40 | .15 | ❏ 184 John Elway | 2.00 | .75 | ❏ 269 Randall Cunningham AP | 1.50 | .60 |
| ❏ 100 Greg Hill | .25 | .08 | ❏ 185 Ed McCaffrey | .40 | .15 | ❏ 270 Steve Young AP | 2.50 | 1.00 |
| ❏ 101 Robert Holcombe | .25 | .08 | ❏ 186 Rod Smith | .40 | .15 | ❏ 271 J.Elway/T.Davis GC | 5.00 | 2.00 |
| ❏ 102 Isaac Bruce | .60 | .25 | ❏ 187 Shannon Sharpe | .40 | .15 | ❏ 272 P.Manning/M.Faulk GC | 5.00 | 2.00 |
| ❏ 103 Amp Lee | .25 | .08 | ❏ 188 Marcus Nash | .25 | .08 | ❏ 273 B.Favre/A.Freeman GC | 6.00 | 2.50 |
| ❏ 104 Az-Zahir Hakim | .40 | .15 | ❏ 189 Brian Griese | .60 | .25 | ❏ 274 T.Aikman/E.Smith GC | 4.00 | 1.50 |
| ❏ 105 Warren Moon | .60 | .25 | ❏ 190 Neil Smith | .40 | .15 | ❏ 275 C.Carter/R.Moss GC | 4.00 | 1.50 |
| ❏ 106 Jeff George | .40 | .15 | ❏ 191 Bubby Brister | .25 | .08 | | | |
| ❏ 107 Rocket Ismail | .40 | .15 | ❏ 192 Ryan Leaf | .60 | .25 | **1999 Score Supplemental** | | |
| ❏ 108 Kordell Stewart | .60 | .25 | ❏ 193 Natrone Means | .40 | .15 | | | |
| ❏ 109 Jerome Bettis | .60 | .25 | ❏ 194 Mikhael Ricks | .25 | .08 | | | |
| ❏ 110 Courtney Hawkins | .25 | .08 | ❏ 195 Junior Seau | .60 | .25 | | | |
| ❏ 111 Chris Fuamatu-Ma'afala | .25 | .08 | ❏ 196 Jim Harbaugh | .40 | .15 | | | |
| ❏ 112 Levon Kirkland | .25 | .08 | ❏ 197 Bryan Still | .25 | .08 | | | |
| ❏ 113 Hines Ward | .60 | .25 | ❏ 198 Freddie Jones | .25 | .08 | | | |
| ❏ 114 Will Blackwell | .25 | .08 | ❏ 199 Andre Rison | .40 | .15 | | | |
| ❏ 115 Corey Dillon | .60 | .25 | ❏ 200 Elvis Grbac | .25 | .08 | | | |
| ❏ 116 Carl Pickens | .40 | .15 | ❏ 201 Byron Bam Morris | .25 | .08 | | | |
| ❏ 117 Neil O'Donnell | .40 | .15 | ❏ 202 Rashaan Shehee | .25 | .08 | | | |
| ❏ 118 Jeff Blake | .40 | .15 | ❏ 203 Kimble Anders | .25 | .08 | | | |
| ❏ 119 Darnay Scott | .25 | .08 | ❏ 204 Donnell Bennett | .25 | .08 | | | |
| ❏ 120 Takeo Spikes | .40 | .15 | ❏ 205 Tony Gonzalez | .60 | .25 | | | |
| ❏ 121 Steve McNair | .60 | .25 | ❏ 206 Derrick Alexander WR | .40 | .15 | | | |
| ❏ 122 Frank Wycheck | .25 | .08 | ❏ 207 Jon Kitna | .60 | .25 | | | |
| ❏ 123 Eddie George | .60 | .25 | ❏ 208 Ricky Watters | .40 | .15 | | | |
| ❏ 124 Chris Sanders | .25 | .08 | ❏ 209 Joey Galloway | .40 | .15 | | | |
| ❏ 125 Yancey Thigpen | .25 | .08 | ❏ 210 Ahman Green | .60 | .25 | | | |
| ❏ 126 Kevin Dyson | .40 | .15 | ❏ 211 Shawn Springs | .25 | .08 | ❏ COMPLETE SET (110) | 25.00 | 10.00 |
| ❏ 127 Blaine Bishop | .25 | .08 | ❏ 212 Michael Sinclair | .25 | .08 | ❏ COMP.FACT.SET (110) | 30.00 | 12.50 |
| ❏ 128 Fred Taylor | .60 | .25 | ❏ 213 Napoleon Kaufman | .60 | .25 | ❏ S1 Chris Greisen RC | 1.00 | .40 |
| ❏ 129 Mark Brunell | .60 | .25 | ❏ 214 Tim Brown | .60 | .25 | ❏ S2 Sherdrick Bonner RC | .60 | .25 |
| ❏ 130 Jimmy Smith | .40 | .15 | ❏ 215 Charles Brown | .25 | .08 | ❏ S3 Joel Makovicka RC | 1.50 | .50 |
| ❏ 131 Keenan McCardell | .40 | .15 | ❏ 216 Harvey Williams | .25 | .08 | ❏ S4 Andy McCullough RC | .60 | .25 |
| | | | | | | ❏ S5 Jeff Paulk RC | .60 | .25 |

| | | |
|---|---|---|
| ☐ S6 Brandon Stokley RC | 2.00 | .75 |
| ☐ S7 Sheldon Jackson RC | 1.00 | .40 |
| ☐ S8 Bobby Collins RC | .60 | .25 |
| ☐ S9 Kamil Loud RC | .60 | .25 |
| ☐ S10 Antoine Winfield RC | 1.00 | .40 |
| ☐ S11 Jerry Azumah RC | 1.00 | .40 |
| ☐ S12 James Allen RC | 1.50 | .60 |
| ☐ S13 Nick Williams RC | 1.00 | .40 |
| ☐ S14 Michael Basnight RC | .60 | .25 |
| ☐ S15 Damon Griffin RC | 1.00 | .40 |
| ☐ S16 Ronnie Powell RC | .60 | .25 |
| ☐ S17 Darrin Chiaverini RC | 1.00 | .40 |
| ☐ S18 Mark Campbell RC | 1.00 | .40 |
| ☐ S19 Mike Lucky RC | 1.00 | .40 |
| ☐ S20 Wane McGarity RC | .60 | .25 |
| ☐ S21 Jason Tucker RC | 1.00 | .40 |
| ☐ S22 Ebenezer Ekuban RC | 1.00 | .40 |
| ☐ S23 Robert Thomas RC | 1.00 | .40 |
| ☐ S24 Dat Nguyen RC | 1.00 | .40 |
| ☐ S25 Olandis Gary RC | 1.50 | .60 |
| ☐ S26 Desmond Clark RC | 1.50 | .60 |
| ☐ S27 Andre Cooper RC | .60 | .25 |
| ☐ S28 Chris Watson RC | .60 | .25 |
| ☐ S29 Al Wilson RC | 1.50 | .60 |
| ☐ S30 Cory Sauter RC | .60 | .25 |
| ☐ S31 Brock Olivo RC | .60 | .25 |
| ☐ S32 Basil Mitchell RC | .60 | .25 |
| ☐ S33 Matt Snider RC | .60 | .25 |
| ☐ S34 Antuan Edwards RC | 1.00 | .40 |
| ☐ S35 Mike McKenzie RC | 1.00 | .40 |
| ☐ S36 Terrence Wilkins RC | 1.00 | .40 |
| ☐ S37 Fernando Bryant RC | 1.00 | .40 |
| ☐ S38 Larry Parker RC | 1.50 | .60 |
| ☐ S39 Autry Denson RC | 1.50 | .60 |
| ☐ S40 Jim Kleinsasser RC | 1.50 | .60 |
| ☐ S41 Michael Bishop RC | 1.50 | .60 |
| ☐ S42 Andy Katzenmoyer | .25 | .08 |
| ☐ S43 Brett Bech RC | .60 | .25 |
| ☐ S44 Sean Bennett RC | .60 | .25 |
| ☐ S45 Dan Campbell RC | .60 | .25 |
| ☐ S46 Ray Lucas RC | 1.50 | .60 |
| ☐ S47 Scott Dreisbach RC | 1.00 | .40 |
| ☐ S48 Cecil Martin RC | 1.00 | .40 |
| ☐ S49 Dameane Douglas RC | 1.00 | .40 |
| ☐ S50 Jed Weaver RC | 1.00 | .40 |
| ☐ S51 Jerame Tuman RC | 1.50 | .60 |
| ☐ S52 Steve Heiden RC | 1.50 | .60 |
| ☐ S53 Jeff Garcia RC | 4.00 | 1.50 |
| ☐ S54 Terry Jackson RC | 1.00 | .40 |
| ☐ S55 Charlie Rogers RC | 1.00 | .40 |
| ☐ S56 Lamar King RC | 1.00 | .40 |
| ☐ S57 Kurt Warner RC | 8.00 | 3.00 |
| ☐ S58 Dre' Bly RC | 1.50 | .60 |
| ☐ S59 Justin Watson RC | .60 | .25 |
| ☐ S60 Rabih Abdullah RC | 1.00 | .40 |
| ☐ S61 Martin Gramatica RC | .60 | .25 |
| ☐ S62 Darnell MacDonald RC | 1.00 | .40 |
| ☐ S63 Anthony McFarland RC | 1.00 | .40 |
| ☐ S64 Larry Brown TE RC | .60 | .25 |
| ☐ S65 Kevin Daft RC | 1.00 | .40 |
| ☐ S66 Mike Sellers | .15 | .05 |
| ☐ S67 Ken Oxendine | .15 | .05 |
| ☐ S68 Errict Rhett | .25 | .08 |
| ☐ S69 Stoney Case | .15 | .05 |
| ☐ S70 Jonathan Linton | .15 | .05 |
| ☐ S71 Marcus Robinson | 1.00 | .40 |
| ☐ S72 Shane Matthews | .25 | .08 |
| ☐ S73 Cade McNown | 1.00 | .40 |
| ☐ S74 Akili Smith | .15 | .05 |
| ☐ S75 Karim Abdul-Jabbar | .25 | .08 |
| ☐ S76 Tim Couch | 1.50 | .60 |
| ☐ S77 Kevin Johnson | .40 | .15 |
| ☐ S78 Ron Rivers | .15 | .05 |
| ☐ S79 Bill Schroeder | .40 | .15 |
| ☐ S80 Edgerrin James | 2.50 | 1.00 |
| ☐ S81 Cecil Collins | .75 | .30 |
| ☐ S82 Matthew Hatchette | .15 | .05 |
| ☐ S83 Daunte Culpepper | 2.50 | 1.00 |
| ☐ S84 Ricky Williams | 1.25 | .50 |
| ☐ S85 Tyrone Wheatley | .40 | .15 |
| ☐ S86 Donovan McNabb | 3.00 | 1.25 |
| ☐ S87 Marshall Faulk | .50 | .20 |
| ☐ S88 Torry Holt | 2.00 | .75 |
| ☐ S89 Stephen Davis | .40 | .15 |
| ☐ S90 Brad Johnson | .40 | .15 |

| | | |
|---|---|---|
| ☐ S91 Jake Plummer SS | .25 | .08 |
| ☐ S92 Emmitt Smith SS | .75 | .30 |
| ☐ S93 Troy Aikman SS | .75 | .30 |
| ☐ S94 John Elway SS | 1.25 | .50 |
| ☐ S95 Terrell Davis SS | .40 | .15 |
| ☐ S96 Barry Sanders SS | 1.25 | .50 |
| ☐ S97 Brett Favre SS | 1.25 | .50 |
| ☐ S98 Antonio Freeman SS | .40 | .15 |
| ☐ S99 Peyton Manning SS | 1.25 | .50 |
| ☐ S100 Fred Taylor SS | .40 | .15 |
| ☐ S101 Mark Brunell SS | .40 | .15 |
| ☐ S102 Dan Marino SS | 1.25 | .50 |
| ☐ S103 Randy Moss SS | 1.00 | .40 |
| ☐ S104 Cris Carter SS | .40 | .15 |
| ☐ S105 Drew Bledsoe SS | .50 | .20 |
| ☐ S106 Terry Glenn SS | .40 | .15 |
| ☐ S107 Keyshawn Johnson SS | .40 | .15 |
| ☐ S108 Jerry Rice SS | .75 | .30 |
| ☐ S109 Steve Young SS | .50 | .20 |
| ☐ S110 Eddie George SS | .40 | .15 |

## 2000 Score

| | | |
|---|---|---|
| ☐ COMP. SET w/o SP's (220) | 20.00 | 7.50 |
| ☐ 1 Michael Pittman | .25 | .08 |
| ☐ 2 Jake Plummer | .40 | .15 |
| ☐ 3 Rob Moore | .40 | .15 |
| ☐ 4 David Boston | .60 | .25 |
| ☐ 5 Frank Sanders | .40 | .15 |
| ☐ 6 Jamal Anderson | .60 | .25 |
| ☐ 7 Chris Chandler | .40 | .15 |
| ☐ 8 Tim Dwight | .60 | .25 |
| ☐ 9 Terance Mathis | .40 | .15 |
| ☐ 10 Shawn Jefferson | .25 | .08 |
| ☐ 11 Ashley Ambrose | .25 | .08 |
| ☐ 12 Peter Boulware | .25 | .08 |
| ☐ 13 Priest Holmes | .75 | .30 |
| ☐ 14 Tony Banks | .40 | .15 |
| ☐ 15 Qadry Ismail | .40 | .15 |
| ☐ 16 Shannon Sharpe | .40 | .15 |
| ☐ 17 Rod Woodson | .40 | .15 |
| ☐ 18 Matt Stover | .25 | .08 |
| ☐ 19 Michael McCrary | .25 | .08 |
| ☐ 20 Doug Flutie | .60 | .25 |
| ☐ 21 Rob Johnson | .40 | .15 |
| ☐ 22 Eric Moulds | .60 | .25 |
| ☐ 23 Peerless Price | .40 | .15 |
| ☐ 24 Jonathan Linton | .25 | .08 |
| ☐ 25 Antowain Smith | .40 | .15 |
| ☐ 26 Jay Riemersma | .25 | .08 |
| ☐ 27 Muhsin Muhammad | .40 | .15 |
| ☐ 28 Tim Biakabutuka | .40 | .15 |
| ☐ 29 Patrick Jeffers | .60 | .25 |
| ☐ 30 Wesley Walls | .40 | .15 |
| ☐ 31 Steve Beuerlein | .40 | .15 |
| ☐ 32 John Kasay | .25 | .08 |
| ☐ 33 Curtis Enis | .25 | .08 |
| ☐ 34 Cade McNown | .60 | .25 |
| ☐ 35 Marcus Robinson | .60 | .25 |
| ☐ 36 Bobby Engram | .25 | .08 |
| ☐ 37 Eddie Kennison | .25 | .08 |
| ☐ 38 Akili Smith | .40 | .15 |
| ☐ 39 Carl Pickens | .40 | .15 |
| ☐ 40 Corey Dillon | .60 | .25 |
| ☐ 41 Damay Scott | .40 | .15 |
| ☐ 42 Errict Rhett | .40 | .15 |
| ☐ 43 Karim Abdul-Jabbar | .40 | .15 |
| ☐ 44 Tim Couch | .40 | .15 |
| ☐ 45 Kevin Johnson | .60 | .25 |

| | | |
|---|---|---|
| ☐ 46 Darrin Chiaverini | .25 | .08 |
| ☐ 47 Terry Kirby | .25 | .08 |
| ☐ 48 Jason Tucker | .25 | .08 |
| ☐ 49 Rocket Ismail | .40 | .15 |
| ☐ 50 Joey Galloway | .40 | .15 |
| ☐ 51 Michael Irvin | .40 | .15 |
| ☐ 52 Troy Aikman | 1.25 | .50 |
| ☐ 53 Emmitt Smith | 1.25 | .50 |
| ☐ 54 David LaFleur | .25 | .08 |
| ☐ 55 Trevor Pryce | .25 | .08 |
| ☐ 56 Brian Griese | .60 | .25 |
| ☐ 57 Olandis Gary | .60 | .25 |
| ☐ 58 Terrell Davis | .60 | .25 |
| ☐ 59 Rod Smith | .40 | .15 |
| ☐ 60 Ed McCaffrey | .60 | .25 |
| ☐ 61 Gus Frerotte | .25 | .08 |
| ☐ 62 Jason Elam | .25 | .08 |
| ☐ 63 Kavika Pittman | .25 | .08 |
| ☐ 64 James Stewart | .40 | .15 |
| ☐ 65 Charlie Batch | .60 | .25 |
| ☐ 66 Johnnie Morton | .40 | .15 |
| ☐ 67 Herman Moore | .40 | .15 |
| ☐ 68 Germane Crowell | .25 | .08 |
| ☐ 69 Barry Sanders | 1.50 | .60 |
| ☐ 70 Chris Claiborne | .25 | .08 |
| ☐ 71 Brett Favre | 2.00 | .75 |
| ☐ 72 Antonio Freeman | .60 | .25 |
| ☐ 73 Dorsey Levens | .40 | .15 |
| ☐ 74 De'Mond Parker | .25 | .08 |
| ☐ 75 Corey Bradford | .40 | .15 |
| ☐ 76 Basil Mitchell | .25 | .08 |
| ☐ 77 Bill Schroeder | .40 | .15 |
| ☐ 78 Peyton Manning | 1.50 | .60 |
| ☐ 79 Marvin Harrison | .60 | .25 |
| ☐ 80 Terrence Wilkins | .25 | .08 |
| ☐ 81 Edgerrin James | 1.00 | .40 |
| ☐ 82 E.G. Green | .25 | .08 |
| ☐ 83 Chad Bratzke | .25 | .08 |
| ☐ 84 Mark Brunell | .60 | .25 |
| ☐ 85 Fred Taylor | .60 | .25 |
| ☐ 86 Jimmy Smith | .40 | .15 |
| ☐ 87 Keenan McCardell | .40 | .15 |
| ☐ 88 Kevin Hardy | .25 | .08 |
| ☐ 89 Aaron Beasley | .25 | .08 |
| ☐ 90 Elvis Grbac | .40 | .15 |
| ☐ 91 Derrick Alexander | .40 | .15 |
| ☐ 92 Tony Gonzalez | .40 | .15 |
| ☐ 93 Donnell Bennett | .25 | .08 |
| ☐ 94 Warren Moon | .60 | .25 |
| ☐ 95 Andre Rison | .40 | .15 |
| ☐ 96 James Hasty | .25 | .08 |
| ☐ 97 Dan Marino | 2.00 | .75 |
| ☐ 98 Thurman Thomas | .40 | .15 |
| ☐ 99 James Johnson | .25 | .08 |
| ☐ 100 O.J. McDuffie | .40 | .15 |
| ☐ 101 Tony Martin | .40 | .15 |
| ☐ 102 Oronde Gadsden | .40 | .15 |
| ☐ 103 Zach Thomas | .60 | .25 |
| ☐ 104 Sam Madison | .25 | .08 |
| ☐ 105 Jay Fiedler | .60 | .25 |
| ☐ 106 Damon Huard | .60 | .25 |
| ☐ 107 Robert Smith | .60 | .25 |
| ☐ 108 Leroy Hoard | .25 | .08 |
| ☐ 109 Randy Moss | 1.25 | .50 |
| ☐ 110 Cris Carter | .60 | .25 |
| ☐ 111 Daunte Culpepper | .75 | .30 |
| ☐ 112 John Randle | .40 | .15 |
| ☐ 113 Randall Cunningham | .60 | .25 |
| ☐ 114 Gary Anderson | .25 | .08 |
| ☐ 115 Drew Bledsoe DP | .75 | .30 |
| ☐ 116 Terry Glenn | .40 | .15 |
| ☐ 117 Kevin Faulk | .40 | .15 |
| ☐ 118 Terry Allen SP | 15.00 | 7.50 |
| ☐ 119 Adam Vinatieri | .60 | .25 |
| ☐ 120 Ty Law | .40 | .15 |
| ☐ 121 Lawyer Milloy | .40 | .15 |
| ☐ 122 Troy Brown | .40 | .15 |
| ☐ 123 Ben Coates | .25 | .08 |
| ☐ 124 Cam Cleeland | .25 | .08 |
| ☐ 125 Jeff Blake | .40 | .15 |
| ☐ 126 Ricky Williams | .60 | .25 |
| ☐ 127 Jake Reed | .40 | .15 |
| ☐ 128 Jake Delhomme RC | 2.50 | 1.00 |
| ☐ 129 Andrew Glover | .25 | .08 |
| ☐ 130 Keith Poole | .25 | .08 |

|  |  | | |
|---|---|---|---|
| ❏ 131 | Joe Horn | .40 | .15 |
| ❏ 132 | Kerry Collins | .40 | .15 |
| ❏ 133 | Joe Montgomery | .25 | .08 |
| ❏ 134 | Sean Bennett | .25 | .08 |
| ❏ 135 | Amani Toomer | .25 | .08 |
| ❏ 136 | Ike Hilliard | .40 | .15 |
| ❏ 137 | Joe Jurevicius | .25 | .08 |
| ❏ 138 | Tiki Barber | .60 | .25 |
| ❏ 139 | Victor Green | .25 | .08 |
| ❏ 140 | Ray Lucas | .40 | .15 |
| ❏ 141 | Vinny Testaverde | .40 | .15 |
| ❏ 142 | Curtis Martin | .60 | .25 |
| ❏ 143 | Wayne Chrebet | .40 | .15 |
| ❏ 144 | Tyrone Wheatley | .40 | .15 |
| ❏ 145 | Rich Gannon | .60 | .25 |
| ❏ 146 | Napoleon Kaufman | .40 | .15 |
| ❏ 147 | Tim Brown | .60 | .25 |
| ❏ 148 | Rickey Dudley | .25 | .08 |
| ❏ 149 | Charles Woodson | .60 | .25 |
| ❏ 150 | James Jett | .40 | .15 |
| ❏ 151 | Duce Staley | .60 | .25 |
| ❏ 152 | Charles Johnson | .40 | .15 |
| ❏ 153 | Donovan McNabb | 1.00 | .40 |
| ❏ 154 | Troy Vincent | .25 | .08 |
| ❏ 155 | Troy Edwards | .25 | .08 |
| ❏ 156 | Jerome Bettis | .60 | .25 |
| ❏ 157 | Kordell Stewart | .25 | .08 |
| ❏ 158 | Richard Huntley | .25 | .08 |
| ❏ 159 | Hines Ward | .60 | .25 |
| ❏ 160 | Levon Kirkland | .25 | .08 |
| ❏ 161 | Ryan Leaf | .40 | .15 |
| ❏ 162 | Jim Harbaugh | .40 | .15 |
| ❏ 163 | Jermaine Fazande | .25 | .08 |
| ❏ 164 | Natrone Means | .25 | .08 |
| ❏ 165 | Junior Seau | .60 | .25 |
| ❏ 166 | Curtis Conway | .40 | .15 |
| ❏ 167 | Freddie Jones | .25 | .08 |
| ❏ 168 | Jeff Graham | .25 | .08 |
| ❏ 169 | Terrell Owens | .60 | .25 |
| ❏ 170 | Jeff Garcia | .60 | .25 |
| ❏ 171 | Jerry Rice | 1.25 | .50 |
| ❏ 172 | Steve Young | .75 | .30 |
| ❏ 173 | Garrison Hearst | .40 | .15 |
| ❏ 174 | Charlie Garner | .40 | .15 |
| ❏ 175 | Fred Beasley | .25 | .08 |
| ❏ 176 | Bryant Young | .25 | .08 |
| ❏ 177 | Derrick Mayes | .40 | .15 |
| ❏ 178 | Sean Dawkins | .25 | .08 |
| ❏ 179 | Jon Kitna | .60 | .25 |
| ❏ 180 | Ricky Watters | .40 | .15 |
| ❏ 181 | Charlie Rogers | .25 | .08 |
| ❏ 182 | Kurt Warner | 1.25 | .50 |
| ❏ 183 | Marshall Faulk | .75 | .30 |
| ❏ 184 | Isaac Bruce | .60 | .25 |
| ❏ 185 | Az-Zahir Hakim | .40 | .15 |
| ❏ 186 | Trent Green | .25 | .08 |
| ❏ 187 | Jeff Wilkins | .25 | .08 |
| ❏ 188 | Torry Holt | .60 | .25 |
| ❏ 189 | London Fletcher RC | .40 | .15 |
| ❏ 190 | Robert Holcombe | .25 | .08 |
| ❏ 191 | Todd Lyght | .25 | .08 |
| ❏ 192 | Keyshawn Johnson | .25 | .08 |
| ❏ 193 | Derrick Brooks | .25 | .08 |
| ❏ 194 | Warren Sapp | .40 | .15 |
| ❏ 195 | Shaun King | .60 | .25 |
| ❏ 196 | Warrick Dunn | .60 | .25 |
| ❏ 197 | Mike Alstott | .60 | .25 |
| ❏ 198 | Jacquez Green | .25 | .08 |
| ❏ 199 | Reidel Anthony | .25 | .08 |
| ❏ 200 | Martin Gramatica | .25 | .08 |
| ❏ 201 | Donnie Abraham | .25 | .08 |
| ❏ 202 | Steve McNair | .60 | .25 |
| ❏ 203 | Eddie George | .60 | .25 |
| ❏ 204 | Jevon Kearse | .60 | .25 |
| ❏ 205 | Frank Wycheck | .25 | .08 |
| ❏ 206 | Kevin Dyson | .40 | .15 |
| ❏ 207 | Yancey Thigpen | .25 | .08 |
| ❏ 208 | Al Del Greco | .25 | .08 |
| ❏ 209 | Jeff George | .40 | .15 |
| ❏ 210 | Adrian Murrell | .25 | .08 |
| ❏ 211 | Brad Johnson | .25 | .08 |
| ❏ 212 | Stephen Davis | .60 | .25 |
| ❏ 213 | Stephen Alexander | .25 | .08 |
| ❏ 214 | Michael Westbrook | .40 | .15 |
| ❏ 215 | Darrell Green | .25 | .08 |
| ❏ 216 | Champ Bailey | .60 | .25 |
| ❏ 217 | Albert Connell | .25 | .08 |
| ❏ 218 | Larry Centers | .25 | .08 |
| ❏ 219 | Bruce Smith | .40 | .15 |
| ❏ 220 | Deion Sanders | .60 | .25 |
| ❏ 221 | Ricky Williams SS | .60 | .25 |
| ❏ 222 | Edgerrin James SS | 1.00 | .40 |
| ❏ 223 | Tim Couch SS | .40 | .15 |
| ❏ 224 | Cade McNown SS | .30 | .10 |
| ❏ 225 | Olandis Gary SS | .75 | .30 |
| ❏ 226 | Torry Holt SS | .75 | .30 |
| ❏ 227 | Donovan McNabb SS | 1.00 | .40 |
| ❏ 228 | Shaun King SS | .25 | .08 |
| ❏ 229 | Kevin Johnson SS | .75 | .30 |
| ❏ 230 | Kurt Warner SS | 1.50 | .60 |
| ❏ 231 | Tony Gonzalez AP | .50 | .20 |
| ❏ 232 | Frank Wycheck AP | .30 | .10 |
| ❏ 233 | Eddie George AP | .75 | .30 |
| ❏ 234 | Mark Brunell AP | .75 | .30 |
| ❏ 235 | Corey Dillon AP | .75 | .30 |
| ❏ 236 | Peyton Manning AP | 2.00 | .75 |
| ❏ 237 | Keyshawn Johnson AP | .75 | .30 |
| ❏ 238 | Rich Gannon AP | .75 | .30 |
| ❏ 239 | Terry Glenn AP | .50 | .20 |
| ❏ 240 | Tony Brackens AP | .30 | .10 |
| ❏ 241 | Edgerrin James AP | 1.00 | .40 |
| ❏ 242 | Tim Brown AP | .75 | .30 |
| ❏ 243 | Michael Strahan AP | .50 | .20 |
| ❏ 244 | Kurt Warner AP | 1.50 | .60 |
| ❏ 245 | Brad Johnson AP | .75 | .30 |
| ❏ 246 | Aeneas Williams AP | .30 | .10 |
| ❏ 247 | Marshall Faulk AP | 1.00 | .40 |
| ❏ 248 | Dexter Coakley AP | .30 | .10 |
| ❏ 249 | Warren Sapp AP | .50 | .20 |
| ❏ 250 | Mike Alstott AP | .75 | .30 |
| ❏ 251 | David Sloan AP | .30 | .10 |
| ❏ 252 | Cris Carter AP | .75 | .30 |
| ❏ 253 | Muhsin Muhammad AP | .75 | .30 |
| ❏ 254 | Isaac Bruce AP | .75 | .30 |
| ❏ 255 | Wesley Walls AP | .30 | .10 |
| ❏ 256 | Steve Beuerlein LL | .50 | .20 |
| ❏ 257 | Kurt Warner LL | 1.50 | .60 |
| ❏ 258 | Peyton Manning LL | 2.00 | .75 |
| ❏ 259 | Brad Johnson LL | .75 | .30 |
| ❏ 260 | Edgerrin James LL | 1.00 | .40 |
| ❏ 261 | Curtis Martin LL | .75 | .30 |
| ❏ 262 | Stephen Davis LL | .75 | .30 |
| ❏ 263 | Emmitt Smith LL | 1.50 | .60 |
| ❏ 264 | Marvin Harrison LL | .75 | .30 |
| ❏ 265 | Jimmy Smith LL | .50 | .20 |
| ❏ 266 | Randy Moss LL | 1.50 | .60 |
| ❏ 267 | Marcus Robinson LL | .75 | .30 |
| ❏ 268 | Kevin Carter LL | .30 | .10 |
| ❏ 269 | Simeon Rice LL | .50 | .20 |
| ❏ 270 | Robert Porcher LL | .30 | .10 |
| ❏ 271 | Jevon Kearse LL | .75 | .30 |
| ❏ 272 | Mike Vanderjagt LL | .30 | .10 |
| ❏ 273 | Olindo Mare LL | .30 | .10 |
| ❏ 274 | Todd Peterson LL | .30 | .10 |
| ❏ 275 | Mike Hollis LL | .30 | .10 |
| ❏ 276 | Mike Anderson RC/500 | 20.00 | 8.00 |
| ❏ 277 | Peter Warrick RC | 2.00 | .75 |
| ❏ 278 | Courtney Brown RC | .75 | .30 |
| ❏ 279 | Plaxico Burress RC | 4.00 | 1.50 |
| ❏ 280 | Corey Simon RC | .75 | .30 |
| ❏ 281 | Thomas Jones RC | 3.00 | 1.25 |
| ❏ 282 | Travis Taylor RC | .75 | .30 |
| ❏ 283 | Shaun Alexander RC | 6.00 | 2.50 |
| ❏ 284 | Patrick Pass RC/500 | 15.00 | 6.00 |
| ❏ 285 | Chris Redman RC | .50 | .20 |
| ❏ 286 | Chad Pennington RC | 5.00 | 2.00 |
| ❏ 287 | Jamal Lewis RC | 5.00 | 2.00 |
| ❏ 288 | Brian Urlacher RC | 8.00 | 3.00 |
| ❏ 289 | Bubba Franks RC | 2.00 | .75 |
| ❏ 290 | Dez White RC | 2.00 | .75 |
| ❏ 291 | Frank Moreau RC/500 | 15.00 | 6.00 |
| ❏ 292 | Ron Dayne RC | 2.00 | .75 |
| ❏ 293 | Sylvester Morris RC | .50 | .20 |
| ❏ 294 | R.Jay Soward RC | 1.50 | .60 |
| ❏ 295 | Curtis Keaton RC | 1.50 | .60 |
| ❏ 296 | Spergon Wynn RC/500 | 15.00 | 6.00 |
| ❏ 297 | Rondell Mealey RC | 1.50 | .60 |
| ❏ 298 | Travis Prentice RC | 1.50 | .60 |
| ❏ 299 | Darrell Jackson RC | 4.00 | 1.50 |
| ❏ 300 | Giovanni Carmazzi RC | 1.50 | .60 |
| ❏ 301 | Anthony Lucas RC | 1.50 | .60 |
| ❏ 302 | Danny Farmer RC | 1.50 | .60 |
| ❏ 303 | Dennis Northcutt RC | 2.00 | .75 |
| ❏ 304 | Troy Walters RC | 2.00 | .75 |
| ❏ 305 | Laveranues Coles RC | 2.50 | 1.00 |
| ❏ 306 | Kwame Cavil RC | 1.50 | .60 |
| ❏ 307 | Tee Martin RC | 2.00 | .75 |
| ❏ 308 | J.R. Redmond RC | 1.50 | .60 |
| ❏ 309 | Tim Rattay RC | 2.00 | .75 |
| ❏ 310 | Jerry Porter RC | 2.50 | 1.00 |
| ❏ 311 | Michael Wiley RC | 1.50 | .60 |
| ❏ 312 | Reuben Droughns RC | 2.50 | 1.00 |
| ❏ 313 | Trung Canidate RC | 1.50 | .60 |
| ❏ 314 | Shyrone Stith RC | 1.50 | .60 |
| ❏ 315 | Marc Bulger RC | 4.00 | 1.50 |
| ❏ 316 | Tom Brady RC | 40.00 | 20.00 |
| ❏ 317 | Doug Johnson RC | 2.00 | .75 |
| ❏ 318 | Todd Husak RC | 2.00 | .75 |
| ❏ 319 | Gari Scott RC | 1.50 | .60 |
| ❏ 320 | Windrell Hayes RC/500 | 15.00 | 6.00 |
| ❏ 321 | Chris Cole RC | 1.50 | .60 |
| ❏ 322 | Sammy Morris RC | 2.00 | .75 |
| ❏ 323 | Trevor Gaylor RC | 1.50 | .60 |
| ❏ 324 | Jarious Jackson RC | 1.50 | .60 |
| ❏ 325 | Doug Chapman RC/500 | 15.00 | 6.00 |
| ❏ 326 | Ron Dugans RC | 1.50 | .60 |
| ❏ 327 | Ron Dixon RC/500 | 15.00 | 6.00 |
| ❏ 328 | Joe Hamilton RC | 1.50 | .60 |
| ❏ 329 | Todd Pinkston RC | 2.00 | .75 |
| ❏ 330 | Chad Morton RC | 2.00 | .75 |

## 2001 Score

| | | | |
|---|---|---|---|
| | COMPLETE SET (330) | 80.00 | 40.00 |
| | COMP.SET w/o SPs (220) | 25.00 | 10.00 |
| ❏ 1 | David Boston | .50 | .20 |
| ❏ 2 | Frank Sanders | .20 | .07 |
| ❏ 3 | Jake Plummer | .30 | .10 |
| ❏ 4 | Michael Pittman | .20 | .07 |
| ❏ 5 | Rob Moore | .20 | .07 |
| ❏ 6 | Thomas Jones | .30 | .10 |
| ❏ 7 | Chris Chandler | .30 | .10 |
| ❏ 8 | Doug Johnson | .20 | .07 |
| ❏ 9 | Jamal Anderson | .50 | .20 |
| ❏ 10 | Tim Dwight | .50 | .20 |
| ❏ 11 | Brandon Stokley | .30 | .10 |
| ❏ 12 | Chris Redman | .20 | .07 |
| ❏ 13 | Jamal Lewis | .75 | .30 |
| ❏ 14 | Qadry Ismail | .30 | .10 |
| ❏ 15 | Ray Lewis | .50 | .20 |
| ❏ 16 | Rod Woodson | .30 | .10 |
| ❏ 17 | Shannon Sharpe | .30 | .10 |
| ❏ 18 | Travis Taylor | .30 | .10 |
| ❏ 19 | Trent Dilfer | .30 | .10 |
| ❏ 20 | Elvis Grbac | .30 | .10 |
| ❏ 21 | Eric Moulds | .30 | .10 |
| ❏ 22 | Jay Riemersma | .20 | .07 |
| ❏ 23 | Peerless Price | .30 | .10 |
| ❏ 24 | Rob Johnson | .30 | .10 |
| ❏ 25 | Sam Cowart | .20 | .07 |
| ❏ 26 | Sammy Morris | .20 | .07 |
| ❏ 27 | Shawn Bryson | .20 | .07 |
| ❏ 28 | Donald Hayes | .20 | .07 |
| ❏ 29 | Muhsin Muhammad | .30 | .10 |
| ❏ 30 | Patrick Jeffers | .30 | .10 |
| ❏ 31 | Reggie White DE | .50 | .20 |
| ❏ 32 | Steve Beuerlein | .30 | .10 |
| ❏ 33 | Tim Biakabutuka | .30 | .10 |
| ❏ 34 | Wesley Walls | .20 | .07 |

|  |  | | |
|---|--------|---|---|
| ❏ 35 | Brian Urlacher | .75 | .30 |
| ❏ 36 | Cade McNown | .20 | .07 |
| ❏ 37 | Dez White | .20 | .07 |
| ❏ 38 | James Allen | .30 | .10 |
| ❏ 39 | Marcus Robinson | .50 | .20 |
| ❏ 40 | Marty Booker | .20 | .07 |
| ❏ 41 | Akili Smith | .20 | .07 |
| ❏ 42 | Corey Dillon | .50 | .20 |
| ❏ 43 | Danny Farmer | .20 | .07 |
| ❏ 44 | Peter Warrick | .50 | .20 |
| ❏ 45 | Ron Dugans | .20 | .07 |
| ❏ 46 | Takeo Spikes | .20 | .07 |
| ❏ 47 | Courtney Brown | .30 | .10 |
| ❏ 48 | Dennis Northcutt | .30 | .10 |
| ❏ 49 | JaJuan Dawson | .20 | .07 |
| ❏ 50 | Kevin Johnson | .30 | .10 |
| ❏ 51 | Tim Couch | .30 | .10 |
| ❏ 52 | Travis Prentice | .20 | .07 |
| ❏ 53 | Anthony Wright | .20 | .07 |
| ❏ 54 | Emmitt Smith | 1.00 | .40 |
| ❏ 55 | James McKnight | .30 | .10 |
| ❏ 56 | Joey Galloway | .30 | .10 |
| ❏ 57 | Rocket Ismail | .30 | .10 |
| ❏ 58 | Randall Cunningham | .50 | .20 |
| ❏ 59 | Troy Aikman | .75 | .30 |
| ❏ 60 | Brian Griese | .50 | .20 |
| ❏ 61 | Ed McCaffrey | .50 | .20 |
| ❏ 62 | Gus Frerotte | .20 | .07 |
| ❏ 63 | John Elway | 1.50 | .60 |
| ❏ 64 | Mike Anderson | .50 | .20 |
| ❏ 65 | Olandis Gary | .30 | .10 |
| ❏ 66 | Rod Smith | .30 | .10 |
| ❏ 67 | Terrell Davis | .50 | .20 |
| ❏ 68 | Barry Sanders | 1.00 | .40 |
| ❏ 69 | Charlie Batch | .50 | .20 |
| ❏ 70 | Germane Crowell | .20 | .07 |
| ❏ 71 | Herman Moore | .30 | .10 |
| ❏ 72 | James Stewart | .30 | .10 |
| ❏ 73 | Johnnie Morton | .30 | .10 |
| ❏ 74 | Robert Porcher | .20 | .07 |
| ❏ 75 | Jim Harbaugh | .30 | .10 |
| ❏ 76 | Ahman Green | .50 | .20 |
| ❏ 77 | Antonio Freeman | .50 | .20 |
| ❏ 78 | Bill Schroeder | .20 | .07 |
| ❏ 79 | Brett Favre | 1.50 | .60 |
| ❏ 80 | Bubba Franks | .30 | .10 |
| ❏ 81 | Dorsey Levens | .30 | .10 |
| ❏ 82 | E.G. Green | .20 | .07 |
| ❏ 83 | Edgerrin James | .60 | .25 |
| ❏ 84 | Jerome Pathon | .30 | .10 |
| ❏ 85 | Ken Dilger | .20 | .07 |
| ❏ 86 | Marcus Pollard | .20 | .07 |
| ❏ 87 | Marvin Harrison | .50 | .20 |
| ❏ 88 | Peyton Manning | 1.25 | .50 |
| ❏ 89 | Terrence Wilkins | .20 | .07 |
| ❏ 90 | Fred Taylor | .50 | .20 |
| ❏ 91 | Hardy Nickerson | .20 | .07 |
| ❏ 92 | Jimmy Smith | .30 | .10 |
| ❏ 93 | Keenan McCardell | .30 | .10 |
| ❏ 94 | Kyle Brady | .20 | .07 |
| ❏ 95 | Mark Brunell | .50 | .20 |
| ❏ 96 | Tony Brackens | .20 | .07 |
| ❏ 97 | Derrick Alexander | .30 | .10 |
| ❏ 98 | Sylvester Morris | .20 | .07 |
| ❏ 99 | Tony Gonzalez | .30 | .10 |
| ❏ 100 | Tony Richardson | .20 | .07 |
| ❏ 101 | Kimble Anders | .20 | .07 |
| ❏ 102 | Warren Moon | .50 | .20 |
| ❏ 103 | Dan Marino | 1.50 | .60 |
| ❏ 104 | Jay Fiedler | .50 | .20 |
| ❏ 105 | Lamar Smith | .30 | .10 |
| ❏ 106 | O.J. McDuffie | .20 | .07 |
| ❏ 107 | Oronde Gadsden | .30 | .10 |
| ❏ 108 | Sam Madison | .20 | .07 |
| ❏ 109 | Thurman Thomas | .20 | .07 |
| ❏ 110 | Tony Martin | .20 | .07 |
| ❏ 111 | Zach Thomas | .50 | .20 |
| ❏ 112 | Cris Carter | .50 | .20 |
| ❏ 113 | Daunte Culpepper | .50 | .20 |
| ❏ 114 | Matthew Hatchette | .20 | .07 |
| ❏ 115 | Randy Moss | 1.00 | .40 |
| ❏ 116 | Robert Smith | .50 | .20 |
| ❏ 117 | Drew Bledsoe | .60 | .25 |
| ❏ 118 | J.R. Redmond | .20 | .07 |
| ❏ 119 | Kevin Faulk | .30 | .10 |
| ❏ 120 | Michael Bishop | .20 | .07 |
| ❏ 121 | Terry Glenn | .30 | .10 |
| ❏ 122 | Troy Brown | .30 | .10 |
| ❏ 123 | Ty Law | .20 | .07 |
| ❏ 124 | Aaron Brooks | .50 | .20 |
| ❏ 125 | Darren Howard | .20 | .07 |
| ❏ 126 | Jake Reed | .30 | .10 |
| ❏ 127 | Jeff Blake | .30 | .10 |
| ❏ 128 | Joe Horn | .30 | .10 |
| ❏ 129 | La'Roi Glover | .20 | .07 |
| ❏ 130 | Ricky Williams | .50 | .20 |
| ❏ 131 | Willie Jackson | .20 | .07 |
| ❏ 132 | Albert Connell | .20 | .07 |
| ❏ 133 | Amani Toomer | .20 | .07 |
| ❏ 134 | Ike Hilliard | .30 | .10 |
| ❏ 135 | Jason Sehorn | .20 | .07 |
| ❏ 136 | Jessie Armstead | .20 | .07 |
| ❏ 137 | Kerry Collins | .30 | .10 |
| ❏ 138 | Michael Strahan | .30 | .10 |
| ❏ 139 | Ron Dayne | .50 | .20 |
| ❏ 140 | Ron Dixon | .20 | .07 |
| ❏ 141 | Tiki Barber | .50 | .20 |
| ❏ 142 | Anthony Becht | .20 | .07 |
| ❏ 143 | Chad Pennington | .75 | .30 |
| ❏ 144 | Curtis Martin | .50 | .20 |
| ❏ 145 | Dedric Ward | .20 | .07 |
| ❏ 146 | Laveranues Coles | .50 | .20 |
| ❏ 147 | Vinny Testaverde | .30 | .10 |
| ❏ 148 | Wayne Chrebet | .30 | .10 |
| ❏ 149 | Andre Rison | .30 | .10 |
| ❏ 150 | Charles Woodson | .20 | .07 |
| ❏ 151 | Darrell Russell | .20 | .07 |
| ❏ 152 | Napoleon Kaufman | .30 | .10 |
| ❏ 153 | Rich Gannon | .50 | .20 |
| ❏ 154 | Tim Brown | .50 | .20 |
| ❏ 155 | Tyrone Wheatley | .30 | .10 |
| ❏ 156 | Chad Lewis | .20 | .07 |
| ❏ 157 | Charles Johnson | .20 | .07 |
| ❏ 158 | Donovan McNabb | .60 | .25 |
| ❏ 159 | Duce Staley | .50 | .20 |
| ❏ 160 | Hugh Douglas | .20 | .07 |
| ❏ 161 | Na Brown | .20 | .07 |
| ❏ 162 | Todd Pinkston | .20 | .07 |
| ❏ 163 | James Thrash | .30 | .10 |
| ❏ 164 | Bobby Shaw | .20 | .07 |
| ❏ 165 | Hines Ward | .50 | .20 |
| ❏ 166 | Jerome Bettis | .50 | .20 |
| ❏ 167 | Kordell Stewart | .30 | .10 |
| ❏ 168 | Levon Kirkland | .20 | .07 |
| ❏ 169 | Plaxico Burress | .50 | .20 |
| ❏ 170 | Richard Huntley | .20 | .07 |
| ❏ 171 | Troy Edwards | .20 | .07 |
| ❏ 172 | Jeff Graham | .20 | .07 |
| ❏ 173 | Junior Seau | .30 | .10 |
| ❏ 174 | Doug Flutie | .50 | .20 |
| ❏ 175 | Charlie Garner | .30 | .10 |
| ❏ 176 | Jeff Garcia | .50 | .20 |
| ❏ 177 | Jerry Rice | 1.00 | .40 |
| ❏ 178 | Steve Young | .50 | .20 |
| ❏ 179 | Terrell Owens | .50 | .20 |
| ❏ 180 | Brock Huard | .20 | .07 |
| ❏ 181 | Darrell Jackson | .50 | .20 |
| ❏ 182 | Derrick Mayes | .30 | .10 |
| ❏ 183 | Ricky Watters | .30 | .10 |
| ❏ 184 | Shaun Alexander | .60 | .25 |
| ❏ 185 | Matt Hasselbeck | .30 | .10 |
| ❏ 186 | John Randle | .30 | .10 |
| ❏ 187 | Az-Zahir Hakim | .20 | .07 |
| ❏ 188 | Isaac Bruce | .50 | .20 |
| ❏ 189 | Kurt Warner | 1.00 | .40 |
| ❏ 190 | Marshall Faulk | .60 | .25 |
| ❏ 191 | Torry Holt | .50 | .20 |
| ❏ 192 | Trent Green | .30 | .10 |
| ❏ 193 | Derrick Brooks | .20 | .07 |
| ❏ 194 | Jacquez Green | .20 | .07 |
| ❏ 195 | John Lynch | .30 | .10 |
| ❏ 196 | Keyshawn Johnson | .50 | .20 |
| ❏ 197 | Mike Alstott | .50 | .20 |
| ❏ 198 | Reidel Anthony | .20 | .07 |
| ❏ 199 | Shaun King | .30 | .10 |
| ❏ 200 | Warren Sapp | .30 | .10 |
| ❏ 201 | Warrick Dunn | .50 | .20 |
| ❏ 202 | Ryan Leaf | .30 | .10 |
| ❏ 203 | Carl Pickens | .30 | .10 |
| ❏ 204 | Derrick Mason | .30 | .10 |
| ❏ 205 | Eddie George | .50 | .20 |
| ❏ 206 | Frank Wycheck | .20 | .07 |
| ❏ 207 | Jevon Kearse | .30 | .10 |
| ❏ 208 | Neil O'Donnell | .20 | .07 |
| ❏ 209 | Steve McNair | .50 | .20 |
| ❏ 210 | Yancey Thigpen | .20 | .07 |
| ❏ 211 | Andre Reed | .30 | .10 |
| ❏ 212 | Brad Johnson | .50 | .20 |
| ❏ 213 | Bruce Smith | .30 | .10 |
| ❏ 214 | Champ Bailey | .50 | .20 |
| ❏ 215 | Darrell Green | .20 | .07 |
| ❏ 216 | Deion Sanders | .50 | .20 |
| ❏ 217 | Irving Fryar | .30 | .10 |
| ❏ 218 | Jeff George | .30 | .10 |
| ❏ 219 | Michael Westbrook | .20 | .07 |
| ❏ 220 | Stephen Davis | .50 | .20 |
| ❏ 221 | Terrell Owens AP | 1.00 | .40 |
| ❏ 222 | Peyton Manning AP | 2.50 | 1.00 |
| ❏ 223 | Stephen Davis AP | 1.00 | .40 |
| ❏ 224 | Marvin Harrison AP | 1.00 | .40 |
| ❏ 225 | Donovan McNabb AP | 1.25 | .50 |
| ❏ 226 | Edgerrin James AP | 1.25 | .50 |
| ❏ 227 | Eric Moulds AP | .60 | .25 |
| ❏ 228 | Daunte Culpepper AP | 1.00 | .40 |
| ❏ 229 | Eddie George AP | 1.00 | .40 |
| ❏ 230 | Cris Carter AP | 1.00 | .40 |
| ❏ 231 | Rich Gannon AP | 1.00 | .40 |
| ❏ 232 | Jeff Garcia AP | 1.00 | .40 |
| ❏ 233 | Jimmy Smith | .60 | .25 |
| ❏ 234 | Tony Gonzalez AP | .60 | .25 |
| ❏ 235 | Torry Holt AP | 1.00 | .40 |
| ❏ 236 | Jevon Kearse AP | .60 | .25 |
| ❏ 237 | Ray Lewis AP | 1.00 | .40 |
| ❏ 238 | Warren Sapp AP | .60 | .25 |
| ❏ 239 | Brian Urlacher AP | 1.50 | .60 |
| ❏ 240 | Champ Bailey AP | .60 | .25 |
| ❏ 241 | Peyton Manning LL | 2.50 | 1.00 |
| ❏ 242 | Jeff Garcia LL | 1.00 | .40 |
| ❏ 243 | Elvis Grbac LL | .60 | .25 |
| ❏ 244 | Daunte Culpepper LL | 1.00 | .40 |
| ❏ 245 | Brett Favre LL | 3.00 | 1.25 |
| ❏ 246 | Edgerrin James LL | 1.25 | .50 |
| ❏ 247 | Robert Smith LL | .60 | .25 |
| ❏ 248 | Eddie George LL | 1.00 | .40 |
| ❏ 249 | Mike Anderson LL | 1.00 | .40 |
| ❏ 250 | Corey Dillon LL | 1.00 | .40 |
| ❏ 251 | Torry Holt LL | 1.00 | .40 |
| ❏ 252 | Rod Smith LL | .60 | .25 |
| ❏ 253 | Isaac Bruce LL | 1.00 | .40 |
| ❏ 254 | Terrell Owens LL | 1.00 | .40 |
| ❏ 255 | Randy Moss LL | 2.00 | .75 |
| ❏ 256 | La'Roi Glover LL | .40 | .15 |
| ❏ 257 | Trace Armstrong LL | .40 | .15 |
| ❏ 258 | Warren Sapp LL | .60 | .25 |
| ❏ 259 | Hugh Douglas LL | .40 | .15 |
| ❏ 260 | Jason Taylor LL | .40 | .15 |
| ❏ 261 | Mike Anderson SS | 1.00 | .40 |
| ❏ 262 | Jamal Lewis SS | 1.25 | .50 |
| ❏ 263 | Sylvester Morris SS | .40 | .15 |
| ❏ 264 | Darrell Jackson SS | 1.00 | .40 |
| ❏ 265 | Peter Warrick SS | 1.00 | .40 |
| ❏ 266 | Ron Dayne SS | 1.00 | .40 |
| ❏ 267 | Shaun Alexander SS | 1.25 | .50 |
| ❏ 268 | Plaxico Burress SS | 1.00 | .40 |
| ❏ 269 | Brian Urlacher SS | 1.50 | .60 |
| ❏ 270 | Courtney Brown SS | .60 | .25 |
| ❏ 271 | Michael Vick RC | 5.00 | 2.00 |
| ❏ 272 | Drew Brees RC | 8.00 | 3.00 |
| ❏ 273 | Chris Weinke RC | 1.00 | .40 |
| ❏ 274 | Quincy Carter RC | 2.00 | .75 |
| ❏ 275 | Sage Rosenfels RC | 1.00 | .40 |
| ❏ 276 | Josh Heupel RC | 2.00 | .75 |
| ❏ 277 | David Rivers RC | 1.25 | .50 |
| ❏ 278 | Ben Leard RC | 1.25 | .50 |
| ❏ 279 | Marques Tuiasosopo RC | 2.00 | .75 |
| ❏ 280 | Mike McMahon RC | 2.00 | .75 |
| ❏ 281 | Deuce McAllister RC | 4.00 | 1.50 |
| ❏ 282 | LaMont Jordan RC | 4.00 | 1.50 |
| ❏ 283 | LaDainian Tomlinson RC | 20.00 | 8.00 |
| ❏ 284 | James Jackson RC | 2.00 | .75 |
| ❏ 285 | Anthony Thomas RC | 2.00 | .75 |
| ❏ 286 | Travis Henry RC | 2.00 | .75 |
| ❏ 287 | Travis Minor RC | 1.25 | .50 |
| ❏ 288 | Rudi Johnson RC | 4.00 | 1.50 |
| ❏ 289 | Michael Bennett RC | 2.00 | .75 |

| | | |
|---|---|---|
| 290 Kevan Barlow RC | 2.00 | .75 |
| 291 Reggie White RC | 1.25 | .50 |
| 292 Moran Norris RC | .75 | .30 |
| 293 Ja'Mar Toombs RC | 1.25 | .50 |
| 294 Heath Evans RC | 1.25 | .50 |
| 295 David Terrell RC | 2.00 | .75 |
| 296 Santana Moss RC | 3.00 | 1.25 |
| 297 Rod Gardner RC | 2.00 | .75 |
| 298 Quincy Morgan RC | 2.00 | .75 |
| 299 Freddie Mitchell RC | 2.00 | .75 |
| 300 Boo Williams RC | 1.25 | .50 |
| 301 Reggie Wayne RC | 4.00 | 1.50 |
| 302 Ronney Daniels RC | .75 | .30 |
| 303 Bobby Newcombe RC | 1.25 | .50 |
| 304 Vinny Sutherland RC | 1.25 | .50 |
| 305 Cedrick Wilson RC | 2.00 | .75 |
| 306 Robert Ferguson RC | 2.00 | .75 |
| 307 Ken-Yon Rambo RC | 1.25 | .50 |
| 308 Alex Bannister RC | 1.25 | .50 |
| 309 Koren Robinson RC | 2.00 | .75 |
| 310 Chad Johnson RC | 5.00 | 2.00 |
| 311 Chris Chambers RC | 3.00 | 1.25 |
| 312 Javon Green RC | 1.25 | .50 |
| 313 Snoop Minnis RC | 1.25 | .50 |
| 314 Scotty Anderson RC | 1.25 | .50 |
| 315 Todd Heap RC | 2.00 | .75 |
| 316 Alge Crumpler RC | 2.50 | 1.00 |
| 317 Marcellus Rivers RC | 1.25 | .50 |
| 318 Rashon Burns RC | .75 | .30 |
| 319 Jamal Reynolds RC | 2.00 | .75 |
| 320 Andre Carter RC | 2.00 | .75 |
| 321 Justin Smith RC | 2.00 | .75 |
| 322 Gerard Warren RC | 2.00 | .75 |
| 323 Tommy Polley RC | 2.00 | .75 |
| 324 Dan Morgan RC | 1.00 | .40 |
| 325 Torrance Marshall RC | 2.00 | .75 |
| 326 Correll Buckhalter RC | 2.50 | 1.00 |
| 327 Derrick Gibson RC | 1.25 | .50 |
| 328 Adam Archuleta RC | 2.00 | .75 |
| 329 Jamar Fletcher RC | 1.25 | .50 |
| 330 Nate Clements RC | 2.00 | .75 |

## 2002 Score

| | | |
|---|---|---|
| COMPLETE SET (330) | 50.00 | 20.00 |
| 1 David Boston | .50 | .20 |
| 2 Arnold Jackson | .20 | .07 |
| 3 MarTay Jenkins | .20 | .07 |
| 4 Thomas Jones | .30 | .10 |
| 5 Kwamie Lassiter | .20 | .07 |
| 6 Michael Pittman | .20 | .07 |
| 7 Jake Plummer | .30 | .10 |
| 8 Chris Chandler | .30 | .10 |
| 9 Alge Crumpler | .30 | .10 |
| 10 Terance Mathis | .20 | .07 |
| 11 Maurice Smith | .30 | .10 |
| 12 Ray Buchanan | .20 | .07 |
| 13 Jamal Anderson | .30 | .10 |
| 14 Keith Brooking | .20 | .07 |
| 15 Michael Vick | 1.00 | .40 |
| 16 Obafemi Ayanbadejo | .20 | .07 |
| 17 Jason Brookins | .20 | .07 |
| 18 Randall Cunningham | .20 | .07 |
| 19 Elvis Grbac | .20 | .07 |
| 20 Todd Heap | .20 | .07 |
| 21 Qadry Ismail | .20 | .07 |
| 22 Shannon Sharpe | .30 | .10 |
| 23 Travis Taylor | .30 | .10 |
| 24 Ray Lewis | .50 | .20 |
| 25 Jamal Lewis | .50 | .20 |
| 26 Larry Centers | .20 | .07 |
| 27 Rob Johnson | .30 | .10 |
| 28 Shawn Bryson | .20 | .07 |
| 29 Eric Moulds | .30 | .10 |
| 30 Peerless Price | .30 | .10 |
| 31 Nate Clements | .20 | .07 |
| 32 Travis Henry | .50 | .20 |
| 33 Isaac Byrd | .20 | .07 |
| 34 Nick Goings | .20 | .07 |
| 35 Donald Hayes | .20 | .07 |
| 36 Richard Huntley | .20 | .07 |
| 37 Muhsin Muhammad | .30 | .10 |
| 38 Steve Smith | .50 | .20 |
| 39 Wesley Walls | .20 | .07 |
| 40 Chris Weinke | .30 | .10 |
| 41 James Allen | .30 | .10 |
| 42 Marty Booker | .20 | .07 |
| 43 Jim Miller | .20 | .07 |
| 44 David Terrell | .50 | .20 |
| 45 Dez White | .20 | .07 |
| 46 Brian Urlacher | .75 | .30 |
| 47 Mike Brown | .50 | .20 |
| 48 Anthony Thomas | .30 | .10 |
| 49 T.J. Houshmandzadeh | .30 | .10 |
| 50 Chad Johnson | .50 | .20 |
| 51 Darnay Scott | .20 | .07 |
| 52 Peter Warrick | .30 | .10 |
| 53 Akili Smith | .20 | .07 |
| 54 Jon Kitna | .30 | .10 |
| 55 Justin Smith | .20 | .07 |
| 56 Corey Dillon | .30 | .10 |
| 57 Benjamin Gay | .30 | .10 |
| 58 Kevin Johnson | .30 | .10 |
| 59 Quincy Morgan | .20 | .07 |
| 60 James Jackson | .20 | .07 |
| 61 Anthony Henry | .20 | .07 |
| 62 Gerard Warren | .20 | .07 |
| 63 Jamir Miller | .20 | .07 |
| 64 Tim Couch | .30 | .10 |
| 65 Quincy Carter | .30 | .10 |
| 66 Joey Galloway | .30 | .10 |
| 67 Troy Hambrick | .20 | .07 |
| 68 Rocket Ismail | .30 | .10 |
| 69 Dexter Coakley | .20 | .07 |
| 70 Darren Woodson | .20 | .07 |
| 71 Emmitt Smith | 1.25 | .50 |
| 72 Mike Anderson | .50 | .20 |
| 73 Terrell Davis | .50 | .20 |
| 74 Kevin Kasper | .20 | .07 |
| 75 Rod Smith | .30 | .10 |
| 76 Ed McCaffrey | .50 | .20 |
| 77 Olandis Gary | .30 | .10 |
| 78 Dwayne Carswell | .20 | .07 |
| 79 Deltha O'Neal | .20 | .07 |
| 80 Brian Griese | .50 | .20 |
| 81 Scotty Anderson | .20 | .07 |
| 82 Johnnie Morton | .30 | .10 |
| 83 Cory Schlesinger | .20 | .07 |
| 84 James Stewart | .30 | .10 |
| 85 Shaun Rogers | .20 | .07 |
| 86 Mike McMahon | .50 | .20 |
| 87 Charlie Batch | .30 | .10 |
| 88 Robert Porcher | .20 | .07 |
| 89 Bubba Franks | .30 | .10 |
| 90 Robert Ferguson | .20 | .07 |
| 91 Antonio Freeman | .30 | .10 |
| 92 Ahman Green | .50 | .20 |
| 93 Bill Schroeder | .30 | .10 |
| 94 Kabeer Gbaja-Biamila | .30 | .10 |
| 95 Jamal Reynolds | .20 | .07 |
| 96 Darren Sharper | .20 | .07 |
| 97 Brett Favre | 1.25 | .50 |
| 98 Marvin Harrison | .50 | .20 |
| 99 Dominic Rhodes | .30 | .10 |
| 100 Edgerrin James | .60 | .25 |
| 101 Reggie Wayne | .50 | .20 |
| 102 Terrence Wilkins | .20 | .07 |
| 103 Ken Dilger | .20 | .07 |
| 104 Peyton Manning | 1.00 | .40 |
| 105 Elvis Joseph | .20 | .07 |
| 106 Stacey Mack | .20 | .07 |
| 107 Fred Taylor | .50 | .20 |
| 108 Keenan McCardell | .20 | .07 |
| 109 Jimmy Smith | .30 | .10 |
| 110 Mark Brunell | .50 | .20 |
| 111 Derrick Alexander | .30 | .10 |
| 112 Tony Gonzalez | .30 | .10 |
| 113 Trent Green | .30 | .10 |
| 114 Snoop Minnis | .20 | .07 |
| 115 Priest Holmes | .60 | .25 |
| 116 Chris Chambers | .50 | .20 |
| 117 Jay Fiedler | .30 | .10 |
| 118 Oronde Gadsden | .30 | .10 |
| 119 Travis Minor | .20 | .07 |
| 120 Lamar Smith | .30 | .10 |
| 121 Zach Thomas | .50 | .20 |
| 122 Michael Bennett | .30 | .10 |
| 123 Todd Bouman | .20 | .07 |
| 124 Cris Carter | .50 | .20 |
| 125 Byron Chamberlain | .20 | .07 |
| 126 Randy Moss | 1.00 | .40 |
| 127 Jake Reed | .30 | .10 |
| 128 Daunte Culpepper | .50 | .20 |
| 129 Drew Bledsoe | .50 | .20 |
| 130 Troy Brown | .30 | .10 |
| 131 David Patten | .20 | .07 |
| 132 J.R. Redmond | .20 | .07 |
| 133 Antowain Smith | .30 | .10 |
| 134 Ty Law | .30 | .10 |
| 135 Richard Seymour | .20 | .07 |
| 136 Adam Vinatieri | .50 | .20 |
| 137 Tom Brady | 1.25 | .50 |
| 138 Joe Horn | .30 | .10 |
| 139 Willie Jackson | .20 | .07 |
| 140 Deuce McAllister | .60 | .25 |
| 141 Boo Williams | .50 | .20 |
| 142 Ricky Williams | .50 | .20 |
| 143 La'Roi Glover | .20 | .07 |
| 144 Sammy Knight | .20 | .07 |
| 145 Aaron Brooks | .50 | .20 |
| 146 Tiki Barber | .50 | .20 |
| 147 Ron Dayne | .30 | .10 |
| 148 Ike Hilliard | .20 | .07 |
| 149 Amani Toomer | .20 | .07 |
| 150 Will Allen | .20 | .07 |
| 151 Michael Strahan | .30 | .10 |
| 152 Jason Sehorn | .20 | .07 |
| 153 Kerry Collins | .30 | .10 |
| 154 Anthony Becht | .20 | .07 |
| 155 Wayne Chrebet | .30 | .10 |
| 156 Laveranues Coles | .30 | .10 |
| 157 LaMont Jordan | .50 | .20 |
| 158 Santana Moss | .50 | .20 |
| 159 Chad Pennington | .60 | .25 |
| 160 John Abraham | .30 | .10 |
| 161 Vinny Testaverde | .30 | .10 |
| 162 Curtis Martin | .50 | .20 |
| 163 Tim Brown | .50 | .20 |
| 164 Rich Gannon | .50 | .20 |
| 165 Charlie Garner | .30 | .10 |
| 166 Jerry Porter | .20 | .07 |
| 167 Marques Tuiasosopo | .30 | .10 |
| 168 Tyrone Wheatley | .20 | .07 |
| 169 Charles Woodson | .30 | .10 |
| 170 Jerry Rice | 1.00 | .40 |
| 171 Correll Buckhalter | .30 | .10 |
| 172 Chad Lewis | .20 | .07 |
| 173 Brian Mitchell | .20 | .07 |
| 174 Freddie Mitchell | .30 | .10 |
| 175 Todd Pinkston | .30 | .10 |
| 176 Duce Staley | .50 | .20 |
| 177 Tony Stewart | .20 | .07 |
| 178 James Thrash | .20 | .07 |
| 179 Hugh Douglas | .20 | .07 |
| 180 Donovan McNabb | .60 | .25 |
| 181 Plaxico Burress | .30 | .10 |
| 182 Chris Fuamatu-Ma'afala | .20 | .07 |
| 183 Kordell Stewart | .30 | .10 |
| 184 Hines Ward | .50 | .20 |
| 185 Amos Zereoue | .50 | .20 |
| 186 Kendrell Bell | .50 | .20 |
| 187 Casey Hampton | .20 | .07 |
| 188 Jerome Bettis | .50 | .20 |
| 189 Drew Brees | .50 | .20 |
| 190 Curtis Conway | .20 | .07 |
| 191 Tim Dwight | .30 | .10 |
| 192 Doug Flutie | .50 | .20 |
| 193 Junior Seau | .20 | .07 |
| 194 Marcellus Wiley | .20 | .07 |

|  |  | | |
|---|---|---|---|
| ❏ 195 | Ryan McNeill | .20 | .07 |
| ❏ 196 | Jeff Graham | .20 | .07 |
| ❏ 197 | LaDainian Tomlinson | .75 | .30 |
| ❏ 198 | Kevan Barlow | .30 | .10 |
| ❏ 199 | Garrison Hearst | .30 | .10 |
| ❏ 200 | Eric Johnson | .30 | .10 |
| ❏ 201 | Terrell Owens | .50 | .20 |
| ❏ 202 | J.J. Stokes | .30 | .10 |
| ❏ 203 | Andre Carter | .20 | .07 |
| ❏ 204 | Jeff Garcia | .50 | .20 |
| ❏ 205 | Trent Dilfer | .30 | .10 |
| ❏ 206 | Matt Hasselbeck | .30 | .10 |
| ❏ 207 | Darrell Jackson | .30 | .10 |
| ❏ 208 | Koren Robinson | .30 | .10 |
| ❏ 209 | Ricky Watters | .30 | .10 |
| ❏ 210 | John Randle | .20 | .07 |
| ❏ 211 | Shaun Alexander | .60 | .25 |
| ❏ 212 | Isaac Bruce | .30 | .10 |
| ❏ 213 | Trung Canidate | .30 | .10 |
| ❏ 214 | Marshall Faulk | .30 | .12 |
| ❏ 215 | Az-Zahir Hakim | .20 | .07 |
| ❏ 216 | Torry Holt | .30 | .10 |
| ❏ 217 | Yo Murphy | .20 | .07 |
| ❏ 218 | Ricky Proehl | .20 | .07 |
| ❏ 219 | Adam Archuleta | .20 | .07 |
| ❏ 220 | Dre Bly | .20 | .07 |
| ❏ 221 | London Fletcher | .20 | .07 |
| ❏ 222 | Tommy Polley | .20 | .07 |
| ❏ 223 | Aeneas Williams | .20 | .07 |
| ❏ 224 | Kurt Warner | .50 | .20 |
| ❏ 225 | Mike Alstott | .50 | .20 |
| ❏ 226 | Warrick Dunn | .50 | .20 |
| ❏ 227 | Jacquez Green | .20 | .07 |
| ❏ 228 | Derrick Brooks | .50 | .20 |
| ❏ 229 | John Lynch | .30 | .10 |
| ❏ 230 | Warren Sapp | .30 | .10 |
| ❏ 231 | Ronde Barber | .20 | .07 |
| ❏ 232 | Brad Johnson | .30 | .10 |
| ❏ 233 | Keyshawn Johnson | .50 | .20 |
| ❏ 234 | Drew Bennett | .50 | .20 |
| ❏ 235 | Kevin Dyson | .30 | .10 |
| ❏ 236 | Eddie George | .50 | .20 |
| ❏ 237 | Derrick Mason | .30 | .10 |
| ❏ 238 | Justin McCareins | .30 | .10 |
| ❏ 239 | Frank Wycheck | .20 | .07 |
| ❏ 240 | Jevon Kearse | .30 | .10 |
| ❏ 241 | Samari Rolle | .20 | .07 |
| ❏ 242 | Steve McNair | .50 | .20 |
| ❏ 243 | Tony Banks | .20 | .07 |
| ❏ 244 | Stephen Davis | .30 | .10 |
| ❏ 245 | Michael Westbrook | .20 | .07 |
| ❏ 246 | Champ Bailey | .30 | .10 |
| ❏ 247 | Darrell Green | .20 | .07 |
| ❏ 248 | Bruce Smith | .20 | .07 |
| ❏ 249 | Fred Smoot | .20 | .07 |
| ❏ 250 | Rod Gardner | .30 | .10 |
| ❏ 251 | David Carr RC | 1.50 | .60 |
| ❏ 252 | Joey Harrington RC | 1.50 | .60 |
| ❏ 253 | Patrick Ramsey RC | 1.25 | .50 |
| ❏ 254 | Kurt Kittner RC | .60 | .25 |
| ❏ 255 | Eric Crouch RC | 1.25 | .50 |
| ❏ 256 | Josh McCown RC | 1.50 | .60 |
| ❏ 257 | David Garrard RC | 2.50 | 1.00 |
| ❏ 258 | Rohan Davey RC | 1.25 | .50 |
| ❏ 259 | Ronald Curry RC | 1.25 | .50 |
| ❏ 260 | Chad Hutchinson RC | .60 | .25 |
| ❏ 261 | William Green RC | 1.25 | .50 |
| ❏ 262 | T.J. Duckett RC | 1.25 | .50 |
| ❏ 263 | Clinton Portis RC | 4.00 | 1.50 |
| ❏ 264 | DeShaun Foster RC | 1.25 | .50 |
| ❏ 265 | Luke Staley RC | .60 | .25 |
| ❏ 266 | Wes Pate RC | .50 | .20 |
| ❏ 267 | Travis Stephens RC | .50 | .25 |
| ❏ 268 | Adrian Peterson RC | 1.50 | .60 |
| ❏ 269 | Zak Kustok RC | 1.25 | .50 |
| ❏ 270 | Maurice Morris RC | 1.25 | .50 |
| ❏ 271 | Lamar Gordon RC | 1.25 | .50 |
| ❏ 272 | Chester Taylor RC | 2.50 | 1.00 |
| ❏ 273 | Najeh Davenport RC | 1.25 | .50 |
| ❏ 274 | Ladell Betts RC | 1.25 | .50 |
| ❏ 275 | Ashley Lelie RC | 2.50 | 1.00 |
| ❏ 276 | Josh Reed RC | 1.25 | .50 |
| ❏ 277 | Cliff Russell RC | .60 | .25 |
| ❏ 278 | Javon Walker RC | 2.00 | .75 |
| ❏ 279 | Ron Johnson RC | .60 | .25 |
| ❏ 280 | Antwaan Randle El RC | 1.50 | .60 |
| ❏ 281 | Andre Davis RC | .60 | .25 |
| ❏ 282 | Marquise Walker RC | .60 | .25 |
| ❏ 283 | Kelly Campbell RC | .60 | .25 |
| ❏ 284 | Tavon Mason RC | .50 | .20 |
| ❏ 285 | Antonio Bryant RC | 1.25 | .50 |
| ❏ 286 | Jabar Gaffney RC | 1.25 | .50 |
| ❏ 287 | Donte Stallworth RC | 2.00 | .75 |
| ❏ 288 | Tim Carter RC | .60 | .25 |
| ❏ 289 | Reche Caldwell RC | 1.25 | .50 |
| ❏ 290 | Freddie Milons RC | .60 | .25 |
| ❏ 291 | Brian Poli-Dixon RC | .60 | .25 |
| ❏ 292 | Brian Westbrook RC | 3.00 | 1.25 |
| ❏ 293 | Josh Scobey RC | 1.25 | .50 |
| ❏ 294 | Jeremy Shockey RC | 2.00 | .75 |
| ❏ 295 | Daniel Graham RC | 1.25 | .50 |
| ❏ 296 | Deion Branch RC | 2.00 | .75 |
| ❏ 297 | Julius Peppers RC | 2.50 | 1.00 |
| ❏ 298 | Kalimba Edwards RC | 1.25 | .50 |
| ❏ 299 | Dwight Freeney RC | 2.00 | .75 |
| ❏ 300 | Terry Charles RC | .60 | .25 |
| ❏ 301 | Alex Brown RC | 1.25 | .50 |
| ❏ 302 | Jason McAddley RC | .60 | .25 |
| ❏ 303 | Michal Lewis RC | 1.25 | .50 |
| ❏ 304 | Dennis Johnson RC | .50 | .20 |
| ❏ 305 | Albert Haynesworth RC | .75 | .30 |
| ❏ 306 | Ryan Sims RC | 1.25 | .50 |
| ❏ 307 | Larry Tripplett RC | .50 | .20 |
| ❏ 308 | Anthony Weaver RC | .60 | .25 |
| ❏ 309 | Wendell Bryant RC | .50 | .20 |
| ❏ 310 | John Henderson RC | 1.25 | .50 |
| ❏ 311 | Alan Harper RC | .50 | .20 |
| ❏ 312 | Napoleon Harris RC | 1.25 | .50 |
| ❏ 313 | Bryan Thomas RC | .60 | .25 |
| ❏ 314 | Andra Davis RC | .60 | .25 |
| ❏ 315 | Levar Fisher RC | .50 | .20 |
| ❏ 316 | Woody Dantzler RC | .60 | .25 |
| ❏ 317 | Robert Thomas RC | 1.25 | .50 |
| ❏ 318 | Quentin Jammer RC | 1.25 | .50 |
| ❏ 319 | Lito Sheppard RC | 1.25 | .50 |
| ❏ 320 | Travis Fisher RC | 1.25 | .50 |
| ❏ 321 | Roy Williams RC | 2.50 | 1.00 |
| ❏ 322 | Phillip Buchanon RC | 1.25 | .50 |
| ❏ 323 | Joseph Jefferson RC | .60 | .25 |
| ❏ 324 | Ed Reed RC | 3.00 | 1.25 |
| ❏ 325 | Lamont Thompson RC | .60 | .25 |
| ❏ 326 | Raonall Smith RC | .60 | .25 |
| ❏ 327 | Mike Rumph RC | 1.25 | .50 |
| ❏ 328 | Rocky Calmus RC | 1.25 | .50 |
| ❏ 329 | Bryant McKinnie RC | .60 | .25 |
| ❏ 330 | Mike Williams RC | .60 | .25 |

## 2003 Score

Clinton Portis

|  |  | | |
|---|---|---|---|
| ❏ | COMPLETE SET (327) | 50.00 | 20.00 |
| ❏ 1 | Jeff Blake | .40 | .15 |
| ❏ 2 | Todd Heap | .40 | .15 |
| ❏ 3 | Ron Johnson | .30 | .12 |
| ❏ 4 | Jamal Lewis | .50 | .20 |
| ❏ 5 | Ray Lewis | .50 | .20 |
| ❏ 6 | Chris Redman | .30 | .12 |
| ❏ 7 | Ed Reed | .50 | .20 |
| ❏ 8 | Travis Taylor | .30 | .12 |
| ❏ 9 | Anthony Weaver | .30 | .12 |
| ❏ 10 | Drew Bledsoe | .50 | .20 |
| ❏ 11 | Larry Centers | .40 | .15 |
| ❏ 12 | Nate Clements | .40 | .15 |
| ❏ 13 | Travis Henry | .40 | .15 |
| ❏ 14 | Eric Moulds | .40 | .15 |
| ❏ 15 | Peerless Price | .30 | .12 |
| ❏ 16 | Josh Reed | .30 | .12 |
| ❏ 17 | Coy Wire | .30 | .12 |
| ❏ 18 | Corey Dillon | .40 | .15 |
| ❏ 19 | T.J. Houshmandzadeh | .50 | .20 |
| ❏ 20 | Chad Johnson | .50 | .20 |
| ❏ 21 | Jon Kitna | .40 | .15 |
| ❏ 22 | Lorenzo Neal | .40 | .15 |
| ❏ 23 | Peter Warrick | .40 | .15 |
| ❏ 24 | Nicolas Luchey RC | .30 | .12 |
| ❏ 25 | Tim Couch | .30 | .12 |
| ❏ 26 | Andre Davis | .30 | .12 |
| ❏ 27 | William Green | .30 | .12 |
| ❏ 28 | Kevin Johnson | .30 | .12 |
| ❏ 29 | Quincy Morgan | .30 | .12 |
| ❏ 30 | Dennis Northcutt | .30 | .12 |
| ❏ 31 | Jamel White | .30 | .12 |
| ❏ 32 | Mike Anderson | .40 | .15 |
| ❏ 33 | Steve Beuerlein | .40 | .15 |
| ❏ 34 | Jason Elam | .30 | .12 |
| ❏ 35 | Olandis Gary | .30 | .12 |
| ❏ 36 | Brian Griese | .40 | .15 |
| ❏ 37 | Ashley Lelie | .30 | .12 |
| ❏ 38 | Ed McCaffrey | .40 | .15 |
| ❏ 39 | Clinton Portis | .60 | .25 |
| ❏ 40 | Shannon Sharpe | .40 | .15 |
| ❏ 41 | Rod Smith | .40 | .15 |
| ❏ 42 | James Allen | .30 | .12 |
| ❏ 43 | Corey Bradford | .30 | .12 |
| ❏ 44 | David Carr | .50 | .20 |
| ❏ 45 | JaJuan Dawson | .30 | .12 |
| ❏ 46 | Jabar Gaffney | .30 | .12 |
| ❏ 47 | Aaron Glenn | .30 | .12 |
| ❏ 48 | Billy Miller | .30 | .12 |
| ❏ 49 | Jonathan Wells | .30 | .12 |
| ❏ 50 | Dwight Freeney | .40 | .15 |
| ❏ 51 | Marvin Harrison | .50 | .20 |
| ❏ 52 | Qadry Ismail | .40 | .15 |
| ❏ 53 | Edgerrin James | .50 | .20 |
| ❏ 54 | Peyton Manning | 1.00 | .40 |
| ❏ 55 | James Mungro | .30 | .12 |
| ❏ 56 | Marcus Pollard | .30 | .12 |
| ❏ 57 | Reggie Wayne | .40 | .15 |
| ❏ 58 | Kyle Brady | .30 | .12 |
| ❏ 59 | Mark Brunell | .40 | .15 |
| ❏ 60 | David Garrard | .50 | .20 |
| ❏ 61 | John Henderson | .40 | .15 |
| ❏ 62 | Stacey Mack | .30 | .12 |
| ❏ 63 | Jimmy Smith | .40 | .15 |
| ❏ 64 | Fred Taylor | .50 | .20 |
| ❏ 65 | Marc Boerigter | .30 | .12 |
| ❏ 66 | Tony Gonzalez | .40 | .15 |
| ❏ 67 | Trent Green | .40 | .15 |
| ❏ 68 | Priest Holmes | .50 | .20 |
| ❏ 69 | Eddie Kennison | .30 | .12 |
| ❏ 70 | Snoop Minnis | .30 | .12 |
| ❏ 71 | Johnnie Morton | .40 | .15 |
| ❏ 72 | Cris Carter | .50 | .20 |
| ❏ 73 | Chris Chambers | .40 | .15 |
| ❏ 74 | Robert Edwards | .40 | .15 |
| ❏ 75 | Jay Fiedler | .40 | .15 |
| ❏ 76 | Ray Lucas | .30 | .12 |
| ❏ 77 | Randy McMichael | .30 | .12 |
| ❏ 78 | Travis Minor | .30 | .12 |
| ❏ 79 | Zach Thomas | .50 | .20 |
| ❏ 80 | Ricky Williams | .40 | .15 |
| ❏ 81 | Tom Brady | 1.25 | .50 |
| ❏ 82 | Deion Branch | .40 | .15 |
| ❏ 83 | Troy Brown | .40 | .15 |
| ❏ 84 | Tedy Bruschi | .50 | .20 |
| ❏ 85 | Kevin Faulk | .40 | .15 |
| ❏ 86 | Daniel Graham | .30 | .12 |
| ❏ 87 | David Patten | .30 | .12 |
| ❏ 88 | Antowain Smith | .40 | .15 |
| ❏ 89 | Adam Vinatieri | .50 | .20 |
| ❏ 90 | Donnie Abraham | .40 | .15 |
| ❏ 91 | Anthony Becht | .40 | .15 |
| ❏ 92 | Wayne Chrebet | .40 | .15 |
| ❏ 93 | Laveranues Coles | .40 | .15 |
| ❏ 94 | LaMont Jordan | .40 | .15 |
| ❏ 95 | Curtis Martin | .50 | .20 |
| ❏ 96 | Chad Morton | .30 | .12 |
| ❏ 97 | Santana Moss | .40 | .15 |
| ❏ 98 | Chad Pennington | .50 | .20 |
| ❏ 99 | Vinny Testaverde | .40 | .15 |

| | | | |
|---|---|---|---|
| ❏ 100 Tim Brown | .50 | .20 |
| ❏ 101 Phillip Buchanon | .30 | .12 |
| ❏ 102 Rich Gannon | .40 | .15 |
| ❏ 103 Charlie Garner | .40 | .15 |
| ❏ 104 Doug Jolley | .30 | .12 |
| ❏ 105 Jerry Porter | .40 | .15 |
| ❏ 106 Jerry Rice | 1.00 | .40 |
| ❏ 107 Marques Tuiasosopo | .30 | .12 |
| ❏ 108 Charles Woodson | .40 | .15 |
| ❏ 109 Rod Woodson | .50 | .20 |
| ❏ 110 Kendrell Bell | .30 | .12 |
| ❏ 111 Jerome Bettis | .50 | .20 |
| ❏ 112 Plaxico Burress | .50 | .20 |
| ❏ 113 Tommy Maddox | .40 | .15 |
| ❏ 114 Joey Porter | .30 | .12 |
| ❏ 115 Antwaan Randle El | .40 | .15 |
| ❏ 116 Kordell Stewart | .40 | .15 |
| ❏ 117 Hines Ward | .50 | .20 |
| ❏ 118 Amos Zereoue | .30 | .12 |
| ❏ 119 Drew Brees | .50 | .20 |
| ❏ 120 Reche Caldwell | .30 | .12 |
| ❏ 121 Curtis Conway | .30 | .12 |
| ❏ 122 Tim Dwight | .30 | .12 |
| ❏ 123 Doug Flutie | .40 | .15 |
| ❏ 124 Quentin Jammer | .30 | .12 |
| ❏ 125 Ben Leber | .30 | .12 |
| ❏ 126 Josh Norman | .30 | .12 |
| ❏ 127 Junior Seau | .40 | .15 |
| ❏ 128 LaDainian Tomlinson | .75 | .30 |
| ❏ 129 Keith Bulluck | .30 | .12 |
| ❏ 130 Rocky Calmus | .30 | .12 |
| ❏ 131 Kevin Carter | .40 | .15 |
| ❏ 132 Kevin Dyson | .40 | .15 |
| ❏ 133 Eddie George | .40 | .15 |
| ❏ 134 Albert Haynesworth | .50 | .20 |
| ❏ 135 Jevon Kearse | .40 | .15 |
| ❏ 136 Derrick Mason | .40 | .15 |
| ❏ 137 Justin McCareins | .30 | .12 |
| ❏ 138 Steve McNair | .50 | .20 |
| ❏ 139 Frank Wycheck | .30 | .12 |
| ❏ 140 David Boston | .30 | .12 |
| ❏ 141 MarTay Jenkins | .30 | .12 |
| ❏ 142 Freddie Jones | .30 | .12 |
| ❏ 143 Thomas Jones | .40 | .15 |
| ❏ 144 Jason McAddley | .30 | .12 |
| ❏ 145 Josh McCown | .40 | .15 |
| ❏ 146 Jake Plummer | .40 | .15 |
| ❏ 147 Marcel Shipp | .30 | .12 |
| ❏ 148 Alge Crumpler | .40 | .15 |
| ❏ 149 T.J. Duckett | .40 | .15 |
| ❏ 150 Warrick Dunn | .40 | .15 |
| ❏ 151 Brian Finneran | .30 | .12 |
| ❏ 152 Trevor Gaylor | .30 | .12 |
| ❏ 153 Shawn Jefferson | .30 | .12 |
| ❏ 154 Michael Vick | .50 | .20 |
| ❏ 155 Randy Fasani | .30 | .12 |
| ❏ 156 DeShaun Foster | .40 | .15 |
| ❏ 157 Muhsin Muhammad | .40 | .15 |
| ❏ 158 Rodney Peete | .30 | .12 |
| ❏ 159 Julius Peppers | .50 | .20 |
| ❏ 160 Lamar Smith | .30 | .15 |
| ❏ 161 Steve Smith | .50 | .20 |
| ❏ 162 Chris Weinke | .40 | .15 |
| ❏ 163 Wesley Walls | .40 | .15 |
| ❏ 164 Marty Booker | .40 | .15 |
| ❏ 165 Mike Brown | .40 | .15 |
| ❏ 166 Chris Chandler | .40 | .15 |
| ❏ 167 Jim Miller | .30 | .15 |
| ❏ 168 Marcus Robinson | .40 | .15 |
| ❏ 169 David Terrell | .30 | .12 |
| ❏ 170 Anthony Thomas | .40 | .15 |
| ❏ 171 Brian Urlacher | .75 | .30 |
| ❏ 172 Dez White | .30 | .12 |
| ❏ 173 Antonio Bryant | .50 | .20 |
| ❏ 174 Quincy Carter | .30 | .12 |
| ❏ 175 Dexter Coakley | .40 | .15 |
| ❏ 176 Joey Galloway | .40 | .15 |
| ❏ 177 La'Roi Glover | .30 | .12 |
| ❏ 178 Troy Hambrick | .30 | .12 |
| ❏ 179 Chad Hutchinson | .30 | .12 |
| ❏ 180 Rocket Ismail | .40 | .15 |
| ❏ 181 Emmitt Smith | 1.25 | .50 |
| ❏ 182 Roy Williams | .50 | .20 |
| ❏ 183 Scotty Anderson | .40 | .15 |
| ❏ 184 Germane Crowell | .30 | .12 |

| | | | |
|---|---|---|---|
| ❏ 185 Az-Zahir Hakim | .30 | .12 |
| ❏ 186 Joey Harrington | .50 | .20 |
| ❏ 187 Cory Schlesinger | .30 | .12 |
| ❏ 188 Bill Schroeder | .30 | .12 |
| ❏ 189 James Stewart | .40 | .15 |
| ❏ 190 Marques Anderson | .30 | .12 |
| ❏ 191 Najeh Davenport | .40 | .15 |
| ❏ 192 Donald Driver | .50 | .20 |
| ❏ 193 Brett Favre | 1.25 | .50 |
| ❏ 194 Bubba Franks | .40 | .15 |
| ❏ 195 Terry Glenn | .40 | .15 |
| ❏ 196 Ahman Green | .50 | .20 |
| ❏ 197 Darren Sharper | .40 | .15 |
| ❏ 198 Javon Walker | .40 | .15 |
| ❏ 199 D'Wayne Bates | .30 | .12 |
| ❏ 200 Michael Bennett | .30 | .12 |
| ❏ 201 Todd Bouman | .30 | .12 |
| ❏ 202 Byron Chamberlain | .30 | .12 |
| ❏ 203 Daunte Culpepper | .50 | .20 |
| ❏ 204 Randy Moss | .60 | .25 |
| ❏ 205 Kelly Campbell | .30 | .12 |
| ❏ 206 Aaron Brooks | .40 | .15 |
| ❏ 207 Charles Grant | .40 | .15 |
| ❏ 208 Joe Horn | .40 | .15 |
| ❏ 209 Michael Lewis | .30 | .12 |
| ❏ 210 Deuce McAllister | .40 | .15 |
| ❏ 211 Jerome Pathon | .30 | .12 |
| ❏ 212 Donte Stallworth | .40 | .15 |
| ❏ 213 Boo Williams | .30 | .12 |
| ❏ 214 Tiki Barber | .50 | .20 |
| ❏ 215 Tim Carter | .30 | .12 |
| ❏ 216 Kerry Collins | .40 | .15 |
| ❏ 217 Ron Dayne | .40 | .15 |
| ❏ 218 Jesse Palmer | .40 | .15 |
| ❏ 219 Will Peterson | .40 | .15 |
| ❏ 220 Jason Sehorn | .40 | .15 |
| ❏ 221 Jeremy Shockey | .50 | .20 |
| ❏ 222 Michael Strahan | .40 | .15 |
| ❏ 223 Amani Toomer | .40 | .15 |
| ❏ 224 Koy Detmer | .30 | .12 |
| ❏ 225 Antonio Freeman | .40 | .15 |
| ❏ 226 Dorsey Levens | .40 | .15 |
| ❏ 227 Chad Lewis | .40 | .15 |
| ❏ 228 Donovan McNabb | .60 | .25 |
| ❏ 229 Freddie Mitchell | .40 | .15 |
| ❏ 230 Duce Staley | .40 | .15 |
| ❏ 231 James Thrash | .30 | .12 |
| ❏ 232 Brian Westbrook | .50 | .20 |
| ❏ 233 Kevan Barlow | .30 | .12 |
| ❏ 234 Andre Carter | .40 | .15 |
| ❏ 235 Jeff Garcia | .50 | .20 |
| ❏ 236 Garrison Hearst | .40 | .15 |
| ❏ 237 Eric Johnson | .40 | .15 |
| ❏ 238 Terrell Owens | .50 | .20 |
| ❏ 239 Jamal Robertson | .30 | .12 |
| ❏ 240 Tai Streets | .30 | .12 |
| ❏ 241 Shaun Alexander | .50 | .20 |
| ❏ 242 Trent Dilfer | .40 | .15 |
| ❏ 243 Bobby Engram | .30 | .12 |
| ❏ 244 Matt Hasselbeck | .40 | .15 |
| ❏ 245 Darrell Jackson | .40 | .15 |
| ❏ 246 Maurice Morris | .30 | .12 |
| ❏ 247 Koren Robinson | .40 | .15 |
| ❏ 248 Jerramy Stevens | .40 | .15 |
| ❏ 249 Isaac Bruce | .50 | .20 |
| ❏ 250 Marc Bulger | .50 | .20 |
| ❏ 251 Marshall Faulk | .50 | .20 |
| ❏ 252 Lamar Gordon | .30 | .12 |
| ❏ 253 Torry Holt | .50 | .20 |
| ❏ 254 Ricky Proehl | .40 | .15 |
| ❏ 255 Kurt Warner | .40 | .15 |
| ❏ 256 Aeneas Williams | .40 | .15 |
| ❏ 257 Mike Alstott | .50 | .20 |
| ❏ 258 Ken Dilger | .40 | .15 |
| ❏ 259 Brad Johnson | .40 | .15 |
| ❏ 260 Keyshawn Johnson | .50 | .20 |
| ❏ 261 Rob Johnson | .40 | .15 |
| ❏ 262 John Lynch | .40 | .15 |
| ❏ 263 Keenan McCardell | .40 | .15 |
| ❏ 264 Michael Pittman | .30 | .12 |
| ❏ 265 Warren Sapp | .40 | .15 |
| ❏ 266 Marquise Walker | .30 | .12 |
| ❏ 267 Champ Bailey | .40 | .15 |
| ❏ 268 Stephen Davis | .40 | .15 |
| ❏ 269 Rod Gardner | .30 | .12 |

| | | | |
|---|---|---|---|
| ❏ 270 Darrell Green | .50 | .20 |
| ❏ 271 Shane Matthews | .30 | .12 |
| ❏ 272 Damerien McCants | .30 | .12 |
| ❏ 273 Patrick Ramsey | .40 | .15 |
| ❏ 274 Bruce Smith | .40 | .15 |
| ❏ 275 Kenny Watson | .30 | .12 |
| ❏ 276 Carson Palmer RC | 5.00 | 2.00 |
| ❏ 277 Byron Leftwich RC | 2.00 | .75 |
| ❏ 278 Kyle Boller RC | 1.25 | .50 |
| ❏ 279 Chris Simms RC | 1.25 | .50 |
| ❏ 280 Dave Ragone RC | .75 | .30 |
| ❏ 281 Rex Grossman RC | 3.00 | 1.25 |
| ❏ 282 Brian St.Pierre RC | 1.25 | .50 |
| ❏ 283 Larry Johnson RC | 3.00 | 1.25 |
| ❏ 284 Lee Suggs RC | 1.00 | .40 |
| ❏ 285 Justin Fargas RC | 1.25 | .50 |
| ❏ 286 Onterrio Smith RC | 1.00 | .40 |
| ❏ 287 Willis McGahee RC | 3.00 | 1.25 |
| ❏ 288 Chris Brown RC | 1.25 | .50 |
| ❏ 289 Musa Smith RC | 1.00 | .40 |
| ❏ 290 Artose Pinner RC | .75 | .30 |
| ❏ 291 Cecil Sapp RC | .75 | .30 |
| ❏ 292 Derek Watson SP RC | 40.00 | 15.00 |
| ❏ 293 LaBrandon Toefield RC | 1.00 | .40 |
| ❏ 294 Charles Rogers RC | 1.00 | .40 |
| ❏ 295 Andre Johnson RC | 2.50 | 1.00 |
| ❏ 296 Taylor Jacobs RC | 1.00 | .40 |
| ❏ 297 Bryant Johnson RC | 1.25 | .50 |
| ❏ 298 Kelley Washington RC | 1.00 | .40 |
| ❏ 299 Brandon Lloyd RC | 1.25 | .50 |
| ❏ 300 Justin Gage RC | 1.00 | .40 |
| ❏ 301 Tyrone Calico RC | 1.00 | .40 |
| ❏ 302 Kevin Curtis RC | 1.50 | .60 |
| ❏ 303 Sam Aiken RC | 1.00 | .40 |
| ❏ 304 Doug Gabriel RC | 1.00 | .40 |
| ❏ 305 Talman Gardner RC | .75 | .30 |
| ❏ 306 Jason Witten RC | 2.50 | 1.00 |
| ❏ 307 Mike Pinkard RC | .75 | .30 |
| ❏ 308 Teyo Johnson RC | 1.00 | .40 |
| ❏ 309 Bennie Joppru RC | .75 | .30 |
| ❏ 310 Dallas Clark RC | 1.25 | .50 |
| ❏ 311 Terrell Suggs RC | 1.50 | .60 |
| ❏ 312 Chris Kelsay RC | 1.00 | .40 |
| ❏ 313 Jerome McDougle RC | .75 | .30 |
| ❏ 314 Andrew Williams RC | .75 | .30 |
| ❏ 315 Jimmy Kennedy RC | .75 | .30 |
| ❏ 316 Jimmy Kennedy RC | 1.00 | .40 |
| ❏ 317 Kevin Williams RC | 1.25 | .50 |
| ❏ 318 Ken Dorsey RC | 1.00 | .40 |
| ❏ 319 William Joseph RC | .75 | .30 |
| ❏ 320 Kenny Peterson RC | 1.00 | .40 |
| ❏ 321 Rien Long RC | .75 | .30 |
| ❏ 322 Boss Bailey RC | 1.00 | .40 |
| ❏ 323 E.J. Henderson SP RC | 40.00 | 15.00 |
| ❏ 324 Terence Newman RC | 1.50 | .60 |
| ❏ 325 Marcus Trufant RC | 1.25 | .50 |
| ❏ 326 Andre Woolfolk RC | 1.00 | .40 |
| ❏ 327 Dennis Weathersby RC | .75 | .30 |
| ❏ 328 Eugene Wilson SP RC | 40.00 | 15.00 |
| ❏ 329 Mike Doss RC | 1.25 | .50 |
| ❏ 330 Rashean Mathis RC | 1.00 | .40 |

## 2004 Score

| | | | |
|---|---|---|---|
| ❏ COMPLETE SET (440) | 80.00 | 40.00 |
| ❏ 1 Emmitt Smith | 1.25 | .50 |
| ❏ 2 Anquan Boldin | .50 | .20 |
| ❏ 3 Bryant Johnson | .40 | .15 |
| ❏ 4 Marcel Shipp | .50 | .20 |

|  |  | | |
|---|--------|---|---|
| ❏ 5 | Josh McCown | .40 | .15 |
| ❏ 6 | Dexter Jackson | .30 | .12 |
| ❏ 7 | Bertrand Berry | .40 | .15 |
| ❏ 8 | Freddie Jones | .30 | .12 |
| ❏ 9 | Duane Starks | .30 | .12 |
| ❏ 10 | Michael Vick | .50 | .20 |
| ❏ 11 | T.J. Duckett | .40 | .15 |
| ❏ 12 | Warrick Dunn | .40 | .15 |
| ❏ 13 | Peerless Price | .40 | .15 |
| ❏ 14 | Alge Crumpler | .40 | .15 |
| ❏ 15 | Brian Finneran | .30 | .12 |
| ❏ 16 | Jason Webster | .30 | .12 |
| ❏ 17 | Dez White | .40 | .15 |
| ❏ 18 | Keith Brooking | .30 | .12 |
| ❏ 19 | Rod Coleman | .30 | .12 |
| ❏ 20 | Jamal Lewis | .40 | .15 |
| ❏ 21 | Kyle Boller | .40 | .15 |
| ❏ 22 | Todd Heap | .40 | .15 |
| ❏ 23 | Jonathan Ogden | .40 | .15 |
| ❏ 24 | Travis Taylor | .30 | .12 |
| ❏ 25 | Ray Lewis | .50 | .20 |
| ❏ 26 | Peter Boulware | .40 | .15 |
| ❏ 27 | Terrell Suggs | .30 | .12 |
| ❏ 28 | Chris McAlister | .30 | .12 |
| ❏ 29 | Ed Reed | .40 | .15 |
| ❏ 30 | Drew Bledsoe | .50 | .20 |
| ❏ 31 | Travis Henry | .40 | .15 |
| ❏ 32 | Eric Moulds | .40 | .15 |
| ❏ 33 | Josh Reed | .50 | .20 |
| ❏ 34 | Willis McGahee | .50 | .20 |
| ❏ 35 | Takeo Spikes | .30 | .12 |
| ❏ 36 | Lawyer Milloy | .40 | .12 |
| ❏ 37 | Troy Vincent | .40 | .15 |
| ❏ 38 | Sam Adams | .30 | .12 |
| ❏ 39 | Nate Clements | .40 | .15 |
| ❏ 40 | Jake Delhomme | .40 | .15 |
| ❏ 41 | Stephen Davis | .40 | .15 |
| ❏ 42 | DeShaun Foster | .40 | .15 |
| ❏ 43 | Muhsin Muhammad | .40 | .15 |
| ❏ 44 | Steve Smith | .50 | .20 |
| ❏ 45 | Ricky Proehl | .40 | .15 |
| ❏ 46 | Julius Peppers | .40 | .15 |
| ❏ 47 | Kris Jenkins | .40 | .15 |
| ❏ 48 | Dan Morgan | .40 | .15 |
| ❏ 49 | Ricky Manning | .30 | .12 |
| ❏ 50 | Brad Hoover | .40 | .15 |
| ❏ 51 | Carson Palmer | .60 | .25 |
| ❏ 52 | Rudi Johnson | .40 | .15 |
| ❏ 53 | Corey Dillon | .40 | .15 |
| ❏ 54 | Chad Johnson | .40 | .15 |
| ❏ 55 | Peter Warrick | .40 | .15 |
| ❏ 56 | Kelley Washington | .30 | .12 |
| ❏ 57 | Kevin Hardy | .40 | .15 |
| ❏ 58 | Tory James | .30 | .12 |
| ❏ 59 | Ickey Woods | .50 | .20 |
| ❏ 60 | Anthony Thomas | .40 | .15 |
| ❏ 61 | Thomas Jones | .40 | .15 |
| ❏ 62 | Rex Grossman | .50 | .20 |
| ❏ 63 | Marty Booker | .40 | .15 |
| ❏ 64 | Justin Gage | .40 | .15 |
| ❏ 65 | David Terrell | .30 | .12 |
| ❏ 66 | Brian Urlacher | .50 | .20 |
| ❏ 67 | Mike Brown | .40 | .15 |
| ❏ 68 | Charles Tillman | .40 | .15 |
| ❏ 69 | Jeff Garcia | .50 | .20 |
| ❏ 70 | Lee Suggs | .50 | .20 |
| ❏ 71 | William Green | .30 | .12 |
| ❏ 72 | Kelly Holcomb | .40 | .15 |
| ❏ 73 | Quincy Morgan | .30 | .12 |
| ❏ 74 | Andre Davis | .30 | .12 |
| ❏ 75 | Dennis Northcutt | .30 | .12 |
| ❏ 76 | Gerard Warren | .30 | .12 |
| ❏ 77 | Courtney Brown | .40 | .15 |
| ❏ 78 | Joey Harrington | .40 | .15 |
| ❏ 79 | Shawn Bryson | .30 | .12 |
| ❏ 80 | Charles Rogers | .40 | .15 |
| ❏ 81 | Mikhael Ricks | .30 | .12 |
| ❏ 82 | Artose Pinner | .30 | .12 |
| ❏ 83 | Az-Zahir Hakim | .30 | .12 |
| ❏ 84 | Dre Bly | .40 | .15 |
| ❏ 85 | Fernando Bryant | .30 | .12 |
| ❏ 86 | Boss Bailey | .30 | .12 |
| ❏ 87 | Tai Streets | .30 | .12 |
| ❏ 88 | Jake Plummer | .40 | .15 |
| ❏ 89 | Quentin Griffin | .40 | .15 |
| ❏ 90 | Mike Anderson | .40 | .15 |
| ❏ 91 | Garrison Hearst | .40 | .15 |
| ❏ 92 | Rod Smith | .40 | .15 |
| ❏ 93 | Ashley Lelie | .40 | .15 |
| ❏ 94 | Shannon Sharpe | .40 | .15 |
| ❏ 95 | Al Wilson | .30 | .12 |
| ❏ 96 | Champ Bailey | .40 | .15 |
| ❏ 97 | Jason Elam | .40 | .15 |
| ❏ 98 | John Lynch | .40 | .15 |
| ❏ 99 | Quincy Carter | .30 | .12 |
| ❏ 100 | Antonio Bryant | .40 | .15 |
| ❏ 101 | Terry Glenn | .40 | .15 |
| ❏ 102 | Keyshawn Johnson | .40 | .15 |
| ❏ 103 | Jason Witten | .50 | .20 |
| ❏ 104 | La'Roi Glover | .40 | .15 |
| ❏ 105 | Dat Nguyen | .30 | .12 |
| ❏ 106 | Dexter Coakley | .30 | .12 |
| ❏ 107 | Terence Newman | .40 | .15 |
| ❏ 108 | Darren Woodson | .40 | .15 |
| ❏ 109 | Roy Williams S | .40 | .15 |
| ❏ 110 | Brett Favre | 1.25 | .50 |
| ❏ 111 | Ahman Green | .50 | .20 |
| ❏ 112 | Najeh Davenport | .40 | .15 |
| ❏ 113 | Donald Driver | .50 | .20 |
| ❏ 114 | Robert Ferguson | .30 | .12 |
| ❏ 115 | Javon Walker | .40 | .15 |
| ❏ 116 | Bubba Franks | .40 | .15 |
| ❏ 117 | Kabeer Gbaja-Biamila | .40 | .15 |
| ❏ 118 | Darren Sharper | .30 | .12 |
| ❏ 119 | Mike McKenzie | .40 | .15 |
| ❏ 120 | Nick Barnett | .40 | .15 |
| ❏ 121 | David Carr | .40 | .15 |
| ❏ 122 | Domanick Davis | .50 | .20 |
| ❏ 123 | Andre Johnson | .50 | .20 |
| ❏ 124 | Corey Bradford | .40 | .15 |
| ❏ 125 | Jabar Gaffney | .40 | .15 |
| ❏ 126 | Billy Miller | .30 | .12 |
| ❏ 127 | Gary Walker | .30 | .12 |
| ❏ 128 | Jamie Sharper | .30 | .12 |
| ❏ 129 | Aaron Glenn | .40 | .15 |
| ❏ 130 | Robaire Smith | .30 | .12 |
| ❏ 131 | Peyton Manning | 1.00 | .40 |
| ❏ 132 | Edgerrin James | .50 | .20 |
| ❏ 133 | Dominic Rhodes | .40 | .15 |
| ❏ 134 | Marvin Harrison | .50 | .20 |
| ❏ 135 | Reggie Wayne | .40 | .15 |
| ❏ 136 | Brandon Stokley | .40 | .15 |
| ❏ 137 | Marcus Pollard | .30 | .12 |
| ❏ 138 | Dallas Clark | .40 | .15 |
| ❏ 139 | Mike Vanderjagt | .30 | .12 |
| ❏ 140 | Dwight Freeney | .50 | .20 |
| ❏ 141 | Mike Doss | .40 | .15 |
| ❏ 142 | Byron Leftwich | .50 | .20 |
| ❏ 143 | Fred Taylor | .40 | .15 |
| ❏ 144 | LaBrandon Toefield | .30 | .12 |
| ❏ 145 | Jimmy Smith | .40 | .15 |
| ❏ 146 | Kevin Johnson | .30 | .12 |
| ❏ 147 | Marcus Stroud | .30 | .12 |
| ❏ 148 | John Henderson | .30 | .12 |
| ❏ 149 | Donovin Darius | .30 | .12 |
| ❏ 150 | Deon Grant | .30 | .12 |
| ❏ 151 | Rashean Mathis | .30 | .12 |
| ❏ 152 | Trent Green | .40 | .15 |
| ❏ 153 | Priest Holmes | .50 | .20 |
| ❏ 154 | Johnnie Morton | .40 | .15 |
| ❏ 155 | Eddie Kennison | .40 | .15 |
| ❏ 156 | Marc Boerigter | .30 | .12 |
| ❏ 157 | Tony Gonzalez | .50 | .20 |
| ❏ 158 | Dante Hall | .40 | .15 |
| ❏ 159 | Tony Richardson | .30 | .12 |
| ❏ 160 | Gary Stills | .30 | .12 |
| ❏ 161 | Daunte Culpepper | .50 | .20 |
| ❏ 162 | Michael Bennett | .40 | .15 |
| ❏ 163 | Moe Williams | .30 | .12 |
| ❏ 164 | Onterrio Smith | .30 | .12 |
| ❏ 165 | Jim Kleinsasser | .30 | .12 |
| ❏ 166 | Antoine Winfield | .40 | .15 |
| ❏ 167 | Nate Burleson | .40 | .15 |
| ❏ 168 | Randy Moss | .60 | .25 |
| ❏ 169 | Marcus Robinson | .30 | .12 |
| ❏ 170 | Chris Hovan | .30 | .12 |
| ❏ 171 | Brian Russell RC | .30 | .12 |
| ❏ 172 | A.J. Feeley | .40 | .15 |
| ❏ 173 | Jay Fiedler | .30 | .12 |
| ❏ 174 | Ricky Williams | .50 | .20 |
| ❏ 175 | Chris Chambers | .40 | .15 |
| ❏ 176 | David Boston | .30 | .12 |
| ❏ 177 | Randy McMichael | .30 | .12 |
| ❏ 178 | Jason Taylor | .50 | .20 |
| ❏ 179 | Adewale Ogunleye | .40 | .15 |
| ❏ 180 | Zach Thomas | .50 | .20 |
| ❏ 181 | Junior Seau | .50 | .20 |
| ❏ 182 | Patrick Surtain | .30 | .12 |
| ❏ 183 | Tom Brady | 1.25 | .50 |
| ❏ 184 | Kevin Faulk | .40 | .15 |
| ❏ 185 | Troy Brown | .40 | .15 |
| ❏ 186 | Deion Branch | .40 | .15 |
| ❏ 187 | David Givens | .40 | .15 |
| ❏ 188 | Bethel Johnson | .30 | .12 |
| ❏ 189 | Richard Seymour | .30 | .12 |
| ❏ 190 | Tedy Bruschi | .50 | .20 |
| ❏ 191 | Ty Law | .40 | .15 |
| ❏ 192 | Rodney Harrison | .40 | .15 |
| ❏ 193 | Willie McGinest | .40 | .15 |
| ❏ 194 | Adam Vinatieri | .50 | .20 |
| ❏ 195 | Aaron Brooks | .40 | .15 |
| ❏ 196 | Deuce McAllister | .50 | .20 |
| ❏ 197 | Joe Horn | .40 | .15 |
| ❏ 198 | Donte Stallworth | .40 | .15 |
| ❏ 199 | Jerome Pathon | .30 | .12 |
| ❏ 200 | Boo Williams | .30 | .12 |
| ❏ 201 | Charles Grant | .30 | .12 |
| ❏ 202 | Darren Howard | .30 | .12 |
| ❏ 203 | Michael Lewis | .40 | .15 |
| ❏ 204 | Johnathan Sullivan | .30 | .12 |
| ❏ 205 | LeCharles Bentley RC | .40 | .15 |
| ❏ 206 | Kerry Collins | .40 | .15 |
| ❏ 207 | Tiki Barber | .50 | .20 |
| ❏ 208 | Amani Toomer | .40 | .15 |
| ❏ 209 | Ike Hilliard | .40 | .15 |
| ❏ 210 | Tim Carter | .30 | .12 |
| ❏ 211 | Jeremy Shockey | .40 | .15 |
| ❏ 212 | Michael Strahan | .40 | .15 |
| ❏ 213 | Will Allen | .30 | .12 |
| ❏ 214 | Will Peterson | .30 | .12 |
| ❏ 215 | William Joseph | .30 | .12 |
| ❏ 216 | Chad Pennington | .50 | .20 |
| ❏ 217 | Curtis Martin | .50 | .20 |
| ❏ 218 | LaMont Jordan | .50 | .20 |
| ❏ 219 | Santana Moss | .40 | .15 |
| ❏ 220 | Justin McCareins | .30 | .12 |
| ❏ 221 | Wayne Chrebet | .40 | .15 |
| ❏ 222 | Anthony Becht | .30 | .12 |
| ❏ 223 | Shaun Ellis | .30 | .12 |
| ❏ 224 | John Abraham | .30 | .12 |
| ❏ 225 | DeWayne Robertson | .30 | .12 |
| ❏ 226 | Rich Gannon | .40 | .15 |
| ❏ 227 | Justin Fargas | .40 | .15 |
| ❏ 228 | Tyrone Wheatley | .40 | .15 |
| ❏ 229 | Jerry Rice | 1.00 | .40 |
| ❏ 230 | Tim Brown | .50 | .20 |
| ❏ 231 | Jerry Porter | .40 | .15 |
| ❏ 232 | Teyo Johnson | .40 | .15 |
| ❏ 233 | Charles Woodson | .50 | .20 |
| ❏ 234 | Phillip Buchanon | .40 | .15 |
| ❏ 235 | Rod Woodson | .50 | .20 |
| ❏ 236 | Warren Sapp | .40 | .15 |
| ❏ 237 | Donovan McNabb | .50 | .20 |
| ❏ 238 | Brian Westbrook | .50 | .20 |
| ❏ 239 | Correll Buckhalter | .40 | .15 |
| ❏ 240 | Chad Lewis | .40 | .15 |
| ❏ 241 | L.J. Smith | .40 | .15 |
| ❏ 242 | Terrell Owens | .50 | .20 |
| ❏ 243 | Todd Pinkston | .30 | .12 |
| ❏ 244 | Freddie Mitchell | .40 | .15 |
| ❏ 245 | Jevon Kearse | .40 | .15 |
| ❏ 246 | Brian Dawkins | .40 | .15 |
| ❏ 247 | Corey Simon | .40 | .15 |
| ❏ 248 | Tommy Maddox | .40 | .15 |
| ❏ 249 | Duce Staley | .40 | .15 |
| ❏ 250 | Jerome Bettis | .50 | .20 |
| ❏ 251 | Hines Ward | .50 | .20 |
| ❏ 252 | Plaxico Burress | .40 | .15 |
| ❏ 253 | Antwaan Randle El | .40 | .15 |
| ❏ 254 | Kendrell Bell | .30 | .12 |
| ❏ 255 | Joey Porter | .40 | .15 |
| ❏ 256 | Alan Faneca | .50 | .20 |
| ❏ 257 | Casey Hampton | .30 | .12 |
| ❏ 258 | Drew Brees | .50 | .20 |
| ❏ 259 | Doug Flutie | .50 | .20 |

|  |  | | |
|---|---|---|---|
| ❑ 260 | LaDainian Tomlinson | .75 | .30 |
| ❑ 261 | Reche Caldwell | .40 | .15 |
| ❑ 262 | Tim Dwight | .40 | .15 |
| ❑ 263 | Eric Parker | .40 | .15 |
| ❑ 264 | Kevin Dyson | .30 | .12 |
| ❑ 265 | Antonio Gates | .50 | .20 |
| ❑ 266 | Quentin Jammer | .30 | .12 |
| ❑ 267 | Zeke Moreno | .30 | .12 |
| ❑ 268 | Tim Rattay | .30 | .12 |
| ❑ 269 | Kevan Barlow | .40 | .15 |
| ❑ 270 | Cedrick Wilson | .30 | .12 |
| ❑ 271 | Brandon Lloyd | .30 | .12 |
| ❑ 272 | Fred Beasley | .30 | .12 |
| ❑ 273 | Andre Carter | .30 | .12 |
| ❑ 274 | Julian Peterson | .40 | .15 |
| ❑ 275 | Ahmed Plummer | .30 | .12 |
| ❑ 276 | Tony Parrish | .30 | .12 |
| ❑ 277 | Bryant Young | .40 | .15 |
| ❑ 278 | Matt Hasselbeck | .50 | .20 |
| ❑ 279 | Shaun Alexander | .50 | .20 |
| ❑ 280 | Maurice Morris | .40 | .15 |
| ❑ 281 | Koren Robinson | .50 | .20 |
| ❑ 282 | Darrell Jackson | .40 | .15 |
| ❑ 283 | Bobby Engram | .40 | .15 |
| ❑ 284 | Grant Wistrom | .30 | .12 |
| ❑ 285 | Chad Brown | .30 | .12 |
| ❑ 286 | Marcus Trufant | .30 | .12 |
| ❑ 287 | Bobby Taylor | .30 | .12 |
| ❑ 288 | Marc Bulger | .40 | .15 |
| ❑ 289 | Kurt Warner | .50 | .20 |
| ❑ 290 | Marshall Faulk | .50 | .20 |
| ❑ 291 | Lamar Gordon | .30 | .12 |
| ❑ 292 | Torry Holt | .50 | .20 |
| ❑ 293 | Isaac Bruce | .40 | .15 |
| ❑ 294 | Leonard Little | .30 | .12 |
| ❑ 295 | Aeneas Williams | .30 | .12 |
| ❑ 296 | Orlando Pace | .30 | .12 |
| ❑ 297 | Tommy Polley | .30 | .12 |
| ❑ 298 | Pisa Tinoisamoa | .30 | .12 |
| ❑ 299 | Brad Johnson | .40 | .15 |
| ❑ 300 | Michael Pittman | .40 | .15 |
| ❑ 301 | Charlie Garner | .40 | .15 |
| ❑ 302 | Mike Alstott | .40 | .15 |
| ❑ 303 | Keenan McCardell | .30 | .12 |
| ❑ 304 | Joey Galloway | .40 | .15 |
| ❑ 305 | Joe Jurevicius | .30 | .12 |
| ❑ 306 | Anthony McFarland | .30 | .12 |
| ❑ 307 | Derrick Brooks | .40 | .15 |
| ❑ 308 | Ronde Barber | .40 | .15 |
| ❑ 309 | Shelton Quarles | .30 | .12 |
| ❑ 310 | Steve McNair | .50 | .20 |
| ❑ 311 | Eddie George | .40 | .15 |
| ❑ 312 | Chris Brown | .40 | .15 |
| ❑ 313 | Derrick Mason | .40 | .15 |
| ❑ 314 | Tyrone Calico | .40 | .15 |
| ❑ 315 | Drew Bennett | .40 | .15 |
| ❑ 316 | Kevin Carter | .30 | .12 |
| ❑ 317 | Keith Bulluck | .30 | .12 |
| ❑ 318 | Samari Rolle | .30 | .12 |
| ❑ 319 | Albert Haynesworth | .30 | .12 |
| ❑ 320 | Erron Kinney | .30 | .12 |
| ❑ 321 | Mark Brunell | .40 | .15 |
| ❑ 322 | Patrick Ramsey | .40 | .15 |
| ❑ 323 | Laveranues Coles | .40 | .15 |
| ❑ 324 | Rod Gardner | .30 | .12 |
| ❑ 325 | Darnerien McCants | .30 | .12 |
| ❑ 326 | Clinton Portis | .50 | .20 |
| ❑ 327 | LaVar Arrington | .30 | .12 |
| ❑ 328 | Shawn Springs | .30 | .12 |
| ❑ 329 | Fred Smoot | .30 | .12 |
| ❑ 330 | James Thrash | .30 | .12 |
| ❑ 331 | Marvin Harrison PB | .30 | .12 |
| ❑ 332 | Steve McNair PB | .30 | .12 |
| ❑ 333 | Ray Lewis PB | .30 | .12 |
| ❑ 334 | Trent Green PB | .25 | .10 |
| ❑ 335 | Peyton Manning PB | .60 | .25 |
| ❑ 336 | Priest Holmes PB | .30 | .12 |
| ❑ 337 | Clinton Portis PB | .30 | .12 |
| ❑ 338 | Torry Holt PB | .30 | .12 |
| ❑ 339 | Anquan Boldin PB | .30 | .12 |
| ❑ 340 | Daunte Culpepper PB | .30 | .12 |
| ❑ 341 | Ahman Green PB | .30 | .12 |
| ❑ 342 | Brian Urlacher PB | .30 | .12 |
| ❑ 343 | Donovan McNabb PB | .30 | .12 |
| ❑ 344 | Marc Bulger PB | .25 | .10 |

|  |  | | |
|---|---|---|---|
| ❑ 345 | Shaun Alexander PB | .30 | .12 |
| ❑ 346 | Peyton Manning LL | .60 | .25 |
| ❑ 347 | Daunte Culpepper LL | .30 | .12 |
| ❑ 348 | Brett Favre LL | .75 | .30 |
| ❑ 349 | Steve McNair LL | .30 | .12 |
| ❑ 350 | Tom Brady LL | .75 | .30 |
| ❑ 351 | Jamal Lewis LL | .25 | .10 |
| ❑ 352 | Deuce McAllister LL | .30 | .12 |
| ❑ 353 | Clinton Portis LL | .30 | .12 |
| ❑ 354 | Ahman Green LL | .30 | .12 |
| ❑ 355 | LaDainian Tomlinson LL | .50 | .20 |
| ❑ 356 | Torry Holt LL | .30 | .12 |
| ❑ 357 | Anquan Boldin LL | .30 | .12 |
| ❑ 358 | Randy Moss LL | .40 | .15 |
| ❑ 359 | Chad Johnson LL | .25 | .10 |
| ❑ 360 | Marvin Harrison LL | .30 | .12 |
| ❑ 361 | Peyton Manning HL | .60 | .25 |
| ❑ 362 | Jamal Lewis HL | .25 | .10 |
| ❑ 363 | Ray Lewis HL | .30 | .12 |
| ❑ 364 | Anquan Boldin HL | .30 | .12 |
| ❑ 365 | Terrell Suggs HL | .20 | .07 |
| ❑ 366 | Jamal Lewis HL | .25 | .10 |
| ❑ 367 | Priest Holmes HL | .30 | .12 |
| ❑ 368 | Tom Brady HL | .75 | .30 |
| ❑ 369 | Marc Bulger HL | .25 | .10 |
| ❑ 370 | Steve McNair HL | .30 | .12 |
| ❑ 371 | Eli Manning RC | 8.00 | 3.00 |
| ❑ 372 | Robert Gallery RC | 1.25 | .50 |
| ❑ 373 | Larry Fitzgerald RC | 4.00 | 1.50 |
| ❑ 374 | Philip Rivers RC | 4.00 | 1.50 |
| ❑ 375 | Sean Taylor RC | 1.25 | .50 |
| ❑ 376 | Kellen Winslow RC | 2.50 | 1.00 |
| ❑ 377 | Roy Williams RC | 3.00 | 1.25 |
| ❑ 378 | DeAngelo Hall RC | 1.25 | .50 |
| ❑ 379 | Reggie Williams RC | 1.25 | .50 |
| ❑ 380 | Dunta Robinson RC | 1.00 | .40 |
| ❑ 381 | Ben Roethlisberger RC | 10.00 | 4.00 |
| ❑ 382 | Jonathan Vilma RC | 1.25 | .50 |
| ❑ 383 | Lee Evans RC | 1.50 | .60 |
| ❑ 384 | Tommie Harris RC | 1.25 | .50 |
| ❑ 385 | Michael Clayton RC | 1.25 | .50 |
| ❑ 386 | D.J. Williams RC | 1.25 | .50 |
| ❑ 387 | Will Smith RC | 1.00 | .40 |
| ❑ 388 | Kenechi Udeze RC | 1.25 | .50 |
| ❑ 389 | Vince Wilfork RC | 1.25 | .50 |
| ❑ 390 | J.P. Losman RC | 1.50 | .60 |
| ❑ 391 | Marcus Tubbs RC | .75 | .30 |
| ❑ 392 | Steven Jackson RC | 4.00 | 1.50 |
| ❑ 393 | Ahmad Carroll RC | 1.25 | .50 |
| ❑ 394 | Chris Perry RC | 1.25 | .50 |
| ❑ 395 | Jason Babin RC | 1.00 | .40 |
| ❑ 396 | Chris Gamble RC | 1.00 | .40 |
| ❑ 397 | Michael Jenkins RC | 1.25 | .50 |
| ❑ 398 | Kevin Jones RC | 1.25 | .50 |
| ❑ 399 | Rashaun Woods RC | .75 | .30 |
| ❑ 400 | Ben Watson RC | 1.25 | .50 |
| ❑ 401 | Karlos Dansby RC | 1.25 | .50 |
| ❑ 402 | Igor Olshansky RC | 1.25 | .50 |
| ❑ 403 | Junior Siavii RC | .75 | .30 |
| ❑ 404 | Teddy Lehman RC | 1.00 | .40 |
| ❑ 405 | Ricardo Colclough RC | 1.25 | .50 |
| ❑ 406 | Daryl Smith RC | 1.00 | .40 |
| ❑ 407 | Ben Troupe RC | 1.00 | .40 |
| ❑ 408 | Tatum Bell RC | 1.25 | .50 |
| ❑ 409 | Travis LaBoy RC | 1.00 | .40 |
| ❑ 410 | Julius Jones RC | 3.00 | 1.25 |
| ❑ 411 | Mewelde Moore RC | 1.25 | .50 |
| ❑ 412 | Drew Henson RC | .75 | .30 |
| ❑ 413 | Dontarrious Thomas RC | 1.00 | .40 |
| ❑ 414 | Keiwan Ratliff RC | .75 | .30 |
| ❑ 415 | Devery Henderson RC | 1.25 | .50 |
| ❑ 416 | Dwan Edwards RC | .75 | .30 |
| ❑ 417 | Michael Boulware RC | 1.25 | .50 |
| ❑ 418 | Darius Watts RC | 1.00 | .40 |
| ❑ 419 | Greg Jones RC | 1.25 | .50 |
| ❑ 420 | Madieu Williams RC | .75 | .30 |
| ❑ 421 | Antwan Odom RC | 1.00 | .40 |
| ❑ 422 | Shawntae Spencer RC | .75 | .30 |
| ❑ 423 | Sean Jones RC | 1.00 | .40 |
| ❑ 424 | Courtney Watson RC | 1.00 | .40 |
| ❑ 425 | Kris Wilson RC | .75 | .30 |
| ❑ 426 | Keary Colbert RC | 1.25 | .50 |
| ❑ 427 | Marquise Hill RC | .75 | .30 |
| ❑ 428 | Darnell Dockett RC | .75 | .30 |
| ❑ 429 | Stuart Schweigert RC | 1.00 | .40 |

|  |  | | |
|---|---|---|---|
| ❑ 430 | Ben Hartsock RC | 1.00 | .40 |
| ❑ 431 | Joey Thomas RC | .75 | .30 |
| ❑ 432 | Randy Starks RC | .75 | .30 |
| ❑ 433 | Keith Smith RC | .75 | .30 |
| ❑ 434 | Derrick Hamilton RC | .75 | .30 |
| ❑ 435 | Bernard Berrian RC | 1.25 | .50 |
| ❑ 436 | Chris Cooley RC | 1.25 | .50 |
| ❑ 437 | Devard Darling RC | 1.00 | .40 |
| ❑ 438 | Matt Schaub RC | 4.00 | 1.50 |
| ❑ 439 | Luke McCown RC | 1.25 | .50 |
| ❑ 440 | Cedric Cobbs RC | 1.00 | .40 |

## 2005 Score

| | | |
|---|---|---|
| ❑ COMPLETE SET (385) | 80.00 | 40.00 |
| ❑ ONE ROOKIE PER PACK | | |
| ❑ 1 Anquan Boldin | .40 | .15 |
| ❑ 2 Bertrand Berry | .30 | .15 |
| ❑ 3 Bryant Johnson | .40 | .15 |
| ❑ 4 Darnell Dockett | .30 | .15 |
| ❑ 5 Freddie Jones | .30 | .15 |
| ❑ 6 Josh McCown | .40 | .15 |
| ❑ 7 Karlos Dansby | .30 | .15 |
| ❑ 8 Larry Fitzgerald | .50 | .20 |
| ❑ 9 Alge Crumpler | .40 | .15 |
| ❑ 10 DeAngelo Hall | .40 | .15 |
| ❑ 11 Keith Brooking | .40 | .15 |
| ❑ 12 Michael Jenkins | .40 | .15 |
| ❑ 13 Michael Vick | .50 | .20 |
| ❑ 14 Peerless Price | .30 | .12 |
| ❑ 15 Rod Coleman | .30 | .12 |
| ❑ 16 T.J. Duckett | .30 | .12 |
| ❑ 17 Warrick Dunn | .40 | .15 |
| ❑ 18 Chris McAlister | .30 | .12 |
| ❑ 19 Clarence Moore | .30 | .12 |
| ❑ 20 Ed Reed | .40 | .15 |
| ❑ 21 Jamal Lewis | .40 | .15 |
| ❑ 22 Jonathan Ogden | .30 | .12 |
| ❑ 23 Kyle Boller | .40 | .15 |
| ❑ 24 Peter Boulware | .30 | .12 |
| ❑ 25 Ray Lewis | .50 | .20 |
| ❑ 26 Terrell Suggs | .30 | .12 |
| ❑ 27 Todd Heap | .40 | .15 |
| ❑ 28 Drew Bledsoe | .50 | .20 |
| ❑ 29 Eric Moulds | .40 | .15 |
| ❑ 30 Josh Reed | .30 | .12 |
| ❑ 31 Lee Evans | .40 | .15 |
| ❑ 32 Nate Clements | .30 | .12 |
| ❑ 33 Takeo Spikes | .30 | .12 |
| ❑ 34 Travis Henry | .40 | .15 |
| ❑ 35 Willis McGahee | .50 | .20 |
| ❑ 36 Dan Morgan | .30 | .12 |
| ❑ 37 DeShaun Foster | .40 | .15 |
| ❑ 38 Jake Delhomme | .50 | .20 |
| ❑ 39 Julius Peppers | .40 | .15 |
| ❑ 40 Keary Colbert | .30 | .12 |
| ❑ 41 Kris Jenkins | .30 | .12 |
| ❑ 42 Muhsin Muhammad | .40 | .15 |
| ❑ 43 Nick Goings | .30 | .12 |
| ❑ 44 Stephen Davis | .45 | .15 |
| ❑ 45 Steve Smith | .50 | .20 |
| ❑ 46 Anthony Thomas | .30 | .12 |
| ❑ 47 Adewale Ogunleye | .30 | .12 |
| ❑ 48 Bernard Berrian | .40 | .15 |
| ❑ 49 Brian Urlacher | .50 | .20 |
| ❑ 50 David Terrell | .30 | .12 |
| ❑ 51 Mike Brown | .30 | .12 |
| ❑ 52 Rex Grossman | .50 | .20 |
| ❑ 53 Thomas Jones | .40 | .15 |

|  |  | | |
|---|---|---|---|
| 54 | Tommie Harris | .30 | .12 |
| 55 | Carson Palmer | .50 | .20 |
| 56 | Chad Johnson | .40 | .15 |
| 57 | Chris Perry | .30 | .12 |
| 58 | Kelley Washington | .30 | .12 |
| 59 | Madieu Williams | .30 | .12 |
| 60 | Peter Warrick | .30 | .12 |
| 61 | Rudi Johnson | .40 | .15 |
| 62 | T.J. Houshmandzadeh | .40 | .15 |
| 63 | Tory James | .30 | .12 |
| 64 | Andre Davis | .30 | .12 |
| 65 | Antonio Bryant | .30 | .12 |
| 66 | Dennis Northcutt | .30 | .12 |
| 67 | Gerard Warren | .30 | .12 |
| 68 | Jeff Garcia | .40 | .15 |
| 69 | Kellen Winslow Jr. | .50 | .20 |
| 70 | Lee Suggs | .40 | .15 |
| 71 | William Green | .30 | .12 |
| 72 | Drew Henson | .40 | .15 |
| 73 | Jason Witten | .40 | .15 |
| 74 | Julius Jones | .50 | .20 |
| 75 | Keyshawn Johnson | .40 | .15 |
| 76 | La'Roi Glover | .40 | .15 |
| 77 | J.P. Losman | .50 | .20 |
| 78 | Roy Williams S | .40 | .15 |
| 79 | Terence Newman | .30 | .12 |
| 80 | Terry Glenn | .30 | .12 |
| 81 | Al Wilson | .30 | .12 |
| 82 | Ashley Lelie | .30 | .12 |
| 83 | Champ Bailey | .40 | .15 |
| 84 | D.J. Williams | .30 | .12 |
| 85 | Jake Plummer | .40 | .15 |
| 86 | Jason Elam | .30 | .12 |
| 87 | John Lynch | .40 | .15 |
| 88 | Reuben Droughns | .30 | .12 |
| 89 | Rod Smith | .40 | .15 |
| 90 | Tatum Bell | .40 | .15 |
| 91 | Trent Dilfer | .30 | .12 |
| 92 | Charles Rogers | .30 | .12 |
| 93 | Dre' Bly | .30 | .12 |
| 94 | Joey Harrington | .50 | .20 |
| 95 | Kevin Jones | .40 | .15 |
| 96 | Roy Williams WR | .50 | .20 |
| 97 | Shawn Bryson | .30 | .12 |
| 98 | Tai Streets | .30 | .12 |
| 99 | Teddy Lehman | .30 | .12 |
| 100 | Ahman Green | .50 | .20 |
| 101 | Brett Favre | 1.25 | .50 |
| 102 | Bubba Franks | .40 | .15 |
| 103 | Darren Sharper | .30 | .12 |
| 104 | Donald Driver | .50 | .20 |
| 105 | Javon Walker | .40 | .15 |
| 106 | Najeh Davenport | .40 | .15 |
| 107 | Nick Barnett | .40 | .15 |
| 108 | Robert Ferguson | .40 | .15 |
| 109 | Aaron Glenn | .30 | .12 |
| 110 | Andre Johnson | .40 | .15 |
| 111 | Corey Bradford | .30 | .12 |
| 112 | David Carr | .40 | .15 |
| 113 | Domanick Davis | .40 | .15 |
| 114 | Dunta Robinson | .30 | .12 |
| 115 | Jabar Gaffney | .30 | .12 |
| 116 | Jamie Sharper | .30 | .12 |
| 117 | Jason Babin | .30 | .12 |
| 118 | Brandon Stokley | .30 | .12 |
| 119 | Dallas Clark | .40 | .15 |
| 120 | Dwight Freeney | .40 | .15 |
| 121 | Edgerrin James | .50 | .20 |
| 122 | Marcus Pollard | .30 | .12 |
| 123 | Marvin Harrison | .50 | .20 |
| 124 | Peyton Manning | .75 | .30 |
| 125 | Reggie Wayne | .40 | .15 |
| 126 | Robert Mathis RC | 1.00 | .40 |
| 127 | Byron Leftwich | .40 | .15 |
| 128 | Daryl Smith | .30 | .12 |
| 129 | Donovan Darius | .30 | .12 |
| 130 | Ernest Wilford | .40 | .15 |
| 131 | Fred Taylor | .50 | .20 |
| 132 | Jimmy Smith | .40 | .15 |
| 133 | John Henderson | .30 | .12 |
| 134 | Marcus Stroud | .30 | .12 |
| 135 | Reggie Williams | .40 | .15 |
| 136 | Dante Hall | .40 | .15 |
| 137 | Eddie Kennison | .30 | .12 |
| 138 | Jared Allen | .40 | .15 |
| 139 | Johnnie Morton | .40 | .15 |
| 140 | Larry Johnson | .50 | .20 |
| 141 | Priest Holmes | .50 | .20 |
| 142 | Samie Parker | .30 | .12 |
| 143 | Tony Gonzalez | .40 | .15 |
| 144 | Trent Green | .40 | .15 |
| 145 | A.J. Feeley | .30 | .12 |
| 146 | Chris Chambers | .40 | .15 |
| 147 | Jason Taylor | .40 | .15 |
| 148 | Junior Seau | .40 | .15 |
| 149 | Marty Booker | .30 | .12 |
| 150 | Patrick Surtain | .30 | .12 |
| 151 | Randy McMichael | .30 | .12 |
| 152 | Sammy Morris | .30 | .12 |
| 153 | Zach Thomas | .50 | .20 |
| 154 | Daunte Culpepper | .50 | .20 |
| 155 | Jim Kleinsasser | .30 | .12 |
| 156 | Kelly Campbell | .30 | .12 |
| 157 | Kevin Williams | .40 | .15 |
| 158 | Marcus Robinson | .40 | .15 |
| 159 | Mewelde Moore | .30 | .12 |
| 160 | Michael Bennett | .40 | .15 |
| 161 | Nate Burleson | .40 | .15 |
| 162 | Onterrio Smith | .30 | .12 |
| 163 | Randy Moss | .50 | .20 |
| 164 | Adam Vinatieri | .50 | .20 |
| 165 | Corey Dillon | .40 | .15 |
| 166 | David Givens | .30 | .12 |
| 167 | David Patten | .30 | .12 |
| 168 | Deion Branch | .40 | .15 |
| 169 | Mike Vrabel | .30 | .12 |
| 170 | Richard Seymour | .30 | .12 |
| 171 | Tedy Bruschi | .50 | .20 |
| 172 | Tom Brady | 1.00 | .40 |
| 173 | Troy Brown | .30 | .12 |
| 174 | Ty Law | .30 | .12 |
| 175 | Aaron Brooks | .30 | .12 |
| 176 | Charles Grant | .30 | .12 |
| 177 | Deuce McAllister | .50 | .20 |
| 178 | Devery Henderson | .40 | .15 |
| 179 | Donte Stallworth | .40 | .15 |
| 180 | Jerome Pathon | .30 | .12 |
| 181 | Joe Horn | .40 | .15 |
| 182 | Will Smith | .30 | .12 |
| 183 | Amani Toomer | .40 | .15 |
| 184 | Eli Manning | 1.00 | .40 |
| 185 | Gibril Wilson | .30 | .12 |
| 186 | Ike Hilliard | .30 | .12 |
| 187 | Jeremy Shockey | .50 | .20 |
| 188 | Michael Strahan | .40 | .15 |
| 189 | Tiki Barber | .50 | .20 |
| 190 | Jamaar Taylor | .30 | .12 |
| 191 | Tim Carter | .30 | .12 |
| 192 | Chad Pennington | .50 | .20 |
| 193 | DeWayne Robertson | .30 | .12 |
| 194 | Curtis Martin | .50 | .20 |
| 195 | John Abraham | .30 | .12 |
| 196 | Jonathan Vilma | .40 | .15 |
| 197 | Justin McCareins | .30 | .12 |
| 198 | LaMont Jordan | .40 | .15 |
| 199 | Santana Moss | .40 | .15 |
| 200 | Shaun Ellis | .30 | .12 |
| 201 | Wayne Chrebet | .40 | .15 |
| 202 | Charles Woodson | .40 | .15 |
| 203 | Doug Jolley | .30 | .12 |
| 204 | Jerry Porter | .40 | .15 |
| 205 | Justin Fargas | .30 | .12 |
| 206 | Kerry Collins | .40 | .15 |
| 207 | Robert Gallery | .30 | .12 |
| 208 | Ronald Curry | .30 | .12 |
| 209 | Sebastian Janikowski | .30 | .12 |
| 210 | Tyrone Wheatley | .30 | .12 |
| 211 | Warren Sapp | .40 | .15 |
| 212 | Brian Dawkins | .40 | .15 |
| 213 | Brian Westbrook | .50 | .20 |
| 214 | Chad Lewis | .30 | .12 |
| 215 | Corey Simon | .30 | .12 |
| 216 | Donovan McNabb | .50 | .20 |
| 217 | Freddie Mitchell | .30 | .12 |
| 218 | Jevon Kearse | .40 | .15 |
| 219 | L.J. Smith | .40 | .15 |
| 220 | Lito Sheppard | .30 | .12 |
| 221 | Terrell Owens | .50 | .20 |
| 222 | Todd Pinkston | .30 | .12 |
| 223 | Alan Faneca | .75 | .30 |
| 224 | Antwaan Randle El | .40 | .15 |
| 225 | Ben Roethlisberger | 1.25 | .50 |
| 226 | Duce Staley | .40 | .15 |
| 227 | Hines Ward | .50 | .20 |
| 228 | James Farrior | .30 | .12 |
| 229 | Jerome Bettis | .50 | .20 |
| 230 | Joey Porter | .40 | .15 |
| 231 | Kendrell Bell | .30 | .12 |
| 232 | Plaxico Burress | .40 | .15 |
| 233 | Troy Polamalu | .60 | .25 |
| 234 | Antonio Gates | .50 | .20 |
| 235 | Reche Caldwell | .30 | .12 |
| 236 | Doug Flutie | .50 | .20 |
| 237 | Drew Brees | .50 | .20 |
| 238 | Eric Parker | .30 | .12 |
| 239 | Keenan McCardell | .40 | .15 |
| 240 | LaDainian Tomlinson | .75 | .30 |
| 241 | Philip Rivers | .50 | .20 |
| 242 | Quentin Jammer | .30 | .12 |
| 243 | Tim Dwight | .30 | .12 |
| 244 | Brandon Lloyd | .30 | .12 |
| 245 | Bryant Young | .30 | .12 |
| 246 | Cedrick Wilson | .30 | .12 |
| 247 | Eric Johnson | .30 | .12 |
| 248 | Julian Peterson | .30 | .12 |
| 249 | Kevan Barlow | .30 | .12 |
| 250 | Rashaun Woods | .30 | .12 |
| 251 | Maurice Hicks RC | .30 | .12 |
| 252 | Tim Rattay | .30 | .12 |
| 253 | Bobby Engram | .40 | .15 |
| 254 | Chad Brown | .30 | .12 |
| 255 | Darrell Jackson | .40 | .15 |
| 256 | Grant Wistrom | .30 | .12 |
| 257 | Jerramy Stevens | .40 | .15 |
| 258 | Koren Robinson | .40 | .15 |
| 259 | Marcus Trufant | .30 | .12 |
| 260 | Matt Hasselbeck | .40 | .15 |
| 261 | Michael Boulware | .30 | .12 |
| 262 | Shaun Alexander | .50 | .20 |
| 263 | Isaac Bruce | .40 | .15 |
| 264 | Leonard Little | .30 | .12 |
| 265 | Marc Bulger | .50 | .20 |
| 266 | Marshall Faulk | .50 | .20 |
| 267 | Orlando Pace | .30 | .12 |
| 268 | Pisa Tinoisamoa | .30 | .12 |
| 269 | Shaun McDonald | .30 | .12 |
| 270 | Steven Jackson | .60 | .25 |
| 271 | Torry Holt | .40 | .15 |
| 272 | Anthony McFarland | .30 | .12 |
| 273 | Brian Griese | .40 | .15 |
| 274 | Charlie Garner | .30 | .12 |
| 275 | Derrick Brooks | .40 | .15 |
| 276 | Joe Jurevicius | .40 | .15 |
| 277 | Joey Galloway | .40 | .15 |
| 278 | Michael Clayton | .40 | .15 |
| 279 | Michael Pittman | .30 | .12 |
| 280 | Mike Alstott | .40 | .15 |
| 281 | Ronde Barber | .40 | .15 |
| 282 | Albert Haynesworth | .30 | .12 |
| 283 | Ben Troupe | .30 | .12 |
| 284 | Billy Volek | .40 | .15 |
| 285 | Chris Brown | .30 | .12 |
| 286 | Derrick Mason | .40 | .15 |
| 287 | Drew Bennett | .40 | .15 |
| 288 | Keith Bulluck | .30 | .12 |
| 289 | Kevin Carter | .30 | .12 |
| 290 | Samari Rolle | .30 | .12 |
| 291 | Steve McNair | .50 | .20 |
| 292 | Tyrone Calico | .40 | .15 |
| 293 | Chris Cooley | .40 | .15 |
| 294 | Clinton Portis | .50 | .20 |
| 295 | Fred Smoot | .30 | .12 |
| 296 | LaVar Arrington | .50 | .20 |
| 297 | Laveranues Coles | .40 | .15 |
| 298 | Patrick Ramsey | .40 | .15 |
| 299 | Rod Gardner | .30 | .12 |
| 300 | Sean Taylor | .40 | .15 |
| 301 | Michael Vick PB | .50 | .20 |
| 302 | Daunte Culpepper PB | .40 | .15 |
| 303 | Donovan McNabb PB | .40 | .15 |
| 304 | Brian Westbrook PB | .40 | .15 |
| 305 | Tiki Barber PB | .40 | .15 |
| 306 | Ahman Green PB | .40 | .15 |
| 307 | Joe Horn PB | .30 | .12 |
| 308 | Javon Walker PB | .30 | .12 |

| | | |
|---|---|---|
| ☐ 309 Torry Holt PB | .30 | .12 |
| ☐ 310 Muhsin Muhammad PB | .30 | .12 |
| ☐ 311 Jason Witten PB | .30 | .12 |
| ☐ 312 Alge Crumpler PB | .30 | .12 |
| ☐ 313 Peyton Manning PB | .60 | .25 |
| ☐ 314 Tom Brady PB | .75 | .30 |
| ☐ 315 Drew Brees PB | .40 | .15 |
| ☐ 316 LaDainian Tomlinson PB | .60 | .25 |
| ☐ 317 Rudi Johnson PB | .30 | .12 |
| ☐ 318 Jerome Bettis PB | .40 | .15 |
| ☐ 319 Marvin Harrison PB | .40 | .15 |
| ☐ 320 Hines Ward PB | .40 | .15 |
| ☐ 321 Andre Johnson PB | .30 | .12 |
| ☐ 322 Chad Johnson PB | .30 | .12 |
| ☐ 323 Tony Gonzalez PB | .30 | .12 |
| ☐ 324 Adam Vinatieri PB | .30 | .12 |
| ☐ 325 David Akers PB | .25 | .10 |
| ☐ 326 Takeo Spikes PB | .25 | .10 |
| ☐ 327 Joey Porter PB | .25 | .10 |
| ☐ 328 Tedy Bruschi PB | .40 | .15 |
| ☐ 329 Ed Reed PB | .30 | .12 |
| ☐ 330 Terrell Owens PB | .40 | .15 |
| ☐ 331 Alex Smith QB RC | 1.50 | .60 |
| ☐ 332 Ronnie Brown RC | 3.00 | 1.25 |
| ☐ 333 Braylon Edwards RC | 3.00 | 1.25 |
| ☐ 334 Cedric Benson RC | 1.00 | .40 |
| ☐ 335 Cadillac Williams RC | 2.00 | .75 |
| ☐ 336 Adam Jones RC | 1.00 | .40 |
| ☐ 337 Troy Williamson RC | 1.00 | .40 |
| ☐ 338 Antrel Rolle RC | 1.00 | .40 |
| ☐ 339 Carlos Rogers RC | 1.00 | .40 |
| ☐ 340 Mike Williams RC | 1.00 | .40 |
| ☐ 341 DeMarcus Ware RC | 1.50 | .60 |
| ☐ 342 Shawne Merriman RC | 1.50 | .60 |
| ☐ 343 Thomas Davis RC | .75 | .30 |
| ☐ 344 Derrick Johnson RC | 1.00 | .40 |
| ☐ 345 Travis Johnson RC | .60 | .25 |
| ☐ 346 David Pollack RC | .75 | .30 |
| ☐ 347 Erasmus James RC | .75 | .30 |
| ☐ 348 Marcus Spears RC | 1.00 | .40 |
| ☐ 349 Matt Jones RC | 1.50 | .60 |
| ☐ 350 Mark Clayton RC | 1.00 | .40 |
| ☐ 351 Fabian Washington RC | 1.00 | .40 |
| ☐ 352 Aaron Rodgers RC | 3.00 | 1.25 |
| ☐ 353 Jason Campbell RC | 2.00 | .75 |
| ☐ 354 Roddy White RC | 1.25 | .50 |
| ☐ 355 Marlin Jackson RC | .75 | .30 |
| ☐ 356 Heath Miller RC | 2.00 | .75 |
| ☐ 357 Mike Patterson RC | .75 | .30 |
| ☐ 358 Reggie Brown RC | 1.00 | .40 |
| ☐ 359 Shaun Cody RC | .75 | .30 |
| ☐ 360 Mark Bradley RC | 1.00 | .40 |
| ☐ 361 J.J. Arrington RC | 1.00 | .40 |
| ☐ 362 Dan Cody RC | 1.00 | .40 |
| ☐ 363 Eric Shelton RC | .75 | .30 |
| ☐ 364 Roscoe Parrish RC | .75 | .30 |
| ☐ 365 Terrence Murphy RC | .60 | .25 |
| ☐ 366 Vincent Jackson RC | 1.00 | .40 |
| ☐ 367 Frank Gore RC | 2.50 | 1.00 |
| ☐ 368 Charlie Frye RC | 1.00 | .40 |
| ☐ 369 Courtney Roby RC | .75 | .30 |
| ☐ 370 Andrew Walter RC | 1.00 | .40 |
| ☐ 371 Vernand Morency RC | 1.00 | .40 |
| ☐ 372 Ryan Moats RC | 1.00 | .40 |
| ☐ 373 Chris Henry RC | 1.00 | .40 |
| ☐ 374 David Greene RC | .75 | .30 |
| ☐ 375 Brandon Jones RC | 1.00 | .40 |
| ☐ 376 Maurice Clarett RC | .75 | .30 |
| ☐ 377 Kyle Orton RC | 1.25 | .50 |
| ☐ 378 Marion Barber RC | 3.00 | 1.25 |
| ☐ 379 Brandon Jacobs RC | 1.25 | .50 |
| ☐ 380 Ciatrick Fason RC | .75 | .30 |
| ☐ 381 Jerome Mathis RC | 1.00 | .40 |
| ☐ 382 Craphonso Thorpe RC | .75 | .30 |
| ☐ 383 Stefan LeFors RC | .75 | .30 |
| ☐ 384 Darren Sproles RC | 1.25 | .50 |
| ☐ 385 Fred Gibson RC | .75 | .30 |

## 2006 Score

| | | |
|---|---|---|
| ☐ 1 Kurt Warner | .40 | .15 |
| ☐ 2 J.J. Arrington | .40 | .15 |
| ☐ 3 Anquan Boldin | .40 | .15 |
| ☐ 4 Larry Fitzgerald | .50 | .20 |
| ☐ 5 Marcel Shipp | .30 | .12 |
| ☐ 6 Bryant Johnson | .25 | .10 |

| | | |
|---|---|---|
| ☐ 7 Bertrand Berry | .25 | .10 |
| ☐ 8 John Navarre | .25 | .10 |
| ☐ 9A Michael Vick | .50 | .20 |
| ☐ 10 Warrick Dunn | .40 | .15 |
| ☐ 11 Roddy White | .30 | .12 |
| ☐ 12 Alge Crumpler | .40 | .15 |
| ☐ 13A T.J. Duckett | .30 | .12 |
| ☐ 14 Michael Jenkins | .40 | .15 |
| ☐ 15 DeAngelo Hall | .40 | .15 |
| ☐ 16 Brian Finneran | .30 | .12 |
| ☐ 17 Kyle Boller | .40 | .15 |
| ☐ 18 Jamal Lewis | .40 | .15 |
| ☐ 19A Chester Taylor | .40 | .15 |
| ☐ 20 Derrick Mason | .40 | .15 |
| ☐ 21 Mark Clayton | .40 | .15 |
| ☐ 22 Todd Heap | .40 | .15 |
| ☐ 23 Ray Lewis | .50 | .20 |
| ☐ 24 Devard Darling | .30 | .12 |
| ☐ 25 J.P. Losman | .40 | .15 |
| ☐ 26 Willis McGahee | .50 | .20 |
| ☐ 27 Lee Evans | .40 | .15 |
| ☐ 28A Eric Moulds | .40 | .15 |
| ☐ 29A Lawyer Milloy | .25 | .10 |
| ☐ 30 Josh Reed | .30 | .12 |
| ☐ 31 Kelly Holcomb | .25 | .10 |
| ☐ 32 Jake Delhomme | .40 | .15 |
| ☐ 33 DeShaun Foster | .40 | .15 |
| ☐ 34 Steve Smith | .50 | .20 |
| ☐ 35 Julius Peppers | .40 | .15 |
| ☐ 36 Drew Carter | .30 | .12 |
| ☐ 37 Chris Gamble | .30 | .12 |
| ☐ 38 Stephen Davis | .40 | .15 |
| ☐ 39 Keary Colbert | .40 | .15 |
| ☐ 40 Nick Goings | .30 | .12 |
| ☐ 41 Eric Shelton | .30 | .12 |
| ☐ 42 Rex Grossman | .50 | .20 |
| ☐ 43 Thomas Jones | .40 | .15 |
| ☐ 44 Cedric Benson | .40 | .15 |
| ☐ 45 Muhsin Muhammad | .40 | .15 |
| ☐ 46 Brian Urlacher | .50 | .20 |
| ☐ 47 Mark Bradley | .30 | .12 |
| ☐ 48 Kyle Orton | .40 | .15 |
| ☐ 49 Tommie Harris | .25 | .10 |
| ☐ 50 Adrian Peterson | .40 | .15 |
| ☐ 51 Bernard Berrian | .40 | .15 |
| ☐ 52 Justin Gage | .30 | .12 |
| ☐ 53 Carson Palmer | .50 | .20 |
| ☐ 54 Rudi Johnson | .40 | .15 |
| ☐ 55 Chad Johnson | .50 | .20 |
| ☐ 56 T.J. Houshmandzadeh | .40 | .15 |
| ☐ 57 Chris Henry | .30 | .12 |
| ☐ 58 Chris Perry | .40 | .15 |
| ☐ 59A Jon Kitna | .40 | .15 |
| ☐ 60 Deltha O'Neal | .30 | .12 |
| ☐ 61 Charlie Frye | .40 | .15 |
| ☐ 62 Reuben Droughns | .40 | .15 |
| ☐ 63 Braylon Edwards | .50 | .20 |
| ☐ 64 Kellen Winslow | .50 | .20 |
| ☐ 65A Antonio Bryant | .40 | .15 |
| ☐ 66A Trent Dilfer | .40 | .15 |
| ☐ 67 Dennis Northcutt | .30 | .12 |
| ☐ 68 Drew Bledsoe | .50 | .20 |
| ☐ 69 Julius Jones | .50 | .20 |
| ☐ 70 Marion Barber | .50 | .20 |
| ☐ 71 Terry Glenn | .40 | .15 |
| ☐ 72A Keyshawn Johnson | .40 | .15 |
| ☐ 73 Roy Williams S | .40 | .15 |
| ☐ 74 Jason Witten | .40 | .15 |

| | | |
|---|---|---|
| ☐ 75 Terence Newman | .30 | .12 |
| ☐ 76 Drew Henson | .25 | .10 |
| ☐ 77 Patrick Crayton | .30 | .12 |
| ☐ 78 Jake Plummer | .40 | .15 |
| ☐ 79A Mike Anderson | .40 | .15 |
| ☐ 80 Tatum Bell | .40 | .15 |
| ☐ 81A Ashley Lelie | .40 | .15 |
| ☐ 82 Rod Smith | .40 | .15 |
| ☐ 83 D.J. Williams | .30 | .12 |
| ☐ 84 Darius Watts | .30 | .12 |
| ☐ 85 Ron Dayne | .40 | .15 |
| ☐ 86A Jeb Putzier | .30 | .12 |
| ☐ 87A Joey Harrington | .30 | .12 |
| ☐ 88 Kevin Jones | .40 | .15 |
| ☐ 89 Roy Williams WR | .50 | .20 |
| ☐ 90 Mike Williams | .50 | .20 |
| ☐ 91 Charles Rogers | .40 | .15 |
| ☐ 92 Teddy Lehman | .25 | .10 |
| ☐ 93 Marcus Pollard | .30 | .12 |
| ☐ 94 Artose Pinner | .25 | .10 |
| ☐ 95 Brett Favre | 1.00 | .40 |
| ☐ 96 Ahman Green | .40 | .15 |
| ☐ 97 Najeh Davenport | .40 | .15 |
| ☐ 98 Samkon Gado | .50 | .20 |
| ☐ 99A Javon Walker | .40 | .15 |
| ☐ 100 Donald Driver | .40 | .15 |
| ☐ 101 Aaron Rodgers | .50 | .20 |
| ☐ 102 Robert Ferguson | .30 | .12 |
| ☐ 103 David Carr | .40 | .15 |
| ☐ 104 Domanick Davis | .40 | .15 |
| ☐ 105 Andre Johnson | .40 | .15 |
| ☐ 106A Jabar Gaffney | .30 | .12 |
| ☐ 107 Jonathan Wells | .25 | .10 |
| ☐ 108 Vernand Morency | .30 | .12 |
| ☐ 109A Corey Bradford | .30 | .12 |
| ☐ 110 Jerome Mathis | .30 | .12 |
| ☐ 111A Peyton Manning | .75 | .30 |
| ☐ 112A Edgerrin James | .40 | .15 |
| ☐ 113 Marvin Harrison | .50 | .20 |
| ☐ 114 Reggie Wayne | .40 | .15 |
| ☐ 115 Dwight Freeney | .40 | .15 |
| ☐ 116 Dallas Clark | .40 | .15 |
| ☐ 117 Dominic Rhodes | .40 | .15 |
| ☐ 118 Jim Sorgi | .25 | .10 |
| ☐ 119 Brandon Stokley | .30 | .12 |
| ☐ 120 Bob Sanders | .40 | .15 |
| ☐ 121 Mike Doss | .25 | .10 |
| ☐ 122 Marlin Jackson | .30 | .12 |
| ☐ 123 Byron Leftwich | .40 | .15 |
| ☐ 124 Fred Taylor | .40 | .15 |
| ☐ 125 Jimmy Smith | .40 | .15 |
| ☐ 126 Matt Jones | .40 | .15 |
| ☐ 127 Ernest Wilford | .30 | .12 |
| ☐ 128 Greg Jones | .30 | .12 |
| ☐ 129 Mike Peterson | .30 | .12 |
| ☐ 130 Reggie Williams | .40 | .15 |
| ☐ 131 Rashean Mathis | .25 | .10 |
| ☐ 132 Trent Green | .40 | .15 |
| ☐ 133 Larry Johnson | .40 | .15 |
| ☐ 134 Priest Holmes | .40 | .15 |
| ☐ 135 Eddie Kennison | .30 | .12 |
| ☐ 136 Tony Gonzalez | .40 | .15 |
| ☐ 137 Kendrell Bell | .30 | .12 |
| ☐ 138 Samie Parker | .30 | .12 |
| ☐ 139 Dante Hall | .40 | .15 |
| ☐ 140A Tony Richardson | .25 | .10 |
| ☐ 141A Gus Frerotte | .25 | .10 |
| ☐ 142 Ronnie Brown | .50 | .20 |
| ☐ 143A Neil Rackers | .25 | .10 |
| ☐ 144 Chris Chambers | .40 | .15 |
| ☐ 145 Zach Thomas | .50 | .20 |
| ☐ 146 Cliff Russell | .25 | .10 |
| ☐ 147A David Bowens | .25 | .10 |
| ☐ 148 Wes Welker | .50 | .20 |
| ☐ 149 Marty Booker | .30 | .12 |
| ☐ 150 Randy McMichael | .30 | .12 |
| ☐ 151A Daunte Culpepper | .50 | .20 |
| ☐ 152 Mewelde Moore | .30 | .12 |
| ☐ 153A Nate Burleson | .40 | .15 |
| ☐ 154 Troy Williamson | .40 | .15 |
| ☐ 155 Koren Robinson | .30 | .12 |
| ☐ 156 Erasmus James | .25 | .10 |
| ☐ 157 Marcus Robinson | .40 | .15 |
| ☐ 158 E.J. Henderson | .30 | .12 |
| ☐ 159 Brad Johnson | .40 | .15 |

|  |  | | |
|---|--------|------|------|
| ❑ 160A | Michael Bennett | .25 | .10 |
| ❑ 161 | Travis Taylor | .30 | .12 |
| ❑ 162 | Tom Brady | .75 | .30 |
| ❑ 163 | Corey Dillon | .40 | .15 |
| ❑ 164 | Deion Branch | .40 | .15 |
| ❑ 165 | Tedy Bruschi | .50 | .20 |
| ❑ 166 | Ben Watson | .30 | .12 |
| ❑ 167 | Daniel Graham | .30 | .12 |
| ❑ 168A | Bethel Johnson | .30 | .12 |
| ❑ 169 | Kevin Faulk | .40 | .15 |
| ❑ 170A | David Givens | .40 | .15 |
| ❑ 171 | Troy Brown | .30 | .12 |
| ❑ 172A | Aaron Brooks | .40 | .15 |
| ❑ 173 | Deuce McAllister | .40 | .15 |
| ❑ 174 | Joe Horn | .40 | .15 |
| ❑ 175A | Donte Stallworth | .40 | .15 |
| ❑ 176A | Antowain Smith | .25 | .10 |
| ❑ 177 | Devery Henderson | .30 | .12 |
| ❑ 178 | Eli Manning | .60 | .25 |
| ❑ 179 | Tiki Barber | .50 | .20 |
| ❑ 180 | Plaxico Burress | .40 | .15 |
| ❑ 181 | Jeremy Shockey | .50 | .20 |
| ❑ 182A | Osi Umenyiora | .40 | .15 |
| ❑ 183 | Gibril Wilson | .25 | .10 |
| ❑ 184 | Brandon Jacobs | .50 | .20 |
| ❑ 185 | Michael Strahan | .40 | .15 |
| ❑ 186A | Will Allen | .25 | .10 |
| ❑ 187 | Amani Toomer | .40 | .15 |
| ❑ 188 | Chad Pennington | .40 | .15 |
| ❑ 189 | Curtis Martin | .50 | .20 |
| ❑ 190 | Laveranues Coles | .40 | .15 |
| ❑ 191 | Jonathan Vilma | .40 | .15 |
| ❑ 192A | Ty Law | .30 | .12 |
| ❑ 193 | Cedric Houston | .30 | .12 |
| ❑ 194 | Justin McCareins | .30 | .12 |
| ❑ 195 | Jerald Sowell | .25 | .10 |
| ❑ 196 | Josh Brown | .25 | .10 |
| ❑ 197 | LaMont Jordan | .40 | .15 |
| ❑ 198 | Randy Moss | .50 | .20 |
| ❑ 199 | Jerry Porter | .40 | .15 |
| ❑ 200 | Doug Gabriel | .30 | .12 |
| ❑ 201 | Johnnie Morant | .25 | .10 |
| ❑ 202 | Zack Crockett | .25 | .10 |
| ❑ 203A | Derrick Burgess | .30 | .12 |
| ❑ 204 | Donovan McNabb | .50 | .20 |
| ❑ 205 | Brian Westbrook | .40 | .15 |
| ❑ 206 | Reggie Brown | .40 | .15 |
| ❑ 207A | Terrell Owens | .50 | .20 |
| ❑ 208 | Ryan Moats | .40 | .15 |
| ❑ 209 | Correll Buckhalter | .30 | .12 |
| ❑ 210 | Jevon Kearse | .40 | .15 |
| ❑ 211 | L.J. Smith | .30 | .12 |
| ❑ 212 | Lamar Gordon | .25 | .10 |
| ❑ 213 | Greg Lewis | .30 | .12 |
| ❑ 214 | Ben Roethlisberger | .75 | .30 |
| ❑ 215 | Willie Parker | .60 | .25 |
| ❑ 216 | Jerome Bettis | .50 | .20 |
| ❑ 217 | Hines Ward | .40 | .15 |
| ❑ 218 | Troy Polamalu | .60 | .25 |
| ❑ 219 | Heath Miller | .40 | .15 |
| ❑ 220A | Antwaan Randle El | .40 | .15 |
| ❑ 221 | Duce Staley | .30 | .12 |
| ❑ 222 | Cedrick Wilson | .30 | .12 |
| ❑ 223 | James Farrior | .30 | .12 |
| ❑ 224A | Drew Brees | .50 | .20 |
| ❑ 225 | LaDainian Tomlinson | .60 | .25 |
| ❑ 226 | Keenan McCardell | .40 | .15 |
| ❑ 227 | Antonio Gates | .50 | .20 |
| ❑ 228 | Shawne Merriman | .50 | .20 |
| ❑ 229 | Philip Rivers | .50 | .20 |
| ❑ 230 | Vincent Jackson | .40 | .15 |
| ❑ 231 | Donnie Edwards | .30 | .12 |
| ❑ 232 | Eric Parker | .30 | .12 |
| ❑ 233A | Reche Caldwell | .30 | .12 |
| ❑ 234 | Alex Smith QB | .50 | .20 |
| ❑ 235 | Frank Gore | .50 | .20 |
| ❑ 236A | Brandon Lloyd | .40 | .15 |
| ❑ 237A | Kevan Barlow | .40 | .15 |
| ❑ 238A | Rashaun Woods | .25 | .10 |
| ❑ 239 | Arnaz Battle | .30 | .12 |
| ❑ 240 | Matt Hasselbeck | .40 | .15 |
| ❑ 241 | Shaun Alexander | .50 | .20 |
| ❑ 242 | Darrell Jackson | .40 | .15 |
| ❑ 243 | Jerramy Stevens | .40 | .15 |
| ❑ 244 | Lofa Tatupu | .40 | .15 |
| ❑ 245 | D.J. Hackett | .40 | .15 |
| ❑ 246 | Bobby Engram | .25 | .10 |
| ❑ 247A | Joe Jurevicius | .40 | .15 |
| ❑ 248 | Maurice Morris | .25 | .10 |
| ❑ 249 | Marc Bulger | .40 | .15 |
| ❑ 250 | Steven Jackson | .50 | .20 |
| ❑ 251 | Torry Holt | .40 | .15 |
| ❑ 252 | Isaac Bruce | .40 | .15 |
| ❑ 253 | Kevin Curtis | .40 | .15 |
| ❑ 254 | Marshall Faulk | .40 | .15 |
| ❑ 255 | Shaun McDonald | .30 | .12 |
| ❑ 256 | Chris Simms | .40 | .15 |
| ❑ 257 | Cadillac Williams | .50 | .20 |
| ❑ 258 | Joey Galloway | .40 | .15 |
| ❑ 259 | Michael Clayton | .40 | .15 |
| ❑ 260 | Derrick Brooks | .40 | .15 |
| ❑ 261 | Ronde Barber | .40 | .15 |
| ❑ 262 | Michael Pittman | .25 | .10 |
| ❑ 263 | Alex Smith TE | .30 | .12 |
| ❑ 264 | Simeon Rice | .30 | .12 |
| ❑ 265A | Steve McNair | .40 | .15 |
| ❑ 266 | Chris Brown | .40 | .15 |
| ❑ 267 | Drew Bennett | .40 | .15 |
| ❑ 268 | Brandon Jones | .30 | .12 |
| ❑ 269 | Adam Jones | .30 | .12 |
| ❑ 270 | Keith Bulluck | .30 | .12 |
| ❑ 271 | Ben Troupe | .30 | .12 |
| ❑ 272 | Jarrett Payton | .25 | .10 |
| ❑ 273 | Tyrone Calico | .30 | .12 |
| ❑ 274 | Bobby Wade | .25 | .10 |
| ❑ 275 | Troy Fleming | .25 | .10 |
| ❑ 276 | Mark Brunell | .40 | .15 |
| ❑ 277 | Clinton Portis | .50 | .20 |
| ❑ 278 | Santana Moss | .40 | .15 |
| ❑ 279 | Jason Campbell | .40 | .15 |
| ❑ 280 | Chris Cooley | .40 | .15 |
| ❑ 281 | Carlos Rogers | .30 | .12 |
| ❑ 282 | Ladell Betts | .40 | .15 |
| ❑ 283A | Patrick Ramsey | .40 | .15 |
| ❑ 284 | Taylor Jacobs | .25 | .10 |
| ❑ 285 | James Thrash | .25 | .10 |
| ❑ 286 | Adrian Wilson | .25 | .10 |
| ❑ 287 | London Fletcher | .30 | .12 |
| ❑ 288 | Lance Briggs | .40 | .15 |
| ❑ 289 | Robert Mathis | .25 | .10 |
| ❑ 290 | Rod Coleman | .25 | .10 |
| ❑ 291 | Bart Scott RC | 1.50 | .60 |
| ❑ 292 | Brian Moorman RC | .40 | .15 |
| ❑ 293 | Shayne Graham RC | .50 | .20 |
| ❑ 294 | Kevin Kaesviharn RC | .40 | .15 |
| ❑ 295 | Leigh Bodden RC | .40 | .15 |
| ❑ 296 | Lousaka Polite RC | .40 | .15 |
| ❑ 297 | Todd Devoe RC | .75 | .30 |
| ❑ 298 | Scottie Vines | .50 | .20 |
| ❑ 299 | Cullen Jenkins RC | .40 | .15 |
| ❑ 300 | Donovan Morgan RC | .40 | .15 |
| ❑ 301 | C.C. Brown | .40 | .15 |
| ❑ 302 | Demarcus Faggins RC | .50 | .20 |
| ❑ 303 | Shantee Orr RC | .40 | .15 |
| ❑ 304 | Vashon Pearson RC | .40 | .15 |
| ❑ 305 | Reggie Hayward RC | .40 | .15 |
| ❑ 306 | Paul Spicer RC | .40 | .15 |
| ❑ 307A | Kenny Wright Jaguars RC | .40 | .15 |
| ❑ 308 | Rich Alexis RC | .40 | .15 |
| ❑ 309 | Terrence Melton RC | .50 | .20 |
| ❑ 310 | Willie Whitehead RC | .40 | .15 |
| ❑ 311A | Kendrick Clancy Giants RC | .40 | .15 |
| ❑ 312 | Mark Brown RC | .50 | .20 |
| ❑ 313 | Tommy Kelly RC | .40 | .15 |
| ❑ 314 | Josh Parry RC | .40 | .15 |
| ❑ 315 | Malcolm Floyd RC | .75 | .30 |
| ❑ 316 | Mike Adams RC | .40 | .15 |
| ❑ 317 | Ben Emanuel RC | .50 | .20 |
| ❑ 318 | Brandon Moore RC | .40 | .15 |
| ❑ 319 | Chartric Darby RC | .40 | .15 |
| ❑ 320 | Bryce Fisher RC | .40 | .15 |
| ❑ 321 | D.D. Lewis RC | .40 | .15 |
| ❑ 322 | Jimmy Williams DB RC | .40 | .15 |
| ❑ 323A | Robert Pollard portrait RC | .40 | .15 |
| ❑ 324A | Chris Johnson Rams RC | .40 | .15 |
| ❑ 325 | Edell Shepherd RC | .40 | .15 |
| ❑ 326 | O.J. Small RC | .40 | .15 |
| ❑ 327A | Brad Kassell Titans RC | .40 | .15 |
| ❑ 328 | M.Leinart/R.Bush | 3.00 | 1.25 |
| ❑ 329 | M.Leinart/V.Young | 2.50 | 1.00 |
| ❑ 330 | White/Leinart/Bush | 3.00 | 1.25 |
| ❑ 331 | Matt Leinart RC | 4.00 | 1.50 |
| ❑ 332A | Chad Greenway RC | 1.25 | .50 |
| ❑ 333A | Devin Aromashodu RC | 1.00 | .40 |
| ❑ 334 | DeAngelo Williams RC | 2.00 | .75 |
| ❑ 335 | Travis Wilson RC | 1.25 | .50 |
| ❑ 336 | Leon Washington RC | 1.25 | .50 |
| ❑ 337 | Maurice Stovall RC | 1.25 | .50 |
| ❑ 338 | Michael Huff SP RC | 1.25 | .50 |
| ❑ 339 | Charlie Whitehurst RC | 1.25 | .50 |
| ❑ 340 | Vince Young RC | 4.00 | 1.50 |
| ❑ 341 | Jerious Norwood RC | 1.50 | .60 |
| ❑ 342A | D'Brickashaw Ferguson RC | 1.25 | .50 |
| ❑ 343A | Taurean Henderson RC | 1.25 | .50 |
| ❑ 344A | Dominique Byrd RC | 1.00 | .40 |
| ❑ 345 | Sinorice Moss SP RC | 1.25 | .50 |
| ❑ 346A | Martin Nance RC | 1.00 | .40 |
| ❑ 347 | Vernon Davis RC | 1.25 | .50 |
| ❑ 348 | Ko Simpson RC | 1.00 | .40 |
| ❑ 349A | Jerome Harrison RC | 1.25 | .50 |
| ❑ 350A | Jay Cutler RC | 5.00 | 2.00 |
| ❑ 350B | Jay Cutler | 5.00 | 2.00 |
| ❑ 351A | Alan Zemaitis RC | 1.25 | .50 |
| ❑ 352A | Haloti Ngata SP RC | 1.25 | .50 |
| ❑ 353A | Greg Lee RC | 1.00 | .40 |
| ❑ 354 | Laurence Maroney RC | 3.00 | 1.25 |
| ❑ 355A | Bobby Carpenter SP RC | 1.25 | .50 |
| ❑ 356A | Jonathan Orr RC | 1.00 | .40 |
| ❑ 357 | Marcedes Lewis RC | 1.25 | .50 |
| ❑ 358A | Brodrick Bunkley SP RC | 1.25 | .50 |
| ❑ 359A | Todd Watkins RC | 1.00 | .40 |
| ❑ 360 | Reggie Bush RC | 5.00 | 2.00 |
| ❑ 361A | Jimmy Williams RC | 1.25 | .50 |
| ❑ 362 | Maurice Drew RC | 2.50 | 1.00 |
| ❑ 363 | Mario Williams RC | 2.00 | .75 |
| ❑ 364 | Derek Hagan RC | 1.25 | .50 |
| ❑ 365 | Santonio Holmes RC | 3.00 | 1.25 |
| ❑ 366A | Tye Hill RC | 1.25 | .50 |
| ❑ 367 | Jason Avant RC | 1.25 | .50 |
| ❑ 368A | Tamba Hali SP RC | 1.25 | .50 |
| ❑ 369 | Joe Klopfenstein RC | 1.00 | .40 |
| ❑ 370 | LenDale White RC | 2.50 | 1.00 |
| ❑ 371A | DeMeco Ryans RC | 1.50 | .60 |
| ❑ 372A | Bruce Gradkowski SP RC | 1.25 | .50 |
| ❑ 373 | A.J. Hawk RC | 2.50 | 1.00 |
| ❑ 374A | Gabe Watson RC | 1.00 | .40 |
| ❑ 375A | Devin Hester SP RC | 2.50 | 1.00 |
| ❑ 376 | Demetrius Williams SP RC | 1.25 | .50 |
| ❑ 377A | Joseph Addai RC | 4.00 | 1.50 |
| ❑ 377B | Joseph Addai | 4.00 | 1.50 |
| ❑ 378A | Leonard Pope RC | 1.25 | .50 |
| ❑ 379 | Omar Jacobs RC | 1.00 | .40 |
| ❑ 380A | Brad Smith SP RC | 1.25 | .50 |
| ❑ 381 | Michael Robinson RC | 1.25 | .50 |
| ❑ 382A | Brodie Croyle RC | 1.50 | .60 |
| ❑ 383A | Anthony Fasano RC | 1.25 | .50 |
| ❑ 384 | Brian Calhoun RC | 1.00 | .40 |
| ❑ 385 | Chad Jackson RC | 1.00 | .40 |
| ❑ 386 | Drew Olson RC | 1.00 | .40 |
| ❑ 387 | Greg Jennings RC | 2.00 | .75 |
| ❑ 388 | Andre Hall RC | 1.25 | .50 |
| ❑ 389 | Mike Espy RC | 1.25 | .50 |
| ❑ 390 | Tim Day RC | 1.00 | .40 |
| ❑ 391 | Brandon Williams RC | 1.25 | .50 |
| ❑ 392 | Mark Anderson RC | 3.00 | 1.25 |
| ❑ 393 | DonTrell Moore RC | 1.25 | .50 |
| ❑ 394 | Kellen Clemens RC | 1.50 | .60 |
| ❑ 395 | Ernie Sims RC | 1.25 | .50 |
| ❑ 396 | Cedric Humes RC | 1.25 | .50 |
| ❑ 397 | Brandon Kirsch RC | 1.25 | .50 |
| ❑ 398 | Tony Scheffler RC | 1.25 | .50 |
| ❑ 399 | Kelly Jennings RC | 1.25 | .50 |
| ❑ 400 | Manny Lawson RC | 1.25 | .50 |
| ❑ 401 | Terrence Whitehead RC | 1.25 | .50 |
| ❑ 402 | Marcus Vick RC | 1.00 | .40 |
| ❑ 403 | De'Arrius Howard RC | 1.25 | .50 |
| ❑ 404 | Wendell Mathis RC | 1.00 | .40 |
| ❑ 405 | Abdul Hodge RC | 1.25 | .50 |
| ❑ 406 | Owen Daniels RC | 1.25 | .50 |
| ❑ 407 | Mike Hass RC | 1.25 | .50 |
| ❑ 408 | Brett Elliott RC | 1.25 | .50 |
| ❑ 409 | Kamerion Wimbley RC | 1.25 | .50 |
| ❑ 410 | Jeremy Bloom RC | 1.00 | .40 |
| ❑ 411 | D.J. Shockley RC | 1.25 | .50 |
| ❑ 412 | Darnell Bing RC | 1.25 | .50 |

|  |  | | |
|---|---|---|---|
| 413 | Miles Austin RC | 1.25 | .50 |
| 414 | D'Qwell Jackson RC | 1.00 | .40 |
| 415 | Tarvaris Jackson RC | 1.25 | .50 |
| 416 | Mathias Kiwanuka RC | 1.50 | .60 |
| 417 | Mike Bell RC | 1.25 | .50 |
| 418 | Paul Pinegar RC | 1.00 | .40 |
| 419 | David Thomas RC | 1.25 | .50 |
| 420 | Hank Baskett RC | 1.25 | .50 |
| 421 | P.J. Daniels RC | 1.00 | .40 |
| 422 | Jon Alston RC | 1.25 | .50 |
| 423 | Reggie McNeal RC | 1.25 | .50 |
| 424 | Brandon Marshall RC | 1.50 | .60 |
| 425 | Gerald Riggs RC | 1.25 | .50 |
| 426 | Delanie Walker RC | 1.00 | .40 |
| 427 | Erik Meyer RC | 1.00 | .40 |
| 428 | Jeff Webb RC | 1.00 | .40 |
| 429 | Skyler Green RC | 1.25 | .50 |
| 430 | Thomas Howard RC | 1.25 | .50 |
| 431 | Ashton Youboty RC | 1.25 | .50 |
| 432 | Cedric Griffin RC | 1.00 | .40 |
| 433 | Donte Whitner RC | 1.25 | .50 |
| 434 | Jason Allen RC | 1.25 | .50 |
| 435 | Pat Watkins RC | 1.25 | .50 |
| 436 | Rocky McIntosh RC | 1.25 | .50 |
| 437 | Ingle Martin RC | 1.25 | .50 |
| 438 | John David Washington RC | 1.00 | .40 |
| 439 | Cory Rodgers RC | 1.25 | .50 |
| 440 | Willie Reid RC | 1.25 | .50 |

## 2007 Score

|  |  | | |
|---|---|---|---|
| 1 | Tony Romo | 1.00 | .40 |
| 2 | Julius Jones | .40 | .15 |
| 3 | Terry Glenn | .50 | .15 |
| 4 | Terrell Owens | .50 | .20 |
| 5 | Jason Witten | .40 | .15 |
| 6 | Marion Barber | .50 | .20 |
| 7 | Patrick Crayton | .30 | .12 |
| 8 | Bradie James | .30 | .12 |
| 9 | DeMarcus Ware | .40 | .15 |
| 10 | Roy Williams S | .40 | .15 |
| 11 | Eli Manning | .50 | .20 |
| 12 | Plaxico Burress | .40 | .15 |
| 13 | Jeremy Shockey | .40 | .15 |
| 14 | Brandon Jacobs | .40 | .15 |
| 15 | Sinorice Moss | .40 | .15 |
| 16 | Antonio Pierce | .30 | .12 |
| 17 | David Tyree | .30 | .12 |
| 18 | Donovan McNabb | .50 | .20 |
| 19 | Brian Westbrook | .40 | .15 |
| 20 | Reggie Brown | .40 | .15 |
| 21 | L.J. Smith | .30 | .12 |
| 22 | Hank Baskett | .40 | .15 |
| 23 | Jeremiah Trotter | .30 | .12 |
| 24 | Trent Cole | .30 | .12 |
| 25 | Lito Sheppard | .30 | .12 |
| 26 | Jason Campbell | .40 | .15 |
| 27 | Clinton Portis | .40 | .15 |
| 28 | Santana Moss | .40 | .15 |
| 29 | Brandon Lloyd | .40 | .15 |
| 30 | Chris Cooley | .30 | .12 |
| 31 | Sean Taylor | .30 | .12 |
| 32 | Lemar Marshall | .30 | .12 |
| 33 | Ladell Betts | .30 | .12 |
| 34 | London Fletcher | .30 | .12 |
| 35 | Rex Grossman | .40 | .15 |
| 36 | Cedric Benson | .40 | .15 |
| 37 | Muhsin Muhammad | .40 | .15 |
| 38 | Bernard Berrian | .30 | .12 |
| 39 | Desmond Clark | .30 | .12 |
| 40 | Lance Briggs | .30 | .12 |
| 41 | Robbie Gould | .30 | .12 |
| 42 | Devin Hester | .50 | .20 |
| 43 | Mark Anderson | .40 | .15 |
| 44 | Brian Urlacher | .50 | .20 |
| 45 | Jon Kitna | .30 | .12 |
| 46 | Kevin Jones | .30 | .12 |
| 47 | Roy Williams WR | .40 | .15 |
| 49 | Cory Redding | .30 | .12 |
| 50 | Ernie Sims | .30 | .12 |
| 51 | Tatum Bell | .30 | .12 |
| 52 | Brian Calhoun | .30 | .12 |
| 53 | Brett Favre | 1.00 | .40 |
| 54 | Vernand Morency | .40 | .15 |
| 55 | Donald Driver | .40 | .15 |
| 56 | Greg Jennings | .40 | .15 |
| 57 | Aaron Kampman | .40 | .15 |
| 58 | Charles Woodson | .40 | .15 |
| 59 | A.J. Hawk | .50 | .20 |
| 60 | Nick Barnett | .30 | .12 |
| 61 | Aaron Rodgers | .50 | .20 |
| 62 | Tarvaris Jackson | .40 | .15 |
| 63 | Chester Taylor | .30 | .12 |
| 64 | Troy Williamson | .30 | .12 |
| 65 | Jim Kleinsasser | .30 | .12 |
| 66 | Dwight Smith | .30 | .12 |
| 67 | Antoine Winfield | .30 | .12 |
| 68 | E.J. Henderson | .30 | .12 |
| 69 | Mewelde Moore | .30 | .12 |
| 70 | Michael Vick | .50 | .20 |
| 71 | Warrick Dunn | .40 | .15 |
| 72 | Joe Horn | .40 | .15 |
| 73 | Michael Jenkins | .30 | .12 |
| 74 | Alge Crumpler | .40 | .15 |
| 75 | DeAngelo Hall | .40 | .15 |
| 76 | Keith Brooking | .30 | .12 |
| 77 | Lawyer Milloy | .30 | .12 |
| 78 | Jerious Norwood | .40 | .15 |
| 79 | Matt Schaub | .40 | .15 |
| 80 | Jake Delhomme | .40 | .15 |
| 81 | DeShaun Foster | .30 | .12 |
| 82 | Steve Smith | .40 | .15 |
| 83 | Keyshawn Johnson | .40 | .15 |
| 84 | Julius Peppers | .40 | .15 |
| 85 | DeAngelo Williams | .50 | .20 |
| 86 | Chris Draft | .30 | .12 |
| 87 | Drew Brees | .40 | .15 |
| 88 | Deuce McAllister | .40 | .15 |
| 89 | Scott Fujita | .30 | .12 |
| 90 | Marques Colston | .50 | .20 |
| 91 | Terrance Copper | .30 | .12 |
| 92 | Will Smith | .30 | .12 |
| 93 | Charles Grant | .30 | .12 |
| 94 | Devery Henderson | .30 | .12 |
| 95 | Reggie Bush | .60 | .25 |
| 96 | Jeff Garcia | .40 | .15 |
| 97 | Cadillac Williams | .40 | .15 |
| 98 | Joey Galloway | .40 | .15 |
| 99 | Michael Clayton | .40 | .15 |
| 100 | Alex Smith TE | .30 | .12 |
| 101 | Ronde Barber | .30 | .12 |
| 102 | Jermaine Phillips | .30 | .12 |
| 103 | Derrick Brooks | .40 | .15 |
| 104 | Matt Leinart | .50 | .20 |
| 105 | Edgerrin James | .40 | .15 |
| 106 | Anquan Boldin | .40 | .15 |
| 107 | Larry Fitzgerald | .50 | .20 |
| 108 | Neil Rackers | .30 | .12 |
| 109 | Adrian Wilson | .30 | .12 |
| 110 | Karlos Dansby | .30 | .12 |
| 111 | Chike Okeafor | .30 | .12 |
| 112 | Marc Bulger | .40 | .15 |
| 113 | Steven Jackson | .50 | .20 |
| 114 | Torry Holt | .40 | .15 |
| 115 | Isaac Bruce | .40 | .15 |
| 116 | Joe Klopfenstein | .30 | .12 |
| 117 | Randy McMichael | .30 | .12 |
| 118 | Will Witherspoon | .30 | .12 |
| 119 | Drew Bennett | .30 | .12 |
| 120 | Alex Smith QB | .50 | .20 |
| 121 | Frank Gore | .50 | .20 |
| 122 | Arnaz Battle | .30 | .12 |
| 123 | Ashley Lelie | .40 | .15 |
| 124 | Vernon Davis | .30 | .15 |
| 125 | Walt Harris | .30 | .12 |
| 126 | Brandon Moore | .30 | .12 |
| 127 | Nate Clements | .30 | .12 |
| 128 | Matt Hasselbeck | .40 | .15 |
| 129 | Shaun Alexander | .40 | .15 |
| 130 | Deion Branch | .40 | .15 |
| 131 | Darrell Jackson | .30 | .12 |
| 132 | Nate Burleson | .30 | .12 |
| 133 | Julian Peterson | .30 | .12 |
| 134 | Lofa Tatupu | .40 | .15 |
| 135 | Mack Strong | .30 | .12 |
| 136 | Josh Brown | .30 | .12 |
| 137 | J.P. Losman | .30 | .12 |
| 138 | Anthony Thomas | .30 | .12 |
| 139 | Lee Evans | .40 | .15 |
| 140 | Josh Reed | .30 | .12 |
| 141 | Roscoe Parrish | .30 | .12 |
| 142 | Aaron Schobel | .30 | .12 |
| 143 | Donte Whitner | .30 | .12 |
| 144 | Shaud Williams | .30 | .12 |
| 145 | Daunte Culpepper | .40 | .15 |
| 146 | Ronnie Brown | .40 | .15 |
| 147 | Chris Chambers | .40 | .15 |
| 148 | Marty Booker | .30 | .12 |
| 149 | Derek Hagan | .30 | .12 |
| 150 | Jason Taylor | .30 | .12 |
| 151 | Vonnie Holliday | .30 | .12 |
| 152 | Zach Thomas | .40 | .15 |
| 153 | Channing Crowder | .30 | .12 |
| 154 | Joey Porter | .30 | .12 |
| 155 | Tom Brady | 1.00 | .40 |
| 156 | Laurence Maroney | .50 | .20 |
| 157 | Chad Jackson | .30 | .12 |
| 158 | Wes Welker | .50 | .20 |
| 159 | Ben Watson | .30 | .12 |
| 160 | Donte Stallworth | .40 | .15 |
| 161 | Rosevelt Colvin | .30 | .12 |
| 162 | Ty Warren | .30 | .12 |
| 163 | Asante Samuel | .30 | .12 |
| 164 | Adalius Thomas | .30 | .12 |
| 165 | Tedy Bruschi | .50 | .20 |
| 166 | Chad Pennington | .40 | .15 |
| 167 | Thomas Jones | .40 | .15 |
| 168 | Laveranues Coles | .40 | .15 |
| 169 | Jerricho Cotchery | .30 | .12 |
| 170 | Chris Baker | .30 | .12 |
| 171 | Bryan Thomas | .30 | .12 |
| 172 | Leon Washington | .40 | .15 |
| 173 | Jonathan Vilma | .40 | .15 |
| 174 | Eric Barton | .30 | .12 |
| 175 | Erik Coleman | .30 | .12 |
| 176 | Steve McNair | .40 | .15 |
| 177 | Willis McGahee | .40 | .15 |
| 178 | Derrick Mason | .40 | .15 |
| 179 | Demetrius Williams | .30 | .12 |
| 180 | Todd Heap | .30 | .12 |
| 181 | Ray Lewis | .50 | .20 |
| 182 | Trevor Pryce | .30 | .12 |
| 183 | Bart Scott | .40 | .15 |
| 184 | Terrell Suggs | .30 | .12 |
| 185 | Mark Clayton | .40 | .15 |
| 186 | Carson Palmer | .50 | .20 |
| 187 | Rudi Johnson | .40 | .15 |
| 188 | Chad Johnson | .40 | .15 |
| 189 | T.J. Houshmandzadeh | .40 | .15 |
| 190 | Robert Geathers | .30 | .12 |
| 191 | Justin Smith | .30 | .12 |
| 192 | Tory James | .30 | .12 |
| 193 | Landon Johnson | .30 | .12 |
| 194 | Shayne Graham | .30 | .12 |
| 195 | Charlie Frye | .40 | .15 |
| 196 | Reuben Droughns | .30 | .12 |
| 197 | Braylon Edwards | .40 | .15 |
| 198 | Travis Wilson | .30 | .12 |
| 199 | Kellen Winslow | .40 | .15 |
| 200 | Kamerion Wimbley | .30 | .12 |
| 201 | Sean Jones | .30 | .12 |
| 202 | Andra Davis | .30 | .12 |
| 203 | Jamal Lewis | .40 | .15 |
| 204 | Ben Roethlisberger | .60 | .25 |
| 205 | Willie Parker | .50 | .20 |
| 206 | Hines Ward | .50 | .20 |
| 207 | Santonio Holmes | .40 | .15 |
| 208 | Heath Miller | .30 | .12 |

|  |  | | |
|---|---|---|---|
| 209 | Troy Polamalu | .50 | .20 |
| 210 | James Farrior | .30 | .12 |
| 211 | Cedrick Wilson | .30 | .12 |
| 212 | Dunta Robinson | .30 | .12 |
| 213 | Ahman Green | .40 | .15 |
| 214 | Andre Johnson | .40 | .15 |
| 215 | Jerome Mathis | .30 | .12 |
| 216 | Owen Daniels | .30 | .12 |
| 217 | DeMeco Ryans | .40 | .15 |
| 218 | Wali Lundy | .30 | .12 |
| 219 | Mario Williams | .40 | .15 |
| 220 | Peyton Manning | .75 | .30 |
| 221 | Joseph Addai | .50 | .20 |
| 222 | Marvin Harrison | .50 | .20 |
| 223 | Reggie Wayne | .40 | .15 |
| 224 | Dallas Clark | .30 | .12 |
| 225 | Robert Mathis | .30 | .12 |
| 226 | Cato June | .30 | .12 |
| 227 | Adam Vinatieri | .40 | .15 |
| 228 | Bob Sanders | .40 | .15 |
| 229 | Dwight Freeney | .40 | .15 |
| 230 | Byron Leftwich | .40 | .15 |
| 231 | Fred Taylor | .40 | .15 |
| 232 | Matt Jones | .30 | .12 |
| 233 | Reggie Williams | .30 | .12 |
| 234 | Marcedes Lewis | .30 | .12 |
| 235 | Bobby McCray | .30 | .12 |
| 236 | Rasheam Mathis | .30 | .12 |
| 237 | Maurice Jones-Drew | .50 | .20 |
| 238 | Ernest Wilford | .30 | .12 |
| 239 | Daryl Smith | .30 | .12 |
| 240 | Vince Young | .40 | .15 |
| 241 | LenDale White | .40 | .15 |
| 242 | Brandon Jones | .30 | .12 |
| 243 | Bo Scaife | .30 | .12 |
| 244 | Keith Bulluck | .30 | .12 |
| 245 | Chris Hope | .30 | .12 |
| 246 | Kyle Vanden Bosch | .30 | .12 |
| 247 | Roydell Williams | .30 | .12 |
| 248 | Jay Cutler | .50 | .20 |
| 249 | Travis Henry | .40 | .15 |
| 250 | Javon Walker | .40 | .15 |
| 251 | Rod Smith | .40 | .15 |
| 252 | Tony Scheffler | .40 | .15 |
| 253 | Elvis Dumervil | .30 | .12 |
| 254 | Champ Bailey | .40 | .15 |
| 255 | Mike Bell | .40 | .15 |
| 256 | Brandon Marshall | .50 | .20 |
| 257 | Al Wilson | .30 | .12 |
| 258 | Trent Green | .40 | .15 |
| 259 | Larry Johnson | .40 | .15 |
| 260 | Eddie Kennison | .30 | .12 |
| 261 | Samie Parker | .30 | .12 |
| 262 | Tony Gonzalez | .40 | .15 |
| 263 | Jared Allen | .30 | .12 |
| 264 | Kawika Mitchell | .30 | .12 |
| 265 | Tamba Hali | .30 | .12 |
| 266 | Dante Hall | .40 | .15 |
| 267 | Brodie Croyle | .50 | .20 |
| 268 | Andrew Walter | .50 | .20 |
| 269 | LaMont Jordan | .40 | .15 |
| 270 | Dominic Rhodes | .40 | .15 |
| 271 | Randy Moss | .50 | .20 |
| 272 | Ronald Curry | .40 | .15 |
| 273 | Courtney Anderson | .30 | .12 |
| 274 | Derrick Burgess | .30 | .12 |
| 275 | Warren Sapp | .40 | .15 |
| 276 | Michael Huff | .40 | .15 |
| 277 | Thomas Howard | .30 | .12 |
| 278 | Kirk Morrison | .30 | .12 |
| 279 | Philip Rivers | .50 | .20 |
| 280 | LaDainian Tomlinson | .60 | .25 |
| 281 | Vincent Jackson | .40 | .15 |
| 282 | Lorenzo Neal | .30 | .12 |
| 283 | Antonio Gates | .40 | .15 |
| 284 | Shawne Merriman | .40 | .15 |
| 285 | Shaun Phillips | .30 | .12 |
| 286 | Michael Turner | .40 | .15 |
| 287 | Jamal Williams | .30 | .12 |
| 288 | Nate Kaeding | .30 | .12 |
| 289 | Michael Okwo RC | 1.00 | .40 |
| 290 | Gary Russell RC | 1.25 | .50 |
| 291 | Josh Wilson RC | 1.00 | .40 |
| 292 | Thomas Clayton RC | 1.00 | .40 |
| 293 | Jerard Rabb RC | 1.00 | .40 |
| 294 | Roy Hall RC | 1.25 | .50 |
| 295 | LaMarr Woodley RC | 1.25 | .50 |
| 296 | Eric Wright RC | 1.25 | .50 |
| 297 | Dan Bazuin RC | 1.00 | .40 |
| 298 | A.J. Davis RC | .75 | .30 |
| 299 | Buster Davis RC | 1.00 | .40 |
| 300 | Stewart Bradley RC | 1.25 | .50 |
| 301 | Toby Korrodi RC | 1.00 | .40 |
| 302 | Marcus McCauley RC | 1.00 | .40 |
| 303 | Demarcus Tank Tyler RC | 1.00 | .40 |
| 304 | Jon Abbate RC | .75 | .30 |
| 305 | Ikaika Alama-Francis RC | 1.25 | .50 |
| 306 | Tim Crowder RC | 1.25 | .50 |
| 307 | D'Juan Woods RC | 1.25 | .50 |
| 308 | Tim Shaw RC | 1.00 | .40 |
| 309 | Fred Bennett RC | .75 | .30 |
| 310 | Victor Abiamiri RC | 1.25 | .50 |
| 311 | Eric Weddle RC | 1.00 | .40 |
| 312 | Danny Ware RC | 1.00 | .40 |
| 313 | Quentin Moses RC | 1.00 | .40 |
| 314 | Ryan McBean RC | 1.25 | .50 |
| 315 | David Harris RC | 1.00 | .40 |
| 316 | David Irons RC | .75 | .30 |
| 317 | Syndric Steptoe RC | 1.00 | .40 |
| 318 | Eric Frampton RC | 1.00 | .40 |
| 319 | Jemalle Cornelius RC | 1.00 | .40 |
| 320 | Earl Everett RC | 1.00 | .40 |
| 321 | Alonzo Coleman RC | 1.25 | .50 |
| 322 | Josh Gattis RC | .75 | .30 |
| 323 | Zak DeOssie RC | 1.00 | .40 |
| 324 | Jon Beason RC | 1.25 | .50 |
| 325 | Joe Staley RC | 1.00 | .40 |
| 326 | Aaron Rouse RC | 1.25 | .50 |
| 327 | Reggie Ball RC | 1.00 | .40 |
| 328 | Rufus Alexander RC | 1.25 | .50 |
| 329 | Dymeion Hughes RC | 1.00 | .40 |
| 330 | Justin Durant RC | 1.00 | .40 |
| 331 | JaMarcus Russell RC | 3.00 | 1.25 |
| 332 | Paul Williams RC | 1.00 | .40 |
| 333 | Kenny Irons RC | 1.25 | .50 |
| 334 | Chris Davis RC | 1.00 | .40 |
| 335 | Darius Walker RC | 1.25 | .50 |
| 336 | Dwayne Bowe RC | 2.50 | 1.00 |
| 337 | Isaiah Stanback RC | 1.25 | .50 |
| 338 | Leon Hall RC | 1.00 | .40 |
| 339 | Sidney Rice RC | 1.25 | .50 |
| 340 | Amobi Okoye RC | 1.25 | .50 |
| 341 | Adrian Peterson RC | 10.00 | 4.00 |
| 342 | LaRon Landry RC | 1.50 | .60 |
| 343 | Lorenzo Booker RC | 1.25 | .50 |
| 344 | Craig Buster Davis RC | 1.25 | .50 |
| 345 | Mike Walker RC | 1.00 | .40 |
| 346 | Zach Miller RC | .75 | .30 |
| 347 | Levi Brown RC | 1.25 | .50 |
| 348 | Brian Leonard RC | 1.25 | .50 |
| 349 | Aundrae Allison RC | 1.00 | .40 |
| 350 | Brandon Siler RC | 1.00 | .40 |
| 351 | Calvin Johnson RC | 3.00 | 1.00 |
| 352 | Gaines Adams RC | 1.25 | .50 |
| 353 | Anthony Gonzalez RC | 2.00 | .75 |
| 354 | John Beck RC | 1.25 | .50 |
| 355 | Joe Thomas RC | 1.25 | .50 |
| 356 | Michael Bush RC | 1.25 | .50 |
| 357 | Courtney Taylor RC | 1.00 | .40 |
| 358 | Lawrence Timmons RC | 1.25 | .50 |
| 359 | Drew Stanton RC | 1.25 | .50 |
| 360 | Chansi Stuckey RC | 1.00 | .40 |
| 361 | Greg Olsen RC | 1.50 | .60 |
| 362 | Rhema McKnight RC | 1.00 | .40 |
| 363 | Antonio Pittman RC | 1.25 | .50 |
| 364 | Kevin Kolb RC | 2.00 | .75 |
| 365 | Alan Branch RC | 1.00 | .40 |
| 366 | Robert Meachem RC | 1.25 | .50 |
| 367 | Troy Smith RC | 1.50 | .60 |
| 368 | Jamaal Anderson RC | 1.00 | .40 |
| 369 | Tony Hunt RC | 1.25 | .50 |
| 370 | David Clowney RC | 1.00 | .40 |
| 371 | Brady Quinn RC | 4.00 | 1.50 |
| 372 | Michael Griffin RC | 1.25 | .50 |
| 373 | Jared Zabransky RC | 1.25 | .50 |
| 374 | Jason Hill RC | 1.25 | .50 |
| 375 | Trent Edwards RC | 3.00 | 1.25 |
| 376 | Dwayne Jarrett RC | 1.25 | .50 |
| 377 | DeShawn Wynn RC | 1.25 | .50 |
| 378 | Patrick Willis RC | 2.50 | 1.00 |
| 379 | Steve Smith USC RC | 1.50 | .60 |
| 380 | David Ball RC | .75 | .30 |
| 381 | Marshawn Lynch RC | 2.50 | 1.00 |
| 382 | Paul Posluszny RC | 1.50 | .60 |
| 383 | Johnnie Lee Higgins RC | 1.00 | .40 |
| 384 | Kolby Smith RC | 1.25 | .50 |
| 385 | Ted Ginn Jr. RC | 2.00 | .75 |
| 386 | Adam Carriker RC | 1.00 | .40 |
| 387 | Tyler Palko RC | 1.25 | .50 |
| 388 | Joel Filani RC | 1.00 | .40 |
| 389 | Garrett Wolfe RC | 1.25 | .50 |
| 390 | Ryne Robinson RC | 1.00 | .40 |
| 391 | Reggie Nelson RC | 1.00 | .40 |
| 392 | Dallas Baker RC | 1.00 | .40 |
| 393 | Dwayne Wright RC | 1.00 | .40 |
| 394 | Scott Chandler RC | 1.00 | .40 |
| 395 | Jordan Kent RC | 1.00 | .40 |
| 396 | Jarvis Moss RC | 1.25 | .50 |
| 397 | Jonathan Wade RC | 1.00 | .40 |
| 398 | Ben Grubbs RC | 1.00 | .40 |
| 399 | Jason Snelling RC | 1.00 | .40 |
| 400 | Jeff Rowe RC | 1.00 | .40 |
| 401 | Aaron Ross RC | 1.25 | .50 |
| 402 | Daniel Sepulveda RC | 1.25 | .50 |
| 403 | Chris Henry RC | 1.25 | .50 |
| 404 | James Jones RC | 1.25 | .50 |
| 405 | Matt Spaeth RC | 1.25 | .50 |
| 406 | Brandon Meriweather RC | 1.25 | .50 |
| 407 | Nate Ilaoa RC | 1.25 | .50 |
| 408 | Mason Crosby RC | 1.25 | .50 |
| 409 | Ray McDonald RC | 1.00 | .40 |
| 410 | Chris Leak RC | 1.00 | .40 |
| 411 | Darrelle Revis RC | 1.25 | .50 |
| 412 | Ahmad Bradshaw RC | 1.50 | .60 |
| 413 | Tyler Thigpen RC | 1.50 | .60 |
| 414 | Justise Hairston RC | 1.00 | .40 |
| 415 | Charles Johnson RC | .75 | .30 |
| 416 | Anthony Spencer RC | 1.25 | .50 |
| 417 | Legedu Naanee RC | 1.25 | .50 |
| 418 | Kenneth Darby RC | 1.25 | .50 |
| 419 | Steve Breaston RC | 1.25 | .50 |
| 420 | Ben Patrick RC | 1.00 | .40 |
| 421 | Chris Houston RC | 1.00 | .40 |
| 422 | Jordan Palmer RC | 1.25 | .50 |
| 423 | Laurent Robinson RC | 1.00 | .40 |
| 424 | Selvin Young RC | 2.00 | .75 |
| 425 | Justin Harrell RC | 1.25 | .50 |
| 426 | Sabby Piscitelli RC | 1.25 | .50 |
| 427 | Yamon Figurs RC | 1.25 | .50 |
| 428 | Brandon Jackson RC | 1.25 | .50 |
| 429 | Jacoby Jones RC | 1.25 | .50 |
| 430 | H.B. Blades RC | 1.00 | .40 |
| 431 | Tanard Jackson RC | .75 | .30 |
| 432 | Matt Gutierrez RC | 1.25 | .50 |
| 433 | Matt Moore RC | 1.25 | .50 |
| 434 | Clifton Dawson RC | 1.25 | .50 |
| 435 | Marcus Mason RC | 1.25 | .50 |
| 436 | Pierre Thomas RC | 4.00 | 1.50 |
| 437 | Dante Rosario RC | 1.25 | .50 |
| 438 | Biren Ealy RC | 1.00 | .40 |
| 439 | John Broussard RC | 1.00 | .40 |
| 440 | Kenton Keith RC | 1.25 | .50 |

## 2008 Score

|  |  | | |
|---|---|---|---|
| 1 | Matt Leinart | .50 | .20 |
| 2 | Kurt Warner | .50 | .20 |
| 3 | Larry Fitzgerald | .50 | .20 |
| 4 | Anquan Boldin | .40 | .15 |

|  |  | | |  |  | | |  |  | | |
|---|---|---|---|---|---|---|---|---|---|---|---|
| ❑ 5 | Edgerrin James | .40 | .15 | ❑ 90 | Selvin Young | .40 | .15 | ❑ 175 | Sidney Rice | .40 | .15 |
| ❑ 6 | Neil Rackers | .30 | .12 | ❑ 91 | Brandon Marshall | .40 | .15 | ❑ 176 | Robert Ferguson | .30 | .12 |
| ❑ 7 | Steve Breaston | .30 | .12 | ❑ 92 | Brandon Stokley | .40 | .15 | ❑ 177 | Darren Sharper | .30 | .12 |
| ❑ 8 | Antrel Rolle | .30 | .12 | ❑ 93 | Champ Bailey | .30 | .12 | ❑ 178 | Visanthe Shiancoe | .30 | .12 |
| ❑ 9 | Karlos Dansby | .30 | .12 | ❑ 94 | John Lynch | .40 | .15 | ❑ 179 | E.J. Henderson | .30 | .12 |
| ❑ 10 | Joey Harrington | .40 | .15 | ❑ 95 | Dre Bly | .30 | .12 | ❑ 180 | Cedric Griffin | .30 | .12 |
| ❑ 11 | Jerious Norwood | .40 | .15 | ❑ 96 | Elvis Dumervil | .40 | .15 | ❑ 181 | Chad Greenway | .30 | .12 |
| ❑ 12 | Roddy White | .40 | .15 | ❑ 97 | Jon Kitna | .40 | .15 | ❑ 182 | Tom Brady | .75 | .30 |
| ❑ 13 | Michael Jenkins | .30 | .12 | ❑ 98 | Tatum Bell | .30 | .12 | ❑ 183 | Randy Moss | .50 | .20 |
| ❑ 14 | Joe Horn | .40 | .15 | ❑ 99 | Shaun McDonald | .30 | .12 | ❑ 184 | Laurence Maroney | .40 | .15 |
| ❑ 15 | Keith Brooking | .30 | .12 | ❑ 100 | Roy Williams WR | .40 | .15 | ❑ 185 | Wes Welker | .50 | .20 |
| ❑ 16 | Lawyer Milloy | .30 | .12 | ❑ 101 | Calvin Johnson | .50 | .20 | ❑ 186 | Sammy Morris | .30 | .12 |
| ❑ 17 | John Abraham | .30 | .12 | ❑ 102 | Mike Furrey | .40 | .15 | ❑ 187 | Kevin Faulk | .40 | .15 |
| ❑ 18 | Michael Turner | .40 | .15 | ❑ 103 | Ernie Sims | .30 | .12 | ❑ 188 | Ben Watson | .30 | .12 |
| ❑ 19 | Troy Smith | .40 | .15 | ❑ 104 | Aveion Cason | .30 | .12 | ❑ 189 | Tedy Bruschi | .50 | .20 |
| ❑ 20 | Willis McGahee | .40 | .15 | ❑ 105 | Aaron Rodgers | .50 | .20 | ❑ 190 | Rodney Harrison | .30 | .12 |
| ❑ 21 | Musa Smith | .30 | .12 | ❑ 106 | Brett Favre | 1.25 | .50 | ❑ 191 | Mike Vrabel | .30 | .12 |
| ❑ 22 | Derrick Mason | .30 | .12 | ❑ 107 | Ryan Grant | .50 | .20 | ❑ 192 | Drew Brees | .50 | .20 |
| ❑ 23 | Mark Clayton | .30 | .12 | ❑ 108 | Greg Jennings | .40 | .15 | ❑ 193 | Reggie Bush | .50 | .20 |
| ❑ 24 | Bart Scott | .30 | .12 | ❑ 109 | Donald Driver | .40 | .15 | ❑ 194 | Deuce McAllister | .40 | .15 |
| ❑ 25 | Demetrius Williams | .30 | .12 | ❑ 110 | Donald Lee | .40 | .15 | ❑ 195 | Marques Colston | .40 | .15 |
| ❑ 26 | Yamon Figurs | .30 | .12 | ❑ 111 | James Jones | .30 | .12 | ❑ 196 | David Patten | .30 | .12 |
| ❑ 27 | Ray Lewis | .50 | .20 | ❑ 112 | Al Harris | .30 | .12 | ❑ 197 | Devery Henderson | .30 | .12 |
| ❑ 28 | Terrell Suggs | .30 | .12 | ❑ 113 | Nick Barnett | .30 | .12 | ❑ 198 | Scott Fujita | .30 | .12 |
| ❑ 29 | Ed Reed | .40 | .15 | ❑ 114 | Charles Woodson | .40 | .15 | ❑ 199 | Roman Harper | .30 | .12 |
| ❑ 30 | Trent Edwards | .50 | .20 | ❑ 115 | Aaron Kampman | .40 | .15 | ❑ 200 | Mike McKenzie | .30 | .12 |
| ❑ 31 | Marshawn Lynch | .50 | .20 | ❑ 116 | Mason Crosby | .40 | .15 | ❑ 201 | Will Smith | .30 | .12 |
| ❑ 32 | Lee Evans | .40 | .15 | ❑ 117 | Matt Schaub | .40 | .15 | ❑ 202 | Billy Miller | .30 | .12 |
| ❑ 33 | Roscoe Parrish | .30 | .12 | ❑ 118 | Ahman Green | .30 | .12 | ❑ 203 | Sammy Knight | .30 | .12 |
| ❑ 34 | Paul Posluszny | .30 | .12 | ❑ 119 | Andre Johnson | .40 | .15 | ❑ 204 | Eli Manning | .50 | .20 |
| ❑ 35 | John DiGiorgio RC | .40 | .15 | ❑ 120 | Kevin Walter | .30 | .12 | ❑ 205 | Plaxico Burress | .40 | .15 |
| ❑ 36 | Angelo Crowell | .30 | .12 | ❑ 121 | Owen Daniels | .30 | .12 | ❑ 206 | Brandon Jacobs | .40 | .15 |
| ❑ 37 | Jabari Greer RC | .30 | .12 | ❑ 122 | Andre Davis | .30 | .12 | ❑ 207 | Ahmad Bradshaw | .40 | .15 |
| ❑ 38 | Chris Kelsay | .30 | .12 | ❑ 123 | DeMeco Ryans | .40 | .15 | ❑ 208 | David Tyree | .40 | .15 |
| ❑ 39 | Fred Jackson RC | .50 | .20 | ❑ 124 | Mario Williams | .40 | .15 | ❑ 209 | Amani Toomer | .40 | .15 |
| ❑ 40 | Matt Moore | .40 | .15 | ❑ 125 | Dunta Robinson | .30 | .12 | ❑ 210 | Jeremy Shockey | .40 | .15 |
| ❑ 41 | Steve Smith | .40 | .15 | ❑ 126 | Chris Brown | .30 | .12 | ❑ 211 | Steve Smith USC | .30 | .12 |
| ❑ 42 | DeAngelo Williams | .40 | .15 | ❑ 127 | Peyton Manning | .75 | .30 | ❑ 212 | Aaron Ross | .30 | .12 |
| ❑ 43 | Brad Hoover | .30 | .12 | ❑ 128 | Joseph Addai | .50 | .20 | ❑ 213 | Antonio Pierce | .30 | .12 |
| ❑ 44 | Dante Rosario | .30 | .12 | ❑ 129 | Marvin Harrison | .50 | .20 | ❑ 214 | Michael Strahan | .40 | .15 |
| ❑ 45 | Julius Peppers | .40 | .15 | ❑ 130 | Reggie Wayne | .40 | .15 | ❑ 215 | Jesse Chatman | .30 | .12 |
| ❑ 46 | Jon Beason | .40 | .15 | ❑ 131 | Dallas Clark | .40 | .15 | ❑ 216 | Calvin Pace | .30 | .12 |
| ❑ 47 | Chris Harris | .30 | .12 | ❑ 132 | Anthony Gonzalez | .40 | .15 | ❑ 217 | Kellen Clemens | .40 | .15 |
| ❑ 48 | D.J. Hackett | .30 | .12 | ❑ 133 | Kenton Keith | .30 | .12 | ❑ 218 | Leon Washington | .30 | .12 |
| ❑ 49 | Jake Delhomme | .40 | .15 | ❑ 134 | Adam Vinatieri | .50 | .20 | ❑ 219 | Jerricho Cotchery | .30 | .12 |
| ❑ 50 | Adrian Peterson | .30 | .12 | ❑ 135 | Bob Sanders | .40 | .15 | ❑ 220 | Laveranues Coles | .40 | .15 |
| ❑ 51 | Mark Anderson | .30 | .12 | ❑ 136 | Kelvin Hayden | .30 | .12 | ❑ 221 | Chris Baker | .30 | .12 |
| ❑ 52 | Desmond Clark | .30 | .12 | ❑ 137 | Freddie Keiaho | .30 | .12 | ❑ 222 | Brad Smith | .30 | .12 |
| ❑ 53 | Greg Olsen | .50 | .20 | ❑ 138 | David Garrard | .40 | .15 | ❑ 223 | Thomas Jones | .40 | .15 |
| ❑ 54 | Devin Hester | .50 | .20 | ❑ 139 | Fred Taylor | .40 | .15 | ❑ 224 | Darrelle Revis | .30 | .12 |
| ❑ 55 | Brian Urlacher | .50 | .20 | ❑ 140 | Maurice Jones-Drew | .40 | .15 | ❑ 225 | David Harris | .30 | .12 |
| ❑ 56 | Jason McKie RC | .40 | .15 | ❑ 141 | Greg Jones | .30 | .12 | ❑ 226 | DeAngelo Hall | .40 | .15 |
| ❑ 57 | Lance Briggs | .30 | .12 | ❑ 142 | Dennis Northcutt | .30 | .12 | ❑ 227 | Drew Carter | .30 | .12 |
| ❑ 58 | Rex Grossman | .30 | .12 | ❑ 143 | Reggie Williams | .40 | .15 | ❑ 228 | Javon Walker | .40 | .15 |
| ❑ 59 | Carson Palmer | .50 | .20 | ❑ 144 | Marcedes Lewis | .30 | .12 | ❑ 229 | JaMarcus Russell | .50 | .20 |
| ❑ 60 | Chad Johnson | .50 | .20 | ❑ 145 | Matt Jones | .40 | .15 | ❑ 230 | Justin Fargas | .40 | .15 |
| ❑ 61 | T.J. Houshmandzadeh | .40 | .15 | ❑ 146 | Reggie Nelson | .30 | .12 | ❑ 231 | Michael Bush | .40 | .15 |
| ❑ 62 | Rudi Johnson | .40 | .15 | ❑ 147 | Cleo Lemon | .30 | .12 | ❑ 232 | Ronald Curry | .40 | .15 |
| ❑ 63 | Kenny Watson | .30 | .12 | ❑ 148 | Jerry Porter | .40 | .15 | ❑ 233 | Zach Miller | .40 | .15 |
| ❑ 64 | Dhani Jones | .30 | .12 | ❑ 149 | Damon Huard | .30 | .12 | ❑ 234 | Thomas Howard | .30 | .12 |
| ❑ 65 | Leon Hall | .30 | .12 | ❑ 150 | Brodie Croyle | .50 | .20 | ❑ 235 | Johnnie Lee Higgins | .30 | .12 |
| ❑ 66 | Johnathan Joseph | .30 | .12 | ❑ 151 | Larry Johnson | .40 | .15 | ❑ 236 | Kirk Morrison | .30 | .12 |
| ❑ 67 | Derek Anderson | .40 | .15 | ❑ 152 | Kolby Smith | .30 | .12 | ❑ 237 | Michael Huff | .30 | .12 |
| ❑ 68 | Brady Quinn | .50 | .20 | ❑ 153 | Tony Gonzalez | .40 | .15 | ❑ 238 | Asante Samuel | .30 | .12 |
| ❑ 69 | Jamal Lewis | .40 | .15 | ❑ 154 | Dwayne Bowe | .40 | .15 | ❑ 239 | Donovan McNabb | .50 | .20 |
| ❑ 70 | Josh Cribbs | .40 | .15 | ❑ 155 | Donnie Edwards | .30 | .12 | ❑ 240 | Brian Westbrook | .40 | .15 |
| ❑ 71 | Kellen Winslow | .40 | .15 | ❑ 156 | Jared Allen | .40 | .15 | ❑ 241 | Correll Buckhalter | .30 | .12 |
| ❑ 72 | Braylon Edwards | .40 | .15 | ❑ 157 | Patrick Surtain | .30 | .12 | ❑ 242 | Kevin Curtis | .30 | .12 |
| ❑ 73 | Joe Jurevicius | .30 | .12 | ❑ 158 | Derrick Johnson | .30 | .12 | ❑ 243 | Reggie Brown | .40 | .15 |
| ❑ 74 | D'Qwell Jackson | .30 | .12 | ❑ 159 | Ernest Wilford | .30 | .12 | ❑ 244 | L.J. Smith | .30 | .12 |
| ❑ 75 | Leigh Bodden | .30 | .12 | ❑ 160 | John Beck | .30 | .12 | ❑ 245 | Greg Lewis | .30 | .12 |
| ❑ 76 | Sean Jones | .30 | .12 | ❑ 161 | Ronnie Brown | .40 | .15 | ❑ 246 | Lito Sheppard | .30 | .12 |
| ❑ 77 | Tony Romo | .75 | .30 | ❑ 162 | Greg Camarillo RC | 1.00 | .40 | ❑ 247 | Omar Gaither | .30 | .12 |
| ❑ 78 | Terrell Owens | .50 | .20 | ❑ 163 | Ted Ginn Jr. | .40 | .15 | ❑ 248 | Ben Roethlisberger | .60 | .25 |
| ❑ 79 | Marion Barber | .50 | .20 | ❑ 164 | Derek Hagan | .30 | .12 | ❑ 249 | Willie Parker | .40 | .15 |
| ❑ 80 | Jason Witten | .40 | .15 | ❑ 165 | Channing Crowder | .30 | .12 | ❑ 250 | Najeh Davenport | .30 | .12 |
| ❑ 81 | Patrick Crayton | .40 | .15 | ❑ 166 | Joey Porter | .30 | .12 | ❑ 251 | Hines Ward | .50 | .20 |
| ❑ 82 | Anthony Henry | .30 | .12 | ❑ 167 | Jason Taylor | .40 | .15 | ❑ 252 | Santonio Holmes | .40 | .15 |
| ❑ 83 | DeMarcus Ware | .40 | .15 | ❑ 168 | Josh McCown | .30 | .12 | ❑ 253 | Heath Miller | .30 | .12 |
| ❑ 84 | Terence Newman | .30 | .12 | ❑ 169 | Bernard Berrian | .40 | .15 | ❑ 254 | Cedrick Wilson | .30 | .12 |
| ❑ 85 | Greg Ellis | .30 | .12 | ❑ 170 | Maurice Hicks | .30 | .12 | ❑ 255 | James Harrison RC | 2.50 | 1.00 |
| ❑ 86 | Zach Thomas | .40 | .15 | ❑ 171 | Tarvaris Jackson | .30 | .12 | ❑ 256 | Ike Taylor | .30 | .12 |
| ❑ 87 | Keary Colbert | .30 | .12 | ❑ 172 | Adrian Peterson | 1.00 | .40 | ❑ 257 | James Farrior | .30 | .12 |
| ❑ 88 | Jay Cutler | .50 | .20 | ❑ 173 | Chester Taylor | .30 | .12 | ❑ 258 | Troy Polamalu | .50 | .20 |
| ❑ 89 | Tony Scheffler | .30 | .12 | ❑ 174 | Bobby Wade | .30 | .12 | ❑ 259 | Philip Rivers | .50 | .20 |

| | | |
|---|---|---|
| ❑ 260 LaDainian Tomlinson | .60 | .25 |
| ❑ 261 Darren Sproles | .30 | .12 |
| ❑ 262 Vincent Jackson | .30 | .12 |
| ❑ 263 Chris Chambers | .40 | .15 |
| ❑ 264 Antonio Gates | .40 | .15 |
| ❑ 265 Craig Buster Davis | .30 | .12 |
| ❑ 266 Malcom Floyd | .30 | .12 |
| ❑ 267 Antonio Cromartie | .30 | .12 |
| ❑ 268 Shawne Merriman | .40 | .15 |
| ❑ 269 DeShaun Foster | .30 | .12 |
| ❑ 270 Alex Smith QB | .40 | .15 |
| ❑ 271 Frank Gore | .40 | .15 |
| ❑ 272 Michael Robinson | .30 | .12 |
| ❑ 273 Vernon Davis | .30 | .12 |
| ❑ 274 Arnaz Battle | .30 | .12 |
| ❑ 275 Isaac Bruce | .40 | .15 |
| ❑ 276 Patrick Willis | .40 | .15 |
| ❑ 277 Nate Clements | .30 | .12 |
| ❑ 278 Jason Hill | .30 | .12 |
| ❑ 279 T.J. Duckett | .30 | .12 |
| ❑ 280 Matt Hasselbeck | .40 | .15 |
| ❑ 281 Julian Peterson | .30 | .12 |
| ❑ 282 Maurice Morris | .30 | .12 |
| ❑ 283 Bobby Engram | .30 | .12 |
| ❑ 284 Nate Burleson | .30 | .12 |
| ❑ 285 Deion Branch | .40 | .15 |
| ❑ 286 Lofa Tatupu | .40 | .15 |
| ❑ 287 Marcus Trufant | .30 | .12 |
| ❑ 288 Darryl Tapp | .30 | .12 |
| ❑ 289 Julius Jones | .40 | .15 |
| ❑ 290 Marc Bulger | .40 | .15 |
| ❑ 291 Steven Jackson | .50 | .20 |
| ❑ 292 Brian Leonard | .30 | .12 |
| ❑ 293 Torry Holt | .40 | .15 |
| ❑ 294 Dante Hall | .30 | .12 |
| ❑ 295 Randy McMichael | .30 | .12 |
| ❑ 296 Drew Bennett | .30 | .12 |
| ❑ 297 Will Witherspoon | .30 | .12 |
| ❑ 298 Tye Hill | .30 | .12 |
| ❑ 299 Corey Chavous | .30 | .12 |
| ❑ 300 Warrick Dunn | .40 | .15 |
| ❑ 301 Brian Griese | .30 | .12 |
| ❑ 302 Jeff Garcia | .40 | .15 |
| ❑ 303 Cadillac Williams | .40 | .15 |
| ❑ 304 Earnest Graham | .40 | .15 |
| ❑ 305 Joey Galloway | .40 | .15 |
| ❑ 306 Ike Hilliard | .30 | .12 |
| ❑ 307 Michael Clayton | .40 | .15 |
| ❑ 308 Derrick Brooks | .40 | .15 |
| ❑ 309 Phillip Buchanon | .30 | .12 |
| ❑ 310 Alex Smith TE | .30 | .12 |
| ❑ 311 Ronde Barber | .30 | .12 |
| ❑ 312 Justin McCareins | .30 | .12 |
| ❑ 313 Jevon Kearse | .40 | .15 |
| ❑ 314 Vince Young | .50 | .20 |
| ❑ 315 LenDale White | .40 | .15 |
| ❑ 316 Justin Gage | .30 | .12 |
| ❑ 317 Roydell Williams | .30 | .12 |
| ❑ 318 Alge Crumpler | .40 | .15 |
| ❑ 319 Brandon Jones | .30 | .12 |
| ❑ 320 Michael Griffin | .30 | .12 |
| ❑ 321 Keith Bulluck | .30 | .12 |
| ❑ 322 Jason Campbell | .40 | .15 |
| ❑ 323 Clinton Portis | .40 | .15 |
| ❑ 324 Ladell Betts | .30 | .12 |
| ❑ 325 Santana Moss | .40 | .15 |
| ❑ 326 Chris Cooley | .40 | .15 |
| ❑ 327 Antwaan Randle El | .30 | .12 |
| ❑ 328 London Fletcher | .30 | .12 |
| ❑ 329 Shawn Springs | .30 | .12 |
| ❑ 330 LaRon Landry | .40 | .15 |
| ❑ 331 Jake Long RC | 1.50 | .60 |
| ❑ 332 Chris Long RC | 1.50 | .60 |
| ❑ 333 Matt Ryan RC | 5.00 | 2.00 |
| ❑ 334 Darren McFadden RC | 3.00 | 1.25 |
| ❑ 335 Glenn Dorsey RC | 1.50 | .60 |
| ❑ 336 Vernon Gholston RC | 1.25 | .50 |
| ❑ 337 Sedrick Ellis RC | 1.25 | .50 |
| ❑ 338 Derrick Harvey RC | 1.00 | .40 |
| ❑ 339 Keith Rivers RC | 1.25 | .50 |
| ❑ 340 Jerod Mayo RC | 2.00 | .75 |
| ❑ 341 Leodis McKelvin RC | 1.25 | .50 |
| ❑ 342 Jonathan Stewart RC | 3.00 | 1.25 |
| ❑ 343 Dominique Rodgers-Cromartie RC | 1.25 | .50 |
| ❑ 344 Joe Flacco RC | 4.00 | 1.50 |

| | | |
|---|---|---|
| ❑ 345 Aqib Talib RC | 1.25 | .50 |
| ❑ 346 Felix Jones RC | 3.00 | 1.25 |
| ❑ 347 Rashard Mendenhall RC | 2.50 | 1.00 |
| ❑ 348 Chris Johnson RC | 3.00 | 1.25 |
| ❑ 349 Mike Jenkins RC | 1.25 | .50 |
| ❑ 350 Antoine Cason RC | 1.25 | .50 |
| ❑ 351 Lawrence Jackson RC | 1.00 | .40 |
| ❑ 352 Kentwan Balmer RC | 1.00 | .40 |
| ❑ 353 Dustin Keller RC | 1.25 | .50 |
| ❑ 354 Kenny Phillips RC | 1.25 | .50 |
| ❑ 355 Phillip Merling RC | 1.00 | .40 |
| ❑ 356 Donnie Avery RC | 1.50 | .60 |
| ❑ 357 Devin Thomas RC | 1.25 | .50 |
| ❑ 358 Brandon Flowers RC | 1.25 | .50 |
| ❑ 359 Jordy Nelson RC | 1.50 | .60 |
| ❑ 360 Curtis Lofton RC | 1.25 | .50 |
| ❑ 361 John Carlson RC | 1.25 | .50 |
| ❑ 362 Tracy Porter RC | 1.00 | .40 |
| ❑ 363 James Hardy RC | 1.25 | .50 |
| ❑ 364 Eddie Royal RC | 2.50 | 1.00 |
| ❑ 365 Matt Forte RC | 3.00 | 1.25 |
| ❑ 366 Jordon Dizon RC | 1.25 | .50 |
| ❑ 367 Jerome Simpson RC | 1.00 | .40 |
| ❑ 368 Fred Davis RC | 1.25 | .50 |
| ❑ 369 DeSean Jackson RC | 2.50 | 1.00 |
| ❑ 370 Calais Campbell RC | 1.00 | .40 |
| ❑ 371 Malcolm Kelly RC | 1.25 | .50 |
| ❑ 372 Quentin Groves RC | 1.00 | .40 |
| ❑ 373 Limas Sweed RC | 1.25 | .50 |
| ❑ 374 Ray Rice RC | 1.50 | .60 |
| ❑ 375 Brian Brohm RC | 1.50 | .60 |
| ❑ 376 Chad Henne RC | 2.00 | .75 |
| ❑ 377 Dexter Jackson RC | 1.25 | .50 |
| ❑ 378 Martellus Bennett RC | 1.25 | .50 |
| ❑ 379 Terrell Thomas RC | 1.00 | .40 |
| ❑ 380 Kevin Smith RC | 2.00 | .75 |
| ❑ 381 Anthony Alridge RC | 1.00 | .40 |
| ❑ 382 Jacob Hester RC | 1.25 | .50 |
| ❑ 383 Earl Bennett RC | 1.25 | .50 |
| ❑ 384 Jamaal Charles RC | 1.50 | .60 |
| ❑ 385 Dan Connor RC | 1.25 | .50 |
| ❑ 386 Reggie Smith RC | 1.00 | .40 |
| ❑ 387 Brad Cottam RC | 1.25 | .50 |
| ❑ 388 Pat Sims RC | 1.00 | .40 |
| ❑ 389 Dantrell Savage RC | 1.25 | .50 |
| ❑ 390 Early Doucet RC | 1.25 | .50 |
| ❑ 391 Harry Douglas RC | 1.25 | .50 |
| ❑ 392 Steve Slaton RC | 2.50 | 1.00 |
| ❑ 393 Jermichael Finley RC | 1.25 | .50 |
| ❑ 394 Kevin O'Connell RC | 1.50 | .60 |
| ❑ 395 Mario Manningham RC | 1.25 | .50 |
| ❑ 396 Andre Caldwell RC | 1.00 | .40 |
| ❑ 397 Will Franklin RC | 1.25 | .50 |
| ❑ 398 Marcus Smith RC | 1.00 | .40 |
| ❑ 399 Martin Rucker RC | 1.00 | .40 |
| ❑ 400 Xavier Adibi RC | 1.00 | .40 |
| ❑ 401 Craig Steltz RC | 1.00 | .40 |
| ❑ 402 Tashard Choice RC | 1.25 | .50 |
| ❑ 403 Lavelle Hawkins RC | 1.00 | .40 |
| ❑ 404 Jacob Tamme RC | 1.00 | .40 |
| ❑ 405 Keenan Burton RC | 1.00 | .40 |
| ❑ 406 John David Booty RC | 1.50 | .60 |
| ❑ 407 Ryan Torain RC | 1.25 | .50 |
| ❑ 408 Tim Hightower RC | 2.50 | 1.00 |
| ❑ 409 Dennis Dixon RC | 1.50 | .60 |
| ❑ 410 Kellen Davis RC | .75 | .30 |
| ❑ 411 Josh Johnson RC | 1.25 | .50 |
| ❑ 412 Erik Ainge RC | 1.25 | .50 |
| ❑ 413 Owen Schmitt RC | 1.00 | .40 |
| ❑ 414 Marcus Thomas RC | 1.00 | .40 |
| ❑ 415 Thomas Brown RC | 1.25 | .50 |
| ❑ 416 Josh Morgan RC | 1.25 | .50 |
| ❑ 417 Kevin Robinson RC | 1.00 | .40 |
| ❑ 418 Colt Brennan RC | 3.00 | 1.25 |
| ❑ 419 Paul Hubbard RC | 1.25 | .50 |
| ❑ 420 Andre Woodson RC | 1.25 | .50 |
| ❑ 421 Mike Hart RC | 1.50 | .60 |
| ❑ 422 Matt Flynn RC | 1.50 | .60 |
| ❑ 423 Chauncey Washington RC | 1.00 | .40 |
| ❑ 424 Caleb Campbell RC | 1.25 | .50 |
| ❑ 425 Peyton Hillis RC | 1.50 | .60 |
| ❑ 426 Justin Forsett RC | 1.25 | .50 |
| ❑ 427 Adrian Arrington RC | 1.00 | .40 |
| ❑ 428 Cory Boyd RC | 1.00 | .40 |
| ❑ 429 Allen Patrick RC | 1.00 | .40 |

| | | |
|---|---|---|
| ❑ 430 Marcus Monk RC | 1.25 | .50 |
| ❑ 431 DJ Hall RC | 1.25 | .50 |
| ❑ 432 Darrell Strong RC | 1.00 | .40 |
| ❑ 433 Jason Rivers RC | 1.25 | .50 |
| ❑ 434 Jed Collins RC | 1.00 | .40 |
| ❑ 435 Paul Smith RC | 1.25 | .50 |
| ❑ 436 Darius Reynaud RC | 1.00 | .40 |
| ❑ 437 Ali Highsmith RC | .75 | .30 |
| ❑ 438 Davone Bess RC | 1.50 | .60 |
| ❑ 439 Erin Henderson RC | 1.00 | .40 |
| ❑ 440 Kalvin McRae RC | 1.00 | .40 |

## 2006 Select

| | | |
|---|---|---|
| ❑ COMP.SET w/o RC's (330) | 50.00 | 25.00 |
| 331-430 RC PRINT RUN 599 SETS | | |
| ❑ 1 Kurt Warner | .60 | .25 |
| ❑ 2 J.J. Arrington | .60 | .25 |
| ❑ 3 Anquan Boldin | .60 | .25 |
| ❑ 4 Larry Fitzgerald | .75 | .30 |
| ❑ 5 Marcel Shipp | .50 | .20 |
| ❑ 6 Bryant Johnson | .40 | .15 |
| ❑ 7 Bertrand Berry | .40 | .15 |
| ❑ 8 John Navarre | .40 | .15 |
| ❑ 9 Michael Vick | .75 | .30 |
| ❑ 10 Warrick Dunn | .60 | .25 |
| ❑ 11 Roddy White | .50 | .20 |
| ❑ 12 Alge Crumpler | .50 | .20 |
| ❑ 13 T.J. Duckett | .60 | .25 |
| ❑ 14 Michael Jenkins | .60 | .25 |
| ❑ 15 DeAngelo Hall | .50 | .20 |
| ❑ 16 Brian Finneran | .50 | .20 |
| ❑ 17 Kyle Boller | .60 | .25 |
| ❑ 18 Jamal Lewis | .60 | .25 |
| ❑ 19 Chester Taylor | .60 | .25 |
| ❑ 20 Derrick Mason | .60 | .25 |
| ❑ 21 Mark Clayton | .60 | .25 |
| ❑ 22 Todd Heap | .60 | .25 |
| ❑ 23 Ray Lewis | .75 | .30 |
| ❑ 24 Devard Darling | .50 | .20 |
| ❑ 25 J.P. Losman | .60 | .25 |
| ❑ 26 Willis McGahee | .75 | .30 |
| ❑ 27 Lee Evans | .60 | .25 |
| ❑ 28 Eric Moulds | .60 | .25 |
| ❑ 29 Lawyer Milloy | .40 | .15 |
| ❑ 30 Josh Reed | .50 | .20 |
| ❑ 31 Kelly Holcomb | .40 | .15 |
| ❑ 32 Jake Delhomme | .60 | .25 |
| ❑ 33 DeShaun Foster | .60 | .25 |
| ❑ 34 Steve Smith | .75 | .30 |
| ❑ 35 Julius Peppers | .60 | .25 |
| ❑ 36 Drew Carter | .50 | .20 |
| ❑ 37 Chris Gamble | .50 | .20 |
| ❑ 38 Stephen Davis | .60 | .25 |
| ❑ 39 Keary Colbert | .50 | .20 |
| ❑ 40 Nick Goings | .40 | .15 |
| ❑ 41 Eric Shelton | .50 | .20 |
| ❑ 42 Rex Grossman | .75 | .30 |
| ❑ 43 Thomas Jones | .60 | .25 |
| ❑ 44 Cedric Benson | .60 | .25 |
| ❑ 45 Muhsin Muhammad | .60 | .25 |
| ❑ 46 Brian Urlacher | .75 | .30 |
| ❑ 47 Mark Bradley | .50 | .20 |
| ❑ 48 Kyle Orton | .50 | .20 |
| ❑ 49 Tommie Harris | .40 | .15 |
| ❑ 50 Adrian Peterson | .60 | .25 |
| ❑ 51 Bernard Berrian | .60 | .25 |
| ❑ 52 Justin Gage | .50 | .20 |
| ❑ 53 Carson Palmer | .75 | .30 |

| # | Player | Hi | Lo |
|---|--------|----|----|
| 54 | Rudi Johnson | .60 | .25 |
| 55 | Chad Johnson | .60 | .25 |
| 56 | T.J. Houshmandzadeh | .60 | .25 |
| 57 | Chris Henry | .50 | .20 |
| 58 | Chris Perry | .60 | .25 |
| 59 | Jon Kitna | .60 | .25 |
| 60 | Deltha O'Neal | .50 | .20 |
| 61 | Charlie Frye | .60 | .25 |
| 62 | Reuben Droughns | .60 | .25 |
| 63 | Braylon Edwards | .75 | .30 |
| 64 | Kellen Winslow | .75 | .30 |
| 65 | Antonio Bryant | .60 | .25 |
| 66 | Trent Dilfer | .60 | .25 |
| 67 | Dennis Northcutt | .50 | .20 |
| 68 | Drew Bledsoe | .75 | .30 |
| 69 | Julius Jones | .75 | .30 |
| 70 | Marion Barber | .75 | .30 |
| 71 | Terry Glenn | .60 | .25 |
| 72 | Keyshawn Johnson | .60 | .25 |
| 73 | Roy Williams S | .60 | .25 |
| 74 | Jason Witten | .60 | .25 |
| 75 | Terence Newman | .50 | .20 |
| 76 | Drew Henson | .60 | .25 |
| 77 | Patrick Crayton | .50 | .20 |
| 78 | Jake Plummer | .60 | .25 |
| 79 | Mike Anderson | .60 | .25 |
| 80 | Tatum Bell | .60 | .25 |
| 81 | Ashley Lelie | .60 | .25 |
| 82 | Rod Smith | .60 | .25 |
| 83 | D.J. Williams | .50 | .20 |
| 84 | Darius Watts | .50 | .20 |
| 85 | Ron Dayne | .60 | .25 |
| 86 | Jeb Putzier | .50 | .20 |
| 87 | Joey Harrington | .50 | .20 |
| 88 | Kevin Jones | .75 | .30 |
| 89 | Roy Williams WR | .75 | .30 |
| 90 | Mike Williams | .75 | .30 |
| 91 | Charles Rogers | .60 | .25 |
| 92 | Teddy Lehman | .40 | .15 |
| 93 | Marcus Pollard | .50 | .20 |
| 94 | Artose Pinner | .40 | .15 |
| 95 | Brett Favre | 1.50 | .60 |
| 96 | Ahman Green | .60 | .25 |
| 97 | Najeh Davenport | .60 | .25 |
| 98 | Samkon Gado | .75 | .30 |
| 99 | Javon Walker | .60 | .25 |
| 100 | Donald Driver | .75 | .30 |
| 101 | Aaron Rodgers | .75 | .30 |
| 102 | Robert Ferguson | .50 | .20 |
| 103 | David Carr | .60 | .25 |
| 104 | Domanick Davis | .60 | .25 |
| 105 | Andre Johnson | .60 | .25 |
| 106 | Jabar Gaffney | .50 | .20 |
| 107 | Jonathan Wells | .40 | .15 |
| 108 | Vernand Morency | .60 | .25 |
| 109 | Corey Bradford | .50 | .20 |
| 110 | Jerome Mathis | .50 | .20 |
| 111 | Peyton Manning | 1.25 | .50 |
| 112 | Edgerrin James | .60 | .25 |
| 113 | Marvin Harrison | .75 | .30 |
| 114 | Reggie Wayne | .60 | .25 |
| 115 | Dwight Freeney | .60 | .25 |
| 116 | Dallas Clark | .60 | .25 |
| 117 | Dominic Rhodes | .60 | .25 |
| 118 | Jim Sorgi | .40 | .15 |
| 119 | Brandon Stokley | .60 | .25 |
| 120 | Bob Sanders | .60 | .25 |
| 121 | Mike Doss | .40 | .15 |
| 122 | Marlin Jackson | .60 | .25 |
| 123 | Byron Leftwich | .60 | .25 |
| 124 | Fred Taylor | .60 | .25 |
| 125 | Jimmy Smith | .60 | .25 |
| 126 | Matt Jones | .60 | .25 |
| 127 | Ernest Wilford | .60 | .25 |
| 128 | Greg Jones | .50 | .20 |
| 129 | Mike Peterson | .50 | .20 |
| 130 | Reggie Williams | .60 | .25 |
| 131 | Rashean Mathis | .40 | .15 |
| 132 | Trent Green | .60 | .25 |
| 133 | Larry Johnson | .60 | .25 |
| 134 | Priest Holmes | .60 | .25 |
| 135 | Eddie Kennison | .50 | .20 |
| 136 | Tony Gonzalez | .60 | .25 |
| 137 | Kendrell Bell | .50 | .20 |
| 138 | Samie Parker | .50 | .20 |
| 139 | Dante Hall | .60 | .25 |
| 140 | Tony Richardson | .40 | .15 |
| 141 | Gus Frerotte | .40 | .15 |
| 142 | Ronnie Brown | .75 | .30 |
| 143 | Neil Rackers | .50 | .20 |
| 144 | Chris Chambers | .60 | .25 |
| 145 | Zach Thomas | .75 | .30 |
| 146 | Cliff Russell | .40 | .15 |
| 147 | David Boston | .40 | .15 |
| 148 | Wes Welker | .75 | .30 |
| 149 | Marty Booker | .50 | .20 |
| 150 | Randy McMichael | .50 | .20 |
| 151 | Daunte Culpepper | .75 | .30 |
| 152 | Mewelde Moore | .50 | .20 |
| 153 | Nate Burleson | .60 | .25 |
| 154 | Troy Williamson | .60 | .25 |
| 155 | Koren Robinson | .50 | .20 |
| 156 | Erasmus James | .40 | .15 |
| 157 | Marcus Robinson | .60 | .25 |
| 158 | E.J. Henderson | .50 | .20 |
| 159 | Brad Johnson | .60 | .25 |
| 160 | Michael Bennett | .40 | .15 |
| 161 | Travis Taylor | .50 | .20 |
| 162 | Tom Brady | 1.25 | .50 |
| 163 | Corey Dillon | .60 | .25 |
| 164 | Deion Branch | .60 | .25 |
| 165 | Tedy Bruschi | .75 | .30 |
| 166 | Ben Watson | .50 | .20 |
| 167 | Daniel Graham | .50 | .20 |
| 168 | Bethel Johnson | .50 | .20 |
| 169 | Kevin Faulk | .60 | .25 |
| 170 | David Givens | .60 | .25 |
| 171 | Troy Brown | .50 | .20 |
| 172 | Aaron Brooks | .60 | .25 |
| 173 | Deuce McAllister | .60 | .25 |
| 174 | Joe Horn | .60 | .25 |
| 175 | Donte Stallworth | .60 | .25 |
| 176 | Antowain Smith | .40 | .15 |
| 177 | Devery Henderson | .50 | .20 |
| 178 | Eli Manning | 1.00 | .40 |
| 179 | Tiki Barber | .75 | .30 |
| 180 | Plaxico Burress | .60 | .25 |
| 181 | Jeremy Shockey | .75 | .30 |
| 182 | Osi Umenyiora | .60 | .25 |
| 183 | Gibril Wilson | .40 | .15 |
| 184 | Brandon Jacobs | .75 | .30 |
| 185 | Michael Strahan | .60 | .25 |
| 186 | Will Allen | .40 | .15 |
| 187 | Amani Toomer | .60 | .25 |
| 188 | Chad Pennington | .75 | .30 |
| 189 | Curtis Martin | .75 | .30 |
| 190 | Laveranues Coles | .60 | .25 |
| 191 | Jonathan Vilma | .60 | .25 |
| 192 | Ty Law | .50 | .20 |
| 193 | Cedric Houston | .50 | .20 |
| 194 | Justin McCareins | .50 | .20 |
| 195 | Jerald Sowell | .40 | .15 |
| 196 | Josh Brown | .40 | .15 |
| 197 | LaMont Jordan | .60 | .25 |
| 198 | Randy Moss | .75 | .30 |
| 199 | Jerry Porter | .60 | .25 |
| 200 | Doug Gabriel | .40 | .15 |
| 201 | Johnnie Morant | .40 | .15 |
| 202 | Zack Crockett | .40 | .15 |
| 203 | Derrick Burgess | .50 | .20 |
| 204 | Donovan McNabb | .75 | .30 |
| 205 | Brian Westbrook | .60 | .25 |
| 206 | Reggie Brown | .60 | .25 |
| 207 | Terrell Owens | .75 | .30 |
| 208 | Ryan Moats | .50 | .20 |
| 209 | Correll Buckhalter | .50 | .20 |
| 210 | Jevon Kearse | .60 | .25 |
| 211 | L.J. Smith | .50 | .20 |
| 212 | Lamar Gordon | .40 | .15 |
| 213 | Greg Lewis | .50 | .20 |
| 214 | Ben Roethlisberger | 1.25 | .50 |
| 215 | Willie Parker | 1.00 | .40 |
| 216 | Jerome Bettis | .75 | .30 |
| 217 | Hines Ward | .75 | .30 |
| 218 | Troy Polamalu | 1.00 | .40 |
| 219 | Heath Miller | .60 | .25 |
| 220 | Antwaan Randle El | .60 | .25 |
| 221 | Duce Staley | .50 | .20 |
| 222 | Cedrick Wilson | .50 | .20 |
| 223 | James Farrior | .50 | .20 |
| 224 | Drew Brees | .75 | .30 |
| 225 | LaDainian Tomlinson | 1.00 | .40 |
| 226 | Keenan McCardell | .60 | .25 |
| 227 | Antonio Gates | .75 | .30 |
| 228 | Shawne Merriman | .60 | .25 |
| 229 | Philip Rivers | .75 | .30 |
| 230 | Vincent Jackson | .60 | .25 |
| 231 | Donnie Edwards | .50 | .20 |
| 232 | Eric Parker | .50 | .20 |
| 233 | Reche Caldwell | .50 | .20 |
| 234 | Alex Smith QB | .75 | .30 |
| 235 | Frank Gore | .75 | .30 |
| 236 | Brandon Lloyd | .60 | .25 |
| 237 | Kevan Barlow | .60 | .25 |
| 238 | Rashaun Woods | .40 | .15 |
| 239 | Arnaz Battle | .50 | .20 |
| 240 | Matt Hasselbeck | .60 | .25 |
| 241 | Shaun Alexander | .75 | .30 |
| 242 | Darrell Jackson | .60 | .25 |
| 243 | Jerramy Stevens | .60 | .25 |
| 244 | Lofa Tatupu | .60 | .25 |
| 245 | D.J. Hackett | .60 | .25 |
| 246 | Bobby Engram | .40 | .15 |
| 247 | Joe Jurevicius | .60 | .25 |
| 248 | Maurice Morris | .40 | .15 |
| 249 | Marc Bulger | .60 | .25 |
| 250 | Steven Jackson | .75 | .30 |
| 251 | Torry Holt | .75 | .30 |
| 252 | Isaac Bruce | .60 | .25 |
| 253 | Kevin Curtis | .60 | .25 |
| 254 | Marshall Faulk | .60 | .25 |
| 255 | Shaun McDonald | .50 | .20 |
| 256 | Chris Simms | .60 | .25 |
| 257 | Cadillac Williams | .75 | .30 |
| 258 | Joey Galloway | .60 | .25 |
| 259 | Michael Clayton | .60 | .25 |
| 260 | Derrick Brooks | .60 | .25 |
| 261 | Ronde Barber | .60 | .25 |
| 262 | Michael Pittman | .40 | .15 |
| 263 | Alex Smith TE | .50 | .20 |
| 264 | Simeon Rice | .50 | .20 |
| 265 | Steve McNair | .60 | .25 |
| 266 | Chris Brown | .60 | .25 |
| 267 | Drew Bennett | .60 | .25 |
| 268 | Brandon Jones | .50 | .20 |
| 269 | Adam Jones | .60 | .25 |
| 270 | Keith Bulluck | .50 | .20 |
| 271 | Ben Troupe | .50 | .20 |
| 272 | Jarrett Payton | .40 | .15 |
| 273 | Tyrone Calico | .50 | .20 |
| 274 | Bobby Wade | .40 | .15 |
| 275 | Troy Fleming | .40 | .15 |
| 276 | Mark Brunell | .60 | .25 |
| 277 | Clinton Portis | .75 | .30 |
| 278 | Santana Moss | .60 | .25 |
| 279 | Jason Campbell | .60 | .25 |
| 280 | Chris Cooley | .60 | .25 |
| 281 | Carlos Rogers | .50 | .20 |
| 282 | Ladell Betts | .60 | .25 |
| 283 | Patrick Ramsey | .60 | .25 |
| 284 | Taylor Jacobs | .60 | .25 |
| 285 | James Thrash | .40 | .15 |
| 286 | Adrian Wilson | .40 | .15 |
| 287 | London Fletcher | .50 | .20 |
| 288 | Lance Briggs | .60 | .25 |
| 289 | Robert Mathis | .40 | .15 |
| 290 | Rod Coleman | .40 | .15 |
| 291 | Bart Scott RC | 2.50 | 1.00 |
| 292 | Brian Moorman RC | .60 | .25 |
| 293 | Shayne Graham RC | .75 | .30 |
| 294 | Kevin Kaesviharn RC | .60 | .25 |
| 295 | Leigh Bodden RC | .60 | .25 |
| 296 | Lousaka Polite RC | .60 | .25 |
| 297 | Todd Devoe RC | 1.25 | .50 |
| 298 | Scottie Vines | .75 | .30 |
| 299 | Cullen Jenkins RC | .60 | .25 |
| 300 | Donovan Morgan RC | .60 | .25 |
| 301 | C.C. Brown | .60 | .25 |
| 302 | Demarcus Faggins RC | .75 | .30 |
| 303 | Shantee Orr RC | .60 | .25 |
| 304 | Vashon Pearson RC | .60 | .25 |
| 305 | Reggie Hayward RC | .60 | .25 |
| 306 | Paul Spicer RC | .60 | .25 |
| 307 | Kenny Wright RC | .60 | .25 |
| 308 | Rich Alexis RC | .60 | .25 |

| | | |
|---|---|---|
| ☐ 309 Terrence Melton RC | .75 | .30 |
| ☐ 310 Willie Whitehead RC | .60 | .25 |
| ☐ 311 Kendrick Clancy RC | .60 | .25 |
| ☐ 312 Mark Brown RC | .75 | .30 |
| ☐ 313 Tommy Kelly RC | .60 | .25 |
| ☐ 314 Josh Parry RC | .60 | .25 |
| ☐ 315 Malcolm Floyd RC | 1.25 | .50 |
| ☐ 316 Mike Adams RC | .60 | .25 |
| ☐ 317 Ben Emanuel RC | .75 | .30 |
| ☐ 318 Brandon Moore RC | .60 | .25 |
| ☐ 319 Chartric Darby RC | .60 | .25 |
| ☐ 320 Bryce Fisher RC | .60 | .25 |
| ☐ 321 D.D. Lewis RC | .60 | .25 |
| ☐ 322 Jimmy Williams DB RC | .60 | .25 |
| ☐ 323 Robert Pollard RC | .60 | .25 |
| ☐ 324 Chris Johnson RC | .60 | .25 |
| ☐ 325 Edell Shepherd RC | .60 | .25 |
| ☐ 326 O.J. Small RC | .60 | .25 |
| ☐ 327 Brad Kassell RC | .60 | .25 |
| ☐ 328 M.Leinart/R.Bush | 5.00 | 2.00 |
| ☐ 329 M.Leinart/V.Young | 4.00 | 1.50 |
| ☐ 330 White/Leinart/Bush | 5.00 | 2.00 |
| ☐ 331 Matt Leinart RC | 20.00 | 8.00 |
| ☐ 332 Chad Greenway RC | 6.00 | 2.50 |
| ☐ 333 Devin Aromashodu RC | 5.00 | 2.00 |
| ☐ 334 DeAngelo Williams RC | 10.00 | 4.00 |
| ☐ 335 Travis Wilson RC | 6.00 | 2.50 |
| ☐ 336 Leon Washington RC | 6.00 | 2.50 |
| ☐ 337 Maurice Stovall RC | 6.00 | 2.50 |
| ☐ 338 Michael Huff RC | 6.00 | 2.50 |
| ☐ 339 Charlie Whitehurst RC | 6.00 | 2.50 |
| ☐ 340 Vince Young RC | 20.00 | 8.00 |
| ☐ 341 Jerious Norwood RC | 8.00 | 3.00 |
| ☐ 342 D'Brickashaw Ferguson RC | 6.00 | 2.50 |
| ☐ 343 Taurean Henderson RC | 6.00 | 2.50 |
| ☐ 344 Dominique Byrd RC | 5.00 | 2.00 |
| ☐ 345 Sinorice Moss RC | 6.00 | 2.50 |
| ☐ 346 Martin Nance RC | 5.00 | 2.00 |
| ☐ 347 Vernon Davis RC | 6.00 | 2.50 |
| ☐ 348 Ko Simpson RC | 5.00 | 2.00 |
| ☐ 349 Jerome Harrison RC | 6.00 | 2.50 |
| ☐ 350 Jay Cutler RC | 25.00 | 10.00 |
| ☐ 351 Alan Zemaitis RC | 6.00 | 2.50 |
| ☐ 352 Haloti Ngata RC | 6.00 | 2.50 |
| ☐ 353 Greg Lee RC | 5.00 | 2.00 |
| ☐ 354 Laurence Maroney RC | 15.00 | 6.00 |
| ☐ 355 Bobby Carpenter RC | 6.00 | 2.50 |
| ☐ 356 Jonathan Orr RC | 5.00 | 2.00 |
| ☐ 357 Marcedes Lewis RC | 6.00 | 2.50 |
| ☐ 358 Brodrick Bunkley RC | 6.00 | 2.50 |
| ☐ 359 Todd Watkins RC | 5.00 | 2.00 |
| ☐ 360 Reggie Bush RC | 50.00 | 20.00 |
| ☐ 361 Jimmy Williams RC | 6.00 | 2.50 |
| ☐ 362 Maurice Drew RC | 12.00 | 5.00 |
| ☐ 363 Mario Williams RC | 10.00 | 4.00 |
| ☐ 364 Derek Hagan RC | 6.00 | 2.50 |
| ☐ 365 Santonio Holmes RC | 15.00 | 6.00 |
| ☐ 366 Tye Hill RC | 6.00 | 2.50 |
| ☐ 367 Jason Avant RC | 6.00 | 2.50 |
| ☐ 368 Tamba Hali RC | 6.00 | 2.50 |
| ☐ 369 Joe Klopfenstein RC | 5.00 | 2.00 |
| ☐ 370 LenDale White RC | 12.00 | 5.00 |
| ☐ 371 DeMeco Ryans RC | 8.00 | 3.00 |
| ☐ 372 Bruce Gradkowski RC | 6.00 | 2.50 |
| ☐ 373 A.J. Hawk RC | 12.00 | 5.00 |
| ☐ 374 Gabe Watson RC | 5.00 | 2.00 |
| ☐ 375 Devin Hester RC | 12.00 | 5.00 |
| ☐ 376 Demetrius Williams RC | 6.00 | 2.50 |
| ☐ 377 Joseph Addai RC | 20.00 | 8.00 |
| ☐ 378 Leonard Pope RC | 6.00 | 2.50 |
| ☐ 379 Omar Jacobs RC | 5.00 | 2.00 |
| ☐ 380 Brad Smith RC | 6.00 | 2.50 |
| ☐ 381 Michael Robinson RC | 6.00 | 2.50 |
| ☐ 382 Brodie Croyle RC | 8.00 | 3.00 |
| ☐ 383 Anthony Fasano RC | 6.00 | 2.50 |
| ☐ 384 Brian Calhoun RC | 5.00 | 2.00 |
| ☐ 385 Chad Jackson RC | 5.00 | 2.00 |
| ☐ 386 Drew Olson RC | 5.00 | 2.00 |
| ☐ 387 Greg Jennings RC | 10.00 | 4.00 |
| ☐ 388 Andre Hall RC | 6.00 | 2.50 |
| ☐ 389 Ryan Gilbert RC | 5.00 | 2.00 |
| ☐ 390 Tim Day RC | 5.00 | 2.00 |
| ☐ 391 Brandon Williams RC | 5.00 | 2.00 |
| ☐ 392 Mark Anderson RC | 15.00 | 6.00 |
| ☐ 393 DonTrell Moore RC | 5.00 | 2.00 |
| ☐ 394 Kellen Clemens RC | 8.00 | 3.00 |
| ☐ 395 Ernie Sims RC | 6.00 | 2.50 |
| ☐ 396 Cedric Humes RC | 6.00 | 2.50 |
| ☐ 397 Brandon Kirsch RC | 6.00 | 2.50 |
| ☐ 398 Tony Scheffler RC | 6.00 | 2.50 |
| ☐ 399 Kelly Jennings RC | 6.00 | 2.50 |
| ☐ 400 Manny Lawson RC | 6.00 | 2.50 |
| ☐ 401 Terrence Whitehead RC | 5.00 | 2.00 |
| ☐ 402 De'Arrius Howard RC | 5.00 | 2.00 |
| ☐ 403 Wendell Mathis RC | 5.00 | 2.00 |
| ☐ 404 Abdul Hodge RC | 6.00 | 2.50 |
| ☐ 405 Owen Daniels RC | 6.00 | 2.50 |
| ☐ 406 Mike Hass RC | 6.00 | 2.50 |
| ☐ 407 Brett Elliott RC | 5.00 | 2.00 |
| ☐ 408 Kamerion Wimbley RC | 6.00 | 2.50 |
| ☐ 409 Jeremy Bloom RC | 6.00 | 2.50 |
| ☐ 410 D.J. Shockley RC | 6.00 | 2.50 |
| ☐ 411 Miles Austin RC | 6.00 | 2.50 |
| ☐ 412 D'Qwell Jackson RC | 5.00 | 2.00 |
| ☐ 413 Tarvaris Jackson RC | 6.00 | 2.50 |
| ☐ 414 Mathias Kiwanuka RC | 8.00 | 3.00 |
| ☐ 415 Mike Bell RC | 6.00 | 2.50 |
| ☐ 416 Paul Pinegar RC | 5.00 | 2.00 |
| ☐ 417 David Thomas RC | 6.00 | 2.50 |
| ☐ 418 Hank Baskett RC | 6.00 | 2.50 |
| ☐ 419 P.J. Daniels RC | 5.00 | 2.00 |
| ☐ 420 Jon Alston RC | 5.00 | 2.00 |
| ☐ 421 Reggie McNeal RC | 5.00 | 2.00 |
| ☐ 422 Brandon Marshall RC | 8.00 | 3.00 |
| ☐ 423 Gerald Riggs RC | 5.00 | 2.00 |
| ☐ 424 Delanie Walker RC | 5.00 | 2.00 |
| ☐ 425 Erik Meyer RC | 5.00 | 2.00 |
| ☐ 426 Jeff Webb RC | 5.00 | 2.00 |
| ☐ 427 Skyler Green RC | 6.00 | 2.50 |
| ☐ 428 Thomas Howard RC | 6.00 | 2.50 |

## 2007 Select

| | | |
|---|---|---|
| ☐ 1 Tony Romo | 1.50 | .60 |
| ☐ 2 Julius Jones | .60 | .25 |
| ☐ 3 Terry Glenn | .60 | .25 |
| ☐ 4 Terrell Owens | .75 | .30 |
| ☐ 5 Jason Witten | .60 | .25 |
| ☐ 6 Marion Barber | .75 | .30 |
| ☐ 7 Patrick Crayton | .50 | .20 |
| ☐ 8 Bradie James | .50 | .20 |
| ☐ 9 DeMarcus Ware | .60 | .25 |
| ☐ 10 Roy Williams S | .60 | .25 |
| ☐ 11 Eli Manning | .75 | .30 |
| ☐ 12 Plaxico Burress | .60 | .25 |
| ☐ 13 Jeremy Shockey | .60 | .25 |
| ☐ 14 Brandon Jacobs | .60 | .25 |
| ☐ 15 Sinorice Moss | .50 | .20 |
| ☐ 16 Antonio Pierce | .50 | .20 |
| ☐ 17 David Tyree | .50 | .20 |
| ☐ 18 Donovan McNabb | .75 | .30 |
| ☐ 19 Brian Westbrook | .60 | .25 |
| ☐ 20 Reggie Brown | .60 | .25 |
| ☐ 21 L.J. Smith | .50 | .20 |
| ☐ 22 Hank Baskett | .60 | .25 |
| ☐ 23 Jeremiah Trotter | .50 | .20 |
| ☐ 24 Trent Cole | .50 | .20 |
| ☐ 25 Lito Sheppard | .50 | .20 |
| ☐ 26 Jason Campbell | .60 | .25 |
| ☐ 27 Clinton Portis | .60 | .25 |
| ☐ 28 Santana Moss | .60 | .25 |
| ☐ 29 Brandon Lloyd | .60 | .25 |
| ☐ 30 Chris Cooley | .50 | .20 |
| ☐ 31 Sean Taylor | .50 | .20 |
| ☐ 32 Lemar Marshall | .50 | .20 |
| ☐ 33 Ladell Betts | .50 | .20 |
| ☐ 34 London Fletcher | .50 | .20 |
| ☐ 35 Rex Grossman | .60 | .25 |
| ☐ 36 Cedric Benson | .60 | .25 |
| ☐ 37 Muhsin Muhammad | .60 | .25 |
| ☐ 38 Bernard Berrian | .50 | .20 |
| ☐ 39 Desmond Clark | .50 | .20 |
| ☐ 40 Lance Briggs | .50 | .20 |
| ☐ 41 Robbie Gould | .50 | .20 |
| ☐ 42 Devin Hester | .75 | .30 |
| ☐ 43 Mark Anderson | .60 | .25 |
| ☐ 44 Brian Urlacher | .75 | .30 |
| ☐ 45 Jon Kitna | .50 | .20 |
| ☐ 46 Kevin Jones | .50 | .20 |
| ☐ 47 Roy Williams WR | .60 | .25 |
| ☐ 48 Mike Furrey | .60 | .25 |
| ☐ 49 Cory Redding | .50 | .20 |
| ☐ 50 Ernie Sims | .50 | .20 |
| ☐ 51 Tatum Bell | .50 | .20 |
| ☐ 52 Brian Calhoun | .50 | .20 |
| ☐ 53 Brett Favre | 1.50 | .60 |
| ☐ 54 Vernand Morency | .60 | .25 |
| ☐ 55 Donald Driver | .60 | .25 |
| ☐ 56 Greg Jennings | .60 | .25 |
| ☐ 57 Aaron Kampman | .60 | .25 |
| ☐ 58 Charles Woodson | .60 | .25 |
| ☐ 59 A.J. Hawk | .75 | .30 |
| ☐ 60 Nick Barnett | .50 | .20 |
| ☐ 61 Aaron Rodgers | .75 | .30 |
| ☐ 62 Tarvaris Jackson | .60 | .25 |
| ☐ 63 Chester Taylor | .50 | .20 |
| ☐ 64 Troy Williamson | .50 | .20 |
| ☐ 65 Jim Kleinsasser | .50 | .20 |
| ☐ 66 Dwight Smith | .50 | .20 |
| ☐ 67 Antoine Winfield | .50 | .20 |
| ☐ 68 E.J. Henderson | .50 | .20 |
| ☐ 69 Mewelde Moore | .50 | .20 |
| ☐ 70 Michael Vick | .75 | .30 |
| ☐ 71 Warrick Dunn | .60 | .25 |
| ☐ 72 Joe Horn | .60 | .25 |
| ☐ 73 Michael Jenkins | .50 | .20 |
| ☐ 74 Alge Crumpler | .60 | .25 |
| ☐ 75 DeAngelo Hall | .60 | .25 |
| ☐ 76 Keith Brooking | .50 | .20 |
| ☐ 77 Lawyer Milloy | .50 | .20 |
| ☐ 78 Jerious Norwood | .60 | .25 |
| ☐ 79 Matt Schaub | .60 | .25 |
| ☐ 80 Jake Delhomme | .50 | .20 |
| ☐ 81 DeShaun Foster | .50 | .20 |
| ☐ 82 Steve Smith | .60 | .25 |
| ☐ 83 Keyshawn Johnson | .60 | .25 |
| ☐ 84 Julius Peppers | .60 | .25 |
| ☐ 85 DeAngelo Williams | .75 | .30 |
| ☐ 86 Chris Draft | .50 | .20 |
| ☐ 87 Drew Brees | .60 | .25 |
| ☐ 88 Deuce McAllister | .60 | .25 |
| ☐ 89 Scott Fujita | .50 | .20 |
| ☐ 90 Marques Colston | .75 | .30 |
| ☐ 91 Terrance Copper | .50 | .20 |
| ☐ 92 Will Smith | .50 | .20 |
| ☐ 93 Charles Grant | .50 | .20 |
| ☐ 94 Devery Henderson | .50 | .20 |
| ☐ 95 Reggie Bush | 1.00 | .40 |
| ☐ 96 Jeff Garcia | .50 | .20 |
| ☐ 97 Cadillac Williams | .60 | .25 |
| ☐ 98 Joey Galloway | .60 | .25 |
| ☐ 99 Michael Clayton | .50 | .20 |
| ☐ 100 Alex Smith TE | .50 | .20 |
| ☐ 101 Ronde Barber | .50 | .20 |
| ☐ 102 Jermaine Phillips | .50 | .20 |
| ☐ 103 Derrick Brooks | .60 | .25 |
| ☐ 104 Matt Leinart | .75 | .30 |
| ☐ 105 Edgerrin James | .60 | .25 |
| ☐ 106 Anquan Boldin | .60 | .25 |
| ☐ 107 Larry Fitzgerald | .75 | .30 |
| ☐ 108 Neil Rackers | .50 | .20 |
| ☐ 109 Adrian Wilson | .50 | .20 |
| ☐ 110 Karlos Dansby | .50 | .20 |
| ☐ 111 Chike Okeafor | .50 | .20 |
| ☐ 112 Marc Bulger | .60 | .25 |
| ☐ 113 Steven Jackson | .75 | .30 |
| ☐ 114 Torry Holt | .60 | .25 |

|  |  | | |
|---|---|---|---|
| 115 | Isaac Bruce | .60 | .25 |
| 116 | Joe Klopfenstein | .50 | .20 |
| 117 | Randy McMichael | .50 | .20 |
| 118 | Will Witherspoon | .50 | .20 |
| 119 | Drew Bennett | .50 | .20 |
| 120 | Alex Smith QB | .75 | .30 |
| 121 | Frank Gore | .75 | .30 |
| 122 | Arnaz Battle | .50 | .20 |
| 123 | Ashley Lelie | .60 | .25 |
| 124 | Vernon Davis | .60 | .25 |
| 125 | Walt Harris | .50 | .20 |
| 126 | Brandon Moore | .50 | .20 |
| 127 | Nate Clements | .50 | .20 |
| 128 | Matt Hasselbeck | .60 | .25 |
| 129 | Shaun Alexander | .60 | .25 |
| 130 | Deion Branch | .60 | .25 |
| 131 | Darrell Jackson | .50 | .20 |
| 132 | Nate Burleson | .50 | .20 |
| 133 | Julian Peterson | .50 | .20 |
| 134 | Lofa Tatupu | .60 | .25 |
| 135 | Mack Strong | .50 | .20 |
| 136 | Josh Brown | .50 | .20 |
| 137 | J.P. Losman | .50 | .20 |
| 138 | Anthony Thomas | .50 | .20 |
| 139 | Lee Evans | .60 | .25 |
| 140 | Josh Reed | .50 | .20 |
| 141 | Roscoe Parrish | .50 | .20 |
| 142 | Aaron Schobel | .50 | .20 |
| 143 | Donte Whitner | .50 | .20 |
| 144 | Shaud Williams | .50 | .20 |
| 145 | Daunte Culpepper | .60 | .25 |
| 146 | Ronnie Brown | .60 | .25 |
| 147 | Chris Chambers | .60 | .25 |
| 148 | Marty Booker | .50 | .20 |
| 149 | Derek Hagan | .50 | .20 |
| 150 | Jason Taylor | .50 | .20 |
| 151 | Vonnie Holliday | .50 | .20 |
| 152 | Zach Thomas | .60 | .25 |
| 153 | Channing Crowder | .50 | .20 |
| 154 | Joey Porter | .50 | .20 |
| 155 | Tom Brady | 1.50 | .60 |
| 156 | Laurence Maroney | .75 | .30 |
| 157 | Chad Jackson | .50 | .20 |
| 158 | Wes Welker | .75 | .30 |
| 159 | Ben Watson | .50 | .20 |
| 160 | Donte Stallworth | .60 | .25 |
| 161 | Rosevelt Colvin | .50 | .20 |
| 162 | Ty Warren | .50 | .20 |
| 163 | Asante Samuel | .50 | .20 |
| 164 | Adalius Thomas | .50 | .20 |
| 165 | Tedy Bruschi | .75 | .30 |
| 166 | Chad Pennington | .60 | .25 |
| 167 | Thomas Jones | .60 | .25 |
| 168 | Laveranues Coles | .60 | .25 |
| 169 | Jerricho Cotchery | .50 | .20 |
| 170 | Chris Baker | .50 | .20 |
| 171 | Bryan Thomas | .50 | .20 |
| 172 | Leon Washington | .60 | .25 |
| 173 | Jonathan Vilma | .60 | .25 |
| 174 | Eric Barton | .50 | .20 |
| 175 | Erik Coleman | .50 | .20 |
| 176 | Steve McNair | .60 | .25 |
| 177 | Willis McGahee | .60 | .25 |
| 178 | Derrick Mason | .60 | .25 |
| 179 | Demetrius Williams | .50 | .20 |
| 180 | Todd Heap | .60 | .25 |
| 181 | Ray Lewis | .75 | .30 |
| 182 | Trevor Pryce | .50 | .20 |
| 183 | Bart Scott | .50 | .20 |
| 184 | Terrell Suggs | .50 | .20 |
| 185 | Mark Clayton | .60 | .25 |
| 186 | Carson Palmer | .75 | .30 |
| 187 | Rudi Johnson | .60 | .25 |
| 188 | Chad Johnson | .60 | .25 |
| 189 | T.J. Houshmandzadeh | .60 | .25 |
| 190 | Robert Geathers | .50 | .20 |
| 191 | Justin Smith | .50 | .20 |
| 192 | Tory James | .50 | .20 |
| 193 | Landon Johnson | .50 | .20 |
| 194 | Shayne Graham | .50 | .20 |
| 195 | Charlie Frye | .60 | .25 |
| 196 | Reuben Droughns | .60 | .25 |
| 197 | Braylon Edwards | .60 | .25 |
| 198 | Travis Wilson | .50 | .20 |
| 199 | Kellen Winslow | .60 | .25 |
| 200 | Kamerion Wimbley | .50 | .20 |
| 201 | Sean Jones | .50 | .20 |
| 202 | Andra Davis | .50 | .20 |
| 203 | Jamal Lewis | .60 | .25 |
| 204 | Ben Roethlisberger | 1.00 | .40 |
| 205 | Willie Parker | .75 | .30 |
| 206 | Hines Ward | .75 | .30 |
| 207 | Santonio Holmes | .60 | .25 |
| 208 | Heath Miller | .60 | .25 |
| 209 | Troy Polamalu | .75 | .30 |
| 210 | James Farrior | .50 | .20 |
| 211 | Cedrick Wilson | .50 | .20 |
| 212 | Dunta Robinson | .50 | .20 |
| 213 | Ahman Green | .60 | .25 |
| 214 | Andre Johnson | .60 | .25 |
| 215 | Jerome Mathis | .50 | .20 |
| 216 | Owen Daniels | .60 | .25 |
| 217 | DeMeco Ryans | .60 | .25 |
| 218 | Wali Lundy | .50 | .20 |
| 219 | Mario Williams | .60 | .25 |
| 220 | Peyton Manning | 1.25 | .50 |
| 221 | Joseph Addai | .75 | .30 |
| 222 | Marvin Harrison | .75 | .30 |
| 223 | Reggie Wayne | .60 | .25 |
| 224 | Dallas Clark | .60 | .25 |
| 225 | Robert Mathis | .50 | .20 |
| 226 | Cato June | .50 | .20 |
| 227 | Adam Vinatieri | .60 | .25 |
| 228 | Bob Sanders | .60 | .25 |
| 229 | Dwight Freeney | .60 | .25 |
| 230 | Byron Leftwich | .60 | .25 |
| 231 | Fred Taylor | .60 | .25 |
| 232 | Matt Jones | .60 | .25 |
| 233 | Reggie Williams | .50 | .20 |
| 234 | Marcedes Lewis | .50 | .20 |
| 235 | Bobby McCray | .50 | .20 |
| 236 | Rashean Mathis | .50 | .20 |
| 237 | Maurice Jones-Drew | .75 | .30 |
| 238 | Ernest Wilford | .50 | .20 |
| 239 | Daryl Smith | .50 | .20 |
| 240 | Vince Young | .75 | .30 |
| 241 | LenDale White | .60 | .25 |
| 242 | Brandon Jones | .50 | .20 |
| 243 | Bo Scaife | .50 | .20 |
| 244 | Keith Bulluck | .50 | .20 |
| 245 | Chris Hope | .50 | .20 |
| 246 | Kyle Vanden Bosch | .50 | .20 |
| 247 | Roydell Williams | .50 | .20 |
| 248 | Jay Cutler | .75 | .30 |
| 249 | Travis Henry | .60 | .25 |
| 250 | Javon Walker | .60 | .25 |
| 251 | Rod Smith | .60 | .25 |
| 252 | Tony Scheffler | .50 | .20 |
| 253 | Elvis Dumervil | .50 | .20 |
| 254 | Champ Bailey | .60 | .25 |
| 255 | Mike Bell | .60 | .25 |
| 256 | Brandon Marshall | .60 | .25 |
| 257 | Al Wilson | .50 | .20 |
| 258 | Trent Green | .50 | .20 |
| 259 | Larry Johnson | .75 | .30 |
| 260 | Eddie Kennison | .50 | .20 |
| 261 | Samie Parker | .50 | .20 |
| 262 | Tony Gonzalez | .60 | .25 |
| 263 | Jared Allen | .50 | .20 |
| 264 | Kawika Mitchell | .50 | .20 |
| 265 | Tamba Hali | .50 | .20 |
| 266 | Dante Hall | .60 | .25 |
| 267 | Brodie Croyle | .75 | .30 |
| 268 | Andrew Walter | .50 | .20 |
| 269 | LaMont Jordan | .60 | .25 |
| 270 | Dominic Rhodes | .50 | .20 |
| 271 | Randy Moss | .75 | .30 |
| 272 | Ronald Curry | .60 | .25 |
| 273 | Courtney Anderson | .50 | .20 |
| 274 | Derrick Burgess | .50 | .20 |
| 275 | Warren Sapp | .60 | .25 |
| 276 | Michael Huff | .60 | .25 |
| 277 | Thomas Howard | .50 | .20 |
| 278 | Kirk Morrison | .50 | .20 |
| 279 | Philip Rivers | .75 | .30 |
| 280 | LaDainian Tomlinson | 1.00 | .40 |
| 281 | Vincent Jackson | .50 | .20 |
| 282 | Lorenzo Neal | .50 | .20 |
| 283 | Antonio Gates | .60 | .25 |
| 284 | Shawne Merriman | .60 | .25 |
| 285 | Shaun Phillips | .50 | .20 |
| 286 | Michael Turner | .60 | .25 |
| 287 | Jamal Williams | .50 | .20 |
| 288 | Nate Kaeding | .50 | .20 |
| 289 | Michael Okwo RC | 1.50 | .60 |
| 290 | Gary Russell RC | 2.00 | .75 |
| 291 | Josh Wilson RC | 1.50 | .60 |
| 292 | Thomas Clayton RC | 1.50 | .60 |
| 293 | Jerard Rabb RC | 1.50 | .60 |
| 294 | Roy Hall RC | 2.00 | .75 |
| 295 | LaMarr Woodley RC | 2.00 | .75 |
| 296 | Eric Wright RC | 2.00 | .75 |
| 297 | Dan Bazuin RC | 1.50 | .60 |
| 298 | A.J. Davis RC | 1.25 | .50 |
| 299 | Buster Davis RC | 1.50 | .60 |
| 300 | Stewart Bradley RC | 2.00 | .75 |
| 301 | Toby Korrodi RC | 1.50 | .60 |
| 302 | Marcus McCauley RC | 1.50 | .60 |
| 303 | DeMarcus Tank Tyler RC | 1.50 | .60 |
| 304 | Jon Abbate RC | 1.25 | .50 |
| 305 | Ikaika Alama-Francis RC | 2.00 | .75 |
| 306 | Tim Crowder RC | 2.00 | .75 |
| 307 | D'Juan Woods RC | 1.50 | .60 |
| 308 | Tim Shaw RC | 1.50 | .60 |
| 309 | Fred Bennett RC | 1.25 | .50 |
| 310 | Victor Abiamiri RC | 2.00 | .75 |
| 311 | Eric Weddle RC | 1.50 | .60 |
| 312 | Danny Ware RC | 1.50 | .60 |
| 313 | Quentin Moses RC | 1.50 | .60 |
| 314 | Ryan McBean RC | 2.00 | .75 |
| 315 | David Harris RC | 1.50 | .60 |
| 316 | David Irons RC | 1.25 | .50 |
| 317 | Syndric Steptoe RC | 1.50 | .60 |
| 318 | Eric Frampton RC | 1.50 | .60 |
| 319 | Jemalle Cornelius RC | 1.50 | .60 |
| 320 | Earl Everett RC | 1.50 | .60 |
| 321 | Alonzo Coleman RC | 1.50 | .60 |
| 322 | Josh Gattis RC | 1.25 | .50 |
| 323 | Zak DeOssie RC | 1.50 | .60 |
| 324 | Jon Beason RC | 2.00 | .75 |
| 325 | Joe Staley RC | 1.50 | .60 |
| 326 | Aaron Rouse RC | 2.00 | .75 |
| 327 | Reggie Ball RC | 1.50 | .60 |
| 328 | Rufus Alexander RC | 2.00 | .75 |
| 329 | Daymeion Hughes RC | 1.50 | .60 |
| 330 | Justin Durant RC | 1.50 | .60 |
| 331 | JaMarcus Russell RC | 15.00 | 6.00 |
| 332 | Paul Williams RC | 5.00 | 2.00 |
| 333 | Kenny Irons RC | 6.00 | 2.50 |
| 334 | Chris Davis RC | 5.00 | 2.00 |
| 335 | Darius Walker RC | 6.00 | 2.50 |
| 336 | Dwayne Bowe RC | 12.00 | 5.00 |
| 337 | Isaiah Stanback RC | 6.00 | 2.50 |
| 338 | Leon Hall RC | 5.00 | 2.00 |
| 339 | Sidney Rice RC | 6.00 | 2.50 |
| 340 | Amobi Okoye RC | 6.00 | 2.50 |
| 341 | Adrian Peterson RC | 50.00 | 20.00 |
| 342 | LaRon Landry RC | 8.00 | 3.00 |
| 343 | Lorenzo Booker RC | 6.00 | 2.50 |
| 344 | Craig Buster Davis RC | 6.00 | 2.50 |
| 345 | Mike Walker RC | 5.00 | 2.00 |
| 346 | Zach Miller RC | 4.00 | 1.50 |
| 347 | Levi Brown RC | 6.00 | 2.50 |
| 348 | Brian Leonard RC | 6.00 | 2.50 |
| 349 | Aundrae Allison RC | 5.00 | 2.00 |
| 350 | Brandon Siler RC | 5.00 | 2.00 |
| 351 | Calvin Johnson RC | 15.00 | 6.00 |
| 352 | Gaines Adams RC | 6.00 | 2.50 |
| 353 | Anthony Gonzalez RC | 10.00 | 4.00 |
| 354 | John Beck RC | 6.00 | 2.50 |
| 355 | Joe Thomas RC | 5.00 | 2.00 |
| 356 | Michael Bush RC | 6.00 | 2.50 |
| 357 | Courtney Taylor RC | 5.00 | 2.00 |
| 358 | Lawrence Timmons RC | 6.00 | 2.50 |
| 359 | Drew Stanton RC | 6.00 | 2.50 |
| 360 | Chansi Stuckey RC | 5.00 | 2.00 |
| 361 | Greg Olsen RC | 8.00 | 3.00 |
| 362 | Rhema McKnight RC | 5.00 | 2.00 |
| 363 | Antonio Pittman RC | 6.00 | 2.50 |
| 364 | Kevin Kolb RC | 10.00 | 4.00 |
| 365 | Alan Branch RC | 5.00 | 2.00 |
| 366 | Robert Meachem RC | 6.00 | 2.50 |
| 367 | Troy Smith RC | 8.00 | 3.00 |
| 368 | Jamaal Anderson RC | 5.00 | 2.00 |
| 369 | Tony Hunt RC | 6.00 | 2.50 |

|  | | | |
|---|---|---|---|
| ❑ 370 | David Clowney RC | 5.00 | 2.00 |
| ❑ 371 | Brady Quinn RC | 20.00 | 8.00 |
| ❑ 372 | Michael Griffin RC | 6.00 | 2.50 |
| ❑ 373 | Jared Zabransky RC | 6.00 | 2.50 |
| ❑ 374 | Jason Hill RC | 6.00 | 2.50 |
| ❑ 375 | Trent Edwards RC | 15.00 | 6.00 |
| ❑ 376 | Dwayne Jarrett RC | 6.00 | 2.50 |
| ❑ 377 | DeShawn Wynn RC | 6.00 | 2.50 |
| ❑ 378 | Patrick Willis RC | 12.00 | 5.00 |
| ❑ 379 | Steve Smith USC RC | 8.00 | 3.00 |
| ❑ 380 | David Ball RC | 4.00 | 1.50 |
| ❑ 381 | Marshawn Lynch RC | 12.00 | 5.00 |
| ❑ 382 | Paul Posluszny RC | 8.00 | 3.00 |
| ❑ 383 | Johnnie Lee Higgins RC | 5.00 | 2.00 |
| ❑ 384 | Kolby Smith RC | 6.00 | 2.50 |
| ❑ 385 | Ted Ginn Jr. RC | 10.00 | 4.00 |
| ❑ 386 | Adam Carriker RC | 5.00 | 2.00 |
| ❑ 387 | Tyler Palko RC | 5.00 | 2.00 |
| ❑ 388 | Joel Filani RC | 5.00 | 2.00 |
| ❑ 389 | Garrett Wolfe RC | 6.00 | 2.50 |
| ❑ 390 | Ryne Robinson RC | 5.00 | 2.00 |
| ❑ 391 | Reggie Nelson RC | 5.00 | 2.00 |
| ❑ 392 | Dallas Baker RC | 5.00 | 2.00 |
| ❑ 393 | Dwayne Wright RC | 5.00 | 2.00 |
| ❑ 394 | Scott Chandler RC | 5.00 | 2.00 |
| ❑ 395 | Jordan Kent RC | 5.00 | 2.00 |
| ❑ 396 | Jarvis Moss RC | 6.00 | 2.50 |
| ❑ 397 | Jonathan Wade RC | 5.00 | 2.00 |
| ❑ 398 | Ben Grubbs RC | 5.00 | 2.00 |
| ❑ 399 | Jason Snelling RC | 5.00 | 2.00 |
| ❑ 400 | Jeff Rowe RC | 5.00 | 2.00 |
| ❑ 401 | Aaron Ross RC | 6.00 | 2.50 |
| ❑ 402 | Jarrett Hicks RC | 5.00 | 2.00 |
| ❑ 403 | Chris Henry RC | 6.00 | 2.50 |
| ❑ 404 | James Jones RC | 6.00 | 2.50 |
| ❑ 405 | Matt Spaeth RC | 6.00 | 2.50 |
| ❑ 406 | Brandon Meriweather RC | 6.00 | 2.50 |
| ❑ 407 | Nate Ilaoa RC | 6.00 | 2.50 |
| ❑ 408 | Brandon Myles RC | 5.00 | 2.00 |
| ❑ 409 | Ray McDonald RC | 5.00 | 2.00 |
| ❑ 410 | Chris Leak RC | 5.00 | 2.00 |
| ❑ 411 | Darrelle Revis RC | 6.00 | 2.50 |
| ❑ 412 | Ahmad Bradshaw RC | 8.00 | 3.00 |
| ❑ 413 | Tyler Thigpen RC | 8.00 | 3.00 |
| ❑ 414 | Justise Hairston RC | 5.00 | 2.00 |
| ❑ 415 | Charles Johnson RC | 4.00 | 1.50 |
| ❑ 416 | Anthony Spencer RC | 6.00 | 2.50 |
| ❑ 417 | Legedu Naanee RC | 6.00 | 2.50 |
| ❑ 418 | Kenneth Darby RC | 6.00 | 2.50 |
| ❑ 419 | Steve Breaston RC | 6.00 | 2.50 |
| ❑ 420 | Ben Patrick RC | 5.00 | 2.00 |
| ❑ 421 | Chris Houston RC | 6.00 | 2.50 |
| ❑ 422 | Jordan Palmer RC | 6.00 | 2.50 |
| ❑ 423 | Laurent Robinson RC | 5.00 | 2.00 |
| ❑ 424 | Selvin Young RC | 10.00 | 4.00 |
| ❑ 425 | Justin Harrell RC | 6.00 | 2.50 |
| ❑ 426 | Sabby Piscitelli RC | 6.00 | 2.50 |
| ❑ 427 | Yamon Figurs RC | 6.00 | 2.50 |
| ❑ 428 | Brandon Jackson RC | 6.00 | 2.50 |
| ❑ 429 | Jacoby Jones RC | 6.00 | 2.50 |
| ❑ 430 | H.B. Blades RC | 5.00 | 2.00 |

## 2008 Select

| # | | | |
|---|---|---|---|
| ❑ 1 | Matt Leinart | .75 | .30 |
| ❑ 2 | Kurt Warner | .75 | .30 |
| ❑ 3 | Larry Fitzgerald | .75 | .30 |
| ❑ 4 | Anquan Boldin | .60 | .25 |
| ❑ 5 | Edgerrin James | .60 | .25 |
| ❑ 6 | Neil Rackers | .50 | .20 |
| ❑ 7 | Steve Breaston | .50 | .20 |
| ❑ 8 | Antrel Rolle | .50 | .20 |
| ❑ 9 | Karlos Dansby | .50 | .20 |
| ❑ 10 | Joey Harrington | .60 | .25 |
| ❑ 11 | Jerious Norwood | .50 | .20 |
| ❑ 12 | Roddy White | .60 | .25 |
| ❑ 13 | Michael Jenkins | .50 | .20 |
| ❑ 14 | Joe Horn | .60 | .25 |
| ❑ 15 | Keith Brooking | .50 | .20 |
| ❑ 16 | Lawyer Milloy | .50 | .20 |
| ❑ 17 | John Abraham | .50 | .20 |
| ❑ 18 | Michael Turner | .60 | .25 |
| ❑ 19 | Troy Smith | .60 | .25 |
| ❑ 20 | Willis McGahee | .50 | .20 |
| ❑ 21 | Musa Smith | .50 | .20 |
| ❑ 22 | Derrick Mason | .50 | .20 |
| ❑ 23 | Mark Clayton | .60 | .25 |
| ❑ 24 | Bart Scott | .50 | .20 |
| ❑ 25 | Demetrius Williams | .50 | .20 |
| ❑ 26 | Yamon Figurs | .50 | .20 |
| ❑ 27 | Ray Lewis | .75 | .30 |
| ❑ 28 | Terrell Suggs | .60 | .25 |
| ❑ 29 | Ed Reed | .60 | .25 |
| ❑ 30 | Trent Edwards | .75 | .30 |
| ❑ 31 | Marshawn Lynch | .75 | .30 |
| ❑ 32 | Lee Evans | .60 | .25 |
| ❑ 33 | Roscoe Parrish | .50 | .20 |
| ❑ 34 | Paul Posluszny | .50 | .20 |
| ❑ 35 | John DiGiorgio RC | .50 | .20 |
| ❑ 36 | Angelo Crowell | .50 | .20 |
| ❑ 37 | Jabari Greer RC | .50 | .20 |
| ❑ 38 | Chris Kelsay | .50 | .20 |
| ❑ 39 | Fred Jackson RC | .75 | .30 |
| ❑ 40 | Matt Moore | .50 | .20 |
| ❑ 41 | Steve Smith | .60 | .25 |
| ❑ 42 | DeAngelo Williams | .60 | .25 |
| ❑ 43 | Brad Hoover | .50 | .20 |
| ❑ 44 | Dante Rosario | .50 | .20 |
| ❑ 45 | Julius Peppers | .60 | .25 |
| ❑ 46 | Jon Beason | .50 | .20 |
| ❑ 47 | Chris Harris | .50 | .20 |
| ❑ 48 | D.J. Hackett | .50 | .20 |
| ❑ 49 | Jake Delhomme | .50 | .20 |
| ❑ 50 | Adrian Peterson | .50 | .20 |
| ❑ 51 | Mark Anderson | .50 | .20 |
| ❑ 52 | Desmond Clark | .50 | .20 |
| ❑ 53 | Greg Olsen | .60 | .25 |
| ❑ 54 | Devin Hester | .75 | .30 |
| ❑ 55 | Brian Urlacher | .60 | .25 |
| ❑ 56 | Jason McKie RC | .50 | .20 |
| ❑ 57 | Lance Briggs | .50 | .20 |
| ❑ 58 | Rex Grossman | .60 | .25 |
| ❑ 59 | Carson Palmer | .75 | .30 |
| ❑ 60 | Chad Johnson | .60 | .25 |
| ❑ 61 | T.J. Houshmandzadeh | .60 | .25 |
| ❑ 62 | Rudi Johnson | .50 | .20 |
| ❑ 63 | Kenny Watson | .50 | .20 |
| ❑ 64 | Dhani Jones | .50 | .20 |
| ❑ 65 | Leon Hall | .50 | .20 |
| ❑ 66 | Johnathan Joseph | .50 | .20 |
| ❑ 67 | Derek Anderson | .60 | .25 |
| ❑ 68 | Brady Quinn | .75 | .30 |
| ❑ 69 | Jamal Lewis | .60 | .25 |
| ❑ 70 | Josh Cribbs | .60 | .25 |
| ❑ 71 | Kellen Winslow | .60 | .25 |
| ❑ 72 | Braylon Edwards | .60 | .25 |
| ❑ 73 | Joe Jurevicius | .50 | .20 |
| ❑ 74 | D'Qwell Jackson | .50 | .20 |
| ❑ 75 | Leigh Bodden | .50 | .20 |
| ❑ 76 | Sean Jones | .50 | .20 |
| ❑ 77 | Tony Romo | 1.25 | .50 |
| ❑ 78 | Terrell Owens | .75 | .30 |
| ❑ 79 | Marion Barber | .75 | .30 |
| ❑ 80 | Jason Witten | .60 | .25 |
| ❑ 81 | Patrick Crayton | .50 | .20 |
| ❑ 82 | Anthony Henry | .50 | .20 |
| ❑ 83 | DeMarcus Ware | .60 | .25 |
| ❑ 84 | Terence Newman | .50 | .20 |
| ❑ 85 | Greg Ellis | .50 | .20 |
| ❑ 86 | Zach Thomas | .60 | .25 |
| ❑ 87 | Keary Colbert | .50 | .20 |
| ❑ 88 | Jay Cutler | .75 | .30 |
| ❑ 89 | Tony Scheffler | .50 | .20 |
| ❑ 90 | Selvin Young | .60 | .25 |
| ❑ 91 | Brandon Marshall | .60 | .25 |
| ❑ 92 | Brandon Stokley | .50 | .20 |
| ❑ 93 | Champ Bailey | .50 | .20 |
| ❑ 94 | John Lynch | .60 | .25 |
| ❑ 95 | Dre Bly | .50 | .20 |
| ❑ 96 | Elvis Dumervil | .50 | .20 |
| ❑ 97 | Jon Kitna | .60 | .25 |
| ❑ 98 | Tatum Bell | .50 | .20 |
| ❑ 99 | Shaun McDonald | .50 | .20 |
| ❑ 100 | Roy Williams WR | .60 | .25 |
| ❑ 101 | Calvin Johnson | .75 | .30 |
| ❑ 102 | Mike Furrey | .50 | .20 |
| ❑ 103 | Ernie Sims | .50 | .20 |
| ❑ 104 | Aveion Cason | .50 | .20 |
| ❑ 105 | Aaron Rodgers | .75 | .30 |
| ❑ 106 | Brett Favre | 2.00 | .75 |
| ❑ 107 | Ryan Grant | .75 | .30 |
| ❑ 108 | Greg Jennings | .60 | .25 |
| ❑ 109 | Donald Driver | .60 | .25 |
| ❑ 110 | Donald Lee | .50 | .20 |
| ❑ 111 | James Jones | .50 | .20 |
| ❑ 112 | Al Harris | .50 | .20 |
| ❑ 113 | Nick Barnett | .50 | .20 |
| ❑ 114 | Charles Woodson | .60 | .25 |
| ❑ 115 | Aaron Kampman | .60 | .25 |
| ❑ 116 | Mason Crosby | .50 | .20 |
| ❑ 117 | Matt Schaub | .60 | .25 |
| ❑ 118 | Ahman Green | .60 | .25 |
| ❑ 119 | Andre Johnson | .60 | .25 |
| ❑ 120 | Kevin Walter | .50 | .20 |
| ❑ 121 | Owen Daniels | .50 | .20 |
| ❑ 122 | Andre Davis | .50 | .20 |
| ❑ 123 | DeMeco Ryans | .60 | .25 |
| ❑ 124 | Mario Williams | .60 | .25 |
| ❑ 125 | Dunta Robinson | .50 | .20 |
| ❑ 126 | Chris Brown | .50 | .20 |
| ❑ 127 | Peyton Manning | 1.25 | .50 |
| ❑ 128 | Joseph Addai | .75 | .30 |
| ❑ 129 | Marvin Harrison | .75 | .30 |
| ❑ 130 | Reggie Wayne | .60 | .25 |
| ❑ 131 | Dallas Clark | .60 | .25 |
| ❑ 132 | Anthony Gonzalez | .60 | .25 |
| ❑ 133 | Kenton Keith | .50 | .20 |
| ❑ 134 | Adam Vinatieri | .75 | .30 |
| ❑ 135 | Bob Sanders | .60 | .25 |
| ❑ 136 | Kelvin Hayden | .50 | .20 |
| ❑ 137 | Freddie Keiaho | .50 | .20 |
| ❑ 138 | David Garrard | .60 | .25 |
| ❑ 139 | Fred Taylor | .60 | .25 |
| ❑ 140 | Maurice Jones-Drew | .60 | .25 |
| ❑ 141 | Greg Jones | .50 | .20 |
| ❑ 142 | Dennis Northcutt | .50 | .20 |
| ❑ 143 | Reggie Williams | .50 | .20 |
| ❑ 144 | Marcedes Lewis | .50 | .20 |
| ❑ 145 | Matt Jones | .50 | .20 |
| ❑ 146 | Reggie Nelson | .50 | .20 |
| ❑ 147 | Cleo Lemon | .50 | .20 |
| ❑ 148 | Jerry Porter | .60 | .25 |
| ❑ 149 | Damon Huard | .50 | .20 |
| ❑ 150 | Brodie Croyle | .75 | .30 |
| ❑ 151 | Larry Johnson | .60 | .25 |
| ❑ 152 | Kolby Smith | .50 | .20 |
| ❑ 153 | Tony Gonzalez | .60 | .25 |
| ❑ 154 | Dwayne Bowe | .60 | .25 |
| ❑ 155 | Donnie Edwards | .50 | .20 |
| ❑ 156 | Jared Allen | .60 | .25 |
| ❑ 157 | Patrick Surtain | .50 | .20 |
| ❑ 158 | Derrick Burgess | .50 | .20 |
| ❑ 159 | Ernest Wilford | .50 | .20 |
| ❑ 160 | John Beck | .50 | .20 |
| ❑ 161 | Ronnie Brown | .60 | .25 |
| ❑ 162 | Greg Camarillo RC | 1.50 | .60 |
| ❑ 163 | Ted Ginn Jr. | .60 | .25 |
| ❑ 164 | Derek Hagan | .50 | .20 |
| ❑ 165 | Channing Crowder | .50 | .20 |
| ❑ 166 | Joey Porter | .50 | .20 |
| ❑ 167 | Jason Taylor | .60 | .25 |
| ❑ 168 | Josh McCown | .50 | .20 |
| ❑ 169 | Bernard Berrian | .60 | .25 |
| ❑ 170 | Maurice Hicks | .50 | .20 |
| ❑ 171 | Tarvaris Jackson | .60 | .25 |
| ❑ 172 | Adrian Peterson | 1.50 | .60 |
| ❑ 173 | Chester Taylor | .50 | .20 |
| ❑ 174 | Bobby Wade | .50 | .20 |
| ❑ 175 | Sidney Rice | .60 | .25 |

|  |  | | |
|---|---|---|---|
| ❏ 176 | Robert Ferguson | .50 | .20 |
| ❏ 177 | Darren Sharper | .50 | .20 |
| ❏ 178 | Visanthe Shiancoe | .50 | .20 |
| ❏ 179 | E.J. Henderson | .50 | .20 |
| ❏ 180 | Cedric Griffin | .50 | .20 |
| ❏ 181 | Chad Greenway | .50 | .20 |
| ❏ 182 | Tom Brady | 1.25 | .50 |
| ❏ 183 | Randy Moss | .75 | .30 |
| ❏ 184 | Laurence Maroney | .60 | .25 |
| ❏ 185 | Wes Welker | .75 | .30 |
| ❏ 186 | Sammy Morris | .50 | .20 |
| ❏ 187 | Kevin Faulk | .60 | .25 |
| ❏ 188 | Ben Watson | .50 | .20 |
| ❏ 189 | Tedy Bruschi | .75 | .30 |
| ❏ 190 | Rodney Harrison | .50 | .20 |
| ❏ 191 | Mike Vrabel | .50 | .20 |
| ❏ 192 | Drew Brees | .75 | .30 |
| ❏ 193 | Reggie Bush | .75 | .30 |
| ❏ 194 | Deuce McAllister | .60 | .25 |
| ❏ 195 | Marques Colston | .50 | .20 |
| ❏ 196 | David Patten | .50 | .20 |
| ❏ 197 | Devery Henderson | .50 | .20 |
| ❏ 198 | Scott Fujita | .50 | .20 |
| ❏ 199 | Roman Harper | .50 | .20 |
| ❏ 200 | Mike McKenzie | .50 | .20 |
| ❏ 201 | Will Smith | .50 | .20 |
| ❏ 202 | Billy Miller | .50 | .20 |
| ❏ 203 | Sammy Knight | .50 | .20 |
| ❏ 204 | Eli Manning | .75 | .30 |
| ❏ 205 | Plaxico Burress | .60 | .25 |
| ❏ 206 | Brandon Jacobs | .60 | .25 |
| ❏ 207 | Ahmad Bradshaw | .60 | .25 |
| ❏ 208 | David Tyree | .60 | .25 |
| ❏ 209 | Amani Toomer | .60 | .25 |
| ❏ 210 | Jeremy Shockey | .60 | .25 |
| ❏ 211 | Steve Smith USC | .50 | .20 |
| ❏ 212 | Aaron Ross | .50 | .20 |
| ❏ 213 | Antonio Pierce | .50 | .20 |
| ❏ 214 | Michael Strahan | .60 | .25 |
| ❏ 215 | Jesse Chatman | .50 | .20 |
| ❏ 216 | Calvin Pace | .50 | .20 |
| ❏ 217 | Kellen Clemens | .50 | .20 |
| ❏ 218 | Leon Washington | .50 | .20 |
| ❏ 219 | Jerricho Cotchery | .50 | .20 |
| ❏ 220 | Laveranues Coles | .60 | .25 |
| ❏ 221 | Chris Baker | .50 | .20 |
| ❏ 222 | Brad Smith | .50 | .20 |
| ❏ 223 | Thomas Jones | .60 | .25 |
| ❏ 224 | Darrelle Revis | .50 | .20 |
| ❏ 225 | David Harris | .50 | .20 |
| ❏ 226 | DeAngelo Hall | .50 | .20 |
| ❏ 227 | Drew Carter | .50 | .20 |
| ❏ 228 | Javon Walker | .60 | .25 |
| ❏ 229 | JaMarcus Russell | .75 | .30 |
| ❏ 230 | Justin Fargas | .50 | .20 |
| ❏ 231 | Michael Bush | .60 | .25 |
| ❏ 232 | Ronald Curry | .60 | .25 |
| ❏ 233 | Zach Miller | .60 | .25 |
| ❏ 234 | Thomas Howard | .50 | .20 |
| ❏ 235 | Johnnie Lee Higgins | .50 | .20 |
| ❏ 236 | Kirk Morrison | .50 | .20 |
| ❏ 237 | Michael Huff | .50 | .20 |
| ❏ 238 | Asante Samuel | .50 | .20 |
| ❏ 239 | Donovan McNabb | .75 | .30 |
| ❏ 240 | Brian Westbrook | .60 | .25 |
| ❏ 241 | Correll Buckhalter | .60 | .25 |
| ❏ 242 | Kevin Curtis | .50 | .20 |
| ❏ 243 | Reggie Brown | .60 | .25 |
| ❏ 244 | L.J. Smith | .50 | .20 |
| ❏ 245 | Greg Lewis | .50 | .20 |
| ❏ 246 | Lito Sheppard | .50 | .20 |
| ❏ 247 | Omar Gaither | .50 | .20 |
| ❏ 248 | Ben Roethlisberger | 1.00 | .40 |
| ❏ 249 | Willie Parker | .60 | .25 |
| ❏ 250 | Najeh Davenport | .50 | .20 |
| ❏ 251 | Hines Ward | .75 | .30 |
| ❏ 252 | Santonio Holmes | .60 | .25 |
| ❏ 253 | Heath Miller | .50 | .20 |
| ❏ 254 | Cedrick Wilson | .50 | .20 |
| ❏ 255 | James Harrison RC | 3.00 | 1.25 |
| ❏ 256 | Ike Taylor | .50 | .20 |
| ❏ 257 | James Farrior | .50 | .20 |
| ❏ 258 | Troy Polamalu | .75 | .30 |
| ❏ 259 | Philip Rivers | .75 | .30 |
| ❏ 260 | LaDainian Tomlinson | 1.00 | .40 |
| ❏ 261 | Darren Sproles | .50 | .20 |
| ❏ 262 | Vincent Jackson | .50 | .20 |
| ❏ 263 | Chris Chambers | .60 | .25 |
| ❏ 264 | Antonio Gates | .60 | .25 |
| ❏ 265 | Craig Buster Davis | .50 | .20 |
| ❏ 266 | Malcom Floyd | .50 | .20 |
| ❏ 267 | Antonio Cromartie | .50 | .20 |
| ❏ 268 | Shawne Merriman | .60 | .25 |
| ❏ 269 | DeShaun Foster | .50 | .20 |
| ❏ 270 | Alex Smith QB | .60 | .25 |
| ❏ 271 | Frank Gore | .60 | .25 |
| ❏ 272 | Michael Robinson | .50 | .20 |
| ❏ 273 | Vernon Davis | .60 | .25 |
| ❏ 274 | Arnaz Battle | .50 | .20 |
| ❏ 275 | Isaac Bruce | .50 | .20 |
| ❏ 276 | Patrick Willis | .60 | .25 |
| ❏ 277 | Nate Clements | .50 | .20 |
| ❏ 278 | Jason Hill | .50 | .20 |
| ❏ 279 | T.J. Duckett | .50 | .20 |
| ❏ 280 | Matt Hasselbeck | .60 | .25 |
| ❏ 281 | Julian Peterson | .50 | .20 |
| ❏ 282 | Maurice Morris | .50 | .20 |
| ❏ 283 | Bobby Engram | .50 | .20 |
| ❏ 284 | Nate Burleson | .50 | .20 |
| ❏ 285 | Deion Branch | .60 | .25 |
| ❏ 286 | Lofa Tatupu | .60 | .25 |
| ❏ 287 | Marcus Trufant | .50 | .20 |
| ❏ 288 | Darryl Tapp | .50 | .20 |
| ❏ 289 | Julius Jones | .60 | .25 |
| ❏ 290 | Marc Bulger | .60 | .25 |
| ❏ 291 | Steven Jackson | .75 | .30 |
| ❏ 292 | Brian Leonard | .50 | .20 |
| ❏ 293 | Torry Holt | .60 | .25 |
| ❏ 294 | Dante Hall | .50 | .20 |
| ❏ 295 | Randy McMichael | .50 | .20 |
| ❏ 296 | Drew Bennett | .50 | .20 |
| ❏ 297 | Will Witherspoon | .50 | .20 |
| ❏ 298 | Tye Hill | .50 | .20 |
| ❏ 299 | Corey Chavous | .50 | .20 |
| ❏ 300 | Warrick Dunn | .60 | .25 |
| ❏ 301 | Brian Griese | .50 | .20 |
| ❏ 302 | Jeff Garcia | .60 | .25 |
| ❏ 303 | Cadillac Williams | .50 | .20 |
| ❏ 304 | Earnest Graham | .50 | .20 |
| ❏ 305 | Joey Galloway | .50 | .20 |
| ❏ 306 | Ike Hilliard | .50 | .20 |
| ❏ 307 | Michael Clayton | .50 | .20 |
| ❏ 308 | Derrick Brooks | .60 | .25 |
| ❏ 309 | Phillip Buchanon | .50 | .20 |
| ❏ 310 | Alex Smith TE | .50 | .20 |
| ❏ 311 | Ronde Barber | .50 | .20 |
| ❏ 312 | Justin McCareins | .50 | .20 |
| ❏ 313 | Jevon Kearse | .50 | .20 |
| ❏ 314 | Vince Young | .75 | .30 |
| ❏ 315 | LenDale White | .60 | .25 |
| ❏ 316 | Justin Gage | .50 | .20 |
| ❏ 317 | Roydell Williams | .50 | .20 |
| ❏ 318 | Alge Crumpler | .50 | .20 |
| ❏ 319 | Brandon Jones | .50 | .20 |
| ❏ 320 | Michael Griffin | .50 | .20 |
| ❏ 321 | Keith Bulluck | .50 | .20 |
| ❏ 322 | Jason Campbell | .60 | .25 |
| ❏ 323 | Clinton Portis | .60 | .25 |
| ❏ 324 | Ladell Betts | .50 | .20 |
| ❏ 325 | Santana Moss | .60 | .25 |
| ❏ 326 | Chris Cooley | .60 | .25 |
| ❏ 327 | Antwaan Randle El | .50 | .20 |
| ❏ 328 | London Fletcher | .50 | .20 |
| ❏ 329 | Shawn Springs | .50 | .20 |
| ❏ 330 | LaRon Landry | .60 | .25 |
| ❏ 331 | Jake Long RC | 5.00 | 2.00 |
| ❏ 332 | Chris Long RC | 5.00 | 2.00 |
| ❏ 333 | Matt Ryan RC | 15.00 | 6.00 |
| ❏ 334 | Darren McFadden RC | 10.00 | 4.00 |
| ❏ 335 | Glenn Dorsey RC | 5.00 | 2.00 |
| ❏ 336 | Vernon Gholston RC | 4.00 | 1.50 |
| ❏ 337 | Sedrick Ellis RC | 4.00 | 1.50 |
| ❏ 338 | Derrick Harvey RC | 3.00 | 1.25 |
| ❏ 339 | Keith Rivers RC | 4.00 | 1.50 |
| ❏ 340 | Jerod Mayo RC | 6.00 | 2.50 |
| ❏ 341 | Leodis McKelvin RC | 4.00 | 1.50 |
| ❏ 342 | Jonathan Stewart RC | 10.00 | 4.00 |
| ❏ 343 | Dominique Rodgers-Cromartie RC | 4.00 | 1.50 |
| ❏ 344 | Joe Flacco RC | 12.00 | 5.00 |
| ❏ 345 | Aqib Talib RC | 4.00 | 1.50 |
| ❏ 346 | Felix Jones RC | 10.00 | 4.00 |
| ❏ 347 | Rashard Mendenhall RC | 8.00 | 3.00 |
| ❏ 348 | Chris Johnson RC | 10.00 | 4.00 |
| ❏ 349 | Mike Jenkins RC | 4.00 | 1.50 |
| ❏ 350 | Antoine Cason RC | 4.00 | 1.50 |
| ❏ 351 | Lawrence Jackson RC | 3.00 | 1.25 |
| ❏ 352 | Kentwan Balmer RC | 3.00 | 1.25 |
| ❏ 353 | Dustin Keller RC | 4.00 | 1.50 |
| ❏ 354 | Kenny Phillips RC | 4.00 | 1.50 |
| ❏ 355 | Phillip Merling RC | 3.00 | 1.25 |
| ❏ 356 | Donnie Avery RC | 5.00 | 2.00 |
| ❏ 357 | Devin Thomas RC | 4.00 | 1.50 |
| ❏ 358 | Brandon Flowers RC | 4.00 | 1.50 |
| ❏ 359 | Jordy Nelson RC | 5.00 | 2.00 |
| ❏ 360 | Curtis Lofton RC | 4.00 | 1.50 |
| ❏ 361 | John Carlson RC | 4.00 | 1.50 |
| ❏ 362 | Tracy Porter RC | 3.00 | 1.25 |
| ❏ 363 | James Hardy RC | 4.00 | 1.50 |
| ❏ 364 | Eddie Royal RC | 8.00 | 3.00 |
| ❏ 365 | Matt Forte RC | 10.00 | 4.00 |
| ❏ 366 | Jordon Dizon RC | 4.00 | 1.50 |
| ❏ 367 | Jerome Simpson RC | 3.00 | 1.25 |
| ❏ 368 | Fred Davis RC | 4.00 | 1.50 |
| ❏ 369 | DeSean Jackson RC | 8.00 | 3.00 |
| ❏ 370 | Calais Campbell RC | 3.00 | 1.25 |
| ❏ 371 | Malcolm Kelly RC | 4.00 | 1.50 |
| ❏ 372 | Quentin Groves RC | 3.00 | 1.25 |
| ❏ 373 | Limas Sweed RC | 5.00 | 2.00 |
| ❏ 374 | Ray Rice RC | 5.00 | 2.00 |
| ❏ 375 | Brian Brohm RC | 5.00 | 2.00 |
| ❏ 376 | Chad Henne RC | 6.00 | 2.50 |
| ❏ 377 | Dexter Jackson RC | 4.00 | 1.50 |
| ❏ 378 | Martellus Bennett RC | 4.00 | 1.50 |
| ❏ 379 | Terrell Thomas RC | 3.00 | 1.25 |
| ❏ 380 | Kevin Smith RC | 6.00 | 2.50 |
| ❏ 381 | Anthony Alridge RC | 3.00 | 1.25 |
| ❏ 382 | Jacob Hester RC | 4.00 | 1.50 |
| ❏ 383 | Earl Bennett RC | 4.00 | 1.50 |
| ❏ 384 | Jamaal Charles RC | 5.00 | 2.00 |
| ❏ 385 | Dan Connor RC | 4.00 | 1.50 |
| ❏ 386 | Reggie Smith RC | 3.00 | 1.25 |
| ❏ 387 | Brad Cottam RC | 4.00 | 1.50 |
| ❏ 388 | Pat Sims RC | 3.00 | 1.25 |
| ❏ 389 | Dartrell Savage RC | 4.00 | 1.50 |
| ❏ 390 | Early Doucet RC | 4.00 | 1.50 |
| ❏ 391 | Harry Douglas RC | 4.00 | 1.50 |
| ❏ 392 | Steve Slaton RC | 8.00 | 3.00 |
| ❏ 393 | Jermichael Finley RC | 4.00 | 1.50 |
| ❏ 394 | Kevin O'Connell RC | 5.00 | 2.00 |
| ❏ 395 | Mario Manningham RC | 3.00 | 1.25 |
| ❏ 396 | Andre Caldwell RC | 3.00 | 1.25 |
| ❏ 397 | Will Franklin RC | 4.00 | 1.50 |
| ❏ 398 | Marcus Smith RC | 3.00 | 1.25 |
| ❏ 399 | Martin Rucker RC | 3.00 | 1.25 |
| ❏ 400 | Xavier Adibi RC | 3.00 | 1.25 |
| ❏ 401 | Craig Steltz RC | 3.00 | 1.25 |
| ❏ 402 | Tashard Choice RC | 4.00 | 1.50 |
| ❏ 403 | Lavelle Hawkins RC | 4.00 | 1.50 |
| ❏ 404 | Jacob Tamme RC | 4.00 | 1.50 |
| ❏ 405 | Keenan Burton RC | 3.00 | 1.25 |
| ❏ 406 | John David Booty RC | 5.00 | 2.00 |
| ❏ 407 | Ryan Torain RC | 4.00 | 1.50 |
| ❏ 408 | Tim Hightower RC | 8.00 | 3.00 |
| ❏ 409 | Dennis Dixon RC | 4.00 | 1.50 |
| ❏ 410 | Kellen Davis RC | 2.50 | 1.00 |
| ❏ 411 | Josh Johnson RC | 4.00 | 1.50 |
| ❏ 412 | Erik Ainge RC | 4.00 | 1.50 |
| ❏ 413 | Owen Schmitt RC | 4.00 | 1.50 |
| ❏ 414 | Marcus Thomas RC | 3.00 | 1.25 |
| ❏ 415 | Thomas Brown RC | 4.00 | 1.50 |
| ❏ 416 | Josh Morgan RC | 4.00 | 1.50 |
| ❏ 417 | Kevin Robinson RC | 3.00 | 1.25 |
| ❏ 418 | Colt Brennan RC | 10.00 | 4.00 |
| ❏ 419 | Paul Hubbard RC | 3.00 | 1.25 |
| ❏ 420 | Andre Woodson RC | 4.00 | 1.50 |
| ❏ 421 | Mike Hart RC | 5.00 | 2.00 |
| ❏ 422 | Matt Flynn RC | 5.00 | 2.00 |
| ❏ 423 | Chauncey Washington RC | 3.00 | 1.25 |
| ❏ 424 | Caleb Campbell RC | 4.00 | 1.50 |
| ❏ 425 | Cory Hillis RC | 5.00 | 2.00 |
| ❏ 426 | Justin Forsett RC | 4.00 | 1.50 |
| ❏ 427 | Adrian Arrington RC | 3.00 | 1.25 |
| ❏ 428 | Cory Boyd RC | 3.00 | 1.25 |
| ❏ 429 | Allen Patrick RC | 3.00 | 1.25 |
| ❏ 430 | Marcus Monk RC | 4.00 | 1.50 |

| | | |
|---|---|---|
| ❏ 431 DJ Hall RC | 4.00 | 1.50 |
| ❏ 432 Darrell Strong RC | 3.00 | 1.25 |
| ❏ 433 Jason Rivers RC | 4.00 | 1.50 |
| ❏ 434 Jed Collins RC | 3.00 | 1.25 |
| ❏ 435 Paul Smith RC | 4.00 | 1.50 |
| ❏ 436 Darius Reynaud RC | 3.00 | 1.25 |
| ❏ 437 Ali Highsmith RC | 2.50 | 1.00 |
| ❏ 438 Davone Bess RC | 5.00 | 2.00 |
| ❏ 439 Erin Henderson RC | 3.00 | 1.25 |
| ❏ 440 Kalvin McRae RC | 3.00 | 1.25 |

## 1993 SP

| | | |
|---|---|---|
| ❏ COMPLETE SET (270) | 60.00 | 25.00 |
| ❏ 1 Curtis Conway FOIL RC | 4.00 | 1.50 |
| ❏ 2 John Copeland FOIL RC | .75 | .30 |
| ❏ 3 Kevin Williams RC WR FOIL | 1.50 | .60 |
| ❏ 4 Dan Williams FOIL RC | .75 | .30 |
| ❏ 5 Patrick Bates FOIL RC | .75 | .30 |
| ❏ 6 Jerome Bettis FOIL RC | 25.00 | 15.00 |
| ❏ 7 O.J. McDuffie FOIL RC | 3.00 | 1.25 |
| ❏ 8 Robert Smith FOIL RC | 8.00 | 3.00 |
| ❏ 9 Drew Bledsoe FOIL RC | 30.00 | 12.50 |
| ❏ 10 Irv Smith FOIL RC | .75 | .30 |
| ❏ 11 Marvin Jones FOIL RC | .75 | .30 |
| ❏ 12 Victor Bailey FOIL RC | .75 | .30 |
| ❏ 13 Garrison Hearst FOIL RC | 8.00 | 3.00 |
| ❏ 14 Natrone Means FOIL RC | 3.00 | 1.25 |
| ❏ 15 Todd Kelly FOIL RC | .75 | .30 |
| ❏ 16 Rick Mirer FOIL RC | 3.00 | 1.25 |
| ❏ 17 Eric Curry FOIL RC | .75 | .30 |
| ❏ 18 Reggie Brooks FOIL RC | 1.50 | .60 |
| ❏ 19 Eric Dickerson | .50 | .20 |
| ❏ 20 Roger Harper RC | .30 | .10 |
| ❏ 21 Michael Haynes | .50 | .20 |
| ❏ 22 Bobby Hebert | .30 | .10 |
| ❏ 23 Lincoln Kennedy RC | .30 | .10 |
| ❏ 24 Chris Miller | .50 | .20 |
| ❏ 25 Mike Pritchard | .50 | .20 |
| ❏ 26 Andre Rison | .50 | .20 |
| ❏ 27 Deion Sanders | 1.50 | .60 |
| ❏ 28 Cornelius Bennett | .30 | .10 |
| ❏ 29 Kenneth Davis | .30 | .10 |
| ❏ 30 Henry Jones | .30 | .10 |
| ❏ 31 Jim Kelly | 1.00 | .40 |
| ❏ 32 John Parrella RC | .30 | .10 |
| ❏ 33 Andre Reed | .50 | .20 |
| ❏ 34 Bruce Smith | 1.00 | .40 |
| ❏ 35 Thomas Smith RC | .50 | .20 |
| ❏ 36 Thurman Thomas | 1.00 | .40 |
| ❏ 37 Neal Anderson | .30 | .10 |
| ❏ 38 Myron Baker RC | .30 | .10 |
| ❏ 39 Mark Carrier DB | .30 | .10 |
| ❏ 40 Richard Dent | .50 | .20 |
| ❏ 41 Chris Gedney RC | .30 | .10 |
| ❏ 42 Jim Harbaugh | 1.00 | .40 |
| ❏ 43 Craig Heyward | .30 | .10 |
| ❏ 44 Carl Simpson RC | .30 | .10 |
| ❏ 45 Alonzo Spellman | .30 | .10 |
| ❏ 46 Derrick Fenner | .30 | .10 |
| ❏ 47 Harold Green | .30 | .10 |
| ❏ 48 David Klingler | .30 | .10 |
| ❏ 49 Ricardo McDonald | .30 | .10 |
| ❏ 50 Tony McGee RC | .50 | .20 |
| ❏ 51 Carl Pickens | .50 | .20 |
| ❏ 52 Steve Tovar RC | .30 | .10 |
| ❏ 53 Alfred Williams | .30 | .10 |
| ❏ 54 Darryl Williams | .30 | .10 |
| ❏ 55 Jerry Ball | .30 | .10 |

| | | |
|---|---|---|
| ❏ 56 Mike Caldwell RC | .30 | .10 |
| ❏ 57 Mark Carrier WR | .50 | .20 |
| ❏ 58 Steve Everitt RC | .30 | .10 |
| ❏ 59 Dan Footman RC | .30 | .10 |
| ❏ 60 Pepper Johnson | .30 | .10 |
| ❏ 61 Bernie Kosar | .50 | .20 |
| ❏ 62 Eric Metcalf | .50 | .20 |
| ❏ 63 Michael Dean Perry | .50 | .20 |
| ❏ 64 Troy Aikman | 2.50 | 1.25 |
| ❏ 65 Charles Haley | .50 | .20 |
| ❏ 66 Michael Irvin | 1.00 | .40 |
| ❏ 67 Robert Jones | .30 | .10 |
| ❏ 68 Derrick Lassic RC | .30 | .10 |
| ❏ 69 Russell Maryland | .30 | .10 |
| ❏ 70 Ken Norton Jr. | .50 | .20 |
| ❏ 71 Darrin Smith RC | .50 | .20 |
| ❏ 72 Emmitt Smith | 5.00 | 2.50 |
| ❏ 73 Steve Atwater | .30 | .10 |
| ❏ 74 Rod Bernstine | .30 | .10 |
| ❏ 75 Jason Elam RC | 1.00 | .40 |
| ❏ 76 John Elway | 5.00 | 2.00 |
| ❏ 77 Simon Fletcher | .30 | .10 |
| ❏ 78 Tommy Maddox | 1.00 | .40 |
| ❏ 79 Glyn Milburn RC | 1.00 | .40 |
| ❏ 80 Derek Russell | .30 | .10 |
| ❏ 81 Shannon Sharpe | 1.00 | .40 |
| ❏ 82 Bennie Blades | .30 | .10 |
| ❏ 83 Willie Green | .30 | .10 |
| ❏ 84 Antonio London RC | .30 | .10 |
| ❏ 85 Ryan McNeil RC | 1.00 | .40 |
| ❏ 86 Herman Moore | 1.00 | .40 |
| ❏ 87 Rodney Peete | .30 | .10 |
| ❏ 88 Barry Sanders | 4.00 | 1.50 |
| ❏ 89 Chris Spielman | .50 | .20 |
| ❏ 90 Pat Swilling | .30 | .10 |
| ❏ 91 Mark Brunell RC | 15.00 | 6.00 |
| ❏ 92 Terrell Buckley | .30 | .10 |
| ❏ 93 Brett Favre | 6.00 | 3.00 |
| ❏ 94 Jackie Harris | .30 | .10 |
| ❏ 95 Sterling Sharpe | 1.00 | .40 |
| ❏ 96 John Stephens | .30 | .10 |
| ❏ 97 Wayne Simmons RC | .30 | .10 |
| ❏ 98 George Teague RC | .50 | .20 |
| ❏ 99 Reggie White | 1.00 | .40 |
| ❏ 100 Micheal Barrow RC | 1.00 | .40 |
| ❏ 101 Cody Carlson | .30 | .10 |
| ❏ 102 Ray Childress | .30 | .10 |
| ❏ 103 Brad Hopkins RC | .30 | .10 |
| ❏ 104 Haywood Jeffires | .50 | .20 |
| ❏ 105 Wilber Marshall | .30 | .10 |
| ❏ 106 Warren Moon | 1.00 | .40 |
| ❏ 107 Webster Slaughter | .30 | .10 |
| ❏ 108 Lorenzo White | .30 | .10 |
| ❏ 109 John Baylor | .30 | .10 |
| ❏ 110 Duane Bickett | .30 | .10 |
| ❏ 111 Quentin Coryatt | .50 | .20 |
| ❏ 112 Steve Emtman | .30 | .10 |
| ❏ 113 Jeff George | 1.00 | .40 |
| ❏ 114 Jessie Hester | .30 | .10 |
| ❏ 115 Anthony Johnson | .50 | .20 |
| ❏ 116 Reggie Langhorne | .30 | .10 |
| ❏ 117 Roosevelt Potts RC | .30 | .10 |
| ❏ 118 Marcus Allen | 1.00 | .40 |
| ❏ 119 J.J. Birden | .30 | .10 |
| ❏ 120 Willie Davis | 1.00 | .40 |
| ❏ 121 Jaime Fields RC | .30 | .10 |
| ❏ 122 Joe Montana | 5.00 | 2.00 |
| ❏ 123 Will Shields RC | 1.00 | .40 |
| ❏ 124 Neil Smith | 1.00 | .40 |
| ❏ 125 Derrick Thomas | 1.00 | .40 |
| ❏ 126 Harvey Williams | .50 | .20 |
| ❏ 127 Tim Brown | 1.00 | .40 |
| ❏ 128 Billy Joe Hobert RC | 1.00 | .40 |
| ❏ 129 Jeff Hostetler | .50 | .20 |
| ❏ 130 Ethan Horton | .30 | .10 |
| ❏ 131 Rocket Ismail | .50 | .20 |
| ❏ 132 Howie Long | 1.00 | .40 |
| ❏ 133 Terry McDaniel | .30 | .10 |
| ❏ 134 Greg Robinson RC | .30 | .10 |
| ❏ 135 Anthony Smith | .30 | .10 |
| ❏ 136 Flipper Anderson | .30 | .10 |
| ❏ 137 Marc Boutte | .30 | .10 |
| ❏ 138 Shane Conlan | .30 | .10 |
| ❏ 139 Troy Drayton RC | .50 | .20 |
| ❏ 140 Henry Ellard | .50 | .20 |

| | | |
|---|---|---|
| ❏ 141 Jim Everett | .50 | .20 |
| ❏ 142 Cleveland Gary | .30 | .10 |
| ❏ 143 Sean Gilbert | .50 | .20 |
| ❏ 144 Robert Young | .30 | .10 |
| ❏ 145 Marco Coleman | .30 | .10 |
| ❏ 146 Bryan Cox | .30 | .10 |
| ❏ 147 Irving Fryar | .50 | .20 |
| ❏ 148 Keith Jackson | .50 | .20 |
| ❏ 149 Terry Kirby RC | 1.00 | .40 |
| ❏ 150 Dan Marino | 5.00 | 2.00 |
| ❏ 151 Scott Mitchell | 1.00 | .40 |
| ❏ 152 Louis Oliver | .30 | .10 |
| ❏ 153 Troy Vincent | .30 | .10 |
| ❏ 154 Anthony Carter | .30 | .10 |
| ❏ 155 Cris Carter | 1.00 | .40 |
| ❏ 156 Roger Craig | .50 | .20 |
| ❏ 157 Chris Doleman | .30 | .10 |
| ❏ 158 Qadry Ismail RC | 2.00 | .75 |
| ❏ 159 Steve Jordan | .30 | .10 |
| ❏ 160 Randall McDaniel | .30 | .10 |
| ❏ 161 Audray McMillian | .30 | .10 |
| ❏ 162 Barry Word | .30 | .10 |
| ❏ 163 Vincent Brown | .30 | .10 |
| ❏ 164 Marv Cook | .30 | .10 |
| ❏ 165 Sam Gash RC | 1.00 | .40 |
| ❏ 166 Pat Harlow | .30 | .10 |
| ❏ 167 Greg McMurtry | .30 | .10 |
| ❏ 168 Todd Rucci RC | .30 | .10 |
| ❏ 169 Leonard Russell | .50 | .20 |
| ❏ 170 Scott Sisson RC | .30 | .10 |
| ❏ 171 Chris Slade RC | .50 | .20 |
| ❏ 172 Morten Andersen | .30 | .10 |
| ❏ 173 Derek Brown RC RBK | .50 | .20 |
| ❏ 174 Reggie Freeman RC | .30 | .10 |
| ❏ 175 Rickey Jackson | .30 | .10 |
| ❏ 176 Eric Martin | .30 | .10 |
| ❏ 177 Wayne Martin | .30 | .10 |
| ❏ 178 Brad Muster | .30 | .10 |
| ❏ 179 Willie Roaf RC | .50 | .20 |
| ❏ 180 Renaldo Turnbull | .30 | .10 |
| ❏ 181 Derek Brown TE | .30 | .10 |
| ❏ 182 Marcus Buckley RC | .30 | .10 |
| ❏ 183 Jarrod Bunch | .30 | .10 |
| ❏ 184 Rodney Hampton | .50 | .20 |
| ❏ 185 Ed McCaffrey | 1.00 | .40 |
| ❏ 186 Kanavis McGhee | .30 | .10 |
| ❏ 187 Mike Sherrard | .30 | .10 |
| ❏ 188 Phil Simms | .50 | .20 |
| ❏ 189 Lawrence Taylor | 1.00 | .40 |
| ❏ 190 Kurt Barber | .30 | .10 |
| ❏ 191 Brian Baldinger | .30 | .10 |
| ❏ 192 Johnny Johnson | .30 | .10 |
| ❏ 193 Ronnie Lott | .50 | .20 |
| ❏ 194 Johnny Mitchell | .30 | .10 |
| ❏ 195 Rob Moore | .50 | .20 |
| ❏ 196 Adrian Murrell RC | 1.00 | .40 |
| ❏ 197 Browning Nagle | .30 | .10 |
| ❏ 198 Marvin Washington | .30 | .10 |
| ❏ 199 Eric Allen | .30 | .10 |
| ❏ 200 Fred Barnett | .50 | .20 |
| ❏ 201 Randall Cunningham | 1.00 | .40 |
| ❏ 202 Byron Evans | .30 | .10 |
| ❏ 203 Tim Harris | .30 | .10 |
| ❏ 204 Seth Joyner | .30 | .10 |
| ❏ 205 Leonard Renfro RC | .30 | .10 |
| ❏ 206 Heath Sherman | .30 | .10 |
| ❏ 207 Clyde Simmons | .30 | .10 |
| ❏ 208 Johnny Bailey | .30 | .10 |
| ❏ 209 Steve Beuerlein | .50 | .20 |
| ❏ 210 Chuck Cecil | .30 | .10 |
| ❏ 211 Larry Centers RC | 1.00 | .40 |
| ❏ 212 Gary Clark | .50 | .20 |
| ❏ 213 Ernest Dye RC | .30 | .10 |
| ❏ 214 Ken Harvey | .30 | .10 |
| ❏ 215 Randal Hill | .30 | .10 |
| ❏ 216 Ricky Proehl | .30 | .10 |
| ❏ 217 Deon Figures RC | .30 | .10 |
| ❏ 218 Barry Foster | .50 | .20 |
| ❏ 219 Kevin Greene | .30 | .10 |
| ❏ 220 Kevin Greene | .30 | .10 |
| ❏ 221 Carlton Haselrig | .30 | .10 |
| ❏ 222 Andre Hastings RC | .50 | .20 |
| ❏ 223 Greg Lloyd | .30 | .10 |
| ❏ 224 Neil O'Donnell | 1.00 | .40 |
| ❏ 225 Rod Woodson | 1.00 | .40 |

| | | | | | | | | | |
|---|---|---|---|---|---|---|---|---|---|
| ❑ 226 | Marion Butts | .30 | .10 | ❑ 20 | David Palmer FOIL RC | 1.25 | .50 | ❑ 105 | Howard Ballard | .15 | .05 |

| Card | Player | Hi | Lo |
|---|---|---|---|
| ❑ 226 | Marion Butts | .30 | .10 |
| ❑ 227 | Darren Carrington RC | .30 | .10 |
| ❑ 228 | Darrien Gordon RC | .30 | .10 |
| ❑ 229 | Ronnie Harmon | .30 | .10 |
| ❑ 230 | Stan Humphries | .50 | .20 |
| ❑ 231 | Anthony Miller | .50 | .20 |
| ❑ 232 | Chris Mims | .30 | .10 |
| ❑ 233 | Leslie O'Neal | .50 | .20 |
| ❑ 234 | Junior Seau | 1.00 | .40 |
| ❑ 235 | Dana Hall | .30 | .10 |
| ❑ 236 | Adrian Hardy | .30 | .10 |
| ❑ 237 | Brent Jones | .50 | .20 |
| ❑ 238 | Tim McDonald | .30 | .10 |
| ❑ 239 | Tom Rathman | .30 | .10 |
| ❑ 240 | Jerry Rice | 3.00 | 1.50 |
| ❑ 241 | Dana Stubblefield RC | 1.00 | .40 |
| ❑ 242 | Ricky Watters | 1.00 | .40 |
| ❑ 243 | Steve Young | 2.50 | 1.25 |
| ❑ 244 | Brian Blades | .50 | .20 |
| ❑ 245 | Ferrell Edmunds | .30 | .10 |
| ❑ 246 | Carlton Gray RC | .30 | .10 |
| ❑ 247 | Cortez Kennedy | .50 | .20 |
| ❑ 248 | Kelvin Martin | .30 | .10 |
| ❑ 249 | Dan McGwire | .30 | .10 |
| ❑ 250 | Jon Vaughn | .30 | .10 |
| ❑ 251 | Chris Warren | .50 | .20 |
| ❑ 252 | John L. Williams | .30 | .10 |
| ❑ 253 | Reggie Cobb | .30 | .10 |
| ❑ 254 | Horace Copeland RC | .50 | .20 |
| ❑ 255 | Lawrence Dawsey | .30 | .10 |
| ❑ 256 | Demetrius DuBose RC | .30 | .10 |
| ❑ 257 | Craig Erickson | .50 | .20 |
| ❑ 258 | Courtney Hawkins | .30 | .10 |
| ❑ 259 | John Lynch RC | 8.00 | 3.00 |
| ❑ 260 | Hardy Nickerson | .50 | .20 |
| ❑ 261 | Lamar Thomas RC | .30 | .10 |
| ❑ 262 | Carl Banks | .30 | .10 |
| ❑ 263 | Tom Carter RC | .50 | .20 |
| ❑ 264 | Brad Edwards | .30 | .10 |
| ❑ 265 | Kurt Gouveia | .30 | .10 |
| ❑ 266 | Desmond Howard | .50 | .20 |
| ❑ 267 | Charles Mann | .30 | .10 |
| ❑ 268 | Art Monk | .50 | .20 |
| ❑ 269 | Mark Rypien | .30 | .10 |
| ❑ 270 | Ricky Sanders | .30 | .10 |
| ❑ P1 | Joe Montana Promo | 5.00 | 2.00 |

## 1994 SP

| Card | Player | Hi | Lo |
|---|---|---|---|
| ❑ | COMPLETE SET (200) | 50.00 | 25.00 |
| ❑ 1 | Dan Wilkinson FOIL RC | 1.25 | .50 |
| ❑ 2 | Heath Shuler FOIL RC | .75 | .30 |
| ❑ 3 | Marshall Faulk FOIL RC | 15.00 | 6.00 |
| ❑ 4 | Willie McGinest FOIL RC | 2.00 | .75 |
| ❑ 5 | Trent Dilfer FOIL RC | 5.00 | 2.00 |
| ❑ 6 | Bryant Young FOIL RC | 2.00 | .75 |
| ❑ 7 | Antonio Langham FOIL RC | .40 | .15 |
| ❑ 8 | John Thierry FOIL RC | .40 | .15 |
| ❑ 9 | Aaron Glenn FOIL RC | 1.25 | .50 |
| ❑ 10 | Charles Johnson FOIL RC | 1.25 | .50 |
| ❑ 11 | Dewayne Washington FOIL RC | .40 | .15 |
| ❑ 12 | Johnnie Morton FOIL RC | 3.00 | 1.25 |
| ❑ 13 | Greg Hill FOIL RC | .75 | .30 |
| ❑ 14 | William Floyd FOIL RC | .75 | .30 |
| ❑ 15 | Derrick Alexander WR FOIL RC | 1.25 | .50 |
| ❑ 16 | Darnay Scott FOIL RC | 1.25 | .50 |
| ❑ 17 | Errict Rhett FOIL RC | 1.25 | .50 |
| ❑ 18 | Charlie Garner FOIL RC | 3.00 | 1.25 |
| ❑ 19 | Thomas Lewis FOIL RC | .40 | .15 |

| Card | Player | Hi | Lo |
|---|---|---|---|
| ❑ 20 | David Palmer FOIL RC | 1.25 | .50 |
| ❑ 21 | Andre Reed | .30 | .10 |
| ❑ 22 | Thurman Thomas | .50 | .20 |
| ❑ 23 | Bruce Smith | .50 | .20 |
| ❑ 24 | Jim Kelly | .50 | .20 |
| ❑ 25 | Cornelius Bennett | .30 | .10 |
| ❑ 26 | Bucky Brooks RC | .15 | .05 |
| ❑ 27 | Jeff Burris RC | .30 | .10 |
| ❑ 28 | Jim Harbaugh | .50 | .20 |
| ❑ 29 | Tony Bennett | .15 | .05 |
| ❑ 30 | Quentin Coryatt | .15 | .05 |
| ❑ 31 | Floyd Turner | .15 | .05 |
| ❑ 32 | Roosevelt Potts | .15 | .05 |
| ❑ 33 | Jeff Herrod | .15 | .05 |
| ❑ 34 | Irving Fryar | .30 | .10 |
| ❑ 35 | Bryan Cox | .15 | .05 |
| ❑ 36 | Dan Marino | 4.00 | 1.50 |
| ❑ 37 | Terry Kirby | .50 | .20 |
| ❑ 38 | Michael Stewart | .15 | .05 |
| ❑ 39 | Bernie Kosar | .30 | .10 |
| ❑ 40 | Aubrey Beavers RC | .15 | .05 |
| ❑ 41 | Vincent Brisby | .30 | .10 |
| ❑ 42 | Ben Coates | .30 | .10 |
| ❑ 43 | Drew Bledsoe | 2.00 | .75 |
| ❑ 44 | Marion Butts | .15 | .05 |
| ❑ 45 | Chris Slade | .15 | .05 |
| ❑ 46 | Michael Timpson | .15 | .05 |
| ❑ 47 | Ray Crittenden RC | .15 | .05 |
| ❑ 48 | Rob Moore | .30 | .10 |
| ❑ 49 | Johnny Mitchell | .15 | .05 |
| ❑ 50 | Art Monk | .30 | .10 |
| ❑ 51 | Boomer Esiason | .30 | .10 |
| ❑ 52 | Ronnie Lott | .30 | .10 |
| ❑ 53 | Ryan Yarborough RC | .15 | .05 |
| ❑ 54 | Carl Pickens | .30 | .10 |
| ❑ 55 | David Klingler | .15 | .05 |
| ❑ 56 | Harold Green | .15 | .05 |
| ❑ 57 | John Copeland | .15 | .05 |
| ❑ 58 | Louis Oliver | .15 | .05 |
| ❑ 59 | Corey Sawyer | .30 | .10 |
| ❑ 60 | Michael Jackson | .30 | .10 |
| ❑ 61 | Mark Rypien | .15 | .05 |
| ❑ 62 | Vinny Testaverde | .30 | .10 |
| ❑ 63 | Eric Metcalf | .30 | .10 |
| ❑ 64 | Eric Turner | .15 | .05 |
| ❑ 65 | Haywood Jeffires | .30 | .10 |
| ❑ 66 | Micheal Barrow | .15 | .05 |
| ❑ 67 | Cody Carlson | .15 | .05 |
| ❑ 68 | Gary Brown | .15 | .05 |
| ❑ 69 | Bucky Richardson | .15 | .05 |
| ❑ 70 | Al Smith | .15 | .05 |
| ❑ 71 | Eric Green | .15 | .05 |
| ❑ 72 | Neil O'Donnell | .50 | .20 |
| ❑ 73 | Barry Foster | .15 | .05 |
| ❑ 74 | Greg Lloyd | .30 | .10 |
| ❑ 75 | Rod Woodson | .30 | .10 |
| ❑ 76 | Byron Bam Morris RC | .30 | .10 |
| ❑ 77 | John L. Williams | .15 | .05 |
| ❑ 78 | Anthony Miller | .30 | .10 |
| ❑ 79 | Mike Pritchard | .15 | .05 |
| ❑ 80 | John Elway | 4.00 | 1.50 |
| ❑ 81 | Shannon Sharpe | .30 | .10 |
| ❑ 82 | Steve Atwater | .15 | .05 |
| ❑ 83 | Simon Fletcher | .15 | .05 |
| ❑ 84 | Glyn Milburn | .30 | .10 |
| ❑ 85 | Mark Collins | .15 | .05 |
| ❑ 86 | Keith Cash | .15 | .05 |
| ❑ 87 | Willie Davis | .30 | .10 |
| ❑ 88 | Joe Montana | 4.00 | 1.50 |
| ❑ 89 | Marcus Allen | .50 | .20 |
| ❑ 90 | Neil Smith | .30 | .10 |
| ❑ 91 | Derrick Thomas | .50 | .20 |
| ❑ 92 | Tim Brown | .50 | .20 |
| ❑ 93 | Jeff Hostetler | .30 | .10 |
| ❑ 94 | Terry McDaniel | .15 | .05 |
| ❑ 95 | Rocket Ismail | .30 | .10 |
| ❑ 96 | Rob Fredrickson RC | .15 | .05 |
| ❑ 97 | Harvey Williams | .30 | .10 |
| ❑ 98 | Steve Wisniewski | .15 | .05 |
| ❑ 99 | Stan Humphries | .30 | .10 |
| ❑ 100 | Natrone Means | .50 | .20 |
| ❑ 101 | Leslie O'Neal | .15 | .05 |
| ❑ 102 | Junior Seau | .50 | .20 |
| ❑ 103 | Ronnie Harmon | .15 | .05 |
| ❑ 104 | Shawn Jefferson | .15 | .05 |

| Card | Player | Hi | Lo |
|---|---|---|---|
| ❑ 105 | Howard Ballard | .15 | .05 |
| ❑ 106 | Rick Mirer | .50 | .20 |
| ❑ 107 | Cortez Kennedy | .30 | .10 |
| ❑ 108 | Chris Warren | .30 | .10 |
| ❑ 109 | Brian Blades | .30 | .10 |
| ❑ 110 | Sam Adams RC | .15 | .05 |
| ❑ 111 | Gary Clark | .30 | .10 |
| ❑ 112 | Steve Beuerlein | .30 | .10 |
| ❑ 113 | Ronald Moore | .15 | .05 |
| ❑ 114 | Eric Swann | .30 | .10 |
| ❑ 115 | Clyde Simmons | .15 | .05 |
| ❑ 116 | Seth Joyner | .15 | .05 |
| ❑ 117 | Troy Aikman | 2.00 | .75 |
| ❑ 118 | Charles Haley | .30 | .10 |
| ❑ 119 | Alvin Harper | .30 | .10 |
| ❑ 120 | Michael Irvin | .50 | .20 |
| ❑ 121 | Daryl Johnston | .30 | .10 |
| ❑ 122 | Emmitt Smith | 3.00 | 1.25 |
| ❑ 123 | Sharte Carver RC | .15 | .05 |
| ❑ 124 | Dave Brown | .30 | .10 |
| ❑ 125 | Rodney Hampton | .30 | .10 |
| ❑ 126 | Dave Meggett | .15 | .05 |
| ❑ 127 | Chris Calloway | .15 | .05 |
| ❑ 128 | Mike Sherrard | .15 | .05 |
| ❑ 129 | Carlton Bailey | .15 | .05 |
| ❑ 130 | Randall Cunningham | .50 | .20 |
| ❑ 131 | William Fuller | .15 | .05 |
| ❑ 132 | Eric Allen | .15 | .05 |
| ❑ 133 | Calvin Williams | .30 | .10 |
| ❑ 134 | Herschel Walker | .30 | .10 |
| ❑ 135 | Bernard Williams RC | .15 | .05 |
| ❑ 136 | Henry Ellard | .30 | .10 |
| ❑ 137 | Ethan Horton | .15 | .05 |
| ❑ 138 | Desmond Howard | .30 | .10 |
| ❑ 139 | Reggie Brooks | .30 | .10 |
| ❑ 140 | John Friesz | .30 | .10 |
| ❑ 141 | Tom Carter | .15 | .05 |
| ❑ 142 | Terry Allen | .30 | .10 |
| ❑ 143 | Adrian Cooper | .15 | .05 |
| ❑ 144 | Qadry Ismail | .50 | .20 |
| ❑ 145 | Warren Moon | .50 | .20 |
| ❑ 146 | Henry Thomas | .15 | .05 |
| ❑ 147 | Todd Steussie RC | .30 | .10 |
| ❑ 148 | Cris Carter | .75 | .30 |
| ❑ 149 | Andy Heck | .15 | .05 |
| ❑ 150 | Curtis Conway | .50 | .20 |
| ❑ 151 | Erik Kramer | .15 | .05 |
| ❑ 152 | Lewis Tillman | .15 | .05 |
| ❑ 153 | Dante Jones | .15 | .05 |
| ❑ 154 | Alonzo Spellman | .30 | .10 |
| ❑ 155 | Herman Moore | .50 | .20 |
| ❑ 156 | Broderick Thomas | .15 | .05 |
| ❑ 157 | Scott Mitchell | .30 | .10 |
| ❑ 158 | Barry Sanders | 3.00 | 1.25 |
| ❑ 159 | Chris Spielman | .30 | .10 |
| ❑ 160 | Pat Swilling | .15 | .05 |
| ❑ 161 | Bennie Blades | .15 | .05 |
| ❑ 162 | Sterling Sharpe | .50 | .20 |
| ❑ 163 | Brett Favre | 4.00 | 1.50 |
| ❑ 164 | Reggie Cobb | .15 | .05 |
| ❑ 165 | Reggie White | .50 | .20 |
| ❑ 166 | Sean Jones | .15 | .05 |
| ❑ 167 | George Teague | .15 | .05 |
| ❑ 168 | LeShon Johnson RC | .30 | .10 |
| ❑ 169 | Courtney Hawkins | .15 | .05 |
| ❑ 170 | Jackie Harris | .15 | .05 |
| ❑ 171 | Craig Erickson | .15 | .05 |
| ❑ 172 | Santana Dotson | .30 | .10 |
| ❑ 173 | Eric Curry | .15 | .05 |
| ❑ 174 | Hardy Nickerson | .15 | .05 |
| ❑ 175 | Derek Brown RBK | .15 | .05 |
| ❑ 176 | Jim Everett | .30 | .10 |
| ❑ 177 | Michael Haynes | .30 | .10 |
| ❑ 178 | Tyrone Hughes | .30 | .10 |
| ❑ 179 | Wayne Martin | .15 | .05 |
| ❑ 180 | Willie Roaf | .15 | .05 |
| ❑ 181 | Irv Smith | .15 | .05 |
| ❑ 182 | Jeff George | .50 | .20 |
| ❑ 183 | Andre Rison | .30 | .10 |
| ❑ 184 | Erric Pegram | .15 | .05 |
| ❑ 185 | Bert Emanuel RC | 1.00 | .40 |
| ❑ 186 | Chris Doleman | .15 | .05 |
| ❑ 187 | Ron George | .15 | .05 |
| ❑ 188 | Chris Miller | .15 | .05 |
| ❑ 189 | Troy Drayton | .15 | .05 |

| | | |
|---|---|---|
| 190 Chris Chandler | .30 | .10 |
| 191 Jerome Bettis | 1.00 | .40 |
| 192 Jimmie Jones | .15 | .05 |
| 193 Sean Gilbert | .15 | .05 |
| 194 Jerry Rice | 2.00 | .75 |
| 195 Brent Jones | .30 | .10 |
| 196 Deion Sanders | 1.00 | .40 |
| 197 Steve Young | 1.50 | .60 |
| 198 Ricky Watters | .30 | .10 |
| 199 Dana Stubblefield | .30 | .10 |
| 200 Ken Norton Jr. | .30 | .10 |
| RB1 Dan Marino RB | 25.00 | 10.00 |
| RB2 Jerry Rice RB | 25.00 | 12.50 |
| P16 Joe Montana Promo | 4.00 | 1.50 |

## 1995 SP

| | | |
|---|---|---|
| COMPLETE SET (200) | 50.00 | 20.00 |
| 1 Ki-Jana Carter FOIL RC | 2.00 | .75 |
| 2 Eric Zeier FOIL RC | 2.00 | .75 |
| 3 Steve McNair FOIL RC | 10.00 | 4.00 |
| 4 Michael Westbrook FOIL RC | 2.00 | .75 |
| 5 Kerry Collins FOIL RC | 6.00 | 2.50 |
| 6 Joey Galloway FOIL RC | 2.00 | .75 |
| 7 Kevin Carter FOIL RC | 2.00 | .75 |
| 8 Mike Mamula FOIL RC | .50 | .20 |
| 9 Kyle Brady FOIL RC | 2.00 | .75 |
| 10 J.J. Stokes FOIL RC | 2.00 | .75 |
| 11 Tyrone Poole RC | 2.00 | .75 |
| 12 Rashaan Salaam FOIL RC | 1.00 | .40 |
| 13 Sherman Williams FOIL RC | .50 | .20 |
| 14 Luther Elliss RC | .50 | .20 |
| 15 James O. Stewart FOIL RC | 3.00 | 1.25 |
| 16 Tamarick Vanover FOIL RC | 2.00 | .75 |
| 17 Napoleon Kaufman FOIL RC | 3.00 | 1.25 |
| 18 Curtis Martin FOIL RC | 12.00 | 6.00 |
| 19 Tyrone Wheatley FOIL RC | 3.00 | 1.25 |
| 20 Frank Sanders FOIL RC | 2.00 | .75 |
| 21 Devin Bush | .20 | .07 |
| 22 Terance Mathis | .40 | .15 |
| 23 Bert Emanuel | .75 | .30 |
| 24 Eric Metcalf | .40 | .15 |
| 25 Craig Heyward | .40 | .15 |
| 26 Jeff George | .40 | .15 |
| 27 Mark Carrier WR | .20 | .07 |
| 28 Pete Metzelaars | .20 | .07 |
| 29 Frank Reich | .20 | .07 |
| 30 Sam Mills | .40 | .15 |
| 31 John Kasay | .20 | .07 |
| 32 Willie Green | .40 | .15 |
| 33 Jeff Graham | .20 | .07 |
| 34 Curtis Conway | .75 | .30 |
| 35 Steve Walsh | .20 | .07 |
| 36 Erik Kramer | .20 | .07 |
| 37 Michael Timpson | .20 | .07 |
| 38 Mark Carrier DB | .20 | .07 |
| 39 Troy Aikman | 2.00 | .75 |
| 40 Michael Irvin | .75 | .30 |
| 41 Charles Haley | .40 | .15 |
| 42 Deion Sanders | 1.25 | .50 |
| 43 Jay Novacek | .20 | .07 |
| 44 Emmitt Smith | 3.00 | 1.25 |
| 45 Herman Moore | .75 | .30 |
| 46 Scott Mitchell UER | .40 | .15 |
| 47 Bennie Blades | .20 | .07 |
| 48 Johnnie Morton | .40 | .15 |
| 49 Chris Spielman | .40 | .15 |
| 50 Barry Sanders | 3.00 | 1.25 |
| 51 Edgar Bennett | .40 | .15 |
| 52 Reggie White | .75 | .30 |
| 53 Sean Jones | .20 | .07 |
| 54 Mark Ingram | .20 | .07 |
| 55 Robert Brooks | .75 | .30 |
| 56 Brett Favre | 4.00 | 1.50 |
| 57 Lovell Pinkney RC | .50 | .20 |
| 58 Chris Miller | .20 | .07 |
| 59 Isaac Bruce | 1.25 | .50 |
| 60 Roman Phifer | .20 | .07 |
| 61 Sean Gilbert | .40 | .15 |
| 62 Jerome Bettis | .75 | .30 |
| 63 Derrick Alexander DE RC | .50 | .20 |
| 64 Cris Carter | .75 | .30 |
| 65 Jake Reed | .40 | .15 |
| 66 Robert Smith | .75 | .30 |
| 67 David Palmer | .40 | .15 |
| 68 Warren Moon | .40 | .15 |
| 69 Ray Zellars RC | 1.00 | .40 |
| 70 Jim Everett | .20 | .07 |
| 71 Michael Haynes | .40 | .15 |
| 72 Quinn Early | .20 | .07 |
| 73 Willie Roaf | .20 | .07 |
| 74 Mario Bates | .40 | .15 |
| 75 Mike Sherrard | .20 | .07 |
| 76 Chris Calloway | .20 | .07 |
| 77 Dave Brown | .40 | .15 |
| 78 Thomas Lewis | .40 | .15 |
| 79 Herschel Walker | .40 | .15 |
| 80 Rodney Hampton | .40 | .15 |
| 81 Fred Barnett | .40 | .15 |
| 82 Calvin Williams | .40 | .15 |
| 83 Randall Cunningham | .75 | .30 |
| 84 Charlie Garner | .75 | .30 |
| 85 Bobby Taylor RC | 3.00 | 1.25 |
| 86 Ricky Watters | .40 | .15 |
| 87 Dave Krieg | .20 | .07 |
| 88 Rob Moore | .40 | .15 |
| 89 Eric Swann | .40 | .15 |
| 90 Clyde Simmons | .20 | .07 |
| 91 Seth Joyner | .20 | .07 |
| 92 Garrison Hearst | .75 | .30 |
| 93 Jerry Rice | 2.00 | .75 |
| 94 Bryant Young | .40 | .15 |
| 95 Brent Jones | .20 | .07 |
| 96 Ken Norton | .40 | .15 |
| 97 William Floyd | .40 | .15 |
| 98 Steve Young | 1.50 | .60 |
| 99 Warren Sapp RC | 5.00 | 2.00 |
| 100 Trent Dilfer | .75 | .30 |
| 101 Alvin Harper | .20 | .07 |
| 102 Hardy Nickerson | .20 | .07 |
| 103 Derrick Brooks RC | 5.00 | 2.00 |
| 104 Errict Rhett | .40 | .15 |
| 105 Henry Ellard | .40 | .15 |
| 106 Ken Harvey | .20 | .07 |
| 107 Gus Frerotte | .40 | .15 |
| 108 Brian Mitchell | .20 | .07 |
| 109 Terry Allen | .40 | .15 |
| 110 Heath Shuler | .40 | .15 |
| 111 Jim Kelly | .75 | .30 |
| 112 Andre Reed | .40 | .15 |
| 113 Bruce Smith | .75 | .30 |
| 114 Darick Holmes RC | 1.00 | .40 |
| 115 Bryce Paup | .40 | .15 |
| 116 Cornelius Bennett | .40 | .15 |
| 117 Carl Pickens | .40 | .15 |
| 118 Darnay Scott | .40 | .15 |
| 119 Jeff Blake RC | 2.00 | .75 |
| 120 Steve Tovar | .20 | .07 |
| 121 Tony McGee | .20 | .07 |
| 122 Dan Wilkinson | .40 | .15 |
| 123 Craig Powell RC | .20 | .07 |
| 124 Vinny Testaverde | .40 | .15 |
| 125 Eric Turner | .20 | .07 |
| 126 Leroy Hoard | .20 | .07 |
| 127 Lorenzo White | .20 | .07 |
| 128 Andre Rison | .40 | .15 |
| 129 Shannon Sharpe | .40 | .15 |
| 130 Terrell Davis RC | 8.00 | 3.00 |
| 131 Anthony Miller | .40 | .15 |
| 132 Mike Pritchard | .20 | .07 |
| 133 Steve Atwater | .20 | .07 |
| 134 John Elway | 4.00 | 1.50 |
| 135 Haywood Jeffires | .20 | .07 |
| 136 Gary Brown | .20 | .07 |
| 137 Al Smith | .20 | .07 |
| 138 Rodney Thomas RC | 1.00 | .40 |
| 139 Chris Chandler | .40 | .15 |
| 140 Mel Gray | .20 | .07 |
| 141 Craig Erickson | .20 | .07 |
| 142 Sean Dawkins | .40 | .15 |
| 143 Ken Dilger RC | 2.00 | .75 |
| 144 Ellis Johnson RC | .50 | .20 |
| 145 Quentin Coryatt | .40 | .15 |
| 146 Marshall Faulk | 2.50 | 1.00 |
| 147 Tony Boselli RC | 2.00 | .75 |
| 148 Rob Johnson RC | 3.00 | 1.25 |
| 149 Desmond Howard | .40 | .15 |
| 150 Steve Beuerlein | .40 | .15 |
| 151 Reggie Cobb | .20 | .07 |
| 152 Jeff Lageman | .20 | .07 |
| 153 Willie Davis | .40 | .15 |
| 154 Marcus Allen | .75 | .30 |
| 155 Neil Smith | .40 | .15 |
| 156 Greg Hill | .40 | .15 |
| 157 Steve Bono | .40 | .15 |
| 158 Derrick Thomas | .75 | .30 |
| 159 Jeff Hostetler | .40 | .15 |
| 160 Harvey Williams | .20 | .07 |
| 161 Rocket Ismail | .40 | .15 |
| 162 Chester McGlockton | .20 | .07 |
| 163 Terry McDaniel | .20 | .07 |
| 164 Tim Brown | .75 | .30 |
| 165 Terry Kirby | .40 | .15 |
| 166 Irving Fryar | .40 | .15 |
| 167 O.J. McDuffie | .75 | .30 |
| 168 Bryan Cox | .20 | .07 |
| 169 Eric Green | .20 | .07 |
| 170 Dan Marino | 4.00 | 1.50 |
| 171 Ben Coates | .40 | .15 |
| 172 Vincent Brisby | .20 | .07 |
| 173 Chris Slade | .20 | .07 |
| 174 Ty Law RC | 4.00 | 1.50 |
| 175 Vincent Brown | .20 | .07 |
| 176 Drew Bledsoe | 1.25 | .50 |
| 177 Johnny Mitchell | .20 | .07 |
| 178 Boomer Esiason | .40 | .15 |
| 179 Wayne Chrebet RC | 6.00 | 3.00 |
| 180 Mo Lewis | .20 | .07 |
| 181 Ronald Moore | .20 | .07 |
| 182 Aaron Glenn | .20 | .07 |
| 183 Mark Brunell RC | 1.00 | .40 |
| 184 Neil O'Donnell | .40 | .15 |
| 185 Charles Johnson | .40 | .15 |
| 186 Greg Lloyd | .20 | .07 |
| 187 Rod Woodson | .40 | .15 |
| 188 Byron Bam Morris | .20 | .07 |
| 189 Terrell Fletcher RC | .50 | .20 |
| 190 Terrance Shaw RC UER | .50 | .20 |
| 191 Stan Humphries | .40 | .15 |
| 192 Junior Seau | .75 | .30 |
| 193 Leslie O'Neal | .40 | .15 |
| 194 Natrone Means | .40 | .15 |
| 195 Christian Fauria RC | 1.00 | .40 |
| 196 Rick Mirer | .40 | .15 |
| 197 Sam Adams | .20 | .07 |
| 198 Cortez Kennedy | .40 | .15 |
| 199 Eugene Robinson | .20 | .07 |
| 200 Chris Warren | .40 | .15 |
| DM1 Dan Marino Tribute | 20.00 | 7.50 |
| JM1 Joe Montana Salute | 20.00 | 7.50 |
| JMAP Joe Montana Promo | 4.00 | 1.50 |
| NNO Dan Marino TRI Jumbo | 25.00 | 10.00 |
| NNO Joe Montana SAL Jumbo | 25.00 | 10.00 |
| P113 Dan Marino Promo | 3.00 | 1.25 |

## 1996 SP

| | | |
|---|---|---|
| COMPLETE SET (188) | 100.00 | 40.00 |
| 1 Keyshawn Johnson RC | 8.00 | 4.00 |
| 2 Kevin Hardy RC | .75 | .30 |
| 3 Simeon Rice RC | 3.00 | 1.25 |
| 4 Jonathan Ogden RC | 1.25 | .50 |
| 5 Eddie George RC | 10.00 | 4.00 |
| 6 Terry Glenn RC | 6.00 | 2.50 |
| 7 Terrell Owens RC | 25.00 | 12.50 |
| 8 Tim Biakabutuka RC | 2.00 | .75 |
| 9 Lawrence Phillips RC | .75 | .30 |
| 10 Alex Molden RC | .40 | .15 |
| 11 Regan Upshaw RC | .40 | .15 |
| 12 Rickey Dudley RC | 1.25 | .50 |

| | | |
|---|---|---|
| ☐ 13 Duane Clemons RC | .40 | .15 |
| ☐ 14 John Mobley RC | .75 | .30 |
| ☐ 15 Eddie Kennison RC | 2.00 | .75 |
| ☐ 16 Karim Abdul-Jabbar RC | 1.25 | .50 |
| ☐ 17 Eric Moulds RC | 6.00 | 2.50 |
| ☐ 18 Marvin Harrison RC | 15.00 | 6.00 |
| ☐ 19 Stepfret Williams RC | .40 | .15 |
| ☐ 20 Stephen Davis RC | 10.00 | 4.00 |
| ☐ 21 Deion Sanders | 1.25 | .50 |
| ☐ 22 Emmitt Smith | 3.00 | 1.25 |
| ☐ 23 Troy Aikman | 2.00 | .75 |
| ☐ 24 Michael Irvin | .75 | .30 |
| ☐ 25 Herschel Walker | .40 | .15 |
| ☐ 26 Kavika Pittman RC | .20 | .07 |
| ☐ 27 Andre Hastings | .20 | .07 |
| ☐ 28 Jerome Bettis | .75 | .30 |
| ☐ 29 Mike Tomczak | .20 | .07 |
| ☐ 30 Kordell Stewart | .75 | .30 |
| ☐ 31 Charles Johnson | .20 | .07 |
| ☐ 32 Greg Lloyd | .40 | .15 |
| ☐ 33 Brett Favre | 4.00 | 1.50 |
| ☐ 34 Mark Chmura | .40 | .15 |
| ☐ 35 Edgar Bennett | .40 | .15 |
| ☐ 36 Robert Brooks | .40 | .15 |
| ☐ 37 Craig Newsome | .20 | .07 |
| ☐ 38 Reggie White | .75 | .30 |
| ☐ 39 Jim Harbaugh | .40 | .15 |
| ☐ 40 Marshall Faulk | 1.00 | .40 |
| ☐ 41 Sean Dawkins | .20 | .07 |
| ☐ 42 Quentin Coryatt | .20 | .07 |
| ☐ 43 Ray Buchanan | .20 | .07 |
| ☐ 44 Ken Dilger | .40 | .15 |
| ☐ 45 Jerry Rice | 2.00 | .75 |
| ☐ 46 J.J. Stokes | .75 | .30 |
| ☐ 47 Steve Young | 1.50 | .60 |
| ☐ 48 Derek Loville | .20 | .07 |
| ☐ 49 Terry Kirby | .40 | .15 |
| ☐ 50 Ken Norton | .20 | .07 |
| ☐ 51 Tamarick Vanover | .40 | .15 |
| ☐ 52 Marcus Allen | .75 | .30 |
| ☐ 53 Steve Bono | .20 | .07 |
| ☐ 54 Neil Smith | .40 | .15 |
| ☐ 55 Derrick Thomas | .75 | .30 |
| ☐ 56 Dale Carter | .20 | .07 |
| ☐ 57 Terance Mathis | .20 | .07 |
| ☐ 58 Eric Metcalf | .20 | .07 |
| ☐ 59 Jamal Anderson RC | 1.50 | .60 |
| ☐ 60 Bert Emanuel | .40 | .15 |
| ☐ 61 Craig Heyward | .20 | .07 |
| ☐ 62 Cornelius Bennett | .20 | .07 |
| ☐ 63 Tony Martin | .40 | .15 |
| ☐ 64 Stan Humphries | .40 | .15 |
| ☐ 65 Andre Coleman | .20 | .07 |
| ☐ 66 Junior Seau | .75 | .30 |
| ☐ 67 Terrell Fletcher | .20 | .07 |
| ☐ 68 John Carney | .20 | .07 |
| ☐ 69 Charlie Jones RC | .40 | .15 |
| ☐ 70 Ricky Watters | .40 | .15 |
| ☐ 71 Charlie Garner | .40 | .15 |
| ☐ 72 Bobby Hoying RC | .75 | .30 |
| ☐ 73 Jason Dunn RC | .20 | .07 |
| ☐ 74 Bobby Taylor | .20 | .07 |
| ☐ 75 Irving Fryar | .40 | .15 |
| ☐ 76 Jim Kelly | .75 | .30 |
| ☐ 77 Thurman Thomas | .75 | .30 |
| ☐ 78 Bruce Smith | .40 | .15 |
| ☐ 79 Bryce Paup | .20 | .07 |
| ☐ 80 Darick Holmes | .20 | .07 |
| ☐ 81 Andre Reed | .40 | .15 |
| ☐ 82 Glyn Milburn | .20 | .07 |
| ☐ 83 Brett Perriman | .20 | .07 |
| ☐ 84 Herman Moore | .40 | .15 |
| ☐ 85 Scott Mitchell | .40 | .15 |
| ☐ 86 Barry Sanders | 3.00 | 1.25 |
| ☐ 87 Johnnie Morton | .40 | .15 |
| ☐ 88 Dan Marino | 4.00 | 1.50 |
| ☐ 89 O.J. McDuffie | .40 | .15 |
| ☐ 90 Stanley Pritchett RC | .20 | .07 |
| ☐ 91 Zach Thomas RC | 5.00 | 2.00 |
| ☐ 92 Daryl Gardener RC | .20 | .07 |
| ☐ 93 Rashaan Salaam | .40 | .15 |
| ☐ 94 Erik Kramer | .20 | .07 |
| ☐ 95 Curtis Conway | .75 | .30 |
| ☐ 96 Bobby Engram RC | .75 | .30 |
| ☐ 97 Walt Harris RC | .20 | .07 |
| ☐ 98 Bryan Cox | .20 | .07 |
| ☐ 99 John Elway | 4.00 | 1.50 |
| ☐ 100 Terrell Davis | 1.50 | .60 |
| ☐ 101 Anthony Miller | .20 | .07 |
| ☐ 102 Shannon Sharpe | .40 | .15 |
| ☐ 103 Tory James RC | .75 | .30 |
| ☐ 104 Jeff Lewis RC | .40 | .15 |
| ☐ 105 Joey Galloway | .75 | .30 |
| ☐ 106 Chris Warren | .40 | .15 |
| ☐ 107 Rick Mirer | .40 | .15 |
| ☐ 108 Cortez Kennedy | .20 | .07 |
| ☐ 109 Michael Sinclair | .20 | .07 |
| ☐ 110 John Friesz | .20 | .07 |
| ☐ 111 Warren Moon | .40 | .15 |
| ☐ 112 Cris Carter | .75 | .30 |
| ☐ 113 Jake Reed | .40 | .15 |
| ☐ 114 Robert Smith | .40 | .15 |
| ☐ 115 John Randle | .40 | .15 |
| ☐ 116 Orlando Thomas | .20 | .07 |
| ☐ 117 Jeff Hostetler | .20 | .07 |
| ☐ 118 Tim Brown | .75 | .30 |
| ☐ 119 Joe Aska | .20 | .07 |
| ☐ 120 Napoleon Kaufman | .75 | .30 |
| ☐ 121 Terry McDaniel | .20 | .07 |
| ☐ 122 Harvey Williams | .20 | .07 |
| ☐ 123 Trent Dilfer | .75 | .30 |
| ☐ 124 Reggie Brooks | .20 | .07 |
| ☐ 125 Alvin Harper | .20 | .07 |
| ☐ 126 Mike Alstott RC | 5.00 | 2.00 |
| ☐ 127 Hardy Nickerson | .20 | .07 |
| ☐ 128 Mario Bates | .20 | .07 |
| ☐ 129 Jim Everett | .20 | .07 |
| ☐ 130 Tyrone Hughes | .20 | .07 |
| ☐ 131 Michael Haynes | .20 | .07 |
| ☐ 132 Eric Allen | .20 | .07 |
| ☐ 133 Isaac Bruce | .75 | .30 |
| ☐ 134 Kevin Carter | .20 | .07 |
| ☐ 135 Leslie O'Neal | .20 | .07 |
| ☐ 136 Tony Banks RC | .75 | .30 |
| ☐ 137 Chris Chandler | .40 | .15 |
| ☐ 138 Steve McNair | 1.50 | .60 |
| ☐ 139 Chris Sanders | .40 | .15 |
| ☐ 140 Ronnie Harmon | .20 | .07 |
| ☐ 141 Willie Davis | .20 | .07 |
| ☐ 142 Michael Westbrook | .75 | .30 |
| ☐ 143 Terry Allen | .40 | .15 |
| ☐ 144 Brian Mitchell | .20 | .07 |
| ☐ 145 Henry Ellard | .20 | .07 |
| ☐ 146 Gus Frerotte | .40 | .15 |
| ☐ 147 Kerry Collins | .75 | .30 |
| ☐ 148 Sam Mills | .20 | .07 |
| ☐ 149 Wesley Walls | .40 | .15 |
| ☐ 150 Kevin Greene | .40 | .15 |
| ☐ 151 Muhsin Muhammad RC | 5.00 | 2.00 |
| ☐ 152 Winslow Oliver | .20 | .07 |
| ☐ 153 Jeff Blake | .75 | .30 |
| ☐ 154 Carl Pickens | .40 | .15 |
| ☐ 155 Darnay Scott | .40 | .15 |
| ☐ 156 Garrison Hearst | .40 | .15 |
| ☐ 157 Marco Battaglia RC | .20 | .07 |
| ☐ 158 Drew Bledsoe | 1.25 | .50 |
| ☐ 159 Curtis Martin | 1.50 | .60 |
| ☐ 160 Shawn Jefferson | .20 | .07 |
| ☐ 161 Ben Coates | .40 | .15 |
| ☐ 162 Lawyer Milloy RC | 2.50 | 1.00 |
| ☐ 163 Tyrone Wheatley | .40 | .15 |
| ☐ 164 Rodney Hampton | .40 | .15 |
| ☐ 165 Chris Calloway | .20 | .07 |
| ☐ 166 Dave Brown | .20 | .07 |
| ☐ 167 Amani Toomer RC | 5.00 | 2.00 |
| ☐ 168 Vinny Testaverde | .40 | .15 |
| ☐ 169 Michael Jackson | .40 | .15 |
| ☐ 170 Eric Turner | .20 | .07 |
| ☐ 171 DeRon Jenkins | .20 | .07 |
| ☐ 172 Jermaine Lewis RC | .75 | .30 |
| ☐ 173 Frank Sanders | .40 | .15 |
| ☐ 174 Rob Moore | .40 | .15 |
| ☐ 175 Kent Graham | .20 | .07 |
| ☐ 176 Leeland McElroy RC | .40 | .15 |
| ☐ 177 Larry Centers | .40 | .15 |
| ☐ 178 Eric Swann | .20 | .07 |
| ☐ 179 Mark Brunell | 1.25 | .50 |
| ☐ 180 Willie Jackson | .40 | .15 |
| ☐ 181 James O. Stewart | .40 | .15 |
| ☐ 182 Natrone Means | .40 | .15 |
| ☐ 183 Tony Brackens RC | .75 | .30 |
| ☐ 184 Adrian Murrell | .40 | .15 |
| ☐ 185 Neil O'Donnell | .40 | .15 |
| ☐ 186 Hugh Douglas | .40 | .15 |
| ☐ 187 Wayne Chrebet | 1.00 | .40 |
| ☐ 188 Alex Van Dyke RC | .40 | .15 |
| ☐ SP13 Dan Marino Promo | 3.00 | 1.25 |

## 1997 SP Authentic

| | | |
|---|---|---|
| ☐ COMPLETE SET (198) | 100.00 | 50.00 |
| ☐ 1 Orlando Pace RC | 2.00 | .75 |
| ☐ 2 Darrell Russell RC | .50 | .20 |
| ☐ 3 Shawn Springs RC | 1.00 | .40 |
| ☐ 4 Peter Boulware RC | 4.00 | 1.50 |
| ☐ 5 Bryant Westbrook RC | 1.00 | .40 |
| ☐ 6 Walter Jones RC | 2.00 | .75 |
| ☐ 7 Ike Hilliard RC | 4.00 | 1.50 |
| ☐ 8 James Farrior RC | 3.00 | 1.25 |
| ☐ 9 Tom Knight RC | .50 | .20 |
| ☐ 10 Warrick Dunn RC | 15.00 | 6.00 |
| ☐ 11 Tony Gonzalez RC | 15.00 | 6.00 |
| ☐ 12 Reinard Wilson RC | 1.00 | .40 |
| ☐ 13 Yatil Green RC | 1.00 | .40 |
| ☐ 14 Reidel Anthony RC | 2.00 | .75 |
| ☐ 15 Kenny Holmes RC | .50 | .20 |
| ☐ 16 Dwayne Rudd RC | .50 | .20 |
| ☐ 17 Renaldo Wynn RC | .50 | .20 |
| ☐ 18 David LaFleur RC | .50 | .20 |
| ☐ 19 Antowain Smith RC | 6.00 | 2.50 |
| ☐ 20 Jim Druckenmiller RC | 1.00 | .40 |
| ☐ 21 Rae Carruth RC | .50 | .20 |
| ☐ 22 Byron Hanspard RC | 1.00 | .40 |
| ☐ 23 Jake Plummer RC | 12.00 | 5.00 |
| ☐ 24 Joey Kent RC | 1.00 | .40 |
| ☐ 25 Corey Dillon RC | 10.00 | 4.00 |
| ☐ 26 Danny Wuerffel RC | 5.00 | 2.00 |
| ☐ 27 Will Blackwell RC | .50 | .20 |
| ☐ 28 Troy Davis RC | 1.00 | .40 |
| ☐ 29 Darnell Autry RC | 1.00 | .40 |
| ☐ 30 Pat Barnes RC | 1.00 | .40 |
| ☐ 31 Kent Graham | .50 | .20 |
| ☐ 32 Simeon Rice | .75 | .30 |
| ☐ 33 Frank Sanders | .75 | .30 |
| ☐ 34 Rob Moore | .75 | .30 |
| ☐ 35 Eric Swann | .50 | .20 |
| ☐ 36 Chris Chandler | .75 | .30 |
| ☐ 37 Jamal Anderson | 1.25 | .50 |
| ☐ 38 Terance Mathis | .75 | .30 |
| ☐ 39 Bert Emanuel | .75 | .30 |
| ☐ 40 Michael Booker | .50 | .20 |
| ☐ 41 Vinny Testaverde | .75 | .30 |

| | | |
|---|---|---|
| ❏ 42 Byron Bam Morris | .50 | .20 |
| ❏ 43 Michael Jackson | .75 | .30 |
| ❏ 44 Derrick Alexander WR | .75 | .30 |
| ❏ 45 Jamie Sharper RC | 2.00 | .75 |
| ❏ 46 Kim Herring RC | .50 | .20 |
| ❏ 47 Todd Collins | .50 | .20 |
| ❏ 48 Thurman Thomas | 1.25 | .50 |
| ❏ 49 Andre Reed | .75 | .30 |
| ❏ 50 Quinn Early | .50 | .20 |
| ❏ 51 Bryce Paup | .50 | .20 |
| ❏ 52 Lonnie Johnson | .50 | .20 |
| ❏ 53 Kerry Collins | 1.25 | .50 |
| ❏ 54 Anthony Johnson | .50 | .20 |
| ❏ 55 Tim Biakabutuka | .75 | .30 |
| ❏ 56 Muhsin Muhammad | .75 | .30 |
| ❏ 57 Sam Mills | .50 | .20 |
| ❏ 58 Wesley Walls | .75 | .30 |
| ❏ 59 Rick Mirer | .50 | .20 |
| ❏ 60 Raymont Harris | .50 | .20 |
| ❏ 61 Curtis Conway | .75 | .30 |
| ❏ 62 Bobby Engram | .75 | .30 |
| ❏ 63 Bryan Cox | .50 | .20 |
| ❏ 64 John Allred RC | .50 | .20 |
| ❏ 65 Jeff Blake | .75 | .30 |
| ❏ 66 Ki-Jana Carter | .50 | .20 |
| ❏ 67 Darnay Scott | .75 | .30 |
| ❏ 68 Carl Pickens | .75 | .30 |
| ❏ 69 Dan Wilkinson | .50 | .20 |
| ❏ 70 Troy Aikman | 2.50 | 1.25 |
| ❏ 71 Emmitt Smith | 4.00 | 2.00 |
| ❏ 72 Michael Irvin | 1.25 | .50 |
| ❏ 73 Deion Sanders | 1.25 | .50 |
| ❏ 74 Anthony Miller | .50 | .20 |
| ❏ 75 Antonio Anderson RC | .50 | .20 |
| ❏ 76 John Elway | 5.00 | 2.00 |
| ❏ 77 Terrell Davis | 1.50 | .60 |
| ❏ 78 Rod Smith WR | 1.25 | .50 |
| ❏ 79 Shannon Sharpe | .75 | .30 |
| ❏ 80 Neil Smith | .75 | .30 |
| ❏ 81 Trevor Pryce RC | 2.00 | .75 |
| ❏ 82 Scott Mitchell | .75 | .30 |
| ❏ 83 Barry Sanders | 4.00 | 1.50 |
| ❏ 84 Herman Moore | .75 | .30 |
| ❏ 85 Johnnie Morton | .75 | .30 |
| ❏ 86 Matt Russell RC | .50 | .20 |
| ❏ 87 Brett Favre | 5.00 | 2.50 |
| ❏ 88 Edgar Bennett | .75 | .30 |
| ❏ 89 Robert Brooks | .75 | .30 |
| ❏ 90 Antonio Freeman | 1.25 | .50 |
| ❏ 91 Reggie White | 1.25 | .50 |
| ❏ 92 Craig Newsome | .50 | .20 |
| ❏ 93 Jim Harbaugh | .75 | .30 |
| ❏ 94 Marshall Faulk | 1.50 | .60 |
| ❏ 95 Sean Dawkins | .50 | .20 |
| ❏ 96 Marvin Harrison | 1.25 | .50 |
| ❏ 97 Quentin Coryatt | .50 | .20 |
| ❏ 98 Tarik Glenn RC | 1.00 | .40 |
| ❏ 99 Mark Brunell | 1.50 | .60 |
| ❏ 100 Natrone Means | .75 | .30 |
| ❏ 101 Keenan McCardell | .75 | .30 |
| ❏ 102 Jimmy Smith | .75 | .30 |
| ❏ 103 Tony Brackens | .50 | .20 |
| ❏ 104 Kevin Hardy | .50 | .20 |
| ❏ 105 Elvis Grbac | .75 | .30 |
| ❏ 106 Marcus Allen | 1.25 | .50 |
| ❏ 107 Greg Hill | .50 | .20 |
| ❏ 108 Derrick Thomas | 1.25 | .50 |
| ❏ 109 Dale Carter | .50 | .20 |
| ❏ 110 Dan Marino | 5.00 | 2.00 |
| ❏ 111 Karim Abdul-Jabbar | .75 | .30 |
| ❏ 112 Brian Manning RC | .50 | .20 |
| ❏ 113 Daryl Gardener | .50 | .20 |
| ❏ 114 Troy Drayton | .50 | .20 |
| ❏ 115 Zach Thomas | 1.25 | .50 |
| ❏ 116 Jason Taylor RC | 20.00 | 10.00 |
| ❏ 117 Brad Johnson | 1.25 | .50 |
| ❏ 118 Robert Smith | .75 | .30 |
| ❏ 119 John Randle | .75 | .30 |
| ❏ 120 Cris Carter | 1.25 | .50 |
| ❏ 121 Jake Reed | .75 | .30 |
| ❏ 122 Randall Cunningham | 1.25 | .50 |
| ❏ 123 Drew Bledsoe | 1.50 | .60 |
| ❏ 124 Curtis Martin | 1.50 | .60 |
| ❏ 125 Terry Glenn | 1.25 | .50 |
| ❏ 126 Willie McGinest | .50 | .20 |

| | | |
|---|---|---|
| ❏ 127 Chris Canty RC | .50 | .20 |
| ❏ 128 Sedrick Shaw RC | 1.00 | .40 |
| ❏ 129 Heath Shuler | .50 | .20 |
| ❏ 130 Mario Bates | .50 | .20 |
| ❏ 131 Ray Zellars | .50 | .20 |
| ❏ 132 Andre Hastings | .50 | .20 |
| ❏ 133 Dave Brown | .50 | .20 |
| ❏ 134 Tyrone Wheatley | .75 | .30 |
| ❏ 135 Rodney Hampton | .75 | .30 |
| ❏ 136 Chris Calloway | .50 | .20 |
| ❏ 137 Tiki Barber RC | 30.00 | 15.00 |
| ❏ 138 Neil O'Donnell | .75 | .30 |
| ❏ 139 Adrian Murrell | .75 | .30 |
| ❏ 140 Wayne Chrebet | 1.25 | .50 |
| ❏ 141 Keyshawn Johnson | 1.25 | .50 |
| ❏ 142 Hugh Douglas | .50 | .20 |
| ❏ 143 Jeff George | .75 | .30 |
| ❏ 144 Napoleon Kaufman | 1.25 | .50 |
| ❏ 145 Tim Brown | 1.25 | .50 |
| ❏ 146 Desmond Howard | .75 | .30 |
| ❏ 147 Rickey Dudley | .75 | .30 |
| ❏ 148 Terry McDaniel | .50 | .20 |
| ❏ 149 Ty Detmer | .75 | .30 |
| ❏ 150 Ricky Watters | .75 | .30 |
| ❏ 151 Chris T. Jones | .50 | .20 |
| ❏ 152 Irving Fryar | .75 | .30 |
| ❏ 153 Mike Mamula | .50 | .20 |
| ❏ 154 Jon Harris RC | .50 | .20 |
| ❏ 155 Kordell Stewart | 1.25 | .50 |
| ❏ 156 Jerome Bettis | 1.25 | .50 |
| ❏ 157 Charles Johnson | .75 | .30 |
| ❏ 158 Greg Lloyd | .50 | .20 |
| ❏ 159 George Jones RC | .50 | .20 |
| ❏ 160 Terrell Fletcher | .50 | .20 |
| ❏ 161 Stan Humphries | .75 | .30 |
| ❏ 162 Tony Martin | .75 | .30 |
| ❏ 163 Eric Metcalf | .75 | .30 |
| ❏ 164 Junior Seau | 1.25 | .50 |
| ❏ 165 Rod Woodson | .75 | .30 |
| ❏ 166 Steve Young | 1.50 | .60 |
| ❏ 167 Terry Kirby | .75 | .30 |
| ❏ 168 Garrison Hearst | .75 | .30 |
| ❏ 169 Jerry Rice | 2.50 | 1.25 |
| ❏ 170 Ken Norton | .50 | .20 |
| ❏ 171 Kevin Greene | .75 | .30 |
| ❏ 172 Lamar Smith | 1.25 | .50 |
| ❏ 173 Warren Moon | 1.25 | .50 |
| ❏ 174 Chris Warren | .75 | .30 |
| ❏ 175 Cortez Kennedy | .75 | .30 |
| ❏ 176 Joey Galloway | .75 | .30 |
| ❏ 177 Tony Banks | .75 | .30 |
| ❏ 178 Isaac Bruce | 1.25 | .50 |
| ❏ 179 Eddie Kennison | .75 | .30 |
| ❏ 180 Kevin Carter | .50 | .20 |
| ❏ 181 Craig Heyward | .50 | .20 |
| ❏ 182 Trent Dilfer | 1.25 | .50 |
| ❏ 183 Errict Rhett | .50 | .20 |
| ❏ 184 Mike Alstott | 1.25 | .50 |
| ❏ 185 Hardy Nickerson | .50 | .20 |
| ❏ 186 Ronde Barber RC | 10.00 | 4.00 |
| ❏ 187 Steve McNair | 1.50 | .60 |
| ❏ 188 Eddie George | 1.25 | .50 |
| ❏ 189 Chris Sanders | .50 | .20 |
| ❏ 190 Blaine Bishop | .50 | .20 |
| ❏ 191 Derrick Mason RC | 12.00 | 5.00 |
| ❏ 192 Gus Frerotte | .50 | .20 |
| ❏ 193 Terry Allen | 1.25 | .50 |
| ❏ 194 Brian Mitchell | .50 | .20 |
| ❏ 195 Alvin Harper | .50 | .20 |
| ❏ 196 Jeff Hostetler | .50 | .20 |
| ❏ 197 Leslie Shepherd | .50 | .20 |
| ❏ 198 Stephen Davis | 1.25 | .50 |
| ❏ A1 Aikman Audio Blue | 4.00 | 1.50 |
| ❏ A2 Aikman Audio Pro Bowl | 10.00 | 4.00 |
| ❏ A3 Aikman Audio White/500 | 30.00 | 15.00 |

## 1998 SP Authentic

| | | |
|---|---|---|
| ❏ COMP.SET w/o SP's (84) | 40.00 | 20.00 |
| ❏ *HAND NUMBERED RCs: .5X TO .8X | | |
| ❏ 1 Andre Wadsworth RC | 25.00 | 10.00 |
| ❏ 2 Corey Chavous RC | 40.00 | 15.00 |
| ❏ 3 Keith Brooking RC | 40.00 | 15.00 |
| ❏ 4 Duane Starks RC | 15.00 | 7.50 |
| ❏ 5 Pat Johnson RC | 25.00 | 10.00 |
| ❏ 6 Jason Peter RC | 15.00 | 7.50 |

| | | |
|---|---|---|
| ❏ 7 Curtis Enis RC | 15.00 | 7.50 |
| ❏ 8 Takeo Spikes RC | 40.00 | 15.00 |
| ❏ 9 Greg Ellis RC | 15.00 | 7.50 |
| ❏ 10 Marcus Nash RC | 15.00 | 7.50 |
| ❏ 11 Brian Griese RC | 50.00 | 20.00 |
| ❏ 12 Germane Crowell RC | 25.00 | 10.00 |
| ❏ 13 Vonnie Holliday RC | 25.00 | 10.00 |
| ❏ 14 Peyton Manning RC | 800.00 | 400.00 |
| ❏ 15 Jerome Pathon RC | 25.00 | 10.00 |
| ❏ 16 Fred Taylor RC | 50.00 | 25.00 |
| ❏ 17 John Avery RC | 25.00 | 10.00 |
| ❏ 18 Randy Moss RC | 150.00 | 75.00 |
| ❏ 19 Robert Edwards RC | 15.00 | 7.50 |
| ❏ 20 Tony Simmons RC | 25.00 | 10.00 |
| ❏ 21 Shaun Williams RC | 25.00 | 10.00 |
| ❏ 22 Joe Jurevicius RC | 40.00 | 15.00 |
| ❏ 23 Charles Woodson RC | 50.00 | 20.00 |
| ❏ 24 Tra Thomas RC | 15.00 | 7.50 |
| ❏ 25 Grant Wistrom RC | 25.00 | 10.00 |
| ❏ 26 Ryan Leaf RC | 40.00 | 15.00 |
| ❏ 27 Ahman Green RC | 50.00 | 20.00 |
| ❏ 28 Jacquez Green RC | 25.00 | 10.00 |
| ❏ 29 Kevin Dyson RC | 40.00 | 15.00 |
| ❏ 30 Stephen Alexander RC | 25.00 | 10.00 |
| ❏ 31 John Elway TW | 20.00 | 7.50 |
| ❏ 32 Jerry Rice TW | 12.00 | 5.00 |
| ❏ 33 Emmitt Smith TW | 20.00 | 7.50 |
| ❏ 34 Steve Young TW | 8.00 | 3.00 |
| ❏ 35 Jerome Bettis TW | 6.00 | 2.50 |
| ❏ 36 Deion Sanders TW | 6.00 | 2.50 |
| ❏ 37 Andre Rison TW | 4.00 | 1.50 |
| ❏ 38 Warren Moon TW | 6.00 | 2.50 |
| ❏ 39 Mark Brunell TW | 6.00 | 2.50 |
| ❏ 40 Ricky Watters TW | 4.00 | 1.50 |
| ❏ 41 Dan Marino TW | 25.00 | 10.00 |
| ❏ 42 Brett Favre TW | 25.00 | 10.00 |
| ❏ 43 Jake Plummer | 1.00 | .40 |
| ❏ 44 Adrian Murrell | .60 | .25 |
| ❏ 45 Eric Swann | .40 | .15 |
| ❏ 46 Jamal Anderson | 1.00 | .40 |
| ❏ 47 Chris Chandler | .60 | .25 |
| ❏ 48 Jim Harbaugh | .60 | .25 |
| ❏ 49 Michael Jackson | .40 | .15 |
| ❏ 50 Jermaine Lewis | .60 | .25 |
| ❏ 51 Rob Johnson | .60 | .25 |
| ❏ 52 Antowain Smith | 1.00 | .40 |
| ❏ 53 Thurman Thomas | 1.00 | .40 |
| ❏ 54 Kerry Collins | .60 | .25 |
| ❏ 55 Fred Lane | .40 | .15 |
| ❏ 56 Rae Carruth | .40 | .15 |
| ❏ 57 Erik Kramer | .40 | .15 |
| ❏ 58 Curtis Conway | .60 | .25 |
| ❏ 59 Corey Dillon | 1.00 | .40 |
| ❏ 60 Neil O'Donnell | .60 | .25 |
| ❏ 61 Carl Pickens | .60 | .25 |
| ❏ 62 Troy Aikman | 2.00 | .75 |
| ❏ 63 Emmitt Smith | 3.00 | 1.25 |
| ❏ 64 Deion Sanders | 1.00 | .40 |
| ❏ 65 Terrell Davis | 1.00 | .40 |
| ❏ 66 John Elway | 4.00 | 1.50 |
| ❏ 67 Rod Smith | .60 | .25 |
| ❏ 68 Scott Mitchell | .60 | .25 |
| ❏ 69 Barry Sanders | 3.00 | 1.25 |
| ❏ 70 Herman Moore | .60 | .25 |
| ❏ 71 Brett Favre | 4.00 | 1.50 |
| ❏ 72 Dorsey Levens | 1.00 | .40 |
| ❏ 73 Antonio Freeman | 1.00 | .40 |
| ❏ 74 Marshall Faulk | 1.25 | .50 |

| | | | |
|---|---|---|---|
| ☐ 75 Marvin Harrison | 1.00 | .40 | |
| ☐ 76 Mark Brunell | 1.00 | .40 | |
| ☐ 77 Keenan McCardell | .60 | .25 | |
| ☐ 78 Jimmy Smith | .60 | .25 | |
| ☐ 79 Andre Rison | .60 | .25 | |
| ☐ 80 Elvis Grbac | .60 | .25 | |
| ☐ 81 Derrick Alexander | .60 | .25 | |
| ☐ 82 Dan Marino | 4.00 | 1.50 | |
| ☐ 83 Karim Abdul-Jabbar | 1.00 | .40 | |
| ☐ 84 O.J. McDuffie | .60 | .25 | |
| ☐ 85 Brad Johnson | 1.00 | .40 | |
| ☐ 86 Cris Carter | 1.00 | .40 | |
| ☐ 87 Robert Smith | 1.00 | .40 | |
| ☐ 88 Drew Bledsoe | 1.50 | .60 | |
| ☐ 89 Terry Glenn | 1.00 | .40 | |
| ☐ 90 Ben Coates | .60 | .25 | |
| ☐ 91 Lamar Smith | .60 | .25 | |
| ☐ 92 Danny Wuerffel | .60 | .25 | |
| ☐ 93 Tiki Barber | 1.00 | .40 | |
| ☐ 94 Danny Kanell | .60 | .25 | |
| ☐ 95 Ike Hilliard | .60 | .25 | |
| ☐ 96 Curtis Martin | 1.00 | .40 | |
| ☐ 97 Keyshawn Johnson | 1.00 | .40 | |
| ☐ 98 Glenn Foley | .60 | .25 | |
| ☐ 99 Jeff George | .60 | .25 | |
| ☐ 100 Tim Brown | 1.00 | .40 | |
| ☐ 101 Napoleon Kaufman | 1.00 | .40 | |
| ☐ 102 Bobby Hoying | .60 | .25 | |
| ☐ 103 Charlie Garner | .60 | .25 | |
| ☐ 104 Irving Fryar | .60 | .25 | |
| ☐ 105 Kordell Stewart | 1.00 | .40 | |
| ☐ 106 Jerome Bettis | 1.00 | .40 | |
| ☐ 107 Charles Johnson | .40 | .15 | |
| ☐ 108 Tony Banks | .60 | .25 | |
| ☐ 109 Isaac Bruce | 1.00 | .40 | |
| ☐ 110 Natrone Means | .60 | .25 | |
| ☐ 111 Junior Seau | 1.00 | .40 | |
| ☐ 112 Steve Young | 1.25 | .50 | |
| ☐ 113 Jerry Rice | 2.00 | .75 | |
| ☐ 114 Garrison Hearst | 1.00 | .40 | |
| ☐ 115 Ricky Watters | .60 | .25 | |
| ☐ 116 Warren Moon | 1.00 | .40 | |
| ☐ 117 Joey Galloway | .60 | .25 | |
| ☐ 118 Trent Dilfer | 1.00 | .40 | |
| ☐ 119 Warrick Dunn | 1.25 | .50 | |
| ☐ 120 Mike Alstott | 1.00 | .40 | |
| ☐ 121 Steve McNair | 1.00 | .40 | |
| ☐ 122 Eddie George | 1.00 | .40 | |
| ☐ 123 Yancey Thigpen | .40 | .15 | |
| ☐ 124 Gus Frerotte | .40 | .15 | |
| ☐ 125 Terry Allen | 1.00 | .40 | |
| ☐ 126 Michael Westbrook | .60 | .25 | |
| ☐ AE13 Dan Marino SAMPLE | 2.00 | .75 | |

### 1999 SP Authentic

| | | |
|---|---|---|
| ☐ COMP.SET w/o SPs (90) | 35.00 | 15.00 |
| ☐ *HAND NUMBERED RCs: .5X TO .8X | | |
| ☐ 1 Jake Plummer | .60 | .25 |
| ☐ 2 Adrian Murrell | .60 | .25 |
| ☐ 3 Frank Sanders | .60 | .25 |
| ☐ 4 Jamal Anderson | 1.00 | .40 |
| ☐ 5 Chris Chandler | .60 | .25 |
| ☐ 6 Terance Mathis | .60 | .25 |
| ☐ 7 Priest Holmes | 1.50 | .60 |
| ☐ 8 Jermaine Lewis | .60 | .25 |
| ☐ 9 Antowain Smith | 1.00 | .40 |
| ☐ 10 Doug Flutie | 1.00 | .40 |
| ☐ 11 Eric Moulds | 1.00 | .40 |

| | | | |
|---|---|---|---|
| ☐ 12 Muhsin Muhammad | .60 | .25 | |
| ☐ 13 Tim Biakabutuka | .60 | .25 | |
| ☐ 14 Wesley Walls | .60 | .25 | |
| ☐ 15 Curtis Enis | .40 | .15 | |
| ☐ 16 Bobby Engram | .60 | .25 | |
| ☐ 17 Corey Dillon | 1.00 | .40 | |
| ☐ 18 Damay Scott | .60 | .25 | |
| ☐ 19 Terry Kirby | .40 | .15 | |
| ☐ 20 Ty Detmer | .60 | .25 | |
| ☐ 21 Troy Aikman | 2.00 | .75 | |
| ☐ 22 Michael Irvin | .60 | .25 | |
| ☐ 23 Emmitt Smith | 2.00 | .75 | |
| ☐ 24 Terrell Davis | 1.00 | .40 | |
| ☐ 25 Brian Griese | 1.00 | .40 | |
| ☐ 26 Rod Smith | .60 | .25 | |
| ☐ 27 Shannon Sharpe | .60 | .25 | |
| ☐ 28 Barry Sanders | 3.00 | 1.25 | |
| ☐ 29 Charlie Batch | 1.00 | .40 | |
| ☐ 30 Herman Moore | .60 | .25 | |
| ☐ 31 Johnnie Morton | .60 | .25 | |
| ☐ 32 Brett Favre | 3.00 | 1.25 | |
| ☐ 33 Antonio Freeman | 1.00 | .40 | |
| ☐ 34 Dorsey Levens | 1.00 | .40 | |
| ☐ 35 Mark Chmura | .60 | .25 | |
| ☐ 36 Peyton Manning | 3.00 | 1.25 | |
| ☐ 37 Marvin Harrison | 1.00 | .40 | |
| ☐ 38 Mark Brunell | 1.00 | .40 | |
| ☐ 39 Fred Taylor | 1.00 | .40 | |
| ☐ 40 Jimmy Smith | .60 | .25 | |
| ☐ 41 Elvis Grbac | .60 | .25 | |
| ☐ 42 Andre Rison | .60 | .25 | |
| ☐ 43 Dan Marino | 3.00 | 1.25 | |
| ☐ 44 O.J. McDuffie | .60 | .25 | |
| ☐ 45 Yatil Green | .40 | .15 | |
| ☐ 46 Randall Cunningham | 1.00 | .40 | |
| ☐ 47 Randy Moss | 3.00 | 1.25 | |
| ☐ 48 Robert Smith | 1.00 | .40 | |
| ☐ 49 Cris Carter | 1.00 | .40 | |
| ☐ 50 Drew Bledsoe | 1.25 | .50 | |
| ☐ 51 Ben Coates | .40 | .15 | |
| ☐ 52 Terry Glenn | 1.00 | .40 | |
| ☐ 53 Eddie Kennison | .60 | .25 | |
| ☐ 54 Cam Cleeland | .40 | .15 | |
| ☐ 55 Ike Hilliard | .40 | .15 | |
| ☐ 56 Gary Brown | .40 | .15 | |
| ☐ 57 Kerry Collins | .60 | .25 | |
| ☐ 58 Vinny Testaverde | .60 | .25 | |
| ☐ 59 Keyshawn Johnson | 1.00 | .40 | |
| ☐ 60 Wayne Chrebet | 1.00 | .40 | |
| ☐ 61 Curtis Martin | 1.00 | .40 | |
| ☐ 62 Tim Brown | 1.00 | .40 | |
| ☐ 63 Napoleon Kaufman | 1.00 | .40 | |
| ☐ 64 Charles Woodson | 1.00 | .40 | |
| ☐ 65 Duce Staley | 1.00 | .40 | |
| ☐ 66 Charles Johnson | .60 | .25 | |
| ☐ 67 Kordell Stewart | .60 | .25 | |
| ☐ 68 Jerome Bettis | 1.00 | .40 | |
| ☐ 69 Marshall Faulk | 1.25 | .50 | |
| ☐ 70 Isaac Bruce | 1.00 | .40 | |
| ☐ 71 Trent Green | 1.00 | .40 | |
| ☐ 72 Jim Harbaugh | .60 | .25 | |
| ☐ 73 Junior Seau | 1.00 | .40 | |
| ☐ 74 Natrone Means | .60 | .25 | |
| ☐ 75 Steve Young | 1.25 | .50 | |
| ☐ 76 Jerry Rice | 2.00 | .75 | |
| ☐ 77 Terrell Owens | 1.00 | .40 | |
| ☐ 78 Lawrence Phillips | .60 | .25 | |
| ☐ 79 Joey Galloway | .60 | .25 | |
| ☐ 80 Ricky Watters | .60 | .25 | |
| ☐ 81 Jon Kitna | 1.00 | .40 | |
| ☐ 82 Warrick Dunn | 1.00 | .40 | |
| ☐ 83 Trent Dilfer | .60 | .25 | |
| ☐ 84 Mike Alstott | 1.00 | .40 | |
| ☐ 85 Eddie George | 1.00 | .40 | |
| ☐ 86 Steve McNair | 1.00 | .40 | |
| ☐ 87 Yancey Thigpen | .40 | .15 | |
| ☐ 88 Brad Johnson | 1.00 | .40 | |
| ☐ 89 Skip Hicks | .40 | .15 | |
| ☐ 90 Michael Westbrook | .60 | .25 | |
| ☐ 91 Ricky Williams RC | 50.00 | 20.00 | |
| ☐ 92 Tim Couch RC | 20.00 | 8.00 | |
| ☐ 93 Akili Smith RC | 12.00 | 5.00 | |
| ☐ 94 Edgerrin James RC | 50.00 | 20.00 | |
| ☐ 95 Donovan McNabb RC | 80.00 | 40.00 | |
| ☐ 96 Torry Holt RC | 50.00 | 20.00 | |

| | | | |
|---|---|---|---|
| ☐ 97 Cade McNown RC | 12.00 | 5.00 | |
| ☐ 98 Shaun King RC | 12.00 | 5.00 | |
| ☐ 99 Daunte Culpepper RC | 40.00 | 15.00 | |
| ☐ 100 Brock Huard RC | 20.00 | 8.00 | |
| ☐ 101 Chris Claiborne RC | 8.00 | 3.00 | |
| ☐ 102 James Johnson RC | 8.00 | 3.00 | |
| ☐ 103 Rob Konrad RC | 20.00 | 8.00 | |
| ☐ 104 Peerless Price RC | 20.00 | 8.00 | |
| ☐ 105 Kevin Faulk RC | 20.00 | 8.00 | |
| ☐ 106 Andy Katzenmoyer RC | 12.00 | 5.00 | |
| ☐ 107 Troy Edwards RC | 12.00 | 5.00 | |
| ☐ 108 Kevin Johnson RC | 12.00 | 5.00 | |
| ☐ 109 Mike Cloud RC | 8.00 | 3.00 | |
| ☐ 110 David Boston RC | 20.00 | 8.00 | |
| ☐ 111 Champ Bailey RC | 30.00 | 12.00 | |
| ☐ 112 D'Wayne Bates RC | 8.00 | 3.00 | |
| ☐ 113 Joe Germaine RC | 12.00 | 5.00 | |
| ☐ 114 Antoine Winfield RC | 12.00 | 5.00 | |
| ☐ 115 Fernando Bryant RC | 8.00 | 3.00 | |
| ☐ 116 Jevon Kearse RC | 30.00 | 12.00 | |
| ☐ 117 Chris McAlister RC | 12.00 | 5.00 | |
| ☐ 118 Brandon Stokley RC | 20.00 | 8.00 | |
| ☐ 119 Karsten Bailey RC | 8.00 | 3.00 | |
| ☐ 120 Daylon McCutcheon RC | 8.00 | 3.00 | |
| ☐ 121 Jermaine Fazande RC | 8.00 | 3.00 | |
| ☐ 122 Joel Makovicka RC | 12.00 | 5.00 | |
| ☐ 123 Ebenezer Ekuban RC | 8.00 | 3.00 | |
| ☐ 124 Joe Montgomery RC | 8.00 | 3.00 | |
| ☐ 125 Sean Bennett RC | 8.00 | 3.00 | |
| ☐ 126 Na Brown RC | 8.00 | 3.00 | |
| ☐ 127 De'Mond Parker RC | 8.00 | 3.00 | |
| ☐ 128 Sedrick Irvin RC | 8.00 | 3.00 | |
| ☐ 129 Terry Jackson RC | 8.00 | 3.00 | |
| ☐ 130 Jeff Paulk RC | 8.00 | 3.00 | |
| ☐ 131 Cecil Collins RC | 8.00 | 3.00 | |
| ☐ 132 Bobby Collins RC | 8.00 | 3.00 | |
| ☐ 133 Amos Zereoue RC | 12.00 | 5.00 | |
| ☐ 134 Travis McGriff RC | 8.00 | 3.00 | |
| ☐ 135 Larry Parker RC | 20.00 | 8.00 | |
| ☐ 136 Wane McGarity RC | 8.00 | 3.00 | |
| ☐ 137 Cecil Martin RC | 8.00 | 3.00 | |
| ☐ 138 Al Wilson RC | 12.00 | 5.00 | |
| ☐ 139 Jim Kleinsasser RC | 12.00 | 5.00 | |
| ☐ 140 Dat Nguyen RC | 12.00 | 5.00 | |
| ☐ 141 Marty Booker RC | 20.00 | 8.00 | |
| ☐ 142 Reginald Kelly RC | 8.00 | 3.00 | |
| ☐ 143 Scott Covington RC | 12.00 | 5.00 | |
| ☐ 144 Antuan Edwards RC | 8.00 | 3.00 | |
| ☐ 145 Craig Yeast RC | 12.00 | 5.00 | |
| ☐ WPA W.Payton AU/100 | 600.00 | 400.00 | |
| ☐ WPSP W.Payton Jsy AU/34 | 1500.00 | 1500.00 | |

### 2000 SP Authentic

| | | |
|---|---|---|
| ☐ COMP.SET w/o SP's (90) | 15.00 | 6.00 |
| ☐ 1 Jake Plummer | .60 | .25 |
| ☐ 2 David Boston | 1.00 | .40 |
| ☐ 3 Frank Sanders | .60 | .25 |
| ☐ 4 Chris Chandler | .60 | .25 |
| ☐ 5 Jamal Anderson | 1.00 | .40 |
| ☐ 6 Shawn Jefferson | .40 | .15 |
| ☐ 7 Tony Banks | .60 | .25 |
| ☐ 8 Shannon Sharpe | .60 | .25 |
| ☐ 9 Rob Johnson | .60 | .25 |
| ☐ 10 Antowain Smith | .60 | .25 |
| ☐ 11 Muhsin Muhammad | .60 | .25 |
| ☐ 12 Steve Beuerlein | .60 | .25 |
| ☐ 13 Cade McNown | .40 | .15 |
| ☐ 14 Curtis Enis | .40 | .15 |

| | | |
|---|---|---|
| ☐ 15 Marcus Robinson | 1.00 | .40 |
| ☐ 16 Akili Smith | .40 | .15 |
| ☐ 17 Corey Dillon | 1.00 | .40 |
| ☐ 18 Tim Couch | .60 | .25 |
| ☐ 19 Kevin Johnson | 1.00 | .40 |
| ☐ 20 Errict Rhett | .40 | .15 |
| ☐ 21 Troy Aikman | 2.00 | .75 |
| ☐ 22 Emmitt Smith | 2.50 | 1.00 |
| ☐ 23 Rocket Ismail | .60 | .25 |
| ☐ 24 Joey Galloway | .60 | .25 |
| ☐ 25 Terrell Davis | 1.00 | .40 |
| ☐ 26 Olandis Gary | 1.00 | .40 |
| ☐ 27 Ed McCaffrey | 1.00 | .40 |
| ☐ 28 Brian Griese | 1.00 | .40 |
| ☐ 29 Charlie Batch | 1.00 | .40 |
| ☐ 30 Germane Crowell | .40 | .15 |
| ☐ 31 James O. Stewart | .60 | .25 |
| ☐ 32 Brett Favre | 3.00 | 1.25 |
| ☐ 33 Antonio Freeman | 1.00 | .40 |
| ☐ 34 Dorsey Levens | .60 | .25 |
| ☐ 35 Peyton Manning | 2.50 | 1.00 |
| ☐ 36 Edgerrin James | 1.50 | .60 |
| ☐ 37 Marvin Harrison | 1.00 | .40 |
| ☐ 38 Mark Brunell | 1.00 | .40 |
| ☐ 39 Fred Taylor | 1.00 | .40 |
| ☐ 40 Jimmy Smith | .60 | .25 |
| ☐ 41 Elvis Grbac | .60 | .25 |
| ☐ 42 Tony Gonzalez | .60 | .25 |
| ☐ 43 James Johnson | .40 | .15 |
| ☐ 44 Oronde Gadsden | .60 | .25 |
| ☐ 45 Damon Huard | 1.00 | .40 |
| ☐ 46 Randy Moss | 2.00 | .75 |
| ☐ 47 Cris Carter | 1.00 | .40 |
| ☐ 48 Daunte Culpepper | 1.25 | .50 |
| ☐ 49 Drew Bledsoe | 1.25 | .50 |
| ☐ 50 Terry Glenn | .60 | .25 |
| ☐ 51 Ricky Williams | 1.00 | .40 |
| ☐ 52 Jeff Blake | .60 | .25 |
| ☐ 53 Keith Poole | .40 | .15 |
| ☐ 54 Kerry Collins | .60 | .25 |
| ☐ 55 Amani Toomer | .60 | .25 |
| ☐ 56 Ike Hilliard | .60 | .25 |
| ☐ 57 Wayne Chrebet | .60 | .25 |
| ☐ 58 Curtis Martin | 1.00 | .40 |
| ☐ 59 Vinny Testaverde | .60 | .25 |
| ☐ 60 Tim Brown | 1.00 | .40 |
| ☐ 61 Rich Gannon | 1.00 | .40 |
| ☐ 62 Tyrone Wheatley | .60 | .25 |
| ☐ 63 Duce Staley | 1.00 | .40 |
| ☐ 64 Donovan McNabb | 1.50 | .60 |
| ☐ 65 Troy Edwards | .40 | .15 |
| ☐ 66 Jerome Bettis | 1.00 | .40 |
| ☐ 67 Kordell Stewart | .60 | .25 |
| ☐ 68 Marshall Faulk | 1.25 | .50 |
| ☐ 69 Kurt Warner | 1.50 | .60 |
| ☐ 70 Isaac Bruce | 1.00 | .40 |
| ☐ 71 Torry Holt | 1.00 | .40 |
| ☐ 72 Ryan Leaf | .60 | .25 |
| ☐ 73 Jim Harbaugh | .60 | .25 |
| ☐ 74 Jermaine Fazande | .40 | .15 |
| ☐ 75 Jerry Rice | 2.00 | .75 |
| ☐ 76 Terrell Owens | 1.00 | .40 |
| ☐ 77 Jeff Garcia | 1.00 | .40 |
| ☐ 78 Ricky Watters | .60 | .25 |
| ☐ 79 Jon Kitna | .60 | .25 |
| ☐ 80 Derrick Mayes | .60 | .25 |
| ☐ 81 Shaun King | .40 | .15 |
| ☐ 82 Mike Alstott | 1.00 | .40 |
| ☐ 83 Keyshawn Johnson | 1.00 | .40 |
| ☐ 84 Warrick Dunn | 1.00 | .40 |
| ☐ 85 Eddie George | 1.00 | .40 |
| ☐ 86 Steve McNair | 1.00 | .40 |
| ☐ 87 Jevon Kearse | 1.00 | .40 |
| ☐ 88 Brad Johnson | 1.00 | .40 |
| ☐ 89 Stephen Davis | 1.00 | .40 |
| ☐ 90 Michael Westbrook | .60 | .25 |
| ☐ 91 Anthony Lucas RC | 8.00 | 3.00 |
| ☐ 92 Avion Black RC | 10.00 | 4.00 |
| ☐ 93 Dante Hall RC | 15.00 | 6.00 |
| ☐ 94 Darrell Jackson RC | 15.00 | 6.00 |
| ☐ 95 Deltha O'Neal RC | 12.00 | 5.00 |
| ☐ 96 Erron Kinney RC | 12.00 | 5.00 |
| ☐ 97 Doug Chapman RC | 10.00 | 4.00 |
| ☐ 98 Frank Murphy RC | 8.00 | 3.00 |
| ☐ 99 Gari Scott RC | 8.00 | 3.00 |

| | | |
|---|---|---|
| ☐ 100 Giovanni Carmazzi RC | 8.00 | 3.00 |
| ☐ 101 JaJuan Dawson RC | 8.00 | 3.00 |
| ☐ 102 Jarious Jackson RC | 10.00 | 4.00 |
| ☐ 103 Rashard Anderson RC | 10.00 | 4.00 |
| ☐ 104 Michael Wiley RC | 10.00 | 4.00 |
| ☐ 105 Spergon Wynn RC | 10.00 | 4.00 |
| ☐ 106 Muneer Moore RC | 8.00 | 3.00 |
| ☐ 107 Ahmed Plummer RC | 12.00 | 5.00 |
| ☐ 108 Chad Morton RC | 12.00 | 5.00 |
| ☐ 109 Rob Morris RC | 10.00 | 4.00 |
| ☐ 110 Ron Dixon RC | 10.00 | 4.00 |
| ☐ 111 Rondell Mealey RC | 8.00 | 3.00 |
| ☐ 112 Sebastian Janikowski RC | 12.00 | 5.00 |
| ☐ 113 Shaun Ellis RC | 12.00 | 5.00 |
| ☐ 114 Rogers Beckett RC | 10.00 | 4.00 |
| ☐ 115 Shyrone Stith RC | 10.00 | 4.00 |
| ☐ 116 Tim Rattay RC | 12.00 | 5.00 |
| ☐ 117 Todd Husak RC | 12.00 | 5.00 |
| ☐ 118 Tom Brady RC | 1200.00 | 600.00 |
| ☐ 119 Trevor Gaylor RC | 10.00 | 4.00 |
| ☐ 120 Windrell Hayes RC | 10.00 | 4.00 |
| ☐ 121 Anthony Becht RC | 12.00 | 5.00 |
| ☐ 122 Brian Urlacher RC | 60.00 | 25.00 |
| ☐ 123 Bubba Franks RC | 12.00 | 5.00 |
| ☐ 124 Chad Pennington RC | 30.00 | 15.00 |
| ☐ 125 Chris Redman RC | 10.00 | 4.00 |
| ☐ 126 Corey Simon RC | 12.00 | 5.00 |
| ☐ 127 Curtis Keaton RC | 10.00 | 4.00 |
| ☐ 128 Danny Farmer RC | 12.00 | 5.00 |
| ☐ 129 Dennis Northcutt RC | 12.00 | 5.00 |
| ☐ 130 Dez White RC | 12.00 | 5.00 |
| ☐ 131 J.R. Redmond RC | 10.00 | 4.00 |
| ☐ 132 Jamal Lewis RC | 30.00 | 12.00 |
| ☐ 133 Jerry Porter RC | 12.00 | 5.00 |
| ☐ 134 Joe Hamilton RC | 10.00 | 4.00 |
| ☐ 135 Laveranues Coles RC | 15.00 | 6.00 |
| ☐ 136 R.Jay Soward RC | 10.00 | 4.00 |
| ☐ 137 Reuben Droughns RC | 12.00 | 5.00 |
| ☐ 138 Ron Dayne RC | 12.00 | 5.00 |
| ☐ 139 Ron Dugans RC | 8.00 | 3.00 |
| ☐ 140 Shaun Alexander RC | 30.00 | 12.00 |
| ☐ 141 Sylvester Morris RC | 10.00 | 4.00 |
| ☐ 142 Tee Martin RC | 12.00 | 5.00 |
| ☐ 143 Thomas Jones RC | 20.00 | 8.00 |
| ☐ 144 Todd Pinkston RC | 12.00 | 5.00 |
| ☐ 145 Travis Prentice RC | 10.00 | 4.00 |
| ☐ 146 Travis Taylor RC | 12.00 | 5.00 |
| ☐ 147 Trung Canidate RC | 10.00 | 4.00 |
| ☐ 148 Courtney Brown RC | 12.00 | 5.00 |
| ☐ 149 Plaxico Burress RC | 30.00 | 12.00 |
| ☐ 150 Peter Warrick RC | 12.00 | 5.00 |
| ☐ 151 Billy Volek RC | 12.00 | 5.00 |
| ☐ 152 Bobby Shaw RC | 8.00 | 3.00 |
| ☐ 153 Brad Hoover RC | 10.00 | 4.00 |
| ☐ 154 Brian Finneran RC | 12.00 | 5.00 |
| ☐ 155 Charles Lee RC | 8.00 | 3.00 |
| ☐ 156 Chris Cole RC | 8.00 | 3.00 |
| ☐ 157 Clint Stoerner RC | 10.00 | 4.00 |
| ☐ 158 Doug Johnson RC | 12.00 | 5.00 |
| ☐ 159 Frank Moreau RC | 10.00 | 4.00 |
| ☐ 160 Jake Delhomme RC | 40.00 | 15.00 |
| ☐ 161 KaRon Coleman RC | 8.00 | 3.00 |
| ☐ 162 Kevin McDougal RC | 8.00 | 3.00 |
| ☐ 163 Larry Foster RC | 8.00 | 3.00 |
| ☐ 164 Mike Anderson RC | 12.00 | 5.00 |
| ☐ 165 Patrick Pass RC | 8.00 | 3.00 |
| ☐ 166 Reggie Jones RC | 8.00 | 3.00 |
| ☐ 167 Sammy Morris RC | 12.00 | 5.00 |
| ☐ 168 Shockmain Davis RC | 8.00 | 3.00 |
| ☐ 169 Terrelle Smith RC | 8.00 | 3.00 |
| ☐ 170 Ronney Jenkins RC | 8.00 | 3.00 |
| ☐ 171 Troy Walters RC | 10.00 | 4.00 |

## 2001 SP Authentic

| | | |
|---|---|---|
| ☐ COMP. SET w/o SP's (90) | 20.00 | 7.50 |
| ☐ 1 Jake Plummer | .60 | .25 |
| ☐ 2 Thomas Jones | .60 | .25 |
| ☐ 3 Frank Sanders | .40 | .15 |
| ☐ 4 Jamal Anderson | 1.00 | .40 |
| ☐ 5 Chris Chandler | .60 | .25 |
| ☐ 6 Tony Martin | .60 | .25 |
| ☐ 7 Jamal Lewis | 1.25 | .50 |
| ☐ 8 Elvis Grbac | .60 | .25 |
| ☐ 9 Travis Taylor | .60 | .25 |
| ☐ 10 Peerless Price | .60 | .25 |

| | | |
|---|---|---|
| ☐ 11 Rob Johnson | .60 | .25 |
| ☐ 12 Eric Moulds | .60 | .25 |
| ☐ 13 Muhsin Muhammad | .60 | .25 |
| ☐ 14 Isaac Byrd | .40 | .15 |
| ☐ 15 Wesley Walls | .40 | .15 |
| ☐ 16 James Allen | .60 | .25 |
| ☐ 17 Marcus Robinson | 1.00 | .40 |
| ☐ 18 Brian Urlacher | 1.25 | .40 |
| ☐ 19 Jon Kitna | .60 | .25 |
| ☐ 20 Peter Warrick | 1.00 | .40 |
| ☐ 21 Corey Dillon | 1.00 | .40 |
| ☐ 22 Kevin Johnson | .60 | .25 |
| ☐ 23 JaJuan Dawson | .40 | .15 |
| ☐ 24 Tim Couch | .60 | .25 |
| ☐ 25 Rocket Ismail | .60 | .25 |
| ☐ 26 Emmitt Smith | 2.00 | .75 |
| ☐ 27 Joey Galloway | .60 | .25 |
| ☐ 28 Terrell Davis | 1.00 | .40 |
| ☐ 29 Mike Anderson | 1.00 | .40 |
| ☐ 30 Brian Griese | 1.00 | .40 |
| ☐ 31 Ed McCaffrey | 1.00 | .40 |
| ☐ 32 Charlie Batch | 1.00 | .40 |
| ☐ 33 James O. Stewart | .60 | .25 |
| ☐ 34 Johnnie Morton | .60 | .25 |
| ☐ 35 Brett Favre | 3.00 | 1.25 |
| ☐ 36 Antonio Freeman | 1.00 | .40 |
| ☐ 37 Bill Schroeder | .40 | .15 |
| ☐ 38 Ahman Green | 1.00 | .40 |
| ☐ 39 Peyton Manning | 2.50 | 1.00 |
| ☐ 40 Edgerrin James | 1.25 | .50 |
| ☐ 41 Marvin Harrison | 1.00 | .40 |
| ☐ 42 Mark Brunell | 1.00 | .40 |
| ☐ 43 Fred Taylor | 1.00 | .40 |
| ☐ 44 Jimmy Smith | .60 | .25 |
| ☐ 45 Tony Gonzalez | .60 | .25 |
| ☐ 46 Trent Green | 1.00 | .40 |
| ☐ 47 Oronde Gadsden | .60 | .25 |
| ☐ 48 Jay Fiedler | 1.00 | .40 |
| ☐ 49 Lamar Smith | .60 | .25 |
| ☐ 50 Randy Moss | 2.00 | .75 |
| ☐ 51 Cris Carter | 1.00 | .40 |
| ☐ 52 Daunte Culpepper | 1.00 | .40 |
| ☐ 53 Drew Bledsoe | 1.25 | .50 |
| ☐ 54 Terry Glenn | .60 | .25 |
| ☐ 55 Antowain Smith | .60 | .25 |
| ☐ 56 Ricky Williams | 1.00 | .40 |
| ☐ 57 Joe Horn | .60 | .25 |
| ☐ 58 Aaron Brooks | 1.00 | .40 |
| ☐ 59 Kerry Collins | .60 | .25 |
| ☐ 60 Tiki Barber | 1.00 | .40 |
| ☐ 61 Ron Dayne | 1.00 | .40 |
| ☐ 62 Vinny Testaverde | .60 | .25 |
| ☐ 63 Wayne Chrebet | .60 | .25 |
| ☐ 64 Curtis Martin | 1.00 | .40 |
| ☐ 65 Tim Brown | 1.00 | .40 |
| ☐ 66 Rich Gannon | 1.00 | .40 |
| ☐ 67 Jerry Rice | 2.00 | .75 |
| ☐ 68 Duce Staley | 1.00 | .40 |
| ☐ 69 Donovan McNabb | 1.25 | .50 |
| ☐ 70 Kordell Stewart | .60 | .25 |
| ☐ 71 Jerome Bettis | 1.00 | .40 |
| ☐ 72 Marshall Faulk | 1.25 | .50 |
| ☐ 73 Kurt Warner | 1.50 | .60 |
| ☐ 74 Isaac Bruce | 1.00 | .40 |
| ☐ 75 Doug Flutie | 1.00 | .40 |
| ☐ 76 Junior Seau | 1.00 | .40 |
| ☐ 77 Jeff Garcia | 1.00 | .40 |
| ☐ 78 Garrison Hearst | .60 | .25 |

|  |  | | |
|---|---|---|---|
| 79 | Terrell Owens | 1.00 | .40 |
| 80 | Ricky Watters | .60 | .25 |
| 81 | Matt Hasselbeck | .60 | .25 |
| 82 | Brad Johnson | 1.00 | .40 |
| 83 | Warrick Dunn | 1.00 | .40 |
| 84 | Mike Alstott | 1.00 | .40 |
| 85 | Kevin Dyson | .60 | .25 |
| 86 | Eddie George | 1.00 | .40 |
| 87 | Steve McNair | 1.00 | .40 |
| 88 | Champ Bailey | .60 | .25 |
| 89 | Michael Westbrook | .60 | .25 |
| 90 | Stephen Davis | 1.00 | .40 |
| 91 | Michael Vick JSY AU | 400.00 | 200.00 |
| 92 | Rod Gardner JSY AU | 60.00 | 30.00 |
| 93 | Freddie Mitchell JSY AU RC | 60.00 | 25.00 |
| 94 | Koren Robinson JSY/500 RC | 50.00 | 20.00 |
| 95 | David Terrell JSY/500 RC | 25.00 | 10.00 |
| 96 | Michael Bennett JSY/500 RC | 40.00 | 15.00 |
| 97 | Robert Ferguson JSY RC | 40.00 | 15.00 |
| 98 | Deuce McAllister JSY RC | 80.00 | 40.00 |
| 99 | Travis Henry JSY RC | 40.00 | 15.00 |
| 100 | Andre Carter JSY RC | 25.00 | 10.00 |
| 101 | Drew Brees JSY RC | 150.00 | 90.00 |
| 102 | Santana Moss JSY/500 RC | 80.00 | 40.00 |
| 103 | Chris Weinke JSY/390 RC | 40.00 | 15.00 |
| 104 | Chad Johnson JSY/160 RC | 300.00 | 150.00 |
| 105 | Reggie Wayne JSY RC | 100.00 | 60.00 |
| 106 | Kevan Barlow JSY/500 RC | 40.00 | 15.00 |
| 107 | Chr Chambers JSY/500 RC | 80.00 | 40.00 |
| 108 | Todd Heap JSY/500 RC | 80.00 | 30.00 |
| 109 | A Thomas JSY/500 RC | 30.00 | 12.50 |
| 110 | James Jackson JSY/500 RC | 25.00 | 10.00 |
| 111 | Rudi Johnson JSY/500 RC | 100.00 | 50.00 |
| 112 | Mike McMahon JSY RC | 25.00 | 10.00 |
| 113 | Josh Heupel JSY RC | 30.00 | 12.00 |
| 114 | Travis Minor JSY RC | 30.00 | 12.50 |
| 115 | Quincy Morgan JSY/500 RC | 30.00 | 12.50 |
| 116 | Dan Morgan JSY/500 RC | 30.00 | 12.50 |
| 117 | Jesse Palmer JSY/500 RC | 50.00 | 20.00 |
| 118 | Sage Rosenfels JSY/300 RC | 50.00 | 20.00 |
| 119 | Marq Tuiasosopo JY RC | 25.00 | 10.00 |
| 120 | L Tomlinson JSY RC | 800.00 | 450.00 |
| 123 | Alge Crumpler AU RC | 30.00 | 15.00 |
| 124 | Arnold Jackson AU RC | 20.00 | 7.50 |
| 125 | Bobby Newcombe AU RC | 20.00 | 7.50 |
| 126 | Brand Manumaleuna AU RC | 20.00 | 7.50 |
| 127 | Cedrick Wilson AU RC | 35.00 | 20.00 |
| 128 | Brian Allen AU RC | 15.00 | 6.00 |
| 129 | Dee Brown AU RC | 25.00 | 10.00 |
| 130 | Darnerien McCants AU RC | 20.00 | 7.50 |
| 131 | Dave Dickenson AU RC | 20.00 | 7.50 |
| 132 | Derrick Blaylock AU RC | 40.00 | 20.00 |
| 133 | Eddie Berlin AU RC | 20.00 | 7.50 |
| 134 | Francis St.Paul AU RC | 20.00 | 7.50 |
| 135 | Jamar Fletcher AU RC | 20.00 | 7.50 |
| 136 | Josh Booty AU RC | 25.00 | 10.00 |
| 137 | Scotty Anderson AU RC | 20.00 | 7.50 |
| 138 | Ken-Yon Rambo AU RC | 20.00 | 7.50 |
| 139 | Kenyatta Walker AU RC | 15.00 | 6.00 |
| 140 | Kevin Kasper AU RC | 25.00 | 10.00 |
| 141 | Snoop Minnis AU RC | 20.00 | 7.50 |
| 142 | Houshmandzadeh AU RC | 60.00 | 35.00 |
| 143 | Quincy Carter AU RC | 25.00 | 10.00 |
| 144 | Ronney Daniels AU RC | 15.00 | 6.00 |
| 145 | Sedrick Hodge AU RC | 15.00 | 6.00 |
| 146 | Steve Smith AU RC | 135.00 | 75.00 |
| 147 | Tim Hasselbeck AU RC | 25.00 | 10.00 |
| 148 | Vinny Sutherland AU RC | 20.00 | 7.50 |
| 149 | Richard Seymour AU RC | 60.00 | 30.00 |
| 150 | Jamie Winborn AU | 20.00 | 7.50 |
| 151 | Gerard Warren RC | 10.00 | 4.00 |
| 152 | Justin Smith RC | 10.00 | 4.00 |
| 153 | David Martin RC | 8.00 | 3.00 |
| 154 | Jamal Reynolds RC | 10.00 | 4.00 |
| 155 | Dominic Rhodes RC | 12.00 | 5.00 |
| 156 | Nate Clements RC | 10.00 | 4.00 |
| 157 | Michael Lewis RC | 10.00 | 4.00 |
| 158 | Andre King RC | 8.00 | 3.00 |
| 159 | Benjamin Gay RC | 10.00 | 4.00 |
| 160 | Correll Buckhalter RC | 15.00 | 6.00 |
| 161 | Roderick Robinson RC | 8.00 | 3.00 |
| 162 | Moran Norris RC | 6.00 | 2.50 |
| 163 | Onome Ojo RC | 8.00 | 3.00 |
| 164 | Will Allen RC | 8.00 | 3.00 |
| 165 | Jonathan Carter RC | 8.00 | 3.00 |
| 166 | LaMont Jordan RC | 20.00 | 8.00 |
| 167 | DeLawrence Grant RC | 6.00 | 2.50 |
| 168 | Derrick Gibson RC | 8.00 | 3.00 |
| 169 | A.J. Feeley RC | 10.00 | 4.00 |
| 170 | Tim Baker RC | 6.00 | 2.50 |
| 171 | Kendrell Bell RC | 10.00 | 4.00 |
| 172 | Zeke Moreno RC | 10.00 | 4.00 |
| 173 | Carlos Polk RC | 8.00 | 3.00 |
| 174 | Ken Lucas RC | 8.00 | 3.00 |
| 175 | Heath Evans RC | 8.00 | 3.00 |
| 176 | Elvis Joseph RC | 8.00 | 3.00 |
| 177 | Damione Lewis RC | 8.00 | 3.00 |
| 178 | Tommy Polley RC | 10.00 | 4.00 |
| 179 | Fred Smoot RC | 10.00 | 4.00 |
| 180 | Jason Brookins RC | 10.00 | 4.00 |
| 181 | Nick Goings RC | 10.00 | 4.00 |
| 182 | Drew Bennett RC | 15.00 | 6.00 |
| 183 | Justin McCareins RC | 15.00 | 6.00 |
| 184 | Kabeer Gbaja-Biamila RC | 15.00 | 6.00 |
| 185 | Edgerton Hartwell RC | 6.00 | 2.50 |
| 186 | Robert Carswell RC | 6.00 | 2.50 |
| 187 | Aaron Schobel RC | 10.00 | 4.00 |
| 188 | Dan Alexander RC | 10.00 | 4.00 |
| 189 | Jamie Winborn RC | 8.00 | 3.00 |
| 190 | Karon Riley RC | 6.00 | 2.50 |
| EG | Eddie George SAMPLE | 3.00 | 1.50 |

## 2002 SP Authentic

|  |  | | |
|---|---|---|---|
| | COMP.SET w/o SP's (90) | 25.00 | 10.00 |
| 1 | Tom Brady | 2.00 | .75 |
| 2 | Antowain Smith | .60 | .25 |
| 3 | Troy Brown | .60 | .25 |
| 4 | Kurt Warner | 1.00 | .40 |
| 5 | Marshall Faulk | 1.00 | .40 |
| 6 | Isaac Bruce | 1.00 | .40 |
| 7 | Kordell Stewart | .60 | .25 |
| 8 | Jerome Bettis | 1.00 | .40 |
| 9 | Plaxico Burress | .60 | .25 |
| 10 | Hines Ward | 1.00 | .40 |
| 11 | Donovan McNabb | 1.25 | .50 |
| 12 | Duce Staley | 1.00 | .40 |
| 13 | Dorsey Levens | .60 | .25 |
| 14 | Antonio Freeman | 1.00 | .40 |
| 15 | Jerry Rice | 2.00 | .75 |
| 16 | Rich Gannon | 1.00 | .40 |
| 17 | Tim Brown | 1.00 | .40 |
| 18 | Jim Miller | .60 | .25 |
| 19 | Marty Booker | .60 | .25 |
| 20 | Brian Urlacher | 1.25 | .50 |
| 21 | Jamal Lewis | 1.00 | .40 |
| 22 | Chris Redman | .40 | .15 |
| 23 | Ray Lewis | 1.00 | .40 |
| 24 | Brett Favre | 2.50 | 1.00 |
| 25 | Ahman Green | 1.00 | .40 |
| 26 | Terry Glenn | .60 | .25 |
| 27 | Keyshawn Johnson | 1.00 | .40 |
| 28 | Keenan McCardell | .40 | .15 |
| 29 | Michael Pittman | .40 | .15 |
| 30 | Curtis Martin | 1.00 | .40 |
| 31 | Vinny Testaverde | .60 | .25 |
| 32 | Chad Pennington | 1.25 | .50 |
| 33 | Wayne Chrebet | .60 | .25 |
| 34 | Terrell Owens | 1.00 | .40 |
| 35 | Garrison Hearst | .60 | .25 |
| 36 | Jay Fiedler | .60 | .25 |
| 37 | Ricky Williams | 1.00 | .40 |
| 38 | Chris Chambers | 1.00 | .40 |
| 39 | Shaun Alexander | 1.25 | .50 |
| 40 | Darrell Jackson | .60 | .25 |
| 41 | Drew Bledsoe | 1.25 | .50 |
| 42 | Travis Henry | 1.00 | .40 |
| 43 | Eric Moulds | .60 | .25 |
| 44 | Stephen Davis | .60 | .25 |
| 45 | Rod Gardner | .60 | .25 |
| 46 | Brian Griese | 1.00 | .40 |
| 47 | Olandis Gary | .60 | .25 |
| 48 | Shannon Sharpe | .60 | .25 |
| 49 | Tim Couch | .60 | .25 |
| 50 | Kevin Johnson | .60 | .25 |
| 51 | Steve McNair | 1.00 | .40 |
| 52 | Eddie George | 1.00 | .40 |
| 53 | Aaron Brooks | 1.00 | .40 |
| 54 | Deuce McAllister | 1.25 | .50 |
| 55 | Joe Horn | .60 | .25 |
| 56 | Michael Vick | 1.50 | .60 |
| 57 | Warrick Dunn | .60 | .25 |
| 58 | Kerry Collins | .60 | .25 |
| 59 | Tiki Barber | 1.00 | .40 |
| 60 | Amani Toomer | .60 | .25 |
| 61 | Jake Plummer | .60 | .25 |
| 62 | David Boston | 1.00 | .40 |
| 63 | Thomas Jones | .60 | .25 |
| 64 | Edgerrin James | 1.25 | .50 |
| 65 | Marvin Harrison | 1.00 | .40 |
| 66 | Mark Brunell | 1.00 | .40 |
| 67 | Jimmy Smith | .60 | .25 |
| 68 | Fred Taylor | 1.00 | .40 |
| 69 | Corey Dillon | .60 | .25 |
| 70 | Jon Kitna | .60 | .25 |
| 71 | Michael Westbrook | .40 | .15 |
| 72 | Trent Green | .60 | .25 |
| 73 | Priest Holmes | 1.25 | .50 |
| 74 | Tony Gonzalez | .60 | .25 |
| 75 | Daunte Culpepper | 1.00 | .40 |
| 76 | Michael Bennett | .60 | .25 |
| 77 | Randy Moss | 1.50 | .60 |
| 78 | Drew Brees | 1.00 | .40 |
| 79 | Curtis Conway | .40 | .15 |
| 80 | Junior Seau | 1.00 | .40 |
| 81 | Quincy Carter | .60 | .25 |
| 82 | Emmitt Smith | 2.50 | 1.00 |
| 83 | Joey Galloway | .60 | .25 |
| 84 | Cory Schlesinger | .40 | .15 |
| 85 | James Stewart | .40 | .15 |
| 86 | Az-Zahir Hakim | .40 | .15 |
| 87 | Rodney Peete | .60 | .25 |
| 88 | Lamar Smith | .60 | .25 |
| 89 | Corey Bradford | .40 | .15 |
| 90 | Jermaine Lewis | .40 | .15 |
| 91 | Peyton Manning AU | 120.00 | 60.00 |
| 92 | Anthony Thomas AU | 25.00 | 12.50 |
| 93 | LaDainian Tomlinson AU | 80.00 | 40.00 |
| 94 | Jeff Garcia AU | 25.00 | 10.00 |
| 95 | Kurt Warner SC | 3.00 | 1.25 |
| 96 | Brett Favre SC | 8.00 | 3.00 |
| 97 | Michael Vick SC | 4.00 | 1.50 |
| 98 | Donovan McNabb SC | 4.00 | 1.50 |
| 99 | Daunte Culpepper SC | 3.00 | 1.25 |
| 100 | Tom Brady SC | 8.00 | 3.00 |
| 101 | Drew Brees SC | 3.00 | 1.25 |
| 102 | Kordell Stewart SC | 2.00 | .75 |
| 103 | Steve McNair SC | 3.00 | 1.25 |
| 104 | Peyton Manning SC | 6.00 | 2.50 |
| 105 | Mark Brunell SC | 3.00 | 1.25 |
| 106 | Jeff Garcia SC | 3.00 | 1.25 |
| 107 | Aaron Brooks SC | 3.00 | 1.25 |
| 108 | Rich Gannon SC | 3.00 | 1.25 |
| 109 | Tim Couch SC | 2.00 | .75 |
| 110 | Jake Plummer SC | 3.00 | 1.25 |
| 111 | Drew Bledsoe SC | 4.00 | 1.50 |
| 112 | Brian Griese SC | 3.00 | 1.25 |
| 113 | Quincy Carter SC | 2.00 | .75 |
| 114 | Vinny Testaverde SC | 2.00 | .75 |
| 115 | Chad Pennington SC | 4.00 | 1.50 |
| 116 | Brad Johnson SC | 2.00 | .75 |
| 117 | Trent Dilfer SC | 2.00 | .75 |
| 118 | Jim Miller SC | 2.00 | .75 |
| 119 | Tommy Maddox SC | 8.00 | 3.00 |
| 120 | Trent Green SC | 2.00 | .75 |
| 121 | Rodney Peete SC | 2.00 | .75 |
| 122 | Jay Fiedler SC | 2.00 | .75 |
| 123 | Kerry Collins SC | 2.00 | .75 |
| 124 | Chris Redman SC | 2.00 | .75 |

| | | | |
|---|---|---|---|
| ❑ 125 Marshall Faulk SS | 4.00 | 1.50 |
| ❑ 126 Donovan McNabb SS | 5.00 | 2.00 |
| ❑ 127 Michael Vick SS | 5.00 | 2.00 |
| ❑ 128 Brett Favre SS | 10.00 | 4.00 |
| ❑ 129 Peyton Manning SS | 8.00 | 3.00 |
| ❑ 130 Kurt Warner SS | 4.00 | 1.50 |
| ❑ 131 Curtis Martin SS | 4.00 | 1.50 |
| ❑ 132 Randy Moss SS | 8.00 | 3.00 |
| ❑ 133 Edgerrin James SS | 5.00 | 2.00 |
| ❑ 134 Jerome Bettis SS | 4.00 | 1.50 |
| ❑ 135 Emmitt Smith SS | 10.00 | 4.00 |
| ❑ 136 LaDainian Tomlinson SS | 6.00 | 2.50 |
| ❑ 137 Jeff Garcia SS | 4.00 | 1.50 |
| ❑ 138 Kordell Stewart SS | 2.50 | 1.00 |
| ❑ 139 Anthony Thomas SS | 2.50 | 1.00 |
| ❑ 140 Tom Brady SS | 10.00 | 4.00 |
| ❑ 141 Daunte Culpepper SS | 4.00 | 1.50 |
| ❑ 142 Drew Bledsoe SS | 5.00 | 2.00 |
| ❑ 143 Ricky Williams SS | 4.00 | 1.50 |
| ❑ 144 Warrick Dunn SS | 4.00 | 1.50 |
| ❑ 145 Steve McNair SS | 4.00 | 1.50 |
| ❑ 146 Rich Gannon SS | 4.00 | 1.50 |
| ❑ 147 Jake Plummer SS | 2.50 | 1.00 |
| ❑ 148 Jerry Rice SS | 8.00 | 3.00 |
| ❑ 149 Mark Brunell SS | 4.00 | 1.50 |
| ❑ 150 Brian Griese SS | 4.00 | 1.50 |
| ❑ 151 Eddie George SS | 4.00 | 1.50 |
| ❑ 152 Tim Couch SS | 2.50 | 1.00 |
| ❑ 153 Keyshawn Johnson SS | 4.00 | 1.50 |
| ❑ 154 Shannon Sharpe SS | 2.50 | 1.00 |
| ❑ 155 Phillip Buchanon RC | 8.00 | 3.00 |
| ❑ 156 Brian Allen RC | 6.00 | 2.50 |
| ❑ 157 Brian Westbrook RC | 40.00 | 25.00 |
| ❑ 158 Lito Sheppard RC | 8.00 | 3.00 |
| ❑ 159 Daryl Jones RC | 5.00 | 2.00 |
| ❑ 160 Javin Hunter RC | 5.00 | 2.00 |
| ❑ 161 Derrick Lewis RC | 5.00 | 2.00 |
| ❑ 162 Javon Walker RC | 15.00 | 6.00 |
| ❑ 163 Tank Williams RC | 6.00 | 2.50 |
| ❑ 164 Shaun Hill RC | 25.00 | 12.50 |
| ❑ 165 Napoleon Harris RC | 6.00 | 2.50 |
| ❑ 166 Herb Haygood RC | 5.00 | 2.50 |
| ❑ 167 Jake Schifino RC | 5.00 | 2.00 |
| ❑ 168 Quentin Jammer RC | 8.00 | 3.00 |
| ❑ 169 Jason McAddley RC | 6.00 | 2.50 |
| ❑ 170 Jerramy Stevens RC | 8.00 | 3.00 |
| ❑ 171 Jesse Chatman RC | 6.00 | 2.50 |
| ❑ 172 Larry Ned RC | 5.00 | 2.50 |
| ❑ 173 Najeh Davenport RC | 8.00 | 3.00 |
| ❑ 174 Lamont Thompson RC | 6.00 | 2.50 |
| ❑ 175 Darrell Hill RC | 5.00 | 2.00 |
| ❑ 176 Ryan Sims RC | 6.00 | 2.50 |
| ❑ 177 Ryan Denney RC | 5.00 | 2.00 |
| ❑ 178 Jamin Elliott RC | 5.00 | 2.00 |
| ❑ 179 Sam Simmons RC | 5.00 | 2.00 |
| ❑ 180 Seth Burford RC | 5.00 | 2.00 |
| ❑ 181 Tellis Redmon RC | 5.00 | 2.00 |
| ❑ 182 Ben Leber RC | 6.00 | 2.50 |
| ❑ 183 Kendall Newson RC | 5.00 | 2.50 |
| ❑ 184 Marques Anderson RC | 6.00 | 2.50 |
| ❑ 185 Adrian Peterson RC | 25.00 | 10.00 |
| ❑ 187 Antwoine Womack AU RC | 20.00 | 7.50 |
| ❑ 188 Brandon Doman AU RC | 20.00 | 7.50 |
| ❑ 189 Craig Nall AU RC | 25.00 | 10.00 |
| ❑ 190 Chad Hutchinson AU RC | 20.00 | 7.50 |
| ❑ 191 Chester Taylor AU RC | 40.00 | 20.00 |
| ❑ 192 Damien Anderson AU RC | 20.00 | 7.50 |
| ❑ 193 Deion Branch AU RC | 50.00 | 25.00 |
| ❑ 194 Dusty Bonner AU RC | 15.00 | 6.00 |
| ❑ 195 Ed Reed AU RC | 50.00 | 30.00 |
| ❑ 196 Eric McCoo AU RC | 15.00 | 6.00 |
| ❑ 197 J.T. O'Sullivan AU RC | 20.00 | 7.50 |
| ❑ 198 Kalimba Edwards AU RC | 25.00 | 10.00 |
| ❑ 199 Jonathan Wells AU RC | 25.00 | 10.00 |
| ❑ 200 Josh Scobey AU RC | 20.00 | 7.50 |
| ❑ 201 Kelly Campbell AU RC | 30.00 | 15.00 |
| ❑ 202 Kurt Kittner AU RC | 20.00 | 7.50 |
| ❑ 203 Lamar Gordon AU RC | 25.00 | 10.00 |
| ❑ 204 Lee Mays AU RC | 20.00 | 7.50 |
| ❑ 205 Leonard Henry AU RC | 20.00 | 7.50 |
| ❑ 206 Luke Staley AU RC | 20.00 | 7.50 |
| ❑ 207 Justin Peelle AU RC | 15.00 | 6.00 |
| ❑ 208 Randy Fasani AU RC | 20.00 | 7.50 |
| ❑ 209 Ricky Williams AU RC | 25.00 | 10.00 |
| ❑ 210 Ronald Curry AU RC | 30.00 | 15.00 |

| | | | |
|---|---|---|---|
| ❑ 211 Travis Stephens AU RC | 20.00 | 7.50 |
| ❑ 212 Wendell Bryant AU RC | 15.00 | 6.00 |
| ❑ 213 Woody Dantzler AU RC | 20.00 | 7.50 |
| ❑ 214 Kahlil Hill AU RC | 20.00 | 7.50 |
| ❑ 215 Donte Stallworth JSY RC | 40.00 | 15.00 |
| ❑ 216 Joey Harrington AU/280 RC | 60.00 | 30.00 |
| ❑ 217 Cliff Russell JSY RC | 20.00 | 8.00 |
| ❑ 218 Clinton Portis JSY RC | 80.00 | 40.00 |
| ❑ 219 Daniel Graham JSY RC | 25.00 | 10.00 |
| ❑ 220 David Garrard JSY RC | 80.00 | 30.00 |
| ❑ 221 DeShaun Foster JSY RC | 50.00 | 20.00 |
| ❑ 222 Julius Peppers JSY RC | 50.00 | 20.00 |
| ❑ 223 Jeremy Shockey JSY RC | 25.00 | 10.00 |
| ❑ 224 Patrick Ramsey JSY RC | 25.00 | 10.00 |
| ❑ 225 Josh Reed JSY RC | 25.00 | 10.00 |
| ❑ 226 LaDell Betts JSY RC | 25.00 | 10.00 |
| ❑ 227 Mike Williams JSY/350 RC | 25.00 | 10.00 |
| ❑ 228 Reche Caldwell JSY RC | 25.00 | 10.00 |
| ❑ 229 Rohan Davey JSY RC | 25.00 | 10.00 |
| ❑ 230 Ron Johnson JSY RC | 20.00 | 8.00 |
| ❑ 231 Roy Williams JSY/350 RC | 40.00 | 15.00 |
| ❑ 232 T.J. Duckett JSY RC | 25.00 | 10.00 |
| ❑ 233 Tim Carter JSY RC | 20.00 | 8.00 |
| ❑ 234 William Green JSY RC | 20.00 | 8.00 |
| ❑ 235 Randle EL JSY AU RC | 60.00 | 25.00 |
| ❑ 237 David Carr JSY AU RC | 60.00 | 20.00 |
| ❑ 238 Andre Davis JSY AU RC | 40.00 | 20.00 |
| ❑ 239 Eric Crouch JSY AU RC | 50.00 | 20.00 |
| ❑ 240 Antonio Bryant JSY AU RC | 40.00 | 20.00 |
| ❑ 241 Jabar Gaffney JSY AU RC | 40.00 | 15.00 |
| ❑ 242 Marquise Walker JSY AU RC | 40.00 | 20.00 |
| ❑ 243 Maurice Morris JSY AU RC | 50.00 | 25.00 |
| ❑ 244 Josh McCown JSY AU RC | 40.00 | 15.00 |
| ❑ AP1 Walter Payton AU/34 | 750.00 | 500.00 |
| ❑ SW1 Walter Payton JSY/150 | 120.00 | 60.00 |
| ❑ SW1 W.Payton Gold JSY/34 | 200.00 | 100.00 |
| ❑ SCPS Payl/Smith JSY/250 | 120.00 | 60.00 |
| ❑ SCPSG Payl/Smith Gld JSY/34 | 300.00 | 175.00 |

**2003 SP Authentic**

| | | | |
|---|---|---|---|
| ❑ COMP.SET w/o SP's (90) | 20.00 | 7.50 |
| ❑ 1 Donovan McNabb | 1.25 | .50 |
| ❑ 2 Tim Couch | .60 | .25 |
| ❑ 3 Joey Harrington | 1.00 | .40 |
| ❑ 4 Brett Favre | 2.50 | 1.00 |
| ❑ 5 Jeff Garcia | 1.00 | .40 |
| ❑ 6 Kerry Collins | .75 | .30 |
| ❑ 7 Michael Vick | 1.00 | .40 |
| ❑ 8 David Carr | 1.00 | .40 |
| ❑ 9 Steve McNair | 1.00 | .40 |
| ❑ 10 Chad Pennington | 1.00 | .40 |
| ❑ 11 Patrick Ramsey | .75 | .30 |
| ❑ 12 Rich Gannon | .75 | .30 |
| ❑ 13 Kurt Warner | 1.00 | .40 |
| ❑ 14 Brad Johnson | .75 | .30 |
| ❑ 15 Jay Fiedler | .75 | .30 |
| ❑ 16 Jake Plummer | .75 | .30 |
| ❑ 17 Mark Brunell | .75 | .30 |
| ❑ 18 Peyton Manning | 2.00 | .75 |
| ❑ 19 Brian Griese | .75 | .30 |
| ❑ 20 Kordell Stewart | .75 | .30 |
| ❑ 21 Kelly Holcomb | .60 | .25 |
| ❑ 22 Josh McCown | .75 | .30 |
| ❑ 23 Matt Hasselbeck | .75 | .30 |
| ❑ 24 Marc Bulger | 1.00 | .40 |
| ❑ 25 Chris Redman | .60 | .25 |
| ❑ 26 Rodney Peete | .60 | .25 |
| ❑ 27 Jake Delhomme | 1.00 | .40 |

| | | | |
|---|---|---|---|
| ❑ 28 Jon Kitna | .75 | .30 |
| ❑ 29 Trent Green | .75 | .30 |
| ❑ 30 Quincy Carter | .60 | .25 |
| ❑ 31 Chad Hutchinson | .60 | .25 |
| ❑ 32 Edgerrin James | 1.00 | .40 |
| ❑ 33 Deuce McAllister | 1.00 | .40 |
| ❑ 34 Ricky Williams | .75 | .30 |
| ❑ 35 Priest Holmes | 1.00 | .40 |
| ❑ 36 Curtis Martin | 1.00 | .40 |
| ❑ 37 Shaun Alexander | 1.00 | .40 |
| ❑ 38 Eddie George | .75 | .30 |
| ❑ 39 Marshall Faulk | 1.00 | .40 |
| ❑ 40 Garrison Hearst | .75 | .30 |
| ❑ 41 Ahman Green | 1.00 | .40 |
| ❑ 42 Corey Dillon | .75 | .30 |
| ❑ 43 Jamal Lewis | 1.00 | .40 |
| ❑ 44 William Green | .60 | .25 |
| ❑ 45 Travis Henry | .75 | .30 |
| ❑ 46 Mike Alstott | 1.00 | .40 |
| ❑ 47 Amos Zereoue | .60 | .25 |
| ❑ 48 Stephen Davis | .75 | .30 |
| ❑ 49 Duce Staley | .75 | .30 |
| ❑ 50 Fred Taylor | 1.00 | .40 |
| ❑ 51 Anthony Thomas | .75 | .30 |
| ❑ 52 Charlie Garner | .75 | .30 |
| ❑ 53 Kevan Barlow | .60 | .25 |
| ❑ 54 Brian Urlacher | 1.50 | .60 |
| ❑ 55 Junior Seau | 1.00 | .40 |
| ❑ 56 Zach Thomas | 1.00 | .40 |
| ❑ 57 Ray Lewis | 1.00 | .40 |
| ❑ 58 Jerry Porter | .75 | .30 |
| ❑ 59 Marty Booker | .75 | .30 |
| ❑ 60 Javon Walker | .75 | .30 |
| ❑ 61 Donald Driver | 1.00 | .40 |
| ❑ 62 Amani Toomer | .75 | .30 |
| ❑ 63 Peerless Price | .60 | .25 |
| ❑ 64 Santana Moss | .75 | .30 |
| ❑ 65 Laveranues Coles | .75 | .30 |
| ❑ 66 Troy Brown | .75 | .30 |
| ❑ 67 Chris Chambers | .75 | .30 |
| ❑ 68 Rod Smith | .75 | .30 |
| ❑ 69 Ashley Lelie | .60 | .25 |
| ❑ 70 Plaxico Burress | 1.00 | .40 |
| ❑ 71 Keyshawn Johnson | 1.00 | .40 |
| ❑ 72 Isaac Bruce | 1.00 | .40 |
| ❑ 73 Torry Holt | 1.00 | .40 |
| ❑ 74 Koren Robinson | .75 | .30 |
| ❑ 75 Derrick Mason | .75 | .30 |
| ❑ 76 Kevin Johnson | .60 | .25 |
| ❑ 77 Andre' Davis | .60 | .25 |
| ❑ 78 Antonio Bryant | 1.00 | .40 |
| ❑ 79 Eric Moulds | .75 | .30 |
| ❑ 80 Jerry Rice | 2.00 | .75 |
| ❑ 81 Tim Brown | 1.00 | .40 |
| ❑ 82 Antwaan Randle El | .75 | .30 |
| ❑ 83 Donte Stallworth | .75 | .30 |
| ❑ 84 Randy Moss | 1.25 | .50 |
| ❑ 85 Chad Johnson | 1.00 | .40 |
| ❑ 86 Hines Ward | 1.00 | .40 |
| ❑ 87 Rod Gardner | .60 | .25 |
| ❑ 88 Marvin Harrison | 1.00 | .40 |
| ❑ 89 David Boston | .60 | .25 |
| ❑ 90 Julius Peppers | 1.00 | .40 |
| ❑ 91 Dewayne White RC | 2.50 | 1.00 |
| ❑ 92 Casey Fitzsimmons RC | 3.00 | 1.25 |
| ❑ 93 Aaron Moorehead RC | 3.00 | 1.25 |
| ❑ 94 Jimmy Farris RC | 2.50 | 1.00 |
| ❑ 95 Eric Parker RC | 4.00 | 1.50 |
| ❑ 96 Michael Haynes RC | 2.50 | 1.00 |
| ❑ 97 J.J. Moses RC | 2.50 | 1.00 |
| ❑ 98 Ken Hamlin RC | 4.00 | 1.50 |
| ❑ 99 William Joseph RC | 2.50 | 1.00 |
| ❑ 100 Alonzo Jackson RC | 2.50 | 1.00 |
| ❑ 101 Tyler Brayton RC | 3.00 | 1.25 |
| ❑ 102 Eddie Moore RC | 2.50 | 1.00 |
| ❑ 103 Cleo Lemon RC | 8.00 | 3.00 |
| ❑ 104 Arlen Harris RC | 2.50 | 1.00 |
| ❑ 105 Cortez Hankton RC | 3.00 | 1.25 |
| ❑ 106 Angelo Crowell RC | 3.00 | 1.25 |
| ❑ 107 Johnathan Sullivan RC | 2.50 | 1.00 |
| ❑ 108 Pisa Tinoisamoa RC | 4.00 | 1.50 |
| ❑ 109 Boss Bailey RC | 3.00 | 1.25 |
| ❑ 110 Tommy Jones RC | 2.50 | 1.00 |
| ❑ 111 E.J. Henderson RC | 3.00 | 1.25 |
| ❑ 112 Jimmy Kennedy RC | 3.00 | 1.25 |

| | | |
|---|---|---|
| ❏ 113 Nnamdi Asomugha RC | 4.00 | 1.50 |
| ❏ 114 Hanik Milligan RC | 2.50 | 1.00 |
| ❏ 115 Sammy Davis RC | 3.00 | 1.25 |
| ❏ 116 Drayton Florence RC | 3.00 | 1.25 |
| ❏ 117 Andre Woolfolk RC | 3.00 | 1.25 |
| ❏ 118 Dennis Weathersby RC | 2.50 | 1.00 |
| ❏ 119 Mike Doss RC | 4.00 | 1.50 |
| ❏ 120 Troy Polamalu RC | 40.00 | 20.00 |
| ❏ 121 Clinton Portis SS | 5.00 | 2.00 |
| ❏ 122 Daunte Culpepper SS | 4.00 | 1.50 |
| ❏ 123 Jeremy Shockey SS | 4.00 | 1.50 |
| ❏ 124 Drew Brees SS | 4.00 | 1.50 |
| ❏ 125 Marshall Faulk SS | 4.00 | 1.50 |
| ❏ 126 Emmitt Smith SS | 10.00 | 4.00 |
| ❏ 127 Terrell Owens SS | 4.00 | 1.50 |
| ❏ 128 Ricky Williams SS | 3.00 | 1.25 |
| ❏ 129 Deuce McAllister SS | 4.00 | 1.50 |
| ❏ 130 Ahman Green SS | 4.00 | 1.50 |
| ❏ 131 Chad Pennington SS | 4.00 | 1.50 |
| ❏ 132 Plaxico Burress SS | 4.00 | 1.50 |
| ❏ 133 Steve McNair SS | 4.00 | 1.50 |
| ❏ 134 Keyshawn Johnson SS | 4.00 | 1.50 |
| ❏ 135 Jeff Garcia SS | 4.00 | 1.50 |
| ❏ 136 Drew Bledsoe SS | 4.00 | 1.50 |
| ❏ 137 Jerry Rice SS | 8.00 | 3.00 |
| ❏ 138 Randy Moss SS | 5.00 | 2.00 |
| ❏ 139 David Carr SS | 4.00 | 1.50 |
| ❏ 140 Joey Harrington SS | 4.00 | 1.50 |
| ❏ 141 Michael Vick SS | 4.00 | 1.50 |
| ❏ 142 Tom Brady SS | 10.00 | 4.00 |
| ❏ 143 Brian Urlacher SS | 6.00 | 2.50 |
| ❏ 144 Brett Favre SS | 10.00 | 4.00 |
| ❏ 145 Kurt Warner SS | 4.00 | 1.50 |
| ❏ 146 LaDainian Tomlinson SS | 6.00 | 2.50 |
| ❏ 147 Aaron Brooks SS | 3.00 | 1.25 |
| ❏ 148 Edgerrin James SS | 4.00 | 1.50 |
| ❏ 149 Peyton Manning SS | 8.00 | 3.00 |
| ❏ 150 Donovan McNabb SS | 5.00 | 2.00 |
| ❏ 151 Jason Gesser RC | 5.00 | 2.00 |
| ❏ 152 Ken Dorsey RC | 5.00 | 2.00 |
| ❏ 153 Jason Johnson RC | 4.00 | 1.50 |
| ❏ 154 Avon Cobourne RC | 4.00 | 1.50 |
| ❏ 155 Andrew Pinnock RC | 5.00 | 2.00 |
| ❏ 156 Kirk Farmer RC | 5.00 | 2.00 |
| ❏ 157 Reno Mahe RC | 5.00 | 2.00 |
| ❏ 158 Lon Sheriff RC | 4.00 | 1.50 |
| ❏ 159 Marquel Blackwell RC | 4.00 | 1.50 |
| ❏ 160 Quentin Griffin RC | 5.00 | 2.00 |
| ❏ 161 Rashean Mathis RC | 5.00 | 2.00 |
| ❏ 162 Lee Suggs RC | 5.00 | 2.00 |
| ❏ 163 Jeremi Johnson RC | 4.00 | 1.50 |
| ❏ 164 Ovie Mughelli RC | 4.00 | 1.50 |
| ❏ 165 Nick Barnett RC | 5.00 | 2.00 |
| ❏ 166 Brock Forsey RC | 5.00 | 2.00 |
| ❏ 167 Malaefou MacKenzie RC | 4.00 | 1.50 |
| ❏ 168 Ahmaad Galloway RC | 5.00 | 2.00 |
| ❏ 169 Cecil Sapp RC | 4.00 | 1.50 |
| ❏ 170 Kerry Carter RC | 4.00 | 1.50 |
| ❏ 171 Dahrran Diedrick RC | 4.00 | 1.50 |
| ❏ 171A Terrence Edwards RC | 4.00 | 1.50 |
| ❏ 172 Joffrey Reynolds RC | 4.00 | 1.50 |
| ❏ 173 Sultan McCullough RC | 4.00 | 1.50 |
| ❏ 174 Brandon Drumm RC | 4.00 | 1.50 |
| ❏ 175 Casey Moore RC | 4.00 | 1.50 |
| ❏ 176 Gerald Hayes RC | 5.00 | 2.00 |
| ❏ 178 Jamal Burke RC | 4.00 | 1.50 |
| ❏ 179 Antonio Chatman RC | 6.00 | 2.50 |
| ❏ 180 Reggie Newhouse RC | 4.00 | 1.50 |
| ❏ 181 Chris Horn RC | 5.00 | 2.00 |
| ❏ 182 Denero Marshall RC | 4.00 | 1.50 |
| ❏ 183 DeAndrew Rubin RC | 4.00 | 1.50 |
| ❏ 184 Taco Wallace RC | 4.00 | 1.50 |
| ❏ 185 Doug Gabriel RC | 5.00 | 2.00 |
| ❏ 186 Willie Ponder RC | 4.00 | 1.50 |
| ❏ 187 David Tyree RC | 6.00 | 2.50 |
| ❏ 188 Kevin Walter RC | 6.00 | 2.50 |
| ❏ 189 Zuriel Smith RC | 4.00 | 1.50 |
| ❏ 190 Keenan Howry RC | 4.00 | 1.50 |
| ❏ 191 C.J. Jones RC | 4.00 | 1.50 |
| ❏ 192 Arnaz Battle RC | 6.00 | 2.50 |
| ❏ 193 Walter Young RC | 4.00 | 1.50 |
| ❏ 194 Anthony Adams RC | 5.00 | 2.00 |
| ❏ 195 Jerome McDougle RC | 4.00 | 1.50 |
| ❏ 196 Will Heller RC | 5.00 | 2.00 |
| ❏ 197 Cecil Moore RC | 4.00 | 1.50 |

| | | |
|---|---|---|
| ❏ 198 Mike Seidman RC | 4.00 | 1.50 |
| ❏ 199 Jason Witten RC | 30.00 | 15.00 |
| ❏ 200 L.J. Smith RC | 6.00 | 2.50 |
| ❏ 201 Bennie Joppru RC | 4.00 | 1.50 |
| ❏ 202 Donald Lee RC | 5.00 | 2.00 |
| ❏ 203 Aaron Walker RC | 5.00 | 2.00 |
| ❏ 204 Antonio Brown RC | 4.00 | 1.50 |
| ❏ 205 George Wrighster RC | 4.00 | 1.50 |
| ❏ 206 Danny Curley RC | 4.00 | 1.50 |
| ❏ 207 Mike Banks RC | 4.00 | 1.50 |
| ❏ 208 Mike Pinkard RC | 4.00 | 1.50 |
| ❏ 209 Ryan Hoag RC | 4.00 | 1.50 |
| ❏ 210 Brad Pyatt RC | 4.00 | 1.50 |
| ❏ 211 Charles Rogers RC | 5.00 | 2.00 |
| ❏ 212 Chris Simms AU/250 RC | 60.00 | 25.00 |
| ❏ 213 Nate Hybl AU RC | 12.00 | 5.00 |
| ❏ 214 Brandon Lloyd AU RC | 15.00 | 6.00 |
| ❏ 215 ReShard Lee AU RC | 10.00 | 4.00 |
| ❏ 216 Dwone Hicks AU RC | 10.00 | 4.00 |
| ❏ 217 Tony Romo AU RC | 600.00 | 300.00 |
| ❏ 218 Brett Engemann AU RC | 10.00 | 4.00 |
| ❏ 219 Nick Maddox AU RC | 10.00 | 4.00 |
| ❏ 220 James MacPherson AU RC | 12.00 | 5.00 |
| ❏ 221 Juston Wood AU RC | 10.00 | 4.00 |
| ❏ 222 Adrian Madise AU RC | 10.00 | 4.00 |
| ❏ 223 Shaun McDonald AU RC | 15.00 | 6.00 |
| ❏ 224 Carl Ford AU RC | 10.00 | 4.00 |
| ❏ 225 Vishante Shiancoe AU RC | 15.00 | 6.00 |
| ❏ 226 Gibran Hamdan AU RC | 10.00 | 4.00 |
| ❏ 227 Brooks Bollinger AU RC | 15.00 | 6.00 |
| ❏ 228 B.J. Askew AU RC | 12.00 | 5.00 |
| ❏ 229 Domanick Davis AU RC | 15.00 | 6.00 |
| ❏ 230 LaBrandon Toefield AU RC | 12.00 | 5.00 |
| ❏ 231 Bobby Wade AU RC | 12.00 | 5.00 |
| ❏ 232 Justin Gage AU RC | 12.00 | 5.00 |
| ❏ 233 Billy McMullen AU RC | 10.00 | 4.00 |
| ❏ 234 David Kircus AU RC | 15.00 | 6.00 |
| ❏ 235 J.R. Tolver AU RC | 12.00 | 5.00 |
| ❏ 236 Sam Aiken AU RC | 12.00 | 5.00 |
| ❏ 237 LaTarence Dunbar AU RC | 10.00 | 4.00 |
| ❏ 238 Kassim Osgood AU RC | 15.00 | 6.00 |
| ❏ 239 Tony Hollings AU RC | 12.00 | 5.00 |
| ❏ 240 Justin Griffith AU RC | 12.00 | 5.00 |
| ❏ 241 Brian St.Pierre JSY AU RC | 20.00 | 8.00 |
| ❏ 242 Kevin Curtis JSY RC | 25.00 | 10.00 |
| ❏ 243 Dallas Clark JSY RC | 30.00 | 12.00 |
| ❏ 244 Willis McGahee JSY RC | 50.00 | 20.00 |
| ❏ 245 Terence Newman JSY AU RC | 25.00 | 10.00 |
| ❏ 246 Justin Fargas JSY AU RC | 40.00 | 15.00 |
| ❏ 247 Artose Pinner JSY RC | 12.00 | 5.00 |
| ❏ 248 Kelley Washington JSY RC | 15.00 | 6.00 |
| ❏ 249 DeWayne Robertson JSY RC | 15.00 | 6.00 |
| ❏ 250 Nate Burleson JSY RC | 15.00 | 6.00 |
| ❏ 251 Kliff Kingsbury JSY RC | 15.00 | 6.00 |
| ❏ 252 Bethel Johnson JSY RC | 15.00 | 6.00 |
| ❏ 253 Anquan Boldin JSY RC | 60.00 | 30.00 |
| ❏ 254 Bryant Johnson JSY AU RC | 40.00 | 15.00 |
| ❏ 255 Terrell Suggs JSY AU RC | 50.00 | 20.00 |
| ❏ 256 Musa Smith JSY RC | 15.00 | 6.00 |
| ❏ 257 Chris Brown JSY RC | 20.00 | 8.00 |
| ❏ 258 Marcus Trufant JSY RC | 20.00 | 8.00 |
| ❏ 259 Troy Johnson JSY RC | 15.00 | 6.00 |
| ❏ 260 Tyrone Calico JSY RC | 15.00 | 6.00 |
| ❏ 261 Dave Ragone JSY AU RC | 25.00 | 10.00 |
| ❏ 262 Kyle Boller JSY AU RC | 40.00 | 15.00 |
| ❏ 263 Onterrio Smith JSY AU RC | 30.00 | 12.00 |
| ❏ 264 Rex Grossman JSY RC | 60.00 | 30.00 |
| ❏ 265 Larry Johnson JSY RC | 60.00 | 30.00 |
| ❏ 266 Seneca Wallace JSY AU RC | 50.00 | 20.00 |
| ❏ 268 Taylor Jacobs JSY AU RC | 30.00 | 12.00 |
| ❏ 269 Byron Leftwich JSY AU RC | 60.00 | 25.00 |
| ❏ 270 Carson Palmer JSY AU RC | 300.00 | 150.00 |

## 2004 SP Authentic

| | | |
|---|---|---|
| ❏ COMP.SET w/o SP's (90) | 25.00 | 10.00 |
| ❏ 151-185 AU RC PRINT RUN 799 | | |
| ❏ 186-200 JSY AU RC PRINT RUN 990 SER.#d SETS | | |
| ❏ 201-206 JSY AU RC PRINT RUN 499 | | |
| ❏ 207-216 JSY AU RC PRINT RUN 299 | | |
| ❏ 1 Josh McCown | .75 | .30 |
| ❏ 2 Anquan Boldin | 1.00 | .40 |
| ❏ 3 Michael Vick | 1.00 | .40 |
| ❏ 4 Peerless Price | .75 | .30 |
| ❏ 5 Todd Heap | .75 | .30 |
| ❏ 6 Kyle Boller | .75 | .30 |

| | | |
|---|---|---|
| ❏ 7 Jamal Lewis | .75 | .30 |
| ❏ 8 Drew Bledsoe | 1.00 | .40 |
| ❏ 9 Travis Henry | .75 | .30 |
| ❏ 10 Eric Moulds | .75 | .30 |
| ❏ 11 Steve Smith | 1.00 | .40 |
| ❏ 12 Stephen Davis | .75 | .30 |
| ❏ 13 Jake Delhomme | .75 | .30 |
| ❏ 14 Rex Grossman | 1.00 | .40 |
| ❏ 15 Brian Urlacher | 1.00 | .40 |
| ❏ 16 Thomas Jones | .75 | .30 |
| ❏ 17 Chad Johnson | .75 | .30 |
| ❏ 18 Rudi Johnson | .75 | .30 |
| ❏ 19 Carson Palmer | 1.25 | .50 |
| ❏ 20 William Green | .60 | .25 |
| ❏ 21 Andre Davis | .60 | .25 |
| ❏ 22 Jeff Garcia | .75 | .30 |
| ❏ 23 Roy Williams | .75 | .30 |
| ❏ 24 Eddie George | .75 | .30 |
| ❏ 25 Keyshawn Johnson | .75 | .30 |
| ❏ 26 Ashley Lelie | .75 | .30 |
| ❏ 27 Jake Plummer | .75 | .30 |
| ❏ 28 Champ Bailey | .75 | .30 |
| ❏ 29 Charles Rogers | .75 | .30 |
| ❏ 30 Joey Harrington | .75 | .30 |
| ❏ 31 Ahman Green | 1.00 | .40 |
| ❏ 32 Brett Favre | 2.50 | 1.00 |
| ❏ 33 Javon Walker | .75 | .30 |
| ❏ 34 David Carr | .75 | .30 |
| ❏ 35 Domanick Davis | 1.00 | .40 |
| ❏ 36 Andre Johnson | 1.00 | .40 |
| ❏ 37 Marvin Harrison | 1.00 | .40 |
| ❏ 38 Edgerrin James | 1.00 | .40 |
| ❏ 39 Peyton Manning | 2.00 | .75 |
| ❏ 40 Byron Leftwich | 1.00 | .40 |
| ❏ 41 Fred Taylor | .75 | .30 |
| ❏ 42 Trent Green | .75 | .30 |
| ❏ 43 Tony Gonzalez | 1.00 | .40 |
| ❏ 44 Priest Holmes | 1.00 | .40 |
| ❏ 45 Ricky Williams | .75 | .30 |
| ❏ 46 Chris Chambers | .75 | .30 |
| ❏ 47 Jay Fiedler | .60 | .25 |
| ❏ 48 Daunte Culpepper | 1.00 | .40 |
| ❏ 49 Randy Moss | 1.25 | .50 |
| ❏ 50 Onterrio Smith | .60 | .25 |
| ❏ 51 Tom Brady | 2.50 | 1.00 |
| ❏ 52 Troy Brown | .75 | .30 |
| ❏ 53 Corey Dillon | .75 | .30 |
| ❏ 54 Deuce McAllister | 1.00 | .40 |
| ❏ 55 Aaron Brooks | .75 | .30 |
| ❏ 56 Joe Horn | .75 | .30 |
| ❏ 57 Amani Toomer | .75 | .30 |
| ❏ 58 Kurt Warner | 1.00 | .40 |
| ❏ 59 Jeremy Shockey | 1.00 | .40 |
| ❏ 60 Chad Pennington | 1.00 | .40 |
| ❏ 61 Santana Moss | .75 | .30 |
| ❏ 62 Curtis Martin | 1.00 | .40 |
| ❏ 63 Rich Gannon | .75 | .30 |
| ❏ 64 Jerry Rice | 2.00 | .75 |
| ❏ 65 Kevin Porter | .75 | .30 |
| ❏ 66 Terrell Owens | 1.00 | .40 |
| ❏ 67 Jevon Kearse | .75 | .30 |
| ❏ 68 Donovan McNabb | 1.00 | .40 |
| ❏ 69 Hines Ward | 1.00 | .40 |
| ❏ 70 Plaxico Burress | .75 | .30 |
| ❏ 71 Tommy Maddox | .75 | .30 |
| ❏ 72 Drew Brees | 1.00 | .40 |
| ❏ 73 LaDainian Tomlinson | 1.50 | .60 |
| ❏ 74 Tim Rattay | .60 | .25 |

| | | |
|---|---|---|
| ❑ 75 Brandon Lloyd | .60 | .25 |
| ❑ 76 Kevan Barlow | .75 | .30 |
| ❑ 77 Shaun Alexander | 1.00 | .40 |
| ❑ 78 Koren Robinson | 1.00 | .40 |
| ❑ 79 Matt Hasselbeck | 1.00 | .40 |
| ❑ 80 Marshall Faulk | 1.00 | .40 |
| ❑ 81 Torry Holt | 1.00 | .40 |
| ❑ 82 Marc Bulger | .75 | .30 |
| ❑ 83 Brad Johnson | .75 | .30 |
| ❑ 84 Joey Galloway | .75 | .30 |
| ❑ 85 Steve McNair | 1.00 | .40 |
| ❑ 86 Derrick Mason | .75 | .30 |
| ❑ 87 Chris Brown | .75 | .30 |
| ❑ 88 Mark Brunell | .75 | .30 |
| ❑ 89 Laveranues Coles | .75 | .30 |
| ❑ 90 Clinton Portis | 1.00 | .40 |
| ❑ 91 Triandos Luke RC | 4.00 | 1.50 |
| ❑ 92 Keith Smith RC | 4.00 | 1.50 |
| ❑ 93 Shaun Phillips RC | 4.00 | 1.50 |
| ❑ 94 D.J. Williams RC | 6.00 | 2.50 |
| ❑ 95 Keiwan Ratliff RC | 4.00 | 1.50 |
| ❑ 96 Madieu Williams RC | 4.00 | 1.50 |
| ❑ 97 Chris Cooley RC | 5.00 | 2.00 |
| ❑ 98 Stuart Schweigert RC | 5.00 | 2.00 |
| ❑ 99 Sloan Thomas RC | 5.00 | 2.00 |
| ❑ 100 Chad Lavalais RC | 4.00 | 1.50 |
| ❑ 101 Jared Allen RC | 8.00 | 3.00 |
| ❑ 102 Brian Jones RC | 4.00 | 1.50 |
| ❑ 103 Matt Ware RC | 6.00 | 2.50 |
| ❑ 104 Daryl Smith RC | 5.00 | 2.00 |
| ❑ 105 J.R. Reed RC | 4.00 | 1.50 |
| ❑ 106 D.J. Hackett RC | 6.00 | 2.50 |
| ❑ 107 Jeris McIntyre RC | 4.00 | 1.50 |
| ❑ 108 Dexter Reid RC | 4.00 | 1.50 |
| ❑ 109 Courtney Anderson RC | 4.00 | 1.50 |
| ❑ 110 Courtney Watson RC | 5.00 | 2.00 |
| ❑ 111 Jimmy Croom RC | 4.00 | 1.50 |
| ❑ 112 Jonathan Smith RC | 4.00 | 1.50 |
| ❑ 113 Vernon Carey RC | 4.00 | 1.50 |
| ❑ 114 Michael Gaines RC | 4.00 | 1.50 |
| ❑ 115 Chris Snee RC | 5.00 | 2.00 |
| ❑ 116 Nathan Vasher RC | 6.00 | 2.50 |
| ❑ 117 Teddy Lehman RC | 5.00 | 2.00 |
| ❑ 118 Marcus Tubbs RC | 4.00 | 1.50 |
| ❑ 119 Ben Utecht RC | 5.00 | 2.00 |
| ❑ 120 Maurice Mann RC | 4.00 | 1.50 |
| ❑ 121 Thomas Tapeh RC | 5.00 | 2.00 |
| ❑ 122 Will Allen RC | 5.00 | 2.00 |
| ❑ 123 Demorrio Williams RC | 6.00 | 2.50 |
| ❑ 124 Ran Carthon RC | 4.00 | 1.50 |
| ❑ 125 Tim Euhus RC | 4.00 | 1.50 |
| ❑ 126 Bradlee Van Pelt RC | 5.00 | 2.00 |
| ❑ 127 Patrick Crayton RC | 8.00 | 3.00 |
| ❑ 128 Ryan Krause RC | 4.00 | 1.50 |
| ❑ 129 Joey Thomas RC | 4.00 | 1.50 |
| ❑ 130 Antwan Odom RC | 5.00 | 2.00 |
| ❑ 131 Karlos Dansby RC | 6.00 | 2.50 |
| ❑ 132 Junior Siavii RC | 4.00 | 1.50 |
| ❑ 133 Jamaar Taylor RC | 4.00 | 1.50 |
| ❑ 134 Kendrick Starling RC | 4.00 | 1.50 |
| ❑ 135 Wes Welker RC | 15.00 | 6.00 |
| ❑ 136 Igor Olshansky RC | 6.00 | 2.50 |
| ❑ 137 Mark Jones RC | 4.00 | 1.50 |
| ❑ 138 Bruce Thornton RC | 4.00 | 1.50 |
| ❑ 139 Michael Boulware RC | 6.00 | 2.50 |
| ❑ 140 Matt Mauck RC | 5.00 | 2.00 |
| ❑ 141 Clarence Moore RC | 5.00 | 2.00 |
| ❑ 142 Derrick Strait RC | 5.00 | 2.00 |
| ❑ 143 Jarrett Payton RC | 5.00 | 2.00 |
| ❑ 144 Dontarrious Thomas RC | 5.00 | 2.00 |
| ❑ 145 Shawntae Spencer RC | 4.00 | 1.50 |
| ❑ 146 Bob Sanders RC | 20.00 | 8.00 |
| ❑ 147 Darnell Dockett RC | 4.00 | 1.50 |
| ❑ 148 Sean Taylor RC | 6.00 | 2.50 |
| ❑ 149 Jason Babin RC | 5.00 | 2.00 |
| ❑ 150 Ricardo Colclough RC | 6.00 | 2.50 |
| ❑ 151 Brandon Chillar AU RC | 12.00 | 5.00 |
| ❑ 152 Clarence Farmer AU RC | 10.00 | 4.00 |
| ❑ 153 B.J. Symons AU RC | 10.00 | 4.00 |
| ❑ 154 John Navarre AU RC | 12.00 | 5.00 |
| ❑ 155 P.K. Sam AU RC | 10.00 | 4.00 |
| ❑ 156 Casey Clausen AU RC | 12.00 | 5.00 |
| ❑ 157 Drew Henson AU RC | 12.00 | 5.00 |
| ❑ 158 Kris Wilson AU RC | 12.00 | 5.00 |
| ❑ 159 Vince Wilfork AU RC | 15.00 | 6.00 |

| | | |
|---|---|---|
| ❑ 160 Michael Turner AU RC | 100.00 | 50.00 |
| ❑ 161 Jonathan Vilma AU RC | 20.00 | 8.00 |
| ❑ 162 Samie Parker AU RC | 12.00 | 5.00 |
| ❑ 163 B.J. Sams AU RC | 12.00 | 5.00 |
| ❑ 164 A.Echemandu AU RC | 12.00 | 5.00 |
| ❑ 165 Ernest Wilford AU RC | 15.00 | 6.00 |
| ❑ 166 Troy Fleming AU RC | 12.00 | 5.00 |
| ❑ 167 Tommie Harris AU RC | 20.00 | 8.00 |
| ❑ 168 Jammal Lord AU RC | 12.00 | 5.00 |
| ❑ 169 Kenechi Udeze AU RC | 15.00 | 6.00 |
| ❑ 170 Chris Gamble AU RC | 15.00 | 6.00 |
| ❑ 171 Carlos Francis AU RC | 12.00 | 5.00 |
| ❑ 172 Mewelde Moore AU RC | 20.00 | 8.00 |
| ❑ 173 Jared Lorenzen AU RC | 12.00 | 5.00 |
| ❑ 174 Jeff Smoker AU RC | 12.00 | 5.00 |
| ❑ 175 Ben Hartsock AU RC | 12.00 | 5.00 |
| ❑ 176 Jerricho Cotchery AU RC | 20.00 | 10.00 |
| ❑ 177 Josh Harris AU RC | 10.00 | 4.00 |
| ❑ 178 Cody Pickett AU RC | 12.00 | 5.00 |
| ❑ 179 Quincy Wilson AU RC | 12.00 | 5.00 |
| ❑ 180 Will Smith AU RC | 12.00 | 5.00 |
| ❑ 181 Ahmad Carroll AU RC | 15.00 | 6.00 |
| ❑ 182 B.J. Johnson AU RC | 10.00 | 4.00 |
| ❑ 183 Dunta Robinson AU RC | 12.00 | 5.00 |
| ❑ 184 Craig Krenzel AU RC | 15.00 | 6.00 |
| ❑ 185 Johnnie Morant AU RC | 12.00 | 5.00 |
| ❑ 186 Cedric Cobbs JSY AU RC | 40.00 | 15.00 |
| ❑ 187 Matt Schaub JSY AU RC | 100.00 | 50.00 |
| ❑ 188 Bernard Berrian JSY AU RC | 50.00 | 20.00 |
| ❑ 189 Devard Darling JSY AU RC | 40.00 | 15.00 |
| ❑ 190 Ben Watson JSY AU RC | 50.00 | 20.00 |
| ❑ 191 Darius Watts JSY AU RC | 40.00 | 15.00 |
| ❑ 192 DeAngelo Hall JSY AU RC | 40.00 | 15.00 |
| ❑ 193 Ben Troupe JSY AU RC | 40.00 | 15.00 |
| ❑ 194 Mich Jenkins JSY AU RC | 50.00 | 20.00 |
| ❑ 195 Keary Colbert JSY AU RC | 50.00 | 20.00 |
| ❑ 196 Robert Gallery JSY AU RC | 50.00 | 20.00 |
| ❑ 197 Greg Jones JSY AU RC | 50.00 | 20.00 |
| ❑ 198 Mich.Clayton JSY AU RC | 40.00 | 15.00 |
| ❑ 199 Luke McCown JSY AU RC | 50.00 | 20.00 |
| ❑ 200 Derrick Hamilton JSY AU RC | 30.00 | 12.00 |
| ❑ 201 Ras.Woods JSY AU RC | 60.00 | 25.00 |
| ❑ 202 Chris Perry JSY AU RC | 60.00 | 25.00 |
| ❑ 203 D.Henderson JSY AU RC | 60.00 | 25.00 |
| ❑ 204 Tatum Bell JSY AU RC | 60.00 | 25.00 |
| ❑ 205 Lee Evans JSY AU RC | 80.00 | 30.00 |
| ❑ 206 J.P. Losman JSY AU RC | 100.00 | 50.00 |
| ❑ 207 Kel.Winslow JSY AU RC | 125.00 | 75.00 |
| ❑ 208 Reg.Williams JSY AU RC | 40.00 | 15.00 |
| ❑ 209 Julius Jones JSY AU RC | 120.00 | 60.00 |
| ❑ 210 S.Jackson JSY AU RC | 250.00 | 125.00 |
| ❑ 211 Kevin Jones JSY AU RC | 80.00 | 30.00 |
| ❑ 212 Roethlisberger JSY AU RC | 600.00 | 450.00 |
| ❑ 213 Philip Rivers JSY AU RC | 350.00 | 200.00 |
| ❑ 215 L.Fitzgerald JSY AU RC | 350.00 | 200.00 |
| ❑ 216 Eli Manning JSY AU RC | 500.00 | 250.00 |

## 2005 SP Authentic

| | | |
|---|---|---|
| ❑ COMP.SET w/ RC's (90) | 25.00 | 10.00 |
| ❑ 91-180 PRINT RUN 750 SER.#'d SETS | | |
| ❑ 181-220/254-257 PRINT RUN 850 SETS | | |
| ❑ 221-253 PRINT RUN 99-899 SER.#'d SETS | | |
| ❑ UNPRICED NFL LOGO PATCHES #'d TO 1 | | |
| ❑ 1 Kurt Warner | 1.00 | .40 |
| ❑ 2 Larry Fitzgerald | 1.00 | .40 |
| ❑ 3 Anquan Boldin | .75 | .30 |
| ❑ 4 Michael Vick | 1.00 | .40 |

| | | |
|---|---|---|
| ❑ 5 Alge Crumpler | .75 | .30 |
| ❑ 6 Warrick Dunn | .75 | .30 |
| ❑ 7 Kyle Boller | .75 | .30 |
| ❑ 8 Jamal Lewis | .75 | .30 |
| ❑ 9 J.P. Losman | 1.00 | .40 |
| ❑ 10 Willis McGahee | 1.00 | .40 |
| ❑ 11 Lee Evans | .75 | .30 |
| ❑ 12 Jake Delhomme | 1.00 | .40 |
| ❑ 13 DeShaun Foster | .75 | .30 |
| ❑ 14 Muhsin Muhammad | .75 | .30 |
| ❑ 15 Walter Payton | 2.50 | 1.00 |
| ❑ 16 Brian Urlacher | 1.00 | .40 |
| ❑ 17 Carson Palmer | 1.00 | .40 |
| ❑ 18 Rudi Johnson | .75 | .30 |
| ❑ 19 Chad Johnson | .75 | .30 |
| ❑ 20 Lee Suggs | .75 | .30 |
| ❑ 21 Antonio Bryant | .60 | .25 |
| ❑ 22 Julius Jones | 1.00 | .40 |
| ❑ 23 Drew Bledsoe | 1.00 | .40 |
| ❑ 24 Keyshawn Johnson | .75 | .30 |
| ❑ 25 Tatum Bell | .75 | .30 |
| ❑ 26 Jake Plummer | .75 | .30 |
| ❑ 27 Roy Williams WR | 1.00 | .40 |
| ❑ 28 Kevin Jones | .75 | .30 |
| ❑ 29 Jeff Garcia | .75 | .30 |
| ❑ 30 Brett Favre | 2.50 | 1.00 |
| ❑ 31 Ahman Green | 1.00 | .40 |
| ❑ 32 Javon Walker | .75 | .30 |
| ❑ 33 David Carr | .75 | .30 |
| ❑ 34 Andre Johnson | .75 | .30 |
| ❑ 35 Domanick Davis | .60 | .25 |
| ❑ 36 Peyton Manning | 1.50 | .60 |
| ❑ 37 Edgerrin James | .75 | .30 |
| ❑ 38 Reggie Wayne | .75 | .30 |
| ❑ 39 Byron Leftwich | .75 | .30 |
| ❑ 40 Fred Taylor | 1.00 | .40 |
| ❑ 41 Jimmy Smith | .75 | .30 |
| ❑ 42 Priest Holmes | 1.00 | .40 |
| ❑ 43 Larry Johnson | 1.00 | .40 |
| ❑ 44 Trent Green | .75 | .30 |
| ❑ 45 Randy McMichael | .60 | .25 |
| ❑ 46 Chris Chambers | .75 | .30 |
| ❑ 47 Ricky Williams | 1.00 | .40 |
| ❑ 48 Daunte Culpepper | 1.00 | .40 |
| ❑ 49 Nate Burleson | .75 | .30 |
| ❑ 50 Tom Brady | 2.00 | .75 |
| ❑ 51 Corey Dillon | .75 | .30 |
| ❑ 52 David Givens | .75 | .30 |
| ❑ 53 Aaron Brooks | .60 | .25 |
| ❑ 54 Deuce McAllister | 1.00 | .40 |
| ❑ 55 Joe Horn | .75 | .30 |
| ❑ 56 Eli Manning | 2.00 | .75 |
| ❑ 57 Jeremy Shockey | 1.00 | .40 |
| ❑ 58 Tiki Barber | 1.00 | .40 |
| ❑ 59 Chad Pennington | 1.00 | .40 |
| ❑ 60 Santana Moss | .75 | .30 |
| ❑ 61 Curtis Martin | 1.00 | .40 |
| ❑ 62 Randy Moss | 1.00 | .40 |
| ❑ 63 LaMont Jordan | .75 | .30 |
| ❑ 64 Kerry Collins | .75 | .30 |
| ❑ 65 Donovan McNabb | 1.00 | .40 |
| ❑ 66 Brian Westbrook | 1.00 | .40 |
| ❑ 67 Terrell Owens | 1.00 | .40 |
| ❑ 68 Ben Roethlisberger | 2.50 | 1.00 |
| ❑ 69 Hines Ward | 1.00 | .40 |
| ❑ 70 Jerome Bettis | 1.00 | .40 |
| ❑ 71 Drew Brees | 1.00 | .40 |
| ❑ 72 Antonio Gates | 1.00 | .40 |
| ❑ 73 LaDainian Tomlinson | 1.50 | .60 |
| ❑ 74 Kevan Barlow | .60 | .25 |
| ❑ 75 Brandon Lloyd | .60 | .25 |
| ❑ 76 Matt Hasselbeck | .75 | .30 |
| ❑ 77 Shaun Alexander | 1.00 | .40 |
| ❑ 78 Darrell Jackson | .75 | .30 |
| ❑ 79 Marc Bulger | .75 | .30 |
| ❑ 80 Steven Jackson | 1.25 | .50 |
| ❑ 81 Torry Holt | .75 | .30 |
| ❑ 82 Brian Griese | .75 | .30 |
| ❑ 83 Michael Clayton | .75 | .30 |
| ❑ 84 Michael Pittman | .60 | .25 |
| ❑ 85 Steve McNair | 1.00 | .40 |
| ❑ 86 Drew Bennett | .75 | .30 |
| ❑ 87 Chris Brown | .75 | .30 |
| ❑ 88 Clinton Portis | 1.00 | .40 |
| ❑ 89 Patrick Ramsey | .75 | .30 |

| | | |
|---|---|---|
| ☐ 90 Laveranues Coles | .75 | .30 |
| ☐ 91 Nehemiah Broughton RC | 5.00 | 2.00 |
| ☐ 92 Madison Hedgecock RC | 6.00 | 2.50 |
| ☐ 93 Damien Nash RC | 5.00 | 2.00 |
| ☐ 94 Michael Boley RC | 4.00 | 1.50 |
| ☐ 95 Lionel Gates RC | 4.00 | 1.50 |
| ☐ 96 Noah Herron RC | 6.00 | 2.50 |
| ☐ 97 Bo Scaife RC | 5.00 | 2.00 |
| ☐ 98 Joel Dreessen RC | 5.00 | 2.00 |
| ☐ 99 Rasheed Marshall RC | 5.00 | 2.00 |
| ☐ 100 Andre Maddox RC | 4.00 | 1.50 |
| ☐ 101 Tab Perry RC | 6.00 | 2.50 |
| ☐ 102 Dante Ridgeway RC | 4.00 | 1.50 |
| ☐ 103 Patrick Estes RC | 4.00 | 1.50 |
| ☐ 104 Billy Bajema RC | 4.00 | 1.50 |
| ☐ 105 Paris Warren RC | 5.00 | 2.00 |
| ☐ 106 LeRon McCoy RC | 4.00 | 1.50 |
| ☐ 107 Adam Bergen RC | 4.00 | 1.50 |
| ☐ 108 Manuel White RC | 5.00 | 2.00 |
| ☐ 109 Stephen Spach RC | 4.00 | 1.50 |
| ☐ 110 Donte Nicholson RC | 5.00 | 2.00 |
| ☐ 111 Brodney Pool RC | 5.00 | 2.00 |
| ☐ 112 Stanford Routt RC | 5.00 | 2.00 |
| ☐ 113 Josh Bullocks RC | 6.00 | 2.50 |
| ☐ 114 Ronald Bartell RC | 5.00 | 2.00 |
| ☐ 115 Nick Collins RC | 6.00 | 2.50 |
| ☐ 116 Darrent Williams RC | 5.00 | 2.00 |
| ☐ 117 Justin Miller RC | 5.00 | 2.00 |
| ☐ 118 Kelvin Hayden RC | 5.00 | 2.00 |
| ☐ 119 Bryant McFadden RC | 5.00 | 2.00 |
| ☐ 120 Oshiomogho Atogwe RC | 4.00 | 1.50 |
| ☐ 121 Stanley Wilson RC | 5.00 | 2.00 |
| ☐ 122 Eric Green RC | 4.00 | 1.50 |
| ☐ 123 Michael Hawkins RC | 4.00 | 1.50 |
| ☐ 124 Marcus Spears RC | 6.00 | 2.50 |
| ☐ 125 Ellis Hobbs RC | 6.00 | 2.50 |
| ☐ 126 Scott Starks RC | 5.00 | 2.00 |
| ☐ 127 Domonique Foxworth RC | 5.00 | 2.00 |
| ☐ 128 Sean Considine RC | 5.00 | 2.00 |
| ☐ 129 James Sanders RC | 4.00 | 1.50 |
| ☐ 130 Travis Daniels RC | 5.00 | 2.00 |
| ☐ 131 Vincent Fuller RC | 5.00 | 2.00 |
| ☐ 132 Marviel Underwood RC | 5.00 | 2.00 |
| ☐ 133 Jerome Carter RC | 4.00 | 1.50 |
| ☐ 134 Kerry Rhodes RC | 6.00 | 2.50 |
| ☐ 135 Fred Amey RC | 5.00 | 2.00 |
| ☐ 136 Eric King RC | 4.00 | 1.50 |
| ☐ 137 Derrick Johnson CB RC | 4.00 | 1.50 |
| ☐ 138 Luis Castillo RC | 6.00 | 2.50 |
| ☐ 139 Shaun Cody RC | 5.00 | 2.00 |
| ☐ 140 Matt Roth RC | 6.00 | 2.50 |
| ☐ 141 Jonathan Babineaux RC | 5.00 | 2.00 |
| ☐ 142 Justin Tuck RC | 15.00 | 6.00 |
| ☐ 143 Sione Pouha RC | 4.00 | 1.50 |
| ☐ 144 Daven Holly RC | 4.00 | 1.50 |
| ☐ 145 Vincent Burns RC | 4.00 | 1.50 |
| ☐ 146 Derrick Johnson RC | 5.00 | 2.00 |
| ☐ 147 Lofa Tatupu RC | 8.00 | 3.00 |
| ☐ 148 Odell Thurman RC | 6.00 | 2.50 |
| ☐ 149 Rick Razzano RC | 4.00 | 1.50 |
| ☐ 150 Channing Crowder RC | 5.00 | 2.00 |
| ☐ 151 Kirk Morrison RC | 5.00 | 2.00 |
| ☐ 152 Alfred Fincher RC | 4.00 | 1.50 |
| ☐ 153 Jordan Beck RC | 5.00 | 2.00 |
| ☐ 154 Darryl Blackstock RC | 4.00 | 1.50 |
| ☐ 155 Leroy Hill RC | 6.00 | 2.50 |
| ☐ 156 Jammal Brown RC | 6.00 | 2.50 |
| ☐ 157 Alex Barron RC | 5.00 | 2.00 |
| ☐ 158 Chris Spencer RC | 6.00 | 2.50 |
| ☐ 159 Logan Mankins RC | 5.00 | 2.00 |
| ☐ 160 David Baas RC | 4.00 | 1.50 |
| ☐ 161 Michael Roos RC | 4.00 | 1.50 |
| ☐ 162 Kurt Campbell RC | 4.00 | 1.50 |
| ☐ 163 Khalif Barnes RC | 4.00 | 1.50 |
| ☐ 164 Antonio Perkins RC | 5.00 | 2.00 |
| ☐ 165 Vonta Leach RC | 4.00 | 1.50 |
| ☐ 166 Brady Poppinga RC | 6.00 | 2.50 |
| ☐ 167 Trent Cole RC | 6.00 | 2.50 |
| ☐ 168 Dave Rayner RC | 4.00 | 1.50 |
| ☐ 169 Bill Swancutt RC | 4.00 | 1.50 |
| ☐ 170 Eric Moore RC | 4.00 | 1.50 |
| ☐ 171 Justin Green RC | 6.00 | 2.50 |
| ☐ 172 Shaun Suisham RC | 4.00 | 1.50 |
| ☐ 173 C.J. Mosley RC | 4.00 | 1.50 |
| ☐ 174 Ryan Riddle RC | 4.00 | 1.50 |

| | | |
|---|---|---|
| ☐ 175 Darrell Shropshire RC | 4.00 | 1.50 |
| ☐ 176 Boomer Grigsby RC | 6.00 | 2.50 |
| ☐ 177 Rian Wallace RC | 5.00 | 2.00 |
| ☐ 178 Lance Mitchell RC | 5.00 | 2.00 |
| ☐ 179 Nick Speegle RC | 4.00 | 1.50 |
| ☐ 180 Tyson Thompson RC | 6.00 | 2.50 |
| ☐ 181 Dan Orlovsky AU RC | 20.00 | 8.00 |
| ☐ 182 Anthony Davis AU RC | 12.00 | 5.00 |
| ☐ 183 Kay-Jay Harris AU RC | 12.00 | 5.00 |
| ☐ 184 Walter Reyes AU RC | 10.00 | 4.00 |
| ☐ 185 Darren Sproles AU RC | 50.00 | 30.00 |
| ☐ 186 Marlin Jackson AU RC | 12.00 | 5.00 |
| ☐ 187 Corey Webster AU RC | 20.00 | 8.00 |
| ☐ 188 Marion Barber AU RC | 150.00 | 75.00 |
| ☐ 189 Chris Henry AU RC | 15.00 | 6.00 |
| ☐ 190 Derek Anderson AU RC | 100.00 | 50.00 |
| ☐ 191 David Pollack AU RC | 12.00 | 5.00 |
| ☐ 192 Anttaj Hawthorne AU RC | 12.00 | 5.00 |
| ☐ 193 David Greene AU RC | 12.00 | 5.00 |
| ☐ 194 Erasmus James AU RC | 12.00 | 5.00 |
| ☐ 195 Ryan Fitzpatrick AU RC | 15.00 | 6.00 |
| ☐ 196 Derrick Johnson AU | 15.00 | 6.00 |
| ☐ 197 Barrett Ruud AU RC | 15.00 | 6.00 |
| ☐ 198 Kevin Burnett AU RC | 12.00 | 5.00 |
| ☐ 200 J.R. Russell AU RC | 10.00 | 4.00 |
| ☐ 201 Larry Brackins AU RC | 10.00 | 4.00 |
| ☐ 202 Thomas Davis AU RC | 12.00 | 5.00 |
| ☐ 203 Fred Gibson AU RC | 12.00 | 5.00 |
| ☐ 204 Craphonso Thorpe AU RC | 12.00 | 5.00 |
| ☐ 205 Brandon Jacobs AU RC | 60.00 | 30.00 |
| ☐ 206 Taylor Stubblefield AU RC | 10.00 | 4.00 |
| ☐ 207 Shawne Merriman AU RC | 50.00 | 25.00 |
| ☐ 208 Travis Johnson AU RC | 10.00 | 4.00 |
| ☐ 209 Adrian McPherson AU RC | 12.00 | 5.00 |
| ☐ 210 Brandon Jones AU RC | 15.00 | 6.00 |
| ☐ 211 Jerome Mathis AU RC | 15.00 | 6.00 |
| ☐ 212 Alex Smith TE AU RC | 15.00 | 6.00 |
| ☐ 213 Fabian Washington AU RC | 15.00 | 6.00 |
| ☐ 214 Mike Nugent AU RC | 12.00 | 5.00 |
| ☐ 215 Chase Lyman AU RC | 10.00 | 4.00 |
| ☐ 216 Roydell Williams AU RC | 12.00 | 5.00 |
| ☐ 217 Matt Cassel AU RC | 80.00 | 50.00 |
| ☐ 218 Alvin Pearman AU RC | 12.00 | 5.00 |
| ☐ 219 DeMarcus Ware AU RC | 40.00 | 20.00 |
| ☐ 220 Mike Patterson AU RC | 12.00 | 5.00 |
| ☐ 221 C.Roby JSY/899 AU RC | 30.00 | 12.00 |
| ☐ 222 E.Shelton JSY/899 AU RC | 30.00 | 12.00 |
| ☐ 223 S.LeFors JSY/899 AU RC | 30.00 | 12.00 |
| ☐ 224 Frank Gore JSY/899 AU RC | 150.00 | 75.00 |
| ☐ 225 Ryan Moats JSY/899 AU RC | 40.00 | 15.00 |
| ☐ 226 A.Walter JSY/899 AU RC | 40.00 | 15.00 |
| ☐ 227 A.Jones JSY/899 AU RC | 40.00 | 15.00 |
| ☐ 228 C.Rogers JSY/899 AU RC | 40.00 | 15.00 |
| ☐ 229 T.Murphy JSY/899 AU RC | 25.00 | 10.00 |
| ☐ 230 Kyle Orton JSY/699 AU RC | 60.00 | 35.00 |
| ☐ 231 C.Fason JSY/899 AU RC | 30.00 | 12.00 |
| ☐ 232 V.Morency JSY/699 AU RC | 40.00 | 15.00 |
| ☐ 233 R.Parrish JSY/699 AU RC | 30.00 | 12.00 |
| ☐ 234 V.Jackson JSY/699 AU RC | 40.00 | 15.00 |
| ☐ 235 M.Bradley JSY/699 AU RC | 40.00 | 15.00 |
| ☐ 236 Re.Brown JSY/599 AU RC | 40.00 | 15.00 |
| ☐ 237 Ro.White JSY/499 AU RC | 80.00 | 50.00 |
| ☐ 238 M.Clayton JSY/499 AU RC | 40.00 | 15.00 |
| ☐ 239 Antrel Rolle JSY/499 AU RC | 50.00 | 20.00 |
| ☐ 240 Maurice Clarett JSY/499 AU | 40.00 | 15.00 |
| ☐ 241 J.Arrington JSY/499 AU RC | 40.00 | 15.00 |
| ☐ 242 Matt Jones JSY/399 AU RC | 60.00 | 25.00 |
| ☐ 243 Ro.Brown JSY/299 AU RC | 250.00 | 125.00 |
| ☐ 244 C.Frye JSY/499 AU RC | 50.00 | 20.00 |
| ☐ 245 J.Campbell JSY/299 AU RC | 175.00 | 100.00 |
| ☐ 246 T.Willmson JSY/299 AU RC | 40.00 | 15.00 |
| ☐ 247 B.Edwrd JSY/299 AU RC | 150.00 | 90.00 |
| ☐ 248 A.Smith QB JSY/299 AU RC | 120.00 | 60.00 |
| ☐ 249 C.White JSY/299 AU RC | 120.00 | 60.00 |
| ☐ 250 H.Miller JSY/299 AU RC | 80.00 | 40.00 |
| ☐ 251 C.Benson JSY/99 AU RC | 60.00 | 30.00 |
| ☐ 252 A.Rodgers JSY/99 AU RC | 500.00 | 300.00 |
| ☐ 253 M.Williams JSY/99 AU | 80.00 | 40.00 |
| ☐ 254 Chris Carr AU RC | 12.00 | 5.00 |
| ☐ 255 Deandra Cobb AU RC | 12.00 | 5.00 |
| ☐ 256 James Kilian AU RC | 10.00 | 4.00 |
| ☐ 257 Airese Currie AU RC | 12.00 | 5.00 |

## 2006 SP Authentic

| | | |
|---|---|---|
| ☐ 1 Edgerrin James | .75 | .30 |
| ☐ 2 Larry Fitzgerald | 1.00 | .40 |
| ☐ 3 Anquan Boldin | .75 | .30 |
| ☐ 4 Michael Vick | 1.00 | .40 |
| ☐ 5 Warrick Dunn | .75 | .30 |
| ☐ 6 Alge Crumpler | .75 | .30 |
| ☐ 7 Steve McNair | .75 | .30 |
| ☐ 8 Jamal Lewis | .75 | .30 |
| ☐ 9 Derrick Mason | .75 | .30 |
| ☐ 10 Willis McGahee | 1.00 | .40 |
| ☐ 11 Lee Evans | .75 | .30 |
| ☐ 12 Jake Delhomme | .75 | .30 |
| ☐ 13 Steve Smith | 1.00 | .40 |
| ☐ 14 DeShaun Foster | .75 | .30 |
| ☐ 15 Rex Grossman | 1.00 | .40 |
| ☐ 16 Thomas Jones | 1.00 | .40 |
| ☐ 17 Brian Urlacher | 1.00 | .40 |
| ☐ 18 Carson Palmer | 1.00 | .40 |
| ☐ 19 Chad Johnson | .75 | .30 |
| ☐ 20 Rudi Johnson | .75 | .30 |
| ☐ 21 Charlie Frye | .75 | .30 |
| ☐ 22 Braylon Edwards | 1.00 | .40 |
| ☐ 23 Reuben Droughns | .75 | .30 |
| ☐ 24 Drew Bledsoe | 1.00 | .40 |
| ☐ 25 Terrell Owens | 1.00 | .40 |
| ☐ 26 Julius Jones | 1.00 | .40 |
| ☐ 27 Jake Plummer | .75 | .30 |
| ☐ 28 Tatum Bell | .75 | .30 |
| ☐ 29 Javon Walker | .75 | .30 |
| ☐ 30 Kevin Jones | 1.00 | .40 |
| ☐ 31 Roy Williams WR | .75 | .30 |
| ☐ 32 Brett Favre | 2.00 | .75 |
| ☐ 33 Donald Driver | .75 | .30 |
| ☐ 34 David Carr | .75 | .30 |
| ☐ 35 Ron Dayne | .75 | .30 |
| ☐ 36 Andre Johnson | .75 | .30 |
| ☐ 37 Peyton Manning | 1.50 | .60 |
| ☐ 38 Marvin Harrison | 1.00 | .40 |
| ☐ 39 Reggie Wayne | .75 | .30 |
| ☐ 40 Byron Leftwich | .75 | .30 |
| ☐ 41 Fred Taylor | .75 | .30 |
| ☐ 42 Matt Jones | .75 | .30 |
| ☐ 43 Trent Green | .75 | .30 |
| ☐ 44 Larry Johnson | .75 | .30 |
| ☐ 45 Tony Gonzalez | .75 | .30 |
| ☐ 46 Daunte Culpepper | 1.00 | .40 |
| ☐ 47 Ronnie Brown | 1.00 | .40 |
| ☐ 48 Chris Chambers | .75 | .30 |
| ☐ 49 Chester Taylor | .75 | .30 |
| ☐ 50 Troy Williamson | .75 | .30 |
| ☐ 51 Tom Brady | 1.50 | .60 |
| ☐ 52 Corey Dillon | .75 | .30 |
| ☐ 53 Troy Brown | .60 | .25 |
| ☐ 54 Drew Brees | 1.00 | .40 |
| ☐ 55 Deuce McAllister | .75 | .30 |
| ☐ 56 Joe Horn | .75 | .30 |
| ☐ 57 Eli Manning | 1.25 | .50 |
| ☐ 58 Tiki Barber | 1.00 | .40 |
| ☐ 59 Plaxico Burress | .75 | .30 |
| ☐ 60 Laveranues Coles | .75 | .30 |
| ☐ 61 Chad Pennington | .75 | .30 |
| ☐ 62 Aaron Brooks | .75 | .30 |
| ☐ 63 Randy Moss | 1.00 | .40 |
| ☐ 64 LaMont Jordan | .75 | .30 |
| ☐ 65 Donovan McNabb | 1.00 | .40 |
| ☐ 66 Brian Westbrook | .75 | .30 |
| ☐ 67 Ben Roethlisberger | 1.50 | .60 |

|  |  | | |
|---|---|---|---|
| ❏ 68 | Willie Parker | 1.25 | .50 |
| ❏ 69 | Hines Ward | 1.00 | .40 |
| ❏ 70 | Philip Rivers | 1.00 | .40 |
| ❏ 71 | LaDainian Tomlinson | 1.25 | .50 |
| ❏ 72 | Antonio Gates | 1.00 | .40 |
| ❏ 73 | Alex Smith QB | 1.00 | .40 |
| ❏ 74 | Frank Gore | 1.00 | .40 |
| ❏ 75 | Antonio Bryant | .75 | .30 |
| ❏ 76 | Matt Hasselbeck | .75 | .30 |
| ❏ 77 | Shaun Alexander | 1.00 | .40 |
| ❏ 78 | Darrell Jackson | .75 | .30 |
| ❏ 79 | Marc Bulger | .75 | .30 |
| ❏ 80 | Steven Jackson | 1.00 | .40 |
| ❏ 81 | Tony Holt | .75 | .30 |
| ❏ 82 | Chris Simms | .75 | .30 |
| ❏ 83 | Cadillac Williams | 1.00 | .40 |
| ❏ 84 | Joey Galloway | .75 | .30 |
| ❏ 85 | Travis Henry | .75 | .30 |
| ❏ 86 | Drew Bennett | .75 | .30 |
| ❏ 87 | David Givens | .75 | .30 |
| ❏ 88 | Mark Brunell | .75 | .30 |
| ❏ 89 | Clinton Portis | 1.00 | .40 |
| ❏ 90 | Santana Moss | .75 | .30 |
| ❏ 91 | Bernard Pollard RC | 10.00 | 4.00 |
| ❏ 92 | Brodie Croyle RC | 15.00 | 6.00 |
| ❏ 93 | Cedric Griffin RC | 10.00 | 4.00 |
| ❏ 94 | Marques Colston RC | 30.00 | 12.00 |
| ❏ 95 | Daniel Bullocks RC | 12.00 | 5.00 |
| ❏ 96 | Darryl Tapp RC | 10.00 | 4.00 |
| ❏ 97 | David Thomas RC | 12.00 | 5.00 |
| ❏ 98 | Montell Owens RC | 10.00 | 4.00 |
| ❏ 99 | DeMeco Ryans RC | 15.00 | 6.00 |
| ❏ 100 | Devin Hester RC | 25.00 | 10.00 |
| ❏ 101 | Donte Whitner RC | 12.00 | 5.00 |
| ❏ 102 | D'Qwell Jackson RC | 10.00 | 4.00 |
| ❏ 103 | Patrick Cobbs RC | 10.00 | 4.00 |
| ❏ 104 | Haloti Ngata RC | 12.00 | 5.00 |
| ❏ 105 | Lawrence Vickers RC | 10.00 | 4.00 |
| ❏ 106 | Jeff King RC | 10.00 | 4.00 |
| ❏ 107 | Jeremy Bloom RC | 10.00 | 4.00 |
| ❏ 108 | Johnathan Joseph RC | 10.00 | 4.00 |
| ❏ 109 | DeDe Dorsey RC | 10.00 | 4.00 |
| ❏ 110 | Marcus Vick RC | 10.00 | 4.00 |
| ❏ 111 | Bobby Carpenter RC | 12.00 | 5.00 |
| ❏ 112 | Manny Lawson RC | 12.00 | 5.00 |
| ❏ 113 | Nick Mangold RC | 12.00 | 5.00 |
| ❏ 114 | Quinn Sypniewski RC | 10.00 | 4.00 |
| ❏ 115 | Richard Marshall RC | 10.00 | 4.00 |
| ❏ 116 | Rocky McIntosh RC | 12.00 | 5.00 |
| ❏ 117 | Roman Harper RC | 10.00 | 4.00 |
| ❏ 118 | Tamba Hali RC | 12.00 | 5.00 |
| ❏ 119 | Tony Scheffler RC | 12.00 | 5.00 |
| ❏ 120 | Wali Lundy RC | 12.00 | 5.00 |
| ❏ 121 | A.J. Nicholson RC | 6.00 | 2.50 |
| ❏ 122 | Abdul Hodge RC | 10.00 | 4.00 |
| ❏ 123 | Adam Jennings RC | 8.00 | 3.00 |
| ❏ 124 | Alan Zemaitis RC | 10.00 | 4.00 |
| ❏ 125 | Andrew Whitworth RC | 6.00 | 2.50 |
| ❏ 126 | Anthony Schlegel RC | 8.00 | 3.00 |
| ❏ 127 | Anthony Smith RC | 10.00 | 4.00 |
| ❏ 128 | Antoine Bethea RC | 10.00 | 4.00 |
| ❏ 129 | Barry Cofield RC | 10.00 | 4.00 |
| ❏ 130 | Brandon Johnson RC | 8.00 | 3.00 |
| ❏ 131 | Calvin Lowry RC | 10.00 | 4.00 |
| ❏ 132 | Shaun Bodiford RC | 8.00 | 3.00 |
| ❏ 133 | Charlie Peprah RC | 8.00 | 3.00 |
| ❏ 134 | Claude Wroten RC | 6.00 | 2.50 |
| ❏ 135 | Clint Ingram RC | 10.00 | 4.00 |
| ❏ 136 | Cortland Finnegan RC | 10.00 | 4.00 |
| ❏ 137 | Daryn Colledge RC | 10.00 | 4.00 |
| ❏ 138 | David Anderson RC | 8.00 | 3.00 |
| ❏ 139 | David Kirtman RC | 8.00 | 3.00 |
| ❏ 140 | Boone Stutz RC | 8.00 | 3.00 |
| ❏ 141 | Delanie Walker RC | 8.00 | 3.00 |
| ❏ 142 | Sam Hurd RC | 15.00 | 6.00 |
| ❏ 143 | Derrick Martin RC | 8.00 | 3.00 |
| ❏ 144 | Willie Andrews RC | 8.00 | 3.00 |
| ❏ 145 | Dusty Dvoracek RC | 10.00 | 4.00 |
| ❏ 146 | Elvis Dumervil RC | 6.00 | 2.50 |
| ❏ 147 | Eric Smith RC | 8.00 | 3.00 |
| ❏ 148 | Freddie Keiaho RC | 8.00 | 3.00 |
| ❏ 149 | Gabe Watson RC | 8.00 | 3.00 |
| ❏ 150 | Gerris Wilkinson RC | 8.00 | 2.50 |
| ❏ 151 | Greg Blue RC | 8.00 | 3.00 |
| ❏ 152 | Guy Whimper RC | 6.00 | 2.50 |
| ❏ 153 | Jamar Williams RC | 8.00 | 3.00 |
| ❏ 154 | James Anderson RC | 6.00 | 2.50 |
| ❏ 155 | Jason Spitz RC | 10.00 | 4.00 |
| ❏ 156 | Jeff Webb RC | 8.00 | 3.00 |
| ❏ 157 | Jeremy Mincey RC | 8.00 | 3.00 |
| ❏ 158 | Jeremy Trueblood RC | 8.00 | 3.00 |
| ❏ 159 | Omar Gaither RC | 8.00 | 3.00 |
| ❏ 160 | Jon Alston RC | 10.00 | 4.00 |
| ❏ 161 | Julian Jenkins RC | 8.00 | 3.00 |
| ❏ 162 | Keith Ellison RC | 8.00 | 3.00 |
| ❏ 163 | Kevin McMahan RC | 8.00 | 3.00 |
| ❏ 164 | Kyle Williams RC | 10.00 | 4.00 |
| ❏ 165 | Leon Williams RC | 8.00 | 3.00 |
| ❏ 166 | Mark Anderson RC | 15.00 | 6.00 |
| ❏ 167 | LaJuan Ramsey RC | 10.00 | 4.00 |
| ❏ 168 | Nate Salley RC | 8.00 | 3.00 |
| ❏ 169 | Rob Ninkovich RC | 8.00 | 3.00 |
| ❏ 170 | Parys Haralson RC | 8.00 | 3.00 |
| ❏ 171 | Pat Watkins RC | 10.00 | 4.00 |
| ❏ 172 | Paul McQuistan RC | 6.00 | 2.50 |
| ❏ 173 | Rashad Butler RC | 6.00 | 2.50 |
| ❏ 174 | Ray Edwards RC | 8.00 | 3.00 |
| ❏ 175 | Reed Doughty RC | 8.00 | 3.00 |
| ❏ 176 | Ronnie Prude RC | 8.00 | 3.00 |
| ❏ 177 | Stephen Tulloch RC | 8.00 | 3.00 |
| ❏ 178 | Tim Jennings RC | 8.00 | 3.00 |
| ❏ 179 | Jarrad Page RC | 10.00 | 4.00 |
| ❏ 180 | Victor Adeyanju RC | 8.00 | 3.00 |
| ❏ 181 | Andre Hall RC | 15.00 | 6.00 |
| ❏ 182 | Anthony Fasano AU RC | 15.00 | 6.00 |
| ❏ 183 | Antonio Cromartie AU RC | 20.00 | 10.00 |
| ❏ 184 | Ashton Youboty AU RC | 15.00 | 6.00 |
| ❏ 185 | Kamerion Wimbley AU RC | 15.00 | 6.00 |
| ❏ 186 | Brad Smith AU RC | 15.00 | 6.00 |
| ❏ 187 | Brodrick Bunkley AU RC | 15.00 | 6.00 |
| ❏ 188 | Bruce Gradkowski AU RC | 15.00 | 6.00 |
| ❏ 189 | Chad Greenway AU RC | 15.00 | 6.00 |
| ❏ 190 | Cory Rodgers AU RC | 15.00 | 6.00 |
| ❏ 191 | D.J. Shockley AU RC | 15.00 | 6.00 |
| ❏ 192 | Daniael Manning AU RC | 15.00 | 6.00 |
| ❏ 193 | Darnell Bing AU RC | 15.00 | 6.00 |
| ❏ 194 | Darrell Hackney AU RC | 15.00 | 6.00 |
| ❏ 195 | D.Ferguson AU RC EXCH | 15.00 | 6.00 |
| ❏ 196 | Dominique Byrd AU RC | 12.00 | 5.00 |
| ❏ 197 | Drew Olson AU RC | 12.00 | 5.00 |
| ❏ 198 | Ernie Sims AU RC | 15.00 | 6.00 |
| ❏ 199 | Garrett Mills AU/99 RC | 100.00 | 50.00 |
| ❏ 200 | Gerald Riggs AU RC | 15.00 | 6.00 |
| ❏ 201 | Greg Jennings AU RC | 50.00 | 20.00 |
| ❏ 202 | Greg Lee AU RC | 12.00 | 5.00 |
| ❏ 203 | Hank Baskett AU RC | 15.00 | 6.00 |
| ❏ 204 | Ingle Martin AU RC | 15.00 | 6.00 |
| ❏ 205 | Jason Allen AU RC | 15.00 | 6.00 |
| ❏ 206 | Jerome Harrison AU RC | 15.00 | 6.00 |
| ❏ 207 | Jimmy Williams AU RC | 15.00 | 6.00 |
| ❏ 208 | John McCargo AU RC | 12.00 | 5.00 |
| ❏ 209 | Josh Betts AU RC | 12.00 | 5.00 |
| ❏ 210 | Leonard Pope AU RC | 15.00 | 6.00 |
| ❏ 211 | Marques Hagans AU RC | 12.00 | 5.00 |
| ❏ 212 | Martin Nance AU RC | 12.00 | 5.00 |
| ❏ 213 | Mathias Kiwanuka AU RC | 20.00 | 8.00 |
| ❏ 214 | Mike Bell AU RC | 15.00 | 6.00 |
| ❏ 215 | Mike Hass AU RC | 15.00 | 6.00 |
| ❏ 216 | Owen Daniels AU RC | 15.00 | 6.00 |
| ❏ 217 | P.J. Daniels AU RC | 12.00 | 5.00 |
| ❏ 218 | Reggie McNeal AU RC | 15.00 | 6.00 |
| ❏ 219 | Skyler Green AU RC | 15.00 | 6.00 |
| ❏ 220 | Terrence Whitehead AU RC | 12.00 | 5.00 |
| ❏ 221 | Thomas Howard AU RC | 15.00 | 6.00 |
| ❏ 222 | Tye Hill AU RC | 15.00 | 6.00 |
| ❏ 223 | Will Blackmon AU RC | 15.00 | 6.00 |
| ❏ 224 | Willie Reid AU RC | 15.00 | 6.00 |
| ❏ 225 | Winston Justice AU RC | 15.00 | 6.00 |
| ❏ 226 | Jay Cutler AU/99 RC | 1200.00 | 800.00 |
| ❏ 227 | Joseph Addai AU/99 RC | 500.00 | 250.00 |
| ❏ 228 | Br.Williams JSY/999 AU RC | 25.00 | 10.00 |
| ❏ 229 | B.Calhoun JSY/999 AU RC | 20.00 | 8.00 |
| ❏ 230 | Ch.Jackson JSY/699 AU RC | 40.00 | 15.00 |
| ❏ 231 | C.Whitehurst JSY/999 AU RC | 25.00 | 10.00 |
| ❏ 232 | DeA.Williams JSY/175 AU RC | 150.00 | 90.00 |
| ❏ 233 | Dem.Williams JSY/999 AU RC | 25.00 | 10.00 |
| ❏ 234 | Derek Hagan JSY/999 AU RC | 25.00 | 10.00 |
| ❏ 235 | Jason Avant JSY/999 AU RC | 25.00 | 10.00 |
| ❏ 236 | J.Norwood JSY/999 AU RC | 30.00 | 12.00 |
| ❏ 237 | J.Klopfenstein JSY/999 AU RC | 20.00 | 8.00 |
| ❏ 238 | K.Clemens JSY/999 AU RC | 40.00 | 20.00 |
| ❏ 239 | K.Jennings JSY/199 AU RC | 80.00 | 40.00 |
| ❏ 240 | L.Maroney JSY/999 AU RC | 120.00 | 50.00 |
| ❏ 241 | L.White JSY/999 AU RC | 120.00 | 50.00 |
| ❏ 242 | L.Washington JSY/999 AU RC | 30.00 | 15.00 |
| ❏ 243 | M.Lewis JSY/699 AU RC | 25.00 | 10.00 |
| ❏ 244 | M.McNeill JSY/260 AU RC | 50.00 | 20.00 |
| ❏ 245 | Ma.Williams JSY/699 AU RC | 50.00 | 20.00 |
| ❏ 246 | Matt Leinart JSY/299 AU RC | 250.00 | 125.00 |
| ❏ 247 | M.Drew JSY/999 AU RC | 120.00 | 60.00 |
| ❏ 248 | M.Stovall JSY/999 AU RC | 25.00 | 10.00 |
| ❏ 249 | Michael Huff JSY/999 AU RC | 50.00 | 20.00 |
| ❏ 250 | M.Robinson JSY/999 AU RC | 25.00 | 10.00 |
| ❏ 251 | Omar Jacobs/750 RC | 10.00 | 4.00 |
| ❏ 252 | Reggie Bush JSY/299 AU RC | 400.00 | 200.00 |
| ❏ 253 | S.Holmes JSY/399 AU RC | 125.00 | 75.00 |
| ❏ 254 | Sinorice Moss JSY/99 AU RC | 150.00 | 75.00 |
| ❏ 255 | T.Jackson JSY/999 AU RC | 35.00 | 20.00 |
| ❏ 256 | Travis Wilson JSY/999 AU RC | 25.00 | 10.00 |
| ❏ 257 | V.Davis JSY/699 AU RC | 30.00 | 12.00 |
| ❏ 258 | Vince Young JSY/270 AU RC | 300.00 | 150.00 |
| ❏ 259 | A.J. Hawk JSY/399 AU RC | 100.00 | 50.00 |
| ❏ 260 | B.Marshall JSY/999 AU RC | 100.00 | 50.00 |

## 2007 SP Authentic

|  |  | | |
|---|---|---|---|
| ❏ 1 | Ahman Green | .60 | .25 |
| ❏ 2 | A.J. Hawk | .75 | .30 |
| ❏ 3 | Alex Smith QB | .75 | .30 |
| ❏ 4 | Andre Johnson | .60 | .25 |
| ❏ 5 | Antonio Gates | .60 | .25 |
| ❏ 6 | Ben Roethlisberger | 1.00 | .40 |
| ❏ 7 | Bernard Berrian | .50 | .20 |
| ❏ 8 | Brandon Jacobs | .60 | .25 |
| ❏ 9 | Braylon Edwards | .60 | .25 |
| ❏ 10 | Brett Favre | 1.50 | .60 |
| ❏ 11 | Brian Urlacher | .75 | .30 |
| ❏ 12 | Brian Westbrook | .60 | .25 |
| ❏ 13 | Brodie Croyle | .60 | .25 |
| ❏ 14 | Byron Leftwich | .60 | .25 |
| ❏ 15 | Cadillac Williams | .75 | .30 |
| ❏ 16 | Carson Palmer | .75 | .30 |
| ❏ 17 | Cedric Benson | .60 | .25 |
| ❏ 18 | Chad Johnson | .75 | .30 |
| ❏ 19 | Chad Pennington | .60 | .25 |
| ❏ 20 | Champ Bailey | .60 | .25 |
| ❏ 21 | Derek Anderson | .60 | .25 |
| ❏ 22 | Chester Taylor | .50 | .20 |
| ❏ 23 | Chris Brown | .50 | .20 |
| ❏ 24 | Chris Chambers | .60 | .25 |
| ❏ 25 | Clinton Portis | .60 | .25 |
| ❏ 26 | Darrell Jackson | .60 | .25 |
| ❏ 27 | Deuce McAllister | .60 | .25 |
| ❏ 28 | Dominic Rhodes | .60 | .25 |
| ❏ 29 | Donald Driver | .60 | .25 |
| ❏ 30 | Donovan McNabb | .75 | .30 |
| ❏ 31 | Donte Stallworth | .60 | .25 |
| ❏ 32 | Drew Brees | .60 | .25 |
| ❏ 33 | Edgerrin James | .60 | .25 |
| ❏ 34 | Eli Manning | .75 | .30 |
| ❏ 35 | Frank Gore | .75 | .30 |
| ❏ 36 | Fred Taylor | .60 | .25 |
| ❏ 37 | Greg Jennings | .60 | .25 |
| ❏ 38 | Hines Ward | .75 | .30 |
| ❏ 39 | Jake Delhomme | .60 | .25 |
| ❏ 40 | Jamal Lewis | .60 | .25 |
| ❏ 41 | Jason Campbell | .60 | .25 |
| ❏ 42 | Jason Taylor | .50 | .20 |
| ❏ 43 | Jason Witten | .60 | .25 |

|  |  | | |
|---|---|---|---|
| 44 | Javon Walker | .60 | .25 |
| 45 | Jay Cutler | .75 | .30 |
| 46 | Jerious Norwood | .60 | .25 |
| 47 | Jerry Porter | .60 | .25 |
| 48 | Jon Kitna | .50 | .20 |
| 49 | Joseph Addai | .75 | .30 |
| 50 | Julius Jones | .60 | .25 |
| 51 | LaDainian Tomlinson | 1.00 | .40 |
| 52 | Larry Johnson | .60 | .25 |
| 53 | Larry Fitzgerald | .75 | .30 |
| 54 | Laurence Maroney | .75 | .30 |
| 55 | Marc Bulger | .60 | .25 |
| 56 | Marion Barber | .75 | .30 |
| 57 | Mark Clayton | .60 | .25 |
| 58 | Marques Colston | .75 | .30 |
| 59 | Marvin Harrison | .75 | .30 |
| 60 | Matt Hasselbeck | .60 | .25 |
| 61 | Matt Jones | .60 | .25 |
| 62 | Matt Leinart | .75 | .30 |
| 63 | Matt Schaub | .60 | .25 |
| 64 | Maurice Jones-Drew | .75 | .30 |
| 65 | Jeff Garcia | .60 | .25 |
| 66 | Mike Alstott | .60 | .25 |
| 67 | David Garrard | .60 | .25 |
| 68 | Peyton Manning | 1.25 | .50 |
| 69 | Philip Rivers | .75 | .30 |
| 70 | Plaxico Burress | .60 | .25 |
| 71 | Randy Moss | .75 | .30 |
| 72 | Reggie Brown | .60 | .25 |
| 73 | Reggie Bush | 1.00 | .40 |
| 74 | Reggie Wayne | .75 | .30 |
| 75 | Rex Grossman | .60 | .25 |
| 76 | Ronnie Brown | .60 | .25 |
| 77 | Roy Williams S | .60 | .25 |
| 78 | Roy Williams WR | .60 | .25 |
| 79 | Rudi Johnson | .60 | .25 |
| 80 | Shaun Alexander | .60 | .25 |
| 81 | Shawne Merriman | .60 | .25 |
| 82 | Steven Jackson | .75 | .30 |
| 83 | Steve McNair | .60 | .25 |
| 84 | Steve Smith | .75 | .30 |
| 85 | T.J. Houshmandzadeh | .60 | .25 |
| 86 | Tarvaris Jackson | .60 | .25 |
| 87 | Tedy Bruschi | .75 | .30 |
| 88 | Terrell Owens | .75 | .30 |
| 89 | Thomas Jones | .60 | .25 |
| 90 | Tom Brady | 1.50 | .60 |
| 91 | Torry Holt | .60 | .25 |
| 92 | Travis Henry | .60 | .25 |
| 93 | Trent Green | .60 | .25 |
| 94 | Vince Young | .75 | .30 |
| 95 | Vincent Jackson | .50 | .20 |
| 96 | Walter Jones | .50 | .20 |
| 97 | Warrick Dunn | .60 | .25 |
| 98 | Willie Parker | .75 | .30 |
| 99 | Willis McGahee | .60 | .25 |
| 100 | Tony Romo | 1.50 | .60 |
| 101 | Deon Anderson RC | 8.00 | 3.00 |
| 102 | Ben Patrick RC | 8.00 | 3.00 |
| 103 | Reagan Mauia RC | 6.00 | 2.50 |
| 104 | Derek Schouman RC | 8.00 | 3.00 |
| 105 | Keyunta Dawson RC | 8.00 | 3.00 |
| 106 | Usama Young RC | 8.00 | 3.00 |
| 107 | Syndric Steptoe RC | 8.00 | 3.00 |
| 108 | Martrez Milner RC | 8.00 | 3.00 |
| 109 | Brandon McDonald RC | 6.00 | 2.50 |
| 110 | Jason Snelling RC | 8.00 | 3.00 |
| 111 | Derek Stanley RC | 8.00 | 3.00 |
| 112 | Ed Johnson RC | 8.00 | 3.00 |
| 113 | Jacob Bender RC | 8.00 | 3.00 |
| 114 | Charles Ali RC | 8.00 | 3.00 |
| 115 | Tanard Jackson RC | 6.00 | 2.50 |
| 116 | Paul Soliai RC | 6.00 | 2.50 |
| 117 | Marvin White RC | 6.00 | 2.50 |
| 118 | Jared Gaither RC | 8.00 | 3.00 |
| 119 | Baraka Atkins RC | 6.00 | 2.50 |
| 120 | Marcus Thomas RC | 6.00 | 2.50 |
| 121 | Fred Bennett RC | 6.00 | 2.50 |
| 122 | Dashon Goldson RC | 6.00 | 2.50 |
| 123 | Kareem Brown RC | 8.00 | 3.00 |
| 124 | Courtney Bryan RC | 6.00 | 2.50 |
| 125 | Joe Cohen RC | 6.00 | 2.50 |
| 126 | Jay Richardson RC | 8.00 | 3.00 |
| 127 | Greg Peterson RC | 8.00 | 3.00 |
| 128 | Dallas Sartz RC | 8.00 | 3.00 |
| 129 | Brandon Harrison RC | 6.00 | 2.50 |
| 130 | Tarell Brown RC | 6.00 | 2.50 |
| 131 | Matt Gutierrez RC | 10.00 | 4.00 |
| 132 | Edmond Miles RC | 8.00 | 3.00 |
| 133 | Clifton Ryan RC | 8.00 | 3.00 |
| 134 | Antwan Barnes RC | 8.00 | 3.00 |
| 135 | Tim Shaw RC | 8.00 | 3.00 |
| 136 | Eric Frampton RC | 8.00 | 3.00 |
| 137 | William Gay RC | 8.00 | 3.00 |
| 138 | Nick Graham RC | 8.00 | 3.00 |
| 139 | Matt Toeaina RC | 8.00 | 3.00 |
| 140 | John Wendling RC | 8.00 | 3.00 |
| 141 | Mason Crosby RC | 10.00 | 4.00 |
| 142 | C.J. Wallace RC | 8.00 | 3.00 |
| 143 | Prescott Burgess RC | 8.00 | 3.00 |
| 144 | Oscar Lua RC | 8.00 | 3.00 |
| 145 | Chase Pittman RC | 8.00 | 3.00 |
| 146 | Zachary Diles RC | 8.00 | 3.00 |
| 147 | Kelvin Smith RC | 8.00 | 3.00 |
| 148 | Marvin Mitchell RC | 8.00 | 3.00 |
| 149 | Trumaine McBride RC | 8.00 | 3.00 |
| 150 | Edgar Jones RC | 8.00 | 3.00 |
| 151 | Abraham Wright RC | 6.00 | 2.50 |
| 152 | Nick Folk RC | 10.00 | 4.00 |
| 153 | Brandon Siler RC | 8.00 | 3.00 |
| 154 | Clint Session RC | 8.00 | 3.00 |
| 155 | Nedu Ndukwe RC | 10.00 | 4.00 |
| 156 | C.J. Wilson RC | 8.00 | 3.00 |
| 157 | Desmond Bishop RC | 8.00 | 3.00 |
| 158 | Melvin Bullitt RC | 8.00 | 3.00 |
| 159 | Courtney Brown RC | 8.00 | 3.00 |
| 160 | Troy Smith RC | 12.00 | 5.00 |
| 161 | Levi Brown RC | 10.00 | 4.00 |
| 162 | Justin Harrell RC | 10.00 | 4.00 |
| 163 | Jarvis Moss RC | 10.00 | 4.00 |
| 164 | Aaron Ross RC | 10.00 | 4.00 |
| 165 | Jon Beason RC | 10.00 | 4.00 |
| 166 | Anthony Spencer RC | 10.00 | 4.00 |
| 167 | Joe Staley RC | 8.00 | 3.00 |
| 168 | Ben Grubbs RC | 8.00 | 3.00 |
| 169 | Arron Sears RC | 8.00 | 3.00 |
| 170 | Eric Weddle RC | 8.00 | 3.00 |
| 171 | Justin Blalock RC | 6.00 | 2.50 |
| 172 | Chris Houston RC | 8.00 | 3.00 |
| 173 | David Harris RC | 8.00 | 3.00 |
| 174 | Justin Durant RC | 8.00 | 3.00 |
| 175 | Turk McBride RC | 8.00 | 3.00 |
| 176 | Josh Wilson RC | 8.00 | 3.00 |
| 177 | Tim Crowder RC | 10.00 | 4.00 |
| 178 | Victor Abiamiri RC | 10.00 | 4.00 |
| 179 | Ikaika Alama-Francis RC | 10.00 | 4.00 |
| 180 | Ryan Kalil RC | 8.00 | 3.00 |
| 181 | Samson Satele RC | 8.00 | 3.00 |
| 182 | Gerald Alexander RC | 6.00 | 2.50 |
| 183 | Corey Graham RC | 8.00 | 3.00 |
| 184 | Sabby Piscitelli RC | 10.00 | 4.00 |
| 185 | Quincy Black RC | 10.00 | 4.00 |
| 186 | Daniel Coats RC | 8.00 | 3.00 |
| 187 | Tony Ugoh RC | 8.00 | 3.00 |
| 188 | David Jones RC | 6.00 | 2.50 |
| 189 | DeMarcus Tank Tyler RC | 8.00 | 3.00 |
| 190 | Chad Nkang RC | 6.00 | 2.50 |
| 191 | Jonathan Wade RC | 8.00 | 3.00 |
| 192 | Brandon Mebane RC | 8.00 | 3.00 |
| 193 | Stewart Bradley RC | 10.00 | 4.00 |
| 194 | Aaron Rouse RC | 10.00 | 4.00 |
| 195 | Michael Okwo RC | 8.00 | 3.00 |
| 196 | Anthony Waters RC | 8.00 | 3.00 |
| 197 | Ray McDonald RC | 8.00 | 3.00 |
| 198 | Clifton Dawson RC | 10.00 | 4.00 |
| 199 | Brian Robison RC | 8.00 | 3.00 |
| 200 | Jay Moore RC | 8.00 | 3.00 |
| 201 | Dante Rosario AU RC | 20.00 | 8.00 |
| 202 | Ahmad Bradshaw AU RC | 40.00 | 15.00 |
| 203 | Roy Hall AU RC | 15.00 | 6.00 |
| 204 | Aundrae Allison AU RC | 12.00 | 5.00 |
| 205 | Brent Celek AU RC | 12.00 | 5.00 |
| 206 | Chansi Stuckey AU RC | 12.00 | 5.00 |
| 207 | Courtney Taylor AU RC | 12.00 | 5.00 |
| 208 | Dallas Baker AU RC | 12.00 | 5.00 |
| 209 | Dwayne Walker AU RC | 15.00 | 6.00 |
| 210 | David Ball AU RC | 10.00 | 4.00 |
| 211 | David Clowney AU RC | 8.00 | 3.00 |
| 212 | David Irons AU RC | 10.00 | 4.00 |
| 213 | Daymeion Hughes AU RC | 12.00 | 5.00 |
| 214 | DeShawn Wynn AU RC | 15.00 | 6.00 |
| 215 | Jordan Kent AU RC | 12.00 | 5.00 |
| 216 | Dwayne Wright AU RC | 12.00 | 5.00 |
| 217 | Eric Wright AU RC | 15.00 | 6.00 |
| 218 | Gary Russell AU RC EXCH | 15.00 | 6.00 |
| 219 | Mike Walker AU RC | 12.00 | 5.00 |
| 220 | Isaiah Stanback AU RC | 15.00 | 6.00 |
| 221 | Jamaal Anderson AU RC | 12.00 | 5.00 |
| 222 | Jared Zabransky AU RC | 15.00 | 6.00 |
| 223 | Jeff Rowe AU RC | 12.00 | 5.00 |
| 224 | Joel Filani AU RC | 12.00 | 5.00 |
| 225 | Jordan Palmer AU RC | 15.00 | 6.00 |
| 226 | Kenneth Darby AU RC | 15.00 | 6.00 |
| 227 | Kolby Smith AU RC | 15.00 | 6.00 |
| 228 | Thomas Clayton AU RC | 12.00 | 5.00 |
| 229 | Steve Breaston AU RC | 30.00 | 15.00 |
| 230 | James Jones AU RC | 15.00 | 6.00 |
| 231 | Marcus McCauley AU RC | 12.00 | 5.00 |
| 232 | Alan Branch AU RC | 12.00 | 5.00 |
| 233 | Michael Griffin AU RC | 15.00 | 6.00 |
| 234 | Paul Posluszny AU RC | 20.00 | 8.00 |
| 235 | Quentin Moses AU RC | 12.00 | 5.00 |
| 236 | Lawrence Timmons AU RC | 15.00 | 6.00 |
| 237 | Scott Chandler AU RC | 12.00 | 5.00 |
| 238 | Jacoby Jones AU RC | 15.00 | 6.00 |
| 239 | Tyler Thigpen AU RC | 40.00 | 20.00 |
| 240 | Laurent Robinson AU RC | 12.00 | 5.00 |
| 241 | John Broussard AU RC | 12.00 | 5.00 |
| 242 | Zach Miller AU RC | 15.00 | 6.00 |
| 243 | Matt Spaeth AU RC | 15.00 | 6.00 |
| 244 | Ryne Robinson AU RC EXCH | 12.00 | 5.00 |
| 245 | Danny Ware AU RC | 12.00 | 5.00 |
| 246 | Legedu Naanee AU RC | 15.00 | 6.00 |
| 247 | Le'Ron McClain AU RC | 30.00 | 15.00 |
| 248 | Kevin Boss AU RC | 30.00 | 15.00 |
| 249 | Orenthal O'Neal AU RC | 10.00 | 4.00 |
| 250 | Amobi Okoye AU RC | 15.00 | 6.00 |
| 251 | Darrelle Revis AU RC | 25.00 | 10.00 |
| 252 | LaRon Landry AU RC | 30.00 | 12.00 |
| 253 | Chris Leak AU RC | 20.00 | 8.00 |
| 254 | Craig Davis AU RC | 25.00 | 10.00 |
| 255 | Leon Hall AU RC | 20.00 | 8.00 |
| 256 | Reggie Nelson AU RC | 20.00 | 8.00 |
| 257 | Adam Carriker AU RC | 20.00 | 8.00 |
| 258 | H.B. Blades AU RC | 20.00 | 8.00 |
| 259 | LaMarr Woodley AU RC | 35.00 | 20.00 |
| 260 | Korey Hall AU RC | 20.00 | 8.00 |
| 261 | Rhema McKnight AU RC | 20.00 | 8.00 |
| 262 | Brandon Meriweather AU RC | 25.00 | 10.00 |
| 263 | Matt Moore AU RC | 40.00 | 15.00 |
| 264 | Kevin Kolb AU RC | 60.00 | 25.00 |
| 265 | Tyler Palko AU RC | 25.00 | 10.00 |
| 266 | Anthony Gonzalez JSY AU RC | 60.00 | 30.00 |
| 267 | Antonio Pittman JSY AU RC | 40.00 | 15.00 |
| 268 | Br.Jackson JSY AU RC | 40.00 | 15.00 |
| 269 | Brian Leonard JSY AU RC | 40.00 | 15.00 |
| 270 | Chris Henry JSY AU RC | 40.00 | 15.00 |
| 271 | Drew Stanton JSY AU RC | 50.00 | 20.00 |
| 273 | Garrett Wolfe JSY AU RC | 40.00 | 15.00 |
| 274 | Greg Olsen JSY AU RC | 50.00 | 20.00 |
| 275 | Jason Hill JSY AU RC | 40.00 | 15.00 |
| 276 | Joe Thomas JSY AU RC | 40.00 | 15.00 |
| 277 | John Beck JSY AU RC | 40.00 | 15.00 |
| 278 | J.Lee Higgins JSY AU RC | 30.00 | 12.00 |
| 279 | Kenny Irons JSY AU RC | 40.00 | 15.00 |
| 280 | Kevin Kolb JSY AU RC | 80.00 | 40.00 |
| 281 | Lorenzo Booker JSY AU RC | 40.00 | 15.00 |
| 282 | Michael Bush JSY AU RC | 40.00 | 15.00 |
| 283 | Patrick Willis JSY AU RC | 60.00 | 30.00 |
| 284 | Paul Williams JSY AU RC | 30.00 | 12.00 |
| 285 | Steve Smith JSY AU RC | 60.00 | 30.00 |
| 286 | Tony Hunt JSY AU RC | 40.00 | 15.00 |
| 287 | Trent Edwards JSY AU RC | 120.00 | 60.00 |
| 288 | Yamon Figurs JSY AU RC | 40.00 | 15.00 |
| 289 | Adrian Peterson JSY AU RC | 700.00 | 400.00 |
| 290 | Brady Quinn JSY AU RC | 250.00 | 125.00 |
| 291 | Calvin Johnson JSY AU RC | 200.00 | 100.00 |
| 292 | JaMarcus Russell JSY AU RC | 150.00 | 75.00 |
| 293 | Marshawn Lynch JSY AU RC | 200.00 | 100.00 |
| 294 | Dwayne Bowe JSY AU RC | 80.00 | 30.00 |
| 295 | Sidney Rice JSY AU RC | 40.00 | 15.00 |
| 296 | Robert Meachem JSY AU RC | 40.00 | 15.00 |
| 297 | Dwayne Jarrett JSY AU RC | 40.00 | 15.00 |
| 298 | Ted Ginn JSY AU RC | 80.00 | 40.00 |

## 2008 SP Authentic

| | | |
|---|---|---|
| ❏ 1 Marshawn Lynch | .75 | .30 |
| ❏ 2 Trent Edwards | .75 | .30 |
| ❏ 3 Roscoe Parrish | .50 | .20 |
| ❏ 4 Jason Taylor | .60 | .25 |
| ❏ 5 Ronnie Brown | .60 | .25 |
| ❏ 6 Chad Pennington | .60 | .25 |
| ❏ 7 Tom Brady | 1.25 | .50 |
| ❏ 8 Laurence Maroney | .60 | .25 |
| ❏ 9 Randy Moss | .75 | .30 |
| ❏ 10 Darrelle Revis | .50 | .20 |
| ❏ 11 Jerricho Cotchery | .50 | .20 |
| ❏ 12 Thomas Jones | .60 | .25 |
| ❏ 13 Ray Lewis | .75 | .30 |
| ❏ 14 Ed Reed | .60 | .25 |
| ❏ 15 Willis McGahee | .60 | .25 |
| ❏ 16 Carson Palmer | .75 | .30 |
| ❏ 17 T.J. Houshmandzadeh | .60 | .25 |
| ❏ 18 Chad Johnson | .60 | .25 |
| ❏ 19 Kellen Winslow | .60 | .25 |
| ❏ 20 Derek Anderson | .60 | .25 |
| ❏ 21 Braylon Edwards | .60 | .25 |
| ❏ 22 Ben Roethlisberger | 1.00 | .40 |
| ❏ 23 Willie Parker | .60 | .25 |
| ❏ 24 Matt Schaub | .60 | .25 |
| ❏ 25 DeMeco Ryans | .60 | .25 |
| ❏ 26 Andre Johnson | .60 | .25 |
| ❏ 27 Darius Walker | .50 | .20 |
| ❏ 28 Peyton Manning | 1.25 | .50 |
| ❏ 29 Reggie Wayne | .60 | .25 |
| ❏ 30 Joseph Addai | .75 | .30 |
| ❏ 31 David Garrard | .60 | .25 |
| ❏ 32 Maurice Jones-Drew | .60 | .25 |
| ❏ 33 Fred Taylor | .60 | .25 |
| ❏ 34 Vince Young | .75 | .30 |
| ❏ 35 LenDale White | .60 | .25 |
| ❏ 36 Alge Crumpler | .60 | .25 |
| ❏ 37 Jay Cutler | .75 | .30 |
| ❏ 38 Brandon Marshall | .60 | .25 |
| ❏ 39 Jason Witten | .60 | .25 |
| ❏ 40 Brodie Croyle | .75 | .30 |
| ❏ 41 Larry Johnson | .60 | .25 |
| ❏ 42 Derrick Johnson | .50 | .20 |
| ❏ 43 JaMarcus Russell | .75 | .30 |
| ❏ 44 Ronald Curry | .60 | .25 |
| ❏ 45 Jeremy Shockey | .60 | .25 |
| ❏ 46 Antonio Gates | .60 | .25 |
| ❏ 47 LaDainian Tomlinson | 1.00 | .40 |
| ❏ 48 Antonio Cromartie | .50 | .20 |
| ❏ 49 Philip Rivers | .75 | .30 |
| ❏ 50 Tony Romo | 1.25 | .50 |
| ❏ 51 Terrell Owens | .75 | .30 |
| ❏ 52 DeMarcus Ware | .60 | .25 |
| ❏ 53 Marion Barber | .75 | .30 |
| ❏ 54 Eli Manning | .75 | .30 |
| ❏ 55 Brandon Jacobs | .60 | .25 |
| ❏ 56 Plaxico Burress | .60 | .25 |
| ❏ 57 Antonio Pierce | .50 | .20 |
| ❏ 58 Donovan McNabb | .75 | .30 |
| ❏ 59 Brian Dawkins | .60 | .25 |
| ❏ 60 Brian Westbrook | .60 | .25 |
| ❏ 61 Chris Cooley | .60 | .25 |
| ❏ 62 Jason Campbell | .60 | .25 |
| ❏ 63 Clinton Portis | .60 | .25 |
| ❏ 64 Brian Urlacher | .60 | .25 |
| ❏ 65 Lance Briggs | .50 | .20 |
| ❏ 66 Devin Hester | .60 | .25 |
| ❏ 67 Roy Williams WR | .60 | .25 |

| | | |
|---|---|---|
| ❏ 68 Calvin Johnson | .75 | .30 |
| ❏ 69 Brett Favre | 3.00 | 1.25 |
| ❏ 70 Aaron Rodgers | .75 | .30 |
| ❏ 71 Ryan Grant | .75 | .30 |
| ❏ 72 Greg Jennings | .60 | .25 |
| ❏ 73 Tarvaris Jackson | .60 | .25 |
| ❏ 74 Adrian Peterson | 1.50 | .60 |
| ❏ 75 Sidney Rice | .60 | .25 |
| ❏ 76 Michael Turner | .60 | .25 |
| ❏ 77 Jerious Norwood | .60 | .25 |
| ❏ 78 Jake Delhomme | .60 | .25 |
| ❏ 79 DeAngelo Williams | .60 | .25 |
| ❏ 80 Steve Smith | .60 | .25 |
| ❏ 81 Julius Peppers | .60 | .25 |
| ❏ 82 Drew Brees | .75 | .30 |
| ❏ 83 Reggie Bush | .75 | .30 |
| ❏ 84 Marques Colston | .60 | .25 |
| ❏ 85 Jonathan Vilma | .60 | .25 |
| ❏ 86 Joey Galloway | .60 | .25 |
| ❏ 87 Jeff Garcia | .60 | .25 |
| ❏ 88 Earnest Graham | .50 | .20 |
| ❏ 89 Kurt Warner | .75 | .30 |
| ❏ 90 Edgerrin James | .60 | .25 |
| ❏ 91 Larry Fitzgerald | .75 | .30 |
| ❏ 92 Anquan Boldin | .60 | .25 |
| ❏ 93 Marc Bulger | .60 | .25 |
| ❏ 94 Steven Jackson | .75 | .30 |
| ❏ 95 Torry Holt | .60 | .25 |
| ❏ 96 J.T. O'Sullivan | .60 | .25 |
| ❏ 97 Frank Gore | .60 | .25 |
| ❏ 98 Nate Clements | .50 | .20 |
| ❏ 99 Matt Hasselbeck | .60 | .25 |
| ❏ 100 Deion Branch | .60 | .25 |
| ❏ 101 Kregg Lumpkin RC | 6.00 | 2.50 |
| ❏ 102 Donovan Woods RC | 5.00 | 2.00 |
| ❏ 103 Joe Mays RC | 5.00 | 2.00 |
| ❏ 104 Anthony Alridge RC | 6.00 | 2.50 |
| ❏ 105 Beau Bell RC | 6.00 | 2.50 |
| ❏ 106 Brad Cottam RC | 8.00 | 3.00 |
| ❏ 107 Brandon Flowers RC | 8.00 | 3.00 |
| ❏ 108 Darrell Strong RC | 6.00 | 2.50 |
| ❏ 109 Mike Tolbert RC | 8.00 | 3.00 |
| ❏ 110 Bryan Kehl RC | 5.00 | 2.00 |
| ❏ 111 Andy Studebaker RC | 5.00 | 2.00 |
| ❏ 112 Duane Brown RC | 6.00 | 2.50 |
| ❏ 113 Mike Humpal RC | 8.00 | 3.00 |
| ❏ 114 Corey Clark RC | 5.00 | 2.00 |
| ❏ 115 Josh Sitton RC | 6.00 | 2.50 |
| ❏ 116 Curtis Lofton RC | 8.00 | 3.00 |
| ❏ 117 Lance Leggett RC | 8.00 | 3.00 |
| ❏ 118 Gary Barnidge RC | 6.00 | 2.50 |
| ❏ 119 Marcus Dixon RC | 5.00 | 2.00 |
| ❏ 120 Dominique Barber RC | 5.00 | 2.00 |
| ❏ 121 Reggie Smith RC | 6.00 | 2.50 |
| ❏ 122 John Sullivan RC | 5.00 | 2.00 |
| ❏ 123 Jabari Arthur RC | 6.00 | 2.50 |
| ❏ 124 Maurice Leggett RC | 6.00 | 2.50 |
| ❏ 125 Jehuu Caulcrick RC | 5.00 | 2.00 |
| ❏ 126 Philip Wheeler RC | 8.00 | 3.00 |
| ❏ 127 Jo-Lonn Dunbar RC | 6.00 | 2.50 |
| ❏ 128 Josh Barrett RC | 5.00 | 2.00 |
| ❏ 129 Danny Amendola RC | 5.00 | 2.00 |
| ❏ 130 Kenny Iwebema RC | 5.00 | 2.00 |
| ❏ 131 Lance Ball RC | 5.00 | 2.00 |
| ❏ 132 Caleb Hanie RC | 6.00 | 2.50 |
| ❏ 133 Chris Chamberlain RC | 5.00 | 2.00 |
| ❏ 134 Marcus Howard RC | 8.00 | 3.00 |
| ❏ 135 Shaheer McBride RC | 5.00 | 2.00 |
| ❏ 136 Orlando Scandrick RC | 8.00 | 3.00 |
| ❏ 137 Quentin Groves RC | 6.00 | 2.50 |
| ❏ 138 Quinn Demps RC | 6.00 | 2.50 |
| ❏ 139 John Greco RC | 6.00 | 2.50 |
| ❏ 140 Jamey Richard RC | 5.00 | 2.00 |
| ❏ 141 Corey Lynch RC | 5.00 | 2.00 |
| ❏ 142 Orlando Scandrick RC | 8.00 | 3.00 |
| ❏ 143 Lex Hilliard RC | 5.00 | 2.00 |
| ❏ 144 Tyrell Johnson RC | 8.00 | 3.00 |
| ❏ 145 Martellus Bennett RC | 8.00 | 3.00 |
| ❏ 146 Simeon Castille RC | 5.00 | 2.00 |
| ❏ 147 Steve Johnson RC | 8.00 | 3.00 |
| ❏ 148 Steven Justice RC | 5.00 | 2.00 |
| ❏ 149 Terrell Thomas RC | 6.00 | 2.50 |
| ❏ 150 Thomas Brown RC | 8.00 | 3.00 |
| ❏ 151 Thomas DeCoud RC | 5.00 | 2.00 |
| ❏ 152 Matthew Slater RC | 8.00 | 3.00 |

| | | |
|---|---|---|
| ❏ 153 Tom Zbikowski RC | 10.00 | 4.00 |
| ❏ 154 Jaymar Johnson RC | 6.00 | 2.50 |
| ❏ 155 Brian Johnston RC | 5.00 | 2.00 |
| ❏ 156 Trevor Laws RC | 8.00 | 3.00 |
| ❏ 157 Will Franklin RC | 8.00 | 3.00 |
| ❏ 158 Xavier Adibi RC | 6.00 | 2.50 |
| ❏ 159 Chaz Schilens RC | 8.00 | 3.00 |
| ❏ 160 Zack Bowman RC | 6.00 | 2.50 |
| ❏ 161 Tim Hightower RC | 15.00 | 6.00 |
| ❏ 162 Barry Richardson RC | 5.00 | 2.00 |
| ❏ 163 Pierre Garcon RC | 8.00 | 3.00 |
| ❏ 164 Tyvon Branch RC | 6.00 | 2.50 |
| ❏ 165 Marcus Henry RC | 6.00 | 2.50 |
| ❏ 166 Carl Nicks RC | 6.00 | 2.50 |
| ❏ 167 Chauncey Washington RC | 6.00 | 2.50 |
| ❏ 168 Chilo Rachal RC | 5.00 | 2.00 |
| ❏ 169 Chris Williams RC | 6.00 | 2.50 |
| ❏ 170 Craig Stevens RC | 6.00 | 2.50 |
| ❏ 171 Jordan Dizon RC | 8.00 | 3.00 |
| ❏ 172 Dantrell Savage RC | 8.00 | 3.00 |
| ❏ 173 Clifton Smith RC | 8.00 | 3.00 |
| ❏ 174 Drew Radovich RC | 6.00 | 2.50 |
| ❏ 175 Jerome Felton RC | 5.00 | 2.00 |
| ❏ 176 Haruki Nakamura RC | 5.00 | 2.00 |
| ❏ 177 Olaniyi Sobomehin RC | 5.00 | 2.00 |
| ❏ 178 Jamie Silva RC | 6.00 | 2.50 |
| ❏ 179 Brandon Carr RC | 6.00 | 2.50 |
| ❏ 180 Jeff Otah RC | 6.00 | 2.50 |
| ❏ 181 William Hayes RC | 5.00 | 2.00 |
| ❏ 182 Jerome Simpson RC | 6.00 | 2.50 |
| ❏ 183 Anthony Collins RC | 5.00 | 2.00 |
| ❏ 184 Alex Hall RC | 6.00 | 2.50 |
| ❏ 185 Branden Albert RC | 8.00 | 3.00 |
| ❏ 186 Jalen Parmele RC | 6.00 | 2.50 |
| ❏ 187 Stanford Keglar RC | 5.00 | 2.00 |
| ❏ 188 Louis Rankin RC | 6.00 | 2.50 |
| ❏ 189 Maurice Purify RC | 8.00 | 3.00 |
| ❏ 190 Darnell Jenkins RC | 6.00 | 2.50 |
| ❏ 191 Pat Sims RC | 6.00 | 2.50 |
| ❏ 192 Patrick Lee RC | 8.00 | 3.00 |
| ❏ 193 Roy Schuening RC | 5.00 | 2.00 |
| ❏ 194 Lynell Hamilton RC | 6.00 | 2.50 |
| ❏ 195 Joey LaRocque RC | 5.00 | 2.00 |
| ❏ 196 Terrence Wheatley RC | 6.00 | 2.50 |
| ❏ 197 Tracy Porter RC | 6.00 | 2.50 |
| ❏ 198 Brett Swain RC | 6.00 | 2.50 |
| ❏ 199 Wesley Woodyard RC | 6.00 | 2.50 |
| ❏ 200 Xavier Omon RC | 8.00 | 3.00 |
| ❏ 201 Allen Patrick RC | 10.00 | 4.00 |
| ❏ 202 Marcus Monk AU RC | 12.00 | 5.00 |
| ❏ 203 Anthony Morelli AU RC | 12.00 | 5.00 |
| ❏ 204 Antoine Cason AU RC | 12.00 | 5.00 |
| ❏ 205 Aqib Talib AU RC | 12.00 | 5.00 |
| ❏ 206 Ben Moffitt AU RC | 8.00 | 3.00 |
| ❏ 207 Chris Long AU RC | 15.00 | 6.00 |
| ❏ 208 Bruce Davis AU RC | 10.00 | 4.00 |
| ❏ 209 Calais Campbell AU RC | 10.00 | 4.00 |
| ❏ 210 Mario Urrutia AU RC | 10.00 | 4.00 |
| ❏ 211 Chevis Jackson AU RC | 10.00 | 4.00 |
| ❏ 212 Chris Ellis AU RC | 10.00 | 4.00 |
| ❏ 213 Josh Morgan AU RC | 12.00 | 5.00 |
| ❏ 214 Craig Steltz AU RC | 10.00 | 4.00 |
| ❏ 215 DJ Hall AU RC | 12.00 | 5.00 |
| ❏ 216 Dan Connor AU RC | 10.00 | 4.00 |
| ❏ 217 Darius Reynaud AU RC | 10.00 | 4.00 |
| ❏ 218 DeJuan Tribble AU RC | 8.00 | 3.00 |
| ❏ 219 DeMario Pressley AU RC | 10.00 | 4.00 |
| ❏ 220 Dennis Keyes AU RC | 10.00 | 4.00 |
| ❏ 221 Derrick Harvey AU RC | 10.00 | 4.00 |
| ❏ 222 Owen Schmitt AU RC | 12.00 | 5.00 |
| ❏ 223 Dwight Lowery AU RC | 8.00 | 3.00 |
| ❏ 224 Erik Ainge AU RC | 15.00 | 6.00 |
| ❏ 225 Erin Henderson AU RC | 10.00 | 4.00 |
| ❏ 226 DaJuan Morgan AU RC | 10.00 | 4.00 |
| ❏ 227 Frank Okam AU RC | 10.00 | 4.00 |
| ❏ 228 Matt Flynn AU RC | 15.00 | 6.00 |
| ❏ 229 Phillip Merling AU RC | 10.00 | 4.00 |
| ❏ 230 Ryan Clady AU RC | 12.00 | 5.00 |
| ❏ 231 Davone Bess AU RC | 20.00 | 8.00 |
| ❏ 232 Fred Davis AU RC | 12.00 | 5.00 |
| ❏ 233 Gosder Cherilus AU RC | 10.00 | 4.00 |
| ❏ 234 Gosder Cherilus AU RC | 10.00 | 4.00 |
| ❏ 235 Tashard Choice AU RC | 25.00 | 10.00 |
| ❏ 236 J Leman AU RC | 10.00 | 4.00 |
| ❏ 237 Jack Ikegwuonu AU RC | 10.00 | 4.00 |
| ❏ 238 Jacob Hester AU RC | 12.00 | 5.00 |

| # | Card | Hi | Lo |
|---|------|----|----|
| 239 | Jacob Tamme AU RC | 12.00 | 5.00 |
| 240 | Sedrick Ellis AU RC | 12.00 | 5.00 |
| 241 | Jermichael Finley AU RC | 12.00 | 5.00 |
| 242 | John Carlson AU RC | 20.00 | 8.00 |
| 243 | Jonathan Goff AU RC | 10.00 | 4.00 |
| 245 | Shawn Crable AU RC | 12.00 | 5.00 |
| 246 | Josh Johnson AU RC | 12.00 | 5.00 |
| 247 | Justin Forsett AU RC | 12.00 | 5.00 |
| 248 | Justin King AU RC | 10.00 | 4.00 |
| 249 | Keenan Burton AU RC | 10.00 | 4.00 |
| 250 | Sam Baker AU RC | 8.00 | 3.00 |
| 251 | Colt Brennan AU/399 RC | 80.00 | 40.00 |
| 252 | Adrian Arrington AU/399 RC | 15.00 | 6.00 |
| 253 | Alex Brink AU/399 RC | 20.00 | 8.00 |
| 254 | Ali Highsmith AU/399 RC | 20.00 | 8.00 |
| 255 | Keith Rivers AU/399 RC | 20.00 | 8.00 |
| 256 | Kellen Davis AU/399 RC | 15.00 | 6.00 |
| 257 | Kenny Phillips AU/399 RC | 20.00 | 8.00 |
| 258 | Geno Hayes AU/399 RC | 15.00 | 6.00 |
| 259 | Paul Smith AU/399 RC | 20.00 | 8.00 |
| 260 | Lavelle Hawkins AU/499 RC | 15.00 | 6.00 |
| 261 | L.Jackson AU/399 RC | 15.00 | 6.00 |
| 262 | Leodis McKelvin AU/399 RC | 20.00 | 8.00 |
| 263 | Andre Woodson AU/399 RC | 20.00 | 8.00 |
| 264 | Mike Hart AU/499 RC | 25.00 | 10.00 |
| 265 | Martin Rucker AU/399 RC | 15.00 | 6.00 |
| 266 | Dennis Dixon AU/399 RC | 30.00 | 12.00 |
| 267 | Paul Hubbard AU/399 RC | 15.00 | 6.00 |
| 268 | Peyton Hillis AU/399 RC | 30.00 | 12.00 |
| 269 | R.Grice-Mullins AU/399 RC | 20.00 | 8.00 |
| 270 | V.Gholston AU/399 RC | 20.00 | 8.00 |
| 271 | Jerome Simpson AU RC | 25.00 | 10.00 |
| 272 | Dexter Jackson JSY AU RC | 30.00 | 12.00 |
| 273 | Donnie Avery JSY AU RC | 40.00 | 15.00 |
| 275 | Jake Long JSY AU RC | 40.00 | 15.00 |
| 276 | D.Keller JSY AU RC EXCH | 30.00 | 12.00 |
| 277 | James Hardy JSY AU RC | 30.00 | 12.00 |
| 278 | Andre Caldwell JSY AU RC | 25.00 | 10.00 |
| 279 | J.Nelson JSY AU RC EXCH | 40.00 | 15.00 |
| 280 | Kevin Smith JSY AU RC | 50.00 | 20.00 |
| 281 | Eddie Royal JSY AU RC | 60.00 | 25.00 |
| 282 | M.Manningham JSY AU RC | 30.00 | 12.00 |
| 283 | Earl Bennett JSY AU RC | 30.00 | 12.00 |
| 284 | H.Douglas JSY AU RC EXCH | 30.00 | 12.00 |
| 285 | Ray Rice JSY AU RC EXCH | 60.00 | 25.00 |
| 286 | Steve Slaton JSY AU RC | 120.00 | 60.00 |
| 288 | C.Johnson JSY AU RC EXCH | 120.00 | 60.00 |
| 289 | Kevin O'Connell JSY AU RC | 60.00 | 25.00 |
| 290 | D.Jackson JSY AU RC EXCH | 60.00 | 25.00 |
| 291 | Early Doucet JSY AU RC EXCH | 30.00 | 12.00 |
| 292 | Felix Jones JSY AU RC | 120.00 | 60.00 |
| 293 | Jamaal Charles JSY AU RC | 40.00 | 15.00 |
| 294 | J.David Booty JSY AU RC | 40.00 | 15.00 |
| 295 | J.Flacco JSY AU RC EXCH | 200.00 | 100.00 |
| 296 | Limas Sweed JSY AU RC | 40.00 | 15.00 |
| 297 | M.Kelly JSY AU RC EXCH | 30.00 | 12.00 |
| 298 | Matt Forte JSY AU RC | 30.00 | 12.00 |
| 299 | D.McFadden JSY AU/499 RC | 175.00 | 100.00 |
| 300 | Matt Ryan JSY AU/499 RC | 500.00 | 250.00 |
| 301 | Brian Brohm JSY AU/499 RC | 50.00 | 20.00 |
| 302 | Chad Henne JSY AU/499 RC | 60.00 | 25.00 |
| 303 | D.Thomas JSY AU/499 RC | 40.00 | 15.00 |
| 304 | R.Mendenhall JSY AU/499 RC | | |
| 305 | J.Stewart JSY AU/499 RC | 100.00 | 40.00 |

## 2008 SP Rookie Edition

| # | Card | Hi | Lo |
|---|------|----|----|
| 1 | Marshawn Lynch | .75 | .30 |
| 2 | Trent Edwards | .75 | .30 |
| 3 | Roscoe Parrish | .50 | .20 |
| 4 | Jason Taylor | .60 | .25 |
| 5 | Ronnie Brown | .60 | .25 |
| 6 | Hines Ward | .75 | .30 |
| 7 | Tom Brady | 1.25 | .50 |
| 8 | Laurence Maroney | .60 | .25 |
| 9 | Randy Moss | .75 | .30 |
| 10 | Thomas Jones | .60 | .25 |
| 11 | Jerricho Cotchery | .50 | .20 |
| 12 | Brett Favre | 4.00 | 1.50 |
| 13 | Ray Lewis | .75 | .30 |
| 14 | Ed Reed | .60 | .25 |
| 15 | Willis McGahee | .60 | .25 |
| 16 | Carson Palmer | .75 | .30 |
| 17 | T.J. Houshmandzadeh | .60 | .25 |
| 18 | Dwayne Bowe | .60 | .25 |
| 19 | Kellen Winslow | .60 | .25 |
| 20 | Derek Anderson | .60 | .25 |
| 21 | Braylon Edwards | .60 | .25 |
| 22 | Ben Roethlisberger | 1.00 | .40 |
| 23 | Willie Parker | .60 | .25 |
| 24 | Wes Welker | .75 | .30 |
| 25 | DeMeco Ryans | .60 | .25 |
| 26 | Andre Johnson | .60 | .25 |
| 27 | Darius Walker | .50 | .20 |
| 28 | Peyton Manning | 1.25 | .50 |
| 29 | Reggie Wayne | .60 | .25 |
| 30 | Joseph Addai | .60 | .25 |
| 31 | David Garrard | .60 | .25 |
| 32 | Maurice Jones-Drew | .60 | .25 |
| 33 | Fred Taylor | .60 | .25 |
| 34 | Vince Young | .75 | .30 |
| 35 | LenDale White | .60 | .25 |
| 36 | Alge Crumpler | .60 | .25 |
| 37 | Jay Cutler | .75 | .30 |
| 38 | Brandon Marshall | .60 | .25 |
| 39 | John Lynch | .60 | .25 |
| 40 | Brodie Croyle | .60 | .25 |
| 41 | Larry Johnson | .60 | .25 |
| 42 | Derrick Johnson | .50 | .20 |
| 43 | JaMarcus Russell | .75 | .30 |
| 44 | Ronald Curry | .60 | .25 |
| 45 | Jake Delhomme | .60 | .25 |
| 46 | Antonio Gates | .60 | .25 |
| 47 | LaDainian Tomlinson | 1.00 | .40 |
| 48 | Antonio Cromartie | .50 | .20 |
| 49 | Philip Rivers | .75 | .30 |
| 50 | Tony Romo | 1.25 | .50 |
| 51 | Terrell Owens | .75 | .30 |
| 52 | DeMarcus Ware | .60 | .25 |
| 53 | Marion Barber | .75 | .30 |
| 54 | Eli Manning | .75 | .30 |
| 55 | Brandon Jacobs | .60 | .25 |
| 56 | Plaxico Burress | .60 | .25 |
| 57 | Antonio Pierce | .50 | .20 |
| 58 | Donovan McNabb | .75 | .30 |
| 59 | Brian Dawkins | .60 | .25 |
| 60 | Brian Westbrook | .60 | .25 |
| 61 | Chris Cooley | .60 | .25 |
| 62 | Jason Campbell | .60 | .25 |
| 63 | Clinton Portis | .60 | .25 |
| 64 | Brian Urlacher | .75 | .30 |
| 65 | Lance Briggs | .50 | .20 |
| 66 | Devin Hester | .75 | .30 |
| 67 | Roy Williams WR | .60 | .25 |
| 68 | Calvin Johnson | .75 | .30 |
| 69 | Ernie Sims | .50 | .20 |
| 70 | Aaron Rodgers | .75 | .30 |
| 71 | Ryan Grant | .75 | .30 |
| 72 | Greg Jennings | .60 | .25 |
| 73 | Tarvaris Jackson | .60 | .25 |
| 74 | Adrian Peterson | 1.50 | .60 |
| 75 | Sidney Rice | .60 | .25 |
| 76 | Michael Turner | .60 | .25 |
| 77 | Roddy White | .60 | .25 |
| 78 | Jason Witten | .60 | .25 |
| 79 | DeAngelo Williams | .60 | .25 |
| 80 | Steve Smith | .60 | .25 |
| 81 | Julius Peppers | .60 | .25 |
| 82 | Drew Brees | .75 | .30 |
| 83 | Reggie Bush | .75 | .30 |
| 84 | Marques Colston | .60 | .25 |
| 85 | Jonathan Vilma | .60 | .25 |
| 86 | Joey Galloway | .60 | .25 |
| 87 | Jeff Garcia | .60 | .25 |
| 88 | Cadillac Williams | .60 | .25 |
| 89 | Kurt Warner | .75 | .30 |
| 90 | Edgerrin James | .60 | .25 |
| 91 | Larry Fitzgerald | .75 | .30 |
| 92 | Anquan Boldin | .60 | .25 |
| 93 | Marc Bulger | .60 | .25 |
| 94 | Steven Jackson | .75 | .30 |
| 95 | Torry Holt | .60 | .25 |
| 96 | J.T. O'Sullivan | .60 | .25 |
| 98 | Nate Clements | .50 | .20 |
| 99 | Matt Hasselbeck | .60 | .25 |
| 100 | Deion Branch | .60 | .25 |
| 101 | Alex Brink RC | 1.50 | .60 |
| 102 | Andre Woodson RC | 1.50 | .60 |
| 103 | Brian Brohm RC | 2.00 | .75 |
| 104 | Dorien Bryant RC | 1.25 | .50 |
| 105 | Colt Brennan RC | 4.00 | 1.50 |
| 106 | Calais Campbell RC | 1.25 | .50 |
| 107 | Chad Henne RC | 2.50 | 1.00 |
| 108 | Chris Johnson RC | 4.00 | 1.50 |
| 109 | Chris Long RC | 2.00 | .75 |
| 110 | Jacob Tamme RC | 1.50 | .60 |
| 111 | Dan Connor RC | 1.50 | .60 |
| 112 | Dennis Dixon RC | 1.50 | .60 |
| 113 | DeSean Jackson RC | 3.00 | 1.25 |
| 114 | Dennis Keyes RC | 1.00 | .40 |
| 115 | Darren McFadden RC | 4.00 | 1.50 |
| 116 | Dominique Rodgers-Cromartie RC | 1.50 | .60 |
| 117 | Devin Thomas RC | 1.50 | .60 |
| 118 | Erik Ainge RC | 1.50 | .60 |
| 119 | Early Doucet RC | 1.50 | .60 |
| 120 | Erin Henderson RC | 1.25 | .50 |
| 121 | Fred Davis RC | 1.50 | .60 |
| 122 | Felix Jones RC | 4.00 | 1.50 |
| 123 | Matt Forte RC | 4.00 | 1.50 |
| 124 | Glenn Dorsey RC | 2.00 | .75 |
| 125 | John David Booty RC | 2.00 | .75 |
| 126 | Jamaal Charles RC | 2.00 | .75 |
| 127 | Joe Flacco RC | 5.00 | 2.00 |
| 128 | Jonathan Goff RC | 1.25 | .50 |
| 129 | Jake Long RC | 2.00 | .75 |
| 130 | Jordy Nelson RC | 2.00 | .75 |
| 131 | Jonathan Stewart RC | 4.00 | 1.50 |
| 132 | Davone Bess RC | 2.00 | .75 |
| 133 | Kalvin McRae RC | 1.25 | .50 |
| 134 | Kenny Phillips RC | 1.50 | .60 |
| 135 | Kevin Smith RC | 2.50 | 1.00 |
| 136 | Leodis McKelvin RC | 1.50 | .60 |
| 137 | Limas Sweed RC | 2.00 | .75 |
| 138 | Matt Flynn RC | 2.00 | .75 |
| 139 | Mike Hart RC | 2.00 | .75 |
| 140 | Aqib Talib RC | 1.50 | .60 |
| 141 | Malcolm Kelly RC | 1.50 | .60 |
| 142 | Mario Manningham RC | 1.50 | .60 |
| 143 | Matt Ryan RC | 6.00 | 2.50 |
| 144 | Paul Smith RC | 1.50 | .60 |
| 145 | Rashard Mendenhall RC | 3.00 | 1.25 |
| 146 | Ray Rice RC | 2.00 | .76 |
| 147 | Sedrick Ellis RC | 1.50 | .60 |
| 148 | Donnie Avery RC | 2.00 | .75 |
| 149 | Tashard Choice RC | 1.50 | .60 |
| 150 | Vernon Gholston RC | 1.50 | .60 |
| 151 | Alex Brink 93 | 2.50 | 1.00 |
| 152 | Andre Caldwell 93 | 2.00 | .75 |
| 153 | Allen Patrick 93 | 2.00 | .75 |
| 154 | Andre Woodson 93 | 2.50 | 1.00 |
| 155 | Brian Brohm 93 | 3.00 | 1.25 |
| 156 | Dorien Bryant 93 | 2.00 | .75 |
| 157 | Colt Brennan 93 | 6.00 | 2.50 |
| 158 | Chris Ellis 93 | 2.00 | .75 |
| 159 | Chad Henne 93 | 4.00 | 1.50 |
| 160 | Chris Johnson 93 | 4.00 | 1.50 |
| 161 | Chris Long 93 | 3.00 | 1.25 |
| 162 | Donnie Avery 93 | 3.00 | 1.25 |
| 163 | Davone Bess 93 | 3.00 | 1.25 |
| 164 | Dan Connor 93 | 2.50 | 1.00 |
| 165 | Dennis Dixon 93 | 2.50 | 1.00 |
| 166 | DeSean Jackson 93 | 2.50 | 1.00 |
| 167 | Darren McFadden 93 | 6.00 | 2.50 |
| 168 | Erik Ainge 93 | 2.50 | 1.00 |
| 169 | Early Doucet 93 | 2.50 | 1.00 |
| 170 | Fred Davis 93 | 2.50 | 1.00 |
| 171 | Felix Jones 93 | 6.00 | 2.50 |
| 172 | Matt Forte 93 | 6.00 | 2.50 |

|  |  | | |
|---|---|---|---|
| ❏ 173 | Geno Hayes 93 | 1.50 | .60 |
| ❏ 174 | Chevis Jackson 93 | 2.00 | .75 |
| ❏ 175 | John David Booty 93 | 3.00 | 1.25 |
| ❏ 176 | Jamaal Charles 93 | 3.00 | 1.25 |
| ❏ 177 | Joe Flacco 93 | 8.00 | 3.00 |
| ❏ 178 | Peyton Hillis 93 | 3.00 | 1.25 |
| ❏ 179 | Jake Long 93 | 3.00 | 1.25 |
| ❏ 180 | Jordy Nelson 93 | 3.00 | 1.25 |
| ❏ 181 | Jonathan Stewart 93 | 6.00 | 2.50 |
| ❏ 182 | Justin Forsett 93 | 2.50 | 1.00 |
| ❏ 183 | Kevin O'Connell 93 | 3.00 | 1.25 |
| ❏ 184 | Kenny Phillips 93 | 2.50 | 1.00 |
| ❏ 185 | Kevin Smith 93 | 4.00 | 1.50 |
| ❏ 186 | Lance Ball 93 | 1.50 | .60 |
| ❏ 187 | Leodis McKelvin 93 | 3.00 | 1.25 |
| ❏ 188 | Limas Sweed 93 | 3.00 | 1.25 |
| ❏ 189 | Marcus Monk 93 | 2.50 | 1.00 |
| ❏ 190 | Matt Flynn 93 | 3.00 | 1.25 |
| ❏ 191 | Mike Hart 93 | 3.00 | 1.25 |
| ❏ 192 | Mike Jenkins 93 | 2.50 | 1.00 |
| ❏ 193 | Malcolm Kelly 93 | 2.50 | 1.00 |
| ❏ 194 | Mario Manningham 93 | 2.50 | 1.00 |
| ❏ 195 | Dre Moore 93 | 2.00 | .75 |
| ❏ 196 | Matt Ryan 93 | 10.00 | 4.00 |
| ❏ 197 | Ryan Clady 93 | 2.50 | 1.00 |
| ❏ 198 | Rashard Mendenhall 93 | 5.00 | 2.00 |
| ❏ 199 | Ray Rice 93 | 3.00 | 1.25 |
| ❏ 200 | Tashard Choice 93 | 2.50 | 1.00 |
| ❏ 201 | Alex Brink 93 | 3.00 | 1.25 |
| ❏ 202 | Aqib Talib 93 | 3.00 | 1.25 |
| ❏ 203 | Andre Woodson 93 | 3.00 | 1.25 |
| ❏ 204 | Brian Brohm 93 | 4.00 | 1.50 |
| ❏ 205 | Dorien Bryant 93 | 2.50 | 1.00 |
| ❏ 206 | Colt Brennan 93 | 8.00 | 3.00 |
| ❏ 207 | Calais Campbell 93 | 3.00 | 1.25 |
| ❏ 208 | Chad Henne 93 | 5.00 | 2.00 |
| ❏ 209 | Chris Johnson 93 | 4.00 | 1.50 |
| ❏ 210 | Chris Long 93 | 4.00 | 1.50 |
| ❏ 211 | Dorytie Avery 93 | 4.00 | 1.50 |
| ❏ 212 | Davone Bess 93 | 4.00 | 1.50 |
| ❏ 213 | Dennis Dixon 93 | 3.00 | 1.25 |
| ❏ 214 | DeSean Jackson 93 | 6.00 | 2.50 |
| ❏ 215 | Darren McFadden 93 | 8.00 | 3.00 |
| ❏ 216 | Dominique Rodgers-Cromartie 93 | 3.00 | 1.25 |
| ❏ 217 | Erik Ainge 93 | 3.00 | 1.25 |
| ❏ 218 | Early Doucet 93 | 3.00 | 1.25 |
| ❏ 219 | Fred Davis 93 | 3.00 | 1.25 |
| ❏ 220 | Felix Jones 93 | 8.00 | 3.00 |
| ❏ 221 | Matt Forte 93 | 8.00 | 3.00 |
| ❏ 222 | Harry Douglas 93 | 4.00 | 1.50 |
| ❏ 223 | John David Booty 93 | 4.00 | 1.50 |
| ❏ 224 | Jamaal Charles 93 | 5.00 | 2.00 |
| ❏ 225 | Joe Flacco 93 | 10.00 | 4.00 |
| ❏ 226 | James Hardy 93 | 4.00 | 1.50 |
| ❏ 227 | Josh Johnson 93 | 3.00 | 1.25 |
| ❏ 228 | Jordy Nelson 93 | 4.00 | 1.50 |
| ❏ 229 | Jonathan Stewart 93 | 8.00 | 3.00 |
| ❏ 230 | Keenan Burton 93 | 2.50 | 1.00 |
| ❏ 231 | Kenny Phillips 93 | 3.00 | 1.25 |
| ❏ 232 | Keith Rivers 93 | 3.00 | 1.25 |
| ❏ 233 | Kevin Smith 93 | 5.00 | 2.00 |
| ❏ 234 | Lavelle Hawkins 93 | 3.00 | 1.25 |
| ❏ 235 | Leodis McKelvin 93 | 3.00 | 1.25 |
| ❏ 236 | Limas Sweed 93 | 4.00 | 1.50 |
| ❏ 237 | Matt Flynn 93 | 4.00 | 1.50 |
| ❏ 238 | Mike Hart 93 | 4.00 | 1.50 |
| ❏ 239 | Adrian Arrington 93 | 2.50 | 1.00 |
| ❏ 240 | Malcolm Kelly 93 | 4.00 | 1.50 |
| ❏ 241 | Mario Manningham 93 | 3.00 | 1.25 |
| ❏ 242 | Matt Ryan 93 | 12.00 | 5.00 |
| ❏ 243 | Phillip Merling 93 | 2.50 | 1.00 |
| ❏ 244 | Darius Reynaud 93 | 2.50 | 1.00 |
| ❏ 245 | Rashard Mendenhall 93 | 6.00 | 2.50 |
| ❏ 246 | Ray Rice 93 | 4.00 | 1.50 |
| ❏ 247 | Ryan Torain 93 | 3.00 | 1.25 |
| ❏ 248 | Thomas Brown 93 | 4.00 | 1.50 |
| ❏ 249 | Tashard Choice 93 | 3.00 | 1.25 |
| ❏ 250 | Vernon Gholston 93 | 4.00 | 1.50 |
| ❏ 251 | Alex Brink 95 | 3.00 | 1.25 |
| ❏ 252 | Allen Patrick 95 | 4.00 | 1.50 |
| ❏ 253 | Aqib Talib 95 | 3.00 | 1.25 |
| ❏ 254 | Andre Woodson 95 | 4.00 | 1.50 |
| ❏ 255 | Brian Brohm 95 | 5.00 | 2.00 |
| ❏ 256 | Dorien Bryant 95 | 3.00 | 1.25 |
| ❏ 257 | Colt Brennan 95 | 10.00 | 4.00 |
| ❏ 258 | Chad Henne 95 | 6.00 | 2.50 |
| ❏ 259 | Chris Johnson 95 | 10.00 | 4.00 |
| ❏ 260 | Chris Long 95 | 5.00 | 2.00 |
| ❏ 261 | Davone Bess 95 | 5.00 | 2.00 |
| ❏ 262 | Dennis Dixon 95 | 4.00 | 1.50 |
| ❏ 263 | DeSean Jackson 95 | 8.00 | 3.00 |
| ❏ 264 | Darren McFadden 95 | 10.00 | 4.00 |
| ❏ 265 | Erik Ainge 95 | 4.00 | 1.50 |
| ❏ 266 | Early Doucet 95 | 4.00 | 1.50 |
| ❏ 267 | Fred Davis 95 | 4.00 | 1.50 |
| ❏ 268 | Felix Jones 95 | 10.00 | 4.00 |
| ❏ 269 | Matt Forte 95 | 10.00 | 4.00 |
| ❏ 270 | Geno Hayes 95 | 2.50 | 1.00 |
| ❏ 271 | Harry Douglas 95 | 4.00 | 1.50 |
| ❏ 272 | John David Booty 95 | 5.00 | 2.00 |
| ❏ 273 | Jamaal Charles 95 | 5.00 | 2.00 |
| ❏ 274 | Joe Flacco 95 | 12.00 | 5.00 |
| ❏ 275 | Peyton Hillis 95 | 4.00 | 1.50 |
| ❏ 276 | Jacob Hester 95 | 4.00 | 1.50 |
| ❏ 277 | Josh Johnson 95 | 4.00 | 1.50 |
| ❏ 278 | Jordy Nelson 95 | 5.00 | 2.00 |
| ❏ 279 | Jonathan Stewart 95 | 10.00 | 4.00 |
| ❏ 280 | Keenan Burton 95 | 3.00 | 1.25 |
| ❏ 281 | Kenny Phillips 95 | 4.00 | 1.50 |
| ❏ 282 | Kevin Smith 95 | 6.00 | 2.50 |
| ❏ 283 | Lance Ball 95 | 2.50 | 1.00 |
| ❏ 284 | Lavelle Hawkins 95 | 3.00 | 1.25 |
| ❏ 285 | Limas Sweed 95 | 5.00 | 2.00 |
| ❏ 286 | Matt Flynn 95 | 4.00 | 1.50 |
| ❏ 287 | Mike Hart 95 | 5.00 | 2.00 |
| ❏ 288 | Adrian Arrington 95 | 3.00 | 1.25 |
| ❏ 289 | Malcolm Kelly 95 | 4.00 | 1.50 |
| ❏ 290 | Mario Manningham 95 | 4.00 | 1.50 |
| ❏ 291 | Marcus Monk 95 | 4.00 | 1.50 |
| ❏ 292 | Matt Ryan 95 | 15.00 | 6.00 |
| ❏ 293 | Mario Urrutia 95 | 3.00 | 1.25 |
| ❏ 294 | Paul Hubbard 95 | 3.00 | 1.25 |
| ❏ 295 | Rashard Mendenhall 95 | 8.00 | 3.00 |
| ❏ 296 | Ray Rice 95 | 5.00 | 2.00 |
| ❏ 297 | Ryan Torain 95 | 3.00 | 1.25 |
| ❏ 298 | Thomas Brown 95 | 4.00 | 1.50 |
| ❏ 299 | Tashard Choice 95 | 4.00 | 1.50 |
| ❏ 300 | Yvenson Bernard 95 | 4.00 | 1.50 |
| ❏ 301 | Alex Brink 96 | 4.00 | 1.50 |
| ❏ 302 | Chevis Jackson 96 | 3.00 | 1.25 |
| ❏ 303 | Andre Caldwell 96 | 3.00 | 1.25 |
| ❏ 304 | Allen Patrick 96 | 3.00 | 1.25 |
| ❏ 305 | Kevin O'Connell 96 | 5.00 | 2.00 |
| ❏ 306 | Andre Woodson 96 | 4.00 | 1.50 |
| ❏ 307 | Brian Brohm 96 | 5.00 | 2.00 |
| ❏ 308 | Mike Jenkins 96 | 4.00 | 1.50 |
| ❏ 309 | Tom Zbikowski 96 | 4.00 | 1.50 |
| ❏ 310 | Dorien Bryant 96 | 3.00 | 1.25 |
| ❏ 311 | Colt Brennan 96 | 10.00 | 4.00 |
| ❏ 312 | Chad Henne 96 | 6.00 | 2.50 |
| ❏ 313 | Chris Johnson 96 | 10.00 | 4.00 |
| ❏ 314 | Chris Long 96 | 5.00 | 2.00 |
| ❏ 315 | Donnie Avery 96 | 5.00 | 2.00 |
| ❏ 316 | Davone Bess 96 | 5.00 | 2.00 |
| ❏ 317 | Dennis Dixon 96 | 4.00 | 1.50 |
| ❏ 318 | DeSean Jackson 96 | 8.00 | 3.00 |
| ❏ 319 | Darren McFadden 96 | 10.00 | 4.00 |
| ❏ 320 | DeMario Pressley 96 | 3.00 | 1.25 |
| ❏ 321 | Dre Moore 96 | 3.00 | 1.25 |
| ❏ 322 | Erik Ainge 96 | 4.00 | 1.50 |
| ❏ 323 | Early Doucet 96 | 4.00 | 1.50 |
| ❏ 324 | Fred Davis 96 | 4.00 | 1.50 |
| ❏ 325 | Felix Jones 96 | 10.00 | 4.00 |
| ❏ 326 | Matt Forte 96 | 10.00 | 4.00 |
| ❏ 327 | Harry Douglas 96 | 4.00 | 1.50 |
| ❏ 328 | John David Booty 96 | 5.00 | 2.00 |
| ❏ 329 | Jamaal Charles 96 | 5.00 | 2.00 |
| ❏ 330 | Joe Flacco 96 | 12.00 | 5.00 |
| ❏ 331 | Jordy Nelson 96 | 5.00 | 2.00 |
| ❏ 332 | Jonathan Stewart 96 | 10.00 | 4.00 |
| ❏ 333 | Kalvin McRae 96 | 3.00 | 1.25 |
| ❏ 334 | Kenny Phillips 96 | 4.00 | 1.50 |
| ❏ 335 | Kevin Smith 96 | 6.00 | 2.50 |
| ❏ 336 | Lavelle Hawkins 96 | 3.00 | 1.25 |
| ❏ 337 | Limas Sweed 96 | 5.00 | 2.00 |
| ❏ 338 | Marcus Monk 96 | 4.00 | 1.50 |
| ❏ 339 | Matt Flynn 96 | 5.00 | 2.00 |
| ❏ 340 | Mike Hart 96 | 5.00 | 2.00 |
| ❏ 341 | Adrian Arrington 96 | 3.00 | 1.25 |
| ❏ 342 | Malcolm Kelly 96 | 4.00 | 1.50 |
| ❏ 343 | Mario Manningham 96 | 4.00 | 1.50 |
| ❏ 344 | Ben Moffitt 96 | 2.50 | 1.00 |
| ❏ 345 | Matt Ryan 96 | 15.00 | 6.00 |
| ❏ 346 | Mario Urrutia 96 | 3.00 | 1.25 |
| ❏ 347 | Rashard Mendenhall 96 | 8.00 | 3.00 |
| ❏ 348 | Ray Rice 96 | 5.00 | 2.00 |
| ❏ 349 | Ryan Torain 96 | 4.00 | 1.50 |
| ❏ 350 | Tashard Choice 96 | 4.00 | 1.50 |
| ❏ 352 | Bob Griese 96 | 3.00 | 1.25 |
| ❏ 353 | Bert Jones 96 | 2.00 | .75 |
| ❏ 354 | Bruce Smith 96 | 2.00 | .75 |
| ❏ 355 | Barry Sanders 96 | 5.00 | 2.00 |
| ❏ 356 | Dick Butkus 96 | 4.00 | 1.50 |
| ❏ 357 | Daryl Johnston 93 | 3.00 | 1.25 |
| ❏ 359 | Franco Harris 96 | 3.00 | 1.25 |
| ❏ 360 | Fran Tarkenton 96 | 3.00 | 1.25 |
| ❏ 363 | Bo Jackson 96 | 4.00 | 1.50 |
| ❏ 365 | John Elway 96 | 5.00 | 2.00 |
| ❏ 366 | Joe Greene 96 | 3.00 | 1.25 |
| ❏ 367 | Jack Ham 96 | 2.50 | 1.00 |
| ❏ 368 | Jerry Kramer 96 | 2.50 | 1.00 |
| ❏ 369 | Jim Kelly 96 | 3.00 | 1.25 |
| ❏ 371 | Joe Namath 96 | 4.00 | 1.50 |
| ❏ 372 | Joe Theismann 96 | 3.00 | 1.25 |
| ❏ 373 | Ken Anderson 96 | 2.50 | 1.00 |
| ❏ 376 | Jerry Rice 96 | 5.00 | 2.00 |
| ❏ 377 | Emmitt Smith 96 | 6.00 | 2.50 |
| ❏ 379 | Ottis Anderson 96 | 2.00 | .75 |
| ❏ 380 | Paul Hornung 96 | 3.00 | 1.25 |
| ❏ 381 | Roger Craig 96 | 2.50 | 1.00 |
| ❏ 382 | Roman Gabriel 96 | 2.50 | 1.00 |
| ❏ 383 | Chuck Bednarik 96 | 2.50 | 1.00 |
| ❏ 384 | Rod Woodson 96 | 3.00 | 1.25 |
| ❏ 385 | Billy Sims 96 | 2.50 | 1.00 |
| ❏ 386 | Archie Manning 96 | 3.00 | 1.25 |
| ❏ 387 | Bart Starr 96 | 5.00 | 2.00 |
| ❏ 388 | Steve Young 96 | 4.00 | 1.50 |
| ❏ 389 | Troy Aikman 96 | 4.00 | 1.50 |
| ❏ 391 | Tom Rathman 96 | 2.50 | 1.00 |
| ❏ 392 | Y.A. Tittle 96 | 3.00 | 1.25 |
| ❏ 394 | Bob Griese 96 | 3.00 | 1.25 |
| ❏ 395 | Bert Jones 96 | 2.00 | .75 |
| ❏ 396 | Bruce Smith 96 | 2.00 | .75 |
| ❏ 397 | Barry Sanders 96 | 5.00 | 2.00 |
| ❏ 398 | Dick Butkus 96 | 4.00 | 1.50 |
| ❏ 399 | Daryl Johnston 93 | 3.00 | 1.25 |
| ❏ 401 | Franco Harris 96 | 3.00 | 1.25 |
| ❏ 402 | Fran Tarkenton 96 | 3.00 | 1.25 |
| ❏ 405 | Bo Jackson 96 | 4.00 | 1.50 |
| ❏ 407 | John Elway 96 | 5.00 | 2.00 |
| ❏ 408 | Joe Greene 96 | 3.00 | 1.25 |
| ❏ 409 | Jack Ham 96 | 2.50 | 1.00 |
| ❏ 410 | Jim Kelly 96 | 3.00 | 1.25 |
| ❏ 411 | Jerry Kramer 96 | 2.50 | 1.00 |
| ❏ 413 | Joe Namath 96 | 4.00 | 1.50 |
| ❏ 414 | Joe Theismann 93 | 3.00 | 1.25 |
| ❏ 415 | Ken Anderson 93 | 2.50 | 1.00 |
| ❏ 418 | Roger Staubach 93 | 4.00 | 1.50 |
| ❏ 419 | Chuck Bednarik 93 | 2.50 | 1.00 |
| ❏ 421 | Ottis Anderson 93 | 2.00 | .75 |
| ❏ 422 | Paul Hornung 93 | 3.00 | 1.25 |
| ❏ 423 | Roger Craig 93 | 2.50 | 1.00 |
| ❏ 424 | Roman Gabriel 93 | 2.50 | 1.00 |
| ❏ 426 | Rod Woodson 93 | 3.00 | 1.25 |
| ❏ 427 | Billy Sims 93 | 2.50 | 1.00 |
| ❏ 428 | Archie Manning 93 | 3.00 | 1.25 |
| ❏ 429 | Bart Starr 93 | 5.00 | 2.00 |
| ❏ 430 | Steve Young 93 | 4.00 | 1.50 |
| ❏ 431 | Troy Aikman 93 | 4.00 | 1.50 |
| ❏ 433 | Tom Rathman 93 | 2.50 | 1.00 |
| ❏ 434 | Y.A. Tittle 93 | 3.00 | 1.25 |

## 1999 SPx

| | | | |
|---|---|---|---|
| ❏ COMPLETE SET (135) | | 2000.00 | 1000.00 |
| ❏ COMP.SET w/o SP's (90) | | 25.00 | 12.50 |
| ❏ *HAND NUMBERED RCs: .5X TO .8X | | | |
| ❏ 1 | Jake Plummer | 1.00 | .40 |
| ❏ 2 | Adrian Murrell | 1.00 | .40 |
| ❏ 3 | Frank Sanders | 1.00 | .40 |
| ❏ 4 | Jamal Anderson | 1.50 | .60 |
| ❏ 5 | Chris Chandler | 1.00 | .40 |
| ❏ 6 | Terance Mathis | 1.00 | .40 |
| ❏ 7 | Tony Banks | 1.00 | .40 |
| ❏ 8 | Priest Holmes | 2.50 | 1.00 |
| ❏ 9 | Jermaine Lewis | 1.00 | .40 |

|  |  | | |
|---|---|---|---|
| ❏ 10 | Antowain Smith | 1.50 | .60 |
| ❏ 11 | Doug Flutie | 1.50 | .60 |
| ❏ 12 | Eric Moulds | 1.50 | .60 |
| ❏ 13 | Tim Biakabutuka | 1.00 | .40 |
| ❏ 14 | Steve Beuerlein | 1.00 | .40 |
| ❏ 15 | Muhsin Muhammad | 1.00 | .40 |
| ❏ 16 | Bobby Engram | 1.00 | .40 |
| ❏ 17 | Curtis Conway | 1.00 | .40 |
| ❏ 18 | Curtis Enis | .60 | .25 |
| ❏ 19 | Corey Dillon | 1.50 | .60 |
| ❏ 20 | Jeff Blake | 1.00 | .40 |
| ❏ 21 | Carl Pickens | 1.00 | .40 |
| ❏ 22 | Ty Detmer | 1.00 | .40 |
| ❏ 23 | Terry Kirby | .60 | .25 |
| ❏ 24 | Leslie Shepherd | .60 | .25 |
| ❏ 25 | Troy Aikman | 3.00 | 1.25 |
| ❏ 26 | Emmitt Smith | 3.00 | 1.25 |
| ❏ 27 | Deion Sanders | 1.50 | .60 |
| ❏ 28 | Terrell Davis | 1.50 | .60 |
| ❏ 29 | Rod Smith | 1.00 | .40 |
| ❏ 30 | Bubby Brister | 1.00 | .40 |
| ❏ 31 | Barry Sanders | 5.00 | 2.00 |
| ❏ 32 | Herman Moore | 1.00 | .40 |
| ❏ 33 | Charlie Batch | 1.50 | .60 |
| ❏ 34 | Brett Favre | 5.00 | 2.00 |
| ❏ 35 | Antonio Freeman | 1.50 | .60 |
| ❏ 36 | Dorsey Levens | 1.50 | .60 |
| ❏ 37 | Peyton Manning | 5.00 | 2.00 |
| ❏ 38 | Marvin Harrison | 1.50 | .60 |
| ❏ 39 | Jerome Pathon | .60 | .25 |
| ❏ 40 | Mark Brunell | 1.50 | .60 |
| ❏ 41 | Jimmy Smith | 1.00 | .40 |
| ❏ 42 | Fred Taylor | 1.50 | .60 |
| ❏ 43 | Elvis Grbac | 1.00 | .40 |
| ❏ 44 | Andre Rison | 1.00 | .40 |
| ❏ 45 | Warren Moon | 1.50 | .60 |
| ❏ 46 | Dan Marino | 5.00 | 2.00 |
| ❏ 47 | Karim Abdul-Jabbar | 1.00 | .40 |
| ❏ 48 | O.J. McDuffie | 1.00 | .40 |
| ❏ 49 | Randall Cunningham | 1.50 | .60 |
| ❏ 50 | Robert Smith | 1.50 | .60 |
| ❏ 51 | Randy Moss | 4.00 | 1.50 |
| ❏ 52 | Drew Bledsoe | 2.00 | .75 |
| ❏ 53 | Terry Glenn | 1.50 | .60 |
| ❏ 54 | Tony Simmons | .60 | .25 |
| ❏ 55 | Danny Wuerffel | .60 | .25 |
| ❏ 56 | Cam Cleeland | .60 | .25 |
| ❏ 57 | Kerry Collins | 1.00 | .40 |
| ❏ 58 | Gary Brown | .60 | .25 |
| ❏ 59 | Ike Hilliard | .60 | .25 |
| ❏ 60 | Vinny Testaverde | 1.00 | .40 |
| ❏ 61 | Curtis Martin | 1.50 | .60 |
| ❏ 62 | Keyshawn Johnson | 1.50 | .60 |
| ❏ 63 | Rich Gannon | 1.00 | .40 |
| ❏ 64 | Napoleon Kaufman | 1.50 | .60 |
| ❏ 65 | Tim Brown | 1.50 | .60 |
| ❏ 66 | Duce Staley | 1.50 | .60 |
| ❏ 67 | Doug Pederson | .60 | .25 |
| ❏ 68 | Charles Johnson | .60 | .25 |
| ❏ 69 | Kordell Stewart | 1.00 | .40 |
| ❏ 70 | Jerome Bettis | 1.50 | .60 |
| ❏ 71 | Trent Green | 1.50 | .60 |
| ❏ 72 | Marshall Faulk | 2.00 | .75 |
| ❏ 73 | Ryan Leaf | 1.50 | .60 |
| ❏ 74 | Natrone Means | 1.00 | .40 |
| ❏ 75 | Jim Harbaugh | 1.00 | .40 |
| ❏ 76 | Steve Young | 2.00 | .75 |
| ❏ 77 | Garrison Hearst | 1.00 | .40 |
| ❏ 78 | Jerry Rice | 3.00 | 1.25 |
| ❏ 79 | Terrell Owens | 1.50 | .60 |
| ❏ 80 | Ricky Watters | 1.00 | .40 |
| ❏ 81 | Joey Galloway | 1.00 | .40 |
| ❏ 82 | Jon Kitna | 1.50 | .60 |
| ❏ 83 | Warrick Dunn | 1.50 | .60 |
| ❏ 84 | Trent Dilfer | 1.00 | .40 |
| ❏ 85 | Mike Alstott | 1.50 | .60 |
| ❏ 86 | Steve McNair | 1.50 | .60 |
| ❏ 87 | Eddie George | 1.50 | .60 |
| ❏ 88 | Yancey Thigpen | .60 | .25 |
| ❏ 89 | Skip Hicks | .60 | .25 |
| ❏ 90 | Michael Westbrook | 1.00 | .40 |
| ❏ 91 | Amos Zereoue RC | 15.00 | 6.00 |
| ❏ 92 | Chris Claiborne AU RC | 25.00 | 10.00 |
| ❏ 93 | Scott Covington RC | 15.00 | 6.00 |
| ❏ 94 | Jeff Paulk RC | 10.00 | 4.00 |
| ❏ 95 | Brandon Stokley AU RC | 40.00 | 15.00 |
| ❏ 96 | Antoine Winfield RC | 12.00 | 5.00 |
| ❏ 97 | Reginald Kelly RC | 10.00 | 4.00 |
| ❏ 98 | Jermaine Fazande AU RC | 15.00 | 6.00 |
| ❏ 99 | Andy Katzenmoyer RC | 12.00 | 5.00 |
| ❏ 100 | Craig Yeast RC | 12.00 | 5.00 |
| ❏ 101 | Joe Montgomery RC | 12.00 | 5.00 |
| ❏ 102 | Darrin Chiaverini RC | 12.00 | 5.00 |
| ❏ 103 | Travis McGriff RC | 10.00 | 4.00 |
| ❏ 104 | Jevon Kearse RC | 30.00 | 12.50 |
| ❏ 105 | Joel Makovicka AU RC | 15.00 | 6.00 |
| ❏ 106 | Aaron Brooks RC | 20.00 | 8.00 |
| ❏ 107 | Chris McAlister RC | 12.00 | 5.00 |
| ❏ 108 | Jim Kleinsasser RC | 15.00 | 6.00 |
| ❏ 109 | Ebenezer Ekuban RC | 12.00 | 5.00 |
| ❏ 110 | Karsten Bailey RC | 12.00 | 5.00 |
| ❏ 111 | Sedrick Irvin AU RC | 12.00 | 5.00 |
| ❏ 112 | D'Wayne Bates AU RC | 12.00 | 5.00 |
| ❏ 113 | Joe Germaine AU RC | 15.00 | 6.00 |
| ❏ 114 | Cecil Collins AU RC | 15.00 | 6.00 |
| ❏ 115 | Mike Cloud RC | 12.00 | 5.00 |
| ❏ 116 | James Johnson RC | 12.00 | 5.00 |
| ❏ 117 | Champ Bailey AU RC | 40.00 | 15.00 |
| ❏ 118 | Rob Konrad RC | 15.00 | 6.00 |
| ❏ 119 | Peerless Price AU RC | 30.00 | 12.50 |
| ❏ 120 | Kevin Faulk AU RC | 25.00 | 10.00 |
| ❏ 121 | Dameane Douglas RC | 10.00 | 4.00 |
| ❏ 122 | Kevin Johnson AU RC | 15.00 | 6.00 |
| ❏ 123 | Troy Edwards AU RC | 25.00 | 10.00 |
| ❏ 124 | Edgerrin James AU RC | 80.00 | 30.00 |
| ❏ 125 | David Boston AU RC | 25.00 | 10.00 |
| ❏ 126 | Michael Bishop AU RC | 25.00 | 10.00 |
| ❏ 127 | Shaun King AU RC SP | 50.00 | 25.00 |
| ❏ 127X | Shaun King EXCH | 10.00 | 4.00 |
| ❏ 128 | Brock Huard AU RC | 15.00 | 6.00 |
| ❏ 129 | Torry Holt AU RC | 60.00 | 30.00 |
| ❏ 130 | Cade McNown AU/500 RC | 40.00 | 15.00 |
| ❏ 131 | Tim Couch AU/500 RC | 40.00 | 15.00 |
| ❏ 132 | Donovan McNabb AU/500 RC | 100.00 | 50.00 |
| ❏ 132X | Donovan McNabb EXCH | 5.00 | 2.00 |
| ❏ 133 | Akili Smith AU/500 RC | 40.00 | 15.00 |
| ❏ 134 | D.Culpepper AU/500 RC | 120.00 | 60.00 |
| ❏ 135 | Ricky Williams AU/500 RC | 60.00 | 30.00 |
| ❏ S8 | Troy Aikman Sample | 2.00 | .75 |

## 2000 SPx

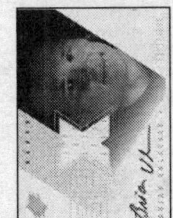

|  |  | | |
|---|---|---|---|
| ❏ COMP.SET w/o SP's (90) | | 20.00 | 7.50 |
| ❏ 1 | Jake Plummer | .60 | .25 |
| ❏ 2 | David Boston | 1.00 | .40 |
| ❏ 3 | Frank Sanders | .60 | .25 |
| ❏ 4 | Chris Chandler | .60 | .25 |
| ❏ 5 | Jamal Anderson | 1.00 | .40 |
| ❏ 6 | Shawn Jefferson | .40 | .15 |
| ❏ 7 | Qadry Ismail | .60 | .25 |
| ❏ 8 | Tony Banks | .60 | .25 |
| ❏ 9 | Shannon Sharpe | .60 | .25 |
| ❏ 10 | Rob Johnson | .60 | .25 |
| ❏ 11 | Eric Moulds | 1.00 | .40 |
| ❏ 12 | Muhsin Muhammad | .60 | .25 |
| ❏ 13 | Steve Beuerlein | .40 | .15 |
| ❏ 14 | Cade McNown | .40 | .15 |
| ❏ 15 | Marcus Robinson | 1.00 | .40 |
| ❏ 16 | Akili Smith | .40 | .15 |
| ❏ 17 | Corey Dillon | 1.00 | .40 |
| ❏ 18 | Darnay Scott | .60 | .25 |
| ❏ 19 | Tim Couch | .60 | .25 |
| ❏ 20 | Kevin Johnson | .40 | .15 |
| ❏ 21 | Errict Rhett | .40 | .15 |
| ❏ 22 | Troy Aikman | 2.00 | .75 |
| ❏ 23 | Emmitt Smith | 2.00 | .75 |
| ❏ 24 | Joey Galloway | .60 | .25 |
| ❏ 25 | Terrell Davis | 1.00 | .40 |
| ❏ 26 | Olandis Gary | 1.00 | .40 |
| ❏ 27 | Brian Griese | 1.00 | .40 |
| ❏ 28 | Charlie Batch | 1.00 | .40 |
| ❏ 29 | Germane Crowell | .40 | .15 |
| ❏ 30 | James Stewart | 1.00 | .40 |
| ❏ 31 | Brett Favre | 3.00 | 1.25 |
| ❏ 32 | Antonio Freeman | 1.00 | .40 |
| ❏ 33 | Dorsey Levens | .60 | .25 |
| ❏ 34 | Peyton Manning | 2.50 | 1.00 |
| ❏ 35 | Edgerrin James | 1.50 | .60 |
| ❏ 36 | Marvin Harrison | 1.00 | .40 |
| ❏ 37 | Mark Brunell | 1.00 | .40 |
| ❏ 38 | Fred Taylor | 1.00 | .40 |
| ❏ 39 | Jimmy Smith | .60 | .25 |
| ❏ 40 | Keenan McCardell | .60 | .25 |
| ❏ 41 | Elvis Grbac | .60 | .25 |
| ❏ 42 | Tony Gonzalez | .60 | .25 |
| ❏ 43 | Tony Martin | .60 | .25 |
| ❏ 44 | Jay Fiedler | 1.00 | .40 |
| ❏ 45 | Damon Huard | 1.00 | .40 |
| ❏ 46 | Randy Moss | 2.00 | .75 |
| ❏ 47 | Robert Smith | 1.00 | .40 |
| ❏ 48 | Cris Carter | 1.00 | .40 |
| ❏ 49 | Daunte Culpepper | 1.25 | .50 |
| ❏ 50 | Drew Bledsoe | 1.25 | .50 |
| ❏ 51 | Terry Glenn | .60 | .25 |
| ❏ 52 | Ricky Williams | 1.00 | .40 |
| ❏ 53 | Jeff Blake | .60 | .25 |
| ❏ 54 | Keith Poole | .40 | .15 |
| ❏ 55 | Kerry Collins | .60 | .25 |
| ❏ 56 | Amani Toomer | .60 | .25 |
| ❏ 57 | Ike Hilliard | .60 | .25 |
| ❏ 58 | Ray Lucas | .60 | .25 |
| ❏ 59 | Curtis Martin | 1.00 | .40 |
| ❏ 60 | Vinny Testaverde | 1.00 | .40 |
| ❏ 61 | Tim Brown | 1.00 | .40 |
| ❏ 62 | Rich Gannon | 1.00 | .40 |
| ❏ 63 | Tyrone Wheatley | .60 | .25 |
| ❏ 64 | Napoleon Kaufman | .60 | .25 |
| ❏ 65 | Duce Staley | 1.00 | .40 |
| ❏ 66 | Donovan McNabb | 1.50 | .60 |
| ❏ 67 | Troy Edwards | .40 | .15 |
| ❏ 68 | Jerome Bettis | 1.00 | .40 |
| ❏ 69 | Kordell Stewart | .60 | .25 |
| ❏ 70 | Marshall Faulk | 1.25 | .50 |
| ❏ 71 | Kurt Warner | 1.50 | .60 |
| ❏ 72 | Isaac Bruce | 1.00 | .40 |
| ❏ 73 | Torry Holt | 1.00 | .40 |
| ❏ 74 | Ryan Leaf | .60 | .25 |
| ❏ 75 | Jim Harbaugh | .60 | .25 |
| ❏ 76 | Jerry Rice | 2.00 | .75 |
| ❏ 77 | Terrell Owens | 1.00 | .40 |
| ❏ 78 | Jeff Garcia | 1.00 | .40 |
| ❏ 79 | Ricky Watters | .60 | .25 |
| ❏ 80 | Jon Kitna | 1.00 | .40 |
| ❏ 81 | Derrick Mayes | .60 | .25 |
| ❏ 82 | Shaun King | .40 | .15 |
| ❏ 83 | Mike Alstott | 1.00 | .40 |
| ❏ 84 | Keyshawn Johnson | 1.00 | .40 |
| ❏ 85 | Eddie George | 1.00 | .40 |
| ❏ 86 | Steve McNair | 1.00 | .40 |
| ❏ 87 | Jevon Kearse | 1.00 | .40 |
| ❏ 88 | Brad Johnson | 1.00 | .40 |
| ❏ 89 | Stephen Davis | 1.00 | .40 |

| | | |
|---|---|---|
| ❏ 90 Michael Westbrook | .60 | .25 |
| ❏ 91 Anthony Lucas RC | 6.00 | 2.50 |
| ❏ 92 Avion Black RC | 8.00 | 3.00 |
| ❏ 93 Corey Moore RC | 6.00 | 2.50 |
| ❏ 94 Chris Cole RC | 8.00 | 3.00 |
| ❏ 95 Chris Hovan RC | 8.00 | 3.00 |
| ❏ 96 Dante Hall RC | 12.00 | 5.00 |
| ❏ 97 Darrell Jackson RC | 12.00 | 5.00 |
| ❏ 98 Deltha O'Neal RC | 10.00 | 4.00 |
| ❏ 99 Doug Chapman RC | 8.00 | 3.00 |
| ❏ 100 Doug Johnson RC | 10.00 | 4.00 |
| ❏ 101 Erron Kinney RC | 8.00 | 3.00 |
| ❏ 102 Frank Moreau RC | 8.00 | 3.00 |
| ❏ 103 Patrick Pass RC | 8.00 | 3.00 |
| ❏ 104 Gari Scott RC | 6.00 | 2.50 |
| ❏ 105 Giovanni Carmazzi RC | 6.00 | 2.50 |
| ❏ 106 JaJuan Dawson RC | 6.00 | 2.50 |
| ❏ 107 James Williams RC | 8.00 | 3.00 |
| ❏ 108 Jarious Jackson RC | 8.00 | 3.00 |
| ❏ 109 John Abraham RC | 12.00 | 5.00 |
| ❏ 110 Keith Bulluck RC | 10.00 | 4.00 |
| ❏ 111 Jonas Lewis RC | 6.00 | 2.50 |
| ❏ 112 Mike Green RC | 8.00 | 3.00 |
| ❏ 113 Rooney Jenkins RC | 8.00 | 3.00 |
| ❏ 114 Michael Wiley RC | 8.00 | 3.00 |
| ❏ 115 Mike Anderson RC | 10.00 | 4.00 |
| ❏ 116 Mareno Philyaw RC | 6.00 | 2.50 |
| ❏ 117 Muneer Moore RC | 6.00 | 2.50 |
| ❏ 118 Paul Smith RC | 8.00 | 3.00 |
| ❏ 119 Raynoch Thompson RC | 8.00 | 3.00 |
| ❏ 120 Rob Morris RC | 8.00 | 3.00 |
| ❏ 121 Ron Dixon RC | 8.00 | 3.00 |
| ❏ 122 Rondell Mealey RC | 6.00 | 2.50 |
| ❏ 123 Sebastian Janikowski RC | 10.00 | 4.00 |
| ❏ 124 Shaun Ellis RC | 10.00 | 4.00 |
| ❏ 125 Charles Lee RC | 8.00 | 3.00 |
| ❏ 126 Shyrone Stith RC | 6.00 | 2.50 |
| ❏ 127 Thomas Hamner RC | 6.00 | 2.50 |
| ❏ 128 Tim Rattay RC | 10.00 | 4.00 |
| ❏ 129 Todd Husak RC | 10.00 | 4.00 |
| ❏ 130 Tom Brady RC | 400.00 | 225.00 |
| ❏ 131 Trevor Gaylor RC | 8.00 | 3.00 |
| ❏ 132 Windrell Hayes RC | 8.00 | 3.00 |
| ❏ 133 Anthony Becht JSY AU RC | 25.00 | 10.00 |
| ❏ 134 Brian Urlacher JSY AU RC | 135.00 | 75.00 |
| ❏ 135 Bubba Franks JSY AU RC | 25.00 | 10.00 |
| ❏ 136 C Pennington JSY AU RC | 50.00 | 20.00 |
| ❏ 137 Chr Redman JSY AU RC | 20.00 | 8.00 |
| ❏ 138 Corey Simon JSY AU RC | 25.00 | 10.00 |
| ❏ 139 Curtis Keaton JSY AU RC | 15.00 | 6.00 |
| ❏ 140 Danny Farmer JSY AU RC | 15.00 | 6.00 |
| ❏ 141 Den Northcutt JSY AU RC | 25.00 | 10.00 |
| ❏ 142 Dez White JSY AU RC | 25.00 | 10.00 |
| ❏ 143 J.R. Redmond JSY AU SP RC | 20.00 | 8.00 |
| ❏ 144 Jamal Lewis JSY AU RC | 50.00 | 20.00 |
| ❏ 145 Jerry Porter JSY AU RC | 30.00 | 12.50 |
| ❏ 146 Joe Hamilton EXCH | 3.00 | 1.25 |
| ❏ 147 Laver Coles JSY AU RC | 40.00 | 15.00 |
| ❏ 148 R.Jay Soward JSY AU RC | 20.00 | 8.00 |
| ❏ 149 Reu Droughns JSY AU RC | 25.00 | 10.00 |
| ❏ 150 Ron Dayne JSY AU RC | 30.00 | 12.50 |
| ❏ 151 Ron Dugans JSY AU RC | 15.00 | 6.00 |
| ❏ 152 Sha Alexander JSY AU RC | 50.00 | 20.00 |
| ❏ 153 Sylvester Morris JSY AU RC | 20.00 | 8.00 |
| ❏ 154 Tee Martin JSY AU RC | 25.00 | 10.00 |
| ❏ 155 Th.Jones JSY AU SP | 150.00 | 75.00 |
| ❏ 156 Todd Pinkston JSY AU RC | 25.00 | 10.00 |
| ❏ 157 Travis Prentice JSY AU RC | 20.00 | 8.00 |
| ❏ 158 Travis Taylor JSY AU SP RC | 25.00 | 10.00 |
| ❏ 159 Trung Canidate JSY AU RC | 20.00 | 8.00 |
| ❏ 160 Courtney Brown JSY AU RC | 30.00 | 12.50 |
| ❏ 161 Peter Warrick JSY AU RC | 30.00 | 12.50 |
| ❏ 162 Plaxico Buress JSY AU RC | 100.00 | 40.00 |
| ❏ S1 Peyton Manning Sample | 4.00 | 1.50 |

## 2001 SPx

| | | |
|---|---|---|
| ❏ COMP.SET w/o SP's (90) | 20.00 | 7.50 |
| ❏ 1 Jake Plummer | .60 | .25 |
| ❏ 2 David Boston | 1.00 | .40 |
| ❏ 3 Jamal Anderson | 1.00 | .40 |
| ❏ 4 Chris Chandler | .60 | .25 |
| ❏ 5 Tony Martin | .60 | .25 |
| ❏ 6 Elvis Grbac | .60 | .25 |
| ❏ 7 Qadry Ismail | .60 | .25 |
| ❏ 8 Ray Lewis | 1.00 | .40 |

| | | |
|---|---|---|
| ❏ 9 Rob Johnson | .60 | .25 |
| ❏ 10 Shawn Bryson | .40 | .15 |
| ❏ 11 Eric Moulds | .60 | .25 |
| ❏ 12 Tim Biakabutuka | .60 | .25 |
| ❏ 13 Jeff Lewis | .40 | .15 |
| ❏ 14 Muhsin Muhammad | .60 | .25 |
| ❏ 15 Shane Matthews | .40 | .15 |
| ❏ 16 Marcus Robinson | .60 | .25 |
| ❏ 17 Brian Urlacher | 1.50 | .60 |
| ❏ 18 Jon Kitna | .40 | .15 |
| ❏ 19 Peter Warrick | 1.00 | .40 |
| ❏ 20 Corey Dillon | 1.00 | .40 |
| ❏ 21 Tim Couch | .60 | .25 |
| ❏ 22 Travis Prentice | .40 | .15 |
| ❏ 23 Kevin Johnson | .60 | .25 |
| ❏ 24 Rocket Ismail | .60 | .25 |
| ❏ 25 Emmitt Smith | 2.00 | .75 |
| ❏ 26 Joey Galloway | .60 | .25 |
| ❏ 27 Terrell Davis | 1.00 | .40 |
| ❏ 28 Brian Griese | 1.00 | .40 |
| ❏ 29 Rod Smith | .60 | .25 |
| ❏ 30 Ed McCaffrey | 1.00 | .40 |
| ❏ 31 Charlie Batch | 1.00 | .40 |
| ❏ 32 Germane Crowell | .40 | .15 |
| ❏ 33 James O. Stewart | .40 | .15 |
| ❏ 34 Brett Favre | 3.00 | 1.25 |
| ❏ 35 Antonio Freeman | 1.00 | .40 |
| ❏ 36 Ahman Green | 1.00 | .40 |
| ❏ 37 Peyton Manning | 2.50 | 1.00 |
| ❏ 38 Edgerrin James | 1.25 | .50 |
| ❏ 39 Marvin Harrison | 1.00 | .40 |
| ❏ 40 Mark Brunell | 1.00 | .40 |
| ❏ 41 Fred Taylor | 1.00 | .40 |
| ❏ 42 Jimmy Smith | .60 | .25 |
| ❏ 43 Tony Gonzalez | .60 | .25 |
| ❏ 44 Trent Green | 1.00 | .40 |
| ❏ 45 Priest Holmes | 1.25 | .50 |
| ❏ 46 Lamar Smith | .60 | .25 |
| ❏ 47 Jay Fiedler | 1.00 | .40 |
| ❏ 48 Oronde Gadsden | .60 | .25 |
| ❏ 49 Daunte Culpepper | 1.00 | .40 |
| ❏ 50 Randy Moss | 2.00 | .75 |
| ❏ 51 Cris Carter | 1.00 | .40 |
| ❏ 52 Drew Bledsoe | 1.25 | .50 |
| ❏ 53 Troy Brown | .60 | .25 |
| ❏ 54 Ricky Williams | 1.00 | .40 |
| ❏ 55 Joe Horn | .60 | .25 |
| ❏ 56 Aaron Brooks | 1.00 | .40 |
| ❏ 57 Albert Connell | .40 | .15 |
| ❏ 58 Kerry Collins | .60 | .25 |
| ❏ 59 Tiki Barber | .60 | .25 |
| ❏ 60 Ron Dayne | 1.00 | .40 |
| ❏ 61 Vinny Testaverde | .60 | .25 |
| ❏ 62 Wayne Chrebet | .60 | .25 |
| ❏ 63 Curtis Martin | 1.00 | .40 |
| ❏ 64 Tim Brown | 1.00 | .40 |
| ❏ 65 Jerry Rice | 2.00 | .75 |
| ❏ 66 Rich Gannon | 1.00 | .40 |
| ❏ 67 Duce Staley | 1.00 | .40 |
| ❏ 68 Donovan McNabb | 1.25 | .50 |
| ❏ 69 Kordell Stewart | .60 | .25 |
| ❏ 70 Jerome Bettis | 1.00 | .40 |
| ❏ 71 Marshall Faulk | 1.25 | .50 |
| ❏ 72 Kurt Warner | 2.00 | .75 |
| ❏ 73 Isaac Bruce | 1.00 | .40 |
| ❏ 74 Torry Holt | 1.00 | .40 |
| ❏ 75 Doug Flutie | 1.00 | .40 |
| ❏ 76 Junior Seau | 1.00 | .40 |

| | | |
|---|---|---|
| ❏ 77 Jeff Garcia | 1.00 | .40 |
| ❏ 78 Garrison Hearst | .60 | .25 |
| ❏ 79 Terrell Owens | 1.00 | .40 |
| ❏ 80 Ricky Watters | .60 | .25 |
| ❏ 81 Matt Hasselbeck | .60 | .25 |
| ❏ 82 Brad Johnson | 1.00 | .40 |
| ❏ 83 Keyshawn Johnson | 1.00 | .40 |
| ❏ 84 Warrick Dunn | 1.00 | .40 |
| ❏ 85 Mike Alstott | 1.00 | .40 |
| ❏ 86 Kevin Dyson | .60 | .25 |
| ❏ 87 Eddie George | 1.00 | .40 |
| ❏ 88 Steve McNair | 1.00 | .40 |
| ❏ 89 Michael Westbrook | .60 | .25 |
| ❏ 90 Stephen Davis | 1.00 | .40 |
| ❏ 91B D McAllister JSY AU/250 RC | 80.00 | 40.00 |
| ❏ 91G D McAllister JSY AU/250 RC | 80.00 | 40.00 |
| ❏ 92B Fr Mitchell JSY AU/250 RC | 30.00 | 12.50 |
| ❏ 92G Fr Mitchell JSY AU/250 RC | 30.00 | 12.50 |
| ❏ 93B Koren Robinson/999 RC | 6.00 | 2.50 |
| ❏ 93G Koren Robinson/999 RC | 6.00 | 2.50 |
| ❏ 94B David Terrell/999 RC | 6.00 | 2.50 |
| ❏ 94G David Terrell/999 RC | 6.00 | 2.50 |
| ❏ 95B M Vick JSY AU/250 RC | 80.00 | 30.00 |
| ❏ 95G M Vick JSY AU/250 RC | 80.00 | 30.00 |
| ❏ 96B M Bennett JSY AU/550 RC | 30.00 | 12.50 |
| ❏ 96G M Bennett JSY AU/550 RC | 30.00 | 12.50 |
| ❏ 97B Robert Ferguson/999 RC | 6.00 | 2.50 |
| ❏ 97G Robert Ferguson/999 RC | 6.00 | 2.50 |
| ❏ 98B Rod Gardner/999 RC | 6.00 | 2.50 |
| ❏ 98G Rod Gardner/999 RC | 6.00 | 2.50 |
| ❏ 99B Travis Henry JSY AU/550 RC | 30.00 | 12.50 |
| ❏ 99G Travis Henry JSY AU/550 RC | 30.00 | 12.50 |
| ❏ 100B C Johnson JSY AU/550 RC | 100.00 | 50.00 |
| ❏ 100G C Johnson JSY AU/550 RC | 100.00 | 50.00 |
| ❏ 101B D.Brees JSY AU/250 RC | 120.00 | 60.00 |
| ❏ 101G D.Brees JSY AU/250 RC | 120.00 | 60.00 |
| ❏ 102B S Moss JSY AU/550 RC | 50.00 | 25.00 |
| ❏ 102G S Moss JSY AU/550 RC | 50.00 | 25.00 |
| ❏ 103B C Weinke JSY AU/550 RC | 25.00 | 10.00 |
| ❏ 103G C Weinke JSY AU/550 RC | 25.00 | 10.00 |
| ❏ 104B R Seymour JSY AU/900 RC | 40.00 | 15.00 |
| ❏ 104G R Seymour JSY AU/900 RC | 40.00 | 15.00 |
| ❏ 105B Reggie Wayne/999 RC | 25.00 | 10.00 |
| ❏ 105G Reggie Wayne/999 RC | 25.00 | 10.00 |
| ❏ 106B K Barlow JSY AU/550 RC | 30.00 | 12.50 |
| ❏ 106G K Barlow JSY AU/550 RC | 30.00 | 12.50 |
| ❏ 107B Chambers JSY AU/900 RC | 50.00 | 25.00 |
| ❏ 107G Chambers JSY AU/900 RC | 50.00 | 25.00 |
| ❏ 108B Todd Heap JSY AU/900 RC | 30.00 | 12.50 |
| ❏ 108G Todd Heap JSY AU/900 RC | 30.00 | 12.50 |
| ❏ 109B A Thomas JSY AU/550 RC | 30.00 | 12.50 |
| ❏ 109G A Thomas JSY AU/550 RC | 30.00 | 12.50 |
| ❏ 110B J Jackson JSY AU/550 RC | 25.00 | 10.00 |
| ❏ 110G J Jackson JSY AU/550 RC | 25.00 | 10.00 |
| ❏ 111B R Johnson JSY AU/900 RC | 60.00 | 30.00 |
| ❏ 111G R Johnson JSY AU/900 RC | 60.00 | 30.00 |
| ❏ 112B McMahon JSY AU/900 RC | 25.00 | 10.00 |
| ❏ 112G McMahon JSY AU/900 RC | 25.00 | 10.00 |
| ❏ 113B J.Heupel JSY AU/900 RC | 80.00 | 30.00 |
| ❏ 113G J.Heupel JSY AU/900 RC | 80.00 | 30.00 |
| ❏ 114B T Minor JSY AU/900 RC | 25.00 | 10.00 |
| ❏ 114G T Minor JSY AU/900 RC | 25.00 | 10.00 |
| ❏ 115B Quincy Morgan/999 RC | 5.00 | 2.00 |
| ❏ 115G Quincy Morgan/999 RC | 5.00 | 2.00 |
| ❏ 116B D Morgan JSY AU/900 RC | 20.00 | 10.00 |
| ❏ 116G D Morgan JSY AU/900 RC | 20.00 | 10.00 |
| ❏ 117B J Palmer JSY AU/900 RC 25.00 | | 10.00 |
| ❏ 117G J Palmer JSY AU/900 RC 25.00 | | 10.00 |
| ❏ 118B S Rosenfels JSY AU/900 RC | 25.00 | 10.00 |
| ❏ 118G S Rosenfels JSY AU/900 RC | 25.00 | 10.00 |
| ❏ 119B Tuiasosopo JSY AU/900 RC | 30.00 | 12.50 |
| ❏ 119G Tuiasosopo JSY AU/900 RC | 30.00 | 12.50 |
| ❏ 120B Damerien McCants/999 RC | 4.00 | 1.50 |
| ❏ 120G Damerien McCants/999 RC | 4.00 | 1.50 |
| ❏ 121B Snoop Minnis/999 RC | 4.00 | 1.50 |
| ❏ 121G Snoop Minnis/999 RC | 4.00 | 1.50 |
| ❏ 122B L.Tomlinson JSY/250 RC | 150.00 | 75.00 |
| ❏ 122G L.Tomlinson JSY/250 RC | 150.00 | 75.00 |
| ❏ 123B Quincy Carter/999 RC | 5.00 | 2.00 |
| ❏ 123G Quincy Carter/999 RC | 5.00 | 2.00 |
| ❏ 124B Arnold Jackson/999 RC | 4.00 | 1.50 |
| ❏ 124G Arnold Jackson/999 RC | 4.00 | 1.50 |
| ❏ 125B Justin McCareins/999 RC | 6.00 | 2.50 |
| ❏ 125G Justin McCareins/999 RC | 6.00 | 2.50 |
| ❏ 126B Eddie Berlin/999 RC | 4.00 | 1.50 |

| Card | Hi | Lo |
|---|---|---|
| ☐ 126G Eddie Berlin/999 RC | 4.00 | 1.50 |
| ☐ 127B Quentin McCord/999 RC | 4.00 | 1.50 |
| ☐ 127G Quentin McCord/999 RC | 4.00 | 1.50 |
| ☐ 128B Vinny Sutherland/999 RC | 4.00 | 1.50 |
| ☐ 128G Vinny Sutherland/999 RC | 4.00 | 1.50 |
| ☐ 129B Willie Middlebrooks/999 RC | 4.00 | 1.50 |
| ☐ 129G Willie Middlebrooks/999 RC | 4.00 | 1.50 |
| ☐ 130B Dan Alexander/999 RC | 5.00 | 2.00 |
| ☐ 130G Dan Alexander/999 RC | 5.00 | 2.00 |
| ☐ 131B Dee Brown/999 RC | 4.00 | 1.50 |
| ☐ 131G Dee Brown/999 RC | 4.00 | 1.50 |
| ☐ 132B Andre Carter/999 RC | 5.00 | 2.00 |
| ☐ 132G Andre Carter/999 RC | 5.00 | 2.00 |
| ☐ 133B Justin Smith/999 RC | 6.00 | 2.50 |
| ☐ 133G Justin Smith/999 RC | 6.00 | 2.50 |
| ☐ 134B Houshmandzadeh/999 RC | 10.00 | 4.00 |
| ☐ 134G Houshmandzadeh/999 RC | 10.00 | 4.00 |
| ☐ 135B Andre King/999 RC | 4.00 | 1.50 |
| ☐ 135G Andre King/999 RC | 4.00 | 1.50 |
| ☐ 136B Nick Goings/999 RC | 6.00 | 2.50 |
| ☐ 136G Nick Goings/999 RC | 6.00 | 2.50 |
| ☐ 137B Scotty Anderson/999 RC | 5.00 | 2.00 |
| ☐ 137G Scotty Anderson/999 RC | 5.00 | 2.00 |
| ☐ 138B David Martin/999 RC | 4.00 | 1.50 |
| ☐ 138G David Martin/999 RC | 4.00 | 1.50 |
| ☐ 139B Derrick Blaylock/999 RC | 6.00 | 2.50 |
| ☐ 139G Derrick Blaylock/999 RC | 6.00 | 2.50 |
| ☐ 140B Onome Ojo/999 RC | 4.00 | 1.50 |
| ☐ 140G Onome Ojo/999 RC | 4.00 | 1.50 |
| ☐ 141B Jonathan Carter/999 RC | 4.00 | 1.50 |
| ☐ 141G Jonathan Carter/999 RC | 4.00 | 1.50 |
| ☐ 142B LaMont Jordan/999 RC | 12.00 | 5.00 |
| ☐ 142G LaMont Jordan/999 RC | 12.00 | 5.00 |
| ☐ 143B Dominic Rhodes/999 RC | 8.00 | 3.00 |
| ☐ 143G Dominic Rhodes/999 RC | 8.00 | 3.00 |
| ☐ 145B A.J. Feeley/999 RC | 6.00 | 2.50 |
| ☐ 145G A.J. Feeley/999 RC | 6.00 | 2.50 |
| ☐ 146B Correll Buckhalter/999 RC | 8.00 | 3.00 |
| ☐ 146G Correll Buckhalter/999 RC | 8.00 | 3.00 |
| ☐ 147B Steve Smith/999 RC | 25.00 | 10.00 |
| ☐ 147G Steve Smith/999 RC | 25.00 | 10.00 |
| ☐ 148B Dave Dickenson/999 RC | 5.00 | 2.00 |
| ☐ 148G Dave Dickenson/999 RC | 5.00 | 2.00 |
| ☐ 149B Cedrick Wilson/999 RC | 6.00 | 2.50 |
| ☐ 149G Cedrick Wilson/999 RC | 6.00 | 2.50 |
| ☐ 150B Jamie Winborn/999 RC | 5.00 | 2.00 |
| ☐ 150G Jamie Winborn/999 RC | 5.00 | 2.00 |
| ☐ 151B Alex Bannister/999 RC | 4.00 | 1.50 |
| ☐ 151G Alex Bannister/999 RC | 4.00 | 1.50 |
| ☐ 152B Heath Evans/999 RC | 5.00 | 2.00 |
| ☐ 152G Heath Evans/999 RC | 5.00 | 2.00 |
| ☐ 153B Josh Booty/999 RC | 5.00 | 2.00 |
| ☐ 153G Josh Booty/999 RC | 5.00 | 2.00 |
| ☐ 154B Adam Archuleta/999 RC | 6.00 | 2.50 |
| ☐ 154G Adam Archuleta/999 RC | 6.00 | 2.50 |
| ☐ 155B Francis St.Paul/999 RC | 4.00 | 1.50 |
| ☐ 155G Francis St.Paul/999 RC | 4.00 | 1.50 |
| ☐ 156B Andre Dyson/999 RC | 4.00 | 1.50 |
| ☐ 156G Andre Dyson/999 RC | 4.00 | 1.50 |
| ☐ RM Randy Moss SAMPLE | 2.00 | .75 |

## 2002 SPx

| Card | Hi | Lo |
|---|---|---|
| ☐ COMP.SET w/o SP's (90) | 20.00 | 7.50 |
| ☐ 1 Drew Bledsoe | 1.25 | .50 |
| ☐ 2 Peerless Price | .60 | .25 |
| ☐ 3 Travis Henry | 1.00 | .40 |
| ☐ 4 Ricky Williams | 1.00 | .40 |
| ☐ 5 Jay Fiedler | .60 | .25 |
| ☐ 6 Tom Brady | 2.50 | 1.00 |
| ☐ 7 Troy Brown | .60 | .25 |
| ☐ 8 Antowain Smith | .60 | .25 |
| ☐ 9 Santana Moss | 1.00 | .40 |
| ☐ 10 Curtis Martin | 1.00 | .40 |
| ☐ 11 Vinny Testaverde | .60 | .25 |
| ☐ 12 Jamal Lewis | 1.00 | .40 |
| ☐ 13 Chris Redman | .40 | .15 |
| ☐ 14 Travis Taylor | .60 | .25 |
| ☐ 15 Corey Dillon | .60 | .25 |
| ☐ 16 T.J. Houshmandzadeh | .60 | .25 |
| ☐ 17 Peter Warrick | .60 | .25 |
| ☐ 18 Courtney Brown | .60 | .25 |
| ☐ 19 Kevin Johnson | .60 | .25 |
| ☐ 20 Tim Couch | .60 | .25 |
| ☐ 21 Hines Ward | 1.00 | .40 |
| ☐ 22 Jerome Bettis | 1.00 | .40 |
| ☐ 23 Kordell Stewart | .60 | .25 |
| ☐ 24 Corey Bradford | .40 | .15 |
| ☐ 25 Jermaine Lewis | .40 | .15 |
| ☐ 26 Edgerrin James | 1.25 | .50 |
| ☐ 27 Marvin Harrison | 1.00 | .40 |
| ☐ 28 Peyton Manning | 2.00 | .75 |
| ☐ 29 Jimmy Smith | .60 | .25 |
| ☐ 30 Mark Brunell | 1.00 | .40 |
| ☐ 31 Fred Taylor | 1.00 | .40 |
| ☐ 32 Eddie George | 1.00 | .40 |
| ☐ 33 Steve McNair | 1.00 | .40 |
| ☐ 34 Brian Griese | 1.00 | .40 |
| ☐ 35 Shannon Sharpe | .60 | .25 |
| ☐ 36 Rod Smith | .60 | .25 |
| ☐ 37 Trent Green | .60 | .25 |
| ☐ 38 Johnnie Morton | .60 | .25 |
| ☐ 39 Priest Holmes | 1.25 | .50 |
| ☐ 40 Jerry Rice | 2.00 | .75 |
| ☐ 41 Rich Gannon | 1.00 | .40 |
| ☐ 42 Tim Brown | 1.00 | .40 |
| ☐ 43 Drew Brees | 1.00 | .40 |
| ☐ 44 Junior Seau | 1.00 | .40 |
| ☐ 45 LaDainian Tomlinson | 1.50 | .60 |
| ☐ 46 Emmitt Smith | 2.50 | 1.00 |
| ☐ 47 Quincy Carter | .60 | .25 |
| ☐ 48 Rocket Ismail | .60 | .25 |
| ☐ 49 Amani Toomer | .60 | .25 |
| ☐ 50 Kerry Collins | .60 | .25 |
| ☐ 51 Ron Dayne | .60 | .25 |
| ☐ 52 Donovan McNabb | 1.25 | .50 |
| ☐ 53 Duce Staley | 1.00 | .40 |
| ☐ 54 Antonio Freeman | 1.00 | .40 |
| ☐ 55 Rod Gardner | .60 | .25 |
| ☐ 56 Stephen Davis | .60 | .25 |
| ☐ 57 Brian Urlacher | 1.50 | .60 |
| ☐ 58 Anthony Thomas | .60 | .25 |
| ☐ 59 Jim Miller | .40 | .15 |
| ☐ 60 Marty Booker | .60 | .25 |
| ☐ 61 Az-Zahir Hakim | .40 | .15 |
| ☐ 62 James Stewart | .60 | .25 |
| ☐ 63 Ahman Green | 1.00 | .40 |
| ☐ 64 Brett Favre | 2.50 | 1.00 |
| ☐ 65 Robert Ferguson | .40 | .15 |
| ☐ 66 Terry Glenn | .60 | .25 |
| ☐ 67 Randy Moss | 2.00 | .75 |
| ☐ 68 Daunte Culpepper | 1.00 | .40 |
| ☐ 69 Michael Bennett | .60 | .25 |
| ☐ 70 Michael Vick | 2.00 | .75 |
| ☐ 71 Warrick Dunn | 1.00 | .40 |
| ☐ 72 Rodney Peete | .60 | .25 |
| ☐ 73 Muhsin Muhammad | .60 | .25 |
| ☐ 74 Aaron Brooks | 1.00 | .40 |
| ☐ 75 Deuce McAllister | 1.25 | .50 |
| ☐ 76 Keyshawn Johnson | 1.00 | .40 |
| ☐ 77 Michael Pittman | .40 | .15 |
| ☐ 78 Brad Johnson | .60 | .25 |
| ☐ 79 Thomas Jones | .60 | .25 |
| ☐ 80 David Boston | 1.00 | .40 |
| ☐ 81 Jake Plummer | .60 | .25 |
| ☐ 82 Terrell Owens | 1.00 | .40 |
| ☐ 83 Garrison Hearst | .60 | .25 |
| ☐ 84 Jeff Garcia | 1.00 | .40 |
| ☐ 85 Darrell Jackson | .60 | .25 |
| ☐ 86 Shaun Alexander | 1.25 | .50 |
| ☐ 87 Trent Dilfer | .60 | .25 |
| ☐ 88 Isaac Bruce | 1.00 | .40 |
| ☐ 89 Kurt Warner | 1.00 | .40 |
| ☐ 90 Marshall Faulk | 1.00 | .40 |
| ☐ 91 Saleem Rasheed RC | 4.00 | 1.50 |
| ☐ 92 Jason McAddley RC | 5.00 | 2.00 |
| ☐ 93 Brandon Doman RC | 4.00 | 1.50 |
| ☐ 94 Mike Rumph RC | 5.00 | 2.00 |
| ☐ 95 Wendell Bryant RC | 4.00 | 1.50 |
| ☐ 96 Bryan Thomas RC | 4.00 | 1.50 |
| ☐ 97 Anthony Weaver RC | 4.00 | 1.50 |
| ☐ 98 Chester Taylor RC | 12.00 | 5.00 |
| ☐ 99 Ed Reed RC | 20.00 | 10.00 |
| ☐ 100 Lamar Gordon RC | 5.00 | 2.00 |
| ☐ 101 Tellis Redmon RC | 4.00 | 1.50 |
| ☐ 102 Ben Leber RC | 4.00 | 1.50 |
| ☐ 103 Javin Hunter RC | 4.00 | 1.50 |
| ☐ 104 Javon Walker RC | 15.00 | 6.00 |
| ☐ 105 Shaun Hill RC | 12.00 | 5.00 |
| ☐ 106 Racinall Smith RC | 4.00 | 1.50 |
| ☐ 107 Darrell Hill RC | 4.00 | 1.50 |
| ☐ 108 Kalimba Edwards RC | 4.00 | 1.50 |
| ☐ 109 Robert Thomas RC | 4.00 | 1.50 |
| ☐ 110 Craig Nall RC | 5.00 | 2.00 |
| ☐ 111 Marques Anderson RC | 5.00 | 2.00 |
| ☐ 112 Najeh Davenport RC | 6.00 | 2.50 |
| ☐ 113 Jonathan Wells RC | 5.00 | 2.00 |
| ☐ 114 Dwight Freeney RC | 20.00 | 7.50 |
| ☐ 115 Larry Tripplett RC | 4.00 | 1.50 |
| ☐ 116 T.J. Duckett RC | 6.00 | 2.50 |
| ☐ 117 John Henderson RC | 6.00 | 2.50 |
| ☐ 118 Albert Haynesworth RC | 6.00 | 2.50 |
| ☐ 119 Tank Williams RC | 5.00 | 2.00 |
| ☐ 120 Ryan Sims RC | 5.00 | 2.00 |
| ☐ 121 Leonard Henry RC | 4.00 | 1.50 |
| ☐ 122 Clinton Portis RC | 50.00 | 20.00 |
| ☐ 123 Josh Reed RC | 6.00 | 2.50 |
| ☐ 124 Chad Hutchinson RC | 8.00 | 3.00 |
| ☐ 125 Deion Branch RC | 12.00 | 5.00 |
| ☐ 126 Rocky Calmus RC | 5.00 | 2.00 |
| ☐ 127 Donte Stallworth RC | 15.00 | 6.00 |
| ☐ 128 Daryl Jones RC | 4.00 | 1.50 |
| ☐ 129 Joey Harrington RC | 15.00 | 6.00 |
| ☐ 130 Napoleon Harris RC | 5.00 | 2.00 |
| ☐ 131 Phillip Buchanon RC | 6.00 | 2.50 |
| ☐ 132 Patrick Ramsey RC | 6.00 | 2.50 |
| ☐ 133 Brian Westbrook RC | 20.00 | 10.00 |
| ☐ 134 Freddie Milons RC | 4.00 | 1.50 |
| ☐ 135 Lito Sheppard RC | 6.00 | 2.50 |
| ☐ 136 Michael Lewis RC | 6.00 | 2.50 |
| ☐ 137 Jamin Elliott RC | 4.00 | 1.50 |
| ☐ 138 Lee Mays RC | 4.00 | 1.50 |
| ☐ 139 Verron Haynes RC | 5.00 | 2.00 |
| ☐ 140 Jesse Chatman RC | 4.00 | 1.50 |
| ☐ 141 Quentin Jammer RC | 6.00 | 2.50 |
| ☐ 142 Seth Burford RC | 4.00 | 1.50 |
| ☐ 143 Julius Peppers RC | 20.00 | 7.50 |
| ☐ 144 William Green RC | 6.00 | 2.50 |
| ☐ 145 DeShaun Foster RC | 6.00 | 2.50 |
| ☐ 146 Daniel Graham RC | 6.00 | 2.50 |
| ☐ 147 David Garrard RC | 20.00 | 10.00 |
| ☐ 148 Reche Caldwell RC | 6.00 | 2.50 |
| ☐ 149 Randy Fasani RC | 5.00 | 2.00 |
| ☐ 150 J.T. O'Sullivan RC | 8.00 | 3.00 |
| ☐ 151 Josh McCown JSY AU RC | 40.00 | 15.00 |
| ☐ 152 Kurt Kittner JSY AU RC | 15.00 | 6.00 |
| ☐ 153 Kahlil Hill JSY AU RC | 15.00 | 6.00 |
| ☐ 154 Ladell Betts JSY AU RC | 30.00 | 12.00 |
| ☐ 155 Ron Johnson JSY AU RC | 15.00 | 6.00 |
| ☐ 156 Maurice Morris JSY AU RC | 25.00 | 10.00 |
| ☐ 157 Andre Davis JSY AU RC | 20.00 | 7.50 |
| ☐ 158 Antonio Bryant JSY AU RC | 25.00 | 10.00 |
| ☐ 159 Roy Williams JSY AU RC | 40.00 | 15.00 |
| ☐ 160 Lam Thompson JSY AU RC | 12.00 | 5.00 |
| ☐ 161 Cliff Russell JSY AU RC | 12.00 | 5.00 |
| ☐ 162 Woody Dantzler JSY AU RC | 15.00 | 6.00 |
| ☐ 163 Travis Stephens JSY AU RC | 15.00 | 6.00 |
| ☐ 164 Tony Fisher JSY AU RC | 15.00 | 6.00 |
| ☐ 165 Eric McCoo JSY AU RC | 12.00 | 5.00 |
| ☐ 166 Eric Crouch JSY AU RC | 25.00 | 10.00 |
| ☐ 167 Rohan Davey JSY AU RC | 15.00 | 6.00 |
| ☐ 168 Marquise Walker JSY AU RC | 25.00 | 10.00 |
| ☐ 169 Jeremy Shockey JSY AU RC | 25.00 | 10.00 |
| ☐ 170 Tim Carter JSY AU RC | 15.00 | 6.00 |
| ☐ 171 Atrews Bell JSY AU RC | 12.00 | 5.00 |
| ☐ 172 Ant Randle El JSY AU RC | 40.00 | 15.00 |
| ☐ 173 Ricky Williams JSY AU RC | 20.00 | 7.50 |
| ☐ 174 Mike Williams JSY AU RC | 15.00 | 6.00 |
| ☐ 175 Adrian Peterson JSY AU RC | 40.00 | 20.00 |

| | | |
|---|---|---|
| ❑ 176 Jab Gaffney JSY AU/650 RC | 25.00 | 10.00 |
| ❑ 177 Ashley Lelie JSY AU/250 RC | 30.00 | 12.50 |
| ❑ 178 David Carr JSY AU/250 RC | 40.00 | 15.00 |

## 2003 SPx

| | | |
|---|---|---|
| ❑ COMP. SET w/o SP's (110) | 25.00 | 10.00 |
| ❑ 1 Peyton Manning | 1.50 | .60 |
| ❑ 2 Aaron Brooks | 1.00 | .40 |
| ❑ 3 Joey Harrington | 1.50 | .60 |
| ❑ 4 Tim Couch | .40 | .15 |
| ❑ 5 Jeff Garcia | 1.00 | .40 |
| ❑ 6 Jay Fiedler | .60 | .25 |
| ❑ 7 Chad Hutchinson | .40 | .15 |
| ❑ 8 Tommy Maddox | .60 | .25 |
| ❑ 9 Drew Brees | 1.00 | .40 |
| ❑ 10 Trent Green | .60 | .25 |
| ❑ 11 Patrick Ramsey | 1.00 | .40 |
| ❑ 12 Daunte Culpepper | 1.00 | .40 |
| ❑ 13 Kurt Warner | 1.00 | .40 |
| ❑ 14 Brad Johnson | .60 | .25 |
| ❑ 15 Rich Gannon | .60 | .25 |
| ❑ 16 Jake Plummer | 1.00 | .40 |
| ❑ 17 Steve McNair | 1.00 | .40 |
| ❑ 18 Mark Brunell | .60 | .25 |
| ❑ 19 Drew Bledsoe | 1.00 | .40 |
| ❑ 20 Kordell Stewart | .60 | .25 |
| ❑ 21 Kelly Holcomb | .60 | .25 |
| ❑ 22 Josh McCown | .60 | .25 |
| ❑ 23 Matt Hasselbeck | .60 | .25 |
| ❑ 24 Marc Bulger | 1.00 | .40 |
| ❑ 25 Chris Redman | .40 | .15 |
| ❑ 26 Rodney Peete | .60 | .25 |
| ❑ 27 Jake Delhomme | .60 | .25 |
| ❑ 28 Jon Kitna | .60 | .25 |
| ❑ 29 Kerry Collins | .60 | .25 |
| ❑ 30 Quincy Carter | .60 | .25 |
| ❑ 31 Ricky Williams | 1.50 | .60 |
| ❑ 32 Clinton Portis | 1.50 | .60 |
| ❑ 33 Deuce McAllister | 1.00 | .40 |
| ❑ 34 Ahman Green | 1.00 | .40 |
| ❑ 35 Priest Holmes | 1.25 | .50 |
| ❑ 36 Curtis Martin | 1.00 | .40 |
| ❑ 37 Michael Bennett | .60 | .25 |
| ❑ 38 Eddie George | .60 | .25 |
| ❑ 39 Marshall Faulk | 1.00 | .40 |
| ❑ 40 Garrison Hearst | .60 | .25 |
| ❑ 41 Shaun Alexander | 1.00 | .40 |
| ❑ 42 Corey Dillon | .60 | .25 |
| ❑ 43 Jamal Lewis | 1.00 | .40 |
| ❑ 44 William Green | .60 | .25 |
| ❑ 45 Travis Henry | .60 | .25 |
| ❑ 46 Randy Moss | 1.50 | .60 |
| ❑ 47 Terrell Owens | 1.00 | .40 |
| ❑ 48 Peerless Price | .60 | .25 |
| ❑ 49 David Boston | .60 | .25 |
| ❑ 50 Eric Moulds | .60 | .25 |
| ❑ 51 Marvin Harrison | 1.00 | .40 |
| ❑ 52 Laveranues Coles | .60 | .25 |
| ❑ 53 Santana Moss | .60 | .25 |
| ❑ 54 Troy Brown | .60 | .25 |
| ❑ 55 Chris Chambers | 1.00 | .40 |
| ❑ 56 Tim Brown | 1.00 | .40 |
| ❑ 57 Rod Smith | .60 | .25 |
| ❑ 58 Hines Ward | 1.00 | .40 |
| ❑ 59 Keyshawn Johnson | 1.00 | .40 |
| ❑ 60 Isaac Bruce | 1.00 | .40 |
| ❑ 61 Torry Holt | 1.00 | .40 |
| ❑ 62 Koren Robinson | .60 | .25 |

| | | |
|---|---|---|
| ❑ 63 Chad Johnson | 1.00 | .40 |
| ❑ 64 Derrick Mason | .60 | .25 |
| ❑ 65 Anquan Bryant | .60 | .25 |
| ❑ 66 Kevin Johnson | .60 | .25 |
| ❑ 67 Todd Heap | .60 | .25 |
| ❑ 68 Tony Gonzalez | .60 | .25 |
| ❑ 69 Jeremy Shockey | 1.50 | .60 |
| ❑ 70 Brian Urlacher | 1.50 | .60 |
| ❑ 71 Emmitt Smith/500 | 20.00 | 7.50 |
| ❑ 72 Edgerrin James/500 | 6.00 | 2.50 |
| ❑ 73 LaDainian Tomlinson/500 | 8.00 | 3.00 |
| ❑ 74 Brett Favre/500 | 20.00 | 7.50 |
| ❑ 75 Donovan McNabb/500 | 8.00 | 3.00 |
| ❑ 76 Tom Brady/500 | 20.00 | 7.50 |
| ❑ 77 Michael Vick/500 | 10.00 | 4.00 |
| ❑ 78 David Carr/500 | 12.00 | 5.00 |
| ❑ 79 Jerry Rice/500 | 15.00 | 6.00 |
| ❑ 80 Chad Pennington/500 | 6.00 | 2.50 |
| ❑ 81 Joey Harrington XCT | 1.50 | .60 |
| ❑ 82 Clinton Portis XCT | 1.50 | .60 |
| ❑ 83 Jeremy Shockey XCT | 1.50 | .60 |
| ❑ 84 David Boston XCT | .60 | .25 |
| ❑ 85 Marshall Faulk XCT | 1.00 | .40 |
| ❑ 86 Emmitt Smith XCT | 2.50 | 1.00 |
| ❑ 87 Terrell Owens XCT | 1.00 | .40 |
| ❑ 88 Randy Moss XCT | 1.50 | .60 |
| ❑ 89 Deuce McAllister XCT | 1.00 | .40 |
| ❑ 90 Ahman Green XCT | 1.00 | .40 |
| ❑ 91 Peerless Price XCT | .60 | .25 |
| ❑ 92 Plaxico Burress XCT | .60 | .25 |
| ❑ 93 Marvin Harrison XCT | 1.00 | .40 |
| ❑ 94 Keyshawn Johnson XCT | 1.00 | .40 |
| ❑ 95 Laveranues Coles XCT | .60 | .25 |
| ❑ 96 Drew Bledsoe XCT | 1.00 | .40 |
| ❑ 97 Eric Moulds XCT | .60 | .25 |
| ❑ 98 Chad Pennington XCT | 1.25 | .50 |
| ❑ 99 Jerry Rice XCT | 2.00 | .75 |
| ❑ 100 David Carr XCT | 1.50 | .60 |
| ❑ 101 Michael Vick XCT | 2.50 | 1.00 |
| ❑ 102 Tom Brady XCT | 2.50 | 1.00 |
| ❑ 103 Donovan McNabb XCT | 1.25 | .50 |
| ❑ 104 Brett Favre XCT | 2.50 | 1.00 |
| ❑ 105 Kurt Warner XCT | 1.00 | .40 |
| ❑ 106 LaDainian Tomlinson XCT | 1.00 | .40 |
| ❑ 107 Drew Brees XCT | 1.00 | .40 |
| ❑ 108 Edgerrin James XCT | 1.00 | .40 |
| ❑ 109 Peyton Manning XCT | 1.50 | .60 |
| ❑ 110 Ricky Williams XCT | 1.00 | .40 |
| ❑ 111 Brooks Bollinger RC | 6.00 | 2.50 |
| ❑ 112 Gibran Hamden RC | 4.00 | 1.50 |
| ❑ 113 Jason Johnson RC | 4.00 | 1.50 |
| ❑ 114 Tony Romo RC | 80.00 | 40.00 |
| ❑ 115 Juston Wood RC | 4.00 | 1.50 |
| ❑ 116 Kirk Farmer RC | 4.00 | 1.50 |
| ❑ 117 Kliff Kingsbury RC | 5.00 | 2.00 |
| ❑ 118 Jason Gesser RC | 6.00 | 2.50 |
| ❑ 119 Brad Banks RC | 4.00 | 1.50 |
| ❑ 120 Rob Adamson RC | 4.00 | 1.50 |
| ❑ 121 Ken Dorsey RC | 6.00 | 2.50 |
| ❑ 122 Curt Anes RC | 4.00 | 1.50 |
| ❑ 123 George Wrighster RC | 5.00 | 2.00 |
| ❑ 124 Brett Engemann RC | 4.00 | 1.50 |
| ❑ 125 Aaron Walker RC | 5.00 | 2.00 |
| ❑ 126 Nate Hybl RC | 6.00 | 2.50 |
| ❑ 127 Chris Simms RC | 8.00 | 3.00 |
| ❑ 128 Marquel Blackwell RC | 4.00 | 1.50 |
| ❑ 129 Domanick Davis RC | 6.00 | 2.50 |
| ❑ 130 Quentin Griffin RC | 6.00 | 2.50 |
| ❑ 131 B.J. Askew RC | 5.00 | 2.00 |
| ❑ 132 Earnest Graham RC | 6.00 | 2.50 |
| ❑ 133 Sultan McCullough RC | 4.00 | 1.50 |
| ❑ 134 Dahrran Diedrick RC | 5.00 | 2.00 |
| ❑ 135 Cecil Sapp RC | 5.00 | 2.00 |
| ❑ 136 LaBrandon Toefield RC | 5.00 | 2.00 |
| ❑ 137 ReShard Lee RC | 5.00 | 2.00 |
| ❑ 138 Dwone Hicks RC | 4.00 | 1.50 |
| ❑ 139 Brock Forsey RC | 6.00 | 2.50 |
| ❑ 140 Bethel Johnson RC | 6.00 | 2.50 |
| ❑ 141 Andrew Pinnock RC | 4.00 | 1.50 |
| ❑ 142 Ahmad Galloway RC | 5.00 | 2.00 |
| ❑ 143 J.T. Wall RC | 4.00 | 1.50 |
| ❑ 144 Tom Lopienski RC | 4.00 | 1.50 |
| ❑ 145 Justin Griffith RC | 4.00 | 1.50 |
| ❑ 146 Lee Suggs RC | 6.00 | 2.50 |
| ❑ 147 Nick Maddox RC | 4.00 | 1.50 |

| | | |
|---|---|---|
| ❑ 148 Jeremi Johnson RC | 4.00 | 1.50 |
| ❑ 149 Doug Gabriel RC | 6.00 | 2.50 |
| ❑ 150 Bobby Wade RC | 6.00 | 2.50 |
| ❑ 151 Justin Gage RC | 6.00 | 2.50 |
| ❑ 152 Arnaz Battle RC | 6.00 | 2.50 |
| ❑ 153 Brandon Lloyd RC | 6.00 | 2.50 |
| ❑ 154 Talman Gardner RC | 5.00 | 2.00 |
| ❑ 155 Kareem Kelly RC | 5.00 | 2.00 |
| ❑ 156 Billy McMullen RC | 4.00 | 1.50 |
| ❑ 157 Antwone Savage RC | 4.00 | 1.50 |
| ❑ 158 J.R. Tolver RC | 4.00 | 1.50 |
| ❑ 159 Kassim Osgood RC | 5.00 | 2.00 |
| ❑ 160 Shaun McDonald RC | 6.00 | 2.50 |
| ❑ 161 Sam Aiken RC | 5.00 | 2.00 |
| ❑ 162 Adrian Madise RC | 4.00 | 1.50 |
| ❑ 163 Charles Rogers RC | 6.00 | 2.50 |
| ❑ 164 David Kircus RC | 5.00 | 2.00 |
| ❑ 165 Zuriel Smith RC | 4.00 | 1.50 |
| ❑ 166 LaTarence Dunbar RC | 4.00 | 1.50 |
| ❑ 167 Willie Ponder RC | 4.00 | 1.50 |
| ❑ 168 David Tyree RC | 8.00 | 3.00 |
| ❑ 169 Kevin Walter RC | 6.00 | 2.50 |
| ❑ 170 Keenan Howry RC | 5.00 | 2.00 |
| ❑ 171 Walter Young RC | 4.00 | 1.50 |
| ❑ 172 DeAndrew Rubin RC | 4.00 | 1.50 |
| ❑ 173 Carl Ford RC | 4.00 | 1.50 |
| ❑ 174 Taco Wallace RC | 4.00 | 1.50 |
| ❑ 175 Travis Anglin RC | 4.00 | 1.50 |
| ❑ 176 Ryan Hoag RC | 4.00 | 1.50 |
| ❑ 177 Ronald Bellamy RC | 4.00 | 1.50 |
| ❑ 178 Terrence Edwards RC | 4.00 | 1.50 |
| ❑ 179 Jerel Myers RC | 4.00 | 1.50 |
| ❑ 180 Mike Bush RC | 4.00 | 1.50 |
| ❑ 181 Dan Curley RC | 4.00 | 1.50 |
| ❑ 182 Carl Morris RC | 4.00 | 1.50 |
| ❑ 183 Reggie Newhouse RC | 4.00 | 1.50 |
| ❑ 184 Troy Polamalu RC | 35.00 | 20.00 |
| ❑ 185 Cecil Moore RC | 4.00 | 1.50 |
| ❑ 186 Bennie Joppru RC | 5.00 | 2.00 |
| ❑ 187 Donald Lee RC | 5.00 | 2.00 |
| ❑ 188 Jason Witten RC | 20.00 | 8.00 |
| ❑ 189 Mike Seidman RC | 5.00 | 2.00 |
| ❑ 190 Vishante Shiancoe RC | 5.00 | 2.00 |
| ❑ 191 Anquan Boldin JSY AU | 50.00 | 20.00 |
| ❑ 192 Kyle Boller JSY AU/450 RC | 40.00 | 15.00 |
| ❑ 193 Chris Brown JSY AU | 40.00 | 15.00 |
| ❑ 194 Nate Burleson JSY AU RC | 30.00 | 12.50 |
| ❑ 195 Tyro Calico JSY AU/450 RC | 40.00 | 15.00 |
| ❑ 196 Dallas Clark JSY AU RC | 40.00 | 20.00 |
| ❑ 197 Kevin Curtis JSY AU RC | 40.00 | 15.00 |
| ❑ 198 Kliff Kingsbury JSY AU RC | 25.00 | 10.00 |
| ❑ 199 Justin Fargas JSY AU RC | 30.00 | 12.50 |
| ❑ 200 Grossman JSY AU/450 RC | 80.00 | 30.00 |
| ❑ 201 Taylor Jacobs JSY AU RC | 25.00 | 10.00 |
| ❑ 202 An Johnson JSY AU/250 RC | 150.00 | 75.00 |
| ❑ 203 Malae MacKenzie JSY AU RC | 15.00 | 6.00 |
| ❑ 204 Bryant Johnson JSY AU RC | 30.00 | 12.50 |
| ❑ 205 Larry Johnson JSY AU RC | 60.00 | 25.00 |
| ❑ 206 T Johnson JSY AU/450 RC | 40.00 | 15.00 |
| ❑ 207 Leftwich JSY AU/250 RC | 50.00 | 20.00 |
| ❑ 208 McGahee JSY AU/450 RC | 100.00 | 50.00 |
| ❑ 210 C.Palmer JSY AU/250 RC | 200.00 | 100.00 |
| ❑ 211 Artose Pinner JSY AU RC | 30.00 | 12.50 |
| ❑ 212 Dave Ragone JSY AU RC | 30.00 | 12.50 |
| ❑ 213 Terrell Suggs JSY AU RC | 40.00 | 15.00 |
| ❑ 215 Onterio Smith JSY AU RC | 30.00 | 12.50 |
| ❑ 216 Musa Smith JSY AU RC | 30.00 | 12.50 |
| ❑ 217 Brian St.Pierre JSY AU RC | 30.00 | 12.50 |
| ❑ 218 Marcus Trufant JSY AU RC | 30.00 | 12.50 |
| ❑ 219 Seneca Wallace JSY AU RC | 30.00 | 12.50 |
| ❑ 220 Kell Washington JSY AU RC | 40.00 | 15.00 |

## 2004 SPx

| | | |
|---|---|---|
| ❑ COMP.SET w/SP's (100) | 30.00 | 15.00 |
| ❑ 191-221 JSY AU #'d TO 1499 UNLESS NOTED | | |
| ❑ 1 Anquan Boldin | 1.00 | .40 |
| ❑ 2 Marcel Shipp | 1.00 | .40 |
| ❑ 3 Josh McCown | .75 | .30 |
| ❑ 4 Peerless Price | .75 | .30 |
| ❑ 5 Michael Vick | 1.00 | .40 |
| ❑ 6 T.J. Duckett | .75 | .30 |
| ❑ 7 Kyle Boller | .75 | .30 |
| ❑ 8 Todd Heap | .75 | .30 |
| ❑ 9 Jamal Lewis | .75 | .30 |

| | | | |
|---|---|---|---|
| ☐ 78 | Tommy Maddox | .75 | .30 |
| ☐ 79 | LaDainian Tomlinson | 1.50 | .60 |
| ☐ 80 | Drew Brees | 1.00 | .40 |
| ☐ 81 | Tim Rattay | .60 | .25 |
| ☐ 82 | Kevan Barlow | .75 | .30 |
| ☐ 83 | Brandon Lloyd | .60 | .25 |
| ☐ 84 | Shaun Alexander | 1.00 | .40 |
| ☐ 85 | Matt Hasselbeck | 1.00 | .40 |
| ☐ 86 | Koren Robinson | 1.00 | .40 |
| ☐ 87 | Marc Bulger | .75 | .30 |
| ☐ 88 | Marshall Faulk | 1.00 | .40 |
| ☐ 89 | Torry Holt | 1.00 | .40 |
| ☐ 90 | Isaac Bruce | .75 | .30 |
| ☐ 91 | Brad Johnson | .75 | .30 |
| ☐ 92 | Keenan McCardell | .60 | .25 |
| ☐ 93 | Derrick Brooks | .75 | .30 |
| ☐ 94 | Steve McNair | 1.00 | .40 |
| ☐ 95 | Chris Brown | .75 | .30 |
| ☐ 96 | Derrick Mason | .75 | .30 |
| ☐ 97 | Clinton Portis | 1.00 | .40 |
| ☐ 98 | Mark Brunell | .75 | .30 |
| ☐ 99 | Laveranues Coles | .75 | .30 |
| ☐ 100 | LaVar Arrington | .75 | .30 |
| ☐ 101 | B.J. Johnson RC | 3.00 | 1.25 |
| ☐ 102 | Craig Krenzel RC | 5.00 | 2.00 |
| ☐ 103 | Will Smith RC | 4.00 | 1.50 |
| ☐ 104 | Jamaar Taylor RC | 3.00 | 1.25 |
| ☐ 105 | Tommie Harris RC | 5.00 | 2.00 |
| ☐ 106 | Shawn Andrews RC | 4.00 | 1.50 |
| ☐ 107 | Kendrick Starling RC | 3.00 | 1.25 |
| ☐ 108 | Jeris McIntyre RC | 3.00 | 1.25 |
| ☐ 109 | Jason Babin RC | 4.00 | 1.50 |
| ☐ 110 | Marcus Tubbs RC | 3.00 | 1.25 |
| ☐ 111 | Triandos Luke RC | 3.00 | 1.25 |
| ☐ 112 | Karlos Dansby RC | 5.00 | 2.00 |
| ☐ 113 | Vernon Carey RC | 3.00 | 1.25 |
| ☐ 114 | Ryan Krause RC | 3.00 | 1.25 |
| ☐ 115 | Daryl Smith RC | 4.00 | 1.50 |
| ☐ 116 | Ricardo Colclough RC | 5.00 | 2.00 |
| ☐ 117 | Michael Boulware RC | 5.00 | 2.00 |
| ☐ 118 | Chris Cooley RC | 5.00 | 2.00 |
| ☐ 119 | Tank Johnson RC | 3.00 | 1.25 |
| ☐ 120 | Marquise Hill RC | 3.00 | 1.25 |
| ☐ 121 | Teddy Lehman RC | 3.00 | 1.25 |
| ☐ 122 | Antwan Odom RC | 4.00 | 1.50 |
| ☐ 123 | Sean Jones RC | 4.00 | 1.50 |
| ☐ 124 | Junior Siavii RC | 3.00 | 1.25 |
| ☐ 125 | Joey Thomas RC | 3.00 | 1.25 |
| ☐ 126 | Shawnte Spencer RC | 3.00 | 1.25 |
| ☐ 127 | Dontarrious Thomas RC | 4.00 | 1.50 |
| ☐ 128 | Travis LaBoy RC | 4.00 | 1.50 |
| ☐ 129 | Justin Jenkins RC | 3.00 | 1.25 |
| ☐ 130 | Dwan Edwards RC | 3.00 | 1.25 |
| ☐ 131 | Derrick Strait RC | 4.00 | 1.50 |
| ☐ 132 | Matt Ware RC | 5.00 | 2.00 |
| ☐ 133 | Jared Lorenzen RC | 4.00 | 1.50 |
| ☐ 134 | Demorrio Williams RC | 5.00 | 2.00 |
| ☐ 135 | Bob Sanders RC | 15.00 | 6.00 |
| ☐ 136 | Justin Smiley RC | 4.00 | 1.50 |
| ☐ 137 | Casey Bramlet RC | 3.00 | 1.25 |
| ☐ 138 | Jake Grove RC | 3.00 | 1.25 |
| ☐ 139 | Thomas Tapeh RC | 4.00 | 1.50 |
| ☐ 140 | Igor Olshansky RC | 5.00 | 2.00 |
| ☐ 141 | Stuart Schweigert RC | 4.00 | 1.50 |
| ☐ 142 | Cody Pickett RC | 3.00 | 1.25 |
| ☐ 143 | Derrick Ward RC | 5.00 | 2.00 |
| ☐ 144 | Gilbert Gardner RC | 3.00 | 1.25 |
| ☐ 145 | D.J. Hackett RC | 5.00 | 2.00 |
| ☐ 146 | Marquis Cooper RC | 3.00 | 1.25 |
| ☐ 147 | Courtney Watson RC | 4.00 | 1.50 |
| ☐ 148 | Jim Sorgi RC | 5.00 | 2.00 |
| ☐ 149 | Caleb Miller RC | 3.00 | 1.25 |
| ☐ 150 | Casey Clausen RC | 3.00 | 1.25 |
| ☐ 151 | Jammal Lord RC | 3.00 | 1.25 |
| ☐ 152 | Sloan Thomas RC | 4.00 | 1.50 |
| ☐ 153 | Keyaron Fox RC | 3.00 | 1.25 |
| ☐ 154 | Adimchinobe Echemandu RC | 4.00 | 1.50 |
| ☐ 155 | Ryan Dinwiddie RC | 3.00 | 1.25 |
| ☐ 156 | Kris Wilson RC | 4.00 | 1.50 |
| ☐ 157 | D.J. Williams RC | 5.00 | 2.00 |
| ☐ 158 | Tim Euhus RC | 3.00 | 1.25 |
| ☐ 159 | Bradlee Van Pelt RC | 4.00 | 1.50 |
| ☐ 160 | Keiwan Ratliff RC | 3.00 | 1.25 |
| ☐ 161 | Darnell Dockett RC | 3.00 | 1.25 |
| ☐ 162 | Troy Fleming RC | 3.00 | 1.25 |

| | | | |
|---|---|---|---|
| ☐ 10 | Travis Henry | .75 | .30 |
| ☐ 11 | Drew Bledsoe | 1.00 | .40 |
| ☐ 12 | Eric Moulds | .75 | .30 |
| ☐ 13 | Jake Delhomme | .75 | .30 |
| ☐ 14 | Steve Smith | 1.00 | .40 |
| ☐ 15 | Stephen Davis | .75 | .30 |
| ☐ 16 | Brian Urlacher | 1.00 | .40 |
| ☐ 17 | Rex Grossman | 1.00 | .40 |
| ☐ 18 | Thomas Jones | .75 | .30 |
| ☐ 19 | Chad Johnson | .75 | .30 |
| ☐ 20 | Carson Palmer | 1.25 | .50 |
| ☐ 21 | Rudi Johnson | .75 | .30 |
| ☐ 22 | William Green | .60 | .25 |
| ☐ 23 | Jeff Garcia | .75 | .30 |
| ☐ 24 | Andre Davis | .60 | .25 |
| ☐ 25 | Roy Williams S | .75 | .30 |
| ☐ 26 | Eddie George | .75 | .30 |
| ☐ 27 | Keyshawn Johnson | .75 | .30 |
| ☐ 28 | Jake Plummer | .75 | .30 |
| ☐ 29 | Ashley Lelie | .75 | .30 |
| ☐ 30 | Quentin Griffin | .75 | .30 |
| ☐ 31 | Charles Rogers | .75 | .30 |
| ☐ 32 | Olandis Gary | .75 | .30 |
| ☐ 33 | Joey Harrington | .75 | .30 |
| ☐ 34 | Brett Favre | 2.50 | 1.00 |
| ☐ 35 | Javon Walker | .75 | .30 |
| ☐ 36 | Ahman Green | 1.00 | .40 |
| ☐ 37 | Andre Johnson | 1.00 | .40 |
| ☐ 38 | Domanick Davis | 1.00 | .40 |
| ☐ 39 | David Carr | .75 | .30 |
| ☐ 40 | Peyton Manning | 2.00 | .75 |
| ☐ 41 | Edgerrin James | 1.00 | .40 |
| ☐ 42 | Marvin Harrison | 1.00 | .40 |
| ☐ 43 | Byron Leftwich | 1.00 | .40 |
| ☐ 44 | Jimmy Smith | .75 | .30 |
| ☐ 45 | Fred Taylor | .75 | .30 |
| ☐ 46 | Trent Green | .75 | .30 |
| ☐ 47 | Priest Holmes | 1.00 | .40 |
| ☐ 48 | Dante Hall | .75 | .30 |
| ☐ 49 | Tony Gonzalez | 1.00 | .40 |
| ☐ 50 | A.J. Feeley | .75 | .30 |
| ☐ 51 | Marty Booker | .75 | .30 |
| ☐ 52 | Chris Chambers | .75 | .30 |
| ☐ 53 | Zach Thomas | 1.00 | .40 |
| ☐ 54 | Randy Moss | 1.25 | .50 |
| ☐ 55 | Daunte Culpepper | 1.00 | .40 |
| ☐ 56 | Onterrio Smith | .60 | .25 |
| ☐ 57 | Troy Brown | .75 | .30 |
| ☐ 58 | Corey Dillon | .75 | .30 |
| ☐ 59 | Tom Brady | 2.50 | 1.00 |
| ☐ 60 | Deuce McAllister | 1.00 | .40 |
| ☐ 61 | Joe Horn | .75 | .30 |
| ☐ 62 | Aaron Brooks | .75 | .30 |
| ☐ 63 | Jeremy Shockey | .75 | .30 |
| ☐ 64 | Kurt Warner | 1.00 | .40 |
| ☐ 65 | Tiki Barber | 1.00 | .40 |
| ☐ 66 | Chad Pennington | 1.00 | .40 |
| ☐ 67 | Curtis Martin | 1.00 | .40 |
| ☐ 68 | Santana Moss | .75 | .30 |
| ☐ 69 | Rich Gannon | .75 | .30 |
| ☐ 70 | Jerry Rice | 2.00 | .75 |
| ☐ 71 | Warren Sapp | .75 | .30 |
| ☐ 72 | Donovan McNabb | 1.00 | .40 |
| ☐ 73 | Terrell Owens | 1.00 | .40 |
| ☐ 74 | Jevon Kearse | .75 | .30 |
| ☐ 75 | Brian Westbrook | 1.00 | .40 |
| ☐ 76 | Hines Ward | .75 | .30 |
| ☐ 77 | Duce Staley | .75 | .30 |

| | | | |
|---|---|---|---|
| ☐ 163 | Tramon Douglas RC | 3.00 | 1.25 |
| ☐ 164 | Jeremy LeSueur RC | 3.00 | 1.25 |
| ☐ 165 | Matt Mauck RC | 4.00 | 1.50 |
| ☐ 166 | Sean Taylor RC | 10.00 | 4.00 |
| ☐ 167 | B.J. Symons RC | 6.00 | 2.50 |
| ☐ 168 | Quincy Wilson RC | 8.00 | 3.00 |
| ☐ 169 | Ernest Wilford RC | 10.00 | 4.00 |
| ☐ 170 | Jerricho Cotchery RC | 10.00 | 4.00 |
| ☐ 171 | Michael Turner RC | 20.00 | 8.00 |
| ☐ 172 | Samie Parker RC | 8.00 | 3.00 |
| ☐ 173 | Andy Hall RC | 8.00 | 3.00 |
| ☐ 174 | Keith Smith RC | 6.00 | 2.50 |
| ☐ 175 | Josh Harris RC | 6.00 | 2.50 |
| ☐ 176 | Maurice Mann RC | 6.00 | 2.50 |
| ☐ 177 | Jonathan Vilma RC | 10.00 | 4.00 |
| ☐ 178 | Jeff Smoker RC | 8.00 | 3.00 |
| ☐ 179 | Ben Hartsock RC | 8.00 | 3.00 |
| ☐ 180 | Chris Gamble RC | 8.00 | 3.00 |
| ☐ 181 | Derrick Hamilton RC | 6.00 | 2.50 |
| ☐ 182 | John Navarre RC | 8.00 | 3.00 |
| ☐ 183 | P.K. Sam RC | 6.00 | 2.50 |
| ☐ 184 | Kenechi Udeze RC | 10.00 | 4.00 |
| ☐ 185 | Mewelde Moore RC | 10.00 | 4.00 |
| ☐ 186 | Carlos Francis RC | 6.00 | 2.50 |
| ☐ 187 | Dunta Robinson RC | 8.00 | 3.00 |
| ☐ 188 | Johnnie Morant RC | 8.00 | 3.00 |
| ☐ 189 | Ahmad Carroll RC | 10.00 | 4.00 |
| ☐ 190 | Vince Wilfork RC | 10.00 | 4.00 |
| ☐ 191 | Tatum Bell JSY AU RC | 20.00 | 8.00 |
| ☐ 192 | Cedric Cobbs JSY AU RC | 15.00 | 6.00 |
| ☐ 193 | Darius Watts JSY AU RC | 15.00 | 6.00 |
| ☐ 194 | Jul.Jones JSY AU/375 RC | 60.00 | 30.00 |
| ☐ 195 | Robert Gallery JSY AU RC | 20.00 | 8.00 |
| ☐ 196 | DeAngelo Hall JSY AU RC | 20.00 | 8.00 |
| ☐ 197 | Ben Watson JSY AU RC | 20.00 | 8.00 |
| ☐ 198 | Ben Troupe JSY AU RC | 15.00 | 6.00 |
| ☐ 199 | Matt Schaub JSY AU RC | 60.00 | 25.00 |
| ☐ 200 | Michael Jenkins JSY AU RC | 20.00 | 8.00 |
| ☐ 201 | Luke McCown JSY AU RC | 20.00 | 8.00 |
| ☐ 202 | Devery Henderson JSY AU RC | 20.00 | 8.00 |
| ☐ 203 | Bernard Berrian JSY AU RC | 20.00 | 8.00 |
| ☐ 204 | Keary Colbert JSY AU RC | 20.00 | 8.00 |
| ☐ 205 | Devard Darling JSY AU RC | 15.00 | 6.00 |
| ☐ 206 | Lee Evans JSY AU RC | 25.00 | 10.00 |
| ☐ 207 | Greg Jones JSY AU RC | 20.00 | 8.00 |
| ☐ 208 | Mich.Clayton JSY AU RC | 20.00 | 8.00 |
| ☐ 209 | Re.Williams JSY AU RC | 20.00 | 8.00 |
| ☐ 210 | C.Perry JSY AU/799 RC | 20.00 | 8.00 |
| ☐ 211 | Rash.Woods JSY AU RC | 12.00 | 5.00 |
| ☐ 212 | J.P. Losman JSY AU RC | 25.00 | 10.00 |
| ☐ 213 | Kevin Jones JSY AU RC | 20.00 | 8.00 |
| ☐ 214 | K.Winslow JSY AU/375 RC | 60.00 | 30.00 |
| ☐ 215 | S.Jackson JSY AU/375 RC | 120.00 | 60.00 |
| ☐ 216 | Hamilton JSY AU RC | 12.00 | 5.00 |
| ☐ 217 | Ro.Will.JSY AU/375 RC | 80.00 | 30.00 |
| ☐ 218 | P.Rivers JSY AU/375 RC | 80.00 | 30.00 |
| ☐ 219 | Fitzgerald JSY AU/100 RC | 225.00 | 150.00 |
| ☐ 220 | Roethlis.JSY AU/375 RC | 300.00 | 175.00 |
| ☐ 221 | Manning JSY AU/375 RC | 250.00 | 125.00 |

## 2005 SPx

| | | | |
|---|---|---|---|
| ☐ COMP.SET w/o SP's (100) | | 30.00 | 15.00 |
| ☐ 101-170 RC PRINT RUN 1199 SER.#'d SETS | | | |
| ☐ 171-200 RC PRINT RUN 499 SER.#'d SETS | | | |
| ☐ JSY AU RC PRINT RUN 150-1275 | | | |
| ☐ UNPRICED NFL LOGO AUTOS #'d OF 1 | | | |
| ☐ 1 | Larry Fitzgerald | 1.00 | .40 |
| ☐ 2 | Anquan Boldin | .75 | .30 |

| | | |
|---|---|---|
| ☐ 3 Josh McCown | .75 | .30 |
| ☐ 4 Michael Vick | 1.00 | .40 |
| ☐ 5 Alge Crumpler | .75 | .30 |
| ☐ 6 Peerless Price | .60 | .25 |
| ☐ 7 Ray Lewis | 1.00 | .40 |
| ☐ 8 Jamal Lewis | .75 | .30 |
| ☐ 9 Kyle Boller | .75 | .30 |
| ☐ 10 J.P. Losman | 1.00 | .40 |
| ☐ 11 Willis McGahee | 1.00 | .40 |
| ☐ 12 Eric Moulds | .75 | .30 |
| ☐ 13 Jake Delhomme | 1.00 | .40 |
| ☐ 14 DeShaun Foster | .75 | .30 |
| ☐ 15 Steve Smith | 1.00 | .40 |
| ☐ 16 Brian Urlacher | 1.00 | .40 |
| ☐ 17 Rex Grossman | 1.00 | .40 |
| ☐ 18 Muhsin Muhammad | .75 | .30 |
| ☐ 19 Carson Palmer | 1.00 | .40 |
| ☐ 20 Rudi Johnson | .75 | .30 |
| ☐ 21 Chad Johnson | .75 | .30 |
| ☐ 22 Julius Jones | .75 | .30 |
| ☐ 23 Keyshawn Johnson | .75 | .30 |
| ☐ 24 Roy Williams S | .75 | .30 |
| ☐ 25 Tatum Bell | .75 | .30 |
| ☐ 26 Jake Plummer | .75 | .30 |
| ☐ 27 Ashley Lelie | .60 | .25 |
| ☐ 28 Roy Williams WR | 1.00 | .40 |
| ☐ 29 Kevin Jones | .75 | .30 |
| ☐ 30 Joey Harrington | 1.00 | .40 |
| ☐ 31 Brett Favre | 2.50 | 1.00 |
| ☐ 32 Ahman Green | 1.00 | .40 |
| ☐ 33 Javon Walker | .75 | .30 |
| ☐ 34 David Carr | .75 | .30 |
| ☐ 35 Andre Johnson | .75 | .30 |
| ☐ 36 Domanick Davis | .60 | .25 |
| ☐ 37 Peyton Manning | 1.50 | .60 |
| ☐ 38 Reggie Wayne | .75 | .30 |
| ☐ 39 Edgerrin James | .75 | .30 |
| ☐ 40 Marvin Harrison | 1.00 | .40 |
| ☐ 41 Byron Leftwich | .75 | .30 |
| ☐ 42 Fred Taylor | 1.00 | .40 |
| ☐ 43 Jimmy Smith | .75 | .30 |
| ☐ 44 Priest Holmes | 1.00 | .40 |
| ☐ 45 Larry Johnson | 1.00 | .40 |
| ☐ 46 Trent Green | .75 | .30 |
| ☐ 47 A.J. Feeley | .60 | .25 |
| ☐ 48 Chris Chambers | .75 | .30 |
| ☐ 49 Randy McMichael | .60 | .25 |
| ☐ 50 Daunte Culpepper | 1.00 | .40 |
| ☐ 51 Nate Burleson | .75 | .30 |
| ☐ 52 Michael Bennett | .75 | .30 |
| ☐ 53 Tom Brady | 2.00 | .75 |
| ☐ 54 Corey Dillon | .75 | .30 |
| ☐ 55 Deion Branch | .75 | .30 |
| ☐ 56 David Givens | .75 | .30 |
| ☐ 57 Aaron Brooks | .60 | .25 |
| ☐ 58 Deuce McAllister | 1.00 | .40 |
| ☐ 59 Joe Horn | .75 | .30 |
| ☐ 60 Eli Manning | 2.00 | .75 |
| ☐ 61 Jeremy Shockey | 1.00 | .40 |
| ☐ 62 Tiki Barber | 1.00 | .40 |
| ☐ 63 Chad Pennington | 1.00 | .40 |
| ☐ 64 Curtis Martin | 1.00 | .40 |
| ☐ 65 Laveranues Coles | .75 | .30 |
| ☐ 66 Kerry Collins | .75 | .30 |
| ☐ 67 Jerry Porter | .75 | .30 |
| ☐ 68 Randy Moss | 1.00 | .40 |
| ☐ 69 Donovan McNabb | 1.00 | .40 |
| ☐ 70 Terrell Owens | 1.00 | .40 |
| ☐ 71 Brian Dawkins | .75 | .30 |
| ☐ 72 Brian Westbrook | 1.00 | .40 |
| ☐ 73 Ben Roethlisberger | 2.50 | 1.00 |
| ☐ 74 Jerome Bettis | 1.00 | .40 |
| ☐ 75 Hines Ward | 1.00 | .40 |
| ☐ 76 Duce Staley | .75 | .30 |
| ☐ 77 Drew Brees | 1.00 | .40 |
| ☐ 78 LaDainian Tomlinson | 1.50 | .60 |
| ☐ 79 Antonio Gates | 1.00 | .40 |
| ☐ 80 Eric Parker | .60 | .25 |
| ☐ 81 Tim Rattay | .60 | .25 |
| ☐ 82 Kevan Barlow | .60 | .25 |
| ☐ 83 Eric Johnson | .60 | .25 |
| ☐ 84 Shaun Alexander | 1.00 | .40 |
| ☐ 85 Darrell Jackson | .75 | .30 |
| ☐ 86 Matt Hasselbeck | .75 | .30 |
| ☐ 87 Marc Bulger | .75 | .30 |

| | | |
|---|---|---|
| ☐ 88 Steven Jackson | 1.25 | .50 |
| ☐ 89 Marshall Faulk | 1.00 | .40 |
| ☐ 90 Torry Holt | .75 | .30 |
| ☐ 91 Michael Pittman | .60 | .25 |
| ☐ 92 Brian Griese | .75 | .30 |
| ☐ 93 Michael Clayton | .75 | .30 |
| ☐ 94 Steve McNair | 1.00 | .40 |
| ☐ 95 Drew Bennett | .75 | .30 |
| ☐ 96 Billy Volek | .75 | .30 |
| ☐ 97 Chris Brown | .75 | .30 |
| ☐ 98 Clinton Portis | 1.00 | .40 |
| ☐ 99 Patrick Ramsey | .75 | .30 |
| ☐ 100 Santana Moss | .75 | .30 |
| ☐ 101 Matt Jones RC | 8.00 | 3.00 |
| ☐ 102 Jonathan Babineaux RC | 4.00 | 1.50 |
| ☐ 103 Darrent Williams RC | 5.00 | 2.00 |
| ☐ 104 Timmy Chang RC | 4.00 | 1.50 |
| ☐ 105 Kelvin Hayden RC | 4.00 | 1.50 |
| ☐ 106 Paris Warren RC | 4.00 | 1.50 |
| ☐ 107 Stanley Wilson RC | 4.00 | 1.50 |
| ☐ 108 Walter Reyes RC | 3.00 | 1.25 |
| ☐ 109 Roydell Williams RC | 4.00 | 1.50 |
| ☐ 110 Chase Lyman RC | 3.00 | 1.25 |
| ☐ 111 Anthony Davis RC | 4.00 | 1.50 |
| ☐ 112 Rasheed Marshall RC | 4.00 | 1.50 |
| ☐ 113 Jerome Carter RC | 3.00 | 1.25 |
| ☐ 114 Mike Nugent RC | 4.00 | 1.50 |
| ☐ 115 Brodney Pool RC | 4.00 | 1.50 |
| ☐ 116 Sean Considine RC | 3.00 | 1.25 |
| ☐ 117 Chris Rix RC | 4.00 | 1.50 |
| ☐ 118 Donte Nicholson RC | 4.00 | 1.50 |
| ☐ 119 Dustin Fox RC | 5.00 | 2.00 |
| ☐ 120 Oshiomogho Atogwe RC | 3.00 | 1.25 |
| ☐ 121 Vincent Fuller RC | 3.00 | 1.25 |
| ☐ 122 Josh Bullocks RC | 5.00 | 2.00 |
| ☐ 123 Ronald Bartell RC | 4.00 | 1.50 |
| ☐ 124 Brock Berlin RC | 4.00 | 1.50 |
| ☐ 125 Fabian Washington RC | 5.00 | 2.00 |
| ☐ 126 Domonique Foxworth RC | 4.00 | 1.50 |
| ☐ 127 Bryant McFadden RC | 4.00 | 1.50 |
| ☐ 128 Marlin Jackson RC | 4.00 | 1.50 |
| ☐ 129 Eric Green RC | 3.00 | 1.25 |
| ☐ 130 Justin Miller RC | 4.00 | 1.50 |
| ☐ 131 Lots Tatupu RC | 6.00 | 2.50 |
| ☐ 132 Justin Tuck RC | 6.00 | 2.50 |
| ☐ 133 Kurt Campbell RC | 3.00 | 1.25 |
| ☐ 134 Darryl Blackstock RC | 4.00 | 1.50 |
| ☐ 135 Kevin Burnett RC | 4.00 | 1.50 |
| ☐ 136 Marviel Underwood RC | 4.00 | 1.50 |
| ☐ 137 Kirk Morrison RC | 5.00 | 2.00 |
| ☐ 138 Alfred Fincher RC | 4.00 | 1.50 |
| ☐ 139 Lance Mitchell RC | 4.00 | 1.50 |
| ☐ 140 Barrett Ruud RC | 4.00 | 1.50 |
| ☐ 141 David Pollack RC | 5.00 | 2.00 |
| ☐ 142 Bill Swancutt RC | 3.00 | 1.25 |
| ☐ 143 DeMarcus Ware RC | 8.00 | 3.00 |
| ☐ 144 Steve Savoy RC | 3.00 | 1.25 |
| ☐ 145 Matt Roth RC | 4.00 | 1.50 |
| ☐ 146 Shaun Cody RC | 4.00 | 1.50 |
| ☐ 147 Dan Cody RC | 4.00 | 1.50 |
| ☐ 148 Jordan Beck RC | 3.00 | 1.25 |
| ☐ 149 Kevin Everett RC | 4.00 | 1.50 |
| ☐ 150 Anttaj Hawthorne RC | 4.00 | 1.50 |
| ☐ 151 Mike Patterson RC | 4.00 | 1.50 |
| ☐ 152 Jerome Collins RC | 4.00 | 1.50 |
| ☐ 153 Dante Ridgeway RC | 3.00 | 1.25 |
| ☐ 154 Bryan Randall RC | 4.00 | 1.50 |
| ☐ 155 Marcus Maxwell RC | 3.00 | 1.25 |
| ☐ 156 Airese Currie RC | 4.00 | 1.50 |
| ☐ 157 Chad Owens RC | 5.00 | 2.00 |
| ☐ 158 Brandon Jacobs RC | 6.00 | 2.50 |
| ☐ 159 Manuel White RC | 4.00 | 1.50 |
| ☐ 160 Ellis Hobbs RC | 5.00 | 2.00 |
| ☐ 161 Lionel Gates RC | 3.00 | 1.25 |
| ☐ 162 Ryan Fitzpatrick RC | 5.00 | 2.00 |
| ☐ 163 Noah Herron RC | 5.00 | 2.00 |
| ☐ 164 Kay-Jay Harris RC | 4.00 | 1.50 |
| ☐ 165 T.A. McLendon RC | 3.00 | 1.25 |
| ☐ 166 Kerry Rhodes RC | 5.00 | 2.00 |
| ☐ 167 Nick Collins RC | 5.00 | 2.00 |
| ☐ 168 Eric Moore RC | 3.00 | 1.25 |
| ☐ 169 Harry Williams RC | 4.00 | 1.50 |
| ☐ 170 Luis Castillo RC | 5.00 | 2.00 |
| ☐ 171 James Kilian RC | 5.00 | 2.00 |
| ☐ 172 Matt Cassel RC | 20.00 | 8.00 |

| | | |
|---|---|---|
| ☐ 173 Alvin Pearman RC | 6.00 | 2.50 |
| ☐ 174 Dan Orlovsky RC | 8.00 | 3.00 |
| ☐ 175 Damien Nash RC | 6.00 | 2.50 |
| ☐ 176 Jason White RC | 8.00 | 3.00 |
| ☐ 177 Craig Bragg RC | 5.00 | 2.00 |
| ☐ 178 Craphonso Thorpe RC | 6.00 | 2.50 |
| ☐ 179 Derrick Johnson RC | 8.00 | 3.00 |
| ☐ 180 Derek Anderson RC | 12.00 | 5.00 |
| ☐ 181 Darren Sproles RC | 10.00 | 4.00 |
| ☐ 182 Cedric Houston RC | 8.00 | 3.00 |
| ☐ 183 Jerome Mathis RC | 8.00 | 3.00 |
| ☐ 184 Larry Brackins RC | 5.00 | 2.00 |
| ☐ 185 Fred Gibson RC | 6.00 | 2.50 |
| ☐ 186 J.R. Russell RC | 5.00 | 2.00 |
| ☐ 187 Alex Smith TE RC | 8.00 | 3.00 |
| ☐ 188 Deandra Cobb RC | 6.00 | 2.50 |
| ☐ 189 Tab Perry RC | 8.00 | 3.00 |
| ☐ 190 Travis Johnson RC | 5.00 | 2.00 |
| ☐ 191A Marion Barber RC | 25.00 | 10.00 |
| ☐ 191B Andrew Walter JSY AU RC | 30.00 | 12.00 |
| ☐ 192A Erasmus James RC | 6.00 | 2.50 |
| ☐ 192B V.Morency JSY AU RC | 30.00 | 12.00 |
| ☐ 193A Marcus Spears RC | 8.00 | 3.00 |
| ☐ 193B Antrel Rolle JSY AU RC | 30.00 | 12.00 |
| ☐ 194A Channing Crowder RC | 6.00 | 2.50 |
| ☐ 194B Adam Jones JSY AU RC | 30.00 | 12.00 |
| ☐ 195A Odell Thurman RC | 8.00 | 3.00 |
| ☐ 195B M.Claret JSY AU/250 | 30.00 | 12.00 |
| ☐ 196A Shawne Merriman RC | 12.00 | 5.00 |
| ☐ 196B Mark Bradley JSY AU RC | 30.00 | 12.00 |
| ☐ 197A Adrian McPherson RC | 6.00 | 2.50 |
| ☐ 197B Eric Shelton JSY AU RC | 25.00 | 10.00 |
| ☐ 198A Chris Henry RC | 8.00 | 3.00 |
| ☐ 198B Kyle Orton JSY AU RC | 40.00 | 15.00 |
| ☐ 199A Thomas Davis RC | 6.00 | 2.50 |
| ☐ 199B Ryan Moats JSY AU RC | 30.00 | 12.00 |
| ☐ 200A Corey Webster RC | 8.00 | 3.00 |
| ☐ 200B Frank Gore JSY AU RC | 80.00 | 30.00 |
| ☐ 201 J.J. Arrington JSY AU RC | 25.00 | 10.00 |
| ☐ 202 M.Williams JSY AU/250 | 40.00 | 15.00 |
| ☐ 203 V.Jackson JSY AU RC | 25.00 | 10.00 |
| ☐ 204 Stefan LeFors JSY AU RC | 20.00 | 8.00 |
| ☐ 206 T.Murphy JSY AU RC | 15.00 | 6.00 |
| ☐ 207 Courtney Roby JSY AU RC | 20.00 | 8.00 |
| ☐ 208 Carlos Rogers JSY AU RC | 25.00 | 10.00 |
| ☐ 209 Charlie Frye JSY AU RC | 25.00 | 10.00 |
| ☐ 210 Mark Clayton JSY AU RC | 25.00 | 10.00 |
| ☐ 211 Roddy White JSY AU RC | 30.00 | 15.00 |
| ☐ 212 Jason Campbell JSY AU RC | 50.00 | 20.00 |
| ☐ 213 Roscoe Parrish JSY AU RC | 20.00 | 8.00 |
| ☐ 214 Reggie Brown JSY AU RC | 25.00 | 10.00 |
| ☐ 215 Heath Miller JSY AU RC | 50.00 | 20.00 |
| ☐ 216 Williamson JSY AU/250 RC | 50.00 | 25.00 |
| ☐ 217 Ciatrick Fason JSY AU RC | 20.00 | 8.00 |
| ☐ 218 C.Benson JSY AU/150 RC | 60.00 | 30.00 |
| ☐ 219 B.Edwards JSY AU/250 RC | 120.00 | 60.00 |
| ☐ 220 Ro.Brown JSY AU/250 RC | 150.00 | 75.00 |
| ☐ 221 C.Williams JSY AU/250 RC | 120.00 | 60.00 |
| ☐ 222 A.Smith QB JSY AU RC | 120.00 | 60.00 |
| ☐ 223 A.Rodgers JSY AU/250 RC | 175.00 | 100.00 |

## 2006 SPx

| | | |
|---|---|---|
| ☐ COMP.SET w/o RC's (90) | 30.00 | 12.50 |
| ☐ 91-180 ROOKIE PRINT RUN 1299 | | |
| ☐ 181-187 RC JSY AU PRINT RUN 399 | | |
| ☐ 181-187 RC JSY AU PRINT RUN 1650 | | |
| ☐ 1 Edgerrin James | .75 | .30 |
| ☐ 2 Kurt Warner | .75 | .30 |

|  |  | | |
|---|---|---|---|
| ❏ 3 | Larry Fitzgerald | 1.00 | .40 |
| ❏ 4 | Michael Vick | 1.00 | .40 |
| ❏ 5 | Warrick Dunn | .75 | .30 |
| ❏ 6 | Michael Jenkins | .75 | .30 |
| ❏ 7 | Jamal Lewis | .75 | .30 |
| ❏ 8 | Kyle Boller | .75 | .30 |
| ❏ 9 | Derrick Mason | .75 | .30 |
| ❏ 10 | Willis McGahee | 1.00 | .40 |
| ❏ 11 | Lee Evans | .75 | .30 |
| ❏ 12 | Jake Delhomme | .75 | .30 |
| ❏ 13 | Steve Smith | 1.00 | .40 |
| ❏ 14 | DeShaun Foster | .75 | .30 |
| ❏ 15 | Rex Grossman | 1.00 | .40 |
| ❏ 16 | Muhsin Muhammad | .75 | .30 |
| ❏ 17 | Thomas Jones | .75 | .30 |
| ❏ 18 | Carson Palmer | 1.00 | .40 |
| ❏ 19 | Chad Johnson | .75 | .30 |
| ❏ 20 | Rudi Johnson | .75 | .30 |
| ❏ 21 | Charlie Frye | .75 | .30 |
| ❏ 22 | Reuben Droughns | .75 | .30 |
| ❏ 23 | Braylon Edwards | 1.00 | .40 |
| ❏ 24 | Drew Bledsoe | 1.00 | .40 |
| ❏ 25 | Terrell Owens | 1.00 | .40 |
| ❏ 26 | Julius Jones | 1.00 | .40 |
| ❏ 27 | Jake Plummer | .75 | .30 |
| ❏ 28 | Tatum Bell | .75 | .30 |
| ❏ 29 | Rod Smith | .75 | .30 |
| ❏ 30 | Kevin Jones | 1.00 | .40 |
| ❏ 31 | Roy Williams WR | 1.00 | .40 |
| ❏ 32 | Brett Favre | 2.00 | .75 |
| ❏ 33 | Ahman Green | .75 | .30 |
| ❏ 34 | Donald Driver | .75 | .30 |
| ❏ 35 | David Carr | .75 | .30 |
| ❏ 36 | Andre Johnson | .75 | .30 |
| ❏ 37 | Peyton Manning | 1.50 | .60 |
| ❏ 38 | Marvin Harrison | 1.00 | .40 |
| ❏ 39 | Reggie Wayne | .75 | .30 |
| ❏ 40 | Byron Leftwich | .75 | .30 |
| ❏ 41 | Fred Taylor | .75 | .30 |
| ❏ 42 | Ernest Wilford | .75 | .30 |
| ❏ 43 | Larry Johnson | .75 | .30 |
| ❏ 44 | Trent Green | .75 | .30 |
| ❏ 45 | Tony Gonzalez | .75 | .30 |
| ❏ 46 | Daunte Culpepper | 1.00 | .40 |
| ❏ 47 | Ronnie Brown | 1.00 | .40 |
| ❏ 48 | Chris Chambers | .75 | .30 |
| ❏ 49 | Troy Williamson | .75 | .30 |
| ❏ 50 | Chester Taylor | .75 | .30 |
| ❏ 51 | Brad Johnson | .75 | .30 |
| ❏ 52 | Tom Brady | 1.50 | .60 |
| ❏ 53 | Deion Branch | .75 | .30 |
| ❏ 54 | Corey Dillon | .75 | .30 |
| ❏ 55 | Drew Brees | 1.00 | .40 |
| ❏ 56 | Deuce McAllister | .75 | .30 |
| ❏ 57 | Donte Stallworth | .75 | .30 |
| ❏ 58 | Eli Manning | 1.25 | .50 |
| ❏ 59 | Tiki Barber | 1.00 | .40 |
| ❏ 60 | Plaxico Burress | .75 | .30 |
| ❏ 61 | Chad Pennington | .75 | .30 |
| ❏ 62 | Curtis Martin | 1.00 | .40 |
| ❏ 63 | Randy Moss | 1.00 | .40 |
| ❏ 64 | LaMont Jordan | .75 | .30 |
| ❏ 65 | Aaron Brooks | .75 | .30 |
| ❏ 66 | Donovan McNabb | 1.00 | .40 |
| ❏ 67 | Brian Westbrook | .75 | .30 |
| ❏ 68 | Ben Roethlisberger | 1.50 | .60 |
| ❏ 69 | Hines Ward | 1.00 | .40 |
| ❏ 70 | Willie Parker | 1.25 | .50 |
| ❏ 71 | LaDainian Tomlinson | 1.25 | .50 |
| ❏ 72 | Philip Rivers | 1.00 | .40 |
| ❏ 73 | Antonio Gates | 1.00 | .40 |
| ❏ 74 | Alex Smith QB | 1.00 | .40 |
| ❏ 75 | Antonio Bryant | .75 | .30 |
| ❏ 76 | Frank Gore | 1.00 | .40 |
| ❏ 77 | Shaun Alexander | 1.00 | .40 |
| ❏ 78 | Matt Hasselbeck | .75 | .30 |
| ❏ 79 | Nate Burleson | .75 | .30 |
| ❏ 80 | Marc Bulger | 1.00 | .40 |
| ❏ 81 | Steven Jackson | 1.00 | .40 |
| ❏ 82 | Torry Holt | .75 | .30 |
| ❏ 83 | Cadillac Williams | 1.00 | .40 |
| ❏ 84 | Joey Galloway | .75 | .30 |
| ❏ 85 | Chris Simms | .75 | .30 |
| ❏ 86 | Billy Volek | .75 | .30 |
| ❏ 87 | Drew Bennett | .75 | .30 |
| ❏ 88 | Clinton Portis | 1.00 | .40 |
| ❏ 89 | Santana Moss | .75 | .30 |
| ❏ 90 | Mark Brunell | .75 | .30 |
| ❏ 91 | Haloti Ngata RC | 10.00 | 4.00 |
| ❏ 92 | Willie Reid RC | 10.00 | 4.00 |
| ❏ 93 | Kamerion Wimbley RC | 10.00 | 4.00 |
| ❏ 94 | Donte Whitner RC | 10.00 | 4.00 |
| ❏ 95 | Ethan Kilmer RC | 10.00 | 4.00 |
| ❏ 96 | Johnathan Joseph RC | 8.00 | 3.00 |
| ❏ 97 | Brodie Croyle RC | 12.00 | 5.00 |
| ❏ 98 | Bobby Carpenter RC | 10.00 | 4.00 |
| ❏ 99 | Antonio Cromartie RC | 10.00 | 4.00 |
| ❏ 100 | Eric Winston RC | 5.00 | 2.00 |
| ❏ 101 | Nick Mangold RC | 8.00 | 3.00 |
| ❏ 102 | Manny Lawson RC | 10.00 | 4.00 |
| ❏ 103 | Claude Wroten RC | 6.00 | 2.50 |
| ❏ 104 | D'Qwell Jackson RC | 8.00 | 3.00 |
| ❏ 105 | Richard Marshall RC | 8.00 | 3.00 |
| ❏ 106 | Tamba Hali RC | 10.00 | 4.00 |
| ❏ 107 | Ko Simpson RC | 8.00 | 3.00 |
| ❏ 108 | Daniel Manning RC | 10.00 | 4.00 |
| ❏ 109 | Gabe Watson RC | 8.00 | 3.00 |
| ❏ 110 | Kelvin McMahan RC | 8.00 | 3.00 |
| ❏ 111 | Jai Lewis RC | 8.00 | 3.00 |
| ❏ 112 | Darryl Tapp RC | 8.00 | 3.00 |
| ❏ 113 | John McCargo RC | 8.00 | 3.00 |
| ❏ 114 | Jeff King RC | 8.00 | 3.00 |
| ❏ 115 | Charles Davis RC | 8.00 | 3.00 |
| ❏ 116 | Calvin Lowry RC | 10.00 | 4.00 |
| ❏ 117 | Delanie Walker RC | 8.00 | 3.00 |
| ❏ 118 | Roman Harper RC | 8.00 | 3.00 |
| ❏ 119 | Nate Salley RC | 8.00 | 3.00 |
| ❏ 120 | Cooper Wallace RC | 8.00 | 3.00 |
| ❏ 121 | Bernard Pollard RC | 8.00 | 3.00 |
| ❏ 122 | Derrick Ross RC | 8.00 | 3.00 |
| ❏ 123 | Ingle Martin RC | 10.00 | 4.00 |
| ❏ 124 | Wali Lundy RC | 8.00 | 3.00 |
| ❏ 125 | Marcus Vick RC | 8.00 | 3.00 |
| ❏ 126 | Cedric Humes RC | 10.00 | 4.00 |
| ❏ 127 | Marques Hagans RC | 8.00 | 3.00 |
| ❏ 128 | Taurean Henderson RC | 10.00 | 4.00 |
| ❏ 129 | Marques Colston RC | 25.00 | 10.00 |
| ❏ 130 | Devin Aromashodu RC | 8.00 | 3.00 |
| ❏ 131 | Jonathan Orr RC | 8.00 | 3.00 |
| ❏ 132 | Skyler Green RC | 10.00 | 4.00 |
| ❏ 133 | Jeff Webb RC | 8.00 | 3.00 |
| ❏ 134 | Jon Alston RC | 10.00 | 4.00 |
| ❏ 135 | Daniel Bullocks RC | 10.00 | 4.00 |
| ❏ 136 | Anthony Schlegel RC | 8.00 | 3.00 |
| ❏ 137 | Adam Jennings RC | 8.00 | 3.00 |
| ❏ 138 | Gerris Wilkinson RC | 6.00 | 2.50 |
| ❏ 139 | James Anderson RC | 6.00 | 2.50 |
| ❏ 140 | Owen Daniels RC | 10.00 | 4.00 |
| ❏ 141 | Ray Edwards RC | 8.00 | 3.00 |
| ❏ 142 | Chris Gocong RC | 8.00 | 3.00 |
| ❏ 143 | Babatunde Oshinowo RC | 8.00 | 3.00 |
| ❏ 144 | Marvin Philip RC | 10.00 | 4.00 |
| ❏ 145 | Stanley McClover RC | 8.00 | 3.00 |
| ❏ 146 | DeMeco Ryans RC | 12.00 | 5.00 |
| ❏ 147 | Tony Scheffler RC | 10.00 | 4.00 |
| ❏ 148 | T.J. Williams RC | 10.00 | 4.00 |
| ❏ 149 | P.J. Daniels RC | 8.00 | 3.00 |
| ❏ 150 | Bennie Brazell RC | 8.00 | 3.00 |
| ❏ 151 | Will Blackmon RC | 10.00 | 4.00 |
| ❏ 152 | Bruce Gradkowski RC | 10.00 | 4.00 |
| ❏ 153 | Drew Olson RC | 8.00 | 3.00 |
| ❏ 154 | Darnell Bing RC | 10.00 | 4.00 |
| ❏ 155 | Darrell Hackney RC | 8.00 | 3.00 |
| ❏ 156 | Cory Rodgers RC | 10.00 | 4.00 |
| ❏ 157 | DonTrell Moore RC | 8.00 | 3.00 |
| ❏ 158 | Ernie Sims RC | 10.00 | 4.00 |
| ❏ 159 | Jay Cutler RC | 40.00 | 15.00 |
| ❏ 160 | D.J. Shockley RC | 10.00 | 4.00 |
| ❏ 161 | Martin Nance RC | 8.00 | 3.00 |
| ❏ 162 | Joseph Addai RC | 30.00 | 12.00 |
| ❏ 163 | Leonard Pope RC | 10.00 | 4.00 |
| ❏ 164 | Anthony Fasano RC | 10.00 | 4.00 |
| ❏ 165 | Mathias Kiwanuka RC | 12.00 | 5.00 |
| ❏ 166 | Greg Jennings RC | 15.00 | 6.00 |
| ❏ 167 | Greg Lee RC | 8.00 | 3.00 |
| ❏ 168 | Jerome Harrison RC | 10.00 | 4.00 |
| ❏ 169 | Jimmy Williams RC | 10.00 | 4.00 |
| ❏ 170 | Josh Betts RC | 8.00 | 3.00 |
| ❏ 171 | Ashton Youboty RC | 10.00 | 4.00 |
| ❏ 172 | Terrence Whitehead RC | 8.00 | 3.00 |
| ❏ 173 | Brad Smith RC | 10.00 | 4.00 |
| ❏ 174 | D'Brickashaw Ferguson RC | 10.00 | 4.00 |
| ❏ 175 | Mike Hass RC | 10.00 | 4.00 |
| ❏ 176 | Reggie McNeal RC | 8.00 | 3.00 |
| ❏ 177 | Dominique Byrd RC | 8.00 | 3.00 |
| ❏ 178 | Winston Justice RC | 10.00 | 4.00 |
| ❏ 179 | Chad Greenway RC | 10.00 | 4.00 |
| ❏ 180 | Tye Hill RC | 10.00 | 4.00 |
| ❏ 181 | Jackson JSY AU RC | 50.00 | 15.00 |
| ❏ 182 | DeA.Williams JSY AU RC | 60.00 | 30.00 |
| ❏ 183 | Vince Young JSY AU RC | 150.00 | 75.00 |
| ❏ 184 | S.Holmes JSY AU RC | 80.00 | 40.00 |
| ❏ 185 | Sinorice Moss JSY AU RC | 40.00 | 15.00 |
| ❏ 186 | Matt Leinart JSY AU RC | 150.00 | 60.00 |
| ❏ 187 | Reggie Bush JSY AU RC | 200.00 | 100.00 |
| ❏ 188 | LenDale White JSY AU RC | 50.00 | 20.00 |
| ❏ 189 | Vernon Davis JSY AU RC | 20.00 | 8.00 |
| ❏ 190 | L.Maroney JSY AU RC | 80.00 | 30.00 |
| ❏ 191 | A.J. Hawk JSY AU RC | 60.00 | 30.00 |
| ❏ 192 | Marcus McNeill JSY AU RC | 15.00 | 6.00 |
| ❏ 193 | Kelly Jennings JSY AU RC | 20.00 | 8.00 |
| ❏ 194 | B.Williams JSY AU RC | 20.00 | 8.00 |
| ❏ 195 | Brian Calhoun JSY AU RC | 15.00 | 6.00 |
| ❏ 196 | Travis Wilson JSY AU RC | 15.00 | 6.00 |
| ❏ 197 | C.Whitehurst JSY AU RC | 20.00 | 8.00 |
| ❏ 198 | Omar Jacobs JSY AU RC | 15.00 | 6.00 |
| ❏ 199 | J.Klopfenstein JSY AU RC | 15.00 | 6.00 |
| ❏ 200 | Derek Hagan JSY AU RC | 20.00 | 8.00 |
| ❏ 201 | Michael Huff JSY AU RC | 20.00 | 8.00 |
| ❏ 202 | Maurice Stovall JSY AU RC | 20.00 | 8.00 |
| ❏ 203 | Maurice Drew JSY AU RC | 50.00 | 25.00 |
| ❏ 204 | Jason Avant JSY AU RC | 20.00 | 8.00 |
| ❏ 205 | K.Clemens JSY AU RC | 30.00 | 12.00 |
| ❏ 206 | J.Norwood JSY AU RC | 40.00 | 20.00 |
| ❏ 207 | T.Jackson JSY AU RC | 25.00 | 10.00 |
| ❏ 208 | B.Marshall JSY AU RC | 30.00 | 15.00 |
| ❏ 209 | Dem.Williams JSY AU RC | 20.00 | 8.00 |
| ❏ 210 | L.Washington JSY AU RC | 30.00 | 12.00 |
| ❏ 211 | M.Robinson JSY AU RC | 20.00 | 8.00 |
| ❏ 212 | Marcedes Lewis JSY AU RC | 20.00 | 8.00 |
| ❏ 213 | Mario Williams JSY AU RC | 30.00 | 12.00 |

## 2007 SPx

|  |  | | |
|---|---|---|---|
| ❏ 1 | Matt Leinart | 1.25 | .50 |
| ❏ 2 | Anquan Boldin | 1.00 | .40 |
| ❏ 3 | Larry Fitzgerald | 1.25 | .50 |
| ❏ 4 | Edgerrin James | 1.00 | .40 |
| ❏ 5 | Michael Vick | 1.25 | .50 |
| ❏ 6 | Warrick Dunn | 1.00 | .40 |
| ❏ 7 | DeAngelo Hall | 1.00 | .40 |
| ❏ 8 | Steve McNair | 1.00 | .40 |
| ❏ 9 | Willis McGahee | 1.00 | .40 |
| ❏ 10 | Ray Lewis | 1.25 | .50 |
| ❏ 11 | J.P. Losman | .75 | .30 |
| ❏ 12 | Lee Evans | 1.00 | .40 |
| ❏ 13 | Anthony Thomas | .75 | .30 |
| ❏ 14 | Jake Delhomme | 1.00 | .40 |
| ❏ 15 | Steve Smith | 1.00 | .40 |
| ❏ 16 | DeAngelo Williams | 1.25 | .50 |
| ❏ 17 | Brian Urlacher | 1.25 | .50 |
| ❏ 18 | Cedric Benson | 1.00 | .40 |
| ❏ 19 | Rex Grossman | 1.00 | .40 |
| ❏ 20 | Carson Palmer | 1.25 | .50 |
| ❏ 21 | Chad Johnson | 1.00 | .40 |
| ❏ 22 | Rudi Johnson | 1.00 | .40 |
| ❏ 23 | Charlie Frye | 1.00 | .40 |
| ❏ 24 | Braylon Edwards | 1.00 | .40 |
| ❏ 25 | Jamal Lewis | 1.00 | .40 |

|  |  | | |
|---|--------|------|------|
| 26 | Tony Romo | 2.50 | 1.00 |
| 27 | Terrell Owens | 1.25 | .50 |
| 28 | Julius Jones | 1.00 | .40 |
| 29 | Marion Barber | 1.25 | .50 |
| 30 | Jay Cutler | 1.25 | .50 |
| 31 | Javon Walker | 1.00 | .40 |
| 32 | Travis Henry | 1.00 | .40 |
| 33 | Roy Williams WR | 1.00 | .40 |
| 34 | Mike Furrey | 1.00 | .40 |
| 35 | Tatum Bell | .75 | .30 |
| 36 | Greg Jennings | 1.00 | .40 |
| 37 | Brett Favre | 2.50 | 1.00 |
| 38 | A.J. Hawk | 1.25 | .50 |
| 39 | Matt Schaub | 1.25 | .50 |
| 40 | Andre Johnson | 1.00 | .40 |
| 41 | Ahman Green | 1.00 | .40 |
| 42 | Peyton Manning | 2.00 | .75 |
| 43 | Marvin Harrison | 1.25 | .50 |
| 44 | Reggie Wayne | 1.25 | .50 |
| 45 | Joseph Addai | 1.25 | .50 |
| 46 | Fred Taylor | 1.00 | .40 |
| 47 | Maurice Jones-Drew | 1.25 | .50 |
| 48 | Byron Leftwich | 1.00 | .40 |
| 49 | Damon Huard | 1.00 | .40 |
| 50 | Larry Johnson | 1.00 | .40 |
| 51 | Tony Gonzalez | 1.00 | .40 |
| 52 | Zach Thomas | 1.00 | .40 |
| 53 | Ronnie Brown | 1.00 | .40 |
| 54 | Chris Chambers | 1.00 | .40 |
| 55 | Tarvaris Jackson | 1.00 | .40 |
| 56 | Chester Taylor | .75 | .30 |
| 57 | Troy Williamson | .75 | .30 |
| 58 | Tom Brady | 2.50 | 1.00 |
| 59 | Donte Stallworth | 1.00 | .40 |
| 60 | Laurence Maroney | 1.25 | .50 |
| 61 | Reggie Bush | 1.50 | .60 |
| 62 | Deuce McAllister | 1.00 | .40 |
| 63 | Drew Brees | 1.25 | .50 |
| 64 | Marques Colston | 1.25 | .50 |
| 65 | Eli Manning | 1.25 | .50 |
| 66 | Plaxico Burress | 1.00 | .40 |
| 67 | Brandon Jacobs | 1.00 | .40 |
| 68 | Chad Pennington | 1.00 | .40 |
| 69 | Thomas Jones | 1.00 | .40 |
| 70 | Laveranues Coles | 1.00 | .40 |
| 71 | LaMont Jordan | 1.00 | .40 |
| 72 | Randy Moss | 1.25 | .50 |
| 73 | Nnamdi Asomugha | .75 | .30 |
| 74 | Donovan McNabb | 1.25 | .50 |
| 75 | Brian Westbrook | 1.00 | .40 |
| 76 | Reggie Brown | 1.00 | .40 |
| 77 | Ben Roethlisberger | 1.50 | .60 |
| 78 | Hines Ward | 1.25 | .50 |
| 79 | Willie Parker | 1.25 | .50 |
| 80 | LaDainian Tomlinson | 1.50 | .60 |
| 81 | Philip Rivers | 1.25 | .50 |
| 82 | Antonio Gates | 1.00 | .40 |
| 83 | Frank Gore | 1.25 | .50 |
| 84 | Alex Smith QB | 1.25 | .50 |
| 85 | Ashley Lelie | 1.00 | .40 |
| 86 | Matt Hasselbeck | 1.00 | .40 |
| 87 | Shaun Alexander | 1.00 | .40 |
| 88 | Deion Branch | 1.00 | .40 |
| 89 | Marc Bulger | 1.00 | .40 |
| 90 | Torry Holt | 1.00 | .40 |
| 91 | Steven Jackson | 1.25 | .50 |
| 92 | Cadillac Williams | 1.00 | .40 |
| 93 | Chris Simms | .75 | .30 |
| 94 | Joey Galloway | 1.00 | .40 |
| 95 | Vince Young | 1.25 | .50 |
| 96 | David Givens | .75 | .30 |
| 97 | LenDale White | 1.00 | .40 |
| 98 | Jason Campbell | 1.00 | .40 |
| 99 | Santana Moss | 1.00 | .40 |
| 100 | Clinton Portis | 1.00 | .40 |
| 101 | Levi Brown RC | 10.00 | 4.00 |
| 102 | Adam Carriker RC | 8.00 | 3.00 |
| 103 | Jarvis Moss RC | 10.00 | 4.00 |
| 104 | Aaron Ross RC | 10.00 | 4.00 |
| 105 | Chris Houston RC | 8.00 | 3.00 |
| 106 | Michael Griffin RC | 10.00 | 4.00 |
| 107 | Justin Harrell RC | 8.00 | 3.00 |
| 108 | Joe Staley RC | 8.00 | 3.00 |
| 109 | Jon Beason RC | 10.00 | 4.00 |
| 110 | Anthony Spencer RC | 10.00 | 4.00 |
| 111 | Ben Grubbs RC | 8.00 | 3.00 |
| 112 | Charles Johnson RC | 6.00 | 2.50 |
| 113 | Marcus McCauley RC | 8.00 | 3.00 |
| 114 | Justin Blalock RC | 6.00 | 2.50 |
| 115 | Tim Crowder RC | 10.00 | 4.00 |
| 116 | Brandon Meriweather RC | 10.00 | 4.00 |
| 117 | Arron Sears RC | 8.00 | 3.00 |
| 118 | Zach Miller RC | 10.00 | 4.00 |
| 119 | Turk McBride RC | 8.00 | 3.00 |
| 120 | Ryan Kalil RC | 8.00 | 3.00 |
| 121 | Tony Ugoh RC | 8.00 | 3.00 |
| 122 | David Harris RC | 8.00 | 3.00 |
| 123 | Jonathan Wade RC | 8.00 | 3.00 |
| 124 | Josh Wilson RC | 8.00 | 3.00 |
| 125 | Demarcus Tank Tyler RC | 8.00 | 3.00 |
| 126 | Tanard Jackson RC | 6.00 | 2.50 |
| 127 | Jordan Kent RC | 8.00 | 3.00 |
| 128 | Ray McDonald RC | 8.00 | 3.00 |
| 129 | Quentin Moses RC | 8.00 | 3.00 |
| 130 | Eric Weddle RC | 8.00 | 3.00 |
| 131 | Victor Abiamiri RC | 10.00 | 4.00 |
| 132 | Josh Beekman RC | 6.00 | 2.50 |
| 133 | Brandon Siler RC | 8.00 | 3.00 |
| 134 | Aundrae Allison RC | 8.00 | 3.00 |
| 135 | Ben Patrick RC | 8.00 | 3.00 |
| 136 | Chris Davis RC | 8.00 | 3.00 |
| 137 | A.J. Davis RC | 6.00 | 2.50 |
| 138 | Scott Chandler RC | 8.00 | 3.00 |
| 139 | Mason Crosby RC | 10.00 | 4.00 |
| 140 | Zak DeOssie RC | 8.00 | 3.00 |
| 141 | Matt Spaeth RC | 10.00 | 4.00 |
| 142 | James Jones RC | 10.00 | 4.00 |
| 143 | Mike Walker RC | 8.00 | 3.00 |
| 144 | Martrez Milner RC | 8.00 | 3.00 |
| 145 | Michael Okwo RC | 8.00 | 3.00 |
| 146 | Steve Breaston RC | 10.00 | 4.00 |
| 147 | Isaiah Stanback RC | 10.00 | 4.00 |
| 148 | Laurent Robinson RC | 8.00 | 3.00 |
| 149 | Brandon Mebane RC | 8.00 | 3.00 |
| 150 | Quinn Pitcock RC | 8.00 | 3.00 |
| 151 | Roy Hall RC | 10.00 | 4.00 |
| 152 | Buster Davis RC | 8.00 | 3.00 |
| 153 | Alan Branch RC | 8.00 | 3.00 |
| 154 | Josh Gattis RC | 6.00 | 2.50 |
| 155 | Aaron Rouse RC | 10.00 | 4.00 |
| 156 | Tim Shaw RC | 8.00 | 3.00 |
| 157 | Sabby Piscitelli RC | 10.00 | 4.00 |
| 158 | Rufus Alexander RC | 10.00 | 4.00 |
| 159 | Marcus Thomas RC | 8.00 | 3.00 |
| 160 | Tarell Brown RC | 6.00 | 2.50 |
| 161 | Chris Leak RC | 15.00 | 6.00 |
| 162 | Amobi Okoye AU RC | 20.00 | 8.00 |
| 163 | Tyler Palko AU RC | 20.00 | 8.00 |
| 164 | Craig Buster Davis AU RC | 20.00 | 8.00 |
| 165 | Courtney Taylor AU RC | 15.00 | 6.00 |
| 166 | Tyrone Moss AU RC | 12.00 | 5.00 |
| 167 | Darrelle Revis AU RC | 20.00 | 8.00 |
| 168 | David Ball AU RC | 12.00 | 5.00 |
| 169 | David Clowney RC | 15.00 | 6.00 |
| 170 | Daymeion Hughes AU RC | 15.00 | 6.00 |
| 171 | DeShawn Wynn AU RC | 20.00 | 8.00 |
| 172 | Drew Tate AU RC | 15.00 | 6.00 |
| 173 | Dwayne Wright AU RC | 15.00 | 6.00 |
| 174 | Eric Wright AU RC | 20.00 | 8.00 |
| 175 | Kenneth Darby AU RC | 20.00 | 8.00 |
| 176 | H.B. Blades AU RC | 15.00 | 6.00 |
| 177 | Jamaal Anderson AU RC | 15.00 | 6.00 |
| 178 | Jared Zabransky AU RC | 20.00 | 8.00 |
| 179 | Rhema McKnight AU RC | 15.00 | 6.00 |
| 180 | Jeff Rowe AU RC | 15.00 | 6.00 |
| 181 | LaRon Landry AU RC | 25.00 | 10.00 |
| 182 | Jordan Palmer AU RC | 20.00 | 8.00 |
| 183 | Kolby Smith AU RC | 20.00 | 8.00 |
| 184 | LaMarr Woodley AU RC | 25.00 | 12.50 |
| 185 | Lawrence Timmons AU RC | 20.00 | 8.00 |
| 186 | Leon Hall AU RC | 15.00 | 6.00 |
| 187 | Matt Moore AU RC | 25.00 | 10.00 |
| 188 | Gary Russell AU RC | 20.00 | 8.00 |
| 189 | Paul Posluszny AU RC | 25.00 | 10.00 |
| 190 | Reggie Nelson AU RC | 15.00 | 6.00 |
| 191 | Antonio Pittman JSY AU RC | 25.00 | 10.00 |
| 192 | A.Gonzalez JSY AU/399 RC | 50.00 | 25.00 |
| 193 | Gaines Adams JSY AU RC | 25.00 | 10.00 |
| 194 | Brandon Jackson JSY AU RC | 25.00 | 10.00 |
| 195 | Brian Leonard JSY AU RC | 25.00 | 10.00 |
| 196 | J.Higgins JSY AU RC | 20.00 | 8.00 |
| 197 | Chris Henry RB JSY AU RC | 25.00 | 10.00 |
| 198 | Patrick Willis JSY AU RC | 50.00 | 20.00 |
| 199 | Drew Stanton JSY AU RC | 25.00 | 10.00 |
| 200 | D.Bowe JSY AU/399 RC | 60.00 | 25.00 |
| 201 | Greg Olsen JSY AU RC | 40.00 | 20.00 |
| 202 | John Beck JSY AU RC | 25.00 | 10.00 |
| 203 | Jason Hill JSY AU RC | 25.00 | 10.00 |
| 204 | Paul Williams JSY AU RC | 20.00 | 8.00 |
| 205 | Joe Thomas JSY AU RC | 25.00 | 10.00 |
| 206 | Lorenzo Booker JSY AU RC | 25.00 | 10.00 |
| 207 | Yamon Figurs JSY AU RC | 25.00 | 10.00 |
| 208 | Kenny Irons JSY AU RC | 25.00 | 10.00 |
| 209 | Kevin Kolb JSY AU/399 RC | 40.00 | 20.00 |
| 210 | Garrett Wolfe JSY AU RC | 25.00 | 10.00 |
| 211 | Michael Bush JSY AU RC | 25.00 | 10.00 |
| 212 | R.Meachem JSY AU/399 RC | 30.00 | 12.00 |
| 213 | Sidney Rice JSY AU/399 RC | 30.00 | 12.00 |
| 214 | Steve Smith JSY AU RC | 30.00 | 15.00 |
| 215 | Tony Hunt JSY AU RC | 25.00 | 10.00 |
| 217 | T.Edwards JSY AU/399 RC | 80.00 | 40.00 |
| 218 | A.Peterson JSY AU/299 RC | 400.00 | 200.00 |
| 219 | B.Quinn JSY AU/299 RC | 150.00 | 75.00 |
| 220 | Ca.Johnson JSY AU/299 RC | 120.00 | 50.00 |
| 221 | D.Jarrett JSY AU/299 RC | 40.00 | 15.00 |
| 222 | J.Russell JSY AU/299 RC | 100.00 | 40.00 |
| 223 | M.Lynch JSY AU/299 RC | 80.00 | 30.00 |
| 224 | Ted Ginn Jr. JSY AU/299 RC | 60.00 | 30.00 |

## 1991 Stadium Club

|  |  | | |
|---|--------|------|------|
| | COMPLETE SET (500) | 60.00 | 30.00 |
| 1 | Pepper Johnson | .20 | .07 |
| 2 | Emmitt Smith | 5.00 | 2.00 |
| 3 | Deion Sanders | 1.50 | .60 |
| 4 | Andre Collins | .20 | .07 |
| 5 | Eric Metcalf | .40 | .15 |
| 6 | Richard Dent | .40 | .15 |
| 7 | Eric Martin | .20 | .07 |
| 8 | Marcus Allen | .75 | .30 |
| 9 | Gary Anderson K | .20 | .07 |
| 10 | Joey Browner | .20 | .07 |
| 11 | Lorenzo White | .20 | .07 |
| 12 | Bruce Smith | .75 | .30 |
| 13 | Mark Boyer | .20 | .07 |
| 14 | Mike Piel | .20 | .07 |
| 15 | Albert Bentley | .20 | .07 |
| 16 | Bennie Blades | .20 | .07 |
| 17 | Jason Staurovsky | .20 | .07 |
| 18 | Anthony Toney | .20 | .07 |
| 19 | Dave Krieg | .40 | .15 |
| 20 | Harvey Williams RC | .75 | .30 |
| 21 | Bubba Paris | .20 | .07 |
| 22 | Tim McGee | .20 | .07 |
| 23 | Brian Noble | .20 | .07 |
| 24 | Vinny Testaverde | .40 | .15 |
| 25 | Doug Widell | .20 | .07 |
| 26 | John Jackson WR RC | .20 | .07 |
| 27 | Marion Butts | .40 | .15 |
| 28 | Deron Cherry | .20 | .07 |
| 29 | Don Warren | .20 | .07 |
| 30 | Rod Woodson | .75 | .30 |
| 31 | Mike Baab | .20 | .07 |
| 32 | Greg Jackson RC | .20 | .07 |
| 33 | Jerry Robinson | .20 | .07 |
| 34 | Dalton Hilliard | .20 | .07 |
| 35 | Brian Jordan | .40 | .15 |
| 36 | James Thornton UER | .20 | .07 |
| 37 | Michael Irvin | .75 | .30 |

|  |  | | |
|---|---|---|---|
| 38 | Billy Joe Tolliver | .20 | .07 |
| 39 | Jeff Herrod | .20 | .07 |
| 40 | Scott Norwood | .20 | .07 |
| 41 | Ferrell Edmunds | .20 | .07 |
| 42 | Andre Waters | .20 | .07 |
| 43 | Kevin Glover | .20 | .07 |
| 44 | Ray Berry | .20 | .07 |
| 45 | Timm Rosenbach | .20 | .07 |
| 46 | Reuben Davis | .20 | .07 |
| 47 | Charles Wilson | .20 | .07 |
| 48 | Todd Marinovich RC | .20 | .07 |
| 49 | Harris Barton | .20 | .07 |
| 50 | Jim Breech | .20 | .07 |
| 51 | Ron Holmes | .20 | .07 |
| 52 | Chris Singleton | .20 | .07 |
| 53 | Pat Leahy | .20 | .07 |
| 54 | Tom Newberry | .20 | .07 |
| 55 | Greg Montgomery | .20 | .07 |
| 56 | Robert Blackmon | .20 | .07 |
| 57 | Jay Hilgenberg | .20 | .07 |
| 58 | Rodney Hampton | .75 | .30 |
| 59 | Brett Perriman | .75 | .30 |
| 60 | Ricky Watters RC | 6.00 | 2.50 |
| 61 | Howie Long | .75 | .30 |
| 62 | Frank Cornish | .40 | .15 |
| 63 | Chris Miller | .40 | .15 |
| 64 | Keith Taylor | .20 | .07 |
| 65 | Tony Paige | .20 | .07 |
| 66 | Gary Zimmerman | .20 | .07 |
| 67 | Mark Royals RC | .20 | .07 |
| 68 | Ernie Jones | .20 | .07 |
| 69 | David Grant | .20 | .07 |
| 70 | Shane Conlan | .20 | .07 |
| 71 | Jerry Rice | 2.50 | 1.00 |
| 72 | Christian Okoye | .20 | .07 |
| 73 | Eddie Murray | .20 | .07 |
| 74 | Reggie White | .75 | .30 |
| 75 | Jeff Graham RC WR | 1.00 | .40 |
| 76 | Mark Jackson | .20 | .07 |
| 77 | David Grayson | .20 | .07 |
| 78 | Dan Stryzinski | .20 | .07 |
| 79 | Sterling Sharpe | .75 | .30 |
| 80 | Cleveland Gary | .20 | .07 |
| 81 | Johnny Meads | .20 | .07 |
| 82 | Howard Cross | .20 | .07 |
| 83 | Ken O'Brien | .20 | .07 |
| 84 | Brian Blades | .40 | .15 |
| 85 | Ethan Horton | .20 | .07 |
| 86 | Bruce Armstrong | .20 | .07 |
| 87 | James Washington RC | .20 | .07 |
| 88 | Eugene Daniel | .20 | .07 |
| 89 | James Lofton | .40 | .15 |
| 90 | Louis Oliver | .20 | .07 |
| 91 | Boomer Esiason | .40 | .15 |
| 92 | Seth Joyner | .40 | .15 |
| 93 | Mark Carrier WR | .75 | .30 |
| 94 | Brett Favre RC UER | 50.00 | 25.00 |
| 95 | Lee Williams | .20 | .07 |
| 96 | Neal Anderson | .40 | .15 |
| 97 | Brent Jones | .75 | .30 |
| 98 | John Alt | .20 | .07 |
| 99 | Rodney Peete | .40 | .15 |
| 100 | Steve Broussard | .20 | .07 |
| 101 | Cedric Mack | .20 | .07 |
| 102 | Pat Swilling | .40 | .15 |
| 103 | Stan Humphries | .75 | .30 |
| 104 | Darrell Thompson | .20 | .07 |
| 105 | Reggie Langhorne | .20 | .07 |
| 106 | Kenny Davidson | .20 | .07 |
| 107 | Jim Everett | .40 | .15 |
| 108 | Keith Millard | .20 | .07 |
| 109 | Garry Lewis | .20 | .07 |
| 110 | Jeff Hostetler | .40 | .15 |
| 111 | Lamar Lathon | .20 | .07 |
| 112 | Johnny Bailey | .20 | .07 |
| 113 | Cornelius Bennett | .40 | .15 |
| 114 | Travis McNeal | .20 | .07 |
| 115 | Jeff Lageman | .20 | .07 |
| 116 | Nick Bell RC | .40 | .15 |
| 117 | Calvin Williams | .40 | .15 |
| 118 | Shawn Lee RC | .20 | .07 |
| 119 | Anthony Munoz | .40 | .15 |
| 120 | Jay Novacek | .75 | .30 |
| 121 | Kevin Fagan | .20 | .07 |
| 122 | Leo Goeas | .20 | .07 |
| 123 | Vance Johnson | .20 | .07 |
| 124 | Brent Williams | .20 | .07 |
| 125 | Clarence Verdin | .20 | .07 |
| 126 | Luis Sharpe | .20 | .07 |
| 127 | Darrell Green | .20 | .07 |
| 128 | Barry Word | .20 | .07 |
| 129 | Steve Walsh | .20 | .07 |
| 130 | Bryan Hinkle | .20 | .07 |
| 131 | Ed West | .20 | .07 |
| 132 | Jeff Campbell | .20 | .07 |
| 133 | Dennis Byrd | .20 | .07 |
| 134 | Nate Odomes | .20 | .07 |
| 135 | Trace Armstrong | .20 | .07 |
| 136 | Jarvis Williams | .20 | .07 |
| 137 | Warren Moon | .75 | .30 |
| 138 | Eric Moten RC | .20 | .07 |
| 139 | Tony Woods | .20 | .07 |
| 140 | Phil Simms | .40 | .15 |
| 141 | Ricky Reynolds | .20 | .07 |
| 142 | Frank Stams | .20 | .07 |
| 143 | Kevin Mack | .20 | .07 |
| 144 | Wade Wilson | .40 | .15 |
| 145 | Shawn Collins | .20 | .07 |
| 146 | Roger Craig | .40 | .15 |
| 147 | Jeff Feagles RC | .20 | .07 |
| 148 | Norm Johnson | .20 | .07 |
| 149 | Terance Mathis | .40 | .15 |
| 150 | Reggie Cobb | .20 | .07 |
| 151 | Chip Banks | .20 | .07 |
| 152 | Darryl Pollard | .20 | .07 |
| 153 | Karl Mecklenburg | .20 | .07 |
| 154 | Ricky Proehl | .20 | .07 |
| 155 | Pete Stoyanovich | .20 | .07 |
| 156 | John Stephens | .20 | .07 |
| 157 | Ron Morris | .20 | .07 |
| 158 | Steve DeBerg | .20 | .07 |
| 159 | Mike Munchak | .40 | .15 |
| 160 | Brett Maxie | .20 | .07 |
| 161 | Don Beebe | .20 | .07 |
| 162 | Martin Mayhew | .20 | .07 |
| 163 | Merril Hoge | .20 | .07 |
| 164 | Kelvin Pritchett RC | .40 | .15 |
| 165 | Jim Jeffcoat | .20 | .07 |
| 166 | Myron Guyton | .20 | .07 |
| 167 | Ickey Woods | .20 | .07 |
| 168 | Andre Ware | .40 | .15 |
| 169 | Gary Plummer | .20 | .07 |
| 170 | Henry Ellard | .40 | .15 |
| 171 | Scott Davis | .20 | .07 |
| 172 | Randall McDaniel | .20 | .07 |
| 173 | Randal Hill RC | .40 | .15 |
| 174 | Anthony Bell | .20 | .07 |
| 175 | Gary Anderson RB | .20 | .07 |
| 176 | Byron Evans | .20 | .07 |
| 177 | Tony Mandarich | .20 | .07 |
| 178 | Jeff George | 1.00 | .40 |
| 179 | Art Monk | .40 | .15 |
| 180 | Mike Kenn | .20 | .07 |
| 181 | Sean Landeta | .20 | .07 |
| 182 | Shaun Gayle | .20 | .07 |
| 183 | Michael Carter | .20 | .07 |
| 184 | Robb Thomas | .20 | .07 |
| 185 | Richmond Webb | .20 | .07 |
| 186 | Carnell Lake | .20 | .07 |
| 187 | Rueben Mayes | .20 | .07 |
| 188 | Issiac Holt | .20 | .07 |
| 189 | Leon Seals | .20 | .07 |
| 190 | Al Smith | .20 | .07 |
| 191 | Steve Atwater | .20 | .07 |
| 192 | Greg McMurtry | .20 | .07 |
| 193 | Al Toon | .40 | .15 |
| 194 | Cortez Kennedy | .75 | .30 |
| 195 | Gill Byrd | .20 | .07 |
| 196 | Del Zander | .20 | .07 |
| 197 | Robert Brown | .20 | .07 |
| 198 | Buford McGee | .20 | .07 |
| 199 | Mervyn Fernandez | .20 | .07 |
| 200 | Mike Dumas RC | .20 | .07 |
| 201 | Rob Burnett RC | .40 | .15 |
| 202 | Brian Mitchell | .40 | .15 |
| 203 | Randall Cunningham | .75 | .30 |
| 204 | Sammie Smith | .20 | .07 |
| 205 | Ken Clarke | .20 | .07 |
| 206 | Floyd Dixon | .20 | .07 |
| 207 | Ken Norton | .40 | .15 |
| 208 | Tony Siragusa RC | .40 | .15 |
| 209 | Louis Lipps | .20 | .07 |
| 210 | Chris Martin | .20 | .07 |
| 211 | Jamie Mueller | .20 | .07 |
| 212 | Dave Waymer | .20 | .07 |
| 213 | Donnell Woolford | .20 | .07 |
| 214 | Paul Gruber | .20 | .07 |
| 215 | Ken Harvey | .40 | .15 |
| 216 | Henry Jones RC | .40 | .15 |
| 217 | Tommy Barnhardt RC | .20 | .07 |
| 218 | Arthur Cox | .20 | .07 |
| 219 | Pat Terrell | .20 | .07 |
| 220 | Curtis Duncan | .20 | .07 |
| 221 | Jeff Jaeger | .20 | .07 |
| 222 | Scott Stephen RC | .20 | .07 |
| 223 | Rob Moore | 1.00 | .40 |
| 224 | Chris Hinton | .20 | .07 |
| 225 | Marv Cook | .20 | .07 |
| 226 | Patrick Hunter RC | .20 | .07 |
| 227 | Earnest Byner | .20 | .07 |
| 228 | Troy Aikman | 3.00 | 1.25 |
| 229 | Kevin Walker RC | .20 | .07 |
| 230 | Keith Jackson | .40 | .15 |
| 231 | Russell Maryland RC | .75 | .30 |
| 232 | Charles Haley | .40 | .15 |
| 233 | Nick Lowery | .20 | .07 |
| 234 | Erik Howard | .20 | .07 |
| 235 | Leonard Smith | .20 | .07 |
| 236 | Tim Irwin | .20 | .07 |
| 237 | Simon Fletcher | .20 | .07 |
| 238 | Thomas Everett | .20 | .07 |
| 239 | Reggie Roby | .20 | .07 |
| 240 | Leroy Hoard | .40 | .15 |
| 241 | Wayne Haddix | .20 | .07 |
| 242 | Gary Clark | .75 | .30 |
| 243 | Eric Andolsek | .20 | .07 |
| 244 | Jim Wahler RC | .20 | .07 |
| 245 | Vaughan Johnson | .20 | .07 |
| 246 | Kevin Butler | .20 | .07 |
| 247 | Steve Tasker | .40 | .15 |
| 248 | LeRoy Butler | .20 | .07 |
| 249 | Darion Conner | .20 | .07 |
| 250 | Eric Turner RC | .40 | .15 |
| 251 | Kevin Ross | .20 | .07 |
| 252 | Stephen Baker | .20 | .07 |
| 253 | Harold Green | .40 | .15 |
| 254 | Rohn Stark | .20 | .07 |
| 255 | Joe Nash | .20 | .07 |
| 256 | Jesse Sapolu | .20 | .07 |
| 257 | Willie Gault | .40 | .15 |
| 258 | Jerome Brown | .20 | .07 |
| 259 | Ken Willis | .20 | .07 |
| 260 | Courtney Hall | .20 | .07 |
| 261 | Hart Lee Dykes | .20 | .07 |
| 262 | William Fuller | .40 | .15 |
| 263 | Stan Thomas | .20 | .07 |
| 264 | Dan Marino | 4.00 | 1.50 |
| 265 | Ron Cox | .20 | .07 |
| 266 | Eric Green | .20 | .07 |
| 267 | Anthony Carter | .40 | .15 |
| 268 | Jerry Ball | .20 | .07 |
| 269 | Ron Hall | .20 | .07 |
| 270 | Dennis Smith | .20 | .07 |
| 271 | Eric Hill | .20 | .07 |
| 272 | Dan McGwire RC | .20 | .07 |
| 273 | Lewis Billups UER | .20 | .07 |
| 274 | Rickey Jackson | .20 | .07 |
| 275 | Jim Sweeney | .20 | .07 |
| 276 | Pat Beach | .20 | .07 |
| 277 | Kevin Porter | .20 | .07 |
| 278 | Mike Sherrard | .20 | .07 |
| 279 | Andy Heck | .20 | .07 |
| 280 | Ron Brown | .20 | .07 |
| 281 | Lawrence Taylor | .75 | .30 |
| 282 | Anthony Pleasant | .20 | .07 |
| 283 | Wes Hopkins | .20 | .07 |
| 284 | Jim Lachey | .20 | .07 |
| 285 | Tim Harris | .20 | .07 |
| 286 | Tory Epps | .20 | .07 |
| 287 | Wendell Davis | .20 | .07 |
| 288 | Bubba McDowell | .20 | .07 |
| 289 | Bubby Brister | .20 | .07 |
| 290 | Chris Zorich RC | .75 | .30 |
| 291 | Mike Merriweather | .20 | .07 |
| 292 | Burt Grossman | .20 | .07 |

|  |  | | |
|---|---|---|---|
| ☐ 293 | Erik McMillan | .20 | .07 |
| ☐ 294 | John Elway | 4.00 | 1.50 |
| ☐ 295 | Toi Cook RC | .20 | .07 |
| ☐ 296 | Tom Rathman | .20 | .07 |
| ☐ 297 | Matt Bahr | .20 | .07 |
| ☐ 298 | Chris Spielman | .40 | .15 |
| ☐ 299 | F.J.Nunn w/Aikman/Emmitt | .40 | .15 |
| ☐ 300 | Jim C. Jensen | .20 | .07 |
| ☐ 301 | David Fulcher UER | .20 | .07 |
| ☐ 302 | Tommy Hodson | .20 | .07 |
| ☐ 303 | Stephone Paige | .20 | .07 |
| ☐ 304 | Greg Townsend | .20 | .07 |
| ☐ 305 | Dean Biasucci | .20 | .07 |
| ☐ 306 | Jimmie Jones | .20 | .07 |
| ☐ 307 | Eugene Marve | .20 | .07 |
| ☐ 308 | Flipper Anderson | .20 | .07 |
| ☐ 309 | Darryl Talley | .20 | .07 |
| ☐ 310 | Mike Croel RC | .20 | .07 |
| ☐ 311 | Thane Gash | .20 | .07 |
| ☐ 312 | Perry Kemp | .20 | .07 |
| ☐ 313 | Heath Sherman | .20 | .07 |
| ☐ 314 | Mike Singletary | .40 | .15 |
| ☐ 315 | Chip Lohmiller | .20 | .07 |
| ☐ 316 | Tunch Ilkin | .20 | .07 |
| ☐ 317 | Junior Seau | 1.25 | .50 |
| ☐ 318 | Mike Gann | .20 | .07 |
| ☐ 319 | Tim McDonald | .20 | .07 |
| ☐ 320 | Kyle Clifton | .20 | .07 |
| ☐ 321 | Dan Owens | .20 | .07 |
| ☐ 322 | Tim Grunhard | .20 | .07 |
| ☐ 323 | Stan Brock | .20 | .07 |
| ☐ 324 | Rodney Holman | .20 | .07 |
| ☐ 325 | Mark Ingram | .40 | .15 |
| ☐ 326 | Browning Nagle RC | .20 | .07 |
| ☐ 327 | Joe Montana | 5.00 | 2.00 |
| ☐ 328 | Carl Lee | .20 | .07 |
| ☐ 329 | John L. Williams | .20 | .07 |
| ☐ 330 | David Griggs | .20 | .07 |
| ☐ 331 | Clarence Kay | .20 | .07 |
| ☐ 332 | Irving Fryar | .40 | .15 |
| ☐ 333 | Doug Smith DT RC** | .40 | .15 |
| ☐ 334 | Kent Hull | .20 | .07 |
| ☐ 335 | Mike Wilcher | .20 | .07 |
| ☐ 336 | Ray Donaldson | .20 | .07 |
| ☐ 337 | Mark Carrier DB UER | .20 | .07 |
| ☐ 338 | Kelvin Martin | .20 | .07 |
| ☐ 339 | Keith Byars | .20 | .07 |
| ☐ 340 | Wilber Marshall | .20 | .07 |
| ☐ 341 | Ronnie Lott | .40 | .15 |
| ☐ 342 | Blair Thomas | .20 | .07 |
| ☐ 343 | Ronnie Harmon | .20 | .07 |
| ☐ 344 | Brian Brennan | .20 | .07 |
| ☐ 345 | Charles McRae RC | .20 | .07 |
| ☐ 346 | Michael Cofer | .20 | .07 |
| ☐ 347 | Keith Willis | .20 | .07 |
| ☐ 348 | Bruce Kozerski | .20 | .07 |
| ☐ 349 | Dave Meggett | .40 | .15 |
| ☐ 350 | John Taylor | .40 | .15 |
| ☐ 351 | Johnny Holland | .20 | .07 |
| ☐ 352 | Steve Christie | .20 | .07 |
| ☐ 353 | Ricky Ervins RC | .40 | .15 |
| ☐ 354 | Robert Massey | .20 | .07 |
| ☐ 355 | Derrick Thomas | .75 | .30 |
| ☐ 356 | Tommy Kane | .20 | .07 |
| ☐ 357 | Melvin Bratton | .20 | .07 |
| ☐ 358 | Bruce Matthews | .40 | .15 |
| ☐ 359 | Mark Duper | .40 | .15 |
| ☐ 360 | Jeff Wright RC | .20 | .07 |
| ☐ 361 | Barry Sanders | 4.00 | 1.50 |
| ☐ 362 | Chuck Webb RC | .20 | .07 |
| ☐ 363 | Darryl Grant | .20 | .07 |
| ☐ 364 | William Roberts | .20 | .07 |
| ☐ 365 | Reggie Rutland | .20 | .07 |
| ☐ 366 | Clay Matthews | .40 | .15 |
| ☐ 367 | Anthony Miller | .40 | .15 |
| ☐ 368 | Mike Prior | .20 | .07 |
| ☐ 369 | Jessie Tuggle | .20 | .07 |
| ☐ 370 | Brad Muster | .20 | .07 |
| ☐ 371 | Jay Schroeder | .20 | .07 |
| ☐ 372 | Greg Lloyd | .75 | .30 |
| ☐ 373 | Mike Cofer | .20 | .07 |
| ☐ 374 | James Brooks | .40 | .15 |
| ☐ 375 | Danny Noonan UER | .20 | .07 |
| ☐ 376 | Latin Berry RC | .20 | .07 |
| ☐ 377 | Brad Baxter | .20 | .07 |
| ☐ 378 | Godfrey Myles RC | .20 | .07 |
| ☐ 379 | Morten Andersen | .20 | .07 |
| ☐ 380 | Keith Woodside | .20 | .07 |
| ☐ 381 | Bobby Humphrey | .20 | .07 |
| ☐ 382 | Mike Golic | .20 | .07 |
| ☐ 383 | Keith McCants | .20 | .07 |
| ☐ 384 | Anthony Thompson | .20 | .07 |
| ☐ 385 | Mark Clayton | .40 | .15 |
| ☐ 386 | Neil Smith | .75 | .30 |
| ☐ 387 | Bryan Millard | .20 | .07 |
| ☐ 388 | Mel Gray UER | .40 | .15 |
| ☐ 389 | Ernest Givins | .40 | .15 |
| ☐ 390 | Reyna Thompson | .20 | .07 |
| ☐ 391 | Eric Bieniemy RC | .20 | .07 |
| ☐ 392 | Jon Hand | .20 | .07 |
| ☐ 393 | Mark Rypien | .40 | .15 |
| ☐ 394 | Bill Romanowski | .20 | .07 |
| ☐ 395 | Thurman Thomas | .75 | .30 |
| ☐ 396 | Jim Harbaugh | .75 | .30 |
| ☐ 397 | Don Mosebar | .20 | .07 |
| ☐ 398 | Andre Rison | .40 | .15 |
| ☐ 399 | Mike Johnson | .20 | .07 |
| ☐ 400 | Dermontti Dawson | .20 | .07 |
| ☐ 401 | Herschel Walker | .40 | .15 |
| ☐ 402 | Joe Prokop | .20 | .07 |
| ☐ 403 | Eddie Brown | .20 | .07 |
| ☐ 404 | Nate Newton | .40 | .15 |
| ☐ 405 | Damone Johnson RC | .20 | .07 |
| ☐ 406 | Jessie Hester | .20 | .07 |
| ☐ 407 | Jim Arnold | .20 | .07 |
| ☐ 408 | Ray Agnew | .20 | .07 |
| ☐ 409 | Michael Brooks | .20 | .07 |
| ☐ 410 | Keith Sims | .20 | .07 |
| ☐ 411 | Carl Banks | .20 | .07 |
| ☐ 412 | Jonathan Hayes | .20 | .07 |
| ☐ 413 | Richard Johnson CB RC | .20 | .07 |
| ☐ 414 | Darryll Lewis RC | .40 | .15 |
| ☐ 415 | Jeff Bryant | .20 | .07 |
| ☐ 416 | Leslie O'Neal | .40 | .15 |
| ☐ 417 | Andre Reed | .40 | .15 |
| ☐ 418 | Charles Mann | .20 | .07 |
| ☐ 419 | Keith DeLong | .20 | .07 |
| ☐ 420 | Bruce Hill | .20 | .07 |
| ☐ 421 | Matt Brock RC | .20 | .07 |
| ☐ 422 | Johnny Johnson | .20 | .07 |
| ☐ 423 | Mark Bortz | .20 | .07 |
| ☐ 424 | Ben Smith | .20 | .07 |
| ☐ 425 | Jeff Cross | .20 | .07 |
| ☐ 426 | Irv Pankey | .20 | .07 |
| ☐ 427 | Hassan Jones | .20 | .07 |
| ☐ 428 | Andre Tippett | .20 | .07 |
| ☐ 429 | Tim Worley | .20 | .07 |
| ☐ 430 | Daniel Stubbs | .20 | .07 |
| ☐ 431 | Max Montoya | .20 | .07 |
| ☐ 432 | Jumbo Elliott | .20 | .07 |
| ☐ 433 | Duane Bickett | .20 | .07 |
| ☐ 434 | Nate Lewis RC | .20 | .07 |
| ☐ 435 | Leonard Russell RC | .75 | .30 |
| ☐ 436 | Hoby Brenner | .20 | .07 |
| ☐ 437 | Ricky Sanders | .20 | .07 |
| ☐ 438 | Pierce Holt | .20 | .07 |
| ☐ 439 | Derrick Fenner | .20 | .07 |
| ☐ 440 | Drew Hill | .20 | .07 |
| ☐ 441 | Will Wolford | .20 | .07 |
| ☐ 442 | Albert Lewis | .20 | .07 |
| ☐ 443 | James Francis | .20 | .07 |
| ☐ 444 | Chris Jacke | .20 | .07 |
| ☐ 445 | Mike Farr | .20 | .07 |
| ☐ 446 | Stephen Braggs | .20 | .07 |
| ☐ 447 | Michael Haynes | .75 | .30 |
| ☐ 448 | Freeman McNeil UER | .20 | .07 |
| ☐ 449 | Kevin Donnalley RC | .20 | .07 |
| ☐ 450 | John Offerdahl | .20 | .07 |
| ☐ 451 | Eric Allen | .20 | .07 |
| ☐ 452 | Keith McKeller | .20 | .07 |
| ☐ 453 | Kevin Greene | .40 | .15 |
| ☐ 454 | Ronnie Lippett | .20 | .07 |
| ☐ 455 | Ray Childress | .20 | .07 |
| ☐ 456 | Mike Saxon | .20 | .07 |
| ☐ 457 | Mark Robinson | .20 | .07 |
| ☐ 458 | Greg Kragen | .20 | .07 |
| ☐ 459 | Steve Jordan | .20 | .07 |
| ☐ 460 | John Johnson RC | .20 | .07 |
| ☐ 461 | Sam Mills | .20 | .07 |
| ☐ 462 | Bo Jackson | 1.00 | .40 |
| ☐ 463 | Mark Collins | .20 | .07 |
| ☐ 464 | Percy Snow | .20 | .07 |
| ☐ 465 | Jeff Bostic | .20 | .07 |
| ☐ 466 | Jacob Green | .20 | .07 |
| ☐ 467 | Dexter Carter | .20 | .07 |
| ☐ 468 | Rich Camarillo | .20 | .07 |
| ☐ 469 | Bill Brooks | .20 | .07 |
| ☐ 470 | John Carney | .20 | .07 |
| ☐ 471 | Don Majkowski | .20 | .07 |
| ☐ 472 | Ralph Tamm RC | .20 | .07 |
| ☐ 473 | Fred Barnett | .75 | .30 |
| ☐ 474 | Jim Covert | .20 | .07 |
| ☐ 475 | Kenneth Davis | .20 | .07 |
| ☐ 476 | Jerry Gray | .20 | .07 |
| ☐ 477 | Broderick Thomas | .20 | .07 |
| ☐ 478 | Chris Doleman | .20 | .07 |
| ☐ 479 | Haywood Jeffires | .40 | .15 |
| ☐ 480 | Craig Heyward | .40 | .15 |
| ☐ 481 | Markus Koch | .20 | .07 |
| ☐ 482 | Tim Krumrie | .20 | .07 |
| ☐ 483 | Robert Clark | .20 | .07 |
| ☐ 484 | Mike Rozier | .20 | .07 |
| ☐ 485 | Danny Villa | .20 | .07 |
| ☐ 486 | Gerald Williams | .20 | .07 |
| ☐ 487 | Steve Wisniewski | .20 | .07 |
| ☐ 488 | J.B. Brown | .20 | .07 |
| ☐ 489 | Eugene Robinson | .20 | .07 |
| ☐ 490 | Ottis Anderson | .40 | .15 |
| ☐ 491 | Tony Stargell | .20 | .07 |
| ☐ 492 | Jack Del Rio | .40 | .15 |
| ☐ 493 | Lamar Rogers RC | .20 | .07 |
| ☐ 494 | Ricky Nattiel | .20 | .07 |
| ☐ 495 | Dan Saleaumua | .20 | .07 |
| ☐ 496 | Checklist 1-100 | .20 | .07 |
| ☐ 497 | Checklist 101-200 | .20 | .07 |
| ☐ 498 | Checklist 201-300 | .20 | .07 |
| ☐ 499 | Checklist 301-400 | .20 | .07 |
| ☐ 500 | Checklist 401-500 | .20 | .07 |

## 1992 Stadium Club

| | | | |
|---|---|---|---|
| ☐ COMPLETE SET (700) | | 200.00 | 100.00 |
| ☐ COMP.SERIES 1 (300) | | 15.00 | 6.00 |
| ☐ COMP.SERIES 2 (300) | | 15.00 | 6.00 |
| ☐ COMP.HIGH SER.(100) | | 175.00 | 100.00 |
| ☐ 1 | Mark Rypien | .10 | .02 |
| ☐ 2 | Carlton Bailey RC | .10 | .02 |
| ☐ 3 | Kevin Glover | .10 | .02 |
| ☐ 4 | Vance Johnson | .10 | .02 |
| ☐ 5 | Jim Jeffcoat | .10 | .02 |
| ☐ 6 | Dan Saleaumua | .10 | .02 |
| ☐ 7 | Darion Conner | .10 | .02 |
| ☐ 8 | Don Maggs | .10 | .02 |
| ☐ 9 | Richard Dent | .15 | .05 |
| ☐ 10 | Mark Murphy | .10 | .02 |
| ☐ 11 | Wesley Carroll | .10 | .02 |
| ☐ 12 | Chris Burkett | .10 | .02 |
| ☐ 13 | Steve Wallace | .10 | .02 |
| ☐ 14 | Jacob Green | .10 | .02 |
| ☐ 15 | Roger Ruzek | .10 | .02 |
| ☐ 16 | J.B. Brown | .10 | .02 |
| ☐ 17 | Dave Meggett | .15 | .05 |
| ☐ 18 | D.J. Johnson | .10 | .02 |
| ☐ 19 | Rich Gannon | .30 | .10 |
| ☐ 20 | Kevin Mack | .10 | .02 |
| ☐ 21A | Reggie Cobb ERR | .10 | .02 |
| ☐ 21B | Reggie Cobb COR | .10 | .02 |
| ☐ 22 | Nate Lewis | .10 | .02 |
| ☐ 23 | Doug Smith | .10 | .02 |

| | | |
|---|---|---|
| ❏ 24 Irving Fryar | .15 | .05 |
| ❏ 25 Anthony Thompson | .10 | .02 |
| ❏ 26 Duane Bickett | .10 | .02 |
| ❏ 27 Don Majkowski | .10 | .02 |
| ❏ 28 Mark Schlereth RC | .10 | .02 |
| ❏ 29 Melvin Jenkins | .10 | .02 |
| ❏ 30 Michael Haynes | .15 | .05 |
| ❏ 31 Greg Lewis | .10 | .02 |
| ❏ 32 Kenneth Davis | .10 | .02 |
| ❏ 33 Derrick Thomas | .30 | .10 |
| ❏ 34 David Williams | .10 | .02 |
| ❏ 35 Neal Anderson | .10 | .02 |
| ❏ 36 Andre Collins | .10 | .02 |
| ❏ 37 Jesse Solomon | .10 | .02 |
| ❏ 38 Barry Sanders | 2.50 | 1.00 |
| ❏ 39 Jeff Gossett | .10 | .02 |
| ❏ 40 Rickey Jackson | .10 | .02 |
| ❏ 41 Ray Berry | .10 | .02 |
| ❏ 42 Leroy Hoard | .15 | .05 |
| ❏ 43 Eric Thomas | .10 | .02 |
| ❏ 44 Brian Washington | .10 | .02 |
| ❏ 45 Pat Terrell | .10 | .02 |
| ❏ 46 Eugene Robinson | .10 | .02 |
| ❏ 47 Luis Sharpe | .10 | .02 |
| ❏ 48 Jerome Brown | .10 | .02 |
| ❏ 49 Mark Collins | .10 | .02 |
| ❏ 50 Johnny Holland | .10 | .02 |
| ❏ 51 Tony Paige | .10 | .02 |
| ❏ 52 Willie Green | .10 | .02 |
| ❏ 53 Steve Atwater | .10 | .02 |
| ❏ 54 Brad Muster | .10 | .02 |
| ❏ 55 Cris Dishman | .10 | .02 |
| ❏ 56 Eddie Anderson | .10 | .02 |
| ❏ 57 Sam Mills | .10 | .02 |
| ❏ 58 Donald Evans | .10 | .02 |
| ❏ 59 Jon Vaughn | .10 | .02 |
| ❏ 60 Marion Butts | .10 | .02 |
| ❏ 61 Rodney Holman | .10 | .02 |
| ❏ 62 Dwayne White RC | .10 | .02 |
| ❏ 63 Martin Mayhew | .10 | .02 |
| ❏ 64 Jonathan Hayes | .10 | .02 |
| ❏ 65 Andre Rison | .15 | .05 |
| ❏ 66 Calvin Williams | .15 | .05 |
| ❏ 67 James Washington | .10 | .02 |
| ❏ 68 Tim Harris | .10 | .02 |
| ❏ 69 Jim Ritcher | .10 | .02 |
| ❏ 70 Johnny Johnson | .10 | .02 |
| ❏ 71 John Offerdahl | .10 | .02 |
| ❏ 72 Herschel Walker | .15 | .05 |
| ❏ 73 Perry Kemp | .10 | .02 |
| ❏ 74 Erik Howard | .10 | .02 |
| ❏ 75 Lamar Lathon | .10 | .02 |
| ❏ 76 Greg Kragen | .10 | .02 |
| ❏ 77 Jay Schroeder | .10 | .02 |
| ❏ 78 Jim Arnold | .10 | .02 |
| ❏ 79 Chris Miller | .15 | .05 |
| ❏ 80 Deron Cherry | .10 | .02 |
| ❏ 81 Jim Harbaugh | .30 | .10 |
| ❏ 82 Gill Fenerty | .10 | .02 |
| ❏ 83 Fred Stokes | .10 | .02 |
| ❏ 84 Roman Phifer | .10 | .02 |
| ❏ 85 Clyde Simmons | .10 | .02 |
| ❏ 86 Vince Newsome | .10 | .02 |
| ❏ 87 Lawrence Dawsey | .15 | .05 |
| ❏ 88 Eddie Brown | .10 | .02 |
| ❏ 89 Greg Montgomery | .10 | .02 |
| ❏ 90 Jeff Lageman | .10 | .02 |
| ❏ 91 Terry Wooden | .10 | .02 |
| ❏ 92 Nate Newton | .10 | .02 |
| ❏ 93 David Richards | .10 | .02 |
| ❏ 94 Derek Russell | .10 | .02 |
| ❏ 95 Steve Jordan | .10 | .02 |
| ❏ 96 Hugh Millen | .10 | .02 |
| ❏ 97 Mark Duper | .10 | .02 |
| ❏ 98 Sean Landeta | .10 | .02 |
| ❏ 99 James Thornton | .10 | .02 |
| ❏ 100 Darrell Green | .10 | .02 |
| ❏ 101 Harris Barton | .10 | .02 |
| ❏ 102 John Alt | .10 | .02 |
| ❏ 103 Mike Farr | .10 | .02 |
| ❏ 104 Bob Golic | .10 | .02 |
| ❏ 105 Gene Atkins | .10 | .02 |
| ❏ 106 Gary Anderson K | .10 | .02 |
| ❏ 107 Norm Johnson | .10 | .02 |
| ❏ 108 Eugene Daniel | .10 | .02 |
| ❏ 109 Kent Hull | .10 | .02 |
| ❏ 110 John Elway | 2.50 | 1.00 |
| ❏ 111 Rich Camarillo | .10 | .02 |
| ❏ 112 Charles Wilson | .10 | .02 |
| ❏ 113 Matt Bahr | .10 | .02 |
| ❏ 114 Mark Carrier WR | .15 | .05 |
| ❏ 115 Richmond Webb | .10 | .02 |
| ❏ 116 Charles Mann | .10 | .02 |
| ❏ 117 Tim McGee | .10 | .02 |
| ❏ 118 Wes Hopkins | .10 | .02 |
| ❏ 119 Mo Lewis | .10 | .02 |
| ❏ 120 Warren Moon | .30 | .10 |
| ❏ 121 Damone Johnson | .10 | .02 |
| ❏ 122 Kevin Gogan | .10 | .02 |
| ❏ 123 Joey Browner | .10 | .02 |
| ❏ 124 Tommy Kane | .10 | .02 |
| ❏ 125 Vincent Brown | .10 | .02 |
| ❏ 126 Barry Word | .10 | .02 |
| ❏ 127 Michael Brooks | .10 | .02 |
| ❏ 128 Jumbo Elliott | .10 | .02 |
| ❏ 129 Marcus Allen | .30 | .10 |
| ❏ 130 Tom Waddle | .10 | .02 |
| ❏ 131 Jim Dombrowski | .10 | .02 |
| ❏ 132 Aeneas Williams | .15 | .05 |
| ❏ 133 Clay Matthews | .15 | .05 |
| ❏ 134 Thurman Thomas | .30 | .10 |
| ❏ 135 Dean Biasucci | .10 | .02 |
| ❏ 136 Moe Gardner | .10 | .02 |
| ❏ 137 James Campen | .10 | .02 |
| ❏ 138 Tim Johnson | .10 | .02 |
| ❏ 139 Erik Kramer | .15 | .05 |
| ❏ 140 Keith McCants | .10 | .02 |
| ❏ 141 John Carney | .10 | .02 |
| ❏ 142 Tunch Ilkin | .10 | .02 |
| ❏ 143 Louis Oliver | .10 | .02 |
| ❏ 144 Bill Maas | .10 | .02 |
| ❏ 145 Wendell Davis | .10 | .02 |
| ❏ 146 Pepper Johnson | .10 | .02 |
| ❏ 147 Howie Long | .30 | .10 |
| ❏ 148 Brett Maxie | .10 | .02 |
| ❏ 149 Tony Casillas | .10 | .02 |
| ❏ 150 Michael Carter | .10 | .02 |
| ❏ 151 Byron Evans | .10 | .02 |
| ❏ 152 Lorenzo White | .10 | .02 |
| ❏ 153 Larry Kelm | .10 | .02 |
| ❏ 154 Andy Heck | .10 | .02 |
| ❏ 155 Harry Newsome | .10 | .02 |
| ❏ 156 Chris Singleton | .10 | .02 |
| ❏ 157 Mike Kenn | .10 | .02 |
| ❏ 158 Jeff Faulkner | .10 | .02 |
| ❏ 159 Ken Lanier | .10 | .02 |
| ❏ 160 Darryl Talley | .10 | .02 |
| ❏ 161 Louie Aguiar RC | .10 | .02 |
| ❏ 162 Danny Copeland | .10 | .02 |
| ❏ 163 Kevin Porter | .10 | .02 |
| ❏ 164 Trace Armstrong | .10 | .02 |
| ❏ 165 Dermontti Dawson | .10 | .02 |
| ❏ 166 Fred McAfee RC | .10 | .02 |
| ❏ 167 Ronnie Lott | .15 | .05 |
| ❏ 168 Tony Mandarich | .10 | .02 |
| ❏ 169 Howard Cross | .10 | .02 |
| ❏ 170 Vestee Jackson | .10 | .02 |
| ❏ 171 Jeff Herrod | .10 | .02 |
| ❏ 172 Randy Hilliard RC | .10 | .02 |
| ❏ 173 Robert Wilson | .10 | .02 |
| ❏ 174 Joe Walter RC | .10 | .02 |
| ❏ 175 Chris Spielman | .15 | .05 |
| ❏ 176 Darryl Henley | .10 | .02 |
| ❏ 177 Jay Hilgenberg | .10 | .02 |
| ❏ 178 John Kidd | .10 | .02 |
| ❏ 179 Doug Widell | .10 | .02 |
| ❏ 180 Seth Joyner | .10 | .02 |
| ❏ 181 Nick Bell | .10 | .02 |
| ❏ 182 Don Griffin | .10 | .02 |
| ❏ 183 Johnny Meads | .10 | .02 |
| ❏ 184 Jeff Bostic | .10 | .02 |
| ❏ 185 Johnny Hector | .10 | .02 |
| ❏ 186 Jessie Tuggle | .10 | .02 |
| ❏ 187 Robb Thomas | .10 | .02 |
| ❏ 188 Shane Conlan | .10 | .02 |
| ❏ 189 Michael Zordich RC | .10 | .02 |
| ❏ 190 Emmitt Smith | 3.00 | 1.50 |
| ❏ 191 Robert Blackmon | .10 | .02 |
| ❏ 192 Carl Lee | .10 | .02 |
| ❏ 193 Harry Galbreath | .10 | .02 |
| ❏ 194 Ed King | .10 | .02 |
| ❏ 195 Stan Thomas | .10 | .02 |
| ❏ 196 Andre Waters | .10 | .02 |
| ❏ 197 Pat Harlow | .10 | .02 |
| ❏ 198 Zefross Moss | .10 | .02 |
| ❏ 199 Bobby Hebert | .10 | .02 |
| ❏ 200 Doug Riesenberg | .10 | .02 |
| ❏ 201 Mike Croel | .10 | .02 |
| ❏ 202 Jeff Jaeger | .10 | .02 |
| ❏ 203 Gary Plummer | .10 | .02 |
| ❏ 204 Chris Jacke | .10 | .02 |
| ❏ 205 Neil O'Donnell | .15 | .05 |
| ❏ 206 Mark Bortz | .10 | .02 |
| ❏ 207 Tim Barnett | .10 | .02 |
| ❏ 208 Jerry Ball | .10 | .02 |
| ❏ 209 Chip Lohmiller | .10 | .02 |
| ❏ 210 Jim Everett | .15 | .05 |
| ❏ 211 Tim McKyer | .10 | .02 |
| ❏ 212 Aaron Craver | .10 | .02 |
| ❏ 213 John L. Williams | .10 | .02 |
| ❏ 214 Simon Fletcher | .10 | .02 |
| ❏ 215 Walter Reeves | .10 | .02 |
| ❏ 216 Terance Mathis | .15 | .05 |
| ❏ 217 Mike Pitts | .10 | .02 |
| ❏ 218 Bruce Matthews | .10 | .02 |
| ❏ 219 Howard Ballard | .10 | .02 |
| ❏ 220 Leonard Russell | .15 | .05 |
| ❏ 221 Michael Stewart | .10 | .02 |
| ❏ 222 Mike Merriweather | .10 | .02 |
| ❏ 223 Ricky Sanders | .10 | .02 |
| ❏ 224 Ray Horton | .10 | .02 |
| ❏ 225 Michael Jackson | .15 | .05 |
| ❏ 226 Bill Romanowski | .10 | .02 |
| ❏ 227 Steve McMichael UER | .15 | .05 |
| ❏ 228 Chris Martin | .10 | .02 |
| ❏ 229 Tim Green | .10 | .02 |
| ❏ 230 Karl Mecklenburg | .10 | .02 |
| ❏ 231 Felix Wright | .10 | .02 |
| ❏ 232 Charles McRae | .10 | .02 |
| ❏ 233 Pete Stoyanovich | .10 | .02 |
| ❏ 234 Stephen Baker | .10 | .02 |
| ❏ 235 Herman Moore | .30 | .10 |
| ❏ 236 Terry McDaniel | .10 | .02 |
| ❏ 237 Dalton Hilliard | .10 | .02 |
| ❏ 238 Gill Byrd | .10 | .02 |
| ❏ 239 Leon Seals | .10 | .02 |
| ❏ 240 Rod Woodson | .30 | .10 |
| ❏ 241 Curtis Duncan | .10 | .02 |
| ❏ 242 Keith Jackson | .15 | .05 |
| ❏ 243 Mark Stepnoski | .15 | .05 |
| ❏ 244 Art Monk | .15 | .05 |
| ❏ 245 Matt Stover | .10 | .02 |
| ❏ 246 John Roper | .10 | .02 |
| ❏ 247 Rodney Hampton | .15 | .05 |
| ❏ 248 Steve Wisniewski | .10 | .02 |
| ❏ 249 Bryan Millard | .10 | .02 |
| ❏ 250 Todd Lyght | .10 | .02 |
| ❏ 251 Marvin Washington | .10 | .02 |
| ❏ 252 Eric Swann | .15 | .05 |
| ❏ 253 Bruce Kozerski | .10 | .02 |
| ❏ 254 Jon Hand | .10 | .02 |
| ❏ 255 Scott Fulhage | .10 | .02 |
| ❏ 256 Chuck Cecil | .10 | .02 |
| ❏ 257 Eric Martin | .10 | .02 |
| ❏ 258 Eric Metcalf | .15 | .05 |
| ❏ 259 T.J. Turner | .10 | .02 |
| ❏ 260 Kirk Lowdermilk | .10 | .02 |
| ❏ 261 Keith McKeller | .10 | .02 |
| ❏ 262 Wymon Henderson | .10 | .02 |
| ❏ 263 David Alexander | .10 | .02 |
| ❏ 264 George Jamison | .10 | .02 |
| ❏ 265 Ken Norton Jr. | .15 | .05 |
| ❏ 266 Jim Lachey | .10 | .02 |
| ❏ 267 Bo Orlando RC | .10 | .02 |
| ❏ 268 Nick Lowery | .10 | .02 |
| ❏ 269 Keith Van Horne | .10 | .02 |
| ❏ 270 Dwight Stone | .10 | .02 |
| ❏ 271 Keith DeLong | .10 | .02 |
| ❏ 272 James Francis | .10 | .02 |
| ❏ 273 Greg McMurtry | .10 | .02 |
| ❏ 274 Ethan Horton | .10 | .02 |
| ❏ 275 Stan Brock | .10 | .02 |
| ❏ 276 Ken Harvey | .10 | .02 |
| ❏ 277 Ronnie Harmon | .10 | .02 |
| ❏ 278 Mike Pritchard | .15 | .05 |
| ❏ 279 Kyle Clifton | .10 | .02 |

|  |  | | |
|---|------|---|---|
| ❏ 280 | Anthony Johnson | .15 | .05 |
| ❏ 281 | Esera Tuaolo | .10 | .02 |
| ❏ 282 | Vernon Turner | .10 | .02 |
| ❏ 283 | David Griggs | .10 | .02 |
| ❏ 284 | Dino Hackett | .10 | .02 |
| ❏ 285 | Carwell Gardner | .10 | .02 |
| ❏ 286 | Ron Hall | .10 | .02 |
| ❏ 287 | Reggie White | .30 | .10 |
| ❏ 288 | Checklist 1-100 | .10 | .02 |
| ❏ 289 | Checklist 101-200 | .10 | .02 |
| ❏ 290 | Checklist 201-300 | .10 | .02 |
| ❏ 291 | Mark Clayton MC | .10 | .02 |
| ❏ 292 | Pat Swilling MC | .10 | .02 |
| ❏ 293 | Ernest Givins MC | .10 | .02 |
| ❏ 294 | Broderick Thomas MC | .10 | .02 |
| ❏ 295 | John Friesz MC | .10 | .02 |
| ❏ 296 | Cornelius Bennett MC | .10 | .02 |
| ❏ 297 | Anthony Carter MC | .15 | .05 |
| ❏ 298 | Earnest Byner MC | .10 | .02 |
| ❏ 299 | Michael Irvin MC | .30 | .10 |
| ❏ 300 | Cortez Kennedy MC | .10 | .02 |
| ❏ 301 | Barry Sanders MC | 1.50 | .60 |
| ❏ 302 | Mike Croel MC | .10 | .02 |
| ❏ 303 | Emmitt Smith MC | 2.00 | .75 |
| ❏ 304 | Leonard Russell MC | .10 | .02 |
| ❏ 305 | Neal Anderson MC | .10 | .02 |
| ❏ 306 | Derrick Thomas MC | .15 | .05 |
| ❏ 307 | Mark Rypien MC | .10 | .02 |
| ❏ 308 | Reggie White MC | .15 | .05 |
| ❏ 309 | Rod Woodson MC | .15 | .05 |
| ❏ 310 | Rodney Hampton MC | .15 | .05 |
| ❏ 311 | Carnell Lake | .10 | .02 |
| ❏ 312 | Robert Delpino | .10 | .02 |
| ❏ 313 | Brian Blades | .15 | .05 |
| ❏ 314 | Marc Spindler | .10 | .02 |
| ❏ 315 | Scott Norwood | .10 | .02 |
| ❏ 316 | Frank Warren | .10 | .02 |
| ❏ 317 | David Treadwell | .10 | .02 |
| ❏ 318 | Steve Broussard | .10 | .02 |
| ❏ 319 | Lorenzo Lynch | .10 | .02 |
| ❏ 320 | Ray Agnew | .10 | .02 |
| ❏ 321 | Derrick Walker | .10 | .02 |
| ❏ 322 | Vinson Smith RC | .10 | .02 |
| ❏ 323 | Gary Clark | .30 | .10 |
| ❏ 324 | Charles Haley | .15 | .05 |
| ❏ 325 | Keith Byars | .10 | .02 |
| ❏ 326 | Winston Moss | .10 | .02 |
| ❏ 327 | Paul McJulien RC UER | .10 | .02 |
| ❏ 328 | Tony Covington | .10 | .02 |
| ❏ 329 | Mark Carrier DB | .10 | .02 |
| ❏ 330 | Mark Tuinei | .10 | .02 |
| ❏ 331 | Tracy Simien RC | .10 | .02 |
| ❏ 332 | Jeff Wright | .10 | .02 |
| ❏ 333 | Bryan Cox | .15 | .05 |
| ❏ 334 | Lonnie Young | .10 | .02 |
| ❏ 335 | Clarence Verdin | .10 | .02 |
| ❏ 336 | Dan Fike | .10 | .02 |
| ❏ 337 | Steve Sewell | .10 | .02 |
| ❏ 338 | Gary Zimmerman | .10 | .02 |
| ❏ 339 | Barney Bussey | .10 | .02 |
| ❏ 340 | William Perry | .15 | .05 |
| ❏ 341 | Jeff Hostetler | .15 | .05 |
| ❏ 342 | Doug Smith | .10 | .02 |
| ❏ 343 | Cleveland Gary | .10 | .02 |
| ❏ 344 | Todd Marinovich | .10 | .02 |
| ❏ 345 | Rich Moran | .10 | .02 |
| ❏ 346 | Tony Woods | .10 | .02 |
| ❏ 347 | Vaughan Johnson | .10 | .02 |
| ❏ 348 | Marv Cook | .10 | .02 |
| ❏ 349 | Pierce Holt | .10 | .02 |
| ❏ 350 | Gerald Williams | .10 | .02 |
| ❏ 351 | Kevin Butler | .10 | .02 |
| ❏ 352 | William White | .10 | .02 |
| ❏ 353 | Henry Rolling | .10 | .02 |
| ❏ 354 | James Joseph | .10 | .02 |
| ❏ 355 | Vinny Testaverde | .15 | .05 |
| ❏ 356 | Scott Radecic | .10 | .02 |
| ❏ 357 | Lee Johnson | .10 | .02 |
| ❏ 358 | Steve Tasker | .15 | .05 |
| ❏ 359 | David Lutz | .10 | .02 |
| ❏ 360 | Audray McMillian UER | .10 | .02 |
| ❏ 361 | Brad Baxter | .10 | .02 |
| ❏ 362 | Mark Dennis | .10 | .02 |
| ❏ 363 | Eric Pegram | .15 | .05 |
| ❏ 364 | Sean Jones | .10 | .02 |
| ❏ 365 | William Roberts | .10 | .02 |
| ❏ 366 | Steve Young | 1.00 | .40 |
| ❏ 367 | Joe Jacoby | .10 | .02 |
| ❏ 368 | Richard Brown RC | .10 | .02 |
| ❏ 369 | Keith Kartz | .10 | .02 |
| ❏ 370 | Freddie Joe Nunn | .10 | .02 |
| ❏ 371 | Darren Comeaux | .10 | .02 |
| ❏ 372 | Larry Brown DB | .10 | .02 |
| ❏ 373 | Haywood Jeffires | .15 | .05 |
| ❏ 374 | Tom Newberry | .10 | .02 |
| ❏ 375 | Steve Bono RC | .30 | .10 |
| ❏ 376 | Kevin Ross | .10 | .02 |
| ❏ 377 | Kelvin Pritchett | .10 | .02 |
| ❏ 378 | Jessie Hester | .10 | .02 |
| ❏ 379 | Mitchell Price | .10 | .02 |
| ❏ 380 | Barry Foster | .15 | .05 |
| ❏ 381 | Reyna Thompson | .10 | .02 |
| ❏ 382 | Cris Carter | .75 | .30 |
| ❏ 383 | Lemuel Stinson | .10 | .02 |
| ❏ 384 | Rod Bernstine | .10 | .02 |
| ❏ 385 | James Lofton | .15 | .05 |
| ❏ 386 | Kevin Murphy | .10 | .02 |
| ❏ 387 | Greg Townsend | .10 | .02 |
| ❏ 388 | Edgar Bennett RC | .30 | .10 |
| ❏ 389 | Rob Moore | .15 | .05 |
| ❏ 390 | Eugene Lockhart | .10 | .02 |
| ❏ 391 | Bern Brostek | .10 | .02 |
| ❏ 392 | Craig Heyward | .15 | .05 |
| ❏ 393 | Ferrell Edmunds | .10 | .02 |
| ❏ 394 | John Kasay | .10 | .02 |
| ❏ 395 | Jesse Sapolu | .10 | .02 |
| ❏ 396 | Jim Breech | .10 | .02 |
| ❏ 397 | Neil Smith | .30 | .10 |
| ❏ 398 | Bryce Paup | .30 | .10 |
| ❏ 399 | Tony Tolbert | .10 | .02 |
| ❏ 400 | Bubby Brister | .10 | .02 |
| ❏ 401 | Dennis Smith | .10 | .02 |
| ❏ 402 | Dan Owens | .10 | .02 |
| ❏ 403 | Steve Beuerlein | .15 | .05 |
| ❏ 404 | Rick Tuten | .10 | .02 |
| ❏ 405 | Eric Allen | .10 | .02 |
| ❏ 406 | Eric Hill | .10 | .02 |
| ❏ 407 | Don Warren | .10 | .02 |
| ❏ 408 | Greg Jackson | .10 | .02 |
| ❏ 409 | Chris Doleman | .10 | .02 |
| ❏ 410 | Anthony Munoz | .15 | .05 |
| ❏ 411 | Michael Young | .10 | .02 |
| ❏ 412 | Cornelius Bennett | .15 | .05 |
| ❏ 413 | Ray Childress | .10 | .02 |
| ❏ 414 | Kevin Call | .10 | .02 |
| ❏ 415 | Burt Grossman | .10 | .02 |
| ❏ 416 | Scott Miller | .10 | .02 |
| ❏ 417 | Tim Newton | .10 | .02 |
| ❏ 418 | Robert Young | .10 | .02 |
| ❏ 419 | Tommy Vardell RC | .10 | .02 |
| ❏ 420 | Michael Walter | .10 | .02 |
| ❏ 421 | Chris Port RC | .10 | .02 |
| ❏ 422 | Carlton Haselrig RC | .10 | .02 |
| ❏ 423 | Rodney Peete | .15 | .05 |
| ❏ 424 | Scott Stephen | .10 | .02 |
| ❏ 425 | Chris Warren | .30 | .10 |
| ❏ 426 | Scott Galbraith RC | .10 | .02 |
| ❏ 427 | Fuad Reveiz UER | .10 | .02 |
| ❏ 428 | Irv Eatman | .10 | .02 |
| ❏ 429 | David Szott | .10 | .02 |
| ❏ 430 | Brent Williams | .10 | .02 |
| ❏ 431 | Mike Heron | .10 | .02 |
| ❏ 432 | Brent Jones | .15 | .05 |
| ❏ 433 | Paul Gruber | .10 | .02 |
| ❏ 434 | Carlos Huerta | .10 | .02 |
| ❏ 435 | Scott Case | .10 | .02 |
| ❏ 436 | Greg Davis | .10 | .02 |
| ❏ 437 | Ken Clarke | .10 | .02 |
| ❏ 438 | Alfred Williams | .10 | .02 |
| ❏ 439 | Jim C. Jensen | .10 | .02 |
| ❏ 440 | Louis Lipps | .10 | .02 |
| ❏ 441 | Larry Roberts | .10 | .02 |
| ❏ 442 | James Jones DT | .10 | .02 |
| ❏ 443 | Don Mosebar | .10 | .02 |
| ❏ 444 | Quinn Early | .15 | .05 |
| ❏ 445 | Robert Brown | .10 | .02 |
| ❏ 446 | Tom Thayer | .10 | .02 |
| ❏ 447 | Michael Irvin | .30 | .10 |
| ❏ 448 | Jarrod Bunch | .10 | .02 |
| ❏ 449 | Riki Ellison | .10 | .02 |
| ❏ 450 | Joe Phillips | .10 | .02 |
| ❏ 451 | Ernest Givins | .15 | .05 |
| ❏ 452 | Glenn Parker | .10 | .02 |
| ❏ 453 | Brett Perriman UER | .30 | .10 |
| ❏ 454 | Jayice Pearson RC | .10 | .02 |
| ❏ 455 | Mark Jackson | .10 | .02 |
| ❏ 456 | Siran Stacy RC | .10 | .02 |
| ❏ 457 | Rufus Porter | .10 | .02 |
| ❏ 458 | Michael Ball | .10 | .02 |
| ❏ 459 | Craig Taylor | .10 | .02 |
| ❏ 460 | George Thomas RC | .10 | .02 |
| ❏ 461 | Alvin Wright | .10 | .02 |
| ❏ 462 | Ron Hallstrom | .10 | .02 |
| ❏ 463 | Mike Mooney RC | .10 | .02 |
| ❏ 464 | Dexter Carter | .10 | .02 |
| ❏ 465 | Marty Carter RC | .10 | .02 |
| ❏ 466 | Pat Swilling | .10 | .02 |
| ❏ 467 | Mike Golic | .10 | .02 |
| ❏ 468 | Reggie Roby | .10 | .02 |
| ❏ 469 | Randall McDaniel | .15 | .05 |
| ❏ 470 | John Stephens | .10 | .02 |
| ❏ 471 | Ricardo McDonald RC | .10 | .02 |
| ❏ 472 | Wilber Marshall | .10 | .02 |
| ❏ 473 | Jim Sweeney | .10 | .02 |
| ❏ 474 | Ernie Jones | .10 | .02 |
| ❏ 475 | Bennie Blades | .10 | .02 |
| ❏ 476 | Don Beebe | .10 | .02 |
| ❏ 477 | Grant Feasel | .10 | .02 |
| ❏ 478 | Ernie Mills | .10 | .02 |
| ❏ 479 | Tony Jones T | .10 | .02 |
| ❏ 480 | Jeff Uhlenhake | .10 | .02 |
| ❏ 481 | Gaston Green | .10 | .02 |
| ❏ 482 | John Taylor | .15 | .05 |
| ❏ 483 | Anthony Smith | .10 | .02 |
| ❏ 484 | Tony Bennett | .10 | .02 |
| ❏ 485 | David Brandon RC | .10 | .02 |
| ❏ 486 | Shawn Jefferson | .10 | .02 |
| ❏ 487 | Christian Okoye | .10 | .02 |
| ❏ 488 | Leonard Marshall | .10 | .02 |
| ❏ 489 | Jay Novacek | .15 | .05 |
| ❏ 490 | Harold Green | .10 | .02 |
| ❏ 491 | Bubba McDowell | .10 | .02 |
| ❏ 492 | Gary Anderson RB | .10 | .02 |
| ❏ 493 | Terrell Buckley RC | .10 | .02 |
| ❏ 494 | Jamie Dukes RC | .10 | .02 |
| ❏ 495 | Morten Andersen | .10 | .02 |
| ❏ 496 | Henry Thomas | .10 | .02 |
| ❏ 497 | Bill Lewis | .10 | .02 |
| ❏ 498 | Jeff Cross | .10 | .02 |
| ❏ 499 | Hardy Nickerson | .15 | .05 |
| ❏ 500 | Henry Ellard | .15 | .05 |
| ❏ 501 | Joe Bowden RC | .10 | .02 |
| ❏ 502 | Brian Noble | .10 | .02 |
| ❏ 503 | Mike Cofer | .10 | .02 |
| ❏ 504 | Jeff Bryant | .10 | .02 |
| ❏ 505 | Lomas Brown | .10 | .02 |
| ❏ 506 | Chip Banks | .10 | .02 |
| ❏ 507 | Keith Traylor | .10 | .02 |
| ❏ 508 | Mark Kelso | .10 | .02 |
| ❏ 509 | Dexter McNabb RC | .10 | .02 |
| ❏ 510 | Gene Chilton RC | .10 | .02 |
| ❏ 511 | George Thornton | .10 | .02 |
| ❏ 512 | Jeff Criswell | .10 | .02 |
| ❏ 513 | Brad Edwards | .10 | .02 |
| ❏ 514 | Ron Heller | .10 | .02 |
| ❏ 515 | Tim Brown | .30 | .10 |
| ❏ 516 | Keith Hamilton RC | .15 | .05 |
| ❏ 517 | Mark Higgs | .10 | .02 |
| ❏ 518 | Tommy Barnhardt | .10 | .02 |
| ❏ 519 | Brian Jordan | .15 | .05 |
| ❏ 520 | Ray Crockett | .10 | .02 |
| ❏ 521 | Karl Wilson | .10 | .02 |
| ❏ 522 | Ricky Reynolds | .10 | .02 |
| ❏ 523 | Max Montoya | .10 | .02 |
| ❏ 524 | David Little | .10 | .02 |
| ❏ 525 | Alonzo Mitz RC | .10 | .02 |
| ❏ 526 | Darryll Lewis | .10 | .02 |
| ❏ 527 | Keith Henderson | .10 | .02 |
| ❏ 528 | LeRoy Butler | .10 | .02 |
| ❏ 529 | Rob Burnett | .10 | .02 |
| ❏ 530 | Chris Chandler | .30 | .10 |
| ❏ 531 | Maury Buford | .10 | .02 |
| ❏ 532 | Mark Ingram | .10 | .02 |
| ❏ 533 | Mike Saxon | .10 | .02 |
| ❏ 534 | Bill Fralic | .10 | .02 |

| | | | | | | |
|---|---|---|---|---|---|---|
| ☐ 535 Craig Patterson RC | .10 | .02 | ☐ 620 Phil Simms | .75 | .30 | **1993 Stadium Club** |
| ☐ 536 John Randle | .15 | .05 | ☐ 621 Troy Vincent RC | .50 | .20 | |
| ☐ 537 Dwayne Harper RC | .10 | .02 | ☐ 622 Jason Hanson RC | .75 | .30 | |
| ☐ 538 Chris Hakel RC | .10 | .02 | ☐ 623 Andre Reed | .75 | .30 | |
| ☐ 539 Maurice Hurst | .10 | .02 | ☐ 624 Russell Maryland | .50 | .20 | |
| ☐ 540 Warren Powers UER | .10 | .02 | ☐ 625 Steve Emtman RC | .50 | .20 | |
| ☐ 541 Will Wolford | .10 | .02 | ☐ 626 Sean Gilbert RC | .75 | .30 | |
| ☐ 542 Dennis Gibson | .10 | .02 | ☐ 627 Dana Hall RC | .50 | .20 | |
| ☐ 543 Jackie Slater | .10 | .02 | ☐ 628 Dan McGwire | .50 | .20 | |
| ☐ 544 Floyd Turner | .10 | .02 | ☐ 629 Lewis Billups | .50 | .20 | |
| ☐ 545 Guy McIntyre | .10 | .02 | ☐ 630 Darryl Williams RC | .50 | .20 | |
| ☐ 546 Eric Green | .10 | .02 | ☐ 631 Dwayne Sabb RC | .50 | .20 | |
| ☐ 547 Rohn Stark | .10 | .02 | ☐ 632 Mark Royals | .50 | .20 | |
| ☐ 548 William Fuller | .10 | .02 | ☐ 633 Cary Conklin | .50 | .20 | |
| ☐ 549 Alvin Harper | .15 | .05 | ☐ 634 Al Toon | .75 | .30 | |
| ☐ 550 Mark Clayton | .15 | .05 | ☐ 635 Junior Seau | 1.50 | .60 | |
| ☐ 551 Natu Tuatagaloa RC | .10 | .02 | ☐ 636 Greg Skrepenak RC UER 68 | .50 | | |
| ☐ 552 Fred Barnett | .30 | .10 | ☐ 637 Deion Sanders | 3.00 | 1.50 | |
| ☐ 553 Bob Whitfield RC | .10 | .02 | ☐ 638 Steve DeOssie | .50 | .20 | ☐ COMPLETE SET (550) 40.00 15.00 |
| ☐ 554 Courtney Hall | .10 | .02 | ☐ 639 Randall Cunningham | 1.50 | .60 | ☐ COMP.SERIES 1 (250) 25.00 10.00 |
| ☐ 555 Brian Mitchell | .15 | .05 | ☐ 640 Jim Kelly | 1.50 | .60 | ☐ COMP.SERIES 2 (250) 15.00 6.00 |
| ☐ 556 Patrick Hunter | .10 | .02 | ☐ 641 Michael Brandon RC | .50 | .20 | ☐ COMP.HIGH SERIES (50) 8.00 4.00 |
| ☐ 557 Rick Bryan | .10 | .02 | ☐ 642 Clayton Holmes RC | .50 | .20 | ☐ COMP.HIGH FACT.SET (51) 12.00 5.00 |
| ☐ 558 Anthony Carter | .15 | .05 | ☐ 643 Webster Slaughter | .50 | .20 | ☐ 1 Sterling Sharpe .20 .07 |
| ☐ 559 Jim Wahler | .10 | .02 | ☐ 644 Ricky Proehl | .50 | .20 | ☐ 2 Chris Burkett .10 .02 |
| ☐ 560 Joe Morris | .10 | .02 | ☐ 645 Jerry Rice | 5.00 | 2.50 | ☐ 3 Santana Dotson .20 .07 |
| ☐ 561 Tony Zendejas | .10 | .02 | ☐ 646 Carl Banks | .50 | .20 | ☐ 4 Michael Jackson .20 .07 |
| ☐ 562 Mervyn Fernandez | .10 | .02 | ☐ 647 J.J.Birden | .50 | .20 | ☐ 5 Neal Anderson .10 .02 |
| ☐ 563 Jamie Williams | .10 | .02 | ☐ 648 Tracy Scroggins RC | .50 | .20 | ☐ 6 Bryan Cox .10 .02 |
| ☐ 564 Darrell Thompson | .10 | .02 | ☐ 649 Alonzo Spellman RC | .75 | .30 | ☐ 7 Dennis Gibson .10 .02 |
| ☐ 565 Adrian Cooper | .10 | .02 | ☐ 650 Joe Montana | 8.00 | 3.00 | ☐ 8 Jeff Graham .20 .07 |
| ☐ 566 Chris Goode | .10 | .02 | ☐ 651 Courtney Hawkins RC | .75 | .30 | ☐ 9 Roger Ruzek .10 .02 |
| ☐ 567 Jeff Davidson RC | .10 | .02 | ☐ 652 Corey Widmer RC | .50 | .20 | ☐ 10 Duane Bickett .10 .02 |
| ☐ 568 James Hasty | .10 | .02 | ☐ 653 Robert Brooks RC | 4.00 | 1.50 | ☐ 11 Charles Mann .10 .02 |
| ☐ 569 Chris Mims RC | .10 | .02 | ☐ 654 Darren Woodson RC | 1.50 | .60 | ☐ 12 Tommy Maddox .40 .15 |
| ☐ 570 Ray Seals RC | .10 | .02 | ☐ 655 Derrick Fenner | .50 | .20 | ☐ 13 Vaughn Dunbar .10 .02 |
| ☐ 571 Myron Guyton | .10 | .02 | ☐ 656 Steve Christie | .50 | .20 | ☐ 14 Gary Plummer .10 .02 |
| ☐ 572 Todd McNair | .10 | .02 | ☐ 657 Chester McGlockton RC | .75 | .30 | ☐ 15 Chris Miller .20 .07 |
| ☐ 573 Andre Tippett | .10 | .02 | ☐ 658 Steve Israel RC | .50 | .20 | ☐ 16 Chris Warren .20 .07 |
| ☐ 574 Kirby Jackson | .10 | .02 | ☐ 659 Robert Harris RC | .50 | .20 | ☐ 17 Alvin Harper .20 .07 |
| ☐ 575 Mel Gray | .15 | .05 | ☐ 660 Dan Marino | 8.00 | 3.00 | ☐ 18 Eric Dickerson .20 .07 |
| ☐ 576 Stephone Paige | .10 | .02 | ☐ 661 Ed McCaffrey | 5.00 | 2.00 | ☐ 19 Mike Jones .10 .02 |
| ☐ 577 Scott Davis | .10 | .02 | ☐ 662 Johnny Mitchell RC | .50 | .20 | ☐ 20 Ernest Givins .20 .07 |
| ☐ 578 John Gesek | .10 | .02 | ☐ 663 Timm Rosenbach | .50 | .20 | ☐ 21 Natrone Means RC .40 .15 |
| ☐ 579 Earnest Byner | .10 | .02 | ☐ 664 Anthony Miller | .75 | .30 | ☐ 22 Doug Riesenberg .10 .02 |
| ☐ 580 John Friesz | .15 | .05 | ☐ 665 Merril Hoge | .50 | .20 | ☐ 23 Barry Word .10 .02 |
| ☐ 581 Al Smith | .10 | .02 | ☐ 666 Eugene Chung RC | .50 | .20 | ☐ 24 Sean Salisbury .10 .02 |
| ☐ 582 Flipper Anderson | .10 | .02 | ☐ 667 Rueben Mayes | .50 | .20 | ☐ 25 Derrick Fenner .10 .02 |
| ☐ 583 Amp Lee RC | .10 | .02 | ☐ 668 Martin Bayless | .50 | .20 | ☐ 26 David Howard .10 .02 |
| ☐ 584 Greg Lloyd | .15 | .05 | ☐ 669 Ashley Ambrose RC | 1.50 | .60 | ☐ 27 Mark Kelso .10 .02 |
| ☐ 585 Cortez Kennedy | .15 | .05 | ☐ 670 Michael Coler UER | .50 | .20 | ☐ 28 Todd Lyght .10 .02 |
| ☐ 586 Keith Sims | .10 | .02 | ☐ 671 Shane Dronett RC | .50 | .20 | ☐ 29 Dana Hall .10 .02 |
| ☐ 587 Terry Allen | .30 | .10 | ☐ 672 Bernie Kosar | .75 | .30 | ☐ 30 Eric Metcalf .20 .07 |
| ☐ 588 David Fulcher | .10 | .02 | ☐ 673 Mike Singletary | .75 | .30 | ☐ 31 Jason Hanson .10 .02 |
| ☐ 589 Chris Hinton | .10 | .02 | ☐ 674 Mike Lodish RC | .50 | .20 | ☐ 32 Dwight Stone .10 .02 |
| ☐ 590 Tim McDonald | .10 | .02 | ☐ 675 Phillippi Sparks RC | .50 | .20 | ☐ 33 Johnny Mitchell .10 .02 |
| ☐ 591 Bruce Armstrong | .10 | .02 | ☐ 676 Joel Steed RC | .50 | .20 | ☐ 34 Reggie Rivers .10 .02 |
| ☐ 592 Sterling Sharpe | .30 | .10 | ☐ 677 Kevin Fagan | .50 | .20 | ☐ 35 Terrell Buckley .10 .02 |
| ☐ 593 Tom Rathman | .10 | .02 | ☐ 678 Randal Hill | .50 | .20 | ☐ 36 Steve McMichael .20 .07 |
| ☐ 594 Bill Brooks | .10 | .02 | ☐ 679 Ken O'Brien | .50 | .20 | ☐ 37 Marty Carter .10 .02 |
| ☐ 595 Broderick Thomas | .10 | .02 | ☐ 680 Lawrence Taylor | 1.50 | .60 | ☐ 38 Seth Joyner .10 .02 |
| ☐ 596 Jim Wilks | .10 | .02 | ☐ 681 Harvey Williams | 1.50 | .60 | ☐ 39 Rohn Stark .10 .02 |
| ☐ 597 Tyrone Braxton UER | .10 | .02 | ☐ 682 Quentin Coryatt RC | .50 | .20 | ☐ 40 Eric Curry RC .20 .07 |
| ☐ 598 Checklist 301-400 UER | .10 | .02 | ☐ 683 Brett Favre | 120.00 | 60.00 | ☐ 41 Tommy Barnhardt .10 .02 |
| ☐ 599 Checklist 401-500 | .10 | .02 | ☐ 684 Robert Jones RC | .50 | .20 | ☐ 42 Karl Mecklenburg .10 .02 |
| ☐ 600 Checklist 501-600 | .10 | .02 | ☐ 685 Michael Dean Perry | .75 | .30 | ☐ 43 Darion Conner .10 .02 |
| ☐ 601 Andre Reed MC | .75 | .30 | ☐ 686 Bruce Smith | 1.50 | .60 | ☐ 44 Ronnie Harmon .10 .02 |
| ☐ 602 Troy Aikman MC | 4.00 | 2.00 | ☐ 687 Troy Auzenne RC | .50 | .20 | ☐ 45 Cortez Kennedy .20 .07 |
| ☐ 603 Dan Marino MC | 6.00 | 2.50 | ☐ 688 Thomas McLemore RC | .50 | .20 | ☐ 46 Tim Brown .40 .15 |
| ☐ 604 Randall Cunningham MC | .75 | .30 | ☐ 689 Dale Carter RC | .75 | .30 | ☐ 47 Bill Lewis .10 .02 |
| ☐ 605 Jim Kelly MC | 1.50 | .60 | ☐ 690 Marc Boutte RC | .50 | .20 | ☐ 48 Randall McDaniel .15 .05 |
| ☐ 606 Deion Sanders MC | 2.00 | .75 | ☐ 691 Jeff George | 1.50 | .60 | ☐ 49 Curtis Duncan .10 .02 |
| ☐ 607 Junior Seau MC | 1.50 | .60 | ☐ 692 Dion Lambert RC | .50 | .20 | ☐ 50 Troy Aikman 1.50 .60 |
| ☐ 608 Jerry Rice MC | 4.00 | 2.00 | ☐ 693 Vaughn Dunbar RC | .50 | .20 | ☐ 51 David Klingler .10 .02 |
| ☐ 609 Bruce Smith MC | .75 | .30 | ☐ 694 Derek Brown TE RC | .50 | .20 | ☐ 52 Brent Jones .20 .07 |
| ☐ 610 Lawrence Taylor MC | 1.50 | .60 | ☐ 695 Troy Aikman | 5.00 | 2.50 | ☐ 53 Dave Krieg .20 .07 |
| ☐ 611 Todd Collins RC | .50 | .20 | ☐ 696 John Fina RC | .50 | .20 | ☐ 54 Bruce Smith .40 .15 |
| ☐ 612 Ty Detmer | 1.50 | .60 | ☐ 697 Kevin Smith RC DB | .50 | .20 | ☐ 55 Vincent Brown .10 .02 |
| ☐ 613 Browning Nagle | .50 | .20 | ☐ 698 Corey Miller RC | .50 | .20 | ☐ 56 O.J.McDuffie RC .40 .15 |
| ☐ 614 Tony Sacca RC UER | .50 | .20 | ☐ 699 Lance Olberding RC | .50 | .20 | ☐ 57 Cleveland Gary .10 .02 |
| ☐ 615 Boomer Esiason | .75 | .30 | ☐ 700 Checklist 601-700 UER | .10 | .02 | ☐ 58 Larry Centers RC .40 .15 |
| ☐ 616 Billy Joe Tolliver | .50 | .20 | ☐ P1 Promo Sheet Natl. | 10.00 | 4.00 | ☐ 59 Pepper Johnson .10 .02 |
| ☐ 617 Leslie O'Neal | .75 | .30 | ☐ P2 Promo Sheet Diam.Day | 12.00 | 5.00 | ☐ 60 Dan Marino 3.00 1.25 |
| ☐ 618 Mark Wheeler RC | .50 | .20 | | | | ☐ 61 Robert Porcher .10 .02 |
| ☐ 619 Eric Dickerson | .75 | .30 | | | | ☐ 62 Jim Harbaugh .40 .15 |

|  |  | | |
|---|---|---|---|
| ❑ 63 | Sam Mills | .10 | .02 |
| ❑ 64 | Gary Anderson RB | .10 | .02 |
| ❑ 65 | Neil O'Donnell | .20 | .07 |
| ❑ 66 | Keith Byars | .10 | .02 |
| ❑ 67 | Jeff Herrod | .10 | .02 |
| ❑ 68 | Marion Butts | .10 | .02 |
| ❑ 69 | Terry McDaniel | .10 | .02 |
| ❑ 70 | John Elway | 3.00 | 1.25 |
| ❑ 71 | Steve Broussard | .10 | .02 |
| ❑ 72 | Kelvin Martin | .10 | .02 |
| ❑ 73 | Tom Carter RC | .20 | .07 |
| ❑ 74 | Bryce Paup | .20 | .07 |
| ❑ 75 | Jim Kelly UER | .20 | .07 |
| ❑ 76 | Bill Romanowski | .10 | .02 |
| ❑ 77 | Andre Collins | .10 | .02 |
| ❑ 78 | Mike Farr | .10 | .02 |
| ❑ 79 | Henry Ellard | .20 | .07 |
| ❑ 80 | Dale Carter | .10 | .02 |
| ❑ 81 | Johnny Bailey | .10 | .02 |
| ❑ 82 | Garrison Hearst RC | 1.50 | .60 |
| ❑ 83 | Brent Williams | .10 | .02 |
| ❑ 84 | Ricardo McDonald | .10 | .02 |
| ❑ 85 | Emmitt Smith | 3.00 | 1.50 |
| ❑ 86 | Vai Sikahema | .10 | .02 |
| ❑ 87 | Jackie Harris | .10 | .02 |
| ❑ 88 | Alonzo Spellman | .10 | .02 |
| ❑ 89 | Mark Wheeler | .10 | .02 |
| ❑ 90 | Dalton Hilliard | .10 | .02 |
| ❑ 91 | Mark Higgs | .10 | .02 |
| ❑ 92 | Aaron Wallace | .10 | .02 |
| ❑ 93 | Earnest Byner | .10 | .02 |
| ❑ 94 | Stanley Richard | .10 | .02 |
| ❑ 95 | Cris Carter | .40 | .15 |
| ❑ 96 | Bobby Houston RC | .10 | .02 |
| ❑ 97 | Craig Heyward | .20 | .07 |
| ❑ 98 | Bernie Kosar | .20 | .07 |
| ❑ 99 | Mike Croel | .10 | .02 |
| ❑ 100 | Deion Sanders | 1.00 | .40 |
| ❑ 101 | Warren Moon | .20 | .07 |
| ❑ 102 | Christian Okoye | .10 | .02 |
| ❑ 103 | Ricky Watters | .40 | .15 |
| ❑ 104 | Eric Swann | .20 | .07 |
| ❑ 105 | Rodney Hampton | .40 | .15 |
| ❑ 106 | Daryl Johnston | .20 | .07 |
| ❑ 107 | Andre Reed | .20 | .07 |
| ❑ 108 | Jerome Bettis RC | 8.00 | 4.00 |
| ❑ 109 | Eugene Daniel | .10 | .02 |
| ❑ 110 | Leonard Russell | .20 | .07 |
| ❑ 111 | Darryl Williams | .10 | .02 |
| ❑ 112 | Rod Woodson | .40 | .15 |
| ❑ 113 | Boomer Esiason | .20 | .07 |
| ❑ 114 | James Hasty | .10 | .02 |
| ❑ 115 | Marc Boutte | .10 | .02 |
| ❑ 116 | Tom Waddle | .10 | .02 |
| ❑ 117 | Lawrence Dawsey | .10 | .02 |
| ❑ 118 | Mark Collins | .10 | .02 |
| ❑ 119 | Willie Gault | .10 | .02 |
| ❑ 120 | Barry Sanders | 2.50 | 1.00 |
| ❑ 121 | Leroy Hoard | .10 | .02 |
| ❑ 122 | Anthony Munoz | .20 | .07 |
| ❑ 123 | Jesse Sapolu | .10 | .02 |
| ❑ 124 | Art Monk | .20 | .07 |
| ❑ 125 | Randal Hill | .10 | .02 |
| ❑ 126 | John Offerdahl | .10 | .02 |
| ❑ 127 | Carlos Jenkins | .10 | .02 |
| ❑ 128 | Al Smith | .10 | .02 |
| ❑ 129 | Michael Irvin | .40 | .15 |
| ❑ 130 | Kenneth Davis | .10 | .02 |
| ❑ 131 | Curtis Conway RC | .75 | .30 |
| ❑ 132 | Steve Atwater | .10 | .02 |
| ❑ 133 | Neil Smith | .40 | .15 |
| ❑ 134 | Steve Everitt RC | .10 | .02 |
| ❑ 135 | Chris Mims | .10 | .02 |
| ❑ 136 | Rickey Jackson | .10 | .02 |
| ❑ 137 | Edgar Bennett | .40 | .15 |
| ❑ 138 | Mike Pritchard | .10 | .02 |
| ❑ 139 | Richard Dent | .20 | .07 |
| ❑ 140 | Barry Foster | .20 | .07 |
| ❑ 141 | Eugene Robinson | .10 | .02 |
| ❑ 142 | Jackie Slater | .10 | .02 |
| ❑ 143 | Paul Gruber | .10 | .02 |
| ❑ 144 | Rob Moore | .20 | .07 |
| ❑ 145 | Robert Smith RC | 2.50 | 1.00 |
| ❑ 146 | Lorenzo White | .10 | .02 |
| ❑ 147 | Tommy Vardell | .10 | .02 |
| ❑ 148 | Dave Meggett | .10 | .02 |
| ❑ 149 | Vince Workman | .10 | .02 |
| ❑ 150 | Terry Allen | .40 | .15 |
| ❑ 151 | Howie Long | .40 | .15 |
| ❑ 152 | Charles Haley | .20 | .07 |
| ❑ 153 | Pete Metzelaars | .10 | .02 |
| ❑ 154 | John Copeland RC | .20 | .07 |
| ❑ 155 | Aeneas Williams | .10 | .02 |
| ❑ 156 | Ricky Sanders | .10 | .02 |
| ❑ 157 | Andre Ware | .10 | .02 |
| ❑ 158 | Tony Paige | .10 | .02 |
| ❑ 159 | Jerome Henderson | .10 | .02 |
| ❑ 160 | Harold Green | .10 | .02 |
| ❑ 161 | Wymon Henderson | .10 | .02 |
| ❑ 162 | Andre Rison | .20 | .07 |
| ❑ 163 | Donald Evans | .10 | .02 |
| ❑ 164 | Todd Scott | .10 | .02 |
| ❑ 165 | Steve Emtman | .10 | .02 |
| ❑ 166 | William Fuller | .10 | .02 |
| ❑ 167 | Michael Dean Perry | .20 | .07 |
| ❑ 168 | Randall Cunningham | .40 | .15 |
| ❑ 169 | Toi Cook | .10 | .02 |
| ❑ 170 | Browning Nagle | .10 | .02 |
| ❑ 171 | Darryl Henley | .10 | .02 |
| ❑ 172 | George Teague RC | .20 | .07 |
| ❑ 173 | Derrick Thomas | .40 | .15 |
| ❑ 174 | Jay Novacek | .20 | .07 |
| ❑ 175 | Mark Carrier DB | .10 | .02 |
| ❑ 176 | Kevin Fagan | .10 | .02 |
| ❑ 177 | Nate Lewis | .10 | .02 |
| ❑ 178 | Courtney Hawkins | .10 | .02 |
| ❑ 179 | Robert Blackmon | .10 | .02 |
| ❑ 180 | Rick Mirer RC | .40 | .15 |
| ❑ 181 | Mike Lodish | .10 | .02 |
| ❑ 182 | Jarrod Bunch | .10 | .02 |
| ❑ 183 | Anthony Smith | .10 | .02 |
| ❑ 184 | Brian Noble | .10 | .02 |
| ❑ 185 | Eric Bieniemy | .10 | .02 |
| ❑ 186 | Keith Jackson | .20 | .07 |
| ❑ 187 | Eric Martin | .10 | .02 |
| ❑ 188 | Vance Johnson | .10 | .02 |
| ❑ 189 | Kevin Mack | .10 | .02 |
| ❑ 190 | Rich Camarillo | .10 | .02 |
| ❑ 191 | Ashley Ambrose | .10 | .02 |
| ❑ 192 | Ray Childress | .10 | .02 |
| ❑ 193 | Jim Arnold | .10 | .02 |
| ❑ 194 | Ricky Ervins | .10 | .02 |
| ❑ 195 | Gary Anderson K | .10 | .02 |
| ❑ 196 | Eric Allen | .10 | .02 |
| ❑ 197 | Roger Craig | .20 | .07 |
| ❑ 198 | Jon Vaughn | .10 | .02 |
| ❑ 199 | Tim McDonald | .10 | .02 |
| ❑ 200 | Broderick Thomas | .10 | .02 |
| ❑ 201 | Jessie Tuggle | .10 | .02 |
| ❑ 202 | Alonzo Mitz | .10 | .02 |
| ❑ 203 | Harvey Williams | .20 | .07 |
| ❑ 204 | Russell Maryland | .10 | .02 |
| ❑ 205 | Marvin Washington | .10 | .02 |
| ❑ 206 | Jim Everett | .20 | .07 |
| ❑ 207 | Trace Armstrong | .10 | .02 |
| ❑ 208 | Steve Young | 1.50 | .60 |
| ❑ 209 | Tony Woods | .10 | .02 |
| ❑ 210 | Brett Favre | 4.00 | 2.00 |
| ❑ 211 | Nate Odomes | .10 | .02 |
| ❑ 212 | Ricky Proehl | .10 | .02 |
| ❑ 213 | Jim Dombrowski | .10 | .02 |
| ❑ 214 | Anthony Carter | .20 | .07 |
| ❑ 215 | Tracy Simien | .10 | .02 |
| ❑ 216 | Clay Matthews | .20 | .07 |
| ❑ 217 | Patrick Bates RC | .10 | .02 |
| ❑ 218 | Jeff George | .40 | .15 |
| ❑ 219 | David Fulcher | .10 | .02 |
| ❑ 220 | Phil Simms | .20 | .07 |
| ❑ 221 | Eugene Chung | .10 | .02 |
| ❑ 222 | Reggie Cobb | .10 | .02 |
| ❑ 223 | Jim Sweeney | .10 | .02 |
| ❑ 224 | Greg Lloyd | .20 | .07 |
| ❑ 225 | Sean Jones | .10 | .02 |
| ❑ 226 | Marvin Jones RC | .10 | .02 |
| ❑ 227 | Bill Brooks | .10 | .02 |
| ❑ 228 | Moe Gardner | .10 | .02 |
| ❑ 229 | Louis Oliver | .10 | .02 |
| ❑ 230 | Flipper Anderson | .10 | .02 |
| ❑ 231 | Marc Spindler | .10 | .02 |
| ❑ 232 | Jerry Rice | 2.00 | .75 |
| ❑ 233 | Chip Lohmiller | .10 | .02 |
| ❑ 234 | Nolan Harrison | .10 | .02 |
| ❑ 235 | Heath Sherman | .10 | .02 |
| ❑ 236 | Reyna Thompson | .10 | .02 |
| ❑ 237 | Derrick Walker | .10 | .02 |
| ❑ 238 | Rufus Porter | .10 | .02 |
| ❑ 239 | Checklist 1-125 | .10 | .02 |
| ❑ 240 | Checklist 126-250 | .10 | .02 |
| ❑ 241 | John Elway MC | 1.50 | .60 |
| ❑ 242 | Troy Aikman MC | .75 | .30 |
| ❑ 243 | Steve Emtman MC | .10 | .02 |
| ❑ 244 | Ricky Watters MC | .20 | .07 |
| ❑ 245 | Barry Foster MC | .10 | .02 |
| ❑ 246 | Dan Marino MC | 1.50 | .60 |
| ❑ 247 | Reggie White MC | .20 | .07 |
| ❑ 248 | Thurman Thomas MC | .20 | .07 |
| ❑ 249 | Broderick Thomas MC | .10 | .02 |
| ❑ 250 | Joe Montana MC | 1.50 | .60 |
| ❑ 251 | Tim Goad | .10 | .02 |
| ❑ 252 | Joe Nash | .10 | .02 |
| ❑ 253 | Anthony Johnson | .20 | .07 |
| ❑ 254 | Carl Pickens | .20 | .07 |
| ❑ 255 | Steve Beuerlein | .20 | .07 |
| ❑ 256 | Anthony Newman | .10 | .02 |
| ❑ 257 | Corey Miller | .10 | .02 |
| ❑ 258 | Steve DeBerg | .10 | .02 |
| ❑ 259 | Johnny Holland | .10 | .02 |
| ❑ 260 | Jerry Ball | .10 | .02 |
| ❑ 261 | Siupeli Malamala RC | .10 | .02 |
| ❑ 262 | Steve Wisniewski | .10 | .02 |
| ❑ 263 | Kelvin Pritchett | .10 | .02 |
| ❑ 264 | Chris Gardocki | .10 | .02 |
| ❑ 265 | Henry Thomas | .10 | .02 |
| ❑ 266 | Arthur Marshall RC | .10 | .02 |
| ❑ 267 | Quinn Early | .20 | .07 |
| ❑ 268 | Jonathan Hayes | .10 | .02 |
| ❑ 269 | Eric Pegram | .20 | .07 |
| ❑ 270 | Clyde Simmons | .10 | .02 |
| ❑ 271 | Eric Moten | .10 | .02 |
| ❑ 272 | Brian Mitchell | .10 | .02 |
| ❑ 273 | Adrian Cooper | .10 | .02 |
| ❑ 274 | Gaston Green | .10 | .02 |
| ❑ 275 | John Taylor | .20 | .07 |
| ❑ 276 | Jeff Uhlenhake | .10 | .02 |
| ❑ 277 | Phil Hansen | .10 | .02 |
| ❑ 278A | Kev.Williams RC WR ERR | .40 | .15 |
| ❑ 278B | Kev.Williams RC WR COR | .40 | .15 |
| ❑ 279 | Robert Massey | .10 | .02 |
| ❑ 280A | Drew Bledsoe RC ERR | 8.00 | 3.00 |
| ❑ 280B | Drew Bledsoe RC COR | 5.00 | 2.00 |
| ❑ 281 | Walter Reeves | .10 | .02 |
| ❑ 282A | Carlton Gray RC ERR | .25 | .08 |
| ❑ 282B | Carlton Gray RC COR | .15 | .05 |
| ❑ 283 | Derek Brown TE | .10 | .02 |
| ❑ 284 | Martin Mayhew | .10 | .02 |
| ❑ 285 | Sean Gilbert | .20 | .07 |
| ❑ 286 | Jessie Hester | .10 | .02 |
| ❑ 287 | Mark Clayton | .10 | .02 |
| ❑ 288 | Blair Thomas | .10 | .02 |
| ❑ 289 | J.J. Birden | .10 | .02 |
| ❑ 290 | Shannon Sharpe | .40 | .15 |
| ❑ 291 | Richard Fain RC | .10 | .02 |
| ❑ 292 | Gene Atkins | .10 | .02 |
| ❑ 293 | Burt Grossman | .10 | .02 |
| ❑ 294 | Chris Doleman | .10 | .02 |
| ❑ 295 | Pat Swilling | .10 | .02 |
| ❑ 296 | Mike Kenn | .10 | .02 |
| ❑ 297 | Merril Hoge | .10 | .02 |
| ❑ 298 | Don Mosebar | .10 | .02 |
| ❑ 299 | Kevin Smith | .20 | .07 |
| ❑ 300 | Darrell Green | .10 | .02 |
| ❑ 301A | Dan Footman RC ERR | .25 | .08 |
| ❑ 301B | Dan Footman RC COR | .15 | .05 |
| ❑ 302 | Vestee Jackson | .10 | .02 |
| ❑ 303 | Carwell Gardner | .10 | .02 |
| ❑ 304 | Amp Lee | .10 | .02 |
| ❑ 305 | Bruce Matthews | .10 | .02 |
| ❑ 306 | Antone Davis | .10 | .02 |
| ❑ 307 | Dean Biasucci | .10 | .02 |
| ❑ 308 | Maurice Hurst | .10 | .02 |
| ❑ 309 | John Kasay | .10 | .02 |
| ❑ 310 | Lawrence Taylor | .20 | .07 |
| ❑ 311 | Ken Harvey | .10 | .02 |
| ❑ 312 | Willie Davis | .20 | .07 |
| ❑ 313 | Tony Bennett | .10 | .02 |

| | | | |
|---|---|---|---|
| ❑ 314 Jay Schroeder | .10 .02 | ❑ 393 Luis Sharpe | .10 .02 |
| ❑ 315 Darren Perry | .10 .02 | ❑ 394 Mike Johnson | .10 .02 |
| ❑ 316A Troy Drayton RC ERR | .25 .08 | ❑ 395 Andre Tippett | .10 .02 |
| ❑ 316B Troy Drayton RC COR | .15 .05 | ❑ 396 Donnel Woolford | .10 .02 |
| ❑ 317A Dan Williams RC ERR | .15 .05 | ❑ 397A Demetrius DuBose RC ERR | .25 .08 |
| ❑ 317B Dan Williams RC COR | .15 .05 | ❑ 397B Demetrius DuBose RC COR | .15 .05 |
| ❑ 318 Michael Haynes | .20 .07 | ❑ 398 Pat Terrell | .10 .02 |
| ❑ 319 Renaldo Turnbull | .10 .02 | ❑ 399 Todd McNair | .10 .02 |
| ❑ 320 Junior Seau | .40 .15 | ❑ 400 Ken Norton | .20 .07 |
| ❑ 321 Ray Crockett | .10 .02 | ❑ 401 Keith Hamilton | .10 .02 |
| ❑ 322 Will Furrer | .10 .02 | ❑ 402 Andy Heck | .10 .02 |
| ❑ 323 Byron Evans | .10 .02 | ❑ 403 Jeff Gossett | .10 .02 |
| ❑ 324 Jim McMahon | .20 .07 | ❑ 404 Dexter McNabb | .10 .02 |
| ❑ 325 Robert Jones | .10 .02 | ❑ 405 Richmond Webb | .10 .02 |
| ❑ 326 Eric Davis | .10 .02 | ❑ 406 Irving Fryar | .20 .07 |
| ❑ 327 Jeff Cross | .10 .02 | ❑ 407 Brian Hansen | .10 .02 |
| ❑ 328 Kyle Clifton | .10 .02 | ❑ 408 David Little | .10 .02 |
| ❑ 329 Haywood Jeffires | .20 .07 | ❑ 409A Glyn Milburn RC ERR | .40 .15 |
| ❑ 330 Jeff Hostetler | .20 .07 | ❑ 409B Glyn Milburn RC COR | .20 .07 |
| ❑ 331 Darryl Talley | .10 .02 | ❑ 410 Doug Dawson | .10 .02 |
| ❑ 332 Keith McCants | .10 .02 | ❑ 411 Scott Mersereau | .10 .02 |
| ❑ 333 Mo Lewis | .10 .02 | ❑ 412 Don Beebe | .10 .02 |
| ❑ 334 Matt Stover | .10 .02 | ❑ 413 Vaughan Johnson | .10 .02 |
| ❑ 335 Ferrell Edmunds | .10 .02 | ❑ 414 Jack Del Rio | .10 .02 |
| ❑ 336 Matt Brock | .10 .02 | ❑ 415A Darrien Gordon RC ERR | .25 .08 |
| ❑ 337 Ernie Mills | .10 .02 | ❑ 415B Darrien Gordon RC COR | .15 .05 |
| ❑ 338 Shane Dronett | .10 .02 | ❑ 416 Mark Schlereth | .10 .02 |
| ❑ 339 Brad Muster | .10 .02 | ❑ 417 Lomas Brown | .10 .02 |
| ❑ 340 Jesse Solomon | .10 .02 | ❑ 418 William Thomas | .10 .02 |
| ❑ 341 John Randle | .20 .07 | ❑ 419 James Francis | .10 .02 |
| ❑ 342 Chris Spielman | .20 .07 | ❑ 420 Quentin Coryatt | .20 .07 |
| ❑ 343 David Whitmore | .10 .02 | ❑ 421 Tyji Armstrong | .10 .02 |
| ❑ 344 Glenn Parker | .10 .02 | ❑ 422 Hugh Millen | .10 .02 |
| ❑ 345 Marco Coleman | .10 .02 | ❑ 423 Adrian White RC | .10 .02 |
| ❑ 346 Kenneth Gant | .10 .02 | ❑ 424 Eddie Anderson | .10 .02 |
| ❑ 347 Cris Dishman | .10 .02 | ❑ 425 Mark Ingram | .10 .02 |
| ❑ 348 Kenny Walker | .10 .02 | ❑ 426 Ken O'Brien | .10 .02 |
| ❑ 349A Roosevelt Potts RC ERR | .25 .08 | ❑ 427 Simon Fletcher | .10 .02 |
| ❑ 349B Roosevelt Potts RC COR | .15 .05 | ❑ 428 Tim McKyer | .10 .02 |
| ❑ 350 Reggie White | .40 .15 | ❑ 429 Leonard Marshall | .10 .02 |
| ❑ 351 Gerald Robinson | .10 .02 | ❑ 430 Eric Green | .10 .02 |
| ❑ 352 Mark Rypien | .10 .02 | ❑ 431 Leonard Harris | .10 .02 |
| ❑ 353 Stan Humphries | .20 .07 | ❑ 432 Darin Jordan RC | .10 .02 |
| ❑ 354 Chris Singleton | .10 .02 | ❑ 433 Erik Howard | .10 .02 |
| ❑ 355 Herschel Walker | .20 .07 | ❑ 434 David Lang | .10 .02 |
| ❑ 356 Ron Hall | .10 .02 | ❑ 435 Eric Turner | .10 .02 |
| ❑ 357 Ethan Horton | .10 .02 | ❑ 436 Michael Cofer | .10 .02 |
| ❑ 358 Anthony Pleasant | .10 .02 | ❑ 437 Jeff Bryant | .10 .02 |
| ❑ 359A Thomas Smith RC ERR | .25 .08 | ❑ 438 Charles McRae | .10 .02 |
| ❑ 359B Thomas Smith RC COR | .15 .05 | ❑ 439 Henry Jones | .10 .02 |
| ❑ 360 Audray McMillian | .10 .02 | ❑ 440 Joe Montana | 3.00 1.25 |
| ❑ 361 D.J. Johnson | .10 .02 | ❑ 441 Morten Andersen | .10 .02 |
| ❑ 362 Ron Heller | .10 .02 | ❑ 442 Jeff Jaeger | .10 .02 |
| ❑ 363 Bern Brostek | .10 .02 | ❑ 443 Leslie O'Neal | .20 .07 |
| ❑ 364 Ronnie Lott | .20 .07 | ❑ 444 LeRoy Butler | .10 .02 |
| ❑ 365 Reggie Johnson | .10 .02 | ❑ 445 Steve Jordan | .10 .02 |
| ❑ 366 Lin Elliott | .10 .02 | ❑ 446 Brad Edwards | .10 .02 |
| ❑ 367 Lemuel Stinson | .10 .02 | ❑ 447 J.B. Brown | .10 .02 |
| ❑ 368 William White | .10 .02 | ❑ 448 Kerry Cash | .10 .02 |
| ❑ 369 Ernie Jones | .10 .02 | ❑ 449 Mark Tuinei | .10 .02 |
| ❑ 370 Tom Rathman | .10 .02 | ❑ 450 Rodney Peete | .10 .02 |
| ❑ 371 Tommy Kane | .10 .02 | ❑ 451 Sheldon White | .10 .02 |
| ❑ 372 David Brandon | .10 .02 | ❑ 452 Wesley Carroll | .10 .02 |
| ❑ 373 Lee Johnson | .10 .02 | ❑ 453 Brad Baxter | .10 .02 |
| ❑ 374 Wade Wilson | .10 .02 | ❑ 454 Mike Pitts | .10 .02 |
| ❑ 375 Nick Lowery | .10 .02 | ❑ 455 Greg Montgomery | .10 .02 |
| ❑ 376 Bubba McDowell | .10 .02 | ❑ 456 Kenny Davidson | .10 .02 |
| ❑ 377A Wayne Simmons RC ERR | .25 .08 | ❑ 457 Scott Fulhage | .10 .02 |
| ❑ 377B Wayne Simmons RC COR | .15 .05 | ❑ 458 Greg Townsend | .10 .02 |
| ❑ 378 Calvin Williams | .20 .07 | ❑ 459 Rod Bernstine | .10 .02 |
| ❑ 379 Courtney Hall | .10 .02 | ❑ 460 Gary Clark | .20 .07 |
| ❑ 380 Troy Vincent | .10 .02 | ❑ 461 Hardy Nickerson | .20 .07 |
| ❑ 381 Tim McGee | .10 .02 | ❑ 462 Sean Landeta | .10 .02 |
| ❑ 382 Russell Freeman RC | .10 .02 | ❑ 463 Rob Burnett | .10 .02 |
| ❑ 383 Steve Tasker | .10 .02 | ❑ 464 Fred Barnett | .20 .07 |
| ❑ 384A Michael Strahan RC ERR | 3.00 1.25 | ❑ 465 John L. Williams | .10 .02 |
| ❑ 384B Michael Strahan RC COR | 2.50 1.00 | ❑ 466 Anthony Miller | .20 .07 |
| ❑ 385 Greg Skrepenak | .10 .02 | ❑ 467 Roman Phifer | .10 .02 |
| ❑ 386 Jake Reed | .20 .07 | ❑ 468 Rich Moran | .10 .02 |
| ❑ 387 Pete Stoyanovich | .10 .02 | ❑ 469A Willie Roaf RC ERR | .25 .08 |
| ❑ 388 Levon Kirkland | .10 .02 | ❑ 469B Willie Roaf RC COR | .15 .05 |
| ❑ 389 Mel Gray | .20 .07 | ❑ 470 William Perry | .20 .07 |
| ❑ 390 Brian Washington | .10 .02 | ❑ 471 Marcus Allen | .40 .15 |
| ❑ 391 Don Griffin | .10 .02 | ❑ 472 Carl Lee | .10 .02 |
| ❑ 392 Desmond Howard | .20 .07 | ❑ 473 Kurt Gouveia | .10 .02 |

| | | |
|---|---|
| ❑ 474 Jarvis Williams | .10 .02 |
| ❑ 475 Alfred Williams | .10 .02 |
| ❑ 476 Mark Stepnoski | .10 .02 |
| ❑ 477 Steve Wallace | .10 .02 |
| ❑ 478 Pat Harlow | .10 .02 |
| ❑ 479 Chip Banks | .10 .02 |
| ❑ 480 Cornelius Bennett | .20 .07 |
| ❑ 481A Ryan McNeil RC ERR | .15 .05 |
| ❑ 481B Ryan McNeil RC COR | .40 .15 |
| ❑ 482 Norm Johnson | .10 .02 |
| ❑ 483 Dermontti Dawson | .10 .02 |
| ❑ 484 Dwayne White | .10 .02 |
| ❑ 485 Derek Russell | .10 .02 |
| ❑ 486 Lionel Washington | .10 .02 |
| ❑ 487 Eric Hill | .10 .02 |
| ❑ 488 Micheal Barrow RC | .40 .15 |
| ❑ 489 Checklist 251-375 UER | .10 .02 |
| ❑ 490 Checklist 376-500 UER | .10 .02 |
| ❑ 491 Emmitt Smith MC | 1.50 .60 |
| ❑ 492 Derrick Thomas MC | .20 .07 |
| ❑ 493 Deion Sanders MC | .40 .15 |
| ❑ 494 Randall Cunningham MC | .20 .07 |
| ❑ 495 Sterling Sharpe MC | .20 .07 |
| ❑ 496 Barry Sanders MC | 1.25 .50 |
| ❑ 497 Thurman Thomas MC | .20 .07 |
| ❑ 498 Brett Favre MC | 2.00 .75 |
| ❑ 499 Vaughan Johnson MC | .10 .02 |
| ❑ 500 Steve Young MC | .75 .30 |
| ❑ 501 Marvin Jones MC | .10 .02 |
| ❑ 502 Reggie Brooks MC RC | .20 .07 |
| ❑ 503 Eric Curry MC | .10 .02 |
| ❑ 504 Drew Bledsoe MC | 2.00 .75 |
| ❑ 505 Glyn Milburn MC | .20 .07 |
| ❑ 506 Jerome Bettis MC | 4.00 1.50 |
| ❑ 507 Robert Smith MC | 1.00 .40 |
| ❑ 508 Dana Stubblefield RC MC | .40 .15 |
| ❑ 509 Tom Carter MC | .20 .07 |
| ❑ 510 Rick Mirer MC | .40 .15 |
| ❑ 511 Russell Copeland RC | .10 .02 |
| ❑ 512 Deon Figures RC | .10 .02 |
| ❑ 513 Tony McGee RC | .20 .07 |
| ❑ 514 Derrick Lassic RC | .10 .02 |
| ❑ 515 Everett Lindsay RC | .10 .02 |
| ❑ 516 Derek Brown RC RBK | .10 .02 |
| ❑ 517 Harold Alexander RC | .10 .02 |
| ❑ 518 Tom Scott OL RC | .10 .02 |
| ❑ 519 Elvis Grbac RC | 3.00 1.25 |
| ❑ 520 Terry Kirby RC | .40 .15 |
| ❑ 521 Doug Pelfrey RC | .10 .02 |
| ❑ 522 Horace Copeland RC | .20 .07 |
| ❑ 523 Irv Smith RC | .10 .02 |
| ❑ 524 Lincoln Kennedy RC | .10 .02 |
| ❑ 525 Jason Elam RC | .40 .15 |
| ❑ 526 Qadry Ismail RC | .40 .15 |
| ❑ 527 Artie Smith RC | .10 .02 |
| ❑ 528 Tyrone Hughes RC | .20 .07 |
| ❑ 529 Lance Gunn RC | .10 .02 |
| ❑ 530 Vincent Brisby RC | .40 .15 |
| ❑ 531 Patrick Robinson RC | .10 .02 |
| ❑ 532 Rocket Ismail | .20 .07 |
| ❑ 533 Willie Beamon RC | .10 .02 |
| ❑ 534 Vaughn Hebron RC | .10 .02 |
| ❑ 535 Darren Drozdov RC | .40 .15 |
| ❑ 536 James Jett RC | .40 .15 |
| ❑ 537 Michael Bates RC | .10 .02 |
| ❑ 538 Tom Rouen RC | .10 .02 |
| ❑ 539 Michael Husted RC | .10 .02 |
| ❑ 540 Greg Robinson RC | .10 .02 |
| ❑ 541 Carl Banks | .10 .02 |
| ❑ 542 Kevin Greene | .20 .07 |
| ❑ 543 Scott Mitchell | .40 .15 |
| ❑ 544 Michael Brooks | .10 .02 |
| ❑ 545 Shane Conlan | .10 .02 |
| ❑ 546 Vinny Testaverde | .20 .07 |
| ❑ 547 Robert Delpino | .10 .02 |
| ❑ 548 Bill Fralic | .10 .02 |
| ❑ 549 Carlton Bailey | .10 .02 |
| ❑ 550 Johnny Johnson | .10 .02 |
| ❑ NNO Jerry Rice RB | 10.00 4.00 |
| ❑ P1 Promo Sheet | 5.00 1.50 |

## 1994 Stadium Club

| | | |
|---|---|
| ❑ COMPLETE SET (630) | 60.00 25.00 |
| ❑ COMP. SERIES 1 (270) | 25.00 10.00 |
| ❑ COMP. SERIES 2 (270) | 25.00 10.00 |

| | | | |
|---|---|---|---|
| ☐ COMP.HIGH SERIES (90) | 10.00 | 5.00 | |
| ☐ 1 Dan Wilkinson RC | .20 | .07 | |
| ☐ 2 Chip Lohmiller | .10 | .02 | |
| ☐ 3 Roosevelt Potts | .10 | .02 | |
| ☐ 4 Martin Mayhew | .10 | .02 | |
| ☐ 5 Shane Conlan | .10 | .02 | |
| ☐ 6 Sam Adams RC | .20 | .07 | |
| ☐ 7 Mike Kenn | .10 | .02 | |
| ☐ 8 Tim Goad | .10 | .02 | |
| ☐ 9 Tony Jones T | .10 | .02 | |
| ☐ 10 Ronald Moore | .10 | .02 | |
| ☐ 11 Mark Bortz | .10 | .02 | |
| ☐ 12 Darren Carrington | .10 | .02 | |
| ☐ 13 Eric Martin | .10 | .02 | |
| ☐ 14 Eric Allen | .10 | .02 | |
| ☐ 15 Aaron Glenn RC | .40 | .15 | |
| ☐ 16 Bryan Cox | .10 | .02 | |
| ☐ 17 Kevin Kirkland | .10 | .02 | |
| ☐ 18 Qadry Ismail | .40 | .15 | |
| ☐ 19 Shane Dronett | .10 | .02 | |
| ☐ 20 Chris Spielman | .20 | .07 | |
| ☐ 21 Rob Fredrickson RC | .20 | .07 | |
| ☐ 22 Wayne Simmons | .10 | .02 | |
| ☐ 23 Glenn Montgomery | .10 | .02 | |
| ☐ 24 Jason Sehorn RC | .60 | .25 | |
| ☐ 25 Nick Lowery | .10 | .02 | |
| ☐ 26 Dennis Brown | .10 | .02 | |
| ☐ 27 Kenneth Davis | .10 | .02 | |
| ☐ 28 Shante Carver RC | .10 | .02 | |
| ☐ 29 Ryan Yarborough RC | .20 | .07 | |
| ☐ 30 Cortez Kennedy | .20 | .07 | |
| ☐ 31 Anthony Pleasant | .10 | .02 | |
| ☐ 32 Jessie Tuggle | .10 | .02 | |
| ☐ 33 Herschel Walker | .20 | .07 | |
| ☐ 34 Andre Collins | .10 | .02 | |
| ☐ 35 William Floyd RC | .40 | .15 | |
| ☐ 36 Harold Green | .10 | .02 | |
| ☐ 37 Courtney Hawkins | .10 | .02 | |
| ☐ 38 Curtis Conway | .40 | .15 | |
| ☐ 39 Ben Coates | .20 | .07 | |
| ☐ 40 Natrone Means | .40 | .15 | |
| ☐ 41 Eric Hill | .10 | .02 | |
| ☐ 42 Keith Kartz | .10 | .02 | |
| ☐ 43 Alexander Wright | .10 | .02 | |
| ☐ 44 Willie Roaf | .10 | .02 | |
| ☐ 45 Vencie Glenn | .10 | .02 | |
| ☐ 46 Ronnie Lott | .20 | .07 | |
| ☐ 47 George Koonce | .10 | .02 | |
| ☐ 48 Rod Woodson | .20 | .07 | |
| ☐ 49 Tim Grunhard | .10 | .02 | |
| ☐ 50 Cody Carlson | .10 | .02 | |
| ☐ 51 Bryant Young RC | .60 | .25 | |
| ☐ 52 Jay Novacek | .20 | .07 | |
| ☐ 53 Darryl Talley | .10 | .02 | |
| ☐ 54 Harry Colon | .10 | .02 | |
| ☐ 55 Dave Meggett | .10 | .02 | |
| ☐ 56 Aubrey Beavers RC | .10 | .02 | |
| ☐ 57 James Folston | .10 | .02 | |
| ☐ 58 Willie Davis | .20 | .07 | |
| ☐ 59 Jason Elam | .20 | .07 | |
| ☐ 60 Eric Metcalf | .20 | .07 | |
| ☐ 61 Bruce Armstrong | .10 | .02 | |
| ☐ 62 Ron Heller | .10 | .02 | |
| ☐ 63 LeRoy Butler | .10 | .02 | |
| ☐ 64 Terry Obee | .10 | .02 | |
| ☐ 65 Kurt Gouveia | .10 | .02 | |
| ☐ 66 Pierce Holt | .10 | .02 | |
| ☐ 67 David Alexander | .10 | .02 | |
| ☐ 68 Deral Boykin | .10 | .02 | |
| ☐ 69 Carl Pickens | .20 | .07 | |
| ☐ 70 Broderick Thomas | .10 | .02 | |
| ☐ 71 Barry Sanders CT | 1.25 | .50 | |
| ☐ 72 Qadry Ismail CT | .40 | .15 | |
| ☐ 73 Thurman Thomas CT | .40 | .15 | |
| ☐ 74 Junior Seau | .40 | .15 | |
| ☐ 75 Vinny Testaverde | .20 | .07 | |
| ☐ 76 Tyrone Hughes | .20 | .07 | |
| ☐ 77 Nate Newton | .10 | .02 | |
| ☐ 78 Eric Swann | .20 | .07 | |
| ☐ 79 Brad Baxter | .10 | .02 | |
| ☐ 80 Dana Stubblefield | .20 | .07 | |
| ☐ 81 Jumbo Elliott | .10 | .02 | |
| ☐ 82 Steve Wisniewski | .10 | .02 | |
| ☐ 83 Eddie Robinson | .10 | .02 | |
| ☐ 84 Isaac Davis | .10 | .02 | |
| ☐ 85 Cris Carter | .60 | .25 | |
| ☐ 86 Mel Gray | .10 | .02 | |
| ☐ 87 Cornelius Bennett | .20 | .07 | |
| ☐ 88 Neil O'Donnell | .40 | .15 | |
| ☐ 89 Jon Hand | .10 | .02 | |
| ☐ 90 John Elway | 3.00 | 1.25 | |
| ☐ 91 Bill Hitchcock | .10 | .02 | |
| ☐ 92 Neil Smith | .20 | .07 | |
| ☐ 93 Joe Johnson RC | .10 | .02 | |
| ☐ 94 Edgar Bennett | .40 | .15 | |
| ☐ 95 Vincent Brown | .10 | .02 | |
| ☐ 96 Tommy Vardell | .10 | .02 | |
| ☐ 97 Donnell Woolford | .10 | .02 | |
| ☐ 98 Lincoln Kennedy | .10 | .02 | |
| ☐ 99 O.J.McDuffie | .40 | .15 | |
| ☐ 100 Heath Shuler RC | .40 | .15 | |
| ☐ 101 Jerry Rice BO | .75 | .30 | |
| ☐ 102 Erik Williams BO | .10 | .02 | |
| ☐ 103 Randall McDaniel BO | .15 | .05 | |
| ☐ 104 Dermontti Dawson BO | .10 | .02 | |
| ☐ 105 Nate Newton BO | .10 | .02 | |
| ☐ 106 Harris Barton BO | .10 | .02 | |
| ☐ 107 Shannon Sharpe BO | .20 | .07 | |
| ☐ 108 Sterling Sharpe BO | .20 | .07 | |
| ☐ 109 Steve Young BO | .60 | .25 | |
| ☐ 110 Emmitt Smith BO | 1.25 | .50 | |
| ☐ 111 Thurman Thomas BO | .40 | .15 | |
| ☐ 112 Kyle Clifton | .10 | .02 | |
| ☐ 113 Desmond Howard | .20 | .07 | |
| ☐ 114 Quinn Early | .20 | .07 | |
| ☐ 115 David Klingler | .10 | .02 | |
| ☐ 116 Bern Brostek | .10 | .02 | |
| ☐ 117 Gary Clark | .20 | .07 | |
| ☐ 118 Courtney Hall | .10 | .02 | |
| ☐ 119 Joe King | .10 | .02 | |
| ☐ 120 Quentin Coryatt | .10 | .02 | |
| ☐ 121 Johnnie Morton RC | 2.00 | .75 | |
| ☐ 122 Andre Reed | .20 | .07 | |
| ☐ 123 Eric Davis | .10 | .02 | |
| ☐ 124 Jack Del Rio | .10 | .02 | |
| ☐ 125 Greg Lloyd | .20 | .07 | |
| ☐ 126 Bubba McDowell | .10 | .02 | |
| ☐ 127 Mark Jackson | .10 | .02 | |
| ☐ 128 Jeff Jaeger | .10 | .02 | |
| ☐ 129 Chris Warren | .20 | .07 | |
| ☐ 130 Tom Waddle | .10 | .02 | |
| ☐ 131 Tony Smith RB | .10 | .02 | |
| ☐ 132 Todd Collins | .10 | .02 | |
| ☐ 133 Mark Bavaro | .10 | .02 | |
| ☐ 134 Joe Phillips | .10 | .02 | |
| ☐ 135 Chris Jacke | .10 | .02 | |
| ☐ 136 Glyn Milburn | .20 | .07 | |
| ☐ 137 Keith Jackson | .20 | .07 | |
| ☐ 138 Steve Tovar | .10 | .02 | |
| ☐ 139 Tim Johnson | .10 | .02 | |
| ☐ 140 Brian Washington | .10 | .02 | |
| ☐ 141 Troy Drayton | .10 | .02 | |
| ☐ 142 Dewayne Washington RC | .20 | .07 | |
| ☐ 143 Erik Williams | .10 | .02 | |
| ☐ 144 Eric Turner | .10 | .02 | |
| ☐ 145 John Taylor | .20 | .07 | |
| ☐ 146 Richard Cooper | .10 | .02 | |
| ☐ 147 Van Malone | .10 | .02 | |
| ☐ 148 Tim Ruddy RC | .10 | .02 | |
| ☐ 149 Henry Jones | .10 | .02 | |
| ☐ 150 Tim Brown | .40 | .15 | |
| ☐ 151 Stan Humphries | .20 | .07 | |
| ☐ 152 Harry Newsome | .10 | .02 | |
| ☐ 153 Craig Erickson | .10 | .02 | |
| ☐ 154 Gary Anderson K | .10 | .02 | |
| ☐ 155 Ray Childress | .10 | .02 | |
| ☐ 156 Howard Cross | .10 | .02 | |
| ☐ 157 Heath Sherman | .10 | .02 | |
| ☐ 158 Terrell Buckley | .10 | .02 | |
| ☐ 159 J.B. Brown | .10 | .02 | |
| ☐ 160 Joe Montana | 3.00 | 1.25 | |
| ☐ 161 David Wyman | .10 | .02 | |
| ☐ 162 Norm Johnson | .10 | .02 | |
| ☐ 163 Rod Stephens | .10 | .02 | |
| ☐ 164 Willie McGinest RC | .40 | .15 | |
| ☐ 165 Barry Sanders | 2.50 | 1.00 | |
| ☐ 166 Marc Logan | .10 | .02 | |
| ☐ 167 Anthony Newman | .10 | .02 | |
| ☐ 168 Russell Maryland | .10 | .02 | |
| ☐ 169 Luis Sharpe | .10 | .02 | |
| ☐ 170 Jim Kelly | .40 | .15 | |
| ☐ 171 Tre Johnson RC | .10 | .02 | |
| ☐ 172 Johnny Mitchell | .10 | .02 | |
| ☐ 173 David Palmer RC | .40 | .15 | |
| ☐ 174 Bob Dahl | .10 | .02 | |
| ☐ 175 Aaron Wallace | .10 | .02 | |
| ☐ 176 Chris Gardocki | .10 | .02 | |
| ☐ 177 Hardy Nickerson | .20 | .07 | |
| ☐ 178 Jeff Query | .10 | .02 | |
| ☐ 179 Leslie O'Neal | .20 | .07 | |
| ☐ 180 Kevin Greene | .20 | .07 | |
| ☐ 181 Alonzo Spellman | .10 | .02 | |
| ☐ 182 Reggie Brooks | .20 | .07 | |
| ☐ 183 Dana Stubblefield | .20 | .07 | |
| ☐ 184 Tyrone Hughes | .20 | .07 | |
| ☐ 185 Drew Bledsoe GE | .40 | .15 | |
| ☐ 186 Ronald Moore GE | .10 | .02 | |
| ☐ 187 Jason Elam GE | .10 | .02 | |
| ☐ 188 Rick Mirer GE | .40 | .15 | |
| ☐ 189 Willie Roaf GE | .10 | .02 | |
| ☐ 190 Jerome Bettis GE | .40 | .15 | |
| ☐ 191 Brad Hopkins | .10 | .02 | |
| ☐ 192 Derek Brown RBK | .10 | .02 | |
| ☐ 193 Nolan Harrison | .10 | .02 | |
| ☐ 194 John Randle | .20 | .07 | |
| ☐ 195 Carlton Bailey | .10 | .02 | |
| ☐ 196 Kevin Williams WR | .20 | .07 | |
| ☐ 197 Greg Hill RC | .40 | .15 | |
| ☐ 198 Mark McMillian | .10 | .02 | |
| ☐ 199 Brad Edwards | .10 | .02 | |
| ☐ 200 Dan Marino | 3.00 | 1.25 | |
| ☐ 201 Ricky Watters | .20 | .07 | |
| ☐ 202 George Teague | .10 | .02 | |
| ☐ 203 Steve Beuerlein | .20 | .07 | |
| ☐ 204 Jeff Burris RC | .20 | .07 | |
| ☐ 205 Steve Atwater | .10 | .02 | |
| ☐ 206 John Thierry RC | .20 | .07 | |
| ☐ 207 Patrick Hunter | .10 | .02 | |
| ☐ 208 Wayne Gandy | .10 | .02 | |
| ☐ 209 Derrick Moore | .10 | .02 | |
| ☐ 210 Phil Simms | .20 | .07 | |
| ☐ 211 Kirk Lowdermilk | .10 | .02 | |
| ☐ 212 Patrick Robinson | .10 | .02 | |
| ☐ 213 Kevin Mitchell | .10 | .02 | |
| ☐ 214 Jonathan Hayes | .10 | .02 | |
| ☐ 215 Michael Dean Perry | .20 | .07 | |
| ☐ 216 John Fina | .10 | .02 | |
| ☐ 217 Anthony Smith | .10 | .02 | |
| ☐ 218 Paul Gruber | .10 | .02 | |
| ☐ 219 Carnell Lake | .10 | .02 | |
| ☐ 220 Carl Lee | .10 | .02 | |
| ☐ 221 Steve Christie | .10 | .02 | |
| ☐ 222 Greg Montgomery | .10 | .02 | |
| ☐ 223 Reggie Brooks | .20 | .07 | |
| ☐ 224 Derrick Thomas | .40 | .15 | |
| ☐ 225 Eric Metcalf | .20 | .07 | |
| ☐ 226 Michael Haynes | .20 | .07 | |
| ☐ 227 Bobby Hebert | .10 | .02 | |
| ☐ 228 Tyrone Hughes | .20 | .07 | |
| ☐ 229 Donald Frank | .10 | .02 | |
| ☐ 230 Vaughan Johnson | .10 | .02 | |
| ☐ 231 Eric Thomas | .10 | .02 | |
| ☐ 232 Ernest Givins | .20 | .07 | |
| ☐ 233 Charles Haley | .20 | .07 | |
| ☐ 234 Darnell Green | .10 | .02 | |
| ☐ 235 Harold Alexander | .10 | .02 | |
| ☐ 236 Dwayne Sabb | .10 | .02 | |
| ☐ 237 Harris Barton | .10 | .02 | |

|  | | |
|---|---|---|
| ❑ 238 Randall Cunningham | .40 | .15 |
| ❑ 239 Ray Buchanan | .10 | .02 |
| ❑ 240 Sterling Sharpe | .20 | .07 |
| ❑ 241 Chris Mims | .10 | .02 |
| ❑ 242 Mark Carrier DB | .10 | .02 |
| ❑ 243 Ricky Proehl | .10 | .02 |
| ❑ 244 Michael Brooks | .10 | .02 |
| ❑ 245 Sean Gilbert | .10 | .02 |
| ❑ 246 David Lutz | .10 | .02 |
| ❑ 247 Kelvin Martin | .10 | .02 |
| ❑ 248 Scottie Graham RC | .20 | .07 |
| ❑ 249 Irving Fryar | .20 | .07 |
| ❑ 250 Ricardo McDonald | .10 | .02 |
| ❑ 251 Marvcus Patton | .10 | .02 |
| ❑ 252 Errict Rhett RC | .40 | .15 |
| ❑ 253 Winston Moss | .10 | .02 |
| ❑ 254 Rod Bernstine | .10 | .02 |
| ❑ 255 Terry Wooden | .10 | .02 |
| ❑ 256 Antonio Langham RC | .20 | .07 |
| ❑ 257 Tommy Barnhardt | .10 | .02 |
| ❑ 258 Marvin Washington | .10 | .02 |
| ❑ 259 Bo Orlando | .10 | .02 |
| ❑ 260 Marcus Allen | .40 | .15 |
| ❑ 261 Mario Bates RC | .40 | .15 |
| ❑ 262 Marco Coleman | .10 | .02 |
| ❑ 263 Doug Riesenberg | .10 | .02 |
| ❑ 264 Jesse Sapolu | .10 | .02 |
| ❑ 265 Dermontti Dawson | .10 | .02 |
| ❑ 266 Fernando Smith RC | .10 | .02 |
| ❑ 267 David Szott | .10 | .02 |
| ❑ 268 Steve Christie | .10 | .02 |
| ❑ 269 Bruce Matthews | .10 | .02 |
| ❑ 270 Michael Irvin | .40 | .15 |
| ❑ 271 Seth Joyner | .10 | .02 |
| ❑ 272 Santana Dotson | .20 | .07 |
| ❑ 273 Vincent Brisby | .20 | .07 |
| ❑ 274 Rohn Stark | .10 | .02 |
| ❑ 275 John Copeland | .10 | .02 |
| ❑ 276 Toby Wright | .10 | .02 |
| ❑ 277 David Griggs | .10 | .02 |
| ❑ 278 Aaron Taylor | .10 | .02 |
| ❑ 279 Chris Doleman | .10 | .02 |
| ❑ 280 Reggie Brooks | .20 | .07 |
| ❑ 281 Flipper Anderson | .10 | .02 |
| ❑ 282 Alvin Harper | .20 | .07 |
| ❑ 283 Chris Hinton | .10 | .02 |
| ❑ 284 Kelvin Pritchett | .10 | .02 |
| ❑ 285 Russell Copeland | .10 | .02 |
| ❑ 286 Dwight Stone | .10 | .02 |
| ❑ 287 Jeff Gossett | .10 | .02 |
| ❑ 288 Larry Allen RC | .40 | .15 |
| ❑ 289 Kevin Mawae RC | .40 | .15 |
| ❑ 290 Mark Collins | .10 | .02 |
| ❑ 291 Chris Zorich | .10 | .02 |
| ❑ 292 Vince Buck | .10 | .02 |
| ❑ 293 Gene Atkins | .10 | .02 |
| ❑ 294 Webster Slaughter | .10 | .02 |
| ❑ 295 Steve Young | 1.25 | .50 |
| ❑ 296 Dan Williams | .10 | .02 |
| ❑ 297 Jessie Armstead | .10 | .02 |
| ❑ 298 Victor Bailey | .10 | .02 |
| ❑ 299 John Carney | .10 | .02 |
| ❑ 300 Emmitt Smith | 2.50 | 1.00 |
| ❑ 301 Bucky Brooks RC | .10 | .02 |
| ❑ 302 Mo Lewis | .10 | .02 |
| ❑ 303 Eugene Daniel | .10 | .02 |
| ❑ 304 Tyji Armstrong | .10 | .02 |
| ❑ 305 Eugene Chung | .10 | .02 |
| ❑ 306 Rocket Ismail | .20 | .07 |
| ❑ 307 Sean Jones | .10 | .02 |
| ❑ 308 Rick Cunningham | .10 | .02 |
| ❑ 309 Ken Harvey | .10 | .02 |
| ❑ 310 Jeff George | .40 | .15 |
| ❑ 311 Jon Vaughn | .10 | .02 |
| ❑ 312 Roy Barker RC | .10 | .02 |
| ❑ 313 Micheal Barrow | .10 | .02 |
| ❑ 314 Ryan McNeil | .10 | .02 |
| ❑ 315 Pete Stoyanovich | .10 | .02 |
| ❑ 316 Darryl Williams | .10 | .02 |
| ❑ 317 Renaldo Turnbull | .10 | .02 |
| ❑ 318 Eric Green | .10 | .02 |
| ❑ 319 Nate Lewis | .10 | .02 |
| ❑ 320 Mike Flores | .10 | .02 |
| ❑ 321 Derek Russell | .10 | .02 |
| ❑ 322 Marcus Spears RC | .10 | .02 |
| ❑ 323 Corey Miller | .10 | .02 |
| ❑ 324 Derrick Thomas | .40 | .15 |
| ❑ 325 Steve Everitt | .10 | .02 |
| ❑ 326 Brent Jones | .20 | .07 |
| ❑ 327 Marshall Faulk RC | 6.00 | 2.50 |
| ❑ 328 Don Beebe | .10 | .02 |
| ❑ 329 Harry Swayne | .10 | .02 |
| ❑ 330 Boomer Esiason | .20 | .07 |
| ❑ 331 Don Mosebar | .10 | .02 |
| ❑ 332 Isaac Bruce RC | 5.00 | 2.00 |
| ❑ 333 Rickey Jackson | .10 | .02 |
| ❑ 334 Daryl Johnston | .20 | .07 |
| ❑ 335 Lorenzo Lynch | .10 | .02 |
| ❑ 336 Brian Blades | .20 | .07 |
| ❑ 337 Michael Timpson | .10 | .02 |
| ❑ 338 Reggie Cobb | .10 | .02 |
| ❑ 339 Joe Walter | .10 | .02 |
| ❑ 340 Barry Foster | .10 | .02 |
| ❑ 341 Richmond Webb | .10 | .02 |
| ❑ 342 Pat Swilling | .10 | .02 |
| ❑ 343 Shaun Gayle | .10 | .02 |
| ❑ 344 Reggie Roby | .10 | .02 |
| ❑ 345 Chris Calloway | .10 | .02 |
| ❑ 346 Doug Dawson | .10 | .02 |
| ❑ 347 Rob Burnett | .10 | .02 |
| ❑ 348 Dana Hall | .10 | .02 |
| ❑ 349 Horace Copeland | .10 | .02 |
| ❑ 350 Shannon Sharpe | .20 | .07 |
| ❑ 351 Rich Miano | .10 | .02 |
| ❑ 352 Henry Thomas | .10 | .02 |
| ❑ 353 Dan Saleaumua | .10 | .02 |
| ❑ 354 Kevin Ross | .10 | .02 |
| ❑ 355 Morten Andersen | .10 | .02 |
| ❑ 356 Anthony Blaylock | .10 | .02 |
| ❑ 357 Stanley Richard | .10 | .02 |
| ❑ 358 Albert Lewis | .10 | .02 |
| ❑ 359 Darren Woodson | .20 | .07 |
| ❑ 360 Drew Bledsoe | 1.00 | .40 |
| ❑ 361 Eric Mahlum | .10 | .02 |
| ❑ 362 Trent Dilfer RC | 1.50 | .60 |
| ❑ 363 William Roberts | .10 | .02 |
| ❑ 364 Robert Brooks | .40 | .15 |
| ❑ 365 Jason Hanson | .10 | .02 |
| ❑ 366 Troy Vincent | .10 | .02 |
| ❑ 367 William Thomas | .10 | .02 |
| ❑ 368 Lonnie Johnson RC | .10 | .02 |
| ❑ 369 Jamir Miller | .10 | .02 |
| ❑ 370 Michael Jackson | .20 | .07 |
| ❑ 371 Charlie Ward CT RC | .40 | .15 |
| ❑ 372 Shannon Sharpe CT | .20 | .07 |
| ❑ 373 Jackie Slater CT | .10 | .02 |
| ❑ 374 Steve Young CT | .60 | .25 |
| ❑ 375 Bobby Wilson | .10 | .02 |
| ❑ 376 Paul Frase | .10 | .02 |
| ❑ 377 Dale Carter | .10 | .02 |
| ❑ 378 Robert Delpino | .10 | .02 |
| ❑ 379 Bert Emanuel RC | .40 | .15 |
| ❑ 380 Rick Mirer | .40 | .15 |
| ❑ 381 Carlos Jenkins | .10 | .02 |
| ❑ 382 Gary Brown | .10 | .02 |
| ❑ 383 Doug Pelfrey | .10 | .02 |
| ❑ 384 Dexter Carter | .10 | .02 |
| ❑ 385 Chris Miller | .10 | .02 |
| ❑ 386 Charles Johnson RC | .40 | .15 |
| ❑ 387 James Joseph | .10 | .02 |
| ❑ 388 Darrin Smith | .10 | .02 |
| ❑ 389 James Jett | .10 | .02 |
| ❑ 390 Junior Seau | .40 | .15 |
| ❑ 391 Chris Slade | .10 | .02 |
| ❑ 392 Jim Harbaugh | .40 | .15 |
| ❑ 393 Herman Moore | .40 | .15 |
| ❑ 394 Thomas Randolph RC | .10 | .02 |
| ❑ 395 Lamar Thomas | .10 | .02 |
| ❑ 396 Reggie Rivers | .10 | .02 |
| ❑ 397 Larry Centers | .40 | .15 |
| ❑ 398 Chad Brown | .10 | .02 |
| ❑ 399 Terry Kirby | .40 | .15 |
| ❑ 400 Bruce Smith | .40 | .15 |
| ❑ 401 Keenan McCardell RC | 2.00 | .75 |
| ❑ 402 Tim McDonald | .10 | .02 |
| ❑ 403 Robert Smith | .40 | .15 |
| ❑ 404 Matt Brock | .10 | .02 |
| ❑ 405 Tony McGee | .10 | .02 |
| ❑ 406 Ethan Horton | .10 | .02 |
| ❑ 407 Michael Haynes | .20 | .07 |
| ❑ 408 Steve Jackson | .10 | .02 |
| ❑ 409 Erik Kramer | .20 | .07 |
| ❑ 410 Jerome Bettis | .60 | .25 |
| ❑ 411 D.J. Johnson | .10 | .02 |
| ❑ 412 John Alt | .10 | .02 |
| ❑ 413 Jeff Lageman | .10 | .02 |
| ❑ 414 Rick Tuten | .10 | .02 |
| ❑ 415 Jeff Robinson | .10 | .02 |
| ❑ 416 Kevin Lee RC | .10 | .02 |
| ❑ 417 Thomas Lewis RC | .20 | .07 |
| ❑ 418 Kerry Cash | .10 | .02 |
| ❑ 419 Chuck Levy RC | .10 | .02 |
| ❑ 420 Mark Ingram | .10 | .02 |
| ❑ 421 Dennis Gibson | .10 | .02 |
| ❑ 422 Tyronne Drakeford | .10 | .02 |
| ❑ 423 James Washington | .10 | .02 |
| ❑ 424 Dante Jones | .10 | .02 |
| ❑ 425 Eugene Robinson | .10 | .02 |
| ❑ 426 Johnny Johnson | .10 | .02 |
| ❑ 427 Brian Mitchell | .10 | .02 |
| ❑ 428 Charles Mincy | .10 | .02 |
| ❑ 429 Mark Carrier WR | .20 | .07 |
| ❑ 430 Vince Workman | .10 | .02 |
| ❑ 431 James Francis | .10 | .02 |
| ❑ 432 Clay Matthews | .10 | .02 |
| ❑ 433 Randall McDaniel | .15 | .05 |
| ❑ 434 Brad Otis | .10 | .02 |
| ❑ 435 Bruce Smith | .40 | .15 |
| ❑ 436 Cortez Kennedy BD | .10 | .02 |
| ❑ 437 John Randle BD | .20 | .07 |
| ❑ 438 Neil Smith BD | .20 | .07 |
| ❑ 439 Cornelius Bennett BD | .20 | .07 |
| ❑ 440 Junior Seau BD | .20 | .07 |
| ❑ 441 Derrick Thomas BD | .20 | .07 |
| ❑ 442 Rod Woodson BD | .20 | .07 |
| ❑ 443 Terry McDaniel BD | .10 | .02 |
| ❑ 444 Tim McDonald BD | .10 | .02 |
| ❑ 445 Mark Carrier DB BD | .10 | .02 |
| ❑ 446 Irv Smith | .10 | .02 |
| ❑ 447 Steve Wallace | .10 | .02 |
| ❑ 448 Cris Dishman | .10 | .02 |
| ❑ 449 Bill Brooks | .10 | .02 |
| ❑ 450 Jeff Hostetler | .20 | .07 |
| ❑ 451 Brentson Buckner RC | .10 | .02 |
| ❑ 452 Ken Ruettgers | .10 | .02 |
| ❑ 453 Marc Boutte | .10 | .02 |
| ❑ 454 John Offerdahl | .10 | .02 |
| ❑ 455 Allen Aldridge | .10 | .02 |
| ❑ 456 Steve Emtman | .10 | .02 |
| ❑ 457 Andre Rison | .20 | .07 |
| ❑ 458 Shawn Jefferson | .10 | .02 |
| ❑ 459 Todd Steussie RC | .20 | .07 |
| ❑ 460 Scott Mitchell | .20 | .07 |
| ❑ 461 Tom Carter | .10 | .02 |
| ❑ 462 Donnell Bennett RC | .40 | .15 |
| ❑ 463 James Jones DT | .10 | .02 |
| ❑ 464 Antone Davis | .10 | .02 |
| ❑ 465 Jim Everett | .20 | .07 |
| ❑ 466 Tony Tolbert | .10 | .02 |
| ❑ 467 Merril Hoge | .10 | .02 |
| ❑ 468 Michael Bates | .10 | .02 |
| ❑ 469 Phil Hansen | .10 | .02 |
| ❑ 470 Rodney Hampton | .20 | .07 |
| ❑ 471 Aeneas Williams | .10 | .02 |
| ❑ 472 Al Del Greco | .10 | .02 |
| ❑ 473 Todd Lyght | .10 | .02 |
| ❑ 474 Joel Steed | .10 | .02 |
| ❑ 475 Merton Hanks | .20 | .07 |
| ❑ 476 Tony Stargell | .10 | .02 |
| ❑ 477 Greg Robinson | .10 | .02 |
| ❑ 478 Roger Duffy | .10 | .02 |
| ❑ 479 Simon Fletcher | .10 | .02 |
| ❑ 480 Reggie White | .40 | .15 |
| ❑ 481 Lee Johnson | .10 | .02 |
| ❑ 482 Wayne Martin | .10 | .02 |
| ❑ 483 Thurman Thomas | .40 | .15 |
| ❑ 484 Warren Moon | .40 | .15 |
| ❑ 485 Sam Rogers RC | .10 | .02 |
| ❑ 486 Erric Pegram | .10 | .02 |
| ❑ 487 Will Wolford | .10 | .02 |
| ❑ 488 Duane Young | .10 | .02 |
| ❑ 489 Keith Hamilton | .10 | .02 |
| ❑ 490 Haywood Jeffires | .20 | .07 |
| ❑ 491 Trace Armstrong | .10 | .02 |
| ❑ 492 J.J. Birden | .10 | .02 |

| □ | | | |
|---|---|---|---|
| 493 | Ricky Ervins | .10 | .02 |
| 494 | Robert Blackmon | .10 | .02 |
| 495 | William Perry | .20 | .07 |
| 496 | Robert Massey | .10 | .02 |
| 497 | Jim Jeffcoat | .10 | .02 |
| 498 | Pat Harlow | .10 | .02 |
| 499 | Jeff Cross | .10 | .02 |
| 500 | Jerry Rice | 1.50 | .60 |
| 501 | Darnay Scott RC | 1.00 | .40 |
| 502 | Clyde Simmons | .10 | .02 |
| 503 | Henry Rolling | .10 | .02 |
| 504 | James Hasty | .10 | .02 |
| 505 | Leroy Thompson | .10 | .02 |
| 506 | Darrell Thompson | .10 | .02 |
| 507 | Tim Bowens RC | .20 | .07 |
| 508 | Gerald Perry | .10 | .02 |
| 509 | Mike Croel | .10 | .02 |
| 510 | Sam Mills | .10 | .02 |
| 511 | Steve Young RZ | .60 | .25 |
| 512 | Hardy Nickerson RZ | .20 | .07 |
| 513 | Cris Carter RZ | .20 | .07 |
| 514 | Boomer Esiason RZ | .10 | .02 |
| 515 | Bruce Smith RZ | .20 | .07 |
| 516 | Emmitt Smith RZ | 1.25 | .50 |
| 517 | Eugene Robinson RZ | .10 | .02 |
| 518 | Gary Brown RZ | .10 | .02 |
| 519 | Jerry Rice RZ | .75 | .30 |
| 520 | Troy Aikman RZ | .75 | .30 |
| 521 | Marcus Allen RZ | .20 | .07 |
| 522 | Junior Seau RZ | .20 | .07 |
| 523 | Sterling Sharpe RZ | .20 | .07 |
| 524 | Dana Stubblefield RZ | .20 | .07 |
| 525 | Tom Carter RZ | .10 | .02 |
| 526 | Pete Metzelaars | .10 | .02 |
| 527 | Russell Freeman | .10 | .02 |
| 528 | Keith Cash | .10 | .02 |
| 529 | Willie Drewrey | .10 | .02 |
| 530 | Randal Hill | .10 | .02 |
| 531 | Pepper Johnson | .10 | .02 |
| 532 | Rob Moore | .20 | .07 |
| 533 | Todd Kelly | .10 | .02 |
| 534 | Keith Byars | .10 | .02 |
| 535 | Mike Fox | .10 | .02 |
| 536 | Brett Favre | 3.00 | 1.25 |
| 537 | Terry McDaniel | .10 | .02 |
| 538 | Darren Perry | .10 | .02 |
| 539 | Maurice Hurst | .10 | .02 |
| 540 | Troy Aikman | 1.50 | .60 |
| 541 | Junior Seau | .40 | .15 |
| 542 | Steve Broussard | .10 | .02 |
| 543 | Lorenzo White | .10 | .02 |
| 544 | Terry McDaniel | .10 | .02 |
| 545 | Henry Thomas | .10 | .02 |
| 546 | Tyrone Hughes | .20 | .07 |
| 547 | Mark Collins | .10 | .02 |
| 548 | Gary Anderson K | .10 | .02 |
| 549 | Darrell Green | .10 | .02 |
| 550 | Jerry Rice | 1.25 | .50 |
| 551 | Cornelius Bennett | .20 | .07 |
| 552 | Aeneas Williams | .10 | .02 |
| 553 | Eric Metcalf | .20 | .07 |
| 554 | Jumbo Elliott | .10 | .02 |
| 555 | Mo Lewis | .10 | .02 |
| 556 | Darren Carrington | .10 | .02 |
| 557 | Kevin Greene | .20 | .07 |
| 558 | John Elway | 2.50 | 1.00 |
| 559 | Eugene Robinson | .10 | .02 |
| 560 | Drew Bledsoe | .75 | .30 |
| 561 | Fred Barnett | .20 | .07 |
| 562 | Bernie Parmalee RC | .40 | .15 |
| 563 | Bryce Paup | .20 | .07 |
| 564 | Donnell Woolford | .10 | .02 |
| 565 | Terance Mathis | .20 | .07 |
| 566 | Santana Dotson | .20 | .07 |
| 567 | Randall McDaniel | .15 | .05 |
| 568 | Stanley Richard | .10 | .02 |
| 569 | Brian Blades | .20 | .07 |
| 570 | Jerome Bettis | .50 | .20 |
| 571 | Neil Smith | .20 | .07 |
| 572 | Andre Reed | .20 | .07 |
| 573 | Michael Bankston | .10 | .02 |
| 574 | Dana Stubblefield | .20 | .07 |
| 575 | Rod Woodson | .20 | .07 |
| 576 | Ken Harvey | .10 | .02 |
| 577 | Andre Rison | .20 | .07 |

| □ | | | |
|---|---|---|---|
| 578 | Darion Conner | .10 | .02 |
| 579 | Michael Strahan | .40 | .15 |
| 580 | Barry Sanders | 2.00 | .75 |
| 581 | Pepper Johnson | .10 | .02 |
| 582 | Lewis Tillman | .10 | .02 |
| 583 | Jeff George | .40 | .15 |
| 584 | Michael Haynes | .20 | .07 |
| 585 | Herschel Walker | .20 | .07 |
| 586 | Tim Brown | .40 | .15 |
| 587 | Jim Kelly | .40 | .15 |
| 588 | Ricky Watters | .20 | .07 |
| 589 | Randall Cunningham | .40 | .15 |
| 590 | Troy Aikman | 1.25 | .50 |
| 591 | Ken Norton Jr. | .20 | .07 |
| 592 | Cortez Kennedy | .20 | .07 |
| 593 | Ricky Ervins | .10 | .02 |
| 594 | Cris Carter | .50 | .20 |
| 595 | Sterling Sharpe | .20 | .07 |
| 596 | John Randle | .20 | .07 |
| 597 | Shannon Sharpe | .20 | .07 |
| 598 | Ray Crittenden RC | .10 | .02 |
| 599 | Barry Foster | .10 | .02 |
| 600 | Deion Sanders | .60 | .25 |
| 601 | Seth Joyner | .10 | .02 |
| 602 | Chris Warren | .20 | .07 |
| 603 | Tom Rathman | .10 | .02 |
| 604 | Brett Favre | 2.50 | 1.00 |
| 605 | Marshall Faulk | 2.00 | .75 |
| 606 | Terry Allen | .20 | .07 |
| 607 | Ben Coates | .20 | .07 |
| 608 | Brian Washington | .10 | .02 |
| 609 | Henry Ellard | .20 | .07 |
| 610 | Dave Meggett | .10 | .02 |
| 611 | Stan Humphries | .20 | .07 |
| 612 | Warren Moon | .40 | .15 |
| 613 | Marcus Allen | .40 | .15 |
| 614 | Ed McDaniel | .10 | .02 |
| 615 | Joe Montana | 2.50 | 1.00 |
| 616 | Jeff Hostetler | .20 | .07 |
| 617 | Johnny Johnson | .10 | .02 |
| 618 | Andre Coleman RC | .10 | .02 |
| 619 | Willie Davis | .20 | .07 |
| 620 | Rick Mirer | .40 | .15 |
| 621 | Dan Marino | 2.50 | 1.00 |
| 622 | Rob Moore | .20 | .07 |
| 623 | Byron Bam Morris RC | .20 | .07 |
| 624 | Natrone Means | .40 | .15 |
| 625 | Steve Young | .75 | .30 |
| 626 | Jim Everett | .20 | .07 |
| 627 | Michael Brooks | .10 | .02 |
| 628 | Dermontti Dawson | .10 | .02 |
| 629 | Reggie White | .40 | .15 |
| 630 | Emmitt Smith | 1.50 | .60 |
| O | Micheal Barrow TSC | 4.00 | 2.00 |
| NNO | Checklist Card 1 | .10 | .02 |
| NNO | Checklist Card 2 | .10 | .02 |
| NNO | Checklist Card 3 | .10 | .02 |

## 1995 Stadium Club

| | | | |
|---|---|---|---|
| □ COMPLETE SET (450) | | 60.00 | 25.00 |
| □ COMP.SERIES 1 (225) | | 30.00 | 12.50 |
| □ COMP.SERIES 2 (225) | | 30.00 | 12.50 |
| □ 1 | Steve Young | 1.25 | .50 |
| □ 2 | Stan Humphries | .20 | .07 |
| □ 3 | Chris Boniol RC | .10 | .02 |
| □ 4 | Darren Perry | .10 | .02 |
| □ 5 | Vinny Testaverde | .20 | .07 |
| □ 6 | Aubrey Beavers | .10 | .02 |

| □ | | | |
|---|---|---|---|
| 7 | Dewayne Washington | .20 | .07 |
| 8 | Marion Butts | .10 | .02 |
| 9 | George Koonce | .10 | .02 |
| 10 | Joe Cain | .10 | .02 |
| 11 | Mike Johnson | .10 | .02 |
| 12 | Dale Carter | .20 | .07 |
| 13 | Greg Biekert | .10 | .02 |
| 14 | Aaron Pierce | .10 | .02 |
| 15 | Aeneas Williams | .10 | .02 |
| 16 | Stephen Grant RC | .10 | .02 |
| 17 | Henry Jones | .10 | .02 |
| 18 | James Williams LB | .10 | .02 |
| 19 | Andy Harmon | .10 | .02 |
| 20 | Anthony Miller | .20 | .07 |
| 21 | Kevin Ross | .10 | .02 |
| 22 | Erik Howard | .10 | .02 |
| 23 | Brian Blades | .20 | .07 |
| 24 | Trent Dilfer | .40 | .15 |
| 25 | Roman Phifer | .10 | .02 |
| 26 | Bruce Kozerski | .10 | .02 |
| 27 | Henry Ellard | .10 | .02 |
| 28 | Rich Camarillo | .10 | .02 |
| 29 | Richmond Webb | .10 | .02 |
| 30 | George Teague | .10 | .02 |
| 31 | Antonio Langham | .10 | .02 |
| 32 | Barry Foster | .20 | .07 |
| 33 | Bruce Armstrong | .10 | .02 |
| 34 | Tim McDonald | .10 | .02 |
| 35 | James Harris DE | .10 | .02 |
| 36 | Lomas Brown | .10 | .02 |
| 37 | Jay Novacek | .20 | .07 |
| 38 | John Thierry | .10 | .02 |
| 39 | John Elliott | .10 | .02 |
| 40 | Terry McDaniel | .10 | .02 |
| 41 | Shawn Lee | .10 | .02 |
| 42 | Shane Dronett | .10 | .02 |
| 43 | Cornelius Bennett | .20 | .07 |
| 44 | Steve Bono | .20 | .07 |
| 45 | Byron Evans | .10 | .02 |
| 46 | Eugene Robinson | .10 | .02 |
| 47 | Tony Bennett | .10 | .02 |
| 48 | Michael Bankston | .10 | .02 |
| 49 | Willie Roaf | .10 | .02 |
| 50 | Bobby Houston | .10 | .02 |
| 51 | Ken Harvey | .10 | .02 |
| 52 | Bruce Matthews | .10 | .02 |
| 53 | Lincoln Kennedy | .10 | .02 |
| 54 | Todd Lyght | .10 | .02 |
| 55 | Paul Gruber | .10 | .02 |
| 56 | Corey Sawyer | .10 | .02 |
| 57 | Myron Guyton | .10 | .02 |
| 58 | John Jackson T | .10 | .02 |
| 59 | Sean Jones | .10 | .02 |
| 60 | Pepper Johnson | .10 | .02 |
| 61 | Steve Walsh | .10 | .02 |
| 62 | Corey Miller | .10 | .02 |
| 63 | Fuad Reveiz | .10 | .02 |
| 64 | Rickey Jackson | .10 | .02 |
| 65 | Scott Mitchell | .20 | .07 |
| 66 | Michael Irvin | .40 | .15 |
| 67 | Andre Reed | .20 | .07 |
| 68 | Mark Seay | .10 | .02 |
| 69 | Keith Byars | .10 | .02 |
| 70 | Marcus Allen | .40 | .15 |
| 71 | Shannon Sharpe | .20 | .07 |
| 72 | Eric Hill | .10 | .02 |
| 73 | James Washington | .10 | .02 |
| 74 | Greg Jackson | .10 | .02 |
| 75 | Chris Warren | .20 | .07 |
| 76 | Will Wolford | .10 | .02 |
| 77 | Anthony Smith | .10 | .02 |
| 78 | Cris Dishman | .10 | .02 |
| 79 | Carl Pickens | .20 | .07 |
| 80 | Tyrone Hughes | .10 | .02 |
| 81 | Chris Miller | .10 | .02 |
| 82 | Clay Matthews | .20 | .07 |
| 83 | Lonnie Marts | .10 | .02 |
| 84 | Jerome Henderson | .10 | .02 |
| 85 | Ben Coates | .20 | .07 |
| 86 | Deon Figures | .10 | .02 |
| 87 | Anthony Pleasant | .10 | .02 |
| 88 | Guy McIntyre | .10 | .02 |
| 89 | Jake Reed | .20 | .07 |
| 90 | Rodney Hampton | .20 | .07 |
| 91 | Santana Dotson | .10 | .02 |

|  |  | | |
|---|---|---|---|
| 92 | Jeff Blackshear | .10 | .02 |
| 93 | Willie Clay | .10 | .02 |
| 94 | Nate Newton | .20 | .07 |
| 95 | Bucky Brooks | .10 | .02 |
| 96 | Lamar Lathon | .10 | .02 |
| 97 | Tim Grunhard | .10 | .02 |
| 98 | Harris Barton | .10 | .02 |
| 99 | Brian Mitchell | .10 | .02 |
| 100 | Natrone Means | .20 | .07 |
| 101 | Sean Dawkins | .20 | .07 |
| 102 | Chris Slade | .10 | .02 |
| 103 | Tom Rathman | .20 | .07 |
| 104 | Fred Barnett | .20 | .07 |
| 105 | Gary Brown | .10 | .02 |
| 106 | Leonard Russell | .10 | .02 |
| 107 | Alfred Williams | .10 | .02 |
| 108 | Kelvin Martin | .10 | .02 |
| 109 | Alexander Wright | .10 | .02 |
| 110 | O.J. McDuffie | .40 | .15 |
| 111 | Mario Bates | .20 | .07 |
| 112 | Tony Casillas | .10 | .02 |
| 113 | Michael Timpson | .10 | .02 |
| 114 | Robert Brooks | .40 | .15 |
| 115 | Rob Burnett | .10 | .02 |
| 116 | Mark Collins | .10 | .02 |
| 117 | Chris Calloway | .10 | .02 |
| 118 | Courtney Hawkins | .10 | .02 |
| 119 | Marcus Patton | .10 | .02 |
| 120 | Greg Lloyd | .20 | .07 |
| 121 | Ryan McNeil | .10 | .02 |
| 122 | Gary Plummer | .10 | .02 |
| 123 | Dwayne Sabb | .10 | .02 |
| 124 | Jessie Hester | .10 | .02 |
| 125 | Terance Mathis | .20 | .07 |
| 126 | Steve Atwater | .10 | .02 |
| 127 | Lorenzo Lynch | .10 | .02 |
| 128 | James Francis | .10 | .02 |
| 129 | John Fina | .10 | .02 |
| 130 | Emmitt Smith | 2.50 | 1.25 |
| 131 | Bryan Cox | .10 | .02 |
| 132 | Robert Blackmon | .10 | .02 |
| 133 | Kenny Davidson | .10 | .02 |
| 134 | Eugene Daniel | .10 | .02 |
| 135 | Vince Buck | .10 | .02 |
| 136 | Leslie O'Neal | .20 | .07 |
| 137 | James Jett | .20 | .07 |
| 138 | Johnny Johnson | .10 | .02 |
| 139 | Michael Zordich | .10 | .02 |
| 140 | Warren Moon | .20 | .07 |
| 141 | William White | .10 | .02 |
| 142 | Carl Banks | .10 | .02 |
| 143 | Marty Carter | .10 | .02 |
| 144 | Keith Hamilton | .10 | .02 |
| 145 | Alvin Harper | .20 | .07 |
| 146 | Corey Harris | .10 | .02 |
| 147 | Elijah Alexander RC | .10 | .02 |
| 148 | Darrell Green | .10 | .02 |
| 149 | Yancey Thigpen RC | .20 | .07 |
| 150 | Deion Sanders | 1.00 | .40 |
| 151 | Burt Grossman | .10 | .02 |
| 152 | J.B. Brown | .10 | .02 |
| 153 | Johnny Bailey | .10 | .02 |
| 154 | Harvey Williams | .10 | .02 |
| 155 | Jeff Blake RC | 1.00 | .40 |
| 156 | Al Smith | .10 | .02 |
| 157 | Chris Doleman | .10 | .02 |
| 158 | Garrison Hearst | .40 | .15 |
| 159 | Bryce Paup | .20 | .07 |
| 160 | Herman Moore | .40 | .15 |
| 161 | Cortez Kennedy | .20 | .07 |
| 162 | Marquez Pope | .10 | .02 |
| 163 | Quinn Early | .10 | .02 |
| 164 | Broderick Thomas | .10 | .02 |
| 165 | Jeff Herrod | .10 | .02 |
| 166 | Robert Jones | .10 | .02 |
| 167 | Mo Lewis | .10 | .02 |
| 168 | Ray Crittenden | .10 | .02 |
| 169 | Raymont Harris | .10 | .02 |
| 170 | Bruce Smith | .40 | .15 |
| 171 | Dana Stubblefield | .20 | .07 |
| 172 | Charles Haley | .20 | .07 |
| 173 | Charles Johnson | .20 | .07 |
| 174 | Shawn Jefferson | .10 | .02 |
| 175 | Leroy Hoard | .10 | .02 |
| 176 | Bernie Parmalee | .10 | .02 |
| 177 | Scottie Graham | .20 | .07 |
| 178 | Edgar Bennett | .20 | .07 |
| 179 | Aubrey Matthews | .10 | .02 |
| 180 | Don Beebe | .10 | .02 |
| 181 | Eric Swann EC SP | .30 | .10 |
| 182 | Jeff George EC SP | .30 | .10 |
| 183 | Jim Kelly EC SP | .60 | .25 |
| 184 | Sam Mills EC SP | .30 | .10 |
| 185 | Mark Carrier DB EC SP | .20 | .07 |
| 186 | Dan Wilkinson EC SP | .30 | .10 |
| 187 | Eric Turner EC SP | .20 | .07 |
| 188 | Troy Aikman EC SP | 2.00 | .75 |
| 189 | John Elway EC SP | 4.00 | 1.50 |
| 190 | Barry Sanders EC SP | 3.00 | 1.25 |
| 191 | Brett Favre EC SP | 4.00 | 2.00 |
| 192 | Micheal Barrow EC SP | .20 | .07 |
| 193 | Marshall Faulk EC SP | 2.50 | 1.00 |
| 194 | Steve Beuerlein EC SP | .30 | .10 |
| 195 | Neil Smith EC SP | .30 | .10 |
| 196 | Jeff Hostetler EC SP | .30 | .10 |
| 197 | Jerome Bettis EC SP | .60 | .25 |
| 198 | Dan Marino EC SP | 4.00 | 1.50 |
| 199 | Cris Carter EC SP | .60 | .25 |
| 200 | Drew Bledsoe EC SP | 1.00 | .40 |
| 201 | Jim Everett EC SP | .30 | .10 |
| 202 | Dave Brown EC SP | .30 | .10 |
| 203 | Boomer Esiason EC SP | .30 | .10 |
| 204 | Randall Cunningham EC SP | .30 | .10 |
| 205 | Rod Woodson EC SP | .30 | .10 |
| 206 | Junior Seau EC SP | .60 | .25 |
| 207 | Jerry Rice EC SP | 2.00 | .75 |
| 208 | Rick Mirer EC SP | .30 | .10 |
| 209 | Errict Rhett EC SP | .30 | .10 |
| 210 | Heath Shuler EC SP | .30 | .10 |
| 211 | Bobby Taylor SP RC | .60 | .25 |
| 212 | Jesse James SP RC | .20 | .07 |
| 213 | Devin Bush SP RC | .20 | .07 |
| 214 | Luther Elliss SP RC | .20 | .07 |
| 215 | Kerry Collins RC SP | 2.50 | 1.00 |
| 216 | Derr. Alexander DE SP RC | .20 | .07 |
| 217 | Rashaan Salaam RC SP | .30 | .10 |
| 218 | J.J. Stokes RC SP | .60 | .25 |
| 219 | Todd Collins RC SP | 2.00 | .75 |
| 220 | Ki-Jana Carter RC SP | .60 | .25 |
| 221 | Kyle Brady RC SP | .60 | .25 |
| 222 | Kevin Carter RC SP | .60 | .25 |
| 223 | Tony Boselli RC SP | .60 | .25 |
| 224 | Scott Gragg SP RC | .20 | .07 |
| 225 | Warren Sapp RC SP | 2.00 | .75 |
| 226 | Ricky Reynolds | .10 | .02 |
| 227 | Roosevelt Potts | .10 | .02 |
| 228 | Jessie Tuggle | .10 | .02 |
| 229 | Anthony Newman | .10 | .02 |
| 230 | Randall Cunningham | .40 | .15 |
| 231 | Jason Elam | .20 | .07 |
| 232 | Darnay Scott | .20 | .07 |
| 233 | Tom Carter | .10 | .02 |
| 234 | Micheal Barrow | .10 | .02 |
| 235 | Steve Tasker | .20 | .07 |
| 236 | Howard Cross | .10 | .02 |
| 237 | Charles Wilson | .10 | .02 |
| 238 | Rob Fredrickson | .10 | .02 |
| 239 | Russell Maryland | .10 | .02 |
| 240 | Dan Marino | 3.00 | 1.25 |
| 241 | Rafael Robinson | .10 | .02 |
| 242 | Ed McDaniel | .10 | .02 |
| 243 | Brett Perriman | .20 | .07 |
| 244 | Chuck Levy | .20 | .07 |
| 245 | Errict Rhett | .20 | .07 |
| 246 | Tracy Simien | .10 | .02 |
| 247 | Steve Everitt | .10 | .02 |
| 248 | John Jurkovic | .10 | .02 |
| 249 | Johnny Mitchell | .20 | .07 |
| 250 | Mark Carrier DB | .10 | .02 |
| 251 | Merton Hanks | .10 | .02 |
| 252 | Joe Johnson | .10 | .02 |
| 253 | Andre Coleman | .10 | .02 |
| 254 | Ray Buchanan | .10 | .02 |
| 255 | Jeff George | .20 | .07 |
| 256 | Shane Conlan | .10 | .02 |
| 257 | Gus Frerotte | .20 | .07 |
| 258 | Doug Pelfrey | .10 | .02 |
| 259 | Glenn Montgomery | .10 | .02 |
| 260 | John Elway | 3.00 | 1.25 |
| 261 | Larry Centers | .20 | .07 |
| 262 | Calvin Williams | .20 | .07 |
| 263 | Gene Atkins | .10 | .02 |
| 264 | Tim Brown | .40 | .15 |
| 265 | Leon Lett | .10 | .02 |
| 266 | Martin Mayhew | .10 | .02 |
| 267 | Arthur Marshall | .10 | .02 |
| 268 | Maurice Hurst | .10 | .02 |
| 269 | Greg Hill | .20 | .07 |
| 270 | Junior Seau | .40 | .15 |
| 271 | Rick Mirer | .20 | .07 |
| 272 | Jack Del Rio | .10 | .02 |
| 273 | Lewis Tillman | .10 | .02 |
| 274 | Renaldo Turnbull | .10 | .02 |
| 275 | Dan Footman | .10 | .02 |
| 276 | John Taylor | .10 | .02 |
| 277 | Russell Copeland | .10 | .02 |
| 278 | Tracy Scroggins | .10 | .02 |
| 279 | Lou Benfatti | .10 | .02 |
| 280 | Rod Woodson | .20 | .07 |
| 281 | Troy Drayton | .10 | .02 |
| 282 | Quentin Coryatt | .20 | .07 |
| 283 | Craig Heyward | .20 | .07 |
| 284 | Jeff Cross | .10 | .02 |
| 285 | Hardy Nickerson | .10 | .02 |
| 286 | Dorsey Levens | .75 | .30 |
| 287 | Derek Russell | .10 | .02 |
| 288 | Seth Joyner | .10 | .02 |
| 289 | Kimble Anders | .20 | .07 |
| 290 | Drew Bledsoe | .75 | .30 |
| 291 | Bryant Young | .20 | .07 |
| 292 | Chris Zorich | .10 | .02 |
| 293 | Michael Strahan | .40 | .15 |
| 294 | Kevin Greene | .20 | .07 |
| 295 | Aaron Glenn | .10 | .02 |
| 296 | Jimmy Spencer RC | .10 | .02 |
| 297 | Eric Turner | .10 | .02 |
| 298 | William Thomas | .10 | .02 |
| 299 | Dan Wilkinson | .20 | .07 |
| 300 | Troy Aikman | 1.50 | .60 |
| 301 | Terry Wooden | .10 | .02 |
| 302 | Heath Shuler | .20 | .07 |
| 303 | Jeff Burris | .10 | .02 |
| 304 | Mark Stepnoski | .10 | .02 |
| 305 | Chris Mims | .10 | .02 |
| 306 | Todd Steussie | .10 | .02 |
| 307 | Johnnie Morton | .20 | .07 |
| 308 | Darryl Talley | .10 | .02 |
| 309 | Nolan Harrison | .10 | .02 |
| 310 | Dave Brown | .20 | .07 |
| 311 | Brent Jones | .10 | .02 |
| 312 | Curtis Conway | .40 | .15 |
| 313 | Ronald Humphrey | .10 | .02 |
| 314 | Richie Anderson RC | .50 | .20 |
| 315 | Jim Everett | .10 | .02 |
| 316 | Willie Davis | .20 | .07 |
| 317 | Ed Cunningham | .10 | .02 |
| 318 | Willie McGinest | .20 | .07 |
| 319 | Sean Gilbert | .20 | .07 |
| 320 | Brett Favre | 3.00 | 1.50 |
| 321 | Bennie Thompson | .10 | .02 |
| 322 | Neil O'Donnell | .20 | .07 |
| 323 | Vince Workman | .10 | .02 |
| 324 | Terry Kirby | .20 | .07 |
| 325 | Simon Fletcher | .10 | .02 |
| 326 | Ricardo McDonald | .10 | .02 |
| 327 | Duane Young | .10 | .02 |
| 328 | Jim Harbaugh | .20 | .07 |
| 329 | D.J. Johnson | .10 | .02 |
| 330 | Boomer Esiason | .20 | .07 |
| 331 | Donnell Woolford | .10 | .02 |
| 332 | Mike Sherrard | .10 | .02 |
| 333 | Tyrone Legette | .10 | .02 |
| 334 | Larry Brown DB | .10 | .02 |
| 335 | William Floyd | .20 | .07 |
| 336 | Reggie Brooks | .20 | .07 |
| 337 | Patrick Bates | .10 | .02 |
| 338 | Jim Jeffcoat | .10 | .02 |
| 339 | Ray Childress | .10 | .02 |
| 340 | Cris Carter | .40 | .15 |
| 341 | Charlie Garner | .40 | .15 |
| 342 | Bill Hitchcock | .10 | .02 |
| 343 | Levon Kirkland | .10 | .02 |
| 344 | Robert Porcher | .10 | .02 |
| 345 | Darryl Williams | .10 | .02 |
| 346 | Vincent Brisby | .10 | .02 |

| | | |
|---|---|---|
| 347 Kenyon Rasheed | .10 | .02 |
| 348 Floyd Turner | .10 | .02 |
| 349 Bob Whitfield | .10 | .02 |
| 350 Jerome Bettis | .40 | .15 |
| 351 Brad Baxter | .10 | .02 |
| 352 Darrin Smith | .10 | .02 |
| 353 Lamar Thomas | .10 | .02 |
| 354 Lorenzo Neal | .10 | .02 |
| 355 Erik Kramer | .10 | .02 |
| 356 Dwayne Harper | .10 | .02 |
| 357 Doug Evans RC | .40 | .15 |
| 358 Jeff Feagles | .10 | .02 |
| 359 Ray Crockett | .10 | .02 |
| 360 Neil Smith | .20 | .07 |
| 361 Troy Vincent | .10 | .02 |
| 362 Don Griffin | .10 | .02 |
| 363 Michael Brooks | .10 | .02 |
| 364 Carlton Gray | .10 | .02 |
| 365 Thomas Smith | .10 | .02 |
| 366 Ken Norton | .20 | .07 |
| 367 Tony McGee | .10 | .02 |
| 368 Eric Metcalf | .20 | .07 |
| 369 Mel Gray | .10 | .02 |
| 370 Barry Sanders | 2.50 | 1.00 |
| 371 Rocket Ismail | .20 | .07 |
| 372 Chad Brown | .20 | .07 |
| 373 Qadry Ismail | .20 | .07 |
| 374 Anthony Prior | .10 | .02 |
| 375 Kevin Lee | .10 | .02 |
| 376 Robert Young | .10 | .02 |
| 377 Kevin Williams WR | .20 | .07 |
| 378 Tydus Winans | .10 | .02 |
| 379 Ricky Watters | .20 | .07 |
| 380 Jim Kelly | .40 | .15 |
| 381 Eric Swann | .20 | .07 |
| 382 Mike Pritchard | .10 | .02 |
| 383 Derek Brown RBK | .10 | .02 |
| 384 Dennis Gibson | .10 | .02 |
| 385 Byron Bam Morris | .10 | .02 |
| 386 Reggie White | .20 | .15 |
| 387 Jeff Graham | .10 | .02 |
| 388 Marshall Faulk | 2.00 | .75 |
| 389 Joe Phillips | .10 | .02 |
| 390 Jeff Hostetler | .20 | .07 |
| 391 Irving Fryar | .20 | .07 |
| 392 Stevon Moore | .10 | .02 |
| 393 Bert Emanuel | .40 | .15 |
| 394 Leon Searcy | .10 | .02 |
| 395 Robert Smith | .40 | .15 |
| 396 Michael Bates | .10 | .02 |
| 397 Thomas Lewis | .20 | .07 |
| 398 Joe Bowden | .10 | .02 |
| 399 Steve Tovar | .10 | .02 |
| 400 Jerry Rice | 1.50 | .60 |
| 401 Toby Wright | .10 | .02 |
| 402 Daryl Johnston | .20 | .07 |
| 403 Vincent Brown | .10 | .02 |
| 404 Marvin Washington | .10 | .02 |
| 405 Chris Spielman | .10 | .02 |
| 406 Willie Jackson ET SP | .30 | .10 |
| 407 Harry Boatswain ET SP | .20 | .07 |
| 408 Kelvin Pritchett ET SP | .20 | .07 |
| 409 Dave Widell ET SP | .20 | .07 |
| 410 Frank Reich ET SP | .20 | .07 |
| 411 Corey Mayfield ET SP RC | .20 | .07 |
| 412 Pete Metzelaars ET SP | .20 | .07 |
| 413 Keith Goganious ET SP | .20 | .07 |
| 414 John Kasay ET SP | .20 | .07 |
| 415 Ernest Givins ET SP | .20 | .07 |
| 416 Randy Baldwin ET SP | .20 | .07 |
| 417 Shawn Bouwens ET SP | .20 | .07 |
| 418 Mike Fox ET SP | .20 | .07 |
| 419 Mark Carrier WR ET SP | .30 | .10 |
| 420 Steve Beuerlein ET SP | .30 | .10 |
| 421 Steve Lofton ET SP | .20 | .07 |
| 422 Jeff Lageman ET SP | .20 | .07 |
| 423 Paul Butcher ET SP | .20 | .07 |
| 424 Mark Brunell ET SP | 1.00 | .40 |
| 425 Vernon Turner ET SP | .20 | .07 |
| 426 Tim McKyer ET SP | .20 | .07 |
| 427 James Williams ET SP | .20 | .07 |
| 428 Tommy Barnhardt ET SP | .20 | .07 |
| 429 Rogerick Green ET SP | .20 | .07 |
| 430 Desmond Howard ET SP | .30 | .10 |
| 431 Darion Conner ET SP | .20 | .07 |

| | | |
|---|---|---|
| 432 Reggie Clark ET SP | .20 | .07 |
| 433 Eric Guliford ET SP | .20 | .07 |
| 434 Rob Johnson ET RC SP | 1.25 | .50 |
| 435 Sam Mills ET SP | .30 | .10 |
| 436 Kordell Stewart RC SP | 2.00 | .75 |
| 437 James O. Stewart RC SP | 1.50 | .60 |
| 438 Zach Wiegert SP | .20 | .07 |
| 439 Ellis Johnson RC SP | .20 | .07 |
| 440 Matt O'Dwyer RC SP | .20 | .07 |
| 441 Anthony Cook RC SP | .20 | .07 |
| 442 Ron Davis RC SP | .20 | .07 |
| 443 Chris Hudson RC SP | .20 | .07 |
| 444 Hugh Douglas RC SP | .60 | .25 |
| 445 Tyrone Poole RC SP | .60 | .25 |
| 446 Korey Stringer RC SP | .60 | .25 |
| 447 Ruben Brown RC SP | .60 | .25 |
| 448 Brian DeMarco RC SP | .20 | .07 |
| 449 Michael Westbrook RC SP | .60 | .25 |
| 450 Steve McNair RC SP | 4.00 | 1.50 |

**1996 Stadium Club**

| | | |
|---|---|---|
| COMPLETE SET (360) | 60.00 | 30.00 |
| COMP.SERIES 1 (180) | 30.00 | 15.00 |
| COMP.SERIES 2 (180) | 30.00 | 15.00 |
| 1 Kyle Brady | .10 | .02 |
| 2 Mickey Washington | .10 | .02 |
| 3 Seth Joyner | .10 | .02 |
| 4 Vinny Testaverde | .25 | .08 |
| 5 Thomas Randolph | .10 | .02 |
| 6 Heath Shuler | .25 | .08 |
| 7 Ty Law | .50 | .20 |
| 8 Blake Brockermeyer | .10 | .02 |
| 9 Darryll Lewis | .10 | .02 |
| 10 Jeff Blake | .50 | .20 |
| 11 Tyrone Hughes | .10 | .02 |
| 12 Horace Copeland | .10 | .02 |
| 13 Roman Phifer | .10 | .02 |
| 14 Eugene Robinson | .10 | .02 |
| 15 Anthony Miller | .25 | .08 |
| 16 Robert Smith | .25 | .08 |
| 17 Chester McGlockton | .10 | .02 |
| 18 Marty Carter | .10 | .02 |
| 19 Scott Mitchell | .25 | .08 |
| 20 O.J. McDuffie | .25 | .08 |
| 21 Stan Humphries | .25 | .08 |
| 22 Eugene Daniel | .10 | .02 |
| 23 Devin Bush | .10 | .02 |
| 24 Darick Holmes | .10 | .02 |
| 25 Ricky Watters | .25 | .08 |
| 26 J.J. Stokes | .50 | .20 |
| 27 George Koonce | .10 | .02 |
| 28 Tamarick Vanover | .25 | .08 |
| 29 Yancey Thigpen | .25 | .08 |
| 30 Troy Aikman | 1.25 | .50 |
| 31 Rashaan Salaam | .25 | .08 |
| 32 Anthony Cook | .10 | .02 |
| 33 Tim McKyer | .10 | .02 |
| 34 Dale Carter | .10 | .02 |
| 35 Marvin Washington | .10 | .02 |
| 36 Terry Allen | .25 | .08 |
| 37 Keith Goganious | .10 | .02 |
| 38 Pepper Johnson | .10 | .02 |
| 39 Dave Brown | .10 | .02 |
| 40 Levon Kirkland | .10 | .02 |
| 41 Ken Dilger | .25 | .08 |
| 42 Harvey Williams | .10 | .02 |
| 43 Robert Blackmon | .10 | .02 |
| 44 Kevin Carter | .10 | .02 |

| | | |
|---|---|---|
| 45 Warren Moon | .25 | .08 |
| 46 Allen Aldridge | .10 | .02 |
| 47 Terance Mathis | .10 | .02 |
| 48 Junior Seau | .50 | .20 |
| 49 William Fuller | .10 | .02 |
| 50 Lee Woodall | .10 | .02 |
| 51 Aeneas Williams | .10 | .02 |
| 52 Thomas Smith | .10 | .02 |
| 53 Chris Slade | .10 | .02 |
| 54 Eric Allen | .10 | .02 |
| 55 David Sloan | .10 | .02 |
| 56 Hardy Nickerson | .10 | .02 |
| 57 Michael Irvin | .50 | .20 |
| 58 Corey Sawyer | .10 | .02 |
| 59 Eric Green | .10 | .02 |
| 60 Reggie White | .50 | .20 |
| 61 Isaac Bruce | .50 | .20 |
| 62 Darrell Green | .10 | .02 |
| 63 Aaron Glenn | .10 | .02 |
| 64 Mark Brunell | .75 | .30 |
| 65 Mark Carrier WR | .10 | .02 |
| 66 Mel Gray | .10 | .02 |
| 67 Phillippi Sparks | .10 | .02 |
| 68 Ernie Mills | .10 | .02 |
| 69 Rick Mirer | .25 | .08 |
| 70 Neil Smith | .25 | .08 |
| 71 Terry McDaniel | .10 | .02 |
| 72 Terrell Davis | 1.00 | .40 |
| 73 Alonzo Spellman | .10 | .02 |
| 74 Jessie Tuggle | .10 | .02 |
| 75 Terry Kirby | .25 | .08 |
| 76 David Palmer | .10 | .02 |
| 77 Calvin Williams | .10 | .02 |
| 78 Shaun Gayle | .10 | .02 |
| 79 Bryant Young | .25 | .08 |
| 80 Jim Harbaugh | .25 | .08 |
| 81 Michael Jackson | .25 | .08 |
| 82 Dave Meggett | .10 | .02 |
| 83 Henry Thomas | .10 | .02 |
| 84 Jim Kelly | .50 | .20 |
| 85 Frank Sanders | .25 | .08 |
| 86 Daryl Johnston | .25 | .08 |
| 87 Alvin Harper | .10 | .02 |
| 88 John Copeland | .10 | .02 |
| 89 Mark Chmura | .25 | .08 |
| 90 Jim Everett | .10 | .02 |
| 91 Bobby Houston | .10 | .02 |
| 92 Willie Jackson | .25 | .08 |
| 93 Carlton Bailey | .10 | .02 |
| 94 Todd Lyght | .10 | .02 |
| 95 Ken Harvey | .10 | .02 |
| 96 Erric Pegram | .10 | .02 |
| 97 Anthony Smith | .10 | .02 |
| 98 Kimble Anders | .25 | .08 |
| 99 Steve McNair | 1.00 | .40 |
| 100 Jeff George | .25 | .08 |
| 101 Michael Timpson | .10 | .02 |
| 102 Brent Jones | .10 | .02 |
| 103 Mike Mamula | .10 | .02 |
| 104 Jeff Cross | .10 | .02 |
| 105 Craig Newsome | .10 | .02 |
| 106 Howard Cross | .10 | .02 |
| 107 Terry Wooden | .10 | .02 |
| 108 Randall McDaniel | .15 | .05 |
| 109 Andre Reed | .25 | .08 |
| 110 Steve Atwater | .10 | .02 |
| 111 Larry Centers | .25 | .08 |
| 112 Tony Bennett | .10 | .02 |
| 113 Drew Bledsoe | .75 | .30 |
| 114 Terrell Fletcher | .10 | .02 |
| 115 Warren Sapp | .10 | .02 |
| 116 Deion Sanders | .75 | .30 |
| 117 Bryce Paup | .10 | .02 |
| 118 Mario Bates | .25 | .08 |
| 119 Steve Tovar | .10 | .02 |
| 120 Barry Sanders | 2.00 | .75 |
| 121 Tony Boselli | .10 | .02 |
| 122 Micheal Barrow | .10 | .02 |
| 123 Sam Mills | .10 | .02 |
| 124 Tim Brown | .50 | .20 |
| 125 Darren Perry | .10 | .02 |
| 126 Brian Blades | .10 | .02 |
| 127 Tyrone Wheatley | .25 | .08 |
| 128 Derrick Thomas | .50 | .20 |
| 129 Edgar Bennett | .25 | .08 |

| | | |
|---|---|---|
| ❏ 130 Cris Carter | .50 | .20 |
| ❏ 131 Stephen Grant | .10 | .02 |
| ❏ 132 Kevin Williams | .10 | .02 |
| ❏ 133 Darnay Scott | .25 | .08 |
| ❏ 134 Rod Stephens | .10 | .02 |
| ❏ 135 Ken Norton | .10 | .02 |
| ❏ 136 Tim Biakabutuka SP RC | .50 | .20 |
| ❏ 137 Willie Anderson SP RC | .10 | .02 |
| ❏ 138 Lawrence Phillips SP RC | .50 | .20 |
| ❏ 139 Jonathan Ogden SP RC | .50 | .20 |
| ❏ 140 Stephen Rice SP RC | 1.25 | .50 |
| ❏ 141 Alex Van Dyke SP RC | .25 | .08 |
| ❏ 142 Jerome Woods SP RC | .10 | .02 |
| ❏ 143 Eric Moulds SP RC | 2.00 | .75 |
| ❏ 144 Mike Alstott SP RC | 1.50 | .60 |
| ❏ 145 Marvin Harrison SP RC | 4.00 | 1.50 |
| ❏ 146 Duane Clemons SP RC | .10 | .02 |
| ❏ 147 Regan Upshaw SP RC | .10 | .02 |
| ❏ 148 Eddie Kennison SP RC | .50 | .20 |
| ❏ 149 John Mobley SP RC | .10 | .02 |
| ❏ 150 Keyshawn Johnson SP RC | 1.50 | .60 |
| ❏ 151 Marco Battaglia SP RC | .10 | .02 |
| ❏ 152 Rickey Dudley SP RC | .50 | .20 |
| ❏ 153 Kevin Hardy SP RC | .50 | .20 |
| ❏ 154 Curtis Martin SM RC | 1.00 | .40 |
| ❏ 155 Dan Marino SM SP | 2.50 | 1.00 |
| ❏ 156 Rashaan Salaam SM SP | .25 | .08 |
| ❏ 157 Joey Galloway SM SP | .50 | .20 |
| ❏ 158 John Elway SM SP | 2.50 | 1.00 |
| ❏ 159 Marshall Faulk SM SP | .60 | .25 |
| ❏ 160 Jerry Rice SM SP | 1.25 | .50 |
| ❏ 161 Darren Bennett SM SP | .10 | .02 |
| ❏ 162 Tamarick Vanover SM SP | .25 | .08 |
| ❏ 163 Orlando Thomas SM SP | .10 | .02 |
| ❏ 164 Jim Kelly SM SP | .50 | .20 |
| ❏ 165 Larry Brown SM SP | .10 | .02 |
| ❏ 166 Errict Rhett SM SP | .25 | .08 |
| ❏ 167 Warren Moon SM SP | .10 | .02 |
| ❏ 168 Hugh Douglas SM SP | .10 | .02 |
| ❏ 169 Jim Everett SM SP | .10 | .02 |
| ❏ 170 AFC Championship Game SP | .10 | .02 |
| ❏ 171 Larry Centers SM SP | .25 | .08 |
| ❏ 172 Marcus Allen GM SP | .50 | .20 |
| ❏ 173 Morten Andersen GM SP | .10 | .02 |
| ❏ 174 Brett Favre GM SP | 1.25 | .50 |
| ❏ 175 Jerry Rice GM SP | 1.25 | .50 |
| ❏ 176 Glyn Milburn GM SP | .10 | .02 |
| ❏ 177 Thurman Thomas GM SP | .25 | .08 |
| ❏ 178 Michael Irvin GM SP | .25 | .08 |
| ❏ 179 Barry Sanders GM SP | 2.00 | .75 |
| ❏ 180 Dan Marino GM SP | 2.50 | 1.00 |
| ❏ 181 Joey Galloway | .50 | .20 |
| ❏ 182 Dwayne Harper | .10 | .02 |
| ❏ 183 Antonio Langham | .10 | .02 |
| ❏ 184 Chris Zorich | .10 | .02 |
| ❏ 185 Willie McGinest | .10 | .02 |
| ❏ 186 Wayne Chrebet | .75 | .30 |
| ❏ 187 Dermontti Dawson | .10 | .02 |
| ❏ 188 Charlie Garner | .25 | .08 |
| ❏ 189 Quentin Coryatt | .10 | .02 |
| ❏ 190 Rodney Hampton | .25 | .08 |
| ❏ 191 Kelvin Pritchett | .10 | .02 |
| ❏ 192 Willie Green | .10 | .02 |
| ❏ 193 Garrison Hearst | .25 | .08 |
| ❏ 194 Tracy Scroggins | .10 | .02 |
| ❏ 195 Rocket Ismail | .10 | .02 |
| ❏ 196 Michael Westbrook | .50 | .20 |
| ❏ 197 Troy Drayton | .10 | .02 |
| ❏ 198 Rob Fredrickson | .10 | .02 |
| ❏ 199 Sean Lumpkin | .10 | .02 |
| ❏ 200 John Elway | 2.50 | 1.00 |
| ❏ 201 Bernie Parmalee | .10 | .02 |
| ❏ 202 Chris Chandler | .25 | .08 |
| ❏ 203 Lake Dawson | .10 | .02 |
| ❏ 204 Orlando Thomas | .10 | .02 |
| ❏ 205 Carl Pickens | .25 | .08 |
| ❏ 206 Kurt Schulz | .10 | .02 |
| ❏ 207 Clay Matthews | .10 | .02 |
| ❏ 208 Winston Moss | .10 | .02 |
| ❏ 209 Sean Dawkins | .10 | .02 |
| ❏ 210 Emmitt Smith | 2.00 | .75 |
| ❏ 211 Mark Carrier DB | .10 | .02 |
| ❏ 212 Clyde Simmons | .10 | .02 |
| ❏ 213 Derrick Brooks | .50 | .20 |
| ❏ 214 William Floyd | .25 | .08 |
| ❏ 215 Aaron Hayden | .10 | .02 |
| ❏ 216 Brian DeMarco | .10 | .02 |
| ❏ 217 Ben Coates | .25 | .08 |
| ❏ 218 Renaldo Turnbull | .10 | .02 |
| ❏ 219 Adrian Murrell | .25 | .08 |
| ❏ 220 Marcus Allen | .50 | .20 |
| ❏ 221 Brett Maxie | .10 | .02 |
| ❏ 222 Trev Alberts | .10 | .02 |
| ❏ 223 Darren Woodson | .25 | .08 |
| ❏ 224 Brian Mitchell | .10 | .02 |
| ❏ 225 Michael Haynes | .10 | .02 |
| ❏ 226 Sean Jones | .10 | .02 |
| ❏ 227 Eric Zeier | .10 | .02 |
| ❏ 228 Herman Moore | .25 | .08 |
| ❏ 229 Shane Conlan | .10 | .02 |
| ❏ 230 Chris Warren | .25 | .08 |
| ❏ 231 Dana Stubblefield | .25 | .08 |
| ❏ 232 Andre Coleman | .10 | .02 |
| ❏ 233 Kordell Stewart UER | .50 | .20 |
| ❏ 234 Ray Crockett | .10 | .02 |
| ❏ 235 Craig Heyward | .10 | .02 |
| ❏ 236 Mike Fox | .10 | .02 |
| ❏ 237 Derek Brown RBK | .10 | .02 |
| ❏ 238 Thomas Lewis | .10 | .02 |
| ❏ 239 Hugh Douglas | .25 | .08 |
| ❏ 240 Tom Carter | .10 | .02 |
| ❏ 241 Toby Wright | .10 | .02 |
| ❏ 242 Jason Belser | .10 | .02 |
| ❏ 243 Rodney Peete | .10 | .02 |
| ❏ 244 Napoleon Kaufman | .50 | .20 |
| ❏ 245 Merton Hanks | .10 | .02 |
| ❏ 246 Kevin Colon | .10 | .02 |
| ❏ 247 Greg Hill | .25 | .08 |
| ❏ 248 Vincent Brisby | .10 | .02 |
| ❏ 249 Eric Hill | .10 | .02 |
| ❏ 250 Brett Favre | 2.50 | 1.00 |
| ❏ 251 Leroy Hoard | .10 | .02 |
| ❏ 252 Eric Guliford | .10 | .02 |
| ❏ 253 Stanley Richard | .25 | .08 |
| ❏ 254 Carlos Jenkins | .10 | .02 |
| ❏ 255 D'Marco Farr | .10 | .02 |
| ❏ 256 Carlton Gray | .10 | .02 |
| ❏ 257 Derek Loville | .10 | .02 |
| ❏ 258 Ray Buchanan | .10 | .02 |
| ❏ 259 Jake Reed | .25 | .08 |
| ❏ 260 Dan Marino | 2.50 | 1.00 |
| ❏ 261 Brad Baxter | .10 | .02 |
| ❏ 262 Pat Swilling | .10 | .02 |
| ❏ 263 Andy Harmon | .10 | .02 |
| ❏ 264 Harold Green | .10 | .02 |
| ❏ 265 Shannon Sharpe | .25 | .08 |
| ❏ 266 Erik Kramer | .10 | .02 |
| ❏ 267 Lamar Lathon | .10 | .02 |
| ❏ 268 Stevon Moore | .10 | .02 |
| ❏ 269 Tony Martin | .25 | .08 |
| ❏ 270 Bruce Smith | .25 | .08 |
| ❏ 271 James Washington | .10 | .02 |
| ❏ 272 Tyrone Poole | .10 | .02 |
| ❏ 273 Eric Swann | .10 | .02 |
| ❏ 274 Dexter Carter | .10 | .02 |
| ❏ 275 Greg Lloyd | .25 | .08 |
| ❏ 276 Michael Zordich | .10 | .02 |
| ❏ 277 Steve Wisniewski | .10 | .02 |
| ❏ 278 Chris Calloway | .10 | .02 |
| ❏ 279 Irv Smith | .10 | .02 |
| ❏ 280 Steve Young | 1.00 | .40 |
| ❏ 281 James O.Stewart | .25 | .08 |
| ❏ 282 Blaine Bishop | .10 | .02 |
| ❏ 283 Rob Moore | .25 | .08 |
| ❏ 284 Eric Metcalf | .10 | .02 |
| ❏ 285 Kerry Collins | .50 | .20 |
| ❏ 286 Dan Wilkinson | .10 | .02 |
| ❏ 287 Curtis Conway | .25 | .08 |
| ❏ 288 Jay Novacek | .10 | .02 |
| ❏ 289 Henry Ellard | .10 | .02 |
| ❏ 290 Curtis Martin | 1.00 | .40 |
| ❏ 291 Brett Perriman | .10 | .02 |
| ❏ 292 Jeff Lageman | .10 | .02 |
| ❏ 293 Trent Dilfer | .50 | .20 |
| ❏ 294 Cortez Kennedy | .10 | .02 |
| ❏ 295 Jeff Hostetler | .10 | .02 |
| ❏ 296 Mark Fields | .10 | .02 |
| ❏ 297 Qadry Ismail | .25 | .08 |
| ❏ 298 Steve Bono | .10 | .02 |
| ❏ 299 Tony Tolbert | .10 | .02 |
| ❏ 300 Jerry Rice | 1.25 | .50 |
| ❏ 301 Marvcus Patton | .10 | .02 |
| ❏ 302 Robert Brooks | .50 | .20 |
| ❏ 303 Terry Ray RC | .10 | .02 |
| ❏ 304 John Thierry | .10 | .02 |
| ❏ 305 Errict Rhett | .25 | .08 |
| ❏ 306 Ricardo McDonald | .10 | .02 |
| ❏ 307 Antonio London | .10 | .02 |
| ❏ 308 Lonnie Johnson | .10 | .02 |
| ❏ 309 Mark Collins | .10 | .02 |
| ❏ 310 Marshall Faulk | .60 | .25 |
| ❏ 311 Anthony Pleasant | .10 | .02 |
| ❏ 312 Howard Griffith | .10 | .02 |
| ❏ 313 Roosevelt Potts | .10 | .02 |
| ❏ 314 Jim Flanigan | .10 | .02 |
| ❏ 315 Omar Ellison RC | .10 | .02 |
| ❏ 316 Boomer Esiason SP | .25 | .08 |
| ❏ 317 Leslie O'Neal SP | .10 | .02 |
| ❏ 318 Jerome Bettis SP | .50 | .20 |
| ❏ 319 Larry Brown SP | .10 | .02 |
| ❏ 320 Neil O'Donnell SP | .25 | .08 |
| ❏ 321 Andre Rison SP | .25 | .08 |
| ❏ 322 Cornelius Bennett SP | .10 | .02 |
| ❏ 323 Quinn Early SP | .10 | .02 |
| ❏ 324 Bryan Cox SP | .10 | .02 |
| ❏ 325 Irving Fryar SP | .25 | .08 |
| ❏ 326 Eddie Robinson SP | .10 | .02 |
| ❏ 327 Chris Doleman SP | .10 | .02 |
| ❏ 328 Sean Gilbert SP | .10 | .02 |
| ❏ 329 Steve Walsh SP | .10 | .02 |
| ❏ 330 Kevin Greene SP | .25 | .08 |
| ❏ 331 Chris Spielman SP | .10 | .02 |
| ❏ 332 Jeff Graham SP | .10 | .02 |
| ❏ 333 Anthony Dorsett SP RC | .10 | .02 |
| ❏ 334 Amani Toomer SP | 1.50 | .60 |
| ❏ 335 Walt Harris SP RC | .10 | .02 |
| ❏ 336 Ray Mickens SP RC | .10 | .02 |
| ❏ 337 Danny Kanell SP RC | .50 | .20 |
| ❏ 338 Daryl Gardener SP RC | .10 | .02 |
| ❏ 339 Jonathan Ogden SP | .25 | .08 |
| ❏ 340 Eddie George SP RC | 2.00 | .75 |
| ❏ 341 Jeff Lewis SP RC | .25 | .08 |
| ❏ 342 Terrell Owens SP RC | 4.00 | 1.50 |
| ❏ 343 Brian Dawkins SP RC | 2.00 | .75 |
| ❏ 344 Tim Biakabutuka SP | .50 | .20 |
| ❏ 345 Marvin Harrison SP | 1.50 | .60 |
| ❏ 346 Lawyer Milloy SP RC | .60 | .25 |
| ❏ 347 Eric Moulds SP | .75 | .30 |
| ❏ 348 Alex Van Dyke SP | .25 | .08 |
| ❏ 349 John Mobley SP | .10 | .02 |
| ❏ 350 Kevin Hardy SP | .50 | .20 |
| ❏ 351 Ray Lewis SP RC | 5.00 | 2.00 |
| ❏ 352 Lawrence Phillips SP | .50 | .20 |
| ❏ 353 Stepfret Williams SP RC | .25 | .08 |
| ❏ 354 Bobby Engram SP RC | .25 | .08 |
| ❏ 355 Leeland McElroy SP RC | .25 | .08 |
| ❏ 356 Marco Battaglia SP | .10 | .02 |
| ❏ 357 Rickey Dudley SP | .50 | .20 |
| ❏ 358 Bobby Hoying SP RC | .50 | .20 |
| ❏ 359 Cedric Jones SP RC | .10 | .02 |
| ❏ 360 Keyshawn Johnson SP | .50 | .20 |
| ❏ P19 Scott Mitchell Prototype | .10 | .02 |
| ❏ P31 Rashaan Salaam Prototype | .75 | .30 |
| ❏ P56 Hardy Nickerson Prototype | .50 | .20 |
| ❏ NNO Checklist Card | .10 | .02 |

**1997 Stadium Club**

|  | | |
|---|---|---|
| ❑ COMPLETE SET (340) | 60.00 | 25.00 |
| ❑ COMP.SERIES 1 (170) | 30.00 | 15.00 |
| ❑ COMP.SERIES 2 (170) | 30.00 | 15.00 |
| ❑ 1 Junior Seau | .75 | .30 |
| ❑ 2 Michael Irvin | .75 | .30 |
| ❑ 3 Marcus Allen | .75 | .30 |
| ❑ 4 Dale Carter | .30 | .10 |
| ❑ 5 Darnell Autry RC | .50 | .20 |
| ❑ 6 Isaac Bruce | .75 | .30 |
| ❑ 7 Darrell Green | .50 | .20 |
| ❑ 8 Joey Galloway | .50 | .20 |
| ❑ 9 Steve Atwater | .30 | .10 |
| ❑ 10 Kordell Stewart | .75 | .30 |
| ❑ 11 Tony Brackens | .30 | .10 |
| ❑ 12 Gus Frerotte | .30 | .10 |
| ❑ 13 Henry Ellard | .30 | .10 |
| ❑ 14 Charles Way | .50 | .20 |
| ❑ 15 Jim Druckenmiller RC | .50 | .20 |
| ❑ 16 Orlando Thomas | .30 | .10 |
| ❑ 17 Terrell Davis | 1.00 | .40 |
| ❑ 18 Jim Schwantz | .30 | .10 |
| ❑ 19 Derrick Thomas | .75 | .30 |
| ❑ 20 Curtis Martin | 1.00 | .40 |
| ❑ 21 Deion Sanders | .75 | .30 |
| ❑ 22 Bruce Smith | .50 | .20 |
| ❑ 23 Jake Reed | .50 | .20 |
| ❑ 24 Leeland McElroy | .30 | .10 |
| ❑ 25 Jerome Bettis | .75 | .30 |
| ❑ 26 Neil Smith | .50 | .20 |
| ❑ 27 Terry Allen | .75 | .30 |
| ❑ 28 Gilbert Brown | .50 | .20 |
| ❑ 29 Steve McNair | 1.00 | .40 |
| ❑ 30 Kerry Collins | .75 | .30 |
| ❑ 31 Thurman Thomas | .75 | .30 |
| ❑ 32 Kenny Holmes RC | .75 | .30 |
| ❑ 33 Karim Abdul-Jabbar | .75 | .30 |
| ❑ 34 Steve Young | 1.00 | .40 |
| ❑ 35 Jerry Rice | 1.50 | .60 |
| ❑ 36 Jeff George | .50 | .20 |
| ❑ 37 Errict Rhett | .30 | .10 |
| ❑ 38 Mike Alstott | .75 | .30 |
| ❑ 39 Tim Brown | .75 | .30 |
| ❑ 40 Keyshawn Johnson | .75 | .30 |
| ❑ 41 Jim Harbaugh | .50 | .20 |
| ❑ 42 Kevin Hardy | .30 | .10 |
| ❑ 43 Kevin Greene | .50 | .20 |
| ❑ 44 Eric Metcalf | .50 | .20 |
| ❑ 45 Troy Aikman | 1.50 | .60 |
| ❑ 46 Marshall Faulk | 1.00 | .40 |
| ❑ 47 Shannon Sharpe | .50 | .20 |
| ❑ 48 Warren Moon | .75 | .30 |
| ❑ 49 Mark Brunell | 1.00 | .40 |
| ❑ 50 Dan Marino | 3.00 | 1.25 |
| ❑ 51 Byron Hanspard RC | .50 | .20 |
| ❑ 52 Chris Chandler | .50 | .20 |
| ❑ 53 Wayne Chrebet | .75 | .30 |
| ❑ 54 Antonio Langham | .30 | .10 |
| ❑ 55 Barry Sanders | 2.50 | 1.00 |
| ❑ 56 Curtis Conway | .50 | .20 |
| ❑ 57 Ricky Watters | .50 | .20 |
| ❑ 58 William Thomas | .30 | .10 |
| ❑ 59 Chris Warren | .50 | .20 |
| ❑ 60 Terry Glenn | .75 | .30 |
| ❑ 61 Peter Boulware RC | .75 | .30 |
| ❑ 62 Chad Cota | .30 | .10 |
| ❑ 63 Eddie Kennison | .50 | .20 |
| ❑ 64 Lamar Smith | .75 | .30 |
| ❑ 65 Brett Favre | 3.00 | 1.50 |
| ❑ 66 Michael Westbrook | .50 | .20 |
| ❑ 67 Larry Centers | .50 | .20 |
| ❑ 68 Trent Dilfer | .75 | .30 |
| ❑ 69 Stevon Moore | .30 | .10 |
| ❑ 70 John Elway | 3.00 | 1.25 |
| ❑ 71 Bryce Paup | .30 | .10 |
| ❑ 72 Quentin Coryatt | .30 | .10 |
| ❑ 73 Rashaan Salaam | .30 | .10 |
| ❑ 74 Thomas Lewis | .30 | .10 |
| ❑ 75 Drew Bledsoe | 1.00 | .40 |
| ❑ 76 Cris Carter | .75 | .30 |
| ❑ 77 Joe Bowden | .30 | .10 |
| ❑ 78 Allen Aldridge | .30 | .10 |
| ❑ 79 Zach Thomas | .75 | .30 |
| ❑ 80 Emmitt Smith | 2.50 | 1.00 |
| ❑ 81 Daryl Johnston | .50 | .20 |
| ❑ 82 Vinny Testaverde | .50 | .20 |
| ❑ 83 James O.Stewart | .50 | .20 |
| ❑ 84 Edgar Bennett | .50 | .20 |
| ❑ 85 Shawn Springs RC | .50 | .20 |
| ❑ 86 Elvis Grbac | .50 | .20 |
| ❑ 87 Levon Kirkland | .30 | .10 |
| ❑ 88 Jeff Graham | .30 | .10 |
| ❑ 89 Terrell Fletcher | .30 | .10 |
| ❑ 90 Eddie George | .75 | .30 |
| ❑ 91 Jessie Tuggle | .30 | .10 |
| ❑ 92 Terrell Owens | 1.00 | .40 |
| ❑ 93 Wayne Martin | .30 | .10 |
| ❑ 94 Dwayne Harper | .30 | .10 |
| ❑ 95 Mark Collins | .30 | .10 |
| ❑ 96 Marvcus Patton | .30 | .10 |
| ❑ 97 Napoleon Kaufman | .75 | .30 |
| ❑ 98 Keenan McCardell | .50 | .20 |
| ❑ 99 Ty Detmer | .50 | .20 |
| ❑ 100 Reggie White | .50 | .20 |
| ❑ 101 William Floyd | .50 | .20 |
| ❑ 102 Scott Mitchell | .50 | .20 |
| ❑ 103 Robert Blackmon | .30 | .10 |
| ❑ 104 Dan Wilkinson | .30 | .10 |
| ❑ 105 Warren Sapp | .50 | .20 |
| ❑ 106 Dave Meggett | .30 | .10 |
| ❑ 107 Brian Mitchell | .30 | .10 |
| ❑ 108 Tyrone Poole | .30 | .10 |
| ❑ 109 Derrick Alexander WR | .50 | .20 |
| ❑ 110 David Palmer | .30 | .10 |
| ❑ 111 James Farrior RC | .75 | .30 |
| ❑ 112 Chad Brown | .30 | .10 |
| ❑ 113 Marty Carter | .30 | .10 |
| ❑ 114 Lawrence Phillips | .30 | .10 |
| ❑ 115 Wesley Walls | .50 | .20 |
| ❑ 116 John Friesz | .30 | .10 |
| ❑ 117 Roman Phifer | .30 | .10 |
| ❑ 118 Jason Sehorn | .50 | .20 |
| ❑ 119 Henry Thomas | .30 | .10 |
| ❑ 120 Natrone Means | .50 | .20 |
| ❑ 121 Ty Law | .30 | .10 |
| ❑ 122 Tony Gonzalez RC | 3.00 | 1.25 |
| ❑ 123 Kevin Williams | .30 | .10 |
| ❑ 124 Regan Upshaw | .30 | .10 |
| ❑ 125 Antonio Freeman | .75 | .30 |
| ❑ 126 Jessie Armstead | .30 | .10 |
| ❑ 127 Pat Barnes RC | .75 | .30 |
| ❑ 128 Charlie Garner | .50 | .20 |
| ❑ 129 Irving Fryar | .50 | .20 |
| ❑ 130 Rickey Dudley | .50 | .20 |
| ❑ 131 Rodney Harrison RC | 1.50 | .60 |
| ❑ 132 Brent Jones | .50 | .20 |
| ❑ 133 Neil O'Donnell | .50 | .20 |
| ❑ 134 Darryll Lewis | .30 | .10 |
| ❑ 135 Jason Belser | .30 | .10 |
| ❑ 136 Mark Chmura | .50 | .20 |
| ❑ 137 Seth Joyner | .30 | .10 |
| ❑ 138 Herschel Walker | .50 | .20 |
| ❑ 139 Santana Dotson | .30 | .10 |
| ❑ 140 Carl Pickens | .50 | .20 |
| ❑ 141 Terance Mathis | .30 | .10 |
| ❑ 142 Walt Harris | .30 | .10 |
| ❑ 143 John Mobley | .30 | .10 |
| ❑ 144 Gabe Northern | .30 | .10 |
| ❑ 145 Herman Moore | .75 | .30 |
| ❑ 146 Michael Jackson | .50 | .20 |
| ❑ 147 Chris Sanders | .30 | .10 |
| ❑ 148 LeShon Johnson | .30 | .10 |
| ❑ 149 Darrell Russell RC | .30 | .10 |
| ❑ 150 Winslow Oliver | .30 | .10 |
| ❑ 151 Tamarick Vanover | .50 | .20 |
| ❑ 152 Tony Martin | .50 | .20 |
| ❑ 153 Lamar Lathon | .30 | .10 |
| ❑ 154 Ray Mickens | .30 | .10 |
| ❑ 155 Derrick Brooks | .75 | .30 |
| ❑ 156 Warrick Dunn RC | 3.00 | 1.25 |
| ❑ 157 Tim McDonald | .30 | .10 |
| ❑ 158 Keith Lyle | .30 | .10 |
| ❑ 159 Terry McDaniel | .30 | .10 |
| ❑ 160 Andre Hastings | .30 | .10 |
| ❑ 161 Phillippi Sparks | .30 | .10 |
| ❑ 162 Tedy Bruschi | 1.50 | .60 |
| ❑ 163 Bryant Westbrook RC | .50 | .20 |
| ❑ 164 Victor Green | .30 | .10 |
| ❑ 165 Jimmy Smith | .50 | .20 |
| ❑ 166 Greg Biekert | .30 | .10 |
| ❑ 167 Frank Sanders | .50 | .20 |
| ❑ 168 Chris Doleman | .30 | .10 |
| ❑ 169 Phil Hansen | .30 | .10 |
| ❑ 170 Walter Jones RC | .75 | .30 |
| ❑ 171 Mark Carrier WR | .30 | .10 |
| ❑ 172 Greg Hill | .30 | .10 |
| ❑ 173 Erik Kramer | .30 | .10 |
| ❑ 174 Chris Spielman | .30 | .10 |
| ❑ 175 Tom Knight RC | .30 | .10 |
| ❑ 176 Sam Mills | .30 | .10 |
| ❑ 177 Robert Smith | .50 | .20 |
| ❑ 178 Dorsey Levens | .75 | .30 |
| ❑ 179 Chris Slade | .30 | .10 |
| ❑ 180 Troy Vincent | .30 | .10 |
| ❑ 181 Mario Bates | .30 | .10 |
| ❑ 182 Ed McCaffrey | .50 | .20 |
| ❑ 183 Mike Mamula | .30 | .10 |
| ❑ 184 Chad Hennings | .30 | .10 |
| ❑ 185 Stan Humphries | .50 | .20 |
| ❑ 186 Reinard Wilson RC | .50 | .20 |
| ❑ 187 Kevin Carter | .30 | .10 |
| ❑ 188 Qadry Ismail | .50 | .20 |
| ❑ 189 Cortez Kennedy | .30 | .10 |
| ❑ 190 Eric Swann | .30 | .10 |
| ❑ 191 Corey Dillon RC | 6.00 | 2.50 |
| ❑ 192 Renaldo Wynn | .30 | .10 |
| ❑ 193 Bobby Hebert | .30 | .10 |
| ❑ 194 Fred Barnett | .30 | .10 |
| ❑ 195 Ray Lewis | 1.25 | .50 |
| ❑ 196 Robert Jones | .30 | .10 |
| ❑ 197 Brian Williams | .30 | .10 |
| ❑ 198 Willie McGinest | .30 | .10 |
| ❑ 199 Jake Plummer RC | 5.00 | 2.00 |
| ❑ 200 Aeneas Williams | .30 | .10 |
| ❑ 201 Ashley Ambrose | .30 | .10 |
| ❑ 202 Cornelius Bennett | .30 | .10 |
| ❑ 203 Mo Lewis | .30 | .10 |
| ❑ 204 James Hasty | .30 | .10 |
| ❑ 205 Carnell Lake | .30 | .10 |
| ❑ 206 Heath Shuler | .30 | .10 |
| ❑ 207 Dana Stubblefield | .30 | .10 |
| ❑ 208 Corey Miller | .30 | .10 |
| ❑ 209 Ike Hilliard RC | 1.25 | .50 |
| ❑ 210 Bryant Young | .30 | .10 |
| ❑ 211 Hardy Nickerson | .30 | .10 |
| ❑ 212 Blaine Bishop | .30 | .10 |
| ❑ 213 Marcus Robertson | .30 | .10 |
| ❑ 214 Tony Bennett | .30 | .10 |
| ❑ 215 Kent Graham | .30 | .10 |
| ❑ 216 Steve Bono | .50 | .20 |
| ❑ 217 Will Blackwell RC | .50 | .20 |
| ❑ 218 Tyrone Braxton | .30 | .10 |
| ❑ 219 Eric Moulds | .75 | .30 |
| ❑ 220 Rod Woodson | .50 | .20 |
| ❑ 221 Anthony Johnson | .30 | .10 |
| ❑ 222 Willie Davis | .30 | .10 |
| ❑ 223 Darrin Smith | .30 | .10 |
| ❑ 224 Rick Mirer | .50 | .20 |
| ❑ 225 Marvin Harrison | .75 | .30 |
| ❑ 226 Terrell Buckley | .30 | .10 |
| ❑ 227 Joe Aska | .30 | .10 |
| ❑ 228 Yatil Green RC | .50 | .20 |
| ❑ 229 William Fuller | .30 | .10 |
| ❑ 230 Eddie Robinson | .30 | .10 |
| ❑ 231 Brian Blades | .30 | .10 |
| ❑ 232 Michael Sinclair | .30 | .10 |
| ❑ 233 Ken Harvey | .30 | .10 |
| ❑ 234 Harvey Williams | .30 | .10 |
| ❑ 235 Simeon Rice | .50 | .20 |
| ❑ 236 Chris T. Jones | .30 | .10 |
| ❑ 237 Bert Emanuel | .50 | .20 |
| ❑ 238 Corey Sawyer | .30 | .10 |
| ❑ 239 Chris Calloway | .30 | .10 |
| ❑ 240 Jeff Blake | .50 | .20 |
| ❑ 241 Alonzo Spellman | .30 | .10 |
| ❑ 242 Bryan Cox | .30 | .10 |
| ❑ 243 Antowain Smith RC | 2.50 | 1.00 |
| ❑ 244 Tim Biakabutuka | .50 | .20 |
| ❑ 245 Ray Crockett | .30 | .10 |
| ❑ 246 Dwayne Rudd | .30 | .10 |
| ❑ 247 Glyn Milburn | .30 | .10 |
| ❑ 248 Gary Plummer | .30 | .10 |
| ❑ 249 O.J. McDuffie | .50 | .20 |
| ❑ 250 Willie Clay | .30 | .10 |
| ❑ 251 Jim Everett | .30 | .10 |
| ❑ 252 Eugene Daniel | .30 | .10 |

| | | |
|---|---|---|
| ❑ 253 Corey Widmer | .30 | .10 |
| ❑ 254 Mel Gray | .30 | .10 |
| ❑ 255 Ken Norton | .30 | .10 |
| ❑ 256 Johnnie Morton | .50 | .20 |
| ❑ 257 Courtney Hawkins | .30 | .10 |
| ❑ 258 Ricardo McDonald | .30 | .10 |
| ❑ 259 Todd Lyght | .30 | .10 |
| ❑ 260 Micheal Barrow | .30 | .10 |
| ❑ 261 Aaron Glenn | .30 | .10 |
| ❑ 262 Jeff Herrod | .30 | .10 |
| ❑ 263 Troy Davis RC | .50 | .20 |
| ❑ 264 Eric Hill | .30 | .10 |
| ❑ 265 Darrien Gordon | .30 | .10 |
| ❑ 266 Lake Dawson | .30 | .10 |
| ❑ 267 John Randle | .50 | .20 |
| ❑ 268 Henry Jones | .30 | .10 |
| ❑ 269 Mickey Washington | .30 | .10 |
| ❑ 270 Amani Toomer | .50 | .20 |
| ❑ 271 Steve Grant | .30 | .10 |
| ❑ 272 Adrian Murrell | .50 | .20 |
| ❑ 273 Derrick Witherspoon | .30 | .10 |
| ❑ 274 Albert Lewis | .30 | .10 |
| ❑ 275 Ben Coates | .50 | .20 |
| ❑ 276 Reidel Anthony RC | .75 | .30 |
| ❑ 277 Jim Schwantz | .30 | .10 |
| ❑ 278 Aaron Hayden | .30 | .10 |
| ❑ 279 Ryan McNeil | .30 | .10 |
| ❑ 280 LeRoy Butler | .30 | .10 |
| ❑ 281 Craig Newsome | .30 | .10 |
| ❑ 282 Bill Romanowski | .30 | .10 |
| ❑ 283 Michael Bankston | .30 | .10 |
| ❑ 284 Kevin Smith | .30 | .10 |
| ❑ 285 Byron Bam Morris | .30 | .10 |
| ❑ 286 Darnay Scott | .50 | .20 |
| ❑ 287 David LaFleur RC | .30 | .10 |
| ❑ 288 Randall Cunningham | .75 | .30 |
| ❑ 289 Eric Davis | .30 | .10 |
| ❑ 290 Todd Collins | .30 | .10 |
| ❑ 291 Steve Tovar | .30 | .10 |
| ❑ 292 Jermaine Lewis | .75 | .30 |
| ❑ 293 Alfred Williams | .30 | .10 |
| ❑ 294 Brad Johnson | .75 | .30 |
| ❑ 295 Charles Johnson | .30 | .20 |
| ❑ 296 Ted Johnson | .30 | .10 |
| ❑ 297 Merton Hanks | .30 | .10 |
| ❑ 298 Andre Coleman | .30 | .10 |
| ❑ 299 Keith Jackson | .50 | .20 |
| ❑ 300 Terry Kirby | .50 | .20 |
| ❑ 301 Tony Banks | .50 | .20 |
| ❑ 302 Terrance Shaw | .30 | .10 |
| ❑ 303 Bobby Engram | .50 | .20 |
| ❑ 304 Hugh Douglas | .30 | .10 |
| ❑ 305 Lawyer Milloy | .50 | .20 |
| ❑ 306 James Jett | .50 | .20 |
| ❑ 307 Joey Kent RC | .75 | .30 |
| ❑ 308 Rodney Hampton | .50 | .20 |
| ❑ 309 Dewayne Washington | .30 | .10 |
| ❑ 310 Kevin Lockett RC | .50 | .20 |
| ❑ 311 Ki-Jana Carter | .30 | .10 |
| ❑ 312 Jeff Lageman | .30 | .10 |
| ❑ 313 Don Beebe | .30 | .10 |
| ❑ 314 Willie Williams | .30 | .10 |
| ❑ 315 Tyrone Wheatley | .50 | .20 |
| ❑ 316 Leslie O'Neal | .30 | .10 |
| ❑ 317 Quinn Early | .30 | .10 |
| ❑ 318 Sean Gilbert | .30 | .10 |
| ❑ 319 Tim Bowens | .30 | .10 |
| ❑ 320 Sean Dawkins | .30 | .10 |
| ❑ 321 Ken Dilger | .30 | .10 |
| ❑ 322 George Koonce | .30 | .10 |
| ❑ 323 Jevon Langford | .30 | .10 |
| ❑ 324 Mike Caldwell | .30 | .10 |
| ❑ 325 Orlando Pace RC | .75 | .30 |
| ❑ 326 Garrison Hearst | .50 | .20 |
| ❑ 327 Mike Tomczak | .30 | .10 |
| ❑ 328 Rob Moore | .50 | .20 |
| ❑ 329 Andre Reed | .50 | .20 |
| ❑ 330 Kimble Anders | .50 | .20 |
| ❑ 331 Qadry Ismail | .50 | .20 |
| ❑ 332 Eric Allen | .30 | .10 |
| ❑ 333 Dave Brown | .30 | .10 |
| ❑ 334 Bennie Blades | .30 | .10 |
| ❑ 335 Jamal Anderson | .75 | .30 |
| ❑ 336 John Lynch | .50 | .20 |
| ❑ 337 Tyrone Hughes | .30 | .10 |

| | | |
|---|---|---|
| ❑ 338 Ronnie Harmon | .30 | .10 |
| ❑ 339 Rae Carruth RC | .30 | .10 |
| ❑ 340 Robert Brooks | .50 | .20 |
| ❑ P1 Antonio Freeman Prototype | .50 | .20 |
| ❑ P20 Curtis Martin Prototype | 1.00 | .40 |
| ❑ P21 Deion Sanders Prototype | .50 | .20 |
| ❑ P30 Kerry Collins Prototype | .75 | .30 |
| ❑ P47 Shannon Sharpe Prototype | .50 | .20 |
| ❑ P84 Edgar Bennett Prototype | .50 | .20 |

**1998 Stadium Club**

| | | |
|---|---|---|
| ❑ COMPLETE SET (195) | 60.00 | 25.00 |
| ❑ 1 Barry Sanders | 2.50 | 1.00 |
| ❑ 2 Tony Martin | .50 | .20 |
| ❑ 3 Fred Lane | .30 | .10 |
| ❑ 4 Darren Woodson | .30 | .10 |
| ❑ 5 Andre Reed | .50 | .20 |
| ❑ 6 Blaine Bishop | .30 | .10 |
| ❑ 7 Robert Brooks | .50 | .20 |
| ❑ 8 Tony Banks | .50 | .20 |
| ❑ 9 Charles Way | .30 | .10 |
| ❑ 10 Mark Brunell | .75 | .30 |
| ❑ 11 Darrell Green | .50 | .20 |
| ❑ 12 Aeneas Williams | .30 | .10 |
| ❑ 13 Rob Johnson | .50 | .20 |
| ❑ 14 Deion Sanders | .75 | .30 |
| ❑ 15 Marshall Faulk | 1.00 | .40 |
| ❑ 16 Stephen Boyd | .30 | .10 |
| ❑ 17 Adrian Murrell | .50 | .20 |
| ❑ 18 Wayne Chrebet | .75 | .30 |
| ❑ 19 Michael Sinclair | .30 | .10 |
| ❑ 20 Dan Marino | 3.00 | 1.25 |
| ❑ 21 Willie Davis | .30 | .10 |
| ❑ 22 Chris Warren | .50 | .20 |
| ❑ 23 John Mobley | .30 | .10 |
| ❑ 24 Shannon Sharpe | .50 | .20 |
| ❑ 25 Thurman Thomas | .75 | .30 |
| ❑ 26 Corey Dillon | .75 | .30 |
| ❑ 27 Zach Thomas | .75 | .30 |
| ❑ 28 James Jett | .50 | .20 |
| ❑ 29 Eric Metcalf | .30 | .10 |
| ❑ 30 Drew Bledsoe | 1.25 | .50 |
| ❑ 31 Scott Greene | .30 | .10 |
| ❑ 32 Simeon Rice | .50 | .20 |
| ❑ 33 Robert Smith | .75 | .30 |
| ❑ 34 Keenan McCardell | .50 | .20 |
| ❑ 35 Jessie Armstead | .30 | .10 |
| ❑ 36 Jerry Rice | 1.50 | .60 |
| ❑ 37 Eric Green | .30 | .10 |
| ❑ 38 Terrell Owens | .75 | .30 |
| ❑ 39 Tim Brown | .75 | .30 |
| ❑ 40 Vinny Testaverde | .50 | .20 |
| ❑ 41 Brian Stablein | .30 | .10 |
| ❑ 42 Bert Emanuel | .50 | .20 |
| ❑ 43 Terry Glenn | .75 | .30 |
| ❑ 44 Chad Cota | .30 | .10 |
| ❑ 45 Jermaine Lewis | .50 | .20 |
| ❑ 46 Derrick Thomas | .75 | .30 |
| ❑ 47 O.J. McDuffie | .50 | .20 |
| ❑ 48 Frank Wycheck | .30 | .10 |
| ❑ 49 Steve Broussard | .30 | .10 |
| ❑ 50 Terrell Davis | .75 | .30 |
| ❑ 51 Eric Allen | .30 | .10 |
| ❑ 52 Napoleon Kaufman | .75 | .30 |
| ❑ 53 Dan Wilkinson | .30 | .10 |
| ❑ 54 Kerry Collins | .50 | .20 |
| ❑ 55 Frank Sanders | .50 | .20 |
| ❑ 56 Jeff Burris | .30 | .10 |

| | | |
|---|---|---|
| ❑ 57 Michael Westbrook | .50 | .20 |
| ❑ 58 Michael McCrary | .30 | .10 |
| ❑ 59 Bobby Hoying | .50 | .20 |
| ❑ 60 Jerome Bettis | .75 | .30 |
| ❑ 61 Amp Lee | .30 | .10 |
| ❑ 62 Levon Kirkland | .30 | .10 |
| ❑ 63 Dana Stubblefield | .30 | .10 |
| ❑ 64 Terance Mathis | .50 | .20 |
| ❑ 65 Mark Chmura | .50 | .20 |
| ❑ 66 Bryant Westbrook | .30 | .10 |
| ❑ 67 Rod Smith | .50 | .20 |
| ❑ 68 Derrick Alexander | .50 | .20 |
| ❑ 69 Jason Taylor | .50 | .20 |
| ❑ 70 Eddie George | .75 | .30 |
| ❑ 71 Elvis Grbac | .50 | .20 |
| ❑ 72 Junior Seau | .75 | .30 |
| ❑ 73 Marvin Harrison | .75 | .30 |
| ❑ 74 Neil O'Donnell | .50 | .20 |
| ❑ 75 Johnnie Morton | .50 | .20 |
| ❑ 76 John Randle | .50 | .20 |
| ❑ 77 Danny Kanell | .50 | .20 |
| ❑ 78 Charlie Garner | .50 | .20 |
| ❑ 79 J.J. Stokes | .50 | .20 |
| ❑ 80 Troy Aikman | 1.50 | .60 |
| ❑ 81 Gus Frerotte | .30 | .10 |
| ❑ 82 Jake Plummer | .75 | .30 |
| ❑ 83 Andre Hastings | .30 | .10 |
| ❑ 84 Steve Atwater | .30 | .10 |
| ❑ 85 Larry Centers | .30 | .10 |
| ❑ 86 Kevin Hardy | .30 | .10 |
| ❑ 87 Willie McGinest | .30 | .10 |
| ❑ 88 Joey Galloway | .50 | .20 |
| ❑ 89 Charles Johnson | .30 | .10 |
| ❑ 90 Warrick Dunn | .75 | .30 |
| ❑ 91 Derrick Rodgers | .30 | .10 |
| ❑ 92 Aaron Glenn | .30 | .10 |
| ❑ 93 Shawn Jefferson | .30 | .10 |
| ❑ 94 Antonio Freeman | .75 | .30 |
| ❑ 95 Jake Reed | .50 | .20 |
| ❑ 96 Reidel Anthony | .50 | .20 |
| ❑ 97 Cris Dishman | .30 | .10 |
| ❑ 98 Jason Sehorn | .50 | .20 |
| ❑ 99 Herman Moore | .50 | .20 |
| ❑ 100 John Elway | 3.00 | 1.25 |
| ❑ 101 Brad Johnson | .75 | .30 |
| ❑ 102 Jeff George | .50 | .20 |
| ❑ 103 Emmitt Smith | 2.50 | 1.00 |
| ❑ 104 Steve McNair | .75 | .30 |
| ❑ 105 Ed McCaffrey | .50 | .20 |
| ❑ 106 Errict Rhett | .50 | .20 |
| ❑ 107 Dorsey Levens | .75 | .30 |
| ❑ 108 Michael Jackson | .30 | .10 |
| ❑ 109 Carl Pickens | .50 | .20 |
| ❑ 110 James Stewart | .50 | .20 |
| ❑ 111 Karim Abdul-Jabbar | .50 | .20 |
| ❑ 112 Jim Harbaugh | .50 | .20 |
| ❑ 113 Yancey Thigpen | .30 | .10 |
| ❑ 114 Chad Brown | .30 | .10 |
| ❑ 115 Chris Sanders | .30 | .10 |
| ❑ 116 Cris Carter | .75 | .30 |
| ❑ 117 Glenn Foley | .50 | .20 |
| ❑ 118 Ben Coates | .50 | .20 |
| ❑ 119 Jamal Anderson | .75 | .30 |
| ❑ 120 Steve Young | 1.00 | .40 |
| ❑ 121 Scott Mitchell | .50 | .20 |
| ❑ 122 Rob Moore | .50 | .20 |
| ❑ 123 Bobby Engram | .50 | .20 |
| ❑ 124 Rod Woodson | .50 | .20 |
| ❑ 125 Terry Allen | .75 | .30 |
| ❑ 126 Warren Sapp | .50 | .20 |
| ❑ 127 Irving Fryar | .50 | .20 |
| ❑ 128 Isaac Bruce | .75 | .30 |
| ❑ 129 Rae Carruth | .30 | .10 |
| ❑ 130 Sean Dawkins | .30 | .10 |
| ❑ 131 Andre Rison | .50 | .20 |
| ❑ 132 Kevin Greene | .50 | .20 |
| ❑ 133 Warren Moon | .75 | .30 |
| ❑ 134 Keyshawn Johnson | .75 | .30 |
| ❑ 135 Jay Graham | .30 | .10 |
| ❑ 136 Mike Alstott | .75 | .30 |
| ❑ 137 Peter Boulware | .30 | .10 |
| ❑ 138 Doug Evans | .30 | .10 |
| ❑ 139 Jimmy Smith | .50 | .20 |
| ❑ 140 Kordell Stewart | .75 | .30 |
| ❑ 141 Tamarick Vanover | .30 | .10 |

|  |  | | |
|---|---|---|---|
| 142 | Chris Slade | .30 | .10 |
| 143 | Freddie Jones | .30 | .10 |
| 144 | Erik Kramer | .30 | .10 |
| 145 | Ricky Watters | .50 | .20 |
| 146 | Chris Chandler | .50 | .20 |
| 147 | Garrison Hearst | .75 | .30 |
| 148 | Trent Dilfer | .75 | .30 |
| 149 | Bruce Smith | .50 | .20 |
| 150 | Brett Favre | 3.00 | 1.25 |
| 151 | Will Blackwell | .30 | .10 |
| 152 | Rickey Dudley | .30 | .10 |
| 153 | Natrone Means | .50 | .20 |
| 154 | Curtis Conway | .50 | .20 |
| 155 | Tony Gonzalez | .50 | .20 |
| 156 | Jeff Blake | .50 | .20 |
| 157 | Michael Irvin | .75 | .30 |
| 158 | Curtis Martin | .75 | .30 |
| 159 | Tim McDonald | .30 | .10 |
| 160 | Wesley Walls | .50 | .20 |
| 161 | Michael Strahan | .50 | .20 |
| 162 | Reggie White | .75 | .30 |
| 163 | Jeff Graham | .30 | .10 |
| 164 | Ray Lewis | .75 | .30 |
| 165 | Antowain Smith | .75 | .30 |
| 166 | Ryan Leaf RC | 2.50 | 1.00 |
| 167 | Jerome Pathon RC | 2.50 | 1.00 |
| 168 | Duane Starks RC | 1.25 | .50 |
| 169 | Brian Simmons RC | 2.00 | .75 |
| 170 | Pat Johnson RC | 2.00 | .75 |
| 171 | Keith Brooking RC | 2.50 | 1.00 |
| 172 | Kevin Dyson RC | 2.50 | 1.00 |
| 173 | Robert Edwards RC | 2.00 | .75 |
| 174 | Grant Wistrom RC | 2.00 | .75 |
| 175 | Curtis Enis RC | 1.25 | .50 |
| 176 | John Avery RC | 2.00 | .75 |
| 177 | Jason Peter RC | 1.25 | .50 |
| 178 | Brian Griese RC | 5.00 | 2.00 |
| 179 | Tavian Banks RC | 2.00 | .75 |
| 180 | Andre Wadsworth RC | 2.00 | .75 |
| 181 | Skip Hicks RC | 2.00 | .75 |
| 182 | Hines Ward RC | 10.00 | 5.00 |
| 183 | Greg Ellis RC | 1.25 | .50 |
| 184 | Robert Holcombe RC | 2.00 | .75 |
| 185 | Joe Jurevicius RC | 2.50 | 1.00 |
| 186 | Takeo Spikes RC | 2.50 | 1.00 |
| 187 | Ahman Green RC | 6.00 | 2.50 |
| 188 | Jacquez Green RC | 2.00 | .75 |
| 189 | Randy Moss RC | 15.00 | 6.00 |
| 190 | Charles Woodson RC | 3.00 | 1.25 |
| 191 | Fred Taylor RC | 4.00 | 1.50 |
| 192 | Marcus Nash RC | 1.25 | .50 |
| 193 | Germane Crowell RC | 2.00 | .75 |
| 194 | Tim Dwight RC | 2.50 | 1.00 |
| 195 | Peyton Manning RC | 25.00 | 10.00 |

## 1999 Stadium Club

| | | | |
|---|---|---|---|
| COMPLETE SET (200) | | 60.00 | 25.00 |
| COMP.SET w/o SP's (175) | | 20.00 | 7.50 |
| UNPRICED 1/1 PRESS PLATES EXIST | | | |
| FOUR DIFF.PP's PRODUCED PER CARD | | | |
| 1 | Dan Marino | 2.50 | 1.00 |
| 2 | Andre Reed | .50 | .20 |
| 3 | Michael Westbrook | .50 | .20 |
| 4 | Isaac Bruce | .75 | .30 |
| 5 | Curtis Martin | .75 | .30 |
| 6 | Courtney Hawkins | .30 | .10 |
| 7 | Charles Way | .30 | .10 |
| 8 | Terrell Owens | .75 | .30 |
| 9 | Warrick Dunn | .75 | .30 |
| 10 | Jake Plummer | .50 | .20 |
| 11 | Chad Brown | .30 | .10 |
| 12 | Yancey Thigpen | .30 | .10 |
| 13 | Lamar Thomas | .30 | .10 |
| 14 | Keenan McCardell | .50 | .20 |
| 15 | Shannon Sharpe | .50 | .20 |
| 16 | Robert Brooks | .50 | .20 |
| 17 | Cameron Cleeland | .30 | .10 |
| 18 | Derrick Thomas | .75 | .30 |
| 19 | Mark Brunell | .75 | .30 |
| 20 | Jamal Anderson | .75 | .30 |
| 21 | Germane Crowell | .30 | .10 |
| 22 | Rod Smith | .50 | .20 |
| 23 | Ty Law | .50 | .20 |
| 24 | Cris Carter | .75 | .30 |
| 25 | Terrell Davis | .75 | .30 |
| 26 | Takeo Spikes | .30 | .10 |
| 27 | Tim Biakabutuka | .50 | .20 |
| 28 | Jermaine Lewis | .50 | .20 |
| 29 | Adrian Murrell | .50 | .20 |
| 30 | Doug Flutie | .75 | .30 |
| 31 | Curtis Enis | .30 | .10 |
| 32 | Skip Hicks | .30 | .10 |
| 33 | Steve McNair | .75 | .30 |
| 34 | Charles Woodson | .75 | .30 |
| 35 | Jessie Armstead | .30 | .10 |
| 36 | Shawn Springs | .30 | .10 |
| 37 | Levon Kirkland | .30 | .10 |
| 38 | Freddie Jones | .30 | .10 |
| 39 | Warren Sapp | .30 | .10 |
| 40 | Emmitt Smith | 1.50 | .60 |
| 41 | Reidel Anthony | .30 | .10 |
| 42 | Tony Simmons | .30 | .10 |
| 43 | Andre Hastings | .30 | .10 |
| 44 | Byron Bam Morris | .30 | .10 |
| 45 | Jimmy Smith | .50 | .20 |
| 46 | Antonio Freeman | .75 | .30 |
| 47 | Herman Moore | .50 | .20 |
| 48 | Muhsin Muhammad | .30 | .10 |
| 49 | Chris Chandler | .50 | .20 |
| 50 | John Elway | 2.50 | 1.00 |
| 51 | Aeneas Williams | .30 | .10 |
| 52 | Bobby Engram | .30 | .10 |
| 53 | Keith Poole | .30 | .10 |
| 54 | Zach Thomas | .75 | .30 |
| 55 | Mike Alstott | .75 | .30 |
| 56 | Junior Seau | .75 | .30 |
| 57 | Aaron Glenn | .30 | .10 |
| 58 | Darrell Green | .30 | .10 |
| 59 | Thurman Thomas | .50 | .20 |
| 60 | Troy Aikman | 1.50 | .60 |
| 61 | Bill Romanowski | .30 | .10 |
| 62 | Wesley Walls | .30 | .10 |
| 63 | Andre Wadsworth | .30 | .10 |
| 64 | Robert Smith | .75 | .30 |
| 65 | Elvis Grbac | .50 | .20 |
| 66 | Terry Fair | .30 | .10 |
| 67 | Ben Coates | .50 | .20 |
| 68 | Bert Emanuel | .30 | .10 |
| 69 | Jacquez Green | .30 | .10 |
| 70 | Barry Sanders | 2.50 | 1.00 |
| 71 | James Jett | .50 | .20 |
| 72 | Gary Brown | .30 | .10 |
| 73 | Stephen Alexander | .30 | .10 |
| 74 | Wayne Chrebet | .50 | .20 |
| 75 | Drew Bledsoe | 1.00 | .40 |
| 76 | John Lynch | .50 | .20 |
| 77 | Jake Reed | .30 | .10 |
| 78 | Marvin Harrison | .75 | .30 |
| 79 | Johnnie Morton | .50 | .20 |
| 80 | Brett Favre | 2.50 | 1.00 |
| 81 | Charlie Batch | .75 | .30 |
| 82 | Antowain Smith | .75 | .30 |
| 83 | Michael Ricks | .30 | .10 |
| 84 | Derrick Mayes | .30 | .10 |
| 85 | John Mobley | .30 | .10 |
| 86 | Ernie Mills | .30 | .10 |
| 87 | Jeff Blake | .50 | .20 |
| 88 | Curtis Conway | .50 | .20 |
| 89 | Bruce Smith | .50 | .20 |
| 90 | Peyton Manning | 2.50 | 1.00 |
| 91 | Tyrone Davis | .30 | .10 |
| 92 | Ray Buchanan | .30 | .10 |
| 93 | Tim Dwight | .75 | .30 |
| 94 | O.J. McDuffie | .50 | .20 |
| 95 | Vonnie Holliday | .30 | .10 |
| 96 | Jon Kitna | .75 | .30 |
| 97 | Trent Dilfer | .50 | .20 |
| 98 | Jerome Bettis | .75 | .30 |
| 99 | Dedric Ward | .30 | .10 |
| 100 | Fred Taylor | .75 | .30 |
| 101 | Ike Hilliard | .30 | .10 |
| 102 | Frank Wycheck | .30 | .10 |
| 103 | Eric Moulds | .75 | .30 |
| 104 | Rob Moore | .50 | .20 |
| 105 | Ed McCaffrey | .50 | .20 |
| 106 | Carl Pickens | .50 | .20 |
| 107 | Priest Holmes | 1.25 | .50 |
| 108 | Kevin Hardy | .30 | .10 |
| 109 | Terry Glenn | .75 | .30 |
| 110 | Keyshawn Johnson | .75 | .30 |
| 111 | Karim Abdul-Jabbar | .50 | .20 |
| 112 | Stephen Boyd | .30 | .10 |
| 113 | Ahman Green | .75 | .30 |
| 114 | Duce Staley | .75 | .30 |
| 115 | Vinny Testaverde | .50 | .20 |
| 116 | Napoleon Kaufman | .75 | .30 |
| 117 | Frank Sanders | .30 | .10 |
| 118 | Peter Boulware | .30 | .10 |
| 119 | Kevin Greene | .30 | .10 |
| 120 | Steve Young | 1.00 | .40 |
| 121 | Darnay Scott | .30 | .10 |
| 122 | Deion Sanders | .75 | .30 |
| 123 | Corey Dillon | .75 | .30 |
| 124 | Randall Cunningham | .75 | .30 |
| 125 | Eddie George | .75 | .30 |
| 126 | Derrick Alexander | .30 | .10 |
| 127 | Mark Chmura | .30 | .10 |
| 128 | Michael Sinclair | .30 | .10 |
| 129 | Rickey Dudley | .30 | .10 |
| 130 | Joey Galloway | .50 | .20 |
| 131 | Michael Strahan | .50 | .20 |
| 132 | Ricky Proehl | .30 | .10 |
| 133 | Natrone Means | .50 | .20 |
| 134 | Dorsey Levens | .75 | .30 |
| 135 | Andre Rison | .30 | .10 |
| 136 | Alonzo Mayes | .30 | .10 |
| 137 | John Randle | .50 | .20 |
| 138 | Terance Mathis | .50 | .20 |
| 139 | Rae Carruth | .30 | .10 |
| 140 | Jerry Rice | 1.50 | .60 |
| 141 | Michael Irvin | .50 | .20 |
| 142 | Oronde Gadsden | .50 | .20 |
| 143 | Jerome Pathon | .50 | .20 |
| 144 | Ricky Watters | .50 | .20 |
| 145 | J.J. Stokes | .50 | .20 |
| 146 | Kordell Stewart | .50 | .20 |
| 147 | Tim Brown | .75 | .30 |
| 148 | Garrison Hearst | .50 | .20 |
| 149 | Tony Gonzalez | .75 | .30 |
| 150 | Randy Moss | 2.00 | .75 |
| 151 | Daunte Culpepper RC | 6.00 | 2.50 |
| 152 | Amos Zereoue RC | 2.00 | .75 |
| 153 | Champ Bailey RC | 2.50 | 1.00 |
| 154 | Peerless Price RC | 2.00 | .75 |
| 155 | Edgerrin James RC | 6.00 | 2.50 |
| 156 | Joe Germaine RC | 1.50 | .60 |
| 157 | David Boston RC | 2.00 | .75 |
| 158 | Kevin Faulk RC | 2.00 | .75 |
| 159 | Troy Edwards RC | 1.50 | .60 |
| 160 | Akili Smith RC | 1.50 | .60 |
| 161 | Kevin Johnson RC | 2.00 | .75 |
| 162 | Rob Konrad RC | 1.50 | .60 |
| 163 | Shaun King RC | 1.50 | .60 |
| 164 | James Johnson RC | 1.50 | .60 |
| 165 | Donovan McNabb RC | 8.00 | 3.00 |
| 166 | Torry Holt RC | 4.00 | 1.50 |
| 167 | Mike Cloud RC | 1.50 | .60 |
| 168 | Sedrick Irvin RC | 1.00 | .40 |
| 169 | Cade McNown RC | 1.50 | .60 |
| 170 | Ricky Williams RC | 3.00 | 1.25 |
| 171 | Karsten Bailey RC | 1.50 | .60 |
| 172 | Cecil Collins RC | 1.00 | .40 |
| 173 | Brock Huard RC | 2.00 | .75 |
| 174 | D'Wayne Bates RC | 1.50 | .60 |
| 175 | Tim Couch RC | 2.00 | .75 |
| 176 | Torrance Small | .30 | .10 |
| 177 | Warren Moon | .75 | .30 |
| 178 | Rocket Ismail | .50 | .20 |

| □ 179 Marshall Faulk | 1.00 | .40 |
| □ 180 Trent Green | .75 | .30 |
| □ 181 Sean Dawkins | .30 | .10 |
| □ 182 Pete Mitchell | .30 | .10 |
| □ 183 Jeff Graham | .30 | .10 |
| □ 184 Eddie Kennison | .50 | .20 |
| □ 185 Kerry Collins | .50 | .20 |
| □ 186 Eric Green | .30 | .10 |
| □ 187 Kyle Brady | .30 | .10 |
| □ 188 Tony Martin | .50 | .20 |
| □ 189 Jim Harbaugh | .50 | .20 |
| □ 190 Erik Kramer | .30 | .10 |
| □ 191 Steve Atwater | .30 | .10 |
| □ 192 Chad Bratzke | .30 | .10 |
| □ 193 Charles Johnson | .30 | .10 |
| □ 194 Damon Gibson | .30 | .10 |
| □ 195 Jeff George | .50 | .20 |
| □ 196 Scott Mitchell | .30 | .10 |
| □ 197 Terry Kirby | .30 | .10 |
| □ 198 Rich Gannon | .75 | .30 |
| □ 199 Chris Spielman | .30 | .10 |
| □ 200 Brad Johnson | .75 | .30 |
| □ PP4 Emmitt Smith PROMO | 3.00 | 1.25 |

## 2000 Stadium Club

| □ COMPLETE SET (175) | 50.00 | 20.00 |
| □ COMP.SET w/o SP's (150) | 20.00 | 7.50 |
| □ 1 Peyton Manning | 1.50 | .60 |
| □ 2 Pete Mitchell | .25 | .08 |
| □ 3 Napoleon Kaufman | .40 | .15 |
| □ 4 Mikhael Ricks | .25 | .08 |
| □ 5 Mike Alstott | .60 | .25 |
| □ 6 Brad Johnson | .40 | .15 |
| □ 7 Tony Gonzalez | .40 | .15 |
| □ 8 Germane Crowell | .25 | .08 |
| □ 9 Marcus Robinson | .60 | .25 |
| □ 10 Stephen Davis | .60 | .25 |
| □ 11 Terance Mathis | .40 | .15 |
| □ 12 Jake Plummer | .40 | .15 |
| □ 13 Qadry Ismail | .40 | .15 |
| □ 14 Cade McNown | .25 | .08 |
| □ 15 Zach Thomas | .60 | .25 |
| □ 16 Curtis Martin | .60 | .25 |
| □ 17 Torrance Small | .25 | .08 |
| □ 18 Steve McNair | .60 | .25 |
| □ 19 Jim Harbaugh | .40 | .15 |
| □ 20 Keyshawn Johnson | .60 | .25 |
| □ 21 Antonio Freeman | .60 | .25 |
| □ 22 Ed McCaffrey | .60 | .25 |
| □ 23 Elvis Grbac | .40 | .15 |
| □ 24 Peerless Price | .40 | .15 |
| □ 25 Jerome Bettis | .60 | .25 |
| □ 26 Yancey Thigpen | .25 | .08 |
| □ 27 Jake Delhomme RC | 3.00 | 1.25 |
| □ 28 Keith Poole | .25 | .08 |
| □ 29 Carl Pickens | .40 | .15 |
| □ 30 Jerry Rice | 1.25 | .50 |
| □ 31 Rob Moore | .40 | .15 |
| □ 32 Reidel Anthony | .25 | .08 |
| □ 33 Jimmy Smith | .40 | .15 |
| □ 34 Ray Lucas | .40 | .15 |
| □ 35 Troy Aikman | 1.25 | .50 |
| □ 36 Steve Beuerlein | .40 | .15 |
| □ 37 Charlie Batch | .60 | .25 |
| □ 38 Derrick Mayes | .40 | .15 |
| □ 39 Tim Brown | .60 | .25 |
| □ 40 Eddie George | .60 | .25 |
| □ 41 O.J. McDuffie | .40 | .15 |

| □ 42 Ike Hilliard | .40 | .15 |
| □ 43 Bill Schroeder | .40 | .15 |
| □ 44 Jim Miller | .25 | .08 |
| □ 45 Chris Chandler | .40 | .15 |
| □ 46 Fred Taylor | .60 | .25 |
| □ 47 Ricky Watters | .40 | .15 |
| □ 48 Tyrone Wheatley | .40 | .15 |
| □ 49 Bruce Smith | .40 | .15 |
| □ 50 Marshall Faulk | .75 | .30 |
| □ 51 Kevin Carter | .25 | .08 |
| □ 52 Champ Bailey | .40 | .15 |
| □ 53 Troy Edwards | .25 | .08 |
| □ 54 Doug Flutie | .60 | .25 |
| □ 55 Charles Johnson | .40 | .15 |
| □ 56 Michael Westbrook | .40 | .15 |
| □ 57 Frank Wycheck | .25 | .08 |
| □ 58 Drew Bledsoe | .75 | .30 |
| □ 59 Terrence Wilkins | .25 | .08 |
| □ 60 Ricky Williams | .60 | .25 |
| □ 61 Rod Smith | .40 | .15 |
| □ 62 Errict Rhett | .40 | .15 |
| □ 63 Vinny Testaverde | .40 | .15 |
| □ 64 Jacquez Green | .25 | .08 |
| □ 65 Curtis Conway | .40 | .15 |
| □ 66 Wayne Chrebet | .40 | .15 |
| □ 67 Albert Connell | .25 | .08 |
| □ 68 Kordell Stewart | .40 | .15 |
| □ 69 Bert Emanuel | .25 | .08 |
| □ 70 Randy Moss | 1.25 | .50 |
| □ 71 Akili Smith | .25 | .08 |
| □ 72 Brian Griese | .60 | .25 |
| □ 73 Frank Sanders | .40 | .15 |
| □ 74 Wesley Walls | .40 | .15 |
| □ 75 Michael Pittman | .25 | .08 |
| □ 76 Steve Young | .75 | .30 |
| □ 77 Jevon Kearse | .60 | .25 |
| □ 78 Az-Zahir Hakim | .40 | .15 |
| □ 79 James Stewart | .40 | .15 |
| □ 80 Brett Favre | 2.00 | .75 |
| □ 81 Dan Marino | 2.00 | .75 |
| □ 82 Joe Horn | .40 | .15 |
| □ 83 Mark Brunell | .60 | .25 |
| □ 84 Eddie Kennison | .40 | .15 |
| □ 85 Deion Sanders | .60 | .25 |
| □ 86 Priest Holmes | .75 | .30 |
| □ 87 Terry Glenn | .40 | .15 |
| □ 88 Olandis Gary | .60 | .25 |
| □ 89 Patrick Jeffers | .60 | .25 |
| □ 90 Emmitt Smith | 1.25 | .50 |
| □ 91 J.J. Stokes | .40 | .15 |
| □ 92 Warrick Dunn | .60 | .25 |
| □ 93 Damon Huard | .25 | .08 |
| □ 94 Herman Moore | .60 | .25 |
| □ 95 Corey Dillon | .60 | .25 |
| □ 96 Joey Galloway | .40 | .15 |
| □ 97 Jamal Anderson | .60 | .25 |
| □ 98 Junior Seau | .60 | .25 |
| □ 99 Robert Smith | .60 | .25 |
| □ 100 Edgerrin James | 1.00 | .40 |
| □ 101 Derrick Alexander | .25 | .08 |
| □ 102 Johnnie Morton | .40 | .15 |
| □ 103 Sean Dawkins | .25 | .08 |
| □ 104 Derrick Brooks | .60 | .25 |
| □ 105 Rickey Dudley | .25 | .08 |
| □ 106 Keenan McCardell | .40 | .15 |
| □ 107 Kerry Collins | .40 | .15 |
| □ 108 Kevin Johnson | .60 | .25 |
| □ 109 Eric Moulds | .60 | .25 |
| □ 110 Terrell Davis | .60 | .25 |
| □ 111 Shawn Jefferson | .25 | .08 |
| □ 112 Donovan McNabb | 1.00 | .40 |
| □ 113 Tony Holt | .60 | .25 |
| □ 114 Marvin Harrison | .60 | .25 |
| □ 115 Amani Toomer | .40 | .15 |
| □ 116 Tony Martin | .40 | .15 |
| □ 117 Curtis Enis | .25 | .08 |
| □ 118 Tiki Barber | .60 | .25 |
| □ 119 Freddie Jones | .25 | .08 |
| □ 120 Muhsin Muhammad | .40 | .15 |
| □ 121 Shaun King | .60 | .25 |
| □ 122 Isaac Bruce | .60 | .25 |
| □ 123 Duce Staley | .60 | .25 |
| □ 124 Hardy Nickerson | .25 | .08 |
| □ 125 Corey Bradford | .40 | .15 |
| □ 126 Kevin Hardy | .25 | .08 |

| □ 127 Hines Ward | .60 | .25 |
| □ 128 Charlie Garner | .40 | .15 |
| □ 129 Warren Sapp | .40 | .15 |
| □ 130 Tim Couch | .40 | .15 |
| □ 131 Kevin Dyson | .40 | .15 |
| □ 132 Rocket Ismail | .40 | .15 |
| □ 133 Tim Dwight | .60 | .25 |
| □ 134 Darnay Scott | .40 | .15 |
| □ 135 Jeff George | .40 | .15 |
| □ 136 Dorsey Levens | .40 | .15 |
| □ 137 Jeff Blake | .40 | .15 |
| □ 138 Jon Kitna | .60 | .25 |
| □ 139 Rich Gannon | .60 | .25 |
| □ 140 Cris Carter | .60 | .25 |
| □ 141 Jeff Graham | .25 | .08 |
| □ 142 James Johnson | .25 | .08 |
| □ 143 Tim Biakabutuka | .40 | .15 |
| □ 144 Bobby Engram | .40 | .15 |
| □ 145 Tony Banks | .40 | .15 |
| □ 146 Shannon Sharpe | .40 | .15 |
| □ 147 Antowain Smith | .40 | .15 |
| □ 148 Terrell Owens | .60 | .25 |
| □ 149 Rob Johnson | .40 | .15 |
| □ 150 Kurt Warner | 1.25 | .50 |
| □ 151 Thomas Jones RC | 4.00 | 1.50 |
| □ 152 Chad Pennington RC | 6.00 | 2.50 |
| □ 153 Ron Dayne RC | 2.50 | 1.00 |
| □ 154 Tee Martin RC | 2.50 | 1.00 |
| □ 155 Reuben Droughns RC | 3.00 | 1.25 |
| □ 156 Jerry Porter RC | 3.00 | 1.25 |
| □ 157 R.Jay Soward RC | 2.00 | .75 |
| □ 158 Sylvester Morris RC | 2.00 | .75 |
| □ 159 Todd Pinkston RC | 2.00 | .75 |
| □ 160 Courtney Brown RC | 2.50 | 1.00 |
| □ 161 Travis Taylor RC | 2.50 | 1.00 |
| □ 162 Ron Dugans RC | 2.00 | .75 |
| □ 163 Laveranues Coles RC | 3.00 | 1.25 |
| □ 164 Joe Hamilton RC | 2.00 | .75 |
| □ 165 Curtis Keaton RC | 2.00 | .75 |
| □ 166 Bubba Franks RC | 2.50 | 1.00 |
| □ 167 Dennis Northcutt RC | 2.50 | 1.00 |
| □ 168 Chris Redman RC | 2.00 | .75 |
| □ 169 Travis Prentice RC | 2.00 | .75 |
| □ 170 Shaun Alexander RC | 8.00 | 3.00 |
| □ 171 Jamal Lewis RC | 6.00 | 2.50 |
| □ 172 Peter Warrick RC | 2.50 | 1.00 |
| □ 173 J.R. Redmond RC | 2.00 | .75 |
| □ 174 Trung Canidate RC | 2.00 | .75 |
| □ 175 Plaxico Burress RC | 5.00 | 2.00 |

## 2001 Stadium Club

| □ COMPLETE SET (175) | 120.00 | 60.00 |
| □ COMP.SET w/o SPs (125) | 20.00 | 7.50 |
| □ 1 Peyton Manning | 1.50 | .60 |
| □ 2 Akili Smith | .25 | .08 |
| □ 3 Brian Griese | .60 | .25 |
| □ 4 Wayne Chrebet | .40 | .15 |
| □ 5 Oronde Gadsden | .40 | .15 |
| □ 6 Marvin Harrison | .60 | .25 |
| □ 7 Charles Johnson | .25 | .08 |
| □ 8 Jay Fiedler | .40 | .15 |
| □ 9 Kerry Collins | .40 | .15 |
| □ 10 Troy Aikman | 1.00 | .40 |
| □ 11 Donovan McNabb | .75 | .30 |
| □ 12 Ike Hilliard | .40 | .15 |
| □ 13 Warrick Dunn | .60 | .25 |
| □ 14 Derrick Alexander | .40 | .15 |
| □ 15 Jake Plummer | .40 | .15 |

|  |  | | |
|---|---|---|---|
| ❑ 16 | Corey Dillon | .60 | .25 |
| ❑ 17 | Ahman Green | .60 | .25 |
| ❑ 18 | Keenan McCardell | .25 | .08 |
| ❑ 19 | Derrick Mason | .40 | .15 |
| ❑ 20 | Jerry Rice | 1.25 | .50 |
| ❑ 21 | Emmitt Smith | 1.25 | .50 |
| ❑ 22 | Dedric Ward | .25 | .08 |
| ❑ 23 | Jamal Anderson | .60 | .25 |
| ❑ 24 | Charlie Garner | .40 | .15 |
| ❑ 25 | Vinny Testaverde | .40 | .15 |
| ❑ 26 | Shaun Alexander | .75 | .30 |
| ❑ 27 | Terry Glenn | .40 | .15 |
| ❑ 28 | Cade McNown | .25 | .08 |
| ❑ 29 | Germane Crowell | .25 | .08 |
| ❑ 30 | Jeff Graham | .25 | .08 |
| ❑ 31 | Rich Gannon | .60 | .25 |
| ❑ 32 | Jevon Kearse | .40 | .15 |
| ❑ 33 | Shannon Sharpe | .40 | .15 |
| ❑ 34 | Marcus Robinson | .60 | .25 |
| ❑ 35 | Rod Smith | .40 | .15 |
| ❑ 36 | Curtis Martin | .60 | .25 |
| ❑ 37 | Robert Smith | .60 | .25 |
| ❑ 38 | Marshall Faulk | .75 | .30 |
| ❑ 39 | Tony Richardson | .25 | .08 |
| ❑ 40 | Travis Prentice | .25 | .08 |
| ❑ 41 | Edgerrin James | .75 | .30 |
| ❑ 42 | Duce Staley | .60 | .25 |
| ❑ 43 | Keyshawn Johnson | .60 | .25 |
| ❑ 44 | Joe Horn | .40 | .15 |
| ❑ 45 | Shawn Bryson | .25 | .08 |
| ❑ 46 | Ray Lewis | .60 | .25 |
| ❑ 47 | Fred Taylor | .60 | .25 |
| ❑ 48 | Jeff George | .40 | .15 |
| ❑ 49 | Sean Dawkins | .25 | .08 |
| ❑ 50 | Daunte Culpepper | .60 | .25 |
| ❑ 51 | Chris Chandler | .40 | .15 |
| ❑ 52 | Tim Couch | .40 | .15 |
| ❑ 53 | Trent Dilfer | .40 | .15 |
| ❑ 54 | Steve McNair | .60 | .25 |
| ❑ 55 | Kordell Stewart | .40 | .15 |
| ❑ 56 | Aaron Brooks | .60 | .25 |
| ❑ 57 | Michael Pittman | .25 | .08 |
| ❑ 58 | Bill Schroeder | .40 | .15 |
| ❑ 59 | Junior Seau | .60 | .25 |
| ❑ 60 | Kurt Warner | 1.25 | .50 |
| ❑ 61 | Drew Bledsoe | .75 | .30 |
| ❑ 62 | Steve Beuerlein | .40 | .15 |
| ❑ 63 | Mike Anderson | .60 | .25 |
| ❑ 64 | Brad Johnson | .60 | .25 |
| ❑ 65 | Tim Brown | .60 | .25 |
| ❑ 66 | Qadry Ismail | .40 | .15 |
| ❑ 67 | Doug Flutie | .60 | .25 |
| ❑ 68 | Terrell Owens | .60 | .25 |
| ❑ 69 | Rocket Ismail | .40 | .15 |
| ❑ 70 | Charlie Batch | .40 | .15 |
| ❑ 71 | Jerome Pathon | .40 | .15 |
| ❑ 72 | Peter Warrick | .60 | .25 |
| ❑ 73 | Hines Ward | .40 | .15 |
| ❑ 74 | Ron Dayne | .60 | .25 |
| ❑ 75 | Lamar Smith | .40 | .15 |
| ❑ 76 | Amani Toomer | .40 | .15 |
| ❑ 77 | Joey Galloway | .40 | .15 |
| ❑ 78 | James Allen | .40 | .15 |
| ❑ 79 | Isaac Bruce | .60 | .25 |
| ❑ 80 | David Boston | .60 | .25 |
| ❑ 81 | James Thrash | .40 | .15 |
| ❑ 82 | Tony Gonzalez | .40 | .15 |
| ❑ 83 | Jason Taylor | .25 | .08 |
| ❑ 84 | Ricky Watters | .40 | .15 |
| ❑ 85 | Terance Mathis | .40 | .15 |
| ❑ 86 | Troy Brown | .40 | .15 |
| ❑ 87 | Mark Brunell | .60 | .25 |
| ❑ 88 | Rob Johnson | .40 | .15 |
| ❑ 89 | Freddie Jones | .25 | .08 |
| ❑ 90 | Eddie George | .60 | .25 |
| ❑ 91 | Tiki Barber | .60 | .25 |
| ❑ 92 | Donald Hayes | .25 | .08 |
| ❑ 93 | Muhsin Muhammad | .40 | .15 |
| ❑ 94 | Johnnie Morton | .40 | .15 |
| ❑ 95 | Warren Sapp | .40 | .15 |
| ❑ 96 | Bobby Shaw | .25 | .08 |
| ❑ 97 | Randy Moss | 1.25 | .50 |
| ❑ 98 | Jerome Bettis | .60 | .25 |
| ❑ 99 | Antonio Freeman | .60 | .25 |
| ❑ 100 | Jamal Lewis | 1.00 | .40 |

|  |  | | |
|---|---|---|---|
| ❑ 101 | Andre Rison | .40 | .15 |
| ❑ 102 | Kevin Faulk | .40 | .15 |
| ❑ 103 | Jon Kitna | .60 | .25 |
| ❑ 104 | Shawn Jefferson | .25 | .08 |
| ❑ 105 | Kevin Johnson | .40 | .15 |
| ❑ 106 | Torry Holt | .60 | .25 |
| ❑ 107 | Cris Carter | .60 | .25 |
| ❑ 108 | Chad Lewis | .25 | .08 |
| ❑ 109 | Stephen Davis | .60 | .25 |
| ❑ 110 | Jeff Blake | .40 | .15 |
| ❑ 111 | Elvis Grbac | .40 | .15 |
| ❑ 112 | Ed McCaffrey | .60 | .25 |
| ❑ 113 | Tim Biakabutuka | .40 | .15 |
| ❑ 114 | Trent Green | .60 | .25 |
| ❑ 115 | Jeff Garcia | .60 | .25 |
| ❑ 116 | Jacquez Green | .25 | .08 |
| ❑ 117 | Shaun King | .25 | .08 |
| ❑ 118 | Jimmy Smith | .40 | .15 |
| ❑ 119 | James Stewart | .40 | .15 |
| ❑ 120 | Brian Urlacher | 1.00 | .40 |
| ❑ 121 | Tyrone Wheatley | .40 | .15 |
| ❑ 122 | J.R. Redmond | .25 | .08 |
| ❑ 123 | Eric Moulds | .40 | .15 |
| ❑ 124 | Ricky Williams | .60 | .25 |
| ❑ 125 | Brett Favre | 2.00 | .75 |
| ❑ 126 | Koren Robinson RC | 2.50 | 1.00 |
| ❑ 127 | Richard Seymour RC | 2.50 | 1.00 |
| ❑ 128 | Jamal Reynolds RC | 2.50 | 1.00 |
| ❑ 129 | Kevin Kasper RC | 2.50 | 1.00 |
| ❑ 130 | LaMont Jordan RC | 5.00 | 2.00 |
| ❑ 131 | Reggie Wayne RC | 5.00 | 2.00 |
| ❑ 132 | Travis Henry RC | 2.50 | 1.00 |
| ❑ 133 | Alge Crumpler RC | 3.00 | 1.25 |
| ❑ 134 | Quincy Carter RC | 2.50 | 1.00 |
| ❑ 135 | Michael Bennett RC | 2.50 | 1.00 |
| ❑ 136 | Jamie Winborn RC | 1.50 | .60 |
| ❑ 137 | Josh Heupel RC | 2.50 | 1.00 |
| ❑ 138 | Will Allen RC | 1.50 | .60 |
| ❑ 139 | Scotty Anderson RC | 1.50 | .60 |
| ❑ 140 | LaDainian Tomlinson RC | 25.00 | 10.00 |
| ❑ 141 | Freddie Mitchell RC | 2.50 | 1.00 |
| ❑ 142 | Gerard Warren RC | 2.50 | 1.00 |
| ❑ 143 | Chad Johnson RC | 6.00 | 2.50 |
| ❑ 144 | Todd Heap RC | 2.50 | 1.00 |
| ❑ 145 | Leonard Davis RC | 1.50 | .60 |
| ❑ 146 | Kevan Barlow RC | 2.50 | 1.00 |
| ❑ 147 | Correll Buckhalter RC | 3.00 | 1.25 |
| ❑ 148 | Fred Smoot RC | 2.50 | 1.00 |
| ❑ 149 | Steve Smith RC | 6.00 | 3.00 |
| ❑ 150 | David Terrell RC | 2.50 | 1.00 |
| ❑ 151 | Chris Chambers RC | 4.00 | 1.50 |
| ❑ 152 | Mike McMahon RC | 2.50 | 1.00 |
| ❑ 153 | Rudi Johnson RC | 5.00 | 2.00 |
| ❑ 154 | Marques Tuiasosopo RC | 2.50 | 1.00 |
| ❑ 155 | Deuce McAllister RC | 5.00 | 2.00 |
| ❑ 156 | Marcus Stroud RC | 2.50 | 1.00 |
| ❑ 157 | Bobby Newcombe RC | 1.50 | .60 |
| ❑ 158 | Rod Gardner RC | 2.50 | 1.00 |
| ❑ 159 | Drew Brees RC | 8.00 | 3.00 |
| ❑ 160 | Jesse Palmer RC | 2.50 | 1.00 |
| ❑ 161 | Derrick Gibson RC | 1.50 | .60 |
| ❑ 162 | James Jackson RC | 2.50 | 1.00 |
| ❑ 163 | Dan Morgan RC | 2.50 | 1.00 |
| ❑ 164 | Michael Vick RC | 5.00 | 2.00 |
| ❑ 165 | Snoop Minnis RC | 1.50 | .60 |
| ❑ 166 | Anthony Thomas RC | 2.50 | 1.00 |
| ❑ 167 | Andre Carter RC | 2.50 | 1.00 |
| ❑ 168 | Travis Minor RC | 1.50 | .60 |
| ❑ 169 | Quincy Morgan RC | 2.50 | 1.00 |
| ❑ 170 | Justin Smith RC | 2.50 | 1.00 |
| ❑ 171 | Tay Cody RC | 1.00 | .40 |
| ❑ 172 | Santana Moss RC | 4.00 | 1.50 |
| ❑ 173 | Sage Rosenfels RC | 2.50 | 1.00 |
| ❑ 174 | Robert Ferguson RC | 2.50 | 1.00 |
| ❑ 175 | Chris Weinke RC | 2.50 | 1.00 |

### 2002 Stadium Club

|  |  | | |
|---|---|---|---|
| ❑ COMP.SET w/o SP's (125) | | 25.00 | 10.00 |
| ❑ 1 | Randy Moss | 1.25 | .50 |
| ❑ 2 | Kordell Stewart | .40 | .15 |
| ❑ 3 | Marvin Harrison | .60 | .25 |
| ❑ 4 | Chris Weinke | .60 | .25 |
| ❑ 5 | James Allen | .40 | .15 |
| ❑ 6 | Michael Pittman | .25 | .08 |
| ❑ 7 | Quincy Carter | .40 | .15 |

|  |  | | |
|---|---|---|---|
| ❑ 8 | Mike Anderson | .60 | .25 |
| ❑ 9 | Mike McMahon | .60 | .25 |
| ❑ 10 | Chris Chambers | .60 | .25 |
| ❑ 11 | Laveranues Coles | .40 | .15 |
| ❑ 12 | Curtis Conway | .25 | .08 |
| ❑ 13 | Brad Johnson | .40 | .15 |
| ❑ 14 | Shaun Alexander | .75 | .30 |
| ❑ 15 | Jerry Rice | 1.25 | .50 |
| ❑ 16 | Rod Gardner | .40 | .15 |
| ❑ 17 | Derrick Mason | .40 | .15 |
| ❑ 18 | Tom Brady | 1.50 | .60 |
| ❑ 19 | Jimmy Smith | .40 | .15 |
| ❑ 20 | Tim Couch | .40 | .15 |
| ❑ 21 | Jim Miller | .25 | .08 |
| ❑ 22 | Eric Moulds | .40 | .15 |
| ❑ 23 | Michael Vick | 1.25 | .50 |
| ❑ 24 | Jon Kitna | .40 | .15 |
| ❑ 25 | Johnnie Morton | .40 | .15 |
| ❑ 26 | Priest Holmes | .75 | .30 |
| ❑ 27 | Aaron Brooks | .60 | .25 |
| ❑ 28 | Duce Staley | .60 | .25 |
| ❑ 29 | LaDainian Tomlinson | 1.00 | .40 |
| ❑ 30 | Lamar Smith | .40 | .15 |
| ❑ 31 | Rod Smith | .40 | .15 |
| ❑ 32 | Richard Huntley | .25 | .08 |
| ❑ 33 | Antonio Freeman | .60 | .25 |
| ❑ 34 | Amani Toomer | .40 | .15 |
| ❑ 35 | Hines Ward | .60 | .25 |
| ❑ 36 | Marshall Faulk | .60 | .25 |
| ❑ 37 | Steve McNair | .60 | .25 |
| ❑ 38 | Tim Brown | .60 | .25 |
| ❑ 39 | Curtis Martin | .60 | .25 |
| ❑ 40 | Kevin Johnson | .40 | .15 |
| ❑ 41 | Rob Johnson | .40 | .15 |
| ❑ 42 | Qadry Ismail | .40 | .15 |
| ❑ 43 | Daunte Culpepper | .60 | .25 |
| ❑ 44 | Willie Jackson | .25 | .08 |
| ❑ 45 | Jeff Garcia | .60 | .25 |
| ❑ 46 | Matt Hasselbeck | .40 | .15 |
| ❑ 47 | Corey Bradford | .25 | .08 |
| ❑ 48 | Snoop Minnis | .25 | .08 |
| ❑ 49 | Ron Dayne | .40 | .15 |
| ❑ 50 | Peyton Manning | 1.25 | .50 |
| ❑ 51 | Drew Bledsoe | .75 | .30 |
| ❑ 52 | Terry Glenn | .40 | .15 |
| ❑ 53 | Warrick Dunn | .60 | .25 |
| ❑ 54 | Mark Brunell | .60 | .25 |
| ❑ 55 | James Stewart | .40 | .15 |
| ❑ 56 | Muhsin Muhammad | .40 | .15 |
| ❑ 57 | Jake Plummer | .40 | .15 |
| ❑ 58 | Terance Mathis | .25 | .08 |
| ❑ 59 | Rocket Ismail | .40 | .15 |
| ❑ 60 | Joe Horn | .40 | .15 |
| ❑ 61 | Wayne Chrebet | .40 | .15 |
| ❑ 62 | James Thrash | .40 | .15 |
| ❑ 63 | Stephen Davis | .40 | .15 |
| ❑ 64 | Isaac Bruce | .60 | .25 |
| ❑ 65 | Peter Warrick | .40 | .15 |
| ❑ 66 | Anthony Thomas | .40 | .15 |
| ❑ 67 | Maurice Smith | .40 | .15 |
| ❑ 68 | Tony Gonzalez | .40 | .15 |
| ❑ 69 | Michael Bennett | .25 | .08 |
| ❑ 70 | Ike Hilliard | .40 | .15 |
| ❑ 71 | Plaxico Burress | .40 | .15 |
| ❑ 72 | Darrell Jackson | .40 | .15 |
| ❑ 73 | Kevan Barlow | .40 | .15 |
| ❑ 74 | Ray Lewis | .60 | .25 |
| ❑ 75 | Emmitt Smith | 1.50 | .60 |

| # | Player | Price | Price |
|---|---|---|---|
| 76 | Bill Schroeder | .40 | .15 |
| 77 | Az-Zahir Hakim | .25 | .08 |
| 78 | Troy Brown | .40 | .15 |
| 79 | Keyshawn Johnson | .60 | .25 |
| 80 | Tim Dwight | .40 | .15 |
| 81 | Peerless Price | .40 | .15 |
| 82 | Marty Booker | .25 | .08 |
| 83 | Terrell Davis | .60 | .25 |
| 84 | Dominic Rhodes | .40 | .15 |
| 85 | Jay Fiedler | .40 | .15 |
| 86 | Rich Gannon | .60 | .25 |
| 87 | Terrell Owens | .60 | .25 |
| 88 | Donald Hayes | .25 | .08 |
| 89 | Thomas Jones | .40 | .15 |
| 90 | Ricky Williams | .60 | .25 |
| 91 | Donovan McNabb | .75 | .30 |
| 92 | Eddie George | .60 | .25 |
| 93 | Germane Crowell | .25 | .08 |
| 94 | David Terrell | .60 | .25 |
| 95 | Alex Van Pelt | .25 | .08 |
| 96 | Antowain Smith | .40 | .15 |
| 97 | Jerome Bettis | .60 | .25 |
| 98 | Mike Alstott | .60 | .25 |
| 99 | Doug Flutie | .60 | .25 |
| 100 | Kurt Warner | .60 | .25 |
| 101 | Cris Carter | .60 | .25 |
| 102 | Oronde Gadsden | .40 | .15 |
| 103 | Ahman Green | .60 | .25 |
| 104 | Corey Dillon | .40 | .15 |
| 105 | Marcus Robinson | .40 | .15 |
| 106 | Shannon Sharpe | .40 | .15 |
| 107 | Kerry Collins | .40 | .15 |
| 108 | Garrison Hearst | .40 | .15 |
| 109 | David Boston | .60 | .25 |
| 110 | Travis Henry | .60 | .25 |
| 111 | James Jackson | .25 | .08 |
| 112 | Fred Taylor | .60 | .25 |
| 113 | Edgerrin James | .75 | .30 |
| 114 | Vinny Testaverde | .40 | .15 |
| 115 | Todd Pinkston | .40 | .15 |
| 116 | Koren Robinson | .40 | .15 |
| 117 | Torry Holt | .60 | .25 |
| 118 | Brian Griese | .60 | .25 |
| 119 | Trent Green | .40 | .15 |
| 120 | James McKnight | .25 | .08 |
| 121 | Charlie Garner | .40 | .15 |
| 122 | Tiki Barber | .60 | .25 |
| 123 | Joey Galloway | .40 | .15 |
| 124 | Quincy Morgan | .25 | .08 |
| 125 | Brett Favre | 1.50 | .60 |
| 126 | Joey Harrington RC | 4.00 | 1.50 |
| 127 | Ashley Lelie RC | 6.00 | 2.00 |
| 128 | Terry Charles RC | 2.50 | 1.00 |
| 129 | Charles Evans RC | 3.00 | 1.25 |
| 130 | Levar Fisher RC | 1.50 | .60 |
| 131 | Larry Tripplett RC | 1.50 | .60 |
| 132 | Quentin Jammer RC | 3.00 | 1.25 |
| 133 | Ron Johnson RC | 2.50 | 1.00 |
| 134 | Maurice Morris RC | 3.00 | 1.25 |
| 135 | Roy Williams RC | 6.00 | 2.50 |
| 136 | Kurt Kittner RC | 2.50 | 1.00 |
| 137 | Dennis Johnson RC | 1.50 | .60 |
| 138 | Seth Burford RC | 2.50 | 1.00 |
| 139 | Michael Lewis RC | 3.00 | 1.25 |
| 140 | William Green RC | 3.00 | 1.25 |
| 141 | Rohan Davey RC | 3.00 | 1.25 |
| 142 | Rocky Calmus RC | 2.50 | 1.00 |
| 143 | Robert Thomas RC | 3.00 | 1.25 |
| 144 | Travis Stephens RC | 2.50 | 1.00 |
| 145 | Ladell Betts RC | 3.00 | 1.25 |
| 146 | Daniel Graham RC | 3.00 | 1.25 |
| 147 | Chester Taylor RC | 6.00 | 2.50 |
| 148 | Tim Carter RC | 2.50 | 1.00 |
| 149 | Lito Sheppard RC | 3.00 | 1.25 |
| 150 | David Carr RC | 4.00 | 1.50 |
| 151 | Alex Brown RC | 3.00 | 1.25 |
| 152 | John Henderson RC | 3.00 | 1.25 |
| 153 | Jamar Martin RC | 2.50 | 1.00 |
| 154 | Raonall Smith RC | 2.50 | 1.00 |
| 155 | Leonard Henry RC | 2.50 | 1.00 |
| 156 | T.J. Duckett RC | 3.00 | 1.25 |
| 157 | Patrick Ramsey RC | 3.00 | 1.25 |
| 158 | Antwaan Randle El RC | 4.00 | 1.50 |
| 159 | Luke Staley RC | 2.50 | 1.00 |
| 160 | Jon McGraw RC | 1.50 | .60 |
| 161 | Phillip Buchanon RC | 3.00 | 1.25 |
| 162 | Dwight Freeney RC | 5.00 | 2.00 |
| 163 | Mike Rumph RC | 3.00 | 1.25 |
| 164 | Albert Haynesworth RC | 3.00 | 1.25 |
| 165 | Antonio Bryant RC | 3.00 | 1.25 |
| 166 | Josh Reed RC | 3.00 | 1.25 |
| 167 | Eric Crouch RC | 3.00 | 1.25 |
| 168 | Reche Caldwell RC | 3.00 | 1.25 |
| 169 | Adrian Peterson RC | 4.00 | 1.50 |
| 170 | Jonathan Wells RC | 3.00 | 1.25 |
| 171 | Wendell Bryant RC | 1.50 | .60 |
| 172 | Tellis Redmon RC | 2.50 | 1.00 |
| 173 | Josh McCown RC | 4.00 | 1.50 |
| 174 | DeShaun Foster RC | 3.00 | 1.25 |
| 175 | Cliff Russell RC | 2.50 | 1.00 |
| 176 | David Garrard RC | 6.00 | 2.50 |
| 177 | Brian Westbrook RC | 8.00 | 3.00 |
| 178 | Anthony Weaver RC | 2.50 | 1.00 |
| 179 | Bryan Thomas RC | 2.50 | 1.00 |
| 180 | Kalimba Edwards RC | 3.00 | 1.25 |
| 181 | Javon Walker RC | 5.00 | 2.00 |
| 182 | Marquise Walker RC | 2.50 | 1.00 |
| 183 | Deion Branch RC | 5.00 | 2.00 |
| 184 | Lamar Gordon RC | 3.00 | 1.25 |
| 185 | Jeremy Shockey RC | 5.00 | 2.00 |
| 186 | Clinton Portis RC | 10.00 | 4.00 |
| 187 | Napoleon Harris RC | 3.00 | 1.25 |
| 188 | Freddie Milons RC | 2.50 | 1.00 |
| 189 | Julius Peppers RC | 6.00 | 2.50 |
| 190 | Andre Davis RC | 2.50 | 1.00 |
| 191 | Travis Fisher RC | 3.00 | 1.25 |
| 192 | Chad Hutchinson RC | 2.50 | 1.00 |
| 193 | Najeh Davenport RC | 3.00 | 1.25 |
| 194 | Ed Reed RC | 8.00 | 3.00 |
| 195 | Donte Stallworth RC | 5.00 | 2.00 |
| 196 | Brandon Doman RC | 2.50 | 1.00 |
| 197 | Zak Kustok RC | 2.50 | 1.00 |
| 198 | Randy Fasani RC | 2.50 | 1.00 |
| 199 | J.T. O'Sullivan RC | 4.00 | 1.50 |
| 200 | Jabar Gaffney RC | 3.00 | 1.25 |

**2008 Stadium Club**

| # | Player | Price | Price |
|---|---|---|---|
| 1 | Drew Brees | 1.25 | .50 |
| 2 | Tom Brady | 2.00 | .75 |
| 3 | Peyton Manning | 2.00 | .75 |
| 4 | Carson Palmer | 1.25 | .50 |
| 5 | Ben Roethlisberger | 1.50 | .60 |
| 6 | Eli Manning | 1.25 | .50 |
| 7 | Tony Romo | 2.00 | .75 |
| 8 | Tarvaris Jackson | 1.00 | .40 |
| 9 | Vince Young | 1.25 | .50 |
| 10 | Steven Jackson | 1.25 | .50 |
| 11 | Willie Parker | 1.00 | .40 |
| 12 | Clinton Portis | 1.00 | .40 |
| 13 | Adrian Peterson | 2.50 | 1.00 |
| 14 | LaDainian Tomlinson | 1.50 | .60 |
| 15 | Marion Barber | 1.25 | .50 |
| 16 | Brian Westbrook | 1.00 | .40 |
| 17 | Fred Taylor | 1.00 | .40 |
| 18 | Marshawn Lynch | 1.25 | .50 |
| 19 | Joseph Addai | 1.00 | .40 |
| 20 | Willis McGahee | 1.00 | .40 |
| 21 | Frank Gore | 1.00 | .40 |
| 22 | Reggie Wayne | 1.00 | .40 |
| 23 | Anquan Boldin | 1.00 | .40 |
| 24 | Randy Moss | 1.25 | .50 |
| 25 | Plaxico Burress | 1.00 | .40 |
| 26 | Terrell Owens | 1.25 | .50 |
| 27 | Andre Johnson | 1.00 | .40 |
| 28 | Larry Fitzgerald | 1.25 | .50 |
| 29 | Braylon Edwards | 1.00 | .40 |
| 30 | Steve Smith | 1.00 | .40 |
| 31 | Jon Kitna | 1.00 | .40 |
| 32 | Matt Hasselbeck | 1.00 | .40 |
| 33 | Derek Anderson | 1.00 | .40 |
| 34 | Jay Cutler | 1.25 | .50 |
| 35 | Kurt Warner | 1.25 | .50 |
| 36 | Donovan McNabb | 1.25 | .50 |
| 37 | Philip Rivers | 1.25 | .50 |
| 38 | Jason Campbell | 1.00 | .40 |
| 39 | David Garrard | 1.00 | .40 |
| 40 | Jeff Garcia | 1.00 | .40 |
| 41 | Marc Bulger | 1.00 | .40 |
| 42 | Jamal Lewis | 1.00 | .40 |
| 43 | Edgerrin James | 1.00 | .40 |
| 44 | Thomas Jones | 1.00 | .40 |
| 45 | Lendale White | 1.00 | .40 |
| 46 | Justin Fargas | .75 | .30 |
| 47 | Brandon Jacobs | 1.00 | .40 |
| 48 | Ryan Grant | 1.25 | .50 |
| 49 | Earnest Graham | .75 | .30 |
| 50 | Chad Johnson | 1.00 | .40 |
| 51 | Brandon Marshall | 1.00 | .40 |
| 52 | Roddy White | 1.00 | .40 |
| 53 | Marques Colston | 1.00 | .40 |
| 54 | Torry Holt | 1.00 | .40 |
| 55 | Wes Welker | 1.25 | .50 |
| 56 | Bobby Engram | .75 | .30 |
| 57 | T.J. Houshmandzadeh | 1.00 | .40 |
| 58 | Jerricho Cotchery | .75 | .30 |
| 59 | Kevin Curtis | .75 | .30 |
| 60 | Derrick Mason | .75 | .30 |
| 61 | Donald Driver | 1.00 | .40 |
| 62 | Jason Witten | 1.00 | .40 |
| 63 | Tony Gonzalez | 1.00 | .40 |
| 64 | Kellen Winslow | 1.00 | .40 |
| 65 | Antonio Gates | 1.00 | .40 |
| 66 | Chris Cooley | 1.00 | .40 |
| 67 | Matt Schaub | 1.00 | .40 |
| 68 | Laurence Maroney | 1.00 | .40 |
| 69 | Joey Galloway | 1.00 | .40 |
| 70 | Jeremy Shockey | 1.00 | .40 |
| 71 | Dwayne Bowe | 1.00 | .40 |
| 72 | Dallas Clark | 1.00 | .40 |
| 73 | Maurice Jones-Drew | 1.00 | .40 |
| 74 | Ray Lewis | 1.25 | .50 |
| 75 | Michael Strahan | 1.00 | .40 |
| 76 | Derrick Brooks | 1.00 | .40 |
| 77 | Ed Reed | 1.00 | .40 |
| 78 | Brian Urlacher | 1.25 | .50 |
| 79 | Jason Taylor | 1.00 | .40 |
| 80 | Bob Sanders | 1.00 | .40 |
| 81 | Patrick Kerney | .75 | .30 |
| 82 | Albert Haynesworth | .75 | .30 |
| 83 | Antonio Cromartie | .75 | .30 |
| 84 | Mike Vrabel | .75 | .30 |
| 85 | DeMarcus Ware | 1.00 | .40 |
| 86 | Ronde Barber | .75 | .30 |
| 87 | James Harrison RC | 8.00 | 3.00 |
| 88 | Patrick Willis | 1.00 | .40 |
| 89 | Mario Williams | 1.00 | .40 |
| 90 | Osi Umenyiora | .75 | .30 |
| 91 | Damon Huard | .75 | .30 |
| 92 | Joey Harrington | .75 | .30 |
| 93 | Roy Williams WR | 1.00 | .40 |
| 94 | Champ Bailey | .75 | .30 |
| 95 | Shawne Merriman | 1.00 | .40 |
| 96 | Chester Taylor | 1.00 | .40 |
| 97 | Ron Dayne | 1.00 | .40 |
| 98 | Santonio Holmes | 1.00 | .40 |
| 99 | Lee Evans | 1.00 | .40 |
| 100 | Chris Chambers | 1.00 | .40 |
| 101 | Matt Ryan RC | 15.00 | 6.00 |
| 102 | Brian Brohm RC | 5.00 | 2.00 |
| 103 | Chad Henne RC | 6.00 | 2.50 |
| 104 | Joe Flacco RC | 12.00 | 5.00 |
| 105 | Andre Woodson RC | 4.00 | 1.50 |
| 106 | John David Booty RC | 5.00 | 2.00 |
| 107 | Josh Johnson RC | 4.00 | 1.50 |
| 108 | Colt Brennan RC | 10.00 | 4.00 |
| 109 | Dennis Dixon RC | 4.00 | 1.50 |
| 110 | Erik Ainge RC | 4.00 | 1.50 |
| 111 | Darren McFadden RC | 10.00 | 4.00 |

|  |  | | |
|---|---|---|---|
| 112 | Rashard Mendenhall RC | 8.00 | 3.00 |
| 113 | Jonathan Stewart RC | 10.00 | 4.00 |
| 114 | Felix Jones RC | 10.00 | 4.00 |
| 115 | Jamaal Charles RC | 5.00 | 2.00 |
| 116 | Ray Rice RC | 5.00 | 2.00 |
| 117 | Chris Johnson RC | 10.00 | 4.00 |
| 118 | Mike Hart RC | 5.00 | 2.00 |
| 119 | Matt Forte RC | 10.00 | 4.00 |
| 120 | Kevin Smith RC | 6.00 | 2.50 |
| 121 | Steve Slaton RC | 8.00 | 3.00 |
| 122 | Malcolm Kelly RC | 4.00 | 1.50 |
| 123 | Limas Sweed RC | 5.00 | 2.00 |
| 124 | DeSean Jackson RC | 8.00 | 3.00 |
| 125 | James Hardy RC | 4.00 | 1.50 |
| 126 | Mario Manningham RC | 4.00 | 1.50 |
| 127 | Devin Thomas RC | 4.00 | 1.50 |
| 128 | Early Doucet RC | 4.00 | 1.50 |
| 129 | Andre Caldwell RC | 3.00 | 1.25 |
| 130 | Jordy Nelson RC | 5.00 | 2.00 |
| 131 | Eddie Royal RC | 8.00 | 3.00 |
| 132 | Earl Bennett RC | 4.00 | 1.50 |
| 133 | Fred Davis RC | 4.00 | 1.50 |
| 134 | Dustin Keller RC | 4.00 | 1.50 |
| 135 | John Carlson RC | 4.00 | 1.50 |
| 136 | Chris Long RC | 5.00 | 2.00 |
| 137 | Jake Long RC | 5.00 | 2.00 |
| 138 | Glenn Dorsey RC | 5.00 | 2.00 |
| 139 | Sedrick Ellis RC | 4.00 | 1.50 |
| 140 | Vernon Gholston RC | 4.00 | 1.50 |
| 141 | Kevin O'Connell RC | 5.00 | 2.00 |
| 142 | Leodis McKelvin RC | 4.00 | 1.50 |
| 143 | Keith Rivers RC | 4.00 | 1.50 |
| 144 | Mike Jenkins RC | 4.00 | 1.50 |
| 145 | Derrick Harvey RC | 3.00 | 1.25 |
| 146 | Phillip Merling RC | 3.00 | 1.25 |
| 147 | Kentwan Balmer RC | 3.00 | 1.25 |
| 148 | Dan Connor RC | 4.00 | 1.50 |
| 149 | Dominique Rodgers-Cromartie RC | 4.00 | 1.50 |
| 150 | Aqib Talib RC | 4.00 | 1.50 |
| 151 | Sam Baker RC | 2.50 | 1.00 |
| 152 | Adarrian Arrington RC | 3.00 | 1.25 |
| 153 | Donnie Avery RC | 5.00 | 2.00 |
| 154 | Marcus Henry RC | 3.00 | 1.25 |
| 155 | Dexter Jackson RC | 4.00 | 1.50 |
| 156 | Jerome Simpson RC | 4.00 | 1.50 |
| 157 | Keenan Burton RC | 3.00 | 1.25 |
| 158 | Tashard Choice RC | 4.00 | 1.50 |
| 159 | Harry Douglas RC | 4.00 | 1.50 |
| 160 | Marcus Griffin RC | 2.50 | 1.00 |
| 161 | DJ Hall RC | 4.00 | 1.50 |
| 162 | Justin Forsett RC | 4.00 | 1.50 |
| 163 | Jaymar Johnson RC | 3.00 | 1.25 |
| 164 | Jacob Hester RC | 4.00 | 1.50 |
| 165 | Ali Highsmith RC | 2.50 | 1.00 |
| 166 | Sam Keller RC | 4.00 | 1.50 |
| 167 | Lance Leggett RC | 4.00 | 1.50 |
| 168 | Xavier Omon RC | 4.00 | 1.50 |
| 169 | Marcus Monk RC | 4.00 | 1.50 |
| 170 | Anthony Morelli RC | 4.00 | 1.50 |
| 171 | Marcus Smith RC | 3.00 | 1.25 |
| 172 | Allen Patrick RC | 3.00 | 1.25 |
| 173 | Kenny Phillips RC | 4.00 | 1.50 |
| 174 | Tyrell Johnson RC | 4.00 | 1.50 |
| 175 | Matt Flynn RC | 5.00 | 2.00 |
| 176 | Martin Rucker RC | 3.00 | 1.25 |
| 177 | Jordon Dizon RC | 4.00 | 1.50 |
| 178 | Owen Schmitt RC | 4.00 | 1.50 |
| 179 | Martellus Bennett RC | 4.00 | 1.50 |
| 180 | Terrence Wheatley RC | 3.00 | 1.25 |
| 181 | Terrell Thomas RC | 3.00 | 1.25 |
| 182 | Kyle Wright RC | 3.00 | 1.25 |
| 183 | Darius Reynaud RC | 3.00 | 1.25 |
| 184 | Chris Williams RC | 3.00 | 1.25 |
| 185 | Jeff Otah RC | 3.00 | 1.25 |
| 186 | Xavier Adibi RC | 3.00 | 1.25 |
| 187 | Jerod Mayo RC | 6.00 | 2.50 |
| 188 | Calais Campbell RC | 3.00 | 1.25 |
| 189 | Charles Godfrey RC | 3.00 | 1.25 |
| 190 | Reggie Smith RC | 3.00 | 1.25 |
| 191 | Pat Sims RC | 3.00 | 1.25 |
| 192 | Curtis Lofton RC | 4.00 | 1.50 |
| 193 | Tracy Porter RC | 3.00 | 1.25 |
| 194 | Patrick Lee RC | 3.00 | 1.25 |
| 195 | Cliff Avril RC | 3.00 | 1.25 |
| 196 | Trevor Laws RC | 4.00 | 1.50 |
| 197 | Lawrence Jackson RC | 3.00 | 1.25 |
| 198 | Antoine Cason RC | 4.00 | 1.50 |
| 199 | Chevis Jackson RC | 3.00 | 1.25 |
| 200 | Justin King RC | 3.00 | 1.25 |

## 1955 Topps All American

JIM THORPE — Railback

|  |  | | |
|---|---|---|---|
| | COMPLETE SET (100) | 3800.00 | 2800.00 |
| | WRAPPER (1-CENT) | 300.00 | 250.00 |
| | WRAPPER (5-CENT) | 250.00 | 200.00 |
| 1 | Herman Hickman RC ! | 125.00 | 65.00 |
| 2 | John Kimbrough | 18.00 | 10.00 |
| 3 | Ed Weir | 18.00 | 10.00 |
| 4 | Erny Pinckert | 18.00 | 10.00 |
| 5 | Bobby Grayson | 18.00 | 10.00 |
| 6 | Nile Kinnick RC UER | 135.00 | 75.00 |
| 7 | Andy Bershak | 18.00 | 10.00 |
| 8 | George Calego RC | 18.00 | 10.00 |
| 9 | Tom Hamilton SP | 30.00 | 20.00 |
| 10 | Bill Dudley | 40.00 | 25.00 |
| 11 | Bobby Dodd SP | 30.00 | 20.00 |
| 12 | Otto Graham | 200.00 | 100.00 |
| 13 | Aaron Rosenberg | 18.00 | 10.00 |
| 14A | Gay.Tinsley RC ERR | 100.00 | 50.00 |
| 14B | Gay.Tinsley RC COR | 25.00 | 15.00 |
| 15 | Ed Kaw SP | 30.00 | 20.00 |
| 16 | Knute Rockne | 275.00 | 175.00 |
| 17 | Bob Reynolds HB | 18.00 | 10.00 |
| 18 | Pudg.Heffelfinger RC SP | 40.00 | 25.00 |
| 19 | Bruce Smith | 40.00 | 25.00 |
| 20 | Sammy Baugh | 200.00 | 125.00 |
| 21A | W.White RC SP ERR | 250.00 | 150.00 |
| 21B | W.White RC SP COR | 100.00 | 60.00 |
| 22 | Brick Muller | 18.00 | 10.00 |
| 23 | Dick Kazmaier RC | 25.00 | 15.00 |
| 24 | Ken Strong | 50.00 | 30.00 |
| 25 | Casimir Myslinski SP | 30.00 | 20.00 |
| 26 | Larry Kelley RC SP | 40.00 | 25.00 |
| 27 | Red Grange UER | 300.00 | 200.00 |
| 28 | Mel Hein RC SP | 100.00 | 60.00 |
| 29 | Leo Nomellini SP | 100.00 | 60.00 |
| 30 | Wes Fesler | 18.00 | 10.00 |
| 31 | George Sauer Sr. RC | 25.00 | 15.00 |
| 32 | Hank Foldberg | 18.00 | 10.00 |
| 33 | Bob Higgins | 18.00 | 10.00 |
| 34 | Davey O'Brien RC | 50.00 | 30.00 |
| 35 | Tom Harmon RC SP | 100.00 | 60.00 |
| 36 | Turk Edwards SP | 60.00 | 35.00 |
| 37 | Jim Thorpe | 400.00 | 275.00 |
| 38 | Amos A. Stagg RC | 75.00 | 40.00 |
| 39 | Jerome Holland RC | 25.00 | 15.00 |
| 40 | Donn Moomaw | 18.00 | 10.00 |
| 41 | Joseph Alexander SP | 30.00 | 20.00 |
| 42 | Eddie Tryon RC SP | 40.00 | 25.00 |
| 43 | George Savitsky | 18.00 | 10.00 |
| 44 | Ed Garbisch | 18.00 | 10.00 |
| 45 | Elmer Oliphant | 18.00 | 10.00 |
| 46 | Arnold Lassman | 18.00 | 10.00 |
| 47 | Bo McMillin RC | 25.00 | 15.00 |
| 48 | Ed Widseth | 18.00 | 10.00 |
| 49 | Don Gordon Zimmerman | 18.00 | 10.00 |
| 50 | Ken Kavanaugh | 25.00 | 15.00 |
| 51 | Duane Purvis SP | 30.00 | 20.00 |
| 52 | Johnny Lujack | 90.00 | 50.00 |
| 53 | John F. Green | 18.00 | 10.00 |
| 54 | Edwin Dooley SP | 30.00 | 20.00 |
| 55 | Frank Merritt SP | 30.00 | 20.00 |
| 56 | Ernie Nevers SP | 125.00 | 75.00 |
| 57 | Vic Hanson SP | 30.00 | 20.00 |
| 58 | Ed Franco | 18.00 | 10.00 |
| 59 | Doc Blanchard SP | 50.00 | 30.00 |
| 60 | Dan Hill | 18.00 | 10.00 |
| 61 | Charles Brickley SP | 30.00 | 20.00 |
| 62 | Harry Newman | 18.00 | 10.00 |
| 63 | Charlie Justice | 35.00 | 20.00 |
| 64 | Benny Friedman SP | 30.00 | 18.00 |
| 65 | Joe Donchess SP | 30.00 | 18.00 |
| 66 | Bruiser Kinard SP | 35.00 | 20.00 |
| 67 | Frankie Albert | 25.00 | 15.00 |
| 68 | Four Horsemen RC SP | 500.00 | 325.00 |
| 69 | Frank Sinkwich RC | 25.00 | 15.00 |
| 70 | Bill Daddio | 18.00 | 10.00 |
| 71 | Bobby Wilson | 18.00 | 10.00 |
| 72 | Chub Peabody | 18.00 | 10.00 |
| 73 | Paul Governali | 25.00 | 15.00 |
| 74 | Gene McEver | 18.00 | 10.00 |
| 75 | Hugh Gallarneau | 18.00 | 10.00 |
| 76 | Angelo Bertelli RC | 25.00 | 15.00 |
| 77 | Bowden Wyatt SP | 30.00 | 20.00 |
| 78 | Jay Berwanger RC SP | 35.00 | 20.00 |
| 79 | Pug Lund | 18.00 | 10.00 |
| 80 | Bennie Oosterbaan | 18.00 | 10.00 |
| 81 | Cotton Warburton | 18.00 | 10.00 |
| 82 | Alex Wojciechowicz | 35.00 | 20.00 |
| 83 | Ted Coy SP | 30.00 | 20.00 |
| 84 | Ace Parker RC SP | 50.00 | 30.00 |
| 85 | Sid Luckman | 150.00 | 90.00 |
| 86 | Albie Booth SP | 30.00 | 20.00 |
| 87 | Adolph Schultz SP | 30.00 | 20.00 |
| 88 | Ralph Kercheval | 18.00 | 10.00 |
| 89 | Marshall Goldberg | 25.00 | 15.00 |
| 90 | Charlie O'Rourke | 18.00 | 10.00 |
| 91 | Bob Odell UER | 18.00 | 10.00 |
| 92 | Biggie Munn | 18.00 | 10.00 |
| 93 | Willie Heston SP | 40.00 | 25.00 |
| 94 | Joe Bernard SP | 40.00 | 25.00 |
| 95 | Chris Cagle SP | 40.00 | 25.00 |
| 96 | Bill Hollenback SP | 40.00 | 25.00 |
| 97 | Don Hutson RC SP | 225.00 | 150.00 |
| 98 | Beattie Feathers SP | 100.00 | 60.00 |
| 99 | Don Whitmire SP | 40.00 | 25.00 |
| 100 | Fats Henry RC SP ! | 200.00 | 100.00 |

## 1956 Topps

|  |  | | |
|---|---|---|---|
| | COMPLETE SET (120) | 1800.00 | 1200.00 |
| | WRAPPER (1-CENT) | 250.00 | 200.00 |
| | WRAPPER (5-CENT) | 50.00 | 40.00 |
| 1 | Johnny Carson SP ! | 80.00 | 40.00 |
| 2 | Gordy Soltau | 6.00 | 3.50 |
| 3 | Frank Varrichione | 6.00 | 3.50 |
| 4 | Eddie Bell | 6.00 | 3.50 |
| 5 | Alex Webster RC | 12.00 | 6.00 |
| 6 | Norm Van Brocklin | 30.00 | 18.00 |
| 7 | Green Bay Packers | 25.00 | 15.00 |
| 8 | Lou Creekmur | 15.00 | 7.50 |
| 9 | Lou Groza | 25.00 | 15.00 |
| 10 | Tom Bienemann SP | 25.00 | 15.00 |
| 11 | George Blanda | 50.00 | 30.00 |
| 12 | Alan Ameche | 12.00 | 6.00 |
| 13 | Vic Janowicz SP | 45.00 | 25.00 |
| 14 | Dick Moegle | 6.00 | 4.00 |
| 15 | Fran Rogel | 6.00 | 3.50 |
| 16 | Harold Giancanelli | 6.00 | 3.50 |
| 17 | Emlen Tunnell | 15.00 | 7.50 |
| 18 | Tank Younger | 12.00 | 6.00 |
| 19 | Billy Howton | 8.00 | 4.00 |
| 20 | Jack Christiansen | 15.00 | 7.50 |

| | | |
|---|---|---|
| 21 Darrel Brewster | 6.00 | 3.50 |
| 22 Chicago Cardinals SP | 100.00 | 60.00 |
| 23 Ed Brown | 8.00 | 4.00 |
| 24 Joe Campanella | 6.00 | 3.50 |
| 25 Leon Heath SP | 22.00 | 12.00 |
| 26 San Francisco 49ers | 18.00 | 10.00 |
| 27 Dick Flanagan | 6.00 | 3.50 |
| 28 Chuck Bednarik | 25.00 | 15.00 |
| 29 Kyle Rote | 12.00 | 6.00 |
| 30 Les Richter | 8.00 | 4.00 |
| 31 Howard Ferguson | 6.00 | 3.50 |
| 32 Dorne Dibble | 6.00 | 3.50 |
| 33 Kenny Konz | 6.00 | 3.50 |
| 34 Dave Mann SP | 25.00 | 15.00 |
| 35 Rick Casares | 12.00 | 6.00 |
| 36 Art Donovan | 30.00 | 18.00 |
| 37 Chuck Drazenovich SP | 22.00 | 12.00 |
| 38 Joe Arenas | 6.00 | 3.50 |
| 39 Lynn Chandnois | 6.00 | 3.50 |
| 40 Philadelphia Eagles | 18.00 | 10.00 |
| 41 Roosevelt Brown RC | 40.00 | 25.00 |
| 42 Tom Fears | 25.00 | 15.00 |
| 43 Gary Knafelc | 6.00 | 3.50 |
| 44 Joe Schmidt RC | 50.00 | 30.00 |
| 45 Cleveland Browns | 18.00 | 10.00 |
| 46 Len Teeuws RC | 25.00 | 15.00 |
| 47 Bill George RC | 35.00 | 20.00 |
| 48 Baltimore Colts | 18.00 | 10.00 |
| 49 Eddie LeBaron SP | 45.00 | 25.00 |
| 50 Hugh McElhenny | 30.00 | 18.00 |
| 51 Ted Marchibroda | 12.00 | 6.00 |
| 52 Adrian Burk | 6.00 | 3.50 |
| 53 Frank Gifford | 60.00 | 35.00 |
| 54 Charley Toogood | 6.00 | 3.50 |
| 55 Tobin Rote | 8.00 | 4.00 |
| 56 Bill Stits | 6.00 | 3.50 |
| 57 Don Colo | 6.00 | 3.50 |
| 58 Ollie Matson SP | 75.00 | 40.00 |
| 59 Harlon Hill | 6.00 | 3.50 |
| 60 Lenny Moore RC ! | 90.00 | 50.00 |
| 61 Wash.Redskins SP | 90.00 | 50.00 |
| 62 Billy Wilson | 6.00 | 3.50 |
| 63 Pittsburgh Steelers | 18.00 | 10.00 |
| 64 Bob Pellegrini | 6.00 | 3.50 |
| 65 Ken MacAfee E | 6.00 | 3.50 |
| 66 Willard Sherman | 6.00 | 3.50 |
| 67 Roger Zatkoff | 6.00 | 3.50 |
| 68 Dave Middleton | 6.00 | 3.50 |
| 69 Ray Renfro | 6.00 | 3.50 |
| 70 Don Stonesifer | 25.00 | 15.00 |
| 71 Stan Jones RC | 40.00 | 25.00 |
| 72 Jim Mutscheller | 6.00 | 3.50 |
| 73 Volney Peters SP | 22.00 | 12.00 |
| 74 Leo Nomellini | 20.00 | 12.00 |
| 75 Ray Mathews | 6.00 | 3.50 |
| 76 Dick Bielski | 6.00 | 3.50 |
| 77 Charley Conerly | 25.00 | 15.00 |
| 78 Elroy Hirsch | 30.00 | 18.00 |
| 79 Bill Forester SP | 6.00 | 3.50 |
| 80 Jim Doran | 6.00 | 3.50 |
| 81 Fred Morrison | 6.00 | 3.50 |
| 82 Jack Simmons SP | 25.00 | 15.00 |
| 83 Bill McColl | 6.00 | 3.50 |
| 84 Bert Rechichar | 6.00 | 3.50 |
| 85 Joe Scudero SP | 22.00 | 12.00 |
| 86 Y.A.Tittle | 50.00 | 30.00 |
| 87 Ernie Stautner | 20.00 | 12.00 |
| 88 Norm Willey | 6.00 | 3.50 |
| 89 Bob Schnelker | 6.00 | 3.50 |
| 90 Dan Towler | 12.00 | 6.00 |
| 91 John Martinkovic | 6.00 | 3.50 |
| 92 Detroit Lions | 18.00 | 10.00 |
| 93 George Ratterman | 8.00 | 4.00 |
| 94 Chuck Ulrich SP | 25.00 | 15.00 |
| 95 Bobby Watkins | 6.00 | 3.50 |
| 96 Buddy Young | 12.00 | 6.00 |
| 97 Billy Wells SP | 22.00 | 12.00 |
| 98 Bob Toneff | 6.00 | 3.50 |
| 99 Bill McPeak | 6.00 | 3.50 |
| 100 Bobby Thomason | 6.00 | 3.50 |
| 101 Roosevelt Grier RC | 50.00 | 30.00 |
| 102 Ron Waller | 6.00 | 3.50 |
| 103 Bobby Dillon | 6.00 | 3.50 |
| 104 Leon Hart | 12.00 | 6.00 |
| 105 Mike McCormack | 15.00 | 7.50 |
| 106 John Olszewski SP | 25.00 | 15.00 |
| 107 Bill Wightkin | 6.00 | 3.50 |
| 108 George Shaw RC | 8.00 | 4.00 |
| 109 Dale Atkeson SP | 22.00 | 12.00 |
| 110 Joe Perry | 25.00 | 15.00 |
| 111 Dale Dodrill | 6.00 | 3.50 |
| 112 Tom Scott | 6.00 | 3.50 |
| 113 New York Giants | 18.00 | 10.00 |
| 114 Los Angeles Rams | 18.00 | 10.00 |
| 115 Al Carmichael | 6.00 | 3.50 |
| 116 Bobby Layne | 50.00 | 30.00 |
| 117 Ed Modzelewski | 6.00 | 3.50 |
| 118 Lamar McHan RC SP | 25.00 | 15.00 |
| 119 Chicago Bears | 18.00 | 10.00 |
| 120 Billy Vessels RC ! | 40.00 | 20.00 |

## 1957 Topps

| | | |
|---|---|---|
| COMPLETE SET (154) | 2200.00 | 1600.00 |
| COMMON CARD (1-88) | 4.00 | 2.50 |
| COMMON CARD (89-154) | 10.00 | 5.00 |
| WRAPPER (1-CENT) | 50.00 | 30.00 |
| WRAPPER (5-CENT) | 75.00 | 50.00 |
| 1 Eddie LeBaron ! | 50.00 | 30.00 |
| 2 Pete Retzlaff RC | 15.00 | 7.50 |
| 3 Mike McCormack | 12.00 | 6.00 |
| 4 Lou Baldacci | 4.00 | 2.50 |
| 5 Gino Marchetti | 20.00 | 10.00 |
| 6 Leo Nomellini | 20.00 | 10.00 |
| 7 Bobby Watkins | 4.00 | 2.50 |
| 8 Dave Middleton | 4.00 | 2.50 |
| 9 Bobby Dillon | 4.00 | 2.50 |
| 10 Les Richter | 6.00 | 3.50 |
| 11 Roosevelt Brown | 20.00 | 10.00 |
| 12 Lavern Torgeson RC | 4.00 | 2.50 |
| 13 Dick Bielski | 4.00 | 2.50 |
| 14 Pat Summerall | 20.00 | 10.00 |
| 15 Jack Butler RC | 10.00 | 5.00 |
| 16 John Henry Johnson | 15.00 | 7.50 |
| 17 Art Spinney | 4.00 | 2.50 |
| 18 Bob St. Clair | 12.00 | 6.00 |
| 19 Perry Jeter | 4.00 | 2.50 |
| 20 Lou Creekmur | 12.00 | 6.00 |
| 21 Dave Hanner | 6.00 | 3.50 |
| 22 Norm Van Brocklin | 30.00 | 18.00 |
| 23 Don Chandler RC | 10.00 | 5.00 |
| 24 Al Dorow | 4.00 | 2.50 |
| 25 Tom Scott | 4.00 | 2.50 |
| 26 Ollie Matson | 20.00 | 12.00 |
| 27 Fran Rogel | 4.00 | 2.50 |
| 28 Lou Groza | 25.00 | 15.00 |
| 29 Billy Vessels | 6.00 | 3.50 |
| 30 Y.A.Tittle | 40.00 | 25.00 |
| 31 George Blanda | 40.00 | 25.00 |
| 32 Bobby Layne | 40.00 | 25.00 |
| 33 Billy Howton | 6.00 | 3.50 |
| 34 Bill Wade | 10.00 | 5.00 |
| 35 Emlen Tunnell | 15.00 | 7.50 |
| 36 Leo Elter | 4.00 | 2.50 |
| 37 Clarence Peaks RC | 6.00 | 3.50 |
| 38 Don Stonesifer | 4.00 | 2.50 |
| 39 George Tarasovic | 4.00 | 2.50 |
| 40 Darrel Brewster | 4.00 | 2.50 |
| 41 Bert Rechichar | 4.00 | 2.50 |
| 42 Billy Wilson | 4.00 | 2.50 |
| 43 Ed Brown | 6.00 | 3.50 |
| 44 Gene Gedman | 4.00 | 2.50 |
| 45 Gary Knafelc | 4.00 | 2.50 |
| 46 Elroy Hirsch | 30.00 | 18.00 |
| 47 Don Heinrich | 6.00 | 3.50 |
| 48 Gene Brito | 4.00 | 2.50 |
| 49 Chuck Bednarik | 25.00 | 15.00 |
| 50 Dave Mann | 4.00 | 2.50 |
| 51 Bill McPeak | 4.00 | 2.50 |
| 52 Kenny Konz | 4.00 | 2.50 |
| 53 Alan Ameche | 10.00 | 5.00 |
| 54 Gordy Soltau | 4.00 | 2.50 |
| 55 Rick Casares | 6.00 | 3.50 |
| 56 Charlie Ane | 4.00 | 2.50 |
| 57 Al Carmichael | 4.00 | 2.50 |
| 58A Willard Sherman ERR | 300.00 | 175.00 |
| 58B Willard Sherman COR | 4.00 | 2.50 |
| 59 Kyle Rote | 10.00 | 5.00 |
| 60 Chuck Drazenovich | 4.00 | 2.50 |
| 61 Bobby Walston | 4.00 | 2.50 |
| 62 John Olszewski | 4.00 | 2.50 |
| 63 Ray Mathews | 4.00 | 2.50 |
| 64 Maurice Bassett | 4.00 | 2.50 |
| 65 Art Donovan | 25.00 | 15.00 |
| 66 Joe Arenas | 4.00 | 2.50 |
| 67 Harlon Hill | 6.00 | 3.50 |
| 68 Yale Lary | 12.00 | 6.00 |
| 69 Bill Forester | 6.00 | 3.50 |
| 70 Bob Boyd | 4.00 | 2.50 |
| 71 Andy Robustelli | 20.00 | 12.00 |
| 72 Sam Baker RC | 6.00 | 3.50 |
| 73 Bob Pellegrini | 4.00 | 2.50 |
| 74 Leo Sanford | 4.00 | 2.50 |
| 75 Sid Watson | 4.00 | 2.50 |
| 76 Ray Renfro | 6.00 | 3.50 |
| 77 Carl Taseff | 4.00 | 2.50 |
| 78 Clyde Conner | 4.00 | 2.50 |
| 79 J.C. Caroline | 4.00 | 2.50 |
| 80 Howard Cassady RC | 15.00 | 7.50 |
| 81 Tobin Rote | 6.00 | 3.50 |
| 82 Ron Waller | 4.00 | 2.50 |
| 83 Jim Patton RC | 6.00 | 3.50 |
| 84 Volney Peters | 4.00 | 2.50 |
| 85 Dick Lane RC | 50.00 | 30.00 |
| 86 Royce Womble | 4.00 | 2.50 |
| 87 Duane Putnam RC | 4.00 | 2.50 |
| 88 Frank Gifford ! | 60.00 | 30.00 |
| 89 Steve Meilinger | 10.00 | 5.00 |
| 90 Buck Lansford | 10.00 | 5.00 |
| 91 Lindon Crow DP | 8.00 | 4.00 |
| 92 Ernie Stautner DP | 25.00 | 12.50 |
| 93 Preston Carpenter RC DP | 8.00 | 4.00 |
| 94 Raymond Berry RC | 135.00 | 75.00 |
| 95 Hugh McElhenny | 30.00 | 18.00 |
| 96 Stan Jones | 25.00 | 15.00 |
| 97 Dorne Dibble | 10.00 | 5.00 |
| 98 Joe Scudero DP | 8.00 | 4.00 |
| 99 Eddie Bell | 10.00 | 5.00 |
| 100 Joe Childress DP | 8.00 | 4.00 |
| 101 Elbert Nickel | 12.00 | 6.00 |
| 102 Walt Michaels | 12.00 | 6.00 |
| 103 Jim Mutscheller DP | 8.00 | 4.00 |
| 104 Earl Morrall RC | 50.00 | 30.00 |
| 105 Larry Strickland | 10.00 | 5.00 |
| 106 Jack Christiansen | 15.00 | 7.50 |
| 107 Fred Cone DP | 8.00 | 4.00 |
| 108 Bud McFadin RC | 12.00 | 6.00 |
| 109 Charley Conerly | 30.00 | 18.00 |
| 110 Tom Runnels DP | 8.00 | 4.00 |
| 111 Ken Keller DP | 8.00 | 4.00 |
| 112 James Root | 10.00 | 5.00 |
| 113 Ted Marchibroda DP | 10.00 | 5.00 |
| 114 Don Paul DB | 10.00 | 5.00 |
| 115 George Shaw | 12.00 | 6.00 |
| 116 Dick Moegle | 10.00 | 5.00 |
| 117 Don Bingham | 10.00 | 5.00 |
| 118 Leon Hart | 14.00 | 7.00 |
| 119 Bart Starr RC | 500.00 | 350.00 |
| 120 Paul Miller DP | 8.00 | 4.00 |
| 121 Alex Webster | 12.00 | 6.00 |
| 122 Ray Wietecha DP | 8.00 | 4.00 |
| 123 Johnny Carson | 10.00 | 5.00 |
| 124 Tom. McDonald RC DP | 30.00 | 18.00 |
| 125 Jerry Tubbs RC | 12.00 | 6.00 |
| 126 Jack Scarbath | 10.00 | 5.00 |
| 127 Ed Modzelewski DP | 8.00 | 4.00 |
| 128 Lenny Moore | 50.00 | 30.00 |
| 129 Joe Perry DP | 25.00 | 15.00 |
| 130 Bill Wightkin | 10.00 | 5.00 |

| | | |
|---|---|---|
| 131 Jim Doran | 10.00 | 5.00 |
| 132 Howard Ferguson UER | 10.00 | 5.00 |
| 133 Tom Wilson | 10.00 | 5.00 |
| 134 Dick James | 10.00 | 5.00 |
| 135 Jimmy Harris | 10.00 - | 5.00 |
| 136 Chuck Ulrich | 10.00 | 5.00 |
| 137 Lynn Chandnois | 10.00 | 5.00 |
| 138 Johnny Unitas RC DP | 450.00 | 300.00 |
| 139 Jim Ridlon DP | 8.00 | 4.00 |
| 140 Zeke Bratkowski DP | 10.00 | 5.00 |
| 141 Ray Krouse | 10.00 | 5.00 |
| 142 John Martinkovic | 10.00 | 5.00 |
| 143 Jim Cason DP | 8.00 | 4.00 |
| 144 Ken MacAfee E | 10.00 | 5.00 |
| 145 Sid Youngelman RC | 12.00 | 6.00 |
| 146 Paul Larson | 10.00 | 5.00 |
| 147 Len Ford | 30.00 | 18.00 |
| 148 Bob Toneff DP | 8.00 | 4.00 |
| 149 Ronnie Knox DP | 8.00 | 4.00 |
| 150 Jim David RC | 12.00 | 6.00 |
| 151 Paul Hornung RC | 400.00 | 250.00 |
| 152 Tank Younger | 14.00 | 7.00 |
| 153 Bill Svoboda DP | 8.00 | 4.00 |
| 154 Fred Morrison ! | 70.00 | 35.00 |
| CL1 Checklist Bazooka SP | 750.00 | 500.00 |
| CL2 Checklist Blony SP | 750.00 | 500.00 |

## 1958 Topps

| | | |
|---|---|---|
| COMPLETE SET (132) | 1250.00 | 850.00 |
| WRAPPER (1-CENT) | 60.00 | 35.00 |
| WRAPPER (5-CENT) | 125.00 | 75.00 |
| 1 Gene Filipski RC ! | 15.00 | 7.50 |
| 2 Bobby Layne | 35.00 | 20.00 |
| 3 Joe Schmidt | 12.00 | 6.00 |
| 4 Bill Barnes | 4.00 | 2.00 |
| 5 Milt Plum RC | 10.00 | 5.00 |
| 6 Billy Howton UER | 5.00 | 2.50 |
| 7 Howard Cassady | 5.00 | 2.50 |
| 8 Jim Dooley | 4.00 | 2.00 |
| 9 Cleveland Browns | 6.00 | 3.00 |
| 10 Lenny Moore | 30.00 | 15.00 |
| 11 Darrel Brewster | 4.00 | 2.00 |
| 12 Alan Ameche | 8.00 | 4.00 |
| 13 Jim David | 4.00 | 2.00 |
| 14 Jim Mutscheller | 4.00 | 2.00 |
| 15 Andy Robustelli | 10.00 | 5.00 |
| 16 Gino Marchetti | 12.00 | 6.00 |
| 17 Ray Renfro | 5.00 | 2.50 |
| 18 Yale Lary | 8.00 | 4.00 |
| 19 Gary Glick | 4.00 | 2.00 |
| 20 Jon Arnett RC | 5.00 | 2.50 |
| 21 Bob Boyd | 4.00 | 2.00 |
| 22 Johnny Unitas UER | 135.00 | 75.00 |
| 23 Zeke Bratkowski | 5.00 | 2.50 |
| 24 Sid Youngelman UER | 4.00 | 2.00 |
| 25 Leo Elter | 4.00 | 2.00 |
| 26 Kenny Konz | 4.00 | 2.00 |
| 27 Washington Redskins | 6.00 | 3.00 |
| 28 Carl Brettschneider | 4.00 | 2.00 |
| 29 Chicago Bears | 6.00 | 3.00 |
| 30 Alex Webster | 5.00 | 2.50 |
| 31 Al Carmichael | 4.00 | 2.00 |
| 32 Bobby Dillon | 4.00 | 2.00 |
| 33 Steve Meilinger | 4.00 | 2.00 |
| 34 Sam Baker | 4.00 | 2.00 |
| 35 Chuck Bednarik | 15.00 | 7.50 |
| 36 Bert Vic Zucco | 4.00 | 2.00 |
| 37 George Tarasovic | 4.00 | 2.00 |
| 38 Bill Wade | 8.00 | 4.00 |
| 39 Dick Stanfel | 5.00 | 2.50 |
| 40 Jerry Norton | 4.00 | 2.50 |
| 41 San Francisco 49ers | 6.00 | 3.00 |
| 42 Emlen Tunnell | 10.00 | 5.00 |
| 43 Jim Doran | 4.00 | 2.00 |
| 44 Ted Marchibroda | 8.00 | 4.00 |
| 45 Chet Hanulak | 4.00 | 2.00 |
| 46 Dale Dodrill | 4.00 | 2.00 |
| 47 Johnny Carson | 4.00 | 2.00 |
| 48 Dick Deschaine | 4.00 | 2.00 |
| 49 Billy Wells UER | 4.00 | 2.00 |
| 50 Larry Morris | 4.00 | 2.00 |
| 51 Jack McClairen | 4.00 | 2.00 |
| 52 Lou Groza | 15.00 | 7.50 |
| 53 Rick Casares | 5.00 | 2.50 |
| 54 Don Chandler | 5.00 | 2.50 |
| 55 Duane Putnam | 4.00 | 2.00 |
| 56 Gary Knafelc | 4.00 | 2.00 |
| 57 Earl Morrall | 10.00 | 5.00 |
| 58 Ron Kramer RC | 5.00 | 2.50 |
| 59 Mike McCormack | 8.00 | 4.00 |
| 60 Gern Nagler | 4.00 | 2.00 |
| 61 New York Giants | 6.00 | 3.00 |
| 62 Jim Brown RC ! | 500.00 | 350.00 |
| 63 Joe Marconi RC | 4.00 | 2.00 |
| 64 R.C. Owens RC UER | 5.00 | 2.50 |
| 65 Jimmy Carr RC | 5.00 | 2.50 |
| 66 Bart Starr UER | 150.00 | 90.00 |
| 67 Tom Wilson | 4.00 | 2.00 |
| 68 Lamar McHan | 4.00 | 2.00 |
| 69 Chicago Cardinals | 6.00 | 3.00 |
| 70 Jack Christiansen | 8.00 | 4.00 |
| 71 Don McIlhenny RC | 4.00 | 2.00 |
| 72 Ron Waller | 4.00 | 2.00 |
| 73 Frank Gifford | 50.00 | 25.00 |
| 74 Bert Rechichar | 4.00 | 2.00 |
| 75 John Henry Johnson | 10.00 | 5.00 |
| 76 Jack Butler | 5.00 | 2.50 |
| 77 Frank Varrichione | 4.00 | 2.00 |
| 78 Ray Mathews | 4.00 | 2.00 |
| 79 Marv Matuszak UER | 4.00 | 2.00 |
| 80 Harlon Hill UER | 4.00 | 2.00 |
| 81 Lou Creekmur | 8.00 | 4.00 |
| 82 Woodley Lewis UER | 4.00 | 2.00 |
| 83 Don Heinrich | 4.00 | 2.00 |
| 84 Charley Conerly | 15.00 | 7.50 |
| 85 Los Angeles Rams | 6.00 | 3.00 |
| 86 Y.A.Tittle | 30.00 | 18.00 |
| 87 Bobby Walston | 4.00 | 2.00 |
| 88 Earl Putman | 4.00 | 2.00 |
| 89 Leo Nomellini | 15.00 | 7.50 |
| 90 Sonny Jurgensen RC | 100.00 | 60.00 |
| 91 Don Paul DB | 4.00 | 2.00 |
| 92 Paige Cothren | 4.00 | 2.00 |
| 93 Joe Perry | 15.00 | 7.50 |
| 94 Tobin Rote | 5.00 | 2.50 |
| 95 Billy Wilson | 4.00 | 2.00 |
| 96 Green Bay Packers | 10.00 | 5.00 |
| 97 Lavern Torgeson | 4.00 | 2.00 |
| 98 Milt Davis | 4.00 | 2.00 |
| 99 Larry Strickland | 4.00 | 2.00 |
| 100 Matt Hazeltine RC | 5.00 | 2.50 |
| 101 Walt Yowarsky | 4.00 | 2.00 |
| 102 Roosevelt Brown | 8.00 | 4.00 |
| 103 Jim Ringo | 10.00 | 5.00 |
| 104 Joe Krupa | 4.00 | 2.00 |
| 105 Les Richter | 5.00 | 2.50 |
| 106 Art Donovan | 20.00 | 12.00 |
| 107 John Olszewski | 4.00 | 2.00 |
| 108 Ken Keller | 4.00 | 2.00 |
| 109 Philadelphia Eagles | 6.00 | 3.00 |
| 110 Baltimore Colts | 6.00 | 3.00 |
| 111 Dick Bielski | 4.00 | 2.00 |
| 112 Eddie LeBaron | 8.00 | 4.00 |
| 113 Gene Brito | 4.00 | 2.00 |
| 114 Willie Galimore RC | 8.00 | 4.00 |
| 115 Detroit Lions | 6.00 | 3.00 |
| 116 Pittsburgh Steelers | 6.00 | 3.00 |
| 117 L.G. Dupre | 4.00 | 2.00 |
| 118 Babe Parilli | 5.00 | 2.50 |
| 119 Bill George | 10.00 | 5.00 |
| 120 Raymond Berry | 40.00 | 25.00 |
| 121 Jim Podoley UER | 4.00 | 2.00 |
| 122 Hugh McElhenny | 15.00 | 7.50 |
| 123 Ed Brown | 5.00 | 2.50 |
| 124 Dick Moegle | 5.00 | 2.50 |
| 125 Tom Scott | 4.00 | 2.00 |
| 126 Tommy McDonald | 12.00 | 6.00 |
| 127 Ollie Matson | 20.00 | 10.00 |
| 128 Preston Carpenter | 4.00 | 2.00 |
| 129 George Blanda | 30.00 | 18.00 |
| 130 Gordy Soltau | 4.00 | 2.00 |
| 131 Dick Nolan RC | 5.00 | 2.50 |
| 132 Don Bosseler RC ! | 20.00 | 10.00 |

## 1959 Topps

| | | |
|---|---|---|
| COMPLETE SET (176) | 900.00 | 600.00 |
| COMMON CARD (1-88) | 3.00 | 1.50 |
| COMMON CARD (89-176) | 2.00 | 1.00 |
| WRAPPER (1-CENT) | 90.00 | 50.00 |
| WRAPPER (1-CENT, REP) | 80.00 | 50.00 |
| WRAPPER (5-CENT) | 80.00 | 50.00 |
| 1 Johnny Unitas ! | 150.00 | 90.00 |
| 2 Gene Brito | 3.00 | 1.50 |
| 3 Detroit Lions CL | 6.00 | 3.00 |
| 4 Max McGee RC | 25.00 | 12.50 |
| 5 Hugh McElhenny | 15.00 | 7.50 |
| 6 Joe Schmidt | 8.00 | 4.00 |
| 7 Kyle Rote | 6.00 | 3.00 |
| 8 Clarence Peaks | 3.00 | 1.50 |
| 9 Steelers Pennant | 3.50 | 1.75 |
| 10 Jim Brown | 150.00 | 90.00 |
| 11 Ray Mathews | 3.00 | 1.50 |
| 12 Bobby Dillon | 3.00 | 1.50 |
| 13 Joe Childress | 3.00 | 1.50 |
| 14 Terry Barr RC | 3.00 | 1.50 |
| 15 Del Shofner RC | 4.00 | 2.00 |
| 16 Bob Pellegrini UER | 3.00 | 1.50 |
| 17 Baltimore Colts CL | 3.00 | 1.50 |
| 18 Preston Carpenter | 3.00 | 1.50 |
| 19 Leo Nomellini | 10.00 | 5.00 |
| 20 Frank Gifford | 40.00 | 25.00 |
| 21 Charlie Ane | 3.00 | 1.50 |
| 22 Jack Butler | 3.00 | 1.50 |
| 23 Bart Starr | 60.00 | 35.00 |
| 24 Cardinals Pennant | 3.50 | 1.75 |
| 25 Bill Barnes | 3.00 | 1.50 |
| 26 Walt Michaels | 4.00 | 2.00 |
| 27 Clyde Conner UER | 3.00 | 1.50 |
| 28 Paige Cothren | 3.00 | 1.50 |
| 29 Roosevelt Grier | 6.00 | 3.00 |
| 30 Alan Ameche | 6.00 | 3.00 |
| 31 Philadelphia Eagles CL | 6.00 | 3.00 |
| 32 Dick Nolan | 4.00 | 2.00 |
| 33 R.C. Owens | 4.00 | 2.00 |
| 34 Dale Dodrill | 3.00 | 1.50 |
| 35 Gene Gedman | 3.00 | 1.50 |
| 36 Gene Lipscomb RC | 10.00 | 5.00 |
| 37 Ray Renfro | 4.00 | 2.00 |
| 38 Browns Pennant | 3.50 | 1.75 |
| 39 Bill Forester | 4.00 | 2.00 |
| 40 Bobby Layne | 25.00 | 15.00 |
| 41 Pat Summerall | 10.00 | 5.00 |
| 42 Jerry Mertens | 3.00 | 1.50 |
| 43 Steve Myhra | 3.00 | 1.50 |
| 44 John Henry Johnson | 8.00 | 4.00 |
| 45 Woodley Lewis UER | 3.00 | 1.50 |
| 46 Green Bay Packers CL | 8.00 | 4.00 |
| 47 Don Owens UER | 3.00 | 1.50 |
| 48 Ed Beatty | 3.00 | 1.50 |
| 49 Don Chandler | 3.00 | 1.50 |
| 50 Ollie Matson | 12.00 | 6.00 |

| | | |
|---|---|---|
| ❑ 51 Sam Huff RC | 50.00 | 30.00 |
| ❑ 52 Tom Miner | 3.00 | 1.50 |
| ❑ 53 Giants Pennant | 3.50 | 1.75 |
| ❑ 54 Kenny Konz | 3.00 | 1.50 |
| ❑ 55 Raymond Berry | 20.00 | 10.00 |
| ❑ 56 Howard Ferguson UER | 3.00 | 1.50 |
| ❑ 57 Chuck Ulrich | 3.00 | 1.50 |
| ❑ 58 Bob St.Clair | 6.00 | 3.00 |
| ❑ 59 Don Burroughs RC | 3.00 | 1.50 |
| ❑ 60 Lou Groza | 15.00 | 7.50 |
| ❑ 61 San Francisco 49ers CL | 6.00 | 3.00 |
| ❑ 62 Andy Nelson | 3.00 | 1.50 |
| ❑ 63 Harold Bradley | 3.00 | 1.50 |
| ❑ 64 Dave Hanner | 4.00 | 2.00 |
| ❑ 65 Charley Conerly | 12.00 | 6.00 |
| ❑ 66 Gene Cronin RC | 3.00 | 1.50 |
| ❑ 67 Duane Putnam | 3.00 | 1.50 |
| ❑ 68 Colts Pennant | 3.50 | 1.75 |
| ❑ 69 Ernie Stautner | 8.00 | 4.00 |
| ❑ 70 Jon Arnett | 4.00 | 2.00 |
| ❑ 71 Ken Panfil | 3.00 | 1.50 |
| ❑ 72 Matt Hazeltine | 3.00 | 1.50 |
| ❑ 73 Harley Sewell | 3.00 | 1.50 |
| ❑ 74 Mike McCormack | 6.00 | 3.00 |
| ❑ 75 Jim Ringo | 8.00 | 4.00 |
| ❑ 76 Los Angeles Rams CL | 6.00 | 3.00 |
| ❑ 77 Bob Gain RC | 3.00 | 1.50 |
| ❑ 78 Buzz Nutter | 3.00 | 1.50 |
| ❑ 79 Jerry Norton | 3.00 | 1.50 |
| ❑ 80 Joe Perry | 12.00 | 6.00 |
| ❑ 81 Carl Brettschneider | 3.00 | 1.50 |
| ❑ 82 Paul Hornung | 60.00 | 30.00 |
| ❑ 83 Eagles Pennant | 3.50 | 1.75 |
| ❑ 84 Les Richter | 4.00 | 2.00 |
| ❑ 85 Howard Cassady | 4.00 | 2.00 |
| ❑ 86 Art Donovan | 15.00 | 7.50 |
| ❑ 87 Jim Patton | 4.00 | 2.00 |
| ❑ 88 Pete Retzlaff | 4.00 | 2.00 |
| ❑ 89 Jim Mutscheller | 2.00 | 1.00 |
| ❑ 90 Zeke Bratkowski | 3.00 | 1.50 |
| ❑ 91 Washington Redskins CL | 6.00 | 3.00 |
| ❑ 92 Art Hunter | 2.00 | 1.00 |
| ❑ 93 Gern Nagler | 2.00 | 1.00 |
| ❑ 94 Chuck Weber | 2.00 | 1.00 |
| ❑ 95 Lew Carpenter UER | 2.00 | 1.00 |
| ❑ 96 Stan Jones | 5.00 | 2.50 |
| ❑ 97 Ralph Guglielmi UER | 3.00 | 1.50 |
| ❑ 98 Packers Pennant | 4.00 | 2.00 |
| ❑ 99 Ray Wietecha | 2.00 | 1.00 |
| ❑ 100 Lenny Moore | 12.00 | 6.00 |
| ❑ 101 Jim Ray Smith RC UER | 3.00 | 1.50 |
| ❑ 102 Abe Woodson RC | 3.00 | 1.50 |
| ❑ 103 Alex Karras RC | 40.00 | 25.00 |
| ❑ 104 Chicago Bears CL | 4.00 | 2.00 |
| ❑ 105 John David Crow RC | 12.00 | 6.00 |
| ❑ 106 Joe Fortunato RC | 2.00 | 1.00 |
| ❑ 107 Babe Parilli | 3.00 | 1.50 |
| ❑ 108 Proverb Jacobs | 2.00 | 1.00 |
| ❑ 109 Gino Marchetti | 8.00 | 4.00 |
| ❑ 110 Bill Wade | 3.00 | 1.50 |
| ❑ 111 49ers Pennant | 3.00 | 1.50 |
| ❑ 112 Karl Rubke | 2.00 | 1.00 |
| ❑ 113 Dave Middleton UER | 2.00 | 1.00 |
| ❑ 114 Roosevelt Brown | 5.00 | 2.50 |
| ❑ 115 Jim Olszewski | 2.00 | 1.00 |
| ❑ 116 Jerry Kramer RC | 30.00 | 18.00 |
| ❑ 117 King Hill RC | 3.00 | 1.50 |
| ❑ 118 Chicago Cardinals CL | 4.00 | 2.00 |
| ❑ 119 Frank Varrichione | 2.00 | 1.00 |
| ❑ 120 Rick Casares | 3.00 | 1.50 |
| ❑ 121 George Strugar | 2.00 | 1.00 |
| ❑ 122 Bill Glass RC | 3.00 | 1.50 |
| ❑ 123 Don Bosseler | 2.00 | 1.00 |
| ❑ 124 John Reger | 2.00 | 1.00 |
| ❑ 125 Jim Ninowski RC | 2.00 | 1.00 |
| ❑ 126 Rams Pennant | 3.00 | 1.50 |
| ❑ 127 Willard Sherman | 2.00 | 1.00 |
| ❑ 128 Bob Schnelker | 2.00 | 1.00 |
| ❑ 129 Ollie Spencer | 2.00 | 1.00 |
| ❑ 130 Y.A.Tittle | 25.00 | 15.00 |
| ❑ 131 Yale Lary | 5.00 | 2.50 |
| ❑ 132 Jim Parker RC | 30.00 | 15.00 |
| ❑ 133 New York Giants CL | 4.00 | 2.00 |
| ❑ 134 Jim Schrader | 2.00 | 1.00 |
| ❑ 135 M.C. Reynolds | 2.00 | 1.00 |
| ❑ 136 Mike Sandusky | 2.00 | 1.00 |
| ❑ 137 Ed Brown | 3.00 | 1.50 |
| ❑ 138 Al Barry | 2.00 | 1.00 |
| ❑ 139 Lions Pennant | 3.00 | 1.50 |
| ❑ 140 Bobby Mitchell RC | 35.00 | 20.00 |
| ❑ 141 Larry Morris | 2.00 | 1.00 |
| ❑ 142 Jim Phillips RC | 3.00 | 1.50 |
| ❑ 143 Jim David | 2.00 | 1.00 |
| ❑ 144 Joe Krupa | 2.00 | 1.00 |
| ❑ 145 Willie Galimore | 3.00 | 1.50 |
| ❑ 146 Pittsburgh Steelers CL | 4.00 | 2.00 |
| ❑ 147 Andy Robustelli | 8.00 | 4.00 |
| ❑ 148 Billy Wilson | 2.00 | 1.00 |
| ❑ 149 Leo Sanford | 2.00 | 1.00 |
| ❑ 150 Eddie LeBaron | 5.00 | 2.50 |
| ❑ 151 Bill McColl | 2.00 | 1.00 |
| ❑ 152 Buck Lansford UER | 2.00 | 1.00 |
| ❑ 153 Bears Pennant | 3.00 | 1.50 |
| ❑ 154 Leo Sugar | 2.00 | 1.00 |
| ❑ 155 Jim Taylor RC UER | 35.00 | 20.00 |
| ❑ 156 Lindon Crow | 2.00 | 1.00 |
| ❑ 157 Jack McClairen | 2.00 | 1.00 |
| ❑ 158 Vince Costello RC UER | 2.00 | 1.00 |
| ❑ 159 Stan Wallace | 2.00 | 1.00 |
| ❑ 160 Mel Triplett RC | 2.00 | 1.00 |
| ❑ 161 Cleveland Browns CL | 4.00 | 2.00 |
| ❑ 162 Dan Currie RC | 3.00 | 1.50 |
| ❑ 163 L.G. Dupre UER | 3.00 | 1.50 |
| ❑ 164 John Morrow UER | 2.00 | 1.00 |
| ❑ 165 Jim Podoley | 2.00 | 1.00 |
| ❑ 166 Bruce Bosley RC | 2.00 | 1.00 |
| ❑ 167 Harlon Hill | 3.00 | 1.50 |
| ❑ 168 Redskins Pennant | 3.00 | 1.50 |
| ❑ 169 Junior Wren | 2.00 | 1.00 |
| ❑ 170 Tobin Rote | 3.00 | 1.50 |
| ❑ 171 Art Spinney | 2.00 | 1.00 |
| ❑ 172 Chuck Drazenovich UER | 2.00 | 1.00 |
| ❑ 173 Bobby Joe Conrad RC | 3.00 | 1.50 |
| ❑ 174 Jesse Richardson | 2.00 | 1.00 |
| ❑ 175 Sam Baker | 2.00 | 1.00 |
| ❑ 176 Tom Tracy RC ! | 8.00 | 4.00 |

**1960 Topps**

| | | |
|---|---|---|
| ❑ COMPLETE SET (132) | 600.00 | 400.00 |
| ❑ WRAPPER (1-CENT) | 80.00 | 50.00 |
| ❑ WRAPPER (1-CENT, REP) | 300.00 | 150.00 |
| ❑ WRAPPER (5-CENT) | 80.00 | 50.00 |
| ❑ 1 Johnny Unitas ! | 80.00 | 40.00 |
| ❑ 2 Alan Ameche | 4.00 | 2.00 |
| ❑ 3 Lenny Moore | 10.00 | 5.00 |
| ❑ 4 Raymond Berry | 12.00 | 6.00 |
| ❑ 5 Jim Parker | 8.00 | 4.00 |
| ❑ 6 George Preas | 2.50 | 1.25 |
| ❑ 7 Art Spinney | 2.50 | 1.25 |
| ❑ 8 Bill Pellington RC | 3.00 | 1.50 |
| ❑ 9 Johnny Sample RC | 3.00 | 1.50 |
| ❑ 10 Gene Lipscomb | 3.00 | 1.50 |
| ❑ 11 Baltimore Colts | 3.00 | 1.50 |
| ❑ 12 Ed Brown | 3.00 | 1.50 |
| ❑ 13 Rick Casares | 3.00 | 1.50 |
| ❑ 14 Willie Galimore | 3.00 | 1.50 |
| ❑ 15 Jim Dooley | 2.50 | 1.25 |
| ❑ 16 Harlon Hill UER | 2.50 | 1.25 |
| ❑ 17 Stan Jones | 4.00 | 2.00 |
| ❑ 18 Bill George | 4.00 | 2.00 |
| ❑ 19 Erich Barnes RC | 3.00 | 1.50 |
| ❑ 20 Doug Atkins | 6.00 | 3.00 |
| ❑ 21 Chicago Bears | 3.00 | 1.50 |
| ❑ 22 Milt Plum | 3.00 | 1.50 |
| ❑ 23 Jim Brown | 100.00 | 60.00 |
| ❑ 24 Sam Baker | 2.50 | 1.25 |
| ❑ 25 Bobby Mitchell | 10.00 | 5.00 |
| ❑ 26 Ray Renfro | 3.00 | 1.50 |
| ❑ 27 Billy Howton | 3.00 | 1.50 |
| ❑ 28 Jim Ray Smith | 2.50 | 1.25 |
| ❑ 29 Jim Shofner RC | 3.00 | 1.50 |
| ❑ 30 Bob Gain | 2.50 | 1.25 |
| ❑ 31 Cleveland Browns | 3.00 | 1.50 |
| ❑ 32 Don Heinrich | 2.50 | 1.25 |
| ❑ 33 Ed Modzelewski UER | 2.50 | 1.25 |
| ❑ 34 Fred Cone | 2.50 | 1.25 |
| ❑ 35 L.G. Dupre | 3.00 | 1.50 |
| ❑ 36 Dick Bielski | 2.50 | 1.25 |
| ❑ 37 Charlie Ane UER | 2.50 | 1.25 |
| ❑ 38 Jerry Tubbs | 2.50 | 1.25 |
| ❑ 39 Doyle Nix | 2.50 | 1.25 |
| ❑ 40 Ray Krouse | 2.50 | 1.25 |
| ❑ 41 Earl Morrall | 4.00 | 2.00 |
| ❑ 42 Howard Cassady | 3.00 | 1.50 |
| ❑ 43 Dave Middleton | 2.50 | 1.25 |
| ❑ 44 Jim Gibbons RC | 2.50 | 1.25 |
| ❑ 45 Darris McCord | 2.50 | 1.25 |
| ❑ 46 Joe Schmidt | 6.00 | 3.00 |
| ❑ 47 Terry Barr | 2.50 | 1.25 |
| ❑ 48 Yale Lary | 4.00 | 2.00 |
| ❑ 49 Gil Mains | 2.50 | 1.25 |
| ❑ 50 Detroit Lions | 3.00 | 1.50 |
| ❑ 51 Bart Starr | 50.00 | 30.00 |
| ❑ 52 Jim Taylor UER | 8.00 | 4.00 |
| ❑ 53 Lew Carpenter | 3.00 | 1.50 |
| ❑ 54 Paul Hornung | 45.00 | 30.00 |
| ❑ 55 Max McGee | 4.00 | 2.00 |
| ❑ 56 Forrest Gregg RC | 40.00 | 25.00 |
| ❑ 57 Jim Ringo | 5.00 | 2.50 |
| ❑ 58 Bill Forester | 3.00 | 1.50 |
| ❑ 59 Dave Hanner | 3.00 | 1.50 |
| ❑ 60 Green Bay Packers | 8.00 | 4.00 |
| ❑ 61 Bill Wade | 3.00 | 1.50 |
| ❑ 62 Frank Ryan RC | 4.00 | 2.00 |
| ❑ 63 Ollie Matson | 10.00 | 5.00 |
| ❑ 64 Jon Arnett | 3.00 | 1.50 |
| ❑ 65 Del Shofner | 3.00 | 1.50 |
| ❑ 66 Jim Phillips | 2.50 | 1.25 |
| ❑ 67 Art Hunter | 2.50 | 1.25 |
| ❑ 68 Les Richter | 3.00 | 1.50 |
| ❑ 69 Lou Michaels RC | 3.00 | 1.50 |
| ❑ 70 John Baker | 2.50 | 1.25 |
| ❑ 71 Los Angeles Rams | 3.00 | 1.50 |
| ❑ 72 Charley Conerly | 8.00 | 4.00 |
| ❑ 73 Mel Triplett | 2.50 | 1.25 |
| ❑ 74 Frank Gifford | 35.00 | 20.00 |
| ❑ 75 Alex Webster | 3.00 | 1.50 |
| ❑ 76 Bob Schnelker | 2.50 | 1.25 |
| ❑ 77 Pat Summerall | 8.00 | 4.00 |
| ❑ 78 Roosevelt Brown | 4.00 | 2.00 |
| ❑ 79 Jim Patton | 2.50 | 1.25 |
| ❑ 80 Sam Huff | 20.00 | 10.00 |
| ❑ 81 Andy Robustelli | 6.00 | 3.00 |
| ❑ 82 New York Giants | 3.00 | 1.50 |
| ❑ 83 Clarence Peaks | 2.50 | 1.25 |
| ❑ 84 Bill Barnes | 2.50 | 1.25 |
| ❑ 85 Pete Retzlaff | 3.00 | 1.50 |
| ❑ 86 Bobby Walston | 2.50 | 1.25 |
| ❑ 87 Chuck Bednarik UER | 8.00 | 4.00 |
| ❑ 88 Bob Pellegrini | 2.50 | 1.25 |
| ❑ 89 Tom Brookshier RC | 3.00 | 1.50 |
| ❑ 90 Marion Campbell | 3.00 | 1.50 |
| ❑ 91 Jesse Richardson | 2.50 | 1.25 |
| ❑ 92 Philadelphia Eagles | 3.00 | 1.50 |
| ❑ 93 Bobby Layne | 30.00 | 18.00 |
| ❑ 94 John Henry Johnson | 6.00 | 3.00 |
| ❑ 95 Tom Tracy UER | 3.00 | 1.50 |
| ❑ 96 Preston Carpenter | 2.50 | 1.25 |
| ❑ 97 Frank Varrichione UER | 2.50 | 1.25 |
| ❑ 98 John Nisby | 2.50 | 1.25 |
| ❑ 99 Dean Derby | 2.50 | 1.25 |
| ❑ 100 George Tarasovic | 2.50 | 1.25 |
| ❑ 101 Ernie Stautner | 5.00 | 2.50 |
| ❑ 102 Pittsburgh Steelers | 3.00 | 1.50 |
| ❑ 103 King Hill | 3.00 | 1.50 |
| ❑ 104 Mal Hammack | 2.50 | 1.25 |
| ❑ 105 John David Crow | 3.00 | 1.50 |
| ❑ 106 Bobby Joe Conrad | 3.00 | 1.50 |

| | | |
|---|---|---|
| ☐ 107 Woodley Lewis | 2.50 | 1.25 |
| ☐ 108 Don Gillis | 2.50 | 1.25 |
| ☐ 109 Carl Brettschneider | 2.50 | 1.25 |
| ☐ 110 Leo Sugar | 2.50 | 1.25 |
| ☐ 111 Frank Fuller | 2.50 | 1.25 |
| ☐ 112 St. Louis Cardinals | 3.00 | 1.50 |
| ☐ 113 Y.A.Tittle | 30.00 | 18.00 |
| ☐ 114 Joe Perry | 8.00 | 4.00 |
| ☐ 115 J.D.Smith RC | 3.00 | 1.50 |
| ☐ 116 Hugh McElhenny | 8.00 | 4.00 |
| ☐ 117 Billy Wilson | 2.50 | 1.25 |
| ☐ 118 Bob St.Clair | 4.00 | 2.00 |
| ☐ 119 Matt Hazeltine | 2.50 | 1.25 |
| ☐ 120 Abe Woodson | 2.50 | 1.25 |
| ☐ 121 Leo Nomellini | 5.00 | 2.50 |
| ☐ 122 San Francisco 49ers | 3.00 | 1.50 |
| ☐ 123 Ralph Guglielmi UER | 2.50 | 1.25 |
| ☐ 124 Don Bosseler | 2.50 | 1.25 |
| ☐ 125 John Olszewski | 2.50 | 1.25 |
| ☐ 126 Bill Anderson UER | 2.50 | 1.25 |
| ☐ 127 Joe Walton RC | 3.00 | 1.50 |
| ☐ 128 Jim Schrader | 2.50 | 1.25 |
| ☐ 129 Ralph Felton | 2.50 | 1.25 |
| ☐ 130 Gary Glick | 2.50 | 1.25 |
| ☐ 131 Bob Toneff | 2.50 | 1.25 |
| ☐ 132 Redskins Team !. | 30.00 | 18.00 |

## 1961 Topps

ALAN AMECHE
FULLBACK-R.C.-BALTIMORE COLTS

| | | |
|---|---|---|
| ☐ COMPLETE SET (198) | 1000.00 | 650.00 |
| ☐ COMMON CARD (1-132) | 2.50 | 1.25 |
| ☐ COMMON CARD (133-198) | 3.00 | 1.50 |
| ☐ WRAPPER (1-CENT) | 350.00 | 200.00 |
| ☐ WRAPPER (1-CENT, REP) | 200.00 | 125.00 |
| ☐ WRAPPER (5-CENT) | 100.00 | 60.00 |
| ☐ 1 Johnny Unitas | 100.00 | 50.00 |
| ☐ 2 Lenny Moore | 12.00 | 6.00 |
| ☐ 3 Alan Ameche | 4.00 | 2.00 |
| ☐ 4 Raymond Berry | 12.00 | 6.00 |
| ☐ 5 Jim Mutscheller | 2.50 | 1.25 |
| ☐ 6 Jim Parker | 5.00 | 2.50 |
| ☐ 7 Gino Marchetti | 6.00 | 3.00 |
| ☐ 8 Gene Lipscomb | 4.00 | 2.00 |
| ☐ 9 Baltimore Colts | 3.00 | 1.50 |
| ☐ 10 Bill Wade | 3.00 | 1.50 |
| ☐ 11 Johnny Morris RC | 6.00 | 3.00 |
| ☐ 12 Rick Casares | 3.00 | 1.50 |
| ☐ 13 Harlon Hill | 2.50 | 1.25 |
| ☐ 14 Stan Jones | 4.00 | 2.00 |
| ☐ 15 Doug Atkins | 5.00 | 2.50 |
| ☐ 16 Bill George | 4.00 | 2.00 |
| ☐ 17 J.C. Caroline | 2.50 | 1.25 |
| ☐ 18 Chicago Bears | 3.00 | 1.50 |
| ☐ 19 Eddie LeBaron IA | 3.00 | 1.50 |
| ☐ 20 Eddie LeBaron | 3.00 | 1.50 |
| ☐ 21 Don McIlhenny | 2.50 | 1.25 |
| ☐ 22 L.G. Dupre | 2.50 | 1.25 |
| ☐ 23 Jim Doran | 2.50 | 1.25 |
| ☐ 24 Billy Howton | 2.50 | 1.25 |
| ☐ 25 Buzz Guy | 2.50 | 1.25 |
| ☐ 26 Jack Patera RC | 3.00 | 1.50 |
| ☐ 27 Tom Franckhauser RC | 2.50 | 1.25 |
| ☐ 28 Cowboys Team | 15.00 | 7.50 |
| ☐ 29 Jim Ninowski | 2.50 | 1.25 |
| ☐ 30 Dan Lewis RC | 2.50 | 1.25 |
| ☐ 31 Nick Pietrosante RC | 3.00 | 1.50 |
| ☐ 32 Gail Cogdill RC | 3.00 | 1.50 |
| ☐ 33 Jim Gibbons | 2.50 | 1.25 |
| ☐ 34 Jim Martin | 2.50 | 1.25 |

| | | |
|---|---|---|
| ☐ 35 Alex Karras | 15.00 | 7.50 |
| ☐ 36 Joe Schmidt | 5.00 | 2.50 |
| ☐ 37 Detroit Lions | 3.00 | 1.50 |
| ☐ 38 Paul Hornung IA | 18.00 | 9.00 |
| ☐ 39 Bart Starr | 40.00 | 20.00 |
| ☐ 40 Paul Hornung | 40.00 | 25.00 |
| ☐ 41 Jim Taylor | 35.00 | 20.00 |
| ☐ 42 Max McGee | 8.00 | 4.00 |
| ☐ 43 Boyd Dowler RC | 8.00 | 4.00 |
| ☐ 44 Jim Ringo | 9.00 | 2.50 |
| ☐ 45 Hank Jordan RC | 30.00 | 18.00 |
| ☐ 46 Bill Forester | 3.00 | 1.50 |
| ☐ 47 Green Bay Packers | 15.00 | 7.50 |
| ☐ 48 Frank Ryan | 3.00 | 1.50 |
| ☐ 49 Jon Arnett | 3.00 | 1.50 |
| ☐ 50 Ollie Matson | 8.00 | 4.00 |
| ☐ 51 Jim Phillips | 2.50 | 1.25 |
| ☐ 52 Del Shofner | 3.00 | 1.50 |
| ☐ 53 Art Hunter | 2.50 | 1.25 |
| ☐ 54 Gene Brito | 2.50 | 1.25 |
| ☐ 55 Lindon Crow | 2.50 | 1.25 |
| ☐ 56 Los Angeles Rams | 3.00 | 1.50 |
| ☐ 57 Johnny Unitas IA | 25.00 | 15.00 |
| ☐ 58 Y.A.Tittle | 30.00 | 18.00 |
| ☐ 59 John Brodie RC | 40.00 | 25.00 |
| ☐ 60 J.D. Smith | 2.50 | 1.25 |
| ☐ 61 R.C. Owens | 2.50 | 1.50 |
| ☐ 62 Clyde Conner | 2.50 | 1.25 |
| ☐ 63 Bob St.Clair | 4.00 | 2.00 |
| ☐ 64 Leo Nomellini | 6.00 | 3.00 |
| ☐ 65 Abe Woodson | 2.50 | 1.25 |
| ☐ 66 San Francisco 49ers | 3.00 | 1.50 |
| ☐ 67 Checklist Card | 40.00 | 25.00 |
| ☐ 68 Milt Plum | 3.00 | 1.50 |
| ☐ 69 Ray Renfro | 3.00 | 1.50 |
| ☐ 70 Bobby Mitchell | 8.00 | 4.00 |
| ☐ 71 Jim Brown | 125.00 | 75.00 |
| ☐ 72 Mike McCormack | 4.00 | 2.00 |
| ☐ 73 Jim Ray Smith | 2.50 | 1.25 |
| ☐ 74 Sam Baker | 2.50 | 1.25 |
| ☐ 75 Walt Michaels | 2.50 | 1.50 |
| ☐ 76 Cleveland Browns | 3.00 | 1.50 |
| ☐ 77 Jim Brown IA | 35.00 | 20.00 |
| ☐ 78 George Shaw | 2.50 | 1.25 |
| ☐ 79 Hugh McElhenny | 8.00 | 4.00 |
| ☐ 80 Clancy Osborne | 2.50 | 1.25 |
| ☐ 81 Dave Middleton | 2.50 | 1.25 |
| ☐ 82 Frank Youso | 2.50 | 1.25 |
| ☐ 83 Don Joyce | 2.50 | 1.25 |
| ☐ 84 Ed Culpepper | 2.50 | 1.25 |
| ☐ 85 Charley Conerly | 8.00 | 4.00 |
| ☐ 86 Mel Triplett | 2.50 | 1.25 |
| ☐ 87 Kyle Rote | 3.00 | 1.50 |
| ☐ 88 Roosevelt Brown | 4.00 | 2.00 |
| ☐ 89 Ray Wietecha | 2.50 | 1.25 |
| ☐ 90 Andy Robustelli | 5.00 | 2.50 |
| ☐ 91 Sam Huff | 8.00 | 4.00 |
| ☐ 92 Jim Patton | 2.50 | 1.25 |
| ☐ 93 New York Giants | 3.00 | 1.50 |
| ☐ 94 Charley Conerly IA | 6.00 | 3.00 |
| ☐ 95 Sonny Jurgensen | 25.00 | 15.00 |
| ☐ 96 Tommy McDonald | 5.00 | 2.50 |
| ☐ 97 Bill Barnes | 2.50 | 1.25 |
| ☐ 98 Bobby Walston | 2.50 | 1.25 |
| ☐ 99 Pete Retzlaff | 3.00 | 1.50 |
| ☐ 100 Jim McCusker | 2.50 | 1.25 |
| ☐ 101 Chuck Bednarik | 8.00 | 4.00 |
| ☐ 102 Tom Brookshier | 3.00 | 1.50 |
| ☐ 103 Philadelphia Eagles | 3.00 | 1.50 |
| ☐ 104 Bobby Layne | 30.00 | 18.00 |
| ☐ 105 John Henry Johnson | 4.00 | 2.00 |
| ☐ 106 Tom Tracy | 3.00 | 1.50 |
| ☐ 107 Buddy Dial RC | 2.50 | 1.25 |
| ☐ 108 Jimmy Orr RC | 4.00 | 2.00 |
| ☐ 109 Mike Sandusky | 2.50 | 1.25 |
| ☐ 110 John Reger | 2.50 | 1.25 |
| ☐ 111 Junior Wren | 2.50 | 1.25 |
| ☐ 112 Pittsburgh Steelers | 3.00 | 1.50 |
| ☐ 113 Bobby Layne IA | 10.00 | 5.00 |
| ☐ 114 John Roach | 2.50 | 1.25 |
| ☐ 115 Sam Etcheverry RC | 3.00 | 1.50 |
| ☐ 116 John David Crow | 3.00 | 1.50 |
| ☐ 117 Mal Hammack | 2.50 | 1.25 |
| ☐ 118 Sonny Randle RC | 3.00 | 1.50 |
| ☐ 119 Leo Sugar | 2.50 | 1.25 |

| | | |
|---|---|---|
| ☐ 120 Jerry Norton | 2.50 | 1.25 |
| ☐ 121 St. Louis Cardinals | 3.00 | 1.50 |
| ☐ 122 Checklist Card | 50.00 | 30.00 |
| ☐ 123 Ralph Guglielmi | 2.50 | 1.25 |
| ☐ 124 Dick James | 2.50 | 1.25 |
| ☐ 125 Don Bosseler | 2.50 | 1.25 |
| ☐ 126 Joe Walton | 2.50 | 1.25 |
| ☐ 127 Bill Anderson | 2.50 | 1.25 |
| ☐ 128 Vince Promuto RC | 2.50 | 1.25 |
| ☐ 129 Bob Toneff | 2.50 | 1.25 |
| ☐ 130 John Paluck | 2.50 | 1.25 |
| ☐ 131 Washington Redskins | 3.00 | 1.50 |
| ☐ 132 Milt Plum IA ! | 2.50 | 1.25 |
| ☐ 133 Abner Haynes ! | 8.00 | 4.00 |
| ☐ 134 Mel Branch UER | 4.00 | 2.00 |
| ☐ 135 Jerry Cornelison UER | 3.00 | 1.50 |
| ☐ 136 Bill Krisher | 3.00 | 1.50 |
| ☐ 137 Paul Miller | 3.00 | 1.50 |
| ☐ 138 Jack Spikes | 4.00 | 2.00 |
| ☐ 139 Johnny Robinson RC | 8.00 | 4.00 |
| ☐ 140 Cotton Davidson RC | 4.00 | 2.00 |
| ☐ 141 Dave Smith RB | 3.00 | 1.50 |
| ☐ 142 Bill Groman | 3.00 | 1.50 |
| ☐ 143 Rich Michael | 3.00 | 1.50 |
| ☐ 144 Mike Dukes | 3.00 | 1.50 |
| ☐ 145 George Blanda | 25.00 | 15.00 |
| ☐ 146 Billy Cannon | 6.00 | 3.00 |
| ☐ 147 Dennit Morris | 3.00 | 1.50 |
| ☐ 148 Jacky Lee UER | 4.00 | 2.00 |
| ☐ 149 Al Dorow | 3.00 | 1.50 |
| ☐ 150 Don Maynard RC | 50.00 | 25.00 |
| ☐ 151 Art Powell RC | 8.00 | 4.00 |
| ☐ 152 Sid Youngelman | 3.00 | 1.50 |
| ☐ 153 Bob Mischak | 3.00 | 1.50 |
| ☐ 154 Larry Grantham | 3.00 | 1.50 |
| ☐ 155 Tom Saidock | 3.00 | 1.50 |
| ☐ 156 Roger Donnahoo | 3.00 | 1.50 |
| ☐ 157 Laverne Torczon | 3.00 | 1.50 |
| ☐ 158 Archie Matsos RC | 4.00 | 2.00 |
| ☐ 159 Elbert Dubenion | 4.00 | 2.00 |
| ☐ 160 Wray Carlton RC | 4.00 | 2.00 |
| ☐ 161 Rich McCabe | 3.00 | 1.50 |
| ☐ 162 Ken Rice | 3.00 | 1.50 |
| ☐ 163 Art Baker RC | 3.00 | 1.50 |
| ☐ 164 Tom Rychlec | 3.00 | 1.50 |
| ☐ 165 Mack Yoho | 3.00 | 1.50 |
| ☐ 166 Jack Kemp | 100.00 | 50.00 |
| ☐ 167 Paul Lowe | 6.00 | 3.00 |
| ☐ 168 Ron Mix | 10.00 | 5.00 |
| ☐ 169 Paul Maguire UER | 6.00 | 3.00 |
| ☐ 170 Volney Peters | 3.00 | 1.50 |
| ☐ 171 Ernie Wright RC | 4.00 | 2.00 |
| ☐ 172 Ron Nery RC | 3.00 | 1.50 |
| ☐ 173 Dave Kocourek RC | 4.00 | 2.00 |
| ☐ 174 Jim Colclough | 3.00 | 1.50 |
| ☐ 175 Babe Parilli | 4.00 | 2.00 |
| ☐ 176 Billy Lott | 3.00 | 1.50 |
| ☐ 177 Fred Bruney | 3.00 | 1.50 |
| ☐ 178 Ross O'Hanley | 3.00 | 1.50 |
| ☐ 179 Walt Cudzik | 3.00 | 1.50 |
| ☐ 180 Charley Leo | 3.00 | 1.50 |
| ☐ 181 Bob Dee | 3.00 | 1.50 |
| ☐ 182 Jim Otto RC | 40.00 | 25.00 |
| ☐ 183 Eddie Macon | 3.00 | 1.50 |
| ☐ 184 Dick Christy | 3.00 | 1.50 |
| ☐ 185 Alan Miller RC | 3.00 | 1.50 |
| ☐ 186 Tom Flores RC | 20.00 | 10.00 |
| ☐ 187 Joe Cannavino | 3.00 | 1.50 |
| ☐ 188 Don Manoukian | 3.00 | 1.50 |
| ☐ 189 Bob Coolbaugh | 3.00 | 1.50 |
| ☐ 190 Lionel Taylor RC | 8.00 | 4.00 |
| ☐ 191 Bud McFadin | 3.00 | 1.50 |
| ☐ 192 Goose Gonsoulin RC | 6.00 | 3.00 |
| ☐ 193 Frank Tripucka | 4.00 | 2.00 |
| ☐ 194 Gene Mingo RC | 4.00 | 2.00 |
| ☐ 195 Eldon Danenhauer | 3.00 | 1.50 |
| ☐ 196 Bob McNamara | 3.00 | 1.50 |
| ☐ 197 Dave Rolle UER | 3.00 | 1.50 |
| ☐ 198 Checklist UER ! | 100.00 | 60.00 |

## 1962 Topps

| | | |
|---|---|---|
| ☐ COMPLETE SET (176) | 2000.00 | 1200.00 |
| ☐ WRAPPER (1-CENT) | 250.00 | 175.00 |
| ☐ WRAPPER (5-CENT,STARS) | 50.00 | 25.00 |
| ☐ WRAPPER (5-CENT,BUCKS) | 40.00 | 25.00 |

|  |  | | |
|---|---|---|---|
| 1 | Johnny Unitas ! | 200.00 | 125.00 |
| 2 | Lenny Moore | 12.00 | 6.00 |
| 3 | Alex Hawkins RC SP | 10.00 | 5.00 |
| 4 | Joe Perry | 8.00 | 4.00 |
| 5 | Raymond Berry SP | 40.00 | 25.00 |
| 6 | Steve Myhra | 4.00 | 2.00 |
| 7 | Tom Gilburg SP | 8.00 | 4.00 |
| 8 | Gino Marchetti | 8.00 | 4.00 |
| 9 | Bill Pellington | 4.00 | 2.00 |
| 10 | Andy Nelson | 4.00 | 2.00 |
| 11 | Wendell Harris SP | 8.00 | 4.00 |
| 12 | Baltimore Colts | 6.00 | 3.00 |
| 13 | Bill Wade SP | 10.00 | 5.00 |
| 14 | Willie Galimore | 5.00 | 2.50 |
| 15 | Johnny Morris SP | 8.00 | 4.00 |
| 16 | Rick Casares | 5.00 | 2.50 |
| 17 | Mike Ditka RC SP | 300.00 | 175.00 |
| 18 | Stan Jones | 6.00 | 3.00 |
| 19 | Roger LeClerc | 4.00 | 2.00 |
| 20 | Angelo Coia | 4.00 | 2.00 |
| 21 | Doug Atkins | 7.00 | 3.50 |
| 22 | Bill George | 6.00 | 3.00 |
| 23 | Richie Petitbon RC | 5.00 | 2.50 |
| 24 | Ronnie Bull RC SP | 6.00 | 3.00 |
| 25 | Chicago Bears | 6.00 | 3.00 |
| 26 | Howard Cassady | 5.00 | 2.50 |
| 27 | Ray Renfro SP | 10.00 | 5.00 |
| 28 | Jim Brown | 175.00 | 100.00 |
| 29 | Rich Kreitling | 4.00 | 2.00 |
| 30 | Jim Ray Smith | 4.00 | 2.00 |
| 31 | John Morrow | 4.00 | 2.00 |
| 32 | Lou Groza | 15.00 | 7.50 |
| 33 | Bob Gain | 4.00 | 2.00 |
| 34 | Bernie Parrish | 4.00 | 2.00 |
| 35 | Jim Shofner | 4.00 | 2.00 |
| 36 | Ernie Davis RC SP | 150.00 | 90.00 |
| 37 | Cleveland Browns | 6.00 | 3.00 |
| 38 | Eddie LeBaron | 5.00 | 2.50 |
| 39 | Don Meredith SP | 100.00 | 60.00 |
| 40 | J.W. Lockett SP | 8.00 | 4.00 |
| 41 | Don Perkins RC | 10.00 | 5.00 |
| 42 | Billy Howton | 5.00 | 2.50 |
| 43 | Dick Bielski | 4.00 | 2.00 |
| 44 | Mike Connelly RC | 4.00 | 2.00 |
| 45 | Jerry Tubbs SP | 8.00 | 4.00 |
| 46 | Don Bishop SP | 8.00 | 4.00 |
| 47 | Dick Moegle | 4.00 | 2.00 |
| 48 | Bobby Plummer SP | 8.00 | 4.00 |
| 49 | Cowboys Team | 20.00 | 12.00 |
| 50 | Milt Plum | 5.00 | 2.50 |
| 51 | Dan Lewis | 4.00 | 2.00 |
| 52 | Nick Pietrosante SP | 8.00 | 4.00 |
| 53 | Gail Cogdill | 4.00 | 2.00 |
| 54 | Jim Gibbons | 4.00 | 2.00 |
| 55 | Jim Martin | 4.00 | 2.00 |
| 56 | Yale Lary | 6.00 | 3.00 |
| 57 | Darris McCord | 4.00 | 2.00 |
| 58 | Alex Karras | 25.00 | 15.00 |
| 59 | Joe Schmidt | 7.00 | 3.50 |
| 60 | Dick Lane | 6.00 | 3.00 |
| 61 | John Lomakoski SP | 8.00 | 4.00 |
| 62 | Detroit Lions SP | 18.00 | 10.00 |
| 63 | Bart Starr SP | 125.00 | 75.00 |
| 64 | Paul Hornung SP | 100.00 | 60.00 |
| 65 | Tom Moore SP | 12.00 | 6.00 |
| 66 | Jim Taylor SP | 50.00 | 30.00 |
| 67 | Max McGee SP | 12.00 | 6.00 |
| 68 | Jim Ringo SP | 15.00 | 7.50 |
| 69 | Fuzzy Thurston RC SP | 25.00 | 15.00 |
| 70 | Forrest Gregg | 7.00 | 3.50 |
| 71 | Boyd Dowler | 6.00 | 3.00 |
| 72 | Hank Jordan SP | 15.00 | 7.50 |
| 73 | Bill Forester SP | 10.00 | 5.00 |
| 74 | Earl Gros SP | 8.00 | 4.00 |
| 75 | Packers Team SP | 40.00 | 25.00 |
| 76 | Checklist SP | 80.00 | 45.00 |
| 77 | Zeke Bratkowski SP | 10.00 | 5.00 |
| 78 | Jon Arnett SP | 10.00 | 5.00 |
| 79 | Ollie Matson SP | 35.00 | 20.00 |
| 80 | Dick Bass SP | 10.00 | 5.00 |
| 81 | Jim Phillips | 4.00 | 2.00 |
| 82 | Carroll Dale RC | 5.00 | 2.50 |
| 83 | Frank Varrichione | 4.00 | 2.00 |
| 84 | Art Hunter | 4.00 | 2.00 |
| 85 | Danny Villanueva RC | 4.00 | 2.00 |
| 86 | Les Richter SP | 8.00 | 4.00 |
| 87 | Lindon Crow | 4.00 | 2.00 |
| 88 | Roman Gabriel SP | 60.00 | 35.00 |
| 89 | Los Angeles Rams SP | 18.00 | 10.00 |
| 90 | Fran Tarkenton SP | 225.00 | 125.00 |
| 91 | Jerry Reichow SP | 8.00 | 4.00 |
| 92 | Hugh McElhenny SP | 30.00 | 18.00 |
| 93 | Mel Triplett SP | 8.00 | 4.00 |
| 94 | Tommy Mason RC SP | 12.00 | 6.00 |
| 95 | Dave Middleton SP | 8.00 | 4.00 |
| 96 | Frank Youso SP | 8.00 | 4.00 |
| 97 | Mike Mercer SP | 8.00 | 4.00 |
| 98 | Rip Hawkins SP | 8.00 | 4.00 |
| 99 | Cliff Livingston SP | 8.00 | 4.00 |
| 100 | Roy Winston RC SP | 8.00 | 4.00 |
| 101 | Vikings Team SP | 25.00 | 15.00 |
| 102 | Y.A.Tittle | 40.00 | 25.00 |
| 103 | Joe Walton | 4.00 | 2.00 |
| 104 | Frank Gifford | 50.00 | 30.00 |
| 105 | Alex Webster | 5.00 | 2.50 |
| 106 | Del Shofner | 5.00 | 2.50 |
| 107 | Don Chandler | 4.00 | 2.00 |
| 108 | Andy Robustelli | 7.00 | 3.50 |
| 109 | Jim Katcavage RC | 4.00 | 2.00 |
| 110 | Sam Huff SP | 40.00 | 25.00 |
| 111 | Erich Barnes | 4.00 | 2.00 |
| 112 | Jim Patton | 4.00 | 2.00 |
| 113 | Jerry Hillebrand SP | 4.00 | 2.00 |
| 114 | New York Giants | 6.00 | 3.00 |
| 115 | Sonny Jurgensen SP | 40.00 | 25.00 |
| 116 | Tommy McDonald | 8.00 | 4.00 |
| 117 | Ted Dean SP | 8.00 | 4.00 |
| 118 | Clarence Peaks | 4.00 | 2.00 |
| 119 | Bobby Walston | 4.00 | 2.00 |
| 120 | Pete Retzlaff SP | 10.00 | 5.00 |
| 121 | Jim Schrader SP | 8.00 | 4.00 |
| 122 | J.D. Smith T | 4.00 | 2.00 |
| 123 | King Hill | 4.00 | 2.00 |
| 124 | Maxie Baughan SP | 5.00 | 2.50 |
| 125 | Pete Case SP | 8.00 | 4.00 |
| 126 | Philadelphia Eagles | 6.00 | 3.00 |
| 127 | Bobby Layne | 40.00 | 25.00 |
| 128 | Tom Tracy | 5.00 | 2.50 |
| 129 | John Henry Johnson | 6.00 | 3.00 |
| 130 | Buddy Dial SP | 10.00 | 5.00 |
| 131 | Preston Carpenter | 4.00 | 2.00 |
| 132 | Lou Michaels SP | 8.00 | 4.00 |
| 133 | Gene Lipscomb SP | 10.00 | 5.00 |
| 134 | Ernie Stautner SP | 20.00 | 12.00 |
| 135 | John Reger SP | 8.00 | 4.00 |
| 136 | Myron Pottios SP | 4.00 | 2.00 |
| 137 | Bob Ferguson SP | 4.00 | 2.00 |
| 138 | Pittsburgh Steelers SP | 18.00 | 10.00 |
| 139 | Sam Etcheverry SP | 5.00 | 2.50 |
| 140 | John David Crow SP | 10.00 | 5.00 |
| 141 | Bobby Joe Conrad SP | 10.00 | 5.00 |
| 142 | Prentice Gautt RC SP | 8.00 | 4.00 |
| 143 | Frank Mestnik | 4.00 | 2.00 |
| 144 | Sonny Randle | 5.00 | 2.50 |
| 145 | Gerry Perry UER | 4.00 | 2.00 |
| 146 | Jerry Norton | 4.00 | 2.00 |
| 147 | Jimmy Hill | 4.00 | 2.00 |
| 148 | Bill Stacy | 4.00 | 2.00 |
| 149 | Fate Echols SP | 8.00 | 4.00 |
| 150 | St. Louis Cardinals | 6.00 | 3.00 |
| 151 | Billy Kilmer SP | 35.00 | 20.00 |
| 152 | John Brodie | 18.00 | 10.00 |
| 153 | J.D. Smith RB | 5.00 | 2.50 |
| 154 | C.R. Roberts SP | 8.00 | 4.00 |
| 155 | Monty Stickles | 4.00 | 2.00 |
| 156 | Clyde Conner UER | 4.00 | 2.00 |
| 157 | Bob St.Clair | 6.00 | 3.00 |
| 158 | Tommy Davis RC | 4.00 | 2.00 |
| 159 | Leo Nomellini | 8.00 | 4.00 |
| 160 | Matt Hazeltine | 4.00 | 2.00 |
| 161 | Abe Woodson | 4.00 | 2.00 |
| 162 | Dave Baker | 4.00 | 2.00 |
| 163 | San Francisco 49ers | 6.00 | 3.00 |
| 164 | Norm Snead RC SP | 30.00 | 18.00 |
| 165 | Dick James | 5.00 | 2.50 |
| 166 | Bobby Mitchell | 8.00 | 4.00 |
| 167 | Sam Horner | 4.00 | 2.00 |
| 168 | Bill Barnes | 4.00 | 2.00 |
| 169 | Bill Anderson | 4.00 | 2.00 |
| 170 | Fred Dugan | 4.00 | 2.00 |
| 171 | John Aveni SP | 8.00 | 4.00 |
| 172 | Bob Toneff | 4.00 | 2.00 |
| 173 | Jim Kerr | 4.00 | 2.00 |
| 174 | Leroy Jackson SP | 8.00 | 4.00 |
| 175 | Washington Redskins | 6.00 | 3.00 |
| 176 | Checklist ! | 100.00 | 60.00 |

## 1963 Topps

| |  | | |
|---|---|---|---|
| | COMPLETE SET (170) | 1350.00 | 850.00 |
| | WRAPPER (1-CENT) | 450.00 | 300.00 |
| | WRAPPER (5-CENT) | 80.00 | 50.00 |
| 1 | Johnny Unitas ! | 135.00 | 75.00 |
| 2 | Lenny Moore | 8.00 | 4.00 |
| 3 | Jimmy Orr | 3.00 | 1.50 |
| 4 | Raymond Berry | 8.00 | 4.00 |
| 5 | Jim Parker | 5.00 | 2.50 |
| 6 | Alex Sandusky | 2.50 | 1.25 |
| 7 | Dick Szymanski RC | 2.50 | 1.25 |
| 8 | Gino Marchetti | 6.00 | 3.00 |
| 9 | Billy Ray Smith RC | 3.00 | 1.50 |
| 10 | Bill Pellington | 2.50 | 1.25 |
| 11 | Bob Boyd RC DB | 2.50 | 1.25 |
| 12 | Baltimore Colts SP | 10.00 | 5.00 |
| 13 | Frank Ryan SP | 8.00 | 4.00 |
| 14 | Jim Brown SP | 200.00 | 100.00 |
| 15 | Ray Renfro SP | 8.00 | 4.00 |
| 16 | Rich Kreitling SP | 6.00 | 3.50 |
| 17 | Mike McCormack SP | 10.00 | 5.00 |
| 18 | Jim Ray Smith SP | 6.00 | 3.50 |
| 19 | Lou Groza SP | 25.00 | 15.00 |
| 20 | Bill Glass SP | 6.00 | 3.50 |
| 21 | Galen Fiss SP | 6.00 | 3.50 |
| 22 | Don Fleming RC SP | 8.00 | 4.00 |
| 23 | Bob Gain SP | 6.00 | 3.50 |
| 24 | Cleveland Browns SP | 10.00 | 5.00 |
| 25 | Milt Plum | 3.00 | 1.50 |
| 26 | Dan Lewis | 2.50 | 1.25 |
| 27 | Nick Pietrosante | 2.50 | 1.25 |
| 28 | Gail Cogdill | 2.50 | 1.25 |
| 29 | Harley Sewell | 2.50 | 1.25 |
| 30 | Jim Gibbons | 2.50 | 1.25 |
| 31 | Carl Brettschneider | 2.50 | 1.25 |
| 32 | Dick Lane | 5.00 | 2.50 |
| 33 | Yale Lary | 5.00 | 2.50 |
| 34 | Roger Brown SP | 3.00 | 1.50 |
| 35 | Joe Schmidt | 6.00 | 3.00 |
| 36 | Detroit Lions SP | 10.00 | 5.00 |
| 37 | Roman Gabriel | 8.00 | 4.00 |
| 38 | Zeke Bratkowski | 3.00 | 1.50 |
| 39 | Dick Bass | 3.00 | 1.50 |
| 40 | Jon Arnett | 3.00 | 1.50 |

| | | | |
|---|---|---|---|
| ❑ 41 Jim Phillips | 2.50 | 1.25 |
| ❑ 42 Frank Varrichione | 2.50 | 1.25 |
| ❑ 43 Danny Villanueva | 2.50 | 1.25 |
| ❑ 44 Deacon Jones RC | 50.00 | 30.00 |
| ❑ 45 Lindon Crow | 2.50 | 1.25 |
| ❑ 46 Marlin McKeever | 2.50 | 1.25 |
| ❑ 47 Ed Meador RC | 2.50 | 1.25 |
| ❑ 48 Los Angeles Rams | 4.00 | 2.00 |
| ❑ 49 Y.A.Tittle SP | 50.00 | 30.00 |
| ❑ 50 Del Shofner SP | 6.00 | 3.50 |
| ❑ 51 Alex Webster SP | 8.00 | 4.00 |
| ❑ 52 Phil King SP | 6.00 | 3.50 |
| ❑ 53 Jack Stroud SP | 6.00 | 3.50 |
| ❑ 54 Darrell Dess SP | 6.00 | 3.50 |
| ❑ 55 Jim Katcavage SP | 6.00 | 3.50 |
| ❑ 56 Roosevelt Grier SP | 10.00 | 5.00 |
| ❑ 57 Erich Barnes SP | 6.00 | 3.50 |
| ❑ 58 Jim Patton SP | 6.00 | 3.50 |
| ❑ 59 Sam Huff SP | 20.00 | 12.00 |
| ❑ 60 New York Giants | 6.00 | 3.50 |
| ❑ 61 Bill Wade | 3.00 | 1.50 |
| ❑ 62 Mike Ditka | 60.00 | 35.00 |
| ❑ 63 Johnny Morris | 2.50 | 1.25 |
| ❑ 64 Roger LeClerc | 2.50 | 1.25 |
| ❑ 65 Roger Davis RC | 2.50 | 1.25 |
| ❑ 66 Joe Marconi | 2.50 | 1.25 |
| ❑ 67 Herman Lee | 2.50 | 1.25 |
| ❑ 68 Doug Atkins | 6.00 | 3.00 |
| ❑ 69 Joe Fortunato | 2.50 | 1.25 |
| ❑ 70 Bill George | 5.00 | 2.50 |
| ❑ 71 Richie Petitbon | 3.00 | 1.50 |
| ❑ 72 Bears Team SP | 10.00 | 5.00 |
| ❑ 73 Eddie LeBaron SP | 10.00 | 5.00 |
| ❑ 74 Don Meredith SP | 60.00 | 35.00 |
| ❑ 75 Don Perkins SP | 10.00 | 5.00 |
| ❑ 76 Amos Marsh SP | 6.00 | 3.50 |
| ❑ 77 Billy Howton SP | 8.00 | 4.00 |
| ❑ 78 Andy Cvercko SP | 6.00 | 3.50 |
| ❑ 79 Sam Baker SP | 6.00 | 3.50 |
| ❑ 80 Jerry Tubbs SP | 6.00 | 3.50 |
| ❑ 81 Don Bishop SP | 6.00 | 3.50 |
| ❑ 82 Bob Lilly RC SP | 175.00 | 100.00 |
| ❑ 83 Jerry Norton SP | 6.00 | 3.50 |
| ❑ 84 Cowboys Team SP | 20.00 | 12.00 |
| ❑ 85 Checklist | 25.00 | 15.00 |
| ❑ 86 Bart Starr | 75.00 | 40.00 |
| ❑ 87 Jim Taylor | 30.00 | 18.00 |
| ❑ 88 Boyd Dowler | 5.00 | 2.50 |
| ❑ 89 Forrest Gregg | 6.00 | 3.00 |
| ❑ 90 Fuzzy Thurston | 6.00 | 3.00 |
| ❑ 91 Jim Ringo | 6.00 | 3.00 |
| ❑ 92 Ron Kramer | 3.00 | 1.50 |
| ❑ 93 Hank Jordan | 6.00 | 3.00 |
| ❑ 94 Bill Forester | 3.00 | 1.50 |
| ❑ 95 Willie Wood RC | 40.00 | 25.00 |
| ❑ 96 Ray Nitschke RC | 135.00 | 75.00 |
| ❑ 97 Green Bay Packers | 15.00 | 7.50 |
| ❑ 98 Fran Tarkenton | 60.00 | 35.00 |
| ❑ 99 Tommy Mason | 3.00 | 1.50 |
| ❑ 100 Mel Triplett | 2.50 | 1.25 |
| ❑ 101 Jerry Reichow | 2.50 | 1.25 |
| ❑ 102 Frank Youso | 2.50 | 1.25 |
| ❑ 103 Hugh McElhenny | 8.00 | 4.00 |
| ❑ 104 Gerald Huth | 2.50 | 1.25 |
| ❑ 105 Ed Sharockman | 2.50 | 1.25 |
| ❑ 106 Rip Hawkins | 2.50 | 1.25 |
| ❑ 107 Jim Marshall RC | 35.00 | 20.00 |
| ❑ 108 Jim Prestel | 2.50 | 1.25 |
| ❑ 109 Minnesota Vikings | 4.00 | 2.00 |
| ❑ 110 Sonny Jurgensen SP | 25.00 | 15.00 |
| ❑ 111 Timmy Brown RC SP | 10.00 | 5.00 |
| ❑ 112 Tommy McDonald SP | 15.00 | 7.50 |
| ❑ 113 Clarence Peaks SP | 6.00 | 3.50 |
| ❑ 114 Pete Retzlaff SP | 8.00 | 4.00 |
| ❑ 115 Jim Schrader SP | 6.00 | 3.50 |
| ❑ 116 Jim McCusker SP | 6.00 | 3.50 |
| ❑ 117 Don Burroughs SP | 6.00 | 3.50 |
| ❑ 118 Maxie Baughan SP | 6.00 | 3.50 |
| ❑ 119 Riley Gunnels SP | 6.00 | 3.50 |
| ❑ 120 Jimmy Carr SP | 6.00 | 3.50 |
| ❑ 121 Philadelphia Eagles SP | 10.00 | 5.00 |
| ❑ 122 Ed Brown SP | 8.00 | 4.00 |
| ❑ 123 John H.Johnson SP | 15.00 | 7.50 |
| ❑ 124 Buddy Dial SP | 6.00 | 3.50 |
| ❑ 125 Bill Red Mack SP | 6.00 | 3.50 |

| | | | |
|---|---|---|---|
| ❑ 126 Preston Carpenter SP | 6.00 | 3.50 |
| ❑ 127 Ray Lemek SP | 6.00 | 3.50 |
| ❑ 128 Buzz Nutter SP | 6.00 | 3.50 |
| ❑ 129 Ernie Stautner SP | 15.00 | 7.50 |
| ❑ 130 Lou Michaels SP | 6.00 | 3.50 |
| ❑ 131 Clendon Thomas RC SP | 6.00 | 3.50 |
| ❑ 132 Tom Bettis SP | 6.00 | 3.50 |
| ❑ 133 Pittsburgh Steelers SP | 10.00 | 5.00 |
| ❑ 134 John Brodie | 8.00 | 4.00 |
| ❑ 135 J.D. Smith | 2.50 | 1.25 |
| ❑ 136 Billy Kilmer | 5.00 | 2.50 |
| ❑ 137 Bernie Casey RC | 3.00 | 1.50 |
| ❑ 138 Tommy Davis | 2.50 | 1.25 |
| ❑ 139 Ted Connolly | 2.50 | 1.25 |
| ❑ 140 Bob St.Clair | 5.00 | 2.50 |
| ❑ 141 Abe Woodson | 2.50 | 1.25 |
| ❑ 142 Matt Hazeltine | 2.50 | 1.25 |
| ❑ 143 Leo Nomellini | 6.00 | 3.00 |
| ❑ 144 Dan Colchico | 2.50 | 1.25 |
| ❑ 145 San Francisco 49ers SP | 10.00 | 5.00 |
| ❑ 146 Charlie Johnson RC | 8.00 | 4.00 |
| ❑ 147 John David Crow | 3.00 | 1.50 |
| ❑ 148 Bobby Joe Conrad | 3.00 | 1.50 |
| ❑ 149 Sonny Randle | 2.50 | 1.25 |
| ❑ 150 Prentice Gautt | 2.50 | 1.25 |
| ❑ 151 Taz Anderson | 2.50 | 1.25 |
| ❑ 152 Ernie McMillan RC | 3.00 | 1.50 |
| ❑ 153 Jimmy Hill | 2.50 | 1.25 |
| ❑ 154 Bill Koman | 2.50 | 1.25 |
| ❑ 155 Larry Wilson RC | 20.00 | 12.00 |
| ❑ 156 Don Owens | 2.50 | 1.25 |
| ❑ 157 St. Louis Cardinals SP | 10.00 | 5.00 |
| ❑ 158 Norm Snead SP | 10.00 | 5.00 |
| ❑ 159 Bobby Mitchell SP | 15.00 | 7.50 |
| ❑ 160 Bill Barnes SP | 6.00 | 3.50 |
| ❑ 161 Fred Dugan SP | 6.00 | 3.50 |
| ❑ 162 Don Bosseler SP | 6.00 | 3.50 |
| ❑ 163 John Nisby SP | 6.00 | 3.50 |
| ❑ 164 Riley Mattson SP | 6.00 | 3.50 |
| ❑ 165 Bob Toneff SP | 6.00 | 3.50 |
| ❑ 166 Rod Breedlove SP | 6.00 | 3.50 |
| ❑ 167 Dick James SP | 6.00 | 3.50 |
| ❑ 168 Claude Crabb SP | 6.00 | 3.50 |
| ❑ 169 Washington Redskins SP | 10.00 | 5.00 |
| ❑ 170 Checklist UER ! | 50.00 | 30.00 |

## 1964 Topps

*LANCE ALWORTH*

| | | | |
|---|---|---|---|
| ❑ COMPLETE SET (176) | 1500.00 | 1000.00 |
| ❑ WRAPPER (1-CENT) | 40.00 | 30.00 |
| ❑ WRAPPER (5-CENT, PENN) | 125.00 | 75.00 |
| ❑ WRAP. (5-CENT, 8-CARD) | 150.00 | 90.00 |
| ❑ 1 Tommy Addison SP | 40.00 | 15.00 |
| ❑ 2 Houston Antwine RC | 4.00 | 2.00 |
| ❑ 3 Nick Buoniconti | 25.00 | 10.00 |
| ❑ 4 Ron Burton SP | 10.00 | 5.00 |
| ❑ 5 Gino Cappelletti | 5.00 | 2.50 |
| ❑ 6 Jim Colclough SP | 6.00 | 3.00 |
| ❑ 7 Bob Dee SP | 6.00 | 3.00 |
| ❑ 8 Larry Eisenhauer | 6.00 | 3.00 |
| ❑ 9 Dick Felt SP | 6.00 | 3.00 |
| ❑ 10 Larry Garron | 4.00 | 2.00 |
| ❑ 11 Art Graham | 4.00 | 2.00 |
| ❑ 12 Ron Hall DB | 4.00 | 2.00 |
| ❑ 13 Charles Long | 4.00 | 2.00 |
| ❑ 14 Don McKinnon | 4.00 | 2.00 |
| ❑ 15 Don Oakes SP | 6.00 | 3.00 |
| ❑ 16 Ross O'Hanley SP | 6.00 | 3.00 |
| ❑ 17 Babe Parilli SP | 10.00 | 5.00 |

| | | | |
|---|---|---|---|
| ❑ 18 Jesse Richardson SP | 6.00 | 3.00 |
| ❑ 19 Jack Rudolph SP | 6.00 | 3.00 |
| ❑ 20 Don Webb RC | 4.00 | 2.00 |
| ❑ 21 Boston Patriots | 6.00 | 3.00 |
| ❑ 22 Ray Abruzzese | 4.00 | 2.00 |
| ❑ 23 Stew Barber RC | 4.00 | 2.00 |
| ❑ 24 Dave Behrman | 4.00 | 2.00 |
| ❑ 25 Al Bemiller | 4.00 | 2.00 |
| ❑ 26 Elbert Dubenion SP | 10.00 | 5.00 |
| ❑ 27 Jim Dunaway RC SP | 6.00 | 3.00 |
| ❑ 28 Booker Edgerson SP | 6.00 | 3.00 |
| ❑ 29 Cookie Gilchrist SP | 25.00 | 15.00 |
| ❑ 30 Jack Kemp SP | 120.00 | 60.00 |
| ❑ 31 Daryle Lamonica RC | 75.00 | 40.00 |
| ❑ 32 Bill Miller | 4.00 | 2.00 |
| ❑ 33 Herb Paterra RC | 4.00 | 2.00 |
| ❑ 34 Ken Rice SP | 6.00 | 3.00 |
| ❑ 35 Ed Rutkowski | 4.00 | 2.00 |
| ❑ 36 George Saimes RC | 4.00 | 2.00 |
| ❑ 37 Tom Sestak | 4.00 | 2.00 |
| ❑ 38 Billy Shaw SP | 15.00 | 7.50 |
| ❑ 39 Mike Stratton | 4.00 | 2.00 |
| ❑ 40 Gene Sykes | 4.00 | 2.00 |
| ❑ 41 John Tracey SP | 6.00 | 3.00 |
| ❑ 42 Sid Youngelman SP | 6.00 | 3.00 |
| ❑ 43 Buffalo Bills | 6.00 | 3.00 |
| ❑ 44 Eldon Danenhauer SP | 6.00 | 3.00 |
| ❑ 45 Jim Fraser SP | 6.00 | 3.00 |
| ❑ 46 Chuck Gavin SP | 6.00 | 3.00 |
| ❑ 47 Goose Gonsoulin SP | 10.00 | 5.00 |
| ❑ 48 Ernie Barnes RC | 4.00 | 2.00 |
| ❑ 49 Tom Janik | 4.00 | 2.00 |
| ❑ 50 Billy Joe RC | 5.00 | 2.50 |
| ❑ 51 Ike Lassiter RC | 4.00 | 2.00 |
| ❑ 52 John McCormick QB SP | 6.00 | 3.00 |
| ❑ 53 Bud McFadin SP | 6.00 | 3.00 |
| ❑ 54 Gene Mingo SP | 6.00 | 3.00 |
| ❑ 55 Charlie Mitchell | 4.00 | 2.00 |
| ❑ 56 John Nocera SP | 6.00 | 3.00 |
| ❑ 57 Tom Nomina | 4.00 | 2.00 |
| ❑ 58 Harold Olson SP | 6.00 | 3.00 |
| ❑ 59 Bob Scarpitto | 4.00 | 2.00 |
| ❑ 60 John Sklopan | 4.00 | 2.00 |
| ❑ 61 Mickey Slaughter | 4.00 | 2.00 |
| ❑ 62 Don Stone | 4.00 | 2.00 |
| ❑ 63 Jerry Sturm | 4.00 | 2.00 |
| ❑ 64 Lionel Taylor SP | 12.00 | 6.00 |
| ❑ 65 Broncos Team SP | 20.00 | 10.00 |
| ❑ 66 Scott Appleton RC | 6.00 | 3.00 |
| ❑ 67 Tony Banfield SP | 6.00 | 3.00 |
| ❑ 68 George Blanda SP | 75.00 | 40.00 |
| ❑ 69 Billy Cannon | 6.00 | 3.00 |
| ❑ 70 Doug Cline SP | 6.00 | 3.00 |
| ❑ 71 Gary Cutsinger SP | 6.00 | 3.00 |
| ❑ 72 Willard Dewveall SP | 6.00 | 3.00 |
| ❑ 73 Don Floyd SP | 6.00 | 3.00 |
| ❑ 74 Freddy Glick SP | 6.00 | 3.00 |
| ❑ 75 Charlie Hennigan SP | 10.00 | 5.00 |
| ❑ 76 Ed Husmann SP | 6.00 | 3.00 |
| ❑ 77 Bobby Jancik SP | 6.00 | 3.00 |
| ❑ 78 Jacky Lee SP | 10.00 | 5.00 |
| ❑ 79 Bob McLeod SP | 6.00 | 3.00 |
| ❑ 80 Rich Michael SP | 6.00 | 3.00 |
| ❑ 81 Larry Onesti SP | 4.00 | 2.00 |
| ❑ 82 Checklist Card UER | 60.00 | 30.00 |
| ❑ 83 Bob Schmidt SP | 6.00 | 3.00 |
| ❑ 84 Walt Suggs SP | 6.00 | 3.00 |
| ❑ 85 Bob Talamini SP | 6.00 | 3.00 |
| ❑ 86 Charley Tolar SP | 6.00 | 3.00 |
| ❑ 87 Don Trull RC | 4.00 | 2.00 |
| ❑ 88 Houston Oilers | 6.00 | 3.00 |
| ❑ 89 Fred Arbanas | 4.00 | 2.00 |
| ❑ 90 Bobby Bell RC | 40.00 | 25.00 |
| ❑ 91 Mel Branch SP | 10.00 | 5.00 |
| ❑ 92 Buck Buchanan RC | 40.00 | 25.00 |
| ❑ 93 Ed Budde RC | 4.00 | 2.00 |
| ❑ 94 Chris Burford SP | 10.00 | 5.00 |
| ❑ 95 Walt Corey RC | 5.00 | 2.50 |
| ❑ 96 Len Dawson SP | 75.00 | 40.00 |
| ❑ 97 Dave Grayson RC | 4.00 | 2.00 |
| ❑ 98 Abner Haynes | 6.00 | 3.00 |
| ❑ 99 Sherrill Headrick SP | 10.00 | 5.00 |
| ❑ 100 E.J. Holub | 4.00 | 2.00 |
| ❑ 101 Bobby Hunt RC | 4.00 | 2.00 |
| ❑ 102 Frank Jackson SP | 6.00 | 3.00 |

|  |  | | |
|---|---|---|---|
| 103 | Curtis McClinton | 5.00 | 2.50 |
| 104 | Jerry Mays SP | 10.00 | 5.00 |
| 105 | Johnny Robinson SP | 12.00 | 6.00 |
| 106 | Jack Spikes SP | 6.00 | 3.00 |
| 107 | Smokey Stover SP | 6.00 | 3.00 |
| 108 | Jim Tyrer RC | 10.00 | 5.00 |
| 109 | Duane Wood SP | 6.00 | 3.00 |
| 110 | Kansas City Chiefs | 6.00 | 3.00 |
| 111 | Dick Christy SP | 6.00 | 3.00 |
| 112 | Dan Ficca SP | 6.00 | 3.00 |
| 113 | Larry Grantham | 4.00 | 2.00 |
| 114 | Curley Johnson SP | 6.00 | 3.00 |
| 115 | Gene Heeter | 4.00 | 2.00 |
| 116 | Jack Klotz | 4.00 | 2.00 |
| 117 | Pete Liske RC | 5.00 | 2.50 |
| 118 | Bob McAdam | 4.00 | 2.00 |
| 119 | Dee Mackey SP | 6.00 | 3.00 |
| 120 | Bill Mathis SP | 10.00 | 5.00 |
| 121 | Don Maynard | 35.00 | 20.00 |
| 122 | Dainard Paulson SP | 6.00 | 3.00 |
| 123 | Gerry Philbin RC | 5.00 | 2.50 |
| 124 | Mark Smolinski SP | 6.00 | 3.00 |
| 125 | Matt Snell RC | 20.00 | 10.00 |
| 126 | Mike Taliaferro | 4.00 | 2.00 |
| 127 | Bake Turner RC SP | 10.00 | 5.00 |
| 128 | Jeff Ware | 4.00 | 2.00 |
| 129 | Clyde Washington | 4.00 | 2.00 |
| 130 | Dick Wood SP | 6.00 | 3.00 |
| 131 | New York Jets | 6.00 | 3.00 |
| 132 | Dalva Allen SP | 6.00 | 3.00 |
| 133 | Dan Birdwell | 4.00 | 2.00 |
| 134 | Dave Costa RC | 4.00 | 2.00 |
| 135 | Dobie Craig | 4.00 | 2.00 |
| 136 | Clem Daniels | 5.00 | 2.50 |
| 137 | Cotton Davidson SP | 10.00 | 5.00 |
| 138 | Claude Gibson | 4.00 | 2.00 |
| 139 | Tom Flores SP | 15.00 | 7.50 |
| 140 | Wayne Hawkins SP | 6.00 | 3.00 |
| 141 | Ken Herock | 4.00 | 2.00 |
| 142 | Jon Jelacic SP | 6.00 | 3.00 |
| 143 | Joe Krakoski | 4.00 | 2.00 |
| 144 | Archie Matsos SP | 6.00 | 3.00 |
| 145 | Mike Mercer | 4.00 | 2.00 |
| 146 | Alan Miller SP | 6.00 | 3.00 |
| 147 | Bob Mischak SP | 6.00 | 3.00 |
| 148 | Jim Otto SP | 30.00 | 18.00 |
| 149 | Clancy Osborne SP | 6.00 | 3.00 |
| 150 | Art Powell SP | 12.00 | 6.00 |
| 151 | Bo Roberson | 4.00 | 2.00 |
| 152 | Fred Williamson SP | 30.00 | 18.00 |
| 153 | Oakland Raiders SP | 6.00 | 3.00 |
| 154 | Chuck Allen RC SP | 10.00 | 5.00 |
| 155 | Lance Alworth | 50.00 | 30.00 |
| 156 | George Blair | 4.00 | 2.00 |
| 157 | Earl Faison | 4.00 | 2.00 |
| 158 | Sam Gruneisen | 4.00 | 2.00 |
| 159 | John Hadl RC | 40.00 | 25.00 |
| 160 | Dick Harris SP | 6.00 | 3.00 |
| 161 | Emil Karas SP | 6.00 | 3.00 |
| 162 | Dave Kocourek SP | 6.00 | 3.00 |
| 163 | Ernie Ladd | 8.00 | 4.00 |
| 164 | Keith Lincoln | 6.00 | 3.00 |
| 165 | Paul Lowe SP | 12.00 | 6.00 |
| 166 | Charley McNeil | 4.00 | 2.00 |
| 167 | Jacque MacKinnon SP RC | 6.00 | 3.00 |
| 168 | Ron Mix SP | 20.00 | 10.00 |
| 169 | Don Norton SP | 6.00 | 3.00 |
| 170 | Don Rogers SP | 6.00 | 3.00 |
| 171 | Tobin Rote SP | 10.00 | 5.00 |
| 172 | Henry Schmidt SP RC | 6.00 | 3.00 |
| 173 | Bud Whitehead | 4.00 | 2.00 |
| 174 | Ernie Wright SP | 10.00 | 5.00 |
| 175 | San Diego Chargers | 6.00 | 3.00 |
| 176 | Checklist SP UER ! | 160.00 | 80.00 |

## 1965 Topps

| | | | |
|---|---|---|---|
| COMPLETE SET (176) | | 4000.00 | 2500.00 |
| WRAPPER (5-CENT) | | 150.00 | 90.00 |
| 1 | Tommy Addison SP | 35.00 | 20.00 |
| 2 | Houston Antwine SP | 12.00 | 7.00 |
| 3 | Nick Buoniconti SP | 30.00 | 18.00 |
| 4 | Ron Burton SP | 20.00 | 10.00 |
| 5 | Gino Cappelletti SP | 20.00 | 10.00 |
| 6 | Jim Colclough | 7.00 | 3.50 |
| 7 | Bob Dee SP | 12.00 | 7.00 |

|  |  | | |
|---|---|---|---|
| 8 | Larry Eisenhauer | 7.00 | 3.50 |
| 9 | J.D. Garrett | 7.00 | 3.50 |
| 10 | Larry Garron | 7.00 | 3.50 |
| 11 | Art Graham SP | 12.00 | 7.00 |
| 12 | Ron Hall DB | 7.00 | 3.50 |
| 13 | Charles Long | 7.00 | 3.50 |
| 14 | Jon Morris RC | 10.00 | 5.00 |
| 15 | Billy Neighbors SP | 12.00 | 7.00 |
| 16 | Ross O'Hanley | 7.00 | 3.50 |
| 17 | Babe Parilli SP | 20.00 | 10.00 |
| 18 | Tony Romeo SP | 12.00 | 7.00 |
| 19 | Jack Rudolph SP | 12.00 | 7.00 |
| 20 | Bob Schmidt | 7.00 | 3.50 |
| 21 | Don Webb SP | 12.00 | 7.00 |
| 22 | Jim Whalen SP | 12.00 | 7.00 |
| 23 | Stew Barber | 7.00 | 3.50 |
| 24 | Glenn Bass SP | 12.00 | 7.00 |
| 25 | Al Bemiller SP | 12.00 | 7.00 |
| 26 | Wray Carlton SP | 12.00 | 7.00 |
| 27 | Tom Day | 7.00 | 3.50 |
| 28 | Elbert Dubenion SP | 15.00 | 7.50 |
| 29 | Jim Dunaway | 7.00 | 3.50 |
| 30 | Pete Gogolak RC SP | 20.00 | 10.00 |
| 31 | Dick Hudson SP | 12.00 | 7.00 |
| 32 | Harry Jacobs SP | 12.00 | 7.00 |
| 33 | Billy Joe SP | 15.00 | 7.50 |
| 34 | Tom Keating RC SP | 12.00 | 7.00 |
| 35 | Jack Kemp SP ! | 150.00 | 75.00 |
| 36 | Daryle Lamonica SP | 50.00 | 30.00 |
| 37 | Paul Maguire SP | 20.00 | 10.00 |
| 38 | Ron McDole SP | 12.00 | 7.00 |
| 39 | George Saimes SP | 12.00 | 7.00 |
| 40 | Tom Sestak SP | 12.00 | 7.00 |
| 41 | Billy Shaw SP | 12.00 | 7.00 |
| 42 | Mike Stratton SP | 12.00 | 7.00 |
| 43 | John Tracey SP | 12.00 | 7.00 |
| 44 | Ernie Warlick | 7.00 | 3.50 |
| 45 | Odell Barry | 7.00 | 3.50 |
| 46 | Willie Brown RC SP | 100.00 | 60.00 |
| 47 | Gerry Bussell SP | 12.00 | 7.00 |
| 48 | Eldon Danenhauer SP | 12.00 | 7.00 |
| 49 | Al Denson SP | 12.00 | 7.00 |
| 50 | Hewritt Dixon RC SP | 15.00 | 7.50 |
| 51 | Cookie Gilchrist SP | 30.00 | 18.00 |
| 52 | Goose Gonsoulin SP | 15.00 | 7.50 |
| 53 | Abner Haynes SP | 20.00 | 10.00 |
| 54 | Jerry Hopkins | 7.00 | 3.50 |
| 55 | Ray Jacobs SP | 12.00 | 7.00 |
| 56 | Jacky Lee SP | 15.00 | 7.50 |
| 57 | John McCormick QB | 7.00 | 3.50 |
| 58 | Bob McCullough SP | 12.00 | 7.00 |
| 59 | John McGeever | 7.00 | 3.50 |
| 60 | Charlie Mitchell SP | 12.00 | 7.00 |
| 61 | Jim Perkins SP | 12.00 | 7.00 |
| 62 | Bob Scarpitto SP | 12.00 | 7.00 |
| 63 | Mickey Slaughter SP | 12.00 | 7.00 |
| 64 | Jerry Sturm SP | 12.00 | 7.00 |
| 65 | Lionel Taylor SP | 20.00 | 10.00 |
| 66 | Scott Appleton SP | 12.00 | 7.00 |
| 67 | Johnny Baker SP | 12.00 | 7.00 |
| 68 | Sonny Bishop SP | 12.00 | 7.00 |
| 69 | George Blanda SP | 125.00 | 75.00 |
| 70 | Sid Blanks SP | 12.00 | 7.00 |
| 71 | Ode Burrell SP | 12.00 | 7.00 |
| 72 | Doug Cline SP | 12.00 | 7.00 |
| 73 | Willard Dewveall | 7.00 | 3.50 |
| 74 | Larry Elkins RC | 7.00 | 3.50 |
| 75 | Don Floyd SP | 12.00 | 7.00 |

|  |  | | |
|---|---|---|---|
| 76 | Freddy Glick | 7.00 | 3.50 |
| 77 | Tom Goode SP | 12.00 | 7.00 |
| 78 | Charlie Hennigan SP | 20.00 | 10.00 |
| 79 | Ed Husmann | 7.00 | 3.50 |
| 80 | Bobby Jancik SP | 12.00 | 7.00 |
| 81 | Bud McFadin SP | 12.00 | 7.00 |
| 82 | Bob McLeod SP | 12.00 | 7.00 |
| 83 | Jim Norton SP | 12.00 | 7.00 |
| 84 | Walt Suggs | 7.00 | 3.50 |
| 85 | Bob Talamini | 7.00 | 3.50 |
| 86 | Charley Tolar SP | 12.00 | 7.00 |
| 87 | Checklist SP ! | 175.00 | 100.00 |
| 88 | Don Trull SP | 12.00 | 7.00 |
| 89 | Fred Arbanas SP | 12.00 | 7.00 |
| 90 | Pete Beathard RC SP | 12.00 | 7.00 |
| 91 | Bobby Bell SP | 40.00 | 25.00 |
| 92 | Mel Branch SP | 12.00 | 7.00 |
| 93 | Tommy Brooker SP | 12.00 | 7.00 |
| 94 | Buck Buchanan SP | 35.00 | 20.00 |
| 95 | Ed Budde SP | 12.00 | 7.00 |
| 96 | Chris Burford SP | 12.00 | 7.00 |
| 97 | Walt Corey | 7.00 | 3.50 |
| 98 | Jerry Cornelison | 7.00 | 3.50 |
| 99 | Len Dawson SP | 100.00 | 60.00 |
| 100 | Jon Gilliam SP | 12.00 | 7.00 |
| 101 | Sherrill Headrick SP UER | 12.00 | 7.00 |
| 102 | Dave Hill SP | 12.00 | 7.00 |
| 103 | E.J. Holub SP | 12.00 | 7.00 |
| 104 | Bobby Hunt SP | 12.00 | 7.00 |
| 105 | Frank Jackson SP | 12.00 | 7.00 |
| 106 | Jerry Mays | 10.00 | 5.00 |
| 107 | Curtis McClinton SP | 15.00 | 7.50 |
| 108 | Bobby Ply SP | 12.00 | 7.00 |
| 109 | Johnny Robinson SP | 15.00 | 7.50 |
| 110 | Jim Tyrer SP | 12.00 | 7.00 |
| 111 | Bill Baird SP | 12.00 | 7.00 |
| 112 | Ralph Baker RC SP | 12.00 | 7.00 |
| 113 | Sam DeLuca SP | 12.00 | 7.00 |
| 114 | Larry Grantham SP | 15.00 | 7.50 |
| 115 | Gene Heeter SP | 12.00 | 7.00 |
| 116 | Winston Hill RC SP | 20.00 | 10.00 |
| 117 | John Huarte SP | 30.00 | 18.00 |
| 118 | Cosmo Iacavazzi SP | 12.00 | 7.00 |
| 119 | Curley Johnson SP | 12.00 | 7.00 |
| 120 | Dee Mackey SP | 7.00 | 3.50 |
| 121 | Don Maynard | 50.00 | 30.00 |
| 122 | Joe Namath RC SP ! | 1800.00 | 1200.00 |
| 123 | Dainard Paulson | 7.00 | 3.50 |
| 124 | Gerry Philbin SP | 12.00 | 7.00 |
| 125 | Sherman Plunkett RC SP | 15.00 | 7.50 |
| 126 | Mark Smolinski | 7.00 | 3.50 |
| 127 | Matt Snell SP | 30.00 | 18.00 |
| 128 | Mike Taliaferro SP | 12.00 | 7.00 |
| 129 | Bake Turner SP | 12.00 | 7.00 |
| 130 | Clyde Washington SP | 12.00 | 7.00 |
| 131 | Verlon Biggs RC SP | 12.00 | 7.00 |
| 132 | Dalva Allen | 7.00 | 3.50 |
| 133 | Fred Biletnikoff RC SP | 225.00 | 150.00 |
| 134 | Billy Cannon SP | 20.00 | 10.00 |
| 135 | Dave Costa SP | 12.00 | 7.00 |
| 136 | Clem Daniels SP | 15.00 | 7.50 |
| 137 | Ben Davidson RC SP | 60.00 | 35.00 |
| 138 | Cotton Davidson SP | 15.00 | 7.50 |
| 139 | Tom Flores SP | 20.00 | 10.00 |
| 140 | Claude Gibson | 7.00 | 3.50 |
| 141 | Wayne Hawkins | 7.00 | 3.50 |
| 142 | Archie Matsos SP | 12.00 | 7.00 |
| 143 | Mike Mercer SP | 12.00 | 7.00 |
| 144 | Bob Mischak SP | 12.00 | 7.00 |
| 145 | Jim Otto | 30.00 | 18.00 |
| 146 | Art Powell UER | 12.00 | 7.00 |
| 147 | Warren Powers DB SP | 12.00 | 7.00 |
| 148 | Ken Rice SP | 12.00 | 7.00 |
| 149 | Bo Roberson SP | 12.00 | 7.00 |
| 150 | Harry Schuh RC | 7.00 | 3.50 |
| 151 | Larry Todd SP | 12.00 | 7.00 |
| 152 | Fred Williamson SP | 30.00 | 15.00 |
| 153 | J.R. Williamson | 7.00 | 3.50 |
| 154 | Chuck Allen | 10.00 | 5.00 |
| 155 | Lance Alworth | 75.00 | 50.00 |
| 156 | Frank Buncom | 7.00 | 3.50 |
| 157 | Steve DeLong RC SP | 12.00 | 7.00 |
| 158 | Earl Faison SP | 15.00 | 7.50 |
| 159 | Kenny Graham SP | 12.00 | 7.00 |
| 160 | George Gross SP | 12.00 | 7.00 |

| | | | |
|---|---|---|---|
| ❏ 161 John Hadl SP | 35.00 | 20.00 | |
| ❏ 162 Emil Karas SP | 12.00 | 7.00 | |
| ❏ 163 Dave Kocourek SP | 12.00 | 7.00 | |
| ❏ 164 Ernie Ladd SP | 20.00 | 10.00 | |
| ❏ 165 Keith Lincoln SP | 20.00 | 10.00 | |
| ❏ 166 Paul Lowe SP | 20.00 | 10.00 | |
| ❏ 167 Jacque MacKinnon | 7.00 | 3.50 | |
| ❏ 168 Ron Mix | 20.00 | 12.00 | |
| ❏ 169 Don Norton SP | 12.00 | 7.00 | |
| ❏ 170 Bob Petrich | 7.00 | 3.50 | |
| ❏ 171 Rick Redman SP | 12.00 | 7.00 | |
| ❏ 172 Pat Shea | 7.00 | 3.50 | |
| ❏ 173 Walt Sweeney RC SP | 15.00 | 7.50 | |
| ❏ 174 Dick Westmoreland RC | 7.00 | 3.50 | |
| ❏ 175 Ernie Wright SP | 20.00 | 10.00 | |
| ❏ 176 Checklist SP ! | 225.00 | 125.00 | |

## 1966 Topps

| | | |
|---|---|---|
| ❏ COMPLETE SET (132) | 1500.00 | 950.00 |
| ❏ WRAPPER (5-CENT) | 60.00 | 30.00 |
| ❏ 1 Tommy Addison ! | 20.00 | 10.00 |
| ❏ 2 Houston Antwine | 5.00 | 3.00 |
| ❏ 3 Nick Buoniconti | 10.00 | 5.00 |
| ❏ 4 Gino Cappelletti | 7.00 | 3.50 |
| ❏ 5 Bob Dee | 5.00 | 3.00 |
| ❏ 6 Larry Garron | 5.00 | 3.00 |
| ❏ 7 Art Graham | 5.00 | 3.00 |
| ❏ 8 Ron Hall DB | 5.00 | 3.00 |
| ❏ 9 Charles Long | 5.00 | 3.00 |
| ❏ 10 Joan Morris | 5.00 | 3.00 |
| ❏ 11 Don Oakes | 5.00 | 3.00 |
| ❏ 12 Babe Parilli | 7.00 | 3.50 |
| ❏ 13 Don Webb | 5.00 | 3.00 |
| ❏ 14 Jim Whalen | 5.00 | 3.00 |
| ❏ 15 Funny Ring Checklist ! | 300.00 | 200.00 |
| ❏ 16 Stew Barber | 5.00 | 3.00 |
| ❏ 17 Glenn Bass | 5.00 | 3.00 |
| ❏ 18 Dave Behrman | 5.00 | 3.00 |
| ❏ 19 Al Bemiller | 5.00 | 3.00 |
| ❏ 20 Butch Byrd RC | 7.00 | 3.50 |
| ❏ 21 Wray Carlton | 5.00 | 3.00 |
| ❏ 22 Tom Day | 5.00 | 3.00 |
| ❏ 23 Elbert Dubenion | 7.00 | 3.50 |
| ❏ 24 Jim Dunaway | 5.00 | 3.00 |
| ❏ 25 Dick Hudson | 5.00 | 3.00 |
| ❏ 26 Jack Kemp | 150.00 | 75.00 |
| ❏ 27 Daryle Lamonica | 20.00 | 12.00 |
| ❏ 28 Tom Sestak | 5.00 | 3.00 |
| ❏ 29 Billy Shaw | 5.00 | 3.00 |
| ❏ 30 Mike Stratton | 5.00 | 3.00 |
| ❏ 31 Eldon Danenhauer | 5.00 | 3.00 |
| ❏ 32 Cookie Gilchrist | 10.00 | 5.00 |
| ❏ 33 Goose Gonsoulin | 7.00 | 3.50 |
| ❏ 34 Wendell Hayes RC | 10.00 | 5.00 |
| ❏ 35 Abner Haynes | 10.00 | 5.00 |
| ❏ 36 Jerry Hopkins | 5.00 | 3.00 |
| ❏ 37 Ray Jacobs | 5.00 | 3.00 |
| ❏ 38 Charlie Janerette | 5.00 | 3.00 |
| ❏ 39 Ray Kubala | 5.00 | 3.00 |
| ❏ 40 John McCormick QB | 5.00 | 3.00 |
| ❏ 41 Leroy Moore | 5.00 | 3.00 |
| ❏ 42 Bob Scarpitto | 5.00 | 3.00 |
| ❏ 43 Mickey Slaughter | 5.00 | 3.00 |
| ❏ 44 Jerry Sturm | 5.00 | 3.00 |
| ❏ 45 Lionel Taylor | 10.00 | 5.00 |
| ❏ 46 Scott Appleton | 5.00 | 3.00 |
| ❏ 47 Johnny Baker | 5.00 | 3.00 |
| ❏ 48 George Blanda | 35.00 | 20.00 |

| | | |
|---|---|---|
| ❏ 49 Sid Blanks | 5.00 | 3.00 |
| ❏ 50 Danny Brabham | 5.00 | 3.00 |
| ❏ 51 Ode Burrell | 5.00 | 3.00 |
| ❏ 52 Gary Cutsinger | 5.00 | 3.00 |
| ❏ 53 Larry Elkins | 5.00 | 3.00 |
| ❏ 54 Don Floyd | 5.00 | 3.00 |
| ❏ 55 Willie Frazier RC | 7.00 | 3.50 |
| ❏ 56 Freddy Glick | 5.00 | 3.00 |
| ❏ 57 Charlie Hennigan | 7.00 | 3.50 |
| ❏ 58 Bobby Jancik | 5.00 | 3.00 |
| ❏ 59 Rich Michael | 5.00 | 3.00 |
| ❏ 60 Don Trull | 7.00 | 3.50 |
| ❏ 61 Checklist | 55.00 | 30.00 |
| ❏ 62 Fred Arbanas | 5.00 | 3.00 |
| ❏ 63 Pete Beathard | 5.00 | 3.00 |
| ❏ 64 Bobby Bell | 10.00 | 5.00 |
| ❏ 65 Ed Budde | 5.00 | 3.00 |
| ❏ 66 Chris Burford | 5.00 | 3.00 |
| ❏ 67 Len Dawson | 40.00 | 25.00 |
| ❏ 68 Jon Gilliam | 5.00 | 3.00 |
| ❏ 69 Sherrill Headrick | 5.00 | 3.00 |
| ❏ 70 E.J. Holub UER | 5.00 | 3.00 |
| ❏ 71 Bobby Hunt | 5.00 | 3.00 |
| ❏ 72 Curtis McClinton | 7.00 | 3.50 |
| ❏ 73 Jerry Mays | 5.00 | 3.00 |
| ❏ 74 Johnny Robinson | 7.00 | 3.50 |
| ❏ 75 Otis Taylor RC | 25.00 | 15.00 |
| ❏ 76 Tom Erlandson | 7.00 | 3.50 |
| ❏ 77 Norm Evans RC | 10.00 | 5.00 |
| ❏ 78 Tom Goode | 7.00 | 3.50 |
| ❏ 79 Mike Hudock | 7.00 | 3.50 |
| ❏ 80 Frank Jackson | 7.00 | 3.50 |
| ❏ 81 Billy Joe | 7.00 | 3.50 |
| ❏ 82 Dave Kocourek | 7.00 | 3.50 |
| ❏ 83 Bo Roberson | 7.00 | 3.50 |
| ❏ 84 Jack Spikes | 7.00 | 3.50 |
| ❏ 85 Jim Warren RC | 7.00 | 3.50 |
| ❏ 86 Willie West RC | 7.00 | 3.50 |
| ❏ 87 Dick Westmoreland | 7.00 | 3.50 |
| ❏ 88 Eddie Wilson | 7.00 | 3.50 |
| ❏ 89 Dick Wood | 7.00 | 3.50 |
| ❏ 90 Verlon Biggs | 7.00 | 3.50 |
| ❏ 91 Sam DeLuca | 5.00 | 3.00 |
| ❏ 92 Winston Hill | 5.00 | 3.00 |
| ❏ 93 Dee Mackey | 5.00 | 3.00 |
| ❏ 94 Bill Mathis | 5.00 | 3.00 |
| ❏ 95 Don Maynard | 30.00 | 18.00 |
| ❏ 96 Joe Namath | 250.00 | 150.00 |
| ❏ 97 Dainard Paulson | 5.00 | 3.00 |
| ❏ 98 Gerry Philbin | 7.00 | 3.50 |
| ❏ 99 Sherman Plunkett | 5.00 | 3.00 |
| ❏ 100 Paul Rochester | 5.00 | 3.00 |
| ❏ 101 George Sauer Jr. RC | 15.00 | 7.50 |
| ❏ 102 Matt Snell | 10.00 | 5.00 |
| ❏ 103 Jim Turner RC | 7.00 | 3.50 |
| ❏ 104 Fred Biletnikoff UER | 50.00 | 30.00 |
| ❏ 105 Bill Budness | 5.00 | 3.00 |
| ❏ 106 Billy Cannon | 10.00 | 5.00 |
| ❏ 107 Clem Daniels | 7.00 | 3.50 |
| ❏ 108 Ben Davidson | 15.00 | 7.50 |
| ❏ 109 Cotton Davidson | 7.00 | 3.50 |
| ❏ 110 Claude Gibson | 5.00 | 3.00 |
| ❏ 111 Wayne Hawkins | 5.00 | 3.00 |
| ❏ 112 Ken Herock | 5.00 | 3.00 |
| ❏ 113 Bob Mischak | 5.00 | 3.00 |
| ❏ 114 Gus Otto | 5.00 | 3.00 |
| ❏ 115 Jim Otto | 20.00 | 12.00 |
| ❏ 116 Art Powell | 10.00 | 5.00 |
| ❏ 117 Harry Schuh | 5.00 | 3.00 |
| ❏ 118 Chuck Allen | 5.00 | 3.00 |
| ❏ 119 Lance Alworth | 40.00 | 25.00 |
| ❏ 120 Frank Buncom | 5.00 | 3.00 |
| ❏ 121 Steve DeLong | 5.00 | 3.00 |
| ❏ 122 John Farris | 5.00 | 3.00 |
| ❏ 123 Kenny Graham | 5.00 | 3.00 |
| ❏ 124 Sam Gruneisen | 5.00 | 3.00 |
| ❏ 125 John Hadl | 10.00 | 5.00 |
| ❏ 126 Walt Sweeney | 5.00 | 3.00 |
| ❏ 127 Keith Lincoln | 10.00 | 5.00 |
| ❏ 128 Ron Mix | 10.00 | 5.00 |
| ❏ 129 Don Norton | 5.00 | 3.00 |
| ❏ 130 Pat Shea | 5.00 | 3.00 |
| ❏ 131 Ernie Wright | 10.00 | 5.00 |
| ❏ 132 Checklist ! | 100.00 | 50.00 |

## 1967 Topps

FRED BILETNIKOFF

| | | |
|---|---|---|
| ❏ COMPLETE SET (132) | 700.00 | 400.00 |
| ❏ WRAPPER (5-CENT) | 60.00 | 30.00 |
| ❏ 1 John Huarte ! | 18.00 | 10.00 |
| ❏ 2 Babe Parilli | 4.00 | 2.00 |
| ❏ 3 Gino Cappelletti | 4.00 | 2.00 |
| ❏ 4 Larry Garron | 3.00 | 1.50 |
| ❏ 5 Tommy Addison | 3.00 | 1.50 |
| ❏ 6 Jon Morris | 3.00 | 1.50 |
| ❏ 7 Houston Antwine | 3.00 | 1.50 |
| ❏ 8 Don Oakes | 3.00 | 1.50 |
| ❏ 9 Larry Eisenhauer | 3.00 | 1.50 |
| ❏ 10 Jim Hunt | 3.00 | 1.50 |
| ❏ 11 Jim Whalen | 3.00 | 1.50 |
| ❏ 12 Art Graham | 3.00 | 1.50 |
| ❏ 13 Nick Buoniconti | 6.00 | 3.00 |
| ❏ 14 Bob Dee | 3.00 | 1.50 |
| ❏ 15 Keith Lincoln | 6.00 | 3.00 |
| ❏ 16 Tom Flores | 4.00 | 2.00 |
| ❏ 17 Art Powell | 4.00 | 2.00 |
| ❏ 18 Stew Barber | 3.00 | 1.50 |
| ❏ 19 Wray Carlton | 3.00 | 1.50 |
| ❏ 20 Elbert Dubenion | 4.00 | 2.00 |
| ❏ 21 Jim Dunaway | 3.00 | 1.50 |
| ❏ 22 Dick Hudson | 3.00 | 1.50 |
| ❏ 23 Harry Jacobs | 3.00 | 1.50 |
| ❏ 24 Jack Kemp | 80.00 | 40.00 |
| ❏ 25 Ron McDole | 3.00 | 1.50 |
| ❏ 26 George Saimes | 3.00 | 1.50 |
| ❏ 27 Tom Sestak | 3.00 | 1.50 |
| ❏ 28 Billy Shaw | 6.00 | 3.00 |
| ❏ 29 Mike Stratton | 3.00 | 1.50 |
| ❏ 30 Nemiah Wilson RC | 3.00 | 1.50 |
| ❏ 31 John McCormick QB | 3.00 | 1.50 |
| ❏ 32 Rex Mirich | 3.00 | 1.50 |
| ❏ 33 Dave Costa | 3.00 | 1.50 |
| ❏ 34 Goose Gonsoulin | 4.00 | 2.00 |
| ❏ 35 Abner Haynes | 6.00 | 3.00 |
| ❏ 36 Wendell Hayes | 4.00 | 2.00 |
| ❏ 37 Archie Matsos | 3.00 | 1.50 |
| ❏ 38 John Bramlett | 3.00 | 1.50 |
| ❏ 39 Jerry Sturm | 3.00 | 1.50 |
| ❏ 40 Max Leetzow | 3.00 | 1.50 |
| ❏ 41 Bob Scarpitto | 3.00 | 1.50 |
| ❏ 42 Lionel Taylor | 6.00 | 3.00 |
| ❏ 43 Al Denson | 3.00 | 1.50 |
| ❏ 44 Miller Farr RC | 3.00 | 1.50 |
| ❏ 45 Don Trull | 4.00 | 2.00 |
| ❏ 46 Jacky Lee | 4.00 | 2.00 |
| ❏ 47 Bobby Jancik | 3.00 | 1.50 |
| ❏ 48 Ode Burrell | 3.00 | 1.50 |
| ❏ 49 Larry Elkins | 3.00 | 1.50 |
| ❏ 50 W.K. Hicks | 3.00 | 1.50 |
| ❏ 51 Sid Blanks | 3.00 | 1.50 |
| ❏ 52 Jim Norton | 3.00 | 1.50 |
| ❏ 53 Bobby Maples RC | 3.00 | 1.50 |
| ❏ 54 Bob Talamini | 3.00 | 1.50 |
| ❏ 55 Walt Suggs | 3.00 | 1.50 |
| ❏ 56 Gary Cutsinger | 3.00 | 1.50 |
| ❏ 57 Danny Brabham | 3.00 | 1.50 |
| ❏ 58 Ernie Ladd | 6.00 | 3.00 |
| ❏ 59 Checklist | 50.00 | 25.00 |
| ❏ 60 Pete Beathard | 3.00 | 1.50 |
| ❏ 61 Len Dawson | 30.00 | 18.00 |
| ❏ 62 Bobby Hunt | 3.00 | 1.50 |
| ❏ 63 Bert Coan | 3.00 | 1.50 |
| ❏ 64 Curtis McClinton | 4.00 | 2.00 |
| ❏ 65 Johnny Robinson | 4.00 | 2.00 |

| | | |
|---|---:|---:|
| 66 E.J. Holub | 3.00 | 1.50 |
| 67 Jerry Mays | 3.00 | 1.50 |
| 68 Jim Tyrer | 4.00 | 2.00 |
| 69 Bobby Bell | 6.00 | 3.00 |
| 70 Fred Arbanas | 3.00 | 1.50 |
| 71 Buck Buchanan | 6.00 | 3.00 |
| 72 Chris Burford | 3.00 | 1.50 |
| 73 Otis Taylor | 6.00 | 3.00 |
| 74 Cookie Gilchrist | 8.00 | 4.00 |
| 75 Earl Faison | 3.00 | 1.50 |
| 76 George Wilson Jr. | 4.00 | 2.00 |
| 77 Rick Norton | 3.00 | 1.50 |
| 78 Frank Jackson | 4.00 | 2.00 |
| 79 Joe Auer | 3.00 | 1.50 |
| 80 Willie West | 3.00 | 1.50 |
| 81 Jim Warren | 3.00 | 1.50 |
| 82 Wahoo McDaniel RC | 50.00 | 30.00 |
| 83 Ernie Park | 3.00 | 1.50 |
| 84 Billy Neighbors | 3.00 | 1.50 |
| 85 Norm Evans | 4.00 | 2.00 |
| 86 Tom Nomina | 3.00 | 1.50 |
| 87 Rich Zecher | 3.00 | 1.50 |
| 88 Dave Kocourek | 3.00 | 1.50 |
| 89 Bill Baird | 3.00 | 1.50 |
| 90 Ralph Baker | 3.00 | 1.50 |
| 91 Verlon Biggs | 3.00 | 1.50 |
| 92 Sam DeLuca | 3.00 | 1.50 |
| 93 Larry Grantham | 4.00 | 2.00 |
| 94 Jim Harris | 3.00 | 1.50 |
| 95 Winston Hill | 3.00 | 1.50 |
| 96 Bill Mathis | 3.00 | 1.50 |
| 97 Don Maynard | 20.00 | 12.00 |
| 98 Joe Namath | 150.00 | 75.00 |
| 99 Gerry Philbin | 4.00 | 2.00 |
| 100 Paul Rochester | 3.00 | 1.50 |
| 101 George Sauer Jr. | 4.00 | 2.00 |
| 102 Matt Snell | 6.00 | 3.00 |
| 103 Daryle Lamonica | 10.00 | 5.00 |
| 104 Glenn Bass | 3.00 | 1.50 |
| 105 Jim Otto | 6.00 | 3.00 |
| 106 Fred Biletnikoff | 30.00 | 18.00 |
| 107 Cotton Davidson | 4.00 | 2.00 |
| 108 Larry Todd | 3.00 | 1.50 |
| 109 Billy Cannon | 6.00 | 3.00 |
| 110 Clem Daniels | 4.00 | 2.00 |
| 111 Dave Grayson | 3.00 | 1.50 |
| 112 Kent McCloughan RC | 3.00 | 1.50 |
| 113 Bob Svihus | 3.00 | 1.50 |
| 114 Ike Lassiter | 3.00 | 1.50 |
| 115 Harry Schuh | 3.00 | 1.50 |
| 116 Ben Davidson | 8.00 | 4.00 |
| 117 Tom Day | 3.00 | 1.50 |
| 118 Scott Appleton | 3.00 | 1.50 |
| 119 Steve Tensi RC | 3.00 | 1.50 |
| 120 John Hadl | 6.00 | 3.00 |
| 121 Paul Lowe | 4.00 | 2.00 |
| 122 Jim Allison | 3.00 | 1.50 |
| 123 Lance Alworth | 35.00 | 20.00 |
| 124 Jacque MacKinnon | 3.00 | 1.50 |
| 125 Ron Mix | 6.00 | 3.00 |
| 126 Bob Petrich | 3.00 | 1.50 |
| 127 Howard Kindig | 3.00 | 1.50 |
| 128 Steve DeLong | 3.00 | 1.50 |
| 129 Chuck Allen | 3.00 | 1.50 |
| 130 Frank Buncom | 3.00 | 1.50 |
| 131 Speedy Duncan RC | 4.00 | 2.00 |
| 132 Checklist ! | 70.00 | 35.00 |

## 1968 Topps

| | | |
|---|---:|---:|
| COMPLETE SET (219) | 550.00 | 350.00 |
| COMMON CARD (1-131) | 1.50 | .75 |
| COMMON CARD (132-219) | 2.00 | 1.00 |
| WRAPPER (5-CENT, SER.1) | 20.00 | 10.00 |
| WRAPPER (5-CENT, SER.2) | 30.00 | 20.00 |
| 1 Bart Starr ! | 40.00 | 25.00 |
| 2 Dick Bass | 2.00 | 1.00 |
| 3 Grady Alderman | 1.50 | .75 |
| 4 Obert Logan | 1.50 | .75 |
| 5 Ernie Koy RC | 2.00 | 1.00 |
| 6 Don Hultz | 1.50 | .75 |
| 7 Earl Gros | 1.50 | .75 |
| 8 Jim Bakken | 1.50 | .75 |
| 9 George Mira | 2.00 | 1.00 |
| 10 Carl Kammerer | 1.50 | .75 |
| 11 Willie Frazier | 1.50 | .75 |
| 12 Kent McCloughan UER | 1.50 | .75 |
| 13 George Sauer Jr. | 2.00 | 1.00 |
| 14 Jack Clancy | 1.50 | .75 |
| 15 Jim Tyrer | 2.00 | 1.00 |
| 16 Bobby Maples | 1.50 | .75 |
| 17 Bo Hickey | 1.50 | .75 |
| 18 Frank Buncom | 1.50 | .75 |
| 19 Keith Lincoln | 2.00 | 1.00 |
| 20 Jim Whalen | 1.50 | .75 |
| 21 Junior Coffey | 1.50 | .75 |
| 22 Billy Ray Smith | 1.50 | .75 |
| 23 Johnny Morris | 1.50 | .75 |
| 24 Ernie Green | 1.50 | .75 |
| 25 Don Meredith | 25.00 | 15.00 |
| 26 Wayne Walker | 2.00 | 1.00 |
| 27 Carroll Dale | 2.00 | 1.00 |
| 28 Bernie Casey | 2.00 | 1.00 |
| 29 Dave Osborn RC | 2.00 | 1.00 |
| 30 Ray Poage | 1.50 | .75 |
| 31 Homer Jones | 1.50 | .75 |
| 32 Sam Baker | 1.50 | .75 |
| 33 Bill Saul | 1.50 | .75 |
| 34 Ken Willard | 2.00 | 1.00 |
| 35 Bobby Mitchell | 4.00 | 2.00 |
| 36 Gary Garrison RC | 2.00 | 1.00 |
| 37 Billy Cannon | 2.00 | 1.00 |
| 38 Ralph Baker | 1.50 | .75 |
| 39 Howard Twilley RC | 4.00 | 2.00 |
| 40 Wendell Hayes | 2.00 | 1.00 |
| 41 Jim Norton | 1.50 | .75 |
| 42 Tom Beer | 1.50 | .75 |
| 43 Chris Burford | 1.50 | .75 |
| 44 Steve Barber | 1.50 | .75 |
| 45 Leroy Mitchell UER | 1.50 | .75 |
| 46 Dan Grimm | 1.50 | .75 |
| 47 Jerry Logan | 1.50 | .75 |
| 48 Andy Livingston | 1.50 | .75 |
| 49 Paul Warfield | 15.00 | 7.50 |
| 50 Don Perkins | 3.00 | 1.50 |
| 51 Ron Kramer | 1.50 | .75 |
| 52 Bob Jeter RC | 2.00 | 1.00 |
| 53 Les Josephson RC | 2.00 | 1.00 |
| 54 Bobby Walden | 1.50 | .75 |
| 55 Checklist | 15.00 | 7.50 |
| 56 Walter Roberts | 1.50 | .75 |
| 57 Henry Carr | 1.50 | .75 |
| 58 Gary Ballman | 1.50 | .75 |
| 59 J.R. Wilburn | 1.50 | .75 |
| 60 Jim Hart RC | 10.00 | 5.00 |
| 61 Jim Johnson | 3.00 | 1.50 |
| 62 Chris Hanburger | 2.00 | 1.00 |
| 63 John Hadl | 3.00 | 1.50 |
| 64 Hewritt Dixon | 2.00 | 1.00 |
| 65 Joe Namath | 80.00 | 50.00 |
| 66 Jim Warren | 1.50 | .75 |
| 67 Curtis McClinton | 2.00 | 1.00 |
| 68 Bob Talamini | 1.50 | .75 |
| 69 Steve Tensi | 1.50 | .75 |
| 70 Dick Van Raaphorst UER | 1.50 | .75 |
| 71 Art Powell | 2.00 | 1.00 |
| 72 Jim Nance RC | 4.00 | 2.00 |
| 73 Bob Riggle | 1.50 | .75 |
| 74 John Mackey | 5.00 | 2.50 |
| 75 Gale Sayers | 40.00 | 25.00 |
| 76 Gene Hickerson | 2.50 | 1.25 |
| 77 Dan Reeves | 10.00 | 5.00 |
| 78 Tom Nowatzke | 1.50 | .75 |
| 79 Elijah Pitts | 3.00 | 1.50 |
| 80 Lamar Lundy | 2.00 | 1.00 |
| 81 Paul Flatley | 1.50 | .75 |
| 82 Dave Whitsell | 1.50 | .75 |
| 83 Spider Lockhart | 2.00 | 1.00 |
| 84 Dave Lloyd | 1.50 | .75 |
| 85 Roy Jefferson | 2.00 | 1.00 |
| 86 Jackie Smith | 6.00 | 3.00 |
| 87 John David Crow | 2.00 | 1.00 |
| 88 Sonny Jurgensen | 6.00 | 3.00 |
| 89 Ron Mix | 3.00 | 1.50 |
| 90 Clem Daniels | 2.00 | 1.00 |
| 91 Cornell Gordon | 1.50 | .75 |
| 92 Tom Goode | 1.50 | .75 |
| 93 Bobby Bell | 3.00 | 1.50 |
| 94 Walt Suggs | 1.50 | .75 |
| 95 Eric Crabtree | 1.50 | .75 |
| 96 Sherrill Headrick | 1.50 | .75 |
| 97 Wray Carlton | 1.50 | .75 |
| 98 Gino Cappelletti | 2.00 | 1.00 |
| 99 Tommy McDonald | 4.00 | 2.00 |
| 100 Johnny Unitas | 35.00 | 20.00 |
| 101 Richie Petitbon | 1.50 | .75 |
| 102 Erich Barnes | 1.50 | .75 |
| 103 Bob Hayes | 10.00 | 5.00 |
| 104 Milt Plum | 2.00 | 1.00 |
| 105 Boyd Dowler | 2.00 | 1.00 |
| 106 Ed Meador | 1.50 | .75 |
| 107 Fred Cox | 1.50 | .75 |
| 108 Steve Stonebreaker RC | 1.50 | .75 |
| 109 Aaron Thomas | 1.50 | .75 |
| 110 Norm Snead | 2.00 | 1.00 |
| 111 Paul Martha RC | 1.50 | .75 |
| 112 Jerry Stovall | 1.50 | .75 |
| 113 Kay McFarland | 1.50 | .75 |
| 114 Pat Richter | 1.50 | .75 |
| 115 Rick Redman | 1.50 | .75 |
| 116 Tom Keating | 1.50 | .75 |
| 117 Matt Snell | 2.00 | 1.00 |
| 118 Dick Westmoreland | 1.50 | .75 |
| 119 Jerry Mays | 1.50 | .75 |
| 120 Sid Blanks | 1.50 | .75 |
| 121 Al Denson | 1.50 | .75 |
| 122 Bobby Hunt | 1.50 | .75 |
| 123 Mike Mercer | 1.50 | .75 |
| 124 Nick Buoniconti | 3.00 | 1.50 |
| 125 Ron Vanderkelen RC | 1.50 | .75 |
| 126 Ordell Braase | 1.50 | .75 |
| 127 Dick Butkus | 45.00 | 30.00 |
| 128 Gary Collins | 2.00 | 1.00 |
| 129 Mel Renfro | 6.00 | 3.00 |
| 130 Alex Karras | 5.00 | 2.50 |
| 131 Herb Adderley ! | 5.00 | 2.50 |
| 132 Roman Gabriel ! | 4.00 | 2.00 |
| 133 Bill Brown | 2.50 | 1.25 |
| 134 Kent Kramer | 2.00 | 1.00 |
| 135 Tucker Frederickson | 2.50 | 1.25 |
| 136 Nate Ramsey | 2.00 | 1.00 |
| 137 Marv Woodson | 2.00 | 1.00 |
| 138 Ken Gray | 2.00 | 1.00 |
| 139 John Brodie | 5.00 | 2.50 |
| 140 Jerry Smith | 2.00 | 1.00 |
| 141 Brad Hubbert | 2.00 | 1.00 |
| 142 George Blanda | 20.00 | 10.00 |
| 143 Pete Lammons RC | 2.00 | 1.00 |
| 144 Doug Moreau | 2.00 | 1.00 |
| 145 E.J. Holub | 2.00 | 1.00 |
| 146 Ode Burrell | 2.00 | 1.00 |
| 147 Bob Scarpitto | 2.00 | 1.00 |
| 148 Andre White | 2.00 | 1.00 |
| 149 Jack Kemp | 50.00 | 30.00 |
| 150 Art Graham | 2.00 | 1.00 |
| 151 Tommy Nobis | 6.00 | 3.00 |
| 152 Willie Richardson RC | 2.50 | 1.25 |
| 153 Jack Concannon | 2.00 | 1.00 |
| 154 Bill Glass | 2.00 | 1.00 |
| 155 Craig Morton RC | 10.00 | 5.00 |
| 156 Pat Studstill | 2.00 | 1.00 |
| 157 Ray Nitschke | 10.00 | 5.00 |
| 158 Roger Brown | 2.00 | 1.00 |
| 159 Joe Kapp RC | 5.00 | 2.50 |
| 160 Jim Taylor | 15.00 | 7.50 |
| 161 Fran Tarkenton | 20.00 | 10.00 |
| 162 Mike Ditka | 30.00 | 18.00 |
| 163 Andy Russell RC | 6.00 | 3.00 |
| 164 Larry Wilson | 4.00 | 2.00 |

|  |  | | |
|---|------|---|---|
| 165 | Tommy Davis | 2.00 | 1.00 |
| 166 | Paul Krause | 4.00 | 2.00 |
| 167 | Speedy Duncan | 2.00 | 1.00 |
| 168 | Fred Biletnikoff | 15.00 | 7.50 |
| 169 | Don Maynard | 10.00 | 5.00 |
| 170 | Frank Emanuel | 2.00 | 1.00 |
| 171 | Len Dawson | 15.00 | 7.50 |
| 172 | Miller Farr | 2.00 | 1.00 |
| 173 | Floyd Little RC | 20.00 | 10.00 |
| 174 | Lonnie Wright | 2.00 | 1.00 |
| 175 | Paul Costa | 2.00 | 1.00 |
| 176 | Don Trull | 2.00 | 1.00 |
| 177 | Jerry Simmons | 2.00 | 1.00 |
| 178 | Tom Matte | 2.50 | 1.25 |
| 179 | Bennie McRae | 2.00 | 1.00 |
| 180 | Jim Kanicki | 2.00 | 1.00 |
| 181 | Bob Lilly | 15.00 | 7.50 |
| 182 | Tom Watkins | 2.00 | 1.00 |
| 183 | Jim Grabowski RC | 4.00 | 2.00 |
| 184 | Jack Snow RC | 4.00 | 2.00 |
| 185 | Gary Cuozzo RC | 2.50 | 1.25 |
| 186 | Billy Kilmer | 4.00 | 2.00 |
| 187 | Jim Katcavage | 2.00 | 1.00 |
| 188 | Floyd Peters | 2.00 | 1.00 |
| 189 | Bill Nelsen | 2.50 | 1.25 |
| 190 | Bobby Joe Conrad | 2.50 | 1.25 |
| 191 | Kermit Alexander | 2.00 | 1.00 |
| 192 | Charley Taylor UER | 6.00 | 3.00 |
| 193 | Lance Alworth | 20.00 | 10.00 |
| 194 | Daryle Lamonica | 5.00 | 2.50 |
| 195 | Al Atkinson | 2.00 | 1.00 |
| 196 | Bob Griese RC | 90.00 | 50.00 |
| 197 | Buck Buchanan | 4.00 | 2.00 |
| 198 | Pete Beathard | 2.00 | 1.00 |
| 199 | Nemiah Wilson | 2.00 | 1.00 |
| 200 | Ernie Wright | 2.00 | 1.00 |
| 201 | George Saimes | 2.00 | 1.00 |
| 202 | John Charles | 2.00 | 1.00 |
| 203 | Randy Johnson | 2.00 | 1.00 |
| 204 | Tony Lorick | 2.00 | 1.00 |
| 205 | Dick Evey | 2.00 | 1.00 |
| 206 | Leroy Kelly | 10.00 | 5.00 |
| 207 | Lee Roy Jordan | 6.00 | 3.00 |
| 208 | Jim Gibbons | 2.00 | 1.00 |
| 209 | Donny Anderson RC | 4.00 | 2.00 |
| 210 | Maxie Baughan | 2.00 | 1.00 |
| 211 | Joe Morrison | 2.00 | 1.00 |
| 212 | Jim Snowden | 2.00 | 1.00 |
| 213 | Lenny Lyles | 2.00 | 1.00 |
| 214 | Bobby Joe Green | 2.00 | 1.00 |
| 215 | Frank Ryan | 2.50 | 1.25 |
| 216 | Cornell Green | 2.50 | 1.25 |
| 217 | Karl Sweetan | 2.00 | 1.00 |
| 218 | Dave Williams | 2.00 | 1.00 |
| 219A | Checklist Green ! | 18.00 | 10.00 |
| 219B | Checklist Blue ! | 20.00 | 12.00 |

## 1969 Topps

GALE SAYERS
CHICAGO BEARS · RUNNING BACK

| | | | |
|---|---|---|---|
| COMPLETE SET (263) | | 550.00 | 350.00 |
| COMMON CARD (1-132) | | 1.50 | .75 |
| COMMON CARD (133-263) | | 2.00 | 1.00 |
| WRAPPER (5-CENT) | | 30.00 | 15.00 |
| 1 | Leroy Kelly ! | 20.00 | 10.00 |
| 2 | Paul Flatley | 1.50 | .75 |
| 3 | Jim Cadile | 1.50 | .75 |
| 4 | Erich Barnes | 1.50 | .75 |
| 5 | Willie Richardson | 1.50 | .75 |
| 6 | Bob Hayes | 8.00 | 4.00 |

|  |  | | |
|---|------|---|---|
| 7 | Bob Jeter | 1.50 | .75 |
| 8 | Jim Colclough | 1.50 | .75 |
| 9 | Sherrill Headrick | 1.50 | .75 |
| 10 | Jim Dunaway | 1.50 | .75 |
| 11 | Bill Munson | 2.00 | 1.00 |
| 12 | Jack Pardee | 2.00 | 1.00 |
| 13 | Jim Lindsey | 1.50 | .75 |
| 14 | Dave Whitsell | 1.50 | .75 |
| 15 | Tucker Frederickson | 1.50 | .75 |
| 16 | Alvin Haymond | 2.00 | 1.00 |
| 17 | Andy Russell | 2.00 | 1.00 |
| 18 | Tom Beer | 1.50 | .75 |
| 19 | Bobby Maples | 1.50 | .75 |
| 20 | Len Dawson | 8.00 | 4.00 |
| 21 | Willis Crenshaw | 1.50 | .75 |
| 22 | Tommy Davis | 1.50 | .75 |
| 23 | Rickie Harris | 1.50 | .75 |
| 24 | Jerry Simmons | 1.50 | .75 |
| 25 | Johnny Unitas | 40.00 | 25.00 |
| 26 | Brian Piccolo RC UER | 80.00 | 50.00 |
| 27 | Bob Matheson | 1.50 | .75 |
| 28 | Howard Twilley | 2.00 | 1.00 |
| 29 | Jim Turner | 2.00 | 1.00 |
| 30 | Pete Banaszak RC | 2.00 | 1.00 |
| 31 | Lance Rentzel RC | 2.00 | 1.00 |
| 32 | Bill Triplett | 1.50 | .75 |
| 33 | Boyd Dowler | 2.00 | 1.00 |
| 34 | Merlin Olsen | 5.00 | 2.50 |
| 35 | Joe Kapp | 3.00 | 1.50 |
| 36 | Dan Abramowicz RC | 4.00 | 2.00 |
| 37 | Spider Lockhart | 2.00 | 1.00 |
| 38 | Tom Day | 1.50 | .75 |
| 39 | Art Graham | 1.50 | .75 |
| 40 | Bob Cappadona | 1.50 | .75 |
| 41 | Gary Ballman | 1.50 | .75 |
| 42 | Clendon Thomas | 1.50 | .75 |
| 43 | Jackie Smith | 4.00 | 2.00 |
| 44 | Wes Wilcox | 3.00 | 1.50 |
| 45 | Jerry Smith | 1.50 | .75 |
| 46 | Dan Grimm | 1.50 | .75 |
| 47 | Tom Matte | 2.00 | 1.00 |
| 48 | John Stofa | 1.50 | .75 |
| 49 | Rex Mirich | 1.50 | .75 |
| 50 | Miller Farr | 1.50 | .75 |
| 51 | Gale Sayers | 40.00 | 25.00 |
| 52 | Bill Nelsen | 2.00 | 1.00 |
| 53 | Bob Lilly | 6.00 | 3.00 |
| 54 | Wayne Walker | 1.50 | .75 |
| 55 | Ray Nitschke | 5.00 | 2.50 |
| 56 | Ed Meador | 1.50 | .75 |
| 57 | Lonnie Warwick | 1.50 | .75 |
| 58 | Wendell Hayes | 1.50 | .75 |
| 59 | Dick Anderson RC | 5.00 | 2.50 |
| 60 | Don Maynard | 6.00 | 3.00 |
| 61 | Tony Lorick | 1.50 | .75 |
| 62 | Pete Gogolak | 1.50 | .75 |
| 63 | Nate Ramsey | 1.50 | .75 |
| 64 | Dick Shiner | 1.50 | .75 |
| 65 | Larry Wilson UER | 3.00 | 1.50 |
| 66 | Ken Willard | 2.00 | 1.00 |
| 67 | Charley Taylor | 5.00 | 2.50 |
| 68 | Billy Cannon | 2.00 | 1.00 |
| 69 | Lance Alworth | 8.00 | 4.00 |
| 70 | Jim Nance | 2.00 | 1.00 |
| 71 | Nick Rassas | 1.50 | .75 |
| 72 | Lenny Lyles | 1.50 | .75 |
| 73 | Bennie McRae | 1.50 | .75 |
| 74 | Bill Glass | 1.50 | .75 |
| 75 | Don Meredith | 25.00 | 15.00 |
| 76 | Dick LeBeau | 1.50 | .75 |
| 77 | Carroll Dale | 2.00 | 1.00 |
| 78 | Ron McDole | 1.50 | .75 |
| 79 | Charley King | 1.50 | .75 |
| 80 | Checklist UER | 15.00 | 7.50 |
| 81 | Dick Bass | 2.00 | 1.00 |
| 82 | Roy Winston | 1.50 | .75 |
| 83 | Don McCall | 1.50 | .75 |
| 84 | Jim Katcavage | 2.00 | 1.00 |
| 85 | Norm Snead | 2.00 | 1.00 |
| 86 | Earl Gros | 1.50 | .75 |
| 87 | Don Brumm | 1.50 | .75 |
| 88 | Sonny Bishop | 1.50 | .75 |
| 89 | Fred Arbanas | 2.00 | 1.00 |
| 90 | Karl Noonan | 1.50 | .75 |
| 91 | Dick Witcher | 1.50 | .75 |

|  |  | | |
|---|------|---|---|
| 92 | Vince Promuto | 1.50 | .75 |
| 93 | Tommy Nobis | 4.00 | 2.00 |
| 94 | Jerry Hill | 1.50 | .75 |
| 95 | Ed O'Bradovich RC | 1.50 | .75 |
| 96 | Ernie Kellerman | 1.50 | .75 |
| 97 | Chuck Howley | 2.00 | 1.00 |
| 98 | Hewritt Dixon | 1.50 | .75 |
| 99 | Ron Mix | 3.00 | 1.50 |
| 100 | Joe Namath | 75.00 | 40.00 |
| 101 | Billy Gambrell | 1.50 | .75 |
| 102 | Elijah Pitts | 2.00 | 1.00 |
| 103 | Billy Truax RC | 2.00 | 1.00 |
| 104 | Ed Sharockman | 1.50 | .75 |
| 105 | Doug Atkins | 3.00 | 1.50 |
| 106 | Greg Larson | 1.50 | .75 |
| 107 | Israel Lang | 1.50 | .75 |
| 108 | Houston Antwine | 1.50 | .75 |
| 109 | Paul Guidry | 1.50 | .75 |
| 110 | Al Denson | 1.50 | .75 |
| 111 | Roy Jefferson | 2.00 | 1.00 |
| 112 | Chuck Latourette | 1.50 | .75 |
| 113 | Jim Johnson | 3.00 | 1.50 |
| 114 | Bobby Mitchell | 4.00 | 2.00 |
| 115 | Randy Johnson | 1.50 | .75 |
| 116 | Lou Michaels | 1.50 | .75 |
| 117 | Rudy Kuechenberg | 1.50 | .75 |
| 118 | Walt Suggs | 1.50 | .75 |
| 119 | Goldie Sellers | 1.50 | .75 |
| 120 | Larry Csonka RC ! | 75.00 | 40.00 |
| 121 | Jim Houston | 1.50 | .75 |
| 122 | Craig Baynham | 1.50 | .75 |
| 123 | Alex Karras | 5.00 | 2.50 |
| 124 | Jim Grabowski | 2.00 | 1.00 |
| 125 | Roman Gabriel | 3.00 | 1.50 |
| 126 | Larry Bowie | 1.50 | .75 |
| 127 | Dave Parks | 2.00 | 1.00 |
| 128 | Ben Davidson | 3.00 | 1.50 |
| 129 | Steve DeLong | 1.50 | .75 |
| 130 | Fred Hill | 1.50 | .75 |
| 131 | Ernie Koy | 2.00 | 1.00 |
| 132A | Checklist no border ! | 15.00 | 7.50 |
| 132B | Checklist bordered ! | 20.00 | 10.00 |
| 133 | Dick Hoak | 2.00 | 1.00 |
| 134 | Larry Stallings RC | 2.00 | 1.00 |
| 135 | Clifton McNeil RC | 2.00 | 1.00 |
| 136 | Walter Rock | 2.00 | 1.00 |
| 137 | Billy Lothridge | 2.00 | 1.00 |
| 138 | Bob Vogel | 2.00 | 1.00 |
| 139 | Dick Butkus | 40.00 | 25.00 |
| 140 | Frank Ryan | 2.50 | 1.25 |
| 141 | Larry Garron | 2.00 | 1.00 |
| 142 | George Saimes | 2.00 | 1.00 |
| 143 | Frank Buncom | 2.00 | 1.00 |
| 144 | Don Perkins | 2.50 | 1.25 |
| 145 | Johnnie Robinson UER | 2.00 | 1.00 |
| 146 | Lee Roy Caffey | 2.00 | 1.00 |
| 147 | Bernie Casey | 2.50 | 1.25 |
| 148 | Billy Martin E | 2.00 | 1.00 |
| 149 | Gene Howard | 2.00 | 1.00 |
| 150 | Fran Tarkenton | 20.00 | 10.00 |
| 151 | Eric Crabtree | 2.00 | 1.00 |
| 152 | W.K. Hicks | 2.00 | 1.00 |
| 153 | Bobby Bell | 4.00 | 2.00 |
| 154 | Sam Baker | 2.00 | 1.00 |
| 155 | Marv Woodson | 2.00 | 1.00 |
| 156 | Dave Williams | 2.00 | 1.00 |
| 157 | Bruce Bosley UER | 2.00 | 1.00 |
| 158 | Carl Kammerer | 2.00 | 1.00 |
| 159 | Jim Burson | 2.00 | 1.00 |
| 160 | Roy Hilton | 2.00 | 1.00 |
| 161 | Bob Griese | 25.00 | 15.00 |
| 162 | Bob Talamini | 2.00 | 1.00 |
| 163 | Jim Otto | 4.00 | 2.00 |
| 164 | Ronnie Bull | 2.00 | 1.00 |
| 165 | Walter Johnson RC | 2.00 | 1.00 |
| 166 | Lee Roy Jordan | 4.00 | 2.00 |
| 167 | Mike Lucci | 2.50 | 1.25 |
| 168 | Willie Wood | 4.00 | 2.00 |
| 169 | Maxie Baughan | 2.50 | 1.25 |
| 170 | Bill Brown | 2.50 | 1.25 |
| 171 | John Hadl | 4.00 | 2.00 |
| 172 | Gino Cappelletti | 2.50 | 1.25 |
| 173 | George Butch Byrd | 2.50 | 1.25 |
| 174 | Steve Stonebreaker | 2.00 | 1.00 |
| 175 | Joe Morrison | 2.00 | 1.00 |

| | | |
|---|---|---|
| ❏ 176 Joe Scarpati | 2.00 | 1.00 |
| ❏ 177 Bobby Walden | 2.00 | 1.00 |
| ❏ 178 Roy Shivers | 2.00 | 1.00 |
| ❏ 179 Kermit Alexander | 2.00 | 1.00 |
| ❏ 180 Pat Richter | 2.00 | 1.00 |
| ❏ 181 Pete Perreault | 2.00 | 1.00 |
| ❏ 182 Pete Duranko | 2.00 | 1.00 |
| ❏ 183 Leroy Mitchell | 2.00 | 1.00 |
| ❏ 184 Jim Simon | 2.00 | 1.00 |
| ❏ 185 Billy Ray Smith | 2.00 | 1.00 |
| ❏ 186 Jack Concannon | 2.00 | 1.00 |
| ❏ 187 Ben Davis | 2.00 | 1.00 |
| ❏ 188 Mike Clark | 2.00 | 1.00 |
| ❏ 189 Jim Gibbons | 2.00 | 1.00 |
| ❏ 190 Dave Robinson | 2.50 | 1.25 |
| ❏ 191 Otis Taylor | 2.50 | 1.25 |
| ❏ 192 Nick Buoniconti | 4.00 | 2.00 |
| ❏ 193 Matt Snell | 2.50 | 1.25 |
| ❏ 194 Bruce Gossett | 2.00 | 1.00 |
| ❏ 195 Mick Tingelhoff | 2.50 | 1.25 |
| ❏ 196 Earl Leggett | 2.00 | 1.00 |
| ❏ 197 Pete Case | 2.00 | 1.00 |
| ❏ 198 Tom Woodeshick RC | 2.00 | 1.00 |
| ❏ 199 Ken Kortas | 2.00 | 1.00 |
| ❏ 200 Jim Hart | 4.00 | 2.00 |
| ❏ 201 Fred Biletnikoff | 10.00 | 5.00 |
| ❏ 202 Jacque MacKinnon | 2.00 | 1.00 |
| ❏ 203 Jim Whalen | 2.00 | 1.00 |
| ❏ 204 Matt Hazeltine | 2.00 | 1.00 |
| ❏ 205 Charlie Gogolak | 2.00 | 1.00 |
| ❏ 206 Ray Ogden | 2.00 | 1.00 |
| ❏ 207 John Mackey | 4.00 | 2.00 |
| ❏ 208 Roosevelt Taylor | 2.00 | 1.00 |
| ❏ 209 Gene Hickerson | 2.50 | 1.25 |
| ❏ 210 Dave Edwards RC | 2.50 | 1.25 |
| ❏ 211 Tom Sestak | 2.00 | 1.00 |
| ❏ 212 Ernie Wright | 2.00 | 1.00 |
| ❏ 213 Dave Costa | 2.00 | 1.00 |
| ❏ 214 Tom Vaughn | 2.00 | 1.00 |
| ❏ 215 Bart Starr | 35.00 | 20.00 |
| ❏ 216 Les Josephson | 2.00 | 1.00 |
| ❏ 217 Fred Cox | 2.00 | 1.00 |
| ❏ 218 Mike Tilleman | 2.00 | 1.00 |
| ❏ 219 Darrell Dess | 2.00 | 1.00 |
| ❏ 220 Dave Lloyd | 2.00 | 1.00 |
| ❏ 221 Pete Beathard | 2.00 | 1.00 |
| ❏ 222 Buck Buchanan | 4.00 | 2.00 |
| ❏ 223 Frank Emanuel | 2.00 | 1.00 |
| ❏ 224 Paul Martha | 2.00 | 1.00 |
| ❏ 225 Johnny Roland | 2.00 | 1.00 |
| ❏ 226 Gary Lewis | 2.00 | 1.00 |
| ❏ 227 Sonny Jurgensen UER | 6.00 | 3.00 |
| ❏ 228 Jim Butler | 2.00 | 1.00 |
| ❏ 229 Mike Curtis RC | 8.00 | 4.00 |
| ❏ 230 Richie Petitbon | 2.00 | 1.00 |
| ❏ 231 George Sauer Jr. | 2.50 | 1.25 |
| ❏ 232 George Blanda | 20.00 | 10.00 |
| ❏ 233 Gary Garrison | 2.00 | 1.00 |
| ❏ 234 Gary Collins | 2.50 | 1.25 |
| ❏ 235 Craig Morton | 4.00 | 2.00 |
| ❏ 236 Tom Nowatzke | 2.00 | 1.00 |
| ❏ 237 Donny Anderson | 2.50 | 1.25 |
| ❏ 238 Deacon Jones | 4.00 | 2.00 |
| ❏ 239 Grady Alderman | 2.00 | 1.00 |
| ❏ 240 Billy Kilmer | 4.00 | 2.00 |
| ❏ 241 Mike Taliaferro | 2.00 | 1.00 |
| ❏ 242 Stew Barber | 2.00 | 1.00 |
| ❏ 243 Bobby Hunt | 2.00 | 1.00 |
| ❏ 244 Homer Jones | 2.00 | 1.00 |
| ❏ 245 Bob Brown OT | 4.00 | 2.00 |
| ❏ 246 Bill Asbury | 2.00 | 1.00 |
| ❏ 247 Charlie Johnson | 2.50 | 1.25 |
| ❏ 248 Chris Hanburger | 2.50 | 1.25 |
| ❏ 249 John Brodie | 6.00 | 3.00 |
| ❏ 250 Earl Morrall | 2.50 | 1.25 |
| ❏ 251 Floyd Little | 5.00 | 2.50 |
| ❏ 252 Jerrel Wilson RC | 2.00 | 1.00 |
| ❏ 253 Jim Keyes | 2.00 | 1.00 |
| ❏ 254 Mel Renfro | 4.00 | 2.00 |
| ❏ 255 Herb Adderley | 4.00 | 2.00 |
| ❏ 256 Jack Snow | 2.00 | 1.00 |
| ❏ 257 Charlie Durkee | 2.00 | 1.00 |
| ❏ 258 Charlie Harper | 2.00 | 1.00 |
| ❏ 259 J.R. Wilburn | 2.00 | 1.00 |
| ❏ 260 Charlie Krueger | 2.00 | 1.00 |

| | | |
|---|---|---|
| ❏ 261 Pete Jacques | 2.00 | 1.00 |
| ❏ 262 Gerry Philbin | 2.00 | 1.00 |
| ❏ 263 Daryle Lamonica ! | 10.00 | 5.00 |

## 1970 Topps

ALAN PAGE · VIKINGS · 88

| | | |
|---|---|---|
| ❏ COMPLETE SET (263) | 475.00 | 300.00 |
| ❏ COMMON CARD (1-132) | 2.50 | 1.00 |
| ❏ COMMON CARD (133-263) | 1.25 | .50 |
| ❏ WRAPPER (10-CENT) | 12.00 | 8.00 |
| ❏ 1 Len Dawson UER ! | 20.00 | 12.00 |
| ❏ 2 Doug Hart | 1.00 | .40 |
| ❏ 3 Verlon Biggs | 1.00 | .40 |
| ❏ 4 Ralph Neely RC | 1.50 | .60 |
| ❏ 5 Harmon Wages | 1.00 | .40 |
| ❏ 6 Dan Conners | 1.00 | .40 |
| ❏ 7 Gino Cappelletti | 1.50 | .60 |
| ❏ 8 Erich Barnes | 1.00 | .40 |
| ❏ 9 Checklist | 10.00 | 5.00 |
| ❏ 10 Bob Griese | 15.00 | 7.50 |
| ❏ 11 Ed Flanagan | 1.00 | .40 |
| ❏ 12 George Seals | 1.00 | .40 |
| ❏ 13 Harry Jacobs | 1.00 | .40 |
| ❏ 14 Mike Haffner | 1.00 | .40 |
| ❏ 15 Bob Vogel | 1.00 | .40 |
| ❏ 16 Bill Peterson | 1.00 | .40 |
| ❏ 17 Spider Lockhart | 1.00 | .40 |
| ❏ 18 Billy Truax | 1.00 | .40 |
| ❏ 19 Jim Beirne | 1.00 | .40 |
| ❏ 20 Leroy Kelly | 6.00 | 3.00 |
| ❏ 21 Dave Lloyd | 1.00 | .40 |
| ❏ 22 Mike Tilleman | 1.00 | .40 |
| ❏ 23 Gary Garrison | 1.00 | .40 |
| ❏ 24 Larry Brown RC | 8.00 | 4.00 |
| ❏ 25 Jan Stenerud RC | 12.00 | 6.00 |
| ❏ 26 Rolf Krueger | 1.00 | .40 |
| ❏ 27 Roland Lakes | 1.00 | .40 |
| ❏ 28 Dick Hoak | 1.00 | .40 |
| ❏ 29 Gene Washington Vik RC | 2.00 | 1.00 |
| ❏ 30 Bart Starr | 20.00 | 10.00 |
| ❏ 31 Dave Grayson | 1.00 | .40 |
| ❏ 32 Jerry Rush | 1.00 | .40 |
| ❏ 33 Len St. Jean | 1.00 | .40 |
| ❏ 34 Randy Edmunds | 1.00 | .40 |
| ❏ 35 Matt Snell | 1.50 | .60 |
| ❏ 36 Paul Costa | 1.00 | .40 |
| ❏ 37 Mike Pyle | 1.00 | .40 |
| ❏ 38 Roy Hilton | 1.00 | .40 |
| ❏ 39 Steve Tensi | 1.00 | .40 |
| ❏ 40 Tommy Nobis | 2.50 | 1.25 |
| ❏ 41 Pete Case | 1.00 | .40 |
| ❏ 42 Andy Rice | 1.00 | .40 |
| ❏ 43 Elvin Bethea RC | 8.00 | 4.00 |
| ❏ 44 Jack Snow | 1.50 | .60 |
| ❏ 45 Mel Renfro | 2.50 | 1.25 |
| ❏ 46 Andy Livingston | 1.00 | .40 |
| ❏ 47 Gary Ballman | 1.00 | .40 |
| ❏ 48 Bob DeMarco | 1.00 | .40 |
| ❏ 49 Steve DeLong | 1.00 | .40 |
| ❏ 50 Daryle Lamonica | 4.00 | 2.00 |
| ❏ 51 Jim Lynch RC | 1.00 | .40 |
| ❏ 52 Mel Farr RC | 1.00 | .40 |
| ❏ 53 Bob Long RC | 1.00 | .40 |
| ❏ 54 John Elliott | 1.00 | .40 |
| ❏ 55 Ray Nitschke | 5.00 | 2.50 |
| ❏ 56 Jim Shorter | 1.00 | .40 |
| ❏ 57 Dave Wilcox | 2.50 | 1.25 |
| ❏ 58 Eric Crabtree | 1.00 | .40 |
| ❏ 59 Alan Page RC | 30.00 | 15.00 |

| | | |
|---|---|---|
| ❏ 60 Jim Nance | 1.50 | .60 |
| ❏ 61 Glen Ray Hines | 1.00 | .40 |
| ❏ 62 John Mackey | 2.50 | 1.25 |
| ❏ 63 Ron McDole | 1.00 | .40 |
| ❏ 64 Tom Beier | 1.00 | .40 |
| ❏ 65 Bill Nelsen | 1.50 | .60 |
| ❏ 66 Paul Flatley | 1.00 | .40 |
| ❏ 67 Sam Brunelli | 1.00 | .40 |
| ❏ 68 Jack Pardee | 1.50 | .60 |
| ❏ 69 Brig Owens | 1.00 | .40 |
| ❏ 70 Gale Sayers | 25.00 | 12.50 |
| ❏ 71 Lee Roy Jordan | 2.50 | 1.25 |
| ❏ 72 Harold Jackson RC | 5.00 | 2.50 |
| ❏ 73 John Hadl | 2.50 | 1.25 |
| ❏ 74 Dave Parks | 1.00 | .40 |
| ❏ 75 Lem Barney RC | 14.00 | 7.00 |
| ❏ 76 Johnny Roland | 1.00 | .40 |
| ❏ 77 Ed Budde | 1.00 | .40 |
| ❏ 78 Ben McGee | 1.00 | .40 |
| ❏ 79 Ken Bowman | 1.00 | .40 |
| ❏ 80 Fran Tarkenton | 15.00 | 7.50 |
| ❏ 81 G.Washington 49er RC | 5.00 | 2.50 |
| ❏ 82 Larry Grantham | 1.00 | .40 |
| ❏ 83 Bill Brown | 1.50 | .60 |
| ❏ 84 John Charles | 1.00 | .40 |
| ❏ 85 Fred Biletnikoff | 7.00 | 3.50 |
| ❏ 86 Royce Berry | 1.00 | .40 |
| ❏ 87 Bob Lilly | 5.00 | 2.50 |
| ❏ 88 Earl Morrall | 1.50 | .60 |
| ❏ 89 Jerry LeVias RC | 1.50 | .60 |
| ❏ 90 O.J. Simpson RC | 80.00 | 40.00 |
| ❏ 91 Mike Howell | 1.00 | .40 |
| ❏ 92 Ken Gray | 1.00 | .40 |
| ❏ 93 Chris Hanburger | 1.00 | .40 |
| ❏ 94 Larry Seiple RC | 1.00 | .40 |
| ❏ 95 Rich Jackson RC | 1.00 | .40 |
| ❏ 96 Rockne Freitas | 1.00 | .40 |
| ❏ 97 Dick Post RC | 1.50 | .60 |
| ❏ 98 Ben Hawkins RC | 1.00 | .40 |
| ❏ 99 Ken Reaves | 1.00 | .40 |
| ❏ 100 Roman Gabriel | 2.50 | 1.25 |
| ❏ 101 Dave Rowe | 1.00 | .40 |
| ❏ 102 Dave Robinson | 1.00 | .40 |
| ❏ 103 Otis Taylor | 1.50 | .60 |
| ❏ 104 Jim Turner | 1.00 | .40 |
| ❏ 105 Joe Morrison | 1.00 | .40 |
| ❏ 106 Dick Evey | 1.00 | .40 |
| ❏ 107 Ray Mansfield | 1.00 | .40 |
| ❏ 108 Grady Alderman | 1.00 | .40 |
| ❏ 109 Bruce Gossett | 1.00 | .40 |
| ❏ 110 Bob Trumpy RC | 4.00 | 2.00 |
| ❏ 111 Jim Hunt | 1.00 | .40 |
| ❏ 112 Larry Stallings | 1.00 | .40 |
| ❏ 113A Lance Rentzel Red | 1.50 | .60 |
| ❏ 113B Lance Rentzel Black | 1.50 | .60 |
| ❏ 114 Bubba Smith RC | 25.00 | 12.50 |
| ❏ 115 Norm Snead | 1.50 | .60 |
| ❏ 116 Jim Otto | 2.50 | 1.25 |
| ❏ 117 Bo Scott RC | 1.00 | .40 |
| ❏ 118 Rick Redman | 1.00 | .40 |
| ❏ 119 George Butch Byrd | 1.00 | .40 |
| ❏ 120 George Webster RC | 1.50 | .60 |
| ❏ 121 Chuck Walton RC | 1.00 | .40 |
| ❏ 122 Dave Costa | 1.00 | .40 |
| ❏ 123 Al Dodd | 1.00 | .40 |
| ❏ 124 Len Hauss | 1.00 | .40 |
| ❏ 125 Deacon Jones | 2.50 | 1.25 |
| ❏ 126 Randy Johnson | 1.00 | .40 |
| ❏ 127 Ralph Heck | 1.00 | .40 |
| ❏ 128 Emerson Boozer RC | 1.50 | .60 |
| ❏ 129 Johnny Robinson | 1.50 | .60 |
| ❏ 130 John Brodie | 5.00 | 2.50 |
| ❏ 131 Gale Gillingham RC | 1.00 | .40 |
| ❏ 132 Checklist DP | 6.00 | 3.00 |
| ❏ 133 Chuck Walker | 1.25 | .50 |
| ❏ 134 Bennie McRae | 1.25 | .50 |
| ❏ 135 Paul Warfield | 7.00 | 3.50 |
| ❏ 136 Dan Darragh | 1.25 | .50 |
| ❏ 137 Paul Robinson RC | 1.25 | .50 |
| ❏ 138 Ed Philpott | 1.25 | .50 |
| ❏ 139 Craig Morton | 3.00 | 1.50 |
| ❏ 140 Tom Dempsey RC | 2.00 | .75 |
| ❏ 141 Al Nelson | 1.25 | .50 |
| ❏ 142 Tom Matte | 2.00 | .75 |
| ❏ 143 Dick Schafrath | 1.25 | .50 |

| | | | | | | | | | | |
|---|---|---|---|---|---|---|---|---|---|---|
| ☐ 144 | Willie Brown | 4.00 | 2.00 | ☐ 229 | Billy Shaw | 3.00 | 1.50 | ☐ 28 Lionel Aldridge RC | .75 | .30 |
| ☐ 145 | Charley Taylor UER | 5.00 | 2.50 | ☐ 230 | Jerry Hillebrand | 1.25 | .50 | ☐ 29 Billy Lothridge | .75 | .30 |
| ☐ 146 | John Huard | 1.25 | .50 | ☐ 231 | Bill Thompson RC | 2.00 | .75 | ☐ 30 Terry Hanratty RC | 1.25 | .50 |
| ☐ 147 | Dave Osborn | 1.25 | .50 | ☐ 232 | Carroll Dale | 2.00 | .75 | ☐ 31 Lee Roy Jordan | 2.00 | .75 |
| ☐ 148 | Gene Mingo | 1.25 | .50 | ☐ 233 | Gene Hickerson | 2.50 | 1.00 | ☐ 32 Rick Volk RC | .75 | .30 |
| ☐ 149 | Larry Hand | 1.25 | .50 | ☐ 234 | Jim Butler | 1.25 | .50 | ☐ 33 Howard Kindig | .75 | .30 |
| ☐ 150 | Joe Namath | 50.00 | 25.00 | ☐ 235 | Greg Cook RC | 1.25 | .50 | ☐ 34 Carl Garrett RC | .75 | .30 |
| ☐ 151 | Tom Mack RC | 10.00 | 5.00 | ☐ 236 | Lee Roy Caffey | 1.25 | .50 | ☐ 35 Bobby Bell | 2.00 | .75 |
| ☐ 152 | Kenny Graham | 1.25 | .50 | ☐ 237 | Merlin Olsen | 4.00 | 2.00 | ☐ 36 Gene Hickerson | 1.50 | .60 |
| ☐ 153 | Don Herrmann | 1.25 | .50 | ☐ 238 | Fred Cox | 1.25 | .50 | ☐ 37 Dave Parks | .75 | .30 |
| ☐ 154 | Bobby Bell | 3.00 | 1.50 | ☐ 239 | Nate Ramsey | 1.25 | .50 | ☐ 38 Paul Martha | .75 | .30 |
| ☐ 155 | Hoyle Granger | 1.25 | .50 | ☐ 240 | Lance Alworth | 7.00 | 3.50 | ☐ 39 George Blanda | 15.00 | 7.50 |
| ☐ 156 | Claude Humphrey RC | 6.00 | 3.00 | ☐ 241 | Chuck Hinton | 1.25 | .50 | ☐ 40 Tom Woodeshick | .75 | .30 |
| ☐ 157 | Clifton McNeil | 1.25 | .50 | ☐ 242 | Jerry Smith | 1.25 | .50 | ☐ 41 Alex Karras | 3.00 | 1.50 |
| ☐ 158 | Mick Tingelhoff | 2.00 | .75 | ☐ 243 | Tony Baker FB | 1.25 | .50 | ☐ 42 Rick Redman | .75 | .30 |
| ☐ 159 | Don Horn RC | 1.25 | .50 | ☐ 244 | Nick Buoniconti | 3.00 | 1.50 | ☐ 43 Zeke Moore | .75 | .30 |
| ☐ 160 | Larry Wilson | 3.00 | 1.50 | ☐ 245 | Jim Johnson | 3.00 | 1.50 | ☐ 44 Jack Snow | 1.25 | .50 |
| ☐ 161 | Tom Neville | 1.25 | .50 | ☐ 246 | Willie Richardson | 1.25 | .50 | ☐ 45 Larry Csonka | 15.00 | 7.50 |
| ☐ 162 | Larry Csonka | 20.00 | 10.00 | ☐ 247 | Fred Dryer RC | 10.00 | 5.00 | ☐ 46 Karl Kassulke | .75 | .30 |
| ☐ 163 | Doug Buffone RC | 1.25 | .50 | ☐ 248 | Bobby Maples | 1.25 | .50 | ☐ 47 Jim Hart | 2.00 | .75 |
| ☐ 164 | Cornell Green | 2.00 | .75 | ☐ 249 | Alex Karras | 4.00 | 2.00 | ☐ 48 Al Atkinson | .75 | .30 |
| ☐ 165 | Haven Moses RC | 2.00 | .75 | ☐ 250 | Joe Kapp | 2.00 | .75 | ☐ 49 Horst Muhlmann RC | .75 | .30 |
| ☐ 166 | Billy Kilmer | 3.00 | 1.50 | ☐ 251 | Ben Davidson | 3.00 | 1.50 | ☐ 50 Sonny Jurgensen | 5.00 | 2.50 |
| ☐ 167 | Tim Rossovich RC | 1.25 | .50 | ☐ 252 | Mike Stratton | 1.25 | .50 | ☐ 51 Ron Johnson RC | 1.25 | .50 |
| ☐ 168 | Bill Bergey RC | 4.00 | 2.00 | ☐ 253 | Les Josephson | 1.25 | .50 | ☐ 52 Cas Banaszek | .75 | .30 |
| ☐ 169 | Gary Collins | 2.00 | .75 | ☐ 254 | Don Maynard | 6.00 | 3.00 | ☐ 53 Bubba Smith | 8.00 | 4.00 |
| ☐ 170 | Floyd Little | 3.00 | 1.50 | ☐ 255 | Houston Antwine | 1.25 | .50 | ☐ 54 Bobby Douglass RC | 1.25 | .50 |
| ☐ 171 | Tom Keating | 1.25 | .50 | ☐ 256 | Mac Percival RC | 1.25 | .50 | ☐ 55 Willie Wood | 2.00 | .75 |
| ☐ 172 | Pat Fischer | 1.25 | .50 | ☐ 257 | George Goeddeke | 1.25 | .50 | ☐ 56 Bake Turner | .75 | .30 |
| ☐ 173 | Walt Sweeney | 1.25 | .50 | ☐ 258 | Homer Jones | 1.25 | .50 | ☐ 57 Mike Morgan LB | .75 | .30 |
| ☐ 174 | Greg Larson | 1.25 | .50 | ☐ 259 | Bob Berry | 1.25 | .50 | ☐ 58 George Butch Byrd | 1.25 | .50 |
| ☐ 175 | Carl Eller | 3.00 | 1.50 | ☐ 260A | Calvin Hill RC Red | 15.00 | 7.50 | ☐ 59 Don Horn | .75 | .30 |
| ☐ 176 | George Sauer Jr. | 2.00 | .75 | ☐ 260B | Calvin Hill RC Black | 20.00 | 10.00 | ☐ 60 Tommy Nobis | 2.00 | .75 |
| ☐ 177 | Jim Hart | 3.00 | 1.50 | ☐ 261 | Willie Wood | 3.00 | 1.50 | ☐ 61 Jan Stenerud | 4.00 | 2.00 |
| ☐ 178 | Bob Brown OT | 3.00 | 1.50 | ☐ 262 | Ed Weisacosky | 1.25 | .50 | ☐ 62 Altie Taylor RC | .75 | .30 |
| ☐ 179 | Mike Garrett UER | 2.00 | .75 | ☐ 263 | Jim Tyrer ! | 3.00 | 1.50 | ☐ 63 Gary Pettigrew | .75 | .30 |
| ☐ 180 | Johnny Unitas | 25.00 | 15.00 | | | | | ☐ 64 Spike Jones RC | .75 | .30 |
| ☐ 181 | Tom Regner | 1.25 | .50 | | **1971 Topps** | | | ☐ 65 Duane Thomas RC | 2.00 | .75 |
| ☐ 182 | Bob Jeter | 1.25 | .50 | | | | | ☐ 66 Marty Domres RC | .75 | .30 |
| ☐ 183 | Gail Cogdill | 1.25 | .50 | | | | | ☐ 67 Dick Anderson | 1.25 | .50 |
| ☐ 184 | Earl Gros | 1.25 | .50 | | | | | ☐ 68 Ken Iman | .75 | .30 |
| ☐ 185 | Dennis Partee | 1.25 | .50 | | | | | ☐ 69 Miller Farr | .75 | .30 |
| ☐ 186 | Charlie Krueger | 1.25 | .50 | | | | | ☐ 70 Daryle Lamonica | 3.00 | 1.50 |
| ☐ 187 | Martin Baccaglio | 1.25 | .50 | | | | | ☐ 71 Alan Page | 12.00 | 6.00 |
| ☐ 188 | Charles Long | 1.25 | .50 | | | | | ☐ 72 Pat Matson | .75 | .30 |
| ☐ 189 | Bob Hayes | 6.00 | 3.00 | | | | | ☐ 73 Emerson Boozer | .75 | .30 |
| ☐ 190 | Dick Butkus | 25.00 | 12.50 | | | | | ☐ 74 Pat Fischer | .75 | .30 |
| ☐ 191 | Al Bemiller | 1.25 | .50 | | | | | ☐ 75 Gary Collins | .75 | .30 |
| ☐ 192 | Dick Westmoreland | 1.25 | .50 | | | | | ☐ 76 John Fuqua RC | 1.25 | .50 |
| ☐ 193 | Joe Scarpati | 1.25 | .50 | | | | | ☐ 77 Bruce Gossett | .75 | .30 |
| ☐ 194 | Ron Snidow | 1.25 | .50 | | | | | ☐ 78 Ed O'Bradovich | .75 | .30 |
| ☐ 195 | Earl McCullouch RC | 1.25 | .50 | | | | | ☐ 79 Bob Tucker RC | 1.25 | .50 |
| ☐ 196 | Jake Kupp | 1.25 | .50 | | | | | ☐ 80 Mike Curtis | .75 | .30 |
| ☐ 197 | Bob Lurtsema | 1.25 | .50 | | | | | ☐ 81 Rich Jackson | .75 | .30 |
| ☐ 198 | Mike Current | 1.25 | .50 | | | | | ☐ 82 Tom Janik | .75 | .30 |
| ☐ 199 | Charlie Smith RB | 1.25 | .50 | | | | | ☐ 83 Gale Gillingham | .75 | .30 |
| ☐ 200 | Sonny Jurgensen | 6.00 | 3.00 | ☐ COMPLETE SET (263) | | 500.00 | 300.00 | ☐ 84 Jim Mitchell TE | .75 | .30 |
| ☐ 201 | Mike Curtis | 2.00 | .75 | ☐ COMMON CARD (1-132) | | .75 | .30 | ☐ 85 Charlie Johnson | 1.25 | .50 |
| ☐ 202 | Aaron Brown RC | 1.25 | .50 | ☐ COMMON CARD (133-263) | | 1.00 | .40 | ☐ 86 Edgar Chandler | .75 | .30 |
| ☐ 203 | Richie Petitbon | 1.25 | .50 | ☐ 1 Johnny Unitas ! | | 30.00 | 15.00 | ☐ 87 Cyril Pinder | .75 | .30 |
| ☐ 204 | Walt Suggs | 1.25 | .50 | ☐ 2 Jim Butler | | .75 | .30 | ☐ 88 Johnnie Robinson | 1.25 | .50 |
| ☐ 205 | Roy Jefferson | 1.25 | .50 | ☐ 3 Marty Schottenheimer RC | | 12.00 | 6.00 | ☐ 89 Ralph Neely | .75 | .30 |
| ☐ 206 | Russ Washington RC | 1.25 | .50 | ☐ 4 Joe O'Donnell | | .75 | .30 | ☐ 90 Dan Abramowicz | .75 | .30 |
| ☐ 207 | Woody Peoples RC | 1.25 | .50 | ☐ 5 Tom Dempsey | | 1.25 | .50 | ☐ 91 Mercury Morris RC | 5.00 | 2.50 |
| ☐ 208 | Dave Williams | 1.25 | .50 | ☐ 6 Chuck Allen | | .75 | .30 | ☐ 92 Steve DeLong | .75 | .30 |
| ☐ 209 | Zeke Dook RC | 1.25 | .50 | ☐ 7 Ernie Kellerman | | .75 | .30 | ☐ 93 Larry Stallings | .75 | .30 |
| ☐ 210 | Tom Woodeshick | 1.25 | .50 | ☐ 8 Walt Garrison RC | | 2.00 | .75 | ☐ 94 Tom Mack | .75 | .30 |
| ☐ 211 | Howard Fest | 1.25 | .50 | ☐ 9 Bill Van Heusen | | .75 | .30 | ☐ 95 Hewritt Dixon | .75 | .30 |
| ☐ 212 | Jack Concannon | 1.25 | .50 | ☐ 10 Lance Alworth | | 8.00 | 4.00 | ☐ 96 Fred Cox | .75 | .30 |
| ☐ 213 | Jim Marshall | 3.00 | 1.50 | ☐ 11 Greg Landry RC | | 2.00 | .75 | ☐ 97 Chris Hanburger | .75 | .30 |
| ☐ 214 | Jon Morris | 1.25 | .50 | ☐ 12 Larry Krause | | .75 | .30 | ☐ 98 Gerry Philbin | .75 | .30 |
| ☐ 215 | Dan Abramowicz | 2.00 | .75 | ☐ 13 Buck Buchanan | | 2.00 | .75 | ☐ 99 Ernie Wright | .75 | .30 |
| ☐ 216 | Paul Martha | 1.25 | .50 | ☐ 14 Roy Gerela RC | | 1.25 | .50 | ☐ 100 John Brodie | 4.00 | 2.00 |
| ☐ 217 | Ken Willard | 1.25 | .50 | ☐ 15 Clifton McNeil | | .75 | .30 | ☐ 101 Tucker Frederickson | .75 | .30 |
| ☐ 218 | Walter Rock | 1.25 | .50 | ☐ 16 Bob Brown OT | | 2.00 | .75 | ☐ 102 Bobby Walden | .75 | .30 |
| ☐ 219 | Garland Boyette | 1.25 | .50 | ☐ 17 Lloyd Mumphord | | .75 | .30 | ☐ 103 Dick Gordon | .75 | .30 |
| ☐ 220 | Buck Buchanan | 3.00 | 1.50 | ☐ 18 Gary Cuozzo | | .75 | .30 | ☐ 104 Walter Johnson | .75 | .30 |
| ☐ 221 | Bill Munson | 2.00 | .75 | ☐ 19 Don Maynard | | 5.00 | 2.50 | ☐ 105 Mike Lucci | 1.25 | .50 |
| ☐ 222 | David Lee RC | 1.25 | .50 | ☐ 20 Larry Wilson | | 2.00 | .75 | ☐ 106 Checklist DP | 6.00 | 3.00 |
| ☐ 223 | Karl Noonan | 1.25 | .50 | ☐ 21 Charlie Smith RB | | .75 | .30 | ☐ 107 Ron Berger | .75 | .30 |
| ☐ 224 | Harry Schuh | 1.25 | .50 | ☐ 22 Ken Avery | | .75 | .30 | ☐ 108 Dan Sullivan | .75 | .30 |
| ☐ 225 | Jackie Smith | 3.00 | 1.50 | ☐ 23 Billy Walik | | .75 | .30 | ☐ 109 George Kunz RC | .75 | .30 |
| ☐ 226 | Gerry Philbin | 1.25 | .50 | ☐ 24 Jim Johnson | | 2.00 | .75 | ☐ 110 Floyd Little | 2.00 | .75 |
| ☐ 227 | Ernie Koy | 1.25 | .50 | ☐ 25 Dick Butkus | | 25.00 | 12.50 | ☐ 111 Zeke Bratkowski | 1.25 | .50 |
| ☐ 228 | Chuck Howley | 2.00 | .75 | ☐ 26 Charley Taylor UER | | 4.00 | 2.00 | ☐ 112 Haven Moses | 1.25 | .50 |
| | | | | ☐ 27 Checklist UER | | 8.00 | 4.00 | | | |

| | | |
|---|---|---|
| ❏ 113 Ken Houston RC | 15.00 | 7.50 |
| ❏ 114 Willie Lanier RC | 15.00 | 7.50 |
| ❏ 115 Larry Brown | 2.00 | .75 |
| ❏ 116 Tim Rossovich | .75 | .30 |
| ❏ 117 Errol Linden | .75 | .30 |
| ❏ 118 Mel Renfro | 2.00 | .75 |
| ❏ 119 Mike Garrett | .75 | .30 |
| ❏ 120 Fran Tarkenton | 15.00 | 7.50 |
| ❏ 121 Garo Yepremian RC | 2.00 | .75 |
| ❏ 122 Glen Condren | .75 | .30 |
| ❏ 123 Johnny Roland | .75 | .30 |
| ❏ 124 Dave Herman | .75 | .30 |
| ❏ 125 Merlin Olsen | 3.00 | 1.50 |
| ❏ 126 Doug Buffone | .75 | .30 |
| ❏ 127 Earl McCullouch | .75 | .30 |
| ❏ 128 Spider Lockhart | .75 | .30 |
| ❏ 129 Ken Willard | .75 | .30 |
| ❏ 130 Gene Washington Vik | .75 | .30 |
| ❏ 131 Mike Phipps RC | 1.25 | .50 |
| ❏ 132 Andy Russell | 1.25 | .50 |
| ❏ 133 Ray Nitschke ! | 4.00 | 2.00 |
| ❏ 134 Jerry Logan | 1.00 | .40 |
| ❏ 135 MacArthur Lane RC | 1.50 | .60 |
| ❏ 136 Jim Turner | 1.00 | .40 |
| ❏ 137 Kent McCloughan | 1.00 | .40 |
| ❏ 138 Paul Guidry | 1.00 | .40 |
| ❏ 139 Otis Taylor | 1.50 | .60 |
| ❏ 140 Virgil Carter RC | 1.00 | .40 |
| ❏ 141 Joe Dawkins | 1.00 | .40 |
| ❏ 142 Steve Preece | 1.00 | .40 |
| ❏ 143 Mike Bragg RC | 1.00 | .40 |
| ❏ 144 Bob Lilly | 5.00 | 2.50 |
| ❏ 145 Joe Kapp | 1.50 | .60 |
| ❏ 146 Al Dodd | 1.00 | .40 |
| ❏ 147 Nick Buoniconti | 2.50 | 1.25 |
| ❏ 148 Speedy Duncan | 1.00 | .40 |
| ❏ 149 Cedrick Hardman RC | 1.00 | .40 |
| ❏ 150 Gale Sayers | 25.00 | 12.50 |
| ❏ 151 Jim Otto | 2.50 | 1.25 |
| ❏ 152 Billy Truax | 1.00 | .40 |
| ❏ 153 John Elliott | 1.00 | .40 |
| ❏ 154 Dick LeBeau | 1.00 | .40 |
| ❏ 155 Bill Bergey | 1.50 | .60 |
| ❏ 156 Terry Bradshaw RC ! | 200.00 | 125.00 |
| ❏ 157 Leroy Kelly | 6.00 | 3.00 |
| ❏ 158 Paul Krause | 2.50 | 1.25 |
| ❏ 159 Ted Vactor | 1.00 | .40 |
| ❏ 160 Bob Griese | 15.00 | 7.50 |
| ❏ 161 Ernie McMillan | 1.00 | .40 |
| ❏ 162 Donny Anderson | 1.50 | .60 |
| ❏ 163 John Pitts | 1.00 | .40 |
| ❏ 164 Dave Costa | 1.00 | .40 |
| ❏ 165 Gene Washington 49er | 1.50 | .60 |
| ❏ 166 John Zook | 1.00 | .40 |
| ❏ 167 Pete Gogolak | 1.00 | .40 |
| ❏ 168 Erich Barnes | 1.00 | .40 |
| ❏ 169 Alvin Reed | 1.00 | .40 |
| ❏ 170 Jim Nance | 1.50 | .60 |
| ❏ 171 Craig Morton | 2.50 | 1.25 |
| ❏ 172 Gary Garrison | 1.00 | .40 |
| ❏ 173 Joe Scarpati | 1.00 | .40 |
| ❏ 174 Adrian Young UER | 1.00 | .40 |
| ❏ 175 John Mackey | 2.50 | 1.25 |
| ❏ 176 Mac Percival | 1.00 | .40 |
| ❏ 177 Preston Pearson RC | 4.00 | 2.00 |
| ❏ 178 Fred Biletnikoff | 8.00 | 4.00 |
| ❏ 179 Mike Battle RC | 1.00 | .40 |
| ❏ 180 Len Dawson | 8.00 | 4.00 |
| ❏ 181 Les Josephson | 1.00 | .40 |
| ❏ 182 Royce Berry | 1.00 | .40 |
| ❏ 183 Herman Weaver | 1.00 | .40 |
| ❏ 184 Norm Snead | 1.50 | .60 |
| ❏ 185 Sam Brunelli | 1.00 | .40 |
| ❏ 186 Jim Kiick RC | 5.00 | 2.50 |
| ❏ 187 Austin Denney | 1.00 | .40 |
| ❏ 188 Roger Wehrli RC | 12.00 | 6.00 |
| ❏ 189 Dave Wilcox | 2.50 | 1.25 |
| ❏ 190 Bob Hayes | 4.00 | 2.00 |
| ❏ 191 Joe Morrison | 1.00 | .40 |
| ❏ 192 Manny Sistrunk | 1.00 | .40 |
| ❏ 193 Don Cockroft RC | 1.00 | .40 |
| ❏ 194 Lee Bouggess | 1.00 | .40 |
| ❏ 195 Bob Berry | 1.00 | .40 |
| ❏ 196 Ron Sellers | 1.00 | .40 |
| ❏ 197 George Webster | 1.00 | .40 |

| | | |
|---|---|---|
| ❏ 198 Hoyle Granger | 1.00 | .40 |
| ❏ 199 Bob Vogel | 1.00 | .40 |
| ❏ 200 Bart Starr | 20.00 | 10.00 |
| ❏ 201 Mike Mercer | 1.00 | .40 |
| ❏ 202 Dave Smith WR | 1.00 | .40 |
| ❏ 203 Lee Roy Caffey | 1.00 | .40 |
| ❏ 204 Mick Tingelhoff | 1.50 | .60 |
| ❏ 205 Matt Snell | 1.50 | .60 |
| ❏ 206 Jim Tyrer | 1.00 | .40 |
| ❏ 207 Willie Brown | 2.50 | 1.25 |
| ❏ 208 Bob Johnson RC | 1.00 | .40 |
| ❏ 209 Deacon Jones | 2.50 | 1.25 |
| ❏ 210 Charlie Sanders RC | 8.00 | 4.00 |
| ❏ 211 Jake Scott RC | 6.00 | 3.00 |
| ❏ 212 Bob Anderson RC | 1.00 | .40 |
| ❏ 213 Charlie Krueger | 1.00 | .40 |
| ❏ 214 Jim Bakken | 1.00 | .40 |
| ❏ 215 Harold Jackson | 1.50 | .60 |
| ❏ 216 Bill Brundige | 1.00 | .40 |
| ❏ 217 Calvin Hill | 5.00 | 2.50 |
| ❏ 218 Claude Humphrey | 1.00 | .40 |
| ❏ 219 Glen Ray Hines | 1.00 | .40 |
| ❏ 220 Bill Nelsen | 1.50 | .60 |
| ❏ 221 Roy Hilton | 1.00 | .40 |
| ❏ 222 Don Herrmann | 1.00 | .40 |
| ❏ 223 John Bramlett | 1.00 | .40 |
| ❏ 224 Ken Ellis | 1.00 | .40 |
| ❏ 225 Dave Osborn | 1.50 | .60 |
| ❏ 226 Edd Hargett RC | 1.00 | .40 |
| ❏ 227 Gene Mingo | 1.00 | .40 |
| ❏ 228 Larry Grantham | 1.00 | .40 |
| ❏ 229 Dick Post | 1.00 | .40 |
| ❏ 230 Roman Gabriel | 2.50 | 1.25 |
| ❏ 231 Mike Eischeid | 1.00 | .40 |
| ❏ 232 Jim Lynch | 1.00 | .40 |
| ❏ 233 Lemar Parrish RC | 1.50 | .60 |
| ❏ 234 Cecil Turner | 1.00 | .40 |
| ❏ 235 Dennis Shaw RC | 1.00 | .40 |
| ❏ 236 Mel Farr | 1.00 | .40 |
| ❏ 237 Curt Knight | 1.00 | .40 |
| ❏ 238 Chuck Howley | 1.50 | .60 |
| ❏ 239 Bruce Taylor RC | 1.00 | .40 |
| ❏ 240 Jerry LeVias | 1.00 | .40 |
| ❏ 241 Bob Lurtsema | 1.00 | .40 |
| ❏ 242 Earl Morrall | 1.50 | .60 |
| ❏ 243 Kermit Alexander | 1.00 | .40 |
| ❏ 244 Jackie Smith | 2.50 | 1.25 |
| ❏ 245 Joe Greene RC | 50.00 | 30.00 |
| ❏ 246 Harmon Wages | 1.00 | .40 |
| ❏ 247 Errol Mann | 1.00 | .40 |
| ❏ 248 Mike McCoy DT RC | 1.00 | .40 |
| ❏ 249 Milt Morin RC | 1.00 | .40 |
| ❏ 250 Joe Namath | 60.00 | 35.00 |
| ❏ 251 Jackie Burkett | 1.00 | .40 |
| ❏ 252 Steve Chomyszak | 1.00 | .40 |
| ❏ 253 Ed Sharockman | 1.00 | .40 |
| ❏ 254 Robert Holmes RC | 1.00 | .40 |
| ❏ 255 John Hadl | 2.50 | 1.25 |
| ❏ 256 Cornell Gordon | 1.00 | .40 |
| ❏ 257 Mark Moseley RC | 1.50 | .60 |
| ❏ 258 Gus Otto | 1.00 | .40 |
| ❏ 259 Mike Taliaferro | 1.00 | .40 |
| ❏ 260 O.J.Simpson | 25.00 | 12.50 |
| ❏ 261 Paul Warfield | 8.00 | 4.00 |
| ❏ 262 Jack Concannon | 1.00 | .40 |
| ❏ 263 Tom Matte ! | 2.50 | 1.25 |

**1972 Topps**

| | | |
|---|---|---|
| ❏ COMPLETE SET (351) | 2500.00 | 1500.00 |
| ❏ COMMON CARD (1-132) | .50 | .25 |
| ❏ COMMON CARD (133-263) | .60 | .30 |
| ❏ COMMON CARD (264-351) | 18.00 | 10.00 |
| ❏ WRAPPER (10-CENT) | 10.00 | 6.00 |
| ❏ WRAPPER SER.3 (10-CENT) | 20.00 | 15.00 |
| ❏ 1 L.Csonka/Litt/Hubb LL | 4.00 | 2.00 |
| ❏ 2 NFC Rushing Leaders | .50 | .25 |
| ❏ 3 B.Griese/Dawson/Cart LL | 2.00 | .75 |
| ❏ 4 R.Staubach/Lan/Kil LL | 5.00 | 2.50 |
| ❏ 5 AFC Receiving Leaders | 1.00 | .40 |
| ❏ 6 NFC Receiving Leaders | .50 | .25 |
| ❏ 7 Yepre/Stener/O'Brien LL | .50 | .25 |
| ❏ 8 NFC Scoring Leaders | .50 | .25 |
| ❏ 9 Jim Kiick | 2.00 | .75 |
| ❏ 10 Otis Taylor | 1.00 | .40 |
| ❏ 11 Bobby Joe Green | .50 | .25 |
| ❏ 12 Ken Ellis | .50 | .25 |
| ❏ 13 John Riggins RC | 20.00 | 10.00 |
| ❏ 14 Dave Parks | .50 | .25 |
| ❏ 15 John Hadl | 2.00 | .75 |
| ❏ 16 Ron Hornsby | .50 | .25 |
| ❏ 17 Chip Myers RC | .50 | .25 |
| ❏ 18 Billy Kilmer | 2.00 | .75 |
| ❏ 19 Fred Hoaglin | .50 | .25 |
| ❏ 20 Carl Eller | 2.00 | .75 |
| ❏ 21 Steve Zabel | .50 | .25 |
| ❏ 22 Vic Washington RC | .50 | .25 |
| ❏ 23 Len St. Jean | .50 | .25 |
| ❏ 24 Bill Thompson | .50 | .25 |
| ❏ 25 Steve Owens RC | 3.00 | 1.25 |
| ❏ 26 Ken Burrough RC | 1.00 | .40 |
| ❏ 27 Mike Clark | .50 | .25 |
| ❏ 28 Willie Brown | 2.00 | .75 |
| ❏ 29 Checklist | 6.00 | 3.00 |
| ❏ 30 Marlin Briscoe RC | .50 | .25 |
| ❏ 31 Jerry Logan | .50 | .25 |
| ❏ 32 Donny Anderson | 1.00 | .40 |
| ❏ 33 Rich McGeorge | .50 | .25 |
| ❏ 34 Charlie Durkee | .50 | .25 |
| ❏ 35 Willie Lanier | 4.00 | 2.00 |
| ❏ 36 Chris Farasopoulos | .50 | .25 |
| ❏ 37 Ron Shanklin RC | .50 | .25 |
| ❏ 38 Forrest Blue RC | .50 | .25 |
| ❏ 39 Ken Reaves | .50 | .25 |
| ❏ 40 Roman Gabriel | 2.00 | .75 |
| ❏ 41 Mac Percival | .50 | .25 |
| ❏ 42 Lem Barney | 3.00 | 1.50 |
| ❏ 43 Nick Buoniconti | 2.00 | .75 |
| ❏ 44 Charlie Gogolak | .50 | .25 |
| ❏ 45 Bill Bradley RC | 1.00 | .40 |
| ❏ 46 Joe Jones DE | .50 | .25 |
| ❏ 47 Dave Williams | .50 | .25 |
| ❏ 48 Pete Athas | .50 | .25 |
| ❏ 49 Virgil Carter | .50 | .25 |
| ❏ 50 Floyd Little | 2.00 | .75 |
| ❏ 51 Curt Knight | .50 | .25 |
| ❏ 52 Bobby Maples | .50 | .25 |
| ❏ 53 Charlie West | .50 | .25 |
| ❏ 54 Marv Hubbard RC | 1.00 | .40 |
| ❏ 55 Archie Manning RC | 20.00 | 10.00 |
| ❏ 56 Jim O'Brien RC | 1.00 | .40 |
| ❏ 57 Wayne Patrick | .50 | .25 |
| ❏ 58 Ken Bowman | .50 | .25 |
| ❏ 59 Roger Wehrli | 1.25 | .50 |
| ❏ 60 Charlie Sanders | 1.25 | .50 |
| ❏ 61 Jan Stenerud | 2.00 | .75 |
| ❏ 62 Willie Ellison | .50 | .25 |
| ❏ 63 Walt Sweeney | .50 | .25 |
| ❏ 64 Ron Smith | .50 | .25 |
| ❏ 65 Jim Plunkett RC | 20.00 | 10.00 |
| ❏ 66 Herb Adderley UER | 2.00 | .75 |
| ❏ 67 Mike Reid RC | 2.00 | .75 |
| ❏ 68 Richard Caster RC | 1.00 | .40 |
| ❏ 69 Dave Wilcox | 2.00 | .75 |
| ❏ 70 Leroy Kelly | 3.00 | 1.50 |
| ❏ 71 Bob Lee RC | .50 | .25 |
| ❏ 72 Verlon Biggs | .50 | .25 |
| ❏ 73 Henry Allison | .50 | .25 |
| ❏ 74 Steve Ramsey | .50 | .25 |
| ❏ 75 Claude Humphrey | 1.00 | .40 |
| ❏ 76 Bob Grim RC | .50 | .25 |
| ❏ 77 John Fuqua | 1.00 | .40 |
| ❏ 78 Ken Houston | 4.00 | 2.00 |
| ❏ 79 Checklist DP | 5.00 | 2.50 |

|  | | |
|---|---|---|
| ❏ 80 Bob Griese | 8.00 | 4.00 |
| ❏ 81 Lance Rentzel | 1.00 | .40 |
| ❏ 82 Ed Podolak RC | 1.00 | .40 |
| ❏ 83 Ike Hill | .50 | .25 |
| ❏ 84 George Farmer | .50 | .25 |
| ❏ 85 John Brockington RC | 2.00 | .75 |
| ❏ 86 Jim Otto | 2.00 | .75 |
| ❏ 87 Richard Neal | .50 | .25 |
| ❏ 88 Jim Hart | 2.00 | .75 |
| ❏ 89 Bob Babich | .50 | .25 |
| ❏ 90 Gene Washington 49er | 1.00 | .40 |
| ❏ 91 John Zook | .50 | .25 |
| ❏ 92 Bobby Duhon | .50 | .25 |
| ❏ 93 Ted Hendricks RC | 15.00 | 7.50 |
| ❏ 94 Rockne Freitas | .50 | .25 |
| ❏ 95 Larry Brown | 2.00 | .75 |
| ❏ 96 Mike Phipps | 1.00 | .40 |
| ❏ 97 Julius Adams | .50 | .25 |
| ❏ 98 Dick Anderson | 1.00 | .40 |
| ❏ 99 Fred Willis | .50 | .25 |
| ❏ 100 Joe Namath | 35.00 | 20.00 |
| ❏ 101 L.C.Greenwood RC | 15.00 | 7.50 |
| ❏ 102 Mark Nordquist | .50 | .25 |
| ❏ 103 Robert Holmes | .50 | .25 |
| ❏ 104 Ron Yary RC | 5.00 | 2.00 |
| ❏ 105 Bob Hayes | 2.50 | 1.00 |
| ❏ 106 Lyle Alzado RC | 15.00 | 7.50 |
| ❏ 107 Bob Berry | .50 | .25 |
| ❏ 108 Phil Villapiano RC | 1.00 | .40 |
| ❏ 109 Dave Elmendorf | .50 | .25 |
| ❏ 110 Gale Sayers | 20.00 | 10.00 |
| ❏ 111 Jim Tyrer | .50 | .25 |
| ❏ 112 Mel Gray RC | 2.00 | .75 |
| ❏ 113 Gerry Philbin | .50 | .25 |
| ❏ 114 Bob James | .50 | .25 |
| ❏ 115 Garo Yepremian | 1.00 | .40 |
| ❏ 116 Dave Robinson | 1.00 | .40 |
| ❏ 117 Jeff Queen | .50 | .25 |
| ❏ 118 Norm Snead | 1.00 | .40 |
| ❏ 119 Jim Nance IA | 1.00 | .40 |
| ❏ 120 Terry Bradshaw IA | 15.00 | 7.50 |
| ❏ 121 Jim Kiick IA | 1.00 | .40 |
| ❏ 122 Roger Staubach IA | 20.00 | 12.00 |
| ❏ 123 Bo Scott IA | .50 | .25 |
| ❏ 124 John Brodie IA | 2.00 | .75 |
| ❏ 125 Rick Volk IA | .50 | .25 |
| ❏ 126 John Riggins IA | 6.00 | 3.00 |
| ❏ 127 Bubba Smith IA | 2.00 | .75 |
| ❏ 128 Roman Gabriel IA | 1.00 | .40 |
| ❏ 129 Calvin Hill IA | 1.00 | .40 |
| ❏ 130 Bill Nelsen IA | .50 | .25 |
| ❏ 131 Tom Matte IA | 1.00 | .40 |
| ❏ 132 Bob Griese IA | 4.00 | 2.00 |
| ❏ 133 AFC Semi-Final | 1.00 | .40 |
| ❏ 134 NFC Semi-Final | 1.00 | .40 |
| ❏ 135 AFC Semi-Final | 1.00 | .40 |
| ❏ 136 NFC Semi-Final | 1.00 | .40 |
| ❏ 137 AFC Title Game/Unitas | 3.00 | 1.50 |
| ❏ 138 NFC Title Game/Bob Lilly | 2.00 | .75 |
| ❏ 139 Super Bowl VI/Staubach | 5.00 | 2.50 |
| ❏ 140 Larry Csonka | 8.00 | 4.00 |
| ❏ 141 Rick Volk | .60 | .30 |
| ❏ 142 Roy Jefferson | 1.00 | .40 |
| ❏ 143 Raymond Chester RC | 1.00 | .40 |
| ❏ 144 Bobby Douglass | .60 | .30 |
| ❏ 145 Bob Lilly | 5.00 | 2.50 |
| ❏ 146 Harold Jackson | 1.00 | .40 |
| ❏ 147 Pete Gogolak | .60 | .30 |
| ❏ 148 Art Malone | .60 | .30 |
| ❏ 149 Ed Flanagan | .60 | .30 |
| ❏ 150 Terry Bradshaw | 40.00 | 25.00 |
| ❏ 151 MacArthur Lane | 1.00 | .40 |
| ❏ 152 Jack Snow | .60 | .30 |
| ❏ 153 Al Beauchamp | .60 | .30 |
| ❏ 154 Bob Anderson | .60 | .30 |
| ❏ 155 Ted Kwalick RC | .60 | .30 |
| ❏ 156 Dan Pastorini RC | 2.00 | .75 |
| ❏ 157 Emmitt Thomas RC | 15.00 | 7.50 |
| ❏ 158 Randy Vataha RC | .60 | .30 |
| ❏ 159 Al Atkinson | .60 | .30 |
| ❏ 160 O.J. Simpson | 15.00 | 7.50 |
| ❏ 161 Jackie Smith | 2.00 | .75 |
| ❏ 162 Ernie Kellerman | .60 | .30 |
| ❏ 163 Dennis Partee | .60 | .30 |
| ❏ 164 Jake Kupp | .60 | .30 |
| ❏ 165 Johnny Unitas | 20.00 | 10.00 |
| ❏ 166 Clint Jones RC | .60 | .30 |
| ❏ 167 Paul Warfield | 6.00 | 3.00 |
| ❏ 168 Roland McDole | .60 | .30 |
| ❏ 169 Daryle Lamonica | 2.00 | .75 |
| ❏ 170 Dick Butkus | 15.00 | 7.50 |
| ❏ 171 Jim Butler | .60 | .30 |
| ❏ 172 Mike McCoy DT | .60 | .30 |
| ❏ 173 Dave Smith WR | .60 | .30 |
| ❏ 174 Greg Landry | 1.00 | .40 |
| ❏ 175 Tom Dempsey | 1.00 | .40 |
| ❏ 176 John Charles | .60 | .30 |
| ❏ 177 Bobby Bell | 2.00 | .75 |
| ❏ 178 Don Horn | .60 | .30 |
| ❏ 179 Bob Trumpy | 2.00 | .75 |
| ❏ 180 Duane Thomas | 1.00 | .40 |
| ❏ 181 Merlin Olsen | 3.00 | 1.50 |
| ❏ 182 Dave Herman | .60 | .30 |
| ❏ 183 Jim Nance | 1.00 | .40 |
| ❏ 184 Pete Beathard | .60 | .30 |
| ❏ 185 Bob Tucker | .60 | .30 |
| ❏ 186 Gene Upshaw RC | 15.00 | 7.50 |
| ❏ 187 Bo Scott | .60 | .30 |
| ❏ 188 J.D.Hill RC | .60 | .30 |
| ❏ 189 Bruce Gossett | .60 | .30 |
| ❏ 190 Bubba Smith | 4.00 | 2.00 |
| ❏ 191 Edd Hargett | .60 | .30 |
| ❏ 192 Gary Garrison | .60 | .30 |
| ❏ 193 Jake Scott | 1.00 | .40 |
| ❏ 194 Fred Cox | .60 | .30 |
| ❏ 195 Sonny Jurgensen | 4.00 | 2.00 |
| ❏ 196 Greg Brezina RC | .60 | .30 |
| ❏ 197 Ed O'Bradovich | .60 | .30 |
| ❏ 198 John Rowser | .60 | .30 |
| ❏ 199 Altie Taylor UER | .60 | .30 |
| ❏ 200 Roger Staubach RC ! | 175.00 | 100.00 |
| ❏ 201 Leroy Keyes RC | .60 | .30 |
| ❏ 202 Garland Boyette | .60 | .30 |
| ❏ 203 Tom Beer | .60 | .30 |
| ❏ 204 Buck Buchanan | 2.00 | .75 |
| ❏ 205 Larry Wilson | 2.00 | .75 |
| ❏ 206 Scott Hunter RC | .60 | .30 |
| ❏ 207 Ron Johnson | .60 | .30 |
| ❏ 208 Sam Brunelli | .60 | .30 |
| ❏ 209 Deacon Jones | 2.00 | .75 |
| ❏ 210 Fred Biletnikoff | 6.00 | 3.00 |
| ❏ 211 Bill Nelsen | 1.00 | .40 |
| ❏ 212 George Nock | .60 | .30 |
| ❏ 213 Dan Abramowicz | 1.00 | .40 |
| ❏ 214 Irv Goode | .60 | .30 |
| ❏ 215 Isiah Robertson RC | 1.00 | .40 |
| ❏ 216 Tom Matte | 1.00 | .40 |
| ❏ 217 Pat Fischer | .60 | .30 |
| ❏ 218 Gene Washington Vik | .60 | .30 |
| ❏ 219 Paul Robinson | .60 | .30 |
| ❏ 220 John Brodie | 4.00 | 2.00 |
| ❏ 221 Manny Fernandez RC | 1.00 | .40 |
| ❏ 222 Errol Mann | .60 | .30 |
| ❏ 223 Dick Gordon | .60 | .30 |
| ❏ 224 Calvin Hill | 2.00 | .75 |
| ❏ 225 Fran Tarkenton | 12.00 | 6.00 |
| ❏ 226 Jim Turner | .60 | .30 |
| ❏ 227 Jim Mitchell TE | .60 | .30 |
| ❏ 228 Pete Liske | .60 | .30 |
| ❏ 229 Carl Garrett | .60 | .30 |
| ❏ 230 Joe Greene | 20.00 | 10.00 |
| ❏ 231 Gale Gillingham | .60 | .30 |
| ❏ 232 Norm Bulaich RC | 1.00 | .40 |
| ❏ 233 Spider Lockhart | .60 | .30 |
| ❏ 234 Ken Willard | .60 | .30 |
| ❏ 235 George Blanda | 12.00 | 6.00 |
| ❏ 236 Wayne Mulligan | .60 | .30 |
| ❏ 237 Dave Lewis | .60 | .30 |
| ❏ 238 Dennis Shaw | .60 | .30 |
| ❏ 239 Fair Hooker | .60 | .30 |
| ❏ 240 Larry Little RC | 15.00 | 7.50 |
| ❏ 241 Mike Garrett | .60 | .30 |
| ❏ 242 Glen Ray Hines | .60 | .30 |
| ❏ 243 Myron Pottios | .60 | .30 |
| ❏ 244 Charlie Joiner RC | 20.00 | 10.00 |
| ❏ 245 Len Dawson | 6.00 | 3.00 |
| ❏ 246 W.K. Hicks | .60 | .30 |
| ❏ 247 Les Josephson | .60 | .30 |
| ❏ 248 Lance Alworth UER | 6.00 | 3.00 |
| ❏ 249 Frank Nunley | .60 | .30 |
| ❏ 250 Mel Farr RC | .60 | .30 |
| ❏ 251 Johnny Unitas IA | 8.00 | 4.00 |
| ❏ 252 George Farmer IA | .60 | .30 |
| ❏ 253 Duane Thomas IA | 1.00 | .40 |
| ❏ 254 John Hadl IA | 2.00 | .75 |
| ❏ 255 Vic Washington IA | .60 | .30 |
| ❏ 256 Don Horn IA | .60 | .30 |
| ❏ 257 L.C.Greenwood IA | 2.00 | .75 |
| ❏ 258 Bob Lee IA | .60 | .30 |
| ❏ 259 Larry Csonka IA | 4.00 | 2.00 |
| ❏ 260 Mike McCoy DT IA | .60 | .30 |
| ❏ 261 Greg Landry IA | 1.00 | .40 |
| ❏ 262 Ray May IA | .60 | .30 |
| ❏ 263 Bobby Douglass IA | .60 | .30 |
| ❏ 264 Charlie Sanders AP ! | 30.00 | 15.00 |
| ❏ 265 Ron Yary AP | 30.00 | 15.00 |
| ❏ 266 Rayfield Wright AP | 40.00 | 20.00 |
| ❏ 267 Larry Little AP | 35.00 | 20.00 |
| ❏ 268 John Niland AP | 30.00 | 15.00 |
| ❏ 269 Forrest Blue AP | 30.00 | 15.00 |
| ❏ 270 Otis Taylor AP | 30.00 | 15.00 |
| ❏ 271 Paul Warfield AP | 50.00 | 30.00 |
| ❏ 272 Bob Griese AP | 70.00 | 40.00 |
| ❏ 273 John Brockington AP | 30.00 | 15.00 |
| ❏ 274 Floyd Little AP | 30.00 | 15.00 |
| ❏ 275 Garo Yepremian AP | 18.00 | 10.00 |
| ❏ 276 Jerrel Wilson AP | 18.00 | 10.00 |
| ❏ 277 Carl Eller AP | 30.00 | 15.00 |
| ❏ 278 Bubba Smith AP | 40.00 | 25.00 |
| ❏ 279 Alan Page AP | 40.00 | 25.00 |
| ❏ 280 Bob Lilly AP | 60.00 | 30.00 |
| ❏ 281 Ted Hendricks AP | 50.00 | 30.00 |
| ❏ 282 Dave Wilcox AP | 30.00 | 15.00 |
| ❏ 283 Willie Lanier AP | 35.00 | 20.00 |
| ❏ 284 Jim Johnson AP | 30.00 | 15.00 |
| ❏ 285 Willie Brown AP | 35.00 | 20.00 |
| ❏ 286 Bill Bradley AP | 18.00 | 10.00 |
| ❏ 287 Ken Houston AP | 35.00 | 20.00 |
| ❏ 288 Mel Farr | 18.00 | 10.00 |
| ❏ 289 Kermit Alexander | 18.00 | 10.00 |
| ❏ 290 John Gilliam RC | 25.00 | 12.50 |
| ❏ 291 Steve Spurrier RC | 100.00 | 50.00 |
| ❏ 292 Walter Johnson | 18.00 | 10.00 |
| ❏ 293 Jack Pardee | 25.00 | 12.50 |
| ❏ 294 Checklist UER | 80.00 | 50.00 |
| ❏ 295 Winston Hill | 18.00 | 10.00 |
| ❏ 296 Hugo Hollas | 18.00 | 10.00 |
| ❏ 297 Ray May RC | 18.00 | 10.00 |
| ❏ 298 Jim Bakken | 18.00 | 10.00 |
| ❏ 299 Larry Carwell | 18.00 | 10.00 |
| ❏ 300 Alan Page | 25.00 | 12.50 |
| ❏ 301 Walt Garrison | 25.00 | 12.50 |
| ❏ 302 Mike Lucci | 25.00 | 12.50 |
| ❏ 303 Nemiah Wilson | 18.00 | 10.00 |
| ❏ 304 Carroll Dale | 18.00 | 10.00 |
| ❏ 305 Jim Kanicki | 18.00 | 10.00 |
| ❏ 306 Preston Pearson | 30.00 | 15.00 |
| ❏ 307 Lemar Parrish | 25.00 | 12.50 |
| ❏ 308 Earl Morrall | 25.00 | 12.50 |
| ❏ 309 Tommy Nobis | 25.00 | 12.50 |
| ❏ 310 Rich Jackson | 18.00 | 10.00 |
| ❏ 311 Doug Cunningham | 18.00 | 10.00 |
| ❏ 312 Jim Marsalis | 18.00 | 10.00 |
| ❏ 313 Jim Beirne | 18.00 | 10.00 |
| ❏ 314 Tom McNeill | 18.00 | 10.00 |
| ❏ 315 Milt Morin | 18.00 | 10.00 |
| ❏ 316 Rayfield Wright RC | 40.00 | 25.00 |
| ❏ 317 Jerry LeVias | 25.00 | 12.50 |
| ❏ 318 Travis Williams RC | 25.00 | 12.50 |
| ❏ 319 Edgar Chandler | 18.00 | 10.00 |
| ❏ 320 Bob Wallace | 18.00 | 10.00 |
| ❏ 321 Delles Howell | 18.00 | 10.00 |
| ❏ 322 Emerson Boozer | 25.00 | 12.50 |
| ❏ 323 George Atkinson RC | 25.00 | 12.50 |
| ❏ 324 Mike Montler | 18.00 | 10.00 |
| ❏ 325 Randy Johnson | 18.00 | 10.00 |
| ❏ 326 Mike Curtis UER | 25.00 | 12.50 |
| ❏ 327 Miller Farr | 18.00 | 10.00 |
| ❏ 328 Horst Muhlmann | 18.00 | 10.00 |
| ❏ 329 John Niland RC | 25.00 | 12.50 |
| ❏ 330 Andy Russell | 30.00 | 15.00 |
| ❏ 331 Mercury Morris | 40.00 | 25.00 |
| ❏ 332 Jim Johnson | 30.00 | 15.00 |
| ❏ 333 Jerrel Wilson | 18.00 | 10.00 |
| ❏ 334 Charley Taylor | 40.00 | 25.00 |

| | | |
|---|---|---|
| 335 Dick LeBeau | 18.00 | 10.00 |
| 336 Jim Marshall | 30.00 | 15.00 |
| 337 Tom Mack | 30.00 | 15.00 |
| 338 Steve Spurrier IA | 60.00 | 30.00 |
| 339 Floyd Little IA | 25.00 | 12.50 |
| 340 Len Dawson IA | 40.00 | 25.00 |
| 341 Dick Butkus IA | 70.00 | 40.00 |
| 342 Larry Brown IA | 25.00 | 12.50 |
| 343 Joe Namath IA | 150.00 | 75.00 |
| 344 Jim Turner IA | 18.00 | 10.00 |
| 345 Doug Cunningham IA | 18.00 | 10.00 |
| 346 Edd Hargett IA | 18.00 | 10.00 |
| 347 Steve Owens IA | 18.00 | 10.00 |
| 348 George Blanda IA | 50.00 | 30.00 |
| 349 Ed Podolak IA | 18.00 | 10.00 |
| 350 Rich Jackson IA | 18.00 | 10.00 |
| 351 Ken Willard IA ! | 40.00 | 25.00 |

## 1973 Topps

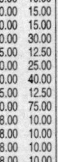

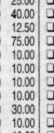

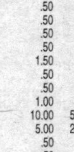
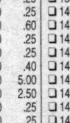
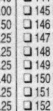

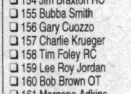
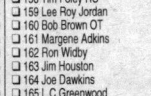
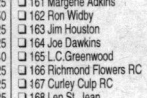

| | | |
|---|---|---|
| COMPLETE SET (528) | 400.00 | 200.00 |
| 1 Simpson/L.Brown LL | 8.00 | 3.00 |
| 2 Passing Leaders | 1.00 | .40 |
| 3 Jackson/Biletnikoff LL | 1.50 | .60 |
| 4 Scoring Leaders | .50 | .25 |
| 5 Interception Leaders | .50 | .25 |
| 6 Punting Leaders | .50 | .25 |
| 7 Bob Trumpy | 1.50 | .60 |
| 8 Mel Tom | .50 | .25 |
| 9 Clarence Ellis | .50 | .25 |
| 10 John Niland | .50 | .25 |
| 11 Randy Jackson | .50 | .25 |
| 12 Greg Landry | 1.50 | .60 |
| 13 Cid Edwards | .50 | .25 |
| 14 Phil Olsen | .50 | .25 |
| 15 Terry Bradshaw | 25.00 | 15.00 |
| 16 Al Cowlings RC | 1.50 | .60 |
| 17 Walker Gillette | .50 | .25 |
| 18 Bob Atkins | .50 | .25 |
| 19 Diron Talbert RC | 1.50 | .60 |
| 20 Jim Johnson | 1.50 | .60 |
| 21 Howard Twilley | 1.00 | .40 |
| 22 Dick Enderle | .50 | .25 |
| 23 Wayne Colman | .50 | .25 |
| 24 John Schmitt | .50 | .25 |
| 25 George Blanda | 10.00 | 5.00 |
| 26 Milt Morin | .50 | .25 |
| 27 Mike Current | .50 | .25 |
| 28 Rex Kern RC | .50 | .25 |
| 29 MacArthur Lane | 1.00 | .40 |
| 30 Alan Page | 3.00 | 1.50 |
| 31 Randy Vataha | .50 | .25 |
| 32 Jim Kearney | .50 | .25 |
| 33 Steve Smith T | .50 | .25 |
| 34 Ken Anderson RC | 15.00 | 7.50 |
| 35 Calvin Hill | 1.50 | .60 |
| 36 Andy Maurer | .50 | .25 |
| 37 Joe Taylor | .50 | .25 |
| 38 Deacon Jones | 1.50 | .60 |
| 39 Mike Weger | .50 | .25 |
| 40 Roy Gerela | 1.00 | .40 |
| 41 Les Josephson | .50 | .25 |
| 42 Dave Washington | .50 | .25 |
| 43 Bill Curry RC | 1.00 | .40 |
| 44 Fred Heron | .50 | .25 |
| 45 John Brodie | 3.00 | 1.50 |
| 46 Roy Winston | .50 | .25 |
| 47 Mike Bragg | .50 | .25 |
| 48 Mercury Morris | 1.50 | .60 |
| 49 Jim Files | .50 | .25 |
| 50 Gene Upshaw RC | 3.00 | 1.50 |
| 51 Hugo Hollas | .50 | .25 |
| 52 Rod Sherman | .50 | .25 |
| 53 Ron Snidow | .50 | .25 |
| 54 Steve Tannen RC | .50 | .25 |
| 55 Jim Carter RC | .50 | .25 |
| 56 Lydell Mitchell RC | 1.50 | .60 |
| 57 Jack Rudnay RC | .50 | .25 |
| 58 Halvor Hagen | .50 | .25 |
| 59 Tom Dempsey | 1.00 | .40 |
| 60 Fran Tarkenton | 10.00 | 5.00 |
| 61 Lance Alworth | 5.00 | 2.50 |
| 62 Vern Holland | .50 | .25 |
| 63 Steve DeLong | .50 | .25 |
| 64 Art Malone | .50 | .25 |
| 65 Isiah Robertson | 1.00 | .40 |
| 66 Jerry Rush | .50 | .25 |
| 67 Bryant Salter | .50 | .25 |
| 68 Checklist 1-132 | 5.00 | 2.50 |
| 69 J.D. Hill | .50 | .25 |
| 70 Forrest Blue | .50 | .25 |
| 71 Myron Pottios | .50 | .25 |
| 72 Norm Thompson RC | .50 | .25 |
| 73 Paul Robinson | .50 | .25 |
| 74 Larry Grantham | .50 | .25 |
| 75 Manny Fernandez | 1.00 | .40 |
| 76 Kent Nix | .50 | .25 |
| 77 Art Shell RC | 15.00 | 7.50 |
| 78 George Saimes | .50 | .25 |
| 79 Don Cockroft | .50 | .25 |
| 80 Bob Tucker | 1.00 | .40 |
| 81 Don McCauley RC | .50 | .25 |
| 82 Bob Brown DT | .50 | .25 |
| 83 Larry Carwell | .50 | .25 |
| 84 Mo Moorman | .50 | .25 |
| 85 John Gilliam | 1.00 | .40 |
| 86 Wade Key | .50 | .25 |
| 87 Ross Brupbacher | .50 | .25 |
| 88 Dave Lewis | .50 | .25 |
| 89 Franco Harris RC | 50.00 | 25.00 |
| 90 Tom Mack | 1.50 | .60 |
| 91 Mike Tilleman | .50 | .25 |
| 92 Carl Mauck | .50 | .25 |
| 93 Larry Hand | .50 | .25 |
| 94 Dave Foley RC | .50 | .25 |
| 95 Frank Nunley | .50 | .25 |
| 96 John Charles | .50 | .25 |
| 97 Jim Bakken | .50 | .25 |
| 98 Pat Fischer | 1.00 | .40 |
| 99 Randy Rasmussen | .50 | .25 |
| 100 Larry Csonka | 6.00 | 3.00 |
| 101 Mike Siani RC | .50 | .25 |
| 102 Tom Roussel | .50 | .25 |
| 103 Clarence Scott RC | .50 | .25 |
| 104 Charlie Johnson | 1.00 | .40 |
| 105 Rick Volk | .50 | .25 |
| 106 Willie Young | .50 | .25 |
| 107 Emmitt Thomas | 1.50 | .60 |
| 108 Jon Morris | .50 | .25 |
| 109 Clarence Williams | .50 | .25 |
| 110 Rayfield Wright | 1.00 | .40 |
| 111 Norm Bulaich | .50 | .25 |
| 112 Mike Eischeid | .50 | .25 |
| 113 Speedy Thomas | .50 | .25 |
| 114 Glen Holloway | .50 | .25 |
| 115 Jack Ham RC | 30.00 | 15.00 |
| 116 Jim Nettles | .50 | .25 |
| 117 Erroll Mann | .50 | .25 |
| 118 John Mackey | 1.50 | .60 |
| 119 George Kunz | .50 | .25 |
| 120 Bob James | .50 | .25 |
| 121 Garland Boyette | .50 | .25 |
| 122 Mel Phillips | .50 | .25 |
| 123 Johnny Roland | .50 | .25 |
| 124 Doug Swift | .50 | .25 |
| 125 Archie Manning | 4.00 | 2.00 |
| 126 Dave Herman | .50 | .25 |
| 127 Carleton Oats | .50 | .25 |
| 128 Bill Van Heusen | .50 | .25 |
| 129 Rich Jackson | .50 | .25 |
| 130 Len Hauss | .50 | .25 |
| 131 Billy Parks RC | .50 | .25 |
| 132 Ray May | .50 | .25 |
| 133 NFC Semi/Staubach | 5.00 | 2.00 |
| 134 AFC Semi/Immac.Rec. | 2.50 | 1.00 |
| 135 NFC Semi-Final | 1.00 | .40 |
| 136 AFC Semi/L.Csonka | 2.00 | .75 |
| 137 NFC Title Game/Kilmer | 1.50 | .60 |
| 138 AFC Title Game | 1.00 | .40 |
| 139 Super Bowl VII | 1.50 | .60 |
| 140 Dwight White RC | 5.00 | 2.00 |
| 141 Jim Marsalis | .50 | .25 |
| 142 Doug Van Horn | .50 | .25 |
| 143 Al Matthews | .50 | .25 |
| 144 Bob Windsor | .50 | .25 |
| 145 Dave Hampton RC | .50 | .25 |
| 146 Horst Muhlmann | .50 | .25 |
| 147 Wally Hilgenberg RC | .50 | .25 |
| 148 Ron Smith | .50 | .25 |
| 149 Coy Bacon RC | 1.00 | .40 |
| 150 Winston Hill | .50 | .25 |
| 151 Ron Jessie RC | 1.00 | .40 |
| 152 Ken Iman | .50 | .25 |
| 153 Ron Saul | .50 | .25 |
| 154 Jim Braxton RC | 1.00 | .40 |
| 155 Bubba Smith | 2.50 | 1.25 |
| 156 Gary Cuozzo | 1.00 | .40 |
| 157 Charlie Krueger | 1.00 | .40 |
| 158 Tim Foley RC | 1.00 | .40 |
| 159 Lee Roy Jordan | 1.50 | .60 |
| 160 Bob Brown OT | 1.50 | .60 |
| 161 Margene Adkins | .50 | .25 |
| 162 Ron Widby | .50 | .25 |
| 163 Jim Houston | .50 | .25 |
| 164 Joe Dawkins | .50 | .25 |
| 165 L.C.Greenwood | 4.00 | 2.00 |
| 166 Richmond Flowers RC | .50 | .25 |
| 167 Curley Culp RC | 1.50 | .60 |
| 168 Len St. Jean | .50 | .25 |
| 169 Walter Rock | .50 | .25 |
| 170 Bill Bradley | 1.00 | .40 |
| 171 Ken Riley RC | 1.50 | .60 |
| 172 Rich Coady | .50 | .25 |
| 173 Don Hansen | .50 | .25 |
| 174 Lionel Aldridge | .50 | .25 |
| 175 Don Maynard | 4.00 | 2.00 |
| 176 Dave Osborn | 1.00 | .40 |
| 177 Jim Bailey | .50 | .25 |
| 178 John Pitts | .50 | .25 |
| 179 Dave Parks | .50 | .25 |
| 180 Chester Marcol RC | .50 | .25 |
| 181 Len Rohde | .50 | .25 |
| 182 Jeff Staggs | .50 | .25 |
| 183 Gene Hickerson | 1.25 | .50 |
| 184 Charlie Evans | .50 | .25 |
| 185 Mel Renfro | 1.50 | .60 |
| 186 Marvin Upshaw | .50 | .25 |
| 187 George Atkinson | 1.00 | .40 |
| 188 Norm Evans | 1.00 | .40 |
| 189 Steve Ramsey | .50 | .25 |
| 190 Dave Chapple | .50 | .25 |
| 191 Gerry Mullins | .50 | .25 |
| 192 John Didion | .50 | .25 |
| 193 Bob Gladieux | .50 | .25 |
| 194 Don Hultz | .50 | .25 |
| 195 Mike Lucci | .50 | .25 |
| 196 John Wilbur | .50 | .25 |
| 197 George Farmer | .50 | .25 |
| 198 Tommy Casanova RC | 1.00 | .40 |
| 199 Russ Washington | .50 | .25 |
| 200 Claude Humphrey | 1.50 | .60 |
| 201 Pat Hughes | .50 | .25 |
| 202 Zeke Moore | .50 | .25 |
| 203 Chip Glass | .50 | .25 |
| 204 Glenn Ressler | .50 | .25 |
| 205 Willie Ellison | .50 | .25 |
| 206 John Leypoldt | .50 | .25 |
| 207 Johnny Fuller | .50 | .25 |
| 208 Bill Hayhoe | .50 | .25 |
| 209 Ed Bell | .50 | .25 |
| 210 Willie Brown | 1.50 | .60 |
| 211 Carl Eller | 1.50 | .60 |
| 212 Mark Nordquist | .50 | .25 |
| 213 Larry Willingham | .50 | .25 |
| 214 Nick Buoniconti | 1.50 | .60 |
| 215 John Hadl | 1.50 | .60 |
| 216 Jethro Pugh RC | 1.50 | .60 |
| 217 Leroy Mitchell | .50 | .25 |
| 218 Billy Newsome | .50 | .25 |

|  | | |
|---|---|---|
| ❏ 219 John McMakin | .50 | .25 |
| ❏ 220 Larry Brown | 1.50 | .60 |
| ❏ 221 Clarence Scott RC | .50 | .25 |
| ❏ 222 Paul Naumoff | .50 | .25 |
| ❏ 223 Ted Fritsch Jr. | .50 | .25 |
| ❏ 224 Checklist 133-264 | 5.00 | 2.50 |
| ❏ 225 Dan Pastorini | 1.50 | .60 |
| ❏ 226 Joe Beauchamp UER | .50 | .25 |
| ❏ 227 Pat Matson | .50 | .25 |
| ❏ 228 Tom McGee DT | .50 | .25 |
| ❏ 229 Mike Phipps | 1.00 | .40 |
| ❏ 230 Harold Jackson | 1.50 | .60 |
| ❏ 231 Willie Williams | .50 | .25 |
| ❏ 232 Spike Jones | .50 | .25 |
| ❏ 233 Jim Tyrer | .50 | .25 |
| ❏ 234 Roy Hilton | .50 | .25 |
| ❏ 235 Phil Villapiano | 1.00 | .40 |
| ❏ 236 Charley Taylor UER | 3.00 | 1.50 |
| ❏ 237 Malcolm Snider | .50 | .25 |
| ❏ 238 Vic Washington | .50 | .25 |
| ❏ 239 Grady Alderman | .50 | .25 |
| ❏ 240 Dick Anderson | 1.00 | .40 |
| ❏ 241 Ron Yankowski | .50 | .25 |
| ❏ 242 Billy Masters | .50 | .25 |
| ❏ 243 Herb Adderley | 1.50 | .60 |
| ❏ 244 David Ray | .50 | .25 |
| ❏ 245 John Riggins | 8.00 | 4.00 |
| ❏ 246 Mike Wagner RC | 3.00 | 1.25 |
| ❏ 247 Don Morrison | .50 | .25 |
| ❏ 248 Earl McCullouch | .50 | .25 |
| ❏ 249 Dennis Wirgowski | .50 | .25 |
| ❏ 250 Chris Hanburger | 1.00 | .40 |
| ❏ 251 Pat Sullivan RC | 1.50 | .60 |
| ❏ 252 Walt Sweeney | .50 | .25 |
| ❏ 253 Willie Alexander | .50 | .25 |
| ❏ 254 Doug Dressler | .50 | .25 |
| ❏ 255 Walter Johnson | .50 | .25 |
| ❏ 256 Ron Hornsby | .50 | .25 |
| ❏ 257 Ben Hawkins | .50 | .25 |
| ❏ 258 Donnie Green RC | .50 | .25 |
| ❏ 259 Fred Hoaglin | .50 | .25 |
| ❏ 260 Jerrel Wilson | .50 | .25 |
| ❏ 261 Horace Jones | .50 | .25 |
| ❏ 262 Woody Peoples | .50 | .25 |
| ❏ 263 Jim Hill RC | .50 | .25 |
| ❏ 264 John Fuqua | .50 | .25 |
| ❏ 265 Donny Anderson KP | 1.00 | .40 |
| ❏ 266 Roman Gabriel KP | 1.50 | .60 |
| ❏ 267 Mike Garrett KP | 1.00 | .40 |
| ❏ 268 Rufus Mayes RC | .50 | .25 |
| ❏ 269 Chip Myrtle | .50 | .25 |
| ❏ 270 Bill Stanfill RC | 1.00 | .40 |
| ❏ 271 Clint Jones | .50 | .25 |
| ❏ 272 Miller Farr | .50 | .25 |
| ❏ 273 Harry Schuh | .50 | .25 |
| ❏ 274 Bob Hayes | 2.00 | .75 |
| ❏ 275 Bobby Douglass | 1.00 | .40 |
| ❏ 276 Gus Hollomon | .50 | .25 |
| ❏ 277 Del Williams | .50 | .25 |
| ❏ 278 Julius Adams | .50 | .25 |
| ❏ 279 Herman Weaver | .50 | .25 |
| ❏ 280 Joe Greene | 8.00 | 4.00 |
| ❏ 281 Wes Chesson | .50 | .25 |
| ❏ 282 Charlie Harraway | .50 | .25 |
| ❏ 283 Paul Guidry | .50 | .25 |
| ❏ 284 Terry Owens RC | .50 | .25 |
| ❏ 285 Jan Stenerud | 1.50 | .60 |
| ❏ 286 Pete Athas | .50 | .25 |
| ❏ 287 Dale Lindsey | .50 | .25 |
| ❏ 288 Jack Tatum RC | 15.00 | 6.00 |
| ❏ 289 Floyd Little | 1.50 | .60 |
| ❏ 290 Bob Johnson | .50 | .25 |
| ❏ 291 Tommy Hart RC | .50 | .25 |
| ❏ 292 Tom Mitchell | .50 | .25 |
| ❏ 293 Walt Patulski RC | .50 | .25 |
| ❏ 294 Jim Skaggs | .50 | .25 |
| ❏ 295 Bob Griese | 6.00 | 3.00 |
| ❏ 296 Mike McCoy DT | .50 | .25 |
| ❏ 297 Mel Gray | 1.00 | .40 |
| ❏ 298 Bobby Bryant | .50 | .25 |
| ❏ 299 Blaine Nye RC | .50 | .25 |
| ❏ 300 Dick Butkus | 12.00 | 6.00 |
| ❏ 301 Charlie Cowan RC | .50 | .25 |
| ❏ 302 Mark Lomas | .50 | .25 |
| ❏ 303 Josh Ashton | .50 | .25 |
| ❏ 304 Happy Feller | .50 | .25 |
| ❏ 305 Ron Shanklin | .50 | .25 |
| ❏ 306 Wayne Rasmussen | .50 | .25 |
| ❏ 307 Jerry Smith | .50 | .25 |
| ❏ 308 Ken Reaves | .50 | .25 |
| ❏ 309 Ron East | .50 | .25 |
| ❏ 310 Otis Taylor | 1.50 | .60 |
| ❏ 311 John Garlington | .50 | .25 |
| ❏ 312 Lyle Alzado | 4.00 | 2.00 |
| ❏ 313 Remi Prudhomme | .50 | .25 |
| ❏ 314 Cornelius Johnson | .50 | .25 |
| ❏ 315 Lemar Parrish | 1.00 | .40 |
| ❏ 316 Jim Kiick | 1.50 | .60 |
| ❏ 317 Steve Zabel | .50 | .25 |
| ❏ 318 Alden Roche | .50 | .25 |
| ❏ 319 Tom Blanchard | .50 | .25 |
| ❏ 320 Fred Biletnikoff | 4.00 | 2.00 |
| ❏ 321 Ralph Neely | 1.00 | .40 |
| ❏ 322 Dan Dierdorf RC | 20.00 | 7.50 |
| ❏ 323 Richard Caster | 1.00 | .40 |
| ❏ 324 Gene Howard | .50 | .25 |
| ❏ 325 Elvin Bethea | 1.50 | .60 |
| ❏ 326 Carl Garrett | 1.00 | .40 |
| ❏ 327 Ron Billingsley | .50 | .25 |
| ❏ 328 Charlie West | .50 | .25 |
| ❏ 329 Tom Neville | .50 | .25 |
| ❏ 330 Ted Kwalick | 1.00 | .40 |
| ❏ 331 Rudy Redmond | .50 | .25 |
| ❏ 332 Henry Davis | .50 | .25 |
| ❏ 333 John Zook | .50 | .25 |
| ❏ 334 Jim Turner | .50 | .25 |
| ❏ 335 Len Dawson | 5.00 | 2.50 |
| ❏ 336 Bob Chandler RC | 1.00 | .40 |
| ❏ 337 Al Beauchamp | .50 | .25 |
| ❏ 338 Tom Matte | 1.00 | .40 |
| ❏ 339 Paul Laaveg | .50 | .25 |
| ❏ 340 Ken Ellis | .50 | .25 |
| ❏ 341 Jim Langer RC | 12.00 | 6.00 |
| ❏ 342 Ron Porter | .50 | .25 |
| ❏ 343 Jack Youngblood RC | 15.00 | 7.50 |
| ❏ 344 Cornell Green | 1.50 | .60 |
| ❏ 345 Marv Hubbard | 1.00 | .40 |
| ❏ 346 Bruce Taylor | .50 | .25 |
| ❏ 347 Sam Havrilak | .50 | .25 |
| ❏ 348 Walt Sumner | .50 | .25 |
| ❏ 349 Steve O'Neal | .50 | .25 |
| ❏ 350 Ron Johnson | 1.00 | .40 |
| ❏ 351 Rockne Freitas | .50 | .25 |
| ❏ 352 Larry Stallings | .50 | .25 |
| ❏ 353 Jim Cadile | .50 | .25 |
| ❏ 354 Ken Burrough | 1.00 | .40 |
| ❏ 355 Jim Plunkett | 4.00 | 2.00 |
| ❏ 356 Dave Long | .50 | .25 |
| ❏ 357 Ralph Anderson | .50 | .25 |
| ❏ 358 Checklist 265-396 | 5.00 | 2.50 |
| ❏ 359 Gene Washington Vik | 1.00 | .40 |
| ❏ 360 Dave Wilcox | 1.50 | .60 |
| ❏ 361 Paul Smith | .50 | .25 |
| ❏ 362 Alvin Wyatt | .50 | .25 |
| ❏ 363 Charlie Smith RB | .50 | .25 |
| ❏ 364 Royce Berry | .50 | .25 |
| ❏ 365 Dave Elmendorf | .50 | .25 |
| ❏ 366 Scott Hunter | 1.00 | .40 |
| ❏ 367 Bob Kuechenberg RC | 3.00 | 1.25 |
| ❏ 368 Pete Gogolak | .50 | .25 |
| ❏ 369 Dave Edwards | .50 | .25 |
| ❏ 370 Lem Barney | 2.50 | 1.25 |
| ❏ 371 Verlon Biggs | .50 | .25 |
| ❏ 372 John Reaves RC | .50 | .25 |
| ❏ 373 Ed Podolak | 1.00 | .40 |
| ❏ 374 Chris Farasopoulos | .50 | .25 |
| ❏ 375 Gary Garrison | .50 | .25 |
| ❏ 376 Tom Funchess | .50 | .25 |
| ❏ 377 Bobby Joe Green | .50 | .25 |
| ❏ 378 Don Brumm | .50 | .25 |
| ❏ 379 Jim O'Brien | .50 | .25 |
| ❏ 380 Paul Krause | 1.50 | .60 |
| ❏ 381 Leroy Kelly | 2.50 | 1.25 |
| ❏ 382 Ray Mansfield | .50 | .25 |
| ❏ 383 Dan Abramowicz | 1.00 | .40 |
| ❏ 384 John Outlaw RC | .50 | .25 |
| ❏ 385 Tommy Nobis | 1.50 | .60 |
| ❏ 386 Tom Domres | .50 | .25 |
| ❏ 387 Ken Willard | .50 | .25 |
| ❏ 388 Mike Stratton | .50 | .25 |
| ❏ 389 Fred Dryer | 2.50 | 1.25 |
| ❏ 390 Jake Scott | 1.50 | .60 |
| ❏ 391 Rich Houston | .50 | .25 |
| ❏ 392 Virgil Carter | .50 | .25 |
| ❏ 393 Tody Smith | .50 | .25 |
| ❏ 394 Ernie Calloway | .50 | .25 |
| ❏ 395 Charlie Sanders | 1.25 | .50 |
| ❏ 396 Fred Willis | .50 | .25 |
| ❏ 397 Curt Knight | .50 | .25 |
| ❏ 398 Nemiah Wilson | .50 | .25 |
| ❏ 399 Carroll Dale | 1.00 | .40 |
| ❏ 400 Joe Namath | 30.00 | 15.00 |
| ❏ 401 Wayne Mulligan | .50 | .25 |
| ❏ 402 Jim Harrison | .50 | .25 |
| ❏ 403 Tim Rossovich | .50 | .25 |
| ❏ 404 David Lee | .50 | .25 |
| ❏ 405 Frank Pitts | .50 | .25 |
| ❏ 406 Jim Marshall | 1.50 | .60 |
| ❏ 407 Bob Brown TE | .50 | .25 |
| ❏ 408 John Rowser | .50 | .25 |
| ❏ 409 Mike Montler | .50 | .25 |
| ❏ 410 Willie Lanier | 1.50 | .60 |
| ❏ 411 Bill Bell K | .50 | .25 |
| ❏ 412 Cedrick Hardman | .50 | .25 |
| ❏ 413 Bob Anderson | .50 | .25 |
| ❏ 414 Earl Morrall | 1.50 | .60 |
| ❏ 415 Ken Houston | 1.50 | .60 |
| ❏ 416 Jack Snow | 1.00 | .40 |
| ❏ 417 Dick Cunningham | .50 | .25 |
| ❏ 418 Greg Larson | .50 | .25 |
| ❏ 419 Mike Bass | 1.00 | .40 |
| ❏ 420 Mike Reid | 1.00 | .40 |
| ❏ 421 Walt Garrison | 1.50 | .60 |
| ❏ 422 Pete Liske | .50 | .25 |
| ❏ 423 Jim Yarbrough | .50 | .25 |
| ❏ 424 Rich McGeorge | .50 | .25 |
| ❏ 425 Bobby Howfield | .50 | .25 |
| ❏ 426 Pete Banaszak | .50 | .25 |
| ❏ 427 Willie Holman | .50 | .25 |
| ❏ 428 Dale Hackbart | .50 | .25 |
| ❏ 429 Fair Hooker | .50 | .25 |
| ❏ 430 Ted Hendricks | 5.00 | 2.50 |
| ❏ 431 Mike Garrett | 1.00 | .40 |
| ❏ 432 Glen Ray Hines | .50 | .25 |
| ❏ 433 Fred Cox | .50 | .25 |
| ❏ 434 Bobby Walden | .50 | .25 |
| ❏ 435 Bobby Bell | 1.50 | .60 |
| ❏ 436 Dave Rowe | .50 | .25 |
| ❏ 437 Bob Berry | .50 | .25 |
| ❏ 438 Bill Thompson | .50 | .25 |
| ❏ 439 Jim Beirne | .50 | .25 |
| ❏ 440 Larry Little | 3.00 | 1.50 |
| ❏ 441 Rocky Thompson | .50 | .25 |
| ❏ 442 Brig Owens | .50 | .25 |
| ❏ 443 Richard Neal | .50 | .25 |
| ❏ 444 Al Nelson | .50 | .25 |
| ❏ 445 Chip Myers | .50 | .25 |
| ❏ 446 Ken Bowman | .50 | .25 |
| ❏ 447 Jim Purnell | .50 | .25 |
| ❏ 448 Altie Taylor | .50 | .25 |
| ❏ 449 Linzy Cole | .50 | .25 |
| ❏ 450 Bob Lilly | 5.00 | 2.50 |
| ❏ 451 Charlie Ford | .50 | .25 |
| ❏ 452 Milt Sunde | .50 | .25 |
| ❏ 453 Doug Wyatt | .50 | .25 |
| ❏ 454 Don Nottingham RC | 1.00 | .40 |
| ❏ 455 Johnny Unitas | 15.00 | 7.50 |
| ❏ 456 Frank Lewis RC | 1.00 | .40 |
| ❏ 457 Roger Wehrli | 1.00 | .40 |
| ❏ 458 Jim Cheyunski | .50 | .25 |
| ❏ 459 Jerry Sherk RC | 1.00 | .40 |
| ❏ 460 Gene Washington 49er | 1.00 | .40 |
| ❏ 461 Jim Otto | 1.50 | .60 |
| ❏ 462 Ed Budde | .50 | .25 |
| ❏ 463 Jim Mitchell TE | 1.00 | .40 |
| ❏ 464 Emerson Boozer | 1.00 | .40 |
| ❏ 465 Garo Yepremian | 1.50 | .60 |
| ❏ 466 Pete Duranko | .50 | .25 |
| ❏ 467 Charlie Joiner | 8.00 | 4.00 |
| ❏ 468 Spider Lockhart | 1.00 | .40 |
| ❏ 469 Marty Domres | .50 | .25 |
| ❏ 470 John Brockington | 1.50 | .60 |
| ❏ 471 Ed Flanagan | .50 | .25 |
| ❏ 472 Roy Jefferson | 1.00 | .40 |
| ❏ 473 Julian Fagan | .50 | .25 |

|  |  | | |
|---|---|---|---|
| ❑ 474 | Bill Brown | 1.00 | .40 |
| ❑ 475 | Roger Staubach | 30.00 | 15.00 |
| ❑ 476 | Jan White RC | .50 | .25 |
| ❑ 477 | Pat Holmes | .50 | .25 |
| ❑ 478 | Bob DeMarco | .50 | .25 |
| ❑ 479 | Merlin Olsen | 2.50 | 1.25 |
| ❑ 480 | Andy Russell | 1.50 | .60 |
| ❑ 481 | Steve Spurrier | 20.00 | 10.00 |
| ❑ 482 | Nate Ramsey | .50 | .25 |
| ❑ 483 | Dennis Partee | .50 | .25 |
| ❑ 484 | Jerry Simmons | .50 | .25 |
| ❑ 485 | Donny Anderson | 1.50 | .60 |
| ❑ 486 | Ralph Baker | .50 | .25 |
| ❑ 487 | Ken Stabler RC ! | 60.00 | 35.00 |
| ❑ 488 | Ernie McMillan | .50 | .25 |
| ❑ 489 | Ken Burrow | .50 | .25 |
| ❑ 490 | Jack Gregory RC | .50 | .25 |
| ❑ 491 | Larry Seiple | 1.00 | .40 |
| ❑ 492 | Mick Tingelhoff | 1.00 | .40 |
| ❑ 493 | Craig Morton | 1.50 | .60 |
| ❑ 494 | Cecil Turner | .50 | .25 |
| ❑ 495 | Steve Owens | 1.50 | .60 |
| ❑ 496 | Rickie Harris | .50 | .25 |
| ❑ 497 | Buck Buchanan | 1.50 | .60 |
| ❑ 498 | Checklist 397-528 | 5.00 | 2.50 |
| ❑ 499 | Billy Kilmer | 1.50 | .60 |
| ❑ 500 | O.J.Simpson | 15.00 | 7.50 |
| ❑ 501 | Bruce Gossett | .50 | .25 |
| ❑ 502 | Art Thoms RC | .50 | .25 |
| ❑ 503 | Larry Kaminski | .50 | .25 |
| ❑ 504 | Larry Smith RB | .50 | .25 |
| ❑ 505 | Bruce Van Dyke | .50 | .25 |
| ❑ 506 | Alvin Reed | .50 | .25 |
| ❑ 507 | Delles Howell | .50 | .25 |
| ❑ 508 | Leroy Keyes | .50 | .25 |
| ❑ 509 | Bo Scott | 1.00 | .40 |
| ❑ 510 | Ron Yary | 1.50 | .60 |
| ❑ 511 | Paul Warfield | 5.00 | 2.50 |
| ❑ 512 | Mac Percival | .50 | .25 |
| ❑ 513 | Essex Johnson | .50 | .25 |
| ❑ 514 | Jackie Smith | 1.50 | .60 |
| ❑ 515 | Norm Snead | 1.50 | .60 |
| ❑ 516 | Charlie Stukes | .50 | .25 |
| ❑ 517 | Reggie Rucker RC | 1.00 | .40 |
| ❑ 518 | Bill Sandeman UER | .50 | .25 |
| ❑ 519 | Mel Farr | 1.00 | .40 |
| ❑ 520 | Raymond Chester | 1.00 | .40 |
| ❑ 521 | Fred Carr RC | 1.00 | .40 |
| ❑ 522 | Jerry LeVias | 1.00 | .40 |
| ❑ 523 | Jim Strong | .50 | .25 |
| ❑ 524 | Roland McDole | .50 | .25 |
| ❑ 525 | Dennis Shaw | .50 | .25 |
| ❑ 526 | Dave Manders | .50 | .25 |
| ❑ 527 | Skip Vanderbundt | .50 | .25 |
| ❑ 528 | Mike Sensibaugh RC ! | 1.50 | .60 |

## 1974 Topps

KEN STABLER  QUARTERBACK
RAIDERS

|  |  | | |
|---|---|---|---|
| ❑ | COMPLETE SET (528) | 300.00 | 175.00 |
| ❑ 1 | O.J.Simpson RB UER | 20.00 | 10.00 |
| ❑ 2 | Blaine Nye | .40 | .20 |
| ❑ 3 | Don Hansen | .40 | .20 |
| ❑ 4 | Ken Bowman | .40 | .20 |
| ❑ 5 | Carl Eller | 1.50 | .60 |
| ❑ 6 | Jerry Smith | .40 | .20 |
| ❑ 7 | Ed Podolak | .40 | .20 |
| ❑ 8 | Mel Gray | 1.50 | .60 |
| ❑ 9 | Pat Matson | .40 | .20 |
| ❑ 10 | Floyd Little | 1.50 | .60 |

|  |  | | |
|---|---|---|---|
| ❑ 11 | Frank Pitts | .40 | .20 |
| ❑ 12 | Vern Den Herder RC | .75 | .30 |
| ❑ 13 | John Fuqua | .75 | .30 |
| ❑ 14 | Jack Tatum | 2.00 | .75 |
| ❑ 15 | Winston Hill | .40 | .20 |
| ❑ 16 | John Beasley | .40 | .20 |
| ❑ 17 | David Lee | .40 | .20 |
| ❑ 18 | Rich Coady | .40 | .20 |
| ❑ 19 | Ken Willard | .40 | .20 |
| ❑ 20 | Coy Bacon | .75 | .30 |
| ❑ 21 | Ben Hawkins | .40 | .20 |
| ❑ 22 | Paul Guidry | .40 | .20 |
| ❑ 23 | Norm Snead HOR | .75 | .30 |
| ❑ 24 | Jim Yarbrough | .40 | .20 |
| ❑ 25 | Jack Reynolds RC | 3.00 | 1.25 |
| ❑ 26 | Josh Ashton | .40 | .20 |
| ❑ 27 | Donnie Green | .40 | .20 |
| ❑ 28 | Bob Hayes | 2.00 | .75 |
| ❑ 29 | John Zook | .40 | .20 |
| ❑ 30 | Bobby Bryant | .40 | .20 |
| ❑ 31 | Scott Hunter | .75 | .30 |
| ❑ 32 | Dan Dierdorf | 6.00 | 3.00 |
| ❑ 33 | Curt Knight | .40 | .20 |
| ❑ 34 | Elmo Wright RC | .40 | .20 |
| ❑ 35 | Essex Johnson | .40 | .20 |
| ❑ 36 | Walt Sumner | .40 | .20 |
| ❑ 37 | Marv Montgomery | .40 | .20 |
| ❑ 38 | Tim Foley | .75 | .30 |
| ❑ 39 | Mike Siani | .40 | .20 |
| ❑ 40 | Joe Greene | 6.00 | 3.00 |
| ❑ 41 | Bobby Howfield | .40 | .20 |
| ❑ 42 | Del Williams | .40 | .20 |
| ❑ 43 | Don McCauley | .40 | .20 |
| ❑ 44 | Randy Jackson | .40 | .20 |
| ❑ 45 | Ron Smith | .40 | .20 |
| ❑ 46 | Gene Washington 49er | .75 | .30 |
| ❑ 47 | Po James | .40 | .20 |
| ❑ 48 | Solomon Freelon | .40 | .20 |
| ❑ 49 | Bob Windsor HOR | .40 | .20 |
| ❑ 50 | John Hadl | 1.50 | .60 |
| ❑ 51 | Greg Larson | .40 | .20 |
| ❑ 52 | Steve Owens | .75 | .30 |
| ❑ 53 | Jim Cheyunski | .40 | .20 |
| ❑ 54 | Rayfield Wright | .75 | .30 |
| ❑ 55 | Dave Hampton | .40 | .20 |
| ❑ 56 | Ron Widby | .40 | .20 |
| ❑ 57 | Milt Sunde | .40 | .20 |
| ❑ 58 | Billy Kilmer | 1.50 | .60 |
| ❑ 59 | Bobby Bell | 1.50 | .60 |
| ❑ 60 | Jim Bakken | .40 | .20 |
| ❑ 61 | Rufus Mayes | .40 | .20 |
| ❑ 62 | Vic Washington | .40 | .20 |
| ❑ 63 | Gene Washington Vik | .75 | .30 |
| ❑ 64 | Clarence Scott | .40 | .20 |
| ❑ 65 | Gene Upshaw | 2.00 | .75 |
| ❑ 66 | Larry Seiple | .75 | .30 |
| ❑ 67 | John McMakin | .40 | .20 |
| ❑ 68 | Ralph Baker | .40 | .20 |
| ❑ 69 | Lydell Mitchell | .75 | .30 |
| ❑ 70 | Archie Manning | 2.50 | 1.25 |
| ❑ 71 | George Farmer | .40 | .20 |
| ❑ 72 | Ron East | .40 | .20 |
| ❑ 73 | Al Nelson | .40 | .20 |
| ❑ 74 | Pat Hughes | .40 | .20 |
| ❑ 75 | Fred Willis | .40 | .20 |
| ❑ 76 | Larry Walton | .40 | .20 |
| ❑ 77 | Tom Neville | .40 | .20 |
| ❑ 78 | Ted Kwalick | .75 | .30 |
| ❑ 79 | Walt Patulski | .40 | .20 |
| ❑ 80 | Jim Niland | .40 | .20 |
| ❑ 81 | Ted Fritsch Jr. | .40 | .20 |
| ❑ 82 | Paul Krause | 1.50 | .60 |
| ❑ 83 | Jack Snow | .75 | .30 |
| ❑ 84 | Mike Bass | .40 | .20 |
| ❑ 85 | Jim Tyrer | .40 | .20 |
| ❑ 86 | Ron Yankowski | .40 | .20 |
| ❑ 87 | Mike Phipps | .75 | .30 |
| ❑ 88 | Al Beauchamp | .40 | .20 |
| ❑ 89 | Riley Odoms RC | 1.50 | .60 |
| ❑ 90 | MacArthur Lane | .40 | .20 |
| ❑ 91 | Art Thoms | .40 | .20 |
| ❑ 92 | Marlin Briscoe | .40 | .20 |
| ❑ 93 | Bruce Van Dyke | .40 | .20 |
| ❑ 94 | Tom Myers RC | .40 | .20 |
| ❑ 95 | Calvin Hill | 1.50 | .60 |

|  |  | | |
|---|---|---|---|
| ❑ 96 | Bruce Laird | .40 | .20 |
| ❑ 97 | Tony McGee DT | .40 | .20 |
| ❑ 98 | Len Rohde | .40 | .20 |
| ❑ 99 | Tom McNeill | .40 | .20 |
| ❑ 100 | Delles Howell | .40 | .20 |
| ❑ 101 | Gary Garrison | .40 | .20 |
| ❑ 102 | Dan Goich | .40 | .20 |
| ❑ 103 | Len St. Jean | .40 | .20 |
| ❑ 104 | Zeke Moore | .40 | .20 |
| ❑ 105 | Ahmad Rashad RC | 20.00 | 10.00 |
| ❑ 106 | Mel Renfro | 1.50 | .60 |
| ❑ 107 | Jim Mitchell TE | .40 | .20 |
| ❑ 108 | Ed Budde | .40 | .20 |
| ❑ 109 | Harry Schuh | .40 | .20 |
| ❑ 110 | Greg Pruitt RC | 4.00 | 2.00 |
| ❑ 111 | Ed Flanagan | .40 | .20 |
| ❑ 112 | Larry Stallings | .40 | .20 |
| ❑ 113 | Chuck Foreman RC | 5.00 | 2.50 |
| ❑ 114 | Royce Berry | .40 | .20 |
| ❑ 115 | Gale Gillingham | .40 | .20 |
| ❑ 116 | Charlie Johnson HOR | 1.50 | .60 |
| ❑ 117 | Checklist 1-132 UER | 4.00 | 2.00 |
| ❑ 118 | Bill Butler | .40 | .20 |
| ❑ 119 | Roy Jefferson | .75 | .30 |
| ❑ 120 | Bobby Douglass | .75 | .30 |
| ❑ 121 | Harold Carmichael RC | 12.00 | 6.00 |
| ❑ 122 | George Kunz AP | .40 | .20 |
| ❑ 123 | Larry Little | 2.00 | .75 |
| ❑ 124 | Forrest Blue AP | .40 | .20 |
| ❑ 125 | Ron Yary | 1.50 | .60 |
| ❑ 126 | Tom Mack AP | 1.50 | .60 |
| ❑ 127 | Bob Tucker AP | .75 | .30 |
| ❑ 128 | Paul Warfield | 4.00 | 2.00 |
| ❑ 129 | Fran Tarkenton | 10.00 | 5.00 |
| ❑ 130 | O.J.Simpson | 12.00 | 6.00 |
| ❑ 131 | Larry Csonka | 6.00 | 3.00 |
| ❑ 132 | Bruce Gossett AP | .40 | .20 |
| ❑ 133 | Bill Stanfill AP | .75 | .30 |
| ❑ 134 | Alan Page | 2.50 | 1.25 |
| ❑ 135 | Paul Smith AP | .40 | .20 |
| ❑ 136 | Claude Humphrey AP | .75 | .30 |
| ❑ 137 | Jack Ham | 10.00 | 5.00 |
| ❑ 138 | Lee Roy Jordan | 1.50 | .60 |
| ❑ 139 | Phil Villapiano AP | .75 | .30 |
| ❑ 140 | Ken Ellis AP | .40 | .20 |
| ❑ 141 | Willie Brown | 1.50 | .60 |
| ❑ 142 | Dick Anderson AP | .75 | .30 |
| ❑ 143 | Bill Bradley AP | .75 | .30 |
| ❑ 144 | Jerrel Wilson AP | .40 | .20 |
| ❑ 145 | Reggie Rucker | .75 | .30 |
| ❑ 146 | Marty Domres | .40 | .20 |
| ❑ 147 | Bob Kowalkowski | .40 | .20 |
| ❑ 148 | John Matuszak AP | 6.00 | 2.50 |
| ❑ 149 | Mike Adamle RC | .75 | .30 |
| ❑ 150 | Johnny Unitas | 15.00 | 7.50 |
| ❑ 151 | Charlie Ford | .40 | .20 |
| ❑ 152 | Bob Klein RC | .40 | .20 |
| ❑ 153 | Jim Merlo | .40 | .20 |
| ❑ 154 | Willie Young | .40 | .20 |
| ❑ 155 | Donny Anderson | .75 | .30 |
| ❑ 156 | Brig Owens | .40 | .20 |
| ❑ 157 | Bruce Jarvis | .40 | .20 |
| ❑ 158 | Ron Carpenter RC | .40 | .20 |
| ❑ 159 | Don Cockroft | .40 | .20 |
| ❑ 160 | Tommy Nobis | 1.50 | .60 |
| ❑ 161 | Craig Morton | 1.50 | .60 |
| ❑ 162 | Jon Staggers | .40 | .20 |
| ❑ 163 | Mike Eischeid | .40 | .20 |
| ❑ 164 | Jerry Sisemore RC | .40 | .20 |
| ❑ 165 | Cedrick Hardman | .40 | .20 |
| ❑ 166 | Bill Thompson | .75 | .30 |
| ❑ 167 | Jim Lynch | .75 | .30 |
| ❑ 168 | Bob Moore | .40 | .20 |
| ❑ 169 | Glen Edwards | .40 | .20 |
| ❑ 170 | Mercury Morris | 1.50 | .60 |
| ❑ 171 | Julius Adams | .40 | .20 |
| ❑ 172 | Cotton Speyrer | .40 | .20 |
| ❑ 173 | Bill Munson | .75 | .30 |
| ❑ 174 | Benny Johnson | .40 | .20 |
| ❑ 175 | Burgess Owens RC | .40 | .20 |
| ❑ 176 | Cid Edwards | .40 | .20 |
| ❑ 177 | Doug Buffone | .40 | .20 |
| ❑ 178 | Charlie Cowan | .40 | .20 |
| ❑ 179 | Bob Newland | .40 | .20 |
| ❑ 180 | Ron Shanklin | .75 | .30 |

|  |  | | |
|---|---|---|---|
| ☐ 181 | Bob Rowe | .40 | .20 |
| ☐ 182 | Len Hauss | .40 | .20 |
| ☐ 183 | Joe DeLamielleure RC | 8.00 | 3.00 |
| ☐ 184 | Sherman White RC | .40 | .20 |
| ☐ 185 | Fair Hooker | .40 | .20 |
| ☐ 186 | Nick Mike-Mayer | .40 | .20 |
| ☐ 187 | Ralph Neely | .40 | .20 |
| ☐ 188 | Rich McGeorge | .40 | .20 |
| ☐ 189 | Ed Marinaro RC | 4.00 | 1.50 |
| ☐ 190 | Dave Wilcox | 1.50 | .60 |
| ☐ 191 | Joe Owens RC | .40 | .20 |
| ☐ 192 | Bill Van Heusen | .40 | .20 |
| ☐ 193 | Jim Kearney | .40 | .20 |
| ☐ 194 | Otis Sistrunk RC | 1.50 | .60 |
| ☐ 195 | Ron Shanklin | .40 | .20 |
| ☐ 196 | Bill Lenkaitis | .40 | .20 |
| ☐ 197 | Tom Drougas | .40 | .20 |
| ☐ 198 | Larry Hand | .40 | .20 |
| ☐ 199 | Mack Alston | .40 | .20 |
| ☐ 200 | Bob Griese | 6.00 | 3.00 |
| ☐ 201 | Earlie Thomas | .40 | .20 |
| ☐ 202 | Carl Gersbach | .40 | .20 |
| ☐ 203 | Jim Harrison | .40 | .20 |
| ☐ 204 | Jake Kupp | .40 | .20 |
| ☐ 205 | Merlin Olsen | 2.00 | .75 |
| ☐ 206 | Spider Lockhart | .75 | .30 |
| ☐ 207 | Walker Gillette | .40 | .20 |
| ☐ 208 | Verlon Biggs | .40 | .20 |
| ☐ 209 | Bob James | .40 | .20 |
| ☐ 210 | Bob Trumpy | 1.50 | .60 |
| ☐ 211 | Jerry Sherk | .40 | .20 |
| ☐ 212 | Andy Maurer | .40 | .20 |
| ☐ 213 | Fred Carr | .40 | .20 |
| ☐ 214 | Mick Tingelhoff | .75 | .30 |
| ☐ 215 | Steve Spurrier | 15.00 | 7.50 |
| ☐ 216 | Richard Harris | .40 | .20 |
| ☐ 217 | Charlie Greer | .40 | .20 |
| ☐ 218 | Buck Buchanan | 1.50 | .60 |
| ☐ 219 | Ray Guy RC | 12.00 | 6.00 |
| ☐ 220 | Franco Harris | 12.00 | 6.00 |
| ☐ 221 | Darryl Stingley RC | 1.50 | .60 |
| ☐ 222 | Rex Kern | .40 | .20 |
| ☐ 223 | Toni Fritsch | .75 | .30 |
| ☐ 224 | Levi Johnson | .40 | .20 |
| ☐ 225 | Bob Kuechenberg | .75 | .30 |
| ☐ 226 | Elvin Bethea | 1.50 | .60 |
| ☐ 227 | Al Woodall RC | .75 | .30 |
| ☐ 228 | Terry Owens | .40 | .20 |
| ☐ 229 | Bivian Lee | .40 | .20 |
| ☐ 230 | Dick Butkus | 10.00 | 5.00 |
| ☐ 231 | Jim Bertelsen RC | .75 | .30 |
| ☐ 232 | John Mendenhall RC | .40 | .20 |
| ☐ 233 | Conrad Dobler RC | 1.50 | .60 |
| ☐ 234 | J.D. Hill | .75 | .30 |
| ☐ 235 | Ken Houston * | 1.50 | .60 |
| ☐ 236 | Dave Lewis | .40 | .20 |
| ☐ 237 | John Garlington | .40 | .20 |
| ☐ 238 | Bill Sandeman | .40 | .20 |
| ☐ 239 | Alden Roche | .40 | .20 |
| ☐ 240 | John Gilliam | .75 | .30 |
| ☐ 241 | Bruce Taylor | .40 | .20 |
| ☐ 242 | Vern Winfield | .40 | .20 |
| ☐ 243 | Bobby Maples | .40 | .20 |
| ☐ 244 | Wendell Hayes | .40 | .20 |
| ☐ 245 | George Blanda | 8.00 | 4.00 |
| ☐ 246 | Dwight White | .75 | .30 |
| ☐ 247 | Sandy Durko | .40 | .20 |
| ☐ 248 | Tom Mitchell | .40 | .20 |
| ☐ 249 | Chuck Walton | .40 | .20 |
| ☐ 250 | Bob Lilly | 4.00 | 2.00 |
| ☐ 251 | Doug Swift | .40 | .20 |
| ☐ 252 | Lynn Dickey RC | 1.50 | .60 |
| ☐ 253 | Jerome Barkum RC | .40 | .20 |
| ☐ 254 | Clint Jones | .40 | .20 |
| ☐ 255 | Billy Newsome | .40 | .20 |
| ☐ 256 | Bob Asher | .40 | .20 |
| ☐ 257 | Joe Scibelli | .40 | .20 |
| ☐ 258 | Tom Blanchard | .40 | .20 |
| ☐ 259 | Norm Thompson | .40 | .20 |
| ☐ 260 | Larry Brown | 1.50 | .60 |
| ☐ 261 | Paul Seymour | .40 | .20 |
| ☐ 262 | Checklist 133-264 | 4.00 | 2.00 |
| ☐ 263 | Doug Dieken RC | .40 | .20 |
| ☐ 264 | Lemar Parrish | .75 | .30 |
| ☐ 265 | Bob Lee UER | .40 | .20 |
| ☐ 266 | Bob Brown DT | .40 | .20 |
| ☐ 267 | Roy Winston | .40 | .20 |
| ☐ 268 | Randy Beisler | .40 | .20 |
| ☐ 269 | Joe Dawkins | .40 | .20 |
| ☐ 270 | Tom Dempsey | .75 | .30 |
| ☐ 271 | Jack Rudnay | .40 | .20 |
| ☐ 272 | Art Shell | 5.00 | 2.50 |
| ☐ 273 | Mike Wagner | .75 | .30 |
| ☐ 274 | Rick Cash | .40 | .20 |
| ☐ 275 | Greg Landry | 1.50 | .60 |
| ☐ 276 | Glenn Ressler | .40 | .20 |
| ☐ 277 | Billy Joe DuPree RC | 3.00 | 1.25 |
| ☐ 278 | Norm Evans | .40 | .20 |
| ☐ 279 | Billy Parks | .40 | .20 |
| ☐ 280 | John Riggins | 6.00 | 3.00 |
| ☐ 281 | Lionel Aldridge | .40 | .20 |
| ☐ 282 | Steve O'Neal | .40 | .20 |
| ☐ 283 | Craig Clemons | .40 | .20 |
| ☐ 284 | Willie Williams | .40 | .20 |
| ☐ 285 | Isiah Robertson | .75 | .30 |
| ☐ 286 | Dennis Shaw | .40 | .20 |
| ☐ 287 | Bill Brundige | .40 | .20 |
| ☐ 288 | John Leypoldt | .40 | .20 |
| ☐ 289 | John DeMarie | .40 | .20 |
| ☐ 290 | Mike Reid | 1.50 | .60 |
| ☐ 291 | Greg Brezina | .40 | .20 |
| ☐ 292 | Willie Buchanon RC | .40 | .20 |
| ☐ 293 | Dave Osborn | .75 | .30 |
| ☐ 294 | Mel Phillips | .40 | .20 |
| ☐ 295 | Haven Moses | .75 | .30 |
| ☐ 296 | Wade Key | .40 | .20 |
| ☐ 297 | Marvin Upshaw | .40 | .20 |
| ☐ 298 | Ray Mansfield | .40 | .20 |
| ☐ 299 | Edgar Chandler | .40 | .20 |
| ☐ 300 | Marv Hubbard | .75 | .30 |
| ☐ 301 | Herman Weaver | .40 | .20 |
| ☐ 302 | Jim Bailey | .40 | .20 |
| ☐ 303 | D.D.Lewis RC | .75 | .30 |
| ☐ 304 | Ken Burrough | .75 | .30 |
| ☐ 305 | Jake Scott | 1.50 | .60 |
| ☐ 306 | Randy Rasmussen | .40 | .20 |
| ☐ 307 | Pettis Norman | .40 | .20 |
| ☐ 308 | Carl Johnson | .40 | .20 |
| ☐ 309 | Joe Taylor | .40 | .20 |
| ☐ 310 | Pete Gogolak | .40 | .20 |
| ☐ 311 | Tony Baker FB | .40 | .20 |
| ☐ 312 | John Richardson | .40 | .20 |
| ☐ 313 | Dave Robinson | .75 | .30 |
| ☐ 314 | Reggie McKenzie RC | 1.50 | .60 |
| ☐ 315 | Isaac Curtis RC | 1.50 | .60 |
| ☐ 316 | Thom Darden | .40 | .20 |
| ☐ 317 | Ken Reaves | .40 | .20 |
| ☐ 318 | Malcolm Snider | .40 | .20 |
| ☐ 319 | Jeff Siemon RC | .75 | .30 |
| ☐ 320 | Dan Abramowicz | .75 | .30 |
| ☐ 321 | Lyle Alzado | 2.00 | .75 |
| ☐ 322 | John Reaves | .40 | .20 |
| ☐ 323 | Morris Stroud | .40 | .20 |
| ☐ 324 | Bobby Walden | .40 | .20 |
| ☐ 325 | Randy Vataha | .40 | .20 |
| ☐ 326 | Nemiah Wilson | .40 | .20 |
| ☐ 327 | Paul Naumoff | .40 | .20 |
| ☐ 328 | O.J.Simpson/Brock. LL | 3.00 | 1.50 |
| ☐ 329 | R.Staubach/Stabler LL | 5.00 | 2.50 |
| ☐ 330 | Harold Carmichael/Will LL | 1.50 | .60 |
| ☐ 331 | Scoring Leaders | .75 | .30 |
| ☐ 332 | Interception Leaders | .75 | .30 |
| ☐ 333 | Punting Leaders | .75 | .30 |
| ☐ 334 | Dennis Nelson | .40 | .20 |
| ☐ 335 | Walt Garrison | .75 | .30 |
| ☐ 336 | Tody Smith | .40 | .20 |
| ☐ 337 | Ed Bell | .40 | .20 |
| ☐ 338 | Bryant Salter | .40 | .20 |
| ☐ 339 | Wayne Colman | .40 | .20 |
| ☐ 340 | Garo Yepremian | .75 | .30 |
| ☐ 341 | Bob Newton | .40 | .20 |
| ☐ 342 | Vince Clements RC | .40 | .20 |
| ☐ 343 | Ken Iman | .40 | .20 |
| ☐ 344 | Jim Tolbert | .40 | .20 |
| ☐ 345 | Chris Hanburger | .75 | .30 |
| ☐ 346 | Dave Foley | .40 | .20 |
| ☐ 347 | Tommy Casanova | .75 | .30 |
| ☐ 348 | John James | .40 | .20 |
| ☐ 349 | Clarence Williams | .40 | .20 |
| ☐ 350 | Leroy Kelly | 1.50 | .60 |
| ☐ 351 | Stu Voigt RC | .75 | .30 |
| ☐ 352 | Skip Vanderbundt | .40 | .20 |
| ☐ 353 | Pete Duranko | .40 | .20 |
| ☐ 354 | John Outlaw | .40 | .20 |
| ☐ 355 | Jan Stenerud | 1.50 | .60 |
| ☐ 356 | Barry Pearson | .40 | .20 |
| ☐ 357 | Brian Dowling RC | .40 | .20 |
| ☐ 358 | Dan Conners | .40 | .20 |
| ☐ 359 | Bob Bell | .40 | .20 |
| ☐ 360 | Rick Volk | .40 | .20 |
| ☐ 361 | Pat Toomay | .75 | .30 |
| ☐ 362 | Bob Gresham | .40 | .20 |
| ☐ 363 | John Schmitt | .40 | .20 |
| ☐ 364 | Mel Rogers | .40 | .20 |
| ☐ 365 | Manny Fernandez | .75 | .30 |
| ☐ 366 | Ernie Jackson | .40 | .20 |
| ☐ 367 | Gary Huff RC | .75 | .30 |
| ☐ 368 | Bob Grim | .40 | .20 |
| ☐ 369 | Ernie McMillan | .40 | .20 |
| ☐ 370 | Dave Elmendorf | .40 | .20 |
| ☐ 371 | Mike Bragg | .40 | .20 |
| ☐ 372 | John Skorupan | .40 | .20 |
| ☐ 373 | Howard Fest | .40 | .20 |
| ☐ 374 | Jerry Tagge RC | .75 | .30 |
| ☐ 375 | Art Malone | .40 | .20 |
| ☐ 376 | Bob Babich | .40 | .20 |
| ☐ 377 | Jim Marshall | 1.50 | .60 |
| ☐ 378 | Bob Hoskins | .40 | .20 |
| ☐ 379 | Don Zimmerman | .40 | .20 |
| ☐ 380 | Ray May | .40 | .20 |
| ☐ 381 | Emmitt Thomas | .75 | .30 |
| ☐ 382 | Terry Hanratty | .75 | .30 |
| ☐ 383 | John Hannah RC | 15.00 | 7.50 |
| ☐ 384 | George Atkinson | .40 | .20 |
| ☐ 385 | Ted Hendricks | 3.00 | 1.50 |
| ☐ 386 | Jim O'Brien | .40 | .20 |
| ☐ 387 | Jethro Pugh | .75 | .30 |
| ☐ 388 | Elbert Drungo | .40 | .20 |
| ☐ 389 | Richard Caster | .75 | .30 |
| ☐ 390 | Deacon Jones | 1.50 | .60 |
| ☐ 391 | Checklist 265-396 | 4.00 | 2.00 |
| ☐ 392 | Jess Phillips | .40 | .20 |
| ☐ 393 | Garry Lyle UER | .40 | .20 |
| ☐ 394 | Jim Files | .40 | .20 |
| ☐ 395 | Jim Hart | 1.50 | .60 |
| ☐ 396 | Dave Chapple | .40 | .20 |
| ☐ 397 | Jim Langer | 2.00 | .75 |
| ☐ 398 | John Wilbur | .40 | .20 |
| ☐ 399 | Dwight Harrison | .40 | .20 |
| ☐ 400 | John Brockington | .75 | .30 |
| ☐ 401 | Ken Anderson | 6.00 | 3.00 |
| ☐ 402 | Mike Tilleman | .40 | .20 |
| ☐ 403 | Charlie Hall | .40 | .20 |
| ☐ 404 | Tommy Hart | .40 | .20 |
| ☐ 405 | Norm Bulaich | .75 | .30 |
| ☐ 406 | Jim Turner | .40 | .20 |
| ☐ 407 | Mo Moorman | .40 | .20 |
| ☐ 408 | Ralph Anderson | .40 | .20 |
| ☐ 409 | Jim Otto | 1.50 | .60 |
| ☐ 410 | Andy Russell | 1.50 | .60 |
| ☐ 411 | Glenn Doughty | .40 | .20 |
| ☐ 412 | Altie Taylor | .40 | .20 |
| ☐ 413 | Marv Bateman | .40 | .20 |
| ☐ 414 | Willie Alexander | .40 | .20 |
| ☐ 415 | Bill Zapalac RC | .40 | .20 |
| ☐ 416 | Russ Washington | .40 | .20 |
| ☐ 417 | Joe Federspiel | .40 | .20 |
| ☐ 418 | Craig Cotton | .40 | .20 |
| ☐ 419 | Randy Johnson | .40 | .20 |
| ☐ 420 | Harold Jackson | 1.50 | .60 |
| ☐ 421 | Roger Wehrli | 1.00 | .40 |
| ☐ 422 | Charlie Harraway | .40 | .20 |
| ☐ 423 | Spike Jones | .40 | .20 |
| ☐ 424 | Bob Johnson | .40 | .20 |
| ☐ 425 | Mike McCoy DT | .40 | .20 |
| ☐ 426 | Dennis Havig | .40 | .20 |
| ☐ 427 | Bob McKay RC | .40 | .20 |
| ☐ 428 | Steve Zabel | .40 | .20 |
| ☐ 429 | Horace Jones | .40 | .20 |
| ☐ 430 | Jim Johnson | 1.50 | .60 |
| ☐ 431 | Roy Gerela | .75 | .30 |
| ☐ 432 | Tom Graham RC | .40 | .20 |
| ☐ 433 | Curley Culp | .75 | .30 |
| ☐ 434 | Ken Mendenhall | .40 | .20 |
| ☐ 435 | Jim Plunkett | 2.50 | 1.25 |

| | | |
|---|---|---|
| ❑ 436 Julian Fagan | .40 | .20 |
| ❑ 437 Mike Garrett | .75 | .30 |
| ❑ 438 Bobby Joe Green | .40 | .20 |
| ❑ 439 Jack Gregory | .40 | .20 |
| ❑ 440 Charlie Sanders | 1.00 | .40 |
| ❑ 441 Bill Curry | .75 | .30 |
| ❑ 442 Bob Pollard | .40 | .20 |
| ❑ 443 David Ray | .40 | .20 |
| ❑ 444 Terry Metcalf RC | 3.00 | 1.50 |
| ❑ 445 Pat Fischer | .75 | .30 |
| ❑ 446 Bob Chandler | .75 | .30 |
| ❑ 447 Bill Bergey | .75 | .30 |
| ❑ 448 Walter Johnson | .40 | .20 |
| ❑ 449 Charle Young RC | 1.50 | .60 |
| ❑ 450 Chester Marcol | .40 | .20 |
| ❑ 451 Ken Stabler | 20.00 | 10.00 |
| ❑ 452 Preston Pearson | 1.50 | .60 |
| ❑ 453 Mike Current | .40 | .20 |
| ❑ 454 Ron Bolton | .40 | .20 |
| ❑ 455 Mark Lomas | .40 | .20 |
| ❑ 456 Raymond Chester | .75 | .30 |
| ❑ 457 Jerry LeVias | .75 | .30 |
| ❑ 458 Skip Butler | .40 | .20 |
| ❑ 459 Mike Livingston RC | .40 | .20 |
| ❑ 460 AFC Semi-Final | .75 | .30 |
| ❑ 461 NFC Semi/Staubach | 4.00 | 2.00 |
| ❑ 462 Playoff Champs/Stabler | 3.00 | 1.50 |
| ❑ 463 SB VIII/L.Csonka | 2.00 | .75 |
| ❑ 464 Wayne Mulligan | .40 | .20 |
| ❑ 465 Horst Muhlmann | .40 | .20 |
| ❑ 466 Milt Morin | .40 | .20 |
| ❑ 467 Don Parish | .40 | .20 |
| ❑ 468 Richard Neal | .40 | .20 |
| ❑ 469 Ron Jessie | .75 | .30 |
| ❑ 470 Terry Bradshaw | 25.00 | 12.50 |
| ❑ 471 Fred Dryer | 1.50 | .60 |
| ❑ 472 Jim Carter | .40 | .20 |
| ❑ 473 Ken Burrow | .40 | .20 |
| ❑ 474 Wally Chambers RC | .75 | .30 |
| ❑ 475 Dan Pastorini | 1.50 | .60 |
| ❑ 476 Don Morrison | .40 | .20 |
| ❑ 477 Carl Mauck | .40 | .20 |
| ❑ 478 Larry Cole RC | .75 | .30 |
| ❑ 479 Jim Kiick | 1.50 | .60 |
| ❑ 480 Willie Lanier | 1.50 | .60 |
| ❑ 481 Don Herrmann | .75 | .30 |
| ❑ 482 George Hunt | .40 | .20 |
| ❑ 483 Bob Howard RC | .40 | .20 |
| ❑ 484 Myron Pottios | .40 | .20 |
| ❑ 485 Jackie Smith | 1.50 | .60 |
| ❑ 486 Vern Holland | .40 | .20 |
| ❑ 487 Jim Braxton | .40 | .20 |
| ❑ 488 Joe Reed | .40 | .20 |
| ❑ 489 Wally Hilgenberg | .40 | .20 |
| ❑ 490 Fred Biletnikoff | 4.00 | 2.00 |
| ❑ 491 Bob DeMarco | .40 | .20 |
| ❑ 492 Mark Nordquist | .40 | .20 |
| ❑ 493 Larry Brooks | .40 | .20 |
| ❑ 494 Pete Athas | .40 | .20 |
| ❑ 495 Emerson Boozer | .75 | .30 |
| ❑ 496 L.C.Greenwood | 2.00 | .75 |
| ❑ 497 Rockne Freitas | .40 | .20 |
| ❑ 498 Checklist 397-528 UER | 4.00 | 2.00 |
| ❑ 499 Joe Schmiesing | .40 | .20 |
| ❑ 500 Roger Staubach | 25.00 | 12.50 |
| ❑ 501 Al Cowlings UER | .75 | .30 |
| ❑ 502 Sam Cunningham RC | 1.50 | .60 |
| ❑ 503 Dennis Partee | .40 | .20 |
| ❑ 504 John Didion | .40 | .20 |
| ❑ 505 Nick Buoniconti | 1.50 | .60 |
| ❑ 506 Carl Garrett | .75 | .30 |
| ❑ 507 Doug Van Horn | .40 | .20 |
| ❑ 508 Jamie Rivers | .40 | .20 |
| ❑ 509 Jack Youngblood | 4.00 | 2.00 |
| ❑ 510 Charley Taylor UER | 2.50 | 1.25 |
| ❑ 511 Ken Riley | 1.50 | .60 |
| ❑ 512 Joe Ferguson RC | 3.00 | 1.25 |
| ❑ 513 Bill Lueck | .40 | .20 |
| ❑ 514 Ray Brown DB RC | 1.50 | .60 |
| ❑ 515 Fred Cox | .40 | .20 |
| ❑ 516 Joe Jones DE | .40 | .20 |
| ❑ 517 Larry Schreiber | .40 | .20 |
| ❑ 518 Dennis Wirgowski | .40 | .20 |
| ❑ 519 Leroy Mitchell | .40 | .20 |
| ❑ 520 Otis Taylor | 1.50 | .60 |
| ❑ 521 Henry Davis | .40 | .20 |
| ❑ 522 Bruce Barnes | .40 | .20 |
| ❑ 523 Charlie Smith RB | .40 | .20 |
| ❑ 524 Bert Jones RC | 5.00 | 2.00 |
| ❑ 525 Lem Barney | 2.00 | .75 |
| ❑ 526 John Fitzgerald RC | .40 | .20 |
| ❑ 527 Tom Funchess | .40 | .20 |
| ❑ 528 Steve Tannen | 1.50 | .60 |

## 1975 Topps

| | | |
|---|---|---|
| ❑ COMPLETE SET (528) | 300.00 | 175.00 |
| ❑ 1 McCutcheon/Armstrong LL | 1.50 | .60 |
| ❑ 2 Jurgensen/K.Anderson LL | 1.50 | .60 |
| ❑ 3 Receiving Leaders | 1.50 | .60 |
| ❑ 4 Scoring Leaders | .75 | .30 |
| ❑ 5 Interception Leaders | .75 | .30 |
| ❑ 6 Punting Leaders | 1.50 | .60 |
| ❑ 7 George Blanda HL | 5.00 | 2.50 |
| ❑ 8 George Blanda | 5.00 | 2.50 |
| ❑ 9 Ralph Baker | .30 | .15 |
| ❑ 10 Don Woods | .30 | .15 |
| ❑ 11 Bob Asher | .30 | .15 |
| ❑ 12 Mel Blount RC | 20.00 | 10.00 |
| ❑ 13 Sam Cunningham | .75 | .30 |
| ❑ 14 Jackie Smith | 1.50 | .60 |
| ❑ 15 Greg Landry | .75 | .30 |
| ❑ 16 Buck Buchanan | 1.50 | .60 |
| ❑ 17 Haven Moses | .75 | .30 |
| ❑ 18 Clarence Ellis | .30 | .15 |
| ❑ 19 Jim Carter | .30 | .15 |
| ❑ 20 Charley Taylor UER | 2.00 | .75 |
| ❑ 21 Jess Phillips | .30 | .15 |
| ❑ 22 Larry Seiple | .30 | .15 |
| ❑ 23 Doug Dieken | .30 | .15 |
| ❑ 24 Ron Saul | .30 | .15 |
| ❑ 25 Isaac Curtis | 1.50 | .60 |
| ❑ 26 Gary Larsen RC | .30 | .15 |
| ❑ 27 Bruce Jarvis | .30 | .15 |
| ❑ 28 Steve Zabel | .30 | .15 |
| ❑ 29 John Mendenhall | .30 | .15 |
| ❑ 30 Rick Volk | .30 | .15 |
| ❑ 31 Checklist 1-132 | 4.00 | 2.00 |
| ❑ 32 Dan Abramowicz | .75 | .30 |
| ❑ 33 Bubba Smith | 1.50 | .60 |
| ❑ 34 David Ray | .30 | .15 |
| ❑ 35 Dan Dierdorf | 4.00 | 2.00 |
| ❑ 36 Randy Rasmussen | .30 | .15 |
| ❑ 37 Bob Howard | .30 | .15 |
| ❑ 38 Gary Huff | .75 | .30 |
| ❑ 39 Rocky Bleier RC | 20.00 | 10.00 |
| ❑ 40 Mel Gray | .75 | .30 |
| ❑ 41 Tony McGee DT | .30 | .15 |
| ❑ 42 Larry Hand | .30 | .15 |
| ❑ 43 Wendell Hayes | .30 | .15 |
| ❑ 44 Doug Wilkerson RC | .30 | .15 |
| ❑ 45 Paul Smith | .30 | .15 |
| ❑ 46 Dave Robinson | .75 | .30 |
| ❑ 47 Bivian Lee | .30 | .15 |
| ❑ 48 Jim Mandich RC | .75 | .30 |
| ❑ 49 Greg Pruitt | 1.50 | .60 |
| ❑ 50 Dan Pastorini | 1.50 | .60 |
| ❑ 51 Ron Pritchard | .30 | .15 |
| ❑ 52 Dan Conners | .30 | .15 |
| ❑ 53 Fred Cox | .30 | .15 |
| ❑ 54 Tony Greene | .30 | .15 |
| ❑ 55 Craig Morton | 1.50 | .60 |
| ❑ 56 Jerry Sisemore | .30 | .15 |
| ❑ 57 Glenn Doughty | .30 | .15 |
| ❑ 58 Larry Schreiber | .30 | .15 |
| ❑ 59 Charlie Waters RC | 4.00 | 2.00 |
| ❑ 60 Jack Youngblood | 1.50 | .60 |
| ❑ 61 Bill Lenkaitis | .30 | .15 |
| ❑ 62 Greg Brezina | .30 | .15 |
| ❑ 63 Bob Pollard | .30 | .15 |
| ❑ 64 Mack Alston | .30 | .15 |
| ❑ 65 Drew Pearson RC | 20.00 | 10.00 |
| ❑ 66 Charlie Stukes | .30 | .15 |
| ❑ 67 Emerson Boozer | .75 | .30 |
| ❑ 68 Dennis Partee | .30 | .15 |
| ❑ 69 Bob Newton | .30 | .15 |
| ❑ 70 Jack Tatum | 1.50 | .60 |
| ❑ 71 Frank Lewis | .30 | .15 |
| ❑ 72 Bob Young | .30 | .15 |
| ❑ 73 Julius Adams | .30 | .15 |
| ❑ 74 Paul Naumoff | .30 | .15 |
| ❑ 75 Otis Taylor | 1.50 | .60 |
| ❑ 76 Dave Hampton | .30 | .15 |
| ❑ 77 Mike Current | .30 | .15 |
| ❑ 78 Brig Owens | .30 | .15 |
| ❑ 79 Bobby Scott | .30 | .15 |
| ❑ 80 Harold Carmichael | 3.00 | 1.50 |
| ❑ 81 Bill Stanfill | .30 | .15 |
| ❑ 82 Bob Babich | .30 | .15 |
| ❑ 83 Vic Washington | .30 | .15 |
| ❑ 84 Mick Tingelhoff | .75 | .30 |
| ❑ 85 Bob Trumpy | 1.50 | .60 |
| ❑ 86 Earl Edwards | .30 | .15 |
| ❑ 87 Ron Hornsby | .30 | .15 |
| ❑ 88 Don McCauley | .30 | .15 |
| ❑ 89 Jim Johnson | 1.50 | .60 |
| ❑ 90 Andy Russell | .75 | .30 |
| ❑ 91 Cornell Green | 1.50 | .60 |
| ❑ 92 Charlie Cowan | .30 | .15 |
| ❑ 93 Jon Staggers | .30 | .15 |
| ❑ 94 Billy Newsome | .30 | .15 |
| ❑ 95 Willie Brown | 1.50 | .60 |
| ❑ 96 Carl Mauck | .30 | .15 |
| ❑ 97 Doug Buffone | .30 | .15 |
| ❑ 98 Preston Pearson | .75 | .30 |
| ❑ 99 Jim Bakken | .30 | .15 |
| ❑ 100 Bob Griese | 5.00 | 2.50 |
| ❑ 101 Bob Windsor | .30 | .15 |
| ❑ 102 Rockne Freitas | .30 | .15 |
| ❑ 103 Jim Marsalis | .30 | .15 |
| ❑ 104 Bill Thompson | .75 | .30 |
| ❑ 105 Ken Burrow | .30 | .15 |
| ❑ 106 Diron Talbert | .30 | .15 |
| ❑ 107 Joe Federspiel | .30 | .15 |
| ❑ 108 Norm Bulaich | .75 | .30 |
| ❑ 109 Bob DeMarco | .30 | .15 |
| ❑ 110 Tom Wittum | .30 | .15 |
| ❑ 111 Larry Hefner | .30 | .15 |
| ❑ 112 Tody Smith | .30 | .15 |
| ❑ 113 Stu Voigt | .30 | .15 |
| ❑ 114 Horst Muhlmann | .30 | .15 |
| ❑ 115 Ahmad Rashad | 6.00 | 3.00 |
| ❑ 116 Joe Dawkins | .30 | .15 |
| ❑ 117 George Kunz | .30 | .15 |
| ❑ 118 D.D.Lewis | .75 | .30 |
| ❑ 119 Levi Johnson | .30 | .15 |
| ❑ 120 Len Dawson | 4.00 | 2.00 |
| ❑ 121 Jim Bertelsen | .30 | .15 |
| ❑ 122 Ed Bell | .30 | .15 |
| ❑ 123 Art Thoms | .30 | .15 |
| ❑ 124 Joe Beauchamp | .30 | .15 |
| ❑ 125 Jack Ham | 6.00 | 3.00 |
| ❑ 126 Carl Garrett | .30 | .15 |
| ❑ 127 Roger Finnie | .30 | .15 |
| ❑ 128 Howard Twilley | .75 | .30 |
| ❑ 129 Bruce Barnes | .30 | .15 |
| ❑ 130 Nate Wright | .30 | .15 |
| ❑ 131 Jerry Tagge | .30 | .15 |
| ❑ 132 Floyd Little | 1.50 | .60 |
| ❑ 133 John Zook | .30 | .15 |
| ❑ 134 Len Hauss | .30 | .15 |
| ❑ 135 Archie Manning | 1.50 | .60 |
| ❑ 136 Po James | .30 | .15 |
| ❑ 137 Walt Sumner | .30 | .15 |
| ❑ 138 Randy Beisler | .30 | .15 |
| ❑ 139 Willie Alexander | .30 | .15 |
| ❑ 140 Garo Yepremian | .75 | .30 |
| ❑ 141 Chip Myers | .30 | .15 |
| ❑ 142 Jim Braxton | .30 | .15 |

|  |  | | |
|---|---|---|---|
| 143 | Doug Van Horn | .30 | .15 |
| 144 | Stan White | .30 | .15 |
| 145 | Roger Staubach | 20.00 | 10.00 |
| 146 | Herman Weaver | .30 | .15 |
| 147 | Marvin Upshaw | .30 | .15 |
| 148 | Bob Klein | .30 | .15 |
| 149 | Earlie Thomas | .30 | .15 |
| 150 | John Brockington | .75 | .30 |
| 151 | Mike Siani | .30 | .15 |
| 152 | Sam Davis RC | .30 | .15 |
| 153 | Mike Wagner | .75 | .30 |
| 154 | Larry Stallings | .30 | .15 |
| 155 | Wally Chambers | .30 | .15 |
| 156 | Randy Vataha | .30 | .15 |
| 157 | Jim Marshall | 1.50 | .60 |
| 158 | Jim Turner | .30 | .15 |
| 159 | Walt Sweeney | .30 | .15 |
| 160 | Ken Anderson | 4.00 | 2.00 |
| 161 | Ray Brown DB | .30 | .15 |
| 162 | John Didion | .30 | .15 |
| 163 | Tom Dempsey | .30 | .15 |
| 164 | Clarence Scott | .30 | .15 |
| 165 | Gene Washington 49er | .75 | .30 |
| 166 | Willie Rodgers RC | .30 | .15 |
| 167 | Doug Swift | .30 | .15 |
| 168 | Rufus Mayes | .30 | .15 |
| 169 | Marv Bateman | .30 | .15 |
| 170 | Lydell Mitchell | .75 | .30 |
| 171 | Ron Smith | .30 | .15 |
| 172 | Bill Munson | .75 | .30 |
| 173 | Bob Grim | .30 | .15 |
| 174 | Ed Budde | .30 | .15 |
| 175 | Bob Lilly UER | 4.00 | 2.00 |
| 176 | Jim Youngblood RC | 1.50 | .60 |
| 177 | Steve Tannen | .30 | .15 |
| 178 | Rich McGeorge | .30 | .15 |
| 179 | Jim Tyrer | .30 | .15 |
| 180 | Forrest Blue | .30 | .15 |
| 181 | Jerry LeVias | .75 | .30 |
| 182 | Joe Gilliam RC | 1.50 | .60 |
| 183 | Jim Otis RC | .75 | .30 |
| 184 | Mel Tom | .30 | .15 |
| 185 | Paul Seymour | .30 | .15 |
| 186 | George Webster | .30 | .15 |
| 187 | Pete Duranko | .30 | .15 |
| 188 | Essex Johnson | .30 | .15 |
| 189 | Bob Lee | .75 | .30 |
| 190 | Gene Upshaw | 1.50 | .60 |
| 191 | Tom Myers | .30 | .15 |
| 192 | Don Zimmerman | .30 | .15 |
| 193 | John Garlington | .30 | .15 |
| 194 | Skip Butler | .30 | .15 |
| 195 | Tom Mitchell | .30 | .15 |
| 196 | Jim Langer | 1.50 | .60 |
| 197 | Ron Carpenter | .30 | .15 |
| 198 | Dave Foley | .30 | .15 |
| 199 | Bert Jones | 1.50 | .60 |
| 200 | Larry Brown | .75 | .30 |
| 201 | Biletnikoff/C.Taylor AP | 2.00 | .75 |
| 202 | All Pro Tackles | .30 | .15 |
| 203 | L.Little/T.Mack AP | 1.50 | .60 |
| 204 | All Pro Centers | .30 | .15 |
| 205 | Hannah/Gillingham AP | 1.50 | .60 |
| 206 | Dan Dierdorf/W.Hill AP | 1.50 | .60 |
| 207 | All Pro Tight Ends | .75 | .30 |
| 208 | F.Tarkenton/Stabler AP | 4.00 | 2.00 |
| 209 | Simpson/McCutch. AP | 3.00 | 1.50 |
| 210 | All Pro Backs | .75 | .30 |
| 211 | All Pro Receivers | .75 | .30 |
| 212 | All Pro Kickers | .30 | .15 |
| 213 | Youngblood/Bethea AP | 1.50 | .60 |
| 214 | All Pro Tackles | .75 | .30 |
| 215 | M.Olsen/M.Reid AP | 1.50 | .60 |
| 216 | Carl Eller/L.Alzado AP | 1.50 | .60 |
| 217 | Hendricks/Villapiano AP | 1.50 | .60 |
| 218 | Willie Lanier/Jordan AP | 1.50 | .60 |
| 219 | All Pro Linebackers | .75 | .30 |
| 220 | All Pro Cornerbacks | .30 | .15 |
| 221 | All Pro Cornerbacks | .30 | .15 |
| 222 | K.Houston/D.Anderson AP | .75 | .30 |
| 223 | Cliff Harris/J.Tatum AP | 1.50 | .60 |
| 224 | All Pro Punters | .75 | .30 |
| 225 | All Pro Returners | .30 | .15 |
| 226 | Ted Kwalick | .30 | .15 |
| 227 | Spider Lockhart | .75 | .30 |
| 228 | Mike Livingston | .30 | .15 |
| 229 | Larry Cole | .30 | .15 |
| 230 | Gary Garrison | .30 | .15 |
| 231 | Larry Brooks | .30 | .15 |
| 232 | Bobby Howfield | .30 | .15 |
| 233 | Fred Carr | .30 | .15 |
| 234 | Norm Evans | .30 | .15 |
| 235 | Dwight White | .75 | .30 |
| 236 | Conrad Dobler | .75 | .30 |
| 237 | Garry Lyle | .30 | .15 |
| 238 | Darryl Stingley | 1.50 | .60 |
| 239 | Tom Graham | .30 | .15 |
| 240 | Chuck Foreman | 1.50 | .60 |
| 241 | Ken Riley | .75 | .30 |
| 242 | Don Morrison | .30 | .15 |
| 243 | Lynn Dickey | .75 | .30 |
| 244 | Don Cockroft | .50 | .15 |
| 245 | Claude Humphrey | .75 | .30 |
| 246 | John Skorupan | .30 | .15 |
| 247 | Raymond Chester | .75 | .30 |
| 248 | Cas Banaszek | .30 | .15 |
| 249 | Art Malone | .30 | .15 |
| 250 | Ed Flanagan | .30 | .15 |
| 251 | Checklist 133-264 | 4.00 | 2.00 |
| 252 | Nemiah Wilson | .30 | .15 |
| 253 | Ron Jessie | .30 | .15 |
| 254 | Jim Lynch | .30 | .15 |
| 255 | Bob Tucker | .75 | .30 |
| 256 | Terry Owens | .30 | .15 |
| 257 | John Fitzgerald | .30 | .15 |
| 258 | Jack Snow | .75 | .30 |
| 259 | Garry Puetz | .30 | .15 |
| 260 | Mike Phipps | .75 | .30 |
| 261 | Al Matthews | .30 | .15 |
| 262 | Bob Kuechenberg | .30 | .15 |
| 263 | Ron Yankowski | .30 | .15 |
| 264 | Ron Shanklin | .30 | .15 |
| 265 | Bobby Douglass | .75 | .30 |
| 266 | Josh Ashton | .30 | .15 |
| 267 | Bill Van Heusen | .30 | .15 |
| 268 | Jeff Siemon | .30 | .15 |
| 269 | Bob Newland | .30 | .15 |
| 270 | Gale Gillingham | .30 | .15 |
| 271 | Zeke Moore | .30 | .15 |
| 272 | Mike Tilleman | .30 | .15 |
| 273 | John Leypoldt | .30 | .15 |
| 274 | Ken Mendenhall | .30 | .15 |
| 275 | Norm Snead | .75 | .30 |
| 276 | Bill Bradley | .75 | .30 |
| 277 | Jerry Smith | .30 | .15 |
| 278 | Clarence Davis | .30 | .15 |
| 279 | Jim Yarbrough | .30 | .15 |
| 280 | Lemar Parrish | .30 | .15 |
| 281 | Bobby Bell | 1.50 | .60 |
| 282 | Lynn Swann RC UER ! | 60.00 | 30.00 |
| 283 | John Hicks | .30 | .15 |
| 284 | Coy Bacon | .75 | .30 |
| 285 | Lee Roy Jordan | 1.50 | .60 |
| 286 | Willie Buchanon | .30 | .15 |
| 287 | Al Woodall | .30 | .15 |
| 288 | Reggie Rucker | .75 | .30 |
| 289 | John Schmitt | .30 | .15 |
| 290 | Carl Eller | 1.50 | .60 |
| 291 | Jake Scott | .75 | .30 |
| 292 | Donny Anderson | .75 | .30 |
| 293 | Charley Wade | .30 | .15 |
| 294 | John Tanner | .30 | .15 |
| 295 | Charlie Johnson | .75 | .30 |
| 296 | Tom Blanchard | .30 | .15 |
| 297 | Curley Culp | .75 | .30 |
| 298 | Jeff Van Note RC | .75 | .30 |
| 299 | Bob James | .30 | .15 |
| 300 | Franco Harris | 8.00 | 4.00 |
| 301 | Tim Berra | .75 | .30 |
| 302 | Bruce Gossett | .30 | .15 |
| 303 | Verlon Biggs | .30 | .15 |
| 304 | Bob Kowalkowski | .30 | .15 |
| 305 | Marv Hubbard | .30 | .15 |
| 306 | Ken Avery | .30 | .15 |
| 307 | Mike Adamle | .30 | .15 |
| 308 | Don Herrmann | .30 | .15 |
| 309 | Chris Fletcher | .30 | .15 |
| 310 | Roman Gabriel | 1.50 | .60 |
| 311 | Billy Joe DuPree | 1.50 | .60 |
| 312 | Fred Dryer | 1.50 | .60 |
| 313 | John Riggins | 5.00 | 2.50 |
| 314 | Bob McKay | .30 | .15 |
| 315 | Ted Hendricks | 1.50 | .60 |
| 316 | Bobby Bryant | .30 | .15 |
| 317 | Don Nottingham | .30 | .15 |
| 318 | John Hannah | 4.00 | 2.00 |
| 319 | Rich Coady | .30 | .15 |
| 320 | Phil Villapiano | .75 | .30 |
| 321 | Jim Plunkett | 1.50 | .60 |
| 322 | Lyle Alzado | 1.50 | .60 |
| 323 | Ernie Jackson | .30 | .15 |
| 324 | Billy Parks | .30 | .15 |
| 325 | Willie Lanier | 1.50 | .60 |
| 326 | John James | .30 | .15 |
| 327 | Joe Ferguson | .75 | .30 |
| 328 | Ernie Holmes RC | 1.50 | .60 |
| 329 | Bruce Laird | .30 | .15 |
| 330 | Chester Marcol | .30 | .15 |
| 331 | Dave Wilcox | 1.50 | .60 |
| 332 | Pat Fischer | .75 | .30 |
| 333 | Steve Owens | .75 | .30 |
| 334 | Royce Berry | .30 | .15 |
| 335 | Russ Washington | .30 | .15 |
| 336 | Walker Gillette | .30 | .15 |
| 337 | Mark Nordquist | .30 | .15 |
| 338 | James Harris RC | 1.50 | .60 |
| 339 | Warren Koegel | .30 | .15 |
| 340 | Emmitt Thomas | .75 | .30 |
| 341 | Walt Garrison | .75 | .30 |
| 342 | Thom Darden | .30 | .15 |
| 343 | Mike Eischeid | .30 | .15 |
| 344 | Ernie McMillan | .30 | .15 |
| 345 | Nick Buoniconti | 1.50 | .60 |
| 346 | George Farmer | .30 | .15 |
| 347 | Sam Adams OL | .30 | .15 |
| 348 | Larry Cipa | .30 | .15 |
| 349 | Bob Moore | .30 | .15 |
| 350 | Otis Armstrong RC | 1.50 | .60 |
| 351 | George Blanda RB | 3.00 | 1.50 |
| 352 | Fred Cox RB | .75 | .30 |
| 353 | Tom Dempsey RB | .75 | .30 |
| 354 | Ken Houston RB | 1.50 | .60 |
| 355 | O.J.Simpson RB | 5.00 | 2.50 |
| 356 | Ron Smith RB | .75 | .30 |
| 357 | Bob Atkins | .30 | .15 |
| 358 | Pat Sullivan | .75 | .30 |
| 359 | Joe DeLamielleure | 2.50 | 1.00 |
| 360 | Lawr. McCutcheon RC | 1.50 | .60 |
| 361 | David Lee | .30 | .15 |
| 362 | Mike McCoy DT | .30 | .15 |
| 363 | Skip Vanderbundt | .30 | .15 |
| 364 | Mark Moseley | .75 | .30 |
| 365 | Lem Barney | 1.50 | .60 |
| 366 | Doug Dressler | .30 | .15 |
| 367 | Dan Fouts RC | 40.00 | 20.00 |
| 368 | Bob Hyland | .30 | .15 |
| 369 | John Outlaw | .30 | .15 |
| 370 | Roy Gerela | .30 | .15 |
| 371 | Isiah Robertson | .75 | .30 |
| 372 | Jerome Barkum | .30 | .15 |
| 373 | Ed Podolak | .30 | .15 |
| 374 | Milt Morin | .30 | .15 |
| 375 | John Niland | .30 | .15 |
| 376 | Checklist 265-396 UER | 4.00 | 2.00 |
| 377 | Ken Iman | .30 | .15 |
| 378 | Manny Fernandez | .75 | .30 |
| 379 | Dave Gallagher | .30 | .15 |
| 380 | Ken Stabler | 15.00 | 7.50 |
| 381 | Mack Herron | .30 | .15 |
| 382 | Bill McClard | .30 | .15 |
| 383 | Ray May | .30 | .15 |
| 384 | Don Hansen | .30 | .15 |
| 385 | Elvin Bethea | 1.50 | .60 |
| 386 | Joe Scibelli | .30 | .15 |
| 387 | Neal Craig | .30 | .15 |
| 388 | Marty Domres | .30 | .15 |
| 389 | Ken Ellis | .30 | .15 |
| 390 | Charle Young | .75 | .30 |
| 391 | Tommy Hart | .30 | .15 |
| 392 | Moses Denson | .30 | .15 |
| 393 | Larry Walton | .30 | .15 |
| 394 | Dave Green | .30 | .15 |
| 395 | Ron Johnson | .75 | .30 |
| 396 | Ed Bradley RC | .30 | .15 |
| 397 | J.T. Thomas | .30 | .15 |

| | | |
|---|---|---|
| ❏ 398 Jim Bailey | .30 | .15 |
| ❏ 399 Barry Pearson | .30 | .15 |
| ❏ 400 Fran Tarkenton | 8.00 | 4.00 |
| ❏ 401 Jack Rudnay | .30 | .15 |
| ❏ 402 Rayfield Wright | .75 | .30 |
| ❏ 403 Roger Wehrli | 1.00 | .40 |
| ❏ 404 Vern Den Herder | .30 | .15 |
| ❏ 405 Fred Biletnikoff | 3.00 | 1.50 |
| ❏ 406 Ken Grandberry | .30 | .15 |
| ❏ 407 Bob Adams | .30 | .15 |
| ❏ 408 Jim Merlo | .30 | .15 |
| ❏ 409 John Pitts | .30 | .15 |
| ❏ 410 Dave Osborn | .75 | .30 |
| ❏ 411 Dennis Havig | .30 | .15 |
| ❏ 412 Bob Johnson | .30 | .15 |
| ❏ 413 Ken Burrough UER | .75 | .30 |
| ❏ 414 Jim Cheyunski | .30 | .15 |
| ❏ 415 MacArthur Lane | .30 | .15 |
| ❏ 416 Joe Theismann RC | 25.00 | 12.50 |
| ❏ 417 Mike Boryla RC | .30 | .15 |
| ❏ 418 Bruce Taylor | .30 | .15 |
| ❏ 419 Chris Hanburger | .75 | .30 |
| ❏ 420 Tom Mack | 1.50 | .60 |
| ❏ 421 Errol Mann | .30 | .15 |
| ❏ 422 Jack Gregory | .30 | .15 |
| ❏ 423 Harrison Davis | .30 | .15 |
| ❏ 424 Burgess Owens | .30 | .15 |
| ❏ 425 Joe Greene | 5.00 | 2.50 |
| ❏ 426 Morris Stroud | .30 | .15 |
| ❏ 427 John DeMarie | .30 | .15 |
| ❏ 428 Mel Renfro | 1.50 | .60 |
| ❏ 429 Cid Edwards | .30 | .15 |
| ❏ 430 Mike Reid | 1.50 | .60 |
| ❏ 431 Jack Mildren RC | .30 | .15 |
| ❏ 432 Jerry Simmons | .30 | .15 |
| ❏ 433 Ron Yary | 1.50 | .60 |
| ❏ 434 Howard Stevens | .30 | .15 |
| ❏ 435 Ray Guy | 2.00 | 1.00 |
| ❏ 436 Tommy Nobis | 1.50 | .60 |
| ❏ 437 Solomon Freelon | .30 | .15 |
| ❏ 438 J.D. Hill | .75 | .30 |
| ❏ 439 Toni Linhart | .30 | .15 |
| ❏ 440 Dick Anderson | .75 | .30 |
| ❏ 441 Guy Morriss | .30 | .15 |
| ❏ 442 Bob Hoskins | .30 | .15 |
| ❏ 443 John Hadl | 1.50 | .60 |
| ❏ 444 Roy Jefferson | .30 | .15 |
| ❏ 445 Charlie Sanders | 1.00 | .40 |
| ❏ 446 Pat Curran | .30 | .15 |
| ❏ 447 David Knight | .30 | .15 |
| ❏ 448 Bob Brown DT | .30 | .15 |
| ❏ 449 Pete Gogolak | .30 | .15 |
| ❏ 450 Terry Metcalf | 1.50 | .60 |
| ❏ 451 Bill Bergey | 1.50 | .60 |
| ❏ 452 Dan Abramowicz HL | .75 | .30 |
| ❏ 453 Otis Armstrong HL | .75 | .30 |
| ❏ 454 Cliff Branch HL | 1.50 | .60 |
| ❏ 455 John James HL | .30 | .15 |
| ❏ 456 Lydell Mitchell HL | .75 | .30 |
| ❏ 457 Lemar Parrish HL | .75 | .30 |
| ❏ 458 Ken Stabler HL | 5.00 | 2.50 |
| ❏ 459 Lynn Swann HL | 8.00 | 4.00 |
| ❏ 460 Emmitt Thomas HL | .30 | .15 |
| ❏ 461 Terry Bradshaw | 20.00 | 10.00 |
| ❏ 462 Jerrel Wilson | .30 | .15 |
| ❏ 463 Walter Johnson | .30 | .15 |
| ❏ 464 Golden Richards | .75 | .30 |
| ❏ 465 Tommy Casanova | .75 | .30 |
| ❏ 466 Randy Jackson | .30 | .15 |
| ❏ 467 Ron Bolton | .30 | .15 |
| ❏ 468 Joe Owens | .30 | .15 |
| ❏ 469 Wally Hilgenberg | .75 | .30 |
| ❏ 470 Riley Odoms | .75 | .30 |
| ❏ 471 Otis Sistrunk | .75 | .30 |
| ❏ 472 Eddie Ray | .30 | .15 |
| ❏ 473 Reggie McKenzie | .75 | .30 |
| ❏ 474 Elbert Drungo | .30 | .15 |
| ❏ 475 Mercury Morris | 1.50 | .60 |
| ❏ 476 Dan Dickel | .30 | .15 |
| ❏ 477 Merritt Kersey | .30 | .15 |
| ❏ 478 Mike Holmes | .30 | .15 |
| ❏ 479 Clarence Williams | .30 | .15 |
| ❏ 480 Billy Kilmer | 1.50 | .60 |
| ❏ 481 Altie Taylor | .30 | .15 |
| ❏ 482 Dave Elmendorf | .30 | .15 |

| | | |
|---|---|---|
| ❏ 483 Bob Rowe | .30 | .15 |
| ❏ 484 Pete Athas | .30 | .15 |
| ❏ 485 Winston Hill | .30 | .15 |
| ❏ 486 Bo Matthews | .30 | .15 |
| ❏ 487 Earl Thomas | .30 | .15 |
| ❏ 488 Jan Stenerud | 1.50 | .60 |
| ❏ 489 Steve Holden | .30 | .15 |
| ❏ 490 Cliff Harris RC | 5.00 | 2.50 |
| ❏ 491 Boobie Clark RC | .75 | .30 |
| ❏ 492 Joe Taylor | .30 | .15 |
| ❏ 493 Tom Neville | .30 | .15 |
| ❏ 494 Wayne Colman | .30 | .15 |
| ❏ 495 Jim Mitchell TE | .30 | .15 |
| ❏ 496 Paul Krause | 1.50 | .60 |
| ❏ 497 Jim Otto | 1.50 | .60 |
| ❏ 498 John Rowser | .30 | .15 |
| ❏ 499 Larry Little | 1.50 | .60 |
| ❏ 500 O.J. Simpson | 10.00 | 5.00 |
| ❏ 501 John Dutton RC | 1.50 | .60 |
| ❏ 502 Pat Hughes | .30 | .15 |
| ❏ 503 Malcolm Snider | .30 | .15 |
| ❏ 504 Fred Willis | .30 | .15 |
| ❏ 505 Harold Jackson | 1.50 | .60 |
| ❏ 506 Mike Bragg | .30 | .15 |
| ❏ 507 Jerry Sherk | .75 | .30 |
| ❏ 508 Mirro Roder | .30 | .15 |
| ❏ 509 Tom Sullivan | .30 | .15 |
| ❏ 510 Jim Hart | 1.50 | .60 |
| ❏ 511 Cedrick Hardman | .30 | .15 |
| ❏ 512 Blaine Nye | .30 | .15 |
| ❏ 513 Elmo Wright | .30 | .15 |
| ❏ 514 Herb Orvis | .30 | .15 |
| ❏ 515 Richard Caster | .75 | .30 |
| ❏ 516 Doug Kotar RC | .30 | .15 |
| ❏ 517 Checklist 397-528 | 4.00 | 2.00 |
| ❏ 518 Jesse Freitas | .30 | .15 |
| ❏ 519 Ken Houston | 1.50 | .60 |
| ❏ 520 Alan Page | 1.50 | .60 |
| ❏ 521 Tim Foley | .75 | .30 |
| ❏ 522 Bill Olds | .30 | .15 |
| ❏ 523 Bobby Maples | .30 | .15 |
| ❏ 524 Cliff Branch RC | 15.00 | 7.50 |
| ❏ 525 Merlin Olsen | 1.50 | .60 |
| ❏ 526 AFC Champs/Brad./Harris | 4.00 | 2.00 |
| ❏ 527 NFC Champs/Foreman | 1.50 | .60 |
| ❏ 528 Super Bowl IX/Bradshaw | 5.00 | 2.50 |

**1976 Topps**

| | | |
|---|---|---|
| ❏ COMPLETE SET (528) | 350.00 | 200.00 |
| ❏ 1 George Blanda RB ! | 5.00 | 2.50 |
| ❏ 2 Neal Colzie RB | .30 | .15 |
| ❏ 3 Chuck Foreman RB | .75 | .30 |
| ❏ 4 Jim Marshall RB | .75 | .30 |
| ❏ 5 Terry Metcalf RB | .75 | .30 |
| ❏ 6 O.J. Simpson RB | 3.00 | 1.50 |
| ❏ 7 Fran Tarkenton RB | 3.00 | 1.50 |
| ❏ 8 Charley Taylor RB | 1.50 | .60 |
| ❏ 9 Ernie Holmes | .75 | .30 |
| ❏ 10 Ken Anderson | 1.50 | .60 |
| ❏ 11 Bobby Bryant | .30 | .15 |
| ❏ 12 Jim Smith | .30 | .15 |
| ❏ 13 David Lee | .30 | .15 |
| ❏ 14 Robert Newhouse RC | 1.50 | .60 |
| ❏ 15 Vern Den Herder | .30 | .15 |
| ❏ 16 John Hannah | 4.00 | 2.00 |
| ❏ 17 J.D. Hill | .75 | .30 |
| ❏ 18 James Harris | .75 | .30 |
| ❏ 19 Willie Buchanon | .30 | .15 |

| | | |
|---|---|---|
| ❏ 20 Charle Young | .75 | .30 |
| ❏ 21 Jim Yarbrough | .30 | .15 |
| ❏ 22 Ronnie Coleman | .30 | .15 |
| ❏ 23 Don Cockroft | .30 | .15 |
| ❏ 24 Willie Lanier | 1.50 | .60 |
| ❏ 25 Fred Biletnikoff | 3.00 | 1.50 |
| ❏ 26 Ron Yankowski | .30 | .15 |
| ❏ 27 Spider Lockhart | .30 | .15 |
| ❏ 28 Bob Johnson | .30 | .15 |
| ❏ 29 J.T. Thomas | .30 | .15 |
| ❏ 30 Ron Yary | 1.50 | .60 |
| ❏ 31 Brad Dusek RC | .30 | .15 |
| ❏ 32 Raymond Chester | .75 | .30 |
| ❏ 33 Larry Little | 1.50 | .60 |
| ❏ 34 Pat Leahy RC | 1.50 | .60 |
| ❏ 35 Steve Bartkowski RC | 4.00 | 2.00 |
| ❏ 36 Tom Myers | .30 | .15 |
| ❏ 37 Bill Van Heusen | .30 | .15 |
| ❏ 38 Russ Washington | .30 | .15 |
| ❏ 39 Tom Sullivan | .30 | .15 |
| ❏ 40 Curley Culp | .75 | .30 |
| ❏ 41 Johnnie Gray | .30 | .15 |
| ❏ 42 Bob Klein | .30 | .15 |
| ❏ 43 Lem Barney | 1.50 | .60 |
| ❏ 44 Harvey Martin RC | 6.00 | 3.00 |
| ❏ 45 Reggie Rucker | .75 | .30 |
| ❏ 46 Neil Clabo | .30 | .15 |
| ❏ 47 Ray Hamilton | .30 | .15 |
| ❏ 48 Joe Ferguson | .75 | .30 |
| ❏ 49 Ed Podolak | .30 | .15 |
| ❏ 50 Ray Guy | 1.50 | .60 |
| ❏ 51 Glen Edwards | .30 | .15 |
| ❏ 52 Jim LeClair | .30 | .15 |
| ❏ 53 Mike Barnes | .30 | .15 |
| ❏ 54 Nat Moore RC | 1.50 | .60 |
| ❏ 55 Billy Kilmer | 1.50 | .60 |
| ❏ 56 Larry Stallings | .30 | .15 |
| ❏ 57 Jack Gregory | .30 | .15 |
| ❏ 58 Steve Mike-Mayer | .30 | .15 |
| ❏ 59 Virgil Livers | .30 | .15 |
| ❏ 60 Jerry Sherk | .75 | .30 |
| ❏ 61 Guy Morriss | .30 | .15 |
| ❏ 62 Barty Smith | .30 | .15 |
| ❏ 63 Jerome Barkum | .30 | .15 |
| ❏ 64 Ira Gordon | .30 | .15 |
| ❏ 65 Paul Krause | 1.50 | .60 |
| ❏ 66 John McMakin | .30 | .15 |
| ❏ 67 Checklist 1 | 3.00 | 1.50 |
| ❏ 68 Charlie Johnson UER | .75 | .30 |
| ❏ 69 Tommy Nobis | 1.50 | .60 |
| ❏ 70 Lydell Mitchell | .75 | .30 |
| ❏ 71 Vern Holland | .30 | .15 |
| ❏ 72 Tim Foley | .75 | .30 |
| ❏ 73 Golden Richards | .75 | .30 |
| ❏ 74 Bryant Salter | .30 | .15 |
| ❏ 75 Terry Bradshaw | 20.00 | 10.00 |
| ❏ 76 Ted Hendricks | 1.50 | .60 |
| ❏ 77 Rich Saul RC | .30 | .15 |
| ❏ 78 John Smith RC | .30 | .15 |
| ❏ 79 Altie Taylor | .30 | .15 |
| ❏ 80 Cedrick Hardman | .30 | .15 |
| ❏ 81 Ken Payne | .30 | .15 |
| ❏ 82 Zeke Moore | .30 | .15 |
| ❏ 83 Alvin Maxson | .30 | .15 |
| ❏ 84 Wally Hilgenberg | .30 | .15 |
| ❏ 85 John Niland | .30 | .15 |
| ❏ 86 Mike Sensibaugh | .30 | .15 |
| ❏ 87 Ron Johnson | .75 | .30 |
| ❏ 88 Winston Hill | .30 | .15 |
| ❏ 89 Charlie Joiner | 4.00 | 2.00 |
| ❏ 90 Roger Wehrli | .75 | .30 |
| ❏ 91 Mike Bragg | .30 | .15 |
| ❏ 92 Dan Dickel | .30 | .15 |
| ❏ 93 Earl Morrall | .75 | .30 |
| ❏ 94 Pat Toomay | .30 | .15 |
| ❏ 95 Gary Garrison | .30 | .15 |
| ❏ 96 Ken Geddes | .30 | .15 |
| ❏ 97 Mike Current | .30 | .15 |
| ❏ 98 Bob Avellini RC | .75 | .30 |
| ❏ 99 Dave Pureifory | .30 | .15 |
| ❏ 100 Franco Harris | 8.00 | 4.00 |
| ❏ 101 Randy Logan | .30 | .15 |

## 1976 Topps

| | | |
|---|---|---|
| ❏ 102 John Fitzgerald | .30 | .15 |
| ❏ 103 Gregg Bingham RC | .75 | .30 |
| ❏ 104 Jim Plunkett | 1.50 | .60 |
| ❏ 105 Carl Eller | 1.50 | .60 |
| ❏ 106 Larry Walton | .30 | .15 |
| ❏ 107 Clarence Scott | .30 | .15 |
| ❏ 108 Skip Vanderbundt | .30 | .15 |
| ❏ 109 Boobie Clark | .75 | .30 |
| ❏ 110 Tom Mack | 1.50 | .60 |
| ❏ 111 Bruce Laird | .30 | .15 |
| ❏ 112 Dave Dalby RC | .30 | .15 |
| ❏ 113 John Leypoldt | .30 | .15 |
| ❏ 114 Barry Pearson | .30 | .15 |
| ❏ 115 Larry Brown | .75 | .30 |
| ❏ 116 Jackie Smith | 1.50 | .60 |
| ❏ 117 Pat Hughes | .30 | .15 |
| ❏ 118 Al Woodall | .30 | .15 |
| ❏ 119 John Zook | .30 | .15 |
| ❏ 120 Jake Scott | .75 | .30 |
| ❏ 121 Rich Glover | .30 | .15 |
| ❏ 122 Ernie Jackson | .30 | .15 |
| ❏ 123 Otis Armstrong | 1.50 | .60 |
| ❏ 124 Bob Grim | .30 | .15 |
| ❏ 125 Jeff Siemon | .75 | .30 |
| ❏ 126 Harold Hart | .30 | .15 |
| ❏ 127 John DeMarie | .30 | .15 |
| ❏ 128 Dan Fouts | 12.00 | 6.00 |
| ❏ 129 Jim Kearney | .30 | .15 |
| ❏ 130 John Dutton | .75 | .30 |
| ❏ 131 Calvin Hill | 1.50 | .60 |
| ❏ 132 Toni Fritsch | .30 | .15 |
| ❏ 133 Ron Jessie | .30 | .15 |
| ❏ 134 Don Nottingham | .30 | .15 |
| ❏ 135 Lemar Parrish | .30 | .15 |
| ❏ 136 Russ Francis RC | 1.50 | .60 |
| ❏ 137 Joe Reed | .30 | .15 |
| ❏ 138 C.L. Whittington | .30 | .15 |
| ❏ 139 Otis Sistrunk | .75 | .30 |
| ❏ 140 Lynn Swann | 20.00 | 10.00 |
| ❏ 141 Jim Carter | .30 | .15 |
| ❏ 142 Mike Montler | .30 | .15 |
| ❏ 143 Walter Johnson | .30 | .15 |
| ❏ 144 Doug Kotar | .30 | .15 |
| ❏ 145 Roman Gabriel | 1.50 | .60 |
| ❏ 146 Billy Newsome | .30 | .15 |
| ❏ 147 Ed Bradley | .30 | .15 |
| ❏ 148 Walter Payton RC | 250.00 | 125.00 |
| ❏ 149 Johnnie Fuller | .30 | .15 |
| ❏ 150 Alan Page | 1.50 | .60 |
| ❏ 151 Frank Grant | .30 | .15 |
| ❏ 152 Dave Green | .30 | .15 |
| ❏ 153 Nelson Munsey | .30 | .15 |
| ❏ 154 Jim Mandich | .30 | .15 |
| ❏ 155 Lawrence McCutcheon | 1.50 | .60 |
| ❏ 156 Steve Ramsey | .30 | .15 |
| ❏ 157 Ed Flanagan | .30 | .15 |
| ❏ 158 Randy White RC | 20.00 | 10.00 |
| ❏ 159 Gerry Mullins | .30 | .15 |
| ❏ 160 Jan Stenerud | 1.50 | .60 |
| ❏ 161 Steve Odom | .30 | .15 |
| ❏ 162 Roger Finnie | .30 | .15 |
| ❏ 163 Norm Snead | .75 | .30 |
| ❏ 164 Jeff Van Note | .75 | .30 |
| ❏ 165 Bill Bergey | 1.50 | .60 |
| ❏ 166 Allen Carter | .30 | .15 |
| ❏ 167 Steve Holden | .30 | .15 |
| ❏ 168 Sherman White | .30 | .15 |
| ❏ 169 Bob Berry | .30 | .15 |
| ❏ 170 Ken Houston | 1.50 | .60 |
| ❏ 171 Bill Olds | .30 | .15 |
| ❏ 172 Larry Seiple | .30 | .15 |
| ❏ 173 Cliff Branch | 4.00 | 2.00 |
| ❏ 174 Reggie McKenzie | .75 | .30 |
| ❏ 175 Dan Pastorini | 1.50 | .60 |
| ❏ 176 Paul Naumoff | .30 | .15 |
| ❏ 177 Checklist 133-264 | 3.00 | 1.50 |
| ❏ 178 Durwood Keeton | .30 | .15 |
| ❏ 179 Earl Thomas | .30 | .15 |
| ❏ 180 L.C.Greenwood | 1.50 | .60 |
| ❏ 181 John Outlaw | .30 | .15 |
| ❏ 182 Frank Nunley | .30 | .15 |
| ❏ 183 Dave Jennings RC | .75 | .30 |
| ❏ 184 MacArthur Lane | .30 | .15 |
| ❏ 185 Chester Marcol | .30 | .15 |
| ❏ 186 J.J. Jones | .30 | .15 |
| ❏ 187 Tom DeLeone | .30 | .15 |
| ❏ 188 Steve Zabel | .30 | .15 |
| ❏ 189 Ken Johnson DT | .30 | .15 |
| ❏ 190 Rayfield Wright | .75 | .30 |
| ❏ 191 Brent McClanahan | .30 | .15 |
| ❏ 192 Pat Fischer | .75 | .30 |
| ❏ 193 Roger Carr RC | .75 | .30 |
| ❏ 194 Manny Fernandez | .75 | .30 |
| ❏ 195 Roy Gerela | .30 | .15 |
| ❏ 196 Dave Elmendorf | .30 | .15 |
| ❏ 197 Bob Kowalkowski | .30 | .15 |
| ❏ 198 Phil Villapiano | .75 | .30 |
| ❏ 199 Will Wynn | .30 | .15 |
| ❏ 200 Terry Metcalf | 1.50 | .60 |
| ❏ 201 Tarkenton/Anderson LL | 2.00 | .75 |
| ❏ 202 Receiving Leaders | .75 | .30 |
| ❏ 203 O.J. Simpson/J.Otis LL | 2.50 | 1.25 |
| ❏ 204 Simpson/Foreman LL | 2.50 | 1.25 |
| ❏ 205 M.Blount/P. Krause LL | 1.50 | .60 |
| ❏ 206 Punting Leaders | .75 | .30 |
| ❏ 207 Ken Ellis | .30 | .15 |
| ❏ 208 Ron Saul | .30 | .15 |
| ❏ 209 Toni Linhart | .30 | .15 |
| ❏ 210 Jim Langer | 1.50 | .60 |
| ❏ 211 Jeff Wright S | .30 | .15 |
| ❏ 212 Moses Denson | .30 | .15 |
| ❏ 213 Earl Edwards | .30 | .15 |
| ❏ 214 Walker Gillette | .30 | .15 |
| ❏ 215 Bob Trumpy | .75 | .30 |
| ❏ 216 Emmitt Thomas | .75 | .30 |
| ❏ 217 Lyle Alzado | 1.50 | .60 |
| ❏ 218 Carl Garrett | .75 | .30 |
| ❏ 219 Van Green | .30 | .15 |
| ❏ 220 Jack Lambert RC | 35.00 | 20.00 |
| ❏ 221 Spike Jones | .30 | .15 |
| ❏ 222 John Hadl | 1.50 | .60 |
| ❏ 223 Billy Johnson RC | 1.50 | .60 |
| ❏ 224 Tony McGee DT | .30 | .15 |
| ❏ 225 Preston Pearson | .75 | .30 |
| ❏ 226 Isiah Robertson | .75 | .30 |
| ❏ 227 Errol Mann | .30 | .15 |
| ❏ 228 Paul Seal | .30 | .15 |
| ❏ 229 Roland Harper RC | .30 | .15 |
| ❏ 230 Ed White RC | .75 | .30 |
| ❏ 231 Joe Theismann | 6.00 | 3.00 |
| ❏ 232 Jim Cheyunski | .30 | .15 |
| ❏ 233 Bill Stanfill | .75 | .30 |
| ❏ 234 Marv Hubbard | .30 | .15 |
| ❏ 235 Tommy Casanova | .75 | .30 |
| ❏ 236 Bob Hyland | .30 | .15 |
| ❏ 237 Jesse Freitas | .30 | .15 |
| ❏ 238 Norm Thompson | .30 | .15 |
| ❏ 239 Charlie Smith WR | .30 | .15 |
| ❏ 240 John James | .30 | .15 |
| ❏ 241 Alden Roche | .30 | .15 |
| ❏ 242 Gordon Jolley | .30 | .15 |
| ❏ 243 Larry Ely | .30 | .15 |
| ❏ 244 Richard Caster | .30 | .15 |
| ❏ 245 Joe Greene | 5.00 | 2.00 |
| ❏ 246 Larry Schreiber | .30 | .15 |
| ❏ 247 Terry Schmidt | .30 | .15 |
| ❏ 248 Jerrel Wilson | .30 | .15 |
| ❏ 249 Marty Domres | .30 | .15 |
| ❏ 250 Isaac Curtis | .75 | .30 |
| ❏ 251 Harold McLinton | .30 | .15 |
| ❏ 252 Fred Dryer | 1.50 | .60 |
| ❏ 253 Bill Lenkaitis | .30 | .15 |
| ❏ 254 Don Hardeman | .30 | .15 |
| ❏ 255 Bob Griese | 4.00 | 2.00 |
| ❏ 256 Oscar Roan RC | .30 | .15 |
| ❏ 257 Randy Gradishar RC | 4.00 | 1.50 |
| ❏ 258 Bob Thomas RC | .30 | .15 |
| ❏ 259 Joe Owens | .30 | .15 |
| ❏ 260 Cliff Harris | 1.50 | .60 |
| ❏ 261 Frank Lewis | .30 | .15 |
| ❏ 262 Mike McCoy DT | .30 | .15 |
| ❏ 263 Rickey Young RC | .30 | .15 |
| ❏ 264 Brian Kelley RC | .30 | .15 |
| ❏ 265 Charlie Sanders | .75 | .30 |
| ❏ 266 Jim Hart | 1.50 | .60 |
| ❏ 267 Greg Gantt | .30 | .15 |
| ❏ 268 John Ward | .30 | .15 |
| ❏ 269 Al Beauchamp | .30 | .15 |
| ❏ 270 Jack Tatum | 1.50 | .60 |
| ❏ 271 Jim Lash | .30 | .15 |
| ❏ 272 Diron Talbert | .30 | .15 |
| ❏ 273 Checklist 265-396 | 3.00 | 1.50 |
| ❏ 274 Steve Spurrier | 8.00 | 3.00 |
| ❏ 275 Greg Pruitt | 1.50 | .60 |
| ❏ 276 Jim Mitchell TE | .30 | .15 |
| ❏ 277 Jack Rudnay | .30 | .15 |
| ❏ 278 Freddie Solomon RC | .75 | .30 |
| ❏ 279 Frank LeMaster | .30 | .15 |
| ❏ 280 Wally Chambers | .30 | .15 |
| ❏ 281 Mike Collier | .30 | .15 |
| ❏ 282 Clarence Williams | .30 | .15 |
| ❏ 283 Mitch Hoopes | .30 | .15 |
| ❏ 284 Ron Bolton | .30 | .15 |
| ❏ 285 Harold Jackson | 1.50 | .60 |
| ❏ 286 Greg Landry | .75 | .30 |
| ❏ 287 Tony Greene | .30 | .15 |
| ❏ 288 Howard Stevens | .30 | .15 |
| ❏ 289 Roy Jefferson | .30 | .15 |
| ❏ 290 Jim Bakken | .30 | .15 |
| ❏ 291 Doug Sutherland | .30 | .15 |
| ❏ 292 Marvin Cobb RC | .30 | .15 |
| ❏ 293 Mack Alston | .30 | .15 |
| ❏ 294 Rod McNeill | .30 | .15 |
| ❏ 295 Gene Upshaw | 1.50 | .60 |
| ❏ 296 Dave Gallagher | .30 | .15 |
| ❏ 297 Larry Ball | .30 | .15 |
| ❏ 298 Ron Howard | .30 | .15 |
| ❏ 299 Don Strock RC | 1.50 | .60 |
| ❏ 300 O.J. Simpson | 8.00 | 4.00 |
| ❏ 301 Ray Mansfield | .30 | .15 |
| ❏ 302 Larry Marshall | .30 | .15 |
| ❏ 303 Dick Himes | .30 | .15 |
| ❏ 304 Ray Wersching RC | .30 | .15 |
| ❏ 305 John Riggins | 4.00 | 2.00 |
| ❏ 306 Bob Parsons | .30 | .15 |
| ❏ 307 Ray Brown DB | .30 | .15 |
| ❏ 308 Len Dawson | 3.00 | 1.50 |
| ❏ 309 Andy Maurer | .30 | .15 |
| ❏ 310 Jack Youngblood | 1.50 | .60 |
| ❏ 311 Essex Johnson | .30 | .15 |
| ❏ 312 Stan White | .30 | .15 |
| ❏ 313 Drew Pearson | 5.00 | 2.00 |
| ❏ 314 Rockne Freitas | .30 | .15 |
| ❏ 315 Mercury Morris | 1.50 | .60 |
| ❏ 316 Willie Alexander | .30 | .15 |
| ❏ 317 Paul Warfield | 3.00 | 1.50 |
| ❏ 318 Bob Chandler | .75 | .30 |
| ❏ 319 Bobby Walden | .30 | .15 |
| ❏ 320 Riley Odoms | .75 | .30 |
| ❏ 321 Mike Boryla | .30 | .15 |
| ❏ 322 Bruce Van Dyke | .30 | .15 |
| ❏ 323 Pete Banaszak | .30 | .15 |
| ❏ 324 Darryl Stingley | 1.50 | .60 |
| ❏ 325 John Mendenhall | .30 | .15 |
| ❏ 326 Dan Dierdorf | 2.00 | .75 |
| ❏ 327 Bruce Taylor | .30 | .15 |
| ❏ 328 Don McCauley | .30 | .15 |
| ❏ 329 John Reaves UER | .30 | .15 |
| ❏ 330 Chris Hanburger | .75 | .30 |
| ❏ 331 NFC Champs/Staubach | 3.00 | 1.50 |
| ❏ 332 AFC Champs/F.Harris | 2.00 | .75 |
| ❏ 333 Super Bowl X/Bradshaw | 2.50 | 1.25 |
| ❏ 334 Godwin Turk | .30 | .15 |
| ❏ 335 Dick Anderson | .75 | .30 |
| ❏ 336 Woody Green | .30 | .15 |
| ❏ 337 Pat Curran | .30 | .15 |
| ❏ 338 Council Rudolph | .30 | .15 |
| ❏ 339 Joe Lavender | .30 | .15 |

| | | |
|---|---|---|
| ☐ 340 John Gilliam | .75 | .30 |
| ☐ 341 Steve Furness RC | .75 | .30 |
| ☐ 342 D.D. Lewis | .75 | .30 |
| ☐ 343 Duane Carrell | .30 | .15 |
| ☐ 344 Jon Morris | .30 | .15 |
| ☐ 345 John Brockington | .75 | .30 |
| ☐ 346 Mike Phipps | .30 | .15 |
| ☐ 347 Lyle Blackwood RC | .30 | .15 |
| ☐ 348 Julius Adams | .30 | .15 |
| ☐ 349 Terry Hermeling | .30 | .15 |
| ☐ 350 Rolland Lawrence RC | .30 | .15 |
| ☐ 351 Glenn Doughty | .30 | .15 |
| ☐ 352 Doug Swift | .30 | .15 |
| ☐ 353 Mike Strachan | .30 | .15 |
| ☐ 354 Craig Morton | 1.50 | .60 |
| ☐ 355 George Blanda | 5.00 | 2.50 |
| ☐ 356 Garry Puetz | .30 | .15 |
| ☐ 357 Carl Mauck | .30 | .15 |
| ☐ 358 Walt Patulski | .30 | .15 |
| ☐ 359 Stu Voigt | .30 | .15 |
| ☐ 360 Fred Carr | .30 | .15 |
| ☐ 361 Po James | .30 | .15 |
| ☐ 362 Otis Taylor | 1.50 | .60 |
| ☐ 363 Jeff West | .30 | .15 |
| ☐ 364 Gary Huff | .75 | .30 |
| ☐ 365 Dwight White | .75 | .30 |
| ☐ 366 Dan Ryczek | .30 | .15 |
| ☐ 367 Jon Keyworth RC | .30 | .15 |
| ☐ 368 Mel Renfro | 1.50 | .60 |
| ☐ 369 Bruce Coslet RC | 1.50 | .60 |
| ☐ 370 Len Hauss | .30 | .15 |
| ☐ 371 Rick Volk | .30 | .15 |
| ☐ 372 Howard Twilley | .75 | .30 |
| ☐ 373 Cullen Bryant RC | .75 | .30 |
| ☐ 374 Bob Babich | .30 | .15 |
| ☐ 375 Herman Weaver | .30 | .15 |
| ☐ 376 Steve Grogan RC | 3.00 | 1.25 |
| ☐ 377 Bubba Smith | 1.50 | .60 |
| ☐ 378 Burgess Owens | .30 | .15 |
| ☐ 379 Al Matthews | .30 | .15 |
| ☐ 380 Art Shell | 1.50 | .60 |
| ☐ 381 Larry Brown | .30 | .15 |
| ☐ 382 Horst Muhlmann | .30 | .15 |
| ☐ 383 Ahmad Rashad | 2.50 | 1.25 |
| ☐ 384 Bobby Maples | .30 | .15 |
| ☐ 385 Jim Marshall | 1.50 | .60 |
| ☐ 386 Joe Dawkins | .30 | .15 |
| ☐ 387 Dennis Partee | .30 | .15 |
| ☐ 388 Eddie McMillan RC | .30 | .15 |
| ☐ 389 Randy Johnson | .30 | .15 |
| ☐ 390 Bob Kuechenberg | .30 | .15 |
| ☐ 391 Rufus Mayes | .30 | .15 |
| ☐ 392 Lloyd Mumphord | .30 | .15 |
| ☐ 393 Ike Harris | .30 | .15 |
| ☐ 394 Dave Hampton | .30 | .15 |
| ☐ 395 Roger Staubach | 20.00 | 10.00 |
| ☐ 396 Doug Buffone | .30 | .15 |
| ☐ 397 Howard Fest | .30 | .15 |
| ☐ 398 Wayne Mulligan | .30 | .15 |
| ☐ 399 Bill Bradley | .75 | .30 |
| ☐ 400 Chuck Foreman | 1.50 | .60 |
| ☐ 401 Jack Snow | .75 | .30 |
| ☐ 402 Bob Howard | .30 | .15 |
| ☐ 403 John Matuszak | 1.50 | .60 |
| ☐ 404 Bill Munson | .75 | .30 |
| ☐ 405 Andy Russell | .75 | .30 |
| ☐ 406 Skip Butler | .30 | .15 |
| ☐ 407 Hugh McKinnis | .30 | .15 |
| ☐ 408 Bob Penchion | .30 | .15 |
| ☐ 409 Mike Bass | .30 | .15 |
| ☐ 410 George Kunz | .30 | .15 |
| ☐ 411 Ron Pritchard | .30 | .15 |
| ☐ 412 Barry Smith | .30 | .15 |
| ☐ 413 Norm Bulaich | .30 | .15 |
| ☐ 414 Marv Bateman | .30 | .15 |
| ☐ 415 Ken Stabler | 12.00 | 6.00 |
| ☐ 416 Conrad Dobler | .75 | .30 |
| ☐ 417 Bob Tucker | .75 | .30 |
| ☐ 418 Gene Washington 49er | .75 | .30 |
| ☐ 419 Ed Marinaro | 1.50 | .60 |
| ☐ 420 Jack Ham | 4.00 | 2.00 |
| ☐ 421 Jim Turner | .30 | .15 |
| ☐ 422 Chris Fletcher | .30 | .15 |
| ☐ 423 Carl Barzilauskas | .30 | .15 |
| ☐ 424 Robert Brazile RC | 1.50 | .60 |
| ☐ 425 Harold Carmichael | 2.00 | .75 |
| ☐ 426 Ron Jaworski RC | 5.00 | 2.00 |
| ☐ 427 Ed Too Tall Jones RC | 20.00 | 10.00 |
| ☐ 428 Larry McCarren | .30 | .15 |
| ☐ 429 Mike Thomas RC | .30 | .15 |
| ☐ 430 Joe DeLamielleure | 1.50 | .60 |
| ☐ 431 Tom Blanchard | .30 | .15 |
| ☐ 432 Ron Carpenter | .30 | .15 |
| ☐ 433 Levi Johnson | .30 | .15 |
| ☐ 434 Sam Cunningham | .75 | .30 |
| ☐ 435 Garo Yepremian | .75 | .30 |
| ☐ 436 Mike Livingston | .30 | .15 |
| ☐ 437 Larry Csonka | 4.00 | 2.00 |
| ☐ 438 Doug Dieken | .75 | .30 |
| ☐ 439 Bill Lueck | .30 | .15 |
| ☐ 440 Tom MacLeod | .30 | .15 |
| ☐ 441 Mick Tingelhoff | .75 | .30 |
| ☐ 442 Terry Hanratty | .75 | .30 |
| ☐ 443 Mike Siani | .30 | .15 |
| ☐ 444 Dwight Harrison | .30 | .15 |
| ☐ 445 Jim Otis | .75 | .30 |
| ☐ 446 Jack Reynolds | .75 | .30 |
| ☐ 447 Jean Fugett RC | .75 | .30 |
| ☐ 448 Dave Beverly | .30 | .15 |
| ☐ 449 Bernard Jackson RC | .30 | .15 |
| ☐ 450 Charley Taylor | 2.00 | .75 |
| ☐ 451 Atlanta Falcons CL | 2.00 | .75 |
| ☐ 452 Baltimore Colts CL | 2.00 | .75 |
| ☐ 453 Buffalo Bills CL | 2.00 | .75 |
| ☐ 454 Chicago Bears CL | 2.00 | .75 |
| ☐ 455 Cincinnati Bengals CL | 2.00 | .75 |
| ☐ 456 Cleveland Browns CL | 2.00 | .75 |
| ☐ 457 Dallas Cowboys CL | 2.00 | .75 |
| ☐ 458 Denver Broncos CL UER | 2.00 | .75 |
| ☐ 459 Detroit Lions CL | 2.00 | .75 |
| ☐ 460 Green Bay Packers CL | 2.00 | .75 |
| ☐ 461 Houston Oilers CL | 2.00 | .75 |
| ☐ 462 Kansas City Chiefs CL | 2.00 | .75 |
| ☐ 463 Los Angeles Rams CL | 2.00 | .75 |
| ☐ 464 Miami Dolphins CL | 2.00 | .75 |
| ☐ 465 Minnesota Vikings CL | 2.00 | .75 |
| ☐ 466 New England Patriots CL | 2.00 | .75 |
| ☐ 467 New Orleans Saints CL | 2.00 | .75 |
| ☐ 468 New York Giants CL | 2.00 | .75 |
| ☐ 469 New York Jets CL | 2.00 | .75 |
| ☐ 470 Oakland Raiders CL | 2.00 | .75 |
| ☐ 471 Philadelphia Eagles CL | 2.00 | .75 |
| ☐ 472 Pittsburgh Steelers CL | 2.00 | .75 |
| ☐ 473 St. Louis Cardinals CL | 2.00 | .75 |
| ☐ 474 San Diego Chargers CL | 2.00 | .75 |
| ☐ 475 San Francisco 49ers CL | 2.00 | .75 |
| ☐ 476 Seattle Seahawks CL | 2.00 | .75 |
| ☐ 477 Tampa Bay Buccaneers CL | 2.00 | .75 |
| ☐ 478 Washington Redskins CL | 2.00 | .75 |
| ☐ 479 Fred Cox | .30 | .15 |
| ☐ 480 Mel Blount | 6.00 | 3.00 |
| ☐ 481 John Bunting RC | .75 | .30 |
| ☐ 482 Ken Mendenhall | .30 | .15 |
| ☐ 483 Will Harrell | .30 | .15 |
| ☐ 484 Marlin Briscoe | .30 | .15 |
| ☐ 485 Archie Manning | 1.50 | .60 |
| ☐ 486 Tody Smith | .30 | .15 |
| ☐ 487 George Hunt | .30 | .15 |
| ☐ 488 Roscoe Word | .30 | .15 |
| ☐ 489 Paul Seymour | .30 | .15 |
| ☐ 490 Lee Roy Jordan | 1.50 | .60 |
| ☐ 491 Chip Myers | .30 | .15 |
| ☐ 492 Norm Evans | .30 | .15 |
| ☐ 493 Jim Bertelsen | .30 | .15 |
| ☐ 494 Mark Moseley | .75 | .30 |
| ☐ 495 George Buehler | .30 | .15 |
| ☐ 496 Charlie Hall | .30 | .15 |
| ☐ 497 Marvin Upshaw | .30 | .15 |
| ☐ 498 Tom Banks RC | .30 | .15 |
| ☐ 499 Randy Vataha | .30 | .15 |
| ☐ 500 Fran Tarkenton | 6.00 | 3.00 |
| ☐ 501 Mike Wagner | .75 | .30 |
| ☐ 502 Art Malone | .30 | .15 |
| ☐ 503 Fred Cook | .30 | .15 |
| ☐ 504 Rich McGeorge | .30 | .15 |
| ☐ 505 Ken Burrough | .75 | .30 |
| ☐ 506 Nick Mike-Mayer | .30 | .15 |
| ☐ 507 Checklist 397-528 | 3.00 | 1.50 |
| ☐ 508 Steve Owens | .75 | .30 |
| ☐ 509 Brad Van Pelt RC | .75 | .30 |
| ☐ 510 Ken Riley | .75 | .30 |
| ☐ 511 Art Thoms | .30 | .15 |
| ☐ 512 Ed Bell | .30 | .15 |
| ☐ 513 Tom Wittum | .30 | .15 |
| ☐ 514 Jim Braxton | .30 | .15 |
| ☐ 515 Nick Buoniconti | 1.50 | .60 |
| ☐ 516 Brian Sipe RC | 6.00 | 2.50 |
| ☐ 517 Jim Lynch | .30 | .15 |
| ☐ 518 Prentice McCray | .30 | .15 |
| ☐ 519 Tom Dempsey | .30 | .15 |
| ☐ 520 Mel Gray | .75 | .30 |
| ☐ 521 Nate Wright | .30 | .15 |
| ☐ 522 Rocky Bleier | 6.00 | 3.00 |
| ☐ 523 Dennis Johnson RC | .30 | .15 |
| ☐ 524 Jerry Sisemore | .30 | .15 |
| ☐ 525 Bert Jones | .75 | .30 |
| ☐ 526 Perry Smith | .30 | .15 |
| ☐ 527 Blaine Nye | .30 | .15 |
| ☐ 528 Bob Moore ! | 1.50 | .60 |

## 1977 Topps

| | | |
|---|---|---|
| ☐ COMPLETE SET (528) | 250.00 | 125.00 |
| ☐ 1 K.Stabler/J.Harris LL | 2.50 | 1.25 |
| ☐ 2 Drew Pearson/M.Lane LL | 1.00 | .40 |
| ☐ 3 W.Payton/Simpson LL | 10.00 | 5.00 |
| ☐ 4 Scoring Leaders | .50 | .20 |
| ☐ 5 Interception Leaders | .50 | .20 |
| ☐ 6 Punting Leaders | .25 | .10 |
| ☐ 7 Mike Phipps | .50 | .20 |
| ☐ 8 Rick Volk | .25 | .10 |
| ☐ 9 Steve Furness | .50 | .20 |
| ☐ 10 Isaac Curtis | .50 | .20 |
| ☐ 11 Nate Wright | .50 | .20 |
| ☐ 12 Jean Fugett | .25 | .10 |
| ☐ 13 Ken Mendenhall | .25 | .10 |
| ☐ 14 Sam Adams OL | 1.00 | .40 |
| ☐ 15 Bill Stanfill | .25 | .10 |
| ☐ 16 John Holland | .25 | .10 |
| ☐ 17 John Holland | .25 | .10 |
| ☐ 18 Pat Haden RC | 2.00 | .75 |
| ☐ 19 Bob Young | .25 | .10 |
| ☐ 20 Wally Chambers | .25 | .10 |
| ☐ 21 Lawrence Gaines | .25 | .10 |
| ☐ 22 Larry McCarren | .25 | .10 |
| ☐ 23 Horst Muhlmann | .25 | .10 |
| ☐ 24 Phil Villapiano | .50 | .20 |
| ☐ 25 Greg Pruitt | .50 | .20 |
| ☐ 26 Ron Howard | .25 | .10 |
| ☐ 27 Craig Morton | 1.00 | .40 |
| ☐ 28 Emmitt Thomas | .25 | .10 |
| ☐ 29 Lee Roy Selmon RC UER | 12.00 | 6.00 |
| ☐ 30 Ed White | .50 | .20 |
| ☐ 31 Harold McLinton | .25 | .10 |
| ☐ 32 Glenn Doughty | .25 | .10 |
| ☐ 33 Bob Kuechenberg | 1.00 | .40 |
| ☐ 34 Duane Carrell | .25 | .10 |
| ☐ 35 Riley Odoms | .25 | .10 |
| ☐ 36 Bobby Scott | .25 | .10 |
| ☐ 37 Nick Mike-Mayer | .25 | .10 |
| ☐ 38 Bill Lenkaitis | .25 | .10 |
| ☐ 39 Roland Harper | .50 | .20 |
| ☐ 40 Tommy Hart | .25 | .10 |
| ☐ 41 Mike Sensibaugh | .25 | .10 |
| ☐ 42 Rusty Jackson | .25 | .10 |
| ☐ 43 Levi Johnson | .25 | .10 |
| ☐ 44 Mike McCoy DT | .25 | .10 |
| ☐ 45 Roger Staubach | 20.00 | 10.00 |
| ☐ 46 Fred Cox | .25 | .10 |
| ☐ 47 Bob Babich | .25 | .10 |
| ☐ 48 Reggie McKenzie | .50 | .20 |
| ☐ 49 Dave Jennings | .25 | .10 |
| ☐ 50 Mike Haynes RC | 10.00 | 4.00 |
| ☐ 51 Larry Brown | .50 | .20 |

| # | Player | Hi | Lo |
|---|---|---|---|
| ☐ 52 | Marvin Cobb | .25 | .10 |
| ☐ 53 | Fred Cook | .25 | .10 |
| ☐ 54 | Freddie Solomon | .50 | .20 |
| ☐ 55 | John Riggins | 2.50 | 1.25 |
| ☐ 56 | John Bunting | .50 | .20 |
| ☐ 57 | Ray Wersching | .25 | .10 |
| ☐ 58 | Mike Livingston | .25 | .10 |
| ☐ 59 | Billy Johnson | .25 | .10 |
| ☐ 60 | Mike Wagner | .25 | .10 |
| ☐ 61 | Waymond Bryant | .25 | .10 |
| ☐ 62 | Jim Otis | .50 | .20 |
| ☐ 63 | Ed Galigher | .25 | .10 |
| ☐ 64 | Randy Vataha | .25 | .10 |
| ☐ 65 | Jim Zorn RC | 5.00 | 2.00 |
| ☐ 66 | Jon Keyworth | .25 | .10 |
| ☐ 67 | Checklist 1-132 | 2.00 | .75 |
| ☐ 68 | Henry Childs | .25 | .10 |
| ☐ 69 | Thom Darden | .25 | .10 |
| ☐ 70 | George Kunz | .25 | .10 |
| ☐ 71 | Lenvil Elliott | .25 | .10 |
| ☐ 72 | Curtis Johnson | .25 | .10 |
| ☐ 73 | Doug Van Horn | .25 | .10 |
| ☐ 74 | Joe Theismann | 4.00 | 2.00 |
| ☐ 75 | Dwight White | .50 | .20 |
| ☐ 76 | Scott Laidlaw | .25 | .10 |
| ☐ 77 | Monte Johnson | .25 | .10 |
| ☐ 78 | Dave Beverly | .25 | .10 |
| ☐ 79 | Jim Mitchell TE | .25 | .10 |
| ☐ 80 | Jack Youngblood | 1.00 | .40 |
| ☐ 81 | Mel Gray | .50 | .20 |
| ☐ 82 | Dwight Harrison | .25 | .10 |
| ☐ 83 | John Hadl | .50 | .20 |
| ☐ 84 | Matt Blair RC | 1.00 | .40 |
| ☐ 85 | Charlie Sanders | .60 | .25 |
| ☐ 86 | Noah Jackson | .25 | .10 |
| ☐ 87 | Ed Marinaro | .50 | .20 |
| ☐ 88 | Bob Howard | .25 | .10 |
| ☐ 89 | John McDaniel | .25 | .10 |
| ☐ 90 | Dan Dierdorf | 1.50 | .60 |
| ☐ 91 | Mark Moseley | .50 | .20 |
| ☐ 92 | Cleo Miller | .25 | .10 |
| ☐ 93 | Andre Tillman | .25 | .10 |
| ☐ 94 | Bruce Taylor | .25 | .10 |
| ☐ 95 | Bert Jones | 1.00 | .40 |
| ☐ 96 | Anthony Davis RC | 1.00 | .40 |
| ☐ 97 | Don Goode | .25 | .10 |
| ☐ 98 | Ray Rhodes RC | 6.00 | 3.00 |
| ☐ 99 | Mike Webster RC | 12.00 | 6.00 |
| ☐ 100 | O.J. Simpson | 6.00 | 3.00 |
| ☐ 101 | Doug Plank RC | .25 | .10 |
| ☐ 102 | Efren Herrera | .50 | .20 |
| ☐ 103 | Charlie Smith WR | .25 | .10 |
| ☐ 104 | Carlos Brown RC | 1.00 | .40 |
| ☐ 105 | Jim Marshall | 1.00 | .40 |
| ☐ 106 | Paul Naumoff | .25 | .10 |
| ☐ 107 | Walter White | .25 | .10 |
| ☐ 108 | John Cappelletti RC | 3.00 | 1.25 |
| ☐ 109 | Chip Myers | .40 | .15 |
| ☐ 110 | Ken Stabler | 10.00 | 5.00 |
| ☐ 111 | Joe Ehrmann | .25 | .10 |
| ☐ 112 | Rick Engles | .25 | .10 |
| ☐ 113 | Jack Dolbin RC | .25 | .10 |
| ☐ 114 | Ron Bolton | .25 | .10 |
| ☐ 115 | Mike Thomas | .25 | .10 |
| ☐ 116 | Mike Fuller | .25 | .10 |
| ☐ 117 | John Hill | .25 | .10 |
| ☐ 118 | Richard Todd RC | 1.00 | .40 |
| ☐ 119 | Duriel Harris RC | 1.00 | .40 |
| ☐ 120 | John James | .25 | .10 |
| ☐ 121 | Lionel Antoine | .25 | .10 |
| ☐ 122 | John Skorupan | .25 | .10 |
| ☐ 123 | Skip Butler | .25 | .10 |
| ☐ 124 | Bob Tucker | .25 | .10 |
| ☐ 125 | Paul Krause | 1.00 | .40 |
| ☐ 126 | Dave Hampton | .25 | .10 |
| ☐ 127 | Tom Wittum | .25 | .10 |
| ☐ 128 | Gary Huff | .50 | .20 |
| ☐ 129 | Emmitt Thomas | .40 | .15 |
| ☐ 130 | Drew Pearson | 2.00 | .75 |
| ☐ 131 | Ron Saul | .25 | .10 |
| ☐ 132 | Steve Niehaus | .25 | .10 |
| ☐ 133 | Fred Carr | .25 | .10 |
| ☐ 134 | Norm Bulaich | .25 | .10 |
| ☐ 135 | Bob Trumpy | .50 | .20 |
| ☐ 136 | Greg Landry | .50 | .20 |
| ☐ 137 | George Buehler | .25 | .10 |
| ☐ 138 | Reggie Rucker | .50 | .20 |
| ☐ 139 | Julius Adams | .25 | .10 |
| ☐ 140 | Jack Ham | 2.50 | 1.25 |
| ☐ 141 | Wayne Morris RC | .25 | .10 |
| ☐ 142 | Marv Bateman | .25 | .10 |
| ☐ 143 | Bobby Maples | .25 | .10 |
| ☐ 144 | Harold Carmichael | 1.00 | .40 |
| ☐ 145 | Bob Avellini | .50 | .20 |
| ☐ 146 | Harry Carson RC | 3.00 | 1.50 |
| ☐ 147 | Lawrence Pillers | .25 | .10 |
| ☐ 148 | Ed Williams RC | .25 | .10 |
| ☐ 149 | Dan Pastorini | .50 | .20 |
| ☐ 150 | Ron Yary | 1.00 | .40 |
| ☐ 151 | Joe Lavender | .25 | .10 |
| ☐ 152 | Pat McInally RC | .50 | .20 |
| ☐ 153 | Lloyd Mumphord | .25 | .10 |
| ☐ 154 | Cullen Bryant | .50 | .20 |
| ☐ 155 | Willie Lanier | 1.00 | .40 |
| ☐ 156 | Gene Washington 49er | .50 | .20 |
| ☐ 157 | Scott Hunter | .25 | .10 |
| ☐ 158 | Jim Merlo | .25 | .10 |
| ☐ 159 | Randy Grossman | .50 | .20 |
| ☐ 160 | Blaine Nye | .25 | .10 |
| ☐ 161 | Ike Harris | .25 | .10 |
| ☐ 162 | Doug Dieken | .25 | .10 |
| ☐ 163 | Guy Morriss | .25 | .10 |
| ☐ 164 | Bob Parsons | .25 | .10 |
| ☐ 165 | Steve Grogan | 1.00 | .40 |
| ☐ 166 | John Brockington | .50 | .20 |
| ☐ 167 | Charlie Joiner | 2.50 | 1.25 |
| ☐ 168 | Ron Carpenter | .25 | .10 |
| ☐ 169 | Jeff Wright S | .25 | .10 |
| ☐ 170 | Chris Hanburger | .50 | .20 |
| ☐ 171 | Roosevelt Leaks RC | .50 | .20 |
| ☐ 172 | Larry Little | 1.00 | .40 |
| ☐ 173 | John Matuszak | .50 | .20 |
| ☐ 174 | Joe Ferguson | .50 | .20 |
| ☐ 175 | Brad Van Pelt | .50 | .20 |
| ☐ 176 | Dexter Bussey RC | .50 | .20 |
| ☐ 177 | Steve Largent RC | 40.00 | 20.00 |
| ☐ 178 | Dewey Selmon | .25 | .10 |
| ☐ 179 | Randy Gradishar | 1.00 | .40 |
| ☐ 180 | Mel Blount | 3.00 | 1.50 |
| ☐ 181 | Dan Neal | .25 | .10 |
| ☐ 182 | Rich Szaro | .25 | .10 |
| ☐ 183 | Mike Boryla | .25 | .10 |
| ☐ 184 | Steve Jones | .25 | .10 |
| ☐ 185 | Paul Warfield | 2.50 | 1.25 |
| ☐ 186 | Greg Buttle RC | .25 | .10 |
| ☐ 187 | Rich McGeorge | .25 | .10 |
| ☐ 188 | Leon Gray RC | .50 | .20 |
| ☐ 189 | John Shinners | .25 | .10 |
| ☐ 190 | Toni Linhart | .25 | .10 |
| ☐ 191 | Robert Miller | .25 | .10 |
| ☐ 192 | Jake Scott | .25 | .10 |
| ☐ 193 | Jon Morris | .25 | .10 |
| ☐ 194 | Randy Crowder | .25 | .10 |
| ☐ 195 | Lynn Swann UER | 18.00 | 10.00 |
| ☐ 196 | Marsh White | .25 | .10 |
| ☐ 197 | Rod Perry RC | 1.00 | .40 |
| ☐ 198 | Willie Hall | .25 | .10 |
| ☐ 199 | Mike Hartenstine | .25 | .10 |
| ☐ 200 | Jim Bakken | .25 | .10 |
| ☐ 201 | Atlanta Falcons CL UER | 1.25 | .50 |
| ☐ 202 | Baltimore Colts CL | 1.25 | .50 |
| ☐ 203 | Buffalo Bills CL | 1.25 | .50 |
| ☐ 204 | Chicago Bears CL | 1.25 | .50 |
| ☐ 205 | Cincinnati Bengals CL | 1.25 | .50 |
| ☐ 206 | Cleveland Browns CL | 1.25 | .50 |
| ☐ 207 | Dallas Cowboys CL | 1.25 | .50 |
| ☐ 208 | Denver Broncos CL | 1.25 | .50 |
| ☐ 209 | Detroit Lions CL | 1.25 | .50 |
| ☐ 210 | Green Bay Packers CL | 1.25 | .50 |
| ☐ 211 | Houston Oilers CL | 1.25 | .50 |
| ☐ 212 | Kansas City Chiefs CL | 1.25 | .50 |
| ☐ 213 | Los Angeles Rams CL | 1.25 | .50 |
| ☐ 214 | Miami Dolphins CL | 1.25 | .50 |
| ☐ 215 | Minnesota Vikings CL | 1.25 | .50 |
| ☐ 216 | New England Patriots CL | 1.25 | .50 |
| ☐ 217 | New Orleans Saints CL | 1.25 | .50 |
| ☐ 218 | New York Giants CL | 1.25 | .50 |
| ☐ 219 | New York Jets CL | 1.25 | .50 |
| ☐ 220 | Oakland Raiders CL | 1.25 | .50 |
| ☐ 221 | Philadelphia Eagles CL | 1.25 | .50 |
| ☐ 222 | Pittsburgh Steelers CL | 1.25 | .50 |
| ☐ 223 | St. Louis Cardinals CL | 1.25 | .50 |
| ☐ 224 | San Diego Chargers CL | 1.25 | .50 |
| ☐ 225 | San Francisco 49ers CL | 1.25 | .50 |
| ☐ 226 | Seattle Seahawks CL | 1.25 | .50 |
| ☐ 227 | Tampa Bay Buccaneers CL | 1.25 | .50 |
| ☐ 228 | Washington Redskins CL | 1.25 | .50 |
| ☐ 229 | Sam Cunningham | .50 | .20 |
| ☐ 230 | Alan Page | 1.00 | .40 |
| ☐ 231 | Eddie Brown S | .25 | .10 |
| ☐ 232 | Stan White | .25 | .10 |
| ☐ 233 | Vern Den Herder | .25 | .10 |
| ☐ 234 | Clarence Davis | .25 | .10 |
| ☐ 235 | Ken Anderson | 1.00 | .40 |
| ☐ 236 | Karl Chandler | .25 | .10 |
| ☐ 237 | Will Harrell | .25 | .10 |
| ☐ 238 | Clarence Scott | .25 | .10 |
| ☐ 239 | Bo Rather | .25 | .10 |
| ☐ 240 | Robert Brazile | .50 | .20 |
| ☐ 241 | Bob Bell | .25 | .10 |
| ☐ 242 | Rolland Lawrence | .25 | .10 |
| ☐ 243 | Tom Sullivan | .25 | .10 |
| ☐ 244 | Larry Brunson | .25 | .10 |
| ☐ 245 | Terry Bradshaw | 20.00 | 10.00 |
| ☐ 246 | Rich Saul | .25 | .10 |
| ☐ 247 | Cleveland Elam | .25 | .10 |
| ☐ 248 | Don Woods | .25 | .10 |
| ☐ 249 | Bruce Laird | .25 | .10 |
| ☐ 250 | Coy Bacon | .50 | .20 |
| ☐ 251 | Russ Francis | 1.00 | .40 |
| ☐ 252 | Jim Braxton | .25 | .10 |
| ☐ 253 | Perry Smith | .25 | .10 |
| ☐ 254 | Jerome Barkum | .25 | .10 |
| ☐ 255 | Garo Yepremian | .50 | .20 |
| ☐ 256 | Checklist 133-264 | 2.00 | .75 |
| ☐ 257 | Tony Galbreath RC | .50 | .20 |
| ☐ 258 | Troy Archer | .25 | .10 |
| ☐ 259 | Brian Sipe | 1.00 | .40 |
| ☐ 260 | Billy Joe DuPree | .50 | .20 |
| ☐ 261 | Bobby Walden | .25 | .10 |
| ☐ 262 | Larry Marshall | .25 | .10 |
| ☐ 263 | Ted Fritsch Jr. | .25 | .10 |
| ☐ 264 | Larry Hand | .25 | .10 |
| ☐ 265 | Tom Mack | 1.00 | .40 |
| ☐ 266 | Ed Bradley | .25 | .10 |
| ☐ 267 | Pat Leahy | .50 | .20 |
| ☐ 268 | Louis Carter | .25 | .10 |
| ☐ 269 | Archie Griffin RC | 6.00 | 3.00 |
| ☐ 270 | Art Shell | 1.00 | .40 |
| ☐ 271 | Stu Voigt | .25 | .10 |
| ☐ 272 | Prentice McCray | .25 | .10 |
| ☐ 273 | MacArthur Lane | .25 | .10 |
| ☐ 274 | Dan Fouts | 6.00 | 3.00 |
| ☐ 275 | Charle Young | .50 | .20 |
| ☐ 276 | Wilbur Jackson RC | .25 | .10 |
| ☐ 277 | John Hicks | .25 | .10 |
| ☐ 278 | Nat Moore | 1.00 | .40 |
| ☐ 279 | Virgil Livers | .25 | .10 |
| ☐ 280 | Curley Culp | .50 | .20 |
| ☐ 281 | Rocky Bleier | 2.50 | 1.25 |
| ☐ 282 | John Zook | .25 | .10 |
| ☐ 283 | Tom DeLeone | .25 | .10 |
| ☐ 284 | Danny White RC | 10.00 | 5.00 |
| ☐ 285 | Otis Armstrong | .50 | .20 |
| ☐ 286 | Larry Walton | .25 | .10 |
| ☐ 287 | Jim Carter | .25 | .10 |
| ☐ 288 | Don McCauley | .25 | .10 |
| ☐ 289 | Frank Grant | .25 | .10 |
| ☐ 290 | Roger Wehrli | .60 | .25 |
| ☐ 291 | Mick Tingelhoff | .50 | .20 |
| ☐ 292 | Bernard Jackson | .25 | .10 |
| ☐ 293 | Tom Owen RC | .25 | .10 |
| ☐ 294 | Mike Esposito | .25 | .10 |
| ☐ 295 | Fred Biletnikoff | 2.50 | 1.25 |
| ☐ 296 | Revie Sorey RC | .25 | .10 |
| ☐ 297 | John McMakin | .25 | .10 |
| ☐ 298 | Dan Ryczek | .25 | .10 |
| ☐ 299 | Wayne Moore | .25 | .10 |
| ☐ 300 | Franco Harris | 4.00 | 2.00 |
| ☐ 301 | Rick Upchurch RC | 1.00 | .40 |
| ☐ 302 | Jim Stienke | .25 | .10 |
| ☐ 303 | Charlie Davis | .25 | .10 |
| ☐ 304 | Don Cockroft | .25 | .10 |
| ☐ 305 | Ken Burrough | .50 | .20 |
| ☐ 306 | Clark Gaines | .25 | .10 |
| ☐ 307 | Bobby Douglass | .25 | .10 |
| ☐ 308 | Ralph Perretta | .25 | .10 |
| ☐ 309 | Wally Hilgenberg | .25 | .10 |
| ☐ 310 | Monte Jackson RC | .50 | .20 |
| ☐ 311 | Chris Bahr RC | .50 | .20 |
| ☐ 312 | Jim Cheyunski | .25 | .10 |

| | | |
|---|---|---|
| ☐ 313 Mike Patrick | .25 | .10 |
| ☐ 314 Ed Too Tall Jones | 5.00 | 2.50 |
| ☐ 315 Bill Bradley | .25 | .10 |
| ☐ 316 Benny Malone | .25 | .10 |
| ☐ 317 Paul Seymour | .25 | .10 |
| ☐ 318 Jim Laslavic | .25 | .10 |
| ☐ 319 Frank Lewis | .50 | .20 |
| ☐ 320 Ray Guy | 1.00 | .40 |
| ☐ 321 Allan Ellis | .25 | .10 |
| ☐ 322 Conrad Dobler | .50 | .20 |
| ☐ 323 Chester Marcol | .25 | .10 |
| ☐ 324 Doug Kotar | .25 | .10 |
| ☐ 325 Lemar Parrish | .25 | .20 |
| ☐ 326 Steve Holden | .25 | .10 |
| ☐ 327 Jeff Van Note | .50 | .20 |
| ☐ 328 Howard Stevens | .25 | .10 |
| ☐ 329 Brad Dusek | .50 | .10 |
| ☐ 330 Joe DeLamielleure | 1.00 | .40 |
| ☐ 331 Jim Plunkett | 1.00 | .40 |
| ☐ 332 Checklist 265-396 | 2.00 | .75 |
| ☐ 333 Lou Piccone | .25 | .10 |
| ☐ 334 Ray Hamilton | .25 | .10 |
| ☐ 335 Jan Stenerud | 1.00 | .40 |
| ☐ 336 Jeris White | .25 | .10 |
| ☐ 337 Sherman Smith RC | .25 | .10 |
| ☐ 338 Dave Green | .25 | .10 |
| ☐ 339 Terry Schmidt | .25 | .10 |
| ☐ 340 Sammie White RC | 1.00 | .40 |
| ☐ 341 Jon Kolb RC | .25 | .10 |
| ☐ 342 Randy White | 8.00 | 4.00 |
| ☐ 343 Bob Klein | .25 | .10 |
| ☐ 344 Bob Kowalkowski | .25 | .10 |
| ☐ 345 Terry Metcalf | .50 | .20 |
| ☐ 346 Joe Danelo | .25 | .10 |
| ☐ 347 Ken Payne | .25 | .10 |
| ☐ 348 Neal Craig | .25 | .10 |
| ☐ 349 Dennis Johnson | .25 | .10 |
| ☐ 350 Bill Bergey | .50 | .20 |
| ☐ 351 Raymond Chester | .25 | .10 |
| ☐ 352 Bob Matheson | .25 | .10 |
| ☐ 353 Mike Kadish | .25 | .10 |
| ☐ 354 Mark Van Eeghen RC | 1.50 | .60 |
| ☐ 355 L.C. Greenwood | 1.00 | .40 |
| ☐ 356 Sam Hunt | .25 | .10 |
| ☐ 357 Darrell Austin | .25 | .10 |
| ☐ 358 Jim Turner | .25 | .10 |
| ☐ 359 Ahmad Rashad | 2.00 | .75 |
| ☐ 360 Walter Payton | 40.00 | 15.00 |
| ☐ 361 Mark Arneson | .25 | .10 |
| ☐ 362 Jerral Wilson | .25 | .10 |
| ☐ 363 Steve Bartkowski | 1.00 | .40 |
| ☐ 364 John Watson | .25 | .10 |
| ☐ 365 Ken Riley | .50 | .20 |
| ☐ 366 Gregg Bingham | .25 | .10 |
| ☐ 367 Golden Richards | .50 | .20 |
| ☐ 368 Clyde Powers | .25 | .10 |
| ☐ 369 Diron Talbert | .25 | .10 |
| ☐ 370 Lydell Mitchell | .50 | .20 |
| ☐ 371 Bob Jackson | .25 | .10 |
| ☐ 372 Jim Mandich | .25 | .10 |
| ☐ 373 Frank LeMaster | .25 | .10 |
| ☐ 374 Benny Ricardo | .25 | .10 |
| ☐ 375 Lawrence McCutcheon | .50 | .20 |
| ☐ 376 Lynn Dickey | .50 | .20 |
| ☐ 377 Phil Wise | .25 | .10 |
| ☐ 378 Tony McGee DT | .25 | .10 |
| ☐ 379 Norm Thompson | .25 | .10 |
| ☐ 380 Dave Casper RC | 4.00 | 1.50 |
| ☐ 381 Glen Edwards | .25 | .10 |
| ☐ 382 Bob Thomas | .25 | .10 |
| ☐ 383 Bob Chandler | .50 | .20 |
| ☐ 384 Rickey Young | .50 | .20 |
| ☐ 385 Carl Eller | 1.00 | .40 |
| ☐ 386 Lyle Alzado | 1.00 | .40 |
| ☐ 387 John Leypoldt | .25 | .10 |
| ☐ 388 Gordon Bell | .25 | .10 |
| ☐ 389 Mike Bragg | .25 | .10 |
| ☐ 390 Jim Langer | 1.00 | .40 |
| ☐ 391 Vern Holland | .25 | .10 |
| ☐ 392 Nelson Munsey | .25 | .10 |
| ☐ 393 Mack Mitchell | .25 | .10 |
| ☐ 394 Tony Adams RC | .25 | .10 |
| ☐ 395 Preston Pearson | .50 | .20 |
| ☐ 396 Emanuel Zanders | .25 | .10 |
| ☐ 397 Vince Papale RC | 20.00 | 8.00 |
| ☐ 398 Joe Fields RC | .50 | .20 |
| ☐ 399 Craig Clemons | .25 | .10 |

| | | |
|---|---|---|
| ☐ 400 Fran Tarkenton | 5.00 | 2.50 |
| ☐ 401 Andy Johnson | .25 | .10 |
| ☐ 402 Willie Buchanon | .25 | .10 |
| ☐ 403 Pat Curran | .25 | .10 |
| ☐ 404 Ray Jarvis | .25 | .10 |
| ☐ 405 Joe Greene | 2.50 | 1.25 |
| ☐ 406 Bill Simpson | .25 | .10 |
| ☐ 407 Ronnie Coleman | .25 | .10 |
| ☐ 408 J.K. McKay RC | .50 | .20 |
| ☐ 409 Pat Fischer | .50 | .20 |
| ☐ 410 John Dutton | .50 | .20 |
| ☐ 411 Boobie Clark | .25 | .10 |
| ☐ 412 Pat Tilley RC | 1.00 | .40 |
| ☐ 413 Don Strock | .50 | .20 |
| ☐ 414 Brian Kelley | .25 | .10 |
| ☐ 415 Gene Upshaw | 1.00 | .40 |
| ☐ 416 Mike Montler | .25 | .10 |
| ☐ 417 Checklist 397-528 | 2.00 | .75 |
| ☐ 418 John Gilliam | .25 | .10 |
| ☐ 419 Brent McClanahan | .25 | .10 |
| ☐ 420 Jerry Sherk | .25 | .10 |
| ☐ 421 Roy Gerela | .25 | .10 |
| ☐ 422 Tim Fox | .50 | .20 |
| ☐ 423 John Ebersole | .25 | .10 |
| ☐ 424 James Scott RC | .25 | .10 |
| ☐ 425 Delvin Williams RC | .25 | .10 |
| ☐ 426 Spike Jones | .25 | .10 |
| ☐ 427 Harvey Martin | 1.00 | .40 |
| ☐ 428 Don Herrmann | .25 | .10 |
| ☐ 429 Calvin Hill | .50 | .20 |
| ☐ 430 Isiah Robertson | .25 | .10 |
| ☐ 431 Tony Greene | .25 | .10 |
| ☐ 432 Bob Johnson | .25 | .10 |
| ☐ 433 Lem Barney | 1.00 | .40 |
| ☐ 434 Eric Torkelson | .25 | .10 |
| ☐ 435 John Mendenhall | .25 | .10 |
| ☐ 436 Larry Seiple | .50 | .20 |
| ☐ 437 Art Kuehn | .25 | .10 |
| ☐ 438 John Vella | .25 | .10 |
| ☐ 439 Greg Latta | .25 | .10 |
| ☐ 440 Roger Carr | .50 | .20 |
| ☐ 441 Doug Sutherland | .25 | .10 |
| ☐ 442 Mike Kruczek RC | .25 | .10 |
| ☐ 443 Steve Zabel | .25 | .10 |
| ☐ 444 Mike Pruitt RC | 1.00 | .40 |
| ☐ 445 Harold Jackson | .50 | .20 |
| ☐ 446 George Jakowenko | .25 | .10 |
| ☐ 447 John Fitzgerald | .25 | .10 |
| ☐ 448 Carey Joyce | .25 | .10 |
| ☐ 449 Jim LeClair | .25 | .10 |
| ☐ 450 Ken Houston | 1.00 | .40 |
| ☐ 451 Steve Grogan RB | .50 | .20 |
| ☐ 452 Jim Marshall RB | .50 | .20 |
| ☐ 453 O.J. Simpson RB | 2.50 | 1.25 |
| ☐ 454 Fran Tarkenton RB | 3.00 | 1.50 |
| ☐ 455 Jim Zorn RB | 1.00 | .40 |
| ☐ 456 Robert Pratt | .25 | .10 |
| ☐ 457 Walker Gillette | .25 | .10 |
| ☐ 458 Charlie Hall | .25 | .10 |
| ☐ 459 Robert Newhouse | .50 | .20 |
| ☐ 460 John Hannah | 1.00 | .40 |
| ☐ 461 Ken Reaves | .25 | .10 |
| ☐ 462 Herman Weaver | .25 | .10 |
| ☐ 463 James Harris | .50 | .20 |
| ☐ 464 Howard Twilley | .50 | .20 |
| ☐ 465 Jeff Siemon | .50 | .20 |
| ☐ 466 John Outlaw | .25 | .10 |
| ☐ 467 Chuck Muncie RC | 1.00 | .40 |
| ☐ 468 Bob Moore | .25 | .10 |
| ☐ 469 Robert Woods | .25 | .10 |
| ☐ 470 Cliff Branch | 2.00 | .75 |
| ☐ 471 Johnnie Gray | .25 | .10 |
| ☐ 472 Don Hardeman | .25 | .10 |
| ☐ 473 Steve Ramsey | .25 | .10 |
| ☐ 474 Steve Mike-Mayer | .25 | .10 |
| ☐ 475 Gary Garrison | .25 | .10 |
| ☐ 476 Walter Johnson | .25 | .10 |
| ☐ 477 Neil Clabo | .25 | .10 |
| ☐ 478 Len Hauss | .25 | .10 |
| ☐ 479 Daryl Stingley | .50 | .20 |
| ☐ 480 Jack Lambert | 8.00 | 4.00 |
| ☐ 481 Mike Adamle | .50 | .20 |
| ☐ 482 David Lee | .25 | .10 |
| ☐ 483 Tom Mullen | .25 | .10 |
| ☐ 484 Claude Humphrey | .25 | .10 |
| ☐ 485 Jim Hart | 1.00 | .40 |
| ☐ 486 Bobby Thompson RB | .25 | .10 |

| | | |
|---|---|---|
| ☐ 487 Jack Rudnay | .25 | .10 |
| ☐ 488 Rich Sowells | .25 | .10 |
| ☐ 489 Reuben Gant | .25 | .10 |
| ☐ 490 Cliff Harris | 1.00 | .40 |
| ☐ 491 Bob Brown DT | .25 | .10 |
| ☐ 492 Don Nottingham | .25 | .10 |
| ☐ 493 Ron Jessie | .25 | .10 |
| ☐ 494 Otis Sistrunk | .50 | .20 |
| ☐ 495 Billy Kilmer | .50 | .20 |
| ☐ 496 Oscar Roan | .25 | .10 |
| ☐ 497 Bill Van Heusen | .25 | .10 |
| ☐ 498 Randy Logan | .25 | .10 |
| ☐ 499 John Smith | .25 | .10 |
| ☐ 500 Chuck Foreman | .50 | .20 |
| ☐ 501 J.T. Thomas | .25 | .10 |
| ☐ 502 Steve Schubert | .25 | .10 |
| ☐ 503 Mike Barnes | .25 | .10 |
| ☐ 504 J.V. Cain | .25 | .10 |
| ☐ 505 Larry Csonka | 3.00 | 1.50 |
| ☐ 506 Elvin Bethea | 1.00 | .40 |
| ☐ 507 Ray Easterling | .25 | .10 |
| ☐ 508 Joe Reed | .25 | .10 |
| ☐ 509 Steve Odom | .25 | .10 |
| ☐ 510 Tommy Casanova | .25 | .10 |
| ☐ 511 Dave Dalby | .25 | .10 |
| ☐ 512 Richard Caster | .25 | .10 |
| ☐ 513 Fred Dryer | 1.00 | .40 |
| ☐ 514 Jeff Kinney | .25 | .10 |
| ☐ 515 Bob Griese | 3.00 | 1.50 |
| ☐ 516 Butch Johnson RC | 1.00 | .40 |
| ☐ 517 Gerald Irons | .25 | .10 |
| ☐ 518 Don Calhoun | .25 | .10 |
| ☐ 519 Jack Gregory | .25 | .10 |
| ☐ 520 Tom Banks | .25 | .10 |
| ☐ 521 Bobby Bryant | .25 | .10 |
| ☐ 522 Reggie Harrison | .25 | .10 |
| ☐ 523 Terry Hermeling | .25 | .10 |
| ☐ 524 David Taylor | .25 | .10 |
| ☐ 525 Brian Baschnagel RC | .50 | .20 |
| ☐ 526 AFC Champ/Stabler | 1.00 | .40 |
| ☐ 527 NFC Championship | .50 | .20 |
| ☐ 528 Super Bowl XI | 1.00 | .40 |

## 1978 Topps

| | | |
|---|---|---|
| ☐ COMPLETE SET (528) | 150.00 | 80.00 |
| ☐ 1 Gary Huff HL ! | 1.00 | .40 |
| ☐ 2 Craig Morton HL | 1.00 | .40 |
| ☐ 3 Walter Payton HL | 8.00 | 3.00 |
| ☐ 4 O.J.Simpson HL | 2.00 | .75 |
| ☐ 5 Fran Tarkenton HL | 2.00 | .75 |
| ☐ 6 Bob Thomas HL | .20 | .07 |
| ☐ 7 Joe Pisarcik | .50 | .20 |
| ☐ 8 Skip Thomas | .20 | .07 |
| ☐ 9 Roosevelt Leaks | .20 | .07 |
| ☐ 10 Ken Houston | 1.00 | .40 |
| ☐ 11 Tom Blanchard | .20 | .07 |
| ☐ 12 Jim Turner | .20 | .07 |
| ☐ 13 Tom DeLeone | .20 | .07 |
| ☐ 14 Jim LeClair | .20 | .07 |
| ☐ 15 Bob Avellini | .50 | .20 |
| ☐ 16 Tony McGee DT | .20 | .07 |
| ☐ 17 James Harris | .50 | .20 |
| ☐ 18 Terry Nelson | .20 | .07 |
| ☐ 19 Rocky Bleier | 2.00 | .75 |
| ☐ 20 Joe DeLamielleure | 1.00 | .40 |
| ☐ 21 Richard Caster | .20 | .07 |
| ☐ 22 A.J.Duhe RC | 1.00 | .40 |
| ☐ 23 John Outlaw | .20 | .07 |
| ☐ 24 Danny White | 1.25 | .50 |

| | | |
|---|---|---|
| ❑ 25 Larry Csonka | 2.50 | 1.00 |
| ❑ 26 David Hill RC | .50 | .20 |
| ❑ 27 Mark Arneson | .20 | .07 |
| ❑ 28 Jack Tatum | .50 | .20 |
| ❑ 29 Norm Thompson | .20 | .07 |
| ❑ 30 Sammie White | .50 | .20 |
| ❑ 31 Dennis Johnson | .20 | .07 |
| ❑ 32 Robin Earl | .20 | .07 |
| ❑ 33 Don Cockroft | .20 | .07 |
| ❑ 34 Bob Johnson | .20 | .07 |
| ❑ 35 John Hannah | 1.00 | .40 |
| ❑ 36 Scott Hunter | .20 | .07 |
| ❑ 37 Ken Burrough | .50 | .20 |
| ❑ 38 Wilbur Jackson | .20 | .07 |
| ❑ 39 Rich McGeorge | .20 | .07 |
| ❑ 40 Lyle Alzado | 1.00 | .40 |
| ❑ 41 John Ebersole | .20 | .07 |
| ❑ 42 Gary Green RC | .20 | .07 |
| ❑ 43 Art Kuehn | .20 | .07 |
| ❑ 44 Glen Edwards | .50 | .20 |
| ❑ 45 Lawrence McCutcheon | .50 | .20 |
| ❑ 46 Duriel Harris | .20 | .07 |
| ❑ 47 Rich Szaro | .20 | .07 |
| ❑ 48 Mike Washington | .20 | .07 |
| ❑ 49 Stan White | .20 | .07 |
| ❑ 50 Dave Casper | 1.00 | .40 |
| ❑ 51 Len Hauss | .20 | .07 |
| ❑ 52 James Scott | .20 | .07 |
| ❑ 53 Brian Sipe | 1.00 | .40 |
| ❑ 54 Gary Shirk | .20 | .07 |
| ❑ 55 Archie Griffin | 1.00 | .40 |
| ❑ 56 Mike Patrick | .20 | .07 |
| ❑ 57 Mario Clark | .20 | .07 |
| ❑ 58 Jeff Siemon | .20 | .07 |
| ❑ 59 Steve Mike-Mayer | .20 | * .07 |
| ❑ 60 Randy White | 4.00 | 2.00 |
| ❑ 61 Darrell Austin | .20 | .07 |
| ❑ 62 Tom Sullivan | .20 | .07 |
| ❑ 63 Johnny Rodgers RC | 1.00 | .40 |
| ❑ 64 Ken Reaves | .20 | .07 |
| ❑ 65 Terry Bradshaw | 12.00 | 6.00 |
| ❑ 66 Fred Steinfort | .20 | .07 |
| ❑ 67 Curley Culp | .50 | .20 |
| ❑ 68 Ted Hendricks | 1.00 | .40 |
| ❑ 69 Raymond Chester | .20 | .07 |
| ❑ 70 Jim Langer | 1.00 | .40 |
| ❑ 71 Calvin Hill | .50 | .20 |
| ❑ 72 Mike Hartenstine | .20 | .07 |
| ❑ 73 Gerald Irons | .20 | .07 |
| ❑ 74 Billy Brooks | .50 | .20 |
| ❑ 75 John Mendenhall | .20 | .07 |
| ❑ 76 Andy Johnson | .20 | .07 |
| ❑ 77 Tom Wittum | .20 | .07 |
| ❑ 78 Lynn Dickey | .50 | .20 |
| ❑ 79 Carl Eller | 1.00 | .40 |
| ❑ 80 Tom Mack | 1.00 | .40 |
| ❑ 81 Clark Gaines | .20 | .07 |
| ❑ 82 Lem Barney | 1.00 | .40 |
| ❑ 83 Mike Montler | .20 | .07 |
| ❑ 84 Jon Kolb | .20 | .07 |
| ❑ 85 Bob Chandler | .20 | .07 |
| ❑ 86 Robert Newhouse | .50 | .20 |
| ❑ 87 Frank LeMaster | .20 | .07 |
| ❑ 88 Jeff West | .20 | .07 |
| ❑ 89 Lyle Blackwood | .50 | .20 |
| ❑ 90 Gene Upshaw | 1.00 | .40 |
| ❑ 91 Frank Grant | .20 | .07 |
| ❑ 92 Tom Hicks | .20 | .07 |
| ❑ 93 Mike Pruitt | .50 | .20 |
| ❑ 94 Chris Bahr | .20 | .07 |
| ❑ 95 Russ Francis | .50 | .20 |
| ❑ 96 Norris Thomas | .20 | .07 |
| ❑ 97 Gary Barbaro RC | .50 | .20 |
| ❑ 98 Jim Merlo | .20 | .07 |
| ❑ 99 Karl Chandler | .20 | .07 |
| ❑ 100 Fran Tarkenton | 4.00 | 1.50 |
| ❑ 101 Abdul Salaam | .20 | .07 |
| ❑ 102 Marv Kellum | .20 | .07 |
| ❑ 103 Herman Weaver | .20 | .07 |
| ❑ 104 Roy Gerela | .20 | .07 |
| ❑ 105 Harold Jackson | .50 | .20 |
| ❑ 106 Dewey Selmon | .20 | .07 |
| ❑ 107 Checklist 1-132 | 1.00 | .40 |
| ❑ 108 Clarence Davis | .20 | .07 |
| ❑ 109 Robert Pratt | .20 | .07 |
| ❑ 110 Harvey Martin | 1.00 | .40 |
| ❑ 111 Brad Dusek | .20 | .07 |
| ❑ 112 Greg Latta | .20 | .07 |
| ❑ 113 Tony Peters | .20 | .07 |
| ❑ 114 Jim Braxton | .20 | .07 |
| ❑ 115 Ken Riley | .50 | .20 |
| ❑ 116 Steve Nelson | .20 | .07 |
| ❑ 117 Rick Upchurch | .50 | .20 |
| ❑ 118 Spike Jones | .20 | .07 |
| ❑ 119 Doug Kotar | .20 | .07 |
| ❑ 120 Bob Griese | 2.50 | 1.00 |
| ❑ 121 Burgess Owens | .20 | .07 |
| ❑ 122 Rolf Benirschke RC | .50 | .20 |
| ❑ 123 Haskel Stanback RC | .20 | .07 |
| ❑ 124 J.T. Thomas | .20 | .07 |
| ❑ 125 Ahmad Rashad | 1.50 | .60 |
| ❑ 126 Rick Kane | .20 | .07 |
| ❑ 127 Elvin Bethea | 1.00 | .40 |
| ❑ 128 Dave Dalby | .20 | .07 |
| ❑ 129 Mike Barnes | .20 | .07 |
| ❑ 130 Isiah Robertson | .20 | .07 |
| ❑ 131 Jim Plunkett | 1.00 | .40 |
| ❑ 132 Allan Ellis | .20 | .07 |
| ❑ 133 Mike Bragg | .20 | .07 |
| ❑ 134 Bob Jackson | .20 | .07 |
| ❑ 135 Coy Bacon | .20 | .07 |
| ❑ 136 John Smith | .20 | .07 |
| ❑ 137 Chuck Muncie | .50 | .20 |
| ❑ 138 Johnnie Gray | .20 | .07 |
| ❑ 139 Jimmy Robinson | .20 | .07 |
| ❑ 140 Tom Banks | .20 | .07 |
| ❑ 141 Marvin Powell RC | .20 | .07 |
| ❑ 142 Jerrel Wilson | .20 | .07 |
| ❑ 143 Ron Howard | .20 | .07 |
| ❑ 144 Rob Lytle RC | .50 | .20 |
| ❑ 145 L.C. Greenwood | 1.00 | .40 |
| ❑ 146 Morris Owens | .20 | .07 |
| ❑ 147 Joe Reed | .20 | .07 |
| ❑ 148 Mike Kadish | .20 | .07 |
| ❑ 149 Phil Villapiano | .20 | .07 |
| ❑ 150 Lydell Mitchell | .50 | .20 |
| ❑ 151 Randy Logan | .20 | .07 |
| ❑ 152 Mike Williams | .20 | .07 |
| ❑ 153 Jeff Van Note | .50 | .20 |
| ❑ 154 Steve Schubert | .20 | .07 |
| ❑ 155 Billy Kilmer | 1.00 | .40 |
| ❑ 156 Boobie Clark | .20 | .07 |
| ❑ 157 Charlie Hall | .20 | .07 |
| ❑ 158 Raymond Clayborn RC | 1.00 | .40 |
| ❑ 159 Jack Gregory | .20 | .07 |
| ❑ 160 Cliff Harris | 1.00 | .40 |
| ❑ 161 Joe Fields | .20 | .07 |
| ❑ 162 Don Nottingham | .20 | .07 |
| ❑ 163 Ed White | .20 | .07 |
| ❑ 164 Toni Fritsch | .20 | .07 |
| ❑ 165 Jack Lambert | 4.00 | 2.00 |
| ❑ 166 NFC Champs/Staubach | .50 | .60 |
| ❑ 167 AFC Champs/Lytle | .50 | .20 |
| ❑ 168 Super Bowl XII/Dorsett | 3.00 | 1.50 |
| ❑ 169 Neal Colzie RC | .20 | .07 |
| ❑ 170 Cleveland Elam | .20 | .07 |
| ❑ 171 David Lee | .20 | .07 |
| ❑ 172 Jim Otis | .20 | .07 |
| ❑ 173 Archie Manning | 1.00 | .40 |
| ❑ 174 Jim Carter | .20 | .07 |
| ❑ 175 Jean Fugett | .20 | .07 |
| ❑ 176 Willie Parker C | .20 | .07 |
| ❑ 177 Haven Moses | .50 | .20 |
| ❑ 178 Horace King RC | .20 | .07 |
| ❑ 179 Bob Thomas | .20 | .07 |
| ❑ 180 Monte Jackson | .20 | .07 |
| ❑ 181 Steve Zabel | .20 | .07 |
| ❑ 182 John Fitzgerald | .20 | .07 |
| ❑ 183 Mike Livingston | .20 | .07 |
| ❑ 184 Larry Poole | .20 | .07 |
| ❑ 185 Isaac Curtis | .50 | .20 |
| ❑ 186 Chuck Ramsey | .20 | .07 |
| ❑ 187 Bob Klein | .20 | .07 |
| ❑ 188 Ray Rhodes | 1.00 | .40 |
| ❑ 189 Otis Sistrunk | .50 | .20 |
| ❑ 190 Bill Bergey | .50 | .20 |
| ❑ 191 Sherman Smith | .50 | .20 |
| ❑ 192 Dave Green | .20 | .07 |
| ❑ 193 Carl Mauck | .20 | .07 |
| ❑ 194 Reggie Harrison | .20 | .07 |
| ❑ 195 Roger Carr | .50 | .20 |
| ❑ 196 Steve Bartkowski | 1.00 | .40 |
| ❑ 197 Ray Wersching | .20 | .07 |
| ❑ 198 Willie Buchanan | .20 | .07 |
| ❑ 199 Neil Clabo | .20 | .07 |
| ❑ 200 Walter Payton UER | 25.00 | 12.50 |
| ❑ 201 Sam Adams OL | .20 | .07 |
| ❑ 202 Larry Gordon | .20 | .07 |
| ❑ 203 Pat Tilley | .50 | .20 |
| ❑ 204 Mack Mitchell | .20 | .07 |
| ❑ 205 Ken Anderson | 1.00 | .40 |
| ❑ 206 Scott Dierking | .20 | .07 |
| ❑ 207 Jack Rudnay | .20 | .07 |
| ❑ 208 Jim Stienke | .20 | .07 |
| ❑ 209 Bill Simpson | .20 | .07 |
| ❑ 210 Errol Mann | .20 | .07 |
| ❑ 211 Bucky Dilts | .20 | .07 |
| ❑ 212 Reuben Gant | .20 | .07 |
| ❑ 213 Thomas Henderson RC | 1.50 | .60 |
| ❑ 214 Steve Furness | .50 | .20 |
| ❑ 215 John Riggins | 2.00 | .75 |
| ❑ 216 Keith Krepfle RC | .20 | .07 |
| ❑ 217 Fred Dean RC | 12.00 | 6.00 |
| ❑ 218 Emanuel Zanders | .20 | .07 |
| ❑ 219 Don Testerman | .20 | .07 |
| ❑ 220 George Kunz | .20 | .07 |
| ❑ 221 Darryl Stingley | .50 | .20 |
| ❑ 222 Ken Sanders | .20 | .07 |
| ❑ 223 Gary Huff | .20 | .07 |
| ❑ 224 Gregg Bingham | .20 | .07 |
| ❑ 225 Jerry Sherk | .20 | .07 |
| ❑ 226 Doug Plank | .20 | .07 |
| ❑ 227 Ed Taylor | .20 | .07 |
| ❑ 228 Emery Moorehead | .20 | .07 |
| ❑ 229 Reggie Williams RC | 1.00 | .40 |
| ❑ 230 Claude Humphrey | .20 | .07 |
| ❑ 231 Randy Cross RC | 2.00 | .75 |
| ❑ 232 Jim Hart | 1.00 | .40 |
| ❑ 233 Bobby Bryant | .20 | .07 |
| ❑ 234 Larry Brown | .20 | .07 |
| ❑ 235 Mark Van Eeghen | .50 | .20 |
| ❑ 236 Terry Hermeling | .20 | .07 |
| ❑ 237 Steve Odom | .20 | .07 |
| ❑ 238 Jan Stenerud | 1.00 | .40 |
| ❑ 239 Andre Tillman | .20 | .07 |
| ❑ 240 Tom Jackson RC | 5.00 | 2.00 |
| ❑ 241 Ken Mendenhall | .20 | .07 |
| ❑ 242 Tim Fox | .20 | .07 |
| ❑ 243 Don Herrmann | .20 | .07 |
| ❑ 244 Eddie McMillan | .20 | .07 |
| ❑ 245 Greg Pruitt | .50 | .20 |
| ❑ 246 J.K. McKay | .20 | .07 |
| ❑ 247 Larry Keller | .20 | .07 |
| ❑ 248 Dave Jennings | .50 | .20 |
| ❑ 249 Bo Harris | .20 | .07 |
| ❑ 250 Revie Sorey | .20 | .07 |
| ❑ 251 Tony Greene | .20 | .07 |
| ❑ 252 Butch Johnson | .50 | .20 |
| ❑ 253 Paul Naumoff | .20 | .07 |
| ❑ 254 Rickey Young | .50 | .20 |
| ❑ 255 Dwight White | .50 | .20 |
| ❑ 256 Joe Lavender | .20 | .07 |
| ❑ 257 Checklist 133-264 | 1.00 | .40 |
| ❑ 258 Ronnie Coleman | .20 | .07 |
| ❑ 259 Charlie Smith WR | .20 | .07 |
| ❑ 260 Ray Guy | 1.00 | .40 |
| ❑ 261 David Taylor | .20 | .07 |
| ❑ 262 Bill Lenkaitis | .20 | .07 |
| ❑ 263 Jim Mitchell TE | .20 | .07 |
| ❑ 264 Delvin Williams | .50 | .20 |
| ❑ 265 Jack Youngblood | 1.00 | .40 |
| ❑ 266 Chuck Crist | .20 | .07 |
| ❑ 267 Richard Todd | .50 | .20 |
| ❑ 268 Dave Logan RC | 1.00 | .40 |
| ❑ 269 Rufus Mayes | .20 | .07 |
| ❑ 270 Brad Van Pelt | .20 | .07 |
| ❑ 271 Chester Marcol | .20 | .07 |
| ❑ 272 J.V. Cain | .20 | .07 |
| ❑ 273 Larry Seiple | .20 | .07 |
| ❑ 274 Brent McClanahan | .20 | .07 |
| ❑ 275 Mike Wagner | .20 | .07 |
| ❑ 276 Diron Talbert | .20 | .07 |
| ❑ 277 Brian Baschnagel | .20 | .07 |
| ❑ 278 Ed Podolak | .20 | .07 |
| ❑ 279 Don Dutton | .20 | .07 |
| ❑ 280 John Dutton | .50 | .20 |
| ❑ 281 Don Calhoun | .20 | .07 |
| ❑ 282 Monte Johnson | .20 | .07 |
| ❑ 283 Ron Jessie | .20 | .07 |
| ❑ 284 Jon Morris | .20 | .07 |
| ❑ 285 Riley Odoms | .20 | .07 |

|  |  | | |
|---|---|---|---|
| ☐ 286 | Marv Bateman | .20 | .07 |
| ☐ 287 | Joe Klecko RC | 1.00 | .40 |
| ☐ 288 | Oliver Davis | .20 | .07 |
| ☐ 289 | John McDaniel | .20 | .07 |
| ☐ 290 | Roger Staubach | 12.00 | 6.00 |
| ☐ 291 | Brian Kelley | .20 | .07 |
| ☐ 292 | Mike Hogan | .20 | .07 |
| ☐ 293 | John Leypoldt | .20 | .07 |
| ☐ 294 | Jack Novak | .20 | .07 |
| ☐ 295 | Joe Greene | 2.00 | .75 |
| ☐ 296 | John Hill | .20 | .07 |
| ☐ 297 | Danny Buggs | .20 | .07 |
| ☐ 298 | Ted Albrecht | .20 | .07 |
| ☐ 299 | Nelson Munsey | .20 | .07 |
| ☐ 300 | Chuck Foreman | .50 | .20 |
| ☐ 301 | Dan Pastorini | .50 | .20 |
| ☐ 302 | Tommy Hart | .20 | .07 |
| ☐ 303 | Dave Beverly | .20 | .07 |
| ☐ 304 | Tony Reed RC | .50 | .20 |
| ☐ 305 | Cliff Branch | 1.50 | .60 |
| ☐ 306 | Clarence Duren | .20 | .07 |
| ☐ 307 | Randy Rasmussen | .20 | .07 |
| ☐ 308 | Oscar Roan | .20 | .07 |
| ☐ 309 | Lenvil Elliott | .20 | .07 |
| ☐ 310 | Dan Dierdorf | 1.00 | .40 |
| ☐ 311 | Johnny Perkins | .20 | .07 |
| ☐ 312 | Rafael Septien RC | .50 | .20 |
| ☐ 313 | Terry Beeson | .20 | .07 |
| ☐ 314 | Lee Roy Selmon | 2.00 | .75 |
| ☐ 315 | Tony Dorsett RC | 40.00 | 25.00 |
| ☐ 316 | Greg Landry | .50 | .20 |
| ☐ 317 | Jake Scott | .20 | .07 |
| ☐ 318 | Dan Peiffer | .20 | .07 |
| ☐ 319 | John Bunting | .50 | .20 |
| ☐ 320 | John Stallworth RC | 20.00 | 10.00 |
| ☐ 321 | Bob Howard | .20 | .07 |
| ☐ 322 | Larry Little | 1.00 | .40 |
| ☐ 323 | Reggie McKenzie | .50 | .20 |
| ☐ 324 | Duane Carrell | .20 | .07 |
| ☐ 325 | Ed Simonini | .20 | .07 |
| ☐ 326 | John Vella | .20 | .07 |
| ☐ 327 | Wesley Walker RC | 3.00 | 1.50 |
| ☐ 328 | Jon Keyworth | .20 | .07 |
| ☐ 329 | Ron Bolton | .20 | .07 |
| ☐ 330 | Tommy Casanova | .20 | .07 |
| ☐ 331 | R.Staubach/B.Griese LL | 4.00 | 2.00 |
| ☐ 332 | A.Rashad/Mitchell LL | 1.00 | .40 |
| ☐ 333 | W.Payton/VanEeghenLL | 3.00 | 1.25 |
| ☐ 334 | W.Payton/E.Mann LL | 3.00 | 1.25 |
| ☐ 335 | Interception Leaders | .20 | .07 |
| ☐ 336 | Punting Leaders | .50 | .20 |
| ☐ 337 | Robert Brazile | .50 | .20 |
| ☐ 338 | Charlie Joiner | 1.50 | .60 |
| ☐ 339 | Joe Ferguson | .50 | .20 |
| ☐ 340 | Bill Thompson | .20 | .07 |
| ☐ 341 | Sam Cunningham | .50 | .20 |
| ☐ 342 | Curtis Johnson | .20 | .07 |
| ☐ 343 | Jim Marshall | 1.00 | .40 |
| ☐ 344 | Charlie Sanders | .50 | .20 |
| ☐ 345 | Willie Hall | .20 | .07 |
| ☐ 346 | Pat Haden | 1.00 | .40 |
| ☐ 347 | Jim Bakken | .20 | .07 |
| ☐ 348 | Bruce Taylor | .20 | .07 |
| ☐ 349 | Barty Smith | .20 | .07 |
| ☐ 350 | Drew Pearson | 1.50 | .60 |
| ☐ 351 | Mike Webster | 2.50 | 1.00 |
| ☐ 352 | Bobby Hammond | .20 | .07 |
| ☐ 353 | Dave Mays | .20 | .07 |
| ☐ 354 | Pat McInally | .20 | .07 |
| ☐ 355 | Toni Linhart | .20 | .07 |
| ☐ 356 | Larry Hand | .20 | .07 |
| ☐ 357 | Ted Fritsch Jr. | .20 | .07 |
| ☐ 358 | Larry Marshall | .20 | .07 |
| ☐ 359 | Waymond Bryant | .20 | .07 |
| ☐ 360 | Louie Kelcher RC | .50 | .20 |
| ☐ 361 | Stanley Morgan RC | 2.00 | .75 |
| ☐ 362 | Bruce Harper RC | .50 | .20 |
| ☐ 363 | Bernard Jackson | .20 | .07 |
| ☐ 364 | Walter White | .20 | .07 |
| ☐ 365 | Ken Stabler | 8.00 | 4.00 |
| ☐ 366 | Fred Dryer | 1.00 | .40 |
| ☐ 367 | Ike Harris | .20 | .07 |
| ☐ 368 | Norm Bulaich | .20 | .07 |
| ☐ 369 | Merv Krakau | .20 | .07 |
| ☐ 370 | John James | .20 | .07 |
| ☐ 371 | Bennie Cunningham RC | .50 | .20 |
| ☐ 372 | Doug Van Horn | .20 | .07 |
| ☐ 373 | Thom Darden | .20 | .07 |
| ☐ 374 | Eddie Edwards RC | .20 | .07 |
| ☐ 375 | Mike Thomas | .20 | .07 |
| ☐ 376 | Fred Cook | .20 | .07 |
| ☐ 377 | Mike Phipps | .50 | .20 |
| ☐ 378 | Paul Krause | 1.00 | .40 |
| ☐ 379 | Harold Carmichael | 1.00 | .40 |
| ☐ 380 | Mike Haynes | 1.00 | .40 |
| ☐ 381 | Wayne Morris | .20 | .07 |
| ☐ 382 | Greg Buttle | .20 | .07 |
| ☐ 383 | Jim Zorn | 1.00 | .40 |
| ☐ 384 | Jack Dolbin | .20 | .07 |
| ☐ 385 | Charlie Waters | .50 | .20 |
| ☐ 386 | Dan Ryczek | .20 | .07 |
| ☐ 387 | Joe Washington RC | 1.00 | .40 |
| ☐ 388 | Checklist 265-396 | 1.00 | .40 |
| ☐ 389 | James Hunter | .20 | .07 |
| ☐ 390 | Billy Johnson | .50 | .20 |
| ☐ 391 | Jim Allen RC | .20 | .07 |
| ☐ 392 | George Buehler | .20 | .07 |
| ☐ 393 | Harry Carson | 1.00 | .40 |
| ☐ 394 | Cleo Miller | .20 | .07 |
| ☐ 395 | Gary Burley | .20 | .07 |
| ☐ 396 | Mark Moseley | .50 | .20 |
| ☐ 397 | Virgil Livers | .20 | .07 |
| ☐ 398 | Joe Ehrmann | .20 | .07 |
| ☐ 399 | Freddie Solomon | .20 | .07 |
| ☐ 400 | O.J.Simpson | 4.00 | 2.00 |
| ☐ 401 | Julius Adams | .20 | .07 |
| ☐ 402 | Artimus Parker | .20 | .07 |
| ☐ 403 | Gene Washington 49er | .50 | .20 |
| ☐ 404 | Herman Edwards | .20 | .07 |
| ☐ 405 | Craig Morton | 1.00 | .40 |
| ☐ 406 | Alan Page | 1.00 | .40 |
| ☐ 407 | Larry McCarren | .20 | .07 |
| ☐ 408 | Tony Galbreath | .50 | .20 |
| ☐ 409 | Roman Gabriel | 1.00 | .40 |
| ☐ 410 | Efren Herrera | .20 | .07 |
| ☐ 411 | Jim Smith RC | .20 | .07 |
| ☐ 412 | Bill Bryant | .20 | .07 |
| ☐ 413 | Doug Dieken | .20 | .07 |
| ☐ 414 | Marvin Cobb | .20 | .07 |
| ☐ 415 | Fred Biletnikoff | 2.00 | .75 |
| ☐ 416 | Joe Theismann | 2.50 | 1.00 |
| ☐ 417 | Roland Harper | .20 | .07 |
| ☐ 418 | Derrel Luce | .20 | .07 |
| ☐ 419 | Ralph Perretta | .20 | .07 |
| ☐ 420 | Louis Wright RC | 1.00 | .40 |
| ☐ 421 | Prentice McCray | .20 | .07 |
| ☐ 422 | Garry Puetz | .20 | .07 |
| ☐ 423 | Alfred Jenkins RC | 1.00 | .40 |
| ☐ 424 | Paul Seymour | .20 | .07 |
| ☐ 425 | Garo Yepremian | .50 | .20 |
| ☐ 426 | Emmitt Thomas | .40 | .15 |
| ☐ 427 | Dexter Bussey | .20 | .07 |
| ☐ 428 | John Sanders | .20 | .07 |
| ☐ 429 | Ed Too Tall Jones | 2.00 | .75 |
| ☐ 430 | Ron Yary | 1.00 | .40 |
| ☐ 431 | Frank Lewis | .50 | .20 |
| ☐ 432 | Jerry Golsteyn | .20 | .07 |
| ☐ 433 | Clarence Scott | .20 | .07 |
| ☐ 434 | Pete Johnson RC | 1.00 | .40 |
| ☐ 435 | Charle Young | .50 | .20 |
| ☐ 436 | Harold McLinton | .20 | .07 |
| ☐ 437 | Noah Jackson | .20 | .07 |
| ☐ 438 | Bruce Laird | .20 | .07 |
| ☐ 439 | John Matuszak | .50 | .20 |
| ☐ 440 | Nat Moore | .50 | .20 |
| ☐ 441 | Leon Gray | .20 | .07 |
| ☐ 442 | Jerome Barkum | .20 | .07 |
| ☐ 443 | Steve Largent | 12.00 | 6.00 |
| ☐ 444 | John Zook | .20 | .07 |
| ☐ 445 | Preston Pearson | .50 | .20 |
| ☐ 446 | Conrad Dobler | .50 | .20 |
| ☐ 447 | Wilbur Summers | .20 | .07 |
| ☐ 448 | Lou Piccone | .20 | .07 |
| ☐ 449 | Ron Jaworski | 1.00 | .40 |
| ☐ 450 | Jack Ham | 1.50 | .60 |
| ☐ 451 | Mick Tingelhoff | .50 | .20 |
| ☐ 452 | Clyde Powers | .20 | .07 |
| ☐ 453 | John Cappelletti | 1.00 | .40 |
| ☐ 454 | Dick Ambrose | .20 | .07 |
| ☐ 455 | Lemar Parrish | .20 | .07 |
| ☐ 456 | Ron Saul | .20 | .07 |
| ☐ 457 | Bob Parsons | .20 | .07 |
| ☐ 458 | Glenn Doughty | .20 | .07 |
| ☐ 459 | Don Woods | .20 | .07 |
| ☐ 460 | Art Shell | 1.00 | .40 |
| ☐ 461 | Sam Hunt | .20 | .07 |
| ☐ 462 | Lawrence Pillers | .20 | .07 |
| ☐ 463 | Henry Childs | .20 | .07 |
| ☐ 464 | Roger Wehrli | .50 | .20 |
| ☐ 465 | Otis Armstrong | .50 | .20 |
| ☐ 466 | Bob Baumhower RC | 2.00 | .75 |
| ☐ 467 | Ray Jarvis | .20 | .07 |
| ☐ 468 | Guy Morriss | .20 | .07 |
| ☐ 469 | Matt Blair | .50 | .20 |
| ☐ 470 | Billy Joe DuPree | .50 | .20 |
| ☐ 471 | Roland Hooks | .20 | .07 |
| ☐ 472 | Joe Danelo | .20 | .07 |
| ☐ 473 | Reggie Rucker | .20 | .07 |
| ☐ 474 | Vern Holland | .20 | .07 |
| ☐ 475 | Mel Blount | 1.50 | .60 |
| ☐ 476 | Eddie Brown S | .20 | .07 |
| ☐ 477 | Bo Rather | .20 | .07 |
| ☐ 478 | Don McCauley | .20 | .07 |
| ☐ 479 | Glen Walker | .20 | .07 |
| ☐ 480 | Randy Gradishar | 1.00 | .40 |
| ☐ 481 | Dave Rowe | .20 | .07 |
| ☐ 482 | Pat Leahy | .50 | .20 |
| ☐ 483 | Mike Fuller | .20 | .07 |
| ☐ 484 | David Lewis RC | .20 | .07 |
| ☐ 485 | Steve Grogan | 1.00 | .40 |
| ☐ 486 | Mel Gray | .50 | .20 |
| ☐ 487 | Eddie Payton RC | 1.00 | .40 |
| ☐ 488 | Checklist 397-528 | 1.00 | .40 |
| ☐ 489 | Stu Voigt | .20 | .07 |
| ☐ 490 | Roland Lawrence | .20 | .07 |
| ☐ 491 | Nick Mike-Mayer | .20 | .07 |
| ☐ 492 | Troy Archer | .20 | .07 |
| ☐ 493 | Benny Malone | .20 | .07 |
| ☐ 494 | Golden Richards | .50 | .20 |
| ☐ 495 | Chris Hanburger | .20 | .07 |
| ☐ 496 | Dwight Harrison | .20 | .07 |
| ☐ 497 | Gary Fencik RC | 1.00 | .40 |
| ☐ 498 | Rich Saul | .20 | .07 |
| ☐ 499 | Dan Fouts | 4.00 | 2.00 |
| ☐ 500 | Franco Harris | 4.00 | 2.00 |
| ☐ 501 | Atlanta Falcons TL | .75 | .30 |
| ☐ 502 | Baltimore Colts TL | .75 | .30 |
| ☐ 503 | Bills TL/O.J.Simpson | 1.50 | .60 |
| ☐ 504 | Bears TL/Walter Payton | 2.00 | .75 |
| ☐ 505 | Bengals TL/Reg.Williams | .75 | .30 |
| ☐ 506 | Cleveland Browns TL | .75 | .30 |
| ☐ 507 | Cowboys TL/T.Dorsett | 2.50 | 1.00 |
| ☐ 508 | Denver Broncos TL | 1.00 | .40 |
| ☐ 509 | Detroit Lions TL | .75 | .30 |
| ☐ 510 | Green Bay Packers TL | 1.00 | .40 |
| ☐ 511 | Houston Oilers TL | .75 | .30 |
| ☐ 512 | Kansas City Chiefs TL | .75 | .30 |
| ☐ 513 | Los Angeles Rams TL | .75 | .30 |
| ☐ 514 | Miami Dolphins TL | 1.00 | .40 |
| ☐ 515 | Minnesota Vikings TL | .75 | .30 |
| ☐ 516 | New England Patriots TL | .75 | .30 |
| ☐ 517 | New Orleans Saints TL | .75 | .30 |
| ☐ 518 | New York Giants TL | .75 | .30 |
| ☐ 519 | Jets TL/Wesley Walker | 1.00 | .40 |
| ☐ 520 | Oakland Raiders TL | 1.00 | .40 |
| ☐ 521 | Philadelphia Eagles TL | .75 | .30 |
| ☐ 522 | Steelers TL/Harris/Blount | 1.00 | .40 |
| ☐ 523 | St.Louis Cardinals TL | .75 | .30 |
| ☐ 524 | San Diego Chargers TL | 1.00 | .40 |
| ☐ 525 | San Francisco 49ers TL | .75 | .30 |
| ☐ 526 | Seahawks TL/S.Largent | 1.50 | .60 |
| ☐ 527 | Tampa Bay Bucs TL | .75 | .30 |
| ☐ 528 | Redskins TL/Ken Houston | 1.00 | .40 |

## 1979 Topps

|  |  | | |
|---|---|---|---|
| ☐ | COMPLETE SET (528) | 150.00 | 75.00 |
| ☐ 1 | Staubach/Bradshaw LL | 8.00 | 4.00 |
| ☐ 2 | S.Largent/R.Young LL | 1.00 | .40 |
| ☐ 3 | E.Campbell/W.Payton LL | 8.00 | 4.00 |
| ☐ 4 | Scoring Leaders | .20 | .07 |
| ☐ 5 | Interception Leaders | .20 | .07 |
| ☐ 6 | Punting Leaders | .20 | .07 |
| ☐ 7 | Johnny Perkins | .20 | .07 |
| ☐ 8 | Charles Phillips | .20 | .07 |
| ☐ 9 | Derrel Luce | .20 | .07 |
| ☐ 10 | John Riggins | 1.25 | .50 |
| ☐ 11 | Chester Marcol | .20 | .07 |
| ☐ 12 | Bernard Jackson | .20 | .07 |
| ☐ 13 | Dave Logan | .20 | .07 |
| ☐ 14 | Bo Harris | .20 | .07 |
| ☐ 15 | Alan Page | 1.00 | .40 |

| | | |
|---|---|---|
| ☐ 16 John Smith | .20 | .07 |
| ☐ 17 Dwight McDonald | .20 | .07 |
| ☐ 18 John Cappelletti | .50 | .20 |
| ☐ 19 Steelers TL/Harris/Dungy | 12.00 | 5.00 |
| ☐ 20 Bill Bergey | .50 | .20 |
| ☐ 21 Jerome Barkum | .20 | .07 |
| ☐ 22 Larry Csonka | 2.50 | 1.00 |
| ☐ 23 Joe Ferguson | .50 | .20 |
| ☐ 24 Ed Too Tall Jones | 1.25 | .50 |
| ☐ 25 Dave Jennings | .50 | .20 |
| ☐ 26 Horace King | .20 | .07 |
| ☐ 27 Steve Little | .50 | .20 |
| ☐ 28 Morris Bradshaw | .20 | .07 |
| ☐ 29 Joe Ehrmann | .20 | .07 |
| ☐ 30 Ahmad Rashad | 1.00 | .40 |
| ☐ 31 Joe Lavender | .20 | .07 |
| ☐ 32 Dan Neal | .20 | .07 |
| ☐ 33 Johnny Evans | .20 | .07 |
| ☐ 34 Pete Johnson | .50 | .20 |
| ☐ 35 Mike Haynes | 1.00 | .40 |
| ☐ 36 Tim Mazzetti | .20 | .07 |
| ☐ 37 Mike Barber RC | .20 | .07 |
| ☐ 38 49ers TL/O.J.Simpson | 1.50 | .60 |
| ☐ 39 Bill Gregory | .20 | .07 |
| ☐ 40 Randy Gradishar | 1.00 | .40 |
| ☐ 41 Richard Todd | .50 | .20 |
| ☐ 42 Henry Marshall | .20 | .07 |
| ☐ 43 John Hill | .20 | .07 |
| ☐ 44 Sidney Thornton | .20 | .07 |
| ☐ 45 Ron Jessie | .20 | .07 |
| ☐ 46 Bob Baumhower | .50 | .20 |
| ☐ 47 Johnnie Gray | .20 | .07 |
| ☐ 48 Doug Williams RC | 6.00 | 3.00 |
| ☐ 49 Don McCauley | .20 | .07 |
| ☐ 50 Ray Guy | .50 | .20 |
| ☐ 51 Bob Klein | .20 | .07 |
| ☐ 52 Golden Richards | .20 | .07 |
| ☐ 53 Mark Miller QB | .20 | .07 |
| ☐ 54 John Sanders | .20 | .07 |
| ☐ 55 Gary Burley | .20 | .07 |
| ☐ 56 Steve Nelson | .20 | .07 |
| ☐ 57 Buffalo Bills TL | .75 | .30 |
| ☐ 58 Bobby Bryant | .20 | .07 |
| ☐ 59 Rick Kane | .20 | .07 |
| ☐ 60 Larry Little | 1.00 | .40 |
| ☐ 61 Ted Fritsch Jr. | .20 | .07 |
| ☐ 62 Larry Mallory | .20 | .07 |
| ☐ 63 Marvin Powell | .20 | .07 |
| ☐ 64 Jim Hart | 1.00 | .40 |
| ☐ 65 Joe Greene | 1.50 | .60 |
| ☐ 66 Walter White | .20 | .07 |
| ☐ 67 Gregg Bingham | .20 | .07 |
| ☐ 68 Errol Mann | .20 | .07 |
| ☐ 69 Bruce Laird | .20 | .07 |
| ☐ 70 Drew Pearson | 1.00 | .40 |
| ☐ 71 Steve Bartkowski | 1.00 | .40 |
| ☐ 72 Ted Albrecht | .20 | .07 |
| ☐ 73 Charlie Hall | .20 | .07 |
| ☐ 74 Pat McInally | .20 | .07 |
| ☐ 75 Bubba Baker RC | 1.00 | .40 |
| ☐ 76 New England Pats TL | .75 | .30 |
| ☐ 77 Steve DeBerg RC | 2.00 | .75 |
| ☐ 78 John Yarno | .20 | .07 |
| ☐ 79 Stu Voigt | .20 | .07 |
| ☐ 80 Frank Corral AP | .20 | .07 |
| ☐ 81 Troy Archer | .20 | .07 |
| ☐ 82 Bruce Harper | .20 | .07 |
| ☐ 83 Tom Jackson | 1.50 | .60 |
| ☐ 84 Larry Brown | .50 | .20 |
| ☐ 85 Wilbert Montgomery RC | 1.00 | .40 |

| | | |
|---|---|---|
| ☐ 86 Butch Johnson | .50 | .20 |
| ☐ 87 Mike Kadish | .20 | .07 |
| ☐ 88 Ralph Perretta | .20 | .07 |
| ☐ 89 David Lee | .20 | .07 |
| ☐ 90 Mark Van Eeghen | .50 | .20 |
| ☐ 91 John McDaniel | .20 | .07 |
| ☐ 92 Gary Fencik | .50 | .20 |
| ☐ 93 Mack Mitchell | .20 | .07 |
| ☐ 94 Cincinnati Bengals TL/Jauron | 1.00 | .40 |
| ☐ 95 Steve Grogan | 1.00 | .40 |
| ☐ 96 Garo Yepremian | .50 | .20 |
| ☐ 97 Barty Smith | .20 | .07 |
| ☐ 98 Frank Reed | .20 | .07 |
| ☐ 99 Jim Clack | .20 | .07 |
| ☐ 100 Chuck Foreman | .50 | .20 |
| ☐ 101 Joe Klecko | 1.00 | .40 |
| ☐ 102 Pat Tilley | .50 | .20 |
| ☐ 103 Conrad Dobler | .50 | .20 |
| ☐ 104 Craig Colquitt | .20 | .07 |
| ☐ 105 Dan Pastorini | .50 | .20 |
| ☐ 106 Rod Perry AP | .20 | .07 |
| ☐ 107 Nick Mike-Mayer | .20 | .07 |
| ☐ 108 John Matuszak | .50 | .20 |
| ☐ 109 David Taylor | .20 | .07 |
| ☐ 110 Billy Joe DuPree | .50 | .20 |
| ☐ 111 Harold McLinton | .20 | .07 |
| ☐ 112 Virgil Livers | .20 | .07 |
| ☐ 113 Cleveland Browns TL | .75 | .30 |
| ☐ 114 Checklist 1-132 | 1.00 | .40 |
| ☐ 115 Ken Anderson | 1.00 | .40 |
| ☐ 116 Bill Lenkaitis | .20 | .07 |
| ☐ 117 Bucky Dilts | .20 | .07 |
| ☐ 118 Tony Greene | .20 | .07 |
| ☐ 119 Bobby Hammond | .20 | .07 |
| ☐ 120 Nat Moore | .50 | .20 |
| ☐ 121 Pat Leahy | .50 | .20 |
| ☐ 122 James Harris | .50 | .20 |
| ☐ 123 Lee Roy Selmon | 1.25 | .50 |
| ☐ 124 Bennie Cunningham | .50 | .20 |
| ☐ 125 Matt Blair AP | .50 | .20 |
| ☐ 126 Jim Allen | .20 | .07 |
| ☐ 127 Alfred Jenkins | .50 | .20 |
| ☐ 128 Arthur Whittington | .20 | .07 |
| ☐ 129 Norm Thompson | .20 | .07 |
| ☐ 130 Pat Haden | 1.00 | .40 |
| ☐ 131 Freddie Solomon | .20 | .07 |
| ☐ 132 Bears TL/W.Payton | 2.00 | .75 |
| ☐ 133 Mark Moseley | .20 | .07 |
| ☐ 134 Cleo Miller | .20 | .07 |
| ☐ 135 Ross Browner RC | .50 | .20 |
| ☐ 136 Don Calhoun | .20 | .07 |
| ☐ 137 David Whitehurst | .20 | .07 |
| ☐ 138 Terry Beeson | .20 | .07 |
| ☐ 139 Ken Stone | .20 | .07 |
| ☐ 140 Brad Van Pelt AP | .20 | .07 |
| ☐ 141 Wesley Walker | 1.00 | .40 |
| ☐ 142 Jan Stenerud | 1.00 | .40 |
| ☐ 143 Henry Childs | .20 | .07 |
| ☐ 144 Otis Armstrong | 1.00 | .40 |
| ☐ 145 Dwight White | .50 | .20 |
| ☐ 146 Steve Wilson | .20 | .07 |
| ☐ 147 Tom Skladany RC | .20 | .07 |
| ☐ 148 Lou Piccone | .20 | .07 |
| ☐ 149 Monte Johnson | .20 | .07 |
| ☐ 150 Joe Washington | .50 | .20 |
| ☐ 151 Eagles TL/W.Montgomery | .75 | .30 |
| ☐ 152 Fred Dean | .75 | .30 |
| ☐ 153 Rolland Lawrence | .20 | .07 |
| ☐ 154 Brian Baschnagel | .20 | .07 |
| ☐ 155 Joe Theismann | 2.00 | .75 |
| ☐ 156 Marvin Cobb | .20 | .07 |
| ☐ 157 Dick Ambrose | .20 | .07 |
| ☐ 158 Mike Patrick | .20 | .07 |
| ☐ 159 Gary Shirk | .20 | .07 |
| ☐ 160 Tony Dorsett | 12.00 | 6.00 |
| ☐ 161 Greg Buttle | .20 | .07 |
| ☐ 162 A.J. Duhe | .50 | .20 |
| ☐ 163 Mick Tingelhoff | .50 | .20 |
| ☐ 164 Ken Burrough | .20 | .07 |
| ☐ 165 Mike Wagner | .20 | .07 |
| ☐ 166 AFC Champs/F.Harris | 1.00 | .40 |
| ☐ 167 NFC Championship | .50 | .20 |
| ☐ 168 Super Bowl XIII/Harris | 1.25 | .50 |
| ☐ 169 Raiders TL/Ted Hendricks | 1.00 | .40 |
| ☐ 170 O.J.Simpson | 4.00 | 1.50 |
| ☐ 171 Doug Nettles | .20 | .07 |
| ☐ 172 Dan Dierdorf | 1.00 | .40 |

| | | |
|---|---|---|
| ☐ 173 Dave Beverly | .20 | .07 |
| ☐ 174 Jim Zorn | 1.00 | .40 |
| ☐ 175 Mike Thomas | .20 | .07 |
| ☐ 176 John Outlaw | .20 | .07 |
| ☐ 177 Jim Turner | .20 | .07 |
| ☐ 178 Freddie Scott | .20 | .07 |
| ☐ 179 Mike Phipps | .50 | .20 |
| ☐ 180 Jack Youngblood | 1.00 | .40 |
| ☐ 181 Sam Hunt | .20 | .07 |
| ☐ 182 Tony Hill RC | 1.00 | .40 |
| ☐ 183 Gary Barbaro | .20 | .07 |
| ☐ 184 Archie Griffin | .50 | .20 |
| ☐ 185 Jerry Sherk | .20 | .07 |
| ☐ 186 Bobby Jackson | .20 | .07 |
| ☐ 187 Don Woods | .20 | .07 |
| ☐ 188 New York Giants TL | .75 | .30 |
| ☐ 189 Raymond Chester | .20 | .07 |
| ☐ 190 Joe DeLamielleure AP | 1.00 | .40 |
| ☐ 191 Tony Galbreath | .50 | .20 |
| ☐ 192 Robert Brazile AP | .50 | .20 |
| ☐ 193 Neil O'Donoghue | .20 | .07 |
| ☐ 194 Mike Webster | 1.00 | .40 |
| ☐ 195 Ed Simonini | .20 | .07 |
| ☐ 196 Benny Malone | .20 | .07 |
| ☐ 197 Tom Wittum | .20 | .07 |
| ☐ 198 Steve Largent | 8.00 | 4.00 |
| ☐ 199 Tommy Hart | .20 | .07 |
| ☐ 200 Fran Tarkenton | 3.00 | 1.50 |
| ☐ 201 Leon Gray AP | .20 | .07 |
| ☐ 202 Leroy Harris | .20 | .07 |
| ☐ 203 Eric Williams LB | .20 | .07 |
| ☐ 204 Thom Darden AP | .20 | .07 |
| ☐ 205 Ken Riley | .50 | .20 |
| ☐ 206 Clark Gaines | .20 | .07 |
| ☐ 207 Kansas City Chiefs TL | .75 | .30 |
| ☐ 208 Joe Danelo | .20 | .07 |
| ☐ 209 Glen Walker | .20 | .07 |
| ☐ 210 Art Shell | 1.00 | .40 |
| ☐ 211 Jon Keyworth | .20 | .07 |
| ☐ 212 Herman Edwards | .20 | .07 |
| ☐ 213 John Fitzgerald | .20 | .07 |
| ☐ 214 Jim Smith | .50 | .20 |
| ☐ 215 Coy Bacon | .50 | .20 |
| ☐ 216 Dennis Johnson RBK RC | .20 | .07 |
| ☐ 217 John Jefferson RC | 3.00 | 1.50 |
| ☐ 218 Gary Weaver | .20 | .07 |
| ☐ 219 Tom Blanchard | .20 | .07 |
| ☐ 220 Bert Jones | 1.00 | .40 |
| ☐ 221 Stanley Morgan | 1.00 | .40 |
| ☐ 222 James Hunter | .20 | .07 |
| ☐ 223 Jim O'Bradovich | .20 | .07 |
| ☐ 224 Carl Mauck | .20 | .07 |
| ☐ 225 Chris Bahr | .20 | .07 |
| ☐ 226 Jets TL/Wesley Walker | .75 | .30 |
| ☐ 227 Roland Harper | .20 | .07 |
| ☐ 228 Randy Dean | .20 | .07 |
| ☐ 229 Bob Jackson | .20 | .07 |
| ☐ 230 Sammie White | .50 | .20 |
| ☐ 231 Mike Dawson | .20 | .07 |
| ☐ 232 Checklist 133-264 | 1.00 | .40 |
| ☐ 233 Ken MacAfee RC | .20 | .07 |
| ☐ 234 Jon Kolb AP | .20 | .07 |
| ☐ 235 Willie Hall | .20 | .07 |
| ☐ 236 Ron Saul AP | .20 | .07 |
| ☐ 237 Haskel Stanback | .20 | .07 |
| ☐ 238 Zenon Andrusyshyn | .20 | .07 |
| ☐ 239 Norris Thomas | .20 | .07 |
| ☐ 240 Rick Upchurch | .50 | .20 |
| ☐ 241 Robert Pratt | .20 | .07 |
| ☐ 242 Julius Adams | .20 | .07 |
| ☐ 243 Rich McGeorge | .20 | .07 |
| ☐ 244 Seahawks TL/S.Largent | 1.25 | .50 |
| ☐ 245 Blair Bush RC | .20 | .07 |
| ☐ 246 Billy Johnson | .50 | .20 |
| ☐ 247 Randy Rasmussen | .20 | .07 |
| ☐ 248 Brian Kelley | .20 | .07 |
| ☐ 249 Mike Pruitt | .50 | .20 |
| ☐ 250 Harold Carmichael | 1.00 | .40 |
| ☐ 251 Mike Hartenstine | .20 | .07 |
| ☐ 252 Robert Newhouse | .50 | .20 |
| ☐ 253 Gary Danielson RC | 1.00 | .40 |
| ☐ 254 Mike Fuller | .20 | .07 |
| ☐ 255 L.C.Greenwood | 1.00 | .40 |
| ☐ 256 Lamar Parrish | 1.00 | .40 |
| ☐ 257 Ike Harris | .20 | .07 |
| ☐ 258 Ricky Bell RC | 1.00 | .40 |
| ☐ 259 Willie Parker C | .20 | .07 |

| | | |
|---|---|---|
| 260 Gene Upshaw | 1.00 | .40 |
| 261 Glenn Doughty | .20 | .07 |
| 262 Steve Zabel | .20 | .07 |
| 263 Atlanta Falcons TL | .75 | .30 |
| 264 Ray Wersching | .20 | .07 |
| 265 Lawrence McCutcheon | .50 | .20 |
| 266 Willie Buchanon AP | .20 | .07 |
| 267 Matt Robinson | .20 | .07 |
| 268 Reggie Rucker | .50 | .20 |
| 269 Doug Van Horn | .20 | .07 |
| 270 Lydell Mitchell | .50 | .20 |
| 271 Vern Holland | .20 | .07 |
| 272 Eason Ramson | .20 | .07 |
| 273 Steve Towle | .20 | .07 |
| 274 Jim Marshall | 1.00 | .40 |
| 275 Mel Blount | 1.25 | .50 |
| 276 Bob Kuziel | .20 | .07 |
| 277 James Scott | .20 | .07 |
| 278 Tony Reed | .20 | .07 |
| 279 Dave Green | .20 | .07 |
| 280 Toni Linhart | .20 | .07 |
| 281 Andy Johnson | .20 | .07 |
| 282 Los Angeles Rams TL | .75 | .30 |
| 283 Phil Villapiano | .20 | .07 |
| 284 Dexter Bussey | .20 | .07 |
| 285 Craig Morton | 1.00 | .40 |
| 286 Guy Morriss | .20 | .07 |
| 287 Lawrence Pillers | .20 | .07 |
| 288 Gerald Irons | .20 | .07 |
| 289 Scott Perry | .20 | .07 |
| 290 Randy White | 2.00 | .75 |
| 291 Jack Gregory | .20 | .07 |
| 292 Bob Chandler | .20 | .07 |
| 293 Rich Szaro | .20 | .07 |
| 294 Sherman Smith | .20 | .07 |
| 295 Tom Banks AP | .20 | .07 |
| 296 Revie Sorey AP | .20 | .07 |
| 297 Ricky Thompson | .20 | .07 |
| 298 Ron Yary | 1.00 | .40 |
| 299 Lyle Blackwood | .20 | .07 |
| 300 Franco Harris | 2.50 | 1.25 |
| 301 Oilers TL/E.Campbell | 3.00 | 1.50 |
| 302 Scott Bull | .20 | .07 |
| 303 Dewey Selmon | .50 | .20 |
| 304 Jack Rudnay | .20 | .07 |
| 305 Fred Biletnikoff | 2.00 | .75 |
| 306 Jeff West | .20 | .07 |
| 307 Shafer Suggs | .20 | .07 |
| 308 Ozzie Newsome RC | 12.00 | 6.00 |
| 309 Boobie Clark | .20 | .07 |
| 310 James Lofton RC | 12.00 | 6.00 |
| 311 Joe Pisarcik | .20 | .07 |
| 312 Bill Simpson AP | .20 | .07 |
| 313 Haven Moses | .50 | .20 |
| 314 Jim Merlo | .20 | .07 |
| 315 Preston Pearson | .50 | .20 |
| 316 Larry Tearry | .20 | .07 |
| 317 Tom Dempsey | .20 | .07 |
| 318 Greg Latta | .20 | .07 |
| 319 Redskins TL/John Riggins | 1.50 | .60 |
| 320 Jack Ham | 1.25 | .50 |
| 321 Harold Jackson | .50 | .20 |
| 322 George Roberts | .20 | .07 |
| 323 Ron Jaworski | 1.00 | .40 |
| 324 Jim Otis | .20 | .07 |
| 325 Roger Carr | .50 | .20 |
| 326 Jack Tatum | .50 | .20 |
| 327 Derrick Gaffney | .20 | .07 |
| 328 Reggie Williams | 1.00 | .40 |
| 329 Doug Dieken | .20 | .07 |
| 330 Efren Herrera | .20 | .07 |
| 331 Earl Campbell RB | 6.00 | 3.00 |
| 332 Tony Galbreath RB | .20 | .07 |
| 333 Bruce Harper RB | .20 | .07 |
| 334 John James RB | .20 | .07 |
| 335 Walter Payton RB | 4.00 | 1.50 |
| 336 Rickey Young RB | .20 | .07 |
| 337 Jeff Van Note | .50 | .20 |
| 338 Chargers TL/J.Jefferson | 1.00 | .40 |
| 339 Stan Walters RC | .20 | .07 |
| 340 Louis Wright | .50 | .20 |
| 341 Horace Ivory | .20 | .07 |
| 342 Andre Tillman | .20 | .07 |
| 343 Greg Coleman RC | 1.00 | .40 |
| 344 Doug English RC | 1.00 | .40 |
| 345 Ted Hendricks | 1.00 | .40 |
| 346 Rich Saul | .20 | .07 |
| 347 Mel Gray | .50 | .20 |
| 348 Toni Fritsch | .20 | .07 |
| 349 Cornell Webster | .20 | .07 |
| 350 Ken Houston | 1.00 | .40 |
| 351 Ron Johnson DB RC | .50 | .20 |
| 352 Doug Kotar | .20 | .07 |
| 353 Brian Sipe | 1.00 | .40 |
| 354 Billy Brooks | .20 | .07 |
| 355 John Dutton | .50 | .20 |
| 356 Don Goode | .20 | .07 |
| 357 Detroit Lions TL | .75 | .30 |
| 358 Reuben Gant | .20 | .07 |
| 359 Bob Parsons | .20 | .07 |
| 360 Cliff Harris | 1.00 | .40 |
| 361 Raymond Clayborn | .50 | .20 |
| 362 Scott Dierking | .20 | .07 |
| 363 Bill Bryan | .20 | .07 |
| 364 Mike Livingston | .20 | .07 |
| 365 Otis Sistrunk | .50 | .20 |
| 366 Charlie Young | .50 | .20 |
| 367 Keith Wortman | .20 | .07 |
| 368 Checklist 265-396 | 1.00 | .40 |
| 369 Mike Michel | .20 | .07 |
| 370 Delvin Williams AP | .20 | .07 |
| 371 Steve Furness | .50 | .20 |
| 372 Emery Moorehead | .20 | .07 |
| 373 Clarence Scott | .20 | .07 |
| 374 Rufus Mayes | .20 | .07 |
| 375 Chris Hanburger | .20 | .07 |
| 376 Baltimore Colts TL | .75 | .30 |
| 377 Bob Avellini | .50 | .20 |
| 378 Jeff Siemon | .20 | .07 |
| 379 Roland Hooks | .20 | .07 |
| 380 Russ Francis | .50 | .20 |
| 381 Roger Wehrli | .50 | .20 |
| 382 Joe Fields | .20 | .07 |
| 383 Archie Manning | 1.00 | .40 |
| 384 Rob Lytle | .20 | .07 |
| 385 Thomas Henderson | .50 | .20 |
| 386 Morris Owens | .20 | .07 |
| 387 Dan Fouts | 3.00 | 1.50 |
| 388 Chuck Crist | .20 | .07 |
| 389 Ed O'Neil | .20 | .07 |
| 390 Earl Campbell RC | 30.00 | 15.00 |
| 391 Randy Grossman | .20 | .07 |
| 392 Monte Jackson | .20 | .07 |
| 393 John Mendenhall | .20 | .07 |
| 394 Miami Dolphins TL | 1.00 | .40 |
| 395 Isaac Curtis | .50 | .20 |
| 396 Mike Bragg | .20 | .07 |
| 397 Doug Plank | .20 | .07 |
| 398 Mike Barnes | .20 | .07 |
| 399 Calvin Hill | .50 | .20 |
| 400 Roger Staubach | 10.00 | 5.00 |
| 401 Doug Beaudoin | .20 | .07 |
| 402 Chuck Ramsey | .20 | .07 |
| 403 Mike Hogan | .20 | .07 |
| 404 Mario Clark | .20 | .07 |
| 405 Riley Odoms | .20 | .07 |
| 406 Carl Eller | 1.00 | .40 |
| 407 Packers TL/J.Lofton | 1.50 | .60 |
| 408 Mark Arneson | .20 | .07 |
| 409 Vince Ferragamo RC | 1.00 | .40 |
| 410 Cleveland Elam | .20 | .07 |
| 411 Donnie Shell RC | 4.00 | 1.50 |
| 412 Ray Rhodes | 1.00 | .40 |
| 413 Don Cockroft | .20 | .07 |
| 414 Don Bass | .50 | .20 |
| 415 Cliff Branch | 1.00 | .40 |
| 416 Diron Talbert | .20 | .07 |
| 417 Tom Hicks | .20 | .07 |
| 418 Roosevelt Leaks | .20 | .07 |
| 419 Charlie Joiner | 1.00 | .40 |
| 420 Lyle Alzado | 1.00 | .40 |
| 421 Sam Cunningham | .20 | .07 |
| 422 Larry Keller | .20 | .07 |
| 423 Jim Mitchell TE | .20 | .07 |
| 424 Randy Logan | .20 | .07 |
| 425 Jim Langer | 1.00 | .40 |
| 426 Gary Green | .20 | .07 |
| 427 Luther Blue | .20 | .07 |
| 428 Dennis Johnson | .20 | .07 |
| 429 Danny White | 1.00 | .40 |
| 430 Roy Gerela | .20 | .07 |
| 431 Jimmy Robinson | .20 | .07 |
| 432 Minnesota Vikings TL | .75 | .30 |
| 433 Oliver Davis | .20 | .07 |
| 434 Lenvil Elliott | .20 | .07 |
| 435 Willie Miller RC | .20 | .07 |
| 436 Brad Dusek | .20 | .07 |
| 437 Bob Thomas | .20 | .07 |
| 438 Ken Mendenhall | .20 | .07 |
| 439 Clarence Davis | .20 | .07 |
| 440 Bob Griese | 2.50 | 1.00 |
| 441 Tony McGee DT | .20 | .07 |
| 442 Ed Taylor | .20 | .07 |
| 443 Ron Howard | .20 | .07 |
| 444 Wayne Morris | .20 | .07 |
| 445 Charlie Waters | .50 | .20 |
| 446 Rick Danmeier | .20 | .07 |
| 447 Paul Naumoff | .20 | .07 |
| 448 Keith Krepfle | .20 | .07 |
| 449 Rusty Jackson | .20 | .07 |
| 450 John Stallworth | 4.00 | 2.00 |
| 451 New Orleans Saints TL | .75 | .30 |
| 452 Ron Mikolajczyk | .20 | .07 |
| 453 Fred Dryer | 1.00 | .40 |
| 454 Jim LeClair | .20 | .07 |
| 455 Greg Pruitt | .50 | .20 |
| 456 Jake Scott | .20 | .07 |
| 457 Steve Schubert | .20 | .07 |
| 458 George Kunz | .20 | .07 |
| 459 Mike Williams | .20 | .07 |
| 460 Dave Casper AP | 1.00 | .40 |
| 461 Sam Adams OL | .20 | .07 |
| 462 Abdul Salaam | .20 | .07 |
| 463 Terdell Middleton | .50 | .20 |
| 464 Mike Wood | .20 | .07 |
| 465 Bill Thompson AP | .20 | .07 |
| 466 Larry Gordon | .20 | .07 |
| 467 Benny Ricardo | .20 | .07 |
| 468 Reggie McKenzie | .50 | .20 |
| 469 Cowboys TL/T.Dorsett | 1.50 | .60 |
| 470 Rickey Young | .50 | .20 |
| 471 Charlie Smith WR | .20 | .07 |
| 472 Al Dixon | .20 | .07 |
| 473 Tom DeLeone | .20 | .07 |
| 474 Louis Breeden | .50 | .20 |
| 475 Jack Lambert | 2.00 | .75 |
| 476 Terry Hermeling | .20 | .07 |
| 477 J.K. McKay | .20 | .07 |
| 478 Stan White | .20 | .07 |
| 479 Terry Nelson | .20 | .07 |
| 480 Walter Payton | 20.00 | 10.00 |
| 481 Dave Dalby | .20 | .07 |
| 482 Burgess Owens | .20 | .07 |
| 483 Rolf Benirschke | .20 | .07 |
| 484 Jack Dolbin | .20 | .07 |
| 485 John Hannah | 1.00 | .40 |
| 486 Checklist 397-528 | 1.00 | .40 |
| 487 Greg Landry | .50 | .20 |
| 488 St. Louis Cardinals TL | .75 | .30 |
| 489 Paul Krause | 1.00 | .40 |
| 490 John James | .20 | .07 |
| 491 Merv Krakau | .20 | .07 |
| 492 Dan Doornink | .20 | .07 |
| 493 Curtis Johnson | .20 | .07 |
| 494 Rafael Septien | .20 | .07 |
| 495 Jean Fugett | .20 | .07 |
| 496 Frank LeMaster | .20 | .07 |
| 497 Allan Ellis | .20 | .07 |
| 498 Billy Waddy RC | .50 | .20 |
| 499 Hank Bauer | .20 | .07 |
| 500 Terry Bradshaw UER | 10.00 | 5.00 |
| 501 Larry McCarren | .20 | .07 |
| 502 Fred Cook | .20 | .07 |
| 503 Chuck Muncie | .50 | .20 |
| 504 Herman Weaver | .20 | .07 |
| 505 Eddie Edwards | .20 | .07 |
| 506 Tony Peters | .20 | .07 |
| 507 Denver Broncos TL | .75 | .30 |
| 508 Jimbo Elrod | .20 | .07 |
| 509 David Hill | .20 | .07 |
| 510 Harvey Martin | .50 | .20 |
| 511 Terry Miller | .20 | .07 |
| 512 June Jones RC | .50 | .20 |
| 513 Randy Cross | 1.00 | .40 |
| 514 Dunel Harris | .20 | .07 |
| 515 Harry Carson | 1.00 | .40 |
| 516 Tim Fox | .20 | .07 |
| 517 John Zook | .20 | .07 |
| 518 Bob Tucker | .20 | .07 |
| 519 Kevin Long RC | .20 | .07 |
| 520 Ken Stabler | 6.00 | 3.00 |

| | | |
|---|---|---|
| ☐ 521 John Bunting | .50 | .20 |
| ☐ 522 Rocky Bleier | 1.25 | .50 |
| ☐ 523 Noah Jackson | .20 | .07 |
| ☐ 524 Cliff Parsley | .20 | .07 |
| ☐ 525 Louie Kelcher AP | .50 | .20 |
| ☐ 526 Bucs TL/Ricky Bell | .75 | .30 |
| ☐ 527 Bob Brudzinski RC | .20 | .07 |
| ☐ 528 Danny Buggs | .20 | .07 |

## 1980 Topps

| | | |
|---|---|---|
| ☐ COMPLETE SET (528) | 75.00 | 40.00 |
| ☐ 1 Ottis Anderson RB | 1.00 | .40 |
| ☐ 2 Harold Carmichael RB | 1.00 | .40 |
| ☐ 3 Dan Fouts RB | 1.00 | .40 |
| ☐ 4 Paul Krause RB | .20 | .07 |
| ☐ 5 Rick Upchurch RB | .50 | .20 |
| ☐ 6 Garo Yepremian RB | .50 | .20 |
| ☐ 7 Harold Jackson | .50 | .20 |
| ☐ 8 Mike Williams | .20 | .07 |
| ☐ 9 Calvin Hill | .50 | .20 |
| ☐ 10 Jack Ham | 1.00 | .40 |
| ☐ 11 Dan Melville | .20 | .07 |
| ☐ 12 Matt Robinson | .20 | .07 |
| ☐ 13 Billy Campfield | .20 | .07 |
| ☐ 14 Phil Tabor | .20 | .07 |
| ☐ 15 Randy Hughes UER | .20 | .07 |
| ☐ 16 Andre Tillman | .20 | .07 |
| ☐ 17 Isaac Curtis | .50 | .20 |
| ☐ 18 Charley Hannah | .20 | .07 |
| ☐ 19 Redskins TL/J.Riggins | 1.00 | .40 |
| ☐ 20 Jim Zorn | .50 | .20 |
| ☐ 21 Brian Baschnagel | .20 | .07 |
| ☐ 22 Jon Keyworth | .20 | .07 |
| ☐ 23 Phil Villapiano | .20 | .07 |
| ☐ 24 Richard Osborne | .20 | .07 |
| ☐ 25 Rich Saul AP | .20 | .07 |
| ☐ 26 Doug Beaudoin | .20 | .07 |
| ☐ 27 Cleveland Elam | .20 | .07 |
| ☐ 28 Charlie Joiner | 1.00 | .40 |
| ☐ 29 Dick Ambrose | .20 | .07 |
| ☐ 30 Mike Reinfeldt RC | .20 | .07 |
| ☐ 31 Matt Bahr RC | 1.00 | .40 |
| ☐ 32 Keith Krepfle | .20 | .07 |
| ☐ 33 Herb Scott | .20 | .07 |
| ☐ 34 Doug Kotar | .20 | .07 |
| ☐ 35 Bob Griese | 1.50 | .60 |
| ☐ 36 Jerry Butler RC | 1.00 | .40 |
| ☐ 37 Rolland Lawrence | .20 | .07 |
| ☐ 38 Gary Weaver | .20 | .07 |
| ☐ 39 Chiefs TL/J.T.Smith | .50 | .20 |
| ☐ 40 Chuck Muncie | .50 | .20 |
| ☐ 41 Mike Hartenstine | .20 | .07 |
| ☐ 42 Sammie White | .20 | .07 |
| ☐ 43 Ken Clark | .20 | .07 |
| ☐ 44 Clarence Harmon | .20 | .07 |
| ☐ 45 Bert Jones | 1.00 | .40 |
| ☐ 46 Mike Washington | .20 | .07 |
| ☐ 47 Joe Fields | .20 | .07 |
| ☐ 48 Mike Wood | .20 | .07 |
| ☐ 49 Oliver Davis | .20 | .07 |
| ☐ 50 Stan Walters AP | .20 | .07 |
| ☐ 51 Riley Odoms | .20 | .07 |
| ☐ 52 Steve Pisarkiewicz | .20 | .07 |
| ☐ 53 Tony Hill | 1.00 | .40 |
| ☐ 54 Scott Perry | .20 | .07 |
| ☐ 55 George Martin RC | .20 | .07 |
| ☐ 56 George Roberts | .20 | .07 |
| ☐ 57 Seahawks TL/S. Largent | 1.00 | .40 |
| ☐ 58 Billy Johnson | .50 | .20 |

| | | |
|---|---|---|
| ☐ 59 Reuben Gant | .20 | .07 |
| ☐ 60 Dennis Harrah RC | .20 | .07 |
| ☐ 61 Rocky Bleier | 1.00 | .40 |
| ☐ 62 Sam Hunt | .20 | .07 |
| ☐ 63 Allan Ellis | .20 | .07 |
| ☐ 64 Ricky Thompson | .20 | .07 |
| ☐ 65 Ken Stabler | 4.00 | 2.00 |
| ☐ 66 Dexter Bussey | .20 | .07 |
| ☐ 67 Ken Mendenhall | .20 | .07 |
| ☐ 68 Woodrow Lowe | .20 | .07 |
| ☐ 69 Thom Darden | .20 | .07 |
| ☐ 70 Randy White | 1.50 | .60 |
| ☐ 71 Ken MacAfee | .20 | .07 |
| ☐ 72 Ron Jaworski | 1.00 | .40 |
| ☐ 73 William Andrews RC | 1.00 | .40 |
| ☐ 74 Jimmy Robinson | .20 | .07 |
| ☐ 75 Roger Wehrli AP | .40 | .15 |
| ☐ 76 Dolphins TL/L.Csonka | 1.00 | .40 |
| ☐ 77 Jack Rudnay | .20 | .07 |
| ☐ 78 James Lofton | 2.00 | .75 |
| ☐ 79 Robert Brazile | .50 | .20 |
| ☐ 80 Russ Francis | .50 | .20 |
| ☐ 81 Ricky Bell | 1.00 | .40 |
| ☐ 82 Bob Avellini | .50 | .20 |
| ☐ 83 Bobby Jackson | .20 | .07 |
| ☐ 84 Mike Bragg | .20 | .07 |
| ☐ 85 Cliff Branch | 1.00 | .40 |
| ☐ 86 Blair Bush | .20 | .07 |
| ☐ 87 Sherman Smith | .20 | .07 |
| ☐ 88 Glen Edwards | .20 | .07 |
| ☐ 89 Don Cockroft | .20 | .07 |
| ☐ 90 Louis Wright | .50 | .20 |
| ☐ 91 Randy Grossman | .20 | .07 |
| ☐ 92 Carl Hairston RC | 1.00 | .40 |
| ☐ 93 Archie Manning | 1.00 | .40 |
| ☐ 94 New York Giants TL | .50 | .20 |
| ☐ 95 Preston Pearson | .50 | .20 |
| ☐ 96 Rusty Chambers | .20 | .07 |
| ☐ 97 Greg Coleman | .20 | .07 |
| ☐ 98 Charle Young | .20 | .07 |
| ☐ 99 Matt Cavanaugh RC | .50 | .20 |
| ☐ 100 Jesse Baker | .20 | .07 |
| ☐ 101 Doug Plank | .20 | .07 |
| ☐ 102 Checklist 1-132 | .75 | .30 |
| ☐ 103 Luther Bradley RC | .20 | .07 |
| ☐ 104 Bob Kuziel | .20 | .07 |
| ☐ 105 Craig Morton | .50 | .20 |
| ☐ 106 Sherman White | .20 | .07 |
| ☐ 107 Jim Breech RC | .50 | .20 |
| ☐ 108 Hank Bauer | .20 | .07 |
| ☐ 109 Tom Blanchard | .20 | .07 |
| ☐ 110 Ozzie Newsome | 2.00 | .75 |
| ☐ 111 Steve Furness | .20 | .07 |
| ☐ 112 Frank LeMaster | .20 | .07 |
| ☐ 113 Cowboys TL/T.Dorsett | 1.00 | .40 |
| ☐ 114 Doug Van Horn | .20 | .07 |
| ☐ 115 Delvin Williams | .20 | .07 |
| ☐ 116 Lyle Blackwood | .20 | .07 |
| ☐ 117 Derrick Gaffney | .20 | .07 |
| ☐ 118 Cornell Webster | .20 | .07 |
| ☐ 119 Sam Cunningham | .50 | .20 |
| ☐ 120 Jim Youngblood AP | .50 | .20 |
| ☐ 121 Bob Thomas | .20 | .07 |
| ☐ 122 Jack Thompson RC | .50 | .20 |
| ☐ 123 Randy Cross | 1.00 | .40 |
| ☐ 124 Karl Lorch RC | .20 | .07 |
| ☐ 125 Mel Gray | .20 | .07 |
| ☐ 126 John James | .20 | .07 |
| ☐ 127 Terdell Middleton | .20 | .07 |
| ☐ 128 Leroy Jones | .20 | .07 |
| ☐ 129 Tom DeLeone | .20 | .07 |
| ☐ 130 John Stallworth | 1.50 | .60 |
| ☐ 131 Jimmie Giles RC | .50 | .20 |
| ☐ 132 Philadelphia Eagles TL | 1.00 | .40 |
| ☐ 133 Gary Green | .20 | .07 |
| ☐ 134 John Dutton | .50 | .20 |
| ☐ 135 Harry Carson | 1.00 | .40 |
| ☐ 136 Bob Kuechenberg | .50 | .20 |
| ☐ 137 Ike Harris | .20 | .07 |
| ☐ 138 Tommy Kramer RC | 1.00 | .40 |
| ☐ 139 Sam Adams OL | .20 | .07 |
| ☐ 140 Doug English | .50 | .20 |
| ☐ 141 Steve Schubert | .20 | .07 |
| ☐ 142 Rusty Jackson | .20 | .07 |
| ☐ 143 Reese McCall | .20 | .07 |
| ☐ 144 Scott Dierking | .20 | .07 |
| ☐ 145 Ken Houston | 1.00 | .40 |

| | | |
|---|---|---|
| ☐ 146 Bob Martin | .20 | .07 |
| ☐ 147 Sam McCullum | .20 | .07 |
| ☐ 148 Tom Banks | .20 | .07 |
| ☐ 149 Willie Buchanon | .20 | .07 |
| ☐ 150 Greg Pruitt | .50 | .20 |
| ☐ 151 Denver Broncos TL | 1.00 | .40 |
| ☐ 152 Don Smith RC | .20 | .07 |
| ☐ 153 Pete Johnson | .50 | .20 |
| ☐ 154 Charlie Smith WR | .20 | .07 |
| ☐ 155 Mel Blount | 1.00 | .40 |
| ☐ 156 John Mendenhall | .20 | .07 |
| ☐ 157 Danny White | 1.00 | .40 |
| ☐ 158 Jimmy Cefalo RC | .50 | .20 |
| ☐ 159 Richard Bishop AP | .20 | .07 |
| ☐ 160 Walter Payton | 12.00 | 6.00 |
| ☐ 161 Dave Dalby | .20 | .07 |
| ☐ 162 Preston Dennard | .20 | .07 |
| ☐ 163 Johnnie Gray | .20 | .07 |
| ☐ 164 Russell Erxleben | .20 | .07 |
| ☐ 165 Toni Fritsch AP | .20 | .07 |
| ☐ 166 Terry Hermeling | .20 | .07 |
| ☐ 167 Roland Hooks | .20 | .07 |
| ☐ 168 Roger Carr | .20 | .07 |
| ☐ 169 San Diego Chargers TL | 1.00 | .40 |
| ☐ 170 Ottis Anderson RC | 4.00 | 1.50 |
| ☐ 171 Brian Sipe | 1.00 | .40 |
| ☐ 172 Leonard Thompson | .20 | .07 |
| ☐ 173 Tony Reed | .20 | .07 |
| ☐ 174 Bob Tucker | .20 | .07 |
| ☐ 175 Joe Greene | 1.00 | .40 |
| ☐ 176 Jack Dolbin | .20 | .07 |
| ☐ 177 Chuck Ramsey | .20 | .07 |
| ☐ 178 Paul Hofer | .20 | .07 |
| ☐ 179 Randy Logan | .20 | .07 |
| ☐ 180 David Lewis AP | .20 | .07 |
| ☐ 181 Duriel Harris | .20 | .07 |
| ☐ 182 June Jones | .50 | .20 |
| ☐ 183 Larry McCarren | .20 | .07 |
| ☐ 184 Ken Johnson RB | .20 | .07 |
| ☐ 185 Charlie Waters | .50 | .20 |
| ☐ 186 Noah Jackson | .20 | .07 |
| ☐ 187 Reggie Williams | .50 | .20 |
| ☐ 188 New England Patriots TL | .50 | .20 |
| ☐ 189 Carl Eller | 1.00 | .40 |
| ☐ 190 Ed White AP | .20 | .07 |
| ☐ 191 Mario Clark | .20 | .07 |
| ☐ 192 Roosevelt Leaks | .20 | .07 |
| ☐ 193 Ted McKnight | .20 | .07 |
| ☐ 194 Danny Buggs | .20 | .07 |
| ☐ 195 Lester Hayes RC | 4.00 | 1.50 |
| ☐ 196 Clarence Scott | .20 | .07 |
| ☐ 197 Saints TL/Wes Chandler | .50 | .20 |
| ☐ 198 Richard Caster | .20 | .07 |
| ☐ 199 Louie Giammona | .20 | .07 |
| ☐ 200 Terry Bradshaw | 8.00 | 3.00 |
| ☐ 201 Ed Newman | .20 | .07 |
| ☐ 202 Fred Dryer | 1.00 | .40 |
| ☐ 203 Dennis Franks | .20 | .07 |
| ☐ 204 Bob Breunig RC | .50 | .20 |
| ☐ 205 Alan Page | 1.00 | .40 |
| ☐ 206 Earnest Gray RC | .20 | .07 |
| ☐ 207 Vikings TL/A.Rashad | 1.00 | .40 |
| ☐ 208 Horace Ivory | .20 | .07 |
| ☐ 209 Isaac Hagins | .20 | .07 |
| ☐ 210 Gary Johnson AP | .20 | .07 |
| ☐ 211 Kevin Long | .20 | .07 |
| ☐ 212 Bill Thompson | .20 | .07 |
| ☐ 213 Don Bass | .20 | .07 |
| ☐ 214 George Starke RC | .20 | .07 |
| ☐ 215 Efren Herrera | .20 | .07 |
| ☐ 216 Theo Bell | .20 | .07 |
| ☐ 217 Monte Jackson | .20 | .07 |
| ☐ 218 Reggie McKenzie | .20 | .07 |
| ☐ 219 Bucky Dilts | .20 | .07 |
| ☐ 220 Lyle Alzado | 1.00 | .40 |
| ☐ 221 Tim Foley | .20 | .07 |
| ☐ 222 Mark Arneson | .20 | .07 |
| ☐ 223 Fred Quillan | .20 | .07 |
| ☐ 224 Benny Ricardo | .20 | .07 |
| ☐ 225 Phil Simms RC | 10.00 | 4.00 |
| ☐ 226 Bears TL/Walter Payton | 1.25 | .50 |
| ☐ 227 Max Runager | .20 | .07 |
| ☐ 228 Barty Smith | .20 | .07 |
| ☐ 229 Jay Saldi | .50 | .20 |
| ☐ 230 John Hannah | 1.00 | .40 |
| ☐ 231 Tim Wilson | .20 | .07 |
| ☐ 232 Jeff Van Note | .20 | .07 |

|  |  | | |
|---|---|---|---|
| 233 | Henry Marshall | .20 | .07 |
| 234 | Diron Talbert | .20 | .07 |
| 235 | Garo Yepremian | .50 | .20 |
| 236 | Larry Brown | .20 | .07 |
| 237 | Clarence Williams RB | .20 | .07 |
| 238 | Burgess Owens | .20 | .07 |
| 239 | Vince Ferragamo | .50 | .20 |
| 240 | Rickey Young | .20 | .07 |
| 241 | Dave Logan | .20 | .07 |
| 242 | Larry Gordon | .20 | .07 |
| 243 | Terry Miller | .20 | .07 |
| 244 | Baltimore Colts TL | 1.00 | .40 |
| 245 | Steve DeBerg | 1.00 | .40 |
| 246 | Checklist 133-264 | .75 | .30 |
| 247 | Greg Latta | .20 | .07 |
| 248 | Raymond Clayborn | .50 | .20 |
| 249 | Jim Clack | .20 | .07 |
| 250 | Drew Pearson | 1.00 | .40 |
| 251 | John Bunting | .50 | .20 |
| 252 | Rob Lytle | .20 | .07 |
| 253 | Jim Hart | 1.00 | .40 |
| 254 | John McDaniel | .20 | .07 |
| 255 | Dave Pear AP | .20 | .07 |
| 256 | Donnie Shell | 1.00 | .40 |
| 257 | Dan Doornink | .20 | .07 |
| 258 | Wallace Francis RC | 1.00 | .40 |
| 259 | Dave Beverly | .20 | .07 |
| 260 | Lee Roy Selmon | 1.00 | .40 |
| 261 | Doug Dieken | .20 | .07 |
| 262 | Gary Davis | .20 | .07 |
| 263 | Bob Rush | .20 | .07 |
| 264 | Buffalo Bills TL | .50 | .20 |
| 265 | Greg Landry | .50 | .20 |
| 266 | Jan Stenerud | 1.00 | .40 |
| 267 | Tom Hicks | .20 | .07 |
| 268 | Pat McInally | .20 | .07 |
| 269 | Tim Fox | .20 | .07 |
| 270 | Harvey Martin | .50 | .20 |
| 271 | Dan Lloyd | .20 | .07 |
| 272 | Mike Barber | .20 | .07 |
| 273 | Wendell Tyler RC | 1.00 | .40 |
| 274 | Jeff Komlo | .20 | .07 |
| 275 | Wes Chandler RC | 1.00 | .40 |
| 276 | Brad Dusek | .20 | .07 |
| 277 | Charlie Johnson NT | .20 | .07 |
| 278 | Dennis Swilley | .20 | .07 |
| 279 | Johnny Evans | .20 | .07 |
| 280 | Jack Lambert | 1.50 | .60 |
| 281 | Vern Den Herder | .20 | .07 |
| 282 | Tampa Bay Bucs TL | 1.00 | .40 |
| 283 | Bob Klein | .20 | .07 |
| 284 | Jim Turner | .20 | .07 |
| 285 | Marvin Powell AP | .50 | .20 |
| 286 | Aaron Kyle | .20 | .07 |
| 287 | Dan Neal | .20 | .07 |
| 288 | Wayne Morris | .20 | .07 |
| 289 | Steve Bartkowski | .50 | .20 |
| 290 | Dave Jennings AP | .50 | .20 |
| 291 | John Smith | .20 | .07 |
| 292 | Bill Gregory | .20 | .07 |
| 293 | Frank Lewis | .20 | .07 |
| 294 | Fred Cook | .20 | .07 |
| 295 | David Hill AP | .20 | .07 |
| 296 | Wade Key | .20 | .07 |
| 297 | Sidney Thornton | .20 | .07 |
| 298 | Charlie Hall | .20 | .07 |
| 299 | Joe Lavender | .20 | .07 |
| 300 | Tom Rafferty RC | .20 | .07 |
| 301 | Mike Renfro RC | .50 | .20 |
| 302 | Wilbur Jackson | .50 | .20 |
| 303 | Packers TL/J.Lofton | 1.00 | .40 |
| 304 | Henry Childs | .20 | .07 |
| 305 | Russ Washington AP | .20 | .07 |
| 306 | Jim LeClair | .20 | .07 |
| 307 | Tommy Hart | .20 | .07 |
| 308 | Gary Barbaro | .20 | .07 |
| 309 | Billy Taylor | .20 | .07 |
| 310 | Ray Guy | .50 | .20 |
| 311 | Don Hasselbeck RC | .50 | .20 |
| 312 | Doug Williams | 1.00 | .40 |
| 313 | Nick Mike-Mayer | .20 | .07 |
| 314 | Don McCauley | .20 | .07 |
| 315 | Wesley Walker | 1.00 | .40 |
| 316 | Dan Dierdorf | 1.00 | .40 |
| 317 | Dave Brown DB RC | .50 | .20 |
| 318 | Leroy Harris | .20 | .07 |
| 319 | Steelers TL/Harris/Lambrt | 1.00 | .40 |
| 320 | Mark Moseley AP UER | .20 | .07 |
| 321 | Mark Dennard | .20 | .07 |
| 322 | Terry Nelson | .20 | .07 |
| 323 | Tom Jackson | 1.00 | .40 |
| 324 | Rick Kane | .20 | .07 |
| 325 | Jerry Sherk | .20 | .07 |
| 326 | Ray Preston | .20 | .07 |
| 327 | Golden Richards | .20 | .07 |
| 328 | Randy Dean | .20 | .07 |
| 329 | Rick Danmeier | .20 | .07 |
| 330 | Tony Dorsett | 6.00 | 3.00 |
| 331 | R.Staubach/Fouts LL | 3.00 | 1.50 |
| 332 | Receiving Leaders | .50 | .20 |
| 333 | Sacks Leaders | 1.00 | .40 |
| 334 | Scoring Leaders | 1.00 | .40 |
| 335 | Interception Leaders | 1.00 | .40 |
| 336 | Punting Leaders | 1.00 | .40 |
| 337 | Freddie Solomon | .20 | .07 |
| 338 | Cincinnati Bengals TL/Jauron | 1.00 | .40 |
| 339 | Ken Stone | .20 | .07 |
| 340 | Greg Buttle AP | .20 | .07 |
| 341 | Bob Baumhower | .50 | .20 |
| 342 | Billy Waddy | .20 | .07 |
| 343 | Cliff Parsley | .20 | .07 |
| 344 | Walter White | .20 | .07 |
| 345 | Mike Thomas | .20 | .07 |
| 346 | Neil O'Donoghue | .20 | .07 |
| 347 | Freddie Scott | .20 | .07 |
| 348 | Joe Ferguson | .50 | .20 |
| 349 | Doug Nettles | .20 | .07 |
| 350 | Mike Webster | 1.00 | .40 |
| 351 | Ron Saul | .20 | .07 |
| 352 | Julius Adams | .20 | .07 |
| 353 | Rafael Septien | .20 | .07 |
| 354 | Cleo Miller | .20 | .07 |
| 355 | Keith Simpson AP | .20 | .07 |
| 356 | Johnny Perkins | .20 | .07 |
| 357 | Jerry Sisemore | .20 | .07 |
| 358 | Arthur Whittington | .20 | .07 |
| 359 | Cardinals TL/Anderson | 1.00 | .40 |
| 360 | Rick Upchurch | .50 | .20 |
| 361 | Kim Bokamper RC | .20 | .07 |
| 362 | Roland Harper | .20 | .07 |
| 363 | Pat Leahy | .20 | .07 |
| 364 | Louis Breeden | .20 | .07 |
| 365 | John Jefferson | 1.00 | .40 |
| 366 | Jerry Eckwood | .20 | .07 |
| 367 | David Whitehurst | .20 | .07 |
| 368 | Willie Parker C | .20 | .07 |
| 369 | Ed Simonini | .20 | .07 |
| 370 | Jack Youngblood | 1.00 | .40 |
| 371 | Don Warren RC | 1.00 | .40 |
| 372 | Andy Johnson | .20 | .07 |
| 373 | D.D. Lewis | .50 | .20 |
| 374A | B.Reece RC ERR | 1.00 | .40 |
| 374B | Beasley Reece RC COR | .50 | .20 |
| 375 | L.C.Greenwood | 1.00 | .40 |
| 376 | Cleveland Browns TL | .50 | .20 |
| 377 | Herman Edwards | .20 | .07 |
| 378 | Rob Carpenter RC RB | .20 | .07 |
| 379 | Herman Weaver | .20 | .07 |
| 380 | Gary Fencik | .20 | .07 |
| 381 | Don Strock | .50 | .20 |
| 382 | Art Shell | 1.00 | .40 |
| 383 | Tim Mazzetti | .20 | .07 |
| 384 | Bruce Harper | .20 | .07 |
| 385 | Al (Bubba) Baker | .50 | .20 |
| 386 | Conrad Dobler | .20 | .07 |
| 387 | Stu Voigt | .20 | .07 |
| 388 | Ken Anderson | 1.00 | .40 |
| 389 | Pat Tilley | .20 | .07 |
| 390 | John Riggins | 1.00 | .40 |
| 391 | Checklist 265-396 | .75 | .30 |
| 392 | Fred Dean | .20 | .07 |
| 393 | Benny Barnes RC | .20 | .07 |
| 394 | Los Angeles Rams TL | .50 | .20 |
| 395 | Brad Van Pelt | .20 | .07 |
| 396 | Eddie Hare | .20 | .07 |
| 397 | John Sciarra RC | .20 | .07 |
| 398 | Bob Jackson | .20 | .07 |
| 399 | John Yarno | .20 | .07 |
| 400 | Franco Harris | 2.00 | .75 |
| 401 | Ray Wersching | .20 | .07 |
| 402 | Virgil Livers | .20 | .07 |
| 403 | Raymond Chester | .20 | .07 |
| 404 | Leon Gray | .20 | .07 |
| 405 | Richard Todd | .50 | .20 |
| 406 | Larry Little | 1.00 | .40 |
| 407 | Ted Fritsch Jr. | .20 | .07 |
| 408 | Larry Mucker | .20 | .07 |
| 409 | Jim Allen | .20 | .07 |
| 410 | Randy Gradishar | 1.00 | .40 |
| 411 | Atlanta Falcons TL | 1.00 | .40 |
| 412 | Louie Kelcher | .50 | .20 |
| 413 | Robert Newhouse | .50 | .20 |
| 414 | Gary Shirk | .20 | .07 |
| 415 | Mike Haynes | 1.00 | .40 |
| 416 | Craig Colquitt | .20 | .07 |
| 417 | Lou Piccone | .20 | .07 |
| 418 | Clay Matthews RC | 2.50 | 1.00 |
| 419 | Marvin Cobb | .20 | .07 |
| 420 | Harold Carmichael | 1.00 | .40 |
| 421 | Uwe Von Schamann | .50 | .20 |
| 422 | Mike Phipps | .50 | .20 |
| 423 | Nolan Cromwell RC | 1.00 | .40 |
| 424 | Glenn Doughty | .20 | .07 |
| 425 | Bob Young AP | .20 | .07 |
| 426 | Tony Galbreath | .20 | .07 |
| 427 | Luke Prestridge RC | .20 | .07 |
| 428 | Terry Beeson | .20 | .07 |
| 429 | Jack Tatum | .50 | .20 |
| 430 | Lemar Parrish AP | .20 | .07 |
| 431 | Chester Marcol | .20 | .07 |
| 432 | Houston Oilers TL | 1.00 | .40 |
| 433 | John Fitzgerald | .20 | .07 |
| 434 | Gary Jeter RC | .50 | .20 |
| 435 | Steve Grogan | 1.00 | .40 |
| 436 | Jon Kolb UER | .20 | .07 |
| 437 | Jim O'Bradovich UER | .20 | .07 |
| 438 | Gerald Irons | .20 | .07 |
| 439 | Jeff West | .20 | .07 |
| 440 | Wilbert Montgomery | .50 | .20 |
| 441 | Norris Thomas | .20 | .07 |
| 442 | James Scott | .20 | .07 |
| 443 | Curtis Brown | .20 | .07 |
| 444 | Ken Fantetti | .20 | .07 |
| 445 | Pat Haden | 1.00 | .40 |
| 446 | Carl Mauck | .20 | .07 |
| 447 | Bruce Laird | .20 | .07 |
| 448 | Otis Armstrong | .50 | .20 |
| 449 | Gene Upshaw | 1.00 | .40 |
| 450 | Steve Largent | 6.00 | 3.00 |
| 451 | Benny Malone | .20 | .07 |
| 452 | Steve Nelson | .20 | .07 |
| 453 | Mark Cotney | .20 | .07 |
| 454 | Joe Danelo | .20 | .07 |
| 455 | Billy Joe DuPree | .50 | .20 |
| 456 | Ron Johnson DB | .20 | .07 |
| 457 | Archie Griffin | .50 | .20 |
| 458 | Reggie Rucker | .20 | .07 |
| 459 | Claude Humphrey | .20 | .07 |
| 460 | Lydell Mitchell | .50 | .20 |
| 461 | Steve Towle | .20 | .07 |
| 462 | Revie Sorey | .20 | .07 |
| 463 | Tom Skladany | .20 | .07 |
| 464 | Clark Gaines | .20 | .07 |
| 465 | Frank Corral | .20 | .07 |
| 466 | Steve Fuller RC | .50 | .20 |
| 467 | Ahmad Rashad | 1.00 | .40 |
| 468 | Oakland Raiders TL | 1.00 | .40 |
| 469 | Brian Peets | .20 | .07 |
| 470 | Pat Donovan AP | .50 | .20 |
| 471 | Ken Burrough | .20 | .07 |
| 472 | Don Calhoun | .20 | .07 |
| 473 | Bill Bryan | .20 | .07 |
| 474 | Terry Jackson | .20 | .07 |
| 475 | Joe Theismann | 1.25 | .50 |
| 476 | Jim Smith | .50 | .20 |
| 477 | Joe DeLamielleure | 1.00 | .40 |
| 478 | Mike Pruitt AP | .50 | .20 |
| 479 | Steve Mike-Mayer | .20 | .07 |
| 480 | Bill Bergey | .50 | .20 |
| 481 | Mike Fuller | .20 | .07 |
| 482 | Bob Parsons | .20 | .07 |
| 483 | Billy Brooks | .20 | .07 |
| 484 | Jerome Barkum | .20 | .07 |
| 485 | Larry Csonka | 1.50 | .60 |
| 486 | John Hill | .20 | .07 |
| 487 | Mike Stensrud | .20 | .07 |
| 488 | Detroit Lions TL | .50 | .20 |
| 489 | Ted Hendricks | 1.00 | .40 |
| 490 | Dan Pastorini | .50 | .20 |
| 491 | Stanley Morgan | 1.00 | .40 |
| 492 | AFC Champs/Bleier | 1.00 | .40 |

| | | |
|---|---|---|
| ☐ 493 NFC Champs/Ferragamo | .50 | .20 |
| ☐ 494 Super Bowl XIV | 1.00 | .40 |
| ☐ 495 Dwight White | .50 | .20 |
| ☐ 496 Haven Moses | .20 | .07 |
| ☐ 497 Guy Morriss | .20 | .07 |
| ☐ 498 Dewey Selmon | .50 | .20 |
| ☐ 499 Dave Butz RC | 1.00 | .40 |
| ☐ 500 Chuck Foreman | .50 | .20 |
| ☐ 501 Chris Bahr | .20 | .07 |
| ☐ 502 Mark Miller QB | .20 | .07 |
| ☐ 503 Tony Greene | .20 | .07 |
| ☐ 504 Brian Kelley | .20 | .07 |
| ☐ 505 Joe Washington | .50 | .20 |
| ☐ 506 Butch Johnson | .20 | .07 |
| ☐ 507 New York Jets TL | .50 | .20 |
| ☐ 508 Steve Little | .20 | .07 |
| ☐ 509 Checklist 397-528 | .75 | .30 |
| ☐ 510 Mark Van Eeghen | .20 | .07 |
| ☐ 511 Gary Danielson | .50 | .20 |
| ☐ 512 Manu Tuiasosopo | .20 | .07 |
| ☐ 513 Paul Coffman RC | .50 | .20 |
| ☐ 514 Cullen Bryant | .20 | .07 |
| ☐ 515 Nat Moore | .50 | .20 |
| ☐ 516 Bill Lenkaitis | .20 | .07 |
| ☐ 517 Lynn Cain RC | .20 | .07 |
| ☐ 518 Gregg Bingham | .20 | .07 |
| ☐ 519 Ted Albrecht | .20 | .07 |
| ☐ 520 Dan Fouts | 2.00 | .75 |
| ☐ 521 Bernard Jackson | .20 | .07 |
| ☐ 522 Coy Bacon | .20 | .07 |
| ☐ 523 Tony Franklin RC | .50 | .20 |
| ☐ 524 Bo Harris | .20 | .07 |
| ☐ 525 Bob Grupp AP | .20 | .07 |
| ☐ 526 San Francisco 49ers TL | 1.00 | .40 |
| ☐ 527 Steve Wilson | .20 | .07 |
| ☐ 528 Bennie Cunningham | .50 | .20 |

## 1981 Topps

| | | |
|---|---|---|
| ☐ COMPLETE SET (528) | 200.00 | 100.00 |
| ☐ 1 Ron Jaworski/B.Sipe LL | .75 | .30 |
| ☐ 2 K.Winslow/Cooper LL | .75 | .30 |
| ☐ 3 Sack Leaders | .40 | .15 |
| ☐ 4 Scoring Leaders | .20 | .07 |
| ☐ 5 Interception Leaders | .40 | .15 |
| ☐ 6 Punting Leaders | .20 | .07 |
| ☐ 7 Don Calhoun | .20 | .07 |
| ☐ 8 Jack Tatum | .40 | .15 |
| ☐ 9 Reggie Rucker | .20 | .07 |
| ☐ 10 Mike Webster | .75 | .30 |
| ☐ 11 Vince Evans RC | .75 | .30 |
| ☐ 12 Ottis Anderson SA | .75 | .30 |
| ☐ 13 Leroy Harris | .20 | .07 |
| ☐ 14 Gordon King | .20 | .07 |
| ☐ 15 Harvey Martin | .40 | .15 |
| ☐ 16 Johnny Lam Jones RC | .40 | .15 |
| ☐ 17 Ken Greene | .20 | .07 |
| ☐ 18 Frank Lewis | .20 | .07 |
| ☐ 19 Seahawks TL/Largent | .75 | .30 |
| ☐ 20 Lester Hayes | .75 | .30 |
| ☐ 21 Uwe Von Schamann | .20 | .07 |
| ☐ 22 Joe Washington | .40 | .15 |
| ☐ 23 Louie Kelcher | .20 | .07 |
| ☐ 24 Willie Miller | .20 | .07 |
| ☐ 25 Steve Grogan | .75 | .30 |
| ☐ 26 John Hill | .20 | .07 |
| ☐ 27 Stan White | .20 | .07 |
| ☐ 28 William Andrews SA | .40 | .15 |
| ☐ 29 Clarence Scott | .20 | .07 |
| ☐ 30 Leon Gray AP | .20 | .07 |

| | | |
|---|---|---|
| ☐ 31 Craig Colquitt | .20 | .07 |
| ☐ 32 Doug Williams | .75 | .30 |
| ☐ 33 Bob Breunig | .40 | .15 |
| ☐ 34 Billy Taylor | .20 | .07 |
| ☐ 35 Harold Carmichael | .75 | .30 |
| ☐ 36 Ray Wersching | .20 | .07 |
| ☐ 37 Dennis Johnson LB RC | .20 | .07 |
| ☐ 38 Archie Griffin | .40 | .15 |
| ☐ 39 Los Angeles Rams TL | .40 | .15 |
| ☐ 40 Gary Fencik | .40 | .15 |
| ☐ 41 Lynn Dickey | .40 | .15 |
| ☐ 42 Steve Bartkowski SA | .40 | .15 |
| ☐ 43 Art Shell | .75 | .30 |
| ☐ 44 Wilbur Jackson | .20 | .07 |
| ☐ 45 Frank Corral | .20 | .07 |
| ☐ 46 Ted McKnight | .20 | .07 |
| ☐ 47 Joe Klecko | .40 | .15 |
| ☐ 48 Dan Doornink | .20 | .07 |
| ☐ 49 Doug Dieken | .20 | .07 |
| ☐ 50 Jerry Robinson RC | .40 | .15 |
| ☐ 51 Wallace Francis | .20 | .07 |
| ☐ 52 Dan Preston RC | .20 | .07 |
| ☐ 53 Jay Saldi | .20 | .07 |
| ☐ 54 Rush Brown | .20 | .07 |
| ☐ 55 Phil Simms | 2.50 | 1.00 |
| ☐ 56 Nick Mike-Mayer | .20 | .07 |
| ☐ 57 Redskins TL/A.Monk | 2.00 | .75 |
| ☐ 58 Mike Renfro | .20 | .07 |
| ☐ 59 Ted Brown SA | .20 | .07 |
| ☐ 60 Steve Nelson | .20 | .07 |
| ☐ 61 Sidney Thornton | .20 | .07 |
| ☐ 62 Kent Hill | .20 | .07 |
| ☐ 63 Don Bessillieu | .20 | .07 |
| ☐ 64 Fred Cook | .20 | .07 |
| ☐ 65 Raymond Chester | .20 | .07 |
| ☐ 66 Rick Kane | .20 | .07 |
| ☐ 67 Mike Fuller | .20 | .07 |
| ☐ 68 Dewey Selmon | .40 | .15 |
| ☐ 69 Charles White RC | .75 | .30 |
| ☐ 70 Jeff Van Note | .20 | .07 |
| ☐ 71 Robert Newhouse | .40 | .15 |
| ☐ 72 Roynell Young RC | .40 | .15 |
| ☐ 73 Lynn Cain SA | .20 | .07 |
| ☐ 74 Mike Friede | .20 | .07 |
| ☐ 75 Earl Cooper RC | .20 | .07 |
| ☐ 76 New Orleans Saints TL | .40 | .15 |
| ☐ 77 Rick Danmeier | .20 | .07 |
| ☐ 78 Darrol Ray | .20 | .07 |
| ☐ 79 Gregg Bingham | .20 | .07 |
| ☐ 80 John Hannah | .75 | .30 |
| ☐ 81 Jack Thompson | .40 | .15 |
| ☐ 82 Rick Upchurch | .40 | .15 |
| ☐ 83 Mike Butler | .20 | .07 |
| ☐ 84 Don Warren | .40 | .15 |
| ☐ 85 Mark Van Eeghen | .20 | .07 |
| ☐ 86 J.T.Smith RC | .75 | .30 |
| ☐ 87 Herman Weaver | .20 | .07 |
| ☐ 88 Terry Bradshaw SA | 2.50 | 1.00 |
| ☐ 89 Charlie Hall | .20 | .07 |
| ☐ 90 Donnie Shell | .75 | .30 |
| ☐ 91 Ike Harris | .20 | .07 |
| ☐ 92 Charlie Johnson NT | .20 | .07 |
| ☐ 93 Rickey Watts | .20 | .07 |
| ☐ 94 New England Patriots TL | .75 | .30 |
| ☐ 95 Drew Pearson | .75 | .30 |
| ☐ 96 Neil O'Donoghue | .20 | .07 |
| ☐ 97 Conrad Dobler | .20 | .07 |
| ☐ 98 Jewerl Thomas RC | .20 | .07 |
| ☐ 99 Mike Barber | .20 | .07 |
| ☐ 100 Billy Sims RC | 3.00 | 1.25 |
| ☐ 101 Vern Den Herder | .20 | .07 |
| ☐ 102 Greg Landry | .40 | .15 |
| ☐ 103 Joe Cribbs SA | .40 | .15 |
| ☐ 104 Mark Murphy S RC | .20 | .07 |
| ☐ 105 Chuck Muncie | .40 | .15 |
| ☐ 106 Alfred Jackson | .40 | .15 |
| ☐ 107 Chris Bahr | .20 | .07 |
| ☐ 108 Gordon Jones | .20 | .07 |
| ☐ 109 Willie Harper RC | .20 | .07 |
| ☐ 110 Dave Jennings | .20 | .07 |
| ☐ 111 Bennie Cunningham | .20 | .07 |
| ☐ 112 Jerry Sisemore | .20 | .07 |
| ☐ 113 Cleveland Browns TL | .75 | .30 |
| ☐ 114 Rickey Young | .20 | .07 |
| ☐ 115 Ken Anderson | .75 | .30 |
| ☐ 116 Randy Gradishar | .75 | .30 |
| ☐ 117 Eddie Lee Ivery RC | .20 | .07 |

| | | |
|---|---|---|
| ☐ 118 Wesley Walker | .75 | .30 |
| ☐ 119 Chuck Foreman | .40 | .15 |
| ☐ 120 Nolan Cromwell UER | .40 | .15 |
| ☐ 121 Curtis Dickey SA | .20 | .07 |
| ☐ 122 Wayne Morris | .20 | .07 |
| ☐ 123 Greg Stemrick | .20 | .07 |
| ☐ 124 Coy Bacon | .20 | .07 |
| ☐ 125 Jim Zorn | .40 | .15 |
| ☐ 126 Henry Childs | .20 | .07 |
| ☐ 127 Checklist 1-132 | .75 | .30 |
| ☐ 128 Len Walterscheid | .20 | .07 |
| ☐ 129 Johnny Evans | .20 | .07 |
| ☐ 130 Gary Barbaro | .20 | .07 |
| ☐ 131 Jim Smith | .20 | .07 |
| ☐ 132 New York Jets TL | .40 | .15 |
| ☐ 133 Curtis Brown | .20 | .07 |
| ☐ 134 D.D. Lewis | .20 | .07 |
| ☐ 135 Jim Plunkett | .75 | .30 |
| ☐ 136 Nat Moore | .40 | .15 |
| ☐ 137 Don McCauley | .20 | .07 |
| ☐ 138 Tony Dorsett SA | .75 | .30 |
| ☐ 139 Julius Adams | .20 | .07 |
| ☐ 140 Ahmad Rashad | .75 | .30 |
| ☐ 141 Rich Saul | .20 | .07 |
| ☐ 142 Ken Fantetti | .20 | .07 |
| ☐ 143 Kenny Johnson | .20 | .07 |
| ☐ 144 Clark Gaines | .20 | .07 |
| ☐ 145 Mark Moseley | .20 | .07 |
| ☐ 146 Vernon Perry RC | .20 | .07 |
| ☐ 147 Jerry Eckwood | .20 | .07 |
| ☐ 148 Freddie Solomon | .20 | .07 |
| ☐ 149 Jerry Sherk | .20 | .07 |
| ☐ 150 Kellen Winslow RC | 8.00 | 4.00 |
| ☐ 151 Packers TL/Lofton | .75 | .30 |
| ☐ 152 Ross Browner | .20 | .07 |
| ☐ 153 Dan Fouts SA | .75 | .30 |
| ☐ 154 Woody Peoples | .20 | .07 |
| ☐ 155 Jack Lambert | 1.00 | .40 |
| ☐ 156 Mike Dennis | .20 | .07 |
| ☐ 157 Rafael Septien | .20 | .07 |
| ☐ 158 Archie Manning | .75 | .30 |
| ☐ 159 Don Hasselbeck | .20 | .07 |
| ☐ 160 Alan Page | .75 | .30 |
| ☐ 161 Arthur Whittington | .20 | .07 |
| ☐ 162 Billy Waddy | .20 | .07 |
| ☐ 163 Horace Belton | .20 | .07 |
| ☐ 164 Luke Prestridge | .20 | .07 |
| ☐ 165 Joe Theismann | 1.00 | .40 |
| ☐ 166 Morris Towns | .20 | .07 |
| ☐ 167 Dave Brown DB | .20 | .07 |
| ☐ 168 Ezra Johnson | .20 | .07 |
| ☐ 169 Tampa Bay Bucs TL | .20 | .07 |
| ☐ 170 Joe DeLamielleure | .75 | .30 |
| ☐ 171 Earnest Gray SA | .20 | .07 |
| ☐ 172 Mike Thomas | .20 | .07 |
| ☐ 173 Jim Haslett RC | 2.00 | .75 |
| ☐ 174 David Woodley RC | .40 | .15 |
| ☐ 175 Al(Bubba) Baker | .40 | .15 |
| ☐ 176 Nesby Glasgow RC | .20 | .07 |
| ☐ 177 Pat Leahy | .20 | .07 |
| ☐ 178 Tom Brahaney | .20 | .07 |
| ☐ 179 Herman Edwards | .20 | .07 |
| ☐ 180 Junior Miller RC | .20 | .07 |
| ☐ 181 Richard Wood RC | .20 | .07 |
| ☐ 182 Lenvil Elliott | .20 | .07 |
| ☐ 183 Sammie White | .40 | .15 |
| ☐ 184 Russell Erxleben | .20 | .07 |
| ☐ 185 Ed Too Tall Jones | 1.00 | .40 |
| ☐ 186 Ray Guy SA | .40 | .15 |
| ☐ 187 Haven Moses | .20 | .07 |
| ☐ 188 New York Giants TL | .40 | .15 |
| ☐ 189 David Whitehurst | .20 | .07 |
| ☐ 190 John Jefferson | .75 | .30 |
| ☐ 191 Terry Beeson | .20 | .07 |
| ☐ 192 Dan Ross RC | .40 | .15 |
| ☐ 193 Dave Williams RB RC | .20 | .07 |
| ☐ 194 Art Monk RC | 15.00 | 7.50 |
| ☐ 195 Roger Wehrli | .40 | .15 |
| ☐ 196 Ricky Feacher | .20 | .07 |
| ☐ 197 Miami Dolphins TL | .75 | .30 |
| ☐ 198 Carl Roaches RC | .20 | .07 |
| ☐ 199 Billy Campfield | .20 | .07 |
| ☐ 200 Ted Hendricks | .75 | .30 |
| ☐ 201 Fred Smerlas RC | .75 | .30 |
| ☐ 202 Walter Payton SA | 3.00 | 1.25 |
| ☐ 203 Luther Bradley | .20 | .07 |
| ☐ 204 Herb Scott | .20 | .07 |

|  |  | | |
|---|------|------|------|
| 205 | Jack Youngblood | .75 | .30 |
| 206 | Danny Pittman | .20 | .07 |
| 207 | Houston Oilers TL | .40 | .15 |
| 208 | Vagas Ferguson RC | .40 | .15 |
| 209 | Mark Dennard | .20 | .07 |
| 210 | Lemar Parrish | .20 | .07 |
| 211 | Bruce Harper | .20 | .07 |
| 212 | Ed Simonini | .20 | .07 |
| 213 | Nick Lowery RC | .75 | .30 |
| 214 | Kevin House RC | .40 | .15 |
| 215 | Mike Kenn RC | .75 | .30 |
| 216 | Joe Montana RC | 150.00 | 75.00 |
| 217 | Joe Senser | .20 | .07 |
| 218 | Lester Hayes SA | .40 | .15 |
| 219 | Gene Upshaw | .75 | .30 |
| 220 | Franco Harris | 1.25 | .50 |
| 221 | Ron Bolton | .20 | .07 |
| 222 | Charles Alexander RC | .40 | .15 |
| 223 | Matt Robinson | .20 | .07 |
| 224 | Ray Oldham | .20 | .07 |
| 225 | George Martin | .20 | .07 |
| 226 | Buffalo Bills TL | .75 | .30 |
| 227 | Tony Franklin | .20 | .07 |
| 228 | George Cumby | .20 | .07 |
| 229 | Butch Johnson | .40 | .15 |
| 230 | Mike Haynes | .75 | .30 |
| 231 | Rob Carpenter | .40 | .15 |
| 232 | Steve Fuller | .40 | .15 |
| 233 | John Sawyer | .20 | .07 |
| 234 | Kenny King SA | .20 | .07 |
| 235 | Jack Ham | 1.00 | .40 |
| 236 | Jimmy Rogers | .20 | .07 |
| 237 | Bob Parsons | .20 | .07 |
| 238 | Marty Lyons RC | .75 | .30 |
| 239 | Pat Tilley | .20 | .07 |
| 240 | Dennis Harrah | .20 | .07 |
| 241 | Thom Darden | .20 | .07 |
| 242 | Rolf Benirschke | .20 | .07 |
| 243 | Gerald Small | .20 | .07 |
| 244 | Atlanta Falcons TL | .75 | .30 |
| 245 | Roger Carr | .20 | .07 |
| 246 | Sherman White | .20 | .07 |
| 247 | Ted Brown | .20 | .07 |
| 248 | Matt Cavanaugh | .40 | .15 |
| 249 | John Dutton | .20 | .07 |
| 250 | Bill Bergey | .40 | .15 |
| 251 | Jim Allen | .20 | .07 |
| 252 | Mike Nelms SA | .20 | .07 |
| 253 | Tom Blanchard | .20 | .07 |
| 254 | Ricky Thompson | .20 | .07 |
| 255 | John Matuszak | .40 | .15 |
| 256 | Randy Grossman | .20 | .07 |
| 257 | Ray Griffin RC | .20 | .07 |
| 258 | Lynn Cain | .20 | .07 |
| 259 | Checklist 133-264 | .75 | .30 |
| 260 | Mike Pruitt | .40 | .15 |
| 261 | Chris Ward RC | .20 | .07 |
| 262 | Fred Steinfort | .20 | .07 |
| 263 | James Owens | .20 | .07 |
| 264 | Bears TL/Payton/Hampton | 1.50 | .60 |
| 265 | Dan Fouts | 1.50 | .60 |
| 266 | Arnold Morgado | .20 | .07 |
| 267 | John Jefferson SA | .75 | .30 |
| 268 | Bill Lenkaitis | .20 | .07 |
| 269 | James Jones COW | .20 | .07 |
| 270 | Brad Van Pelt | .20 | .07 |
| 271 | Steve Largent | 2.50 | 1.25 |
| 272 | Elvin Bethea | .75 | .30 |
| 273 | Cullen Bryant | .20 | .07 |
| 274 | Gary Danielson | .40 | .15 |
| 275 | Tony Galbreath | .20 | .07 |
| 276 | Dave Butz | .40 | .15 |
| 277 | Steve Mike-Mayer | .20 | .07 |
| 278 | Ron Johnson DB | .20 | .07 |
| 279 | Tom DeLeone | .20 | .07 |
| 280 | Ron Jaworski | .75 | .30 |
| 281 | Mel Gray | .20 | .07 |
| 282 | San Diego Chargers TL | .75 | .30 |
| 283 | Mark Brammer RC | .20 | .07 |
| 284 | Alfred Jenkins SA | .40 | .15 |
| 285 | Greg Buttle | .20 | .07 |
| 286 | Randy Hughes | .20 | .07 |
| 287 | Delvin Williams | .20 | .07 |
| 288 | Brian Baschnagel | .20 | .07 |
| 289 | Gary Jeter | .20 | .07 |
| 290 | Stanley Morgan | .75 | .30 |
| 291 | Gerry Ellis | .20 | .07 |
| 292 | Al Richardson | .20 | .07 |
| 293 | Jimmie Giles | .20 | .07 |
| 294 | Dave Jennings SA | .20 | .07 |
| 295 | Wilbert Montgomery | .40 | .15 |
| 296 | Dave Pureifory | .20 | .07 |
| 297 | Greg Hawthorne | .20 | .07 |
| 298 | Dick Ambrose | .20 | .07 |
| 299 | Terry Hermeling | .20 | .07 |
| 300 | Danny White | .75 | .30 |
| 301 | Ken Burrough | .20 | .07 |
| 302 | Paul Hofer | .20 | .07 |
| 303 | Denver Broncos TL | .75 | .30 |
| 304 | Eddie Payton | .40 | .15 |
| 305 | Isaac Curtis | .40 | .15 |
| 306 | Benny Ricardo | .20 | .07 |
| 307 | Riley Odoms | .20 | .07 |
| 308 | Bob Chandler | .20 | .07 |
| 309 | Larry Heater | .20 | .07 |
| 310 | Art Still RC | .75 | .30 |
| 311 | Harold Jackson | .40 | .15 |
| 312 | Charlie Joiner SA | .75 | .30 |
| 313 | Jeff Nixon | .20 | .07 |
| 314 | Aundra Thompson | .20 | .07 |
| 315 | Richard Todd | .40 | .15 |
| 316 | Dan Hampton RC | 3.00 | 1.25 |
| 317 | Doug Marsh | .20 | .07 |
| 318 | Louie Giammona | .20 | .07 |
| 319 | 49ers TL/Dwight Clark | .75 | .30 |
| 320 | Manu Tuiasosopo | .20 | .07 |
| 321 | Rich Milot | .20 | .07 |
| 322 | Mike Guman RC | .20 | .07 |
| 323 | Bob Kuechenberg | .40 | .15 |
| 324 | Tom Skladany | .20 | .07 |
| 325 | Dave Logan | .20 | .07 |
| 326 | Bruce Laird | .20 | .07 |
| 327 | James Jones COW SA | .20 | .07 |
| 328 | Joe Danelo | .20 | .07 |
| 329 | Kenny King RC | .40 | .15 |
| 330 | Pat Donovan | .20 | .07 |
| 331 | Earl Cooper RB | .40 | .15 |
| 332 | John Jefferson RB | .75 | .30 |
| 333 | Kenny King RB | .40 | .15 |
| 334 | Rod Martin RB | .40 | .15 |
| 335 | Jim Plunkett RB | .75 | .30 |
| 336 | Bill Thompson RB | .20 | .07 |
| 337 | John Cappelletti | .40 | .15 |
| 338 | Lions TL/Billy Sims | .75 | .30 |
| 339 | Don Smith | .20 | .07 |
| 340 | Rod Perry | .20 | .07 |
| 341 | David Lewis | .20 | .07 |
| 342 | Mark Gastineau RC | 1.00 | .40 |
| 343 | Steve Largent SA | .75 | .30 |
| 344 | Charle Young | .20 | .07 |
| 345 | Toni Fritsch | .20 | .07 |
| 346 | Matt Blair | .40 | .15 |
| 347 | Don Bass | .20 | .07 |
| 348 | Jim Jensen RC | .40 | .15 |
| 349 | Karl Lorch | .20 | .07 |
| 350 | Brian Sipe | .40 | .15 |
| 351 | Theo Bell | .20 | .07 |
| 352 | Sam Adams OL | .20 | .07 |
| 353 | Paul Coffman | .20 | .07 |
| 354 | Eric Harris | .20 | .07 |
| 355 | Tony Hill | .40 | .15 |
| 356 | J.T. Turner | .20 | .07 |
| 357 | Frank LeMaster | .20 | .07 |
| 358 | Jim Jodat | .20 | .07 |
| 359 | Raiders TL/Hendricks | .75 | .30 |
| 360 | Joe Cribbs RC | .75 | .30 |
| 361 | James Lofton SA | .75 | .30 |
| 362 | Dexter Bussey | .20 | .07 |
| 363 | Bobby Jackson | .20 | .07 |
| 364 | Steve DeBerg | .75 | .30 |
| 365 | Ottis Anderson | .75 | .30 |
| 366 | Tom Myers | .20 | .07 |
| 367 | John James | .20 | .07 |
| 368 | Reese McCall | .20 | .07 |
| 369 | Jack Reynolds | .40 | .15 |
| 370 | Gary Johnson | .20 | .07 |
| 371 | Jimmy Cefalo | .20 | .07 |
| 372 | Horace Ivory | .20 | .07 |
| 373 | Garo Yepremian | .20 | .07 |
| 374 | Brian Kelley | .20 | .07 |
| 375 | Terry Bradshaw | 8.00 | 3.00 |
| 376 | Cowboys TL/Tony Dorsett | .75 | .30 |
| 377 | Randy Logan | .20 | .07 |
| 378 | Tim Wilson | .20 | .07 |
| 379 | Archie Manning SA | .75 | .30 |
| 380 | Revie Sorey | .20 | .07 |
| 381 | Randy Holloway | .20 | .07 |
| 382 | Henry Lawrence | .20 | .07 |
| 383 | Pat McInally | .40 | .15 |
| 384 | Kevin Long | .20 | .07 |
| 385 | Louis Wright | .40 | .15 |
| 386 | Leonard Thompson | .20 | .07 |
| 387 | Jan Stenerud | .40 | .15 |
| 388 | Raymond Butler RC | .20 | .07 |
| 389 | Checklist 265-396 | .75 | .30 |
| 390 | Steve Bartkowski | .40 | .15 |
| 391 | Clarence Harmon | .20 | .07 |
| 392 | Wilbert Montgomery SA | .40 | .15 |
| 393 | Billy Joe DuPree | .40 | .15 |
| 394 | Kansas City Chiefs TL | .40 | .15 |
| 395 | Earnest Gray | .20 | .07 |
| 396 | Ray Hamilton | .20 | .07 |
| 397 | Brenard Wilson | .20 | .07 |
| 398 | Calvin Hill | .40 | .15 |
| 399 | Robin Cole | .20 | .07 |
| 400 | Walter Payton | 12.00 | 6.00 |
| 401 | Jim Hart | .75 | .30 |
| 402 | Ron Yary | .40 | .15 |
| 403 | Cliff Branch | .75 | .30 |
| 404 | Roland Hooks | .20 | .07 |
| 405 | Ken Stabler | 3.00 | 1.50 |
| 406 | Chuck Ramsey | .20 | .07 |
| 407 | Mike Nelms RC | .20 | .07 |
| 408 | Ron Jaworski SA | .40 | .15 |
| 409 | James Hunter | .20 | .07 |
| 410 | Lee Roy Selmon | .75 | .30 |
| 411 | Baltimore Colts TL | .40 | .15 |
| 412 | Henry Marshall | .20 | .07 |
| 413 | Preston Pearson | .40 | .15 |
| 414 | Richard Bishop | .20 | .07 |
| 415 | Greg Pruitt | .40 | .15 |
| 416 | Matt Bahr | .40 | .15 |
| 417 | Tom Mullady | .20 | .07 |
| 418 | Glen Edwards | .20 | .07 |
| 419 | Sam McCullum | .20 | .07 |
| 420 | Stan Walters | .20 | .07 |
| 421 | George Roberts | .20 | .07 |
| 422 | Dwight Clark RC | 5.00 | 2.00 |
| 423 | Pat Thomas RC | .20 | .07 |
| 424 | Bruce Harper SA | .20 | .07 |
| 425 | Craig Morton | .40 | .15 |
| 426 | Derrick Gaffney | .20 | .07 |
| 427 | Pete Johnson | .20 | .07 |
| 428 | Wes Chandler | .75 | .30 |
| 429 | Burgess Owens | .20 | .07 |
| 430 | James Lofton | 2.00 | .75 |
| 431 | Tony Reed | .20 | .07 |
| 432 | Vikings TL/A.Rashad | .75 | .30 |
| 433 | Ron Springs RC | .40 | .15 |
| 434 | Tim Fox | .20 | .07 |
| 435 | Ozzie Newsome | 2.00 | .75 |
| 436 | Steve Furness | .20 | .07 |
| 437 | Will Lewis | .20 | .07 |
| 438 | Mike Hartenstine | .20 | .07 |
| 439 | John Bunting | .20 | .07 |
| 440 | Eddie Murray RC | .75 | .30 |
| 441 | Mike Pruitt SA | .40 | .15 |
| 442 | Larry Swider | .20 | .07 |
| 443 | Steve Freeman | .20 | .07 |
| 444 | Bruce Hardy RC | .20 | .07 |
| 445 | Pat Haden | .40 | .15 |
| 446 | Curtis Dickey RC | .40 | .15 |
| 447 | Doug Wilkerson | .20 | .07 |
| 448 | Alfred Jenkins | .40 | .15 |
| 449 | Dave Dalby | .20 | .07 |
| 450 | Robert Brazile | .40 | .15 |
| 451 | Bobby Hammond | .20 | .07 |
| 452 | Raymond Clayborn | .20 | .07 |
| 453 | Jim Miller P RC | .20 | .07 |
| 454 | Roy Simmons | .20 | .07 |
| 455 | Charlie Waters | .40 | .15 |
| 456 | Ricky Bell | .75 | .30 |
| 457 | Ahmad Rashad SA | .75 | .30 |
| 458 | Don Cockroft | .20 | .07 |
| 459 | Keith Krepfle | .20 | .07 |
| 460 | Marvin Powell | .20 | .07 |
| 461 | Tommy Kramer | .75 | .30 |
| 462 | Jim LeClair | .20 | .07 |
| 463 | Freddie Scott | .20 | .07 |
| 464 | Rob Lytle | .20 | .07 |
| 465 | Johnnie Gray | .20 | .07 |

| | | | | | | | | | |
|---|---|---|---|---|---|---|---|---|---|
| ❑ 466 Doug France RC | .20 | .07 | ❑ 4 Stump Mitchell RB | .15 | .05 | ❑ 91 Steve Watson IA | .15 | .05 |
| ❑ 467 Carlos Carson RC | .40 | .15 | ❑ 5 George Rogers RB | .75 | .30 | ❑ 92 Houston Oilers TL | .15 | .05 |
| ❑ 468 Cardinals TL/O.Anderson | .75 | .30 | ❑ 6 Dan Ross RB | .15 | .05 | ❑ 93 Mike Barber | .15 | .05 |
| ❑ 469 Efren Herrera | .20 | .07 | ❑ 7 AFC Champs/K.Anderson | .75 | .30 | ❑ 94 Elvin Bethea | .75 | .30 |
| ❑ 470 Randy White | 1.25 | .50 | ❑ 8 NFC Champs/E.Cooper | .75 | .30 | ❑ 95 Gregg Bingham | .15 | .05 |
| ❑ 471 Richard Caster | .20 | .07 | ❑ 9 Super Bowl XVI/A.Munoz | .75 | .30 | ❑ 96 Robert Brazile | .15 | .05 |
| ❑ 472 Andy Johnson | .20 | .07 | ❑ 10 Baltimore Colts TL | .15 | .05 | ❑ 97 Ken Burrough | .15 | .05 |
| ❑ 473 Billy Sims SA | .75 | .30 | ❑ 11 Raymond Butler | .15 | .05 | ❑ 98 Toni Fritsch | .15 | .05 |
| ❑ 474 Joe Lavender | .20 | .07 | ❑ 12 Roger Carr | .15 | .05 | ❑ 99 Leon Gray | .15 | .05 |
| ❑ 475 Harry Carson | .40 | .15 | ❑ 13 Curtis Dickey | .40 | .15 | ❑ 100 Gifford Nielsen RC | .40 | .15 |
| ❑ 476 John Stallworth | 1.00 | .40 | ❑ 14 Zachary Dixon | .15 | .05 | ❑ 101 Vernon Perry | .15 | .05 |
| ❑ 477 Bob Thomas | .20 | .07 | ❑ 15 Nesby Glasgow | .15 | .05 | ❑ 102 Mike Reinfeldt | .15 | .05 |
| ❑ 478 Keith Wright RC | .20 | .07 | ❑ 16 Bert Jones | .75 | .30 | ❑ 103 Mike Renfro | .40 | .15 |
| ❑ 479 Ken Stone | .20 | .07 | ❑ 17 Bruce Laird | .15 | .05 | ❑ 104 Carl Roaches | .15 | .05 |
| ❑ 480 Carl Hairston | .40 | .15 | ❑ 18 Reese McCall | .15 | .05 | ❑ 105 Ken Stabler | 2.00 | .75 |
| ❑ 481 Reggie McKenzie | .20 | .07 | ❑ 19 Randy McMillan | .15 | .05 | ❑ 106 Greg Stemrick | .15 | .05 |
| ❑ 482 Bob Griese | 1.50 | .60 | ❑ 20 Ed Simonini | .15 | .05 | ❑ 107 J.C. Wilson | .15 | .05 |
| ❑ 483 Mike Bragg | .20 | .07 | ❑ 21 Buffalo Bills TL | .40 | .15 | ❑ 108 Tim Wilson | .15 | .05 |
| ❑ 484 Scott Dierking | .20 | .07 | ❑ 22 Mark Brammer | .15 | .05 | ❑ 109 Kansas City Chiefs TL | .15 | .05 |
| ❑ 485 David Hill | .20 | .07 | ❑ 23 Curtis Brown | .15 | .05 | ❑ 110 Gary Barbaro | .15 | .05 |
| ❑ 486 Brian Sipe SA | .40 | .15 | ❑ 24 Jerry Butler | .15 | .05 | ❑ 111 Brad Budde RC | .15 | .05 |
| ❑ 487 Rod Martin RC | .40 | .15 | ❑ 25 Mario Clark | .15 | .05 | ❑ 112 Joe Delaney RC | .75 | .30 |
| ❑ 488 Cincinnati Bengals TL | .20 | .07 | ❑ 26 Joe Cribbs | .40 | .15 | ❑ 113 Joe Delaney IA | .40 | .15 |
| ❑ 489 Preston Dennard | .20 | .07 | ❑ 27 Joe Cribbs IA | .40 | .15 | ❑ 114 Steve Fuller | .15 | .05 |
| ❑ 490 John Smith | .20 | .07 | ❑ 28 Jim Haslett | .75 | .30 | ❑ 115 Gary Green | .15 | .05 |
| ❑ 491 Mike Reinfeldt | .20 | .07 | ❑ 30 Frank Lewis | .15 | .05 | ❑ 116 James Hadnot | .15 | .05 |
| ❑ 492 NFC Champs/Jaworski | .75 | .30 | ❑ 31 Frank Lewis IA | .15 | .05 | ❑ 117 Eric Harris | .15 | .05 |
| ❑ 493 AFC Champs/Plunkett | .75 | .30 | ❑ 32 Shane Nelson | .15 | .05 | ❑ 118 Billy Jackson | .15 | .05 |
| ❑ 494 Super Bowl XVI/J.Plunkett | .75 | .30 | ❑ 33 Charles Romes | .15 | .05 | ❑ 119 Bill Kenney RC | .15 | .05 |
| ❑ 495 Joe Greene | 1.00 | .40 | ❑ 34 Bill Simpson | .15 | .05 | ❑ 120 Nick Lowery | .75 | .30 |
| ❑ 496 Charlie Joiner | .75 | .30 | ❑ 35 Fred Smerlas | .15 | .05 | ❑ 121 Nick Lowery IA | .40 | .15 |
| ❑ 497 Rolland Lawrence | .20 | .07 | ❑ 36 Bengals TL/C.Collinsworth | .40 | .15 | ❑ 122 Henry Marshall | .15 | .05 |
| ❑ 498 Al(Bubba) Baker SA | .40 | .15 | ❑ 37 Charles Alexander | .15 | .05 | ❑ 123 J.T.Smith | .40 | .15 |
| ❑ 499 Brad Dusek | .20 | .07 | ❑ 38 Ken Anderson | .75 | .30 | ❑ 124 Art Still | .40 | .15 |
| ❑ 500 Tony Dorsett | 4.00 | 2.00 | ❑ 39 Ken Anderson IA | .75 | .30 | ❑ 125 Miami Dolphins TL | .40 | .15 |
| ❑ 501 Robin Earl | .20 | .07 | ❑ 40 Jim Breech | .15 | .05 | ❑ 126 Bob Baumhower | .40 | .15 |
| ❑ 502 Theotis Brown RC | .20 | .07 | ❑ 41 Jim Breech IA | .15 | .05 | ❑ 127 Glenn Blackwood RC | .15 | .05 |
| ❑ 503 Joe Ferguson | .40 | .15 | ❑ 42 Louis Breeden | .15 | .05 | ❑ 128 Jimmy Cefalo | .15 | .05 |
| ❑ 504 Beasley Reece | .20 | .07 | ❑ 43 Ross Browner | .15 | .05 | ❑ 129 A.J. Duhe | .15 | .05 |
| ❑ 505 Lyle Alzado | .75 | .30 | ❑ 44 Cris Collinsworth RC | 2.00 | .75 | ❑ 130 Andra Franklin RC | .15 | .05 |
| ❑ 506 Tony Nathan RC | .75 | .30 | ❑ 45 Cris Collinsworth IA | .75 | .30 | ❑ 131 Duriel Harris | .15 | .05 |
| ❑ 507 Philadelphia Eagles TL | .40 | .15 | ❑ 46 Isaac Curtis | .15 | .05 | ❑ 132 Nat Moore | .40 | .15 |
| ❑ 508 Herb Orvis | .20 | .07 | ❑ 47 Pete Johnson | .15 | .05 | ❑ 133 Tony Nathan | .15 | .05 |
| ❑ 509 Clarence Williams RB | .20 | .07 | ❑ 48 Pete Johnson IA | .15 | .05 | ❑ 134 Ed Newman | .15 | .05 |
| ❑ 510 Ray Guy | .40 | .15 | ❑ 49 Steve Kreider | .15 | .05 | ❑ 135 Earnie Rhone | .15 | .05 |
| ❑ 511 Jeff Komlo | .20 | .07 | ❑ 50 Pat McInally | .15 | .05 | ❑ 136 Don Strock | .15 | .05 |
| ❑ 512 Freddie Solomon SA | .20 | .07 | ❑ 51 Anthony Munoz RC | 8.00 | 4.00 | ❑ 137 Tommy Vigorito | .15 | .05 |
| ❑ 513 Tim Mazzetti | .20 | .07 | ❑ 52 Dan Ross | .40 | .15 | ❑ 138 Uwe Von Schamann | .15 | .05 |
| ❑ 514 Elvis Peacock RC | .20 | .07 | ❑ 53 David Verser RC | .15 | .05 | ❑ 139 Uwe Von Schamann IA | .15 | .05 |
| ❑ 515 Russ Francis | .40 | .15 | ❑ 54 Reggie Williams | .40 | .15 | ❑ 140 David Woodley | .40 | .15 |
| ❑ 516 Roland Harper | .20 | .07 | ❑ 55 Browns TL/O.Newsome | .40 | .15 | ❑ 141 New England Pats TL | .15 | .05 |
| ❑ 517 Checklist 397-528 | .75 | .30 | ❑ 56 Lyle Alzado | .75 | .30 | ❑ 142 Julius Adams | .15 | .05 |
| ❑ 518 Billy Johnson | .40 | .15 | ❑ 57 Dick Ambrose | .15 | .05 | ❑ 143 Richard Bishop | .15 | .05 |
| ❑ 519 Dan Dierdorf | .75 | .30 | ❑ 58 Ron Bolton | .15 | .05 | ❑ 144 Matt Cavanaugh | .15 | .05 |
| ❑ 520 Fred Dean | .40 | .15 | ❑ 59 Steve Cox | .15 | .05 | ❑ 145 Raymond Clayborn | .15 | .05 |
| ❑ 521 Jerry Butler | .20 | .07 | ❑ 60 Joe DeLamielleure | .75 | .30 | ❑ 146 Tony Collins RC | .15 | .05 |
| ❑ 522 Ron Saul | .20 | .07 | ❑ 61 Tom DeLeone | .15 | .05 | ❑ 147 Vagas Ferguson | .15 | .05 |
| ❑ 523 Charlie Smith WR | .20 | .07 | ❑ 62 Doug Dieken | .15 | .05 | ❑ 148 Tim Fox | .15 | .05 |
| ❑ 524 Kellen Winslow SA | 3.00 | 1.50 | ❑ 63 Ricky Feacher | .15 | .05 | ❑ 149 Steve Grogan | .40 | .15 |
| ❑ 525 Bert Jones | .40 | .15 | ❑ 64 Don Goode | .15 | .05 | ❑ 150 John Hannah | .75 | .30 |
| ❑ 526 Steelers TL/Fr.Harris | .75 | .30 | ❑ 65 Robert L.Jackson RC | .15 | .05 | ❑ 151 John Hannah | .40 | .15 |
| ❑ 527 Duriel Harris | .20 | .07 | ❑ 66 Dave Logan | .15 | .05 | ❑ 152 Don Hasselbeck | .15 | .05 |
| ❑ 528 William Andrews | .75 | .30 | ❑ 67 Ozzie Newsome | 1.00 | .40 | ❑ 153 Mike Haynes | .40 | .15 |
| | | | ❑ 68 Ozzie Newsome IA | .75 | .30 | ❑ 154 Harold Jackson | .40 | .15 |
| **1982 Topps** | | | ❑ 69 Greg Pruitt | .40 | .15 | ❑ 155 Andy Johnson | .15 | .05 |
| | | | ❑ 70 Mike Pruitt | .40 | .15 | ❑ 156 Stanley Morgan | .40 | .15 |
| | | | ❑ 71 Mike Pruitt IA | .40 | .15 | ❑ 157 Stanley Morgan IA | .40 | .15 |
| | | | ❑ 72 Reggie Rucker | .15 | .05 | ❑ 158 Steve Nelson | .15 | .05 |
| | | | ❑ 73 Clarence Scott | .15 | .05 | ❑ 159 Rod Shoate | .15 | .05 |
| | | | ❑ 74 Brian Sipe | .40 | .15 | ❑ 160 Jets TL/F.McNeil | .40 | .15 |
| | | | ❑ 75 Charles White | .40 | .15 | ❑ 161 Dan Alexander RC | .15 | .05 |
| | | | ❑ 76 Denver Broncos TL | .40 | .15 | ❑ 162 Mike Augustyniak | .15 | .05 |
| | | | ❑ 77 Rubin Carter | .15 | .05 | ❑ 163 Jerome Barkum | .15 | .05 |
| | | | ❑ 78 Steve Foley | .15 | .05 | ❑ 164 Greg Buttle | .15 | .05 |
| | | | ❑ 79 Randy Gradishar | .40 | .15 | ❑ 165 Scott Dierking | .15 | .05 |
| | | | ❑ 80 Tom Jackson | .75 | .30 | ❑ 166 Joe Fields | .15 | .05 |
| | | | ❑ 81 Craig Morton | .40 | .15 | ❑ 167 Mark Gastineau | .40 | .15 |
| | | | ❑ 82 Craig Morton IA | .40 | .15 | ❑ 168 Mark Gastineau IA | .40 | .15 |
| | | | ❑ 83 Riley Odoms | .15 | .05 | ❑ 169 Bruce Harper | .15 | .05 |
| | | | ❑ 84 Rick Parros | .15 | .05 | ❑ 170 Johnny Lam Jones | .15 | .05 |
| | | | ❑ 85 Dave Preston | .15 | .05 | ❑ 171 Joe Klecko | .40 | .15 |
| ❑ COMPLETE SET (528) | 80.00 | 40.00 | ❑ 86 Tony Reed | .15 | .05 | ❑ 172 Joe Klecko IA | .40 | .15 |
| ❑ 1 Ken Anderson RB | .75 | .30 | ❑ 87 Bob Swenson RC | .15 | .05 | ❑ 173 Pat Leahy | .15 | .05 |
| ❑ 2 Dan Fouts RB | .75 | .30 | ❑ 88 Bill Thompson | .15 | .05 | ❑ 174 Pat Leahy IA | .15 | .05 |
| ❑ 3 LeRoy Irvin RB | .15 | .05 | ❑ 89 Rick Upchurch | .40 | .15 | ❑ 175 Marty Lyons | .40 | .15 |
| | | | ❑ 90 Steve Watson RC | .40 | .15 | ❑ 176 Freeman McNeil RC | .75 | .30 |
| | | | | | | ❑ 177 Marvin Powell | .15 | .05 |

| Column 1 | | |
|---|---|---|
| ☐ 178 Chuck Ramsey | .15 | .05 |
| ☐ 179 Darrol Ray | .15 | .05 |
| ☐ 180 Abdul Salaam | .15 | .05 |
| ☐ 181 Richard Todd | .40 | .15 |
| ☐ 182 Richard Todd IA | .40 | .15 |
| ☐ 183 Wesley Walker | .40 | .15 |
| ☐ 184 Chris Ward | .15 | .05 |
| ☐ 185 Oakland Raiders TL | .40 | .15 |
| ☐ 186 Cliff Branch | .75 | .30 |
| ☐ 187 Bob Chandler | .15 | .05 |
| ☐ 188 Ray Guy | .40 | .15 |
| ☐ 189 Lester Hayes | .40 | .15 |
| ☐ 190 Ted Hendricks | .75 | .30 |
| ☐ 191 Monte Jackson | .15 | .05 |
| ☐ 192 Derrick Jensen | .15 | .05 |
| ☐ 193 Kenny King | .15 | .05 |
| ☐ 194 Rod Martin | .15 | .05 |
| ☐ 195 John Matuszak | .40 | .15 |
| ☐ 196 Matt Millen RC | 1.50 | .60 |
| ☐ 197 Derrick Ramsey | .15 | .05 |
| ☐ 198 Art Shell | .75 | .30 |
| ☐ 199 Mark Van Eeghen | .15 | .05 |
| ☐ 200 Arthur Whittington | .15 | .05 |
| ☐ 201 Marc Wilson RC | .40 | .15 |
| ☐ 202 Steelers TL/Fr.Harris | .75 | .30 |
| ☐ 203 Mel Blount | .75 | .30 |
| ☐ 204 Terry Bradshaw | 5.00 | 2.00 |
| ☐ 205 Terry Bradshaw IA | 1.25 | .50 |
| ☐ 206 Craig Colquitt | .15 | .05 |
| ☐ 207 Bennie Cunningham | .15 | .05 |
| ☐ 208 Russell Davis RC | .15 | .05 |
| ☐ 209 Gary Dunn | .15 | .05 |
| ☐ 210 Jack Ham | .75 | .30 |
| ☐ 211 Franco Harris | 1.00 | .40 |
| ☐ 212 Franco Harris IA | .75 | .30 |
| ☐ 213 Jack Lambert | .75 | .30 |
| ☐ 214 Jack Lambert IA | .75 | .30 |
| ☐ 215 Mark Malone RC | .75 | .30 |
| ☐ 216 Frank Pollard RC | .15 | .05 |
| ☐ 217 Donnie Shell | .75 | .30 |
| ☐ 218 Jim Smith | .15 | .05 |
| ☐ 219 John Stallworth | .75 | .30 |
| ☐ 220 John Stallworth IA | .75 | .30 |
| ☐ 221 David Trout | .15 | .05 |
| ☐ 222 Mike Webster | .75 | .30 |
| ☐ 223 San Diego Chargers TL | .40 | .15 |
| ☐ 224 Rolf Benirschke | .15 | .05 |
| ☐ 225 Rolf Benirschke IA | .15 | .05 |
| ☐ 226 James Brooks RC | .75 | .30 |
| ☐ 227 Willie Buchanon | .15 | .05 |
| ☐ 228 Wes Chandler | .75 | .30 |
| ☐ 229 Wes Chandler IA | .40 | .15 |
| ☐ 230 Dan Fouts | 1.00 | .40 |
| ☐ 231 Dan Fouts IA | .75 | .30 |
| ☐ 232 Gary Johnson | .15 | .05 |
| ☐ 233 Charlie Joiner | .75 | .30 |
| ☐ 234 Charlie Joiner IA | .75 | .30 |
| ☐ 235 Louie Kelcher | .15 | .05 |
| ☐ 236 Chuck Muncie | .40 | .15 |
| ☐ 237 Chuck Muncie IA | .15 | .05 |
| ☐ 238 George Roberts | .15 | .05 |
| ☐ 239 Ed White | .15 | .05 |
| ☐ 240 Doug Wilkerson | .15 | .05 |
| ☐ 241 Kellen Winslow | 2.00 | .75 |
| ☐ 242 Kellen Winslow IA | .75 | .30 |
| ☐ 243 Seahawks TL/S.Largent | .75 | .30 |
| ☐ 244 Theotis Brown | .15 | .05 |
| ☐ 245 Dan Doornink | .15 | .05 |
| ☐ 246 John Harris | .15 | .05 |
| ☐ 247 Efren Herrera | .15 | .05 |
| ☐ 248 David Hughes | .15 | .05 |
| ☐ 249 Steve Largent | 2.00 | .75 |
| ☐ 250 Steve Largent IA | .75 | .30 |
| ☐ 251 Sam McCullum | .15 | .05 |
| ☐ 252 Sherman Smith | .15 | .05 |
| ☐ 253 Manu Tuiasosopo | .15 | .05 |
| ☐ 254 John Yarno | .15 | .05 |
| ☐ 255 Jim Zorn | .40 | .15 |
| ☐ 256 Jim Zorn IA | .40 | .15 |
| ☐ 257 J.Montana/Anderson LL | 4.00 | 1.50 |
| ☐ 258 Kellen Winslow/Clark LL | .75 | .30 |
| ☐ 259 QB Sack Leaders | .15 | .05 |
| ☐ 260 Scoring Leaders | .40 | .15 |
| ☐ 261 Interception Leaders | .40 | .15 |
| ☐ 262 Punting Leaders | .15 | .05 |
| ☐ 263 Brothers: Bahr | .15 | .05 |
| ☐ 264 Brothers: Blackwood | .40 | .15 |

| Column 2 | | |
|---|---|---|
| ☐ 265 Brothers: Brock | .15 | .05 |
| ☐ 266 Brothers: Griffin | .40 | .15 |
| ☐ 267 Brothers: Hannah | .75 | .30 |
| ☐ 268 Brothers: Jackson | .15 | .05 |
| ☐ 269 Walter/Eddie Payton | 1.00 | .40 |
| ☐ 270 Brothers: Selmon | .75 | .30 |
| ☐ 271 Atlanta Falcons TL | .40 | .15 |
| ☐ 272 William Andrews | .40 | .15 |
| ☐ 273 William Andrews IA | .40 | .15 |
| ☐ 274 Steve Bartkowski | .40 | .15 |
| ☐ 275 Steve Bartkowski IA | .40 | .15 |
| ☐ 276 Bobby Butler RC | .15 | .05 |
| ☐ 277 Lynn Cain | .15 | .05 |
| ☐ 278 Wallace Francis | .15 | .05 |
| ☐ 279 Alfred Jackson | .15 | .05 |
| ☐ 280 John James | .15 | .05 |
| ☐ 281 Alfred Jenkins | .15 | .05 |
| ☐ 282 Alfred Jenkins IA | .15 | .05 |
| ☐ 283 Kenny Johnson | .15 | .05 |
| ☐ 284 Mike Kenn | .75 | .30 |
| ☐ 285 Fulton Kuykendall | .15 | .05 |
| ☐ 286 Mick Luckhurst RC | .15 | .05 |
| ☐ 287 Mick Luckhurst IA | .15 | .05 |
| ☐ 288 Junior Miller | .15 | .05 |
| ☐ 289 Al Richardson | .15 | .05 |
| ☐ 290 R.C.Thielemann RC | .15 | .05 |
| ☐ 291 Jeff Van Note | .15 | .05 |
| ☐ 292 Bears TL/Walter Payton | .75 | .30 |
| ☐ 293 Brian Baschnagel | .15 | .05 |
| ☐ 294 Robin Earl | .15 | .05 |
| ☐ 295 Vince Evans | .40 | .15 |
| ☐ 296 Gary Fencik | .15 | .05 |
| ☐ 297 Dan Hampton | .75 | .30 |
| ☐ 298 Noah Jackson | .15 | .05 |
| ☐ 299 Ken Margerum | .15 | .05 |
| ☐ 300 Jim Osborne | .15 | .05 |
| ☐ 301 Bob Parsons | .15 | .05 |
| ☐ 302 Walter Payton | 10.00 | 4.00 |
| ☐ 303 Walter Payton IA | 3.00 | 1.25 |
| ☐ 304 Revie Sorey | .15 | .05 |
| ☐ 305 Matt Suhey RC | .75 | .30 |
| ☐ 306 Rickey Watts | .15 | .05 |
| ☐ 307 Cowboys TL/Dorsett | .75 | .30 |
| ☐ 308 Bob Breunig | .15 | .05 |
| ☐ 309 Doug Cosbie RC | .15 | .05 |
| ☐ 310 Pat Donovan | .15 | .05 |
| ☐ 311 Tony Dorsett | 1.50 | .60 |
| ☐ 312 Tony Dorsett IA | .75 | .30 |
| ☐ 313 Michael Downs RC | .15 | .05 |
| ☐ 314 Billy Joe DuPree | .40 | .15 |
| ☐ 315 John Dutton | .15 | .05 |
| ☐ 316 Tony Hill | .40 | .15 |
| ☐ 317 Butch Johnson | .40 | .15 |
| ☐ 318 Ed Too Tall Jones | .75 | .30 |
| ☐ 319 James Jones COW | .15 | .05 |
| ☐ 320 Harvey Martin | .40 | .15 |
| ☐ 321 Drew Pearson | .75 | .30 |
| ☐ 322 Herb Scott | .15 | .05 |
| ☐ 323 Rafael Septien | .15 | .05 |
| ☐ 324 Rafael Septien IA | .15 | .05 |
| ☐ 325 Ron Springs | .40 | .15 |
| ☐ 326 Dennis Thurman RC | .15 | .05 |
| ☐ 327 Everson Walls RC | .75 | .30 |
| ☐ 328 Everson Walls IA | .75 | .30 |
| ☐ 329 Danny White | .75 | .30 |
| ☐ 330 Danny White IA | .40 | .15 |
| ☐ 331 Randy White | .75 | .30 |
| ☐ 332 Randy White IA | .75 | .30 |
| ☐ 333 Detroit Lions TL | .40 | .15 |
| ☐ 334 Jim Allen | .15 | .05 |
| ☐ 335 Al(Bubba) Baker | .40 | .15 |
| ☐ 336 Dexter Bussey | .15 | .05 |
| ☐ 337 Doug English | .40 | .15 |
| ☐ 338 Ken Fantetti | .15 | .05 |
| ☐ 339 William Gay | .15 | .05 |
| ☐ 340 David Hill | .15 | .05 |
| ☐ 341 Eric Hipple RC | .15 | .05 |
| ☐ 342 Rick Kane | .15 | .05 |
| ☐ 343 Eddie Murray | .75 | .30 |
| ☐ 344 Eddie Murray IA | .40 | .15 |
| ☐ 345 Ray Oldham | .15 | .05 |
| ☐ 346 Dave Pureifory | .15 | .05 |
| ☐ 347 Freddie Scott | .15 | .05 |
| ☐ 348 Freddie Scott IA | .15 | .05 |
| ☐ 349 Billy Sims | .75 | .30 |
| ☐ 350 Billy Sims IA | .75 | .30 |
| ☐ 351 Tom Skladany | .15 | .05 |

| Column 3 | | |
|---|---|---|
| ☐ 352 Leonard Thompson | .15 | .05 |
| ☐ 353 Stan White | .15 | .05 |
| ☐ 354 Packers TL/Lofton | .75 | .30 |
| ☐ 355 Paul Coffman | .15 | .05 |
| ☐ 356 George Cumby | .15 | .05 |
| ☐ 357 Lynn Dickey | .15 | .05 |
| ☐ 358 Lynn Dickey IA | .15 | .05 |
| ☐ 359 Gerry Ellis | .15 | .05 |
| ☐ 360 Maurice Harvey | .15 | .05 |
| ☐ 361 Harlan Huckleby | .15 | .05 |
| ☐ 362 John Jefferson | .75 | .30 |
| ☐ 363 Mark Lee RC | .15 | .05 |
| ☐ 364 James Lofton | 1.00 | .40 |
| ☐ 365 James Lofton IA | .75 | .30 |
| ☐ 366 Jan Stenerud | .40 | .15 |
| ☐ 367 Jan Stenerud IA | .40 | .15 |
| ☐ 368 Rich Wingo | .15 | .05 |
| ☐ 369 Los Angeles Rams TL | .40 | .15 |
| ☐ 370 Frank Corral | .15 | .05 |
| ☐ 371 Nolan Cromwell | .40 | .15 |
| ☐ 372 Nolan Cromwell IA | .40 | .15 |
| ☐ 373 Preston Dennard | .15 | .05 |
| ☐ 374 Mike Fanning | .15 | .05 |
| ☐ 375 Doug France | .15 | .05 |
| ☐ 376 Mike Guman | .15 | .05 |
| ☐ 377 Pat Haden | .40 | .15 |
| ☐ 378 Dennis Harrah | .15 | .05 |
| ☐ 379 Drew Hill RC | .75 | .30 |
| ☐ 380 LeRoy Irvin RC | .15 | .05 |
| ☐ 381 Cody Jones | .15 | .05 |
| ☐ 382 Rod Perry | .15 | .05 |
| ☐ 383 Rich Saul | .15 | .05 |
| ☐ 384 Pat Thomas | .15 | .05 |
| ☐ 385 Wendell Tyler | .40 | .15 |
| ☐ 386 Wendell Tyler IA | .15 | .05 |
| ☐ 387 Billy Waddy | .15 | .05 |
| ☐ 388 Jack Youngblood | .75 | .30 |
| ☐ 389 Minnesota Vikings TL | .15 | .05 |
| ☐ 390 Matt Blair | .15 | .05 |
| ☐ 391 Ted Brown | .15 | .05 |
| ☐ 392 Ted Brown IA | .15 | .05 |
| ☐ 393 Rick Danmeier | .15 | .05 |
| ☐ 394 Tommy Kramer | .40 | .15 |
| ☐ 395 Mark Mullaney | .15 | .05 |
| ☐ 396 Eddie Payton | .15 | .05 |
| ☐ 397 Ahmad Rashad | .75 | .30 |
| ☐ 398 Joe Senser | .15 | .05 |
| ☐ 399 Joe Senser IA | .15 | .05 |
| ☐ 400 Sammie White | .40 | .15 |
| ☐ 401 Sammie White IA | .15 | .05 |
| ☐ 402 Ron Yary | .75 | .30 |
| ☐ 403 Rickey Young | .15 | .05 |
| ☐ 404 Saints TL/Ric.Jackson | .40 | .15 |
| ☐ 405 Russell Erxleben | .15 | .05 |
| ☐ 406 Elois Grooms | .15 | .05 |
| ☐ 407 Jack Holmes | .15 | .05 |
| ☐ 408 Archie Manning | .75 | .30 |
| ☐ 409 Derland Moore | .15 | .05 |
| ☐ 410 George Rogers RC | .75 | .30 |
| ☐ 411 George Rogers IA | .40 | .15 |
| ☐ 412 Toussaint Tyler | .15 | .05 |
| ☐ 413 Dave Waymer RC | .15 | .05 |
| ☐ 414 Wayne Wilson | .15 | .05 |
| ☐ 415 New York Giants TL | .15 | .05 |
| ☐ 416 Scott Brunner RC | .15 | .05 |
| ☐ 417 Rob Carpenter | .15 | .05 |
| ☐ 418 Harry Carson | .40 | .15 |
| ☐ 419 Bill Currier | .15 | .05 |
| ☐ 420 Joe Danelo | .15 | .05 |
| ☐ 421 Joe Danelo IA | .15 | .05 |
| ☐ 422 Mark Haynes RC | .40 | .15 |
| ☐ 423 Terry Jackson | .15 | .05 |
| ☐ 424 Dave Jennings | .15 | .05 |
| ☐ 425 Gary Jeter | .15 | .05 |
| ☐ 426 Brian Kelley | .15 | .05 |
| ☐ 427 George Martin | .15 | .05 |
| ☐ 428 Curtis McGriff | .15 | .05 |
| ☐ 429 Bill Neill | .15 | .05 |
| ☐ 430 Johnny Perkins | .15 | .05 |
| ☐ 431 Beasley Reece | .15 | .05 |
| ☐ 432 Gary Shirk | .15 | .05 |
| ☐ 433 Phil Simms | 2.00 | .75 |
| ☐ 434 Lawrence Taylor RC | 20.00 | 7.50 |
| ☐ 435 Lawrence Taylor IA | 10.00 | 4.00 |
| ☐ 436 Brad Van Pelt | .15 | .05 |
| ☐ 437 Philadelphia Eagles TL | .40 | .15 |
| ☐ 438 John Bunting | .15 | .05 |

| | | |
|---|---|---|
| 439 Billy Campfield | .15 | .05 |
| 440 Harold Carmichael | .75 | .30 |
| 441 Harold Carmichael IA | .75 | .30 |
| 442 Herman Edwards | .15 | .05 |
| 443 Tony Franklin | .15 | .05 |
| 444 Tony Franklin IA | .15 | .05 |
| 445 Carl Hairston | .15 | .05 |
| 446 Dennis Harrison | .15 | .05 |
| 447 Ron Jaworski | .75 | .30 |
| 448 Charlie Johnson NT | .15 | .05 |
| 449 Keith Krepfle | .15 | .05 |
| 450 Frank LeMaster | .15 | .05 |
| 451 Randy Logan | .15 | .05 |
| 452 Wilbert Montgomery | .40 | .15 |
| 453 Wilbert Montgomery IA | .40 | .15 |
| 454 Hubie Oliver | .15 | .05 |
| 455 Jerry Robinson | .15 | .05 |
| 456 Jerry Robinson IA | .15 | .05 |
| 457 Jerry Sisemore | .15 | .05 |
| 458 Charlie Smith WR | .15 | .05 |
| 459 Stan Walters | .15 | .05 |
| 460 Brenard Wilson | .15 | .05 |
| 461 Roynell Young | .15 | .05 |
| 462 Cardinals TL/O.Anderson | .40 | .15 |
| 463 Ottis Anderson | .75 | .30 |
| 464 Ottis Anderson IA | .75 | .30 |
| 465 Carl Birdsong | .15 | .05 |
| 466 Rush Brown | .15 | .05 |
| 467 Mel Gray | .40 | .15 |
| 468 Ken Greene | .15 | .05 |
| 469 Jim Hart | .75 | .30 |
| 470 E.J.Junior RC | .40 | .15 |
| 471 Neil Lomax RC | .75 | .30 |
| 472 Stump Mitchell RC | .75 | .30 |
| 473 Wayne Morris | .15 | .05 |
| 474 Neil O'Donoghue | .15 | .05 |
| 475 Pat Tilley | .15 | .05 |
| 476 Pat Tilley IA | .15 | .05 |
| 477 49ers TL/Dwight Clark | .40 | .15 |
| 478 Dwight Clark | .75 | .30 |
| 479 Dwight Clark IA | .75 | .30 |
| 480 Earl Cooper | .15 | .05 |
| 481 Randy Cross | .40 | .15 |
| 482 Johnny Davis RC | .15 | .05 |
| 483 Fred Dean | .30 | .10 |
| 484 Fred Dean IA | .15 | .05 |
| 485 Dwight Hicks RC | .75 | .30 |
| 486 Ronnie Lott RC | 20.00 | 7.50 |
| 487 Ronnie Lott IA | 6.00 | 3.00 |
| 488 Joe Montana | 20.00 | 7.50 |
| 489 Joe Montana | 12.00 | 5.00 |
| 490 Ricky Patton | .15 | .05 |
| 491 Jack Reynolds | .40 | .15 |
| 492 Freddie Solomon | .15 | .05 |
| 493 Ray Wersching | .15 | .05 |
| 494 Charle Young | .15 | .05 |
| 495 Tampa Bay Bucs TL | .15 | .05 |
| 496 Cedric Brown | .15 | .05 |
| 497 Neal Colzie | .15 | .05 |
| 498 Jerry Eckwood | .15 | .05 |
| 499 Jimmie Giles | .40 | .15 |
| 500 Hugh Green RC | .75 | .30 |
| 501 Kevin House | .15 | .05 |
| 502 Kevin House IA | .15 | .05 |
| 503 Cecil Johnson | .15 | .05 |
| 504 James Owens | .15 | .05 |
| 505 Lee Roy Selmon | .75 | .30 |
| 506 Mike Washington | .15 | .05 |
| 507 James Wilder RC | .40 | .15 |
| 508 Doug Williams | .75 | .30 |
| 509 Redskins TL/Monk | .75 | .30 |
| 510 Perry Brooks | .15 | .05 |
| 511 Dave Butz | .40 | .15 |
| 512 Wilbur Jackson | .15 | .05 |
| 513 Joe Lavender | .15 | .05 |
| 514 Terry Metcalf | .40 | .15 |
| 515 Art Monk ~ | 3.00 | 1.25 |
| 516 Mark Moseley | .15 | .05 |
| 517 Mark Murphy | .15 | .05 |
| 518 Mike Nelms | .15 | .05 |
| 519 Lemar Parrish | .15 | .05 |
| 520 John Riggins | .75 | .30 |
| 521 Joe Theismann | .75 | .30 |
| 522 Ricky Thompson | .15 | .05 |
| 523 Don Warren UER | .15 | .05 |
| 524 Joe Washington | .40 | .15 |
| 525 Checklist 1-132 | .50 | .20 |

| | | |
|---|---|---|
| 526 Checklist 133-264 | .50 | .20 |
| 527 Checklist 265-396 | .50 | .20 |
| 528 Checklist 397-528 | .50 | .20 |

## 1983 Topps

| | | |
|---|---|---|
| COMPLETE SET (396) | 60.00 | 30.00 |
| 1 Ken Anderson RB | .60 | .25 |
| 2 Tony Dorsett RB | .60 | .25 |
| 3 Dan Fouts RB | .60 | .25 |
| 4 Joe Montana RB | 3.00 | 1.50 |
| 5 Mark Moseley RB | .30 | .10 |
| 6 Mike Nelms RB | .10 | .02 |
| 7 Darrol Ray RB | .10 | .02 |
| 8 John Riggins RB | .60 | .25 |
| 9 Fulton Walker RB | .10 | .02 |
| 10 NFC Champs/Riggins | .60 | .25 |
| 11 AFC Championship | .30 | .10 |
| 12 Super Bowl XVII/J.Riggins | .60 | .25 |
| 13 Atlanta Falcons TL | .30 | .10 |
| 14 William Andrews DP | .30 | .10 |
| 15 Steve Bartkowski | .30 | .10 |
| 16 Bobby Butler | .10 | .02 |
| 17 Buddy Curry | .10 | .02 |
| 18 Alfred Jackson DP | .10 | .02 |
| 19 Alfred Jenkins | .10 | .02 |
| 20 Kenny Johnson | .10 | .02 |
| 21 Mike Kenn | .10 | .02 |
| 22 Mick Luckhurst | .10 | .02 |
| 23 Junior Miller | .10 | .02 |
| 24 Al Richardson | .10 | .02 |
| 25 Gerald Riggs RC DP | .30 | .10 |
| 26 R.C. Thielemann | .10 | .02 |
| 27 Jeff Van Note | .10 | .02 |
| 28 Bears TL/W.Payton | 1.00 | .40 |
| 29 Brian Baschnagel | .10 | .02 |
| 30 Dan Hampton | .60 | .25 |
| 31 Mike Hartenstine | .10 | .02 |
| 32 Noah Jackson | .10 | .02 |
| 33 Jim McMahon RC | 8.00 | 4.00 |
| 34 Emery Moorehead DP | .10 | .02 |
| 35 Bob Parsons | .10 | .02 |
| 36 Walter Payton | 6.00 | 3.00 |
| 37 Terry Schmidt | .10 | .02 |
| 38 Mike Singletary RC | 8.00 | 4.00 |
| 39 Matt Suhey DP | .30 | .10 |
| 40 Rickey Watts DP | .10 | .02 |
| 41 Otis Wilson RC DP | .30 | .10 |
| 42 Cowboys TL/Tony Dorsett | .60 | .25 |
| 43 Bob Breunig | .30 | .10 |
| 44 Doug Cosbie | .10 | .02 |
| 45 Pat Donovan | .10 | .02 |
| 46 Tony Dorsett | 1.00 | .40 |
| 47 Tony Hill | .30 | .10 |
| 48 Butch Johnson DP | .30 | .10 |
| 49 Ed Too Tall Jones DP | .60 | .25 |
| 50 Harvey Martin DP | .30 | .10 |
| 51 Drew Pearson | .30 | .10 |
| 52 Rafael Septien | .10 | .02 |
| 53 Ron Springs DP | .10 | .02 |
| 54 Dennis Thurman | .10 | .02 |
| 55 Everson Walls | .10 | .02 |
| 56 Danny White DP | .60 | .25 |
| 57 Randy White | .60 | .25 |
| 58 Detroit Lions TL | .30 | .10 |
| 59 Al(Bubba) Baker DP | .10 | .02 |
| 60 Dexter Bussey DP | .10 | .02 |
| 61 Gary Danielson DP | .10 | .02 |
| 62 Keith Dorney DP | .10 | .02 |
| 63 Doug English | .10 | .02 |

| | | |
|---|---|---|
| 64 Ken Fantetti DP | .10 | .02 |
| 65 Alvin Hall DP | .10 | .02 |
| 66 David Hill DP | .10 | .02 |
| 67 Eric Hipple | .10 | .02 |
| 68 Eddie Murray DP | .30 | .10 |
| 69 Freddie Scott | .10 | .02 |
| 70 Billy Sims DP | .30 | .10 |
| 71 Tom Skladany DP | .10 | .02 |
| 72 Leonard Thompson DP | .10 | .02 |
| 73 Bobby Watkins | .10 | .02 |
| 74 Green Bay Packers TL | .10 | .02 |
| 75 John Anderson | .10 | .02 |
| 76 Paul Coffman | .10 | .02 |
| 77 Lynn Dickey | .10 | .02 |
| 78 Mike Douglass DP | .10 | .02 |
| 79 Eddie Lee Ivery | .10 | .02 |
| 80 John Jefferson DP | .60 | .25 |
| 81 Ezra Johnson | .10 | .02 |
| 82 Mark Lee | .10 | .02 |
| 83 James Lofton | .60 | .25 |
| 84 Larry McCarren | .10 | .02 |
| 85 Jan Stenerud DP | .30 | .10 |
| 86 Los Angeles Rams TL | .10 | .02 |
| 87 Bill Bain DP | .10 | .02 |
| 88 Nolan Cromwell | .30 | .10 |
| 89 Preston Dennard | .10 | .02 |
| 90 Vince Ferragamo DP | .30 | .10 |
| 91 Mike Guman | .10 | .02 |
| 92 Kent Hill | .10 | .02 |
| 93 Mike Lansford RC DP | .10 | .02 |
| 94 Rod Perry | .10 | .02 |
| 95 Pat Thomas DP | .10 | .02 |
| 96 Jack Youngblood | .60 | .25 |
| 97 Minnesota Vikings TL | .10 | .02 |
| 98 Matt Blair | .10 | .02 |
| 99 Ted Brown | .10 | .02 |
| 100 Greg Coleman | .10 | .02 |
| 101 Randy Holloway | .10 | .02 |
| 102 Tommy Kramer | .30 | .10 |
| 103 Doug Martin DP | .10 | .02 |
| 104 Mark Mullaney | .10 | .02 |
| 105 Joe Senser | .10 | .02 |
| 106 Willie Teal DP | .10 | .02 |
| 107 Sammie White | .30 | .10 |
| 108 Rickey Young | .10 | .02 |
| 109 New Orleans Saints TL | .10 | .02 |
| 110 Stan Brock RC | .10 | .02 |
| 111 Bruce Clark RC | .10 | .02 |
| 112 Russell Erxleben DP | .10 | .02 |
| 113 Russell Gary | .10 | .02 |
| 114 Jeff Groth DP | .10 | .02 |
| 115 John Hill DP | .10 | .02 |
| 116 Derland Moore | .10 | .02 |
| 117 George Rogers | .30 | .10 |
| 118 Ken Stabler | 1.50 | .60 |
| 119 Wayne Wilson | .10 | .02 |
| 120 New York Giants TL | .10 | .02 |
| 121 Scott Brunner | .10 | .02 |
| 122 Rob Carpenter | .10 | .02 |
| 123 Harry Carson | .30 | .10 |
| 124 Joe Danelo DP | .10 | .02 |
| 125 Earnest Gray | .10 | .02 |
| 126 Mark Haynes DP | .30 | .10 |
| 127 Terry Jackson | .10 | .02 |
| 128 Dave Jennings | .10 | .02 |
| 129 Brian Kelley | .10 | .02 |
| 130 George Martin | .10 | .02 |
| 131 Tom Mullady | .10 | .02 |
| 132 Johnny Perkins | .10 | .02 |
| 133 Lawrence Taylor | 5.00 | 2.00 |
| 134 Brad Van Pelt | .10 | .02 |
| 135 Butch Woolfolk DP RC | .10 | .02 |
| 136 Philadelphia Eagles TL | .10 | .02 |
| 137 Harold Carmichael | .60 | .25 |
| 138 Herman Edwards | .10 | .02 |
| 139 Tony Franklin DP | .10 | .02 |
| 140 Carl Hairston DP | .10 | .02 |
| 141 Dennis Harrison DP | .10 | .02 |
| 142 Ron Jaworski DP | .30 | .10 |
| 143 Frank LeMaster | .10 | .02 |
| 144 Wilbert Montgomery DP | .30 | .10 |
| 145 Guy Morriss | .10 | .02 |
| 146 Jerry Robinson | .10 | .02 |
| 147 Max Runager | .10 | .02 |
| 148 Ron Smith DP RC | .10 | .02 |
| 149 John Spagnola | .10 | .02 |
| 150 Stan Walters DP | .10 | .02 |

| | | |
|---|---|---|
| ☐ 151 Roynell Young DP | .10 | .02 |
| ☐ 152 Cardinals TL/O.Anderson | .30 | .10 |
| ☐ 153 Ottis Anderson | .60 | .25 |
| ☐ 154 Carl Birdsong | .10 | .02 |
| ☐ 155 Dan Dierdorf DP | .60 | .25 |
| ☐ 156 Roy Green RC | .60 | .25 |
| ☐ 157 Elois Grooms | .10 | .02 |
| ☐ 158 Neil Lomax DP | .30 | .10 |
| ☐ 159 Wayne Morris | .10 | .02 |
| ☐ 160 Tootie Robbins RC | .10 | .02 |
| ☐ 161 Luis Sharpe RC | .10 | .02 |
| ☐ 162 Pat Tilley | .10 | .02 |
| ☐ 163 San Francisco 49ers TL | .10 | .02 |
| ☐ 164 Dwight Clark | .60 | .25 |
| ☐ 165 Randy Cross | .30 | .10 |
| ☐ 166 Russ Francis | .30 | .10 |
| ☐ 167 Dwight Hicks | .10 | .02 |
| ☐ 168 Ronnie Lott | 2.50 | 1.25 |
| ☐ 169 Joe Montana DP | 10.00 | 4.00 |
| ☐ 170 Jeff Moore | .10 | .02 |
| ☐ 171 Renaldo Nehemiah RC DP | .60 | .25 |
| ☐ 172 Freddie Solomon | .10 | .02 |
| ☐ 173 Ray Wersching DP | .10 | .02 |
| ☐ 174 Tampa Bay Bucs TL | .10 | .02 |
| ☐ 175 Cedric Brown | .10 | .02 |
| ☐ 176 Bill Capece | .10 | .02 |
| ☐ 177 Neal Colzie | .10 | .02 |
| ☐ 178 Jimmie Giles | .10 | .02 |
| ☐ 179 Hugh Green | .30 | .10 |
| ☐ 180 Kevin House DP | .10 | .02 |
| ☐ 181 James Owens | .10 | .02 |
| ☐ 182 Lee Roy Selmon | .60 | .25 |
| ☐ 183 Mike Washington | .10 | .02 |
| ☐ 184 James Wilder | .10 | .02 |
| ☐ 185 Doug Williams DP | .30 | .10 |
| ☐ 186 Redskins TL/John Riggins | .60 | .25 |
| ☐ 187 Jeff Bostic RC DP | 1.00 | .40 |
| ☐ 188 Charlie Brown RC | .30 | .10 |
| ☐ 189 Vernon Dean DP RC | .10 | .02 |
| ☐ 190 Joe Jacoby RC | 3.00 | 1.25 |
| ☐ 191 Dexter Manley RC | .30 | .10 |
| ☐ 192 Rich Milot | .10 | .02 |
| ☐ 193 Art Monk TL | 1.00 | .40 |
| ☐ 194 Mark Moseley DP | .10 | .02 |
| ☐ 195 Mike Nelms | .10 | .02 |
| ☐ 196 Neal Olkewicz DP | .10 | .02 |
| ☐ 197 Tony Peters | .10 | .02 |
| ☐ 198 John Riggins DP | .60 | .25 |
| ☐ 199 Joe Theismann | .60 | .25 |
| ☐ 200 Don Warren | .10 | .02 |
| ☐ 201 Jeris White DP | .10 | .02 |
| ☐ 202 J.Theismann/K.Anderson LL | .60 | .25 |
| ☐ 203 Receiving Leaders | .10 | .02 |
| ☐ 204 Tony Dorsett/F.McNeil LL | .60 | .25 |
| ☐ 205 M.Allen/W.Tyler LL | 1.25 | .50 |
| ☐ 206 Interception Leaders | .30 | .10 |
| ☐ 207 Punting Leaders | .10 | .02 |
| ☐ 208 Baltimore Colts TL | .10 | .02 |
| ☐ 209 Matt Bouza | .10 | .02 |
| ☐ 210 Johnie Cooks RC DP | .10 | .02 |
| ☐ 211 Curtis Dickey | .10 | .02 |
| ☐ 212 Nesby Glasgow DP | .10 | .02 |
| ☐ 213 Derrick Hatchett | .10 | .02 |
| ☐ 214 Randy McMillan | .10 | .02 |
| ☐ 215 Mike Pagel RC | .30 | .10 |
| ☐ 216 Rohn Stark RC DP | .30 | .10 |
| ☐ 217 Donnell Thompson RC DP | .10 | .02 |
| ☐ 218 Leo Wisniewski DP | .10 | .02 |
| ☐ 219 Buffalo Bills TL | .30 | .10 |
| ☐ 220 Curtis Brown | .10 | .02 |
| ☐ 221 Jerry Butler | .10 | .02 |
| ☐ 222 Greg Cater DP | .10 | .02 |
| ☐ 223 Joe Cribbs | .30 | .10 |
| ☐ 224 Joe Ferguson | .30 | .10 |
| ☐ 225 Roosevelt Leaks | .10 | .02 |
| ☐ 226 Frank Lewis | .10 | .02 |
| ☐ 227 Eugene Marve RC | .10 | .02 |
| ☐ 228 Fred Smerlas DP | .10 | .02 |
| ☐ 229 Ben Williams DP | .10 | .02 |
| ☐ 230 Cincinnati Bengals TL | .10 | .02 |
| ☐ 231 Charles Alexander | .10 | .02 |
| ☐ 232 Ken Anderson DP | .60 | .25 |
| ☐ 233 Jim Breech DP | .10 | .02 |
| ☐ 234 Ross Browner | .10 | .02 |
| ☐ 235 Cris Collinsworth DP | .60 | .25 |
| ☐ 236 Isaac Curtis | .10 | .02 |
| ☐ 237 Pete Johnson | .10 | .02 |

| | | |
|---|---|---|
| ☐ 238 Steve Kreider DP | .10 | .02 |
| ☐ 239 Max Montoya RC DP | .10 | .02 |
| ☐ 240 Anthony Munoz | 1.00 | .40 |
| ☐ 241 Ken Riley | .10 | .02 |
| ☐ 242 Dan Ross | .10 | .02 |
| ☐ 243 Reggie Williams | .30 | .10 |
| ☐ 244 Cleveland Browns TL | .30 | .10 |
| ☐ 245 Chip Banks RC DP | .30 | .10 |
| ☐ 246 Tom Cousineau RC DP | .10 | .02 |
| ☐ 247 Joe DeLamielleure DP | .30 | .10 |
| ☐ 248 Doug Dieken DP | .10 | .02 |
| ☐ 249 Hanford Dixon RC | .10 | .02 |
| ☐ 250 Ricky Feacher DP | .10 | .02 |
| ☐ 251 Lawrence Johnson DP | .10 | .02 |
| ☐ 252 Dave Logan DP | .10 | .02 |
| ☐ 253 Paul McDonald DP | .10 | .02 |
| ☐ 254 Ozzie Newsome DP | .60 | .25 |
| ☐ 255 Mike Pruitt | .30 | .10 |
| ☐ 256 Clarence Scott DP | .10 | .02 |
| ☐ 257 Brian Sipe DP | .30 | .10 |
| ☐ 258 Dwight Walker DP | .10 | .02 |
| ☐ 259 Charles White | .30 | .10 |
| ☐ 260 Denver Broncos TL | .30 | .10 |
| ☐ 261 Steve DeBerg DP | .30 | .10 |
| ☐ 262 Randy Gradishar DP | .30 | .10 |
| ☐ 263 Rulon Jones RC DP | .10 | .02 |
| ☐ 264 Rich Karlis DP | .10 | .02 |
| ☐ 265 Don Latimer | .10 | .02 |
| ☐ 266 Rick Parros DP | .10 | .02 |
| ☐ 267 Luke Prestridge | .10 | .02 |
| ☐ 268 Rick Upchurch | .30 | .10 |
| ☐ 269 Steve Watson DP | .10 | .02 |
| ☐ 270 Gerald Willhite DP | .10 | .02 |
| ☐ 271 Houston Oilers TL | .10 | .02 |
| ☐ 272 Harold Bailey | .10 | .02 |
| ☐ 273 Jesse Baker DP | .10 | .02 |
| ☐ 274 Gregg Bingham DP | .10 | .02 |
| ☐ 275 Robert Brazile DP | .10 | .02 |
| ☐ 276 Donnie Craft | .10 | .02 |
| ☐ 277 Daryl Hunt | .10 | .02 |
| ☐ 278 Archie Manning DP | .30 | .10 |
| ☐ 279 Gifford Nielsen | .10 | .02 |
| ☐ 280 Mike Renfro | .10 | .02 |
| ☐ 281 Carl Roaches DP | .10 | .02 |
| ☐ 282 Kansas City Chiefs TL | .30 | .10 |
| ☐ 283 Gary Barbaro | .10 | .02 |
| ☐ 284 Joe Delaney | .10 | .02 |
| ☐ 285 Jeff Gossett RC | .60 | .25 |
| ☐ 286 Gary Green DP | .10 | .02 |
| ☐ 287 Eric Harris DP | .10 | .02 |
| ☐ 288 Billy Jackson DP | .10 | .02 |
| ☐ 289 Bill Kenney DP | .10 | .02 |
| ☐ 290 Nick Lowery | .60 | .25 |
| ☐ 291 Henry Marshall | .10 | .02 |
| ☐ 292 Art Still DP | .10 | .02 |
| ☐ 293 Raiders TL/M.Allen | 2.00 | .75 |
| ☐ 294 Marcus Allen RC DP | 15.00 | 6.00 |
| ☐ 295 Lyle Alzado | .60 | .25 |
| ☐ 296 Chris Bahr DP | .10 | .02 |
| ☐ 297 Cliff Branch | .60 | .25 |
| ☐ 298 Todd Christensen RC | .75 | .30 |
| ☐ 299 Ray Guy | .30 | .10 |
| ☐ 300 Frank Hawkins DP | .10 | .02 |
| ☐ 301 Lester Hayes DP | .10 | .02 |
| ☐ 302 Ted Hendricks DP | .60 | .25 |
| ☐ 303 Kenny King DP | .10 | .02 |
| ☐ 304 Rod Martin | .10 | .02 |
| ☐ 305 Matt Millen DP | .60 | .25 |
| ☐ 306 Burgess Owens | .10 | .02 |
| ☐ 307 Jim Plunkett | .60 | .25 |
| ☐ 308 Miami Dolphins TL | .10 | .02 |
| ☐ 309 Bob Baumhower | .10 | .02 |
| ☐ 310 Glenn Blackwood | .10 | .02 |
| ☐ 311 Lyle Blackwood DP | .10 | .02 |
| ☐ 312 A.J. Duhe | .10 | .02 |
| ☐ 313 Andra Franklin | .10 | .02 |
| ☐ 314 Duriel Harris | .10 | .02 |
| ☐ 315 Bob Kuechenberg DP | .30 | .10 |
| ☐ 316 Don McNeal | .10 | .02 |
| ☐ 317 Tony Nathan | .30 | .10 |
| ☐ 318 Ed Newman | .10 | .02 |
| ☐ 319 Earnie Rhone DP | .10 | .02 |
| ☐ 320 Joe Rose DP | .10 | .02 |
| ☐ 321 Don Strock DP | .10 | .02 |
| ☐ 322 Uwe Von Schamann | .10 | .02 |
| ☐ 323 David Woodley DP | .30 | .10 |
| ☐ 324 New England Pats TL | .10 | .02 |

| | | |
|---|---|---|
| ☐ 325 Julius Adams | .10 | .02 |
| ☐ 326 Pete Brock | .10 | .02 |
| ☐ 327 Rich Camarillo RC DP | .10 | .02 |
| ☐ 328 Tony Collins DP | .10 | .02 |
| ☐ 329 Steve Grogan | .30 | .10 |
| ☐ 330 John Hannah | .60 | .25 |
| ☐ 331 Don Hasselbeck | .10 | .02 |
| ☐ 332 Mike Haynes | .30 | .10 |
| ☐ 333 Roland James RC | .10 | .02 |
| ☐ 334A Stanley Morgan ERR IL | .60 | .25 |
| ☐ 334B Stanley Morgan COR | .30 | .10 |
| ☐ 335 Steve Nelson | .10 | .02 |
| ☐ 336 Kenneth Sims DP | .10 | .02 |
| ☐ 337 Mark Van Eeghen | .30 | .10 |
| ☐ 338 New York Jets TL | .30 | .10 |
| ☐ 339 Greg Buttle | .10 | .02 |
| ☐ 340 Joe Fields | .10 | .02 |
| ☐ 341 Mark Gastineau DP | .30 | .10 |
| ☐ 342 Bruce Harper | .10 | .02 |
| ☐ 343 Bobby Jackson | .10 | .02 |
| ☐ 344 Bobby Jones | .10 | .02 |
| ☐ 345 Johnny Lam Jones DP | .10 | .02 |
| ☐ 346 Joe Klecko | .30 | .10 |
| ☐ 347 Marty Lyons | .10 | .02 |
| ☐ 348 Freeman McNeil | .60 | .25 |
| ☐ 349 Lance Mehl RC | .10 | .02 |
| ☐ 350 Marvin Powell DP | .10 | .02 |
| ☐ 351 Darrol Ray DP | .10 | .02 |
| ☐ 352 Abdul Salaam | .10 | .02 |
| ☐ 353 Richard Todd | .30 | .10 |
| ☐ 354 Wesley Walker | .30 | .10 |
| ☐ 355 Steelers TL/Franco Harris | .60 | .25 |
| ☐ 356 Gary Anderson K RC DP | 6.00 | 3.00 |
| ☐ 357 Mel Blount DP | .60 | .25 |
| ☐ 358 Terry Bradshaw DP | 1.50 | .60 |
| ☐ 359 Larry Brown | .10 | .02 |
| ☐ 360 Bennie Cunningham | .10 | .02 |
| ☐ 361 Gary Dunn | .10 | .02 |
| ☐ 362 Franco Harris | .75 | .30 |
| ☐ 363 Jack Lambert | .60 | .25 |
| ☐ 364 Frank Pollard | .10 | .02 |
| ☐ 365 Donnie Shell | .30 | .10 |
| ☐ 366 John Stallworth | .60 | .25 |
| ☐ 367 Loren Toews | .10 | .02 |
| ☐ 368 Mike Webster DP | .60 | .25 |
| ☐ 369 Dwayne Woodruff RC | .10 | .02 |
| ☐ 370 San Diego Chargers TL | .30 | .10 |
| ☐ 371 Rolf Benirschke DP | .10 | .02 |
| ☐ 372 James Brooks | .60 | .25 |
| ☐ 373 Wes Chandler | .30 | .10 |
| ☐ 374 Dan Fouts DP | .60 | .25 |
| ☐ 375 Tim Fox | .10 | .02 |
| ☐ 376 Gary Johnson | .10 | .02 |
| ☐ 377 Charlie Joiner DP | .60 | .25 |
| ☐ 378 Louie Kelcher | .10 | .02 |
| ☐ 379 Chuck Muncie | .10 | .02 |
| ☐ 380 Cliff Thrift | .10 | .02 |
| ☐ 381 Doug Wilkerson | .10 | .02 |
| ☐ 382 Kellen Winslow | .75 | .30 |
| ☐ 383 Seattle Seahawks TL | .10 | .02 |
| ☐ 384 Kenny Easley RC | .60 | .25 |
| ☐ 385 Jacob Green RC | .30 | .10 |
| ☐ 386 John Harris | .10 | .02 |
| ☐ 387 Michael Jackson | .10 | .02 |
| ☐ 388 Norm Johnson RC | .10 | .02 |
| ☐ 389 Steve Largent | 1.25 | .50 |
| ☐ 390 Keith Simpson | .10 | .02 |
| ☐ 391 Sherman Smith | .10 | .02 |
| ☐ 392 Jeff West DP | .10 | .02 |
| ☐ 393 Jim Zorn DP | .30 | .10 |
| ☐ 394 Checklist 1-132 | .50 | .20 |
| ☐ 395 Checklist 133-264 | .50 | .20 |
| ☐ 396 Checklist 265-396 | .50 | .20 |

### 1984 Topps

| | | |
|---|---|---|
| ☐ COMPLETE SET (396) | 200.00 | 100.00 |
| ☐ COMP.FACT.SET (396) | 350.00 | 200.00 |
| ☐ 1 Eric Dickerson RB | .25 | .08 |
| ☐ 2 Ali Haji-Sheikh RB | .25 | .08 |
| ☐ 3 Franco Harris RB | .50 | .20 |
| ☐ 4 Mark Moseley RB | .25 | .08 |
| ☐ 5 John Riggins RB | .50 | .20 |
| ☐ 6 Jan Stenerud RB | .25 | .08 |
| ☐ 7 AFC Champs/M.Allen | .50 | .20 |
| ☐ 8 NFC Champs/Riggins | .25 | .10 |
| ☐ 9 Super Bowl XVIII/Allen UER | .50 | .20 |
| ☐ 10 Indianapolis Colts TL | .10 | .02 |

| | | |
|---|---|---|
| ☐ 11 Raul Allegre RC | .10 | .02 |
| ☐ 12 Curtis Dickey | .25 | .08 |
| ☐ 13 Ray Donaldson RC | .25 | .08 |
| ☐ 14 Nesby Glasgow | .10 | .02 |
| ☐ 15 Chris Hinton RC | .50 | .20 |
| ☐ 16 Vernon Maxwell RC | .10 | .02 |
| ☐ 17 Randy McMillan | .10 | .02 |
| ☐ 18 Mike Pagel | .25 | .08 |
| ☐ 19 Rohn Stark | .25 | .08 |
| ☐ 20 Leo Wisniewski | .10 | .02 |
| ☐ 21 Buffalo Bills TL | .25 | .08 |
| ☐ 22 Jerry Butler | .10 | .02 |
| ☐ 23 Joe Danelo | .10 | .02 |
| ☐ 24 Joe Ferguson | .25 | .08 |
| ☐ 25 Steve Freeman | .10 | .02 |
| ☐ 26 Roosevelt Leaks | .10 | .02 |
| ☐ 27 Frank Lewis | .10 | .02 |
| ☐ 28 Eugene Marve | .10 | .02 |
| ☐ 29 Booker Moore | .10 | .02 |
| ☐ 30 Fred Smerlas | .10 | .02 |
| ☐ 31 Ben Williams | .10 | .02 |
| ☐ 32 Cincinnati Bengals TL | .25 | .08 |
| ☐ 33 Charles Alexander | .10 | .02 |
| ☐ 34 Ken Anderson | .50 | .20 |
| ☐ 35 Ken Anderson IR | .50 | .20 |
| ☐ 36 Jim Breech | .10 | .02 |
| ☐ 37 Cris Collinsworth | .50 | .20 |
| ☐ 38 Cris Collinsworth IR | .25 | .08 |
| ☐ 39 Isaac Curtis | .25 | .08 |
| ☐ 40 Eddie Edwards | .10 | .02 |
| ☐ 41 Ray Horton RC | .10 | .02 |
| ☐ 42 Pete Johnson | .25 | .08 |
| ☐ 43 Steve Kreider | .10 | .02 |
| ☐ 44 Max Montoya | .10 | .02 |
| ☐ 45 Anthony Munoz | .50 | .20 |
| ☐ 46 Reggie Williams | .25 | .08 |
| ☐ 47 Cleveland Browns TL | .25 | .08 |
| ☐ 48 Matt Bahr | .25 | .08 |
| ☐ 49 Chip Banks | .25 | .08 |
| ☐ 50 Tom Cousineau | .10 | .02 |
| ☐ 51 Joe DeLamielleure | .50 | .20 |
| ☐ 52 Doug Dieken | .10 | .02 |
| ☐ 53 Bob Golic RC | .50 | .20 |
| ☐ 54 Bobby Jones | .10 | .02 |
| ☐ 55 Dave Logan | .10 | .02 |
| ☐ 56 Clay Matthews | .50 | .20 |
| ☐ 57 Paul McDonald | .10 | .02 |
| ☐ 58 Ozzie Newsome | .50 | .20 |
| ☐ 59 Ozzie Newsome IR | .25 | .08 |
| ☐ 60 Mike Pruitt | .25 | .08 |
| ☐ 61 Denver Broncos TL | .25 | .08 |
| ☐ 62 Barney Chavous RC | .10 | .02 |
| ☐ 63 John Elway RC ! | 60.00 | 30.00 |
| ☐ 64 Steve Foley | .10 | .02 |
| ☐ 65 Tom Jackson | .50 | .20 |
| ☐ 66 Rich Karlis | .10 | .02 |
| ☐ 67 Luke Prestridge | .10 | .02 |
| ☐ 68 Zach Thomas WR | .10 | .02 |
| ☐ 69 Rick Upchurch | .25 | .08 |
| ☐ 70 Steve Watson | .25 | .08 |
| ☐ 71 Sammy Winder RC | .50 | .20 |
| ☐ 72 Louis Wright | .25 | .08 |
| ☐ 73 Houston Oilers TL | .10 | .02 |
| ☐ 74 Jesse Baker | .10 | .02 |
| ☐ 75 Gregg Bingham | .10 | .02 |
| ☐ 76 Robert Brazile | .25 | .08 |
| ☐ 77 Steve Brown RC | .10 | .02 |
| ☐ 78 Chris Dressel | .10 | .02 |
| ☐ 79 Doug France | .10 | .02 |
| ☐ 80 Florian Kempf | .10 | .02 |

| | | |
|---|---|---|
| ☐ 81 Carl Roaches | .25 | .08 |
| ☐ 82 Tim Smith WR RC | .25 | .08 |
| ☐ 83 Willie Tullis | .10 | .02 |
| ☐ 84 Kansas City Chiefs TL | .10 | .02 |
| ☐ 85 Mike Bell RC | .10 | .02 |
| ☐ 86 Theotis Brown | .10 | .02 |
| ☐ 87 Carlos Carson | .50 | .20 |
| ☐ 88 Carlos Carson IR | .25 | .08 |
| ☐ 89 Deron Cherry RC | .25 | .08 |
| ☐ 90 Gary Green | .10 | .02 |
| ☐ 91 Billy Jackson | .10 | .02 |
| ☐ 92 Bill Kenney | .25 | .08 |
| ☐ 93 Bill Kenney IR | .25 | .08 |
| ☐ 94 Nick Lowery | .25 | .08 |
| ☐ 95 Henry Marshall | .10 | .02 |
| ☐ 96 Art Still | .10 | .02 |
| ☐ 97 Los Angeles Raiders TL | .25 | .08 |
| ☐ 98 Marcus Allen | 5.00 | 2.50 |
| ☐ 99 Marcus Allen IR | 2.50 | 1.00 |
| ☐ 100 Lyle Alzado | .25 | .08 |
| ☐ 101 Lyle Alzado IR | .25 | .08 |
| ☐ 102 Chris Bahr | .10 | .02 |
| ☐ 103 Malcolm Barnwell RC | .10 | .02 |
| ☐ 104 Cliff Branch | .50 | .20 |
| ☐ 105 Todd Christensen | .50 | .20 |
| ☐ 106 Todd Christensen IR | .50 | .20 |
| ☐ 107 Ray Guy | .50 | .20 |
| ☐ 108 Frank Hawkins | .10 | .02 |
| ☐ 109 Lester Hayes | .25 | .08 |
| ☐ 110 Ted Hendricks | .50 | .20 |
| ☐ 111 Howie Long RC | 15.00 | 6.00 |
| ☐ 112 Rod Martin | .25 | .08 |
| ☐ 113 Vann McElroy RC | .10 | .02 |
| ☐ 114 Jim Plunkett | .50 | .20 |
| ☐ 115 Greg Pruitt | .25 | .08 |
| ☐ 116 Dolphins TL/M.Duper | .50 | .20 |
| ☐ 117 Bob Baumhower | .10 | .02 |
| ☐ 118 Doug Betters RC | .10 | .02 |
| ☐ 119 A.J. Duhe | .10 | .02 |
| ☐ 120 Mark Duper RC | .50 | .20 |
| ☐ 121 Andra Franklin | .10 | .02 |
| ☐ 122 William Judson | .10 | .02 |
| ☐ 123 Dan Marino RC ! | 60.00 | 30.00 |
| ☐ 124 Dan Marino IR | 12.00 | 5.00 |
| ☐ 125 Nat Moore | .25 | .08 |
| ☐ 126 Ed Newman | .10 | .02 |
| ☐ 127 Reggie Roby RC | .25 | .08 |
| ☐ 128 Gerald Small | .10 | .02 |
| ☐ 129 Dwight Stephenson RC | 5.00 | 2.00 |
| ☐ 130 Uwe Von Schamann | .10 | .02 |
| ☐ 131 New England Pats TL | .10 | .02 |
| ☐ 132 Rich Camarillo | .25 | .08 |
| ☐ 133 Tony Collins | .25 | .08 |
| ☐ 134 Tony Collins IR | .10 | .02 |
| ☐ 135 Bob Cryder | .10 | .02 |
| ☐ 136 Steve Grogan | .25 | .08 |
| ☐ 137 John Hannah | .50 | .20 |
| ☐ 138 Brian Holloway RC | .10 | .02 |
| ☐ 139 Roland James | .10 | .02 |
| ☐ 140 Stanley Morgan | .50 | .20 |
| ☐ 141 Rick Sanford | .10 | .02 |
| ☐ 142 Mosi Tatupu RC | .10 | .02 |
| ☐ 143 Andre Tippett RC | 5.00 | 2.00 |
| ☐ 144 New York Jets TL | .10 | .02 |
| ☐ 145 Jerome Barkum | .10 | .02 |
| ☐ 146 Mark Gastineau | .25 | .08 |
| ☐ 147 Mark Gastineau IR | .25 | .08 |
| ☐ 148 Bruce Harper | .10 | .02 |
| ☐ 149 Johnny Lam Jones | .10 | .02 |
| ☐ 150 Joe Klecko | .25 | .08 |
| ☐ 151 Pat Leahy | .25 | .08 |
| ☐ 152 Freeman McNeil | .25 | .08 |
| ☐ 153 Lance Mehl | .10 | .02 |
| ☐ 154 Marvin Powell | .10 | .02 |
| ☐ 155 Darrol Ray UER | .10 | .02 |
| ☐ 156 Pat Ryan RC | .10 | .02 |
| ☐ 157 Kirk Springs | .10 | .02 |
| ☐ 158 Wesley Walker | .25 | .08 |
| ☐ 159 Steelers TL/F.Harris | .50 | .20 |
| ☐ 160 Walter Abercrombie RC | .25 | .08 |
| ☐ 161 Gary Anderson K | .50 | .20 |
| ☐ 162 Terry Bradshaw | 2.00 | .75 |
| ☐ 163 Craig Colquitt | .10 | .02 |
| ☐ 164 Bennie Cunningham | .10 | .02 |
| ☐ 165 Franco Harris | .50 | .20 |
| ☐ 166 Franco Harris IR | .50 | .20 |
| ☐ 167 Jack Lambert | .50 | .20 |

| | | |
|---|---|---|
| ☐ 168 Jack Lambert IR | .50 | .20 |
| ☐ 169 Frank Pollard | .10 | .02 |
| ☐ 170 Donnie Shell | .25 | .08 |
| ☐ 171 Mike Webster | .25 | .08 |
| ☐ 172 Keith Willis RC | .10 | .02 |
| ☐ 173 Rick Woods | .10 | .02 |
| ☐ 174 Chargers TL/K.Winslow | .50 | .20 |
| ☐ 175 Rolf Benirschke | .10 | .02 |
| ☐ 176 James Brooks | .25 | .08 |
| ☐ 177 Maury Buford | .10 | .02 |
| ☐ 178 Wes Chandler | .25 | .08 |
| ☐ 179 Dan Fouts | .60 | .25 |
| ☐ 180 Dan Fouts IR | .50 | .20 |
| ☐ 181 Charlie Joiner | .50 | .20 |
| ☐ 182 Linden King | .10 | .02 |
| ☐ 183 Chuck Muncie | .25 | .08 |
| ☐ 184 Billy Ray Smith RC | .50 | .20 |
| ☐ 185 Danny Walters RC | .10 | .02 |
| ☐ 186 Kellen Winslow | .60 | .25 |
| ☐ 187 Kellen Winslow IR | .50 | .20 |
| ☐ 188 Seahawks TL/C.Warner | .50 | .20 |
| ☐ 189 Steve August | .10 | .02 |
| ☐ 190 Dave Brown DB | .10 | .02 |
| ☐ 191 Zachary Dixon | .10 | .02 |
| ☐ 192 Kenny Easley | .25 | .08 |
| ☐ 193 Jacob Green | .10 | .02 |
| ☐ 194 Norm Johnson | .25 | .08 |
| ☐ 195 Dave Krieg | 1.50 | .60 |
| ☐ 196 Steve Largent | 1.00 | .40 |
| ☐ 197 Steve Largent IR | .50 | .20 |
| ☐ 198 Curt Warner RC | .50 | .20 |
| ☐ 199 Curt Warner IR | .50 | .20 |
| ☐ 200 Jeff West | .10 | .02 |
| ☐ 201 Charle Young | .10 | .02 |
| ☐ 202 D.Marino/Bartkow. LL | 6.00 | 2.50 |
| ☐ 203 Receiving Leaders | .25 | .08 |
| ☐ 204 Eric Dickerson/Warner LL | .50 | .20 |
| ☐ 205 Scoring Leaders | .10 | .02 |
| ☐ 206 Interception Leaders | .10 | .02 |
| ☐ 207 Punting Leaders | .10 | .02 |
| ☐ 208 Atlanta Falcons TL | .25 | .08 |
| ☐ 209 William Andrews | .25 | .08 |
| ☐ 210 William Andrews IR | .25 | .08 |
| ☐ 211 Stacey Bailey RC | .10 | .02 |
| ☐ 212 Steve Bartkowski | .50 | .20 |
| ☐ 213 Steve Bartkowski IR | .25 | .08 |
| ☐ 214 Ralph Giacomarro | .10 | .02 |
| ☐ 215 Billy Johnson | .25 | .08 |
| ☐ 216 Mike Kenn | .25 | .08 |
| ☐ 217 Mick Luckhurst | .10 | .02 |
| ☐ 218 Gerald Riggs | .50 | .20 |
| ☐ 219 R.C. Thielemann | .10 | .02 |
| ☐ 220 Jeff Van Note | .25 | .08 |
| ☐ 221 Bears TL/W.Payton | .75 | .30 |
| ☐ 222 Jim Covert RC | .50 | .20 |
| ☐ 223 Leslie Frazier | .10 | .02 |
| ☐ 224 Willie Gault RC | .50 | .20 |
| ☐ 225 Mike Hartenstine | .10 | .02 |
| ☐ 226 Noah Jackson UER | .10 | .02 |
| ☐ 227 Jim McMahon | 1.25 | .50 |
| ☐ 228 Walter Payton | 6.00 | 2.50 |
| ☐ 229 Walter Payton IR | 1.25 | .50 |
| ☐ 230 Mike Richardson RC | .10 | .02 |
| ☐ 231 Terry Schmidt | .10 | .02 |
| ☐ 232 Mike Singletary | 1.25 | .50 |
| ☐ 233 Matt Suhey | .25 | .08 |
| ☐ 234 Bob Thomas | .10 | .02 |
| ☐ 235 Cowboys TL/T.Dorsett | .50 | .20 |
| ☐ 236 Bob Breunig | .10 | .02 |
| ☐ 237 Doug Cosbie | .25 | .08 |
| ☐ 238 Tony Dorsett | 1.00 | .40 |
| ☐ 239 Tony Dorsett IR | .50 | .20 |
| ☐ 240 John Dutton | .10 | .02 |
| ☐ 241 Tony Hill | .25 | .08 |
| ☐ 242 Ed Too Tall Jones | .50 | .20 |
| ☐ 243 Drew Pearson | .50 | .20 |
| ☐ 244 Rafael Septien | .10 | .02 |
| ☐ 245 Ron Springs | .10 | .02 |
| ☐ 246 Dennis Thurman | .10 | .02 |
| ☐ 247 Everson Walls | .50 | .20 |
| ☐ 248 Danny White | .50 | .20 |
| ☐ 249 Randy White | .50 | .20 |
| ☐ 250 Detroit Lions TL | .25 | .08 |
| ☐ 251 Jeff Chadwick RC | .25 | .08 |
| ☐ 252 Garry Cobb | .10 | .02 |
| ☐ 253 Doug English | .25 | .08 |
| ☐ 254 William Gay | .10 | .02 |

|  | | |  | | |  | | |
|---|---|---|---|---|---|---|---|---|
| 255 Eric Hipple | .25 | .08 | 342 Roy Green | .25 | .08 | 11 Fred Bohannon | 2.00 | .75 |
| 256 James Jones FB RC | .25 | .08 | 343 Roy Green IR | .25 | .08 | 12 Joe Cribbs | 4.00 | 2.00 |
| 257 Bruce McNorton | .10 | .02 | 344 Curtis Greer RC | .10 | .02 | 13 Joey Jones | 2.00 | .75 |
| 258 Eddie Murray | .25 | .08 | 345 Neil Lomax | .25 | .08 | 14 Scott Norwood XRC | 2.50 | 1.25 |
| 259 Ulysses Norris | .10 | .02 | 346 Doug Marsh | .10 | .02 | 15 Jim Smith | 2.50 | 1.25 |
| 260 Billy Sims | .50 | .20 | 347 Stump Mitchell | .25 | .08 | 16 Cliff Stoudt | 4.00 | 2.00 |
| 261 Billy Sims IR | .25 | .08 | 348 Lionel Washington RC | .25 | .08 | 17 Vince Evans | 4.00 | 2.00 |
| 262 Leonard Thompson | .10 | .02 | 349 49ers TL/D.Clark | .25 | .08 | 18 Vagas Ferguson | 2.00 | .75 |
| 263 Packers TL/J.Lofton | .50 | .20 | 350 Dwaine Board | .10 | .02 | 19 John Gillen | 2.00 | .75 |
| 264 John Anderson | .10 | .02 | 351 Dwight Clark | .50 | .20 | 20 Kris Haines | 2.00 | .75 |
| 265 Paul Coffman | .25 | .08 | 352 Dwight Clark IR | .25 | .08 | 21 Glenn Hyde | 2.00 | .75 |
| 266 Lynn Dickey | .25 | .08 | 353 Roger Craig RC ! | 3.00 | 1.25 | 22 Mark Keel | 2.00 | .75 |
| 267 Gerry Ellis | .10 | .02 | 354 Fred Dean | .25 | .08 | 23 Gary Lewis XRC | 2.00 | .75 |
| 268 John Jefferson | .50 | .20 | 355 Fred Dean IR w/Marino | .50 | .20 | 24 Doug Plank | 2.00 | .75 |
| 269 John Jefferson IR | .50 | .20 | 356 Dwight Hicks | .25 | .08 | 25 Neil Balholm | 2.00 | .75 |
| 270 Ezra Johnson | .10 | .02 | 357 Ronnie Lott | 1.50 | .60 | 26 David Dumars | 2.00 | .75 |
| 271 Tim Lewis RC | .10 | .02 | 358 Joe Montana | 10.00 | 4.00 | 27 David Martin XRC | 2.00 | .75 |
| 272 James Lofton | .50 | .20 | 359 Joe Montana IR | 3.00 | 1.50 | 28 Craig Penrose | 2.00 | .75 |
| 273 James Lofton IR | .50 | .20 | 360 Freddie Solomon | .10 | .02 | 29 Dave Stalls | 2.00 | .75 |
| 274 Larry McCarren | .10 | .02 | 361 Wendell Tyler | .10 | .02 | 30 Harry Sydney XRC | 2.00 | .75 |
| 275 Jan Stenerud | .25 | .08 | 362 Ray Wersching | .10 | .02 | 31 Vincent White | 2.00 | .75 |
| 276 Rams TL/E.Dickerson | .50 | .20 | 363 Eric Wright RC | .25 | .08 | 32 George Yarno | 2.00 | .75 |
| 277 Mike Barber | .10 | .02 | 364 Tampa Bay Bucs TL | .10 | .02 | 33 Kiki DeAyala | 2.00 | .75 |
| 278 Jim Collins | .10 | .02 | 365 Gerald Carter | .10 | .02 | 34 Sam Harrell | 2.00 | .75 |
| 279 Nolan Cromwell | .25 | .08 | 366 Hugh Green | .25 | .08 | 35 Mike Hawkins | 2.00 | .75 |
| 280 Eric Dickerson RC | 10.00 | 4.00 | 367 Kevin House | .25 | .08 | 36 Jim Kelly XRC | 80.00 | 40.00 |
| 281 Eric Dickerson IR | 2.00 | .75 | 368 Michael Morton RC | .10 | .02 | 37 Mark Rush | 2.00 | .75 |
| 282 George Farmer South. | .10 | .02 | 369 James Owens | .10 | .02 | 38 Ricky Sanders XRC | 6.00 | 3.00 |
| 283 Vince Ferragamo | .25 | .08 | 370 Booker Reese | .10 | .02 | 39 Paul Bergmann | 2.00 | .75 |
| 284 Kent Hill | .10 | .02 | 371 Lee Roy Selmon | .50 | .20 | 40 Tom Dinkel | 2.00 | .75 |
| 285 John Misko | .10 | .02 | 372 Jack Thompson | .25 | .08 | 41 Wyatt Henderson | 2.00 | .75 |
| 286 Jackie Slater RC | 4.00 | 1.50 | 373 James Wilder | .25 | .08 | 42 Vaughan Johnson XRC | 2.50 | 1.25 |
| 287 Jack Youngblood | .25 | .08 | 374 Steve Wilson | .10 | .02 | 43 Willie McClendon Geor. | 2.00 | .75 |
| 288 Minnesota Vikings TL | .10 | .02 | 375 Redskins TL/J.Riggins | .50 | .20 | 44 Matt Robinson | 2.00 | .75 |
| 289 Ted Brown | .25 | .08 | 376 Jeff Bostic | .10 | .02 | 45 George Achica | 2.00 | .75 |
| 290 Greg Coleman | .10 | .02 | 377 Charlie Brown | .50 | .20 | 46 Mark Adickes | 2.00 | .75 |
| 291 Steve Dils | .10 | .02 | 378 Charlie Brown IR | .25 | .08 | 47 Howard Carson | 2.00 | .75 |
| 292 Tony Galbreath | .10 | .02 | 379 Dave Butz | .25 | .08 | 48 Kevin Nelson | 2.00 | .75 |
| 293 Tommy Kramer | .25 | .08 | 380 Darrell Green RC | 12.00 | 6.00 | 49 Jeff Partridge | 2.00 | .75 |
| 294 Doug Martin | .10 | .02 | 381 Russ Grimm RC | 1.00 | .40 | 50 Jo Jo Townsell | 2.50 | 1.25 |
| 295 Darrin Nelson | .25 | .08 | 382 Joe Jacoby | .25 | .08 | 51 Eddie Weaver | 2.00 | .75 |
| 296 Benny Ricardo | .10 | .02 | 383 Dexter Manley | .25 | .08 | 52 Steve Young XRC | 120.00 | 60.00 |
| 297 John Swain | .10 | .02 | 384 Art Monk | 1.00 | .40 | 53 Derrick Crawford | 2.00 | .75 |
| 298 John Turner | .10 | .02 | 385 Mark Moseley | .25 | .08 | 54 Walter Lewis | 2.00 | .75 |
| 299 New Orleans Saints TL | .25 | .08 | 386 Mark Murphy | .10 | .02 | 55 Phil McKinnely | 2.00 | .75 |
| 300 Morten Andersen RC | 1.50 | .60 | 387 Mike Nelms | .10 | .02 | 56 Vic Minore | 2.00 | .75 |
| 301 Russell Erxleben | .10 | .02 | 388 John Riggins | .50 | .20 | 57 Gary Shirk | 2.00 | .75 |
| 302 Jeff Groth | .10 | .02 | 389 John Riggins IR | .50 | .20 | 58 Reggie White XRC | 60.00 | 30.00 |
| 303 Rickey Jackson RC | .50 | .20 | 390 Joe Theismann | .50 | .20 | 59 Anthony Carter XRC | 12.00 | 5.00 |
| 304 Johnnie Poe RC | .10 | .02 | 391 Joe Theismann IR | .50 | .20 | 60 John Corker | 2.00 | .75 |
| 305 George Rogers | .25 | .08 | 392 Don Warren | .25 | .08 | 61 David Greenwood | 2.00 | .75 |
| 306 Richard Todd | .25 | .08 | 393 Joe Washington | .25 | .08 | 62 Bobby Hebert XRC | 4.00 | 2.00 |
| 307 Jim Wilks RC | .10 | .02 | 394 Checklist 1-132 | .30 | .10 | 63 Derek Holloway | 2.00 | .75 |
| 308 Dave Wilson RC | .10 | .02 | 395 Checklist 133-264 | .30 | .10 | 64 Ken Lacy | 2.00 | .75 |
| 309 Wayne Wilson | .10 | .02 | 396 Checklist 265-396 | .30 | .10 | 65 Tyrone McGriff | 2.00 | .75 |
| 310 New York Giants TL | .10 | .02 | | | | 66 Ray Pinney | 2.00 | .75 |
| 311 Leon Bright | .10 | .02 | | | | 67 Gary Barbaro | 2.00 | .75 |
| 312 Scott Brunner | .10 | .02 | | | | 68 Sam Bowers | 2.00 | .75 |
| 313 Rob Carpenter | .10 | .02 | **1984 Topps USFL** | | | 69 Clarence Collins | 2.00 | .75 |
| 314 Harry Carson | .25 | .08 | | | | 70 Willie Harper | 2.00 | .75 |
| 315 Earnest Gray | .10 | .02 | | | | 71 Jim LeClair | 2.00 | .75 |
| 316 Ali Haji-Sheikh RC | .10 | .02 | | | | 72 Bobby Leopold XRC | 2.00 | .75 |
| 317 Mark Haynes | .10 | .02 | | | | 73 Brian Sipe | 4.00 | 2.00 |
| 318 Dave Jennings | .10 | .02 | | | | 74 Herschel Walker XRC | 25.00 | 12.50 |
| 319 Brian Kelley | .10 | .02 | | | | 75 Junior Ah You XRC | 2.00 | .75 |
| 320 Phil Simms | .75 | .30 | | | | 76 Marcus Dupree XRC | 6.00 | 2.50 |
| 321 Lawrence Taylor | 3.00 | 1.50 | | | | 77 Marcus Marek | 2.00 | .75 |
| 322 Lawrence Taylor IR | 1.50 | .60 | | | | 78 Tim Mazzetti | 2.00 | .75 |
| 323 Brad Van Pelt | .10 | .02 | | | | 79 Mike Robinson XRC | 2.00 | .75 |
| 324 Butch Woolfolk | .10 | .02 | | | | 80 Dan Ross | 4.00 | 2.00 |
| 325 Eagles TL/M.Quick | .25 | .08 | | | | 81 Mark Schellen | 2.00 | .75 |
| 326 Harold Carmichael | .25 | .08 | | | | 82 Johnnie Walton | 2.00 | .75 |
| 327 Herman Edwards | .10 | .02 | | | | 83 Gordon Banks | 2.00 | .75 |
| 328 Michael Haddix RC | .10 | .02 | | | | 84 Fred Besana | 2.00 | .75 |
| 329 Dennis Harrison | .10 | .02 | COMP.FACT.SET (132) | 300.00 | 150.00 | 85 Dave Browning | 2.00 | .75 |
| 330 Ron Jaworski | .25 | .08 | COMPLETE SET (132) | 300.00 | 150.00 | 86 Eric Jordan | 2.00 | .75 |
| 331 Wilbert Montgomery | .25 | .08 | 1 Luther Bradley | 2.00 | .75 | 87 Frank Manumaleuga | 2.00 | .75 |
| 332 Hubie Oliver | .10 | .02 | 2 Frank Corral | 2.00 | .75 | 88 Gary Plummer XRC | 4.00 | 2.00 |
| 333 Mike Quick RC | .50 | .20 | 3 Trumaine Johnson | 2.00 | .75 | 89 Stan Talley | 2.00 | .75 |
| 334 Jerry Robinson | .10 | .02 | 4 Greg Landry | 2.50 | 1.25 | 90 Arthur Whittington | 2.00 | .75 |
| 335 Max Runager | .10 | .02 | 5 Kit Lathrop | 2.00 | .75 | 91 Terry Beeson | 2.00 | .75 |
| 336 Michael Williams | .10 | .02 | 6 Kevin Long | 2.00 | .75 | 92 Mel Gray | 4.00 | 2.00 |
| 337 Cardinals TL/O.Anderson | .25 | .08 | 7 Tim Spencer | 2.00 | .75 | 93 Mike Katolin | 2.00 | .75 |
| 338 Ottis Anderson | .50 | .20 | 8 Stan White | 2.00 | .75 | 94 Dewey McClain | 2.00 | .75 |
| 339 Al(Bubba) Baker | .25 | .08 | 9 Buddy Aydelette | 2.00 | .75 | 95 Sidney Thornton | 2.00 | .75 |
| 340 Carl Birdsong | .10 | .02 | 10 Tom Banks | 2.00 | .75 | 96 Doug Williams | 4.00 | 2.00 |
| 341 David Galloway | .10 | .02 | | | | 97 Kelvin Bryant XRC | 4.00 | 2.00 |

| | | |
|---|---|---|
| ☐ 98 John Bunting | 2.00 | .75 |
| ☐ 99 Irv Eatman XRC | 2.50 | 1.25 |
| ☐ 100 Scott Fitzkee | 2.00 | .75 |
| ☐ 101 Chuck Fusina | 2.00 | .75 |
| ☐ 102 Sean Landeta XRC | 2.50 | 1.25 |
| ☐ 103 David Trout | 2.00 | .75 |
| ☐ 104 Scott Woerner | 2.00 | .75 |
| ☐ 105 Glenn Carano | 2.00 | .75 |
| ☐ 106 Ron Crosby | 2.00 | .75 |
| ☐ 107 Jerry Holmes | 2.00 | .75 |
| ☐ 108 Bruce Huther | 2.00 | .75 |
| ☐ 109 Mike Rozier XRC | 4.00 | 2.00 |
| ☐ 110 Larry Swider | 2.00 | .75 |
| ☐ 111 Danny Buggs | 2.00 | .75 |
| ☐ 112 Putt Choate | 2.00 | .75 |
| ☐ 113 Rich Garza | 2.00 | .75 |
| ☐ 114 Joey Hackett | 2.00 | .75 |
| ☐ 115 Rick Neuheisel XRC | 4.00 | 2.00 |
| ☐ 116 Mike St. Clair | 2.00 | .75 |
| ☐ 117 Gary Anderson XRC RB | 4.00 | 2.00 |
| ☐ 118 Zenon Andrusyshyn | 2.00 | .75 |
| ☐ 119 Doug Beaudoin | 2.00 | .75 |
| ☐ 120 Mike Butler | 2.00 | .75 |
| ☐ 121 Willie Gillespie | 2.00 | .75 |
| ☐ 122 Fred Nordgren | 2.00 | .75 |
| ☐ 123 John Reaves | 2.00 | .75 |
| ☐ 124 Eric Truvillion | 2.00 | .75 |
| ☐ 125 Reggie Collier | 2.00 | .75 |
| ☐ 126 Mike Guess | 2.00 | .75 |
| ☐ 127 Mike Hohensee | 2.00 | .75 |
| ☐ 128 Craig James XRC | 8.00 | 3.00 |
| ☐ 129 Eric Robinson | 2.00 | .75 |
| ☐ 130 Billy Taylor | 2.00 | .75 |
| ☐ 131 Joey Walters | 2.00 | .75 |
| ☐ 132 Checklist 1-132 | 2.50 | 1.25 |

## 1985 Topps

| | | |
|---|---|---|
| ☐ COMPLETE SET (396) | 60.00 | 35.00 |
| ☐ COMP.FACT.SET (396) | 75.00 | 40.00 |
| ☐ 1 Mark Clayton RB | .50 | .20 |
| ☐ 2 Eric Dickerson RB | .50 | .20 |
| ☐ 3 Charlie Joiner RB | .50 | .20 |
| ☐ 4 Dan Marino RB | 6.00 | 3.00 |
| ☐ 5 Art Monk RB | .50 | .20 |
| ☐ 6 Walter Payton RB | 1.00 | .40 |
| ☐ 7 NFC Champs/Suhey | .25 | .08 |
| ☐ 8 AFC Championship | .25 | .08 |
| ☐ 9 Super Bowl XIX | .25 | .08 |
| ☐ 10 Atlanta Falcons TL | .10 | .02 |
| ☐ 11 William Andrews | .25 | .08 |
| ☐ 12 Stacey Bailey | .10 | .02 |
| ☐ 13 Steve Bartkowski | .50 | .20 |
| ☐ 14 Rick Bryan RC | .10 | .02 |
| ☐ 15 Alfred Jackson | .10 | .02 |
| ☐ 16 Kenny Johnson | .10 | .02 |
| ☐ 17 Mike Kenn | .10 | .02 |
| ☐ 18 Mike Pitts RC | .10 | .02 |
| ☐ 19 Gerald Riggs | .25 | .08 |
| ☐ 20 Sylvester Stamps | .10 | .02 |
| ☐ 21 R.C. Thielemann | .10 | .02 |
| ☐ 22 Bears TL/W.Payton | .75 | .30 |
| ☐ 23 Todd Bell RC | .10 | .02 |
| ☐ 24 Richard Dent RC | 4.00 | 1.50 |
| ☐ 25 Gary Fencik | .25 | .08 |
| ☐ 26 Dave Finzer | .10 | .02 |
| ☐ 27 Leslie Frazier | .10 | .02 |
| ☐ 28 Steve Fuller | .25 | .08 |
| ☐ 29 Willie Gault | .50 | .20 |
| ☐ 30 Dan Hampton | .50 | .20 |

| | | |
|---|---|---|
| ☐ 31 Jim McMahon | .75 | .30 |
| ☐ 32 Steve McMichael RC | .50 | .20 |
| ☐ 33 Walter Payton | 6.00 | 2.50 |
| ☐ 34 Mike Singletary | .75 | .30 |
| ☐ 35 Matt Suhey | .10 | .02 |
| ☐ 36 Bob Thomas | .10 | .02 |
| ☐ 37 Cowboys TL/Dorsett | .50 | .20 |
| ☐ 38 Bill Bates RC | 1.00 | .40 |
| ☐ 39 Doug Cosbie | .25 | .08 |
| ☐ 40 Tony Dorsett | .75 | .30 |
| ☐ 41 Michael Downs | .10 | .02 |
| ☐ 42 Mike Hegman RC UER | .10 | .02 |
| ☐ 43 Tony Hill | .25 | .08 |
| ☐ 44 Gary Hogeboom RC | .10 | .02 |
| ☐ 45 Jim Jeffcoat RC | .50 | .20 |
| ☐ 46 Ed Too Tall Jones | .50 | .20 |
| ☐ 47 Mike Renfro | .10 | .02 |
| ☐ 48 Rafael Septien | .10 | .02 |
| ☐ 49 Dennis Thurman | .10 | .02 |
| ☐ 50 Everson Walls | .25 | .08 |
| ☐ 51 Danny White | .25 | .08 |
| ☐ 52 Randy White | .50 | .20 |
| ☐ 53 Detroit Lions TL | .10 | .02 |
| ☐ 54 Jeff Chadwick | .10 | .02 |
| ☐ 55 Michael Cofer RC | .10 | .02 |
| ☐ 56 Gary Danielson | .10 | .02 |
| ☐ 57 Keith Dorney | .10 | .02 |
| ☐ 58 Doug English | .25 | .08 |
| ☐ 59 William Gay | .10 | .02 |
| ☐ 60 Ken Jenkins | .10 | .02 |
| ☐ 61 James Jones FB | .25 | .08 |
| ☐ 62 Eddie Murray | .25 | .08 |
| ☐ 63 Billy Sims | .50 | .20 |
| ☐ 64 Leonard Thompson | .10 | .02 |
| ☐ 65 Bobby Watkins | .10 | .02 |
| ☐ 66 Green Bay Packers TL | .10 | .02 |
| ☐ 67 Paul Coffman | .10 | .02 |
| ☐ 68 Lynn Dickey | .25 | .08 |
| ☐ 69 Mike Douglass | .10 | .02 |
| ☐ 70 Tom Flynn RC | .10 | .02 |
| ☐ 71 Eddie Lee Ivery | .10 | .02 |
| ☐ 72 Ezra Johnson | .10 | .02 |
| ☐ 73 Mark Lee | .10 | .02 |
| ☐ 74 Tim Lewis | .10 | .02 |
| ☐ 75 James Lofton | .50 | .20 |
| ☐ 76 Bucky Scribner | .10 | .02 |
| ☐ 77 Rams TL/Dickerson | .50 | .20 |
| ☐ 78 Nolan Cromwell | .25 | .08 |
| ☐ 79 Eric Dickerson | 1.25 | .50 |
| ☐ 80 Henry Ellard RC | 2.50 | 1.00 |
| ☐ 81 Kent Hill | .10 | .02 |
| ☐ 82 LeRoy Irvin | .25 | .08 |
| ☐ 83 Jeff Kemp RC | .25 | .08 |
| ☐ 84 Mike Lansford | .10 | .02 |
| ☐ 85 Barry Redden | .10 | .02 |
| ☐ 86 Jackie Slater | .50 | .20 |
| ☐ 87 Doug Smith C RC | .25 | .08 |
| ☐ 88 Jack Youngblood | .25 | .08 |
| ☐ 89 Minnesota Vikings TL | .10 | .02 |
| ☐ 90 Alfred Anderson RC | .10 | .02 |
| ☐ 91 Ted Brown | .10 | .02 |
| ☐ 92 Greg Coleman | .10 | .02 |
| ☐ 93 Tommy Hannon | .10 | .02 |
| ☐ 94 Tommy Kramer | .25 | .08 |
| ☐ 95 Leo Lewis RC | .25 | .08 |
| ☐ 96 Doug Martin | .10 | .02 |
| ☐ 97 Darrin Nelson | .25 | .06 |
| ☐ 98 Jan Stenerud | .25 | .08 |
| ☐ 99 Sammie White | .25 | .08 |
| ☐ 100 New Orleans Saints TL | .10 | .02 |
| ☐ 101 Morten Andersen | .50 | .20 |
| ☐ 102 Hoby Brenner RC | .25 | .08 |
| ☐ 103 Bruce Clark | .10 | .02 |
| ☐ 104 Hokie Gajan | .10 | .02 |
| ☐ 105 Brian Hansen RC | .10 | .02 |
| ☐ 106 Rickey Jackson | .50 | .20 |
| ☐ 107 George Rogers | .25 | .08 |
| ☐ 108 Dave Wilson | .10 | .02 |
| ☐ 109 Tyrone Young | .10 | .02 |
| ☐ 110 New York Giants TL | .25 | .08 |
| ☐ 111 Carl Banks RC | .50 | .20 |
| ☐ 112 Jim Burt RC | .50 | .20 |
| ☐ 113 Rob Carpenter | .10 | .02 |
| ☐ 114 Harry Carson | .25 | .08 |
| ☐ 115 Earnest Gray | .10 | .02 |
| ☐ 116 Ali Haji-Sheikh | .25 | .08 |
| ☐ 117 Mark Haynes | .25 | .08 |

| | | |
|---|---|---|
| ☐ 118 Bobby Johnson | .10 | .02 |
| ☐ 119 Lionel Manuel RC | .25 | .08 |
| ☐ 120 Joe Morris RC | .50 | .20 |
| ☐ 121 Zeke Mowatt RC | .25 | .08 |
| ☐ 122 Jeff Rutledge RC | .10 | .02 |
| ☐ 123 Phil Simms | .50 | .20 |
| ☐ 124 Lawrence Taylor | 1.50 | .60 |
| ☐ 125 Philadelphia Eagles TL | .10 | .02 |
| ☐ 126 Greg Brown | .10 | .02 |
| ☐ 127 Ray Ellis | .10 | .02 |
| ☐ 128 Dennis Harrison | .10 | .02 |
| ☐ 129 Wes Hopkins RC | .25 | .08 |
| ☐ 130 Mike Horan RC | .10 | .02 |
| ☐ 131 Kenny Jackson RC | .10 | .02 |
| ☐ 132 Ron Jaworski | .25 | .08 |
| ☐ 133 Paul McFadden | .10 | .02 |
| ☐ 134 Wilbert Montgomery | .25 | .08 |
| ☐ 135 Mike Quick | .50 | .20 |
| ☐ 136 John Spagnola | .10 | .02 |
| ☐ 137 St.Louis Cardinals TL | .10 | .02 |
| ☐ 138 Ottis Anderson | .50 | .20 |
| ☐ 139 Al(Bubba) Baker | .25 | .08 |
| ☐ 140 Roy Green | .25 | .08 |
| ☐ 141 Curtis Greer | .10 | .02 |
| ☐ 142 E.J.Junior | .10 | .02 |
| ☐ 143 Neil Lomax | .25 | .08 |
| ☐ 144 Stump Mitchell | .25 | .08 |
| ☐ 145 Neil O'Donoghue | .10 | .02 |
| ☐ 146 Pat Tilley | .10 | .02 |
| ☐ 147 Lionel Washington | .10 | .02 |
| ☐ 148 49ers TL/J.Montana | 1.25 | .50 |
| ☐ 149 Dwaine Board | .10 | .02 |
| ☐ 150 Dwight Clark | .50 | .20 |
| ☐ 151 Roger Craig | 1.00 | .40 |
| ☐ 152 Randy Cross | .25 | .08 |
| ☐ 153 Fred Dean | .25 | .08 |
| ☐ 154 Keith Fahnhorst RC | .10 | .02 |
| ☐ 155 Dwight Hicks | .10 | .02 |
| ☐ 156 Ronnie Lott | .50 | .20 |
| ☐ 157 Joe Montana | 10.00 | 4.00 |
| ☐ 158 Renaldo Nehemiah | .25 | .08 |
| ☐ 159 Fred Quillan | .10 | .02 |
| ☐ 160 Jack Reynolds | .10 | .02 |
| ☐ 161 Freddie Solomon | .10 | .02 |
| ☐ 162 Keena Turner RC | .10 | .02 |
| ☐ 163 Wendell Tyler | .10 | .02 |
| ☐ 164 Ray Wersching | .10 | .02 |
| ☐ 165 Carlton Williamson | .10 | .02 |
| ☐ 166 Tampa Bay Bucs TL | .25 | .08 |
| ☐ 167 Gerald Carter | .10 | .02 |
| ☐ 168 Mark Cotney | .10 | .02 |
| ☐ 169 Steve DeBerg | .50 | .20 |
| ☐ 170 Sean Farrell RC | .25 | .08 |
| ☐ 171 Hugh Green | .25 | .08 |
| ☐ 172 Kevin House | .25 | .08 |
| ☐ 173 David Logan | .10 | .02 |
| ☐ 174 Michael Morton | .10 | .02 |
| ☐ 175 Lee Roy Selmon | .50 | .20 |
| ☐ 176 James Wilder | .10 | .02 |
| ☐ 177 Redskins TL/J.Riggins | .50 | .20 |
| ☐ 178 Charlie Brown | .10 | .02 |
| ☐ 179 Monte Coleman RC | .10 | .02 |
| ☐ 180 Vernon Dean | .10 | .02 |
| ☐ 181 Darrell Green | .50 | .20 |
| ☐ 182 Russ Grimm | .25 | .08 |
| ☐ 183 Joe Jacoby | .25 | .08 |
| ☐ 184 Dexter Manley | .25 | .08 |
| ☐ 185 Art Monk | .50 | .20 |
| ☐ 186 Mark Moseley | .25 | .08 |
| ☐ 187 Calvin Muhammad | .10 | .02 |
| ☐ 188 Mike Nelms | .10 | .02 |
| ☐ 189 John Riggins | .50 | .20 |
| ☐ 190 Joe Theismann | .50 | .20 |
| ☐ 191 Joe Washington | .25 | .08 |
| ☐ 192 D.Marino/Montana LL | 10.00 | 4.00 |
| ☐ 193 Art Monk/O.Newsome LL | .25 | .08 |
| ☐ 194 E.Dickerson/Jackson LL | .50 | .20 |
| ☐ 195 Scoring Leaders | .10 | .02 |
| ☐ 196 Interception Leaders | .10 | .02 |
| ☐ 197 Punting Leaders | .10 | .02 |
| ☐ 198 Bills TL/Greg Bell | .10 | .02 |
| ☐ 199 Greg Bell RC | .25 | .08 |
| ☐ 200 Preston Dennard | .10 | .02 |
| ☐ 201 Joe Ferguson | .25 | .08 |
| ☐ 202 Byron Franklin | .10 | .02 |
| ☐ 203 Steve Freeman | .10 | .02 |
| ☐ 204 Jim Haslett | .25 | .08 |

| Card | Price | |
|---|---|---|
| ☐ 205 Charles Romes | .10 | .02 |
| ☐ 206 Fred Smerlas | .10 | .02 |
| ☐ 207 Darryl Talley RC | .50 | .20 |
| ☐ 208 Van Williams | .10 | .02 |
| ☐ 209 Cincinnati Bengals TL | .25 | .08 |
| ☐ 210 Ken Anderson | .50 | .20 |
| ☐ 211 Jim Breech | .10 | .02 |
| ☐ 212 Louis Breeden | .10 | .02 |
| ☐ 213 James Brooks | .25 | .08 |
| ☐ 214 Ross Browner | .25 | .08 |
| ☐ 215 Eddie Edwards | .10 | .02 |
| ☐ 216 M.L. Harris | .10 | .02 |
| ☐ 217 Bobby Kemp | .10 | .02 |
| ☐ 218 Larry Kinnebrew RC | .10 | .02 |
| ☐ 219 Anthony Munoz | .50 | .20 |
| ☐ 220 Reggie Williams | .25 | .08 |
| ☐ 221 Cleveland Browns TL | .10 | .02 |
| ☐ 222 Matt Bahr | .25 | .08 |
| ☐ 223 Chip Banks | .10 | .02 |
| ☐ 224 Reggie Camp | .10 | .02 |
| ☐ 225 Tom Cousineau | .10 | .02 |
| ☐ 226 Joe DeLamielleure | .50 | .20 |
| ☐ 227 Ricky Feacher | .10 | .02 |
| ☐ 228 Boyce Green RC | .10 | .02 |
| ☐ 229 Al Gross | .10 | .02 |
| ☐ 230 Clay Matthews | .50 | .20 |
| ☐ 231 Paul McDonald | .10 | .02 |
| ☐ 232 Ozzie Newsome | .50 | .20 |
| ☐ 233 Mike Pruitt | .25 | .08 |
| ☐ 234 Don Rogers DB | .10 | .02 |
| ☐ 235 Broncos TL/J.Elway | 2.50 | 1.00 |
| ☐ 236 Rubin Carter | .10 | .02 |
| ☐ 237 Barney Chavous | .10 | .02 |
| ☐ 238 John Elway | 12.00 | 5.00 |
| ☐ 239 Steve Foley | .10 | .02 |
| ☐ 240 Mike Harden RC | .10 | .02 |
| ☐ 241 Tom Jackson | .50 | .20 |
| ☐ 242 Butch Johnson | .10 | .02 |
| ☐ 243 Rulon Jones | .10 | .02 |
| ☐ 244 Rich Karlis | .10 | .02 |
| ☐ 245 Steve Watson | .25 | .08 |
| ☐ 246 Gerald Willhite | .10 | .02 |
| ☐ 247 Sammy Winder | .25 | .08 |
| ☐ 248 Houston Oilers TL | .10 | .02 |
| ☐ 249 Jesse Baker | .10 | .02 |
| ☐ 250 Carter Hartwig | .10 | .02 |
| ☐ 251 Warren Moon RC | 15.00 | 6.00 |
| ☐ 252 Larry Moriarty RC | .10 | .02 |
| ☐ 253 Mike Munchak RC | 3.00 | 1.25 |
| ☐ 254 Carl Roaches | .10 | .02 |
| ☐ 255 Tim Smith | .25 | .08 |
| ☐ 256 Willie Tullis | .10 | .02 |
| ☐ 257 Jamie Williams RC | .25 | .08 |
| ☐ 258 Indianapolis Colts TL | .10 | .02 |
| ☐ 259 Raymond Butler | .10 | .02 |
| ☐ 260 Johnie Cooks | .10 | .02 |
| ☐ 261 Eugene Daniel RC | .10 | .02 |
| ☐ 262 Curtis Dickey | .25 | .08 |
| ☐ 263 Chris Hinton | .25 | .08 |
| ☐ 264 Vernon Maxwell | .10 | .02 |
| ☐ 265 Randy McMillan | .10 | .02 |
| ☐ 266 Art Schlichter RC | .50 | .20 |
| ☐ 267 Rohn Stark | .25 | .08 |
| ☐ 268 Leo Wisniewski | .10 | .02 |
| ☐ 269 Kansas City Chiefs TL | .10 | .02 |
| ☐ 270 Jim Arnold | .10 | .02 |
| ☐ 271 Mike Bell | .10 | .02 |
| ☐ 272 Todd Blackledge RC | .25 | .08 |
| ☐ 273 Carlos Carson | .25 | .08 |
| ☐ 274 Deron Cherry | .25 | .08 |
| ☐ 275 Herman Heard RC | .10 | .02 |
| ☐ 276 Bill Kenney | .25 | .08 |
| ☐ 277 Nick Lowery | .50 | .20 |
| ☐ 278 Bill Maas RC | .10 | .02 |
| ☐ 279 Henry Marshall | .10 | .02 |
| ☐ 280 Art Still | .10 | .02 |
| ☐ 281 Raiders TL/M.Allen | .50 | .20 |
| ☐ 282 Marcus Allen | 2.50 | 1.00 |
| ☐ 283 Lyle Alzado | .25 | .08 |
| ☐ 284 Chris Bahr | .10 | .02 |
| ☐ 285 Malcolm Barnwell | .10 | .02 |
| ☐ 286 Cliff Branch | .50 | .20 |
| ☐ 287 Todd Christensen | .50 | .20 |
| ☐ 288 Ray Guy | .50 | .20 |
| ☐ 289 Lester Hayes | .25 | .08 |
| ☐ 290 Mike Haynes | .25 | .08 |
| ☐ 291 Henry Lawrence | .10 | .02 |
| ☐ 292 Howie Long | 2.00 | .75 |
| ☐ 293 Rod Martin | .25 | .08 |
| ☐ 294 Vann McElroy | .10 | .02 |
| ☐ 295 Matt Millen | .25 | .08 |
| ☐ 296 Bill Pickel RC | .10 | .02 |
| ☐ 297 Jim Plunkett | .50 | .20 |
| ☐ 298 Dokie Williams RC | .10 | .02 |
| ☐ 299 Marc Wilson | .25 | .08 |
| ☐ 300 Dolphins TL/Duper | .25 | .08 |
| ☐ 301 Bob Baumhower | .10 | .02 |
| ☐ 302 Doug Betters | .10 | .02 |
| ☐ 303 Glenn Blackwood | .10 | .02 |
| ☐ 304 Lyle Blackwood | .25 | .08 |
| ☐ 305 Kim Bokamper | .10 | .02 |
| ☐ 306 Charles Bowser RC | .10 | .02 |
| ☐ 307 Jimmy Cefalo | .10 | .02 |
| ☐ 308 Mark Clayton RC | .75 | .30 |
| ☐ 309 A.J. Duhe | .10 | .02 |
| ☐ 310 Mark Duper | .50 | .20 |
| ☐ 311 Andra Franklin | .10 | .02 |
| ☐ 312 Bruce Hardy | .10 | .02 |
| ☐ 313 Pete Johnson | .25 | .08 |
| ☐ 314 Dan Marino | 12.00 | 5.00 |
| ☐ 315 Tony Nathan | .25 | .08 |
| ☐ 316 Ed Newman | .10 | .02 |
| ☐ 317 Reggie Roby | .50 | .20 |
| ☐ 318 Dwight Stephenson | 1.00 | .40 |
| ☐ 319 Uwe Von Schamann | .10 | .02 |
| ☐ 320 New England Pats TL | .10 | .02 |
| ☐ 321 Raymond Clayborn | .25 | .08 |
| ☐ 322 Tony Collins | .25 | .08 |
| ☐ 323 Tony Eason RC | .50 | .20 |
| ☐ 324 Tony Franklin | .10 | .02 |
| ☐ 325 Irving Fryar RC | 5.00 | 2.00 |
| ☐ 326 John Hannah | .50 | .20 |
| ☐ 327 Brian Holloway | .10 | .02 |
| ☐ 328 Craig James RC | .75 | .30 |
| ☐ 329 Stanley Morgan | .25 | .08 |
| ☐ 330 Steve Nelson | .10 | .02 |
| ☐ 331 Derrick Ramsey | .10 | .02 |
| ☐ 332 Stephen Starring RC | .25 | .08 |
| ☐ 333 Mosi Tatupu | .10 | .02 |
| ☐ 334 Andre Tippett | .50 | .20 |
| ☐ 335 New York Jets TL | .25 | .08 |
| ☐ 336 Russell Carter RC | .10 | .02 |
| ☐ 337 Mark Gastineau | .25 | .08 |
| ☐ 338 Bruce Harper | .10 | .02 |
| ☐ 339 Bobby Humphery RC | .10 | .02 |
| ☐ 340 Johnny Lam Jones | .10 | .02 |
| ☐ 341 Joe Klecko | .25 | .08 |
| ☐ 342 Pat Leahy | .10 | .02 |
| ☐ 343 Marty Lyons | .25 | .08 |
| ☐ 344 Freeman McNeil | .25 | .08 |
| ☐ 345 Lance Mehl | .10 | .02 |
| ☐ 346 Ken O'Brien RC | .50 | .20 |
| ☐ 347 Marvin Powell | .10 | .02 |
| ☐ 348 Pat Ryan | .10 | .02 |
| ☐ 349 Mickey Shuler RC | .10 | .02 |
| ☐ 350 Wesley Walker | .25 | .08 |
| ☐ 351 Pittsburgh Steelers TL | .25 | .08 |
| ☐ 352 Walter Abercrombie | .10 | .02 |
| ☐ 353 Gary Anderson K | .25 | .08 |
| ☐ 354 Robin Cole | .10 | .02 |
| ☐ 355 Bennie Cunningham | .10 | .02 |
| ☐ 356 Rich Erenberg | .10 | .02 |
| ☐ 357 Jack Lambert | .50 | .20 |
| ☐ 358 Louis Lipps RC | .50 | .20 |
| ☐ 359 Mark Malone | .25 | .08 |
| ☐ 360 Mike Merriweather RC | .10 | .02 |
| ☐ 361 Frank Pollard | .10 | .02 |
| ☐ 362 Donnie Shell | .25 | .08 |
| ☐ 363 John Stallworth | .50 | .20 |
| ☐ 364 Sam Washington | .10 | .02 |
| ☐ 365 Mike Webster | .25 | .08 |
| ☐ 366 Dwayne Woodruff | .10 | .02 |
| ☐ 367 San Diego Chargers TL | .10 | .02 |
| ☐ 368 Rolf Benirschke | .10 | .02 |
| ☐ 369 Gill Byrd RC | .50 | .20 |
| ☐ 370 Wes Chandler | .25 | .08 |
| ☐ 371 Bobby Duckworth | .10 | .02 |
| ☐ 372 Dan Fouts | .50 | .20 |
| ☐ 373 Mike Green | .10 | .02 |
| ☐ 374 Pete Holohan RC | .10 | .02 |
| ☐ 375 Earnest Jackson RC | .25 | .08 |
| ☐ 376 Lionel James RC | .25 | .08 |
| ☐ 377 Charlie Joiner | .50 | .20 |
| ☐ 378 Billy Ray Smith | .25 | .08 |
| ☐ 379 Kellen Winslow | .50 | .20 |
| ☐ 380 Seattle Seahawks TL | .25 | .08 |
| ☐ 381 Dave Brown DB | .10 | .02 |
| ☐ 382 Jeff Bryant | .10 | .02 |
| ☐ 383 Dan Doornink | .10 | .02 |
| ☐ 384 Kenny Easley | .25 | .08 |
| ☐ 385 Jacob Green | .25 | .08 |
| ☐ 386 David Hughes | .10 | .02 |
| ☐ 387 Norm Johnson | .10 | .02 |
| ☐ 388 Dave Krieg | .50 | .20 |
| ☐ 389 Steve Largent | 1.00 | .40 |
| ☐ 390 Joe Nash RC | .10 | .02 |
| ☐ 391 Daryl Turner RC | .10 | .02 |
| ☐ 392 Curt Warner | .50 | .20 |
| ☐ 393 Fredd Young RC | .25 | .08 |
| ☐ 394 Checklist 1-132 | .25 | .08 |
| ☐ 395 Checklist 133-264 | .25 | .08 |
| ☐ 396 Checklist 265-396 | .25 | .08 |

## 1985 Topps USFL

| Card | Price | |
|---|---|---|
| ☐ COMP.FACT.SET (132) | 120.00 | 60.00 |
| ☐ COMPLETE SET (132) | 120.00 | 60.00 |
| ☐ 1 Case DeBruijn | .50 | .20 |
| ☐ 2 Mike Katolin | .50 | .20 |
| ☐ 3 Bruce Laird | .50 | .20 |
| ☐ 4 Kit Lathrop | .50 | .20 |
| ☐ 5 Kevin Long | .50 | .20 |
| ☐ 6 Karl Lorch | .50 | .20 |
| ☐ 7 Dave Tipton DT | .50 | .20 |
| ☐ 8 Doug Williams | 2.00 | .75 |
| ☐ 9 Luis Zendejas XRC | .50 | .20 |
| ☐ 10 Kelvin Bryant | 1.00 | .40 |
| ☐ 11 Willie Collier | .50 | .20 |
| ☐ 12 Irv Eatman | .50 | .20 |
| ☐ 13 Scott Fitzkee | .50 | .20 |
| ☐ 14 William Fuller XRC | 3.00 | 1.25 |
| ☐ 15 Chuck Fusina | .50 | .20 |
| ☐ 16 Pete Kugler | .50 | .20 |
| ☐ 17 Garcia Lane | .50 | .20 |
| ☐ 18 Mike Lush | .50 | .20 |
| ☐ 19 Sam Mills XRC | 5.00 | 2.00 |
| ☐ 20 Buddy Aydelette | .50 | .20 |
| ☐ 21 Joe Cribbs | 2.00 | .75 |
| ☐ 22 David Dumars | .50 | .20 |
| ☐ 23 Robin Earl | .50 | .20 |
| ☐ 24 Joey Jones | .50 | .20 |
| ☐ 25 Leon Perry RB | .50 | .20 |
| ☐ 26 Dave Pureifory | .50 | .20 |
| ☐ 27 Bill Roe | .50 | .20 |
| ☐ 28 Doug Smith DT XRC | 2.00 | .75 |
| ☐ 29 Cliff Stoudt | 1.00 | .40 |
| ☐ 30 Jeff Delaney | .50 | .20 |
| ☐ 31 Vince Evans | 1.00 | .40 |
| ☐ 32 Leonard Harris XRC | .50 | .20 |
| ☐ 33 Bill Johnson RB | .50 | .20 |
| ☐ 34 Marc Lewis XRC | .50 | .20 |
| ☐ 35 David Martin | .50 | .20 |
| ☐ 36 Bruce Thornton | .50 | .20 |
| ☐ 37 Craig Walls | .50 | .20 |
| ☐ 38 Vincent White | .50 | .20 |
| ☐ 39 Luther Bradley | .50 | .20 |
| ☐ 40 Pete Catan | .50 | .20 |
| ☐ 41 Kiki DeAyala | .50 | .20 |
| ☐ 42 Toni Fritsch | .50 | .20 |
| ☐ 43 Sam Harrell | .50 | .20 |
| ☐ 44 Richard Johnson WR XRC | 1.00 | .40 |
| ☐ 45 Jim Kelly | 20.00 | 10.00 |
| ☐ 46 Gerald McNeil XRC | .50 | .20 |
| ☐ 47 Clarence Verdin XRC | 2.00 | .75 |

| | | |
|---|---|---|
| ❑ 48 Dale Walters | .50 | .20 |
| ❑ 49 Gary Clark XRC | 6.00 | 2.50 |
| ❑ 50 Tom Dinkel | .50 | .20 |
| ❑ 51 Mike Edwards LB | .50 | .20 |
| ❑ 52 Brian Franco | .50 | .20 |
| ❑ 53 Bob Gruber | .50 | .20 |
| ❑ 54 Robbie Mahfouz | .50 | .20 |
| ❑ 55 Mike Rozier | 2.00 | .75 |
| ❑ 56 Brian Sipe | 1.00 | .40 |
| ❑ 57 J.T. Turner | .50 | .20 |
| ❑ 58 Howard Carson | .50 | .20 |
| ❑ 59 Wymon Henderson XRC | .50 | .20 |
| ❑ 60 Kevin Nelson | .50 | .20 |
| ❑ 61 Jeff Partridge | .50 | .20 |
| ❑ 62 Ben Rudolph | .50 | .20 |
| ❑ 63 Jo Jo Townsell | 1.00 | .40 |
| ❑ 64 Eddie Weaver | .50 | .20 |
| ❑ 65 Steve Young | 30.00 | 15.00 |
| ❑ 66 Tony Zendejas XRC | 1.00 | .40 |
| ❑ 67 Mossy Cade | .50 | .20 |
| ❑ 68 Leonard Coleman XRC | .50 | .20 |
| ❑ 69 John Corker | .50 | .20 |
| ❑ 70 Derrick Crawford | .50 | .20 |
| ❑ 71 Art Kuehn | .50 | .20 |
| ❑ 72 Walter Lewis | .50 | .20 |
| ❑ 73 Tyrone McGriff | .50 | .20 |
| ❑ 74 Tim Spencer | 1.00 | .40 |
| ❑ 75 Reggie White | 25.00 | 12.50 |
| ❑ 76 Gizmo Williams XRC | 2.00 | .75 |
| ❑ 77 Sam Bowers | .50 | .20 |
| ❑ 78 Maurice Carthon XRC | 2.00 | .75 |
| ❑ 79 Clarence Collins | .50 | .20 |
| ❑ 80 Doug Flutie XRC | 30.00 | 12.50 |
| ❑ 81 Freddie Gilbert DE | .50 | .20 |
| ❑ 82 Kerry Justin | .50 | .20 |
| ❑ 83 Dave Lapham | .50 | .20 |
| ❑ 84 Rick Partridge | .50 | .20 |
| ❑ 85 Roger Ruzek XRC | 1.00 | .40 |
| ❑ 86 Herschel Walker | 8.00 | 3.00 |
| ❑ 87 Gordon Banks | .50 | .20 |
| ❑ 88 Monte Bennett | .50 | .20 |
| ❑ 89 Albert Bentley XRC | 1.00 | .40 |
| ❑ 90 Novo Bojovic | .50 | .20 |
| ❑ 91 Dave Browning | .50 | .20 |
| ❑ 92 Anthony Carter | 2.00 | .75 |
| ❑ 93 Bobby Hebert | 2.00 | .75 |
| ❑ 94 Ray Pinney | .50 | .20 |
| ❑ 95 Stan Talley | .50 | .20 |
| ❑ 96 Ruben Vaughan | .50 | .20 |
| ❑ 97 Curtis Bledsoe | .50 | .20 |
| ❑ 98 Reggie Collier | .50 | .20 |
| ❑ 99 Jerry Doerger | .50 | .20 |
| ❑ 100 Jerry Golsteyn | .50 | .20 |
| ❑ 101 Bob Niziolek | .50 | .20 |
| ❑ 102 Joel Patten | .50 | .20 |
| ❑ 103 Ricky Simmons | .50 | .20 |
| ❑ 104 Joey Walters | .50 | .20 |
| ❑ 105 Marcus Dupree | 1.00 | .40 |
| ❑ 106 Jeff Gossett | 1.00 | .40 |
| ❑ 107 Frank Lockett | .50 | .20 |
| ❑ 108 Marcus Marek | .50 | .20 |
| ❑ 109 Kenny Neil | .50 | .20 |
| ❑ 110 Robert Pennywell | .50 | .20 |
| ❑ 111 Matt Robinson | .50 | .20 |
| ❑ 112 Dan Ross | 1.00 | .40 |
| ❑ 113 Doug Woodward | .50 | .20 |
| ❑ 114 Danny Buggs | .50 | .20 |
| ❑ 115 Putt Choate | .50 | .20 |
| ❑ 116 Greg Fields | .50 | .20 |
| ❑ 117 Ken Hartley | .50 | .20 |
| ❑ 118 Nick Mike-Mayer | .50 | .20 |
| ❑ 119 Rick Neuheisel | 2.00 | .75 |
| ❑ 120 Peter Raeford | .50 | .20 |
| ❑ 121 Gary Worthy | .50 | .20 |
| ❑ 122 Gary Anderson RB | 1.00 | .40 |
| ❑ 123 Zenon Andrusyshyn | .50 | .20 |
| ❑ 124 Greg Boone | .50 | .20 |
| ❑ 125 Mike Butler | .50 | .20 |
| ❑ 126 Mike Clark | .50 | .20 |
| ❑ 127 Willie Gillespie | .50 | .20 |
| ❑ 128 James Harrell | .50 | .20 |
| ❑ 129 Marvin Harvey | .50 | .20 |
| ❑ 130 John Reaves | 1.00 | .40 |
| ❑ 131 Eric Truvillion | .50 | .20 |
| ❑ 132 Checklist 1-132 | .50 | .40 |

### 1986 Topps

| | | |
|---|---|---|
| ❑ COMPLETE SET (396) | 120.00 | 60.00 |
| ❑ COMP.FACT.SET (396) | 225.00 | 150.00 |
| ❑ 1 Marcus Allen RB | .75 | .30 |
| ❑ 2 Eric Dickerson RB | .50 | .20 |
| ❑ 3 Lionel James RB | .50 | .20 |
| ❑ 4 Steve Largent RB | .50 | .20 |
| ❑ 5 George Martin RB | .10 | .02 |
| ❑ 6 Stephone Paige RB | .10 | .02 |
| ❑ 7 Walter Payton RB | .75 | .30 |
| ❑ 8 Super Bowl XX | .50 | .20 |
| ❑ 9 Bears TL/W.Payton | .60 | .25 |
| ❑ 10 Jim McMahon | .50 | .20 |
| ❑ 11 Walter Payton | 5.00 | 2.00 |
| ❑ 12 Matt Suhey | .10 | .02 |
| ❑ 13 Willie Gault | .25 | .08 |
| ❑ 14 Dennis McKinnon RC | .10 | .02 |
| ❑ 15 Emery Moorehead | .10 | .02 |
| ❑ 16 Jim Covert | .10 | .02 |
| ❑ 17 Jay Hilgenberg RC | .25 | .08 |
| ❑ 18 Kevin Butler RC | .25 | .08 |
| ❑ 19 Richard Dent | .75 | .30 |
| ❑ 20 William Perry RC | .50 | .20 |
| ❑ 21 Steve McMichael RC | .50 | .20 |
| ❑ 22 Dan Hampton | .50 | .20 |
| ❑ 23 Otis Wilson | .10 | .02 |
| ❑ 24 Mike Singletary | .60 | .25 |
| ❑ 25 Wilber Marshall RC | .50 | .20 |
| ❑ 26 Leslie Frazier | .10 | .02 |
| ❑ 27 Dave Duerson RC | .25 | .08 |
| ❑ 28 Gary Fencik | .10 | .02 |
| ❑ 29 Patriots TL | .50 | .20 |
| ❑ 30 Tony Eason | .10 | .02 |
| ❑ 31 Steve Grogan | .25 | .08 |
| ❑ 32 Craig James | .50 | .20 |
| ❑ 33 Tony Collins | .10 | .02 |
| ❑ 34 Irving Fryar | 1.25 | .50 |
| ❑ 35 Brian Holloway | .10 | .02 |
| ❑ 36 John Hannah | .50 | .20 |
| ❑ 37 Tony Franklin | .10 | .02 |
| ❑ 38 Garin Veris RC | .10 | .02 |
| ❑ 39 Andre Tippett | .25 | .08 |
| ❑ 40 Steve Nelson | .10 | .02 |
| ❑ 41 Raymond Clayborn | .10 | .02 |
| ❑ 42 Fred Marion RC | .10 | .02 |
| ❑ 43 Rich Camarillo | .10 | .02 |
| ❑ 44 Dolphins TL/D.Marino | 2.00 | .75 |
| ❑ 45 Dan Marino | 8.00 | 4.00 |
| ❑ 46 Tony Nathan | .25 | .08 |
| ❑ 47 Ron Davenport RC | .10 | .02 |
| ❑ 48 Mark Duper | .50 | .20 |
| ❑ 49 Mark Clayton | .50 | .20 |
| ❑ 50 Nat Moore | .25 | .08 |
| ❑ 51 Bruce Hardy | .10 | .02 |
| ❑ 52 Roy Foster | .10 | .02 |
| ❑ 53 Dwight Stephenson | .75 | .30 |
| ❑ 54 Fuad Reveiz RC | .25 | .08 |
| ❑ 55 Bob Baumhower | .10 | .02 |
| ❑ 56 Mike Charles | .10 | .02 |
| ❑ 57 Hugh Green | .25 | .08 |
| ❑ 58 Glenn Blackwood | .10 | .02 |
| ❑ 59 Reggie Roby | .25 | .08 |
| ❑ 60 Raiders TL/M.Allen | .50 | .20 |
| ❑ 61 Marc Wilson | .10 | .02 |
| ❑ 62 Marcus Allen | 1.50 | .60 |
| ❑ 63 Dokie Williams | .10 | .02 |
| ❑ 64 Todd Christensen | .50 | .20 |
| ❑ 65 Chris Bahr | .10 | .02 |
| ❑ 66 Fulton Walker | .10 | .02 |

| | | |
|---|---|---|
| ❑ 67 Howie Long | 1.25 | .50 |
| ❑ 68 Bill Pickel | .10 | .02 |
| ❑ 69 Ray Guy | .50 | .20 |
| ❑ 70 Greg Townsend RC | .50 | .20 |
| ❑ 71 Rod Martin | .25 | .08 |
| ❑ 72 Matt Millen | .25 | .08 |
| ❑ 73 Mike Haynes | .25 | .08 |
| ❑ 74 Lester Hayes | .25 | .08 |
| ❑ 75 Vann McElroy | .10 | .02 |
| ❑ 76 Rams TL/ Dickerson | .50 | .20 |
| ❑ 77 Dieter Brock RC | .25 | .08 |
| ❑ 78 Eric Dickerson | .75 | .30 |
| ❑ 79 Henry Ellard | 1.00 | .40 |
| ❑ 80 Ron Brown RC | .25 | .08 |
| ❑ 81 Tony Hunter RC | .10 | .02 |
| ❑ 82 Kent Hill AP | .10 | .02 |
| ❑ 83 Doug Smith | .10 | .02 |
| ❑ 84 Dennis Harrah | .10 | .02 |
| ❑ 85 Jackie Slater | .50 | .20 |
| ❑ 86 Mike Lansford | .10 | .02 |
| ❑ 87 Gary Jeter | .25 | .08 |
| ❑ 88 Mike Wilcher | .10 | .02 |
| ❑ 89 Jim Collins | .10 | .02 |
| ❑ 90 LeRoy Irvin | .25 | .08 |
| ❑ 91 Gary Green | .10 | .02 |
| ❑ 92 Nolan Cromwell | .25 | .08 |
| ❑ 93 Dale Hatcher RC | .10 | .02 |
| ❑ 94 Jets TL | .25 | .08 |
| ❑ 95 Ken O'Brien | .50 | .20 |
| ❑ 96 Freeman McNeil | .25 | .08 |
| ❑ 97 Tony Paige RC | .10 | .02 |
| ❑ 98 Johnny Lam Jones | .10 | .02 |
| ❑ 99 Wesley Walker | .25 | .08 |
| ❑ 100 Kurt Sohn | .10 | .02 |
| ❑ 101 Al Toon RC | .50 | .20 |
| ❑ 102 Mickey Shuler | .10 | .02 |
| ❑ 103 Marvin Powell | .10 | .02 |
| ❑ 104 Pat Leahy | .10 | .02 |
| ❑ 105 Mark Gastineau | .25 | .08 |
| ❑ 106 Joe Klecko | .25 | .08 |
| ❑ 107 Marty Lyons | .10 | .02 |
| ❑ 108 Lance Mehl | .10 | .02 |
| ❑ 109 Bobby Jackson | .10 | .02 |
| ❑ 110 Dave Jennings | .10 | .02 |
| ❑ 111 Broncos TL | .25 | .08 |
| ❑ 112 John Elway | 8.00 | 4.00 |
| ❑ 113 Sammy Winder | .25 | .08 |
| ❑ 114 Gerald Willhite | .10 | .02 |
| ❑ 115 Steve Watson | .10 | .02 |
| ❑ 116 Vance Johnson RC | .50 | .20 |
| ❑ 117 Rich Karlis | .10 | .02 |
| ❑ 118 Rulon Jones | .10 | .02 |
| ❑ 119 Karl Mecklenburg RC | .50 | .20 |
| ❑ 120 Louis Wright | .10 | .02 |
| ❑ 121 Mike Harden | .10 | .02 |
| ❑ 122 Dennis Smith RC | .50 | .20 |
| ❑ 123 Steve Foley | .10 | .02 |
| ❑ 124 Cowboys TL | .25 | .08 |
| ❑ 125 Danny White | .50 | .20 |
| ❑ 126 Tony Dorsett | .60 | .25 |
| ❑ 127 Timmy Newsome | .10 | .02 |
| ❑ 128 Mike Renfro | .10 | .02 |
| ❑ 129 Tony Hill | .25 | .08 |
| ❑ 130 Doug Cosbie | .25 | .08 |
| ❑ 131 Rafael Septien | .10 | .02 |
| ❑ 132 Ed Too Tall Jones | .50 | .20 |
| ❑ 133 Randy White | .50 | .20 |
| ❑ 134 Jim Jeffcoat | .50 | .20 |
| ❑ 135 Everson Walls | .25 | .08 |
| ❑ 136 Dennis Thurman | .10 | .02 |
| ❑ 137 Giants TL | .25 | .08 |
| ❑ 138 Phil Simms | .50 | .20 |
| ❑ 139 Joe Morris | .25 | .08 |
| ❑ 140 George Adams RC | .10 | .02 |
| ❑ 141 Lionel Manuel | .25 | .08 |
| ❑ 142 Bobby Johnson | .10 | .02 |
| ❑ 143 Phil McConkey RC | .25 | .08 |
| ❑ 144 Mark Bavaro RC | .50 | .20 |
| ❑ 145 Zeke Mowatt | .10 | .02 |
| ❑ 146 Brad Benson RC | .10 | .02 |
| ❑ 147 Bart Oates RC | .25 | .08 |
| ❑ 148 Leonard Marshall RC | .50 | .20 |
| ❑ 149 Jim Burt | .25 | .08 |
| ❑ 150 George Martin | .10 | .02 |
| ❑ 151 Lawrence Taylor | 1.25 | .50 |
| ❑ 152 Harry Carson | .50 | .20 |
| ❑ 153 Elvis Patterson RC | .10 | .02 |

|  |  | | |
|---|---|---|---|
| 154 | Sean Landeta RC | .25 | .08 |
| 155 | 49ers TL/Roger Craig | .50 | .20 |
| 156 | Joe Montana | 8.00 | 4.00 |
| 157 | Roger Craig | .50 | .20 |
| 158 | Wendell Tyler | .10 | .02 |
| 159 | Carl Monroe | .10 | .02 |
| 160 | Dwight Clark | .25 | .08 |
| 161 | Jerry Rice RC ! | 80.00 | 40.00 |
| 162 | Randy Cross | .25 | .08 |
| 163 | Keith Fahnhorst | .10 | .02 |
| 164 | Jeff Stover | .10 | .02 |
| 165 | Michael Carter RC | .10 | .02 |
| 166 | Dwaine Board | .10 | .02 |
| 167 | Eric Wright | .25 | .08 |
| 168 | Ronnie Lott | .75 | .30 |
| 169 | Carlton Williamson | .10 | .02 |
| 170 | Redskins TL | .25 | .08 |
| 171 | Joe Theismann | .50 | .20 |
| 172 | Jay Schroeder RC | .50 | .20 |
| 173 | George Rogers | .25 | .08 |
| 174 | Ken Jenkins | .10 | .02 |
| 175 | Art Monk | .50 | .20 |
| 176 | Gary Clark RC | 2.00 | .75 |
| 177 | Joe Jacoby | .25 | .08 |
| 178 | Russ Grimm | .25 | .08 |
| 179 | Mark Moseley | .10 | .02 |
| 180 | Dexter Manley | .25 | .08 |
| 181 | Charles Mann RC | .50 | .20 |
| 182 | Vernon Dean | .10 | .02 |
| 183 | Raphel Cherry RC | .10 | .02 |
| 184 | Curtis Jordan | .10 | .02 |
| 185 | Browns TL/Kosar | .50 | .20 |
| 186 | Gary Danielson | .25 | .08 |
| 187 | Bernie Kosar RC | 3.00 | 1.25 |
| 188 | Kevin Mack RC | .50 | .20 |
| 189 | Earnest Byner RC | .75 | .30 |
| 190 | Glen Young | .10 | .02 |
| 191 | Ozzie Newsome | .50 | .20 |
| 192 | Mike Baab | .10 | .02 |
| 193 | Cody Risien | .25 | .08 |
| 194 | Bob Golic | .25 | .08 |
| 195 | Reggie Camp | .10 | .02 |
| 196 | Chip Banks | .25 | .08 |
| 197 | Tom Cousineau | .10 | .02 |
| 198 | Frank Minnifield RC | .10 | .02 |
| 199 | Al Gross | .10 | .02 |
| 200 | Seahawks TL | .25 | .08 |
| 201 | Dave Krieg | .50 | .20 |
| 202 | Curt Warner | .25 | .08 |
| 203 | Steve Largent | .60 | .25 |
| 204 | Norm Johnson | .10 | .02 |
| 205 | Daryl Turner | .10 | .02 |
| 206 | Jacob Green | .10 | .02 |
| 207 | Joe Nash | .10 | .02 |
| 208 | Jeff Bryant | .10 | .02 |
| 209 | Randy Edwards | .10 | .02 |
| 210 | Fredd Young | .10 | .02 |
| 211 | Kenny Easley | .25 | .08 |
| 212 | John Harris | .10 | .02 |
| 213 | Packers TL | .25 | .08 |
| 214 | Lynn Dickey | .25 | .08 |
| 215 | Gerry Ellis | .10 | .02 |
| 216 | Eddie Lee Ivery | .10 | .02 |
| 217 | Jessie Clark | .10 | .02 |
| 218 | James Lofton | .50 | .20 |
| 219 | Paul Coffman | .10 | .02 |
| 220 | Alphonso Carreker | .10 | .02 |
| 221 | Ezra Johnson | .10 | .02 |
| 222 | Mike Douglass | .10 | .02 |
| 223 | Tim Lewis | .10 | .02 |
| 224 | Mark Murphy RC CB | .10 | .02 |
| 225 | Joe Montana/K.O'Brien LL | 1.00 | .40 |
| 226 | Receiving Leaders | .25 | .08 |
| 227 | Marcus Allen/G.Riggs LL | .50 | .20 |
| 228 | Scoring Leaders | .25 | .08 |
| 229 | Interception Leaders | .10 | .02 |
| 230 | Chargers TL/Dan Fouts | .25 | .08 |
| 231 | Dan Fouts | .50 | .20 |
| 232 | Lionel James | .10 | .02 |
| 233 | Gary Anderson RB RC | .25 | .08 |
| 234 | Tim Spencer RC | .25 | .08 |
| 235 | Wes Chandler | .25 | .08 |
| 236 | Charlie Joiner | .50 | .20 |
| 237 | Kellen Winslow | .50 | .20 |
| 238 | Jim Lachey RC | .50 | .20 |
| 239 | Bob Thomas | .10 | .02 |
| 240 | Jeffery Dale | .10 | .02 |
| 241 | Ralf Mojsiejenko | .10 | .02 |
| 242 | Lions TL | .10 | .02 |
| 243 | Eric Hipple | .10 | .02 |
| 244 | Billy Sims | .25 | .08 |
| 245 | James Jones FB | .10 | .02 |
| 246 | Pete Mandley RC | .10 | .02 |
| 247 | Leonard Thompson | .10 | .02 |
| 248 | Lomas Brown RC | .25 | .08 |
| 249 | Eddie Murray | .25 | .08 |
| 250 | Curtis Green | .10 | .02 |
| 251 | William Gay | .10 | .02 |
| 252 | Jimmy Williams | .10 | .02 |
| 253 | Bobby Watkins | .10 | .02 |
| 254 | Bengals TL/B.Esiason | .50 | .20 |
| 255 | Boomer Esiason RC | 6.00 | 2.50 |
| 256 | James Brooks | .25 | .08 |
| 257 | Larry Kinnebrew | .10 | .02 |
| 258 | Cris Collinsworth | .25 | .08 |
| 259 | Mike Martin | .10 | .02 |
| 260 | Eddie Brown RC | .50 | .20 |
| 261 | Anthony Munoz | .50 | .20 |
| 262 | Jim Breech | .10 | .02 |
| 263 | Ross Browner | .25 | .08 |
| 264 | Carl Zander | .10 | .02 |
| 265 | James Griffin | .10 | .02 |
| 266 | Robert Jackson | .10 | .02 |
| 267 | Pat McInally | .10 | .02 |
| 268 | Eagles TL | .50 | .20 |
| 269 | Ron Jaworski | .25 | .08 |
| 270 | Earnest Jackson | .25 | .08 |
| 271 | Mike Quick | .25 | .08 |
| 272 | John Spagnola | .10 | .02 |
| 273 | Mark Dennard | .10 | .02 |
| 274 | Paul McFadden | .10 | .02 |
| 275 | Reggie White RC | 15.00 | 7.50 |
| 276 | Greg Brown | .10 | .02 |
| 277 | Herman Edwards | .10 | .02 |
| 278 | Roynell Young | .10 | .02 |
| 279 | Wes Hopkins | .10 | .02 |
| 280 | Steelers TL | .25 | .08 |
| 281 | Mark Malone | .25 | .08 |
| 282 | Frank Pollard | .10 | .02 |
| 283 | Walter Abercrombie | .10 | .02 |
| 284 | Louis Lipps | .50 | .20 |
| 285 | John Stallworth | .50 | .20 |
| 286 | Mike Webster | .25 | .08 |
| 287 | Gary Anderson K | .25 | .08 |
| 288 | Keith Willis | .10 | .02 |
| 289 | Mike Merriweather | .10 | .02 |
| 290 | Dwayne Woodruff | .10 | .02 |
| 291 | Donnie Shell | .25 | .08 |
| 292 | Vikings TL | .25 | .08 |
| 293 | Tommy Kramer | .25 | .08 |
| 294 | Darrin Nelson | .10 | .02 |
| 295 | Ted Brown | .25 | .08 |
| 296 | Buster Rhymes | .10 | .02 |
| 297 | Anthony Carter RC | 1.00 | .40 |
| 298 | Steve Jordan RC | .50 | .20 |
| 299 | Keith Millard RC | .50 | .20 |
| 300 | Joey Browner RC | .50 | .20 |
| 301 | John Turner | .10 | .02 |
| 302 | Greg Coleman | .10 | .02 |
| 303 | Chiefs TL | .10 | .02 |
| 304 | Bill Kenney | .10 | .02 |
| 305 | Herman Heard | .10 | .02 |
| 306 | Stephone Paige RC | .50 | .20 |
| 307 | Carlos Carson | .25 | .08 |
| 308 | Nick Lowery | .25 | .08 |
| 309 | Mike Bell | .10 | .02 |
| 310 | Bill Maas | .10 | .02 |
| 311 | Art Still | .10 | .02 |
| 312 | Albert Lewis RC | .50 | .20 |
| 313 | Deron Cherry | .25 | .08 |
| 314 | Colts TL | .10 | .02 |
| 315 | Mike Pagel | .10 | .02 |
| 316 | Randy McMillan | .10 | .02 |
| 317 | Albert Bentley RC | .25 | .08 |
| 318 | George Wonsley RC | .10 | .02 |
| 319 | Robbie Martin | .10 | .02 |
| 320 | Pat Beach | .10 | .02 |
| 321 | Chris Hinton | .25 | .08 |
| 322 | Duane Bickett RC | .50 | .20 |
| 323 | Eugene Daniel | .10 | .02 |
| 324 | Cliff Odom RC | .10 | .02 |
| 325 | Rohn Stark | .25 | .08 |
| 326 | Cardinals TL | .10 | .02 |
| 327 | Neil Lomax | .25 | .08 |
| 328 | Stump Mitchell | .25 | .08 |
| 329 | Ottis Anderson | .50 | .20 |
| 330 | J.T.Smith | .25 | .08 |
| 331 | Pat Tilley | .10 | .02 |
| 332 | Roy Green | .25 | .08 |
| 333 | Lance Smith RC | .10 | .02 |
| 334 | Curtis Greer | .10 | .02 |
| 335 | Freddie Joe Nunn RC | .25 | .08 |
| 336 | E.J. Junior | .25 | .08 |
| 337 | Lonnie Young RC | .10 | .02 |
| 338 | Saints TL | .10 | .02 |
| 339 | Bobby Hebert RC | .50 | .20 |
| 340 | Dave Wilson | .10 | .02 |
| 341 | Wayne Wilson | .10 | .02 |
| 342 | Hoby Brenner | .25 | .08 |
| 343 | Stan Brock | .25 | .08 |
| 344 | Morten Andersen | .50 | .20 |
| 345 | Bruce Clark | .10 | .02 |
| 346 | Rickey Jackson | .50 | .20 |
| 347 | Dave Waymer | .10 | .02 |
| 348 | Brian Hansen | .10 | .02 |
| 349 | Oilers TL/W.Moon | .50 | .20 |
| 350 | Warren Moon | 3.00 | 1.50 |
| 351 | Mike Rozier RC | .50 | .20 |
| 352 | Butch Woolfolk | .10 | .02 |
| 353 | Drew Hill | .50 | .20 |
| 354 | Willie Drewrey RC | .10 | .02 |
| 355 | Tim Smith | .25 | .08 |
| 356 | Mike Munchak | .50 | .20 |
| 357 | Ray Childress RC | .50 | .20 |
| 358 | Frank Bush | .10 | .02 |
| 359 | Steve Brown | .10 | .02 |
| 360 | Falcons TL | .25 | .08 |
| 361 | David Archer RC | .25 | .08 |
| 362 | Gerald Riggs | .25 | .08 |
| 363 | William Andrews | .25 | .08 |
| 364 | Billy Johnson | .25 | .08 |
| 365 | Arthur Cox | .10 | .02 |
| 366 | Mike Kenn | .10 | .02 |
| 367 | Bill Fralic RC | .25 | .08 |
| 368 | Mick Luckhurst | .10 | .02 |
| 369 | Rick Bryan | .10 | .02 |
| 370 | Bobby Butler | .10 | .02 |
| 371 | Rick Donnelly RC | .10 | .02 |
| 372 | Buccaneers TL | .10 | .02 |
| 373 | Steve DeBerg | .50 | .20 |
| 374 | Steve Young RC | 20.00 | 10.00 |
| 375 | James Wilder | .10 | .02 |
| 376 | Kevin House | .10 | .02 |
| 377 | Gerald Carter | .10 | .02 |
| 378 | Jimmie Giles | .25 | .08 |
| 379 | Sean Farrell | .10 | .02 |
| 380 | Donald Igwebuike | .10 | .02 |
| 381 | David Logan | .10 | .02 |
| 382 | Jeremiah Castille RC | .10 | .02 |
| 383 | Bills TL | .25 | .08 |
| 384 | Bruce Mathison RC | .10 | .02 |
| 385 | Joe Cribbs | .25 | .08 |
| 386 | Greg Bell | .25 | .08 |
| 387 | Jerry Butler | .10 | .02 |
| 388 | Andre Reed RC | 6.00 | 2.50 |
| 389 | Bruce Smith RC | 8.00 | 4.00 |
| 390 | Fred Smerlas | .10 | .02 |
| 391 | Darryl Talley | .50 | .20 |
| 392 | Jim Haslett | .25 | .08 |
| 393 | Charles Romes | .10 | .02 |
| 394 | Checklist 1-132 | .20 | .07 |
| 395 | Checklist 133-264 | .20 | .07 |
| 396 | Checklist 265-396 | .20 | .07 |

## 1987 Topps

| | | | |
|---|---|---|---|
| | COMPLETE SET (396) | 30.00 | 15.00 |
| | COMP.FACT.SET (396) | 80.00 | 50.00 |
| 1 | Super Bowl XXI | .50 | .20 |
| 2 | Todd Christensen RB | .25 | .08 |
| 3 | Dave Jennings RB | .10 | .02 |
| 4 | Charlie Joiner RB | .10 | .02 |
| 5 | Steve Largent RB | .50 | .20 |
| 6 | Dan Marino RB | 2.00 | .75 |
| 7 | Donnie Shell RB | .25 | .08 |
| 8 | Phil Simms RB | .25 | .08 |
| 9 | New York Giants TL | .25 | .08 |
| 10 | Joe Morris | .25 | .08 |
| 11 | Joe Morris | .10 | .02 |
| 12 | Maurice Carthon RC | .25 | .08 |
| 13 | Lee Rouson | .10 | .02 |
| 14 | Bobby Johnson | .10 | .02 |

| | | |
|---|---|---|
| ☐ 85 Ozzie Newsome | .50 | .20 |
| ☐ 86 Jeff Gossett | .25 | .08 |
| ☐ 87 Cody Risien | .10 | .02 |
| ☐ 88 Reggie Camp | .10 | .02 |
| ☐ 89 Bob Golic | .10 | .02 |
| ☐ 90 Carl Hairston | .10 | .02 |
| ☐ 91 Chip Banks | .10 | .02 |
| ☐ 92 Frank Minnifield | .10 | .02 |
| ☐ 93 Hanford Dixon | .10 | .02 |
| ☐ 94 Gerald McNeil RC | .10 | .02 |
| ☐ 95 Dave Puzzuoli | .10 | .02 |
| ☐ 96 Patriots TL | .10 | .02 |
| ☐ 97 Tony Eason | .25 | .08 |
| ☐ 98 Craig James | .25 | .08 |
| ☐ 99 Tony Collins | .10 | .02 |
| ☐ 100 Mosi Tatupu | .10 | .02 |
| ☐ 101 Stanley Morgan | .25 | .08 |
| ☐ 102 Irving Fryar | .50 | .20 |
| ☐ 103 Stephen Starring | .10 | .02 |
| ☐ 104 Tony Franklin | .10 | .02 |
| ☐ 105 Rich Camarillo | .10 | .02 |
| ☐ 106 Garin Veris | .10 | .02 |
| ☐ 107 Andre Tippett | .25 | .08 |
| ☐ 108 Don Blackmon | .10 | .02 |
| ☐ 109 Ronnie Lippett RC | .10 | .02 |
| ☐ 110 Raymond Clayborn | .10 | .02 |
| ☐ 111 49ers TL/R.Craig | .25 | .08 |
| ☐ 112 Joe Montana | 6.00 | 2.50 |
| ☐ 113 Roger Craig | .50 | .20 |
| ☐ 114 Joe Cribbs | .25 | .08 |
| ☐ 115 Jerry Rice | 6.00 | 2.50 |
| ☐ 116 Dwight Clark | .25 | .08 |
| ☐ 117 Ray Wersching | .10 | .02 |
| ☐ 118 Max Runager | .10 | .02 |
| ☐ 119 Jeff Stover | .10 | .02 |
| ☐ 120 Dwaine Board | .10 | .02 |
| ☐ 121 Tim McKyer RC | .25 | .08 |
| ☐ 122 Don Griffin RC | .10 | .02 |
| ☐ 123 Ronnie Lott | .50 | .20 |
| ☐ 124 Tom Holmoe | .10 | .02 |
| ☐ 125 Charles Haley RC | 2.00 | .75 |
| ☐ 126 Jets TL | .10 | .02 |
| ☐ 127 Ken O'Brien | .25 | .08 |
| ☐ 128 Pat Ryan | .10 | .02 |
| ☐ 129 Freeman McNeil | .25 | .08 |
| ☐ 130 Johnny Hector RC | .10 | .02 |
| ☐ 131 Al Toon | .50 | .20 |
| ☐ 132 Wesley Walker | .25 | .08 |
| ☐ 133 Mickey Shuler | .10 | .02 |
| ☐ 134 Pat Leahy | .10 | .02 |
| ☐ 135 Mark Gastineau | .25 | .08 |
| ☐ 136 Joe Klecko | .25 | .08 |
| ☐ 137 Marty Lyons | .10 | .02 |
| ☐ 138 Bob Crable | .10 | .02 |
| ☐ 139 Lance Mehl | .10 | .02 |
| ☐ 140 Dave Jennings | .10 | .02 |
| ☐ 141 Harry Hamilton RC | .10 | .02 |
| ☐ 142 Lester Lyles | .10 | .02 |
| ☐ 143 Bobby Humphery UER | .10 | .02 |
| ☐ 144 Rams TL/E.Dickerson | .50 | .20 |
| ☐ 145 Jim Everett RC | 1.25 | .50 |
| ☐ 146 Eric Dickerson | .50 | .20 |
| ☐ 147 Barry Redden | .10 | .02 |
| ☐ 148 Ron Brown | .25 | .08 |
| ☐ 149 Kevin House | .10 | .02 |
| ☐ 150 Henry Ellard | .50 | .20 |
| ☐ 151 Doug Smith | .10 | .02 |
| ☐ 152 Dennis Harrah | .10 | .02 |
| ☐ 153 Jackie Slater | .25 | .08 |
| ☐ 154 Gary Jeter | .10 | .02 |
| ☐ 155 Carl Ekern | .10 | .02 |
| ☐ 156 Mike Wilcher | .10 | .02 |
| ☐ 157 Jerry Gray RC | .10 | .02 |
| ☐ 158 LeRoy Irvin | .10 | .02 |
| ☐ 159 Nolan Cromwell | .25 | .08 |
| ☐ 160 Chiefs TL | .10 | .02 |
| ☐ 161 Bill Kenney | .10 | .02 |
| ☐ 162 Stephone Paige | .25 | .08 |
| ☐ 163 Henry Marshall | .10 | .02 |
| ☐ 164 Carlos Carson | .10 | .02 |
| ☐ 165 Nick Lowery | .25 | .08 |
| ☐ 166 Irv Eatman RC | .10 | .02 |
| ☐ 167 Brad Budde | .10 | .02 |
| ☐ 168 Art Still | .10 | .02 |
| ☐ 169 Bill Maas | .10 | .02 |
| ☐ 170 Lloyd Burruss RC | .10 | .02 |
| ☐ 171 Deron Cherry | .10 | .02 |

| | | |
|---|---|---|
| ☐ 172 Seahawks TL | .25 | .08 |
| ☐ 173 Dave Krieg | .50 | .20 |
| ☐ 174 Curt Warner | .25 | .08 |
| ☐ 175 John L.Williams RC | .50 | .20 |
| ☐ 176 Bobby Joe Edmonds RC | .25 | .08 |
| ☐ 177 Steve Largent | .60 | .25 |
| ☐ 178 Bruce Scholtz | .10 | .02 |
| ☐ 179 Norm Johnson | .10 | .02 |
| ☐ 180 Jacob Green | .10 | .02 |
| ☐ 181 Fredd Young | .10 | .02 |
| ☐ 182 Dave Brown DB | .10 | .02 |
| ☐ 183 Kenny Easley | .10 | .02 |
| ☐ 184 Bengals TL | .25 | .08 |
| ☐ 185 Boomer Esiason | .50 | .20 |
| ☐ 186 James Brooks | .25 | .08 |
| ☐ 187 Larry Kinnebrew | .10 | .02 |
| ☐ 188 Cris Collinsworth | .25 | .08 |
| ☐ 189 Eddie Brown | .50 | .20 |
| ☐ 190 Tim McGee RC | .50 | .20 |
| ☐ 191 Jim Breech | .10 | .02 |
| ☐ 192 Anthony Munoz | .50 | .20 |
| ☐ 193 Max Montoya | .10 | .02 |
| ☐ 194 Eddie Edwards | .10 | .02 |
| ☐ 195 Ross Browner | .25 | .08 |
| ☐ 196 Emanuel King | .10 | .02 |
| ☐ 197 Louis Breeden | .10 | .02 |
| ☐ 198 Vikings TL | .10 | .02 |
| ☐ 199 Tommy Kramer | .25 | .08 |
| ☐ 200 Darrin Nelson | .10 | .02 |
| ☐ 201 Allen Rice | .10 | .02 |
| ☐ 202 Anthony Carter | .50 | .20 |
| ☐ 203 Leo Lewis | .10 | .02 |
| ☐ 204 Steve Jordan | .50 | .20 |
| ☐ 205 Chuck Nelson RC | .10 | .02 |
| ☐ 206 Greg Coleman | .10 | .02 |
| ☐ 207 Gary Zimmerman RC | 2.50 | 1.00 |
| ☐ 208 Doug Martin | .10 | .02 |
| ☐ 209 Keith Millard | .10 | .02 |
| ☐ 210 Issiac Holt RC | .10 | .02 |
| ☐ 211 Joey Browner | .25 | .08 |
| ☐ 212 Rufus Bess | .10 | .02 |
| ☐ 213 Raiders TL/M.Allen | .50 | .20 |
| ☐ 214 Jim Plunkett | .50 | .20 |
| ☐ 215 Marcus Allen | 1.00 | .40 |
| ☐ 216 Napoleon McCallum RC | .25 | .08 |
| ☐ 217 Dokie Williams | .10 | .02 |
| ☐ 218 Todd Christensen | .50 | .20 |
| ☐ 219 Chris Bahr | .10 | .02 |
| ☐ 220 Howie Long | .60 | .25 |
| ☐ 221 Bill Pickel | .10 | .02 |
| ☐ 222 Sean Jones RC | .50 | .20 |
| ☐ 223 Lester Hayes | .25 | .08 |
| ☐ 224 Mike Haynes | .25 | .08 |
| ☐ 225 Vann McElroy | .10 | .02 |
| ☐ 226 Fulton Walker | .10 | .02 |
| ☐ 227 Dan Marino/T.Kramer LL | 1.25 | .50 |
| ☐ 228 J.Rice/Christensen LL | 1.25 | .50 |
| ☐ 229 Eric Dickerson/Warner LL | .50 | .20 |
| ☐ 230 Scoring Leaders | .25 | .08 |
| ☐ 231 Interception Leaders | .50 | .20 |
| ☐ 232 Dolphins TL | .25 | .08 |
| ☐ 233 Dan Marino | 6.00 | 2.50 |
| ☐ 234 Lorenzo Hampton RC | .10 | .02 |
| ☐ 235 Tony Nathan | .25 | .08 |
| ☐ 236 Mark Duper | .50 | .20 |
| ☐ 237 Mark Clayton | .50 | .20 |
| ☐ 238 Nat Moore | .25 | .08 |
| ☐ 239 Bruce Hardy | .10 | .02 |
| ☐ 240 Reggie Roby | .10 | .02 |
| ☐ 241 Roy Foster | .10 | .02 |
| ☐ 242 Dwight Stephenson | .25 | .08 |
| ☐ 243 Hugh Green | .10 | .02 |
| ☐ 244 John Offerdahl RC | .50 | .20 |
| ☐ 245 Mark Brown | .10 | .02 |
| ☐ 246 Doug Betters | .10 | .02 |
| ☐ 247 Bob Baumhower | .10 | .02 |
| ☐ 248 Falcons TL | .10 | .02 |
| ☐ 249 David Archer | .50 | .20 |
| ☐ 250 Gerald Riggs | .25 | .08 |
| ☐ 251 William Andrews | .25 | .08 |
| ☐ 252 Charlie Brown | .10 | .02 |
| ☐ 253 Arthur Cox | .10 | .02 |
| ☐ 254 Rick Donnelly | .10 | .02 |
| ☐ 255 Bill Fralic | .10 | .02 |
| ☐ 256 Mike Gann RC | .10 | .02 |
| ☐ 257 Rick Bryan | .10 | .02 |
| ☐ 258 Bret Clark | .10 | .02 |

| | | |
|---|---|---|
| ☐ 15 Lionel Manuel | .10 | .02 |
| ☐ 16 Phil McConkey | .10 | .02 |
| ☐ 17 Mark Bavaro | .50 | .20 |
| ☐ 18 Zeke Mowatt | .10 | .02 |
| ☐ 19 Raul Allegre | .10 | .02 |
| ☐ 20 Sean Landeta | .10 | .02 |
| ☐ 21 Brad Benson | .10 | .02 |
| ☐ 22 Jim Burt | .10 | .02 |
| ☐ 23 Leonard Marshall | .50 | .20 |
| ☐ 24 Carl Banks | .50 | .20 |
| ☐ 25 Harry Carson | .10 | .02 |
| ☐ 26 Lawrence Taylor | .75 | .30 |
| ☐ 27 Terry Kinard RC | .10 | .02 |
| ☐ 28 Pepper Johnson RC | .50 | .20 |
| ☐ 29 Erik Howard RC | .10 | .02 |
| ☐ 30 Broncos TL | .10 | .02 |
| ☐ 31 John Elway | 6.00 | 2.50 |
| ☐ 32 Gerald Willhite | .10 | .02 |
| ☐ 33 Sammy Winder | .25 | .08 |
| ☐ 34 Ken Bell | .10 | .02 |
| ☐ 35 Steve Watson | .10 | .02 |
| ☐ 36 Rich Karlis | .10 | .02 |
| ☐ 37 Keith Bishop | .10 | .02 |
| ☐ 38 Rulon Jones | .10 | .02 |
| ☐ 39 Karl Mecklenburg | .50 | .20 |
| ☐ 40 Louis Wright | .10 | .02 |
| ☐ 41 Mike Harden | .10 | .02 |
| ☐ 42 Dennis Smith | .25 | .08 |
| ☐ 43 Bears TL/W.Payton | .50 | .20 |
| ☐ 44 Jim McMahon | .50 | .20 |
| ☐ 45 Doug Flutie RC | 8.00 | 3.00 |
| ☐ 46 Walter Payton | 4.00 | 1.50 |
| ☐ 47 Matt Suhey | .10 | .02 |
| ☐ 48 Willie Gault | .25 | .08 |
| ☐ 49 Dennis Gentry RC | .10 | .02 |
| ☐ 50 Kevin Butler | .10 | .02 |
| ☐ 51 Jim Covert | .10 | .02 |
| ☐ 52 Jay Hilgenberg | .25 | .08 |
| ☐ 53 Dan Hampton | .50 | .20 |
| ☐ 54 Steve McMichael | .50 | .20 |
| ☐ 55 William Perry | .50 | .20 |
| ☐ 56 Richard Dent | .50 | .20 |
| ☐ 57 Otis Wilson | .10 | .02 |
| ☐ 58 Mike Singletary | .50 | .20 |
| ☐ 59 Wilber Marshall | .50 | .20 |
| ☐ 60 Mike Richardson | .10 | .02 |
| ☐ 61 Dave Duerson | .10 | .02 |
| ☐ 62 Gary Fencik | .10 | .02 |
| ☐ 63 Redskins TL | .25 | .08 |
| ☐ 64 Jay Schroeder | .25 | .08 |
| ☐ 65 George Rogers | .25 | .08 |
| ☐ 66 Kelvin Bryant RC | .25 | .08 |
| ☐ 67 Ken Jenkins | .10 | .02 |
| ☐ 68 Gary Clark | .50 | .20 |
| ☐ 69 Art Monk | .50 | .20 |
| ☐ 70 Clint Didier RC | .10 | .02 |
| ☐ 71 Steve Cox | .10 | .02 |
| ☐ 72 Joe Jacoby | .10 | .02 |
| ☐ 73 Russ Grimm | .10 | .02 |
| ☐ 74 Charles Mann | .25 | .08 |
| ☐ 75 Dave Butz | .10 | .02 |
| ☐ 76 Dexter Manley | .10 | .02 |
| ☐ 77 Darrell Green | .50 | .20 |
| ☐ 78 Curtis Jordan | .10 | .02 |
| ☐ 79 Browns TL | .10 | .02 |
| ☐ 80 Bernie Kosar | .50 | .20 |
| ☐ 81 Curtis Dickey | .10 | .02 |
| ☐ 82 Kevin Mack | .25 | .08 |
| ☐ 83 Herman Fontenot | .10 | .02 |
| ☐ 84 Brian Brennan RC | .10 | .02 |

| | | |
|---|---|---|
| ☐ 259 Mike Pitts | .10 | .02 |
| ☐ 260 Cowboys TL/T.Dorsett | .50 | .20 |
| ☐ 261 Danny White | .50 | .20 |
| ☐ 262 Steve Pelluer RC | .10 | .02 |
| ☐ 263 Tony Dorsett UER | .50 | .20 |
| ☐ 264 Herschel Walker RC | 2.50 | 1.00 |
| ☐ 265 Timmy Newsome | .10 | .02 |
| ☐ 266 Tony Hill | .25 | .08 |
| ☐ 267 Mike Sherrard RC | .50 | .20 |
| ☐ 268 Jim Jeffcoat | .50 | .20 |
| ☐ 269 Ron Fellows | .10 | .02 |
| ☐ 270 Bill Bates | .50 | .20 |
| ☐ 271 Michael Downs | .10 | .02 |
| ☐ 272 Saints TL/B.Hebert | .25 | .08 |
| ☐ 273 Dave Wilson | .10 | .02 |
| ☐ 274 Rueben Mayes RC UER | .10 | .02 |
| ☐ 275 Hoby Brenner | .10 | .02 |
| ☐ 276 Eric Martin RC | .50 | .20 |
| ☐ 277 Morten Andersen | .25 | .08 |
| ☐ 278 Brian Hansen | .10 | .02 |
| ☐ 279 Rickey Jackson | .50 | .20 |
| ☐ 280 Dave Waymer | .10 | .02 |
| ☐ 281 Bruce Clark | .10 | .02 |
| ☐ 282 Jumpy Geathers RC | .25 | .08 |
| ☐ 283 Steelers TL | .25 | .08 |
| ☐ 284 Mark Malone | .25 | .08 |
| ☐ 285 Earnest Jackson | .10 | .02 |
| ☐ 286 Walter Abercrombie | .10 | .02 |
| ☐ 287 Louis Lipps | .25 | .08 |
| ☐ 288 John Stallworth UER | .50 | .20 |
| ☐ 289 Gary Anderson K | .10 | .02 |
| ☐ 290 Keith Willis | .10 | .02 |
| ☐ 291 Mike Merriweather | .10 | .02 |
| ☐ 292 Lupe Sanchez | .10 | .02 |
| ☐ 293 Donnie Shell | .25 | .08 |
| ☐ 294 Eagles TL/K.Byars | .50 | .20 |
| ☐ 295 Mike Reichenbach | .10 | .02 |
| ☐ 296 Randall Cunningham RC | 6.00 | 3.00 |
| ☐ 297 Keith Byars RC | .75 | .30 |
| ☐ 298 Mike Quick | .25 | .08 |
| ☐ 299 Kenny Jackson | .10 | .02 |
| ☐ 300 John Teltschik RC | .10 | .02 |
| ☐ 301 Reggie White | 3.00 | 1.50 |
| ☐ 302 Ken Clarke | .10 | .02 |
| ☐ 303 Greg Brown | .10 | .02 |
| ☐ 304 Roynell Young | .10 | .02 |
| ☐ 305 Andre Waters RC | .50 | .20 |
| ☐ 306 Oilers TL/W.Moon | .50 | .20 |
| ☐ 307 Warren Moon | 1.50 | .60 |
| ☐ 308 Mike Rozier | .25 | .08 |
| ☐ 309 Drew Hill | .25 | .08 |
| ☐ 310 Ernest Givins RC | .50 | .20 |
| ☐ 311 Lee Johnson RC | .10 | .02 |
| ☐ 312 Kent Hill | .10 | .02 |
| ☐ 313 Dean Steinkuhler RC | .25 | .08 |
| ☐ 314 Ray Childress | .25 | .08 |
| ☐ 315 John Grimsley RC | .10 | .02 |
| ☐ 316 Jesse Baker | .10 | .02 |
| ☐ 317 Lions TL | .10 | .02 |
| ☐ 318 Chuck Long RC | .25 | .08 |
| ☐ 319 James Jones FB | .10 | .02 |
| ☐ 320 Garry James | .10 | .02 |
| ☐ 321 Jeff Chadwick | .10 | .02 |
| ☐ 322 Leonard Thompson | .10 | .02 |
| ☐ 323 Pete Mandley | .10 | .02 |
| ☐ 324 Jimmie Giles | .25 | .08 |
| ☐ 325 Herman Hunter | .10 | .02 |
| ☐ 326 Keith Ferguson | .10 | .02 |
| ☐ 327 Devon Mitchell | .10 | .02 |
| ☐ 328 Cardinals TL | .10 | .02 |
| ☐ 329 Neil Lomax | .25 | .08 |
| ☐ 330 Stump Mitchell | .10 | .02 |
| ☐ 331 Earl Ferrell | .10 | .02 |
| ☐ 332 Vai Sikahema RC | .25 | .08 |
| ☐ 333 Ron Wolfley RC | .10 | .02 |
| ☐ 334 J.T.Smith | .25 | .08 |
| ☐ 335 Roy Green | .25 | .08 |
| ☐ 336 Al(Bubba) Baker | .10 | .02 |
| ☐ 337 Freddie Joe Nunn | .10 | .02 |
| ☐ 338 Cedric Mack | .10 | .02 |
| ☐ 339 Chargers TL | .25 | .08 |
| ☐ 340 Dan Fouts | .50 | .20 |
| ☐ 341 Gary Anderson RB UER | .50 | .20 |
| ☐ 342 Wes Chandler | .25 | .08 |
| ☐ 343 Kellen Winslow | .50 | .20 |
| ☐ 344 Ralf Mojsiejenko | .10 | .02 |
| ☐ 345 Rolf Benirschke | .10 | .02 |

| | | |
|---|---|---|
| ☐ 346 Lee Williams RC | .25 | .08 |
| ☐ 347 Leslie O'Neal RC | 1.00 | .40 |
| ☐ 348 Billy Ray Smith | .25 | .08 |
| ☐ 349 Gill Byrd | .25 | .08 |
| ☐ 350 Packers TL | .10 | .02 |
| ☐ 351 Randy Wright | .10 | .02 |
| ☐ 352 Kenneth Davis RC | .50 | .20 |
| ☐ 353 Gerry Ellis | .10 | .02 |
| ☐ 354 James Lofton | .50 | .20 |
| ☐ 355 Phillip Epps RC | .10 | .02 |
| ☐ 356 Walter Stanley RC | .10 | .02 |
| ☐ 357 Eddie Lee Ivery | .10 | .02 |
| ☐ 358 Tim Harris RC | .50 | .20 |
| ☐ 359 Mark Lee UER | .10 | .02 |
| ☐ 360 Mossy Cade | .10 | .02 |
| ☐ 361 Bills TL/J.Kelly | 1.00 | .40 |
| ☐ 362 Jim Kelly RC | 10.00 | 4.00 |
| ☐ 363 Robb Riddick RC | .10 | .02 |
| ☐ 364 Greg Bell | .10 | .02 |
| ☐ 365 Andre Reed | 1.25 | .50 |
| ☐ 366 Pete Metzelaars RC | .50 | .20 |
| ☐ 367 Sean McNanie | .10 | .02 |
| ☐ 368 Fred Smerlas | .10 | .02 |
| ☐ 369 Bruce Smith | 2.00 | .75 |
| ☐ 370 Darryl Talley | .25 | .08 |
| ☐ 371 Charles Romes | .10 | .02 |
| ☐ 372 Colts TL | .10 | .02 |
| ☐ 373 Jack Trudeau RC | .25 | .08 |
| ☐ 374 Gary Hogeboom | .10 | .02 |
| ☐ 375 Randy McMillan | .10 | .02 |
| ☐ 376 Albert Bentley | .10 | .02 |
| ☐ 377 Matt Bouza | .10 | .02 |
| ☐ 378 Bill Brooks RC | .75 | .30 |
| ☐ 379 Rohn Stark | .10 | .02 |
| ☐ 380 Chris Hinton | .10 | .02 |
| ☐ 381 Ray Donaldson | .10 | .02 |
| ☐ 382 Jon Hand RC | .10 | .02 |
| ☐ 383 Buccaneers TL | .10 | .02 |
| ☐ 384 Steve Young | 5.00 | 2.00 |
| ☐ 385 James Wilder | .10 | .02 |
| ☐ 386 Frank Garcia | .10 | .02 |
| ☐ 387 Gerald Carter | .10 | .02 |
| ☐ 388 Phil Freeman | .10 | .02 |
| ☐ 389 Calvin Magee | .10 | .02 |
| ☐ 390 Donald Igwebuike | .10 | .02 |
| ☐ 391 David Logan | .10 | .02 |
| ☐ 392 Jeff Davis | .10 | .02 |
| ☐ 393 Chris Washington | .10 | .02 |
| ☐ 394 Checklist 1-132 | .10 | .02 |
| ☐ 395 Checklist 133-264 | .10 | .02 |
| ☐ 396 Checklist 265-396 | .10 | .02 |

**1988 Topps**

| | | |
|---|---|---|
| ☐ COMPLETE SET (396) | 20.00 | 7.50 |
| ☐ COMP.FACT.SET (396) | 30.00 | 15.00 |
| ☐ 1 Super Bowl XXII | .20 | .07 |
| ☐ 2 Vencie Glenn RB | .10 | .02 |
| ☐ 3 Steve Largent RB | .40 | .15 |
| ☐ 4 Joe Montana RB | .75 | .30 |
| ☐ 5 Walter Payton RB | .75 | .30 |
| ☐ 6 Jerry Rice RB | .75 | .30 |
| ☐ 7 Redskins TL | .20 | .07 |
| ☐ 8 Doug Williams | .20 | .07 |
| ☐ 9 George Rogers | .20 | .07 |
| ☐ 10 Kelvin Bryant | .20 | .07 |
| ☐ 11 Timmy Smith SR | .20 | .07 |
| ☐ 12 Art Monk | .40 | .15 |
| ☐ 13 Gary Clark | .40 | .15 |
| ☐ 14 Ricky Sanders RC | .40 | .15 |

| | | |
|---|---|---|
| ☐ 15 Steve Cox | .10 | .02 |
| ☐ 16 Joe Jacoby | .10 | .02 |
| ☐ 17 Charles Mann | .20 | .07 |
| ☐ 18 Dave Butz | .20 | .07 |
| ☐ 19 Darrell Green | .20 | .07 |
| ☐ 20 Dexter Manley | .10 | .02 |
| ☐ 21 Barry Wilburn | .10 | .02 |
| ☐ 22 Broncos TL | .10 | .02 |
| ☐ 23 John Elway | 2.00 | .75 |
| ☐ 24 Sammy Winder | .10 | .02 |
| ☐ 25 Vance Johnson | .20 | .07 |
| ☐ 26 Mark Jackson RC | .40 | .15 |
| ☐ 27 Ricky Nattiel RC | .10 | .02 |
| ☐ 28 Clarence Kay | .10 | .02 |
| ☐ 29 Rich Karlis | .10 | .02 |
| ☐ 30 Keith Bishop | .10 | .02 |
| ☐ 31 Mike Horan | .10 | .02 |
| ☐ 32 Rulon Jones | .10 | .02 |
| ☐ 33 Karl Mecklenburg | .20 | .07 |
| ☐ 34 Jim Ryan | .10 | .02 |
| ☐ 35 Mark Haynes | .10 | .02 |
| ☐ 36 Mike Harden | .10 | .02 |
| ☐ 37 49ers TL | .40 | .15 |
| ☐ 38 Joe Montana | 2.00 | .75 |
| ☐ 39 Steve Young | 1.00 | .40 |
| ☐ 40 Roger Craig | .20 | .07 |
| ☐ 41 Tom Rathman RC | .40 | .15 |
| ☐ 42 Joe Cribbs | .20 | .07 |
| ☐ 43 Jerry Rice | 2.00 | .75 |
| ☐ 44 Mike Wilson RC | .10 | .02 |
| ☐ 45 Ron Heller TE RC | .10 | .02 |
| ☐ 46 Ray Wersching | .10 | .02 |
| ☐ 47 Michael Carter | .10 | .02 |
| ☐ 48 Dwaine Board | .10 | .02 |
| ☐ 49 Michael Walter | .10 | .02 |
| ☐ 50 Don Griffin | .10 | .02 |
| ☐ 51 Ronnie Lott | .40 | .15 |
| ☐ 52 Charles Haley | .40 | .15 |
| ☐ 53 Dana McLemore | .10 | .02 |
| ☐ 54 Saints TL | .20 | .07 |
| ☐ 55 Bobby Hebert | .20 | .07 |
| ☐ 56 Rueben Mayes | .10 | .02 |
| ☐ 57 Dalton Hilliard RC | .10 | .02 |
| ☐ 58 Eric Martin | .20 | .07 |
| ☐ 59 John Tice RC | .10 | .02 |
| ☐ 60 Brad Edelman | .10 | .02 |
| ☐ 61 Morten Andersen | .20 | .07 |
| ☐ 62 Brian Hansen | .10 | .02 |
| ☐ 63 Mel Gray RC | .40 | .15 |
| ☐ 64 Rickey Jackson | .20 | .07 |
| ☐ 65 Sam Mills RC | .75 | .30 |
| ☐ 66 Pat Swilling RC | .40 | .15 |
| ☐ 67 Dave Waymer | .10 | .02 |
| ☐ 68 Bears TL | .20 | .07 |
| ☐ 69 Jim McMahon | .40 | .15 |
| ☐ 70 Mike Tomczak RC | .10 | .02 |
| ☐ 71 Neal Anderson RC | .40 | .15 |
| ☐ 72 Willie Gault | .20 | .07 |
| ☐ 73 Dennis Gentry | .10 | .02 |
| ☐ 74 Dennis McKinnon | .10 | .02 |
| ☐ 75 Kevin Butler | .10 | .02 |
| ☐ 76 Jim Covert | .10 | .02 |
| ☐ 77 Jay Hilgenberg | .20 | .07 |
| ☐ 78 Steve McMichael | .20 | .07 |
| ☐ 79 William Perry | .20 | .07 |
| ☐ 80 Richard Dent | .40 | .15 |
| ☐ 81 Ron Rivera RC | .20 | .07 |
| ☐ 82 Mike Singletary | .40 | .15 |
| ☐ 83 Dan Hampton | .40 | .15 |
| ☐ 84 Dave Duerson | .10 | .02 |
| ☐ 85 Browns TL | .10 | .02 |
| ☐ 86 Bernie Kosar | .40 | .15 |
| ☐ 87 Earnest Byner | .40 | .15 |
| ☐ 88 Kevin Mack | .20 | .07 |
| ☐ 89 Webster Slaughter RC | .40 | .15 |
| ☐ 90 Gerald McNeil | .10 | .02 |
| ☐ 91 Brian Brennan | .10 | .02 |
| ☐ 92 Ozzie Newsome | .40 | .15 |
| ☐ 93 Cody Risien | .10 | .02 |
| ☐ 94 Bob Golic | .10 | .02 |
| ☐ 95 Carl Hairston | .10 | .02 |
| ☐ 96 Mike Johnson RC | .10 | .02 |
| ☐ 97 Clay Matthews | .20 | .07 |
| ☐ 98 Frank Minnifield | .10 | .02 |
| ☐ 99 Hanford Dixon | .10 | .02 |
| ☐ 100 Dave Puzzuoli | .10 | .02 |
| ☐ 101 Felix Wright RC | .10 | .02 |

|  |  | | |
|---|---|---|---|
| ❏ 102 | Oilers TL/Moon | .40 | .15 |
| ❏ 103 | Warren Moon | .50 | .20 |
| ❏ 104 | Mike Rozier | .10 | .02 |
| ❏ 105 | Alonzo Highsmith RC | .20 | .07 |
| ❏ 106 | Drew Hill | .20 | .07 |
| ❏ 107 | Ernest Givins | .40 | .15 |
| ❏ 108 | Curtis Duncan RC | .40 | .15 |
| ❏ 109 | Tony Zendejas RC | .10 | .02 |
| ❏ 110 | Mike Munchak | .40 | .15 |
| ❏ 111 | Kent Hill | .10 | .02 |
| ❏ 112 | Ray Childress | .20 | .07 |
| ❏ 113 | Al Smith RC | .20 | .07 |
| ❏ 114 | Keith Bostic RC | .10 | .02 |
| ❏ 115 | Jeff Donaldson | .10 | .02 |
| ❏ 116 | Colts TL/Dickerson | .40 | .15 |
| ❏ 117 | Jack Trudeau | .10 | .02 |
| ❏ 118 | Eric Dickerson | .40 | .15 |
| ❏ 119 | Albert Bentley | .10 | .02 |
| ❏ 120 | Matt Bouza | .10 | .02 |
| ❏ 121 | Bill Brooks | .40 | .15 |
| ❏ 122 | Dean Biasucci RC | .10 | .02 |
| ❏ 123 | Chris Hinton | .10 | .02 |
| ❏ 124 | Ray Donaldson | .10 | .02 |
| ❏ 125 | Ron Solt RC | .10 | .02 |
| ❏ 126 | Donnell Thompson | .10 | .02 |
| ❏ 127 | Barry Krauss RC | .10 | .02 |
| ❏ 128 | Duane Bickett | .10 | .02 |
| ❏ 129 | Mike Prior RC | .10 | .02 |
| ❏ 130 | Seahawks TL | .20 | .07 |
| ❏ 131 | Dave Krieg | .20 | .07 |
| ❏ 132 | Curt Warner | .20 | .07 |
| ❏ 133 | John L. Williams | .40 | .15 |
| ❏ 134 | Bobby Joe Edmonds | .10 | .02 |
| ❏ 135 | Steve Largent | .40 | .15 |
| ❏ 136 | Raymond Butler | .10 | .02 |
| ❏ 137 | Norm Johnson | .10 | .02 |
| ❏ 138 | Ruben Rodriguez | .10 | .02 |
| ❏ 139 | Blair Bush | .10 | .02 |
| ❏ 140 | Jacob Green | .10 | .02 |
| ❏ 141 | Joe Nash | .10 | .02 |
| ❏ 142 | Jeff Bryant | .10 | .02 |
| ❏ 143 | Fredd Young | .10 | .02 |
| ❏ 144 | Brian Bosworth RC | 1.50 | .60 |
| ❏ 145 | Kenny Easley | .10 | .02 |
| ❏ 146 | Vikings TL | .20 | .07 |
| ❏ 147 | Wade Wilson RC | .40 | .15 |
| ❏ 148 | Tommy Kramer | .10 | .02 |
| ❏ 149 | Darrin Nelson | .10 | .02 |
| ❏ 150 | D.J.Dozier RC | .20 | .07 |
| ❏ 151 | Anthony Carter | .20 | .07 |
| ❏ 152 | Leo Lewis | .10 | .02 |
| ❏ 153 | Steve Jordan | .20 | .07 |
| ❏ 154 | Gary Zimmerman | .30 | .14 |
| ❏ 155 | Chuck Nelson | .10 | .02 |
| ❏ 156 | Henry Thomas RC | .40 | .15 |
| ❏ 157 | Chris Doleman RC | .40 | .15 |
| ❏ 158 | Scott Studwell RC | .10 | .02 |
| ❏ 159 | Jesse Solomon RC | .10 | .02 |
| ❏ 160 | Joey Browner | .10 | .02 |
| ❏ 161 | Neal Guggemos | .10 | .02 |
| ❏ 162 | Steelers TL | .20 | .07 |
| ❏ 163 | Mark Malone | .10 | .02 |
| ❏ 164 | Walter Abercrombie | .10 | .02 |
| ❏ 165 | Earnest Jackson | .10 | .02 |
| ❏ 166 | Frank Pollard | .10 | .02 |
| ❏ 167 | Dwight Stone RC | .20 | .07 |
| ❏ 168 | Gary Anderson K | .10 | .02 |
| ❏ 169 | Harry Newsome RC | .10 | .02 |
| ❏ 170 | Keith Willis | .10 | .02 |
| ❏ 171 | Keith Gary | .10 | .02 |
| ❏ 172 | David Little RC | .20 | .07 |
| ❏ 173 | Mike Merriweather | .10 | .02 |
| ❏ 174 | Dwayne Woodruff | .10 | .02 |
| ❏ 175 | Patriots TL | .40 | .15 |
| ❏ 176 | Steve Grogan | .20 | .07 |
| ❏ 177 | Tony Eason | .20 | .07 |
| ❏ 178 | Tony Collins | .20 | .07 |
| ❏ 179 | Mosi Tatupu | .10 | .02 |
| ❏ 180 | Stanley Morgan | .20 | .07 |
| ❏ 181 | Irving Fryar | .40 | .15 |
| ❏ 182 | Stephen Starring | .10 | .02 |
| ❏ 183 | Tony Franklin | .10 | .02 |
| ❏ 184 | Rich Camarillo | .10 | .02 |
| ❏ 185 | Garin Veris | .10 | .02 |
| ❏ 186 | Andre Tippett | .20 | .07 |
| ❏ 187 | Ronnie Lippett | .10 | .02 |
| ❏ 188 | Fred Marion | .10 | .02 |
| ❏ 189 | Dolphins TL/D.Marino | .75 | .30 |
| ❏ 190 | Dan Marino | 2.00 | .75 |
| ❏ 191 | Troy Stradford RC | .20 | .07 |
| ❏ 192 | Lorenzo Hampton | .10 | .02 |
| ❏ 193 | Mark Duper | .20 | .07 |
| ❏ 194 | Mark Clayton | .20 | .07 |
| ❏ 195 | Reggie Roby | .20 | .07 |
| ❏ 196 | Dwight Stephenson | .40 | .15 |
| ❏ 197 | T.J. Turner RC | .10 | .02 |
| ❏ 198 | John Bosa RC | .10 | .02 |
| ❏ 199 | Jackie Shipp | .10 | .02 |
| ❏ 200 | John Offerdahl | .20 | .07 |
| ❏ 201 | Mark Brown | .10 | .02 |
| ❏ 202 | Paul Lankford | .10 | .02 |
| ❏ 203 | Chargers TL | .40 | .15 |
| ❏ 204 | Tim Spencer | .10 | .02 |
| ❏ 205 | Gary Anderson RB | .20 | .07 |
| ❏ 206 | Curtis Adams | .10 | .02 |
| ❏ 207 | Lionel James | .10 | .02 |
| ❏ 208 | Chip Banks | .10 | .02 |
| ❏ 209 | Kellen Winslow | .40 | .15 |
| ❏ 210 | Ralf Mojsiejenko | .10 | .02 |
| ❏ 211 | Jim Lachey | .20 | .07 |
| ❏ 212 | Lee Williams | .10 | .02 |
| ❏ 213 | Billy Ray Smith | .10 | .02 |
| ❏ 214 | Vencie Glenn RC | .20 | .07 |
| ❏ 215 | J.Montana/B.Kosar LL | .50 | .20 |
| ❏ 216 | Receiving Leaders | .20 | .07 |
| ❏ 217 | Eric Dickerson/C.White L | .20 | .07 |
| ❏ 218 | Jerry Rice/J.Breech LL | .40 | .15 |
| ❏ 219 | Interception Leaders | .10 | .02 |
| ❏ 220 | Bills TL/Jim Kelly | .40 | .15 |
| ❏ 221 | Jim Kelly | .75 | .30 |
| ❏ 222 | Ronnie Harmon RC | .10 | .02 |
| ❏ 223 | Robb Riddick | .10 | .02 |
| ❏ 224 | Andre Reed | .40 | .15 |
| ❏ 225 | Chris Burkett RC | .10 | .02 |
| ❏ 226 | Pete Metzelaars | .40 | .15 |
| ❏ 227 | Bruce Smith | .50 | .20 |
| ❏ 228 | Darryl Talley | .20 | .07 |
| ❏ 229 | Eugene Marve | .10 | .02 |
| ❏ 230 | Cornelius Bennett RC | .75 | .30 |
| ❏ 231 | Mark Kelso RC | .10 | .02 |
| ❏ 232 | Shane Conlan RC | .40 | .15 |
| ❏ 233 | Eagles TL/R.Cunningham | .40 | .15 |
| ❏ 234 | Randall Cunningham | 1.00 | .40 |
| ❏ 235 | Keith Byars | .40 | .15 |
| ❏ 236 | Anthony Toney RC | .10 | .02 |
| ❏ 237 | Mike Quick | .20 | .07 |
| ❏ 238 | Kenny Jackson | .10 | .02 |
| ❏ 239 | John Spagnola | .10 | .02 |
| ❏ 240 | Paul McFadden | .10 | .02 |
| ❏ 241 | Reggie White | .60 | .25 |
| ❏ 242 | Ken Clarke | .10 | .02 |
| ❏ 243 | Mike Pitts | .10 | .02 |
| ❏ 244 | Clyde Simmons RC | .40 | .15 |
| ❏ 245 | Seth Joyner RC | .40 | .15 |
| ❏ 246 | Andre Waters | .40 | .15 |
| ❏ 247 | Jerome Brown RC | .40 | .15 |
| ❏ 248 | Cardinals TL | .10 | .02 |
| ❏ 249 | Neil Lomax | .20 | .07 |
| ❏ 250 | Stump Mitchell | .10 | .02 |
| ❏ 251 | Earl Ferrell | .10 | .02 |
| ❏ 252 | Val Sikahema | .10 | .02 |
| ❏ 253 | J.T. Smith | .20 | .07 |
| ❏ 254 | Roy Green | .20 | .07 |
| ❏ 255 | Robert Awalt RC | .20 | .07 |
| ❏ 256 | Freddie Joe Nunn | .10 | .02 |
| ❏ 257 | Leonard Smith RC | .10 | .02 |
| ❏ 258 | Travis Curtis | .10 | .02 |
| ❏ 259 | Cowboys TL/H.Walker | .40 | .15 |
| ❏ 260 | Danny White | .40 | .15 |
| ❏ 261 | Herschel Walker | .40 | .15 |
| ❏ 262 | Tony Dorsett | .40 | .15 |
| ❏ 263 | Doug Cosbie | .10 | .02 |
| ❏ 264 | Roger Ruzek RC | .10 | .02 |
| ❏ 265 | Darryl Clack | .10 | .02 |
| ❏ 266 | Ed Too Tall Jones | .40 | .15 |
| ❏ 267 | Jim Jeffcoat | .10 | .02 |
| ❏ 268 | Everson Walls | .10 | .02 |
| ❏ 269 | Bill Bates | .20 | .07 |
| ❏ 270 | Michael Downs | .10 | .02 |
| ❏ 271 | Giants TL | .10 | .02 |
| ❏ 272 | Phil Simms | .40 | .15 |
| ❏ 273 | Joe Morris | .20 | .07 |
| ❏ 274 | Lee Rouson | .10 | .02 |
| ❏ 275 | George Adams | .10 | .02 |
| ❏ 276 | Lionel Manuel | .10 | .02 |
| ❏ 277 | Mark Bavaro | .20 | .07 |
| ❏ 278 | Raul Allegre | .10 | .02 |
| ❏ 279 | Sean Landeta | .10 | .02 |
| ❏ 280 | Erik Howard | .10 | .02 |
| ❏ 281 | Leonard Marshall | .20 | .07 |
| ❏ 282 | Carl Banks | .20 | .07 |
| ❏ 283 | Pepper Johnson | .20 | .07 |
| ❏ 284 | Harry Carson | .20 | .07 |
| ❏ 285 | Lawrence Taylor | .40 | .15 |
| ❏ 286 | Terry Kinard | .10 | .02 |
| ❏ 287 | Rams TL/Everett | .40 | .15 |
| ❏ 288 | Jim Everett | .40 | .15 |
| ❏ 289 | Charles White | .20 | .07 |
| ❏ 290 | Ron Brown | .20 | .07 |
| ❏ 291 | Henry Ellard | .40 | .15 |
| ❏ 292 | Mike Lansford | .10 | .02 |
| ❏ 293 | Dale Hatcher | .10 | .02 |
| ❏ 294 | Doug Smith | .10 | .02 |
| ❏ 295 | Jackie Slater | .20 | .07 |
| ❏ 296 | Jim Collins | .10 | .02 |
| ❏ 297 | Jerry Gray | .10 | .02 |
| ❏ 298 | LeRoy Irvin | .10 | .02 |
| ❏ 299 | Nolan Cromwell | .20 | .07 |
| ❏ 300 | Kevin Greene RC | 1.25 | .50 |
| ❏ 301 | Jets TL | .20 | .07 |
| ❏ 302 | Ken O'Brien | .20 | .07 |
| ❏ 303 | Freeman McNeil | .20 | .07 |
| ❏ 304 | Johnny Hector | .10 | .02 |
| ❏ 305 | Al Toon | .20 | .07 |
| ❏ 306 | JoJo Townsell RC | .10 | .02 |
| ❏ 307 | Mickey Shuler | .10 | .02 |
| ❏ 308 | Pat Leahy | .10 | .02 |
| ❏ 309 | Roger Vick | .10 | .02 |
| ❏ 310 | Alex Gordon RC | .10 | .02 |
| ❏ 311 | Troy Benson | .10 | .02 |
| ❏ 312 | Bob Crable | .10 | .02 |
| ❏ 313 | Harry Hamilton | .10 | .02 |
| ❏ 314 | Packers TL | .10 | .02 |
| ❏ 315 | Randy Wright | .10 | .02 |
| ❏ 316 | Kenneth Davis | .20 | .07 |
| ❏ 317 | Phillip Epps | .10 | .02 |
| ❏ 318 | Walter Stanley | .10 | .02 |
| ❏ 319 | Frankie Neal | .10 | .02 |
| ❏ 320 | Don Bracken | .10 | .02 |
| ❏ 321 | Brian Noble RC | .20 | .07 |
| ❏ 322 | Johnny Holland RC | .20 | .07 |
| ❏ 323 | Tim Harris | .20 | .07 |
| ❏ 324 | Mark Murphy | .10 | .02 |
| ❏ 325 | Raiders TL/B.Jackson | .50 | .20 |
| ❏ 326 | Marc Wilson | .10 | .02 |
| ❏ 327 | Bo Jackson RC | 5.00 | 2.00 |
| ❏ 328 | Marcus Allen | .40 | .15 |
| ❏ 329 | James Lofton | .40 | .15 |
| ❏ 330 | Todd Christensen | .20 | .07 |
| ❏ 331 | Chris Bahr | .10 | .02 |
| ❏ 332 | Stan Talley | .10 | .02 |
| ❏ 333 | Howie Long | .40 | .15 |
| ❏ 334 | Sean Jones | .40 | .15 |
| ❏ 335 | Matt Millen | .20 | .07 |
| ❏ 336 | Stacey Toran | .10 | .02 |
| ❏ 337 | Vann McElroy | .10 | .02 |
| ❏ 338 | Greg Townsend | .20 | .07 |
| ❏ 339 | Bengals TL/Esiason | .40 | .15 |
| ❏ 340 | Boomer Esiason | .40 | .15 |
| ❏ 341 | Larry Kinnebrew | .10 | .02 |
| ❏ 342 | Stanford Jennings RC | .10 | .02 |
| ❏ 343 | Eddie Brown | .20 | .07 |
| ❏ 344 | Jim Breech | .10 | .02 |
| ❏ 345 | Anthony Munoz | .40 | .15 |
| ❏ 346 | Scott Fulhage RC | .10 | .02 |
| ❏ 347 | Tim Krumrie RC | .10 | .02 |
| ❏ 348 | Reggie Williams | .20 | .07 |
| ❏ 349 | David Fulcher RC | .20 | .07 |
| ❏ 350 | Buccaneers TL | .10 | .02 |
| ❏ 351 | Frank Garcia | .10 | .02 |
| ❏ 352 | Vinny Testaverde RC | 4.00 | 1.50 |
| ❏ 353 | James Wilder | .10 | .02 |
| ❏ 354 | Jeff Smith RBK | .10 | .02 |
| ❏ 355 | Gerald Carter | .10 | .02 |
| ❏ 356 | Calvin Magee | .10 | .02 |
| ❏ 357 | Donald Igwebuike | .10 | .02 |
| ❏ 358 | Ron Holmes RC | .10 | .02 |
| ❏ 359 | Chris Washington | .10 | .02 |
| ❏ 360 | Ervin Randle | .10 | .02 |
| ❏ 361 | Chiefs TL | .10 | .02 |
| ❏ 362 | Bill Kenney | .10 | .02 |

|  | | |
|---|---|---|
| ❏ 363 Christian Okoye RC | .40 | .15 |
| ❏ 364 Paul Palmer | .10 | .02 |
| ❏ 365 Stephone Paige | .20 | .07 |
| ❏ 366 Carlos Carson | .10 | .02 |
| ❏ 367 Kelly Goodburn RC | .10 | .02 |
| ❏ 368 Bill Maas | .10 | .02 |
| ❏ 369 Mike Bell | .10 | .02 |
| ❏ 370 Dino Hackett RC | .10 | .02 |
| ❏ 371 Deron Cherry | .10 | .02 |
| ❏ 372 Lions TL | .10 | .02 |
| ❏ 373 Chuck Long | .20 | .07 |
| ❏ 374 Gary James | .10 | .02 |
| ❏ 375 James Jones FB | .10 | .02 |
| ❏ 376 Pete Mandley | .10 | .02 |
| ❏ 377 Gary Lee RC | .10 | .02 |
| ❏ 378 Eddie Murray | .10 | .02 |
| ❏ 379 Jim Arnold | .10 | .02 |
| ❏ 380 Dennis Gibson RC | .10 | .02 |
| ❏ 381 Michael Cofer LB | .10 | .02 |
| ❏ 382 James Griffin | .10 | .02 |
| ❏ 383 Falcons TL | .10 | .02 |
| ❏ 384 Scott Campbell | .10 | .02 |
| ❏ 385 Gerald Riggs | .20 | .07 |
| ❏ 386 Floyd Dixon RC | .10 | .02 |
| ❏ 387 Rick Donnelly | .10 | .02 |
| ❏ 388 Bill Fralic | .20 | .07 |
| ❏ 389 Major Everett | .10 | .02 |
| ❏ 390 Mike Gann | .10 | .02 |
| ❏ 391 Tony Casillas RC | .20 | .07 |
| ❏ 392 Rick Bryan | .10 | .02 |
| ❏ 393 John Rade RC | .10 | .02 |
| ❏ 394 Checklist 1-132 | .10 | .02 |
| ❏ 395 Checklist 133-264 | .10 | .02 |
| ❏ 396 Checklist 265-396 | .10 | .02 |

## 1989 Topps

JERRY RICE
TOPPS ALL PRO

|  | | |
|---|---|---|
| ❏ COMPLETE SET (396) | 20.00 | 7.50 |
| ❏ COMP.FACT.SET (396) | 25.00 | 10.00 |
| ❏ 1 Super Bowl XXIII/Montana | .50 | .20 |
| ❏ 2 Tim Brown RB | .50 | .20 |
| ❏ 3 Eric Dickerson RB | .25 | .08 |
| ❏ 4 Steve Largent RB | .25 | .08 |
| ❏ 5 Dan Marino RB | .75 | .30 |
| ❏ 6 49ers TL/Montana | .50 | .20 |
| ❏ 7 Jerry Rice | 1.50 | .60 |
| ❏ 8 Roger Craig | .25 | .08 |
| ❏ 9 Ronnie Lott | .10 | .02 |
| ❏ 10 Michael Carter | .10 | .02 |
| ❏ 11 Charles Haley | .25 | .08 |
| ❏ 12 Joe Montana | 2.00 | .75 |
| ❏ 13 John Taylor RC | .10 | .02 |
| ❏ 14 Michael Walter | .10 | .02 |
| ❏ 15 Mike Cofer K RC | .10 | .02 |
| ❏ 16 Tom Rathman | .10 | .02 |
| ❏ 17 Daniel Stubbs RC | .10 | .02 |
| ❏ 18 Keena Turner | .10 | .02 |
| ❏ 19 Tim McKyer | .10 | .02 |
| ❏ 20 Larry Roberts | .10 | .02 |
| ❏ 21 Jeff Fuller | .10 | .02 |
| ❏ 22 Bubba Paris | .10 | .02 |
| ❏ 23 Bengals Team UER | .10 | .02 |
| ❏ 24 Eddie Brown | .10 | .02 |
| ❏ 25 Boomer Esiason | .25 | .08 |
| ❏ 26 Tim Krumrie | .10 | .02 |
| ❏ 27 Ickey Woods RC | .10 | .02 |
| ❏ 28 Anthony Munoz | .10 | .02 |
| ❏ 29 Tim McGee | .10 | .02 |
| ❏ 30 Max Montoya | .10 | .02 |
| ❏ 31 David Grant | .10 | .02 |
| ❏ 32 Rodney Holman RC | .10 | .02 |
| ❏ 33 David Fulcher | .10 | .02 |
| ❏ 34 Jim Skow | .10 | .02 |
| ❏ 35 James Brooks | .10 | .02 |
| ❏ 36 Reggie Williams | .10 | .02 |
| ❏ 37 Eric Thomas RC | .10 | .02 |
| ❏ 38 Stanford Jennings | .10 | .02 |
| ❏ 39 Jim Breech | .10 | .02 |
| ❏ 40 Bills TL/Jim Kelly | .25 | .08 |
| ❏ 41 Shane Conlan | .10 | .02 |
| ❏ 42 Scott Norwood RC | .10 | .02 |
| ❏ 43 Cornelius Bennett | .10 | .02 |
| ❏ 44 Bruce Smith | .25 | .08 |
| ❏ 45 Thurman Thomas RC | 1.25 | .50 |
| ❏ 46 Jim Kelly | .50 | .20 |
| ❏ 47 John Kidd | .10 | .02 |
| ❏ 48 Kent Hull RC | .10 | .02 |
| ❏ 49 Art Still | .10 | .02 |
| ❏ 50 Fred Smerlas | .10 | .02 |
| ❏ 51A Derrick Burroughs | .10 | .02 |
| ❏ 51B Derrick Burroughs | .10 | .02 |
| ❏ 52 Andre Reed | .25 | .08 |
| ❏ 53 Robb Riddick | .10 | .02 |
| ❏ 54 Chris Burkett | .10 | .02 |
| ❏ 55 Ronnie Harmon | .10 | .02 |
| ❏ 56 Mark Kelso UER | .10 | .02 |
| ❏ 57 Bears Team | .10 | .02 |
| ❏ 58 Mike Singletary | .10 | .02 |
| ❏ 59 Jay Hilgenberg UER | .10 | .02 |
| ❏ 60 Richard Dent | .10 | .02 |
| ❏ 61 Ron Rivera RC | .10 | .02 |
| ❏ 62 Jim McMahon | .10 | .02 |
| ❏ 63 Mike Tomczak | .10 | .02 |
| ❏ 64 Neal Anderson | .10 | .02 |
| ❏ 65 Dennis Gentry | .10 | .02 |
| ❏ 66 Dan Hampton | .10 | .02 |
| ❏ 67 David Tate | .10 | .02 |
| ❏ 68 Thomas Sanders RC | .10 | .02 |
| ❏ 69 Steve McMichael | .10 | .02 |
| ❏ 70 Dennis McKinnon | .10 | .02 |
| ❏ 71 Brad Muster RC | .10 | .02 |
| ❏ 72 Vestee Jackson RC | .10 | .02 |
| ❏ 73 Dave Duerson | .10 | .02 |
| ❏ 74 Vikings Team | .10 | .02 |
| ❏ 75 Joey Browner | .10 | .02 |
| ❏ 76 Carl Lee RC | .10 | .02 |
| ❏ 77 Gary Zimmerman | .20 | .07 |
| ❏ 78 Hassan Jones RC | .10 | .02 |
| ❏ 79 Anthony Carter | .10 | .02 |
| ❏ 80 Ray Berry | .10 | .02 |
| ❏ 81 Steve Jordan | .10 | .02 |
| ❏ 82 Issiac Holt | .10 | .02 |
| ❏ 83 Wade Wilson | .10 | .02 |
| ❏ 84 Chris Doleman | .10 | .02 |
| ❏ 85 Alfred Anderson | .10 | .02 |
| ❏ 86 Keith Millard | .10 | .02 |
| ❏ 87 Darrin Nelson | .10 | .02 |
| ❏ 88 D.J. Dozier | .10 | .02 |
| ❏ 89 Scott Studwell | .10 | .02 |
| ❏ 90 Oilers Team | .10 | .02 |
| ❏ 91 Bruce Matthews RC | .75 | .30 |
| ❏ 92 Curtis Duncan | .10 | .02 |
| ❏ 93 Warren Moon | .25 | .08 |
| ❏ 94 Johnny Meads RC | .10 | .02 |
| ❏ 95 Drew Hill | .10 | .02 |
| ❏ 96 Alonzo Highsmith | .10 | .02 |
| ❏ 97 Mike Munchak | .10 | .02 |
| ❏ 98 Mike Rozier | .10 | .02 |
| ❏ 99 Tony Zendejas | .10 | .02 |
| ❏ 100 Jeff Donaldson | .10 | .02 |
| ❏ 101 Ray Childress | .10 | .02 |
| ❏ 102 Sean Jones | .10 | .02 |
| ❏ 103 Ernest Givins | .10 | .02 |
| ❏ 104 William Fuller RC | .25 | .08 |
| ❏ 105 Allen Pinkett RC | .10 | .02 |
| ❏ 106 Eagles TL/R.Cunningham | .10 | .02 |
| ❏ 107 Keith Jackson RC | .25 | .08 |
| ❏ 108 Reggie White | .25 | .08 |
| ❏ 109 Clyde Simmons | .10 | .02 |
| ❏ 110 John Teltschik | .10 | .02 |
| ❏ 111 Wes Hopkins | .10 | .02 |
| ❏ 112 Keith Byars | .10 | .02 |
| ❏ 113 Jerome Brown | .10 | .02 |
| ❏ 114 Mike Quick | .10 | .02 |
| ❏ 115 Randall Cunningham | .40 | .15 |
| ❏ 116 Anthony Toney | .10 | .02 |
| ❏ 117 Ron Johnson WR | .10 | .02 |
| ❏ 118 Terry Hoage | .10 | .02 |
| ❏ 119 Seth Joyner | .10 | .02 |
| ❏ 120 Eric Allen RC | .25 | .08 |
| ❏ 121 Cris Carter RC | 1.50 | .60 |
| ❏ 122 Rams Team | .10 | .02 |
| ❏ 123 Tom Newberry RC | .10 | .02 |
| ❏ 124 Pete Holohan | .10 | .02 |
| ❏ 125 Robert Delpino RC UER | .10 | .02 |
| ❏ 126 Carl Ekern | .10 | .02 |
| ❏ 127 Greg Bell | .10 | .02 |
| ❏ 128 Mike Lansford | .10 | .02 |
| ❏ 129 Jim Everett | .10 | .02 |
| ❏ 130 Mike Wilcher | .10 | .02 |
| ❏ 131 Jerry Gray | .10 | .02 |
| ❏ 132 Dale Hatcher | .10 | .02 |
| ❏ 133 Doug Smith | .10 | .02 |
| ❏ 134 Kevin Greene | .25 | .08 |
| ❏ 135 Jackie Slater | .10 | .02 |
| ❏ 136 Aaron Cox RC | .10 | .02 |
| ❏ 137 Henry Ellard | .25 | .08 |
| ❏ 138 Browns Team | .10 | .02 |
| ❏ 139 Frank Minnifield | .10 | .02 |
| ❏ 140 Webster Slaughter | .10 | .02 |
| ❏ 141 Bernie Kosar | .10 | .02 |
| ❏ 142 Charles Buchanan | .10 | .02 |
| ❏ 143 Clay Matthews | .10 | .02 |
| ❏ 144 Reggie Langhorne RC | .10 | .02 |
| ❏ 145 Hanford Dixon | .10 | .02 |
| ❏ 146 Brian Brennan | .10 | .02 |
| ❏ 147 Earnest Byner | .10 | .02 |
| ❏ 148 Michael Dean Perry RC | .10 | .02 |
| ❏ 149 Kevin Mack | .10 | .02 |
| ❏ 150 Matt Bahr | .10 | .02 |
| ❏ 151 Ozzie Newsome | .10 | .02 |
| ❏ 152 Saints Team | .10 | .02 |
| ❏ 153 Morten Andersen | .10 | .02 |
| ❏ 154 Pat Swilling | .10 | .02 |
| ❏ 155 Sam Mills | .10 | .02 |
| ❏ 156 Lonzell Hill | .10 | .02 |
| ❏ 157 Dalton Hilliard | .10 | .02 |
| ❏ 158 Craig Heyward RC | .10 | .02 |
| ❏ 159 Vaughan Johnson RC | .10 | .02 |
| ❏ 160 Rueben Mayes | .10 | .02 |
| ❏ 161 Gene Atkins RC | .10 | .02 |
| ❏ 162 Bobby Hebert | .10 | .02 |
| ❏ 163 Rickey Jackson | .10 | .02 |
| ❏ 164 Eric Martin | .10 | .02 |
| ❏ 165 Giants Team | .10 | .02 |
| ❏ 166 Lawrence Taylor | .25 | .08 |
| ❏ 167 Bart Oates | .10 | .02 |
| ❏ 168 Carl Banks | .10 | .02 |
| ❏ 169 Eric Moore RC | .10 | .02 |
| ❏ 170 Sheldon White RC | .10 | .02 |
| ❏ 171 Mark Collins RC | .10 | .02 |
| ❏ 172 Phil Simms | .10 | .02 |
| ❏ 173 Jim Burt | .10 | .02 |
| ❏ 174 Stephen Baker RC | .10 | .02 |
| ❏ 175 Mark Bavaro | .10 | .02 |
| ❏ 176 Pepper Johnson | .10 | .02 |
| ❏ 177 Lionel Manuel | .10 | .02 |
| ❏ 178 Joe Morris | .10 | .02 |
| ❏ 179 Jumbo Elliott RC | .10 | .02 |
| ❏ 180 Gary Reasons RC | .10 | .02 |
| ❏ 181 Seahawks Team | .10 | .02 |
| ❏ 182 Brian Blades RC | .25 | .08 |
| ❏ 183 Steve Largent | .25 | .08 |
| ❏ 184 Rufus Porter RC | .10 | .02 |
| ❏ 185 Ruben Rodriguez | .10 | .02 |
| ❏ 186 Curt Warner | .10 | .02 |
| ❏ 187 Paul Moyer | .10 | .02 |
| ❏ 188 Dave Krieg | .10 | .02 |
| ❏ 189 Jacob Green | .10 | .02 |
| ❏ 190 John L.Williams | .10 | .02 |
| ❏ 191 Eugene Robinson RC | .10 | .02 |
| ❏ 192 Brian Bosworth | .10 | .02 |
| ❏ 193 Patriots Team | .10 | .02 |
| ❏ 194 John Stephens RC | .10 | .02 |
| ❏ 195 Robert Perryman RC | .10 | .02 |
| ❏ 196 Andre Tippett | .10 | .02 |
| ❏ 197 Fred Marion | .10 | .02 |
| ❏ 198 Doug Flutie | 1.00 | .40 |
| ❏ 199 Stanley Morgan | .10 | .02 |
| ❏ 200 Johnny Rembert RC | .10 | .02 |
| ❏ 201 Tony Eason | .10 | .02 |
| ❏ 202 Marvin Allen | .10 | .02 |
| ❏ 203 Raymond Clayborn | .10 | .02 |
| ❏ 204 Irving Fryar | .25 | .08 |

| | | |
|---|---|---|
| ❑ 205 Colts Team | .10 | .02 |
| ❑ 206 Eric Dickerson | .10 | .02 |
| ❑ 207 Chris Hinton | .10 | .02 |
| ❑ 208 Duane Bickett | .10 | .02 |
| ❑ 209 Chris Chandler RC | 1.00 | .40 |
| ❑ 210 Jon Hand | .10 | .02 |
| ❑ 211 Ray Donaldson | .10 | .02 |
| ❑ 212 Dean Biasucci | .10 | .02 |
| ❑ 213 Bill Brooks | .10 | .02 |
| ❑ 214 Chris Goode RC | .10 | .02 |
| ❑ 215 Clarence Verdin RC | .10 | .02 |
| ❑ 216 Albert Bentley | .10 | .02 |
| ❑ 217 Passing Leaders | .10 | .02 |
| ❑ 218 Receiving Leaders | .10 | .02 |
| ❑ 219 Eric Dickerson/Walker LL | .10 | .02 |
| ❑ 220 Scoring Leaders | .10 | .02 |
| ❑ 221 Interception Leaders | .10 | .02 |
| ❑ 222 Jets Team | .10 | .02 |
| ❑ 223 Erik McMillan RC | .10 | .02 |
| ❑ 224 James Hasty RC | .10 | .02 |
| ❑ 225 Al Toon | .10 | .02 |
| ❑ 226 John Booty RC | .10 | .02 |
| ❑ 227 Johnny Hector | .10 | .02 |
| ❑ 228 Ken O'Brien | .10 | .02 |
| ❑ 229 Marty Lyons | .10 | .02 |
| ❑ 230 Mickey Shuler | .10 | .02 |
| ❑ 231 Robin Cole | .10 | .02 |
| ❑ 232 Freeman McNeil | .10 | .02 |
| ❑ 233 Marion Barber RC | .20 | .07 |
| ❑ 234 Jo Jo Townsell | .10 | .02 |
| ❑ 235 Wesley Walker | .10 | .02 |
| ❑ 236 Roger Vick | .10 | .02 |
| ❑ 237 Pat Leahy | .10 | .02 |
| ❑ 238 Broncos TL/Elway | .50 | .20 |
| ❑ 239 Mike Horan | .10 | .02 |
| ❑ 240 Tony Dorsett | .25 | .08 |
| ❑ 241 John Elway | 2.00 | .75 |
| ❑ 242 Mark Jackson | .10 | .02 |
| ❑ 243 Sammy Winder | .10 | .02 |
| ❑ 244 Rich Karlis | .10 | .02 |
| ❑ 245 Vance Johnson | .10 | .02 |
| ❑ 246 Steve Sewell RC | .10 | .02 |
| ❑ 247 Karl Mecklenburg UER | .10 | .02 |
| ❑ 248 Rulon Jones | .10 | .02 |
| ❑ 249 Simon Fletcher RC | .10 | .02 |
| ❑ 250 Redskins Team | .10 | .02 |
| ❑ 251 Chip Lohmiller RC | .10 | .02 |
| ❑ 252 Jamie Morris | .10 | .02 |
| ❑ 253 Mark Rypien RC UER | .10 | .02 |
| ❑ 254 Barry Wilburn | .10 | .02 |
| ❑ 255 Mark May RC | .10 | .02 |
| ❑ 256 Wilber Marshall | .10 | .02 |
| ❑ 257 Charles Mann | .10 | .02 |
| ❑ 258 Gary Clark | .25 | .08 |
| ❑ 259 Doug Williams | .10 | .02 |
| ❑ 260 Art Monk | .10 | .02 |
| ❑ 261 Kelvin Bryant | .10 | .02 |
| ❑ 262 Dexter Manley | .10 | .02 |
| ❑ 263 Ricky Sanders | .10 | .02 |
| ❑ 264 Raiders Team | .25 | .08 |
| ❑ 265 Tim Brown RC | 1.50 | .60 |
| ❑ 266 Jay Schroeder | .10 | .02 |
| ❑ 267 Marcus Allen | .25 | .08 |
| ❑ 268 Mike Haynes | .10 | .02 |
| ❑ 269 Bo Jackson | .30 | .10 |
| ❑ 270 Steve Beuerlein RC | .60 | .25 |
| ❑ 271 Vann McElroy | .10 | .02 |
| ❑ 272 Willie Gault | .10 | .02 |
| ❑ 273 Howie Long | .25 | .08 |
| ❑ 274 Greg Townsend | .10 | .02 |
| ❑ 275 Mike Wise DE | .10 | .02 |
| ❑ 276 Cardinals Team | .10 | .02 |
| ❑ 277 Luis Sharpe | .10 | .02 |
| ❑ 278 Scott Dill | .10 | .02 |
| ❑ 279 Vai Sikahema | .10 | .02 |
| ❑ 280 Ron Wolfley | .10 | .02 |
| ❑ 281 David Galloway | .10 | .02 |
| ❑ 282 Jay Novacek RC | .25 | .08 |
| ❑ 283 Neil Lomax | .10 | .02 |
| ❑ 284 Robert Awalt | .10 | .02 |
| ❑ 285 Cedric Mack | .10 | .02 |
| ❑ 286 Freddie Joe Nunn | .10 | .02 |
| ❑ 287 J.T. Smith | .10 | .02 |
| ❑ 288 Stump Mitchell | .10 | .02 |
| ❑ 289 Roy Green | .10 | .02 |
| ❑ 290 Dolphins TL/Marino | .50 | .20 |
| ❑ 291 Jarvis Williams RC | .10 | .02 |

| | | |
|---|---|---|
| ❑ 292 Troy Stradford | .10 | .02 |
| ❑ 293 Dan Marino | 2.00 | .75 |
| ❑ 294 T.J. Turner | .10 | .02 |
| ❑ 295 John Offerdahl | .10 | .02 |
| ❑ 296 Ferrell Edmunds RC | .10 | .02 |
| ❑ 297 Scott Schwedes | .10 | .02 |
| ❑ 298 Lorenzo Hampton | .10 | .02 |
| ❑ 299 Jim C.Jensen RC | .10 | .02 |
| ❑ 300 Brian Sochia | .10 | .02 |
| ❑ 301 Reggie Roby | .10 | .02 |
| ❑ 302 Mark Clayton | .10 | .02 |
| ❑ 303 Chargers Team | .10 | .02 |
| ❑ 304 Lee Williams | .10 | .02 |
| ❑ 305 Gary Plummer RC | .10 | .02 |
| ❑ 306 Gary Anderson RB | .10 | .02 |
| ❑ 307 Gill Byrd | .10 | .02 |
| ❑ 308 Jamie Holland RC | .10 | .02 |
| ❑ 309 Billy Ray Smith | .10 | .02 |
| ❑ 310 Lionel James | .10 | .02 |
| ❑ 311 Mark Vlasic RC | .10 | .02 |
| ❑ 312 Curtis Adams | .10 | .02 |
| ❑ 313 Anthony Miller RC | .25 | .08 |
| ❑ 314 Steelers Team | .10 | .02 |
| ❑ 315 Bubby Brister RC | .25 | .08 |
| ❑ 316 David Little | .10 | .02 |
| ❑ 317 Tunch Ilkin RC | .10 | .02 |
| ❑ 318 Louis Lipps | .10 | .02 |
| ❑ 319 Warren Williams RC | .10 | .02 |
| ❑ 320 Dwight Stone | .10 | .02 |
| ❑ 321 Merril Hoge RC | .10 | .02 |
| ❑ 322 Thomas Everett RC | .10 | .02 |
| ❑ 323 Rod Woodson RC | 1.00 | .40 |
| ❑ 324 Gary Anderson K | .10 | .02 |
| ❑ 325 Buccaneers Team | .10 | .02 |
| ❑ 326 Donnie Elder | .10 | .02 |
| ❑ 327 Vinny Testaverde | .30 | .10 |
| ❑ 328 Harry Hamilton | .10 | .02 |
| ❑ 329 James Wilder | .10 | .02 |
| ❑ 330 Lars Tate | .10 | .02 |
| ❑ 331 Mark Carrier RC WR | .25 | .08 |
| ❑ 332 Bruce Hill RC | .10 | .02 |
| ❑ 333 Paul Gruber RC | .10 | .02 |
| ❑ 334 Ricky Reynolds | .10 | .02 |
| ❑ 335 Eugene Marve | .10 | .02 |
| ❑ 336 Falcons Team | .10 | .02 |
| ❑ 337 Aundray Bruce RC | .10 | .02 |
| ❑ 338 John Rade | .10 | .02 |
| ❑ 339 Scott Case RC | .10 | .02 |
| ❑ 340 Robert Moore | .10 | .02 |
| ❑ 341 Chris Miller RC | .25 | .08 |
| ❑ 342 Gerald Riggs | .10 | .02 |
| ❑ 343 Gene Lang | .10 | .02 |
| ❑ 344 Marcus Cotton | .10 | .02 |
| ❑ 345 Rick Donnelly | .10 | .02 |
| ❑ 346 John Settle RC | .10 | .02 |
| ❑ 347 Bill Fralic | .10 | .02 |
| ❑ 348 Chiefs Team | .10 | .02 |
| ❑ 349 Steve DeBerg | .10 | .02 |
| ❑ 350 Mike Stensrud | .10 | .02 |
| ❑ 351 Dino Hackett | .10 | .02 |
| ❑ 352 Deron Cherry | .10 | .02 |
| ❑ 353 Christian Okoye | .10 | .02 |
| ❑ 354 Bill Maas | .10 | .02 |
| ❑ 355 Carlos Carson | .10 | .02 |
| ❑ 356 Albert Lewis | .10 | .02 |
| ❑ 357 Paul Palmer | .10 | .02 |
| ❑ 358 Nick Lowery | .10 | .02 |
| ❑ 359 Stephone Paige | .10 | .02 |
| ❑ 360 Lions Team | .10 | .02 |
| ❑ 361 Chris Spielman RC | .25 | .08 |
| ❑ 362 Jim Arnold | .10 | .02 |
| ❑ 363 Devon Mitchell | .10 | .02 |
| ❑ 364 Mike Cofer | .10 | .02 |
| ❑ 365 Bennie Blades RC | .10 | .02 |
| ❑ 366 James Jones FB | .10 | .02 |
| ❑ 367 Garry James | .10 | .02 |
| ❑ 368 Pete Mandley | .10 | .02 |
| ❑ 369 Keith Ferguson | .10 | .02 |
| ❑ 370 Dennis Gibson | .10 | .02 |
| ❑ 371 Packers Team UER | .10 | .02 |
| ❑ 372 Brent Fullwood RC | .10 | .02 |
| ❑ 373 Don Majkowski RC | .10 | .02 |
| ❑ 374 Tim Harris | .10 | .02 |
| ❑ 375 Keith Woodside RC | .10 | .02 |
| ❑ 376 Mark Murphy | .10 | .02 |
| ❑ 377 Dave Brown DB | .10 | .02 |
| ❑ 378 Perry Kemp RC | .10 | .02 |

| | | |
|---|---|---|
| ❑ 379 Sterling Sharpe RC | .75 | .30 |
| ❑ 380 Chuck Cecil RC | .10 | .02 |
| ❑ 381 Walter Stanley | .10 | .02 |
| ❑ 382 Cowboys Team | .10 | .02 |
| ❑ 383 Michael Irvin RC | 1.50 | .60 |
| ❑ 384 Bill Bates | .10 | .02 |
| ❑ 385 Herschel Walker | .25 | .08 |
| ❑ 386 Darryl Clack | .10 | .02 |
| ❑ 387 Danny Noonan | .10 | .02 |
| ❑ 388 Eugene Lockhart RC | .10 | .02 |
| ❑ 389 Ed Too Tall Jones | .10 | .02 |
| ❑ 390 Steve Pelluer | .10 | .02 |
| ❑ 391 Ray Alexander | .10 | .02 |
| ❑ 392 Nate Newton RC | .10 | .02 |
| ❑ 393 Garry Cobb | .10 | .02 |
| ❑ 394 Checklist 1-132 | .10 | .02 |
| ❑ 395 Checklist 133-264 | .10 | .02 |
| ❑ 396 Checklist 265-396 | .10 | .02 |

## 1989 Topps Traded

| | | |
|---|---|---|
| ❑ COMP.FACT.SET (132) | 15.00 | 6.00 |
| ❑ 1T Eric Ball RC | .15 | .05 |
| ❑ 2T Tony Mandarich RC | .15 | .05 |
| ❑ 3T Shawn Collins RC | .15 | .05 |
| ❑ 4T Ray Bentley RC | .10 | .02 |
| ❑ 5T Tony Casillas | .15 | .05 |
| ❑ 6T Al Del Greco RC | .15 | .05 |
| ❑ 7T Dan Saleaumua RC | .15 | .05 |
| ❑ 8T Keith Bishop | .10 | .02 |
| ❑ 9T Rodney Peete RC | .50 | .20 |
| ❑ 10T Lorenzo White RC | .25 | .08 |
| ❑ 11T Steve Smith RC | .10 | .02 |
| ❑ 12T Pete Mandley | .10 | .02 |
| ❑ 13T Mervyn Fernandez RC | .10 | .02 |
| ❑ 14T Flipper Anderson RC | .25 | .08 |
| ❑ 15T Louis Oliver RC | .15 | .05 |
| ❑ 16T Rick Fenney | .10 | .02 |
| ❑ 17T Gary Jeter | .10 | .02 |
| ❑ 18T Greg Cox | .10 | .02 |
| ❑ 19T Bubba McDowell RC | .10 | .02 |
| ❑ 20T Ron Heller | .10 | .02 |
| ❑ 21T Tim McDonald RC | .15 | .05 |
| ❑ 22T Jerrol Williams RC | .10 | .02 |
| ❑ 23T Marion Butts RC | .25 | .08 |
| ❑ 24T Steve Young | .75 | .30 |
| ❑ 25T Mike Merriweather | .15 | .05 |
| ❑ 26T Richard Johnson | .10 | .02 |
| ❑ 27T Gerald Riggs | .15 | .05 |
| ❑ 28T Dave Waymer | .10 | .02 |
| ❑ 29T Issiac Holt | .10 | .02 |
| ❑ 30T Deion Sanders RC | 1.50 | .60 |
| ❑ 31T Todd Blackledge | .15 | .05 |
| ❑ 32T Jeff Cross RC | .15 | .05 |
| ❑ 33T Steve Wisniewski RC | .25 | .08 |
| ❑ 34T Ron Brown | .10 | .02 |
| ❑ 35T Rod Bernstine RC | .15 | .05 |
| ❑ 36T Jeff Uhlenhake RC | .10 | .02 |
| ❑ 37T Donnell Woolford RC | .25 | .08 |
| ❑ 38T Bob Gagliano RC | .10 | .02 |
| ❑ 39T Ezra Johnson | .10 | .02 |
| ❑ 40T Ron Jaworski | .25 | .08 |
| ❑ 41T Lawyer Tillman RC | .15 | .05 |
| ❑ 42T Lorenzo Lynch RC | .10 | .02 |
| ❑ 43T Mike Alexander | .10 | .02 |
| ❑ 44T Tim Worley RC | .15 | .05 |
| ❑ 45T Guy Bingham | .10 | .02 |
| ❑ 46T Cleveland Gary RC | .15 | .05 |
| ❑ 47T Danny Peebles | .10 | .02 |
| ❑ 48T Clarence Weathers RC | .25 | .08 |

**1990 Topps**

| | | |
|---|---|---|
| ❑ 49T Jeff Lageman RC | .25 | .08 |
| ❑ 50T Eric Metcalf RC | .25 | .08 |
| ❑ 51T Myron Guyton RC | .15 | .05 |
| ❑ 52T Steve Atwater RC | .25 | .08 |
| ❑ 53T John Fourcade RC | .15 | .05 |
| ❑ 54T Randall McDaniel RC | 1.50 | .60 |
| ❑ 55T Al Noga RC | .10 | .02 |
| ❑ 56T Sammie Smith RC | .15 | .05 |
| ❑ 57T Jesse Solomon RC | .10 | .02 |
| ❑ 58T Greg Kragen RC | .10 | .02 |
| ❑ 59T Don Beebe RC | .25 | .08 |
| ❑ 60T Hart Lee Dykes RC | .10 | .02 |
| ❑ 61T Trace Armstrong RC | .15 | .05 |
| ❑ 62T Steve Pelluer RC | .10 | .02 |
| ❑ 63T Barry Krauss RC | .10 | .02 |
| ❑ 64T Kevin Murphy RC | .10 | .02 |
| ❑ 65T Steve Tasker RC | .25 | .08 |
| ❑ 66T Jessie Small RC | .15 | .05 |
| ❑ 67T Dave Meggett RC | .25 | .08 |
| ❑ 68T Dean Hamel | .10 | .02 |
| ❑ 69T Jim Covert | .15 | .05 |
| ❑ 70T Troy Aikman RC | 5.00 | 2.00 |
| ❑ 71T Raul Allegre | .10 | .02 |
| ❑ 72T Chris Jacke RC | .10 | .02 |
| ❑ 73T Leslie O'Neal | .15 | .05 |
| ❑ 74T Keith Taylor RC | .10 | .02 |
| ❑ 75T Steve Walsh RC | .25 | .08 |
| ❑ 76T Tracy Rocker | .10 | .02 |
| ❑ 77T Robert Massey RC | .10 | .02 |
| ❑ 78T Bryan Wagner | .10 | .02 |
| ❑ 79T Steve DeOssie | .15 | .05 |
| ❑ 80T Carnell Lake RC | .25 | .08 |
| ❑ 81T Frank Reich RC | .25 | .08 |
| ❑ 82T Tyrone Braxton | .15 | .05 |
| ❑ 83T Barry Sanders RC | 6.00 | 2.50 |
| ❑ 84T Pete Stoyanovich | .15 | .05 |
| ❑ 85T Paul Palmer | .10 | .02 |
| ❑ 86T Billy Joe Tolliver RC | .15 | .05 |
| ❑ 87T Eric Hill RC | .10 | .02 |
| ❑ 88T Gerald McNeil | .10 | .02 |
| ❑ 89T Bill Hawkins RC | .10 | .02 |
| ❑ 90T Derrick Thomas RC | 1.25 | .50 |
| ❑ 91T Jim Harbaugh RC | .75 | .30 |
| ❑ 92T Brian Williams OL RC | .10 | .02 |
| ❑ 93T Jack Trudeau | .10 | .02 |
| ❑ 94T Leonard Smith | .10 | .02 |
| ❑ 95T Gary Hogeboom | .10 | .02 |
| ❑ 96T A.J. Johnson RC | .10 | .02 |
| ❑ 97T Jim McMahon | .15 | .05 |
| ❑ 98T David Williams RC | .10 | .02 |
| ❑ 99T Rohn Stark | .10 | .02 |
| ❑ 100T Sean Landeta | .15 | .05 |
| ❑ 101T Tim Johnson RC | .15 | .05 |
| ❑ 102T Andre Rison RC | .75 | .30 |
| ❑ 103T Earnest Byner | .15 | .05 |
| ❑ 104T Don McPherson RC | .10 | .02 |
| ❑ 105T Zefross Moss RC | .10 | .02 |
| ❑ 106T Frank Stams RC | .10 | .02 |
| ❑ 107T Courtney Hall RC | .10 | .02 |
| ❑ 108T Marc Logan RC | .10 | .02 |
| ❑ 109T James Lofton | .25 | .08 |
| ❑ 110T Lewis Tillman RC | .15 | .05 |
| ❑ 111T Irv Pankey RC | .10 | .02 |
| ❑ 112T Ralf Mojsiejenko | .10 | .02 |
| ❑ 113T Bobby Humphrey RC | .10 | .02 |
| ❑ 114T Chris Burkett | .10 | .02 |
| ❑ 115T Greg Lloyd RC | .25 | .08 |
| ❑ 116T Matt Millen | .15 | .05 |
| ❑ 117T Carl Zander | .10 | .02 |
| ❑ 118T Wayne Martin RC | .25 | .08 |
| ❑ 119T Mike Saxon | .10 | .02 |
| ❑ 120T Herschel Walker | .25 | .08 |
| ❑ 121T Andy Heck RC | .10 | .02 |
| ❑ 122T Mark Robinson | .10 | .02 |
| ❑ 123T Keith Van Horne RC | .10 | .02 |
| ❑ 124T Ricky Hunley | .10 | .02 |
| ❑ 125T Timm Rosenbach RC | .15 | .05 |
| ❑ 126T Steve Grogan | .25 | .08 |
| ❑ 127T Stephen Braggs RC | .10 | .02 |
| ❑ 128T Terry Long | .10 | .02 |
| ❑ 129T Evan Cooper | .10 | .02 |
| ❑ 130T Robert Lyles | .10 | .02 |
| ❑ 131T Mike Webster | .25 | .08 |
| ❑ 132T Checklist 1-132 | .10 | .02 |

| | | |
|---|---|---|
| ❑ COMPLETE SET (528) | 25.00 | 10.00 |
| ❑ COMP.FACT.SET (528) | 30.00 | 13.50 |
| ❑ 1 Joe Montana RB | .50 | .20 |
| ❑ 2 Flipper Anderson RB | .05 | .01 |
| ❑ 3 Troy Aikman RB | .40 | .15 |
| ❑ 4 Kevin Butler RB | .05 | .01 |
| ❑ 5 Super Bowl XXIV | .05 | .01 |
| ❑ 6 Dexter Carter RC | .05 | .01 |
| ❑ 7 Matt Millen | .10 | .02 |
| ❑ 8 Jerry Rice | .75 | .30 |
| ❑ 9 Ronnie Lott | .10 | .02 |
| ❑ 10 John Taylor | .10 | .02 |
| ❑ 11 Guy McIntyre | .05 | .01 |
| ❑ 12 Roger Craig | .10 | .02 |
| ❑ 13 Joe Montana | 1.25 | .50 |
| ❑ 14 Brent Jones RC | .25 | .08 |
| ❑ 15 Tom Rathman | .05 | .01 |
| ❑ 16 Harris Barton | .05 | .01 |
| ❑ 17 Charles Haley | .10 | .02 |
| ❑ 18 Pierce Holt RC | .05 | .01 |
| ❑ 19 Michael Carter | .05 | .01 |
| ❑ 20 Chet Brooks | .05 | .01 |
| ❑ 21 Eric Wright | .05 | .01 |
| ❑ 22 Mike Cofer | .05 | .01 |
| ❑ 23 Jim Fahnhorst | .05 | .01 |
| ❑ 24 Keena Turner | .05 | .01 |
| ❑ 25 Don Griffin | .05 | .01 |
| ❑ 26 Kevin Fagan RC | .05 | .01 |
| ❑ 27 Bubba Paris | .05 | .01 |
| ❑ 28 Barry Sanders/C.Okoye LL | .50 | .20 |
| ❑ 29 Steve Atwater | .05 | .01 |
| ❑ 30 Tyrone Braxton | .05 | .01 |
| ❑ 31 Ron Holmes | .05 | .01 |
| ❑ 32 Bobby Humphrey | .05 | .01 |
| ❑ 33 Greg Kragen | .05 | .01 |
| ❑ 34 David Treadwell | .05 | .01 |
| ❑ 35 Karl Mecklenburg | .05 | .01 |
| ❑ 36 Dennis Smith | .05 | .01 |
| ❑ 37 John Elway | 1.25 | .50 |
| ❑ 38 Vance Johnson | .05 | .01 |
| ❑ 39 Simon Fletcher UER | .05 | .01 |
| ❑ 40 Jim Junga | .05 | .01 |
| ❑ 41 Mark Jackson | .05 | .01 |
| ❑ 42 Melvin Bratton RC | .05 | .01 |
| ❑ 43 Wymon Henderson RC | .05 | .01 |
| ❑ 44 Ken Bell | .05 | .01 |
| ❑ 45 Sammy Winder | .05 | .01 |
| ❑ 46 Alphonso Carreker | .05 | .01 |
| ❑ 47 Orson Mobley RC | .05 | .01 |
| ❑ 48 Rodney Hampton RC | .25 | .08 |
| ❑ 49 Dave Meggett | .10 | .02 |
| ❑ 50 Myron Guyton | .05 | .01 |
| ❑ 51 Phil Simms | .10 | .02 |
| ❑ 52 Lawrence Taylor | .25 | .08 |
| ❑ 53 Carl Banks | .05 | .01 |
| ❑ 54 Pepper Johnson | .05 | .01 |
| ❑ 55 Leonard Marshall | .05 | .01 |
| ❑ 56 Mark Collins | .05 | .01 |
| ❑ 57 Erik Howard | .05 | .01 |
| ❑ 58 Eric Dorsey RC | .05 | .01 |
| ❑ 59 Ottis Anderson | .10 | .02 |
| ❑ 60 Mark Bavaro | .05 | .01 |
| ❑ 61 Odessa Turner RC | .05 | .01 |
| ❑ 62 Gary Reasons | .05 | .01 |
| ❑ 63 Mauricio Carthon | .05 | .01 |
| ❑ 64 Lionel Manuel | .05 | .01 |
| ❑ 65 Sean Landeta | .05 | .01 |
| ❑ 66 Perry Williams | .05 | .01 |

| | | |
|---|---|---|
| ❑ 67 Pat Terrell RC | .05 | .01 |
| ❑ 68 Flipper Anderson | .05 | .01 |
| ❑ 69 Jackie Slater | .05 | .01 |
| ❑ 70 Tom Newberry | .05 | .01 |
| ❑ 71 Jerry Gray | .05 | .01 |
| ❑ 72 Henry Ellard | .10 | .02 |
| ❑ 73 Doug Smith | .05 | .01 |
| ❑ 74 Kevin Greene | .10 | .02 |
| ❑ 75 Jim Everett | .10 | .02 |
| ❑ 76 Mike Lansford | .05 | .01 |
| ❑ 77 Greg Bell | .05 | .01 |
| ❑ 78 Pete Holohan | .05 | .01 |
| ❑ 79 Robert Delpino | .05 | .01 |
| ❑ 80 Mike Wilcher | .05 | .01 |
| ❑ 81 Mike Piel | .05 | .01 |
| ❑ 82 Mel Owens | .05 | .01 |
| ❑ 83 Michael Stewart RC | .05 | .01 |
| ❑ 84 Ben Smith RC | .05 | .01 |
| ❑ 85 Keith Jackson | .10 | .02 |
| ❑ 86 Reggie White | .25 | .08 |
| ❑ 87 Eric Allen | .05 | .01 |
| ❑ 88 Jerome Brown | .05 | .01 |
| ❑ 89 Robert Drummond | .05 | .01 |
| ❑ 90 Anthony Toney | .05 | .01 |
| ❑ 91 Keith Byars | .05 | .01 |
| ❑ 92 Cris Carter | .50 | .20 |
| ❑ 93 Randall Cunningham | .25 | .08 |
| ❑ 94 Ron Johnson WR | .05 | .01 |
| ❑ 95 Mike Quick | .05 | .01 |
| ❑ 96 Clyde Simmons | .05 | .01 |
| ❑ 97 Mike Pitts | .05 | .01 |
| ❑ 98 Izel Jenkins RC | .05 | .01 |
| ❑ 99 Seth Joyner | .10 | .02 |
| ❑ 100 Mike Schad | .05 | .01 |
| ❑ 101 Wes Hopkins | .05 | .01 |
| ❑ 102 Kirk Lowdermilk | .05 | .01 |
| ❑ 103 Rick Fenney | .05 | .01 |
| ❑ 104 Randall McDaniel | .15 | .05 |
| ❑ 105 Herschel Walker | .10 | .02 |
| ❑ 106 Al Noga | .05 | .01 |
| ❑ 107 Gary Zimmerman | .10 | .02 |
| ❑ 108 Chris Doleman | .05 | .01 |
| ❑ 109 Keith Millard | .05 | .01 |
| ❑ 110 Carl Lee | .05 | .01 |
| ❑ 111 Joey Browner | .05 | .01 |
| ❑ 112 Steve Jordan | .05 | .01 |
| ❑ 113 Reggie Rutland RC | .05 | .01 |
| ❑ 114 Wade Wilson | .10 | .02 |
| ❑ 115 Anthony Carter | .10 | .02 |
| ❑ 116 Rich Karlis | .05 | .01 |
| ❑ 117 Hassan Jones | .05 | .01 |
| ❑ 118 Henry Thomas | .05 | .01 |
| ❑ 119 Scott Studwell | .05 | .01 |
| ❑ 120 Ralf Mojsiejenko | .05 | .01 |
| ❑ 121 Earnest Byner | .10 | .02 |
| ❑ 122 Gerald Riggs | .10 | .02 |
| ❑ 123 Tracy Rocker | .05 | .01 |
| ❑ 124 A.J. Johnson | .05 | .01 |
| ❑ 125 Charles Mann | .05 | .01 |
| ❑ 126 Art Monk | .10 | .02 |
| ❑ 127 Ricky Sanders | .05 | .01 |
| ❑ 128 Gary Clark | .25 | .08 |
| ❑ 129 Jim Lachey | .05 | .01 |
| ❑ 130 Martin Mayhew RC | .05 | .01 |
| ❑ 131 Ravin Caldwell | .05 | .01 |
| ❑ 132 Don Warren | .05 | .01 |
| ❑ 133 Mark Rypien | .10 | .02 |
| ❑ 134 Ed Simmons RC | .05 | .01 |
| ❑ 135 Darryl Grant | .05 | .01 |
| ❑ 136 Darrell Green | .10 | .02 |
| ❑ 137 Chip Lohmiller | .05 | .01 |
| ❑ 138 Tony Bennett RC | .25 | .08 |
| ❑ 139 Tony Mandarich | .05 | .01 |
| ❑ 140 Sterling Sharpe | .25 | .08 |
| ❑ 141 Tim Harris | .05 | .01 |
| ❑ 142 Don Majkowski | .05 | .01 |
| ❑ 143 Rich Moran RC | .05 | .01 |
| ❑ 144 Jeff Query | .05 | .01 |
| ❑ 145 Brent Fullwood | .05 | .01 |
| ❑ 146 Chris Jacke | .05 | .01 |
| ❑ 147 Keith Woodside | .05 | .01 |
| ❑ 148 Perry Kemp | .05 | .01 |
| ❑ 149 Herman Fontenot | .05 | .01 |
| ❑ 150 Dave Brown DB | .05 | .01 |
| ❑ 151 Brian Noble | .05 | .01 |
| ❑ 152 Johnny Holland | .05 | .01 |
| ❑ 153 Mark Murphy | .05 | .01 |

|  |  | | |
|---|---|---|---|
| ❏ 154 | Bob Nelson NT | .05 | .01 |
| ❏ 155 | Darrell Thompson RC | .05 | .01 |
| ❏ 156 | Lawyer Tillman | .05 | .01 |
| ❏ 157 | Eric Metcalf | .25 | .08 |
| ❏ 158 | Webster Slaughter | .10 | .02 |
| ❏ 159 | Frank Minnifield | .05 | .01 |
| ❏ 160 | Brian Brennan | .05 | .01 |
| ❏ 161 | Thane Gash RC | .05 | .01 |
| ❏ 162 | Robert Banks DE | .05 | .01 |
| ❏ 163 | Bernie Kosar | .10 | .02 |
| ❏ 164 | David Grayson | .05 | .01 |
| ❏ 165 | Kevin Mack | .05 | .01 |
| ❏ 166 | Mike Johnson | .05 | .01 |
| ❏ 167 | Tim Manoa | .05 | .01 |
| ❏ 168 | Ozzie Newsome | .10 | .02 |
| ❏ 169 | Felix Wright | .05 | .01 |
| ❏ 170A | Al Baker Omg. | .10 | .02 |
| ❏ 170B | Al Baker Wht. | .10 | .02 |
| ❏ 171 | Reggie Langhorne | .10 | .02 |
| ❏ 172 | Clay Matthews | .10 | .02 |
| ❏ 173 | Andrew Stewart | .05 | .01 |
| ❏ 174 | Barry Foster RC | .25 | .08 |
| ❏ 175 | Tim Worley | .05 | .01 |
| ❏ 176 | Tim Johnson | .05 | .01 |
| ❏ 177 | Cantell Lake | .05 | .01 |
| ❏ 178 | Greg Lloyd | .25 | .08 |
| ❏ 179 | Rod Woodson | .25 | .08 |
| ❏ 180 | Tunch Ilkin | .05 | .01 |
| ❏ 181 | Dermontti Dawson | .10 | .02 |
| ❏ 182 | Gary Anderson K | .05 | .01 |
| ❏ 183 | Bubby Brister | .05 | .01 |
| ❏ 184 | Louis Lipps | .10 | .02 |
| ❏ 185 | Merril Hoge | .05 | .01 |
| ❏ 186 | Mike Mularkey | .05 | .01 |
| ❏ 187 | Derek Hill | .05 | .01 |
| ❏ 188 | Rodney Carter | .05 | .01 |
| ❏ 189 | Dwayne Woodruff | .05 | .01 |
| ❏ 190 | Keith Willis | .05 | .01 |
| ❏ 191 | Jerry Olsavsky | .05 | .01 |
| ❏ 192 | Mark Stock | .05 | .01 |
| ❏ 193 | Sacks Leaders | .05 | .01 |
| ❏ 194 | Leonard Smith | .05 | .01 |
| ❏ 195 | Darryl Talley | .05 | .01 |
| ❏ 196 | Mark Kelso | .05 | .01 |
| ❏ 197 | Kent Hull | .05 | .01 |
| ❏ 198 | Nate Odomes RC | .10 | .02 |
| ❏ 199 | Pete Metzelaars | .05 | .01 |
| ❏ 200 | Don Beebe | .10 | .02 |
| ❏ 201 | Ray Bentley | .05 | .01 |
| ❏ 202 | Steve Tasker | .10 | .02 |
| ❏ 203 | Scott Norwood | .05 | .01 |
| ❏ 204 | Andre Reed | .25 | .08 |
| ❏ 205 | Bruce Smith | .25 | .08 |
| ❏ 206 | Thurman Thomas | .25 | .08 |
| ❏ 207 | Jim Kelly | .25 | .08 |
| ❏ 208 | Cornelius Bennett | .10 | .02 |
| ❏ 209 | Shane Conlan | .05 | .01 |
| ❏ 210 | Larry Kinnebrew | .05 | .01 |
| ❏ 211 | Jeff Alm RC | .05 | .01 |
| ❏ 212 | Robert Lyles | .05 | .01 |
| ❏ 213 | Bubba McDowell | .05 | .01 |
| ❏ 214 | Mike Munchak | .10 | .02 |
| ❏ 215 | Bruce Matthews | .10 | .02 |
| ❏ 216 | Warren Moon | .25 | .08 |
| ❏ 217 | Drew Hill | .05 | .01 |
| ❏ 218 | Ray Childress | .05 | .01 |
| ❏ 219 | Steve Brown | .05 | .01 |
| ❏ 220 | Alonzo Highsmith | .05 | .01 |
| ❏ 221 | Allen Pinkett | .05 | .01 |
| ❏ 222 | Sean Jones | .10 | .02 |
| ❏ 223 | Johnny Meads | .05 | .01 |
| ❏ 224 | John Grimsley | .05 | .01 |
| ❏ 225 | Haywood Jeffires RC | .25 | .08 |
| ❏ 226 | Curtis Duncan | .05 | .01 |
| ❏ 227 | Greg Montgomery RC | .05 | .01 |
| ❏ 228 | Ernest Givins | .10 | .02 |
| ❏ 229 | Joe Montana/B.Esiason LL | .30 | .10 |
| ❏ 230 | Robert Massey | .05 | .01 |
| ❏ 231 | John Fourcade | .05 | .01 |
| ❏ 232 | Dalton Hilliard | .05 | .01 |
| ❏ 233 | Vaughan Johnson | .05 | .01 |
| ❏ 234 | Hoby Brenner | .05 | .01 |
| ❏ 235 | Pat Swilling | .10 | .02 |
| ❏ 236 | Kevin Haverdink | .05 | .01 |
| ❏ 237 | Bobby Hebert | .05 | .01 |
| ❏ 238 | Sam Mills | .10 | .02 |
| ❏ 239 | Eric Martin | .05 | .01 |
| ❏ 240 | Lonzell Hill | .05 | .01 |
| ❏ 241 | Steve Trapilo | .05 | .01 |
| ❏ 242 | Rickey Jackson | .10 | .02 |
| ❏ 243 | Craig Heyward | .10 | .02 |
| ❏ 244 | Rueben Mayes | .05 | .01 |
| ❏ 245 | Morten Andersen | .05 | .01 |
| ❏ 246 | Percy Snow RC | .05 | .01 |
| ❏ 247 | Pete Mandley | .05 | .01 |
| ❏ 248 | Derrick Thomas | .25 | .08 |
| ❏ 249 | Dan Saleaumua | .05 | .01 |
| ❏ 250 | Todd McNair RC | .05 | .01 |
| ❏ 251 | Leonard Griffin | .05 | .01 |
| ❏ 252 | Jonathan Hayes | .05 | .01 |
| ❏ 253 | Christian Okoye | .05 | .01 |
| ❏ 254 | Albert Lewis | .05 | .01 |
| ❏ 255 | Nick Lowery | .05 | .01 |
| ❏ 256 | Kevin Ross | .05 | .01 |
| ❏ 257 | Steve DeBerg UER | .05 | .01 |
| ❏ 258 | Stephone Paige | .05 | .01 |
| ❏ 259 | James Saxon RC | .05 | .01 |
| ❏ 260 | Herman Heard | .05 | .01 |
| ❏ 261 | Deron Cherry | .05 | .01 |
| ❏ 262 | Dino Hackett | .05 | .01 |
| ❏ 263 | Neil Smith | .25 | .08 |
| ❏ 264 | Steve Pelluer | .05 | .01 |
| ❏ 265 | Eric Thomas | .05 | .01 |
| ❏ 266 | Eric Ball | .05 | .01 |
| ❏ 267 | Leon White | .05 | .01 |
| ❏ 268 | Tim Krumrie | .05 | .01 |
| ❏ 269 | Jason Buck | .05 | .01 |
| ❏ 270 | Boomer Esiason | .10 | .02 |
| ❏ 271 | Carl Zander | .05 | .01 |
| ❏ 272 | Eddie Brown | .05 | .01 |
| ❏ 273 | David Fulcher | .05 | .01 |
| ❏ 274 | Tim McGee | .05 | .01 |
| ❏ 275 | James Brooks | .10 | .02 |
| ❏ 276 | Rickey Dixon RC | .05 | .01 |
| ❏ 277 | Ickey Woods | .05 | .01 |
| ❏ 278 | Anthony Munoz | .10 | .02 |
| ❏ 279 | Rodney Holman | .05 | .01 |
| ❏ 280 | Mike Alexander | .05 | .01 |
| ❏ 281 | Mervyn Fernandez | .05 | .01 |
| ❏ 282 | Steve Wisniewski | .10 | .02 |
| ❏ 283 | Steve Smith | .05 | .01 |
| ❏ 284 | Howie Long | .25 | .08 |
| ❏ 285 | Bo Jackson | .30 | .10 |
| ❏ 286 | Mike Dyal | .05 | .01 |
| ❏ 287 | Thomas Benson | .05 | .01 |
| ❏ 288 | Willie Gault | .10 | .02 |
| ❏ 289 | Marcus Allen | .25 | .08 |
| ❏ 290 | Greg Townsend | .10 | .02 |
| ❏ 291 | Steve Beuerlein | .10 | .02 |
| ❏ 292 | Scott Davis | .05 | .01 |
| ❏ 293 | Eddie Anderson RC | .05 | .01 |
| ❏ 294 | Terry McDaniel | .05 | .01 |
| ❏ 295 | Tim Brown | .25 | .08 |
| ❏ 296 | Bob Golic | .05 | .01 |
| ❏ 297 | Jeff Jaeger RC | .05 | .01 |
| ❏ 298 | Jeff George RC | .50 | .20 |
| ❏ 299 | Chip Banks | .05 | .01 |
| ❏ 300 | Andre Rison UER | .25 | .08 |
| ❏ 301 | Rohn Stark | .05 | .01 |
| ❏ 302 | Keith Taylor | .05 | .01 |
| ❏ 303 | Jack Trudeau | .05 | .01 |
| ❏ 304 | Chris Hinton | .05 | .01 |
| ❏ 305 | Ray Donaldson | .05 | .01 |
| ❏ 306 | Jeff Herrod RC | .05 | .01 |
| ❏ 307 | Clarence Verdin | .05 | .01 |
| ❏ 308 | Jon Hand | .05 | .01 |
| ❏ 309 | Bill Brooks | .05 | .01 |
| ❏ 310 | Albert Bentley | .05 | .01 |
| ❏ 311 | Mike Prior | .05 | .01 |
| ❏ 312 | Pat Beach | .05 | .01 |
| ❏ 313 | Eugene Daniel | .05 | .01 |
| ❏ 314 | Duane Bickett | .05 | .01 |
| ❏ 315 | Dean Biasucci | .05 | .01 |
| ❏ 316 | Richmond Webb RC | .05 | .01 |
| ❏ 317 | Jeff Cross | .05 | .01 |
| ❏ 318 | Louis Oliver | .05 | .01 |
| ❏ 319 | Sammie Smith | .05 | .01 |
| ❏ 320 | Pete Stoyanovich | .05 | .01 |
| ❏ 321 | John Offerdahl | .05 | .01 |
| ❏ 322 | Ferrell Edmunds | .05 | .01 |
| ❏ 323 | Dan Marino | 1.25 | .50 |
| ❏ 324 | Andre Brown | .05 | .01 |
| ❏ 325 | Reggie Roby | .05 | .01 |
| ❏ 326 | Jarvis Williams | .05 | .01 |
| ❏ 327 | Roy Foster | .05 | .01 |
| ❏ 328 | Mark Clayton | .10 | .02 |
| ❏ 329 | Brian Sochia | .05 | .01 |
| ❏ 330 | Mark Duper | .10 | .02 |
| ❏ 331 | T.J. Turner | .05 | .01 |
| ❏ 332 | Jeff Uhlenhake | .05 | .01 |
| ❏ 333 | Jim C.Jensen | .05 | .01 |
| ❏ 334 | Cortez Kennedy RC | .25 | .08 |
| ❏ 335 | Andy Heck | .05 | .01 |
| ❏ 336 | Rufus Porter | .05 | .01 |
| ❏ 337 | Brian Blades | .10 | .02 |
| ❏ 338 | Dave Krieg | .10 | .02 |
| ❏ 339 | John L. Williams | .05 | .01 |
| ❏ 340 | David Wyman | .05 | .01 |
| ❏ 341 | Paul Skansi RC | .05 | .01 |
| ❏ 342 | Eugene Robinson | .05 | .01 |
| ❏ 343 | Joe Nash | .05 | .01 |
| ❏ 344 | Jacob Green | .05 | .01 |
| ❏ 345 | Jeff Bryant | .05 | .01 |
| ❏ 346 | Ruben Rodriguez | .05 | .01 |
| ❏ 347 | Norm Johnson | .05 | .01 |
| ❏ 348 | Darren Comeaux | .05 | .01 |
| ❏ 349 | Andre Ware RC | .10 | .02 |
| ❏ 350 | Richard Johnson | .05 | .01 |
| ❏ 351 | Rodney Peete | .10 | .02 |
| ❏ 352 | Barry Sanders | 1.25 | .50 |
| ❏ 353 | Chris Spielman | .25 | .08 |
| ❏ 354 | Eddie Murray | .05 | .01 |
| ❏ 355 | Jerry Ball | .05 | .01 |
| ❏ 356 | Mel Gray | .10 | .02 |
| ❏ 357 | Eric Williams RC | .05 | .01 |
| ❏ 358 | Robert Clark RC | .05 | .01 |
| ❏ 359 | Jason Phillips | .05 | .01 |
| ❏ 360 | Terry Taylor RC | .05 | .01 |
| ❏ 361 | Bennie Blades | .05 | .01 |
| ❏ 362 | Michael Cofer | .05 | .01 |
| ❏ 363 | Jim Arnold | .05 | .01 |
| ❏ 364 | Marc Spindler RC | .05 | .01 |
| ❏ 365 | Jim Covert | .05 | .01 |
| ❏ 366 | Jim Harbaugh | .25 | .08 |
| ❏ 367 | Neal Anderson | .10 | .02 |
| ❏ 368 | Mike Singletary | .10 | .02 |
| ❏ 369 | John Roper | .05 | .01 |
| ❏ 370 | Steve McMichael | .10 | .02 |
| ❏ 371 | Dennis Gentry | .05 | .01 |
| ❏ 372 | Brad Muster | .05 | .01 |
| ❏ 373 | Ron Morris | .05 | .01 |
| ❏ 374 | James Thornton | .05 | .01 |
| ❏ 375 | Kevin Butler | .05 | .01 |
| ❏ 376 | Richard Dent | .10 | .02 |
| ❏ 377 | Dan Hampton | .10 | .02 |
| ❏ 378 | Jay Hilgenberg | .05 | .01 |
| ❏ 379 | Donnell Woolford | .05 | .01 |
| ❏ 380 | Trace Armstrong | .05 | .01 |
| ❏ 381 | Junior Seau RC | 1.25 | .50 |
| ❏ 382 | Rod Bernstine | .05 | .01 |
| ❏ 383 | Marion Butts | .10 | .02 |
| ❏ 384 | Burt Grossman | .05 | .01 |
| ❏ 385 | Darrin Nelson | .05 | .01 |
| ❏ 386 | Leslie O'Neal | .10 | .02 |
| ❏ 387 | Billy Joe Tolliver | .05 | .01 |
| ❏ 388 | Courtney Hall | .05 | .01 |
| ❏ 389 | Lee Williams | .05 | .01 |
| ❏ 390 | Anthony Miller | .25 | .08 |
| ❏ 391 | Gill Byrd | .05 | .01 |
| ❏ 392 | Wayne Walker WR | .05 | .01 |
| ❏ 393 | Billy Ray Smith | .05 | .01 |
| ❏ 394 | Vencie Glenn | .05 | .01 |
| ❏ 395 | Tim Spencer | .05 | .01 |
| ❏ 396 | Gary Plummer | .05 | .01 |
| ❏ 397 | Arthur Cox | .05 | .01 |
| ❏ 398 | Jamie Holland | .05 | .01 |
| ❏ 399 | Keith McCants RC | .05 | .01 |
| ❏ 400 | Kevin Murphy | .05 | .01 |
| ❏ 401 | Danny Peebles | .05 | .01 |
| ❏ 402 | Mark Robinson | .05 | .01 |
| ❏ 403 | Broderick Thomas | .05 | .01 |
| ❏ 404 | Ron Hall | .05 | .01 |
| ❏ 405 | Mark Carrier WR | .25 | .08 |
| ❏ 406 | Paul Gruber | .05 | .01 |
| ❏ 407 | Vinny Testaverde | .10 | .02 |
| ❏ 408 | Bruce Hill | .05 | .01 |
| ❏ 409 | Lars Tate | .05 | .01 |
| ❏ 410 | Harry Hamilton | .05 | .01 |
| ❏ 411 | Ricky Reynolds | .05 | .01 |
| ❏ 412 | Donald Igwebuike | .05 | .01 |
| ❏ 413 | Reuben Davis | .05 | .01 |

|  |  | | |
|---|------|------|------|
| 414 | William Howard | .05 | .01 |
| 415 | Winston Moss RC | .05 | .01 |
| 416 | Chris Singleton RC | .05 | .01 |
| 417 | Hart Lee Dykes | .05 | .01 |
| 418 | Steve Grogan | .10 | .02 |
| 419 | Bruce Armstrong | .05 | .01 |
| 420 | Robert Perryman | .05 | .01 |
| 421 | Andre Tippett | .05 | .01 |
| 422 | Sammy Martin | .05 | .01 |
| 423 | Stanley Morgan | .05 | .01 |
| 424 | Cedric Jones | .05 | .01 |
| 425 | Sean Farrell | .05 | .01 |
| 426 | Marc Wilson | .05 | .01 |
| 427 | John Stephens | .05 | .01 |
| 428 | Eric Sievers RC | .05 | .01 |
| 429 | Maurice Hurst RC | .05 | .01 |
| 430 | Johnny Rembert | .05 | .01 |
| 431 | Jerry Rice/Andre Reed LL | .30 | .10 |
| 432 | Eric Hill | .05 | .01 |
| 433 | Gary Hogeboom | .05 | .01 |
| 434 | Timm Rosenbach UER | .05 | .01 |
| 435 | Tim McDonald | .05 | .01 |
| 436 | Rich Camarillo | .05 | .01 |
| 437 | Luis Sharpe | .05 | .01 |
| 438 | J.T. Smith | .05 | .01 |
| 439 | Roy Green | .10 | .02 |
| 440 | Ernie Jones RC | .05 | .01 |
| 441 | Robert Awalt | .05 | .01 |
| 442 | Vai Sikahema | .05 | .01 |
| 443 | Joe Wolf | .05 | .01 |
| 444 | Stump Mitchell | .05 | .01 |
| 445 | David Galloway | .05 | .01 |
| 446 | Ron Wolfley | .05 | .01 |
| 447 | Freddie Joe Nunn | .05 | .01 |
| 448 | Blair Thomas RC | .10 | .02 |
| 449 | Jeff Lageman | .05 | .01 |
| 450 | Tony Eason | .05 | .01 |
| 451 | Erik McMillan | .05 | .01 |
| 452 | Jim Sweeney | .05 | .01 |
| 453 | Ken O'Brien | .05 | .01 |
| 454 | Johnny Hector | .05 | .01 |
| 455 | Jo Jo Townsell | .05 | .01 |
| 456 | Roger Vick | .05 | .01 |
| 457 | James Hasty | .05 | .01 |
| 458 | Dennis Byrd RC | .10 | .02 |
| 459 | Ron Stallworth | .05 | .01 |
| 460 | Mickey Shuler | .05 | .01 |
| 461 | Bobby Humphery | .05 | .01 |
| 462 | Kyle Clifton | .05 | .01 |
| 463 | Al Toon | .10 | .02 |
| 464 | Freeman McNeil | .05 | .01 |
| 465 | Pat Leahy | .05 | .01 |
| 466 | Scott Case | .05 | .01 |
| 467 | Shawn Collins | .05 | .01 |
| 468 | Floyd Dixon | .05 | .01 |
| 469 | Deion Sanders | .50 | .20 |
| 470 | Tony Casillas | .05 | .01 |
| 471 | Michael Haynes RC | .25 | .08 |
| 472 | Chris Miller | .25 | .08 |
| 473 | John Settle | .05 | .01 |
| 474 | Aundray Bruce | .05 | .01 |
| 475 | Gene Lang | .05 | .01 |
| 476 | Tim Gordon RC | .05 | .01 |
| 477 | Scott Fulhage | .05 | .01 |
| 478 | Bill Fralic | .05 | .01 |
| 479 | Jessie Tuggle RC | .05 | .01 |
| 480 | Marcus Cotton | .05 | .01 |
| 481 | Steve Walsh | .10 | .02 |
| 482 | Troy Aikman | .75 | .30 |
| 483 | Ray Horton | .05 | .01 |
| 484 | Tony Tolbert RC | .10 | .02 |
| 485 | Steve Folsom | .05 | .01 |
| 486 | Ken Norton Jr. RC | .25 | .08 |
| 487 | Kelvin Martin RC | .05 | .01 |
| 488 | Jack Del Rio | .10 | .02 |
| 489 | Daryl Johnston RC | 1.00 | .40 |
| 490 | Bill Bates | .10 | .02 |
| 491 | Jim Jeffcoat | .05 | .01 |
| 492 | Vince Albritton | .05 | .01 |
| 493 | Eugene Lockhart | .05 | .01 |
| 494 | Mike Saxon | .05 | .01 |
| 495 | James Dixon | .05 | .01 |
| 496 | Willie Broughton | .05 | .01 |
| 497 | Checklist 1-132 | .05 | .01 |
| 498 | Checklist 133-264 | .05 | .01 |
| 499 | Checklist 265-396 | .05 | .01 |
| 500 | Checklist 397-528 | .05 | .01 |
| 501 | Bears Team | .10 | .02 |
| 502 | Bengals Team | .05 | .01 |
| 503 | Bills Team | .05 | .01 |
| 504 | Broncos Team | .05 | .01 |
| 505 | Browns Team | .05 | .01 |
| 506 | Buccaneers Team | .05 | .01 |
| 507 | Cardinals Team | .05 | .01 |
| 508 | Chargers Team | .05 | .01 |
| 509 | Chiefs Team | .05 | .01 |
| 510 | Colts Team | .05 | .01 |
| 511 | Cowboys TL/Aikman | .30 | .10 |
| 512 | Dolphins Team | .05 | .01 |
| 513 | Eagles Team | .05 | .01 |
| 514 | Falcons Team | .05 | .01 |
| 515 | 49ers TL/Montana/Craig | .30 | .10 |
| 516 | Giants Team | .05 | .01 |
| 517 | Jets Team | .05 | .01 |
| 518 | Lions Team | .05 | .01 |
| 519 | Oilers TL/Moon | .10 | .02 |
| 520 | Packers Team | .05 | .01 |
| 521 | Patriots Team | .05 | .01 |
| 522 | Raiders TL/Bo Jackson | .10 | .02 |
| 523 | Rams Team | .05 | .01 |
| 524 | Redskins Team | .05 | .01 |
| 525 | Saints Team | .05 | .01 |
| 526 | Seahawks Team | .05 | .01 |
| 527 | Steelers Team | .05 | .01 |
| 528 | Vikings Team | .05 | .01 |

## 1990 Topps Traded

|  |  | | |
|---|------|------|------|
| | COMP.FACT.SET (132) | 15.00 | 6.00 |
| 1T | Gerald McNeil | .05 | .01 |
| 2T | Andre Rison | .25 | .08 |
| 3T | Steve Walsh | .05 | .01 |
| 4T | Lorenzo White | .10 | .02 |
| 5T | Max Montoya | .05 | .01 |
| 6T | William Roberts RC | .05 | .01 |
| 7T | Alonzo Highsmith | .05 | .01 |
| 8T | Chris Hinton | .05 | .01 |
| 9T | Stanley Morgan | .10 | .02 |
| 10T | Mickey Shuler | .05 | .01 |
| 11T | Bobby Humphrey | .05 | .01 |
| 12T | Gary Anderson RB | .05 | .01 |
| 13T | Mike Tomczak | .05 | .01 |
| 14T | Anthony Pleasant RC | .10 | .02 |
| 15T | Walter Stanley | .05 | .01 |
| 16T | Greg Bell | .05 | .01 |
| 17T | Tony Martin RC | .75 | .30 |
| 18T | Terry Kinard | .05 | .01 |
| 19T | Cris Carter | .50 | .20 |
| 20T | James Wilder | .05 | .01 |
| 21T | Jerry Kauric | .05 | .01 |
| 22T | Irving Fryar | .25 | .08 |
| 23T | Ken Harvey RC | .25 | .08 |
| 24T | James Williams DB RC | .05 | .01 |
| 25T | Ron Cox RC | .05 | .01 |
| 26T | Andre Ware | .25 | .08 |
| 27T | Emmitt Smith RC | 12.00 | 5.00 |
| 28T | Junior Seau | .75 | .30 |
| 29T | Mark Carrier RC DB | .25 | .08 |
| 30T | Rodney Hampton | .25 | .08 |
| 31T | Rob Moore RC | .50 | .20 |
| 32T | Bern Brostek RC | .05 | .01 |
| 33T | Dexter Carter | .10 | .02 |
| 34T | Blair Thomas | .10 | .02 |
| 35T | Harold Green RC | .25 | .08 |
| 36T | Darrell Thompson | .05 | .01 |
| 37T | Eric Green RC | .25 | .08 |
| 38T | Renaldo Turnbull RC | .05 | .01 |
| 39T | Leroy Hoard RC | .25 | .08 |
| 40T | Anthony Thompson | .10 | .02 |
| 41T | Jeff George | .25 | .08 |
| 42T | Alexander Wright RC | .05 | .01 |
| 43T | Richmond Webb | .05 | .01 |
| 44T | Cortez Kennedy RC | .25 | .08 |
| 45T | Ray Agnew RC | .05 | .01 |
| 46T | Percy Snow | .05 | .01 |
| 47T | Chris Singleton | .05 | .01 |
| 48T | James Francis RC | .10 | .02 |
| 49T | Tony Bennett | .10 | .02 |
| 50T | Reggie Cobb RC | .10 | .02 |
| 51T | Barry Foster | .25 | .08 |
| 52T | Ben Smith | .05 | .01 |
| 53T | Anthony Smith RC | .25 | .08 |
| 54T | Steve Christie RC | .05 | .01 |
| 55T | Johnny Bailey RC | .10 | .02 |
| 56T | Alan Grant RC | .05 | .01 |
| 57T | Eric Floyd RC | .05 | .01 |
| 58T | Robert Blackmon RC | .05 | .01 |
| 59T | Brent Williams | .05 | .01 |
| 60T | Raymond Clayborn | .05 | .01 |
| 61T | Dave Duerson | .05 | .01 |
| 62T | Derrick Fenner RC | .10 | .02 |
| 63T | Ken Willis | .05 | .01 |
| 64T | Brad Baxter RC | .10 | .02 |
| 65T | Tony Paige | .05 | .01 |
| 66T | Jay Schroeder | .05 | .01 |
| 67T | Jim Breech | .05 | .01 |
| 68T | Barry Word RC | .10 | .02 |
| 69T | Anthony Dilweg FTC | .05 | .01 |
| 70T | Rich Gannon RC | 2.00 | .75 |
| 71T | Stan Humphries RC | .25 | .08 |
| 72T | Jay Novacek | .25 | .08 |
| 73T | Tommy Kane RC | .05 | .01 |
| 74T | Everson Walls | .05 | .01 |
| 75T | Mike Rozier | .10 | .02 |
| 76T | Robb Thomas | .05 | .01 |
| 77T | Terance Mathis RC | .75 | .30 |
| 78T | LeRoy Irvin | .05 | .01 |
| 79T | Jeff Donaldson | .05 | .01 |
| 80T | Ethan Horton RC | .10 | .02 |
| 81T | J.B. Brown RC | .05 | .01 |
| 82T | Joe Kelly | .05 | .01 |
| 83T | John Carney RC | .05 | .01 |
| 84T | Dan Stryzinski RC | .05 | .01 |
| 85T | John Kidd | .05 | .01 |
| 86T | Al Smith | .10 | .02 |
| 87T | Travis McNeal | .05 | .01 |
| 88T | Reyna Thompson RC | .05 | .01 |
| 89T | Rick Donnelly | .05 | .01 |
| 90T | Marv Cook RC | .10 | .02 |
| 91T | Mike Farr RC | .05 | .01 |
| 92T | Daniel Stubbs | .05 | .01 |
| 93T | Jeff Campbell RC | .05 | .01 |
| 94T | Tim McKyer | .05 | .01 |
| 95T | Ian Beckles RC | .05 | .01 |
| 96T | Lemuel Stinson | .05 | .01 |
| 97T | Frank Cornish | .05 | .01 |
| 98T | Riki Ellison | .05 | .01 |
| 99T | Jamie Mueller RC | .05 | .01 |
| 100T | Brian Hansen | .05 | .01 |
| 101T | Warren Powers RC | .05 | .01 |
| 102T | Howard Cross RC | .05 | .01 |
| 103T | Tim Grunhard RC | .05 | .01 |
| 104T | Johnny Johnson RC | .25 | .08 |
| 105T | Calvin Williams RC | .25 | .08 |
| 106T | Keith McCants | .05 | .01 |
| 107T | Lamar Lathon RC | .10 | .02 |
| 108T | Steve Broussard RC | .10 | .02 |
| 109T | Glenn Parker RC | .05 | .01 |
| 110T | Alton Montgomery RC | .05 | .01 |
| 111T | Jim McMahon | .10 | .02 |
| 112T | Aaron Wallace RC | .05 | .01 |
| 113T | Keith Sims RC | .05 | .01 |
| 114T | Ervin Randle | .05 | .01 |
| 115T | Walter Wilson | .05 | .01 |
| 116T | Terry Wooden RC | .05 | .01 |
| 117T | Bernard Clark | .05 | .01 |
| 118T | Tony Stargell RC | .05 | .01 |
| 119T | Jimmie Jones RC | .05 | .01 |
| 120T | Andre Collins RC | .10 | .02 |
| 121T | Ricky Proehl RC | .25 | .08 |
| 122T | Darion Conner RC | .10 | .02 |
| 123T | Jeff Rutledge | .05 | .01 |
| 124T | Heath Sherman RC | .10 | .02 |
| 125T | Tommie Agee RC | .05 | .01 |

| | | |
|---|---|---|
| ❏ 126T Tory Epps RC | .05 | .01 |
| ❏ 127T Tommy Hodson RC | .05 | .01 |
| ❏ 128T Jessie Hester RC | .05 | .01 |
| ❏ 129T Alfred Oglesby RC | .05 | .01 |
| ❏ 130T Chris Chandler | .25 | .08 |
| ❏ 131T Fred Barnett RC | .25 | .08 |
| ❏ 132T Checklist 1-132 | .05 | .01 |

## 1991 Topps

| | | |
|---|---|---|
| ❏ COMPLETE SET (660) | 20.00 | 10.00 |
| ❏ COMP.FACT.SET (660) | 30.00 | 15.00 |
| ❏ 1 Super Bowl XXV | .05 | .01 |
| ❏ 2 Roger Craig HL | .10 | .01 |
| ❏ 3 Derrick Thomas HL | .10 | .02 |
| ❏ 4 Pete Stoyanovich HL | .05 | .01 |
| ❏ 5 Ottis Anderson HL | .10 | .02 |
| ❏ 6 Jerry Rice HL | .50 | .20 |
| ❏ 7 Warren Moon HL | .10 | .02 |
| ❏ 8 Warren Moon/J.Everett LL | .10 | .02 |
| ❏ 9 B.Sanders/T.Thomas LL | .40 | .15 |
| ❏ 10 J.Rice/H.Jeffires LL | .30 | .10 |
| ❏ 11 M.Carrier/R.Johnson DB LL | .05 | .01 |
| ❏ 12 Derrick Thomas/C.Haley L | .10 | .02 |
| ❏ 13 Jumbo Elliott | .05 | .01 |
| ❏ 14 Leonard Marshall | .05 | .01 |
| ❏ 15 William Roberts | .05 | .01 |
| ❏ 16 Lawrence Taylor | .25 | .08 |
| ❏ 17 Mark Ingram | .10 | .02 |
| ❏ 18 Rodney Hampton | .25 | .08 |
| ❏ 19 Carl Banks | .05 | .01 |
| ❏ 20 Ottis Anderson | .10 | .02 |
| ❏ 21 Mark Collins | .05 | .01 |
| ❏ 22 Pepper Johnson | .05 | .01 |
| ❏ 23 Dave Meggett | .10 | .02 |
| ❏ 24 Reyna Thompson | .05 | .01 |
| ❏ 25 Stephen Baker | .05 | .01 |
| ❏ 26 Mike Fox | .05 | .01 |
| ❏ 27 Maurice Carthon UER | .05 | .01 |
| ❏ 28 Jeff Hostetler | .25 | .08 |
| ❏ 29 Greg Jackson RC | .05 | .01 |
| ❏ 30 Sean Landeta | .05 | .01 |
| ❏ 31 Bart Oates | .05 | .01 |
| ❏ 32 Phil Simms | .10 | .02 |
| ❏ 33 Erik Howard | .05 | .01 |
| ❏ 34 Myron Guyton | .05 | .01 |
| ❏ 35 Mark Bavaro | .05 | .01 |
| ❏ 36 Jarrod Bunch RC | .10 | .02 |
| ❏ 37 Will Wolford | .05 | .01 |
| ❏ 38 Ray Bentley | .05 | .01 |
| ❏ 39 Nate Odomes | .05 | .01 |
| ❏ 40 Scott Norwood | .05 | .01 |
| ❏ 41 Darryl Talley | .05 | .01 |
| ❏ 42 Carwell Gardner | .05 | .01 |
| ❏ 43 James Lofton | .10 | .02 |
| ❏ 44 Shane Conlan | .05 | .01 |
| ❏ 45 Steve Tasker | .10 | .02 |
| ❏ 46 James Williams | .05 | .01 |
| ❏ 47 Kent Hull | .05 | .01 |
| ❏ 48 Al Edwards | .05 | .01 |
| ❏ 49 Frank Reich | .10 | .02 |
| ❏ 50 Leon Seals | .05 | .01 |
| ❏ 51 Keith McKeller | .05 | .01 |
| ❏ 52 Thurman Thomas | .25 | .08 |
| ❏ 53 Leonard Smith | .05 | .01 |
| ❏ 54 Andre Reed | .10 | .02 |
| ❏ 55 Kenneth Davis | .05 | .01 |
| ❏ 56 Jeff Wright RC | .05 | .01 |
| ❏ 57 Jamie Mueller | .05 | .01 |
| ❏ 58 Jim Ritcher | .05 | .01 |
| ❏ 59 Bruce Smith | .25 | .08 |
| ❏ 60 Ted Washington RC | .05 | .01 |
| ❏ 61 Guy McIntyre | .05 | .01 |
| ❏ 62 Michael Carter | .05 | .01 |
| ❏ 63 Pierce Holt | .05 | .01 |
| ❏ 64 Darryl Pollard | .05 | .01 |
| ❏ 65 Mike Sherrard | .05 | .01 |
| ❏ 66 Dexter Carter | .05 | .01 |
| ❏ 67 Bubba Paris | .05 | .01 |
| ❏ 68 Harry Sydney | .05 | .01 |
| ❏ 69 Tom Rathman | .05 | .01 |
| ❏ 70 Jesse Sapolu | .05 | .01 |
| ❏ 71 Mike Cofer | .05 | .01 |
| ❏ 72 Keith DeLong | .05 | .01 |
| ❏ 73 Joe Montana | 1.25 | .50 |
| ❏ 74 Bill Romanowski | .05 | .01 |
| ❏ 75 John Taylor | .10 | .02 |
| ❏ 76 Brent Jones | .25 | .08 |
| ❏ 77 Harris Barton | .05 | .01 |
| ❏ 78 Charles Haley | .10 | .02 |
| ❏ 79 Eric Davis | .05 | .01 |
| ❏ 80 Kevin Fagan | .05 | .01 |
| ❏ 81 Jerry Rice | .75 | .30 |
| ❏ 82 Dave Waymer | .05 | .01 |
| ❏ 83 Todd Marinovich RC | .10 | .02 |
| ❏ 84 Steve Smith | .05 | .01 |
| ❏ 85 Tim Brown | .25 | .08 |
| ❏ 86 Ethan Horton | .05 | .01 |
| ❏ 87 Marcus Allen | .25 | .08 |
| ❏ 88 Terry McDaniel | .05 | .01 |
| ❏ 89 Thomas Benson | .05 | .01 |
| ❏ 90 Roger Craig | .10 | .02 |
| ❏ 91 Don Mosebar | .05 | .01 |
| ❏ 92 Aaron Wallace | .05 | .01 |
| ❏ 93 Eddie Anderson | .05 | .01 |
| ❏ 94 Willie Gault | .10 | .02 |
| ❏ 95 Howie Long | .25 | .08 |
| ❏ 96 Jay Schroeder | .05 | .01 |
| ❏ 97 Ronnie Lott | .10 | .02 |
| ❏ 98 Bob Golic | .05 | .01 |
| ❏ 99 Bo Jackson | .30 | .10 |
| ❏ 100 Max Montoya | .05 | .01 |
| ❏ 101 Scott Davis | .05 | .01 |
| ❏ 102 Greg Townsend | .05 | .01 |
| ❏ 103 Garry Lewis | .05 | .01 |
| ❏ 104 Mervyn Fernandez | .05 | .01 |
| ❏ 105 Steve Wisniewski UER | .05 | .01 |
| ❏ 106 Jeff Jaeger | .05 | .01 |
| ❏ 107 Nick Bell RC | .05 | .01 |
| ❏ 108 Mark Dennis RC | .05 | .01 |
| ❏ 109 Jarvis Williams | .05 | .01 |
| ❏ 110 Mark Clayton | .10 | .02 |
| ❏ 111 Harry Galbreath | .05 | .01 |
| ❏ 112 Dan Marino | 1.25 | .50 |
| ❏ 113 Louis Oliver | .05 | .01 |
| ❏ 114 Pete Stoyanovich | .05 | .01 |
| ❏ 115 Ferrell Edmunds | .05 | .01 |
| ❏ 116 Jeff Cross | .05 | .01 |
| ❏ 117 Richmond Webb | .05 | .01 |
| ❏ 118 Jim C. Jensen | .05 | .01 |
| ❏ 119 Keith Sims | .05 | .01 |
| ❏ 120 Mark Duper | .10 | .02 |
| ❏ 121 Shawn Lee RC | .05 | .01 |
| ❏ 122 Reggie Roby | .05 | .01 |
| ❏ 123 Jeff Uhlenhake | .05 | .01 |
| ❏ 124 Sammie Smith | .05 | .01 |
| ❏ 125 John Offerdahl | .05 | .01 |
| ❏ 126 Hugh Green | .05 | .01 |
| ❏ 127 Tony Paige | .05 | .01 |
| ❏ 128 David Griggs | .05 | .01 |
| ❏ 129 J.B. Brown | .05 | .01 |
| ❏ 130 Harvey Williams RC | .25 | .08 |
| ❏ 131 John Alt | .05 | .01 |
| ❏ 132 Albert Lewis | .05 | .01 |
| ❏ 133 Robb Thomas | .05 | .01 |
| ❏ 134 Neil Smith | .25 | .08 |
| ❏ 135 Stephone Paige | .05 | .01 |
| ❏ 136 Nick Lowery | .05 | .01 |
| ❏ 137 Steve DeBerg | .05 | .01 |
| ❏ 138 Rich Baldinger RC | .05 | .01 |
| ❏ 139 Percy Snow | .05 | .01 |
| ❏ 140 Kevin Porter | .05 | .01 |
| ❏ 141 Chris Martin | .05 | .01 |
| ❏ 142 Deron Cherry | .05 | .01 |
| ❏ 143 Derrick Thomas | .25 | .08 |
| ❏ 144 Tim Grunhard | .05 | .01 |
| ❏ 145 Todd McNair | .05 | .01 |
| ❏ 146 David Szott | .05 | .01 |
| ❏ 147 Dan Saleaumua | .05 | .01 |
| ❏ 148 Jonathan Hayes | .05 | .01 |
| ❏ 149 Christian Okoye | .05 | .01 |
| ❏ 150 Dino Hackett | .05 | .01 |
| ❏ 151 Bryan Barker RC | .05 | .01 |
| ❏ 152 Kevin Ross | .05 | .01 |
| ❏ 153 Barry Word | .05 | .01 |
| ❏ 154 Stan Thomas | .05 | .01 |
| ❏ 155 Brad Muster | .05 | .01 |
| ❏ 156 Donnell Woolford | .05 | .01 |
| ❏ 157 Neal Anderson | .10 | .02 |
| ❏ 158 Jim Covert | .05 | .01 |
| ❏ 159 Jim Harbaugh | .25 | .08 |
| ❏ 160 Shaun Gayle | .05 | .01 |
| ❏ 161 William Perry | .10 | .02 |
| ❏ 162 Ron Morris | .05 | .01 |
| ❏ 163 Mark Bortz | .05 | .01 |
| ❏ 164 James Thornton | .05 | .01 |
| ❏ 165 Ron Rivera | .05 | .01 |
| ❏ 166 Kevin Butler | .05 | .01 |
| ❏ 167 Jay Hilgenberg | .05 | .01 |
| ❏ 168 Peter Tom Willis | .05 | .01 |
| ❏ 169 Johnny Bailey | .05 | .01 |
| ❏ 170 Ron Cox | .05 | .01 |
| ❏ 171 Keith Van Horne | .05 | .01 |
| ❏ 172 Mark Carrier DB | .10 | .02 |
| ❏ 173 Richard Dent | .10 | .02 |
| ❏ 174 Wendell Davis | .05 | .01 |
| ❏ 175 Trace Armstrong | .05 | .01 |
| ❏ 176 Mike Singletary | .10 | .02 |
| ❏ 177 Chris Zorich RC | .25 | .08 |
| ❏ 178 Gerald Riggs | .05 | .01 |
| ❏ 179 Jeff Bostic | .05 | .01 |
| ❏ 180 Kurt Gouveia RC | .05 | .01 |
| ❏ 181 Stan Humphries | .25 | .08 |
| ❏ 182 Chip Lohmiller | .05 | .01 |
| ❏ 183 Raleigh McKenzie RC | .05 | .01 |
| ❏ 184 Alvin Walton | .05 | .01 |
| ❏ 185 Earnest Byner | .05 | .01 |
| ❏ 186 Markus Koch | .05 | .01 |
| ❏ 187 Art Monk | .10 | .02 |
| ❏ 188 Ed Simmons | .05 | .01 |
| ❏ 189 Bobby Wilson RC | .05 | .01 |
| ❏ 190 Charles Mann | .05 | .01 |
| ❏ 191 Darrell Green | .10 | .02 |
| ❏ 192 Mark Rypien | .10 | .02 |
| ❏ 193 Ricky Sanders | .05 | .01 |
| ❏ 194 Jim Lachey | .05 | .01 |
| ❏ 195 Martin Mayhew | .05 | .01 |
| ❏ 196 Gary Clark | .25 | .08 |
| ❏ 197 Wilber Marshall | .05 | .01 |
| ❏ 198 Darryl Grant | .05 | .01 |
| ❏ 199 Don Warren | .05 | .01 |
| ❏ 200 Ricky Ervins RC UER | .10 | .02 |
| ❏ 201 Eric Allen | .05 | .01 |
| ❏ 202 Anthony Toney | .05 | .01 |
| ❏ 203 Ben Smith UER | .05 | .01 |
| ❏ 204 David Alexander | .05 | .01 |
| ❏ 205 Jerome Brown | .05 | .01 |
| ❏ 206 Mike Golic | .05 | .01 |
| ❏ 207 Roger Ruzek | .05 | .01 |
| ❏ 208 Andre Waters | .05 | .01 |
| ❏ 209 Fred Barnett | .25 | .08 |
| ❏ 210 Randall Cunningham | .25 | .08 |
| ❏ 211 Mike Schad | .05 | .01 |
| ❏ 212 Reggie White | .25 | .08 |
| ❏ 213 Mike Bellamy | .05 | .01 |
| ❏ 214 Jeff Feagles RC | .05 | .01 |
| ❏ 215 Wes Hopkins | .05 | .01 |
| ❏ 216 Clyde Simmons | .05 | .01 |
| ❏ 217 Keith Byars | .05 | .01 |
| ❏ 218 Seth Joyner | .10 | .02 |
| ❏ 219 Byron Evans | .05 | .01 |
| ❏ 220 Keith Jackson | .10 | .02 |
| ❏ 221 Calvin Williams | .10 | .02 |
| ❏ 222 Mike Dumas RC | .05 | .01 |
| ❏ 223 Ray Childress | .05 | .01 |
| ❏ 224 Ernest Givins | .05 | .01 |
| ❏ 225 Lamar Lathon | .05 | .01 |
| ❏ 226 Greg Montgomery | .05 | .01 |
| ❏ 227 Mike Munchak | .10 | .02 |
| ❏ 228 Al Smith | .05 | .01 |
| ❏ 229 Bubba McDowell | .05 | .01 |
| ❏ 230 Haywood Jeffires | .10 | .02 |
| ❏ 231 Drew Hill | .05 | .01 |
| ❏ 232 William Fuller | .10 | .02 |

|  | | |
|---|---|---|
| ☐ 233 Warren Moon | .25 | .08 |
| ☐ 234 Doug Smith DT RC | .10 | .02 |
| ☐ 235 Cris Dishman RC | .05 | .01 |
| ☐ 236 Teddy Garcia RC | .05 | .01 |
| ☐ 237 Richard Johnson CB RC | .05 | .01 |
| ☐ 238 Bruce Matthews | .10 | .02 |
| ☐ 239 Gerald McNeil | .05 | .01 |
| ☐ 240 Johnny Meads | .05 | .01 |
| ☐ 241 Curtis Duncan | .05 | .01 |
| ☐ 242 Sean Jones | .10 | .02 |
| ☐ 243 Lorenzo White | .05 | .01 |
| ☐ 244 Rob Carpenter RC WR | .05 | .01 |
| ☐ 245 Bruce Reimers | .05 | .01 |
| ☐ 246 Ickey Woods | .05 | .01 |
| ☐ 247 Lewis Billups | .05 | .01 |
| ☐ 248 Boomer Esiason | .10 | .02 |
| ☐ 249 Tim Krumrie | .05 | .01 |
| ☐ 250 David Fulcher | .05 | .01 |
| ☐ 251 Jim Breech | .05 | .01 |
| ☐ 252 Mitchell Price RC | .05 | .01 |
| ☐ 253 Carl Zander | .05 | .01 |
| ☐ 254 Barney Bussey RC | .05 | .01 |
| ☐ 255 Leon White | .05 | .01 |
| ☐ 256 Eddie Brown | .05 | .01 |
| ☐ 257 James Francis | .05 | .01 |
| ☐ 258 Harold Green | .10 | .02 |
| ☐ 259 Anthony Munoz | .10 | .02 |
| ☐ 260 James Brooks | .10 | .02 |
| ☐ 261 Kevin Walker RC UER | .05 | .01 |
| ☐ 262 Bruce Kozerski | .05 | .01 |
| ☐ 263 David Grant | .05 | .01 |
| ☐ 264 Tim McGee | .05 | .01 |
| ☐ 265 Rodney Holman | .05 | .01 |
| ☐ 266 Dan McGwire RC | .05 | .01 |
| ☐ 267 Andy Heck | .05 | .01 |
| ☐ 268 Dave Krieg | .10 | .02 |
| ☐ 269 David Wyman | .05 | .01 |
| ☐ 270 Robert Blackmon | .05 | .01 |
| ☐ 271 Grant Feasel | .05 | .01 |
| ☐ 272 Patrick Hunter RC | .05 | .01 |
| ☐ 273 Travis McNeal | .05 | .01 |
| ☐ 274 John L. Williams | .05 | .01 |
| ☐ 275 Tony Woods | .05 | .01 |
| ☐ 276 Derrick Fenner | .05 | .01 |
| ☐ 277 Jacob Green | .05 | .01 |
| ☐ 278 Brian Blades | .10 | .02 |
| ☐ 279 Eugene Robinson | .05 | .01 |
| ☐ 280 Terry Wooden | .05 | .01 |
| ☐ 281 Jeff Bryant | .05 | .01 |
| ☐ 282 Norm Johnson | .05 | .01 |
| ☐ 283 Joe Nash UER | .05 | .01 |
| ☐ 284 Rick Donnelly | .05 | .01 |
| ☐ 285 Chris Warren | .25 | .08 |
| ☐ 286 Tommy Kane | .05 | .01 |
| ☐ 287 Cortez Kennedy | .25 | .08 |
| ☐ 288 Ernie Mills RC | .10 | .02 |
| ☐ 289 Dermontti Dawson | .05 | .01 |
| ☐ 290 Tunch Ilkin | .05 | .01 |
| ☐ 291 Tim Worley | .05 | .01 |
| ☐ 292 David Little | .05 | .01 |
| ☐ 293 Gary Anderson K | .05 | .01 |
| ☐ 294 Chris Calloway | .05 | .01 |
| ☐ 295 Carnell Lake | .05 | .01 |
| ☐ 296 Dan Stryzinski | .05 | .01 |
| ☐ 297 Rod Woodson | .25 | .08 |
| ☐ 298 John Jackson T RC | .05 | .01 |
| ☐ 299 Bubby Brister | .05 | .01 |
| ☐ 300 Thomas Everett | .05 | .01 |
| ☐ 301 Merril Hoge | .05 | .01 |
| ☐ 302 Eric Green | .10 | .02 |
| ☐ 303 Greg Lloyd | .25 | .08 |
| ☐ 304 Gerald Williams | .05 | .01 |
| ☐ 305 Bryan Hinkle | .05 | .01 |
| ☐ 306 Keith Willis | .05 | .01 |
| ☐ 307 Louis Lipps | .05 | .01 |
| ☐ 308 Donald Evans | .05 | .01 |
| ☐ 309 D.J. Johnson | .05 | .01 |
| ☐ 310 Wesley Carroll RC | .05 | .01 |
| ☐ 311 Eric Martin | .05 | .01 |
| ☐ 312 Brett Maxie | .05 | .01 |
| ☐ 313 Rickey Jackson | .05 | .01 |
| ☐ 314 Robert Massey | .05 | .01 |
| ☐ 315 Pat Swilling | .10 | .02 |
| ☐ 316 Morten Andersen | .05 | .01 |
| ☐ 317 Toi Cook RC | .05 | .01 |
| ☐ 318 Sam Mills | .05 | .01 |
| ☐ 319 Steve Walsh | .05 | .01 |
| ☐ 320 Tommy Barnhardt RC | .05 | .01 |
| ☐ 321 Vince Buck | .05 | .01 |
| ☐ 322 Joel Hilgenberg | .05 | .01 |
| ☐ 323 Rueben Mayes | .05 | .01 |
| ☐ 324 Renaldo Turnbull | .05 | .01 |
| ☐ 325 Brett Perriman | .25 | .08 |
| ☐ 326 Vaughan Johnson | .05 | .01 |
| ☐ 327 Gill Fenerty | .05 | .01 |
| ☐ 328 Stan Brock | .05 | .01 |
| ☐ 329 Dalton Hilliard | .05 | .01 |
| ☐ 330 Hoby Brenner | .05 | .01 |
| ☐ 331 Craig Heyward | .10 | .02 |
| ☐ 332 Jon Hand | .05 | .01 |
| ☐ 333 Duane Bickett | .05 | .01 |
| ☐ 334 Jessie Hester | .05 | .01 |
| ☐ 335 Rohn Stark | .05 | .01 |
| ☐ 336 Zefross Moss | .05 | .01 |
| ☐ 337 Bill Brooks | .05 | .01 |
| ☐ 338 Clarence Verdin | .05 | .01 |
| ☐ 339 Mike Prior | .05 | .01 |
| ☐ 340 Chip Banks | .05 | .01 |
| ☐ 341 Dean Biasucci | .05 | .01 |
| ☐ 342 Ray Donaldson | .05 | .01 |
| ☐ 343 Jeff Herrod | .05 | .01 |
| ☐ 344 Donnell Thompson | .05 | .01 |
| ☐ 345 Chris Goode | .05 | .01 |
| ☐ 346 Eugene Daniel | .05 | .01 |
| ☐ 347 Pat Beach | .05 | .01 |
| ☐ 348 Keith Taylor | .05 | .01 |
| ☐ 349 Jeff George | .25 | .08 |
| ☐ 350 Tony Siragusa RC | .10 | .02 |
| ☐ 351 Randy Dixon | .05 | .01 |
| ☐ 352 Albert Bentley | .05 | .01 |
| ☐ 353 Russell Maryland RC | .25 | .08 |
| ☐ 354 Mike Saxon | .05 | .01 |
| ☐ 355 Godfrey Myles RC UER | .05 | .01 |
| ☐ 356 Mark Stepnoski RC | .10 | .02 |
| ☐ 357 James Washington RC | .05 | .01 |
| ☐ 358 Jay Novacek | .25 | .08 |
| ☐ 359 Kelvin Martin | .05 | .01 |
| ☐ 360 Emmitt Smith UER | 2.50 | 1.00 |
| ☐ 361 Jim Jeffcoat | .05 | .01 |
| ☐ 362 Alexander Wright | .05 | .01 |
| ☐ 363 James Dixon UER | .05 | .01 |
| ☐ 364 Alonzo Highsmith | .05 | .01 |
| ☐ 365 Daniel Stubbs | .05 | .01 |
| ☐ 366 Jack Del Rio | .10 | .02 |
| ☐ 367 Mark Tuinei RC | .05 | .01 |
| ☐ 368 Michael Irvin | .25 | .08 |
| ☐ 369 John Gesek RC | .05 | .01 |
| ☐ 370 Ken Norton | .05 | .01 |
| ☐ 371 Troy Aikman | .75 | .30 |
| ☐ 372 Jimmie Jones | .05 | .01 |
| ☐ 373 Nate Newton | .10 | .02 |
| ☐ 374 Issiac Holt | .05 | .01 |
| ☐ 375 Alvin Harper RC | .25 | .08 |
| ☐ 376 Todd Kalis | .05 | .01 |
| ☐ 377 Wade Wilson | .10 | .02 |
| ☐ 378 Joey Browner | .05 | .01 |
| ☐ 379 Chris Doleman | .05 | .01 |
| ☐ 380 Hassan Jones | .05 | .01 |
| ☐ 381 Henry Thomas | .05 | .01 |
| ☐ 382 Darrell Fullington | .05 | .01 |
| ☐ 383 Steve Jordan | .05 | .01 |
| ☐ 384 Gary Zimmerman | .10 | .02 |
| ☐ 385 Ray Berry | .05 | .01 |
| ☐ 386 Cris Carter | .50 | .20 |
| ☐ 387 Mike Merriweather | .05 | .01 |
| ☐ 388 Carl Lee | .05 | .01 |
| ☐ 389 Keith Millard | .05 | .01 |
| ☐ 390 Reggie Rutland RC | .10 | .02 |
| ☐ 391 Anthony Carter | .10 | .02 |
| ☐ 392 Mark Dusbabek | .05 | .01 |
| ☐ 393 Kirk Lowdermilk | .05 | .01 |
| ☐ 394 Al Noga UER | .05 | .01 |
| ☐ 395 Herschel Walker | .10 | .02 |
| ☐ 396 Randall McDaniel | .10 | .02 |
| ☐ 397 Herman Moore RC | .25 | .08 |
| ☐ 398 Eddie Murray | .05 | .01 |
| ☐ 399 Lomas Brown | .05 | .01 |
| ☐ 400 Marc Spindler | .05 | .01 |
| ☐ 401 Bennie Blades | .05 | .01 |
| ☐ 402 Kevin Glover | .05 | .01 |
| ☐ 403 Aubrey Matthews RC | .05 | .01 |
| ☐ 404 Michael Cofer | .05 | .01 |
| ☐ 405 Robert Clark | .05 | .01 |
| ☐ 406 Eric Andolsek | .05 | .01 |
| ☐ 407 William White | .05 | .01 |
| ☐ 408 Rodney Peete | .10 | .02 |
| ☐ 409 Mel Gray | .10 | .02 |
| ☐ 410 Jim Arnold | .05 | .01 |
| ☐ 411 Jeff Campbell | .05 | .01 |
| ☐ 412 Chris Spielman | .10 | .02 |
| ☐ 413 Jerry Ball | .05 | .01 |
| ☐ 414 Dan Owens | .05 | .01 |
| ☐ 415 Barry Sanders | 1.25 | .50 |
| ☐ 416 Andre Ware | .10 | .02 |
| ☐ 417 Stanley Richard RC | .05 | .01 |
| ☐ 418 Gill Byrd | .05 | .01 |
| ☐ 419 John Kidd | .05 | .01 |
| ☐ 420 Sam Seale | .05 | .01 |
| ☐ 421 Gary Plummer | .05 | .01 |
| ☐ 422 Anthony Miller | .10 | .02 |
| ☐ 423 Ronnie Harmon | .05 | .01 |
| ☐ 424 Frank Cornish | .05 | .01 |
| ☐ 425 Marion Butts | .10 | .02 |
| ☐ 426 Leo Goeas | .05 | .01 |
| ☐ 427 Junior Seau | .25 | .08 |
| ☐ 428 Courtney Hall | .05 | .01 |
| ☐ 429 Leslie O'Neal | .10 | .02 |
| ☐ 430 Martin Bayless | .05 | .01 |
| ☐ 431 John Carney | .05 | .01 |
| ☐ 432 Lee Williams | .05 | .01 |
| ☐ 433 Arthur Cox | .05 | .01 |
| ☐ 434 Burt Grossman | .05 | .01 |
| ☐ 435 Nate Lewis RC | .05 | .01 |
| ☐ 436 Rod Bernstine | .05 | .01 |
| ☐ 437 Henry Rolling RC | .05 | .01 |
| ☐ 438 Billy Joe Tolliver | .05 | .01 |
| ☐ 439 Vinnie Clark RC | .05 | .01 |
| ☐ 440 Brian Noble | .05 | .01 |
| ☐ 441 Charles Wilson | .05 | .01 |
| ☐ 442 Don Majkowski | .05 | .01 |
| ☐ 443 Tim Harris | .05 | .01 |
| ☐ 444 Scott Stephen RC | .05 | .01 |
| ☐ 445 Perry Kemp | .05 | .01 |
| ☐ 446 Darrell Thompson | .05 | .01 |
| ☐ 447 Chris Jacke | .05 | .01 |
| ☐ 448 Mark Murphy | .05 | .01 |
| ☐ 449 Ed West | .05 | .01 |
| ☐ 450 LeRoy Butler | .10 | .02 |
| ☐ 451 Keith Woodside | .05 | .01 |
| ☐ 452 Tony Bennett | .10 | .02 |
| ☐ 453 Mark Lee | .05 | .01 |
| ☐ 454 James Campen RC | .05 | .01 |
| ☐ 455 Robert Brown | .05 | .01 |
| ☐ 456 Sterling Sharpe | .25 | .08 |
| ☐ 457A T.Mandarich ERR Bronc. | 2.50 | 1.25 |
| ☐ 457B T.Mandarich COR Packers | .05 | .01 |
| ☐ 458 Johnny Holland | .05 | .01 |
| ☐ 459 Matt Brock RC | .05 | .01 |
| ☐ 460A Esera Tuaolo RC ERR | 2.50 | 1.25 |
| ☐ 460B Esera Tuaolo RC COR | .05 | .01 |
| ☐ 461 Freeman McNeil | .05 | .01 |
| ☐ 462 Terance Mathis UER 460 | .25 | .08 |
| ☐ 463 Rob Moore | .25 | .08 |
| ☐ 464 Darrell Davis RC | .05 | .01 |
| ☐ 465 Chris Burkett | .05 | .01 |
| ☐ 466 Jeff Criswell | .05 | .01 |
| ☐ 467 Tony Stargell | .05 | .01 |
| ☐ 468 Ken O'Brien | .05 | .01 |
| ☐ 469 Erik McMillan | .05 | .01 |
| ☐ 470 Jeff Lageman UER | .05 | .01 |
| ☐ 471 Pat Leahy | .05 | .01 |
| ☐ 472 Dennis Byrd | .05 | .01 |
| ☐ 473 Jim Sweeney | .05 | .01 |
| ☐ 474 Brad Baxter | .05 | .01 |
| ☐ 475 Joe Kelly | .05 | .01 |
| ☐ 476 Al Toon | .10 | .02 |
| ☐ 477 Joe Prokop | .05 | .01 |
| ☐ 478 Mark Boyer | .05 | .01 |
| ☐ 479 Kyle Clifton | .05 | .01 |
| ☐ 480 James Hasty | .05 | .01 |
| ☐ 481 Browning Nagle RC | .25 | .08 |
| ☐ 482 Gary Anderson RB | .05 | .01 |
| ☐ 483 Mark Carrier WR | .25 | .08 |
| ☐ 484 Ricky Reynolds | .05 | .01 |
| ☐ 485 Bruce Hill | .05 | .01 |
| ☐ 486 Steve Christie | .05 | .01 |
| ☐ 487 Paul Gruber | .05 | .01 |
| ☐ 488 Jesse Anderson | .05 | .01 |
| ☐ 489 Reggie Cobb | .05 | .01 |
| ☐ 490 Harry Hamilton | .05 | .01 |
| ☐ 491 Vinny Testaverde | .10 | .02 |

| | | |
|---|---|---|
| ☐ 492 Mark Royals RC | .05 | .01 |
| ☐ 493 Keith McCants | .05 | .01 |
| ☐ 494 Ron Hall | .05 | .01 |
| ☐ 495 Ian Beckles | .05 | .01 |
| ☐ 496 Mark Robinson | .05 | .01 |
| ☐ 497 Reuben Davis | .05 | .01 |
| ☐ 498 Wayne Haddix | .05 | .01 |
| ☐ 499 Kevin Murphy | .05 | .01 |
| ☐ 500 Eugene Marve | .05 | .01 |
| ☐ 501 Broderick Thomas | .05 | .01 |
| ☐ 502 Eric Swann RC UER | .25 | .08 |
| ☐ 503 Ernie Jones | .05 | .01 |
| ☐ 504 Rich Camarillo | .05 | .01 |
| ☐ 505 Tim McDonald | .05 | .01 |
| ☐ 506 Freddie Joe Nunn | .05 | .01 |
| ☐ 507 Tim Jorden RC | .05 | .01 |
| ☐ 508 Johnny Johnson | .05 | .01 |
| ☐ 509 Eric Hill | .05 | .01 |
| ☐ 510 Derek Kennard | .05 | .01 |
| ☐ 511 Ricky Proehl | .05 | .01 |
| ☐ 512 Bill Lewis | .05 | .01 |
| ☐ 513 Roy Green | .05 | .01 |
| ☐ 514 Anthony Bell | .05 | .01 |
| ☐ 515 Timm Rosenbach | .05 | .01 |
| ☐ 516 Jim Wahler RC | .05 | .01 |
| ☐ 517 Anthony Thompson | .05 | .01 |
| ☐ 518 Ken Harvey | .10 | .02 |
| ☐ 519 Luis Sharpe | .05 | .01 |
| ☐ 520 Walter Reeves | .05 | .01 |
| ☐ 521 Lonnie Young | .05 | .01 |
| ☐ 522 Rod Saddler | .05 | .01 |
| ☐ 523 Todd Lyght RC | .05 | .01 |
| ☐ 524 Alvin Wright | .05 | .01 |
| ☐ 525 Flipper Anderson | .05 | .01 |
| ☐ 526 Jackie Slater | .05 | .01 |
| ☐ 527 Damone Johnson RC | .05 | .01 |
| ☐ 528 Cleveland Gary | .05 | .01 |
| ☐ 529 Mike Piel | .05 | .01 |
| ☐ 530 Buford McGee | .05 | .01 |
| ☐ 531 Michael Stewart | .05 | .01 |
| ☐ 532 Jim Everett | .10 | .02 |
| ☐ 533 Mike Wilcher | .05 | .01 |
| ☐ 534 Irv Pankey | .05 | .01 |
| ☐ 535 Bern Brostek | .05 | .01 |
| ☐ 536 Henry Ellard | .10 | .02 |
| ☐ 537 Doug Smith | .05 | .01 |
| ☐ 538 Larry Kelm | .05 | .01 |
| ☐ 539 Pat Terrell | .05 | .01 |
| ☐ 540 Tom Newberry | .05 | .01 |
| ☐ 541 Jerry Gray | .05 | .01 |
| ☐ 542 Kevin Greene | .10 | .02 |
| ☐ 543 Duval Love RC | .05 | .01 |
| ☐ 544 Frank Stams | .05 | .01 |
| ☐ 545 Mike Croel RC | .05 | .01 |
| ☐ 546 Mark Jackson | .05 | .01 |
| ☐ 547 Greg Kragen | .05 | .01 |
| ☐ 548 Karl Mecklenburg | .05 | .01 |
| ☐ 549 Simon Fletcher | .05 | .01 |
| ☐ 550 Bobby Humphrey | .05 | .01 |
| ☐ 551 Ken Lanier | .05 | .01 |
| ☐ 552 Vance Johnson | .05 | .01 |
| ☐ 553 Ron Holmes | .05 | .01 |
| ☐ 554 John Elway | 1.25 | .50 |
| ☐ 555 Melvin Bratton | .05 | .01 |
| ☐ 556 Dennis Smith | .05 | .01 |
| ☐ 557 Ricky Nattiel | .05 | .01 |
| ☐ 558 Clarence Kay | .05 | .01 |
| ☐ 559 Michael Brooks | .05 | .01 |
| ☐ 560 Mike Horan | .05 | .01 |
| ☐ 561 Warren Powers | .05 | .01 |
| ☐ 562 Keith Kartz | .05 | .01 |
| ☐ 563 Shannon Sharpe | .50 | .20 |
| ☐ 564 Wymon Henderson | .05 | .01 |
| ☐ 565 Steve Atwater | .05 | .01 |
| ☐ 566 David Treadwell | .05 | .01 |
| ☐ 567 Bruce Pickens RC | .05 | .01 |
| ☐ 568 Jessie Tuggle | .05 | .01 |
| ☐ 569 Chris Hinton | .05 | .01 |
| ☐ 570 Keith Jones | .05 | .01 |
| ☐ 571 Bill Fralic | .05 | .01 |
| ☐ 572 Mike Rozier | .05 | .01 |
| ☐ 573 Scott Fulhage | .05 | .01 |
| ☐ 574 Floyd Dixon | .05 | .01 |
| ☐ 575 Andre Rison | .10 | .02 |
| ☐ 576 Darion Conner | .05 | .01 |
| ☐ 577 Brian Jordan | .10 | .02 |
| ☐ 578 Michael Haynes | .25 | .08 |

| | | |
|---|---|---|
| ☐ 579 Oliver Barnett | .05 | .01 |
| ☐ 580 Shawn Collins | .05 | .01 |
| ☐ 581 Tim Green | .05 | .01 |
| ☐ 582 Deion Sanders | .40 | .15 |
| ☐ 583 Mike Kenn | .05 | .01 |
| ☐ 584 Mike Gann | .05 | .01 |
| ☐ 585 Chris Miller | .10 | .02 |
| ☐ 586 Tory Epps | .05 | .01 |
| ☐ 587 Steve Broussard | .05 | .01 |
| ☐ 588 Gary Wilkins | .05 | .01 |
| ☐ 589 Eric Turner RC | .10 | .02 |
| ☐ 590 Thane Gash | .05 | .01 |
| ☐ 591 Clay Matthews | .10 | .02 |
| ☐ 592 Mike Johnson | .05 | .01 |
| ☐ 593 Raymond Clayborn | .05 | .01 |
| ☐ 594 Leroy Hoard | .10 | .02 |
| ☐ 595 Reggie Langhorne | .05 | .01 |
| ☐ 596 Mike Baab | .05 | .01 |
| ☐ 597 Anthony Pleasant | .05 | .01 |
| ☐ 598 David Grayson | .05 | .01 |
| ☐ 599 Rob Burnett RC | .10 | .02 |
| ☐ 600 Frank Minnifield | .05 | .01 |
| ☐ 601 Gregg Rakoczy | .05 | .01 |
| ☐ 602 Eric Metcalf UER | .25 | .08 |
| ☐ 603 Paul Farren | .05 | .01 |
| ☐ 604 Brian Brennan | .05 | .01 |
| ☐ 605 Tony Jones T RC | .05 | .01 |
| ☐ 606 Stephen Braggs | .05 | .01 |
| ☐ 607 Kevin Mack | .05 | .01 |
| ☐ 608 Pat Harlow RC | .05 | .01 |
| ☐ 609 Marv Cook | .05 | .01 |
| ☐ 610 John Stephens | .05 | .01 |
| ☐ 611 Ed Reynolds | .05 | .01 |
| ☐ 612 Tim Goad | .05 | .01 |
| ☐ 613 Chris Singleton | .05 | .01 |
| ☐ 614 Bruce Armstrong | .05 | .01 |
| ☐ 615 Tommy Hodson | .05 | .01 |
| ☐ 616 Sammy Martin | .05 | .01 |
| ☐ 617 Andre Tippett | .05 | .01 |
| ☐ 618 Johnny Rembert | .05 | .01 |
| ☐ 619 Maurice Hurst | .05 | .01 |
| ☐ 620 Vincent Brown | .05 | .01 |
| ☐ 621 Ray Agnew | .05 | .01 |
| ☐ 622 Ronnie Lippett | .05 | .01 |
| ☐ 623 Greg McMurtry | .05 | .01 |
| ☐ 624 Brent Williams | .05 | .01 |
| ☐ 625 Jason Staurovsky | .05 | .01 |
| ☐ 626 Marvin Allen | .05 | .01 |
| ☐ 627 Hart Lee Dykes | .05 | .01 |
| ☐ 628 Atlanta Falcons | .05 | .01 |
| ☐ 629 Buffalo Bills | .05 | .01 |
| ☐ 630 Chicago Bears | .10 | .02 |
| ☐ 631 Cincinnati Bengals | .05 | .01 |
| ☐ 632 Cleveland Browns | .05 | .01 |
| ☐ 633 Dallas Cowboys | .05 | .01 |
| ☐ 634 Denver Broncos | .05 | .01 |
| ☐ 635 Detroit Lions | .05 | .01 |
| ☐ 636 Green Bay Packers | .05 | .01 |
| ☐ 637 Oilers TL/Warren Moon | .10 | .02 |
| ☐ 638 Colts TL/Jeff George | .05 | .01 |
| ☐ 639 Kansas City Chiefs | .05 | .01 |
| ☐ 640 Los Angeles Raiders | .05 | .01 |
| ☐ 641 Los Angeles Rams | .05 | .01 |
| ☐ 642 Miami Dolphins | .05 | .01 |
| ☐ 643 Minnesota Vikings | .10 | .02 |
| ☐ 644 New Eng. Patriots | .05 | .01 |
| ☐ 645 New Orleans Saints | .05 | .01 |
| ☐ 646 New York Giants | .05 | .01 |
| ☐ 647 New York Jets | .05 | .01 |
| ☐ 648 Eagles TL/R.Cunningham | .05 | .01 |
| ☐ 649 Phoenix Cardinals | .05 | .01 |
| ☐ 650 Pittsburgh Steelers | .05 | .01 |
| ☐ 651 San Diego Chargers | .05 | .01 |
| ☐ 652 San Francisco 49ers | .05 | .01 |
| ☐ 653 Seattle Seahawks | .05 | .01 |
| ☐ 654 Tampa Bay Buccaneers | .05 | .01 |
| ☐ 655 Washington Redskins | .05 | .01 |
| ☐ 656 Checklist 1-132 | .05 | .01 |
| ☐ 657 Checklist 132-264 | .05 | .01 |
| ☐ 658 Checklist 265-396 | .05 | .01 |
| ☐ 659 Checklist 397-528 | .05 | .01 |
| ☐ 660 Checklist 529-660 | .05 | .01 |

## 1992 Topps

| | | |
|---|---|---|
| ☐ COMPLETE SET (759) | 50.00 | 25.00 |
| ☐ COMP.FACT.SET (680) | 80.00 | 40.00 |
| ☐ COMP.SERIES 1 (330) | 20.00 | 10.00 |

| | | |
|---|---|---|
| ☐ COMP.SERIES 2 (330) | 20.00 | 10.00 |
| ☐ COMP.HIGH SER.(99) | 10.00 | 5.00 |
| ☐ COMP.FACT.HIGH SET (113) | 12.00 | 5.00 |
| ☐ 1 Tim McGee | .05 | .01 |
| ☐ 2 Rich Camarillo | .05 | .01 |
| ☐ 3 Anthony Johnson | .10 | .02 |
| ☐ 4 Larry Kelm | .05 | .01 |
| ☐ 5 Irving Fryar | .10 | .02 |
| ☐ 6 Joey Browner | .05 | .01 |
| ☐ 7 Michael Walter | .05 | .01 |
| ☐ 8 Cortez Kennedy | .10 | .02 |
| ☐ 9 Reyna Thompson | .05 | .01 |
| ☐ 10 John Friesz | .10 | .02 |
| ☐ 11 Leroy Hoard | .10 | .02 |
| ☐ 12 Steve McMichael | .10 | .02 |
| ☐ 13 Marvin Washington | .05 | .01 |
| ☐ 14 Clyde Simmons | .05 | .01 |
| ☐ 15 Stephone Paige | .05 | .01 |
| ☐ 16 Mike Utley | .10 | .02 |
| ☐ 17 Tunch Ilkin | .05 | .01 |
| ☐ 18 Lawrence Dawsey | .10 | .02 |
| ☐ 19 Vance Johnson | .05 | .01 |
| ☐ 20 Bryce Paup | .25 | .08 |
| ☐ 21 Jeff Wright | .05 | .01 |
| ☐ 22 Gill Fenerty | .05 | .01 |
| ☐ 23 Lamar Lathon | .05 | .01 |
| ☐ 24 Danny Copeland | .05 | .01 |
| ☐ 25 Marcus Allen | .25 | .08 |
| ☐ 26 Tim Green | .05 | .01 |
| ☐ 27 Pete Stoyanovich | .05 | .01 |
| ☐ 28 Alvin Harper | .10 | .02 |
| ☐ 29 Roy Foster | .05 | .01 |
| ☐ 30 Eugene Daniel | .05 | .01 |
| ☐ 31 Luis Sharpe | .05 | .01 |
| ☐ 32 Terry Wooden | .05 | .01 |
| ☐ 33 Jim Breech | .05 | .01 |
| ☐ 34 Randy Hilliard RC | .05 | .01 |
| ☐ 35 Roman Phifer | .05 | .01 |
| ☐ 36 Erik Howard | .05 | .01 |
| ☐ 37 Chris Singleton | .05 | .01 |
| ☐ 38 Matt Stover | .05 | .01 |
| ☐ 39 Tim Irwin | .05 | .01 |
| ☐ 40 Karl Mecklenburg | .05 | .01 |
| ☐ 41 Joe Phillips | .05 | .01 |
| ☐ 42 Bill Jones RC | .05 | .01 |
| ☐ 43 Mark Carrier DB | .05 | .01 |
| ☐ 44 George Jamison | .05 | .01 |
| ☐ 45 Rob Taylor | .05 | .01 |
| ☐ 46 Jeff Jaeger | .05 | .01 |
| ☐ 47 Don Majkowski | .05 | .01 |
| ☐ 48 Al Edwards | .05 | .01 |
| ☐ 49 Curtis Duncan | .05 | .01 |
| ☐ 50 Sam Mills | .05 | .01 |
| ☐ 51 Terance Mathis | .10 | .02 |
| ☐ 52 Brian Mitchell | .10 | .02 |
| ☐ 53 Mike Pritchard | .10 | .02 |
| ☐ 54 Calvin Williams | .10 | .02 |
| ☐ 55 Hardy Nickerson | .10 | .02 |
| ☐ 56 Nate Newton | .05 | .01 |
| ☐ 57 Steve Wallace | .05 | .01 |
| ☐ 58 John Offerdahl | .05 | .01 |
| ☐ 59 Aeneas Williams | .05 | .01 |
| ☐ 60 Lee Johnson | .05 | .01 |
| ☐ 61 Ricardo McDonald RC | .05 | .01 |
| ☐ 62 David Richards | .05 | .01 |
| ☐ 63 Paul Gruber | .05 | .01 |
| ☐ 64 Greg McMurtry | .05 | .01 |
| ☐ 65 Jay Hilgenberg | .05 | .01 |
| ☐ 66 Tim Grunhard | .05 | .01 |
| ☐ 67 Dwayne White RC | .05 | .01 |

|  |  | | |
|---|---|---|---|
| ❑ 68 | Don Beebe | .05 | .01 |
| ❑ 69 | Simon Fletcher | .05 | .01 |
| ❑ 70 | Warren Moon | .25 | .08 |
| ❑ 71 | Chris Jacke | .05 | .01 |
| ❑ 72 | Steve Wisniewski UER | .05 | .01 |
| ❑ 73 | Mike Cofer | .05 | .01 |
| ❑ 74 | Tim Johnson UER | .05 | .01 |
| ❑ 75 | T.J. Turner | .05 | .01 |
| ❑ 76 | Scott Case | .05 | .01 |
| ❑ 77 | Michael Jackson | .10 | .02 |
| ❑ 78 | Jon Hand | .05 | .01 |
| ❑ 79 | Stan Brock | .05 | .01 |
| ❑ 80 | Robert Blackmon | .05 | .01 |
| ❑ 81 | D.J. Johnson | .05 | .01 |
| ❑ 82 | Damone Johnson | .05 | .01 |
| ❑ 83 | Marc Spindler | .05 | .01 |
| ❑ 84 | Larry Brown DB | .05 | .01 |
| ❑ 85 | Ray Berry | .05 | .01 |
| ❑ 86 | Andre Waters | .05 | .01 |
| ❑ 87 | Carlos Huerta | .05 | .01 |
| ❑ 88 | Brad Muster | .05 | .01 |
| ❑ 89 | Chuck Cecil | .05 | .01 |
| ❑ 90 | Nick Lowery | .05 | .01 |
| ❑ 91 | Cornelius Bennett | .10 | .02 |
| ❑ 92 | Jessie Tuggle | .05 | .01 |
| ❑ 93 | Mark Schlereth | .05 | .01 |
| ❑ 94 | Vestee Jackson | .05 | .01 |
| ❑ 95 | Eric Bieniemy | .05 | .01 |
| ❑ 96 | Jeff Hostetler | .10 | .02 |
| ❑ 97 | Ken Lanier | .05 | .01 |
| ❑ 98 | Wayne Haddix | .05 | .01 |
| ❑ 99 | Lorenzo White | .05 | .01 |
| ❑ 100 | Mervyn Fernandez | .05 | .01 |
| ❑ 101 | Brent Williams | .05 | .01 |
| ❑ 102 | Ian Beckles | .05 | .01 |
| ❑ 103 | Harris Barton | .05 | .01 |
| ❑ 104 | Edgar Bennett RC | .25 | .08 |
| ❑ 105 | Mike Pitts | .05 | .01 |
| ❑ 106 | Fuad Reveiz | .05 | .01 |
| ❑ 107 | Vernon Turner | .05 | .01 |
| ❑ 108 | Tracy Hayworth RC | .05 | .01 |
| ❑ 109 | Checklist 1-110 | .05 | .01 |
| ❑ 110 | Tom Waddle | .05 | .01 |
| ❑ 111 | Fred Stokes | .05 | .01 |
| ❑ 112 | Howard Ballard | .05 | .01 |
| ❑ 113 | David Szott | .05 | .01 |
| ❑ 114 | Tim McKyer | .05 | .01 |
| ❑ 115 | Kyle Clifton | .05 | .01 |
| ❑ 116 | Tony Bennett | .05 | .01 |
| ❑ 117 | Joel Hilgenberg | .05 | .01 |
| ❑ 118 | Dwayne Harper | .05 | .01 |
| ❑ 119 | Mike Baab | .05 | .01 |
| ❑ 120 | Mark Clayton | .10 | .02 |
| ❑ 121 | Eric Swann | .10 | .02 |
| ❑ 122 | Neil O'Donnell | .10 | .02 |
| ❑ 123 | Mike Munchak | .05 | .01 |
| ❑ 124 | Howie Long | .25 | .08 |
| ❑ 125 | John Elway | 1.25 | .50 |
| ❑ 126 | Joe Prokop | .05 | .01 |
| ❑ 127 | Pepper Johnson | .05 | .01 |
| ❑ 128 | Richard Dent | .10 | .02 |
| ❑ 129 | Robert Porcher RC | .25 | .08 |
| ❑ 130 | Earnest Byner | .05 | .01 |
| ❑ 131 | Kent Hull | .05 | .01 |
| ❑ 132 | Mike Merriweather | .05 | .01 |
| ❑ 133 | Scott Fulhage | .05 | .01 |
| ❑ 134 | Kevin Porter | .05 | .01 |
| ❑ 135 | Tony Casillas | .05 | .01 |
| ❑ 136 | Dean Biasucci | .05 | .01 |
| ❑ 137 | Ben Smith | .05 | .01 |
| ❑ 138 | Bruce Kozerski | .05 | .01 |
| ❑ 139 | Jeff Campbell | .05 | .01 |
| ❑ 140 | Kevin Greene | .10 | .02 |
| ❑ 141 | Gary Plummer | .05 | .01 |
| ❑ 142 | Vincent Brown | .05 | .01 |
| ❑ 143 | Ron Hall | .05 | .01 |
| ❑ 144 | Louie Aguiar RC | .05 | .01 |
| ❑ 145 | Mark Duper | .05 | .01 |
| ❑ 146 | Jesse Sapolu | .05 | .01 |
| ❑ 147 | Jeff Gossett | .05 | .01 |
| ❑ 148 | Brian Noble | .05 | .01 |
| ❑ 149 | Derek Russell | .05 | .01 |
| ❑ 150 | Carlton Bailey RC | .05 | .01 |
| ❑ 151 | Kelly Goodburn | .05 | .01 |
| ❑ 152 | Audray McMillian UER | .05 | .01 |
| ❑ 153 | Neal Anderson | .05 | .01 |
| ❑ 154 | Bill Maas | .05 | .01 |
| ❑ 155 | Rickey Jackson | .05 | .01 |
| ❑ 156 | Chris Miller | .10 | .02 |
| ❑ 157 | Darren Comeaux | .05 | .01 |
| ❑ 158 | David Williams | .05 | .01 |
| ❑ 159 | Rich Gannon | .25 | .08 |
| ❑ 160 | Kevin Mack | .05 | .01 |
| ❑ 161 | Jim Arnold | .05 | .01 |
| ❑ 162 | Reggie White | .25 | .08 |
| ❑ 163 | Leonard Russell | .10 | .02 |
| ❑ 164 | Doug Smith | .05 | .01 |
| ❑ 165 | Tony Mandarich | .05 | .01 |
| ❑ 166 | Greg Lloyd | .10 | .02 |
| ❑ 167 | Jumbo Elliott | .05 | .01 |
| ❑ 168 | Jonathan Hayes | .05 | .01 |
| ❑ 169 | Jim Ritcher | .05 | .01 |
| ❑ 170 | Mike Kenn | .05 | .01 |
| ❑ 171 | James Washington | .05 | .01 |
| ❑ 172 | Tim Harris | .05 | .01 |
| ❑ 173 | James Thornton | .05 | .01 |
| ❑ 174 | John Brandes RC | .05 | .01 |
| ❑ 175 | Fred McAfee RC | .05 | .01 |
| ❑ 176 | Henry Rolling | .05 | .01 |
| ❑ 177 | Tony Paige | .05 | .01 |
| ❑ 178 | Jay Schroeder | .05 | .01 |
| ❑ 179 | Jeff Herrod | .05 | .01 |
| ❑ 180 | Emmitt Smith | 1.50 | .60 |
| ❑ 181 | Wymon Henderson | .05 | .01 |
| ❑ 182 | Rob Moore | .10 | .02 |
| ❑ 183 | Robert Wilson | .05 | .01 |
| ❑ 184 | Michael Zordich RC | .05 | .01 |
| ❑ 185 | Jim Harbaugh | .25 | .08 |
| ❑ 186 | Vince Workman | .05 | .01 |
| ❑ 187 | Ernest Givins | .10 | .02 |
| ❑ 188 | Herschel Walker | .10 | .02 |
| ❑ 189 | Dan Fike | .05 | .01 |
| ❑ 190 | Seth Joyner | .05 | .01 |
| ❑ 191 | Steve Young | .60 | .25 |
| ❑ 192 | Dennis Gibson | .05 | .01 |
| ❑ 193 | Darryl Talley | .05 | .01 |
| ❑ 194 | Emile Harry | .05 | .01 |
| ❑ 195 | Bill Fralic | .05 | .01 |
| ❑ 196 | Michael Stewart | .05 | .01 |
| ❑ 197 | James Francis | .05 | .01 |
| ❑ 198 | Jerome Henderson | .05 | .01 |
| ❑ 199 | John L. Williams | .05 | .01 |
| ❑ 200 | Rod Woodson | .25 | .08 |
| ❑ 201 | Mike Farr | .05 | .01 |
| ❑ 202 | Greg Montgomery | .05 | .01 |
| ❑ 203 | Andre Collins | .05 | .01 |
| ❑ 204 | Scott Miller | .05 | .01 |
| ❑ 205 | Clay Matthews | .10 | .02 |
| ❑ 206 | Ethan Horton | .05 | .01 |
| ❑ 207 | Rich Miano | .05 | .01 |
| ❑ 208 | Chris Mims RC | .05 | .01 |
| ❑ 209 | Anthony Morgan | .05 | .01 |
| ❑ 210 | Rodney Hampton | .10 | .02 |
| ❑ 211 | Chris Hinton | .05 | .01 |
| ❑ 212 | Esera Tuaolo | .05 | .01 |
| ❑ 213 | Shane Conlan | .05 | .01 |
| ❑ 214 | John Carney | .05 | .01 |
| ❑ 215 | Kenny Walker | .05 | .01 |
| ❑ 216 | Scott Radecic | .05 | .01 |
| ❑ 217 | Chris Martin | .05 | .01 |
| ❑ 218 | Checklist 111-220 UER | .05 | .01 |
| ❑ 219 | Wesley Carroll | .05 | .01 |
| ❑ 220 | Bill Romanowski | .05 | .01 |
| ❑ 221 | Reggie Cobb | .05 | .01 |
| ❑ 222 | Alfred Anderson | .05 | .01 |
| ❑ 223 | Cleveland Gary | .05 | .01 |
| ❑ 224 | Eddie Blake RC | .05 | .01 |
| ❑ 225 | Chris Spielman | .10 | .02 |
| ❑ 226 | John Roper | .05 | .01 |
| ❑ 227 | George Thomas RC | .05 | .01 |
| ❑ 228 | Jeff Faulkner | .05 | .01 |
| ❑ 229 | Chip Lohmiller UER | .05 | .01 |
| ❑ 230 | Hugh Millen | .05 | .01 |
| ❑ 231 | Ray Horton | .05 | .01 |
| ❑ 232 | James Campen | .05 | .01 |
| ❑ 233 | Howard Cross | .05 | .01 |
| ❑ 234 | Keith McKeller | .05 | .01 |
| ❑ 235 | Dino Hackett | .05 | .01 |
| ❑ 236 | Jerome Brown | .05 | .01 |
| ❑ 237 | Andy Heck | .05 | .01 |
| ❑ 238 | Rodney Holman | .05 | .01 |
| ❑ 239 | Bruce Matthews | .05 | .01 |
| ❑ 240 | Jeff Lageman | .05 | .01 |
| ❑ 241 | Bobby Hebert | .05 | .01 |
| ❑ 242 | Gary Anderson K | .05 | .01 |
| ❑ 243 | Mark Bortz | .05 | .01 |
| ❑ 244 | Rich Moran | .05 | .01 |
| ❑ 245 | Jeff Uhlenhake | .05 | .01 |
| ❑ 246 | Ricky Sanders | .05 | .01 |
| ❑ 247 | Clarence Kay | .05 | .01 |
| ❑ 248 | Ed King | .05 | .01 |
| ❑ 249 | Eddie Anderson | .05 | .01 |
| ❑ 250 | Amp Lee RC | .05 | .01 |
| ❑ 251 | Norm Johnson | .05 | .01 |
| ❑ 252 | Michael Carter | .05 | .01 |
| ❑ 253 | Felix Wright | .05 | .01 |
| ❑ 254 | Leon Seals | .05 | .01 |
| ❑ 255 | Nate Lewis | .05 | .01 |
| ❑ 256 | Kevin Call | .05 | .01 |
| ❑ 257 | Darryl Henley | .05 | .01 |
| ❑ 258 | Jon Vaughn | .05 | .01 |
| ❑ 259 | Matt Bahr | .05 | .01 |
| ❑ 260 | Johnny Johnson | .05 | .01 |
| ❑ 261 | Ken Norton | .10 | .02 |
| ❑ 262 | Wendell Davis | .05 | .01 |
| ❑ 263 | Eugene Robinson | .05 | .01 |
| ❑ 264 | David Treadwell | .05 | .01 |
| ❑ 265 | Michael Haynes | .10 | .02 |
| ❑ 266 | Robb Thomas | .05 | .01 |
| ❑ 267 | Nate Odomes | .05 | .01 |
| ❑ 268 | Martin Mayhew | .05 | .01 |
| ❑ 269 | Perry Kemp | .05 | .01 |
| ❑ 270 | Jerry Ball | .05 | .01 |
| ❑ 271 | Tommy Vardell RC | .05 | .01 |
| ❑ 272 | Ernie Mills | .05 | .01 |
| ❑ 273 | Mo Lewis | .05 | .01 |
| ❑ 274 | Roger Ruzek | .05 | .01 |
| ❑ 275 | Steve Smith | .05 | .01 |
| ❑ 276 | Bo Orlando RC | .05 | .01 |
| ❑ 277 | Louis Oliver | .05 | .01 |
| ❑ 278 | Toi Cook | .05 | .01 |
| ❑ 279 | Eddie Brown | .05 | .01 |
| ❑ 280 | Keith McCants | .05 | .01 |
| ❑ 281 | Rob Burnett | .05 | .01 |
| ❑ 282 | Keith DeLong | .05 | .01 |
| ❑ 283 | Stan Thomas UER | .05 | .01 |
| ❑ 284 | Robert Brown | .05 | .01 |
| ❑ 285 | John Alt | .05 | .01 |
| ❑ 286 | Randy Dixon | .05 | .01 |
| ❑ 287 | Siran Stacy RC | .05 | .01 |
| ❑ 288 | Ray Agnew | .05 | .01 |
| ❑ 289 | Darion Conner | .05 | .01 |
| ❑ 290 | Kirk Lowdermilk | .05 | .01 |
| ❑ 291 | Greg Jackson | .05 | .01 |
| ❑ 292 | Ken Harvey | .05 | .01 |
| ❑ 293 | Jacob Green | .05 | .01 |
| ❑ 294 | Mark Tuinei | .05 | .01 |
| ❑ 295 | Mark Rypien | .05 | .01 |
| ❑ 296 | Gerald Robinson RC | .05 | .01 |
| ❑ 297 | Broderick Thompson | .05 | .01 |
| ❑ 298 | Doug Widell | .05 | .01 |
| ❑ 299 | Carwell Gardner | .05 | .01 |
| ❑ 300 | Barry Sanders | 1.25 | .50 |
| ❑ 301 | Eric Metcalf | .10 | .02 |
| ❑ 302 | Eric Thomas | .05 | .01 |
| ❑ 303 | Terrell Buckley RC | .05 | .01 |
| ❑ 304 | Byron Evans | .05 | .01 |
| ❑ 305 | Johnny Hector | .05 | .01 |
| ❑ 306 | Steve Broussard | .05 | .01 |
| ❑ 307 | Gene Atkins | .05 | .01 |
| ❑ 308 | Terry McDaniel | .05 | .01 |
| ❑ 309 | Charles McRae | .05 | .01 |
| ❑ 310 | Jim Lachey | .05 | .01 |
| ❑ 311 | Pat Harlow | .05 | .01 |
| ❑ 312 | Kevin Butler | .05 | .01 |
| ❑ 313 | Scott Stephen | .05 | .01 |
| ❑ 314 | Dermontti Dawson | .05 | .01 |
| ❑ 315 | Johnny Meads | .05 | .01 |
| ❑ 316 | Checklist 221-330 | .05 | .01 |
| ❑ 317 | Aaron Craver | .05 | .01 |
| ❑ 318 | Michael Brooks | .05 | .01 |
| ❑ 319 | Guy McIntyre | .05 | .01 |
| ❑ 320 | Thurman Thomas | .25 | .08 |
| ❑ 321 | Courtney Hall | .05 | .01 |
| ❑ 322 | Dan Saleaumua | .05 | .01 |
| ❑ 323 | Vinson Smith RC | .05 | .01 |
| ❑ 324 | Steve Jordan | .05 | .01 |
| ❑ 325 | Walter Reeves | .05 | .01 |
| ❑ 326 | Erik Kramer | .10 | .02 |
| ❑ 327 | Duane Bickett | .05 | .01 |
| ❑ 328 | Tom Newberry | .05 | .01 |

| | | |
|---|---|---|
| ❏ 329 John Kasay | .05 | .01 |
| ❏ 330 Dave Meggett | .10 | .02 |
| ❏ 331 Kevin Ross | .05 | .01 |
| ❏ 332 Keith Hamilton RC | .10 | .02 |
| ❏ 333 Dwight Stone | .05 | .01 |
| ❏ 334 Mel Gray | .10 | .02 |
| ❏ 335 Harry Galbreath | .05 | .01 |
| ❏ 336 William Perry | .10 | .02 |
| ❏ 337 Brian Blades | .10 | .02 |
| ❏ 338 Randall McDaniel | .10 | .02 |
| ❏ 339 Pat Coleman RC | .05 | .01 |
| ❏ 340 Michael Irvin | .25 | .08 |
| ❏ 341 Checklist 331-440 | .05 | .01 |
| ❏ 342 Chris Mohr | .05 | .01 |
| ❏ 343 Greg Davis | .05 | .01 |
| ❏ 344 Dave Cadigan | .05 | .01 |
| ❏ 345 Art Monk | .10 | .02 |
| ❏ 346 Tim Goad | .05 | .01 |
| ❏ 347 Vinnie Clark | .05 | .01 |
| ❏ 348 David Fulcher | .05 | .01 |
| ❏ 349 Craig Heyward | .10 | .02 |
| ❏ 350 Ronnie Lott | .10 | .02 |
| ❏ 351 Dexter Carter | .05 | .01 |
| ❏ 352 Mark Jackson | .05 | .01 |
| ❏ 353 Brian Jordan | .10 | .02 |
| ❏ 354 Ray Donaldson | .05 | .01 |
| ❏ 355 Jim Price | .05 | .01 |
| ❏ 356 Rod Bernstine | .05 | .01 |
| ❏ 357 Tony Mayberry RC | .05 | .01 |
| ❏ 358 Richard Brown RC | .05 | .01 |
| ❏ 359 David Alexander | .05 | .01 |
| ❏ 360 Haywood Jeffires | .10 | .02 |
| ❏ 361 Henry Thomas | .05 | .01 |
| ❏ 362 Jeff Graham | .25 | .08 |
| ❏ 363 Don Warren | .05 | .01 |
| ❏ 364 Scott Davis | .05 | .01 |
| ❏ 365 Harlon Barnett | .05 | .01 |
| ❏ 366 Mark Collins | .05 | .01 |
| ❏ 367 Rick Tuten | .05 | .01 |
| ❏ 368 Lonnie Marts RC | .05 | .01 |
| ❏ 369 Dennis Smith | .05 | .01 |
| ❏ 370 Steve Tasker | .10 | .02 |
| ❏ 371 Robert Massey | .05 | .01 |
| ❏ 372 Ricky Reynolds | .05 | .01 |
| ❏ 373 Alvin Wright | .05 | .01 |
| ❏ 374 Kelvin Martin | .05 | .01 |
| ❏ 375 Vince Buck | .05 | .01 |
| ❏ 376 John Kidd | .05 | .01 |
| ❏ 377 William White | .05 | .01 |
| ❏ 378 Bryan Cox | .10 | .02 |
| ❏ 379 Jamie Dukes RC | .05 | .01 |
| ❏ 380 Anthony Munoz | .10 | .02 |
| ❏ 381 Mark Gunn RC | .05 | .01 |
| ❏ 382 Keith Henderson | .05 | .01 |
| ❏ 383 Charles Wilson | .05 | .01 |
| ❏ 384 Shawn McCarthy RC | .05 | .01 |
| ❏ 385 Ernie Jones | .05 | .01 |
| ❏ 386 Nick Bell | .05 | .01 |
| ❏ 387 Derrick Walker | .05 | .01 |
| ❏ 388 Mark Stepnoski | .10 | .02 |
| ❏ 389 Broderick Thomas | .05 | .01 |
| ❏ 390 Reggie Roby | .05 | .01 |
| ❏ 391 Bubba McDowell | .05 | .01 |
| ❏ 392 Eric Martin | .05 | .01 |
| ❏ 393 Toby Caston RC | .05 | .01 |
| ❏ 394 Bern Brostek | .05 | .01 |
| ❏ 395 Christian Okoye | .05 | .01 |
| ❏ 396 Frank Minnifield | .05 | .01 |
| ❏ 397 Mike Golic | .05 | .01 |
| ❏ 398 Grant Feasel | .05 | .01 |
| ❏ 399 Michael Ball | .05 | .01 |
| ❏ 400 Mike Croel | .05 | .01 |
| ❏ 401 Maury Buford | .05 | .01 |
| ❏ 402 Jeff Bostic UER | .05 | .01 |
| ❏ 403 Sean Landeta | .05 | .01 |
| ❏ 404 Terry Allen | .25 | .08 |
| ❏ 405 Donald Evans | .05 | .01 |
| ❏ 406 Don Mosebar | .05 | .01 |
| ❏ 407 D.J. Dozier | .05 | .01 |
| ❏ 408 Bruce Pickens | .05 | .01 |
| ❏ 409 Jim Dombrowski | .05 | .01 |
| ❏ 410 Deron Cherry | .05 | .01 |
| ❏ 411 Richard Johnson CB | .05 | .01 |
| ❏ 412 Alexander Wright | .05 | .01 |
| ❏ 413 Tom Rathman | .05 | .01 |
| ❏ 414 Mark Dennis | .05 | .01 |
| ❏ 415 Phil Hansen | .05 | .01 |

| | | |
|---|---|---|
| ❏ 416 Lonnie Young | .05 | .01 |
| ❏ 417 Burt Grossman | .05 | .01 |
| ❏ 418 Tony Covington | .05 | .01 |
| ❏ 419 John Stephens | .05 | .01 |
| ❏ 420 Jim Everett | .10 | .02 |
| ❏ 421 Johnny Holland | .05 | .01 |
| ❏ 422 Mike Barber RC WR | .05 | .01 |
| ❏ 423 Carl Lee | .05 | .01 |
| ❏ 424 Craig Patterson RC | .05 | .01 |
| ❏ 425 Greg Townsend | .05 | .01 |
| ❏ 426 Brett Perriman | .25 | .08 |
| ❏ 427 Morten Andersen | .05 | .01 |
| ❏ 428 John Gesek | .05 | .01 |
| ❏ 429 Bryan Barker | .05 | .01 |
| ❏ 430 John Taylor | .10 | .02 |
| ❏ 431 Donnell Woolford | .05 | .01 |
| ❏ 432 Ron Holmes | .05 | .01 |
| ❏ 433 Lee Williams | .05 | .01 |
| ❏ 434 Alfred Oglesby | .05 | .01 |
| ❏ 435 Jarrod Bunch | .05 | .01 |
| ❏ 436 Carlton Haselrig RC | .05 | .01 |
| ❏ 437 Rufus Porter | .05 | .01 |
| ❏ 438 Rohn Stark | .05 | .01 |
| ❏ 439 Tony Jones T | .05 | .01 |
| ❏ 440 Andre Rison | .10 | .02 |
| ❏ 441 Eric Hill | .05 | .01 |
| ❏ 442 Jesse Solomon | .05 | .01 |
| ❏ 443 Jackie Slater | .05 | .01 |
| ❏ 444 Donnie Elder | .05 | .01 |
| ❏ 445 Brett Maxie | .05 | .01 |
| ❏ 446 Max Montoya | .05 | .01 |
| ❏ 447 Will Wolford | .05 | .01 |
| ❏ 448 Craig Taylor | .05 | .01 |
| ❏ 449 Jimmie Jones | .05 | .01 |
| ❏ 450 Anthony Carter | .10 | .02 |
| ❏ 451 Brian Bollinger RC | .05 | .01 |
| ❏ 452 Checklist 441-550 | .05 | .01 |
| ❏ 453 Brad Edwards | .05 | .01 |
| ❏ 454 Gene Chilton RC | .05 | .01 |
| ❏ 455 Eric Allen | .05 | .01 |
| ❏ 456 William Roberts | .05 | .01 |
| ❏ 457 Eric Green | .05 | .01 |
| ❏ 458 Irv Eatman | .05 | .01 |
| ❏ 459 Derrick Thomas | .25 | .08 |
| ❏ 460 Tommy Kane | .05 | .01 |
| ❏ 461 LeRoy Butler | .05 | .01 |
| ❏ 462 Oliver Barnett | .05 | .01 |
| ❏ 463 Anthony Smith | .05 | .01 |
| ❏ 464 Cris Dishman | .05 | .01 |
| ❏ 465 Pat Terrell | .05 | .01 |
| ❏ 466 Greg Kragen | .05 | .01 |
| ❏ 467 Rodney Peete | .10 | .02 |
| ❏ 468 Willie Drewrey | .05 | .01 |
| ❏ 469 Jim Wilks | .05 | .01 |
| ❏ 470 Vince Newsome | .05 | .01 |
| ❏ 471 Chris Gardocki | .05 | .01 |
| ❏ 472 Chris Chandler | .25 | .08 |
| ❏ 473 George Thornton | .05 | .01 |
| ❏ 474 Albert Lewis | .05 | .01 |
| ❏ 475 Kevin Glover | .05 | .01 |
| ❏ 476 Joe Bowden RC | .05 | .01 |
| ❏ 477 Harry Sydney | .05 | .01 |
| ❏ 478 Bob Golic | .05 | .01 |
| ❏ 479 Tony Zendejas | .05 | .01 |
| ❏ 480 Brad Baxter | .05 | .01 |
| ❏ 481 Steve Beuerlein | .10 | .02 |
| ❏ 482 Mark Higgs | .05 | .01 |
| ❏ 483 Drew Hill | .05 | .01 |
| ❏ 484 Bryan Millard | .05 | .01 |
| ❏ 485 Mark Kelso | .05 | .01 |
| ❏ 486 David Grant | .05 | .01 |
| ❏ 487 Gary Zimmerman | .05 | .01 |
| ❏ 488 Leonard Marshall | .05 | .01 |
| ❏ 489 Keith Jackson | .10 | .02 |
| ❏ 490 Sterling Sharpe | .25 | .08 |
| ❏ 491 Ferrell Edmunds | .05 | .01 |
| ❏ 492 Wilber Marshall | .05 | .01 |
| ❏ 493 Charles Haley | .10 | .02 |
| ❏ 494 Riki Ellison | .05 | .01 |
| ❏ 495 Bill Brooks | .05 | .01 |
| ❏ 496 Bill Hawkins | .05 | .01 |
| ❏ 497 Erik Williams | .05 | .01 |
| ❏ 498 Leon Searcy RC | .05 | .01 |
| ❏ 499 Mike Horan | .05 | .01 |
| ❏ 500 Pat Swilling | .05 | .01 |
| ❏ 501 Maurice Hurst | .05 | .01 |
| ❏ 502 William Fuller | .05 | .01 |

| | | |
|---|---|---|
| ❏ 503 Tim Newton | .05 | .01 |
| ❏ 504 Lorenzo Lynch | .05 | .01 |
| ❏ 505 Tim Barnett | .05 | .01 |
| ❏ 506 Tom Thayer | .05 | .01 |
| ❏ 507 Chris Burkett | .05 | .01 |
| ❏ 508 Ronnie Harmon | .05 | .01 |
| ❏ 509 James Brooks | .10 | .02 |
| ❏ 510 Bennie Blades | .05 | .01 |
| ❏ 511 Roger Craig | .10 | .02 |
| ❏ 512 Tony Woods | .05 | .01 |
| ❏ 513 Greg Lewis | .05 | .01 |
| ❏ 514 Eric Pegram | .10 | .02 |
| ❏ 515 Elvis Patterson | .05 | .01 |
| ❏ 516 Jeff Cross | .05 | .01 |
| ❏ 517 Myron Guyton | .05 | .01 |
| ❏ 518 Jay Novacek | .10 | .02 |
| ❏ 519 Leo Barker RC | .05 | .01 |
| ❏ 520 Keith Byars | .05 | .01 |
| ❏ 521 Dalton Hilliard | .05 | .01 |
| ❏ 522 Ted Washington | .05 | .01 |
| ❏ 523 Dexter McNabb RC | .05 | .01 |
| ❏ 524 Frank Reich | .10 | .02 |
| ❏ 525 Henry Ellard | .05 | .01 |
| ❏ 526 Barry Foster | .10 | .02 |
| ❏ 527 Barry Word | .05 | .01 |
| ❏ 528 Gary Anderson RB | .05 | .01 |
| ❏ 529 Reggie Rutland | .05 | .01 |
| ❏ 530 Stephen Baker | .05 | .01 |
| ❏ 531 John Flannery | .05 | .01 |
| ❏ 532 Steve Wright | .05 | .01 |
| ❏ 533 Eric Sanders | .05 | .01 |
| ❏ 534 Bob Whitfield RC | .05 | .01 |
| ❏ 535 Gaston Green | .05 | .01 |
| ❏ 536 Anthony Pleasant | .05 | .01 |
| ❏ 537 Jeff Bryant | .05 | .01 |
| ❏ 538 Jarvis Williams | .05 | .01 |
| ❏ 539 Jim Morrisey | .05 | .01 |
| ❏ 540 Andre Tippett | .05 | .01 |
| ❏ 541 Gill Byrd | .05 | .01 |
| ❏ 542 Raleigh McKenzie | .05 | .01 |
| ❏ 543 Jim Sweeney | .05 | .01 |
| ❏ 544 David Lutz | .05 | .01 |
| ❏ 545 Wayne Martin | .05 | .01 |
| ❏ 546 Karl Wilson | .05 | .01 |
| ❏ 547 Pierce Holt | .05 | .01 |
| ❏ 548 Doug Smith | .05 | .01 |
| ❏ 549 Nolan Harrison RC | .05 | .01 |
| ❏ 550 Freddie Joe Nunn | .05 | .01 |
| ❏ 551 Eric Moore | .05 | .01 |
| ❏ 552 Cris Carter | .50 | .20 |
| ❏ 553 Kevin Gogan | .05 | .01 |
| ❏ 554 Harold Green | .05 | .01 |
| ❏ 555 Kenneth Davis | .05 | .01 |
| ❏ 556 Travis McNeal | .05 | .01 |
| ❏ 557 Jim C. Jensen | .05 | .01 |
| ❏ 558 Willie Green | .05 | .01 |
| ❏ 559 Scott Galbraith RC | .05 | .01 |
| ❏ 560 Louis Lipps | .05 | .01 |
| ❏ 561 Matt Brock | .05 | .01 |
| ❏ 562 Mike Prior | .05 | .01 |
| ❏ 563 Checklist 551-660 | .05 | .01 |
| ❏ 564 Robert Delpino | .05 | .01 |
| ❏ 565 Vinny Testaverde | .10 | .02 |
| ❏ 566 Willie Gault | .05 | .01 |
| ❏ 567 Quinn Early | .10 | .02 |
| ❏ 568 Eric Moten | .05 | .01 |
| ❏ 569 Lance Smith | .05 | .01 |
| ❏ 570 Darrell Green | .05 | .01 |
| ❏ 571 Moe Gardner | .05 | .01 |
| ❏ 572 Steve Atwater | .05 | .01 |
| ❏ 573 Ray Childress | .05 | .01 |
| ❏ 574 Dave Krieg | .10 | .02 |
| ❏ 575 Bruce Armstrong | .05 | .01 |
| ❏ 576 Fred Barnett | .25 | .08 |
| ❏ 577 Don Griffin | .05 | .01 |
| ❏ 578 David Brandon RC | .05 | .01 |
| ❏ 579 Robert Young | .05 | .01 |
| ❏ 580 Keith Van Horne | .05 | .01 |
| ❏ 581 Jeff Criswell | .05 | .01 |
| ❏ 582 Lewis Tillman | .05 | .01 |
| ❏ 583 Bubby Brister | .05 | .01 |
| ❏ 584 Aaron Wallace | .05 | .01 |
| ❏ 585 Chris Doleman | .05 | .01 |
| ❏ 586 Marty Carter RC | .05 | .01 |
| ❏ 587 Chris Warren | .25 | .08 |
| ❏ 588 David Griggs | .05 | .01 |
| ❏ 589 Darrell Thompson | .05 | .01 |

### 1993 Topps

|  |  | | |
|---|---|---|---|
| ☐ 590 | Marion Butts | .05 | .01 |
| ☐ 591 | Scott Norwood | .05 | .01 |
| ☐ 592 | Lomas Brown | .05 | .01 |
| ☐ 593 | Daryl Johnston | .25 | .08 |
| ☐ 594 | Alonzo Mitz RC | .05 | .01 |
| ☐ 595 | Tommy Barnhardt | .05 | .01 |
| ☐ 596 | Tim Jorden | .05 | .01 |
| ☐ 597 | Neil Smith | .25 | .08 |
| ☐ 598 | Todd Marinovich | .05 | .01 |
| ☐ 599 | Sean Jones | .05 | .01 |
| ☐ 600 | Clarence Verdin | .05 | .01 |
| ☐ 601 | Trace Armstrong | .05 | .01 |
| ☐ 602 | Steve Bono RC | .25 | .08 |
| ☐ 603 | Mark Ingram | .05 | .01 |
| ☐ 604 | Flipper Anderson | .05 | .01 |
| ☐ 605 | James Jones DT | .05 | .01 |
| ☐ 606 | Al Noga | .05 | .01 |
| ☐ 607 | Rick Bryan | .05 | .01 |
| ☐ 608 | Eugene Lockhart | .05 | .01 |
| ☐ 609 | Charles Mann | .05 | .01 |
| ☐ 610 | James Hasty | .05 | .01 |
| ☐ 611 | Jeff Feagles | .05 | .01 |
| ☐ 612 | Tim Brown | .25 | .08 |
| ☐ 613 | David Little | .05 | .01 |
| ☐ 614 | Keith Sims | .05 | .01 |
| ☐ 615 | Kevin Murphy | .05 | .01 |
| ☐ 616 | Ray Crockett | .05 | .01 |
| ☐ 617 | Jim Jeffcoat | .05 | .01 |
| ☐ 618 | Patrick Hunter | .05 | .01 |
| ☐ 619 | Keith Kartz | .05 | .01 |
| ☐ 620 | Peter Tom Willis | .05 | .01 |
| ☐ 621 | Vaughan Johnson | .05 | .01 |
| ☐ 622 | Shawn Jefferson | .05 | .01 |
| ☐ 623 | Anthony Thompson | .05 | .01 |
| ☐ 624 | John Rienstra | .05 | .01 |
| ☐ 625 | Don Maggs | .05 | .01 |
| ☐ 626 | Todd Lyght | .05 | .01 |
| ☐ 627 | Brent Jones | .10 | .02 |
| ☐ 628 | Todd McNair | .05 | .01 |
| ☐ 629 | Winston Moss | .05 | .01 |
| ☐ 630 | Mark Carrier WR | .10 | .02 |
| ☐ 631 | Dan Owens | .05 | .01 |
| ☐ 632 | Sammie Smith UER | .05 | .01 |
| ☐ 633 | James Lofton | .05 | .01 |
| ☐ 634 | Paul McJulien RC | .05 | .01 |
| ☐ 635 | Tony Tolbert | .05 | .01 |
| ☐ 636 | Carnell Lake | .05 | .01 |
| ☐ 637 | Gary Clark | .25 | .08 |
| ☐ 638 | Brian Washington | .05 | .01 |
| ☐ 639 | Jessie Hester | .05 | .01 |
| ☐ 640 | Doug Riesenberg | .05 | .01 |
| ☐ 641 | Joe Walter RC | .05 | .01 |
| ☐ 642 | John Rade | .05 | .01 |
| ☐ 643 | Wes Hopkins | .05 | .01 |
| ☐ 644 | Kelly Stouffer | .05 | .01 |
| ☐ 645 | Marv Cook | .05 | .01 |
| ☐ 646 | Ken Clarke | .05 | .01 |
| ☐ 647 | Bobby Humphrey UER | .05 | .01 |
| ☐ 648 | Tim McDonald | .05 | .01 |
| ☐ 649 | Donald Frank RC | .05 | .01 |
| ☐ 650 | Richmond Webb | .05 | .01 |
| ☐ 651 | Lemuel Stinson | .05 | .01 |
| ☐ 652 | Merton Hanks | .10 | .02 |
| ☐ 653 | Frank Warren | .05 | .01 |
| ☐ 654 | Thomas Benson | .05 | .01 |
| ☐ 655 | Al Smith | .05 | .01 |
| ☐ 656 | Steve DeBerg | .05 | .01 |
| ☐ 657 | Jayice Pearson RC | .05 | .01 |
| ☐ 658 | Joe Morris | .05 | .01 |
| ☐ 659 | Fred Strickland | .05 | .01 |
| ☐ 660 | Kelvin Pritchett | .05 | .01 |
| ☐ 661 | Lewis Billups | .05 | .01 |
| ☐ 662 | Todd Collins RC | .05 | .01 |
| ☐ 663 | Corey Miller RC | .05 | .01 |
| ☐ 664 | Levon Kirkland RC | .05 | .01 |
| ☐ 665 | Jerry Rice | .75 | .30 |
| ☐ 666 | Mike Lodish RC | .05 | .01 |
| ☐ 667 | Chuck Smith RC | .05 | .01 |
| ☐ 668 | Lance Olberding RC | .05 | .01 |
| ☐ 669 | Kevin Smith RC DB | .05 | .01 |
| ☐ 670 | Dale Carter RC | .10 | .02 |
| ☐ 671 | Sean Gilbert RC | .05 | .01 |
| ☐ 672 | Ken O'Brien | .05 | .01 |
| ☐ 673 | Ricky Proehl | .05 | .01 |
| ☐ 674 | Junior Seau | .25 | .08 |
| ☐ 675 | Courtney Hawkins RC | .10 | .02 |
| ☐ 676 | Eddie Robinson RC | .05 | .01 |

|  |  | | |
|---|---|---|---|
| ☐ 677 | Tommy Jeter RC | .05 | .01 |
| ☐ 678 | Jeff George | .25 | .08 |
| ☐ 679 | Cary Conklin | .05 | .01 |
| ☐ 680 | Rueben Mayes | .05 | .01 |
| ☐ 681 | Sean Lumpkin RC | .05 | .01 |
| ☐ 682 | Dan Marino | 1.25 | .50 |
| ☐ 683 | Ed McDaniel RC | .05 | .01 |
| ☐ 684 | Greg Skrepenak RC | .05 | .01 |
| ☐ 685 | Tracy Scroggins RC | .05 | .01 |
| ☐ 686 | Tommy Maddox RC | 2.00 | .75 |
| ☐ 687 | Mike Singletary | .10 | .02 |
| ☐ 688 | Patrick Rowe RC | .05 | .01 |
| ☐ 689 | Phillippi Sparks RC | .05 | .01 |
| ☐ 690 | Joel Steed RC | .05 | .01 |
| ☐ 691 | Kevin Fagan | .05 | .01 |
| ☐ 692 | Deion Sanders | .50 | .20 |
| ☐ 693 | Bruce Smith | .25 | .08 |
| ☐ 694 | David Klingler RC | .05 | .01 |
| ☐ 695 | Clayton Holmes RC | .05 | .01 |
| ☐ 696 | Brett Favre | 6.00 | 2.50 |
| ☐ 697 | Marc Boutte RC | .05 | .01 |
| ☐ 698 | Dwayne Sabb RC | .05 | .01 |
| ☐ 699 | Ed McCaffrey | .30 | .10 |
| ☐ 700 | Randall Cunningham | .25 | .08 |
| ☐ 701 | Quentin Coryatt RC | .05 | .01 |
| ☐ 702 | Bernie Kosar | .10 | .02 |
| ☐ 703 | Vaughn Dunbar RC | .05 | .01 |
| ☐ 704 | Browning Nagle | .05 | .01 |
| ☐ 705 | Mark Wheeler RC | .05 | .01 |
| ☐ 706 | Paul Siever RC | .05 | .01 |
| ☐ 707 | Anthony Miller | .10 | .02 |
| ☐ 708 | Corey Widmer RC | .05 | .01 |
| ☐ 709 | Eric Dickerson | .10 | .02 |
| ☐ 710 | Martin Bayless | .05 | .01 |
| ☐ 711 | Jason Hanson RC | .10 | .02 |
| ☐ 712 | Michael Dean Perry | .10 | .02 |
| ☐ 713 | Billy Joe Tolliver UER | .05 | .01 |
| ☐ 714 | Chad Hennings RC | .10 | .02 |
| ☐ 715 | Bucky Richardson RC | .05 | .01 |
| ☐ 716 | Steve Israel RC | .05 | .01 |
| ☐ 717 | Robert Harris RC | .05 | .01 |
| ☐ 718 | Timm Rosenbach | .05 | .01 |
| ☐ 719 | Joe Montana | 1.25 | .50 |
| ☐ 720 | Derek Brown TE RC | .05 | .01 |
| ☐ 721 | Robert Brooks RC | .75 | .30 |
| ☐ 722 | Boomer Esiason | .10 | .02 |
| ☐ 723 | Troy Auzenne RC | .05 | .01 |
| ☐ 724 | John Fina RC | .05 | .01 |
| ☐ 725 | Chris Crooms RC | .05 | .01 |
| ☐ 726 | Eugene Chung RC | .05 | .01 |
| ☐ 727 | Darren Woodson RC | .25 | .08 |
| ☐ 728 | Leslie O'Neal | .10 | .02 |
| ☐ 729 | Dan McGwire | .05 | .01 |
| ☐ 730 | Al Toon | .10 | .02 |
| ☐ 731 | Michael Brandon RC | .05 | .01 |
| ☐ 732 | Steve DeOssie | .05 | .01 |
| ☐ 733 | Jim Kelly | .25 | .08 |
| ☐ 734 | Webster Slaughter | .05 | .01 |
| ☐ 735 | Tony Smith RBK RC | .05 | .01 |
| ☐ 736 | Shane Collins RC | .05 | .01 |
| ☐ 737 | Randal Hill | .05 | .01 |
| ☐ 738 | Chris Holder RC | .05 | .01 |
| ☐ 739 | Russell Maryland | .10 | .02 |
| ☐ 740 | Carl Pickens RC | .25 | .08 |
| ☐ 741 | Andre Reed | .10 | .02 |
| ☐ 742 | Steve Emtman RC | .05 | .01 |
| ☐ 743 | Carl Banks | .05 | .01 |
| ☐ 744 | Troy Aikman | .75 | .30 |
| ☐ 745 | Mark Royals | .05 | .01 |
| ☐ 746 | J.J.Birden | .05 | .01 |
| ☐ 747 | Michael Cofer | .05 | .01 |
| ☐ 748 | Darryl Ashmore RC | .05 | .01 |
| ☐ 749 | Dion Lambert RC | .05 | .01 |
| ☐ 750 | Phil Simms | .10 | .02 |
| ☐ 751 | Reggie E.White RC | .25 | .08 |
| ☐ 752 | Harvey Williams | .25 | .08 |
| ☐ 753 | Ty Detmer | .25 | .08 |
| ☐ 754 | Tony Brooks RC | .05 | .01 |
| ☐ 755 | Steve Christie | .05 | .01 |
| ☐ 756 | Lawrence Taylor | .25 | .08 |
| ☐ 757 | Merril Hoge | .05 | .01 |
| ☐ 758 | Robert Jones RC | .05 | .01 |
| ☐ 759 | Checklist 661-759 | .05 | .01 |

### 1993 Topps

|  |  | | |
|---|---|---|---|
| ☐ | COMPLETE SET (660) | 30.00 | 12.00 |
| ☐ | COMP.FACT.SET (673) | 125.00 | 75.00 |
| ☐ | COMP.SERIES 1 (330) | 15.00 | 6.00 |
| ☐ | COMP.SERIES 2 (330) | 15.00 | 6.00 |
| ☐ 1 | Art Monk RB | .10 | .02 |
| ☐ 2 | Jerry Rice RB | .50 | .20 |
| ☐ 3 | Stanley Richard | .05 | .01 |
| ☐ 4 | Ron Hall | .05 | .01 |
| ☐ 5 | Daryl Johnston | .25 | .08 |
| ☐ 6 | Wendell Davis | .05 | .01 |
| ☐ 7 | Vaughn Dunbar | .05 | .01 |
| ☐ 8 | Mike Jones | .05 | .01 |
| ☐ 9 | Anthony Johnson | .10 | .02 |
| ☐ 10 | Chris Miller | .10 | .02 |
| ☐ 11 | Kyle Clifton | .05 | .01 |
| ☐ 12 | Curtis Conway RC | .40 | .15 |
| ☐ 13 | Lionel Washington | .05 | .01 |
| ☐ 14 | Reggie Johnson | .05 | .01 |
| ☐ 15 | David Little | .05 | .01 |
| ☐ 16 | Nick Lowery | .05 | .01 |
| ☐ 17 | Darryl Williams | .05 | .01 |
| ☐ 18 | Brent Jones | .10 | .02 |
| ☐ 19 | Bruce Matthews | .10 | .02 |
| ☐ 20 | Heath Sherman | .05 | .01 |
| ☐ 21 | John Kasay UER | .05 | .01 |
| ☐ 22 | Troy Drayton RC | .10 | .02 |
| ☐ 23 | Eric Metcalf | .10 | .02 |
| ☐ 24 | Andre Tippett | .10 | .02 |
| ☐ 25 | Rodney Hampton | .10 | .02 |
| ☐ 26 | Henry Jones | .05 | .01 |
| ☐ 27 | Jim Everett | .10 | .02 |
| ☐ 28 | Steve Jordan | .05 | .01 |
| ☐ 29 | LeRoy Butler | .05 | .01 |
| ☐ 30 | Troy Vincent | .05 | .01 |
| ☐ 31 | Nate Lewis | .05 | .01 |
| ☐ 32 | Rickey Jackson | .10 | .02 |
| ☐ 33 | Darion Conner | .05 | .01 |
| ☐ 34 | Tom Carter RC | .10 | .02 |
| ☐ 35 | Jeff George | .25 | .08 |
| ☐ 36 | Larry Centers RC | .25 | .08 |
| ☐ 37 | Reggie Cobb | .05 | .01 |
| ☐ 38 | Mike Saxon | .05 | .01 |
| ☐ 39 | Brad Baxter | .05 | .01 |
| ☐ 40 | Reggie White | .25 | .08 |
| ☐ 41 | Haywood Jeffires | .10 | .02 |
| ☐ 42 | Alfred Williams | .05 | .01 |
| ☐ 43 | Aaron Wallace | .05 | .01 |
| ☐ 44 | Tracy Simien | .05 | .01 |
| ☐ 45 | Pat Harlow | .05 | .01 |
| ☐ 46 | D.J. Johnson | .05 | .01 |
| ☐ 47 | Don Griffin | .05 | .01 |
| ☐ 48 | Flipper Anderson | .10 | .02 |
| ☐ 49 | Keith Kartz | .05 | .01 |
| ☐ 50 | Bernie Kosar | .10 | .02 |
| ☐ 51 | Kent Hull | .05 | .01 |
| ☐ 52 | Erik Howard | .05 | .01 |
| ☐ 53 | Pierce Holt | .05 | .01 |
| ☐ 54 | Dwayne Harper | .05 | .01 |
| ☐ 55 | Bennie Blades | .05 | .01 |
| ☐ 56 | Mark Duper | .05 | .01 |
| ☐ 57 | Brian Noble | .05 | .01 |
| ☐ 58 | Jeff Feagles | .05 | .01 |
| ☐ 59 | Michael Haynes | .10 | .02 |
| ☐ 60 | Junior Seau | .25 | .08 |
| ☐ 61 | Gaston Green AB | .10 | .02 |
| ☐ 62 | Jon Hand | .05 | .01 |
| ☐ 63 | Lin Elliott RC | .05 | .01 |
| ☐ 64 | Dana Stubblefield RC | .25 | .08 |

|  |  | | |
|---|--------|---|---|
| 65 | Vaughan Johnson | .05 | .01 |
| 66 | Mo Lewis | .05 | .01 |
| 67 | Aeneas Williams | .10 | .01 |
| 68 | David Fulcher | .05 | .01 |
| 69 | Chip Lohmiller | .05 | .01 |
| 70 | Greg Townsend | .10 | .02 |
| 71 | Simon Fletcher | .05 | .01 |
| 72 | Sean Salisbury | .10 | .01 |
| 73 | Christian Okoye | .10 | .02 |
| 74 | Jim Arnold | .05 | .01 |
| 75 | Bruce Smith | .25 | .08 |
| 76 | Fred Barnett | .10 | .02 |
| 77 | Bill Romanowski | .10 | .02 |
| 78 | Dermontti Dawson | .05 | .01 |
| 79 | Bern Brostek | .05 | .01 |
| 80 | Warren Moon | .25 | .08 |
| 81 | Bill Fralic | .05 | .01 |
| 82 | Lomas Brown FP | .05 | .01 |
| 83 | Duane Bickett FP | .05 | .01 |
| 84 | Neil Smith FP | .10 | .02 |
| 85 | Reggie White FP | .10 | .02 |
| 86 | Tim McDonald FP | .05 | .01 |
| 87 | Leslie O'Neal FP | .05 | .01 |
| 88 | Steve Young FP | .40 | .15 |
| 89 | Paul Gruber FP | .05 | .01 |
| 90 | Wilber Marshall FP | .05 | .01 |
| 91 | Trace Armstrong | .05 | .01 |
| 92 | Bobby Houston RC | .05 | .01 |
| 93 | George Thornton | .05 | .01 |
| 94 | Keith McCants | .05 | .01 |
| 95 | Ricky Sanders | .05 | .01 |
| 96 | Jackie Harris | .05 | .01 |
| 97 | Todd Marinovich | .05 | .01 |
| 98 | Henry Thomas | .05 | .01 |
| 99 | Jeff Wright | .05 | .01 |
| 100 | John Elway | 1.50 | .60 |
| 101 | Garrison Hearst RC | .75 | .30 |
| 102 | Roy Foster | .05 | .01 |
| 103 | David Lang | .05 | .01 |
| 104 | Matt Stover | .05 | .01 |
| 105 | Lawrence Taylor | .25 | .08 |
| 106 | Pete Stoyanovich | .05 | .01 |
| 107 | Jessie Tuggle | .05 | .01 |
| 108 | William White | .05 | .01 |
| 109 | Andy Harmon RC | .10 | .02 |
| 110 | John L. Williams | .05 | .01 |
| 111 | Jon Vaughn | .05 | .01 |
| 112 | John Alt | .05 | .01 |
| 113 | Chris Jacke | .05 | .01 |
| 114 | Jim Breech | .05 | .01 |
| 115 | Eric Martin | .05 | .01 |
| 116 | Derrick Walker | .05 | .01 |
| 117 | Ricky Ervins | .05 | .01 |
| 118 | Roger Craig | .10 | .02 |
| 119 | Jeff Gossett | .05 | .01 |
| 120 | Emmitt Smith | 1.50 | .60 |
| 121 | Bob Whitfield | .05 | .01 |
| 122 | Alonzo Spellman | .05 | .01 |
| 123 | David Klingler | .25 | .08 |
| 124 | Tommy Maddox | .25 | .08 |
| 125 | Robert Porcher | .05 | .01 |
| 126 | Edgar Bennett | .25 | .08 |
| 127 | Harvey Williams | .10 | .02 |
| 128 | Dave Brown RC | .25 | .08 |
| 129 | Johnny Mitchell | .05 | .01 |
| 130 | Drew Bledsoe RC | 2.50 | 1.00 |
| 131 | Zefross Moss | .05 | .01 |
| 132 | Nate Odomes | .05 | .01 |
| 133 | Rufus Porter | .05 | .01 |
| 134 | Jackie Slater | .10 | .01 |
| 135 | Steve Young | .75 | .30 |
| 136 | Chris Calloway | .05 | .01 |
| 137 | Steve Atwater | .05 | .01 |
| 138 | Mark Carrier DB | .05 | .01 |
| 139 | Marvin Washington | .05 | .01 |
| 140 | Barry Foster | .10 | .02 |
| 141 | Ricky Reynolds | .05 | .01 |
| 142 | Bubba McDowell | .05 | .01 |
| 143 | Dan Footman RC | .05 | .01 |
| 144 | Richmond Webb | .05 | .01 |
| 145 | Mike Pritchard | .10 | .02 |
| 146 | Chris Spielman | .05 | .01 |
| 147 | Dave Krieg | .10 | .02 |
| 148 | Nick Bell | .05 | .01 |
| 149 | Vincent Brown | .05 | .01 |
| 150 | Seth Joyner | .05 | .01 |
| 151 | Tommy Kane | .05 | .01 |
| 152 | Carlton Gray RC | .05 | .01 |
| 153 | Harry Newsome | .05 | .01 |
| 154 | Rohn Stark | .05 | .01 |
| 155 | Shannon Sharpe | .25 | .08 |
| 156 | Charles Haley | .10 | .02 |
| 157 | Cornelius Bennett | .10 | .02 |
| 158 | Doug Riesenberg | .05 | .01 |
| 159 | Amp Lee | .05 | .01 |
| 160 | Sterling Sharpe UER | .25 | .08 |
| 161 | Alonzo Mitz | .05 | .01 |
| 162 | Pat Terrell | .05 | .01 |
| 163 | Mark Schlereth | .05 | .01 |
| 164 | Gary Anderson K | .05 | .01 |
| 165 | Quinn Early | .10 | .02 |
| 166 | Jerome Bettis RC | 5.00 | 2.50 |
| 167 | Lawrence Dawsey | .05 | .01 |
| 168 | Derrick Thomas | .25 | .08 |
| 169 | Rodney Peete | .05 | .01 |
| 170 | Jim Kelly | .25 | .08 |
| 171 | Deion Sanders TL | .25 | .08 |
| 172 | Richard Dent TL | .05 | .01 |
| 173 | Emmitt Smith TL | .75 | .30 |
| 174 | Barry Sanders TL | .60 | .25 |
| 175 | Sterling Sharpe TL | .10 | .02 |
| 176 | Cleveland Gary TL | .05 | .01 |
| 177 | Terry Allen TL | .10 | .02 |
| 178 | Vaughan Johnson TL | .05 | .01 |
| 179 | Rodney Hampton TL | .05 | .01 |
| 180 | Randall Cunningham TL | .10 | .02 |
| 181 | Ricky Proehl TL | .05 | .01 |
| 182 | Jerry Rice TL | .50 | .20 |
| 183 | Reggie Cobb TL | .05 | .01 |
| 184 | Earnest Byner TL | .05 | .01 |
| 185 | Jeff Lageman | .05 | .01 |
| 186 | Carlos Jenkins | .05 | .01 |
| 187 | G.Heart/Dye/Moore/Cole. | .40 | .15 |
| 188 | Todd Lyght | .05 | .01 |
| 189 | Carl Simpson RC | .05 | .01 |
| 190 | Barry Sanders | 1.25 | .50 |
| 191 | Jim Harbaugh | .25 | .08 |
| 192 | Roger Ruzek | .05 | .01 |
| 193 | Brent Williams | .05 | .01 |
| 194 | Chip Banks | .05 | .01 |
| 195 | Mike Croel | .05 | .01 |
| 196 | Marion Butts | .10 | .02 |
| 197 | James Washington | .05 | .01 |
| 198 | John Offerdahl | .05 | .01 |
| 199 | Tom Rathman | .05 | .01 |
| 200 | Joe Montana | 1.50 | .60 |
| 201 | Pepper Johnson | .10 | .02 |
| 202 | Cris Dishman | .05 | .01 |
| 203 | Adrian White RC | .05 | .01 |
| 204 | Reggie Brooks RC | .10 | .02 |
| 205 | Cortez Kennedy | .10 | .02 |
| 206 | Robert Massey | .05 | .01 |
| 207 | Toi Cook | .05 | .01 |
| 208 | Harry Sydney | .05 | .01 |
| 209 | Lincoln Kennedy RC | .05 | .01 |
| 210 | Randall McDaniel | .15 | .05 |
| 211 | Eugene Daniel | .05 | .01 |
| 212 | Rob Burnett | .05 | .01 |
| 213 | Steve Broussard | .05 | .01 |
| 214 | Brian Washington | .05 | .01 |
| 215 | Leonard Renfro RC | .05 | .01 |
| 216 | Audray McMillian LL | .05 | .01 |
| 217 | Sterling Sharpe/Miller L | .05 | .01 |
| 218 | Clyde Simmons LL | .05 | .01 |
| 219 | Emmitt Smith/B.Foster LL | .40 | .15 |
| 220 | Steve Young/W.Moon LL | .10 | .02 |
| 221 | Mel Gray | .10 | .02 |
| 222 | Luis Sharpe | .05 | .01 |
| 223 | Eric Moten | .05 | .01 |
| 224 | Alvin Harper | .10 | .02 |
| 225 | Steve Wallace | .05 | .01 |
| 226 | Mark Higgs | .05 | .01 |
| 227 | Eugene Lockhart | .05 | .01 |
| 228 | Sean Jones | .05 | .01 |
| 229 | J.Lynch RC/Thom/DuBose | .60 | .25 |
| 230 | Jimmy Williams | .05 | .01 |
| 231 | Demetrius DuBose RC | .05 | .01 |
| 232 | John Roper | .05 | .01 |
| 233 | Keith Hamilton | .05 | .01 |
| 234 | Donald Evans | .05 | .01 |
| 235 | Kenneth Davis | .10 | .02 |
| 236 | John Copeland RC | .10 | .02 |
| 237 | Leonard Russell | .10 | .02 |
| 238 | Ken Harvey | .05 | .01 |
| 239 | Dale Carter | .05 | .01 |
| 240 | Anthony Pleasant | .05 | .01 |
| 241 | Darrell Green | .10 | .02 |
| 242 | Natrone Means RC | .25 | .08 |
| 243 | Rob Moore | .10 | .02 |
| 244 | Chris Doleman | .05 | .01 |
| 245 | J.B. Brown | .05 | .01 |
| 246 | Ray Crockett | .05 | .01 |
| 247 | John Taylor | .10 | .02 |
| 248 | Russell Maryland | .05 | .01 |
| 249 | Brett Favre | 2.00 | .75 |
| 250 | Carl Pickens | .10 | .02 |
| 251 | Andy Heck | .05 | .01 |
| 252 | Jerome Henderson | .05 | .01 |
| 253 | Deion Sanders | .50 | .20 |
| 254 | Steve Emtman | .05 | .01 |
| 255 | Calvin Williams | .10 | .02 |
| 256 | Sean Gilbert | .10 | .02 |
| 257 | Don Beebe | .05 | .01 |
| 258 | Robert Smith RC | 1.25 | .50 |
| 259 | Robert Blackmon | .05 | .01 |
| 260 | Jim Kelly TL | .10 | .02 |
| 261 | Harold Green TL UER | .05 | .01 |
| 262 | Clay Matthews TL | .05 | .01 |
| 263 | John Elway TL | .75 | .30 |
| 264 | Warren Moon TL | .10 | .02 |
| 265 | Jeff George TL | .10 | .02 |
| 266 | Derrick Thomas TL | .10 | .02 |
| 267 | Howie Long TL | .05 | .01 |
| 268 | Dan Marino TL | .75 | .30 |
| 269 | Jon Vaughn TL | .05 | .01 |
| 270 | Chris Burkett TL | .05 | .01 |
| 271 | Barry Foster TL | .05 | .01 |
| 272 | Marion Butts TL | .05 | .01 |
| 273 | Chris Warren TL | .05 | .01 |
| 274 | M.Strahan RC/M.Buck. | 2.00 | .75 |
| 275 | Tony Casillas | .05 | .01 |
| 276 | Jarrod Bunch | .05 | .01 |
| 277 | Eric Green | .05 | .01 |
| 278 | Stan Brock | .05 | .01 |
| 279 | Chester McGlockton | .10 | .02 |
| 280 | Ricky Watters | .25 | .08 |
| 281 | Dan Saleaumua | .05 | .01 |
| 282 | Rich Camarillo | .05 | .01 |
| 283 | Cris Carter | .25 | .08 |
| 284 | Rick Mirer RC | .25 | .08 |
| 285 | Matt Brock | .05 | .01 |
| 286 | Burt Grossman | .05 | .01 |
| 287 | Andre Collins | .05 | .01 |
| 288 | Mark Jackson | .05 | .01 |
| 289 | Dan Marino | 1.50 | .60 |
| 290 | Cornelius Bennett FG | .05 | .01 |
| 291 | Steve Atwater FG | .05 | .01 |
| 292 | Bryan Cox FG | .05 | .01 |
| 293 | Sam Mills FG | .05 | .01 |
| 294 | Pepper Johnson FG | .05 | .01 |
| 295 | Seth Joyner FG | .05 | .01 |
| 296 | Chris Spielman FG | .05 | .01 |
| 297 | Junior Seau FG | .10 | .02 |
| 298 | Cortez Kennedy FG | .05 | .01 |
| 299 | Broderick Thomas FG | .05 | .01 |
| 300 | Todd McNair | .05 | .01 |
| 301 | Nate Newton | .10 | .02 |
| 302 | Michael Walter | .05 | .01 |
| 303 | Clyde Simmons | .05 | .01 |
| 304 | Ernie Mills | .05 | .01 |
| 305 | Steve Wisniewski | .05 | .01 |
| 306 | Coleman Rudolph RC | .05 | .01 |
| 307 | Thurman Thomas | .25 | .08 |
| 308 | Reggie Roby | .05 | .01 |
| 309 | Eric Swann | .10 | .02 |
| 310 | Mark Wheeler | .05 | .01 |
| 311 | Jeff Herrod | .05 | .01 |
| 312 | Leroy Hoard | .10 | .02 |
| 313 | Patrick Bates RC | .05 | .01 |
| 314 | Earnest Byner | .05 | .01 |
| 315 | Dave Meggett | .10 | .02 |
| 316 | George Teague RC | .10 | .02 |
| 317 | Ray Childress | .10 | .02 |
| 318 | Mike Kenn | .05 | .01 |
| 319 | Jason Hanson | .05 | .01 |
| 320 | Gary Clark | .10 | .02 |
| 321 | Chris Gardocki | .05 | .01 |
| 322 | Ken Norton | .10 | .02 |
| 323 | Eric Curry RC | .05 | .01 |
| 324 | Byron Evans | .05 | .01 |

|  |  | | |
|---|---|---|---|
| ❏ 326 | O.J.McDuffie RC | .25 | .08 |
| ❏ 327 | Dwight Stone | .05 | .01 |
| ❏ 328 | Tommy Barnhardt | .05 | .01 |
| ❏ 329 | Checklist 1-165 | .05 | .01 |
| ❏ 330 | Checklist 166-329 | .05 | .01 |
| ❏ 331 | Erik Williams | .05 | .01 |
| ❏ 332 | Phil Hansen | .05 | .01 |
| ❏ 333 | Martin Harrison RC | .05 | .01 |
| ❏ 334 | Mark Ingram | .05 | .01 |
| ❏ 335 | Mark Rypien | .10 | .02 |
| ❏ 336 | Anthony Miller | .10 | .02 |
| ❏ 337 | Antone Davis | .05 | .01 |
| ❏ 338 | Mike Munchak | .10 | .02 |
| ❏ 339 | Wayne Martin | .05 | .01 |
| ❏ 340 | Joe Montana | 1.50 | .60 |
| ❏ 341 | Deon Figures RC | .05 | .01 |
| ❏ 342 | Ed McDaniel | .05 | .01 |
| ❏ 343 | Chris Burkett | .05 | .01 |
| ❏ 344 | Tony Smith RB | .05 | .01 |
| ❏ 345 | James Lofton | .10 | .02 |
| ❏ 346 | Courtney Hawkins | .05 | .01 |
| ❏ 347 | Dennis Smith | .05 | .01 |
| ❏ 348 | Anthony Morgan | .05 | .01 |
| ❏ 349 | Chris Goode | .05 | .01 |
| ❏ 350 | Phil Simms | .10 | .02 |
| ❏ 351 | Patrick Hunter | .05 | .01 |
| ❏ 352 | Brett Perriman | .25 | .08 |
| ❏ 353 | Corey Miller | .05 | .01 |
| ❏ 354 | Harry Galbreath | .05 | .01 |
| ❏ 355 | Mark Carrier WR | .10 | .02 |
| ❏ 356 | Troy Drayton | .10 | .02 |
| ❏ 357 | Greg Davis | .05 | .01 |
| ❏ 358 | Tim Krumrie | .05 | .01 |
| ❏ 359 | Tim McDonald | .05 | .01 |
| ❏ 360 | Webster Slaughter | .05 | .01 |
| ❏ 361 | Steve Christie | .05 | .01 |
| ❏ 362 | Courtney Hall | .05 | .01 |
| ❏ 363 | Charles Mann | .05 | .01 |
| ❏ 364 | Vestee Jackson | .05 | .01 |
| ❏ 365 | Robert Jones | .05 | .01 |
| ❏ 366 | Rich Miano | .05 | .01 |
| ❏ 367 | Morten Andersen | .10 | .02 |
| ❏ 368 | Jeff Graham | .10 | .02 |
| ❏ 369 | Martin Mayhew | .05 | .01 |
| ❏ 370 | Anthony Carter | .10 | .02 |
| ❏ 371 | Greg Kragen | .05 | .01 |
| ❏ 372 | Ron Cox | .05 | .01 |
| ❏ 373 | Perry Williams | .05 | .01 |
| ❏ 374 | Willie Gault | .10 | .02 |
| ❏ 375 | Chris Warren | .10 | .02 |
| ❏ 376 | Reyna Thompson | .05 | .01 |
| ❏ 377 | Bennie Thompson | .05 | .01 |
| ❏ 378 | Kevin Mack | .05 | .01 |
| ❏ 379 | Clarence Verdin | .05 | .01 |
| ❏ 380 | Marc Boutte | .05 | .01 |
| ❏ 381 | Marvin Jones RC | .05 | .01 |
| ❏ 382 | Greg Jackson | .05 | .01 |
| ❏ 383 | Steve Bono | .10 | .02 |
| ❏ 384 | Terrell Buckley | .05 | .01 |
| ❏ 385 | Garrison Hearst | .25 | .08 |
| ❏ 386 | Mike Brim | .05 | .01 |
| ❏ 387 | Jesse Sapolu | .05 | .01 |
| ❏ 388 | Carl Lee | .05 | .01 |
| ❏ 389 | Jeff Cross | .05 | .01 |
| ❏ 390 | Karl Mecklenburg | .10 | .02 |
| ❏ 391 | Chad Hennings | .05 | .01 |
| ❏ 392 | Oliver Barnett | .05 | .01 |
| ❏ 393 | Dalton Hilliard | .05 | .01 |
| ❏ 394 | Broderick Thompson | .05 | .01 |
| ❏ 395 | Rocket Ismail | .10 | .02 |
| ❏ 396 | John Kidd | .05 | .01 |
| ❏ 397 | Eddie Anderson | .05 | .01 |
| ❏ 398 | Lamar Lathon | .05 | .01 |
| ❏ 399 | Darren Perry | .05 | .01 |
| ❏ 400 | Drew Bledsoe | 1.25 | .50 |
| ❏ 401 | Ferrell Edmunds | .05 | .01 |
| ❏ 402 | Lomas Brown | .05 | .01 |
| ❏ 403 | Drew Hill | .10 | .02 |
| ❏ 404 | David Whitmore | .05 | .01 |
| ❏ 405 | Mike Johnson | .05 | .01 |
| ❏ 406 | Paul Gruber | .05 | .01 |
| ❏ 407 | Kirk Lowdermilk | .05 | .01 |
| ❏ 408 | Curtis Conway | .25 | .08 |
| ❏ 409 | Bryce Paup | .10 | .02 |
| ❏ 410 | Boomer Esiason | .10 | .02 |
| ❏ 411 | Jay Schroeder | .05 | .01 |
| ❏ 412 | Anthony Newman | .05 | .01 |
| ❏ 413 | Ernie Jones | .05 | .01 |
| ❏ 414 | Carlton Bailey | .05 | .01 |
| ❏ 415 | Kenneth Gant | .05 | .01 |
| ❏ 416 | Todd Scott | .05 | .01 |
| ❏ 417 | Anthony Smith | .05 | .01 |
| ❏ 418 | Erik McMillan | .05 | .01 |
| ❏ 419 | Ronnie Harmon | .05 | .01 |
| ❏ 420 | Andre Reed | .10 | .02 |
| ❏ 421 | Wymon Henderson | .05 | .01 |
| ❏ 422 | Carnell Lake | .05 | .01 |
| ❏ 423 | Al Noga | .05 | .01 |
| ❏ 424 | Curtis Duncan | .05 | .01 |
| ❏ 425 | Mike Gann | .05 | .01 |
| ❏ 426 | Eugene Robinson | .10 | .02 |
| ❏ 427 | Scott Mersereau | .05 | .01 |
| ❏ 428 | Chris Singleton | .05 | .01 |
| ❏ 429 | Gerald Robinson | .05 | .01 |
| ❏ 430 | Pat Swilling | .10 | .02 |
| ❏ 431 | Ed McCaffrey | .05 | .01 |
| ❏ 432 | Neal Anderson | .10 | .02 |
| ❏ 433 | Joe Phillips | .05 | .01 |
| ❏ 434 | Jerry Ball | .05 | .01 |
| ❏ 435 | Tyronne Stowe | .05 | .01 |
| ❏ 436 | Dana Stubblefield | .25 | .08 |
| ❏ 437 | Eric Curry | .05 | .01 |
| ❏ 438 | Derrick Fenner | .05 | .01 |
| ❏ 439 | Mark Clayton | .10 | .02 |
| ❏ 440 | Quentin Coryatt | .10 | .02 |
| ❏ 441 | Willie Roaf RC | .10 | .02 |
| ❏ 442 | Ernest Dye | .05 | .01 |
| ❏ 443 | Jeff Jaeger | .05 | .01 |
| ❏ 444 | Stan Humphries | .10 | .02 |
| ❏ 445 | Johnny Johnson | .05 | .01 |
| ❏ 446 | Larry Brown DB | .05 | .01 |
| ❏ 447 | Kurt Gouveia | .05 | .01 |
| ❏ 448 | Qadry Ismail RC | .25 | .08 |
| ❏ 449 | Dan Footman | .05 | .01 |
| ❏ 450 | Tom Waddle | .05 | .01 |
| ❏ 451 | Kelvin Martin | .05 | .01 |
| ❏ 452 | Kanavis McGhee | .05 | .01 |
| ❏ 453 | Herman Moore | .25 | .08 |
| ❏ 454 | Jesse Solomon | .05 | .01 |
| ❏ 455 | Shane Conlan | .05 | .01 |
| ❏ 456 | Joel Steed | .05 | .01 |
| ❏ 457 | Charles Arbuckle | .05 | .01 |
| ❏ 458 | Shane Dronett | .05 | .01 |
| ❏ 459 | Steve Tasker | .10 | .02 |
| ❏ 460 | Herschel Walker | .10 | .02 |
| ❏ 461 | Willie Davis | .25 | .08 |
| ❏ 462 | Al Smith | .05 | .01 |
| ❏ 463 | O.J.McDuffie | .25 | .08 |
| ❏ 464 | Kevin Fagan | .05 | .01 |
| ❏ 465 | Hardy Nickerson | .10 | .02 |
| ❏ 466 | Leonard Marshall | .10 | .02 |
| ❏ 467 | John Baylor | .05 | .01 |
| ❏ 468 | Jay Novacek | .10 | .02 |
| ❏ 469 | Wayne Simmons RC | .05 | .01 |
| ❏ 470 | Tommy Vardell | .05 | .01 |
| ❏ 471 | Cleveland Gary | .05 | .01 |
| ❏ 472 | Mark Collins | .10 | .02 |
| ❏ 473 | Craig Heyward | .10 | .02 |
| ❏ 474 | John Copeland UER | .10 | .02 |
| ❏ 475 | Jeff Hostetler | .10 | .02 |
| ❏ 476 | Brian Mitchell | .10 | .02 |
| ❏ 477 | Natrone Means | .25 | .08 |
| ❏ 478 | Brad Muster | .05 | .01 |
| ❏ 479 | David Lutz | .05 | .01 |
| ❏ 480 | Andre Rison | .10 | .02 |
| ❏ 481 | Michael Zordich | .05 | .01 |
| ❏ 482 | Jim McMahon | .10 | .02 |
| ❏ 483 | Carlton Gray | .05 | .01 |
| ❏ 484 | Chris Mohr | .05 | .01 |
| ❏ 485 | Ernest Givins | .10 | .02 |
| ❏ 486 | Tony Tolbert | .05 | .01 |
| ❏ 487 | Vai Sikahema | .05 | .01 |
| ❏ 488 | Larry Webster | .05 | .01 |
| ❏ 489 | James Hasty | .05 | .01 |
| ❏ 490 | Reggie White | .25 | .08 |
| ❏ 491 | Reggie Rivers RC | .05 | .01 |
| ❏ 492 | Roman Phifer | .05 | .01 |
| ❏ 493 | Lewon Kirkland | .05 | .01 |
| ❏ 494 | Demetrius DuBose | .05 | .01 |
| ❏ 495 | William Perry | .10 | .02 |
| ❏ 496 | Clay Matthews | .10 | .02 |
| ❏ 497 | Aaron Jones | .05 | .01 |
| ❏ 498 | Jack Trudeau | .05 | .01 |
| ❏ 499 | Michael Brooks | .05 | .01 |
| ❏ 500 | Jerry Rice | 1.00 | .40 |
| ❏ 501 | Lonnie Marts | .05 | .01 |
| ❏ 502 | Tim McGee | .10 | .02 |
| ❏ 503 | Kelvin Pritchett | .10 | .02 |
| ❏ 504 | Bobby Hebert | .10 | .02 |
| ❏ 505 | Audray McMillian | .05 | .01 |
| ❏ 506 | Chuck Cecil | .05 | .01 |
| ❏ 507 | Leonard Renfro | .05 | .01 |
| ❏ 508 | Ethan Horton | .05 | .01 |
| ❏ 509 | Kevin Smith | .10 | .02 |
| ❏ 510 | Louis Oliver | .05 | .01 |
| ❏ 511 | John Stephens | .05 | .01 |
| ❏ 512 | Browning Nagle | .05 | .01 |
| ❏ 513 | Ricardo McDonald | .05 | .01 |
| ❏ 514 | Leslie O'Neal | .10 | .02 |
| ❏ 515 | Lorenzo White | .05 | .01 |
| ❏ 516 | Thomas Smith RC | .10 | .02 |
| ❏ 517 | Tony Woods | .05 | .01 |
| ❏ 518 | Darryl Henley | .05 | .01 |
| ❏ 519 | Robert Delpino | .05 | .01 |
| ❏ 520 | Rod Woodson | .25 | .08 |
| ❏ 521 | Phillippi Sparks | .05 | .01 |
| ❏ 522 | Jessie Hester | .05 | .01 |
| ❏ 523 | Shaun Gayle | .05 | .01 |
| ❏ 524 | Brad Edwards | .05 | .01 |
| ❏ 525 | Randall Cunningham | .25 | .08 |
| ❏ 526 | Marv Cook | .05 | .01 |
| ❏ 527 | Dennis Gibson | .05 | .01 |
| ❏ 528 | Erric Pegram | .10 | .02 |
| ❏ 529 | Terry McDaniel | .05 | .01 |
| ❏ 530 | Troy Aikman | .75 | .30 |
| ❏ 531 | Irving Fryar | .10 | .02 |
| ❏ 532 | Blair Thomas | .05 | .01 |
| ❏ 533 | Jim Wilks | .05 | .01 |
| ❏ 534 | Michael Jackson | .10 | .02 |
| ❏ 535 | Eric Davis | .05 | .01 |
| ❏ 536 | James Campen | .05 | .01 |
| ❏ 537 | Steve Beuerlein | .10 | .02 |
| ❏ 538 | Robert Smith | .50 | .20 |
| ❏ 539 | J.J. Birden | .05 | .01 |
| ❏ 540 | Broderick Thomas | .05 | .01 |
| ❏ 541 | Darryl Talley | .05 | .01 |
| ❏ 542 | Russell Freeman RC | .05 | .01 |
| ❏ 543 | David Alexander | .05 | .01 |
| ❏ 544 | Chris Mims | .05 | .01 |
| ❏ 545 | Coleman Rudolph | .05 | .01 |
| ❏ 546 | Steve McMichael | .10 | .02 |
| ❏ 547 | David Williams | .05 | .01 |
| ❏ 548 | Chris Hinton | .05 | .01 |
| ❏ 549 | Jim Jeffcoat | .05 | .01 |
| ❏ 550 | Howie Long | .25 | .06 |
| ❏ 551 | Roosevelt Potts RC | .05 | .01 |
| ❏ 552 | Bryan Cox | .05 | .01 |
| ❏ 553 | David Richards UER | .05 | .01 |
| ❏ 554 | Reggie Brooks | .10 | .02 |
| ❏ 555 | Neil O'Donnell | .25 | .08 |
| ❏ 556 | Irv Smith RC | .05 | .01 |
| ❏ 557 | Henry Ellard | .10 | .02 |
| ❏ 558 | Steve DeBerg | .10 | .02 |
| ❏ 559 | Jim Sweeney | .05 | .01 |
| ❏ 560 | Harold Green | .05 | .01 |
| ❏ 561 | Darrell Thompson | .05 | .01 |
| ❏ 562 | Vinny Testaverde | .10 | .02 |
| ❏ 563 | Bubby Brister | .05 | .01 |
| ❏ 564 | Sean Landeta | .05 | .01 |
| ❏ 565 | Neil Smith | .25 | .08 |
| ❏ 566 | Craig Erickson | .05 | .01 |
| ❏ 567 | Jim Ritcher | .05 | .01 |
| ❏ 568 | Don Mosebar | .05 | .01 |
| ❏ 569 | John Gesek | .05 | .01 |
| ❏ 570 | Gary Plummer | .05 | .01 |
| ❏ 571 | Norm Johnson | .05 | .01 |
| ❏ 572 | Ron Heller | .05 | .01 |
| ❏ 573 | Carl Simpson | .05 | .01 |
| ❏ 574 | Greg Montgomery | .05 | .01 |
| ❏ 575 | Dana Hall | .05 | .01 |
| ❏ 576 | Vencie Glenn | .05 | .01 |
| ❏ 577 | Dean Biasucci | .05 | .01 |
| ❏ 578 | Rod Bernstine UER | .05 | .01 |
| ❏ 579 | Randal Hill | .05 | .01 |
| ❏ 580 | Sam Mills | .10 | .02 |
| ❏ 581 | Santana Dotson | .10 | .02 |
| ❏ 582 | Greg Lloyd | .10 | .02 |
| ❏ 583 | Eric Thomas | .05 | .01 |
| ❏ 584 | Henry Rolling | .05 | .01 |
| ❏ 585 | Tony Bennett | .05 | .01 |
| ❏ 586 | Sheldon White | .05 | .01 |

| | | |
|---|---|---|
| ❏ 587 Mark Kelso | .10 | .02 |
| ❏ 588 Marc Spindler | .05 | .01 |
| ❏ 589 Greg McMurtry | .05 | .01 |
| ❏ 590 Art Monk | .10 | .02 |
| ❏ 591 Marco Coleman | .05 | .01 |
| ❏ 592 Tony Jones T | .05 | .01 |
| ❏ 593 Melvin Jenkins | .05 | .01 |
| ❏ 594 Kevin Ross | .05 | .01 |
| ❏ 595 William Fuller | .05 | .01 |
| ❏ 596 James Joseph | .05 | .01 |
| ❏ 597 Lamar McGriggs RC | .05 | .01 |
| ❏ 598 Gill Byrd | .05 | .01 |
| ❏ 599 Alexander Wright | .05 | .01 |
| ❏ 600 Rick Mirer | .25 | .08 |
| ❏ 601 Richard Dent | .10 | .02 |
| ❏ 602 Thomas Everett | .05 | .01 |
| ❏ 603 Jack Del Rio | .10 | .02 |
| ❏ 604 Jerome Bettis | 2.50 | 1.00 |
| ❏ 605 Ronnie Lott | .10 | .02 |
| ❏ 606 Marty Carter | .05 | .01 |
| ❏ 607 Arthur Marshall RC | .05 | .01 |
| ❏ 608 Lee Johnson | .05 | .01 |
| ❏ 609 Bruce Armstrong | .05 | .01 |
| ❏ 610 Ricky Proehl | .10 | .02 |
| ❏ 611 Will Wolford | .05 | .01 |
| ❏ 612 Mike Prior | .05 | .01 |
| ❏ 613 George Jamison | .05 | .01 |
| ❏ 614 Gene Atkins | .05 | .01 |
| ❏ 615 Merril Hoge | .10 | .02 |
| ❏ 616 Desmond Howard | .10 | .02 |
| ❏ 617 Jarvis Williams | .05 | .01 |
| ❏ 618 Marcus Allen | .25 | .08 |
| ❏ 619 Gary Brown | .05 | .01 |
| ❏ 620 Bill Brooks | .05 | .01 |
| ❏ 621 Eric Allen | .05 | .01 |
| ❏ 622 Todd Kelly | .05 | .01 |
| ❏ 623 Michael Dean Perry | .10 | .02 |
| ❏ 624 David Braxton | .05 | .01 |
| ❏ 625 Mike Sherrard | .05 | .01 |
| ❏ 626 Jeff Bryant | .05 | .01 |
| ❏ 627 Eric Bieniemy | .05 | .01 |
| ❏ 628 Tim Brown | .25 | .08 |
| ❏ 629 Troy Auzenne | .05 | .01 |
| ❏ 630 Michael Irvin | .25 | .08 |
| ❏ 631 Maurice Hurst | .05 | .01 |
| ❏ 632 Duane Bickett | .05 | .01 |
| ❏ 633 George Teague | .10 | .02 |
| ❏ 634 Vince Workman | .05 | .01 |
| ❏ 635 Renaldo Turnbull | .05 | .01 |
| ❏ 636 Johnny Bailey | .05 | .01 |
| ❏ 637 Dan Williams RC | .05 | .01 |
| ❏ 638 James Thornton | .05 | .01 |
| ❏ 639 Terry Allen | .25 | .08 |
| ❏ 640 Kevin Greene | .10 | .02 |
| ❏ 641 Tony Zendejas | .05 | .01 |
| ❏ 642 Scott Kowalkowski RC | .05 | .01 |
| ❏ 643 Jeff Query UER | .05 | .01 |
| ❏ 644 Brian Blades | .10 | .02 |
| ❏ 645 Keith Jackson | .10 | .02 |
| ❏ 646 Monte Coleman | .05 | .01 |
| ❏ 647 Guy McIntyre | .05 | .01 |
| ❏ 648 Barry Word | .05 | .01 |
| ❏ 649 Steve Everitt RC | .05 | .01 |
| ❏ 650 Patrick Bates | .05 | .01 |
| ❏ 651 Marcus Robertson RC | .05 | .01 |
| ❏ 652 John Carney | .05 | .01 |
| ❏ 653 Derek Brown TE | .05 | .01 |
| ❏ 654 Carwell Gardner | .05 | .01 |
| ❏ 655 Moe Gardner | .05 | .01 |
| ❏ 656 Andre Ware | .10 | .02 |
| ❏ 657 Keith Van Horne | .05 | .01 |
| ❏ 658 Hugh Millen | .05 | .01 |
| ❏ 659 Checklist 330-495 | .05 | .01 |
| ❏ 660 Checklist 496-660 | .05 | .01 |

## 1994 Topps

| | | |
|---|---|---|
| ❏ COMPLETE SET (660) | 80.00 | 40.00 |
| ❏ COMP.FACT.SET | 80.00 | 45.00 |
| ❏ COMP.SERIES 1 (330) | 25.00 | 12.50 |
| ❏ COMP.SERIES 2 (330) | 25.00 | 12.50 |
| ❏ 1 Emmitt Smith | 1.50 | .60 |
| ❏ 2 Russell Copeland | .05 | .01 |
| ❏ 3 Jesse Sapolu | .05 | .01 |
| ❏ 4 David Szott | .05 | .01 |
| ❏ 5 Rodney Hampton | .10 | .02 |
| ❏ 6 Bubba McDowell | .05 | .01 |
| ❏ 7 Bryce Paup | .10 | .02 |

| | | |
|---|---|---|
| ❏ 8 Winston Moss | .05 | .01 |
| ❏ 9 Brett Perriman | .10 | .02 |
| ❏ 10 Rod Woodson | .10 | .02 |
| ❏ 11 John Randle | .10 | .02 |
| ❏ 12 David Wyman | .05 | .01 |
| ❏ 13 Jeff Cross | .05 | .01 |
| ❏ 14 Richard Cooper | .05 | .01 |
| ❏ 15 Johnny Mitchell | .05 | .01 |
| ❏ 16 David Alexander | .05 | .01 |
| ❏ 17 Ronnie Harmon | .05 | .01 |
| ❏ 18 Tyronne Stowe UER | .05 | .01 |
| ❏ 19 Chris Zorich | .05 | .01 |
| ❏ 20 Rob Burnett | .05 | .01 |
| ❏ 21 Harold Alexander | .05 | .01 |
| ❏ 22 Rod Stephens | .05 | .01 |
| ❏ 23 Mark Wheeler | .05 | .01 |
| ❏ 24 Dwayne Sabb | .05 | .01 |
| ❏ 25 Troy Drayton | .05 | .01 |
| ❏ 26 Kurt Gouveia | .05 | .01 |
| ❏ 27 Warren Moon | .25 | .08 |
| ❏ 28 Jeff Query | .05 | .01 |
| ❏ 29 Chuck Levy RC | .05 | .01 |
| ❏ 30 Bruce Smith | .25 | .08 |
| ❏ 31 Doug Riesenberg | .05 | .01 |
| ❏ 32 Willie Drewrey | .05 | .01 |
| ❏ 33 Nate Newton UER | .05 | .01 |
| ❏ 34 James Jett | .05 | .01 |
| ❏ 35 George Teague | .05 | .01 |
| ❏ 36 Marc Spindler | .05 | .01 |
| ❏ 37 Jack Del Rio | .05 | .01 |
| ❏ 38 Dale Carter | .05 | .01 |
| ❏ 39 Steve Atwater | .05 | .01 |
| ❏ 40 Herschel Walker | .10 | .02 |
| ❏ 41 James Hasty | .05 | .01 |
| ❏ 42 Seth Joyner | .05 | .01 |
| ❏ 43 Keith Jackson | .05 | .01 |
| ❏ 44 Tommy Vardell | .05 | .01 |
| ❏ 45 Antonio Langham RC | .10 | .02 |
| ❏ 46 Derek Brown RBK | .05 | .01 |
| ❏ 47 John Wojciechowski | .05 | .01 |
| ❏ 48 Horace Copeland | .05 | .01 |
| ❏ 49 Luis Sharpe | .05 | .01 |
| ❏ 50 Pat Harlow | .05 | .01 |
| ❏ 51 David Palmer RC | .25 | .08 |
| ❏ 52 Tony Smith RB | .05 | .01 |
| ❏ 53 Tim Johnson | .05 | .01 |
| ❏ 54 Anthony Newman | .05 | .01 |
| ❏ 55 Terry Wooden | .05 | .01 |
| ❏ 56 Derrick Fenner | .05 | .01 |
| ❏ 57 Mike Fox | .05 | .01 |
| ❏ 58 Brad Hopkins | .05 | .01 |
| ❏ 59 Daryl Johnston UER | .10 | .02 |
| ❏ 60 Steve Young | .75 | .30 |
| ❏ 61 Scottie Graham RC | .10 | .02 |
| ❏ 62 Nolan Harrison | .05 | .01 |
| ❏ 63 David Richards | .05 | .01 |
| ❏ 64 Chris Mohr | .05 | .01 |
| ❏ 65 Hardy Nickerson | .10 | .02 |
| ❏ 66 Heath Sherman | .05 | .01 |
| ❏ 67 Ronnie Fryar | .10 | .02 |
| ❏ 68 Ray Buchanan UER | .05 | .01 |
| ❏ 69 Jay Taylor | .05 | .01 |
| ❏ 70 Shannon Sharpe | .10 | .02 |
| ❏ 71 Vinny Testaverde | .10 | .02 |
| ❏ 72 Renaldo Turnbull | .05 | .01 |
| ❏ 73 Dwight Stone | .05 | .01 |
| ❏ 74 Willie McGinest RC | .25 | .08 |
| ❏ 75 Darrell Green | .05 | .01 |
| ❏ 76 Kyle Clifton | .05 | .01 |
| ❏ 77 Leo Goeas | .05 | .01 |

| | | |
|---|---|---|
| ❏ 78 Ken Ruettgers | .05 | .01 |
| ❏ 79 Craig Heyward | .10 | .02 |
| ❏ 80 Andre Rison | .10 | .02 |
| ❏ 81 Chris Mims | .05 | .01 |
| ❏ 82 Gary Clark | .10 | .02 |
| ❏ 83 Ricardo McDonald | .05 | .01 |
| ❏ 84 Patrick Hunter | .05 | .01 |
| ❏ 85 Bruce Matthews | .05 | .01 |
| ❏ 86 Russell Maryland | .05 | .01 |
| ❏ 87 Gary Anderson K | .05 | .01 |
| ❏ 88 Brad Edwards | .05 | .01 |
| ❏ 89 Carlton Bailey | .05 | .01 |
| ❏ 90 Qadry Ismail | .25 | .08 |
| ❏ 91 Terry McDaniel | .05 | .01 |
| ❏ 92 Willie Green | .05 | .01 |
| ❏ 93 Cornelius Bennett | .10 | .02 |
| ❏ 94 Paul Gruber | .05 | .01 |
| ❏ 95 Pete Stoyanovich | .05 | .01 |
| ❏ 96 Merton Hanks | .10 | .02 |
| ❏ 97 Tre Johnson RC | .05 | .01 |
| ❏ 98 Jonathan Hayes | .05 | .01 |
| ❏ 99 Jason Elam | .10 | .02 |
| ❏ 100 Jerome Bettis | .50 | .20 |
| ❏ 101 Ronnie Lott | .10 | .02 |
| ❏ 102 Maurice Hurst | .05 | .01 |
| ❏ 103 Kirk Lowdermilk | .05 | .01 |
| ❏ 104 Tony Jones T | .05 | .01 |
| ❏ 105 Steve Beuerlein | .10 | .02 |
| ❏ 106 Isaac Davis RC | .05 | .01 |
| ❏ 107 Vaughan Johnson | .05 | .01 |
| ❏ 108 Terrell Buckley | .05 | .01 |
| ❏ 109 Pierce Holt | .05 | .01 |
| ❏ 110 Alonzo Spellman | .05 | .01 |
| ❏ 111 Patrick Robinson | .05 | .01 |
| ❏ 112 Cortez Kennedy | .10 | .02 |
| ❏ 113 Kevin Williams WR | .10 | .02 |
| ❏ 114 Danny Copeland | .05 | .01 |
| ❏ 115 Chris Doleman | .05 | .01 |
| ❏ 116 Jerry Rice LL | .50 | .20 |
| ❏ 117 Neil Smith LL | .10 | .02 |
| ❏ 118 Emmitt Smith LL | .75 | .30 |
| ❏ 119 E.Robinson/Odomes LL | .05 | .01 |
| ❏ 120 Steve Young LL | .25 | .08 |
| ❏ 121 Carnell Lake | .05 | .01 |
| ❏ 122 Ernest Givins UER | .10 | .02 |
| ❏ 123 Henry Jones | .05 | .01 |
| ❏ 124 Michael Brooks | .05 | .01 |
| ❏ 125 Jason Hanson | .05 | .01 |
| ❏ 126 Andy Harmon | .05 | .01 |
| ❏ 127 Errict Rhett RC | .25 | .08 |
| ❏ 128 Harris Barton | .05 | .01 |
| ❏ 129 Greg Robinson | .05 | .01 |
| ❏ 130 Derrick Thomas | .25 | .08 |
| ❏ 131 Keith Kartz | .05 | .01 |
| ❏ 132 Lincoln Kennedy | .05 | .01 |
| ❏ 133 Leslie O'Neal | .05 | .01 |
| ❏ 134 Tim Goad | .05 | .01 |
| ❏ 135 Rohn Stark | .05 | .01 |
| ❏ 136 O.J.McDuffie | .25 | .08 |
| ❏ 137 Donnell Woolford | .05 | .01 |
| ❏ 138 Jamir Miller RC | .10 | .02 |
| ❏ 139 Eric Thomas UER | .05 | .01 |
| ❏ 140 Willie Roaf | .05 | .01 |
| ❏ 141 Wayne Gandy RC | .05 | .01 |
| ❏ 142 Mike Brim | .05 | .01 |
| ❏ 143 Kelvin Martin | .05 | .01 |
| ❏ 144 Edgar Bennett | .25 | .08 |
| ❏ 145 Michael Dean Perry | .10 | .02 |
| ❏ 146 Shante Carver RC | .05 | .01 |
| ❏ 147 Jessie Armstead UER | .05 | .01 |
| ❏ 148 Mo Elewonibi | .05 | .01 |
| ❏ 149 Dana Stubblefield | .10 | .02 |
| ❏ 150 Cody Carlson | .05 | .01 |
| ❏ 151 Vencie Glenn | .05 | .01 |
| ❏ 152 Levon Kirkland | .05 | .01 |
| ❏ 153 Derrick Moore | .05 | .01 |
| ❏ 154 John Fina | .05 | .01 |
| ❏ 155 Jeff Hostetler | .10 | .02 |
| ❏ 156 Courtney Hawkins | .05 | .01 |
| ❏ 157 Todd Collins | .05 | .01 |
| ❏ 158 Neil Smith | .10 | .02 |
| ❏ 159 Simon Fletcher | .05 | .01 |
| ❏ 160 Dan Marino | 2.00 | .75 |
| ❏ 161 Sam Adams RC | .10 | .02 |
| ❏ 162 Marvin Washington | .05 | .01 |
| ❏ 163 John Copeland | .05 | .01 |
| ❏ 164 Eugene Robinson | .05 | .01 |

|  |  | | |
|---|---|---|---|
| 165 | Mark Carrier DB | .05 | .01 |
| 166 | Mike Kenn | .05 | .01 |
| 167 | Tyrone Hughes | .10 | .02 |
| 168 | Darren Carrington | .05 | .01 |
| 169 | Shane Conlan | .05 | .01 |
| 170 | Ricky Proehl | .05 | .01 |
| 171 | Jeff Herrod | .05 | .01 |
| 172 | Mark Carrier WR | .10 | .02 |
| 173 | George Koonce | .05 | .01 |
| 174 | Desmond Howard | .10 | .02 |
| 175 | Dave Meggett | .05 | .01 |
| 176 | Charles Haley | .10 | .02 |
| 177 | Steve Wisniewski | .05 | .01 |
| 178 | Dermontti Dawson | .05 | .01 |
| 179 | Tim McDonald | .05 | .01 |
| 180 | Broderick Thomas | .05 | .01 |
| 181 | Bernard Dafney | .05 | .01 |
| 182 | Bo Orlando | .05 | .01 |
| 183 | Andre Reed | .10 | .02 |
| 184 | Randall Cunningham | .25 | .08 |
| 185 | Chris Spielman | .05 | .01 |
| 186 | Keith Byars | .05 | .01 |
| 187 | Ben Coates | .10 | .02 |
| 188 | Tracy Simien | .05 | .01 |
| 189 | Carl Pickens | .10 | .02 |
| 190 | Reggie White | .25 | .08 |
| 191 | Norm Johnson | .05 | .01 |
| 192 | Brian Washington | .05 | .01 |
| 193 | Stan Humphries | .10 | .02 |
| 194 | Fred Stokes | .05 | .01 |
| 195 | Dan Williams | .05 | .01 |
| 196 | John Elway TOG | .75 | .30 |
| 197 | Eric Allen TOG | .05 | .01 |
| 198 | Hardy Nickerson TOG | .10 | .02 |
| 199 | Jerome Bettis TOG | .25 | .08 |
| 200 | Troy Aikman TOG | .50 | .20 |
| 201 | Thurman Thomas TOG | .10 | .02 |
| 202 | Cornelius Bennett TOG UER | .10 | .02 |
| 203 | Michael Irvin TOG | .10 | .02 |
| 204 | Jim Kelly TOG | .10 | .02 |
| 205 | Junior Seau TOG | .10 | .02 |
| 206 | Heath Shuler RC UER | .25 | .08 |
| 207 | Howard Cross UER | .05 | .01 |
| 208 | Pat Swilling | .05 | .01 |
| 209 | Pete Metzelaars | .05 | .01 |
| 210 | Tony McGee | .05 | .01 |
| 211 | Neil O'Donnell | .25 | .08 |
| 212 | Eugene Chung | .05 | .01 |
| 213 | J.B. Brown | .05 | .01 |
| 214 | Marcus Allen | .25 | .08 |
| 215 | Harry Newsome | .05 | .01 |
| 216 | Greg Hill RC | .25 | .08 |
| 217 | Ryan Yarborough | .05 | .01 |
| 218 | Marty Carter | .05 | .01 |
| 219 | Bern Brostek | .05 | .01 |
| 220 | Boomer Esiason | .10 | .02 |
| 221 | Vince Buck | .05 | .01 |
| 222 | Jim Jeffcoat | .05 | .01 |
| 223 | Bob Dahl | .05 | .01 |
| 224 | Marion Butts | .05 | .01 |
| 225 | Ronald Moore | .05 | .01 |
| 226 | Robert Blackmon | .05 | .01 |
| 227 | Curtis Conway | .25 | .08 |
| 228 | Jon Hand | .05 | .01 |
| 229 | Shane Dronett | .05 | .01 |
| 230 | Erik Williams UER | .05 | .01 |
| 231 | Dennis Brown | .05 | .01 |
| 232 | Ray Childress | .05 | .01 |
| 233 | Johnnie Morton RC | .50 | .20 |
| 234 | Kent Hull | .05 | .01 |
| 235 | John Elliott | .05 | .01 |
| 236 | Ron Heller | .05 | .01 |
| 237 | J.J. Birden | .05 | .01 |
| 238 | Thomas Randolph RC | .05 | .01 |
| 239 | Chip Lohmiller | .05 | .01 |
| 240 | Tim Brown | .25 | .08 |
| 241 | Steve Tovar | .05 | .01 |
| 242 | Moe Gardner | .05 | .01 |
| 243 | Vincent Brown | .05 | .01 |
| 244 | Tony Zendejas | .05 | .01 |
| 245 | Eric Allen | .05 | .01 |
| 246 | Joe King RC | .05 | .01 |
| 247 | Mo Lewis | .05 | .01 |
| 248 | Rod Bernstine | .05 | .01 |
| 249 | Tom Waddle | .10 | .02 |
| 250 | Junior Seau | .25 | .08 |
| 251 | Eric Metcalf | .10 | .02 |
| 252 | Cris Carter | .50 | .20 |
| 253 | Bill Hitchcock | .05 | .01 |
| 254 | Zefross Moss | .05 | .01 |
| 255 | Morten Andersen | .05 | .01 |
| 256 | Keith Rucker RC | .05 | .01 |
| 257 | Chris Jacke | .05 | .01 |
| 258 | Richmond Webb | .05 | .01 |
| 259 | Herman Moore | .25 | .08 |
| 260 | Phil Simms | .10 | .02 |
| 261 | Mark Tuinei | .05 | .01 |
| 262 | Don Beebe | .05 | .01 |
| 263 | Marc Logan | .05 | .01 |
| 264 | Willie Davis | .10 | .02 |
| 265 | David Klingler | .05 | .01 |
| 266 | Martin Mayhew UER | .05 | .01 |
| 267 | Mark Bavaro | .05 | .01 |
| 268 | Greg Lloyd | .10 | .02 |
| 269 | Al Del Greco | .05 | .01 |
| 270 | Reggie Brooks | .10 | .02 |
| 271 | Greg Townsend | .05 | .01 |
| 272 | Rohn Stark CAL | .05 | .01 |
| 273 | Marcus Allen CAL | .10 | .02 |
| 274 | Ronnie Lott CAL | .10 | .02 |
| 275 | Dan Marino CAL | .75 | .30 |
| 276 | Sean Gilbert | .05 | .01 |
| 277 | LeRoy Butler | .05 | .01 |
| 278 | Troy Auzenne | .05 | .01 |
| 279 | Eric Swann | .10 | .02 |
| 280 | Quentin Coryatt | .05 | .01 |
| 281 | Anthony Pleasant | .05 | .01 |
| 282 | Brad Baxter | .05 | .01 |
| 283 | Carl Lee | .05 | .01 |
| 284 | Courtney Hall | .05 | .01 |
| 285 | Quinn Early | .10 | .02 |
| 286 | Eddie Robinson | .05 | .01 |
| 287 | Marco Coleman | .05 | .01 |
| 288 | Harold Green | .05 | .01 |
| 289 | Santana Dotson | .10 | .02 |
| 290 | Robert Porcher | .05 | .01 |
| 291 | Joe Phillips | .05 | .01 |
| 292 | Mark McMillian | .05 | .01 |
| 293 | Eric Davis | .05 | .01 |
| 294 | Mark Jackson | .05 | .01 |
| 295 | Darryl Talley | .05 | .01 |
| 296 | Curtis Duncan | .05 | .01 |
| 297 | Bruce Armstrong | .05 | .01 |
| 298 | Eric Hill | .05 | .01 |
| 299 | Andre Collins | .05 | .01 |
| 300 | Jay Novacek | .10 | .02 |
| 301 | Roosevelt Potts | .05 | .01 |
| 302 | Eric Martin | .05 | .01 |
| 303 | Chris Warren | .10 | .02 |
| 304 | Deral Boykin RC | .05 | .01 |
| 305 | Jessie Tuggle | .05 | .01 |
| 306 | Glyn Milburn | .10 | .02 |
| 307 | Terry Obee | .05 | .01 |
| 308 | Eric Turner | .05 | .01 |
| 309 | Dewayne Washington RC | .10 | .02 |
| 310 | Sterling Sharpe | .10 | .02 |
| 311 | Jeff Gossett | .05 | .01 |
| 312 | John Carney | .05 | .01 |
| 313 | Aaron Glenn RC | .25 | .08 |
| 314 | Nick Lowery | .05 | .01 |
| 315 | Thurman Thomas | .25 | .08 |
| 316 | Troy Aikman MG | .50 | .20 |
| 317 | Thurman Thomas MG | .10 | .02 |
| 318 | Michael Irvin MG | .10 | .02 |
| 319 | Steve Beuerlein MG | .10 | .02 |
| 320 | Jerry Rice | 1.00 | .40 |
| 321 | Alexander Wright | .05 | .01 |
| 322 | Michael Bates | .05 | .01 |
| 323 | Greg Davis | .05 | .01 |
| 324 | Mark Bortz | .05 | .01 |
| 325 | Kevin Greene | .10 | .02 |
| 326 | Wayne Simmons | .05 | .01 |
| 327 | Wayne Martin | .05 | .01 |
| 328 | Michael Irvin UER | .25 | .08 |
| 329 | Checklist Card | .05 | .01 |
| 330 | Checklist Card | .05 | .01 |
| 331 | Doug Pelfrey | .05 | .01 |
| 332 | Myron Guyton | .05 | .01 |
| 333 | Howard Ballard | .05 | .01 |
| 334 | Ricky Ervins | .05 | .01 |
| 335 | Steve Emtman | .05 | .01 |
| 336 | Eric Curry | .05 | .01 |
| 337 | Bert Emanuel RC | .25 | .08 |
| 338 | Darryl Ashmore | .05 | .01 |
| 339 | Stevon Moore | .05 | .01 |
| 340 | Garrison Hearst | .25 | .08 |
| 341 | Vance Johnson | .05 | .01 |
| 342 | Anthony Johnson | .10 | .02 |
| 343 | Merril Hoge | .05 | .01 |
| 344 | William Thomas | .05 | .01 |
| 345 | Scott Mitchell | .10 | .02 |
| 346 | Jim Everett | .10 | .02 |
| 347 | Ray Crockett | .05 | .01 |
| 348 | Bryan Cox | .05 | .01 |
| 349 | Charles Johnson RC | .25 | .08 |
| 350 | Randall McDaniel | .10 | .02 |
| 351 | Micheal Barrow | .05 | .01 |
| 352 | Darrell Thompson | .05 | .01 |
| 353 | Kevin Gogan | .05 | .01 |
| 354 | Brad Daluiso | .05 | .01 |
| 355 | Mark Collins | .05 | .01 |
| 356 | Bryant Young RC | .40 | .15 |
| 357 | Steve Christie | .05 | .01 |
| 358 | Derek Kennard | .05 | .01 |
| 359 | Jon Vaughn | .05 | .01 |
| 360 | Drew Bledsoe 3X | .75 | .30 |
| 361 | Randy Baldwin | .05 | .01 |
| 362 | Kevin Ross | .05 | .01 |
| 363 | Reuben Davis | .05 | .01 |
| 364 | Chris Miller | .05 | .01 |
| 365 | Tim McGee | .05 | .01 |
| 366 | Tony Woods | .05 | .01 |
| 367 | Dean Biasucci | .05 | .01 |
| 368 | George Jamison | .05 | .01 |
| 369 | Lorenzo Lynch | .05 | .01 |
| 370 | Johnny Johnson | .05 | .01 |
| 371 | Greg Kragen | .05 | .01 |
| 372 | Vinson Smith | .05 | .01 |
| 373 | Vince Workman | .05 | .01 |
| 374 | Allen Aldridge | .05 | .01 |
| 375 | Terry Kirby | .25 | .08 |
| 376 | Mario Bates RC | .25 | .08 |
| 377 | Dixon Edwards | .05 | .01 |
| 378 | Leon Searcy | .05 | .01 |
| 379 | Eric Guilford RC | .05 | .01 |
| 380 | Gary Brown | .05 | .01 |
| 381 | Phil Hansen | .05 | .01 |
| 382 | Keith Hamilton | .05 | .01 |
| 383 | John Alt | .05 | .01 |
| 384 | John Taylor | .10 | .02 |
| 385 | Reggie Cobb | .05 | .01 |
| 386 | Rob Fredrickson RC | .10 | .02 |
| 387 | Pepper Johnson | .05 | .01 |
| 388 | Kevin Lee RC | .05 | .01 |
| 389 | Stanley Richard | .05 | .01 |
| 390 | Jackie Slater | .05 | .01 |
| 391 | Darrick Brilz | .05 | .01 |
| 392 | John Gesek | .05 | .01 |
| 393 | Kelvin Pritchett | .05 | .01 |
| 394 | Aeneas Williams | .05 | .01 |
| 395 | Henry Ford | .05 | .01 |
| 396 | Eric Mahlum | .05 | .01 |
| 397 | Tom Rouen | .05 | .01 |
| 398 | Vinnie Clark | .05 | .01 |
| 399 | Jim Sweeney | .05 | .01 |
| 400 | Troy Aikman | 1.00 | .40 |
| 401 | Toi Cook | .05 | .01 |
| 402 | Dan Saleaumua | .05 | .01 |
| 403 | Andy Heck | .05 | .01 |
| 404 | Deon Figures | .05 | .01 |
| 405 | Henry Thomas | .05 | .01 |
| 406 | Glenn Montgomery | .05 | .01 |
| 407 | Trent Differ RC | 1.00 | .40 |
| 408 | Eddie Murray | .05 | .01 |
| 409 | Gene Atkins | .05 | .01 |
| 410 | Mike Sherrard | .05 | .01 |
| 411 | Don Mosebar | .05 | .01 |
| 412 | Thomas Smith | .05 | .01 |
| 413 | Ken Norton Jr. | .10 | .02 |
| 414 | Robert Brooks | .25 | .08 |
| 415 | Jeff Lageman | .05 | .01 |
| 416 | Tony Siragusa | .05 | .01 |
| 417 | Brian Blades | .10 | .02 |
| 418 | Matt Stover | .05 | .01 |
| 419 | Jesse Solomon | .05 | .01 |
| 420 | Reggie Roby | .05 | .01 |
| 421 | Shawn Jefferson | .05 | .01 |
| 422 | Marc Boutte | .05 | .01 |
| 423 | William White | .05 | .01 |
| 424 | Clyde Simmons | .05 | .01 |
| 425 | Anthony Miller | .10 | .02 |

| □ | | | |
|---|---|---|---|
| 426 | Brent Jones | .10 | .02 |
| 427 | Tim Grunhard | .05 | .01 |
| 428 | Alfred Williams | .05 | .01 |
| 429 | Roy Barker RC | .05 | .01 |
| 430 | Dante Jones | .05 | .01 |
| 431 | Leroy Thompson | .05 | .01 |
| 432 | Marcus Robertson | .05 | .01 |
| 433 | Thomas Lewis RC | .10 | .02 |
| 434 | Sean Jones | .05 | .01 |
| 435 | Michael Haynes | .10 | .02 |
| 436 | Albert Lewis | .05 | .01 |
| 437 | Tim Bowens RC | .10 | .02 |
| 438 | Marcus Patton | .05 | .01 |
| 439 | Rich Miano | .05 | .01 |
| 440 | Craig Erickson | .05 | .01 |
| 441 | Larry Allen RC | .25 | .08 |
| 442 | Fernando Smith | .05 | .01 |
| 443 | D.J. Johnson | .05 | .01 |
| 444 | Leonard Russell | .05 | .01 |
| 445 | Marshall Faulk RC | 5.00 | 2.00 |
| 446 | Najee Mustafaa | .05 | .01 |
| 447 | Brian Hansen | .05 | .01 |
| 448 | Isaac Bruce RC | 4.00 | 2.00 |
| 449 | Kevin Scott | .05 | .01 |
| 450 | Natrone Means UER | .25 | .08 |
| 451 | Tracy Rogers RC | .05 | .01 |
| 452 | Mike Croel | .05 | .01 |
| 453 | Anthony Edwards | .05 | .01 |
| 454 | Brentson Buckner RC | .05 | .01 |
| 455 | Tom Carter | .05 | .01 |
| 456 | Burt Grossman | .05 | .01 |
| 457 | Jimmy Spencer RC | .05 | .01 |
| 458 | Rocket Ismail | .10 | .02 |
| 459 | Fred Strickland | .05 | .01 |
| 460 | Jeff Burris RC | .10 | .02 |
| 461 | Adrian Hardy | .05 | .01 |
| 462 | Lamar McGriggs | .05 | .01 |
| 463 | Webster Slaughter | .05 | .01 |
| 464 | Demetrius DuBose | .05 | .01 |
| 465 | Dave Brown | .10 | .02 |
| 466 | Kenneth Gant | .05 | .01 |
| 467 | Erik Kramer | .10 | .02 |
| 468 | Mark Ingram | .05 | .01 |
| 469 | Roman Phifer | .05 | .01 |
| 470 | Steve Young | .50 | .20 |
| 471 | Nick Lowery | .05 | .01 |
| 472 | Irving Fryar | .10 | .02 |
| 473 | Art Monk | .10 | .02 |
| 474 | Mel Gray | .05 | .01 |
| 475 | Reggie White | .25 | .08 |
| 476 | Eric Ball | .05 | .01 |
| 477 | Dwayne Harper | .05 | .01 |
| 478 | Will Shields | .05 | .01 |
| 479 | Roger Harper | .05 | .01 |
| 480 | Rick Mirer | .25 | .08 |
| 481 | Vincent Brisby | .10 | .02 |
| 482 | John Jurkovic | .05 | .01 |
| 483 | Michael Jackson | .10 | .02 |
| 484 | Ed Cunningham | .05 | .01 |
| 485 | Brad Ottis | .05 | .01 |
| 486 | Sterling Palmer RC | .05 | .01 |
| 487 | Tony Bennett | .05 | .01 |
| 488 | Mike Pritchard | .05 | .01 |
| 489 | Bucky Brooks RC | .05 | .01 |
| 490 | Troy Vincent | .05 | .01 |
| 491 | Eric Green | .05 | .01 |
| 492 | Van Malone | .05 | .01 |
| 493 | Marcus Spears RC | .05 | .01 |
| 494 | Brian Williams OL | .05 | .01 |
| 495 | Robert Smith | .25 | .08 |
| 496 | Haywood Jeffires | .10 | .02 |
| 497 | Darrin Smith | .05 | .01 |
| 498 | Tommy Barnhardt | .05 | .01 |
| 499 | Anthony Smith | .05 | .01 |
| 500 | Ricky Watters | .10 | .02 |
| 501 | Antone Davis | .05 | .01 |
| 502 | David Braxton | .05 | .01 |
| 503 | Donnell Bennett RC | .05 | .01 |
| 504 | Donald Evans | .05 | .01 |
| 505 | Lewis Tillman | .05 | .01 |
| 506 | Lance Smith | .05 | .01 |
| 507 | Aaron Taylor | .05 | .01 |
| 508 | Ricky Sanders | .05 | .01 |
| 509 | Dennis Smith | .05 | .01 |
| 510 | Barry Foster | .05 | .01 |
| 511 | Stan Brock | .05 | .01 |
| 512 | Henry Rolling | .05 | .01 |
| 513 | Walter Reeves | .05 | .01 |
| 514 | John Booty | .05 | .01 |
| 515 | Kenneth Davis | .05 | .01 |
| 516 | Cris Dishman | .05 | .01 |
| 517 | Bill Lewis | .05 | .01 |
| 518 | Jeff Bryant | .05 | .01 |
| 519 | Brian Mitchell | .05 | .01 |
| 520 | Joe Montana | 2.00 | .75 |
| 521 | Keith Sims | .05 | .01 |
| 522 | Harry Colon | .05 | .01 |
| 523 | Leon Lett | .05 | .01 |
| 524 | Carlos Jenkins | .05 | .01 |
| 525 | Victor Bailey | .05 | .01 |
| 526 | Harvey Williams | .10 | .02 |
| 527 | Irv Smith | .05 | .01 |
| 528 | Jason Sehorn RC | .40 | .15 |
| 529 | John Thierry RC | .05 | .01 |
| 530 | Brett Favre | 2.00 | .75 |
| 531 | Sean Dawkins RC | .25 | .08 |
| 532 | Eric Pegram | .05 | .01 |
| 533 | Jimmy Williams | .05 | .01 |
| 534 | Michael Timpson | .05 | .01 |
| 535 | Flipper Anderson | .05 | .01 |
| 536 | John Parrella | .05 | .01 |
| 537 | Freddie Joe Nunn | .05 | .01 |
| 538 | Doug Dawson | .05 | .01 |
| 539 | Michael Stewart | .05 | .01 |
| 540 | John Elway | 2.00 | .75 |
| 541 | Ronnie Lott | .10 | .02 |
| 542 | Barry Sanders TOG | .75 | .30 |
| 543 | Andre Reed TOG | .10 | .02 |
| 544 | Deion Sanders TOG | .75 | .30 |
| 545 | Dan Marino TOG | .75 | .30 |
| 546 | Carlton Bailey TOG | .05 | .01 |
| 547 | Emmitt Smith TOG | .75 | .30 |
| 548 | Alvin Harper TOG | .10 | .02 |
| 549 | Eric Metcalf TOG | .05 | .01 |
| 550 | Jerry Rice TOG | .50 | .20 |
| 551 | Derrick Thomas TOG | .25 | .08 |
| 552 | Mark Collins TOG | .05 | .01 |
| 553 | Eric Turner TOG | .05 | .01 |
| 554 | Sterling Sharpe TOG | .10 | .02 |
| 555 | Steve Young TOG | .25 | .08 |
| 556 | Darnay Scott RC | .50 | .20 |
| 557 | Joel Steed | .05 | .01 |
| 558 | Dennis Gibson | .05 | .01 |
| 559 | Charles Mincy | .05 | .01 |
| 560 | Rickey Jackson | .05 | .01 |
| 561 | Dave Cadigan | .05 | .01 |
| 562 | Rick Tuten | .05 | .01 |
| 563 | Mike Caldwell | .05 | .01 |
| 564 | Todd Steussie RC | .10 | .02 |
| 565 | Kevin Smith | .05 | .01 |
| 566 | Arthur Marshall | .05 | .01 |
| 567 | Aaron Wallace | .05 | .01 |
| 568 | Calvin Williams | .10 | .02 |
| 569 | Todd Kelly | .05 | .01 |
| 570 | Barry Sanders | 1.50 | .60 |
| 571 | Shaun Gayle | .05 | .01 |
| 572 | Will Wolford | .05 | .01 |
| 573 | Ethan Horton | .05 | .01 |
| 574 | Chris Slade | .05 | .01 |
| 575 | Jeff Wright | .05 | .01 |
| 576 | Toby Wright | .05 | .01 |
| 577 | Lamar Thomas | .05 | .01 |
| 578 | Chris Singleton | .05 | .01 |
| 579 | Ed West | .05 | .01 |
| 580 | Jeff George | .25 | .08 |
| 581 | Kevin Mitchell | .05 | .01 |
| 582 | Chad Brown | .05 | .01 |
| 583 | Rich Camarillo | .05 | .01 |
| 584 | Gary Zimmerman | .05 | .01 |
| 585 | Randal Hill | .05 | .01 |
| 586 | Keith Cash | .05 | .01 |
| 587 | Sam Mills | .05 | .01 |
| 588 | Shawn Lee | .05 | .01 |
| 589 | Kent Graham | .05 | .01 |
| 590 | Steve Everitt | .05 | .01 |
| 591 | Rob Moore | .10 | .02 |
| 592 | Kevin Mawae RC | .25 | .08 |
| 593 | Jerry Ball | .05 | .01 |
| 594 | Larry Brown DB | .05 | .01 |
| 595 | Tim Krumrie | .05 | .01 |
| 596 | Aubrey Beavers RC | .05 | .01 |
| 597 | Chris Hinton | .05 | .01 |
| 598 | Greg Montgomery | .05 | .01 |
| 599 | Jimmie Jones | .05 | .01 |
| 600 | Jim Kelly | .25 | .08 |
| 601 | Joe Johnson RC | .05 | .01 |
| 602 | Tim Irwin | .05 | .01 |
| 603 | Steve Jackson | .05 | .01 |
| 604 | James Williams RC LB | .05 | .01 |
| 605 | Blair Thomas | .05 | .01 |
| 606 | Danan Hughes | .05 | .01 |
| 607 | Russell Freeman | .05 | .01 |
| 608 | Andre Hastings | .10 | .02 |
| 609 | Ken Harvey | .05 | .01 |
| 610 | Jim Harbaugh | .25 | .08 |
| 611 | Emmitt Smith MG | .75 | .30 |
| 612 | Andre Rison MG | .10 | .02 |
| 613 | Steve Young MG | .25 | .08 |
| 614 | Anthony Miller MG | .05 | .01 |
| 615 | Barry Sanders MG | .75 | .30 |
| 616 | Bernie Kosar | .10 | .02 |
| 617 | Chris Gardocki | .05 | .01 |
| 618 | William Floyd RC | .25 | .08 |
| 619 | Matt Brock | .05 | .01 |
| 620 | Dan Wilkinson RC | .10 | .02 |
| 621 | Tony Meola RC | .10 | .02 |
| 622 | Tony Tolbert | .05 | .01 |
| 623 | Mike Zandofsky | .05 | .01 |
| 624 | William Fuller | .05 | .01 |
| 625 | Steve Jordan | .05 | .01 |
| 626 | Mike Johnson | .05 | .01 |
| 627 | Ferrell Edmunds | .05 | .01 |
| 628 | Gene Williams | .05 | .01 |
| 629 | Willie Beamon | .05 | .01 |
| 630 | Gerald Perry | .05 | .01 |
| 631 | John Baylor | .05 | .01 |
| 632 | Carwell Gardner | .05 | .01 |
| 633 | Thomas Everett | .05 | .01 |
| 634 | Lamar Lathon | .05 | .01 |
| 635 | Michael Bankston | .05 | .01 |
| 636 | Ray Crittenden RC | .05 | .01 |
| 637 | Kimble Anders | .10 | .02 |
| 638 | Robert Delpino | .05 | .01 |
| 639 | Darren Perry | .05 | .01 |
| 640 | Byron Evans | .05 | .01 |
| 641 | Mark Higgs | .05 | .01 |
| 642 | Lorenzo Neal | .05 | .01 |
| 643 | Henry Ellard | .10 | .02 |
| 644 | Trace Armstrong | .05 | .01 |
| 645 | Greg McMurtry | .05 | .01 |
| 646 | Steve McMichael | .10 | .02 |
| 647 | Terance Mathis | .10 | .02 |
| 648 | Eric Beinemy | .05 | .01 |
| 649 | Bobby Houston | .05 | .01 |
| 650 | Alvin Harper | .10 | .02 |
| 651 | James Folston RC | .05 | .01 |
| 652 | Mel Gray | .05 | .01 |
| 653 | Adrian Cooper | .05 | .01 |
| 654 | Dexter Carter | .05 | .01 |
| 655 | Don Griffin | .05 | .01 |
| 656 | Corey Widmer | .05 | .01 |
| 657 | Lee Johnson | .05 | .01 |
| 658 | Nate Odomes | .05 | .01 |
| 659 | Checklist Card | .05 | .01 |
| 660 | Checklist Card | .05 | .01 |
| P1 | Promo Sheet | 4.00 | 1.50 |
| P2 | Promo Sheet Special Effects | 4.00 | 1.50 |

## 1995 Topps

PR. MINNESOTA VIKINGS

| □ COMPLETE SET (468) | 40.00 | 15.00 |
|---|---|---|
| □ COMP.FACT SET (478) | 60.00 | 30.00 |
| □ COMP SERIES 1 (248) | 20.00 | 8.00 |
| □ COMP SERIES 2 (220) | 20.00 | 8.00 |

|  |  | | |
|---|------|---|---|
| ❏ 1 | Barry Sanders TYC | .75 | .30 |
| ❏ 2 | Chris Warren TYC | .20 | .07 |
| ❏ 3 | Jerry Rice TYC | .50 | .20 |
| ❏ 4 | Emmitt Smith TYC | .75 | .30 |
| ❏ 5 | Henry Ellard TYC | .20 | .07 |
| ❏ 6 | Natrone Means TYC | .20 | .07 |
| ❏ 7 | Terance Mathis TYC | .20 | .07 |
| ❏ 8 | Tim Brown TYC | .20 | .07 |
| ❏ 9 | Andre Reed TYC | .20 | .07 |
| ❏ 10 | Marshall Faulk TYC | .60 | .25 |
| ❏ 11 | Irving Fryar TYC | .20 | .07 |
| ❏ 12 | Cris Carter TYC | .30 | .10 |
| ❏ 13 | Michael Irvin TYC | .30 | .10 |
| ❏ 14 | Jake Reed TYC | .20 | .07 |
| ❏ 15 | Ben Coates TYC | .20 | .07 |
| ❏ 16 | Herman Moore TYC | .30 | .10 |
| ❏ 17 | Carl Pickens TYC | .20 | .07 |
| ❏ 18 | Fred Barnett TYC | .20 | .07 |
| ❏ 19 | Sterling Sharpe TYC | .20 | .07 |
| ❏ 20 | Anthony Miller TYC | .20 | .07 |
| ❏ 21 | Thurman Thomas TYC | .30 | .10 |
| ❏ 22 | Andre Rison TYC | .20 | .07 |
| ❏ 23 | Brian Blades TYC | .20 | .07 |
| ❏ 24 | Rodney Hampton TYC | .20 | .07 |
| ❏ 25 | Terry Allen TYC | .20 | .07 |
| ❏ 26 | Jerome Bettis TYC | .30 | .10 |
| ❏ 27 | Errict Rhett TYC | .20 | .07 |
| ❏ 28 | Rob Moore TYC | .20 | .07 |
| ❏ 29 | Shannon Sharpe TYC | .20 | .07 |
| ❏ 30 | Drew Bledsoe TYC | .30 | .10 |
| ❏ 31 | Dan Marino TYC | 1.00 | .40 |
| ❏ 32 | Warren Moon TYC | .40 | .15 |
| ❏ 33 | Steve Young TYC | .40 | .15 |
| ❏ 34 | Brett Favre TYC | 1.00 | .40 |
| ❏ 35 | Jim Everett TYC | .20 | .02 |
| ❏ 36 | Jeff George TYC | .20 | .07 |
| ❏ 37 | John Elway TYC | 1.00 | .40 |
| ❏ 38 | Jeff Hostetler TYC | .20 | .07 |
| ❏ 39 | Randall Cunningham TYC | .20 | .10 |
| ❏ 40 | Sam Humphries TYC | .20 | .07 |
| ❏ 41 | Jim Kelly TYC | .30 | .10 |
| ❏ 42 | Tommy Barnhardt | .10 | .02 |
| ❏ 43 | Bob Whitfield | .10 | .02 |
| ❏ 44 | William Thomas | .10 | .02 |
| ❏ 45 | Glyn Milburn | .10 | .02 |
| ❏ 46 | Steve Christie | .10 | .02 |
| ❏ 47 | Kevin Mawae | .10 | .02 |
| ❏ 48 | Vencie Glenn | .10 | .02 |
| ❏ 49 | Eric Curry | .10 | .02 |
| ❏ 50 | Jeff Hostetler | .20 | .07 |
| ❏ 51 | Tyronne Stowe | .10 | .02 |
| ❏ 52 | Steve Jackson | .10 | .02 |
| ❏ 53 | Ben Coleman | .10 | .02 |
| ❏ 54 | Brad Baxter | .10 | .02 |
| ❏ 55 | Darryl Williams | .10 | .02 |
| ❏ 56 | Troy Drayton | .10 | .02 |
| ❏ 57 | George Teague | .10 | .02 |
| ❏ 58 | Calvin Williams | .20 | .07 |
| ❏ 59 | Jeff Cross | .10 | .02 |
| ❏ 60 | Leroy Hoard | .10 | .02 |
| ❏ 61 | John Carney | .10 | .02 |
| ❏ 62 | Daryl Johnston | .20 | .07 |
| ❏ 63 | Jim Jeffcoat | .10 | .02 |
| ❏ 64 | Matt Stover | .10 | .02 |
| ❏ 65 | LeRoy Butler | .10 | .02 |
| ❏ 66 | Curtis Conway | .30 | .10 |
| ❏ 67 | O.J. McDuffie | .30 | .10 |
| ❏ 68 | Robert Massey | .10 | .02 |
| ❏ 69 | Ed McDaniel | .10 | .02 |
| ❏ 70 | William Floyd | .30 | .10 |
| ❏ 71 | Willie Davis | .20 | .07 |
| ❏ 72 | William Roberts | .10 | .02 |
| ❏ 73 | Chester McGlockton | .20 | .07 |
| ❏ 74 | D.J. Johnson | .10 | .02 |
| ❏ 75 | Rondell Jones | .10 | .02 |
| ❏ 76 | Morten Andersen | .10 | .02 |
| ❏ 77 | Glenn Parker | .10 | .02 |
| ❏ 78 | William Fuller | .10 | .02 |
| ❏ 79 | Ray Buchanan | .10 | .02 |
| ❏ 80 | Maurice Hurst | .10 | .02 |
| ❏ 81 | Wayne Gandy | .10 | .02 |
| ❏ 82 | Marcus Turner | .10 | .02 |
| ❏ 83 | Greg Davis | .10 | .02 |
| ❏ 84 | Terry Wooden | .10 | .02 |
| ❏ 85 | Thomas Everett | .10 | .02 |
| ❏ 86 | Steve Broussard | .10 | .02 |
| ❏ 87 | Tom Carter | .10 | .02 |
| ❏ 88 | Glenn Montgomery | .10 | .02 |
| ❏ 89 | Larry Allen | .20 | .07 |
| ❏ 90 | Donnell Woolford | .10 | .02 |
| ❏ 91 | John Alt | .10 | .02 |
| ❏ 92 | Phil Hansen | .10 | .02 |
| ❏ 93 | Seth Joyner | .10 | .02 |
| ❏ 94 | Michael Brooks | .10 | .02 |
| ❏ 95 | Randall McDaniel | .15 | .05 |
| ❏ 96 | Tydus Winans | .10 | .02 |
| ❏ 97 | Rob Fredrickson | .10 | .02 |
| ❏ 98 | Ray Crockett | .10 | .02 |
| ❏ 99 | Courtney Hall | .10 | .02 |
| ❏ 100 | Merton Hanks | .10 | .02 |
| ❏ 101 | Aaron Glenn | .10 | .02 |
| ❏ 102 | Roosevelt Potts | .10 | .02 |
| ❏ 103 | Leon Lett | .10 | .02 |
| ❏ 104 | Jessie Tuggle | .10 | .02 |
| ❏ 105 | Martin Mayhew | .10 | .02 |
| ❏ 106 | Willie Roaf | .10 | .02 |
| ❏ 107 | Todd Lyght | .10 | .02 |
| ❏ 108 | Ernest Givins | .10 | .02 |
| ❏ 109 | Tony McGee | .10 | .02 |
| ❏ 110 | Barry Sanders | 1.50 | .60 |
| ❏ 111 | Dermontti Dawson | .20 | .07 |
| ❏ 112 | Rick Tuten | .10 | .02 |
| ❏ 113 | Vincent Brisby | .10 | .02 |
| ❏ 114 | Charlie Garner | .30 | .10 |
| ❏ 115 | Irving Fryar | .20 | .07 |
| ❏ 116 | Stevon Moore | .10 | .02 |
| ❏ 117 | Matt Darby | .10 | .02 |
| ❏ 118 | Howard Cross | .10 | .02 |
| ❏ 119 | John Gesek | .10 | .02 |
| ❏ 120 | Jack Del Rio | .10 | .02 |
| ❏ 121 | Marcus Allen | .30 | .10 |
| ❏ 122 | Torrance Small | .10 | .02 |
| ❏ 123 | Chris Mims | .10 | .02 |
| ❏ 124 | Don Mosebar | .10 | .02 |
| ❏ 125 | Carl Pickens | .20 | .07 |
| ❏ 126 | Tom Rouen | .10 | .02 |
| ❏ 127 | Garrison Hearst | .30 | .10 |
| ❏ 128 | Charles Johnson | .20 | .07 |
| ❏ 129 | Derek Brown RBK | .10 | .02 |
| ❏ 130 | Troy Aikman | 1.00 | .40 |
| ❏ 131 | Troy Vincent | .10 | .02 |
| ❏ 132 | Ken Ruettgers | .10 | .02 |
| ❏ 133 | Michael Jackson | .20 | .07 |
| ❏ 134 | Dennis Gibson | .10 | .02 |
| ❏ 135 | Brett Perriman | .20 | .07 |
| ❏ 136 | Jeff Graham | .10 | .02 |
| ❏ 137 | Chad Brown | .10 | .02 |
| ❏ 138 | Ken Norton Jr. | .20 | .07 |
| ❏ 139 | Chris Slade | .10 | .02 |
| ❏ 140 | Dave Brown | .20 | .07 |
| ❏ 141 | Bert Emanuel | .30 | .10 |
| ❏ 142 | Renaldo Turnbull | .10 | .02 |
| ❏ 143 | Jim Harbaugh | .20 | .07 |
| ❏ 144 | Micheal Barrow | .10 | .02 |
| ❏ 145 | Vincent Brown | .10 | .02 |
| ❏ 146 | Bryant Young | .20 | .07 |
| ❏ 147 | Boomer Esiason | .20 | .07 |
| ❏ 148 | Sean Gilbert | .10 | .02 |
| ❏ 149 | Greg Truitt | .10 | .02 |
| ❏ 150 | Rod Woodson | .20 | .07 |
| ❏ 151 | Robert Porcher | .10 | .02 |
| ❏ 152 | Joe Phillips | .10 | .02 |
| ❏ 153 | Gary Zimmerman | .10 | .02 |
| ❏ 154 | Bruce Smith | .20 | .07 |
| ❏ 155 | Randall Cunningham | .30 | .10 |
| ❏ 156 | Fred Strickland | .10 | .02 |
| ❏ 157 | Derrick Alexander WR | .30 | .10 |
| ❏ 158 | James Williams LB | .10 | .02 |
| ❏ 159 | Scott Dill | .10 | .02 |
| ❏ 160 | Tim Bowens | .10 | .02 |
| ❏ 161 | Floyd Turner | .10 | .02 |
| ❏ 162 | Ronnie Harmon | .10 | .02 |
| ❏ 163 | Wayne Martin | .10 | .02 |
| ❏ 164 | John Randle | .20 | .07 |
| ❏ 165 | Larry Centers | .20 | .07 |
| ❏ 166 | Larry Brown DB | .10 | .02 |
| ❏ 167 | Albert Lewis | .10 | .02 |
| ❏ 168 | Michael Strahan | .30 | .10 |
| ❏ 169 | Reggie Brooks | .20 | .07 |
| ❏ 170 | Craig Heyward | .20 | .07 |
| ❏ 171 | Pat Harlow | .10 | .02 |
| ❏ 172 | Eugene Robinson | .10 | .02 |
| ❏ 173 | Shane Conlan | .10 | .02 |
| ❏ 174 | Bennie Blades | .10 | .02 |
| ❏ 175 | Neil O'Donnell | .20 | .07 |
| ❏ 176 | Steve Tovar | .10 | .02 |
| ❏ 177 | Donald Evans | .10 | .02 |
| ❏ 178 | Brent Jones | .10 | .02 |
| ❏ 179 | Ray Childress | .10 | .02 |
| ❏ 180 | Reggie White | .30 | .10 |
| ❏ 181 | David Alexander | .10 | .02 |
| ❏ 182 | Greg Hill | .20 | .07 |
| ❏ 183 | Vinny Testaverde | .20 | .07 |
| ❏ 184 | Jeff Burris | .10 | .02 |
| ❏ 185 | Hardy Nickerson | .10 | .02 |
| ❏ 186 | Terry Kirby | .20 | .07 |
| ❏ 187 | Kirk Lowdermilk | .10 | .02 |
| ❏ 188 | Eric Swann | .20 | .07 |
| ❏ 189 | Chris Zorich | .10 | .02 |
| ❏ 190 | Simon Fletcher | .10 | .02 |
| ❏ 191 | Qadry Ismail | .20 | .07 |
| ❏ 192 | Heath Shuler | .20 | .07 |
| ❏ 193 | Michael Haynes | .20 | .07 |
| ❏ 194 | Mike Sherrard | .10 | .02 |
| ❏ 195 | Nolan Harrison | .10 | .02 |
| ❏ 196 | Marcus Robertson | .10 | .02 |
| ❏ 197 | Kevin Williams WR | .20 | .07 |
| ❏ 198 | Moe Gardner | .10 | .02 |
| ❏ 199 | Rick Mirer | .20 | .07 |
| ❏ 200 | Junior Seau | .30 | .10 |
| ❏ 201 | Byron Bam Morris | .10 | .02 |
| ❏ 202 | Willie McGinest | .20 | .07 |
| ❏ 203 | Chris Spielman | .20 | .07 |
| ❏ 204 | Darnay Scott | .20 | .07 |
| ❏ 205 | Jesse Sapolu | .10 | .02 |
| ❏ 206 | Marvin Washington | .10 | .02 |
| ❏ 207 | Anthony Newman | .10 | .02 |
| ❏ 208 | Cortez Kennedy | .20 | .07 |
| ❏ 209 | Quentin Coryatt | .20 | .07 |
| ❏ 210 | Neil Smith | .20 | .07 |
| ❏ 211 | Keith Sims | .10 | .02 |
| ❏ 212 | Sean Jones | .10 | .02 |
| ❏ 213 | Tony Jones T | .10 | .02 |
| ❏ 214 | Lewis Tillman | .10 | .02 |
| ❏ 215 | Darren Woodson | .20 | .07 |
| ❏ 216 | Jason Hanson | .10 | .02 |
| ❏ 217 | John Taylor | .10 | .02 |
| ❏ 218 | Shawn Lee | .10 | .02 |
| ❏ 219 | Kevin Greene | .20 | .07 |
| ❏ 220 | Jerry Rice | 1.00 | .40 |
| ❏ 221 | Ki-Jana Carter RC | .30 | .10 |
| ❏ 222 | Tony Boselli RC | .30 | .10 |
| ❏ 223 | Michael Westbrook RC | .30 | .10 |
| ❏ 224 | Kerry Collins RC | 2.00 | .75 |
| ❏ 225 | Kevin Carter RC | .30 | .10 |
| ❏ 226 | Kyle Brady RC | .30 | .10 |
| ❏ 227 | J.J. Stokes RC | .30 | .10 |
| ❏ 228 | Derrick Alexander DE RC | .10 | .02 |
| ❏ 229 | Warren Sapp RC | 1.50 | .60 |
| ❏ 230 | Ruben Brown RC | .30 | .10 |
| ❏ 231 | Hugh Douglas RC | .30 | .10 |
| ❏ 232 | Luther Elliss RC | .10 | .02 |
| ❏ 233 | Rashaan Salaam RC | .20 | .07 |
| ❏ 234 | Tyrone Poole RC | .30 | .10 |
| ❏ 235 | Korey Stringer RC | .20 | .07 |
| ❏ 236 | Devin Bush RC | .10 | .02 |
| ❏ 237 | Cory Raymer RC | .10 | .02 |
| ❏ 238 | Zach Wiegert RC | .10 | .02 |
| ❏ 239 | Ron Davis RC | .10 | .02 |
| ❏ 240 | Todd Collins RC | 1.25 | .50 |
| ❏ 241 | Bobby Taylor RC | .30 | .10 |
| ❏ 242 | Patrick Riley RC | .10 | .02 |
| ❏ 243 | Scott Gragg | .10 | .02 |
| ❏ 244 | Marvcus Patton | .10 | .02 |
| ❏ 245 | Alvin Harper | .10 | .02 |
| ❏ 246 | Ricky Watters | .20 | .07 |
| ❏ 247 | Checklist 1 | .10 | .02 |
| ❏ 248 | Checklist 2 | .10 | .02 |
| ❏ 249 | Terance Mathis | .20 | .07 |
| ❏ 250 | Mark Carrier DB | .10 | .02 |
| ❏ 251 | Elijah Alexander | .10 | .02 |
| ❏ 252 | George Koonce | .10 | .02 |
| ❏ 253 | Tony Bennett | .10 | .02 |
| ❏ 254 | Steve Wisniewski | .10 | .02 |
| ❏ 255 | Bernie Parmalee | .20 | .07 |
| ❏ 256 | Dwayne Sabb | .10 | .02 |
| ❏ 257 | Lorenzo Neal | .10 | .02 |
| ❏ 258 | Corey Miller | .10 | .02 |
| ❏ 259 | Fred Barnett | .20 | .07 |
| ❏ 260 | Greg Gloyd | .20 | .07 |
| ❏ 261 | Robert Blackmon | .10 | .02 |

| | | |
|---|---|---|
| ❑ 262 Ken Harvey | .10 | .02 |
| ❑ 263 Eric Hill | .10 | .02 |
| ❑ 264 Russell Copeland | .10 | .02 |
| ❑ 265 Jeff Blake RC | .75 | .30 |
| ❑ 266 Carl Banks | .10 | .02 |
| ❑ 267 Jay Novacek | .20 | .07 |
| ❑ 268 Mel Gray | .10 | .02 |
| ❑ 269 Kimble Anders | .10 | .02 |
| ❑ 270 Cris Carter | .30 | .10 |
| ❑ 271 Johnny Mitchell | .10 | .02 |
| ❑ 272 Shawn Jefferson | .10 | .02 |
| ❑ 273 Doug Brien | .10 | .02 |
| ❑ 274 Sean Landeta | .10 | .02 |
| ❑ 275 Scott Mitchell | .20 | .07 |
| ❑ 276 Charles Wilson | .10 | .02 |
| ❑ 277 Anthony Smith | .10 | .02 |
| ❑ 278 Anthony Miller | .20 | .07 |
| ❑ 279 Steve Walsh | .10 | .02 |
| ❑ 280 Drew Bledsoe | .60 | .25 |
| ❑ 281 Jamir Miller | .10 | .02 |
| ❑ 282 Robert Brooks | .30 | .10 |
| ❑ 283 Sean Lumpkin | .10 | .02 |
| ❑ 284 Bryan Cox | .10 | .02 |
| ❑ 285 Byron Evans | .10 | .02 |
| ❑ 286 Chris Doleman | .10 | .02 |
| ❑ 287 Anthony Pleasant | .10 | .02 |
| ❑ 288 Stephen Grant RC | .10 | .02 |
| ❑ 289 Doug Riesenberg | .10 | .02 |
| ❑ 290 Natrone Means | .20 | .07 |
| ❑ 291 Henry Thomas | .10 | .02 |
| ❑ 292 Mike Pritchard | .10 | .02 |
| ❑ 293 Courtney Hawkins | .10 | .02 |
| ❑ 294 Bill Bates | .20 | .07 |
| ❑ 295 Jerome Bettis | .30 | .10 |
| ❑ 296 Russell Maryland | .10 | .02 |
| ❑ 297 Stanley Richard | .10 | .02 |
| ❑ 298 William White | .10 | .02 |
| ❑ 299 Dan Wilkinson | .20 | .07 |
| ❑ 300 Steve Young | .75 | .30 |
| ❑ 301 Gary Brown | .10 | .02 |
| ❑ 302 Jake Reed | .20 | .07 |
| ❑ 303 Carlton Gray | .10 | .02 |
| ❑ 304 Levon Kirkland | .10 | .02 |
| ❑ 305 Shannon Sharpe | .20 | .07 |
| ❑ 306 Luis Sharpe | .10 | .02 |
| ❑ 307 Marshall Faulk | 1.25 | .50 |
| ❑ 308 Stan Humphries | .20 | .07 |
| ❑ 309 Chris Calloway | .10 | .02 |
| ❑ 310 Tim Brown | .30 | .10 |
| ❑ 311 Steve Everitt | .10 | .02 |
| ❑ 312 Raymont Harris | .10 | .02 |
| ❑ 313 Tim McDonald | .10 | .02 |
| ❑ 314 Trent Dilfer | .30 | .10 |
| ❑ 315 Jim Everett | .10 | .02 |
| ❑ 316 Ray Crittenden | .10 | .02 |
| ❑ 317 Jim Kelly | .30 | .10 |
| ❑ 318 Andre Reed | .20 | .07 |
| ❑ 319 Chris Miller | .10 | .02 |
| ❑ 320 Bobby Houston | .10 | .02 |
| ❑ 321 Charles Haley | .10 | .02 |
| ❑ 322 James Francis | .10 | .02 |
| ❑ 323 Bernard Williams | .10 | .02 |
| ❑ 324 Michael Bates | .10 | .02 |
| ❑ 325 Brian Mitchell | .10 | .02 |
| ❑ 326 Mike Johnson | .10 | .02 |
| ❑ 327 Eric Bieniemy | .10 | .02 |
| ❑ 328 Aubrey Beavers | .10 | .02 |
| ❑ 329 Dale Carter | .20 | .07 |
| ❑ 330 Emmitt Smith | 1.50 | .60 |
| ❑ 331 Darren Perry | .10 | .02 |
| ❑ 332 Marquez Pope | .10 | .02 |
| ❑ 333 Clyde Simmons | .10 | .02 |
| ❑ 334 Corey Croom | .10 | .02 |
| ❑ 335 Thomas Randolph | .10 | .02 |
| ❑ 336 Harvey Williams | .10 | .02 |
| ❑ 337 Michael Timpson | .10 | .02 |
| ❑ 338 Eugene Daniel | .10 | .02 |
| ❑ 339 Shane Dronett | .10 | .02 |
| ❑ 340 Eric Turner | .10 | .02 |
| ❑ 341 Eric Metcalf | .20 | .07 |
| ❑ 342 Leslie O'Neal | .20 | .07 |
| ❑ 343 Mark Wheeler | .10 | .02 |
| ❑ 344 Mark Pike | .10 | .02 |
| ❑ 345 Brett Favre | 2.00 | .75 |
| ❑ 346 Johnny Bailey | .10 | .02 |
| ❑ 347 Henry Ellard | .20 | .07 |
| ❑ 348 Chris Gardocki | .10 | .02 |

| | | |
|---|---|---|
| ❑ 349 Henry Jones | .10 | .02 |
| ❑ 350 Dan Marino | 2.00 | .75 |
| ❑ 351 Lake Dawson | .20 | .07 |
| ❑ 352 Mark McMillian | .10 | .02 |
| ❑ 353 Deion Sanders | .60 | .25 |
| ❑ 354 Antonio London | .10 | .02 |
| ❑ 355 Cris Dishman | .10 | .02 |
| ❑ 356 Ricardo McDonald | .10 | .02 |
| ❑ 357 Dexter Carter | .10 | .02 |
| ❑ 358 Kevin Smith | .10 | .02 |
| ❑ 359 Yancey Thigpen RC | .20 | .07 |
| ❑ 360 Chris Warren | .20 | .07 |
| ❑ 361 Quinn Early | .20 | .07 |
| ❑ 362 John Mangum | .10 | .02 |
| ❑ 363 Santana Dotson | .10 | .02 |
| ❑ 364 Rocket Ismail | .20 | .07 |
| ❑ 365 Aeneas Williams | .10 | .02 |
| ❑ 366 Dan Williams | .10 | .02 |
| ❑ 367 Sean Dawkins | .20 | .07 |
| ❑ 368 Pepper Johnson | .10 | .02 |
| ❑ 369 Roman Phifer | .10 | .02 |
| ❑ 370 Rodney Hampton | .20 | .07 |
| ❑ 371 Darrell Green | .10 | .02 |
| ❑ 372 Michael Zordich | .10 | .02 |
| ❑ 373 Andre Coleman | .10 | .02 |
| ❑ 374 Wayne Simmons | .10 | .02 |
| ❑ 375 Michael Irvin | .30 | .10 |
| ❑ 376 Clay Matthews | .20 | .07 |
| ❑ 377 Dewayne Washington | .20 | .07 |
| ❑ 378 Keith Byars | .10 | .02 |
| ❑ 379 Todd Collins LB | .30 | .10 |
| ❑ 380 Mark Collins | .10 | .02 |
| ❑ 381 Joel Steed | .10 | .02 |
| ❑ 382 Bart Oates | .10 | .02 |
| ❑ 383 Al Smith | .10 | .02 |
| ❑ 384 Rafael Robinson | .10 | .02 |
| ❑ 385 Mo Lewis | .10 | .02 |
| ❑ 386 Aubrey Matthews | .10 | .02 |
| ❑ 387 Corey Sawyer | .10 | .02 |
| ❑ 388 Bucky Brooks | .10 | .02 |
| ❑ 389 Erik Kramer | .10 | .02 |
| ❑ 390 Tyrone Hughes | .20 | .07 |
| ❑ 391 Terry McDaniel | .10 | .02 |
| ❑ 392 Craig Erickson | .10 | .02 |
| ❑ 393 Mike Flores | .10 | .02 |
| ❑ 394 Harry Swayne | .10 | .02 |
| ❑ 395 Irving Spikes | .20 | .07 |
| ❑ 396 Lorenzo Lynch | .10 | .02 |
| ❑ 397 Antonio Langham | .10 | .02 |
| ❑ 398 Edgar Bennett | .20 | .07 |
| ❑ 399 Thomas Lewis | .20 | .07 |
| ❑ 400 John Elway | 2.00 | .75 |
| ❑ 401 Jeff George | .20 | .07 |
| ❑ 402 Errict Rhett | .20 | .07 |
| ❑ 403 Bill Romanowski | .10 | .02 |
| ❑ 404 Alexander Wright | .10 | .02 |
| ❑ 405 Warren Moon | .20 | .07 |
| ❑ 406 Eddie Robinson | .10 | .02 |
| ❑ 407 John Copeland | .10 | .02 |
| ❑ 408 Robert Jones | .10 | .02 |
| ❑ 409 Steve Bono | .20 | .07 |
| ❑ 410 Cornelius Bennett | .20 | .07 |
| ❑ 411 Ben Coates | .20 | .07 |
| ❑ 412 Dana Stubblefield | .10 | .02 |
| ❑ 413 Darryl Talley | .10 | .02 |
| ❑ 414 Brian Blades | .20 | .07 |
| ❑ 415 Herman Moore | .30 | .10 |
| ❑ 416 Nick Lowery | .10 | .02 |
| ❑ 417 Donnell Bennett | .10 | .02 |
| ❑ 418 Van Malone | .10 | .02 |
| ❑ 419 Pete Stoyanovich | .10 | .02 |
| ❑ 420 Joe Montana | 2.00 | .75 |
| ❑ 421 Steve Young | .50 | .20 |
| ❑ 422 Steve Young | .50 | .20 |
| ❑ 423 Steve Young | .50 | .20 |
| ❑ 424 Steve Young | .50 | .20 |
| ❑ 425 Steve Young | .50 | .20 |
| ❑ 426 Rod Stephens | .10 | .02 |
| ❑ 427 Ellis Johnson RC UER | .10 | .02 |
| ❑ 428 Kordell Stewart RC | 1.25 | .50 |
| ❑ 429 James O. Stewart RC | 1.00 | .40 |
| ❑ 430 Steve McNair RC | 2.50 | 1.00 |
| ❑ 431 Brian DeMarco | .10 | .02 |
| ❑ 432 Matt O'Dwyer | .10 | .02 |
| ❑ 433 Lorenzo Styles RC | .10 | .02 |
| ❑ 434 Anthony Cook RC | .10 | .02 |
| ❑ 435 Jesse James | .10 | .02 |

| | | |
|---|---|---|
| ❑ 436 Darryl Pounds RC | .10 | .02 |
| ❑ 437 Derrick Graham | .10 | .02 |
| ❑ 438 Vernon Turner | .10 | .02 |
| ❑ 439 Carlton Bailey | .10 | .02 |
| ❑ 440 Darion Conner | .10 | .02 |
| ❑ 441 Randy Baldwin | .10 | .02 |
| ❑ 442 Tim McKyer | .10 | .02 |
| ❑ 443 Sam Mills | .20 | .07 |
| ❑ 444 Rob Christian | .10 | .02 |
| ❑ 445 Steve Lofton | .10 | .02 |
| ❑ 446 Lamar Lathon | .10 | .02 |
| ❑ 447 Tony Smith RB | .10 | .02 |
| ❑ 448 Don Beebe | .10 | .02 |
| ❑ 449 Barry Foster | .20 | .07 |
| ❑ 450 Frank Reich | .10 | .02 |
| ❑ 451 Pete Metzelaars | .10 | .02 |
| ❑ 452 Reggie Cobb | .10 | .02 |
| ❑ 453 Jeff Lageman | .10 | .02 |
| ❑ 454 Derek Brown TE | .10 | .02 |
| ❑ 455 Desmond Howard | .20 | .07 |
| ❑ 456 Vinnie Clark | .10 | .02 |
| ❑ 457 Keith Goganious | .10 | .02 |
| ❑ 458 Shawn Bouwens | .10 | .02 |
| ❑ 459 Rob Johnson RC | .75 | .30 |
| ❑ 460 Steve Beuerlein | .20 | .07 |
| ❑ 461 Mark Brunell | .60 | .25 |
| ❑ 462 Harry Colon | .10 | .02 |
| ❑ 463 Chris Hudson | .10 | .02 |
| ❑ 464 Darren Carrington | .10 | .02 |
| ❑ 465 Ernest Givins | .10 | .02 |
| ❑ 466 Kelvin Pritchett | .10 | .02 |
| ❑ 467 Checklist (249-358) | .10 | .02 |
| ❑ 468 Checklist (358-468) | .10 | .02 |

## 1996 Topps

| | | |
|---|---|---|
| ❑ COMPLETE SET (440) | 40.00 | 20.00 |
| ❑ COMP.FACT.SET (448) | 60.00 | 35.00 |
| ❑ COMP.CER.FACT.SET (445) | 40.00 | 20.00 |
| ❑ 1 Troy Aikman | 1.00 | .40 |
| ❑ 2 Kevin Greene | .20 | .07 |
| ❑ 3 Robert Brooks | .30 | .10 |
| ❑ 4 Eugene Daniel | .10 | .02 |
| ❑ 5 Rodney Peete | .10 | .02 |
| ❑ 6 James Hasty | .10 | .02 |
| ❑ 7 Tim McDonald | .10 | .02 |
| ❑ 8 Darick Holmes | .10 | .02 |
| ❑ 9 Morten Andersen | .10 | .02 |
| ❑ 10 Junior Seau | .30 | .10 |
| ❑ 11 Brett Perriman | .10 | .02 |
| ❑ 12 Eric Green | .10 | .02 |
| ❑ 13 Jim Flanigan | .10 | .02 |
| ❑ 14 Cortez Kennedy | .10 | .02 |
| ❑ 15 Orlando Thomas | .10 | .02 |
| ❑ 16 Anthony Miller | .20 | .07 |
| ❑ 17 Sean Gilbert | .10 | .02 |
| ❑ 18 Rob Fredrickson | .10 | .02 |
| ❑ 19 Willie Green | .10 | .02 |
| ❑ 20 Jeff Blake | .30 | .10 |
| ❑ 21 Trent Dilfer | .30 | .10 |
| ❑ 22 Chris Chandler | .20 | .07 |
| ❑ 23 Renaldo Turnbull | .10 | .02 |
| ❑ 24 Dave Meggett | .10 | .02 |
| ❑ 25 Heath Shuler | .20 | .07 |
| ❑ 26 Michael Jackson | .20 | .07 |
| ❑ 27 Thomas Randolph | .10 | .02 |
| ❑ 28 Keith Goganious | .10 | .02 |
| ❑ 29 Seth Joyner | .10 | .02 |
| ❑ 30 Wayne Chrebet | .60 | .25 |
| ❑ 31 Craig Newsome | .10 | .02 |

|  |  | | |
|---|---|---|---|
| 32 | William Fuller | .10 | .02 |
| 33 | Merton Hanks | .10 | .02 |
| 34 | Dale Carter | .10 | .02 |
| 35 | Quentin Coryatt | .10 | .02 |
| 36 | Robert Jones | .10 | .02 |
| 37 | Eric Metcalf | .10 | .02 |
| 38 | Byron Bam Morris | .10 | .02 |
| 39 | Bill Brooks | .10 | .02 |
| 40 | Barry Sanders | 1.50 | .60 |
| 41 | Michael Haynes | .10 | .02 |
| 42 | Joey Galloway | .30 | .10 |
| 43 | Robert Smith | .20 | .07 |
| 44 | John Thierry | .10 | .02 |
| 45 | Bryan Cox | .10 | .02 |
| 46 | Anthony Parker | .10 | .02 |
| 47 | Harvey Williams | .10 | .02 |
| 48 | Terrell Davis | .75 | .30 |
| 49 | Darnay Scott | .10 | .02 |
| 50 | Kerry Collins | .30 | .10 |
| 51 | Cris Dishman | .10 | .02 |
| 52 | Dwayne Harper | .10 | .02 |
| 53 | Warren Sapp | .10 | .02 |
| 54 | Will Moore | .10 | .02 |
| 55 | Earnest Byner | .10 | .02 |
| 56 | Aaron Glenn | .10 | .02 |
| 57 | Michael Westbrook | .30 | .10 |
| 58 | Vencie Glenn | .10 | .02 |
| 59 | Rob Moore | .20 | .07 |
| 60 | Mark Brunell | .60 | .25 |
| 61 | Craig Heyward | .10 | .02 |
| 62 | Eric Allen | .10 | .02 |
| 63 | Bill Romanowski | .10 | .02 |
| 64 | Dana Stubblefield | .20 | .07 |
| 65 | Steve Beno | .10 | .02 |
| 66 | George Koonce | .10 | .02 |
| 67 | Larry Brown | .10 | .02 |
| 68 | Warren Moon | .20 | .07 |
| 69 | Eric Pegram | .10 | .02 |
| 70 | Jim Kelly | .30 | .10 |
| 71 | Jason Belser | .10 | .02 |
| 72 | Henry Thomas | .10 | .02 |
| 73 | Mark Carrier DB | .10 | .02 |
| 74 | Terry Wooden | .10 | .02 |
| 75 | Terry McDaniel | .10 | .02 |
| 76 | O.J. McDuffie | .20 | .07 |
| 77 | Dan Wilkinson | .10 | .02 |
| 78 | Blake Brockermeyer | .10 | .02 |
| 79 | Michael Barrow | .10 | .02 |
| 80 | Dave Brown | .10 | .02 |
| 81 | Todd Lyght | .10 | .02 |
| 82 | Henry Ellard | .10 | .02 |
| 83 | Jeff Lageman | .10 | .02 |
| 84 | Anthony Pleasant | .10 | .02 |
| 85 | Aeneas Williams | .10 | .02 |
| 86 | Vincent Brisby | .10 | .02 |
| 87 | Terrell Fletcher | .10 | .02 |
| 88 | Brad Baxter | .10 | .02 |
| 89 | Shannon Sharpe | .20 | .07 |
| 90 | Errict Rhett | .20 | .07 |
| 91 | Michael Zordich | .10 | .02 |
| 92 | Dan Saleaumua | .10 | .02 |
| 93 | Devin Bush | .10 | .02 |
| 94 | Wayne Simmons | .10 | .02 |
| 95 | Tyrone Hughes | .10 | .02 |
| 96 | John Randle | .10 | .02 |
| 97 | Tony Tolbert | .10 | .02 |
| 98 | Yancey Thigpen | .20 | .07 |
| 99 | J.J. Stokes | .30 | .10 |
| 100 | Marshall Faulk | .40 | .15 |
| 101 | Barry Minter | .10 | .02 |
| 102 | Glenn Foley | .20 | .07 |
| 103 | Chester McGlockton | .10 | .02 |
| 104 | Carlton Gray | .10 | .02 |
| 105 | Terry Kirby | .20 | .07 |
| 106 | Darryll Lewis | .10 | .02 |
| 107 | Thomas Smith | .10 | .02 |
| 108 | Mike Fox | .10 | .02 |
| 109 | Antonio Langham | .10 | .02 |
| 110 | Drew Bledsoe | .60 | .25 |
| 111 | Troy Drayton | .10 | .02 |
| 112 | Marcus Patton | .10 | .02 |
| 113 | Tyrone Wheatley | .20 | .07 |
| 114 | Desmond Howard | .20 | .07 |
| 115 | Johnny Mitchell | .10 | .02 |
| 116 | Dave Krieg | .10 | .02 |
| 117 | Natrone Means | .20 | .07 |
| 118 | Herman Moore | .20 | .07 |
| 119 | Darren Woodson | .20 | .07 |
| 120 | Ricky Watters | .20 | .07 |
| 121 | Emmitt Smith TYC | .75 | .30 |
| 122 | Barry Sanders TYC | .75 | .30 |
| 123 | Curtis Martin TYC | .30 | .10 |
| 124 | Chris Warren TYC | .20 | .07 |
| 125 | Terry Allen TYC | .20 | .07 |
| 126 | Ricky Watters TYC | .20 | .07 |
| 127 | Errict Rhett TYC | .20 | .07 |
| 128 | Rodney Hampton TYC | .10 | .02 |
| 129 | Terrell Davis TYC | .30 | .10 |
| 130 | Harvey Williams TYC | .10 | .02 |
| 131 | Craig Heyward TYC | .10 | .02 |
| 132 | Marshall Faulk TYC | .30 | .10 |
| 133 | Rashaan Salaam TYC | .20 | .07 |
| 134 | Garrison Hearst TYC | .20 | .07 |
| 135 | Edgar Bennett TYC | .20 | .07 |
| 136 | Thurman Thomas TYC | .20 | .07 |
| 137 | Brian Washington | .10 | .02 |
| 138 | Derek Loville | .10 | .02 |
| 139 | Curtis Conway | .30 | .10 |
| 140 | Isaac Bruce | .30 | .10 |
| 141 | Ricardo McDonald | .10 | .02 |
| 142 | Bruce Armstrong | .10 | .02 |
| 143 | Will Wolford | .10 | .02 |
| 144 | Thurman Thomas | .30 | .10 |
| 145 | Mel Gray | .10 | .02 |
| 146 | Napoleon Kaufman | .30 | .10 |
| 147 | Terry Allen | .20 | .07 |
| 148 | Chris Calloway | .10 | .02 |
| 149 | Harry Colon | .10 | .02 |
| 150 | Pepper Johnson | .10 | .02 |
| 151 | Marco Coleman | .10 | .02 |
| 152 | Shawn Jefferson | .10 | .02 |
| 153 | Larry Centers | .20 | .07 |
| 154 | Lamar Lathon | .10 | .02 |
| 155 | Mark Chmura | .20 | .07 |
| 156 | Dermontti Dawson | .10 | .02 |
| 157 | Alvin Harper | .10 | .02 |
| 158 | Randall McDaniel | .15 | .05 |
| 159 | Allen Aldridge | .10 | .02 |
| 160 | Chris Warren | .20 | .07 |
| 161 | Jessie Tuggle | .10 | .02 |
| 162 | Sean Lumpkin | .10 | .02 |
| 163 | Bobby Houston | .10 | .02 |
| 164 | Dexter Carter | .10 | .02 |
| 165 | Erik Kramer | .10 | .02 |
| 166 | Brock Marion | .10 | .02 |
| 167 | Toby Wright | .10 | .02 |
| 168 | John Copeland | .10 | .02 |
| 169 | Sean Dawkins | .10 | .02 |
| 170 | Tim Brown | .30 | .10 |
| 171 | Darion Conner | .10 | .02 |
| 172 | Aaron Hayden RC | .10 | .02 |
| 173 | Charlie Garner | .20 | .07 |
| 174 | Anthony Cook | .10 | .02 |
| 175 | Derrick Thomas | .30 | .10 |
| 176 | Willie McGinest | .10 | .02 |
| 177 | Thomas Lewis | .10 | .02 |
| 178 | Sherman Williams | .10 | .02 |
| 179 | Cornelius Bennett | .10 | .02 |
| 180 | Frank Sanders | .30 | .10 |
| 181 | Leroy Hoard | .10 | .02 |
| 182 | Bernie Parmalee | .10 | .02 |
| 183 | Sterling Palmer | .10 | .02 |
| 184 | Kelvin Pritchett | .10 | .02 |
| 185 | Kordell Stewart | .30 | .10 |
| 186 | Brent Jones | .10 | .02 |
| 187 | Robert Blackmon | .10 | .02 |
| 188 | Adrian Murrell | .20 | .07 |
| 189 | Edgar Bennett | .20 | .07 |
| 190 | Rashaan Salaam | .20 | .07 |
| 191 | Ellis Johnson | .10 | .02 |
| 192 | Andre Coleman | .10 | .02 |
| 193 | Will Shields | .10 | .02 |
| 194 | Derrick Brooks | .30 | .10 |
| 195 | Carl Pickens | .20 | .07 |
| 196 | Carlton Bailey | .10 | .02 |
| 197 | Terance Mathis | .20 | .07 |
| 198 | Carlos Jenkins | .10 | .02 |
| 199 | Derrick Alexander | .10 | .02 |
| 200 | Deion Sanders | .60 | .25 |
| 201 | Glyn Milburn | .10 | .02 |
| 202 | Chris Sanders | .20 | .07 |
| 203 | Rocket Ismail | .10 | .02 |
| 204 | Fred Barnett | .10 | .02 |
| 205 | Quinn Early | .10 | .02 |
| 206 | Henry Jones | .10 | .02 |
| 207 | Herschel Walker | .20 | .07 |
| 208 | James Washington | .10 | .02 |
| 209 | Lee Woodall | .10 | .02 |
| 210 | Neil Smith | .20 | .07 |
| 211 | Tony Bennett | .10 | .02 |
| 212 | Ernie Mills | .10 | .02 |
| 213 | Clyde Simmons | .10 | .02 |
| 214 | Chris Slade | .10 | .02 |
| 215 | Tony Boselli | .10 | .02 |
| 216 | Ryan McNeil | .10 | .02 |
| 217 | Rob Burnett | .10 | .02 |
| 218 | Stan Humphries | .20 | .07 |
| 219 | Rick Mirer | .20 | .07 |
| 220 | Troy Vincent | .10 | .02 |
| 221 | Sean Jones | .10 | .02 |
| 222 | Marty Carter | .10 | .02 |
| 223 | Boomer Esiason | .20 | .07 |
| 224 | Charles Haley | .20 | .07 |
| 225 | Sam Mills | .10 | .02 |
| 226 | Greg Biekert | .10 | .02 |
| 227 | Bryant Young | .10 | .02 |
| 228 | Ken Dilger | .20 | .07 |
| 229 | Levon Kirkland | .10 | .02 |
| 230 | Brian Mitchell | .10 | .02 |
| 231 | Hardy Nickerson | .10 | .02 |
| 232 | Elvis Grbac | .20 | .07 |
| 233 | Kurt Schulz | .10 | .02 |
| 234 | Chris Doleman | .10 | .02 |
| 235 | Tamarick Vanover | .20 | .07 |
| 236 | Jesse Campbell | .10 | .02 |
| 237 | William Thomas | .10 | .02 |
| 238 | Shane Conlan | .10 | .02 |
| 239 | Jason Elam | .20 | .07 |
| 240 | Steve McNair | .75 | .30 |
| 241 | Jerry Rice TYC | .50 | .20 |
| 242 | Isaac Bruce TYC | .30 | .10 |
| 243 | Herman Moore TYC | .20 | .07 |
| 244 | Michael Irvin TYC | .20 | .07 |
| 245 | Robert Brooks TYC | .30 | .10 |
| 246 | Brett Perriman TYC | .10 | .02 |
| 247 | Cris Carter TYC | .30 | .10 |
| 248 | Tim Brown TYC | .20 | .07 |
| 249 | Yancey Thigpen TYC | .20 | .07 |
| 250 | Jeff Graham TYC | .10 | .02 |
| 251 | Carl Pickens TYC | .20 | .07 |
| 252 | Tony Martin TYC | .10 | .02 |
| 253 | Eric Metcalf TYC | .10 | .02 |
| 254 | Jake Reed TYC | .20 | .07 |
| 255 | Quinn Early TYC | .10 | .02 |
| 256 | Anthony Miller TYC | .20 | .07 |
| 257 | Joey Galloway TYC | .30 | .10 |
| 258 | Bert Emanuel TYC | .20 | .07 |
| 259 | Terance Mathis TYC | .10 | .02 |
| 260 | Curtis Conway TYC | .20 | .07 |
| 261 | Henry Ellard TYC | .10 | .02 |
| 262 | Mark Carrier TYC | .10 | .02 |
| 263 | Brian Blades TYC | .10 | .02 |
| 264 | William Roaf | .10 | .02 |
| 265 | Ed McDaniel | .10 | .02 |
| 266 | Nate Newton | .10 | .02 |
| 267 | Brett Maxie | .10 | .02 |
| 268 | Anthony Smith | .10 | .02 |
| 269 | Mickey Washington | .10 | .02 |
| 270 | Jerry Rice | 1.00 | .40 |
| 271 | Shaun Gayle | .10 | .02 |
| 272 | Gilbert Brown RC | .30 | .10 |
| 273 | Mark Bruener | .10 | .02 |
| 274 | Eugene Robinson | .10 | .02 |
| 275 | Marvin Washington | .10 | .02 |
| 276 | Keith Sims | .10 | .02 |
| 277 | Ashley Ambrose | .10 | .02 |
| 278 | Garrison Hearst | .20 | .07 |
| 279 | Donnell Woolford | .10 | .02 |
| 280 | Cris Carter | .30 | .10 |
| 281 | Curtis Martin | .75 | .30 |
| 282 | Scott Mitchell | .20 | .07 |
| 283 | Steven Moore | .10 | .02 |
| 284 | Roman Phifer | .10 | .02 |
| 285 | Ken Harvey | .10 | .02 |
| 286 | Rodney Hampton | .20 | .07 |
| 287 | Willie Davis | .10 | .02 |
| 288 | Yonel Jourdain | .10 | .02 |
| 289 | Brian DeMarco | .10 | .02 |
| 290 | Reggie White | .30 | .10 |
| 291 | Kevin Williams | .10 | .02 |
| 292 | Gary Plummer | .10 | .02 |

| | | |
|---|---|---|
| ☐ 293 Terrance Shaw | .10 | .02 |
| ☐ 294 Calvin Williams | .10 | .02 |
| ☐ 295 Eddie Robinson | .10 | .02 |
| ☐ 296 Tony McGee | .10 | .02 |
| ☐ 297 Clay Matthews | .10 | .02 |
| ☐ 298 Joe Cain | .10 | .02 |
| ☐ 299 Tim McKyer | .10 | .02 |
| ☐ 300 Greg Lloyd | .20 | .07 |
| ☐ 301 Steve Wisniewski | .10 | .02 |
| ☐ 302 Ray Buchanan | .10 | .02 |
| ☐ 303 Lake Dawson | .10 | .02 |
| ☐ 304 Kevin Carter | .10 | .02 |
| ☐ 305 Phillippi Sparks | .10 | .02 |
| ☐ 306 Emmitt Smith | 1.50 | .60 |
| ☐ 307 Ruben Brown | .10 | .02 |
| ☐ 308 Tom Carter | .10 | .02 |
| ☐ 309 William Floyd | .20 | .07 |
| ☐ 310 Jim Everett | .10 | .02 |
| ☐ 311 Vincent Brown | .10 | .02 |
| ☐ 312 Dennis Gibson | .10 | .02 |
| ☐ 313 Lorenzo Lynch | .10 | .02 |
| ☐ 314 Corey Harris | .10 | .02 |
| ☐ 315 James O.Stewart | .20 | .07 |
| ☐ 316 Kyle Brady | .10 | .02 |
| ☐ 317 Irving Fryar | .20 | .07 |
| ☐ 318 Jake Reed | .20 | .07 |
| ☐ 319 Vinny Testaverde | .20 | .07 |
| ☐ 320 John Elway | 2.00 | .75 |
| ☐ 321 Tracy Scroggins | .10 | .02 |
| ☐ 322 Chris Spielman | .10 | .02 |
| ☐ 323 Horace Copeland | .10 | .02 |
| ☐ 324 Chris Zorich | .10 | .02 |
| ☐ 325 Mike Mamula | .10 | .02 |
| ☐ 326 Henry Ford | .10 | .02 |
| ☐ 327 Steve Walsh | .10 | .02 |
| ☐ 328 Stanley Richard | .20 | .07 |
| ☐ 329 Mike Jones | .10 | .02 |
| ☐ 330 Jim Harbaugh | .20 | .07 |
| ☐ 331 Darren Perry | .10 | .02 |
| ☐ 332 Ken Norton | .10 | .02 |
| ☐ 333 Kimble Anders | .20 | .07 |
| ☐ 334 Harold Green | .10 | .02 |
| ☐ 335 Tyrone Poole | .10 | .02 |
| ☐ 336 Mark Fields | .10 | .02 |
| ☐ 337 Darren Bennett | .10 | .02 |
| ☐ 338 Mike Sherrard | .10 | .02 |
| ☐ 339 Terry Ray | .10 | .02 |
| ☐ 340 Bruce Smith | .10 | .02 |
| ☐ 341 Daryl Johnston | .20 | .07 |
| ☐ 342 Vinnie Clark | .10 | .02 |
| ☐ 343 Mike Caldwell | .10 | .02 |
| ☐ 344 Vinson Smith | .10 | .02 |
| ☐ 345 Mo Lewis | .10 | .02 |
| ☐ 346 Brian Blades | .10 | .02 |
| ☐ 347 Rod Stephens | .10 | .02 |
| ☐ 348 David Palmer | .10 | .02 |
| ☐ 349 Blaine Bishop | .10 | .02 |
| ☐ 350 Jeff George | .20 | .07 |
| ☐ 351 George Teague | .10 | .02 |
| ☐ 352 Jeff Hostetler | .10 | .02 |
| ☐ 353 Michael Strahan | .10 | .02 |
| ☐ 354 Eric Davis | .10 | .02 |
| ☐ 355 Jerome Bettis | .30 | .10 |
| ☐ 356 Irv Smith | .10 | .02 |
| ☐ 357 Jeff Herrod | .10 | .02 |
| ☐ 358 Jay Novacek | .10 | .02 |
| ☐ 359 Bryce Paup | .10 | .02 |
| ☐ 360 Neil O'Donnell | .20 | .07 |
| ☐ 361 Eric Swann | .10 | .02 |
| ☐ 362 Corey Sawyer | .10 | .02 |
| ☐ 363 Ty Law | .30 | .10 |
| ☐ 364 Bo Orlando | .10 | .02 |
| ☐ 365 Marcus Allen | .30 | .10 |
| ☐ 366 Mark McMillian | .10 | .02 |
| ☐ 367 Mark Carrier WR | .10 | .02 |
| ☐ 368 Jackie Harris | .10 | .02 |
| ☐ 369 Steve Atwater | .10 | .02 |
| ☐ 370 Steve Young | .75 | .30 |
| ☐ 371 Brett Favre TYC | 1.00 | .40 |
| ☐ 372 Scott Mitchell TYC | .10 | .02 |
| ☐ 373 Warren Moon TYC | .10 | .02 |
| ☐ 374 Jeff George TYC | .10 | .02 |
| ☐ 375 Jim Everett TYC | .10 | .02 |
| ☐ 376 John Elway TYC | 1.00 | .40 |
| ☐ 377 Erik Kramer TYC | .10 | .02 |
| ☐ 378 Jeff Blake TYC | .20 | .07 |
| ☐ 379 Dan Marino TYC | 1.00 | .40 |

| | | |
|---|---|---|
| ☐ 380 Dave Krieg TYC | .10 | .02 |
| ☐ 381 Drew Bledsoe TYC | .30 | .10 |
| ☐ 382 Stan Humphries TYC | .10 | .02 |
| ☐ 383 Troy Aikman TYC | .50 | .20 |
| ☐ 384 Steve Young TYC | .30 | .10 |
| ☐ 385 Jim Kelly TYC | .30 | .10 |
| ☐ 386 Steve Bono TYC | .10 | .02 |
| ☐ 387 David Sloan | .10 | .02 |
| ☐ 388 Jeff Graham | .10 | .02 |
| ☐ 389 Hugh Douglas | .20 | .07 |
| ☐ 390 Dan Marino | 2.00 | .75 |
| ☐ 391 Winston Moss | .10 | .02 |
| ☐ 392 Darrell Green | .10 | .02 |
| ☐ 393 Mark Stepnoski | .10 | .02 |
| ☐ 394 Bert Emanuel | .20 | .07 |
| ☐ 395 Eric Zeier | .10 | .02 |
| ☐ 396 Willie Jackson | .10 | .02 |
| ☐ 397 Qadry Ismail | .20 | .07 |
| ☐ 398 Michael Brooks | .10 | .02 |
| ☐ 399 D'Marco Farr | .10 | .02 |
| ☐ 400 Brett Favre | 2.00 | .75 |
| ☐ 401 Carnell Lake | .10 | .02 |
| ☐ 402 Pat Swilling | .10 | .02 |
| ☐ 403 Stephen Grant | .10 | .02 |
| ☐ 404 Steve Tasker | .10 | .02 |
| ☐ 405 Ben Coates | .20 | .07 |
| ☐ 406 Steve Tovar | .10 | .02 |
| ☐ 407 Tony Martin | .20 | .07 |
| ☐ 408 Greg Hill | .20 | .07 |
| ☐ 409 Eric Guliford | .10 | .02 |
| ☐ 410 Michael Irvin | .30 | .10 |
| ☐ 411 Eric Hill | .10 | .02 |
| ☐ 412 Mario Bates | .20 | .07 |
| ☐ 413 Brian Stablein RC | .10 | .02 |
| ☐ 414 Marcus Jones RC | .10 | .02 |
| ☐ 415 Reggie Brown LB RC | .10 | .02 |
| ☐ 416 Lawrence Phillips RC | .30 | .10 |
| ☐ 417 Alex Van Dyke RC | .20 | .07 |
| ☐ 418 Daryl Gardener RC | .10 | .02 |
| ☐ 419 Mike Alstott RC | 1.00 | .40 |
| ☐ 420 Kevin Hardy RC | .30 | .10 |
| ☐ 421 Rickey Dudley RC | .30 | .10 |
| ☐ 422 Jerome Woods RC | .10 | .02 |
| ☐ 423 Eric Moulds RC | 1.25 | .50 |
| ☐ 424 Cedric Jones RC | .10 | .02 |
| ☐ 425 Simeon Rice RC | .75 | .30 |
| ☐ 426 Marvin Harrison RC | 2.50 | 1.00 |
| ☐ 427 Tim Biakabutaka RC | .30 | .10 |
| ☐ 428 Duane Clemons RC | .10 | .02 |
| ☐ 429 Alex Molden RC | .10 | .02 |
| ☐ 430 Keyshawn Johnson RC | 1.00 | .40 |
| ☐ 431 Willie Anderson RC | .10 | .02 |
| ☐ 432 John Mobley RC | .10 | .02 |
| ☐ 433 Leeland McElroy RC | .20 | .07 |
| ☐ 434 Regan Upshaw RC | .10 | .02 |
| ☐ 435 Eddie George RC | 1.25 | .50 |
| ☐ 436 Jonathan Ogden RC | .30 | .10 |
| ☐ 437 Eddie Kennison RC | .30 | .10 |
| ☐ 438 Jermane Mayberry RC | .10 | .02 |
| ☐ 439 Checklist 1 of 2 | .10 | .02 |
| ☐ 440 Checklist 2 of 2 | .10 | .02 |
| ☐ P1 Joe Namath/Steve Young Promo | 15.00 | 7.50 |
| ☐ P1R Joe Namath Promo Steve Young | 20.00 | 10.00 |

**1997 Topps**

| | | |
|---|---|---|
| ☐ COMPLETE SET (415) | 40.00 | 20.00 |
| ☐ COMP.FACT.SET (424) | 70.00 | 40.00 |
| ☐ 1 Brett Favre | 2.00 | .75 |

| | | |
|---|---|---|
| ☐ 2 Lawyer Milloy | .30 | .10 |
| ☐ 3 Tim Biakabutaka | .30 | .10 |
| ☐ 4 Clyde Simmons | .20 | .07 |
| ☐ 5 Deion Sanders | .50 | .20 |
| ☐ 6 Anthony Miller | .20 | .07 |
| ☐ 7 Marquez Pope | .20 | .07 |
| ☐ 8 Mike Tomczak | .20 | .07 |
| ☐ 9 William Thomas | .20 | .07 |
| ☐ 10 Marshall Faulk | .60 | .25 |
| ☐ 11 John Randle | .30 | .10 |
| ☐ 12 Jim Kelly | .50 | .20 |
| ☐ 13 Steve Bono | .30 | .10 |
| ☐ 14 Rod Stephens | .20 | .07 |
| ☐ 15 Stan Humphries | .20 | .07 |
| ☐ 16 Terrell Buckley | .20 | .07 |
| ☐ 17 Ki-Jana Carter | .20 | .07 |
| ☐ 18 Marcus Robertson | .20 | .07 |
| ☐ 19 Corey Harris | .20 | .07 |
| ☐ 20 Rashaan Salaam | .20 | .07 |
| ☐ 21 Rickey Dudley | .30 | .10 |
| ☐ 22 Jamir Miller | .20 | .07 |
| ☐ 23 Martin Mayhew | .20 | .07 |
| ☐ 24 Jason Sehorn | .30 | .10 |
| ☐ 25 Isaac Bruce | .50 | .20 |
| ☐ 26 Johnnie Morton | .30 | .10 |
| ☐ 27 Antonio Langham | .20 | .07 |
| ☐ 28 Cornelius Bennett | .20 | .07 |
| ☐ 29 Joe Johnson | .20 | .07 |
| ☐ 30 Keyshawn Johnson | .50 | .20 |
| ☐ 31 Willie Green | .20 | .07 |
| ☐ 32 Craig Newsome | .20 | .07 |
| ☐ 33 Brock Marion | .20 | .07 |
| ☐ 34 Corey Fuller | .20 | .07 |
| ☐ 35 Ben Coates | .30 | .10 |
| ☐ 36 Ty Detmer | .30 | .10 |
| ☐ 37 Charles Johnson | .20 | .07 |
| ☐ 38 Willie Jackson | .20 | .07 |
| ☐ 39 Tyronne Drakeford | .20 | .07 |
| ☐ 40 Gus Frerotte | .20 | .07 |
| ☐ 41 Robert Blackmon | .20 | .07 |
| ☐ 42 Andre Coleman | .20 | .07 |
| ☐ 43 Mario Bates | .20 | .07 |
| ☐ 44 Chris Calloway | .20 | .07 |
| ☐ 45 Terry McDaniel | .20 | .07 |
| ☐ 46 Anthony Davis | .20 | .07 |
| ☐ 47 Stanley Pritchett | .20 | .07 |
| ☐ 48 Ray Buchanan | .20 | .07 |
| ☐ 49 Chris Chandler | .30 | .10 |
| ☐ 50 Ashley Ambrose | .20 | .07 |
| ☐ 51 Tyrone Braxton | .20 | .07 |
| ☐ 52 Pepper Johnson | .20 | .07 |
| ☐ 53 Frank Sanders | .30 | .10 |
| ☐ 54 Clay Matthews | .20 | .07 |
| ☐ 55 Bruce Smith | .30 | .10 |
| ☐ 56 Jermaine Lewis | .50 | .20 |
| ☐ 57 Mark Carrier WR UER | .20 | .07 |
| ☐ 58 Jeff Graham | .20 | .07 |
| ☐ 59 Keith Lyle | .20 | .07 |
| ☐ 60 Trent Dilfer | .50 | .20 |
| ☐ 61 Trace Armstrong | .20 | .07 |
| ☐ 62 Jeff Herrod | .20 | .07 |
| ☐ 63 Tyrone Wheatley | .30 | .10 |
| ☐ 64 Torrance-Small | .20 | .07 |
| ☐ 65 Chris Warren | .30 | .10 |
| ☐ 66 Terry Kirby | .20 | .07 |
| ☐ 67 Erric Pegram | .20 | .07 |
| ☐ 68 Sean Gilbert | .20 | .07 |
| ☐ 69 Greg Biekert | .20 | .07 |
| ☐ 70 Ricky Watters | .30 | .10 |
| ☐ 71 Chris Hudson | .20 | .07 |
| ☐ 72 Tamarick Vanover | .30 | .10 |
| ☐ 73 Orlando Thomas | .20 | .07 |
| ☐ 74 Jimmy Spencer | .20 | .07 |
| ☐ 75 John Mobley | .20 | .07 |
| ☐ 76 Henry Thomas | .20 | .07 |
| ☐ 77 Santana Dotson | .20 | .07 |
| ☐ 78 Boomer Esiason | .30 | .10 |
| ☐ 79 Bobby Hebert | .20 | .07 |
| ☐ 80 Kerry Collins | .50 | .20 |
| ☐ 81 Bobby Engram | .30 | .10 |
| ☐ 82 Kevin Smith | .20 | .07 |
| ☐ 83 Rick Mirer | .30 | .10 |
| ☐ 84 Ted Johnson | .20 | .07 |
| ☐ 85 Derrick Alexander WR | .30 | .10 |
| ☐ 86 Hugh Douglas | .20 | .07 |
| ☐ 87 Rodney Harrison RC | 1.00 | .40 |
| ☐ 88 Roman Phifer | .20 | .07 |

|  |  | | |
|---|---|---|---|
| ❑ 89 | Warren Moon | .50 | .20 |
| ❑ 90 | Thurman Thomas | .50 | .20 |
| ❑ 91 | Michael McCrary | .20 | .07 |
| ❑ 92 | Dana Stubblefield | .20 | .07 |
| ❑ 93 | Andre Hastings UER | .20 | .07 |
| ❑ 94 | William Fuller | .20 | .07 |
| ❑ 95 | Jeff Hostetler | .20 | .07 |
| ❑ 96 | Danny Kanell | .20 | .07 |
| ❑ 97 | Mark Fields | .20 | .07 |
| ❑ 98 | Eddie Robinson | .20 | .07 |
| ❑ 99 | Daryl Gardener | .20 | .07 |
| ❑ 100 | Drew Bledsoe | .60 | .25 |
| ❑ 101 | Winslow Oliver | .20 | .07 |
| ❑ 102 | Raymont Harris | .20 | .07 |
| ❑ 103 | LeShon Johnson | .20 | .07 |
| ❑ 104 | Byron Bam Morris | .20 | .07 |
| ❑ 105 | Herman Moore | .30 | .10 |
| ❑ 106 | Keith Jackson | .20 | .07 |
| ❑ 107 | Chris Penn | .20 | .07 |
| ❑ 108 | Robert Griffith RC | .20 | .07 |
| ❑ 109 | Jeff Burris | .20 | .07 |
| ❑ 110 | Troy Aikman | 1.00 | .40 |
| ❑ 111 | Allen Aldridge | .20 | .07 |
| ❑ 112 | Mel Gray | .20 | .07 |
| ❑ 113 | Aaron Bailey | .20 | .07 |
| ❑ 114 | Michael Strahan | .30 | .10 |
| ❑ 115 | Adrian Murrell | .30 | .10 |
| ❑ 116 | Chris Mims | .20 | .07 |
| ❑ 117 | Robert Jones | .20 | .07 |
| ❑ 118 | Derrick Brooks | .50 | .20 |
| ❑ 119 | Tom Carter | .20 | .07 |
| ❑ 120 | Carl Pickens | .30 | .10 |
| ❑ 121 | Tony Brackens | .20 | .07 |
| ❑ 122 | O.J. McDuffie | .30 | .10 |
| ❑ 123 | Napoleon Kaufman | .50 | .20 |
| ❑ 124 | Chris T. Jones | .20 | .07 |
| ❑ 125 | Kordell Stewart | .50 | .20 |
| ❑ 126 | Ray Zellars | .20 | .07 |
| ❑ 127 | Jessie Tuggle | .20 | .07 |
| ❑ 128 | Greg Kragen | .20 | .07 |
| ❑ 129 | Brett Perriman | .20 | .07 |
| ❑ 130 | Steve Young | .60 | .25 |
| ❑ 131 | Willie Clay | .20 | .07 |
| ❑ 132 | Kimble Anders | .30 | .10 |
| ❑ 133 | Eugene Daniel | .20 | .07 |
| ❑ 134 | Jevon Langford | .20 | .07 |
| ❑ 135 | Shannon Sharpe | .30 | .10 |
| ❑ 136 | Wayne Simmons | .20 | .07 |
| ❑ 137 | Leeland McElroy | .20 | .07 |
| ❑ 138 | Mike Caldwell | .20 | .07 |
| ❑ 139 | Eric Moulds | .50 | .20 |
| ❑ 140 | Eddie George | .50 | .20 |
| ❑ 141 | Jamal Anderson | .50 | .20 |
| ❑ 142 | Michael Timpson | .20 | .07 |
| ❑ 143 | Tony Tolbert | .20 | .07 |
| ❑ 144 | Robert Smith | .30 | .10 |
| ❑ 145 | Mike Alstott | .50 | .20 |
| ❑ 146 | Gary Jones | .20 | .07 |
| ❑ 147 | Terrance Shaw | .20 | .07 |
| ❑ 148 | Carlton Gray | .20 | .07 |
| ❑ 149 | Kevin Carter | .20 | .07 |
| ❑ 150 | Darrell Green | .30 | .10 |
| ❑ 151 | David Dunn | .20 | .07 |
| ❑ 152 | Ken Norton | .20 | .07 |
| ❑ 153 | Chad Brown | .20 | .07 |
| ❑ 154 | Pat Swilling | .20 | .07 |
| ❑ 155 | Irving Fryar | .30 | .10 |
| ❑ 156 | Michael Haynes | .20 | .07 |
| ❑ 157 | Shawn Jefferson | .20 | .07 |
| ❑ 158 | Stephen Grant | .20 | .07 |
| ❑ 159 | James O.Stewart | .30 | .10 |
| ❑ 160 | Derrick Thomas | .50 | .20 |
| ❑ 161 | Tim Bowens | .20 | .07 |
| ❑ 162 | Dixon Edwards | .20 | .07 |
| ❑ 163 | Micheal Barrow | .20 | .07 |
| ❑ 164 | Antonio Freeman | .50 | .20 |
| ❑ 165 | Terrell Davis | .60 | .25 |
| ❑ 166 | Henry Ellard | .30 | .10 |
| ❑ 167 | Daryl Johnston | .30 | .10 |
| ❑ 168 | Bryan Cox | .20 | .07 |
| ❑ 169 | Chad Cota | .20 | .07 |
| ❑ 170 | Vinny Testaverde | .30 | .10 |
| ❑ 171 | Andre Reed | .30 | .10 |
| ❑ 172 | Larry Centers | .30 | .10 |
| ❑ 173 | Craig Heyward | .20 | .07 |
| ❑ 174 | Glyn Milburn | .20 | .07 |
| ❑ 175 | Hardy Nickerson | .20 | .07 |
| ❑ 176 | Corey Miller | .20 | .07 |
| ❑ 177 | Bobby Houston | .20 | .07 |
| ❑ 178 | Marco Coleman | .20 | .07 |
| ❑ 179 | Winston Moss | .20 | .07 |
| ❑ 180 | Tony Banks | .30 | .10 |
| ❑ 181 | Jeff Lageman | .20 | .07 |
| ❑ 182 | Jason Belser | .20 | .07 |
| ❑ 183 | James Jett | .30 | .10 |
| ❑ 184 | Wayne Martin | .20 | .07 |
| ❑ 185 | Dave Meggett | .20 | .07 |
| ❑ 186 | Terrell Owens | .60 | .25 |
| ❑ 187 | Willie Williams | .20 | .07 |
| ❑ 188 | Eric Turner | .20 | .07 |
| ❑ 189 | Chuck Smith | .20 | .07 |
| ❑ 190 | Simeon Rice | .30 | .10 |
| ❑ 191 | Kevin Greene | .30 | .10 |
| ❑ 192 | Lance Johnstone | .20 | .07 |
| ❑ 193 | Marty Carter | .20 | .07 |
| ❑ 194 | Ricardo McDonald | .20 | .07 |
| ❑ 195 | Michael Irvin | .50 | .20 |
| ❑ 196 | George Koonce | .20 | .07 |
| ❑ 197 | Robert Porcher | .20 | .07 |
| ❑ 198 | Mark Collins | .20 | .07 |
| ❑ 199 | Louis Oliver | .20 | .07 |
| ❑ 200 | John Elway | 2.00 | .75 |
| ❑ 201 | Jake Reed | .30 | .10 |
| ❑ 202 | Rodney Hampton | .30 | .10 |
| ❑ 203 | Aaron Glenn | .20 | .07 |
| ❑ 204 | Mike Mamula | .20 | .07 |
| ❑ 205 | Terry Allen | .50 | .20 |
| ❑ 206 | John Lynch | .30 | .10 |
| ❑ 207 | Todd Lyght | .20 | .07 |
| ❑ 208 | Dean Wells | .20 | .07 |
| ❑ 209 | Aaron Hayden | .20 | .07 |
| ❑ 210 | Blaine Bishop | .20 | .07 |
| ❑ 211 | Bert Emanuel | .30 | .10 |
| ❑ 212 | Mark Carrier DB UER | .20 | .07 |
| ❑ 213 | Dale Carter | .20 | .07 |
| ❑ 214 | Jimmy Smith | .30 | .10 |
| ❑ 215 | Jim Harbaugh | .30 | .10 |
| ❑ 216 | Jeff George | .30 | .10 |
| ❑ 217 | Anthony Newman | .20 | .07 |
| ❑ 218 | Ty Law | .30 | .10 |
| ❑ 219 | Brent Jones | .20 | .07 |
| ❑ 220 | Emmitt Smith | 1.50 | .60 |
| ❑ 221 | Bennie Blades | .20 | .07 |
| ❑ 222 | Alfred Williams | .20 | .07 |
| ❑ 223 | Eugene Robinson | .20 | .07 |
| ❑ 224 | Fred Barnett | .20 | .07 |
| ❑ 225 | Errict Rhett | .20 | .07 |
| ❑ 226 | Leslie O'Neal | .20 | .07 |
| ❑ 227 | Michael Sinclair | .20 | .07 |
| ❑ 228 | Marcus Patton | .20 | .07 |
| ❑ 229 | Darrien Gordon | .20 | .07 |
| ❑ 230 | Jerome Bettis | .50 | .20 |
| ❑ 231 | Troy Vincent | .20 | .07 |
| ❑ 232 | Ray Mickens | .20 | .07 |
| ❑ 233 | Lonnie Johnson | .20 | .07 |
| ❑ 234 | Charles Way | .20 | .07 |
| ❑ 235 | Chris Sanders | .20 | .07 |
| ❑ 236 | Bracy Walker | .20 | .07 |
| ❑ 237 | Dave Krieg UER | .20 | .07 |
| ❑ 238 | Kent Graham | .20 | .07 |
| ❑ 239 | Ray Lewis | .75 | .30 |
| ❑ 240 | Cris Carter | .50 | .20 |
| ❑ 241 | Elvis Grbac | .30 | .10 |
| ❑ 242 | Eric Davis | .20 | .07 |
| ❑ 243 | Harvey Williams | .20 | .07 |
| ❑ 244 | Eric Allen | .20 | .07 |
| ❑ 245 | Bryant Young | .20 | .07 |
| ❑ 246 | Terrell Fletcher | .20 | .07 |
| ❑ 247 | Darren Perry | .20 | .07 |
| ❑ 248 | Ken Harvey | .20 | .07 |
| ❑ 249 | Marvin Washington | .20 | .07 |
| ❑ 250 | Marcus Allen | .50 | .20 |
| ❑ 251 | Darrin Smith | .20 | .07 |
| ❑ 252 | James Francis | .20 | .07 |
| ❑ 253 | Michael Jackson | .30 | .10 |
| ❑ 254 | Ryan McNeil | .20 | .07 |
| ❑ 255 | Mark Chmura | .30 | .10 |
| ❑ 256 | Keenan McCardell | .20 | .07 |
| ❑ 257 | Tony Bennett | .20 | .07 |
| ❑ 258 | Irving Spikes | .20 | .07 |
| ❑ 259 | Jason Dunn | .20 | .07 |
| ❑ 260 | Joey Galloway | .30 | .10 |
| ❑ 261 | Eddie Kennison | .30 | .10 |
| ❑ 262 | Lonnie Marts | .20 | .07 |
| ❑ 263 | Thomas Lewis | .20 | .07 |
| ❑ 264 | Tedy Bruschi | 1.00 | .40 |
| ❑ 265 | Steve Atwater | .20 | .07 |
| ❑ 266 | Dorsey Levens | .50 | .20 |
| ❑ 267 | Kurt Schulz | .20 | .07 |
| ❑ 268 | Rob Moore | .30 | .10 |
| ❑ 269 | Walt Harris | .20 | .07 |
| ❑ 270 | Steve McNair | .60 | .25 |
| ❑ 271 | Bill Romanowski | .20 | .07 |
| ❑ 272 | Sean Dawkins | .20 | .07 |
| ❑ 273 | Don Beebe | .20 | .07 |
| ❑ 274 | Fernando Smith | .20 | .07 |
| ❑ 275 | Willie McGinest | .20 | .07 |
| ❑ 276 | Levon Kirkland | .20 | .07 |
| ❑ 277 | Tony Martin | .30 | .10 |
| ❑ 278 | Warren Sapp | .30 | .10 |
| ❑ 279 | Lamar Smith | .50 | .20 |
| ❑ 280 | Mark Brunell | .60 | .25 |
| ❑ 281 | Jim Everett | .20 | .07 |
| ❑ 282 | Victor Green | .20 | .07 |
| ❑ 283 | Mike Jones | .20 | .07 |
| ❑ 284 | Charlie Garner | .30 | .10 |
| ❑ 285 | Karim Abdul-Jabbar | .30 | .10 |
| ❑ 286 | Michael Westbrook | .30 | .10 |
| ❑ 287 | Lawrence Phillips | .30 | .10 |
| ❑ 288 | Amani Toomer | .30 | .10 |
| ❑ 289 | Neil Smith | .30 | .10 |
| ❑ 290 | Barry Sanders | 1.50 | .60 |
| ❑ 291 | Willie Davis | .20 | .07 |
| ❑ 292 | Bo Orlando | .20 | .07 |
| ❑ 293 | Alonzo Spellman | .20 | .07 |
| ❑ 294 | Eric Hill | .20 | .07 |
| ❑ 295 | Wesley Walls | .30 | .10 |
| ❑ 296 | Todd Collins | .20 | .07 |
| ❑ 297 | Steven Moore | .20 | .07 |
| ❑ 298 | Eric Metcalf | .30 | .10 |
| ❑ 299 | Darren Woodson | .20 | .07 |
| ❑ 300 | Jerry Rice | 1.00 | .40 |
| ❑ 301 | Scott Mitchell | .30 | .10 |
| ❑ 302 | Ray Crockett | .20 | .07 |
| ❑ 303 | Jim Schwartz RC UER | .20 | .07 |
| ❑ 304 | Steve Tovar | .20 | .07 |
| ❑ 305 | Terance Mathis | .30 | .10 |
| ❑ 306 | Earnest Byner | .20 | .07 |
| ❑ 307 | Chris Spielman | .20 | .07 |
| ❑ 308 | Curtis Conway | .30 | .10 |
| ❑ 309 | Cris Dishman | .20 | .07 |
| ❑ 310 | Marvin Harrison | .50 | .20 |
| ❑ 311 | Sam Mills | .20 | .07 |
| ❑ 312 | Brent Alexander RC | .20 | .07 |
| ❑ 313 | Shawn Moore RC | .20 | .07 |
| ❑ 314 | Dewayne Washington | .20 | .07 |
| ❑ 315 | Terry Glenn | .50 | .20 |
| ❑ 316 | Winfred Tubbs | .20 | .07 |
| ❑ 317 | Dave Brown | .20 | .07 |
| ❑ 318 | Neil O'Donnell | .30 | .10 |
| ❑ 319 | Anthony Parker | .20 | .07 |
| ❑ 320 | Junior Seau | .50 | .20 |
| ❑ 321 | Brian Mitchell | .20 | .07 |
| ❑ 322 | Regan Upshaw | .20 | .07 |
| ❑ 323 | Darryl Williams | .20 | .07 |
| ❑ 324 | Chris Doleman | .20 | .07 |
| ❑ 325 | Rod Woodson | .30 | .10 |
| ❑ 326 | Derrick Witherspoon | .20 | .07 |
| ❑ 327 | Chester McGlockton | .20 | .07 |
| ❑ 328 | Mickey Washington | .20 | .07 |
| ❑ 329 | Greg Hill | .20 | .07 |
| ❑ 330 | Reggie White | .50 | .20 |
| ❑ 331 | John Copeland | .20 | .07 |
| ❑ 332 | Doug Evans | .20 | .07 |
| ❑ 333 | Lamar Lathon | .20 | .07 |
| ❑ 334 | Mark Maddox | .20 | .07 |
| ❑ 335 | Natrone Means | .30 | .10 |
| ❑ 336 | Corey Widmer | .20 | .07 |
| ❑ 337 | Terry Wooden | .20 | .07 |
| ❑ 338 | Merton Hanks | .20 | .07 |
| ❑ 339 | Cortez Kennedy | .30 | .10 |
| ❑ 340 | Tyrone Hughes | .20 | .07 |
| ❑ 341 | Tim Brown | .50 | .20 |
| ❑ 342 | John Jurkovic | .20 | .07 |
| ❑ 343 | Carnell Lake | .20 | .07 |
| ❑ 344 | Stanley Richard | .20 | .07 |
| ❑ 345 | Darryl Lewis | .20 | .07 |
| ❑ 346 | Dan Wilkinson | .20 | .07 |
| ❑ 347 | Broderick Thomas | .20 | .07 |
| ❑ 348 | Brian Williams | .20 | .07 |
| ❑ 349 | Eric Swann | .20 | .07 |

| | | |
|---|---|---|
| ❏ 350 Dan Marino | 2.00 | .75 |
| ❏ 351 Anthony Johnson | .20 | .07 |
| ❏ 352 Joe Cain | .20 | .07 |
| ❏ 353 Quinn Early | .20 | .07 |
| ❏ 354 Seth Joyner | .20 | .07 |
| ❏ 355 Garrison Hearst | .30 | .10 |
| ❏ 356 Edgar Bennett | .30 | .10 |
| ❏ 357 Brian Washington | .20 | .07 |
| ❏ 358 Kevin Hardy | .20 | .07 |
| ❏ 359 Quentin Coryatt | .20 | .07 |
| ❏ 360 Tim McDonald | .20 | .07 |
| ❏ 361 Brian Blades | .20 | .07 |
| ❏ 362 Courtney Hawkins | .20 | .07 |
| ❏ 363 Ray Farmer | .20 | .07 |
| ❏ 364 Jessie Armstead | .20 | .07 |
| ❏ 365 Curtis Martin | .60 | .25 |
| ❏ 366 Zach Thomas | .50 | .20 |
| ❏ 367 Frank Wycheck | .30 | .10 |
| ❏ 368 Darnay Scott | .30 | .10 |
| ❏ 369 Percy Ellsworth RC | .20 | .07 |
| ❏ 370 Desmond Howard | .30 | .10 |
| ❏ 371 Aeneas Williams | .20 | .07 |
| ❏ 372 Bryce Paup | .20 | .07 |
| ❏ 373 Michael Bates | .20 | .07 |
| ❏ 374 Brad Johnson | .50 | .20 |
| ❏ 375 Jeff Blake | .30 | .10 |
| ❏ 376 Donnell Woolford UER | .20 | .07 |
| ❏ 377 Mo Lewis | .20 | .07 |
| ❏ 378 Phillippi Sparks | .20 | .07 |
| ❏ 379 Michael Bankston | .20 | .07 |
| ❏ 380 LeRoy Butler | .20 | .07 |
| ❏ 381 Tyrone Poole | .20 | .07 |
| ❏ 382 Wayne Chrebet | .50 | .20 |
| ❏ 383 Chris Slade | .20 | .07 |
| ❏ 384 Checklist 1 (1-208) | .20 | .07 |
| ❏ 385 Checklist 2 (209-415) | .20 | .07 |
| ❏ 386 Will Blackwell RC | .30 | .10 |
| ❏ 387 Tom Knight RC SP | .20 | .07 |
| ❏ 388 Darnell Autry RC SP | .50 | .20 |
| ❏ 389 Bryant Westbrook RC SP | .20 | .07 |
| ❏ 390 David LaFleur RC SP | .30 | .10 |
| ❏ 391 Antowain Smith RC SP | 2.50 | 1.00 |
| ❏ 392 Kevin Lockett RC SP | .20 | .07 |
| ❏ 393 Rae Carruth RC SP | .30 | .10 |
| ❏ 394 Renaldo Wynn RC SP | .30 | .10 |
| ❏ 395 Jim Druckenmiller RC SP | .50 | .20 |
| ❏ 396 Kenny Holmes RC SP | .75 | .30 |
| ❏ 397 Shawn Springs RC SP | .50 | .20 |
| ❏ 398 Troy Davis RC SP | .50 | .20 |
| ❏ 399 Dwayne Rudd RC SP | .75 | .30 |
| ❏ 400 Orlando Pace RC SP | .75 | .30 |
| ❏ 401 Byron Hanspard RC SP | .50 | .20 |
| ❏ 402 Corey Dillon RC SP | 6.00 | 2.50 |
| ❏ 403 Walter Jones RC SP | .75 | .30 |
| ❏ 404 Reidel Anthony RC SP | .75 | .30 |
| ❏ 405 Peter Boulware RC SP | .75 | .30 |
| ❏ 406 Reinard Wilson RC SP | .50 | .20 |
| ❏ 407 Pat Barnes RC SP | .75 | .30 |
| ❏ 408 Yatil Green RC SP | .75 | .30 |
| ❏ 409 Joey Kent RC SP | .75 | .30 |
| ❏ 410 Ike Hilliard RC SP | 1.50 | .60 |
| ❏ 411 Jake Plummer SP RC | 5.00 | 2.00 |
| ❏ 412 Darrell Russell RC SP | .30 | .10 |
| ❏ 413 James Farrior RC SP | .75 | .30 |
| ❏ 414 Tony Gonzalez RC SP | 3.00 | 1.25 |
| ❏ 415 Warrick Dunn RC SP | 3.00 | 1.25 |
| ❏ P40 Gus Frerotte PROMO | .25 | .08 |
| ❏ P170 Vinny Testaverde PROMO | .25 | .08 |
| ❏ P240 Cris Carter PROMO | .40 | .15 |
| ❏ P250 Marcus Allen PROMO | .40 | .15 |
| ❏ P285 Karim Abdul-Jabbar PROMO | .25 | .08 |
| ❏ P356 Edgar Bennett PROMO | .25 | .08 |

## 1998 Topps

| | | |
|---|---|---|
| ❏ COMPLETE SET (360) | 60.00 | 30.00 |
| ❏ COMP.FACT.SET (360) | 80.00 | 40.00 |
| ❏ 1 Barry Sanders | 1.50 | .60 |
| ❏ 2 Derrick Rodgers | .20 | .07 |
| ❏ 3 Chris Calloway | .20 | .07 |
| ❏ 4 Bruce Armstrong | .20 | .07 |
| ❏ 5 Horace Copeland | .20 | .07 |
| ❏ 6 Chad Brown | .20 | .07 |
| ❏ 7 Ken Harvey | .20 | .07 |
| ❏ 8 Levon Kirkland | .20 | .07 |
| ❏ 9 Glenn Foley | .30 | .10 |
| ❏ 10 Corey Dillon | .50 | .20 |
| ❏ 11 Sean Dawkins | .20 | .07 |

| | | |
|---|---|---|
| ❏ 12 Curtis Conway | .30 | .10 |
| ❏ 13 Chris Chandler | .30 | .10 |
| ❏ 14 Kerry Collins | .30 | .10 |
| ❏ 15 Jonathan Ogden | .20 | .07 |
| ❏ 16 Sam Shade | .20 | .07 |
| ❏ 17 Vaughn Hebron | .20 | .07 |
| ❏ 18 Quentin Coryatt | .20 | .07 |
| ❏ 19 Jerris McPhail | .20 | .07 |
| ❏ 20 Warrick Dunn | .50 | .20 |
| ❏ 21 Wayne Martin | .20 | .07 |
| ❏ 22 Chad Lewis | .30 | .10 |
| ❏ 23 Danny Kanell | .30 | .10 |
| ❏ 24 Shawn Springs | .20 | .07 |
| ❏ 25 Emmitt Smith | 1.50 | .60 |
| ❏ 26 Todd Lyght | .20 | .07 |
| ❏ 27 Donnie Edwards | .20 | .07 |
| ❏ 28 Charlie Jones | .20 | .07 |
| ❏ 29 Willie McGinest | .20 | .07 |
| ❏ 30 Steve Young | .60 | .25 |
| ❏ 31 Darrell Russell | .20 | .07 |
| ❏ 32 Gary Anderson | .20 | .07 |
| ❏ 33 Stanley Richard | .20 | .07 |
| ❏ 34 Leslie O'Neal | .20 | .07 |
| ❏ 35 Dermontti Dawson | .20 | .07 |
| ❏ 36 Jeff Brady | .20 | .07 |
| ❏ 37 Kimble Anders | .30 | .10 |
| ❏ 38 Glyn Milburn | .20 | .07 |
| ❏ 39 Greg Hill | .20 | .07 |
| ❏ 40 Freddie Jones | .30 | .10 |
| ❏ 41 Bobby Engram | .30 | .10 |
| ❏ 42 Aeneas Williams | .20 | .07 |
| ❏ 43 Antowain Smith | .50 | .20 |
| ❏ 44 Reggie White | .50 | .20 |
| ❏ 45 Rae Carruth | .20 | .07 |
| ❏ 46 Leon Johnson | .20 | .07 |
| ❏ 47 Bryant Young | .20 | .07 |
| ❏ 48 Jamie Asher | .20 | .07 |
| ❏ 49 Hardy Nickerson | .20 | .07 |
| ❏ 50 Jerome Bettis | .50 | .20 |
| ❏ 51 Michael Strahan | .30 | .10 |
| ❏ 52 John Randle | .30 | .10 |
| ❏ 53 Kevin Hardy | .20 | .07 |
| ❏ 54 Eric Bjornson | .20 | .07 |
| ❏ 55 Morten Andersen UER | .20 | .07 |
| ❏ 56 Larry Centers | .20 | .07 |
| ❏ 57 Bryce Paup | .20 | .07 |
| ❏ 58 John Mobley | .20 | .07 |
| ❏ 59 Michael Bates | .20 | .07 |
| ❏ 60 Tim Brown | .50 | .20 |
| ❏ 61 Doug Evans | .20 | .07 |
| ❏ 62 Will Shields | .20 | .07 |
| ❏ 63 Jeff Graham | .20 | .07 |
| ❏ 64 Henry Jones | .20 | .07 |
| ❏ 65 Steve Broussard | .20 | .07 |
| ❏ 66 Blaine Bishop | .20 | .07 |
| ❏ 67 Ernie Conwell | .20 | .07 |
| ❏ 68 Heath Shuler | .20 | .07 |
| ❏ 69 Eric Metcalf | .20 | .07 |
| ❏ 70 Terry Glenn | .50 | .20 |
| ❏ 71 James Hasty | .20 | .07 |
| ❏ 72 Robert Porcher | .20 | .07 |
| ❏ 73 Keenan McCardell | .30 | .10 |
| ❏ 74 Tyrone Hughes | .20 | .07 |
| ❏ 75 Troy Aikman | 1.00 | .40 |
| ❏ 76 Peter Boulware | .20 | .07 |
| ❏ 77 Rob Johnson | .30 | .10 |
| ❏ 78 Erik Kramer | .20 | .07 |
| ❏ 79 Kevin Smith | .20 | .07 |
| ❏ 80 Andre Rison | .30 | .10 |
| ❏ 81 Jim Harbaugh | .30 | .10 |

| | | |
|---|---|---|
| ❏ 82 Chris Hudson | .20 | .07 |
| ❏ 83 Ray Zellars | .20 | .07 |
| ❏ 84 Jeff George | .30 | .10 |
| ❏ 85 Willie Davis | .20 | .07 |
| ❏ 86 Jason Gildon | .20 | .07 |
| ❏ 87 Robert Brooks | .30 | .10 |
| ❏ 88 Chad Cota | .20 | .07 |
| ❏ 89 Simeon Rice | .30 | .10 |
| ❏ 90 Mark Brunell | .50 | .20 |
| ❏ 91 Jay Graham | .20 | .07 |
| ❏ 92 Scott Greene | .20 | .07 |
| ❏ 93 Jeff Blake | .30 | .10 |
| ❏ 94 Jason Belser | .20 | .07 |
| ❏ 95 Derrick Alexander DE | .20 | .07 |
| ❏ 96 Ty Law | .30 | .10 |
| ❏ 97 Charles Johnson | .20 | .07 |
| ❏ 98 James Jett | .30 | .10 |
| ❏ 99 Darrell Green | .30 | .10 |
| ❏ 100 Brett Favre | 2.00 | .75 |
| ❏ 101 George Jones | .20 | .07 |
| ❏ 102 Derrick Mason | .30 | .10 |
| ❏ 103 Sam Adams | .20 | .07 |
| ❏ 104 Lawrence Phillips | .20 | .07 |
| ❏ 105 Randall Hill | .20 | .07 |
| ❏ 106 John Mangum | .20 | .07 |
| ❏ 107 Natrone Means | .30 | .10 |
| ❏ 108 Bill Romanowski | .20 | .07 |
| ❏ 109 Terance Mathis | .30 | .10 |
| ❏ 110 Bruce Smith | .30 | .10 |
| ❏ 111 Pete Mitchell | .20 | .07 |
| ❏ 112 Duane Clemons | .20 | .07 |
| ❏ 113 Willie Clay | .20 | .07 |
| ❏ 114 Eric Allen | .20 | .07 |
| ❏ 115 Troy Drayton | .20 | .07 |
| ❏ 116 Derrick Thomas | .50 | .20 |
| ❏ 117 Charles Way | .20 | .07 |
| ❏ 118 Wayne Chrebet | .50 | .20 |
| ❏ 119 Bobby Hoying | .30 | .10 |
| ❏ 120 Michael Jackson | .20 | .07 |
| ❏ 121 Gary Zimmerman | .20 | .07 |
| ❏ 122 Yancey Thigpen | .20 | .07 |
| ❏ 123 Dana Stubblefield | .20 | .07 |
| ❏ 124 Keith Lyle | .20 | .07 |
| ❏ 125 Marco Coleman | .20 | .07 |
| ❏ 126 Karl Williams | .20 | .07 |
| ❏ 127 Stephen Davis | .20 | .07 |
| ❏ 128 Chris Sanders | .20 | .07 |
| ❏ 129 Cris Dishman | .20 | .07 |
| ❏ 130 Jake Plummer | .50 | .20 |
| ❏ 131 Darryl Williams | .20 | .07 |
| ❏ 132 Merton Hanks | .20 | .07 |
| ❏ 133 Torrance Small | .20 | .07 |
| ❏ 134 Aaron Glenn | .20 | .07 |
| ❏ 135 Chester McGlockton | .20 | .07 |
| ❏ 136 William Thomas | .20 | .07 |
| ❏ 137 Kordell Stewart | .50 | .20 |
| ❏ 138 Jason Taylor | .30 | .10 |
| ❏ 139 Lake Dawson | .20 | .07 |
| ❏ 140 Carl Pickens | .30 | .10 |
| ❏ 141 Eugene Robinson | .20 | .07 |
| ❏ 142 Ed McCaffrey | .30 | .10 |
| ❏ 143 Lamar Lathon | .20 | .07 |
| ❏ 144 Ray Buchanan | .20 | .07 |
| ❏ 145 Thurman Thomas | .50 | .20 |
| ❏ 146 Andre Reed | .30 | .10 |
| ❏ 147 Wesley Walls | .30 | .10 |
| ❏ 148 Rob Moore | .30 | .10 |
| ❏ 149 Darren Woodson | .20 | .07 |
| ❏ 150 Eddie George | .50 | .20 |
| ❏ 151 Michael Irvin | .30 | .10 |
| ❏ 152 Johnnie Morton | .30 | .10 |
| ❏ 153 Ken Dilger | .20 | .07 |
| ❏ 154 Tony Boselli | .20 | .07 |
| ❏ 155 Randall McDaniel | .20 | .07 |
| ❏ 156 Mark Fields | .20 | .07 |
| ❏ 157 Phillippi Sparks | .20 | .07 |
| ❏ 158 Troy Davis | .30 | .10 |
| ❏ 159 Troy Vincent | .20 | .07 |
| ❏ 160 Cris Carter | .50 | .20 |
| ❏ 161 Amp Lee | .20 | .07 |
| ❏ 162 Will Blackwell | .20 | .07 |
| ❏ 163 Chad Scott | .20 | .07 |
| ❏ 164 Henry Ellard | .30 | .10 |
| ❏ 165 Robert Jones | .20 | .07 |
| ❏ 166 Garrison Hearst | .50 | .20 |
| ❏ 167 James McKnight | .50 | .20 |
| ❏ 168 Rodney Harrison | .30 | .10 |

|  |  | | |
|---|--------|---|---|
| 169 | Adrian Murrell | .30 | .10 |
| 170 | Rod Smith WR | .30 | .10 |
| 171 | Desmond Howard | .30 | .10 |
| 172 | Ben Coates | .20 | .07 |
| 173 | David Palmer | .20 | .07 |
| 174 | Zach Thomas | .50 | .20 |
| 175 | Dale Carter | .20 | .07 |
| 176 | Mark Chmura | .30 | .10 |
| 177 | Elvis Grbac | .30 | .10 |
| 178 | Jason Hanson | .20 | .07 |
| 179 | Walt Harris | .20 | .07 |
| 180 | Ricky Watters | .30 | .10 |
| 181 | Ray Lewis | .50 | .20 |
| 182 | Lonnie Johnson | .20 | .07 |
| 183 | Marvin Harrison | .50 | .20 |
| 184 | Dorsey Levens | .50 | .20 |
| 185 | Tony Gonzalez | .20 | .07 |
| 186 | Andre Hastings | .20 | .07 |
| 187 | Kevin Turner | .20 | .07 |
| 188 | Mo Lewis | .20 | .07 |
| 189 | Jason Sehorn | .30 | .10 |
| 190 | Drew Bledsoe | .75 | .30 |
| 191 | Michael Sinclair | .20 | .07 |
| 192 | William Floyd | .20 | .07 |
| 193 | Kenny Holmes | .20 | .07 |
| 194 | Marcus Patton | .20 | .07 |
| 195 | Warren Sapp | .30 | .10 |
| 196 | Junior Seau | .50 | .20 |
| 197 | Ryan McNeil | .20 | .07 |
| 198 | Tyrone Wheatley | .30 | .10 |
| 199 | Robert Smith | .50 | .20 |
| 200 | Terrell Davis | .20 | .07 |
| 201 | Brett Perriman | .20 | .07 |
| 202 | Tamarick Vanover | .20 | .07 |
| 203 | Stephen Boyd | .20 | .07 |
| 204 | Zack Crockett | .20 | .07 |
| 205 | Sherman Williams | .20 | .07 |
| 206 | Neil Smith | .30 | .10 |
| 207 | Jermaine Lewis | .30 | .10 |
| 208 | Kevin Williams | .20 | .07 |
| 209 | Byron Hanspard | .20 | .07 |
| 210 | Warren Moon | .50 | .20 |
| 211 | Tony McGee | .20 | .07 |
| 212 | Raymont Harris | .20 | .07 |
| 213 | Eric Davis | .20 | .07 |
| 214 | Darrien Gordon | .20 | .07 |
| 215 | James Stewart | .30 | .10 |
| 216 | Derrick Mayes | .30 | .10 |
| 217 | Brad Johnson | .50 | .20 |
| 218 | Karim Abdul-Jabbar UER | .50 | .20 |
| 219 | Hugh Douglas | .20 | .07 |
| 220 | Terry Allen | .50 | .20 |
| 221 | Rhett Hall | .20 | .07 |
| 222 | Terrell Fletcher | .20 | .07 |
| 223 | Carnell Lake | .20 | .07 |
| 224 | Darryll Lewis | .20 | .07 |
| 225 | Chris Slade | .20 | .07 |
| 226 | Michael Westbrook | .30 | .10 |
| 227 | Willie Williams | .20 | .07 |
| 228 | Tony Banks | .30 | .10 |
| 229 | Keyshawn Johnson | .50 | .20 |
| 230 | Mike Alstott | .50 | .20 |
| 231 | Tiki Barber | .50 | .20 |
| 232 | Jake Reed | .30 | .10 |
| 233 | Eric Swann | .20 | .07 |
| 234 | Eric Moulds | .50 | .20 |
| 235 | Vinny Testaverde | .30 | .10 |
| 236 | Jessie Tuggle | .20 | .07 |
| 237 | Ryan Wetnight RC | .20 | .07 |
| 238 | Tyrone Poole | .20 | .07 |
| 239 | Bryant Westbrook | .20 | .07 |
| 240 | Steve McNair | .50 | .20 |
| 241 | Jimmy Smith | .30 | .10 |
| 242 | Dewayne Washington | .20 | .07 |
| 243 | Robert Harris | .20 | .07 |
| 244 | Rod Woodson | .30 | .10 |
| 245 | Reidel Anthony | .30 | .10 |
| 246 | Jessie Armstead | .20 | .07 |
| 247 | O.J. McDuffie | .30 | .10 |
| 248 | Carlton Gray | .20 | .07 |
| 249 | LeRoy Butler | .20 | .07 |
| 250 | Jerry Rice | 1.00 | .40 |
| 251 | Frank Sanders | .30 | .10 |
| 252 | Todd Collins | .20 | .07 |
| 253 | Fred Lane | .20 | .07 |
| 254 | David Dunn | .20 | .07 |
| 255 | Michael Barrow | .20 | .07 |
| 256 | Luther Elliss | .20 | .07 |
| 257 | Scott Mitchell | .30 | .10 |
| 258 | Dave Meggett | .20 | .07 |
| 259 | Rickey Dudley | .20 | .07 |
| 260 | Isaac Bruce | .50 | .20 |
| 261 | Tony Martin | .30 | .10 |
| 262 | Leslie Shepherd | .20 | .07 |
| 263 | Derrick Brooks | .50 | .20 |
| 264 | Greg Lloyd | .20 | .07 |
| 265 | Terrell Buckley | .20 | .07 |
| 266 | Antonio Freeman | .50 | .20 |
| 267 | Tony Brackens | .20 | .07 |
| 268 | Mark McMillian | .20 | .07 |
| 269 | Dexter Coakley | .20 | .07 |
| 270 | Dan Marino | 2.00 | .75 |
| 271 | Bryan Cox | .20 | .07 |
| 272 | Leeland McElroy | .20 | .07 |
| 273 | Jeff Burris | .20 | .07 |
| 274 | Eric Green | .20 | .07 |
| 275 | Damay Scott | .30 | .10 |
| 276 | Greg Clark | .20 | .07 |
| 277 | Mario Bates | .30 | .10 |
| 278 | Eric Turner | .20 | .07 |
| 279 | Neil O'Donnell | .30 | .10 |
| 280 | Herman Moore | .30 | .10 |
| 281 | Gary Brown | .20 | .07 |
| 282 | Terrell Owens | .50 | .20 |
| 283 | Frank Wycheck | .20 | .07 |
| 284 | Trent Dilfer | .50 | .20 |
| 285 | Curtis Martin | .50 | .20 |
| 286 | Ricky Proehl | .20 | .07 |
| 287 | Steve Atwater | .20 | .07 |
| 288 | Aaron Bailey | .20 | .07 |
| 289 | William Henderson | .30 | .10 |
| 290 | Marcus Allen | .50 | .20 |
| 291 | Tom Knight | .20 | .07 |
| 292 | Quinn Early | .20 | .07 |
| 293 | Michael McCrary | .20 | .07 |
| 294 | Bert Emanuel | .30 | .10 |
| 295 | Tom Carter | .20 | .07 |
| 296 | Kevin Glover | .20 | .07 |
| 297 | Marshall Faulk | .60 | .25 |
| 298 | Harvey Williams | .20 | .07 |
| 299 | Chris Warren | .30 | .10 |
| 300 | John Elway | 2.00 | .75 |
| 301 | Eddie Kennison | .30 | .10 |
| 302 | Gus Frerotte | .20 | .07 |
| 303 | Regan Upshaw | .20 | .07 |
| 304 | Kevin Gogan | .20 | .07 |
| 305 | Napoleon Kaufman | .50 | .20 |
| 306 | Charlie Garner | .30 | .10 |
| 307 | Shawn Jefferson | .20 | .07 |
| 308 | Tommy Vardell | .20 | .07 |
| 309 | Mike Hollis | .20 | .07 |
| 310 | Irving Fryar | .30 | .10 |
| 311 | Shannon Sharpe | .30 | .10 |
| 312 | Byron Bam Morris | .20 | .07 |
| 313 | Jamal Anderson | .50 | .20 |
| 314 | Chris Gedney | .20 | .07 |
| 315 | Chris Spielman | .20 | .07 |
| 316 | Derrick Alexander WR | .30 | .10 |
| 317 | O.J. Santiago | .20 | .07 |
| 318 | Anthony Miller | .30 | .10 |
| 319 | Ki-Jana Carter | .30 | .10 |
| 320 | Deion Sanders | .50 | .20 |
| 321 | Joey Galloway | .30 | .10 |
| 322 | J.J. Stokes | .30 | .10 |
| 323 | Rodney Thomas | .20 | .07 |
| 324 | John Lynch | .30 | .10 |
| 325 | Mike Pritchard | .20 | .07 |
| 326 | Terrance Shaw | .20 | .07 |
| 327 | Ted Johnson | .20 | .07 |
| 328 | Ashley Ambrose | .20 | .07 |
| 329 | Checklist 1 | .20 | .07 |
| 330 | Checklist 2 | .20 | .07 |
| 331 | Jerome Bettis RC | 2.50 | 1.00 |
| 332 | Ryan Leaf RC | 2.50 | 1.00 |
| 333 | Duane Starks RC | 1.25 | .50 |
| 334 | Brian Simmons RC | 2.00 | .75 |
| 335 | Keith Brooking RC | 2.50 | 1.00 |
| 336 | Robert Edwards RC | 2.00 | .75 |
| 337 | Curtis Enis RC | 1.25 | .50 |
| 338 | John Avery RC | 2.00 | .75 |
| 339 | Fred Taylor RC | 4.00 | 1.50 |
| 340 | Germane Crowell RC | 2.00 | .75 |
| 341 | Hines Ward RC | 10.00 | 4.00 |
| 342 | Marcus Nash RC | 1.25 | .50 |
| 343 | Jacquez Green RC | 2.00 | .75 |
| 344 | Joe Jurevicius RC | 2.50 | 1.00 |
| 345 | Greg Ellis RC | 1.25 | .50 |
| 346 | Brian Griese RC | 5.00 | 2.00 |
| 347 | Tavian Banks RC | 2.00 | .75 |
| 348 | Robert Holcombe RC | 2.00 | .75 |
| 349 | Skip Hicks RC | 2.00 | .75 |
| 350 | Ahman Green RC | 6.00 | 2.50 |
| 351 | Takeo Spikes RC | 2.50 | 1.00 |
| 352 | Randy Moss RC | 15.00 | 6.00 |
| 353 | Andre Wadsworth RC | 2.00 | .75 |
| 354 | Jason Peter RC | 1.25 | .50 |
| 355 | Grant Wistrom RC | 2.00 | .75 |
| 356 | Charles Woodson RC | 3.00 | 1.25 |
| 357 | Kevin Dyson RC | 2.50 | 1.00 |
| 358 | Pat Johnson RC | 2.00 | .75 |
| 359 | Tim Dwight RC | 2.50 | 1.00 |
| 360 | Peyton Manning RC | 25.00 | 10.00 |

## 1999 Topps

|  |  | | |
|---|--------|---|---|
| | COMPLETE SET (357) | 50.00 | 20.00 |
| | COMP.SET w/o SPs (330) | 20.00 | 10.00 |
| 1 | Terrell Davis | .60 | .25 |
| 2 | Adrian Murrell | .40 | .15 |
| 3 | Ernie Mills | .25 | .08 |
| 4 | Jimmy Hitchcock | .25 | .08 |
| 5 | Charlie Garner | .40 | .15 |
| 6 | Blaine Bishop | .25 | .08 |
| 7 | Junior Seau | .60 | .25 |
| 8 | Andre Rison | .40 | .15 |
| 9 | Jake Reed | .25 | .08 |
| 10 | Cris Carter | .60 | .25 |
| 11 | Torrance Small | .25 | .08 |
| 12 | Ronald McKinnon | .25 | .08 |
| 13 | Tyrone Davis | .25 | .08 |
| 14 | Warren Moon | .60 | .25 |
| 15 | Jo Jo Johnson | .25 | .08 |
| 16 | Bert Emanuel | .40 | .15 |
| 17 | Brad Culpepper | .25 | .08 |
| 18 | Henry Jones | .25 | .08 |
| 19 | Jonathan Ogden | .25 | .08 |
| 20 | Terrell Owens | .60 | .25 |
| 21 | Derrick Mason | .40 | .15 |
| 22 | Jon Ritchie | .25 | .08 |
| 23 | Eric Metcalf | .25 | .08 |
| 24 | Kevin Carter | .25 | .08 |
| 25 | Fred Taylor | .60 | .25 |
| 26 | DeWayne Washington | .25 | .08 |
| 27 | William Thomas | .25 | .08 |
| 28 | Jason Taylor | .40 | .15 |
| 29 | Doug Flutie | .60 | .25 |
| 30 | Doug Flutie | .60 | .25 |
| 31 | Michael Sinclair | .25 | .08 |
| 32 | Yancey Thigpen | .25 | .08 |
| 33 | Damay Scott | .25 | .08 |
| 34 | Amani Toomer | .25 | .08 |
| 35 | Edgar Bennett | .25 | .08 |
| 36 | LeRoy Butler | .25 | .08 |
| 37 | Jessie Tuggle | .25 | .08 |
| 38 | Andrew Glover | .25 | .08 |
| 39 | Tim McDonald | .25 | .08 |
| 40 | Marshall Faulk | .75 | .30 |
| 41 | Ray Mickens | .25 | .08 |
| 42 | Kimble Anders | .40 | .15 |
| 43 | Trent Green | .60 | .25 |
| 44 | Dermontti Dawson | .25 | .08 |
| 45 | Greg Ellis | .25 | .08 |
| 46 | Hugh Douglas | .25 | .08 |
| 47 | Amp Lee | .25 | .08 |

|  |  | | |
|---|---|---|---|
| ☐ 48 | Lamar Thomas | .25 | .08 |
| ☐ 49 | Curtis Conway | .40 | .15 |
| ☐ 50 | Emmitt Smith | 1.25 | .50 |
| ☐ 51 | Elvis Grbac | .40 | .15 |
| ☐ 52 | Tony Simmons | .25 | .08 |
| ☐ 53 | Darrin Smith | .25 | .08 |
| ☐ 54 | Donovin Darius | .25 | .08 |
| ☐ 55 | Corey Chavous | .25 | .08 |
| ☐ 56 | Phillippi Sparks | .25 | .08 |
| ☐ 57 | Luther Elliss | .25 | .08 |
| ☐ 58 | Tim Dwight | .60 | .25 |
| ☐ 59 | Andre Hastings | .25 | .08 |
| ☐ 60 | Dan Marino | 2.00 | .75 |
| ☐ 61 | Micheal Barrow | .25 | .08 |
| ☐ 62 | Corey Fuller | .25 | .08 |
| ☐ 63 | Bill Romanowski | .25 | .08 |
| ☐ 64 | Derrick Rodgers | .40 | .15 |
| ☐ 65 | Natrone Means | .40 | .15 |
| ☐ 66 | Peter Boulware | .25 | .08 |
| ☐ 67 | Brian Mitchell | .25 | .08 |
| ☐ 68 | Cornelius Bennett | .25 | .08 |
| ☐ 69 | Dedric Ward | .25 | .08 |
| ☐ 70 | Drew Bledsoe | .75 | .30 |
| ☐ 71 | Freddie Jones | .25 | .08 |
| ☐ 72 | Derrick Thomas | .60 | .25 |
| ☐ 73 | Willie Davis | .25 | .08 |
| ☐ 74 | Larry Centers | .25 | .08 |
| ☐ 75 | Mark Brunell | .60 | .25 |
| ☐ 76 | Chuck Smith | .25 | .08 |
| ☐ 77 | Desmond Howard | .40 | .15 |
| ☐ 78 | Sedrick Shaw | .25 | .08 |
| ☐ 79 | Tiki Barber | .25 | .08 |
| ☐ 80 | Curtis Martin | .60 | .25 |
| ☐ 81 | Barry Minter | .25 | .08 |
| ☐ 82 | Skip Hicks | .25 | .08 |
| ☐ 83 | O.J. Santiago | .25 | .08 |
| ☐ 84 | Ed McCaffrey | .40 | .15 |
| ☐ 85 | Terrell Buckley | .25 | .08 |
| ☐ 86 | Charlie Jones | .25 | .08 |
| ☐ 87 | Pete Mitchell | .25 | .08 |
| ☐ 88 | La'Roi Glover RC | .60 | .25 |
| ☐ 89 | Eric Davis | .25 | .08 |
| ☐ 90 | John Elway | 2.00 | .75 |
| ☐ 91 | Kavika Pittman | .25 | .08 |
| ☐ 92 | Fred Lane | .25 | .08 |
| ☐ 93 | Warren Sapp | .25 | .08 |
| ☐ 94 | Lorenzo Bromell RC | .60 | .25 |
| ☐ 95 | Lawyer Milloy | .40 | .15 |
| ☐ 96 | Aeneas Williams | .25 | .08 |
| ☐ 97 | Michael McCrary | .25 | .08 |
| ☐ 98 | Rickey Dudley | .25 | .08 |
| ☐ 99 | Bryce Paup | .25 | .08 |
| ☐ 100 | Jamal Anderson | .60 | .25 |
| ☐ 101 | D'Marco Farr | .25 | .08 |
| ☐ 102 | Johnnie Morton | .40 | .15 |
| ☐ 103 | Jeff Graham | .25 | .08 |
| ☐ 104 | Sam Cowart | .25 | .08 |
| ☐ 105 | Bryant Young | .25 | .08 |
| ☐ 106 | Jermaine Lewis | .40 | .15 |
| ☐ 107 | Chad Bratzke | .25 | .08 |
| ☐ 108 | Jeff Burris | .25 | .08 |
| ☐ 109 | Roell Preston | .25 | .08 |
| ☐ 110 | Vinny Testaverde | .40 | .15 |
| ☐ 111 | Ruben Brown | .25 | .08 |
| ☐ 112 | Darryll Lewis | .25 | .08 |
| ☐ 113 | Billy Davis | .25 | .08 |
| ☐ 114 | Bryant Westbrook | .25 | .08 |
| ☐ 115 | Stephen Alexander | .25 | .08 |
| ☐ 116 | Terrell Fletcher | .25 | .08 |
| ☐ 117 | Terry Glenn | .60 | .25 |
| ☐ 118 | Rod Smith | .40 | .15 |
| ☐ 119 | Carl Pickens | .40 | .15 |
| ☐ 120 | Tim Brown | .60 | .25 |
| ☐ 121 | Mikhael Ricks | .25 | .08 |
| ☐ 122 | Jason Gildon | .25 | .08 |
| ☐ 123 | Charles Way | .25 | .08 |
| ☐ 124 | Rob Moore | .40 | .15 |
| ☐ 125 | Jerome Bettis | .60 | .25 |
| ☐ 126 | Kerry Collins | .40 | .15 |
| ☐ 127 | Bruce Smith | .40 | .15 |
| ☐ 128 | James Hasty | .25 | .08 |
| ☐ 129 | Ken Norton Jr. | .25 | .08 |
| ☐ 130 | Charles Woodson | .60 | .25 |
| ☐ 131 | Tony McGee | .25 | .08 |
| ☐ 132 | Kevin Turner | .25 | .08 |
| ☐ 133 | Jerome Pathon | .25 | .08 |
| ☐ 134 | Garrison Hearst | .40 | .15 |
| ☐ 135 | Craig Newsome | .25 | .08 |
| ☐ 136 | Hardy Nickerson | .25 | .08 |
| ☐ 137 | Ray Lewis | .60 | .25 |
| ☐ 138 | Derrick Alexander | .25 | .08 |
| ☐ 139 | Phil Hansen | .25 | .08 |
| ☐ 140 | Joey Galloway | .40 | .15 |
| ☐ 141 | Oronde Gadsden | .40 | .15 |
| ☐ 142 | Herman Moore | .40 | .15 |
| ☐ 143 | Bobby Taylor | .25 | .08 |
| ☐ 144 | Mario Bates | .25 | .08 |
| ☐ 145 | Kevin Dyson | .40 | .15 |
| ☐ 146 | Aaron Glenn | .25 | .08 |
| ☐ 147 | Ed McDaniel | .25 | .08 |
| ☐ 148 | Terry Allen | .40 | .15 |
| ☐ 149 | Ike Hilliard | .25 | .08 |
| ☐ 150 | Steve Young | .75 | .30 |
| ☐ 151 | Eugene Robinson | .25 | .08 |
| ☐ 152 | John Mobley | .25 | .08 |
| ☐ 153 | Kevin Hardy | .25 | .08 |
| ☐ 154 | Lance Johnstone | .25 | .08 |
| ☐ 155 | Willie McGinest | .25 | .08 |
| ☐ 156 | Gary Anderson | .25 | .08 |
| ☐ 157 | Dexter Coakley | .25 | .08 |
| ☐ 158 | Mark Fields | .25 | .08 |
| ☐ 159 | Steve McNair | .60 | .25 |
| ☐ 160 | Corey Dillon | .60 | .25 |
| ☐ 161 | Zach Thomas | .60 | .25 |
| ☐ 162 | Kent Graham | .25 | .08 |
| ☐ 163 | Tony Parrish | .25 | .08 |
| ☐ 164 | Sam Gash | .25 | .08 |
| ☐ 165 | Kyle Brady | .25 | .08 |
| ☐ 166 | Donnell Bennett | .25 | .08 |
| ☐ 167 | Tony Martin | .40 | .15 |
| ☐ 168 | Michael Bates | .25 | .08 |
| ☐ 169 | Bobby Engram | .40 | .15 |
| ☐ 170 | Jimmy Smith | .40 | .15 |
| ☐ 171 | Vonnie Holliday | .25 | .08 |
| ☐ 172 | Simeon Rice | .40 | .15 |
| ☐ 173 | Kevin Greene | .25 | .08 |
| ☐ 174 | Mike Alstott | .60 | .25 |
| ☐ 175 | Eddie George | .60 | .25 |
| ☐ 176 | Michael Jackson | .25 | .08 |
| ☐ 177 | Neil O'Donnell | .40 | .15 |
| ☐ 178 | Sean Dawkins | .25 | .08 |
| ☐ 179 | Courtney Hawkins | .25 | .08 |
| ☐ 180 | Michael Irvin | .40 | .15 |
| ☐ 181 | Thurman Thomas | .40 | .15 |
| ☐ 182 | Cam Cleeland | .25 | .08 |
| ☐ 183 | Ellis Johnson | .25 | .08 |
| ☐ 184 | Will Blackwell | .25 | .08 |
| ☐ 185 | Ty Law | .40 | .15 |
| ☐ 186 | Merton Hanks | .25 | .08 |
| ☐ 187 | Dan Wilkinson | .25 | .08 |
| ☐ 188 | Andre Wadsworth | .25 | .08 |
| ☐ 189 | Troy Vincent | .25 | .08 |
| ☐ 190 | Frank Sanders | .40 | .15 |
| ☐ 191 | Stephen Boyd | .25 | .08 |
| ☐ 192 | Jason Elam | .25 | .08 |
| ☐ 193 | Kordell Stewart | .40 | .15 |
| ☐ 194 | Ted Johnson | .25 | .08 |
| ☐ 195 | Glyn Milburn | .25 | .08 |
| ☐ 196 | Gary Brown | .25 | .08 |
| ☐ 197 | Travis Hall | .25 | .08 |
| ☐ 198 | John Randle | .40 | .15 |
| ☐ 199 | Jay Riemersma | .25 | .08 |
| ☐ 200 | Barry Sanders | 2.00 | .75 |
| ☐ 201 | Chris Spielman | .25 | .08 |
| ☐ 202 | Rod Woodson | .40 | .15 |
| ☐ 203 | Darrell Russell | .25 | .08 |
| ☐ 204 | Tony Boselli | .25 | .08 |
| ☐ 205 | Darren Woodson | .25 | .08 |
| ☐ 206 | Muhsin Muhammad | .40 | .15 |
| ☐ 207 | Jim Harbaugh | .40 | .15 |
| ☐ 208 | Isaac Bruce | .60 | .25 |
| ☐ 209 | Mo Lewis | .25 | .08 |
| ☐ 210 | Dorsey Levens | .60 | .25 |
| ☐ 211 | Frank Wycheck | .25 | .08 |
| ☐ 212 | Napoleon Kaufman | .60 | .25 |
| ☐ 213 | Walt Harris | .25 | .08 |
| ☐ 214 | Leon Lett | .25 | .08 |
| ☐ 215 | Karim Abdul-Jabbar | .40 | .15 |
| ☐ 216 | Carnell Lake | .25 | .08 |
| ☐ 217 | Byron Bam Morris | .25 | .08 |
| ☐ 218 | John Avery | .25 | .08 |
| ☐ 219 | Chris Slade | .25 | .08 |
| ☐ 220 | Robert Smith | .60 | .25 |
| ☐ 221 | Mike Pritchard | .25 | .08 |
| ☐ 222 | Ty Detmer | .40 | .15 |
| ☐ 223 | Randall Cunningham | .60 | .25 |
| ☐ 224 | Alonzo Mayes | .25 | .08 |
| ☐ 225 | Jake Plummer | .40 | .15 |
| ☐ 226 | Derrick Mayes | .25 | .08 |
| ☐ 227 | Jeff Brady | .25 | .08 |
| ☐ 228 | John Lynch | .40 | .15 |
| ☐ 229 | Steve Atwater | .25 | .08 |
| ☐ 230 | Warrick Dunn | .60 | .25 |
| ☐ 231 | Shawn Jefferson | .25 | .08 |
| ☐ 232 | Erik Kramer | .25 | .08 |
| ☐ 233 | Ken Dilger | .25 | .08 |
| ☐ 234 | Ryan Leaf | .60 | .25 |
| ☐ 235 | Ray Buchanan | .25 | .08 |
| ☐ 236 | Kevin Williams | .25 | .08 |
| ☐ 237 | Ricky Watters | .40 | .15 |
| ☐ 238 | Dwayne Rudd | .25 | .08 |
| ☐ 239 | Duce Staley | .60 | .25 |
| ☐ 240 | Charlie Batch | .60 | .25 |
| ☐ 241 | Tim Biakabutuka | .40 | .15 |
| ☐ 242 | Tony Gonzalez | .60 | .25 |
| ☐ 243 | Bryan Still | .25 | .08 |
| ☐ 244 | Donnie Edwards | .25 | .08 |
| ☐ 245 | Troy Aikman | 1.25 | .50 |
| ☐ 246 | Tony Banks | .40 | .15 |
| ☐ 247 | Curtis Enis | .25 | .08 |
| ☐ 248 | Chris Chandler | .40 | .15 |
| ☐ 249 | James Jett | .40 | .15 |
| ☐ 250 | Brett Favre | 2.00 | .75 |
| ☐ 251 | Keith Poole | .25 | .08 |
| ☐ 252 | Ricky Proehl | .25 | .08 |
| ☐ 253 | Shannon Sharpe | .40 | .15 |
| ☐ 254 | Robert Jones | .25 | .08 |
| ☐ 255 | Chad Brown | .25 | .08 |
| ☐ 256 | Ben Coates | .40 | .15 |
| ☐ 257 | Jacquez Green | .25 | .08 |
| ☐ 258 | Jessie Armstead | .25 | .08 |
| ☐ 259 | Dale Carter | .25 | .08 |
| ☐ 260 | Antowain Smith | .60 | .25 |
| ☐ 261 | Mark Chmura | .25 | .08 |
| ☐ 262 | Michael Westbrook | .40 | .15 |
| ☐ 263 | Marvin Harrison | .60 | .25 |
| ☐ 264 | Darrien Gordon | .25 | .08 |
| ☐ 265 | Rodney Harrison | .25 | .08 |
| ☐ 266 | Charles Johnson | .25 | .08 |
| ☐ 267 | Roman Phifer | .25 | .08 |
| ☐ 268 | Reidel Anthony | .40 | .15 |
| ☐ 269 | Jerry Rice | 1.25 | .50 |
| ☐ 270 | Eric Moulds | .60 | .25 |
| ☐ 271 | Robert Porcher | .25 | .08 |
| ☐ 272 | Deion Sanders | .60 | .25 |
| ☐ 273 | Germane Crowell | .25 | .08 |
| ☐ 274 | Randy Moss | 1.50 | .60 |
| ☐ 275 | Antonio Freeman | .60 | .25 |
| ☐ 276 | Trent Dilfer | .40 | .15 |
| ☐ 277 | Eric Turner | .25 | .08 |
| ☐ 278 | Jeff George | .40 | .15 |
| ☐ 279 | Levon Kirkland | .25 | .08 |
| ☐ 280 | O.J. McDuffie | .40 | .15 |
| ☐ 281 | Takeo Spikes | .25 | .08 |
| ☐ 282 | Jim Flanigan | .25 | .08 |
| ☐ 283 | Chris Warren | .25 | .08 |
| ☐ 284 | J.J. Stokes | .40 | .15 |
| ☐ 285 | Bryan Cox | .25 | .08 |
| ☐ 286 | Sam Madison | .25 | .08 |
| ☐ 287 | Priest Holmes | 1.00 | .40 |
| ☐ 288 | Keenan McCardell | .40 | .15 |
| ☐ 289 | Michael Strahan | .40 | .15 |
| ☐ 290 | Robert Edwards | .25 | .08 |
| ☐ 291 | Tommy Vardell | .25 | .08 |
| ☐ 292 | Wayne Chrebet | .40 | .15 |
| ☐ 293 | Chris Calloway | .25 | .08 |
| ☐ 294 | Wesley Walls | .40 | .15 |
| ☐ 295 | Derrick Brooks | .60 | .25 |
| ☐ 296 | Trace Armstrong | .25 | .08 |
| ☐ 297 | Brian Simmons | .25 | .08 |
| ☐ 298 | Darrell Green | .25 | .08 |
| ☐ 299 | Robert Brooks | .40 | .15 |
| ☐ 300 | Peyton Manning | 2.00 | .75 |
| ☐ 301 | Dana Stubblefield | .25 | .08 |
| ☐ 302 | Shawn Springs | .25 | .08 |
| ☐ 303 | Leslie Shepherd | .25 | .08 |
| ☐ 304 | Ken Harvey | .25 | .08 |
| ☐ 305 | Jon Kitna | .60 | .25 |
| ☐ 306 | Terance Mathis | .25 | .08 |
| ☐ 307 | Andre Reed | .40 | .15 |
| ☐ 308 | Jackie Harris | .25 | .08 |

| ❏ 309 Rich Gannon | .60 | .25 |
| ❏ 310 Keyshawn Johnson | .60 | .25 |
| ❏ 311 Victor Green | .25 | .08 |
| ❏ 312 Eric Allen | .25 | .08 |
| ❏ 313 Terry Fair | .25 | .08 |
| ❏ 314 Jason Elam SH | .25 | .08 |
| ❏ 315 Garrison Hearst SH | .40 | .15 |
| ❏ 316 Jake Plummer SH | .40 | .15 |
| ❏ 317 Randall Cunningham SH | .60 | .25 |
| ❏ 318 Randy Moss SH | .75 | .30 |
| ❏ 319 Jamal Anderson SH | .60 | .25 |
| ❏ 320 John Elway SH | 1.00 | .40 |
| ❏ 321 Doug Flutie SH | .40 | .15 |
| ❏ 322 Emmitt Smith SH | .75 | .30 |
| ❏ 323 Terrell Davis SH | .75 | .30 |
| ❏ 324 Jerris McPhail | .25 | .08 |
| ❏ 325 Damon Gibson | .25 | .08 |
| ❏ 326 Jim Pyne | .25 | .08 |
| ❏ 327 Antonio Langham | .25 | .08 |
| ❏ 328 Freddie Solomon | .25 | .08 |
| ❏ 329 Ricky Williams RC | 4.00 | 1.50 |
| ❏ 330 Daunte Culpepper RC | 8.00 | 3.00 |
| ❏ 331 Chris Claiborne RC | 1.25 | .50 |
| ❏ 332 Amos Zereoue RC | 2.50 | 1.00 |
| ❏ 333 Chris McAlister RC | 2.00 | .75 |
| ❏ 334 Kevin Faulk RC | 2.50 | 1.00 |
| ❏ 335 James Johnson RC | 2.00 | .75 |
| ❏ 336 Mike Cloud RC | 2.00 | .75 |
| ❏ 337 Jevon Kearse RC | 4.00 | 1.50 |
| ❏ 338 Akili Smith RC | 2.00 | .75 |
| ❏ 339 Edgerrin James RC | 8.00 | 3.00 |
| ❏ 340 Cecil Collins RC | 1.25 | .50 |
| ❏ 341 Donovan McNabb RC | 10.00 | 4.00 |
| ❏ 342 Kevin Johnson RC | 2.50 | 1.00 |
| ❏ 343 Torry Holt RC | 5.00 | 2.00 |
| ❏ 344 Rob Konrad RC | 1.25 | .50 |
| ❏ 345 Tim Couch RC | 2.50 | 1.00 |
| ❏ 346 David Boston RC | 2.50 | 1.00 |
| ❏ 347 Karsten Bailey RC | 2.00 | .75 |
| ❏ 348 Troy Edwards RC | 2.50 | .75 |
| ❏ 349 Sedrick Irvin RC | 1.25 | .50 |
| ❏ 350 Shaun King RC | 2.00 | .75 |
| ❏ 351 Peerless Price RC | 2.50 | 1.00 |
| ❏ 352 Brock Huard RC | 2.50 | 1.00 |
| ❏ 353 Cade McNown RC | 2.00 | .75 |
| ❏ 354 Champ Bailey RC | 3.00 | 1.25 |
| ❏ 355 D'Wayne Bates RC | 2.00 | .75 |
| ❏ 356 Checklist Card | .25 | .08 |
| ❏ 357 Checklist Card | .25 | .08 |

## 2000 Topps

| COMPLETE SET (400) | 60.00 | 25.00 |
| COMP.SET w/o SP's (360) | 20.00 | 7.50 |
| SBMVP STATED ODDS 1:1287 HTA | | |
| ❏ 1 Kurt Warner | 1.25 | .50 |
| ❏ 2 Darrell Russell | .25 | .08 |
| ❏ 3 Tai Streets | .25 | .08 |
| ❏ 4 Bryant Young | .25 | .08 |
| ❏ 5 Kent Graham | .25 | .08 |
| ❏ 6 Shawn Jefferson | .25 | .08 |
| ❏ 7 Wesley Walls | .25 | .08 |
| ❏ 8 Jessie Armstead | .25 | .08 |
| ❏ 9 Dedric Ward | .25 | .08 |
| ❏ 10 Emmitt Smith | 1.25 | .50 |
| ❏ 11 James Stewart | .40 | .15 |
| ❏ 12 Frank Sanders | .25 | .08 |
| ❏ 13 Ray Buchanan | .25 | .08 |
| ❏ 14 Olindo Mare | .25 | .08 |
| ❏ 15 Andre Reed | .40 | .15 |

| ❏ 16 Curtis Conway | .40 | .15 |
| ❏ 17 Patrick Jeffers | .60 | .25 |
| ❏ 18 Greg Hill | .25 | .08 |
| ❏ 19 John Unitas | .60 | .25 |
| ❏ 20 Brett Favre | 2.00 | .75 |
| ❏ 21 Jerome Pathon | .40 | .15 |
| ❏ 22 Jason Tucker | .25 | .08 |
| ❏ 23 Charles Johnson | .40 | .15 |
| ❏ 24 Brian Mitchell | .25 | .08 |
| ❏ 25 Billy Miller | .25 | .08 |
| ❏ 26 Jay Fiedler | .60 | .25 |
| ❏ 27 Marcus Pollard | .25 | .08 |
| ❏ 28 De'Mond Parker | .25 | .08 |
| ❏ 29 Leslie Shepherd | .25 | .08 |
| ❏ 30 Fred Taylor | .60 | .25 |
| ❏ 31 Michael Pittman | .25 | .08 |
| ❏ 32 Ricky Watters | .40 | .15 |
| ❏ 33 Derrick Brooks | .60 | .25 |
| ❏ 34 Junior Seau | .60 | .25 |
| ❏ 35 Troy Vincent | .25 | .08 |
| ❏ 36 Eric Allen | .25 | .08 |
| ❏ 37 Pete Mitchell | .25 | .08 |
| ❏ 38 Tony Simmons | .25 | .08 |
| ❏ 39 Az-Zahir Hakim | .40 | .15 |
| ❏ 40 Dan Marino | 2.00 | .75 |
| ❏ 41 Mac Cody | .25 | .08 |
| ❏ 42 Scott Dreisbach | .25 | .08 |
| ❏ 43 Al Wilson | .25 | .08 |
| ❏ 44 Luther Broughton RC | .40 | .15 |
| ❏ 45 Wane McGarity | .25 | .08 |
| ❏ 46 Stephen Boyd | .25 | .08 |
| ❏ 47 Michael Strahan | .40 | .15 |
| ❏ 48 Chris Chandler | .40 | .15 |
| ❏ 49 Tony Martin | .40 | .15 |
| ❏ 50 Edgerrin James | 1.00 | .40 |
| ❏ 51 John Randle | .40 | .15 |
| ❏ 52 Warrick Dunn | .60 | .25 |
| ❏ 53 Elvis Grbac | .40 | .15 |
| ❏ 54 Champ Bailey | .40 | .15 |
| ❏ 55 Kyle Brady | .25 | .08 |
| ❏ 56 John Lynch | .40 | .15 |
| ❏ 57 Kevin Carter | .25 | .08 |
| ❏ 58 Mike Pritchard | .25 | .08 |
| ❏ 59 Deon Mitchell RC | .40 | .15 |
| ❏ 60 Randy Moss | 1.25 | .50 |
| ❏ 61 Jermaine Fazande | .25 | .08 |
| ❏ 62 Donovan McNabb | 1.00 | .40 |
| ❏ 63 Richard Huntley | .25 | .08 |
| ❏ 64 Rich Gannon | .60 | .25 |
| ❏ 65 Aaron Glenn | .25 | .08 |
| ❏ 66 Amani Toomer | .25 | .08 |
| ❏ 67 Andre Hastings | .25 | .08 |
| ❏ 68 Ricky Williams | .60 | .25 |
| ❏ 69 Sam Madison | .25 | .08 |
| ❏ 70 Drew Bledsoe | .75 | .30 |
| ❏ 71 Eric Moulds | .60 | .25 |
| ❏ 72 Justin Armour | .25 | .08 |
| ❏ 73 Jamal Anderson | .60 | .25 |
| ❏ 74 Mario Bates | .25 | .08 |
| ❏ 75 Sam Gash | .25 | .08 |
| ❏ 76 Macey Brooks | .25 | .08 |
| ❏ 77 Tremain Mack | .25 | .08 |
| ❏ 78 David LaFleur | .25 | .08 |
| ❏ 79 Dexter Coakley | .25 | .08 |
| ❏ 80 Cris Carter | .60 | .25 |
| ❏ 81 Byron Chamberlain | .25 | .08 |
| ❏ 82 David Sloan | .25 | .08 |
| ❏ 83 Mike Devlin RC | .25 | .08 |
| ❏ 84 Jimmy Smith | .40 | .15 |
| ❏ 85 Derrick Alexander | .40 | .15 |
| ❏ 86 Damon Huard | .60 | .25 |
| ❏ 87 Jake Reed | .40 | .15 |
| ❏ 88 Darrell Green | .25 | .08 |
| ❏ 89 Derrick Mason | .40 | .15 |
| ❏ 90 Curtis Martin | .60 | .25 |
| ❏ 91 Donnie Abraham | .25 | .08 |
| ❏ 92 D'Marco Farr | .25 | .08 |
| ❏ 93 Ahman Green | .60 | .25 |
| ❏ 94 Shane Matthews | .40 | .15 |
| ❏ 95 Torrance Small | .25 | .08 |
| ❏ 96 Duce Staley | .60 | .25 |
| ❏ 97 Jon Ritchie | .25 | .08 |
| ❏ 98 Victor Green | .25 | .08 |
| ❏ 99 Kerry Collins | .40 | .15 |
| ❏ 100 Peyton Manning | 1.50 | .60 |
| ❏ 101 Ben Coates | .25 | .08 |
| ❏ 102 Thurman Thomas | .40 | .15 |

| ❏ 103 Cornelius Bennett | .25 | .08 |
| ❏ 104 Terance Mathis | .40 | .15 |
| ❏ 105 Adrian Murrell | .40 | .15 |
| ❏ 106 Donald Hayes | .25 | .08 |
| ❏ 107 Terry Kirby | .25 | .08 |
| ❏ 108 James Allen | .40 | .15 |
| ❏ 109 Ty Law | .40 | .15 |
| ❏ 110 Tim Brown | .60 | .25 |
| ❏ 111 Chad Bratzke | .25 | .08 |
| ❏ 112 Deion Sanders | .60 | .25 |
| ❏ 113 James Johnson | .25 | .08 |
| ❏ 114 Tony Richardson RC | .40 | .15 |
| ❏ 115 Tony Brackens | .25 | .08 |
| ❏ 116 Ken Dilger | .25 | .08 |
| ❏ 117 Albert Connell | .25 | .08 |
| ❏ 118 Neil O'Donnell | .25 | .08 |
| ❏ 119 Selucio Sanford EP RC | .60 | .25 |
| ❏ 120 Steve Young | .75 | .30 |
| ❏ 121 Tony Home | .25 | .08 |
| ❏ 122 Charlie Rogers | .25 | .08 |
| ❏ 123 J.J. Stokes | .40 | .15 |
| ❏ 124 Kenny Bynum | .25 | .08 |
| ❏ 125 Jeff Graham | .25 | .08 |
| ❏ 126 Ike Hilliard | .40 | .15 |
| ❏ 127 Ray Lucas | .40 | .15 |
| ❏ 128 Terry Glenn | .40 | .15 |
| ❏ 129 Rickey Dudley | .25 | .08 |
| ❏ 130 Joey Galloway | .40 | .15 |
| ❏ 131 Brian Dawkins | .60 | .25 |
| ❏ 132 Rob Moore | .40 | .15 |
| ❏ 133 Bob Christian | .25 | .08 |
| ❏ 134 Anthony Wright RC | 2.00 | .75 |
| ❏ 135 Antowain Smith | .40 | .15 |
| ❏ 136 Kevin Johnson | .60 | .25 |
| ❏ 137 Scott Covington | .25 | .08 |
| ❏ 138 D'Wayne Bates | .25 | .08 |
| ❏ 139 Sam Cowart | .25 | .08 |
| ❏ 140 Isaac Bruce | .60 | .25 |
| ❏ 141 Tony McGee | .25 | .08 |
| ❏ 142 Dale Carter | .25 | .08 |
| ❏ 143 Matt Hasselbeck | .40 | .15 |
| ❏ 144 Torry Holt | .60 | .25 |
| ❏ 145 Daunte Culpepper | .75 | .30 |
| ❏ 146 Yatil Green | .25 | .08 |
| ❏ 147 Chris Howard | .25 | .08 |
| ❏ 148 Irving Fryar | .40 | .15 |
| ❏ 149 Derrick Mayes | .25 | .08 |
| ❏ 150 Warren Sapp | .40 | .15 |
| ❏ 151 Ricky Proehl | .25 | .08 |
| ❏ 152 Eric Kresser EP | .50 | .20 |
| ❏ 153 Jeff Garcia | .60 | .25 |
| ❏ 154 Froddie Jones | .25 | .08 |
| ❏ 155 Mike Cloud | .25 | .08 |
| ❏ 156 Wayne Chrebet | .40 | .15 |
| ❏ 157 Joe Montgomery | .25 | .08 |
| ❏ 158 Shannon Sharpe | .40 | .15 |
| ❏ 159 Eddie Kennison | .25 | .08 |
| ❏ 160 Eddie George | .60 | .25 |
| ❏ 161 Jay Riemersma | .25 | .08 |
| ❏ 162 Peter Boulware | .25 | .08 |
| ❏ 163 Aeneas Williams | .25 | .08 |
| ❏ 164 Jim Miller | .25 | .08 |
| ❏ 165 Jamir Miller | .25 | .08 |
| ❏ 166 Tim Biakabutuka | .40 | .15 |
| ❏ 167 Kordell Stewart | .40 | .15 |
| ❏ 168 Charlie Garner | .40 | .15 |
| ❏ 169 Germane Crowell | .25 | .08 |
| ❏ 170 Stephen Davis | .60 | .25 |
| ❏ 171 Jeff George | .40 | .15 |
| ❏ 172 Mark Brunell | .60 | .25 |
| ❏ 173 Stephen Alexander | .25 | .08 |
| ❏ 174 Mike Alstott | .40 | .15 |
| ❏ 175 Terry Allen | .40 | .15 |
| ❏ 176 Ed McCaffrey | .60 | .25 |
| ❏ 177 Bobby Engram | .25 | .08 |
| ❏ 178 Andre Cooper | .25 | .08 |
| ❏ 179 Kevin Faulk | .40 | .15 |
| ❏ 180 Errict Rhett | .40 | .15 |
| ❏ 181 Jammi German | .25 | .08 |
| ❏ 182 Oronde Gadsden | .40 | .15 |
| ❏ 183 Jevon Kearse | .60 | .25 |
| ❏ 184 Herman Moore | .40 | .15 |
| ❏ 185 Terrence Wilkins | .25 | .08 |
| ❏ 186 Rocket Ismail | .40 | .15 |
| ❏ 187 Patrick Johnson | .25 | .08 |
| ❏ 188 Simeon Rice | .25 | .08 |
| ❏ 189 Mo Lewis | .25 | .08 |

| | | |
|---|---|---|
| ☐ 190 Qadry Ismail | .40 | .15 |
| ☐ 191 Terry Jackson | .25 | .08 |
| ☐ 192 Rashaan Shehee | .25 | .08 |
| ☐ 193 Charles Woodson | .40 | .15 |
| ☐ 194 Akili Smith | .40 | .15 |
| ☐ 195 Yancey Thigpen | .25 | .08 |
| ☐ 196 Michael Westbrook | .40 | .15 |
| ☐ 197 Donnell Bennett | .25 | .08 |
| ☐ 198 Sedrick Irvin | .25 | .08 |
| ☐ 199 Keenan McCardell | .40 | .15 |
| ☐ 200 Marshall Faulk | .75 | .30 |
| ☐ 201 Jeff Blake | .40 | .15 |
| ☐ 202 Rob Johnson | .40 | .15 |
| ☐ 203 Vinny Testaverde | .40 | .15 |
| ☐ 204 Andy Katzenmoyer | .25 | .08 |
| ☐ 205 Michael Basnight | .25 | .08 |
| ☐ 206 Lance Schulters | .25 | .08 |
| ☐ 207 Shaun King | .25 | .08 |
| ☐ 208 Bill Schroeder | .40 | .15 |
| ☐ 209 Skip Hicks | .25 | .08 |
| ☐ 210 Jake Plummer | .40 | .15 |
| ☐ 211 Leroy Hoard | .25 | .08 |
| ☐ 212 Reggie Barlow | .25 | .08 |
| ☐ 213 E.G. Green | .25 | .08 |
| ☐ 214 Fred Lane | .25 | .08 |
| ☐ 215 Antonio Freeman | .60 | .25 |
| ☐ 216 Grant Wistrom | .25 | .08 |
| ☐ 217 Kevin Dyson | .40 | .15 |
| ☐ 218 Mikhael Ricks | .25 | .08 |
| ☐ 219 Rod Woodson | .40 | .15 |
| ☐ 220 Tim Dwight | .60 | .25 |
| ☐ 221 Darnay Scott | .40 | .15 |
| ☐ 222 Curtis Enis | .25 | .08 |
| ☐ 223 Sean Bennett | .25 | .08 |
| ☐ 224 Napoleon Kaufman | .40 | .15 |
| ☐ 225 Jonathan Linton | .25 | .08 |
| ☐ 226 Jim Harbaugh | .40 | .15 |
| ☐ 227 Hardy Nickerson | .25 | .08 |
| ☐ 228 Todd Lyght | .25 | .08 |
| ☐ 229 Dorsey Levens | .40 | .15 |
| ☐ 230 Steve Beuerlein | .40 | .15 |
| ☐ 231 Marty Booker | .25 | .08 |
| ☐ 232 Andre Wadsworth | .25 | .08 |
| ☐ 233 James Hasty | .25 | .08 |
| ☐ 234 Shawn Bryson | .25 | .08 |
| ☐ 235 Larry Centers | .25 | .08 |
| ☐ 236 Charlie Batch | .60 | .25 |
| ☐ 237 Steve McNair | .60 | .25 |
| ☐ 238 Darrin Chiaverini | .25 | .08 |
| ☐ 239 Jerome Bettis | .60 | .25 |
| ☐ 240 Muhsin Muhammad | .40 | .15 |
| ☐ 241 Terrell Fletcher | .25 | .08 |
| ☐ 242 Jon Kitna | .60 | .25 |
| ☐ 243 Frank Wycheck | .25 | .08 |
| ☐ 244 Tony Gonzalez | .40 | .15 |
| ☐ 245 Ron Rivers | .25 | .08 |
| ☐ 246 Olandis Gary | .60 | .25 |
| ☐ 247 Jermaine Lewis | .25 | .08 |
| ☐ 248 Joe Jurevicius | .25 | .08 |
| ☐ 249 Richie Anderson | .25 | .08 |
| ☐ 250 Marcus Robinson | .60 | .25 |
| ☐ 251 Shawn Springs | .25 | .08 |
| ☐ 252 William Floyd | .25 | .08 |
| ☐ 253 Bobby Shaw RC | .60 | .25 |
| ☐ 254 Glyn Milburn | .25 | .08 |
| ☐ 255 Brian Griese | .60 | .25 |
| ☐ 256 Donnie Edwards | .25 | .08 |
| ☐ 257 Joe Horn | .40 | .15 |
| ☐ 258 Cameron Cleeland | .25 | .08 |
| ☐ 259 Glenn Foley | .25 | .08 |
| ☐ 260 Corey Dillon | .60 | .25 |
| ☐ 261 Troy Brown | .40 | .15 |
| ☐ 262 Stoney Case | .25 | .08 |
| ☐ 263 Kevin Williams | .25 | .08 |
| ☐ 264 London Fletcher RC | .25 | .08 |
| ☐ 265 O.J. McDuffie | .40 | .15 |
| ☐ 266 Jonathan Quinn | .25 | .08 |
| ☐ 267 Trent Dilfer | .40 | .15 |
| ☐ 268 Dameyune Craig | .25 | .08 |
| ☐ 269 Terrell Owens | .60 | .25 |
| ☐ 270 Tim Couch | .40 | .15 |
| ☐ 271 Dameane Douglas | .25 | .08 |
| ☐ 272 Moses Moreno | .25 | .08 |
| ☐ 273 Bruce Smith | .40 | .15 |
| ☐ 274 Peerless Price | .40 | .15 |
| ☐ 275 Sam Games | .25 | .08 |
| ☐ 276 Natrone Means | .25 | .08 |

| | | |
|---|---|---|
| ☐ 277 Na Brown | .25 | .08 |
| ☐ 278 Dave Moore | .25 | .08 |
| ☐ 279 Chris Sanders | .25 | .08 |
| ☐ 280 Troy Aikman | 1.25 | .50 |
| ☐ 281 Cecil Collins | .25 | .08 |
| ☐ 282 Matthew Hatchette | .25 | .08 |
| ☐ 283 Bill Romanowski | .25 | .08 |
| ☐ 284 Basil Mitchell | .25 | .08 |
| ☐ 285 Tony Banks | .40 | .15 |
| ☐ 286 Jake Delhomme RC | 3.00 | 1.25 |
| ☐ 287 Keyshawn Johnson | .60 | .25 |
| ☐ 288 Dexter McCleon RC | .60 | .25 |
| ☐ 289 Corey Bradford | .40 | .15 |
| ☐ 290 Terrell Davis | .60 | .25 |
| ☐ 291 Johnnie Morton | .40 | .15 |
| ☐ 292 Kevin Lockett | .25 | .08 |
| ☐ 293 Robert Smith | .60 | .25 |
| ☐ 294 Jeff Lewis | .25 | .08 |
| ☐ 295 Wali Rainer | .25 | .08 |
| ☐ 296 Troy Edwards | .25 | .08 |
| ☐ 297 Keith Poole | .25 | .08 |
| ☐ 298 Priest Holmes | .75 | .30 |
| ☐ 299 David Boston | .60 | .25 |
| ☐ 300 Marvin Harrison | .60 | .25 |
| ☐ 301 Levon Kirkland | .25 | .08 |
| ☐ 302 Robert Holcombe | .25 | .08 |
| ☐ 303 Autry Denson | .25 | .08 |
| ☐ 304 Kevin Hardy | .25 | .08 |
| ☐ 305 Rod Smith | .40 | .15 |
| ☐ 306 Robert Porcher | .25 | .08 |
| ☐ 307 Cade McNown | .25 | .08 |
| ☐ 308 Craig Yeast | .25 | .08 |
| ☐ 309 Doug Flutie | .60 | .25 |
| ☐ 310 Jerry Rice | 1.25 | .50 |
| ☐ 311 Brad Johnson | .60 | .25 |
| ☐ 312 Tiki Barber | .60 | .25 |
| ☐ 313 Will Blackwell | .25 | .08 |
| ☐ 314 Sean Dawkins | .25 | .08 |
| ☐ 315 Jacquez Green | .25 | .08 |
| ☐ 316 Zach Thomas | .60 | .25 |
| ☐ 317 Gus Frerotte | .25 | .08 |
| ☐ 318 Chris Warren | .25 | .08 |
| ☐ 319 Carl Pickens | .40 | .15 |
| ☐ 320 Tyrone Wheatley HL | .25 | .08 |
| ☐ 321 Kurt Warner HL | .60 | .25 |
| ☐ 322 Dan Marino HL | 1.00 | .40 |
| ☐ 323 Cris Carter HL | .40 | .15 |
| ☐ 324 Brett Favre HL | 1.00 | .40 |
| ☐ 325 Marshall Faulk HL | .60 | .25 |
| ☐ 326 Jevon Kearse HL | .40 | .15 |
| ☐ 327 Edgerrin James HL | .60 | .25 |
| ☐ 328 Emmitt Smith HL | .60 | .25 |
| ☐ 329 Andre Reed HL | .25 | .08 |
| ☐ 330 K.Dyson/F.Wycheck HL | .25 | .08 |
| ☐ 331 Olindo Mare MM | .25 | .08 |
| ☐ 332 Marcus Coleman MM | .25 | .08 |
| ☐ 333 James Johnson MM | .25 | .08 |
| ☐ 334 Ray Lucas MM | .40 | .15 |
| ☐ 335 Dedric Ward MM | .25 | .08 |
| ☐ 336 Richie Cunningham MM | .25 | .08 |
| ☐ 337 James Hasty MM | .25 | .08 |
| ☐ 338 Sedrick Shaw MM | .25 | .08 |
| ☐ 339 Kurt Warner MM | .60 | .25 |
| ☐ 340 Marshall Faulk MM | .60 | .25 |
| ☐ 341 Brian Shay EP | .50 | .20 |
| ☐ 342 L.C. Stevens EP | .50 | .20 |
| ☐ 343 Corey Thomas EP | .50 | .20 |
| ☐ 344 Scott Milanovich EP | .60 | .25 |
| ☐ 345 Pat Barnes EP | .60 | .25 |
| ☐ 346 Danny Wuerffel EP | .60 | .25 |
| ☐ 347 Kevin Daft EP | .50 | .20 |
| ☐ 348 Ron Powlus EP RC | 1.00 | .40 |
| ☐ 349 Tony Graziani EP | .60 | .25 |
| ☐ 350 Norman Miller EP RC | .50 | .20 |
| ☐ 351 Cory Sauter EP | .50 | .20 |
| ☐ 352 Marcus Crandell EP RC | .60 | .25 |
| ☐ 353 Sean Morey EP RC | .60 | .25 |
| ☐ 354 Jeff Ogden EP | .50 | .20 |
| ☐ 355 Ted White EP | .50 | .20 |
| ☐ 356 Jim Kubiak EP | .60 | .25 |
| ☐ 357 Aaron Stecker EP RC | 1.00 | .40 |
| ☐ 358 Romeo Powell EP | .50 | .20 |
| ☐ 359 Matt Lytle EP RC | .50 | .20 |
| ☐ 360 Kendrick Nord EP RC | .50 | .20 |
| ☐ 361 Tim Rattay RC | 2.50 | 1.00 |
| ☐ 362 Rob Morris RC | 2.50 | 1.00 |
| ☐ 363 Chris Samuels RC | 2.00 | .75 |

| | | |
|---|---|---|
| ☐ 364 Todd Husak RC | 2.50 | 1.00 |
| ☐ 365 Ahmed Plummer RC | 2.50 | 1.00 |
| ☐ 366 Frank Murphy RC | 2.00 | .75 |
| ☐ 367 Michael Wiley RC | 2.50 | 1.00 |
| ☐ 368 Giovanni Carmazzi RC | 2.00 | .75 |
| ☐ 369 Anthony Becht RC | 2.50 | 1.00 |
| ☐ 370 John Abraham RC | 2.50 | 1.00 |
| ☐ 371 Shaun Alexander RC | 8.00 | 3.00 |
| ☐ 372 Thomas Jones RC | 4.00 | 1.50 |
| ☐ 373 Courtney Brown RC | 1.00 | .40 |
| ☐ 374 Curtis Keaton RC | 2.00 | .75 |
| ☐ 375 Jerry Porter RC | 3.00 | 1.25 |
| ☐ 376 Corey Simon RC | 1.00 | .40 |
| ☐ 377 Dez White RC | 2.50 | 1.00 |
| ☐ 378 Jamal Lewis RC | 6.00 | 2.50 |
| ☐ 379 Ron Dayne RC | 2.50 | 1.00 |
| ☐ 380 R.Jay Soward RC | 2.50 | 1.00 |
| ☐ 381 Tee Martin RC | 2.50 | 1.00 |
| ☐ 382 Shaun Ellis RC | 2.50 | 1.00 |
| ☐ 383 Brian Urlacher RC | 10.00 | 4.00 |
| ☐ 384 Reuben Droughns RC | 4.00 | 1.50 |
| ☐ 385 Travis Taylor RC | 1.00 | .40 |
| ☐ 386 Plaxico Burress RC | 5.00 | 2.00 |
| ☐ 387 Chad Pennington RC | 6.00 | 2.50 |
| ☐ 388 Sylvester Morris RC | 2.50 | 1.00 |
| ☐ 389 Ron Dugans RC | 2.00 | .75 |
| ☐ 390 Joe Hamilton RC | 2.50 | 1.00 |
| ☐ 391 Chris Redman RC | .60 | .25 |
| ☐ 392 Trung Canidate RC | 2.50 | 1.00 |
| ☐ 393 J.R. Redmond RC | 2.50 | 1.00 |
| ☐ 394 Danny Farmer RC | 2.50 | 1.00 |
| ☐ 395 Todd Pinkston RC | 2.50 | 1.00 |
| ☐ 396 Dennis Northcutt RC | 2.50 | 1.00 |
| ☐ 397 Laveranues Coles RC | 3.00 | 1.25 |
| ☐ 398 Bubba Franks RC | 2.50 | 1.00 |
| ☐ 399 Travis Prentice RC | 2.50 | 1.00 |
| ☐ 400 Peter Warrick RC | 2.50 | 1.00 |
| ☐ SBMVP Kurt Warner FB AU | 120.00 | 50.00 |

## 2001 Topps

| | | |
|---|---|---|
| ☐ COMPLETE SET (385) | 75.00 | 45.00 |
| ☐ 1 Marshall Faulk | .75 | .30 |
| ☐ 2 Lawyer Milloy | .40 | .15 |
| ☐ 3 Rich Gannon | .60 | .25 |
| ☐ 4 Rod Smith | .40 | .15 |
| ☐ 5 David Boston | .60 | .25 |
| ☐ 6 Jeremy McDaniel | .25 | .08 |
| ☐ 7 Joey Galloway | .40 | .15 |
| ☐ 8 Ron Dixon | .25 | .08 |
| ☐ 9 Terrell Fletcher | .25 | .08 |
| ☐ 10 Deion Sanders | .60 | .25 |
| ☐ 11 Jevon Kearse | .40 | .15 |
| ☐ 12 Charles Woodson | .40 | .15 |
| ☐ 13 Brian Walker | .25 | .08 |
| ☐ 14 Mike Peterson | .25 | .08 |
| ☐ 15 Marcus Robinson | .60 | .25 |
| ☐ 16 Duane Starks | .25 | .08 |
| ☐ 17 KaRon Coleman | .25 | .08 |
| ☐ 18 Randy Moss | 1.25 | .50 |
| ☐ 19 Reggie Jones | .25 | .08 |
| ☐ 20 Derrick Brooks | .60 | .25 |
| ☐ 21 Eddie George | .60 | .25 |
| ☐ 22 Wayne Chrebet | .40 | .15 |
| ☐ 23 Kevin Hardy | .25 | .08 |
| ☐ 24 Bill Schroeder | .40 | .15 |
| ☐ 25 Doug Flutie | .60 | .25 |
| ☐ 26 Tim Dwight | .60 | .25 |
| ☐ 27 Eddie Kennison | .40 | .15 |
| ☐ 28 Reggie Kelly | .25 | .08 |

| | | |
|---|---|---|
| ❑ 290 Edgerrin James | .75 | .30 |
| ❑ 291 Takeo Spikes | .25 | .08 |
| ❑ 292 John Lynch | .40 | .15 |
| ❑ 293 Sam Madison | .25 | .08 |
| ❑ 294 Stephen Boyd | .25 | .08 |
| ❑ 295 Tony Siragusa | .25 | .08 |
| ❑ 296 Robert Porcher | .25 | .08 |
| ❑ 297 Donnel Bennett | .25 | .08 |
| ❑ 298 Hardy Nickerson | .25 | .08 |
| ❑ 299 Jonathan Quinn | .25 | .08 |
| ❑ 300 Rob Morris | .25 | .08 |
| ❑ 301 E.G. Green | .25 | .08 |
| ❑ 302 David Sloan | .25 | .08 |
| ❑ 303 Jason Tucker | .25 | .08 |
| ❑ 304 Darrin Chiaverini | .25 | .08 |
| ❑ 305 Wali Rainer | .25 | .08 |
| ❑ 306 Jerry Azumah | .25 | .08 |
| ❑ 307 Jonathan Linton | .25 | .08 |
| ❑ 308 Dameyune Craig | .25 | .08 |
| ❑ 309 Courtney Brown | .25 | .08 |
| ❑ 310 Jammi German | .25 | .08 |
| ❑ 311 Michael Vick RC | 3.00 | 1.25 |
| ❑ 312 Jamar Fletcher RC | .75 | .30 |
| ❑ 313 Will Allen RC | .75 | .30 |
| ❑ 314 Jamal Reynolds RC | 1.25 | .50 |
| ❑ 315 Quincy Morgan RC | 1.25 | .50 |
| ❑ 316 Eric Kelly RC | .50 | .20 |
| ❑ 317 Michael Stone RC | .50 | .20 |
| ❑ 318 Rod Gardner RC | 1.25 | .50 |
| ❑ 319 Ken-Yon Rambo RC | .75 | .30 |
| ❑ 320 Eric Westmoreland RC | .75 | .30 |
| ❑ 321 Steve Smith RC | 3.00 | 1.50 |
| ❑ 322 George Layne RC | .75 | .30 |
| ❑ 323 Justin McCareins RC | 1.25 | .50 |
| ❑ 324 Adam Archuleta RC | 1.25 | .50 |
| ❑ 325 Justin Smith RC | 1.25 | .50 |
| ❑ 326 David Terrell RC | 1.25 | .50 |
| ❑ 327 Correll Buckhalter RC | 1.50 | .60 |
| ❑ 328 Drew Brees RC | 5.00 | 2.00 |
| ❑ 329 Chris Barnes RC | .75 | .30 |
| ❑ 330 Santana Moss RC | 2.00 | .75 |
| ❑ 331 Josh Heupel RC | 1.25 | .50 |
| ❑ 332 Cedrick Wilson RC | 1.25 | .50 |
| ❑ 333 Gerard Warren RC | 1.25 | .50 |
| ❑ 334 Jamie Henderson RC | .75 | .30 |
| ❑ 335 Onomo Ojo RC | .75 | .30 |
| ❑ 336 Marcus Stroud RC | 1.25 | .50 |
| ❑ 337 Quincy Carter RC | 1.25 | .50 |
| ❑ 338 Koren Robinson RC | 1.25 | .50 |
| ❑ 339 Ryan Pickett RC | .50 | .20 |
| ❑ 340 Chad Johnson RC | 3.00 | 1.25 |
| ❑ 341 Nate Clements RC | 1.25 | .50 |
| ❑ 342 Jesse Palmer RC | 1.25 | .50 |
| ❑ 343 Snoop Minnis RC | .75 | .30 |
| ❑ 344 Reggie Wayne RC | 2.50 | 1.00 |
| ❑ 345 Kevin Kasper RC | 1.25 | .50 |
| ❑ 346 Will Peterson RC | .75 | .30 |
| ❑ 347 Marques Tuiasosopo RC | 1.25 | .50 |
| ❑ 348 Sage Rosenfels RC | 1.25 | .50 |
| ❑ 349 Dan Alexander RC | 1.25 | .50 |
| ❑ 350 LaDainian Tomlinson RC | 25.00 | 10.00 |
| ❑ 351 Dan Morgan RC | 1.25 | .50 |
| ❑ 352 Scotty Anderson RC | .75 | .30 |
| ❑ 353 Deuce McAllister RC | 2.50 | 1.00 |
| ❑ 354 Todd Heap RC | 1.25 | .50 |
| ❑ 355 Tony Dixon RC | .75 | .30 |
| ❑ 356 Chris Chambers RC | 2.00 | .75 |
| ❑ 357 Eddie Berlin RC | .75 | .30 |
| ❑ 358 Anthony Thomas RC | 1.25 | .50 |
| ❑ 359 James Jackson RC | 1.25 | .50 |
| ❑ 360 Richard Seymour RC | 1.25 | .50 |
| ❑ 361 Andre Carter RC | 1.25 | .50 |
| ❑ 362 Bobby Newcombe RC | .75 | .30 |
| ❑ 363 Robert Ferguson RC | 1.25 | .50 |
| ❑ 364 Jonathan Carter RC | .75 | .30 |
| ❑ 365 Damione Lewis RC | .75 | .30 |
| ❑ 366 Damerien McCants RC | .75 | .30 |
| ❑ 367 Tim Hasselbeck RC | 1.25 | .50 |
| ❑ 368 Derrick Gibson RC | .75 | .30 |
| ❑ 369 Rudi Johnson RC | 2.50 | 1.00 |
| ❑ 370 Alge Crumpler RC | 1.50 | .60 |
| ❑ 371 Derrick Blaylock RC | 1.25 | .50 |
| ❑ 372 Moran Norris RC | .50 | .20 |
| ❑ 373 Travis Minor RC | .75 | .30 |
| ❑ 374 LaMont Jordan RC | 2.50 | 1.00 |
| ❑ 375 Kevan Barlow RC | 1.25 | .50 |
| ❑ 376 Freddie Mitchell RC | 1.25 | .50 |

| | | |
|---|---|---|
| ❑ 377 Shaun Rogers RC | 1.25 | .50 |
| ❑ 378 Tay Cody RC | .50 | .20 |
| ❑ 379 Travis Henry RC | 1.25 | .50 |
| ❑ 380 Chris Weinke RC | 1.25 | .50 |
| ❑ 381 Willie Middlebrooks RC | .75 | .30 |
| ❑ 382 Rashard Casey RC | .75 | .30 |
| ❑ 383 Mike McMahon RC | 1.25 | .50 |
| ❑ 384 Michael Bennett RC | 1.25 | .50 |
| ❑ 385 Jabari Holloway RC | .75 | .30 |
| ❑ SBMVP Ray Lewis FB AU | 250.00 | 150.00 |

## 2002 Topps

| | | |
|---|---|---|
| ❑ COMPLETE SET (385) | 50.00 | 20.00 |
| ❑ 1 Kurt Warner | .60 | .25 |
| ❑ 2 Jeff Graham | .25 | .08 |
| ❑ 3 Todd Bouman | .25 | .08 |
| ❑ 4 Duce Staley | .60 | .25 |
| ❑ 5 Jon Kitna | .40 | .15 |
| ❑ 6 Shannon Sharpe | .40 | .15 |
| ❑ 7 Darrell Jackson | .40 | .15 |
| ❑ 8 Michael Pittman | .25 | .08 |
| ❑ 9 Tony Gonzalez | .40 | .15 |
| ❑ 10 Wayne Chrebet | .40 | .15 |
| ❑ 11 Jevon Kearse | .40 | .15 |
| ❑ 12 Bill Schroeder | .25 | .08 |
| ❑ 13 Jeremy McDaniel | .25 | .08 |
| ❑ 14 Todd Pinkston | .25 | .08 |
| ❑ 15 Maurice Smith | .40 | .15 |
| ❑ 16 Charlie Batch | .40 | .15 |
| ❑ 17 Olandis Gary | .40 | .15 |
| ❑ 18 Ron Dugans | .25 | .08 |
| ❑ 19 Brian Urlacher | 1.00 | .40 |
| ❑ 20 Amani Toomer | .40 | .15 |
| ❑ 21 Tim Couch | .40 | .15 |
| ❑ 22 Derrick Brooks | .60 | .25 |
| ❑ 23 Frank Sanders | .25 | .08 |
| ❑ 24 James Williams | .25 | .08 |
| ❑ 25 Lamar Smith | .40 | .15 |
| ❑ 26 Darrick Vaughn | .25 | .08 |
| ❑ 27 Cris Carter | .60 | .25 |
| ❑ 28 Roland Williams | .25 | .08 |
| ❑ 29 Bobby Shaw | .25 | .08 |
| ❑ 30 Jerome Pathon | .40 | .15 |
| ❑ 31 Rod Woodson | .40 | .15 |
| ❑ 32 Ronney Jenkins | .25 | .08 |
| ❑ 33 Chris Chandler | .40 | .15 |
| ❑ 34 Dez White | .25 | .08 |
| ❑ 35 Rod Smith | .40 | .15 |
| ❑ 36 Troy Brown | .40 | .15 |
| ❑ 37 JaJuan Dawson | .25 | .08 |
| ❑ 38 Reidel Anthony | .25 | .08 |
| ❑ 39 Mike Green | .25 | .08 |
| ❑ 40 Steve Smith | .60 | .25 |
| ❑ 41 Willie Jackson | .25 | .08 |
| ❑ 42 MarTay Jenkins | .25 | .08 |
| ❑ 43 Reggie Germany | .25 | .08 |
| ❑ 44 Desmond Howard | .40 | .15 |
| ❑ 45 Fred Taylor | .60 | .25 |
| ❑ 46 Scotty Anderson | .25 | .08 |
| ❑ 47 John Lynch | .40 | .15 |
| ❑ 48 Amos Zereoue | .60 | .25 |
| ❑ 49 Damay Scott | .25 | .08 |
| ❑ 50 Anthony Thomas | .40 | .15 |
| ❑ 51 Jeff Garcia | .60 | .25 |
| ❑ 52 Charlie Garner | .40 | .15 |
| ❑ 53 Drew Bledsoe | .60 | .25 |
| ❑ 54 Donnie Edwards | .25 | .08 |
| ❑ 55 Corey Bradford | .25 | .08 |
| ❑ 56 Desmond Clark | .25 | .08 |

| | | |
|---|---|---|
| ❑ 57 Courtney Brown | .40 | .15 |
| ❑ 58 Wesley Walls | .25 | .08 |
| ❑ 59 Chad Brown | .25 | .08 |
| ❑ 60 Shawn Jefferson | .25 | .08 |
| ❑ 61 Corey Dillon | .40 | .15 |
| ❑ 62 Johnnie Morton | .40 | .15 |
| ❑ 63 Marcus Pollard | .25 | .08 |
| ❑ 64 Jason Taylor | .25 | .08 |
| ❑ 65 Kevin Faulk | .40 | .15 |
| ❑ 66 Shane Matthews | .25 | .08 |
| ❑ 67 Hines Ward | .60 | .25 |
| ❑ 68 Garrison Hearst | .40 | .15 |
| ❑ 69 Trung Canidate | .40 | .15 |
| ❑ 70 Tony Banks | .25 | .08 |
| ❑ 71 Matt Hasselbeck | .40 | .15 |
| ❑ 72 Correll Buckhalter | .40 | .15 |
| ❑ 73 Ron Dayne | .40 | .15 |
| ❑ 74 Zach Thomas | .60 | .25 |
| ❑ 75 Emmitt Smith | 1.50 | .60 |
| ❑ 76 Peter Warrick | .40 | .15 |
| ❑ 77 Rob Johnson | .40 | .15 |
| ❑ 78 Michael Strahan | .40 | .15 |
| ❑ 79 Ray Lewis | .60 | .25 |
| ❑ 80 Jamir Miller | .25 | .08 |
| ❑ 81 Brian Griese | .60 | .25 |
| ❑ 82 Stacey Mack | .25 | .08 |
| ❑ 83 Michael Bennett | .40 | .15 |
| ❑ 84 Ricky Williams | 1.00 | .40 |
| ❑ 85 Jamal Lewis | .60 | .25 |
| ❑ 86 Doug Flutie | .60 | .25 |
| ❑ 87 Jonathan Quinn | .25 | .08 |
| ❑ 88 Mike Alstott | .60 | .25 |
| ❑ 89 Samari Rolle | .25 | .08 |
| ❑ 90 LaMont Jordan | .60 | .25 |
| ❑ 91 Dominic Rhodes | .40 | .15 |
| ❑ 92 Quincy Carter | .40 | .15 |
| ❑ 93 Marcus Robinson | .40 | .15 |
| ❑ 94 Travis Henry | .60 | .25 |
| ❑ 95 Jason Brookins | .25 | .08 |
| ❑ 96 Nick Goings | .25 | .08 |
| ❑ 97 Brian Finneran | .25 | .08 |
| ❑ 98 Dorsey Levens | .40 | .15 |
| ❑ 99 Reggie Swinton | .25 | .08 |
| ❑ 100 Chris Chambers | .60 | .25 |
| ❑ 101 Kordell Stewart | .40 | .15 |
| ❑ 102 Tai Streets | .25 | .08 |
| ❑ 103 Chris Redman | .25 | .08 |
| ❑ 104 Jacquez Green | .25 | .08 |
| ❑ 105 Rod Gardner | .40 | .15 |
| ❑ 106 Kevin Kasper | .25 | .08 |
| ❑ 107 Anthony Henry | .25 | .08 |
| ❑ 108 Dan Morgan | .25 | .08 |
| ❑ 109 Ronald McKinnon | .25 | .08 |
| ❑ 110 Qadry Ismail | .40 | .15 |
| ❑ 111 Chad Johnson | .60 | .25 |
| ❑ 112 James Stewart | .40 | .15 |
| ❑ 113 Terrence Wilkins | .25 | .08 |
| ❑ 114 Joey Galloway | .40 | .15 |
| ❑ 115 Deuce McAllister | .75 | .30 |
| ❑ 116 Joe Jurevicius | .25 | .08 |
| ❑ 117 Tyrone Wheatley | .40 | .15 |
| ❑ 118 Jason Gildon | .25 | .08 |
| ❑ 119 LaDainian Tomlinson | 1.00 | .40 |
| ❑ 120 Grant Wistrom | .25 | .08 |
| ❑ 121 Eddie George | .60 | .25 |
| ❑ 122 Laveranues Coles | .40 | .15 |
| ❑ 123 Antowain Smith | .40 | .15 |
| ❑ 124 Larry Parker | .25 | .08 |
| ❑ 125 Bubba Franks | .40 | .15 |
| ❑ 126 Troy Hambrick | .25 | .08 |
| ❑ 127 Jamal Reynolds | .25 | .08 |
| ❑ 128 Doug Chapman | .25 | .08 |
| ❑ 129 Freddie Mitchell | .40 | .15 |
| ❑ 130 Tim Dwight | .40 | .15 |
| ❑ 131 Erron Kinney | .25 | .08 |
| ❑ 132 James Allen | .40 | .15 |
| ❑ 133 Eric Moulds | .40 | .15 |
| ❑ 134 Keenan McCardell | .25 | .08 |
| ❑ 135 David Sloan | .25 | .08 |
| ❑ 136 Dennis Northcutt | .40 | .15 |
| ❑ 137 Kevan Barlow | .40 | .15 |
| ❑ 138 Bobby Engram | .25 | .08 |
| ❑ 139 Champ Bailey | .40 | .15 |
| ❑ 140 Donald Hayes | .25 | .08 |
| ❑ 141 Brandon Bennett | .25 | .08 |
| ❑ 142 Deltha O'Neal | .25 | .08 |
| ❑ 143 James Jackson | .25 | .08 |

|  |  | | |
|---|---|---|---|
| 144 | Shaun Rogers | .25 | .08 |
| 145 | Joe Johnson | .25 | .08 |
| 146 | Ricky Watters | .40 | .15 |
| 147 | Warrick Dunn | .60 | .25 |
| 148 | Steve McNair | .60 | .25 |
| 149 | Marvin Harrison | .60 | .25 |
| 150 | Kendrell Bell | .60 | .25 |
| 151 | Jim Miller | .25 | .08 |
| 152 | Terry Allen | .25 | .08 |
| 153 | Jake Plummer | .40 | .15 |
| 154 | James McKnight | .25 | .08 |
| 155 | Curtis Martin | .60 | .25 |
| 156 | Keyshawn Johnson | .60 | .25 |
| 157 | Kevin Lockett | .25 | .08 |
| 158 | Jeremiah Trotter | .25 | .08 |
| 159 | Derrick Alexander | .40 | .15 |
| 160 | Brandon Stokley | .25 | .08 |
| 161 | J.J. Stokes | .40 | .15 |
| 162 | Drew Bennett | .25 | .08 |
| 163 | Drew Brees | .60 | .25 |
| 164 | Tim Brown | .60 | .25 |
| 165 | Daunte Culpepper | .60 | .25 |
| 166 | Rocket Ismail | .40 | .15 |
| 167 | Alex Van Pelt | .40 | .15 |
| 168 | Arnold Jackson | .25 | .08 |
| 169 | Oronde Gadsden | .40 | .15 |
| 170 | Isaac Bruce | .60 | .25 |
| 171 | Warren Sapp | .40 | .15 |
| 172 | Michael Westbrook | .25 | .08 |
| 173 | John Abraham | .40 | .15 |
| 174 | Jessie Armstead | .25 | .08 |
| 175 | Brock Marion | .25 | .08 |
| 176 | Brett Favre | 1.50 | .60 |
| 177 | Benjamin Gay | .40 | .15 |
| 178 | Muhsin Muhammad | .40 | .15 |
| 179 | Reggie Wayne | .60 | .25 |
| 180 | Kailee Wong | .25 | .08 |
| 181 | Rich Gannon | .60 | .25 |
| 182 | Chris Fuamatu-Ma'afala | .25 | .08 |
| 183 | Shaun Alexander | .75 | .30 |
| 184 | Kevin Dyson | .40 | .15 |
| 185 | Kwamie Lassiter | .25 | .08 |
| 186 | Elvis Joseph | .25 | .08 |
| 187 | Trent Dilfer | .40 | .15 |
| 188 | Marty Booker | .25 | .08 |
| 189 | Travis Taylor | .40 | .15 |
| 190 | Michael Vick | 1.25 | .50 |
| 191 | Mike McMahon | .60 | .25 |
| 192 | Jay Fiedler | .40 | .15 |
| 193 | Zack Bronson | .25 | .08 |
| 194 | Derrick Mason | .40 | .15 |
| 195 | Anthony Becht | .25 | .08 |
| 196 | Ahman Green | .60 | .25 |
| 197 | Alge Crumpler | .40 | .15 |
| 198 | Thomas Jones | .60 | .25 |
| 199 | Tiki Barber | .60 | .25 |
| 200 | Donovan McNabb | .75 | .30 |
| 201 | Andre Carter | .25 | .08 |
| 202 | Stephen Davis | .40 | .15 |
| 203 | Troy Edwards | .25 | .08 |
| 204 | Lawyer Milloy | .40 | .15 |
| 205 | Peyton Manning | 1.25 | .50 |
| 206 | James Farrior | .25 | .08 |
| 207 | Gerard Warren | .25 | .08 |
| 208 | Peerless Price | .40 | .15 |
| 209 | Avion Black | .25 | .08 |
| 210 | Marcellus Wiley | .25 | .08 |
| 211 | Torry Holt | .60 | .25 |
| 212 | A.J. Feeley | .60 | .25 |
| 213 | Travis Minor | .25 | .08 |
| 214 | Darren Sharper | .25 | .08 |
| 215 | Jerry Porter | .25 | .08 |
| 216 | Randall Cunningham | .25 | .08 |
| 217 | Chris Weinke | .40 | .15 |
| 218 | Mike Anderson | .60 | .25 |
| 219 | Snoop Minnis | .25 | .08 |
| 220 | David Martin | .25 | .08 |
| 221 | Vinny Sutherland | .25 | .08 |
| 222 | Ki-Jana Carter | .25 | .08 |
| 223 | Kevin Swayne | .25 | .08 |
| 224 | Mark Brunell | .60 | .25 |
| 225 | Quincy Morgan | .40 | .15 |
| 226 | David Terrell | .60 | .25 |
| 227 | Terance Mathis | .25 | .08 |
| 228 | Frank Wycheck | .25 | .08 |
| 229 | Az-Zahir Hakim | .25 | .08 |
| 230 | Freddie Jones | .25 | .08 |
| 231 | Jerry Rice | 1.25 | .50 |
| 232 | Ike Hilliard | .40 | .15 |
| 233 | Terrell Davis | .60 | .25 |
| 234 | Shawn Bryson | .25 | .08 |
| 235 | David Boston | .60 | .25 |
| 236 | Edgerrin James | .75 | .30 |
| 237 | Trent Green | .40 | .15 |
| 238 | Charlie Rogers | .25 | .08 |
| 239 | Vinny Testaverde | .40 | .15 |
| 240 | Koren Robinson | .40 | .15 |
| 241 | Ronde Barber | .25 | .08 |
| 242 | Dwayne Carswell | .25 | .08 |
| 243 | Dedric Ward | .25 | .08 |
| 244 | Richard Huntley | .25 | .08 |
| 245 | Jamal Anderson | .40 | .15 |
| 246 | Ryan Leaf | .40 | .15 |
| 247 | Priest Holmes | .75 | .30 |
| 248 | Tom Brady | 1.50 | .60 |
| 249 | Charles Woodson | .40 | .15 |
| 250 | Jerome Bettis | .60 | .25 |
| 251 | Tommy Polley | .25 | .08 |
| 252 | Anthony Wright | .25 | .08 |
| 253 | Chad Pennington | .75 | .30 |
| 254 | David Patten | .25 | .08 |
| 255 | Antonio Freeman | .40 | .15 |
| 256 | Jamel White | .25 | .08 |
| 257 | Jermaine Lewis | .25 | .08 |
| 258 | Aaron Brooks | .60 | .25 |
| 259 | Ron Dixon | .25 | .08 |
| 260 | James Thrash | .40 | .15 |
| 261 | Junior Seau | .40 | .15 |
| 262 | Byron Chamberlain | .25 | .08 |
| 263 | Ed McCaffrey | .40 | .15 |
| 264 | Nate Clements | .25 | .08 |
| 265 | Tony Martin | .25 | .08 |
| 266 | Germane Crowell | .25 | .08 |
| 267 | Terrell Owens | .60 | .25 |
| 268 | Marshall Faulk | .60 | .25 |
| 269 | Dat Nguyen | .25 | .08 |
| 270 | Elvis Grbac | .25 | .08 |
| 271 | Dante Hall | .40 | .15 |
| 272 | Sylvester Morris | .25 | .08 |
| 273 | Mike Brown | .25 | .08 |
| 274 | Kevin Johnson | .40 | .15 |
| 275 | Jimmy Smith | .40 | .15 |
| 276 | Randy Moss | 1.25 | .50 |
| 277 | Kerry Collins | .40 | .15 |
| 278 | Santana Moss | .40 | .15 |
| 279 | Plaxico Burress | .40 | .15 |
| 280 | Brad Johnson | .40 | .15 |
| 281 | Curtis Conway | .25 | .08 |
| 282 | Eric Johnson | .25 | .08 |
| 283 | Joe Horn | .40 | .15 |
| 284 | Peter Boulware | .25 | .08 |
| 285 | Larry Foster | .25 | .08 |
| 286 | Nate Jacquet | .25 | .08 |
| 287 | Terry Glenn | .40 | .15 |
| 288 | Jarious Jackson | .25 | .08 |
| 289 | Hugh Douglas | .25 | .08 |
| 290 | Chad Lewis | .25 | .08 |
| 291 | Ahman Green WW | .40 | .15 |
| 292 | Peyton Manning WW | .60 | .25 |
| 293 | Kurt Warner WW | .40 | .15 |
| 294 | Daunte Culpepper WW | .60 | .25 |
| 295 | Tom Brady WW | .75 | .30 |
| 296 | Rod Gardner WW | .25 | .08 |
| 297 | Corey Dillon WW | .40 | .15 |
| 298 | Priest Holmes WW | .50 | .20 |
| 299 | Shaun Alexander WW | .50 | .20 |
| 300 | Randy Moss WW | .60 | .25 |
| 301 | Eric Moulds WW | .25 | .08 |
| 302 | Brett Favre WW | .75 | .30 |
| 303 | Todd Bouman WW | .25 | .08 |
| 304 | Dominic Rhodes WW | .40 | .15 |
| 305 | Marvin Harrison WW | .40 | .15 |
| 306 | Torry Holt WW | .60 | .25 |
| 307 | Derrick Mason WW | .25 | .08 |
| 308 | Jerry Rice WW | .60 | .25 |
| 309 | Donovan McNabb WW | .40 | .15 |
| 310 | Marshall Faulk WW | .40 | .15 |
| 311 | David Carr RC | 1.50 | .60 |
| 312 | Quentin Jammer RC | 1.25 | .50 |
| 313 | Mike Williams RC | 1.00 | .40 |
| 314 | Rocky Calmus RC | 1.25 | .50 |
| 315 | Travis Fisher RC | 1.25 | .50 |
| 316 | Dwight Freeney RC | 2.00 | .75 |
| 317 | Jeremy Shockey RC | 2.00 | .75 |
| 318 | Marquise Walker RC | 1.00 | .40 |
| 319 | Eric Crouch RC | 1.25 | .50 |
| 320 | DeShaun Foster RC | 1.25 | .50 |
| 321 | Roy Williams RC | 2.50 | 1.00 |
| 322 | Andre Davis RC | 1.00 | .40 |
| 323 | Alex Brown RC | 1.25 | .50 |
| 324 | Michael Lewis RC | 1.25 | .50 |
| 325 | Terry Charles RC | 1.00 | .40 |
| 326 | Clinton Portis RC | 5.00 | 2.00 |
| 327 | Dennis Johnson RC | .60 | .25 |
| 328 | Lito Sheppard RC | 1.25 | .50 |
| 329 | Ryan Sims RC | 1.25 | .50 |
| 330 | Raonall Smith RC | 1.00 | .40 |
| 331 | Albert Haynesworth RC | 1.25 | .50 |
| 332 | Eddie Freeman RC | .60 | .25 |
| 333 | Levi Jones RC | 1.00 | .40 |
| 334 | Josh McCown RC | 1.50 | .60 |
| 335 | Cliff Russell RC | 1.00 | .40 |
| 336 | Maurice Morris RC | 1.25 | .50 |
| 337 | Antwaan Randle El RC | 1.50 | .60 |
| 338 | Ladell Betts RC | 1.25 | .50 |
| 339 | Daniel Graham RC | 1.25 | .50 |
| 340 | David Garrard RC | 2.50 | 1.00 |
| 341 | Antonio Bryant RC | 1.25 | .50 |
| 342 | Patrick Ramsey RC | 1.25 | .50 |
| 343 | Kelly Campbell RC | 1.00 | .40 |
| 344 | Will Overstreet RC | .60 | .25 |
| 345 | Ryan Denney RC | 1.00 | .40 |
| 346 | John Henderson RC | 1.25 | .50 |
| 347 | Freddie Milons RC | 1.00 | .40 |
| 348 | Tim Carter RC | 1.00 | .40 |
| 349 | Kurt Kittner RC | 1.00 | .40 |
| 350 | Joey Harrington RC | 1.50 | .60 |
| 351 | Ricky Williams RC | 1.25 | .50 |
| 352 | Bryant McKinnie RC | 1.00 | .40 |
| 353 | Ed Reed RC | 3.00 | 1.25 |
| 354 | Josh Reed RC | 1.25 | .50 |
| 355 | Seth Burford RC | 1.00 | .40 |
| 356 | Javon Walker RC | 2.00 | .75 |
| 357 | Jamar Martin RC | 1.00 | .40 |
| 358 | Leonard Henry RC | 1.00 | .40 |
| 359 | Julius Peppers RC | 2.50 | 1.00 |
| 360 | Jabar Gaffney RC | 1.25 | .50 |
| 361 | Kalimba Edwards RC | 1.25 | .50 |
| 362 | Napoleon Harris RC | 1.25 | .50 |
| 363 | Ashley Lelie RC | 2.50 | 1.00 |
| 364 | Anthony Weaver RC | 1.00 | .40 |
| 365 | Bryan Thomas RC | 1.00 | .40 |
| 366 | Wendell Bryant RC | .60 | .25 |
| 367 | Damien Anderson RC | 1.00 | .40 |
| 368 | Travis Stephens RC | 1.00 | .40 |
| 369 | Rohan Davey RC | 1.25 | .50 |
| 370 | Mike Pearson RC | .60 | .25 |
| 371 | Marc Colombo RC | .60 | .25 |
| 372 | Phillip Buchanon RC | 1.25 | .50 |
| 373 | T.J. Duckett RC | 1.25 | .50 |
| 374 | Ron Johnson RC | 1.00 | .40 |
| 375 | Larry Tripplett RC | .60 | .25 |
| 376 | Randy Fasani RC | 1.00 | .40 |
| 377 | Keyuo Craver RC | 1.00 | .40 |
| 378 | Marquand Manuel RC | .60 | .25 |
| 379 | Jonathan Wells RC | 1.25 | .50 |
| 380 | Reche Caldwell RC | 1.25 | .50 |
| 381 | Luke Staley RC | 1.00 | .40 |
| 382 | Donte Stallworth RC | 2.00 | .75 |
| 383 | Levar Fisher RC | .60 | .25 |
| 384 | Lamar Gordon RC | 1.25 | .50 |
| 385 | William Green RC | 1.25 | .50 |
| | SBMVP Tom Brady FB AU/150 | 500.00 | 350.00 |

## 2003 Topps

|  |  | | |
|---|---|---|---|
| | COMPLETE SET (385) | 60.00 | 25.00 |
| 1 | Michael Vick | .60 | .25 |
| 2 | Wesley Walls | .50 | .20 |
| 3 | Josh Reed | .40 | .15 |
| 4 | Josh McCown | .50 | .20 |
| 5 | James Stewart | .50 | .20 |
| 6 | Deltha O'Neal | .40 | .15 |
| 7 | Quincy Morgan | .40 | .15 |
| 8 | Tony Fisher | .40 | .15 |
| 9 | Corey Bradford | .40 | .15 |
| 10 | Byron Chamberlain | .40 | .15 |
| 11 | James McKnight | .40 | .15 |
| 12 | Fred Taylor | .60 | .25 |
| 13 | David Patten | .40 | .15 |
| 14 | Jerome Bettis | .60 | .25 |
| 15 | Jerry Porter | .50 | .20 |

MICHAEL VICK

| | | | |
|---|---|---|---|
| ❏ 16 Anthony Becht | .50 | .20 | |
| ❏ 17 Steve McNair | .60 | .25 | |
| ❏ 18 Stephen Davis | .50 | .20 | |
| ❏ 19 Terrence Wilkins | .40 | .15 | |
| ❏ 20 Jamie Martin | .40 | .15 | |
| ❏ 21 Tai Streets | .40 | .15 | |
| ❏ 22 Frank Wycheck | .40 | .15 | |
| ❏ 23 Sammy Knight | .40 | .15 | |
| ❏ 24 Marcus Pollard | .40 | .15 | |
| ❏ 25 Jamie Sharper | .40 | .15 | |
| ❏ 26 T.J. Houshmandzadeh | .60 | .25 | |
| ❏ 27 Javin Hunter | .50 | .20 | |
| ❏ 28 Alge Crumpler | .50 | .20 | |
| ❏ 29 Chris Weinke | .50 | .20 | |
| ❏ 30 David Terrell | .40 | .15 | |
| ❏ 31 Troy Hambrick | .40 | .15 | |
| ❏ 32 Bubba Franks | .50 | .20 | |
| ❏ 33 Todd Bouman | .40 | .15 | |
| ❏ 34 Trent Green | .50 | .20 | |
| ❏ 35 Mark Brunell | .50 | .20 | |
| ❏ 36 James Thrash | .40 | .15 | |
| ❏ 37 Donnie Edwards | .40 | .15 | |
| ❏ 38 Mike Alstott | .60 | .25 | |
| ❏ 39 Bobby Engram | .40 | .15 | |
| ❏ 40 Deuce McAllister | .60 | .25 | |
| ❏ 41 Santana Moss | .50 | .20 | |
| ❏ 42 Kordell Stewart | .50 | .20 | |
| ❏ 43 Jason Taylor | .50 | .20 | |
| ❏ 44 Corey Dillon | .50 | .20 | |
| ❏ 45 Damien Anderson | .40 | .15 | |
| ❏ 46 Rodney Peete | .40 | .15 | |
| ❏ 47 Jeff Blake | .50 | .20 | |
| ❏ 48 Mike McMahon | .40 | .15 | |
| ❏ 49 Ed McCaffrey | .50 | .20 | |
| ❏ 50 Priest Holmes | .60 | .25 | |
| ❏ 51 Moe Williams | .40 | .15 | |
| ❏ 52 Brian Dawkins | .50 | .20 | |
| ❏ 53 Tim Brown | .60 | .25 | |
| ❏ 54 Curtis Martin | .50 | .20 | |
| ❏ 55 Charles Stackhouse | .40 | .15 | |
| ❏ 56 Derrius Thompson | .40 | .15 | |
| ❏ 57 John Simon | .40 | .15 | |
| ❏ 58 Joe Jurevicius | .50 | .20 | |
| ❏ 59 Jonathan Wells | .40 | .15 | |
| ❏ 60 William Green | .40 | .15 | |
| ❏ 61 Ken-Yon Rambo | .40 | .15 | |
| ❏ 62 Frank Sanders | .40 | .15 | |
| ❏ 63 Chester Taylor | .50 | .20 | |
| ❏ 64 Keith Brooking | .50 | .20 | |
| ❏ 65 Bill Schroeder | .40 | .15 | |
| ❏ 66 Travis Minor | .40 | .15 | |
| ❏ 67 Eric Parker RC | .75 | .30 | |
| ❏ 68 Phillip Buchanon | .40 | .15 | |
| ❏ 69 Amos Zereoue | .40 | .15 | |
| ❏ 70 Warren Sapp | .50 | .20 | |
| ❏ 71 Ladell Betts | .50 | .20 | |
| ❏ 72 Lamar Gordon | .40 | .15 | |
| ❏ 73 Koren Robinson | .50 | .20 | |
| ❏ 74 Ron Dayne | .50 | .20 | |
| ❏ 75 Donovan McNabb | .75 | .30 | |
| ❏ 76 Edgerrin James | .60 | .25 | |
| ❏ 77 Stacey Mack | .40 | .15 | |
| ❏ 78 Justin Smith | .50 | .20 | |
| ❏ 79 Kelly Holcomb | .50 | .20 | |
| ❏ 80 Thomas Jones | .50 | .20 | |
| ❏ 81 Randy McMichael | .50 | .20 | |
| ❏ 82 Daunte Culpepper | .60 | .25 | |
| ❏ 83 Tommy Maddox | .50 | .20 | |
| ❏ 84 Tyrone Wheatley | .50 | .20 | |
| ❏ 85 Kevin Dyson | .50 | .20 | |

| | | |
|---|---|---|
| ❏ 86 Rod Gardner | .40 | .15 |
| ❏ 87 Wayne Chrebet | .50 | .20 |
| ❏ 88 Marc Boerigter | .40 | .15 |
| ❏ 89 Darnay Scott | .50 | .20 |
| ❏ 90 T.J. Duckett | .50 | .20 |
| ❏ 91 Marcel Shipp | .40 | .15 |
| ❏ 92 Ross Tucker | .40 | .15 |
| ❏ 93 Drew Bledsoe | .60 | .25 |
| ❏ 94 Scotty Anderson | .50 | .20 |
| ❏ 95 Rod Smith | .50 | .20 |
| ❏ 96 Jim Kleinsasser | .40 | .15 |
| ❏ 97 Peyton Manning | 1.25 | .50 |
| ❏ 98 Junior Seau | .60 | .25 |
| ❏ 99 Darrell Jackson | .50 | .20 |
| ❏ 100 Brett Favre | 1.50 | .60 |
| ❏ 101 Ashley Lelie | .40 | .15 |
| ❏ 102 Jajuan Dawson | .40 | .15 |
| ❏ 103 Kyle Brady | .40 | .15 |
| ❏ 104 Kevin Faulk | .50 | .20 |
| ❏ 105 Jeremy Shockey | .60 | .25 |
| ❏ 106 Hines Ward | .60 | .25 |
| ❏ 107 Jeff Garcia | .60 | .25 |
| ❏ 108 Shane Matthews | .40 | .15 |
| ❏ 109 Javon Kearse | .50 | .20 |
| ❏ 110 Eddie Kennison | .40 | .15 |
| ❏ 111 Quincy Carter | .40 | .15 |
| ❏ 112 Brian Urlacher | 1.00 | .40 |
| ❏ 113 Charlie Rogers | .40 | .15 |
| ❏ 114 Robert Ferguson | .40 | .15 |
| ❏ 115 Christian Fauria | .40 | .15 |
| ❏ 116 Brian Westbrook | .60 | .25 |
| ❏ 117 Antwaan Randle El | .50 | .20 |
| ❏ 118 Eddie George | .50 | .20 |
| ❏ 119 Derrick Brooks | .50 | .20 |
| ❏ 120 Isaac Bruce | .60 | .25 |
| ❏ 121 Joe Horn | .50 | .20 |
| ❏ 122 Jermaine Lewis | .40 | .15 |
| ❏ 123 Jon Kitna | .50 | .20 |
| ❏ 124 David Boston | .40 | .15 |
| ❏ 125 Todd Heap | .50 | .20 |
| ❏ 126 Lamar Smith | .50 | .20 |
| ❏ 127 Marcus Robinson | .50 | .20 |
| ❏ 128 Germane Crowell | .40 | .15 |
| ❏ 129 Kevin Johnson | .40 | .15 |
| ❏ 130 Cris Carter | .50 | .20 |
| ❏ 131 Drew Brees | .60 | .25 |
| ❏ 132 Champ Bailey | .50 | .20 |
| ❏ 133 Brian Finneran | .40 | .15 |
| ❏ 134 Mike Anderson | .50 | .20 |
| ❏ 135 Derek Ross | .40 | .15 |
| ❏ 136 Javon Walker | .50 | .20 |
| ❏ 137 D'Wayne Bates | .40 | .15 |
| ❏ 138 Chad Lewis | .50 | .20 |
| ❏ 139 Charlie Garner | .50 | .20 |
| ❏ 140 Laveranues Coles | .50 | .20 |
| ❏ 141 Ron Dixon | .40 | .15 |
| ❏ 142 Rob Johnson | .50 | .20 |
| ❏ 143 Shaun Alexander | .60 | .25 |
| ❏ 144 Kevan Barlow | .50 | .20 |
| ❏ 145 Aaron Brooks | .50 | .20 |
| ❏ 146 Jay Foreman | .40 | .15 |
| ❏ 147 Mike Peterson | .40 | .15 |
| ❏ 148 Brandon Bennett | .40 | .15 |
| ❏ 149 Jake Plummer | .50 | .20 |
| ❏ 150 Emmitt Smith | 1.50 | .60 |
| ❏ 151 Mikhael Ricks | .40 | .15 |
| ❏ 152 Terry Glenn | .50 | .20 |
| ❏ 153 Michael Bennett | .50 | .20 |
| ❏ 154 Deion Branch | .50 | .20 |
| ❏ 155 Justin McCareins | .50 | .20 |
| ❏ 156 Keyshawn Johnson | .60 | .25 |
| ❏ 157 Marc Bulger | .60 | .25 |
| ❏ 158 Matt Hasselbeck | .50 | .20 |
| ❏ 159 Garrison Hearst | .50 | .20 |
| ❏ 160 Jamel White | .40 | .15 |
| ❏ 161 Doug Johnson | .40 | .15 |
| ❏ 162 Larry Centers | .50 | .20 |
| ❏ 163 Dee Brown | .40 | .15 |
| ❏ 164 Dez White | .40 | .15 |
| ❏ 165 Brian Griese | .50 | .20 |
| ❏ 166 Johnnie Morton | .50 | .20 |
| ❏ 167 Oronde Gadsden | .40 | .15 |
| ❏ 168 Chad Morton | .40 | .15 |
| ❏ 169 Rod Woodson | .60 | .25 |
| ❏ 170 Ricky Proehl | .50 | .20 |
| ❏ 171 Tim Dwight | .40 | .15 |
| ❏ 172 Patrick Ramsey | .50 | .20 |

| | | |
|---|---|---|
| ❏ 173 Donald Driver | .60 | .25 |
| ❏ 174 Joey Harrington | .60 | .25 |
| ❏ 175 Ricky Williams | .50 | .20 |
| ❏ 176 David Givens | .50 | .20 |
| ❏ 177 Antonio Freeman | .50 | .20 |
| ❏ 178 Dwight Freeney | .50 | .20 |
| ❏ 179 Jabar Gaffney | .40 | .15 |
| ❏ 180 Leon Johnson | .40 | .15 |
| ❏ 181 Freddie Jones | .40 | .15 |
| ❏ 182 Ron Johnson | .40 | .15 |
| ❏ 183 Duce Staley | .50 | .20 |
| ❏ 184 Charles Woodson | .50 | .20 |
| ❏ 185 Trung Canidate | .40 | .15 |
| ❏ 186 Jerome Pathon | .40 | .15 |
| ❏ 187 Jimmy Smith | .50 | .20 |
| ❏ 188 Reggie Wayne | .50 | .20 |
| ❏ 189 Chad Johnson | .60 | .25 |
| ❏ 190 Steve Beuerlein | .50 | .20 |
| ❏ 191 Joey Galloway | .50 | .20 |
| ❏ 192 Chris Walsh | .40 | .15 |
| ❏ 193 Ty Law | .50 | .20 |
| ❏ 194 Ike Hilliard | .50 | .20 |
| ❏ 195 Curtis Conway | .50 | .20 |
| ❏ 196 Kenny Watson | .40 | .15 |
| ❏ 197 Brad Johnson | .50 | .20 |
| ❏ 198 Shawn Jefferson | .40 | .15 |
| ❏ 199 Jamal Lewis | .60 | .25 |
| ❏ 200 Terrell Owens | .60 | .25 |
| ❏ 201 Todd Pinkston | .40 | .15 |
| ❏ 202 Maurice Morris | .40 | .15 |
| ❏ 203 Dante Hall | .50 | .20 |
| ❏ 204 Jeremiah Trotter UER | .50 | .20 |
| ❏ 205 Keenan McCardell | .50 | .20 |
| ❏ 206 Antonio Bryant | .60 | .25 |
| ❏ 207 Trevor Gaylor | .40 | .15 |
| ❏ 208 Eric Moulds | .50 | .20 |
| ❏ 209 Jim Miller | .50 | .20 |
| ❏ 210 Kabeer Gbaja-Biamila | .50 | .20 |
| ❏ 211 James Mungro | .40 | .15 |
| ❏ 212 Troy Brown | .50 | .20 |
| ❏ 213 J.J. Stokes | .50 | .20 |
| ❏ 214 Rich Gannon | .50 | .20 |
| ❏ 215 Chad Pennington | .60 | .25 |
| ❏ 216 Michael Strahan | .50 | .20 |
| ❏ 217 David Garrard | .60 | .25 |
| ❏ 218 Chris Chambers | .50 | .20 |
| ❏ 219 Antowain Smith | .50 | .20 |
| ❏ 220 Olandis Gary | .50 | .20 |
| ❏ 221 Jason McAddley | .40 | .15 |
| ❏ 222 Brandon Stokley | .50 | .20 |
| ❏ 223 Derrick Alexander | .40 | .15 |
| ❏ 224 Hugh Douglas | .50 | .20 |
| ❏ 225 Danny Wuerffel | .50 | .20 |
| ❏ 226 Derrick Mason | .50 | .20 |
| ❏ 227 Michael Pittman | .40 | .15 |
| ❏ 228 Torry Holt | .60 | .25 |
| ❏ 229 Bobby Shaw | .40 | .15 |
| ❏ 230 Tony Gonzalez | .50 | .20 |
| ❏ 231 Ed Hartwell | .40 | .15 |
| ❏ 232 Kris Mangum RC | .40 | .15 |
| ❏ 233 Martay Jenkins | .40 | .15 |
| ❏ 234 Marty Booker | .50 | .20 |
| ❏ 235 London Fletcher | .40 | .15 |
| ❏ 236 Shannon Sharpe | .50 | .20 |
| ❏ 237 Zach Thomas | .60 | .25 |
| ❏ 238 Plaxico Burress | .60 | .25 |
| ❏ 239 Trent Dilfer | .50 | .20 |
| ❏ 240 Kurt Warner | .60 | .25 |
| ❏ 241 Vinny Testaverde | .50 | .20 |
| ❏ 242 Al Wilson | .50 | .20 |
| ❏ 243 Chris Redman | .40 | .15 |
| ❏ 244 Warrick Dunn | .50 | .20 |
| ❏ 245 Jay Fiedler | .50 | .20 |
| ❏ 246 A.J. Feeley | .40 | .15 |
| ❏ 247 LaMont Jordan | .50 | .20 |
| ❏ 248 Kerry Collins | .50 | .20 |
| ❏ 249 Michael Lewis | .40 | .15 |
| ❏ 250 Jerry Rice | 1.25 | .50 |
| ❏ 251 Simeon Rice | .50 | .20 |
| ❏ 252 Reche Caldwell | .40 | .15 |
| ❏ 253 Randy Moss | .75 | .30 |
| ❏ 254 Az-Zahir Hakim | .50 | .20 |
| ❏ 255 Nate Wayne | .40 | .15 |
| ❏ 256 James Allen | .40 | .15 |
| ❏ 257 Qadry Ismail | .50 | .20 |
| ❏ 258 Tom Brady | 1.50 | .60 |
| ❏ 259 Brian Kelly | .40 | .15 |

| □ | | | |
|---|---|---|---|
| □ 260 Ray Lucas | .40 | .15 | |
| □ 261 Amani Toomer | .50 | .20 | |
| □ 262 Travis Henry | .50 | .20 | |
| □ 263 Chris Chandler | .40 | .15 | |
| □ 264 Peter Warrick | .50 | .20 | |
| □ 265 Ray Lewis | .40 | .15 | |
| □ 266 Sam Cowart | .40 | .15 | |
| □ 267 Donte Stallworth | .50 | .20 | |
| □ 268 David Carr | .60 | .25 | |
| □ 269 Andre Davis | .40 | .15 | |
| □ 270 Jake Delhomme | .60 | .25 | |
| □ 271 Travis Taylor | .40 | .15 | |
| □ 272 Steve Smith | .60 | .25 | |
| □ 273 Tiki Barber | .60 | .25 | |
| □ 274 Chad Hutchinson | .40 | .15 | |
| □ 275 Marshall Faulk | .60 | .25 | |
| □ 276 Chris Claiborne | .40 | .15 | |
| □ 277 Billy Miller | .40 | .15 | |
| □ 278 Peerless Price | .40 | .15 | |
| □ 279 Ed Reed | .60 | .25 | |
| □ 280 Ahman Green | .60 | .25 | |
| □ 281 Roy Williams | .60 | .25 | |
| □ 282 Dennis Northcutt | .40 | .15 | |
| □ 283 Julius Peppers | .60 | .25 | |
| □ 284 John Davis | .40 | .15 | |
| □ 285 LaDainian Tomlinson | 1.00 | .40 | |
| □ 286 Muhsin Muhammad | .50 | .20 | |
| □ 287 Tim Couch | .40 | .15 | |
| □ 288 Clinton Portis | .75 | .30 | |
| □ 289 Anthony Thomas | .50 | .20 | |
| □ 290 Marvin Harrison | .60 | .25 | |
| □ 291 Priest Holmes WW | .40 | .15 | |
| □ 292 Drew Bledsoe WW | .40 | .15 | |
| □ 293 Tom Brady WW | 1.00 | .40 | |
| □ 294 Shaun Alexander WW | .40 | .15 | |
| □ 295 Brett Favre WW | 1.00 | .40 | |
| □ 296 Travis Henry WW | .30 | .12 | |
| □ 297 Marshall Faulk WW | .40 | .15 | |
| □ 298 Terrell Owens WW | .40 | .15 | |
| □ 299 Jeff Garcia WW | .40 | .15 | |
| □ 300 Plaxico Burress WW | .40 | .15 | |
| □ 301 Donovan McNabb WW | .50 | .20 | |
| □ 302 Ricky Williams WW | .30 | .12 | |
| □ 303 Michael Vick WW | .50 | .20 | |
| □ 304 Steve Smith WW | .40 | .15 | |
| □ 305 Marvin Harrison WW | .40 | .15 | |
| □ 306 Chad Pennington WW | .40 | .15 | |
| □ 307 Jeremy Shockey WW | .40 | .15 | |
| □ 308 Tommy Maddox WW | .30 | .12 | |
| □ 309 Steve Martin WW | .40 | .15 | |
| □ 310 Rich Gannon WW | .30 | .12 | |
| □ 311 Carson Palmer RC | 5.00 | 2.00 | |
| □ 312 Keenan Howry RC | .75 | .30 | |
| □ 313 Michael Haynes RC | .75 | .30 | |
| □ 314 Terrell Suggs RC | 1.50 | .60 | |
| □ 315 Rashean Mathis RC | 1.00 | .40 | |
| □ 316 Chris Kelsay RC | 1.00 | .40 | |
| □ 317 Brad Banks RC | 1.00 | .40 | |
| □ 318 Jordan Gross RC | .75 | .30 | |
| □ 319 Lee Suggs RC | 1.00 | .40 | |
| □ 320 Kliff Kingsbury RC | 1.00 | .40 | |
| □ 321 William Joseph RC | .75 | .30 | |
| □ 322 Kelley Washington RC | 1.00 | .40 | |
| □ 323 Jerome McDougle RC | .75 | .30 | |
| □ 324 Osi Umenyiora RC | 2.00 | .75 | |
| □ 325 Chris Simms RC | 1.25 | .50 | |
| □ 326 Alonzo Jackson RC | 1.25 | .50 | |
| □ 327 L.J. Smith RC | 1.25 | .50 | |
| □ 328 Mike Doss RC | 1.25 | .50 | |
| □ 329 Bobby Wade RC | 1.00 | .40 | |
| □ 330 Ken Hamlin RC | 1.25 | .50 | |
| □ 331 Brandon Lloyd RC | 1.25 | .50 | |
| □ 332 Justin Fargas RC | 1.25 | .50 | |
| □ 333 DeWayne Robertson RC | 1.00 | .40 | |
| □ 334 Bryant Johnson RC | 1.25 | .50 | |
| □ 335 Boss Bailey RC | 1.00 | .40 | |
| □ 336 Onterrio Smith RC | 1.00 | .40 | |
| □ 337 Doug Gabriel RC | 1.00 | .40 | |
| □ 338 Jimmy Kennedy RC | 1.00 | .40 | |
| □ 339 B.J. Askew RC | 1.00 | .40 | |
| □ 340 Taylor Jacobs RC | 1.00 | .40 | |
| □ 341 Dallas Clark RC | 1.25 | .50 | |
| □ 342 DeWayne White RC | .75 | .30 | |
| □ 343 Arnaz Battle RC | 1.25 | .50 | |
| □ 344 Kareem Kelly RC | .75 | .30 | |
| □ 345 Terry Pierce RC | .75 | .30 | |
| □ 346 Billy McMullen RC | .75 | .30 | |

| □ 347 Taiman Gardner RC | .75 | .30 |
|---|---|---|
| □ 348 Anquan Boldin RC | 3.00 | 1.25 |
| □ 349 Travis Anglin RC | .75 | .30 |
| □ 350 Byron Leftwich RC | 2.00 | .75 |
| □ 351 Marcus Trufant RC | 1.25 | .50 |
| □ 352 Sam Aiken RC | 1.00 | .40 |
| □ 353 LaBrandon Toefield RC | 1.00 | .40 |
| □ 354 J.R. Tolver RC | 1.00 | .40 |
| □ 355 Charles Rogers RC | 1.00 | .40 |
| □ 356 Chaun Thompson RC | .75 | .30 |
| □ 357 Chris Brown RC | 1.25 | .50 |
| □ 358 Justin Gage RC | 1.00 | .40 |
| □ 359 Kevin Williams RC | 1.25 | .50 |
| □ 360 Willis McGahee RC | 3.00 | 1.25 |
| □ 361 Victor Hobson RC | .75 | .30 |
| □ 362 Brian St.Pierre RC | 1.25 | .50 |
| □ 363 Nate Burleson RC | 1.00 | .40 |
| □ 364 Calvin Pace RC | 1.00 | .40 |
| □ 365 Larry Johnson RC | 3.00 | 1.25 |
| □ 366 Andre Woolfolk RC | 1.00 | .40 |
| □ 367 Tyrone Calico RC | 1.00 | .40 |
| □ 368 Seneca Wallace RC | 1.25 | .50 |
| □ 369 Domanick Davis RC | 1.25 | .50 |
| □ 370 Rex Grossman RC | 4.00 | 1.50 |
| □ 371 Artose Pinner RC | .75 | .30 |
| □ 372 Jason Witten RC | 2.50 | 1.00 |
| □ 373 Bennie Joppru RC | .75 | .30 |
| □ 374 Bethel Johnson RC | 1.00 | .40 |
| □ 375 Kyle Boller RC | 1.25 | .50 |
| □ 376 Shaun McDonald RC | 1.25 | .50 |
| □ 377 Musa Smith RC | 1.00 | .40 |
| □ 378 Ken Dorsey RC | 1.00 | .40 |
| □ 379 Johnathan Sullivan RC | .75 | .30 |
| □ 380 Andre Johnson RC | 2.50 | 1.00 |
| □ 381 Nick Barnett RC | 1.00 | .40 |
| □ 382 Teyo Johnson RC | 1.00 | .40 |
| □ 383 Terence Newman RC | 1.50 | .60 |
| □ 384 Kevin Curtis RC | 1.50 | .60 |
| □ 385 Dave Ragone RC | 1.00 | .40 |
| □ MVP Dex.Jackson FB AU/250 | 120.00 | 50.00 |
| □ RH Dexter Jackson RH | 2.00 | .75 |
| □ RHA Dexter Jackson RH AU | 150.00 | 75.00 |

### 2004 Topps

| □ COMPLETE SET (385) | 60.00 | 30.00 |
|---|---|---|
| □ RH38 STATED ODDS 1:36 H/HTA/W | | |
| □ RH38A ODDS 1:13,494H, 1:3895HTA | | |
| □ SBMVP ODDS | | |
| 1:35,787H,1:10,710HTA,1:33,984R | | |
| □ 1 Peyton Manning | 1.25 | .50 |
| □ 2 Curtis Conway | .50 | .20 |
| □ 3 Tim Brown | .60 | .25 |
| □ 4 David Givens | .50 | .20 |
| □ 5 Dorsey Levens | .50 | .20 |
| □ 6 Jamal Robertson | .40 | .15 |
| □ 7 Doug Flutie | .60 | .25 |
| □ 8 Lamar Gordon | .40 | .15 |
| □ 9 Leonard Little | .40 | .15 |
| □ 10 Patrick Ramsey | .50 | .20 |
| □ 11 Justin McCareins | .40 | .15 |
| □ 12 Charles Lee | .40 | .15 |
| □ 13 Matt Hasselbeck | .60 | .25 |
| □ 14 Chris Chambers | .50 | .20 |
| □ 15 Derrick Blaylock | .40 | .15 |
| □ 16 Shannon Sharpe | .50 | .20 |
| □ 17 Bubba Franks | .50 | .20 |
| □ 18 London Fletcher | .40 | .15 |
| □ 19 Eric Moulds | .50 | .20 |
| □ 20 Anquan Boldin | .60 | .25 |

| □ 21 Brian Urlacher | .60 | .25 |
|---|---|---|
| □ 22 Stephen Davis | .50 | .20 |
| □ 23 Mikhael Ricks | .40 | .15 |
| □ 24 Jason Taylor | .50 | .20 |
| □ 25 Michael Vick | .60 | .25 |
| □ 26 Dante Hall | .50 | .20 |
| □ 27 Marcus Pollard | .40 | .15 |
| □ 28 Rick Mirer | .50 | .20 |
| □ 29 David Tyree | .60 | .25 |
| □ 30 Chad Pennington | .60 | .25 |
| □ 31 Kevan Barlow | .50 | .20 |
| □ 32 James Farrior | .40 | .15 |
| □ 33 James Thrash | .40 | .15 |
| □ 34 Darnerien McCants | .50 | .20 |
| □ 35 L.J. Smith | .50 | .20 |
| □ 36 Tommy Maddox | .50 | .20 |
| □ 37 Tedy Bruschi | .60 | .25 |
| □ 38 Moe Williams | .40 | .15 |
| □ 39 Todd Bouman | .40 | .15 |
| □ 40 Domanick Davis | .60 | .25 |
| □ 41 Dwight Freeney | .60 | .25 |
| □ 42 Kyle Brady | .50 | .20 |
| □ 43 LaVar Arrington | .60 | .25 |
| □ 44 Troy Hambrick | .40 | .15 |
| □ 45 Jake Plummer | .60 | .25 |
| □ 46 Freddie Jones | .40 | .15 |
| □ 47 Chester Taylor | .60 | .25 |
| □ 48 Willis McGahee | .60 | .25 |
| □ 49 Bobby Wade | .50 | .20 |
| □ 50 Steve McNair | .60 | .25 |
| □ 51 Joe Jurevicius | .40 | .15 |
| □ 52 Ladell Betts | .50 | .20 |
| □ 53 LaMont Jordan | .60 | .25 |
| □ 54 Kerry Collins | .50 | .20 |
| □ 55 Hines Ward | .60 | .25 |
| □ 56 Scott Fujita | .40 | .15 |
| □ 57 Kevin Johnson | .40 | .15 |
| □ 58 Troy Brown | .50 | .20 |
| □ 59 Jerome Pathon | .40 | .15 |
| □ 60 Andre Johnson | .60 | .25 |
| □ 61 DeShaun Foster | .50 | .20 |
| □ 62 Terrell Suggs | .60 | .25 |
| □ 63 Marcel Shipp | .60 | .25 |
| □ 64 Allen Rossum | .40 | .15 |
| □ 65 Kyle Boller | .50 | .20 |
| □ 66 Terence Newman | .50 | .20 |
| □ 67 Javon Walker | .50 | .20 |
| □ 68 Shawn Bryson | .40 | .15 |
| □ 69 Travis Minor | .40 | .15 |
| □ 70 Terrell Owens | .60 | .25 |
| □ 71 Kassim Osgood | .40 | .15 |
| □ 72 Bobby Engram | .50 | .20 |
| □ 73 Drew Bennett | .50 | .20 |
| □ 74 Rock Cartwright | .40 | .15 |
| □ 75 Ahman Green | .60 | .25 |
| □ 76 Steve Beuerlein | .50 | .20 |
| □ 77 Takeo Spikes | .40 | .15 |
| □ 78 Dez White | .40 | .15 |
| □ 79 Tim Couch | .60 | .25 |
| □ 80 Travis Henry | .50 | .20 |
| □ 81 T.J. Duckett | .50 | .20 |
| □ 82 LaBrandon Toefield | .40 | .15 |
| □ 83 Randy McMichael | .50 | .20 |
| □ 84 Jonathan Carter | .40 | .15 |
| □ 85 Jerry Rice | 1.25 | .50 |
| □ 86 Maurice Morris | .50 | .20 |
| □ 87 Kurt Warner | .60 | .25 |
| □ 88 Josh Scobey | .40 | .15 |
| □ 89 Travis Taylor | .40 | .15 |
| □ 90 Fred Taylor | .50 | .20 |
| □ 91 Zach Thomas | .60 | .25 |
| □ 92 Kelly Campbell | .40 | .15 |
| □ 93 Tim Carter | .40 | .15 |
| □ 94 Marques Tuiasosopo | .40 | .15 |
| □ 95 Laveranues Coles | .50 | .20 |
| □ 96 Chris Brown | .50 | .20 |
| □ 97 Thomas Jones | .50 | .20 |
| □ 98 Dane Looker | .50 | .20 |
| □ 99 Ross Tucker | .40 | .15 |
| □ 100 Priest Holmes | .60 | .25 |
| □ 101 Troy Walters | .40 | .15 |
| □ 102 Jamie Sharper | .40 | .15 |
| □ 103 Quincy Morgan | .40 | .15 |
| □ 104 Aveion Cason | .40 | .15 |
| □ 105 Joey Galloway | .50 | .20 |
| □ 106 Bill Schroeder | .40 | .15 |
| □ 107 Tony Fisher | .40 | .15 |

|  |  | | |
|---|--------|------|------|
| ❏ 108 | Adewale Ogunleye | .50 | .20 |
| ❏ 109 | Justin Fargas | .50 | .20 |
| ❏ 110 | Daunte Culpepper | .60 | .20 |
| ❏ 111 | Donnie Edwards | .50 | .20 |
| ❏ 112 | Jed Weaver | .40 | .15 |
| ❏ 113 | Arlen Harris | .50 | .20 |
| ❏ 114 | Keenan McCardell | .40 | .15 |
| ❏ 115 | Chad Johnson | .50 | .20 |
| ❏ 116 | Marty Booker | .50 | .20 |
| ❏ 117 | Anthony Wright | .40 | .15 |
| ❏ 118 | Brian Finneran | .40 | .15 |
| ❏ 119 | Robert Ferguson | .50 | .20 |
| ❏ 120 | Ricky Williams | .60 | .25 |
| ❏ 121 | Shaun Ellis | .50 | .20 |
| ❏ 122 | Brian Westbrook | .60 | .25 |
| ❏ 123 | Sam Cowart | .40 | .15 |
| ❏ 124 | Tim Rattay | .40 | .15 |
| ❏ 125 | LaDainian Tomlinson | 1.00 | .40 |
| ❏ 126 | Simeon Rice | .50 | .20 |
| ❏ 127 | Jason Witten | .60 | .25 |
| ❏ 128 | Lee Suggs | .60 | .25 |
| ❏ 129 | Keith Brooking | .40 | .15 |
| ❏ 130 | Rex Grossman | .50 | .20 |
| ❏ 131 | Kelley Washington | .40 | .15 |
| ❏ 132 | Antonio Bryant | .50 | .20 |
| ❏ 133 | Dallas Clark | .50 | .20 |
| ❏ 134 | Stacey Mack | .40 | .15 |
| ❏ 135 | Charles Rogers | .50 | .20 |
| ❏ 136 | Donte' Stallworth | .50 | .20 |
| ❏ 137 | Deion Branch | .50 | .20 |
| ❏ 138 | Nate Burleson | .50 | .20 |
| ❏ 139 | Ike Hilliard | .50 | .20 |
| ❏ 140 | Randy Moss | .75 | .30 |
| ❏ 141 | Michael Strahan | .50 | .20 |
| ❏ 142 | John Abraham | .40 | .15 |
| ❏ 143 | Tim Dwight | .50 | .20 |
| ❏ 144 | Isaac Bruce | .50 | .20 |
| ❏ 145 | Brad Johnson | .50 | .20 |
| ❏ 146 | Trung Canidate | .40 | .15 |
| ❏ 147 | Warrick Dunn | .50 | .20 |
| ❏ 148 | Josh McCown | .50 | .20 |
| ❏ 149 | Muhsin Muhammad | .50 | .20 |
| ❏ 150 | Donovan McNabb | .60 | .25 |
| ❏ 151 | Tai Streets | .40 | .15 |
| ❏ 152 | Antonio Gates | .60 | .25 |
| ❏ 153 | Antwaan Randle El | .50 | .20 |
| ❏ 154 | Doug Jolley | .40 | .15 |
| ❏ 155 | Shaun Alexander | .60 | .25 |
| ❏ 156 | William Green | .40 | .15 |
| ❏ 157 | Carson Palmer | .75 | .30 |
| ❏ 158 | Quentin Griffin | .50 | .20 |
| ❏ 159 | Az-Zahir Hakim | .40 | .15 |
| ❏ 160 | Edgerrin James | .60 | .25 |
| ❏ 161 | Gus Frerotte | .50 | .20 |
| ❏ 162 | Brandon Lloyd | .40 | .15 |
| ❏ 163 | Brian Griese | .50 | .20 |
| ❏ 164 | Boo Williams | .40 | .15 |
| ❏ 165 | Santana Moss | .50 | .20 |
| ❏ 166 | Tyrone Wheatley | .50 | .20 |
| ❏ 167 | Eric Parker | .50 | .20 |
| ❏ 168 | Amos Zereoue | .40 | .15 |
| ❏ 169 | Hula Mili | .40 | .15 |
| ❏ 170 | Marshall Faulk | .60 | .25 |
| ❏ 171 | Tyrone Calico | .50 | .20 |
| ❏ 172 | Tim Hasselbeck | .50 | .20 |
| ❏ 173 | Anthony Becht | .40 | .15 |
| ❏ 174 | Larry Johnson | 1.00 | .40 |
| ❏ 175 | Marvin Harrison | .60 | .25 |
| ❏ 176 | Tony Gonzalez | .50 | .20 |
| ❏ 177 | Wayne Chrebet | .50 | .20 |
| ❏ 178 | Mike Barrow | .40 | .15 |
| ❏ 179 | Bethel Johnson | .40 | .15 |
| ❏ 180 | Deuce McAllister | .60 | .25 |
| ❏ 181 | Drew Brees | .60 | .25 |
| ❏ 182 | Teyo Johnson | .50 | .20 |
| ❏ 183 | Garrison Hearst | .50 | .20 |
| ❏ 184 | Todd Pinkston | .40 | .15 |
| ❏ 185 | Jeff Garcia | .60 | .25 |
| ❏ 186 | Darnell Jackson | .50 | .20 |
| ❏ 187 | Billy Volek | .50 | .20 |
| ❏ 188 | Ray Lewis | .60 | .25 |
| ❏ 189 | Ricky Proehl | .50 | .20 |
| ❏ 190 | Rudi Johnson | .50 | .20 |
| ❏ 191 | Emmitt Smith | 1.50 | .60 |
| ❏ 192 | Cedrick Wilson | .40 | .15 |
| ❏ 193 | Julius Peppers | .50 | .20 |
| ❏ 194 | Peter Warrick | .50 | .20 |
| ❏ 195 | Trent Green | .50 | .20 |
| ❏ 196 | Derrius Thompson | .40 | .15 |
| ❏ 197 | Onterrio Smith | .40 | .15 |
| ❏ 198 | Jerome Bettis | .60 | .25 |
| ❏ 199 | Keyshawn Johnson | .50 | .20 |
| ❏ 200 | Jamal Lewis | .50 | .20 |
| ❏ 201 | Alge Crumpler | .50 | .20 |
| ❏ 202 | Justin Gage | .50 | .20 |
| ❏ 203 | Mike Rucker | .40 | .15 |
| ❏ 204 | Michael Bennett | .50 | .20 |
| ❏ 205 | Jimmy Smith | .50 | .20 |
| ❏ 206 | Ricky Williams TT | .40 | .15 |
| ❏ 207 | Corey Bradford | .40 | .15 |
| ❏ 208 | Jerry Porter | .50 | .20 |
| ❏ 209 | Erron Kinney | .40 | .15 |
| ❏ 210 | Marc Bulger | .50 | .20 |
| ❏ 211 | Jeff Blake | .50 | .20 |
| ❏ 212 | Terry Jones | .40 | .15 |
| ❏ 213 | Kordell Stewart | .50 | .20 |
| ❏ 214 | Andra Davis | .40 | .15 |
| ❏ 215 | David Carr | .50 | .20 |
| ❏ 216 | Nick Barnett | .50 | .20 |
| ❏ 217 | Mark Brunell | .50 | .20 |
| ❏ 218 | Daniel Graham | .40 | .15 |
| ❏ 219 | Jim Kleinsasser | .40 | .15 |
| ❏ 220 | Aaron Brooks | .50 | .20 |
| ❏ 221 | Plaxico Burress | .50 | .20 |
| ❏ 222 | Correll Buckhalter | .50 | .20 |
| ❏ 223 | Jevon Kearse | .50 | .20 |
| ❏ 224 | Michael Pittman | .50 | .20 |
| ❏ 225 | Clinton Portis | .60 | .25 |
| ❏ 226 | Corey Dillon | .50 | .20 |
| ❏ 227 | Steve Smith | .60 | .25 |
| ❏ 228 | David Thornton | .40 | .15 |
| ❏ 229 | Eddie Kennison | .50 | .20 |
| ❏ 230 | Amani Toomer | .40 | .15 |
| ❏ 231 | Artose Pinner | .40 | .15 |
| ❏ 232 | Kelly Holcomb | .50 | .20 |
| ❏ 233 | Jay Fiedler | .40 | .15 |
| ❏ 234 | Ernie Conwell | .40 | .15 |
| ❏ 235 | Torry Holt | .60 | .25 |
| ❏ 236 | Eddie George | .50 | .20 |
| ❏ 237 | Jeremy Shockey | .50 | .20 |
| ❏ 238 | Troy Edwards | .40 | .15 |
| ❏ 239 | Antowain Smith | .50 | .20 |
| ❏ 240 | Jon Kitna | .50 | .20 |
| ❏ 241 | Bryant Johnson | .50 | .20 |
| ❏ 242 | Todd Heap | .50 | .20 |
| ❏ 243 | Doug Johnson | .40 | .15 |
| ❏ 244 | Ashley Lelie | .50 | .20 |
| ❏ 245 | Byron Leftwich | .60 | .25 |
| ❏ 246 | Shawn Barber | .40 | .15 |
| ❏ 247 | Duce Staley | .50 | .20 |
| ❏ 248 | Rod Gardner | .40 | .15 |
| ❏ 249 | Warren Sapp | .50 | .20 |
| ❏ 250 | Brett Favre | 1.50 | .60 |
| ❏ 251 | Olandis Gary | .50 | .20 |
| ❏ 252 | Reggie Wayne | .50 | .20 |
| ❏ 253 | Billy Miller | .40 | .15 |
| ❏ 254 | Johnnie Morton | .50 | .20 |
| ❏ 255 | Joe Horn | .50 | .20 |
| ❏ 256 | Curtis Martin | .60 | .25 |
| ❏ 257 | Freddie Mitchell | .40 | .15 |
| ❏ 258 | Charlie Garner | .50 | .20 |
| ❏ 259 | Marcus Robinson | .50 | .20 |
| ❏ 260 | Derrick Mason | .50 | .20 |
| ❏ 261 | Bobby Shaw | .40 | .15 |
| ❏ 262 | Desmond Clark | .50 | .20 |
| ❏ 263 | James Jackson | .40 | .15 |
| ❏ 264 | Josh Reed | .60 | .25 |
| ❏ 265 | David Boston | .40 | .15 |
| ❏ 266 | Drew Bledsoe | .50 | .20 |
| ❏ 267 | Brock Forsey | .40 | .15 |
| ❏ 268 | Dat Nguyen | .40 | .15 |
| ❏ 269 | Mike Anderson | .50 | .20 |
| ❏ 270 | Anthony Thomas | .50 | .20 |
| ❏ 271 | Najeh Davenport | .50 | .20 |
| ❏ 272 | Jabar Gaffney | .50 | .20 |
| ❏ 273 | Tiki Barber | .60 | .25 |
| ❏ 274 | Rich Gannon | .50 | .20 |
| ❏ 275 | Tom Brady | 1.50 | .60 |
| ❏ 276 | Terry Glenn | .50 | .20 |
| ❏ 277 | Dennis Northcutt | .40 | .15 |
| ❏ 278 | A.J. Feeley | .50 | .20 |
| ❏ 279 | Peerless Price | .50 | .20 |
| ❏ 280 | Jake Delhomme | .50 | .20 |
| ❏ 281 | Kevin Faulk | .50 | .20 |
| ❏ 282 | Quincy Carter | .40 | .15 |
| ❏ 283 | Andre' Davis | .40 | .15 |
| ❏ 284 | Tony Hollings | .40 | .15 |
| ❏ 285 | Joey Harrington | .50 | .20 |
| ❏ 286 | Richie Anderson | .40 | .15 |
| ❏ 287 | Donald Driver | .60 | .25 |
| ❏ 288 | Koren Robinson | .60 | .25 |
| ❏ 289 | Tony Banks | .50 | .20 |
| ❏ 290 | Rod Smith | .50 | .20 |
| ❏ 291 | Anquan Boldin WW | .40 | .15 |
| ❏ 292 | Jamal Lewis WW | .30 | .12 |
| ❏ 293 | Priest Holmes WW | .40 | .15 |
| ❏ 294 | Peyton Manning WW | .75 | .30 |
| ❏ 295 | Marvin Harrison WW | .40 | .15 |
| ❏ 296 | Steve McNair WW | .40 | .15 |
| ❏ 297 | Travis Henry WW | .30 | .12 |
| ❏ 298 | Torry Holt WW | .40 | .15 |
| ❏ 299 | Tom Brady WW | 1.00 | .40 |
| ❏ 300 | Ahman Green WW | .40 | .15 |
| ❏ 301 | Donovan McNabb WW | .40 | .15 |
| ❏ 302 | Deuce McAllister WW | .40 | .15 |
| ❏ 303 | Domanick Davis WW | .40 | .15 |
| ❏ 304 | Clinton Portis WW | .40 | .15 |
| ❏ 305 | Rudi Johnson WW | .30 | .12 |
| ❏ 306 | Brett Favre WW | 1.00 | .40 |
| ❏ 307 | LaDainian Tomlinson WW | .60 | .25 |
| ❏ 308 | Steve Smith WW | .40 | .15 |
| ❏ 309 | Edgerrin James WW | .40 | .15 |
| ❏ 310 | Ty Law WW | .30 | .12 |
| ❏ 311 | Ben Roethlisberger RC | 15.00 | 6.00 |
| ❏ 312 | Ahmad Carroll RC | 1.50 | .60 |
| ❏ 313 | Johnnie Morant RC | 1.25 | .60 |
| ❏ 314 | Greg Jones RC | 1.50 | .60 |
| ❏ 315 | Michael Clayton RC | 1.50 | .60 |
| ❏ 316 | Josh Harris RC | 1.00 | .40 |
| ❏ 317 | Tatum Bell RC | 1.50 | .60 |
| ❏ 318 | Robert Gallery RC | 1.50 | .60 |
| ❏ 319 | B.J. Symons RC | 1.00 | .40 |
| ❏ 320 | Roy Williams RC | 4.00 | 1.50 |
| ❏ 321 | DeAngelo Hall RC | 1.50 | .60 |
| ❏ 322 | Jeff Smoker RC | 1.25 | .50 |
| ❏ 323 | Lee Evans RC | 2.00 | .75 |
| ❏ 324 | Michael Jenkins RC | 1.50 | .60 |
| ❏ 325 | Steven Jackson RC | 5.00 | 2.00 |
| ❏ 326 | Will Smith RC | 1.25 | .50 |
| ❏ 327 | Vince Wilfork RC | 1.50 | .60 |
| ❏ 328 | Ben Troupe RC | 1.25 | .50 |
| ❏ 329 | Chris Gamble RC | 1.25 | .50 |
| ❏ 330 | Kevin Jones RC | 1.50 | .60 |
| ❏ 331 | Jonathan Vilma RC | 1.50 | .60 |
| ❏ 332 | Dontarrious Thomas RC | 1.25 | .50 |
| ❏ 333 | Michael Boulware RC | 1.50 | .60 |
| ❏ 334 | Mewelde Moore RC | 1.50 | .60 |
| ❏ 335 | Drew Henson RC | 1.00 | .40 |
| ❏ 336 | D.J. Williams RC | 1.50 | .60 |
| ❏ 337 | Ernest Wilford RC | 1.50 | .60 |
| ❏ 338 | John Navarre RC | 1.25 | .50 |
| ❏ 339 | Jerricho Cotchery RC | 1.50 | .60 |
| ❏ 340 | Derrick Hamilton RC | 1.00 | .40 |
| ❏ 341 | Carlos Francis RC | 1.00 | .40 |
| ❏ 342 | Ben Watson RC | 1.50 | .60 |
| ❏ 343 | Reggie Williams RC | 1.50 | .60 |
| ❏ 344 | Devard Darling RC | 1.25 | .50 |
| ❏ 345 | Chris Perry RC | 1.50 | .60 |
| ❏ 346 | Derrick Strait RC | 1.25 | .50 |
| ❏ 347 | Sean Taylor RC | 5.00 | 2.00 |
| ❏ 348 | Michael Turner RC | 3.00 | 1.25 |
| ❏ 349 | Keary Colbert RC | 1.50 | .60 |
| ❏ 350 | Eli Manning RC | 12.00 | 5.00 |
| ❏ 351 | Julius Jones RC | 4.00 | 1.50 |
| ❏ 352 | Jason Babin RC | 1.25 | .50 |
| ❏ 353 | Cody Pickett RC | 1.25 | .50 |
| ❏ 354 | Kenechi Udeze RC | 1.25 | .50 |
| ❏ 355 | Rashaun Woods RC | 1.00 | .40 |
| ❏ 356 | Matt Schaub RC | 5.00 | 2.00 |
| ❏ 357 | Tommie Harris RC | 1.50 | .60 |
| ❏ 358 | Dwan Edwards RC | 1.00 | .40 |
| ❏ 359 | Shawn Andrews RC | 1.25 | .50 |
| ❏ 360 | Larry Fitzgerald RC | 5.00 | 2.00 |
| ❏ 361 | P.K. Sam RC | 1.00 | .40 |
| ❏ 362 | Teddy Lehman RC | 1.25 | .50 |
| ❏ 363 | Darius Watts RC | 1.25 | .50 |
| ❏ 364 | D.J. Hackett RC | 1.25 | .50 |
| ❏ 365 | Cedric Cobbs RC | 1.25 | .50 |
| ❏ 366 | Antwan Odom RC | 1.25 | .50 |
| ❏ 367 | Marquise Hill RC | 1.00 | .40 |
| ❏ 368 | Luke McCown RC | 1.50 | .60 |

| | | |
|---|---|---|
| ❏ 369 Triandos Luke RC | 1.00 | .40 |
| ❏ 370 Kellen Winslow RC | 3.00 | 1.25 |
| ❏ 371 Derek Abney RC | 1.00 | .40 |
| ❏ 372 Chris Cooley RC | 1.50 | .60 |
| ❏ 373 Dunta Robinson RC | 1.25 | .50 |
| ❏ 374 Sean Jones RC | 1.25 | .50 |
| ❏ 375 Philip Rivers RC | 5.00 | 2.00 |
| ❏ 376 Craig Krenzel RC | 1.50 | .60 |
| ❏ 377 Daryl Smith RC | 1.25 | .50 |
| ❏ 378 Samie Parker RC | 1.25 | .50 |
| ❏ 379 Ben Hartsock RC | 1.25 | .50 |
| ❏ 380 J.P. Losman RC | 2.00 | .75 |
| ❏ 381 Karlos Dansby RC | 1.50 | .60 |
| ❏ 382 Ricardo Colclough RC | 1.50 | .60 |
| ❏ 383 Bernard Berrian RC | 1.50 | .60 |
| ❏ 384 Junior Siavii RC | 1.50 | .60 |
| ❏ 385 Devery Henderson RC | 1.50 | .60 |
| ❏ TB38 Tom Brady RH | 6.00 | 2.50 |
| ❏ RHTBR2 Tom Brady RH AU | 500.00 | 300.00 |
| ❏ SBMVP Tom Brady RH AU/99 | 500.00 | 350.00 |

## 2005 Topps

| | | |
|---|---|---|
| ❏ COMP.COWBOYS SET (445) | 50.00 | 25.00 |
| ❏ COMP.EAGLES SET (445) | 50.00 | 25.00 |
| ❏ COMP.FACT.SET (445) | 50.00 | 25.00 |
| ❏ COMP.PACKERS SET (445) | 50.00 | 25.00 |
| ❏ COMP.RAIDERS SET (445) | 50.00 | 25.00 |
| ❏ COMP.SB XL SET (445) | 80.00 | 50.00 |
| ❏ COMPLETE SET (440) | 50.00 | 25.00 |
| ❏ RH39 STATED ODDS 1:275 HOB/HTA/RET | | |
| ❏ RH39A 1:62,233H, 1:15,547HTA, 1:51,346R | | |
| ❏ SBMVP 1:27,629H, 1:7774HTA, 1:43,632R | | |
| ❏ UNPRICED PLATINUM PRINT RUN 1 SET | | |
| ❏ 1 Brian Westbrook | .60 | .25 |
| ❏ 2 Tim Rattay | .40 | .15 |
| ❏ 3 Dominick Davis | .40 | .15 |
| ❏ 4 Lee Suggs | .50 | .20 |
| ❏ 5 Keith Brooking | .40 | .15 |
| ❏ 6 Rex Grossman | .60 | .25 |
| ❏ 7 Chad Johnson | .50 | .20 |
| ❏ 8 Willis McGahee | .60 | .25 |
| ❏ 9 Eli Manning | 1.25 | .50 |
| ❏ 10 Tom Brady | 1.25 | .50 |
| ❏ 11 Ray Lewis | .60 | .25 |
| ❏ 12 Terrence Newman | .40 | .15 |
| ❏ 13 Daunte Culpepper | .60 | .25 |
| ❏ 14 Marvin Harrison | .60 | .25 |
| ❏ 15 Greg Jones | .40 | .15 |
| ❏ 16 Anquan Boldin | .50 | .20 |
| ❏ 17 Julius Peppers | .50 | .20 |
| ❏ 18 Kevin Jones | .50 | .20 |
| ❏ 19 Javon Walker | .50 | .20 |
| ❏ 20 Michael Lewis | .40 | .15 |
| ❏ 21 Jamaar Taylor | .40 | .15 |
| ❏ 22 Hines Ward | .60 | .25 |
| ❏ 23 Drew Brees | .60 | .25 |
| ❏ 24 Marcus Trufant | .40 | .15 |
| ❏ 25 Derrick Brooks | .40 | .15 |
| ❏ 26 Sean Taylor | .50 | .20 |
| ❏ 27 Dernius Thompson | .40 | .15 |
| ❏ 28 Nick Barnett | .40 | .15 |
| ❏ 29 Dante Hall | .50 | .20 |
| ❏ 30 Mike Cloud | .40 | .15 |
| ❏ 31 Jake Plummer | .50 | .20 |
| ❏ 32 Donte Stallworth | .50 | .20 |
| ❏ 33 Shaun Ellis | .40 | .15 |
| ❏ 34 Jeremy Shockey | .60 | .25 |
| ❏ 35 Teyo Johnson | .40 | .15 |
| ❏ 36 Adam Archuleta | .40 | .15 |
| ❏ 37 Darius Watts | .40 | .15 |
| ❏ 38 Michael Pittman | .40 | .15 |
| ❏ 39 Drew Bennett | .50 | .20 |
| ❏ 40 Aaron Stecker | .40 | .15 |
| ❏ 41 Artose Pinner | .40 | .15 |
| ❏ 42 Dane Looker | .40 | .15 |
| ❏ 43 Jeff Garcia | .50 | .20 |
| ❏ 44 Travis Taylor | .40 | .15 |
| ❏ 45 Najeh Davenport | .50 | .20 |
| ❏ 46 Walter Jones | .40 | .15 |
| ❏ 47 Donnie Edwards | .40 | .15 |
| ❏ 48 Terrell Owens | .60 | .25 |
| ❏ 49 Matt Birk | .40 | .15 |
| ❏ 50 Chris Baker | .40 | .15 |
| ❏ 51 Brandon Lloyd | .40 | .15 |
| ❏ 52 Marshall Faulk | .60 | .25 |
| ❏ 53 Jonathan Vilma | .50 | .20 |
| ❏ 54 Dallas Clark | .50 | .20 |
| ❏ 55 David Carr | .50 | .20 |
| ❏ 56 Jerricho Cotchery | .50 | .20 |
| ❏ 57 Deuce McAllister | .60 | .25 |
| ❏ 58 Donald Driver | .60 | .25 |
| ❏ 59 Jeff Smoker | .40 | .15 |
| ❏ 60 Champ Bailey | .50 | .20 |
| ❏ 61 Jason Witten | .50 | .20 |
| ❏ 62 T.J. Houshmandzadeh | .50 | .20 |
| ❏ 63 Jay Fiedler | .40 | .15 |
| ❏ 64 Philip Rivers | .60 | .25 |
| ❏ 65 Jake Delhomme | .60 | .25 |
| ❏ 66 Terrence McGee RC | .40 | .15 |
| ❏ 67 Chester Taylor | .50 | .20 |
| ❏ 68 Tommy Maddox | .50 | .20 |
| ❏ 69 Bryant Johnson | .50 | .20 |
| ❏ 70 Justin Gage | .50 | .20 |
| ❏ 71 Troy Hambrick | .40 | .15 |
| ❏ 72 Kerry Collins | .50 | .20 |
| ❏ 73 Jeb Putzier | .40 | .15 |
| ❏ 74 Keary Colbert | .40 | .15 |
| ❏ 75 Jason Elam | .40 | .15 |
| ❏ 76 Jerramy Stevens | .40 | .15 |
| ❏ 77 Clinton Portis | .60 | .25 |
| ❏ 78 Sam Aiken | .40 | .15 |
| ❏ 79 Trent Green | .50 | .20 |
| ❏ 80 Dat Nguyen | .40 | .15 |
| ❏ 81 Ladell Betts | .40 | .15 |
| ❏ 82 Peter Warrick | .50 | .20 |
| ❏ 83 Dominic Rhodes | .40 | .15 |
| ❏ 84 Jason Taylor | .50 | .20 |
| ❏ 85 Antwaan Randle El | .50 | .20 |
| ❏ 86 Michael Jenkins | .50 | .20 |
| ❏ 87 Adam Vinatieri | .60 | .25 |
| ❏ 88 Mark Brunell | .50 | .20 |
| ❏ 89 Brian Finneran | .40 | .15 |
| ❏ 90 Ernie Conwell | .40 | .15 |
| ❏ 91 Chad Pennington | .60 | .25 |
| ❏ 92 Dan Morgan | .40 | .15 |
| ❏ 93 Kelly Holcomb | .40 | .15 |
| ❏ 94 Ronde Barber | .50 | .20 |
| ❏ 95 Torry Holt | .50 | .20 |
| ❏ 96 Bubba Franks | .40 | .15 |
| ❏ 97 Keyshawn Johnson | .50 | .20 |
| ❏ 98 J.P. Losman | .60 | .25 |
| ❏ 99 Ed Reed | .50 | .20 |
| ❏ 100 Chris McAlister | .40 | .15 |
| ❏ 101 Jamie Sharper | .40 | .15 |
| ❏ 102 Chad Lewis | .40 | .15 |
| ❏ 103 Chris Brown | .50 | .20 |
| ❏ 104 Marc Boerigter | .40 | .15 |
| ❏ 105 Zach Thomas | .60 | .25 |
| ❏ 106 Byron Leftwich | .50 | .20 |
| ❏ 107 Tatum Bell | .50 | .20 |
| ❏ 108 Tai Streets | .40 | .15 |
| ❏ 109 Tory James | .40 | .15 |
| ❏ 110 Cedrick Wilson | .40 | .15 |
| ❏ 111 Darrell Jackson | .50 | .20 |
| ❏ 112 Ben Roethlisberger | 1.50 | .60 |
| ❏ 113 Quentin Jammer | .40 | .15 |
| ❏ 114 Maurice Morris | .40 | .15 |
| ❏ 115 Simeon Rice | .40 | .15 |
| ❏ 116 Tyrone Calico | .50 | .20 |
| ❏ 117 Patrick Ramsey | .50 | .20 |
| ❏ 118 Marcus Robinson | .50 | .20 |
| ❏ 119 Reggie Wayne | .50 | .20 |
| ❏ 120 Kevin Faulk | .50 | .20 |
| ❏ 121 Nate Burleson | .50 | .20 |
| ❏ 122 Aaron Brooks | .50 | .20 |
| ❏ 123 Willie Roaf | .40 | .15 |
| ❏ 124 Fred Taylor | .60 | .25 |
| ❏ 125 Dwight Freeney | .50 | .20 |
| ❏ 126 Olin Kreutz | .50 | .20 |
| ❏ 127 Dunta Robinson | .40 | .15 |
| ❏ 128 Warren Sapp | .50 | .20 |
| ❏ 129 Chris Perry | .40 | .15 |
| ❏ 130 Desmond Clark | .40 | .15 |
| ❏ 131 Takeo Spikes | .40 | .15 |
| ❏ 132 B.J. Sams | .40 | .15 |
| ❏ 133 Bertrand Berry | .40 | .15 |
| ❏ 134 Drew Henson | .50 | .20 |
| ❏ 135 Robert Ferguson | .50 | .20 |
| ❏ 136 Julius Jones | .60 | .25 |
| ❏ 137 Jeremiah Trotter | .40 | .15 |
| ❏ 138 Chris Simms | .50 | .20 |
| ❏ 139 Damenen McCants | .40 | .15 |
| ❏ 140 Robert Gallery | .40 | .15 |
| ❏ 141 Michael Strahan | .50 | .20 |
| ❏ 142 Reggie Williams | .50 | .20 |
| ❏ 143 Tony Gonzalez | .50 | .20 |
| ❏ 144 Priest Holmes | .60 | .25 |
| ❏ 145 Luke McCown | .40 | .15 |
| ❏ 146 Alien Rossum | .40 | .15 |
| ❏ 147 Eric Moulds | .50 | .20 |
| ❏ 148 Jonathan Wells | .40 | .15 |
| ❏ 149 Randy McMichael | .40 | .15 |
| ❏ 150 John Abraham | .40 | .15 |
| ❏ 151 Doug Gabriel | .40 | .15 |
| ❏ 152 Tiki Barber | .60 | .25 |
| ❏ 153 Marcel Shipp | .40 | .15 |
| ❏ 154 LaDainian Tomlinson | 1.00 | .40 |
| ❏ 155 Richard Seymour | .50 | .20 |
| ❏ 156 Mike Vanderjagt | .40 | .15 |
| ❏ 157 Roy Williams WR | .60 | .25 |
| ❏ 158 William Green | .40 | .15 |
| ❏ 159 DeAngelo Hall | .50 | .20 |
| ❏ 160 Josh McCown | .50 | .20 |
| ❏ 161 Terrell Suggs | .50 | .20 |
| ❏ 162 Brian Dawkins | .50 | .20 |
| ❏ 163 Lee Evans | .50 | .20 |
| ❏ 164 Nick Goings | .40 | .15 |
| ❏ 165 Carson Palmer | .50 | .20 |
| ❏ 166 Charles Woodson | .50 | .20 |
| ❏ 167 Keenan McCardell | .40 | .15 |
| ❏ 168 Kevan Barlow | .40 | .15 |
| ❏ 169 Matt Hasselbeck | .50 | .20 |
| ❏ 170 Steven Jackson | .75 | .30 |
| ❏ 171 Ben Troupe | .40 | .15 |
| ❏ 172 Jamal Lewis | .50 | .20 |
| ❏ 173 Sammy Morris | .40 | .15 |
| ❏ 174 Troy Polamalu | .75 | .30 |
| ❏ 175 Donovan McNabb | .60 | .25 |
| ❏ 176 Curtis Martin | .60 | .25 |
| ❏ 177 David Givens | .50 | .20 |
| ❏ 178 Kenedh Udeze | .40 | .15 |
| ❏ 179 A.J. Feeley | .40 | .15 |
| ❏ 180 Eddie Kennison | .40 | .15 |
| ❏ 181 LaBrandon Toefield | .40 | .15 |
| ❏ 182 Jabar Gaffney | .40 | .15 |
| ❏ 183 Bethel Johnson | .40 | .15 |
| ❏ 184 Eddie Drummond | .40 | .15 |
| ❏ 185 Rod Smith | .50 | .20 |
| ❏ 186 La'Roi Glover | .50 | .20 |
| ❏ 187 Onterrio Smith | .40 | .15 |
| ❏ 188 Antonio Bryant | .40 | .15 |
| ❏ 189 Lee Mays | .40 | .15 |
| ❏ 190 Michael Vick | .60 | .25 |
| ❏ 191 Samie Parker | .40 | .15 |
| ❏ 192 London Fletcher | .40 | .15 |
| ❏ 193 DeShaun Foster | .50 | .20 |
| ❏ 194 Rashaun Woods | .40 | .15 |
| ❏ 195 Marc Bulger | .50 | .20 |
| ❏ 196 Adrian Peterson | .50 | .20 |
| ❏ 197 Justin McCareins | .40 | .15 |
| ❏ 198 Corey Dillon | .50 | .20 |
| ❏ 199 James Farrior | .40 | .15 |
| ❏ 200 Antonio Gates | .60 | .25 |
| ❏ 201 Todd Pinkston | .40 | .15 |
| ❏ 202 Randy Hymes | .40 | .15 |
| ❏ 203 Peyton Manning | 1.00 | .40 |
| ❏ 204 Ahman Green | .60 | .25 |
| ❏ 205 Charles Rogers | .40 | .15 |
| ❏ 206 John Lynch | .50 | .20 |
| ❏ 207 Larry Fitzgerald | .50 | .20 |
| ❏ 208 Jonathan Ogden | .40 | .15 |
| ❏ 209 Michael Bennett | .40 | .15 |
| ❏ 210 DeWayne Robertson | .40 | .15 |

|  |  | | |
|---|---|---|---|
| ❏ 211 | Justin Fargas | .50 | .20 |
| ❏ 212 | Duce Staley | .50 | .20 |
| ❏ 213 | Koren Robinson | .50 | .20 |
| ❏ 214 | Billy Volek | .50 | .20 |
| ❏ 215 | Laveranues Coles | .50 | .20 |
| ❏ 216 | Michael Clayton | .50 | .20 |
| ❏ 217 | Amani Toomer | .50 | .20 |
| ❏ 218 | Thomas Jones | .50 | .20 |
| ❏ 219 | Todd Heap | .50 | .20 |
| ❏ 220 | Ken Lucas | .40 | .15 |
| ❏ 221 | Donovin Darius | .40 | .15 |
| ❏ 222 | Ashley Lelie | .40 | .15 |
| ❏ 223 | Warrick Dunn | .50 | .20 |
| ❏ 224 | Doug Jolley | .40 | .15 |
| ❏ 225 | Jimmy Smith | .50 | .20 |
| ❏ 226 | Quentin Griffin | .50 | .20 |
| ❏ 227 | Isaac Bruce | .50 | .20 |
| ❏ 228 | Ronald Curry | .50 | .20 |
| ❏ 229 | Corey Bradford | .50 | .20 |
| ❏ 230 | LaVar Arrington | .60 | .25 |
| ❏ 231 | William Henderson | .50 | .20 |
| ❏ 232 | Brandon Stokley | .40 | .15 |
| ❏ 233 | Alge Crumpler | .50 | .20 |
| ❏ 234 | Joe Horn | .50 | .20 |
| ❏ 235 | Bernard Berrian | .50 | .20 |
| ❏ 236 | Michael Boulware | .40 | .15 |
| ❏ 237 | Brett Favre | 1.50 | .60 |
| ❏ 238 | Dennis Northcutt | .40 | .15 |
| ❏ 239 | Muhsin Muhammad | .50 | .20 |
| ❏ 240 | Shawn Springs | .40 | .15 |
| ❏ 241 | Kelly Campbell | .50 | .20 |
| ❏ 242 | Johnnie Morton | .50 | .20 |
| ❏ 243 | Derrick Blaylock | .40 | .15 |
| ❏ 244 | Chris Chambers | .50 | .20 |
| ❏ 245 | Joey Harrington | .50 | .20 |
| ❏ 246 | Brian Urlacher | .60 | .25 |
| ❏ 247 | T.J. Duckett | .40 | .15 |
| ❏ 248 | Quincy Morgan | .40 | .15 |
| ❏ 249 | Darren Sharper | .40 | .15 |
| ❏ 250 | L.J. Smith | .50 | .20 |
| ❏ 251 | Steve McNair | .60 | .25 |
| ❏ 252 | Eric Parker | .40 | .15 |
| ❏ 253 | Jerome Bettis | .50 | .20 |
| ❏ 254 | LaMont Jordan | .50 | .20 |
| ❏ 255 | Tedy Bruschi | .60 | .25 |
| ❏ 256 | Ernest Wilford | .50 | .20 |
| ❏ 257 | Reuben Droughns | .40 | .15 |
| ❏ 258 | Lito Sheppard | .50 | .20 |
| ❏ 259 | Steve Smith | .60 | .25 |
| ❏ 260 | Shaun Alexander | .60 | .25 |
| ❏ 261 | Kevin Curtis | .40 | .15 |
| ❏ 262 | Drew Bledsoe | .60 | .25 |
| ❏ 263 | Derrick Mason | .50 | .20 |
| ❏ 264 | Jevon Kearse | .50 | .20 |
| ❏ 265 | Jerry Porter | .50 | .20 |
| ❏ 266 | Edgerrin James | .50 | .20 |
| ❏ 267 | Santana Moss | .50 | .20 |
| ❏ 268 | Kyle Boller | .50 | .20 |
| ❏ 269 | Travis Henry | .50 | .20 |
| ❏ 270 | Stephen Davis | .50 | .20 |
| ❏ 271 | Gibril Wilson | .40 | .15 |
| ❏ 272 | Plaxico Burress | .50 | .20 |
| ❏ 273 | Deion Branch | .50 | .20 |
| ❏ 274 | Larry Johnson | .60 | .25 |
| ❏ 275 | Rudi Johnson | .60 | .25 |
| ❏ 276 | Andre Johnson | .50 | .20 |
| ❏ 277 | David Akers | .40 | .15 |
| ❏ 278 | Randy Moss | .60 | .25 |
| ❏ 279 | Roy Williams S | .50 | .20 |
| ❏ 280 | Antoine Winfield | .50 | .20 |
| ❏ 281 | Antonio Pierce | .40 | .15 |
| ❏ 282 | Keith Bulluck | .40 | .15 |
| ❏ 283 | Correll Buckhalter | .50 | .20 |
| ❏ 284 | Troy Vincent | .50 | .20 |
| ❏ 285 | D.J. Williams | .40 | .15 |
| ❏ 286 | Matt Schaub | .60 | .25 |
| ❏ 287 | Clarence Moore | .40 | .15 |
| ❏ 288 | Billy Miller | .40 | .15 |
| ❏ 289 | Terrence Holt | .40 | .15 |
| ❏ 290 | Tony Hollings | .40 | .15 |
| ❏ 291 | E.J. Henderson | .40 | .15 |
| ❏ 292 | Fred Smoot | .40 | .15 |
| ❏ 293 | Patrick Crayton | .60 | .25 |
| ❏ 294 | Mike Alstott | .50 | .20 |
| ❏ 295 | Mewelde Moore | .40 | .15 |
| ❏ 296 | Shawn Bryson | .40 | .15 |
| ❏ 297 | David Garrard | .50 | .20 |
| ❏ 298 | Kurt Warner | .60 | .25 |
| ❏ 299 | Nate Clements | .50 | .20 |
| ❏ 300 | Kellen Winslow | .60 | .25 |
| ❏ 301 | Eric Johnson | .40 | .15 |
| ❏ 302 | Peerless Price | .40 | .15 |
| ❏ 303 | Joey Galloway | .40 | .15 |
| ❏ 304 | Sebastian Janikowski | .40 | .15 |
| ❏ 305 | Jason McAddley | .40 | .15 |
| ❏ 306 | Chris Gamble | .40 | .15 |
| ❏ 307 | Brian Griese | .50 | .20 |
| ❏ 308 | Greg Lewis | .50 | .20 |
| ❏ 309 | Wes Welker | .60 | .25 |
| ❏ 310 | Jesse Chatman | .40 | .15 |
| ❏ 311 | Curtis Martin LL | .60 | .25 |
| ❏ 312 | Daunte Culpepper LL | .50 | .20 |
| ❏ 313 | Muhsin Muhammad LL | .40 | .15 |
| ❏ 314 | Shaun Alexander LL | .50 | .20 |
| ❏ 315 | Trent Green LL | .40 | .15 |
| ❏ 316 | Joe Horn LL | .40 | .15 |
| ❏ 317 | Corey Dillon LL | .40 | .15 |
| ❏ 318 | Peyton Manning LL | .75 | .30 |
| ❏ 319 | Javon Walker LL | .40 | .15 |
| ❏ 320 | Edgerrin James LL | .40 | .15 |
| ❏ 321 | Jake Scott GM | .40 | .15 |
| ❏ 322 | John Elway GM | 1.25 | .50 |
| ❏ 323 | Dwight Clark GM | .50 | .20 |
| ❏ 324 | Lawrence Taylor GM | .60 | .25 |
| ❏ 325 | Joe Namath GM | 1.00 | .40 |
| ❏ 326 | Richard Dent GM | .50 | .20 |
| ❏ 327 | Peyton Manning GM | 1.00 | .40 |
| ❏ 328 | Don Maynard GM | .50 | .20 |
| ❏ 329 | Joe Greene GM | .50 | .20 |
| ❏ 330 | Roger Staubach GM | 1.00 | .40 |
| ❏ 331 | Daunte Culpepper AP | .50 | .20 |
| ❏ 332 | Peyton Manning AP | .75 | .30 |
| ❏ 333 | Tiki Barber AP | .50 | .20 |
| ❏ 334 | Antonio Gates AP | .50 | .20 |
| ❏ 335 | Marvin Harrison AP | .50 | .20 |
| ❏ 336 | Lito Sheppard AP | .40 | .15 |
| ❏ 337 | LaDainian Tomlinson AP | .75 | .30 |
| ❏ 338 | Muhsin Muhammad AP | .40 | .15 |
| ❏ 339 | Allen Rossum AP | .30 | .12 |
| ❏ 340 | Dwight Freeney AP | .40 | .15 |
| ❏ 341 | Jerome Bettis AP | .50 | .20 |
| ❏ 342 | Alge Crumpler AP | .40 | .15 |
| ❏ 343 | Ed Reed AP | .40 | .15 |
| ❏ 344 | Ronde Barber AP | .40 | .15 |
| ❏ 345 | Takeo Spikes AP | .30 | .12 |
| ❏ 346 | Rudi Johnson AP | .40 | .15 |
| ❏ 347 | Adam Vinatieri AP | .50 | .20 |
| ❏ 348 | Tony Holt AP | .40 | .15 |
| ❏ 349 | Chad Johnson AP | .40 | .15 |
| ❏ 350 | Brian Westbrook AP | .50 | .20 |
| ❏ 351 | Michael Vick AP | .50 | .20 |
| ❏ 352 | Tom Brady AP | 1.00 | .40 |
| ❏ 353 | Donovan McNabb AP | .50 | .20 |
| ❏ 354 | Ahman Green AP | .50 | .20 |
| ❏ 355 | Andre Johnson AP | .40 | .15 |
| ❏ 356 | Drew Brees AP | .50 | .20 |
| ❏ 357 | Hines Ward AP | .50 | .20 |
| ❏ 358 | Deion Branch PH | .40 | .15 |
| ❏ 359 | Philadelphia Eagles PH | .50 | .20 |
| ❏ 360 | Tom Brady PH | 1.00 | .40 |
| ❏ 361 | Taylor Stubblefield RC | 1.00 | .50 |
| ❏ 362 | Dan Cody RC | 1.50 | .60 |
| ❏ 363 | Ryan Claridge RC | 1.00 | .40 |
| ❏ 364 | David Pollack RC | 1.25 | .50 |
| ❏ 365 | Craig Bragg RC | 1.00 | .40 |
| ❏ 366 | Alvin Pearman RC | 1.25 | .50 |
| ❏ 367 | Marcus Maxwell RC | 1.00 | .40 |
| ❏ 368 | Brock Berlin RC | 1.25 | .50 |
| ❏ 369 | Khalif Barnes RC | 1.00 | .40 |
| ❏ 370 | Eric King RC | 1.00 | .40 |
| ❏ 371 | Alex Smith TE RC | 1.50 | .60 |
| ❏ 372 | Dante Ridgeway RC | 1.00 | .40 |
| ❏ 373 | Shaun Cody RC | 1.25 | .50 |
| ❏ 374 | Donte Nicholson RC | 1.25 | -.50 |
| ❏ 375 | Lionel Gates RC | 1.00 | .40 |
| ❏ 376 | Fabian Washington RC | 1.50 | .60 |
| ❏ 377 | Brandon Jacobs RC | 2.00 | .75 |
| ❏ 378 | Noah Herron RC | 1.50 | .60 |
| ❏ 379 | Derrick Johnson RC | 1.50 | .60 |
| ❏ 380 | Derrick Johnson RC | 1.50 | .60 |
| ❏ 381 | J.R. Russell RC | 1.50 | .60 |
| ❏ 382 | Adrian McPherson RC | 1.25 | .50 |
| ❏ 383 | Marcus Spears RC | 1.50 | .60 |
| ❏ 384 | Justin Miller RC | 1.25 | .50 |
| ❏ 385 | Marion Barber RC | 5.00 | 2.00 |
| ❏ 386 | Anthony Davis RC | 1.25 | .50 |
| ❏ 387 | Chad Owens RC | 1.50 | .60 |
| ❏ 388 | Craphonso Thorpe RC | 1.25 | .50 |
| ❏ 389 | Travis Johnson RC | 1.00 | .40 |
| ❏ 390 | Erasmus James RC | 1.25 | .50 |
| ❏ 391 | Mike Patterson RC | 1.25 | .50 |
| ❏ 392 | Alphonso Hodge RC | 1.00 | .40 |
| ❏ 393 | Airese Currie RC | 1.25 | .50 |
| ❏ 394 | Justin Tuck RC | 2.00 | .75 |
| ❏ 395 | Dan Orlovsky RC | 1.50 | .60 |
| ❏ 396 | Thomas Davis RC | 1.25 | .50 |
| ❏ 397 | Derek Anderson RC | 2.50 | 1.00 |
| ❏ 398 | Matt Roth RC | 1.50 | .60 |
| ❏ 399 | Darryl Blackstock RC | 1.00 | .40 |
| ❏ 400 | Chris Henry RC | 1.50 | .60 |
| ❏ 401 | Rasheed Marshall RC | 1.25 | .50 |
| ❏ 402 | Anttaj Hawthorne RC | 1.25 | .50 |
| ❏ 403 | Bryant McFadden RC | 1.25 | .50 |
| ❏ 404 | Darren Sproles RC | 2.00 | .75 |
| ❏ 405 | Oshiomogho Atogwe RC | 1.50 | .60 |
| ❏ 406 | Fred Gibson RC | 1.25 | .50 |
| ❏ 407 | J.J. Arrington RC | 1.50 | .60 |
| ❏ 408 | Cedric Benson RC | 1.50 | .60 |
| ❏ 409 | Mark Bradley RC | 1.50 | .60 |
| ❏ 410 | Reggie Brown RC | 1.50 | .60 |
| ❏ 411 | Ronnie Brown RC | 5.00 | 2.00 |
| ❏ 412 | Jason Campbell RC | 3.00 | 1.25 |
| ❏ 413 | Maurice Clarett RC | 1.25 | .50 |
| ❏ 414 | Mark Clayton RC | 1.50 | .60 |
| ❏ 415 | Braylon Edwards RC | 5.00 | 2.00 |
| ❏ 416 | Ciatrick Fason RC | 1.25 | .50 |
| ❏ 417 | Charlie Frye RC | 1.50 | .60 |
| ❏ 418 | Frank Gore RC | 4.00 | 1.50 |
| ❏ 419 | David Greene RC | 1.25 | .50 |
| ❏ 420 | Vincent Jackson RC | 1.50 | .60 |
| ❏ 421 | Adam Jones RC | 1.50 | .60 |
| ❏ 422 | Matt Jones RC | 2.50 | 1.00 |
| ❏ 423 | Stefan LeFors RC | 1.25 | .50 |
| ❏ 424 | Heath Miller RC | 3.00 | 1.25 |
| ❏ 425 | Ryan Moats RC | 1.50 | .60 |
| ❏ 426 | Vernand Morency RC | 1.50 | .60 |
| ❏ 427 | Terrence Murphy RC | 1.00 | .40 |
| ❏ 428 | Kyle Orton RC | 2.00 | .75 |
| ❏ 429 | Roscoe Parrish RC | 1.25 | .50 |
| ❏ 430 | Courtney Roby RC | 1.25 | .50 |
| ❏ 431 | Aaron Rodgers RC | 5.00 | 2.00 |
| ❏ 432 | Carlos Rogers RC | 1.50 | .60 |
| ❏ 433 | Antrel Rolle RC | 1.50 | .60 |
| ❏ 434 | Eric Shelton RC | 1.25 | .50 |
| ❏ 435 | Alex Smith QB RC | 2.50 | 1.00 |
| ❏ 436 | Andrew Walter RC | 1.50 | .60 |
| ❏ 437 | Roddy White RC | 2.00 | .75 |
| ❏ 438 | Cadillac Williams RC | 3.00 | 1.25 |
| ❏ 439 | Mike Williams RC | 1.50 | .60 |
| ❏ 440 | Troy Williamson RC | 1.50 | .60 |
| ❏ RHDB | Deion Branch RH | 5.00 | 2.00 |
| ❏ RHDBA | Deion Branch RH AU | 350.00 | 200.00 |
| ❏ SBMVP | D.Branch FB AU/200 | 150.00 | 60.00 |

## 2006 Topps

|  |  | | |
|---|---|---|---|
| ❏ | COMPLETE SET (385) | 50.00 | 25.00 |
| ❏ 1 | Jonathan Vilma | .50 | .20 |
| ❏ 2 | Mewelde Moore | .40 | .15 |
| ❏ 3 | Shaun McDonald | .40 | .15 |
| ❏ 4 | Marcus Pollard | .40 | .15 |
| ❏ 5 | Marcus Robinson | .40 | .15 |
| ❏ 6 | David Garrard | .60 | .25 |
| ❏ 7 | Chris Gamble | .40 | .15 |

|  |  | | |
|---|---|---|---|
| ❑ 8 | Rex Grossman | .60 | .25 |
| ❑ 9 | Lee Suggs | .50 | .20 |
| ❑ 10 | Steve McNair | .60 | .25 |
| ❑ 11 | Chester Taylor | .50 | .20 |
| ❑ 12 | Randy Moss | .60 | .25 |
| ❑ 13 | Jeremy Shockey | .60 | .25 |
| ❑ 14 | Tedy Bruschi | .60 | .25 |
| ❑ 15 | Walter Jones | .40 | .15 |
| ❑ 16 | Troy Polamalu | .75 | .30 |
| ❑ 17 | Ladell Betts | .50 | .20 |
| ❑ 18 | DeMarcus Ware | .50 | .20 |
| ❑ 19 | Erron Kinney | .40 | .15 |
| ❑ 20 | Trent Cole | .40 | .15 |
| ❑ 21 | Charlie Adams | .40 | .15 |
| ❑ 22 | Brandon Jacobs | .60 | .25 |
| ❑ 23 | Nathan Vasher | .40 | .15 |
| ❑ 24 | Shawne Merriman | .50 | .20 |
| ❑ 25 | Drew Carter | .40 | .15 |
| ❑ 26 | Clinton Portis | .60 | .25 |
| ❑ 27 | Alex Brown | .40 | .15 |
| ❑ 28 | Osi Umenyiora | .50 | .20 |
| ❑ 29 | Willie Parker | .75 | .30 |
| ❑ 30 | Lofa Tatupu | .50 | .20 |
| ❑ 31 | Odell Thurman | .40 | .15 |
| ❑ 32 | Scottie Vines | .40 | .15 |
| ❑ 33 | Sam Gado | .60 | .25 |
| ❑ 34 | Todd DeVoe | .60 | .25 |
| ❑ 35 | Keith Brooking | .40 | .15 |
| ❑ 36 | Eddie Kennison | .40 | .15 |
| ❑ 37 | Mike Williams | .60 | .25 |
| ❑ 38 | Adam Jones | .40 | .15 |
| ❑ 39 | Charlie Frye | .50 | .20 |
| ❑ 40 | Reggie Wayne | .50 | .20 |
| ❑ 41 | Donte Stallworth | .50 | .20 |
| ❑ 42 | Vincent Jackson | .50 | .20 |
| ❑ 43 | Alex Smith QB | .60 | .25 |
| ❑ 44 | Greg Lewis | .40 | .15 |
| ❑ 45 | Billy Volek | .40 | .15 |
| ❑ 46 | Dominique Foxworth | .40 | .15 |
| ❑ 47 | Terrell Owens | .60 | .25 |
| ❑ 48 | Josh McCown | .50 | .20 |
| ❑ 49 | Simeon Rice | .40 | .15 |
| ❑ 50 | Curtis Martin | .60 | .25 |
| ❑ 51 | Peyton Manning | 1.00 | .40 |
| ❑ 52 | Nick Barnett | .50 | .20 |
| ❑ 53 | Marion Barber | .60 | .25 |
| ❑ 54 | Chris McAlister | .40 | .15 |
| ❑ 55 | Jerramy Stevens | .50 | .20 |
| ❑ 56 | Jerome Bettis | .60 | .25 |
| ❑ 57 | Chris Brown | .50 | .20 |
| ❑ 58 | LeRon McCoy | .40 | .15 |
| ❑ 59 | John Abraham | .40 | .15 |
| ❑ 60 | LaMont Jordan | .50 | .20 |
| ❑ 61 | Jason Taylor | .50 | .20 |
| ❑ 62 | Michael Clayton | .50 | .20 |
| ❑ 63 | Jake Plummer | .50 | .20 |
| ❑ 64 | Travis Taylor | .40 | .15 |
| ❑ 65 | Samie Parker | .40 | .15 |
| ❑ 66 | Carlos Rogers | .40 | .15 |
| ❑ 67 | Kevin Faulk | .50 | .20 |
| ❑ 68 | Alvin Pearman | .40 | .15 |
| ❑ 69 | Derrick Johnson | .50 | .20 |
| ❑ 70 | Cedric Benson | .50 | .20 |
| ❑ 71 | J.P. Losman | .50 | .20 |
| ❑ 72 | Julius Peppers | .50 | .20 |
| ❑ 73 | DeAngelo Hall | .50 | .20 |
| ❑ 74 | Joey Galloway | .50 | .20 |
| ❑ 75 | Marcus Trufant | .40 | .15 |
| ❑ 76 | Frisman Jackson | .40 | .15 |
| ❑ 77 | Jason Campbell | .50 | .20 |
| ❑ 78 | Ron Dayne | .50 | .20 |
| ❑ 79 | Ashley Lelie | .50 | .20 |
| ❑ 80 | Drew Bennett | .50 | .20 |
| ❑ 81 | Brandon Lloyd | .50 | .20 |
| ❑ 82 | Trent Dilfer | .50 | .20 |
| ❑ 83 | Marty Booker | .40 | .15 |
| ❑ 84 | Aaron Rodgers | .60 | .25 |
| ❑ 85 | Deltha O'Neal | .50 | .20 |
| ❑ 86 | Jon Kitna | .50 | .20 |
| ❑ 87 | Doug Gabriel | .40 | .15 |
| ❑ 88 | Keenan McCardell | .50 | .20 |
| ❑ 89 | Brian Griese | .50 | .20 |
| ❑ 90 | Michael Jenkins | .50 | .20 |
| ❑ 91 | Brian Westbrook | .50 | .20 |
| ❑ 92 | Terrence Holt | .40 | .15 |
| ❑ 93 | Justin Gage | .40 | .15 |
| ❑ 94 | Shayne Graham | .40 | .15 |
| ❑ 95 | D.J. Hackett | .50 | .20 |
| ❑ 96 | Kevan Barlow | .50 | .20 |
| ❑ 97 | Bob Sanders | .50 | .20 |
| ❑ 98 | Charles Rogers | .50 | .20 |
| ❑ 99 | Kevin Curtis | .50 | .20 |
| ❑ 100 | LaDainian Tomlinson | .75 | .30 |
| ❑ 101 | Plaxico Burress | .50 | .20 |
| ❑ 102 | Kyle Boller | .50 | .20 |
| ❑ 103 | Donald Driver | .50 | .20 |
| ❑ 104 | Jerome Mathis | .40 | .15 |
| ❑ 105 | Takeo Spikes | .40 | .15 |
| ❑ 106 | Tony Gonzalez | .50 | .20 |
| ❑ 107 | Keary Colbert | .50 | .20 |
| ❑ 108 | Derrick Burgess | .40 | .15 |
| ❑ 109 | T.J. Duckett | .40 | .15 |
| ❑ 110 | Chris Chambers | .40 | .15 |
| ❑ 111 | Cadillac Williams | .60 | .25 |
| ❑ 112 | Jerricho Cotchery | .40 | .15 |
| ❑ 113 | Ernest Wilford | .50 | .20 |
| ❑ 114 | Torry Holt | .50 | .20 |
| ❑ 115 | Corey Dillon | .50 | .20 |
| ❑ 116 | Chris Simms | .50 | .20 |
| ❑ 117 | Philip Rivers | .60 | .25 |
| ❑ 118 | LaVar Arrington | .60 | .25 |
| ❑ 119 | Andrew Walter | .50 | .20 |
| ❑ 120 | Joe Jurevicius | .50 | .20 |
| ❑ 121 | Kyle Vanden Bosch | .40 | .15 |
| ❑ 122 | London Fletcher | .40 | .15 |
| ❑ 123 | Deuce McAllister | .50 | .20 |
| ❑ 124 | Cedrick Wilson | .40 | .15 |
| ❑ 125 | Jason Witten | .50 | .20 |
| ❑ 126 | Troy Williamson | .50 | .20 |
| ❑ 127 | Dominic Rhodes | .50 | .20 |
| ❑ 128 | Koren Robinson | .40 | .15 |
| ❑ 129 | Eli Manning | .75 | .30 |
| ❑ 130 | Brian Finneran | .40 | .15 |
| ❑ 131 | Fabian Washington | .40 | .15 |
| ❑ 132 | Michael Boulware | .40 | .15 |
| ❑ 133 | Bernard Berrian | .50 | .20 |
| ❑ 134 | Stephen Davis | .50 | .20 |
| ❑ 135 | Reggie Brown | .50 | .20 |
| ❑ 136 | Chad Johnson | .50 | .20 |
| ❑ 137 | Ronnie Brown | .60 | .25 |
| ❑ 138 | Amani Toomer | .50 | .20 |
| ❑ 139 | Deion Branch | .50 | .20 |
| ❑ 140 | Darren Sproles | .50 | .20 |
| ❑ 141 | L.J. Smith | .40 | .15 |
| ❑ 142 | Amaz Battle | .40 | .15 |
| ❑ 143 | Jerry Porter | .50 | .20 |
| ❑ 144 | Terry Glenn | .50 | .20 |
| ❑ 145 | Mike Vrabel | .50 | .20 |
| ❑ 146 | Chad Pennington | .50 | .20 |
| ❑ 147 | Allen Rossum | .40 | .15 |
| ❑ 148 | Greg Jones | .40 | .15 |
| ❑ 149 | Jake Delhomme | .50 | .20 |
| ❑ 150 | Tom Brady | 1.00 | .40 |
| ❑ 151 | Neil Rackers | .40 | .15 |
| ❑ 152 | Charles Woodson | .50 | .20 |
| ❑ 153 | Carson Palmer | .60 | .25 |
| ❑ 154 | Kerry Collins | .50 | .20 |
| ❑ 155 | Brian Urlacher | .60 | .25 |
| ❑ 156 | Kevin Jones | .50 | .20 |
| ❑ 157 | Eric Parker | .40 | .15 |
| ❑ 158 | Daniel Graham | .40 | .15 |
| ❑ 159 | Dallas Clark | .50 | .20 |
| ❑ 160 | Matt Schaub | .50 | .20 |
| ❑ 161 | Drew Brees | .60 | .25 |
| ❑ 162 | Andre Johnson | .50 | .20 |
| ❑ 163 | Ray Lewis | .60 | .25 |
| ❑ 164 | Cato June | .40 | .15 |
| ❑ 165 | J.J. Arrington | .50 | .20 |
| ❑ 166 | Warren Sapp | .50 | .20 |
| ❑ 167 | T.J. Houshmandzadeh | .50 | .20 |
| ❑ 168 | Donnie Edwards | .40 | .15 |
| ❑ 169 | Thomas Jones | .50 | .20 |
| ❑ 170 | Mark Clayton | .50 | .20 |
| ❑ 171 | Kyle Orton | .40 | .15 |
| ❑ 172 | Najeh Davenport | .50 | .20 |
| ❑ 173 | Dan Morgan | .40 | .15 |
| ❑ 174 | David Pollack | .50 | .20 |
| ❑ 175 | D.J. Williams | .50 | .20 |
| ❑ 176 | Julius Jones | .50 | .20 |
| ❑ 177 | Roy Williams WR | .60 | .25 |
| ❑ 178 | Willis McGahee | .60 | .25 |
| ❑ 179 | Keyshawn Johnson | .50 | .20 |
| ❑ 180 | Dennis Northcutt | .40 | .15 |
| ❑ 181 | Courtney Roby | .40 | .15 |
| ❑ 182 | Jonathan Ogden | .40 | .15 |
| ❑ 183 | Kellen Winslow | .60 | .25 |
| ❑ 184 | Matt Jones | .50 | .20 |
| ❑ 185 | Robert Gallery | .40 | .15 |
| ❑ 186 | Mike Anderson | .50 | .20 |
| ❑ 187 | Frank Gore | .60 | .25 |
| ❑ 188 | Jimmy Smith | .50 | .20 |
| ❑ 189 | Antonio Pierce | .40 | .15 |
| ❑ 190 | Todd Heap | .50 | .20 |
| ❑ 191 | Champ Bailey | .50 | .20 |
| ❑ 192 | Roddy White | .40 | .15 |
| ❑ 193 | Rod Smith | .50 | .20 |
| ❑ 194 | Brian Dawkins | .50 | .20 |
| ❑ 195 | Larry Johnson | .50 | .20 |
| ❑ 196 | Ed Reed | .50 | .20 |
| ❑ 197 | Marc Bulger | .50 | .20 |
| ❑ 198 | Zach Thomas | .60 | .25 |
| ❑ 199 | Cedric Houston | .40 | .15 |
| ❑ 200 | Brett Favre | 1.25 | .50 |
| ❑ 201 | Mark Brunell | .50 | .20 |
| ❑ 202 | Edgerrin James | .50 | .20 |
| ❑ 203 | Ronald Curry | .50 | .20 |
| ❑ 204 | Antonio Gates | .60 | .25 |
| ❑ 205 | Roscoe Parrish | .40 | .15 |
| ❑ 206 | Steve Smith | .60 | .25 |
| ❑ 207 | Reuben Droughns | .50 | .20 |
| ❑ 208 | Michael Vick | .60 | .25 |
| ❑ 209 | Chris Cooley | .50 | .20 |
| ❑ 210 | Chris Perry | .50 | .20 |
| ❑ 211 | Muhsin Muhammad | .50 | .20 |
| ❑ 212 | Trent Green | .50 | .20 |
| ❑ 213 | Matt Hasselbeck | .50 | .20 |
| ❑ 214 | Ben Roethlisberger | 1.00 | .40 |
| ❑ 215 | Tyrone Calico | .40 | .15 |
| ❑ 216 | Jamal Lewis | .50 | .20 |
| ❑ 217 | Antwaan Randle El | .50 | .20 |
| ❑ 218 | Byron Leftwich | .50 | .20 |
| ❑ 219 | Priest Holmes | .50 | .20 |
| ❑ 220 | Anquan Boldin | .50 | .20 |
| ❑ 221 | Drew Bledsoe | .60 | .25 |
| ❑ 222 | Randy McMichael | .40 | .15 |
| ❑ 223 | Tatum Bell | .50 | .20 |
| ❑ 224 | Daunte Culpepper | .60 | .25 |
| ❑ 225 | David Carr | .50 | .20 |
| ❑ 226 | Mark Bradley | .40 | .15 |
| ❑ 227 | Lee Evans | .50 | .20 |
| ❑ 228 | Domanick Davis | .50 | .20 |
| ❑ 229 | Robert Ferguson | .40 | .15 |
| ❑ 230 | Peter Warrick | .50 | .20 |
| ❑ 231 | Heath Miller | .50 | .20 |
| ❑ 232 | Derrick Brooks | .50 | .20 |
| ❑ 233 | Isaac Bruce | .50 | .20 |
| ❑ 234 | Aaron Brooks | .50 | .20 |
| ❑ 235 | Nate Burleson | .50 | .20 |
| ❑ 236 | Braylon Edwards | .60 | .25 |
| ❑ 237 | Ben Watson | .40 | .15 |
| ❑ 238 | Hines Ward | .60 | .25 |
| ❑ 239 | Shaun Alexander | .60 | .25 |
| ❑ 240 | Kurt Warner | .60 | .25 |
| ❑ 241 | Warrick Dunn | .50 | .20 |
| ❑ 242 | Rodney Harrison | .40 | .15 |
| ❑ 243 | Dante Hall | .50 | .20 |
| ❑ 244 | Tiki Barber | .60 | .25 |
| ❑ 245 | Santana Moss | .50 | .20 |
| ❑ 246 | Fred Taylor | .50 | .20 |
| ❑ 247 | Laveranues Coles | .50 | .20 |
| ❑ 248 | Darren Sharper | .40 | .15 |
| ❑ 249 | Brandon Stokley | .50 | .20 |
| ❑ 250 | Alge Crumpler | .50 | .20 |
| ❑ 251 | Derrick Mason | .50 | .20 |
| ❑ 252 | Antonio Bryant | .50 | .20 |
| ❑ 253 | Antrel Rolle | .40 | .15 |
| ❑ 254 | Eric Moulds | .50 | .20 |
| ❑ 255 | Bubba Franks | .40 | .15 |
| ❑ 256 | Joe Horn | .50 | .20 |
| ❑ 257 | Dunta Robinson | .50 | .20 |
| ❑ 258 | Larry Fitzgerald | .60 | .25 |
| ❑ 259 | Roy Williams S | .50 | .20 |
| ❑ 260 | Javon Walker | .50 | .20 |
| ❑ 261 | Alex Smith TE | .40 | .15 |
| ❑ 262 | Travis Henry | .50 | .20 |
| ❑ 263 | Luke McCown | .40 | .15 |
| ❑ 264 | James Farrior | .40 | .15 |
| ❑ 265 | Darrell Jackson | .50 | .20 |
| ❑ 266 | Marvin Harrison | .60 | .25 |
| ❑ 267 | Patrick Ramsey | .50 | .20 |
| ❑ 268 | Ernie Conwell | .40 | .15 |

| | | |
|---|---|---|
| ❑ 269 Ahman Green | .50 | .20 |
| ❑ 270 Ryan Moats | .50 | .20 |
| ❑ 271 Donovan McNabb | .60 | .25 |
| ❑ 272 Steven Jackson | .60 | .25 |
| ❑ 273 Ronde Barber | .50 | .20 |
| ❑ 274 Michael Strahan | .50 | .20 |
| ❑ 275 Dwight Freeney | .50 | .20 |
| ❑ 276 DeShaun Foster | .50 | .20 |
| ❑ 277 Terence Newman | .40 | .15 |
| ❑ 278 Rudi Johnson | .50 | .20 |
| ❑ 279 Shaun Alexander LL | .40 | .15 |
| ❑ 280 Tom Brady LL | .60 | .25 |
| ❑ 281 Steve Smith LL | .40 | .15 |
| ❑ 282 Tiki Barber LL | .40 | .15 |
| ❑ 283 Trent Green LL | .30 | .12 |
| ❑ 284 Santana Moss LL | .30 | .12 |
| ❑ 285 Larry Johnson LL | .30 | .12 |
| ❑ 286 Brett Favre LL | .75 | .30 |
| ❑ 287 Chad Johnson AP | .30 | .12 |
| ❑ 288 Peyton Manning AP | .60 | .25 |
| ❑ 289 Matt Hasselbeck AP | .30 | .12 |
| ❑ 290 Edgerrin James AP | .30 | .12 |
| ❑ 291 Shaun Alexander AP | .40 | .15 |
| ❑ 292 Larry Johnson AP | .30 | .12 |
| ❑ 293 Tiki Barber AP | .40 | .15 |
| ❑ 294 Marvin Harrison AP | .40 | .15 |
| ❑ 295 Santana Moss AP | .30 | .12 |
| ❑ 296 Chad Johnson AP | .30 | .12 |
| ❑ 297 Alge Crumpler AP | .30 | .12 |
| ❑ 298 LaDainian Tomlinson AP | .50 | .20 |
| ❑ 299 Derrick Brooks AP | .40 | .15 |
| ❑ 300 Antonio Gates AP | .40 | .15 |
| ❑ 301 Steve Smith AP | .40 | .15 |
| ❑ 302 Shawne Merriman AP | .30 | .12 |
| ❑ 303 Michael Vick AP | .40 | .15 |
| ❑ 304 Tony Gonzalez AP | .30 | .12 |
| ❑ 305 Jake Delhomme AP | .30 | .12 |
| ❑ 306 Steve McNair AP | .30 | .12 |
| ❑ 307 Larry Fitzgerald AP | .40 | .15 |
| ❑ 308 Ben Roethlisberger HL | .60 | .25 |
| ❑ 309 Seattle Seahawks HL | .60 | .25 |
| ❑ 310 Pittsburgh Steelers HL | .60 | .25 |
| ❑ 311 Tamba Hali RC | 1.50 | .60 |
| ❑ 312 Haloti Ngata RC | 1.50 | .60 |
| ❑ 313 Mike Hass RC | 1.50 | .60 |
| ❑ 314 Manny Lawson RC | 1.50 | .60 |
| ❑ 315 Reggie McNeal RC | 1.25 | .50 |
| ❑ 316 Kelly Jennings RC | 1.50 | .60 |
| ❑ 317 Jason Allen RC | 1.50 | .60 |
| ❑ 318 Joe Klopfenstein RC | 1.25 | .50 |
| ❑ 319 Willie Reid RC | 1.50 | .60 |
| ❑ 320 Brad Smith RC | 1.50 | .60 |
| ❑ 321 Bruce Gradkowski RC | 1.50 | .60 |
| ❑ 322 Ashton Youboty RC | 1.50 | .60 |
| ❑ 323 Abdul Hodge RC | 1.50 | .60 |
| ❑ 324 P.J. Daniels RC | 1.25 | .50 |
| ❑ 325 D'Qwell Jackson RC | 1.50 | .60 |
| ❑ 326 Johnathan Joseph RC | 1.25 | .50 |
| ❑ 327 Antonio Cromartie RC | 1.50 | .60 |
| ❑ 328 Elvis Dumervil RC | 1.00 | .40 |
| ❑ 329 Tye Hill RC | 1.50 | .60 |
| ❑ 330 Mathias Kiwanuka RC | 2.00 | .75 |
| ❑ 331 Leonard Pope RC | 1.50 | .60 |
| ❑ 332 DeMeco Ryans RC | 2.00 | .75 |
| ❑ 333 Brodrick Bunkley RC | 1.50 | .60 |
| ❑ 334 Devin Hester RC | 3.00 | 1.25 |
| ❑ 335 Thomas Howard RC | 1.50 | .60 |
| ❑ 336 Cory Rodgers RC | 1.50 | .60 |
| ❑ 337 Ernie Sims RC | 1.50 | .60 |
| ❑ 338 Todd Watkins RC | 1.25 | .50 |
| ❑ 339 Rocky McIntosh RC | 1.50 | .60 |
| ❑ 340 Donte Whitner RC | 1.50 | .60 |
| ❑ 341 Anthony Schlegel RC | 1.25 | .50 |
| ❑ 342 Kamerion Wimbley RC | 1.50 | .60 |
| ❑ 343 Wali Lundy RC | 1.50 | .60 |
| ❑ 344 Bobby Carpenter RC | 1.50 | .60 |
| ❑ 345 Jimmy Williams RC | 1.50 | .60 |
| ❑ 346 Michael Robinson RC | 1.50 | .60 |
| ❑ 347 Brandon Williams RC | 1.50 | .60 |
| ❑ 348 Skyler Green RC | 1.50 | .60 |
| ❑ 349 Jerious Norwood RC | 2.00 | .75 |
| ❑ 350 Travis Wilson RC | 1.50 | .60 |
| ❑ 351 Mario Williams RC | 2.50 | 1.00 |
| ❑ 352 Santonio Holmes RC | 4.00 | 1.50 |
| ❑ 353 Vince Young RC | 5.00 | 2.00 |
| ❑ 354 Matt Leinart RC | 5.00 | 2.00 |
| ❑ 355 D'Brickashaw Ferguson RC | 1.50 | .60 |

| | | |
|---|---|---|
| ❑ 356 Michael Huff RC | 1.50 | .60 |
| ❑ 357 Chad Greenway RC | 1.50 | .60 |
| ❑ 358 Chad Jackson RC | 1.25 | .50 |
| ❑ 359A Reggie Bush RC | 6.00 | 2.50 |
| ❑ 359B Reggie Bush RC | 6.00 | 2.50 |
| ❑ 360 A.J. Hawk RC | 3.00 | 1.25 |
| ❑ 361 DeAngelo Williams RC | 2.50 | 1.00 |
| ❑ 362 Derek Hagan RC | 1.50 | .60 |
| ❑ 363 Vernon Davis RC | 1.50 | .60 |
| ❑ 364 Joseph Addai RC | 5.00 | 2.00 |
| ❑ 365 Jay Cutler RC | 6.00 | 2.50 |
| ❑ 366 Jason Avant RC | 1.50 | .60 |
| ❑ 367 Brian Calhoun RC | 1.25 | .50 |
| ❑ 368 LenDale White RC | 3.00 | 1.25 |
| ❑ 369 Greg Jennings RC | 2.50 | 1.00 |
| ❑ 370 Charlie Whitehurst RC | 1.50 | .60 |
| ❑ 371 Sinorice Moss RC | 1.50 | .60 |
| ❑ 372 Maurice Stovall RC | 1.50 | .60 |
| ❑ 373 Laurence Maroney RC | 4.00 | 1.50 |
| ❑ 374 Brodie Croyle RC | 2.00 | .75 |
| ❑ 375 Demetrius Williams RC | 1.50 | .60 |
| ❑ 376 Jerome Harrison RC | 1.50 | .60 |
| ❑ 377 Maurice Drew RC | 3.00 | 1.25 |
| ❑ 378 Kellen Clemens RC | 2.00 | .75 |
| ❑ 379 Marcedes Lewis RC | 1.50 | .60 |
| ❑ 380 Leon Washington RC | 1.50 | .60 |
| ❑ 381 Anthony Fasano RC | 1.50 | .60 |
| ❑ 382 Jeremy Bloom RC | 1.25 | .50 |
| ❑ 383 Omar Jacobs RC | 1.25 | .50 |
| ❑ 384 Tarvaris Jackson RC | 1.50 | .60 |
| ❑ 385 Brandon Marshall RC | 2.00 | .75 |

## 2007 Topps

| | | |
|---|---|---|
| ❑ COMPLETE SET (440) | 50.00 | 25.00 |
| ❑ 1 Matt Leinart | .50 | .20 |
| ❑ 2 Kurt Warner | .50 | .20 |
| ❑ 3 Matt Schaub | .50 | .20 |
| ❑ 4 Michael Vick | .60 | .25 |
| ❑ 5 Kyle Boller | .40 | .15 |
| ❑ 6 Steve McNair | .50 | .20 |
| ❑ 7 J.P. Losman | .50 | .20 |
| ❑ 8 Jake Delhomme | .50 | .20 |
| ❑ 9 Rex Grossman | .50 | .20 |
| ❑ 10 Brian Griese | .50 | .20 |
| ❑ 11 Carson Palmer | .60 | .25 |
| ❑ 12 Charlie Frye | .50 | .20 |
| ❑ 13 Drew Bledsoe | .60 | .25 |
| ❑ 14 Tony Romo | 1.25 | .50 |
| ❑ 15 Joey Harrington | .50 | .20 |
| ❑ 16 Jay Cutler | .60 | .25 |
| ❑ 17 Jon Kitna | .40 | .15 |
| ❑ 18 Aaron Rodgers | .40 | .15 |
| ❑ 19 Brett Favre | 1.25 | .50 |
| ❑ 20 David Carr | .50 | .20 |
| ❑ 21 Peyton Manning | 1.00 | .40 |
| ❑ 22 David Garrard | .50 | .20 |
| ❑ 23 Byron Leftwich | .50 | .20 |
| ❑ 24 Trent Green | .50 | .20 |
| ❑ 25 Damon Huard | .50 | .20 |
| ❑ 26 Daunte Culpepper | .50 | .20 |
| ❑ 27 Tarvaris Jackson | .50 | .20 |
| ❑ 28 Tom Brady | 1.25 | .50 |
| ❑ 29 Drew Brees | .50 | .20 |
| ❑ 30 Eli Manning | .60 | .25 |
| ❑ 31 Chad Pennington | .50 | .20 |
| ❑ 32 Andrew Walter | .40 | .15 |
| ❑ 33 Aaron Brooks | .40 | .15 |
| ❑ 34 Donovan McNabb | .60 | .25 |
| ❑ 35 Jeff Garcia | .50 | .20 |

| | | |
|---|---|---|
| ❑ 36 Ben Roethlisberger | .75 | .30 |
| ❑ 37 Philip Rivers | .60 | .25 |
| ❑ 38 Alex Smith QB | .50 | .20 |
| ❑ 39 Matt Hasselbeck | .50 | .20 |
| ❑ 40 Seneca Wallace | .40 | .15 |
| ❑ 41 Marc Bulger | .50 | .20 |
| ❑ 42 Chris Simms | .40 | .15 |
| ❑ 43 Bruce Gradkowski | .40 | .15 |
| ❑ 44 Vince Young | .50 | .25 |
| ❑ 45 Jason Campbell | .50 | .20 |
| ❑ 46 Jared Lorenzen | .40 | .15 |
| ❑ 47 Mark Brunell | .50 | .20 |
| ❑ 48 J.J. Arrington | .50 | .20 |
| ❑ 49 Edgerrin James | .50 | .20 |
| ❑ 50 Jerious Norwood | .50 | .20 |
| ❑ 51 Warrick Dunn | .50 | .20 |
| ❑ 52 Mike Anderson | .50 | .20 |
| ❑ 53 Jamal Lewis | .50 | .20 |
| ❑ 54 Willis McGahee | .50 | .20 |
| ❑ 55 DeShaun Foster | .50 | .20 |
| ❑ 56 DeAngelo Williams | .60 | .25 |
| ❑ 57 Cedric Benson | .50 | .20 |
| ❑ 58 Thomas Jones | .50 | .20 |
| ❑ 59 Chris Perry | .40 | .15 |
| ❑ 60 Rudi Johnson | .50 | .20 |
| ❑ 61 Reuben Droughns | .50 | .20 |
| ❑ 62 Jerome Harrison | .40 | .15 |
| ❑ 63 Marion Barber | .50 | .20 |
| ❑ 64 Julius Jones | .50 | .20 |
| ❑ 65 Tatum Bell | .40 | .15 |
| ❑ 66 Mike Bell | .50 | .20 |
| ❑ 67 Kevin Jones | .40 | .15 |
| ❑ 68 Brian Calhoun | .40 | .15 |
| ❑ 69 Ahman Green | .50 | .20 |
| ❑ 70 Vernand Morency | .50 | .20 |
| ❑ 71 Ron Dayne | .50 | .20 |
| ❑ 72 Wali Lundy | .40 | .15 |
| ❑ 73 Dominic Rhodes | .50 | .20 |
| ❑ 74 Joseph Addai | .60 | .25 |
| ❑ 75 Fred Taylor | .50 | .20 |
| ❑ 76 Maurice Jones-Drew | .60 | .25 |
| ❑ 77 Larry Johnson | .60 | .25 |
| ❑ 78 Sammy Morris | .40 | .15 |
| ❑ 79 Ronnie Brown | .50 | .20 |
| ❑ 80 Mewelde Moore | .40 | .15 |
| ❑ 81 Chester Taylor | .40 | .15 |
| ❑ 82 Kevin Faulk | .40 | .15 |
| ❑ 83 Corey Dillon | .50 | .20 |
| ❑ 84 Laurence Maroney | .50 | .20 |
| ❑ 85 Deuce McAllister | .50 | .20 |
| ❑ 86 Reggie Bush | .75 | .30 |
| ❑ 87 Brandon Jacobs | .50 | .20 |
| ❑ 88 Anthony Thomas | .40 | .15 |
| ❑ 89 Cedric Houston | .40 | .15 |
| ❑ 90 Leon Washington | .50 | .20 |
| ❑ 91 Kevan Barlow | .50 | .20 |
| ❑ 92 LaMont Jordan | .50 | .20 |
| ❑ 93 Justin Fargas | .40 | .15 |
| ❑ 94 Brian Westbrook | .50 | .20 |
| ❑ 95 Correll Buckhalter | .50 | .20 |
| ❑ 96 Willie Parker | .60 | .25 |
| ❑ 97 Najeh Davenport | .40 | .15 |
| ❑ 98 LaDainian Tomlinson | .75 | .30 |
| ❑ 99 Darren Sproles | .50 | .20 |
| ❑ 100 Frank Gore | .60 | .25 |
| ❑ 101 Michael Robinson | .50 | .20 |
| ❑ 102 Shaun Alexander | .50 | .20 |
| ❑ 103 Maurice Morris | .40 | .15 |
| ❑ 104 Steven Jackson | .60 | .25 |
| ❑ 105 Stephen Davis | .50 | .20 |
| ❑ 106 Cadillac Williams | .50 | .20 |
| ❑ 107 Travis Henry | .50 | .20 |
| ❑ 108 LenDale White | .50 | .20 |
| ❑ 109 Ladell Betts | .40 | .15 |
| ❑ 110 Clinton Portis | .50 | .20 |
| ❑ 111 Michael Turner | .50 | .20 |
| ❑ 112 T.J. Duckett | .40 | .15 |
| ❑ 113 Anquan Boldin | .50 | .20 |
| ❑ 114 Larry Fitzgerald | .60 | .25 |
| ❑ 115 Bryant Johnson | .40 | .15 |
| ❑ 116 Michael Jenkins | .40 | .15 |
| ❑ 117 Ashley Lelie | .50 | .20 |
| ❑ 118 Roddy White | .50 | .20 |
| ❑ 119 Mark Clayton | .50 | .20 |
| ❑ 120 Derrick Mason | .40 | .15 |
| ❑ 121 Demetrius Williams | .40 | .15 |
| ❑ 122 Peerless Price | .40 | .15 |

| | | |
|---|---|---|
| ❏ 123 Lee Evans | .50 | .20 |
| ❏ 124 Drew Carter | .40 | .15 |
| ❏ 125 Keyshawn Johnson | .50 | .20 |
| ❏ 126 Steve Smith | .50 | .20 |
| ❏ 127 Bernard Berrian | .40 | .15 |
| ❏ 128 Mark Bradley | .40 | .15 |
| ❏ 129 Muhsin Muhammad | .50 | .20 |
| ❏ 130 Chad Johnson | .50 | .20 |
| ❏ 131 T.J. Houshmandzadeh | .50 | .20 |
| ❏ 132 Chris Henry | .40 | .15 |
| ❏ 133 Joe Jurevicius | .40 | .15 |
| ❏ 134 Braylon Edwards | .50 | .20 |
| ❏ 135 Terrell Owens | .60 | .25 |
| ❏ 136 Terry Glenn | .50 | .20 |
| ❏ 137 Skyler Green | .40 | .15 |
| ❏ 138 Rod Smith | .40 | .15 |
| ❏ 139 Javon Walker | .50 | .20 |
| ❏ 140 Brandon Marshall | .50 | .20 |
| ❏ 141 Mike Furrey | .40 | .15 |
| ❏ 142 Mike Williams | .40 | .15 |
| ❏ 143 Roy Williams WR | .50 | .20 |
| ❏ 144 Donald Driver | .50 | .20 |
| ❏ 145 Greg Jennings | .50 | .20 |
| ❏ 146 Andre Johnson | .50 | .20 |
| ❏ 147 Eric Moulds | .50 | .20 |
| ❏ 148 Reggie Wayne | .50 | .20 |
| ❏ 149 Marvin Harrison | .60 | .25 |
| ❏ 150 Ernest Wilford | .40 | .15 |
| ❏ 151 Matt Jones | .50 | .20 |
| ❏ 152 Reggie Williams | .50 | .20 |
| ❏ 153 Eddie Kennison | .40 | .15 |
| ❏ 154 Samie Parker | .40 | .15 |
| ❏ 155 Marty Booker | .40 | .15 |
| ❏ 156 Chris Chambers | .50 | .20 |
| ❏ 157 Wes Welker | .60 | .25 |
| ❏ 158 Travis Taylor | .40 | .15 |
| ❏ 159 Troy Williamson | .40 | .15 |
| ❏ 160 Reche Caldwell | .40 | .15 |
| ❏ 161 Chad Jackson | .50 | .20 |
| ❏ 162 Devery Henderson | .50 | .20 |
| ❏ 163 Joe Horn | .50 | .20 |
| ❏ 164 Marques Colston | .60 | .25 |
| ❏ 165 Plaxico Burress | .50 | .20 |
| ❏ 166 Amani Toomer | .50 | .20 |
| ❏ 167 Sinorice Moss | .40 | .15 |
| ❏ 168 Jerricho Cotchery | .40 | .15 |
| ❏ 169 Laveranues Coles | .50 | .20 |
| ❏ 170 Randy Moss | .60 | .25 |
| ❏ 171 Ronald Curry | .50 | .20 |
| ❏ 172 Donte Stallworth | .50 | .20 |
| ❏ 173 Reggie Brown | .50 | .20 |
| ❏ 174 Hines Ward | .60 | .25 |
| ❏ 175 Nate Washington | .40 | .15 |
| ❏ 176 Santonio Holmes | .50 | .20 |
| ❏ 177 Keenan McCardell | .40 | .15 |
| ❏ 178 Eric Parker | .40 | .15 |
| ❏ 179 Amaz Battle | .40 | .15 |
| ❏ 180 Antonio Bryant | .50 | .20 |
| ❏ 181 D.J. Hackett | .40 | .15 |
| ❏ 182 Deion Branch | .50 | .20 |
| ❏ 183 Darrell Jackson | .50 | .20 |
| ❏ 184 Kevin Curtis | .40 | .15 |
| ❏ 185 Torry Holt | .50 | .20 |
| ❏ 186 Isaac Bruce | .50 | .20 |
| ❏ 187 Michael Clayton | .50 | .20 |
| ❏ 188 Joey Galloway | .50 | .20 |
| ❏ 189 Drew Bennett | .40 | .15 |
| ❏ 190 Bobby Wade | .40 | .15 |
| ❏ 191 Antwaan Randle El | .50 | .20 |
| ❏ 192 Santana Moss | .50 | .20 |
| ❏ 193 Roscoe Parrish | .40 | .15 |
| ❏ 194 Leonard Pope | .40 | .15 |
| ❏ 195 Alge Crumpler | .40 | .15 |
| ❏ 196 Todd Heap | .50 | .20 |
| ❏ 197 Desmond Clark | .40 | .15 |
| ❏ 198 Kellen Winslow | .50 | .20 |
| ❏ 199 Jason Witten | .50 | .20 |
| ❏ 200 Marcus Pollard | .40 | .15 |
| ❏ 201 Bubba Franks | .40 | .15 |
| ❏ 202 Dallas Clark | .40 | .15 |
| ❏ 203 George Wrighster | .40 | .15 |
| ❏ 204 Tony Gonzalez | .50 | .20 |
| ❏ 205 Randy McMichael | .40 | .15 |
| ❏ 206 Jermaine Wiggins | .40 | .15 |
| ❏ 207 Ben Watson | .50 | .20 |
| ❏ 208 Ernie Conwell | .40 | .15 |
| ❏ 209 Jeremy Shockey | .50 | .20 |
| ❏ 210 L.J. Smith | .40 | .15 |
| ❏ 211 Heath Miller | .40 | .15 |
| ❏ 212 Antonio Gates | .50 | .20 |
| ❏ 213 Vernon Davis | .50 | .20 |
| ❏ 214 Jerramy Stevens | .40 | .15 |
| ❏ 215 Joe Klopfenstein | .40 | .15 |
| ❏ 216 Alex Smith TE | .40 | .15 |
| ❏ 217 Bo Scaife | .40 | .15 |
| ❏ 218 Anthony Becht | .40 | .15 |
| ❏ 219 Chris Cooley | .50 | .20 |
| ❏ 220 Robbie Gould | .40 | .15 |
| ❏ 221 Adam Vinatieri | .50 | .20 |
| ❏ 222 Devin Hester | .60 | .25 |
| ❏ 223 Justin Miller | .40 | .15 |
| ❏ 224 Sean Taylor | .40 | .15 |
| ❏ 225 DeAngelo Hall | .50 | .20 |
| ❏ 226 Chris McAlister | .40 | .15 |
| ❏ 227 Nate Clements | .40 | .15 |
| ❏ 228 Chris Gamble | .40 | .15 |
| ❏ 229 Ricky Manning | .40 | .15 |
| ❏ 230 Charles Tillman | .40 | .15 |
| ❏ 231 Deltha O'Neal | .40 | .15 |
| ❏ 232 Terence Newman | .40 | .15 |
| ❏ 233 Champ Bailey | .50 | .20 |
| ❏ 234 Charles Woodson | .50 | .20 |
| ❏ 235 Dunta Robinson | .40 | .15 |
| ❏ 236 Rasheah Mathis | .40 | .15 |
| ❏ 237 Antoine Winfield | .40 | .15 |
| ❏ 238 Asante Samuel | .40 | .15 |
| ❏ 239 Nnamdi Asomugha | .40 | .15 |
| ❏ 240 Lito Sheppard | .40 | .15 |
| ❏ 241 Walt Harris | .40 | .15 |
| ❏ 242 Tye Hill | .40 | .15 |
| ❏ 243 Ronde Barber | .40 | .15 |
| ❏ 244 Quentin Jammer | .40 | .15 |
| ❏ 245 Ed Reed | .50 | .20 |
| ❏ 246 Roy Williams S | .50 | .20 |
| ❏ 247 Troy Polamalu | .50 | .25 |
| ❏ 248 Brian Dawkins | .50 | .20 |
| ❏ 249 Terrell Suggs | .40 | .15 |
| ❏ 250 Aaron Schobel | .40 | .15 |
| ❏ 251 Julius Peppers | .50 | .20 |
| ❏ 252 Alex Brown | .40 | .15 |
| ❏ 253 Kamerion Wimbley | .40 | .15 |
| ❏ 254 DeMarcus Ware | .50 | .20 |
| ❏ 255 Elvis Dumervil | .40 | .15 |
| ❏ 256 Mario Williams | .50 | .20 |
| ❏ 257 Dwight Freeney | .50 | .20 |
| ❏ 258 Tamba Hali | .40 | .15 |
| ❏ 259 Jason Taylor | .50 | .20 |
| ❏ 260 Michael Strahan | .50 | .20 |
| ❏ 261 Aaron Kampman | .50 | .20 |
| ❏ 262 Derrick Burgess | .40 | .15 |
| ❏ 263 Leonard Little | .40 | .15 |
| ❏ 264 Ty Warren | .40 | .15 |
| ❏ 265 Warren Sapp | .50 | .20 |
| ❏ 266 Luis Castillo | .40 | .15 |
| ❏ 267 Keith Brooking | .40 | .15 |
| ❏ 268 Ray Lewis | .60 | .25 |
| ❏ 269 London Fletcher | .40 | .15 |
| ❏ 270 Brian Urlacher | .60 | .25 |
| ❏ 271 Ernie Sims | .40 | .15 |
| ❏ 272 A.J. Hawk | .60 | .25 |
| ❏ 273 DeMeco Ryans | .50 | .20 |
| ❏ 274 Cato June | .40 | .15 |
| ❏ 275 Derrick Johnson LB | .40 | .15 |
| ❏ 276 Zach Thomas | .50 | .20 |
| ❏ 277 Antonio Pierce | .40 | .15 |
| ❏ 278 Jonathan Vilma | .50 | .20 |
| ❏ 279 James Farrior | .40 | .15 |
| ❏ 280 Shawne Merriman | .50 | .20 |
| ❏ 281 Lofa Tatupu | .50 | .20 |
| ❏ 282 Derrick Brooks | .50 | .20 |
| ❏ 283 Jonathan Ogden | .40 | .15 |
| ❏ 284 Steve Hutchinson | .40 | .15 |
| ❏ 285 Walter Jones | .40 | .15 |
| ❏ 286 JaMarcus Russell RC | 4.00 | 1.50 |
| ❏ 287 Brady Quinn RC | 5.00 | 2.00 |
| ❏ 288 Drew Stanton RC | 1.50 | .60 |
| ❏ 289 Troy Smith RC | 2.00 | .75 |
| ❏ 290 Kevin Kolb RC | 2.50 | 1.00 |
| ❏ 291 Trent Edwards RC | 4.00 | 1.50 |
| ❏ 292 John Beck RC | 1.50 | .60 |
| ❏ 293 Jordan Palmer RC | 1.50 | .60 |
| ❏ 294 Chris Leak RC | 1.25 | .50 |
| ❏ 295 Isaiah Stanback RC | 1.50 | .60 |
| ❏ 296 Tyler Palko RC | 1.50 | .60 |
| ❏ 297 Jared Zabransky RC | 1.50 | .60 |
| ❏ 298 Jeff Rowe RC | 1.25 | .60 |
| ❏ 299 Zac Taylor RC | 1.50 | .60 |
| ❏ 300 Lester Ricard RC | 3.00 | 1.25 |
| ❏ 301 Adrian Peterson RC | 12.00 | 5.00 |
| ❏ 302 Marshawn Lynch RC | 3.00 | 1.25 |
| ❏ 303 Brandon Jackson RC | 1.50 | .60 |
| ❏ 304 Michael Bush RC | 1.50 | .60 |
| ❏ 305 Kenny Irons RC | 1.50 | .60 |
| ❏ 306 Antonio Pittman RC | 1.50 | .60 |
| ❏ 307 Tony Hunt RC | 1.50 | .60 |
| ❏ 308 Darius Walker RC | 1.50 | .60 |
| ❏ 309 Dwayne Wright RC | 1.25 | .50 |
| ❏ 310 Lorenzo Booker RC | 1.50 | .60 |
| ❏ 311 Kenneth Darby RC | 1.50 | .60 |
| ❏ 312 Chris Henry RC | 1.50 | .60 |
| ❏ 313 Selvin Young RC | 2.50 | 1.00 |
| ❏ 314 Brian Leonard RC | 1.50 | .60 |
| ❏ 315 Ahmad Bradshaw RC | 2.00 | .75 |
| ❏ 316 Gary Russell RC | 1.50 | .60 |
| ❏ 317 Kolby Smith RC | 1.50 | .60 |
| ❏ 318 Thomas Clayton RC | 1.25 | .50 |
| ❏ 319 Garrett Wolfe RC | 1.50 | .60 |
| ❏ 320 Calvin Johnson RC | 4.00 | 1.50 |
| ❏ 321 Ted Ginn Jr. RC | 2.50 | 1.00 |
| ❏ 322 Dwayne Jarrett RC | 1.50 | .60 |
| ❏ 323 Dwayne Bowe RC | 3.00 | 1.25 |
| ❏ 324 Sidney Rice RC | 1.50 | .60 |
| ❏ 325 Robert Meachem RC | 1.50 | .60 |
| ❏ 326 Anthony Gonzalez RC | 2.50 | 1.00 |
| ❏ 327 Craig Buster Davis RC | 1.50 | .60 |
| ❏ 328 Aundrae Allison RC | 1.25 | .50 |
| ❏ 329 Chansi Stuckey RC | 1.25 | .50 |
| ❏ 330 David Clowney RC | 1.25 | .50 |
| ❏ 331 Steve Smith USC RC | 2.00 | .75 |
| ❏ 332 Courtney Taylor RC | 1.25 | .50 |
| ❏ 333 Paul Williams RC | 1.25 | .50 |
| ❏ 334 Johnnie Lee Higgins RC | 1.25 | .50 |
| ❏ 335 Rhema McKnight RC | 1.25 | .50 |
| ❏ 336 Jason Hill RC | 1.50 | .60 |
| ❏ 337 Dallas Baker RC | 1.25 | .50 |
| ❏ 338 Greg Olsen RC | 2.00 | .75 |
| ❏ 339 Yamon Figurs RC | 1.50 | .60 |
| ❏ 340 Scott Chandler RC | 1.25 | .50 |
| ❏ 341 Matt Spaeth RC | 1.50 | .60 |
| ❏ 342 Ben Patrick RC | 1.25 | .50 |
| ❏ 343 Clark Harris RC | 1.50 | .60 |
| ❏ 344 Martrez Milner RC | 1.25 | .50 |
| ❏ 345 Joe Newton RC | 1.50 | .60 |
| ❏ 346 Alan Branch RC | 1.25 | .50 |
| ❏ 347 Amobi Okoye RC | 1.50 | .60 |
| ❏ 348 DeMarcus Tank Tyler RC | 1.25 | .50 |
| ❏ 349 Justin Harrell RC | 1.50 | .60 |
| ❏ 350 Brandon Mebane RC | 1.25 | .50 |
| ❏ 351 Gaines Adams RC | 1.50 | .60 |
| ❏ 352 Jamaal Anderson RC | 1.50 | .60 |
| ❏ 353 Adam Carriker RC | 1.25 | .50 |
| ❏ 354 Jarvis Moss RC | 1.50 | .60 |
| ❏ 355 Charles Johnson RC | 1.00 | .40 |
| ❏ 356 Anthony Spencer RC | 1.50 | .60 |
| ❏ 357 Quentin Moses RC | 1.25 | .50 |
| ❏ 358 LaMarr Woodley RC | 1.50 | .60 |
| ❏ 359 Victor Abiarmi RC | 1.50 | .60 |
| ❏ 360 Ray McDonald RC | 1.25 | .50 |
| ❏ 361 Tim Crowder RC | 1.50 | .50 |
| ❏ 362 Patrick Willis RC | 3.00 | 1.25 |
| ❏ 363 Brandon Siler RC | 1.25 | .50 |
| ❏ 364 David Harris RC | 1.25 | .50 |
| ❏ 365 Buster Davis RC | 1.50 | .60 |
| ❏ 366 Lawrence Timmons RC | 1.50 | .60 |
| ❏ 367 Paul Posluszny RC | 2.00 | .75 |
| ❏ 368 Jon Beason RC | 1.50 | .60 |
| ❏ 369 Rufus Alexander RC | 1.50 | .60 |
| ❏ 370 Earl Everett RC | 1.25 | .50 |
| ❏ 371 Stewart Bradley RC | 1.50 | .60 |
| ❏ 372 Prescott Burgess RC | 1.25 | .50 |
| ❏ 373 Leon Hall RC | 1.50 | .60 |
| ❏ 374 Darrelle Revis RC | 1.50 | .60 |
| ❏ 375 Aaron Ross RC | 1.50 | .60 |
| ❏ 376 Daymeion Hughes RC | 1.25 | .50 |
| ❏ 377 Marcus McCauley RC | 1.25 | .50 |
| ❏ 378 Chris Houston RC | 1.25 | .50 |
| ❏ 379 Tanard Jackson RC | 1.00 | .40 |
| ❏ 380 Jonathan Wade RC | 1.25 | .50 |
| ❏ 381 Josh Wilson RC | 1.25 | .50 |
| ❏ 382 Eric Wright RC | 1.50 | .60 |
| ❏ 383 A.J. Davis RC | 1.00 | .40 |
| ❏ 384 David Irons RC | 1.00 | .40 |
| ❏ 385 LaRon Landry RC | 2.00 | .75 |
| ❏ 386 Reggie Nelson RC | 1.25 | .50 |

|  |  | | |
|---|---|---|---|
| ❏ 387 | Michael Griffin RC | 1.50 | .60 |
| ❏ 388 | Brandon Meriweather RC | 1.50 | .60 |
| ❏ 389 | Eric Weddle RC | 1.25 | .50 |
| ❏ 390 | Aaron Rouse RC | 1.50 | .60 |
| ❏ 391 | Josh Gattis RC | 1.00 | .40 |
| ❏ 392 | Joe Thomas RC | 1.50 | .60 |
| ❏ 393 | Lavi Brown RC | 1.50 | .60 |
| ❏ 394 | Tony Ugoh RC | 1.25 | .50 |
| ❏ 395 | Ryan Kalil RC | 1.25 | .50 |
| ❏ 396 | Peyton Manning LL | .75 | .30 |
| ❏ 397 | Marc Bulger LL | .50 | .20 |
| ❏ 398 | LaDainian Tomlinson LL | .60 | .25 |
| ❏ 399 | Larry Johnson LL | .40 | .15 |
| ❏ 400 | Frank Gore LL | .50 | .20 |
| ❏ 401 | Chad Johnson LL | .40 | .15 |
| ❏ 402 | Marvin Harrison LL | .50 | .20 |
| ❏ 403 | Reggie Wayne LL | .40 | .15 |
| ❏ 404 | LaDainian Tomlinson LL | .60 | .25 |
| ❏ 405 | Peyton Manning PB | .75 | .30 |
| ❏ 406 | Marvin Harrison PB | .50 | .20 |
| ❏ 407 | LaDainian Tomlinson PB | .60 | .25 |
| ❏ 408 | Reggie Wayne PB | .40 | .15 |
| ❏ 409 | Antonio Gates PB | .40 | .15 |
| ❏ 410 | Jeff Saturday PB | .30 | .12 |
| ❏ 411 | Jason Taylor PB | .30 | .12 |
| ❏ 412 | Shawne Merriman PB | .40 | .15 |
| ❏ 413 | Champ Bailey PB | .40 | .15 |
| ❏ 414 | Troy Polamalu PB | .50 | .20 |
| ❏ 415 | Drew Brees PB | .50 | .20 |
| ❏ 416 | Frank Gore PB | .50 | .20 |
| ❏ 417 | Tony Gonzalez PB | .40 | .15 |
| ❏ 418 | Steve Smith PB | .40 | .15 |
| ❏ 419 | Walter Jones PB | .30 | .12 |
| ❏ 420 | Devin Hester PB | .50 | .20 |
| ❏ 421 | Julius Peppers PB | .40 | .15 |
| ❏ 422 | Tony Romo PB | 1.00 | .40 |
| ❏ 423 | Ronde Barber PB | .30 | .12 |
| ❏ 424 | Larry Johnson PB | .40 | .15 |
| ❏ 425 | LaDainian Tomlinson MVP | .60 | .25 |
| ❏ 426 | Vince Young OROY | .50 | .20 |
| ❏ 427 | DeMeco Ryans DROY | .40 | .15 |
| ❏ 428 | P.Manning/R.Wayne PSH | .75 | .30 |
| ❏ 429 | Drew Brees LL | .40 | .15 |
| ❏ 430 | Asante Samuel PSH | .30 | .12 |
| ❏ 431 | New Orleans Saints PSH | .40 | .15 |
| ❏ 432 | Reggie Bush PSH | .60 | .25 |
| ❏ 433 | Peyton Manning PSH | .75 | .30 |
| ❏ 434 | Robbie Gould PSH | .30 | .12 |
| ❏ 435 | T.Jones/C.Benson PSH | .40 | .15 |
| ❏ 436 | Joseph Addai PSH | .50 | .20 |
| ❏ 437 | Tom Brady PSH | 1.00 | .40 |
| ❏ 438 | Colts Defense PSH | .40 | .15 |
| ❏ 439 | Adam Vinatieri PSH | .40 | .15 |
| ❏ 440 | Devin Hester PSH | .50 | .20 |
| ❏ RH41 | Peyton Manning RH | 6.00 | 2.50 |
| ❏ RH41A | Peyton Manning RH AU | 350.00 | 250.00 |
| ❏ SBMVP | P.Manning MVP FB/25 | 200.00 | 125.00 |

## 2008 Topps

| | | | |
|---|---|---|---|
| ❏ COMP.FACT.SET (445) | | 50.00 | 30.00 |
| ❏ COMP.COWBOY SET (445) | | 50.00 | 30.00 |
| ❏ COMP.GIANTS SET (445) | | 50.00 | 30.00 |
| ❏ COMP.PACKER SET (445) | | 50.00 | 30.00 |
| ❏ COMP.PATRIOT SET (445) | | 50.00 | 30.00 |
| ❏ COMPLETE SET (440) | | 50.00 | 25.00 |
| ❏ 1 | Drew Brees | .60 | .25 |
| ❏ 2 | Jon Kitna | .50 | .20 |
| ❏ 3 | Tom Brady | 1.00 | .40 |
| ❏ 4 | Chad Pennington | .50 | .20 |
| ❏ 5 | Steve McNair | .50 | .20 |
| ❏ 6 | Josh McCown | .40 | .15 |
| ❏ 7 | Matt Hasselbeck | .50 | .20 |

|  |  | | |
|---|---|---|---|
| ❏ 8 | David Garrard | .50 | .20 |
| ❏ 9 | Jay Cutler | .60 | .25 |
| ❏ 10 | Matt Schaub | .50 | .20 |
| ❏ 11 | Daunte Culpepper | .50 | .20 |
| ❏ 12 | Kellen Clemens | .50 | .20 |
| ❏ 13 | John Beck | .40 | .15 |
| ❏ 14 | Trent Edwards | .40 | .15 |
| ❏ 15 | Brodie Croyle | .50 | .20 |
| ❏ 16 | Trent Dilfer | .50 | .20 |
| ❏ 17 | Chris Redman | .40 | .15 |
| ❏ 18 | Peyton Manning | 1.00 | .40 |
| ❏ 19 | Carson Palmer | .60 | .25 |
| ❏ 20 | Ben Roethlisberger | .75 | .30 |
| ❏ 21 | Eli Manning | .60 | .25 |
| ❏ 22 | Tony Romo | 1.00 | .40 |
| ❏ 23 | Donovan McNabb | .60 | .25 |
| ❏ 24 | Joey Harrington | .40 | .15 |
| ❏ 25 | Jeff Garcia | .50 | .20 |
| ❏ 26 | Derek Anderson | .50 | .20 |
| ❏ 27 | Rex Grossman | .50 | .20 |
| ❏ 28 | Kyle Boller | .40 | .15 |
| ❏ 29 | Sage Rosenfels | .40 | .15 |
| ❏ 30 | JaMarcus Russell | .60 | .25 |
| ❏ 31 | Gus Frerotte | .40 | .15 |
| ❏ 32 | Luke McCown | .40 | .15 |
| ❏ 33 | Marc Bulger | .50 | .20 |
| ❏ 34A | Brett Favre | 1.50 | .60 |
| ❏ 34B | Brett Favre Lombardi | 300.00 | 150.00 |
| ❏ 34C | B.Favre Tractor Packers | 300.00 | 175.00 |
| ❏ 34D | Brett Favre Jets | 12.00 | 5.00 |
| ❏ 34E | B.Favre Tractor Jets/500 | 100.00 | 50.00 |
| ❏ 35 | Philip Rivers | | .25 |
| ❏ 36 | Vince Young | .60 | .25 |
| ❏ 37 | Kurt Warner | .50 | .20 |
| ❏ 38 | Cleo Lemon | .40 | .15 |
| ❏ 39 | Damon Huard | .40 | .15 |
| ❏ 40 | Jason Campbell | .50 | .20 |
| ❏ 41 | Brian Griese | .40 | .15 |
| ❏ 42 | Tarvaris Jackson | .50 | .20 |
| ❏ 43 | J.P. Losman | .40 | .15 |
| ❏ 44 | Troy Smith | .50 | .20 |
| ❏ 45 | Brady Quinn | .60 | .25 |
| ❏ 46 | Trent Green | .50 | .20 |
| ❏ 47 | Quinn Gray | .40 | .15 |
| ❏ 48 | Alex Smith QB | .50 | .20 |
| ❏ 49 | Todd Collins | .50 | .20 |
| ❏ 50 | Matt Moore | .50 | .20 |
| ❏ 51 | A.J. Feeley | .40 | .15 |
| ❏ 52 | Matt Leinart | .60 | .25 |
| ❏ 53 | Jake Delhomme | .50 | .20 |
| ❏ 54 | Steven Jackson | .60 | .25 |
| ❏ 55 | Willie Parker | .50 | .20 |
| ❏ 56 | Derrick Ward | .50 | .20 |
| ❏ 57 | Julius Jones | .50 | .20 |
| ❏ 58 | DeShaun Foster | .50 | .20 |
| ❏ 59 | Shaun Alexander | .50 | .20 |
| ❏ 60 | Reggie Bush | .60 | .25 |
| ❏ 61 | Clinton Portis | .50 | .20 |
| ❏ 62 | Ron Dayne | .50 | .20 |
| ❏ 63 | Maurice Jones-Drew | .50 | .20 |
| ❏ 64 | Warrick Dunn | .50 | .20 |
| ❏ 65 | Adrian Peterson | 1.25 | .50 |
| ❏ 66 | Brian Leonard | .40 | .15 |
| ❏ 67 | Jerious Norwood | .40 | .15 |
| ❏ 68 | Thomas Jones | .50 | .20 |
| ❏ 69 | LaDainian Tomlinson | .75 | .30 |
| ❏ 70 | Cedric Benson | .40 | .15 |
| ❏ 71 | Marion Barber | .60 | .25 |
| ❏ 72 | Brian Westbrook | .50 | .20 |
| ❏ 73 | LenDale White | .50 | .20 |
| ❏ 74 | Ronnie Brown | .50 | .20 |
| ❏ 75 | Travis Henry | .50 | .20 |
| ❏ 76 | Kenny Watson | .40 | .15 |
| ❏ 77 | Fred Taylor | .50 | .20 |
| ❏ 78 | Ryan Grant | .50 | .20 |
| ❏ 79 | Marshawn Lynch | .60 | .25 |
| ❏ 80 | Selvin Young | .40 | .15 |
| ❏ 81 | Joseph Addai | .50 | .20 |
| ❏ 82 | Laurence Maroney | .50 | .20 |
| ❏ 83 | Brandon Jacobs | .50 | .20 |
| ❏ 84 | Willis McGahee | .50 | .20 |
| ❏ 85 | Frank Gore | .50 | .20 |
| ❏ 86 | Edgerrin James | .50 | .20 |
| ❏ 87 | Kevin Jones | .40 | .15 |
| ❏ 88 | DeAngelo Williams | .50 | .20 |
| ❏ 89 | Jamal Lewis | .50 | .20 |
| ❏ 90 | Chester Taylor | .40 | .15 |
| ❏ 91 | Earnest Graham | .40 | .15 |
| ❏ 92 | Justin Fargas | .40 | .15 |
| ❏ 93 | Kolby Smith | .40 | .15 |
| ❏ 94 | Maurice Morris | .40 | .15 |

|  |  | | |
|---|---|---|---|
| ❏ 95 | Larry Johnson | .50 | .20 |
| ❏ 96 | LaMont Jordan | .40 | .15 |
| ❏ 97 | Kenton Keith | .40 | .15 |
| ❏ 98 | Jesse Chatman | .40 | .15 |
| ❏ 99 | Adrian Peterson Bears | .40 | .15 |
| ❏ 100 | Najeh Davenport | .40 | .15 |
| ❏ 101 | Rudi Johnson | .50 | .20 |
| ❏ 102 | Chris Brown | .40 | .15 |
| ❏ 103 | Aaron Stecker | .40 | .15 |
| ❏ 104 | Sammy Morris | .40 | .15 |
| ❏ 105 | Leon Washington | .40 | .15 |
| ❏ 106 | T.J. Duckett | .40 | .15 |
| ❏ 107 | Ladell Betts | .40 | .15 |
| ❏ 108 | Michael Turner | .50 | .20 |
| ❏ 109 | Correll Buckhalter | .50 | .20 |
| ❏ 110 | Ahmad Bradshaw | .50 | .20 |
| ❏ 111 | Greg Jennings | .50 | .20 |
| ❏ 112 | Torry Holt | .50 | .20 |
| ❏ 113 | T.J. Houshmandzadeh | .50 | .20 |
| ❏ 114 | Jerricho Cotchery | .40 | .15 |
| ❏ 115 | Derrick Mason | .40 | .15 |
| ❏ 116 | Kevin Curtis | .40 | .15 |
| ❏ 117 | Kevin Walter | .40 | .15 |
| ❏ 118 | Joey Galloway | .50 | .20 |
| ❏ 119 | Anquan Boldin | .50 | .20 |
| ❏ 120 | Santonio Holmes | .50 | .20 |
| ❏ 121 | Lee Evans | .50 | .20 |
| ❏ 122 | Dwayne Bowe | .50 | .20 |
| ❏ 123 | Laurent Robinson | .40 | .15 |
| ❏ 124 | Wes Welker | .60 | .25 |
| ❏ 125 | Roy Williams WR | .50 | .20 |
| ❏ 126 | Randy Moss | .60 | .25 |
| ❏ 127 | Plaxico Burress | .50 | .20 |
| ❏ 128 | Terrell Owens | .60 | .25 |
| ❏ 129 | Andre Johnson | .50 | .20 |
| ❏ 130 | Roddy White | .50 | .20 |
| ❏ 131 | Brandon Marshall | .50 | .20 |
| ❏ 132 | Donald Driver | .50 | .20 |
| ❏ 133 | Hines Ward | .60 | .25 |
| ❏ 134 | Ike Hilliard | .40 | .15 |
| ❏ 135 | James Jones | .40 | .15 |
| ❏ 136 | Calvin Johnson | .60 | .25 |
| ❏ 137 | Marques Colston | .50 | .20 |
| ❏ 138 | Reggie Wayne | .50 | .20 |
| ❏ 139 | Chad Johnson | .50 | .20 |
| ❏ 140 | Amani Toomer | .50 | .20 |
| ❏ 141 | Bernard Berrian | .50 | .20 |
| ❏ 142 | Steve Smith | .50 | .20 |
| ❏ 143 | Larry Fitzgerald | .60 | .25 |
| ❏ 144 | Chris Chambers | .50 | .20 |
| ❏ 145 | Braylon Edwards | .50 | .20 |
| ❏ 146 | David Patten | .40 | .15 |
| ❏ 147 | Bobby Engram | .40 | .15 |
| ❏ 148 | Shaun McDonald | .40 | .15 |
| ❏ 149 | Anthony Gonzalez | .50 | .20 |
| ❏ 150 | Sidney Rice | .50 | .20 |
| ❏ 151 | Santana Moss | .50 | .20 |
| ❏ 152 | Reggie Brown | .50 | .20 |
| ❏ 153 | Justin Gage | .40 | .15 |
| ❏ 154 | Isaac Bruce | .50 | .20 |
| ❏ 155 | Antwaan Randle El | .50 | .20 |
| ❏ 156 | Roydell Williams | .40 | .15 |
| ❏ 157 | Ronald Curry | .40 | .15 |
| ❏ 158 | Jerry Porter | .50 | .20 |
| ❏ 159 | Patrick Crayton | .50 | .20 |
| ❏ 160 | Donte Stallworth | .50 | .20 |
| ❏ 161 | Nate Burleson | .40 | .15 |
| ❏ 162 | Mike Furrey | .40 | .15 |
| ❏ 163 | Deion Branch | .50 | .20 |
| ❏ 164 | Bobby Wade | .40 | .15 |
| ❏ 165 | Laveranues Coles | .50 | .20 |
| ❏ 166 | Brandon Stokley | .40 | .15 |
| ❏ 167 | Reggie Williams | .50 | .20 |
| ❏ 168 | Vincent Jackson | .40 | .15 |
| ❏ 169 | Joe Jurevicius | .40 | .15 |
| ❏ 170 | Dennis Northcutt | .40 | .15 |
| ❏ 171 | Arnaz Battle | .40 | .15 |
| ❏ 172 | Steve Smith USC | .50 | .20 |
| ❏ 173 | Ted Ginn Jr. | .50 | .20 |
| ❏ 174 | Antonio Gates | .60 | .25 |
| ❏ 175 | Chris Cooley | .50 | .20 |
| ❏ 176 | Owen Daniels | .40 | .15 |
| ❏ 177 | Kellen Winslow | .50 | .20 |
| ❏ 178 | Tony Gonzalez | .50 | .20 |
| ❏ 179 | Jason Witten | .50 | .20 |
| ❏ 180 | Greg Olsen | .50 | .20 |
| ❏ 181 | Jeremy Shockey | .50 | .20 |
| ❏ 182 | Dallas Clark | .50 | .20 |
| ❏ 183 | Donald Lee | .40 | .15 |
| ❏ 184 | Heath Miller | .40 | .15 |
| ❏ 185 | Tony Scheffler | .40 | .15 |

|  |  | | |
|---|---|---|---|
| ❏ 186 | Desmond Clark | .40 | .15 |
| ❏ 187 | Vernon Davis | .40 | .15 |
| ❏ 188 | Alge Crumpler | .40 | .15 |
| ❏ 189 | Zach Miller | .50 | .20 |
| ❏ 190 | Randy McMichael | .40 | .15 |
| ❏ 191 | Bo Scaife | .40 | .15 |
| ❏ 192 | Chris Baker | .40 | .15 |
| ❏ 193 | Jeff King | .40 | .15 |
| ❏ 194 | Marcedes Lewis | .40 | .15 |
| ❏ 195 | Ben Watson | .40 | .15 |
| ❏ 196 | Albert Haynesworth | .40 | .15 |
| ❏ 197 | Kevin Williams | .40 | .15 |
| ❏ 198 | Pat Williams | .40 | .15 |
| ❏ 199 | Tommie Harris | .40 | .15 |
| ❏ 200 | Darnell Dockett | .40 | .15 |
| ❏ 201 | Vince Wilfork | .40 | .15 |
| ❏ 202 | Jamal Williams | .40 | .15 |
| ❏ 203 | Casey Hampton | .40 | .15 |
| ❏ 204 | Amobi Okoye | .40 | .15 |
| ❏ 205 | Patrick Kerney | .40 | .15 |
| ❏ 206 | Gaines Adams | .40 | .15 |
| ❏ 207 | Osi Umenyiora | .40 | .15 |
| ❏ 208 | Mario Williams | .50 | .20 |
| ❏ 209 | Jared Allen | .50 | .20 |
| ❏ 210 | Trent Cole | .40 | .15 |
| ❏ 211 | Aaron Kampman | .50 | .20 |
| ❏ 212 | Kyle Vanden Bosch | .40 | .15 |
| ❏ 213 | Elvis Dumervil | .50 | .20 |
| ❏ 214 | Jason Taylor | .50 | .20 |
| ❏ 215 | Aaron Schobel | .40 | .15 |
| ❏ 216 | Andre Carter | .40 | .15 |
| ❏ 217 | John Abraham | .40 | .15 |
| ❏ 218 | Justin Tuck | .50 | .20 |
| ❏ 219 | Michael Strahan | .40 | .15 |
| ❏ 220 | Kabeer Gbaja-Biamila | .40 | .15 |
| ❏ 221 | Adewale Ogunleye | .40 | .15 |
| ❏ 222 | Julius Peppers | .50 | .20 |
| ❏ 223 | Tamba Hali | .40 | .15 |
| ❏ 224 | Luis Castillo | .40 | .15 |
| ❏ 225 | Jon Beason | .40 | .15 |
| ❏ 226 | D.J. Williams | .40 | .15 |
| ❏ 227 | Ernie Sims | .40 | .15 |
| ❏ 228 | DeMarcus Ware | .50 | .20 |
| ❏ 229 | Nick Barnett | .40 | .15 |
| ❏ 230 | Patrick Willis | .50 | .20 |
| ❏ 231 | Mike Vrabel | .40 | .15 |
| ❏ 232 | Shawne Merriman | .50 | .20 |
| ❏ 233 | Greg Ellis | .40 | .15 |
| ❏ 234 | Thomas Howard | .40 | .15 |
| ❏ 235 | Brian Urlacher | .60 | .25 |
| ❏ 236 | Keith Bulluck | .40 | .15 |
| ❏ 237 | London Fletcher | .40 | .15 |
| ❏ 238 | DeMeco Ryans | .50 | .20 |
| ❏ 239 | David Harris | .40 | .15 |
| ❏ 240 | Angelo Crowell | .40 | .15 |
| ❏ 241 | James Harrison RC | 3.00 | 1.25 |
| ❏ 242 | Julian Peterson | .40 | .15 |
| ❏ 243 | Lance Briggs | .40 | .15 |
| ❏ 244 | Lofa Tatupu | .40 | .15 |
| ❏ 245 | Ray Lewis | .60 | .25 |
| ❏ 246 | Shaun Phillips | .40 | .15 |
| ❏ 247 | Antonio Pierce | .40 | .15 |
| ❏ 248 | Antonio Cromartie | .40 | .15 |
| ❏ 249 | Marcus Trufant | .40 | .15 |
| ❏ 250 | Asante Samuel | .40 | .15 |
| ❏ 251 | Anthony Henry | .40 | .15 |
| ❏ 252 | Leigh Bodden | .40 | .15 |
| ❏ 253 | Antrel Rolle | .40 | .15 |
| ❏ 254 | Roderick Hood | .40 | .15 |
| ❏ 255 | DeAngelo Hall | .40 | .15 |
| ❏ 256 | Dre Bly | .40 | .15 |
| ❏ 257 | Leon Hall | .40 | .15 |
| ❏ 258 | Ronde Barber | .40 | .15 |
| ❏ 259 | Al Harris | .40 | .15 |
| ❏ 260 | Terence Newman | .40 | .15 |
| ❏ 261 | Champ Bailey | .50 | .20 |
| ❏ 262 | Aaron Ross | .40 | .15 |
| ❏ 263 | Bob Sanders | .50 | .20 |
| ❏ 264 | Reggie Nelson | .40 | .15 |
| ❏ 265 | Marvin Harrison | .60 | .25 |
| ❏ 266 | Ed Reed | .50 | .20 |
| ❏ 267 | O.J. Atogwe | .40 | .15 |
| ❏ 268 | Ken Hamlin | .40 | .15 |
| ❏ 269 | Kerry Rhodes | .40 | .15 |
| ❏ 270 | Clinton Hart | .40 | .15 |
| ❏ 271 | Atari Bigby | .40 | .15 |
| ❏ 272 | Sean Jones | .40 | .15 |
| ❏ 273 | Darren Sharper | .40 | .15 |
| ❏ 274 | Roy Williams S | .50 | .20 |
| ❏ 275 | Troy Polamalu | .60 | .25 |
| ❏ 276 | John Lynch | .40 | .15 |
| ❏ 277 | Antoine Bethea | .40 | .15 |
| ❏ 278 | LaRon Landry | .50 | .20 |
| ❏ 279 | Walter Jones | .40 | .15 |
| ❏ 280 | Jonathan Vilma | .50 | .20 |
| ❏ 281 | Joe Thomas | .50 | .20 |
| ❏ 282 | Nick Folk | .40 | .15 |
| ❏ 283 | Rob Bironas | .40 | .15 |
| ❏ 284 | Devin Hester | .60 | .25 |
| ❏ 285 | Josh Cribbs | .50 | .20 |
| ❏ 286 | Tom Brady LL | .75 | .30 |
| ❏ 287 | Drew Brees LL | .50 | .20 |
| ❏ 288 | Tony Romo LL | .75 | .30 |
| ❏ 289 | LaDainian Tomlinson LL | .60 | .25 |
| ❏ 290 | Adrian Peterson LL | 1.00 | .40 |
| ❏ 291 | Brian Westbrook LL | .40 | .15 |
| ❏ 292 | Reggie Wayne LL | .40 | .15 |
| ❏ 293 | Randy Moss LL | .50 | .20 |
| ❏ 294 | Chad Johnson LL | .50 | .20 |
| ❏ 295 | Randy Moss PB | .50 | .20 |
| ❏ 296 | Matt Hasselbeck PB | .40 | .15 |
| ❏ 297 | Tony Romo PB | .75 | .30 |
| ❏ 298 | Adrian Peterson PB | 1.00 | .40 |
| ❏ 299 | Marion Barber PB | .40 | .15 |
| ❏ 300 | Brian Westbrook PB | .40 | .15 |
| ❏ 301 | Larry Fitzgerald PB | .50 | .20 |
| ❏ 302 | Terrell Owens PB | .50 | .20 |
| ❏ 303 | Osi Umenyiora PB | .40 | .15 |
| ❏ 304 | Lofa Tatupu PB | .40 | .15 |
| ❏ 305 | Jason Witten PB | .40 | .15 |
| ❏ 306 | Torry Holt PB | .40 | .15 |
| ❏ 307 | Donald Driver PB | .40 | .15 |
| ❏ 308 | Peyton Manning PB | .75 | .30 |
| ❏ 309 | Ben Roethlisberger PB | .60 | .25 |
| ❏ 310 | Joseph Addai PB | .50 | .20 |
| ❏ 311 | Reggie Wayne PB | .40 | .15 |
| ❏ 312 | Braylon Edwards PB | .40 | .15 |
| ❏ 313 | Devin Hester PB | .50 | .20 |
| ❏ 314 | Champ Bailey PB | .30 | .12 |
| ❏ 315 | Ed Reed PB | .40 | .15 |
| ❏ 316 | Eli Manning PSH | .50 | .20 |
| ❏ 317 | David Tyree PSH | .40 | .15 |
| ❏ 318 | Plaxico Burress PSH | .40 | .15 |
| ❏ 319 | Lawrence Tynes PSH | .40 | .15 |
| ❏ 320 | Patriots Defense PSH | .50 | .20 |
| ❏ 321 | R.W. McQuarters PSH | .40 | .15 |
| ❏ 322 | Ryan Grant PSH | .50 | .20 |
| ❏ 323 | Philip Rivers PSH | .50 | .20 |
| ❏ 324 | David Garrard PSH | .40 | .15 |
| ❏ 325 | Laurence Maroney PSH | .40 | .15 |
| ❏ 326 | Seattle Seahawks PSH | .40 | .15 |
| ❏ 327 | San Diego Chargers PSH | .40 | .15 |
| ❏ 328 | Tom Brady MVP | .75 | .30 |
| ❏ 329 | Adrian Peterson OROY | 1.00 | .40 |
| ❏ 330 | Patrick Willis DROY | .40 | .15 |
| ❏ 331 | Matt Ryan RC | 6.00 | 2.50 |
| ❏ 331B | Matt Ryan No Helm | 100.00 | 60.00 |
| ❏ 332 | Brian Brohm RC | 2.00 | .75 |
| ❏ 332B | Brian Brohm No Helm | 50.00 | 20.00 |
| ❏ 333 | Andre Woodson RC | 1.50 | .60 |
| ❏ 334 | Chad Henne RC | 2.50 | 1.00 |
| ❏ 335 | Joe Flacco RC | 5.00 | 2.00 |
| ❏ 336 | John David Booty RC | 2.00 | .75 |
| ❏ 337 | Colt Brennan RC | 4.00 | 1.50 |
| ❏ 338 | Dennis Dixon RC | 1.50 | .60 |
| ❏ 339 | Erik Ainge RC | 1.50 | .60 |
| ❏ 340 | Josh Johnson RC | 1.50 | .60 |
| ❏ 341 | Kevin O'Connell RC | 2.00 | .75 |
| ❏ 342 | Matt Flynn RC | 2.00 | .75 |
| ❏ 343 | Sam Keller RC | 1.50 | .60 |
| ❏ 344 | Harry Douglas RC | 1.50 | .60 |
| ❏ 345 | Anthony Morelli RC | 1.50 | .60 |
| ❏ 346 | Darren McFadden RC | 4.00 | 1.50 |
| ❏ 346B | Darren McFadden FB | 80.00 | 40.00 |
| ❏ 347 | Rashard Mendenhall RC | 3.00 | 1.25 |
| ❏ 347B | Rashard Mendenhall FB | 50.00 | 20.00 |
| ❏ 348 | Jonathan Stewart RC | 4.00 | 1.50 |
| ❏ 348B | Jonathan Stewart No Helm | 50.00 | 25.00 |
| ❏ 349 | Felix Jones RC | 4.00 | 1.50 |
| ❏ 350 | Jamaal Charles RC | 4.00 | 1.50 |
| ❏ 351 | Chris Johnson RC | 4.00 | 1.50 |
| ❏ 352 | Ray Rice RC | 2.00 | .75 |
| ❏ 353 | Mike Hart RC | 2.00 | .75 |
| ❏ 354 | Kevin Smith RC | 2.50 | 1.00 |
| ❏ 355 | Steve Slaton RC | 3.00 | 1.25 |
| ❏ 356 | Matt Forte RC | 4.00 | 1.50 |
| ❏ 357 | Tashard Choice RC | 1.50 | .60 |
| ❏ 358 | Dominique Rodgers-Cromartie RC | 1.50 | .60 |
| ❏ 359 | Cory Boyd RC | 1.25 | .50 |
| ❏ 360 | Allen Patrick RC | 1.25 | .50 |
| ❏ 361 | Thomas Brown RC | 1.50 | .60 |
| ❏ 362 | Justin Forsett RC | 1.50 | .60 |
| ❏ 363 | DeSean Jackson RC | 3.00 | 1.25 |
| ❏ 364 | Malcolm Kelly RC | 1.50 | .60 |
| ❏ 365 | Limas Sweed RC UER 362 | 2.00 | .75 |
| ❏ 366 | Mario Manningham RC | 1.50 | .60 |
| ❏ 367 | James Hardy RC | 1.50 | .60 |
| ❏ 368 | Early Doucet RC | 1.50 | .60 |
| ❏ 369 | Donnie Avery RC | 2.00 | .75 |
| ❏ 370 | Dexter Jackson RC | 1.50 | .60 |
| ❏ 371 | Devin Thomas RC | 1.50 | .60 |
| ❏ 372 | Jordy Nelson RC | 2.00 | .75 |
| ❏ 373 | Keenan Burton RC | 1.25 | .50 |
| ❏ 374 | Chris Williams RC | 1.25 | .50 |
| ❏ 375 | Earl Bennett RC | 1.50 | .60 |
| ❏ 376 | Jerome Simpson RC | 1.50 | .60 |
| ❏ 377 | Andre Caldwell RC | 1.25 | .50 |
| ❏ 378 | Josh Morgan RC | 1.50 | .60 |
| ❏ 379 | Fred Davis RC | 1.50 | .60 |
| ❏ 380 | John Carlson RC | 1.50 | .60 |
| ❏ 381 | Martellus Bennett RC | 1.50 | .60 |
| ❏ 382 | Martin Rucker RC | 1.25 | .50 |
| ❏ 383 | Jermichael Finley RC | 1.50 | .60 |
| ❏ 384 | Dustin Keller RC | 1.50 | .60 |
| ❏ 385 | Jacob Tamme RC | 1.50 | .60 |
| ❏ 386 | Kellen Davis RC | 1.00 | .40 |
| ❏ 387 | Jake Long RC | 2.00 | .75 |
| ❏ 388 | Sam Baker RC | 1.00 | .40 |
| ❏ 389 | Jeff Otah RC | 1.25 | .50 |
| ❏ 390 | Owen Schmitt RC | 1.50 | .60 |
| ❏ 391 | Chevis Jackson RC | 1.25 | .50 |
| ❏ 392 | Jacob Hester RC | 1.50 | .60 |
| ❏ 393 | Glenn Dorsey RC | 2.00 | .75 |
| ❏ 394 | Sedrick Ellis RC | 1.50 | .60 |
| ❏ 395 | Kentwan Balmer RC | 1.25 | .50 |
| ❏ 396 | Pat Sims RC | 1.25 | .50 |
| ❏ 397 | Marcus Harrison RC | 1.50 | .60 |
| ❏ 398 | Dre Moore RC | 1.25 | .50 |
| ❏ 399 | Red Bryant RC | 1.00 | .40 |
| ❏ 400 | Trevor Laws RC | 1.50 | .60 |
| ❏ 401 | Chris Long RC | 2.00 | .75 |
| ❏ 402 | Vernon Gholston RC | 1.25 | .50 |
| ❏ 403 | Derrick Harvey RC | 1.25 | .50 |
| ❏ 404 | Calais Campbell RC | 1.25 | .50 |
| ❏ 405 | Terrence Wheatley RC | 1.25 | .50 |
| ❏ 406 | Philip Merling RC | 1.25 | .50 |
| ❏ 407 | Chris Ellis RC | 1.25 | .50 |
| ❏ 408 | Lawrence Jackson RC | 1.25 | .50 |
| ❏ 409 | Dan Connor RC | 1.50 | .60 |
| ❏ 410 | Curtis Lofton RC | 1.50 | .60 |
| ❏ 411 | Jerod Mayo RC | 2.50 | 1.00 |
| ❏ 412 | Tavares Gooden RC | 1.25 | .50 |
| ❏ 413 | Beau Bell RC | 1.25 | .50 |
| ❏ 414 | Philip Wheeler RC | 1.25 | .50 |
| ❏ 415 | Vince Hall RC | 1.00 | .40 |
| ❏ 416 | Jonathan Goff RC | 1.25 | .50 |
| ❏ 417 | Keith Rivers RC | 1.50 | .60 |
| ❏ 418 | Ali Highsmith RC | 1.00 | .40 |
| ❏ 419 | Xavier Adibi RC | 1.25 | .50 |
| ❏ 420 | Erin Henderson RC | 1.25 | .50 |
| ❏ 421 | Bruce Davis RC | 1.50 | .60 |
| ❏ 422 | Jordon Dizon RC | 1.50 | .60 |
| ❏ 423 | Shawn Crable RC | 1.50 | .60 |
| ❏ 424 | Geno Hayes RC | 1.00 | .40 |
| ❏ 425 | Mike Jenkins RC | 1.50 | .60 |
| ❏ 426 | Aqib Talib RC | 1.50 | .60 |
| ❏ 427 | Leodis McKelvin RC | 1.50 | .60 |
| ❏ 428 | Terrell Thomas RC | 1.25 | .50 |
| ❏ 429 | Reggie Smith RC | 1.25 | .50 |
| ❏ 430 | Antoine Cason RC | 1.50 | .60 |
| ❏ 431 | Patrick Lee RC | 1.50 | .60 |
| ❏ 432 | Tracy Porter RC | 1.25 | .50 |
| ❏ 433 | Kenny Phillips RC | 1.50 | .60 |
| ❏ 434 | Simeon Castille RC | 1.50 | .60 |
| ❏ 435 | Eddie Royal RC | 3.00 | 1.25 |
| ❏ 436 | Thomas DeCoud RC | 1.00 | .40 |
| ❏ 437 | Marcus Griffin RC | 1.00 | .40 |
| ❏ 438 | Charles Godfrey RC | 1.25 | .50 |
| ❏ 439 | Tyrell Johnson RC | 1.50 | .60 |
| ❏ 440 | Jamar Adams RC | 1.00 | .40 |
| ❏ RH42 | Eli Manning RH | 6.00 | 2.50 |
| ❏ RHA42 | Eli Manning RH AU | 400.00 | 250.00 |
| ❏ SBAEM | Eli Manning FB AU | 350.00 | 200.00 |
| ❏ SBEM | Eli Manning FB/99 | 80.00 | 40.00 |

## 1996 Topps Chrome

|  |  | | |
|---|---|---|---|
| ❏ | COMPLETE SET (165) | 100.00 | 40.00 |
| ❏ 1 | Troy Aikman | 2.50 | 1.00 |
| ❏ 2 | Kevin Greene | .50 | .20 |
| ❏ 3 | Robert Brooks | 1.00 | .40 |
| ❏ 4 | Junior Seau | 1.00 | .40 |
| ❏ 5 | Brett Perriman | .20 | .07 |

| | | |
|---|---|---|
| ❏ 79 Deion Sanders | 1.25 | .50 |
| ❏ 80 Glyn Milburn | .20 | .07 |
| ❏ 81 Lee Woodall | .20 | .07 |
| ❏ 82 Neil Smith | .50 | .20 |
| ❏ 83 Stan Humphries | .50 | .20 |
| ❏ 84 Rick Mirer | .50 | .20 |
| ❏ 85 Troy Vincent | .20 | .07 |
| ❏ 86 Sam Mills | .20 | .07 |
| ❏ 87 Brian Mitchell | .20 | .07 |
| ❏ 88 Hardy Nickerson | .20 | .07 |
| ❏ 89 Tamarick Vanover | .50 | .20 |
| ❏ 90 Steve McNair | 1.50 | .60 |
| ❏ 91 Jerry Rice TYC | 1.00 | .40 |
| ❏ 92 Isaac Bruce TYC | 1.00 | .40 |
| ❏ 93 Herman Moore TYC | .50 | .20 |
| ❏ 94 Cris Carter TYC | 1.00 | .40 |
| ❏ 95 Tim Brown TYC | .50 | .20 |
| ❏ 96 Carl Pickens TYC | .50 | .20 |
| ❏ 97 Joey Galloway TYC | 1.00 | .40 |
| ❏ 98 Jerry Rice | 2.50 | 1.00 |
| ❏ 99 Cris Carter | 1.00 | .40 |
| ❏ 100 Curtis Martin | 1.50 | .60 |
| ❏ 101 Scott Mitchell | .50 | .20 |
| ❏ 102 Ken Harvey | .20 | .07 |
| ❏ 103 Rodney Hampton | .50 | .20 |
| ❏ 104 Reggie White | 1.00 | .40 |
| ❏ 105 Eddie Robinson | .20 | .07 |
| ❏ 106 Greg Lloyd | .50 | .20 |
| ❏ 107 Phillippi Sparks | .20 | .07 |
| ❏ 108 Emmitt Smith | 4.00 | 1.50 |
| ❏ 109 Tom Carter | .20 | .07 |
| ❏ 110 Jim Everett | .20 | .07 |
| ❏ 111 James O.Stewart | .50 | .20 |
| ❏ 112 Kyle Brady | .20 | .07 |
| ❏ 113 Irving Fryar | .50 | .20 |
| ❏ 114 Vinny Testaverde | .50 | .20 |
| ❏ 115 John Elway | 5.00 | 2.00 |
| ❏ 116 Chris Spielman | .20 | .07 |
| ❏ 117 Mike Mamula | .20 | .07 |
| ❏ 118 Jim Harbaugh | .50 | .20 |
| ❏ 119 Ken Norton | .20 | .07 |
| ❏ 120 Bruce Smith | .50 | .20 |
| ❏ 121 Daryl Johnston | .50 | .20 |
| ❏ 122 Blaine Bishop | .20 | .07 |
| ❏ 123 Jeff George | .50 | .20 |
| ❏ 124 Jeff Hostetler | .20 | .07 |
| ❏ 125 Jerome Bettis | 1.00 | .40 |
| ❏ 126 Jay Novacek | .20 | .07 |
| ❏ 127 Bryce Paup | .20 | .07 |
| ❏ 128 Neil O'Donnell | .50 | .20 |
| ❏ 129 Marcus Allen | 1.00 | .40 |
| ❏ 130 Steve Young | 1.50 | .60 |
| ❏ 131 Brett Favre TYC | 2.00 | .75 |
| ❏ 132 Scott Mitchell TYC | .20 | .07 |
| ❏ 133 John Elway TYC | 2.00 | .75 |
| ❏ 134 Jeff Blake TYC | .50 | .20 |
| ❏ 135 Dan Marino TYC | 2.00 | .75 |
| ❏ 136 Drew Bledsoe TYC | 1.00 | .40 |
| ❏ 137 Troy Aikman TYC | 1.00 | .40 |
| ❏ 138 Steve Young TYC | 1.00 | .40 |
| ❏ 139 Jim Kelly TYC | 1.00 | .40 |
| ❏ 140 Jeff Graham | .20 | .07 |
| ❏ 141 Hugh Douglas | .50 | .20 |
| ❏ 142 Dan Marino | 5.00 | 2.00 |
| ❏ 143 Darnell Green | .20 | .07 |
| ❏ 144 Eric Zeier | .20 | .07 |
| ❏ 145 Brett Favre | 5.00 | 2.00 |
| ❏ 146 Carnell Lake | .20 | .07 |
| ❏ 147 Ben Coates | .50 | .20 |
| ❏ 148 Tony Martin | .50 | .20 |
| ❏ 149 Michael Irvin | 1.00 | .40 |
| ❏ 150 Lawrence Phillips RC | 1.00 | .40 |
| ❏ 151 Alex Van Dyke RC | 1.50 | .60 |
| ❏ 152 Kevin Hardy RC | 1.50 | .60 |
| ❏ 153 Rickey Dudley RC | 5.00 | 2.00 |
| ❏ 154 Eric Moulds RC | 10.00 | 5.00 |
| ❏ 155 Simeon Rice RC | 4.00 | 1.50 |
| ❏ 156 Marvin Harrison RC | 30.00 | 15.00 |
| ❏ 157 Tim Biakabutuka RC | 4.00 | 1.50 |
| ❏ 158 Duane Clemons RC | 1.00 | .40 |
| ❏ 159 Keyshawn Johnson RC | 12.00 | 5.00 |
| ❏ 160 John Mobley RC | 1.50 | .60 |
| ❏ 161 Leeland McElroy RC | 1.50 | .60 |
| ❏ 162 Eddie George RC | 12.00 | 6.00 |
| ❏ 163 Jonathan Ogden RC | 2.00 | .75 |
| ❏ 164 Eddie Kennison RC | 5.00 | 2.00 |
| ❏ 165 Checklist | .20 | .07 |

| | | |
|---|---|---|
| ❏ COMPLETE SET (165) | 60.00 | 30.00 |
| ❏ 1 Brett Favre | 6.00 | 2.50 |
| ❏ 2 Tim Biakabutuka | 1.00 | .40 |
| ❏ 3 Deion Sanders | 1.50 | .60 |
| ❏ 4 Marshall Faulk | 2.00 | .75 |
| ❏ 5 John Randle | 1.00 | .40 |
| ❏ 6 Stan Humphries | 1.00 | .40 |
| ❏ 7 Ki-Jana Carter | .60 | .25 |
| ❏ 8 Rashaan Salaam | .60 | .25 |
| ❏ 9 Rickey Dudley | 1.00 | .40 |
| ❏ 10 Isaac Bruce | 1.50 | .60 |
| ❏ 11 Keyshawn Johnson | 1.50 | .60 |
| ❏ 12 Ben Coates | 1.00 | .40 |
| ❏ 13 Ty Detmer | 1.00 | .40 |
| ❏ 14 Gus Frerotte | .60 | .25 |
| ❏ 15 Mario Bates | .60 | .25 |
| ❏ 16 Chris Calloway | .60 | .25 |
| ❏ 17 Frank Sanders | 1.00 | .40 |
| ❏ 18 Bruce Smith | 1.00 | .40 |
| ❏ 19 Jeff Graham | .60 | .25 |
| ❏ 20 Trent Dilfer | 1.50 | .60 |
| ❏ 21 Tyrone Wheatley | 1.00 | .40 |
| ❏ 22 Chris Warren | 1.00 | .40 |
| ❏ 23 Terry Kirby | 1.00 | .40 |
| ❏ 24 Tony Gonzalez RC | 8.00 | 3.00 |
| ❏ 25 Ricky Watters | 1.00 | .40 |
| ❏ 26 Tamarick Vanover | 1.00 | .40 |
| ❏ 27 Kerry Collins | 1.50 | .60 |
| ❏ 28 Bobby Engram | 1.00 | .40 |
| ❏ 29 Derrick Alexander WR | 1.00 | .40 |
| ❏ 30 Hugh Douglas | .60 | .25 |
| ❏ 31 Thurman Thomas | 1.50 | .60 |
| ❏ 32 Drew Bledsoe | 2.00 | .75 |
| ❏ 33 LeShon Johnson | .60 | .25 |
| ❏ 34 Byron Bam Morris | .60 | .25 |
| ❏ 35 Herman Moore | 1.00 | .40 |
| ❏ 36 Troy Aikman | 3.00 | 1.25 |
| ❏ 37 Mel Gray | .60 | .25 |
| ❏ 38 Adrian Murrell | 1.00 | .40 |
| ❏ 39 Carl Pickens | 1.00 | .40 |
| ❏ 40 Tony Brackens | .60 | .25 |
| ❏ 41 O.J. McDuffie | 1.00 | .40 |
| ❏ 42 Napoleon Kaufman | 1.50 | .60 |
| ❏ 43 Chris T. Jones | .60 | .25 |
| ❏ 44 Kordell Stewart | 2.00 | .75 |
| ❏ 45 Steve Young | 2.00 | .75 |
| ❏ 46 Shannon Sharpe | 1.00 | .40 |
| ❏ 47 Leeland McElroy | .60 | .25 |
| ❏ 48 Eric Moulds | 1.50 | .60 |
| ❏ 49 Eddie George | 1.50 | .60 |
| ❏ 50 Jamal Anderson | 1.50 | .60 |
| ❏ 51 Robert Smith | 1.00 | .40 |
| ❏ 52 Mike Alstott | 1.50 | .60 |
| ❏ 53 Darrell Green | 1.00 | .40 |
| ❏ 54 Irving Fryar | 1.00 | .40 |
| ❏ 55 Derrick Thomas | 1.50 | .60 |
| ❏ 56 Antonio Freeman | 2.00 | .75 |
| ❏ 57 Terrell Davis | 2.00 | .75 |
| ❏ 58 Henry Ellard | .60 | .25 |
| ❏ 59 Daryl Johnston | .60 | .25 |
| ❏ 60 Bryan Cox | .60 | .25 |
| ❏ 61 Vinny Testaverde | 1.00 | .40 |
| ❏ 62 Andre Reed | 1.00 | .40 |
| ❏ 63 Larry Centers | 1.00 | .40 |
| ❏ 64 Hardy Nickerson | .60 | .25 |
| ❏ 65 Tony Banks | 1.00 | .40 |
| ❏ 66 Dave Meggett | .60 | .25 |
| ❏ 67 Simeon Rice | 1.00 | .40 |
| ❏ 68 Warrick Dunn | 10.00 | 4.00 |
| ❏ 69 Michael Irvin | 1.50 | .60 |
| ❏ 70 John Elway | 6.00 | 2.50 |

| | | |
|---|---|---|
| ❏ 6 Cortez Kennedy | .20 | .07 |
| ❏ 7 Orlando Thomas | .20 | .07 |
| ❏ 8 Anthony Miller | .50 | .20 |
| ❏ 9 Jeff Blake | 1.00 | .40 |
| ❏ 10 Trent Dilfer | 1.00 | .40 |
| ❏ 11 Heath Shuler | .50 | .20 |
| ❏ 12 Michael Jackson | .50 | .20 |
| ❏ 13 Merton Hanks | .20 | .07 |
| ❏ 14 Dale Carter | .20 | .07 |
| ❏ 15 Eric Metcalf | .20 | .07 |
| ❏ 16 Barry Sanders | 4.00 | 1.50 |
| ❏ 17 Joey Galloway | 1.00 | .40 |
| ❏ 18 Bryan Cox | .20 | .07 |
| ❏ 19 Harvey Williams | .20 | .07 |
| ❏ 20 Terrell Davis | 1.50 | .60 |
| ❏ 21 Danny Scott | .50 | .20 |
| ❏ 22 Kerry Collins | 1.00 | .40 |
| ❏ 23 Warren Sapp | .20 | .07 |
| ❏ 24 Michael Westbrook | 1.00 | .40 |
| ❏ 25 Mark Brunell | 1.50 | .60 |
| ❏ 26 Craig Heyward | .20 | .07 |
| ❏ 27 Eric Allen | .20 | .07 |
| ❏ 28 Dana Stubblefield | .50 | .20 |
| ❏ 29 Steve Bono | .20 | .07 |
| ❏ 30 Larry Brown | .20 | .07 |
| ❏ 31 Warren Moon | .50 | .20 |
| ❏ 32 Jim Kelly | 1.00 | .40 |
| ❏ 33 Terry McDaniel | .20 | .07 |
| ❏ 34 Dan Wilkinson | .20 | .07 |
| ❏ 35 Dave Brown | .20 | .07 |
| ❏ 36 Todd Lyght | .20 | .07 |
| ❏ 37 Aeneas Williams | .20 | .07 |
| ❏ 38 Shannon Sharpe | .50 | .20 |
| ❏ 39 Errict Rhett | .50 | .20 |
| ❏ 40 Yancey Thigpen | .50 | .20 |
| ❏ 41 J.J. Stokes | 1.00 | .40 |
| ❏ 42 Marshall Faulk | 1.25 | .50 |
| ❏ 43 Chester McGlockton | .20 | .07 |
| ❏ 44 Darryll Lewis | .20 | .07 |
| ❏ 45 Drew Bledsoe | 1.50 | .60 |
| ❏ 46 Tyrone Wheatley | .50 | .20 |
| ❏ 47 Herman Moore | .50 | .20 |
| ❏ 48 Darren Woodson | .20 | .07 |
| ❏ 49 Ricky Watters | .50 | .20 |
| ❏ 50 Emmitt Smith TYC | 1.50 | .60 |
| ❏ 51 Barry Sanders TYC | 1.50 | .60 |
| ❏ 52 Curtis Martin TYC | 1.00 | .40 |
| ❏ 53 Chris Warren TYC | .50 | .40 |
| ❏ 54 Errict Rhett TYC | .50 | .20 |
| ❏ 55 Rodney Hampton TYC | .50 | .20 |
| ❏ 56 Terrell Davis TYC | 1.00 | .40 |
| ❏ 57 Marshall Faulk TYC | 1.00 | .40 |
| ❏ 58 Rashaan Salaam TYC | .50 | .20 |
| ❏ 59 Curtis Conway | 1.00 | .40 |
| ❏ 60 Isaac Bruce | 1.00 | .40 |
| ❏ 61 Thurman Thomas | 1.00 | .40 |
| ❏ 62 Terry Allen | .50 | .20 |
| ❏ 63 Lamar Lathon | .20 | .07 |
| ❏ 64 Mark Chmura | .50 | .20 |
| ❏ 65 Chris Warren | .50 | .20 |
| ❏ 66 Jessie Tuggle | .20 | .07 |
| ❏ 67 Erik Kramer | .20 | .07 |
| ❏ 68 Tim Brown | 1.00 | .40 |
| ❏ 69 Derrick Thomas | 1.00 | .40 |
| ❏ 70 Willie McGinest | .20 | .07 |
| ❏ 71 Frank Sanders | .50 | .20 |
| ❏ 72 Bernie Parmalee | .20 | .07 |
| ❏ 73 Kordell Stewart | 1.00 | .40 |
| ❏ 74 Brent Jones | .50 | .20 |
| ❏ 75 Edgar Bennett | .50 | .20 |
| ❏ 76 Rashaan Salaam | .50 | .20 |
| ❏ 77 Carl Pickens | .50 | .20 |
| ❏ 78 Terance Mathis | .20 | .07 |

|  |  | | |
|---|---|---|---|
| ❏ 71 | Jake Reed | 1.00 | .40 |
| ❏ 72 | Rodney Hampton | 1.00 | .40 |
| ❏ 73 | Aaron Glenn | .60 | .25 |
| ❏ 74 | Terry Allen | 1.50 | .60 |
| ❏ 75 | Blaine Bishop | .60 | .25 |
| ❏ 76 | Bert Emanuel | 1.00 | .40 |
| ❏ 77 | Mark Carrier WR | .60 | .25 |
| ❏ 78 | Jimmy Smith | 1.00 | .40 |
| ❏ 79 | Jim Harbaugh | 1.00 | .40 |
| ❏ 80 | Brent Jones | .60 | .25 |
| ❏ 81 | Emmitt Smith | 5.00 | 2.00 |
| ❏ 82 | Fred Barnett | .60 | .25 |
| ❏ 83 | Errict Rhett | .60 | .25 |
| ❏ 84 | Michael Sinclair | .60 | .25 |
| ❏ 85 | Jerome Bettis | 1.50 | .60 |
| ❏ 86 | Chris Sanders | .60 | .25 |
| ❏ 87 | Kent Graham | .60 | .25 |
| ❏ 88 | Cris Carter | 1.50 | .60 |
| ❏ 89 | Harvey Williams | .60 | .25 |
| ❏ 90 | Eric Allen | .60 | .25 |
| ❏ 91 | Bryant Young | .60 | .25 |
| ❏ 92 | Marcus Allen | 1.50 | .60 |
| ❏ 93 | Michael Jackson | 1.00 | .40 |
| ❏ 94 | Mark Chmura | 1.00 | .40 |
| ❏ 95 | Keenan McCardell | 1.00 | .40 |
| ❏ 96 | Joey Galloway | 1.00 | .40 |
| ❏ 97 | Eddie Kennison | 1.00 | .40 |
| ❏ 98 | Steve Atwater | .60 | .25 |
| ❏ 99 | Dorsey Levens | 1.50 | .60 |
| ❏ 100 | Rob Moore | 1.00 | .40 |
| ❏ 101 | Steve McNair | 2.00 | .75 |
| ❏ 102 | Sean Dawkins | .60 | .25 |
| ❏ 103 | Don Beebe | .60 | .25 |
| ❏ 104 | Willie McGinest | .60 | .25 |
| ❏ 105 | Tony Martin | 1.00 | .40 |
| ❏ 106 | Mark Brunell | 2.00 | .75 |
| ❏ 107 | Karim Abdul-Jabbar | 1.50 | .60 |
| ❏ 108 | Michael Westbrook | 1.00 | .40 |
| ❏ 109 | Lawrence Phillips | .60 | .25 |
| ❏ 110 | Barry Sanders | 5.00 | 2.00 |
| ❏ 111 | Willie Davis | .60 | .25 |
| ❏ 112 | Wesley Walls | 1.00 | .40 |
| ❏ 113 | Todd Collins | .60 | .25 |
| ❏ 114 | Jerry Rice | 3.00 | 1.25 |
| ❏ 115 | Scott Mitchell | 1.00 | .40 |
| ❏ 116 | Terance Mathis | 1.00 | .40 |
| ❏ 117 | Chris Spielman | .60 | .25 |
| ❏ 118 | Curtis Conway | 1.00 | .40 |
| ❏ 119 | Marvin Harrison | 1.50 | .60 |
| ❏ 120 | Terry Glenn | 1.50 | .60 |
| ❏ 121 | Dave Brown | .60 | .25 |
| ❏ 122 | Neil O'Donnell | 1.00 | .40 |
| ❏ 123 | Junior Seau | 1.50 | .60 |
| ❏ 124 | Reggie White | 1.50 | .60 |
| ❏ 125 | Lamar Lathon | .60 | .25 |
| ❏ 126 | Natrone Means | 1.50 | .60 |
| ❏ 127 | Tim Brown | 1.50 | .60 |
| ❏ 128 | Eric Swann | .60 | .25 |
| ❏ 129 | Dan Marino | 6.00 | 2.50 |
| ❏ 130 | Anthony Johnson | .60 | .25 |
| ❏ 131 | Edgar Bennett | 1.00 | .40 |
| ❏ 132 | Kevin Hardy | .60 | .25 |
| ❏ 133 | Brian Blades | .60 | .25 |
| ❏ 134 | Curtis Martin | 2.00 | .75 |
| ❏ 135 | Zach Thomas | 1.50 | .60 |
| ❏ 136 | Darnay Scott | 1.00 | .40 |
| ❏ 137 | Desmond Howard | 1.00 | .40 |
| ❏ 138 | Aeneas Williams | .60 | .25 |
| ❏ 139 | Bryce Paup | .60 | .25 |
| ❏ 140 | Brad Johnson | 1.50 | .60 |
| ❏ 141 | Jeff Blake | 1.00 | .40 |
| ❏ 142 | Wayne Chrebet | 1.50 | .60 |
| ❏ 143 | Will Blackwell RC | 1.25 | .50 |
| ❏ 144 | Tom Knight RC | .60 | .25 |
| ❏ 145 | Darnell Autry RC | 1.00 | .40 |
| ❏ 146 | Bryant Westbrook RC | .60 | .25 |
| ❏ 147 | David LaFleur RC | .75 | .30 |
| ❏ 148 | Antowain Smith RC | 8.00 | 3.00 |
| ❏ 149 | Rae Carruth RC | 1.00 | .40 |
| ❏ 150 | Jim Druckenmiller RC | 1.00 | .40 |
| ❏ 151 | Shawn Springs RC | .75 | .30 |
| ❏ 152 | Troy Davis RC | 1.25 | .50 |
| ❏ 153 | Orlando Pace RC | 2.00 | .75 |
| ❏ 154 | Byron Hanspard RC | 1.25 | .50 |
| ❏ 155 | Corey Dillon RC | 10.00 | 4.00 |
| ❏ 156 | Reidel Anthony RC | 2.00 | .75 |
| ❏ 157 | Peter Boulware RC | 2.00 | .75 |
| ❏ 158 | Reinard Wilson RC | 1.25 | .50 |
| ❏ 159 | Pat Barnes RC | 2.00 | .75 |
| ❏ 160 | Joey Kent RC | 2.00 | .75 |
| ❏ 161 | Ike Hilliard RC | 3.00 | 1.25 |
| ❏ 162 | Jake Plummer RC | 8.00 | 3.00 |
| ❏ 163 | Darrell Russell RC | .75 | .30 |
| ❏ 164 | Checklist Card | .60 | .25 |
| ❏ 165 | Checklist Card | .60 | .25 |

## 1998 Topps Chrome

|  |  | | |
|---|---|---|---|
| ❏ | COMPLETE SET (165) | 120.00 | 50.00 |
| ❏ 1 | Barry Sanders | 4.00 | 1.50 |
| ❏ 2 | Duane Starks RC | 2.00 | .75 |
| ❏ 3 | J.J. Stokes | .75 | .30 |
| ❏ 4 | Joey Galloway | .75 | .30 |
| ❏ 5 | Deion Sanders | 1.25 | .50 |
| ❏ 6 | Anthony Miller | .50 | .20 |
| ❏ 7 | Jamal Anderson | 1.25 | .50 |
| ❏ 8 | Shannon Sharpe | .75 | .30 |
| ❏ 9 | Irving Fryar | .50 | .20 |
| ❏ 10 | Curtis Martin | 1.25 | .50 |
| ❏ 11 | Shawn Jefferson | .50 | .20 |
| ❏ 12 | Charlie Garner | .75 | .30 |
| ❏ 13 | Robert Edwards RC | 3.00 | 1.25 |
| ❏ 14 | Napoleon Kaufman | 1.25 | .50 |
| ❏ 15 | Gus Frerotte | .50 | .20 |
| ❏ 16 | John Elway | 5.00 | 2.00 |
| ❏ 17 | Jerome Pathon RC | 4.00 | 1.50 |
| ❏ 18 | Marshall Faulk | 1.50 | .60 |
| ❏ 19 | Michael McCrary | .50 | .20 |
| ❏ 20 | Marcus Allen | 1.25 | .50 |
| ❏ 21 | Trent Dilfer | .75 | .30 |
| ❏ 22 | Frank Wycheck | .50 | .20 |
| ❏ 23 | Terrell Owens | 1.25 | .50 |
| ❏ 24 | Herman Moore | .75 | .30 |
| ❏ 25 | Neil O'Donnell | .75 | .30 |
| ❏ 26 | Darnay Scott | .75 | .30 |
| ❏ 27 | Keith Brooking RC | 4.00 | 1.50 |
| ❏ 28 | Eric Green | .50 | .20 |
| ❏ 29 | Dan Marino | 5.00 | 2.00 |
| ❏ 30 | Antonio Freeman | 1.25 | .50 |
| ❏ 31 | Tony Martin | .75 | .30 |
| ❏ 32 | Isaac Bruce | 1.25 | .50 |
| ❏ 33 | Rickey Dudley | .50 | .20 |
| ❏ 34 | Scott Mitchell | .75 | .30 |
| ❏ 35 | Randy Moss RC | 25.00 | 10.00 |
| ❏ 36 | Fred Lane | .75 | .30 |
| ❏ 37 | Frank Sanders | .75 | .30 |
| ❏ 38 | Jerry Rice | 2.50 | 1.00 |
| ❏ 39 | O.J. McDuffie | .75 | .30 |
| ❏ 40 | Jessie Armstead | .50 | .20 |
| ❏ 41 | Reidel Anthony | .75 | .30 |
| ❏ 42 | Steve McNair | 1.25 | .50 |
| ❏ 43 | Jake Reed | .75 | .30 |
| ❏ 44 | Charles Woodson RC | 5.00 | 2.00 |
| ❏ 45 | Tiki Barber | 1.25 | .50 |
| ❏ 46 | Mike Alstott | 1.25 | .50 |
| ❏ 47 | Keyshawn Johnson | .75 | .30 |
| ❏ 48 | Tony Banks | .75 | .30 |
| ❏ 49 | Michael Westbrook | .75 | .30 |
| ❏ 50 | Chris Slade | .50 | .20 |
| ❏ 51 | Terry Allen | 1.25 | .50 |
| ❏ 52 | Karim Abdul-Jabbar | 1.25 | .50 |
| ❏ 53 | Brad Johnson | 1.25 | .50 |
| ❏ 54 | Tony McGee | .50 | .20 |
| ❏ 55 | Kevin Dyson RC | 4.00 | 1.50 |
| ❏ 56 | Warren Moon | 1.25 | .50 |
| ❏ 57 | Byron Hanspard | .50 | .20 |
| ❏ 58 | Jermaine Lewis | .75 | .30 |
| ❏ 59 | Neil Smith | .75 | .30 |
| ❏ 60 | Tamarick Vanover | .50 | .20 |
| ❏ 61 | Terrell Davis | 1.25 | .50 |
| ❏ 62 | Robert Smith | .75 | .30 |
| ❏ 63 | Junior Seau | 1.25 | .50 |
| ❏ 64 | Warren Sapp | .75 | .30 |
| ❏ 65 | Michael Sinclair | .50 | .20 |
| ❏ 66 | Ryan Leaf RC | 4.00 | 1.50 |
| ❏ 67 | Drew Bledsoe | 2.00 | .75 |
| ❏ 68 | Jason Sehorn | .75 | .30 |
| ❏ 69 | Andre Hastings | .50 | .20 |
| ❏ 70 | Tony Gonzalez | 1.25 | .50 |
| ❏ 71 | Dorsey Levens | 1.25 | .50 |
| ❏ 72 | Ray Lewis | 1.25 | .50 |
| ❏ 73 | Grant Wistrom RC | 3.00 | 1.25 |
| ❏ 74 | Elvis Grbac | .75 | .30 |
| ❏ 75 | Mark Chmura | .75 | .30 |
| ❏ 76 | Zach Thomas | 1.25 | .50 |
| ❏ 77 | Ben Coates | .75 | .30 |
| ❏ 78 | Rod Smith WR | .75 | .30 |
| ❏ 79 | Andre Wadsworth RC | 3.00 | 1.25 |
| ❏ 80 | Garrison Hearst | 1.25 | .50 |
| ❏ 81 | Will Blackwell | .50 | .20 |
| ❏ 82 | Cris Carter | 1.25 | .50 |
| ❏ 83 | Mark Fields | .50 | .20 |
| ❏ 84 | Ken Dilger | .50 | .20 |
| ❏ 85 | Johnnie Morton | .75 | .30 |
| ❏ 86 | Michael Irvin | 1.25 | .50 |
| ❏ 87 | Eddie George | 1.25 | .50 |
| ❏ 88 | Rob Moore | .75 | .30 |
| ❏ 89 | Takeo Spikes RC | 4.00 | 1.50 |
| ❏ 90 | Wesley Walls | .75 | .30 |
| ❏ 91 | Andre Reed | .75 | .30 |
| ❏ 92 | Thurman Thomas | 1.25 | .50 |
| ❏ 93 | Ed McCaffrey | .75 | .30 |
| ❏ 94 | Carl Pickens | .75 | .30 |
| ❏ 95 | Jason Taylor | .75 | .30 |
| ❏ 96 | Kordell Stewart | 1.25 | .50 |
| ❏ 97 | Greg Ellis RC | 2.00 | .75 |
| ❏ 98 | Aaron Glenn | .50 | .20 |
| ❏ 99 | Jake Plummer | 1.25 | .50 |
| ❏ 100 | Checklist | .50 | .20 |
| ❏ 101 | Chris Sanders | .50 | .20 |
| ❏ 102 | Michael Jackson | .50 | .20 |
| ❏ 103 | Bobby Hoying | .50 | .20 |
| ❏ 104 | Wayne Chrebet | 1.25 | .50 |
| ❏ 105 | Charles Way | .50 | .20 |
| ❏ 106 | Derrick Thomas | 1.25 | .50 |
| ❏ 107 | Troy Drayton | .50 | .20 |
| ❏ 108 | Robert Holcombe RC | 3.00 | 1.25 |
| ❏ 109 | Pete Mitchell | .50 | .20 |
| ❏ 110 | Bruce Smith | .75 | .30 |
| ❏ 111 | Terance Mathis | .75 | .30 |
| ❏ 112 | Lawrence Phillips | .50 | .20 |
| ❏ 113 | Brett Favre | 5.00 | 2.00 |
| ❏ 114 | Darrell Green | .75 | .30 |
| ❏ 115 | Charles Johnson | .50 | .20 |
| ❏ 116 | Jeff Blake | .75 | .30 |
| ❏ 117 | Mark Brunell | 1.25 | .50 |
| ❏ 118 | Simeon Rice | .75 | .30 |
| ❏ 119 | Robert Brooks | .75 | .30 |
| ❏ 120 | Jacquez Green RC | 3.00 | 1.25 |
| ❏ 121 | Willie Davis | .50 | .20 |
| ❏ 122 | Jeff George | .75 | .30 |
| ❏ 123 | Andre Rison | .50 | .20 |
| ❏ 124 | Erik Kramer | .50 | .20 |
| ❏ 125 | Peter Boulware | .50 | .20 |
| ❏ 126 | Marcus Nash RC | 2.00 | .75 |
| ❏ 127 | Troy Aikman | 2.50 | 1.00 |
| ❏ 128 | Keenan McCardell | .75 | .30 |
| ❏ 129 | Bryant Westbrook | .50 | .20 |
| ❏ 130 | Terry Glenn | 1.25 | .50 |
| ❏ 131 | Blaine Bishop | .50 | .20 |
| ❏ 132 | Tim Brown | 1.25 | .50 |
| ❏ 133 | Brian Griese RC | 8.00 | 3.00 |
| ❏ 134 | John Mobley | .50 | .20 |
| ❏ 135 | Larry Centers | .50 | .20 |
| ❏ 136 | Eric Bjornson | .50 | .20 |
| ❏ 137 | Kevin Hardy | .50 | .20 |
| ❏ 138 | John Randle | .75 | .30 |
| ❏ 139 | Michael Strahan | .75 | .30 |
| ❏ 140 | Jerome Bettis | 1.25 | .50 |
| ❏ 141 | Rae Carruth | .50 | .20 |
| ❏ 142 | Reggie White | 1.25 | .50 |
| ❏ 143 | Antowain Smith | 1.25 | .50 |
| ❏ 144 | Aeneas Williams | .50 | .20 |
| ❏ 145 | Bobby Engram | .75 | .30 |
| ❏ 146 | Germane Crowell RC | 3.00 | 1.25 |
| ❏ 147 | Freddie Jones | .50 | .20 |
| ❏ 148 | Kimble Anders | .75 | .30 |
| ❏ 149 | Steve Young | 1.50 | .60 |
| ❏ 150 | Willie McGinest | .50 | .20 |
| ❏ 151 | Emmitt Smith | 4.00 | 1.50 |
| ❏ 152 | Fred Taylor RC | 6.00 | 2.50 |
| ❏ 153 | Danny Kanell | .75 | .30 |
| ❏ 154 | Warrick Dunn | 1.25 | .50 |
| ❏ 155 | Kerry Collins | .75 | .30 |
| ❏ 156 | Chris Chandler | .75 | .30 |

| | | |
|---|---|---|
| ☐ 157 Curtis Conway | .75 | .30 |
| ☐ 158 Curtis Enis RC | 2.00 | .75 |
| ☐ 159 Corey Dillon | 1.25 | .50 |
| ☐ 160 Glenn Foley | .75 | .30 |
| ☐ 161 Marvin Harrison | 1.25 | .50 |
| ☐ 162 Chad Brown | .50 | .20 |
| ☐ 163 Derrick Rodgers | .50 | .20 |
| ☐ 164 Levon Kirkland | .50 | .20 |
| ☐ 165 Peyton Manning RC | 50.00 | 20.00 |

## 1999 Topps Chrome

| | | |
|---|---|---|
| ☐ COMPLETE SET (165) | 150.00 | 60.00 |
| ☐ COMP.SET w/o SP's (135) | 50.00 | 25.00 |
| ☐ 1 Randy Moss | 3.00 | 1.25 |
| ☐ 2 Keyshawn Johnson | 1.25 | .50 |
| ☐ 3 Priest Holmes | 2.00 | .75 |
| ☐ 4 Warren Moon | 1.25 | .50 |
| ☐ 5 Joey Galloway | .75 | .30 |
| ☐ 6 Zach Thomas | 1.25 | .50 |
| ☐ 7 Cam Cleeland | .50 | .20 |
| ☐ 8 Jim Harbaugh | .75 | .30 |
| ☐ 9 Napoleon Kaufman | 1.25 | .50 |
| ☐ 10 Fred Taylor | 1.25 | .50 |
| ☐ 11 Mark Brunell | 1.25 | .50 |
| ☐ 12 Shannon Sharpe | .75 | .30 |
| ☐ 13 Jacquez Green | .50 | .20 |
| ☐ 14 Adrian Murrell | .75 | .30 |
| ☐ 15 Cris Carter | 1.25 | .50 |
| ☐ 16 Jerome Pathon | .50 | .20 |
| ☐ 17 Drew Bledsoe | 1.50 | .60 |
| ☐ 18 Curtis Martin | 1.25 | .50 |
| ☐ 19 Johnnie Morton | .75 | .30 |
| ☐ 20 Doug Flutie | 1.25 | .50 |
| ☐ 21 Carl Pickens | .75 | .30 |
| ☐ 22 Jerome Bettis | 1.25 | .50 |
| ☐ 23 Derrick Alexander | .50 | .20 |
| ☐ 24 Antowain Smith | 1.25 | .50 |
| ☐ 25 Barry Sanders | 4.00 | 1.50 |
| ☐ 26 Riedel Anthony | .75 | .30 |
| ☐ 27 Wayne Chrebet | .75 | .30 |
| ☐ 28 Terance Mathis | .75 | .30 |
| ☐ 29 Shawn Springs | .50 | .20 |
| ☐ 30 Emmitt Smith | 2.50 | 1.00 |
| ☐ 31 Robert Smith | 1.25 | .50 |
| ☐ 32 Charles Johnson | .50 | .20 |
| ☐ 33 Mike Alstott | 1.25 | .50 |
| ☐ 34 Ike Hilliard | .75 | .30 |
| ☐ 35 Ricky Watters | .75 | .30 |
| ☐ 36 Charles Woodson | 1.25 | .50 |
| ☐ 37 Rod Smith | .75 | .30 |
| ☐ 38 Pete Mitchell | .50 | .20 |
| ☐ 39 Derrick Thomas | 1.25 | .50 |
| ☐ 40 Dan Marino | 4.00 | 1.50 |
| ☐ 41 Darnay Scott | .50 | .20 |
| ☐ 42 Jake Reed | .50 | .20 |
| ☐ 43 Chris Chandler | .75 | .30 |
| ☐ 44 Dorsey Levens | 1.25 | .50 |
| ☐ 45 Kordell Stewart | .75 | .30 |
| ☐ 46 Eddie George | 1.25 | .50 |
| ☐ 47 Corey Dillon | 1.25 | .50 |
| ☐ 48 Rich Gannon | 1.25 | .50 |
| ☐ 49 Chris Spielman | .50 | .20 |
| ☐ 50 Jerry Rice | 2.50 | 1.00 |
| ☐ 51 Trent Dilfer | .50 | .20 |
| ☐ 52 Mark Chmura | .50 | .20 |
| ☐ 53 Jimmy Smith | .75 | .30 |
| ☐ 54 Isaac Bruce | 1.25 | .50 |
| ☐ 55 Karim Abdul-Jabbar | 1.25 | .50 |
| ☐ 56 Sedrick Shaw | .50 | .20 |
| ☐ 57 Jake Plummer | 1.25 | .50 |
| ☐ 58 Tony Gonzalez | 1.25 | .50 |
| ☐ 59 Ben Coates | .75 | .30 |

| | | |
|---|---|---|
| ☐ 60 John Elway | 4.00 | 1.50 |
| ☐ 61 Bruce Smith | .75 | .30 |
| ☐ 62 Tim Brown | 1.25 | .50 |
| ☐ 63 Tim Dwight | 1.25 | .50 |
| ☐ 64 Yancey Thigpen | .50 | .20 |
| ☐ 65 Terrell Owens | 1.25 | .50 |
| ☐ 66 Kyle Brady | .50 | .20 |
| ☐ 67 Tony Martin | .75 | .30 |
| ☐ 68 Michael Strahan | .75 | .30 |
| ☐ 69 Deion Sanders | 1.25 | .50 |
| ☐ 70 Steve Young | 1.50 | .60 |
| ☐ 71 Dale Carter | .50 | .20 |
| ☐ 72 Ty Law | .75 | .30 |
| ☐ 73 Frank Wycheck | .50 | .20 |
| ☐ 74 Marshall Faulk | 1.50 | .60 |
| ☐ 75 Vinny Testaverde | .75 | .30 |
| ☐ 76 Chad Brown | .50 | .20 |
| ☐ 77 Natrone Means | .75 | .30 |
| ☐ 78 Bert Emanuel | .75 | .30 |
| ☐ 79 Kerry Collins | .75 | .30 |
| ☐ 80 Randall Cunningham | 1.25 | .50 |
| ☐ 81 Garrison Hearst | .75 | .30 |
| ☐ 82 Curtis Enis | .50 | .20 |
| ☐ 83 Steve Atwater | .50 | .20 |
| ☐ 84 Kevin Greene | .50 | .20 |
| ☐ 85 Steve McNair | 1.25 | .50 |
| ☐ 86 Andre Reed | .75 | .30 |
| ☐ 87 J.J. Stokes | .75 | .30 |
| ☐ 88 Eric Moulds | 1.25 | .50 |
| ☐ 89 Marvin Harrison | 1.25 | .50 |
| ☐ 90 Troy Aikman | 2.50 | 1.00 |
| ☐ 91 Herman Moore | .75 | .30 |
| ☐ 92 Michael Irvin | .75 | .30 |
| ☐ 93 Frank Sanders | .75 | .30 |
| ☐ 94 Duce Staley | 1.25 | .50 |
| ☐ 95 James Jett | .75 | .30 |
| ☐ 96 Ricky Proehl | .50 | .20 |
| ☐ 97 Andre Rison | .75 | .30 |
| ☐ 98 Leslie Shepherd | .50 | .20 |
| ☐ 99 Trent Green | 1.25 | .50 |
| ☐ 100 Terrell Davis | 1.25 | .50 |
| ☐ 101 Freddie Jones | .50 | .20 |
| ☐ 102 Skip Hicks | .50 | .20 |
| ☐ 103 Jeff Graham | .50 | .20 |
| ☐ 104 Rob Moore | .75 | .30 |
| ☐ 105 Torrance Small | .50 | .20 |
| ☐ 106 Antonio Freeman | 1.25 | .50 |
| ☐ 107 Robert Brooks | .75 | .30 |
| ☐ 108 Jon Kitna | 1.25 | .50 |
| ☐ 109 Curtis Conway | .75 | .30 |
| ☐ 110 Brett Favre | 4.00 | 1.50 |
| ☐ 111 Warrick Dunn | 1.25 | .50 |
| ☐ 112 Elvis Grbac | .75 | .30 |
| ☐ 113 Corey Fuller | .50 | .20 |
| ☐ 114 Rickey Dudley | .50 | .20 |
| ☐ 115 Jamal Anderson | 1.25 | .50 |
| ☐ 116 Terry Glenn | 1.25 | .50 |
| ☐ 117 Rocket Ismail | .75 | .30 |
| ☐ 118 John Randle | .75 | .30 |
| ☐ 119 Chris Calloway | .50 | .20 |
| ☐ 120 Peyton Manning | 4.00 | 1.50 |
| ☐ 121 Keenan McCardell | .75 | .30 |
| ☐ 122 O.J. McDuffie | .75 | .30 |
| ☐ 123 Ed McCaffrey | .75 | .30 |
| ☐ 124 Charlie Batch | 1.25 | .50 |
| ☐ 125 Jason Elam SH | .50 | .20 |
| ☐ 126 Randy Moss SH | 1.50 | .60 |
| ☐ 127 John Elway SH | 2.00 | .75 |
| ☐ 128 Emmitt Smith SH | 1.25 | .50 |
| ☐ 129 Terrell Davis SH | 1.25 | .50 |
| ☐ 130 Jerris McPhail | .50 | .20 |
| ☐ 131 Damon Gibson | .50 | .20 |
| ☐ 132 Jim Pyne | .50 | .20 |
| ☐ 133 Antonio Langham | .50 | .20 |
| ☐ 134 Freddie Solomon | .50 | .20 |
| ☐ 135 Ricky Williams RC | 10.00 | 4.00 |
| ☐ 136 Daunte Culpepper RC | 20.00 | 10.00 |
| ☐ 137 Chris Claiborne RC | 2.00 | .75 |
| ☐ 138 Amos Zereoue RC | 5.00 | 2.00 |
| ☐ 139 Chris McAlister RC | 4.00 | 1.50 |
| ☐ 140 Kevin Faulk RC | 5.00 | 2.00 |
| ☐ 141 James Johnson RC | 4.00 | 1.50 |
| ☐ 142 Mike Cloud RC | 4.00 | 1.50 |
| ☐ 143 Jevon Kearse RC | 10.00 | 4.00 |
| ☐ 144 Akili Smith RC | 4.00 | 1.50 |
| ☐ 145 Edgerrin James RC | 20.00 | 10.00 |
| ☐ 146 Cecil Collins RC | 2.00 | .75 |
| ☐ 147 Donovan McNabb RC | 25.00 | 12.50 |
| ☐ 148 Kevin Johnson RC | 5.00 | 2.00 |
| ☐ 149 Torry Holt RC | 15.00 | 6.00 |
| ☐ 150 Rob Konrad RC | 5.00 | 2.00 |

| | | |
|---|---|---|
| ☐ 151 Tim Couch RC | 5.00 | 2.00 |
| ☐ 152 David Boston RC | 5.00 | 2.00 |
| ☐ 153 Karsten Bailey RC | 4.00 | 1.50 |
| ☐ 154 Troy Edwards RC | 4.00 | 1.50 |
| ☐ 155 Sedrick Irvin RC | 2.00 | .75 |
| ☐ 156 Shaun King RC | 4.00 | 1.50 |
| ☐ 157 Peerless Price RC | 5.00 | 2.00 |
| ☐ 158 Brock Huard RC | 5.00 | 2.00 |
| ☐ 159 Cade McNown RC | 4.00 | 1.50 |
| ☐ 160 Champ Bailey RC | 8.00 | 3.00 |
| ☐ 161 D'Wayne Bates RC | 4.00 | 1.50 |
| ☐ 162 Joe Germaine RC | 4.00 | 1.50 |
| ☐ 163 Andy Katzenmoyer RC | 4.00 | 1.50 |
| ☐ 164 Antoine Winfield RC | 4.00 | 1.50 |
| ☐ 165 Checklist Card | .50 | .20 |

## 2000 Topps Chrome

| | | |
|---|---|---|
| ☐ COMPLETE SET (270) | 800.00 | 400.00 |
| ☐ COMP.SET w/o SP's (180) | 50.00 | 25.00 |
| ☐ 1 Daunte Culpepper | 1.50 | .60 |
| ☐ 2 Troy Edwards | .40 | .15 |
| ☐ 3 Terrell Owens | 1.25 | .50 |
| ☐ 4 Ricky Proehl | .40 | .15 |
| ☐ 5 Shaun King | .40 | .15 |
| ☐ 6 Jeff George | .60 | .25 |
| ☐ 7 Champ Bailey | .60 | .25 |
| ☐ 8 Amani Toomer | .40 | .15 |
| ☐ 9 Stephen Boyd | .40 | .15 |
| ☐ 10 Thurman Thomas | .60 | .25 |
| ☐ 11 Patrick Jeffers | 1.25 | .50 |
| ☐ 12 Jake Plummer | .60 | .25 |
| ☐ 13 Peter Boulware | .40 | .15 |
| ☐ 14 Darrin Chiaverini | .40 | .15 |
| ☐ 15 Olandis Gary | 1.25 | .50 |
| ☐ 16 Peyton Manning | 3.00 | 1.25 |
| ☐ 17 Joe Horn | .60 | .25 |
| ☐ 18 Wayne Chrebet | .60 | .25 |
| ☐ 19 Freddie Jones | .40 | .15 |
| ☐ 20 Kurt Warner | 2.50 | 1.00 |
| ☐ 21 Mike Alstott | 1.25 | .50 |
| ☐ 22 Stephen Davis | 1.25 | .50 |
| ☐ 23 Tim Brown | 1.25 | .50 |
| ☐ 24 Damon Huard | 1.25 | .50 |
| ☐ 25 Terry Glenn | .60 | .25 |
| ☐ 26 Ricky Williams | 1.25 | .50 |
| ☐ 27 Tim Dwight | 1.25 | .50 |
| ☐ 28 Jay Riemersma | .40 | .15 |
| ☐ 29 Carl Pickens | .60 | .25 |
| ☐ 30 Brett Favre | 4.00 | 1.50 |
| ☐ 31 Oronde Gadsden | .60 | .25 |
| ☐ 32 Steve McNair | 1.25 | .50 |
| ☐ 33 Michael Pittman | .40 | .15 |
| ☐ 34 Emmitt Smith | 2.50 | 1.00 |
| ☐ 35 Mark Brunell | 1.25 | .50 |
| ☐ 36 Ed McCaffrey | 1.25 | .50 |
| ☐ 37 Tyrone Wheatley | .60 | .25 |
| ☐ 38 Sean Dawkins | .40 | .15 |
| ☐ 39 Jevon Kearse | 1.25 | .50 |
| ☐ 40 Tai Streets | .40 | .15 |
| ☐ 41 Keyshawn Johnson | 1.25 | .50 |
| ☐ 42 Germane Crowell | .40 | .15 |
| ☐ 43 Yatil Green | .40 | .15 |
| ☐ 44 Anthony Wright RC | 4.00 | 1.50 |
| ☐ 45 Jerry Rice | 2.50 | 1.00 |
| ☐ 46 Az-Zahir Hakim | .60 | .25 |
| ☐ 47 Stephen Alexander | .40 | .15 |
| ☐ 48 Zach Thomas | 1.25 | .50 |
| ☐ 49 Tony Simmons | .40 | .15 |
| ☐ 50 Jessie Armstead | .40 | .15 |
| ☐ 51 Kordell Stewart | .60 | .25 |
| ☐ 52 Cade McNown | .60 | .25 |
| ☐ 53 Tony Gonzalez | .60 | .25 |

|  |  | | |
|---|---|---|---|
| 54 | John Randle | .60 | .25 |
| 55 | Donovan McNabb | 2.00 | .75 |
| 56 | Warrick Dunn | 1.25 | .50 |
| 57 | Dorsey Levens | .60 | .25 |
| 58 | Erict Rhett | .50 | .25 |
| 59 | Priest Holmes | 1.50 | .60 |
| 60 | Terrell Davis | 1.25 | .50 |
| 61 | Natrone Means | .40 | .15 |
| 62 | Brad Johnson | 1.25 | .50 |
| 63 | Rickey Dudley | .40 | .15 |
| 64 | Moses Moreno | .40 | .15 |
| 65 | Randy Moss | 2.50 | 1.00 |
| 66 | Joe Montgomery | .40 | .15 |
| 67 | Johnnie Morton | .60 | .25 |
| 68 | Peerless Price | .60 | .25 |
| 69 | Rocket Ismail | .60 | .25 |
| 70 | David Boston | 1.25 | .50 |
| 71 | Fred Taylor | 1.25 | .50 |
| 72 | Jermaine Fazande | .40 | .15 |
| 73 | Elvis Grbac | .60 | .25 |
| 74 | Derrick Mayes | .60 | .25 |
| 75 | Yancey Thigpen | .40 | .15 |
| 76 | Ike Hilliard | .60 | .25 |
| 77 | Muhsin Muhammad | .60 | .25 |
| 78 | Shawn Jefferson | .40 | .15 |
| 79 | Rod Smith | .60 | .25 |
| 80 | Darnay Scott | .40 | .15 |
| 81 | Cam Cleeland | .40 | .15 |
| 82 | Steve Young | 1.50 | .60 |
| 83 | E.G. Green | .40 | .15 |
| 84 | Robert Smith | 1.25 | .50 |
| 85 | Jermaine Lewis | .60 | .25 |
| 86 | Tim Biakabutuka | .60 | .25 |
| 87 | Jerome Pathon | .60 | .25 |
| 88 | Kent Graham | .40 | .15 |
| 89 | Bruce Smith | .60 | .25 |
| 90 | Isaac Bruce | 1.25 | .50 |
| 91 | Curtis Enis | .40 | .15 |
| 92 | Bert Emanuel | .40 | .15 |
| 93 | Keith Poole | .40 | .15 |
| 94 | Troy Aikman | 2.50 | 1.00 |
| 95 | Rich Gannon | 1.25 | .50 |
| 96 | Michael Westbrook | .60 | .25 |
| 97 | Albert Connell | .40 | .15 |
| 98 | James Johnson | .40 | .15 |
| 99 | Jeff Blake | .60 | .25 |
| 100 | Joey Galloway | .60 | .25 |
| 101 | Rob Moore | .60 | .25 |
| 102 | Chris Chandler | .60 | .25 |
| 103 | Fred Lane | .40 | .15 |
| 104 | Eddie Kennison | .40 | .15 |
| 105 | Kevin Hardy | .40 | .15 |
| 106 | Napoleon Kaufman | .60 | .25 |
| 107 | Kevin Dyson | .60 | .25 |
| 108 | Keenan McCardell | .60 | .25 |
| 109 | Drew Bledsoe | 1.50 | .60 |
| 110 | Kevin Johnson | 1.25 | .50 |
| 111 | Terance Mathis | .60 | .25 |
| 112 | Gus Frerotte | .40 | .15 |
| 113 | Matthew Hatchette | .40 | .15 |
| 114 | Herman Moore | .60 | .25 |
| 115 | Curtis Martin | 1.25 | .50 |
| 116 | Jacquez Green | .40 | .15 |
| 117 | Jake Reed | .40 | .15 |
| 118 | Antonio Freeman | 1.25 | .50 |
| 119 | Jim Miller | .40 | .15 |
| 120 | Frank Sanders | .60 | .25 |
| 121 | Brian Griese | 1.25 | .50 |
| 122 | Troy Brown | .60 | .25 |
| 123 | Jeff Graham | .40 | .15 |
| 124 | Marshall Faulk | 1.50 | .60 |
| 125 | Vinny Testaverde | .40 | .15 |
| 126 | Frank Wycheck | .40 | .15 |
| 127 | Kerry Collins | .60 | .25 |
| 128 | Jay Fiedler | .60 | .25 |
| 129 | Cris Carter | 1.25 | .50 |
| 130 | Jason Tucker | .40 | .15 |
| 131 | Antowain Smith | .60 | .25 |
| 132 | Tony Banks | .60 | .25 |
| 133 | Terrence Wilkins | .40 | .15 |
| 134 | Tony Martin | .40 | .15 |
| 135 | Richard Huntley | .40 | .15 |
| 136 | J.J. Stokes | .60 | .25 |
| 137 | Ricky Watters | .60 | .25 |
| 138 | Pete Mitchell | .40 | .15 |
| 139 | Jimmy Smith | .60 | .25 |
| 140 | Doug Flutie | 1.25 | .50 |
| 141 | Corey Bradford | .40 | .15 |
| 142 | Curtis Conway | .60 | .25 |
| 143 | Pete Mitchell | .40 | .15 |
| 144 | Torry Holt | 1.25 | .50 |
| 145 | Warren Sapp | .60 | .25 |
| 146 | Duce Staley | 1.25 | .50 |
| 147 | Mikhael Ricks | .40 | .15 |
| 148 | Edgerrin James | 2.00 | .75 |
| 149 | Charlie Batch | 1.25 | .50 |
| 150 | Rob Johnson | .60 | .25 |
| 151 | Jamal Anderson | 1.25 | .50 |
| 152 | Tim Couch | .60 | .25 |
| 153 | O.J. McDuffie | .60 | .25 |
| 154 | Charles Woodson | .60 | .25 |
| 155 | Jake Delhomme RC | 12.00 | 5.00 |
| 156 | Eddie George | 1.25 | .50 |
| 157 | Jim Harbaugh | .60 | .25 |
| 158 | Jon Kitna | 1.25 | .50 |
| 159 | Derrick Alexander | .60 | .25 |
| 160 | Marvin Harrison | 1.25 | .50 |
| 161 | James Stewart | .60 | .25 |
| 162 | Qadry Ismail | .60 | .25 |
| 163 | Wesley Walls | .40 | .15 |
| 164 | Steve Beuerlein | .60 | .25 |
| 165 | Marcus Robinson | 1.25 | .50 |
| 166 | Bill Schroeder | .60 | .25 |
| 167 | Charles Johnson | .60 | .25 |
| 168 | Charlie Garner | .60 | .25 |
| 169 | Eric Moulds | 1.25 | .50 |
| 170 | Jerome Bettis | 1.25 | .50 |
| 171 | Tai Streets | .40 | .15 |
| 172 | Akili Smith | .40 | .15 |
| 173 | Jonathan Linton | .40 | .15 |
| 174 | Corey Dillon | 1.25 | .50 |
| 175 | Junior Seau | 1.25 | .50 |
| 176 | Jonathan Quinn | .40 | .15 |
| 177 | Bobby Engram | .40 | .15 |
| 178 | Shannon Sharpe | .60 | .25 |
| 179 | Michael Basnight | .40 | .15 |
| 180 | Sedrick Irvin | .40 | .15 |
| 181 | Sammy Morris RC | 12.00 | 5.00 |
| 182 | Ron Dixon RC | 10.00 | 4.00 |
| 183 | Trevor Gaylor RC | 10.00 | 4.00 |
| 184 | Chris Cole RC | 8.00 | 3.00 |
| 185 | Deltha O'Neal RC | 15.00 | 6.00 |
| 186 | Sebastian Janikowski RC | 15.00 | 6.00 |
| 187 | Kwame Cavil RC | 8.00 | 3.00 |
| 188 | Chad Morton RC | 15.00 | 6.00 |
| 189 | Terrelle Smith RC | 10.00 | 4.00 |
| 190 | Frank Moreau RC | 10.00 | 4.00 |
| 191 | Kurt Warner HL | 1.50 | .60 |
| 192 | Dan Marino HL | 2.50 | 1.00 |
| 193 | Cris Carter HL | .60 | .25 |
| 194 | Brett Favre HL | 2.50 | 1.00 |
| 195 | Marshall Faulk HL | 1.25 | .50 |
| 196 | Jevon Kearse HL | .60 | .25 |
| 197 | Edgerrin James HL | 1.50 | .60 |
| 198 | Emmitt Smith HL | 1.50 | .60 |
| 199 | Andre Reed HL | .40 | .15 |
| 200 | K.Dyson/F.Wycheck HL | .40 | .15 |
| 201 | Olindo Mare MM | .40 | .15 |
| 202 | Marcus Coleman MM | .40 | .15 |
| 203 | James Johnson MM | .40 | .15 |
| 204 | Ray Lucas MM | .60 | .25 |
| 205 | Dedric Ward MM | .40 | .15 |
| 206 | Richie Cunningham MM | .40 | .15 |
| 207 | James Hasty MM | .40 | .15 |
| 208 | Sedrick Shaw MM | .40 | .15 |
| 209 | Kurt Warner MM | 1.50 | .60 |
| 210 | Marshall Faulk MM | 1.25 | .50 |
| 211 | Brian Shay EP | 1.00 | .40 |
| 212 | L.C. Stevens EP | 1.00 | .40 |
| 213 | Corey Thomas EP | 1.00 | .40 |
| 214 | Scott Milanovich EP | 1.50 | .60 |
| 215 | Pat Barnes EP | 1.00 | .40 |
| 216 | Danny Wuerffel EP | 1.50 | .60 |
| 217 | Kevin Daft EP | 1.00 | .40 |
| 218 | Ron Powlus EP RC | 2.00 | .75 |
| 219 | Eric Kresser EP | 1.00 | .40 |
| 220 | Norman Miller EP RC | 1.00 | .40 |
| 221 | Cory Sauter EP | 1.00 | .40 |
| 222 | Marcus Crandell EP RC | 1.50 | .60 |
| 223 | Sean Morey EP RC | 1.50 | .60 |
| 224 | Jeff Ogden EP | 1.50 | .60 |
| 225 | Ted White EP | 1.00 | .40 |
| 226 | Jim Kubiak EP | 1.00 | .40 |
| 227 | Aaron Stecker EP RC | 2.00 | .75 |
| 228 | Ronnie Powell EP | 1.00 | .40 |
| 229 | Matt Lytle EP RC | 1.50 | .60 |
| 230 | Kendrick Nord EP RC | 1.00 | .40 |
| 231 | Tim Rattay RC | 15.00 | 6.00 |
| 232 | Rob Morris RC | 10.00 | 4.00 |
| 233 | Chris Samuels RC | 10.00 | 4.00 |
| 234 | Todd Husak RC | 15.00 | 6.00 |
| 235 | Ahmed Plummer RC | 15.00 | 6.00 |
| 236 | Frank Murphy RC | 8.00 | 3.00 |
| 237 | Michael Wiley RC | 10.00 | 4.00 |
| 238 | Giovanni Carmazzi RC | 8.00 | 3.00 |
| 239 | Antonio Becht RC | 15.00 | 6.00 |
| 240 | John Abraham RC | 20.00 | 7.50 |
| 241 | Shaun Alexander RC | 30.00 | 12.50 |
| 242 | Thomas Jones RC | 30.00 | 12.50 |
| 243 | Courtney Brown RC | 15.00 | 6.00 |
| 244 | Curtis Keaton RC | 10.00 | 4.00 |
| 245 | Jerry Porter RC | 25.00 | 10.00 |
| 246 | Corey Simon RC | 15.00 | 6.00 |
| 247 | Dez White RC | 15.00 | 6.00 |
| 248 | Jamal Lewis RC | 30.00 | 12.50 |
| 249 | Ron Dayne RC | 15.00 | 6.00 |
| 250 | R.Jay Soward RC | 10.00 | 4.00 |
| 251 | Tee Martin RC | 15.00 | 6.00 |
| 252 | Shaun Ellis RC | 15.00 | 6.00 |
| 253 | Brian Urlacher RC | 50.00 | 20.00 |
| 254 | Reuben Droughns RC | 15.00 | 6.00 |
| 255 | Travis Taylor RC | 15.00 | 6.00 |
| 256 | Plaxico Burress RC | 30.00 | 12.50 |
| 257 | Chad Pennington RC | 30.00 | 12.50 |
| 258 | Sylvester Morris RC | 10.00 | 4.00 |
| 259 | Ron Dugans RC | 8.00 | 3.00 |
| 260 | Joe Hamilton RC | 10.00 | 4.00 |
| 261 | Chris Redman RC | 10.00 | 4.00 |
| 262 | Trung Canidate RC | 10.00 | 4.00 |
| 263 | J.R. Redmond RC | 10.00 | 4.00 |
| 264 | Danny Farmer RC | 10.00 | 4.00 |
| 265 | Todd Pinkston RC | 15.00 | 6.00 |
| 266 | Dennis Northcutt RC | 15.00 | -6.00 |
| 267 | Laveranues Coles RC | 20.00 | 7.50 |
| 268 | Bubba Franks RC | 15.00 | 6.00 |
| 269 | Travis Prentice RC | 10.00 | 4.00 |
| 270 | Peter Warrick RC | 15.00 | 6.00 |

## 2001 Topps Chrome

|  |  | | |
|---|---|---|---|
| | COMP.SET w/o SP's (210) | 50.00 | 20.00 |
| 1 | Randy Moss | 2.50 | 1.00 |
| 2 | Desmond Howard | .50 | .20 |
| 3 | Shawn Bryson | .50 | .20 |
| 4 | Lamar Smith | .75 | .30 |
| 5 | Peter Warrick | 1.25 | .50 |
| 6 | Hines Ward | 1.25 | .50 |
| 7 | J.R. Redmond | .50 | .20 |
| 8 | Reidel Anthony | .50 | .20 |
| 9 | Rich Gannon | 1.25 | .50 |
| 10 | Ed McCaffrey | 1.25 | .50 |
| 11 | Jamal White | .50 | .20 |
| 12 | Michael Pittman | .50 | .20 |
| 13 | Rob Johnson | .75 | .30 |
| 14 | Tim Couch | .75 | .30 |
| 15 | Stephen Alexander | .50 | .20 |
| 16 | Ricky Watters | .75 | .30 |
| 17 | Kerry Collins | .75 | .30 |
| 18 | Ricky Williams | 1.25 | .50 |
| 19 | Joey Galloway | .75 | .30 |
| 20 | Chris Chandler | .75 | .30 |
| 21 | Marty Booker | .50 | .20 |
| 22 | Mark Brunell | 1.25 | .50 |
| 23 | Antonio Freeman | .50 | .20 |
| 24 | Richie Anderson | .50 | .20 |
| 25 | Amani Toomer | .75 | .30 |
| 26 | Trent Green | 1.25 | .50 |
| 27 | Terrell Fletcher | .50 | .20 |
| 28 | Kevin Lockett | .50 | .20 |
| 29 | Ron Dixon | .50 | .20 |
| 30 | Charlie Batch | .50 | .20 |
| 31 | Oronde Gadsden | .75 | .30 |
| 32 | Dorsey Levens | .75 | .30 |
| 33 | Jamal Lewis | 2.00 | .75 |
| 34 | Craig Yeast | .50 | .20 |

|  |  | | |
|---|---|---|---|
| 35 | Muhsin Muhammad | .75 | .30 |
| 36 | Willie Jackson | .50 | .20 |
| 37 | Isaac Bruce | 1.25 | .50 |
| 38 | Frank Wycheck | .50 | .20 |
| 39 | Troy Brown | .75 | .30 |
| 40 | Anthony Wright | .50 | .20 |
| 41 | Zach Thomas | 1.25 | .50 |
| 42 | Qadry Ismail | .75 | .30 |
| 43 | Jake Plummer | .75 | .30 |
| 44 | Keenan McCardell | .50 | .20 |
| 45 | Charles Johnson | .50 | .20 |
| 46 | Brett Favre | 4.00 | 1.50 |
| 47 | Jacquez Green | .50 | .20 |
| 48 | Matt Hasselbeck | .75 | .30 |
| 49 | Tiki Barber | 1.25 | .50 |
| 50 | Jeff Garcia | 1.25 | .50 |
| 51 | Shawn Jefferson | .50 | .20 |
| 52 | Kevin Johnson | .75 | .30 |
| 53 | Terrence Wilkins | .50 | .20 |
| 54 | Mike Anderson | .75 | .30 |
| 55 | Tim Brown | 1.25 | .50 |
| 56 | Champ Bailey | 1.25 | .50 |
| 57 | Jimmy Smith | .75 | .30 |
| 58 | Trent Dilfer | .75 | .30 |
| 59 | James Allen | .75 | .30 |
| 60 | David Boston | 1.25 | .50 |
| 61 | Jeremiah Trotter | .75 | .30 |
| 62 | Freddie Jones | .50 | .20 |
| 63 | Deion Sanders | 1.25 | .50 |
| 64 | Darrell Jackson | 1.25 | .50 |
| 65 | David Patten | .50 | .20 |
| 66 | Jeremy McDaniel | .50 | .20 |
| 67 | Jay Fiedler | .75 | .30 |
| 68 | Chad Lewis | .50 | .20 |
| 69 | Rocket Ismail | .75 | .30 |
| 70 | Cade McNown | .75 | .30 |
| 71 | Jevon Kearse | .75 | .30 |
| 72 | Jermaine Fazande | .50 | .20 |
| 73 | Junior Seau | .75 | .30 |
| 74 | Rod Smith | .75 | .30 |
| 75 | Jermaine Lewis | .50 | .20 |
| 76 | Dennis Northcutt | .75 | .30 |
| 77 | Charlie Garner | .50 | .20 |
| 78 | Charles Woodson | .75 | .30 |
| 79 | Wayne Chrebet | .75 | .30 |
| 80 | Ahman Green | .75 | .30 |
| 81 | Donald Hayes | .50 | .20 |
| 82 | Terance Mathis | .50 | .20 |
| 83 | Warrick Dunn | 1.25 | .50 |
| 84 | Chris Sanders | .50 | .20 |
| 85 | Albert Connell | .50 | .20 |
| 86 | Robert Griffith | .50 | .20 |
| 87 | Germane Crowell | .50 | .20 |
| 88 | Tony Banks | .75 | .30 |
| 89 | Travis Taylor | .75 | .30 |
| 90 | Akili Smith | .75 | .30 |
| 91 | Michael Westbrook | .75 | .30 |
| 92 | Doug Flutie | 1.25 | .50 |
| 93 | Ike Hilliard | .75 | .30 |
| 94 | Terry Glenn | .75 | .30 |
| 95 | Leslie Shepherd | .50 | .20 |
| 96 | Az-Zahir Hakim | .50 | .20 |
| 97 | La'Roi Glover | .50 | .20 |
| 98 | Peyton Manning | 3.00 | 1.25 |
| 99 | Jackie Harris | .50 | .20 |
| 100 | Edgerrin James | 1.50 | .60 |
| 101 | Peerless Price | .75 | .30 |
| 102 | Jamal Anderson | 1.25 | .50 |
| 103 | Keyshawn Johnson | 1.25 | .50 |
| 104 | Derrick Mason | .75 | .30 |
| 105 | J.J. Stokes | .75 | .30 |
| 106 | Kevin Faulk | .75 | .30 |
| 107 | Tony Richardson | .50 | .20 |
| 108 | James Stewart | .75 | .30 |
| 109 | Tim Biakabutuka | .75 | .30 |
| 110 | Jon Kitna | 1.25 | .50 |
| 111 | Thomas Jones | .75 | .30 |
| 112 | Steve McNair | 1.25 | .50 |
| 113 | Sean Dawkins | .50 | .20 |
| 114 | Jerome Bettis | 1.25 | .50 |
| 115 | Donovan McNabb | 1.50 | .60 |
| 116 | Bill Schroeder | .75 | .30 |
| 117 | Rod Woodson | .75 | .30 |
| 118 | James McKnight | .50 | .20 |
| 119 | Daunte Culpepper | 1.25 | .50 |
| 120 | Todd Husak | .50 | .20 |
| 121 | Shaun King | .50 | .20 |
| 122 | Tyrone Wheatley | .50 | .20 |
| 123 | Curtis Martin | 1.25 | .50 |
| 124 | Terrell Davis | .50 | .50 |
| 125 | Steve Beuerlein | .75 | .30 |

|  |  | | |
|---|---|---|---|
| 126 | Brad Johnson | 1.25 | .50 |
| 127 | Joe Horn | .75 | .30 |
| 128 | Fred Taylor | 1.25 | .50 |
| 129 | Brian Urlacher | 2.00 | .75 |
| 130 | Ray Lewis | 1.25 | .50 |
| 131 | Marshall Faulk | 1.50 | .60 |
| 132 | Curtis Conway | .50 | .20 |
| 133 | Jason Sehorn | .50 | .20 |
| 134 | Jerome Pathon | .75 | .30 |
| 135 | Derrick Alexander | .75 | .30 |
| 136 | Jerry Rice | 2.50 | 1.00 |
| 137 | Jeff George | .75 | .30 |
| 138 | Johnnie Morton | .75 | .30 |
| 139 | Eric Moulds | .75 | .30 |
| 140 | Duce Staley | 1.25 | .50 |
| 141 | Vinny Testaverde | .75 | .30 |
| 142 | Eddie George | 1.25 | .50 |
| 143 | Shaun Alexander | 1.50 | .60 |
| 144 | Drew Bledsoe | 1.50 | .60 |
| 145 | Emmitt Smith | 2.50 | 1.00 |
| 146 | Marvin Harrison | 1.25 | .50 |
| 147 | Frank Sanders | .50 | .20 |
| 148 | Aaron Shea | .50 | .20 |
| 149 | Cris Carter | 1.25 | .50 |
| 150 | Tony Gonzalez | .75 | .30 |
| 151 | Marcus Robinson | 1.25 | .50 |
| 152 | Danny Farmer | .50 | .20 |
| 153 | Warren Sapp | .75 | .30 |
| 154 | Kurt Warner | 2.50 | 1.00 |
| 155 | Jessie Armstead | .50 | .20 |
| 156 | Lawyer Milloy | .75 | .30 |
| 157 | Brian Griese | 1.25 | .50 |
| 158 | Jason Taylor | .75 | .30 |
| 159 | Jeff Lewis | .50 | .20 |
| 160 | Travis Prentice | .50 | .20 |
| 161 | Tim Dwight | 1.25 | .50 |
| 162 | Kyle Brady | .75 | .30 |
| 163 | Bubba Franks | .75 | .30 |
| 164 | James Thrash | .75 | .30 |
| 165 | Bobby Shaw | .50 | .20 |
| 166 | Ron Dayne | 1.25 | .50 |
| 167 | Mike Alstott | 1.25 | .50 |
| 168 | Bruce Smith | .50 | .20 |
| 169 | Jeff Graham | .50 | .20 |
| 170 | Jeff Blake | .75 | .30 |
| 171 | Laveranues Coles | 1.25 | .50 |
| 172 | Herman Moore | .75 | .30 |
| 173 | Shannon Sharpe | .75 | .30 |
| 174 | Corey Dillon | 1.25 | .50 |
| 175 | Ken Dilger | .50 | .20 |
| 176 | Eddie Kennison | .50 | .20 |
| 177 | Andre Rison | .75 | .30 |
| 178 | Stephen Davis | 1.25 | .50 |
| 179 | Torry Holt | 1.25 | .50 |
| 180 | Samari Rolle | .75 | .30 |
| 181 | Michael Strahan | .75 | .30 |
| 182 | Plaxico Burress | 1.25 | .50 |
| 183 | Darnell Autry | .50 | .20 |
| 184 | Wesley Walls | .75 | .30 |
| 185 | Elvis Grbac | .75 | .30 |
| 186 | Marcus Pollard | .50 | .20 |
| 187 | Keith Poole | .50 | .20 |
| 188 | Ryan Leaf | .75 | .30 |
| 189 | Terrell Owens | 1.25 | .50 |
| 190 | Dedric Ward | .50 | .20 |
| 191 | Donald Driver | .75 | .30 |
| 192 | Larry Foster | .50 | .20 |
| 193 | Priest Holmes | 1.50 | .60 |
| 194 | Sammy Morris | .50 | .20 |
| 195 | Reggie Jones | .50 | .20 |
| 196 | Kordell Stewart | .75 | .30 |
| 197 | Sylvester Morris | .50 | .20 |
| 198 | Aaron Brooks | 1.25 | .50 |
| 199 | Tai Streets | .50 | .20 |
| 200 | Chad Pennington | 2.00 | .75 |
| 201 | Terrell Owens SH | 1.25 | .50 |
| 202 | Marshall Faulk SH | 1.25 | .50 |
| 203 | Mike Anderson SH | .75 | .30 |
| 204 | Cris Carter SH | 1.25 | .50 |
| 205 | Corey Dillon SH | 1.25 | .50 |
| 206 | Daunte Culpepper SH | 1.25 | .50 |
| 207 | Peyton Manning SH | 1.50 | .60 |
| 208 | Torry Holt SH | .75 | .30 |
| 209 | Marvin Harrison SH | 1.25 | .50 |
| 210 | Edgerrin James SH | 1.25 | .50 |
| 211 | Sam Madison | .50 | .20 |
| 212 | Jonathan Quinn | .50 | .20 |
| 213 | Rob Morris | .50 | .20 |
| 214 | E.G. Green | .50 | .20 |
| 215 | David Sloan | .50 | .20 |
| 216 | Jason Tucker | .50 | .20 |

|  |  | | |
|---|---|---|---|
| 217 | Wali Rainer | .50 | .20 |
| 218 | Jerry Azumah | .50 | .20 |
| 219 | Dameyune Craig | .50 | .20 |
| 220 | Jammi German | .50 | .20 |
| 221 | LaDainian Tomlinson RC | 250.00 | 125.00 |
| 222 | Quincy Morgan RC | 20.00 | 7.50 |
| 223 | Steve Smith RC | 40.00 | 20.00 |
| 224 | Santana Moss RC | 30.00 | 12.50 |
| 225 | Koren Robinson RC | 20.00 | 7.50 |
| 226 | Kevin Kasper RC | 20.00 | 7.50 |
| 227 | Jamie Henderson RC | 12.00 | 5.00 |
| 228 | Adam Archuleta RC | 20.00 | 7.50 |
| 229 | Drew Brees RC | 80.00 | 40.00 |
| 230 | Michael Stone RC | 8.00 | 3.00 |
| 231 | Jamar Fletcher RC | 12.00 | 5.00 |
| 232 | Eric Westmoreland RC | 12.00 | 5.00 |
| 233 | Chris Barnes RC | 12.00 | 5.00 |
| 234 | Gerard Warren RC | 20.00 | 7.50 |
| 235 | Snoop Minnis RC | 12.00 | 5.00 |
| 236 | Chris Chambers RC | 25.00 | 12.50 |
| 237 | Damerien McCants RC | 12.00 | 5.00 |
| 238 | Kevan Barlow RC | 20.00 | 7.50 |
| 239 | Mike McMahon RC | 20.00 | 7.50 |
| 240 | Jabari Holloway RC | 12.00 | 5.00 |
| 241 | Travis Henry RC | 20.00 | 7.50 |
| 242 | Derrick Blaylock RC | 20.00 | 7.50 |
| 243 | Tim Hasselbeck RC | 20.00 | 7.50 |
| 244 | Andre Carter RC | 20.00 | 7.50 |
| 245 | Sage Rosenfels RC | 20.00 | 7.50 |
| 246 | Cedrick Wilson RC | 20.00 | 7.50 |
| 247 | Scotty Anderson RC | 12.00 | 5.00 |
| 248 | Ken-Yon Rambo RC | 12.00 | 5.00 |
| 249 | Marques Tuiasosopo RC | 20.00 | 7.50 |
| 250 | Reggie Wayne RC | 30.00 | 15.00 |
| 251 | Onome Ojo RC | 12.00 | 5.00 |
| 252 | James Jackson RC | 20.00 | 7.50 |
| 253 | Moran Norris RC | 8.00 | 3.00 |
| 254 | Rashard Casey RC | 12.00 | 5.00 |
| 255 | Rudi Johnson RC | 40.00 | 15.00 |
| 256 | Willie Middlebrooks RC | 12.00 | 5.00 |
| 257 | Freddie Mitchell RC | 20.00 | 7.50 |
| 258 | Deuce McAllister RC | 40.00 | 20.00 |
| 259 | Chad Johnson RC | 50.00 | 20.00 |
| 260 | David Terrell RC | 20.00 | 7.50 |
| 261 | Jamal Reynolds RC | 20.00 | 7.50 |
| 262 | Michael Vick RC | 50.00 | 20.00 |
| 263 | Marcus Stroud RC | 20.00 | 7.50 |
| 264 | Dan Alexander RC | 20.00 | 7.50 |
| 265 | Jonathan Carter RC | 12.00 | 5.00 |
| 266 | Bobby Newcombe RC | 12.00 | 5.00 |
| 267 | Eddie Berlin RC | 12.00 | 5.00 |
| 268 | LaMont Jordan RC | 40.00 | 15.00 |
| 269 | Michael Bennett RC | 20.00 | 7.50 |
| 270 | Shaun Rogers RC | 20.00 | 7.50 |
| 271 | Travis Minor RC | 12.00 | 5.00 |
| 272 | Jesse Palmer RC | 20.00 | 7.50 |
| 273 | Derrick Gibson RC | 12.00 | 5.00 |
| 274 | Chris Weinke RC | 20.00 | 7.50 |
| 275 | Nate Clements RC | 20.00 | 7.50 |
| 276 | Eric Kelly RC | 8.00 | 3.00 |
| 277 | Justin Smith RC | 20.00 | 7.50 |
| 278 | Ryan Pickett RC | 8.00 | 3.00 |
| 279 | Anthony Thomas RC | 20.00 | 7.50 |
| 280 | Will Allen RC | 12.00 | 5.00 |
| 281 | Quincy Carter RC | 20.00 | 7.50 |
| 282 | Richard Seymour RC | 20.00 | 7.50 |
| 283 | Dan Morgan RC | 20.00 | 7.50 |
| 284 | Tay Cody RC | 8.00 | 3.00 |
| 285 | Alge Crumpler RC | 25.00 | 10.00 |
| 286 | Robert Ferguson RC | 20.00 | 7.50 |
| 287 | Will Peterson RC | 12.00 | 5.00 |
| 288 | Tony Dixon RC | 12.00 | 5.00 |
| 289 | Correll Buckhalter RC | 20.00 | 7.50 |
| 290 | Rod Gardner RC | 20.00 | 7.50 |
| 291 | Justin McCareins RC | 20.00 | 7.50 |
| 292 | Josh Heupel RC | 20.00 | 7.50 |
| 293 | Todd Heap RC | 20.00 | 7.50 |
| 294 | Damione Lewis RC | 12.00 | 5.00 |
| 295 | George Layne RC | 12.00 | 5.00 |
| 296 | Jamie Winborn RC | 12.00 | 5.00 |
| 297 | Billy Baber RC | 8.00 | 3.00 |
| 298 | T.J. Houshmandzadeh RC | 25.00 | 10.00 |
| 299 | Aaron Schobel RC | 20.00 | 7.50 |
| 300 | Gary Baxter RC | 12.00 | 5.00 |
| 301 | DeLawrence Grant RC | 8.00 | 3.00 |
| 302 | Morlon Greenwood RC | 12.00 | 5.00 |
| 303 | Chad Morton RC | 20.00 | 7.50 |
| 304 | Torrance Marshall RC | 20.00 | 7.50 |
| 305 | David Martin RC | 12.00 | 5.00 |
| 306 | Anthony Henry RC | 20.00 | 7.50 |
| 307 | Derrick Burgess RC | 20.00 | 7.50 |

|  |  | | |
|---|--------|------|------|
| 308 | Andre Dyson RC | 8.00 | 3.00 |
| 309 | Ryan Helming RC | 8.00 | 3.00 |
| 310 | Fred Smoot RC | 20.00 | 7.50 |
| 311 | Arther Love RC | 8.00 | 3.00 |
| 312 | John Capel RC | 12.00 | 5.00 |
| 313 | Brandon Spoon RC | 12.00 | 5.00 |
| 314 | Karon Riley RC | 8.00 | 3.00 |
| 315 | Andre King RC | 12.00 | 5.00 |
| 316 | Quentin McCord RC | 12.00 | 5.00 |
| 317 | Zeke Moreno RC | 20.00 | 7.50 |
| 318 | Francis St. Paul RC | 12.00 | 5.00 |
| 319 | Richmond Flowers RC | 12.00 | 5.00 |
| 320 | Derek Combs RC | 12.00 | 5.00 |

## 2002 Topps Chrome

|  |  | | |
|---|--------|------|------|
| | COMP.SET w/o SPs (165) | 50.00 | 20.00 |
| 1 | Anthony Thomas | .75 | .30 |
| 2 | Jake Plummer | .75 | .30 |
| 3 | Maurice Smith | .75 | .30 |
| 4 | Jamal Lewis | 1.25 | .50 |
| 5 | Ray Lewis | 1.25 | .50 |
| 6 | Alex Van Pelt | .50 | .20 |
| 7 | Chris Weinke | .75 | .30 |
| 8 | Corey Dillon | .75 | .30 |
| 9 | Quincy Morgan | .50 | .20 |
| 10 | Rocket Ismail | .75 | .30 |
| 11 | Brian Griese | .75 | .30 |
| 12 | Johnnie Morton | .75 | .30 |
| 13 | Edgerrin James | 1.50 | .60 |
| 14 | Keenan McCardell | .50 | .20 |
| 15 | Travis Minor | .50 | .20 |
| 16 | Sylvester Morris | .50 | .20 |
| 17 | Randy Moss | 2.50 | 1.00 |
| 18 | Drew Bledsoe | 1.50 | .60 |
| 19 | Willie Jackson | .50 | .20 |
| 20 | Michael Strahan | .75 | .30 |
| 21 | Santana Moss | 1.25 | .50 |
| 22 | Duce Staley | .75 | .30 |
| 23 | Kendrell Bell | 1.25 | .50 |
| 24 | LaDainian Tomlinson | 2.00 | .75 |
| 25 | Terrell Owens | 1.25 | .50 |
| 26 | Shaun Alexander | 1.50 | .60 |
| 27 | Trung Canidate | .75 | .30 |
| 28 | Mike Alstott | 1.25 | .50 |
| 29 | Kevin Dyson | .75 | .30 |
| 30 | Rod Gardner | .75 | .30 |
| 31 | David Boston | 1.25 | .50 |
| 32 | Michael Vick | 2.50 | 1.00 |
| 33 | Qadry Ismail | .75 | .30 |
| 34 | Peerless Price | .75 | .30 |
| 35 | Rob Johnson | .75 | .30 |
| 36 | Marcus Robinson | .75 | .30 |
| 37 | Peter Warrick | .75 | .30 |
| 38 | Kevin Johnson | .75 | .30 |
| 39 | Ed McCaffrey | 1.25 | .50 |
| 40 | Shaun Rogers | .50 | .20 |
| 41 | Marvin Harrison | 1.25 | .50 |
| 42 | Priest Holmes | 1.50 | .60 |
| 43 | Oronde Gadsden | .75 | .30 |
| 44 | Terry Glenn | .75 | .30 |
| 45 | Ike Hilliard | .75 | .30 |
| 46 | Charles Woodson | .75 | .30 |
| 47 | Freddie Mitchell | .75 | .30 |
| 48 | Drew Brees | 1.25 | .50 |
| 49 | Jeff Garcia | 1.25 | .50 |
| 50 | Kurt Warner | 2.50 | 1.00 |
| 51 | Keyshawn Johnson | 1.25 | .50 |
| 52 | Jevon Kearse | .75 | .30 |
| 53 | Stephen Davis | .75 | .30 |
| 54 | Shannon Sharpe | .75 | .30 |
| 55 | Eric Moulds | .75 | .30 |
| 56 | Muhsin Muhammad | .75 | .30 |
| 57 | Brian Urlacher | 2.00 | .75 |
| 58 | Chad Johnson | 1.25 | .50 |
| 59 | Tim Couch | .75 | .30 |
| 60 | Mike Anderson | 1.25 | .50 |
| 61 | James Stewart | .75 | .30 |
| 62 | Corey Bradford | .50 | .20 |
| 63 | Reggie Wayne | 1.25 | .50 |
| 64 | Mark Brunell | 1.25 | .50 |
| 65 | Trent Green | .75 | .30 |
| 66 | Zach Thomas | 1.25 | .50 |
| 67 | Michael Bennett | .75 | .30 |
| 68 | Troy Brown | .75 | .30 |
| 69 | Amani Toomer | .75 | .30 |
| 70 | Curtis Martin | 1.25 | .50 |
| 71 | Tim Brown | 1.25 | .50 |
| 72 | Correll Buckhalter | .75 | .30 |
| 73 | Kordell Stewart | .75 | .30 |
| 74 | Junior Seau | 1.25 | .50 |
| 75 | Kevan Barlow | .75 | .30 |
| 76 | Matt Hasselbeck | .75 | .30 |
| 77 | Marshall Faulk | 1.25 | .50 |
| 78 | Warren Sapp | .75 | .30 |
| 79 | Frank Wycheck | .50 | .20 |
| 80 | Michael Westbrook | .50 | .20 |
| 81 | Travis Henry | 1.25 | .50 |
| 82 | David Terrell | 1.25 | .50 |
| 83 | Jon Kitna | .75 | .30 |
| 84 | James Jackson | .50 | .20 |
| 85 | Joey Galloway | .75 | .30 |
| 86 | Rod Smith | .75 | .30 |
| 87 | Germane Crowell | .50 | .20 |
| 88 | Bill Schroeder | .75 | .30 |
| 89 | Dominic Rhodes | .75 | .30 |
| 90 | Fred Taylor | 1.25 | .50 |
| 91 | Snoop Minnis | .50 | .20 |
| 92 | Chris Chambers | 1.25 | .50 |
| 93 | Daunte Culpepper | 1.25 | .50 |
| 94 | Deuce McAllister | 1.50 | .60 |
| 95 | Kerry Collins | .75 | .30 |
| 96 | John Abraham | .75 | .30 |
| 97 | Rich Gannon | 1.25 | .50 |
| 98 | Tiki Barber | 1.25 | .50 |
| 99 | Hines Ward | 1.25 | .50 |
| 100 | Tom Brady | 3.00 | 1.25 |
| 101 | Tim Dwight | .75 | .30 |
| 102 | Garrison Hearst | .75 | .30 |
| 103 | Darrell Jackson | .75 | .30 |
| 104 | Isaac Bruce | 1.25 | .50 |
| 105 | Brad Johnson | .75 | .30 |
| 106 | Steve McNair | 1.25 | .50 |
| 107 | Champ Bailey | .75 | .30 |
| 108 | Emmitt Smith | 3.00 | 1.25 |
| 109 | Mike McMahon | 1.25 | .50 |
| 110 | Terrell Davis | 1.25 | .50 |
| 111 | Antonio Freeman | .75 | .30 |
| 112 | Jimmy Smith | .75 | .30 |
| 113 | Tony Gonzalez | .75 | .30 |
| 114 | Jay Fiedler | .75 | .30 |
| 115 | Cris Carter | 1.25 | .50 |
| 116 | David Patten | .50 | .20 |
| 117 | Joe Horn | .75 | .30 |
| 118 | Laveranues Coles | .75 | .30 |
| 119 | Charlie Garner | .75 | .30 |
| 120 | Donovan McNabb | 1.50 | .60 |
| 121 | Jerome Bettis | 1.25 | .50 |
| 122 | Curtis Conway | .50 | .20 |
| 123 | Az-Zahir Hakim | .50 | .20 |
| 124 | Warrick Dunn | 1.25 | .50 |
| 125 | Eddie George | 1.25 | .50 |
| 126 | Quincy Carter | .75 | .30 |
| 127 | Ahman Green | 1.25 | .50 |
| 128 | Peyton Manning | 2.50 | 1.00 |
| 129 | James McKnight | .50 | .20 |
| 130 | Antowain Smith | .75 | .30 |
| 131 | Ricky Williams | 8.00 | 3.00 |
| 132 | Chad Pennington | 1.50 | .60 |
| 133 | Jerry Rice | 2.50 | 1.00 |
| 134 | Todd Pinkston | .75 | .30 |
| 135 | Plaxico Burress | 1.25 | .50 |
| 136 | Doug Flutie | 1.25 | .50 |
| 137 | Koren Robinson | .75 | .30 |
| 138 | Torry Holt | 1.25 | .50 |
| 139 | Aaron Brooks | 1.25 | .50 |
| 140 | Ron Dayne | .75 | .30 |
| 141 | Vinny Testaverde | .75 | .30 |
| 142 | Brett Favre | 3.00 | 1.25 |
| 143 | James Thrash | .75 | .30 |
| 144 | Wayne Chrebet | .75 | .30 |
| 145 | Derrick Mason | .75 | .30 |
| 146 | Ahman Green WWU | .75 | .30 |
| 147 | Peyton Manning WWU | 1.25 | .50 |
| 148 | Kurt Warner WWU | .75 | .30 |
| 149 | Daunte Culpepper WWU | .75 | .30 |
| 150 | Tom Brady WWU | 1.50 | .60 |
| 151 | Rod Gardner WWU | .75 | .30 |
| 152 | Corey Dillon WWU | .75 | .30 |
| 153 | Priest Holmes WWU | 1.00 | .40 |
| 154 | Shaun Alexander WWU | 1.00 | .40 |
| 155 | Randy Moss WWU | 1.25 | .50 |
| 156 | Eric Moulds WWU | .75 | .30 |
| 157 | Brett Favre WWU | 1.50 | .60 |
| 158 | Todd Bouman WWU | .50 | .20 |
| 159 | Dominic Rhodes WWU | .50 | .20 |
| 160 | Marvin Harrison WWU | .75 | .30 |
| 161 | Torry Holt WWU | 1.25 | .50 |
| 162 | Derrick Mason WWU | .50 | .20 |
| 163 | Jerry Rice WWU | 1.25 | .50 |
| 164 | Donovan McNabb WWU | 1.25 | .50 |
| 165 | Marshall Faulk WWU | 1.25 | .50 |
| 166 | David Carr RC | 15.00 | 6.00 |
| 167 | Quentin Jammer RC | 10.00 | 4.00 |
| 168 | Mike Williams RC | 8.00 | 3.00 |
| 169 | Rocky Calmus RC | 10.00 | 4.00 |
| 170 | Travis Fisher RC | 10.00 | 4.00 |
| 171 | Dwight Freeney RC | 15.00 | 6.00 |
| 172 | Jeremy Shockey RC | 20.00 | 8.00 |
| 173 | Marquise Walker RC | 8.00 | 3.00 |
| 174 | Eric Crouch RC | 10.00 | 4.00 |
| 175 | DeShaun Foster RC | 10.00 | 4.00 |
| 176 | Roy Williams RC | 20.00 | 7.50 |
| 177 | Andre Davis RC | 8.00 | 3.00 |
| 178 | Alex Brown RC | 10.00 | 4.00 |
| 179 | Michael Lewis RC | 10.00 | 4.00 |
| 180 | Terry Charles RC | 8.00 | 3.00 |
| 181 | Clinton Portis RC | 40.00 | 15.00 |
| 182 | Dennis Johnson RC | 5.00 | 2.00 |
| 183 | Lito Sheppard RC | 10.00 | 4.00 |
| 184 | Ryan Sims RC | 10.00 | 4.00 |
| 185 | Raonall Smith RC | 8.00 | 3.00 |
| 186 | Albert Haynesworth RC | 10.00 | 4.00 |
| 187 | Eddie Freeman RC | 5.00 | 2.00 |
| 188 | Levi Jones RC | 8.00 | 3.00 |
| 189 | Josh McCown RC | 12.00 | 5.00 |
| 190 | Cliff Russell RC | 8.00 | 3.00 |
| 191 | Maurice Morris RC | 10.00 | 4.00 |
| 192 | Antwaan Randle El RC | 12.00 | 5.00 |
| 193 | Ladell Betts RC | 10.00 | 4.00 |
| 194 | Daniel Graham RC | 10.00 | 4.00 |
| 195 | David Garrard RC | 20.00 | 7.50 |
| 196 | Antonio Bryant RC | 10.00 | 4.00 |
| 197 | Patrick Ramsey RC | 10.00 | 4.00 |
| 198 | Kelly Campbell RC | 8.00 | 3.00 |
| 199 | Will Overstreet RC | 5.00 | 2.00 |
| 200 | Ryan Denney RC | 8.00 | 3.00 |
| 201 | John Henderson RC | 10.00 | 4.00 |
| 202 | Freddie Milons RC | 8.00 | 3.00 |
| 203 | Tim Carter RC | 8.00 | 3.00 |
| 204 | Kurt Kittner RC | 8.00 | 3.00 |
| 205 | Joey Harrington RC | 12.00 | 5.00 |
| 206 | Ricky Williams RC | 8.00 | 3.00 |
| 207 | Bryant McKinnie RC | 8.00 | 3.00 |
| 208 | Ed Reed RC | 25.00 | 10.00 |
| 209 | Josh Reed RC | 10.00 | 4.00 |
| 210 | Seth Burford RC | 8.00 | 3.00 |
| 211 | Javon Walker RC | 15.00 | 6.00 |
| 212 | Jamar Martin RC | 8.00 | 3.00 |
| 213 | Leonard Henry RC | 8.00 | 3.00 |
| 214 | Julius Peppers RC | 20.00 | 7.50 |
| 215 | Jabar Gaffney RC | 10.00 | 4.00 |
| 216 | Kalimba Edwards RC | 10.00 | 4.00 |
| 217 | Napoleon Harris RC | 10.00 | 4.00 |
| 218 | Ashley Lelie RC | 20.00 | 7.50 |
| 219 | Anthony Weaver RC | 8.00 | 3.00 |
| 220 | Bryan Thomas RC | 8.00 | 3.00 |
| 221 | Wendell Bryant RC | 5.00 | 2.00 |
| 222 | Damien Anderson RC | 8.00 | 3.00 |
| 223 | Travis Stephens RC | 8.00 | 3.00 |
| 224 | Rohan Davey RC | 10.00 | 4.00 |
| 225 | Mike Pearson RC | 5.00 | 2.00 |
| 226 | Marc Colombo RC | 5.00 | 2.00 |
| 227 | Phillip Buchanon RC | 10.00 | 4.00 |
| 228 | T.J. Duckett RC | 10.00 | 4.00 |
| 229 | Ron Johnson RC | 8.00 | 3.00 |
| 230 | Larry Tripplett RC | 5.00 | 2.00 |
| 231 | Randy Fasani RC | 8.00 | 3.00 |
| 232 | Keyuo Craver RC | 8.00 | 3.00 |
| 233 | Marquand Manuel RC | 5.00 | 2.00 |
| 234 | Jonathan Wells RC | 10.00 | 4.00 |
| 235 | Reche Caldwell RC | 10.00 | 4.00 |
| 236 | Luke Staley RC | 8.00 | 3.00 |
| 237 | Donte Stallworth RC | 15.00 | 6.00 |
| 238 | Levar Fisher RC | 10.00 | 4.00 |

| | | | |
|---|---|---|---|
| ❑ 239 Lamar Gordon RC | 10.00 | 4.00 |
| ❑ 240 William Green RC | 10.00 | 4.00 |
| ❑ 241 Dusty Bonner RC | 5.00 | 2.00 |
| ❑ 242 Craig Nall RC | 10.00 | 4.00 |
| ❑ 243 Eric McCoo RC | 5.00 | 2.00 |
| ❑ 244 David Thornton RC | 5.00 | 2.00 |
| ❑ 245 Terry Jones RC | 8.00 | 3.00 |
| ❑ 246 Lee Mays RC | 10.00 | 4.00 |
| ❑ 247 Bryan Fletcher RC | 5.00 | 2.00 |
| ❑ 248 Verron Haynes RC | 10.00 | 4.00 |
| ❑ 249 Zak Kustok RC | 10.00 | 4.00 |
| ❑ 250 Chad Hutchinson RC | 8.00 | 3.00 |
| ❑ 251 Andra Davis RC | 8.00 | 3.00 |
| ❑ 252 Wes Pate RC | 5.00 | 2.00 |
| ❑ 253 Jon McGraw RC | 5.00 | 2.00 |
| ❑ 254 Howard Green RC | 5.00 | 2.00 |
| ❑ 255 Daryl Jones RC | 8.00 | 3.00 |
| ❑ 256 David Priestley RC | 8.00 | 3.00 |
| ❑ 257 Marques Anderson RC | 10.00 | 4.00 |
| ❑ 258 Roosevelt Williams RC | 5.00 | 2.00 |
| ❑ 259 Major Applewhite RC | 10.00 | 4.00 |
| ❑ 260 Ronald Curry RC | 10.00 | 4.00 |
| ❑ 261 Adrian Peterson RC | 12.00 | 5.00 |
| ❑ 262 Tellis Redmon RC | 8.00 | 3.00 |
| ❑ 263 Chester Taylor RC | 20.00 | 7.50 |
| ❑ 264 Deion Branch RC | 15.00 | 6.00 |
| ❑ 265 Tank Williams RC | 5.00 | 2.00 |

## 2003 Topps Chrome

PRIEST HOLMES

| | | | |
|---|---|---|---|
| ❑ COMP.SET w/o SP's (165) | 40.00 | 15.00 |
| ❑ 1 Michael Vick | 3.00 | 1.25 |
| ❑ 2 Josh Reed | .75 | .30 |
| ❑ 3 James Stewart | .75 | .30 |
| ❑ 4 Quincy Morgan | .75 | .30 |
| ❑ 5 Corey Bradford | .50 | .20 |
| ❑ 6 Fred Taylor | 1.25 | .50 |
| ❑ 7 David Patten | .75 | .30 |
| ❑ 8 Jerome Bettis | 1.25 | .50 |
| ❑ 9 Jerry Porter | .75 | .30 |
| ❑ 10 Steve McNair | 1.25 | .50 |
| ❑ 11 Stephen Davis | .75 | .30 |
| ❑ 12 Frank Wycheck | .50 | .20 |
| ❑ 13 Marcus Pollard | .50 | .20 |
| ❑ 14 David Terrell | .75 | .30 |
| ❑ 15 Bubba Franks | .75 | .30 |
| ❑ 16 Trent Green | .75 | .30 |
| ❑ 17 Mark Brunell | .75 | .30 |
| ❑ 18 James Thrash | .50 | .20 |
| ❑ 19 Mike Alstott | 1.25 | .50 |
| ❑ 20 Deuce McAllister | 1.25 | .50 |
| ❑ 21 Santana Moss | .75 | .30 |
| ❑ 22 Jason Taylor | .50 | .20 |
| ❑ 23 Corey Dillon | .75 | .30 |
| ❑ 24 Jeff Blake | .50 | .20 |
| ❑ 25 Ed McCaffrey | 1.25 | .50 |
| ❑ 26 Priest Holmes | 1.50 | .60 |
| ❑ 27 Tim Brown | 1.25 | .50 |
| ❑ 28 Curtis Martin | 1.25 | .50 |
| ❑ 29 Derrius Thompson | .50 | .20 |
| ❑ 30 Jonathan Wells | .50 | .20 |
| ❑ 31 William Green | .50 | .20 |
| ❑ 32 Bill Schroeder | .75 | .30 |
| ❑ 33 Amos Zereoue | .75 | .30 |
| ❑ 34 Warren Sapp | .75 | .30 |
| ❑ 35 Koren Robinson | .75 | .30 |
| ❑ 36 Donovan McNabb | 1.50 | .60 |
| ❑ 37 Edgerrin James | 1.25 | .50 |
| ❑ 38 Kelly Holcomb | .75 | .30 |
| ❑ 39 Daunte Culpepper | 1.25 | .50 |
| ❑ 40 Tommy Maddox | 1.25 | .50 |
| ❑ 41 Rod Gardner | .75 | .30 |

| | | | |
|---|---|---|---|
| ❑ 42 T.J. Duckett | .75 | .30 |
| ❑ 43 Drew Bledsoe | 1.25 | .50 |
| ❑ 44 Rod Smith | .75 | .30 |
| ❑ 45 Peyton Manning | 2.00 | .75 |
| ❑ 46 Darrell Jackson | .75 | .30 |
| ❑ 47 Brett Favre | 3.00 | 1.25 |
| ❑ 48 Ashley Lelie | 1.25 | .50 |
| ❑ 49 Jeremy Shockey | 2.00 | .75 |
| ❑ 50 Hines Ward | 1.25 | .50 |
| ❑ 51 Jeff Garcia | 1.25 | .50 |
| ❑ 52 Eddie Kennison | .50 | .20 |
| ❑ 53 Brian Urlacher | 2.00 | .75 |
| ❑ 54 Antwaan Randle El | 1.25 | .50 |
| ❑ 55 Eddie George | .75 | .30 |
| ❑ 56 Derrick Brooks | .75 | .30 |
| ❑ 57 Isaac Bruce | .75 | .30 |
| ❑ 58 Joe Horn | .75 | .30 |
| ❑ 59 Jon Kitna | .75 | .30 |
| ❑ 60 David Boston | .75 | .30 |
| ❑ 61 Todd Heap | .75 | .30 |
| ❑ 62 Lamar Smith | .50 | .20 |
| ❑ 63 Germane Crowell | .50 | .20 |
| ❑ 64 Kevin Johnson | .75 | .30 |
| ❑ 65 Drew Brees | 1.25 | .50 |
| ❑ 66 Chad Lewis | .50 | .20 |
| ❑ 67 Charlie Garner | .75 | .30 |
| ❑ 68 Laveranues Coles | .75 | .30 |
| ❑ 69 Shaun Alexander | 1.25 | .50 |
| ❑ 70 Kevan Barlow | .75 | .30 |
| ❑ 71 Aaron Brooks | 1.25 | .50 |
| ❑ 72 Jake Plummer | .75 | .30 |
| ❑ 73 Emmitt Smith | 3.00 | 1.25 |
| ❑ 74 Terry Glenn | .50 | .20 |
| ❑ 75 Michael Bennett | .75 | .30 |
| ❑ 76 Deion Branch | 1.25 | .50 |
| ❑ 77 Keyshawn Johnson | 1.25 | .50 |
| ❑ 78 Marc Bulger | 1.25 | .50 |
| ❑ 79 Matt Hasselbeck | .75 | .30 |
| ❑ 80 Garrison Hearst | .75 | .30 |
| ❑ 81 Brian Griese | 1.25 | .50 |
| ❑ 82 Johnnie Morton | .75 | .30 |
| ❑ 83 Patrick Ramsey | 1.25 | .50 |
| ❑ 84 Donald Driver | .75 | .30 |
| ❑ 85 Joey Harrington | 2.00 | .75 |
| ❑ 86 Ricky Williams | 1.25 | .50 |
| ❑ 87 Jabar Gaffney | .75 | .30 |
| ❑ 88 Duce Staley | .75 | .30 |
| ❑ 89 Jimmy Smith | .75 | .30 |
| ❑ 90 Reggie Wayne | .75 | .30 |
| ❑ 91 Chad Johnson | 1.25 | .50 |
| ❑ 92 Steve Beuerlein | .50 | .20 |
| ❑ 93 Joey Galloway | .75 | .30 |
| ❑ 94 Curtis Conway | .50 | .20 |
| ❑ 95 Brad Johnson | .75 | .30 |
| ❑ 96 Jamal Lewis | 1.25 | .50 |
| ❑ 97 Terrell Owens | 1.25 | .50 |
| ❑ 98 Todd Pinkston | .75 | .30 |
| ❑ 99 Keenan McCardell | .75 | .30 |
| ❑ 100 Antonio Bryant | .75 | .30 |
| ❑ 101 Eric Moulds | .75 | .30 |
| ❑ 102 Jim Miller | .50 | .20 |
| ❑ 103 Troy Brown | .75 | .30 |
| ❑ 104 Rich Gannon | 1.25 | .50 |
| ❑ 105 Chad Pennington | 1.50 | .60 |
| ❑ 106 Michael Strahan | .75 | .30 |
| ❑ 107 Chris Chambers | 1.25 | .50 |
| ❑ 108 Antowain Smith | .75 | .30 |
| ❑ 109 Derrick Mason | .75 | .30 |
| ❑ 110 Michael Pittman | .50 | .20 |
| ❑ 111 Torry Holt | 1.25 | .50 |
| ❑ 112 Tony Gonzalez | .75 | .30 |
| ❑ 113 Marty Booker | .75 | .30 |
| ❑ 114 Shannon Sharpe | .50 | .20 |
| ❑ 115 Zach Thomas | 1.25 | .50 |
| ❑ 116 Plaxico Burress | .75 | .30 |
| ❑ 117 Kurt Warner | 1.25 | .50 |
| ❑ 118 Warrick Dunn | .75 | .30 |
| ❑ 119 Jay Fiedler | .75 | .30 |
| ❑ 120 LaMont Jordan | 1.25 | .50 |
| ❑ 121 Kerry Collins | .75 | .30 |
| ❑ 122 Jerry Rice | 2.50 | 1.00 |
| ❑ 123 Randy Moss | 2.00 | .75 |
| ❑ 124 Tom Brady | 3.00 | 1.25 |
| ❑ 125 Amani Toomer | .75 | .30 |
| ❑ 126 Travis Henry | .75 | .30 |
| ❑ 127 Chris Chandler | .50 | .20 |
| ❑ 128 Ray Lewis | 1.25 | .50 |

| | | | |
|---|---|---|---|
| ❑ 129 Donte Stallworth | 1.25 | .50 |
| ❑ 130 David Carr | 2.00 | .75 |
| ❑ 131 Andre Davis | .50 | .20 |
| ❑ 132 Travis Taylor | .75 | .30 |
| ❑ 133 Steve Smith | 1.25 | .50 |
| ❑ 134 Tiki Barber | 1.25 | .50 |
| ❑ 135 Chad Hutchinson | .50 | .20 |
| ❑ 136 Marshall Faulk | 1.25 | .50 |
| ❑ 137 Peerless Price | .75 | .30 |
| ❑ 138 Ahman Green | 1.25 | .50 |
| ❑ 139 Julius Peppers | 1.25 | .50 |
| ❑ 140 LaDainian Tomlinson | 1.25 | .50 |
| ❑ 141 Muhsin Muhammad | .75 | .30 |
| ❑ 142 Tim Couch | .50 | .20 |
| ❑ 143 Clinton Portis | 2.00 | .75 |
| ❑ 144 Anthony Thomas | .75 | .30 |
| ❑ 145 Marvin Harrison | 1.25 | .50 |
| ❑ 146 Priest Holmes WW | .75 | .30 |
| ❑ 147 Drew Bledsoe WW | .75 | .30 |
| ❑ 148 Tom Brady WW | 1.25 | .50 |
| ❑ 149 Shaun Alexander WW | .75 | .30 |
| ❑ 150 Brett Favre WW | 1.25 | .50 |
| ❑ 151 Travis Henry WW | .50 | .20 |
| ❑ 152 Marshall Faulk WW | .75 | .30 |
| ❑ 153 Terrell Owens WW | .50 | .20 |
| ❑ 154 Jeff Garcia WW | .50 | .20 |
| ❑ 155 Plaxico Burress WW | .50 | .20 |
| ❑ 156 Donovan McNabb WW | .75 | .30 |
| ❑ 157 Ricky Williams WW | .75 | .30 |
| ❑ 158 Michael Vick WW | 1.50 | .60 |
| ❑ 159 Steve Smith WW | .75 | .30 |
| ❑ 160 Marvin Harrison WW | .50 | .20 |
| ❑ 161 Chad Pennington WW | .75 | .30 |
| ❑ 162 Jeremy Shockey WW | .75 | .30 |
| ❑ 163 Tommy Maddox WW | .50 | .20 |
| ❑ 164 Steve McNair WW | .50 | .20 |
| ❑ 165 Rich Gannon WW | .50 | .20 |
| ❑ 166 Carson Palmer RC | 30.00 | 15.00 |
| ❑ 167 J.R. Tolver RC | 6.00 | 2.50 |
| ❑ 168 Michael Haynes RC | 8.00 | 3.00 |
| ❑ 169 Terrell Suggs RC | 12.00 | 5.00 |
| ❑ 170 Rashean Mathis RC | 6.00 | 2.50 |
| ❑ 171 Chris Kelsay RC | 8.00 | 3.00 |
| ❑ 172 Brad Banks RC | 6.00 | 2.50 |
| ❑ 173 Jordan Gross RC | 6.00 | 2.50 |
| ❑ 174 Lee Suggs RC | 8.00 | 3.00 |
| ❑ 175 Kliff Kingsbury RC | 6.00 | 2.50 |
| ❑ 176 William Joseph RC | 8.00 | 3.00 |
| ❑ 177 Kelley Washington RC | 8.00 | 3.00 |
| ❑ 178 Jerome McDougle RC | 8.00 | 3.00 |
| ❑ 179 Keenan Howry RC | 8.00 | 3.00 |
| ❑ 180 Chris Simms RC | 12.00 | 5.00 |
| ❑ 181 Alonzo Jackson RC | 6.00 | 2.50 |
| ❑ 182 L.J. Smith RC | 8.00 | 3.00 |
| ❑ 183 Mike Doss RC | 8.00 | 3.00 |
| ❑ 184 Bobby Wade RC | 8.00 | 3.00 |
| ❑ 185 Ken Hamlin RC | 8.00 | 3.00 |
| ❑ 186 Brandon Lloyd RC | 8.00 | 3.00 |
| ❑ 187 Justin Fargas RC | 8.00 | 3.00 |
| ❑ 188 DeWayne Robertson RC | 8.00 | 3.00 |
| ❑ 189 Bryant Johnson RC | 8.00 | 3.00 |
| ❑ 190 Boss Bailey RC | 8.00 | 3.00 |
| ❑ 191 Onterrio Smith RC | 8.00 | 3.00 |
| ❑ 192 Doug Gabriel RC | 8.00 | 3.00 |
| ❑ 193 Jimmy Kennedy RC | 8.00 | 3.00 |
| ❑ 194 B.J. Askew RC | 8.00 | 3.00 |
| ❑ 195 Taylor Jacobs RC | 6.00 | 2.50 |
| ❑ 196 Dallas Clark RC | 8.00 | 3.00 |
| ❑ 197 DeWayne White RC | 6.00 | 2.50 |
| ❑ 198 Arnaz Battle RC | 8.00 | 3.00 |
| ❑ 199 Kareem Kelly RC | 6.00 | 2.50 |
| ❑ 200 Talman Gardner RC | 8.00 | 3.00 |
| ❑ 201 Billy McMullen RC | 6.00 | 2.50 |
| ❑ 202 Travis Anglin RC | 4.00 | 1.50 |
| ❑ 203 Anquan Boldin RC | 20.00 | 10.00 |
| ❑ 204 Osi Umenyiora RC | 12.00 | 5.00 |
| ❑ 205 Byron Leftwich RC | 15.00 | 6.00 |
| ❑ 206 Marcus Trufant RC | 8.00 | 3.00 |
| ❑ 207 Sam Aiken RC | 6.00 | 2.50 |
| ❑ 208 LaBrandon Toefield RC | 8.00 | 3.00 |
| ❑ 209 Terry Pierce RC | 6.00 | 2.50 |
| ❑ 210 Charles Rogers RC | 8.00 | 3.00 |
| ❑ 211 Chaun Thompson RC | 4.00 | 1.50 |
| ❑ 212 Chris Brown RC | 8.00 | 3.00 |
| ❑ 213 Justin Gage RC | 8.00 | 3.00 |
| ❑ 214 Kevin Williams RC | 8.00 | 3.00 |
| ❑ 215 Willis McGahee RC | 20.00 | 7.50 |

| | | |
|---|---|---|
| ☐ 216 Victor Hobson RC | 8.00 | 3.00 |
| ☐ 217 Brian St.Pierre RC | 8.00 | 3.00 |
| ☐ 218 Nate Burleson RC | 8.00 | 3.00 |
| ☐ 219 Calvin Pace RC | 6.00 | 2.50 |
| ☐ 220 Larry Johnson RC | 20.00 | 8.00 |
| ☐ 221 Andre Woolfolk RC | 8.00 | 3.00 |
| ☐ 222 Tyrone Calico RC | 8.00 | 3.00 |
| ☐ 223 Seneca Wallace RC | 8.00 | 3.00 |
| ☐ 224 Domanick Davis RC | 8.00 | 3.00 |
| ☐ 225 Rex Grossman RC | 25.00 | 10.00 |
| ☐ 226 Artose Pinner RC | 8.00 | 3.00 |
| ☐ 227 Jason Witten RC | 15.00 | 6.00 |
| ☐ 228 Bennie Joppru RC | 8.00 | 3.00 |
| ☐ 229 Bethel Johnson RC | 8.00 | 3.00 |
| ☐ 230 Kyle Boller RC | 8.00 | 3.00 |
| ☐ 231 Shaun McDonald RC | 8.00 | 3.00 |
| ☐ 232 Musa Smith RC | 8.00 | 3.00 |
| ☐ 233 Ken Dorsey RC | 8.00 | 3.00 |
| ☐ 234 Johnathan Sullivan RC | 6.00 | 2.50 |
| ☐ 235 Andre Johnson RC | 15.00 | 6.00 |
| ☐ 236 Nick Barnett RC | 8.00 | 3.00 |
| ☐ 237 Teyo Johnson RC | 8.00 | 3.00 |
| ☐ 238 Terrence Newman RC | 15.00 | 6.00 |
| ☐ 239 Kevin Curtis RC | 10.00 | 4.00 |
| ☐ 240 Dave Ragone RC | 8.00 | 3.00 |
| ☐ 241 Ty Warren RC | 8.00 | 3.00 |
| ☐ 242 Walter Young RC | 4.00 | 1.50 |
| ☐ 243 Kevin Walter RC | 6.00 | 2.50 |
| ☐ 244 Carl Ford RC | 4.00 | 1.50 |
| ☐ 245 Cecil Sapp RC | 6.00 | 2.50 |
| ☐ 246 Sultan McCullough RC | 6.00 | 2.50 |
| ☐ 247 Eugene Wilson RC | 8.00 | 3.00 |
| ☐ 248 Ricky Manning RC | 8.00 | 3.00 |
| ☐ 249 Andrew Williams RC | 6.00 | 2.50 |
| ☐ 250 Juston Wood RC | 4.00 | 1.50 |
| ☐ 251 Cory Redding RC | 6.00 | 2.50 |
| ☐ 252 Charles Tillman RC | 10.00 | 4.00 |
| ☐ 253 Terrence Edwards RC | 6.00 | 2.50 |
| ☐ 254 Adrian Madise RC | 6.00 | 2.50 |
| ☐ 255 David Kircus RC | 8.00 | 3.00 |
| ☐ 256 Zuriel Smith RC | 4.00 | 1.50 |
| ☐ 257 Earnest Graham RC | 8.00 | 3.00 |
| ☐ 258 Ronald Bellamy RC | 4.00 | 1.50 |
| ☐ 259 John Anderson RC | 4.00 | 1.50 |
| ☐ 260 David Tyree RC | 6.00 | 2.50 |
| ☐ 261 Malaefou MacKenzie RC | 4.00 | 1.50 |
| ☐ 262 Ahrriaad Galloway RC | 6.00 | 2.50 |
| ☐ 263 Brooks Bollinger RC | 8.00 | 3.00 |
| ☐ 264 Gibran Hamdan RC | 6.00 | 2.50 |
| ☐ 265 Taco Wallace RC | 6.00 | 2.50 |
| ☐ 266 LaTarence Dunbar RC | 6.00 | 2.50 |
| ☐ 267 Justin Griffith RC | 6.00 | 2.50 |
| ☐ 268 Bradie James RC | 8.00 | 3.00 |
| ☐ 269 Danny Curley RC | 4.00 | 1.50 |
| ☐ 270 Kenny Peterson RC | 6.00 | 2.50 |
| ☐ 271 DeAndrew Rubin RC | 4.00 | 1.50 |
| ☐ 272 Ryan Hoag RC | 4.00 | 1.50 |
| ☐ 273 Rien Long RC | 4.00 | 1.50 |
| ☐ 274 Troy Polamalu RC | 30.00 | 15.00 |
| ☐ 275 Terrence Holt RC | 6.00 | 2.50 |

**2004 Topps Chrome**

| | | |
|---|---|---|
| ☐ COMP.SET w/o SPs (165) | 30.00 | 12.50 |
| ☐ 1 Peyton Manning | 2.00 | .75 |
| ☐ 2 Patrick Ramsey | .75 | .30 |
| ☐ 3 Justin McCareins | .60 | .25 |
| ☐ 4 Matt Hasselbeck | 1.00 | .40 |
| ☐ 5 Chris Chambers | .75 | .30 |
| ☐ 6 Bubba Franks | .75 | .30 |

| | | |
|---|---|---|
| ☐ 7 Eric Moulds | .75 | .30 |
| ☐ 8 Anquan Boldin | 1.00 | .40 |
| ☐ 9 Brian Urlacher | 1.00 | .40 |
| ☐ 10 Stephen Davis | .75 | .30 |
| ☐ 11 Michael Vick | 1.00 | .40 |
| ☐ 12 Dante Hall | .75 | .30 |
| ☐ 13 Chad Pennington | 1.00 | .40 |
| ☐ 14 Kevan Barlow | .75 | .30 |
| ☐ 15 Tommy Maddox | .75 | .30 |
| ☐ 16 Domanick Davis | 1.00 | .40 |
| ☐ 17 Dwight Freeney | 1.00 | .40 |
| ☐ 18 LaVar Arrington | .75 | .30 |
| ☐ 19 Troy Hambrick | .60 | .25 |
| ☐ 20 Jake Plummer | .75 | .30 |
| ☐ 21 Willis McGahee | 1.00 | .40 |
| ☐ 22 Steve McNair | 1.00 | .40 |
| ☐ 23 Kerry Collins | .75 | .30 |
| ☐ 24 Hines Ward | 1.00 | .40 |
| ☐ 25 Terrell Owens | 1.00 | .40 |
| ☐ 26 Jerome Pathon | .60 | .25 |
| ☐ 27 Andre Johnson | 1.00 | .40 |
| ☐ 28 DeShaun Foster | .75 | .30 |
| ☐ 29 Terrell Suggs | .60 | .25 |
| ☐ 30 Marcel Shipp | 1.00 | .40 |
| ☐ 31 Kyle Boller | .75 | .30 |
| ☐ 32 Javon Walker | .75 | .30 |
| ☐ 33 Ahman Green | 1.00 | .40 |
| ☐ 34 Travis Henry | .75 | .30 |
| ☐ 35 Randy McMichael | .60 | .25 |
| ☐ 36 Jerry Rice | 2.00 | .75 |
| ☐ 37 Travis Taylor | .60 | .25 |
| ☐ 38 Fred Taylor | .75 | .30 |
| ☐ 39 Zach Thomas | 1.00 | .40 |
| ☐ 40 Marques Tuiasosopo | .60 | .25 |
| ☐ 41 Laveranues Coles | .75 | .30 |
| ☐ 42 Thomas Jones | .75 | .30 |
| ☐ 43 Jamie Sharper | .60 | .25 |
| ☐ 44 Quincy Morgan | .60 | .25 |
| ☐ 45 Troy Brown | .75 | .30 |
| ☐ 46 Joey Galloway | .75 | .30 |
| ☐ 47 Justin Fargas | .75 | .30 |
| ☐ 48 Daunte Culpepper | 1.00 | .40 |
| ☐ 49 Keenan McCardell | .60 | .25 |
| ☐ 50 Priest Holmes | 1.00 | .40 |
| ☐ 51 Chad Johnson | .75 | .30 |
| ☐ 52 Marty Booker | .75 | .30 |
| ☐ 53 Tim Rattay | .60 | .25 |
| ☐ 54 Brian Westbrook | 1.00 | .40 |
| ☐ 55 Ricky Williams | 1.00 | .40 |
| ☐ 56 Lee Suggs | 1.00 | .40 |
| ☐ 57 Keith Brooking | .60 | .25 |
| ☐ 58 Rex Grossman | 1.00 | .40 |
| ☐ 59 Dallas Clark | .75 | .30 |
| ☐ 60 Charles Rogers | .75 | .30 |
| ☐ 61 Donte' Stallworth | .75 | .30 |
| ☐ 62 Deion Branch | .75 | .30 |
| ☐ 63 Ike Hilliard | .75 | .30 |
| ☐ 64 Michael Strahan | .75 | .30 |
| ☐ 65 Randy Moss | 1.25 | .50 |
| ☐ 66 Isaac Bruce | .75 | .30 |
| ☐ 67 Brad Johnson | .75 | .30 |
| ☐ 68 Warrick Dunn | .75 | .30 |
| ☐ 69 Josh McCown | .75 | .30 |
| ☐ 70 Donovan McNabb | 1.00 | .40 |
| ☐ 71 Shaun Alexander | 1.00 | .40 |
| ☐ 72 William Green | .60 | .25 |
| ☐ 73 Carson Palmer | 1.25 | .50 |
| ☐ 74 Quentin Griffin | .75 | .30 |
| ☐ 75 LaDainian Tomlinson | 1.50 | .60 |
| ☐ 76 Edgerrin James | 1.00 | .40 |
| ☐ 77 Santana Moss | .75 | .30 |
| ☐ 78 Marshall Faulk | 1.00 | .40 |
| ☐ 79 Tyrone Calico | .75 | .30 |
| ☐ 80 Marvin Harrison | 1.00 | .40 |
| ☐ 81 Tony Gonzalez | 1.00 | .40 |
| ☐ 82 Deuce McAllister | 1.00 | .40 |
| ☐ 83 Drew Brees | 1.00 | .40 |
| ☐ 84 Todd Pinkston | .60 | .25 |
| ☐ 85 Jeff Garcia | 1.00 | .40 |
| ☐ 86 Darrell Jackson | .75 | .30 |
| ☐ 87 Ray Lewis | 1.00 | .40 |
| ☐ 88 Billy Volek | .75 | .30 |
| ☐ 89 Rudi Johnson | .75 | .30 |
| ☐ 90 Julius Peppers | .75 | .30 |
| ☐ 91 Peter Warrick | .75 | .30 |
| ☐ 92 Trent Green | .75 | .30 |
| ☐ 93 Onterrio Smith | .60 | .25 |

| | | |
|---|---|---|
| ☐ 94 Jerome Bettis | 1.00 | .40 |
| ☐ 95 Keyshawn Johnson | .75 | .30 |
| ☐ 96 Jamal Lewis | .75 | .30 |
| ☐ 97 Alge Crumpler | .75 | .30 |
| ☐ 98 Michael Bennett | .75 | .30 |
| ☐ 99 Jimmy Smith | .75 | .30 |
| ☐ 100 Brett Favre | 2.50 | 1.00 |
| ☐ 101 Jerry Porter | .75 | .30 |
| ☐ 102 Marc Bulger | .75 | .30 |
| ☐ 103 David Carr | .75 | .30 |
| ☐ 104 Mark Brunell | .75 | .30 |
| ☐ 105 Aaron Brooks | .75 | .30 |
| ☐ 106 Plaxico Burress | .75 | .30 |
| ☐ 107 Correll Buckhalter | .75 | .30 |
| ☐ 108 Jevon Kearse | .75 | .30 |
| ☐ 109 Michael Pittman | .75 | .30 |
| ☐ 110 Clinton Portis | 1.00 | .40 |
| ☐ 111 Corey Dillon | .75 | .30 |
| ☐ 112 Steve Smith | 1.00 | .40 |
| ☐ 113 Eddie Kennison | .75 | .30 |
| ☐ 114 Amani Toomer | .75 | .30 |
| ☐ 115 Kelly Holcomb | .75 | .30 |
| ☐ 116 Torry Holt | 1.00 | .40 |
| ☐ 117 Eddie George | .75 | .30 |
| ☐ 118 Jeremy Shockey | .75 | .30 |
| ☐ 119 Jon Kitna | .75 | .30 |
| ☐ 120 Todd Heap | .75 | .30 |
| ☐ 121 Ashley Lelie | .75 | .30 |
| ☐ 122 Byron Leftwich | 1.00 | .40 |
| ☐ 123 Duce Staley | .75 | .30 |
| ☐ 124 Rod Gardner | .60 | .25 |
| ☐ 125 Tom Brady | 2.50 | 1.00 |
| ☐ 126 Reggie Wayne | .75 | .30 |
| ☐ 127 Joe Horn | .75 | .30 |
| ☐ 128 Curtis Martin | 1.00 | .40 |
| ☐ 129 Charlie Garner | .75 | .30 |
| ☐ 130 Derrick Mason | .75 | .30 |
| ☐ 131 Marcus Robinson | .75 | .30 |
| ☐ 132 David Boston | .60 | .25 |
| ☐ 133 Drew Bledsoe | 1.00 | .40 |
| ☐ 134 Anthony Thomas | .75 | .30 |
| ☐ 135 Tiki Barber | 1.00 | .40 |
| ☐ 136 Terry Glenn | .75 | .30 |
| ☐ 137 A.J. Feeley | .75 | .30 |
| ☐ 138 Peerless Price | .75 | .30 |
| ☐ 139 Jake Delhomme | .75 | .30 |
| ☐ 140 Kevin Faulk | .75 | .30 |
| ☐ 141 Quincy Carter | .60 | .25 |
| ☐ 142 Joey Harrington | .75 | .30 |
| ☐ 143 Donald Driver | 1.00 | .40 |
| ☐ 144 Koren Robinson | 1.00 | .40 |
| ☐ 145 Rod Smith | .75 | .30 |
| ☐ 146 Anquan Boldin WW | .60 | .25 |
| ☐ 147 Jamal Lewis WW | .50 | .20 |
| ☐ 148 Priest Holmes WW | .60 | .25 |
| ☐ 149 Peyton Manning WW | 1.25 | .50 |
| ☐ 150 Marvin Harrison WW | .60 | .25 |
| ☐ 151 Steve McNair WW | .60 | .25 |
| ☐ 152 Travis Henry WW | .50 | .20 |
| ☐ 153 Torry Holt WW | .60 | .25 |
| ☐ 154 Tom Brady WW | 1.50 | .60 |
| ☐ 155 Ahman Green WW | .60 | .25 |
| ☐ 156 Donovan McNabb WW | .60 | .25 |
| ☐ 157 Deuce McAllister WW | .60 | .25 |
| ☐ 158 Domanick Davis WW | .60 | .25 |
| ☐ 159 Clinton Portis WW | .60 | .25 |
| ☐ 160 Rudi Johnson WW | .50 | .20 |
| ☐ 161 Brett Favre WW | 1.50 | .60 |
| ☐ 162 LaDainian Tomlinson WW | 1.00 | .40 |
| ☐ 163 Steve Smith WW | .60 | .25 |
| ☐ 164 Edgerrin James WW | .60 | .25 |
| ☐ 165 Ty Law WW | .50 | .20 |
| ☐ 166 Ben Roethlisberger RC | 40.00 | 15.00 |
| ☐ 167 Ahmad Carroll RC | 5.00 | 2.00 |
| ☐ 168 Johnnie Morant RC | 4.00 | 1.50 |
| ☐ 169 Greg Jones RC | 5.00 | 2.00 |
| ☐ 170 Michael Clayton RC | 3.00 | 1.25 |
| ☐ 171 Josh Harris RC | 3.00 | 1.25 |
| ☐ 172 Tatum Bell RC | 5.00 | 2.00 |
| ☐ 173 Robert Gallery RC | 5.00 | 2.00 |
| ☐ 174 B.J. Symons RC | 3.00 | 1.25 |
| ☐ 175 Roy Williams RC | 12.00 | 5.00 |
| ☐ 176 DeAngelo Hall RC | 5.00 | 2.00 |
| ☐ 177 Jeff Smoker RC | 4.00 | 1.50 |
| ☐ 178 Lee Evans RC | 6.00 | 2.50 |
| ☐ 179 Michael Jenkins RC | 5.00 | 2.00 |
| ☐ 180 Steven Jackson RC | 15.00 | 6.00 |

| | | |
|---|---|---|
| ❏ 181 Will Smith RC | 4.00 | 1.50 |
| ❏ 182 Vince Wilfork RC | 5.00 | 2.00 |
| ❏ 183 Ben Troupe RC | 4.00 | 1.50 |
| ❏ 184 Chris Gamble RC | 4.00 | 1.50 |
| ❏ 185 Kevin Jones RC | 5.00 | 2.00 |
| ❏ 186 Jonathan Vilma RC | 5.00 | 2.00 |
| ❏ 187 Dontarrious Thomas RC | 5.00 | 2.00 |
| ❏ 188 Michael Boulware RC | 5.00 | 2.00 |
| ❏ 189 Mewelde Moore RC | 5.00 | 2.00 |
| ❏ 190 Drew Henson RC | 3.00 | 1.25 |
| ❏ 191 D.J. Williams RC | 5.00 | 2.00 |
| ❏ 192 Ernest Wilford RC | 5.00 | 2.00 |
| ❏ 193 John Navarre RC | 4.00 | 1.50 |
| ❏ 194 Jerricho Cotchery RC | 5.00 | 2.00 |
| ❏ 195 Derrick Hamilton RC | 3.00 | 1.25 |
| ❏ 196 Carlos Francis RC | 3.00 | 1.25 |
| ❏ 197 Ben Watson RC | 5.00 | 2.00 |
| ❏ 198 Reggie Williams RC | 5.00 | 2.00 |
| ❏ 199 Devard Darling RC | 4.00 | 1.50 |
| ❏ 200 Chris Perry RC | 5.00 | 2.00 |
| ❏ 201 Derrick Strait RC | 4.00 | 1.50 |
| ❏ 202 Sean Taylor RC | 5.00 | 2.00 |
| ❏ 203 Michael Turner RC | 10.00 | 4.00 |
| ❏ 204 Keary Colbert RC | 5.00 | 2.00 |
| ❏ 205 Eli Manning RC | 30.00 | 12.00 |
| ❏ 206 Julius Jones RC | 12.00 | 5.00 |
| ❏ 207 Jason Babin RC | 4.00 | 1.50 |
| ❏ 208 Cody Pickett RC | 4.00 | 1.50 |
| ❏ 209 Kenechi Udeze RC | 5.00 | 2.00 |
| ❏ 210 Rashaun Woods RC | 3.00 | 1.25 |
| ❏ 211 Matt Schaub RC | 15.00 | 6.00 |
| ❏ 212 Tommie Harris RC | 5.00 | 2.00 |
| ❏ 213 Dwan Edwards RC | 3.00 | 1.25 |
| ❏ 214 Shawn Andrews RC | 4.00 | 1.50 |
| ❏ 215 Larry Fitzgerald RC | 15.00 | 6.00 |
| ❏ 216 P.K. Sam RC | 3.00 | 1.25 |
| ❏ 217 Teddy Lehman RC | 4.00 | 1.50 |
| ❏ 218 Darius Watts RC | 4.00 | 1.50 |
| ❏ 219 D.J. Hackett RC | 5.00 | 2.00 |
| ❏ 220 Cedric Cobbs RC | 4.00 | 1.50 |
| ❏ 221 Antwan Odom RC | 4.00 | 1.50 |
| ❏ 222 Marquise Hill RC | 3.00 | 1.25 |
| ❏ 223 Luke Mecown RC | 5.00 | 2.00 |
| ❏ 224 Triandos Luke RC | 3.00 | 1.25 |
| ❏ 225 Kellen Winslow RC | 10.00 | 4.00 |
| ❏ 226 Derek Abney RC | 4.00 | 1.50 |
| ❏ 227 Chris Cooley RC | 5.00 | 2.00 |
| ❏ 228 Dunta Robinson RC | 4.00 | 1.50 |
| ❏ 229 Sean Jones RC | 4.00 | 1.50 |
| ❏ 230 Philip Rivers RC | 15.00 | 6.00 |
| ❏ 231 Craig Krenzel RC | 5.00 | 2.00 |
| ❏ 232 Daryl Smith RC | 4.00 | 1.50 |
| ❏ 233 Samie Parker RC | 4.00 | 1.50 |
| ❏ 234 Ben Hartsock RC | 4.00 | 1.50 |
| ❏ 235 J.P. Losman RC | 6.00 | 2.50 |
| ❏ 236 Karlos Dansby RC | 5.00 | 2.00 |
| ❏ 237 Ricardo Colclough RC | 5.00 | 2.00 |
| ❏ 238 Bernard Berrian RC | 5.00 | 2.00 |
| ❏ 239 Junior Siavii RC | 3.00 | 1.25 |
| ❏ 240 Devery Henderson RC | 5.00 | 2.00 |
| ❏ 241 Adimchinobe Echemandu RC | 4.00 | 1.50 |
| ❏ 242 Patrick Crayton RC | 6.00 | 2.50 |
| ❏ 243 Marcus Tubbs RC | 4.00 | 1.50 |
| ❏ 244 Jamaar Taylor RC | 3.00 | 1.25 |
| ❏ 245 Andy Hall RC | 4.00 | 1.50 |
| ❏ 246 Darnell Dockett RC | 3.00 | 1.25 |
| ❏ 247 Darrion Scott RC | 4.00 | 1.50 |
| ❏ 248 Jim Sorgi RC | 5.00 | 2.00 |
| ❏ 249 Jeff Dugan RC | 3.00 | 1.25 |
| ❏ 250 Ryan Krause RC | 3.00 | 1.25 |
| ❏ 251 Nate Lawrie RC | 3.00 | 1.25 |
| ❏ 252 Casey Bramlet RC | 4.00 | 1.50 |
| ❏ 253 Donnell Washington RC | 4.00 | 1.50 |
| ❏ 254 Jonathan Smith RC | 3.00 | 1.25 |
| ❏ 255 Tank Johnson RC | 4.00 | 1.50 |
| ❏ 256 Keith Smith RC | 3.00 | 1.25 |
| ❏ 257 Brandon Miree RC | 3.00 | 1.25 |
| ❏ 258 Michael Gaines RC | 3.00 | 1.25 |
| ❏ 259 Keiwan Ratliff RC | 3.00 | 1.25 |
| ❏ 260 Stuart Schweigert RC | 4.00 | 1.50 |
| ❏ 261 Derrick Ward RC | 5.00 | 2.00 |
| ❏ 262 Matt Ware RC | 5.00 | 2.00 |
| ❏ 263 Tim Anderson RC | 4.00 | 1.50 |
| ❏ 264 Bradlee Van Pelt RC | 3.00 | 1.25 |
| ❏ 265 Shawntae Spencer RC | 3.00 | 1.25 |
| ❏ 266 Joey Thomas RC | 3.00 | 1.25 |
| ❏ 267 Maurice Mann RC | 3.00 | 1.25 |

| | | |
|---|---|---|
| ❏ 268 Tim Euhus RC | 3.00 | 1.25 |
| ❏ 269 Matt Mauck RC | 4.00 | 1.50 |
| ❏ 270 Sloan Thomas RC | 4.00 | 1.50 |
| ❏ 271 Jeris McIntyre RC | 3.00 | 1.25 |
| ❏ 272 Randy Starks RC | 3.00 | 1.25 |
| ❏ 273 Clarence Moore RC | 4.00 | 1.50 |
| ❏ 274 Drew Carter RC | 5.00 | 2.00 |
| ❏ 275 Sean Ryan RC | 3.00 | 1.25 |
| ❏ RH38 Tom Brady RH | 5.00 | 2.00 |

## 2005 Topps Chrome

| | | |
|---|---|---|
| ❏ COMPLETE SET (275) | 150.00 | 75.00 |
| ❏ COMP.SET w/o RC's (165) | 30.00 | 12.50 |
| ❏ ROOKIE STATED ODDS 1:2 HOB/RET | | |
| ❏ RH STATED ODDS 1:288 HOB/RET | | |
| ❏ RH REFRACT.ODDS 1:17,884 H, 1:22,080 R | | |
| ❏ 1 Deuce McAllister | 1.00 | .40 |
| ❏ 2 Sean Taylor | .75 | .30 |
| ❏ 3 Koren Robinson | .75 | .30 |
| ❏ 4 Tiki Barber | 1.00 | .40 |
| ❏ 5 LaDainian Tomlinson | 1.50 | .60 |
| ❏ 6 Lee Evans | .75 | .30 |
| ❏ 7 Aaron Brooks | .60 | .25 |
| ❏ 8 LaMont Jordan | .75 | .30 |
| ❏ 9 Dante Hall | .75 | .30 |
| ❏ 10 Daunte Culpepper | 1.00 | .40 |
| ❏ 11 Thomas Jones | .75 | .30 |
| ❏ 12 Warrick Dunn | .75 | .30 |
| ❏ 13 Willis McGahee | 1.00 | .40 |
| ❏ 14 Ed Reed | .75 | .30 |
| ❏ 15 Derrick Mason | .75 | .30 |
| ❏ 16 Jason Witten | .75 | .30 |
| ❏ 17 Chad Johnson | .75 | .30 |
| ❏ 18 Amani Toomer | .75 | .30 |
| ❏ 19 Joey Harrington | 1.00 | .40 |
| ❏ 20 Brian Urlacher | 1.00 | .40 |
| ❏ 21 Brian Westbrook | 1.00 | .40 |
| ❏ 22 Matt Hasselbeck | .75 | .30 |
| ❏ 23 Michael Vick | 1.00 | .40 |
| ❏ 24 Kevin Jones | .75 | .30 |
| ❏ 25 Julius Peppers | .75 | .30 |
| ❏ 26 Michael Clayton | .75 | .30 |
| ❏ 27 Javon Walker | .75 | .30 |
| ❏ 28 Santana Moss | .75 | .30 |
| ❏ 29 Travis Henry | .75 | .30 |
| ❏ 30 Stephen Davis | .75 | .30 |
| ❏ 31 Larry Johnson | 1.00 | .40 |
| ❏ 32 Terrell Owens | 1.00 | .40 |
| ❏ 33 Ray Lewis | .75 | .30 |
| ❏ 34 Jake Plummer | .75 | .30 |
| ❏ 35 Philip Rivers | 1.00 | .40 |
| ❏ 36 Eli Manning | 2.00 | .75 |
| ❏ 37 Tedy Bruschi | 1.00 | .40 |
| ❏ 38 Adam Vinatieri | 1.00 | .40 |
| ❏ 39 J.P. Losman | 1.00 | .40 |
| ❏ 40 Zach Thomas | 1.00 | .40 |
| ❏ 41 Deion Branch | .75 | .30 |
| ❏ 42 Andre Johnson | .75 | .30 |
| ❏ 43 Marshall Faulk | 1.00 | .40 |
| ❏ 44 Bertrand Berry | .60 | .25 |
| ❏ 45 Terrell Suggs | .75 | .30 |
| ❏ 46 Tom Brady | 2.00 | .75 |
| ❏ 47 Ashley Lelie | .60 | .25 |
| ❏ 48 Jonathan Wells | .60 | .25 |
| ❏ 49 Randy McMichael | .60 | .25 |
| ❏ 50 Charles Rogers | .60 | .25 |
| ❏ 51 Larry Fitzgerald | 1.00 | .40 |
| ❏ 52 Hines Ward | 1.00 | .40 |
| ❏ 53 Jason Taylor | .75 | .30 |

| | | |
|---|---|---|
| ❏ 54 Ronde Barber | .75 | .30 |
| ❏ 55 T.J. Houshmandzadeh | .75 | .30 |
| ❏ 56 Keary Colbert | .60 | .25 |
| ❏ 57 DeAngelo Hall | .75 | .30 |
| ❏ 58 Chris Brown | .75 | .30 |
| ❏ 59 Chris Perry | .60 | .25 |
| ❏ 60 Steven Jackson | 1.25 | .50 |
| ❏ 61 Kyle Boller | .75 | .30 |
| ❏ 62 Rudi Johnson | .75 | .30 |
| ❏ 63 Roy Williams S | .75 | .30 |
| ❏ 64 Onterrio Smith | .60 | .25 |
| ❏ 65 Roy Williams WR | 1.00 | .40 |
| ❏ 66 Jerry Porter | .75 | .30 |
| ❏ 67 Edgerrin James | .75 | .30 |
| ❏ 68 Randy Moss | 1.00 | .40 |
| ❏ 69 Brian Griese | .75 | .30 |
| ❏ 70 Donovan McNabb | 1.00 | .40 |
| ❏ 71 Joe Horn | .75 | .30 |
| ❏ 72 Muhsin Muhammad | .75 | .30 |
| ❏ 73 Johnnie Morton | .75 | .30 |
| ❏ 74 Chad Pennington | 1.00 | .40 |
| ❏ 75 Torry Holt | .75 | .30 |
| ❏ 76 Marc Bulger | .75 | .30 |
| ❏ 77 Duce Staley | .75 | .30 |
| ❏ 78 Todd Heap | .75 | .30 |
| ❏ 79 Lee Suggs | .75 | .30 |
| ❏ 80 Patrick Ramsey | .75 | .30 |
| ❏ 81 Drew Bennett | .75 | .30 |
| ❏ 82 Michael Strahan | .75 | .30 |
| ❏ 83 Priest Holmes | 1.00 | .40 |
| ❏ 84 DeShaun Foster | .75 | .30 |
| ❏ 85 Corey Dillon | .75 | .30 |
| ❏ 86 Antonio Gates | 1.00 | .40 |
| ❏ 87 Trent Green | .75 | .30 |
| ❏ 88 Brandon Stokley | .60 | .25 |
| ❏ 89 Alge Crumpler | .75 | .30 |
| ❏ 90 Keyshawn Johnson | .75 | .30 |
| ❏ 91 Byron Leftwich | .75 | .30 |
| ❏ 92 Dunta Robinson | .60 | .25 |
| ❏ 93 Ben Roethlisberger | 2.50 | 1.00 |
| ❏ 94 Rod Smith | .75 | .30 |
| ❏ 95 Robert Gallery | .60 | .25 |
| ❏ 96 Tony Gonzalez | .75 | .30 |
| ❏ 97 Steve McNair | 1.00 | .40 |
| ❏ 98 Jeremy Shockey | 1.00 | .40 |
| ❏ 99 Dominic Rhodes | .75 | .30 |
| ❏ 100 Michael Jenkins | .75 | .30 |
| ❏ 101 Jake Delhomme | 1.00 | .40 |
| ❏ 102 Jerome Bettis | 1.00 | .40 |
| ❏ 103 Jevon Kearse | .75 | .30 |
| ❏ 104 Plaxico Burress | .75 | .30 |
| ❏ 105 Dwight Freeney | .75 | .30 |
| ❏ 106 Marcus Robinson | .75 | .30 |
| ❏ 107 Rex Grossman | 1.00 | .40 |
| ❏ 108 Drew Henson | .60 | .25 |
| ❏ 109 Julius Jones | 1.00 | .40 |
| ❏ 110 Jamal Lewis | .75 | .30 |
| ❏ 111 Justin McCareins | .60 | .25 |
| ❏ 112 Billy Volek | .75 | .30 |
| ❏ 113 Curtis Martin | 1.00 | .40 |
| ❏ 114 Tatum Bell | .75 | .30 |
| ❏ 115 Domanick Davis | .60 | .25 |
| ❏ 116 Marvin Harrison | 1.00 | .40 |
| ❏ 117 Anquan Boldin | .75 | .30 |
| ❏ 118 Jimmy Smith | .75 | .30 |
| ❏ 119 Drew Brees | 1.00 | .40 |
| ❏ 120 Donte Stallworth | .75 | .30 |
| ❏ 121 Nate Burleson | .75 | .30 |
| ❏ 122 Fred Taylor | 1.00 | .40 |
| ❏ 123 Takeo Spikes | .60 | .25 |
| ❏ 124 Jonathan Ogden | .60 | .25 |
| ❏ 125 Michael Bennett | .75 | .30 |
| ❏ 126 Clinton Portis | 1.00 | .40 |
| ❏ 127 Ahman Green | 1.00 | .40 |
| ❏ 128 Drew Bledsoe | 1.00 | .40 |
| ❏ 129 Darrell Jackson | .75 | .30 |
| ❏ 130 Jonathan Vilma | .75 | .30 |
| ❏ 131 David Carr | .75 | .30 |
| ❏ 132 Champ Bailey | .75 | .30 |
| ❏ 133 Derrick Blaylock | .60 | .25 |
| ❏ 134 T.J. Duckett | .60 | .25 |
| ❏ 135 Shaun Alexander | 1.00 | .40 |
| ❏ 136 Peyton Manning | 1.50 | .60 |
| ❏ 137 Isaac Bruce | .75 | .30 |
| ❏ 138 LaVar Arrington | .75 | .30 |
| ❏ 139 Brett Favre | 2.50 | 1.00 |
| ❏ 140 Allen Rossum | .60 | .25 |

| | | |
|---|---|---|
| ❏ 141 Eric Moulds | .75 | .30 |
| ❏ 142 Carson Palmer | 1.00 | .40 |
| ❏ 143 Laveranues Coles | .75 | .30 |
| ❏ 144 Chester Taylor | .75 | .30 |
| ❏ 145 Reggie Wayne | .75 | .30 |
| ❏ 146 Curtis Martin LL | .75 | .30 |
| ❏ 147 Daunte Culpepper LL | .75 | .30 |
| ❏ 148 Muhsin Muhammad LL | .60 | .25 |
| ❏ 149 Shaun Alexander LL | .75 | .30 |
| ❏ 150 Trent Green LL | .60 | .25 |
| ❏ 151 Joe Horn LL | .60 | .25 |
| ❏ 152 Corey Dillon LL | .60 | .25 |
| ❏ 153 Peyton Manning LL | 1.25 | .50 |
| ❏ 154 Javon Walker LL | .60 | .25 |
| ❏ 155 Edgerrin James LL | .60 | .25 |
| ❏ 156 Jake Scott GM | .50 | .20 |
| ❏ 157 John Elway GM | 1.50 | .60 |
| ❏ 158 Dwight Clark GM | .60 | .25 |
| ❏ 159 Lawrence Taylor GM | .75 | .30 |
| ❏ 160 Joe Namath GM | 1.25 | .50 |
| ❏ 161 Richard Dent GM | .60 | .25 |
| ❏ 162 Peyton Manning GM | 1.25 | .50 |
| ❏ 163 Don Maynard GM | .60 | .25 |
| ❏ 164 Joe Greene GM | .75 | .30 |
| ❏ 165 Roger Staubach GM | 1.25 | .50 |
| ❏ 166 J.J. Arrington RC | 5.00 | 2.00 |
| ❏ 167 Cedric Benson RC | 5.00 | 2.00 |
| ❏ 168 Mark Bradley RC | 5.00 | 2.00 |
| ❏ 169 Reggie Brown RC | 5.00 | 2.00 |
| ❏ 170 Ronnie Brown RC | 15.00 | 6.00 |
| ❏ 171 Jason Campbell RC | 10.00 | 4.00 |
| ❏ 172 Maurice Clarett RC | 4.00 | 1.50 |
| ❏ 173 Mark Clayton RC | 5.00 | 2.00 |
| ❏ 174 Braylon Edwards RC | 15.00 | 6.00 |
| ❏ 175 Ciatrick Fason RC | 4.00 | 1.50 |
| ❏ 176 Charlie Frye RC | 5.00 | 2.00 |
| ❏ 177 Frank Gore RC | 12.00 | 5.00 |
| ❏ 178 David Greene RC | 4.00 | 1.50 |
| ❏ 179 Vincent Jackson RC | 5.00 | 2.00 |
| ❏ 180 Adam Jones RC | 5.00 | 2.00 |
| ❏ 181 Matt Jones RC | 8.00 | 3.00 |
| ❏ 182 Stefan LeFors RC | 4.00 | 1.50 |
| ❏ 183 Heath Miller RC | 10.00 | 4.00 |
| ❏ 184 Ryan Moats RC | 5.00 | 2.00 |
| ❏ 185 Vernand Morency RC | 4.00 | 1.50 |
| ❏ 186 Terrence Murphy RC | 3.00 | 1.25 |
| ❏ 187 Kyle Orton RC | 6.00 | 2.50 |
| ❏ 188 Roscoe Parrish RC | 4.00 | 1.50 |
| ❏ 189 Courtney Roby RC | 4.00 | 1.50 |
| ❏ 190 Aaron Rodgers RC | 15.00 | 6.00 |
| ❏ 191 Carlos Rogers RC | 5.00 | 2.00 |
| ❏ 192 Antrel Rolle RC | 5.00 | 2.00 |
| ❏ 193 Eric Shelton RC | 4.00 | 1.50 |
| ❏ 194 Alex Smith QB RC | 8.00 | 3.00 |
| ❏ 195 Andrew Walter RC | 5.00 | 2.00 |
| ❏ 196 Roddy White RC | 6.00 | 2.50 |
| ❏ 197 Cadillac Williams RC | 10.00 | 4.00 |
| ❏ 198 Mike Williams RC | 5.00 | 2.00 |
| ❏ 199 Troy Williamson RC | 5.00 | 2.00 |
| ❏ 200 Taylor Stubblefield RC | 3.00 | 1.25 |
| ❏ 201 Dan Cody RC | 5.00 | 2.00 |
| ❏ 202 David Pollack RC | 4.00 | 1.50 |
| ❏ 203 Craig Bragg RC | 3.00 | 1.25 |
| ❏ 204 Alvin Pearman RC | 4.00 | 1.50 |
| ❏ 205 Marcus Maxwell RC | 3.00 | 1.25 |
| ❏ 206 Brock Berlin RC | 4.00 | 1.50 |
| ❏ 207 Khalif Barnes RC | 3.00 | 1.25 |
| ❏ 208 Eric King RC | 3.00 | 1.25 |
| ❏ 209 Alex Smith TE RC | 5.00 | 2.00 |
| ❏ 210 Dante Ridgeway RC | 3.00 | 1.25 |
| ❏ 211 Shaun Cody RC | 4.00 | 1.50 |
| ❏ 212 Donte Nicholson RC | 4.00 | 1.50 |
| ❏ 213 DeMarcus Ware RC | 8.00 | 3.00 |
| ❏ 214 Lionel Gates RC | 3.00 | 1.25 |
| ❏ 215 Fabian Washington RC | 5.00 | 2.00 |
| ❏ 216 Brandon Jacobs RC | 6.00 | 2.50 |
| ❏ 217 Noah Herron RC | 5.00 | 2.00 |
| ❏ 218 Derrick Johnson RC | 5.00 | 2.00 |
| ❏ 219 J.R. Russell RC | 3.00 | 1.25 |
| ❏ 220 Adrian McPherson RC | 4.00 | 1.50 |
| ❏ 221 Marcus Spears RC | 5.00 | 2.00 |
| ❏ 222 Justin Miller RC | 4.00 | 1.50 |
| ❏ 223 Marion Barber RC | 15.00 | 6.00 |
| ❏ 224 Anthony Davis RC | 4.00 | 1.50 |
| ❏ 225 Chad Owens RC | 5.00 | 2.00 |
| ❏ 226 Craphonso Thorpe RC | 4.00 | 1.50 |
| ❏ 227 Travis Johnson RC | 3.00 | 1.25 |
| ❏ 228 Erasmus James RC | 4.00 | 1.50 |
| ❏ 229 Mike Patterson RC | 4.00 | 1.50 |
| ❏ 230 Airese Currie RC | 4.00 | 1.50 |
| ❏ 231 Justin Tuck RC | 6.00 | 2.50 |
| ❏ 232 Dan Orlovsky RC | 5.00 | 2.00 |
| ❏ 233 Thomas Davis RC | 4.00 | 1.50 |
| ❏ 234 Derek Anderson RC | 8.00 | 3.00 |
| ❏ 235 Matt Roth RC | 5.00 | 2.00 |
| ❏ 236 Chris Henry RC | 5.00 | 2.00 |
| ❏ 237 Rasheed Marshall RC | 4.00 | 1.50 |
| ❏ 238 Bryant McFadden RC | 4.00 | 1.50 |
| ❏ 239 Darren Sproles RC | 6.00 | 2.50 |
| ❏ 240 Fred Gibson RC | 4.00 | 1.50 |
| ❏ 241 Barrett Ruud RC | 5.00 | 2.00 |
| ❏ 242 Kelvin Hayden RC | 4.00 | 1.50 |
| ❏ 243 Ryan Fitzpatrick RC | 5.00 | 2.00 |
| ❏ 244 Patrick Estes RC | 3.00 | 1.25 |
| ❏ 245 Zach Tuiasosopo RC | 3.00 | 1.25 |
| ❏ 246 Luis Castillo RC | 5.00 | 2.00 |
| ❏ 247 Lance Mitchell RC | 4.00 | 1.50 |
| ❏ 248 Ronald Bartell RC | 4.00 | 1.50 |
| ❏ 249 Jerome Mathis RC | 5.00 | 2.00 |
| ❏ 250 Marlin Jackson RC | 4.00 | 1.50 |
| ❏ 251 James Kilian RC | 3.00 | 1.25 |
| ❏ 252 Roydell Williams RC | 4.00 | 1.50 |
| ❏ 253 Joel Dreessen RC | 4.00 | 1.50 |
| ❏ 254 Paris Warren RC | 4.00 | 1.50 |
| ❏ 255 Dustin Fox RC | 5.00 | 2.00 |
| ❏ 256 Ellis Hobbs RC | 5.00 | 2.00 |
| ❏ 257 Mike Nugent RC | 4.00 | 1.50 |
| ❏ 258 Channing Crowder RC | 4.00 | 1.50 |
| ❏ 259 Kerry Rhodes RC | 5.00 | 2.00 |
| ❏ 260 Jerome Collins RC | 4.00 | 1.50 |
| ❏ 261 Stanford Routt RC | 4.00 | 1.50 |
| ❏ 262 Madison Hedgecock RC | 4.00 | 1.50 |
| ❏ 263 Rian Wallace RC | 4.00 | 1.50 |
| ❏ 264 Larry Brackins RC | 3.00 | 1.25 |
| ❏ 265 Manuel White RC | 4.00 | 1.50 |
| ❏ 266 Corey Webster RC | 5.00 | 2.00 |
| ❏ 267 Eric Moore RC | 3.00 | 1.25 |
| ❏ 268 Kirk Morrison RC | 5.00 | 2.00 |
| ❏ 269 Atiyyah Ellison RC | 3.00 | 1.25 |
| ❏ 270 Travis Daniels RC | 4.00 | 1.50 |
| ❏ 271 Boomer Grigsby RC | 5.00 | 2.00 |
| ❏ 272 Alex Barron RC | 3.00 | 1.25 |
| ❏ 273 Tab Perry RC | 5.00 | 2.00 |
| ❏ 274 Cedric Houston RC | 5.00 | 2.00 |
| ❏ 275 Kevin Burnett RC | 4.00 | 1.50 |
| ❏ RH39 Deion Branch RH | 5.00 | 2.00 |
| ❏ RH39R Deion Branch RH/100 | 15.00 | 6.00 |

## 2006 Topps Chrome

| | | |
|---|---|---|
| ❏ 1 Jonathan Vilma | .75 | .30 |
| ❏ 2 Chester Taylor | .75 | .30 |
| ❏ 3 Troy Polamalu | 1.25 | .50 |
| ❏ 4 Nathan Vasher | .60 | .25 |
| ❏ 5 Clinton Portis | 1.00 | .40 |
| ❏ 6 Willie Parker | 1.25 | .50 |
| ❏ 7 Lofa Tatupu | .75 | .30 |
| ❏ 8 Peyton Manning | 1.50 | .60 |
| ❏ 9 LaMont Jordan | .75 | .30 |
| ❏ 10 Jason Taylor | .75 | .30 |
| ❏ 11 Travis Taylor | .60 | .25 |
| ❏ 12 Derrick Johnson | .75 | .30 |
| ❏ 13 Jason Campbell | .75 | .30 |
| ❏ 14 Aaron Rodgers | 1.00 | .40 |
| ❏ 15 Deltha O'Neal | .60 | .25 |
| ❏ 16 LaDainian Tomlinson | 1.25 | .50 |
| ❏ 17 Keary Colbert | .75 | .30 |

| | | |
|---|---|---|
| ❏ 18 Chris Chambers | .75 | .30 |
| ❏ 19 Chris Simms | .75 | .30 |
| ❏ 20 Troy Williamson | .75 | .30 |
| ❏ 21 Chad Johnson | .75 | .30 |
| ❏ 22 Jake Delhomme | .75 | .30 |
| ❏ 23 Willis McGahee | 1.00 | .40 |
| ❏ 24 Roddy White | .60 | .25 |
| ❏ 25 Rod Smith | .75 | .30 |
| ❏ 26 Zach Thomas | 1.00 | .40 |
| ❏ 27 Antonio Gates | 1.00 | .40 |
| ❏ 28 Michael Vick | 1.00 | .40 |
| ❏ 29 Antwaan Randle El | .75 | .30 |
| ❏ 30 Drew Bledsoe | 1.00 | .40 |
| ❏ 31 Randy McMichael | .60 | .25 |
| ❏ 32 Heath Miller | .75 | .30 |
| ❏ 33 Fred Taylor | .75 | .30 |
| ❏ 34 Alge Crumpler | .75 | .30 |
| ❏ 35 Roy Williams S | .75 | .30 |
| ❏ 36 Ryan Moats | .75 | .30 |
| ❏ 37 Dwight Freeney | .75 | .30 |
| ❏ 38 Jeremy Shockey | 1.00 | .40 |
| ❏ 39 Shawne Merriman | .75 | .30 |
| ❏ 40 Charlie Frye | .75 | .30 |
| ❏ 41 Reggie Wayne | .75 | .30 |
| ❏ 42 Alex Smith QB | 1.00 | .40 |
| ❏ 43 Jerome Bettis | 1.00 | .40 |
| ❏ 44 Chris Brown | .75 | .30 |
| ❏ 45 Michael Clayton | .75 | .30 |
| ❏ 46 Carlos Rogers | .60 | .25 |
| ❏ 47 DeAngelo Hall | .75 | .30 |
| ❏ 48 Drew Bennett | .75 | .30 |
| ❏ 49 Brandon Lloyd | .75 | .30 |
| ❏ 50 Corey Dillon | .75 | .30 |
| ❏ 51 Eli Manning | 1.25 | .50 |
| ❏ 52 Jerry Porter | .75 | .30 |
| ❏ 53 Carson Palmer | 1.00 | .40 |
| ❏ 54 Kevin Jones | 1.00 | .40 |
| ❏ 55 Andre Johnson | .75 | .30 |
| ❏ 56 Ray Lewis | 1.00 | .40 |
| ❏ 57 Kyle Orton | .60 | .25 |
| ❏ 58 Julius Jones | .75 | .30 |
| ❏ 59 Roy Williams WR | 1.00 | .40 |
| ❏ 60 Jonathan Ogden | .60 | .25 |
| ❏ 61 Antonio Pierce | .60 | .25 |
| ❏ 62 Larry Johnson | .75 | .30 |
| ❏ 63 Muhsin Muhammad | .75 | .30 |
| ❏ 64 Trent Green | .75 | .30 |
| ❏ 65 Tatum Bell | .75 | .30 |
| ❏ 66 Lee Evans | .75 | .30 |
| ❏ 67 Braylon Edwards | 1.00 | .40 |
| ❏ 68 Hines Ward | 1.00 | .40 |
| ❏ 69 Warrick Dunn | .75 | .30 |
| ❏ 70 Antonio Bryant | .75 | .30 |
| ❏ 71 Mewelde Moore | .60 | .25 |
| ❏ 72 Samkon Gado | 1.00 | .40 |
| ❏ 73 Mike Williams | 1.00 | .40 |
| ❏ 74 Marion Barber | .75 | .30 |
| ❏ 75 Samie Parker | .60 | .25 |
| ❏ 76 Julius Peppers | .75 | .30 |
| ❏ 77 Brian Westbrook | .75 | .30 |
| ❏ 78 Kevan Barlow | .75 | .30 |
| ❏ 79 Kyle Boller | .75 | .30 |
| ❏ 80 Deion Edwards | .60 | .25 |
| ❏ 81 Courtney Roby | .60 | .25 |
| ❏ 82 Marc Bulger | .75 | .30 |
| ❏ 83 Steve Smith | 1.00 | .40 |
| ❏ 84 Ben Roethlisberger | 1.50 | .60 |
| ❏ 85 Byron Leftwich | .75 | .30 |
| ❏ 86 Isaac Bruce | .75 | .30 |
| ❏ 87 Kurt Warner | .75 | .30 |
| ❏ 88 Tiki Barber | 1.00 | .40 |
| ❏ 89 Derrick Mason | .75 | .30 |
| ❏ 90 Joe Horn | .75 | .30 |
| ❏ 91 Donovan McNabb | 1.00 | .40 |
| ❏ 92 DeShaun Foster | .75 | .30 |
| ❏ 93 Rex Grossman | 1.00 | .40 |
| ❏ 94 Randy Moss | 1.00 | .40 |
| ❏ 95 Tedy Bruschi | 1.00 | .40 |
| ❏ 96 Tony Gonzalez | .75 | .30 |
| ❏ 97 Cadillac Williams | 1.00 | .40 |
| ❏ 98 Torry Holt | .75 | .30 |
| ❏ 99 Philip Rivers | 1.00 | .40 |
| ❏ 100 Deuce McAllister | .75 | .30 |
| ❏ 101 Jason Witten | .75 | .30 |
| ❏ 102 Reggie Brown | .75 | .30 |
| ❏ 103 Ronnie Brown | 1.00 | .40 |
| ❏ 104 Deion Branch | .75 | .30 |

| □ | | | |
|---|---|---|---|
| 105 | Terry Glenn | .75 | .30 |
| 106 | Tom Brady | 1.50 | .60 |
| 107 | Dallas Clark | .75 | .30 |
| 108 | Mark Clayton | .75 | .30 |
| 109 | D.J. Williams | .60 | .25 |
| 110 | Matt Jones | .75 | .30 |
| 111 | Ed Reed | .75 | .30 |
| 112 | Reuben Droughns | .75 | .30 |
| 113 | Matt Hasselbeck | .75 | .30 |
| 114 | Anquan Boldin | .75 | .30 |
| 115 | David Carr | .75 | .30 |
| 116 | Domanick Davis | .75 | .30 |
| 117 | Nate Burleson | .75 | .30 |
| 118 | Shaun Alexander | 1.00 | .40 |
| 119 | Dante Hall | .75 | .30 |
| 120 | Santana Moss | .75 | .30 |
| 121 | Brandon Stokley | .75 | .30 |
| 122 | Larry Fitzgerald | 1.00 | .40 |
| 123 | Marvin Harrison | 1.00 | .40 |
| 124 | Steve McNair | .75 | .30 |
| 125 | Osi Umenyiora | .75 | .30 |
| 126 | Odell Thurman | .60 | .25 |
| 127 | Josh McCown | .75 | .30 |
| 128 | Curtis Martin | 1.00 | .40 |
| 129 | Jake Plummer | .75 | .30 |
| 130 | Cedric Benson | .75 | .30 |
| 131 | J.P. Losman | .75 | .30 |
| 132 | Joey Galloway | .75 | .30 |
| 133 | Brian Griese | .75 | .30 |
| 134 | Plaxico Burress | .75 | .30 |
| 135 | Brian Urlacher | 1.00 | .40 |
| 136 | T.J. Houshmandzadeh | .75 | .30 |
| 137 | Todd Heap | .75 | .30 |
| 138 | Champ Bailey | .75 | .30 |
| 139 | Mark Brunell | .75 | .30 |
| 140 | Chris Cooley | .75 | .30 |
| 141 | Priest Holmes | .75 | .30 |
| 142 | Aaron Brooks | .75 | .30 |
| 143 | Steven Jackson | 1.00 | .40 |
| 144 | Michael Strahan | .75 | .30 |
| 145 | Rudi Johnson | .75 | .30 |
| 146 | Terrell Owens | 1.00 | .40 |
| 147 | John Abraham | .60 | .25 |
| 148 | Jon Kitna | .75 | .30 |
| 149 | LaVar Arrington | 1.00 | .40 |
| 150 | Joe Jurevicius | .75 | .30 |
| 151 | Dominic Rhodes | .75 | .30 |
| 152 | Chad Pennington | .75 | .30 |
| 153 | Charles Woodson | .75 | .30 |
| 154 | Kerry Collins | .75 | .30 |
| 155 | Drew Brees | 1.00 | .40 |
| 156 | Keyshawn Johnson | .75 | .30 |
| 157 | Mike Anderson | .75 | .30 |
| 158 | Jimmy Smith | .75 | .30 |
| 159 | Brett Favre | 2.00 | .75 |
| 160 | Edgerrin James | .75 | .30 |
| 161 | Jamal Lewis | .75 | .30 |
| 162 | Daunte Culpepper | 1.00 | .40 |
| 163 | Eric Moulds | .75 | .30 |
| 164 | Patrick Ramsey | .75 | .30 |
| 165 | Ahman Green | .75 | .30 |
| 166 | Kamerion Wimbley RC | 5.00 | 2.00 |
| 167 | Bobby Carpenter RC | 5.00 | 2.00 |
| 168 | Abdul Hodge RC | 5.00 | 2.00 |
| 169 | A.J. Daniels RC | 4.00 | 1.50 |
| 170 | D'Qwell Jackson RC | 4.00 | 1.50 |
| 171 | Johnathan Joseph RC | 4.00 | 1.50 |
| 172 | Antonio Cromartie RC | 5.00 | 2.00 |
| 173 | Elvis Dumervil RC | 3.00 | 1.25 |
| 174 | Tamba Hali RC | 5.00 | 2.00 |
| 175 | Derek Hagan RC | 5.00 | 2.00 |
| 176 | Haloti Ngata RC | 5.00 | 2.00 |
| 177 | Manny Lawson RC | 5.00 | 2.00 |
| 178 | Kelly Jennings RC | 5.00 | 2.00 |
| 179 | Jason Allen RC | 5.00 | 2.00 |
| 180 | Mathias Kiwanuka RC | 6.00 | 2.50 |
| 181 | Marques Hagans RC | 4.00 | 1.50 |
| 182 | Devin Aromashodu RC | 4.00 | 1.50 |
| 183 | Brandon Johnson RC | 4.00 | 1.50 |
| 184 | Ingle Martin RC | 5.00 | 2.00 |
| 185 | Claude Wroten RC | 3.00 | 1.25 |
| 186 | Tye Hill RC | 5.00 | 2.00 |
| 187 | Ashton Youboty RC | 5.00 | 2.00 |
| 188 | DeMeco Ryans RC | 6.00 | 2.50 |
| 189 | Abdul Buckley RC | 5.00 | 2.00 |
| 190 | Thomas Howard RC | 5.00 | 2.00 |
| 191 | Ernie Sims RC | 5.00 | 2.00 |
| 192 | Rocky McIntosh RC | 5.00 | 2.00 |
| 193 | Donte Whitner RC | 5.00 | 2.00 |
| 194 | Anthony Schlegel RC | 4.00 | 1.50 |
| 195 | Jimmy Williams RC | 5.00 | 2.00 |
| 196 | Brett Basanez RC | 5.00 | 2.00 |
| 197 | Ben Obomanu RC | 4.00 | 1.50 |
| 198 | Jonathan Orr RC | 4.00 | 1.50 |
| 199 | Andre Hall RC | 5.00 | 2.00 |
| 200 | James Anderson RC | 3.00 | 1.25 |
| 201 | Darnell Bing RC | 5.00 | 2.00 |
| 202 | Jovon Bouknight RC | 4.00 | 1.50 |
| 203 | Gabe Watson RC | 4.00 | 1.50 |
| 204 | Garrett Mills RC | 5.00 | 2.00 |
| 205 | Jeff Webb RC | 4.00 | 1.50 |
| 206 | Kevin McMahan RC | 4.00 | 1.50 |
| 207 | D.J. Shockley RC | 5.00 | 2.00 |
| 208 | A.J. Nicholson RC | 3.00 | 1.25 |
| 209 | Cedric Humes RC | 5.00 | 2.00 |
| 210 | Winston Justice RC | 5.00 | 2.00 |
| 211 | Lawrence Vickers RC | 4.00 | 1.50 |
| 212 | Daniel Bullocks RC | 5.00 | 2.00 |
| 213 | Tim Day RC | 4.00 | 1.50 |
| 214 | Ko Simpson RC | 4.00 | 1.50 |
| 215 | Dusty Dvoracek RC | 5.00 | 2.00 |
| 216 | Davin Joseph RC | 4.00 | 1.50 |
| 217 | Dominique Byrd RC | 4.00 | 1.50 |
| 218 | Marcus Vick RC | 5.00 | 2.00 |
| 219 | John McCargo RC | 4.00 | 1.50 |
| 220 | Danieal Manning RC | 5.00 | 2.00 |
| 221 | Reggie Bush RC | 20.00 | 8.00 |
| 222 | A.J. Hawk RC | 10.00 | 4.00 |
| 223 | Vince Young RC | 15.00 | 6.00 |
| 224 | Matt Leinart RC | 15.00 | 6.00 |
| 225 | Kellen Clemens RC | 6.00 | 2.50 |
| 226 | Sinorice Moss RC | 5.00 | 2.00 |
| 227 | Laurence Maroney RC | 12.00 | 5.00 |
| 228 | DeAngelo Williams RC | 8.00 | 3.00 |
| 229 | Jay Cutler RC | 20.00 | 8.00 |
| 230 | LenDale White RC | 10.00 | 4.00 |
| 231 | Leonard Pope RC | 5.00 | 2.00 |
| 232 | Chad Greenway RC | 5.00 | 2.00 |
| 233 | Chad Jackson RC | 4.00 | 1.50 |
| 234 | Vernon Davis RC | 5.00 | 2.00 |
| 235 | Todd Watkins RC | 5.00 | 2.00 |
| 236 | David Thomas RC | 5.00 | 2.00 |
| 237 | Marcedes Lewis RC | 5.00 | 2.00 |
| 238 | Leon Washington RC | 5.00 | 2.00 |
| 239 | Will Blackmon RC | 5.00 | 2.00 |
| 240 | Michael Huff RC | 5.00 | 2.00 |
| 241 | Jerious Norwood RC | 6.00 | 2.50 |
| 242 | Reggie McNeal RC | 4.00 | 1.50 |
| 243 | Wali Lundy RC | 5.00 | 2.00 |
| 244 | Santonio Holmes RC | 12.00 | 5.00 |
| 245 | Jerome Harrison RC | 5.00 | 2.00 |
| 246 | Brace Gradkowski RC | 5.00 | 2.00 |
| 247 | Maurice Drew RC | 10.00 | 4.00 |
| 248 | Brandon Williams RC | 5.00 | 2.00 |
| 249 | Anthony Fasano RC | 5.00 | 2.00 |
| 250 | Omar Jacobs RC | 4.00 | 1.50 |
| 251 | Domenik Hixon RC | 6.00 | 2.50 |
| 252 | Devin Hester RC | 10.00 | 4.00 |
| 253 | Maurice Stovall RC | 5.00 | 2.00 |
| 254 | Tarvaris Jackson RC | 5.00 | 2.00 |
| 255 | Michael Robinson RC | 5.00 | 2.00 |
| 256 | Mario Williams RC | 8.00 | 3.00 |
| 257 | Jason Avant RC | 5.00 | 2.00 |
| 258 | Brian Calhoun RC | 4.00 | 1.50 |
| 259 | Skyler Green RC | 5.00 | 2.00 |
| 260 | Greg Jennings RC | 8.00 | 3.00 |
| 261 | Charlie Whitehurst RC | 5.00 | 2.00 |
| 262 | Mike Hass RC | 5.00 | 2.00 |
| 263 | Brandon Marshall RC | 6.00 | 2.50 |
| 264 | Drew Olson RC | 5.00 | 2.00 |
| 265 | Demetrius Williams RC | 5.00 | 2.00 |
| 266 | Travis Wilson RC | 5.00 | 2.00 |
| 267 | Joe Klopfenstein RC | 4.00 | 1.50 |
| 268 | Joseph Addai RC | 15.00 | 6.00 |
| 269 | Brad Smith RC | 5.00 | 2.00 |
| 270 | Willie Reid RC | 5.00 | 2.00 |
| RH40 | Hines Ward RH | 6.00 | 2.50 |

## 2007 Topps Chrome

| □ | | | |
|---|---|---|---|
| TC1 | Matt Leinart | 1.00 | .40 |
| TC2 | J.P. Losman | .60 | .25 |
| TC3 | Carson Palmer | 1.00 | .40 |
| TC4 | Jay Cutler | 1.00 | .40 |
| TC5 | Peyton Manning | 1.50 | .60 |
| TC6 | Tom Brady | 2.00 | .75 |
| TC7 | Chad Pennington | .75 | .30 |
| TC8 | Philip Rivers | 1.00 | .40 |
| TC9 | Marc Bulger | .75 | .30 |
| TC10 | Edgerrin James | .75 | .30 |
| TC11 | Willis McGahee | .75 | .30 |
| TC12 | Thomas Jones | .75 | .30 |
| TC13 | Marion Barber | 1.00 | .40 |
| TC14 | Fred Taylor | .75 | .30 |
| TC15 | Chester Taylor | .60 | .25 |
| TC16 | Reggie Bush | 1.25 | .50 |
| TC17 | Willie Parker | 1.00 | .40 |
| TC18 | Shaun Alexander | .75 | .30 |
| TC19 | LenDale White | .75 | .30 |
| TC20 | Larry Fitzgerald | 1.00 | .40 |
| TC21 | Lee Evans | .75 | .30 |
| TC22 | Muhsin Muhammad | .75 | .30 |
| TC23 | Rod Smith | .75 | .30 |
| TC24 | Andre Johnson | .75 | .30 |
| TC25 | Matt Jones | .75 | .30 |
| TC26 | Devery Henderson | .50 | .25 |
| TC27 | Plaxico Burress | .75 | .30 |
| TC28 | Randy Moss | 1.00 | .40 |
| TC29 | Santonio Holmes | .75 | .30 |
| TC30 | Torry Holt | .75 | .30 |
| TC31 | Antwaan Randle El | .60 | .25 |
| TC32 | Todd Heap | .60 | .25 |
| TC33 | Tony Gonzalez | .75 | .30 |
| TC34 | Heath Miller | .60 | .25 |
| TC35 | Alex Smith TE | .75 | .30 |
| TC36 | Champ Bailey | .75 | .30 |
| TC37 | Roy Williams S | .75 | .30 |
| TC38 | Julius Peppers | .75 | .30 |
| TC39 | Jason Taylor | .60 | .25 |
| TC40 | Brian Urlacher | 1.00 | .40 |
| TC41 | Marc Bulger LL | .75 | .30 |
| TC42 | Frank Gore LL | .75 | .30 |
| TC43 | Reggie Wayne LL | .60 | .25 |
| TC44 | Peyton Manning PB | 1.25 | .50 |
| TC45 | Reggie Wayne PB | .60 | .25 |
| TC46 | Jason Taylor PB | .50 | .20 |
| TC47 | Troy Polamalu PB | .75 | .30 |
| TC48 | Tony Gonzalez PB | .60 | .25 |
| TC49 | Devin Hester PB | .75 | .30 |
| TC50 | LaDainian Tomlinson MVP | 1.00 | .40 |
| TC51 | P.Manning/R.Wayne PSH | 1.25 | .50 |
| TC52 | New Orleans Saints PSH | .60 | .25 |
| TC53 | Peyton Manning PSH | 1.25 | .50 |
| TC54 | T.Jones/C.Benson PSH | .75 | .30 |
| TC55 | Colts Defense PSH | .60 | .25 |
| TC56 | Steve McNair | .75 | .30 |
| TC57 | Rex Grossman | .75 | .30 |
| TC58 | Tony Romo | 2.00 | .75 |
| TC59 | David Carr | .75 | .30 |
| TC60 | Tarvaris Jackson | .75 | .30 |
| TC61 | Eli Manning | 1.00 | .40 |
| TC62 | Ben Roethlisberger | 1.25 | .50 |
| TC63 | Matt Hasselbeck | .75 | .30 |
| TC64 | Jason Campbell | .75 | .30 |
| TC65 | Warrick Dunn | .75 | .30 |
| TC66 | Jamal Lewis | .75 | .30 |
| TC67 | Cedric Benson | .75 | .30 |
| TC68 | Reuben Droughns | .75 | .30 |
| TC69 | Joseph Addai | 1.00 | .40 |
| TC70 | Ronnie Brown | .75 | .30 |
| TC71 | Deuce McAllister | .75 | .30 |
| TC72 | Brian Westbrook | .75 | .30 |
| TC73 | Frank Gore | 1.00 | .40 |
| TC74 | Cadillac Williams | .75 | .30 |
| TC75 | Anquan Boldin | .75 | .30 |

| | | | | | | | | | |
|---|---|---|---|---|---|---|---|---|---|
| ☐ TC76 Mark Clayton | .75 | .30 | ☐ TC163 Robbie Gould PSH | .50 | .20 | ☐ TC250 Aaron Ross RC | 5.00 | 2.00 |
| ☐ TC77 Bernard Berrian | .60 | .25 | ☐ TC164 Joseph Addai PSH | .75 | .30 | ☐ TC251 Daymeion Hughes RC | 4.00 | 1.50 |
| ☐ TC78 Braylon Edwards | .75 | .30 | ☐ TC165 Adam Vinatieri PSH | .60 | .25 | ☐ TC252 Marcus McCauley RC | 4.00 | 1.50 |
| ☐ TC79 Donald Driver | .75 | .30 | ☐ TC166 JaMarcus Russell RC | 12.00 | 5.00 | ☐ TC253 Chris Houston RC | 4.00 | 1.50 |
| ☐ TC80 Marvin Harrison | 1.00 | .40 | ☐ TC167 Brady Quinn RC | 15.00 | 6.00 | ☐ TC254 Tanard Jackson RC | 3.00 | 1.25 |
| ☐ TC81 Troy Williamson | .60 | .25 | ☐ TC168 Drew Stanton RC | 5.00 | 2.00 | ☐ TC255 Jonathan Wade RC | 4.00 | 1.50 |
| ☐ TC82 Marques Colston | .75 | .30 | ☐ TC169 Troy Smith RC | 6.00 | 2.50 | ☐ TC256 Josh Wilson RC | 4.00 | 1.50 |
| ☐ TC83 Laveranues Coles | .75 | .30 | ☐ TC170 Kevin Kolb RC | 8.00 | 3.00 | ☐ TC257 Eric Wright RC | 5.00 | 2.00 |
| ☐ TC84 Hines Ward | 1.00 | .40 | ☐ TC171 Trent Edwards RC | 12.00 | 5.00 | ☐ TC258 David Irons RC | 3.00 | 1.25 |
| ☐ TC85 Deion Branch | .75 | .30 | ☐ TC172 John Beck RC | 5.00 | 2.00 | ☐ TC259 Laron Landry RC | 6.00 | 2.50 |
| ☐ TC86 Alge Crumpler | .75 | .30 | ☐ TC173 Jordan Palmer RC | 5.00 | 2.00 | ☐ TC260 Reggie Nelson RC | 4.00 | 1.50 |
| ☐ TC87 Kellen Winslow | .75 | .30 | ☐ TC174 Chris Leak RC | 4.00 | 1.50 | ☐ TC261 Michael Griffin RC | 5.00 | 2.00 |
| ☐ TC88 Dallas Clark | .60 | .25 | ☐ TC175 Isaiah Stanback RC | 5.00 | 2.00 | ☐ TC262 Brandon Meriweather RC | 5.00 | 2.00 |
| ☐ TC89 L.J. Smith | .60 | .25 | ☐ TC176 Tyler Palko RC | 5.00 | 2.00 | ☐ TC263 Eric Weddle RC | 4.00 | 1.50 |
| ☐ TC90 Vernon Davis | .75 | .30 | ☐ TC177 Jared Zabransky RC | 5.00 | 2.00 | ☐ TC264 Joe Thomas RC | 5.00 | 2.00 |
| ☐ TC91 Sean Taylor | .60 | .25 | ☐ TC178 Jeff Rowe RC | 4.00 | 1.50 | ☐ TC265 Levi Brown RC | 5.00 | 2.00 |
| ☐ TC92 Ronde Barber | .60 | .25 | ☐ TC179 Zac Taylor RC | 5.00 | 2.00 | ☐ RH41 Peyton Manning RH | 5.00 | 2.00 |
| ☐ TC93 Brian Dawkins | .75 | .30 | ☐ TC180 Lester Ricard RC | 10.00 | 4.00 | | | |
| ☐ TC94 Dwight Freeney | .75 | .30 | ☐ TC181 Adrian Peterson RC | 40.00 | 15.00 | | | |
| ☐ TC95 Ray Lewis | 1.00 | .40 | ☐ TC182 Marshawn Lynch RC | 20.00 | 8.00 | | | |
| ☐ TC96 Peyton Manning LL | 1.25 | .50 | ☐ TC183 Brandon Jackson RC | 5.00 | 2.00 | | | |
| ☐ TC97 Larry Johnson LL | .60 | .25 | ☐ TC184 Michael Bush RC | 5.00 | 2.00 | | | |
| ☐ TC98 Marvin Harrison LL | .75 | .30 | ☐ TC185 Kenny Irons RC | 5.00 | 2.00 | | | |
| ☐ TC99 LaDainian Tomlinson PB | 1.00 | .40 | ☐ TC186 Antonio Pittman RC | 5.00 | 2.00 | | | |
| ☐ TC100 Jeff Saturday PB | .50 | .20 | ☐ TC187 Tony Hunt RC | 5.00 | 2.00 | | | |
| ☐ TC101 Champ Bailey PB | .60 | .25 | ☐ TC188 Darius Walker RC | 5.00 | 2.00 | | | |
| ☐ TC102 Frank Gore PB | .75 | .30 | ☐ TC189 Dwayne Wright RC | 4.00 | 1.50 | | | |
| ☐ TC103 Walter Jones PB | .50 | .20 | ☐ TC190 Lorenzo Booker RC | 5.00 | 2.00 | | | |
| ☐ TC104 Tony Romo PB | 1.50 | .60 | ☐ TC191 Kenneth Darby RC | 5.00 | 2.00 | | | |
| ☐ TC105 Ronde Barber PB | .50 | .20 | ☐ TC192 Chris Henry RB RC | 5.00 | 2.00 | | | |
| ☐ TC106 Larry Johnson PB | .60 | .25 | ☐ TC193 Selvin Young RC | 8.00 | 3.00 | | | |
| ☐ TC107 Vince Young OROY | .75 | .30 | ☐ TC194 Brian Leonard RC | 5.00 | 2.00 | | | |
| ☐ TC108 Akeem Samuel PSH | .50 | .20 | ☐ TC195 Ahmad Bradshaw RC | 6.00 | 2.50 | | | |
| ☐ TC109 Tom Brady PSH | 1.50 | .60 | ☐ TC196 Gary Russell RC | 5.00 | 2.00 | | | |
| ☐ TC110 Devin Hester PSH | .75 | .30 | ☐ TC197 Kolby Smith RC | 5.00 | 2.00 | | | |
| ☐ TC111 Michael Vick SP | 100.00 | 60.00 | ☐ TC198 Thomas Clayton RC | 4.00 | 1.50 | | | |
| ☐ TC112 Jake Delhomme | .75 | .30 | ☐ TC199 Garrett Wolfe RC | 5.00 | 2.00 | ☐ **2008 Topps Chrome** | | |
| ☐ TC113 Charlie Frye | .75 | .30 | ☐ TC200 Calvin Johnson RC | 12.00 | 5.00 | | | |
| ☐ TC114 Brett Favre | 2.00 | .75 | ☐ TC201 Ted Ginn Jr. RC | 8.00 | 3.00 | | | |
| ☐ TC115 Trent Green | .75 | .30 | ☐ TC202 Dwayne Jarrett RC | 5.00 | 2.00 | | | |
| ☐ TC116 Drew Brees | .75 | .30 | ☐ TC203 Dwayne Bowe RC | 10.00 | 4.00 | | | |
| ☐ TC117 Donovan McNabb | 1.00 | .40 | ☐ TC204 Sidney Rice RC | 5.00 | 2.00 | | | |
| ☐ TC118 Alex Smith QB | 1.00 | .40 | ☐ TC205 Robert Meachem RC | 5.00 | 2.00 | | | |
| ☐ TC119 Vince Young | 1.00 | .40 | ☐ TC206 Anthony Gonzalez RC | 8.00 | 3.00 | | | |
| ☐ TC120 DeAngelo Williams | .75 | .30 | ☐ TC207 Craig Buster Davis RC | 5.00 | 2.00 | | | |
| ☐ TC121 Rudi Johnson | .75 | .30 | ☐ TC208 Aundrae Allison RC | 4.00 | 1.50 | | | |
| ☐ TC122 Julius Jones | .75 | .30 | ☐ TC209 Chansi Stuckey RC | 4.00 | 1.50 | | | |
| ☐ TC123 Larry Johnson | .75 | .30 | ☐ TC210 David Clowney RC | 4.00 | 1.50 | | | |
| ☐ TC124 Laurence Maroney | 1.00 | .40 | ☐ TC211 Steve Smith USC RC | 6.00 | 2.50 | | | |
| ☐ TC125 Brandon Jacobs | .75 | .30 | ☐ TC212 Courtney Taylor RC | 5.00 | 2.00 | | | |
| ☐ TC126 LaDainian Tomlinson | 1.25 | .50 | ☐ TC213 Paul Williams RC | 4.00 | 1.50 | | | |
| ☐ TC127 Steven Jackson | 1.00 | .40 | ☐ TC214 Johnnie Lee Higgins RC | 4.00 | 1.50 | | | |
| ☐ TC128 Clinton Portis | .75 | .30 | ☐ TC215 Rhema McKnight RC | 4.00 | 1.50 | | | |
| ☐ TC129 Michael Jenkins | .75 | .30 | ☐ TC216 Jason Hill RC | 5.00 | 2.00 | ☐ TC1 Drew Brees | 1.00 | .40 |
| ☐ TC130 Steve Smith | .75 | .30 | ☐ TC217 Dallas Baker RC | 4.00 | 1.50 | ☐ TC2 Jon Kitna | .75 | .30 |
| ☐ TC131 Chad Johnson | .75 | .30 | ☐ TC218 Greg Olsen RC | 6.00 | 2.50 | ☐ TC3 Tom Brady | 1.50 | .60 |
| ☐ TC132 Roy Williams WR | .75 | .30 | ☐ TC219 Yamon Figurs RC | 5.00 | 2.00 | ☐ TC4 Chad Pennington | .75 | .30 |
| ☐ TC133 Reggie Wayne | .75 | .30 | ☐ TC220 Scott Chandler RC | 4.00 | 1.50 | ☐ TC5 Matt Hasselbeck | .75 | .30 |
| ☐ TC134 Reggie Williams | .75 | .30 | ☐ TC221 Matt Spaeth RC | 5.00 | 2.00 | ☐ TC6 David Garrard | .75 | .30 |
| ☐ TC135 Chris Chambers | .75 | .30 | ☐ TC222 Ben Patrick RC | 4.00 | 1.50 | ☐ TC7 Jay Cutler | 1.00 | .40 |
| ☐ TC136 Sinorice Moss | .75 | .30 | ☐ TC223 Clark Harris RC | 4.00 | 1.50 | ☐ TC8 Matt Schaub | .75 | .30 |
| ☐ TC137 Reggie Brown | .75 | .30 | ☐ TC224 Martrez Milner RC | 4.00 | 1.50 | ☐ TC9 Trent Edwards | 1.00 | .40 |
| ☐ TC138 Anaz Battle | .60 | .25 | ☐ TC225 Alan Branch RC | 4.00 | 1.50 | ☐ TC10 Peyton Manning | 1.50 | .60 |
| ☐ TC139 Michael Clayton | .75 | .30 | ☐ TC226 Amobi Okoye RC | 5.00 | 2.00 | ☐ TC11 Carson Palmer | 1.25 | .50 |
| ☐ TC140 Santana Moss | .75 | .30 | ☐ TC227 DeMarcus Tank Tyler RC | 4.00 | 1.50 | ☐ TC12 Ben Roethlisberger | 1.25 | .50 |
| ☐ TC141 Desmond Clark | .60 | .25 | ☐ TC228 Justin Harrell RC | 5.00 | 2.00 | ☐ TC13 Eli Manning | 1.00 | .40 |
| ☐ TC142 Jeremy Shockey | .75 | .30 | ☐ TC229 Gaines Adams RC | 5.00 | 2.00 | ☐ TC14 Tony Romo | 1.50 | .60 |
| ☐ TC143 Antonio Gates | .75 | .30 | ☐ TC230 Jamaal Anderson RC | 5.00 | 2.00 | ☐ TC15 Donovan McNabb | .75 | .30 |
| ☐ TC144 Chris Cooley | .75 | .30 | ☐ TC231 Adam Carriker RC | 4.00 | 1.50 | ☐ TC16 Joey Harrington | .75 | .30 |
| ☐ TC145 Devin Hester | 1.00 | .40 | ☐ TC232 Jarvis Moss RC | 5.00 | 2.00 | ☐ TC17 Jeff Garcia | .75 | .30 |
| ☐ TC146 Asante Samuel | .60 | .25 | ☐ TC233 Charles Johnson RC | 3.00 | 1.25 | ☐ TC18 Derek Anderson | .75 | .30 |
| ☐ TC147 Troy Polamalu | .75 | .30 | ☐ TC234 Anthony Spencer RC | 5.00 | 2.00 | ☐ TC19 Kyle Boller | .60 | .25 |
| ☐ TC148 DeMarcus Ware | .75 | .30 | ☐ TC235 Quentin Moses RC | 4.00 | 1.50 | ☐ TC20 Sage Rosenfels | .60 | .25 |
| ☐ TC149 Michael Strahan | .75 | .30 | ☐ TC236 LaMarr Woodley RC | 5.00 | 2.00 | ☐ TC21 Marc Bulger | .75 | .30 |
| ☐ TC150 A.J. Hawk | .75 | .30 | ☐ TC237 Victor Abiamiri RC | 5.00 | 2.00 | ☐ TC22 Brett Favre | 2.50 | 1.00 |
| ☐ TC151 LaDainian Tomlinson LL | 1.00 | .40 | ☐ TC238 Ray McDonald RC | 4.00 | 1.50 | ☐ TC23 Philip Rivers | 1.00 | .40 |
| ☐ TC152 Chad Johnson LL | .75 | .30 | ☐ TC239 Tim Crowder RC | 5.00 | 2.00 | ☐ TC24 Vince Young | 1.00 | .40 |
| ☐ TC153 LaDainian Tomlinson LL | 1.00 | .40 | ☐ TC240 Patrick Willis RC | 10.00 | 4.00 | ☐ TC25 Kurt Warner | 1.00 | .40 |
| ☐ TC154 Marvin Harrison PB | .75 | .30 | ☐ TC241 David Harris RC | 4.00 | 1.50 | ☐ TC26 Cleo Lemon | .60 | .25 |
| ☐ TC155 Antonio Gates PB | .60 | .25 | ☐ TC242 Buster Davis RC | 4.00 | 1.50 | ☐ TC27 Damon Huard | .60 | .25 |
| ☐ TC156 Shawne Merriman PB | .60 | .25 | ☐ TC243 Lawrence Timmons RC | 5.00 | 2.00 | ☐ TC28 Jason Campbell | .75 | .30 |
| ☐ TC157 Drew Brees PB | .75 | .30 | ☐ TC244 Paul Posluszny RC | 6.00 | 2.50 | ☐ TC29 Brian Griese | .60 | .25 |
| ☐ TC158 Steve Smith PB | .60 | .25 | ☐ TC245 Jon Beason RC | 5.00 | 2.00 | ☐ TC30 Tarvaris Jackson | .75 | .30 |
| ☐ TC159 Julius Peppers PB | .60 | .25 | ☐ TC246 Rufus Alexander RC | 4.00 | 1.50 | ☐ TC31 Steven Jackson | 1.00 | .40 |
| ☐ TC160 DeMeco Ryans DROY | .60 | .25 | ☐ TC247 Prescott Burgess RC | 4.00 | 1.50 | ☐ TC32 Willie Parker | .75 | .30 |
| ☐ TC161 Drew Brees PSH | .60 | .25 | ☐ TC248 Leon Hall RC | 4.00 | 1.50 | ☐ TC33 DeShaun Foster | .75 | .30 |
| ☐ TC162 Reggie Bush PSH | 1.25 | .50 | ☐ TC249 Darrelle Revis RC | 5.00 | 2.00 | ☐ TC34 Shaun Alexander | .75 | .30 |
| | | | | | | ☐ TC35 Clinton Portis | .75 | .30 |
| | | | | | | ☐ TC36 Ron Dayne | .75 | .30 |
| | | | | | | ☐ TC37 Maurice Jones-Drew | .75 | .30 |
| | | | | | | ☐ TC38 Warrick Dunn | .75 | .30 |
| | | | | | | ☐ TC39 Adrian Peterson | 2.00 | .75 |
| | | | | | | ☐ TC40 Thomas Jones | .75 | .30 |
| | | | | | | ☐ TC41 LaDainian Tomlinson | 1.25 | .50 |
| | | | | | | ☐ TC42 Marion Barber | 1.00 | .40 |
| | | | | | | ☐ TC43 Brian Westbrook | .75 | .30 |
| | | | | | | ☐ TC44 LenDale White | .75 | .30 |
| | | | | | | ☐ TC45 Kenny Watson | .60 | .25 |
| | | | | | | ☐ TC46 Fred Taylor | .75 | .30 |
| | | | | | | ☐ TC47 Ryan Grant | 1.00 | .40 |
| | | | | | | ☐ TC48 Marshawn Lynch | 1.00 | .40 |
| | | | | | | ☐ TC49 Selvin Young | .75 | .30 |
| | | | | | | ☐ TC50 Joseph Addai | 1.00 | .40 |

RASHARD MENDENHALL

TC51 Laurence Maroney .75 .30
TC52 Brandon Jacobs .75 .30
TC53 Willis McGahee .75 .30
TC54 Frank Gore .75 .30
TC55 Edgerrin James .75 .30
TC56 DeAngelo Williams .75 .30
TC57 Jamal Lewis .75 .30
TC58 Chester Taylor .60 .25
TC59 Earnest Graham .60 .25
TC60 Justin Fargas .60 .25
TC61 Greg Jennings .75 .30
TC62 Torry Holt .75 .30
TC63 T.J. Houshmandzadeh .75 .30
TC64 Jerricho Cotchery .60 .25
TC65 Derrick Mason .60 .25
TC66 Kevin Curtis .60 .25
TC67 Joey Galloway .75 .30
TC68 Anquan Boldin .75 .30
TC69 Santonio Holmes .75 .30
TC70 Lee Evans .75 .30
TC71 Dwayne Bowe .75 .30
TC72 Wes Welker 1.00 .40
TC73 Roy Williams WR .75 .30
TC74 Randy Moss 1.00 .40
TC75 Plaxico Burress .75 .30
TC76 Terrell Owens 1.00 .40
TC77 Andre Johnson .75 .30
TC78 Roddy White .75 .30
TC79 Brandon Marshall .75 .30
TC80 Donald Driver .75 .30
TC81 Marques Colston .75 .30
TC82 Reggie Wayne .75 .30
TC83 Chad Johnson .75 .30
TC84 Bernard Berrian .75 .30
TC85 Steve Smith .75 .30
TC86 Larry Fitzgerald 1.00 .40
TC87 Braylon Edwards .75 .30
TC88 Bobby Engram .60 .25
TC89 Shaun McDonald .60 .25
TC90 Santana Moss .75 .30
TC91 Antonio Gates .75 .30
TC92 Chris Cooley .75 .30
TC93 Owen Daniels .60 .25
TC94 Kellen Winslow .75 .30
TC95 Tony Gonzalez .75 .30
TC96 Jason Witten .75 .30
TC97 Jeremy Shockey .75 .30
TC98 Dallas Clark .75 .30
TC99 Donald Lee .60 .25
TC100 Heath Miller .60 .25
TC101 Tony Scheffler .60 .25
TC102 Desmond Clark .60 .25
TC103 Vernon Davis .60 .25
TC104 Alge Crumpler .75 .30
TC105 Zach Miller .75 .30
TC106 Patrick Kerney .60 .25
TC107 Osi Umenyiora .60 .25
TC108 Mario Williams .75 .30
TC109 Jared Allen .75 .30
TC110 Michael Strahan .75 .30
TC111 Ernie Sims .60 .25
TC112 DeMarcus Ware .75 .30
TC113 Patrick Willis .75 .30
TC114 Shawne Merriman .75 .30
TC115 Brian Urlacher 1.00 .40
TC116 Ray Lewis 1.00 .40
TC117 Antonio Cromartie .60 .25
TC118 Champ Bailey .60 .25
TC119 Bob Sanders .75 .30
TC120 Ed Reed .75 .30
TC121 Tom Brady LL 1.25 .50
TC122 Drew Brees LL .75 .30
TC123 Tony Romo LL 1.25 .50
TC124 LaDainian Tomlinson LL 1.00 .40
TC125 Adrian Peterson LL 1.50 .60
TC126 Brian Westbrook LL .60 .25
TC127 Reggie Wayne LL .60 .25
TC128 Randy Moss LL .75 .30
TC129 Chad Johnson LL .60 .25
TC130 Randy Moss LL .75 .30
TC131 Matt Hasselbeck AP .60 .25
TC132 Tony Romo AP 1.25 .50
TC133 Adrian Peterson AP 1.50 .60
TC134 Marion Barber AP .75 .30
TC135 Brian Westbrook AP .60 .25
TC136 Larry Fitzgerald AP .75 .30
TC137 Terrell Owens AP .75 .30

TC138 Osi Umenyiora AP .50 .20
TC139 Lofa Tatupu AP .60 .25
TC140 Jason Witten AP .60 .25
TC141 Torry Holt AP .60 .25
TC142 Donald Driver AP .60 .25
TC143 Peyton Manning AP 1.25 .50
TC144 Ben Roethlisberger AP 1.00 .40
TC145 Joseph Addai AP .75 .30
TC146 Reggie Wayne AP .60 .25
TC147 Braylon Edwards AP .60 .25
TC148 Devin Hester AP .75 .30
TC149 Champ Bailey AP .60 .25
TC150 Ed Reed AP .60 .25
TC151 Eli Manning PSH .75 .30
TC152 David Tyree PSH .60 .25
TC153 Plaxico Burress PSH .60 .25
TC154 Lawrence Tynes PSH .50 .20
TC155 Patriots defense PSH .50 .20
TC156 R.W. McQuarters PSH .50 .20
TC157 Ryan Grant PSH .75 .30
TC158 Philip Rivers PSH .75 .30
TC159 David Garrard PSH .60 .25
TC160 Laurence Maroney PSH .60 .25
TC161 Seahawks PSH .60 .25
TC162 Chargers defense PSH .50 .20
TC163 Tom Brady MVP 1.25 .50
TC164 Adrian Peterson OROY 1.50 .60
TC165 Patrick Willis DROY .60 .25
TC166 Matt Ryan RC 12.00 5.00
TC167 Brian Brohm RC 4.00 1.50
TC168 Andre Woodson RC 3.00 1.25
TC169 Chad Henne RC 5.00 2.00
TC170 Joe Flacco RC 10.00 4.00
TC171 John David Booty RC 4.00 1.50
TC172 Colt Brennan RC 8.00 3.00
TC173 Dennis Dixon RC 3.00 1.25
TC174 Erik Ainge RC 3.00 1.25
TC175 Josh Johnson RC 3.00 1.25
TC176 Kevin O'Connell RC 4.00 1.50
TC177 Matt Flynn RC 4.00 1.50
TC178 Sam Keller RC 3.00 1.25
TC179 Harry Douglas RC 3.00 1.25
TC180 Anthony Morelli RC 3.00 1.25
TC181 Darren McFadden RC 8.00 3.00
TC182 Rashard Mendenhall RC 6.00 3.00
TC183 Jonathan Stewart RC 8.00 3.00
TC184 Felix Jones RC 8.00 3.00
TC185 Jamaal Charles RC 4.00 1.50
TC186 Chris Johnson RC 8.00 3.00
TC187 Ray Rice RC 4.00 1.50
TC188 Mike Hart RC 4.00 1.50
TC189 Kevin Smith RC 5.00 2.00
TC190 Steve Slaton RC 6.00 2.50
TC191 Matt Forte RC 8.00 3.00
TC192 Tashard Choice RC 3.00 1.25
TC193 Dominique Rodgers-Cromartie RC 3.00 1.25
TC194 Cory Boyd RC 2.50 1.00
TC195 Allen Patrick RC 2.50 1.00
TC196 Thomas Brown RC 3.00 1.25
TC197 Justin Forsett RC 3.00 1.25
TC198 DeSean Jackson RC 6.00 2.50
TC199 Malcolm Kelly RC 3.00 1.25
TC200 Limas Sweed RC 4.00 1.50
TC201 Mario Manningham RC 3.00 1.25
TC202 James Hardy RC 3.00 1.25
TC203 Early Doucet RC 3.00 1.25
TC204 Donnie Avery RC 4.00 1.50
TC205 Dexter Jackson RC 3.00 1.25
TC206 Devin Thomas RC 3.00 1.25
TC207 Jordy Nelson RC 4.00 1.50
TC208 Keenan Burton RC 2.50 1.00
TC209 Chris Williams RC 2.50 1.00
TC210 Earl Bennett RC 3.00 1.25
TC211 Jerome Simpson RC 2.50 1.00
TC212 Andre Caldwell RC 2.50 1.00
TC213 Josh Morgan RC 3.00 1.25
TC214 Fred Davis RC 3.00 1.25
TC215 John Carlson RC 3.00 1.25
TC216 Martellus Bennett RC 3.00 1.25
TC217 Martin Rucker RC 2.50 1.00
TC218 Jermichael Finley RC 3.00 1.25
TC219 Dustin Keller RC 3.00 1.25
TC220 Jacob Tamme RC 2.50 1.00
TC221 Kellen Davis RC 2.00 .75
TC222 Jake Long RC 4.00 1.50
TC223 Sam Baker RC 2.00 .75

TC224 Jeff Otah RC 2.50 1.00
TC225 Owen Schmitt RC 3.00 1.25
TC226 Chevis Jackson RC 2.50 1.00
TC227 Jacob Hester RC 3.00 1.25
TC228 Glenn Dorsey RC 4.00 1.50
TC229 Sedrick Ellis RC 2.50 1.00
TC230 Kentwan Balmer RC 2.50 1.00
TC231 Pat Sims RC 2.50 1.00
TC232 Marcus Harrison RC 3.00 1.25
TC233 Dre Moore RC 2.50 1.00
TC234 Red Bryant RC 2.00 .75
TC235 Trevor Laws RC 3.00 1.25
TC236 Chris Long RC 4.00 1.50
TC237 Vernon Gholston RC 3.00 1.25
TC238 Derrick Harvey RC 2.50 1.00
TC239 Calais Campbell RC 2.50 1.00
TC240 Terrence Wheatley RC 2.50 1.00
TC241 Phillip Merling RC 2.50 1.00
TC242 Chris Ellis RC 2.50 1.00
TC243 Lawrence Jackson RC 3.00 1.25
TC244 Dan Connor RC 3.00 1.25
TC245 Curtis Lofton RC 3.00 1.25
TC246 Jerod Mayo RC 5.00 2.00
TC247 Tavares Gooden RC 2.50 1.00
TC248 Beau Bell RC 2.50 1.00
TC249 Philip Wheeler RC 2.50 1.00
TC250 Vince Hall RC 2.00 .75
TC251 Jonathan Goff RC 2.50 1.00
TC252 Keith Rivers RC 3.00 1.25
TC253 Ali Highsmith RC 2.00 .75
TC254 Xavier Adibi RC 2.50 1.00
TC255 Erin Henderson RC 2.50 1.00
TC256 Bruce Davis RC 3.00 1.00
TC257 Jordon Dizon RC 3.00 1.25
TC258 Shawn Crable RC 3.00 1.25
TC259 Geno Hayes RC 2.00 .75
TC260 Mike Jenkins RC 3.00 1.25
TC261 Aqib Talib RC 3.00 1.25
TC262 Leodis McKelvin RC 3.00 1.25
TC263 Terrell Thomas RC 2.50 1.00
TC264 Reggie Smith RC 2.50 1.00
TC265 Antoine Cason RC 3.00 1.25
TC266 Patrick Lee RC 2.50 1.00
TC267 Tracy Porter RC 2.50 1.00
TC268 Kenny Phillips RC 3.00 1.25
TC269 Simeon Castille RC 3.00 1.25
TC270 Eddie Royal RC 6.00 2.50
TC271 Thomas DeCoud RC 2.00 .75
TC272 Marcus Griffin RC 2.00 .75
TC273 Charles Godfrey RC 2.50 1.00
TC274 Tyrell Johnson RC 2.50 1.00
TC275 Jamar Adams RC 2.50 1.00
RH242 Eli Manning RH 2.50 1.00

## 2003 Topps Draft Picks and Prospects

COMPLETE SET (165) 50.00 25.00
1 Priest Holmes 1.25 .50
2 Tommy Maddox 1.00 .40
3 Donald Driver .60 .25
4 Drew Bledsoe 1.00 .40
5 Tiki Barber 1.00 .40
6 Terrell Owens 1.00 .40
7 Rich Gannon .60 .25
8 Isaac Bruce 1.00 .40
9 Stephen Davis .60 .25
10 Peyton Manning 1.50 .60
11 Tony Gonzalez .60 .25
12 Marty Booker .60 .25

| | | |
|---|---|---|
| 13 Warrick Dunn | .60 | .25 |
| 14 Jimmy Smith | .60 | .25 |
| 15 Troy Brown | .60 | .25 |
| 16 Jerry Rice | 2.00 | .75 |
| 17 Curtis Conway | .40 | .15 |
| 18 Kurt Warner | 1.00 | .40 |
| 19 Steve McNair | 1.00 | .40 |
| 20 Edgerrin James | 1.00 | .40 |
| 21 Aaron Brooks | 1.00 | .40 |
| 22 Joey Galloway | .60 | .25 |
| 23 Peerless Price | .60 | .25 |
| 24 Torry Holt | 1.00 | .40 |
| 25 Derrick Mason | .60 | .25 |
| 26 Curtis Martin | 1.00 | .40 |
| 27 Daunte Culpepper | 1.00 | .40 |
| 28 Ahman Green | 1.00 | .40 |
| 29 Tim Couch | .40 | .15 |
| 30 Ricky Williams | 1.00 | .40 |
| 31 Darrell Jackson | .60 | .25 |
| 32 Keyshawn Johnson | 1.00 | .40 |
| 33 Jeff Garcia | 1.00 | .40 |
| 34 Charlie Garner | .60 | .25 |
| 35 Randy Moss | 1.50 | .60 |
| 36 Rod Smith | .60 | .25 |
| 37 Jamal Lewis | 1.00 | .40 |
| 38 Corey Dillon | .60 | .25 |
| 39 Marvin Harrison | 1.00 | .40 |
| 40 Joe Horn | .60 | .25 |
| 41 Laveranues Coles | .60 | .25 |
| 42 Hines Ward | 1.00 | .40 |
| 43 Brad Johnson | .60 | .25 |
| 44 Eddie George | .60 | .25 |
| 45 Donovan McNabb | 1.25 | .50 |
| 46 Marshall Faulk | 1.00 | .40 |
| 47 Amani Toomer | .60 | .25 |
| 48 Trent Green | .60 | .25 |
| 49 Emmitt Smith | 2.50 | 1.00 |
| 50 Brett Favre | 2.50 | 1.00 |
| 51 Brian Griese | 1.00 | .40 |
| 52 Eric Moulds | .60 | .25 |
| 53 Plaxico Burress | .60 | .25 |
| 54 Fred Taylor | 1.00 | .40 |
| 55 Tom Brady | 2.50 | 1.00 |
| 56 Michael Vick | 2.00 | .75 |
| 57 Andre Davis | .40 | .15 |
| 58 Chris Chambers | 1.00 | .40 |
| 59 Javon Walker | .60 | .25 |
| 60 Marc Bulger | 1.00 | .40 |
| 61 LaDainian Tomlinson | 1.00 | .40 |
| 62 Chad Pennington | 1.25 | .50 |
| 63 Marc Boerigter | .60 | .25 |
| 64 Rod Gardner | .60 | .25 |
| 65 DeShaun Foster | .40 | .15 |
| 66 Chris Redman | .40 | .15 |
| 67 Chad Hutchinson | .40 | .15 |
| 68 Deion Branch | 1.00 | .40 |
| 69 Jeremy Shockey | 1.50 | .60 |
| 70 Shaun Alexander | 1.00 | .40 |
| 71 Derrius Thompson | .40 | .15 |
| 72 A.J. Feeley | .60 | .25 |
| 73 Reggie Wayne | .60 | .25 |
| 74 William Green | .60 | .25 |
| 75 Julius Peppers | 1.00 | .40 |
| 76 Travis Henry | .60 | .25 |
| 77 Marcel Shipp | .60 | .25 |
| 78 Michael Bennett | .60 | .25 |
| 79 Maurice Morris | .40 | .15 |
| 80 Josh Reed | .60 | .25 |
| 81 David Terrell | .60 | .25 |
| 82 Drew Brees | 1.00 | .40 |
| 83 Jonathan Wells | .40 | .15 |
| 84 Anthony Thomas | .60 | .25 |
| 85 Quincy Morgan | .60 | .25 |
| 86 Jerry Porter | .60 | .25 |
| 87 Ron Johnson | .40 | .15 |
| 88 Najeh Davenport | .40 | .15 |
| 89 Lamar Gordon | .40 | .15 |
| 90 Joey Harrington | 1.50 | .60 |
| 91 Donte Stallworth | 1.00 | .40 |
| 92 Kenny Watson | .40 | .15 |
| 93 LaMont Jordan | .60 | .25 |
| 94 Antonio Bryant | .60 | .25 |
| 95 Steve Smith | .60 | .25 |
| 96 T.J. Duckett | .60 | .25 |
| 97 Patrick Ramsey | .60 | .25 |
| 98 Santana Moss | .60 | .25 |
| 99 Chad Johnson | 1.00 | .40 |

| | | |
|---|---|---|
| 100 Clinton Portis | 1.50 | .60 |
| 101 Reche Caldwell | .40 | .15 |
| 102 Kevan Barlow | .60 | .25 |
| 103 Deuce McAllister | 1.00 | .40 |
| 104 Koren Robinson | .40 | .15 |
| 105 Todd Heap | .60 | .25 |
| 106 Jabar Gaffney | .60 | .25 |
| 107 Randy McMichael | .60 | .25 |
| 108 Dwight Freeney | .60 | .25 |
| 109 Antwaan Randle El | 1.00 | .40 |
| 110 David Carr | 1.50 | .60 |
| 111 Carson Palmer RC | 6.00 | 2.50 |
| 112 Dahrran Diedrick RC | 1.50 | .60 |
| 113 Kyle Boller RC | 1.50 | .60 |
| 114 Terrell Suggs RC | 2.50 | 1.00 |
| 115 Rien Long RC | .75 | .30 |
| 116 Justin Gage RC | 1.50 | .60 |
| 117 William Joseph RC | 1.50 | .60 |
| 118 Chris Simms RC | 2.50 | 1.00 |
| 119 Alvon Cobourne RC | .75 | .30 |
| 120 Victor Hobson RC | 1.50 | .60 |
| 121 Jason Gesser RC | 1.50 | .60 |
| 122 Ronald Bellamy RC | 1.25 | .50 |
| 123 Terence Newman RC | 3.00 | 1.25 |
| 124 Terrence Edwards RC | 1.25 | .50 |
| 125 Sultan McCullough RC | 1.25 | .50 |
| 126 Kareem Kelly RC | 1.25 | .50 |
| 127 Jason Witten RC | 2.50 | 1.00 |
| 128 Mike Doss RC | 1.50 | .60 |
| 129 Seneca Wallace RC | 1.50 | .60 |
| 130 Chris Brown RC | 1.50 | .60 |
| 131 Larry Johnson RC | 4.00 | 1.50 |
| 132 Taylor Jacobs RC | 1.25 | .50 |
| 133 Jerome McDougle RC | 1.50 | .60 |
| 134 Kelley Washington RC | 1.50 | .60 |
| 135 Brad Banks RC | 1.50 | .60 |
| 136 DeWayne White RC | 1.25 | .50 |
| 137 LaBrandon Toefield RC | 1.50 | .60 |
| 138 Brian St.Pierre RC | 1.50 | .60 |
| 139 Kindal Moorehead RC | 1.25 | .50 |
| 140 Willis McGahee RC | 4.00 | 1.50 |
| 141 Jimmy Kennedy RC | 1.50 | .60 |
| 142 Talman Gardner RC | 1.50 | .60 |
| 143 Chris Kelsay RC | 1.50 | .60 |
| 144 Cory Redding RC | 1.25 | .50 |
| 145 Dave Ragone RC | 1.50 | .60 |
| 146 Earnest Graham RC | 1.50 | .60 |
| 147 Andre Johnson RC | 3.00 | 1.00 |
| 148 Boss Bailey RC | 1.50 | .60 |
| 149 Sam Aiken RC | 1.25 | .50 |
| 150 Byron Leftwich RC | 3.00 | 1.25 |
| 151 Teyo Johnson RC | 1.50 | .60 |
| 152 Quentin Griffin RC | 1.50 | .60 |
| 153 Justin Fargas RC | 1.50 | .60 |
| 154 Bradie James RC | 1.50 | .60 |
| 155 Andre Woolfolk RC | 1.50 | .60 |
| 156 Marcus Trufant RC | 1.50 | .60 |
| 157 Ken Dorsey RC | 1.50 | .60 |
| 158 Onterrio Smith RC | 1.50 | .60 |
| 159 Bryant Johnson RC | 1.50 | .60 |
| 160 Charles Rogers RC | 1.50 | .60 |
| 161 Kliff Kingsbury RC | 1.25 | .50 |
| 162 Michael Haynes RC | 1.50 | .60 |
| 163 Bennie Joppru RC | 1.50 | .60 |
| 164 Brandon Lloyd RC | 1.50 | .60 |
| 165 Jarret Johnson RC | 1.25 | .50 |

## 2004 Topps Draft Picks and Prospects

| | | |
|---|---|---|
| COMPLETE SET (165) | 80.00 | 40.00 |
| 1 Steve McNair | 1.00 | .40 |
| 2 Stephen Davis | .75 | .30 |
| 3 Chris Chambers | .75 | .30 |
| 4 Curtis Martin | 1.00 | .40 |
| 5 Shaun Alexander | 1.00 | .40 |
| 6 Jon Kitna | .75 | .30 |
| 7 Jimmy Smith | .75 | .30 |
| 8 Travis Henry | .75 | .30 |
| 9 Torry Holt | 1.00 | .40 |
| 10 Jamal Lewis | .75 | .30 |
| 11 Clinton Portis | 1.00 | .40 |
| 12 Aaron Brooks | .75 | .30 |
| 13 Plaxico Burress | .75 | .30 |
| 14 Trent Green | .75 | .30 |
| 15 Chad Johnson | .75 | .30 |
| 16 Jake Delhomme | .75 | .30 |
| 17 David Boston | .60 | .25 |
| 18 Joe Horn | .75 | .30 |
| 19 Ahman Green | 1.00 | .40 |
| 20 Fred Taylor | .75 | .30 |
| 21 Terrell Owens | 1.00 | .40 |
| 22 Brad Johnson | .75 | .30 |
| 23 Laveranues Coles | .75 | .30 |
| 24 Ricky Williams | 1.00 | .40 |
| 25 Peyton Manning | 2.00 | .75 |
| 26 Hines Ward | 1.00 | .40 |
| 27 Matt Hasselbeck | 1.00 | .40 |
| 28 Marshall Faulk | 1.00 | .40 |
| 29 Tony Gonzalez | 1.00 | .40 |
| 30 Marvin Harrison | 1.00 | .40 |
| 31 Eric Moulds | .75 | .30 |
| 32 Chad Pennington | 1.00 | .40 |
| 33 Jerry Porter | .75 | .30 |
| 34 Jeff Garcia | 1.00 | .40 |
| 35 Derrick Mason | .75 | .30 |
| 36 Anthony Thomas | .75 | .30 |
| 37 Drew Bledsoe | 1.00 | .40 |
| 38 Jake Plummer | .75 | .30 |
| 39 Tiki Barber | 1.00 | .40 |
| 40 Brett Favre | 2.50 | 1.00 |
| 41 Joey Harrington | .75 | .30 |
| 42 Daunte Culpepper | 1.00 | .40 |
| 43 LaVar Arrington | .75 | .30 |
| 44 Santana Moss | .75 | .30 |
| 45 David Carr | .75 | .30 |
| 46 Randy Moss | 1.25 | .50 |
| 47 LaDainian Tomlinson | 1.50 | .60 |
| 48 Deuce McAllister | 1.00 | .40 |
| 49 Amani Toomer | .75 | .30 |
| 50 Donovan McNabb | 1.00 | .40 |
| 51 Priest Holmes | 1.00 | .40 |
| 52 Corey Dillon | .75 | .30 |
| 53 Tom Brady | 2.50 | 1.00 |
| 54 Edgerrin James | 1.00 | .40 |
| 55 Michael Vick | 1.00 | .40 |
| 56 Anquan Boldin | 1.00 | .40 |
| 57 Robert Ferguson | .60 | .25 |
| 58 Onterrio Smith | .60 | .25 |
| 59 Marques Tuiasosopo | .60 | .25 |
| 60 Rudi Johnson | .75 | .30 |
| 61 Alge Crumpler | .75 | .30 |
| 62 Antonio Bryant | .75 | .30 |
| 63 LaMont Jordan | 1.00 | .40 |
| 64 Lamar Gordon | .60 | .25 |
| 65 Tim Rattay | .60 | .25 |
| 66 Antwaan Randle El | .75 | .30 |
| 67 Ladell Betts | .75 | .30 |
| 68 LaBrandon Toefield | .60 | .25 |
| 69 Ashley Lelie | .75 | .30 |
| 70 Marc Bulger | .75 | .30 |
| 71 Reggie Wayne | .75 | .30 |
| 72 William Green | .60 | .25 |
| 73 Josh Reed | 1.00 | .40 |
| 74 T.J. Duckett | .75 | .30 |
| 75 Andre Johnson | 1.00 | .40 |
| 76 Deion Branch | .75 | .30 |
| 77 Tyrone Calico | .75 | .30 |
| 78 Jeremy Shockey | .75 | .30 |
| 79 Najeh Davenport | .75 | .30 |
| 80 Byron Leftwich | 1.00 | .40 |
| 81 Correll Buckhalter | .75 | .30 |
| 82 Justin McCareins | .60 | .25 |
| 83 Carson Palmer | 1.25 | .50 |
| 84 Brandon Johnson | .75 | .30 |
| 85 Patrick Ramsey | .75 | .30 |
| 86 Justin Fargas | .75 | .30 |

| | | |
|---|---|---|
| ❑ 87 Dallas Clark | .75 | .30 |
| ❑ 88 Kelly Campbell | .60 | .25 |
| ❑ 89 DeShaun Foster | .75 | .30 |
| ❑ 90 Charles Rogers | .75 | .30 |
| ❑ 91 Donte' Stallworth | .75 | .30 |
| ❑ 92 Dante Hall | .75 | .30 |
| ❑ 93 Randy McMichael | .60 | .25 |
| ❑ 94 Marcel Shipp | 1.00 | .40 |
| ❑ 95 Kyle Boller | .75 | .30 |
| ❑ 96 Steve Smith | 1.00 | .40 |
| ❑ 97 Brian Westbrook | 1.00 | .40 |
| ❑ 98 Kevan Barlow | .75 | .30 |
| ❑ 99 Darrenen McCants | .60 | .25 |
| ❑ 100 Domanick Davis | 1.00 | .40 |
| ❑ 101 Andre' Davis | .60 | .25 |
| ❑ 102 Nate Burleson | .75 | .30 |
| ❑ 103 Larry Johnson | 1.50 | .60 |
| ❑ 104 Drew Brees | 1.00 | .40 |
| ❑ 105 Koren Robinson | 1.00 | .40 |
| ❑ 106 Quincy Carter | .60 | .25 |
| ❑ 107 Javon Walker | .75 | .30 |
| ❑ 108 Willis McGahee | 1.00 | .40 |
| ❑ 109 Chris Simms | .75 | .30 |
| ❑ 110 Rex Grossman | 1.00 | .40 |
| ❑ 111 Steven Jackson RC | 6.00 | 2.50 |
| ❑ 112 Greg Jones RC | 2.00 | .75 |
| ❑ 113 Brandon Everage RC | 1.25 | .50 |
| ❑ 114 DeAngelo Hall RC | 2.00 | .75 |
| ❑ 115 Tatum Bell RC | 2.00 | .75 |
| ❑ 116 B.J. Symons RC | 1.25 | .50 |
| ❑ 117 Michael Clayton RC | 2.00 | .75 |
| ❑ 118 Jared Lorenzen RC | 1.50 | .60 |
| ❑ 119 Josh Harris RC | 1.25 | .50 |
| ❑ 120 Roy Williams RC | 5.00 | 2.00 |
| ❑ 121 Mewelde Moore RC | 2.00 | .75 |
| ❑ 122 Jeff Smoker RC | 1.50 | .60 |
| ❑ 123 Lee Evans RC | 2.50 | 1.00 |
| ❑ 124 Michael Jenkins RC | 2.00 | .75 |
| ❑ 125 Drew Henson RC | 1.25 | .50 |
| ❑ 126 Ben Watson RC | 2.00 | .75 |
| ❑ 127 Jerricho Cotchery RC | 2.00 | .75 |
| ❑ 128 Ben Troupe RC | 1.50 | .60 |
| ❑ 129 Chris Gamble RC | 1.50 | .60 |
| ❑ 130 Kevin Jones RC | 2.00 | .75 |
| ❑ 131 Cody Pickett RC | 1.50 | .60 |
| ❑ 132 J.P. Losman RC | 2.50 | 1.00 |
| ❑ 133 Michael Boulware RC | 2.00 | .75 |
| ❑ 134 Julius Jones RC | 5.00 | 2.00 |
| ❑ 135 Keary Colbert RC | 2.00 | .75 |
| ❑ 136 Vince Wilfork RC | 2.00 | .75 |
| ❑ 137 Ernest Wilford RC | 2.00 | .75 |
| ❑ 138 John Navarre RC | 1.50 | .60 |
| ❑ 139 D.J. Williams RC | 2.00 | .75 |
| ❑ 140 Larry Fitzgerald RC | 6.00 | 2.50 |
| ❑ 141 Quincy Wilson RC | 1.50 | .60 |
| ❑ 142 James Newson RC | 2.00 | .75 |
| ❑ 143 Reggie Williams RC | 2.00 | .75 |
| ❑ 144 Devard Darling RC | 1.50 | .60 |
| ❑ 145 Chris Perry RC | 2.00 | .75 |
| ❑ 146 Derrick Strait RC | 1.50 | .60 |
| ❑ 147 Teddy Lehman RC | 1.50 | .60 |
| ❑ 148 Michael Turner RC | 4.00 | 1.50 |
| ❑ 149 Will Smith RC | 1.50 | .60 |
| ❑ 150 Eli Manning RC | 15.00 | 6.00 |
| ❑ 151 Cedric Cobbs RC | 1.50 | .60 |
| ❑ 152 Eli Roberson UER RC | 2.00 | .75 |
| ❑ 153 Matt Schaub RC | 6.00 | 2.50 |
| ❑ 154 Derrick Knight RC | 1.25 | .50 |
| ❑ 155 Rashaun Woods RC | 1.25 | .50 |
| ❑ 156 Jonathan Vilma RC | 2.00 | .75 |
| ❑ 157 Tommie Harris RC | 2.00 | .75 |
| ❑ 158 Dwan Edwards RC | 1.25 | .50 |
| ❑ 159 Will Poole RC | 2.00 | .75 |
| ❑ 160 Mike Williams RC | 1.50 | .60 |
| ❑ 161 Philip Rivers RC | 6.00 | 2.50 |
| ❑ 162 Sean Taylor RC | 2.00 | .75 |
| ❑ 163 Darius Watts RC | 1.50 | .60 |
| ❑ 164 Casey Clausen RC | 1.50 | .60 |
| ❑ 165 Ben Roethlisberger RC | 20.00 | 8.00 |

## 2005 Topps Draft Picks and Prospects

| | | |
|---|---|---|
| ❑ COMP.SET w/AU's (165) | 40.00 | 15.00 |
| ❑ COMP.SET w/o RC's (110) | 25.00 | 10.00 |
| ❑ ONE ROOKIE PER PACK | | |
| ❑ DRAFT PICK AUTO ODDS 1:1179H, 1:1182R | | |

| | | |
|---|---|---|
| ❑ UNPRICED GOLD SUPERFRACTORS #'d TO 1 | | |
| ❑ UNPRICED PRINTING PLATES #'d TO 1 | | |
| ❑ 1 Marvin Harrison | 1.00 | .40 |
| ❑ 2 Rudi Johnson | .75 | .30 |
| ❑ 3 Matt Hasselbeck | .75 | .30 |
| ❑ 4 Plaxico Burress | .75 | .30 |
| ❑ 5 Chad Pennington | 1.00 | .40 |
| ❑ 6 Jamal Lewis | .75 | .30 |
| ❑ 7 Terrell Owens | 1.00 | .40 |
| ❑ 8 LaDainian Tomlinson | 1.50 | .60 |
| ❑ 9 Tiki Barber | 1.00 | .40 |
| ❑ 10 Dante Hall | .75 | .30 |
| ❑ 11 Peyton Manning | 1.50 | .60 |
| ❑ 12 Marshall Faulk | 1.00 | .40 |
| ❑ 13 Donovan McNabb | 1.00 | .40 |
| ❑ 14 Randy Moss | 1.00 | .40 |
| ❑ 15 Muhsin Muhammad | .75 | .30 |
| ❑ 16 Deuce McAllister | 1.00 | .40 |
| ❑ 17 Fred Taylor | 1.00 | .40 |
| ❑ 18 Jake Plummer | .75 | .30 |
| ❑ 19 Javon Walker | .75 | .30 |
| ❑ 20 Tony Gonzalez | .75 | .30 |
| ❑ 21 Michael Vick | 1.00 | .40 |
| ❑ 22 Brett Favre | 2.50 | 1.00 |
| ❑ 23 Joe Horn | .75 | .30 |
| ❑ 24 Jeremy Shockey | 1.00 | .40 |
| ❑ 25 Laveranues Coles | .75 | .30 |
| ❑ 26 Trent Green | .75 | .30 |
| ❑ 27 Alge Crumpler | .75 | .30 |
| ❑ 28 Curtis Martin | 1.00 | .40 |
| ❑ 29 Torry Holt | .75 | .30 |
| ❑ 30 Daunte Culpepper | 1.00 | .40 |
| ❑ 31 Aaron Brooks | .60 | .25 |
| ❑ 32 Priest Holmes | 1.00 | .40 |
| ❑ 33 Eric Moulds | .75 | .30 |
| ❑ 34 Jerome Bettis | 1.00 | .40 |
| ❑ 35 David Carr | .75 | .30 |
| ❑ 36 Chad Johnson | .75 | .30 |
| ❑ 37 Ahman Green | .75 | .30 |
| ❑ 38 Clinton Portis | .75 | .30 |
| ❑ 39 Drew Brees | 1.00 | .40 |
| ❑ 40 Darrell Jackson | .75 | .30 |
| ❑ 41 Corey Dillon | .75 | .30 |
| ❑ 42 Reggie Wayne | .75 | .30 |
| ❑ 43 Shaun Alexander | 1.00 | .40 |
| ❑ 44 Hines Ward | 1.00 | .40 |
| ❑ 45 Tom Brady | 2.00 | .75 |
| ❑ 46 Isaac Bruce | .75 | .30 |
| ❑ 47 Byron Leftwich | .75 | .30 |
| ❑ 48 Chris Chambers | .75 | .30 |
| ❑ 49 Marc Bulger | .75 | .30 |
| ❑ 50 Edgerrin James | .75 | .30 |
| ❑ 51 Jake Delhomme | 1.00 | .40 |
| ❑ 52 Koren Robinson | .75 | .30 |
| ❑ 53 Brian Westbrook | 1.00 | .40 |
| ❑ 54 Reuben Droughns | .60 | .25 |
| ❑ 55 Joey Harrington | .75 | .30 |
| ❑ 56 Eli Manning | 2.00 | .75 |
| ❑ 57 Julius Jones | 1.00 | .40 |
| ❑ 58 Nick Goings | .60 | .25 |
| ❑ 59 T.J. Houshmandzadeh | .75 | .30 |
| ❑ 60 Ben Roethlisberger | 2.50 | 1.00 |
| ❑ 61 Charles Rogers | .75 | .30 |
| ❑ 62 Billy Volek | .75 | .30 |
| ❑ 63 Drew Henson | .60 | .25 |
| ❑ 64 Andre Johnson | .75 | .30 |
| ❑ 65 Carson Palmer | 1.00 | .40 |
| ❑ 66 Anquan Boldin | .75 | .30 |
| ❑ 67 Lee Suggs | .75 | .30 |
| ❑ 68 Jerry Porter | .75 | .30 |

| | | |
|---|---|---|
| ❑ 69 J.P. Losman | 1.00 | .40 |
| ❑ 70 Nate Burleson | .75 | .30 |
| ❑ 71 Lee Evans | .75 | .30 |
| ❑ 72 Tatum Bell | .75 | .30 |
| ❑ 73 Chester Taylor | .75 | .30 |
| ❑ 74 Philip Rivers | 1.00 | .40 |
| ❑ 75 Rex Grossman | 1.00 | .40 |
| ❑ 76 Willis McGahee | 1.00 | .40 |
| ❑ 77 Antonio Gates | 1.00 | .40 |
| ❑ 78 Steven Jackson | 1.25 | .50 |
| ❑ 79 Roy Williams WR | 1.00 | .40 |
| ❑ 80 Chris Simms | .75 | .30 |
| ❑ 81 Najeh Davenport | .75 | .30 |
| ❑ 82 Kevin Jones | .75 | .30 |
| ❑ 83 Jason Witten | .75 | .30 |
| ❑ 84 Brandon Lloyd | .60 | .25 |
| ❑ 85 Larry Johnson | 1.00 | .40 |
| ❑ 86 Ronald Curry | .75 | .30 |
| ❑ 87 Chris Brown | .75 | .30 |
| ❑ 88 Kyle Boller | .75 | .30 |
| ❑ 89 Chris Perry | .60 | .25 |
| ❑ 90 Keary Colbert | .60 | .25 |
| ❑ 91 Sean Taylor | .75 | .30 |
| ❑ 92 Greg Jones | .60 | .25 |
| ❑ 93 Larry Fitzgerald | 1.00 | .40 |
| ❑ 94 Michael Clayton | .75 | .30 |
| ❑ 95 Mewelde Moore | .60 | .25 |
| ❑ 96 Drew Bennett | .75 | .30 |
| ❑ 97 Reggie Williams | .75 | .30 |
| ❑ 98 Quentin Griffin | .75 | .30 |
| ❑ 99 Josh McCown | .75 | .30 |
| ❑ 100 Santana Moss | .75 | .30 |
| ❑ 101 Kellen Winslow | 1.00 | .40 |
| ❑ 102 Michael Jenkins | .75 | .30 |
| ❑ 103 Dunta Robinson | .60 | .25 |
| ❑ 104 Luke McCown | .60 | .25 |
| ❑ 105 Brandon Stokley | .60 | .25 |
| ❑ 106 Derrick Blaylock | .60 | .25 |
| ❑ 107 Ernest Wilford | .75 | .30 |
| ❑ 108 Domanick Davis | .60 | .25 |
| ❑ 109 Jonathan Vilma | .75 | .30 |
| ❑ 110 Dwight Freeney | .75 | .30 |
| ❑ 111 Alex Smith QB AU RC | 120.00 | 60.00 |
| ❑ 112 Derrick Johnson AU RC | 60.00 | 25.00 |
| ❑ 113 Charlie Frye AU RC | 50.00 | 20.00 |
| ❑ 114 Ronnie Brown AU RC | 120.00 | 60.00 |
| ❑ 115 Mike Williams AU | 50.00 | 20.00 |
| ❑ 116 Erasmus James RC | 1.50 | .60 |
| ❑ 117 Alex Smith TE RC | 2.00 | .75 |
| ❑ 118 Dan Orlovsky RC | 2.00 | .75 |
| ❑ 119 Eric Shelton RC | 1.50 | .60 |
| ❑ 120 Reggie Brown RC | 2.00 | .75 |
| ❑ 121 Carlos Rogers RC | 2.00 | .75 |
| ❑ 122 Dan Cody RC | 2.00 | .75 |
| ❑ 123 J.J. Arrington RC | 2.00 | .75 |
| ❑ 124 Travis Johnson RC | 1.25 | .50 |
| ❑ 125 Antrel Rolle RC | 2.00 | .75 |
| ❑ 126 Andrew Walter RC | 2.00 | .75 |
| ❑ 127 Craphonso Thorpe RC | 1.50 | .60 |
| ❑ 128 Bryan Randall RC | 1.50 | .60 |
| ❑ 129 Anttaj Hawthorne RC | 1.50 | .60 |
| ❑ 130 David Pollack RC | 1.50 | .60 |
| ❑ 131 Heath Miller RC | 4.00 | 1.50 |
| ❑ 132 Charles Frederick RC | 1.50 | .60 |
| ❑ 133 Anthony Davis RC | 1.50 | .60 |
| ❑ 134 Chris Rix RC | 1.50 | .60 |
| ❑ 135 T.A. McLendon RC | 1.25 | .50 |
| ❑ 136 David Greene RC | 1.50 | .60 |
| ❑ 137 Timmy Chang RC | 1.50 | .60 |
| ❑ 138 Marcus Spears RC | 2.00 | .75 |
| ❑ 139 Airese Currie RC | 1.50 | .60 |
| ❑ 140 Chris Henry RC | 2.00 | .75 |
| ❑ 141 Josh Davis RC | 1.25 | .50 |
| ❑ 142 Jason Campbell RC | 4.00 | 1.50 |
| ❑ 143 Barrett Ruud RC | 2.00 | .75 |
| ❑ 144 Courtney Roby RC | 1.50 | .60 |
| ❑ 145 Mike Patterson RC | 1.50 | .60 |
| ❑ 146 Jason White RC | 2.00 | .75 |
| ❑ 147 Fred Gibson RC | 1.50 | .60 |
| ❑ 148 Marion Barber RC | 6.00 | 2.50 |
| ❑ 149 Braylon Edwards RC | 6.00 | 2.50 |
| ❑ 150 Cadillac Williams RC | 4.00 | 1.50 |
| ❑ 151 Kyle Orton RC | 2.50 | 1.00 |
| ❑ 152 Aaron Rodgers RC | 6.00 | 2.50 |
| ❑ 153 Alvin Pearman RC | 1.50 | .60 |
| ❑ 154 Stefan LeFors RC | 1.50 | .60 |
| ❑ 155 Marlin Jackson RC | 1.50 | .60 |

| | | | |
|---|---|---|---|
| ☐ 156 Taylor Stubblefield RC | 1.25 | .50 |
| ☐ 157 Ciatrick Fason RC | 1.50 | .60 |
| ☐ 158 Kay-Jay Harris RC | 1.50 | .60 |
| ☐ 159 Frank Gore RC | 5.00 | 2.00 |
| ☐ 160 Vernand Morency RC | .20 | .75 |
| ☐ 161 Adam Jones RC | 2.00 | .75 |
| ☐ 162 Troy Williamson RC | 2.00 | .75 |
| ☐ 163 Roddy White RC | 2.50 | 1.00 |
| ☐ 164 Thomas Davis RC | 2.00 | .75 |
| ☐ 165 Mark Clayton RC | 2.00 | .75 |
| ☐ 166 Craig Bragg RC | 1.25 | .50 |
| ☐ 167 Noah Herron RC | 2.00 | .75 |
| ☐ 168 Darren Sproles RC | 2.50 | 1.00 |
| ☐ 169 Terrence Murphy RC | 1.25 | .50 |
| ☐ 170 Walter Reyes RC | 1.25 | .50 |

## 2006 Topps Draft Picks and Prospects

| | | |
|---|---|---|
| ☐ COMP SET w/o SP's (165) | 30.00 | 12.50 |
| ☐ COMP SET w/o RC's (110) | 15.00 | 6.00 |
| ☐ ONE ROOKIE CARD PER PACK | | |
| ☐ 166-175 ROOKIE AU/199 ODDS 1:282 | | |
| ☐ 1 Plaxico Burress | .75 | .30 |
| ☐ 2 Ahman Green | .75 | .30 |
| ☐ 3 Domanick Davis | .75 | .30 |
| ☐ 4 Andre Johnson | .75 | .30 |
| ☐ 5 Donovan McNabb | 1.00 | .40 |
| ☐ 6 Marvin Harrison | 1.00 | .40 |
| ☐ 7 Michael Vick | 1.00 | .40 |
| ☐ 8 Priest Holmes | .75 | .30 |
| ☐ 9 Torry Holt | .75 | .30 |
| ☐ 10 Marc Bulger | .75 | .30 |
| ☐ 11 Ben Roethlisberger | 1.50 | .60 |
| ☐ 12 Larry Fitzgerald | 1.00 | .40 |
| ☐ 13 Peyton Manning | 1.50 | .60 |
| ☐ 14 Chris Perry | .75 | .30 |
| ☐ 15 Antonio Gates | 1.00 | .40 |
| ☐ 16 Eli Manning | 1.25 | .50 |
| ☐ 17 Brett Favre | 2.00 | .75 |
| ☐ 18 Reggie Brown | .75 | .30 |
| ☐ 19 Curtis Martin | 1.00 | .40 |
| ☐ 20 Charlie Frye | .75 | .30 |
| ☐ 21 Tom Brady | 1.50 | .60 |
| ☐ 22 Cadillac Williams | 1.00 | .40 |
| ☐ 23 Trent Green | .75 | .30 |
| ☐ 24 Matt Jones | .75 | .30 |
| ☐ 25 Anquan Boldin | .75 | .30 |
| ☐ 26 Larry Johnson | .75 | .30 |
| ☐ 27 Rudi Johnson | ..75 | .30 |
| ☐ 28 Marion Barber | 1.00 | .40 |
| ☐ 29 Jake Delhomme | .75 | .30 |
| ☐ 30 Philip Rivers | 1.00 | .40 |
| ☐ 31 Fred Taylor | .75 | .30 |
| ☐ 32 Frank Gore | 1.00 | .40 |
| ☐ 33 Shaun Alexander | 1.00 | .40 |
| ☐ 34 Chris Simms | .75 | .30 |
| ☐ 35 LaDainian Tomlinson | 1.25 | .50 |
| ☐ 36 Troy Williamson | .75 | .30 |
| ☐ 37 Clinton Portis | .75 | .30 |
| ☐ 38 Kyle Orton | .60 | .25 |
| ☐ 39 Tony Gonzalez | .75 | .30 |
| ☐ 40 Mark Clayton | .75 | .30 |
| ☐ 41 Steve Smith | 1.00 | .40 |
| ☐ 42 Heath Miller | .75 | .30 |
| ☐ 43 Warrick Dunn | .75 | .30 |
| ☐ 44 Alex Smith TE | .60 | .25 |
| ☐ 45 Chris Brown | .75 | .30 |
| ☐ 46 Billy Volek | .75 | .30 |
| ☐ 47 Tiki Barber | 1.00 | .40 |

| | | |
|---|---|---|
| ☐ 48 Julius Jones | 1.00 | .40 |
| ☐ 49 Drew Bledsoe | 1.00 | .40 |
| ☐ 50 Charles Rogers | .75 | .30 |
| ☐ 51 Jake Plummer | .75 | .30 |
| ☐ 52 Greg Jones | .60 | .25 |
| ☐ 53 Chad Johnson | .75 | .30 |
| ☐ 54 Braylon Edwards | 1.00 | .40 |
| ☐ 55 Carson Palmer | 1.00 | .40 |
| ☐ 56 Scottie Vines | .60 | .25 |
| ☐ 57 Keary Colbert | .75 | .30 |
| ☐ 58 Alex Smith QB | 1.00 | .40 |
| ☐ 59 Roy Williams WR | 1.00 | .40 |
| ☐ 60 Roddy White | .60 | .25 |
| ☐ 61 Willis McGahee | 1.00 | .40 |
| ☐ 62 Michael Clayton | .75 | .30 |
| ☐ 63 Edgerrin James | .75 | .30 |
| ☐ 64 Aaron Rodgers | .75 | .30 |
| ☐ 65 Byron Leftwich | .75 | .30 |
| ☐ 66 Tatum Bell | .75 | .30 |
| ☐ 67 Daunte Culpepper | 1.00 | .40 |
| ☐ 68 Chris Henry | .60 | .25 |
| ☐ 69 Corey Dillon | .75 | .30 |
| ☐ 70 Ronnie Brown | 1.00 | .40 |
| ☐ 71 Kevin Jones | 1.00 | .40 |
| ☐ 72 J.P. Losman | .75 | .30 |
| ☐ 73 Steven Jackson | 1.00 | .40 |
| ☐ 74 Mike Williams | 1.00 | .40 |
| ☐ 75 Jeremy Shockey | 1.00 | .40 |
| ☐ 76 DeMarcus Ware | .75 | .30 |
| ☐ 77 LaMont Jordan | .75 | .30 |
| ☐ 78 Cedric Benson | .75 | .30 |
| ☐ 79 Ricky Williams | .60 | .25 |
| ☐ 80 Brandon Jones | .60 | .25 |
| ☐ 81 Brian Westbrook | .75 | .30 |
| ☐ 82 Willie Parker | 1.25 | .50 |
| ☐ 83 Hines Ward | 1.00 | .40 |
| ☐ 84 Ernest Wilford | .75 | .30 |
| ☐ 85 Matt Hasselbeck | .75 | .30 |
| ☐ 86 Jason Campbell | .75 | .30 |
| ☐ 87 Joey Galloway | .75 | .30 |
| ☐ 88 Odell Thurman | .60 | .25 |
| ☐ 89 Santana Moss | .75 | .30 |
| ☐ 90 Courtney Roby | .60 | .25 |
| ☐ 91 Deuce McAllister | .75 | .30 |
| ☐ 92 Derrick Johnson | .75 | .30 |
| ☐ 93 Drew Brees | 1.00 | .40 |
| ☐ 94 Michael Jenkins | .75 | .30 |
| ☐ 95 Jerome Bettis | 1.00 | .40 |
| ☐ 96 Osi Umenyiora | .75 | .30 |
| ☐ 97 Reggie Wayne | .75 | .30 |
| ☐ 98 Ryan Moats | .75 | .30 |
| ☐ 99 Randy Moss | 1.00 | .40 |
| ☐ 100 Samie Parker | .60 | .25 |
| ☐ 101 Mark Bradley | .60 | .25 |
| ☐ 102 Samkon Gado | 1.00 | .40 |
| ☐ 103 Matt Schaub | .75 | .30 |
| ☐ 104 Shaun McDonald | .60 | .25 |
| ☐ 105 D.J. Hackett | .75 | .30 |
| ☐ 106 Mewelde Moore | .60 | .25 |
| ☐ 107 Chester Taylor | .75 | .30 |
| ☐ 108 Greg Lewis | .60 | .25 |
| ☐ 109 Chris Cooley | .75 | .30 |
| ☐ 110 Todd DeVoe RC | 1.00 | .40 |
| ☐ 111 Joel Klopfenstein RC | 2.00 | .75 |
| ☐ 112 Devin Hester RC | 5.00 | 2.00 |
| ☐ 113 Brad Smith RC | 2.50 | 1.00 |
| ☐ 114 Jason Avant RC | 2.50 | 1.00 |
| ☐ 115 Michael Robinson RC | 2.50 | 1.00 |
| ☐ 116 Kellen Clemens RC | 3.00 | 1.25 |
| ☐ 117 Anthony Fasano RC | 2.50 | 1.00 |
| ☐ 118 Leon Washington RC | 2.50 | 1.00 |
| ☐ 119 Laurence Maroney RC | 6.00 | 2.50 |
| ☐ 120 Martin Nance RC | 2.00 | .75 |
| ☐ 121 Demetrius Williams RC | 2.50 | 1.00 |
| ☐ 122 A.J. Nicholson RC | 1.50 | .60 |
| ☐ 123 Jimmy Williams RC | 2.50 | 1.00 |
| ☐ 124 Michael Huff RC | 2.50 | 1.00 |
| ☐ 125 Chad Jackson RC | 2.50 | 1.00 |
| ☐ 126 Mike Hass RC | 2.50 | 1.00 |
| ☐ 127 Brodie Croyle RC | 3.00 | 1.25 |
| ☐ 128 Jerome Harrison RC | 2.50 | 1.00 |
| ☐ 129 Hank Baskett RC | 6.00 | 2.50 |
| ☐ 130 Santonio Holmes RC | 6.00 | 2.50 |
| ☐ 131 Chad Greenway RC | 2.50 | 1.00 |
| ☐ 132 Mario Williams RC | 4.00 | 1.50 |
| ☐ 133 Charlie Whitehurst RC | 2.50 | 1.00 |
| ☐ 134 Darrell Hackney RC | 2.00 | .75 |

| | | |
|---|---|---|
| ☐ 135 DeMeco Ryans RC | 3.00 | 1.25 |
| ☐ 136 Mathias Kiwanuka RC | 3.00 | 1.25 |
| ☐ 137 Omar Jacobs RC | 2.00 | .75 |
| ☐ 138 Bruce Gradkowski RC | 2.50 | 1.00 |
| ☐ 139 Drew Olson RC | 2.00 | .75 |
| ☐ 140 Maurice Stovall RC | 2.50 | 1.00 |
| ☐ 141 Greg Jennings RC | 4.00 | 1.50 |
| ☐ 142 D'Brickashaw Ferguson RC | 2.00 | 1.00 |
| ☐ 143 Manny Lawson RC | 2.50 | 1.00 |
| ☐ 144 Tamba Hali RC | 2.50 | 1.00 |
| ☐ 145 Vernon Davis RC | 2.50 | 1.00 |
| ☐ 146 Greg Lee RC | 2.00 | .75 |
| ☐ 147 Dominique Byrd RC | 2.00 | .75 |
| ☐ 148 Leonard Pope RC | 2.50 | 1.00 |
| ☐ 149 Bobby Carpenter RC | 2.50 | 1.00 |
| ☐ 150 Haloti Ngata RC | 2.50 | 1.00 |
| ☐ 151 Marcedes Lewis RC | 2.50 | 1.00 |
| ☐ 152 Ernie Sims RC | 2.50 | 1.00 |
| ☐ 153 Ashton Youboty RC | 2.50 | 1.00 |
| ☐ 154 D.J. Shockley RC | 2.50 | 1.00 |
| ☐ 155 Paul Pinegar RC | 2.00 | .75 |
| ☐ 156 Maurice Drew RC | 5.00 | 2.00 |
| ☐ 157 Jeremy Bloom RC | 2.00 | .75 |
| ☐ 158 Cory Rodgers RC | 2.50 | 1.00 |
| ☐ 159 Abdul Hodge RC | 2.50 | 1.00 |
| ☐ 160 Tye Hill RC | 2.50 | 1.00 |
| ☐ 161 D'Qwell Jackson RC | 2.00 | .75 |
| ☐ 162 Jonathan Orr RC | 2.00 | .75 |
| ☐ 163 Antonio Cromartie RC | 2.50 | 1.00 |
| ☐ 164 Todd Watkins RC | 2.00 | .75 |
| ☐ 165 Gerald Riggs RC | 2.50 | 1.00 |
| ☐ 166 Matt Leinart AU RC | 120.00 | 60.00 |
| ☐ 167 Reggie Bush AU RC | 150.00 | 75.00 |
| ☐ 168 DeAngelo Williams AU RC | 80.00 | 40.00 |
| ☐ 169 A.J. Hawk AU RC | 120.00 | 60.00 |
| ☐ 170 Vince Young AU RC | 120.00 | 60.00 |
| ☐ 171 Derek Hagan AU RC | 40.00 | 20.00 |
| ☐ 172 Joseph Addai AU RC | 135.00 | 75.00 |
| ☐ 173 Jay Cutler AU RC | 150.00 | 75.00 |
| ☐ 174 Sinorice Moss AU RC | 50.00 | 25.00 |
| ☐ 175 LenDale White AU RC | 80.00 | 40.00 |
| ☐ RBML R.Bush/Leinart AU/25 | 250.00 | 125.00 |

## 2007 Topps Draft Picks and Prospects

| | | |
|---|---|---|
| ☐ 1 Donovan McNabb | 1.00 | .40 |
| ☐ 2 Larry Johnson | .75 | .30 |
| ☐ 3 Willis-McGahee | .75 | .30 |
| ☐ 4 Tom Brady | 2.00 | .75 |
| ☐ 5 Anquan Boldin | .75 | .30 |
| ☐ 6 Steve Smith | .75 | .30 |
| ☐ 7 Philip Rivers | 1.00 | .40 |
| ☐ 8 LaDainian Tomlinson | 1.25 | .50 |
| ☐ 9 Reuben Droughns | .75 | .30 |
| ☐ 10 Julius Jones | .75 | .30 |
| ☐ 11 Drew Brees | .75 | .30 |
| ☐ 12 Chad Johnson | .75 | .30 |
| ☐ 13 Ronnie Brown | .75 | .30 |
| ☐ 14 Brett Favre | 2.00 | .75 |
| ☐ 15 J.P. Losman | .60 | .25 |
| ☐ 16 Clinton Portis | .75 | .30 |
| ☐ 17 Edgerrin James | .75 | .30 |
| ☐ 18 Andre Johnson | .75 | .30 |
| ☐ 19 Fred Taylor | .75 | .30 |
| ☐ 20 Marc Bulger | .75 | .30 |
| ☐ 21 Peyton Manning | 1.50 | .60 |
| ☐ 22 Reggie Wayne | .75 | .30 |
| ☐ 23 Hines Ward | 1.00 | .40 |
| ☐ 24 Michael Vick | 1.00 | .40 |

| | | |
|---|---|---|
| ❑ 25 Santana Moss | .75 | .30 |
| ❑ 26 Torry Holt | .75 | .30 |
| ❑ 27 Jake Delhomme | .75 | .30 |
| ❑ 28 Brian Westbrook | .75 | .30 |
| ❑ 29 Tony Gonzalez | .75 | .30 |
| ❑ 30 Larry Fitzgerald | 1.00 | .40 |
| ❑ 31 Matt Hasselbeck | .75 | .30 |
| ❑ 32 Kevin Jones | .60 | .25 |
| ❑ 33 Willie Parker | 1.00 | .40 |
| ❑ 34 Jeremy Shockey | .75 | .30 |
| ❑ 35 Marvin Harrison | 1.00 | .40 |
| ❑ 36 Warrick Dunn | .75 | .30 |
| ❑ 37 Ahman Green | .75 | .30 |
| ❑ 38 Ben Roethlisberger | 1.25 | .50 |
| ❑ 39 Randy Moss | 1.00 | .40 |
| ❑ 40 Rudi Johnson | .75 | .30 |
| ❑ 41 Carson Palmer | 1.00 | .40 |
| ❑ 42 Trent Green | .75 | .30 |
| ❑ 43 Plaxico Burress | .75 | .30 |
| ❑ 44 Steven Jackson | 1.00 | .40 |
| ❑ 45 Deuce McAllister | .75 | .30 |
| ❑ 46 Antonio Gates | .75 | .30 |
| ❑ 47 Cadillac Williams | .75 | .30 |
| ❑ 48 Eli Manning | 1.00 | .40 |
| ❑ 49 Rex Grossman | .75 | .30 |
| ❑ 50 Shaun Alexander | .75 | .30 |
| ❑ 51 DeAngelo Williams | 1.00 | .40 |
| ❑ 52 Joseph Addai | 1.00 | .40 |
| ❑ 53 Vince Young | 1.00 | .40 |
| ❑ 54 Matt Leinart | 1.00 | .40 |
| ❑ 55 Sinorice Moss | .75 | .30 |
| ❑ 56 Matt Jones | .75 | .30 |
| ❑ 57 Tony Romo | 2.00 | .75 |
| ❑ 58 Jay Cutler | 1.00 | .40 |
| ❑ 59 Marques Colston | 1.00 | .40 |
| ❑ 60 Vernon Davis | .75 | .30 |
| ❑ 61 Cedric Benson | .75 | .30 |
| ❑ 62 Mario Williams | .75 | .30 |
| ❑ 63 Hank Baskett | .75 | .30 |
| ❑ 64 Alex Smith QB | 1.00 | .40 |
| ❑ 65 Jason Campbell | .75 | .30 |
| ❑ 66 Mike Furrey | .75 | .30 |
| ❑ 67 Greg Jennings | .75 | .30 |
| ❑ 68 Laurence Maroney | 1.00 | .40 |
| ❑ 69 Charlie Frye | .75 | .30 |
| ❑ 70 Michael Robinson | .75 | .30 |
| ❑ 71 Michael Huff | .75 | .30 |
| ❑ 72 A.J. Hawk | 1.00 | .40 |
| ❑ 73 Marion Barber | 1.00 | .40 |
| ❑ 74 Santonio Holmes | .75 | .30 |
| ❑ 75 Kellen Winslow | .75 | .30 |
| ❑ 76 Reggie Bush | 1.25 | .50 |
| ❑ 77 Charlie Whitehurst | .60 | .25 |
| ❑ 78 Brad Smith | .60 | .25 |
| ❑ 79 Leon Washington | .75 | .30 |
| ❑ 80 Wali Lundy | .60 | .25 |
| ❑ 81 Owen Daniels | .60 | .25 |
| ❑ 82 Devin Hester | 1.00 | .40 |
| ❑ 83 Chad Jackson | .75 | .30 |
| ❑ 84 Braylon Edwards | .75 | .30 |
| ❑ 85 Bruce Gradkowski | .60 | .25 |
| ❑ 86 Tarvaris Jackson | .75 | .30 |
| ❑ 87 Derek Hagan | .60 | .25 |
| ❑ 88 Mike Bell | .75 | .30 |
| ❑ 89 Frank Gore | 1.00 | .40 |
| ❑ 90 LenDale White | .75 | .30 |
| ❑ 91 Chris Henry | .60 | .25 |
| ❑ 92 Kellen Clemens | .60 | .25 |
| ❑ 93 Nate Washington | .60 | .25 |
| ❑ 94 Jerious Norwood | .75 | .30 |
| ❑ 95 Maurice Jones-Drew | 1.00 | .40 |
| ❑ 96 Mark Clayton | .75 | .30 |
| ❑ 97 Jason Avant | .60 | .25 |
| ❑ 98 Mathias Kiwanuka | .60 | .25 |
| ❑ 99 Brandon Jacobs | .75 | .30 |
| ❑ 100 Chris Cooley | .60 | .25 |
| ❑ 101 Brady Quinn RC | 8.00 | 3.00 |
| ❑ 102 Michael Bush RC | 2.50 | 1.00 |
| ❑ 103 Leon Hall RC | 2.00 | .75 |
| ❑ 104 Jason Hill RC | 2.50 | 1.00 |
| ❑ 105 Patrick Willis RC | 5.00 | 2.00 |
| ❑ 106 Brian Leonard RC | 2.50 | 1.00 |
| ❑ 107 Gaines Adams RC | 2.50 | 1.00 |
| ❑ 108 Kenneth Darby RC | 2.50 | 1.00 |
| ❑ 109 Marcus McCauley RC | 2.00 | .75 |
| ❑ 110 Paul Posluszny RC | 3.00 | 1.25 |
| ❑ 111 Drew Stanton RC | 2.50 | 1.00 |

| | | |
|---|---|---|
| ❑ 112 Troy Smith RC | 3.00 | 1.25 |
| ❑ 113 Garrett Wolfe RC | 2.50 | 1.00 |
| ❑ 114 Chris Leak RC | 2.00 | .75 |
| ❑ 115 Joe Thomas RC | 2.50 | 1.00 |
| ❑ 116 Paul Williams RC | 2.00 | .75 |
| ❑ 117 LaRon Landry RC | 3.00 | 1.25 |
| ❑ 118 Aundrae Allison RC | 2.50 | 1.00 |
| ❑ 119 Kenny Irons RC | 2.50 | 1.00 |
| ❑ 120 Kevin Kolb RC | 4.00 | 1.50 |
| ❑ 121 Tyler Palko RC | 2.50 | 1.00 |
| ❑ 122 Steve Smith USC RC | 3.00 | 1.25 |
| ❑ 123 Steve Breaston RC | 2.50 | 1.00 |
| ❑ 124 Tyrone Moss RC | 1.50 | .60 |
| ❑ 125 LaMarr Woodley RC | 2.50 | 1.00 |
| ❑ 126 Brandon Meriweather RC | 2.50 | 1.00 |
| ❑ 127 Rhema McKnight RC | 2.00 | .75 |
| ❑ 128 Daymeion Hughes RC | 2.00 | .75 |
| ❑ 129 Jared Zabransky RC | 2.50 | 1.00 |
| ❑ 130 Chansi Stuckey RC | 2.00 | .75 |
| ❑ 131 Arnobi Okoye RC | 2.50 | 1.00 |
| ❑ 132 Calvin Johnson RC | 6.00 | 2.50 |
| ❑ 133 Marshawn Lynch RC | 5.00 | 2.00 |
| ❑ 134 Ted Ginn Jr. RC | 4.00 | 1.50 |
| ❑ 135 Adrian Peterson RC | 20.00 | 8.00 |
| ❑ 136 Dwayne Jarrett RC | 2.50 | 1.00 |
| ❑ 137 Greg Olsen RC | 3.00 | 1.25 |
| ❑ 138 Adam Carriker RC | 2.00 | .75 |
| ❑ 139 Darius Walker RC | 2.50 | 1.00 |
| ❑ 140 Robert Meachem RC | 2.50 | 1.00 |
| ❑ 141 Jordan Palmer RC | 2.50 | 1.00 |
| ❑ 142 JaMarcus Russell RC | 6.00 | 2.50 |
| ❑ 143 DeShawn Wynn RC | 2.50 | 1.00 |
| ❑ 144 Zach Miller RC | 1.50 | .60 |
| ❑ 145 Lorenzo Booker RC | 2.50 | 1.00 |
| ❑ 146 Selvin Young RC | 4.00 | 1.50 |
| ❑ 147 Courtney Lewis RC | 2.00 | .75 |
| ❑ 148 Tony Hunt RC | 2.50 | 1.00 |
| ❑ 149 Dwayne Bowe RC | 5.00 | 2.00 |
| ❑ 150 Aaron Ross RC | 2.50 | 1.00 |
| ❑ 151 Antonio Pittman RC | 2.50 | 1.00 |
| ❑ 152 Anthony Gonzalez RC | 4.00 | 1.50 |
| ❑ 153 John Beck RC | 2.50 | 1.00 |
| ❑ 155 Lawrence Timmons RC | 2.50 | 1.00 |

## 2008 Topps Letterman

| | | |
|---|---|---|
| ❑ 1 Drew Brees | 2.50 | 1.00 |
| ❑ 2 Tom Brady | 2.50 | 1.50 |
| ❑ 3 Peyton Manning | 4.00 | 1.50 |
| ❑ 4 Carson Palmer | 2.50 | 1.00 |
| ❑ 5 Ben Roethlisberger | 3.00 | 1.25 |
| ❑ 6 Eli Manning | 2.50 | 1.00 |
| ❑ 7 Tony Romo | 4.00 | 1.50 |
| ❑ 8 Vince Young | 2.50 | 1.00 |
| ❑ 9 Matt Hasselbeck | 2.00 | .75 |
| ❑ 10 Derek Anderson | 2.00 | .75 |
| ❑ 11 Jay Cutler | 2.50 | 1.00 |
| ❑ 12 Philip Rivers | 2.50 | 1.00 |
| ❑ 13 Steven Jackson | 2.50 | 1.00 |
| ❑ 14 Willie Parker | 2.00 | .75 |
| ❑ 15 Clinton Portis | 2.00 | .75 |
| ❑ 16 Peyton Manning | 5.00 | 2.00 |
| ❑ 17 LaDainian Tomlinson | 3.00 | 1.25 |
| ❑ 18 Marion Barber | 2.50 | 1.00 |
| ❑ 19 Brian Westbrook | 2.00 | .75 |
| ❑ 20 Fred Taylor | 2.00 | .75 |
| ❑ 21 Marshawn Lynch | 2.50 | 1.00 |
| ❑ 22 Joseph Addai | 2.50 | 1.00 |
| ❑ 23 Willis McGahee | 2.00 | .75 |
| ❑ 24 Frank Gore | 2.00 | .75 |

| | | |
|---|---|---|
| ❑ 25 Larry Johnson | 2.00 | .75 |
| ❑ 26 Brandon Jacobs | 2.00 | .75 |
| ❑ 27 Ryan Grant | 2.50 | 1.00 |
| ❑ 28 Chester Taylor | 1.50 | .60 |
| ❑ 29 Laurence Maroney | 2.00 | .75 |
| ❑ 30 Thomas Jones | 2.00 | .75 |
| ❑ 31 Chad Johnson | 2.00 | .75 |
| ❑ 32 Reggie Wayne | 2.00 | .75 |
| ❑ 33 Anquan Boldin | 2.00 | .75 |
| ❑ 34 Randy Moss | 2.50 | 1.00 |
| ❑ 35 Plaxico Burress | 2.00 | .75 |
| ❑ 36 Terrell Owens | 2.50 | 1.00 |
| ❑ 37 Andre Johnson | 2.00 | .75 |
| ❑ 38 Larry Fitzgerald | 2.50 | 1.00 |
| ❑ 39 Braylon Edwards | 2.00 | .75 |
| ❑ 40 Steve Smith | 2.00 | .75 |
| ❑ 41 T.J. Houshmandzadeh | 2.00 | .75 |
| ❑ 42 Torry Holt | 2.00 | .75 |
| ❑ 43 Brandon Marshall | 2.00 | .75 |
| ❑ 44 Wes Welker | 2.50 | 1.00 |
| ❑ 45 Dwayne Bowe | 2.00 | .75 |
| ❑ 46 Terry Bradshaw | 5.00 | 2.00 |
| ❑ 47 Brett Favre | 15.00 | 6.00 |
| ❑ 48 John Elway | 5.00 | 2.00 |
| ❑ 49 Lawrence Taylor | 3.00 | 1.25 |
| ❑ 50 Joe Namath | 4.00 | 1.50 |
| ❑ 51 Matt Ryan RC | 15.00 | 6.00 |
| ❑ 52 Brian Brohm RC | 5.00 | 2.00 |
| ❑ 53 Chad Henne RC | 6.00 | 2.50 |
| ❑ 54 Joe Flacco RC | 12.00 | 5.00 |
| ❑ 55 Andre Woodson RC | 4.00 | 1.50 |
| ❑ 56 John David Booty RC | 4.00 | 1.50 |
| ❑ 57 Josh Johnson RC | 4.00 | 1.50 |
| ❑ 58 Colt Brennan RC | 10.00 | 4.00 |
| ❑ 59 Dennis Dixon RC | 4.00 | 1.50 |
| ❑ 60 Erik Ainge RC | 4.00 | 1.50 |
| ❑ 61 Kevin O'Connell RC | 5.00 | 2.00 |
| ❑ 62 Darren McFadden RC | 10.00 | 4.00 |
| ❑ 63 Rashard Mendenhall RC | 8.00 | 3.00 |
| ❑ 64 Jonathan Stewart RC | 10.00 | 4.00 |
| ❑ 65 Felix Jones RC | 10.00 | 4.00 |
| ❑ 66 Jamaal Charles RC | 5.00 | 2.00 |
| ❑ 67 Ray Rice RC | 5.00 | 2.00 |
| ❑ 68 Chris Johnson RC | 10.00 | 4.00 |
| ❑ 69 Mike Hart RC | 5.00 | 2.00 |
| ❑ 70 Matt Forte RC | 10.00 | 4.00 |
| ❑ 71 Kevin Smith RC | 6.00 | 2.50 |
| ❑ 72 Steve Slaton RC | 8.00 | 3.00 |
| ❑ 73 Malcolm Kelly RC | 4.00 | 1.50 |
| ❑ 74 Limas Sweed RC | 5.00 | 2.00 |
| ❑ 75 DeSean Jackson RC | 8.00 | 3.00 |
| ❑ 76 James Hardy RC | 4.00 | 1.50 |
| ❑ 77 Mario Manningham RC | 4.00 | 1.50 |
| ❑ 78 Devin Thomas RC | 4.00 | 1.50 |
| ❑ 79 Early Doucet RC | 4.00 | 1.50 |
| ❑ 80 Andre Caldwell RC | 3.00 | 1.25 |
| ❑ 81 Jordy Nelson RC | 5.00 | 2.00 |
| ❑ 82 Eddie Royal RC | 8.00 | 3.00 |
| ❑ 83 Earl Bennett RC | 4.00 | 1.50 |
| ❑ 84 Donnie Avery RC | 5.00 | 2.00 |
| ❑ 85 Dexter Jackson RC | 4.00 | 1.50 |
| ❑ 86 Jerome Simpson RC | 3.00 | 1.25 |
| ❑ 87 Harry Douglas RC | 4.00 | 1.50 |
| ❑ 88 Keenan Burton RC | 3.00 | 1.25 |
| ❑ 89 Marcus Smith RC | 3.00 | 1.25 |
| ❑ 90 Dustin Keller RC | 4.00 | 1.50 |
| ❑ 91 John Carlson RC | 4.00 | 1.50 |
| ❑ 92 Jake Long RC | 5.00 | 2.00 |
| ❑ 93 Chris Long RC | 5.00 | 2.00 |
| ❑ 94 Vernon Gholston RC | 4.00 | 1.50 |
| ❑ 95 Glenn Dorsey RC | 5.00 | 2.00 |
| ❑ 96 Sedrick Ellis RC | 4.00 | 1.50 |
| ❑ 97 Keith Rivers RC | 4.00 | 1.50 |
| ❑ 98 Leodis McKelvin RC | 4.00 | 1.50 |
| ❑ 99 Dominique Rodgers-Cromartie RC | 4.00 | 1.50 |
| ❑ 100 Aqib Talib RC | 4.00 | 1.50 |

## 2008 Topps Mayo

| | | |
|---|---|---|
| ❑ COMPLETE SET (330) | 120.00 | 60.00 |
| ❑ COMP.SET w/o SP's (275) | 40.00 | 20.00 |
| ❑ 1 Drew Brees | .75 | .30 |
| ❑ 2 Kyle Orton SP | 2.50 | 1.00 |
| ❑ 3 LenDale White SP | 3.00 | 1.25 |
| ❑ 4 Shaun McDonald | .50 | .20 |
| ❑ 5 Buddy Wade | .50 | .20 |
| ❑ 6 Javon Walker | .60 | .25 |
| ❑ 7 Owen Daniels | .50 | .20 |

|  |  | | |
|---|------|------|------|
| ☐ 8 | Justin Tuck SP | 3.00 | 1.25 |
| ☐ 9 | Amobi Okoye | .50 | .20 |
| ☐ 10 | Rich Eisen | .50 | .20 |
| ☐ 11 | Fred Taylor SP | 3.00 | 1.25 |
| ☐ 12 | Ryan Torain SP RC | 3.00 | 1.25 |
| ☐ 13 | Steve Slaton RC | 5.00 | 2.00 |
| ☐ 14 | Jake Long SP RC | 4.00 | 1.50 |
| ☐ 15 | Peyton Manning | 1.25 | .50 |
| ☐ 16 | Jon Kitna | .60 | .25 |
| ☐ 17 | Ryan Grant | .75 | .30 |
| ☐ 18 | Brandon Stokley | .60 | .25 |
| ☐ 19 | Troy Williamson SP | 2.50 | 1.00 |
| ☐ 20 | Reggie Brown | .60 | .25 |
| ☐ 21 | Zach Miller | .60 | .25 |
| ☐ 22 | Aaron Kampman SP | 3.00 | 1.25 |
| ☐ 23 | Albert Haynesworth | .50 | .20 |
| ☐ 24 | Matt Cassel | .75 | .30 |
| ☐ 25 | Selvin Young SP | 3.00 | 1.25 |
| ☐ 26 | Will Franklin SP RC | 3.00 | 1.25 |
| ☐ 27 | Matt Forte RC | 6.00 | 2.50 |
| ☐ 28 | Glenn Dorsey SP | 3.00 | 1.25 |
| ☐ 29 | Marc Bulger | .60 | .25 |
| ☐ 30 | Jeff Garcia | .60 | .25 |
| ☐ 31 | DeAngelo Williams | .50 | .20 |
| ☐ 32 | Roydell Williams | .50 | .20 |
| ☐ 33 | Sidney Rice | .50 | .20 |
| ☐ 34 | James Jones SP | 2.50 | 1.00 |
| ☐ 35 | L.J. Smith | .50 | .20 |
| ☐ 36 | Aaron Schobel | .50 | .20 |
| ☐ 37 | Tommie Harris | .50 | .20 |
| ☐ 38 | Tyler Thigpen | .50 | .20 |
| ☐ 39 | LaDainian Tomlinson SP | 5.00 | 2.00 |
| ☐ 40 | Marcus Smith SP RC | 2.50 | 1.00 |
| ☐ 41 | Tashard Choice RC | 2.50 | 1.00 |
| ☐ 42 | Chris Long RC | 3.00 | 1.25 |
| ☐ 43 | Matt Moore SP | 3.00 | 1.25 |
| ☐ 44 | Chris Redman | .50 | .20 |
| ☐ 45 | Laurence Maroney | .60 | .25 |
| ☐ 46 | Larry Fitzgerald | .75 | .30 |
| ☐ 47 | Donte Stallworth | .60 | .25 |
| ☐ 48 | Marty Booker | .50 | .20 |
| ☐ 49 | Greg Olsen | .60 | .25 |
| ☐ 50 | Terrell Suggs | .50 | .20 |
| ☐ 51 | Kevin Williams | .50 | .20 |
| ☐ 52 | Derrick Ward | .60 | .25 |
| ☐ 53 | Steven Jackson SP | 4.00 | 1.50 |
| ☐ 54 | Adrian Arrington SP RC | 2.50 | 1.00 |
| ☐ 55 | Tim Hightower RC | 5.00 | 2.00 |
| ☐ 56 | Chauncey Washington RC | 2.00 | .75 |
| ☐ 57 | Joe Thomas | .60 | .25 |
| ☐ 58 | Matt Leinart SP | 4.00 | 1.50 |
| ☐ 59 | Jamal Lewis | .60 | .25 |
| ☐ 60 | Braylon Edwards | .60 | .25 |
| ☐ 61 | Steve Smith USC | .60 | .25 |
| ☐ 62 | Mark Bradley | .50 | .20 |
| ☐ 63 | Leonard Pope | .50 | .20 |
| ☐ 64 | Dwight Freeney | .60 | .25 |
| ☐ 65 | Adam Carriker | .50 | .20 |
| ☐ 66 | Devery Henderson | .50 | .20 |
| ☐ 67 | Willis McGahee SP | 3.00 | 1.25 |
| ☐ 68 | Fred Davis SP RC | 3.00 | 1.25 |
| ☐ 69 | Harry Douglas RC | 2.50 | 1.00 |
| ☐ 70 | Anthony Alridge SP RC | 2.50 | 1.00 |
| ☐ 71 | Rex Grossman | .60 | .25 |
| ☐ 72 | Kellen Clemens | .60 | .25 |
| ☐ 73 | Justin Fargas | .60 | .25 |
| ☐ 74 | Steve Smith | .60 | .25 |
| ☐ 75 | Hines Ward | .75 | .30 |
| ☐ 76 | Muhsin Muhammad | .50 | .20 |
| ☐ 77 | Randy McMichael | .50 | .20 |
| ☐ 78 | Tamba Hali | .50 | .20 |
| ☐ 79 | Archie Manning | .75 | .30 |
| ☐ 80 | Orville Wright | .50 | .20 |
| ☐ 81 | Michael Turner SP | 3.00 | 1.25 |
| ☐ 82 | Paul Smith SP | 2.50 | 1.00 |
| ☐ 83 | DeSean Jackson RC | 5.00 | 2.00 |
| ☐ 84 | Josh McCown | .50 | .20 |
| ☐ 85 | John Beck | .60 | .25 |
| ☐ 86 | LaMont Jordan SP | 3.00 | 1.25 |
| ☐ 87 | Greg Jennings | .60 | .25 |
| ☐ 88 | Deion Branch | .60 | .25 |
| ☐ 89 | David Patten | .50 | .20 |
| ☐ 90 | Bob Sanders | .60 | .25 |
| ☐ 91 | Luis Castillo | .50 | .20 |
| ☐ 92 | Troy Aikman | 1.00 | .40 |
| ☐ 93 | Le'Ron McClain | .75 | .30 |
| ☐ 94 | Todd Heap SP | 2.50 | 1.00 |
| ☐ 95 | Kyle Wright RC | 2.00 | .75 |
| ☐ 96 | Malcolm Kelly RC | 2.50 | 1.00 |
| ☐ 97 | Vince Young | .75 | .30 |
| ☐ 98 | Troy Smith | .60 | .25 |
| ☐ 99 | Reggie Bush | .75 | .30 |
| ☐ 100 | Jerricho Cotchery | .50 | .20 |
| ☐ 101 | Jerry Porter | .60 | .25 |
| ☐ 102 | Ike Hilliard | .50 | .20 |
| ☐ 103 | Ed Reed | .60 | .25 |
| ☐ 104 | John Abraham | .50 | .20 |
| ☐ 105 | Sterling Sharpe | .60 | .25 |
| ☐ 106 | Brodie Croyle | .75 | .30 |
| ☐ 107 | Jeremy Shockey SP | 3.00 | 1.25 |
| ☐ 108 | Andre Woodson RC | 2.50 | 1.00 |
| ☐ 109 | Limas Sweed RC | 3.00 | 1.25 |
| ☐ 110 | Jay Cutler | .75 | .30 |
| ☐ 111 | Adrian Peterson | 1.50 | .60 |
| ☐ 112 | Larry Johnson | .60 | .25 |
| ☐ 113 | Joey Galloway | .60 | .25 |
| ☐ 114 | Reggie Williams | .50 | .20 |
| ☐ 115 | Justin McCareins | .50 | .20 |
| ☐ 116 | Roy Williams S | .60 | .25 |
| ☐ 117 | Julius Peppers | .60 | .25 |
| ☐ 118 | Terry Bradshaw | 1.25 | .50 |
| ☐ 119 | James Harrison RC | 12.00 | 5.00 |
| ☐ 120 | Heath Miller RC | 2.50 | 1.00 |
| ☐ 121 | Chad Henne RC | 4.00 | 1.50 |
| ☐ 122 | Mario Manningham RC | 2.50 | 1.00 |
| ☐ 123 | J.P. Losman | .50 | .20 |
| ☐ 124 | Willie Parker | .60 | .25 |
| ☐ 125 | Rudi Johnson | .60 | .25 |
| ☐ 126 | Lee Evans | .60 | .25 |
| ☐ 127 | Marvin Harrison | .75 | .30 |
| ☐ 128 | Isaac Bruce | .60 | .25 |
| ☐ 129 | Kerry Rhodes | .50 | .20 |
| ☐ 130 | Brian Urlacher SP | 4.00 | 1.50 |
| ☐ 131 | John Elway | 1.25 | .50 |
| ☐ 132 | LaMarr Woodley | .60 | .25 |
| ☐ 133 | Calvin Johnson SP | 4.00 | 1.50 |
| ☐ 134 | Joe Flacco RC | 8.00 | 3.00 |
| ☐ 135 | James Hardy SP RC | 3.00 | 1.25 |
| ☐ 136 | Jason Campbell | .60 | .25 |
| ☐ 137 | DeShaun Foster | .60 | .25 |
| ☐ 138 | Ahmad Bradshaw | .60 | .25 |
| ☐ 139 | Roy Williams WR | .60 | .25 |
| ☐ 140 | Amani Toomer | .60 | .25 |
| ☐ 141 | Bryant Johnson | .50 | .20 |
| ☐ 142 | Troy Polamalu | .75 | .30 |
| ☐ 143 | DeMarcus Ware | .60 | .25 |
| ☐ 144 | Dan Marino | 1.50 | .60 |
| ☐ 145 | Grover Cleveland | .50 | .20 |
| ☐ 146 | Plaxico Burress SP | 3.00 | 1.25 |
| ☐ 147 | Colt Brennan RC | 6.00 | 2.50 |
| ☐ 148 | Early Doucet RC | 2.50 | 1.00 |
| ☐ 149 | Matt Hasselbeck | .60 | .25 |
| ☐ 150 | Jerious Norwood | .60 | .25 |
| ☐ 151 | Leon Washington | .50 | .20 |
| ☐ 152 | Amaz Battle | .50 | .20 |
| ☐ 153 | Ted Ginn Jr. | .60 | .25 |
| ☐ 154 | Drew Bennett | .50 | .20 |
| ☐ 155 | Brian Dawkins | .60 | .25 |
| ☐ 156 | Patrick Willis | .60 | .25 |
| ☐ 157 | Sonny Jurgensen | .60 | .25 |
| ☐ 158 | Susan B. Anthony | .50 | .20 |
| ☐ 159 | Terrell Owens SP | 4.00 | 1.50 |
| ☐ 160 | Dennis Dixon RC | 2.50 | 1.00 |
| ☐ 161 | Donnie Avery RC | 3.00 | 1.25 |
| ☐ 162 | Matt Schaub | .60 | .25 |
| ☐ 163 | Kerry Collins | .60 | .25 |
| ☐ 164 | Ronnie Brown | .60 | .25 |
| ☐ 165 | Bobby Engram | .50 | .20 |
| ☐ 166 | Laveranues Coles | .60 | .25 |
| ☐ 167 | Antonio Gates | .60 | .25 |
| ☐ 168 | LaRon Landry | .60 | .25 |
| ☐ 169 | Ray Lewis | .75 | .30 |
| ☐ 170 | Joe Namath | 1.00 | .40 |
| ☐ 171 | William Cody | .50 | .20 |
| ☐ 172 | Andre Johnson SP | 3.00 | 1.25 |
| ☐ 173 | Erik Ainge SP | 2.50 | 1.00 |
| ☐ 174 | Dexter Jackson RC | 2.50 | 1.00 |
| ☐ 175 | Philip Rivers | .75 | .30 |
| ☐ 176 | Marion Barber | .75 | .30 |
| ☐ 177 | Chris Perry | .50 | .20 |
| ☐ 178 | Torry Holt | .60 | .25 |
| ☐ 179 | Anthony Gonzalez | .60 | .25 |
| ☐ 180 | Kellen Winslow | .60 | .25 |
| ☐ 181 | Adrian Wilson | .50 | .20 |
| ☐ 182 | Shawne Merriman | .60 | .25 |
| ☐ 183 | Lawrence Taylor | .75 | .30 |
| ☐ 184 | William Rockefeller | .50 | .20 |
| ☐ 185 | Brandon Marshall SP | 3.00 | 1.25 |
| ☐ 186 | Josh Johnson RC | 2.50 | 1.00 |
| ☐ 187 | Devin Thomas RC | 2.50 | 1.00 |
| ☐ 188 | Chad Pennington | .60 | .25 |
| ☐ 189 | Brian Westbrook | .60 | .25 |
| ☐ 190 | Ahman Green | .50 | .20 |
| ☐ 191 | Derrick Mason | .50 | .20 |
| ☐ 192 | Ernest Wilford | .50 | .20 |
| ☐ 193 | Tony Scheffler | .50 | .20 |
| ☐ 194 | Champ Bailey | .50 | .20 |
| ☐ 195 | DeMeco Ryans | .50 | .20 |
| ☐ 196 | Gale Sayers | 1.00 | .40 |
| ☐ 197 | Gus Frerotte | .50 | .20 |
| ☐ 198 | Dwayne Bowe SP | 3.00 | 1.25 |
| ☐ 199 | Kevin O'Connell RC | 3.00 | 1.25 |
| ☐ 200 | Jordy Nelson RC | 3.00 | 1.25 |
| ☐ 201 | Trent Edwards | .75 | .30 |
| ☐ 202 | Kolby Smith | .50 | .20 |
| ☐ 203 | Brian Leonard | .60 | .25 |
| ☐ 204 | Mike Furrey | .60 | .25 |
| ☐ 205 | Jabar Gaffney | .50 | .20 |
| ☐ 206 | Donald Lee | .60 | .25 |
| ☐ 207 | Antonio Cromartie | .60 | .25 |
| ☐ 208 | Joey Porter | .50 | .20 |
| ☐ 209 | Norman Rockwell | .50 | .20 |
| ☐ 210 | Tom Brady SP | 6.00 | 2.50 |
| ☐ 211 | Nate Burleson SP | 2.50 | 1.00 |
| ☐ 212 | Funkmaster Flex SP | 2.50 | 1.00 |
| ☐ 213 | Keenan Burton RC | 2.00 | .75 |
| ☐ 214 | Donovan McNabb | .75 | .30 |
| ☐ 215 | Marshawn Lynch | .75 | .30 |
| ☐ 216 | Earnest Graham | .50 | .20 |
| ☐ 217 | Donald Driver | .60 | .25 |
| ☐ 218 | Mark Clayton | .60 | .25 |
| ☐ 219 | Vernon Davis | .60 | .25 |
| ☐ 220 | Asante Samuel | .50 | .20 |
| ☐ 221 | Mike Vrabel | .50 | .20 |
| ☐ 222 | King Edward VIII | .50 | .20 |
| ☐ 223 | Warren Haynes SP | 2.50 | 1.00 |
| ☐ 224 | Antwaan Randle El SP | 2.50 | 1.00 |
| ☐ 225 | Darren McFadden RC | 6.00 | 2.50 |
| ☐ 226 | Earl Bennett RC | 2.50 | 1.00 |
| ☐ 227 | Derek Anderson | .60 | .25 |
| ☐ 228 | Joseph Addai | .75 | .30 |
| ☐ 229 | Julius Jones | .60 | .25 |
| ☐ 230 | T.J. Houshmandzadeh | .60 | .25 |
| ☐ 231 | Kevin Walter | .50 | .20 |
| ☐ 232 | Chris Cooley | .60 | .25 |
| ☐ 233 | Leon Hall | .50 | .20 |
| ☐ 234 | D.J. Williams | .50 | .20 |
| ☐ 235 | Guglielmo Marconi | .50 | .20 |
| ☐ 236 | David Garrard SP | 3.00 | 1.25 |
| ☐ 237 | Vincent Jackson SP | 2.50 | 1.00 |
| ☐ 238 | Jonathan Stewart RC | 6.00 | 2.50 |
| ☐ 239 | Jerome Simpson RC | 2.00 | .75 |
| ☐ 240 | Kyle Boller | .50 | .20 |
| ☐ 241 | Warrick Dunn | .60 | .25 |
| ☐ 242 | Ricky Williams | .60 | .25 |
| ☐ 243 | Kevin Curtis | .50 | .20 |
| ☐ 244 | Justin Gage | .50 | .20 |
| ☐ 245 | Tony Gonzalez | .60 | .25 |
| ☐ 246 | DeAngelo Hall | .50 | .20 |
| ☐ 247 | Antonio Pierce | .50 | .20 |
| ☐ 248 | Claude Monet | .50 | .20 |
| ☐ 249 | Carson Palmer SP | 4.00 | 1.50 |
| ☐ 250 | Laurent Robinson SP | 2.50 | 1.00 |
| ☐ 251 | Felix Jones RC | 6.00 | 2.50 |

| | | |
|---|---|---|
| ☐ 252 Andre Caldwell RC | 2.00 | .75 |
| ☐ 253 JaMarcus Russell | .75 | .30 |
| ☐ 254 Frank Gore | .60 | .25 |
| ☐ 255 Dominic Rhodes | .50 | .20 |
| ☐ 256 Santonio Holmes | .50 | .20 |
| ☐ 257 J.T. O'Sullivan | .60 | .25 |
| ☐ 258 Dallas Clark | .60 | .25 |
| ☐ 259 Terence Newman | .50 | .20 |
| ☐ 260 Ernie Sims | .50 | .20 |
| ☐ 261 Paul Gauguin | .50 | .20 |
| ☐ 262 Ben Roethlisberger SP | 5.00 | 2.00 |
| ☐ 263 Chris Chambers SP | 3.00 | 1.25 |
| ☐ 264 John David Booty RC | 3.00 | 1.25 |
| ☐ 265 Eddie Royal RC | 5.00 | 2.00 |
| ☐ 266 Brady Quinn | .75 | .30 |
| ☐ 267 Maurice Jones-Drew | .60 | .25 |
| ☐ 268 Deuce McAllister | .60 | .25 |
| ☐ 269 Wes Welker | .75 | .30 |
| ☐ 270 Darrell Jackson | .50 | .20 |
| ☐ 271 Jason Witten | .60 | .25 |
| ☐ 272 Nate Clements | .50 | .20 |
| ☐ 273 A.J. Hawk | .60 | .25 |
| ☐ 274 Dr. John Harvey Kellogg | .50 | .20 |
| ☐ 275 Eli Manning SP | 4.00 | 1.50 |
| ☐ 276 Matt Ryan SP RC | 12.00 | 5.00 |
| ☐ 277 Jamaal Charles RC | 3.00 | 1.25 |
| ☐ 278 Lavelle Hawkins RC | 2.00 | .75 |
| ☐ 279 Jake Delhomme | .60 | .25 |
| ☐ 280 Thomas Jones | .60 | .25 |
| ☐ 281 Chad Johnson | .60 | .25 |
| ☐ 282 Roddy White | .60 | .25 |
| ☐ 283 Devard Darling | .50 | .20 |
| ☐ 284 Alge Crumpler | .60 | .25 |
| ☐ 285 Jared Allen | .60 | .25 |
| ☐ 286 Jonathan Vilma | .60 | .25 |
| ☐ 287 Milton Hershey | .50 | .20 |
| ☐ 288 Tony Romo SP | 6.00 | 2.50 |
| ☐ 289 Brian Brohm SP RC | 4.00 | 1.50 |
| ☐ 290 Chris Johnson RC | 6.00 | 2.50 |
| ☐ 291 Vernon Gholston RC | 2.50 | 1.00 |
| ☐ 292 Alex Smith QB | .50 | .20 |
| ☐ 293 Brandon Jacobs | .60 | .25 |
| ☐ 294 Reggie Wayne | .60 | .25 |
| ☐ 295 Marques Colston | .60 | .25 |
| ☐ 296 Ronald Curry | .60 | .25 |
| ☐ 297 Ben Watson | .50 | .20 |
| ☐ 298 Mario Williams | .60 | .25 |
| ☐ 299 Derrick Brooks | .60 | .25 |
| ☐ 300 Thomas Edison | .50 | .20 |
| ☐ 301 Brett Favre SP | 10.00 | 4.00 |
| ☐ 302 Anthony Morelli SP RC | 3.00 | 1.25 |
| ☐ 303 Ray Rice RC | 3.00 | 1.25 |
| ☐ 304 Dustin Keller RC | 2.50 | 1.00 |
| ☐ 305 Aaron Rodgers | .75 | .30 |
| ☐ 306 Edgerrin James | .60 | .25 |
| ☐ 307 Anquan Boldin | .60 | .25 |
| ☐ 308 Bernard Berrian | .60 | .25 |
| ☐ 309 Dennis Northcutt | .50 | .20 |
| ☐ 310 Marcedes Lewis | .50 | .20 |
| ☐ 311 Jason Taylor | .60 | .25 |
| ☐ 312 Lofa Tatupu | .60 | .25 |
| ☐ 313 Arthur Conan Doyle | .50 | .20 |
| ☐ 314 Kurt Warner SP | 4.00 | 1.50 |
| ☐ 315 Rashard Mendenhall SP RC | 6.00 | 2.50 |
| ☐ 316 Mike Hart SP RC | 4.00 | 1.50 |
| ☐ 317 Owen Schmitt RC | 2.50 | 1.00 |
| ☐ 318 Tarvaris Jackson | .60 | .25 |
| ☐ 319 Chester Taylor | .50 | .20 |
| ☐ 320 Randy Moss | .75 | .30 |
| ☐ 321 Santana Moss | .60 | .25 |
| ☐ 322 Patrick Crayton | .60 | .25 |
| ☐ 323 Chris Baker | .50 | .20 |
| ☐ 324 Osi Umenyiora | .50 | .20 |
| ☐ 325 Shaun Rogers | .50 | .20 |
| ☐ 326 Rudyard Kipling | .50 | .20 |
| ☐ 327 Clinton Portis SP | 3.00 | 1.25 |
| ☐ 328 Xavier Omon SP RC | 3.00 | 1.25 |
| ☐ 329 Kevin Smith RC | 4.00 | 1.50 |
| ☐ 330 Jacob Hester RC | 2.50 | 1.00 |

## 2008 Topps Rookie Progression

| | | |
|---|---|---|
| ☐ COMPLETE SET (220) | 70.00 | 35.00 |
| ☐ 1 Drew Brees | 1.00 | .40 |
| ☐ 2 Jon Kitna | .75 | .30 |
| ☐ 3 Tom Brady | 1.50 | .60 |

| | | |
|---|---|---|
| ☐ 4 Chad Pennington | .75 | .30 |
| ☐ 5 Steve McNair | .75 | .30 |
| ☐ 6 Josh McCown | .60 | .25 |
| ☐ 7 Matt Hasselbeck | .75 | .30 |
| ☐ 8 David Garrard | .75 | .30 |
| ☐ 9 Jay Cutler | 1.00 | .40 |
| ☐ 10 Matt Schaub | .75 | .30 |
| ☐ 11 Daunte Culpepper | .75 | .30 |
| ☐ 12 Kellen Clemens | .75 | .30 |
| ☐ 13 John Beck | .60 | .25 |
| ☐ 14 Trent Edwards | 1.00 | .40 |
| ☐ 15 Steven Jackson | 1.00 | .40 |
| ☐ 16 Willie Parker | .75 | .30 |
| ☐ 17 Derrick Ward | .75 | .30 |
| ☐ 18 Julius Jones | .75 | .30 |
| ☐ 19 DeShaun Foster | .75 | .30 |
| ☐ 20 Shaun Alexander | .75 | .30 |
| ☐ 21 Reggie Bush | 1.00 | .40 |
| ☐ 22 Clinton Portis | .75 | .30 |
| ☐ 23 Ron Dayne | .75 | .30 |
| ☐ 24 Maurice Jones-Drew | .75 | .30 |
| ☐ 25 Warrick Dunn | .75 | .30 |
| ☐ 26 Adrian Peterson | 2.00 | .75 |
| ☐ 27 Brian Leonard | .60 | .25 |
| ☐ 28 Greg Jennings | .75 | .30 |
| ☐ 29 Torry Holt | .75 | .30 |
| ☐ 30 T.J. Houshmandzadeh | .75 | .30 |
| ☐ 31 Jerricho Cotchery | .60 | .25 |
| ☐ 32 Derrick Mason | .60 | .25 |
| ☐ 33 Kevin Curtis | .60 | .25 |
| ☐ 34 Kevin Walter | .60 | .25 |
| ☐ 35 Joey Galloway | .75 | .30 |
| ☐ 36 Anquan Boldin | .75 | .30 |
| ☐ 37 Santonio Holmes | .75 | .30 |
| ☐ 38 Lee Evans | .75 | .30 |
| ☐ 39 Dwayne Bowe | .75 | .30 |
| ☐ 40 Laurent Robinson | .60 | .25 |
| ☐ 41 Antonio Gates | .75 | .30 |
| ☐ 42 Chris Cooley | .75 | .30 |
| ☐ 43 Owen Daniels | .60 | .25 |
| ☐ 44 Patrick Kerney | .60 | .25 |
| ☐ 45 Gaines Adams | .60 | .25 |
| ☐ 46 Jon Beason | .60 | .25 |
| ☐ 47 Antonio Cromartie | .60 | .25 |
| ☐ 48 Bob Sanders | .75 | .30 |
| ☐ 49 Reggie Nelson | .60 | .25 |
| ☐ 50 John Elway | 2.00 | .75 |
| ☐ 51 Allen Patrick RC | 1.50 | .60 |
| ☐ 52 Steve Young | 1.50 | .60 |
| ☐ 53 Bruce Davis RC | 2.00 | .75 |
| ☐ 54 Cliff Avril RC | 1.50 | .60 |
| ☐ 55 Chevis Jackson RC | 1.50 | .60 |
| ☐ 56 Peyton Manning | 1.50 | .60 |
| ☐ 57 Carson Palmer | 1.00 | .40 |
| ☐ 58 Ben Roethlisberger | 1.25 | .50 |
| ☐ 59 Eli Manning | 1.00 | .40 |
| ☐ 60 Tony Romo | 1.50 | .60 |
| ☐ 61 Donovan McNabb | 1.00 | .40 |
| ☐ 62 Joey Harrington | .75 | .30 |
| ☐ 63 Jeff Garcia | .75 | .30 |
| ☐ 64 Derek Anderson | .75 | .30 |
| ☐ 65 Rex Grossman | .75 | .30 |
| ☐ 66 Kyle Boller | .60 | .25 |
| ☐ 67 Sage Rosenfels | .60 | .25 |
| ☐ 68 JaMarcus Russell | 1.00 | .40 |
| ☐ 69 Anthony Morelli | .75 | .30 |
| ☐ 70 Thomas Jones | .75 | .30 |
| ☐ 71 LaDainian Tomlinson | 1.25 | .50 |
| ☐ 72 Cedric Benson | .60 | .25 |
| ☐ 73 Marion Barber | 1.00 | .40 |

| | | |
|---|---|---|
| ☐ 74 Brian Westbrook | .75 | .30 |
| ☐ 75 LenDale White | .75 | .30 |
| ☐ 76 Ronnie Brown | .75 | .30 |
| ☐ 77 Travis Henry | .75 | .30 |
| ☐ 78 Kenny Watson | .60 | .25 |
| ☐ 79 Fred Taylor | .75 | .30 |
| ☐ 80 Ryan Grant | 1.00 | .40 |
| ☐ 81 Marshawn Lynch | 1.00 | .40 |
| ☐ 82 Selvin Young | .75 | .30 |
| ☐ 83 Wes Welker | 1.00 | .40 |
| ☐ 84 Roy Williams WR | .75 | .30 |
| ☐ 85 Randy Moss | 1.00 | .40 |
| ☐ 86 Plaxico Burress | .75 | .30 |
| ☐ 87 Terrell Owens | 1.00 | .40 |
| ☐ 88 Andre Johnson | .75 | .30 |
| ☐ 89 Roddy White | .75 | .30 |
| ☐ 90 Brandon Marshall | .75 | .30 |
| ☐ 91 Donald Driver | .75 | .30 |
| ☐ 92 Hines Ward | 1.00 | .40 |
| ☐ 93 Ike Hilliard | .60 | .25 |
| ☐ 94 James Jones | .60 | .25 |
| ☐ 95 Calvin Johnson | 1.00 | .40 |
| ☐ 96 Kellen Winslow | .75 | .30 |
| ☐ 97 Tony Gonzalez | .75 | .30 |
| ☐ 98 Osi Umenyiora | .60 | .25 |
| ☐ 99 Mario Williams | .75 | .30 |
| ☐ 100 D.J. Williams | .60 | .25 |
| ☐ 101 Ernie Sims | .60 | .25 |
| ☐ 102 Marcus Trufant | .60 | .25 |
| ☐ 103 Sean Taylor | .75 | .30 |
| ☐ 104 Troy Aikman | 1.50 | .60 |
| ☐ 105 Dan Marino | 2.50 | 1.00 |
| ☐ 106 Dantrell Savage RC | 2.00 | .75 |
| ☐ 107 DJ Hall RC | 2.00 | .75 |
| ☐ 108 Eddie Royal RC | 4.00 | 1.50 |
| ☐ 109 Harry Douglas RC | 2.00 | .75 |
| ☐ 110 Marcus Griffin RC | 1.25 | .50 |
| ☐ 111 Marc Bulger | .75 | .30 |
| ☐ 112 Peyton Hillis RC | 2.50 | 1.00 |
| ☐ 113 Philip Rivers | 1.00 | .40 |
| ☐ 114 Vince Young | 1.00 | .40 |
| ☐ 115 Kurt Warner | 1.00 | .40 |
| ☐ 116 Cleo Lemon | .60 | .25 |
| ☐ 117 Damon Huard | .60 | .25 |
| ☐ 118 Jason Campbell | .75 | .30 |
| ☐ 119 Brian Griese | .60 | .25 |
| ☐ 120 Tarvaris Jackson | .75 | .30 |
| ☐ 121 J.P. Losman | .60 | .25 |
| ☐ 122 Troy Smith | .75 | .30 |
| ☐ 123 Brady Quinn | 1.00 | .40 |
| ☐ 124 Joseph Addai | 1.00 | .40 |
| ☐ 125 Laurence Maroney | .75 | .30 |
| ☐ 126 Brandon Jacobs | .75 | .30 |
| ☐ 127 Willis McGahee | .75 | .30 |
| ☐ 128 Frank Gore | .75 | .30 |
| ☐ 129 Edgerrin James | .75 | .30 |
| ☐ 130 Kevin Jones | .60 | .25 |
| ☐ 131 DeAngelo Williams | .75 | .30 |
| ☐ 132 Jamal Lewis | .75 | .30 |
| ☐ 133 Chester Taylor | .60 | .25 |
| ☐ 134 Earnest Graham | .60 | .25 |
| ☐ 135 Justin Fargas | .60 | .25 |
| ☐ 136 Kolby Smith | .60 | .25 |
| ☐ 137 Marques Colston | .75 | .30 |
| ☐ 138 Reggie Wayne | .75 | .30 |
| ☐ 139 Chad Johnson | .75 | .30 |
| ☐ 140 Amani Toomer | .75 | .30 |
| ☐ 141 Bernard Berrian | .75 | .30 |
| ☐ 142 Steve Smith | .75 | .30 |
| ☐ 143 Larry Fitzgerald | 1.00 | .40 |
| ☐ 144 Chris Chambers | .75 | .30 |
| ☐ 145 Braylon Edwards | .75 | .30 |
| ☐ 146 David Patten | .60 | .25 |
| ☐ 147 Bobby Engram | .60 | .25 |
| ☐ 148 Shaun McDonald | .60 | .25 |
| ☐ 149 Anthony Gonzalez | .75 | .30 |
| ☐ 150 Sidney Rice | .75 | .30 |
| ☐ 151 Jason Witten | .75 | .30 |
| ☐ 152 Greg Olsen | .75 | .30 |
| ☐ 153 Jared Allen | .75 | .30 |
| ☐ 154 DeMarcus Ware | .75 | .30 |
| ☐ 155 Nick Barnett | .60 | .25 |
| ☐ 156 Patrick Willis | .75 | .30 |
| ☐ 157 Ed Reed | .60 | .25 |
| ☐ 158 Asante Samuel | .60 | .25 |
| ☐ 159 Rafael Little RC | 1.50 | .60 |
| ☐ 160 Joe Montana | 2.50 | 1.00 |

| | | |
|---|---|---|
| ☐ 161 Lawrence Jackson RC | 1.50 | .60 |
| ☐ 162 Chauncey Washington RC | 1.50 | .60 |
| ☐ 163 Keenan Burton RC | 1.50 | .60 |
| ☐ 164 John Carlson RC | 2.00 | .75 |
| ☐ 165 Dorien Bryant RC | 1.50 | .60 |
| ☐ 166 Adarius Bowman RC | 1.50 | .60 |
| ☐ 167 Ali Highsmith RC | 1.25 | .50 |
| ☐ 168 Andre Woodson RC | 2.00 | .75 |
| ☐ 169 Darren McFadden RC | 5.00 | 2.00 |
| ☐ 170 Brian Brohm RC | 2.50 | 1.00 |
| ☐ 171 Brandon Flowers RC | 2.00 | .75 |
| ☐ 172 Matt Ryan RC | 8.00 | 3.00 |
| ☐ 173 Calais Campbell RC | 1.50 | .60 |
| ☐ 174 Quentin Groves RC | 1.50 | .60 |
| ☐ 175 Curtis Lofton RC | 2.00 | .75 |
| ☐ 176 Justin Forsett RC | 2.00 | .75 |
| ☐ 177 Lavelle Hawkins RC | 1.50 | .60 |
| ☐ 178 DeSean Jackson RC | 4.00 | 1.50 |
| ☐ 179 Dan Connor RC | 2.00 | .75 |
| ☐ 180 Dennis Dixon RC | 2.00 | .75 |
| ☐ 181 Derrick Harvey RC | 1.50 | .60 |
| ☐ 182 Erik Ainge RC | 2.00 | .75 |
| ☐ 183 Earl Bennett RC | 2.00 | .75 |
| ☐ 184 Early Doucet RC | 2.00 | .75 |
| ☐ 185 Erin Henderson RC | 1.50 | .60 |
| ☐ 186 Felix Jones RC | 5.00 | 2.00 |
| ☐ 187 James Hardy RC | 2.00 | .75 |
| ☐ 188 Jonathan Stewart RC | 5.00 | 2.00 |
| ☐ 189 Kenny Phillips RC | 2.00 | .75 |
| ☐ 190 Keith Rivers RC | 2.00 | .75 |
| ☐ 191 Kevin Smith RC | 3.00 | 1.25 |
| ☐ 192 Mike Jenkins RC | 2.00 | .75 |
| ☐ 193 Malcom Kelly RC | 2.00 | .75 |
| ☐ 194 Mike Hart RC | 2.50 | 1.00 |
| ☐ 195 Chad Henne RC | 3.00 | 1.25 |
| ☐ 196 Jake Long RC | 2.50 | 1.00 |
| ☐ 197 Mario Manningham RC | 2.00 | .75 |
| ☐ 198 Rashard Mendenhall RC | 4.00 | 1.50 |
| ☐ 199 Reggie Smith RC | 1.50 | .60 |
| ☐ 200 Ray Rice RC | 2.50 | 1.00 |
| ☐ 201 Steve Slaton RC | 4.00 | 1.50 |
| ☐ 202 Tracy Porter RC | 1.50 | .60 |
| ☐ 203 Jerod Mayo RC | 3.00 | 1.25 |
| ☐ 204 John David Booty RC | 2.50 | 1.00 |
| ☐ 205 Fred Davis RC | 2.00 | .75 |
| ☐ 206 Sedrick Ellis RC | 2.00 | .75 |
| ☐ 207 Chris Johnson RC | 5.00 | 2.00 |
| ☐ 208 Andre Caldwell RC | 1.50 | .60 |
| ☐ 209 Tashard Choice RC | 2.00 | .75 |
| ☐ 210 Glenn Dorsey RC | 2.50 | 1.00 |
| ☐ 211 Vernon Gholston RC | 2.00 | .75 |
| ☐ 212 Chris Long RC | 2.50 | 1.00 |
| ☐ 213 Xavier Adibi RC | 1.50 | .60 |
| ☐ 214 Donnie Avery RC | 2.50 | 1.00 |
| ☐ 215 Colt Brennan RC | 5.00 | 2.00 |
| ☐ 216 Kentwan Balmer RC | 1.50 | .60 |
| ☐ 217 Jamaal Charles RC | 2.50 | 1.00 |
| ☐ 218 Limas Sweed RC | 2.50 | 1.00 |
| ☐ 219 Matt Forte RC | 5.00 | 2.00 |
| ☐ 220 Owen Schmitt RC | 2.00 | .75 |

## 2003 Topps Total

Ricky
WILLIAMS

| | | |
|---|---|---|
| ☐ COMPLETE SET (550) | 80.00 | 40.00 |
| ☐ 1 Rich Gannon | .50 | .20 |
| ☐ 2 Travis Henry | .50 | .20 |
| ☐ 3 Brian Finneran | .30 | .10 |
| ☐ 4 Ed Hartwell | .30 | .10 |
| ☐ 5 Az-Zahir Hakim | .30 | .10 |
| ☐ 6 Rodney Peete | .30 | .10 |

| | | |
|---|---|---|
| ☐ 7 David Terrell | .50 | .20 |
| ☐ 8 Matt Schobel | .30 | .10 |
| ☐ 9 Andre Davis | .30 | .10 |
| ☐ 10 Dexter Coakley | .30 | .10 |
| ☐ 11 Rod Smith | .50 | .20 |
| ☐ 12 Damerien McCants | .30 | .10 |
| ☐ 13 Robert Ferguson | .30 | .10 |
| ☐ 14 Kailee Wong | .30 | .10 |
| ☐ 15 James Mungro | .30 | .10 |
| ☐ 16 Fred Taylor | .75 | .30 |
| ☐ 17 Tony Gonzalez | .50 | .20 |
| ☐ 18 Randall Godfrey | .30 | .10 |
| ☐ 19 Robert Thomas | .30 | .10 |
| ☐ 20 Rohan Davey | .50 | .20 |
| ☐ 21 Terrell Owens | .75 | .30 |
| ☐ 22 Ron Dayne | .30 | .10 |
| ☐ 23 Charlie Batch | .30 | .10 |
| ☐ 24 Brian Westbrook | .50 | .20 |
| ☐ 25 Plaxico Burress | .50 | .20 |
| ☐ 26 Reche Caldwell | .30 | .10 |
| ☐ 27 Fred Beasley | .30 | .10 |
| ☐ 28 Anthony Simmons | .30 | .10 |
| ☐ 29 Rod Woodson | .50 | .20 |
| ☐ 30 Derrick Brooks | .50 | .20 |
| ☐ 31 Shaun Ellis | .30 | .10 |
| ☐ 32 Ladell Betts | .50 | .20 |
| ☐ 33 Russell Davis | .30 | .10 |
| ☐ 34 Warrick Dunn | .50 | .20 |
| ☐ 35 Jeremy Shockey | 1.25 | .50 |
| ☐ 36 Alex Van Pelt | .30 | .10 |
| ☐ 37 Todd Bouman | .30 | .10 |
| ☐ 38 Kelly Campbell | .30 | .10 |
| ☐ 39 Justin Smith | .30 | .10 |
| ☐ 40 Jamel White | .30 | .10 |
| ☐ 41 La'Roi Glover | .30 | .10 |
| ☐ 42 Ian Gold | .30 | .10 |
| ☐ 43 Robert Porcher | .30 | .10 |
| ☐ 44 Jermaine Lewis | .30 | .10 |
| ☐ 45 Marvin Harrison | .75 | .30 |
| ☐ 46 Darren Sharper | .30 | .10 |
| ☐ 47 Jamie Sharper | .30 | .10 |
| ☐ 48 Tony Richardson | .30 | .10 |
| ☐ 49 Moe Williams | .30 | .10 |
| ☐ 50 Ricky Williams | .75 | .30 |
| ☐ 51 Ty Law | .50 | .20 |
| ☐ 52 Donte Stallworth | .50 | .20 |
| ☐ 53 Shannon Sharpe | .50 | .20 |
| ☐ 54 Santana Moss | .50 | .20 |
| ☐ 55 Charlie Garner | .50 | .20 |
| ☐ 56 Brian Dawkins | .50 | .20 |
| ☐ 57 Dan Campbell | .30 | .10 |
| ☐ 58 William Green | .50 | .20 |
| ☐ 59 Ron Dugans | .30 | .10 |
| ☐ 60 Darrell Jackson | .50 | .20 |
| ☐ 61 Marc Bulger | .75 | .30 |
| ☐ 62 Joe Jurevicius | .30 | .10 |
| ☐ 63 Erron Kinney | .30 | .10 |
| ☐ 64 Champ Bailey | .50 | .20 |
| ☐ 65 Peerless Price | .50 | .20 |
| ☐ 66 Gary Baxter | .30 | .10 |
| ☐ 67 Chris Redman | .30 | .10 |
| ☐ 68 London Fletcher | .30 | .10 |
| ☐ 69 Dee Brown | .30 | .10 |
| ☐ 70 Anthony Thomas | .50 | .20 |
| ☐ 71 Jake Delhomme | .75 | .30 |
| ☐ 72 Dorsey Levens | .30 | .10 |
| ☐ 73 Roy Williams | .75 | .30 |
| ☐ 74 Ashley Lelie | .75 | .30 |
| ☐ 75 Joey Harrington | 1.25 | .50 |
| ☐ 76 William Henderson | .30 | .10 |
| ☐ 77 Corey Bradford | .30 | .10 |
| ☐ 78 Reggie Wayne | .50 | .20 |
| ☐ 79 Kyle Brady | .30 | .10 |
| ☐ 80 Trent Green | .50 | .20 |
| ☐ 81 Bill Romanowski | .30 | .10 |
| ☐ 82 Chike Okeafor RC | 1.25 | .50 |
| ☐ 83 David Patten | .30 | .10 |
| ☐ 84 Terrelle Smith | .30 | .10 |
| ☐ 85 Kerry Collins | .50 | .20 |
| ☐ 86 Derrick Mason | .50 | .20 |
| ☐ 87 Trung Canidate | .30 | .10 |
| ☐ 88 A.J. Feeley | .50 | .20 |
| ☐ 89 Jason Gildon | .30 | .10 |
| ☐ 90 Doug Flutie | .75 | .30 |
| ☐ 91 Tai Streets | .30 | .10 |
| ☐ 92 Keith Newman | .30 | .10 |
| ☐ 93 Adam Archuleta | .30 | .10 |

| | | |
|---|---|---|
| ☐ 94 Simeon Rice | .50 | .20 |
| ☐ 95 Eddie George | .50 | .20 |
| ☐ 96 Frank Sanders | .30 | .10 |
| ☐ 97 Freddie Jones | .30 | .10 |
| ☐ 98 Charles Johnson | .30 | .10 |
| ☐ 99 Keith Traylor | .30 | .10 |
| ☐ 100 Drew Bledsoe | .75 | .30 |
| ☐ 101 Muhsin Muhammad | .50 | .20 |
| ☐ 102 Marques Anderson | .30 | .10 |
| ☐ 103 Donald Hayes | .30 | .10 |
| ☐ 104 Quincy Morgan | .50 | .20 |
| ☐ 105 Chad Hutchinson | .30 | .10 |
| ☐ 106 Mike Anderson | .50 | .20 |
| ☐ 107 Randy McMichael | .50 | .20 |
| ☐ 108 Vonnie Holliday | .30 | .10 |
| ☐ 109 Marcus Coleman | .30 | .10 |
| ☐ 110 Edgerrin James | .75 | .30 |
| ☐ 111 Michael Lewis | .30 | .10 |
| ☐ 112 Wayne Chrebet | .50 | .20 |
| ☐ 113 Antwaan Randle El | .75 | .30 |
| ☐ 114 Byron Chamberlain | .30 | .10 |
| ☐ 115 Jeff Garcia | .75 | .30 |
| ☐ 116 Kim Herring | .30 | .10 |
| ☐ 117 Kenny Holmes | .30 | .10 |
| ☐ 118 John Lynch | .50 | .20 |
| ☐ 119 Doug Jolley | .30 | .10 |
| ☐ 120 Duce Staley | .50 | .20 |
| ☐ 121 Kordell Stewart | .50 | .20 |
| ☐ 122 Stephen Alexander | .30 | .10 |
| ☐ 123 Andre Carter | .30 | .10 |
| ☐ 124 Bobby Engram | .30 | .10 |
| ☐ 125 Marshall Faulk | .75 | .30 |
| ☐ 126 Peter Sirmon RC | .50 | .20 |
| ☐ 127 Alge Crumpler | .30 | .10 |
| ☐ 128 Kenny Watson | .30 | .10 |
| ☐ 129 Duane Starks | .30 | .10 |
| ☐ 130 Jeff Blake | .30 | .10 |
| ☐ 131 Todd Heap | .50 | .20 |
| ☐ 132 Bobby Shaw | .30 | .10 |
| ☐ 133 Ricky Proehl | .30 | .10 |
| ☐ 134 John Abraham | .30 | .10 |
| ☐ 135 T.J. Houshmandzadeh | .50 | .20 |
| ☐ 136 Brian Urlacher | 1.25 | .50 |
| ☐ 137 Darren Woodson | .30 | .10 |
| ☐ 138 Steve Beuerlein | .30 | .10 |
| ☐ 139 Cory Schlesinger | .30 | .10 |
| ☐ 140 Ahman Green | .75 | .30 |
| ☐ 141 Jabar Gaffney | .50 | .20 |
| ☐ 142 Eddie Drummond | .30 | .10 |
| ☐ 143 Stacey Mack | .30 | .10 |
| ☐ 144 Johnnie Morton | .50 | .20 |
| ☐ 145 Chris Chambers | .75 | .30 |
| ☐ 146 Jim Kleinsasser | .30 | .10 |
| ☐ 147 Tebucky Jones | .30 | .10 |
| ☐ 148 Marcus Pollard | .30 | .10 |
| ☐ 149 Tony Brackens | .30 | .10 |
| ☐ 150 Chad Pennington | 1.00 | .40 |
| ☐ 151 Kevin Faulk | .30 | .10 |
| ☐ 152 Michael Lewis | .30 | .10 |
| ☐ 153 Mark Bruener | .30 | .10 |
| ☐ 154 Tim Dwight | .50 | .20 |
| ☐ 155 Jerry Rice | 1.50 | .60 |
| ☐ 156 Trent Dilfer | .50 | .20 |
| ☐ 157 Jon Ritchie | .30 | .10 |
| ☐ 158 Michael Pittman | .30 | .10 |
| ☐ 159 Lamar Gordon | .30 | .10 |
| ☐ 160 Rod Gardner | .50 | .20 |
| ☐ 161 Ken Dilger | .30 | .10 |
| ☐ 162 Doug Johnson | .30 | .10 |
| ☐ 163 Peter Boulware | .50 | .20 |
| ☐ 164 Jevon Kearse | .50 | .20 |
| ☐ 165 Julius Peppers | .75 | .30 |
| ☐ 166 Chris Chandler | .30 | .10 |
| ☐ 167 Lorenzo Neal | .30 | .10 |
| ☐ 168 Kevin Johnson | .30 | .10 |
| ☐ 169 Kevin Hardy | .30 | .10 |
| ☐ 170 KaRon Coleman | .30 | .10 |
| ☐ 171 James Stewart | .30 | .10 |
| ☐ 172 Tony Fisher | .30 | .10 |
| ☐ 173 Billy Miller | .30 | .10 |
| ☐ 174 Phillip Crosby | .30 | .10 |
| ☐ 175 Priest Holmes | 1.00 | .40 |
| ☐ 176 Elvis Joseph | .30 | .10 |
| ☐ 177 Bryan Gilmore | .30 | .10 |
| ☐ 178 D'Wayne Bates | .30 | .10 |
| ☐ 179 Quincy Carter | .50 | .20 |
| ☐ 180 Joe Horn | .50 | .20 |

|  |  | | |
|---|---|---|---|
| 181 | Anthony Henry | .30 | .10 |
| 182 | Anthony Becht | .30 | .10 |
| 183 | Mike Peterson | .30 | .10 |
| 184 | James Thrash | .30 | .10 |
| 185 | Jerome Bettis | .75 | .30 |
| 186 | Marcellus Wiley | .30 | .10 |
| 187 | Tim Rattay | .50 | .20 |
| 188 | Maurice Morris | .50 | .20 |
| 189 | Jason Taylor | .30 | .10 |
| 190 | Keyshawn Johnson | .75 | .30 |
| 191 | John Simon | .30 | .10 |
| 192 | Fred Smoot | .30 | .10 |
| 193 | Wendell Bryant | .30 | .10 |
| 194 | Brandon Stokley | .50 | .20 |
| 195 | Kurt Warner | .75 | .30 |
| 196 | Steve Smith | .75 | .30 |
| 197 | Dez White | .30 | .10 |
| 198 | Jim Miller | .30 | .10 |
| 199 | Robert Griffith | .30 | .10 |
| 200 | Michael Vick | 2.00 | .75 |
| 201 | Antonio Bryant | .50 | .20 |
| 202 | Laveranues Coles | .50 | .20 |
| 203 | Kalimba Edwards | .30 | .10 |
| 204 | Bubba Franks | .50 | .20 |
| 205 | David Carr | 1.25 | .50 |
| 206 | Dwight Freeney | .50 | .20 |
| 207 | Eric Johnson | .50 | .20 |
| 208 | Reggie Tongue | .30 | .10 |
| 209 | Cam Cleeland | .30 | .10 |
| 210 | Michael Bennett | .50 | .20 |
| 211 | Antowain Smith | .50 | .20 |
| 212 | Warren Sapp | .50 | .20 |
| 213 | Ike Hilliard | .30 | .10 |
| 214 | Olandis Gary | .50 | .20 |
| 215 | Tim Brown | .75 | .30 |
| 216 | Kevin Dyson | .50 | .20 |
| 217 | Eddie Kennison | .30 | .10 |
| 218 | Junior Seau | .75 | .30 |
| 219 | Donnie Edwards | .30 | .10 |
| 220 | Shaun Alexander | .75 | .30 |
| 221 | Terrence Wilkins | .30 | .10 |
| 222 | Garrison Hearst | .50 | .20 |
| 223 | Keith Bulluck | .30 | .10 |
| 224 | Zeron Flemister | .30 | .10 |
| 225 | Jake Plummer | .50 | .20 |
| 226 | Chad Johnson | .75 | .30 |
| 227 | Travis Taylor | .50 | .20 |
| 228 | Josh Reed | .50 | .20 |
| 229 | James Farrior | .30 | .10 |
| 230 | Marty Booker | .50 | .20 |
| 231 | Todd Pinkston | .50 | .20 |
| 232 | Dennis Northcutt | .50 | .20 |
| 233 | Troy Hambrick | .30 | .10 |
| 234 | Roland Williams | .30 | .10 |
| 235 | Bill Schroeder | .50 | .20 |
| 236 | Javon Walker | .50 | .20 |
| 237 | Kevin Swayne | .30 | .10 |
| 238 | Dominic Rhodes | .50 | .20 |
| 239 | David Garrard | .30 | .10 |
| 240 | Mike Maslowski RC | .30 | .10 |
| 241 | Travis Minor | .30 | .10 |
| 242 | Terry Glenn | .50 | .20 |
| 243 | Deion Branch | .75 | .30 |
| 244 | Adrian Peterson | .50 | .20 |
| 245 | Tiki Barber | .75 | .30 |
| 246 | Ray Lewis | .75 | .30 |
| 247 | Marques Tuiasosopo | .50 | .20 |
| 248 | Chad Lewis | .30 | .10 |
| 249 | Takeo Spikes | .30 | .10 |
| 250 | LaDainian Tomlinson | .75 | .30 |
| 251 | Stephen Davis | .50 | .20 |
| 252 | Koren Robinson | .50 | .20 |
| 253 | Daylon McCutcheon | .30 | .10 |
| 254 | Rob Johnson | .30 | .10 |
| 255 | Donovan McNabb | 1.00 | .50 |
| 256 | Derrius Thompson | .30 | .10 |
| 257 | Marcel Shipp | .50 | .20 |
| 258 | Keith Brooking | .50 | .20 |
| 259 | Chris McAlister | .30 | .10 |
| 260 | Eric Moulds | .50 | .20 |
| 261 | Amos Zereoue | .50 | .20 |
| 262 | Drew Brees | .75 | .30 |
| 263 | Jon Kitna | .50 | .20 |
| 264 | Brad Johnson | .50 | .20 |
| 265 | Emmitt Smith | 2.00 | 1.00 |
| 266 | Trevor Pryce | .30 | .10 |
| 267 | Mike McMahon | .50 | .20 |
| 268 | Patrick Ramsey | .75 | .30 |
| 269 | Jonathan Wells | .50 | .10 |
| 270 | Mark Brunell | .50 | .20 |
| 271 | Marc Boerigter | .50 | .20 |
| 272 | Rob Konrad | .30 | .10 |
| 273 | Derrick Alexander | .50 | .10 |
| 274 | Joey Galloway | .50 | .20 |
| 275 | Peyton Manning | 1.25 | .50 |
| 276 | Najeh Davenport | .30 | .10 |
| 277 | Jesse Palmer | .30 | .10 |
| 278 | LaMont Jordan | .75 | .30 |
| 279 | Ernie Conwell | .30 | .10 |
| 280 | Hines Ward | .75 | .30 |
| 281 | Freddie Mitchell | .50 | .20 |
| 282 | Curtis Conway | .30 | .10 |
| 283 | Cedrick Wilson | .30 | .10 |
| 284 | Troy Brown | .50 | .20 |
| 285 | Torry Holt | .50 | .20 |
| 286 | Mike Alstott | .75 | .30 |
| 287 | Frank Wycheck | .30 | .10 |
| 288 | Jeremiah Trotter | .30 | .10 |
| 289 | Tyrone Wheatley | .30 | .10 |
| 290 | David Boston | .50 | .20 |
| 291 | Jay Fiedler | .50 | .20 |
| 292 | Troy Walters | .30 | .10 |
| 293 | Warrick Holdman | .30 | .10 |
| 294 | Peter Warrick | .50 | .20 |
| 295 | Tim Couch | .75 | .30 |
| 296 | Aaron Glenn | .30 | .10 |
| 297 | Deuce McAllister | .75 | .30 |
| 298 | Michael Strahan | .50 | .20 |
| 299 | Tom Brady | 2.00 | .75 |
| 300 | Brett Favre | 2.00 | .75 |
| 301 | Isaac Bruce | .50 | .20 |
| 302 | Jimmy Smith | .50 | .20 |
| 303 | Dante Hall | .50 | .20 |
| 304 | James McKnight | .30 | .10 |
| 305 | Daunte Culpepper | .75 | .30 |
| 306 | Lawyer Milloy | .30 | .10 |
| 307 | Jerome Pathon | .30 | .10 |
| 308 | Steve McNair | .75 | .30 |
| 309 | Vinny Testaverde | .50 | .20 |
| 310 | Tommy Maddox | .75 | .30 |
| 311 | Amani Toomer | .50 | .20 |
| 312 | Aaron Brooks | .75 | .30 |
| 313 | Gus Frerotte | .30 | .10 |
| 314 | Kevan Barlow | .50 | .20 |
| 315 | Matt Hasselbeck | .50 | .20 |
| 316 | Clinton Portis | 1.25 | .50 |
| 317 | Keenan McCardell | .50 | .20 |
| 318 | Zach Thomas | .75 | .30 |
| 319 | Curtis Martin | .75 | .30 |
| 320 | Jamal Lewis | .75 | .30 |
| 321 | T.J. Duckett | .50 | .20 |
| 322 | Jerry Porter | .50 | .20 |
| 323 | Randy Moss | 1.25 | .50 |
| 324 | Rosevelt Colvin | .30 | .10 |
| 325 | Corey Dillon | .50 | .20 |
| 326 | Kelly Holcomb | .50 | .20 |
| 327 | Josh McCown | .50 | .20 |
| 328 | Ed McCaffrey | .50 | .20 |
| 329 | Mikhael Ricks | .30 | .10 |
| 330 | Donald Driver | .50 | .20 |
| 331 | Darling/Thompson/McKinnon | .30 | .10 |
| 332 | Hall/Carpenter/Buchanon | .30 | .10 |
| 333 | Thomas/Weaver/Gregg RC | 1.00 | .40 |
| 334 | Winfield/Wire/Clements | .30 | .10 |
| 335 | Morgan/Fields/Witherspoon | .50 | .20 |
| 336 | Brown/Robinson RC/Daniels | .50 | .20 |
| 337 | Freed RC/Thornton/Williams RC | .50 | .20 |
| 338 | Taylor RC/Little/Holmes | .30 | .10 |
| 339 | Ekuban/Ellis/Myers | .30 | .10 |
| 340 | Gard/Dalton RC/Berry RC | 1.25 | .50 |
| 341 | Green/Curry RC/Holmes | .30 | .10 |
| 342 | Hunt RC/KGB/Walker RC | .75 | .30 |
| 343 | Walker/Deloach RC/Payne | .30 | .10 |
| 344 | Bratzke/Washington/Morris | .30 | .10 |
| 345 | Henderson/Coleman/Stroud | .50 | .20 |
| 346 | Hicks/Browning RC/Sims | .50 | .20 |
| 347 | A.Ogunleye RC/Chester RC | 2.00 | .75 |
| 348 | Robbins/Mixon/Johnstone | .30 | .10 |
| 349 | Pfeifer/Johnson/Bruschi | .30 | .10 |
| 350 | Grant/Chase RC/Howard | .50 | .20 |
| 351 | Short/Jones RC/Barrow | .30 | .10 |
| 352 | Jones/Lewis/Cowart | .30 | .10 |
| 353 | Barton/Parrella/Harris | .30 | .10 |
| 354 | Wiling/Simon/Walker | .30 | .10 |
| 355 | Smith/Hamp/von Oel | 1.00 | .40 |
| 356 | Williams RC/Fisk/Johnson | .50 | .20 |
| 357 | Smith/Ulbrich/Peterson | .30 | .10 |
| 358 | Cochran RC/Eaton/Randle | .50 | .20 |
| 359 | Lewis/Wistrom/Little | .30 | .10 |
| 360 | Rudd/Spires/Quarles RC | .75 | .30 |
| 361 | Haynesworth/Carter/Smith | .30 | .10 |
| 362 | Smith/Armstead/Upshaw | .30 | .10 |
| 363 | Ad.Wilson/Dex.Jackson RC | .75 | .30 |
| 364 | F.Wakefield/K.Vanden | .30 | .10 |
| 365 | K.Kasper/J.McAddley | .30 | .10 |
| 366 | B.Smith/P.Kerney | .30 | .10 |
| 367 | M.Jenkins/T.Gaylor | .30 | .10 |
| 368 | C.Draft/M.Stewart | .30 | .10 |
| 369 | J.Hunter/R.Johnson | .30 | .10 |
| 370 | C.Fuller/E.Reed | .50 | .20 |
| 371 | A.Schobel/J.Posey RC | .30 | .10 |
| 372 | P.Williams/S.Adams | .30 | .10 |
| 373 | D.Grant/M.Minter | .30 | .10 |
| 374 | B.Buckner/K.Jenkins | .30 | .10 |
| 375 | R.Howard RC/T.Cousin RC | .30 | .10 |
| 376 | M.Brown/M.Green | .50 | .20 |
| 377 | J.Azumah/R.W.McQuarters | .30 | .10 |
| 378 | B.Simmons/S.Foley | .30 | .10 |
| 379 | A.Hawkins/J.Burris | .30 | .10 |
| 380 | Jo.Armour RC/M.Manuel | .30 | .10 |
| 381 | G.Warren/O.Roye | .30 | .10 |
| 382 | C.Brown/K.Lang | .30 | .10 |
| 383 | D.Ross/M.Edwards | .30 | .10 |
| 384 | A.Singleton RC/D.Nguyen | .50 | .20 |
| 385 | A.Wilson/J.Mobley | .30 | .10 |
| 386 | D.O'Neal/K.Kennedy | .30 | .10 |
| 387 | L.Elliss/S.Rogers | .30 | .10 |
| 388 | C.Cash/D.Bly | .30 | .10 |
| 389 | B.Walker/C.Harris | .30 | .10 |
| 390 | H.Navies RC/N.Diggs | .30 | .10 |
| 391 | A.Harris/M.McKenzie | .30 | .10 |
| 392 | C.Clemons/J.Foreman | .30 | .10 |
| 393 | E.Brown/M.Stevens | .30 | .10 |
| 394 | B.Scioli/L.Tripplett | .30 | .10 |
| 395 | D.Macklin/W.Harris | .30 | .10 |
| 396 | A.Ayodele/H.Douglas | .30 | .10 |
| 397 | F.Bryant/J.Craft RC | .30 | .10 |
| 398 | D.Darius/M.McCree | .30 | .10 |
| 399 | S.Fujita/S.Barber | .50 | .20 |
| 400 | E.Warfield RC/W.Bartee | .75 | .30 |
| 401 | G.Wesley/J.Woods | .30 | .10 |
| 402 | P.Sutrain/S.Madison | .30 | .10 |
| 403 | G.Mario/S.Knight | .30 | .10 |
| 404 | G.Biekert/H.Crockett | .30 | .10 |
| 405 | C.Claiborne/C.Hovan | .30 | .10 |
| 406 | C.Chavous/K.Irvin | .30 | .10 |
| 407 | C.Fauria/D.Graham | .30 | .10 |
| 408 | O.Smith/R.Harrison | .30 | .10 |
| 409 | A.Pleasant/R.Seymour | .30 | .10 |
| 410 | D.Smith/S.Hodge | .30 | .10 |
| 411 | A.Ambrose/D.Carter | .30 | .10 |
| 412 | M.Mitchell/D.Rodgers | .30 | .10 |
| 413 | W.Allen/W.Peterson | .30 | .10 |
| 414 | C.Griffin/K.Hamilton | .30 | .10 |
| 415 | O.Stoutmire/S.Williams | .30 | .10 |
| 416 | A.Beasley/D.Abraham | .30 | .10 |
| 417 | J.McGraw/S.Garnes | .30 | .10 |
| 418 | C.Woodson/P.Buchanon | .50 | .20 |
| 419 | T.Bryant/T.Armstrong | .30 | .10 |
| 420 | B.Taylor/T.Vincent | .30 | .10 |
| 421 | C.Emmons/N.Wayne | .30 | .10 |
| 422 | B.Alexander/C.Hope | .50 | .20 |
| 423 | J.Porter/K.Bell | .75 | .30 |
| 424 | C.Scott/D.Washington | .30 | .10 |
| 425 | B.Leber/R.McNeil | .30 | .10 |
| 426 | Q.Jammer/T.Cody | .30 | .10 |
| 427 | A.Plummer/J.Webster | .30 | .10 |
| 428 | T.Parrish/Z.Bronson | .30 | .10 |
| 429 | I.Mili/J.Stevens | .30 | .10 |
| 430 | K.Lucas/S.Springs | .30 | .10 |
| 431 | C.Brown/O.Huff | .30 | .10 |
| 432 | J.Duncan/T.Polley | .30 | .10 |
| 433 | A.Williams/T.Fisher | .30 | .10 |
| 434 | B.Kelly/R.Barber | .30 | .10 |
| 435 | A.Stecker/K.Williams | .30 | .10 |
| 436 | D.Bennett/J.McCareins | .50 | .20 |
| 437 | L.Schulters/T.Williams | .30 | .10 |
| 438 | A.Dyson/S.Rolle | .30 | .10 |
| 439 | I.Ohalete/M.Bowen | .30 | .10 |
| 440 | B.Noble/D.Wilkinson | .30 | .10 |
| 441 | Charles Rogers RC | 1.25 | .50 |

| | | |
|---|---|---|
| ❑ 442 Jimmy Kennedy RC | 1.25 | .50 |
| ❑ 443 Kelley Washington RC | 1.25 | .50 |
| ❑ 444 Trent Smith RC | 1.00 | .40 |
| ❑ 445 Rashean Mathis RC | 1.00 | .40 |
| ❑ 446 Brian St.Pierre RC | 1.25 | .50 |
| ❑ 447 Bethel Johnson RC | 1.25 | .50 |
| ❑ 448 Alonzo Jackson RC | 1.00 | .40 |
| ❑ 449 Anaz Battle RC | 1.25 | .50 |
| ❑ 450 Carson Palmer RC | 6.00 | 2.50 |
| ❑ 451 Michael Haynes RC | 1.25 | .50 |
| ❑ 452 LaBrandon Toefield RC | 1.25 | .50 |
| ❑ 453 Earnest Graham RC | 1.25 | .50 |
| ❑ 454 Walter Young RC | .60 | .25 |
| ❑ 455 Terry Pierce RC | 1.00 | .40 |
| ❑ 456 Talman Gardner RC | 1.25 | .50 |
| ❑ 457 J.T. Wall RC | .60 | .25 |
| ❑ 458 DeWayne Robertson RC | 1.25 | .50 |
| ❑ 459 Bradie James RC | 1.25 | .50 |
| ❑ 460 Andre Johnson RC | 2.50 | 1.00 |
| ❑ 461 Bobby Wade RC | 1.25 | .50 |
| ❑ 462 Chris Davis RC | 1.00 | .40 |
| ❑ 463 Kliff Kingsbury RC | 1.00 | .40 |
| ❑ 464 Osi Umenyiora RC | 2.00 | .75 |
| ❑ 465 Domanick Davis RC | 1.25 | .50 |
| ❑ 466 Sam Aiken RC | 1.00 | .40 |
| ❑ 467 Ty Warren RC | 1.25 | .50 |
| ❑ 468 Terence Newman RC | 2.50 | 1.00 |
| ❑ 469 Zuriel Smith RC | .60 | .25 |
| ❑ 470 Willis McGahee RC | 3.00 | 1.25 |
| ❑ 471 David Kircus RC | 1.25 | .50 |
| ❑ 472 Billy McMullen RC | 1.00 | .40 |
| ❑ 473 Antwoine Sanders RC | .60 | .25 |
| ❑ 474 Adrian Madise RC | 1.00 | .40 |
| ❑ 475 Byron Leftwich RC | 2.50 | 1.00 |
| ❑ 476 Justin Gage RC | 1.25 | .50 |
| ❑ 477 Jason Witten RC | 2.50 | 1.00 |
| ❑ 478 Lee Suggs RC | 1.25 | .50 |
| ❑ 479 Kareem Kelly RC | 1.00 | .40 |
| ❑ 480 Rex Grossman RC | 4.00 | 1.50 |
| ❑ 481 Nate Burleson RC | 1.25 | .50 |
| ❑ 482 Chris Brown RC | 1.25 | .50 |
| ❑ 483 Julian Battle RC | 1.00 | .40 |
| ❑ 484 Carl Ford RC | .60 | .25 |
| ❑ 485 Angelo Crowell RC | 1.00 | .40 |
| ❑ 486 Bennie Joppru RC | 1.25 | .50 |
| ❑ 487 Aaron Walker RC | 1.00 | .40 |
| ❑ 488 Brandon Green RC | 1.00 | .40 |
| ❑ 489 L.J. Smith RC | 1.25 | .50 |
| ❑ 490 Ken Dorsey RC | 1.25 | .50 |
| ❑ 491 Eugene Wilson RC | 1.25 | .50 |
| ❑ 492 Chaun Thompson RC | .60 | .25 |
| ❑ 493 Kevin Curtis RC | 1.50 | .60 |
| ❑ 494 Marcus Trufant RC | 1.25 | .50 |
| ❑ 495 Andrew Williams RC | 1.00 | .40 |
| ❑ 496 Visanthe Shiancoe RC | 1.00 | .40 |
| ❑ 497 Terrence Edwards RC | 1.00 | .40 |
| ❑ 498 Rien Long RC | 1.00 | .40 |
| ❑ 499 Nick Barnett RC | 1.25 | .50 |
| ❑ 500 Larry Johnson RC | 4.00 | 1.50 |
| ❑ 501 Ken Hamlin RC | 1.25 | .50 |
| ❑ 502 Johnathan Sullivan RC | 1.00 | .40 |
| ❑ 503 Jeremi Johnson RC | .60 | .25 |
| ❑ 504 William Joseph RC | 1.25 | .50 |
| ❑ 505 Boss Bailey RC | 1.25 | .50 |
| ❑ 506 Anquan Boldin RC | 3.00 | 1.25 |
| ❑ 507 Dave Ragone RC | 1.25 | .50 |
| ❑ 508 DeJuan Groce RC | 1.25 | .50 |
| ❑ 509 Rashad Moore RC | 1.00 | .40 |
| ❑ 510 Mike Doss RC | 1.25 | .50 |
| ❑ 511 Kenny Peterson RC | 1.00 | .40 |
| ❑ 512 Justin Griffith RC | 1.25 | .50 |
| ❑ 513 Jordan Gross RC | 1.25 | .50 |
| ❑ 514 Terrence Holt RC | 1.00 | .40 |
| ❑ 515 Seneca Wallace RC | 1.25 | .50 |
| ❑ 516 Ovie Mughelli RC | .60 | .25 |
| ❑ 517 Jerome McDougle RC | 1.25 | .50 |
| ❑ 518 Kevin Williams RC | 1.25 | .50 |
| ❑ 519 Musa Smith RC | 1.25 | .50 |
| ❑ 520 Teyo Johnson RC | 1.25 | .50 |
| ❑ 521 Victor Hobson RC | 1.25 | .50 |
| ❑ 522 Cory Redding RC | 1.00 | .40 |
| ❑ 523 Cecil Sapp RC | 1.25 | .50 |
| ❑ 524 Brandon Lloyd RC | 1.25 | .50 |
| ❑ 525 Chris Simms RC | 2.00 | .75 |
| ❑ 526 Artose Pinner RC | 1.25 | .50 |
| ❑ 527 DeWayne White RC | 1.00 | .40 |
| ❑ 528 Doug Gabriel RC | 1.25 | .50 |

| | | |
|---|---|---|
| ❑ 529 Calvin Pace RC | 1.00 | .40 |
| ❑ 530 Onterrio Smith RC | 1.25 | .50 |
| ❑ 531 Terrell Suggs RC | 2.00 | .75 |
| ❑ 532 Ronald Bellamy RC | 1.00 | .40 |
| ❑ 533 Jimmy Wilkerson RC | 1.00 | .40 |
| ❑ 534 Travis Anglin RC | .60 | .25 |
| ❑ 535 Tyrone Calico RC | 1.25 | .50 |
| ❑ 536 Keenan Howry RC | 1.25 | .50 |
| ❑ 537 Gibran Hamdan RC | .60 | .25 |
| ❑ 538 Bryant Johnson RC | 1.25 | .50 |
| ❑ 539 Brad Banks RC | 1.00 | .40 |
| ❑ 540 Justin Fargas RC | 1.25 | .50 |
| ❑ 541 B.J. Askew RC | 1.25 | .50 |
| ❑ 542 J.R. Tolver RC | 1.00 | .40 |
| ❑ 543 Tully Banta-Cain RC | 1.00 | .40 |
| ❑ 544 Shaun McDonald RC | 1.25 | .50 |
| ❑ 545 Taylor Jacobs RC | 1.00 | .40 |
| ❑ 546 Ricky Manning RC | 1.00 | .40 |
| ❑ 547 Dallas Clark RC | 1.25 | .50 |
| ❑ 548 Juston Wood RC | .60 | .25 |
| ❑ 549 Andre Woolfolk RC | 1.25 | .50 |
| ❑ 550 Kyle Boller RC | 1.25 | .50 |
| ❑ CL1 Checklist Card 1 | .10 | .02 |
| ❑ CL2 Checklist Card 2 | .10 | .02 |
| ❑ CL3 Checklist Card 3 | .10 | .02 |
| ❑ CL4 Checklist Card 4 | .10 | .02 |

## 2004 Topps Total

| | | |
|---|---|---|
| ❑ COMPLETE SET (440) | 80.00 | 40.00 |
| ❑ 1 Donovan McNabb | .75 | .30 |
| ❑ 2 Zach Thomas | .75 | .30 |
| ❑ 3 Randy Moss | 1.00 | .40 |
| ❑ 4 Kerry Collins | .50 | .20 |
| ❑ 5 Hines Ward | .75 | .30 |
| ❑ 6 Tyrone Calico | .60 | .25 |
| ❑ 7 Patrick Ramsey | .60 | .25 |
| ❑ 8 Jeff Garcia | .75 | .30 |
| ❑ 9 Aveion Cason | .50 | .20 |
| ❑ 10 Stephen Davis | .60 | .25 |
| ❑ 11 Marcel Shipp | .75 | .30 |
| ❑ 12 T.J. Duckett | .60 | .25 |
| ❑ 13 Chris McAlister | .50 | .20 |
| ❑ 14 Peter Warrick | .60 | .25 |
| ❑ 15 Ahman Green | .75 | .30 |
| ❑ 16 Deion Branch | .60 | .25 |
| ❑ 17 David Boston | .50 | .20 |
| ❑ 18 Wayne Chrebet | .60 | .25 |
| ❑ 19 Michael Strahan | .60 | .25 |
| ❑ 20 Anaz Battle | .50 | .20 |
| ❑ 21 Darrell Jackson | .60 | .25 |
| ❑ 22 Chris Chandler | .60 | .25 |
| ❑ 23 Charlie Garner | .50 | .20 |
| ❑ 24 James Thrash | .50 | .20 |
| ❑ 25 LaDainian Tomlinson | 1.25 | .50 |
| ❑ 26 Jerry Porter | .60 | .25 |
| ❑ 27 Jerome Pathon | .50 | .20 |
| ❑ 28 Jerome Bettis | .75 | .30 |
| ❑ 29 Eddie George | .60 | .25 |
| ❑ 30 Jamal Lewis | .60 | .25 |
| ❑ 31 Ricky Proehl | .60 | .25 |
| ❑ 32 Josh Reed | .75 | .30 |
| ❑ 33 David Terrell | .50 | .20 |
| ❑ 34 Antonio Bryant | .60 | .25 |
| ❑ 35 Domanick Davis | .75 | .30 |
| ❑ 36 Artose Pinner | .50 | .20 |
| ❑ 37 Jed Weaver | .50 | .20 |
| ❑ 38 Johnnie Morton | .60 | .25 |
| ❑ 39 Troy Edwards | .50 | .20 |
| ❑ 40 Marvin Harrison | .75 | .30 |

| | | |
|---|---|---|
| ❑ 41 Chris Hovan | .50 | .20 |
| ❑ 42 Boo Williams | .50 | .20 |
| ❑ 43 Ike Hilliard | .60 | .25 |
| ❑ 44 Sam Cowart | .50 | .20 |
| ❑ 45 Shaun Alexander | .75 | .30 |
| ❑ 46 Freddie Mitchell | .60 | .25 |
| ❑ 47 Garrison Hearst | .60 | .25 |
| ❑ 48 Joe Jurevicius | .50 | .20 |
| ❑ 49 Freddie Jones | .50 | .20 |
| ❑ 50 Michael Vick | .75 | .30 |
| ❑ 51 Mike Rucker | .50 | .20 |
| ❑ 52 Carson Palmer | 1.00 | .40 |
| ❑ 53 Az-Zahir Hakim | .50 | .20 |
| ❑ 54 Billy Miller | .50 | .20 |
| ❑ 55 Chad Pennington | .75 | .30 |
| ❑ 56 Charles Woodson | .75 | .30 |
| ❑ 57 Andre Carter | .50 | .20 |
| ❑ 58 Maurice Morris | .60 | .25 |
| ❑ 59 Leonard Little | .50 | .20 |
| ❑ 60 Travis Henry | .60 | .25 |
| ❑ 61 Thomas Jones | .60 | .25 |
| ❑ 62 Dennis Northcutt | .50 | .20 |
| ❑ 63 Quentin Griffin | .60 | .25 |
| ❑ 64 Joey Harrington | .60 | .25 |
| ❑ 65 Edgerrin James | .75 | .30 |
| ❑ 66 Cortez Hankton | .50 | .20 |
| ❑ 67 Jason Taylor | .60 | .25 |
| ❑ 68 Eddie Kennison | .60 | .25 |
| ❑ 69 Ty Law | .60 | .25 |
| ❑ 70 Aaron Brooks | .60 | .25 |
| ❑ 71 Antonio Gates | .75 | .30 |
| ❑ 72 Antwaan Randle El | .60 | .25 |
| ❑ 73 Kevan Barlow | .60 | .25 |
| ❑ 74 Chris Brown | .60 | .25 |
| ❑ 75 Clinton Portis | .75 | .30 |
| ❑ 76 Rod Gardner | .50 | .20 |
| ❑ 77 Isaac Bruce | .60 | .25 |
| ❑ 78 Mike Alstott | .60 | .25 |
| ❑ 79 Brian Westbrook | .75 | .30 |
| ❑ 80 Amani Toomer | .60 | .25 |
| ❑ 81 Justin Fargas | .60 | .25 |
| ❑ 82 Michael Bennett | .60 | .25 |
| ❑ 83 Dante Hall | .60 | .25 |
| ❑ 84 Marcus Pollard | .50 | .20 |
| ❑ 85 Fred Taylor | .60 | .25 |
| ❑ 86 Tai Streets | .50 | .20 |
| ❑ 87 Robert Ferguson | .50 | .20 |
| ❑ 88 Roy Williams S | .60 | .25 |
| ❑ 89 Lee Suggs | .75 | .30 |
| ❑ 90 Chad Johnson | .75 | .30 |
| ❑ 91 DeShaun Foster | .60 | .25 |
| ❑ 92 Alge Crumpler | .60 | .25 |
| ❑ 93 Travis Taylor | .50 | .20 |
| ❑ 94 London Fletcher | .50 | .20 |
| ❑ 95 Priest Holmes | .75 | .30 |
| ❑ 96 A.J. Feeley | .60 | .25 |
| ❑ 97 Kevin Faulk | .50 | .20 |
| ❑ 98 Shaun Ellis | .50 | .20 |
| ❑ 99 Tim Dwight | .60 | .25 |
| ❑ 100 Peyton Manning | 1.50 | .60 |
| ❑ 101 Dane Looker | .60 | .25 |
| ❑ 102 Mark Brunell | .60 | .25 |
| ❑ 103 Bryant Johnson | .50 | .20 |
| ❑ 104 Kelley Washington | .50 | .20 |
| ❑ 105 Rex Grossman | .75 | .30 |
| ❑ 106 William Green | .50 | .20 |
| ❑ 107 Keyshawn Johnson | .60 | .25 |
| ❑ 108 Trevor Pryce | .50 | .20 |
| ❑ 109 Donald Driver | .75 | .30 |
| ❑ 110 David Carr | .60 | .25 |
| ❑ 111 Marcus Robinson | .50 | .20 |
| ❑ 112 Justin McCareins | .50 | .20 |
| ❑ 113 Tim Brown | .75 | .30 |
| ❑ 114 James Farrior | .50 | .20 |
| ❑ 115 Deuce McAllister | .75 | .30 |
| ❑ 116 Simeon Rice | .60 | .25 |
| ❑ 117 Koren Robinson | .75 | .30 |
| ❑ 118 Kassim Osgood | .50 | .20 |
| ❑ 119 Tim Rattay | .60 | .25 |
| ❑ 120 Laveranues Coles | .60 | .25 |
| ❑ 121 Brian Finneran | .50 | .20 |
| ❑ 122 Todd Heap | .60 | .25 |
| ❑ 123 Bobby Shaw | .50 | .20 |
| ❑ 124 Anthony Thomas | .60 | .25 |
| ❑ 125 Brett Favre | 2.00 | .75 |
| ❑ 126 Dwight Freeney | .75 | .30 |
| ❑ 127 Randy McMichael | .50 | .20 |

|  |  | | |
|---|------|---|---|
| ❑ 128 | David Givens | .60 | .25 |
| ❑ 129 | Rich Gannon | .60 | .25 |
| ❑ 130 | Tiki Barber | .75 | .30 |
| ❑ 131 | Terrell Owens | .75 | .30 |
| ❑ 132 | Drew Bennett | .60 | .25 |
| ❑ 133 | Shawn Bryson | .50 | .20 |
| ❑ 134 | Jabar Gaffney | .60 | .25 |
| ❑ 135 | Jake Delhomme | .60 | .25 |
| ❑ 136 | Warrick Dunn | .60 | .25 |
| ❑ 137 | Brandon Lloyd | .50 | .20 |
| ❑ 138 | Brad Johnson | .60 | .25 |
| ❑ 139 | Jon Kitna | .60 | .25 |
| ❑ 140 | Marshall Faulk | .75 | .30 |
| ❑ 141 | Javon Walker | .60 | .25 |
| ❑ 142 | Nate Burleson | .60 | .25 |
| ❑ 143 | Jimmy Smith | .60 | .25 |
| ❑ 144 | Adewale Ogunleye | .50 | .20 |
| ❑ 145 | Trent Green | .60 | .25 |
| ❑ 146 | Richard Seymour | .60 | .25 |
| ❑ 147 | Donte' Stallworth | .60 | .25 |
| ❑ 148 | Curtis Martin | .75 | .30 |
| ❑ 149 | Todd Pinkston | .50 | .20 |
| ❑ 150 | Steve McNair | .75 | .30 |
| ❑ 151 | Josh McCown | .60 | .25 |
| ❑ 152 | Ray Lewis | .75 | .30 |
| ❑ 153 | Muhsin Muhammad | .60 | .25 |
| ❑ 154 | Quincy Morgan | .50 | .20 |
| ❑ 155 | Jake Plummer | .60 | .25 |
| ❑ 156 | Jason Witten | .75 | .30 |
| ❑ 157 | Dallas Clark | .60 | .25 |
| ❑ 158 | Onterrio Smith | .60 | .25 |
| ❑ 159 | Jeremy Shockey | .60 | .25 |
| ❑ 160 | Ricky Williams | .75 | .30 |
| ❑ 161 | Jevon Kearse | .60 | .25 |
| ❑ 162 | Plaxico Burress | .60 | .25 |
| ❑ 163 | Drew Brees | .75 | .30 |
| ❑ 164 | Bobby Engram | .60 | .25 |
| ❑ 165 | Torry Holt | .75 | .30 |
| ❑ 166 | Ladell Betts | .60 | .25 |
| ❑ 167 | Kelly Holcomb | .60 | .25 |
| ❑ 168 | Vinny Testaverde | .60 | .25 |
| ❑ 169 | Marty Booker | .60 | .25 |
| ❑ 170 | Rudi Johnson | .60 | .25 |
| ❑ 171 | Andra Davis | .50 | .20 |
| ❑ 172 | Kurt Warner | .75 | .30 |
| ❑ 173 | Troy Brown | .60 | .25 |
| ❑ 174 | Jerry Rice | 1.50 | .60 |
| ❑ 175 | Daunte Culpepper | .75 | .30 |
| ❑ 176 | Darren Sharper | .50 | .20 |
| ❑ 177 | Charles Rogers | .60 | .25 |
| ❑ 178 | Ashley Lelie | .60 | .25 |
| ❑ 179 | Correll Buckhalter | .60 | .25 |
| ❑ 180 | Anquan Boldin | .75 | .30 |
| ❑ 181 | Terrell Suggs | .50 | .20 |
| ❑ 182 | Reggie Wayne | .60 | .25 |
| ❑ 183 | Duce Staley | .60 | .25 |
| ❑ 184 | Donnie Edwards | .50 | .20 |
| ❑ 185 | Joe Horn | .60 | .25 |
| ❑ 186 | LaVar Arrington | .60 | .25 |
| ❑ 187 | Keenan McCardell | .50 | .20 |
| ❑ 188 | Cedrick Wilson | .50 | .20 |
| ❑ 189 | Bubba Franks | .50 | .20 |
| ❑ 190 | Santana Moss | .60 | .25 |
| ❑ 191 | Peerless Price | .50 | .20 |
| ❑ 192 | Kyle Boller | .60 | .25 |
| ❑ 193 | Julius Peppers | .60 | .25 |
| ❑ 194 | Drew Bledsoe | .75 | .30 |
| ❑ 195 | Marc Bulger | .60 | .25 |
| ❑ 196 | Brian Urlacher | .75 | .30 |
| ❑ 197 | Andre' Davis | .50 | .20 |
| ❑ 198 | Terry Glenn | .60 | .25 |
| ❑ 199 | Champ Bailey | .60 | .25 |
| ❑ 200 | Tom Brady | 2.00 | .75 |
| ❑ 201 | Chris Chambers | .60 | .25 |
| ❑ 202 | Tommy Maddox | .60 | .25 |
| ❑ 203 | Derrick Brooks | .60 | .25 |
| ❑ 204 | Corey Dillon | .60 | .25 |
| ❑ 205 | Matt Hasselbeck | .75 | .30 |
| ❑ 206 | Keith Brooking | .50 | .20 |
| ❑ 207 | Steve Smith | .75 | .30 |
| ❑ 208 | Tony Gonzalez | .75 | .30 |
| ❑ 209 | Joey Galloway | .60 | .25 |
| ❑ 210 | Derrick Mason | .60 | .25 |
| ❑ 211 | Quincy Carter | .50 | .20 |
| ❑ 212 | Rod Smith | .60 | .25 |
| ❑ 213 | Andre Johnson | .75 | .30 |
| ❑ 214 | Rod Woodson | .60 | .25 |

|  |  | | |
|---|------|---|---|
| ❑ 215 | Byron Leftwich | .75 | .30 |
| ❑ 216 | Kevin Dyson | .50 | .20 |
| ❑ 217 | Keith Bulluck | .50 | .20 |
| ❑ 218 | Eric Moulds | .60 | .25 |
| ❑ 219 | Jamie Sharper | .50 | .20 |
| ❑ 220 | Takeo Spikes | .50 | .20 |
| ❑ 221 | C.Pace/F.Wakefield | .50 | .20 |
| ❑ 222 | B.Smith/P.Kerney | .60 | .25 |
| ❑ 223 | E.Reed/G.Baxter | .60 | .25 |
| ❑ 224 | A.Schobel/J.Posey | .50 | .20 |
| ❑ 225 | K.Jenkins/B.Buckner | .60 | .25 |
| ❑ 226 | J.Smith/D.Clemons | .50 | .20 |
| ❑ 227 | M.Haynes/B.Robinson | .50 | .20 |
| ❑ 228 | C.Brown/G.Warren | .60 | .25 |
| ❑ 229 | T.Newman/D.Woodson | .60 | .25 |
| ❑ 230 | R.Johnson/M.Fatafehi | .50 | .20 |
| ❑ 231 | R.Porcher/J.Hall RC | .50 | .20 |
| ❑ 232 | K.Gbaja-Biamila/C.Hunt | .60 | .25 |
| ❑ 233 | A.Glenn/M.Coleman | .50 | .20 |
| ❑ 234 | N.Harper RC/J.Jefferson | .50 | .20 |
| ❑ 235 | H.Douglas/T.Brackens | .50 | .20 |
| ❑ 236 | V.Holliday/E.Hicks | .50 | .20 |
| ❑ 237 | S.Knight/A.Freeman | .50 | .20 |
| ❑ 238 | S.Martin/N.Rogers | .50 | .20 |
| ❑ 239 | R.Colvin/W.McGinest | .60 | .25 |
| ❑ 240 | O.Stoutmire/S.Williams | .50 | .20 |
| ❑ 241 | E.Barton/V.Hobson | .50 | .20 |
| ❑ 242 | W.Sapp/T.Washington | .60 | .25 |
| ❑ 243 | C.Simon/D.Walker | .50 | .20 |
| ❑ 244 | T.Polamalu/M.Logan | 2.50 | 1.00 |
| ❑ 245 | J.Williams/A.Dingle RC | .50 | .20 |
| ❑ 246 | B.Young/B.Whiting | .50 | .20 |
| ❑ 247 | K.Hamlin/D.Robinson RC | .50 | .20 |
| ❑ 248 | D.Lewis/R.Pickett | .50 | .20 |
| ❑ 249 | A.McFarland/G.Spires | .50 | .20 |
| ❑ 250 | A.Haynesworth/R.Long | .50 | .20 |
| ❑ 251 | I.Ohalete/M.Brown | .50 | .20 |
| ❑ 252 | B.Berry/K.King | .60 | .25 |
| ❑ 253 | E.Johnson/E.Jasper | .50 | .20 |
| ❑ 254 | C.Tillman/J.Azumah | .60 | .25 |
| ❑ 255 | M.Wiley/L.Glover | .50 | .20 |
| ❑ 256 | S.Rogers/D.Wilkinson | .50 | .20 |
| ❑ 257 | G.Walker/R.Smith | .50 | .20 |
| ❑ 258 | M.Doss/I.Bashir | .60 | .25 |
| ❑ 259 | M.Stroud/J.Henderson | .50 | .20 |
| ❑ 260 | R.Sims/J.Browning | .50 | .20 |
| ❑ 261 | J.Seau/M.Greenwood | .75 | .30 |
| ❑ 262 | K.Williams/K.Mixon | .50 | .20 |
| ❑ 263 | T.Warren/K.Traylor | .50 | .20 |
| ❑ 264 | W.Allen/W.Peterson | .50 | .20 |
| ❑ 265 | D.Barrett/R.Tongue | .50 | .20 |
| ❑ 266 | P.Buchanon/D.Gibson | .50 | .20 |
| ❑ 267 | L.Sheppard/S.Brown | .50 | .20 |
| ❑ 268 | B.Taylor/M.Trufant | .60 | .25 |
| ❑ 269 | M.Washington/M.Barrow | .60 | .25 |
| ❑ 270 | C.Draft/M.Stewart | .50 | .20 |
| ❑ 271 | M.Brown/M.Green | .60 | .25 |
| ❑ 272 | E.Brown/M.McCree | .50 | .20 |
| ❑ 273 | P.Surtain/S.Madison | .50 | .20 |
| ❑ 274 | B.Dawkins/M.Lewis | .60 | .25 |
| ❑ 275 | S.Springs/F.Smoot | .50 | .20 |
| ❑ 276 | McKinnon/Fisher/Thompson | .50 | .20 |
| ❑ 277 | Webster/McBride RC/Scott | .50 | .20 |
| ❑ 278 | Boulware/Hartwell/Thomas | .60 | .25 |
| ❑ 279 | Vincent/Miloy/Clements | .60 | .25 |
| ❑ 280 | Witherspoon/Morgan/Fields | .60 | .25 |
| ❑ 281 | Simmons/Hardy/Webster | .60 | .25 |
| ❑ 282 | Odom RC/Brown/Briggs | 2.50 | 1.00 |
| ❑ 283 | Holdman/Thompson/Lang | .50 | .20 |
| ❑ 284 | Nguyen/Coakley/Singleton | .50 | .20 |
| ❑ 285 | Wilson/Spragan RC/Holland | .50 | .20 |
| ❑ 286 | Holmes/J.Davis RC/Bailey | .50 | .20 |
| ❑ 287 | Barnett/Diggs/Navies | .60 | .25 |
| ❑ 288 | Foreman/Peek/Wong | .50 | .20 |
| ❑ 289 | Brock RC/Reagor/Tripplett | .50 | .20 |
| ❑ 290 | Ayodele/Favors/Peterson | .50 | .20 |
| ❑ 291 | Barber/Maslowski/Fujita | .50 | .20 |
| ❑ 292 | Claiborne/Henderson/Nattiel | .60 | .25 |
| ❑ 293 | Bruschi/Phifer/Vrabel | .75 | .30 |
| ❑ 294 | Grant/Howard/Sullivan | .50 | .20 |
| ❑ 295 | Robbins/Joseph/Umenyiora | .50 | .20 |
| ❑ 296 | Abra/Krause/Fergus RC | 1.25 | .50 |
| ❑ 297 | Harris/Rudd/Brayton | .50 | .20 |
| ❑ 298 | Simoneau/Warner/Jones | .50 | .20 |
| ❑ 299 | Porter/Bell/Haggans RC | 1.00 | .40 |
| ❑ 300 | Jammer/Davis/Florence | .50 | .20 |
| ❑ 301 | Peterson/Ulbrich/Smith | .60 | .25 |

|  |  | | |
|---|------|---|---|
| ❑ 302 | Simmons/Huff/Brown | .50 | .20 |
| ❑ 303 | Tinoisamoa/Polley/Thomas | .50 | .20 |
| ❑ 304 | Quarles/Wyms/Nece | .50 | .20 |
| ❑ 305 | Carter/Hall/Sirmon | .60 | .25 |
| ❑ 306 | Griffin/Daniels/Wynn | .50 | .20 |
| ❑ 307 | Jackson/Wilson/Macklin | .50 | .20 |
| ❑ 308 | Gregg/Douglas/Weaver | .50 | .20 |
| ❑ 309 | Williams/Denney/Adams | .50 | .20 |
| ❑ 310 | Hawkins/Minter/Manning | .50 | .20 |
| ❑ 311 | James/Herring/Beckett | .50 | .20 |
| ❑ 312 | Griffith/Little/Henry | .50 | .20 |
| ❑ 313 | Lynch/Ferg.RC/Hern.RC | .60 | .25 |
| ❑ 314 | Bly/Marion/Bryant | .50 | .20 |
| ❑ 315 | Harris/Roman/McKenzie | .50 | .20 |
| ❑ 316 | Thorn/Morris/Brackett RC | .75 | .30 |
| ❑ 317 | Mathis/Darius/Bolden RC | .50 | .20 |
| ❑ 318 | Warfield/Wesley/Woods | .50 | .20 |
| ❑ 319 | Winfield/Russell RC/Chavous | .60 | .25 |
| ❑ 320 | Harrison/Wilson/Poole | .60 | .25 |
| ❑ 321 | Rodgers/Ruff/Hodge | .50 | .20 |
| ❑ 322 | Green/Greisen/Emmons | .50 | .20 |
| ❑ 323 | Von Oelhoffen/Smith/Hampton | .50 | .20 |
| ❑ 324 | Godfrey/Foley/Lober | .50 | .20 |
| ❑ 325 | Plummer/Parrish/Rumph | .50 | .20 |
| ❑ 326 | Okeafor/Wistrom/Moore | .60 | .25 |
| ❑ 327 | Archuleta/Williams/Butler | .50 | .20 |
| ❑ 328 | Barber/Smith/Phillips | .50 | .20 |
| ❑ 329 | Dyson/Schulters/Williams | .50 | .20 |
| ❑ 330 | Thomas/Bellamy/Jones | .50 | .20 |
| ❑ 331 | Philip Rivers RC | 5.00 | 2.00 |
| ❑ 332 | Dwan Edwards RC | 1.00 | .40 |
| ❑ 333 | Ben Watson RC | 1.50 | .60 |
| ❑ 334 | Karlos Dansby RC | 1.50 | .60 |
| ❑ 335 | Cedric Cobbs RC | 1.25 | .50 |
| ❑ 336 | Chris Perry RC | 1.50 | .60 |
| ❑ 337 | Darius Watts RC | 1.25 | .50 |
| ❑ 338 | Ricardo Colclough RC | 1.50 | .60 |
| ❑ 339 | Derrick Hamilton RC | 1.00 | .40 |
| ❑ 340 | Devard Darling RC | 1.25 | .50 |
| ❑ 341 | Daryl Smith RC | 1.25 | .50 |
| ❑ 342 | Luke McCown RC | 1.50 | .60 |
| ❑ 343 | Dunta Robinson RC | 1.25 | .50 |
| ❑ 344 | Keith Smith RC | 1.00 | .40 |
| ❑ 345 | Ben Hartsock RC | 1.25 | .50 |
| ❑ 346 | J.P. Losman RC | 2.00 | .75 |
| ❑ 347 | Chris Cooley RC | 1.50 | .60 |
| ❑ 348 | Keary Colbert RC | 1.50 | .60 |
| ❑ 349 | Tommie Harris RC | 1.50 | .60 |
| ❑ 350 | Eli Manning RC | 10.00 | 4.00 |
| ❑ 351 | Kevin Jones RC | 1.50 | .60 |
| ❑ 352 | Lee Evans RC | 2.00 | .75 |
| ❑ 353 | D.J. Williams RC | 1.50 | .60 |
| ❑ 354 | Ben Troupe RC | 1.25 | .50 |
| ❑ 355 | Mewelde Moore RC | 1.50 | .60 |
| ❑ 356 | Michael Clayton RC | 1.50 | .60 |
| ❑ 357 | Michael Jenkins RC | 1.50 | .60 |
| ❑ 358 | Adimchinobe Echemandu RC | 1.25 | .50 |
| ❑ 359 | Rashaun Woods RC | 1.00 | .40 |
| ❑ 360 | Bernard Berrian RC | 1.50 | .60 |
| ❑ 361 | Carlos Francis RC | 1.00 | .40 |
| ❑ 362 | Roy Williams RC | 4.00 | 1.50 |
| ❑ 363 | Sean Taylor RC | 1.50 | .60 |
| ❑ 364 | Steven Jackson RC | 5.00 | 2.00 |
| ❑ 365 | Tatum Bell RC | 1.50 | .60 |
| ❑ 366 | Jonathan Vilma RC | 1.50 | .60 |
| ❑ 367 | Derrick Strait RC | 1.25 | .50 |
| ❑ 368 | Andy Hall RC | 1.25 | .50 |
| ❑ 369 | Jason Babin RC | 1.25 | .50 |
| ❑ 370 | Will Smith RC | 1.25 | .50 |
| ❑ 371 | Kenechi Udeze RC | 1.25 | .50 |
| ❑ 372 | Vince Wilfork RC | 1.50 | .60 |
| ❑ 373 | Ahmad Carroll RC | 1.25 | .50 |
| ❑ 374 | Marquise Hill RC | 1.00 | .40 |
| ❑ 375 | Ben Roethlisberger RC | 12.00 | 5.00 |
| ❑ 376 | Chris Gamble RC | 1.25 | .50 |
| ❑ 377 | Junior Siavii RC | 1.00 | .40 |
| ❑ 378 | Teddy Lehman RC | 1.25 | .50 |
| ❑ 379 | Antwan Odom RC | 1.25 | .50 |
| ❑ 380 | DeAngelo Hall RC | 1.50 | .60 |
| ❑ 381 | Nathan Vasher RC | 1.50 | .60 |
| ❑ 382 | B.J. Symons RC | 1.00 | .40 |
| ❑ 383 | Reggie Williams RC | 1.50 | .60 |
| ❑ 384 | Michael Boulware RC | 1.50 | .60 |
| ❑ 385 | Matt Schaub RC | 5.00 | 2.00 |
| ❑ 386 | Sean Jones RC | 1.00 | .40 |
| ❑ 387 | Courtney Watson RC | 1.00 | .40 |
| ❑ 388 | Nathaniel Adibi RC | 1.00 | .40 |

| | | |
|---|---|---|
| ☐ 389 Devery Henderson RC | 1.50 | .60 |
| ☐ 390 Greg Jones RC | 1.50 | .60 |
| ☐ 391 Joey Thomas RC | 1.00 | .40 |
| ☐ 392 Drew Carter RC | 1.50 | .60 |
| ☐ 393 Julius Jones RC | 4.00 | 1.50 |
| ☐ 394 Keyaron Fox RC | 1.25 | .50 |
| ☐ 395 Darrion Scott RC | 1.25 | .50 |
| ☐ 396 Rich Gardner RC | 1.25 | .50 |
| ☐ 397 Jeff Smoker RC | 1.25 | .50 |
| ☐ 398 Will Poole RC | 1.50 | .60 |
| ☐ 399 Samie Parker RC | 1.25 | .50 |
| ☐ 400 Larry Fitzgerald RC | 5.00 | 2.00 |
| ☐ 401 Jerricho Cotchery RC | 1.50 | .60 |
| ☐ 402 Ernest Wilford RC | 1.50 | .60 |
| ☐ 403 Johnnie Morant RC | 1.25 | .50 |
| ☐ 404 Craig Krenzel RC | 1.50 | .60 |
| ☐ 405 Michael Turner RC | 3.00 | 1.25 |
| ☐ 406 D.J. Hackett RC | 1.50 | .60 |
| ☐ 407 P.K. Sam RC | 1.00 | .40 |
| ☐ 408 Triandos Luke RC | 1.00 | .40 |
| ☐ 409 Josh Harris RC | 1.00 | .40 |
| ☐ 410 Drew Henson RC | 1.00 | .40 |
| ☐ 411 Jim Navarre RC | 1.25 | .50 |
| ☐ 412 Cody Pickett RC | 1.25 | .50 |
| ☐ 413 Clarence Moore RC | 1.25 | .50 |
| ☐ 414 Michael Gaines RC | 1.00 | .40 |
| ☐ 415 Derek Abney RC | 1.00 | .40 |
| ☐ 416 Dontarrious Thomas RC | 1.25 | .50 |
| ☐ 417 Reggie Torbor RC | 1.00 | .40 |
| ☐ 418 Ryan Krause RC | 1.00 | .40 |
| ☐ 419 Travis LaBoy RC | 1.25 | .50 |
| ☐ 420 Kellen Winslow RC | 3.00 | 1.25 |
| ☐ 421 Keiwan Ratliff RC | 1.00 | .40 |
| ☐ 422 Gilbert Gardner RC | 1.00 | .40 |
| ☐ 423 Jamaar Taylor RC | 1.00 | .40 |
| ☐ 424 Matt Ware RC | 1.50 | .60 |
| ☐ 425 Stuart Schweigert RC | 1.25 | .50 |
| ☐ 426 Marcus Tubbs RC | 1.25 | .50 |
| ☐ 427 Brandon Chillar RC | 1.25 | .50 |
| ☐ 428 Shawntae Spencer RC | 1.00 | .40 |
| ☐ 429 Marquis Cooper RC | 1.50 | .60 |
| ☐ 430 Derrick Ward RC | 1.50 | .60 |
| ☐ 431 Tim Euhus RC | 1.00 | .40 |
| ☐ 432 Patrick Crayton RC | 2.00 | .75 |
| ☐ 433 Caleb Miller RC | 1.00 | .40 |
| ☐ 434 Donnell Washington RC | 1.25 | .50 |
| ☐ 435 Thomas Tapeh RC | 1.25 | .50 |
| ☐ 436 Randy Starks RC | 1.00 | .40 |
| ☐ 437 Sloan Thomas RC | 1.25 | .50 |
| ☐ 438 Maurice Mann RC | 1.00 | .40 |
| ☐ 439 Jim Sorgi RC | 1.50 | .60 |
| ☐ 440 Nate Lawrie RC | 1.00 | .40 |

## 2005 Topps Total

| | | |
|---|---|---|
| ☐ COMPLETE SET (550) | 80.00 | 30.00 |
| ☐ COMP.PACKERS TIN (20) | 20.00 | 10.00 |
| ☐ COMP.STEELERS TIN (20) | 20.00 | 10.00 |
| ☐ 1 Michael Vick | .75 | .30 |
| ☐ 2 O.Kreutz/J.Mitchell RC | .60 | .25 |
| ☐ 3 Re.Williams/Garrard/T.Edwards | .50 | .20 |
| ☐ 4 Terence Newman | .50 | .20 |
| ☐ 5 D.Clay/C.Baker | .50 | .20 |
| ☐ 6 D.Clark/S.Will.RC/B.Hamilton | .50 | .20 |
| ☐ 7 Terrell Owens | .75 | .30 |
| ☐ 8 I.Ohalete/A.Wilson | .50 | .20 |
| ☐ 9 G.Walker/Payne/Rob.Smith | .50 | .20 |
| ☐ 10 Quentin Jammer | .50 | .20 |
| ☐ 11 Ke.Smith/D.Bly | .50 | .20 |
| ☐ 12 C.Taylor/Ogden/B.Sams | .60 | .25 |

| | | |
|---|---|---|
| ☐ 13 Torry Holt | .60 | .25 |
| ☐ 14 W.Henderson/N.Davenport | .60 | .25 |
| ☐ 15 J.Siavii/Hicks/J.Allen | .50 | .20 |
| ☐ 16 Keith Bulluck | .50 | .20 |
| ☐ 17 K.Irvin/C.Chavous | .50 | .20 |
| ☐ 18 F.Jackson/A.Bryant/A.Davis | .50 | .20 |
| ☐ 19 Michael Pittman | .50 | .20 |
| ☐ 20 Vanderjagt/H.Smith RC | .50 | .20 |
| ☐ 21 J.Winborn/Ulbrich/D.Smith | .50 | .20 |
| ☐ 22 Reggie Wayne | .60 | .25 |
| ☐ 23 S.Lechler/Janikowski | .50 | .20 |
| ☐ 24 K.Mathis RC/J.Webster/B.Scott | .50 | .20 |
| ☐ 25 Daunte Culpepper | .75 | .30 |
| ☐ 26 W.Peterson/W.Allen | .50 | .20 |
| ☐ 27 T.Walter/F.Adams/L.Allen | .50 | .20 |
| ☐ 28 Tauscher/M.Flanagan/Clifton RC | .50 | .20 |
| ☐ 29 Jerome Bettis | .75 | .30 |
| ☐ 30 M.Brown/R.McQuarters | .50 | .20 |
| ☐ 31 Andre Johnson | .60 | .25 |
| ☐ 32 Tofield/G.Jones/Fuamatu-Ma/Afala | .50 | .20 |
| ☐ 33 G.Lewis/B.McMullen | .60 | .25 |
| ☐ 34 Kyle Boller | .60 | .25 |
| ☐ 35 Kacyvenski/T.White RC/Bates | .50 | .20 |
| ☐ 36 Chris Brown | .60 | .25 |
| ☐ 37 J.Phillips/B.Kelly | .50 | .20 |
| ☐ 38 Saturday RC/Diem RC/Ta.Glenn | .75 | .30 |
| ☐ 39 Clinton Portis | .75 | .30 |
| ☐ 40 M.Scifres/N.Kaeding | .50 | .20 |
| ☐ 41 Ke.Williams/Udeze/Johnstone | .50 | .20 |
| ☐ 42 Tony Parrish | .50 | .20 |
| ☐ 43 D.Armstrong/J.Gaffney | .50 | .20 |
| ☐ 44 F.Bryant/C.Cash/Te.Holt | .50 | .20 |
| ☐ 45 Kerry Collins | .60 | .25 |
| ☐ 46 M.Strong/M.Morris | .50 | .20 |
| ☐ 47 Robertson/J.Abraham/S.Ellis | .50 | .20 |
| ☐ 48 Darrell Jackson | .60 | .25 |
| ☐ 49 P.Price/A.Rossum | .50 | .20 |
| ☐ 50 A.Henry/N.Jones RC/Frazier RC | .50 | .20 |
| ☐ 51 Steven Jackson | .50 | .20 |
| ☐ 52 R.Sims/J.Browning | .50 | .20 |
| ☐ 53 Robbins/Umenyiora/W.Joseph | .75 | .30 |
| ☐ 54 Billy Volek | .60 | .25 |
| ☐ 55 A.Ayodele/Da.Smith | .50 | .20 |
| ☐ 56 I.Scott RC/Odom/T.Johnson | .50 | .20 |
| ☐ 57 Onterrio Smith | .50 | .20 |
| ☐ 58 M.Stover/D.Zastudil RC | .50 | .20 |
| ☐ 59 Hunt/Obaja-Biamila/Kampman RC | .75 | .30 |
| ☐ 60 Dante Hall | .60 | .25 |
| ☐ 61 J.Peterson/B.Young | .50 | .20 |
| ☐ 62 Hardwick/Olivea RC/Oben | .50 | .20 |
| ☐ 63 Chad Pennington | .75 | .30 |
| ☐ 64 D.Clark/A.Moorehead | .60 | .25 |
| ☐ 65 B.Taylor/K.Richard RC | .50 | .20 |
| ☐ 66 K.Walker/J.Wade RC | .50 | .20 |
| ☐ 67 Jeremy Shockey | .75 | .30 |
| ☐ 68 Daylon McCutcheon | .50 | .20 |
| ☐ 69 Coakley/Claiborne/Tinoisamoa | .50 | .20 |
| ☐ 70 Roy Williams WR | .75 | .30 |
| ☐ 71 L.Schulters/Ta.Williams | .50 | .20 |
| ☐ 72 S.Brown/Hood RC/Wynn | .75 | .30 |
| ☐ 73 Sean Taylor | .60 | .25 |
| ☐ 74 J.Little/B.Chillar | .50 | .20 |
| ☐ 75 Boiman/R.Starks/Clauss RC | .50 | .20 |
| ☐ 76 Lee Suggs | .60 | .25 |
| ☐ 77 P.Crayton/T.Glenn | .75 | .30 |
| ☐ 78 Dansby/Darling/G.Hayes | .50 | .20 |
| ☐ 79 Nick Barnett | .60 | .25 |
| ☐ 80 R.Coleman/A.Lake RC | .50 | .20 |
| ☐ 81 Berrian/J.Gage/D.Clark | .60 | .25 |
| ☐ 82 Dominic Rhodes | .60 | .25 |
| ☐ 83 C.Moore/R.Hymes | .50 | .20 |
| ☐ 84 Fraley RC/Runyan/T.Thomas | .50 | .20 |
| ☐ 85 Philip Rivers | .75 | .30 |
| ☐ 86 A.Harris/A.Carroll | .50 | .20 |
| ☐ 87 B.Sanders/Doss/J.Jefferson | .50 | .20 |
| ☐ 88 Cesaire RC/Ja.Will/Dingle | .50 | .20 |
| ☐ 89 Eric Moulds | .60 | .25 |
| ☐ 90 P.Zellner RC/R.Davis | .50 | .20 |
| ☐ 91 K.Wong/Babin/A.Peek | .50 | .20 |
| ☐ 92 Tony Richardson | .50 | .20 |
| ☐ 93 G.Wesley/J.Woods | .50 | .20 |
| ☐ 94 Fabini/Goodwin RC/K.Mawae | .50 | .20 |
| ☐ 95 Tatum Bell | .60 | .25 |
| ☐ 96 K.Lewis RC/C.Emmons | .50 | .20 |
| ☐ 97 J.Galloway/W.Heller | .50 | .20 |
| ☐ 98 Tom Brady | 1.50 | .60 |
| ☐ 99 R.Babers/B.Walker | .50 | .20 |

| | | |
|---|---|---|
| ☐ 100 Mickens/McGraw/Buckley | .50 | .20 |
| ☐ 101 Zach Thomas | .75 | .30 |
| ☐ 102 Co.Brown RC/A.Weaver | .50 | .20 |
| ☐ 103 A.Will/J.Butler/K.Garrett | .50 | .20 |
| ☐ 104 Troy Polamalu | 1.00 | .40 |
| ☐ 105 W.Sapp/T.Washington | .60 | .25 |
| ☐ 106 T.Johnson/Crockett/Morant | .50 | .20 |
| ☐ 107 Chris McAlister | .50 | .20 |
| ☐ 108 C.Stanley RC/K.Brown | .50 | .20 |
| ☐ 109 Drew Henson | .50 | .20 |
| ☐ 110 James Hall | .50 | .20 |
| ☐ 111 S.Player/N.Rackers | .50 | .20 |
| ☐ 112 D.Watts/A.Lelie | .50 | .20 |
| ☐ 113 J.David/N.Harper | .50 | .20 |
| ☐ 114 R.Curry/D.Gabriel | .60 | .25 |
| ☐ 115 R.Colclough/W.Williams | .50 | .20 |
| ☐ 116 C.Tillman/J.Azumah | .50 | .20 |
| ☐ 117 M.Kennoaldu RC/Ad.Thomas | .50 | .20 |
| ☐ 118 M.Roman/J.Thomas | .50 | .20 |
| ☐ 119 D.Henderson/M.Lewis | .50 | .20 |
| ☐ 120 M.Furrey/Manumaleuna | .75 | .30 |
| ☐ 121 R.Mahe/C.Buckhalter | .50 | .20 |
| ☐ 122 E.Kinney/T.Fleming | .50 | .20 |
| ☐ 123 W.Dunn/T.Duckett | .60 | .25 |
| ☐ 124 T.Euhus/M.Campbell | .50 | .20 |
| ☐ 125 P.Hunter/A.Glenn | .50 | .20 |
| ☐ 126 R.Tongue/D.Barrett | .50 | .20 |
| ☐ 127 S.Morris/L.Gordon | .50 | .20 |
| ☐ 128 R.Clark RC/S.Springs | 1.50 | .60 |
| ☐ 129 J.Miller/A.Vinatieri | .75 | .30 |
| ☐ 130 E.Warfield/W.Bartee | .50 | .20 |
| ☐ 131 Me.Moore/M.Bennett | .60 | .25 |
| ☐ 132 N.Goings/B.Hoover | .50 | .20 |
| ☐ 133 Q.Harris/D.Macklin | .50 | .20 |
| ☐ 134 E.Drummond/R.Swinton | .50 | .20 |
| ☐ 135 J.Fargas/A.Whitted | .60 | .25 |
| ☐ 136 N.Clements/T.McGee RC | .50 | .20 |
| ☐ 137 T.Hollings/J.Wells | .50 | .20 |
| ☐ 138 D.Cooper RC/K.Thomas RC | .50 | .20 |
| ☐ 139 P.Dawson/D.Frost RC | .50 | .20 |
| ☐ 140 J.McCown/J.Navarre | .60 | .25 |
| ☐ 141 G.Ellis/K.Coleman | .50 | .20 |
| ☐ 142 G.Wilson/B.Alexander | .60 | .25 |
| ☐ 143 A.Woolfolk/L.Thompson | .50 | .20 |
| ☐ 144 E.Cornwell/B.Williams | .50 | .20 |
| ☐ 145 D.Akers/Di.Johnson RC | .50 | .20 |
| ☐ 146 Hillenmeyer RC/L.Briggs | 1.25 | .50 |
| ☐ 147 R.Mathis RC/G.Brackett | .50 | .20 |
| ☐ 148 J.Rice/R.Alexander | 1.50 | .60 |
| ☐ 149 E.Coleman/D.Strait | .50 | .20 |
| ☐ 150 J.Hartwig RC/B.Troupe | .50 | .20 |
| ☐ 151 S.Davis/D.Florence | .50 | .20 |
| ☐ 152 P.Buchanon/M.Coleman | .50 | .20 |
| ☐ 153 S.Heiden/A.Shea | .50 | .20 |
| ☐ 154 T.Spikes/L.Fletcher | .50 | .20 |
| ☐ 155 T.Laboy/A.Odom | .50 | .20 |
| ☐ 156 A.Toomer/M.Cloud | .60 | .25 |
| ☐ 157 L.Tynes/C.Horn | .50 | .20 |
| ☐ 158 N.Diggs/P.Lenon RC | .50 | .20 |
| ☐ 159 R.Long/A.Hawesworth | .50 | .20 |
| ☐ 160 B.Askew/J.Sowell | .50 | .20 |
| ☐ 161 John Carney | | |
|     Mitch Berger | | .20 |
| ☐ 162 K.Campbell/J.Wiggins | .60 | .25 |
| ☐ 163 Jerramy Stevens | .60 | .25 |
| ☐ 164 Willis McGahee | .75 | .30 |
| ☐ 165 Ed Reed | .60 | .25 |
| ☐ 166 Muhsin Muhammad | .60 | .25 |
| ☐ 167 Donovin Darius | .50 | .20 |
| ☐ 168 E.J. Henderson | .50 | .20 |
| ☐ 169 Tony Banks | .50 | .20 |
| ☐ 170 Fred Taylor | .75 | .30 |
| ☐ 171 Jeremiah Trotter | .50 | .20 |
| ☐ 172 Adam Archuleta | .50 | .20 |
| ☐ 173 Marcus Trufant | .60 | .25 |
| ☐ 174 Steve McNair | .75 | .30 |
| ☐ 175 Ben Roethlisberger | 2.00 | .75 |
| ☐ 176 Derrick Blaylock | .50 | .20 |
| ☐ 177 Michael Strahan | .60 | .25 |
| ☐ 178 Robert Gallery | .50 | .20 |
| ☐ 179 Drew Brees | .75 | .30 |
| ☐ 180 David Kircus | .50 | .20 |
| ☐ 181 Robert Ferguson | .60 | .25 |
| ☐ 182 Jim Sorgi | .50 | .20 |
| ☐ 183 Alge Crumpler | .60 | .25 |
| ☐ 184 DeShaun Foster | .50 | .20 |
| ☐ 185 Reuben Droughns | .50 | .20 |

|  |  | | |
|---|---|---|---|
| ❑ 186 | Charles Grant | .50 | .20 |
| ❑ 187 | Jason Taylor | .60 | .25 |
| ❑ 188 | James Thrash | .60 | .25 |
| ❑ 189 | LaDainian Tomlinson | 1.25 | .50 |
| ❑ 190 | Tim Rattay | .50 | .20 |
| ❑ 191 | Jeff Garcia | .60 | .25 |
| ❑ 192 | Jerricho Cotchery | .60 | .25 |
| ❑ 193 | Chris Simms | .60 | .25 |
| ❑ 194 | Jevon Kearse | .60 | .25 |
| ❑ 195 | Kyle Brady | .50 | .20 |
| ❑ 196 | Trent Green | .60 | .25 |
| ❑ 197 | Antoine Winfield | .50 | .20 |
| ❑ 198 | Deion Branch | .60 | .25 |
| ❑ 199 | Rudi Johnson | .60 | .25 |
| ❑ 200 | Lee Evans | .75 | .30 |
| ❑ 201 | Stephen Davis | .50 | .20 |
| ❑ 202 | Darnell Dockett | .50 | .20 |
| ❑ 203 | Kurt Warner | .75 | .30 |
| ❑ 204 | Quincy Morgan | .50 | .20 |
| ❑ 205 | Daimon Shelton | .50 | .20 |
| ❑ 206 | Champ Bailey | .60 | .25 |
| ❑ 207 | Jamal Lewis | .60 | .25 |
| ❑ 208 | Brett Favre | 2.00 | .75 |
| ❑ 209 | Charles Woodson | .60 | .25 |
| ❑ 210 | Koren Robinson | .50 | .20 |
| ❑ 211 | Chris Chambers | .60 | .25 |
| ❑ 212 | Dave Ragone | .50 | .20 |
| ❑ 213 | Travis Minor | .50 | .20 |
| ❑ 214 | Simeon Rice | .50 | .20 |
| ❑ 215 | Tommy Maddox | .60 | .25 |
| ❑ 216 | Aaron Stecker | .50 | .20 |
| ❑ 217 | Dwight Freeney | .60 | .25 |
| ❑ 218 | Thomas Jones | .60 | .25 |
| ❑ 219 | Patrick Ramsey | .60 | .25 |
| ❑ 220 | Travis Taylor | .50 | .20 |
| ❑ 221 | Chris Weinke | .50 | .20 |
| ❑ 222 | Marc Bulger | .60 | .25 |
| ❑ 223 | James Farrior | .50 | .20 |
| ❑ 224 | Billy Miller | .50 | .20 |
| ❑ 225 | Mike Peterson | .50 | .20 |
| ❑ 226 | Eddie Kennison | .50 | .20 |
| ❑ 227 | Aaron Brooks | .60 | .25 |
| ❑ 228 | Plaxico Burress | .60 | .25 |
| ❑ 229 | Jerry Porter | .60 | .25 |
| ❑ 230 | Joey Harrington | .75 | .30 |
| ❑ 231 | Bubba Franks | .60 | .25 |
| ❑ 232 | Michael Jenkins | .60 | .25 |
| ❑ 233 | Larry Fitzgerald | .75 | .30 |
| ❑ 234 | Troy Vincent | .50 | .20 |
| ❑ 235 | Chad Johnson | .60 | .25 |
| ❑ 236 | Roy Williams S | .60 | .25 |
| ❑ 237 | Corey Dillon | .60 | .25 |
| ❑ 238 | Donovan McNabb | .75 | .30 |
| ❑ 239 | Marcus Robinson | .60 | .25 |
| ❑ 240 | Derrick Brooks | .60 | .25 |
| ❑ 241 | David Bowens RC | .50 | .20 |
| ❑ 242 | Renaldo Wynn | .50 | .20 |
| ❑ 243 | Kevan Barlow | .50 | .20 |
| ❑ 244 | Antonio Gates | .75 | .30 |
| ❑ 245 | Duce Staley | .60 | .25 |
| ❑ 246 | Ernest Wilford | .60 | .25 |
| ❑ 247 | Kevin Jones | .60 | .25 |
| ❑ 248 | Julius Peppers | .60 | .25 |
| ❑ 249 | Terrell Suggs | .60 | .25 |
| ❑ 250 | Bertrand Berry | .50 | .20 |
| ❑ 251 | Brian Simmons | .50 | .20 |
| ❑ 252 | Jake Plummer | .60 | .25 |
| ❑ 253 | Brian Urlacher | .75 | .30 |
| ❑ 254 | Justin McCareins | .50 | .20 |
| ❑ 255 | L.J. Smith | .60 | .25 |
| ❑ 256 | Matt Hasselbeck | .75 | .30 |
| ❑ 257 | Rashaun Woods | .50 | .20 |
| ❑ 258 | Rodney Harrison | .60 | .25 |
| ❑ 259 | Brandon Stokley | .50 | .20 |
| ❑ 260 | Tony Gonzalez | .60 | .25 |
| ❑ 261 | J.P. Losman | .75 | .30 |
| ❑ 262 | DeAngelo Hall | .60 | .25 |
| ❑ 263 | Jake Delhomme | .75 | .30 |
| ❑ 264 | Shaun Rogers | .50 | .20 |
| ❑ 265 | Donald Driver | .75 | .30 |
| ❑ 266 | Will Smith | .50 | .20 |
| ❑ 267 | Brian Westbrook | .60 | .25 |
| ❑ 268 | A.J. Feeley | .50 | .20 |
| ❑ 269 | Marshall Faulk | .75 | .30 |
| ❑ 270 | Marques Tuiasosopo | .50 | .20 |
| ❑ 271 | Curtis Martin | .75 | .30 |
| ❑ 272 | Jason Witten | .60 | .25 |
| ❑ 273 | Kellen Winslow | .75 | .30 |
| ❑ 274 | Corey Bradford | .60 | .25 |
| ❑ 275 | Samari Rolle | .50 | .20 |
| ❑ 276 | Anquan Boldin | .60 | .25 |
| ❑ 277 | Adrian Peterson | .60 | .25 |
| ❑ 278 | Javon Walker | .60 | .25 |
| ❑ 279 | Fred Smoot | .50 | .20 |
| ❑ 280 | Mike Alstott | .60 | .25 |
| ❑ 281 | Randy McMichael | .50 | .20 |
| ❑ 282 | Jay Fiedler | .50 | .20 |
| ❑ 283 | Jamie Sharper | .50 | .20 |
| ❑ 284 | Eli Manning | 1.50 | .60 |
| ❑ 285 | Todd Pinkston | .50 | .20 |
| ❑ 286 | La'Roi Glover | .60 | .25 |
| ❑ 287 | Chris Perry | .60 | .25 |
| ❑ 288 | David Carr | .60 | .25 |
| ❑ 289 | Bryant Johnson | .60 | .25 |
| ❑ 290 | Ray Lewis | .75 | .30 |
| ❑ 291 | Tommie Harris | .60 | .25 |
| ❑ 292 | Joe Horn | .60 | .25 |
| ❑ 293 | Rod Smith | .60 | .25 |
| ❑ 294 | Michael Clayton | .60 | .25 |
| ❑ 295 | Tyrone Calico | .50 | .20 |
| ❑ 296 | Santana Moss | .60 | .25 |
| ❑ 297 | Hines Ward | .75 | .30 |
| ❑ 298 | Jonathan Vilma | .60 | .25 |
| ❑ 299 | Randy Moss | .75 | .30 |
| ❑ 300 | Donte Stallworth | .60 | .25 |
| ❑ 301 | Isaac Bruce | .60 | .25 |
| ❑ 302 | Brian Griese | .60 | .25 |
| ❑ 303 | Dennis Northcutt | .50 | .20 |
| ❑ 304 | Michael Green | .50 | .20 |
| ❑ 305 | Marvin Harrison | .75 | .30 |
| ❑ 306 | Jimmy Smith | .60 | .25 |
| ❑ 307 | Patrick Kerney | .50 | .20 |
| ❑ 308 | Todd Heap | .60 | .25 |
| ❑ 309 | Dan Morgan | .50 | .20 |
| ❑ 310 | Charles Rogers | .60 | .25 |
| ❑ 311 | Dunta Robinson | .50 | .20 |
| ❑ 312 | Deuce McAllister | .75 | .30 |
| ❑ 313 | Ronde Barber | .50 | .20 |
| ❑ 314 | Brandon Lloyd | .50 | .20 |
| ❑ 315 | Tiki Barber | .75 | .30 |
| ❑ 316 | LaMont Jordan | .60 | .25 |
| ❑ 317 | Lito Sheppard | .50 | .20 |
| ❑ 318 | Laveranues Coles | .60 | .25 |
| ❑ 319 | Drew Bennett | .60 | .25 |
| ❑ 320 | Julius Jones | .75 | .30 |
| ❑ 321 | Ahman Green | .75 | .30 |
| ❑ 322 | Domanick Davis | .50 | .20 |
| ❑ 323 | Byron Leftwich | .60 | .25 |
| ❑ 324 | Nate Burleson | .60 | .25 |
| ❑ 325 | David Givens | .60 | .25 |
| ❑ 326 | Trent Dilfer | .60 | .25 |
| ❑ 327 | T.J. Houshmandzadeh | .50 | .20 |
| ❑ 328 | Keith Brooking | .50 | .20 |
| ❑ 329 | Derrick Mason | .60 | .25 |
| ❑ 330 | Ken Lucas | .50 | .20 |
| ❑ 331 | Rex Grossman | .75 | .30 |
| ❑ 332 | Edgerrin James | .75 | .30 |
| ❑ 333 | Priest Holmes | .75 | .30 |
| ❑ 334 | Donnie Edwards | .50 | .20 |
| ❑ 335 | Pierson Prioleau RC | .50 | .20 |
| ❑ 336 | Shaun Alexander | .75 | .30 |
| ❑ 337 | D.J. Williams | .60 | .25 |
| ❑ 338 | Peyton Manning | 1.25 | .50 |
| ❑ 339 | Carson Palmer | .75 | .30 |
| ❑ 340 | Keyshawn Johnson | .60 | .25 |
| ❑ 341 | Tory James | .50 | .20 |
| ❑ 342 | Drew Bledsoe | .75 | .30 |
| ❑ 343 | Chris Gamble | .50 | .20 |
| ❑ 344 | Mi. Lewis/B. Dawkins | .60 | .25 |
| ❑ 345 | Forney/McClure RC/Weiner RC | .50 | .20 |
| ❑ 346 | R. Smart/Kasay/J. Kyle | .50 | .20 |
| ❑ 347 | J. Ferguson/Reeves/Nguyen | .50 | .20 |
| ❑ 348 | Crocker/Lehan RC/M. Jameson | .50 | .20 |
| ❑ 349 | Tyree/Ja. Taylor/T. Carter | .50 | .20 |
| ❑ 350 | H. Thomas/D. Jones/Simoneau | .50 | .20 |
| ❑ 351 | Royal/McCants/T. Jacobs | .50 | .20 |
| ❑ 352 | Webber/D. Thompson/Gilmore | .50 | .20 |
| ❑ 353 | D. Lewis/Pickett/Ty. Jackson | .50 | .20 |
| ❑ 354 | F. Brown/F. Thomas/J. Harbaugh | .50 | .20 |
| ❑ 355 | Asomugha/M. Anderson/Schweiger | .50 | .20 |
| ❑ 356 | M. Stroud/J. Hender/Favors | .50 | .20 |
| ❑ 357 | W. Shields/Roaf/B. Waters RC | .50 | .20 |
| ❑ 358 | Hamilton/Nalen/Lepsis | .50 | .20 |
| ❑ 359 | J. Smith/Geathers/D. Clemons | .50 | .20 |
| ❑ 360 | Wire/R. Baker/L. Milloy | .60 | .25 |
| ❑ 361 | Ayanbadejo/J. Scobey/Hambrick | .50 | .20 |
| ❑ 362 | St. Smith/Proehl/Colbert | .75 | .30 |
| ❑ 363 | N. Harris/D. Thomas/Offord | .50 | .20 |
| ❑ 364 | L. Neal/M. Turner/Pinnock | .75 | .30 |
| ❑ 365 | Faneca/M. Smith RC/Hartings | 1.25 | .50 |
| ❑ 366 | E. Moore/Pope/Ayanbadejo RC | .60 | .25 |
| ❑ 367 | A. Plummer/Jo. Hanson RC/Spencer | .50 | .20 |
| ❑ 368 | L. Betts/Brunell/C. Morton | .60 | .25 |
| ❑ 369 | Pace/Timmerman/McCollum | .50 | .20 |
| ❑ 370 | B. Thomas/Barton/Hobson | .50 | .20 |
| ❑ 371 | S. Barber/K. Fox/K. Mitchell | .50 | .20 |
| ❑ 372 | K. Edwards/Wilkinson/Redding | .50 | .20 |
| ❑ 373 | Co. Jackson RC/Lang/McKinley | .50 | .20 |
| ❑ 374 | Bannan/R. Edwards/S. Adams | .50 | .20 |
| ❑ 375 | M. Schaub/D. White/Finneran | .75 | .30 |
| ❑ 376 | Short/A. Wallace RC/K. Jenkins | .50 | .20 |
| ❑ 377 | Leach/Carswell/Putzier | .50 | .20 |
| ❑ 378 | Vrabel/T. Johnson/Bruschi | .75 | .30 |
| ❑ 379 | Kiel/Je. Wilson RC/Fletcher | .50 | .20 |
| ❑ 380 | Engelber/To. Brown RC/A. Adams | .50 | .20 |
| ❑ 381 | Quarles/Gooch/D. White | .50 | .20 |
| ❑ 382 | Madison/W. Poole/R. Howard | .50 | .20 |
| ❑ 383 | Schneck RC/Gardocki/J. Reed | .50 | .20 |
| ❑ 384 | J. Mitchell RC/Gross/Brzezinski RC | .50 | .20 |
| ❑ 385 | Greisen/B. Green/A. Pierce | .50 | .20 |
| ❑ 386 | C. Simon/D. Walker/McDougle | .50 | .20 |
| ❑ 387 | D. Graham/Fauria/B. Watson | .60 | .25 |
| ❑ 388 | E. Johnson/R. John/M. Coleman | .50 | .20 |
| ❑ 389 | June/D. Thornton/Hutchins | .60 | .25 |
| ❑ 390 | Teague/R. Tucker/M. Will. T | .50 | .20 |
| ❑ 391 | M. Haynes/A. Brown/Ogunleye | .50 | .20 |
| ❑ 392 | Ulmer/R. Smith/De. Williams | .50 | .20 |
| ❑ 393 | K. Faulk/Pass/Be. Johnson | .60 | .25 |
| ❑ 394 | Tobeck RC/W. Jones/S. Hutchin | .50 | .20 |
| ❑ 395 | V. Holliday/Y. Bell RC/K. Carter | .50 | .20 |
| ❑ 396 | L. Foote/J. Porter/Al. Jackson | .50 | .20 |
| ❑ 397 | Looker/K. Curtis/S. McDonald | .50 | .20 |
| ❑ 398 | L. Marshall RC/C. Griffin/D. Evans | .60 | .25 |
| ❑ 399 | D. Klecko/Izzo/R. Colvin | .50 | .20 |
| ❑ 400 | M. Holland/Bentley/Gandy | .50 | .20 |
| ❑ 401 | Petitgout/McKenzie RC/J. Whittle RC | .50 | .20 |
| ❑ 402 | Sykes RC/Fatafehi/A. Wilson | .50 | .20 |
| ❑ 403 | Meester RC/Ma. Will/Manuwai RC | .50 | .20 |
| ❑ 404 | M. Schobel/K. Washing/Warrick | .50 | .20 |
| ❑ 405 | M. Minter/R. Manning/C. Branch | .50 | .20 |
| ❑ 406 | Jo. Reed/Jo. Smith/Aiken | .50 | .20 |
| ❑ 407 | Birk/Liwienski/McKinnie | .50 | .20 |
| ❑ 408 | Godfrey/Foley/Leber | .50 | .20 |
| ❑ 409 | McFarland/Wyms/G. Spires | .50 | .20 |
| ❑ 410 | E. Perry/Do. Lee/Booker | .50 | .20 |
| ❑ 411 | Von Oelhoffen/Hoke RC/Aa. Smith | .60 | .25 |
| ❑ 412 | B. Mitchell/Wistrom/Ra. Moore | .50 | .20 |
| ❑ 413 | J. Green/Wilfork/T. Warren | .60 | .25 |
| ❑ 414 | Middlebrooks/Lynch/N. Ferguson | .60 | .25 |
| ❑ 415 | Reagor/R. Brock/Jo. Williams | .50 | .20 |
| ❑ 416 | J. Dunn/S. Parker/La. Johnson | .75 | .30 |
| ❑ 417 | La. Johnson/M. Wilkins RC/C. Miller | .50 | .20 |
| ❑ 418 | Buckner/Moorehead/M. Rucker | .50 | .20 |
| ❑ 419 | Denney/Kelsay/A. Schobel | .50 | .20 |
| ❑ 420 | Singleton/B. James/K. O'Neil RC | .50 | .20 |
| ❑ 421 | C. Thompson/Boyer/An. Davis | .50 | .20 |
| ❑ 422 | D. Grant/Richardson RC/R. Mathis | .50 | .20 |
| ❑ 423 | Schlesinger/Brown/Pinner | .50 | .20 |
| ❑ 424 | S. Johnson RC/R. Davis/Ru. Jones | .50 | .20 |
| ❑ 425 | Phifer/Banta-Cain/McGinest | .60 | .25 |
| ❑ 426 | McCardell/Osgood/E. Parker | .60 | .25 |
| ❑ 427 | C. Woodard/Bernard/A. Cochran | .50 | .20 |
| ❑ 428 | A. Battle/A. Walker/E. Johnson | .50 | .20 |
| ❑ 429 | Salave'a/Po/RC/Wash/L. Arrington | .75 | .30 |
| ❑ 430 | I. Mays/C. Wilson/Randle El | .60 | .25 |
| ❑ 431 | D. Starks/E. Wilson/R. Gay | .50 | .20 |
| ❑ 432 | Q. Griffin/M. Anderson/C. Sapp | .60 | .25 |
| ❑ 433 | J. Thornton/L. Moore RC/Powell | .50 | .20 |
| ❑ 434 | M. Gaines/Hankton/Seidman | .50 | .20 |
| ❑ 435 | M. Ragan RC/Posey/A. Crowell | .50 | .20 |
| ❑ 436 | O'Neal/M. Williams/K. Ratliff | .50 | .20 |
| ❑ 437 | M. Light/Koppen RC/S. Neal RC | .50 | .20 |
| ❑ 438 | C. Watson/D. Rodgers/J. Allen | .50 | .20 |
| ❑ 439 | M. Boulware/Hamlin/Bierria | .50 | .20 |

| | | |
|---|---|---|
| 440 T.Rogers RC/Unck RC/Roye | .50 | .20 |
| 441 Frank Gore RC | 4.00 | 1.50 |
| 442 Mike Patterson RC | 1.25 | .50 |
| 443 DeMarcus Ware RC | 2.50 | 1.00 |
| 444 Chris Henry RC | 1.50 | .60 |
| 445 Thomas Davis RC | 1.25 | .50 |
| 446 Justin Miller RC | 1.25 | .50 |
| 447 Shaun Cody RC | 1.25 | .50 |
| 448 Alex Barron RC | 1.00 | .40 |
| 449 Brock Berlin RC | 1.25 | .50 |
| 450 Travis Johnson RC | 1.00 | .40 |
| 451 Jerome Mathis RC | 1.50 | .60 |
| 452 Lance Mitchell RC | 1.25 | .50 |
| 453 Martin Jackson RC | 1.25 | .50 |
| 454 Charlie Frye RC | 1.50 | .60 |
| 455 Luis Castillo RC | 1.50 | .60 |
| 456 Fred Gibson RC | 1.25 | .50 |
| 457 Dustin Fox RC | 1.50 | .60 |
| 458 Ryan Fitzpatrick RC | 1.50 | .60 |
| 459 Dan Orlovsky RC | 1.50 | .60 |
| 460 Justin Tuck RC | 2.00 | .75 |
| 461 Corey Webster RC | 1.50 | .60 |
| 462 Travis Daniels RC | 1.25 | .50 |
| 463 J.J. Arrington RC | 1.50 | .60 |
| 464 David Greene RC | 1.25 | .50 |
| 465 Alvin Pearman RC | 1.25 | .50 |
| 466 Manuel White RC | 1.25 | .50 |
| 467 Paris Warren RC | 1.25 | .50 |
| 468 Patrick Estes RC | 1.00 | .40 |
| 469 Cedric Houston RC | 1.50 | .60 |
| 470 David Pollack RC | 1.25 | .50 |
| 471 Craig Bragg RC | 1.00 | .40 |
| 472 Vincent Jackson RC | 1.50 | .60 |
| 473 Adam Jones RC | 1.50 | .60 |
| 474 Matt Jones RC | 2.50 | 1.00 |
| 475 Stefan LeFors RC | 1.25 | .50 |
| 476 Heath Miller RC | 3.00 | 1.25 |
| 477 Ryan Moats RC | 1.50 | .60 |
| 478 Vernand Morency RC | 1.50 | .60 |
| 479 Terrence Murphy RC | 1.00 | .40 |
| 480 Kyle Orton RC | 2.00 | .75 |
| 481 Roscoe Parrish RC | 1.25 | .50 |
| 482 Courtney Roby RC | 1.25 | .50 |
| 483 Aaron Rodgers RC | 5.00 | 2.00 |
| 484 Carlos Rogers RC | 1.50 | .60 |
| 485 Antrel Rolle RC | 1.50 | .60 |
| 486 Eric Shelton RC | 1.25 | .50 |
| 487 Alex Smith QB RC | 2.50 | 1.00 |
| 488 Andrew Walter RC | 1.50 | .60 |
| 489 Roddy White RC | 2.00 | .75 |
| 490 Cadillac Williams RC | 3.00 | 1.25 |
| 491 Mike Williams | 1.50 | .60 |
| 492 Troy Williamson RC | 1.50 | .60 |
| 493 Kirk Morrison RC | 1.50 | .60 |
| 494 Tab Perry RC | 1.50 | .60 |
| 495 Chad Owens RC | 1.50 | .60 |
| 496 Lofa Tatupu RC | 2.00 | .75 |
| 497 Craphonso Thorpe RC | 1.25 | .50 |
| 498 Ryan Riddle RC | 1.00 | .40 |
| 499 Marcus Maxwell RC | 1.00 | .40 |
| 500 Barrett Ruud RC | 1.50 | .60 |
| 501 Stanley Wilson RC | 1.25 | .50 |
| 502 Mike Nugent RC | 1.25 | .50 |
| 503 Eric King RC | 1.25 | .50 |
| 504 Darryl Blackstock RC | 1.00 | .40 |
| 505 Attiyah Ellison RC | 1.00 | .40 |
| 506 Donte Nicholson RC | 1.25 | .50 |
| 507 Airese Currie RC | 1.25 | .50 |
| 508 Larry Brackins RC | 1.50 | .60 |
| 509 Joel Dreessen RC | 1.25 | .50 |
| 510 Cedric Benson RC | 1.50 | .60 |
| 511 Mark Bradley RC | 1.50 | .60 |
| 512 Reggie Brown RC | 1.50 | .60 |
| 513 Ronnie Brown RC | 5.00 | 2.00 |
| 514 Jason Campbell RC | 3.00 | 1.25 |
| 515 Maurice Clarett RC | 1.25 | .50 |
| 516 Mark Clayton RC | 1.50 | .60 |
| 517 Braylon Edwards RC | 5.00 | 2.00 |
| 518 Ciatrick Fason RC | 1.25 | .50 |
| 519 Dan Cody RC | 1.00 | .40 |
| 520 Taylor Stubblefield RC | 1.00 | .40 |
| 521 J.R. Russell RC | 1.25 | .50 |
| 522 Rian Wallace RC | 1.25 | .50 |
| 523 Anthony Davis RC | 1.50 | .50 |

| | | |
|---|---|---|
| 524 Derek Anderson RC | 2.50 | 1.00 |
| 525 Boomer Grigsby RC | 1.50 | .60 |
| 526 Rasheed Marshall RC | 1.25 | .50 |
| 527 Adrian McPherson RC | 1.25 | .50 |
| 528 Noah Herron RC | 1.50 | .60 |
| 529 Bryant McFadden RC | 1.25 | .50 |
| 530 Lionel Gates RC | 1.00 | .40 |
| 531 Matt Roth RC | 1.50 | .60 |
| 532 Derrick Johnson RC | 1.50 | .60 |
| 533 Stanford Routt RC | 1.25 | .50 |
| 534 Brandon Jacobs RC | 2.00 | .75 |
| 535 Kevin Burnett RC | 1.25 | .50 |
| 536 Ryan Claridge RC | 1.00 | .40 |
| 537 James Kilian RC | 1.00 | .40 |
| 538 Oshiomogho Atogwe RC | 1.00 | .40 |
| 539 Fabian Washington RC | 1.50 | .60 |
| 540 Marion Barber RC | 5.00 | 2.00 |
| 541 Anttaj Hawthorne RC | 1.25 | .50 |
| 542 Zach Tuiasosopo RC | 1.00 | .40 |
| 543 Ellis Hobbs RC | 1.50 | .60 |
| 544 Alex Smith TE RC | 1.50 | .60 |
| 545 Erasmus James RC | 1.25 | .50 |
| 546 Channing Crowder RC | 1.25 | .50 |
| 547 Kelvin Hayden RC | 1.25 | .50 |
| 548 Darren Sproles RC | 2.00 | .75 |
| 549 Marcus Spears RC | 1.50 | .60 |
| 550 Dante Ridgeway RC | 1.25 | .50 |
| CL1 Checklist 1 | .10 | .02 |
| CL2 Checklist 2 | .10 | .02 |
| CL3 Checklist 3 | .10 | .02 |
| CL4 Checklist 4 | .10 | .02 |
| BR1 Ben Roethlisberger Jumbo | 6.00 | 3.00 |
| VL1 Vince Lombardi Jumbo | 6.00 | 3.00 |

### 2006 Topps Total

| | | |
|---|---|---|
| 1 C.Webster/S.Madison | .50 | .20 |
| 2 Randy Moss | .75 | .30 |
| 3 Garcia/Parry/Detmer | .60 | .25 |
| 4 Matt Jones | .60 | .25 |
| 5 C.Brown/G.Earl | .60 | .25 |
| 6 Anderson/Steinbach/Braham | .50 | .20 |
| 7 DeAngelo Hall | .60 | .25 |
| 8 J.P. Losman | .60 | .25 |
| 9 Kevin Jones | .75 | .30 |
| 10 K.Dorsey/F.Gore | .75 | .30 |
| 11 Nichol/Pearson RC/Allen | .60 | .25 |
| 12 Brandon Lloyd | .60 | .25 |
| 13 Jeremiah Trotter | .50 | .20 |
| 14 Stone/Grove/Sims | .50 | .20 |
| 15 Drew Brees | .75 | .30 |
| 16 Jason Taylor | .60 | .25 |
| 17 Tony Gonzalez | .60 | .25 |
| 18 Brandon Stokley | .50 | .20 |
| 19 Jake Plummer | .60 | .25 |
| 20 Braylon Edwards | .75 | .30 |
| 21 Berrian/Maynard/Gould RC | .50 | .20 |
| 22 B.Sams/M.Stover | .50 | .20 |
| 23 Darling/Huff/Dansby | .50 | .20 |
| 24 Julius Peppers | .60 | .25 |
| 25 Ferguson/Spears/Ellis | .50 | .20 |
| 26 D.Lee/D.Martin | .50 | .20 |
| 27 B.Johnson/B.Johnson | .60 | .25 |
| 28 Bethel Johnson | .50 | .20 |
| 29 Ellis/Robertson/Thomas | .50 | .20 |
| 30 Willie Parker | 1.00 | .40 |
| 31 E.Shepherd/I.Hilliard | .50 | .20 |
| 32 Troupe/Scaife/Mauck | .50 | .20 |

| | | |
|---|---|---|
| 33 Marc Bulger | .60 | .25 |
| 34 M.Trufant/M.Boulware | .50 | .20 |
| 35 Hardwick/Oben/Olivea | .50 | .20 |
| 36 Ray Lewis | .75 | .30 |
| 37 S.Lefors/C.Weinke | .50 | .20 |
| 38 Kaesviharn/Pollack/Ohalete | .50 | .20 |
| 39 G.Jones/A.Pearman | .50 | .20 |
| 40 Allen/Hicks/Sims | .50 | .20 |
| 41 Tiki Barber | .75 | .30 |
| 42 N.Asomugha/F.Washington | .50 | .20 |
| 43 Lewis/Adams/Emanuel | .50 | .20 |
| 44 Rodney Harrison | .50 | .20 |
| 45 H.Smith/A.Vinatieri | .60 | .25 |
| 46 Orlovsky/Kitna/Bryson | .50 | .20 |
| 47 Bubba Franks | .50 | .20 |
| 48 A.Wilson/I.Gold | .50 | .20 |
| 49 Davis/Thompson/McGinest | .50 | .20 |
| 50 Nathan Vasher | .50 | .20 |
| 51 J.Greer/T.Vincent | .50 | .20 |
| 52 Rossum/Ptrsn/Koenen RC | .50 | .20 |
| 53 DeMarcus Ware | .60 | .25 |
| 54 L.Diamond RC/Booker | .50 | .20 |
| 55 McKinnie/Birk/Hutchinson | .50 | .20 |
| 56 Cole/Kearse/Patterson | .50 | .20 |
| 57 Tubbs/Wistrom/Fisher | .50 | .20 |
| 58 Curtis Martin | .75 | .30 |
| 59 D.Macklin/A.Rolle | .50 | .20 |
| 60 Lejeune/Howard/Bell | .50 | .20 |
| 61 Reggie Brown | .60 | .25 |
| 62 M.McKenzie/F.Thomas | .50 | .20 |
| 63 Fletcher/Hartsock/Sorgi | .50 | .20 |
| 64 Larry Fitzgerald | .75 | .30 |
| 65 E.Moulds/V.Morency | .50 | .20 |
| 66 Williams/Barnes/Naeole | .50 | .20 |
| 67 Trent Green | .60 | .25 |
| 68 D.Sproles/M.Turner | .60 | .25 |
| 69 Chillar/Glover/Tinoisamoa | .60 | .25 |
| 70 Chris Gamble | .50 | .20 |
| 71 A.Jones/M.Waddell | .50 | .20 |
| 72 Marshall/Washington/Daniels | .50 | .20 |
| 73 Hines Ward | .75 | .30 |
| 74 S.Knight/P.Surtain | .50 | .20 |
| 75 McKinney/Wade/Wiegert | .50 | .20 |
| 76 Rod Smith | .60 | .25 |
| 77 D.Henson/T.Romo | 5.00 | 2.00 |
| 78 Franklin RC/Gregg/Pryce | .50 | .20 |
| 79 David Garrard | .75 | .30 |
| 80 D.Smith/M.Peterson | .50 | .20 |
| 81 Bowens/Traylor/Roth | .50 | .20 |
| 82 Simeon Rice | .50 | .20 |
| 83 M.Douglas/B.Young | .50 | .20 |
| 84 Thornton/Reynolds RC/Sirmon | .50 | .20 |
| 85 T.J. Houshmandzadeh | .60 | .25 |
| 86 L.Betts/J.Campbell | .60 | .25 |
| 87 Smith/Hartings/Faneca | .50 | .20 |
| 88 Antonio Pierce | .50 | .20 |
| 89 C.Kluwe/R.Longwell | .50 | .20 |
| 90 Thomas/Manning/Poppinga | .50 | .20 |
| 91 Willis McGahee | .75 | .30 |
| 92 K.Smith/T.Holt | .60 | .25 |
| 93 Wilson/Samuel/Hobbs | .50 | .20 |
| 94 Pace/Timmerman/Barron | .50 | .20 |
| 95 Fred Taylor | .60 | .25 |
| 96 M.Doss/B.Sanders | .50 | .20 |
| 97 Joe/Briggs/Ayanbadejo | .50 | .20 |
| 98 Daunte Culpepper | .75 | .30 |
| 99 C.Perry/T.Perry | .60 | .25 |
| 100 Whitted/Janikowski/Lechler | .50 | .20 |
| 101 Julius Jones | .75 | .30 |
| 102 C.Lavalais/R.Coleman | .50 | .20 |
| 103 Rucker/Ciurciu RC/Wallace | .50 | .20 |
| 104 Rex Grossman | .75 | .30 |
| 105 Danta Robinson | .60 | .25 |
| 106 Bockwoldt/Craft/Gleason | .50 | .20 |
| 107 Chad Pennington | .60 | .25 |
| 108 Heath Miller | .60 | .25 |
| 109 D.Hackett/N.Burleson | .50 | .20 |
| 110 Drew Bennett | .60 | .25 |
| 111 Williams/Godfrey/Castillo | .50 | .20 |
| 112 Doug Gabriel | .50 | .20 |
| 113 A.Toomer/B.Jacobs | .60 | .25 |
| 114 Travis Taylor | .50 | .20 |
| 115 Terrell Suggs | .60 | .25 |
| 116 Todd Heap | .60 | .25 |

|  |  | | |
|---|------|------|------|
| ❑ 117 | Reese/Williams/Boley | .50 | .20 |
| ❑ 118 | Odell Thurman | .50 | .20 |
| ❑ 119 | D.Watts/S.Alexander | .50 | .20 |
| ❑ 120 | Scobee/Hanson RC/Toefield | .50 | .20 |
| ❑ 121 | Donovan McNabb | .75 | .30 |
| ❑ 122 | A.Smith TE/A.Becht | .50 | .20 |
| ❑ 123 | Adam Archuleta | .50 | .20 |
| ❑ 124 | J.J. Arrington | .60 | .25 |
| ❑ 125 | Johnson/Simmons/Miller | .50 | .20 |
| ❑ 126 | Andruzzi/Bentley/Tucker | .50 | .20 |
| ❑ 127 | Aaron Rodgers | .75 | .30 |
| ❑ 128 | Brown/Gardner/Hobson | .50 | .20 |
| ❑ 129 | Antonio Bryant | .60 | .25 |
| ❑ 130 | Isaac Bruce | .50 | .20 |
| ❑ 131 | Quarles/Nece/Ruud | .50 | .20 |
| ❑ 132 | Williams/Elam/Sauerbrun | .50 | .20 |
| ❑ 133 | B.Hoover/N.Goings | .50 | .20 |
| ❑ 134 | Ward/Carter/Rolle | .50 | .20 |
| ❑ 135 | Dante Hall | .60 | .25 |
| ❑ 136 | Tom Brady | 1.25 | .50 |
| ❑ 137 | R.Moats/C.Buckhalter | .60 | .25 |
| ❑ 138 | Amaz Battle | .50 | .20 |
| ❑ 139 | Bernard/Hill/Lewis RC | .50 | .20 |
| ❑ 140 | Kampman/Gbaja-Biamila/Jenkins | .60 | .25 |
| ❑ 141 | Fowler RC/James/Burnett | .50 | .20 |
| ❑ 142 | Warrick Dunn | .60 | .25 |
| ❑ 143 | Eli Manning | 1.00 | .40 |
| ❑ 144 | Clark/Brayton/Morrison | .50 | .20 |
| ❑ 145 | Zach Thomas | .75 | .30 |
| ❑ 146 | Anderson/Babin/Greenwood | .50 | .20 |
| ❑ 147 | Ron Dayne | .60 | .25 |
| ❑ 148 | D.Zastudil/P.Dawson | .50 | .20 |
| ❑ 149 | Williams/Mosley/Johnson | .50 | .20 |
| ❑ 150 | Donte Stallworth | .60 | .25 |
| ❑ 151 | Shawne Merriman | .60 | .25 |
| ❑ 152 | Thompson/Hentrich/Bironas | .50 | .20 |
| ❑ 153 | Clinton Portis | .75 | .30 |
| ❑ 154 | R.Curry/J.Morant | .50 | .20 |
| ❑ 155 | Dwight Freeney | .60 | .25 |
| ❑ 156 | B.Russell/D.McCutcheon | .50 | .20 |
| ❑ 157 | Brown/Green/Tillman | .50 | .20 |
| ❑ 158 | Takeo Spikes | .50 | .20 |
| ❑ 159 | Kurt Warner | .60 | .25 |
| ❑ 160 | Jonathan Vilma | .60 | .25 |
| ❑ 161 | James Farrior | .50 | .20 |
| ❑ 162 | D.Florence/Q.Jammer | .50 | .20 |
| ❑ 163 | Kevan Barlow | .60 | .25 |
| ❑ 164 | Haggans/Hampton/Smith | .50 | .20 |
| ❑ 165 | Walter Jones | .50 | .20 |
| ❑ 166 | Rayburn/Jacox RC/Holland | .50 | .20 |
| ❑ 167 | Byron Leftwich | .60 | .25 |
| ❑ 168 | Mike Williams WR | .75 | .30 |
| ❑ 169 | Jason Witten | .60 | .25 |
| ❑ 170 | Dennis Northcutt | .50 | .20 |
| ❑ 171 | Baker/Clements/Wire | .50 | .20 |
| ❑ 172 | Ronnie Cruz | .50 | .20 |
| ❑ 173 | E.Henderson/E.James | .50 | .20 |
| ❑ 174 | LaMont Jordan | .60 | .25 |
| ❑ 175 | Tyrone Calico | .50 | .20 |
| ❑ 176 | Nalen/Foster/Hamilton | .50 | .20 |
| ❑ 177 | Sam Gado | .75 | .30 |
| ❑ 178 | Randy McMichael | .50 | .20 |
| ❑ 179 | Brown/Sheppard/Ware | .60 | .25 |
| ❑ 180 | L.Little/A.Hargrove | .50 | .20 |
| ❑ 181 | Cadillac Williams | .75 | .30 |
| ❑ 182 | Feely/Morton/Tyree | .50 | .20 |
| ❑ 183 | Dallas Clark | .60 | .25 |
| ❑ 184 | Faggins/Sanders/Coleman | .50 | .20 |
| ❑ 185 | V.Holliday/K.Carter | .50 | .20 |
| ❑ 186 | Smith/Ulbrich/Winborn | .50 | .20 |
| ❑ 187 | S.Player/N.Rackers | .50 | .20 |
| ❑ 188 | Steve Smith | .75 | .30 |
| ❑ 189 | Cassel/Graham/Watson | .75 | .30 |
| ❑ 190 | J.Porter/L.Foote | .50 | .20 |
| ❑ 191 | Jamal Lewis | .60 | .25 |
| ❑ 192 | Michael Jenkins | .60 | .25 |
| ❑ 193 | Michael Strahan | .60 | .25 |
| ❑ 194 | Kyle Vanden Bosch | .50 | .20 |
| ❑ 195 | Shields/Roaf/Waters | .50 | .20 |
| ❑ 196 | Terry Glenn | .60 | .25 |
| ❑ 197 | Griffith/Green/Wilson | .50 | .20 |
| ❑ 198 | Philip Rivers | .75 | .30 |
| ❑ 199 | Tuck/Joseph/Robbins | .60 | .25 |
| ❑ 200 | LaDainian Tomlinson | 1.00 | .40 |
| ❑ 201 | J.David/N.Harper | .50 | .20 |
| ❑ 202 | Hall/Bailey/Rogers | .50 | .20 |
| ❑ 203 | Donald Driver | .60 | .25 |
| ❑ 204 | Reuben Droughns | .50 | .20 |
| ❑ 205 | Wahle/Gross/Wharton | .50 | .20 |
| ❑ 206 | Jonathan Ogden | .50 | .20 |
| ❑ 207 | J.Bullocks/D.Smith | .50 | .20 |
| ❑ 208 | Nugent/Miller/Graham RC | .50 | .20 |
| ❑ 209 | Matt Hasselbeck | .60 | .25 |
| ❑ 210 | Derrick Brooks | .60 | .25 |
| ❑ 211 | Foxworth/Lynch/Ferguson | .50 | .20 |
| ❑ 212 | Stewart/Unck/Fisk | .50 | .20 |
| ❑ 213 | M.Will.TI/Anderson RC/Villarrial | .50 | .20 |
| ❑ 214 | Saturday/Glenn/Diem | .50 | .20 |
| ❑ 215 | Larry Johnson | .60 | .25 |
| ❑ 216 | Marcus Robinson | .60 | .25 |
| ❑ 217 | Aaron Brooks | .60 | .25 |
| ❑ 218 | Smith/Bartrum/Spach | .50 | .20 |
| ❑ 219 | Steven Jackson | .75 | .30 |
| ❑ 220 | Roy Williams WR | .75 | .30 |
| ❑ 221 | L.Polite/P.Crayton | .50 | .20 |
| ❑ 222 | Carson Palmer | .75 | .30 |
| ❑ 223 | Brown/Kreutz/Tait | .50 | .20 |
| ❑ 224 | Javon Walker | .60 | .25 |
| ❑ 225 | J.Payton/T.Henry | .60 | .25 |
| ❑ 226 | K.Rhodes/E.Coleman | .50 | .20 |
| ❑ 227 | Ronnie Brown | .75 | .30 |
| ❑ 228 | David Carr | .60 | .25 |
| ❑ 229 | Terence Newman | .50 | .20 |
| ❑ 230 | Grigsby/Bell/Mitchell | .50 | .20 |
| ❑ 231 | M.Vrabel/R.Colvin | .50 | .20 |
| ❑ 232 | Heitmann/Smiley/Harris | .50 | .20 |
| ❑ 233 | Joey Galloway | .50 | .20 |
| ❑ 234 | Keith Bulluck | .50 | .20 |
| ❑ 235 | Hall/Frost/Brown | .50 | .20 |
| ❑ 236 | Dockett/Smith/Okeafor | .50 | .20 |
| ❑ 237 | Mike Anderson | .60 | .25 |
| ❑ 238 | Kellen Winslow | .75 | .30 |
| ❑ 239 | Tatum Bell | .60 | .25 |
| ❑ 240 | A.Pinner/C.Schlesinger | .50 | .20 |
| ❑ 241 | Roman/Underwood/Collins | .50 | .20 |
| ❑ 242 | Reggie Wayne | .60 | .25 |
| ❑ 243 | Reggie Williams | .50 | .20 |
| ❑ 244 | Pope/Spragan/Crowder | .50 | .20 |
| ❑ 245 | Courtney Watson | .50 | .20 |
| ❑ 246 | G.Lewis/B.McMullen | .50 | .20 |
| ❑ 247 | Troy Polamalu | 1.00 | .40 |
| ❑ 248 | Smoker/Faulk/Looker | .60 | .25 |
| ❑ 249 | Keyshawn Johnson | .60 | .25 |
| ❑ 250 | J.Babineaux/C.Davis | .50 | .20 |
| ❑ 251 | Marcel Shipp | .50 | .20 |
| ❑ 252 | Brian Urlacher | .75 | .30 |
| ❑ 253 | Haynesworth/LaBoy/Starks | .50 | .20 |
| ❑ 254 | Derrick Burgess | .50 | .20 |
| ❑ 255 | Harris/Thomas/Leber | .50 | .20 |
| ❑ 256 | Henderson/Stroud/Hayward | .50 | .20 |
| ❑ 257 | Travis Minor | .50 | .20 |
| ❑ 258 | Rivera/Petitti/Johnson | .50 | .20 |
| ❑ 259 | D.J. Williams | .50 | .20 |
| ❑ 260 | Terrell Owens | .75 | .30 |
| ❑ 261 | C.Wilson/D.Kreider | .50 | .20 |
| ❑ 262 | Antonio Gates | .75 | .30 |
| ❑ 263 | Ronde Barber | .60 | .25 |
| ❑ 264 | Bryant Johnson | .40 | .15 |
| ❑ 265 | Brett Favre | 1.50 | .60 |
| ❑ 266 | C.Stanley/K.Brown | .50 | .20 |
| ❑ 267 | McKenzie/Petitgout/O'Hara | 1.00 | .40 |
| ❑ 268 | Chris Cooley | .60 | .25 |
| ❑ 269 | Steve McNair | .60 | .25 |
| ❑ 270 | Smith/Thornton/Geathers | .50 | .20 |
| ❑ 271 | McClure/Forney/Lehr RC | .50 | .20 |
| ❑ 272 | B.Sapp RC/McCleon/Warf | .40 | .15 |
| ❑ 273 | Jeremy Shockey | .60 | .25 |
| ❑ 274 | Chad Johnson | .60 | .25 |
| ❑ 275 | Vincent RC/Flynn RC/Mulitalo | .50 | .20 |
| ❑ 276 | Deuce McAllister | .60 | .25 |
| ❑ 277 | Sapp/Kelly/Hamilton | .50 | .20 |
| ❑ 278 | B.Manumaleuna/R.Fitzpatrick | .60 | .25 |
| ❑ 279 | Spires/White/Wyms | .50 | .20 |
| ❑ 280 | Josh McCown | .60 | .25 |
| ❑ 281 | Derrick Johnson LB | .60 | .25 |
| ❑ 282 | T.Bryant/C.Grant | .50 | .20 |
| ❑ 283 | C.Houston/D.Blaylock | .50 | .20 |
| ❑ 284 | David Givens | .60 | .25 |
| ❑ 285 | Lindell/McGee/Moorman | .50 | .20 |
| ❑ 286 | Charlie Frye | .60 | .25 |
| ❑ 287 | Ahman Green | .60 | .25 |
| ❑ 288 | Darren Sharper | .50 | .20 |
| ❑ 289 | Justin McCareins | .50 | .20 |
| ❑ 290 | Lofa Tatupu | .60 | .25 |
| ❑ 291 | Brock/Reagor/Thomas | .50 | .20 |
| ❑ 292 | Muhsin Muhammad | .60 | .25 |
| ❑ 293 | Derrick Mason | .60 | .25 |
| ❑ 294 | Jones/Mare/Welker | .75 | .30 |
| ❑ 295 | Stecker/Henderson/Conwell | .50 | .20 |
| ❑ 296 | Mawae/Roos/Olson | .50 | .20 |
| ❑ 297 | M.Bradley/A.Peterson | .50 | .20 |
| ❑ 298 | John Abraham | .50 | .20 |
| ❑ 299 | Dockery/Rabach/Samuels | .50 | .20 |
| ❑ 300 | Peyton Manning | 1.25 | .50 |
| ❑ 301 | Alge Crumpler | .60 | .25 |
| ❑ 302 | Mathis/Richardson/Grant | .50 | .20 |
| ❑ 303 | Tedy Bruschi | .60 | .25 |
| ❑ 304 | Snee/Diehl RC/Whittle | 1.00 | .40 |
| ❑ 305 | J.Stevens/P.Warrick | .50 | .20 |
| ❑ 306 | Trent Dilfer | .60 | .25 |
| ❑ 307 | Marion Barber | .75 | .30 |
| ❑ 308 | Robert Ferguson | .50 | .20 |
| ❑ 309 | Chester Taylor | .60 | .25 |
| ❑ 310 | Jerry Porter | .60 | .25 |
| ❑ 311 | Bunning/Walker/Wade | .50 | .20 |
| ❑ 312 | DeShaun Foster | .60 | .25 |
| ❑ 313 | R.Parrish/K.Holcomb | .50 | .20 |
| ❑ 314 | Chris Brown | .60 | .25 |
| ❑ 315 | Woody/Backus/Raiola | .50 | .20 |
| ❑ 316 | Andre Johnson | .60 | .25 |
| ❑ 317 | S.Graham/K.Larson | .50 | .20 |
| ❑ 318 | Mangum/Gaines/Shelton | .50 | .20 |
| ❑ 319 | Ben Roethlisberger | 1.25 | .50 |
| ❑ 320 | T.Devoe/C.Adams | .50 | .20 |
| ❑ 321 | Jake Delhomme | .60 | .25 |
| ❑ 322 | Chris Chambers | .60 | .25 |
| ❑ 323 | Chris Simms | .60 | .25 |
| ❑ 324 | Ed Reed | .60 | .25 |
| ❑ 325 | Charles Rogers | .60 | .25 |
| ❑ 326 | Eddie Kennison | .50 | .20 |
| ❑ 327 | Seymour/Warren/Wilfork | .50 | .20 |
| ❑ 328 | Lorenzo Neal | .50 | .20 |
| ❑ 329 | Taylor Jacobs | .50 | .20 |
| ❑ 330 | K.Mathis/L.Milloy | .50 | .20 |
| ❑ 331 | Glenn/Henry/Reeves | .50 | .20 |
| ❑ 332 | B.Dawkins/M.Lewis | .60 | .25 |
| ❑ 333 | Edgerrin James | .60 | .25 |
| ❑ 334 | Lee Evans | .60 | .25 |
| ❑ 335 | Pat Williams | .50 | .20 |
| ❑ 336 | Arrington/Torbor/Moore | .75 | .30 |
| ❑ 337 | Roy Williams S | .60 | .25 |
| ❑ 338 | Joe Horn | .60 | .25 |
| ❑ 339 | Keenan McCardell | .60 | .25 |
| ❑ 340 | Lee RC/Nedney/Hicks | .50 | .20 |
| ❑ 341 | Mark Brunell | .60 | .25 |
| ❑ 342 | Jimmy Smith | .60 | .25 |
| ❑ 343 | Deltha O'Neal | .50 | .20 |
| ❑ 344 | Chris McAlister | .50 | .20 |
| ❑ 345 | T.Williamson/J.Kleinsasser | .50 | .20 |
| ❑ 346 | N.Herron/A.Thurman | .50 | .20 |
| ❑ 347 | A.Brown/A.Ogunleye | .50 | .20 |
| ❑ 348 | Michael Vick | .75 | .30 |
| ❑ 349 | Laveranues Coles | .60 | .25 |
| ❑ 350 | Alex Smith QB | .75 | .30 |
| ❑ 351 | Billy Volek | .60 | .25 |
| ❑ 352 | Cato June | .60 | .25 |
| ❑ 353 | J.Jurevicius/F.Jackson | .50 | .20 |
| ❑ 354 | Keary Colbert | .50 | .20 |
| ❑ 355 | Griffith/Schaub/White | .50 | .20 |
| ❑ 356 | Smith/Payne/Walker | .50 | .20 |
| ❑ 357 | Samie Parker | .50 | .20 |
| ❑ 358 | Plaxico Burress | .60 | .25 |
| ❑ 359 | R.Bartell/D.Atogwe | .50 | .20 |
| ❑ 360 | C.Rcby/R.Williams | .50 | .20 |
| ❑ 361 | Springs/Harris/Prioleau | .50 | .20 |
| ❑ 362 | A.Crowell/L.Fletcher | .50 | .20 |
| ❑ 363 | Nick Barnett | .60 | .25 |
| ❑ 364 | Antoine Winfield | .50 | .20 |
| ❑ 365 | Will Smith | .60 | .25 |
| ❑ 366 | J.Jackson/B.Askew | .50 | .20 |
| ❑ 367 | Brian Westbrook | .60 | .25 |
| ❑ 368 | Jerome Mathis | .50 | .20 |

|  |  | | |
|---|---|---|---|
| ❏ 369 | C.Moore/D.Darling | .50 | .20 |
| ❏ 370 | Eric Parker | .50 | .20 |
| ❏ 371 | Bly/Wilson/Kennedy | .50 | .20 |
| ❏ 372 | Champ Bailey | .60 | .25 |
| ❏ 373 | Cedric Benson | .60 | .25 |
| ❏ 374 | Gray RC/Tobeck/Locklear | .50 | .20 |
| ❏ 375 | L.Tynes/D.Colquitt | .50 | .20 |
| ❏ 376 | Dan Morgan | .50 | .20 |
| ❏ 377 | Posey/Schobel/Kelsay | .50 | .20 |
| ❏ 378 | Ekuban/Brown/Myers | .50 | .20 |
| ❏ 379 | Reed/Colclough/Gardocki | .50 | .20 |
| ❏ 380 | M.Pollard/S.Vines | .50 | .20 |
| ❏ 381 | McQuarters/Butler/Deloatch | .50 | .20 |
| ❏ 382 | Fred Smoot | .50 | .20 |
| ❏ 383 | Walter/Anderson/Crockett | .60 | .25 |
| ❏ 384 | Dominic Rhodes | .50 | .20 |
| ❏ 385 | T.Thompson/M.Vanderjagt | .60 | .25 |
| ❏ 386 | Sullivan/Melton/Bryant | .50 | .20 |
| ❏ 387 | M.Scifres/N.Kaeding | .50 | .20 |
| ❏ 388 | Erron Kinney | .50 | .20 |
| ❏ 389 | Bergen/Edwards/McCoy | .50 | .20 |
| ❏ 390 | B.Jones/K.Brady | .60 | .25 |
| ❏ 391 | McKinley/Pool/Baxter | .50 | .20 |
| ❏ 392 | Jackson/Giordano/Hayden | .50 | .20 |
| ❏ 393 | Keith Brooking | .50 | .20 |
| ❏ 394 | Josh Reed | .50 | .20 |
| ❏ 395 | Thomas Jones | .60 | .25 |
| ❏ 396 | D.Johnson CB/S.Spencer | .50 | .20 |
| ❏ 397 | Woolfolk/Clauss/Gardner | .50 | .20 |
| ❏ 398 | Kyle Boller | .60 | .25 |
| ❏ 399 | P.Pass/K.Faulk | .60 | .25 |
| ❏ 400 | Routt/Schweigert/Riddle | .50 | .20 |
| ❏ 401 | Donnie Edwards | .50 | .20 |
| ❏ 402 | Michael Clayton | .60 | .25 |
| ❏ 403 | Kasay/Kyle/Robertson | .50 | .20 |
| ❏ 404 | A.Carroll/A.Harris | .50 | .20 |
| ❏ 405 | Priest Holmes | .60 | .25 |
| ❏ 406 | Jabar Gaffney | .50 | .20 |
| ❏ 407 | Mewelde Moore | .50 | .20 |
| ❏ 408 | Torry Holt | .60 | .25 |
| ❏ 409 | Mark Clayton | .60 | .25 |
| ❏ 410 | Shaun Alexander | .75 | .30 |
| ❏ 411 | T.Tillman/T.Daniels | .50 | .20 |
| ❏ 412 | Deion Branch | .50 | .20 |
| ❏ 413 | Fraley/Andrews/Darilek RC | .50 | .20 |
| ❏ 414 | Anquan Boldin | .60 | .25 |
| ❏ 415 | T.James/K.Ratliff | .50 | .20 |
| ❏ 416 | Ernest Wilford | .50 | .20 |
| ❏ 417 | Moore/Jones/Kendall | .50 | .20 |
| ❏ 418 | Brian Griese | .50 | .20 |
| ❏ 419 | B.Kelly/J.Phillips | .50 | .20 |
| ❏ 420 | Patrick Ramsey | .50 | .20 |
| ❏ 421 | Corey Dillon | .60 | .25 |
| ❏ 422 | Santana Moss | .60 | .25 |
| ❏ 423 | Thomas/Edwards/Boulware | .60 | .25 |
| ❏ 424 | Ashley Lelie | .60 | .25 |
| ❏ 425 | G.Wilson/W.Demps | .75 | .30 |
| ❏ 426 | Darrell Jackson | .50 | .20 |
| ❏ 427 | Williams/Udeze/Scott | .50 | .20 |
| ❏ 428 | K.Lucas/M.Minter | .50 | .20 |
| ❏ 429 | Lee Suggs | .60 | .25 |
| ❏ 430 | Kaczur/Mruczkowski/Gorin | .50 | .20 |
| ❏ 431 | Robert Gallery | .50 | .20 |
| ❏ 432 | Osgood/Feeley/Jackson | .60 | .25 |
| ❏ 433 | Domanick Davis | .60 | .25 |
| ❏ 434 | Osi Umenyiora | .60 | .25 |
| ❏ 435 | Drew Bledsoe | .75 | .30 |
| ❏ 436 | J.Gage/E.Berlin | .50 | .20 |
| ❏ 437 | Rudi Johnson | .60 | .25 |
| ❏ 438 | J.Fargas/M.Tuiasosopo | .60 | .25 |
| ❏ 439 | Antwaan Randle El | .60 | .25 |
| ❏ 440 | Marvin Harrison | .75 | .30 |
| ❏ 441 | Brandon Marshall RC | 2.00 | .75 |
| ❏ 442 | Wali Lundy RC | 1.50 | .60 |
| ❏ 443 | Bruce Gradkowski RC | 1.50 | .60 |
| ❏ 444 | Leonard Pope RC | 1.50 | .60 |
| ❏ 445 | Omar Jacobs RC | 1.25 | .50 |
| ❏ 446 | Travis Wilson RC | 1.50 | .60 |
| ❏ 447 | Derek Hagan RC | 1.50 | .60 |
| ❏ 448 | Devin Hester RC | 3.00 | 1.25 |
| ❏ 449 | Willie Reid RC | 1.50 | .60 |
| ❏ 450 | A.J. Hawk RC | 3.00 | 1.25 |
| ❏ 451 | DeAngelo Williams RC | 2.50 | 1.00 |
| ❏ 452 | Ashton Youboty RC | 1.50 | .60 |

|  |  | | |
|---|---|---|---|
| ❏ 453 | Abdul Hodge RC | 1.50 | .60 |
| ❏ 454 | Leon Washington RC | 1.50 | .60 |
| ❏ 455 | D'Qwell Jackson RC | 1.50 | .60 |
| ❏ 456 | Johnathan Joseph RC | 1.25 | .50 |
| ❏ 457 | Antonio Cromartie RC | 1.50 | .60 |
| ❏ 458 | Michael Robinson RC | 1.50 | .60 |
| ❏ 459 | Tye Hill RC | 1.50 | .60 |
| ❏ 460 | Mathias Kiwanuka RC | 2.00 | .75 |
| ❏ 461 | Vince Young RC | 5.00 | 2.00 |
| ❏ 462 | DeMeco Ryans RC | 2.00 | .75 |
| ❏ 463 | Brodrick Bunkley RC | 1.50 | .60 |
| ❏ 464 | Jay Cutler RC | 6.00 | 2.50 |
| ❏ 465 | Brad Smith RC | 1.50 | .60 |
| ❏ 466 | Elvis Dumervil RC | 1.00 | .40 |
| ❏ 467 | Cory Rodgers RC | 1.50 | .60 |
| ❏ 468 | Davin Joseph RC | 1.25 | .50 |
| ❏ 469 | Rocky McIntosh RC | 1.50 | .60 |
| ❏ 470 | Jason Avant RC | 1.50 | .60 |
| ❏ 471 | Anthony Schlegel RC | 1.25 | .50 |
| ❏ 472 | Kamerion Wimbley RC | 1.50 | .60 |
| ❏ 473 | Joseph Addai RC | 5.00 | 2.00 |
| ❏ 474 | Ernie Sims RC | 1.50 | .60 |
| ❏ 475 | Jimmy Williams RC | 1.50 | .60 |
| ❏ 476 | LenDale White RC | 3.00 | 1.25 |
| ❏ 477 | Brandon Williams RC | 1.50 | .60 |
| ❏ 478 | Ko Simpson RC | 1.25 | .50 |
| ❏ 479 | Jerious Norwood RC | 2.00 | .75 |
| ❏ 480 | P.J. Daniels RC | 1.25 | .50 |
| ❏ 481 | Mario Williams RC | 2.50 | 1.00 |
| ❏ 482 | Santonio Holmes RC | 4.00 | 1.50 |
| ❏ 483 | Joe Klopfenstein RC | 1.25 | .50 |
| ❏ 484 | Matt Leinart RC | 5.00 | 2.00 |
| ❏ 485 | Daniead Manning RC | 1.50 | .60 |
| ❏ 486 | Andre Hall RC | 1.50 | .60 |
| ❏ 487 | Chad Greenway RC | 1.25 | .50 |
| ❏ 488 | Chad Jackson RC | 1.25 | .50 |
| ❏ 489 | Skyler Green RC | 1.50 | .60 |
| ❏ 490 | Donte Whitner RC | 1.50 | .60 |
| ❏ 491 | Bobby Carpenter RC | 1.50 | .60 |
| ❏ 492 | Jovon Bouknight RC | 1.25 | .50 |
| ❏ 493 | Vernon Davis RC | 2.00 | .75 |
| ❏ 494 | Kevin McMahan RC | 1.25 | .50 |
| ❏ 495 | D.J. Shockley RC | 1.50 | .60 |
| ❏ 496 | A.J. Nicholson RC | 1.00 | .40 |
| ❏ 497 | Brian Calhoun RC | 1.25 | .50 |
| ❏ 498 | Tim Day RC | 1.25 | .50 |
| ❏ 499 | Devin Aromashodu RC | 1.50 | .60 |
| ❏ 500 | Charlie Whitehurst RC | 1.50 | .60 |
| ❏ 501 | Sinorice Moss RC | 1.50 | .60 |
| ❏ 502 | Maurice Stovall RC | 1.50 | .60 |
| ❏ 503 | Laurence Maroney RC | 4.00 | 1.50 |
| ❏ 504 | James Anderson RC | 1.00 | .40 |
| ❏ 505 | Darnell Bing RC | 1.50 | .60 |
| ❏ 506 | Jerome Harrison RC | 1.50 | .60 |
| ❏ 507 | Daniel Bullocks RC | 1.50 | .60 |
| ❏ 508 | Will Blackmon RC | 1.50 | .60 |
| ❏ 509 | Marcedes Lewis RC | 1.50 | .60 |
| ❏ 510 | Lawrence Vickers RC | 1.25 | .50 |
| ❏ 511 | Marques Hagans RC | 1.25 | .50 |
| ❏ 512 | Jeremy Bloom RC | 1.25 | .50 |
| ❏ 513 | Dominique Byrd RC | 1.25 | .50 |
| ❏ 514 | Tarvaris Jackson RC | 1.50 | .60 |
| ❏ 515 | Dusty Dvoracek RC | 1.50 | .60 |
| ❏ 516 | Brodie Croyle RC | 2.00 | .75 |
| ❏ 517 | Demetrius Williams RC | 1.50 | .60 |
| ❏ 518 | Jason Allen RC | 1.50 | .60 |
| ❏ 519 | Mike Hass RC | 1.50 | .60 |
| ❏ 520 | Nick Mangold RC | 1.25 | .50 |
| ❏ 521 | Brett Basanez RC | 1.50 | .60 |
| ❏ 522 | Ben Obomanu RC | 1.25 | .50 |
| ❏ 523 | Tamba Hali RC | 1.50 | .60 |
| ❏ 524 | Gabe Watson RC | 1.25 | .50 |
| ❏ 525 | Kelly Jennings RC | 1.50 | .60 |
| ❏ 526 | Reggie Bush RC | 6.00 | 2.50 |
| ❏ 527 | Bernard Pollard RC | .75 | .30 |
| ❏ 528 | Reggie McNeal RC | 1.25 | .50 |
| ❏ 529 | Jonathan Orr RC | 1.25 | .50 |
| ❏ 530 | Haloti Ngata RC | 1.50 | .60 |
| ❏ 531 | David Thomas RC | 1.50 | .60 |
| ❏ 532 | Ingle Martin RC | 1.50 | .60 |
| ❏ 533 | Anthony Fasano RC | 1.50 | .60 |
| ❏ 534 | Winston Justice RC | 1.50 | .60 |
| ❏ 535 | Manny Lawson RC | 1.50 | .60 |
| ❏ 536 | Kellen Clemens RC | 2.00 | .75 |

|  |  | | |
|---|---|---|---|
| ❏ 537 | Adam Jennings RC | 1.25 | .50 |
| ❏ 538 | Thomas Howard RC | 1.50 | .60 |
| ❏ 539 | Cedric Humes RC | 1.50 | .60 |
| ❏ 540 | Garrett Mills RC | 1.50 | .60 |
| ❏ 541 | Jeff Webb RC | 1.25 | .50 |
| ❏ 542 | Michael Huff RC | 1.50 | .60 |
| ❏ 543 | Gerris Wilkinson RC | 1.00 | .40 |
| ❏ 544 | Maurice Drew RC | 3.00 | 1.25 |
| ❏ 545 | John McCargo RC | 1.25 | .50 |
| ❏ 546 | Todd Watkins RC | 1.25 | .50 |
| ❏ 547 | Marcus Vick RC | 1.25 | .50 |
| ❏ 548 | Greg Jennings RC | 2.50 | 1.00 |
| ❏ 549 | P.J. Pope RC | 1.50 | .60 |
| ❏ 550 | D'Brickashaw Ferguson RC | 1.50 | .60 |

### 2007 Topps Total

|  |  | | |
|---|---|---|---|
| ❏ 1 | Cadillac Williams | .60 | .25 |
| ❏ 2 | Marcel Shipp/Troy Walters | .50 | .20 |
| ❏ 3 | Kerry Collins/Brandon Jones | .50 | .20 |
| ❏ 4 | J.J. Arrington | .50 | .20 |
| ❏ 5 | Albert Haynesworth | .50 | .20 |
| ❏ 6 | DeAngelo Hall | .60 | .25 |
| ❏ 7 | Eric Vanden Bosch/Travis LaBoy /Andre Woolfolk | .50 | .20 |
| ❏ 8 | Kyle Boller/Justin Green /Demetrius Williams | .50 | .20 |
| ❏ 9 | Anquan Boldin | .60 | .25 |
| ❏ 10 | Anthony Thomas | .50 | .20 |
| ❏ 11 | Orlando Huff/Leonard Pope /Darnell Dockett | .50 | .20 |
| ❏ 12 | Mike Rucker/Kris Jenkins | .50 | .20 |
| ❏ 13 | Musa Smith/Mike Anderson | .50 | .25 |
| ❏ 14 | DeShaun Foster | .60 | .25 |
| ❏ 15 | Mark Clayton | .60 | .25 |
| ❏ 16 | Mike Minter | | |
| | Ken Lucas | | |
| | Richard Marshall | .50 | .20 |
| ❏ 17 | Ed Reed | .60 | .25 |
| ❏ 18 | Devin Hester | .75 | .30 |
| ❏ 19 | Brian Moorman | | |
| | Craig Nall | | |
| | Rian Lindell | .50 | .20 |
| ❏ 20 | Jamal Lewis | .60 | .25 |
| ❏ 21 | Chris Gamble | .50 | .20 |
| ❏ 22 | Kenny Wright | | |
| | Leigh Bodden | | |
| | Tim Carter | .50 | .20 |
| ❏ 23 | Tommie Harris | | |
| | Tank Johnson | .50 | .20 |
| ❏ 24 | Ryan Tucker | | |
| | Kevin Shaffer RC | | |
| | Hank Fraley | .50 | .20 |
| ❏ 25 | Brad Maynard | | |
| | Robbie Gould | | |
| | Adrian Peterson Bears | .50 | .20 |
| ❏ 26 | Terence Newman | | |
| | Anthony Henry | .50 | .20 |
| ❏ 27 | T.J. Houshmandzadeh | .60 | .25 |
| ❏ 28 | Travis Henry | .60 | .25 |
| ❏ 29 | Julius Jones | .60 | .25 |
| ❏ 30 | Kyle Johnson | | |
| | Nick Ferguson | | |
| | Dre Bly | .50 | .20 |
| ❏ 31 | Leonard Davis | | |
| | Marco Rivera | | |
| | Andre Gurode | .50 | .20 |
| ❏ 32 | Aaron Kampman | | |

| | | |
|---|---|---|
| Kabeer Gbaja-Biamila | .60 | .25 |
| ❑ 33 Demetrin Veal RC | | |
| Gerard Warren | .50 | .20 |
| ❑ 34 Brett Favre | 1.50 | .60 |
| ❑ 35 Mike Bell | .60 | .25 |
| ❑ 36 Ron Dayne | .60 | .25 |
| ❑ 37 Jon Kitna | .50 | .20 |
| ❑ 38 Kris Brown | | |
| Dexter Wynn | | |
| Samkon Gado | .50 | .20 |
| ❑ 39 Daniel Bullocks | | |
| Fernando Bryant | | |
| Kenoy Kennedy | .50 | .20 |
| ❑ 40 Peyton Manning | 1.25 | .50 |
| ❑ 41 Matt Schaub | .60 | .25 |
| ❑ 42 Matt Jones | .60 | .25 |
| ❑ 43 Jim Sorgi | | |
| Ben Utecht | .50 | .20 |
| ❑ 44 Dennis Northcutt | | |
| Josh Scobee | | |
| Alvin Pearman | .50 | .20 |
| ❑ 45 Dallas Clark | .50 | .20 |
| ❑ 46 Kris Wilson | | |
| Michael Bennett | .50 | .20 |
| ❑ 47 Jeff Saturday | | |
| Tarik Glenn | | |
| Ryan Diem | .50 | .20 |
| ❑ 48 Daunte Culpepper | .60 | .25 |
| ❑ 49 Damon Huard | .60 | .25 |
| ❑ 50 Bryant McKinnie | | |
| Matt Birk | | |
| Steve Hutchinson | .50 | .20 |
| ❑ 51 Ty Law | .60 | .25 |
| ❑ 52 Rosevelt Colvin | | |
| Mike Vrabel | .50 | .20 |
| ❑ 53 Brian Waters | | |
| Casey Wiegmann | | |
| Will Shields | .50 | .20 |
| ❑ 54 Chad Jackson | .50 | .20 |
| ❑ 55 Bobby Wade | | |
| Tony Richardson | .50 | .20 |
| ❑ 56 Tedy Bruschi | .75 | .30 |
| ❑ 57 Antoine Winfield | .50 | .20 |
| ❑ 58 Jammal Brown | | |
| Jeff Faine | | |
| Jon Stinchcomb | .50 | .20 |
| ❑ 59 Matt Light | | |
| Logan Mankins | | |
| Dan Koppen | .50 | .20 |
| ❑ 60 Michael Strahan | .60 | .25 |
| ❑ 61 Marques Colston | .75 | .30 |
| ❑ 62 Johnnie Morant | | |
| Ronald Curry | .60 | .25 |
| ❑ 63 Will Demps/Gibril Wilson | .50 | .20 |
| ❑ 64 Warren Sapp | .60 | .25 |
| ❑ 65 William Joseph | | |
| Fred Robbins | | |
| Barry Cofield | .50 | .20 |
| ❑ 66 Chris Carr | | |
| Sebastian Janikowski | | |
| Shane Lechler | .50 | .20 |
| ❑ 67 Cedric Houston | .50 | .20 |
| ❑ 68 Nate Washington | .50 | .20 |
| ❑ 69 Jonathan Vilma | .60 | .25 |
| ❑ 70 Willie Parker | .75 | .30 |
| ❑ 71 Sheldon Brown | | |
| Lito Sheppard | .50 | .20 |
| ❑ 72 Najeh Davenport | | |
| Charlie Batch | | |
| Dan Kreider | .50 | .20 |
| ❑ 73 Jevon Kearse | .60 | .25 |
| ❑ 74 Luis Castillo | | |
| Jamal Williams | .50 | .20 |
| ❑ 75 Darren Howard | | |
| Jerome McDougle | | |
| Trent Cole | .50 | .20 |
| ❑ 76 Vernon Davis | .60 | .25 |
| ❑ 77 Antonio Gates | .75 | .25 |
| ❑ 78 Chris Gray | | |
| Chris Spencer | | |
| Walter Jones | .50 | .20 |
| ❑ 79 Terrence Kiel | | |
| Drayton Florence | | |
| Marlon McCree | .50 | .20 |

| | | |
|---|---|---|
| ❑ 80 Victor Adeyanju | | |
| La'Roi Glover | .50 | .20 |
| ❑ 81 Ashley Lelie | .60 | .25 |
| ❑ 82 Torry Holt | .60 | .25 |
| ❑ 83 Maurice Morris | | |
| Mack Strong | .50 | .20 |
| ❑ 84 Jermaine Phillips | | |
| Will Allen | | |
| Shelton Quarles | .50 | .20 |
| ❑ 85 Shaun Alexander | .60 | .25 |
| ❑ 86 Vince Young | .75 | .30 |
| ❑ 87 Orlando Pace | | |
| Alex Barron | | |
| Andy McCollum | .50 | .20 |
| ❑ 88 Brandon Lloyd | .60 | .25 |
| ❑ 89 Joey Galloway | .60 | .25 |
| ❑ 90 Neil Rackers | | |
| Scott Player | .50 | .20 |
| ❑ 91 Peter Sirmon | | |
| David Thornton | .50 | .20 |
| ❑ 92 Bryant Johnson | .50 | .20 |
| ❑ 93 Bo Scaife | | |
| Cortland Finnegan | | |
| Reynaldo Hill | .50 | .20 |
| ❑ 94 John Abraham | .50 | .20 |
| ❑ 95 Jason Campbell | .60 | .25 |
| ❑ 96 Kelly Gregg | | |
| Bart Scott | | |
| Haloti Ngata | .60 | .25 |
| ❑ 97 Adrian Wilson | .50 | .20 |
| ❑ 98 Drew Carter | | |
| Keary Colbert | .50 | .20 |
| ❑ 99 Michael Jenkins | | |
| D.J. Shockley | | |
| Roddy White | .60 | .25 |
| ❑ 100 Jake Delhomme | .60 | .25 |
| ❑ 101 Terrell Suggs | | |
| Trevor Pryce | .50 | .20 |
| ❑ 102 Thomas Davis | | |
| James Anderson | | |
| Dan Morgan | .50 | .20 |
| ❑ 103 Todd Heap | .50 | .20 |
| ❑ 104 Bernard Berrian | .50 | .20 |
| ❑ 105 Peerless Price | .50 | .20 |
| ❑ 106 Chris Henry | .50 | .20 |
| ❑ 107 Daimon Shelton | | |
| Robert Royal | | |
| Ryan Neufeld | .50 | .20 |
| ❑ 108 Kellen Winslow | .60 | .25 |
| ❑ 109 Rex Grossman | .60 | .25 |
| ❑ 110 Kamerion Wimbley | | |
| D'Qwell Jackson | | |
| Andra Davis | .50 | .20 |
| ❑ 111 Levi Jones | | |
| Willie Anderson | .50 | .20 |
| ❑ 112 Bradie James | | |
| Akin Ayodele | | |
| ❑ 113 Deltha O'Neal | .50 | .20 |
| ❑ 114 Javon Walker | .60 | .25 |
| ❑ 115 Jeremi Johnson | | |
| Doug Johnson | | |
| Reggie Kelly | .50 | .20 |
| ❑ 116 Quincy Morgan | | |
| Jason Elam | | |
| Paul Ernster | .50 | .20 |
| ❑ 117 Roy Williams S | .60 | .25 |
| ❑ 118 Donald Driver | .60 | .25 |
| ❑ 119 Miles Austin | | |
| Mat McBriar | | |
| Sam Hurd | .50 | .20 |
| ❑ 120 Dunta Robinson | | |
| Dexter McCleon | .50 | .20 |
| ❑ 121 Devale Ellis RC | | |
| Shaun McDonald | .50 | .20 |
| ❑ 122 Wali Lundy | .50 | .20 |
| ❑ 123 Tatum Bell | .50 | .20 |
| ❑ 124 Owen Daniels | | |
| Mark Bruener | | |
| Jeb Putzier | .50 | .20 |
| ❑ 125 Marquand Manuel | | |
| Nick Collins | | |
| Al Harris | .50 | .20 |
| ❑ 126 Morton Greenwood | | |
| Shawn Barber | | |

| | | |
|---|---|---|
| Shantee Orr | .50 | .20 |
| ❑ 127 Ahman Green | .60 | .25 |
| ❑ 128 Marvin Harrison | .75 | .30 |
| ❑ 129 Josh Thomas | | |
| Corey Simon | | |
| Raheem Brock | .50 | .20 |
| ❑ 130 Chris Naeole | | |
| Brad Meester | | |
| Maurice Williams | .50 | .20 |
| ❑ 131 Marcus Stroud | | |
| John Henderson | .50 | .20 |
| ❑ 132 Kendrell Bell | | |
| Derrick Johnson | .50 | .20 |
| ❑ 133 Byron Leftwich | .60 | .25 |
| ❑ 134 Trent Green | .60 | .25 |
| ❑ 135 Samie Parker | .50 | .20 |
| ❑ 136 Mewelde Moore | .50 | .20 |
| ❑ 137 Chris Chambers | .60 | .25 |
| ❑ 138 Chris Kluwe/Artose Pinner | | |
| /Ryan Longwell | .50 | .20 |
| ❑ 139 Travis Daniels/Michael Lehan | | |
| /Keith Adams | .50 | .20 |
| ❑ 140 Richard Seymour | .50 | .20 |
| ❑ 141 Jim Kleinsasser/Brooks Bollinger | .50 | .20 |
| ❑ 142 Fred Thomas/Mike McKenzie | .50 | .20 |
| ❑ 143 Darren Sharper | .50 | .20 |
| ❑ 144 Will Smith | .50 | .20 |
| ❑ 145 Ellis Hobbs/Asante Samuel | | |
| /Chad Scott | .50 | .20 |
| ❑ 146 Brian Simmons/Scott Shanle | | |
| /Scott Fujita | .50 | .20 |
| ❑ 147 Devery Henderson | .50 | .20 |
| ❑ 148 Jeremy Shockey | .60 | .25 |
| ❑ 149 Antonio Pierce/Reggie Torbor | .50 | .20 |
| ❑ 150 Zack Crockett/Justin Fargas | .50 | .20 |
| ❑ 151 Jerricho Cotchery | .50 | .20 |
| ❑ 152 Dominic Rhodes | .60 | .25 |
| ❑ 153 D'Brickashaw Ferguson | | |
| /Nick Mangold/Pete Kendall | .50 | .20 |
| ❑ 154 Nnamdi Asomugha/Fabian | | |
| Washington/Stuart Schweigert | .50 | .20 |
| ❑ 155 Andrew Walter | .50 | .20 |
| ❑ 156 Cedrick Wilson | .50 | .20 |
| ❑ 157 Dirk Johnson/David Akers | | |
| /Reno Mahe | .50 | .20 |
| ❑ 158 Troy Polamalu | .75 | .30 |
| ❑ 159 Casey Hampton/Aaron Smith | .50 | .20 |
| ❑ 160 Alan Faneca/Max Starks | | |
| /Marvel Smith | .50 | .20 |
| ❑ 161 Shawne Merriman | .60 | .25 |
| ❑ 162 Shaun Phillips/Randall Godfrey | .50 | .20 |
| ❑ 163 Jonas Jennings/Larry Allen | | |
| /Kwame Harris | .50 | .20 |
| ❑ 164 Nate Clements | .50 | .20 |
| ❑ 165 Marcus Pollard/Seneca Wallace | .50 | .20 |
| ❑ 166 Marcus Trufant/Jordan Babineaux/Kelly | | |
| Jennings | .50 | .20 |
| ❑ 167 Nate Burleson | .50 | .20 |
| ❑ 168 Isaac Bruce | .60 | .25 |
| ❑ 169 Deion Branch | .60 | .25 |
| ❑ 170 Alex Smith TE/Anthony Becht | .50 | .20 |
| ❑ 171 Brandon Chillar/Pisa Tinoisamoa | | |
| /Will Witherspoon | .50 | .20 |
| ❑ 172 Mark Jones/Matt Bryant | | |
| /Josh Bidwell | .50 | .20 |
| ❑ 173 Michael Clayton | .60 | .25 |
| ❑ 174 LenDale White | .60 | .25 |
| ❑ 175 Lamont Thompson/Chris Hope | .50 | .20 |
| ❑ 176 Chris Cooley | .50 | .20 |
| ❑ 177 Santana Moss | .60 | .25 |
| ❑ 178 Chike Okeafor/Bertrand Berry | .50 | .20 |
| ❑ 179 Chris Samuels/Jon Jansen | | |
| /Randy Thomas | .50 | .20 |
| ❑ 180 Matt Leinart | .75 | .30 |
| ❑ 181 Michael Vick | .75 | .30 |
| ❑ 182 Antrel Rolle/Roderick Hood | | |
| /Terrence Holt | .50 | .20 |
| ❑ 183 Michael Koenen/Morten Andersen | | |
| /Allen Rossum | .50 | .20 |
| ❑ 184 Joe Horn | .60 | .25 |
| ❑ 185 Chris McAlister/Samari Rolle | .50 | .20 |
| ❑ 186 Steve McNair | .60 | .25 |
| ❑ 187 Roscoe Parrish | .50 | .20 |
| ❑ 188 Sam Koch/Jonathan Ogden | | |

| | | |
|---|---|---|
| /Matt Stover | .50 | .20 |
| ❑ 189 J.P. Losman | .50 | .20 |
| ❑ 190 John Kasay/Jason Baker | .50 | .20 |
| ❑ 191 Kiwaukee Thomas/Ko Simpson | | |
| /Donte Whitner | .50 | .20 |
| ❑ 192 Steve Smith | .60 | .25 |
| ❑ 193 Cedric Benson | .60 | .25 |
| ❑ 194 Rashied Davis | .50 | .20 |
| ❑ 195 Bryan Robinson/Justin Smith | .50 | .20 |
| ❑ 196 Mark Bradley/Brian Griese | | |
| /Desmond Clark | | .25 |
| ❑ 197 Dexter Jackson/Keiwan | | |
| Ratliff/Johnathan Joseph | .50 | .20 |
| ❑ 198 Carson Palmer | .75 | .30 |
| ❑ 199 Joe Jurevicius | .50 | .20 |
| ❑ 200 Willie McGinest | .50 | .20 |
| ❑ 201 Terry Glenn | .60 | .25 |
| ❑ 202 Joshua Cribbs/Phil Dawson | | |
| /Dave Zastudil | | .20 |
| ❑ 203 DeMarcus Ware/Greg Ellis | | |
| /Marcus Spears | | .25 |
| ❑ 204 Bobby Carpenter/Aaron Glenn | .50 | .20 |
| ❑ 205 Cory Redding/Shaun Rogers | .50 | .20 |
| ❑ 206 Champ Bailey | .60 | .25 |
| ❑ 207 T.J. Duckett | .50 | .20 |
| ❑ 208 Damien Woody/Dominic Raiola | | |
| /Jeff Backus | .50 | .20 |
| ❑ 209 Kevin Jones | .50 | .20 |
| ❑ 210 Greg Jennings | .60 | .25 |
| ❑ 211 Cullen Jenkins/Corey Williams | | |
| /Ryan Pickett | .50 | .20 |
| ❑ 212 Anthony Weaver/Jason Babin | .50 | .20 |
| ❑ 213 Andre Johnson | .60 | .25 |
| ❑ 214 Kevin Walter/Jameel Cook | | |
| /Derrick Lewis | .50 | .20 |
| ❑ 215 Hunter Smith/Terrence Wilkins | | |
| /Adam Vinatieri | .60 | .25 |
| ❑ 216 Bob Sanders | .60 | .25 |
| ❑ 217 Greg Jones/David Garrard | .60 | .25 |
| ❑ 218 Reggie Wayne | .60 | .25 |
| ❑ 219 Fred Taylor | .60 | .25 |
| ❑ 220 Eddie Kennison | .50 | .20 |
| ❑ 221 Marty Booker | .50 | .20 |
| ❑ 222 Jeff Webb/Rod Gardner | | |
| /Dustin Colquitt | .50 | .20 |
| ❑ 223 Ronnie Brown | .60 | .25 |
| ❑ 224 Channing Crowder/Joey Porter | .50 | .20 |
| ❑ 225 Jason Allen/Renaldo Hill | | |
| /Yeremiah Bell | .50 | .20 |
| ❑ 226 Tarvaris Jackson | .60 | .25 |
| ❑ 227 Kevin Williams/Pat Williams | .50 | .20 |
| ❑ 228 Kenechi Udeze/Darrion Scott | | |
| /Dwight Smith | .50 | .20 |
| ❑ 229 Tom Brady | 1.50 | .60 |
| ❑ 230 Roman Harper/Josh Bullocks | .50 | .20 |
| ❑ 231 James Sanders/Rodney | | |
| Harrison/Stephen Gostkowski | .50 | .20 |
| ❑ 232 Terrance Copper | .50 | .20 |
| ❑ 233 Brandon Jacobs | .60 | .25 |
| ❑ 234 Drew Brees | .75 | .30 |
| ❑ 235 Bryan Thomas/Shaun Ellis | .50 | .20 |
| ❑ 236 Amani Toomer | .60 | .25 |
| ❑ 237 Justin Miller | .50 | .20 |
| ❑ 238 Jared Lorenzen/David Tyree | | |
| /Sinorice Moss | .60 | .25 |
| ❑ 239 Brad Smith/Chris Baker | .50 | .20 |
| ❑ 240 Derrick Burgess/Tyler Brayton | .50 | .20 |
| ❑ 241 Jerry Porter | .60 | .25 |
| ❑ 242 Michael Huff | .60 | .25 |
| ❑ 243 Jeremiah Trotter | .50 | .20 |
| ❑ 244 Kirk Morrison/Sam Williams | | |
| /Thomas Howard | .50 | .20 |
| ❑ 245 Shawn Andrews/William Thomas | | |
| /Jon Runyan | .50 | .20 |
| ❑ 246 Santonio Holmes | .60 | .25 |
| ❑ 247 Jerame Tuman/Heath Miller | .50 | .20 |
| ❑ 248 Eric Parker | .50 | .20 |
| ❑ 249 Quentin Jammer | .50 | .20 |
| ❑ 250 Marcus McNeill/Nick Hardwick | | |
| /Mike Goff | .50 | .20 |
| ❑ 251 Mark Roman/Jeff Ulbrich | | |
| /Shawntae Spencer | .50 | .20 |
| ❑ 252 Walt Harris/Michael Lewis | .50 | .20 |
| ❑ 253 LeRoy Hill/Lofa Tatupu | .60 | .25 |

| | | |
|---|---|---|
| ❑ 254 Bryant Young | .50 | .20 |
| ❑ 255 Darrell Jackson | .60 | .25 |
| ❑ 256 Deon Grant/Brian Russell | | |
| /Michael Boulware | .50 | .20 |
| ❑ 257 Drew Bennett | .50 | .20 |
| ❑ 258 Steven Jackson | .75 | .30 |
| ❑ 259 Dane Looker/Gus Frerotte | | |
| /Corey Chavous | .50 | .20 |
| ❑ 260 Ike Hilliard/Michael Pittman | .50 | .20 |
| ❑ 261 Simeon Rice | .50 | .20 |
| ❑ 262 Roydell Williams | .50 | .20 |
| ❑ 263 Mark Brunell/James Thrash | .60 | .25 |
| ❑ 264 Ben Troupe/Kevin Mawae | | |
| /Erron Kinney | .50 | .20 |
| ❑ 265 Clinton Portis | .60 | .25 |
| ❑ 266 Larry Fitzgerald | .75 | .30 |
| ❑ 267 Carlos Rogers/Fred Smoot | | |
| /Shawn Springs | .50 | .20 |
| ❑ 268 Gerald Hayes/Calvin Pace | | |
| /Karlos Dansby | .50 | .20 |
| ❑ 269 Warrick Dunn | .60 | .25 |
| ❑ 270 Keith Brooking/Brian Finneran | .50 | .20 |
| ❑ 271 Kynan Forney/Wayne Gandy | | |
| /Todd McClure | .50 | .20 |
| ❑ 272 Jerious Norwood | .50 | .20 |
| ❑ 273 Josh Reed/Shaud Williams | .50 | .20 |
| ❑ 274 Willis McGahee | .60 | .25 |
| ❑ 275 Terrence McGee | .50 | .20 |
| ❑ 276 Ronnie Prude/Jarret Johnson | | |
| /Dawan Landry | .50 | .20 |
| ❑ 277 Lee Evans | .60 | .25 |
| ❑ 278 Keyshawn Johnson | .60 | .25 |
| ❑ 279 Jordan Gross/Mike Wahle | | |
| /Will Montgomery | .50 | .20 |
| ❑ 280 Alex Brown/Adewale Ogunleye | .50 | .20 |
| ❑ 281 Muhsin Muhammad | .50 | .20 |
| ❑ 282 Olin Kreutz/John Tait/Fred Miller | .50 | .20 |
| ❑ 283 Glenn Holt RC/Kyle Larson | | |
| /Shayne Graham | .50 | .20 |
| ❑ 284 Chris Perry | .50 | .25 |
| ❑ 285 Derek Anderson/Ken Dorsey | .50 | .20 |
| ❑ 286 Chad Johnson | .60 | .25 |
| ❑ 287 Charlie Frye | .60 | .25 |
| ❑ 288 Orpheus Roye/Ted Washington | | |
| /Robaire Smith | .50 | .20 |
| ❑ 289 Jason Witten | .60 | .25 |
| ❑ 290 Tony Romo | 1.50 | .60 |
| ❑ 291 D.J. Williams/Ian Gold/Al Wilson | .50 | .20 |
| ❑ 292 Ebenezer Ekuban/Kenard Lang | .50 | .20 |
| ❑ 293 Paris Lenon/Boss Bailey | .50 | .20 |
| ❑ 294 Rod Smith | .60 | .25 |
| ❑ 295 Mike Furrey | .60 | .25 |
| ❑ 296 Nick Harris/Jason Hanson | | |
| /Eddie Drummond | .50 | .20 |
| ❑ 297 Robert Ferguson | .50 | .20 |
| ❑ 298 Charles Woodson | .60 | .25 |
| ❑ 299 Chad Clifton/Mark Tauscher | | |
| /Rob Davis | .50 | .20 |
| ❑ 300 Travis Johnson/C.C. Brown | | |
| /Glenn Earl | .50 | .20 |
| ❑ 301 Mario Williams | .60 | .25 |
| ❑ 302 Anthony McFarland | | |
| /Robert Mathis | .50 | .20 |
| ❑ 303 George Wrighster/Marcedes Lewis | .50 | .20 |
| ❑ 304 Joseph Addai | .75 | .30 |
| ❑ 305 Maurice Jones-Drew | .75 | .30 |
| ❑ 306 Ernest Wilford | .50 | .20 |
| ❑ 307 Donovin Darius/Nick Greisen | | |
| /Mike Peterson | .50 | .20 |
| ❑ 308 Larry Johnson | .60 | .25 |
| ❑ 309 Derek Hagan | .50 | .20 |
| ❑ 310 Ron Edwards/James Reed | | |
| /Jimmy Wilkerson | .50 | .20 |
| ❑ 311 Zach Thomas | .60 | .25 |
| ❑ 312 Vonnie Holliday/Keith Traylor | .50 | .20 |
| ❑ 313 Jason Rader/L.J. Shelton | | |
| /Cleo Lemon | .50 | .20 |
| ❑ 314 Chester Taylor | .50 | .20 |
| ❑ 315 Jabar Gaffney/Reche Caldwell | .50 | .20 |
| ❑ 316 E.J. Henderson/Dontarrious Thomas/Ben | | |
| Leber | .50 | .20 |
| ❑ 317 Donte Stallworth | .60 | .25 |
| ❑ 318 Jamie Martin/Mike Karney | .50 | .20 |
| ❑ 319 Hollis Thomas/Brian Young | | |

| | | |
|---|---|---|
| Charles Grant | .50 | .20 |
| ❑ 320 Reuben Droughns | .60 | .25 |
| ❑ 321 Eli Manning | .75 | .30 |
| ❑ 322 Corey Webster/R.W. McQuarters | | |
| /Sam Madison | | .50 | .20 |
| ❑ 323 Erik Coleman/Kerry Rhodes | .50 | .20 |
| ❑ 324 Chad Pennington | .60 | .25 |
| ❑ 325 DeWayne Robertson | | |
| /Kimo Von Oelhoffen/Andre Dyson | .50 | .20 |
| ❑ 326 Courtney Anderson | | |
| /Robert Gallery/Randal Williams | .50 | .20 |
| ❑ 327 Randy Moss | .75 | .30 |
| ❑ 328 Brodrick Bunkley/Mike Patterson | .50 | .20 |
| ❑ 329 Correll Buckhalter | .60 | .25 |
| ❑ 330 Donovan McNabb | .75 | .30 |
| ❑ 331 Chris Gardocki/Jeff Reed | .50 | .20 |
| ❑ 332 Vincent Jackson | .50 | .20 |
| ❑ 333 Ben Roethlisberger | 1.00 | .40 |
| ❑ 334 Philip Rivers | .75 | .30 |
| ❑ 335 Larry Foote/Clark Haggans | | |
| /James Farrior | .50 | .20 |
| ❑ 336 Billy Volek/Brandon Manumaleuna | | |
| /Nate Kaeding | .50 | .20 |
| ❑ 337 Alex Smith QB | .75 | .30 |
| ❑ 338 Marques Douglas/Manny Lawson | .50 | .20 |
| ❑ 339 Maurice Hicks/Joe Nedney | | |
| /Andy Lee | .50 | .20 |
| ❑ 340 D.J. Hackett | .50 | .20 |
| ❑ 341 Julian Peterson | .50 | .20 |
| ❑ 342 Patrick Kerney/Bryce Fisher | | |
| /Rocky Bernard | .50 | .20 |
| ❑ 343 Randy McMichael/Joe Klopfenstein | .50 | .20 |
| ❑ 344 Leonard Little | .50 | .20 |
| ❑ 345 Jeff Garcia | .60 | .25 |
| ❑ 346 Cato June/Derrick Brooks | .50 | .20 |
| ❑ 347 Mike Alstott | .60 | .25 |
| ❑ 348 Keith Bulluck | .50 | .20 |
| ❑ 349 Kevin Carter/Greg Spires | | |
| /Chris Hovan | .50 | .20 |
| ❑ 350 Courtney Roby/Craig Hentrich | | |
| /Rob Bironas | .50 | .20 |
| ❑ 351 London Fletcher | | |
| /Marcus Washington | .50 | .20 |
| ❑ 352 Edgerrin James | .60 | .25 |
| ❑ 353 Antwaan Randle El | .50 | .20 |
| ❑ 354 Obafemi Ayanbadejo/Kurt Warner | | |
| /Sean Morey | .50 | .20 |
| ❑ 355 Renaldo Wynn/Phillip Daniels | | |
| /Andre Carter | .50 | .20 |
| ❑ 356 Roy Williams WR | .60 | .25 |
| ❑ 357 Alge Crumpler | .60 | .25 |
| ❑ 358 Brian Dawkins | .60 | .25 |
| ❑ 359 Chris Crocker/Lawyer Milloy/Jimmy | | |
| Williams | .50 | .20 |
| ❑ 360 Reggie Bush | 1.00 | .40 |
| ❑ 361 Chris Kelsay/Angelo Crowell | .50 | .20 |
| ❑ 362 Sean Taylor | .60 | .25 |
| ❑ 363 Aaron Schobel | .50 | .20 |
| ❑ 364 Rock Cartwright/Ladell Betts | | |
| /Mike Sellers | .50 | .20 |
| ❑ 365 DeAngelo Williams | .75 | .30 |
| ❑ 366 Grady Jackson/Rod Coleman | .50 | .20 |
| ❑ 367 David Carr/Brad Hoover | | |
| /Michael Gaines | .60 | .25 |
| ❑ 368 Derrick Mason | .50 | .20 |
| ❑ 369 Brian Urlacher | .75 | .30 |
| ❑ 370 Ray Lewis | .75 | .30 |
| ❑ 371 Robert Geathers | | |
| /Madieu Williams/Landon Johnson | .50 | .20 |
| ❑ 372 Langston Walker/Jason Peters | | |
| /Derrick Dockery | .50 | .20 |
| ❑ 373 Jason Wright/Jerome Harrison | .50 | .20 |
| ❑ 374 Julius Peppers | .60 | .25 |
| ❑ 375 Braylon Edwards | .60 | .25 |
| ❑ 376 Lance Briggs/Mark Anderson | .50 | .20 |
| ❑ 377 Jay Cutler | .75 | .30 |
| ❑ 378 Nathan Vasher/Charles Tillman | | |
| /Ricky Manning Jr | .50 | .20 |
| ❑ 379 Brandon Marshall | | |
| /Daniel Graham/Patrick Ramsey | .60 | .25 |
| ❑ 380 Rudi Johnson | .60 | .25 |
| ❑ 381 Ernie Sims | .50 | .20 |
| ❑ 382 Marion Barber | .75 | .30 |
| ❑ 383 Bubba Franks/Aaron Rodgers | .75 | .30 |

|  |  | | |
|---|---|---|---|
| ❑ 384 | Terrell Owens | .75 | .30 |
| ❑ 385 | Vernand Morency | .60 | .25 |
| ❑ 386 | Brad Johnson/Anthony Fasano /Patrick Crayton | .60 | .25 |
| ❑ 387 | Nick Barnett/Will Blackmon /Abdul Hodge | .60 | .25 |
| ❑ 388 | John Engelberger/Elvis Dumervil | .50 | .20 |
| ❑ 389 | DeMeco Ryans RC | .60 | .25 |
| ❑ 390 | John Lynch | .60 | .25 |
| ❑ 391 | Rasheam Mathis | .50 | .20 |
| ❑ 392 | Shawn Bryson/Brian Calhoun /Dan Campbell | .50 | .20 |
| ❑ 393 | Brian Williams/Paul Spicer /Reggie Hayward | .50 | .20 |
| ❑ 394 | A.J. Hawk | .75 | .30 |
| ❑ 395 | Tamba Hali/Jared Allen | .50 | .20 |
| ❑ 396 | Gary Brackett/Rob Morris | .50 | .20 |
| ❑ 397 | Jason Taylor | .50 | .20 |
| ❑ 398 | Dwight Freeney | .60 | .25 |
| ❑ 399 | Donnie Spragan/Matt Roth /Travares Tillman | .50 | .20 |
| ❑ 400 | Marlin Jackson/Matt Giordano /Antoine Bethea | .50 | .20 |
| ❑ 401 | Ty Warren/Vince Wilfork | .50 | .20 |
| ❑ 402 | Reggie Williams | .60 | .25 |
| ❑ 403 | Wes Welker | .75 | .30 |
| ❑ 404 | Tony Gonzalez | .60 | .25 |
| ❑ 405 | Laurence Maroney | .75 | .30 |
| ❑ 406 | Patrick Surtain/Greg Wesley /Sammy Knight | .50 | .20 |
| ❑ 407 | Steve Weatherford/Michael Lewis /John Carney | .50 | .20 |
| ❑ 408 | Will Allen/Andre Goodman | .50 | .20 |
| ❑ 409 | Plaxico Burress | .60 | .25 |
| ❑ 410 | Troy Williamson | .50 | .20 |
| ❑ 411 | Victor Hobson/Eric Barton | .50 | .20 |
| ❑ 412 | Ben Watson/Matt Cassel /Kevin Faulk | .75 | .30 |
| ❑ 413 | Justin McCareins/Mike Nugent /Ben Graham | .50 | .20 |
| ❑ 414 | Deuce McAllister | .60 | .25 |
| ❑ 415 | LaMont Jordan | .60 | .25 |
| ❑ 416 | Osi Umenyiora/Mathias Kiwanuka | .50 | .20 |
| ❑ 417 | Reggie Brown | .60 | .25 |
| ❑ 418 | Shaun O'Hara/Kareem McKenzie /Chris Snee | .50 | .20 |
| ❑ 419 | Hines Ward | .75 | .30 |
| ❑ 420 | Leon Washington | .50 | .20 |
| ❑ 421 | Ike Taylor/Deshea Townsend /Bryant McFadden | .50 | .20 |
| ❑ 422 | Laveranues Coles | .50 | .20 |
| ❑ 423 | Lorenzo Neal/Michael Turner | .60 | .25 |
| ❑ 424 | Dhani Jones/Takeo Spikes | .50 | .20 |
| ❑ 425 | Frank Gore | .75 | .30 |
| ❑ 426 | Brian Westbrook | .60 | .25 |
| ❑ 427 | Michael Robinson/Moran Norris /Trent Dilfer | .60 | .25 |
| ❑ 428 | Kevin Curtis/Hank Baskett /Greg Lewis | .50 | .20 |
| ❑ 429 | Fakhir Brown/Tye Hill | .50 | .20 |
| ❑ 430 | LaDainian Tomlinson | 1.00 | .40 |
| ❑ 431 | Marc Bulger | .60 | .25 |
| ❑ 432 | Matt Wilhelm/Igor Olshansky /Antonio Cromartie | .50 | .20 |
| ❑ 433 | Chris Simms | .50 | .20 |
| ❑ 434 | Derek Smith/LB/Tully Banta-Cain | .50 | .20 |
| ❑ 435 | Ronde Barber/Brian Kelly /Phillip Buchanon | .50 | .20 |
| ❑ 436 | Arnaz Battle | .50 | .20 |
| ❑ 437 | David Givens | .50 | .20 |
| ❑ 438 | Matt Hasselbeck | .60 | .25 |
| ❑ 439 | Cornelius Griffin/Rocky McIntosh | .50 | .20 |
| ❑ 440 | Dominique Byrd/Jeff Wilkins /Aaron Walker | .50 | .20 |
| ❑ 441 | JaMarcus Russell RC | 4.00 | 1.50 |
| ❑ 442 | Brady Quinn RC | 5.00 | 2.00 |
| ❑ 443 | Drew Stanton RC | 1.50 | .60 |
| ❑ 444 | Troy Smith RC | 2.00 | .75 |
| ❑ 445 | Kevin Kolb RC | 2.50 | 1.00 |
| ❑ 446 | Trent Edwards RC | 4.00 | 1.50 |
| ❑ 447 | John Beck RC | 1.50 | .60 |
| ❑ 448 | Jordan Palmer RC | 1.50 | .60 |
| ❑ 449 | Chris Leak RC | 1.25 | .50 |
| ❑ 450 | Isiah Stanback RC | 1.50 | .60 |

|  |  | | |
|---|---|---|---|
| ❑ 451 | Tyler Palko RC | 1.50 | .60 |
| ❑ 452 | Jared Zabransky RC | 1.50 | .60 |
| ❑ 453 | Jeff Rowe RC | 1.25 | .50 |
| ❑ 454 | Zac Taylor RC | 1.50 | .60 |
| ❑ 455 | Lester Ricard RC | 3.00 | 1.25 |
| ❑ 456 | Adrian Peterson RC | 12.00 | 5.00 |
| ❑ 457 | Marshawn Lynch RC | 3.00 | 1.25 |
| ❑ 458 | Brandon Jackson RC | 1.50 | .60 |
| ❑ 459 | Michael Bush RC | 1.50 | .60 |
| ❑ 460 | Kenny Irons RC | 1.50 | .60 |
| ❑ 461 | Antonio Pittman RC | 1.50 | .60 |
| ❑ 462 | Tony Hunt RC | 1.50 | .60 |
| ❑ 463 | Darius Walker RC | 1.50 | .60 |
| ❑ 464 | Dwayne Wright RC | 1.25 | .50 |
| ❑ 465 | Lorenzo Booker RC | 1.50 | .60 |
| ❑ 466 | Kenneth Darby RC | 1.50 | .60 |
| ❑ 467 | Chris Henry RC | 1.50 | .60 |
| ❑ 468 | Selvin Young RC | 2.50 | 1.00 |
| ❑ 469 | Brian Leonard RC | 1.50 | .60 |
| ❑ 470 | Ahmad Bradshaw RC | 2.00 | .75 |
| ❑ 471 | Gary Russell RC | 1.50 | .60 |
| ❑ 472 | Kolby Smith RC | 1.50 | .60 |
| ❑ 473 | Thomas Clayton RC | 1.25 | .50 |
| ❑ 474 | Garrett Wolfe RC | 1.50 | .60 |
| ❑ 475 | Calvin Johnson RC | 4.00 | 1.50 |
| ❑ 476 | Ted Ginn Jr. RC | 2.50 | 1.00 |
| ❑ 477 | Dwayne Jarrett RC | 1.50 | .60 |
| ❑ 478 | Dwayne Bowe RC | 3.00 | 1.25 |
| ❑ 479 | Sidney Rice RC | 1.50 | .60 |
| ❑ 480 | Robert Meachem RC | 1.50 | .60 |
| ❑ 481 | Anthony Gonzalez RC | 2.50 | 1.00 |
| ❑ 482 | Craig Buster Davis RC | 1.50 | .60 |
| ❑ 483 | Aundrae Allison RC | 1.25 | .50 |
| ❑ 484 | Chansi Stuckey RC | 1.25 | .50 |
| ❑ 485 | David Clowney RC | 1.25 | .50 |
| ❑ 486 | Steve Smith RC | 2.00 | .75 |
| ❑ 487 | Courtney Taylor RC | 1.25 | .50 |
| ❑ 488 | Paul Williams RC | 1.25 | .50 |
| ❑ 489 | Johnnie Lee Higgins RC | 1.25 | .50 |
| ❑ 490 | Rhema McKnight RC | 1.25 | .50 |
| ❑ 491 | Jason Hill RC | 1.50 | .60 |
| ❑ 492 | Dallas Baker RC | 1.25 | .50 |
| ❑ 493 | Greg Olsen RC | 2.00 | .75 |
| ❑ 494 | Yamon Figurs RC | 1.50 | .60 |
| ❑ 495 | Scott Chandler RC | 1.25 | .50 |
| ❑ 496 | Matt Spaeth RC | 1.50 | .60 |
| ❑ 497 | Ben Patrick RC | 1.25 | .50 |
| ❑ 498 | Clark Harris RC | 1.25 | .50 |
| ❑ 499 | Martrez Milner RC | 1.25 | .50 |
| ❑ 500 | Joe Newton RC | 1.25 | .50 |
| ❑ 501 | Alan Branch RC | 1.25 | .50 |
| ❑ 502 | Amobi Okoye RC | 1.50 | .60 |
| ❑ 503 | DeMarcus Tank Tyler RC | 1.50 | .60 |
| ❑ 504 | Justin Harrell RC | 1.50 | .60 |
| ❑ 505 | Brandon Mebane RC | 1.25 | .50 |
| ❑ 506 | Gaines Adams RC | 1.50 | .60 |
| ❑ 507 | Jamaal Anderson RC | 1.25 | .50 |
| ❑ 508 | Adam Carriker RC | 1.25 | .50 |
| ❑ 509 | Jarvis Moss RC | 1.50 | .60 |
| ❑ 510 | Charles Johnson RC | 1.00 | .40 |
| ❑ 511 | Anthony Spencer RC | 1.50 | .60 |
| ❑ 512 | Quentin Moses RC | 1.25 | .50 |
| ❑ 513 | LaMarr Woodley RC | 1.50 | .60 |
| ❑ 514 | Victor Abiamiri RC | 1.25 | .50 |
| ❑ 515 | Ray McDonald RC | 1.25 | .50 |
| ❑ 516 | Tim Crowder RC | 1.50 | .60 |
| ❑ 517 | Patrick Willis RC | 3.00 | 1.25 |
| ❑ 518 | Brandon Siler RC | 1.25 | .50 |
| ❑ 519 | David Harris RC | 1.25 | .50 |
| ❑ 520 | Buster Davis RC | 1.25 | .50 |
| ❑ 521 | Lawrence Timmons RC | 1.50 | .60 |
| ❑ 522 | Paul Posluszny RC | 2.00 | .75 |
| ❑ 523 | Jon Beason RC | 1.50 | .60 |
| ❑ 524 | Rufus Alexander RC | 1.50 | .60 |
| ❑ 525 | Earl Everett RC | 1.25 | .50 |
| ❑ 526 | Stewart Bradley RC | 1.25 | .50 |
| ❑ 527 | Prescott Burgess RC | 1.25 | .50 |
| ❑ 528 | Leon Hall RC | 1.50 | .60 |
| ❑ 529 | Darrelle Revis RC | 1.50 | .60 |
| ❑ 530 | Aaron Ross RC | 1.50 | .60 |
| ❑ 531 | Daymeion Hughes RC | 1.25 | .50 |
| ❑ 532 | Marcus McCauley RC | 1.25 | .50 |
| ❑ 533 | Chris Houston RC | 1.25 | .50 |
| ❑ 534 | Tanard Jackson RC | 1.00 | .40 |

|  |  | | |
|---|---|---|---|
| ❑ 535 | Jonathan Wade RC | 1.25 | .50 |
| ❑ 536 | Josh Wilson RC | 1.25 | .50 |
| ❑ 537 | Eric Wright RC | 1.50 | .60 |
| ❑ 538 | A.J. Davis RC | 1.00 | .40 |
| ❑ 539 | David Irons RC | 1.00 | .40 |
| ❑ 540 | LaRon Landry RC | 2.00 | .75 |
| ❑ 541 | Reggie Nelson RC | 1.25 | .50 |
| ❑ 542 | Michael Griffin RC | 1.50 | .60 |
| ❑ 543 | Brandon Meriweather RC | 1.50 | .60 |
| ❑ 544 | Eric Weddle RC | 1.25 | .50 |
| ❑ 545 | Aaron Rouse RC | 1.50 | .60 |
| ❑ 546 | Josh Gattis RC | 1.00 | .40 |
| ❑ 547 | Joe Thomas RC | 1.50 | .60 |
| ❑ 548 | Levi Brown RC | 1.50 | .60 |
| ❑ 549 | Tony Ugoh RC | 1.25 | .50 |
| ❑ 550 | Ryan Kalil RC | 1.25 | .50 |

## 2005 Topps Turkey Red

| | | | |
|---|---|---|---|
| ❑ COMPLETE SET (299) | | 250.00 | 125.00 |
| ❑ COMP.SET w/o SP's (249). | | 60.00 | 25.00 |
| ❑ SP STATED ODDS 1:4 | | | |
| ❑ UNPRICED WOOD/1 ODDS 1:2072H, 1:2089R | | | |
| ❑ 1A | Eli Manning | 2.00 | .75 |
| ❑ 1B | Eli Manning Ad Back | 10.00 | 4.00 |
| ❑ 2 | Clinton Portis | 1.00 | .40 |
| ❑ 3 | Charles Woodson | .75 | .30 |
| ❑ 4A | Ray Lewis | 1.00 | .40 |
| ❑ 4B | Ray Lewis Ad Back | 5.00 | 2.00 |
| ❑ 5 | Michael Clayton | .75 | .30 |
| ❑ 6 | Eric Moulds | .75 | .30 |
| ❑ 7 | Derrick Blaylock | .60 | .25 |
| ❑ 8 | Carson Palmer | 1.00 | .40 |
| ❑ 9 | Zach Thomas | 1.00 | .40 |
| ❑ 10 | Dallas Clark | .75 | .30 |
| ❑ 11 | DeAngelo Hall | .75 | .30 |
| ❑ 12 | Terrell Owens | 1.00 | .40 |
| ❑ 13 | Brian Griese | .75 | .30 |
| ❑ 14 | Dunta Robinson | .60 | .25 |
| ❑ 15 | Kevan Barlow | .60 | .25 |
| ❑ 16 | Jake Plummer | .75 | .30 |
| ❑ 17 | James Farrior | .60 | .25 |
| ❑ 18A | Peyton Manning | 1.50 | .60 |
| ❑ 18B | Peyton Manning Ad Back | 8.00 | 3.00 |
| ❑ 19 | Michael Bennett | .75 | .30 |
| ❑ 20 | Brian Urlacher | 1.00 | .40 |
| ❑ 21 | Dante Hall | .75 | .30 |
| ❑ 22 | Deion Branch | .75 | .30 |
| ❑ 23 | Billy Volek | .75 | .30 |
| ❑ 24 | Donald Driver | 1.00 | .40 |
| ❑ 25 | LaDainian Tomlinson CL | 1.25 | .50 |
| ❑ 26 | Donte Stallworth CL | .60 | .25 |
| ❑ 27 | Joey Galloway | .75 | .30 |
| ❑ 28 | Joey Harrington | 1.00 | .40 |
| ❑ 29 | T.J. Houshmandzadeh | .75 | .30 |
| ❑ 30 | LaDainian Tomlinson | 1.50 | .60 |
| ❑ 31 | Darius Watts | .60 | .25 |
| ❑ 32 | Chris Gamble | .60 | .25 |
| ❑ 33 | Javon Walker | .75 | .30 |
| ❑ 34 | Kevin Curtis | .75 | .30 |
| ❑ 35 | Steven Jackson | 1.25 | .50 |
| ❑ 36 | J.P. Losman | .75 | .30 |
| ❑ 37A | Champ Bailey | .75 | .30 |
| ❑ 37B | Champ Bailey Ad Back | 4.00 | 1.50 |
| ❑ 38 | Tiki Barber | 1.00 | .40 |
| ❑ 39 | LaVar Arrington | .75 | .30 |
| ❑ 40 | Byron Leftwich | .75 | .30 |

|  |  | | |
|---|---|---|---|
| ❑ 41 | Edgerrin James | .75 | .30 |
| ❑ 42 | DeShaun Foster | .75 | .30 |
| ❑ 43 | Darrell Jackson | .75 | .30 |
| ❑ 44 | Julius Peppers | .75 | .30 |
| ❑ 45 | David Carr | .75 | .30 |
| ❑ 46 | Drew Bennett | .75 | .30 |
| ❑ 47 | Antonio Gates | 1.00 | .40 |
| ❑ 48A | Deuce McAllister | 1.00 | .40 |
| ❑ 48B | Deuce McAllister Ad Back | 5.00 | 2.00 |
| ❑ 49 | Patrick Ramsey | .75 | .30 |
| ❑ 50 | Antonio Bryant | .60 | .25 |
| ❑ 51 | Quentin Jammer | .60 | .25 |
| ❑ 52 | Chris Brown | .75 | .30 |
| ❑ 53 | Eddie Kennison | .75 | .30 |
| ❑ 54 | Steve McNair | 1.00 | .40 |
| ❑ 55 | Corey Bradford | .75 | .30 |
| ❑ 56 | Chris Perry | .60 | .25 |
| ❑ 57 | Curtis Martin | 1.00 | .40 |
| ❑ 58 | Mewelde Moore | .60 | .25 |
| ❑ 59 | Travis Taylor | .60 | .25 |
| ❑ 60 | Chad Pennington | 1.00 | .40 |
| ❑ 61 | Chad Johnson | .75 | .30 |
| ❑ 62 | Kyle Boller | .75 | .30 |
| ❑ 63 | Tyrone Calico | .75 | .30 |
| ❑ 64 | Michael Pittman | .60 | .25 |
| ❑ 65 | Kerry Collins | .75 | .30 |
| ❑ 66 | Keary Colbert | .60 | .25 |
| ❑ 67 | LaMont Jordan CL | .60 | .25 |
| ❑ 68 | Robert Gallery | .75 | .30 |
| ❑ 69 | Derrick Mason | .75 | .30 |
| ❑ 70 | Brian Dawkins | .75 | .30 |
| ❑ 71 | Chris Simms | .75 | .30 |
| ❑ 72 | Marc Bulger | .75 | .30 |
| ❑ 73 | Stephen Davis | .75 | .30 |
| ❑ 74 | Kurt Warner | 1.00 | .40 |
| ❑ 75 | Todd Heap | .75 | .30 |
| ❑ 76 | Domanick Davis CL | .50 | .20 |
| ❑ 77 | Shaun Alexander | 1.00 | .40 |
| ❑ 78 | Jerry Porter | .75 | .30 |
| ❑ 79 | Chester Taylor | .75 | .30 |
| ❑ 80A | Michael Vick | 1.00 | .40 |
| ❑ 80B | Michael Vick Ad Back | 5.00 | 2.00 |
| ❑ 81 | Justin McCareins | .75 | .30 |
| ❑ 82 | Fred Taylor | 1.00 | .40 |
| ❑ 83 | Laveranues Coles | .75 | .30 |
| ❑ 84 | Steve Smith | 1.00 | .40 |
| ❑ 85 | Sean Taylor | .75 | .30 |
| ❑ 86 | Marvin Harrison | 1.00 | .40 |
| ❑ 87 | Ashley Lelie | .60 | .25 |
| ❑ 88 | Willis McGahee | 1.00 | .40 |
| ❑ 89 | Terence Newman | .60 | .25 |
| ❑ 90 | Joe Horn | .75 | .30 |
| ❑ 91 | Lee Suggs | .75 | .30 |
| ❑ 92 | Keyshawn Johnson | .75 | .30 |
| ❑ 93 | Desmond Clark | .60 | .25 |
| ❑ 94 | T.J. Duckett | .60 | .25 |
| ❑ 95 | Reggie Wayne | .75 | .30 |
| ❑ 96 | Donte Stallworth | .75 | .30 |
| ❑ 97 | Clarence Moore | .60 | .25 |
| ❑ 98 | Jason Witten | .75 | .30 |
| ❑ 99 | Jake Delhomme | 1.00 | .40 |
| ❑ 100 | Julius Jones | 1.00 | .40 |
| ❑ 101 | Ben Troupe | .60 | .25 |
| ❑ 102 | Hines Ward | 1.00 | .40 |
| ❑ 103 | Domanick Davis | .60 | .25 |
| ❑ 104 | B.J. Sams | .60 | .25 |
| ❑ 105 | Marcus Robinson | .75 | .30 |
| ❑ 106 | Devery Henderson | .60 | .25 |
| ❑ 107 | Matt Hasselbeck | .75 | .30 |
| ❑ 108 | Antonio Pierce | .60 | .25 |
| ❑ 109 | Santana Moss | .75 | .30 |
| ❑ 110 | Adam Vinatieri | 1.00 | .40 |
| ❑ 111 | Michael Strahan | .75 | .30 |
| ❑ 112 | Greg Jones | .60 | .25 |
| ❑ 113 | Drew Brees | 1.00 | .40 |
| ❑ 114 | Marcus Robinson | .75 | .30 |
| ❑ 115 | Michael Jenkins | .75 | .30 |
| ❑ 116 | Randy McMichael | .60 | .25 |
| ❑ 117 | Jonathan Vilma | .75 | .30 |
| ❑ 118 | Greg Lewis | .75 | .30 |
| ❑ 119 | Ernest Wilford | .75 | .30 |
| ❑ 120 | Warrick Dunn | .75 | .30 |
| ❑ 121 | Shaun Alexander CL | .75 | .30 |
| ❑ 122 | Donnie Edwards | .60 | .25 |
| ❑ 123 | Antwaan Randle El | .75 | .30 |
| ❑ 124 | Rod Smith | .75 | .30 |
| ❑ 125 | Ed Reed | .75 | .30 |
| ❑ 126 | Muhsin Muhammad | .75 | .30 |
| ❑ 127 | L.J. Smith | .75 | .30 |
| ❑ 128 | Chris Chambers | .75 | .30 |
| ❑ 129 | Matt Schaub | 1.00 | .40 |
| ❑ 130 | Andre Johnson | .75 | .30 |
| ❑ 131 | Thomas Jones | .75 | .30 |
| ❑ 132 | Robert Ferguson | .75 | .30 |
| ❑ 133 | Jeremy Shockey | 1.00 | .40 |
| ❑ 134 | William Green | .60 | .25 |
| ❑ 135A | Ben Roethlisberger | 2.50 | 1.00 |
| ❑ 135B | Ben Roethlisberger Ad Back | 12.00 | 5.00 |
| ❑ 136A | Donovan McNabb | 1.00 | .40 |
| ❑ 136B | Donovan McNabb Ad Back | 5.00 | 2.00 |
| ❑ 137 | Duce Staley | .75 | .30 |
| ❑ 138 | Larry Fitzgerald | 1.00 | .40 |
| ❑ 139 | Charles Rogers | .60 | .25 |
| ❑ 140 | Mark Brunell | .75 | .30 |
| ❑ 141 | Kevin Jones | .75 | .30 |
| ❑ 142 | LaMont Jordan | .75 | .30 |
| ❑ 143 | Aaron Brooks | .60 | .25 |
| ❑ 144 | Brian Westbrook | 1.00 | .40 |
| ❑ 145 | Larry Johnson | 1.00 | .40 |
| ❑ 146 | Tommy Maddox | .75 | .30 |
| ❑ 147 | Corey Dillon | .75 | .30 |
| ❑ 148 | William Henderson | .75 | .30 |
| ❑ 149 | Tony Hollings | .60 | .25 |
| ❑ 150 | Lee Evans | .75 | .30 |
| ❑ 151 | Kelly Holcomb | .60 | .25 |
| ❑ 152 | Reuben Droughns | .60 | .25 |
| ❑ 153 | Keenan McCardell | .75 | .30 |
| ❑ 154 | Ricky Williams | .75 | .30 |
| ❑ 155 | Rashaun Woods | .60 | .25 |
| ❑ 156 | D.J. Williams | .60 | .25 |
| ❑ 157 | Tom Brady | 2.00 | .75 |
| ❑ 158 | Eric Parker | .60 | .25 |
| ❑ 159 | Mike Anderson | .60 | .25 |
| ❑ 160 | Roy Williams WR | 1.00 | .40 |
| ❑ 161 | Mike Vanderjagt | .60 | .25 |
| ❑ 162 | Ronald Curry | .75 | .30 |
| ❑ 163 | Priest Holmes | 1.00 | .40 |
| ❑ 164 | Bernard Berrian | .75 | .30 |
| ❑ 165 | Brian Finneran | .60 | .25 |
| ❑ 166 | Tony Gonzalez | .75 | .30 |
| ❑ 167 | Chris McAlister | .60 | .25 |
| ❑ 168 | Gus Frerotte | .50 | .20 |
| ❑ 169 | Bryant Johnson | .75 | .30 |
| ❑ 170 | Jay Fiedler | .60 | .25 |
| ❑ 171 | Bubba Franks | .75 | .30 |
| ❑ 172 | Tony Romo | 10.00 | 5.00 |
| ❑ 173 | Jamal Lewis | .75 | .30 |
| ❑ 174 | Torry Holt | .75 | .30 |
| ❑ 175 | Ladell Betts | .75 | .30 |
| ❑ 176 | Bertrand Berry | .60 | .25 |
| ❑ 177 | Josh McCown | .75 | .30 |
| ❑ 178 | Jonathan Wells | .60 | .25 |
| ❑ 179 | Plaxico Burress | .75 | .30 |
| ❑ 180 | Rudi Johnson | .75 | .30 |
| ❑ 181 | Cedric Benson RC | 2.00 | .75 |
| ❑ 182 | Carlos Rogers RC | 2.00 | .75 |
| ❑ 183 | Terrence Murphy RC | 1.25 | .50 |
| ❑ 184 | Frank Gore RC | 5.00 | 2.00 |
| ❑ 185 | Vincent Jackson RC | 2.00 | .75 |
| ❑ 186 | Ciatrick Fason RC | 1.50 | .60 |
| ❑ 187 | Alex Smith QB RC | 3.00 | 1.25 |
| ❑ 188 | Mike Williams RC | 2.00 | .75 |
| ❑ 189 | Kyle Orton RC | 2.50 | 1.00 |
| ❑ 190A | Ronnie Brown RC | 6.00 | 2.50 |
| ❑ 190B | Ronnie Brown | 10.00 | 4.00 |
| ❑ 191 | Charlie Frye RC | 2.00 | .75 |
| ❑ 192 | Mark Bradley RC | 2.00 | .75 |
| ❑ 193 | Antrel Rolle RC | 2.00 | .75 |
| ❑ 194 | Roscoe Parrish RC | 1.50 | .60 |
| ❑ 195 | Ryan Moats RC | 2.00 | .75 |
| ❑ 196 | Andrew Walter RC | 2.00 | .75 |
| ❑ 197 | Troy Williamson RC | 2.00 | .75 |
| ❑ 198 | Cadillac Williams RC | 4.00 | 1.50 |
| ❑ 199 | Adam Jones RC | 2.00 | .75 |
| ❑ 200 | Braylon Edwards RC | 6.00 | 2.50 |
| ❑ 201 | Vernand Morency RC | 2.00 | .75 |
| ❑ 202 | Ryan Fitzpatrick RC | 2.00 | .75 |
| ❑ 203 | Heath Miller RC | 4.00 | 1.50 |
| ❑ 204 | Eric Shelton RC | 1.50 | .60 |
| ❑ 205 | Jason Campbell RC | 3.00 | 1.25 |
| ❑ 206 | David Pollack RC | 1.50 | .60 |
| ❑ 207 | Stefan LeFors RC | 1.50 | .60 |
| ❑ 208 | DeMarcus Ware RC | 3.00 | 1.25 |
| ❑ 209 | J.J. Arrington RC | 2.00 | .75 |
| ❑ 210 | Marion Barber RC | 6.00 | 2.50 |
| ❑ 211 | Samkon Gado RC | 2.00 | .75 |
| ❑ 212 | Roddy White RC | 2.50 | 1.00 |
| ❑ 213 | Brandon Jacobs RC | 2.50 | 1.00 |
| ❑ 214 | Mark Clayton RC | 2.00 | .75 |
| ❑ 215 | Alex Smith TE RC | 2.00 | .75 |
| ❑ 216 | Darren Sproles RC | 2.50 | 1.00 |
| ❑ 217 | Fabian Washington RC | 2.00 | .75 |
| ❑ 218 | Brandon Jones RC | 2.00 | .75 |
| ❑ 219 | Derrick Johnson RC | 2.00 | .75 |
| ❑ 220 | Dan Orlovsky RC | 2.00 | .75 |
| ❑ 221 | Aaron Rodgers RC | 6.00 | 2.50 |
| ❑ 222 | Cedric Houston RC | 2.00 | .75 |
| ❑ 223 | Reggie Brown RC | 2.00 | .75 |
| ❑ 224 | Scottie Vines RC | 2.00 | .75 |
| ❑ 225 | Willie Parker | 8.00 | 3.00 |
| ❑ 226 | Matt Jones RC | 3.00 | 1.25 |
| ❑ 227 | Odell Thurman RC | 2.00 | .75 |
| ❑ 228 | Alvin Pearman RC | 1.50 | .60 |
| ❑ 229 | Chris Henry RC | 2.00 | .75 |
| ❑ 230 | Courtney Roby RC | 1.50 | .60 |
| ❑ 231 | Isaac Bruce | .75 | .30 |
| ❑ 232 | Warrick Dunn CL | .60 | .25 |
| ❑ 233 | Willis McGahee CL | .75 | .30 |
| ❑ 234 | Marcus Pollard | .60 | .25 |
| ❑ 235 | Jason Taylor | .75 | .30 |
| ❑ 236 | Joe Namath | 6.00 | 2.50 |
| ❑ 237 | Joe Montana | 10.00 | 4.00 |
| ❑ 238 | Barry Sanders | 6.00 | 2.50 |
| ❑ 239 | Jim Brown | 5.00 | 2.00 |
| ❑ 240 | Terry Bradshaw | 6.00 | 2.50 |
| ❑ 241 | Ahman Green | 1.00 | .40 |
| ❑ 242 | Tiki Barber CL | .75 | .30 |
| ❑ 243 | Julius Jones CL | .75 | .30 |
| ❑ 244 | Daunte Culpepper | 1.00 | .40 |
| ❑ 245 | Edgerrin James CL | .60 | .25 |
| ❑ 246 | Trent Green | 6.00 | 2.50 |
| ❑ 247 | Dwight Freeney | 6.00 | 2.50 |
| ❑ 248A | Brett Favre | 12.00 | 5.00 |
| ❑ 248B | Brett Favre Ad Back | 15.00 | 6.00 |
| ❑ 249 | Marshall Faulk | 8.00 | 3.00 |
| ❑ 250 | Jerome Bettis | 8.00 | 3.00 |
| ❑ 251 | Nate Burleson | 6.00 | 2.50 |
| ❑ 252 | Brandon Lloyd | 5.00 | 2.00 |
| ❑ 253 | Randy Moss | 8.00 | 3.00 |
| ❑ 254 | Drew Bledsoe | 8.00 | 3.00 |
| ❑ 255 | Brandon Stokley | 5.00 | 2.00 |
| ❑ 256 | Takeo Spikes | 5.00 | 2.00 |
| ❑ 257 | Philip Rivers | 8.00 | 3.00 |
| ❑ 258 | Lito Sheppard | 6.00 | 2.50 |
| ❑ 259 | Jimmy Smith | 6.00 | 2.50 |
| ❑ 260 | Tatum Bell | 5.00 | 2.00 |
| ❑ 261 | Allen Rossum | 5.00 | 2.00 |
| ❑ 262 | Amani Toomer | 5.00 | 2.00 |
| ❑ 263 | Jabar Gaffney | 5.00 | 2.00 |
| ❑ 264 | Jonathan Ogden | 5.00 | 2.00 |
| ❑ 265 | John Abraham | 5.00 | 2.00 |
| ❑ 266 | Aaron Stecker | 5.00 | 2.00 |
| ❑ 267 | Jason Elam | 5.00 | 2.00 |
| ❑ 268 | Najeh Davenport | 6.00 | 2.50 |
| ❑ 269 | Alge Crumpler | 6.00 | 2.50 |
| ❑ 270 | Roy Williams S | 6.00 | 2.50 |
| ❑ 271 | Trent Dilfer | 6.00 | 2.50 |
| ❑ 272 | Anquan Boldin | 6.00 | 2.50 |
| ❑ 273 | Artose Pinner | 5.00 | 2.00 |
| ❑ 274 | David Garrard | 8.00 | 3.00 |
| ❑ 275 | Terry Glenn | 5.00 | 2.00 |
| ❑ 276 | Adam Archuleta | 5.00 | 2.00 |
| ❑ 277 | Jeremiah Trotter | 5.00 | 2.00 |
| ❑ 278 | Travis Henry | 5.00 | 2.00 |
| ❑ 279 | Rex Grossman | 8.00 | 3.00 |
| ❑ 280 | Maurice Morris | 5.00 | 2.00 |
| ❑ 281 | Mike Alstott | 6.00 | 2.50 |
| ❑ 282 | Justin Gage | 5.00 | 2.00 |
| ❑ 283 | Dennis Northcutt | 5.00 | 2.00 |
| ❑ 284 | David Givens | 5.00 | 2.00 |
| ❑ 285 | Dominic Rhodes | 6.00 | 2.50 |
| ❑ 286 | Gerald Ford | 5.00 | 2.00 |

| | | |
|---|---|---|
| ❏ 287 Ronald Reagan | 5.00 | 2.00 |
| ❏ 288 John F. Kennedy | 5.00 | 2.00 |
| ❏ 289 Ulysses S. Grant | 5.00 | 2.00 |
| ❏ CL1 Jumbo Checklist 1 | 1.00 | .40 |
| ❏ CL2 Jumbo Checklist 2 | 1.00 | .40 |

## 2006 Topps Turkey Red

| | | |
|---|---|---|
| ❏ 1 LaVar Arrington | .75 | .30 |
| ❏ 2 Heath Miller | .60 | .25 |
| ❏ 3 Antwaan Randle El | .60 | .25 |
| ❏ 4 Derrick Mason | .60 | .25 |
| ❏ 5 Deshaun Foster | .60 | .25 |
| ❏ 6 Andre Johnson | .60 | .25 |
| ❏ 7 Jonathan Vilma | .60 | .25 |
| ❏ 8 Trent Dilfer | .60 | .25 |
| ❏ 9 Tatum Bell | .60 | .25 |
| ❏ 10 Bubba Franks | .50 | .20 |
| ❏ 11 T.J. Houshmandzadeh | .60 | .25 |
| ❏ 12 Adam Vinatieri | .60 | .25 |
| ❏ 13 Quentin Jammer | .50 | .20 |
| ❏ 14 Jim Kleinsasser | .50 | .20 |
| ❏ 15 Priest Holmes | .60 | .25 |
| ❏ 16 Courtney Roby | .50 | .20 |
| ❏ 17 Chris Simms | .60 | .25 |
| ❏ 18 Terry Glenn | .60 | .25 |
| ❏ 19 Jonathan Ogden | .50 | .20 |
| ❏ 20 Andrew Walter | .60 | .25 |
| ❏ 21 Lito Sheppard | .60 | .25 |
| ❏ 22 Kevan Barlow | .60 | .25 |
| ❏ 23 Santana Moss | .60 | .25 |
| ❏ 24 Kelly Holcomb | .40 | .15 |
| ❏ 25 Thomas Jones | .60 | .25 |
| ❏ 26 Dennis Northcutt | .50 | .20 |
| ❏ 27 Najeh Davenport | .60 | .25 |
| ❏ 28 Edgerrin James | .60 | .25 |
| ❏ 29 Kevin Curtis | .50 | .20 |
| ❏ 30 Brian Griese | .60 | .25 |
| ❏ 31 Jason Taylor | .50 | .20 |
| ❏ 32 T.J. Duckett | .50 | .20 |
| ❏ 33 Antonio Bryant | .60 | .25 |
| ❏ 34 Donald Driver | .60 | .25 |
| ❏ 35 Brian Westbrook | .60 | .25 |
| ❏ 36 Lofa Tatupu | .60 | .25 |
| ❏ 37 Ben Troupe | .50 | .20 |
| ❏ 38 Chris Cooley | .60 | .25 |
| ❏ 39 Josh McCown | .60 | .25 |
| ❏ 40 Chris Perry | .60 | .25 |
| ❏ 41 Joe Horn | .60 | .25 |
| ❏ 42 Kyle Boller | .60 | .25 |
| ❏ 43 Keyshawn Johnson | .60 | .25 |
| ❏ 44 Frank Gore | .75 | .30 |
| ❏ 45 Terence Newman | .50 | .20 |
| ❏ 46 Devery Henderson | .50 | .20 |
| ❏ 47 Michael Strahan | .60 | .25 |
| ❏ 48 Ladell Betts | .50 | .20 |
| ❏ 49 Patrick Ramsey | .60 | .25 |
| ❏ 50 Anquan Boldin | .60 | .25 |
| ❏ 51 Nathan Vasher | .50 | .20 |
| ❏ 52 Dominic Rhodes | .60 | .25 |
| ❏ 53 Travis Minor | .50 | .20 |
| ❏ 54 Torry Holt | .60 | .25 |
| ❏ 55 Sam Gado | .75 | .30 |
| ❏ 56 Fred Taylor | .60 | .25 |
| ❏ 57 Braylon Edwards | .75 | .30 |
| ❏ 58 Tyrone Calico | .50 | .20 |
| ❏ 59 Derrick Burgess | .50 | .20 |
| ❏ 60 Chester Taylor | .60 | .25 |

| | | |
|---|---|---|
| ❏ 61 Julius Peppers | .60 | .25 |
| ❏ 62 L.J. Smith | .50 | .20 |
| ❏ 63 Keenan McCardell | .60 | .25 |
| ❏ 64 Lee Evans | .60 | .25 |
| ❏ 65 Champ Bailey | .60 | .25 |
| ❏ 66 Alex Smith QB | .75 | .30 |
| ❏ 67 Tedy Bruschi | .75 | .30 |
| ❏ 68 Roddy White | .50 | .20 |
| ❏ 69 Marty Booker | .50 | .20 |
| ❏ 70 Fred Smoot | .50 | .20 |
| ❏ 71 A.J. Feeley | .50 | .20 |
| ❏ 72 Kellen Winslow | .75 | .30 |
| ❏ 73 Curtis Martin | .75 | .30 |
| ❏ 74 Ronald Curry | .60 | .25 |
| ❏ 75 Sam Madison | .50 | .20 |
| ❏ 76 Keary Colbert | .60 | .25 |
| ❏ 77 Marcus Pollard | .50 | .20 |
| ❏ 78 James Farrior | .50 | .20 |
| ❏ 79 Travis Henry | .60 | .25 |
| ❏ 80 Samari Rolle | .50 | .20 |
| ❏ 81 Rodney Harrison | .60 | .25 |
| ❏ 82 Matt Schaub | .60 | .25 |
| ❏ 83 Philip Rivers | .75 | .30 |
| ❏ 84 DeMarcus Ware | .60 | .25 |
| ❏ 85 Reggie Wayne | .60 | .25 |
| ❏ 86 Derrick Johnson | .60 | .25 |
| ❏ 87 Travis Taylor | .60 | .25 |
| ❏ 88 Antonio Pierce | .50 | .20 |
| ❏ 89 Jamal Lewis | .60 | .25 |
| ❏ 90 Aaron Brooks | .60 | .25 |
| ❏ 91 Michael Pittman | .40 | .15 |
| ❏ 92 Jerricho Cotchery | .50 | .20 |
| ❏ 93 Shayne Graham | .50 | .20 |
| ❏ 94 Dante Hall | .60 | .25 |
| ❏ 95 Warrick Dunn | .60 | .25 |
| ❏ 96 Mewelde Moore | .50 | .20 |
| ❏ 97 Brandon Lloyd | .60 | .25 |
| ❏ 98 Chris Gamble | .50 | .20 |
| ❏ 99 Odell Thurman | .60 | .25 |
| ❏ 100 Osi Umenyiora | .60 | .25 |
| ❏ 101 Jerry Porter | .60 | .25 |
| ❏ 102 Brandon Stokley | .60 | .25 |
| ❏ 103 Clinton Portis | .75 | .30 |
| ❏ 104 Quentin Jammer | .50 | .20 |
| ❏ 105 Reuben Droughns | .60 | .25 |
| ❏ 106 Jason Campbell | .60 | .25 |
| ❏ 107 LaBrandon Toefield | .40 | .15 |
| ❏ 108 Nate Burleson | .60 | .25 |
| ❏ 109 Antrel Rolle | .60 | .25 |
| ❏ 110A Steve McNair PS | .60 | .25 |
| ❏ 110B Steve McNair YS | .60 | .25 |
| ❏ 111A Chad Johnson PBB | .60 | .25 |
| ❏ 111B Chad Johnson No PBB | .60 | .25 |
| ❏ 112 Steven Jackson | .75 | .30 |
| ❏ 113 Ron Dayne | .60 | .25 |
| ❏ 114 Deion Branch | .60 | .25 |
| ❏ 115 Ed Reed | .60 | .25 |
| ❏ 116 Ty Law | .50 | .20 |
| ❏ 117 Drew Bledsoe | .75 | .30 |
| ❏ 118 Chris McAlister | .50 | .20 |
| ❏ 119 Plaxico Burress | .60 | .25 |
| ❏ 120 Aaron Rodgers | .75 | .30 |
| ❏ 121 Tony Gonzalez | .60 | .25 |
| ❏ 122 David Givens | .60 | .25 |
| ❏ 123 Michael Vick | .75 | .30 |
| ❏ 124 Antonio Gates | .75 | .30 |
| ❏ 125 Darrell Jackson | .60 | .25 |
| ❏ 126 Javon James | .50 | .20 |
| ❏ 127 LaDainian Tomlinson CL | .75 | .30 |
| ❏ 128 Chad Pennington | .60 | .25 |
| ❏ 129 Kevin Faulk | .60 | .25 |
| ❏ 130 Isaac Bruce | .60 | .25 |
| ❏ 131 Tom Brady CL | 1.00 | .40 |
| ❏ 132 Deuce McAllister | .60 | .25 |
| ❏ 133 Laveranues Coles | .60 | .25 |
| ❏ 134 Domino Edwards | .50 | .20 |
| ❏ 135 Brian Urlacher CL | .60 | .25 |
| ❏ 136 Dallas Clark | .60 | .25 |
| ❏ 137 Drew Bennett | .60 | .25 |
| ❏ 138 Domanick Davis | .60 | .25 |
| ❏ 139 Cadillac Williams CL | .60 | .25 |
| ❏ 140 David Garrard | .75 | .30 |
| ❏ 141 Shaun Alexander CL | .60 | .25 |
| ❏ 142 Troy Williamson | .60 | .25 |

| | | |
|---|---|---|
| ❏ 143 Steve Smith CL | .60 | .25 |
| ❏ 144 Jake Plummer | .60 | .25 |
| ❏ 145 Carson Palmer CL | .60 | .25 |
| ❏ 146 DeAngelo Hall | .60 | .25 |
| ❏ 147 Michael Vick CL | .60 | .25 |
| ❏ 148 Kyle Vanden Bosch | .50 | .20 |
| ❏ 149 Larry Johnson CL | .50 | .20 |
| ❏ 150 LaDainian Tomlinson | 1.00 | .40 |
| ❏ 151 Dunta Robinson | .60 | .25 |
| ❏ 152 Muhsin Muhammad | .60 | .25 |
| ❏ 153 Steven Jackson CL | .60 | .25 |
| ❏ 154 David Pollack | .60 | .25 |
| ❏ 155 Mark Brunell | .60 | .25 |
| ❏ 156 Donovan McNabb | .75 | .30 |
| ❏ 157 Jeremy Shockey | .75 | .30 |
| ❏ 158 Corey Dillon | .60 | .25 |
| ❏ 159 Mark Clayton | .60 | .25 |
| ❏ 160 Vincent Jackson | .60 | .25 |
| ❏ 161 Kurt Warner | .60 | .25 |
| ❏ 162 Marcus Robinson | .60 | .25 |
| ❏ 163 Takeo Spikes | .50 | .20 |
| ❏ 164 Charles Rogers | .60 | .25 |
| ❏ 165 J.P. Losman | .60 | .25 |
| ❏ 166 Matt Jones | .60 | .25 |
| ❏ 167 Rod Smith | .60 | .25 |
| ❏ 168 Steve Smith | .75 | .30 |
| ❏ 169 Michael Vick | .75 | .30 |
| ❏ 170 Mike Vanderjagt | .40 | .15 |
| ❏ 171 Amani Toomer | .60 | .25 |
| ❏ 172 Deltha O'Neal | .50 | .20 |
| ❏ 173 Michael Jenkins | .60 | .25 |
| ❏ 174 David Carr | .60 | .25 |
| ❏ 175 Chris Brown | .60 | .25 |
| ❏ 176 Kevin Jones | .75 | .30 |
| ❏ 177 Roy Williams S | .60 | .25 |
| ❏ 178 Marvin Harrison | .75 | .30 |
| ❏ 179 Drew Brees | .75 | .30 |
| ❏ 180 John Abraham | .60 | .25 |
| ❏ 181 Joseph Addai RC SP | 15.00 | 6.00 |
| ❏ 182 Sinorice Moss RC SP | 5.00 | 2.00 |
| ❏ 183A Vince Young PS RC | 6.00 | 2.50 |
| ❏ 183B Vince Young OS SP | 15.00 | 6.00 |
| ❏ 184 Vernon Davis RC SP | 5.00 | 2.00 |
| ❏ 185 Brandon Williams RC SP | 5.00 | 2.00 |
| ❏ 186 Derek Hagan RC SP | 5.00 | 2.00 |
| ❏ 187 Brian Calhoun RC SP | 4.00 | 1.50 |
| ❏ 188 Mario Williams RC SP | 8.00 | 3.00 |
| ❏ 189 DeAngelo Williams RC SP | 8.00 | 3.00 |
| ❏ 190 Jay Cutler RC SP | 20.00 | 8.00 |
| ❏ 191 A.J. Hawk RC SP | 10.00 | 4.00 |
| ❏ 192 Reggie Bush RC SP | 8.00 | 3.00 |
| ❏ 193 Laurence Maroney RC SP | 12.00 | 5.00 |
| ❏ 194 D'Brickashaw Ferguson RC SP | 5.00 | 2.00 |
| ❏ 195 Jason Avant RC SP | 5.00 | 2.00 |
| ❏ 196 Brodie Croyle RC SP | 6.00 | 2.50 |
| ❏ 197 Michael Huff RC SP | 5.00 | 2.00 |
| ❏ 198 LenDale White RC SP | 10.00 | 4.00 |
| ❏ 199 Marcedes Lewis RC SP | 5.00 | 2.00 |
| ❏ 200 Travis Wilson RC SP | 5.00 | 2.00 |
| ❏ 201 Haloti Ngata RC SP | 5.00 | 2.00 |
| ❏ 202 Greg Jennings RC SP | 8.00 | 3.00 |
| ❏ 203 Leon Washington RC SP | 5.00 | 2.00 |
| ❏ 204 Tamba Hali RC SP | 5.00 | 2.00 |
| ❏ 205 Santonio Holmes RC SP | 12.00 | 5.00 |
| ❏ 206 Jerome Harrison RC SP | 5.00 | 2.00 |
| ❏ 207 Tarvaris Jackson RC SP | 5.00 | 2.00 |
| ❏ 208 Mathias Kiwanuka RC SP | 6.00 | 2.50 |
| ❏ 209 Omar Jacobs RC SP | 4.00 | 1.50 |
| ❏ 210 Alan Zemaitis RC SP | 5.00 | 2.00 |
| ❏ 211 Demetrius Williams RC SP | 5.00 | 2.00 |
| ❏ 212 Bobby Carpenter RC SP | 5.00 | 2.00 |
| ❏ 213 Tye Hill RC SP | 5.00 | 2.00 |
| ❏ 214 Chad Jackson RC SP | 4.00 | 1.50 |
| ❏ 215 Joe Klopfenstein RC SP | 4.00 | 1.50 |
| ❏ 216 Kamerion Wimbley RC SP | 5.00 | 2.00 |
| ❏ 217 Michael Robinson RC SP | 5.00 | 2.00 |
| ❏ 218 David Thomas RC SP | 5.00 | 2.00 |
| ❏ 219 Charlie Whitehurst RC SP | 5.00 | 2.00 |
| ❏ 220 Jerious Norwood RC SP | 6.00 | 2.50 |
| ❏ 221 Bruce Gradkowski RC SP | 5.00 | 2.00 |
| ❏ 222 Kellen Clemens RC SP | 6.00 | 2.50 |
| ❏ 223 Thomas Howard RC SP | 5.00 | 2.00 |
| ❏ 224 Anthony Fasano RC SP | 5.00 | 2.00 |
| ❏ 225 Maurice Drew RC SP | 10.00 | 4.00 |

- ❏ 226 Antonio Cromartie RC SP 5.00 2.00
- ❏ 227 Mike Bell RC SP 5.00 2.00
- ❏ 228 D'Qwell Jackson RC SP 4.00 1.50
- ❏ 229A Matt Leinart TIB RC 6.00 2.50
- ❏ 229B Matt Leinart SIB RC 15.00 6.00
- ❏ 230 Maurice Stovall RC SP 5.00 2.00
- ❏ 231A Carson Palmer BJ .75 .30
- ❏ 231A Carson Palmer WJ .75 .30
- ❏ 232 Courtney Anderson .40 .15
- ❏ 233 D.J. Williams .50 .20
- ❏ 234 Chris Chambers .60 .25
- ❏ 235 Zach Thomas .75 .30
- ❏ 236 Reggie Brown .60 .25
- ❏ 237 Cadillac Williams .60 .25
- ❏ 238 Randy McMichael .50 .20
- ❏ 239 Brian Urlacher .75 .30
- ❏ 240 Cedric Houston .50 .20
- ❏ 241 Marc Bulger .60 .25
- ❏ 242 Mike Anderson .60 .25
- ❏ 243 Allen Rossum .50 .20
- ❏ 244 William Henderson .50 .20
- ❏ 245 Eddie Kennison .50 .20
- ❏ 246 Adam Archuleta .60 .25
- ❏ 247 Ryan Moats .60 .25
- ❏ 248 D.J. Hackett .60 .25
- ❏ 249 Marion Barber .75 .30
- ❏ 250 Mike Alstott .75 .30
- ❏ 251 Shawne Merriman .60 .25
- ❏ 252 Byron Leftwich .60 .25
- ❏ 253 Dan Morgan .50 .20
- ❏ 254 Ronnie Brown .75 .30
- ❏ 255 Mark Bradley .50 .20
- ❏ 256 Mike Williams .60 .25
- ❏ 257 Ronde Barber .60 .25
- ❏ 258 Bernard Berrian .60 .25
- ❏ 259 Gibril Wilson .40 .15
- ❏ 260 Scottie Vines .50 .20
- ❏ 261 Rex Grossman .75 .30
- ❏ 262 Daniel Graham .50 .20
- ❏ 263 Ernest Wilford .60 .25
- ❏ 264 Javon Walker .60 .25
- ❏ 265 Corey Webster .40 .15
- ❏ 266 Jon Kitna .60 .25
- ❏ 267 Amaz Battle .50 .20
- ❏ 268 Robert Ferguson SP 4.00 1.50
- ❏ 269 Cedric Benson .60 .25
- ❏ 270 Michael Clayton .60 .25
- ❏ 271 Brandon Jacobs .75 .30
- ❏ 272 Jason Witten SP 5.00 2.00
- ❏ 273A Randy Moss BS .75 .30
- ❏ 273B Randy Moss SS .75 .30
- ❏ 274 Daunte Culpepper SP 6.00 2.50
- ❏ 275 Ronnie Brown .60 .25
- ❏ 276 Dwight Freeney .60 .25
- ❏ 277 LaMont Jordan .50 .20
- ❏ 278 Jeremiah Trotter .50 .20
- ❏ 279A Hines Ward PO sky .75 .30
- ❏ 279B Hines Ward BY sky .75 .30
- ❏ 280A Tom Brady PBB 1.25 .50
- ❏ 280B Tom Brady No PBB 1.25 .50
- ❏ 281 Charles Woodson .60 .25
- ❏ 282A Shaun Alexander GJ .75 .30
- ❏ 282B Shaun Alexander WJ .75 .30
- ❏ 283 Eric Moulds .60 .25
- ❏ 284A Ben Roethlisberger BS 1.25 .50
- ❏ 284B Ben Roethlisberger PS 1.25 .50
- ❏ 285 Matt Hasselbeck .60 .25
- ❏ 286 Willis McGahee .75 .30
- ❏ 287 Carlos Rogers .50 .20
- ❏ 288 Brett Favre 1.50 .60
- ❏ 289 Larry Fitzgerald .75 .30
- ❏ 290 Billy Volek .60 .25
- ❏ 291 Julius Jones .75 .30
- ❏ 292 Trent Green .60 .25
- ❏ 293 Ashley Lelie .60 .25
- ❏ 294 Eli Manning 1.00 .40
- ❏ 295 Alge Crumpler .60 .25
- ❏ 296 Rudi Johnson .60 .25
- ❏ 297 Troy Polamalu 1.00 .40
- ❏ 298 Roy Williams WR .75 .30
- ❏ 299 Willie Parker 1.00 .40
- ❏ 300 Jake Delhomme .60 .25
- ❏ 301 Champ Bailey .60 .25
- ❏ 302 Ahman Green .60 .25

- ❏ 303 Robert Gallery .50 .20
- ❏ 304 Todd Heap .60 .25
- ❏ 305 Joey Harrington .50 .20
- ❏ 306 Terrell Owens .75 .30
- ❏ 307 Joey Galloway .60 .25
- ❏ 308A Larry Johnson OS .60 .25
- ❏ 308A Larry Johnson PS .60 .25
- ❏ 309 Brian Dawkins .60 .25
- ❏ 310 Ray Lewis .75 .30
- ❏ 311A Tiki Barber OS .75 .30
- ❏ 311B Tiki Barber BS SP 6.00 2.50
- ❏ 312 Donte Stallworth .60 .25
- ❏ 313 Eric Parker .50 .20
- ❏ 314 Charlie Frye .60 .25
- ❏ 315A Peyton Manning BYS 1.25 .50
- ❏ 315B Peyton Manning OS SP 40.00 15.00

## 2008 UD Masterpieces

- ❏ 1 Donnie Avery RC 2.50 1.00
- ❏ 2 Adrian Peterson 2.50 1.00
- ❏ 3 D.Tyree/E.Manning 1.25 .50
- ❏ 4 Alan Ameche .75 .30
- ❏ 5 Bart Starr 2.00 .75
- ❏ 6 Barry Sanders 2.00 .75
- ❏ 7 Ben Roethlisberger 1.50 .60
- ❏ 8 Brett Favre 3.00 1.25
- ❏ 9 Bob Sanders 1.00 .40
- ❏ 10 Brett Favre 3.00 1.25
- ❏ 11 Brian Urlacher 1.25 .50
- ❏ 12 Earl Bennett RC 2.00 .75
- ❏ 13 Champ Bailey .75 .30
- ❏ 14 Chuck Bednarik 1.00 .40
- ❏ 15 Dan Marino 2.50 1.00
- ❏ 16 Brian Bosworth 1.25 .50
- ❏ 17 Devin Thomas RC 2.00 .75
- ❏ 18 Andre Caldwell RC 1.50 .60
- ❏ 19 Desmond Howard .75 .30
- ❏ 20 Devin Hester 1.25 .50
- ❏ 21 Dick Butkus 1.50 .60
- ❏ 22 Harry Douglas RC 2.00 .75
- ❏ 23 Don Shula .75 .30
- ❏ 24 Donovan McNabb 1.25 .50
- ❏ 25 Kevin O'Connell RC 2.50 1.00
- ❏ 26 Doug Flutie 1.00 .40
- ❏ 27 Drew Pearson 1.00 .40
- ❏ 28 Dwight Clark 1.00 .40
- ❏ 29 Early Doucet RC 2.00 .75
- ❏ 30 Ed Podolak .75 .30
- ❏ 31 Eli Manning 1.25 .50
- ❏ 32 Joe Flacco RC 6.00 2.50
- ❏ 33 James Hardy RC 2.00 .75
- ❏ 34 Franco Harris 1.25 .50
- ❏ 35 Frank Reich .75 .30
- ❏ 36 Dexter Jackson RC 2.00 .75
- ❏ 37 Gale Sayers 1.50 .60
- ❏ 38 Chris Johnson RC 5.00 2.00
- ❏ 39 Herm Edwards .75 .30
- ❏ 40 Howard Cosell 1.00 .40
- ❏ 41 Dustin Keller RC 2.00 .75
- ❏ 42 Jamaal Charles RC 2.50 1.00
- ❏ 43 Jim Brown 1.50 .60
- ❏ 44 Jim Thorpe 1.50 .60
- ❏ 45 Joe Montana 2.50 1.00
- ❏ 46 Joe Montana 2.50 1.00
- ❏ 47 Joe Namath 2.50 1.00
- ❏ 48 John David Booty RC 2.50 1.00
- ❏ 49 John Elway 2.00 .75
- ❏ 50 Johnny Unitas 2.00 .75

- ❏ 51 Jordy Nelson RC 2.50 1.00
- ❏ 52 Kellen Winslow Sr. 1.00 .40
- ❏ 53 Eddie Royal RC 4.00 1.50
- ❏ 54 Kevin Dyson .75 .30
- ❏ 55 Kevin Dyson .75 .30
- ❏ 56 Kevin Smith RC 4.00 1.50
- ❏ 57 LaDainian Tomlinson 1.50 .60
- ❏ 58 Limas Sweed RC 2.50 1.00
- ❏ 60 Malcolm Kelly RC 2.00 .75
- ❏ 61 Mario Manningham RC 2.00 .75
- ❏ 62 Marvin Harrison 1.25 .50
- ❏ 63 Jerome Simpson RC 1.50 .60
- ❏ 64 Matt Forte RC 5.00 2.00
- ❏ 67 Paul Hornung 1.25 .50
- ❏ 68 Peyton Manning 2.00 .75
- ❏ 69 Randy Moss 1.25 .50
- ❏ 71 Ray Rice RC 1.50 .60
- ❏ 72 Red Grange 1.50 .60
- ❏ 73 Lester Hayes 1.00 .40
- ❏ 74 Sammy Baugh 1.25 .50
- ❏ 75 Adrian Peterson 2.50 1.00
- ❏ 76 Steve Slaton RC 4.00 1.50
- ❏ 77 Billy Sims 1.00 .40
- ❏ 78 Jack Lambert 1.25 .50
- ❏ 79 Scott Norwood .75 .30
- ❏ 80 Snow Plow Game .75 .30
- ❏ 81 Terrell Owens 1.25 .50
- ❏ 82 Terry Bradshaw 2.00 .75
- ❏ 83 Tom Brady 2.00 .75
- ❏ 84 Tom Brady 2.00 .75
- ❏ 85 Tony Romo 2.00 .75
- ❏ 86 Vince Lombardi 2.00 .75
- ❏ 87 Vince Young 1.25 .50
- ❏ 88 Walter Payton 2.50 1.00
- ❏ 89 Wes Welker 1.25 .50
- ❏ 90 Y.A. Tittle 1.25 .50
- ❏ 91 Peterson/Butkus TW 10.00 4.00
- ❏ 92 Unitas/P.Mann TW 12.00 5.00
- ❏ 93 Favre/Manning TW 10.00 4.00
- ❏ 94 R.Moss/M.Blount TW 8.00 3.00
- ❏ 95 Horn/Mont/Theis/Quinn TW 12.00 5.00
- ❏ 96 B.Sanders/Swann TW 10.00 4.00
- ❏ 97 Hornung/Favre TW 10.00 4.00
- ❏ 98 Tarkenton/Peterson TW 10.00 4.00
- ❏ 99 E.Manning/Tittle TW 10.00 4.00
- ❏ 101 Rashard Mendenhall SP RC 6.00 2.50
- ❏ 102 Brian Brohm SP RC 4.00 1.50
- ❏ 103 Chad Henne SP RC 5.00 2.00
- ❏ 104 Jake Long SP RC 4.00 1.50
- ❏ 105 Felix Jones SP RC 8.00 3.00
- ❏ 106 Darren McFadden SP RC 8.00 3.00
- ❏ 107 DeSean Jackson SP RC 6.00 2.50
- ❏ 108 Glenn Dorsey SP RC 4.00 1.50
- ❏ 109 Jonathan Stewart SP RC 8.00 3.00
- ❏ 110 Matt Ryan SP RC 12.00 5.00

## 1991 Ultra

- ❏ COMPLETE SET (300) 20.00 7.50
- ❏ 1 Don Beebe .05 .01
- ❏ 2 Shane Conlan .05 .01
- ❏ 3 Pete Metzelaars .05 .01
- ❏ 4 Jamie Mueller .05 .01
- ❏ 5 Scott Norwood .05 .01
- ❏ 6 Andre Reed .10 .02
- ❏ 7 Leon Seals .05 .01
- ❏ 8 Bruce Smith .25 .08

|  |  | | |
|---|---|---|---|
| ❑ 9 | Leonard Smith | .05 | .01 |
| ❑ 10 | Thurman Thomas | .25 | .08 |
| ❑ 11 | Lewis Billups | .05 | .01 |
| ❑ 12 | Jim Breech | .05 | .01 |
| ❑ 13 | James Brooks | .10 | .02 |
| ❑ 14 | Eddie Brown | .05 | .01 |
| ❑ 15 | Boomer Esiason | .10 | .02 |
| ❑ 16 | David Fulcher | .05 | .01 |
| ❑ 17 | Rodney Holman | .05 | .01 |
| ❑ 18 | Bruce Kozerski | .05 | .01 |
| ❑ 19 | Tim Krumrie | .05 | .01 |
| ❑ 20 | Tim McGee | .05 | .01 |
| ❑ 21 | Anthony Munoz | .10 | .02 |
| ❑ 22 | Leon White | .05 | .01 |
| ❑ 23 | Ickey Woods | .05 | .01 |
| ❑ 24 | Carl Zander | .05 | .01 |
| ❑ 25 | Brian Brennan | .05 | .01 |
| ❑ 26 | Thane Gash | .05 | .01 |
| ❑ 27 | Leroy Hoard | .10 | .02 |
| ❑ 28 | Mike Johnson | .05 | .01 |
| ❑ 29 | Reggie Langhorne | .05 | .01 |
| ❑ 30 | Kevin Mack | .05 | .01 |
| ❑ 31 | Clay Matthews | .10 | .02 |
| ❑ 32 | Eric Metcalf | .10 | .02 |
| ❑ 33 | Steve Atwater | .05 | .01 |
| ❑ 34 | Melvin Bratton | .05 | .01 |
| ❑ 35 | John Elway | 1.25 | .50 |
| ❑ 36 | Bobby Humphrey | .05 | .01 |
| ❑ 37 | Mark Jackson | .05 | .01 |
| ❑ 38 | Vance Johnson | .05 | .01 |
| ❑ 39 | Ricky Nattiel | .05 | .01 |
| ❑ 40 | Steve Sewell | .05 | .01 |
| ❑ 41 | Dennis Smith | .05 | .01 |
| ❑ 42 | David Treadwell | .05 | .01 |
| ❑ 43 | Michael Young | .05 | .01 |
| ❑ 44 | Ray Childress | .05 | .01 |
| ❑ 45 | Cris Dishman RC | .05 | .01 |
| ❑ 46 | William Fuller | .10 | .02 |
| ❑ 47 | Ernest Givins | .10 | .02 |
| ❑ 48 | John Grimsley UER | .05 | .01 |
| ❑ 49 | Drew Hill | .05 | .01 |
| ❑ 50 | Haywood Jeffires | .10 | .02 |
| ❑ 51 | Sean Jones | .10 | .02 |
| ❑ 52 | Johnny Meads | .05 | .01 |
| ❑ 53 | Warren Moon | .25 | .08 |
| ❑ 54 | Al Smith | .05 | .01 |
| ❑ 55 | Lorenzo White | .05 | .01 |
| ❑ 56 | Albert Bentley | .05 | .01 |
| ❑ 57 | Duane Bickett | .05 | .01 |
| ❑ 58 | Bill Brooks | .05 | .01 |
| ❑ 59 | Jeff George | .25 | .08 |
| ❑ 60 | Mike Prior | .05 | .01 |
| ❑ 61 | Rohn Stark | .05 | .01 |
| ❑ 62 | Jack Trudeau | .05 | .01 |
| ❑ 63 | Clarence Verdin | .05 | .01 |
| ❑ 64 | Steve DeBerg | .05 | .01 |
| ❑ 65 | Emile Harry | .05 | .01 |
| ❑ 66 | Albert Lewis | .05 | .01 |
| ❑ 67 | Nick Lowery UER | .05 | .01 |
| ❑ 68 | Todd McNair | .05 | .01 |
| ❑ 69 | Christian Okoye | .05 | .01 |
| ❑ 70 | Stephone Paige | .05 | .01 |
| ❑ 71 | Kevin Porter UER | .05 | .01 |
| ❑ 72 | Derrick Thomas | .25 | .08 |
| ❑ 73 | Robb Thomas | .05 | .01 |
| ❑ 74 | Barry Word | .05 | .01 |
| ❑ 75 | Marcus Allen | .25 | .08 |
| ❑ 76 | Eddie Anderson | .05 | .01 |
| ❑ 77 | Tim Brown | .25 | .08 |
| ❑ 78 | Mervyn Fernandez | .05 | .01 |
| ❑ 79 | Willie Gault | .10 | .02 |
| ❑ 80 | Ethan Horton | .05 | .01 |
| ❑ 81 | Howie Long | .25 | .08 |
| ❑ 82 | Vance Mueller | .05 | .01 |
| ❑ 83 | Jay Schroeder | .05 | .01 |
| ❑ 84 | Steve Smith | .05 | .01 |
| ❑ 85 | Greg Townsend | .05 | .01 |
| ❑ 86 | Mark Clayton | .10 | .02 |
| ❑ 87 | Jim C. Jensen | .05 | .01 |
| ❑ 88 | Dan Marino | 1.25 | .50 |
| ❑ 89 | Tim McKyer UER | .05 | .01 |
| ❑ 90 | John Offerdahl | .05 | .01 |
| ❑ 91 | Louis Oliver | .05 | .01 |
| ❑ 92 | Reggie Roby | .05 | .01 |
| ❑ 93 | Sammie Smith | .05 | .01 |
| ❑ 94 | Hart Lee Dykes | .05 | .01 |
| ❑ 95 | Irving Fryar | .10 | .02 |
| ❑ 96 | Tommy Hodson | .05 | .01 |
| ❑ 97 | Maurice Hurst | .05 | .01 |
| ❑ 98 | John Stephens | .05 | .01 |
| ❑ 99 | Andre Tippett | .05 | .01 |
| ❑ 100 | Mark Boyer | .05 | .01 |
| ❑ 101 | Kyle Clifton | .05 | .01 |
| ❑ 102 | James Hasty | .05 | .01 |
| ❑ 103 | Erik McMillan | .05 | .01 |
| ❑ 104 | Rob Moore | .25 | .08 |
| ❑ 105 | Joe Mott | .05 | .01 |
| ❑ 106 | Ken O'Brien | .05 | .01 |
| ❑ 107 | Ron Stallworth UER | .05 | .01 |
| ❑ 108 | Al Toon | .10 | .02 |
| ❑ 109 | Gary Anderson K | .05 | .01 |
| ❑ 110 | Bubby Brister | .05 | .01 |
| ❑ 111 | Thomas Everett | .05 | .01 |
| ❑ 112 | Merril Hoge | .05 | .01 |
| ❑ 113 | Louis Lipps | .05 | .01 |
| ❑ 114 | Greg Lloyd | .25 | .08 |
| ❑ 115 | Hardy Nickerson | .10 | .02 |
| ❑ 116 | Dwight Stone | .05 | .01 |
| ❑ 117 | Rod Woodson | .25 | .08 |
| ❑ 118 | Tim Worley | .05 | .01 |
| ❑ 119 | Rod Bernstine | .05 | .01 |
| ❑ 120 | Marion Butts | .10 | .02 |
| ❑ 121 | Gill Byrd | .05 | .01 |
| ❑ 122 | Arthur Cox | .05 | .01 |
| ❑ 123 | Burt Grossman | .05 | .01 |
| ❑ 124 | Ronnie Harmon | .05 | .01 |
| ❑ 125 | Anthony Miller | .10 | .02 |
| ❑ 126 | Leslie O'Neal | .10 | .02 |
| ❑ 127 | Gary Plummer | .05 | .01 |
| ❑ 128 | Sam Seale | .05 | .01 |
| ❑ 129 | Junior Seau | .25 | .08 |
| ❑ 130 | Broderick Thompson | .05 | .01 |
| ❑ 131 | Billy Joe Tolliver | .05 | .01 |
| ❑ 132 | Brian Blades | .10 | .02 |
| ❑ 133 | Jeff Bryant | .05 | .01 |
| ❑ 134 | Derrick Fenner | .05 | .01 |
| ❑ 135 | Jacob Green | .05 | .01 |
| ❑ 136 | Andy Heck | .05 | .01 |
| ❑ 137 | Patrick Hunter RC UER | .05 | .01 |
| ❑ 138 | Norm Johnson | .05 | .01 |
| ❑ 139 | Tommy Kane | .05 | .01 |
| ❑ 140 | Dave Krieg | .10 | .02 |
| ❑ 141 | John L. Williams | .05 | .01 |
| ❑ 142 | Terry Wooden | .05 | .01 |
| ❑ 143 | Steve Broussard | .05 | .01 |
| ❑ 144 | Keith Jones | .05 | .01 |
| ❑ 145 | Brian Jordan | .10 | .02 |
| ❑ 146 | Chris Miller | .10 | .02 |
| ❑ 147 | John Rade | .05 | .01 |
| ❑ 148 | Andre Rison | .10 | .02 |
| ❑ 149 | Mike Rozier | .05 | .01 |
| ❑ 150 | Deion Sanders | .40 | .15 |
| ❑ 151 | Neal Anderson | .10 | .02 |
| ❑ 152 | Trace Armstrong | .05 | .01 |
| ❑ 153 | Kevin Butler | .05 | .01 |
| ❑ 154 | Mark Carrier DB | .10 | .02 |
| ❑ 155 | Richard Dent | .10 | .02 |
| ❑ 156 | Dennis Gentry | .05 | .01 |
| ❑ 157 | Jim Harbaugh | .25 | .08 |
| ❑ 158 | Brad Muster | .05 | .01 |
| ❑ 159 | William Perry | .10 | .02 |
| ❑ 160 | Mike Singletary | .10 | .02 |
| ❑ 161 | Lemuel Stinson | .05 | .01 |
| ❑ 162 | Troy Aikman | .75 | .30 |
| ❑ 163 | Michael Irvin | .25 | .08 |
| ❑ 164 | Mike Saxon | .05 | .01 |
| ❑ 165 | Emmitt Smith | 2.50 | 1.00 |
| ❑ 166 | Jerry Ball | .05 | .01 |
| ❑ 167 | Michael Cofer | .05 | .01 |
| ❑ 168 | Rodney Peete | .10 | .02 |
| ❑ 169 | Barry Sanders | 1.25 | .50 |
| ❑ 170 | Robert Brown | .05 | .01 |
| ❑ 171 | Anthony Dilweg | .05 | .01 |
| ❑ 172 | Tim Harris | .05 | .01 |
| ❑ 173 | Johnny Holland | .05 | .01 |
| ❑ 174 | Perry Kemp | .05 | .01 |
| ❑ 175 | Don Majkowski | .05 | .01 |
| ❑ 176 | Brian Noble | .05 | .01 |
| ❑ 177 | Jeff Query | .05 | .01 |
| ❑ 178 | Sterling Sharpe | .25 | .08 |
| ❑ 179 | Charles Wilson | .05 | .01 |
| ❑ 180 | Keith Woodside | .05 | .01 |
| ❑ 181 | Flipper Anderson UER | .05 | .01 |
| ❑ 182 | Bern Brostek | .05 | .01 |
| ❑ 183 | Pat Carter RC | .05 | .01 |
| ❑ 184 | Aaron Cox | .05 | .01 |
| ❑ 185 | Henry Ellard | .10 | .02 |
| ❑ 186 | Jim Everett | .10 | .02 |
| ❑ 187 | Cleveland Gary | .05 | .01 |
| ❑ 188 | Jerry Gray | .05 | .01 |
| ❑ 189 | Kevin Greene | .10 | .02 |
| ❑ 190 | Mike Wilcher | .05 | .01 |
| ❑ 191 | Alfred Anderson | .05 | .01 |
| ❑ 192 | Joey Browner | .05 | .01 |
| ❑ 193 | Anthony Carter | .10 | .02 |
| ❑ 194 | Chris Doleman | .05 | .01 |
| ❑ 195 | Rick Fenney | .05 | .01 |
| ❑ 196 | Darrell Fullington | .05 | .01 |
| ❑ 197 | Rich Gannon | .25 | .08 |
| ❑ 198 | Hassan Jones | .05 | .01 |
| ❑ 199 | Steve Jordan | .05 | .01 |
| ❑ 200 | Mike Merriweather | .05 | .01 |
| ❑ 201 | Al Noga | .05 | .01 |
| ❑ 202 | Herschel Walker | .10 | .02 |
| ❑ 203 | Wade Wilson | .10 | .02 |
| ❑ 204 | Morten Andersen | .05 | .01 |
| ❑ 205 | Gene Atkins | .05 | .01 |
| ❑ 206 | Toi Cook RC | .05 | .01 |
| ❑ 207 | Craig Heyward | .10 | .02 |
| ❑ 208 | Dalton Hilliard | .05 | .01 |
| ❑ 209 | Vaughan Johnson | .05 | .01 |
| ❑ 210 | Eric Martin | .05 | .01 |
| ❑ 211 | Brett Perriman | .25 | .08 |
| ❑ 212 | Pat Swilling | .10 | .02 |
| ❑ 213 | Steve Walsh | .05 | .01 |
| ❑ 214 | Ottis Anderson | .10 | .02 |
| ❑ 215 | Carl Banks | .05 | .01 |
| ❑ 216 | Maurice Carthon | .05 | .01 |
| ❑ 217 | Mark Collins | .05 | .01 |
| ❑ 218 | Rodney Hampton | .25 | .08 |
| ❑ 219 | Erik Howard | .05 | .01 |
| ❑ 220 | Mark Ingram | .10 | .02 |
| ❑ 221 | Pepper Johnson | .05 | .01 |
| ❑ 222 | Dave Meggett | .10 | .02 |
| ❑ 223 | Phil Simms | .10 | .02 |
| ❑ 224 | Lawrence Taylor | .25 | .08 |
| ❑ 225 | Lewis Tillman | .05 | .01 |
| ❑ 226 | Everson Walls | .05 | .01 |
| ❑ 227 | Fred Barnett | .25 | .08 |
| ❑ 228 | Jerome Brown | .05 | .01 |
| ❑ 229 | Keith Byars | .05 | .01 |
| ❑ 230 | Randall Cunningham | .25 | .08 |
| ❑ 231 | Byron Evans | .05 | .01 |
| ❑ 232 | Wes Hopkins | .05 | .01 |
| ❑ 233 | Keith Jackson | .10 | .02 |
| ❑ 234 | Heath Sherman | .05 | .01 |
| ❑ 235 | Anthony Toney | .05 | .01 |
| ❑ 236 | Reggie White | .25 | .08 |
| ❑ 237 | Rich Camarillo | .05 | .01 |
| ❑ 238 | Ken Harvey | .10 | .02 |
| ❑ 239 | Eric Hill | .05 | .01 |
| ❑ 240 | Johnny Johnson | .05 | .01 |
| ❑ 241 | Ernie Jones | .05 | .01 |
| ❑ 242 | Tim McDonald | .05 | .01 |
| ❑ 243 | Timm Rosenbach | .05 | .01 |
| ❑ 244 | Jay Taylor | .05 | .01 |
| ❑ 245 | Dexter Carter | .05 | .01 |
| ❑ 246 | Mike Cofer | .05 | .01 |
| ❑ 247 | Kevin Fagan | .05 | .01 |
| ❑ 248 | Don Griffin | .05 | .01 |
| ❑ 249 | Charles Haley | .10 | .02 |
| ❑ 250 | Brent Jones | .25 | .08 |
| ❑ 251 | Joe Montana UER | 1.25 | .50 |
| ❑ 252 | Darryl Pollard | .05 | .01 |
| ❑ 253 | Tom Rathman | .05 | .01 |
| ❑ 254 | Jerry Rice | .75 | .30 |
| ❑ 255 | John Taylor | .10 | .02 |
| ❑ 256 | Steve Young | .75 | .30 |
| ❑ 257 | Gary Anderson RB | .05 | .01 |
| ❑ 258 | Mark Carrier WR | .25 | .08 |
| ❑ 259 | Chris Chandler | .25 | .08 |
| ❑ 260 | Reggie Cobb | .05 | .01 |

| | | |
|---|---|---|
| ☐ 261 Reuben Davis | .05 | .01 |
| ☐ 262 Willie Drewrey | .05 | .01 |
| ☐ 263 Ron Hall | .05 | .01 |
| ☐ 264 Eugene Marve | .05 | .01 |
| ☐ 265 Winston Moss UER | .05 | .01 |
| ☐ 266 Vinny Testaverde | .10 | .02 |
| ☐ 267 Broderick Thomas | .05 | .01 |
| ☐ 268 Jeff Bostic | .05 | .01 |
| ☐ 269 Earnest Byner | .05 | .01 |
| ☐ 270 Gary Clark | .25 | .08 |
| ☐ 271 Darrell Green | .05 | .01 |
| ☐ 272 Jim Lachey | .05 | .01 |
| ☐ 273 Wilber Marshall | .05 | .01 |
| ☐ 274 Art Monk | .10 | .02 |
| ☐ 275 Gerald Riggs | .05 | .01 |
| ☐ 276 Mark Rypien | .10 | .02 |
| ☐ 277 Ricky Sanders | .05 | .01 |
| ☐ 278 Alvin Walton | .05 | .01 |
| ☐ 279 Nick Bell RC | .05 | .01 |
| ☐ 280 Eric Bieniemy RC | .05 | .01 |
| ☐ 281 Jarrod Bunch RC | .05 | .01 |
| ☐ 282 Mike Croel RC | .05 | .01 |
| ☐ 283 Brett Favre RC | 10.00 | 5.00 |
| ☐ 284 Moe Gardner RC | .05 | .01 |
| ☐ 285 Pat Harlow RC | .05 | .01 |
| ☐ 286 Randal Hill RC | .10 | .02 |
| ☐ 287 Todd Marinovich RC | .05 | .01 |
| ☐ 288 Russell Maryland RC | .25 | .08 |
| ☐ 289 Dan McGwire RC | .05 | .01 |
| ☐ 290 Ernie Mills RC UER | .10 | .02 |
| ☐ 291 Herman Moore RC | .25 | .08 |
| ☐ 292 Godfrey Myles RC | .05 | .01 |
| ☐ 293 Browning Nagle RC | .10 | .02 |
| ☐ 294 Mike Pritchard RC | .25 | .08 |
| ☐ 295 Esera Tuaolo RC | .05 | .01 |
| ☐ 296 Mark Vander Poel RC | .05 | .01 |
| ☐ 297 Ricky Watters RC | 1.50 | .60 |
| ☐ 298 Chris Zorich RC | .25 | .08 |
| ☐ 299 Checklist Card | .10 | .02 |
| ☐ 300 Checklist Card | .10 | .02 |

## 1991 Ultra Update

| | | |
|---|---|---|
| ☐ COMP.FACT.SET (100) | 25.00 | 10.00 |
| ☐ U1 Brett Favre | 15.00 | 7.50 |
| ☐ U2 Moe Gardner | .10 | .02 |
| ☐ U3 Tim McKyer | .10 | .02 |
| ☐ U4 Bruce Pickens RC | .10 | .02 |
| ☐ U5 Mike Pritchard | .40 | .15 |
| ☐ U6 Cornelius Bennett | .20 | .07 |
| ☐ U7 Phil Hansen RC | .10 | .02 |
| ☐ U8 Henry Jones RC | .20 | .07 |
| ☐ U9 Mark Kelso | .10 | .02 |
| ☐ U10 James Lofton | .20 | .07 |
| ☐ U11 Anthony Morgan RC | .10 | .02 |
| ☐ U12 Stan Thomas | .10 | .02 |
| ☐ U13 Chris Zorich | .20 | .07 |
| ☐ U14 Reggie Rembert | .10 | .02 |
| ☐ U15 Alfred Williams RC | .10 | .02 |
| ☐ U16 Michael Jackson RC WR | .40 | .15 |
| ☐ U17 Ed King RC | .10 | .02 |
| ☐ U18 Joe Morris | .10 | .02 |
| ☐ U19 Vince Newsome | .10 | .02 |
| ☐ U20 Tony Casillas | .10 | .02 |
| ☐ U21 Russell Maryland | .40 | .15 |
| ☐ U22 Jay Novacek | .40 | .15 |
| ☐ U23 Mike Croel | .10 | .02 |
| ☐ U24 Gaston Green | .10 | .02 |

| | | |
|---|---|---|
| ☐ U25 Kenny Walker RC | .10 | .02 |
| ☐ U26 Melvin Jenkins RC | .10 | .02 |
| ☐ U27 Herman Moore RC | .40 | .15 |
| ☐ U28 Kelvin Pritchett RC | .20 | .07 |
| ☐ U29 Chris Spielman | .20 | .07 |
| ☐ U30 Vinnie Clark RC | .10 | .02 |
| ☐ U31 Allen Rice | .10 | .02 |
| ☐ U32 Vai Sikahema | .10 | .02 |
| ☐ U33 Esera Tuaolo | .10 | .02 |
| ☐ U34 Mike Dumas RC | .10 | .02 |
| ☐ U35 John Flannery RC | .10 | .02 |
| ☐ U36 Allen Pinkett | .10 | .02 |
| ☐ U37 Tim Barnett RC | .10 | .02 |
| ☐ U38 Dan Saleaumua | .10 | .02 |
| ☐ U39 Harvey Williams RC | .40 | .15 |
| ☐ U40 Nick Bell | .10 | .02 |
| ☐ U41 Roger Craig | .20 | .07 |
| ☐ U42 Ronnie Lott | .20 | .07 |
| ☐ U43 Todd Marinovich | .10 | .02 |
| ☐ U44 Robert Delpino | .10 | .02 |
| ☐ U45 Todd Lyght RC | .10 | .02 |
| ☐ U46 Robert Young RC | .20 | .07 |
| ☐ U47 Aaron Craver RC | .10 | .02 |
| ☐ U48 Mark Higgs RC | .10 | .02 |
| ☐ U49 Vestee Jackson | .10 | .02 |
| ☐ U50 Cari Lee | .10 | .02 |
| ☐ U51 Felix Wright | .10 | .02 |
| ☐ U52 Darrell Fullington | .10 | .02 |
| ☐ U53 Pat Harlow | .10 | .02 |
| ☐ U54 Eugene Lockhart | .10 | .02 |
| ☐ U55 Hugh Millen RC | .10 | .02 |
| ☐ U56 Leonard Russell RC | .40 | .15 |
| ☐ U57 Jon Vaughn RC | .10 | .02 |
| ☐ U58 Quinn Early | .20 | .07 |
| ☐ U59 Bobby Hebert | .10 | .02 |
| ☐ U60 Rickey Jackson | .10 | .02 |
| ☐ U61 Sam Mills | .20 | .07 |
| ☐ U62 Jarrod Bunch | .10 | .02 |
| ☐ U63 John Elliott | .10 | .02 |
| ☐ U64 Jeff Hostetler | .20 | .07 |
| ☐ U65 Ed McCaffrey RC | 6.00 | 2.50 |
| ☐ U66 Kanavis McGhee RC | .10 | .02 |
| ☐ U67 Mo Lewis RC | .20 | .07 |
| ☐ U68 Browning Nagle | .10 | .02 |
| ☐ U69 Blair Thomas | .10 | .02 |
| ☐ U70 Antone Davis RC | .10 | .02 |
| ☐ U71 Brad Goebel RC | .10 | .02 |
| ☐ U72 Jim McMahon | .20 | .07 |
| ☐ U73 Clyde Simmons | .10 | .02 |
| ☐ U74 Randal Hill UER U71 | .20 | .07 |
| ☐ U75 Eric Swann RC | .40 | .15 |
| ☐ U76 Tom Tupa | .10 | .02 |
| ☐ U77 Jeff Graham RC WR | .40 | .15 |
| ☐ U78 Eric Green | .10 | .02 |
| ☐ U79 Neil O'Donnell RC | .40 | .15 |
| ☐ U80 Huey Richardson RC | .10 | .02 |
| ☐ U81 Eric Bieniemy | .10 | .02 |
| ☐ U82 John Friesz | .40 | .15 |
| ☐ U83 Eric Moten RC | .10 | .02 |
| ☐ U84 Stanley Richard RC | .10 | .02 |
| ☐ U85 Todd Bowles | .10 | .02 |
| ☐ U86 Merton Hanks RC | .40 | .15 |
| ☐ U87 Tim Harris | .10 | .02 |
| ☐ U88 Pierce Holt | .10 | .02 |
| ☐ U89 Ted Washington RC | .10 | .02 |
| ☐ U90 John Kasay RC | .20 | .07 |
| ☐ U91 Dan McGwire | .10 | .02 |
| ☐ U92 Lawrence Dawsey RC | .20 | .07 |
| ☐ U93 Charles McRae RC | .10 | .02 |
| ☐ U94 Jesse Solomon | .10 | .02 |
| ☐ U95 Robert Wilson RC | .10 | .02 |
| ☐ U96 Ricky Ervins RC | .20 | .07 |
| ☐ U97 Charles Mann | .10 | .02 |
| ☐ U98 Bobby Wilson RC | .10 | .02 |
| ☐ U99 Jerry Rice PV | 1.50 | .60 |
| ☐ U100 Nick Bell/J.McMahon CL | .10 | .02 |

## 1992 Ultra

| | | |
|---|---|---|
| ☐ COMPLETE SET (450) | 15.00 | 6.00 |
| ☐ 1 Steve Broussard | .10 | .02 |
| ☐ 2 Rick Bryan | .10 | .02 |
| ☐ 3 Scott Case | .10 | .02 |
| ☐ 4 Darion Conner | .10 | .02 |
| ☐ 5 Bill Fralic | .10 | .02 |

| | | |
|---|---|---|
| ☐ 6 Moe Gardner | .10 | .02 |
| ☐ 7 Tim Green | .10 | .02 |
| ☐ 8 Michael Haynes | .20 | .07 |
| ☐ 9 Chris Hinton | .10 | .02 |
| ☐ 10 Mike Kenn | .10 | .02 |
| ☐ 11 Tim McKyer | .10 | .02 |
| ☐ 12 Chris Miller | .20 | .07 |
| ☐ 13 Erric Pegram | .20 | .07 |
| ☐ 14 Mike Pritchard | .20 | .07 |
| ☐ 15 Andre Rison | .20 | .07 |
| ☐ 16 Jessie Tuggle | .10 | .02 |
| ☐ 17 Carlton Bailey RC | .10 | .02 |
| ☐ 18 Howard Ballard | .10 | .02 |
| ☐ 19 Cornelius Bennett | .20 | .07 |
| ☐ 20 Shane Conlan | .10 | .02 |
| ☐ 21 Kenneth Davis | .10 | .02 |
| ☐ 22 Kent Hull | .10 | .02 |
| ☐ 23 Mark Kelso | .10 | .02 |
| ☐ 24 James Lofton | .20 | .07 |
| ☐ 25 Keith McKeller | .10 | .02 |
| ☐ 26 Nate Odomes | .10 | .02 |
| ☐ 27 Jim Ritcher | .10 | .02 |
| ☐ 28 Leon Seals | .10 | .02 |
| ☐ 29 Darryl Talley | .10 | .02 |
| ☐ 30 Steve Tasker | .20 | .07 |
| ☐ 31 Thurman Thomas | .40 | .15 |
| ☐ 32 Will Wolford | .10 | .02 |
| ☐ 33 Jeff Wright | .10 | .02 |
| ☐ 34 Neal Anderson | .10 | .02 |
| ☐ 35 Trace Armstrong | .10 | .02 |
| ☐ 36 Mark Carrier DB | .10 | .02 |
| ☐ 37 Wendell Davis | .10 | .02 |
| ☐ 38 Richard Dent | .20 | .07 |
| ☐ 39 Shaun Gayle | .10 | .02 |
| ☐ 40 Jim Harbaugh | .40 | .15 |
| ☐ 41 Jay Hilgenberg | .10 | .02 |
| ☐ 42 Darren Lewis | .10 | .02 |
| ☐ 43 Steve McMichael | .20 | .07 |
| ☐ 44 Anthony Morgan | .10 | .02 |
| ☐ 45 Brad Muster | .10 | .02 |
| ☐ 46 William Perry | .20 | .07 |
| ☐ 47 John Roper | .10 | .02 |
| ☐ 48 Lemuel Stinson | .10 | .02 |
| ☐ 49 Tom Waddle | .10 | .02 |
| ☐ 50 Donnell Woolford | .10 | .02 |
| ☐ 51 Leo Barker RC | .10 | .02 |
| ☐ 52 Eddie Brown | .10 | .02 |
| ☐ 53 James Francis | .10 | .02 |
| ☐ 54 David Fulcher RC | .10 | .02 |
| ☐ 55 David Grant | .10 | .02 |
| ☐ 56 Harold Green | .10 | .02 |
| ☐ 57 Rodney Holman | .10 | .02 |
| ☐ 58 Lee Johnson | .10 | .02 |
| ☐ 59 Tim Krumrie | .10 | .02 |
| ☐ 60 Tim McGee | .10 | .02 |
| ☐ 61 Alonzo Mitz RC | .10 | .02 |
| ☐ 62 Anthony Munoz | .20 | .07 |
| ☐ 63 Alfred Williams | .10 | .02 |
| ☐ 64 Stephen Braggs | .10 | .02 |
| ☐ 65 Richard Brown RC | .10 | .02 |
| ☐ 66 Randy Hilliard RC | .10 | .02 |
| ☐ 67 Leroy Hoard | .20 | .07 |
| ☐ 68 Michael Jackson | .20 | .07 |
| ☐ 69 Mike Johnson | .10 | .02 |
| ☐ 70 James Jones DT | .10 | .02 |
| ☐ 71 Tony Jones T | .10 | .02 |
| ☐ 72 Ed King | .10 | .02 |

|  |  | | |
|---|--------|------|------|
| 73 | Kevin Mack | .10 | .02 |
| 74 | Clay Matthews | .20 | .07 |
| 75 | Eric Metcalf | .20 | .07 |
| 76 | Vince Newsome | .10 | .02 |
| 77 | Steve Beuerlein | .20 | .07 |
| 78 | Larry Brown DB | .10 | .02 |
| 79 | Tony Casillas | .10 | .02 |
| 80 | Alvin Harper | .20 | .07 |
| 81 | Issiac Holt | .10 | .02 |
| 82 | Ray Horton | .10 | .02 |
| 83 | Michael Irvin | .40 | .15 |
| 84 | Daryl Johnston | .40 | .15 |
| 85 | Kelvin Martin | .10 | .02 |
| 86 | Ken Norton | .20 | .07 |
| 87 | Jay Novacek | .20 | .07 |
| 88 | Emmitt Smith | 3.00 | 1.50 |
| 89 | Vinson Smith RC | .10 | .02 |
| 90 | Mark Stepnoski | .20 | .07 |
| 91 | Tony Tolbert | .10 | .02 |
| 92 | Alexander Wright | .10 | .02 |
| 93 | Steve Atwater | .10 | .02 |
| 94 | Tyrone Braxton | .10 | .02 |
| 95 | Michael Brooks | .10 | .02 |
| 96 | Mike Croel | .10 | .02 |
| 97 | John Elway | 2.50 | 1.00 |
| 98 | Simon Fletcher | .10 | .02 |
| 99 | Gaston Green | .10 | .02 |
| 100 | Mark Jackson | .10 | .02 |
| 101 | Keith Kartz | .10 | .02 |
| 102 | Greg Kragen | .10 | .02 |
| 103 | Greg Lewis | .10 | .02 |
| 104 | Karl Mecklenburg | .10 | .02 |
| 105 | Derek Russell | .10 | .02 |
| 106 | Steve Sewell | .10 | .02 |
| 107 | Dennis Smith | .10 | .02 |
| 108 | David Treadwell | .10 | .02 |
| 109 | Kenny Walker | .10 | .02 |
| 110 | Michael Young | .10 | .02 |
| 111 | Jerry Ball | .10 | .02 |
| 112 | Bennie Blades | .10 | .02 |
| 113 | Lomas Brown | .10 | .02 |
| 114 | Scott Conover RC | .10 | .02 |
| 115 | Ray Crockett | .10 | .02 |
| 116 | Mel Gray | .20 | .07 |
| 117 | Willie Green | .10 | .02 |
| 118 | Erik Kramer | .20 | .07 |
| 119 | Dan Owens | .10 | .02 |
| 120 | Rodney Peete | .20 | .07 |
| 121 | Brett Perriman | .40 | .15 |
| 122 | Barry Sanders | 2.50 | 1.00 |
| 123 | Chris Spielman | .20 | .07 |
| 124 | Marc Spindler | .10 | .02 |
| 125 | William White | .10 | .02 |
| 126 | Tony Bennett | .10 | .02 |
| 127 | Matt Brock | .10 | .02 |
| 128 | LeRoy Butler | .10 | .02 |
| 129 | Chuck Cecil | .10 | .02 |
| 130 | Johnny Holland | .10 | .02 |
| 131 | Perry Kemp | .10 | .02 |
| 132 | Don Majkowski | .10 | .02 |
| 133 | Tony Mandarich | .10 | .02 |
| 134 | Brian Noble | .10 | .02 |
| 135 | Bryce Paup | .40 | .15 |
| 136 | Sterling Sharpe | .40 | .15 |
| 137 | Darrell Thompson | .10 | .02 |
| 138 | Mike Tomczak | .10 | .02 |
| 139 | Vince Workman | .10 | .02 |
| 140 | Ray Childress | .10 | .02 |
| 141 | Cris Dishman | .10 | .02 |
| 142 | Curtis Duncan | .10 | .02 |
| 143 | William Fuller | .10 | .02 |
| 144 | Ernest Givins | .20 | .07 |
| 145 | Haywood Jeffires | .20 | .07 |
| 146 | Sean Jones | .10 | .02 |
| 147 | Lamar Lathon | .10 | .02 |
| 148 | Bruce Matthews | .10 | .02 |
| 149 | Bubba McDowell | .10 | .02 |
| 150 | Johnny Meads | .10 | .02 |
| 151 | Warren Moon | .40 | .15 |
| 152 | Mike Munchak | .20 | .07 |
| 153 | Bo Orlando RC | .10 | .02 |
| 154 | Al Smith | .10 | .02 |
| 155 | Doug Smith | .10 | .02 |
| 156 | Lorenzo White | .10 | .02 |
| 157 | Chip Banks | .10 | .02 |
| 158 | Duane Bickett | .10 | .02 |
| 159 | Bill Brooks | .10 | .02 |
| 160 | Eugene Daniel | .10 | .02 |
| 161 | Jon Hand | .10 | .02 |
| 162 | Jeff Herrod | .10 | .02 |
| 163 | Jessie Hester | .10 | .02 |
| 164 | Scott Radecic | .10 | .02 |
| 165 | Rohn Stark | .10 | .02 |
| 166 | Clarence Verdin | .10 | .02 |
| 167 | John Alt | .10 | .02 |
| 168 | Tim Barnett | .10 | .02 |
| 169 | Tim Grunhard | .10 | .02 |
| 170 | Dino Hackett | .10 | .02 |
| 171 | Jonathan Hayes | .10 | .02 |
| 172 | Bill Maas | .10 | .02 |
| 173 | Chris Martin | .10 | .02 |
| 174 | Christian Okoye | .10 | .02 |
| 175 | Stephone Paige | .10 | .02 |
| 176 | Jayice Pearson RC | .10 | .02 |
| 177 | Kevin Porter | .10 | .02 |
| 178 | Kevin Ross | .10 | .02 |
| 179 | Dan Saleaumua | .10 | .02 |
| 180 | Tracy Simien RC | .10 | .02 |
| 181 | Neil Smith | .40 | .15 |
| 182 | Derrick Thomas | .40 | .15 |
| 183 | Robb Thomas | .10 | .02 |
| 184 | Barry Word | .10 | .02 |
| 185 | Marcus Allen | .40 | .15 |
| 186 | Eddie Anderson | .10 | .02 |
| 187 | Nick Bell | .10 | .02 |
| 188 | Tim Brown | .40 | .15 |
| 189 | Mervyn Fernandez | .10 | .02 |
| 190 | Willie Gault | .20 | .07 |
| 191 | Jeff Gossett | .10 | .02 |
| 192 | Ethan Horton | .10 | .02 |
| 193 | Jeff Jaeger | .10 | .02 |
| 194 | Howie Long | .40 | .15 |
| 195 | Ronnie Lott | .20 | .07 |
| 196 | Todd Marinovich | .10 | .02 |
| 197 | Don Mosebar | .10 | .02 |
| 198 | Jay Schroeder | .10 | .02 |
| 199 | Anthony Smith | .10 | .02 |
| 200 | Greg Townsend | .10 | .02 |
| 201 | Lionel Washington | .10 | .02 |
| 202 | Steve Wisniewski | .10 | .02 |
| 203 | Flipper Anderson | .10 | .02 |
| 204 | Robert Delpino | .10 | .02 |
| 205 | Henry Ellard | .20 | .07 |
| 206 | Jim Everett | .20 | .07 |
| 207 | Kevin Greene | .20 | .07 |
| 208 | Darryl Henley | .10 | .02 |
| 209 | Damone Johnson | .10 | .02 |
| 210 | Larry Kelm | .10 | .02 |
| 211 | Todd Lyght | .10 | .02 |
| 212 | Jackie Slater | .10 | .02 |
| 213 | Michael Stewart | .10 | .02 |
| 214 | Pat Terrell | .10 | .02 |
| 215 | Robert Young | .10 | .02 |
| 216 | Mark Clayton | .20 | .07 |
| 217 | Bryan Cox | .20 | .07 |
| 218 | Jeff Cross | .10 | .02 |
| 219 | Mark Duper | .10 | .02 |
| 220 | Harry Galbreath | .10 | .02 |
| 221 | David Griggs | .10 | .02 |
| 222 | Mark Higgs | .10 | .02 |
| 223 | Vestee Jackson | .10 | .02 |
| 224 | John Offerdahl | .10 | .02 |
| 225 | Louis Oliver | .10 | .02 |
| 226 | Tony Paige | .10 | .02 |
| 227 | Reggie Roby | .10 | .02 |
| 228 | Pete Stoyanovich | .10 | .02 |
| 229 | Richmond Webb | .10 | .02 |
| 230 | Terry Allen | .40 | .15 |
| 231 | Ray Berry | .10 | .02 |
| 232 | Anthony Carter | .20 | .07 |
| 233 | Cris Carter | .75 | .30 |
| 234 | Chris Doleman | .10 | .02 |
| 235 | Rich Gannon | .40 | .15 |
| 236 | Steve Jordan | .10 | .02 |
| 237 | Carl Lee | .10 | .02 |
| 238 | Randall McDaniel | .10 | .05 |
| 239 | Mike Merriweather | .10 | .02 |
| 240 | Harry Newsome | .10 | .02 |
| 241 | John Randle | .20 | .07 |
| 242 | Henry Thomas | .10 | .02 |
| 243 | Bruce Armstrong | .10 | .02 |
| 244 | Vincent Brown | .10 | .02 |
| 245 | Marv Cook | .10 | .02 |
| 246 | Irving Fryar | .20 | .07 |
| 247 | Pat Harlow | .10 | .02 |
| 248 | Maurice Hurst | .10 | .02 |
| 249 | Eugene Lockhart | .10 | .02 |
| 250 | Greg McMurtry | .10 | .02 |
| 251 | Hugh Millen | .10 | .02 |
| 252 | Leonard Russell | .20 | .07 |
| 253 | Chris Singleton | .10 | .02 |
| 254 | Andre Tippett | .10 | .02 |
| 255 | Jon Vaughn | .10 | .02 |
| 256 | Morten Andersen | .10 | .02 |
| 257 | Gene Atkins | .10 | .02 |
| 258 | Wesley Carroll | .10 | .02 |
| 259 | Jim Dombrowski | .10 | .02 |
| 260 | Quinn Early | .20 | .07 |
| 261 | Bobby Hebert | .10 | .02 |
| 262 | Joel Hilgenberg | .10 | .02 |
| 263 | Rickey Jackson | .10 | .02 |
| 264 | Vaughan Johnson | .10 | .02 |
| 265 | Eric Martin | .10 | .02 |
| 266 | Brett Maxie | .10 | .02 |
| 267 | Fred McAfee RC | .10 | .02 |
| 268 | Sam Mills | .10 | .02 |
| 269 | Pat Swilling | .10 | .02 |
| 270 | Floyd Turner | .10 | .02 |
| 271 | Steve Walsh | .10 | .02 |
| 272 | Stephen Baker | .10 | .02 |
| 273 | Jarrod Bunch | .10 | .02 |
| 274 | Mark Collins | .10 | .02 |
| 275 | John Elliott | .10 | .02 |
| 276 | Myron Guyton | .10 | .02 |
| 277 | Rodney Hampton | .20 | .07 |
| 278 | Jeff Hostetler | .20 | .07 |
| 279 | Mark Ingram | .10 | .02 |
| 280 | Pepper Johnson | .10 | .02 |
| 281 | Sean Landeta | .10 | .02 |
| 282 | Leonard Marshall | .10 | .02 |
| 283 | Kanavis McGhee | .10 | .02 |
| 284 | Dave Meggett | .20 | .07 |
| 285 | Bart Oates | .10 | .02 |
| 286 | Phil Simms | .20 | .07 |
| 287 | Reyna Thompson | .10 | .02 |
| 288 | Lewis Tillman | .10 | .02 |
| 289 | Brad Baxter | .10 | .02 |
| 290 | Mike Brim RC | .10 | .02 |
| 291 | Chris Burkett | .10 | .02 |
| 292 | Kyle Clifton | .10 | .02 |
| 293 | James Hasty | .10 | .02 |
| 294 | Joe Kelly | .10 | .02 |
| 295 | Jeff Lageman | .10 | .02 |
| 296 | Mo Lewis | .10 | .02 |
| 297 | Erik McMillan | .10 | .02 |
| 298 | Scott Mersereau | .10 | .02 |
| 299 | Rob Moore | .20 | .07 |
| 300 | Tony Stargell | .10 | .02 |
| 301 | Jim Sweeney | .10 | .02 |
| 302 | Marvin Washington | .10 | .02 |
| 303 | Lonnie Young | .10 | .02 |
| 304 | Eric Allen | .10 | .02 |
| 305 | Fred Barnett | .40 | .15 |
| 306 | Keith Byars | .10 | .02 |
| 307 | Byron Evans | .10 | .02 |
| 308 | Wes Hopkins | .10 | .02 |
| 309 | Keith Jackson | .20 | .07 |
| 310 | James Joseph | .10 | .02 |
| 311 | Seth Joyner | .10 | .02 |
| 312 | Roger Ruzek | .10 | .02 |
| 313 | Clyde Simmons | .10 | .02 |
| 314 | William Thomas | .10 | .02 |
| 315 | Reggie White | .40 | .15 |
| 316 | Calvin Williams | .10 | .02 |
| 317 | Rich Camarillo | .10 | .02 |
| 318 | Jeff Faulkner | .10 | .02 |
| 319 | Ken Harvey | .10 | .02 |
| 320 | Eric Hill | .10 | .02 |
| 321 | Johnny Johnson | .10 | .02 |
| 322 | Ernie Jones | .10 | .02 |
| 323 | Tim McDonald | .10 | .02 |
| 324 | Freddie Joe Nunn | .10 | .02 |

| | | | |
|---|---|---|---|
| ☐ 325 Luis Sharpe | .10 | .02 |
| ☐ 326 Eric Swann | .20 | .07 |
| ☐ 327 Aeneas Williams | .20 | .07 |
| ☐ 328 Michael Zordich RC | .10 | .02 |
| ☐ 329 Gary Anderson K | .10 | .02 |
| ☐ 330 Bubby Brister | .10 | .02 |
| ☐ 331 Barry Foster | .20 | .07 |
| ☐ 332 Eric Green | .10 | .02 |
| ☐ 333 Bryan Hinkle | .10 | .02 |
| ☐ 334 Tunch Ilkin | .10 | .02 |
| ☐ 335 Carnell Lake | .10 | .02 |
| ☐ 336 Louis Lipps | .10 | .02 |
| ☐ 337 David Little | .10 | .02 |
| ☐ 338 Greg Lloyd | .20 | .07 |
| ☐ 339 Neil O'Donnell | .20 | .07 |
| ☐ 340 Rod Woodson | .40 | .15 |
| ☐ 341 Rod Bernstine | .10 | .02 |
| ☐ 342 Marion Butts | .10 | .02 |
| ☐ 343 Gill Byrd | .10 | .02 |
| ☐ 344 John Friesz | .20 | .07 |
| ☐ 345 Burt Grossman | .10 | .02 |
| ☐ 346 Courtney Hall | .10 | .02 |
| ☐ 347 Ronnie Harmon | .10 | .02 |
| ☐ 348 Shawn Jefferson | .10 | .02 |
| ☐ 349 Nate Lewis | .10 | .02 |
| ☐ 350 Craig McEwen RC | .10 | .02 |
| ☐ 351 Eric Moten | .10 | .02 |
| ☐ 352 Gary Plummer | .10 | .02 |
| ☐ 353 Henry Rolling | .10 | .02 |
| ☐ 354 Broderick Thompson | .10 | .02 |
| ☐ 355 Derrick Walker | .10 | .02 |
| ☐ 356 Harris Barton | .10 | .02 |
| ☐ 357 Steve Bono RC | .40 | .15 |
| ☐ 358 Todd Bowles | .10 | .02 |
| ☐ 359 Dexter Carter | .10 | .02 |
| ☐ 360 Michael Carter | .10 | .02 |
| ☐ 361 Keith DeLong | .10 | .02 |
| ☐ 362 Charles Haley | .20 | .07 |
| ☐ 363 Merton Hanks | .20 | .07 |
| ☐ 364 Tim Harris | .10 | .02 |
| ☐ 365 Brent Jones | .20 | .07 |
| ☐ 366 Guy McIntyre | .10 | .02 |
| ☐ 367 Tom Rathman | .10 | .02 |
| ☐ 368 Bill Romanowski | .10 | .02 |
| ☐ 369 Jesse Sapolu | .10 | .02 |
| ☐ 370 John Taylor | .20 | .07 |
| ☐ 371 Steve Young | 1.50 | .60 |
| ☐ 372 Robert Blackmon | .10 | .02 |
| ☐ 373 Brian Blades | .20 | .07 |
| ☐ 374 Jacob Green | .10 | .02 |
| ☐ 375 Dwayne Harper | .10 | .02 |
| ☐ 376 Andy Heck | .10 | .02 |
| ☐ 377 Tommy Kane | .10 | .02 |
| ☐ 378 John Kasay | .10 | .02 |
| ☐ 379 Cortez Kennedy | .20 | .07 |
| ☐ 380 Bryan Millard | .10 | .02 |
| ☐ 381 Rufus Porter | .10 | .02 |
| ☐ 382 Eugene Robinson | .10 | .02 |
| ☐ 383 John L. Williams | .10 | .02 |
| ☐ 384 Terry Wooden | .10 | .02 |
| ☐ 385 Gary Anderson RB | .10 | .02 |
| ☐ 386 Ian Beckles | .10 | .02 |
| ☐ 387 Mark Carrier WR | .20 | .07 |
| ☐ 388 Reggie Cobb | .10 | .02 |
| ☐ 389 Tony Covington | .10 | .02 |
| ☐ 390 Lawrence Dawsey | .20 | .07 |
| ☐ 391 Ron Hall | .10 | .02 |
| ☐ 392 Keith McCants | .10 | .02 |
| ☐ 393 Charles McRae | .10 | .02 |
| ☐ 394 Tim Newton | .10 | .02 |
| ☐ 395 Jesse Solomon | .10 | .02 |
| ☐ 396 Vinny Testaverde | .20 | .07 |
| ☐ 397 Broderick Thomas | .10 | .02 |
| ☐ 398 Robert Wilson | .10 | .02 |
| ☐ 399 Earnest Byner | .10 | .02 |
| ☐ 400 Gary Clark | .40 | .15 |
| ☐ 401 Andre Collins | .10 | .02 |
| ☐ 402 Brad Edwards | .10 | .02 |
| ☐ 403 Kurt Gouveia | .10 | .02 |
| ☐ 404 Darrell Green | .10 | .02 |
| ☐ 405 Joe Jacoby | .10 | .02 |
| ☐ 406 Jim Lachey | .10 | .02 |
| ☐ 407 Chip Lohmiller | .10 | .02 |
| ☐ 408 Charles Mann | .10 | .02 |

| | | |
|---|---|---|
| ☐ 409 Wilber Marshall | .10 | .02 |
| ☐ 410 Brian Mitchell | .20 | .07 |
| ☐ 411 Art Monk | .20 | .07 |
| ☐ 412 Mark Rypien | .10 | .02 |
| ☐ 413 Ricky Sanders | .10 | .02 |
| ☐ 414 Mark Schlereth RC | .10 | .02 |
| ☐ 415 Fred Stokes | .10 | .02 |
| ☐ 416 Bobby Wilson | .10 | .02 |
| ☐ 417 Corey Barlow RC | .10 | .02 |
| ☐ 418 Edgar Bennett RC | .40 | .15 |
| ☐ 419 Eddie Blake RC | .10 | .02 |
| ☐ 420 Terrell Buckley RC | .10 | .02 |
| ☐ 421 Willie Clay RC | .10 | .02 |
| ☐ 422 Rodney Culver RC | .10 | .02 |
| ☐ 423 Ed Cunningham RC | .10 | .02 |
| ☐ 424 Mark D'Onofrio RC | .10 | .02 |
| ☐ 425 Matt Darby RC | .10 | .02 |
| ☐ 426 Charles Davenport RC | .10 | .02 |
| ☐ 427 Will Furrer RC | .10 | .02 |
| ☐ 428 Keith Goganious RC | .10 | .02 |
| ☐ 429 Mario Bailey RC | .10 | .02 |
| ☐ 430 Chris Hakel RC | .10 | .02 |
| ☐ 431 Keith Hamilton RC | .20 | .07 |
| ☐ 432 Aaron Pierce RC | .10 | .02 |
| ☐ 433 Amp Lee RC | .10 | .02 |
| ☐ 434 Scott Lockwood RC | .10 | .02 |
| ☐ 435 Ricardo McDonald RC | .10 | .02 |
| ☐ 436 Dexter McNabb RC | .10 | .02 |
| ☐ 437 Chris Mims RC | .10 | .02 |
| ☐ 438 Mike Mooney RC | .10 | .02 |
| ☐ 439 Ray Roberts RC | .10 | .02 |
| ☐ 440 Patrick Rowe RC | .10 | .02 |
| ☐ 441 Leon Searcy RC | .10 | .02 |
| ☐ 442 Siran Stacy RC | .10 | .02 |
| ☐ 443 Kevin Turner RC | .10 | .02 |
| ☐ 444 Tommy Vardell RC | .10 | .02 |
| ☐ 445 Bob Whitfield RC | .10 | .02 |
| ☐ 446 Darryl Williams RC | .10 | .02 |
| ☐ 447 Checklist 1-110 | .10 | .02 |
| ☐ 448 Checklist 111-224 | .10 | .02 |
| ☐ 449 Checklist 230-340 UER | .10 | .02 |
| ☐ 450 Checklist 341-450 | .10 | .02 |
| ☐ AD Super Bowl XXVII Strip | 2.00 | .75 |

**1993 Ultra**

| | | |
|---|---|---|
| ☐ COMPLETE SET (500) | 20.00 | 7.50 |
| ☐ 1 Vinnie Clark | .10 | .02 |
| ☐ 2 Darion Conner | .10 | .02 |
| ☐ 3 Eric Dickerson | .20 | .07 |
| ☐ 4 Moe Gardner | .10 | .02 |
| ☐ 5 Tim Green | .10 | .02 |
| ☐ 6 Roger Harper RC | .10 | .02 |
| ☐ 7 Michael Haynes | .20 | .07 |
| ☐ 8 Bobby Hebert | .10 | .02 |
| ☐ 9 Chris Hinton | .10 | .02 |
| ☐ 10 Pierce Holt | .10 | .02 |
| ☐ 11 Mike Kenn | .10 | .02 |
| ☐ 12 Lincoln Kennedy RC | .10 | .02 |
| ☐ 13 Chris Miller | .20 | .07 |
| ☐ 14 Mike Pritchard | .20 | .07 |
| ☐ 15 Andre Rison | .20 | .07 |
| ☐ 16 Deion Sanders | .75 | .30 |
| ☐ 17 Tony Smith RB | .10 | .02 |
| ☐ 18 Jessie Tuggle | .10 | .02 |
| ☐ 19 Howard Ballard | .10 | .02 |
| ☐ 20 Don Beebe | .10 | .02 |
| ☐ 21 Cornelius Bennett | .20 | .07 |

| | | |
|---|---|---|
| ☐ 22 Bill Brooks | .10 | .02 |
| ☐ 23 Kenneth Davis | .10 | .02 |
| ☐ 24 Phil Hansen | .10 | .02 |
| ☐ 25 Henry Jones | .10 | .02 |
| ☐ 26 Jim Kelly | .40 | .15 |
| ☐ 27 Nate Odomes | .10 | .02 |
| ☐ 28 John Parrella RC | .10 | .02 |
| ☐ 29 Andre Reed | .20 | .07 |
| ☐ 30 Frank Reich | .20 | .07 |
| ☐ 31 Jim Ritcher | .10 | .02 |
| ☐ 32 Bruce Smith | .40 | .15 |
| ☐ 33 Thomas Smith RC | .20 | .07 |
| ☐ 34 Darryl Talley | .10 | .02 |
| ☐ 35 Steve Tasker | .10 | .02 |
| ☐ 36 Thurman Thomas | .40 | .15 |
| ☐ 37 Jeff Wright | .10 | .02 |
| ☐ 38 Neal Anderson | .10 | .02 |
| ☐ 39 Trace Armstrong | .10 | .02 |
| ☐ 40 Mark Carrier DB | .10 | .02 |
| ☐ 41 Curtis Conway RC | .75 | .30 |
| ☐ 42 Wendell Davis | .10 | .02 |
| ☐ 43 Richard Dent | .20 | .07 |
| ☐ 44 Shaun Gayle | .10 | .02 |
| ☐ 45 Jim Harbaugh | .40 | .15 |
| ☐ 46 Craig Heyward | .20 | .07 |
| ☐ 47 Darren Lewis | .10 | .02 |
| ☐ 48 Steve McMichael | .10 | .02 |
| ☐ 49 William Perry | .20 | .07 |
| ☐ 50 Carl Simpson RC | .10 | .02 |
| ☐ 51 Alonzo Spellman | .10 | .02 |
| ☐ 52 Keith Van Horne | .10 | .02 |
| ☐ 53 Tom Waddle | .10 | .02 |
| ☐ 54 Donnell Woolford | .10 | .02 |
| ☐ 55 John Copeland RC | .20 | .07 |
| ☐ 56 Derrick Fenner | .10 | .02 |
| ☐ 57 James Francis | .10 | .02 |
| ☐ 58 Harold Green | .10 | .02 |
| ☐ 59 David Klingler | .10 | .02 |
| ☐ 60 Tim Krumrie | .10 | .02 |
| ☐ 61 Ricardo McDonald | .10 | .02 |
| ☐ 62 Tony McGee RC | .20 | .07 |
| ☐ 63 Carl Pickens | .20 | .07 |
| ☐ 64 Lamar Rogers | .10 | .02 |
| ☐ 65 Jay Schroeder | .10 | .02 |
| ☐ 66 Daniel Stubbs | .10 | .02 |
| ☐ 67 Steve Tovar RC | .10 | .02 |
| ☐ 68 Alfred Williams | .10 | .02 |
| ☐ 69 Darryl Williams | .10 | .02 |
| ☐ 70 Jerry Ball | .10 | .02 |
| ☐ 71 David Brandon | .10 | .02 |
| ☐ 72 Rob Burnett | .10 | .02 |
| ☐ 73 Mark Carrier WR | .20 | .07 |
| ☐ 74 Steve Everitt RC | .10 | .02 |
| ☐ 75 Dan Footman RC | .10 | .02 |
| ☐ 76 Leroy Hoard | .20 | .07 |
| ☐ 77 Michael Jackson | .20 | .07 |
| ☐ 78 Mike Johnson | .10 | .02 |
| ☐ 79 Bernie Kosar | .20 | .07 |
| ☐ 80 Clay Matthews | .20 | .07 |
| ☐ 81 Eric Metcalf | .20 | .07 |
| ☐ 82 Michael Dean Perry | .20 | .07 |
| ☐ 83 Vinny Testaverde | .20 | .07 |
| ☐ 84 Tommy Vardell | .10 | .02 |
| ☐ 85 Tony Alonzo | 1.50 | .60 |
| ☐ 86 Larry Brown DB | .10 | .02 |
| ☐ 87 Tony Casillas | .10 | .02 |
| ☐ 88 Thomas Everett | .10 | .02 |
| ☐ 89 Charles Haley | .20 | .07 |
| ☐ 90 Alvin Harper | .20 | .07 |
| ☐ 91 Michael Irvin | .40 | .15 |
| ☐ 92 Jim Jeffcoat | .10 | .02 |
| ☐ 93 Daryl Johnston | .40 | .15 |
| ☐ 94 Robert Jones | .10 | .02 |
| ☐ 95 Leon Lett RC | .20 | .07 |
| ☐ 96 Russell Maryland | .10 | .02 |
| ☐ 97 Nate Newton | .20 | .07 |
| ☐ 98 Ken Norton | .20 | .07 |
| ☐ 99 Jay Novacek | .20 | .07 |
| ☐ 100 Darrin Smith RC | .20 | .07 |
| ☐ 101 Emmitt Smith | 3.00 | 1.25 |
| ☐ 102 Kevin Smith | .20 | .07 |
| ☐ 103 Mark Stepnoski | .10 | .02 |
| ☐ 104 Tony Tolbert | .10 | .02 |
| ☐ 105 Kevin Williams RC WR | .40 | .15 |

|  |  | | |
|---|---|---|---|
| 106 | Steve Atwater | .10 | .02 |
| 107 | Rod Bernstine | .10 | .02 |
| 108 | Mike Croel | .10 | .02 |
| 109 | Robert Delpino | .10 | .02 |
| 110 | Shane Dronett | .10 | .02 |
| 111 | John Elway | 3.00 | 1.25 |
| 112 | Simon Fletcher | .10 | .02 |
| 113 | Greg Kragen | .10 | .02 |
| 114 | Tommy Maddox | .40 | .15 |
| 115 | Arthur Marshall RC | .10 | .02 |
| 116 | Karl Mecklenburg | .10 | .02 |
| 117 | Glyn Milburn RC | .40 | .15 |
| 118 | Reggie Rivers RC | .10 | .02 |
| 119 | Shannon Sharpe | .40 | .15 |
| 120 | Dennis Smith | .10 | .02 |
| 121 | Kenny Walker | .10 | .02 |
| 122 | Dan Williams RC | .10 | .02 |
| 123 | Bennie Blades | .10 | .02 |
| 124 | Lomas Brown | .10 | .02 |
| 125 | Bill Fralic | .10 | .02 |
| 126 | Mel Gray | .20 | .07 |
| 127 | Willie Green | .10 | .02 |
| 128 | Jason Hanson | .10 | .02 |
| 129 | Antonio London RC | .10 | .02 |
| 130 | Ryan McNeil RC | .40 | .15 |
| 131 | Herman Moore | .40 | .15 |
| 132 | Rodney Peete | .10 | .02 |
| 133 | Brett Perriman | .40 | .15 |
| 134 | Kelvin Pritchett | .10 | .02 |
| 135 | Barry Sanders | 2.50 | 1.00 |
| 136 | Tracy Scroggins | .10 | .02 |
| 137 | Chris Spielman | .20 | .07 |
| 138 | Pat Swilling | .10 | .02 |
| 139 | Andre Ware | .10 | .02 |
| 140 | Edgar Bennett | .40 | .15 |
| 141 | Tony Bennett | .10 | .02 |
| 142 | Matt Brock | .10 | .02 |
| 143 | Terrell Buckley | .10 | .02 |
| 144 | LeRoy Butler | .10 | .02 |
| 145 | Mark Clayton | .10 | .02 |
| 146 | Brett Favre | 4.00 | 1.50 |
| 147 | Jackie Harris | .10 | .02 |
| 148 | Johnny Holland | .10 | .02 |
| 149 | Bill Maas | .10 | .02 |
| 150 | Brian Noble | .10 | .02 |
| 151 | Bryce Paup | .20 | .07 |
| 152 | Ken Ruettgers | .10 | .02 |
| 153 | Sterling Sharpe | .40 | .15 |
| 154 | Wayne Simmons RC | .10 | .02 |
| 155 | John Stephens | .10 | .02 |
| 156 | George Teague RC | .20 | .07 |
| 157 | Reggie White | .40 | .15 |
| 158 | Micheal Barrow RC | .10 | .02 |
| 159 | Cody Carlson | .10 | .02 |
| 160 | Ray Childress | .10 | .02 |
| 161 | Cris Dishman | .10 | .02 |
| 162 | Curtis Duncan | .10 | .02 |
| 163 | William Fuller | .10 | .02 |
| 164 | Ernest Givins | .20 | .07 |
| 165 | Brad Hopkins RC | .10 | .02 |
| 166 | Haywood Jeffires | .20 | .07 |
| 167 | Lamar Lathon | .10 | .02 |
| 168 | Wilber Marshall | .10 | .02 |
| 169 | Bruce Matthews | .10 | .02 |
| 170 | Bubba McDowell | .10 | .02 |
| 171 | Warren Moon | .40 | .15 |
| 172 | Mike Munchak | .20 | .07 |
| 173 | Eddie Robinson | .10 | .02 |
| 174 | Al Smith | .10 | .02 |
| 175 | Lorenzo White | .10 | .02 |
| 176 | Lee Williams | .10 | .02 |
| 177 | Chip Banks | .10 | .02 |
| 178 | John Baylor | .10 | .02 |
| 179 | Duane Bickett | .10 | .02 |
| 180 | Kerry Cash | .10 | .02 |
| 181 | Quentin Coryatt | .20 | .07 |
| 182 | Rodney Culver | .10 | .02 |
| 183 | Steve Emtman | .10 | .02 |
| 184 | Jeff George | .40 | .15 |
| 185 | Jeff Herrod | .10 | .02 |
| 186 | Jessie Hester | .10 | .02 |
| 187 | Anthony Johnson | .20 | .07 |
| 188 | Reggie Langhorne | .10 | .02 |
| 189 | Roosevelt Potts RC | .10 | .02 |
| 190 | Rohn Stark | .10 | .02 |
| 191 | Clarence Verdin | .10 | .02 |
| 192 | Will Wolford | .10 | .02 |
| 193 | Marcus Allen | .40 | .15 |
| 194 | John Alt | .10 | .02 |
| 195 | Tim Barnett | .10 | .02 |
| 196 | J.J. Birden | .10 | .02 |
| 197 | Dale Carter | .10 | .02 |
| 198 | Willie Davis | .40 | .15 |
| 199 | Jaime Fields RC | .10 | .02 |
| 200 | Dave Krieg | .20 | .07 |
| 201 | Nick Lowery | .10 | .02 |
| 202 | Charles Mincy RC | .10 | .02 |
| 203 | Joe Montana | 3.00 | 1.25 |
| 204 | Christian Okoye | .10 | .02 |
| 205 | Dan Saleaumua | .10 | .02 |
| 206 | Will Shields RC | .40 | .15 |
| 207 | Tracy Simien | .10 | .02 |
| 208 | Neil Smith | .40 | .15 |
| 209 | Derrick Thomas | .40 | .15 |
| 210 | Harvey Williams | .20 | .07 |
| 211 | Barry Word | .10 | .02 |
| 212 | Eddie Anderson | .10 | .02 |
| 213 | Patrick Bates RC | .10 | .02 |
| 214 | Nick Bell | .10 | .02 |
| 215 | Tim Brown | .40 | .15 |
| 216 | Willie Gault | .10 | .02 |
| 217 | Gaston Green | .10 | .02 |
| 218 | Billy Joe Hobert RC | .40 | .15 |
| 219 | Ethan Horton | .10 | .02 |
| 220 | Jeff Hostetler | .20 | .07 |
| 221 | James Lofton | .20 | .07 |
| 222 | Howie Long | .40 | .15 |
| 223 | Todd Marinovich | .10 | .02 |
| 224 | Terry McDaniel | .10 | .02 |
| 225 | Winston Moss | .10 | .02 |
| 226 | Anthony Smith | .10 | .02 |
| 227 | Greg Townsend | .10 | .02 |
| 228 | Aaron Wallace | .10 | .02 |
| 229 | Lionel Washington | .10 | .02 |
| 230 | Steve Wisniewski | .10 | .02 |
| 231 | Flipper Anderson | .10 | .02 |
| 232 | Jerome Bettis RC | 8.00 | 4.00 |
| 233 | Marc Boutte | .10 | .02 |
| 234 | Shane Conlan | .10 | .02 |
| 235 | Troy Drayton RC | .20 | .07 |
| 236 | Henry Ellard | .20 | .07 |
| 237 | Jim Everett | .20 | .07 |
| 238 | Cleveland Gary | .10 | .02 |
| 239 | Sean Gilbert | .20 | .07 |
| 240 | Darryl Henley | .10 | .02 |
| 241 | David Lang | .10 | .02 |
| 242 | Todd Lyght | .10 | .02 |
| 243 | Anthony Newman | .10 | .02 |
| 244 | Roman Phifer | .10 | .02 |
| 245 | Gerald Robinson | .10 | .02 |
| 246 | Henry Rolling | .10 | .02 |
| 247 | Jackie Slater | .10 | .02 |
| 248 | Keith Byars | .10 | .02 |
| 249 | Marco Coleman | .10 | .02 |
| 250 | Bryan Cox | .10 | .02 |
| 251 | Jeff Cross | .10 | .02 |
| 252 | Irving Fryar | .20 | .07 |
| 253 | Mark Higgs | .10 | .02 |
| 254 | Dwight Hollier RC | .10 | .02 |
| 255 | Mark Ingram | .10 | .02 |
| 256 | Keith Jackson | .20 | .07 |
| 257 | Terry Kirby RC | .40 | .15 |
| 258 | Dan Marino | 3.00 | 1.25 |
| 259 | O.J. McDuffie RC | .40 | .15 |
| 260 | John Offerdahl | .10 | .02 |
| 261 | Louis Oliver | .10 | .02 |
| 262 | Pete Stoyanovich | .10 | .02 |
| 263 | Troy Vincent | .10 | .02 |
| 264 | Richmond Webb | .10 | .02 |
| 265 | Jarvis Williams | .10 | .02 |
| 266 | Terry Allen | .40 | .15 |
| 267 | Anthony Carter | .20 | .07 |
| 268 | Cris Carter | .40 | .15 |
| 269 | Roger Craig | .20 | .07 |
| 270 | Jack Del Rio | .10 | .02 |
| 271 | Chris Doleman | .10 | .02 |
| 272 | Qadry Ismail RC | .40 | .15 |
| 273 | Steve Jordan | .10 | .02 |
| 274 | Randall McDaniel | .15 | .05 |
| 275 | Audray McMillian | .10 | .02 |
| 276 | John Randle | .20 | .07 |
| 277 | Sean Salisbury | .10 | .02 |
| 278 | Todd Scott | .10 | .02 |
| 279 | Robert Smith RC | 2.50 | 1.00 |
| 280 | Henry Thomas | .10 | .02 |
| 281 | Ray Agnew | .10 | .02 |
| 282 | Bruce Armstrong | .10 | .02 |
| 283 | Drew Bledsoe RC | 5.00 | 2.00 |
| 284 | Vincent Brisby RC | .40 | .15 |
| 285 | Vincent Brown | .10 | .02 |
| 286 | Eugene Chung | .10 | .02 |
| 287 | Marv Cook | .10 | .02 |
| 288 | Pat Harlow | .10 | .02 |
| 289 | Jerome Henderson | .10 | .02 |
| 290 | Greg McMurtry | .10 | .02 |
| 291 | Leonard Russell | .20 | .07 |
| 292 | Chris Singleton | .10 | .02 |
| 293 | Chris Slade RC | .20 | .07 |
| 294 | Andre Tippett | .10 | .02 |
| 295 | Brent Williams | .10 | .02 |
| 296 | Scott Zolak | .10 | .02 |
| 297 | Morten Andersen | .10 | .02 |
| 298 | Gene Atkins | .10 | .02 |
| 299 | Mike Buck | .10 | .02 |
| 300 | Toi Cook | .10 | .02 |
| 301 | Jim Dombrowski | .10 | .02 |
| 302 | Vaughn Dunbar | .10 | .02 |
| 303 | Quinn Early | .20 | .07 |
| 304 | Joel Hilgenberg | .10 | .02 |
| 305 | Dalton Hilliard | .10 | .02 |
| 306 | Rickey Jackson | .10 | .02 |
| 307 | Vaughan Johnson | .10 | .02 |
| 308 | Reginald Jones | .10 | .02 |
| 309 | Eric Martin | .10 | .02 |
| 310 | Wayne Martin | .10 | .02 |
| 311 | Sam Mills | .10 | .02 |
| 312 | Brad Muster | .10 | .02 |
| 313 | Willie Roaf RC | .20 | .07 |
| 314 | Irv Smith RC | .10 | .02 |
| 315 | Wade Wilson | .10 | .02 |
| 316 | Carlton Bailey | .10 | .02 |
| 317 | Michael Brooks | .10 | .02 |
| 318 | Derek Brown TE | .10 | .02 |
| 319 | Marcus Buckley RC | .10 | .02 |
| 320 | Jarrod Bunch | .10 | .02 |
| 321 | Mark Collins | .10 | .02 |
| 322 | Eric Dorsey | .10 | .02 |
| 323 | Rodney Hampton | .20 | .07 |
| 324 | Mark Jackson | .10 | .02 |
| 325 | Pepper Johnson | .10 | .02 |
| 326 | Ed McCaffrey | .40 | .15 |
| 327 | Dave Meggett | .10 | .02 |
| 328 | Bart Oates | .10 | .02 |
| 329 | Mike Sherrard | .10 | .02 |
| 330 | Phil Simms | .20 | .07 |
| 331 | Michael Strahan RC | 3.00 | 1.25 |
| 332 | Lawrence Taylor | .40 | .15 |
| 333 | Brad Baxter | .10 | .02 |
| 334 | Chris Burkett | .10 | .02 |
| 335 | Kyle Clifton | .10 | .02 |
| 336 | Boomer Esiason | .20 | .07 |
| 337 | James Hasty | .10 | .02 |
| 338 | Johnny Johnson | .10 | .02 |
| 339 | Marvin Jones RC | .10 | .02 |
| 340 | Jeff Lageman | .10 | .02 |
| 341 | Mo Lewis | .10 | .02 |
| 342 | Ronnie Lott | .20 | .07 |
| 343 | Leonard Marshall | .10 | .02 |
| 344 | Johnny Mitchell | .10 | .02 |
| 345 | Rob Moore | .20 | .07 |
| 346 | Browning Nagle | .10 | .02 |
| 347 | Coleman Rudolph RC | .10 | .02 |
| 348 | Blair Thomas | .10 | .02 |
| 349 | Eric Thomas | .10 | .02 |
| 350 | Brian Washington | .10 | .02 |
| 351 | Marvin Washington | .10 | .02 |
| 352 | Eric Allen | .10 | .02 |
| 353 | Victor Bailey RC | .10 | .02 |
| 354 | Fred Barnett | .20 | .07 |
| 355 | Mark Bavaro | .10 | .02 |
| 356 | Randall Cunningham | .40 | .19 |
| 357 | Byron Evans | .10 | .02 |

|  |  | | |
|---|---|---|---|
| 358 | Andy Harmon RC | .20 | .07 |
| 359 | Tim Harris | .10 | .02 |
| 360 | Lester Holmes | .10 | .02 |
| 361 | Seth Joyner | .10 | .02 |
| 362 | Keith Millard | .10 | .02 |
| 363 | Leonard Renfro RC | .10 | .02 |
| 364 | Heath Sherman | .10 | .02 |
| 365 | Vai Sikahema | .10 | .02 |
| 366 | Clyde Simmons | .10 | .02 |
| 367 | William Thomas | .10 | .02 |
| 368 | Herschel Walker | .20 | .07 |
| 369 | Andre Waters | .10 | .02 |
| 370 | Calvin Williams | .20 | .07 |
| 371 | Johnny Bailey | .10 | .02 |
| 372 | Steve Beuerlein | .20 | .07 |
| 373 | Rich Camarillo | .10 | .02 |
| 374 | Chuck Cecil | .10 | .02 |
| 375 | Chris Chandler | .20 | .07 |
| 376 | Gary Clark | .20 | .07 |
| 377 | Ben Coleman RC | .10 | .02 |
| 378 | Ernest Dye RC | .10 | .02 |
| 379 | Ken Harvey | .10 | .02 |
| 380 | Garrison Hearst RC | 1.50 | .60 |
| 381 | Randal Hill | .10 | .02 |
| 382 | Robert Massey | .10 | .02 |
| 383 | Freddie Joe Nunn | .10 | .02 |
| 384 | Ricky Proehl | .10 | .02 |
| 385 | Luis Sharpe | .10 | .02 |
| 386 | Tyronne Stowe | .10 | .02 |
| 387 | Eric Swann | .20 | .07 |
| 388 | Aeneas Williams | .10 | .02 |
| 389 | Chad Brown RC LB | .20 | .07 |
| 390 | Dermontti Dawson | .10 | .02 |
| 391 | Donald Evans | .10 | .02 |
| 392 | Deon Figures RC | .10 | .02 |
| 393 | Barry Foster | .20 | .07 |
| 394 | Jeff Graham | .20 | .07 |
| 395 | Eric Green | .20 | .07 |
| 396 | Kevin Greene | .20 | .07 |
| 397 | Carlton Haselrig | .10 | .02 |
| 398 | Andre Hastings RC | .20 | .07 |
| 399 | D.J. Johnson | .10 | .02 |
| 400 | Carnell Lake | .10 | .02 |
| 401 | Greg Lloyd | .20 | .07 |
| 402 | Neil O'Donnell | .40 | .15 |
| 403 | Darren Perry | .10 | .02 |
| 404 | Mike Tomczak | .10 | .02 |
| 405 | Rod Woodson | .40 | .15 |
| 406 | Eric Bieniemy | .10 | .02 |
| 407 | Marion Butts | .10 | .02 |
| 408 | Gill Byrd | .10 | .02 |
| 409 | Darren Carrington RC | .10 | .02 |
| 410 | Darrien Gordon RC | .10 | .02 |
| 411 | Burt Grossman | .10 | .02 |
| 412 | Courtney Hall | .10 | .02 |
| 413 | Ronnie Harmon | .10 | .02 |
| 414 | Stan Humphries | .20 | .07 |
| 415 | Nate Lewis | .10 | .02 |
| 416 | Natrone Means RC | .40 | .15 |
| 417 | Anthony Miller | .20 | .07 |
| 418 | Chris Mims | .10 | .02 |
| 419 | Leslie O'Neal | .10 | .02 |
| 420 | Gary Plummer | .10 | .02 |
| 421 | Stanley Richard | .10 | .02 |
| 422 | Junior Seau | .40 | .15 |
| 423 | Harry Swayne | .10 | .02 |
| 424 | Jerrol Williams | .10 | .02 |
| 425 | Harris Barton | .10 | .02 |
| 426 | Steve Bono | .20 | .07 |
| 427 | Kevin Fagan | .10 | .02 |
| 428 | Don Griffin | .10 | .02 |
| 429 | Dana Hall | .10 | .02 |
| 430 | Adrian Hardy | .10 | .02 |
| 431 | Brent Jones | .20 | .07 |
| 432 | Todd Kelly RC | .10 | .02 |
| 433 | Amp Lee | .10 | .02 |
| 434 | Tim McDonald | .10 | .02 |
| 435 | Guy McIntyre | .10 | .02 |
| 436 | Tom Rathman | .10 | .02 |
| 437 | Jerry Rice | 2.00 | .75 |
| 438 | Bill Romanowski | .10 | .02 |
| 439 | Dana Stubblefield RC | .40 | .15 |
| 440 | John Taylor | .20 | .07 |
| 441 | Steve Wallace | .10 | .02 |
| 442 | Michael Walter | .10 | .02 |
| 443 | Ricky Watters | .40 | .15 |
| 444 | Steve Young | 1.50 | .60 |
| 445 | Robert Blackmon | .10 | .02 |
| 446 | Brian Blades | .20 | .07 |
| 447 | Jeff Bryant | .10 | .02 |
| 448 | Ferrell Edmunds | .10 | .02 |
| 449 | Carlton Gray RC | .10 | .02 |
| 450 | Dwayne Harper | .10 | .02 |
| 451 | Andy Heck | .10 | .02 |
| 452 | Tommy Kane | .10 | .02 |
| 453 | Cortez Kennedy | .20 | .07 |
| 454 | Kelvin Martin | .10 | .02 |
| 455 | Dan McGwire | .10 | .02 |
| 456 | Rick Mirer RC | .40 | .15 |
| 457 | Rufus Porter | .10 | .02 |
| 458 | Ray Roberts | .10 | .02 |
| 459 | Eugene Robinson | .10 | .02 |
| 460 | Chris Warren | .20 | .07 |
| 461 | John L. Williams | .10 | .02 |
| 462 | Gary Anderson RB | .10 | .02 |
| 463 | Tyji Armstrong | .10 | .02 |
| 464 | Reggie Cobb | .10 | .02 |
| 465 | Eric Curry RC | .10 | .02 |
| 466 | Lawrence Dawsey | .10 | .02 |
| 467 | Steve DeBerg | .10 | .02 |
| 468 | Santana Dotson | .20 | .07 |
| 469 | Demetrius DuBose RC | .10 | .02 |
| 470 | Paul Gruber | .10 | .02 |
| 471 | Ron Hall | .10 | .02 |
| 472 | Courtney Hawkins | .10 | .02 |
| 473 | Hardy Nickerson | .20 | .07 |
| 474 | Ricky Reynolds | .10 | .02 |
| 475 | Broderick Thomas | .10 | .02 |
| 476 | Mark Wheeler | .10 | .02 |
| 477 | Jimmy Williams | .10 | .02 |
| 478 | Carl Banks | .10 | .02 |
| 479 | Reggie Brooks RC | .20 | .07 |
| 480 | Earnest Byner | .10 | .02 |
| 481 | Tom Carter RC | .20 | .07 |
| 482 | Andre Collins | .10 | .02 |
| 483 | Brad Edwards | .10 | .02 |
| 484 | Ricky Ervins | .10 | .02 |
| 485 | Kurt Gouveia | .10 | .02 |
| 486 | Darrell Green | .10 | .02 |
| 487 | Desmond Howard | .20 | .07 |
| 488 | Jim Lachey | .10 | .02 |
| 489 | Chip Lohmiller | .10 | .02 |
| 490 | Charles Mann | .10 | .02 |
| 491 | Tim McGee | .10 | .02 |
| 492 | Brian Mitchell | .20 | .07 |
| 493 | Art Monk | .20 | .07 |
| 494 | Mark Rypien | .10 | .02 |
| 495 | Ricky Sanders | .10 | .02 |
| 496 | Checklist 1-126 | .10 | .02 |
| 497 | Checklist 127-254 | .10 | .02 |
| 498 | Checklist 255-382 | .10 | .02 |
| 499 | Checklist 383-500 | .10 | .02 |
| 500 | Inserts Checklist | .10 | .02 |

## 1994 Ultra

| | | | |
|---|---|---|---|
| | COMPLETE SET (525) | 25.00 | 10.00 |
| | COMP.SERIES 1 (325) | 12.00 | 5.00 |
| | COMP.SERIES 2 (200) | 12.00 | 5.00 |
| 1 | Steve Beuerlein | .20 | .07 |
| 2 | Gary Clark | .20 | .07 |
| 3 | Randal Hill | .10 | .02 |
| 4 | Seth Joyner | .10 | .02 |
| 5 | Jamir Miller RC | .20 | .07 |
| 6 | Ronald Moore | .10 | .02 |
| 7 | Luis Sharpe | .10 | .02 |
| 8 | Clyde Simmons | .10 | .02 |
| 9 | Eric Swann | .20 | .07 |
| 10 | Aeneas Williams | .10 | .02 |
| 11 | Chris Doleman | .10 | .02 |
| 12 | Bert Emanuel RC | .40 | .15 |
| 13 | Moe Gardner | .10 | .02 |
| 14 | Jeff George | .40 | .15 |
| 15 | Roger Harper | .10 | .02 |
| 16 | Pierce Holt | .10 | .02 |
| 17 | Lincoln Kennedy | .10 | .02 |
| 18 | Erric Pegram | .10 | .02 |
| 19 | Andre Rison | .20 | .07 |
| 20 | Deion Sanders | .75 | .30 |
| 21 | Jessie Tuggle | .10 | .02 |
| 22 | Cornelius Bennett | .20 | .07 |
| 23 | Bill Brooks | .10 | .02 |
| 24 | Jeff Burris RC | .20 | .07 |
| 25 | Kent Hull | .10 | .02 |
| 26 | Henry Jones | .10 | .02 |
| 27 | Jim Kelly | .40 | .15 |
| 28 | Marvcus Patton | .10 | .02 |
| 29 | Andre Reed | .20 | .07 |
| 30 | Bruce Smith | .40 | .15 |
| 31 | Thomas Smith | .10 | .02 |
| 32 | Thurman Thomas | .40 | .15 |
| 33 | Jeff Wright | .10 | .02 |
| 34 | Trace Armstrong | .10 | .02 |
| 35 | Mark Carrier DB | .10 | .02 |
| 36 | Dante Jones | .10 | .02 |
| 37 | Erik Kramer | .20 | .07 |
| 38 | Terry Obee | .10 | .02 |
| 39 | Alonzo Spellman | .10 | .02 |
| 40 | John Thierry RC | .10 | .02 |
| 41 | Tom Waddle | .10 | .02 |
| 42 | Donnell Woolford | .10 | .02 |
| 43 | Tim Worley | .10 | .02 |
| 44 | Chris Zorich | .10 | .02 |
| 45 | John Copeland | .10 | .02 |
| 46 | Harold Green | .10 | .02 |
| 47 | David Klingler | .10 | .02 |
| 48 | Ricardo McDonald | .10 | .02 |
| 49 | Tony McGee | .10 | .02 |
| 50 | Louis Oliver | .10 | .02 |
| 51 | Carl Pickens | .20 | .07 |
| 52 | Darnay Scott RC | .75 | .30 |
| 53 | Steve Tovar | .10 | .02 |
| 54 | Dan Wilkinson RC | .20 | .07 |
| 55 | Darryl Williams | .10 | .02 |
| 56 | Derrick Alexander WR RC | .40 | .15 |
| 57 | Michael Jackson | .20 | .07 |
| 58 | Tony Jones T | .10 | .02 |
| 59 | Antonio Langham RC | .20 | .07 |
| 60 | Eric Metcalf | .20 | .07 |
| 61 | Stevon Moore | .10 | .02 |
| 62 | Michael Dean Perry | .20 | .07 |
| 63 | Anthony Pleasant | .10 | .02 |
| 64 | Vinny Testaverde | .20 | .07 |
| 65 | Eric Turner | .10 | .02 |
| 66 | Tommy Vardell | .10 | .02 |
| 67 | Troy Aikman | 1.50 | .60 |
| 68 | Larry Brown DB | .10 | .02 |
| 69 | Shante Carver RC | .10 | .02 |
| 70 | Charles Haley | .20 | .07 |
| 71 | Michael Irvin | .40 | .15 |
| 72 | Leon Lett | .10 | .02 |
| 73 | Nate Newton | .10 | .02 |
| 74 | Jay Novacek | .20 | .07 |
| 75 | Darrin Smith | .10 | .02 |
| 76 | Emmitt Smith | 2.50 | 1.00 |
| 77 | Tony Tolbert | .10 | .02 |
| 78 | Erik Williams | .10 | .02 |
| 79 | Kevin Williams WR | .20 | .07 |
| 80 | Steve Atwater | .10 | .02 |
| 81 | Rod Bernstine | .10 | .02 |
| 82 | Ray Crockett | .10 | .02 |
| 83 | Mike Croel | .10 | .02 |
| 84 | Shane Dronett | .20 | .07 |
| 85 | Jason Elam | .10 | .02 |
| 86 | John Elway | 3.00 | 1.25 |
| 87 | Simon Fletcher | .10 | .02 |

|  |  | | |
|---|---|---|---|
| 88 | Glyn Milburn | .20 | .07 |
| 89 | Anthony Miller | .20 | .07 |
| 90 | Shannon Sharpe | .20 | .07 |
| 91 | Gary Zimmerman | .10 | .02 |
| 92 | Bennie Blades | .10 | .02 |
| 93 | Lomas Brown | .10 | .02 |
| 94 | Mel Gray | .10 | .02 |
| 95 | Jason Hanson | .10 | .02 |
| 96 | Ryan McNeil | .10 | .02 |
| 97 | Scott Mitchell | .20 | .07 |
| 98 | Herman Moore | .40 | .15 |
| 99 | Johnnie Morton RC | 1.50 | .60 |
| 100 | Robert Porcher | .10 | .02 |
| 101 | Barry Sanders | 2.50 | 1.00 |
| 102 | Chris Spielman | .20 | .07 |
| 103 | Pat Swilling | .10 | .02 |
| 104 | Edgar Bennett | .40 | .15 |
| 105 | Terrell Buckley | .10 | .02 |
| 106 | Reggie Cobb | .10 | .02 |
| 107 | Brett Favre | 3.00 | 1.25 |
| 108 | Sean Jones | .10 | .02 |
| 109 | Ken Ruettgers | .10 | .02 |
| 110 | Sterling Sharpe | .20 | .07 |
| 111 | Wayne Simmons | .10 | .02 |
| 112 | Aaron Taylor RC | .10 | .02 |
| 113 | George Teague | .10 | .02 |
| 114 | Reggie White | .40 | .15 |
| 115 | Micheal Barrow | .10 | .02 |
| 116 | Gary Brown | .10 | .02 |
| 117 | Cody Carlson | .10 | .02 |
| 118 | Ray Childress | .10 | .02 |
| 119 | Cris Dishman | .10 | .02 |
| 120 | Henry Ford RC | .10 | .02 |
| 121 | Haywood Jeffires | .20 | .07 |
| 122 | Bruce Matthews | .10 | .02 |
| 123 | Bubba McDowell | .10 | .02 |
| 124 | Marcus Robertson | .10 | .02 |
| 125 | Eddie Robinson | .10 | .02 |
| 126 | Webster Slaughter | .10 | .02 |
| 127 | Trev Alberts RC | .20 | .07 |
| 128 | Tony Bennett | .10 | .02 |
| 129 | Ray Buchanan | .10 | .02 |
| 130 | Quentin Coryatt | .10 | .02 |
| 131 | Eugene Daniel | .10 | .02 |
| 132 | Steve Emtman | .10 | .02 |
| 133 | Marshall Faulk RC | 6.00 | 2.50 |
| 134 | Jim Harbaugh | .40 | .15 |
| 135 | Roosevelt Potts | .10 | .02 |
| 136 | Rohn Stark | .10 | .02 |
| 137 | Marcus Allen | .40 | .15 |
| 138 | Donnell Bennett RC | .40 | .15 |
| 139 | Dale Carter | .10 | .02 |
| 140 | Tony Casillas | .10 | .02 |
| 141 | Mark Collins | .10 | .02 |
| 142 | Willie Davis | .20 | .07 |
| 143 | Tim Grunhard | .10 | .02 |
| 144 | Greg Hill RC | .40 | .15 |
| 145 | Joe Montana | 3.00 | 1.25 |
| 146 | Tracy Simien | .10 | .02 |
| 147 | Neil Smith | .20 | .07 |
| 148 | Derrick Thomas | .40 | .15 |
| 149 | Tim Brown | .40 | .15 |
| 150 | James Folston RC | .10 | .02 |
| 151 | Rob Fredrickson RC | .20 | .07 |
| 152 | Jeff Hostetler | .20 | .07 |
| 153 | Rocket Ismail | .20 | .07 |
| 154 | James Jett | .10 | .02 |
| 155 | Terry McDaniel | .10 | .02 |
| 156 | Winston Moss | .10 | .02 |
| 157 | Greg Robinson | .10 | .02 |
| 158 | Anthony Smith | .10 | .02 |
| 159 | Steve Wisniewski | .10 | .02 |
| 160 | Flipper Anderson | .10 | .02 |
| 161 | Jerome Bettis | .60 | .25 |
| 162 | Isaac Bruce RC | 4.00 | 2.00 |
| 163 | Shane Conlan | .10 | .02 |
| 164 | Wayne Gandy RC | .10 | .02 |
| 165 | Sean Gilbert | .10 | .02 |
| 166 | Todd Lyght | .10 | .02 |
| 167 | Chris Miller | .10 | .02 |
| 168 | Anthony Newman | .10 | .02 |
| 169 | Roman Phifer | .10 | .02 |
| 170 | Jackie Slater | .10 | .02 |
| 171 | Gene Atkins | .10 | .02 |
| 172 | Aubrey Beavers RC | .10 | .02 |
| 173 | Tim Bowens RC | .20 | .07 |
| 174 | J.B. Brown | .10 | .02 |
| 175 | Marco Coleman | .10 | .02 |
| 176 | Bryan Cox | .10 | .02 |
| 177 | Irving Fryar | .20 | .07 |
| 178 | Terry Kirby | .40 | .15 |
| 179 | Dan Marino | 3.00 | 1.25 |
| 180 | Troy Vincent | .10 | .02 |
| 181 | Richmond Webb | .10 | .02 |
| 182 | Terry Allen | .20 | .07 |
| 183 | Cris Carter | .75 | .30 |
| 184 | Jack Del Rio | .10 | .02 |
| 185 | Vencie Glenn | .10 | .02 |
| 186 | Randall McDaniel | .15 | .05 |
| 187 | Warren Moon | .40 | .15 |
| 188 | David Palmer RC | .40 | .15 |
| 189 | John Randle | .20 | .07 |
| 190 | Todd Scott | .10 | .02 |
| 191 | Todd Steussie RC | .20 | .07 |
| 192 | Henry Thomas | .10 | .02 |
| 193 | Dewayne Washington RC | .20 | .07 |
| 194 | Bruce Armstrong | .10 | .02 |
| 195 | Harlon Barnett | .10 | .02 |
| 196 | Drew Bledsoe | 1.00 | .40 |
| 197 | Vincent Brisby | .20 | .07 |
| 198 | Vincent Brown | .10 | .02 |
| 199 | Marion Butts | .10 | .02 |
| 200 | Ben Coates | .20 | .07 |
| 201 | Todd Collins | .10 | .02 |
| 202 | Maurice Hurst | .10 | .02 |
| 203 | Willie McGinest RC | .40 | .15 |
| 204 | Ricky Reynolds | .10 | .02 |
| 205 | Chris Slade | .10 | .02 |
| 206 | Mario Bates RC | .40 | .15 |
| 207 | Derek Brown RBK | .10 | .02 |
| 208 | Vince Buck | .10 | .02 |
| 209 | Quinn Early | .10 | .02 |
| 210 | Jim Everett | .20 | .07 |
| 211 | Michael Haynes | .20 | .07 |
| 212 | Tyrone Hughes | .20 | .07 |
| 213 | Joe Johnson RC | .10 | .02 |
| 214 | Vaughan Johnson | .10 | .02 |
| 215 | Willie Roaf | .10 | .02 |
| 216 | Renaldo Turnbull | .10 | .02 |
| 217 | Michael Brooks | .10 | .02 |
| 218 | Dave Brown | .20 | .07 |
| 219 | Howard Cross | .10 | .02 |
| 220 | Stacey Dillard | .10 | .02 |
| 221 | Jumbo Elliott | .10 | .02 |
| 222 | Keith Hamilton | .10 | .02 |
| 223 | Rodney Hampton | .20 | .07 |
| 224 | Thomas Lewis RC | .20 | .07 |
| 225 | Dave Meggett | .10 | .02 |
| 226 | Corey Miller | .10 | .02 |
| 227 | Thomas Randolph RC | .10 | .02 |
| 228 | Mike Sherrard | .10 | .02 |
| 229 | Kyle Clifton | .10 | .02 |
| 230 | Boomer Esiason | .20 | .07 |
| 231 | Aaron Glenn RC | .40 | .15 |
| 232 | James Hasty | .10 | .02 |
| 233 | Bobby Houston | .10 | .02 |
| 234 | Johnny Johnson | .10 | .02 |
| 235 | Mo Lewis | .10 | .02 |
| 236 | Ronnie Lott | .20 | .07 |
| 237 | Rob Moore | .20 | .07 |
| 238 | Marvin Washington | .10 | .02 |
| 239 | Ryan Yarborough RC | .10 | .02 |
| 240 | Eric Allen | .10 | .02 |
| 241 | Victor Bailey | .10 | .02 |
| 242 | Fred Barnett | .20 | .07 |
| 243 | Mark Bavaro | .10 | .02 |
| 244 | Randall Cunningham | .40 | .15 |
| 245 | Byron Evans | .10 | .02 |
| 246 | William Fuller | .10 | .02 |
| 247 | Andy Harmon | .10 | .02 |
| 248 | William Perry | .20 | .07 |
| 249 | Herschel Walker | .20 | .07 |
| 250 | Bernard Williams RC | .10 | .02 |
| 251 | Dermontti Dawson | .10 | .02 |
| 252 | Deon Figures | .10 | .02 |
| 253 | Barry Foster | .20 | .07 |
| 254 | Kevin Greene | .20 | .07 |
| 255 | Charles Johnson RC | .40 | .15 |
| 256 | Levon Kirkland | .10 | .02 |
| 257 | Greg Lloyd | .20 | .07 |
| 258 | Neil O'Donnell | .40 | .15 |
| 259 | Darren Perry | .10 | .02 |
| 260 | Dwight Stone | .10 | .02 |
| 261 | Rod Woodson | .20 | .07 |
| 262 | John Carney | .10 | .02 |
| 263 | Isaac Davis RC | .10 | .02 |
| 264 | Courtney Hall | .10 | .02 |
| 265 | Ronnie Harmon | .10 | .02 |
| 266 | Stan Humphries | .20 | .07 |
| 267 | Vance Johnson | .10 | .02 |
| 268 | Natrone Means | .40 | .15 |
| 269 | Chris Mims | .10 | .02 |
| 270 | Leslie O'Neal | .10 | .02 |
| 271 | Stanley Richard | .10 | .02 |
| 272 | Junior Seau | .40 | .15 |
| 273 | Harris Barton | .10 | .02 |
| 274 | Dennis Brown | .10 | .02 |
| 275 | Eric Davis | .10 | .02 |
| 276 | William Floyd RC | .40 | .15 |
| 277 | John Johnson | .10 | .02 |
| 278 | Tim McDonald | .10 | .02 |
| 279 | Ken Norton Jr. | .20 | .07 |
| 280 | Jerry Rice | 1.50 | .60 |
| 281 | Jesse Sapolu | .10 | .02 |
| 282 | Dana Stubblefield | .20 | .07 |
| 283 | Ricky Watters | .20 | .07 |
| 284 | Bryant Young RC | .60 | .25 |
| 285 | Steve Young | 1.00 | .40 |
| 286 | Sam Adams RC | .20 | .07 |
| 287 | Brian Blades | .10 | .02 |
| 288 | Ferrell Edmunds | .10 | .02 |
| 289 | Patrick Hunter | .10 | .02 |
| 290 | Cortez Kennedy | .20 | .07 |
| 291 | Rick Mirer | .40 | .15 |
| 292 | Nate Odomes | .10 | .02 |
| 293 | Ray Roberts | .10 | .02 |
| 294 | Eugene Robinson | .10 | .02 |
| 295 | Rod Stephens | .10 | .02 |
| 296 | Chris Warren | .20 | .07 |
| 297 | Marty Carter | .10 | .02 |
| 298 | Horace Copeland | .10 | .02 |
| 299 | Eric Curry | .10 | .02 |
| 300 | Santana Dotson | .20 | .07 |
| 301 | Craig Erickson | .10 | .02 |
| 302 | Paul Gruber | .10 | .02 |
| 303 | Courtney Hawkins | .10 | .02 |
| 304 | Martin Mayhew | .10 | .02 |
| 305 | Hardy Nickerson | .20 | .07 |
| 306 | Errict Rhett RC | .40 | .15 |
| 307 | Vince Workman | .10 | .02 |
| 308 | Reggie Brooks | .10 | .02 |
| 309 | Tom Carter | .10 | .02 |
| 310 | Andre Collins | .10 | .02 |
| 311 | Brad Edwards | .10 | .02 |
| 312 | Kurt Gouveia | .10 | .02 |
| 313 | Darrell Green | .10 | .02 |
| 314 | Ethan Horton | .10 | .02 |
| 315 | Desmond Howard | .20 | .07 |
| 316 | Tre Johnson RC | .10 | .02 |
| 317 | Sterling Palmer RC | .10 | .02 |
| 318 | Heath Shuler RC | .40 | .15 |
| 319 | Tyronne Stowe | .10 | .02 |
| 320 | NFL 75th Anniversary | .10 | .02 |
| 321 | Checklist | .10 | .02 |
| 322 | Checklist | .10 | .02 |
| 323 | Checklist | .10 | .02 |
| 324 | Checklist | .10 | .02 |
| 325 | Checklist | .10 | .02 |
| 326 | Garrison Hearst | .40 | .15 |
| 327 | Eric Hill | .10 | .02 |
| 328 | Seth Joyner | .10 | .02 |
| 329 | Jim McMahon | .20 | .07 |
| 330 | Jamir Miller | .10 | .02 |
| 331 | Ricky Proehl | .10 | .02 |
| 332 | Clyde Simmons | .10 | .02 |
| 333 | Chris Dishman | .10 | .02 |
| 334 | Bert Emanuel | .40 | .15 |
| 335 | Jeff George | .40 | .15 |
| 336 | D.J. Johnson | .10 | .02 |
| 337 | Terance Mathis | .20 | .07 |
| 338 | Clay Matthews | .10 | .02 |
| 339 | Tony Smith RB | .10 | .02 |

| | | | | | |
|---|---|---|---|---|---|
| ❑ 340 Don Beebe | .10 | .02 | ❑ 424 Tom Rathman | .10 | .02 |
| ❑ 341 Bucky Brooks RC | .10 | .02 | ❑ 425 Harvey Williams | .20 | .07 |
| ❑ 342 Jeff Burris | .20 | .02 | ❑ 426 Isaac Bruce | 1.50 | .60 |
| ❑ 343 Kenneth Davis | .10 | .02 | ❑ 427 Troy Drayton | .10 | .02 |
| ❑ 344 Phil Hansen | .10 | .02 | ❑ 428 Wayne Gandy | .10 | .02 |
| ❑ 345 Pete Metzelaars | .10 | .02 | ❑ 429 Fred Stokes | .10 | .02 |
| ❑ 346 Darryl Talley | .10 | .02 | ❑ 430 Robert Young | .10 | .02 |
| ❑ 347 Joe Cain | .10 | .02 | ❑ 431 Gene Atkins | .10 | .02 |
| ❑ 348 Curtis Conway | .40 | .15 | ❑ 432 Aubrey Beavers | .10 | .02 |
| ❑ 349 Shaun Gayle | .10 | .02 | ❑ 433 Tim Bowens | .20 | .07 |
| ❑ 350 Chris Gedney | .10 | .02 | ❑ 434 Keith Byars | .10 | .02 |
| ❑ 351 Erik Kramer | .20 | .07 | ❑ 435 Jeff Cross | .10 | .02 |
| ❑ 352 Vinson Smith | .10 | .02 | ❑ 436 Mark Ingram | .10 | .02 |
| ❑ 353 John Thierry | .10 | .02 | ❑ 437 Keith Jackson | .10 | .02 |
| ❑ 354 Lewis Tillman | .10 | .02 | ❑ 438 Michael Stewart | .10 | .02 |
| ❑ 355 Mike Brim | .10 | .02 | ❑ 439 Chris Hinton | .10 | .02 |
| ❑ 356 Derrick Fenner | .10 | .02 | ❑ 440 Qadry Ismail | .40 | .15 |
| ❑ 357 James Francis | .10 | .02 | ❑ 441 Carlos Jenkins | .10 | .02 |
| ❑ 358 Louis Oliver | .10 | .02 | ❑ 442 Warren Moon | .40 | .15 |
| ❑ 359 Darnay Scott | .40 | .15 | ❑ 443 David Palmer | .20 | .07 |
| ❑ 360 Dan Wilkinson | .20 | .07 | ❑ 444 Jake Reed | .20 | .07 |
| ❑ 361 Alfred Williams | .10 | .02 | ❑ 445 Robert Smith | .40 | .15 |
| ❑ 362 Derrick Alexander WR | .40 | .15 | ❑ 446 Todd Steussie | .20 | .07 |
| ❑ 363 Rob Burnett | .10 | .02 | ❑ 447 Dewayne Washington | .20 | .07 |
| ❑ 364 Mark Carrier WR | .20 | .07 | ❑ 448 Marion Butts | .10 | .02 |
| ❑ 365 Steve Everitt | .10 | .02 | ❑ 449 Tim Goad | .10 | .02 |
| ❑ 366 Leroy Hoard | .10 | .02 | ❑ 450 Myron Guyton | .10 | .02 |
| ❑ 367 Pepper Johnson | .10 | .02 | ❑ 451 Kevin Lee RC | .10 | .02 |
| ❑ 368 Antonio Langham | .20 | .07 | ❑ 452 Willie McGinest | .40 | .15 |
| ❑ 369 Shante Carver | .10 | .02 | ❑ 453 Ricky Reynolds | .10 | .02 |
| ❑ 370 Alvin Harper | .20 | .07 | ❑ 454 Michael Timpson | .10 | .02 |
| ❑ 371 Daryl Johnston | .20 | .07 | ❑ 455 Morten Andersen | .10 | .02 |
| ❑ 372 Russell Maryland | .10 | .02 | ❑ 456 Jim Everett | .20 | .07 |
| ❑ 373 Kevin Smith | .10 | .02 | ❑ 457 Michael Haynes | .20 | .07 |
| ❑ 374 Mark Stepnoski | .10 | .02 | ❑ 458 Joe Johnson | .10 | .02 |
| ❑ 375 Darren Woodson | .20 | .07 | ❑ 459 Wayne Martin | .10 | .02 |
| ❑ 376 Allen Aldridge RC | .10 | .02 | ❑ 460 Sam Mills | .10 | .02 |
| ❑ 377 Ray Crockett | .10 | .02 | ❑ 461 Irv Smith | .10 | .02 |
| ❑ 378 Karl Mecklenburg | .10 | .02 | ❑ 462 Carlton Bailey | .10 | .02 |
| ❑ 379 Anthony Miller | .20 | .07 | ❑ 463 Chris Calloway | .10 | .02 |
| ❑ 380 Mike Pritchard | .10 | .02 | ❑ 464 Mark Jackson | .10 | .02 |
| ❑ 381 Leonard Russell | .10 | .02 | ❑ 465 Thomas Lewis | .20 | .07 |
| ❑ 382 Dennis Smith | .10 | .02 | ❑ 466 Thomas Randolph | .10 | .02 |
| ❑ 383 Anthony Carter | .20 | .07 | ❑ 467 Stevie Anderson RC | .10 | .02 |
| ❑ 384 Van Malone RC | .10 | .02 | ❑ 468 Brad Baxter | .10 | .02 |
| ❑ 385 Robert Massey | .10 | .02 | ❑ 469 Aaron Glenn | .20 | .07 |
| ❑ 386 Scott Mitchell | .20 | .07 | ❑ 470 Jeff Lageman | .10 | .02 |
| ❑ 387 Johnnie Morton | .60 | .25 | ❑ 471 Johnny Mitchell | .10 | .02 |
| ❑ 388 Brett Perriman | .20 | .07 | ❑ 472 Art Monk | .20 | .07 |
| ❑ 389 Tracy Scroggins | .10 | .02 | ❑ 473 William Fuller | .10 | .02 |
| ❑ 390 Robert Brooks | .40 | .15 | ❑ 474 Charlie Garner RC | 1.25 | .50 |
| ❑ 391 LeRoy Butler | .10 | .02 | ❑ 475 Vaughn Hebron | .10 | .02 |
| ❑ 392 Reggie Cobb | .10 | .02 | ❑ 476 Bill Romanowski | .10 | .02 |
| ❑ 393 Sean Jones | .10 | .02 | ❑ 477 William Thomas | .10 | .02 |
| ❑ 394 George Koonce | .10 | .02 | ❑ 478 Greg Townsend | .10 | .02 |
| ❑ 395 Steve McMichael | .10 | .02 | ❑ 479 Bernard Williams | .10 | .02 |
| ❑ 396 Bryce Paup | .20 | .07 | ❑ 480 Calvin Williams | .20 | .07 |
| ❑ 397 Aaron Taylor | .10 | .02 | ❑ 481 Eric Green | .10 | .02 |
| ❑ 398 Henry Ford | .10 | .02 | ❑ 482 Charles Johnson | .40 | .15 |
| ❑ 399 Ernest Givins | .10 | .02 | ❑ 483 Carnell Lake | .10 | .02 |
| ❑ 400 Jeremy Nunley RC | .10 | .02 | ❑ 484 Byron Bam Morris | .20 | .07 |
| ❑ 401 Bo Orlando | .10 | .02 | ❑ 485 John L. Williams | .10 | .02 |
| ❑ 402 Al Smith | .10 | .02 | ❑ 486 Darren Carrington | .10 | .02 |
| ❑ 403 Barron Wortham RC | .10 | .02 | ❑ 487 Andre Coleman RC | .10 | .02 |
| ❑ 404 Trev Alberts | .20 | .07 | ❑ 488 Isaac Davis | .10 | .02 |
| ❑ 405 Tony Bennett | .10 | .02 | ❑ 489 Dwayne Harper | .10 | .02 |
| ❑ 406 Kerry Cash | .10 | .02 | ❑ 490 Tony Martin | .40 | .15 |
| ❑ 407 Sean Dawkins RC | .40 | .15 | ❑ 491 Mark Seay RC | .40 | .15 |
| ❑ 408 Marshall Faulk | 2.00 | .75 | ❑ 492 Richard Dent | .20 | .07 |
| ❑ 409 Jim Harbaugh | .40 | .15 | ❑ 493 William Floyd | .40 | .15 |
| ❑ 410 Jeff Herrod | .10 | .02 | ❑ 494 Rickey Jackson | .10 | .02 |
| ❑ 411 Kimble Anders | .20 | .07 | ❑ 495 Brent Jones | .20 | .07 |
| ❑ 412 Donnell Bennett | .20 | .07 | ❑ 496 Ken Norton Jr. | .20 | .07 |
| ❑ 413 J.J. Birden | .10 | .02 | ❑ 497 Gary Plummer | .10 | .02 |
| ❑ 414 Mark Collins | .10 | .02 | ❑ 498 Deion Sanders | .75 | .30 |
| ❑ 415 Lake Dawson RC | .40 | .15 | ❑ 499 John Taylor | .20 | .07 |
| ❑ 416 Greg Hill | .40 | .15 | ❑ 500 Lee Woodall RC | .10 | .02 |
| ❑ 417 Charles Mincy | .10 | .02 | ❑ 501 Bryant Young | .60 | .25 |
| ❑ 418 Greg Biekert | .10 | .02 | ❑ 502 Sam Adams | .20 | .07 |
| ❑ 419 Rob Fredrickson | .20 | .07 | ❑ 503 Howard Ballard | .10 | .02 |
| ❑ 420 Nolan Harrison | .10 | .02 | ❑ 504 Michael Bates | .10 | .02 |
| ❑ 421 Jeff Jaeger | .10 | .02 | ❑ 505 Robert Blackmon | .10 | .02 |
| ❑ 422 Albert Lewis | .10 | .02 | ❑ 506 John Kasay | .10 | .02 |
| ❑ 423 Chester McGlockton | .10 | .02 | ❑ 507 Kelvin Martin | .10 | .02 |

| | | |
|---|---|---|
| ❑ 508 Kevin Mawae RC | .40 | .15 |
| ❑ 509 Rufus Porter | .10 | .02 |
| ❑ 510 Lawrence Dawsey | .10 | .02 |
| ❑ 511 Trent Dilfer RC | 1.25 | .50 |
| ❑ 512 Thomas Everett | .10 | .02 |
| ❑ 513 Jackie Harris | .10 | .02 |
| ❑ 514 Errict Rhett | .20 | .07 |
| ❑ 515 Henry Ellard | .20 | .07 |
| ❑ 516 John Friesz | .10 | .02 |
| ❑ 517 Ken Harvey | .10 | .02 |
| ❑ 518 Ethan Horton | .10 | .02 |
| ❑ 519 Tre Johnson | .10 | .02 |
| ❑ 520 Jim Lachey | .10 | .02 |
| ❑ 521 Heath Shuler | .40 | .15 |
| ❑ 522 Tony Woods | .10 | .02 |
| ❑ 523 Checklist | .10 | .02 |
| ❑ 524 Checklist | .10 | .02 |
| ❑ 525 Checklist | .10 | .02 |

## 1995 Ultra

| | | |
|---|---|---|
| ❑ COMPLETE SET (550) | 50.00 | 20.00 |
| ❑ COMP.SERIES 1 (350) | 25.00 | 10.00 |
| ❑ COMP.SERIES 2 (200) | 25.00 | 10.00 |
| ❑ 1 Michael Bankston | .10 | .02 |
| ❑ 2 Larry Centers | .20 | .07 |
| ❑ 3 Garrison Hearst | .40 | .15 |
| ❑ 4 Eric Hill | .10 | .02 |
| ❑ 5 Seth Joyner | .10 | .02 |
| ❑ 6 Lorenzo Lynch | .10 | .02 |
| ❑ 7 Jamir Miller | .10 | .02 |
| ❑ 8 Clyde Simmons | .10 | .02 |
| ❑ 9 Eric Swann | .20 | .07 |
| ❑ 10 Aeneas Williams | .10 | .02 |
| ❑ 11 Devin Bush RC | .10 | .02 |
| ❑ 12 Ron Davis RC | .10 | .02 |
| ❑ 13 Chris Doleman | .10 | .02 |
| ❑ 14 Bert Emanuel | .40 | .15 |
| ❑ 15 Jeff George | .20 | .07 |
| ❑ 16 Roger Harper | .10 | .02 |
| ❑ 17 Craig Heyward | .10 | .02 |
| ❑ 18 Pierce Holt | .10 | .02 |
| ❑ 19 D.J. Johnson | .10 | .02 |
| ❑ 20 Terance Mathis | .20 | .07 |
| ❑ 21 Chuck Smith | .10 | .02 |
| ❑ 22 Jessie Tuggle | .10 | .02 |
| ❑ 23 Cornelius Bennett | .20 | .07 |
| ❑ 24 Ruben Brown RC | .40 | .15 |
| ❑ 25 Jeff Burris | .10 | .02 |
| ❑ 26 Matt Darby | .10 | .02 |
| ❑ 27 Phil Hansen | .10 | .02 |
| ❑ 28 Henry Jones | .10 | .02 |
| ❑ 29 Jim Kelly | .40 | .15 |
| ❑ 30 Mark Maddox RC | .10 | .02 |
| ❑ 31 Andre Reed | .20 | .07 |
| ❑ 32 Bruce Smith | .40 | .15 |
| ❑ 33 Don Beebe | .10 | .02 |
| ❑ 34 Kerry Collins RC | 2.00 | .75 |
| ❑ 35 Darion Conner | .10 | .02 |
| ❑ 36 Pete Metzelaars | .10 | .02 |
| ❑ 37 Sam Mills | .20 | .07 |
| ❑ 38 Tyrone Poole RC | .40 | .15 |
| ❑ 39 Joe Cain | .10 | .02 |
| ❑ 40 Mark Carrier DB | .10 | .02 |
| ❑ 41 Curtis Conway | .40 | .15 |
| ❑ 42 Jeff Graham | .10 | .02 |
| ❑ 43 Raymont Harris | .10 | .02 |
| ❑ 44 Erik Kramer | .10 | .02 |

|  |  | | |
|---|--------|----|----|
| 45 | Rashaan Salaam RC | .20 | .07 |
| 46 | Lewis Tillman | .10 | .02 |
| 47 | Donnell Woolford | .10 | .02 |
| 48 | Chris Zorich | .10 | .02 |
| 49 | Jeff Blake RC | .75 | .30 |
| 50 | Mike Brim | .10 | .02 |
| 51 | Ki-Jana Carter RC | .40 | .15 |
| 52 | James Francis | .10 | .02 |
| 53 | Carl Pickens | .20 | .07 |
| 54 | Damay Scott | .10 | .02 |
| 55 | Steve Tovar | .10 | .02 |
| 56 | Dan Wilkinson | .20 | .07 |
| 57 | Alfred Williams | .10 | .02 |
| 58 | Darryl Williams | .10 | .02 |
| 59 | Derrick Alexander WR | .40 | .15 |
| 60 | Rob Burnett | .10 | .02 |
| 61 | Steve Everitt | .10 | .02 |
| 62 | Leroy Hoard | .10 | .02 |
| 63 | Michael Jackson | .20 | .07 |
| 64 | Pepper Johnson | .10 | .02 |
| 65 | Tony Jones T | .10 | .02 |
| 66 | Antonio Langham | .10 | .02 |
| 67 | Anthony Pleasant | .10 | .02 |
| 68 | Craig Powell RC | .10 | .02 |
| 69 | Vinny Testaverde | .20 | .07 |
| 70 | Eric Turner | .10 | .02 |
| 71 | Troy Aikman | 1.50 | .60 |
| 72 | Charles Haley | .20 | .07 |
| 73 | Michael Irvin | .40 | .15 |
| 74 | Daryl Johnston | .20 | .07 |
| 75 | Robert Jones | .10 | .02 |
| 76 | Leon Lett | .10 | .02 |
| 77 | Russell Maryland | .10 | .02 |
| 78 | Jay Novacek | .20 | .07 |
| 79 | Darrin Smith | .10 | .02 |
| 80 | Emmitt Smith | 2.50 | 1.25 |
| 81 | Kevin Smith | .10 | .02 |
| 82 | Erik Williams | .10 | .02 |
| 83 | Kevin Williams WR | .20 | .07 |
| 84 | Sherman Williams RC | .10 | .02 |
| 85 | Darren Woodson | .20 | .07 |
| 86 | Elijah Alexander RC | .10 | .02 |
| 87 | Steve Atwater | .10 | .02 |
| 88 | Ray Crockett | .10 | .02 |
| 89 | Shane Dronett | .10 | .02 |
| 90 | Jason Elam | .20 | .07 |
| 91 | John Elway | 3.00 | 1.25 |
| 92 | Simon Fletcher | .10 | .02 |
| 93 | Glyn Milburn | .10 | .02 |
| 94 | Anthony Miller | .20 | .07 |
| 95 | Leonard Russell | .20 | .07 |
| 96 | Shannon Sharpe | .20 | .07 |
| 97 | Bennie Blades | .10 | .02 |
| 98 | Lomas Brown | .10 | .02 |
| 99 | Willie Clay | .10 | .02 |
| 100 | Luther Elliss RC | .10 | .02 |
| 101 | Mike Johnson | .10 | .02 |
| 102 | Robert Massey | .10 | .02 |
| 103 | Scott Mitchell | .20 | .07 |
| 104 | Herman Moore | .40 | .15 |
| 105 | Brett Perriman | .20 | .07 |
| 106 | Robert Porcher | .10 | .02 |
| 107 | Barry Sanders | 2.50 | 1.00 |
| 108 | Chris Spielman | .20 | .07 |
| 109 | Edgar Bennett | .20 | .07 |
| 110 | Robert Brooks | .40 | .15 |
| 111 | LeRoy Butler | .10 | .02 |
| 112 | Brett Favre | 3.00 | 1.50 |
| 113 | Sean Jones | .10 | .02 |
| 114 | John Jurkovic | .10 | .02 |
| 115 | George Koonce | .10 | .02 |
| 116 | Wayne Simmons | .10 | .02 |
| 117 | George Teague | .10 | .02 |
| 118 | Reggie White | .40 | .15 |
| 119 | Micheal Barrow | .10 | .02 |
| 120 | Gary Brown | .10 | .02 |
| 121 | Cody Carlson | .10 | .02 |
| 122 | Ray Childress | .10 | .02 |
| 123 | Cris Dishman | .10 | .02 |
| 124 | Bruce Matthews | .10 | .02 |
| 125 | Steve McNair RC | 3.00 | 1.25 |
| 126 | Marcus Robertson | .10 | .02 |
| 127 | Webster Slaughter | .10 | .02 |
| 128 | Al Smith | .10 | .02 |
| 129 | Tony Bennett | .10 | .02 |
| 130 | Ray Buchanan | .10 | .02 |
| 131 | Quentin Coryatt | .20 | .07 |
| 132 | Sean Dawkins | .20 | .07 |
| 133 | Marshall Faulk | 2.00 | .75 |
| 134 | Stephen Grant RC | .10 | .02 |
| 135 | Jim Harbaugh | .20 | .07 |
| 136 | Jeff Herrod | .10 | .02 |
| 137 | Ellis Johnson RC | .10 | .02 |
| 138 | Tony Siragusa | .10 | .02 |
| 139 | Steve Beuerlein | .20 | .07 |
| 140 | Tony Boselli RC | .40 | .15 |
| 141 | Darren Carrington | .10 | .02 |
| 142 | Reggie Cobb | .10 | .02 |
| 143 | Kelvin Martin | .10 | .02 |
| 144 | Kelvin Pritchett | .10 | .02 |
| 145 | Joel Smeenge | .10 | .02 |
| 146 | James O. Stewart RC | 1.25 | .50 |
| 147 | Marcus Allen | .40 | .15 |
| 148 | Kimble Anders | .20 | .07 |
| 149 | Dale Carter | .20 | .07 |
| 150 | Mark Collins | .10 | .02 |
| 151 | Willie Davis | .20 | .07 |
| 152 | Lake Dawson | .20 | .07 |
| 153 | Greg Hill | .20 | .07 |
| 154 | Trezelle Jenkins RC | .10 | .02 |
| 155 | Darren Mickell | .10 | .02 |
| 156 | Tracy Simien | .10 | .02 |
| 157 | Neil Smith | .20 | .07 |
| 158 | William White | .10 | .02 |
| 159 | Joe Aska RC | .10 | .02 |
| 160 | Greg Biekert | .10 | .02 |
| 161 | Tim Brown | .40 | .15 |
| 162 | Rob Fredrickson | .10 | .02 |
| 163 | Andrew Glover RC | .10 | .02 |
| 164 | Jeff Hostetler | .20 | .07 |
| 165 | Rocket Ismail | .20 | .07 |
| 166 | Napoleon Kaufman RC | 1.25 | .50 |
| 167 | Terry McDaniel | .10 | .02 |
| 168 | Chester McGlockton | .20 | .07 |
| 169 | Anthony Smith | .10 | .02 |
| 170 | Harvey Williams | .10 | .02 |
| 171 | Steve Wisniewski | .10 | .02 |
| 172 | Gene Atkins | .10 | .02 |
| 173 | Aubrey Beavers | .10 | .02 |
| 174 | Tim Bowens | .10 | .02 |
| 175 | Bryan Cox | .10 | .02 |
| 176 | Jeff Cross | .10 | .02 |
| 177 | Irving Fryar | .20 | .07 |
| 178 | Dan Marino | 3.00 | 1.25 |
| 179 | O.J. McDuffie | .40 | .15 |
| 180 | Billy Milner RC | .10 | .02 |
| 181 | Bernie Parmalee | .20 | .07 |
| 182 | Troy Vincent | .10 | .02 |
| 183 | Richmond Webb | .10 | .02 |
| 184 | Derrick Alexander DE RC | .10 | .02 |
| 185 | Cris Carter | .40 | .15 |
| 186 | Jack Del Rio | .10 | .02 |
| 187 | Qadry Ismail | .20 | .07 |
| 188 | Ed McDaniel | .10 | .02 |
| 189 | Randall McDaniel | .15 | .05 |
| 190 | Warren Moon | .20 | .07 |
| 191 | John Randle | .20 | .07 |
| 192 | Mike Reed | .20 | .07 |
| 193 | Fuad Reveiz | .10 | .02 |
| 194 | Korey Stringer RC | .20 | .07 |
| 195 | Dewayne Washington | .20 | .07 |
| 196 | Bruce Armstrong | .10 | .02 |
| 197 | Drew Bledsoe | 1.00 | .40 |
| 198 | Vincent Brisby | .10 | .02 |
| 199 | Vincent Brown | .10 | .02 |
| 200 | Marion Butts | .10 | .02 |
| 201 | Ben Coates | .20 | .07 |
| 202 | Myron Guyton | .10 | .02 |
| 203 | Maurice Hurst | .10 | .02 |
| 204 | Mike Jones | .10 | .02 |
| 205 | Ty Law RC | 1.50 | .60 |
| 206 | Willie McGinest | .20 | .07 |
| 207 | Chris Slade | .10 | .02 |
| 208 | Mario Bates | .20 | .07 |
| 209 | Quinn Early | .20 | .07 |
| 210 | Jim Everett | .10 | .02 |
| 211 | Mark Fields RC | .40 | .15 |
| 212 | Michael Haynes | .20 | .07 |
| 213 | Tyrone Hughes | .20 | .07 |
| 214 | Joe Johnson | .10 | .02 |
| 215 | Wayne Martin | .10 | .02 |
| 216 | Willie Roaf | .10 | .02 |
| 217 | Irv Smith | .10 | .02 |
| 218 | Jimmy Spencer | .10 | .02 |
| 219 | Winfred Tubbs | .10 | .02 |
| 220 | Renaldo Turnbull | .10 | .02 |
| 221 | Michael Brooks | .10 | .02 |
| 222 | Dave Brown | .20 | .07 |
| 223 | Chris Calloway | .10 | .02 |
| 224 | Howard Cross | .10 | .02 |
| 225 | John Elliott | .10 | .02 |
| 226 | Keith Hamilton | .10 | .02 |
| 227 | Rodney Hampton | .20 | .07 |
| 228 | Thomas Lewis | .20 | .07 |
| 229 | Thomas Randolph | .10 | .02 |
| 230 | Mike Sherrard | .10 | .02 |
| 231 | Michael Strahan | .40 | .15 |
| 232 | Tyrone Wheatley RC | 1.25 | .50 |
| 233 | Brad Baxter | .10 | .02 |
| 234 | Kyle Brady RC | .40 | .15 |
| 235 | Kyle Clifton | .10 | .02 |
| 236 | Hugh Douglas RC | .40 | .15 |
| 237 | Boomer Esiason | .20 | .07 |
| 238 | Aaron Glenn | .10 | .02 |
| 239 | Bobby Houston | .10 | .02 |
| 240 | Johnny Johnson | .10 | .02 |
| 241 | Mo Lewis | .10 | .02 |
| 242 | Johnny Mitchell | .10 | .02 |
| 243 | Marvin Washington | .10 | .02 |
| 244 | Fred Barnett | .20 | .07 |
| 245 | Randall Cunningham | .40 | .15 |
| 246 | William Fuller | .10 | .02 |
| 247 | Charlie Garner | .40 | .15 |
| 248 | Andy Harmon | .10 | .02 |
| 249 | Greg Jackson | .10 | .02 |
| 250 | Mike Mamula RC | .20 | .07 |
| 251 | Bill Romanowski | .10 | .02 |
| 252 | Bobby Taylor RC | .40 | .15 |
| 253 | William Thomas | .10 | .02 |
| 254 | Calvin Williams | .20 | .07 |
| 255 | Michael Zordich | .10 | .02 |
| 256 | Chad Brown | .20 | .07 |
| 257 | Mark Bruener | .20 | .07 |
| 258 | Dermontti Dawson | .20 | .07 |
| 259 | Barry Foster | .20 | .07 |
| 260 | Kevin Greene | .20 | .07 |
| 261 | Charles Johnson | .20 | .07 |
| 262 | Carnell Lake | .10 | .02 |
| 263 | Greg Lloyd | .20 | .07 |
| 264 | Byron Bam Morris | .10 | .02 |
| 265 | Neil O'Donnell | .20 | .07 |
| 266 | Darren Perry | .10 | .02 |
| 267 | Ray Seals | .10 | .02 |
| 268 | Kordell Stewart RC | 1.50 | .60 |
| 269 | John L. Williams | .10 | .02 |
| 270 | Rod Woodson | .20 | .07 |
| 271 | Jerome Bettis | .40 | .15 |
| 272 | Isaac Bruce | .75 | .30 |
| 273 | Kevin Carter RC | .40 | .15 |
| 274 | Shane Conlan | .10 | .02 |
| 275 | Troy Drayton | .10 | .02 |
| 276 | Sean Gilbert | .20 | .07 |
| 277 | Todd Lyght | .10 | .02 |
| 278 | Chris Miller | .10 | .02 |
| 279 | Anthony Newman | .10 | .02 |
| 280 | Roman Phifer | .10 | .02 |
| 281 | Robert Young | .10 | .02 |
| 282 | John Carney | .10 | .02 |
| 283 | Andre Coleman | .10 | .02 |
| 284 | Courtney Hall | .10 | .02 |
| 285 | Ronnie Harmon | .10 | .02 |
| 286 | Dwayne Harper | .10 | .02 |
| 287 | Stan Humphries | .20 | .07 |
| 288 | Shawn Jefferson | .10 | .02 |
| 289 | Tony Martin | .20 | .07 |
| 290 | Natrone Means | .20 | .07 |
| 291 | Chris Mims | .10 | .02 |
| 292 | Leslie O'Neal | .20 | .07 |
| 293 | Junior Seau | .40 | .15 |
| 294 | Mark Seay | .20 | .07 |
| 295 | Eric Davis | .10 | .02 |
| 296 | William Floyd | .20 | .07 |

|  |  | | |
|---|---|---|---|
| 297 | Merton Hanks | .10 | .02 |
| 298 | Brent Jones | .10 | .02 |
| 299 | Ken Norton Jr. | .20 | .07 |
| 300 | Gary Plummer | .10 | .02 |
| 301 | Jerry Rice | 1.50 | .60 |
| 302 | Deion Sanders | 1.00 | .40 |
| 303 | Jesse Sapolu | .10 | .02 |
| 304 | J.J. Stokes RC | .40 | .15 |
| 305 | Dana Stubblefield | .20 | .07 |
| 306 | John Taylor | .10 | .02 |
| 307 | Steve Wallace | .10 | .02 |
| 308 | Lee Woodall | .10 | .02 |
| 309 | Bryant Young | .20 | .07 |
| 310 | Steve Young | 1.25 | .50 |
| 311 | Sam Adams | .10 | .02 |
| 312 | Howard Ballard | .10 | .02 |
| 313 | Robert Blackmon | .10 | .02 |
| 314 | Brian Blades | .20 | .07 |
| 315 | Joey Galloway RC | 1.50 | .60 |
| 316 | Carlton Gray | .10 | .02 |
| 317 | Cortez Kennedy | .20 | .07 |
| 318 | Rick Mirer | .20 | .07 |
| 319 | Eugene Robinson | .10 | .02 |
| 320 | Chris Warren | .20 | .07 |
| 321 | Terry Wooden | .10 | .02 |
| 322 | Derrick Brooks RC | 1.50 | .60 |
| 323 | Lawrence Dawsey | .10 | .02 |
| 324 | Trent Dilfer | .40 | .15 |
| 325 | Santana Dotson | .10 | .02 |
| 326 | Thomas Everett | .10 | .02 |
| 327 | Paul Gruber | .10 | .02 |
| 328 | Jackie Harris | .10 | .02 |
| 329 | Courtney Hawkins | .10 | .02 |
| 330 | Martin Mayhew | .10 | .02 |
| 331 | Hardy Nickerson | .10 | .02 |
| 332 | Errict Rhett | .20 | .07 |
| 333 | Warren Sapp RC | 1.50 | .60 |
| 334 | Charles Wilson | .10 | .02 |
| 335 | Reggie Brooks | .20 | .07 |
| 336 | Tom Carter | .10 | .02 |
| 337 | Henry Ellard | .20 | .07 |
| 338 | Ricky Ervins | .10 | .02 |
| 339 | Darrell Green | .10 | .02 |
| 340 | Ken Harvey | .10 | .02 |
| 341 | Brian Mitchell | .10 | .02 |
| 342 | Cory Raymer RC | .10 | .02 |
| 343 | Heath Shuler | .20 | .07 |
| 344 | Michael Westbrook RC | .40 | .15 |
| 345 | Tony Woods | .10 | .02 |
| 346 | Checklist | .10 | .02 |
| 347 | Checklist | .10 | .02 |
| 348 | Checklist | .10 | .02 |
| 349 | Checklist | .10 | .02 |
| 350 | Checklist | .10 | .02 |
| 351 | Checklist | .10 | .02 |
| 352 | Checklist | .10 | .02 |
| 353 | Dave Krieg | .10 | .02 |
| 354 | Rob Moore | .20 | .07 |
| 355 | J.J. Birden | .10 | .02 |
| 356 | Eric Metcalf | .10 | .02 |
| 357 | Bryce Paup | .20 | .07 |
| 358 | Willie Green | .20 | .07 |
| 359 | Derrick Moore | .10 | .02 |
| 360 | Michael Timpson | .10 | .02 |
| 361 | Eric Bieniemy | .10 | .02 |
| 362 | Keenan McCardell | .40 | .15 |
| 363 | Andre Rison | .20 | .07 |
| 364 | Lorenzo White | .10 | .02 |
| 365 | Deion Sanders | 1.00 | .40 |
| 366 | Wade Wilson | .10 | .02 |
| 367 | Aaron Craver | .10 | .02 |
| 368 | Michael Dean Perry | .10 | .02 |
| 369 | Rod Smith WR RC | 12.00 | 5.00 |
| 370 | Henry Thomas | .10 | .02 |
| 371 | Mark Ingram | .10 | .02 |
| 372 | Chris Chandler | .10 | .02 |
| 373 | Mel Gray | .10 | .02 |
| 374 | Flipper Anderson | .10 | .02 |
| 375 | Craig Erickson | .10 | .02 |
| 376 | Mark Brunell | 1.00 | .40 |
| 377 | Ernest Givins | .10 | .02 |
| 378 | Randy Jordan | .10 | .02 |
| 379 | Webster Slaughter | .10 | .02 |
| 380 | Tamarick Vanover RC | .40 | .15 |
| 381 | Gary Clark | .10 | .02 |
| 382 | Steve Emtman | .10 | .02 |
| 383 | Eric Green | .10 | .02 |
| 384 | Louis Oliver | .10 | .02 |
| 385 | Robert Smith | .40 | .15 |
| 386 | Dave Meggett | .10 | .02 |
| 387 | Eric Allen | .10 | .02 |
| 388 | Wesley Walls | .20 | .07 |
| 389 | Herschel Walker | .20 | .07 |
| 390 | Ronald Moore | .10 | .02 |
| 391 | Adrian Murrell | .20 | .07 |
| 392 | Charles Wilson | .10 | .02 |
| 393 | Derrick Fenner | .10 | .02 |
| 394 | Pat Swilling | .10 | .02 |
| 395 | Kelvin Martin | .10 | .02 |
| 396 | Rodney Peete | .10 | .02 |
| 397 | Ricky Watters | .20 | .07 |
| 398 | Eric Pegram | .20 | .07 |
| 399 | Leonard Russell | .10 | .02 |
| 400 | Alexander Wright | .10 | .02 |
| 401 | Darrien Gordon | .10 | .02 |
| 402 | Alfred Pupunu | .10 | .02 |
| 403 | Elvis Grbac | .40 | .15 |
| 404 | Derek Loville | .10 | .02 |
| 405 | Steve Broussard | .10 | .02 |
| 406 | Ricky Proehl | .10 | .02 |
| 407 | Bobby Joe Edmonds | .10 | .02 |
| 408 | Alvin Harper | .10 | .02 |
| 409 | Dave Moore RC | .10 | .02 |
| 410 | Terry Allen | .20 | .07 |
| 411 | Gus Frerotte | .20 | .07 |
| 412 | Leslie Shepherd RC | .20 | .07 |
| 413 | Stoney Case RC | .10 | .02 |
| 414 | Frank Sanders RC | .40 | .15 |
| 415 | Roell Preston RC | .20 | .07 |
| 416 | Lorenzo Styles RC | .10 | .02 |
| 417 | Justin Armour RC | .10 | .02 |
| 418 | Todd Collins RC | 1.25 | .50 |
| 419 | Darick Holmes RC | .20 | .07 |
| 420 | Kerry Collins | .75 | .30 |
| 421 | Tyrone Poole | .20 | .07 |
| 422 | Rashaan Salaam | .20 | .07 |
| 423 | Todd Sauerbrun RC | .10 | .02 |
| 424 | Ki-Jana Carter | .40 | .15 |
| 425 | David Dunn RC | .10 | .02 |
| 426 | Ernest Hunter RC | .10 | .02 |
| 427 | Eric Zeier RC | .40 | .15 |
| 428 | Eric Bjornson RC | .10 | .02 |
| 429 | Sherman Williams | .10 | .02 |
| 430 | Terrell Davis RC | 2.50 | 1.00 |
| 431 | Luther Elliss | .10 | .02 |
| 432 | Kez McCorvey RC | .10 | .02 |
| 433 | Antonio Freeman RC | 1.25 | .50 |
| 434 | Craig Newsome RC | .10 | .02 |
| 435 | Steve McNair | 1.50 | .60 |
| 436 | Chris Sanders RC | .20 | .07 |
| 437 | Zack Crockett RC | .20 | .07 |
| 438 | Ellis Johnson | .10 | .02 |
| 439 | Tony Boselli | .40 | .15 |
| 440 | James O. Stewart | .40 | .15 |
| 441 | Trezelle Jenkins | .10 | .02 |
| 442 | Tamarick Vanover | .40 | .15 |
| 443 | Derrick Alexander DE | .10 | .02 |
| 444 | Chad May RC | .10 | .02 |
| 445 | James A.Stewart RC | .10 | .02 |
| 446 | Ty Law | .40 | .15 |
| 447 | Curtis Martin RC | 3.00 | 1.25 |
| 448 | Will Moore RC | .10 | .02 |
| 449 | Mark Fields | .10 | .02 |
| 450 | Ray Zellars RC | .20 | .07 |
| 451 | Charles Way RC | .10 | .02 |
| 452 | Tyrone Wheatley | .40 | .15 |
| 453 | Kyle Brady | .40 | .15 |
| 454 | Wayne Chrebet RC | 2.50 | 1.00 |
| 455 | Hugh Douglas | .20 | .07 |
| 456 | Chris T.Jones RC | .10 | .02 |
| 457 | Mike Mamula | .10 | .02 |
| 458 | Fred McCrary RC | .10 | .02 |
| 459 | Mark Bruener | .20 | .07 |
| 460 | Mark Bruener | .20 | .07 |
| 461 | Kordell Stewart | .60 | .25 |
| 462 | Kevin Carter | .20 | .07 |
| 463 | Lovell Pinkney RC | .10 | .02 |
| 464 | Johnny Thomas WR RC | .10 | .02 |
| 465 | Terrell Fletcher RC | .10 | .02 |
| 466 | Jimmy Oliver RC | .10 | .02 |
| 467 | J.J. Stokes | .40 | .15 |
| 468 | Christian Fauria RC | .20 | .07 |
| 469 | Joey Galloway | .60 | .25 |
| 470 | Derrick Brooks | .60 | .25 |
| 471 | Warren Sapp | .40 | .15 |
| 472 | Michael Westbrook | .40 | .15 |
| 473 | Garrison Hearst ES | .40 | .15 |
| 474 | Jeff George ES | .20 | .07 |
| 475 | Terance Mathis ES | .20 | .07 |
| 476 | Andre Reed ES | .20 | .07 |
| 477 | Bruce Smith ES | .40 | .15 |
| 478 | Lamar Lathon ES | .10 | .02 |
| 479 | Curtis Conway ES | .40 | .15 |
| 480 | Jeff Blake ES | .40 | .15 |
| 481 | Carl Pickens ES | .20 | .07 |
| 482 | Eric Turner ES | .10 | .02 |
| 483 | Troy Aikman ES | .75 | .30 |
| 484 | Michael Irvin ES | .40 | .15 |
| 485 | Emmitt Smith ES | 1.25 | .50 |
| 486 | John Elway ES | 1.50 | .60 |
| 487 | Shannon Sharpe ES | .20 | .07 |
| 488 | Herman Moore ES | .40 | .15 |
| 489 | Barry Sanders ES | 1.25 | .50 |
| 490 | Brett Favre ES | 1.50 | .60 |
| 491 | Reggie White ES | .40 | .15 |
| 492 | Haywood Jeffires ES | .10 | .02 |
| 493 | Sean Dawkins ES | .10 | .02 |
| 494 | Marshall Faulk ES | 1.00 | .40 |
| 495 | Desmond Howard ES | .20 | .07 |
| 496 | Steve Bono ES | .20 | .07 |
| 497 | Derrick Thomas ES | .40 | .15 |
| 498 | Irving Fryar ES | .20 | .07 |
| 499 | Terry Kirby ES | .20 | .07 |
| 500 | Dan Marino ES | 1.50 | .60 |
| 501 | O.J. McDuffie ES | .40 | .15 |
| 502 | Cris Carter ES | .40 | .15 |
| 503 | Warren Moon ES | .20 | .07 |
| 504 | Jake Reed ES | .20 | .07 |
| 505 | Drew Bledsoe ES | .40 | .15 |
| 506 | Ben Coates ES | .20 | .07 |
| 507 | Jim Everett ES | .10 | .02 |
| 508 | Rodney Hampton ES | .20 | .07 |
| 509 | Mo Lewis ES | .10 | .02 |
| 510 | Tim Brown ES | .40 | .15 |
| 511 | Jeff Hostetler ES | .20 | .07 |
| 512 | Rocket Ismail ES | .20 | .07 |
| 513 | Chester McGlockton ES | .20 | .07 |
| 514 | Fred Barnett ES | .20 | .07 |
| 515 | Greg Lloyd ES | .20 | .07 |
| 516 | Byron Bam Morris ES | .10 | .02 |
| 517 | Rod Woodson ES | .20 | .07 |
| 518 | Jerome Bettis ES | .40 | .15 |
| 519 | Isaac Bruce ES | .40 | .15 |
| 520 | Stan Humphries ES | .20 | .07 |
| 521 | Natrone Means ES | .20 | .07 |
| 522 | Junior Seau ES | .40 | .15 |
| 523 | William Floyd ES | .20 | .07 |
| 524 | Jerry Rice ES | .75 | .30 |
| 525 | Steve Young ES | .60 | .25 |
| 526 | Cortez Kennedy ES | .20 | .07 |
| 527 | Rick Mirer ES | .20 | .07 |
| 528 | Chris Warren ES | .20 | .07 |
| 529 | Trent Dilfer ES | .40 | .15 |
| 530 | Errict Rhett ES | .20 | .07 |
| 531 | Darrell Green ES | .10 | .02 |
| 532 | Heath Shuler ES | .20 | .07 |
| 533 | Stoney Case ES | .10 | .02 |
| 534 | Eric Zeier ES | .20 | .07 |
| 535 | Kerry Collins RO | .40 | .15 |
| 536 | Steve McNair RO | 1.25 | .50 |
| 537 | Kordell Stewart RO | .60 | .25 |
| 538 | Rob Johnson RO RC | 1.00 | .40 |
| 539 | Eric Ball EE | .10 | .02 |
| 540 | Darrick Brownlow EE | .10 | .02 |
| 541 | Paul Butcher EE | .10 | .02 |
| 542 | Carlester Crumpler EE | .10 | .02 |
| 543 | Maurice Douglas EE | .10 | .02 |
| 544 | Keith Elias EE RC | .10 | .02 |
| 545 | Kenneth Gant EE | .10 | .02 |
| 546 | Corey Harris EE | .10 | .02 |
| 547 | Andre Hastings EE | .20 | .07 |
| 548 | Thomas Homco EE | .10 | .02 |

| | | |
|---|---|---|
| ❑ 549 Lenny McGill EE | .10 | .02 |
| ❑ 550 Mark Pike EE | .10 | .02 |
| ❑ P1 Promo Sheet | 2.00 | .75 |
| ❑ P264 Byron Bam Morris Prototype | 1.00 | .40 |

## 1996 Ultra

| | | |
|---|---|---|
| ❑ COMPLETE SET (200) | 25.00 | 10.00 |
| ❑ 1 Larry Centers | .10 | .08 |
| ❑ 2 Garrison Hearst | .25 | .08 |
| ❑ 3 Rob Moore | .25 | .08 |
| ❑ 4 Eric Swann | .10 | .02 |
| ❑ 5 Aeneas Williams | .10 | .02 |
| ❑ 6 Bert Emanuel | .25 | .08 |
| ❑ 7 Jeff George | .25 | .08 |
| ❑ 8 Craig Heyward | .10 | .02 |
| ❑ 9 Terance Mathis | .10 | .02 |
| ❑ 10 Eric Metcalf | .10 | .02 |
| ❑ 11 Cornelius Bennett | .10 | .02 |
| ❑ 12 Darick Holmes | .10 | .02 |
| ❑ 13 Jim Kelly | .50 | .20 |
| ❑ 14 Bryce Paup | .10 | .02 |
| ❑ 15 Bruce Smith | .25 | .08 |
| ❑ 16 Mark Carrier WR | .10 | .02 |
| ❑ 17 Kerry Collins | .50 | .20 |
| ❑ 18 Lamar Lathon | .10 | .02 |
| ❑ 19 Derrick Moore | .10 | .02 |
| ❑ 20 Tyrone Poole | .10 | .02 |
| ❑ 21 Curtis Conway | .50 | .20 |
| ❑ 22 Jeff Graham | .10 | .02 |
| ❑ 23 Raymont Harris | .25 | .08 |
| ❑ 24 Erik Kramer | .10 | .02 |
| ❑ 25 Rashaan Salaam | .25 | .08 |
| ❑ 26 Jeff Blake | .50 | .20 |
| ❑ 27 Ki-Jana Carter | .25 | .08 |
| ❑ 28 Carl Pickens | .25 | .08 |
| ❑ 29 Damay Scott | .25 | .08 |
| ❑ 30 Dan Wilkinson | .10 | .02 |
| ❑ 31 Leroy Hoard | .10 | .02 |
| ❑ 32 Michael Jackson | .25 | .08 |
| ❑ 33 Andre Rison | .25 | .08 |
| ❑ 34 Vinny Testaverde | .25 | .08 |
| ❑ 35 Eric Turner | .10 | .02 |
| ❑ 36 Troy Aikman | 1.25 | .50 |
| ❑ 37 Charles Haley | .10 | .02 |
| ❑ 38 Michael Irvin | .50 | .20 |
| ❑ 39 Daryl Johnston | .25 | .08 |
| ❑ 40 Jay Novacek | .25 | .08 |
| ❑ 41 Deion Sanders | .75 | .30 |
| ❑ 42 Emmitt Smith | 2.00 | .75 |
| ❑ 43 Steve Atwater | .10 | .02 |
| ❑ 44 Terrell Davis | 1.00 | .40 |
| ❑ 45 John Elway | 2.50 | 1.00 |
| ❑ 46 Anthony Miller | .25 | .08 |
| ❑ 47 Shannon Sharpe | .25 | .08 |
| ❑ 48 Scott Mitchell | .25 | .08 |
| ❑ 49 Herman Moore | .25 | .08 |
| ❑ 50 Johnnie Morton | .25 | .08 |
| ❑ 51 Brett Perriman | .10 | .02 |
| ❑ 52 Barry Sanders | 2.00 | .75 |
| ❑ 53 Chris Spielman | .10 | .02 |
| ❑ 54 Edgar Bennett | .25 | .08 |
| ❑ 55 Robert Brooks | .50 | .20 |
| ❑ 56 Mark Chmura | .25 | .08 |
| ❑ 57 Brett Favre | 2.50 | 1.00 |
| ❑ 58 Reggie White | .50 | .20 |
| ❑ 59 Mel Gray | .10 | .02 |
| ❑ 60 Haywood Jeffires | .10 | .02 |

| | | |
|---|---|---|
| ❑ 61 Steve McNair | 1.00 | .40 |
| ❑ 62 Chris Sanders | .25 | .08 |
| ❑ 63 Rodney Thomas | .10 | .02 |
| ❑ 64 Quentin Coryatt | .10 | .02 |
| ❑ 65 Sean Dawkins | .10 | .02 |
| ❑ 66 Ken Dilger | .25 | .08 |
| ❑ 67 Marshall Faulk | .60 | .25 |
| ❑ 68 Jim Harbaugh | .25 | .08 |
| ❑ 69 Tony Boselli | .10 | .02 |
| ❑ 70 Mark Brunell | .75 | .30 |
| ❑ 71 Desmond Howard | .25 | .08 |
| ❑ 72 Jimmy Smith | .50 | .20 |
| ❑ 73 James O. Stewart | .50 | .20 |
| ❑ 74 Marcus Allen | .50 | .20 |
| ❑ 75 Steve Bono | .10 | .02 |
| ❑ 76 Lake Dawson | .10 | .02 |
| ❑ 77 Neil Smith | .25 | .08 |
| ❑ 78 Derrick Thomas | .50 | .20 |
| ❑ 79 Tamarick Vanover | .25 | .08 |
| ❑ 80 Bryan Cox | .10 | .02 |
| ❑ 81 Irving Fryar | .25 | .08 |
| ❑ 82 Eric Green | .10 | .02 |
| ❑ 83 Dan Marino | 2.50 | 1.00 |
| ❑ 84 O.J. McDuffie | .25 | .08 |
| ❑ 85 Bernie Parmalee | .10 | .02 |
| ❑ 86 Cris Carter | .50 | .20 |
| ❑ 87 Qadry Ismail | .25 | .08 |
| ❑ 88 Warren Moon | .25 | .08 |
| ❑ 89 Jake Reed | .25 | .08 |
| ❑ 90 Robert Smith | .25 | .08 |
| ❑ 91 Drew Bledsoe | .75 | .30 |
| ❑ 92 Vincent Brisby | .10 | .02 |
| ❑ 93 Ben Coates | .25 | .08 |
| ❑ 94 Curtis Martin | 1.00 | .40 |
| ❑ 95 Willie McGinest | .10 | .02 |
| ❑ 96 Dave Meggett | .10 | .02 |
| ❑ 97 Mario Bates | .25 | .08 |
| ❑ 98 Quinn Early | .10 | .02 |
| ❑ 99 Jim Everett | .10 | .02 |
| ❑ 100 Michael Haynes | .10 | .02 |
| ❑ 101 Renaldo Turnbull | .10 | .02 |
| ❑ 102 Dave Brown | .10 | .02 |
| ❑ 103 Rodney Hampton | .25 | .08 |
| ❑ 104 Mike Sherrard | .10 | .02 |
| ❑ 105 Phillippi Sparks | .10 | .02 |
| ❑ 106 Tyrone Wheatley | .25 | .08 |
| ❑ 107 Hugh Douglas | .25 | .08 |
| ❑ 108 Boomer Esiason | .25 | .08 |
| ❑ 109 Aaron Glenn | .10 | .02 |
| ❑ 110 Mo Lewis | .10 | .02 |
| ❑ 111 Johnny Mitchell | .10 | .02 |
| ❑ 112 Tim Brown | .50 | .20 |
| ❑ 113 Jeff Hostetler | .10 | .02 |
| ❑ 114 Rocket Ismail | .10 | .02 |
| ❑ 115 Chester McGlockton | .10 | .02 |
| ❑ 116 Harvey Williams | .10 | .02 |
| ❑ 117 Fred Barnett | .10 | .02 |
| ❑ 118 William Fuller | .10 | .02 |
| ❑ 119 Charlie Garner | .25 | .08 |
| ❑ 120 Ricky Watters | .25 | .08 |
| ❑ 121 Calvin Williams | .10 | .02 |
| ❑ 122 Kevin Greene | .25 | .08 |
| ❑ 123 Greg Lloyd | .25 | .08 |
| ❑ 124 Byron Bam Morris | .10 | .02 |
| ❑ 125 Neil O'Donnell | .25 | .08 |
| ❑ 126 Erric Pegram | .10 | .02 |
| ❑ 127 Kordell Stewart | .50 | .20 |
| ❑ 128 Yancey Thigpen | .25 | .08 |
| ❑ 129 Rod Woodson | .25 | .08 |
| ❑ 130 Jerome Bettis | .50 | .20 |
| ❑ 131 Isaac Bruce | .50 | .20 |
| ❑ 132 Troy Drayton | .10 | .02 |
| ❑ 133 Sean Gilbert | .10 | .02 |
| ❑ 134 Chris Miller | .10 | .02 |
| ❑ 135 Andre Coleman | .10 | .02 |
| ❑ 136 Ronnie Harmon | .10 | .02 |
| ❑ 137 Aaron Hayden RC | .10 | .02 |
| ❑ 138 Stan Humphries | .25 | .08 |
| ❑ 139 Natrone Means | .25 | .08 |
| ❑ 140 Junior Seau | .50 | .20 |
| ❑ 141 William Floyd | .25 | .08 |
| ❑ 142 Merton Hanks | .10 | .02 |
| ❑ 143 Brent Jones | .25 | .08 |
| ❑ 144 Derek Loville | .10 | .02 |

| | | |
|---|---|---|
| ❑ 145 Jerry Rice | 1.25 | .50 |
| ❑ 146 J.J. Stokes | .50 | .20 |
| ❑ 147 Steve Young | 1.00 | .40 |
| ❑ 148 Brian Blades | .10 | .02 |
| ❑ 149 Joey Galloway | .50 | .20 |
| ❑ 150 Cortez Kennedy | .10 | .02 |
| ❑ 151 Rick Mirer | .25 | .08 |
| ❑ 152 Chris Warren | .25 | .08 |
| ❑ 153 Derrick Brooks | .50 | .20 |
| ❑ 154 Trent Dilfer | .50 | .20 |
| ❑ 155 Alvin Harper | .10 | .02 |
| ❑ 156 Jackie Harris | .10 | .02 |
| ❑ 157 Hardy Nickerson | .10 | .02 |
| ❑ 158 Errict Rhett | .25 | .08 |
| ❑ 159 Terry Allen | .25 | .08 |
| ❑ 160 Henry Ellard | .10 | .02 |
| ❑ 161 Brian Mitchell | .10 | .02 |
| ❑ 162 Heath Shuler | .25 | .08 |
| ❑ 163 Michael Westbrook | .50 | .20 |
| ❑ 164 Tim Biakabutuka RC | .50 | .20 |
| ❑ 165 Tony Brackens RC | .50 | .20 |
| ❑ 166 Rickey Dudley RC | .50 | .20 |
| ❑ 167 Bobby Engram RC | .50 | .20 |
| ❑ 168 Daryl Gardener RC | .10 | .02 |
| ❑ 169 Eddie George RC | 1.50 | .60 |
| ❑ 170 Terry Glenn RC | 1.25 | .50 |
| ❑ 171 Kevin Hardy RC | .50 | .20 |
| ❑ 172 Keyshawn Johnson RC | 1.25 | .50 |
| ❑ 173 Cedric Jones RC | .10 | .02 |
| ❑ 174 Leeland McElroy RC | .25 | .08 |
| ❑ 175 Jonathan Ogden RC | .50 | .20 |
| ❑ 176 Lawrence Phillips RC | .50 | .20 |
| ❑ 177 Simeon Rice RC | 1.25 | .50 |
| ❑ 178 Regan Upshaw RC | .10 | .02 |
| ❑ 179 Justin Armour FI | .10 | .02 |
| ❑ 180 Kyle Brady FI | .10 | .02 |
| ❑ 181 Devin Bush FI | .10 | .02 |
| ❑ 182 Kevin Carter FI | .10 | .02 |
| ❑ 183 Wayne Chrebet FI | .75 | .30 |
| ❑ 184 Napoleon Kaufman FI | .50 | .20 |
| ❑ 185 Frank Sanders FI | .25 | .08 |
| ❑ 186 Warren Sapp FI | .10 | .02 |
| ❑ 187 Eric Zeier FI | .10 | .02 |
| ❑ 188 Ray Zellars FI | .10 | .02 |
| ❑ 189 Bill Brooks SW | .10 | .02 |
| ❑ 190 Chris Calloway SW | .10 | .02 |
| ❑ 191 Zack Crockett SW | .10 | .02 |
| ❑ 192 Antonio Freeman SW | .50 | .20 |
| ❑ 193 Tyrone Hughes SW | .10 | .02 |
| ❑ 194 Daryl Johnston SW | .25 | .08 |
| ❑ 195 Tony Martin SW | .10 | .02 |
| ❑ 196 Keenan McCardell SW | .50 | .20 |
| ❑ 197 Glyn Milburn SW | .10 | .02 |
| ❑ 198 David Palmer SW | .10 | .02 |
| ❑ 199 Checklist | .10 | .02 |
| ❑ 200 Checklist | .10 | .02 |
| ❑ P1 Promo Sheet | 2.00 | .75 |

## 1997 Ultra

| | | |
|---|---|---|
| ❑ COMPLETE SET (350) | 80.00 | 40.00 |
| ❑ COMP.SERIES 1 (200) | 30.00 | 15.00 |
| ❑ COMP.SERIES 2 (150) | 50.00 | 25.00 |
| ❑ 1 Brett Favre | 2.50 | 1.25 |
| ❑ 2 Ricky Watters | .40 | .15 |
| ❑ 3 Dan Marino | 2.50 | 1.00 |
| ❑ 4 Bryan Still | .25 | .08 |
| ❑ 5 Chester McGlockton | .25 | .08 |

|  |  | | |
|---|------|---|---|
| ☐ 6 | Tim Biakabutuka | .40 | .15 |
| ☐ 7 | Dave Brown | .25 | .08 |
| ☐ 8 | Mike Alstott | .60 | .25 |
| ☐ 9 | O.J. McDuffie | .40 | .15 |
| ☐ 10 | Mark Brunell | .75 | .30 |
| ☐ 11 | Michael Bates | .25 | .08 |
| ☐ 12 | Tyrone Wheatley | .40 | .15 |
| ☐ 13 | Eddie George | .60 | .25 |
| ☐ 14 | Kevin Greene | .40 | .15 |
| ☐ 15 | Jerris McPhail | .25 | .08 |
| ☐ 16 | Harvey Williams | .25 | .08 |
| ☐ 17 | Eric Swann | .25 | .08 |
| ☐ 18 | Carl Pickens | .40 | .15 |
| ☐ 19 | Terrell Davis | .75 | .30 |
| ☐ 20 | Charles Way | .25 | .08 |
| ☐ 21 | Jamie Asher | .25 | .08 |
| ☐ 22 | Qadry Ismail | .40 | .15 |
| ☐ 23 | Lawrence Phillips | .25 | .08 |
| ☐ 24 | John Friesz | .25 | .08 |
| ☐ 25 | Dorsey Levens | .60 | .25 |
| ☐ 26 | Willie McGinest | .25 | .08 |
| ☐ 27 | Chris T. Jones | .25 | .08 |
| ☐ 28 | Cortez Kennedy | .25 | .08 |
| ☐ 29 | Raymont Harris | .25 | .08 |
| ☐ 30 | William Roaf | .25 | .08 |
| ☐ 31 | Ted Johnson | .25 | .08 |
| ☐ 32 | Tony Martin | .40 | .15 |
| ☐ 33 | Jim Everett | .25 | .08 |
| ☐ 34 | Ray Zellars | .25 | .08 |
| ☐ 35 | Derrick Alexander WR | .40 | .15 |
| ☐ 36 | Leonard Russell | .25 | .08 |
| ☐ 37 | William Thomas | .25 | .08 |
| ☐ 38 | Karim Abdul-Jabbar | .40 | .15 |
| ☐ 39 | Kevin Turner | .25 | .08 |
| ☐ 40 | Robert Brooks | .40 | .15 |
| ☐ 41 | Kent Graham | .25 | .08 |
| ☐ 42 | Tony Brackens | .25 | .08 |
| ☐ 43 | Rodney Hampton | .40 | .15 |
| ☐ 44 | Drew Bledsoe | .75 | .30 |
| ☐ 45 | Barry Sanders | 2.00 | .75 |
| ☐ 46 | Tim Brown | .60 | .25 |
| ☐ 47 | Reggie White | .60 | .25 |
| ☐ 48 | Terry Allen | .60 | .25 |
| ☐ 49 | Jim Harbaugh | .40 | .15 |
| ☐ 50 | John Elway | 2.50 | 1.00 |
| ☐ 51 | William Floyd | .40 | .15 |
| ☐ 52 | Michael Jackson | .40 | .15 |
| ☐ 53 | Larry Centers | .40 | .15 |
| ☐ 54 | Emmitt Smith | 2.00 | .75 |
| ☐ 55 | Bruce Smith | .40 | .15 |
| ☐ 56 | Terrell Owens | .75 | .30 |
| ☐ 57 | Deion Sanders | .60 | .25 |
| ☐ 58 | Neil O'Donnell | .40 | .15 |
| ☐ 59 | Kordell Stewart | .60 | .25 |
| ☐ 60 | Bobby Engram | .40 | .15 |
| ☐ 61 | Keenan McCardell | .40 | .15 |
| ☐ 62 | Ben Coates | .40 | .15 |
| ☐ 63 | Curtis Martin | .75 | .30 |
| ☐ 64 | Hugh Douglas | .25 | .08 |
| ☐ 65 | Eric Moulds | .60 | .25 |
| ☐ 66 | Derrick Thomas | .60 | .25 |
| ☐ 67 | Byron Bam Morris | .25 | .08 |
| ☐ 68 | Bryan Cox | .25 | .08 |
| ☐ 69 | Rob Moore | .40 | .15 |
| ☐ 70 | Michael Haynes | .25 | .08 |
| ☐ 71 | Brian Mitchell | .25 | .08 |
| ☐ 72 | Alex Molden | .25 | .08 |
| ☐ 73 | Steve Young | .75 | .30 |
| ☐ 74 | Andre Reed | .40 | .15 |
| ☐ 75 | Michael Westbrook | .40 | .15 |
| ☐ 76 | Eric Metcalf | .40 | .15 |
| ☐ 77 | Tony Banks | .40 | .15 |
| ☐ 78 | Ken Dilger | .25 | .08 |
| ☐ 79 | John Henry Mills RC | .25 | .08 |
| ☐ 80 | Ashley Ambrose | .25 | .08 |
| ☐ 81 | Jason Dunn | .25 | .08 |
| ☐ 82 | Trent Dilfer | .60 | .25 |
| ☐ 83 | Wayne Chrebet | .60 | .25 |
| ☐ 84 | Ty Detmer | .40 | .15 |
| ☐ 85 | Aeneas Williams | .25 | .08 |
| ☐ 86 | Frank Wycheck | .25 | .08 |
| ☐ 87 | Jessie Tuggle | .25 | .08 |
| ☐ 88 | Steve McNair | .75 | .30 |
| ☐ 89 | Chris Slade | .25 | .08 |
| ☐ 90 | Anthony Johnson | .25 | .08 |
| ☐ 91 | Simeon Rice | .40 | .15 |
| ☐ 92 | Mike Tomczak | .25 | .08 |
| ☐ 93 | Sean Jones | .25 | .08 |
| ☐ 94 | Wesley Walls | .40 | .15 |
| ☐ 95 | Thurman Thomas | .60 | .25 |
| ☐ 96 | Scott Mitchell | .40 | .15 |
| ☐ 97 | Desmond Howard | .40 | .15 |
| ☐ 98 | Chris Warren | .40 | .15 |
| ☐ 99 | Glyn Milburn | .25 | .08 |
| ☐ 100 | Vinny Testaverde | .40 | .15 |
| ☐ 101 | James O.Stewart | .40 | .15 |
| ☐ 102 | Iheanyi Uwaezuoke | .25 | .08 |
| ☐ 103 | Stan Humphries | .40 | .15 |
| ☐ 104 | Terance Mathis | .40 | .15 |
| ☐ 105 | Thomas Lewis | .25 | .08 |
| ☐ 106 | Eddie Kennison | .40 | .15 |
| ☐ 107 | Rashaan Salaam | .25 | .08 |
| ☐ 108 | Curtis Conway | .40 | .15 |
| ☐ 109 | Chris Sanders | .25 | .08 |
| ☐ 110 | Marcus Allen | .60 | .25 |
| ☐ 111 | Gilbert Brown | .40 | .15 |
| ☐ 112 | Jason Sehorn | .40 | .15 |
| ☐ 113 | Zach Thomas | .60 | .25 |
| ☐ 114 | Bobby Hebert | .25 | .08 |
| ☐ 115 | Herman Moore | .40 | .15 |
| ☐ 116 | Ray Lewis | 1.00 | .40 |
| ☐ 117 | Darnay Scott | .40 | .15 |
| ☐ 118 | Jamal Anderson | .60 | .25 |
| ☐ 119 | Keyshawn Johnson | .60 | .25 |
| ☐ 120 | Adrian Murrell | .40 | .15 |
| ☐ 121 | Sam Mills | .25 | .08 |
| ☐ 122 | Irving Fryar | .40 | .15 |
| ☐ 123 | Ki-Jana Carter | .25 | .08 |
| ☐ 124 | Gus Frerotte | .25 | .08 |
| ☐ 125 | Terry Glenn | .60 | .25 |
| ☐ 126 | Quentin Coryatt | .25 | .08 |
| ☐ 127 | Robert Smith | .40 | .15 |
| ☐ 128 | Jeff Blake | .40 | .15 |
| ☐ 129 | Natrone Means | .40 | .15 |
| ☐ 130 | Isaac Bruce | .60 | .25 |
| ☐ 131 | Lamar Lathon | .25 | .08 |
| ☐ 132 | Johnnie Morton | .40 | .15 |
| ☐ 133 | Jerry Rice | 1.25 | .50 |
| ☐ 134 | Errict Rhett | .25 | .08 |
| ☐ 135 | Junior Seau | .60 | .25 |
| ☐ 136 | Joey Galloway | .40 | .15 |
| ☐ 137 | Napoleon Kaufman | .60 | .25 |
| ☐ 138 | Troy Aikman | 1.25 | .50 |
| ☐ 139 | Kevin Hardy | .25 | .08 |
| ☐ 140 | Jimmy Smith | .40 | .15 |
| ☐ 141 | Edgar Bennett | .40 | .15 |
| ☐ 142 | Hardy Nickerson | .25 | .08 |
| ☐ 143 | Greg Lloyd | .25 | .08 |
| ☐ 144 | Dale Carter | .25 | .08 |
| ☐ 145 | Jake Reed | .40 | .15 |
| ☐ 146 | Cris Carter | .60 | .25 |
| ☐ 147 | Todd Collins | .25 | .08 |
| ☐ 148 | Mel Gray | .25 | .08 |
| ☐ 149 | Lawyer Milloy | .40 | .15 |
| ☐ 150 | Kimble Anders | .40 | .15 |
| ☐ 151 | Darick Holmes | .25 | .08 |
| ☐ 152 | Bert Emanuel | .40 | .15 |
| ☐ 153 | Marshall Faulk | .75 | .30 |
| ☐ 154 | Frank Sanders | .40 | .15 |
| ☐ 155 | Leeland McElroy | .25 | .08 |
| ☐ 156 | Rickey Dudley | .40 | .15 |
| ☐ 157 | Tamarick Vanover | .25 | .08 |
| ☐ 158 | Kerry Collins | .60 | .25 |
| ☐ 159 | Jeff Graham | .25 | .08 |
| ☐ 160 | Jerome Bettis | .60 | .25 |
| ☐ 161 | Greg Hill | .25 | .08 |
| ☐ 162 | John Mobley | .25 | .08 |
| ☐ 163 | Michael Irvin | .60 | .25 |
| ☐ 164 | Marvin Harrison | .60 | .25 |
| ☐ 165 | Jim Schwantz RC | .25 | .08 |
| ☐ 166 | Jermaine Lewis | .25 | .08 |
| ☐ 167 | Levon Kirkland | .25 | .08 |
| ☐ 168 | Nilo Silvan | .25 | .08 |
| ☐ 169 | Ken Norton | .25 | .08 |
| ☐ 170 | Yancey Thigpen | .40 | .15 |
| ☐ 171 | Antonio Freeman | .60 | .25 |
| ☐ 172 | Terry Kirby | .40 | .15 |
| ☐ 173 | Brad Johnson | .60 | .25 |
| ☐ 174 | Reidel Anthony RC | .60 | .25 |
| ☐ 175 | Tiki Barber RC | 5.00 | 2.00 |
| ☐ 176 | Pat Barnes RC | .60 | .25 |
| ☐ 177 | Michael Booker RC | .25 | .08 |
| ☐ 178 | Peter Boulware RC | .60 | .25 |
| ☐ 179 | Rae Carruth RC | .25 | .08 |
| ☐ 180 | Troy Davis RC | .40 | .15 |
| ☐ 181 | Corey Dillon RC | 5.00 | 2.00 |
| ☐ 182 | Jim Druckenmiller RC | .40 | .15 |
| ☐ 183 | Warrick Dunn RC | 2.50 | 1.00 |
| ☐ 184 | James Farrior RC | .60 | .25 |
| ☐ 185 | Yatil Green RC | .40 | .15 |
| ☐ 186 | Walter Jones RC | .60 | .25 |
| ☐ 187 | Tom Knight RC | .25 | .08 |
| ☐ 188 | Sam Madison RC | .60 | .25 |
| ☐ 189 | Tyrus Mcleod RC | .25 | .08 |
| ☐ 190 | Orlando Pace RC | .60 | .25 |
| ☐ 191 | Jake Plummer RC | 4.00 | 1.50 |
| ☐ 192 | Dwayne Rudd RC | .60 | .25 |
| ☐ 193 | Darrell Russell RC | .25 | .08 |
| ☐ 194 | Sedrick Shaw RC | .40 | .15 |
| ☐ 195 | Shawn Springs RC | .40 | .15 |
| ☐ 196 | Bryant Westbrook RC | .25 | .08 |
| ☐ 197 | Danny Wuerffel RC | .60 | .25 |
| ☐ 198 | Reinard Wilson RC | .40 | .15 |
| ☐ 199 | Checklist | .25 | .08 |
| ☐ 200 | Checklist | .25 | .08 |
| ☐ 201 | Rick Mirer | .60 | .25 |
| ☐ 202 | Torrance Small | .25 | .08 |
| ☐ 203 | Ricky Proehl | .25 | .08 |
| ☐ 204 | Will Blackwell RC | .40 | .15 |
| ☐ 205 | Warrick Dunn | 1.25 | .50 |
| ☐ 206 | Rob Johnson | .40 | .15 |
| ☐ 207 | Jim Schwantz | .25 | .08 |
| ☐ 208 | Ike Hilliard RC | 1.25 | .50 |
| ☐ 209 | Chris Canty RC | .25 | .08 |
| ☐ 210 | Chris Boniol | .25 | .08 |
| ☐ 211 | Jim Druckenmiller | .25 | .08 |
| ☐ 212 | Tony Gonzalez RC | 2.50 | 1.00 |
| ☐ 213 | Scottie Graham | .25 | .08 |
| ☐ 214 | Byron Hanspard RC | .40 | .15 |
| ☐ 215 | Gary Brown | .25 | .08 |
| ☐ 216 | Darrell Russell | .25 | .08 |
| ☐ 217 | Sedrick Shaw | .40 | .15 |
| ☐ 218 | Boomer Esiason | .40 | .15 |
| ☐ 219 | Peter Boulware | .40 | .15 |
| ☐ 220 | Willie Green | .25 | .08 |
| ☐ 221 | Dietrich Jells | .25 | .08 |
| ☐ 222 | Freddie Jones RC | .40 | .15 |
| ☐ 223 | Eric Metcalf | .40 | .15 |
| ☐ 224 | John Henry Mills | .25 | .08 |
| ☐ 225 | Michael Timpson | .25 | .08 |
| ☐ 226 | Danny Wuerffel | .60 | .25 |
| ☐ 227 | Daimon Shelton RC | .25 | .08 |
| ☐ 228 | Henry Ellard | .25 | .08 |
| ☐ 229 | Flipper Anderson | .25 | .08 |
| ☐ 230 | Hunter Goodwin RC | .25 | .08 |
| ☐ 231 | Jay Graham RC | .40 | .15 |
| ☐ 232 | Duce Staley RC | 6.00 | 2.50 |
| ☐ 233 | Lamar Thomas | .25 | .08 |
| ☐ 234 | Rod Woodson | .40 | .15 |
| ☐ 235 | Zack Crockett | .25 | .08 |
| ☐ 236 | Ernie Mills | .25 | .08 |
| ☐ 237 | Kyle Brady | .25 | .08 |
| ☐ 238 | Jesse Campbell | .25 | .08 |
| ☐ 239 | Anthony Miller | .25 | .08 |
| ☐ 240 | Michael Haynes | .25 | .08 |
| ☐ 241 | Qadry Ismail | .40 | .15 |
| ☐ 242 | Tom Knight | .25 | .08 |
| ☐ 243 | Brian Manning RC | .25 | .08 |
| ☐ 244 | Derrick Mayes | .40 | .15 |
| ☐ 245 | Jamie Sharper RC | .40 | .15 |
| ☐ 246 | Sherman Williams | .25 | .08 |
| ☐ 247 | Yatil Green | .40 | .15 |
| ☐ 248 | Howard Griffith | .25 | .08 |
| ☐ 249 | Brian Blades | .25 | .08 |
| ☐ 250 | Mark Chmura | .40 | .15 |
| ☐ 251 | Chris Darkins | .25 | .08 |
| ☐ 252 | Willie Clay | .25 | .08 |
| ☐ 253 | Quinn Early | .25 | .08 |
| ☐ 254 | Marc Edwards RC | .25 | .08 |
| ☐ 255 | Charlie Jones | .25 | .08 |
| ☐ 256 | Jake Plummer | 1.50 | .60 |
| ☐ 257 | Heath Shuler | .25 | .08 |

| | | |
|---|---|---|
| ❏ 258 Fred Barnett | .25 | .08 |
| ❏ 259 William Henderson | .40 | .15 |
| ❏ 260 Michael Booker | .25 | .08 |
| ❏ 261 Chad Brown | .25 | .08 |
| ❏ 262 Garrison Hearst | .40 | .15 |
| ❏ 263 Leon Johnson RC | .40 | .15 |
| ❏ 264 Antowain Smith RC | 2.00 | .75 |
| ❏ 265 Darnell Autry RC | .40 | .15 |
| ❏ 266 Craig Heyward | .25 | .08 |
| ❏ 267 Walter Jones | .25 | .08 |
| ❏ 268 Dexter Coakley RC | .60 | .25 |
| ❏ 269 Mercury Hayes | .25 | .08 |
| ❏ 270 Brett Perriman | .25 | .08 |
| ❏ 271 Chris Spielman | .25 | .08 |
| ❏ 272 Kevin Greene | .40 | .15 |
| ❏ 273 Kevin Lockett RC | .40 | .15 |
| ❏ 274 Troy Davis | .25 | .08 |
| ❏ 275 Brent Jones | .25 | .08 |
| ❏ 276 Chris Chandler | .40 | .15 |
| ❏ 277 Bryant Westbrook | .40 | .15 |
| ❏ 278 Desmond Howard | .40 | .15 |
| ❏ 279 Tyrone Hughes | .25 | .08 |
| ❏ 280 Kez McCorvey | .25 | .08 |
| ❏ 281 Stephen Davis | .60 | .25 |
| ❏ 282 Steve Everitt | .25 | .08 |
| ❏ 283 Andre Hastings | .25 | .08 |
| ❏ 284 Marcus Robinson RC | 5.00 | 2.00 |
| ❏ 285 Donnell Woolford | .25 | .08 |
| ❏ 286 Mario Bates | .25 | .08 |
| ❏ 287 Corey Dillon | 2.00 | .75 |
| ❏ 288 Jackie Harris | .25 | .08 |
| ❏ 289 Lorenzo Neal | .25 | .08 |
| ❏ 290 Anthony Pleasant | .25 | .08 |
| ❏ 291 Andre Rison | .40 | .15 |
| ❏ 292 Amani Toomer | .25 | .08 |
| ❏ 293 Eric Turner | .25 | .08 |
| ❏ 294 Elvis Grbac | .25 | .08 |
| ❏ 295 Cris Dishman | .25 | .08 |
| ❏ 296 Tom Carter | .25 | .08 |
| ❏ 297 Mark Carrier DB | .25 | .08 |
| ❏ 298 Orlando Pace | .40 | .15 |
| ❏ 299 Jay Riemersma RC | .25 | .08 |
| ❏ 300 Daryl Johnston | .40 | .15 |
| ❏ 301 Joey Kent RC | .60 | .25 |
| ❏ 302 Ronnie Harmon | .40 | .15 |
| ❏ 303 Rocket Ismail | .40 | .15 |
| ❏ 304 Terrell Davis | .75 | .30 |
| ❏ 305 Sean Dawkins | .25 | .08 |
| ❏ 306 Jeff George | .40 | .15 |
| ❏ 307 David Palmer | .25 | .08 |
| ❏ 308 Dwayne Rudd | .25 | .08 |
| ❏ 309 J.J. Stokes | .40 | .15 |
| ❏ 310 James Farrior | .40 | .15 |
| ❏ 311 William Fuller | .25 | .08 |
| ❏ 312 George Jones RC | .40 | .15 |
| ❏ 313 John Allred RC | .25 | .08 |
| ❏ 314 Tony Graziani RC | .60 | .25 |
| ❏ 315 Jeff Hostetler | .25 | .08 |
| ❏ 316 Keith Poole RC | .60 | .25 |
| ❏ 317 Neil Smith | .40 | .15 |
| ❏ 318 Steve Tasker | .25 | .08 |
| ❏ 319 Mike Vrabel RC | 15.00 | 6.00 |
| ❏ 320 Pat Barnes | .60 | .25 |
| ❏ 321 James Hundon RC | .60 | .25 |
| ❏ 322 O.J. Santiago RC | .40 | .15 |
| ❏ 323 Billy Davis RC | .25 | .08 |
| ❏ 324 Shawn Springs | .40 | .15 |
| ❏ 325 Reinard Wilson | .25 | .08 |
| ❏ 326 Charles Johnson | .40 | .15 |
| ❏ 327 Micheal Barrow | .25 | .08 |
| ❏ 328 Derrick Mason RC | 3.00 | 1.25 |
| ❏ 329 Muhsin Muhammad | .25 | .08 |
| ❏ 330 David LaFleur RC | .25 | .08 |
| ❏ 331 Reidel Anthony | .40 | .15 |
| ❏ 332 Tiki Barber | 2.00 | .75 |
| ❏ 333 Ray Buchanan | .25 | .08 |
| ❏ 334 John Elway | 2.50 | 1.00 |
| ❏ 335 Alvin Harper | .25 | .08 |
| ❏ 336 Damon Jones RC | .40 | .15 |
| ❏ 337 Dedric Ward RC | .40 | .15 |
| ❏ 338 Jim Everett | .25 | .08 |
| ❏ 339 Jon Harris | .25 | .08 |
| ❏ 340 Warren Moon | .60 | .25 |
| ❏ 341 Rae Carruth | .25 | .08 |

| | | |
|---|---|---|
| ❏ 342 John Mobley | .25 | .08 |
| ❏ 343 Tyrone Poole | .25 | .08 |
| ❏ 344 Mike Cherry RC | .25 | .08 |
| ❏ 345 Horace Copeland | .25 | .08 |
| ❏ 346 Deon Figures | .25 | .08 |
| ❏ 347 Antwuan Wyatt RC | .25 | .08 |
| ❏ 348 Tommy Vardell | .25 | .08 |
| ❏ 349 Checklist (201-324) | .25 | .08 |
| ❏ 350 Checklist (325-350/inserts) | .25 | .08 |
| ❏ S1A T.Davis Sample AU | 80.00 | 40.00 |
| ❏ AU3 Dan Marino AU | 100.00 | 40.00 |
| ❏ S1 Terrell Davis Sample | 3.00 | 1.25 |

**1998 Ultra**

| | | |
|---|---|---|
| ❏ COMPLETE SET (425) | 120.00 | 50.00 |
| ❏ COMP.SERIES 1 (225) | 80.00 | 30.00 |
| ❏ COMP.SERIES 2 (200) | 50.00 | 25.00 |
| ❏ 1 Barry Sanders | 2.50 | 1.00 |
| ❏ 2 Brett Favre | 3.00 | 1.50 |
| ❏ 3 Napoleon Kaufman | .75 | .30 |
| ❏ 4 Robert Smith | .75 | .30 |
| ❏ 5 Terry Allen | .75 | .30 |
| ❏ 6 Vinny Testaverde | .50 | .20 |
| ❏ 7 William Floyd | .30 | .10 |
| ❏ 8 Carl Pickens | .50 | .20 |
| ❏ 9 Antonio Freeman | .75 | .30 |
| ❏ 10 Ben Coates | .50 | .20 |
| ❏ 11 Elvis Grbac | .50 | .20 |
| ❏ 12 Kerry Collins | .50 | .20 |
| ❏ 13 Orlando Pace | .30 | .10 |
| ❏ 14 Steve Broussard | .30 | .10 |
| ❏ 15 Terance Mathis | .30 | .10 |
| ❏ 16 Tiki Barber | .75 | .30 |
| ❏ 17 Cris Carter | .75 | .30 |
| ❏ 18 Eric Green | .30 | .10 |
| ❏ 19 Eric Metcalf | .30 | .10 |
| ❏ 20 Jeff George | .50 | .20 |
| ❏ 21 Leslie Shepherd | .30 | .10 |
| ❏ 22 Natrone Means | .50 | .20 |
| ❏ 23 Scott Mitchell | .50 | .20 |
| ❏ 24 Adrian Murrell | .50 | .20 |
| ❏ 25 Gilbert Brown | .30 | .10 |
| ❏ 26 Jimmy Smith | .50 | .20 |
| ❏ 27 Mark Brunell | .30 | .10 |
| ❏ 28 Troy Aikman | 1.50 | .60 |
| ❏ 29 Warrick Dunn | .75 | .30 |
| ❏ 30 Jay Graham | .30 | .10 |
| ❏ 31 Craig Whelihan RC | .30 | .10 |
| ❏ 32 Ed McCaffrey | .50 | .20 |
| ❏ 33 Jamie Asher | .30 | .10 |
| ❏ 34 John Randle | .50 | .20 |
| ❏ 35 Michael Jackson | .30 | .10 |
| ❏ 36 Rickey Dudley | .30 | .10 |
| ❏ 37 Sean Dawkins | .30 | .10 |
| ❏ 38 Andre Rison | .50 | .20 |
| ❏ 39 Bert Emanuel | .30 | .10 |
| ❏ 40 Jeff Blake | .50 | .20 |
| ❏ 41 Curtis Conway | .50 | .20 |
| ❏ 42 Eddie Kennison | .50 | .20 |
| ❏ 43 James McKnight | .25 | .08 |
| ❏ 44 Rae Carruth | .30 | .10 |
| ❏ 45 Tito Wooten RC | .30 | .10 |
| ❏ 46 Cris Dishman | .30 | .10 |
| ❏ 47 Ernie Conwell | .30 | .10 |
| ❏ 48 Fred Lane | .30 | .10 |
| ❏ 49 Jamal Anderson | .75 | .30 |
| ❏ 50 Lake Dawson | .30 | .10 |

| | | |
|---|---|---|
| ❏ 51 Michael Strahan | .50 | .20 |
| ❏ 52 Reggie White | .75 | .30 |
| ❏ 53 Trent Dilfer | .75 | .30 |
| ❏ 54 Troy Brown | .50 | .20 |
| ❏ 55 Wesley Walls | .50 | .20 |
| ❏ 56 Chidi Ahanotu | .30 | .10 |
| ❏ 57 Dwayne Rudd | .30 | .10 |
| ❏ 58 Jerry Rice | 1.50 | .60 |
| ❏ 59 Johnnie Morton | .50 | .20 |
| ❏ 60 Sherman Williams | .30 | .10 |
| ❏ 61 Steve McNair | .75 | .30 |
| ❏ 62 Will Blackwell | .30 | .10 |
| ❏ 63 Chris Chandler | .50 | .20 |
| ❏ 64 Dexter Coakley | .30 | .10 |
| ❏ 65 Horace Copeland | .30 | .10 |
| ❏ 66 Jerald Moore | .30 | .10 |
| ❏ 67 Leon Johnson | .30 | .10 |
| ❏ 68 Mark Chmura | .50 | .20 |
| ❏ 69 Micheal Barrow | .30 | .10 |
| ❏ 70 Muhsin Muhammad | .50 | .20 |
| ❏ 71 Terry Glenn | .75 | .30 |
| ❏ 72 Tony Brackens | .30 | .10 |
| ❏ 73 Chad Scott | .30 | .10 |
| ❏ 74 Glenn Foley | .50 | .20 |
| ❏ 75 Keenan McCardell | .50 | .20 |
| ❏ 76 Peter Boulware | .30 | .10 |
| ❏ 77 Reidel Anthony | .50 | .20 |
| ❏ 78 William Henderson | .50 | .20 |
| ❏ 79 Tony Martin | .50 | .20 |
| ❏ 80 Tony Gonzalez | .75 | .30 |
| ❏ 81 Charlie Jones | .30 | .10 |
| ❏ 82 Chris Gedney | .30 | .10 |
| ❏ 83 Chris Calloway | .30 | .10 |
| ❏ 84 Dale Carter | .30 | .10 |
| ❏ 85 Ki-Jana Carter | .50 | .20 |
| ❏ 86 Shawn Springs | .30 | .10 |
| ❏ 87 Antowain Smith | .75 | .30 |
| ❏ 88 Eric Turner | .30 | .10 |
| ❏ 89 John Mobley | .30 | .10 |
| ❏ 90 Ken Dilger | .30 | .10 |
| ❏ 91 Bobby Hoying | .50 | .20 |
| ❏ 92 Curtis Martin | .75 | .30 |
| ❏ 93 Drew Bledsoe | 1.25 | .50 |
| ❏ 94 Gary Brown | .30 | .10 |
| ❏ 95 Marvin Harrison | .75 | .30 |
| ❏ 96 Todd Collins | .30 | .10 |
| ❏ 97 Chris Warren | .50 | .20 |
| ❏ 98 Danny Kanell | .50 | .20 |
| ❏ 99 Tony McGee | .30 | .10 |
| ❏ 100 Rod Smith | .50 | .20 |
| ❏ 101 Frank Sanders | .50 | .20 |
| ❏ 102 Irving Fryar | .50 | .20 |
| ❏ 103 Marcus Allen | .75 | .30 |
| ❏ 104 Marshall Faulk | 1.00 | .40 |
| ❏ 105 Bruce Smith | .50 | .20 |
| ❏ 106 Charlie Garner | .50 | .20 |
| ❏ 107 Paul Justin | .30 | .10 |
| ❏ 108 Randal Hill | .30 | .10 |
| ❏ 109 Erik Kramer | .30 | .10 |
| ❏ 110 Rob Moore | .50 | .20 |
| ❏ 111 Shannon Sharpe | .50 | .20 |
| ❏ 112 Warren Moon | .75 | .30 |
| ❏ 113 Zach Thomas | .75 | .30 |
| ❏ 114 Dan Marino | 3.00 | 1.50 |
| ❏ 115 Duce Staley | 1.00 | .40 |
| ❏ 116 Eric Swann | .30 | .10 |
| ❏ 117 Kenny Holmes | .30 | .10 |
| ❏ 118 Merton Hanks | .30 | .10 |
| ❏ 119 Raymont Harris | .30 | .10 |
| ❏ 120 Terrell Davis | .75 | .30 |
| ❏ 121 Thurman Thomas | .75 | .30 |
| ❏ 122 Wayne Martin | .30 | .10 |
| ❏ 123 Charles Way | .30 | .10 |
| ❏ 124 Chuck Smith | .30 | .10 |
| ❏ 125 Corey Dillon | .75 | .30 |
| ❏ 126 Darnell Autry | .30 | .10 |
| ❏ 127 Isaac Bruce | .75 | .30 |
| ❏ 128 Joey Galloway | .50 | .20 |
| ❏ 129 Kimble Anders | .50 | .20 |
| ❏ 130 Aeneas Williams | .30 | .10 |
| ❏ 131 Andre Hastings | .30 | .10 |
| ❏ 132 Chad Lewis | .30 | .10 |
| ❏ 133 J.J. Stokes | .50 | .20 |
| ❏ 134 John Elway | 3.00 | 1.25 |

|  |  | | |
|---|---|---|---|
| 135 | Karim Abdul-Jabbar | .75 | .30 |
| 136 | Ken Harvey | .30 | .10 |
| 137 | Robert Brooks | .50 | .20 |
| 138 | Rodney Thomas | .30 | .10 |
| 139 | James Stewart | .50 | .20 |
| 140 | Billy Joe Hobert | .30 | .10 |
| 141 | Frank Wycheck | .30 | .10 |
| 142 | Jake Plummer | .75 | .30 |
| 143 | Jerris McPhail | .30 | .10 |
| 144 | Kordell Stewart | .75 | .30 |
| 145 | Terrell Owens | .75 | .30 |
| 146 | Willie Green | .30 | .10 |
| 147 | Anthony Miller | .30 | .10 |
| 148 | Courtney Hawkins | .30 | .10 |
| 149 | Larry Centers | .30 | .10 |
| 150 | Gus Frerotte | .30 | .10 |
| 151 | O.J. McDuffie | .50 | .20 |
| 152 | Ray Zellars | .30 | .10 |
| 153 | Terry Kirby | .30 | .10 |
| 154 | Tommy Vardell | .30 | .10 |
| 155 | Willie Davis | .30 | .10 |
| 156 | Chris Canty | .30 | .10 |
| 157 | Byron Hanspard | .30 | .10 |
| 158 | Chris Penn | .30 | .10 |
| 159 | Damon Jones | .30 | .10 |
| 160 | Derrick Mayes | .50 | .20 |
| 161 | Emmitt Smith | 2.50 | 1.25 |
| 162 | Keyshawn Johnson | .75 | .30 |
| 163 | Mike Alstott | .75 | .30 |
| 164 | Tom Carter | .30 | .10 |
| 165 | Tony Banks | .50 | .20 |
| 166 | Bryant Westbrook | .30 | .10 |
| 167 | Chris Sanders | .30 | .10 |
| 168 | Deion Sanders | .75 | .30 |
| 169 | Garrison Hearst | .75 | .30 |
| 170 | Jason Taylor | .50 | .20 |
| 171 | Jerome Bettis | .75 | .30 |
| 172 | John Lynch | .50 | .20 |
| 173 | Troy Davis | .30 | .10 |
| 174 | Freddie Jones | .30 | .10 |
| 175 | Herman Moore | .50 | .20 |
| 176 | Jake Reed | .50 | .20 |
| 177 | Mark Brunell | .75 | .30 |
| 178 | Ray Lewis | .75 | .30 |
| 179 | Stephen Davis | .30 | .10 |
| 180 | Tim Brown | .75 | .30 |
| 181 | Willie McGinest | .30 | .10 |
| 182 | Andre Reed | .50 | .20 |
| 183 | Darrien Gordon | .30 | .10 |
| 184 | David Palmer | .30 | .10 |
| 185 | James Jett | .50 | .20 |
| 186 | Junior Seau | .75 | .30 |
| 187 | Zack Crockett | .30 | .10 |
| 188 | Brad Johnson | .75 | .30 |
| 189 | Charles Johnson | .30 | .10 |
| 190 | Eddie George | .75 | .30 |
| 191 | Jermaine Lewis | .50 | .20 |
| 192 | Michael Irvin | .75 | .30 |
| 193 | Reggie Brown LB | .30 | .10 |
| 194 | Steve Young | 1.00 | .40 |
| 195 | Warren Sapp | .50 | .20 |
| 196 | Wayne Chrebet | .75 | .30 |
| 197 | David Dunn | .30 | .10 |
| 198 | Dorsey Levens CL | .50 | .20 |
| 199 | Troy Aikman CL | .75 | .30 |
| 200 | John Elway CL | .75 | .30 |
| 201 | Peyton Manning RC | 30.00 | 12.00 |
| 202 | Ryan Leaf RC | 3.00 | 1.25 |
| 203 | Charles Woodson RC | 4.00 | 1.50 |
| 204 | Andre Wadsworth RC | 2.50 | 1.00 |
| 205 | Brian Simmons RC | 2.50 | 1.00 |
| 206 | Curtis Enis RC | 1.50 | .60 |
| 207 | Randy Moss RC | 20.00 | 8.00 |
| 208 | Germane Crowell RC | 2.50 | 1.00 |
| 209 | Greg Ellis RC | .50 | .20 |
| 210 | Kevin Dyson RC | 3.00 | 1.25 |
| 211 | Skip Hicks RC | 2.50 | 1.00 |
| 212 | Alonzo Mayes RC | 1.50 | .60 |
| 213 | Robert Edwards RC | 2.50 | 1.00 |
| 214 | Fred Taylor RC | 5.00 | 2.00 |
| 215 | Robert Holcombe RC | 2.50 | 1.00 |
| 216 | John Dutton RC | 1.50 | .60 |
| 217 | Vonnie Holliday RC | 2.50 | 1.00 |
| 218 | Tim Dwight RC | 3.00 | 1.25 |
| 219 | Tavian Banks RC | 2.50 | 1.00 |
| 220 | Marcus Nash RC | 1.50 | .60 |
| 221 | Jason Peter RC | 1.50 | .60 |
| 222 | Michael Myers RC | 1.50 | .60 |
| 223 | Takeo Spikes RC | 3.00 | 1.25 |
| 224 | Kivuusama Mays RC | 1.50 | .60 |
| 225 | Jacquez Green RC | 2.50 | 1.00 |
| 226 | Doug Flutie | .75 | .30 |
| 227 | Ike Hilliard | .50 | .20 |
| 228 | Craig Heyward | .30 | .10 |
| 229 | Kevin Hardy | .30 | .10 |
| 230 | Jason Dunn | .30 | .10 |
| 231 | Billy Davis | .30 | .10 |
| 232 | Chester McGlockton | .30 | .10 |
| 233 | Sean Gilbert | .30 | .10 |
| 234 | Bert Emanuel | .50 | .20 |
| 235 | Keith Byars | .30 | .10 |
| 236 | Tyrone Wheatley | .50 | .20 |
| 237 | Ricky Proehl | .30 | .10 |
| 238 | Michael Bates | .30 | .10 |
| 239 | Derrick Alexander | .50 | .20 |
| 240 | Harvey Williams | .30 | .10 |
| 241 | Mike Pritchard | .30 | .10 |
| 242 | Paul Justin | .30 | .10 |
| 243 | Jeff Hostetler | .30 | .10 |
| 244 | Eric Moulds | .75 | .30 |
| 245 | Jeff Burris | .30 | .10 |
| 246 | Gary Brown | .30 | .10 |
| 247 | Anthony Johnson | .30 | .10 |
| 248 | Dan Wilkinson | .30 | .10 |
| 249 | Chris Warren | .50 | .20 |
| 250 | Chris Darkins | .30 | .10 |
| 251 | Eric Metcalf | .30 | .10 |
| 252 | Pat Swilling | .30 | .10 |
| 253 | Lamar Smith | .50 | .20 |
| 254 | Quinn Early | .30 | .10 |
| 255 | Carlester Crumpler | .30 | .10 |
| 256 | Eric Bieniemy | .30 | .10 |
| 257 | Aaron Bailey | .30 | .10 |
| 258 | Neil O'Donnell | .50 | .20 |
| 259 | Rod Woodson | .50 | .20 |
| 260 | Ricky Whittle | .30 | .10 |
| 261 | Iheanyi Uwaezuoke | .30 | .10 |
| 262 | Heath Shuler | .30 | .10 |
| 263 | Darren Sharper | .50 | .20 |
| 264 | John Henry Mills | .30 | .10 |
| 265 | Marco Battaglia | .30 | .10 |
| 266 | Yancey Thigpen | .30 | .10 |
| 267 | Irv Smith | .30 | .10 |
| 268 | Jamie Sharper | .30 | .10 |
| 269 | Marcus Robinson | 5.00 | 2.00 |
| 270 | Dorsey Levens | .75 | .30 |
| 271 | Qadry Ismail | .50 | .20 |
| 272 | Desmond Howard | .50 | .20 |
| 273 | Webster Slaughter | .30 | .10 |
| 274 | Eugene Robinson | .30 | .10 |
| 275 | Bill Romanowski | .30 | .10 |
| 276 | Vincent Brisby | .30 | .10 |
| 277 | Errict Rhett | .50 | .20 |
| 278 | Albert Connell | .30 | .10 |
| 279 | Thomas Lewis | .30 | .10 |
| 280 | John Farquhar | .30 | .10 |
| 281 | Marc Edwards | .30 | .10 |
| 282 | Tyrone Davis | .30 | .10 |
| 283 | Eric Allen | .30 | .10 |
| 284 | Aaron Glenn | .30 | .10 |
| 285 | Roosevelt Potts | .30 | .10 |
| 286 | Kez McCorvey | .30 | .10 |
| 287 | Joey Kent | .50 | .20 |
| 288 | Jim Druckenmiller | .30 | .10 |
| 289 | Sean Dawkins | .30 | .10 |
| 290 | Edgar Bennett | .30 | .10 |
| 291 | Vinny Testaverde | .50 | .20 |
| 292 | Chris Slade | .30 | .10 |
| 293 | Lamar Lathon | .30 | .10 |
| 294 | Jackie Harris | .30 | .10 |
| 295 | Jim Harbaugh | .50 | .20 |
| 296 | Rob Fredrickson | .30 | .10 |
| 297 | Ty Detmer | .50 | .20 |
| 298 | Karl Williams | .30 | .10 |
| 299 | Troy Drayton | .30 | .10 |
| 300 | Curtis Martin | .75 | .30 |
| 301 | Tamarick Vanover | .30 | .10 |
| 302 | Lorenzo Neal | .30 | .10 |
| 303 | John Hall | .30 | .10 |
| 304 | Kevin Greene | .50 | .20 |
| 305 | Bryan Still | .30 | .10 |
| 306 | Neil Smith | .50 | .20 |
| 307 | Greg Lloyd | .30 | .10 |
| 308 | Shawn Jefferson | .30 | .10 |
| 309 | Aaron Taylor | .30 | .10 |
| 310 | Sedrick Shaw | .30 | .10 |
| 311 | O.J. Santiago | .30 | .10 |
| 312 | Kevin Abrams | .30 | .10 |
| 313 | Dana Stubblefield | .30 | .10 |
| 314 | Daryl Johnston | .50 | .20 |
| 315 | Bryan Cox | .30 | .10 |
| 316 | Jeff Graham | .30 | .10 |
| 317 | Mario Bates | .50 | .20 |
| 318 | Adrian Murrell | .50 | .20 |
| 319 | Greg Hill | .30 | .10 |
| 320 | Jahine Arnold | .30 | .10 |
| 321 | Justin Armour | .30 | .10 |
| 322 | Ricky Watters | .50 | .20 |
| 323 | Lamont Warren | .30 | .10 |
| 324 | Mack Strong | .75 | .30 |
| 325 | Damay Scott | .30 | .10 |
| 326 | Brian Mitchell | .50 | .20 |
| 327 | Rob Johnson | .50 | .20 |
| 328 | Kent Graham | .30 | .10 |
| 329 | Hugh Douglas | .30 | .10 |
| 330 | Simeon Rice | .50 | .20 |
| 331 | Rick Mirer | .30 | .10 |
| 332 | Randall Cunningham | .75 | .30 |
| 333 | Steve Atwater | .30 | .10 |
| 334 | Latario Rachal | .30 | .10 |
| 335 | Tony Martin | .50 | .20 |
| 336 | Leroy Hoard | .30 | .10 |
| 337 | Howard Griffith | .30 | .10 |
| 338 | Kevin Lockett | .30 | .10 |
| 339 | William Floyd | .30 | .10 |
| 340 | Jerry Ellison | .30 | .10 |
| 341 | Kyle Brady | .30 | .10 |
| 342 | Michael Westbrook | .50 | .20 |
| 343 | Kevin Turner | .30 | .10 |
| 344 | David LaFleur | .30 | .10 |
| 345 | Robert Jones | .30 | .10 |
| 346 | Dave Brown | .30 | .10 |
| 347 | Kevin Williams | .30 | .10 |
| 348 | Amani Toomer | .50 | .20 |
| 349 | Amp Lee | .30 | .10 |
| 350 | Bryce Paup | .30 | .10 |
| 351 | Dewayne Washington | .30 | .10 |
| 352 | Mercury Hayes | .30 | .10 |
| 353 | Tim Biakabutuka | .50 | .20 |
| 354 | Ray Crockett | .30 | .10 |
| 355 | Ted Washington | .30 | .10 |
| 356 | Pete Mitchell | .30 | .10 |
| 357 | Billy Jenkins RC | .30 | .10 |
| 358 | Troy Aikman CL | .75 | .30 |
| 359 | Drew Bledsoe CL | .75 | .30 |
| 360 | Steve Young CL | .75 | .30 |
| 361 | Antonio Freeman NG | .50 | .20 |
| 362 | Antowain Smith NG | .50 | .20 |
| 363 | Barry Sanders NG | 1.50 | .60 |
| 364 | Bobby Hoying NG | .30 | .10 |
| 365 | Brett Favre NG | 2.00 | .75 |
| 366 | Corey Dillon NG | .50 | .20 |
| 367 | Dan Marino NG | 2.00 | .75 |
| 368 | Drew Bledsoe NG | .75 | .30 |
| 369 | Eddie George NG | .75 | .30 |
| 370 | Emmitt Smith NG | 1.50 | .60 |
| 371 | Herman Moore NG | .50 | .20 |
| 372 | Jake Plummer NG | .50 | .20 |
| 373 | Jerome Bettis NG | .50 | .20 |
| 374 | Jerry Rice NG | 1.00 | .40 |
| 375 | Joey Galloway NG | .50 | .20 |
| 376 | John Elway NG | 2.00 | .75 |
| 377 | Kordell Stewart NG | .50 | .20 |
| 378 | Mark Brunell NG | .50 | .20 |
| 379 | Keyshawn Johnson NG | .50 | .20 |
| 380 | Steve Young NG | .75 | .30 |
| 381 | Steve McNair NG | .50 | .20 |
| 382 | Terrell Davis NG | .75 | .30 |
| 383 | Tim Brown NG | .50 | .20 |
| 384 | Troy Aikman NG | 1.00 | .40 |
| 385 | Warrick Dunn NG | .75 | .30 |
| 386 | Ryan Leaf | 3.00 | 1.25 |

| | | |
|---|---|---|
| ❏ 387 Tony Simmons RC | 2.00 | .75 |
| ❏ 388 Rodney Williams RC | 1.25 | .50 |
| ❏ 389 John Avery RC | 2.00 | .75 |
| ❏ 390 Shaun Williams RC | 2.00 | .75 |
| ❏ 391 Anthony Simmons RC | 2.00 | .75 |
| ❏ 392 Rashaan Shehee RC | 2.00 | .75 |
| ❏ 393 Robert Holcombe | 2.00 | .75 |
| ❏ 394 Larry Shannon RC | 1.25 | .50 |
| ❏ 395 Skip Hicks | 2.00 | .75 |
| ❏ 396 Rod Rutledge RC | 1.25 | .50 |
| ❏ 397 Donald Hayes RC | 1.25 | .50 |
| ❏ 398 Curtis Enis | 1.25 | .50 |
| ❏ 399 Mikhael Ricks RC | 2.00 | .75 |
| ❏ 400 Brian Griese RC | 6.00 | 2.50 |
| ❏ 401 Michael Pittman RC | 4.00 | 1.50 |
| ❏ 402 Jacquez Green | 2.00 | .75 |
| ❏ 403 Jerome Pathon RC | 3.00 | 1.25 |
| ❏ 404 Ahman Green RC | 8.00 | 3.00 |
| ❏ 405 Marcus Nash | 1.25 | .50 |
| ❏ 406 Randy Moss | 15.00 | 6.00 |
| ❏ 407 Terry Fair RC | 2.00 | .75 |
| ❏ 408 Jammi German RC | 1.25 | .50 |
| ❏ 409 Stephen Alexander RC | 2.00 | .75 |
| ❏ 410 Grant Wistrom RC | 2.00 | .75 |
| ❏ 411 Charlie Batch RC | 3.00 | 1.25 |
| ❏ 412 Fred Taylor | 4.00 | 1.50 |
| ❏ 413 Pat Johnson RC | 2.00 | .75 |
| ❏ 414 Robert Edwards | 2.00 | .75 |
| ❏ 415 Keith Brooking RC | 3.00 | 1.25 |
| ❏ 416 Peyton Manning | 25.00 | 10.00 |
| ❏ 417 Duane Starks RC | 1.25 | .50 |
| ❏ 418 Andre Wadsworth | 2.00 | .75 |
| ❏ 419 Brian Alford RC | 1.25 | .50 |
| ❏ 420 Brian Kelly RC | 2.00 | .75 |
| ❏ 421 Joe Jurevicius RC | 3.00 | 1.25 |
| ❏ 422 Tebucky Jones RC | 1.25 | .50 |
| ❏ 423 R.W. McQuarters RC | 2.00 | .75 |
| ❏ 424 Kevin Dyson | 2.50 | 1.00 |
| ❏ 425 Charles Woodson | 3.00 | 1.25 |
| ❏ R1 Reggie White COMM | .60 | .25 |
| ❏ P20 Jeff George Promo | .75 | .30 |

**1999 Ultra**

| | | |
|---|---|---|
| ❏ COMPLETE SET (300) | 80.00 | 30.00 |
| ❏ COMP.SET w/o SP's (250) | 20.00 | 8.00 |
| ❏ 1 Terrell Davis | .75 | .30 |
| ❏ 2 Courtney Hawkins | .30 | .10 |
| ❏ 3 Cris Carter | .75 | .30 |
| ❏ 4 Damay Scott | .30 | .10 |
| ❏ 5 Darrell Green | .50 | .20 |
| ❏ 6 Jimmy Smith | .50 | .20 |
| ❏ 7 Doug Flutie | .75 | .30 |
| ❏ 8 Michael Jackson | .30 | .10 |
| ❏ 9 Warren Sapp | .50 | .20 |
| ❏ 10 Greg Hill | .30 | .10 |
| ❏ 11 Karim Abdul-Jabbar | .50 | .20 |
| ❏ 12 Greg Ellis | .30 | .10 |
| ❏ 13 Dan Marino | 2.50 | 1.00 |
| ❏ 14 Napoleon Kaufman | .75 | .30 |
| ❏ 15 Peyton Manning | 2.50 | 1.00 |
| ❏ 16 Simeon Rice | .50 | .20 |
| ❏ 17 Tony Simmons | .30 | .10 |
| ❏ 18 Carlester Crumpler | .30 | .10 |
| ❏ 19 Charles Johnson | .30 | .10 |
| ❏ 20 Derrick Alexander | .30 | .10 |
| ❏ 21 Kent Graham | .30 | .10 |
| ❏ 22 Randall Cunningham | .75 | .30 |

| | | |
|---|---|---|
| ❏ 23 Trent Green | .75 | .30 |
| ❏ 24 Chris Spielman | .30 | .10 |
| ❏ 25 Carl Pickens | .50 | .20 |
| ❏ 26 Bill Romanowski | .30 | .10 |
| ❏ 27 Jermaine Lewis | .50 | .20 |
| ❏ 28 Ahman Green | .75 | .30 |
| ❏ 29 Bryan Still | .30 | .10 |
| ❏ 30 Dorsey Levens | .50 | .20 |
| ❏ 31 Frank Wycheck | .30 | .10 |
| ❏ 32 Jerome Bettis | .75 | .30 |
| ❏ 33 Reidel Anthony | .50 | .20 |
| ❏ 34 Robert Jones | .30 | .10 |
| ❏ 35 Terry Glenn | .75 | .30 |
| ❏ 36 Tim Brown | .75 | .30 |
| ❏ 37 Eric Metcalf | .30 | .10 |
| ❏ 38 Kevin Greene | .50 | .20 |
| ❏ 39 Takeo Spikes | .30 | .10 |
| ❏ 40 Brian Mitchell | .30 | .10 |
| ❏ 41 Duane Starks | .30 | .10 |
| ❏ 42 Eddie George | .75 | .30 |
| ❏ 43 Joe Jurevicius | .50 | .20 |
| ❏ 44 Kimble Anders | .30 | .10 |
| ❏ 45 Kordell Stewart | .50 | .20 |
| ❏ 46 Leroy Hoard | .30 | .10 |
| ❏ 47 Rod Smith | .50 | .20 |
| ❏ 48 Terrell Owens | .75 | .30 |
| ❏ 49 Ty Detmer | .50 | .20 |
| ❏ 50 Charles Woodson | .75 | .30 |
| ❏ 51 Andre Rison | .50 | .20 |
| ❏ 52 Chris Slade | .30 | .10 |
| ❏ 53 Frank Sanders | .50 | .20 |
| ❏ 54 Michael Irvin | .50 | .20 |
| ❏ 55 Jerome Pathon | .30 | .10 |
| ❏ 56 Desmond Howard | .30 | .10 |
| ❏ 57 Billy Davis | .30 | .10 |
| ❏ 58 Anthony Simmons | .30 | .10 |
| ❏ 59 James Jett | .50 | .20 |
| ❏ 60 Jake Plummer | .50 | .20 |
| ❏ 61 John Avery | .30 | .10 |
| ❏ 62 Marvin Harrison | .75 | .30 |
| ❏ 63 Merton Hanks | .30 | .10 |
| ❏ 64 Ricky Proehl | .30 | .10 |
| ❏ 65 Steve Beuerlein | .30 | .10 |
| ❏ 66 Willie McGinest | .30 | .10 |
| ❏ 67 Bryce Paup | .30 | .10 |
| ❏ 68 Brett Favre | 2.50 | 1.00 |
| ❏ 69 Brian Griese | .75 | .30 |
| ❏ 70 Curtis Martin | .75 | .30 |
| ❏ 71 Drew Bledsoe | 1.00 | .40 |
| ❏ 72 Jim Harbaugh | .50 | .20 |
| ❏ 73 Joey Galloway | .50 | .20 |
| ❏ 74 Natrone Means | .50 | .20 |
| ❏ 75 O.J. McDuffie | .50 | .20 |
| ❏ 76 Tiki Barber | .75 | .30 |
| ❏ 77 Wesley Walls | .50 | .20 |
| ❏ 78 Will Blackwell | .30 | .10 |
| ❏ 79 Bert Emanuel | .50 | .20 |
| ❏ 80 J.J. Stokes | .50 | .20 |
| ❏ 81 Steve McNair | .75 | .30 |
| ❏ 82 Adrian Murrell | .50 | .20 |
| ❏ 83 Dexter Coakley | .30 | .10 |
| ❏ 84 Jeff George | .50 | .20 |
| ❏ 85 Marshall Faulk | 1.00 | .40 |
| ❏ 86 Tim Biakabutuka | .50 | .20 |
| ❏ 87 Troy Drayton | .30 | .10 |
| ❏ 88 Ty Law | .50 | .20 |
| ❏ 89 Brian Simmons | .30 | .10 |
| ❏ 90 Eric Allen | .30 | .10 |
| ❏ 91 Jon Kitna | .75 | .30 |
| ❏ 92 Junior Seau | .75 | .30 |
| ❏ 93 Kevin Turner | .30 | .10 |
| ❏ 94 Larry Centers | .30 | .10 |
| ❏ 95 Robert Edwards | .50 | .20 |
| ❏ 96 Rocket Ismail | .50 | .20 |
| ❏ 97 Sam Madison | .30 | .10 |
| ❏ 98 Stephen Alexander | .30 | .10 |
| ❏ 99 Trent Dilfer | .50 | .20 |
| ❏ 100 Vonnie Holliday | .50 | .20 |
| ❏ 101 Charlie Garner | .50 | .20 |
| ❏ 102 Deion Sanders | .75 | .30 |
| ❏ 103 Jamal Anderson | .75 | .30 |
| ❏ 104 Mike Vanderjagt | .30 | .10 |
| ❏ 105 Aeneas Williams | .30 | .10 |
| ❏ 106 Daryl Johnston | .50 | .20 |

| | | |
|---|---|---|
| ❏ 107 Hugh Douglas | .30 | .10 |
| ❏ 108 Torrance Small | .30 | .10 |
| ❏ 109 Amani Toomer | .30 | .10 |
| ❏ 110 Amp Lee | .30 | .10 |
| ❏ 111 Germane Crowell | .30 | .10 |
| ❏ 112 Marco Battaglia | .30 | .10 |
| ❏ 113 Michael Westbrook | .50 | .20 |
| ❏ 114 Randy Moss | 2.00 | .75 |
| ❏ 115 Ricky Watters | .50 | .20 |
| ❏ 116 Rob Johnson | .50 | .20 |
| ❏ 117 Tony Gonzalez | .75 | .30 |
| ❏ 118 Charles Way | .30 | .10 |
| ❏ 119 Chris Penn | .30 | .10 |
| ❏ 120 Eddie Kennison | .50 | .20 |
| ❏ 121 Elvis Grbac | .50 | .20 |
| ❏ 122 Eric Moulds | .75 | .30 |
| ❏ 123 Terry Fair | .30 | .10 |
| ❏ 124 Tony Banks | .50 | .20 |
| ❏ 125 Chris Chandler | .50 | .20 |
| ❏ 126 Emmitt Smith | 1.50 | .60 |
| ❏ 127 Herman Moore | .50 | .20 |
| ❏ 128 Irv Smith | .30 | .10 |
| ❏ 129 Kyle Brady | .30 | .10 |
| ❏ 130 Lamont Warren | .30 | .10 |
| ❏ 131 Troy Davis | .30 | .10 |
| ❏ 132 Andre Reed | .50 | .20 |
| ❏ 133 Justin Armour | .30 | .10 |
| ❏ 134 James Hasty | .30 | .10 |
| ❏ 135 Johnnie Morton | .50 | .20 |
| ❏ 136 Reggie Barlow | .30 | .10 |
| ❏ 137 Robert Holcombe | .30 | .10 |
| ❏ 138 Sean Dawkins | .30 | .10 |
| ❏ 139 Steve Atwater | .30 | .10 |
| ❏ 140 Tim Dwight | .75 | .30 |
| ❏ 141 Wayne Chrebet | .50 | .20 |
| ❏ 142 Alonzo Mayes | .30 | .10 |
| ❏ 143 Mark Brunell | .75 | .30 |
| ❏ 144 Antowain Smith | .75 | .30 |
| ❏ 145 Byron Bam Morris | .30 | .10 |
| ❏ 146 Isaac Bruce | .75 | .30 |
| ❏ 147 Bryan Cox | .30 | .10 |
| ❏ 148 Bryant Westbrook | .30 | .10 |
| ❏ 149 Duce Staley | .75 | .30 |
| ❏ 150 Barry Sanders | 2.50 | 1.00 |
| ❏ 151 La'Roi Glover RC | .75 | .30 |
| ❏ 152 Ray Crockett | .30 | .10 |
| ❏ 153 Tony Brackens | .30 | .10 |
| ❏ 154 Roy Barker | .30 | .10 |
| ❏ 155 Kerry Collins | .50 | .20 |
| ❏ 156 Andre Wadsworth | .30 | .10 |
| ❏ 157 Cameron Cleeland | .30 | .10 |
| ❏ 158 Koy Detmer | .30 | .10 |
| ❏ 159 Marcus Pollard | .30 | .10 |
| ❏ 160 Patrick Jeffers RC | 6.00 | 2.50 |
| ❏ 161 Aaron Glenn | .30 | .10 |
| ❏ 162 Andre Hastings | .30 | .10 |
| ❏ 163 Bruce Smith | .50 | .20 |
| ❏ 164 David Palmer | .30 | .10 |
| ❏ 165 Erik Kramer | .30 | .10 |
| ❏ 166 Orlando Pace | .30 | .10 |
| ❏ 167 Robert Brooks | .50 | .20 |
| ❏ 168 Shawn Springs | .30 | .10 |
| ❏ 169 Terance Mathis | .30 | .10 |
| ❏ 170 Chris Calloway | .30 | .10 |
| ❏ 171 Gilbert Brown | .30 | .10 |
| ❏ 172 Charlie Jones | .30 | .10 |
| ❏ 173 Curtis Enis | .50 | .20 |
| ❏ 174 Eugene Robinson | .30 | .10 |
| ❏ 175 Garrison Hearst | .50 | .20 |
| ❏ 176 Jason Elam | .30 | .10 |
| ❏ 177 John Randle | .50 | .20 |
| ❏ 178 Keith Poole | .30 | .10 |
| ❏ 179 Kevin Hardy | .30 | .10 |
| ❏ 180 Keyshawn Johnson | .75 | .30 |
| ❏ 181 O.J. Santiago | .30 | .10 |
| ❏ 182 Jacquez Green | .30 | .10 |
| ❏ 183 Bobby Engram | .50 | .20 |
| ❏ 184 Damon Jones | .30 | .10 |
| ❏ 185 Freddie Jones | .50 | .20 |
| ❏ 186 Jake Reed | .30 | .10 |
| ❏ 187 Jerry Rice | 1.50 | .60 |
| ❏ 188 Joey Kent | .30 | .10 |
| ❏ 189 Lamar Smith | .30 | .10 |
| ❏ 190 John Elway | 2.50 | 1.00 |

|  |  | | |
|---|---|---|---|
| ❑ 191 | Leon Johnson | .30 | .10 |
| ❑ 192 | Mark Chmura | .50 | .20 |
| ❑ 193 | Peter Boulware | .30 | .10 |
| ❑ 194 | Zach Thomas | .75 | .30 |
| ❑ 195 | Marc Edwards | .30 | .10 |
| ❑ 196 | Mike Alstott | .75 | .30 |
| ❑ 197 | Yancey Thigpen | .30 | .10 |
| ❑ 198 | Oronde Gadsden | .50 | .20 |
| ❑ 199 | Rae Carruth | .30 | .10 |
| ❑ 200 | Troy Aikman | 1.50 | .60 |
| ❑ 201 | Shawn Jefferson | .30 | .10 |
| ❑ 202 | Rob Moore | .50 | .20 |
| ❑ 203 | Rickey Dudley | .30 | .10 |
| ❑ 204 | Jason Taylor | .30 | .10 |
| ❑ 205 | Curtis Conway | .50 | .20 |
| ❑ 206 | Darrien Gordon | .30 | .10 |
| ❑ 207 | Eric Green | .30 | .10 |
| ❑ 208 | Jessie Armstead | .30 | .10 |
| ❑ 209 | Keenan McCardell | .50 | .20 |
| ❑ 210 | Robert Smith | .75 | .30 |
| ❑ 211 | Mo Lewis | .30 | .10 |
| ❑ 212 | Ryan Leaf | .75 | .30 |
| ❑ 213 | Steve Young | 1.00 | .40 |
| ❑ 214 | Tyrone Davis | .30 | .10 |
| ❑ 215 | Chad Brown | .30 | .10 |
| ❑ 216 | Ike Hilliard | .30 | .10 |
| ❑ 217 | Jimmy Hitchcock | .30 | .10 |
| ❑ 218 | Kevin Dyson | .50 | .20 |
| ❑ 219 | Levon Kirkland | .30 | .10 |
| ❑ 220 | Neil O'Donnell | .50 | .20 |
| ❑ 221 | Ray Lewis | .75 | .30 |
| ❑ 222 | Shannon Sharpe | .50 | .20 |
| ❑ 223 | Skip Hicks | .30 | .10 |
| ❑ 224 | Brad Johnson | .75 | .30 |
| ❑ 225 | Charlie Batch | .75 | .30 |
| ❑ 226 | Corey Dillon | .75 | .30 |
| ❑ 227 | Dale Carter | .30 | .10 |
| ❑ 228 | John Mobley | .30 | .10 |
| ❑ 229 | Hines Ward | .75 | .30 |
| ❑ 230 | Leslie Shepherd | .30 | .10 |
| ❑ 231 | Michael Strahan | .50 | .20 |
| ❑ 232 | R.W. McQuarters | .30 | .10 |
| ❑ 233 | Mike Pritchard | .30 | .10 |
| ❑ 234 | Antonio Freeman | .75 | .30 |
| ❑ 235 | Ben Coates | .50 | .20 |
| ❑ 236 | Michael Bates | .30 | .10 |
| ❑ 237 | Ed McCaffrey | .50 | .20 |
| ❑ 238 | Gary Brown | .30 | .10 |
| ❑ 239 | Mark Bruener | .30 | .10 |
| ❑ 240 | Mikhael Ricks | .30 | .10 |
| ❑ 241 | Muhsin Muhammad | .50 | .20 |
| ❑ 242 | Priest Holmes | 1.25 | .50 |
| ❑ 243 | Stephen Davis | .75 | .30 |
| ❑ 244 | Vinny Testaverde | .50 | .20 |
| ❑ 245 | Warrick Dunn | .75 | .30 |
| ❑ 246 | Derrick Mayes | .30 | .10 |
| ❑ 247 | Fred Taylor | .75 | .30 |
| ❑ 248 | Drew Bledsoe CL | .50 | .20 |
| ❑ 249 | Eddie George CL | .50 | .20 |
| ❑ 250 | Steve Young CL | .50 | .20 |
| ❑ 251 | Jamal Anderson BB | .60 | .25 |
| ❑ 252 | D.Gordon/Romanowski BB | .30 | .10 |
| ❑ 253 | Shannon Sharpe BB | .30 | .10 |
| ❑ 254 | Terrell Davis BB | 1.00 | .40 |
| ❑ 255 | Rod Smith BB | .30 | .10 |
| ❑ 256 | Rod Smith BB | .30 | .10 |
| ❑ 257 | John Elway BB | 5.00 | 2.00 |
| ❑ 258 | Tim Dwight BB | .60 | .25 |
| ❑ 259 | Elway/McC/Griff/Dav. BB | 3.00 | 1.25 |
| ❑ 260 | John Elway BB | 5.00 | 2.00 |
| ❑ 261 | Ricky Williams RC | 6.00 | 2.50 |
| ❑ 262 | Tim Couch RC | 3.00 | 1.25 |
| ❑ 263 | Chris Claiborne RC | 1.50 | .60 |
| ❑ 264 | Champ Bailey RC | 5.00 | 2.00 |
| ❑ 265 | Torry Holt RC | 8.00 | 3.00 |
| ❑ 266 | Donovan McNabb RC | 15.00 | 6.00 |
| ❑ 267 | David Boston RC | 3.00 | 1.25 |
| ❑ 268 | Chris McAlister RC | 2.50 | 1.00 |
| ❑ 269 | Brock Huard RC | 3.00 | 1.25 |
| ❑ 270 | Daunte Culpepper RC | 12.00 | 5.00 |
| ❑ 271 | Matt Stinchcomb RC | 1.50 | .60 |
| ❑ 272 | Edgerrin James RC | 12.00 | 5.00 |
| ❑ 273 | Jevon Kearse RC | 6.00 | 2.50 |
| ❑ 274 | Ebenezer Ekuban RC | 2.50 | 1.00 |
| ❑ 275 | Kris Farris RC | 1.50 | .60 |
| ❑ 276 | Chris Terry RC | 1.50 | .60 |
| ❑ 277 | Jerame Tuman RC | 3.00 | 1.25 |
| ❑ 278 | Akili Smith RC | 2.50 | 1.00 |
| ❑ 279 | Aaron Gibson RC | 1.50 | .60 |
| ❑ 280 | Rahim Abdullah RC | 2.50 | 1.00 |
| ❑ 281 | Peerless Price RC | 3.00 | 1.25 |
| ❑ 282 | Antoine Winfield RC | 2.50 | 1.00 |
| ❑ 283 | Antuan Edwards RC | 1.50 | .60 |
| ❑ 284 | Rob Konrad RC | 3.00 | 1.25 |
| ❑ 285 | Troy Edwards RC | 2.50 | 1.00 |
| ❑ 286 | John Thornton RC | 1.50 | .60 |
| ❑ 287 | James Johnson RC | 2.50 | 1.00 |
| ❑ 288 | Gary Stills RC | 1.50 | .60 |
| ❑ 289 | Mike Peterson RC | 2.50 | 1.00 |
| ❑ 290 | Kevin Faulk RC | 3.00 | 1.25 |
| ❑ 291 | Jared DeVries RC | 1.50 | .60 |
| ❑ 292 | Martin Gramatica RC | 1.50 | .60 |
| ❑ 293 | Montae Reagor RC | 1.50 | .60 |
| ❑ 294 | Andy Katzenmoyer RC | 2.50 | 1.00 |
| ❑ 295 | Sedrick Irvin RC | 1.50 | .60 |
| ❑ 296 | D'Wayne Bates RC | 2.50 | 1.00 |
| ❑ 297 | Amos Zereoue RC | 3.00 | 1.25 |
| ❑ 298 | Dre' Bly RC | 3.00 | 1.25 |
| ❑ 299 | Kevin Johnson RC | 3.00 | 1.25 |
| ❑ 300 | Cade McNown RC | 2.50 | 1.00 |
| ❑ P247 | Fred Taylor Promo | 2.00 | .75 |

## 2000 Ultra

|  |  | | |
|---|---|---|---|
| ❑ | COMPLETE SET (249) | 100.00 | 40.00 |
| ❑ | COMP.SET w/o SP's (220) | 20.00 | 7.50 |
| ❑ 1 | Kurt Warner | 1.50 | .60 |
| ❑ 2 | Derrick Alexander | .50 | .20 |
| ❑ 3 | Aaron Craver | .30 | .10 |
| ❑ 4 | Kevin Faulk | .50 | .20 |
| ❑ 5 | Marcus Robinson | .75 | .30 |
| ❑ 6 | Tony Banks | .50 | .20 |
| ❑ 7 | Jon Ritchie | .30 | .10 |
| ❑ 8 | Torry Holt | .75 | .30 |
| ❑ 9 | Joe Horn | .50 | .20 |
| ❑ 10 | Eddie George | .75 | .30 |
| ❑ 11 | Michael Westbrook | .50 | .20 |
| ❑ 12 | Gus Frerotte | .30 | .10 |
| ❑ 13 | Tim Brown | .75 | .30 |
| ❑ 14 | Tamarick Vanover | .30 | .10 |
| ❑ 15 | David Sloan | .30 | .10 |
| ❑ 16 | Darnay Scott | .30 | .10 |
| ❑ 17 | Junior Seau | .50 | .20 |
| ❑ 18 | Warren Sapp | .50 | .20 |
| ❑ 19 | Priest Holmes | 1.00 | .40 |
| ❑ 20 | Jerry Rice | 1.50 | .60 |
| ❑ 21 | Cade McNown | .50 | .20 |
| ❑ 22 | Johnnie Morton | .50 | .20 |
| ❑ 23 | Vinny Testaverde | .50 | .20 |
| ❑ 24 | James Jett | .30 | .10 |
| ❑ 25 | Tony Gonzalez | .50 | .20 |
| ❑ 26 | Charlie Batch | .75 | .30 |
| ❑ 27 | Tony Simmons | .30 | .10 |
| ❑ 28 | James Stewart | .50 | .20 |
| ❑ 29 | Corey Dillon | .75 | .30 |
| ❑ 30 | Ricky Williams RC | .75 | .30 |
| ❑ 31 | Ryan Leaf | .50 | .20 |
| ❑ 32 | Terry Allen | .50 | .20 |
| ❑ 33 | Freddie Jones | .30 | .10 |
| ❑ 34 | Terry Kirby | .30 | .10 |
| ❑ 35 | Charles Johnson | .50 | .20 |
| ❑ 36 | William Henderson | .50 | .20 |
| ❑ 37 | Stephen Alexander | .30 | .10 |
| ❑ 38 | Moe Williams | .50 | .20 |
| ❑ 39 | David Boston | .75 | .30 |
| ❑ 40 | Emmitt Smith | 1.50 | .60 |
| ❑ 41 | Ken Oxendine | .30 | .10 |
| ❑ 42 | Byron Hanspard | .30 | .10 |
| ❑ 43 | Dwight Stone | .30 | .10 |
| ❑ 44 | Jim Harbaugh | .50 | .20 |
| ❑ 45 | Curtis Enis | .30 | .10 |
| ❑ 46 | Peerless Price | .50 | .20 |
| ❑ 47 | Terance Mathis | .50 | .20 |
| ❑ 48 | Mike Alstott | .75 | .30 |
| ❑ 49 | Rod Smith | .50 | .20 |
| ❑ 50 | Marshall Faulk | 1.00 | .40 |
| ❑ 51 | Derrick Mayes | .50 | .20 |
| ❑ 52 | Keenan McCardell | .50 | .20 |
| ❑ 53 | Curtis Martin | .50 | .20 |
| ❑ 54 | Bobby Engram | .30 | .10 |
| ❑ 55 | Carl Pickens | .50 | .20 |
| ❑ 56 | Robert Smith | .75 | .30 |
| ❑ 57 | Ike Hilliard | .50 | .20 |
| ❑ 58 | Reidel Anthony | .50 | .20 |
| ❑ 59 | Jeff Graham | .30 | .10 |
| ❑ 60 | Mark Brunell | .75 | .30 |
| ❑ 61 | Joe Montgomery | .30 | .10 |
| ❑ 62 | Ed McCaffrey | .75 | .30 |
| ❑ 63 | Kenny Bynum | .30 | .10 |
| ❑ 64 | Curtis Conway | .50 | .20 |
| ❑ 65 | Trent Dilfer | .50 | .20 |
| ❑ 66 | Jake Reed | .50 | .20 |
| ❑ 67 | Jake Plummer | .75 | .30 |
| ❑ 68 | Tony Martin | .50 | .20 |
| ❑ 69 | Yatil Green | .30 | .10 |
| ❑ 70 | Keyshawn Johnson | .75 | .30 |
| ❑ 71 | Leroy Hoard | .30 | .10 |
| ❑ 72 | Skip Hicks | .30 | .10 |
| ❑ 73 | Marvin Harrison | .75 | .30 |
| ❑ 74 | Steve Beuerlein | .50 | .20 |
| ❑ 75 | Will Blackwell | .30 | .10 |
| ❑ 76 | Derek Loville | .30 | .10 |
| ❑ 77 | Warrick Dunn | .75 | .30 |
| ❑ 78 | Amos Zereoue | .75 | .30 |
| ❑ 79 | Ray Lucas | .50 | .20 |
| ❑ 80 | Randy Moss | 1.50 | .60 |
| ❑ 81 | Wesley Walls | .30 | .10 |
| ❑ 82 | Jimmy Smith | .50 | .20 |
| ❑ 83 | Kordell Stewart | .50 | .20 |
| ❑ 84 | Brian Griese | .75 | .30 |
| ❑ 85 | Martin Gramatica | .30 | .10 |
| ❑ 86 | Chris Chandler | .50 | .20 |
| ❑ 87 | Reggie Barlow | .30 | .10 |
| ❑ 88 | Jeff George | .50 | .20 |
| ❑ 89 | Tavian Banks | .30 | .10 |
| ❑ 90 | Muhsin Muhammad | .50 | .20 |
| ❑ 91 | Steve McNair | .75 | .30 |
| ❑ 92 | Hines Ward | .75 | .30 |
| ❑ 93 | Brian Mitchell | .30 | .10 |
| ❑ 94 | Daunte Culpepper | 1.00 | .40 |
| ❑ 95 | Tim Dwight | .75 | .30 |
| ❑ 96 | Terrence Wilkins | .30 | .10 |
| ❑ 97 | Fred Lane | .30 | .10 |
| ❑ 98 | Brett Favre | 2.50 | 1.00 |
| ❑ 99 | Richie Anderson | .50 | .20 |
| ❑ 100 | Jamal Anderson | .75 | .30 |
| ❑ 101 | Doug Flutie | .75 | .30 |
| ❑ 102 | Charles Woodson | .50 | .20 |
| ❑ 103 | Jacquez Green | .30 | .10 |
| ❑ 104 | Olandis Gary | .75 | .30 |
| ❑ 105 | Steve Young | 1.00 | .40 |
| ❑ 106 | Wayne Chrebet | .50 | .20 |
| ❑ 107 | Karim Abdul-Jabbar | .50 | .20 |
| ❑ 108 | Andre Rison | .50 | .20 |
| ❑ 109 | Eddie Kennison | .30 | .10 |
| ❑ 110 | Jevon Kearse | .75 | .30 |
| ❑ 111 | Tony Richardson RC | .50 | .20 |
| ❑ 112 | Jake Delhomme RC | 3.00 | 1.25 |
| ❑ 113 | Errict Rhett | .50 | .20 |
| ❑ 114 | Akili Smith | .30 | .10 |
| ❑ 115 | Tyrone Wheatley | .50 | .20 |
| ❑ 116 | Corey Bradford | .50 | .20 |
| ❑ 117 | J.J. Stokes | .50 | .20 |
| ❑ 118 | Simeon Rice | .30 | .10 |
| ❑ 119 | Brad Johnson | .75 | .30 |
| ❑ 120 | Edgerrin James | 1.25 | .50 |

|  |  | | |
|---|---|---|---|
| ❏ 121 | Amani Toomer | .30 | .10 |
| ❏ 122 | O.J. McDuffie | .50 | .20 |
| ❏ 123 | Az-Zahir Hakim | .50 | .20 |
| ❏ 124 | Troy Edwards | .30 | .10 |
| ❏ 125 | Tim Biakabutuka | .50 | .20 |
| ❏ 126 | Jason Tucker | .30 | .10 |
| ❏ 127 | Charles Way | .30 | .10 |
| ❏ 128 | Terrell Davis | .75 | .30 |
| ❏ 129 | Garrison Hearst | .50 | .20 |
| ❏ 130 | Fred Taylor | .75 | .30 |
| ❏ 131 | Robert Holcombe | .30 | .10 |
| ❏ 132 | Frank Sanders | .50 | .20 |
| ❏ 133 | Morten Andersen | .30 | .10 |
| ❏ 134 | Cris Carter | .75 | .30 |
| ❏ 135 | Patrick Jeffers | .75 | .30 |
| ❏ 136 | Antonio Freeman | .75 | .30 |
| ❏ 137 | Jonathan Linton | .30 | .10 |
| ❏ 138 | Rashaan Shehee | .30 | .10 |
| ❏ 139 | Luther Broughton RC | .50 | .20 |
| ❏ 140 | Tim Couch | .50 | .20 |
| ❏ 141 | Keith Poole | .30 | .10 |
| ❏ 142 | Champ Bailey | .50 | .20 |
| ❏ 143 | Yancey Thigpen | .30 | .10 |
| ❏ 144 | Joey Galloway | .50 | .20 |
| ❏ 145 | Mac Cody | .30 | .10 |
| ❏ 146 | Damon Huard | .75 | .30 |
| ❏ 147 | Dorsey Levens | .50 | .20 |
| ❏ 148 | Donovan McNabb | 1.25 | .50 |
| ❏ 149 | Jamie Asher | .30 | .10 |
| ❏ 150 | Peyton Manning | 2.00 | .75 |
| ❏ 151 | Leslie Shepherd | .30 | .10 |
| ❏ 152 | Charlie Rogers | .30 | .10 |
| ❏ 153 | Tony Horne | .30 | .10 |
| ❏ 154 | Jim Miller | .30 | .10 |
| ❏ 155 | Richard Huntley | .30 | .10 |
| ❏ 156 | Germane Crowell | .30 | .10 |
| ❏ 157 | Natrone Means | .30 | .10 |
| ❏ 158 | Justin Armour | .30 | .10 |
| ❏ 159 | Drew Bledsoe | 1.00 | .40 |
| ❏ 160 | Dedric Ward | .30 | .10 |
| ❏ 161 | Allen Rossum | .30 | .10 |
| ❏ 162 | Ricky Watters | .50 | .20 |
| ❏ 163 | Kerry Collins | .50 | .20 |
| ❏ 164 | James Johnson | .30 | .10 |
| ❏ 165 | Elvis Grbac | .50 | .20 |
| ❏ 166 | Larry Centers | .30 | .10 |
| ❏ 167 | Rob Moore | .50 | .20 |
| ❏ 168 | Jay Riemersma | .30 | .10 |
| ❏ 169 | Bill Schroeder | .30 | .10 |
| ❏ 170 | Deion Sanders | .75 | .30 |
| ❏ 171 | Jerome Bettis | .75 | .30 |
| ❏ 172 | Dan Marino | 2.50 | 1.00 |
| ❏ 173 | Terrell Owens | .75 | .30 |
| ❏ 174 | Kevin Carter | .30 | .10 |
| ❏ 175 | Lamar Smith | .30 | .10 |
| ❏ 176 | Ken Dilger | .30 | .10 |
| ❏ 177 | Napoleon Kaufman | .50 | .20 |
| ❏ 178 | Kevin Williams | .30 | .10 |
| ❏ 179 | Tremain Mack | .30 | .10 |
| ❏ 180 | Troy Aikman | 1.50 | .60 |
| ❏ 181 | Glyn Milburn | .30 | .10 |
| ❏ 182 | Pete Mitchell | .30 | .10 |
| ❏ 183 | Cameron Cleeland | .30 | .10 |
| ❏ 184 | Qadry Ismail | .50 | .20 |
| ❏ 185 | Michael Pittman | .30 | .10 |
| ❏ 186 | Kevin Dyson | .50 | .20 |
| ❏ 187 | Matt Hasselbeck | .50 | .20 |
| ❏ 188 | Kevin Johnson | .75 | .30 |
| ❏ 189 | Rich Gannon | .75 | .30 |
| ❏ 190 | Stephen Davis | .75 | .30 |
| ❏ 191 | Frank Wycheck | .30 | .10 |
| ❏ 192 | Eric Moulds | .75 | .30 |
| ❏ 193 | Jon Kitna | .75 | .30 |
| ❏ 194 | Mario Bates | .30 | .10 |
| ❏ 195 | Na Brown | .30 | .10 |
| ❏ 196 | Jeff Blake | .50 | .20 |
| ❏ 197 | Charles Evans | .30 | .10 |
| ❏ 198 | Oronde Gadsden | .50 | .20 |
| ❏ 199 | Donnell Bennett | .30 | .10 |
| ❏ 200 | Isaac Bruce | .75 | .30 |
| ❏ 201 | Olindo Mare | .30 | .10 |
| ❏ 202 | Darnell McDonald | .30 | .10 |
| ❏ 203 | Charlie Garner | .50 | .20 |
| ❏ 204 | Shawn Jefferson | .30 | .10 |
| ❏ 205 | Adrian Murrell | .50 | .20 |
| ❏ 206 | Peter Boulware | .30 | .10 |
| ❏ 207 | LeShon Johnson | .30 | .10 |
| ❏ 208 | Herman Moore | .50 | .20 |
| ❏ 209 | Duce Staley | .75 | .30 |
| ❏ 210 | Sean Dawkins | .30 | .10 |
| ❏ 211 | Antowain Smith | .50 | .20 |
| ❏ 212 | Albert Connell | .30 | .10 |
| ❏ 213 | Jeff Garcia | .75 | .30 |
| ❏ 214 | Kimble Anders | .30 | .10 |
| ❏ 215 | Shaun King | .30 | .10 |
| ❏ 216 | Rocket Ismail | .50 | .20 |
| ❏ 217 | Andrew Glover | .30 | .10 |
| ❏ 218 | Rickey Dudley | .30 | .10 |
| ❏ 219 | Michael Basnight | .30 | .10 |
| ❏ 220 | Terry Glenn | .50 | .20 |
| ❏ 221 | Peter Warrick RC | 3.00 | 1.25 |
| ❏ 222 | Ron Dayne RC | 3.00 | 1.25 |
| ❏ 223 | Thomas Jones RC | 5.00 | 2.00 |
| ❏ 224 | Joe Hamilton RC | 2.50 | 1.00 |
| ❏ 225 | Tim Rattay RC | 3.00 | 1.25 |
| ❏ 226 | Chad Pennington RC | 8.00 | 3.00 |
| ❏ 227 | Dennis Northcutt RC | 2.50 | 1.00 |
| ❏ 228 | Troy Walters RC | 3.00 | 1.25 |
| ❏ 229 | Travis Prentice RC | 2.50 | 1.00 |
| ❏ 230 | Shaun Alexander RC | 10.00 | 4.00 |
| ❏ 231 | J.R. Redmond RC | 2.50 | 1.00 |
| ❏ 232 | Chris Redman RC | 2.50 | 1.00 |
| ❏ 233 | Tee Martin RC | 3.00 | 1.25 |
| ❏ 234 | Tom Brady RC | 50.00 | 20.00 |
| ❏ 235 | Travis Taylor RC | 3.00 | 1.25 |
| ❏ 236 | R.Jay Soward RC | 2.50 | 1.00 |
| ❏ 237 | Jamal Lewis RC | 8.00 | 3.00 |
| ❏ 238 | Giovanni Carmazzi RC | 2.00 | .75 |
| ❏ 239 | Dez White RC | 3.00 | 1.25 |
| ❏ 240 | LaVar Arrington RC SP | 50.00 | 20.00 |
| ❏ 241 | Laveranues Coles RC | 4.00 | 1.50 |
| ❏ 242 | Sherrod Gideon RC | 2.00 | .75 |
| ❏ 243 | Trung Canidate RC | 2.50 | 1.00 |
| ❏ 244 | Michael Wiley RC | 2.50 | 1.00 |
| ❏ 245 | Anthony Lucas RC | 2.00 | .75 |
| ❏ 246 | Darrell Jackson RC | 6.00 | 2.50 |
| ❏ 247 | Plaxico Burress RC | 4.00 | 1.50 |
| ❏ 248 | Reuben Droughns RC | 4.00 | 1.50 |
| ❏ 249 | Marc Bulger RC | 6.00 | 2.50 |
| ❏ 250 | Danny Farmer RC | 2.50 | 1.00 |

## 2001 Ultra

|  |  | | |
|---|---|---|---|
| ❏ | COMP.SET w/o SP's (250) | 25.00 | 10.00 |
| ❏ 1 | Daunte Culpepper | .75 | .30 |
| ❏ 2 | Kurt Warner | 1.50 | .60 |
| ❏ 3 | Emmitt Smith | 1.50 | .60 |
| ❏ 4 | Eddie George | .75 | .30 |
| ❏ 5 | Ron Dayne | .75 | .30 |
| ❏ 6 | Zach Thomas | .75 | .30 |
| ❏ 7 | Itula Mili | .30 | .10 |
| ❏ 8 | Jake Reed | .50 | .20 |
| ❏ 9 | James Stewart | .50 | .20 |
| ❏ 10 | Terrence Wilkins | .30 | .10 |
| ❏ 11 | Jeff Blake | .50 | .20 |
| ❏ 12 | Kerry Collins | .50 | .20 |
| ❏ 13 | Christian Fauria | .30 | .10 |
| ❏ 14 | Jackie Harris | .30 | .10 |
| ❏ 15 | Jon Johnson | .50 | .20 |
| ❏ 16 | Tony Martin | .50 | .20 |
| ❏ 17 | Joey Galloway | .50 | .20 |
| ❏ 18 | Junior Seau | .75 | .30 |
| ❏ 19 | Jason Tucker | .30 | .10 |
| ❏ 20 | Steve Beuerlein | .30 | .10 |
| ❏ 21 | Mike Cloud | .30 | .10 |
| ❏ 22 | Kevin Faulk | .50 | .20 |
| ❏ 23 | Az-Zahir Hakim | .30 | .10 |
| ❏ 24 | Charles Johnson | .30 | .10 |
| ❏ 25 | Curtis Martin | .75 | .30 |
| ❏ 26 | Eric Moulds | .50 | .20 |
| ❏ 27 | Bill Schroeder | .50 | .20 |
| ❏ 28 | Amani Toomer | .30 | .10 |
| ❏ 29 | Obafemi Ayanbadejo | .30 | .10 |
| ❏ 30 | Aaron Shea | .30 | .10 |
| ❏ 31 | Ken Dilger | .30 | .10 |
| ❏ 32 | Terry Glenn | .30 | .10 |
| ❏ 33 | Rocket Ismail | .50 | .20 |
| ❏ 34 | Dorsey Levens | .30 | .10 |
| ❏ 35 | Brian Mitchell | .30 | .10 |
| ❏ 36 | Tony Richardson | .30 | .10 |
| ❏ 37 | Sam Madison | .30 | .10 |
| ❏ 38 | Darren Sharper | .30 | .10 |
| ❏ 39 | Derrick Alexander | .50 | .20 |
| ❏ 40 | Aaron Brooks | .75 | .30 |
| ❏ 41 | Casey Crawford | .30 | .10 |
| ❏ 42 | Terrell Fletcher | .30 | .10 |
| ❏ 43 | William Henderson | .30 | .10 |
| ❏ 44 | Thomas Jones | .50 | .20 |
| ❏ 45 | Keenan McCardell | .30 | .10 |
| ❏ 46 | Chad Pennington | 1.25 | .50 |
| ❏ 47 | Akili Smith | .30 | .10 |
| ❏ 48 | Hines Ward | .75 | .30 |
| ❏ 49 | Champ Bailey | .50 | .20 |
| ❏ 50 | Cris Carter | .75 | .30 |
| ❏ 51 | Corey Dillon | .75 | .30 |
| ❏ 52 | Tony Gonzalez | .50 | .20 |
| ❏ 53 | Darrell Jackson | .75 | .30 |
| ❏ 54 | Chad Lewis | .30 | .10 |
| ❏ 55 | Dave Moore | .30 | .10 |
| ❏ 56 | Jay Riemersma | .30 | .10 |
| ❏ 57 | J.J. Stokes | .50 | .20 |
| ❏ 58 | Frank Wycheck | .30 | .10 |
| ❏ 59 | Tiki Barber | .75 | .30 |
| ❏ 60 | Tony Carter | .30 | .10 |
| ❏ 61 | Rickey Dudley | .30 | .10 |
| ❏ 62 | John Lynch | .50 | .20 |
| ❏ 63 | Larry Foster | .30 | .10 |
| ❏ 64 | Willie Jackson | .30 | .10 |
| ❏ 65 | Jamal Lewis | 1.25 | .50 |
| ❏ 66 | Herman Moore | .50 | .20 |
| ❏ 67 | Andre Rison | .50 | .20 |
| ❏ 68 | Michael Strahan | .50 | .20 |
| ❏ 69 | Charlie Batch | .75 | .30 |
| ❏ 70 | Larry Centers | .30 | .10 |
| ❏ 71 | Ron Dugans | .30 | .10 |
| ❏ 72 | Jeff Graham | .30 | .10 |
| ❏ 73 | Edgerrin James | 1.00 | .40 |
| ❏ 74 | Jermaine Lewis | .30 | .10 |
| ❏ 75 | Charles Woodson | .50 | .20 |
| ❏ 76 | Chris Redman | .30 | .10 |
| ❏ 77 | Jon Ritchie | .30 | .10 |
| ❏ 78 | Fred Taylor | .75 | .30 |
| ❏ 79 | Jamal Anderson | .75 | .30 |
| ❏ 80 | Isaac Bruce | .75 | .30 |
| ❏ 81 | Terrell Davis | .75 | .30 |
| ❏ 82 | Rich Gannon | .75 | .30 |
| ❏ 83 | Joe Horn | .50 | .20 |
| ❏ 84 | Eddie Kennison | .50 | .20 |
| ❏ 85 | Steve McNair | .50 | .20 |
| ❏ 86 | Travis Prentice | .30 | .10 |
| ❏ 87 | Rod Smith | .50 | .20 |
| ❏ 88 | Ricky Watters | .50 | .20 |
| ❏ 89 | Michael Bates | .30 | .10 |
| ❏ 90 | Byron Chamberlain | .30 | .10 |
| ❏ 91 | Warrick Dunn | .75 | .30 |
| ❏ 92 | Elvis Grbac | .50 | .20 |
| ❏ 93 | Patrick Jeffers | .30 | .10 |
| ❏ 94 | Ray Lewis | .75 | .30 |
| ❏ 95 | Sammy Morris | .30 | .10 |
| ❏ 96 | Marcus Robinson | .75 | .30 |
| ❏ 97 | Travis Taylor | .50 | .20 |
| ❏ 98 | Fred Beasley | .30 | .10 |
| ❏ 99 | Chris Chandler | .50 | .20 |
| ❏ 100 | Tim Dwight | .75 | .30 |
| ❏ 101 | Ahman Green | .75 | .30 |
| ❏ 102 | Shawn Jefferson | .30 | .10 |

| | | |
|---|---|---|
| ❏ 103 Jeremy McDaniel | .30 | .10 |
| ❏ 104 Sylvester Morris | .30 | .10 |
| ❏ 105 John Randle | .30 | .10 |
| ❏ 106 Vinny Testaverde | .50 | .20 |
| ❏ 107 Anthony Becht | .30 | .10 |
| ❏ 108 Wayne Chrebet | .50 | .20 |
| ❏ 109 Stephen Boyd | .30 | .10 |
| ❏ 110 Jacquez Green | .30 | .10 |
| ❏ 111 MarTay Jenkins | .30 | .10 |
| ❏ 112 Jason Gildon | .30 | .10 |
| ❏ 113 Chad Morton | .30 | .10 |
| ❏ 114 Deion Sanders | .75 | .30 |
| ❏ 115 Yancey Thigpen | .30 | .10 |
| ❏ 116 Marty Booker | .30 | .10 |
| ❏ 117 Curtis Conway | .50 | .20 |
| ❏ 118 Jermaine Fazande | .30 | .10 |
| ❏ 119 Matthew Hatchette | .30 | .10 |
| ❏ 120 Pat Johnson | .30 | .10 |
| ❏ 121 Terance Mathis | .50 | .20 |
| ❏ 122 Terrell Owens | .75 | .30 |
| ❏ 123 Corey Simon | .50 | .20 |
| ❏ 124 Darrick Vaughn | .30 | .10 |
| ❏ 125 Drew Bledsoe | 1.00 | .40 |
| ❏ 126 Albert Connell | .30 | .10 |
| ❏ 127 Brett Favre | 2.50 | 1.00 |
| ❏ 128 Marvin Harrison | .75 | .30 |
| ❏ 129 Keyshawn Johnson | .75 | .30 |
| ❏ 130 Derrick Mason | .50 | .20 |
| ❏ 131 Dennis Northcutt | .50 | .20 |
| ❏ 132 Shannon Sharpe | .50 | .20 |
| ❏ 133 Brian Urlacher | 1.25 | .50 |
| ❏ 134 Mike Anderson | .75 | .30 |
| ❏ 135 Mark Bruener | .30 | .10 |
| ❏ 136 Sean Dawkins | .30 | .10 |
| ❏ 137 Jeff Garcia | .75 | .30 |
| ❏ 138 Tony Horne | .30 | .10 |
| ❏ 139 Shaun King | .30 | .10 |
| ❏ 140 Cade McNown | .30 | .10 |
| ❏ 141 Peerless Price | .50 | .20 |
| ❏ 142 R.Jay Soward | .30 | .10 |
| ❏ 143 Tyrone Wheatley | .50 | .20 |
| ❏ 144 Richie Anderson | .30 | .10 |
| ❏ 145 Mark Brunell | .75 | .30 |
| ❏ 146 JaJuan Dawson | .30 | .10 |
| ❏ 147 Charlie Garner | .50 | .20 |
| ❏ 148 Desmond Howard | .30 | .10 |
| ❏ 149 Jon Kitna | .50 | .20 |
| ❏ 150 Duane Starks | .30 | .10 |
| ❏ 151 J.R. Redmond | .30 | .10 |
| ❏ 152 Duce Staley | .75 | .30 |
| ❏ 153 Dez White | .30 | .10 |
| ❏ 154 David Boston | .75 | .30 |
| ❏ 155 Tim Couch | .50 | .20 |
| ❏ 156 Jay Fiedler | .75 | .30 |
| ❏ 157 Jessie Armstead | .30 | .10 |
| ❏ 158 Rob Johnson | .50 | .20 |
| ❏ 159 Brad Johnson | .75 | .30 |
| ❏ 160 Derrick Mayes | .30 | .10 |
| ❏ 161 Jerome Pathon | .50 | .20 |
| ❏ 162 David Sloan | .30 | .10 |
| ❏ 163 Wesley Walls | .30 | .10 |
| ❏ 164 Shaun Alexander | 1.00 | .40 |
| ❏ 165 Derrick Brooks | .75 | .30 |
| ❏ 166 Germane Crowell | .30 | .10 |
| ❏ 167 Doug Flutie | .75 | .30 |
| ❏ 168 Ike Hilliard | .50 | .20 |
| ❏ 169 Hugh Douglas | .30 | .10 |
| ❏ 170 Wane McGarity | .30 | .10 |
| ❏ 171 Michael Pittman | .30 | .10 |
| ❏ 172 Shawn Bryson | .30 | .10 |
| ❏ 173 Richard Huntley | .30 | .10 |
| ❏ 174 Darnell Autry | .30 | .10 |
| ❏ 175 Plaxico Burress | .75 | .30 |
| ❏ 176 Trent Dilfer | .50 | .20 |
| ❏ 177 Jeff George | .50 | .20 |
| ❏ 178 Qadry Ismail | .50 | .20 |
| ❏ 179 Ryan Leaf | .50 | .20 |
| ❏ 180 Jim Miller | .30 | .10 |
| ❏ 181 Jerry Rice | 1.50 | .60 |
| ❏ 182 Kordell Stewart | .50 | .20 |
| ❏ 183 Ricky Williams | .75 | .30 |
| ❏ 184 James Allen | .30 | .10 |
| ❏ 185 Courtney Brown | .50 | .20 |
| ❏ 186 Reidel Anthony | .30 | .10 |
| ❏ 187 Bubba Franks | .50 | .20 |
| ❏ 188 Priest Holmes | 1.00 | .40 |
| ❏ 189 Napoleon Kaufman | .30 | .10 |
| ❏ 190 Trevor Pryce | .30 | .10 |
| ❏ 191 Jake Plummer | .50 | .20 |
| ❏ 192 Jimmy Smith | .50 | .20 |
| ❏ 193 Michael Wiley | .30 | .10 |
| ❏ 194 Brock Huard | .30 | .10 |
| ❏ 195 Troy Brown | .50 | .20 |
| ❏ 196 Stephen Davis | .75 | .30 |
| ❏ 197 Orronde Gadsden | .50 | .20 |
| ❏ 198 Brad Hoover | .30 | .10 |
| ❏ 199 La'Roi Glover | .30 | .10 |
| ❏ 200 Donovan McNabb | 1.00 | .40 |
| ❏ 201 Jerry Porter | .50 | .20 |
| ❏ 202 Robert Smith | .50 | .20 |
| ❏ 203 Justin Watson | .30 | .10 |
| ❏ 204 Tim Biakabutuka | .50 | .20 |
| ❏ 205 Laveranues Coles | .75 | .30 |
| ❏ 206 Marshall Faulk | 1.00 | .40 |
| ❏ 207 Jim Harbaugh | .50 | .20 |
| ❏ 208 Doug Johnson | .30 | .10 |
| ❏ 209 Tee Martin | .50 | .20 |
| ❏ 210 Muhsin Muhammad | .50 | .20 |
| ❏ 211 Darnay Scott | .30 | .10 |
| ❏ 212 Jeremiah Trotter | .50 | .20 |
| ❏ 213 Troy Aikman | 1.25 | .50 |
| ❏ 214 Kyle Brady | .30 | .10 |
| ❏ 215 Sam Gash | .30 | .10 |
| ❏ 216 Darren Howard | .30 | .10 |
| ❏ 217 Donald Hayes | .30 | .10 |
| ❏ 218 Freddie Jones | .30 | .10 |
| ❏ 219 Ed McCaffrey | .75 | .30 |
| ❏ 220 David Patten | .30 | .10 |
| ❏ 221 Brian Griese | .75 | .30 |
| ❏ 222 Dedric Ward | .30 | .10 |
| ❏ 223 Jerome Bettis | .75 | .30 |
| ❏ 224 Greg Clark | .30 | .10 |
| ❏ 225 Bobby Engram | .50 | .20 |
| ❏ 226 Matt Hasselbeck | .50 | .20 |
| ❏ 227 James Jett | .30 | .10 |
| ❏ 228 Peyton Manning | 2.00 | .75 |
| ❏ 229 Randy Moss | 1.50 | .60 |
| ❏ 230 Warren Sapp | .50 | .20 |
| ❏ 231 James Thrash | .30 | .20 |
| ❏ 232 Mike Alstott | .75 | .30 |
| ❏ 233 Tim Brown | .75 | .30 |
| ❏ 234 Randall Cunningham | .75 | .30 |
| ❏ 235 Antonio Freeman | .75 | .30 |
| ❏ 236 Torry Holt | .75 | .30 |
| ❏ 237 Jevon Kearse | .50 | .20 |
| ❏ 238 James McKnight | .50 | .20 |
| ❏ 239 Marcus Pollard | .30 | .10 |
| ❏ 240 Lamar Smith | .50 | .20 |
| ❏ 241 Peter Warrick | .75 | .30 |
| ❏ 242 Donnell Bennett | .30 | .10 |
| ❏ 243 Joe Johnson | .30 | .10 |
| ❏ 244 Troy Edwards | .30 | .10 |
| ❏ 245 Trent Green | .75 | .30 |
| ❏ 246 Jason Taylor | .50 | .20 |
| ❏ 247 Aeneas Williams | .30 | .10 |
| ❏ 248 Johnnie Morton | .50 | .20 |
| ❏ 249 Frank Sanders | .30 | .10 |
| ❏ 250 Jason Sehorn | .30 | .10 |
| ❏ 251 Chris Weinke RC | 6.00 | 2.50 |
| ❏ 252 Bobby Newcombe RC | 4.00 | 1.50 |
| ❏ 253 LaDainian Tomlinson RC | 40.00 | 20.00 |
| ❏ 254 Chad Johnson RC | 15.00 | 6.00 |
| ❏ 255 Derrick Gibson RC | 4.00 | 1.50 |
| ❏ 256 Sage Rosenfels RC | 6.00 | 2.50 |
| ❏ 257 LaMont Jordan RC | 12.00 | 5.00 |
| ❏ 258 Mike McMahon RC | 6.00 | 2.50 |
| ❏ 259 Vinny Sutherland RC | 4.00 | 1.50 |
| ❏ 260 Drew Brees RC | 20.00 | 10.00 |
| ❏ 261 Deuce McAllister RC | 12.00 | 5.00 |
| ❏ 262 Kevan Barlow RC | 6.00 | 2.50 |
| ❏ 263 Jamar Fletcher RC | 4.00 | 1.50 |
| ❏ 264 Gerard Warren RC | 6.00 | 2.50 |
| ❏ 265 Todd Heap RC | 6.00 | 2.50 |
| ❏ 266 Travis Henry RC | 6.00 | 2.50 |
| ❏ 267 Quincy Morgan RC | 6.00 | 2.50 |
| ❏ 268 Anthony Thomas RC | 6.00 | 2.50 |
| ❏ 269 Andre Carter RC | 6.00 | 2.50 |
| ❏ 270 Freddie Mitchell RC | 6.00 | 2.50 |

| | | |
|---|---|---|
| ❏ 271 Richard Seymour RC | 6.00 | 2.50 |
| ❏ 272 Josh Booty RC | 6.00 | 2.50 |
| ❏ 273 Robert Ferguson RC | 6.00 | 2.50 |
| ❏ 274 Marques Tuiasosopo RC | 6.00 | 2.50 |
| ❏ 275 Reggie Wayne RC | 12.00 | 5.00 |
| ❏ 276 Jabari Holloway RC | 4.00 | 1.50 |
| ❏ 277 Rudi Johnson RC | 12.00 | 5.00 |
| ❏ 278 Michael Bennett RC | 6.00 | 2.50 |
| ❏ 279 Snoop Minnis RC | 4.00 | 1.50 |
| ❏ 280 Dan Morgan RC | 6.00 | 2.50 |
| ❏ 281 Rod Gardner RC | 6.00 | 2.50 |
| ❏ 282 Jesse Palmer RC | 6.00 | 2.50 |
| ❏ 283 Michael Vick RC | 12.00 | 5.00 |
| ❏ 284 Chris Chambers RC | 10.00 | 4.00 |
| ❏ 285 James Jackson RC | 6.00 | 2.50 |
| ❏ 286 David Terrell RC | 6.00 | 2.50 |
| ❏ 287 Koren Robinson RC | 6.00 | 2.50 |
| ❏ 288 Travis Minor RC | 4.00 | 1.50 |
| ❏ 289 Santana Moss RC | 10.00 | 4.00 |
| ❏ 290 Josh Heupel RC | 6.00 | 2.50 |
| ❏ 291 Jamal Reynolds RC | 6.00 | 2.50 |
| ❏ 292 Ken-Yon Rambo RC | 4.00 | 1.50 |
| ❏ 293 Cedrick Wilson RC | 6.00 | 2.50 |
| ❏ 294 Alge Crumpler RC | 8.00 | 3.00 |
| ❏ 295 Fred Smoot RC | 6.00 | 2.50 |
| ❏ 296 Dan Alexander RC | 6.00 | 2.50 |
| ❏ 297 Tim Hasselbeck RC | 6.00 | 2.50 |
| ❏ 298 Will Allen RC | 4.00 | 1.50 |
| ❏ 299 Keith Adams RC | 4.00 | 1.50 |
| ❏ 300 Heath Evans RC | 4.00 | 1.50 |
| ❏ 301 Quincy Carter RC | 6.00 | 2.50 |
| ❏ 302 Derrick Blaylock RC | 6.00 | 2.50 |
| ❏ 303 Correll Buckhalter RC | 6.00 | 2.50 |
| ❏ 304 A.J. Feeley RC | 6.00 | 2.50 |
| ❏ 305 Milton Wynn RC | 4.00 | 1.50 |
| ❏ 306 Kevin Kasper RC | 6.00 | 2.50 |
| ❏ 307 Justin McCareins RC | 6.00 | 2.50 |
| ❏ 308 Dave Dickenson RC | 4.00 | 1.50 |
| ❏ 309 Steve Smith RC | 15.00 | 7.50 |
| ❏ 310 Moran Norris RC | 2.50 | 1.00 |

## 2002 Ultra

| | | |
|---|---|---|
| ❏ COMP.SET w/o SP's (200) | 25.00 | 10.00 |
| ❏ 1 Donovan McNabb | 1.00 | .40 |
| ❏ 2 Chad Pennington | 1.00 | .40 |
| ❏ 3 Shaun Alexander | 1.00 | .40 |
| ❏ 4 Corey Dillon | .50 | .20 |
| ❏ 5 Kurt Warner | .75 | .30 |
| ❏ 6 Ed McCaffrey | .75 | .30 |
| ❏ 7 Hugh Douglas | .30 | .10 |
| ❏ 8 Tony Gonzalez | .50 | .20 |
| ❏ 9 Travis Taylor | .50 | .20 |
| ❏ 10 Tony Boselli | .30 | .10 |
| ❏ 11 Chad Scott | .30 | .10 |
| ❏ 12 Ernie Conwell | .30 | .10 |
| ❏ 13 Brad Johnson | .50 | .20 |
| ❏ 14 Donald Hayes | .30 | .10 |
| ❏ 15 Emmitt Smith | 2.00 | .75 |
| ❏ 16 Jimmy Smith | .50 | .20 |
| ❏ 17 Anthony Becht | .30 | .10 |
| ❏ 18 Rod Gardner | .50 | .20 |
| ❏ 19 Muhsin Muhammad | .50 | .20 |
| ❏ 20 Troy Hambrick | .30 | .10 |
| ❏ 21 Keenan McCardell | .30 | .10 |
| ❏ 22 Laveranues Coles | .50 | .20 |
| ❏ 23 Kevin Dyson | .50 | .20 |
| ❏ 24 Grant Wistrom | .30 | .10 |

|  |  | | |
|---|---|---|---|
| ☐ 25 | Eric Moulds | .50 | .20 |
| ☐ 26 | Nate Clements | .30 | .10 |
| ☐ 27 | Terrell Davis | .75 | .30 |
| ☐ 28 | Aaron Glenn | .30 | .10 |
| ☐ 29 | Eric Hicks | .30 | .10 |
| ☐ 30 | Tiki Barber | .75 | .30 |
| ☐ 31 | Jake Plummer | .50 | .20 |
| ☐ 32 | Junior Seau | .75 | .30 |
| ☐ 33 | Marshall Faulk | .75 | .30 |
| ☐ 34 | Warrick Dunn | .75 | .30 |
| ☐ 35 | Bill Gramatica | .30 | .10 |
| ☐ 36 | Tim Couch | .50 | .20 |
| ☐ 37 | Kabeer Gbaja-Biamila | .50 | .20 |
| ☐ 38 | Kailee Wong | .30 | .10 |
| ☐ 39 | David Patten | .30 | .10 |
| ☐ 40 | Correll Buckhalter | .50 | .20 |
| ☐ 41 | Troy Brown | .50 | .20 |
| ☐ 42 | Drew Bledsoe | 1.00 | .40 |
| ☐ 43 | Travis Henry | .75 | .30 |
| ☐ 44 | Jim Miller | .30 | .10 |
| ☐ 45 | Rod Smith | .50 | .20 |
| ☐ 46 | Tai Streets | .30 | .10 |
| ☐ 47 | Snoop Minnis | .30 | .10 |
| ☐ 48 | Ron Dayne | .50 | .20 |
| ☐ 49 | Tyrone Wheatley | .50 | .20 |
| ☐ 50 | LaDainian Tomlinson | 1.25 | .50 |
| ☐ 51 | Akili Smith | .30 | .10 |
| ☐ 52 | Warren Sapp | .50 | .20 |
| ☐ 53 | Adam Archuleta | .30 | .10 |
| ☐ 54 | Chris Fuamatu-Ma'afala | .30 | .10 |
| ☐ 55 | Marty Booker | .30 | .10 |
| ☐ 56 | Trevor Pryce | .30 | .10 |
| ☐ 57 | Peyton Manning | 1.50 | .60 |
| ☐ 58 | Lamar Smith | .50 | .20 |
| ☐ 59 | Amani Toomer | .50 | .20 |
| ☐ 60 | Greg Biekert | .30 | .10 |
| ☐ 61 | Marcellus Wiley | .30 | .10 |
| ☐ 62 | Ahmed Plummer | .30 | .10 |
| ☐ 63 | Mike Alstott | .75 | .30 |
| ☐ 64 | Gary Walker | .30 | .10 |
| ☐ 65 | Champ Bailey | .50 | .20 |
| ☐ 66 | Chris Redman | .30 | .10 |
| ☐ 67 | David Terrell | .75 | .30 |
| ☐ 68 | Mike McMahon | .75 | .30 |
| ☐ 69 | Marvin Harrison | .75 | .30 |
| ☐ 70 | Jay Fiedler | .50 | .20 |
| ☐ 71 | JaJuan Dawson | .30 | .10 |
| ☐ 72 | Charlie Garner | .50 | .20 |
| ☐ 73 | Curtis Conway | .30 | .10 |
| ☐ 74 | J.J. Stokes | .50 | .20 |
| ☐ 75 | Ronde Barber | .30 | .10 |
| ☐ 76 | Alge Crumpler | .50 | .20 |
| ☐ 77 | Jamir Miller | .30 | .10 |
| ☐ 78 | Brett Favre | 2.00 | .75 |
| ☐ 79 | Randy Moss | 1.50 | .60 |
| ☐ 80 | Joe Horn | .50 | .20 |
| ☐ 81 | Hines Ward | .75 | .30 |
| ☐ 82 | Lawyer Milloy | .50 | .20 |
| ☐ 83 | Aeneas Williams | .30 | .10 |
| ☐ 84 | Chris McAlister | .30 | .10 |
| ☐ 85 | Anthony Thomas | .50 | .20 |
| ☐ 86 | Johnnie Morton | .50 | .20 |
| ☐ 87 | Edgerrin James | 1.00 | .40 |
| ☐ 88 | Chris Chambers | .75 | .30 |
| ☐ 89 | Michael Strahan | .50 | .20 |
| ☐ 90 | Charles Woodson | .50 | .20 |
| ☐ 91 | Tim Dwight | .50 | .20 |
| ☐ 92 | Kevan Barlow | .50 | .20 |
| ☐ 93 | Donnie Abraham | .30 | .10 |
| ☐ 94 | Peter Boulware | .30 | .10 |
| ☐ 95 | Marcus Robinson | .50 | .20 |
| ☐ 96 | Shaun Rogers | .30 | .10 |
| ☐ 97 | Dominic Rhodes | .50 | .20 |
| ☐ 98 | Zach Thomas | .75 | .30 |
| ☐ 99 | Kerry Collins | .50 | .20 |
| ☐ 100 | Tim Brown | .75 | .30 |
| ☐ 101 | Garrison Hearst | .50 | .20 |
| ☐ 102 | Steve McNair | .75 | .30 |
| ☐ 103 | Fred Smoot | .30 | .10 |
| ☐ 104 | Isaac Bruce | .75 | .30 |
| ☐ 105 | Jamal Lewis | .75 | .30 |
| ☐ 106 | Brian Urlacher | 1.25 | .50 |
| ☐ 107 | Takeo Spikes | .30 | .10 |
| ☐ 108 | Marcus Pollard | .30 | .10 |
| ☐ 109 | Jason Taylor | .30 | .10 |
| ☐ 110 | Deuce McAllister | 1.00 | .40 |
| ☐ 111 | Jerry Rice | 1.50 | .60 |
| ☐ 112 | Terrell Owens | .75 | .30 |
| ☐ 113 | Eddie George | .75 | .30 |
| ☐ 114 | Rob Morris | .30 | .10 |
| ☐ 115 | Mike Brown | .75 | .30 |
| ☐ 116 | Joey Galloway | .50 | .20 |
| ☐ 117 | Fred Taylor | .75 | .30 |
| ☐ 118 | Rich Gannon | .75 | .30 |
| ☐ 119 | Chris Chandler | .50 | .20 |
| ☐ 120 | Koren Robinson | .50 | .20 |
| ☐ 121 | Dan Morgan | .30 | .10 |
| ☐ 122 | Rocket Ismail | .50 | .20 |
| ☐ 123 | Mark Brunell | .75 | .30 |
| ☐ 124 | John Abraham | .50 | .20 |
| ☐ 125 | Stephen Davis | .50 | .20 |
| ☐ 126 | Patrick Kerney | .30 | .10 |
| ☐ 127 | Anthony Henry | .30 | .10 |
| ☐ 128 | Scotty Anderson | .30 | .10 |
| ☐ 129 | Oronde Gadsden | .30 | .10 |
| ☐ 130 | Willie Jackson | .30 | .10 |
| ☐ 131 | Kendrell Bell | .75 | .30 |
| ☐ 132 | Ray Lewis | .75 | .30 |
| ☐ 133 | Quincy Carter | .50 | .20 |
| ☐ 134 | James Stewart | .50 | .20 |
| ☐ 135 | Travis Minor | .30 | .10 |
| ☐ 136 | Kyle Turley | .30 | .10 |
| ☐ 137 | Jason Gildon | .30 | .10 |
| ☐ 138 | David Boston | .75 | .30 |
| ☐ 139 | Justin Smith | .30 | .10 |
| ☐ 140 | Jamie Sharper | .30 | .10 |
| ☐ 141 | Antowain Smith | .50 | .20 |
| ☐ 142 | Freddie Mitchell | .50 | .20 |
| ☐ 143 | Frank Sanders | .30 | .10 |
| ☐ 144 | Kevin Johnson | .50 | .20 |
| ☐ 145 | Darren Sharper | .30 | .10 |
| ☐ 146 | Eric Johnson | .30 | .10 |
| ☐ 147 | Ty Law | .75 | .30 |
| ☐ 148 | James Thrash | .50 | .20 |
| ☐ 149 | Matt Hasselbeck | .50 | .20 |
| ☐ 150 | Peerless Price | .50 | .20 |
| ☐ 151 | T.J. Houshmandzadeh | .50 | .20 |
| ☐ 152 | Mike Anderson | .75 | .30 |
| ☐ 153 | Jermaine Lewis | .30 | .10 |
| ☐ 154 | Trent Green | .50 | .20 |
| ☐ 155 | Ron Dixon | .30 | .10 |
| ☐ 156 | Duce Staley | .75 | .30 |
| ☐ 157 | Drew Brees | .75 | .30 |
| ☐ 158 | Torry Holt | .75 | .30 |
| ☐ 159 | Keyshawn Johnson | .75 | .30 |
| ☐ 160 | Michael Vick | 1.50 | .60 |
| ☐ 161 | Benjamin Gay | .30 | .10 |
| ☐ 162 | Bill Schroeder | .50 | .20 |
| ☐ 163 | Byron Chamberlain | .30 | .10 |
| ☐ 164 | Tedy Bruschi | .75 | .30 |
| ☐ 165 | Kordell Stewart | .50 | .20 |
| ☐ 166 | Deltha O'Neal | .30 | .10 |
| ☐ 167 | Quincy Morgan | .30 | .10 |
| ☐ 168 | Bubba Franks | .50 | .20 |
| ☐ 169 | Daunte Culpepper | .75 | .30 |
| ☐ 170 | Ricky Williams | 4.00 | 1.50 |
| ☐ 171 | Plaxico Burress | .50 | .20 |
| ☐ 172 | Trent Dilfer | .50 | .20 |
| ☐ 173 | Steve Smith | .75 | .30 |
| ☐ 174 | Greg Ellis | .30 | .10 |
| ☐ 175 | Tony Brackens | .30 | .10 |
| ☐ 176 | Santana Moss | .75 | .30 |
| ☐ 177 | Frank Wycheck | .30 | .10 |
| ☐ 178 | Michael Pittman | .30 | .10 |
| ☐ 179 | Peter Warrick | .50 | .20 |
| ☐ 180 | Antonio Freeman | .75 | .30 |
| ☐ 181 | Tom Brady | 2.00 | .75 |
| ☐ 182 | Bobby Taylor | .30 | .10 |
| ☐ 183 | Jeff Garcia | .75 | .30 |
| ☐ 184 | Darrell Jackson | .50 | .20 |
| ☐ 185 | Chris Weinke | .30 | .10 |
| ☐ 186 | Darren Woodson | .30 | .10 |
| ☐ 187 | Hardy Nickerson | .30 | .10 |
| ☐ 188 | Wayne Chrebet | .50 | .20 |
| ☐ 189 | Samari Rolle | .30 | .10 |
| ☐ 190 | Jamal Anderson | .50 | .20 |
| ☐ 191 | James Jackson | .30 | .10 |
| ☐ 192 | Ahman Green | .75 | .30 |
| ☐ 193 | Michael Bennett | .50 | .20 |
| ☐ 194 | Aaron Brooks | .75 | .30 |
| ☐ 195 | Jerome Bettis | .75 | .30 |
| ☐ 196 | Jay Riemersma | .30 | .10 |
| ☐ 197 | Brian Griese | .75 | .30 |
| ☐ 198 | Priest Holmes | 1.00 | .40 |
| ☐ 199 | Curtis Martin | .75 | .30 |
| ☐ 200 | Derrick Mason | .50 | .20 |
| ☐ 201 | Antonio Bryant RC | 5.00 | 2.00 |
| ☐ 202 | David Carr RC | 6.00 | 2.50 |
| ☐ 203 | Eric Crouch RC | 5.00 | 2.00 |
| ☐ 204 | Freddie Milons RC | 4.00 | 1.50 |
| ☐ 205 | Najeh Davenport RC | 5.00 | 2.00 |
| ☐ 206 | Rohan Davey RC | 5.00 | 2.00 |
| ☐ 207 | T.J. Duckett RC | 5.00 | 2.00 |
| ☐ 208 | DeShaun Foster RC | 5.00 | 2.00 |
| ☐ 209 | Jabar Gaffney RC | 5.00 | 2.00 |
| ☐ 210 | William Green RC | 5.00 | 2.00 |
| ☐ 211 | Joey Harrington RC | 6.00 | 2.50 |
| ☐ 212 | Travis Stephens RC | 4.00 | 1.50 |
| ☐ 213 | Julius Peppers RC | 10.00 | 4.00 |
| ☐ 214 | Adrian Peterson RC | 6.00 | 2.50 |
| ☐ 215 | Josh Reed RC | 5.00 | 2.00 |
| ☐ 216 | Mike Williams RC | 5.00 | 2.00 |
| ☐ 217 | Javon Walker RC | 8.00 | 3.00 |
| ☐ 218 | Marquise Walker RC | 4.00 | 1.50 |
| ☐ 219 | Patrick Ramsey RC | 5.00 | 2.00 |
| ☐ 220 | Lamar Gordon RC | 5.00 | 2.00 |
| ☐ 221 | David Garrard RC | 10.00 | 4.00 |
| ☐ 222 | Major Applewhite RC | 5.00 | 2.00 |
| ☐ 223 | Andre Davis RC | 4.00 | 1.50 |
| ☐ 224 | Roy Williams RC | 10.00 | 4.00 |
| ☐ 225 | Tim Carter RC | 4.00 | 1.50 |
| ☐ 226 | Ron Johnson RC | 4.00 | 1.50 |
| ☐ 227 | Randy Fasani RC | 4.00 | 1.50 |
| ☐ 228 | Ashley Lelie RC | 5.00 | 2.00 |
| ☐ 229 | Ladell Betts RC | 5.00 | 2.00 |
| ☐ 230 | Antwaan Randle El RC | 5.00 | 2.00 |
| ☐ 231 | Jonathan Wells RC | 5.00 | 2.00 |
| ☐ 232 | Brian Westbrook RC | 12.00 | 5.00 |
| ☐ 233 | Clinton Portis RC | 15.00 | 6.00 |
| ☐ 234 | Luke Staley RC | 4.00 | 1.50 |
| ☐ 235 | Cliff Russell RC | 4.00 | 1.50 |
| ☐ 236 | Jeremy Shockey RC | 8.00 | 3.00 |
| ☐ 237 | Donte Stallworth RC | 8.00 | 3.00 |
| ☐ 238 | Daniel Graham RC | 5.00 | 2.00 |
| ☐ 239 | Reche Caldwell RC | 5.00 | 2.00 |
| ☐ 240 | Ryan Sims RC | 5.00 | 2.00 |

## 2003 Ultra

|  |  | | |
|---|---|---|---|
| ☐ COMP.SET w/o SP's (160) | | 30.00 | 12.50 |
| ☐ 1 | Rich Gannon | .50 | .20 |
| ☐ 2 | Warren Sapp | .50 | .20 |
| ☐ 3 | Steve McNair | .75 | .30 |
| ☐ 4 | Donovan McNabb | 1.00 | .40 |
| ☐ 5 | Chad Pennington | 1.00 | .40 |
| ☐ 6 | Michael Vick | 2.00 | .75 |
| ☐ 7 | Hines Ward | .75 | .30 |
| ☐ 8 | Terrell Owens | .75 | .30 |
| ☐ 9 | Brett Favre | 2.00 | .75 |
| ☐ 10 | Jeremy Shockey | 1.25 | .50 |
| ☐ 11 | William Green | .50 | .20 |
| ☐ 12 | Marvin Harrison | .75 | .30 |
| ☐ 13 | Mark Brunell | .50 | .20 |
| ☐ 14 | Todd Heap | .50 | .20 |
| ☐ 15 | Tim Couch | .30 | .10 |
| ☐ 16 | Javon Walker | .50 | .20 |

| | | |
|---|---|---|
| ❏ 17 Zach Thomas | .50 | .20 |
| ❏ 18 Brian Westbrook | .50 | .20 |
| ❏ 19 Matt Hasselbeck | .50 | .20 |
| ❏ 20 Jevon Kearse | .50 | .20 |
| ❏ 21 David Boston | .50 | .20 |
| ❏ 22 Michael Bennett | .50 | .20 |
| ❏ 23 James Mungro | .30 | .10 |
| ❏ 24 Antowain Smith | .50 | .20 |
| ❏ 25 Laveranues Coles | .50 | .20 |
| ❏ 26 Curtis Conway | .30 | .10 |
| ❏ 27 Peerless Price | .50 | .20 |
| ❏ 28 Michael Strahan | .50 | .20 |
| ❏ 29 Tommy Maddox | .75 | .30 |
| ❏ 30 Dennis Northcutt | .50 | .20 |
| ❏ 31 Rod Gardner | .50 | .20 |
| ❏ 32 Marcel Shipp | .50 | .20 |
| ❏ 33 Quincy Morgan | .50 | .20 |
| ❏ 34 Reggie Wayne | .50 | .20 |
| ❏ 35 Troy Brown | .30 | .10 |
| ❏ 36 John Abraham | .30 | .10 |
| ❏ 37 Tim Dwight | .50 | .20 |
| ❏ 38 Jamal Lewis | .75 | .30 |
| ❏ 39 Chad Hutchinson | .30 | .10 |
| ❏ 40 Jerramy Stevens | .30 | .10 |
| ❏ 41 Deion Branch | .75 | .30 |
| ❏ 42 Jake Plummer | .50 | .20 |
| ❏ 43 Junior Seau | .75 | .30 |
| ❏ 44 T.J. Duckett | .50 | .20 |
| ❏ 45 Emmitt Smith | 2.00 | .75 |
| ❏ 46 Edgerrin James | .75 | .30 |
| ❏ 47 David Patten | .30 | .10 |
| ❏ 48 Charlie Garner | .50 | .20 |
| ❏ 49 Quentin Jammer | .30 | .10 |
| ❏ 50 Corey Dillon | .50 | .20 |
| ❏ 51 Rod Smith | .50 | .20 |
| ❏ 52 Marc Boerigter | .50 | .20 |
| ❏ 53 Michael Lewis | .30 | .10 |
| ❏ 54 Kendrell Bell | .50 | .20 |
| ❏ 55 Isaac Bruce | .75 | .30 |
| ❏ 56 Warrick Dunn | .50 | .20 |
| ❏ 57 Antonio Bryant | .50 | .20 |
| ❏ 58 Peyton Manning | 1.25 | .50 |
| ❏ 59 Ty Law | .50 | .20 |
| ❏ 60 Jerry Rice | 1.50 | .60 |
| ❏ 61 Jeff Garcia | .75 | .30 |
| ❏ 62 Joey Galloway | .50 | .20 |
| ❏ 63 Aaron Glenn | .30 | .10 |
| ❏ 64 Aaron Brooks | .50 | .20 |
| ❏ 65 Tim Brown | .75 | .30 |
| ❏ 66 David Terrell | .50 | .20 |
| ❏ 67 Fred Smoot | .30 | .10 |
| ❏ 68 Brian Finneran | .30 | .10 |
| ❏ 69 Roy Williams | .75 | .30 |
| ❏ 70 Corey Bradford | .30 | .10 |
| ❏ 71 Deuce McAllister | .75 | .30 |
| ❏ 72 Jerry Porter | .50 | .20 |
| ❏ 73 Kevan Barlow | .50 | .20 |
| ❏ 74 Keith Brooking | .30 | .10 |
| ❏ 75 Brian Urlacher | 1.25 | .50 |
| ❏ 76 Jabar Gaffney | .50 | .20 |
| ❏ 77 Randy Moss | 1.25 | .50 |
| ❏ 78 Charles Woodson | .50 | .20 |
| ❏ 79 Darrell Jackson | .50 | .20 |
| ❏ 80 John Lynch | .50 | .20 |
| ❏ 81 Chester Taylor | .30 | .10 |
| ❏ 82 Anthony Thomas | .50 | .20 |
| ❏ 83 Jonathan Wells | .30 | .10 |
| ❏ 84 Daunte Culpepper | .75 | .30 |
| ❏ 85 Phillip Buchanon | .30 | .10 |
| ❏ 86 Koren Robinson | .30 | .10 |
| ❏ 87 Ronde Barber | .30 | .10 |
| ❏ 88 Julius Peppers | .75 | .30 |
| ❏ 89 Clinton Portis | 1.25 | .50 |
| ❏ 90 Jay Fiedler | .50 | .20 |
| ❏ 91 Donte Stallworth | .75 | .30 |
| ❏ 92 Marc Bulger | .75 | .30 |
| ❏ 93 Joe Jurevicius | .30 | .10 |
| ❏ 94 Jon Kitna | .50 | .20 |
| ❏ 95 Ricky Williams | .75 | .30 |
| ❏ 96 Joe Horn | .50 | .20 |
| ❏ 97 Jerome Bettis | .75 | .30 |
| ❏ 98 Kurt Warner | .75 | .30 |
| ❏ 99 Travis Henry | .50 | .20 |
| ❏ 100 Ahman Green | .75 | .30 |
| ❏ 101 Jimmy Smith | .50 | .20 |
| ❏ 102 Curtis Martin | .75 | .30 |
| ❏ 103 Simeon Rice | .50 | .20 |
| ❏ 104 Patrick Ramsey | .75 | .30 |
| ❏ 105 Josh Reed | .50 | .20 |
| ❏ 106 James Stewart | .50 | .20 |
| ❏ 107 Trent Green | .50 | .20 |
| ❏ 108 Randy McMichael | .50 | .20 |
| ❏ 109 Amos Zereoue | .50 | .20 |
| ❏ 110 Keyshawn Johnson | .75 | .30 |
| ❏ 111 DeShaun Foster | .30 | .10 |
| ❏ 112 Kevin Johnson | .50 | .20 |
| ❏ 113 Dwight Freeney | .50 | .20 |
| ❏ 114 Tom Brady | 2.00 | .75 |
| ❏ 115 Santana Moss | .50 | .20 |
| ❏ 116 LaDainian Tomlinson | .75 | .30 |
| ❏ 117 Joey Harrington | 1.25 | .50 |
| ❏ 118 Priest Holmes | 1.00 | .40 |
| ❏ 119 Amani Toomer | .50 | .20 |
| ❏ 120 Plaxico Burress | .50 | .20 |
| ❏ 121 Brad Johnson | .50 | .20 |
| ❏ 122 Champ Bailey | .50 | .20 |
| ❏ 123 Muhsin Muhammad | .50 | .20 |
| ❏ 124 Ashley Lelie | .50 | .20 |
| ❏ 125 Tony Gonzalez | .50 | .20 |
| ❏ 126 Kerry Collins | .50 | .20 |
| ❏ 127 Antwaan Randle El | .75 | .30 |
| ❏ 128 Torry Holt | .75 | .30 |
| ❏ 129 Ladell Betts | .50 | .20 |
| ❏ 130 Travis Taylor | .50 | .20 |
| ❏ 131 Marty Booker | .50 | .20 |
| ❏ 132 Patrick Surtain | .30 | .10 |
| ❏ 133 Duce Staley | .50 | .20 |
| ❏ 134 Shaun Alexander | .75 | .30 |
| ❏ 135 Eddie George | .50 | .20 |
| ❏ 136 Eric Moulds | .50 | .20 |
| ❏ 137 David Carr | 1.25 | .50 |
| ❏ 138 Fred Taylor | .75 | .30 |
| ❏ 139 Wayne Chrebet | .50 | .20 |
| ❏ 140 Bobby Taylor | .30 | .10 |
| ❏ 141 Derrick Brooks | .50 | .20 |
| ❏ 142 Stephen Davis | .50 | .20 |
| ❏ 143 Ray Lewis | .75 | .30 |
| ❏ 144 Kelly Holcomb | .50 | .20 |
| ❏ 145 Terry Glenn | .30 | .10 |
| ❏ 146 Jason Taylor | .50 | .20 |
| ❏ 147 Todd Pinkston | .30 | .10 |
| ❏ 148 Derrick Mason | .50 | .20 |
| ❏ 149 Chad Johnson | .75 | .30 |
| ❏ 150 Ed McCaffrey | .50 | .20 |
| ❏ 151 Tiki Barber | .75 | .30 |
| ❏ 152 Drew Brees | .75 | .30 |
| ❏ 153 Marshall Faulk | .75 | .30 |
| ❏ 154 Drew Bledsoe | .75 | .30 |
| ❏ 155 Andre Davis | .30 | .10 |
| ❏ 156 Donald Driver | .50 | .20 |
| ❏ 157 Chris Chambers | .75 | .30 |
| ❏ 158 Brian Dawkins | .50 | .20 |
| ❏ 159 Garrison Hearst | .50 | .20 |
| ❏ 160 Frank Wycheck | .30 | .10 |
| ❏ 161 Carson Palmer RC | 15.00 | 6.00 |
| ❏ 162 Byron Leftwich RC | 8.00 | 3.00 |
| ❏ 163 Charles Rogers RC | 4.00 | 1.50 |
| ❏ 164 Andre Johnson RC | 8.00 | 3.00 |
| ❏ 165 Chris Simms RC | 6.00 | 2.50 |
| ❏ 166 Rex Grossman RC | 12.00 | 5.00 |
| ❏ 167 Brandon Lloyd RC | 4.00 | 1.50 |
| ❏ 168 Lee Suggs RC | 4.00 | 1.50 |
| ❏ 169 Larry Johnson RC | 10.00 | 4.00 |
| ❏ 170 Onterrio Smith RC | 4.00 | 1.50 |
| ❏ 171 Dave Ragone RC | 4.00 | 1.50 |
| ❏ 172 Taylor Jacobs RC | 3.00 | 1.25 |
| ❏ 173 Kelley Washington RC | 4.00 | 1.50 |
| ❏ 174 Bryant Johnson RC | 4.00 | 1.50 |
| ❏ 175 Kyle Boller RC | 6.00 | 2.50 |
| ❏ 176 Ken Dorsey RC | 4.00 | 1.50 |
| ❏ 177 Kliff Kingsbury RC | 3.00 | 1.25 |
| ❏ 178 Jason Gesser RC | 4.00 | 1.50 |
| ❏ 179 Brian St.Pierre RC | 4.00 | 1.50 |
| ❏ 180 Brad Banks RC | 3.00 | 1.25 |
| ❏ 181 Seneca Wallace RC | 4.00 | 1.50 |
| ❏ 182 Tony Romo RC | 25.00 | 12.50 |
| ❏ 183 Terrell Suggs RC | 6.00 | 2.50 |
| ❏ 184 Terence Newman RC | 8.00 | 3.00 |
| ❏ 185 Willis McGahee RC | 10.00 | 4.00 |
| ❏ 186 Justin Fargas RC | 4.00 | 1.50 |
| ❏ 187 Musa Smith RC | 4.00 | 1.50 |
| ❏ 188 Earnest Graham RC | 4.00 | 1.50 |
| ❏ 189 Chris Brown RC | 4.00 | 1.50 |
| ❏ 190 LaBrandon Toefield RC | 4.00 | 1.50 |
| ❏ 191 Bennie Joppru RC | 4.00 | 1.50 |
| ❏ 192 Jason Witten RC | 8.00 | 3.00 |
| ❏ 193 Anquan Boldin RC | 10.00 | 4.00 |
| ❏ 194 Talman Gardner RC | 4.00 | 1.50 |
| ❏ 195 Justin Gage RC | 4.00 | 1.50 |
| ❏ 196 Sam Aiken RC | 3.00 | 1.25 |
| ❏ 197 Kevin Curtis RC | 5.00 | 2.00 |
| ❏ 198 Terrence Edwards RC | 3.00 | 1.25 |
| ❏ U199 DeWayne Robertson RC | 4.00 | 1.50 |
| ❏ U200 Kevin Williams RC | 4.00 | 1.50 |
| ❏ U201 Marcus Trufant RC | 4.00 | 1.50 |
| ❏ U202 Jimmy Kennedy RC | 4.00 | 1.50 |
| ❏ U203 Ty Warren RC | 4.00 | 1.50 |
| ❏ U204 Michael Haynes RC | 4.00 | 1.50 |
| ❏ U205 Jerome McDougle RC | 4.00 | 1.50 |
| ❏ U206 Dallas Clark RC | 4.00 | 1.50 |
| ❏ U207 William Joseph RC | 4.00 | 1.50 |
| ❏ U208 Andre Woolfolk RC | 4.00 | 1.50 |
| ❏ U209 Bethel Johnson RC | 4.00 | 1.50 |
| ❏ U210 Teyo Johnson RC | 4.00 | 1.50 |
| ❏ U211 Tyrone Calico RC | 4.00 | 1.50 |
| ❏ U212 L.J. Smith RC | 4.00 | 1.50 |
| ❏ U213 Nate Burleson RC | 4.00 | 1.50 |
| ❏ U214 B.J. Askew RC | 4.00 | 1.50 |
| ❏ U215 Billy McMullen RC | 4.00 | 1.50 |
| ❏ U216 Domanick Davis RC | 4.00 | 1.50 |
| ❏ U217 Doug Gabriel RC | 4.00 | 1.50 |
| ❏ U218 Quentin Griffin RC | 4.00 | 1.50 |

## 2004 Ultra

| | | |
|---|---|---|
| ❏ COMP.SET w/o L13's (218) | 60.00 | 25.00 |
| ❏ COMP.SET w/o SP's (200) | 30.00 | 12.50 |
| ❏ COMP.UPDATE SET (21) | 40.00 | 15.00 |
| ❏ L13 201-213 ROOKIE ODDS 1:100H,1:530R | | |
| ❏ L13 ROOKIE PRINT RUN 500 SER.#'d SETS | | |
| ❏ 214-232 ROOKIE STATED ODDS 1:100R | | |
| ❏ U234-U254 ODDS 2:1 TRADITION HOT PACK | | |
| ❏ 1 Michael Vick | .75 | .30 |
| ❏ 2 Kelley Washington | .50 | .20 |
| ❏ 3 Rex Grossman | .75 | .30 |
| ❏ 4 Boss Bailey | .50 | .20 |
| ❏ 5 Johnnie Morton | .60 | .25 |
| ❏ 6 Michael Strahan | .60 | .25 |
| ❏ 7 Joey Porter | .50 | .20 |
| ❏ 8 Keenan McCardell | .50 | .20 |
| ❏ 9 Quincy Carter | .50 | .20 |
| ❏ 10 Travis Henry | .60 | .25 |
| ❏ 11 Bertrand Berry | .60 | .25 |
| ❏ 12 Marvin Harrison | .75 | .30 |
| ❏ 13 Ty Law | .60 | .25 |
| ❏ 14 Phillip Buchanon | .60 | .25 |
| ❏ 15 Kevan Barlow | .60 | .25 |
| ❏ 16 Eddie George | .60 | .25 |
| ❏ 17 Drew Bledsoe | .75 | .30 |
| ❏ 18 Antonio Bryant | .60 | .25 |
| ❏ 19 Marcus Pollard | .50 | .20 |
| ❏ 20 Brian Russell RC | .50 | .20 |
| ❏ 21 Santana Moss | .60 | .25 |
| ❏ 22 Julian Peterson | .60 | .25 |
| ❏ 23 Justin McCareins | .50 | .20 |
| ❏ 24 Ed Reed | .60 | .25 |

| | | |
|---|---|---|
| ❏ 25 Charles Tillman | .60 | .25 |
| ❏ 26 Dat Nguyen | .50 | .20 |
| ❏ 27 Ricky Manning | .50 | .20 |
| ❏ 28 Dwight Freeney | .75 | .30 |
| ❏ 29 Zach Thomas | .75 | .30 |
| ❏ 30 Tiki Barber | .75 | .30 |
| ❏ 31 Jay Riemersma | .50 | .20 |
| ❏ 32 Joe Jurevicius | .50 | .20 |
| ❏ 33 Marcel Shipp | .75 | .30 |
| ❏ 34 Justin Gage | .60 | .25 |
| ❏ 35 Charles Rogers | .60 | .25 |
| ❏ 36 Eddie Kennison | .60 | .25 |
| ❏ 37 Deion Branch | .60 | .25 |
| ❏ 38 Matt Hasselbeck | .75 | .30 |
| ❏ 39 L.J. Smith | .60 | .25 |
| ❏ 40 Jamal Lewis | .60 | .25 |
| ❏ 41 Muhsin Muhammad | .60 | .25 |
| ❏ 42 Terence Newman | .60 | .25 |
| ❏ 43 Jabar Gaffney | .60 | .25 |
| ❏ 44 Junior Seau | .75 | .30 |
| ❏ 45 Jeremy Shockey | .60 | .25 |
| ❏ 46 Hines Ward | .75 | .30 |
| ❏ 47 Brad Johnson | .60 | .25 |
| ❏ 48 Kyle Boller | .60 | .25 |
| ❏ 49 Steve Smith | .75 | .30 |
| ❏ 50 Quincy Morgan | .50 | .20 |
| ❏ 51 Corey Bradford | .60 | .25 |
| ❏ 52 Ricky Williams | .75 | .30 |
| ❏ 53 Amani Toomer | .60 | .25 |
| ❏ 54 Plaxico Burress | .60 | .25 |
| ❏ 55 Derrick Brooks | .60 | .25 |
| ❏ 56 Dre Bly | .50 | .20 |
| ❏ 57 Terrell Suggs | .60 | .25 |
| ❏ 58 DeShaun Foster | .60 | .25 |
| ❏ 59 Andre Davis | .50 | .20 |
| ❏ 60 Rod Smith | .60 | .25 |
| ❏ 61 Andre Johnson | .75 | .30 |
| ❏ 62 Randy McMichael | .50 | .20 |
| ❏ 63 Ike Hilliard | .60 | .25 |
| ❏ 64 Antwaan Randle El | .60 | .25 |
| ❏ 65 Warren Sapp | .60 | .25 |
| ❏ 66 LaBrandon Toefield | .50 | .20 |
| ❏ 67 Chad Johnson | .75 | .30 |
| ❏ 68 Javon Walker | .60 | .25 |
| ❏ 69 Jimmy Smith | .60 | .25 |
| ❏ 70 Donte Stallworth | .60 | .25 |
| ❏ 71 Brian Dawkins | .60 | .25 |
| ❏ 72 Leonard Little | .50 | .20 |
| ❏ 73 Ladell Betts | .60 | .25 |
| ❏ 74 Ray Lewis | .75 | .30 |
| ❏ 75 Stephen Davis | .60 | .25 |
| ❏ 76 Dennis Northcutt | .50 | .20 |
| ❏ 77 Ashley Lelie | .60 | .25 |
| ❏ 78 Billy Miller | .50 | .20 |
| ❏ 79 Chris Chambers | .60 | .25 |
| ❏ 80 John Abraham | .50 | .20 |
| ❏ 81 Quentin Jammer | .50 | .20 |
| ❏ 82 Isaac Bruce | .60 | .25 |
| ❏ 83 Peerless Price | .60 | .25 |
| ❏ 84 Jake Delhomme | .60 | .25 |
| ❏ 85 Lee Suggs | .60 | .25 |
| ❏ 86 Shannon Sharpe | .60 | .25 |
| ❏ 87 Domanick Davis | .75 | .30 |
| ❏ 88 Daunte Culpepper | .75 | .30 |
| ❏ 89 Shaun Ellis | .50 | .20 |
| ❏ 90 Drew Brees | .75 | .30 |
| ❏ 91 Torry Holt | .75 | .30 |
| ❏ 92 Alge Crumpler | .60 | .25 |
| ❏ 93 Mike Rucker | .50 | .20 |
| ❏ 94 Tim Couch | .60 | .25 |
| ❏ 95 Quentin Griffin | .60 | .25 |
| ❏ 96 David Carr | .60 | .25 |
| ❏ 97 Moe Williams | .50 | .20 |
| ❏ 98 Chad Pennington | .75 | .30 |
| ❏ 99 LaDainian Tomlinson | 1.25 | .50 |
| ❏ 100 Adam Archuleta | .50 | .20 |
| ❏ 101 Julius Peppers | .60 | .25 |
| ❏ 102 Clinton Portis | .75 | .30 |
| ❏ 103 Marcus Stroud | .50 | .20 |
| ❏ 104 Tom Brady | 2.00 | .75 |
| ❏ 105 Teyo Johnson | .60 | .25 |
| ❏ 106 Terrell Owens | .75 | .30 |
| ❏ 107 Keith Bulluck | .60 | .25 |
| ❏ 108 Eric Moulds | .60 | .25 |

| | | |
|---|---|---|
| ❏ 109 Jake Plummer | .60 | .25 |
| ❏ 110 Reggie Wayne | .60 | .25 |
| ❏ 111 Tedy Bruschi | .75 | .30 |
| ❏ 112 Rich Gannon | .60 | .25 |
| ❏ 113 Tony Parrish | .50 | .20 |
| ❏ 114 Steve McNair | .75 | .30 |
| ❏ 115 T.J. Duckett | .60 | .25 |
| ❏ 116 Peter Warrick | .60 | .25 |
| ❏ 117 Donald Driver | .75 | .30 |
| ❏ 118 Fred Taylor | .60 | .25 |
| ❏ 119 Joe Horn | .60 | .25 |
| ❏ 120 Jerry Porter | .60 | .25 |
| ❏ 121 Marc Bulger | .60 | .25 |
| ❏ 122 Trung Canidate | .50 | .20 |
| ❏ 123 Warrick Dunn | .60 | .25 |
| ❏ 124 Kelly Holcomb | .60 | .25 |
| ❏ 125 Robert Ferguson | .50 | .20 |
| ❏ 126 Byron Leftwich | .75 | .30 |
| ❏ 127 Michael Lewis | .60 | .25 |
| ❏ 128 Jerry Rice | 1.50 | .60 |
| ❏ 129 Marshall Faulk | .75 | .30 |
| ❏ 130 Patrick Ramsey | .60 | .25 |
| ❏ 131 Josh McCown | .60 | .25 |
| ❏ 132 Anthony Thomas | .60 | .25 |
| ❏ 133 Joey Harrington | .60 | .25 |
| ❏ 134 Dante Hall | .60 | .25 |
| ❏ 135 Daniel Graham | .50 | .20 |
| ❏ 136 Richard Seymour | .50 | .20 |
| ❏ 137 Brandon Lloyd | .50 | .20 |
| ❏ 138 Anquan Boldin | .75 | .30 |
| ❏ 139 Jon Kitna | .60 | .25 |
| ❏ 140 Nick Barnett | .60 | .25 |
| ❏ 141 Priest Holmes | .75 | .30 |
| ❏ 142 Bethel Johnson | .50 | .20 |
| ❏ 143 Shaun Alexander | .75 | .30 |
| ❏ 144 Todd Heap | .60 | .25 |
| ❏ 145 Brian Urlacher | .75 | .30 |
| ❏ 146 Peyton Manning | 1.50 | .60 |
| ❏ 147 Jason Taylor | .75 | .30 |
| ❏ 148 Kerry Collins | .60 | .25 |
| ❏ 149 Tommy Maddox | .60 | .25 |
| ❏ 150 Charles Lee | .50 | .20 |
| ❏ 151 Tim Rattay | .50 | .20 |
| ❏ 152 Carson Palmer | 1.00 | .40 |
| ❏ 153 Brett Favre | 2.00 | .75 |
| ❏ 154 Trent Green | .60 | .25 |
| ❏ 155 Aaron Brooks | .60 | .25 |
| ❏ 156 Brian Westbrook | .75 | .30 |
| ❏ 157 Itula Mili | .50 | .20 |
| ❏ 158 Keith Brooking | .50 | .20 |
| ❏ 159 Rudi Johnson | .60 | .25 |
| ❏ 160 Najeh Davenport | .60 | .25 |
| ❏ 161 Kevin Johnson | .50 | .20 |
| ❏ 162 Boo Williams | .50 | .20 |
| ❏ 163 Corey Simon | .60 | .25 |
| ❏ 164 Darrell Jackson | .60 | .25 |
| ❏ 165 Darnerien McCants | .50 | .20 |
| ❏ 166 Willis McGahee | .75 | .30 |
| ❏ 167 Terry Glenn | .60 | .25 |
| ❏ 168 Dallas Clark | .60 | .25 |
| ❏ 169 Randy Moss | 1.00 | .40 |
| ❏ 170 Charles Woodson | .75 | .30 |
| ❏ 171 Jeff Garcia | .75 | .30 |
| ❏ 172 Chris Brown | .60 | .25 |
| ❏ 173 Emmitt Smith | 2.00 | .75 |
| ❏ 174 Marty Booker | .60 | .25 |
| ❏ 175 Artose Pinner | .50 | .20 |
| ❏ 176 Tony Gonzalez | .75 | .30 |
| ❏ 177 Troy Brown | .60 | .25 |
| ❏ 178 Freddie Mitchell | .50 | .20 |
| ❏ 179 Marcus Trufant | .50 | .20 |
| ❏ 180 London Fletcher | .50 | .20 |
| ❏ 181 Roy Williams S | .75 | .30 |
| ❏ 182 Edgerrin James | .75 | .30 |
| ❏ 183 Michael Bennett | .60 | .25 |
| ❏ 184 Jerald Sowell | .50 | .20 |
| ❏ 185 David Boston | .60 | .25 |
| ❏ 186 Derrick Mason | .60 | .25 |
| ❏ 187 Bryant Johnson | .60 | .25 |
| ❏ 188 Corey Dillon | .60 | .25 |
| ❏ 189 Ahman Green | .75 | .30 |
| ❏ 190 Vonnie Holliday | .50 | .20 |
| ❏ 191 Deuce McAllister | .75 | .30 |
| ❏ 192 Donovan McNabb | .75 | .30 |

| | | |
|---|---|---|
| ❏ 193 Koren Robinson | .75 | .30 |
| ❏ 194 Laveranues Coles | .60 | .25 |
| ❏ 195 Takeo Spikes | .50 | .20 |
| ❏ 196 Richie Anderson | .50 | .20 |
| ❏ 197 Onterrio Smith | .50 | .20 |
| ❏ 198 Curtis Martin | .75 | .30 |
| ❏ 199 Antonio Gates | .75 | .30 |
| ❏ 200 Champ Bailey | .60 | .25 |
| ❏ 201 Eli Manning L13 RC | 60.00 | 25.00 |
| ❏ 202 Philip Rivers L13 RC | 40.00 | 15.00 |
| ❏ 203 Roy Williams L13 RC | 30.00 | 12.00 |
| ❏ 204 Drew Henson L13 RC | 8.00 | 3.00 |
| ❏ 205 Chris Perry L13 RC | 12.00 | 5.00 |
| ❏ 206 Larry Fitzgerald L13 RC | 40.00 | 15.00 |
| ❏ 207 Rashaun Woods L13 RC | 8.00 | 3.00 |
| ❏ 208 Reggie Williams L13 RC | 12.00 | 5.00 |
| ❏ 209 Mike Williams L13 RC | 10.00 | 4.00 |
| ❏ 210 Kellen Winslow L13 RC | 25.00 | 10.00 |
| ❏ 211 Steven Jackson L13 RC | 40.00 | 15.00 |
| ❏ 212 Kevin Jones L13 RC | 12.00 | 5.00 |
| ❏ 213 Ben Roethlisberger L13 RC | 80.00 | 30.00 |
| ❏ 214 Michael Turner RC | 6.00 | 2.50 |
| ❏ 215 Tatum Bell RC | 3.00 | 1.25 |
| ❏ 216 Quincy Wilson RC | 2.50 | 1.00 |
| ❏ 217 Devery Henderson RC | 3.00 | 1.25 |
| ❏ 218 Ernest Wilford RC | 3.00 | 1.25 |
| ❏ 219 Cody Pickett RC | 2.50 | 1.00 |
| ❏ 220 Ryan Dinwiddie RC | 2.50 | 1.00 |
| ❏ 221 J.P. Losman RC | 4.00 | 1.50 |
| ❏ 222 Derrick Knight RC | 2.00 | .75 |
| ❏ 223 Michael Jenkins RC | 3.00 | 1.25 |
| ❏ 224 Greg Jones RC | 3.00 | 1.25 |
| ❏ 225 Cedric Cobbs RC | 2.50 | 1.00 |
| ❏ 226 Will Poole RC | 3.00" | 1.25 |
| ❏ 227 Michael Clayton RC | 3.00 | 1.25 |
| ❏ 228 Sean Taylor RC | 3.00 | 1.25 |
| ❏ 229 Will Smith RC | 2.50 | 1.00 |
| ❏ 230 Jonathan Vilma RC | 3.00 | 1.25 |
| ❏ 231 Lee Evans RC | 4.00 | 1.50 |
| ❏ 232 Julius Jones RC | 8.00 | 3.00 |
| ❏ U234 D.J. Williams RC | 3.00 | 1.25 |
| ❏ U235 Mewelde Moore RC | 3.00 | 1.25 |
| ❏ U236 Ben Watson RC | 3.00 | 1.25 |
| ❏ U237 Robert Gallery RC | 3.00 | 1.25 |
| ❏ U238 DeAngelo Hall RC | 3.00 | 1.25 |
| ❏ U239 Luke McCown RC | 3.00 | 1.25 |
| ❏ U240 Ben Troupe RC | 2.50 | 1.00 |
| ❏ U241 Keary Colbert RC | 3.00 | 1.25 |
| ❏ U242 Matt Schaub RC | 10.00 | 4.00 |
| ❏ U243 Kenechi Udeze RC | 3.00 | 1.25 |
| ❏ U244 Jeff Smoker RC | 2.50 | 1.00 |
| ❏ U245 Derrick Hamilton RC | 2.00 | .75 |
| ❏ U246 Bernard Berrian RC | 3.00 | 1.25 |
| ❏ U247 Devard Darling RC | 2.50 | 1.00 |
| ❏ U248 Johnnie Morant RC | 2.50 | 1.00 |
| ❏ U249 Vince Wilfork RC | 3.00 | 1.25 |
| ❏ U250 Jerricho Cotchery RC | 3.00 | 1.25 |
| ❏ U251 Darius Watts RC | 2.50 | 1.00 |
| ❏ U252 Carlos Francis RC | 2.00 | .75 |
| ❏ U253 P.K. Sam RC | 2.00 | .75 |

### 2005 Ultra

| | | |
|---|---|---|
| ❏ COMP.SET w/o RC's (200) | 30.00 | 12.50 |
| ❏ 201-213 L13 PRINT RUN 599 SER.#'d SETS | | |
| ❏ OVERALL ROOKIE ODDS 1:4 HOB, 1:5 RET | | |
| ❏ 1 Peyton Manning | 1.25 | .50 |
| ❏ 2 Brian Westbrook | .75 | .30 |

|  |  | | |
|---|---|---|---|
| 3 | Daunte Culpepper | .75 | .30 |
| 4 | Marvin Harrison | .75 | .30 |
| 5 | Edgerrin James | .60 | .25 |
| 6 | Reggie Wayne | .60 | .25 |
| 7 | Michael Vick | .75 | .30 |
| 8 | Donte Stallworth | .60 | .25 |
| 9 | Brian Urlacher | .75 | .30 |
| 10 | Hines Ward | .75 | .30 |
| 11 | Charles Rogers | .50 | .20 |
| 12 | Roy Williams WR | .75 | .30 |
| 13 | Julius Peppers | .60 | .25 |
| 14 | Eric Moulds | .60 | .25 |
| 15 | Ray Lewis | .75 | .30 |
| 16 | Byron Leftwich | .60 | .25 |
| 17 | Fred Taylor | .75 | .30 |
| 18 | Andre Johnson | .60 | .25 |
| 19 | Travis Henry | .60 | .25 |
| 20 | Tom Brady | 1.50 | .60 |
| 21 | Drew Bledsoe | .75 | .30 |
| 22 | Tiki Barber | .75 | .30 |
| 23 | Larry Fitzgerald | .75 | .30 |
| 24 | Jeff Garcia | .60 | .25 |
| 25 | Rex Grossman | .75 | .30 |
| 26 | Larry Johnson | .75 | .30 |
| 27 | Curtis Martin | .75 | .30 |
| 28 | Chad Pennington | .75 | .30 |
| 29 | Dwight Freeney | .60 | .25 |
| 30 | Peerless Price | .50 | .20 |
| 31 | Rich Gannon | .60 | .25 |
| 32 | Matt Hasselbeck | .60 | .25 |
| 33 | Clinton Portis | .75 | .30 |
| 34 | Jerry Rice | 1.50 | .60 |
| 35 | Jeremy Shockey | .75 | .30 |
| 36 | Tony Gonzalez | .60 | .25 |
| 37 | Deuce McAllister | .75 | .30 |
| 38 | Shaun Alexander | .75 | .30 |
| 39 | Peter Warrick | .50 | .20 |
| 40 | Isaac Bruce | .60 | .25 |
| 41 | Antonio Bryant | .50 | .20 |
| 42 | Mike Alstott | .60 | .25 |
| 43 | Domanick Davis | .60 | .25 |
| 44 | Jake Delhomme | .75 | .30 |
| 45 | Santana Moss | .60 | .25 |
| 46 | Ahman Green | .75 | .30 |
| 47 | David Carr | .60 | .25 |
| 48 | Kyle Boller | .60 | .25 |
| 49 | Chris Chambers | .60 | .25 |
| 50 | Quentin Griffin | .60 | .25 |
| 51 | Donovan McNabb | .75 | .30 |
| 52 | Eli Manning | 1.50 | .60 |
| 53 | Julius Jones | .75 | .30 |
| 54 | Sean Taylor | .60 | .25 |
| 55 | Javon Walker | .60 | .25 |
| 56 | Randy Moss | .75 | .30 |
| 57 | Thomas Jones | .60 | .25 |
| 58 | Joey Harrington | .60 | .25 |
| 59 | Michael Boulware | .50 | .20 |
| 60 | Marshall Faulk | .75 | .30 |
| 61 | Tony Parrish | .50 | .20 |
| 62 | Bertrand Berry | .50 | .20 |
| 63 | Alge Crumpler | .60 | .25 |
| 64 | Aaron Brooks | .50 | .20 |
| 65 | Muhsin Muhammad | .60 | .25 |
| 66 | Simeon Rice | .50 | .20 |
| 67 | Corey Dillon | .60 | .25 |
| 68 | Willis McGahee | .75 | .30 |
| 69 | Ben Roethlisberger | 2.00 | .75 |
| 70 | Chad Johnson | .60 | .25 |
| 71 | Jamal Lewis | .60 | .25 |
| 72 | Drew Brees | .75 | .30 |
| 73 | LaDainian Tomlinson | 1.25 | .50 |
| 74 | Reuben Droughns | .50 | .20 |
| 75 | Priest Holmes | .75 | .30 |
| 76 | Jerry Porter | .60 | .25 |
| 77 | Chris Brown | .60 | .25 |
| 78 | Steve McNair | .75 | .30 |
| 79 | Troy Brown | .50 | .20 |
| 80 | Jerome Bettis | .75 | .30 |
| 81 | Patrick Kerney | .60 | .25 |
| 82 | Terrell Owens | .75 | .30 |
| 83 | Brett Favre | 2.00 | .75 |
| 84 | Carson Palmer | .75 | .30 |
| 85 | Jake Plummer | .60 | .25 |
| 86 | Tedy Bruschi | .75 | .30 |
| 87 | Plaxico Burress | .60 | .25 |
| 88 | Jonathan Vilma | .60 | .25 |
| 89 | Ed Reed | .60 | .25 |
| 90 | Brian Dawkins | .60 | .25 |
| 91 | Anquan Boldin | .60 | .25 |
| 92 | Vinny Testaverde | .60 | .25 |
| 93 | David Givens | .60 | .25 |
| 94 | Rudi Johnson | .60 | .25 |
| 95 | Philip Rivers | .75 | .30 |
| 96 | Jimmy Smith | .60 | .25 |
| 97 | Emmitt Smith | 1.50 | .60 |
| 98 | Eric Johnson | .50 | .20 |
| 99 | Jeremiah Trotter | .50 | .20 |
| 100 | Duce Staley | .60 | .25 |
| 101 | Warrick Dunn | .60 | .25 |
| 102 | Nate Burleson | .60 | .25 |
| 103 | Marc Bulger | .60 | .25 |
| 104 | Joe Horn | .60 | .25 |
| 105 | Rodney Harrison | .60 | .25 |
| 106 | Zach Thomas | .75 | .30 |
| 107 | Michael Clayton | .60 | .25 |
| 108 | Derrick Brooks | .60 | .25 |
| 109 | Michael Lewis | .50 | .20 |
| 110 | Kurt Warner | .75 | .30 |
| 111 | Jason Witten | .60 | .25 |
| 112 | Roy Williams S | .60 | .25 |
| 113 | Kabeer Gbaja-Biamila | .75 | .30 |
| 114 | Torry Holt | .60 | .25 |
| 115 | Tim Rattay | .50 | .20 |
| 116 | Josh McCown | .60 | .25 |
| 117 | Brian Griese | .60 | .25 |
| 118 | Patrick Ramsey | .60 | .25 |
| 119 | A.J. Feeley | .50 | .20 |
| 120 | Kerry Collins | .60 | .25 |
| 121 | Trent Green | .60 | .25 |
| 122 | Billy Volek | .50 | .20 |
| 123 | Travis Taylor | .50 | .20 |
| 124 | T.J. Houshmandzadeh | .60 | .25 |
| 125 | James Farrior | .50 | .20 |
| 126 | Bryan Scott | .50 | .20 |
| 127 | Lito Sheppard | .60 | .25 |
| 128 | David Patten | .50 | .20 |
| 129 | Antwaan Randle El | .60 | .25 |
| 130 | Antonio Gates | .75 | .30 |
| 131 | Brandon Stokley | .50 | .20 |
| 132 | Keyshawn Johnson | .60 | .25 |
| 133 | Amani Toomer | .50 | .20 |
| 134 | Shawn Springs | .50 | .20 |
| 135 | Eddie George | .60 | .25 |
| 136 | Kevin Jones | .60 | .25 |
| 137 | Darrell Jackson | .60 | .25 |
| 138 | Ricky Manning | .50 | .20 |
| 139 | Laveranues Coles | .60 | .25 |
| 140 | Champ Bailey | .60 | .25 |
| 141 | Rod Smith | .60 | .25 |
| 142 | Ashley Lelie | .50 | .20 |
| 143 | Charles Woodson | .60 | .25 |
| 144 | Drew Bennett | .60 | .25 |
| 145 | Derrick Mason | .60 | .25 |
| 146 | Donovin Darius | .50 | .20 |
| 147 | Dennis Northcutt | .50 | .20 |
| 148 | Jamie Sharper | .50 | .20 |
| 149 | Steven Jackson | 1.00 | .40 |
| 150 | David Terrell | .50 | .20 |
| 151 | Onterrio Smith | .50 | .20 |
| 152 | Donald Driver | .75 | .30 |
| 153 | Antoine Winfield | .60 | .25 |
| 154 | Michael Pittman | .60 | .25 |
| 155 | Dan Morgan | .50 | .20 |
| 156 | Troy Polamalu | 1.00 | .40 |
| 157 | Willie McGinest | .60 | .25 |
| 158 | Justin McCareins | .60 | .25 |
| 159 | Allen Rossum | .50 | .20 |
| 160 | Deion Branch | .60 | .25 |
| 161 | Deion Sanders | 1.00 | .40 |
| 162 | Josh Reed | .50 | .20 |
| 163 | Lee Evans | .60 | .25 |
| 164 | Lee Suggs | .60 | .25 |
| 165 | Dante Hall | .60 | .25 |
| 166 | Eddie Kennison | .50 | .20 |
| 167 | Ken Dorsey | .50 | .20 |
| 168 | Andre Dyson | .50 | .20 |
| 169 | Keith Bulluck | .50 | .20 |
| 170 | Todd Pinkston | .50 | .20 |
| 171 | Jevon Kearse | .60 | .25 |
| 172 | Dunta Robinson | .50 | .20 |
| 173 | Steve Smith | .75 | .30 |
| 174 | Koren Robinson | .60 | .25 |
| 175 | Freddie Mitchell | .50 | .20 |
| 176 | L.J. Smith | .60 | .25 |
| 177 | Kevin Curtis | .60 | .25 |
| 178 | Marcus Robinson | .60 | .25 |
| 179 | Kellen Winslow | .75 | .30 |
| 180 | Reggie Williams | .60 | .25 |
| 181 | Bubba Franks | .60 | .25 |
| 182 | J.P. Losman | .75 | .30 |
| 183 | Chris Perry | .50 | .20 |
| 184 | Michael Jenkins | .60 | .25 |
| 185 | T.J. Duckett | .50 | .20 |
| 186 | Rashaun Woods | .50 | .20 |
| 187 | Ben Watson | .60 | .25 |
| 188 | Bryant Johnson | .60 | .25 |
| 189 | Dallas Clark | .60 | .25 |
| 190 | William Green | .50 | .20 |
| 191 | Daniel Graham | .60 | .25 |
| 192 | Jerramy Stevens | .60 | .25 |
| 193 | DeShaun Foster | .60 | .25 |
| 194 | Nick Goings | .50 | .20 |
| 195 | Ronald Curry | .60 | .25 |
| 196 | Kevan Barlow | .50 | .20 |
| 197 | Kevin Faulk | .60 | .25 |
| 198 | Eric Parker | .50 | .20 |
| 199 | Keenan McCardell | .60 | .25 |
| 200 | LaMont Jordan | .60 | .25 |
| 201 | Alex Smith QB L13 RC | 40.00 | 15.00 |
| 202 | Aaron Rodgers L13 RC | 60.00 | 25.00 |
| 203 | Cedric Benson L13 RC | 20.00 | 7.50 |
| 204 | Braylon Edwards L13 RC | 40.00 | 20.00 |
| 205 | Ronnie Brown L13 RC | 60.00 | 30.00 |
| 206 | Cadillac Williams L13 RC | 40.00 | 15.00 |
| 207 | Troy Williamson L13 RC | 20.00 | 7.50 |
| 208 | Mark Clayton L13 RC | 20.00 | 7.50 |
| 209 | Charlie Frye L13 RC | 15.00 | 6.00 |
| 210 | Mike Williams L13 RC | 15.00 | 6.00 |
| 211 | Marion Barber L13 RC | 40.00 | 15.00 |
| 212 | Eric Shelton L13 RC | 15.00 | 6.00 |
| 213 | Antrel Rolle L13 RC | 15.00 | 6.00 |
| 214 | Heath Miller RC | 10.00 | 4.00 |
| 215 | Dan Cody RC | 5.00 | 2.00 |
| 216 | Adam Jones RC | 5.00 | 2.00 |
| 217 | Derrick Johnson RC | 5.00 | 2.00 |
| 218 | Alex Smith TE RC | 5.00 | 2.00 |
| 219 | Kyle Orton RC | 6.00 | 2.50 |
| 220 | David Pollack RC | 4.00 | 1.50 |
| 221 | Erasmus James RC | 4.00 | 1.50 |
| 222 | Justin Tuck RC | 6.00 | 2.50 |
| 223 | Jason Campbell RC | 10.00 | 4.00 |
| 224 | Dan Orlovsky RC | 5.00 | 2.00 |
| 225 | Thomas Davis RC | 4.00 | 1.50 |
| 226 | J.J. Arrington RC | 5.00 | 2.00 |
| 227 | Roddy White RC | 6.00 | 2.50 |
| 228 | David Greene RC | 4.00 | 1.50 |
| 229 | Ciatrick Fason RC | 4.00 | 1.50 |
| 230 | Chris Henry RC | 5.00 | 2.00 |
| 231 | Reggie Brown RC | 5.00 | 2.00 |
| 232 | Vernand Morency RC | 5.00 | 2.00 |
| 233 | Carlos Rogers RC | 5.00 | 2.00 |
| 234 | Ryan Moats RC | 5.00 | 2.00 |
| 235 | Roscoe Parrish RC | 4.00 | 1.50 |
| 236 | Terrence Murphy RC | 3.00 | 1.25 |
| 237 | Shawne Merriman RC | 8.00 | 3.00 |
| 238 | Courtney Roby RC | 4.00 | 1.50 |
| 239 | Mark Bradley RC | 5.00 | 2.00 |
| 240 | Marcus Spears RC | 5.00 | 2.00 |
| 241 | Justin Miller RC | 4.00 | 1.50 |
| 242 | Matt Jones RC | 8.00 | 3.00 |
| 243 | DeMarcus Ware RC | 8.00 | 3.00 |
| 244 | Fabian Washington RC | 5.00 | 2.00 |
| 245 | Marlin Jackson RC | 4.00 | 1.50 |
| 246 | Corey Webster RC | 5.00 | 2.00 |
| 247 | Brandon Jacobs RC | 6.00 | 2.50 |
| 248 | Frank Gore RC | 12.00 | 5.00 |

## 2006 Ultra

|  |  | | |
|---|---|---|---|
| 1 | Larry Fitzgerald | .75 | .30 |
| 2 | Anquan Boldin | .60 | .25 |
| 3 | Kurt Warner | .60 | .25 |
| 4 | Bryant Johnson | .40 | .15 |

|  |  | | |
|---|---|---|---|
| ❑ 5 | Marcel Shipp | .50 | .20 |
| ❑ 6 | J.J. Arrington | .60 | .25 |
| ❑ 7 | Michael Vick | .75 | .30 |
| ❑ 8 | Warrick Dunn | .60 | .25 |
| ❑ 9 | T.J. Duckett | .50 | .20 |
| ❑ 10 | Alge Crumpler | .60 | .25 |
| ❑ 11 | Michael Jenkins | .60 | .25 |
| ❑ 12 | DeAngelo Hall | .60 | .25 |
| ❑ 13 | Kyle Boller | .60 | .25 |
| ❑ 14 | Jamal Lewis | .60 | .25 |
| ❑ 15 | Todd Heap | .60 | .25 |
| ❑ 16 | Derrick Mason | .60 | .25 |
| ❑ 17 | Ray Lewis | .75 | .30 |
| ❑ 18 | Terrell Suggs | .60 | .25 |
| ❑ 19 | J.P. Losman | .60 | .25 |
| ❑ 20 | Willis McGahee | .75 | .30 |
| ❑ 21 | Eric Moulds | .60 | .25 |
| ❑ 22 | Lee Evans | .60 | .25 |
| ❑ 23 | Roscoe Parrish | .50 | .20 |
| ❑ 24 | Kelly Holcomb | .40 | .15 |
| ❑ 25 | Jake Delhomme | .60 | .25 |
| ❑ 26 | Steve Smith | .75 | .30 |
| ❑ 27 | Stephen Davis | .60 | .25 |
| ❑ 28 | Julius Peppers | .60 | .25 |
| ❑ 29 | DeShaun Foster | .60 | .25 |
| ❑ 30 | Keary Colbert | .60 | .25 |
| ❑ 31 | Chris Gamble | .50 | .20 |
| ❑ 32 | Kyle Orton | .50 | .20 |
| ❑ 33 | Thomas Jones | .60 | .25 |
| ❑ 34 | Rex Grossman | .75 | .30 |
| ❑ 35 | Muhsin Muhammad | .60 | .25 |
| ❑ 36 | Brian Urlacher | .75 | .30 |
| ❑ 37 | Adrian Peterson | .60 | .25 |
| ❑ 38 | Carson Palmer | .75 | .30 |
| ❑ 39 | Chad Johnson | .60 | .25 |
| ❑ 40 | Rudi Johnson | .60 | .25 |
| ❑ 41 | Chris Perry | .60 | .25 |
| ❑ 42 | T.J. Houshmandzadeh | .60 | .25 |
| ❑ 43 | Chris Henry | .50 | .20 |
| ❑ 44 | Dellha O'Neal | .50 | .20 |
| ❑ 45 | Trent Dilfer | .60 | .25 |
| ❑ 46 | Reuben Droughns | .60 | .25 |
| ❑ 47 | Antonio Bryant | .60 | .25 |
| ❑ 48 | Braylon Edwards | .75 | .30 |
| ❑ 49 | Charlie Frye | .60 | .25 |
| ❑ 50 | Dennis Northcutt | .50 | .20 |
| ❑ 51 | Drew Bledsoe | .75 | .30 |
| ❑ 52 | Julius Jones | .75 | .30 |
| ❑ 53 | Keyshawn Johnson | .60 | .25 |
| ❑ 54 | Jason Witten | .60 | .25 |
| ❑ 55 | Roy Williams S. | .60 | .25 |
| ❑ 56 | Marion Barber | .75 | .30 |
| ❑ 57 | Terry Glenn | .60 | .25 |
| ❑ 58 | Jake Plummer | .60 | .25 |
| ❑ 59 | Mike Anderson | .60 | .25 |
| ❑ 60 | Champ Bailey | .60 | .25 |
| ❑ 61 | Tatum Bell | .60 | .25 |
| ❑ 62 | Rod Smith | .60 | .25 |
| ❑ 63 | Ashley Lelie | .60 | .25 |
| ❑ 64 | Joey Harrington | .50 | .20 |
| ❑ 65 | Kevin Jones | .75 | .30 |
| ❑ 66 | Roy Williams WR | .75 | .30 |
| ❑ 67 | Mike Williams | .75 | .30 |
| ❑ 68 | Marcus Pollard | .50 | .20 |
| ❑ 69 | Jeff Garcia | .60 | .25 |
| ❑ 70 | Brett Favre | 1.50 | .60 |
| ❑ 71 | Javon Walker | .60 | .25 |
| ❑ 72 | Donald Driver | .60 | .25 |
| ❑ 73 | Samkon Gado | .75 | .30 |
| ❑ 74 | Najeh Davenport | .60 | .25 |
| ❑ 75 | Robert Ferguson | .50 | .20 |
| ❑ 76 | David Carr | .60 | .25 |
| ❑ 77 | Domanick Davis | .60 | .25 |
| ❑ 78 | Andre Johnson | .60 | .25 |
| ❑ 79 | Jabar Gaffney | .50 | .20 |
| ❑ 80 | Corey Bradford | .50 | .20 |
| ❑ 81 | Dunta Robinson | .60 | .25 |
| ❑ 82 | Peyton Manning | 1.25 | .50 |
| ❑ 83 | Edgerrin James | .60 | .25 |
| ❑ 84 | Marvin Harrison | .75 | .30 |
| ❑ 85 | Reggie Wayne | .60 | .25 |
| ❑ 86 | Dallas Clark | .60 | .25 |
| ❑ 87 | Dwight Freeney | .60 | .25 |
| ❑ 88 | Cato June | .60 | .25 |
| ❑ 89 | Byron Leftwich | .60 | .25 |
| ❑ 90 | Fred Taylor | .60 | .25 |
| ❑ 91 | Jimmy Smith | .60 | .25 |
| ❑ 92 | Matt Jones | .60 | .25 |
| ❑ 93 | Ernest Wilford | .60 | .25 |
| ❑ 94 | Greg Jones | .50 | .20 |
| ❑ 95 | Trent Green | .60 | .25 |
| ❑ 96 | Priest Holmes | .60 | .25 |
| ❑ 97 | Larry Johnson | .60 | .25 |
| ❑ 98 | Tony Gonzalez | .60 | .25 |
| ❑ 99 | Dante Hall | .60 | .25 |
| ❑ 100 | Eddie Kennison | .50 | .20 |
| ❑ 101 | Gus Frerotte | .40 | .15 |
| ❑ 102 | Chris Chambers | .60 | .25 |
| ❑ 103 | Ronnie Brown | .75 | .30 |
| ❑ 104 | Ricky Williams | .50 | .20 |
| ❑ 105 | Randy McMichael | .50 | .20 |
| ❑ 106 | Zach Thomas | .75 | .30 |
| ❑ 107 | Daunte Culpepper | .75 | .30 |
| ❑ 108 | Nate Burleson | .60 | .25 |
| ❑ 109 | Michael Bennett | .40 | .15 |
| ❑ 110 | Mewelde Moore | .60 | .25 |
| ❑ 111 | Troy Williamson | .60 | .25 |
| ❑ 112 | Travis Taylor | .50 | .20 |
| ❑ 113 | Jermaine Wiggins | .40 | .15 |
| ❑ 114 | Tom Brady | 1.25 | .50 |
| ❑ 115 | Corey Dillon | .60 | .25 |
| ❑ 116 | Deion Branch | .60 | .25 |
| ❑ 117 | Tedy Bruschi | .75 | .30 |
| ❑ 118 | David Givens | .60 | .25 |
| ❑ 119 | Patrick Pass | .40 | .15 |
| ❑ 120 | Aaron Brooks | .60 | .25 |
| ❑ 121 | Deuce McAllister | .60 | .25 |
| ❑ 122 | Joe Horn | .60 | .25 |
| ❑ 123 | Donte Stallworth | .60 | .25 |
| ❑ 124 | Antowain Smith | .40 | .15 |
| ❑ 125 | Devery Henderson | .50 | .20 |
| ❑ 126 | Eli Manning | 1.00 | .40 |
| ❑ 127 | Tiki Barber | .75 | .30 |
| ❑ 128 | Jeremy Shockey | .75 | .30 |
| ❑ 129 | Plaxico Burress | .60 | .25 |
| ❑ 130 | Amani Toomer | .60 | .25 |
| ❑ 131 | Michael Strahan | .60 | .25 |
| ❑ 132 | Chad Pennington | .60 | .25 |
| ❑ 133 | Curtis Martin | .75 | .30 |
| ❑ 134 | Jonathan Vilma | .60 | .25 |
| ❑ 135 | Laveranues Coles | .60 | .25 |
| ❑ 136 | Justin McCareins | .50 | .20 |
| ❑ 137 | Ty Law | .50 | .20 |
| ❑ 138 | Kerry Collins | .60 | .25 |
| ❑ 139 | LaMont Jordan | .60 | .25 |
| ❑ 140 | Randy Moss | .75 | .30 |
| ❑ 141 | Jerry Porter | .60 | .25 |
| ❑ 142 | Doug Gabriel | .50 | .20 |
| ❑ 143 | Zack Crockett | .40 | .15 |
| ❑ 144 | Donovan McNabb | .75 | .30 |
| ❑ 145 | Brian Westbrook | .60 | .25 |
| ❑ 146 | Terrell Owens | .75 | .30 |
| ❑ 147 | Jevon Kearse | .60 | .25 |
| ❑ 148 | L.J. Smith | .50 | .20 |
| ❑ 149 | Greg Lewis | .50 | .20 |
| ❑ 150 | Ben Roethlisberger | 1.25 | .50 |
| ❑ 151 | Willie Parker | 1.00 | .40 |
| ❑ 152 | Hines Ward | .75 | .30 |
| ❑ 153 | Jerome Bettis | .75 | .30 |
| ❑ 154 | Antwaan Randle El | .60 | .25 |
| ❑ 155 | Heath Miller | .60 | .25 |
| ❑ 156 | Joey Porter | .50 | .20 |
| ❑ 157 | Drew Brees | .75 | .30 |
| ❑ 158 | LaDainian Tomlinson | 1.00 | .40 |
| ❑ 159 | Antonio Gates | .75 | .30 |
| ❑ 160 | Keenan McCardell | .60 | .25 |
| ❑ 161 | Donnie Edwards | .50 | .20 |
| ❑ 162 | Shawne Merriman | .60 | .25 |
| ❑ 163 | Eric Parker | .60 | .25 |
| ❑ 164 | Alex Smith | .75 | .30 |
| ❑ 165 | Kevan Barlow | .60 | .25 |
| ❑ 166 | Frank Gore | .75 | .30 |
| ❑ 167 | Brandon Lloyd | .60 | .25 |
| ❑ 168 | Eric Johnson | .50 | .20 |
| ❑ 169 | Julian Peterson | .50 | .20 |
| ❑ 170 | Matt Hasselbeck | .60 | .25 |
| ❑ 171 | Shaun Alexander | .75 | .30 |
| ❑ 172 | Darrell Jackson | .60 | .25 |
| ❑ 173 | Joe Jurevicius | .60 | .25 |
| ❑ 174 | Jerramy Stevens | .60 | .25 |
| ❑ 175 | D.J. Hackett | .60 | .25 |
| ❑ 176 | Marc Bulger | .60 | .25 |
| ❑ 177 | Steven Jackson | .75 | .30 |
| ❑ 178 | Torry Holt | .60 | .25 |
| ❑ 179 | Isaac Bruce | .60 | .25 |
| ❑ 180 | Kevin Curtis | .60 | .25 |
| ❑ 181 | Marshall Faulk | .60 | .25 |
| ❑ 182 | Chris Simms | .60 | .25 |
| ❑ 183 | Cadillac Williams | .75 | .30 |
| ❑ 184 | Michael Pittman | .40 | .15 |
| ❑ 185 | Michael Clayton | .60 | .25 |
| ❑ 186 | Joey Galloway | .60 | .25 |
| ❑ 187 | Brian Griese | .60 | .25 |
| ❑ 188 | Steve McNair | .60 | .25 |
| ❑ 189 | Chris Brown | .60 | .25 |
| ❑ 190 | Drew Bennett | .60 | .25 |
| ❑ 191 | Travis Henry | .60 | .25 |
| ❑ 192 | Ben Troupe | .50 | .20 |
| ❑ 193 | Billy Volek | .60 | .25 |
| ❑ 194 | Erron Kinney | .50 | .20 |
| ❑ 195 | Mark Brunell | .60 | .25 |
| ❑ 196 | Santana Moss | .60 | .25 |
| ❑ 197 | Clinton Portis | .75 | .30 |
| ❑ 198 | Chris Cooley | .60 | .25 |
| ❑ 199 | Ladell Betts | .60 | .25 |
| ❑ 200 | Sean Taylor | .60 | .25 |
| ❑ 201 | Matt Leinart L13 RC | 80.00 | 40.00 |
| ❑ 202 | Vince Young L13 RC | 100.00 | 50.00 |
| ❑ 203 | Reggie Bush L13 RC | 100.00 | 50.00 |
| ❑ 204 | D'Brick Ferguson L13 RC | 25.00 | 10.00 |
| ❑ 205 | DeAngelo Williams L13 RC | 40.00 | 15.00 |
| ❑ 206 | Jay Cutler L13 RC | 80.00 | 40.00 |
| ❑ 207 | A.J. Hawk L13 RC | 60.00 | 25.00 |
| ❑ 208 | Mario Williams L13 RC | 40.00 | 15.00 |
| ❑ 209 | Santonio Holmes L13 RC | 40.00 | 20.00 |
| ❑ 210 | Chad Greenway L13 RC | 30.00 | 15.00 |
| ❑ 211 | Laurence Maroney L13 RC | 60.00 | 30.00 |
| ❑ 212 | LenDale White L13 RC | 50.00 | 20.00 |
| ❑ 213 | Sinorice Moss L13 RC | 40.00 | 20.00 |
| ❑ 214 | A.J. Nicholson RC | 3.00 | 1.25 |
| ❑ 215 | Abdul Hodge RC | 5.00 | 2.00 |
| ❑ 216 | Jeremy Bloom RC | 4.00 | 1.50 |
| ❑ 217 | Anthony Fasano RC | 5.00 | 2.00 |
| ❑ 218 | Bobby Carpenter RC | 5.00 | 2.00 |
| ❑ 219 | Brian Calhoun RC | 4.00 | 1.50 |
| ❑ 220 | Brodie Croyle RC | 6.00 | 2.50 |
| ❑ 221 | Chad Jackson RC | 4.00 | 1.50 |
| ❑ 222 | Charlie Whitehurst RC | 5.00 | 2.00 |
| ❑ 223 | Claude Wroten RC | 3.00 | 1.25 |
| ❑ 224 | Darnell Bing RC | 5.00 | 2.00 |
| ❑ 225 | Darrell Hackney RC | 4.00 | 1.50 |
| ❑ 226 | David Thomas RC | 5.00 | 2.00 |
| ❑ 227 | Demetrius Williams RC | 5.00 | 2.00 |
| ❑ 228 | Derek Hagan RC | 5.00 | 2.00 |
| ❑ 229 | Devin Hester RC | 10.00 | 4.00 |
| ❑ 230 | Dominique Byrd RC | 4.00 | 1.50 |
| ❑ 231 | D'Qwell Jackson RC | 4.00 | 1.50 |
| ❑ 232 | Elvis Dumervil RC | 3.00 | 1.25 |
| ❑ 233 | Haloti Ngata RC | 5.00 | 2.00 |
| ❑ 234 | Hank Baskett RC | 5.00 | 2.00 |
| ❑ 235 | Jason Avant RC | 5.00 | 2.00 |
| ❑ 236 | Jerome Harrison RC | 5.00 | 2.00 |
| ❑ 237 | Jimmy Williams RC | 5.00 | 2.00 |
| ❑ 238 | Joe Klopfenstein RC | 4.00 | 1.50 |
| ❑ 239 | Joseph Addai RC | 15.00 | 6.00 |

|  |  | | |
|---|---|---|---|
| ☐ 240 | Kellen Clemens RC | 6.00 | 2.50 |
| ☐ 241 | Cory Rodgers RC | 5.00 | 2.00 |
| ☐ 242 | Leon Washington RC | 5.00 | 2.00 |
| ☐ 243 | Leonard Pope RC | 5.00 | 2.00 |
| ☐ 244 | Marcedes Lewis RC | 5.00 | 2.00 |
| ☐ 245 | Martin Nance RC | 4.00 | 1.50 |
| ☐ 246 | Mathias Kiwanuka RC | 6.00 | 2.50 |
| ☐ 247 | Maurice Drew RC | 10.00 | 4.00 |
| ☐ 248 | Maurice Stovall RC | 5.00 | 2.00 |
| ☐ 249 | Michael Huff RC | 5.00 | 2.00 |
| ☐ 250 | Mike Hass RC | 5.00 | 2.00 |
| ☐ 251 | Omar Jacobs RC | 4.00 | 1.50 |
| ☐ 252 | Orien Harris RC | 4.00 | 1.50 |
| ☐ 253 | Owen Daniels RC | 5.00 | 2.00 |
| ☐ 254 | Reggie McNeal RC | 4.00 | 1.50 |
| ☐ 255 | DeMeco Ryans RC | 6.00 | 2.50 |
| ☐ 256 | Tamba Hali RC | 5.00 | 2.00 |
| ☐ 257 | Ernie Sims RC | 5.00 | 2.00 |
| ☐ 258 | Thomas Howard RC | 5.00 | 2.00 |
| ☐ 259 | Todd Watkins RC | 4.00 | 1.50 |
| ☐ 260 | Travis Wilson RC | 5.00 | 2.00 |
| ☐ 261 | Greg Lee RC | 4.00 | 1.50 |
| ☐ 262 | Tye Hill RC | 5.00 | 2.00 |
| ☐ 263 | Vernon Davis RC | 5.00 | 2.00 |

## 2007 Ultra

| | | | |
|---|---|---|---|
| ☐ COMP.SET w/o RCs (200) | | 40.00 | 15.00 |
| ☐ HOBBY PRODUCED WITH SILVER HOLO-FOIL | | | |
| ☐ 1 | Bryant Johnson | .75 | .30 |
| ☐ 2 | Matt Leinart | 1.25 | .50 |
| ☐ 3 | Edgerrin James | 1.00 | .40 |
| ☐ 4 | Larry Fitzgerald | 1.25 | .50 |
| ☐ 5 | Anquan Boldin | 1.00 | .40 |
| ☐ 6 | Jerious Norwood | 1.00 | .40 |
| ☐ 7 | Roddy White | 1.00 | .40 |
| ☐ 8 | Keith Brooking | .75 | .30 |
| ☐ 9 | DeAngelo Hall | 1.00 | .40 |
| ☐ 10 | Michael Vick | 1.25 | .50 |
| ☐ 11 | Warrick Dunn | 1.00 | .40 |
| ☐ 12 | Alge Crumpler | 1.00 | .40 |
| ☐ 13 | Terrell Suggs | .75 | .30 |
| ☐ 14 | Derrick Mason | .75 | .30 |
| ☐ 15 | Todd Heap | 1.00 | .40 |
| ☐ 16 | Ray Lewis | 1.25 | .50 |
| ☐ 17 | Steve McNair | 1.00 | .40 |
| ☐ 18 | Willis McGahee | 1.00 | .40 |
| ☐ 19 | Mark Clayton | 1.00 | .40 |
| ☐ 20 | Aaron Schobel | .75 | .30 |
| ☐ 21 | Terrence McGee | .75 | .30 |
| ☐ 22 | J.P. Losman | 1.00 | .40 |
| ☐ 23 | Anthony Thomas | .75 | .30 |
| ☐ 24 | Lee Evans | 1.00 | .40 |
| ☐ 25 | Keyshawn Johnson | 1.00 | .40 |
| ☐ 26 | DeAngelo Williams | 1.25 | .50 |
| ☐ 27 | Julius Peppers | 1.00 | .40 |
| ☐ 28 | Jake Delhomme | 1.00 | .40 |
| ☐ 29 | DeShaun Foster | 1.00 | .40 |
| ☐ 30 | Steve Smith | 1.00 | .40 |
| ☐ 31 | Mark Anderson | .75 | .30 |
| ☐ 32 | Devin Hester | 1.25 | .50 |
| ☐ 33 | Bernard Berrian | .75 | .30 |
| ☐ 34 | Muhsin Muhammad | .75 | .30 |
| ☐ 35 | Rex Grossman | 1.00 | .40 |
| ☐ 36 | Cedric Benson | 1.00 | .40 |
| ☐ 37 | Brian Urlacher | 1.25 | .50 |
| ☐ 38 | Reggie Kelly | .75 | .30 |
| ☐ 39 | Carson Palmer | 1.25 | .50 |
| ☐ 40 | Rudi Johnson | 1.00 | .40 |
| ☐ 41 | Chad Johnson | 1.00 | .40 |
| ☐ 42 | T.J. Houshmandzadeh | 1.00 | .40 |
| ☐ 43 | Jamal Lewis | 1.00 | .40 |
| ☐ 44 | Charlie Frye | 1.00 | .40 |
| ☐ 45 | Braylon Edwards | 1.00 | .40 |
| ☐ 46 | Kellen Winslow | 1.00 | .40 |
| ☐ 47 | DeMarcus Ware | 1.00 | .40 |
| ☐ 48 | Roy Williams S | 1.00 | .40 |
| ☐ 49 | Jason Witten | 1.00 | .40 |
| ☐ 50 | Marion Barber | 1.25 | .50 |
| ☐ 51 | Tony Romo | 2.50 | 1.00 |
| ☐ 52 | Julius Jones | 1.00 | .40 |
| ☐ 53 | Terrell Owens | 1.25 | .50 |
| ☐ 54 | Terry Glenn | 1.00 | .40 |
| ☐ 55 | Rod Smith | 1.00 | .40 |
| ☐ 56 | Mike Bell | 1.00 | .40 |
| ☐ 57 | Jason Elam | .75 | .30 |
| ☐ 58 | Jay Cutler | 1.25 | .50 |
| ☐ 59 | Champ Bailey | 1.00 | .40 |
| ☐ 60 | Javon Walker | 1.00 | .40 |
| ☐ 61 | Tatum Bell | .75 | .30 |
| ☐ 62 | Jason Hanson | .75 | .30 |
| ☐ 63 | Jon Kitna | .75 | .30 |
| ☐ 64 | Kevin Jones | .75 | .30 |
| ☐ 65 | Roy Williams WR | 1.00 | .40 |
| ☐ 66 | Mike Furrey | 1.00 | .40 |
| ☐ 67 | Charles Woodson | 1.00 | .40 |
| ☐ 68 | Aaron Kampman | 1.00 | .40 |
| ☐ 69 | Bubba Franks | .75 | .30 |
| ☐ 70 | Brett Favre | 2.50 | 1.00 |
| ☐ 71 | Greg Jennings | 1.00 | .40 |
| ☐ 72 | Donald Driver | 1.00 | .40 |
| ☐ 73 | Ron Dayne | 1.00 | .40 |
| ☐ 74 | DeMeco Ryans | 1.00 | .40 |
| ☐ 75 | Jeb Putzier | .75 | .30 |
| ☐ 76 | Matt Schaub | 1.00 | .40 |
| ☐ 77 | Ahman Green | 1.00 | .40 |
| ☐ 78 | Andre Johnson | 1.00 | .40 |
| ☐ 79 | Terrence Wilkins | .75 | .30 |
| ☐ 80 | Bob Sanders | 1.00 | .40 |
| ☐ 81 | Dwight Freeney | 1.00 | .40 |
| ☐ 82 | Dallas Clark | .75 | .30 |
| ☐ 83 | Adam Vinatieri | 1.00 | .40 |
| ☐ 84 | Peyton Manning | 2.00 | .75 |
| ☐ 85 | Joseph Addai | 1.25 | .50 |
| ☐ 86 | Marvin Harrison | 1.25 | .50 |
| ☐ 87 | Reggie Wayne | 1.00 | .40 |
| ☐ 88 | Rashean Mathis | .75 | .30 |
| ☐ 89 | Matt Jones | 1.00 | .40 |
| ☐ 90 | Fred Taylor | 1.00 | .40 |
| ☐ 91 | Byron Leftwich | 1.00 | .40 |
| ☐ 92 | David Garrard | 1.00 | .40 |
| ☐ 93 | Reggie Williams | 1.00 | .40 |
| ☐ 94 | Maurice Jones-Drew | 1.25 | .50 |
| ☐ 95 | Damon Huard | 1.00 | .40 |
| ☐ 96 | Dante Hall | 1.00 | .40 |
| ☐ 97 | Eddie Kennison | .75 | .30 |
| ☐ 98 | Trent Green | 1.00 | .40 |
| ☐ 99 | Larry Johnson | 1.00 | .40 |
| ☐ 100 | Tony Gonzalez | 1.00 | .40 |
| ☐ 101 | Jason Taylor | .75 | .30 |
| ☐ 102 | Randy McMichael | .75 | .30 |
| ☐ 103 | Zach Thomas | 1.00 | .40 |
| ☐ 104 | Daunte Culpepper | 1.00 | .40 |
| ☐ 105 | Ronnie Brown | 1.00 | .40 |
| ☐ 106 | Chris Chambers | 1.00 | .40 |
| ☐ 107 | Troy Williamson | .75 | .30 |
| ☐ 108 | Tony Richardson | .75 | .30 |
| ☐ 109 | Tarvaris Jackson | 1.00 | .40 |
| ☐ 110 | Chester Taylor | .75 | .30 |
| ☐ 111 | Travis Taylor | .75 | .30 |
| ☐ 112 | Richard Seymour | .75 | .30 |
| ☐ 113 | Reche Caldwell | .75 | .30 |
| ☐ 114 | Tedy Bruschi | 1.25 | .50 |
| ☐ 115 | Ben Watson | .75 | .30 |
| ☐ 116 | Tom Brady | 2.50 | 1.00 |
| ☐ 117 | Laurence Maroney | 1.25 | .50 |
| ☐ 118 | Asante Samuel | .75 | .30 |
| ☐ 119 | Michael Lewis | .75 | .30 |
| ☐ 120 | Devery Henderson | .75 | .30 |
| ☐ 121 | Mike Karney | .75 | .30 |
| ☐ 122 | Will Smith | .75 | .30 |
| ☐ 123 | Drew Brees | 1.00 | .40 |
| ☐ 124 | Deuce McAllister | 1.00 | .40 |
| ☐ 125 | Reggie Bush | 1.50 | .60 |
| ☐ 126 | Marques Colston | 1.25 | .50 |
| ☐ 127 | Michael Strahan | 1.00 | .40 |
| ☐ 128 | Reuben Droughns | 1.00 | .40 |
| ☐ 129 | Jeremy Shockey | 1.25 | .50 |
| ☐ 130 | Eli Manning | 1.25 | .50 |
| ☐ 131 | Brandon Jacobs | 1.00 | .40 |
| ☐ 132 | Plaxico Burress | 1.00 | .40 |
| ☐ 133 | Jonathan Vilma | 1.00 | .40 |
| ☐ 134 | Jerricho Cotchery | .75 | .30 |
| ☐ 135 | Thomas Jones | 1.00 | .40 |
| ☐ 136 | Chad Pennington | 1.00 | .40 |
| ☐ 137 | Leon Washington | 1.00 | .40 |
| ☐ 138 | Laveranues Coles | 1.00 | .40 |
| ☐ 139 | Dominic Rhodes | 1.00 | .40 |
| ☐ 140 | Andrew Walter | .75 | .30 |
| ☐ 141 | Randy Moss | 1.25 | .50 |
| ☐ 142 | Ronald Curry | 1.00 | .40 |
| ☐ 143 | LaMont Jordan | 1.00 | .40 |
| ☐ 144 | Justin Fargas | .75 | .30 |
| ☐ 145 | David Akers | .75 | .30 |
| ☐ 146 | Correll Buckhalter | 1.00 | .40 |
| ☐ 147 | Brian Dawkins | 1.00 | .40 |
| ☐ 148 | L.J. Smith | .75 | .30 |
| ☐ 149 | Donovan McNabb | 1.25 | .50 |
| ☐ 150 | Brian Westbrook | 1.00 | .40 |
| ☐ 151 | Reggie Brown | 1.00 | .40 |
| ☐ 152 | Cedrick Wilson | .75 | .30 |
| ☐ 153 | Aaron Smith | .75 | .30 |
| ☐ 154 | Troy Polamalu | 1.25 | .50 |
| ☐ 155 | Ben Roethlisberger | 1.50 | .60 |
| ☐ 156 | Willie Parker | 1.25 | .50 |
| ☐ 157 | Hines Ward | 1.25 | .50 |
| ☐ 158 | Santonio Holmes | 1.00 | .40 |
| ☐ 159 | Eric Parker | .75 | .30 |
| ☐ 160 | Leslie O'Neal | .75 | .30 |
| ☐ 161 | Shawne Merriman | 1.25 | .50 |
| ☐ 162 | Philip Rivers | 1.25 | .50 |
| ☐ 163 | LaDainian Tomlinson | 1.50 | .60 |
| ☐ 164 | Antonio Gates | 1.00 | .40 |
| ☐ 165 | Matt Harris | .75 | .30 |
| ☐ 166 | Vernon Davis | 1.00 | .40 |
| ☐ 167 | Alex Smith QB | 1.25 | .50 |
| ☐ 168 | Frank Gore | 1.25 | .50 |
| ☐ 169 | Arnaz Battle | .75 | .30 |
| ☐ 170 | Maurice Morris | .75 | .30 |
| ☐ 171 | Julian Peterson | .75 | .30 |
| ☐ 172 | D.J. Hackett | .75 | .30 |
| ☐ 173 | Lofa Tatupu | 1.00 | .40 |
| ☐ 174 | Darrell Jackson | 1.00 | .40 |
| ☐ 175 | Matt Hasselbeck | 1.00 | .40 |
| ☐ 176 | Shaun Alexander | 1.00 | .40 |
| ☐ 177 | Deion Branch | 1.00 | .40 |
| ☐ 178 | Tye Hill | .75 | .30 |
| ☐ 179 | Isaac Bruce | 1.00 | .40 |
| ☐ 180 | Marc Bulger | 1.00 | .40 |
| ☐ 181 | Steven Jackson | 1.25 | .50 |
| ☐ 182 | Torry Holt | 1.00 | .40 |
| ☐ 183 | Drew Bennett | .75 | .30 |
| ☐ 184 | Jeff Garcia | 1.00 | .40 |
| ☐ 185 | Michael Clayton | 1.00 | .40 |
| ☐ 186 | Derrick Brooks | 1.00 | .40 |
| ☐ 187 | Cadillac Williams | 1.00 | .40 |
| ☐ 188 | Joey Galloway | 1.00 | .40 |
| ☐ 189 | Ronde Barber | .75 | .30 |
| ☐ 190 | Chris Simms | .75 | .30 |
| ☐ 191 | Keith Bulluck | .75 | .30 |
| ☐ 192 | LenDale White | .75 | .30 |
| ☐ 193 | David Givens | .75 | .30 |
| ☐ 194 | Vince Young | 1.25 | .50 |
| ☐ 195 | Ladell Betts | .75 | .30 |
| ☐ 196 | Chris Cooley | .75 | .30 |
| ☐ 197 | Antwaan Randle El | .75 | .30 |
| ☐ 198 | Jason Campbell | 1.00 | .40 |
| ☐ 199 | Clinton Portis | 1.00 | .40 |
| ☐ 200 | Santana Moss | 1.00 | .40 |
| ☐ 201 | JaMarcus Russell L13 RC | 25.00 | 10.00 |
| ☐ 202 | Brady Quinn L13 RC | 30.00 | 12.00 |
| ☐ 203 | Calvin Johnson L13 RC | 25.00 | 10.00 |
| ☐ 204 | Joe Thomas L13 RC | 10.00 | 4.00 |
| ☐ 205 | Adrian Peterson L13 RC | 80.00 | 30.00 |
| ☐ 206 | Marshawn Lynch L13 RC | 20.00 | 8.00 |

|  |  | | |
|---|---|---|---|
| 207 | Ted Ginn Jr. L13 RC | 15.00 | 6.00 |
| 208 | Leon Hall L13 RC | 8.00 | 3.00 |
| 209 | Dwayne Bowe L13 RC | 20.00 | 8.00 |
| 210 | Steve Smith USC L13 RC | 12.00 | 5.00 |
| 211 | Robert Meachem L13 RC | 10.00 | 4.00 |
| 212 | LaRon Landry L13 RC | 12.00 | 5.00 |
| 213 | Dwayne Jarrett L13 RC | 10.00 | 4.00 |
| 214 | Darius Walker RC | 6.00 | 2.50 |
| 215 | Chris Leak RC | 5.00 | 2.00 |
| 216 | Darrelle Revis RC | 6.00 | 2.50 |
| 217 | Paul Posluszny RC | 8.00 | 3.00 |
| 218 | Daymeion Hughes RC | 5.00 | 2.00 |
| 219 | LaMarr Woodley RC | 6.00 | 2.50 |
| 220 | Garrett Wolfe RC | 6.00 | 2.50 |
| 221 | DeShawn Wynn RC | 6.00 | 2.50 |
| 222 | Alan Branch RC | 5.00 | 2.00 |
| 223 | Greg Olsen RC | 8.00 | 3.00 |
| 224 | Tyler Palko RC | 6.00 | 2.50 |
| 225 | Jordan Palmer RC | 6.00 | 2.50 |
| 226 | Drew Stanton RC | 6.00 | 2.50 |
| 227 | Jamaal Anderson RC | 5.00 | 2.00 |
| 228 | Eric Wright RC | 6.00 | 2.50 |
| 229 | Quentin Moses RC | 5.00 | 2.00 |
| 230 | Patrick Willis RC | 12.00 | 5.00 |
| 231 | Troy Smith RC | 8.00 | 3.00 |
| 232 | Amobi Okoye RC | 6.00 | 2.50 |
| 233 | Lawrence Timmons RC | 6.00 | 2.50 |
| 234 | H.B. Blades RC | 5.00 | 2.00 |
| 235 | Jared Zabransky RC | 5.00 | 2.00 |
| 236 | John Beck RC | 8.00 | 3.00 |
| 237 | Kevin Kolb RC | 10.00 | 4.00 |
| 238 | Matt Moore RC | 6.00 | 2.50 |
| 239 | Trent Edwards RC | 15.00 | 6.00 |
| 240 | Antonio Pittman RC | 6.00 | 2.50 |
| 241 | Brandon Jackson RC | 6.00 | 2.50 |
| 242 | Chris Henry RC | 6.00 | 2.50 |
| 243 | Dwayne Wright RC | 5.00 | 2.00 |
| 244 | Brian Leonard RC | 6.00 | 2.50 |
| 245 | Kenneth Darby RC | 5.00 | 2.00 |
| 246 | Kenny Irons RC | 6.00 | 2.50 |
| 247 | Kolby Smith RC | 5.00 | 2.00 |
| 248 | Lorenzo Booker RC | 6.00 | 2.50 |
| 249 | Drew Tate RC | 5.00 | 2.00 |
| 250 | Tanard Jackson RC | 4.00 | 1.50 |
| 251 | Michael Bush RC | 6.00 | 2.50 |
| 252 | Selvin Young RC | 10.00 | 4.00 |
| 253 | Tony Hunt RC | 6.00 | 2.50 |
| 254 | Tyrone Moss RC | 5.00 | 2.00 |
| 255 | Reggie Nelson RC | 6.00 | 2.50 |
| 256 | Zach Miller RC | 4.00 | 1.50 |
| 257 | Antonio Gonzalez RC | 10.00 | 4.00 |
| 258 | Adam Carriker RC | 5.00 | 2.00 |
| 259 | Sidney Rice RC | 6.00 | 2.50 |
| 260 | Aundrae Allison RC | 5.00 | 2.00 |
| 261 | Chansi Stuckey RC | 5.00 | 2.00 |
| 262 | Courtney Taylor RC | 5.00 | 2.00 |
| 263 | Craig Buster Davis RC | 6.00 | 2.50 |
| 264 | Dallas Baker RC | 5.00 | 2.00 |
| 265 | David Clowney RC | 5.00 | 2.00 |
| 266 | David Ball RC | 4.00 | 1.50 |
| 267 | Jason Hill RC | 6.00 | 2.50 |
| 268 | Johnnie Lee Higgins RC | 5.00 | 2.00 |
| 269 | Rhema McKnight RC | 5.00 | 2.00 |
| 270 | Gaines Adams RC | 5.00 | 2.00 |
| 271 | Mike Walker RC | 5.00 | 2.00 |
| 272 | Steve Breaston RC | 6.00 | 2.50 |
| 273 | Gary Russell RC | 5.00 | 2.00 |
| 274 | Marcus McCauley RC | 5.00 | 2.00 |
| 275 | Jarvis Moss RC | 5.00 | 2.00 |
| 276 | Syvelle Newton RC | 5.00 | 2.00 |
| 277 | DeMarcus Tank Tyler RC | 5.00 | 2.00 |
| 278 | Alvin Banks RC | 5.00 | 2.00 |
| 279 | Joel Filani RC | 5.00 | 2.00 |
| 280 | Chris Davis RC | 5.00 | 2.00 |
| 281 | Matt Trannon RC | 5.00 | 2.00 |
| 282 | Ryan Kalil RC | 5.00 | 2.00 |
| 283 | Levi Brown RC | 5.00 | 2.00 |
| 284 | Anthony Spencer RC | 6.00 | 2.50 |
| 285 | Brandon Meriweather RC | 5.00 | 2.00 |
| 286 | Chris Houston RC | 5.00 | 2.00 |
| 287 | Michael Griffin RC | 6.00 | 2.50 |
| 288 | Jon Beason RC | 6.00 | 2.50 |
| 289 | Legedu Naanee RC | 5.00 | 2.00 |
| 290 | Eric Weddle RC | 5.00 | 2.00 |
| 291 | Isaiah Stanback RC | 6.00 | 2.50 |
| 292 | Aaron Ross RC | 6.00 | 2.50 |
| 293 | Sabby Piscitelli RC | 6.00 | 2.50 |
| 294 | Charles Johnson RC | 4.00 | 1.50 |
| 295 | Buster Davis RC | 5.00 | 2.00 |
| 296 | Justin Harrell RC | 6.00 | 2.50 |
| 297 | Stewart Bradley RC | 4.00 | 1.50 |
| 298 | A.J. Davis RC | 4.00 | 1.50 |
| 299 | David Irons RC | 4.00 | 1.50 |
| 300 | Scott Chandler RC | 5.00 | 2.00 |

## 1991 Upper Deck

| | | |
|---|---|---|
| COMPLETE SET (700) | 15.00 | 6.00 |
| COMP.FACT.SET (700) | 25.00 | 10.00 |
| COMP.SERIES 1 SET (500) | 10.00 | 4.00 |
| COMP.SERIES 2 SET (200) | 5.00 | 2.00 |
| COMP.FACT.SERIES 2 (200) | 6.00 | 2.50 |

|  |  | | |
|---|---|---|---|
| 1 | Dan McGwire CL | .05 | .01 |
| 2 | Eric Bieniemy RC | .05 | .01 |
| 3 | Mike Dumas RC | .05 | .01 |
| 4 | Mike Croel RC | .05 | .01 |
| 5 | Russell Maryland RC | .25 | .08 |
| 6 | Charles McRae RC | .05 | .01 |
| 7 | Dan McGwire RC | .05 | .01 |
| 8 | Mike Pritchard RC | .25 | .08 |
| 9 | Ricky Watters RC | 1.50 | .60 |
| 10 | Chris Zorich RC | .25 | .08 |
| 11 | Browning Nagle RC | .05 | .01 |
| 12 | Wesley Carroll RC | .05 | .01 |
| 13 | Brett Favre RC | 10.00 | 5.00 |
| 14 | Rob Carpenter RC WR | .25 | .08 |
| 15 | Eric Swann RC | .25 | .08 |
| 16 | Stanley Richard RC | .05 | .01 |
| 17 | Herman Moore RC | .25 | .08 |
| 18 | Todd Marinovich RC | .05 | .01 |
| 19 | Aaron Craver RC | .05 | .01 |
| 20 | Chuck Webb RC | .05 | .01 |
| 21 | Todd Lyght RC | .05 | .01 |
| 22 | Greg Lewis RC | .05 | .01 |
| 23 | Eric Turner RC | .10 | .02 |
| 24 | Alvin Harper RC | .25 | .08 |
| 25 | Jarrod Bunch RC | .05 | .01 |
| 26 | Bruce Pickens RC | .05 | .01 |
| 27 | Harvey Williams RC | .25 | .08 |
| 28 | Randal Hill RC | .10 | .02 |
| 29 | Nick Bell RC | .05 | .01 |
| 30 | Jim Everett AT | .10 | .02 |
| 31 | R.Cunningham/Jackson AT | .05 | .01 |
| 32 | Steve DeBerg AT | .05 | .01 |
| 33 | Warren Moon/D.Hill AT | .10 | .02 |
| 34 | D.Marino/M.Clayton AT | .50 | .20 |
| 35 | J.Montana/J.Rice AT | .50 | .20 |
| 36 | Percy Snow | .05 | .01 |
| 37 | Kelvin Martin | .05 | .01 |
| 38 | Scott Case | .05 | .01 |
| 39 | John Gesek RC | .05 | .01 |
| 40 | Barry Word | .05 | .01 |
| 41 | Cornelius Bennett | .10 | .02 |
| 42 | Mike Kenn | .05 | .01 |
| 43 | Andre Reed | .10 | .02 |
| 44 | Bobby Hebert | .05 | .01 |
| 45 | William Perry | .10 | .02 |
| 46 | Dennis Byrd | .05 | .01 |
| 47 | Martin Mayhew | .05 | .01 |
| 48 | Issiac Holt | .05 | .01 |
| 49 | William White | .05 | .01 |
| 50 | JoJo Townsell | .05 | .01 |
| 51 | Jarvis Williams | .05 | .01 |
| 52 | Joey Browner | .05 | .01 |
| 53 | Pat Terrell | .05 | .01 |
| 54 | Joe Montana 3X UER | 1.25 | .50 |
| 55 | Jeff Herrod | .05 | .01 |
| 56 | Cris Carter | .50 | .20 |
| 57 | Jerry Rice | .75 | .30 |
| 58 | Brett Perriman | .25 | .08 |
| 59 | Kevin Fagan | .05 | .01 |
| 60 | Wayne Haddix | .05 | .01 |
| 61 | Tommy Kane | .05 | .01 |
| 62 | Pat Beach | .05 | .01 |
| 63 | Jeff Lageman | .05 | .01 |
| 64 | Hassan Jones | .05 | .01 |
| 65 | Bennie Blades | .05 | .01 |
| 66 | Tim McGee | .05 | .01 |
| 67 | Robert Blackmon | .05 | .01 |
| 68 | Fred Stokes RC | .05 | .01 |
| 69 | Barney Bussey RC | .05 | .01 |
| 70 | Eric Metcalf | .10 | .02 |
| 71 | Mark Kelso | .05 | .01 |
| 72 | Neal Anderson TC | .05 | .01 |
| 73 | Boomer Esiason TC | .10 | .02 |
| 74 | Thurman Thomas TC | .25 | .08 |
| 75 | John Elway TC | .50 | .20 |
| 76 | Eric Metcalf TC | .10 | .02 |
| 77 | Vinny Testaverde TC | .10 | .02 |
| 78 | Johnny Johnson TC | .05 | .01 |
| 79 | Anthony Miller TC | .10 | .02 |
| 80 | Derrick Thomas TC | .10 | .02 |
| 81 | Jeff George TC | .10 | .02 |
| 82 | Troy Aikman TC | .40 | .15 |
| 83 | Dan Marino TC | .50 | .20 |
| 84 | Randall Cunningham TC | .10 | .02 |
| 85 | Deion Sanders TC | .05 | .01 |
| 86 | Jerry Rice TC | .40 | .15 |
| 87 | Lawrence Taylor TC | .10 | .02 |
| 88 | Al Toon TC | .05 | .01 |
| 89 | Barry Sanders TC | .50 | .20 |
| 90 | Warren Moon TC | .10 | .02 |
| 91 | Don Majkowski TC | .05 | .01 |
| 92 | Andre Tippett TC | .05 | .01 |
| 93 | Bo Jackson TC | .30 | .10 |
| 94 | Jim Everett TC | .05 | .01 |
| 95 | Art Monk TC | .10 | .02 |
| 96 | Morten Andersen TC | .05 | .01 |
| 97 | John L. Williams TC | .05 | .01 |
| 98 | Rod Woodson TC | .10 | .02 |
| 99 | Herschel Walker TC | .10 | .02 |
| 100 | Checklist 1-100 | .05 | .01 |
| 101 | Steve Young | .75 | .30 |
| 102 | Jim Lachey | .05 | .01 |
| 103 | Tom Rathman | .05 | .01 |
| 104 | Earnest Byner | .05 | .01 |
| 105 | Karl Mecklenburg | .05 | .01 |
| 106 | Wes Hopkins | .05 | .01 |
| 107 | Michael Irvin | .25 | .08 |
| 108 | Burt Grossman | .05 | .01 |
| 109 | Jay Novacek UER | .25 | .08 |
| 110 | Ben Smith | .05 | .01 |
| 111 | Rod Woodson | .25 | .08 |
| 112 | Ernie Jones | .05 | .01 |
| 113 | Bryan Hinkle | .05 | .01 |
| 114 | Vai Sikahema | .05 | .01 |
| 115 | Bubby Brister | .05 | .01 |
| 116 | Brian Blades | .10 | .02 |
| 117 | Don Majkowski | .05 | .01 |
| 118 | Rod Bernstine | .05 | .01 |
| 119 | Brian Noble | .05 | .01 |
| 120 | Eugene Robinson | .05 | .01 |
| 121 | John Taylor | .10 | .02 |
| 122 | Vance Johnson | .05 | .01 |
| 123 | Art Monk | .25 | .08 |
| 124 | John Elway | 1.25 | .50 |
| 125 | Dexter Carter | .05 | .01 |
| 126 | Anthony Miller | .10 | .02 |
| 127 | Keith Jackson | .10 | .02 |
| 128 | Albert Lewis | .05 | .01 |
| 129 | Billy Ray Smith | .05 | .01 |
| 130 | Clyde Simmons | .05 | .01 |
| 131 | Merril Hoge | .05 | .01 |
| 132 | Ricky Proehl | .05 | .01 |
| 133 | Tim McDonald | .05 | .01 |
| 134 | Louis Lipps | .05 | .01 |

| | | | | | | | | |
|---|---|---|---|---|---|---|---|---|
| ☐ 135 Ken Harvey | .10 | .02 | ☐ 219 Wade Wilson | .10 | .02 | ☐ 303 Jerry Ball | .05 | .01 |
| ☐ 136 Sterling Sharpe | .10 | .02 | ☐ 220 Billy Joe Tolliver | .05 | .01 | ☐ 304 Dwight Stone UER | .05 | .01 |
| ☐ 137 Gill Byrd | .05 | .01 | ☐ 221 Harold Green | .10 | .02 | ☐ 305 Rodney Peete | .10 | .02 |
| ☐ 138 Tim Harris | .05 | .01 | ☐ 222 Al(Bubba) Baker | .10 | .02 | ☐ 306 Mike Baab | .05 | .01 |
| ☐ 139 Derrick Fenner | .05 | .01 | ☐ 223 Carl Zander | .05 | .01 | ☐ 307 Tim Worley | .05 | .01 |
| ☐ 140 Johnny Holland | .05 | .01 | ☐ 224 Thane Gash | .05 | .01 | ☐ 308 Paul Farren | .05 | .01 |
| ☐ 141 Ricky Sanders | .05 | .01 | ☐ 225 Kevin Mack | .05 | .01 | ☐ 309 Carnell Lake | .05 | .01 |
| ☐ 142 Bobby Humphrey | .05 | .01 | ☐ 226 Morten Andersen | .05 | .01 | ☐ 310 Clay Matthews | .10 | .02 |
| ☐ 143 Roger Craig | .10 | .02 | ☐ 227 Dennis Gentry | .05 | .01 | ☐ 311 Alton Montgomery | .05 | .01 |
| ☐ 144 Steve Atwater | .05 | .01 | ☐ 228 Vince Buck | .05 | .01 | ☐ 312 Ernest Givins | .10 | .02 |
| ☐ 145 Ickey Woods | .05 | .01 | ☐ 229 Mike Singletary | .10 | .02 | ☐ 313 Mike Horan | .05 | .01 |
| ☐ 146 Randall Cunningham | .25 | .08 | ☐ 230 Rueben Mayes | .05 | .01 | ☐ 314 Sean Jones | .10 | .02 |
| ☐ 147 Marion Butts | .10 | .02 | ☐ 231 Mark Carrier WR | .25 | .08 | ☐ 315 Leonard Smith | .05 | .01 |
| ☐ 148 Reggie White | .25 | .08 | ☐ 232 Tony Mandarich | .05 | .01 | ☐ 316 Carl Banks | .05 | .01 |
| ☐ 149 Ronnie Harmon | .05 | .01 | ☐ 233 Al Toon | .10 | .02 | ☐ 317 Jerome Brown | .05 | .01 |
| ☐ 150 Mike Saxon | .05 | .01 | ☐ 234 Renaldo Turnbull | .05 | .01 | ☐ 318 Everson Walls | .05 | .01 |
| ☐ 151 Greg Townsend | .05 | .01 | ☐ 235 Broderick Thomas | .05 | .01 | ☐ 319 Ron Heller | .05 | .01 |
| ☐ 152 Troy Aikman | .75 | .30 | ☐ 236 Anthony Carter | .10 | .02 | ☐ 320 Mark Collins | .05 | .01 |
| ☐ 153 Shane Conlan | .05 | .01 | ☐ 237 Flipper Anderson | .05 | .01 | ☐ 321 Eddie Murray | .05 | .01 |
| ☐ 154 Deion Sanders | .40 | .15 | ☐ 238 Jerry Robinson | .05 | .01 | ☐ 322 Jim Harbaugh | .25 | .08 |
| ☐ 155 Bo Jackson | .30 | .10 | ☐ 239 Vince Newsome | .05 | .01 | ☐ 323 Mel Gray | .10 | .02 |
| ☐ 156 Jeff Hostetler | .10 | .02 | ☐ 240 Keith Millard | .05 | .01 | ☐ 324 Keith Van Horne | .05 | .01 |
| ☐ 157 Albert Bentley | .05 | .01 | ☐ 241 Reggie Langhorne | .05 | .01 | ☐ 325 Lomas Brown | .05 | .01 |
| ☐ 158 James Williams | .05 | .01 | ☐ 242 James Francis | .05 | .01 | ☐ 326 Carl Lee | .05 | .01 |
| ☐ 159 Bill Brooks | .05 | .01 | ☐ 243 Felix Wright | .05 | .01 | ☐ 327 Ken O'Brien | .05 | .01 |
| ☐ 160 Nick Lowery | .05 | .01 | ☐ 244 Neal Anderson | .10 | .02 | ☐ 328 Dermontti Dawson | .05 | .01 |
| ☐ 161 Ottis Anderson | .10 | .02 | ☐ 245 Boomer Esiason | .10 | .02 | ☐ 329 Brad Baxter | .05 | .01 |
| ☐ 162 Kevin Greene | .10 | .02 | ☐ 246 Pat Swilling | .10 | .02 | ☐ 330 Chris Doleman | .05 | .01 |
| ☐ 163 Neil Smith | .25 | .08 | ☐ 247 Richard Dent | .10 | .02 | ☐ 331 Louis Oliver | .05 | .01 |
| ☐ 164 Jim Everett | .10 | .02 | ☐ 248 Craig Heyward | .10 | .02 | ☐ 332 Frank Stams | .05 | .01 |
| ☐ 165 Derrick Thomas | .25 | .08 | ☐ 249 Ron Morris | .05 | .01 | ☐ 333 Mike Munchak | .10 | .02 |
| ☐ 166 John L. Williams | .05 | .01 | ☐ 250 Eric Martin | .05 | .01 | ☐ 334 Fred Strickland | .05 | .01 |
| ☐ 167 Timm Rosenbach | .05 | .01 | ☐ 251 Jim C. Jensen | .05 | .01 | ☐ 335 Mark Duper | .10 | .02 |
| ☐ 168 Leslie O'Neal | .10 | .02 | ☐ 252 Anthony Toney | .05 | .01 | ☐ 336 Jacob Green | .05 | .01 |
| ☐ 169 Clarence Verdin | .05 | .01 | ☐ 253 Sammie Smith | .05 | .01 | ☐ 337 Tony Paige | .05 | .01 |
| ☐ 170 Dave Krieg | .10 | .02 | ☐ 254 Calvin Williams | .10 | .02 | ☐ 338 Jeff Bryant | .05 | .01 |
| ☐ 171 Steve Broussard | .05 | .01 | ☐ 255 Dan Marino | 1.25 | .50 | ☐ 339 Lemuel Stinson | .05 | .01 |
| ☐ 172 Emmitt Smith | 2.50 | 1.00 | ☐ 256 Warren Moon | .25 | .08 | ☐ 340 David Wyman | .05 | .01 |
| ☐ 173 Andre Rison | .10 | .02 | ☐ 257 Tommie Agee | .05 | .01 | ☐ 341 Lee Williams | .05 | .01 |
| ☐ 174 Bruce Smith | .25 | .08 | ☐ 258 Haywood Jeffires | .10 | .02 | ☐ 342 Trace Armstrong | .05 | .01 |
| ☐ 175 Mark Clayton | .10 | .02 | ☐ 259 Eugene Lockhart | .05 | .01 | ☐ 343 Junior Seau | .25 | .08 |
| ☐ 176 Christian Okoye | .05 | .01 | ☐ 260 Drew Hill | .05 | .01 | ☐ 344 John Roper | .05 | .01 |
| ☐ 177 Duane Bickett | .05 | .01 | ☐ 261 Vinny Testaverde | .10 | .02 | ☐ 345 Jeff George | .25 | .08 |
| ☐ 178 Stephone Paige | .05 | .01 | ☐ 262 Jim Arnold | .05 | .01 | ☐ 346 Herschel Walker | .10 | .02 |
| ☐ 179 Fredd Young | .05 | .01 | ☐ 263 Steve Christie | .05 | .01 | ☐ 347 Sam Clancy | .05 | .01 |
| ☐ 180 Mervyn Fernandez | .05 | .01 | ☐ 264 Chris Spielman | .10 | .02 | ☐ 348 Steve Jordan | .05 | .01 |
| ☐ 181 Phil Simms | .10 | .02 | ☐ 265 Reggie Cobb | .05 | .01 | ☐ 349 Nate Odomes | .05 | .01 |
| ☐ 182 Pete Holohan | .05 | .01 | ☐ 266 John Stephens | .05 | .01 | ☐ 350 Martin Bayless | .05 | .01 |
| ☐ 183 Pepper Johnson | .05 | .01 | ☐ 267 Jay Hilgenberg | .05 | .01 | ☐ 351 Brent Jones | .25 | .08 |
| ☐ 184 Jackie Slater | .05 | .01 | ☐ 268 Brent Williams | .05 | .01 | ☐ 352 Ray Agnew | .05 | .01 |
| ☐ 185 Stephen Baker | .05 | .01 | ☐ 269 Rodney Hampton | .25 | .08 | ☐ 353 Charles Haley | .10 | .02 |
| ☐ 186 Frank Cornish | .05 | .01 | ☐ 270 Irving Fryar | .10 | .02 | ☐ 354 Andre Tippett | .05 | .01 |
| ☐ 187 Dave Waymer | .05 | .01 | ☐ 271 Terry McDaniel | .05 | .01 | ☐ 355 Ronnie Lott | .10 | .02 |
| ☐ 188 Terance Mathis | .10 | .02 | ☐ 272 Reggie Roby | .05 | .01 | ☐ 356 Thurman Thomas | .25 | .08 |
| ☐ 189 Darryl Talley | .05 | .01 | ☐ 273 Allen Pinkett | .05 | .01 | ☐ 357 Fred Barnett | .25 | .08 |
| ☐ 190 James Hasty | .05 | .01 | ☐ 274 Tim McKyer | .05 | .01 | ☐ 358 James Lofton | .10 | .02 |
| ☐ 191 Jay Schroeder | .05 | .01 | ☐ 275 Bob Golic | .05 | .01 | ☐ 359 William Frizzell RC | .05 | .01 |
| ☐ 192 Kenneth Davis | .05 | .01 | ☐ 276 Wilber Marshall | .05 | .01 | ☐ 360 Keith McKeller | .05 | .01 |
| ☐ 193 Chris Miller | .10 | .02 | ☐ 277 Ray Childress | .05 | .01 | ☐ 361 Rodney Holman | .05 | .01 |
| ☐ 194 Scott Davis | .05 | .01 | ☐ 278 Charles Mann | .05 | .01 | ☐ 362 Henry Ellard | .10 | .02 |
| ☐ 195 Tim Green | .05 | .01 | ☐ 279 Cris Dishman RC | .05 | .01 | ☐ 363 David Fulcher | .05 | .01 |
| ☐ 196 Dan Saleaumua | .05 | .01 | ☐ 280 Mark Rypien | .10 | .02 | ☐ 364 Jerry Gray | .05 | .01 |
| ☐ 197 Rohn Stark | .05 | .01 | ☐ 281 Michael Cofer | .05 | .01 | ☐ 365 James Brooks | .10 | .02 |
| ☐ 198 John Alt | .05 | .01 | ☐ 282 Keith Byars | .05 | .01 | ☐ 366 Tony Stargell | .05 | .01 |
| ☐ 199 Steve Tasker | .10 | .02 | ☐ 283 Mike Rozier | .05 | .01 | ☐ 367 Keith McCants | .05 | .01 |
| ☐ 200 Checklist 101-200 | .05 | .01 | ☐ 284 Seth Joyner | .10 | .02 | ☐ 368 Lewis Billups | .05 | .01 |
| ☐ 201 Freddie Joe Nunn | .05 | .01 | ☐ 285 Jessie Tuggle | .05 | .01 | ☐ 369 Ervin Randle | .05 | .01 |
| ☐ 202 Jim Breech | .05 | .01 | ☐ 286 Mark Bavaro | .05 | .01 | ☐ 370 Pat Leahy | .05 | .01 |
| ☐ 203 Roy Green | .05 | .01 | ☐ 287 Eddie Anderson | .05 | .01 | ☐ 371 Bruce Armstrong | .05 | .01 |
| ☐ 204 Gary Anderson RB | .05 | .01 | ☐ 288 Sean Landeta | .05 | .01 | ☐ 372 Steve DeBerg | .10 | .02 |
| ☐ 205 Rich Camarillo | .05 | .01 | ☐ 289 Howie Long/George Brett | .25 | .08 | ☐ 373 Guy McIntyre | .05 | .01 |
| ☐ 206 Mark Bortz | .05 | .01 | ☐ 290 Reyna Thompson | .05 | .01 | ☐ 374 Deron Cherry | .05 | .01 |
| ☐ 207 Eddie Brown | .05 | .01 | ☐ 291 Ferrell Edmunds | .05 | .01 | ☐ 375 Fred Marion | .05 | .01 |
| ☐ 208 Brad Muster | .05 | .01 | ☐ 292 Willie Gault | .10 | .02 | ☐ 376 Michael Haddix | .05 | .01 |
| ☐ 209 Anthony Munoz | .10 | .02 | ☐ 293 John Offerdahl | .05 | .01 | ☐ 377 Kent Hull | .05 | .01 |
| ☐ 210 Dalton Hilliard | .05 | .01 | ☐ 294 Tim Brown | .25 | .08 | ☐ 378 Jerry Holmes | .05 | .01 |
| ☐ 211 Erik McMillan | .05 | .01 | ☐ 295 Bruce Matthews | .05 | .01 | ☐ 379 Jim Ritcher | .05 | .01 |
| ☐ 212 Perry Kemp | .05 | .01 | ☐ 296 Kevin Ross | .05 | .01 | ☐ 380 Ed West | .05 | .01 |
| ☐ 213 Jim Thornton | .05 | .01 | ☐ 297 Lorenzo White | .05 | .01 | ☐ 381 Richmond Webb | .05 | .01 |
| ☐ 214 Anthony Dilweg | .05 | .01 | ☐ 298 Dino Hackett | .05 | .01 | ☐ 382 Mark Jackson | .05 | .01 |
| ☐ 215 Cleveland Gary | .05 | .01 | ☐ 299 Curtis Duncan | .05 | .01 | ☐ 383 Tom Newberry | .05 | .01 |
| ☐ 216 Leo Goeas | .05 | .01 | ☐ 300 Checklist 201-300 | .05 | .01 | ☐ 384 Ricky Nattiel | .05 | .01 |
| ☐ 217 Mike Merriweather | .05 | .01 | ☐ 301 Andre Ware | .10 | .02 | ☐ 385 Keith Sims | .05 | .01 |
| ☐ 218 Courtney Hall | .05 | .01 | ☐ 302 David Little | .05 | .01 | ☐ 386 Ron Hall | .05 | .01 |

| | | | | | | | | |
|---|---|---|---|---|---|---|---|---|
| ☐ 387 Ken Norton | .10 | .02 | ☐ 471 Randall Cunningham TM | .10 | .02 | ☐ 555 John Friesz | .25 | .08 |
| ☐ 388 Paul Gruber | .05 | .01 | ☐ 472 Johnny Johnson TM | .05 | .01 | ☐ 556 Cody Carlson RC | .05 | .01 |
| ☐ 389 Daniel Stubbs | .05 | .01 | ☐ 473 Rod Woodson TM | .10 | .02 | ☐ 557 Eric Allen | .05 | .01 |
| ☐ 390 Ian Beckles | .05 | .01 | ☐ 474 Anthony Miller MVP | .10 | .02 | ☐ 558 Thomas Benson | .05 | .01 |
| ☐ 391 Hoby Brenner | .05 | .01 | ☐ 475 Jerry Rice TM | .40 | .15 | ☐ 559 Scott Mersereau RC | .05 | .01 |
| ☐ 392 Tory Epps | .05 | .01 | ☐ 476 John L.Williams MVP | .05 | .01 | ☐ 560 Lionel Washington | .05 | .01 |
| ☐ 393 Sam Mills | .05 | .01 | ☐ 477 Wayne Haddix MVP | .05 | .01 | ☐ 561 Brian Brennan | .05 | .01 |
| ☐ 394 Chris Hinton | .05 | .01 | ☐ 478 Earnest Byner MVP | .05 | .01 | ☐ 562 Jim Jeffcoat | .05 | .01 |
| ☐ 395 Steve Walsh | .05 | .01 | ☐ 479 Doug Widell | .05 | .01 | ☐ 563 Jeff Jaeger | .05 | .01 |
| ☐ 396 Simon Fletcher | .05 | .01 | ☐ 480 Tommy Hodson | .05 | .01 | ☐ 564 D.J. Johnson | .05 | .01 |
| ☐ 397 Tony Bennett | .10 | .02 | ☐ 481 Shawn Collins | .05 | .01 | ☐ 565 Danny Villa | .05 | .01 |
| ☐ 398 Aundray Bruce | .05 | .01 | ☐ 482 Rickey Jackson | .05 | .01 | ☐ 566 Don Beebe | .05 | .01 |
| ☐ 399 Mark Murphy | .05 | .01 | ☐ 483 Tony Casillas | .05 | .01 | ☐ 567 Michael Haynes | .25 | .08 |
| ☐ 400 Checklist 301-400 | .05 | .01 | ☐ 484 Vaughan Johnson | .05 | .01 | ☐ 568 Brett Faryniarz RC | .05 | .01 |
| ☐ 401 Barry Sanders SL | .50 | .20 | ☐ 485 Floyd Dixon | .05 | .01 | ☐ 569 Mike Prior | .05 | .01 |
| ☐ 402 Jerry Rice SL | .40 | .15 | ☐ 486 Eric Green | .05 | .01 | ☐ 570 John Davis RC | .05 | .01 |
| ☐ 403 Warren Moon SL | .10 | .02 | ☐ 487 Harry Hamilton | .05 | .01 | ☐ 571 Vernon Turner RC | .05 | .01 |
| ☐ 404 Derrick Thomas SL | .10 | .02 | ☐ 488 Gary Anderson K | .05 | .01 | ☐ 572 Michael Brooks | .05 | .01 |
| ☐ 405 Nick Lowery LL | .05 | .01 | ☐ 489 Bruce Hill | .05 | .01 | ☐ 573 Mike Gann | .05 | .01 |
| ☐ 406 Mark Carrier DB LL | .05 | .01 | ☐ 490 Gerald Williams | .05 | .01 | ☐ 574 Ron Holmes | .05 | .01 |
| ☐ 407 Michael Carter | .05 | .01 | ☐ 491 Cortez Kennedy | .25 | .08 | ☐ 575 Gary Plummer | .05 | .01 |
| ☐ 408 Chris Singleton | .05 | .01 | ☐ 492 Chet Brooks | .05 | .01 | ☐ 576 Bill Romanowski | .05 | .01 |
| ☐ 409 Matt Millen | .10 | .02 | ☐ 493 Dwayne Harper RC | .05 | .01 | ☐ 577 Chris Jacke | .05 | .01 |
| ☐ 410 Ronnie Lippett | .05 | .01 | ☐ 494 Don Griffin | .05 | .01 | ☐ 578 Gary Reasons | .05 | .01 |
| ☐ 411 E.J. Junior | .05 | .01 | ☐ 495 Andy Heck | .05 | .01 | ☐ 579 Tim Jorden RC | .05 | .01 |
| ☐ 412 Ray Donaldson | .05 | .01 | ☐ 496 David Treadwell | .05 | .01 | ☐ 580 Tim McKyer | .05 | .01 |
| ☐ 413 Keith Willis | .05 | .01 | ☐ 497 Irv Pankey | .05 | .01 | ☐ 581 Johnnie Jackson RC | .05 | .01 |
| ☐ 414 Jessie Hester | .05 | .01 | ☐ 498 Dennis Smith | .05 | .01 | ☐ 582 Ethan Horton | .05 | .01 |
| ☐ 415 Jeff Cross | .05 | .01 | ☐ 499 Marcus Dupree | .05 | .01 | ☐ 583 Pete Stoyanovich | .05 | .01 |
| ☐ 416 Greg Jackson RC | .05 | .01 | ☐ 500 Checklist 401-500 | .05 | .01 | ☐ 584 Jeff Query | .05 | .01 |
| ☐ 417 Alvin Walton | .05 | .01 | ☐ 501 Wendell Davis | .05 | .01 | ☐ 585 Frank Reich | .10 | .02 |
| ☐ 418 Bart Oates | .05 | .01 | ☐ 502 Matt Bahr | .05 | .01 | ☐ 586 Riki Ellison | .05 | .01 |
| ☐ 419 Chip Lohmiller | .05 | .01 | ☐ 503 Rob Burnett RC | .10 | .02 | ☐ 587 Eric Hill | .05 | .01 |
| ☐ 420 John Elliott | .05 | .01 | ☐ 504 Maurice Carthon | .05 | .01 | ☐ 588 Anthony Shelton RC | .05 | .01 |
| ☐ 421 Randall McDaniel | .10 | .02 | ☐ 505 Donnell Woolford | .05 | .01 | ☐ 589 Steve Smith | .05 | .01 |
| ☐ 422 Richard Johnson CB RC | .05 | .01 | ☐ 506 Howard Ballard | .05 | .01 | ☐ 590 Garth Jax RC | .05 | .01 |
| ☐ 423 Al Noga | .05 | .01 | ☐ 507 Mark Boyer | .05 | .01 | ☐ 591 Greg Davis RC | .05 | .01 |
| ☐ 424 Lamar Lathon | .05 | .01 | ☐ 508 Eugene Marve | .05 | .01 | ☐ 592 Bill Maas | .05 | .01 |
| ☐ 425 Rick Fenney | .05 | .01 | ☐ 509 Joe Kelly | .05 | .01 | ☐ 593 Henry Rolling RC | .05 | .01 |
| ☐ 426 Jack Del Rio | .10 | .02 | ☐ 510 Will Wolford | .05 | .01 | ☐ 594 Keith Jones | .05 | .01 |
| ☐ 427 Don Mosebar | .05 | .01 | ☐ 511 Robert Clark | .05 | .01 | ☐ 595 Tootie Robbins | .05 | .01 |
| ☐ 428 Luis Sharpe | .05 | .01 | ☐ 512 Matt Brock RC | .05 | .01 | ☐ 596 Brian Jordan | .10 | .02 |
| ☐ 429 Steve Wisniewski | .05 | .01 | ☐ 513 Chris Warren | .25 | .08 | ☐ 597 Derrick Walker RC | .05 | .01 |
| ☐ 430 Jimmie Jones | .05 | .01 | ☐ 514 Ken Willis | .05 | .01 | ☐ 598 Jonathan Hayes | .05 | .01 |
| ☐ 431 Freeman McNeil | .05 | .01 | ☐ 515 George Jamison RC | .05 | .01 | ☐ 599 Nate Lewis RC | .05 | .01 |
| ☐ 432 Ron Rivera | .05 | .01 | ☐ 516 Rufus Porter | .05 | .01 | ☐ 600 Checklist 501-600 | .05 | .01 |
| ☐ 433 Hart Lee Dykes | .05 | .01 | ☐ 517 Mark Higgs RC | .05 | .01 | ☐ 601 Croel/Lewis/Tray/Walk CL | .05 | .01 |
| ☐ 434 Mark Carrier DB | .10 | .02 | ☐ 518 Thomas Everett | .05 | .01 | ☐ 602 James Jones RC DT | .05 | .01 |
| ☐ 435 Rob Moore | .25 | .08 | ☐ 519 Robert Brown | .05 | .01 | ☐ 603 Tim Barnett RC | .05 | .01 |
| ☐ 436 Gary Clark | .25 | .08 | ☐ 520 Gene Atkins | .05 | .01 | ☐ 604 Ed King RC | .05 | .01 |
| ☐ 437 Heath Sherman | .05 | .01 | ☐ 521 Hardy Nickerson | .10 | .02 | ☐ 605 Shane Curry RF | .05 | .01 |
| ☐ 438 Darrell Green | .05 | .01 | ☐ 522 Johnny Bailey | .05 | .01 | ☐ 606 Mike Croel | .05 | .01 |
| ☐ 439 Jessie Small | .05 | .01 | ☐ 523 William Frizzell | .05 | .01 | ☐ 607 Bryan Cox RC | .25 | .08 |
| ☐ 440 Monte Coleman | .05 | .01 | ☐ 524 Steve McMichael | .10 | .02 | ☐ 608 Shawn Jefferson RC | .10 | .02 |
| ☐ 441 Leonard Marshall | .05 | .01 | ☐ 525 Kevin Porter | .05 | .01 | ☐ 609 Kenny Walker RC | .05 | .01 |
| ☐ 442 Richard Johnson | .05 | .01 | ☐ 526 Carwell Gardner | .05 | .01 | ☐ 610 Michael Jackson RC WR | .25 | .08 |
| ☐ 443 Dave Meggett | .10 | .02 | ☐ 527 Eugene Daniel | .05 | .01 | ☐ 611 Jon Vaughn RC | .05 | .01 |
| ☐ 444 Barry Sanders | 1.25 | .50 | ☐ 528 Vestee Jackson | .05 | .01 | ☐ 612 Greg Lewis | .05 | .01 |
| ☐ 445 Lawrence Taylor | .25 | .08 | ☐ 529 Chris Goode | .05 | .01 | ☐ 613 Joe Valerio RF | .05 | .01 |
| ☐ 446 Marcus Allen | .25 | .08 | ☐ 530 Leon Seals | .05 | .01 | ☐ 614 Pat Harlow RC | .05 | .01 |
| ☐ 447 Johnny Johnson | .05 | .01 | ☐ 531 Darion Conner | .05 | .01 | ☐ 615 Henry Jones | .10 | .02 |
| ☐ 448 Aaron Wallace | .05 | .01 | ☐ 532 Stan Brock | .05 | .01 | ☐ 616 Jeff Graham RC WR | .25 | .08 |
| ☐ 449 Anthony Thompson | .05 | .01 | ☐ 533 Kirby Jackson RC | .05 | .01 | ☐ 617 Darryll Lewis | .10 | .02 |
| ☐ 450 D.Marino/S.DeBerg CL | .40 | .15 | ☐ 534 Marv Cook | .05 | .01 | ☐ 618 Keith Traylor RC | .05 | .01 |
| ☐ 451 Andre Rison TM | .10 | .02 | ☐ 535 Bill Fralic | .05 | .01 | ☐ 619 Scott Miller RF | .05 | .01 |
| ☐ 452 Thurman Thomas TM | .10 | .02 | ☐ 536 Keith Woodside | .05 | .01 | ☐ 620 Nick Bell | .05 | .01 |
| ☐ 453 Neal Anderson MVP | .05 | .01 | ☐ 537 Hugh Green | .05 | .01 | ☐ 621 John Flannery RC | .05 | .01 |
| ☐ 454 Boomer Esiason MVP | .05 | .01 | ☐ 538 Grant Feasel | .05 | .01 | ☐ 622 Leonard Russell RC | .10 | .02 |
| ☐ 455 Eric Metcalf MVP | .10 | .02 | ☐ 539 Bubba McDowell | .05 | .01 | ☐ 623 Alfred Williams RC | .05 | .01 |
| ☐ 456 Emmitt Smith TM | 1.25 | .50 | ☐ 540 Val Sikahema | .05 | .01 | ☐ 624 Browning Nagle | .10 | .02 |
| ☐ 457 Bobby Humphrey MVP | .05 | .01 | ☐ 541 Aaron Cox | .05 | .01 | ☐ 625 Harvey Williams | .10 | .02 |
| ☐ 458 Barry Sanders MVP | .50 | .20 | ☐ 542 Roger Craig | .10 | .02 | ☐ 626 Dan McGwire | .10 | .02 |
| ☐ 459 Sterling Sharpe TM | .10 | .02 | ☐ 543 Rob Harlow RC | .05 | .01 | ☐ 627 Favre/Pritchard/Pegram CL | .50 | .20 |
| ☐ 460 Warren Moon TM | .10 | .02 | ☐ 544 Ronnie Lott | .10 | .02 | ☐ 628 William Thomas RC | .05 | .01 |
| ☐ 461 Albert Bentley MVP | .05 | .01 | ☐ 545 Robert Delpino | .05 | .01 | ☐ 629 Lawrence Dawsey RC | .10 | .02 |
| ☐ 462 Steve DeBerg MVP | .05 | .01 | ☐ 546 Greg McMurtry | .05 | .01 | ☐ 630 Aeneas Williams RC | .25 | .08 |
| ☐ 463 Greg Townsend MVP | .05 | .01 | ☐ 547 Jim Morrissey RC | .05 | .01 | ☐ 631 Stan Thomas RF | .05 | .01 |
| ☐ 464 Henry Ellard MVP | .10 | .02 | ☐ 548 Johnny Rembert | .05 | .01 | ☐ 632 Randal Hill | .05 | .01 |
| ☐ 465 Dan Marino TM | .50 | .20 | ☐ 549 Markus Paul RC | .05 | .01 | ☐ 633 Moe Gardner RC | .05 | .01 |
| ☐ 466 Anthony Carter MVP | .10 | .02 | ☐ 550 Karl Wilson RC | .05 | .01 | ☐ 634 Alvin Harper | .10 | .02 |
| ☐ 467 John Stephens MVP | .05 | .01 | ☐ 551 Gaston Green | .05 | .01 | ☐ 635 Esera Tuaolo RC | .05 | .01 |
| ☐ 468 Pat Swilling MVP | .05 | .01 | ☐ 552 Willie Drewrey | .05 | .01 | ☐ 636 Russell Maryland | .10 | .02 |
| ☐ 469 Ottis Anderson MVP | .10 | .02 | ☐ 553 Michael Young | .05 | .01 | ☐ 637 Anthony Morgan RC | .05 | .01 |
| ☐ 470 Dennis Byrd MVP | .05 | .01 | ☐ 554 Tom Tupa | .05 | .01 | ☐ 638 Eric Pegram RC | .25 | .08 |

| | | |
|---|---|---|
| ❏ 639 Herman Moore | .25 | .08 |
| ❏ 640 Ricky Ervins RC | .10 | .02 |
| ❏ 641 Kelvin Pritchett RC | .10 | .02 |
| ❏ 642 Roman Phifer RC | .05 | .01 |
| ❏ 643 Antone Davis RC | .05 | .01 |
| ❏ 644 Mike Pritchard | .10 | .02 |
| ❏ 645 Vinnie Clark RC | .05 | .01 |
| ❏ 646 Jake Reed RC | .50 | .20 |
| ❏ 647 Brett Favre | 4.00 | 1.50 |
| ❏ 648 Todd Lyght | .05 | .01 |
| ❏ 649 Bruce Pickens RC | .05 | .01 |
| ❏ 650 Darren Lewis RC | .05 | .01 |
| ❏ 651 Wesley Carroll | .05 | .01 |
| ❏ 652 James Joseph RC | .10 | .02 |
| ❏ 653 Robert Delpino RC | .05 | .01 |
| ❏ 654 Deion Sanders/V.Glenn AR | .05 | .01 |
| ❏ 655 J.Rice/T.McDaniels AR | .30 | .10 |
| ❏ 656 B.Sanders/D.Thomas AR | .50 | .20 |
| ❏ 657 Ken Tippins AR | .05 | .01 |
| ❏ 658 Christian Okoye AR | .05 | .01 |
| ❏ 659 Rich Gannon | .25 | .08 |
| ❏ 660 Johnny Meads | .05 | .01 |
| ❏ 661 J.J.Birden RC | .10 | .02 |
| ❏ 662 Bruce Kozerski | .05 | .01 |
| ❏ 663 Felix Wright | .05 | .01 |
| ❏ 664 Al Smith | .05 | .01 |
| ❏ 665 Stan Humphries | .25 | .08 |
| ❏ 666 Alfred Anderson | .05 | .01 |
| ❏ 667 Nate Newton | .10 | .02 |
| ❏ 668 Vince Workman RC | .10 | .02 |
| ❏ 669 Ricky Reynolds | .05 | .01 |
| ❏ 670 Bryce Paup RC | .25 | .08 |
| ❏ 671 Gill Fenerty | .05 | .01 |
| ❏ 672 Darrell Thompson | .05 | .01 |
| ❏ 673 Anthony Smith | .05 | .01 |
| ❏ 674 Darryl Henley RC | .05 | .01 |
| ❏ 675 Brett Maxie | .05 | .01 |
| ❏ 676 Craig Taylor RC | .05 | .01 |
| ❏ 677 Steve Wallace | .10 | .02 |
| ❏ 678 Jeff Feagles RC | .05 | .01 |
| ❏ 679 James Washington RC | .05 | .01 |
| ❏ 680 Tim Harris | .05 | .01 |
| ❏ 681 Dennis Gibson | .05 | .01 |
| ❏ 682 Toi Cook RC | .05 | .01 |
| ❏ 683 Lorenzo Lynch | .05 | .01 |
| ❏ 684 Brad Edwards RC | .05 | .01 |
| ❏ 685 Ray Crockett RC | .05 | .01 |
| ❏ 686 Harris Barton | .05 | .01 |
| ❏ 687 Byron Evans | .05 | .01 |
| ❏ 688 Eric Thomas | .05 | .01 |
| ❏ 689 Jeff Criswell | .05 | .01 |
| ❏ 690 Eric Ball | .05 | .01 |
| ❏ 691 Brian Mitchell | .10 | .02 |
| ❏ 692 Quinn Early | .10 | .02 |
| ❏ 693 Aaron Jones | .05 | .01 |
| ❏ 694 Jim Dombrowski | .05 | .01 |
| ❏ 695 Jeff Bostic | .05 | .01 |
| ❏ 696 Tony Casillas | .05 | .01 |
| ❏ 697 Ken Lanier | .05 | .01 |
| ❏ 698 Henry Thomas | .05 | .01 |
| ❏ 699 Steve Beuerlein | .10 | .02 |
| ❏ 700 Checklist 601-700 | .05 | .01 |
| ❏ 1P Joe Montana Promo | 15.00 | 1.00 |
| ❏ 500P Barry Sanders Promo | 2.00 | .75 |
| ❏ SP1 Darrell Green Fastest | .50 | .20 |
| ❏ SP2 Don Shula 300th Win | 2.00 | .75 |

## 1992 Upper Deck

| | | |
|---|---|---|
| ❏ COMPLETE SET (620) | 15.00 | 6.00 |
| ❏ COMP.SERIES 1 (400) | 10.00 | 4.00 |
| ❏ COMP.SERIES 2 (220) | 5.00 | 2.50 |
| ❏ 1 Bennett/Buckley/McNabb C | .10 | .02 |
| ❏ 2 Edgar Bennett RC | .25 | .08 |
| ❏ 3 Eddie Blake RC | .05 | .01 |
| ❏ 4 Brian Bollinger RC | .05 | .01 |
| ❏ 5 Joe Bowden RC | .05 | .01 |
| ❏ 6 Terrell Buckley RC | .10 | .02 |
| ❏ 7 Willie Clay RC | .05 | .01 |
| ❏ 8 Ed Cunningham RC | .05 | .01 |
| ❏ 9 Matt Darby RC | .05 | .01 |
| ❏ 10 Will Furrer RC | .05 | .01 |
| ❏ 11 Chris Hakel RC | .05 | .01 |
| ❏ 12 Carlos Huerta | .05 | .01 |
| ❏ 13 Amp Lee RC | .05 | .01 |

| | | |
|---|---|---|
| ❏ 14 Ricardo McDonald RC | .05 | .01 |
| ❏ 15 Dexter McNabb RC | .05 | .01 |
| ❏ 16 Chris Mims RC | .05 | .01 |
| ❏ 17 Derrick Moore RC | .10 | .02 |
| ❏ 18 Mark D'Onofrio RC | .05 | .01 |
| ❏ 19 Patrick Rowe RC | .05 | .01 |
| ❏ 20 Leon Searcy RC | .05 | .01 |
| ❏ 21 Torrance Small RC | .10 | .02 |
| ❏ 22 Jimmy Smith RC | 3.00 | 1.25 |
| ❏ 23 Tony Smith RC WR | .05 | .01 |
| ❏ 24 Siran Stacy RC | .05 | .01 |
| ❏ 25 Kevin Turner RC | .05 | .01 |
| ❏ 26 Tommy Vardell RC | .05 | .01 |
| ❏ 27 Bob Whitfield RC | .05 | .01 |
| ❏ 28 Darryl Williams RC | .05 | .01 |
| ❏ 29 Jeff Sydner RC | .05 | .01 |
| ❏ 30 Mike Croel/L.Russell CL | .05 | .01 |
| ❏ 31 Todd Marinovich ART | .05 | .01 |
| ❏ 32 Leonard Russell ART | .05 | .01 |
| ❏ 33 Nick Bell ART | .05 | .01 |
| ❏ 34 Alvin Harper ART | .05 | .01 |
| ❏ 35 Mike Pritchard ART | .05 | .01 |
| ❏ 36 Lawrence Dawsey AR | .05 | .01 |
| ❏ 37 Tim Barnett AR | .05 | .01 |
| ❏ 38 John Flannery AR | .05 | .01 |
| ❏ 39 Stan Thomas AR | .05 | .01 |
| ❏ 40 Ed King AR | .05 | .01 |
| ❏ 41 Charles McRae AR | .05 | .01 |
| ❏ 42 Eric Moten AR | .05 | .01 |
| ❏ 43 Moe Gardner AR | .05 | .01 |
| ❏ 44 Kenny Walker AR | .05 | .01 |
| ❏ 45 Esera Tuaolo AR | .05 | .01 |
| ❏ 46 Alfred Williams AR | .05 | .01 |
| ❏ 47 Bryan Cox AR | .05 | .01 |
| ❏ 48 Mo Lewis AR | .05 | .01 |
| ❏ 49 Mike Croel ART | .05 | .01 |
| ❏ 50 Stanley Richard AR | .05 | .01 |
| ❏ 51 Tony Covington AR | .05 | .01 |
| ❏ 52 Larry Brown DB AR | .05 | .01 |
| ❏ 53 Aeneas Williams AR | .05 | .01 |
| ❏ 54 John Kasay AR | .05 | .01 |
| ❏ 55 Jon Vaughn ART | .05 | .01 |
| ❏ 56 David Fulcher | .05 | .01 |
| ❏ 57 Barry Foster | .10 | .02 |
| ❏ 58 Terry Wooden | .05 | .01 |
| ❏ 59 Gary Anderson K | .05 | .01 |
| ❏ 60 Alfred Williams | .05 | .01 |
| ❏ 61 Robert Blackmon | .05 | .01 |
| ❏ 62 Brian Noble | .05 | .01 |
| ❏ 63 Terry Allen | .25 | .08 |
| ❏ 64 Darrell Green | .05 | .01 |
| ❏ 65 Darren Comeaux | .05 | .01 |
| ❏ 66 Rob Burnett | .05 | .01 |
| ❏ 67 Jarrod Bunch | .05 | .01 |
| ❏ 68 Michael Jackson RC | .10 | .02 |
| ❏ 69 Greg Lloyd | .10 | .02 |
| ❏ 70 Richard Brown RC | .05 | .01 |
| ❏ 71 Harold Green | .05 | .01 |
| ❏ 72 William Fuller | .05 | .01 |
| ❏ 73 Mark Carrier DB TC | .05 | .01 |
| ❏ 74 David Fulcher TC | .05 | .01 |
| ❏ 75 Cornelius Bennett TC | .05 | .01 |
| ❏ 76 Steve Atwater TC | .05 | .01 |
| ❏ 77 Kevin Mack TC | .05 | .01 |
| ❏ 78 Mark Carrier WR TC | .05 | .01 |
| ❏ 79 Tim McDonald TC | .05 | .01 |
| ❏ 80 Marion Butts TC | .05 | .01 |

| | | |
|---|---|---|
| ❏ 81 Christian Okoye TC | .05 | .01 |
| ❏ 82 Jeff Herrod TC | .05 | .01 |
| ❏ 83 Emmitt Smith TC | .60 | .25 |
| ❏ 84 Mark Duper TC | .05 | .01 |
| ❏ 85 Keith Jackson TC | .05 | .01 |
| ❏ 86 Andre Rison TC | .10 | .02 |
| ❏ 87 John Taylor TC | .05 | .01 |
| ❏ 88 Rodney Hampton TC | .10 | .02 |
| ❏ 89 Rob Moore TC | .05 | .01 |
| ❏ 90 Chris Spielman TC | .05 | .01 |
| ❏ 91 Haywood Jeffires TC | .05 | .01 |
| ❏ 92 Sterling Sharpe TC | .10 | .02 |
| ❏ 93 Irving Fryar TC | .05 | .01 |
| ❏ 94 Marcus Allen TC | .10 | .02 |
| ❏ 95 Henry Ellard TC | .05 | .01 |
| ❏ 96 Mark Rypien TC | .05 | .01 |
| ❏ 97 Pat Swilling TC | .05 | .01 |
| ❏ 98 Brian Blades TC | .05 | .01 |
| ❏ 99 Eric Green TC | .05 | .01 |
| ❏ 100 Anthony Carter TC | .05 | .01 |
| ❏ 101 Burt Grossman | .05 | .01 |
| ❏ 102 Gary Anderson RB | .05 | .01 |
| ❏ 103 Neil Smith | .25 | .08 |
| ❏ 104 Jeff Feagles | .05 | .01 |
| ❏ 105 Shane Conlan | .05 | .01 |
| ❏ 106 Jay Novacek | .10 | .02 |
| ❏ 107 Bill Brooks | .05 | .01 |
| ❏ 108 Mark Ingram | .05 | .01 |
| ❏ 109 Anthony Munoz | .10 | .02 |
| ❏ 110 Wendell Davis | .05 | .01 |
| ❏ 111 Jim Everett | .10 | .02 |
| ❏ 112 Bruce Matthews | .05 | .01 |
| ❏ 113 Mark Higgs | .05 | .01 |
| ❏ 114 Chris Warren | .10 | .02 |
| ❏ 115 Brad Baxter | .05 | .01 |
| ❏ 116 Greg Townsend | .05 | .01 |
| ❏ 117 Al Smith | .05 | .01 |
| ❏ 118 Jeff Cross | .05 | .01 |
| ❏ 119 Terry McDaniel | .05 | .01 |
| ❏ 120 Ernest Givins | .10 | .02 |
| ❏ 121 Fred Barnett | .10 | .02 |
| ❏ 122 Flipper Anderson | .05 | .01 |
| ❏ 123 Floyd Turner | .05 | .01 |
| ❏ 124 Stephen Baker | .05 | .01 |
| ❏ 125 Tim Johnson | .05 | .01 |
| ❏ 126 Brent Jones | .10 | .02 |
| ❏ 127 Leonard Marshall | .05 | .01 |
| ❏ 128 Jim Price | .05 | .01 |
| ❏ 129 Jessie Hester | .05 | .01 |
| ❏ 130 Mark Carrier WR | .10 | .02 |
| ❏ 131 Bubba McDowell | .05 | .01 |
| ❏ 132 Andre Tippett | .05 | .01 |
| ❏ 133 James Hasty | .05 | .01 |
| ❏ 134 Mel Gray | .10 | .02 |
| ❏ 135 Christian Okoye | .05 | .01 |
| ❏ 136 Earnest Byner | .05 | .01 |
| ❏ 137 Ferrell Edmunds | .05 | .01 |
| ❏ 138 Henry Ellard | .10 | .02 |
| ❏ 139 Rob Moore | .10 | .02 |
| ❏ 140 Brian Jordan | .10 | .02 |
| ❏ 141 Clarence Verdin | .05 | .01 |
| ❏ 142 Cornelius Bennett | .05 | .01 |
| ❏ 143 John Taylor | .10 | .02 |
| ❏ 144 Derrick Thomas | .25 | .08 |
| ❏ 145 Thurman Thomas | .25 | .08 |
| ❏ 146 Warren Moon | .25 | .08 |
| ❏ 147 Vinny Testaverde | .10 | .02 |
| ❏ 148 Steve Bono RC | .25 | .08 |
| ❏ 149 Robb Thomas | .05 | .01 |
| ❏ 150 John Friesz | .05 | .01 |
| ❏ 151 Richard Dent | .10 | .02 |
| ❏ 152 Eddie Anderson | .05 | .01 |
| ❏ 153 Kevin Greene | .10 | .02 |
| ❏ 154 Marion Butts | .05 | .01 |
| ❏ 155 Barry Sanders | 1.25 | .50 |
| ❏ 156 Andre Rison | .10 | .02 |
| ❏ 157 Ronnie Lott | .10 | .02 |
| ❏ 158 Eric Allen | .05 | .01 |
| ❏ 159 Mark Clayton | .10 | .02 |
| ❏ 160 Terance Mathis | .05 | .01 |
| ❏ 161 Darryl Talley | .05 | .01 |
| ❏ 162 Eric Metcalf | .10 | .02 |
| ❏ 163 Reggie Cobb | .05 | .01 |
| ❏ 164 Ernie Jones | .05 | .01 |

|  |  | | |
|---|---|---|---|
| 165 | David Griggs | .05 | .01 |
| 166 | Tom Rathman | .05 | .01 |
| 167 | Bubby Brister | .10 | .01 |
| 168 | Broderick Thomas | .05 | .01 |
| 169 | Chris Doleman | .05 | .01 |
| 170 | Charles Haley | .10 | .02 |
| 171 | Michael Haynes | .10 | .02 |
| 172 | Rodney Hampton | .10 | .02 |
| 173 | Nick Bell | .05 | .01 |
| 174 | Gene Atkins | .05 | .01 |
| 175 | Mike Merriweather | .05 | .01 |
| 176 | Reggie Roby | .05 | .01 |
| 177 | Bennie Blades | .05 | .01 |
| 178 | John L. Williams | .05 | .01 |
| 179 | Rodney Peete | .10 | .02 |
| 180 | Greg Montgomery | .05 | .01 |
| 181 | Vince Newsome | .05 | .01 |
| 182 | Andre Collins | .05 | .01 |
| 183 | Erik Kramer | .10 | .02 |
| 184 | Bryan Hinkle | .05 | .01 |
| 185 | Reggie White | .25 | .08 |
| 186 | Bruce Armstrong | .05 | .01 |
| 187 | Anthony Carter | .10 | .02 |
| 188 | Pat Swilling | .05 | .01 |
| 189 | Robert Delpino | .05 | .01 |
| 190 | Brent Williams | .05 | .01 |
| 191 | Johnny Johnson | .05 | .01 |
| 192 | Aaron Craver | .05 | .01 |
| 193 | Vincent Brown | .05 | .01 |
| 194 | Herschel Walker | .10 | .02 |
| 195 | Tim McDonald | .05 | .01 |
| 196 | Gaston Green | .05 | .01 |
| 197 | Brian Blades | .05 | .01 |
| 198 | Rod Bernstine | .05 | .01 |
| 199 | Brett Perriman | .10 | .02 |
| 200 | John Elway | 1.25 | .50 |
| 201 | Michael Carter | .05 | .01 |
| 202 | Mark Carrier DB | .05 | .01 |
| 203 | Cris Carter | .50 | .20 |
| 204 | Kyle Clifton | .05 | .01 |
| 205 | Alvin Wright | .05 | .01 |
| 206 | Andre Ware | .05 | .01 |
| 207 | Dave Waymer | .05 | .01 |
| 208 | Darren Lewis | .05 | .01 |
| 209 | Joey Browner | .05 | .01 |
| 210 | Rich Miano | .05 | .01 |
| 211 | Marcus Allen | .25 | .08 |
| 212 | Steve Broussard | .05 | .01 |
| 213 | Joel Hilgenberg | .05 | .01 |
| 214 | Bo Orlando RC | .05 | .01 |
| 215 | Clay Matthews | .10 | .02 |
| 216 | Chris Hinton | .05 | .01 |
| 217 | Al Edwards | .05 | .01 |
| 218 | Tim Brown | .25 | .08 |
| 219 | Sam Mills | .05 | .01 |
| 220 | Don Majkowski | .05 | .01 |
| 221 | James Francis | .05 | .01 |
| 222 | Steve Hendrickson RC | .05 | .01 |
| 223 | James Thornton | .05 | .01 |
| 224 | Byron Evans | .05 | .01 |
| 225 | Pepper Johnson | .05 | .01 |
| 226 | Darryl Henley | .05 | .01 |
| 227 | Simon Fletcher | .05 | .01 |
| 228 | Hugh Millen | .05 | .01 |
| 229 | Tim McGee | .05 | .01 |
| 230 | Richmond Webb | .05 | .01 |
| 231 | Tony Bennett | .05 | .01 |
| 232 | Nate Odomes | .05 | .01 |
| 233 | Scott Case | .05 | .01 |
| 234 | Dalton Hilliard | .05 | .01 |
| 235 | Paul Gruber | .05 | .01 |
| 236 | Jeff Lageman | .05 | .01 |
| 237 | Tony Mandarich | .05 | .01 |
| 238 | Cris Dishman | .05 | .01 |
| 239 | Steve Walsh | .05 | .01 |
| 240 | Moe Gardner | .05 | .01 |
| 241 | Bill Romanowski | .05 | .01 |
| 242 | Chris Zorich | .10 | .02 |
| 243 | Stephone Paige | .05 | .01 |
| 244 | Mike Croel | .05 | .01 |
| 245 | Leonard Russell | .05 | .01 |
| 246 | Mark Rypien | .05 | .01 |
| 247 | Aeneas Williams | .05 | .01 |
| 248 | Steve Atwater | .05 | .01 |
| 249 | Michael Stewart | .05 | .01 |
| 250 | Pierce Holt | .05 | .01 |
| 251 | Kevin Mack | .05 | .01 |
| 252 | Sterling Sharpe | .25 | .08 |
| 253 | Lawrence Dawsey | .10 | .02 |
| 254 | Emmitt Smith | 1.50 | .60 |
| 255 | Todd Marinovich | .05 | .01 |
| 256 | Neal Anderson | .05 | .01 |
| 257 | Mo Lewis | .05 | .01 |
| 258 | Vance Johnson | .05 | .01 |
| 259 | Rickey Jackson | .05 | .01 |
| 260 | Esera Tuaolo | .05 | .01 |
| 261 | Wilber Marshall | .05 | .01 |
| 262 | Keith Henderson | .05 | .01 |
| 263 | William Thomas | .05 | .01 |
| 264 | Rickey Dixon | .05 | .01 |
| 265 | Dave Meggett | .10 | .02 |
| 266 | Gerald Riggs | .05 | .01 |
| 267 | Tim Harris | .05 | .01 |
| 268 | Ken Harvey | .05 | .01 |
| 269 | Clyde Simmons | .05 | .01 |
| 270 | Irving Fryar | .10 | .02 |
| 271 | Darion Conner | .05 | .01 |
| 272 | Vince Workman | .05 | .01 |
| 273 | Jim Harbaugh | .25 | .08 |
| 274 | Lorenzo White | .05 | .01 |
| 275 | Bobby Hebert | .05 | .01 |
| 276 | Duane Bickett | .05 | .01 |
| 277 | Jeff Bryant | .05 | .01 |
| 278 | Scott Stephen | .05 | .01 |
| 279 | Bob Golic | .05 | .01 |
| 280 | Steve McMichael | .10 | .02 |
| 281 | Jeff Graham | .25 | .08 |
| 282 | Keith Jackson | .10 | .02 |
| 283 | Howard Ballard | .05 | .01 |
| 284 | Michael Brooks | .05 | .01 |
| 285 | Freeman McNeil | .10 | .02 |
| 286 | Rodney Holman | .05 | .01 |
| 287 | Eric Bieniemy | .05 | .01 |
| 288 | Seth Joyner | .05 | .01 |
| 289 | Carwell Gardner | .05 | .01 |
| 290 | Brian Mitchell | .10 | .02 |
| 291 | Chris Miller | .10 | .02 |
| 292 | Ray Berry | .05 | .01 |
| 293 | Matt Brock | .05 | .01 |
| 294 | Eric Thomas | .05 | .01 |
| 295 | John Kasay | .05 | .01 |
| 296 | Jay Hilgenberg | .05 | .01 |
| 297 | Darrell Thompson | .05 | .01 |
| 298 | Rich Gannon | .25 | .08 |
| 299 | Steve Young | .60 | .25 |
| 300 | Mike Kenn | .05 | .01 |
| 301 | Emmitt Smith SL | .60 | .25 |
| 302 | Haywood Jeffires SL | .05 | .01 |
| 303 | Michael Irvin SL | .25 | .08 |
| 304 | Warren Moon SL | .10 | .02 |
| 305 | Chip Lohmiller SL | .05 | .01 |
| 306 | Barry Sanders SL | .50 | .20 |
| 307 | Ronnie Lott SL | .10 | .02 |
| 308 | Pat Swilling SL | .05 | .01 |
| 309 | Thurman Thomas SL | .10 | .02 |
| 310 | Reggie Roby SL | .05 | .01 |
| 311 | Moon/Irvin/T.Thomas CL | .10 | .02 |
| 312 | Jacob Green | .05 | .01 |
| 313 | Stephen Braggs | .05 | .01 |
| 314 | Haywood Jeffires | .10 | .02 |
| 315 | Freddie Joe Nunn | .05 | .01 |
| 316 | Gary Clark | .10 | .02 |
| 317 | Tim Barnett | .05 | .01 |
| 318 | Mark Duper | .05 | .01 |
| 319 | Eric Green | .05 | .01 |
| 320 | Robert Wilson | .05 | .01 |
| 321 | Michael Ball | .05 | .01 |
| 322 | Eric Martin | .05 | .01 |
| 323 | Alexander Wright | .05 | .01 |
| 324 | Jessie Tuggle | .05 | .01 |
| 325 | Ronnie Harmon | .05 | .01 |
| 326 | Jeff Hostetler | .10 | .02 |
| 327 | Eugene Daniel | .05 | .01 |
| 328 | Ken Norton Jr. | .10 | .02 |
| 329 | Reyna Thompson | .05 | .01 |
| 330 | Jerry Ball | .05 | .01 |
| 331 | Leroy Hoard | .10 | .02 |
| 332 | Chris Martin | .05 | .01 |
| 333 | Keith McKeller | .05 | .01 |
| 334 | Brian Washington | .05 | .01 |
| 335 | Eugene Robinson | .05 | .01 |
| 336 | Maurice Hurst | .05 | .01 |
| 337 | Dan Saleaumua | .05 | .01 |
| 338 | Neil O'Donnell | .10 | .02 |
| 339 | Dexter Davis | .05 | .01 |
| 340 | Keith McCants | .05 | .01 |
| 341 | Steve Beuerlein | .10 | .02 |
| 342 | Roman Phifer | .05 | .01 |
| 343 | Bryan Cox | .10 | .02 |
| 344 | Art Monk | .10 | .02 |
| 345 | Michael Irvin | .25 | .08 |
| 346 | Vaughan Johnson | .05 | .01 |
| 347 | Jeff Herrod | .05 | .01 |
| 348 | Stanley Richard | .05 | .01 |
| 349 | Michael Young | .05 | .01 |
| 350 | Rod.Hampton/R.Cobb CL | .10 | .02 |
| 351 | Jim Harbaugh MVP | .10 | .02 |
| 352 | David Fulcher MVP | .05 | .01 |
| 353 | Thurman Thomas MVP | .10 | .02 |
| 354 | Gaston Green MVP | .05 | .01 |
| 355 | Leroy Hoard MVP | .05 | .01 |
| 356 | Reggie Cobb MVP | .05 | .01 |
| 357 | Tim McDonald MVP | .05 | .01 |
| 358 | Ronnie Harmon MVP UER | .05 | .01 |
| 359 | Derrick Thomas MVP | .10 | .02 |
| 360 | Jeff Herrod MVP | .05 | .01 |
| 361 | Michael Irvin MVP | .25 | .08 |
| 362 | Mark Higgs MVP | .05 | .01 |
| 363 | Reggie White MVP | .10 | .02 |
| 364 | Chris Miller MVP | .05 | .01 |
| 365 | Steve Young MVP | .30 | .10 |
| 366 | Rodney Hampton MVP | .10 | .02 |
| 367 | Jeff Lageman MVP | .05 | .01 |
| 368 | Barry Sanders MVP | .50 | .20 |
| 369 | Haywood Jeffires MVP | .05 | .01 |
| 370 | Tony Bennett MVP | .05 | .01 |
| 371 | Leonard Russell MVP | .05 | .01 |
| 372 | Jeff Jaeger MVP | .05 | .01 |
| 373 | Robert Delpino MVP | .05 | .01 |
| 374 | Mark Rypien MVP | .05 | .01 |
| 375 | Pat Swilling MVP | .05 | .01 |
| 376 | Cortez Kennedy MVP | .10 | .02 |
| 377 | Eric Green MVP | .05 | .01 |
| 378 | Cris Carter MVP | .10 | .02 |
| 379 | John Roper | .05 | .01 |
| 380 | Barry Word | .05 | .01 |
| 381 | Shawn Jefferson | .05 | .01 |
| 382 | Tony Casillas | .05 | .01 |
| 383 | John Baylor RC | .05 | .01 |
| 384 | Al Noga | .05 | .01 |
| 385 | Charles Mann | .05 | .01 |
| 386 | Gill Byrd | .05 | .01 |
| 387 | Chris Singleton | .05 | .01 |
| 388 | James Joseph | .05 | .01 |
| 389 | Larry Brown DB | .05 | .01 |
| 390 | Chris Spielman | .10 | .02 |
| 391 | Anthony Thompson | .05 | .01 |
| 392 | Karl Mecklenburg | .05 | .01 |
| 393 | Joe Kelly | .05 | .01 |
| 394 | Kanavis McGhee | .05 | .01 |
| 395 | Bill Maas | .05 | .01 |
| 396 | Marv Cook | .05 | .01 |
| 397 | Louis Lipps | .05 | .01 |
| 398 | Marty Carter RC | .05 | .01 |
| 399 | Louis Oliver | .05 | .01 |
| 400 | Eric Swann | .10 | .02 |
| 401 | Troy Auzenne RC | .05 | .01 |
| 402 | Kurt Barber | .05 | .01 |
| 403 | Marc Boutte RC | .05 | .01 |
| 404 | Dale Carter | .10 | .02 |
| 405 | Marco Coleman | .05 | .01 |
| 406 | Quentin Coryatt | .05 | .01 |
| 407 | Shane Dronett RC | .05 | .01 |
| 408 | Vaughn Dunbar | .05 | .01 |
| 409 | Steve Emtman | .05 | .01 |
| 410 | Dana Hall RC | .05 | .01 |
| 411 | Jason Hanson RC | .10 | .02 |
| 412 | Courtney Hawkins RC | .05 | .01 |
| 413 | Terrell Buckley | .05 | .01 |
| 414 | Robert Jones RC | .05 | .01 |
| 415 | David Klingler | .05 | .01 |
| 416 | Tommy Maddox | 1.50 | .60 |

| | | |
|---|---|---|
| ☐ 417 Johnny Mitchell RC | .05 | .01 |
| ☐ 418 Carl Pickens | .10 | .02 |
| ☐ 419 Tracy Scroggins RC | .05 | .01 |
| ☐ 420 Tony Sacca RC | .05 | .01 |
| ☐ 421 Kevin Smith DB | .05 | .01 |
| ☐ 422 Alonzo Spellman | .10 | .02 |
| ☐ 423 Troy Vincent RC | .05 | .01 |
| ☐ 424 Sean Gilbert RC | .10 | .02 |
| ☐ 425 Larry Webster RC | .05 | .01 |
| ☐ 426 Carl Pickens/Klingler CL | .10 | .02 |
| ☐ 427 Bill Fralic | .05 | .01 |
| ☐ 428 Kevin Murphy | .05 | .01 |
| ☐ 429 Lemuel Stinson | .05 | .01 |
| ☐ 430 Harris Barton | .05 | .01 |
| ☐ 431 Dino Hackett | .05 | .01 |
| ☐ 432 John Stephens | .05 | .01 |
| ☐ 433 Keith Jennings RC | .05 | .01 |
| ☐ 434 Derrick Fenner | .05 | .01 |
| ☐ 435 Kenneth Gant RC | .05 | .01 |
| ☐ 436 Willie Gault | .10 | .02 |
| ☐ 437 Steve Jordan | .05 | .01 |
| ☐ 438 Charles Haley | .10 | .02 |
| ☐ 439 Keith Kartz | .05 | .01 |
| ☐ 440 Nate Lewis | .05 | .01 |
| ☐ 441 Doug Widell | .05 | .01 |
| ☐ 442 William White | .05 | .01 |
| ☐ 443 Eric Hill | .05 | .01 |
| ☐ 444 Melvin Jenkins | .05 | .01 |
| ☐ 445 David Wyman | .05 | .01 |
| ☐ 446 Ed West | .05 | .01 |
| ☐ 447 Brad Muster | .05 | .01 |
| ☐ 448 Ray Childress | .05 | .01 |
| ☐ 449 Kevin Ross | .05 | .01 |
| ☐ 450 Johnnie Jackson S | .05 | .01 |
| ☐ 451 Tracy Simien RC | .05 | .01 |
| ☐ 452 Don Mosebar | .05 | .01 |
| ☐ 453 Jay Hilgenberg | .05 | .01 |
| ☐ 454 Wes Hopkins | .05 | .01 |
| ☐ 455 Jay Schroeder | .05 | .01 |
| ☐ 456 Jeff Bostic | .05 | .01 |
| ☐ 457 Bryce Paup | .25 | .08 |
| ☐ 458 Dave Waymer | .05 | .01 |
| ☐ 459 Toi Cook | .05 | .01 |
| ☐ 460 Anthony Smith | .05 | .01 |
| ☐ 461 Don Griffin | .05 | .01 |
| ☐ 462 Bill Hawkins | .05 | .01 |
| ☐ 463 Courtney Hall | .05 | .01 |
| ☐ 464 Jeff Uhlenhake | .05 | .01 |
| ☐ 465 Mike Sherrard | .05 | .01 |
| ☐ 466 James Jones DT | .05 | .01 |
| ☐ 467 Jerrol Williams | .05 | .01 |
| ☐ 468 Eric Ball | .05 | .01 |
| ☐ 469 Randall McDaniel | .10 | .02 |
| ☐ 470 Alvin Harper | .10 | .02 |
| ☐ 471 Tom Waddle | .05 | .01 |
| ☐ 472 Tony Woods | .05 | .01 |
| ☐ 473 Kelvin Martin | .05 | .01 |
| ☐ 474 Jon Vaughn | .05 | .01 |
| ☐ 475 Gill Fenerty | .05 | .01 |
| ☐ 476 Aundray Bruce | .05 | .01 |
| ☐ 477 Morten Andersen | .05 | .01 |
| ☐ 478 Lamar Lathon | .05 | .01 |
| ☐ 479 Steve DeOssie | .05 | .01 |
| ☐ 480 Marvin Washington | .05 | .01 |
| ☐ 481 Herschel Walker | .10 | .02 |
| ☐ 482 Howie Long | .25 | .08 |
| ☐ 483 Calvin Williams | .10 | .02 |
| ☐ 484 Brett Favre | 2.50 | 1.25 |
| ☐ 485 Johnny Bailey | .05 | .01 |
| ☐ 486 Jeff Gossett | .05 | .01 |
| ☐ 487 Carnell Lake | .05 | .01 |
| ☐ 488 Michael Zordich RC | .05 | .01 |
| ☐ 489 Henry Rolling | .05 | .01 |
| ☐ 490 Steve Smith | .05 | .01 |
| ☐ 491 Vestee Jackson | .05 | .01 |
| ☐ 492 Ray Crockett | .05 | .01 |
| ☐ 493 Dexter Carter | .05 | .01 |
| ☐ 494 Nick Lowery | .05 | .01 |
| ☐ 495 Cortez Kennedy | .10 | .02 |
| ☐ 496 Cleveland Gary | .05 | .01 |
| ☐ 497 Kelly Stouffer | .05 | .01 |
| ☐ 498 Carl Carter | .05 | .01 |
| ☐ 499 Shannon Sharpe | .25 | .08 |
| ☐ 500 Roger Craig | .10 | .02 |

| | | |
|---|---|---|
| ☐ 501 Willie Drewrey | .05 | .01 |
| ☐ 502 Mark Schlereth RC | .05 | .01 |
| ☐ 503 Tony Martin | .10 | .02 |
| ☐ 504 Tom Newberry | .05 | .01 |
| ☐ 505 Ron Hall | .05 | .01 |
| ☐ 506 Scott Miller | .05 | .01 |
| ☐ 507 Donnell Woolford | .05 | .01 |
| ☐ 508 Dave Krieg | .10 | .02 |
| ☐ 509 Erric Pegram | .10 | .02 |
| ☐ 510 Checklist 401-510 | .05 | .01 |
| ☐ 511 Barry Sanders SBK | .60 | .25 |
| ☐ 512 Thurman Thomas SBK | .10 | .02 |
| ☐ 513 Warren Moon SBK | .10 | .02 |
| ☐ 514 John Elway SBK | .50 | .20 |
| ☐ 515 Ronnie Lott SBK | .10 | .02 |
| ☐ 516 Emmitt Smith SBK | .60 | .25 |
| ☐ 517 Andre Rison SBK | .10 | .02 |
| ☐ 518 Steve Atwater SBK | .05 | .01 |
| ☐ 519 Steve Young SBK | .30 | .10 |
| ☐ 520 Mark Rypien SBK | .05 | .01 |
| ☐ 521 Rich Camarillo | .05 | .01 |
| ☐ 522 Mark Bavaro | .05 | .01 |
| ☐ 523 Brad Edwards | .05 | .01 |
| ☐ 524 Chad Hennings RC | .10 | .02 |
| ☐ 525 Tony Paige | .05 | .01 |
| ☐ 526 Shawn Moore | .05 | .01 |
| ☐ 527 Sidney Johnson RC | .05 | .01 |
| ☐ 528 Sanjay Beach RC | .05 | .01 |
| ☐ 529 Kelvin Pritchett | .05 | .01 |
| ☐ 530 Jerry Holmes | .05 | .01 |
| ☐ 531 Al Del Greco | .05 | .01 |
| ☐ 532 Bob Gagliano | .05 | .01 |
| ☐ 533 Drew Hill | .05 | .01 |
| ☐ 534 Donald Frank RC | .05 | .01 |
| ☐ 535 Pio Sagapolutele RC | .05 | .01 |
| ☐ 536 Jackie Slater | .05 | .01 |
| ☐ 537 Vernon Turner | .05 | .01 |
| ☐ 538 Bobby Humphrey | .05 | .01 |
| ☐ 539 Audray McMillian | .05 | .01 |
| ☐ 540 Gary Brown RC | .25 | .08 |
| ☐ 541 Wesley Carroll | .05 | .01 |
| ☐ 542 Nate Newton | .05 | .01 |
| ☐ 543 Vai Sikahema | .05 | .01 |
| ☐ 544 Chris Chandler | .25 | .08 |
| ☐ 545 Nolan Harrison RC | .05 | .01 |
| ☐ 546 Mark Green | .05 | .01 |
| ☐ 547 Ricky Watters | .25 | .08 |
| ☐ 548 J.J. Birden | .05 | .01 |
| ☐ 549 Cody Carlson | .05 | .01 |
| ☐ 550 Tim Green | .05 | .01 |
| ☐ 551 Mark Jackson | .05 | .01 |
| ☐ 552 Vince Buck | .05 | .01 |
| ☐ 553 George Jamison | .05 | .01 |
| ☐ 554 Anthony Pleasant | .05 | .01 |
| ☐ 555 Reggie Johnson | .05 | .01 |
| ☐ 556 John Jackson WR | .05 | .01 |
| ☐ 557 Ian Beckles | .05 | .01 |
| ☐ 558 Buford McGee | .05 | .01 |
| ☐ 559 Fuad Reveiz UER | .05 | .01 |
| ☐ 560 Joe Montana | 1.25 | .50 |
| ☐ 561 Phil Simms | .10 | .02 |
| ☐ 562 Greg McMurtry | .05 | .01 |
| ☐ 563 Gerald Williams | .05 | .01 |
| ☐ 564 Dave Cadigan | .05 | .01 |
| ☐ 565 Rufus Porter | .05 | .01 |
| ☐ 566 Jim Kelly | .25 | .08 |
| ☐ 567 Deion Sanders | .50 | .20 |
| ☐ 568 Mike Singletary | .10 | .02 |
| ☐ 569 Boomer Esiason | .10 | .02 |
| ☐ 570 Andre Reed | .10 | .02 |
| ☐ 571 James Washington | .05 | .01 |
| ☐ 572 Jack Del Rio | .05 | .01 |
| ☐ 573 Gerald Perry | .05 | .01 |
| ☐ 574 Vinnie Clark | .05 | .01 |
| ☐ 575 Mike Piel | .05 | .01 |
| ☐ 576 Michael Dean Perry | .10 | .02 |
| ☐ 577 Ricky Proehl | .05 | .01 |
| ☐ 578 Leslie O'Neal | .10 | .02 |
| ☐ 579 Russell Maryland | .10 | .02 |
| ☐ 580 Eric Dickerson | .10 | .02 |
| ☐ 581 Fred Strickland | .05 | .01 |
| ☐ 582 Nick Lowery | .05 | .01 |
| ☐ 583 Joe Milinichik RC | .05 | .01 |
| ☐ 584 Mark Vlasic | .05 | .01 |

| | | |
|---|---|---|
| ☐ 585 James Lofton | .10 | .02 |
| ☐ 586 Bruce Smith | .25 | .08 |
| ☐ 587 Harvey Williams | .10 | .02 |
| ☐ 588 Bernie Kosar | .10 | .02 |
| ☐ 589 Carl Banks | .05 | .01 |
| ☐ 590 Jeff George | .25 | .08 |
| ☐ 591 Fred Jones RC | .05 | .01 |
| ☐ 592 Todd Scott | .05 | .01 |
| ☐ 593 Keith Jones | .05 | .01 |
| ☐ 594A Tootie Robbins ERR | .05 | .01 |
| ☐ 594B Tootie Robbins COR | .05 | .01 |
| ☐ 595 Todd Philcox RC | .05 | .01 |
| ☐ 596 Browning Nagle | .05 | .01 |
| ☐ 597 Troy Aikman | .75 | .30 |
| ☐ 598 Dan Marino | 1.25 | .50 |
| ☐ 599 Lawrence Taylor | .25 | .08 |
| ☐ 600 Webster Slaughter | .05 | .01 |
| ☐ 601 Aaron Cox | .05 | .01 |
| ☐ 602 Matt Stover | .05 | .01 |
| ☐ 603 Keith Sims | .05 | .01 |
| ☐ 604 Dennis Smith | .05 | .01 |
| ☐ 605 Kevin Porter | .05 | .01 |
| ☐ 606 Anthony Miller | .10 | .02 |
| ☐ 607 Ken O'Brien | .05 | .01 |
| ☐ 608 Randall Cunningham | .25 | .08 |
| ☐ 609 Timm Rosenbach | .05 | .01 |
| ☐ 610 Junior Seau | .25 | .08 |
| ☐ 611 Johnny Rembert | .05 | .01 |
| ☐ 612 Rick Tuten | .05 | .01 |
| ☐ 613 Willie Green | .05 | .01 |
| ☐ 614 Sean Salisbury RC**/C | .05 | .01 |
| ☐ 615 Martin Bayless | .05 | .01 |
| ☐ 616 Jerry Rice | .75 | .30 |
| ☐ 617 Randal Hill | .05 | .01 |
| ☐ 618 Dan McGwire | .05 | .01 |
| ☐ 619 Merril Hoge | .05 | .01 |
| ☐ 620 Checklist 571-620 | .05 | .01 |
| ☐ A560 Joe Montana Blowup UDA | 15.00 | 6.00 |
| ☐ A598 Dan Marino Blowup UDA | 15.00 | 6.00 |
| ☐ SP3 James Lofton Yardage | .75 | .30 |
| ☐ SP4 Art Monk Catches | .50 | .20 |

## 1992 Upper Deck Gold

| | | |
|---|---|---|
| ☐ COMPLETE SET (50) | 12.00 | 5.00 |
| ☐ G1 Steve Emtman RC | .10 | .02 |
| ☐ G2 Carl Pickens RC | .30 | .10 |
| ☐ G3 Dale Carter RC | .30 | .10 |
| ☐ G4 Greg Skrepenak RC | .10 | .02 |
| ☐ G5 Kevin Smith RC DB | .15 | .05 |
| ☐ G6 Marco Coleman RC | .15 | .05 |
| ☐ G7 David Klingler RC | .15 | .05 |
| ☐ G8 Phillippi Sparks RC | .10 | .02 |
| ☐ G9 Tommy Maddox RC | 1.50 | .60 |
| ☐ G10 Quentin Coryatt RC | .15 | .05 |
| ☐ G11 Ty Detmer | .30 | .10 |
| ☐ G12 Vaughn Dunbar RC | .10 | .02 |
| ☐ G13 Ashley Ambrose RC | .30 | .10 |
| ☐ G14 Kurt Barber RC | .10 | .02 |
| ☐ G15 Chester McGlockton RC | .30 | .10 |
| ☐ G16 Todd Collins RC | .10 | .02 |
| ☐ G17 Steve Israel RC | .10 | .02 |
| ☐ G18 Marquez Pope RC | .10 | .02 |
| ☐ G19 Alonzo Spellman RC | .15 | .05 |
| ☐ G20 Tracy Scroggins RC | .10 | .02 |
| ☐ G21 Jim Kelly QC | .30 | .10 |
| ☐ G22 Troy Aikman QC | .60 | .25 |
| ☐ G23 Randall Cunningham QC | .30 | .10 |

| | | |
|---|---|---|
| G24 Bernie Kosar QC | .15 | .05 |
| G25 Dan Marino QC | 1.00 | .40 |
| G26 Andre Reed | .15 | .05 |
| G27 Deion Sanders | .50 | .20 |
| G28 Randal Hill | .10 | .02 |
| G29 Eric Dickerson | .15 | .05 |
| G30 Jim Kelly | .30 | .10 |
| G31 Bernie Kosar | .15 | .05 |
| G32 Mike Singletary | .15 | .05 |
| G33 Anthony Miller | .15 | .05 |
| G34 Harvey Williams | .30 | .10 |
| G35 Dan McGwire | .30 | .10 |
| G36 Joe Montana | 1.25 | .50 |
| G37 Dan McGwire | .10 | .02 |
| G38 Al Toon | .15 | .05 |
| G39 Carl Banks | .10 | .02 |
| G40 Troy Aikman | .75 | .30 |
| G41 Junior Seau | .30 | .10 |
| G42 Jeff George | .30 | .10 |
| G43 Michael Dean Perry | .15 | .05 |
| G44 Lawrence Taylor | .30 | .10 |
| G45 Dan Marino | 1.25 | .50 |
| G46 Jerry Rice | .75 | .30 |
| G47 Boomer Esiason | .15 | .05 |
| G48 Bruce Smith | .30 | .10 |
| G49 Leslie O'Neal | .15 | .05 |
| G50 Checklist Card | .10 | .02 |

## 1993 Upper Deck

Barry Foster RB

| | | |
|---|---|---|
| COMPLETE SET (530) | 25.00 | 10.00 |
| 1 Mirer/Hearst/Con/Ken CL | .25 | .08 |
| 2 Eric Curry RC | .05 | .01 |
| 3 Rick Mirer RC | .25 | .08 |
| 4 Dan Williams RC | .05 | .01 |
| 5 Marvin Jones RC | .05 | .01 |
| 6 Willie Roaf RC | .10 | .02 |
| 7 Reggie Brooks RC | .10 | .02 |
| 8 Horace Copeland RC | .10 | .02 |
| 9 Lincoln Kennedy RC | .05 | .01 |
| 10 Curtis Conway RC | .40 | .15 |
| 11 Drew Bledsoe RC | 2.50 | 1.00 |
| 12 Patrick Bates RC | .05 | .01 |
| 13 Wayne Simmons RC | .05 | .01 |
| 14 Irv Smith RC | .05 | .01 |
| 15 Robert Smith RC | 1.25 | .50 |
| 16 O.J.McDuffie RC | .25 | .08 |
| 17 Darrien Gordon RC | .05 | .01 |
| 18 John Copeland RC | .10 | .02 |
| 19 Derek Brown RC RBK | .05 | .01 |
| 20 Jerome Bettis RC | 5.00 | 2.50 |
| 21 Deon Figures RC | .05 | .01 |
| 22 Glyn Milburn RC | .25 | .08 |
| 23 Garrison Hearst RC | .75 | .30 |
| 24 Qadry Ismail RC | .25 | .08 |
| 25 Terry Kirby RC | .25 | .08 |
| 26 Lamar Thomas RC | .05 | .01 |
| 27 Tom Carter RC | .10 | .02 |
| 28 Andre Hastings RC | .10 | .02 |
| 29 George Teague RC | .10 | .02 |
| 30 Tommy Maddox CL | .05 | .01 |
| 31 David Klingler ART | .05 | .01 |
| 32 Tommy Maddox ART | .10 | .02 |
| 33 Vaughn Dunbar ART | .05 | .01 |
| 34 Rodney Culver ART | .05 | .01 |
| 35 Carl Pickens ART | .10 | .02 |
| 36 Courtney Hawkins ART | .05 | .01 |
| 37 Tyji Armstrong ART | .05 | .01 |

| | | |
|---|---|---|
| 38 Ray Roberts ART | .05 | .01 |
| 39 Troy Auzenne ART | .05 | .01 |
| 40 Shane Dronett ART | .05 | .01 |
| 41 Chris Mims ART | .05 | .01 |
| 42 Sean Gilbert ART | .05 | .01 |
| 43 Steve Emtman ART | .05 | .01 |
| 44 Robert Jones ART | .05 | .01 |
| 45 Marco Coleman ART | .05 | .01 |
| 46 Ricardo McDonald ART | .05 | .01 |
| 47 Quentin Coryatt ART | .10 | .02 |
| 48 Dana Hall ART | .05 | .01 |
| 49 Darren Perry ART | .05 | .01 |
| 50 Darryl Williams ART | .05 | .01 |
| 51 Kevin Smith ART | .05 | .01 |
| 52 Terrell Buckley ART | .05 | .01 |
| 53 Troy Vincent ART | .05 | .01 |
| 54 Lin Elliott ART | .05 | .01 |
| 55 Dale Carter ART | .05 | .01 |
| 56 Steve Atwater HIT | .05 | .01 |
| 57 Junior Seau HIT | .10 | .02 |
| 58 Ronnie Lott HIT | .05 | .01 |
| 59 Louis Oliver HIT | .05 | .01 |
| 60 Cortez Kennedy HIT | .05 | .01 |
| 61 Pat Swilling HIT | .05 | .01 |
| 62 Hitmen Checklist | .05 | .01 |
| 63 Curtis Conway TC | .25 | .08 |
| 64 Alfred Williams TC | .05 | .01 |
| 65 Jim Kelly TC | .10 | .02 |
| 66 Simon Fletcher TC | .05 | .01 |
| 67 Eric Metcalf TC | .05 | .01 |
| 68 Lawrence Dawsey TC | .05 | .01 |
| 69 Garrison Hearst TC | .25 | .08 |
| 70 Anthony Miller TC | .05 | .01 |
| 71 Neil Smith TC | .05 | .01 |
| 72 Jeff George TC | .10 | .02 |
| 73 Emmitt Smith TC | .75 | .30 |
| 74 Dan Marino TC | .75 | .30 |
| 75 Clyde Simmons TC | .05 | .01 |
| 76 Deion Sanders TC | .25 | .08 |
| 77 Ricky Watters TC | .10 | .02 |
| 78 Rodney Hampton TC | .10 | .02 |
| 79 Brad Baxter TC | .05 | .01 |
| 80 Barry Sanders TC | .60 | .25 |
| 81 Warren Moon TC | .10 | .02 |
| 82 Brett Favre TC | 1.00 | .40 |
| 83 Drew Bledsoe TC | 1.25 | .50 |
| 84 Tim Brown TC | .10 | .02 |
| 85 Cleveland Gary TC | .05 | .01 |
| 86 Earnest Byner TC | .05 | .01 |
| 87 Wayne Martin TC | .05 | .01 |
| 88 Rick Mirer TC | .25 | .08 |
| 89 Barry Foster TC | .10 | .02 |
| 90 Terry Allen TC | .10 | .02 |
| 91 Vinnie Clark | .05 | .01 |
| 92 Howard Ballard | .05 | .01 |
| 93 Eric Ball | .05 | .01 |
| 94 Marc Boutte | .05 | .01 |
| 95 Larry Centers RC | .25 | .08 |
| 96 Gary Brown | .05 | .01 |
| 97 Hugh Millen | .05 | .01 |
| 98 Anthony Newman RC | .05 | .01 |
| 99 Darrell Thompson | .05 | .01 |
| 100 George Jamison | .05 | .01 |
| 101 James Francis | .05 | .01 |
| 102 Leonard Harris | .05 | .01 |
| 103 Lomas Brown | .05 | .01 |
| 104 James Lofton | .10 | .02 |
| 105 Jamie Dukes | .05 | .01 |
| 106 Quinn Early | .10 | .02 |
| 107 Ernie Jones | .05 | .01 |
| 108 Torrance Small | .05 | .01 |
| 109 Michael Carter | .05 | .01 |
| 110 Aeneas Williams | .05 | .01 |
| 111 Renaldo Turnbull | .05 | .01 |
| 112 Al Smith | .05 | .01 |
| 113 Troy Auzenne | .05 | .01 |
| 114 Stephen Baker | .05 | .01 |
| 115 Daniel Stubbs | .05 | .01 |
| 116 Dana Hall | .05 | .01 |
| 117 Lawrence Taylor | .25 | .08 |
| 118 Ron Hall | .05 | .01 |
| 119 Derrick Fenner | .05 | .01 |
| 120 Martin Mayhew | .05 | .01 |
| 121 Jay Schroeder | .05 | .01 |

| | | |
|---|---|---|
| 122 Michael Zordich | .05 | .01 |
| 123 Ed McCaffrey | .25 | .08 |
| 124 John Stephens | .05 | .01 |
| 125 Brad Edwards | .05 | .01 |
| 126 Don Griffin | .05 | .01 |
| 127 Broderick Thomas | .05 | .01 |
| 128 Ted Washington | .05 | .01 |
| 129 Haywood Jeffires | .10 | .02 |
| 130 Gary Plummer | .05 | .01 |
| 131 Mark Wheeler | .05 | .01 |
| 132 Ty Detmer | .25 | .08 |
| 133 Derrick Walker | .05 | .01 |
| 134 Henry Ellard | .10 | .02 |
| 135 Neal Anderson | .05 | .01 |
| 136 Bruce Smith | .25 | .08 |
| 137 Cris Carter | .25 | .08 |
| 138 Vaughn Dunbar | .05 | .01 |
| 139 Dan Marino | 1.50 | .60 |
| 140 Troy Aikman | .75 | .30 |
| 141 Randall Cunningham | .25 | .08 |
| 142 Daryl Johnston | .25 | .08 |
| 143 Mark Clayton | .05 | .01 |
| 144 Rich Gannon | .25 | .08 |
| 145 Nate Newton | .10 | .02 |
| 146 Willie Gault | .05 | .01 |
| 147 Brian Washington | .05 | .01 |
| 148 Fred Barnett | .10 | .02 |
| 149 Gill Byrd | .05 | .01 |
| 150 Art Monk | .10 | .02 |
| 151 Stan Humphries | .05 | .01 |
| 152 Charles Mann | .05 | .01 |
| 153 Greg Lloyd | .10 | .02 |
| 154 Marvin Washington | .05 | .01 |
| 155 Bernie Kosar | .05 | .01 |
| 156 Pete Metzelaars | .05 | .01 |
| 157 Chris Hinton | .05 | .01 |
| 158 Jim Harbaugh | .25 | .08 |
| 159 Willie Davis | .25 | .08 |
| 160 Leroy Thompson | .05 | .01 |
| 161 Scott Miller | .05 | .01 |
| 162 Eugene Robinson | .05 | .01 |
| 163 David Little | .05 | .01 |
| 164 Pierce Holt | .05 | .01 |
| 165 James Hasty | .05 | .01 |
| 166 Dave Krieg | .10 | .02 |
| 167 Gerald Williams | .05 | .01 |
| 168 Kyle Clifton | .05 | .01 |
| 169 Bill Brooks | .05 | .01 |
| 170 Vance Johnson | .05 | .01 |
| 171 Greg Townsend | .05 | .01 |
| 172 Jason Belser | .05 | .01 |
| 173 Brett Perriman | .25 | .08 |
| 174 Steve Jordan | .05 | .01 |
| 175 Kelvin Martin | .05 | .01 |
| 176 Greg Kragen | .05 | .01 |
| 177 Kerry Cash | .05 | .01 |
| 178 Chester McGlockton | .05 | .01 |
| 179 Jim Kelly | .25 | .08 |
| 180 Todd McNair | .05 | .01 |
| 181 Leroy Hoard | .10 | .02 |
| 182 Seth Joyner | .05 | .01 |
| 183 Sam Gash RC | .25 | .08 |
| 184 Joe Nash | .05 | .01 |
| 185 Lin Elliott RC | .05 | .01 |
| 186 Robert Porcher | .05 | .01 |
| 187 Tommy Hodson | .05 | .01 |
| 188 Greg Lewis | .05 | .01 |
| 189 Dan Saleaumua | .05 | .01 |
| 190 Chris Goode | .05 | .01 |
| 191 Henry Thomas | .05 | .01 |
| 192 Bobby Hebert | .05 | .01 |
| 193 Clay Matthews | .10 | .02 |
| 194 Mark Carrier WR | .10 | .02 |
| 195 Anthony Pleasant | .05 | .01 |
| 196 Eric Dorsey | .05 | .01 |
| 197 Clarence Verdin | .05 | .01 |
| 198 Marc Spindler | .05 | .01 |
| 199 Tommy Maddox | .25 | .08 |
| 200 Wendell Davis | .05 | .01 |
| 201 John Fina | .05 | .01 |
| 202 Alonzo Spellman | .05 | .01 |
| 203 Darryl Williams | .05 | .01 |
| 204 Mike Croel | .05 | .01 |
| 205 Ken Norton Jr. | .10 | .02 |

| | | | | | | | | | |
|---|---|---|---|---|---|---|---|---|---|
| ❏ 206 Mel Gray | .10 | .02 | ❏ 290 Michael Dean Perry | .10 | .02 | ❏ 374 Brad Baxter | .05 | .01 |
| ❏ 207 Chuck Cecil | .05 | .01 | ❏ 291 Richard Dent | .10 | .02 | ❏ 375 Ernest Givins | .10 | .02 |
| ❏ 208 John Flannery | .05 | .01 | ❏ 292 Howie Long | .25 | .08 | ❏ 376 Keith Byars | .05 | .01 |
| ❏ 209 Chip Banks | .05 | .01 | ❏ 293 Chris Mims | .05 | .01 | ❏ 377 Eric Bieniemy | .05 | .01 |
| ❏ 210 Chris Martin | .05 | .01 | ❏ 294 Kurt Barber | .05 | .01 | ❏ 378 Mike Brim | .05 | .01 |
| ❏ 211 Dennis Brown | .05 | .01 | ❏ 295 Wilber Marshall | .05 | .01 | ❏ 379 Darren Lewis | .05 | .01 |
| ❏ 212 Vinny Testaverde | .10 | .02 | ❏ 296 Ethan Horton | .05 | .01 | ❏ 380 Heath Sherman | .05 | .01 |
| ❏ 213 Nick Bell | .05 | .01 | ❏ 297 Tony Bennett | .05 | .01 | ❏ 381 Leonard Russell | .10 | .02 |
| ❏ 214 Robert Delpino | .05 | .01 | ❏ 298 Johnny Johnson | .05 | .01 | ❏ 382 Brent Jones | .10 | .02 |
| ❏ 215 Mark Higgs | .05 | .01 | ❏ 299 Craig Heyward | .10 | .02 | ❏ 383 David Whitmore | .05 | .01 |
| ❏ 216 Al Noga | .05 | .01 | ❏ 300 Steve Israel | .05 | .01 | ❏ 384 Ray Roberts | .05 | .01 |
| ❏ 217 Andre Tippett | .05 | .01 | ❏ 301 Kenneth Gant | .05 | .01 | ❏ 385 John Offerdahl | .05 | .01 |
| ❏ 218 Pat Swilling | .05 | .01 | ❏ 302 Eugene Chung | .05 | .01 | ❏ 386 Keith McCants | .05 | .01 |
| ❏ 219 Phil Simms | .10 | .02 | ❏ 303 Harvey Williams | .10 | .02 | ❏ 387 John Baylor | .05 | .01 |
| ❏ 220 Ricky Proehl | .05 | .01 | ❏ 304 Jarrod Bunch | .05 | .01 | ❏ 388 Amp Lee | .05 | .01 |
| ❏ 221 William Thomas | .05 | .01 | ❏ 305 Darren Perry | .05 | .01 | ❏ 389 Chris Warren | .10 | .02 |
| ❏ 222 Jeff Graham | .10 | .02 | ❏ 306 Steve Christie | .05 | .01 | ❏ 390 Herman Moore | .25 | .08 |
| ❏ 223 Darion Conner | .05 | .01 | ❏ 307 John Randle | .10 | .02 | ❏ 391 Johnny Bailey | .05 | .01 |
| ❏ 224 Mark Carrier DB | .05 | .01 | ❏ 308 Warren Moon | .25 | .08 | ❏ 392 Tim Johnson | .05 | .01 |
| ❏ 225 Willie Green | .05 | .01 | ❏ 309 Charles Haley | .10 | .02 | ❏ 393 Eric Metcalf | .10 | .02 |
| ❏ 226 Reggie Rivers RC | .05 | .01 | ❏ 310 Tony Smith RB | .05 | .01 | ❏ 394 Chris Chandler | .10 | .02 |
| ❏ 227 Andre Reed | .10 | .02 | ❏ 311 Steve Broussard | .05 | .01 | ❏ 395 Mark Rypien | .05 | .01 |
| ❏ 228 Deion Sanders | .50 | .20 | ❏ 312 Alfred Williams | .05 | .01 | ❏ 396 Christian Okoye | .05 | .01 |
| ❏ 229 Chris Doleman | .05 | .01 | ❏ 313 Terrell Buckley | .05 | .01 | ❏ 397 Shannon Sharpe | .25 | .08 |
| ❏ 230 Jerry Ball | .05 | .01 | ❏ 314 Trace Armstrong | .05 | .01 | ❏ 398 Eric Hill | .05 | .01 |
| ❏ 231 Eric Dickerson | .10 | .02 | ❏ 315 Brian Mitchell | .10 | .02 | ❏ 399 David Lang | .05 | .01 |
| ❏ 232 Carlos Jenkins | .05 | .01 | ❏ 316 Steve Atwater | .05 | .01 | ❏ 400 Bruce Matthews | .05 | .01 |
| ❏ 233 Mike Johnson | .05 | .01 | ❏ 317 Nate Lewis | .05 | .01 | ❏ 401 Harold Green | .05 | .01 |
| ❏ 234 Marco Coleman | .05 | .01 | ❏ 318 Richard Brown | .05 | .01 | ❏ 402 Mo Lewis | .05 | .01 |
| ❏ 235 Leslie O'Neal | .10 | .02 | ❏ 319 Rufus Porter | .05 | .01 | ❏ 403 Terry McDaniel | .05 | .01 |
| ❏ 236 Browning Nagle | .05 | .01 | ❏ 320 Pat Harlow | .05 | .01 | ❏ 404 Wesley Carroll | .05 | .01 |
| ❏ 237 Carl Pickens | .10 | .02 | ❏ 321 Anthony Smith | .05 | .01 | ❏ 405 Richmond Webb | .05 | .01 |
| ❏ 238 Steve Emtman | .05 | .01 | ❏ 322 Jack Del Rio | .05 | .01 | ❏ 406 Andre Rison | .10 | .02 |
| ❏ 239 Alvin Harper | .10 | .02 | ❏ 323 Darryl Talley | .05 | .01 | ❏ 407 Lonnie Young | .05 | .01 |
| ❏ 240 Keith Jackson | .10 | .02 | ❏ 324 Sam Mills | .05 | .01 | ❏ 408 Tommy Vardell | .05 | .01 |
| ❏ 241 Jerry Rice | 1.00 | .40 | ❏ 325 Chris Miller | .10 | .02 | ❏ 409 Gene Atkins | .05 | .01 |
| ❏ 242 Cortez Kennedy | .10 | .02 | ❏ 326 Ken Harvey | .05 | .01 | ❏ 410 Sean Salisbury | .05 | .01 |
| ❏ 243 Tyji Armstrong | .05 | .01 | ❏ 327 Rod Woodson | .25 | .08 | ❏ 411 Kenneth Davis | .05 | .01 |
| ❏ 244 Troy Vincent | .05 | .01 | ❏ 328 Tony Tolbert | .05 | .01 | ❏ 412 John L. Williams | .05 | .01 |
| ❏ 245 Randal Hill | .05 | .01 | ❏ 329 Todd Kinchen | .05 | .01 | ❏ 413 Roman Phifer | .05 | .01 |
| ❏ 246 Robert Blackmon | .05 | .01 | ❏ 330 Brian Noble | .05 | .01 | ❏ 414 Bennie Blades | .05 | .01 |
| ❏ 247 Junior Seau | .25 | .08 | ❏ 331 Dave Meggett | .05 | .01 | ❏ 415 Tim Brown | .25 | .08 |
| ❏ 248 Sterling Sharpe | .25 | .08 | ❏ 332 Chris Spielman | .05 | .01 | ❏ 416 Lorenzo White | .05 | .01 |
| ❏ 249 Thurman Thomas | .25 | .08 | ❏ 333 Barry Word | .05 | .01 | ❏ 417 Tony Casillas | .05 | .01 |
| ❏ 250 David Klingler | .05 | .01 | ❏ 334 Jessie Hester | .05 | .01 | ❏ 418 Tom Waddle | .05 | .01 |
| ❏ 251 Jeff George | .25 | .08 | ❏ 335 Michael Jackson | .10 | .02 | ❏ 419 David Fulcher | .05 | .01 |
| ❏ 252 Anthony Miller | .10 | .02 | ❏ 336 Mitchell Price | .05 | .01 | ❏ 420 Jessie Tuggle | .05 | .01 |
| ❏ 253 Earnest Byner | .05 | .01 | ❏ 337 Michael Irvin | .25 | .08 | ❏ 421 Emmitt Smith SL | .75 | .30 |
| ❏ 254 Eric Swann | .10 | .02 | ❏ 338 Simon Fletcher | .05 | .01 | ❏ 422 Clyde Simmons SL | .05 | .01 |
| ❏ 255 Jeff Herrod | .05 | .01 | ❏ 339 Keith Jennings | .05 | .01 | ❏ 423 Sterling Sharpe SL | .10 | .02 |
| ❏ 256 Eddie Robinson | .05 | .01 | ❏ 340 Vai Sikahema | .05 | .01 | ❏ 424 Sterling Sharpe SL | .10 | .02 |
| ❏ 257 Eric Allen | .05 | .01 | ❏ 341 Roger Craig | .10 | .02 | ❏ 425 Emmitt Smith SL | .75 | .30 |
| ❏ 258 John Taylor | .10 | .02 | ❏ 342 Ricky Watters | .25 | .08 | ❏ 426 Dan Marino SL | .75 | .30 |
| ❏ 259 Sean Gilbert | .10 | .02 | ❏ 343 Reggie Cobb | .05 | .01 | ❏ 427 Henry Jones SL | .05 | .01 |
| ❏ 260 Ray Childress | .05 | .01 | ❏ 344 Kanavis McGhee | .05 | .01 | ❏ 428 Thurman Thomas SL | .10 | .02 |
| ❏ 261 Michael Haynes | .10 | .02 | ❏ 345 Barry Foster | .10 | .02 | ❏ 429 Greg Montgomery SL | .05 | .01 |
| ❏ 262 Greg McMurtry | .05 | .01 | ❏ 346 Marion Butts | .05 | .01 | ❏ 430 Pete Stoyanovich SL | .05 | .01 |
| ❏ 263 Bill Romanowski | .05 | .01 | ❏ 347 Bryan Cox | .05 | .01 | ❏ 431 Emmitt Smith BB | .40 | .15 |
| ❏ 264 Todd Lyght | .05 | .01 | ❏ 348 Wayne Martin | .05 | .01 | ❏ 432 Steve Young BB | .40 | .15 |
| ❏ 265 Clyde Simmons | .05 | .01 | ❏ 349 Jim Everett | .10 | .02 | ❏ 433 Jerry Rice BB | .50 | .20 |
| ❏ 266 Webster Slaughter | .05 | .01 | ❏ 350 Nate Odomes | .05 | .01 | ❏ 434 Ricky Watters BB | .10 | .02 |
| ❏ 267 J.J. Birden | .05 | .01 | ❏ 351 Anthony Johnson | .10 | .02 | ❏ 435 Barry Foster BB | .05 | .01 |
| ❏ 268 Aaron Wallace | .05 | .01 | ❏ 352 Rodney Hampton | .10 | .02 | ❏ 436 Cortez Kennedy BB | .05 | .01 |
| ❏ 269 Carl Banks | .05 | .01 | ❏ 353 Terry Allen | .25 | .08 | ❏ 437 Warren Moon BB | .10 | .02 |
| ❏ 270 Ricardo McDonald | .05 | .01 | ❏ 354 Derrick Thomas | .25 | .08 | ❏ 438 Thurman Thomas BB | .10 | .02 |
| ❏ 271 Michael Brooks | .05 | .01 | ❏ 355 Calvin Williams | .10 | .02 | ❏ 439 Brett Favre BB | 1.00 | .40 |
| ❏ 272 Dale Carter | .05 | .01 | ❏ 356 Pepper Johnson | .05 | .01 | ❏ 440 Andre Rison BB | .10 | .02 |
| ❏ 273 Mike Pritchard | .10 | .02 | ❏ 357 John Elway | 1.50 | .60 | ❏ 441 Barry Sanders BB | .60 | .25 |
| ❏ 274 Derek Brown TE | .05 | .01 | ❏ 358 Steve Young | .75 | .30 | ❏ 442 Chris Berman CL | .05 | .01 |
| ❏ 275 Burt Grossman | .05 | .01 | ❏ 359 Emmitt Smith | 1.50 | .60 | ❏ 443 Moe Gardner | .05 | .01 |
| ❏ 276 Mark Schlereth | .05 | .01 | ❏ 360 Brett Favre | 2.00 | .75 | ❏ 444 Robert Jones | .05 | .01 |
| ❏ 277 Karl Mecklenburg | .05 | .01 | ❏ 361 Cody Carlson | .05 | .01 | ❏ 445 Reggie Langhorne | .05 | .01 |
| ❏ 278 Rickey Jackson | .05 | .01 | ❏ 362 Vincent Brown | .05 | .01 | ❏ 446 Flipper Anderson | .05 | .01 |
| ❏ 279 Ricky Ervins | .05 | .01 | ❏ 363 Gary Anderson RB | .05 | .01 | ❏ 447 James Washington | .05 | .01 |
| ❏ 280 Jeff Bryant | .05 | .01 | ❏ 364 Jon Vaughn | .05 | .01 | ❏ 448 Aaron Craver | .05 | .01 |
| ❏ 281 Eric Martin | .05 | .01 | ❏ 365 Todd Marinovich | .05 | .01 | ❏ 449 Jack Trudeau | .05 | .01 |
| ❏ 282 Carlton Haselrig | .05 | .01 | ❏ 366 Carnell Lake | .05 | .01 | ❏ 450 Neil Smith | .25 | .08 |
| ❏ 283 Kevin Mack | .05 | .01 | ❏ 367 Kurt Gouveia | .05 | .01 | ❏ 451 Chris Burkett | .05 | .01 |
| ❏ 284 Brad Muster | .05 | .01 | ❏ 368 Lawrence Dawsey | .05 | .01 | ❏ 452 Russell Maryland | .05 | .01 |
| ❏ 285 Kelvin Pritchett | .05 | .01 | ❏ 369 Neil O'Donnell | .25 | .08 | ❏ 453 Drew Hill | .05 | .01 |
| ❏ 286 Courtney Hawkins | .05 | .01 | ❏ 370 Duane Bickett | .05 | .01 | ❏ 454 Barry Sanders | 1.25 | .50 |
| ❏ 287 Levon Kirkland | .05 | .01 | ❏ 371 Ronnie Harmon | .05 | .01 | ❏ 455 Jeff Cross | .05 | .01 |
| ❏ 288 Steve DeBerg | .05 | .01 | ❏ 372 Rodney Peete | .05 | .01 | ❏ 456 Bennie Thompson | .05 | .01 |
| ❏ 289 Edgar Bennett | .25 | .08 | ❏ 373 Cornelius Bennett | .10 | .02 | ❏ 457 Marcus Allen | .25 | .08 |

| | | |
|---|---|---|
| 458 Tracy Scroggins | .05 | .01 |
| 459 LeRoy Butler | .05 | .01 |
| 460 Joe Montana | 1.50 | .60 |
| 461 Eddie Anderson | .05 | .01 |
| 462 Tim McDonald- | .05 | .01 |
| 463 Ronnie Lott | .10 | .02 |
| 464 Gaston Green | .05 | .01 |
| 465 Shane Conlan | .05 | .01 |
| 466 Leonard Marshall | .05 | .01 |
| 467 Melvin Jenkins | .05 | .01 |
| 468 Don Beebe | .05 | .01 |
| 469 Johnny Mitchell | .05 | .01 |
| 470 Darryl Henley | .05 | .01 |
| 471 Boomer Esiason | .10 | .02 |
| 472 Mark Kelso | .05 | .01 |
| 473 John Booty | .05 | .01 |
| 474 Pete Stoyanovich | .05 | .01 |
| 475 Thomas Smith RC | .10 | .02 |
| 476 Carlton Gray RC | .05 | .01 |
| 477 Dana Stubblefield RC | .25 | .08 |
| 478 Ryan McNeil RC | .25 | .08 |
| 479 Natrone Means RC | .25 | .08 |
| 480 Carl Simpson RC | .05 | .01 |
| 481 Robert O'Neal RC | .05 | .01 |
| 482 Demetrius DuBose RC | .05 | .01 |
| 483 Darrin Smith RC | .10 | .02 |
| 484 Micheal Barrow RC | .25 | .08 |
| 485 Chris Slade RC | .10 | .02 |
| 486 Steve Tovar RC | .05 | .01 |
| 487 Ron George RC | .05 | .01 |
| 488 Steve Tasker | .10 | .02 |
| 489 Will Furrer | .05 | .01 |
| 490 Reggie White | .25 | .08 |
| 491 Sean Jones | .05 | .01 |
| 492 Gary Clark | .10 | .02 |
| 493 Donnell Woolford | .05 | .01 |
| 494 Steve Beuerlein | .10 | .02 |
| 495 Anthony Carter | .10 | .02 |
| 496 Louis Oliver | .05 | .01 |
| 497 Chris Zorich | .05 | .01 |
| 498 David Brandon | .05 | .01 |
| 499 Bubba McDowell | .05 | .01 |
| 500 Adrian Cooper | .05 | .01 |
| 501 Bill Johnson | .05 | .01 |
| 502 Shawn Jefferson | .05 | .01 |
| 503 Siran Stacy | .05 | .01 |
| 504 James Jones DT | .05 | .01 |
| 505 Tom Rathman | .05 | .01 |
| 506 Vince Buck | .05 | .01 |
| 507 Kent Graham RC | .25 | .08 |
| 508 Darren Carrington RC | .05 | .01 |
| 509 Rickey Dixon | .05 | .01 |
| 510 Toi Cook | .05 | .01 |
| 511 Steve Smith | .05 | .01 |
| 512 Eric Green | .05 | .01 |
| 513 Phillippi Sparks | .05 | .01 |
| 514 Lee Williams | .05 | .01 |
| 515 Gary Reasons | .05 | .01 |
| 516 Shane Dronett | .05 | .01 |
| 517 Jay Novacek | .10 | .02 |
| 518 Kevin Greene | .10 | .02 |
| 519 Derek Russell | .05 | .01 |
| 520 Quentin Coryatt | .10 | .02 |
| 521 Santana Dotson | .10 | .02 |
| 522 Donald Frank | .05 | .01 |
| 523 Mike Prior | .05 | .01 |
| 524 Dwight Hollier RC | .05 | .01 |
| 525 Eric Davis | .05 | .01 |
| 526 Dalton Hilliard | .05 | .01 |
| 527 Rodney Culver | .05 | .01 |
| 528 Jeff Hostetler | .10 | .02 |
| 529 Ernie Mills | .05 | .01 |
| 530 Craig Erickson | .10 | .02 |
| P231 Eric Dickerson Promo | 1.25 | .50 |

### 1994 Upper Deck

| | | |
|---|---|---|
| COMPLETE SET (330) | 25.00 | 12.50 |
| 1 Dan Wilkinson RC | .20 | .07 |
| 2 Antonio Langham RC | .20 | .07 |
| 3 Derrick Alexander WR RC | .40 | .15 |
| 4 Charles Johnson RC | .40 | .15 |
| 5 Bucky Brooks RC | .10 | .02 |
| 6 Trev Alberts RC | .20 | .07 |
| 7 Marshall Faulk RC | 6.00 | 2.50 |

| | | |
|---|---|---|
| 8 Willie McGinest RC | .40 | .15 |
| 9 Aaron Glenn RC | .40 | .15 |
| 10 Ryan Yarborough RC | .10 | .02 |
| 11 Greg Hill RC | .40 | .15 |
| 12 Sam Adams RC | .20 | .07 |
| 13 John Thierry RC | .10 | .02 |
| 14 Johnnie Morton RC | .75 | .30 |
| 15 LeShon Johnson RC | .20 | .07 |
| 16 David Palmer RC | .50 | |
| 17 Trent Dilfer RC | 1.25 | .50 |
| 18 Jamir Miller RC | .20 | .07 |
| 19 Thomas Lewis RC | .20 | .07 |
| 20 Heath Shuler RC | .40 | .15 |
| 21 Wayne Gandy | .10 | .02 |
| 22 Isaac Bruce RC | 4.00 | 2.00 |
| 23 Joe Johnson RC | .10 | .02 |
| 24 Mario Bates RC | .40 | .15 |
| 25 Bryant Young RC | .60 | .25 |
| 26 William Floyd RC | .40 | .15 |
| 27 Errict Rhett RC | .40 | .15 |
| 28 Chuck Levy RC | .10 | .02 |
| 29 Darnay Scott RC | .75 | .30 |
| 30 Rob Fredrickson RC | .20 | .07 |
| 31 Jamir Miller HW | .10 | .02 |
| 32 Thomas Lewis HW | .10 | .02 |
| 33 John Thierry HW | .10 | .02 |
| 34 Sam Adams HW | .10 | .02 |
| 35 Joe Johnson HW | .10 | .02 |
| 36 Bryant Young HW | .30 | .10 |
| 37 Wayne Gandy HW | .10 | .02 |
| 38 LeShon Johnson HW | .10 | .02 |
| 39 Mario Bates HW | .20 | .07 |
| 40 Greg Hill HW | .20 | .07 |
| 41 Andy Heck | .10 | .02 |
| 42 Warren Moon | .40 | .15 |
| 43 Jim Everett | .20 | .07 |
| 44 Bill Romanowski | .10 | .02 |
| 45 Michael Haynes | .20 | .07 |
| 46 Chris Doleman | .10 | .02 |
| 47 Merril Hoge | .10 | .02 |
| 48 Chris Miller | .10 | .02 |
| 49 Clyde Simmons | .10 | .02 |
| 50 Jeff George | .40 | .15 |
| 51 Jeff Burris RC | .20 | .07 |
| 52 Ethan Horton | .10 | .02 |
| 53 Scott Mitchell | .20 | .07 |
| 54 Howard Ballard | .10 | .02 |
| 55 Lewis Tillman | .10 | .02 |
| 56 Marion Butts | .10 | .02 |
| 57 Erik Kramer | .20 | .07 |
| 58 Ken Norton Jr. | .20 | .07 |
| 59 Anthony Miller | .20 | .07 |
| 60 Chris Hinton | .10 | .02 |
| 61 Ricky Proehl | .10 | .02 |
| 62 Craig Heyward | .20 | .07 |
| 63 Darryl Talley | .10 | .02 |
| 64 Tim Worley | .10 | .02 |
| 65 Derrick Fenner | .10 | .02 |
| 66 Jerry Ball | .10 | .02 |
| 67 Darrin Smith | .10 | .02 |
| 68 Mike Croel | .10 | .02 |
| 69 Ray Crockett | .10 | .02 |
| 70 Tony Bennett | .10 | .02 |
| 71 Webster Slaughter | .10 | .02 |
| 72 Anthony Johnson | .20 | .07 |
| 73 Charles Mincy | .10 | .02 |
| 74 Calvin Jones RC | .10 | .02 |

| | | |
|---|---|---|
| 75 Henry Ellard | .20 | .07 |
| 76 Troy Vincent | .10 | .02 |
| 77 Sean Salisbury | .10 | .02 |
| 78 Pat Harlow | .10 | .02 |
| 79 James Williams RC LB | .10 | .02 |
| 80 Dave Brown | .20 | .07 |
| 81 Kent Graham | .20 | .07 |
| 82 Seth Joyner | .10 | .02 |
| 83 Deon Figures | .10 | .02 |
| 84 Stanley Richard | .10 | .02 |
| 85 Tom Rathman | .10 | .02 |
| 86 Rod Stephens | .10 | .02 |
| 87 Ray Seals | .10 | .02 |
| 88 Andre Collins | .10 | .02 |
| 89 Cornelius Bennett | .20 | .07 |
| 90 Richard Dent | .20 | .07 |
| 91 Louis Oliver | .10 | .02 |
| 92 Rodney Peete | .10 | .02 |
| 93 Jackie Harris | .10 | .02 |
| 94 Tracy Simien | .10 | .02 |
| 95 Greg Townsend | .10 | .02 |
| 96 Michael Stewart | .10 | .02 |
| 97 Irving Fryar | .20 | .07 |
| 98 Todd Collins | .10 | .02 |
| 99 Irv Smith | .10 | .02 |
| 100 Chris Calloway | .10 | .02 |
| 101 Kevin Greene | .20 | .07 |
| 102 John Friesz | .10 | .02 |
| 103 Steve Bono | .20 | .07 |
| 104 Brian Blades | .20 | .07 |
| 105 Reggie Cobb | .10 | .02 |
| 106 Eric Swann | .10 | .02 |
| 107 Mike Pritchard | .10 | .02 |
| 108 Bill Brooks | .10 | .02 |
| 109 Jim Harbaugh | .40 | .15 |
| 110 David Whitmore | .10 | .02 |
| 111 Eddie Anderson | .10 | .02 |
| 112 Ray Crittenden RC | .10 | .02 |
| 113 Mark Collins | .10 | .02 |
| 114 Brian Washington | .10 | .02 |
| 115 Barry Foster | .20 | .07 |
| 116 Gary Plummer | .10 | .02 |
| 117 Marc Logan | .10 | .02 |
| 118 John L. Williams | .10 | .02 |
| 119 Marty Carter | .10 | .02 |
| 120 Kurt Gouveia | .10 | .02 |
| 121 Ronald Moore | .10 | .02 |
| 122 Pierce Holt | .10 | .02 |
| 123 Henry Jones | .10 | .02 |
| 124 Donnell Woolford | .10 | .02 |
| 125 Steve Tovar | .10 | .02 |
| 126 Anthony Pleasant | .10 | .02 |
| 127 Jay Novacek | .20 | .07 |
| 128 Dan Williams | .10 | .02 |
| 129 Barry Sanders | 2.50 | 1.00 |
| 130 Robert Brooks | .40 | .15 |
| 131 Lorenzo White | .10 | .02 |
| 132 Kerry Cash | .10 | .02 |
| 133 Joe Montana | 3.00 | 1.25 |
| 134 Jeff Hostetler | .20 | .07 |
| 135 Jerome Bettis | .60 | .25 |
| 136 Dan Marino | 3.00 | 1.25 |
| 137 Vencie Glenn | .10 | .02 |
| 138 Vincent Brown | .10 | .02 |
| 139 Rickey Jackson | .10 | .02 |
| 140 Carlton Bailey | .10 | .02 |
| 141 Jeff Lageman | .10 | .02 |
| 142 William Thomas | .10 | .02 |
| 143 Neil O'Donnell | .40 | .15 |
| 144 Shawn Jefferson | .10 | .02 |
| 145 Steve Young | 1.00 | .40 |
| 146 Chris Warren | .20 | .07 |
| 147 Courtney Hawkins | .10 | .02 |
| 148 Brad Edwards | .10 | .02 |
| 149 O.J.McDuffie | .40 | .15 |
| 150 David Lang | .10 | .02 |
| 151 Chuck Cecil | .10 | .02 |
| 152 Norm Johnson | .10 | .02 |
| 153 Pete Metzelaars | .10 | .02 |
| 154 Shaun Gayle | .10 | .02 |
| 155 Alfred Williams | .10 | .02 |
| 156 Eric Turner | .10 | .02 |
| 157A Emmitt Smith ERR 1900 | 2.50 | 1.00 |
| 157B Emmitt Smith COR | 2.50 | 1.00 |

| | | |
|---|---|---|
| ❑ 158 Steve Atwater | .10 | .02 |
| ❑ 159 Robert Porcher | .10 | .02 |
| ❑ 160 Edgar Bennett | .40 | .15 |
| ❑ 161 Bubba McDowell | .10 | .02 |
| ❑ 162 Jeff Herrod | .10 | .02 |
| ❑ 163 Keith Cash | .10 | .02 |
| ❑ 164 Patrick Bates | .10 | .02 |
| ❑ 165 Todd Lyght | .10 | .02 |
| ❑ 166 Mark Higgs | .10 | .02 |
| ❑ 167 Carlos Jenkins | .10 | .02 |
| ❑ 168 Drew Bledsoe | 1.00 | .40 |
| ❑ 169 Wayne Martin | .10 | .02 |
| ❑ 170 Mike Sherrard | .10 | .02 |
| ❑ 171 Ronnie Lott | .20 | .07 |
| ❑ 172 Fred Barnett | .20 | .07 |
| ❑ 173 Eric Green | .10 | .02 |
| ❑ 174 Leslie O'Neal | .10 | .02 |
| ❑ 175 Brent Jones | .20 | .07 |
| ❑ 176 Jon Vaughn | .10 | .02 |
| ❑ 177 Vince Workman | .10 | .02 |
| ❑ 178 Ron Middleton | .10 | .02 |
| ❑ 179 Terry McDaniel | .10 | .02 |
| ❑ 180 Willie Davis | .20 | .07 |
| ❑ 181 Gary Clark | .20 | .07 |
| ❑ 182 Bobby Hebert | .10 | .02 |
| ❑ 183 Russell Copeland | .10 | .02 |
| ❑ 184 Chris Gedney | .10 | .02 |
| ❑ 185 Tony McGee | .10 | .02 |
| ❑ 186 Rob Burnett | .10 | .02 |
| ❑ 187 Charles Haley | .10 | .02 |
| ❑ 188 Shannon Sharpe | .20 | .07 |
| ❑ 189 Mel Gray | .10 | .02 |
| ❑ 190 George Teague | .10 | .02 |
| ❑ 191 Ernest Givins | .20 | .07 |
| ❑ 192 Ray Buchanan | .10 | .02 |
| ❑ 193 J.J. Birden | .10 | .02 |
| ❑ 194 Tim Brown | .40 | .15 |
| ❑ 195 Tim Lester | .10 | .02 |
| ❑ 196 Marco Coleman | .10 | .02 |
| ❑ 197 Randall McDaniel | .15 | .05 |
| ❑ 198 Bruce Armstrong | .10 | .02 |
| ❑ 199 Willie Roaf | .20 | .07 |
| ❑ 200 Greg Jackson | .10 | .02 |
| ❑ 201 Johnny Mitchell | .10 | .02 |
| ❑ 202 Calvin Williams | .20 | .07 |
| ❑ 203 Jeff Graham | .10 | .02 |
| ❑ 204 Darren Carrington | .10 | .02 |
| ❑ 205 Jerry Rice | 1.50 | .60 |
| ❑ 206 Cortez Kennedy | .20 | .07 |
| ❑ 207 Charles Wilson | .10 | .02 |
| ❑ 208 James Jenkins TE RC | .10 | .02 |
| ❑ 209 Ray Childress | .10 | .02 |
| ❑ 210 LeRoy Butler | .10 | .02 |
| ❑ 211 Randal Hill | .10 | .02 |
| ❑ 212 Lincoln Kennedy | .10 | .02 |
| ❑ 213 Kenneth Davis | .10 | .02 |
| ❑ 214 Terry Obee | .10 | .02 |
| ❑ 215 Ricardo McDonald | .10 | .02 |
| ❑ 216 Pepper Johnson | .10 | .02 |
| ❑ 217 Alvin Harper | .20 | .07 |
| ❑ 218 John Elway | 3.00 | 1.25 |
| ❑ 219 Derrick Moore | .10 | .02 |
| ❑ 220 Terrell Buckley | .10 | .02 |
| ❑ 221 Haywood Jeffires | .20 | .07 |
| ❑ 222 Jessie Hester | .10 | .02 |
| ❑ 223 Kimble Anders | .20 | .07 |
| ❑ 224 Rocket Ismail | .20 | .07 |
| ❑ 225 Roman Phifer | .10 | .02 |
| ❑ 226 Bryan Cox | .10 | .02 |
| ❑ 227 Cris Carter | .75 | .30 |
| ❑ 228 Sam Gash | .10 | .02 |
| ❑ 229 Renaldo Turnbull | .10 | .02 |
| ❑ 230 Rodney Hampton | .20 | .07 |
| ❑ 231 Johnny Johnson | .10 | .02 |
| ❑ 232 Tim Harris | .10 | .02 |
| ❑ 233 Leroy Thompson | .10 | .02 |
| ❑ 234 Junior Seau | .40 | .15 |
| ❑ 235 Tim McDonald | .10 | .02 |
| ❑ 236 Eugene Robinson | .10 | .02 |
| ❑ 237 Lawrence Dawsey | .10 | .02 |
| ❑ 238 Tim Johnson | .10 | .02 |
| ❑ 239 Jason Elam | .20 | .07 |
| ❑ 240 Willie Green | .10 | .02 |
| ❑ 241 Larry Centers | .40 | .15 |

| | | |
|---|---|---|
| ❑ 242 Erric Pegram | .10 | .02 |
| ❑ 243 Bruce Smith | .40 | .15 |
| ❑ 244 Alonzo Spellman | .10 | .02 |
| ❑ 245 Carl Pickens | .20 | .07 |
| ❑ 246 Michael Jackson | .20 | .07 |
| ❑ 247 Kevin Williams WR | .20 | .07 |
| ❑ 248 Glyn Milburn | .20 | .07 |
| ❑ 249 Herman Moore | .40 | .15 |
| ❑ 250 Brett Favre | 3.00 | 1.25 |
| ❑ 251 Al Smith | .10 | .02 |
| ❑ 252 Roosevelt Potts | .10 | .02 |
| ❑ 253 Marcus Allen | .40 | .15 |
| ❑ 254 Anthony Smith | .10 | .02 |
| ❑ 255 Sean Gilbert | .10 | .02 |
| ❑ 256 Keith Byars | .10 | .02 |
| ❑ 257 Scottie Graham RC | .20 | .07 |
| ❑ 258 Leonard Russell | .10 | .02 |
| ❑ 259 Eric Martin | .10 | .02 |
| ❑ 260 Jarrod Bunch | .10 | .02 |
| ❑ 261 Rob Moore | .20 | .07 |
| ❑ 262 Herschel Walker | .20 | .07 |
| ❑ 263 Levon Kirkland | .10 | .02 |
| ❑ 264 Chris Mims | .10 | .02 |
| ❑ 265 Ricky Watters | .20 | .07 |
| ❑ 266 Rick Mirer | .40 | .15 |
| ❑ 267 Santana Dotson | .20 | .07 |
| ❑ 268 Reggie Brooks | .20 | .07 |
| ❑ 269 Garrison Hearst | .40 | .15 |
| ❑ 270 Thurman Thomas | .40 | .15 |
| ❑ 271 Johnny Bailey | .10 | .02 |
| ❑ 272 Andre Rison | .20 | .07 |
| ❑ 273 Jim Kelly | .40 | .15 |
| ❑ 274 Mark Carrier DB | .10 | .02 |
| ❑ 275 David Klingler | .10 | .02 |
| ❑ 276 Eric Metcalf | .20 | .07 |
| ❑ 277 Troy Aikman UER | 1.50 | .60 |
| ❑ 278 Simon Fletcher | .10 | .02 |
| ❑ 279 Pat Swilling | .10 | .02 |
| ❑ 280 Sterling Sharpe | .20 | .07 |
| ❑ 281 Cody Carlson | .10 | .02 |
| ❑ 282 Steve Emtman | .10 | .02 |
| ❑ 283 Neil Smith | .20 | .07 |
| ❑ 284 James Jett | .10 | .02 |
| ❑ 285 Shane Conlan | .10 | .02 |
| ❑ 286 Keith Jackson | .10 | .02 |
| ❑ 287 Qadry Ismail | .40 | .15 |
| ❑ 288 Chris Slade | .10 | .02 |
| ❑ 289 Derek Brown RBK | .10 | .02 |
| ❑ 290 Phil Simms | .20 | .07 |
| ❑ 291 Boomer Esiason | .20 | .07 |
| ❑ 292 Eric Allen | .10 | .02 |
| ❑ 293 Rod Woodson | .20 | .07 |
| ❑ 294 Ronnie Harmon | .10 | .02 |
| ❑ 295 John Taylor | .20 | .07 |
| ❑ 296 Ferrell Edmunds | .10 | .02 |
| ❑ 297 Craig Erickson | .10 | .02 |
| ❑ 298 Brian Mitchell | .10 | .02 |
| ❑ 299 Dante Jones | .10 | .02 |
| ❑ 300 John Copeland | .10 | .02 |
| ❑ 301 Steve Beuerlein | .20 | .07 |
| ❑ 302 Deion Sanders | .75 | .30 |
| ❑ 303 Andre Reed | .20 | .07 |
| ❑ 304 Curtis Conway | .40 | .15 |
| ❑ 305 Harold Green | .10 | .02 |
| ❑ 306 Vinny Testaverde | .20 | .07 |
| ❑ 307 Michael Irvin | .40 | .15 |
| ❑ 308 Rod Bernstine | .10 | .02 |
| ❑ 309 Chris Spielman | .10 | .02 |
| ❑ 310 Reggie White | .40 | .15 |
| ❑ 311 Gary Brown | .10 | .02 |
| ❑ 312 Quentin Coryatt | .10 | .02 |
| ❑ 313 Derrick Thomas | .40 | .15 |
| ❑ 314 Greg Robinson | .10 | .02 |
| ❑ 315 Troy Drayton | .10 | .02 |
| ❑ 316 Terry Kirby | .40 | .15 |
| ❑ 317 John Randle | .20 | .07 |
| ❑ 318 Ben Coates | .20 | .07 |
| ❑ 319 Tyrone Hughes | .20 | .07 |
| ❑ 320 Corey Miller | .10 | .02 |
| ❑ 321 Brad Baxter | .10 | .02 |
| ❑ 322 Randall Cunningham | .40 | .15 |
| ❑ 323 Greg Lloyd | .20 | .07 |
| ❑ 324 Stan Humphries | .20 | .07 |
| ❑ 325 Dana Stubblefield | .20 | .07 |

| | | |
|---|---|---|
| ❑ 326 Kelvin Martin | .10 | .02 |
| ❑ 327 Hardy Nickerson | .20 | .07 |
| ❑ 328 Desmond Howard | .20 | .07 |
| ❑ 329 Mark Carrier WR | .20 | .07 |
| ❑ 330 Daryl Johnston | .20 | .07 |
| ❑ P19 Joe Montana Promo | 2.50 | 1.00 |

**1995 Upper Deck**

*Dahdin at Rod Woodson XX*

| | | |
|---|---|---|
| ❑ COMPLETE SET (300) | 30.00 | 12.50 |
| ❑ 1 Ki-Jana Carter RC | .40 | .15 |
| ❑ 2 Tony Boselli RC | .40 | .15 |
| ❑ 3 Steve McNair RC | 4.00 | 1.50 |
| ❑ 4 Michael Westbrook RC | .40 | .15 |
| ❑ 5 Kerry Collins RC | 2.00 | .75 |
| ❑ 6 Kevin Carter RC | .40 | .15 |
| ❑ 7 James A.Stewart RC | .10 | .02 |
| ❑ 8 Joey Galloway RC | 2.00 | .75 |
| ❑ 9 Kyle Brady RC | .40 | .15 |
| ❑ 10 J.J. Stokes RC | .40 | .15 |
| ❑ 11 Derrick Alexander DE RC | .10 | .02 |
| ❑ 12 Warren Sapp RC | 2.00 | .75 |
| ❑ 13 Mark Fields RC | .40 | .15 |
| ❑ 14 Tyrone Wheatley RC | 1.50 | .60 |
| ❑ 15 Napoleon Kaufman RC | 1.50 | .60 |
| ❑ 16 James O. Stewart RC | 1.50 | .60 |
| ❑ 17 Luther Elliss RC | .10 | .02 |
| ❑ 18 Rashaan Salaam RC | .20 | .07 |
| ❑ 19 Jimmy Oliver RC | .10 | .02 |
| ❑ 20 Mark Bruener RC | .20 | .07 |
| ❑ 21 Derrick Brooks RC | 2.00 | .75 |
| ❑ 22 Christian Fauria RC | .20 | .07 |
| ❑ 23 Ray Zellars RC | .20 | .07 |
| ❑ 24 Todd Collins RC | 1.25 | .50 |
| ❑ 25 Sherman Williams RC | .10 | .02 |
| ❑ 26 Frank Sanders RC | .40 | .15 |
| ❑ 27 Rodney Thomas RC | .20 | .07 |
| ❑ 28 Rob Johnson RC | 1.25 | .50 |
| ❑ 29 Steve Stenstrom RC | .10 | .02 |
| ❑ 30 Curtis Martin RC | 4.00 | 1.50 |
| ❑ 31 Gary Clark | .10 | .02 |
| ❑ 32 Troy Aikman | 1.50 | .60 |
| ❑ 33 Mike Sherrard | .10 | .02 |
| ❑ 34 Fred Barnett | .20 | .07 |
| ❑ 35 Henry Ellard | .20 | .07 |
| ❑ 36 Terry Allen | .20 | .07 |
| ❑ 37 Jeff Graham | .10 | .02 |
| ❑ 38 Herman Moore | .40 | .15 |
| ❑ 39 Brett Favre | 3.00 | 1.25 |
| ❑ 40 Trent Dilfer | .40 | .15 |
| ❑ 41 Derek Brown RBK | .10 | .02 |
| ❑ 42 Andre Rison | .20 | .07 |
| ❑ 43 Flipper Anderson | .10 | .02 |
| ❑ 44 Jerry Rice | 1.50 | .60 |
| ❑ 45 Andre Reed | .20 | .07 |
| ❑ 46 Sean Dawkins | .20 | .07 |
| ❑ 47 Irving Fryar | .20 | .07 |
| ❑ 48 Vincent Brisby | .10 | .02 |
| ❑ 49 Rob Moore | .20 | .07 |
| ❑ 50 Carl Pickens | .20 | .07 |
| ❑ 51 Vinny Testaverde | .20 | .07 |
| ❑ 52 Ray Childress | .10 | .02 |
| ❑ 53 Eric Green | .10 | .02 |
| ❑ 54 Anthony Miller | .20 | .07 |
| ❑ 55 Lake Dawson | .20 | .07 |
| ❑ 56 Tim Brown | .40 | .15 |
| ❑ 57 Stan Humphries | .20 | .07 |
| ❑ 58 Rick Mirer | .20 | .07 |

|  |  | | |
|---|---|---|---|
| ❏ 59 | Randal Hill | .10 | .02 |
| ❏ 60 | Charles Haley | .20 | .07 |
| ❏ 61 | Chris Calloway | .10 | .02 |
| ❏ 62 | Calvin Williams | .20 | .07 |
| ❏ 63 | Ethan Horton | .10 | .02 |
| ❏ 64 | Cris Carter | .40 | .15 |
| ❏ 65 | Curtis Conway | .40 | .15 |
| ❏ 66 | Scott Mitchell | .20 | .07 |
| ❏ 67 | Edgar Bennett | .20 | .07 |
| ❏ 68 | Craig Erickson | .10 | .02 |
| ❏ 69 | Jim Everett | .10 | .02 |
| ❏ 70 | Terance Mathis | .20 | .07 |
| ❏ 71 | Robert Young | .10 | .02 |
| ❏ 72 | Brent Jones | .10 | .02 |
| ❏ 73 | Bill Brooks | .20 | .07 |
| ❏ 74 | Marshall Faulk | 2.00 | .75 |
| ❏ 75 | O.J. McDuffie | .40 | .15 |
| ❏ 76 | Ben Coates | .20 | .07 |
| ❏ 77 | Johnny Mitchell | .10 | .02 |
| ❏ 78 | Darnay Scott | .20 | .07 |
| ❏ 79 | Derrick Alexander WR | .40 | .15 |
| ❏ 80 | Lorenzo White | .10 | .02 |
| ❏ 81 | Charles Johnson | .20 | .07 |
| ❏ 82 | John Elway | 3.00 | 1.25 |
| ❏ 83 | Willie Davis | .20 | .07 |
| ❏ 84 | James Jett | .20 | .07 |
| ❏ 85 | Mark Seay | .10 | .02 |
| ❏ 86 | Brian Blades | .20 | .07 |
| ❏ 87 | Ronald Moore | .10 | .02 |
| ❏ 88 | Alvin Harper | .10 | .02 |
| ❏ 89 | Dave Brown | .20 | .07 |
| ❏ 90 | Randall Cunningham | .40 | .15 |
| ❏ 91 | Heath Shuler | .20 | .07 |
| ❏ 92 | Jake Reed | .20 | .07 |
| ❏ 93 | Donnell Woolford | .10 | .02 |
| ❏ 94 | Barry Sanders | 2.50 | 1.00 |
| ❏ 95 | Reggie White | .40 | .15 |
| ❏ 96 | Lawrence Dawsey | .10 | .02 |
| ❏ 97 | Michael Haynes | .20 | .07 |
| ❏ 98 | Bert Emanuel | .40 | .15 |
| ❏ 99 | Troy Drayton | .10 | .02 |
| ❏ 100 | Steve Young | 1.25 | .50 |
| ❏ 101 | Bruce Smith | .40 | .15 |
| ❏ 102 | Roosevelt Potts | .10 | .02 |
| ❏ 103 | Dan Marino | 3.00 | 1.25 |
| ❏ 104 | Michael Timpson | .10 | .02 |
| ❏ 105 | Boomer Esiason | .20 | .07 |
| ❏ 106 | David Klingler | .20 | .07 |
| ❏ 107 | Eric Metcalf | .20 | .07 |
| ❏ 108 | Gary Brown | .10 | .02 |
| ❏ 109 | Neil O'Donnell | .40 | .15 |
| ❏ 110 | Shannon Sharpe | .20 | .07 |
| ❏ 111 | Joe Montana | 3.00 | 1.25 |
| ❏ 112 | Jeff Hostetler | .20 | .07 |
| ❏ 113 | Ronnie Harmon | .10 | .02 |
| ❏ 114 | Chris Warren | .20 | .07 |
| ❏ 115 | Larry Centers | .20 | .07 |
| ❏ 116 | Michael Irvin | .40 | .15 |
| ❏ 117 | Rodney Hampton | .20 | .07 |
| ❏ 118 | Herschel Walker | .20 | .07 |
| ❏ 119 | Reggie Brooks | .20 | .07 |
| ❏ 120 | Qadry Ismail | .20 | .07 |
| ❏ 121 | Chris Zorich | .10 | .02 |
| ❏ 122 | Chris Spielman | .20 | .07 |
| ❏ 123 | Sean Jones | .10 | .02 |
| ❏ 124 | Errict Rhett | .20 | .07 |
| ❏ 125 | Tyrone Hughes | .20 | .07 |
| ❏ 126 | Jeff George | .20 | .07 |
| ❏ 127 | Chris Miller | .10 | .02 |
| ❏ 128 | Ricky Watters | .20 | .07 |
| ❏ 129 | Jim Kelly | .40 | .15 |
| ❏ 130 | Tony Bennett | .10 | .02 |
| ❏ 131 | Terry Kirby | .20 | .07 |
| ❏ 132 | Drew Bledsoe | 1.00 | .40 |
| ❏ 133 | Johnny Johnson | .10 | .02 |
| ❏ 134 | Dan Wilkinson | .20 | .07 |
| ❏ 135 | Leroy Hoard | .10 | .02 |
| ❏ 136 | Darryll Lewis | .10 | .02 |
| ❏ 137 | Barry Foster | .20 | .07 |
| ❏ 138 | Shane Dronett | .10 | .02 |
| ❏ 139 | Marcus Allen | .40 | .15 |
| ❏ 140 | Harvey Williams | .10 | .02 |
| ❏ 141 | Tony Martin | .20 | .07 |
| ❏ 142 | Rod Stephens | .10 | .02 |
| ❏ 143 | Eric Swann | .20 | .07 |
| ❏ 144 | Daryl Johnston | .20 | .07 |
| ❏ 145 | Dave Meggett | .10 | .02 |
| ❏ 146 | Charlie Garner | .40 | .15 |
| ❏ 147 | Ken Harvey | .10 | .02 |
| ❏ 148 | Warren Moon | .20 | .07 |
| ❏ 149 | Steve Walsh | .10 | .02 |
| ❏ 150 | Pat Swilling | .10 | .02 |
| ❏ 151 | Terrell Buckley | .10 | .02 |
| ❏ 152 | Courtney Hawkins | .10 | .02 |
| ❏ 153 | Willie Roaf | .10 | .02 |
| ❏ 154 | Chris Doleman | .10 | .02 |
| ❏ 155 | Jerome Bettis | .40 | .15 |
| ❏ 156 | Dana Stubblefield | .20 | .07 |
| ❏ 157 | Cornelius Bennett | .20 | .07 |
| ❏ 158 | Quentin Coryatt | .20 | .07 |
| ❏ 159 | Bryan Cox | .10 | .02 |
| ❏ 160 | Marion Butts | .10 | .02 |
| ❏ 161 | Aaron Glenn | .10 | .02 |
| ❏ 162 | Louis Oliver | .10 | .02 |
| ❏ 163 | Eric Turner | .10 | .02 |
| ❏ 164 | Cris Dishman | .10 | .02 |
| ❏ 165 | John L. Williams | .10 | .02 |
| ❏ 166 | Simon Fletcher | .10 | .02 |
| ❏ 167 | Neil Smith | .20 | .07 |
| ❏ 168 | Chester McGlockton | .20 | .07 |
| ❏ 169 | Natrone Means | .20 | .07 |
| ❏ 170 | Sam Adams | .10 | .02 |
| ❏ 171 | Clyde Simmons | .10 | .02 |
| ❏ 172 | Jay Novacek | .20 | .07 |
| ❏ 173 | Keith Hamilton | .10 | .02 |
| ❏ 174 | William Fuller | .10 | .02 |
| ❏ 175 | Tom Carter | .10 | .02 |
| ❏ 176 | John Randle | .20 | .07 |
| ❏ 177 | Lewis Tillman | .10 | .02 |
| ❏ 178 | Mel Gray | .10 | .02 |
| ❏ 179 | George Teague | .10 | .02 |
| ❏ 180 | Hardy Nickerson | .10 | .02 |
| ❏ 181 | Mario Bates | .20 | .07 |
| ❏ 182 | D.J. Johnson | .10 | .02 |
| ❏ 183 | Sean Gilbert | .20 | .07 |
| ❏ 184 | Bryant Young | .20 | .07 |
| ❏ 185 | Jeff Burris | .10 | .02 |
| ❏ 186 | Floyd Turner | .10 | .02 |
| ❏ 187 | Troy Vincent | .10 | .02 |
| ❏ 188 | Willie McGinest | .20 | .07 |
| ❏ 189 | James Hasty | .10 | .02 |
| ❏ 190 | Jeff Blake RC | 1.00 | .40 |
| ❏ 191 | Stevon Moore | .10 | .02 |
| ❏ 192 | Ernest Givins | .10 | .02 |
| ❏ 193 | Byron Bam Morris | .20 | .07 |
| ❏ 194 | Ray Crockett | .10 | .02 |
| ❏ 195 | Dale Carter | .20 | .07 |
| ❏ 196 | Terry McDaniel | .10 | .02 |
| ❏ 197 | Leslie O'Neal | .20 | .07 |
| ❏ 198 | Cortez Kennedy | .20 | .07 |
| ❏ 199 | Seth Joyner | .10 | .02 |
| ❏ 200 | Emmitt Smith | 2.50 | 1.00 |
| ❏ 201 | Thomas Lewis | .20 | .07 |
| ❏ 202 | Andy Harmon | .10 | .02 |
| ❏ 203 | Ricky Ervins | .10 | .02 |
| ❏ 204 | Fuad Reveiz | .10 | .02 |
| ❏ 205 | John Thierry | .10 | .02 |
| ❏ 206 | Bennie Blades | .10 | .02 |
| ❏ 207 | LeShon Johnson | .10 | .02 |
| ❏ 208 | Charles Wilson | .10 | .02 |
| ❏ 209 | Joe Johnson | .10 | .02 |
| ❏ 210 | Chuck Smith | .10 | .02 |
| ❏ 211 | Roman Phifer | .10 | .02 |
| ❏ 212 | Ken Norton Jr. | .20 | .07 |
| ❏ 213 | Bucky Brooks | .10 | .02 |
| ❏ 214 | Ray Buchanan | .10 | .02 |
| ❏ 215 | Tim Bowens | .10 | .02 |
| ❏ 216 | Vincent Brown | .10 | .02 |
| ❏ 217 | Marcus Turner | .10 | .02 |
| ❏ 218 | Derrick Fenner | .10 | .02 |
| ❏ 219 | Antonio Langham | .10 | .02 |
| ❏ 220 | Cody Carlson | .10 | .02 |
| ❏ 221 | Greg Lloyd | .20 | .07 |
| ❏ 222 | Steve Atwater | .10 | .02 |
| ❏ 223 | Donnell Bennett | .20 | .07 |
| ❏ 224 | Rocket Ismail | .20 | .07 |
| ❏ 225 | John Carney | .10 | .02 |
| ❏ 226 | Eugene Robinson | .10 | .02 |
| ❏ 227 | Aeneas Williams | .10 | .02 |
| ❏ 228 | Darrin Smith | .10 | .02 |
| ❏ 229 | Phillippi Sparks | .10 | .02 |
| ❏ 230 | Eric Allen | .10 | .02 |
| ❏ 231 | Brian Mitchell | .10 | .02 |
| ❏ 232 | David Palmer | .20 | .07 |
| ❏ 233 | Mark Carrier DB | .20 | .07 |
| ❏ 234 | Dave Krieg | .20 | .07 |
| ❏ 235 | Robert Brooks | .40 | .15 |
| ❏ 236 | Eric Curry | .10 | .02 |
| ❏ 237 | Wayne Martin | .10 | .02 |
| ❏ 238 | Craig Heyward | .20 | .07 |
| ❏ 239 | Isaac Bruce | .75 | .30 |
| ❏ 240 | Deion Sanders | 1.00 | .40 |
| ❏ 241 | Steve Tasker | .20 | .07 |
| ❏ 242 | Jim Harbaugh | .20 | .07 |
| ❏ 243 | Aubrey Beavers | .10 | .02 |
| ❏ 244 | Chris Slade | .10 | .02 |
| ❏ 245 | Mo Lewis | .10 | .02 |
| ❏ 246 | Alfred Williams | .10 | .02 |
| ❏ 247 | Michael Dean Perry | .10 | .02 |
| ❏ 248 | Marcus Robertson | .10 | .02 |
| ❏ 249 | Kevin Greene | .20 | .07 |
| ❏ 250 | Leonard Russell | .10 | .02 |
| ❏ 251 | Greg Hill | .20 | .07 |
| ❏ 252 | Rob Fredrickson | .10 | .02 |
| ❏ 253 | Junior Seau | .40 | .15 |
| ❏ 254 | Rick Tuten | .10 | .02 |
| ❏ 255 | Garrison Hearst | .40 | .15 |
| ❏ 256 | Russell Maryland | .10 | .02 |
| ❏ 257 | Michael Brooks | .10 | .02 |
| ❏ 258 | Bernard Williams | .10 | .02 |
| ❏ 259 | Reggie Roby | .10 | .02 |
| ❏ 260 | Dewayne Washington | .20 | .07 |
| ❏ 261 | Raymont Harris | .20 | .07 |
| ❏ 262 | Brett Perriman | .20 | .07 |
| ❏ 263 | LeRoy Butler | .10 | .02 |
| ❏ 264 | Santana Dotson | .10 | .02 |
| ❏ 265 | Irv Smith | .10 | .02 |
| ❏ 266 | Ron George | .10 | .02 |
| ❏ 267 | Marquez Pope | .10 | .02 |
| ❏ 268 | William Floyd | .20 | .07 |
| ❏ 269 | Matt Darby | .10 | .02 |
| ❏ 270 | Jeff Herrod | .10 | .02 |
| ❏ 271 | Bernie Parmalee | .20 | .07 |
| ❏ 272 | Leroy Thompson | .10 | .02 |
| ❏ 273 | Ronnie Lott | .20 | .07 |
| ❏ 274 | Steve Tovar | .10 | .02 |
| ❏ 275 | Michael Jackson | .20 | .07 |
| ❏ 276 | Al Smith | .10 | .02 |
| ❏ 277 | Rod Woodson | .20 | .07 |
| ❏ 278 | Glyn Milburn | .10 | .02 |
| ❏ 279 | Kimble Anders | .20 | .07 |
| ❏ 280 | Anthony Smith | .10 | .02 |
| ❏ 281 | Andre Coleman | .10 | .02 |
| ❏ 282 | Terry Wooden | .10 | .02 |
| ❏ 283 | Mickey Washington | .10 | .02 |
| ❏ 284 | Steve Beuerlein | .20 | .07 |
| ❏ 285 | Mark Brunell | 1.00 | .40 |
| ❏ 286 | Keith Goganious | .10 | .02 |
| ❏ 287 | Desmond Howard | .20 | .07 |
| ❏ 288 | Darren Carrington | .10 | .02 |
| ❏ 289 | Derek Brown TE | .10 | .02 |
| ❏ 290 | Reggie Cobb | .10 | .02 |
| ❏ 291 | Jeff Lageman | .10 | .02 |
| ❏ 292 | Lamar Lathon | .10 | .02 |
| ❏ 293 | Sam Mills | .20 | .07 |
| ❏ 294 | Carlton Bailey | .10 | .02 |
| ❏ 295 | Mark Carrier WR | .20 | .07 |
| ❏ 296 | Willie Green | .10 | .02 |
| ❏ 297 | Frank Reich | .20 | .07 |
| ❏ 298 | Don Beebe | .10 | .02 |
| ❏ 299 | Tim McKyer | .10 | .02 |
| ❏ 300 | Pete Metzelaars | .10 | .02 |
| ❏ A19 | Joe Montana | 15.00 | 6.00 |
| ❏ A103 | Dan Marino | 15.00 | 6.00 |
| ❏ P1 | Joe Montana Promo | 2.00 | .75 |
| ❏ P2 | Joe Montana Promo Numbered 19 | 2.00 | .75 |
| ❏ P3 | Marshall Faulk Promo | 1.00 | .40 |

## 1996 Upper Deck

| | | | |
|---|---|---|---|
| ❏ | COMPLETE SET (300) | 30.00 | 12.50 |
| ❏ 1 | Keyshawn Johnson RC | 1.25 | .50 |

| | | |
|---|---|---|
| ☐ 2 Kevin Hardy RC | .50 | .20 |
| ☐ 3 Simeon Rice RC | 1.25 | .50 |
| ☐ 4 Jonathan Ogden RC | .50 | .20 |
| ☐ 5 Cedric Jones RC | .10 | .02 |
| ☐ 6 Lawrence Phillips RC | .50 | .20 |
| ☐ 7 Tim Biakabutuka RC | .50 | .20 |
| ☐ 8 Terry Glenn RC | 1.25 | .50 |
| ☐ 9 Rickey Dudley RC | .50 | .20 |
| ☐ 10 Willie Anderson RC | .10 | .02 |
| ☐ 11 Alex Molden RC | .10 | .02 |
| ☐ 12 Regan Upshaw RC | .10 | .02 |
| ☐ 13 Walt Harris RC | .10 | .02 |
| ☐ 14 Eddie George RC | 1.50 | .60 |
| ☐ 15 John Mobley RC | .10 | .02 |
| ☐ 16 Duane Clemons RC | .10 | .02 |
| ☐ 17 Eddie Kennison RC | .50 | .20 |
| ☐ 18 Marvin Harrison RC | 3.00 | 1.25 |
| ☐ 19 Daryl Gardener RC | .10 | .02 |
| ☐ 20 Leeland McElroy RC | .25 | .08 |
| ☐ 21 Eric Moulds RC | 1.50 | .60 |
| ☐ 22 Alex Van Dyke RC | .25 | .08 |
| ☐ 23 Mike Alstott RC | 1.25 | .50 |
| ☐ 24 Jeff Lewis RC | .10 | .02 |
| ☐ 25 Bobby Engram RC | .50 | .20 |
| ☐ 26 Derrick Mayes RC | .50 | .20 |
| ☐ 27 Karim Abdul-Jabbar RC | .50 | .20 |
| ☐ 28 Bobby Hoying RC | .50 | .20 |
| ☐ 29 Stepfret Williams RC | .25 | .08 |
| ☐ 30 Chris Darkins RC | .10 | .02 |
| ☐ 31 Stephen Davis RC | 2.00 | .75 |
| ☐ 32 Danny Kanell RC | .25 | .08 |
| ☐ 33 Tony Brackens RC | .50 | .20 |
| ☐ 34 Leslie O'Neal | .10 | .02 |
| ☐ 35 Chris Doleman | .10 | .02 |
| ☐ 36 Larry Brown | .10 | .02 |
| ☐ 37 Ronnie Harmon | .10 | .02 |
| ☐ 38 Chris Spielman | .10 | .02 |
| ☐ 39 John Jurkovic | .10 | .02 |
| ☐ 40 Shawn Jefferson | .10 | .02 |
| ☐ 41 William Floyd | .25 | .08 |
| ☐ 42 Eric Davis | .10 | .02 |
| ☐ 43 Willie Clay | .10 | .02 |
| ☐ 44 Marco Coleman | .10 | .02 |
| ☐ 45 Lorenzo White | .10 | .02 |
| ☐ 46 Neil O'Donnell | .25 | .08 |
| ☐ 47 Natrone Means | .25 | .08 |
| ☐ 48 Cornelius Bennett | .10 | .02 |
| ☐ 49 Steve Walsh | .10 | .02 |
| ☐ 50 Jerome Bettis | .50 | .20 |
| ☐ 51 Boomer Esiason | .25 | .08 |
| ☐ 52 Glyn Milburn | .10 | .02 |
| ☐ 53 Kevin Greene | .25 | .08 |
| ☐ 54 Seth Joyner | .10 | .02 |
| ☐ 55 Jeff Graham | .10 | .02 |
| ☐ 56 Darren Woodson | .25 | .08 |
| ☐ 57 Dale Carter | .10 | .02 |
| ☐ 58 Lorenzo Lynch | .10 | .02 |
| ☐ 59 Tim Brown | .50 | .20 |
| ☐ 60 Jerry Rice | 1.25 | .50 |
| ☐ 61 Garrison Hearst | .25 | .08 |
| ☐ 62 Eric Metcalf | .10 | .02 |
| ☐ 63 Leroy Hoard | .10 | .02 |
| ☐ 64 Thurman Thomas | .25 | .08 |
| ☐ 65 Sam Mills | .10 | .02 |
| ☐ 66 Curtis Conway | .50 | .20 |
| ☐ 67 Carl Pickens | .25 | .08 |
| ☐ 68 Deion Sanders | .75 | .30 |

| | | |
|---|---|---|
| ☐ 69 Shannon Sharpe | .25 | .08 |
| ☐ 70 Herman Moore | .25 | .08 |
| ☐ 71 Robert Brooks | .50 | .20 |
| ☐ 72 Rodney Thomas | .10 | .02 |
| ☐ 73 Ken Dilger | .25 | .08 |
| ☐ 74 Mark Brunell | .75 | .30 |
| ☐ 75 Marcus Allen | .50 | .20 |
| ☐ 76 Dan Marino | 2.50 | 1.00 |
| ☐ 77 Robert Smith | .25 | .08 |
| ☐ 78 Drew Bledsoe | .75 | .30 |
| ☐ 79 Jim Everett | .10 | .02 |
| ☐ 80 Rodney Hampton | .25 | .08 |
| ☐ 81 Adrian Murrell | .25 | .08 |
| ☐ 82 Daryl Hobbs RC | .10 | .02 |
| ☐ 83 Ricky Watters | .25 | .08 |
| ☐ 84 Yancey Thigpen | .25 | .08 |
| ☐ 85 Roman Phifer | .10 | .02 |
| ☐ 86 Tony Martin | .25 | .08 |
| ☐ 87 Dana Stubblefield | .25 | .08 |
| ☐ 88 Joey Galloway | .50 | .20 |
| ☐ 89 Errict Rhett | .25 | .08 |
| ☐ 90 Terry Allen | .25 | .08 |
| ☐ 91 Aeneas Williams | .10 | .02 |
| ☐ 92 Craig Heyward | .10 | .02 |
| ☐ 93 Vinny Testaverde | .25 | .08 |
| ☐ 94 Bryce Paup | .10 | .02 |
| ☐ 95 Kerry Collins | .50 | .20 |
| ☐ 96 Rashaan Salaam | .25 | .08 |
| ☐ 97 Dan Wilkinson | .10 | .02 |
| ☐ 98 Jay Novacek | .10 | .02 |
| ☐ 99 John Elway | 2.50 | 1.00 |
| ☐ 100 Bennie Blades | .10 | .02 |
| ☐ 101 Edgar Bennett | .25 | .08 |
| ☐ 102 Darryll Lewis | .10 | .02 |
| ☐ 103 Marshall Faulk | .60 | .25 |
| ☐ 104 Bryan Schwartz | .10 | .02 |
| ☐ 105 Tamarick Vanover | .25 | .08 |
| ☐ 106 Terry Kirby | .25 | .08 |
| ☐ 107 John Randle | .25 | .08 |
| ☐ 108 Ted Johnson RC | .50 | .20 |
| ☐ 109 Mario Bates | .25 | .08 |
| ☐ 110 Phillippi Sparks | .10 | .02 |
| ☐ 111 Marvin Washington | .10 | .02 |
| ☐ 112 Terry McDaniel | .10 | .02 |
| ☐ 113 Bobby Taylor | .10 | .02 |
| ☐ 114 Carnell Lake | .10 | .02 |
| ☐ 115 Troy Drayton | .10 | .02 |
| ☐ 116 Darren Bennett | .10 | .02 |
| ☐ 117 J.J. Stokes | .50 | .20 |
| ☐ 118 Rick Mirer | .25 | .08 |
| ☐ 119 Jackie Harris | .10 | .02 |
| ☐ 120 Ken Harvey | .10 | .02 |
| ☐ 121 Rob Moore | .25 | .08 |
| ☐ 122 Jeff George | .25 | .08 |
| ☐ 123 Andre Rison | .25 | .08 |
| ☐ 124 Darick Holmes | .10 | .02 |
| ☐ 125 Tim McKyer | .10 | .02 |
| ☐ 126 Alonzo Spellman | .10 | .02 |
| ☐ 127 Jeff Blake | .50 | .20 |
| ☐ 128 Kevin Williams | .10 | .02 |
| ☐ 129 Anthony Miller | .25 | .08 |
| ☐ 130 Barry Sanders | 2.00 | .75 |
| ☐ 131 Brett Favre | 2.50 | 1.25 |
| ☐ 132 Steve McNair | 1.00 | .40 |
| ☐ 133 Jim Harbaugh | .25 | .08 |
| ☐ 134 Desmond Howard | .25 | .08 |
| ☐ 135 Steve Bono | .10 | .02 |
| ☐ 136 Bernie Parmalee | .10 | .02 |
| ☐ 137 Warren Moon | .25 | .08 |
| ☐ 138 Curtis Martin | 1.00 | .40 |
| ☐ 139 Irv Smith | .10 | .02 |
| ☐ 140 Thomas Lewis | .10 | .02 |
| ☐ 141 Kyle Brady | .10 | .02 |
| ☐ 142 Napoleon Kaufman | .50 | .20 |
| ☐ 143 Mike Mamula | .10 | .02 |
| ☐ 144 Erric Pegram | .10 | .02 |
| ☐ 145 Isaac Bruce | .50 | .20 |
| ☐ 146 Andre Coleman | .10 | .02 |
| ☐ 147 Merton Hanks | .10 | .02 |
| ☐ 148 Brian Blades | .10 | .02 |
| ☐ 149 Hardy Nickerson | .10 | .02 |
| ☐ 150 Michael Westbrook | .50 | .20 |
| ☐ 151 Larry Centers | .25 | .08 |
| ☐ 152 Morten Andersen | .10 | .02 |

| | | |
|---|---|---|
| ☐ 153 Michael Jackson | .25 | .08 |
| ☐ 154 Bruce Smith | .25 | .08 |
| ☐ 155 Derrick Moore | .10 | .02 |
| ☐ 156 Mark Carrier DB | .10 | .02 |
| ☐ 157 John Copeland | .10 | .02 |
| ☐ 158 Emmitt Smith | 2.00 | .75 |
| ☐ 159 Jason Elam | .25 | .08 |
| ☐ 160 Scott Mitchell | .25 | .08 |
| ☐ 161 Mark Chmura | .25 | .08 |
| ☐ 162 Blaine Bishop | .10 | .02 |
| ☐ 163 Tony Bennett | .10 | .02 |
| ☐ 164 Pete Mitchell | .25 | .08 |
| ☐ 165 Dan Saleaumua | .10 | .02 |
| ☐ 166 Pete Stoyanovich | .10 | .02 |
| ☐ 167 Cris Carter | .50 | .20 |
| ☐ 168 Vince Brisby | .10 | .02 |
| ☐ 169 Wayne Martin | .10 | .02 |
| ☐ 170 Tyrone Wheatley | .25 | .08 |
| ☐ 171 Mo Lewis | .10 | .02 |
| ☐ 172 Harvey Williams | .10 | .02 |
| ☐ 173 Calvin Williams | .10 | .02 |
| ☐ 174 Norm Johnson | .10 | .02 |
| ☐ 175 Mark Rypien | .10 | .02 |
| ☐ 176 Stan Humphries | .25 | .08 |
| ☐ 177 Derek Loville | .10 | .02 |
| ☐ 178 Christian Fauria | .10 | .02 |
| ☐ 179 Warren Sapp | .10 | .02 |
| ☐ 180 Henry Ellard | .10 | .02 |
| ☐ 181 Jamir Miller | .10 | .02 |
| ☐ 182 Jessie Tuggle | .10 | .02 |
| ☐ 183 Stevon Moore | .10 | .02 |
| ☐ 184 Jim Kelly | .50 | .20 |
| ☐ 185 Mark Carrier | .10 | .02 |
| ☐ 186 Chris Zorich | .10 | .02 |
| ☐ 187 Harold Green | .10 | .02 |
| ☐ 188 Chris Boniol | .10 | .02 |
| ☐ 189 Allen Aldridge | .10 | .02 |
| ☐ 190 Brett Perriman | .10 | .02 |
| ☐ 191 Chris Jacke | .10 | .02 |
| ☐ 192 Todd McNair | .10 | .02 |
| ☐ 193 Floyd Turner | .10 | .02 |
| ☐ 194 Jeff Lageman | .10 | .02 |
| ☐ 195 Derrick Thomas | .50 | .20 |
| ☐ 196 Eric Green | .10 | .02 |
| ☐ 197 Orlando Thomas | .10 | .02 |
| ☐ 198 Ben Coates | .25 | .08 |
| ☐ 199 Tyrone Hughes | .10 | .02 |
| ☐ 200 Dave Brown | .10 | .02 |
| ☐ 201 Brad Baxter | .10 | .02 |
| ☐ 202 Chester McGlockton | .10 | .02 |
| ☐ 203 Rodney Peete | .10 | .02 |
| ☐ 204 Willie Williams | .10 | .02 |
| ☐ 205 Kevin Carter | .10 | .02 |
| ☐ 206 Aaron Hayden RC | .10 | .02 |
| ☐ 207 Steve Young | 1.00 | .40 |
| ☐ 208 Chris Warren | .25 | .08 |
| ☐ 209 Eric Curry | .10 | .02 |
| ☐ 210 Brian Mitchell | .10 | .02 |
| ☐ 211 Frank Sanders | .25 | .08 |
| ☐ 212 Terance Mathis UER | .10 | .02 |
| ☐ 213 Eric Turner | .10 | .02 |
| ☐ 214 Bill Brooks | .10 | .02 |
| ☐ 215 John Kasay | .10 | .02 |
| ☐ 216 Erik Kramer | .10 | .02 |
| ☐ 217 Danny Scott | .25 | .08 |
| ☐ 218 Charles Haley | .10 | .02 |
| ☐ 219 Steve Atwater | .10 | .02 |
| ☐ 220 Jason Hanson | .10 | .02 |
| ☐ 221 LeRoy Butler | .10 | .02 |
| ☐ 222 Cris Dishman | .10 | .02 |
| ☐ 223 Sean Dawkins | .10 | .02 |
| ☐ 224 James O. Stewart | .25 | .08 |
| ☐ 225 Greg Hill | .25 | .08 |
| ☐ 226 Jeff Cross | .10 | .02 |
| ☐ 227 Qadry Ismail | .25 | .08 |
| ☐ 228 Dave Meggett | .10 | .02 |
| ☐ 229 Eric Allen | .10 | .02 |
| ☐ 230 Chris Calloway | .10 | .02 |
| ☐ 231 Wayne Chrebet | .75 | .30 |
| ☐ 232 Jeff Hostetler | .10 | .02 |
| ☐ 233 Andy Harmon | .10 | .02 |
| ☐ 234 Greg Lloyd | .25 | .08 |
| ☐ 235 Toby Wright | .10 | .02 |
| ☐ 236 Junior Seau | .50 | .20 |

| | | |
|---|---|---|
| 237 Bryant Young | .25 | .08 |
| 238 Robert Blackmon | .10 | .02 |
| 239 Trent Dilfer | .50 | .20 |
| 240 Leslie Shepherd | .10 | .02 |
| 241 Eric Swann | .10 | .02 |
| 242 Bert Emanuel | .25 | .08 |
| 243 Antonio Langham | .10 | .02 |
| 244 Steve Christie | .10 | .02 |
| 245 Tyrone Poole | .10 | .02 |
| 246 Jim Flanigan | .10 | .02 |
| 247 Tony McGee | .10 | .02 |
| 248 Michael Irvin | .50 | .20 |
| 249 Byron Bam Morris | .10 | .02 |
| 250 Terrell Davis | 1.00 | .40 |
| 251 Johnnie Morton | .25 | .08 |
| 252 Sean Jones | .10 | .02 |
| 253 Chris Sanders | .25 | .08 |
| 254 Quentin Coryatt | .10 | .02 |
| 255 Willie Jackson | .25 | .08 |
| 256 Mark Collins | .10 | .02 |
| 257 Randal Hill | .10 | .02 |
| 258 David Palmer | .10 | .02 |
| 259 Will Moore | .10 | .02 |
| 260 Michael Haynes | .10 | .02 |
| 261 Mike Sherrard | .10 | .02 |
| 262 William Thomas | .10 | .02 |
| 263 Kordell Stewart | .50 | .20 |
| 264 D'Marco Farr | .10 | .02 |
| 265 Terrell Fletcher | .10 | .02 |
| 266 Lee Woodall | .10 | .02 |
| 267 Eugene Robinson | .10 | .02 |
| 268 Alvin Harper | .10 | .02 |
| 269 Gus Frerotte | .25 | .08 |
| 270 Antonio Freeman | .50 | .20 |
| 271 Clyde Simmons | .10 | .02 |
| 272 Chuck Smith | .10 | .02 |
| 273 Steve Tasker | .10 | .02 |
| 274 Kevin Butler | .10 | .02 |
| 275 Steve Tovar | .10 | .02 |
| 276 Troy Aikman | 1.25 | .50 |
| 277 Aaron Craver | .10 | .02 |
| 278 Henry Thomas | .10 | .02 |
| 279 Craig Newsome | .10 | .02 |
| 280 Brent Jones | .10 | .02 |
| 281 Micheal Barrow | .10 | .02 |
| 282 Ray Buchanan | .10 | .02 |
| 283 Jimmy Smith | .50 | .20 |
| 284 Neil Smith | .25 | .08 |
| 285 O.J. McDuffie | .25 | .08 |
| 286 Jake Reed | .25 | .08 |
| 287 Ty Law | .50 | .20 |
| 288 Torrance Small | .10 | .02 |
| 289 Hugh Douglas | .10 | .02 |
| 290 Pat Swilling | .10 | .02 |
| 291 Charlie Garner | .25 | .08 |
| 292 Ernie Mills | .10 | .02 |
| 293 John Carney | .10 | .02 |
| 294 Ken Norton | .10 | .02 |
| 295 Cortez Kennedy | .10 | .02 |
| 296 Derrick Brooks | .50 | .20 |
| 297 Heath Shuler | .25 | .08 |
| 298 Reggie White | .50 | .20 |
| 299 Kimble Anders | .25 | .08 |
| 300 Willie McGinest | .10 | .02 |
| P96 Dan Marino Promo | 2.00 | .75 |
| MS1 Dan Marino | 5.00 | 2.00 |
| MS2 Dan Marino | 5.00 | 2.00 |
| P13 Dan Marino Promo | 2.50 | 1.00 |

## 1997 Upper Deck

| | | |
|---|---|---|
| COMPLETE SET (300) | 40.00 | 20.00 |
| 1 Orlando Pace RC | .60 | .25 |
| 2 Darrell Russell RC | .25 | .08 |
| 3 Shawn Springs RC | .40 | .15 |
| 4 Bryant Westbrook RC | .25 | .08 |
| 5 Ike Hilliard RC | 1.25 | .50 |
| 6 Peter Boulware RC | .60 | .25 |
| 7 Tom Knight RC | .25 | .08 |
| 8 Yatil Green RC | .40 | .15 |
| 9 Tony Gonzalez RC | 2.50 | 1.00 |
| 10 Reidel Anthony RC | .60 | .25 |
| 11 Warrick Dunn RC | 2.50 | 1.00 |
| 12 Kenny Holmes RC | .60 | .25 |
| 13 Jim Druckenmiller RC | .40 | .15 |

| | | |
|---|---|---|
| 14 James Farrior RC | .60 | .25 |
| 15 David LaFleur RC | .25 | .08 |
| 16 Antowain Smith RC | 2.00 | .75 |
| 17 Rae Carruth RC | .25 | .08 |
| 18 Dwayne Rudd RC | .60 | .25 |
| 19 Jake Plummer RC | 4.00 | 1.50 |
| 20 Reinard Wilson RC | .40 | .15 |
| 21 Byron Hanspard RC | .40 | .15 |
| 22 Will Blackwell RC | .40 | .15 |
| 23 Troy Davis RC | .40 | .15 |
| 24 Corey Dillon RC | 5.00 | 2.00 |
| 25 Joey Kent RC | .60 | .25 |
| 26 Renaldo Wynn RC | .25 | .08 |
| 27 Pat Barnes RC | .60 | .25 |
| 28 Kevin Lockett RC | .40 | .15 |
| 29 Darnell Autry RC | .40 | .15 |
| 30 Walter Jones RC | .60 | .25 |
| 31 Trevor Pryce RC | .60 | .25 |
| 32 Dan Marino SRF | 1.25 | .50 |
| 33 Steve Young SRF | .25 | .08 |
| 34 John Elway SRF | 1.25 | .50 |
| 35 Jerry Rice SRF | .60 | .25 |
| 36 Tim Brown SRF | .60 | .25 |
| 37 Deion Sanders SRF | .60 | .25 |
| 38 Troy Aikman SRF | .60 | .25 |
| 39 Barry Sanders SRF | 1.00 | .40 |
| 40 Emmitt Smith SRF | 1.00 | .40 |
| 41 Junior Seau SRF | .60 | .25 |
| 42 Neil Smith | .40 | .15 |
| 43 Brett Perriman | .25 | .08 |
| 44 Jim Everett | .25 | .08 |
| 45 Qadry Ismail | .40 | .15 |
| 46 Dana Stubblefield | .25 | .08 |
| 47 Bryant Young | .25 | .08 |
| 48 Ken Norton Jr. | .25 | .08 |
| 49 Terrell Owens | .75 | .30 |
| 50 Jerry Rice | 1.25 | .50 |
| 51 Steve Young | .75 | .30 |
| 52 Terry Kirby | .40 | .15 |
| 53 Chris Doleman | .25 | .08 |
| 54 Lee Woodall | .25 | .08 |
| 55 Merton Hanks | .25 | .08 |
| 56 Garrison Hearst | .40 | .15 |
| 57 Rashaan Salaam | .25 | .08 |
| 58 Raymont Harris | .25 | .08 |
| 59 Curtis Conway | .40 | .15 |
| 60 Bobby Engram | .40 | .15 |
| 61 Bryan Cox | .25 | .08 |
| 62 Walt Harris | .25 | .08 |
| 63 Tyrone Hughes | .25 | .08 |
| 64 Rick Mirer | .40 | .15 |
| 65 Jeff Blake | .40 | .15 |
| 66 Carl Pickens | .40 | .15 |
| 67 Darnay Scott | .40 | .15 |
| 68 Tony McGee | .25 | .08 |
| 69 Ki-Jana Carter | .40 | .15 |
| 70 Ashley Ambrose | .25 | .08 |
| 71 Dan Wilkinson | .25 | .08 |
| 72 Chris Spielman | .25 | .08 |
| 73 Todd Collins | .25 | .08 |
| 74 Andre Reed | .40 | .15 |
| 75 Quinn Early | .25 | .08 |
| 76 Eric Moulds | .60 | .25 |
| 77 Darick Holmes | .25 | .08 |
| 78 Thurman Thomas | .60 | .25 |
| 79 Bruce Smith | .40 | .15 |
| 80 Bryce Paup | .25 | .08 |

| | | |
|---|---|---|
| 81 John Elway | 2.50 | 1.00 |
| 82 Terrell Davis | .75 | .30 |
| 83 Anthony Miller | .25 | .08 |
| 84 Shannon Sharpe | .40 | .15 |
| 85 Alfred Williams | .25 | .08 |
| 86 John Mobley | .25 | .08 |
| 87 Tory James | .25 | .08 |
| 88 Steve Atwater | .25 | .08 |
| 89 Darrien Gordon | .25 | .08 |
| 90 Mike Alstott | .60 | .25 |
| 91 Errict Rhett | .25 | .08 |
| 92 Trent Dilfer | .60 | .25 |
| 93 Courtney Hawkins | .25 | .08 |
| 94 Warren Sapp | .40 | .15 |
| 95 Regan Upshaw | .25 | .08 |
| 96 Hardy Nickerson | .25 | .08 |
| 97 Donnie Abraham RC | .60 | .25 |
| 98 Larry Centers | .40 | .15 |
| 99 Aeneas Williams | .25 | .08 |
| 100 Kent Graham UER | .25 | .08 |
| 101 Rob Moore | .40 | .15 |
| 102 Frank Sanders | .40 | .15 |
| 103 Leeland McElroy | .25 | .08 |
| 104 Eric Swann | .25 | .08 |
| 105 Simeon Rice | .40 | .15 |
| 106 Seth Joyner | .25 | .08 |
| 107 Stan Humphries | .40 | .15 |
| 108 Tony Martin | .25 | .08 |
| 109 Charlie Jones | .25 | .08 |
| 110 Andre Coleman UER 103 | .25 | .08 |
| 111 Terrell Fletcher | .25 | .08 |
| 112 Junior Seau | .60 | .25 |
| 113 Eric Metcalf | .25 | .08 |
| 114 Chris Penn | .25 | .08 |
| 115 Marcus Allen | .60 | .25 |
| 116 Greg Hill | .25 | .08 |
| 117 Tamarick Vanover | .40 | .15 |
| 118 Lake Dawson | .25 | .08 |
| 119 Derrick Thomas | .60 | .25 |
| 120 Dale Carter | .25 | .08 |
| 121 Elvis Grbac | .40 | .15 |
| 122 Aaron Bailey | .25 | .08 |
| 123 Jim Harbaugh | .40 | .15 |
| 124 Marshall Faulk | .75 | .30 |
| 125 Sean Dawkins | .25 | .08 |
| 126 Marvin Harrison | .60 | .25 |
| 127 Ken Dilger | .25 | .08 |
| 128 Tony Bennett | .25 | .08 |
| 129 Jeff Herrod | .25 | .08 |
| 130 Chris Gardocki | .25 | .08 |
| 131 Cary Blanchard | .25 | .08 |
| 132 Troy Aikman | 1.25 | .50 |
| 133 Emmitt Smith | 2.00 | .75 |
| 134 Sherman Williams | .25 | .08 |
| 135 Michael Irvin | .60 | .25 |
| 136 Eric Bjornson | .25 | .08 |
| 137 Herschel Walker | .40 | .15 |
| 138 Tony Tolbert | .25 | .08 |
| 139 Deion Sanders | .60 | .25 |
| 140 Daryl Johnston | .40 | .15 |
| 141 Dan Marino | 2.50 | 1.00 |
| 142 O.J. McDuffie | .40 | .15 |
| 143 Troy Drayton | .25 | .08 |
| 144 Karim Abdul-Jabbar | .40 | .15 |
| 145 Stanley Pritchett | .25 | .08 |
| 146 Fred Barnett | .25 | .08 |
| 147 Zach Thomas | .60 | .25 |
| 148 Shawn Wooden RC | .25 | .08 |
| 149 Ty Detmer | .40 | .15 |
| 150 Derrick Witherspoon | .25 | .08 |
| 151 Ricky Watters | .40 | .15 |
| 152 Charlie Garner | .40 | .15 |
| 153 Chris T. Jones | .25 | .08 |
| 154 Irving Fryar | .40 | .15 |
| 155 Mike Mamula | .25 | .08 |
| 156 Troy Vincent | .25 | .08 |
| 157 Bobby Taylor | .25 | .08 |
| 158 Chris Boniol | .25 | .08 |
| 159 Devin Bush | .25 | .08 |
| 160 Bert Emanuel | .40 | .15 |
| 161 Jamal Anderson | .60 | .25 |
| 162 Terance Mathis | .25 | .08 |
| 163 Cornelius Bennett | .25 | .08 |
| 164 Ray Buchanan | .25 | .08 |

|  |  | | |
|---|---|---|---|
| 165 | Chris Chandler | .40 | .15 |
| 166 | Dave Brown | .25 | .08 |
| 167 | Danny Kanell | .25 | .08 |
| 168 | Rodney Hampton | .40 | .15 |
| 169 | Tyrone Wheatley | .40 | .15 |
| 170 | Amani Toomer | .40 | .15 |
| 171 | Chris Calloway | .25 | .08 |
| 172 | Thomas Lewis | .25 | .08 |
| 173 | Phillippi Sparks | .25 | .08 |
| 174 | Mark Brunell | .75 | .30 |
| 175 | Keenan McCardell | .40 | .15 |
| 176 | Willie Jackson | .25 | .08 |
| 177 | Jimmy Smith | .60 | .25 |
| 178 | Pete Mitchell | .25 | .08 |
| 179 | Natrone Means | .40 | .15 |
| 180 | Kevin Hardy | .25 | .08 |
| 181 | Tony Brackens | .25 | .08 |
| 182 | James O. Stewart | .25 | .08 |
| 183 | Wayne Chrebet | .60 | .25 |
| 184 | Keyshawn Johnson | .60 | .25 |
| 185 | Adrian Murrell | .40 | .15 |
| 186 | Neil O'Donnell | .40 | .15 |
| 187 | Hugh Douglas | .25 | .08 |
| 188 | Mo Lewis | .25 | .08 |
| 189 | Marvin Washington | .25 | .08 |
| 190 | Aaron Glenn | .25 | .08 |
| 191 | Barry Sanders | 2.00 | .75 |
| 192 | Scott Mitchell | .40 | .15 |
| 193 | Herman Moore | .40 | .15 |
| 194 | Johnnie Morton | .40 | .15 |
| 195 | Glyn Milburn | .25 | .08 |
| 196 | Reggie Brown LB | .40 | .15 |
| 197 | Jason Hanson | .25 | .08 |
| 198 | Steve McNair | .75 | .30 |
| 199 | Eddie George | .60 | .25 |
| 200 | Ronnie Harmon | .25 | .08 |
| 201 | Chris Sanders | .25 | .08 |
| 202 | Willie Davis | .25 | .08 |
| 203 | Frank Wycheck | .25 | .08 |
| 204 | Darryll Lewis | .25 | .08 |
| 205 | Blaine Bishop | .25 | .08 |
| 206 | Robert Brooks | .40 | .15 |
| 207 | Brett Favre | 2.50 | 1.25 |
| 208 | Edgar Bennett | .40 | .15 |
| 209 | Dorsey Levens | .40 | .15 |
| 210 | Derrick Mayes | .25 | .08 |
| 211 | Antonio Freeman | .60 | .25 |
| 212 | Mark Chmura | .40 | .15 |
| 213 | Reggie White | .60 | .25 |
| 214 | Gilbert Brown | .40 | .15 |
| 215 | LeRoy Butler | .25 | .08 |
| 216 | Craig Newsome | .25 | .08 |
| 217 | Kerry Collins | .60 | .25 |
| 218 | Wesley Walls | .40 | .15 |
| 219 | Muhsin Muhammad | .40 | .15 |
| 220 | Anthony Johnson | .25 | .08 |
| 221 | Tim Biakabutuka | .40 | .15 |
| 222 | Kevin Greene | .25 | .08 |
| 223 | Sam Mills | .25 | .08 |
| 224 | John Kasay | .25 | .08 |
| 225 | Micheal Barrow | .25 | .08 |
| 226 | Drew Bledsoe | .75 | .30 |
| 227 | Curtis Martin | .75 | .30 |
| 228 | Terry Glenn | .60 | .25 |
| 229 | Ben Coates | .40 | .15 |
| 230 | Shawn Jefferson | .25 | .08 |
| 231 | Willie McGinest | .25 | .08 |
| 232 | Ted Johnson | .25 | .08 |
| 233 | Lawyer Milloy | .40 | .15 |
| 234 | Ty Law | .40 | .15 |
| 235 | Willie Clay | .25 | .08 |
| 236 | Tim Brown | .60 | .25 |
| 237 | Rickey Dudley | .40 | .15 |
| 238 | Napoleon Kaufman | .60 | .25 |
| 239 | Chester McGlockton | .25 | .08 |
| 240 | Rob Fredrickson | .25 | .08 |
| 241 | Terry McDaniel | .25 | .08 |
| 242 | Desmond Howard | .40 | .15 |
| 243 | Jeff George | .40 | .15 |
| 244 | Isaac Bruce | .60 | .25 |
| 245 | Tony Banks | .40 | .15 |
| 246 | Lawrence Phillips UER 247 | .25 | .08 |
| 247 | Kevin Carter | .25 | .08 |
| 248 | Roman Phifer | .25 | .08 |

|  |  | | |
|---|---|---|---|
| 249 | Keith Lyle | .25 | .08 |
| 250 | Eddie Kennison | .40 | .15 |
| 251 | Craig Heyward | .25 | .08 |
| 252 | Vinny Testaverde | .40 | .15 |
| 253 | Derrick Alexander WR | .40 | .15 |
| 254 | Michael Jackson | .40 | .15 |
| 255 | Byron Bam Morris | .25 | .08 |
| 256 | Eric Green | .25 | .08 |
| 257 | Ray Lewis | 1.00 | .40 |
| 258 | Antonio Langham | .25 | .08 |
| 259 | Michael McCrary | .25 | .08 |
| 260 | Gus Frerotte | .25 | .08 |
| 261 | Terry Allen | .60 | .25 |
| 262 | Brian Mitchell | .25 | .08 |
| 263 | Michael Westbrook | .40 | .15 |
| 264 | Sean Gilbert | .25 | .08 |
| 265 | Rich Owens | .25 | .08 |
| 266 | Ken Harvey | .25 | .08 |
| 267 | Jeff Hostetler | .25 | .08 |
| 268 | Michael Haynes | .25 | .08 |
| 269 | Mario Bates | .25 | .08 |
| 270 | Renaldo Turnbull UER 273 | .25 | .08 |
| 271 | Ray Zellars | .25 | .08 |
| 272 | Joe Johnson | .25 | .08 |
| 273 | Eric Allen | .25 | .08 |
| 274 | Heath Shuler | .25 | .08 |
| 275 | Daryl Hobbs | .25 | .08 |
| 276 | John Friesz | .25 | .08 |
| 277 | Brian Blades | .25 | .08 |
| 278 | Joey Galloway | .40 | .15 |
| 279 | Chris Warren | .40 | .15 |
| 280 | Lamar Smith | .60 | .25 |
| 281 | Cortez Kennedy | .25 | .08 |
| 282 | Chad Brown | .25 | .08 |
| 283 | Warren Moon | .60 | .25 |
| 284 | Jerome Bettis | .60 | .25 |
| 285 | Charles Johnson | .40 | .15 |
| 286 | Kordell Stewart | .60 | .25 |
| 287 | Eric Pegram | .25 | .08 |
| 288 | Norm Johnson | .25 | .08 |
| 289 | Levon Kirkland | .25 | .08 |
| 290 | Greg Lloyd | .25 | .08 |
| 291 | Carnell Lake | .25 | .08 |
| 292 | Brad Johnson | .60 | .25 |
| 293 | Cris Carter | .40 | .15 |
| 294 | Jake Reed | .40 | .15 |
| 295 | Robert Smith | .40 | .15 |
| 296 | Derrick Alexander DE | .25 | .08 |
| 297 | John Randle | .40 | .15 |
| 298 | Dixon Edwards | .25 | .08 |
| 299 | Orlanda Thomas | .25 | .08 |
| 300 | Dewayne Washington | .25 | .08 |

## 1998 Upper Deck

| | | |
|---|---|---|
| COMPLETE SET (255) | 200.00 | 75.00 |
| COMP.SET w/o SP's (213) | 25.00 | 12.50 |
| 1 Peyton Manning RC | 50.00 | 20.00 |
| 2 Ryan Leaf RC | 5.00 | 2.00 |
| 3 Andre Wadsworth RC | 3.00 | 1.25 |
| 4 Charles Woodson RC | 6.00 | 2.50 |
| 5 Curtis Enis RC | 2.50 | 1.00 |
| 6 Grant Wistrom RC | 3.00 | 1.25 |
| 7 Greg Ellis RC | 2.50 | 1.00 |
| 8 Fred Taylor RC | 8.00 | 3.00 |
| 9 Duane Starks RC | 2.50 | 1.00 |
| 10 Keith Brooking RC | 5.00 | 2.00 |
| 11 Takeo Spikes RC | 5.00 | 2.00 |

|  |  | | |
|---|---|---|---|
| 12 | Jason Peter RC | 2.50 | 1.00 |
| 13 | Anthony Simmons RC | 3.00 | 1.25 |
| 14 | Kevin Dyson RC | 5.00 | 2.00 |
| 15 | Brian Simmons RC | 3.00 | 1.25 |
| 16 | Robert Edwards RC | 3.00 | 1.25 |
| 17 | Randy Moss RC | 30.00 | 12.00 |
| 18 | John Avery RC | 3.00 | 1.25 |
| 19 | Marcus Nash RC | 2.50 | 1.00 |
| 20 | Jerome Pathon RC | 5.00 | 2.00 |
| 21 | Jacquez Green RC | 3.00 | 1.25 |
| 22 | Robert Holcombe RC | 3.00 | 1.25 |
| 23 | Pat Johnson RC | 3.00 | 1.25 |
| 24 | Germane Crowell RC | 3.00 | 1.25 |
| 25 | Joe Jurevicius RC | 5.00 | 2.00 |
| 26 | Skip Hicks RC | 3.00 | 1.25 |
| 27 | Ahman Green RC | 12.00 | 5.00 |
| 28 | Brian Griese RC | 10.00 | 4.00 |
| 29 | Hines Ward RC | 20.00 | 10.00 |
| 30 | Tavian Banks RC | 3.00 | 1.25 |
| 31 | Tony Simmons RC | 3.00 | 1.25 |
| 32 | Victor Riley RC | 2.50 | 1.00 |
| 33 | Rashaan Shehee RC | 3.00 | 1.25 |
| 34 | R.W. McQuarters RC | 3.00 | 1.25 |
| 35 | Flozell Adams RC | 2.50 | 1.00 |
| 36 | Ja Thomas RC | 2.50 | 1.00 |
| 37 | Greg Favors RC | 3.00 | 1.25 |
| 38 | Jon Ritchie RC | 3.00 | 1.25 |
| 39 | Jesse Haynes RC | 2.50 | 1.00 |
| 40 | Ryan Sutter RC | 2.50 | 1.00 |
| 41 | Mo Collins RC | 2.50 | 1.00 |
| 42 | Tim Dwight RC | 5.00 | 2.00 |
| 43 | Chris Chandler | .40 | .15 |
| 44 | Byron Hanspard | .25 | .08 |
| 45 | Jessie Tuggle | .25 | .08 |
| 46 | Jamal Anderson | .60 | .25 |
| 47 | Terance Mathis | .40 | .15 |
| 48 | Morten Andersen | .25 | .08 |
| 49 | Jake Plummer | .60 | .25 |
| 50 | Mario Bates | .40 | .15 |
| 51 | Frank Sanders | .40 | .15 |
| 52 | Adrian Murrell | .40 | .15 |
| 53 | Simeon Rice | .40 | .15 |
| 54 | Aeneas Williams | .25 | .08 |
| 55 | Eric Swann UER | .25 | .08 |
| 56 | Jim Harbaugh | .40 | .15 |
| 57 | Michael Jackson | .25 | .08 |
| 58 | Peter Boulware | .25 | .08 |
| 59 | Errict Rhett | .40 | .15 |
| 60 | Jermaine Lewis | .40 | .15 |
| 61 | Eric Zeier | .40 | .15 |
| 62 | Rod Woodson | .40 | .15 |
| 63 | Rob Johnson | .60 | .25 |
| 64 | Antowain Smith | .60 | .25 |
| 65 | Bruce Smith | .40 | .15 |
| 66 | Eric Moulds | .60 | .25 |
| 67 | Andre Reed | .40 | .15 |
| 68 | Thurman Thomas | .60 | .25 |
| 69 | Lonnie Johnson | .25 | .08 |
| 70 | Kerry Collins | .40 | .15 |
| 71 | Kevin Greene | .25 | .08 |
| 72 | Fred Lane | .25 | .08 |
| 73 | Rae Carruth | .25 | .08 |
| 74 | Michael Bates | .25 | .08 |
| 75 | William Floyd | .25 | .08 |
| 76 | Sean Gilbert | .25 | .08 |
| 77 | Erik Kramer | .25 | .08 |
| 78 | Edgar Bennett | .25 | .08 |
| 79 | Curtis Conway | .40 | .15 |
| 80 | Darnell Autry | .25 | .08 |
| 81 | Ryan Wetnight RC | .25 | .08 |
| 82 | Walt Harris | .25 | .08 |
| 83 | Bobby Engram | .40 | .15 |
| 84 | Jeff Blake | .40 | .15 |
| 85 | Carl Pickens | .40 | .15 |
| 86 | Darnay Scott | .40 | .15 |
| 87 | Corey Dillon | .60 | .25 |
| 88 | Reinard Wilson | .25 | .08 |
| 89 | Ashley Ambrose | .25 | .08 |
| 90 | Troy Aikman | 1.25 | .50 |
| 91 | Michael Irvin | .60 | .25 |
| 92 | Emmitt Smith | 2.00 | .75 |
| 93 | Deion Sanders | .60 | .25 |
| 94 | David LaFleur | .25 | .08 |
| 95 | Chris Warren | .40 | .15 |

|  |  | | |
|---|---|---|---|
| 96 | Darren Woodson | .25 | .08 |
| 97 | John Elway | 2.50 | 1.00 |
| 98 | Terrell Davis | .60 | .25 |
| 99 | Rod Smith | .40 | .15 |
| 100 | Shannon Sharpe | .40 | .15 |
| 101 | Ed McCaffrey | .40 | .15 |
| 102 | Steve Atwater | .25 | .08 |
| 103 | John Mobley | .25 | .08 |
| 104 | Darrien Gordon | .25 | .08 |
| 105 | Barry Sanders | 2.00 | .75 |
| 106 | Scott Mitchell | .40 | .15 |
| 107 | Herman Moore | .40 | .15 |
| 108 | Johnnie Morton | .40 | .15 |
| 109 | Robert Porcher | .25 | .08 |
| 110 | Bryant Westbrook | .25 | .08 |
| 111 | Tommy Vardell | .25 | .08 |
| 112 | Brett Favre | 2.50 | 1.00 |
| 113 | Dorsey Levens | .60 | .25 |
| 114 | Reggie White | .60 | .25 |
| 115 | Antonio Freeman | .60 | .25 |
| 116 | Robert Brooks | .40 | .15 |
| 117 | Mark Chmura | .40 | .15 |
| 118 | Derrick Mayes | .40 | .15 |
| 119 | Gilbert Brown | .25 | .08 |
| 120 | Marshall Faulk | .75 | .30 |
| 121 | Jeff Burris | .25 | .08 |
| 122 | Marvin Harrison | .60 | .25 |
| 123 | Quentin Coryatt | .25 | .08 |
| 124 | Ken Dilger | .25 | .08 |
| 125 | Zack Crockett | .25 | .08 |
| 126 | Mark Brunell | .60 | .25 |
| 127 | Bryce Paup | .25 | .08 |
| 128 | Tony Brackens | .25 | .08 |
| 129 | Renaldo Wynn | .25 | .08 |
| 130 | Keenan McCardell | .40 | .15 |
| 131 | Jimmy Smith | .40 | .15 |
| 132 | Kevin Hardy | .25 | .08 |
| 133 | Elvis Grbac | .25 | .08 |
| 134 | Tamarick Vanover | .25 | .08 |
| 135 | Chester McGlockton | .25 | .08 |
| 136 | Andre Rison | .40 | .15 |
| 137 | Derrick Alexander | .40 | .15 |
| 138 | Tony Gonzalez | .60 | .25 |
| 139 | Derrick Thomas | .60 | .25 |
| 140 | Dan Marino | 2.50 | 1.00 |
| 141 | Karim Abdul-Jabbar | .60 | .25 |
| 142 | O.J. McDuffie | .40 | .15 |
| 143 | Yatil Green | .25 | .08 |
| 144 | Charles Jordan | .25 | .08 |
| 145 | Brock Marion | .25 | .08 |
| 146 | Zach Thomas | .60 | .25 |
| 147 | Brad Johnson | .40 | .15 |
| 148 | Cris Carter | .60 | .25 |
| 149 | Jake Reed | .40 | .15 |
| 150 | Robert Smith | .60 | .25 |
| 151 | John Randle | .25 | .08 |
| 152 | Dwayne Rudd | .25 | .08 |
| 153 | Randall Cunningham | .60 | .25 |
| 154 | Drew Bledsoe | 1.00 | .40 |
| 155 | Terry Glenn | .60 | .25 |
| 156 | Ben Coates | .40 | .15 |
| 157 | Willie Clay | .25 | .08 |
| 158 | Chris Slade | .25 | .08 |
| 159 | Derrick Cullors RC | .25 | .08 |
| 160 | Ty Law | .40 | .15 |
| 161 | Danny Wuerffel | .25 | .08 |
| 162 | Andre Hastings | .25 | .08 |
| 163 | Troy Davis | .25 | .08 |
| 164 | Billy Joe Hobert | .25 | .08 |
| 165 | Eric Guliford | .25 | .08 |
| 166 | Mark Fields | .25 | .08 |
| 167 | Alex Molden | .25 | .08 |
| 168 | Danny Kanell | .40 | .15 |
| 169 | Tiki Barber | .60 | .25 |
| 170 | Charles Way | .25 | .08 |
| 171 | Amani Toomer | .40 | .15 |
| 172 | Michael Strahan | .40 | .15 |
| 173 | Jessie Armstead | .25 | .08 |
| 174 | Jason Sehorn | .25 | .08 |
| 175 | Glenn Foley | .40 | .15 |
| 176 | Curtis Martin | .60 | .25 |
| 177 | Aaron Glenn | .25 | .08 |
| 178 | Keyshawn Johnson | .60 | .25 |
| 179 | James Farrior | .25 | .08 |
| 180 | Wayne Chrebet | .60 | .25 |
| 181 | Keith Byars | .25 | .08 |
| 182 | Jeff George | .40 | .15 |
| 183 | Napoleon Kaufman | .60 | .25 |
| 184 | Tim Brown | .60 | .25 |
| 185 | Darrell Russell | .25 | .08 |
| 186 | Rickey Dudley | .25 | .08 |
| 187 | James Jett | .40 | .15 |
| 188 | Desmond Howard | .40 | .15 |
| 189 | Bobby Hoying | .40 | .15 |
| 190 | Charlie Garner | .40 | .15 |
| 191 | Irving Fryar | .40 | .15 |
| 192 | Chris T. Jones | .25 | .08 |
| 193 | Mike Mamula | .25 | .08 |
| 194 | Troy Vincent | .25 | .08 |
| 195 | Kordell Stewart | .60 | .25 |
| 196 | Jerome Bettis | .60 | .25 |
| 197 | Will Blackwell | .25 | .08 |
| 198 | Levon Kirkland | .25 | .08 |
| 199 | Carnell Lake | .25 | .08 |
| 200 | Charles Johnson | .25 | .08 |
| 201 | Greg Lloyd | .25 | .08 |
| 202 | Donnell Woolford | .25 | .08 |
| 203 | Tony Banks | .40 | .15 |
| 204 | Amp Lee | .25 | .08 |
| 205 | Isaac Bruce | .60 | .25 |
| 206 | Eddie Kennison | .40 | .15 |
| 207 | Ryan McNeil | .25 | .08 |
| 208 | Mike Jones | .25 | .08 |
| 209 | Ernie Conwell | .25 | .08 |
| 210 | Natrone Means | .40 | .15 |
| 211 | Junior Seau | .60 | .25 |
| 212 | Tony Martin | .40 | .15 |
| 213 | Freddie Jones | .25 | .08 |
| 214 | Bryan Still | .25 | .08 |
| 215 | Rodney Harrison | .40 | .15 |
| 216 | Steve Young | .75 | .30 |
| 217 | Jerry Rice | 1.25 | .50 |
| 218 | Garrison Hearst | .60 | .25 |
| 219 | J.J. Stokes | .40 | .15 |
| 220 | Ken Norton | .25 | .08 |
| 221 | Greg Clark | .25 | .08 |
| 222 | Terrell Owens | .60 | .25 |
| 223 | Bryant Young | .25 | .08 |
| 224 | Warren Moon | .60 | .25 |
| 225 | Jon Kitna | .60 | .25 |
| 226 | Ricky Watters | .40 | .15 |
| 227 | Chad Brown | .25 | .08 |
| 228 | Joey Galloway | .40 | .15 |
| 229 | Shawn Springs | .25 | .08 |
| 230 | Cortez Kennedy | .25 | .08 |
| 231 | Trent Dilfer | .60 | .25 |
| 232 | Warrick Dunn | .60 | .25 |
| 233 | Mike Alstott | .60 | .25 |
| 234 | Warren Sapp | .40 | .15 |
| 235 | Bert Emanuel | .40 | .15 |
| 236 | Reidel Anthony | .40 | .15 |
| 237 | Hardy Nickerson | .25 | .08 |
| 238 | Derrick Brooks | .60 | .25 |
| 239 | Steve McNair | .60 | .25 |
| 240 | Yancey Thigpen | .25 | .08 |
| 241 | Anthony Dorsett | .25 | .08 |
| 242 | Blaine Bishop | .25 | .08 |
| 243 | Kenny Holmes | .25 | .08 |
| 244 | Eddie George | .60 | .25 |
| 245 | Chris Sanders | .25 | .08 |
| 246 | Gus Frerotte | .40 | .15 |
| 247 | Terry Allen | .60 | .25 |
| 248 | Dana Stubblefield | .25 | .08 |
| 249 | Michael Westbrook | .40 | .15 |
| 250 | Darrell Green | .40 | .15 |
| 251 | Brian Mitchell | .25 | .08 |
| 252 | Ken Harvey | .25 | .08 |
| CL1 | Troy Aikman CL | .60 | .25 |
| CL2 | Dan Marino CL | .75 | .30 |
| CL3 | Herman Moore CL | .40 | .15 |

## 1999 Upper Deck

| | | | |
|---|---|---|---|
| COMPLETE SET (270) | | 100.00 | 50.00 |
| COMP.SET w/o SP's (225) | | 25.00 | 12.50 |
| 1 | Jake Plummer | .50 | .20 |
| 2 | Adrian Murrell | .50 | .20 |
| 3 | Rob Moore | .50 | .20 |
| 4 | Larry Centers | .30 | .10 |
| 5 | Simeon Rice | .50 | .20 |
| 6 | Andre Wadsworth | .30 | .10 |
| 7 | Frank Sanders | .50 | .20 |
| 8 | Tim Dwight | .75 | .30 |
| 9 | Ray Buchanan | .30 | .10 |
| 10 | Chris Chandler | .50 | .20 |
| 11 | Jamal Anderson | .75 | .30 |
| 12 | O.J. Santiago | .30 | .10 |
| 13 | Danny Kanell | .30 | .10 |
| 14 | Terance Mathis | .50 | .20 |
| 15 | Priest Holmes | 1.25 | .50 |
| 16 | Tony Banks | .50 | .20 |
| 17 | Ray Lewis | .75 | .30 |
| 18 | Patrick Johnson | .30 | .10 |
| 19 | Michael Jackson | .30 | .10 |
| 20 | Michael McCrary | .30 | .10 |
| 21 | Jermaine Lewis | .50 | .20 |
| 22 | Eric Moulds | .75 | .30 |
| 23 | Doug Flutie | .75 | .30 |
| 24 | Antowain Smith | .75 | .30 |
| 25 | Rob Johnson | .50 | .20 |
| 26 | Bruce Smith | .50 | .20 |
| 27 | Andre Reed | .50 | .20 |
| 28 | Thurman Thomas | .50 | .20 |
| 29 | Fred Lane | .30 | .10 |
| 30 | Wesley Walls | .50 | .20 |
| 31 | Tim Biakabutuka | .30 | .10 |
| 32 | Kevin Greene | .30 | .10 |
| 33 | Steve Beuerlein | .30 | .10 |
| 34 | Muhsin Muhammad | .30 | .10 |
| 35 | Rae Carruth | .30 | .10 |
| 36 | Bobby Engram | .30 | .10 |
| 37 | Curtis Enis | .50 | .20 |
| 38 | Edgar Bennett | .30 | .10 |
| 39 | Erik Kramer | .30 | .10 |
| 40 | Steve Stenstrom | .30 | .10 |
| 41 | Alonzo Mayes | .30 | .10 |
| 42 | Curtis Conway | .50 | .20 |
| 43 | Tony McGee | .30 | .10 |
| 44 | Darnay Scott | .30 | .10 |
| 45 | Jeff Blake | .50 | .20 |
| 46 | Corey Dillon | .75 | .30 |
| 47 | Ki-Jana Carter | .30 | .10 |
| 48 | Takeo Spikes | .30 | .10 |
| 49 | Carl Pickens | .50 | .20 |
| 50 | Ty Detmer | .30 | .10 |
| 51 | Leslie Shepherd | .30 | .10 |
| 52 | Terry Kirby | .30 | .10 |
| 53 | Marquez Pope | .30 | .10 |
| 54 | Antonio Langham | .30 | .10 |
| 55 | Jamir Miller | .30 | .10 |
| 56 | Derrick Alexander DT | .30 | .10 |
| 57 | Troy Aikman | 1.50 | .60 |
| 58 | Rocket Ismail | .50 | .20 |
| 59 | Emmitt Smith | 1.50 | .60 |
| 60 | Michael Irvin | .50 | .20 |
| 61 | David LaFleur | .30 | .10 |
| 62 | Chris Warren | .30 | .10 |
| 63 | Deion Sanders | .75 | .30 |
| 64 | Greg Ellis | .30 | .10 |
| 65 | John Elway | 2.50 | 1.00 |
| 66 | Bubby Brister | .30 | .10 |
| 67 | Terrell Davis | .75 | .30 |
| 68 | Ed McCaffrey | .50 | .20 |
| 69 | John Mobley | .30 | .10 |
| 70 | Bill Romanowski | .30 | .10 |
| 71 | Rod Smith | .50 | .20 |

|  |  | | |
|---|---|---|---|
| ❏ 72 | Shannon Sharpe | .50 | .20 |
| ❏ 73 | Charlie Batch | .75 | .30 |
| ❏ 74 | Germane Crowell | .30 | .10 |
| ❏ 75 | Johnnie Morton | .30 | .10 |
| ❏ 76 | Barry Sanders | 2.50 | 1.00 |
| ❏ 77 | Robert Porcher | .30 | .10 |
| ❏ 78 | Stephen Boyd | .30 | .10 |
| ❏ 79 | Herman Moore | .75 | .30 |
| ❏ 80 | Brett Favre | 2.50 | 1.00 |
| ❏ 81 | Mark Chmura | .30 | .10 |
| ❏ 82 | Antonio Freeman | .75 | .30 |
| ❏ 83 | Robert Brooks | .50 | .20 |
| ❏ 84 | Vonnie Holliday | .30 | .10 |
| ❏ 85 | Bill Schroeder | .75 | .30 |
| ❏ 86 | Dorsey Levens | .75 | .30 |
| ❏ 87 | Santana Dotson | .30 | .10 |
| ❏ 88 | Peyton Manning | 2.50 | 1.00 |
| ❏ 89 | Jerome Pathon | .30 | .10 |
| ❏ 90 | Marvin Harrison | .75 | .30 |
| ❏ 91 | Ellis Johnson | .30 | .10 |
| ❏ 92 | Ken Dilger | .30 | .10 |
| ❏ 93 | E.G. Green | .30 | .10 |
| ❏ 94 | Jeff Burris | .30 | .10 |
| ❏ 95 | Mark Brunell | .75 | .30 |
| ❏ 96 | Fred Taylor | .75 | .30 |
| ❏ 97 | Jimmy Smith | .50 | .20 |
| ❏ 98 | James Stewart | .50 | .20 |
| ❏ 99 | Kyle Brady | .30 | .10 |
| ❏ 100 | Dave Thomas RC | .30 | .10 |
| ❏ 101 | Keenan McCardell | .50 | .20 |
| ❏ 102 | Elvis Grbac | .75 | .30 |
| ❏ 103 | Tony Gonzalez | .75 | .30 |
| ❏ 104 | Andre Rison | .50 | .20 |
| ❏ 105 | Donnell Bennett | .30 | .10 |
| ❏ 106 | Derrick Thomas | .75 | .30 |
| ❏ 107 | Warren Moon | .75 | .30 |
| ❏ 108 | Derrick Alexander WR | .50 | .20 |
| ❏ 109 | Dan Marino | 2.50 | 1.00 |
| ❏ 110 | O.J. McDuffie | .50 | .20 |
| ❏ 111 | Karim Abdul-Jabbar | .50 | .20 |
| ❏ 112 | John Avery | .30 | .10 |
| ❏ 113 | Sam Madison | .30 | .10 |
| ❏ 114 | Jason Taylor | .30 | .10 |
| ❏ 115 | Zach Thomas | .75 | .30 |
| ❏ 116 | Randall Cunningham | .75 | .30 |
| ❏ 117 | Randy Moss | 2.00 | .75 |
| ❏ 118 | Cris Carter | .75 | .30 |
| ❏ 119 | Jake Reed | .50 | .20 |
| ❏ 120 | Matthew Hatchette | .30 | .10 |
| ❏ 121 | John Randle | .50 | .20 |
| ❏ 122 | Robert Smith | .75 | .30 |
| ❏ 123 | Drew Bledsoe | 1.00 | .40 |
| ❏ 124 | Ben Coates | .75 | .30 |
| ❏ 125 | Terry Glenn | .75 | .30 |
| ❏ 126 | Ty Law | .50 | .20 |
| ❏ 127 | Tony Simmons | .30 | .10 |
| ❏ 128 | Ted Johnson | .30 | .10 |
| ❏ 129 | Tony Carter | .30 | .10 |
| ❏ 130 | Willie McGinest | .30 | .10 |
| ❏ 131 | Danny Wuerffel | .30 | .10 |
| ❏ 132 | Cameron Cleeland | .50 | .20 |
| ❏ 133 | Eddie Kennison | .50 | .20 |
| ❏ 134 | Joe Johnson | .30 | .10 |
| ❏ 135 | Andre Hastings | .30 | .10 |
| ❏ 136 | La'Roi Glover RC | .75 | .30 |
| ❏ 137 | Kent Graham | .30 | .10 |
| ❏ 138 | Tiki Barber | .75 | .30 |
| ❏ 139 | Gary Brown | .30 | .10 |
| ❏ 140 | Ike Hilliard | .30 | .10 |
| ❏ 141 | Jason Sehorn | .30 | .10 |
| ❏ 142 | Michael Strahan | .50 | .20 |
| ❏ 143 | Amani Toomer | .50 | .20 |
| ❏ 144 | Kerry Collins | .50 | .20 |
| ❏ 145 | Vinny Testaverde | .50 | .20 |
| ❏ 146 | Wayne Chrebet | .50 | .20 |
| ❏ 147 | Curtis Martin | .75 | .30 |
| ❏ 148 | Mo Lewis | .30 | .10 |
| ❏ 149 | Aaron Glenn | .30 | .10 |
| ❏ 150 | Steve Atwater | .30 | .10 |
| ❏ 151 | Keyshawn Johnson | .75 | .30 |
| ❏ 152 | James Farrior | .30 | .10 |
| ❏ 153 | Rich Gannon | .50 | .20 |
| ❏ 154 | Tim Brown | .75 | .30 |
| ❏ 155 | Darrell Russell | .30 | .10 |
| ❏ 156 | Rickey Dudley | .30 | .10 |
| ❏ 157 | Charles Woodson | .75 | .30 |
| ❏ 158 | James Jett | .50 | .20 |
| ❏ 159 | Napoleon Kaufman | .75 | .30 |
| ❏ 160 | Duce Staley | .75 | .30 |
| ❏ 161 | Doug Pederson | .30 | .10 |
| ❏ 162 | Bobby Hoying | .50 | .20 |
| ❏ 163 | Koy Detmer | .30 | .10 |
| ❏ 164 | Kevin Turner | .30 | .10 |
| ❏ 165 | Charles Johnson | .30 | .10 |
| ❏ 166 | Mike Mamula | .30 | .10 |
| ❏ 167 | Jerome Bettis | .75 | .30 |
| ❏ 168 | Courtney Hawkins | .30 | .10 |
| ❏ 169 | Will Blackwell | .30 | .10 |
| ❏ 170 | Kordell Stewart | .50 | .20 |
| ❏ 171 | Richard Huntley | .30 | .10 |
| ❏ 172 | Levon Kirkland | .30 | .10 |
| ❏ 173 | Hines Ward | .75 | .30 |
| ❏ 174 | Trent Green | .75 | .30 |
| ❏ 175 | Marshall Faulk | 1.00 | .40 |
| ❏ 176 | Az-Zahir Hakim | .30 | .10 |
| ❏ 177 | Amp Lee | .30 | .10 |
| ❏ 178 | Robert Holcombe | .30 | .10 |
| ❏ 179 | Isaac Bruce | .75 | .30 |
| ❏ 180 | Kevin Carter | .30 | .10 |
| ❏ 181 | Jim Harbaugh | .50 | .20 |
| ❏ 182 | Junior Seau | .75 | .30 |
| ❏ 183 | Natrone Means | .50 | .20 |
| ❏ 184 | Ryan Leaf | .75 | .30 |
| ❏ 185 | Charlie Jones | .30 | .10 |
| ❏ 186 | Rodney Harrison | .30 | .10 |
| ❏ 187 | Mikhael Ricks | .30 | .10 |
| ❏ 188 | Steve Young | 1.00 | .40 |
| ❏ 189 | Terrell Owens | .75 | .30 |
| ❏ 190 | Jerry Rice | 1.50 | .60 |
| ❏ 191 | J.J. Stokes | .50 | .20 |
| ❏ 192 | Irv Smith | .30 | .10 |
| ❏ 193 | Bryant Young | .30 | .10 |
| ❏ 194 | Garrison Hearst | .50 | .20 |
| ❏ 195 | Jon Kitna | .75 | .30 |
| ❏ 196 | Ahman Green | .75 | .30 |
| ❏ 197 | Joey Galloway | .50 | .20 |
| ❏ 198 | Ricky Watters | .50 | .20 |
| ❏ 199 | Chad Brown | .30 | .10 |
| ❏ 200 | Shawn Springs | .30 | .10 |
| ❏ 201 | Mike Pritchard | .30 | .10 |
| ❏ 202 | Trent Dilfer | .50 | .20 |
| ❏ 203 | Reidel Anthony | .50 | .20 |
| ❏ 204 | Bert Emanuel | .30 | .10 |
| ❏ 205 | Warrick Dunn | .75 | .30 |
| ❏ 206 | Jacquez Green | .30 | .10 |
| ❏ 207 | Hardy Nickerson | .30 | .10 |
| ❏ 208 | Mike Alstott | .75 | .30 |
| ❏ 209 | Eddie George | .75 | .30 |
| ❏ 210 | Steve McNair | .75 | .30 |
| ❏ 211 | Kevin Dyson | .50 | .20 |
| ❏ 212 | Frank Wycheck | .30 | .10 |
| ❏ 213 | Jackie Harris | .30 | .10 |
| ❏ 214 | Blaine Bishop | .30 | .10 |
| ❏ 215 | Yancey Thigpen | .30 | .10 |
| ❏ 216 | Brad Johnson | .75 | .30 |
| ❏ 217 | Rodney Peete | .30 | .10 |
| ❏ 218 | Michael Westbrook | .50 | .20 |
| ❏ 219 | Skip Hicks | .30 | .10 |
| ❏ 220 | Brian Mitchell | .30 | .10 |
| ❏ 221 | Dan Wilkinson | .30 | .10 |
| ❏ 222 | Dana Stubblefield | .30 | .10 |
| ❏ 223 | Kordell Stewart CL | .50 | .20 |
| ❏ 224 | Fred Taylor CL | .75 | .30 |
| ❏ 225 | Warrick Dunn CL | .50 | .20 |
| ❏ 226 | Champ Bailey RC | 3.00 | 1.25 |
| ❏ 227 | Chris McAlister RC | 1.50 | .60 |
| ❏ 228 | Jevon Kearse RC | 4.00 | 1.50 |
| ❏ 229 | Ebenezer Ekuban RC | 1.50 | .60 |
| ❏ 230 | Chris Claiborne RC | 1.50 | .60 |
| ❏ 231 | Andy Katzenmoyer RC | 1.50 | .60 |
| ❏ 232 | Tim Couch RC | 2.00 | .75 |
| ❏ 233 | Daunte Culpepper RC | 10.00 | 4.00 |
| ❏ 234 | Akili Smith RC | 1.50 | .60 |
| ❏ 235 | Donovan McNabb RC | 12.00 | 5.00 |
| ❏ 236 | Sean Bennett RC | 1.00 | .40 |
| ❏ 237 | Brock Huard RC | 2.00 | .75 |
| ❏ 238 | Cade McNown RC | 1.50 | .60 |
| ❏ 239 | Shaun King RC | 1.50 | .60 |
| ❏ 240 | Joe Germaine RC | 1.50 | .60 |
| ❏ 241 | Ricky Williams RC | 5.00 | 2.00 |
| ❏ 242 | Edgerrin James RC | 10.00 | 4.00 |
| ❏ 243 | Sedrick Irvin RC | 1.00 | .40 |
| ❏ 244 | Kevin Faulk RC | 2.00 | .75 |
| ❏ 245 | Rob Konrad RC | 2.00 | .75 |
| ❏ 246 | James Johnson RC | 1.50 | .60 |
| ❏ 247 | Amos Zereoue RC | 2.00 | .75 |
| ❏ 248 | Torry Holt RC | 6.00 | 2.50 |
| ❏ 249 | D'Wayne Bates RC | 1.50 | .60 |
| ❏ 250 | David Boston RC | 2.00 | .75 |
| ❏ 251 | Dameane Douglas RC | 2.00 | .75 |
| ❏ 252 | Troy Edwards RC | 1.50 | .60 |
| ❏ 253 | Kevin Johnson RC | 2.00 | .75 |
| ❏ 254 | Peerless Price RC | 2.00 | .75 |
| ❏ 255 | Antoine Winfield RC | 1.50 | .60 |
| ❏ 256 | Mike Cloud RC | 1.50 | .60 |
| ❏ 257 | Joe Montgomery RC | 1.50 | .60 |
| ❏ 258 | Jermaine Fazande RC | 1.50 | .60 |
| ❏ 259 | Scott Covington RC | 2.00 | .75 |
| ❏ 260 | Aaron Brooks RC | 5.00 | 2.00 |
| ❏ 261 | Patrick Kerney RC | 2.00 | .75 |
| ❏ 262 | Cecil Collins RC | 1.00 | .40 |
| ❏ 263 | Chris Greisen RC | 1.50 | .60 |
| ❏ 264 | Craig Yeast RC | 1.50 | .60 |
| ❏ 265 | Karsten Bailey RC | 1.50 | .60 |
| ❏ 266 | Reginald Kelly RC | 1.00 | .40 |
| ❏ 267 | Al Wilson RC | 1.50 | .60 |
| ❏ 268 | Jeff Paulk RC | 1.00 | .40 |
| ❏ 269 | Jim Kleinsasser RC | 2.00 | .75 |
| ❏ 270 | Darrin Chiaverini RC | 1.50 | .60 |

## 2000 Upper Deck

|  |  | | |
|---|---|---|---|
| ❏ | COMPLETE SET (1-270) | 120.00 | 60.00 |
| ❏ | COMP.SET w/o SPs (222) | 30.00 | 12.50 |
| ❏ 1 | Jake Plummer | .30 | .10 |
| ❏ 2 | Michael Pittman | .30 | .10 |
| ❏ 3 | Rob Moore | .50 | .20 |
| ❏ 4 | David Boston | .75 | .30 |
| ❏ 5 | Frank Sanders | .50 | .20 |
| ❏ 6 | Aeneas Williams | .30 | .10 |
| ❏ 7 | Kwamie Lassiter | .30 | .10 |
| ❏ 8 | Rob Fredrickson | .30 | .10 |
| ❏ 9 | Tim Dwight | .75 | .30 |
| ❏ 10 | Chris Chandler | .30 | .10 |
| ❏ 11 | Jamal Anderson | .75 | .30 |
| ❏ 12 | Shawn Jefferson | .30 | .10 |
| ❏ 13 | Ken Oxendine | .30 | .10 |
| ❏ 14 | Terance Mathis | .50 | .20 |
| ❏ 15 | Bob Christian | .30 | .10 |
| ❏ 16 | Qadry Ismail | .30 | .10 |
| ❏ 17 | Jermaine Lewis | .50 | .20 |
| ❏ 18 | Rod Woodson | .50 | .20 |
| ❏ 19 | Michael McCrary | .30 | .10 |
| ❏ 20 | Tony Banks | .50 | .20 |
| ❏ 21 | Peter Boulware | .30 | .10 |
| ❏ 22 | Shannon Sharpe | .50 | .20 |
| ❏ 23 | Peerless Price | .50 | .20 |
| ❏ 24 | Rob Johnson | .50 | .20 |
| ❏ 25 | Eric Moulds | .75 | .30 |
| ❏ 26 | Doug Flutie | .75 | .30 |
| ❏ 27 | Jay Riemersma | .30 | .10 |
| ❏ 28 | Antowain Smith | .50 | .20 |
| ❏ 29 | Jonathan Linton | .30 | .10 |
| ❏ 30 | Muhsin Muhammad | .50 | .20 |
| ❏ 31 | Patrick Jeffers | .75 | .30 |
| ❏ 32 | Steve Beuerlein | .50 | .20 |

|  |  | | |
|---|--------|------|------|
| 33 | Natrone Means | .30 | .10 |
| 34 | Tim Biakabutuka | .50 | .20 |
| 35 | Michael Bates | .30 | .10 |
| 36 | Chuck Smith | .30 | .10 |
| 37 | Wesley Walls | .30 | .10 |
| 38 | Cade McNown | .30 | .10 |
| 39 | Curtis Enis | .30 | .10 |
| 40 | Marcus Robinson | .75 | .30 |
| 41 | Eddie Kennison | .50 | .20 |
| 42 | Bobby Engram | .50 | .20 |
| 43 | Glyn Milburn | .30 | .10 |
| 44 | Marty Booker | .50 | .20 |
| 45 | Akili Smith | .30 | .10 |
| 46 | Corey Dillon | .75 | .30 |
| 47 | Darnay Scott | .50 | .20 |
| 48 | Tremain Mack | .30 | .10 |
| 49 | Damon Griffin | .30 | .10 |
| 50 | Takeo Spikes | .30 | .10 |
| 51 | Tony McGee | .30 | .10 |
| 52 | Tim Couch | .50 | .20 |
| 53 | Kevin Johnson | .75 | .30 |
| 54 | Darrin Chiaverini | .30 | .10 |
| 55 | Jamir Miller | .30 | .10 |
| 56 | Errict Rhett | .30 | .10 |
| 57 | Terry Kirby | .30 | .10 |
| 58 | Marc Edwards | .30 | .10 |
| 59 | Troy Aikman | 1.50 | .60 |
| 60 | Emmitt Smith | 1.50 | .60 |
| 61 | Rocket Ismail | .50 | .20 |
| 62 | Jason Tucker | .30 | .10 |
| 63 | Dexter Coakley | .30 | .10 |
| 64 | Joey Galloway | .75 | .30 |
| 65 | Wane McGarity | .30 | .10 |
| 66 | Terrell Davis | .75 | .30 |
| 67 | Olandis Gary | .75 | .30 |
| 68 | Brian Griese | .75 | .30 |
| 69 | Gus Frerotte | .30 | .10 |
| 70 | Byron Chamberlain | .30 | .10 |
| 71 | Ed McCaffrey | .75 | .30 |
| 72 | Rod Smith | .50 | .20 |
| 73 | Al Wilson | .30 | .10 |
| 74 | Charlie Batch | .75 | .30 |
| 75 | Germane Crowell | .30 | .10 |
| 76 | Sedrick Irvin | .30 | .10 |
| 77 | Johnnie Morton | .50 | .20 |
| 78 | Robert Porcher | .30 | .10 |
| 79 | Herman Moore | .50 | .20 |
| 80 | James Stewart | .50 | .20 |
| 81 | Brett Favre | 2.50 | 1.00 |
| 82 | Antonio Freeman | .75 | .30 |
| 83 | Bill Schroeder | .50 | .20 |
| 84 | Dorsey Levens | .50 | .20 |
| 85 | Corey Bradford | .50 | .20 |
| 86 | De'Mond Parker | .30 | .10 |
| 87 | Vonnie Holliday | .30 | .10 |
| 88 | Peyton Manning | 2.00 | .75 |
| 89 | Edgerrin James | 1.25 | .50 |
| 90 | Marvin Harrison | .75 | .30 |
| 91 | Ken Dilger | .30 | .10 |
| 92 | Terrence Wilkins | .30 | .10 |
| 93 | Marcus Pollard | .30 | .10 |
| 94 | Fred Lane | .30 | .10 |
| 95 | Mark Brunell | .75 | .30 |
| 96 | Fred Taylor | .75 | .30 |
| 97 | Jimmy Smith | .50 | .20 |
| 98 | Keenan McCardell | .50 | .20 |
| 99 | Carnell Lake | .30 | .10 |
| 100 | Tavian Banks | .30 | .10 |
| 101 | Kyle Brady | .30 | .10 |
| 102 | Hardy Nickerson | .30 | .10 |
| 103 | Elvis Grbac | .50 | .20 |
| 104 | Tony Gonzalez | .50 | .20 |
| 105 | Derrick Alexander WR | .50 | .20 |
| 106 | Donnell Bennett | .30 | .10 |
| 107 | Mike Cloud | .30 | .10 |
| 108 | Donnie Edwards | .30 | .10 |
| 109 | Jay Fiedler | .75 | .30 |
| 110 | James Johnson | .30 | .10 |
| 111 | Tony Martin | .50 | .20 |
| 112 | Damon Huard | .75 | .30 |
| 113 | O.J. McDuffie | .50 | .20 |
| 114 | Thurman Thomas | .50 | .20 |
| 115 | Zach Thomas | .75 | .30 |
| 116 | Oronde Gadsden | .50 | .20 |
| 117 | Randy Moss | 1.50 | .60 |
| 118 | Robert Smith | .75 | .30 |
| 119 | Cris Carter | .75 | .30 |
| 120 | Matthew Hatchette | .30 | .10 |
| 121 | Daunte Culpepper | 1.00 | .40 |
| 122 | Leroy Hoard | .30 | .10 |
| 123 | Drew Bledsoe | 1.00 | .40 |
| 124 | Terry Glenn | .50 | .20 |
| 125 | Troy Brown | .50 | .20 |
| 126 | Kevin Faulk | .30 | .10 |
| 127 | Lawyer Milloy | .50 | .20 |
| 128 | Ricky Williams | .75 | .30 |
| 129 | Keith Poole | .30 | .10 |
| 130 | Jake Reed | .50 | .20 |
| 131 | Cam Cleeland | .30 | .10 |
| 132 | Jeff Blake | .50 | .20 |
| 133 | Andrew Glover | .30 | .10 |
| 134 | Kerry Collins | .50 | .20 |
| 135 | Amani Toomer | .50 | .20 |
| 136 | Joe Montgomery | .30 | .10 |
| 137 | Ike Hilliard | .50 | .20 |
| 138 | Tiki Barber | .75 | .30 |
| 139 | Pete Mitchell | .30 | .10 |
| 140 | Ray Lucas | .50 | .20 |
| 141 | Mo Lewis | .30 | .10 |
| 142 | Curtis Martin | .75 | .30 |
| 143 | Vinny Testaverde | .50 | .20 |
| 144 | Wayne Chrebet | .50 | .20 |
| 145 | Dedric Ward | .30 | .10 |
| 146 | Tim Brown | .75 | .30 |
| 147 | Rich Gannon | .75 | .30 |
| 148 | Tyrone Wheatley | .50 | .20 |
| 149 | Napoleon Kaufman | .50 | .20 |
| 150 | Charles Woodson | .50 | .20 |
| 151 | Darrell Russell | .30 | .10 |
| 152 | James Jett | .30 | .10 |
| 153 | Rickey Dudley | .30 | .10 |
| 154 | Jon Ritchie | .30 | .10 |
| 155 | Duce Staley | .75 | .30 |
| 156 | Donovan McNabb | 1.25 | .50 |
| 157 | Torrance Small | .30 | .10 |
| 158 | Allen Rossum | .30 | .10 |
| 159 | Mike Mamula | .30 | .10 |
| 160 | Na Brown | .30 | .10 |
| 161 | Charles Johnson | .50 | .20 |
| 162 | Kent Graham | .30 | .10 |
| 163 | Troy Edwards | .30 | .10 |
| 164 | Jerome Bettis | .75 | .30 |
| 165 | Hines Ward | .75 | .30 |
| 166 | Kordell Stewart | .50 | .20 |
| 167 | Levon Kirkland | .30 | .10 |
| 168 | Richard Huntley | .30 | .10 |
| 169 | Marshall Faulk | 1.00 | .40 |
| 170 | Kurt Warner | 1.50 | .60 |
| 171 | Torry Holt | .75 | .30 |
| 172 | Isaac Bruce | .75 | .30 |
| 173 | Kevin Carter | .30 | .10 |
| 174 | Az-Zahir Hakim | .50 | .20 |
| 175 | Ricky Proehl | .30 | .10 |
| 176 | Jermaine Fazande | .30 | .10 |
| 177 | Curtis Conway | .50 | .20 |
| 178 | Freddie Jones | .30 | .10 |
| 179 | Junior Seau | .75 | .30 |
| 180 | Jeff Graham | .30 | .10 |
| 181 | Jim Harbaugh | .50 | .20 |
| 182 | Rodney Harrison | .30 | .10 |
| 183 | Steve Young | 1.00 | .40 |
| 184 | Jerry Rice | 1.50 | .60 |
| 185 | Charlie Garner | .50 | .20 |
| 186 | Terrell Owens | .75 | .30 |
| 187 | Jeff Garcia | .75 | .30 |
| 188 | Fred Beasley | .30 | .10 |
| 189 | J.J. Stokes | .50 | .20 |
| 190 | Ricky Watters | .50 | .20 |
| 191 | Jon Kitna | .75 | .30 |
| 192 | Derrick Mayes | .50 | .20 |
| 193 | Sean Dawkins | .30 | .10 |
| 194 | Charlie Rogers | .30 | .10 |
| 195 | Mike Pritchard | .30 | .10 |
| 196 | Cortez Kennedy | .30 | .10 |
| 197 | Christian Fauria | .30 | .10 |
| 198 | Warrick Dunn | .75 | .30 |
| 199 | Shaun King | .50 | .20 |
| 200 | Mike Alstott | .75 | .30 |
| 201 | Warren Sapp | .50 | .20 |
| 202 | Jacquez Green | .30 | .10 |
| 203 | Reidel Anthony | .30 | .10 |
| 204 | Dave Moore | .30 | .10 |
| 205 | Keyshawn Johnson | .75 | .30 |
| 206 | Eddie George | .75 | .30 |
| 207 | Steve McNair | .75 | .30 |
| 208 | Kevin Dyson | .50 | .20 |
| 209 | Jevon Kearse | .75 | .30 |
| 210 | Yancey Thigpen | .30 | .10 |
| 211 | Frank Wycheck | .30 | .10 |
| 212 | Isaac Byrd | .30 | .10 |
| 213 | Neil O'Donnell | .30 | .10 |
| 214 | Brad Johnson | .75 | .30 |
| 215 | Stephen Davis | .75 | .30 |
| 216 | Michael Westbrook | .50 | .20 |
| 217 | Albert Connell | .30 | .10 |
| 218 | Brian Mitchell | .30 | .10 |
| 219 | Bruce Smith | .50 | .20 |
| 220 | Stephen Alexander | .30 | .10 |
| 221 | Jeff George | .50 | .20 |
| 222 | Adrian Murrell | .30 | .10 |
| 223 | Courtney Brown RC | 4.00 | 1.50 |
| 224 | John Engelberger RC | 2.50 | 1.00 |
| 225 | Deltha O'Neal RC | 4.00 | 1.50 |
| 226 | Corey Simon RC | 4.00 | 1.50 |
| 227 | R.Jay Soward RC | 2.50 | 1.00 |
| 228 | Marc Bulger RC | 8.00 | 3.00 |
| 229 | Raynoch Thompson RC | 2.50 | 1.00 |
| 230 | Deon Grant RC | 2.50 | 1.00 |
| 231 | Darrell Jackson RC | 8.00 | 3.00 |
| 232 | Chris Cole RC | 2.50 | 1.00 |
| 233 | Trevor Gaylor RC | 2.50 | 1.00 |
| 234 | John Abraham RC | 4.00 | 1.50 |
| 235 | Chris Redman RC | 2.50 | 1.00 |
| 236 | Joe Hamilton RC | 2.50 | 1.00 |
| 237 | Chad Pennington RC | 10.00 | 4.00 |
| 238 | Tee Martin RC | 4.00 | 1.50 |
| 239 | Giovanni Carmazzi RC | 2.00 | .75 |
| 240 | Tim Rattay RC | 4.00 | 1.50 |
| 241 | Ron Dayne RC | 4.00 | 1.50 |
| 242 | Shaun Alexander RC | 12.00 | 5.00 |
| 243 | Thomas Jones RC | 6.00 | 2.50 |
| 244 | Reuben Droughns RC | 4.00 | 1.50 |
| 245 | Jamal Lewis RC | 10.00 | 4.00 |
| 246 | Michael Wiley RC | 2.50 | 1.00 |
| 247 | J.R. Redmond RC | 2.50 | 1.00 |
| 248 | Travis Prentice RC | 2.50 | 1.00 |
| 249 | Todd Husak RC | 4.00 | 1.50 |
| 250 | Trung Canidate RC | 2.50 | 1.00 |
| 251 | Brian Urlacher RC | 15.00 | 6.00 |
| 252 | Anthony Becht RC | 4.00 | 1.50 |
| 253 | Bubba Franks RC | 4.00 | 1.50 |
| 254 | Tom Brady RC | 60.00 | 30.00 |
| 255 | Peter Warrick RC | 4.00 | 1.50 |
| 256 | Plaxico Burress RC | 8.00 | 3.00 |
| 257 | Sylvester Morris RC | 2.50 | 1.00 |
| 258 | Dez White RC | 4.00 | 1.50 |
| 259 | Travis Taylor RC | 4.00 | 1.50 |
| 260 | Todd Pinkston RC | 4.00 | 1.50 |
| 261 | Dennis Northcutt RC | 4.00 | 1.50 |
| 262 | Jerry Porter RC | 5.00 | 2.00 |
| 263 | Laveranues Coles RC | 5.00 | 2.00 |
| 264 | Danny Farmer RC | 2.50 | 1.00 |
| 265 | Curtis Keaton RC | 2.50 | 1.00 |
| 266 | Sherrod Gideon RC | 2.00 | .75 |
| 267 | Ron Dugans RC | 2.00 | .75 |
| 268 | Steve McNair CL | .50 | .20 |
| 269 | Jake Plummer CL | .50 | .20 |
| 270 | Antonio Freeman CL | .50 | .20 |

## 2001 Upper Deck

| | | | |
|---|---|------|------|
| | COMPLETE SET (280) | 300.00 | 150.00 |
| | COMP.SET w/o SPs (180) | 25.00 | 10.00 |
| 1 | Jake Plummer | .50 | .20 |
| 2 | David Boston | .75 | .30 |
| 3 | Thomas Jones | .50 | .20 |
| 4 | Frank Sanders | .30 | .10 |
| 5 | Eric Zeier | .30 | .10 |
| 6 | Jamal Anderson | .75 | .30 |
| 7 | Chris Chandler | .50 | .20 |
| 8 | Shawn Jefferson | .30 | .10 |
| 9 | Darrick Vaughn | .50 | .20 |
| 10 | Terance Mathis | .50 | .20 |

| | | | |
|---|---|---|---|
| ❏ 11 Jamal Lewis | 1.25 | .50 | |
| ❏ 12 Shannon Sharpe | .50 | .20 | |
| ❏ 13 Elvis Grbac | .50 | .20 | |
| ❏ 14 Ray Lewis | .75 | .30 | |
| ❏ 15 Qadry Ismail | .50 | .20 | |
| ❏ 16 Chris Redman | .30 | .10 | |
| ❏ 17 Rob Johnson | .75 | .30 | |
| ❏ 18 Eric Moulds | .75 | .30 | |
| ❏ 19 Sammy Morris | .30 | .10 | |
| ❏ 20 Shawn Bryson | .30 | .10 | |
| ❏ 21 Jeremy McDaniel | .30 | .10 | |
| ❏ 22 Muhsin Muhammad | .50 | .20 | |
| ❏ 23 Brad Hoover | .30 | .10 | |
| ❏ 24 Tim Biakabutuka | .50 | .20 | |
| ❏ 25 Steve Beuerlein | .30 | .10 | |
| ❏ 26 Jeff Lewis | .30 | .10 | |
| ❏ 27 Wesley Walls | .30 | .10 | |
| ❏ 28 Cade McNown | .30 | .10 | |
| ❏ 29 James Allen | .50 | .20 | |
| ❏ 30 Marcus Robinson | .75 | .30 | |
| ❏ 31 Brian Urlacher | 1.25 | .50 | |
| ❏ 32 Bobby Engram | .30 | .10 | |
| ❏ 33 Peter Warrick | .75 | .30 | |
| ❏ 34 Corey Dillon | .75 | .30 | |
| ❏ 35 Akili Smith | .30 | .10 | |
| ❏ 36 Danny Farmer | .30 | .10 | |
| ❏ 37 Ron Dugans | .30 | .10 | |
| ❏ 38 Jon Kitna | .75 | .30 | |
| ❏ 39 Tim Couch | .50 | .20 | |
| ❏ 40 Kevin Johnson | .50 | .20 | |
| ❏ 41 Travis Prentice | .30 | .10 | |
| ❏ 42 Spergon Wynn | .30 | .10 | |
| ❏ 43 Errict Rhett | .30 | .10 | |
| ❏ 44 Dennis Northcutt | .50 | .20 | |
| ❏ 45 Courtney Brown | .50 | .20 | |
| ❏ 46 Tony Banks | .30 | .10 | |
| ❏ 47 Emmitt Smith | 1.50 | .60 | |
| ❏ 48 Joey Galloway | .50 | .20 | |
| ❏ 49 Rocket Ismail | .50 | .20 | |
| ❏ 50 Randall Cunningham | .75 | .30 | |
| ❏ 51 James McKnight | .50 | .20 | |
| ❏ 52 Terrell Davis | .75 | .30 | |
| ❏ 53 Mike Anderson | .75 | .30 | |
| ❏ 54 Brian Griese | .75 | .30 | |
| ❏ 55 Rod Smith | .50 | .20 | |
| ❏ 56 Ed McCaffrey | .75 | .30 | |
| ❏ 57 Eddie Kennison | .50 | .20 | |
| ❏ 58 Olandis Gary | .50 | .20 | |
| ❏ 59 Charlie Batch | .75 | .30 | |
| ❏ 60 Germane Crowell | .30 | .10 | |
| ❏ 61 James O. Stewart | .30 | .10 | |
| ❏ 62 Johnnie Morton | .50 | .20 | |
| ❏ 63 Brett Favre | 2.50 | 1.00 | |
| ❏ 64 Antonio Freeman | .75 | .30 | |
| ❏ 65 Dorsey Levens | .50 | .20 | |
| ❏ 66 Ahman Green | .75 | .30 | |
| ❏ 67 Bill Schroeder | .50 | .20 | |
| ❏ 68 Peyton Manning | 2.00 | .75 | |
| ❏ 69 Edgerrin James | 1.00 | .40 | |
| ❏ 70 Marvin Harrison | .75 | .30 | |
| ❏ 71 Jerome Pathon | .50 | .20 | |
| ❏ 72 Ken Dilger | .30 | .10 | |
| ❏ 73 Mark Brunell | .75 | .30 | |
| ❏ 74 Fred Taylor | .75 | .30 | |
| ❏ 75 Jimmy Smith | .75 | .30 | |
| ❏ 76 Keenan McCardell | .30 | .10 | |
| ❏ 77 R.Jay Soward | .30 | .10 | |

| | | | |
|---|---|---|---|
| ❏ 78 Todd Collins | .30 | .10 | |
| ❏ 79 Tony Gonzalez | .50 | .20 | |
| ❏ 80 Derrick Alexander | .50 | .20 | |
| ❏ 81 Tony Richardson | .30 | .10 | |
| ❏ 82 Sylvester Morris | .30 | .10 | |
| ❏ 83 Oronde Gadsden | .50 | .20 | |
| ❏ 84 Lamar Smith | .50 | .20 | |
| ❏ 85 Jay Fiedler | .75 | .30 | |
| ❏ 86 Jason Taylor | .30 | .10 | |
| ❏ 87 Ray Lucas | .30 | .10 | |
| ❏ 88 O.J. McDuffie | .30 | .10 | |
| ❏ 89 Randy Moss | 1.50 | .60 | |
| ❏ 90 Cris Carter | .75 | .30 | |
| ❏ 91 Daunte Culpepper | .75 | .30 | |
| ❏ 92 Moe Williams | .50 | .20 | |
| ❏ 93 Troy Walters | .30 | .10 | |
| ❏ 94 Drew Bledsoe | 1.00 | .40 | |
| ❏ 95 Terry Glenn | .50 | .20 | |
| ❏ 96 Kevin Faulk | .50 | .20 | |
| ❏ 97 J.R. Redmond | .30 | .10 | |
| ❏ 98 Troy Brown | .50 | .20 | |
| ❏ 99 Ricky Williams | .75 | .30 | |
| ❏ 100 Jeff Blake | .50 | .20 | |
| ❏ 101 Joe Horn | .50 | .20 | |
| ❏ 102 Albert Connell | .30 | .10 | |
| ❏ 103 Aaron Brooks | .75 | .30 | |
| ❏ 104 Chad Morton | .30 | .10 | |
| ❏ 105 Kerry Collins | .50 | .20 | |
| ❏ 106 Amani Toomer | .50 | .20 | |
| ❏ 107 Ron Dayne | .75 | .30 | |
| ❏ 108 Tiki Barber | .75 | .30 | |
| ❏ 109 Ike Hilliard | .50 | .20 | |
| ❏ 110 Ron Dixon | .30 | .10 | |
| ❏ 111 Jason Sehorn | .50 | .20 | |
| ❏ 112 Vinny Testaverde | .50 | .20 | |
| ❏ 113 Wayne Chrebet | .50 | .20 | |
| ❏ 114 Curtis Martin | .75 | .30 | |
| ❏ 115 Dedric Ward | .30 | .10 | |
| ❏ 116 Laveranues Coles | .75 | .30 | |
| ❏ 117 Windrell Hayes | .30 | .10 | |
| ❏ 118 Tim Brown | .75 | .30 | |
| ❏ 119 Rich Gannon | .75 | .30 | |
| ❏ 120 Tyrone Wheatley | .50 | .20 | |
| ❏ 121 Charlie Garner | .50 | .20 | |
| ❏ 122 Andre Rison | .50 | .20 | |
| ❏ 123 Charles Woodson | .50 | .20 | |
| ❏ 124 Trace Armstrong | .30 | .10 | |
| ❏ 125 Duce Staley | .75 | .30 | |
| ❏ 126 Donovan McNabb | 1.00 | .40 | |
| ❏ 127 Darnell Autry | .30 | .10 | |
| ❏ 128 Charles Johnson | .30 | .10 | |
| ❏ 129 Torrance Small | .30 | .10 | |
| ❏ 130 Kordell Stewart | .75 | .30 | |
| ❏ 131 Jerome Bettis | .75 | .30 | |
| ❏ 132 Plaxico Burress | .75 | .30 | |
| ❏ 133 Bobby Shaw | .30 | .10 | |
| ❏ 134 Troy Edwards | .50 | .20 | |
| ❏ 135 Marshall Faulk | 1.00 | .40 | |
| ❏ 136 Kurt Warner | 1.50 | .60 | |
| ❏ 137 Isaac Bruce | .75 | .30 | |
| ❏ 138 Torry Holt | .75 | .30 | |
| ❏ 139 Trent Green | .75 | .30 | |
| ❏ 140 Az-Zahir Hakim | .50 | .20 | |
| ❏ 141 Junior Seau | .75 | .30 | |
| ❏ 142 Curtis Conway | .50 | .20 | |
| ❏ 143 Doug Flutie | .75 | .30 | |
| ❏ 144 Jeff Graham | .30 | .10 | |
| ❏ 145 Freddie Jones | .30 | .10 | |
| ❏ 146 Marcellus Wiley | .30 | .10 | |
| ❏ 147 Jeff Garcia | .75 | .30 | |
| ❏ 148 Jerry Rice | 1.50 | .60 | |
| ❏ 149 Fred Beasley | .30 | .10 | |
| ❏ 150 Terrell Owens | .75 | .30 | |
| ❏ 151 J.J. Stokes | .50 | .20 | |
| ❏ 152 Garrison Hearst | .50 | .20 | |
| ❏ 153 Ricky Watters | .30 | .10 | |
| ❏ 154 Shaun Alexander | 1.00 | .40 | |
| ❏ 155 Matt Hasselbeck | .50 | .20 | |
| ❏ 156 Brock Huard | .30 | .10 | |
| ❏ 157 Darrell Jackson | .75 | .30 | |
| ❏ 158 John Randle | .30 | .10 | |
| ❏ 159 Warrick Dunn | .75 | .30 | |
| ❏ 160 Shaun King | .50 | .20 | |
| ❏ 161 Ryan Leaf | .50 | .20 | |

| | | | |
|---|---|---|---|
| ❏ 162 Mike Alstott | .75 | .30 | |
| ❏ 163 Jacquez Green | .30 | .10 | |
| ❏ 164 Brad Johnson | .75 | .30 | |
| ❏ 165 Keyshawn Johnson | .75 | .30 | |
| ❏ 166 Eddie George | .75 | .30 | |
| ❏ 167 Steve McNair | .75 | .30 | |
| ❏ 168 Neil O'Donnell | .30 | .10 | |
| ❏ 169 Derrick Mason | .50 | .20 | |
| ❏ 170 Frank Wycheck | .30 | .10 | |
| ❏ 171 Kevin Dyson | .50 | .20 | |
| ❏ 172 Jevon Kearse | .50 | .20 | |
| ❏ 173 Jeff George | .50 | .20 | |
| ❏ 174 Stephen Davis | .75 | .30 | |
| ❏ 175 Larry Centers | .30 | .10 | |
| ❏ 176 Michael Westbrook | .50 | .20 | |
| ❏ 177 Stephen Alexander | .50 | .20 | |
| ❏ 178 Ron Dayne | .75 | .30 | |
| ❏ 179 Donovan McNabb | 1.00 | .40 | |
| ❏ 180 Jimmy Smith | .50 | .20 | |
| ❏ 181 Adam Archuleta RC | 5.00 | 2.00 | |
| ❏ 182 A.J. Feeley RC | 5.00 | 2.00 | |
| ❏ 183 Alex Bannister RC | 3.00 | 1.25 | |
| ❏ 184 Alge Crumpler RC | 6.00 | 2.50 | |
| ❏ 185 Andre Carter RC | 5.00 | 2.00 | |
| ❏ 186 Andre Dyson RC | 2.00 | .75 | |
| ❏ 187 Anthony Thomas RC | 5.00 | 2.00 | |
| ❏ 188 Arther Love RC | 2.00 | .75 | |
| ❏ 189 Bobby Newcombe RC | 3.00 | 1.25 | |
| ❏ 190 Brandon Spoon RC | 5.00 | 2.00 | |
| ❏ 191 Carlos Polk RC | 2.00 | .75 | |
| ❏ 192 Casey Hampton RC | 5.00 | 2.00 | |
| ❏ 193 Cedrick Wilson RC | 5.00 | 2.00 | |
| ❏ 194 Chad Johnson RC | 12.00 | 5.00 | |
| ❏ 195 Chris Chambers RC | 8.00 | 3.00 | |
| ❏ 196 Chris Taylor RC | 3.00 | 1.25 | |
| ❏ 197 Chris Weinke RC | 5.00 | 2.00 | |
| ❏ 198 Correll Buckhalter RC | 6.00 | 2.50 | |
| ❏ 199 Damione Lewis RC | 3.00 | 1.25 | |
| ❏ 200 Dan Alexander RC | 5.00 | 2.00 | |
| ❏ 201 Dan Morgan RC | 5.00 | 2.00 | |
| ❏ 202 Willie Middlebrooks RC | 3.00 | 1.25 | |
| ❏ 203 David Terrell RC | 5.00 | 2.00 | |
| ❏ 204 Derrick Gibson RC | 3.00 | 1.25 | |
| ❏ 205 Deuce McAllister RC | 10.00 | 4.00 | |
| ❏ 206 Drew Brees RC | 20.00 | 10.00 | |
| ❏ 207 Edgerton Hartwell RC | 2.00 | .75 | |
| ❏ 208 Fred Smoot RC | 5.00 | 2.00 | |
| ❏ 209 Freddie Mitchell RC | 5.00 | 2.00 | |
| ❏ 210 Gary Baxter RC | 3.00 | 1.25 | |
| ❏ 211 Gerard Warren RC | 5.00 | 2.00 | |
| ❏ 212 Hakim Akbar RC | 2.00 | .75 | |
| ❏ 213 Heath Evans RC | 3.00 | 1.25 | |
| ❏ 214 Jabari Holloway RC | 3.00 | 1.25 | |
| ❏ 215 Jamal Reynolds RC | 5.00 | 2.00 | |
| ❏ 216 Jamar Fletcher RC | 3.00 | 1.25 | |
| ❏ 217 James Jackson RC | 5.00 | 2.00 | |
| ❏ 218 Jamie Winborn RC | 3.00 | 1.25 | |
| ❏ 219 Jesse Palmer RC | 5.00 | 2.00 | |
| ❏ 220 Josh Booty RC | 5.00 | 2.00 | |
| ❏ 221 Josh Heupel RC | 5.00 | 2.00 | |
| ❏ 222 Justin Smith RC | 5.00 | 2.00 | |
| ❏ 223 Karon Riley RC | 2.00 | .75 | |
| ❏ 224 Ken Lucas RC | 3.00 | 1.25 | |
| ❏ 225 Kenyatta Walker RC | 2.00 | .75 | |
| ❏ 226 Ken-Yon Rambo RC | 3.00 | 1.25 | |
| ❏ 227 Kevan Barlow RC | 5.00 | 2.00 | |
| ❏ 228 Kevin Kasper RC | 5.00 | 2.00 | |
| ❏ 229 Koren Robinson RC | 5.00 | 2.00 | |
| ❏ 230 LaDainian Tomlinson RC | 60.00 | 30.00 | |
| ❏ 231 LaMont Jordan RC | 10.00 | 4.00 | |
| ❏ 232 Leonard Davis RC | 3.00 | 1.25 | |
| ❏ 233 Marcus Stroud RC | 5.00 | 2.00 | |
| ❏ 234 Marques Tuiasosopo RC | 5.00 | 2.00 | |
| ❏ 235 Snoop Minnis RC | 3.00 | 1.25 | |
| ❏ 236 Michael Bennett RC | 5.00 | 2.00 | |
| ❏ 237 Michael Stone RC | 2.00 | .75 | |
| ❏ 238 Mike McMahon RC | 5.00 | 2.00 | |
| ❏ 239 Michael Vick RC | 12.00 | 5.00 | |
| ❏ 240 Moran Norris RC | 2.00 | .75 | |
| ❏ 241 Morlon Greenwood RC | 3.00 | 1.25 | |
| ❏ 242 Nate Clements RC | 5.00 | 2.00 | |
| ❏ 243 Orlando Huff RC | 2.00 | .75 | |
| ❏ 244 Quincy Morgan RC | 5.00 | 2.00 | |
| ❏ 245 Reggie Wayne RC | 10.00 | 4.00 | |

|  |  | | |
|---|------|------|------|
| 246 | Richard Seymour RC | 5.00 | 2.00 |
| 247 | Robert Ferguson RC | 5.00 | 2.00 |
| 248 | Rod Gardner RC | 5.00 | 2.00 |
| 249 | Rudi Johnson RC | 10.00 | 4.00 |
| 250 | Sage Rosenfels RC | 5.00 | 2.00 |
| 251 | Santana Moss RC | 8.00 | 3.00 |
| 252 | Scotty Anderson RC | 3.00 | 1.00 |
| 253 | Sedrick Hodge RC | 2.00 | .75 |
| 254 | Shaun Rogers RC | 5.00 | 2.00 |
| 255 | Steve Hutchinson RC | 3.00 | 1.25 |
| 256 | T.J. Houshmandzadeh RC | 6.00 | 2.50 |
| 257 | Tay Cody RC | 2.00 | .75 |
| 258 | George Layne RC | 3.00 | 1.25 |
| 259 | Todd Heap RC | 5.00 | 2.00 |
| 260 | Tommy Polley RC | 5.00 | 2.00 |
| 261 | Tony Dixon RC | 3.00 | 1.25 |
| 262 | Brian Allen RC | 2.00 | .75 |
| 263 | Torrance Marshall RC | 5.00 | 2.00 |
| 264 | Travis Henry RC | 5.00 | 2.00 |
| 265 | Travis Minor RC | 3.00 | 1.25 |
| 266 | Vinny Sutherland RC | 3.00 | 1.25 |
| 267 | Will Allen RC | 3.00 | 1.25 |
| 268 | Derrick Blaylock RC | 5.00 | 2.00 |
| 269 | Zeke Moreno RC | 5.00 | 2.00 |
| 270 | Chris Barnes RC | 3.00 | 1.25 |
| 271 | Dee Brown RC | 5.00 | 2.00 |
| 272 | Reggie White RC | 3.00 | 1.25 |
| 273 | Derek Combs RC | 3.00 | 1.25 |
| 274 | Steve Smith RC | 12.00 | 6.00 |
| 275 | John Capel RC | 3.00 | 1.25 |
| 276 | Justin McCareins RC | 5.00 | 2.00 |
| 277 | Darnerien McCants RC | 3.00 | 1.25 |
| 278 | Eddie Berlin RC | 3.00 | 1.25 |
| 279 | Francis St. Paul RC | 3.00 | 1.25 |
| 280 | Quincy Carter RC | 5.00 | 2.00 |

## 2002 Upper Deck

|  |  | | |
|---|------|------|------|
|  | COMP.SET w/o SP's (180) | 25.00 | 10.00 |
| 1 | Jake Plummer | .50 | .20 |
| 2 | Marcel Shipp | .75 | .30 |
| 3 | David Boston | .75 | .30 |
| 4 | Arnold Jackson | .30 | .10 |
| 5 | Frank Sanders | .30 | .10 |
| 6 | Freddie Jones | .30 | .10 |
| 7 | Michael Vick | 1.50 | .60 |
| 8 | Jamal Anderson | .50 | .20 |
| 9 | Warrick Dunn | .75 | .30 |
| 10 | Maurice Smith | .30 | .10 |
| 11 | Shawn Jefferson | .30 | .10 |
| 12 | Chris Redman | .30 | .10 |
| 13 | Jeff Blake | .30 | .10 |
| 14 | Jamal Lewis | .75 | .30 |
| 15 | Travis Taylor | .50 | .20 |
| 16 | Ray Lewis | .75 | .30 |
| 17 | Chris McAlister | .30 | .10 |
| 18 | Drew Bledsoe | 1.00 | .40 |
| 19 | Travis Henry | .75 | .30 |
| 20 | Larry Centers | .30 | .10 |
| 21 | Eric Moulds | .50 | .20 |
| 22 | Reggie Germany | .30 | .10 |
| 23 | Peerless Price | .50 | .20 |
| 24 | Chris Weinke | .50 | .20 |
| 25 | Lamar Smith | .50 | .20 |
| 26 | Nick Goings | .30 | .10 |
| 27 | Muhsin Muhammad | .50 | .20 |
| 28 | Isaac Byrd | .30 | .10 |
| 29 | Wesley Walls | .30 | .10 |
| 30 | Jim Miller | .30 | .10 |
| 31 | Anthony Thomas | .50 | .20 |
| 32 | Dez White | .30 | .10 |
| 33 | David Terrell | .75 | .30 |
| 34 | Marty Booker | .50 | .20 |
| 35 | Brian Urlacher | 1.25 | .50 |
| 36 | Jon Kitna | .50 | .20 |
| 37 | Corey Dillon | .50 | .20 |
| 38 | Peter Warrick | .50 | .20 |
| 39 | Darnay Scott | .30 | .10 |
| 40 | Chad Johnson | .75 | .30 |
| 41 | Tim Couch | .50 | .20 |
| 42 | James Jackson | .30 | .10 |
| 43 | JaJuan Dawson | .30 | .10 |
| 44 | Kevin Johnson | .50 | .20 |
| 45 | Quincy Morgan | .30 | .10 |
| 46 | Courtney Brown | .50 | .20 |
| 47 | Quincy Carter | .50 | .20 |
| 48 | Emmitt Smith | 2.00 | .75 |
| 49 | Joey Galloway | .50 | .20 |
| 50 | Rocket Ismail | .50 | .20 |
| 51 | Ken-Yon Rambo | .30 | .10 |
| 52 | Brian Griese | .75 | .30 |
| 53 | Terrell Davis | .75 | .30 |
| 54 | Mike Anderson | .75 | .30 |
| 55 | Shannon Sharpe | .50 | .20 |
| 56 | Ed McCaffrey | .75 | .30 |
| 57 | Rod Smith | .50 | .20 |
| 58 | Mike McMahon | .75 | .30 |
| 59 | James Stewart | .50 | .20 |
| 60 | Az-Zahir Hakim | .30 | .10 |
| 61 | Desmond Howard | .30 | .10 |
| 62 | Germane Crowell | .30 | .10 |
| 63 | Brett Favre | 2.00 | .75 |
| 64 | Ahman Green | .75 | .30 |
| 65 | Antonio Freeman | .75 | .30 |
| 66 | Terry Glenn | .50 | .20 |
| 67 | Kabeer Gbaja-Biamila | .50 | .20 |
| 68 | Kent Graham | .30 | .10 |
| 69 | James Allen | .50 | .20 |
| 70 | Corey Bradford | .30 | .10 |
| 71 | Jermaine Lewis | .30 | .10 |
| 72 | Jamie Sharper | .30 | .10 |
| 73 | Peyton Manning | 1.50 | .60 |
| 74 | Edgerrin James | 1.00 | .40 |
| 75 | Dominic Rhodes | .50 | .20 |
| 76 | Marvin Harrison | .75 | .30 |
| 77 | Qadry Ismail | .50 | .20 |
| 78 | Mark Brunell | .75 | .30 |
| 79 | Fred Taylor | .75 | .30 |
| 80 | Stacey Mack | .30 | .10 |
| 81 | Jimmy Smith | .50 | .20 |
| 82 | Keenan McCardell | .30 | .10 |
| 83 | Trent Green | .50 | .20 |
| 84 | Priest Holmes | 1.00 | .40 |
| 85 | Derrick Alexander | .50 | .20 |
| 86 | Johnnie Morton | .50 | .20 |
| 87 | Snoop Minnis | .30 | .10 |
| 88 | Tony Gonzalez | .50 | .20 |
| 89 | Jay Fiedler | .50 | .20 |
| 90 | Ricky Williams | 2.50 | 1.00 |
| 91 | Chris Chambers | .75 | .30 |
| 92 | Oronde Gadsden | .30 | .10 |
| 93 | Zach Thomas | .75 | .30 |
| 94 | Daunte Culpepper | .75 | .30 |
| 95 | Michael Bennett | .50 | .20 |
| 96 | Randy Moss | 1.50 | .60 |
| 97 | Sean Dawkins | .30 | .10 |
| 98 | Tom Brady | 2.00 | .75 |
| 99 | Antowain Smith | .50 | .20 |
| 100 | David Patten | .30 | .10 |
| 101 | Troy Brown | .50 | .20 |
| 102 | Adam Vinatieri | .75 | .30 |
| 103 | Aaron Brooks | .75 | .30 |
| 104 | Deuce McAllister | 1.00 | .40 |
| 105 | Jake Reed | .50 | .20 |
| 106 | Jerome Pathon | .30 | .10 |
| 107 | Joe Horn | .50 | .20 |
| 108 | Kyle Turley | .30 | .10 |
| 109 | Kerry Collins | .50 | .20 |
| 110 | Ron Dayne | .50 | .20 |
| 111 | Tiki Barber | .75 | .30 |
| 112 | Amani Toomer | .50 | .20 |
| 113 | Ike Hilliard | .50 | .20 |
| 114 | Michael Strahan | .50 | .20 |
| 115 | Vinny Testaverde | .50 | .20 |
| 116 | Chad Pennington | 1.00 | .40 |
| 117 | Curtis Martin | .75 | .30 |
| 118 | Santana Moss | .75 | .30 |
| 119 | Laveranues Coles | .50 | .20 |
| 120 | Wayne Chrebet | .50 | .20 |
| 121 | Rich Gannon | .75 | .30 |
| 122 | Charlie Garner | .50 | .20 |
| 123 | Jerry Rice | 1.50 | .60 |
| 124 | Tim Brown | .75 | .30 |
| 125 | Charles Woodson | .50 | .20 |
| 126 | Donovan McNabb | 1.00 | .40 |
| 127 | Duce Staley | .75 | .30 |
| 128 | Correll Buckhalter | .50 | .20 |
| 129 | Freddie Mitchell | .50 | .20 |
| 130 | James Thrash | .50 | .20 |
| 131 | Todd Pinkston | .50 | .20 |
| 132 | Kordell Stewart | .50 | .20 |
| 133 | Jerome Bettis | .75 | .30 |
| 134 | Chris Fuamatu-Ma'afala | .30 | .10 |
| 135 | Hines Ward | .75 | .30 |
| 136 | Plaxico Burress | .50 | .20 |
| 137 | Kendrell Bell | .75 | .30 |
| 138 | Doug Flutie | .75 | .30 |
| 139 | Drew Brees | .75 | .30 |
| 140 | LaDainian Tomlinson | 1.25 | .50 |
| 141 | Curtis Conway | .30 | .10 |
| 142 | Tim Dwight | .50 | .20 |
| 143 | Junior Seau | .50 | .20 |
| 144 | Jeff Garcia | .75 | .30 |
| 145 | Garrison Hearst | .50 | .20 |
| 146 | Kevan Barlow | .50 | .20 |
| 147 | Terrell Owens | .75 | .30 |
| 148 | J.J. Stokes | .50 | .20 |
| 149 | Trent Dilfer | .50 | .20 |
| 150 | Shaun Alexander | 1.00 | .40 |
| 151 | Ricky Watters | .50 | .20 |
| 152 | Bobby Engram | .30 | .10 |
| 153 | Koren Robinson | .50 | .20 |
| 154 | Kurt Warner | .75 | .30 |
| 155 | Marshall Faulk | .75 | .30 |
| 156 | Isaac Bruce | .75 | .30 |
| 157 | Ricky Proehl | .30 | .10 |
| 158 | Terrence Wilkins | .30 | .10 |
| 159 | Torry Holt | .75 | .30 |
| 160 | Brad Johnson | .50 | .20 |
| 161 | Shaun King | .30 | .10 |
| 162 | Rob Johnson | .50 | .20 |
| 163 | Mike Alstott | .75 | .30 |
| 164 | Michael Pittman | .30 | .10 |
| 165 | Keyshawn Johnson | .75 | .30 |
| 166 | Steve McNair | .75 | .30 |
| 167 | Eddie George | .75 | .30 |
| 168 | Derrick Mason | .50 | .20 |
| 169 | Kevin Dyson | .50 | .20 |
| 170 | Frank Wycheck | .30 | .10 |
| 171 | Jevon Kearse | .50 | .20 |
| 172 | Danny Wuerffel | .50 | .20 |
| 173 | Stephen Davis | .50 | .20 |
| 174 | Michael Westbrook | .30 | .10 |
| 175 | Rod Gardner | .50 | .20 |
| 176 | Champ Bailey | .50 | .20 |
| 177 | Darrell Green | .30 | .10 |
| 178 | Kurt Warner CL | .50 | .20 |
| 179 | Brett Favre CL | 1.00 | .40 |
| 180 | Randy Moss CL | .75 | .30 |
| 181 | David Boston SS | 4.00 | 1.50 |
| 182 | Jake Plummer SS | 2.50 | 1.00 |
| 183 | Michael Vick SS | 8.00 | 3.00 |
| 184 | Drew Bledsoe SS | 5.00 | 2.00 |
| 185 | Anthony Thomas SS | 2.50 | 1.00 |
| 186 | Tim Couch SS | 2.50 | 1.00 |
| 187 | Emmitt Smith SS | 10.00 | 4.00 |
| 188 | Ahman Green SS | 4.00 | 1.50 |
| 189 | Brett Favre SS | 10.00 | 4.00 |
| 190 | Edgerrin James SS | 5.00 | 2.00 |
| 191 | Peyton Manning SS | 8.00 | 3.00 |
| 192 | Mark Brunell SS | 4.00 | 1.50 |
| 193 | Daunte Culpepper SS | 8.00 | 3.00 |
| 194 | Randy Moss SS | 8.00 | 3.00 |
| 195 | Tom Brady SS | 10.00 | 4.00 |
| 196 | Aaron Brooks SS | 4.00 | 1.50 |
| 197 | Ricky Williams SS | 4.00 | 1.50 |

| | | |
|---|---|---|
| ☐ 198 Curtis Martin SS | 4.00 | 1.50 |
| ☐ 199 Jerry Rice SS | 8.00 | 3.00 |
| ☐ 200 Donovan McNabb SS | 5.00 | 2.00 |
| ☐ 201 Jerome Bettis SS | 4.00 | 1.50 |
| ☐ 202 Kordell Stewart SS | 2.50 | 1.00 |
| ☐ 203 LaDainian Tomlinson SS | 6.00 | 2.50 |
| ☐ 204 Jeff Garcia SS | 4.00 | 1.50 |
| ☐ 205 Terrell Owens SS | 4.00 | 1.50 |
| ☐ 206 Shaun Alexander SS | 5.00 | 2.00 |
| ☐ 207 Kurt Warner SS | 4.00 | 1.50 |
| ☐ 208 Marshall Faulk SS | 4.00 | 1.50 |
| ☐ 209 Keyshawn Johnson SS | 4.00 | 1.50 |
| ☐ 210 Steve McNair SS | 4.00 | 1.50 |
| ☐ 211 Damien Anderson RC | 5.00 | 2.00 |
| ☐ 212 Jason McAddley RC | 5.00 | 2.00 |
| ☐ 213 Josh McCown RC | 8.00 | 3.00 |
| ☐ 214 Josh Scobey RC | 4.00 | 1.50 |
| ☐ 215 Preston Parsons RC | 3.00 | 1.25 |
| ☐ 216 Dusty Bonner RC | 3.00 | 1.25 |
| ☐ 217 Kahlil Hill RC | 5.00 | 2.00 |
| ☐ 218 Kurt Kittner RC | 5.00 | 2.00 |
| ☐ 219 T.J. Duckett RC | 6.00 | 2.50 |
| ☐ 220 Chester Taylor RC | 6.00 | 2.50 |
| ☐ 221 Kalimba Edwards RC | 6.00 | 2.50 |
| ☐ 223 Ron Johnson RC | 5.00 | 2.00 |
| ☐ 224 Tellis Redmon RC | 5.00 | 2.00 |
| ☐ 225 Wes Pate RC | 3.00 | 1.25 |
| ☐ 226 David Priestley RC | 5.00 | 2.00 |
| ☐ 227 Josh Reed RC | 6.00 | 2.50 |
| ☐ 228 Mike Williams RC | 5.00 | 2.00 |
| ☐ 229 Ryan Denney RC | 5.00 | 2.00 |
| ☐ 230 DeShaun Foster RC | 6.00 | 2.50 |
| ☐ 231 Julius Peppers RC | 12.00 | 5.00 |
| ☐ 232 Randy Fasani RC | 5.00 | 2.00 |
| ☐ 233 Adrian Peterson RC | 8.00 | 3.00 |
| ☐ 234 Alex Brown RC | 6.00 | 2.50 |
| ☐ 235 Gavin Hoffman RC | 3.00 | 1.25 |
| ☐ 236 Levi Jones RC | 5.00 | 2.00 |
| ☐ 237 Andre Davis RC | 5.00 | 2.00 |
| ☐ 238 Andre Davis RC | 5.00 | 2.00 |
| ☐ 239 William Green RC | 6.00 | 2.50 |
| ☐ 240 Antonio Bryant RC | 6.00 | 2.50 |
| ☐ 241 Chad Hutchinson RC | 6.00 | 2.50 |
| ☐ 242 Roy Williams RC | 12.00 | 5.00 |
| ☐ 243 Woody Dantzler RC | 5.00 | 2.00 |
| ☐ 244 Ashley Lelie RC | 12.00 | 5.00 |
| ☐ 245 Clinton Portis RC | 20.00 | 7.50 |
| ☐ 246 Lamont Thompson RC | 5.00 | 2.00 |
| ☐ 247 James Mungro RC | 6.00 | 2.50 |
| ☐ 248 Joey Harrington RC | 8.00 | 3.00 |
| ☐ 249 Luke Staley RC | 5.00 | 2.00 |
| ☐ 250 Craig Nall RC | 6.00 | 2.50 |
| ☐ 251 Javon Walker RC | 10.00 | 4.00 |
| ☐ 252 Najeh Davenport RC | 6.00 | 2.50 |
| ☐ 253 David Carr RC | 8.00 | 3.00 |
| ☐ 254 Saleem Rasheed RC | 6.00 | 2.50 |
| ☐ 255 Mike Rumph RC | 6.00 | 2.50 |
| ☐ 256 Jabar Gaffney RC | 6.00 | 2.50 |
| ☐ 257 Jonathan Wells RC | 6.00 | 2.50 |
| ☐ 258 Dwight Freeney RC | 10.00 | 4.00 |
| ☐ 259 Larry Tripplett RC | 3.00 | 1.25 |
| ☐ 260 David Garrard RC | 12.00 | 5.00 |
| ☐ 261 John Henderson RC | 6.00 | 2.50 |
| ☐ 262 Ryan Sims RC | 6.00 | 2.50 |
| ☐ 263 Leonard Henry RC | 5.00 | 2.00 |
| ☐ 264 Brian Allen RC | 5.00 | 2.00 |
| ☐ 265 Atrews Bell RC | 3.00 | 1.25 |
| ☐ 266 Bryant McKinnie RC | 5.00 | 2.00 |
| ☐ 267 Kelly Campbell RC | 5.00 | 2.00 |
| ☐ 268 Raonall Smith RC | 5.00 | 2.00 |
| ☐ 269 Antwoine Womack RC | 5.00 | 2.00 |
| ☐ 270 Daniel Graham RC | 6.00 | 2.50 |
| ☐ 271 Deion Branch RC | 10.00 | 4.00 |
| ☐ 272 Sam Simmons RC | 3.00 | 1.25 |
| ☐ 273 Rohan Davey RC | 6.00 | 2.50 |
| ☐ 274 Charles Grant RC | 6.00 | 2.50 |
| ☐ 275 Derrick Lewis RC | 3.00 | 1.25 |
| ☐ 276 Donte Stallworth RC | 10.00 | 4.00 |
| ☐ 277 J.T. O'Sullivan RC | 8.00 | 3.00 |
| ☐ 278 Keyuo Craver RC | 5.00 | 2.00 |
| ☐ 279 Ricky Williams RC | 5.00 | 2.00 |
| ☐ 280 Bryan Thomas RC | 5.00 | 2.00 |
| ☐ 281 Jeremy Shockey RC | 10.00 | 4.00 |
| ☐ 282 Tim Carter RC | 5.00 | 2.00 |
| ☐ 283 Larry Ned RC | 2.50 | 1.00 |
| ☐ 284 Ronald Harris RC | 4.00 | 1.50 |
| ☐ 285 Phillip Buchanon RC | 6.00 | 2.50 |
| ☐ 286 Ronald Curry RC | 6.00 | 2.50 |
| ☐ 287 Brian Westbrook RC | 15.00 | 6.00 |
| ☐ 288 Freddie Milons RC | 5.00 | 2.00 |
| ☐ 289 Lito Sheppard RC | 6.00 | 2.50 |
| ☐ 290 Antwaan Randle El RC | 8.00 | 3.00 |
| ☐ 291 Lee Mays RC | 2.50 | 1.00 |
| ☐ 292 Daryl Jones RC | 5.00 | 2.00 |
| ☐ 293 Justin Peelle RC | 3.00 | 1.25 |
| ☐ 294 Quentin Jammer RC | 4.00 | 1.50 |
| ☐ 295 Reche Caldwell RC | 6.00 | 2.50 |
| ☐ 296 Seth Burford RC | 5.00 | 2.00 |
| ☐ 297 Terry Charles RC | 5.00 | 2.00 |
| ☐ 298 Brandon Doman RC | 5.00 | 2.00 |
| ☐ 299 Maurice Morris RC | 6.00 | 2.50 |
| ☐ 300 Eric Crouch RC | 6.00 | 2.50 |
| ☐ 301 Lamar Gordon RC | 6.00 | 2.50 |
| ☐ 302 Marquise Walker RC | 5.00 | 2.00 |
| ☐ 303 Tracey Wistrom RC | 5.00 | 2.00 |
| ☐ 304 Travis Stephens RC | 5.00 | 2.00 |
| ☐ 305 Herb Haygood RC | 3.00 | 1.25 |
| ☐ 306 Albert Haynesworth RC | 6.00 | 2.50 |
| ☐ 307 Rocky Calmus RC | 6.00 | 2.50 |
| ☐ 308 Cliff Russell RC | 5.00 | 2.00 |
| ☐ 309 Ladell Betts RC | 6.00 | 2.50 |
| ☐ 310A Patrick Ramsey RC | 6.00 | 2.50 |
| ☐ 310B Ed Reed RC | 15.00 | 6.00 |

## 2003 Upper Deck

| | | |
|---|---|---|
| ☐ COMP.SET w/o SP's (180) | 25.00 | 10.00 |
| ☐ 1 Brad Johnson | .60 | .25 |
| ☐ 2 Derrick Brooks | .50 | .25 |
| ☐ 3 Simeon Rice | .60 | .25 |
| ☐ 4 Warren Sapp | .60 | .25 |
| ☐ 5 Thomas Jones | .60 | .25 |
| ☐ 6 Mike Alstott | .75 | .30 |
| ☐ 7 Michael Pittman | .50 | .20 |
| ☐ 8 Tim Brown | .75 | .30 |
| ☐ 9 Rich Gannon | .60 | .25 |
| ☐ 10 Charlie Garner | .60 | .25 |
| ☐ 11 Jerry Porter | .60 | .25 |
| ☐ 12 Phillip Buchanon | .50 | .20 |
| ☐ 13 Charles Woodson | .60 | .25 |
| ☐ 14 James Thrash | .50 | .20 |
| ☐ 15 Duce Staley | .60 | .25 |
| ☐ 16 Brian Westbrook | .75 | .30 |
| ☐ 17 Correll Buckhalter | .60 | .25 |
| ☐ 18 Koy Detmer | .50 | .20 |
| ☐ 19 Brian Dawkins | .60 | .25 |
| ☐ 20 Jon Ritchie | .50 | .20 |
| ☐ 21 Ahman Green | .75 | .30 |
| ☐ 22 Donald Driver | .75 | .30 |
| ☐ 23 Bubba Franks | .60 | .25 |
| ☐ 24 Javon Walker | .60 | .25 |
| ☐ 25 Kabeer Gbaja-Biamila | .60 | .25 |
| ☐ 26 Robert Ferguson | .50 | .20 |
| ☐ 27 Eddie George | .60 | .25 |
| ☐ 28 Jevon Kearse | .60 | .25 |
| ☐ 29 Billy Volek | .60 | .25 |
| ☐ 30 Frank Wycheck | .50 | .20 |
| ☐ 31 Derrick Mason | .60 | .25 |
| ☐ 32 Tommy Maddox | .60 | .25 |
| ☐ 33 Jerome Bettis | .75 | .30 |
| ☐ 34 Antwan Randle El | .60 | .25 |
| ☐ 35 Amos Zereoue | .50 | .20 |
| ☐ 36 Hines Ward | .75 | .30 |
| ☐ 37 Jeff Garcia | .75 | .30 |
| ☐ 38 Terrell Owens | .75 | .30 |
| ☐ 39 Tim Rattay | .50 | .20 |
| ☐ 40 Brandon Doman | .50 | .20 |
| ☐ 41 Tai Streets | .50 | .20 |
| ☐ 42 Garrison Hearst | .60 | .25 |
| ☐ 43 Kerry Collins | .60 | .25 |
| ☐ 44 Tiki Barber | .75 | .30 |
| ☐ 45 Amani Toomer | .60 | .25 |
| ☐ 46 Jesse Palmer | .50 | .20 |
| ☐ 47 Tim Carter | .50 | .20 |
| ☐ 48 Michael Strahan | .60 | .25 |
| ☐ 49 Ike Hilliard | .60 | .25 |
| ☐ 50 Marvin Harrison | .75 | .30 |
| ☐ 51 Peyton Manning | 1.50 | .60 |
| ☐ 52 Marcus Pollard | .50 | .20 |
| ☐ 53 James Mungro | .50 | .20 |
| ☐ 54 Reggie Wayne | .60 | .25 |
| ☐ 55 Peerless Price | .60 | .25 |
| ☐ 56 Warrick Dunn | .60 | .25 |
| ☐ 57 T.J. Duckett | .60 | .25 |
| ☐ 58 Keith Brooking | .60 | .25 |
| ☐ 59 Doug Johnson | .50 | .20 |
| ☐ 60 Brian Finneran | .50 | .20 |
| ☐ 61 Chad Pennington | .75 | .30 |
| ☐ 62 Curtis Martin | .75 | .30 |
| ☐ 63 Marvin Jones | .50 | .20 |
| ☐ 64 Wayne Chrebet | .60 | .25 |
| ☐ 65 LaMont Jordan | .60 | .25 |
| ☐ 66 Curtis Conway | .50 | .20 |
| ☐ 67 Vinny Testaverde | .50 | .20 |
| ☐ 68 Tim Couch | .50 | .20 |
| ☐ 69 William Green | .50 | .20 |
| ☐ 70 Andre Davis | .50 | .20 |
| ☐ 71 Quincy Morgan | .50 | .20 |
| ☐ 72 Dennis Northcutt | .50 | .20 |
| ☐ 73 Kelly Holcomb | .60 | .25 |
| ☐ 74 Jake Plummer | .60 | .25 |
| ☐ 75 Mike Anderson | .50 | .20 |
| ☐ 76 Ashley Lelie | .50 | .20 |
| ☐ 77 Ed McCaffrey | .60 | .25 |
| ☐ 78 Shannon Sharpe | .60 | .25 |
| ☐ 79 Rod Smith | .60 | .25 |
| ☐ 80 Terrell Davis | .75 | .30 |
| ☐ 81 Antowain Smith | .60 | .25 |
| ☐ 82 Kevin Faulk | .60 | .25 |
| ☐ 83 David Patten | .60 | .25 |
| ☐ 84 Deion Branch | .60 | .25 |
| ☐ 85 Troy Brown | .60 | .25 |
| ☐ 86 Rohan Davey | .50 | .20 |
| ☐ 87 Jay Fiedler | .50 | .20 |
| ☐ 88 Randy McMichael | .50 | .20 |
| ☐ 89 Derrius Thompson | .50 | .20 |
| ☐ 90 Jason Taylor | .60 | .25 |
| ☐ 91 Zach Thomas | .75 | .30 |
| ☐ 92 Ricky Williams | .75 | .30 |
| ☐ 93 Deuce McAllister | .75 | .30 |
| ☐ 94 Donte Stallworth | .60 | .25 |
| ☐ 95 Jerome Pathon | .50 | .20 |
| ☐ 96 Michael Lewis | .50 | .20 |
| ☐ 97 Joe Horn | .60 | .25 |
| ☐ 98 Priest Holmes | .75 | .30 |
| ☐ 99 Johnnie Morton | .50 | .20 |
| ☐ 100 Eddie Kennison | .50 | .20 |
| ☐ 101 Dante Hall | .60 | .25 |
| ☐ 102 Tony Gonzalez | .60 | .25 |
| ☐ 103 Marc Boerigter | .50 | .20 |
| ☐ 104 Drew Brees | .75 | .30 |
| ☐ 105 David Boston | .60 | .25 |
| ☐ 106 Reche Caldwell | .50 | .20 |
| ☐ 107 Tim Dwight | .60 | .25 |
| ☐ 108 Doug Flutie | .75 | .30 |
| ☐ 109 Drew Bledsoe | .75 | .30 |
| ☐ 110 Eric Moulds | .60 | .25 |
| ☐ 111 Alex Van Pelt | .50 | .20 |
| ☐ 112 Charles Johnson | .50 | .20 |
| ☐ 113 Takeo Spikes | .60 | .25 |
| ☐ 114 Josh Reed | .60 | .25 |
| ☐ 115 Ladell Betts | .60 | .25 |
| ☐ 116 Laveranues Coles | .60 | .25 |
| ☐ 117 Champ Bailey | .60 | .25 |
| ☐ 118 Trung Canidate | .50 | .20 |
| ☐ 119 Kenny Watson | .50 | .20 |

| | | | |
|---|---|---|---|
| ❑ 120 Rod Gardner | | .50 | .20 |
| ❑ 121 Kurt Warner | | .75 | .30 |
| ❑ 122 Lamar Gordon | | .50 | .20 |
| ❑ 123 Shaun McDonald RC | | 1.00 | .40 |
| ❑ 124 Marc Bulger | | .75 | .30 |
| ❑ 125 Isaac Bruce | | .75 | .30 |
| ❑ 126 Torry Holt | | .75 | .30 |
| ❑ 127 Matt Hasselbeck | | .60 | .25 |
| ❑ 128 Maurice Morris | | .50 | .20 |
| ❑ 129 Bobby Engram | | .50 | .20 |
| ❑ 130 Darrell Jackson | | .60 | .25 |
| ❑ 131 Koren Robinson | | .60 | .25 |
| ❑ 132 Chris Redman | | .50 | .20 |
| ❑ 133 Todd Heap | | .60 | .25 |
| ❑ 134 Travis Taylor | | .50 | .20 |
| ❑ 135 Ron Johnson | | .50 | .20 |
| ❑ 136 Ray Lewis | | .75 | .30 |
| ❑ 137 Jake Delhomme | | .75 | .30 |
| ❑ 138 Muhsin Muhammad | | .60 | .25 |
| ❑ 139 Stephen Davis | | .60 | .25 |
| ❑ 140 Julius Peppers | | .75 | .30 |
| ❑ 141 Rodney Peete | | .50 | .20 |
| ❑ 142 Mark Brunell | | .60 | .25 |
| ❑ 143 Jimmy Smith | | .60 | .25 |
| ❑ 144 Kyle Brady | | .50 | .20 |
| ❑ 145 Kevin Lockett | | .50 | .20 |
| ❑ 146 David Garrard | | .75 | .30 |
| ❑ 147 Fred Taylor | | .75 | .30 |
| ❑ 148 Michael Bennett | | .60 | .25 |
| ❑ 149 Ronald Bellamy RC | | .75 | .30 |
| ❑ 150 Randy Moss | | 1.00 | .40 |
| ❑ 151 D'Wayne Bates | | .50 | .20 |
| ❑ 152 Josh McCown | | .50 | .20 |
| ❑ 153 Marquise Walker | | .50 | .20 |
| ❑ 154 Jeff Blake | | .50 | .20 |
| ❑ 155 Freddie Jones | | .50 | .20 |
| ❑ 156 Marcel Shipp | | .50 | .20 |
| ❑ 157 Troy Hambrick | | .50 | .20 |
| ❑ 158 Joey Galloway | | .60 | .25 |
| ❑ 159 Terry Glenn | | .60 | .25 |
| ❑ 160 Roy Williams | | .75 | .30 |
| ❑ 161 Antonio Bryant | | .75 | .30 |
| ❑ 162 Quincy Carter | | .60 | .25 |
| ❑ 163 Anthony Thomas | | .60 | .25 |
| ❑ 164 Marty Booker | | .60 | .25 |
| ❑ 165 Dez White | | .50 | .20 |
| ❑ 166 Adrian Peterson | | .50 | .20 |
| ❑ 167 Kordell Stewart | | .60 | .25 |
| ❑ 168 David Terrell | | .50 | .20 |
| ❑ 169 Jabar Gaffney | | .50 | .20 |
| ❑ 170 Bennie Joppru RC | | .50 | .20 |
| ❑ 171 Corey Bradford | | .50 | .20 |
| ❑ 172 David Carr | | .75 | .30 |
| ❑ 173 James Stewart | | .60 | .25 |
| ❑ 174 Ty Detmer | | .50 | .20 |
| ❑ 175 Az-Zahir Hakim | | .50 | .20 |
| ❑ 176 Bill Schroeder | | .50 | .20 |
| ❑ 177 Jon Kitna | | .60 | .25 |
| ❑ 178 Chad Johnson | | .75 | .30 |
| ❑ 179 Ron Dugans | | .50 | .20 |
| ❑ 180 Peter Warrick | | .60 | .25 |
| ❑ 181 Brett Favre SS | | 8.00 | 3.00 |
| ❑ 182 Emmitt Smith SS | | 8.00 | 3.00 |
| ❑ 183 LaDainian Tomlinson SS | | 5.00 | 2.00 |
| ❑ 184 Joey Harrington SS | | 3.00 | 1.25 |
| ❑ 185 Brian Urlacher SS | | 5.00 | 2.00 |
| ❑ 186 Daunte Culpepper SS | | 3.00 | 1.25 |
| ❑ 187 Jamal Lewis SS | | 3.00 | 1.25 |
| ❑ 188 Shaun Alexander SS | | 3.00 | 1.25 |
| ❑ 189 Marshall Faulk SS | | 3.00 | 1.25 |
| ❑ 190 Travis Henry SS | | 2.50 | 1.00 |
| ❑ 191 Trent Green SS | | 2.50 | 1.00 |
| ❑ 192 Aaron Brooks SS | | 2.50 | 1.00 |
| ❑ 193 Chris Chambers SS | | 2.50 | 1.00 |
| ❑ 194 Tom Brady SS | | 8.00 | 3.00 |
| ❑ 195 Clinton Portis SS | | 4.00 | 1.50 |
| ❑ 196 Kevin Johnson SS | | 2.00 | .75 |
| ❑ 197 Santana Moss SS | | 2.50 | 1.00 |
| ❑ 198 Michael Vick SS | | 3.00 | 1.25 |
| ❑ 199 Edgerrin James SS | | 3.00 | 1.25 |
| ❑ 200 Jeremy Shockey SS | | 3.00 | 1.25 |
| ❑ 201 Kevan Barlow SS | | 2.00 | .75 |
| ❑ 202 Plaxico Burress SS | | 3.00 | 1.25 |
| ❑ 203 Steve McNair SS | | 3.00 | 1.25 |

| | | | |
|---|---|---|---|
| ❑ 204 Donovan McNabb SS | | 4.00 | 1.50 |
| ❑ 205 Jerry Rice SS | | 6.00 | 2.50 |
| ❑ 206 Keyshawn Johnson SS | | 3.00 | 1.25 |
| ❑ 207 Patrick Ramsey SS | | 2.50 | 1.00 |
| ❑ 208 Stephen Davis SS | | 2.50 | 1.00 |
| ❑ 209 Corey Dillon SS | | 2.50 | 1.00 |
| ❑ 210 Chad Hutchinson SS | | 2.00 | .75 |
| ❑ 211 Brad Banks RC | | 4.00 | 1.50 |
| ❑ 212 Kliff Kingsbury RC | | 4.00 | 1.50 |
| ❑ 213 Jason Gesser RC | | 4.00 | 1.50 |
| ❑ 214 Jason Johnson RC | | 3.00 | 1.25 |
| ❑ 215 Brian St.Pierre RC | | 5.00 | 2.00 |
| ❑ 216 Ken Dorsey RC | | 4.00 | 1.50 |
| ❑ 217 Seneca Wallace RC | | 5.00 | 2.00 |
| ❑ 218 Brooks Bollinger RC | | 5.00 | 2.00 |
| ❑ 219 Chris Brown RC | | 5.00 | 2.00 |
| ❑ 220 B.J. Askew RC | | 4.00 | 1.50 |
| ❑ 221 Earnest Graham RC | | 5.00 | 2.00 |
| ❑ 222 Quentin Griffin RC | | 4.00 | 1.50 |
| ❑ 223 Musa Smith RC | | 4.00 | 1.50 |
| ❑ 224 Antoine Riner RC | | 3.00 | 1.25 |
| ❑ 225 Domanick Davis RC | | 5.00 | 2.00 |
| ❑ 226 Anquan Boldin RC | | 12.00 | 5.00 |
| ❑ 227 Talman Gardner RC | | 3.00 | 1.25 |
| ❑ 228 Brandon Lloyd RC | | 5.00 | 2.00 |
| ❑ 229 Bryant Johnson RC | | 5.00 | 2.00 |
| ❑ 230 Kareem Kelly RC | | 3.00 | 1.25 |
| ❑ 231 Arnaz Battle RC | | 5.00 | 2.00 |
| ❑ 232 Keenan Howry RC | | 3.00 | 1.25 |
| ❑ 233 Justin Gage RC | | 4.00 | 1.50 |
| ❑ 234 Tyrone Calico RC | | 4.00 | 1.50 |
| ❑ 235 Teyo Johnson RC | | 4.00 | 1.50 |
| ❑ 236 Malaefou MacKenzie RC | | 3.00 | 1.25 |
| ❑ 237 Terrence Newman RC | | 6.00 | 2.50 |
| ❑ 238 Marcus Trufant RC | | 5.00 | 2.00 |
| ❑ 239 Mike Doss RC | | 5.00 | 2.00 |
| ❑ 240 Terrell Suggs RC | | 6.00 | 2.50 |
| ❑ 241 Carson Palmer RC | | 30.00 | 12.00 |
| ❑ 242 Byron Leftwich RC | | 12.00 | 5.00 |
| ❑ 243 Rex Grossman RC | | 20.00 | 8.00 |
| ❑ 244 Kyle Boller RC | | 8.00 | 3.00 |
| ❑ 245 Dave Ragone RC | | 5.00 | 2.00 |
| ❑ 246 Chris Simms RC | | 8.00 | 3.00 |
| ❑ 247 Larry Johnson RC | | 20.00 | 8.00 |
| ❑ 248 Lee Suggs RC | | 6.00 | 2.50 |
| ❑ 249 Justin Fargas RC | | 8.00 | 3.00 |
| ❑ 250 Onterrio Smith RC | | 6.00 | 2.50 |
| ❑ 251 Willis McGahee RC | | 20.00 | 8.00 |
| ❑ 252 Charles Rogers RC | | 6.00 | 2.50 |
| ❑ 253 Andre Johnson RC | | 15.00 | 6.00 |
| ❑ 254 Taylor Jacobs RC | | 6.00 | 2.50 |
| ❑ 255 Kelley Washington RC | | 6.00 | 2.50 |
| ❑ 256 Tony Romo RC | | 40.00 | 20.00 |
| ❑ 257 Jerel Myers RC | | 4.00 | 1.50 |
| ❑ 258 Kirk Farmer RC | | 5.00 | 2.00 |
| ❑ 259 Kevin Walter RC | | 6.00 | 2.50 |
| ❑ 260 Gibran Hamdan RC | | 4.00 | 1.50 |
| ❑ 261 Juston Wood RC | | 4.00 | 1.50 |
| ❑ 262 Travis Anglin RC | | 4.00 | 1.50 |
| ❑ 263 Marquel Blackwell RC | | 4.00 | 1.50 |
| ❑ 264 Jason Thomas RC | | 4.00 | 1.50 |
| ❑ 265 Carl Ford RC | | 4.00 | 1.50 |
| ❑ 266 Walter Young RC | | 4.00 | 1.50 |
| ❑ 267 Sultan McCullough RC | | 4.00 | 1.50 |
| ❑ 268 Dahrran Diedrick RC | | 4.00 | 1.50 |
| ❑ 269 Cecil Sapp RC | | 4.00 | 1.50 |
| ❑ 270 Doug Gabriel RC | | 5.00 | 2.00 |
| ❑ 271 LaBrandon Toefield RC | | 5.00 | 2.00 |
| ❑ 272 Adrian Madise RC | | 4.00 | 1.50 |
| ❑ 273 J.R. Tolver RC | | 5.00 | 2.00 |
| ❑ 274 Kevin Curtis RC | | 8.00 | 3.00 |
| ❑ 275 Bobby Wade RC | | 5.00 | 2.00 |
| ❑ 276 Sam Aiken RC | | 5.00 | 2.00 |
| ❑ 277 Mike Bush RC | | 4.00 | 1.50 |
| ❑ 278 Billy McMullen RC | | 4.00 | 1.50 |
| ❑ 279 Bethel Johnson RC | | 4.00 | 1.50 |
| ❑ 280 David Kircus RC | | 6.00 | 2.50 |
| ❑ 281 Zuriel Smith RC | | 4.00 | 1.50 |
| ❑ 282 LaTarence Dunbar RC | | 4.00 | 1.50 |
| ❑ 283 Nate Burleson RC | | 5.00 | 2.00 |
| ❑ 284 Antwone Savage RC | | 4.00 | 1.50 |
| ❑ 285 Terrence Edwards RC | | 4.00 | 1.50 |

## 2004 Upper Deck

| | | | |
|---|---|---|---|
| ❑ COMPLETE SET (275) | | 135.00 | 75.00 |
| ❑ COMP.SET w/o SP's (250) | | 60.00 | 30.00 |
| ❑ COMP.SET w/o RC's (200) | | 25.00 | 10.00 |
| ❑ 201-225 ROOKIE STATED ODDS 1:8 | | | |
| ❑ 226-275 ROOKIE STATED ODDS 1:1 | | | |
| ❑ UNPRICED PRINT PLATE PRINT RUN 1 SET | | | |
| | | 1 SET | |
| ❑ 1 Anquan Boldin | | .75 | .30 |
| ❑ 2 Josh McCown | | .60 | .25 |
| ❑ 3 Emmitt Smith | | 2.00 | .75 |
| ❑ 4 Freddie Jones | | .50 | .20 |
| ❑ 5 Marcel Shipp | | .50 | .20 |
| ❑ 6 Shaun King | | .50 | .20 |
| ❑ 7 Michael Vick | | .75 | .30 |
| ❑ 8 T.J. Duckett | | .60 | .25 |
| ❑ 9 Peerless Price | | .60 | .25 |
| ❑ 10 Warrick Dunn | | .60 | .25 |
| ❑ 11 Keith Brooking | | .60 | .25 |
| ❑ 12 Brian Finneran | | .50 | .20 |
| ❑ 13 Anthony Wright | | .60 | .25 |
| ❑ 14 Kyle Boller | | .60 | .25 |
| ❑ 15 Jamal Lewis | | .60 | .25 |
| ❑ 16 Todd Heap | | .60 | .25 |
| ❑ 17 Ray Lewis | | .75 | .30 |
| ❑ 18 Terrell Suggs | | .50 | .20 |
| ❑ 19 Travis Taylor | | .50 | .20 |
| ❑ 20 Drew Bledsoe | | .75 | .30 |
| ❑ 21 Willis McGahee | | .60 | .25 |
| ❑ 22 Eric Moulds | | .60 | .25 |
| ❑ 23 Travis Henry | | .60 | .25 |
| ❑ 24 Takeo Spikes | | .50 | .20 |
| ❑ 25 Josh Reed | | .75 | .30 |
| ❑ 26 Lawyer Milloy | | .60 | .25 |
| ❑ 27 Stephen Davis | | .60 | .25 |
| ❑ 28 Jake Delhomme | | .60 | .25 |
| ❑ 29 Steve Smith | | .75 | .30 |
| ❑ 30 DeShaun Foster | | .60 | .25 |
| ❑ 31 Dan Morgan | | .50 | .20 |
| ❑ 32 Julius Peppers | | .60 | .25 |
| ❑ 33 Rod Smart | | .60 | .25 |
| ❑ 34 Rex Grossman | | .75 | .30 |
| ❑ 35 Thomas Jones | | .60 | .25 |
| ❑ 36 Marty Booker | | .60 | .25 |
| ❑ 37 Anthony Thomas | | .60 | .25 |
| ❑ 38 Brian Urlacher | | .75 | .30 |
| ❑ 39 Justin Gage | | .50 | .20 |
| ❑ 40 Chad Johnson | | .75 | .30 |
| ❑ 41 Carson Palmer | | 1.00 | .40 |
| ❑ 42 Peter Warrick | | .60 | .25 |
| ❑ 43 Jon Kitna | | .60 | .25 |
| ❑ 44 Kelley Washington | | .50 | .20 |
| ❑ 45 Rudi Johnson | | .60 | .25 |
| ❑ 46 Jeff Garcia | | .75 | .30 |
| ❑ 47 Dennis Northcutt | | .60 | .25 |
| ❑ 48 Lee Suggs | | .75 | .30 |
| ❑ 49 Andre Davis | | .50 | .20 |
| ❑ 50 Quincy Morgan | | .60 | .25 |
| ❑ 51 Kelly Holcomb | | .60 | .25 |
| ❑ 52 Keyshawn Johnson | | .50 | .20 |
| ❑ 53 Quincy Carter | | .50 | .20 |
| ❑ 54 Antonio Bryant | | .60 | .25 |
| ❑ 55 Terry Glenn | | .60 | .25 |
| ❑ 56 Terrence Newman | | .60 | .25 |
| ❑ 57 Roy Williams | | .60 | .25 |
| ❑ 58 Champ Bailey | | .60 | .25 |
| ❑ 59 Jake Plummer | | .60 | .25 |

| | | |
|---|---|---|
| ❏ 60 Quentin Griffin | .60 | .25 |
| ❏ 61 John Lynch | .60 | .25 |
| ❏ 62 Rod Smith | .60 | .25 |
| ❏ 63 Ashley Lelie | .60 | .25 |
| ❏ 64 Joey Harrington | .60 | .25 |
| ❏ 65 Az-Zahir Hakim | .60 | .20 |
| ❏ 66 Charles Rogers | .60 | .20 |
| ❏ 67 Tai Streets | .50 | .20 |
| ❏ 68 Shawn Bryson | .50 | .20 |
| ❏ 69 Artose Pinner | .50 | .20 |
| ❏ 70 Brett Favre | 2.00 | .75 |
| ❏ 71 Nick Barnett | .60 | .25 |
| ❏ 72 Ahman Green | .75 | .30 |
| ❏ 73 Kabeer Gbaja-Biamila | .60 | .25 |
| ❏ 74 Javon Walker | .60 | .25 |
| ❏ 75 Donald Driver | .75 | .30 |
| ❏ 76 Tim Couch | .60 | .25 |
| ❏ 77 David Carr | .60 | .25 |
| ❏ 78 Corey Bradford | .60 | .25 |
| ❏ 79 J.J. Moses | .50 | .20 |
| ❏ 80 Domanick Davis | .75 | .30 |
| ❏ 81 Jabar Gaffney | .60 | .25 |
| ❏ 82 Andre Johnson | .75 | .30 |
| ❏ 83 Marvin Harrison | .75 | .30 |
| ❏ 84 Peyton Manning | 1.50 | .60 |
| ❏ 85 Dallas Clark | .60 | .25 |
| ❏ 86 Edgerrin James | .75 | .30 |
| ❏ 87 Reggie Wayne | .60 | .25 |
| ❏ 88 Dwight Freeney | .75 | .30 |
| ❏ 89 Byron Leftwich | .60 | .25 |
| ❏ 90 LaBrandon Toefield | .50 | .20 |
| ❏ 91 Fred Taylor | .60 | .25 |
| ❏ 92 Troy Edwards | .60 | .25 |
| ❏ 93 Jimmy Smith | .60 | .25 |
| ❏ 94 Kyle Brady | .60 | .25 |
| ❏ 95 Trent Green | .60 | .25 |
| ❏ 96 Tony Gonzalez | .75 | .30 |
| ❏ 97 Dante Hall | .60 | .25 |
| ❏ 98 Priest Holmes | .75 | .30 |
| ❏ 99 Eddie Kennison | .60 | .25 |
| ❏ 100 Johnnie Morton | .60 | .25 |
| ❏ 101 Jay Fiedler | .50 | .20 |
| ❏ 102 Junior Seau | .75 | .30 |
| ❏ 103 Ricky Williams | .75 | .30 |
| ❏ 104 Chris Chambers | .60 | .25 |
| ❏ 105 Zach Thomas | .75 | .30 |
| ❏ 106 David Boston | .50 | .20 |
| ❏ 107 A.J. Feeley | .50 | .20 |
| ❏ 108 Daunte Culpepper | .75 | .30 |
| ❏ 109 Onterrio Smith | .50 | .20 |
| ❏ 110 Randy Moss | 1.00 | .40 |
| ❏ 111 Moe Williams | .50 | .20 |
| ❏ 112 Michael Bennett | .60 | .25 |
| ❏ 113 Jim Kleinsasser | .50 | .20 |
| ❏ 114 Tom Brady | 2.00 | .75 |
| ❏ 115 Kevin Faulk | .60 | .25 |
| ❏ 116 Deion Branch | .60 | .25 |
| ❏ 117 Corey Dillon | .60 | .25 |
| ❏ 118 Troy Brown | .60 | .25 |
| ❏ 119 Adam Vinatieri | .75 | .30 |
| ❏ 120 Tedy Bruschi | .75 | .30 |
| ❏ 121 Aaron Brooks | .60 | .25 |
| ❏ 122 Deuce McAllister | .75 | .30 |
| ❏ 123 Donte' Stallworth | .60 | .25 |
| ❏ 124 Joe Horn | .60 | .25 |
| ❏ 125 Jerome Pathon | .50 | .20 |
| ❏ 126 Boo Williams | .50 | .20 |
| ❏ 127 Jeremy Shockey | .75 | .30 |
| ❏ 128 Kurt Warner | .75 | .30 |
| ❏ 129 Amani Toomer | .60 | .25 |
| ❏ 130 Tiki Barber | .75 | .30 |
| ❏ 131 Ike Hilliard | .60 | .25 |
| ❏ 132 Michael Strahan | .60 | .25 |
| ❏ 133 Chad Pennington | .75 | .30 |
| ❏ 134 Santana Moss | .60 | .25 |
| ❏ 135 Wayne Chrebet | .60 | .25 |
| ❏ 136 Curtis Martin | .75 | .30 |
| ❏ 137 LaMont Jordan | .75 | .30 |
| ❏ 138 Justin McCareins | .50 | .20 |
| ❏ 139 Jerry Rice | 1.50 | .60 |
| ❏ 140 Rich Gannon | .60 | .25 |
| ❏ 141 Tim Brown | .75 | .30 |
| ❏ 142 Jerry Porter | .60 | .25 |
| ❏ 143 Warren Sapp | .60 | .25 |
| ❏ 144 Charles Woodson | .75 | .30 |
| ❏ 145 Donovan McNabb | .75 | .30 |
| ❏ 146 Brian Westbrook | .75 | .30 |
| ❏ 147 Todd Pinkston | .50 | .20 |
| ❏ 148 Jevon Kearse | .60 | .25 |
| ❏ 149 Freddie Mitchell | .50 | .20 |
| ❏ 150 Correll Buckhalter | .60 | .25 |
| ❏ 151 Terrell Owens | .75 | .30 |
| ❏ 152 Tommy Maddox | .60 | .25 |
| ❏ 153 Duce Staley | .60 | .25 |
| ❏ 154 Plaxico Burress | .60 | .25 |
| ❏ 155 Hines Ward | .75 | .30 |
| ❏ 156 Antwaan Randle El | .60 | .25 |
| ❏ 157 Jerome Bettis | .75 | .30 |
| ❏ 158 Kendrell Bell | .50 | .20 |
| ❏ 159 LaDainian Tomlinson | 1.25 | .50 |
| ❏ 160 Doug Flutie | .75 | .30 |
| ❏ 161 Quentin Jammer | .50 | .20 |
| ❏ 162 Drew Brees | .75 | .30 |
| ❏ 163 Reche Caldwell | .60 | .25 |
| ❏ 164 Tim Dwight | .60 | .25 |
| ❏ 165 Tim Rattay | .50 | .20 |
| ❏ 166 Kevan Barlow | .60 | .25 |
| ❏ 167 Brandon Lloyd | .60 | .25 |
| ❏ 168 Cedrick Wilson | .50 | .20 |
| ❏ 169 Julian Peterson | .60 | .25 |
| ❏ 170 Ahmed Plummer | .50 | .20 |
| ❏ 171 Matt Hasselbeck | .75 | .30 |
| ❏ 172 Koren Robinson | .75 | .30 |
| ❏ 173 Shaun Alexander | .75 | .30 |
| ❏ 174 Darrell Jackson | .60 | .25 |
| ❏ 175 Marcus Trufant | .50 | .20 |
| ❏ 176 Bobby Engram | .60 | .25 |
| ❏ 177 Marc Bulger | .60 | .25 |
| ❏ 178 Torry Holt | .75 | .30 |
| ❏ 179 Marshall Faulk | .75 | .30 |
| ❏ 180 Orlando Pace | .60 | .25 |
| ❏ 181 Isaac Bruce | .60 | .25 |
| ❏ 182 Kyle Turley | .50 | .20 |
| ❏ 183 Brad Johnson | .60 | .25 |
| ❏ 184 Charlie Garner | .60 | .25 |
| ❏ 185 Keenan McCardell | .50 | .20 |
| ❏ 186 Mike Alstott | .75 | .30 |
| ❏ 187 Derrick Brooks | .60 | .25 |
| ❏ 188 Brian Griese | .60 | .25 |
| ❏ 189 Steve McNair | .75 | .30 |
| ❏ 190 Chris Brown | .60 | .25 |
| ❏ 191 Eddie George | .60 | .25 |
| ❏ 192 Tyrone Calico | .60 | .25 |
| ❏ 193 Derrick Mason | .60 | .25 |
| ❏ 194 Drew Bennett | .60 | .25 |
| ❏ 195 Mark Brunell | .60 | .25 |
| ❏ 196 LaVar Arrington | .60 | .25 |
| ❏ 197 Clinton Portis | .75 | .30 |
| ❏ 198 Laveranues Coles | .60 | .25 |
| ❏ 199 Patrick Ramsey | .60 | .25 |
| ❏ 200 Rod Gardner | .60 | .25 |
| ❏ 201 Eli Manning RC | 30.00 | 12.00 |
| ❏ 202 Larry Fitzgerald RC | 15.00 | 6.00 |
| ❏ 203 Michael Jenkins RC | 5.00 | 2.00 |
| ❏ 204 Ben Roethlisberger RC | 40.00 | 15.00 |
| ❏ 205 Philip Rivers RC | 15.00 | 6.00 |
| ❏ 206 Kellen Winslow RC | 10.00 | 4.00 |
| ❏ 207 Kevin Jones RC | 5.00 | 2.00 |
| ❏ 208 Steven Jackson RC | 15.00 | 6.00 |
| ❏ 209 Reggie Williams RC | 5.00 | 2.00 |
| ❏ 210 Chris Perry RC | 5.00 | 2.00 |
| ❏ 211 Roy Williams RC | 12.00 | 5.00 |
| ❏ 212 Rashaun Woods RC | 3.00 | 1.25 |
| ❏ 213 Chris Gamble RC | 4.00 | 1.50 |
| ❏ 214 Sean Taylor RC | 5.00 | 2.00 |
| ❏ 215 Robert Gallery RC | 5.00 | 2.00 |
| ❏ 216 Ben Troupe RC | 4.00 | 1.50 |
| ❏ 217 Lee Evans RC | 6.00 | 2.50 |
| ❏ 218 Michael Clayton RC | 5.00 | 2.00 |
| ❏ 219 J.P. Losman RC | 6.00 | 2.50 |
| ❏ 220 Devery Henderson RC | 5.00 | 2.00 |
| ❏ 221 Drew Henson RC | 3.00 | 1.25 |
| ❏ 222 DeAngelo Hall RC | 5.00 | 2.00 |
| ❏ 223 Julius Jones RC | 12.00 | 5.00 |
| ❏ 224 Ben Watson RC | 5.00 | 2.00 |
| ❏ 225 Greg Jones RC | 5.00 | 2.00 |
| ❏ 226 D.J. Williams RC | 1.50 | .60 |
| ❏ 227 Tommie Harris RC | 1.50 | .60 |
| ❏ 228 Shawn Andrews RC | 1.25 | .50 |
| ❏ 229 Vince Wilfork RC | 1.50 | .60 |
| ❏ 230 Dunta Robinson RC | 1.25 | .50 |
| ❏ 231 Will Smith RC | 1.25 | .50 |
| ❏ 232 Jonathan Vilma RC | 1.50 | .60 |
| ❏ 233 Ricardo Colclough RC | 1.50 | .60 |
| ❏ 234 Ahmad Carroll RC | 1.50 | .60 |
| ❏ 235 Karlos Dansby RC | 1.50 | .60 |
| ❏ 236 Matt Ware RC | 1.50 | .60 |
| ❏ 237 Jim Sorgi RC | 1.50 | .60 |
| ❏ 238 Will Poole RC | 1.50 | .60 |
| ❏ 239 Derrick Strait RC | 1.25 | .50 |
| ❏ 240 Andy Hall RC | 1.25 | .50 |
| ❏ 241 Nathan Vasher RC | 1.50 | .60 |
| ❏ 242 D.J. Hackett RC | 1.25 | .50 |
| ❏ 243 Jason Babin RC | 1.25 | .50 |
| ❏ 244 Derrick Hamilton RC | 1.00 | .40 |
| ❏ 245 Michael Boulware RC | 1.50 | .60 |
| ❏ 246 Michael Turner RC | 3.00 | 1.25 |
| ❏ 247 Sean Jones RC | 1.25 | .50 |
| ❏ 248 Ernest Wilford RC | 1.50 | .60 |
| ❏ 249 Cedric Cobbs RC | 1.25 | .50 |
| ❏ 250 Tatum Bell RC | 1.50 | .60 |
| ❏ 251 Bernard Berrian RC | 1.50 | .60 |
| ❏ 252 Vernon Carey RC | 1.00 | .40 |
| ❏ 253 Kenechi Udeze RC | 1.50 | .60 |
| ❏ 254 P.K. Sam RC | 1.00 | .40 |
| ❏ 255 Ben Hartsock RC | 1.25 | .50 |
| ❏ 256 Chris Cooley RC | 1.50 | .60 |
| ❏ 257 Josh Harris RC | 1.00 | .40 |
| ❏ 258 Cody Pickett RC | 1.25 | .50 |
| ❏ 259 Carlos Francis RC | 1.25 | .50 |
| ❏ 260 Devard Darling RC | 1.25 | .50 |
| ❏ 261 Johnnie Morant RC | 1.25 | .50 |
| ❏ 262 John Navarre RC | 1.25 | .50 |
| ❏ 263 Kris Wilson RC | 1.25 | .50 |
| ❏ 264 Jerricho Cotchery RC | 1.50 | .60 |
| ❏ 265 Darius Watts RC | 1.25 | .50 |
| ❏ 266 Quincy Wilson RC | 1.25 | .50 |
| ❏ 267 Maurice Mann RC | 1.00 | .40 |
| ❏ 268 Samie Parker RC | 1.25 | .50 |
| ❏ 269 B.J. Symons RC | 1.00 | .40 |
| ❏ 270 Matt Schaub RC | 5.00 | 2.00 |
| ❏ 271 Jeff Smoker RC | 1.25 | .50 |
| ❏ 272 Craig Krenzel RC | 1.50 | .60 |
| ❏ 273 Luke McCown RC | 1.50 | .60 |
| ❏ 274 Mewelde Moore RC | 1.50 | .60 |
| ❏ 275 Keary Colbert RC | 1.50 | .60 |

## 2005 Upper Deck

| | | |
|---|---|---|
| ❏ COMPLETE SET (275) | 250.00 | 125.00 |
| ❏ COMP.SET w/o SP's (250) | 60.00 | 30.00 |
| ❏ COMP.SET w/ RC's (200) | 30.00 | 12.50 |
| ❏ 201-225 ROOKIE STATED ODDS 1:8 | | |
| ❏ 226-275 ROOKIE STATED ODDS 1:1 | | |
| ❏ 1 Larry Fitzgerald | .75 | .30 |
| ❏ 2 Anquan Boldin | .60 | .25 |
| ❏ 3 Kurt Warner | .75 | .30 |
| ❏ 4 Josh McCown | .60 | .25 |
| ❏ 5 Bryant Johnson | .60 | .25 |
| ❏ 6 Duane Starks | .50 | .20 |
| ❏ 7 Michael Vick | .75 | .30 |
| ❏ 8 Warrick Dunn | .60 | .25 |
| ❏ 9 T.J. Duckett | .50 | .20 |
| ❏ 10 Peerless Price | .50 | .20 |
| ❏ 11 Alge Crumpler | .60 | .25 |
| ❏ 12 Patrick Kerney | .60 | .25 |

|  |  | | |
|---|---|---|---|
| 13 | Ed Reed | .60 | .25 |
| 14 | Ray Lewis | .75 | .30 |
| 15 | Kyle Boller | .60 | .25 |
| 16 | Ma'Ake Kemoeatu RC | .40 | .20 |
| 17 | Jamal Lewis | .60 | .25 |
| 18 | Derrick Mason | .60 | .25 |
| 19 | J.P. Losman | .75 | .30 |
| 20 | Willis McGahee | .75 | .30 |
| 21 | Lawyer Milloy | .60 | .25 |
| 22 | Lee Evans | .60 | .25 |
| 23 | Eric Moulds | .60 | .25 |
| 24 | Takeo Spikes | .50 | .20 |
| 25 | Jake Delhomme | .75 | .30 |
| 26 | DeShaun Foster | .60 | .25 |
| 27 | Keary Colbert | .50 | .20 |
| 28 | Stephen Davis | .60 | .25 |
| 29 | Nick Goings | .50 | .20 |
| 30 | Julius Peppers | .60 | .25 |
| 31 | Rex Grossman | .75 | .30 |
| 32 | Brian Urlacher | .75 | .30 |
| 33 | Thomas Jones | .60 | .25 |
| 34 | Muhsin Muhammad | .60 | .25 |
| 35 | Anthony Thomas | .50 | .20 |
| 36 | Bernard Berrian | .60 | .25 |
| 37 | Carson Palmer | .75 | .30 |
| 38 | Chad Johnson | .60 | .25 |
| 39 | Peter Warrick | .50 | .20 |
| 40 | T.J. Houshmandzadeh | .60 | .25 |
| 41 | Rudi Johnson | .60 | .25 |
| 42 | Justin Smith | .50 | .20 |
| 43 | Jeff Garcia | .60 | .25 |
| 44 | Lee Suggs | .60 | .25 |
| 45 | William Green | .50 | .20 |
| 46 | Kellen Winslow | .75 | .30 |
| 47 | Dennis Northcutt | .50 | .20 |
| 48 | Antonio Bryant | .50 | .20 |
| 49 | Julius Jones | .75 | .30 |
| 50 | Drew Bledsoe | .75 | .30 |
| 51 | Keyshawn Johnson | .60 | .25 |
| 52 | Al Johnson | .50 | .20 |
| 53 | Jason Witten | .75 | .30 |
| 54 | Roy Williams S | .60 | .25 |
| 55 | Jake Plummer | .60 | .25 |
| 56 | Champ Bailey | .60 | .25 |
| 57 | Tatum Bell | .60 | .25 |
| 58 | Reuben Droughns | .60 | .25 |
| 59 | Ashley Lelie | .50 | .20 |
| 60 | Rod Smith | .60 | .25 |
| 61 | Kevin Jones | .75 | .30 |
| 62 | Roy Williams WR | .75 | .30 |
| 63 | Charles Rogers | .50 | .20 |
| 64 | Joey Harrington | .75 | .30 |
| 65 | Az-Zahir Hakim | .50 | .20 |
| 66 | Dre Bly | .50 | .20 |
| 67 | Brett Favre | 2.00 | .75 |
| 68 | Javon Walker | .60 | .25 |
| 69 | Ahman Green | .75 | .30 |
| 70 | Donald Driver | .75 | .30 |
| 71 | Robert Ferguson | .60 | .25 |
| 72 | Nick Barnett | .60 | .25 |
| 73 | David Carr | .60 | .25 |
| 74 | Domanick Davis | .50 | .20 |
| 75 | Andre Johnson | .60 | .25 |
| 76 | Jabar Gaffney | .50 | .20 |
| 77 | Dunta Robinson | .50 | .20 |
| 78 | Jamie Sharper | .50 | .20 |
| 79 | Peyton Manning | 1.25 | .50 |
| 80 | Edgerrin James | .60 | .25 |
| 81 | Marvin Harrison | .75 | .30 |
| 82 | Reggie Wayne | .60 | .25 |
| 83 | Brandon Stokley | .60 | .25 |
| 84 | Dwight Freeney | .60 | .25 |
| 85 | Byron Leftwich | .60 | .25 |
| 86 | Fred Taylor | .75 | .30 |
| 87 | Jimmy Smith | .60 | .25 |
| 88 | Greg Jones | .50 | .20 |
| 89 | Donovin Darius | .50 | .20 |
| 90 | Reggie Williams | .60 | .25 |
| 91 | Priest Holmes | .75 | .30 |
| 92 | Larry Johnson | .75 | .30 |
| 93 | Tony Gonzalez | .60 | .25 |
| 94 | Trent Green | .60 | .25 |
| 95 | Eddie Kennison | .60 | .25 |
| 96 | Johnnie Morton | .60 | .25 |
| 97 | Jason Taylor | .60 | .25 |
| 98 | A.J. Feeley | .50 | .25 |
| 99 | Sammy Morris | .50 | .25 |
| 100 | Chris Chambers | .60 | .25 |
| 101 | Randy McMichael | .50 | .20 |
| 102 | Zach Thomas | .75 | .30 |
| 103 | Antoine Winfield | .60 | .25 |
| 104 | Daunte Culpepper | .75 | .30 |
| 105 | Michael Bennett | .60 | .25 |
| 106 | Nate Burleson | .60 | .25 |
| 107 | Onterrio Smith | .50 | .20 |
| 108 | Marcus Robinson | .60 | .25 |
| 109 | Tom Brady | 1.50 | .60 |
| 110 | Corey Dillon | .60 | .25 |
| 111 | David Givens | .60 | .25 |
| 112 | David Patten | .50 | .20 |
| 113 | Adam Vinatieri | .75 | .30 |
| 114 | Troy Brown | .50 | .20 |
| 115 | Aaron Brooks | .50 | .20 |
| 116 | Deuce McAllister | .75 | .30 |
| 117 | Joe Horn | .60 | .25 |
| 118 | Donte Stallworth | .60 | .25 |
| 119 | Charles Grant | .50 | .20 |
| 120 | Jerome Pathon | .50 | .20 |
| 121 | Eli Manning | 1.50 | .60 |
| 122 | Tiki Barber | .75 | .30 |
| 123 | Amani Toomer | .60 | .25 |
| 124 | Jeremy Shockey | .75 | .30 |
| 125 | Michael Strahan | .60 | .25 |
| 126 | Plaxico Burress | .60 | .25 |
| 127 | Chad Pennington | .75 | .30 |
| 128 | Curtis Martin | .75 | .30 |
| 129 | Laveranues Coles | .60 | .25 |
| 130 | Wayne Chrebet | .60 | .25 |
| 131 | Jonathan Vilma | .60 | .25 |
| 132 | Justin McCareins | .50 | .20 |
| 133 | Kerry Collins | .60 | .25 |
| 134 | Jerry Porter | .60 | .25 |
| 135 | LaMont Jordan | .60 | .25 |
| 136 | Randy Moss | .75 | .30 |
| 137 | Barry Sims | .50 | .20 |
| 138 | Warren Sapp | .60 | .25 |
| 139 | Donovan McNabb | .75 | .30 |
| 140 | Brian Westbrook | .75 | .30 |
| 141 | Terrell Owens | .75 | .30 |
| 142 | Jevon Kearse | .60 | .25 |
| 143 | Brian Dawkins | .60 | .25 |
| 144 | Ben Roethlisberger | 2.00 | .75 |
| 145 | Jerome Bettis | .75 | .30 |
| 146 | Duce Staley | .60 | .25 |
| 147 | Cedrick Wilson | .50 | .20 |
| 148 | Hines Ward | .75 | .30 |
| 149 | Antwaan Randle El | .60 | .25 |
| 150 | Troy Polamalu | 1.00 | .40 |
| 151 | Philip Rivers | .75 | .30 |
| 152 | Drew Brees | .75 | .30 |
| 153 | LaDainian Tomlinson | 1.25 | .50 |
| 154 | Antonio Gates | .75 | .30 |
| 155 | Reche Caldwell | .50 | .20 |
| 156 | Eric Parker | .50 | .20 |
| 157 | Kevan Barlow | .50 | .20 |
| 158 | Tim Rattay | .50 | .20 |
| 159 | Eric Johnson | .50 | .20 |
| 160 | Rashaun Woods | .50 | .20 |
| 161 | Brandon Lloyd | .50 | .20 |
| 162 | Julian Peterson | .50 | .20 |
| 163 | Matt Hasselbeck | .60 | .25 |
| 164 | Shaun Alexander | .75 | .30 |
| 165 | Michael Boulware | .50 | .20 |
| 166 | Darrell Jackson | .60 | .25 |
| 167 | Koren Robinson | .60 | .25 |
| 168 | Marcus Trufant | .50 | .20 |
| 169 | Marc Bulger | .60 | .25 |
| 170 | Steven Jackson | 1.00 | .40 |
| 171 | Marshall Faulk | .75 | .30 |
| 172 | Issac Bruce | .60 | .25 |
| 173 | Torry Holt | .75 | .30 |
| 174 | Michael Clayton | .60 | .25 |
| 175 | Michael Pittman | .50 | .20 |
| 176 | Brian Griese | .60 | .25 |
| 177 | Joey Galloway | .60 | .25 |
| 178 | Derrick Brooks | .60 | .25 |
| 179 | Josh Savage RC | .50 | .20 |
| 180 | Steve McNair | .75 | .30 |
| 181 | Chris Brown | .60 | .25 |
| 182 | Billy Volek | .50 | .25 |
| 183 | Ben Troupe | .50 | .25 |
| 184 | Drew Bennett | .60 | .25 |
| 185 | Clinton Portis | .75 | .30 |
| 186 | Mark Brunell | .60 | .25 |
| 187 | Patrick Ramsey | .60 | .25 |
| 188 | Sean Taylor | .60 | .25 |
| 189 | LaVar Arrington | .75 | .30 |
| 190 | Santana Moss | .60 | .25 |
| 191 | David Terrell | .50 | .20 |
| 192 | Deion Branch | .60 | .25 |
| 193 | Chester Taylor | .60 | .25 |
| 194 | Derrick Blaylock | .50 | .20 |
| 195 | Shaun Ellis | .50 | .20 |
| 196 | Terrell Suggs | .60 | .25 |
| 197 | Charles Woodson | .60 | .25 |
| 198 | Jason Elam | .50 | .20 |
| 199 | Lawrence Tynes RC | .60 | .25 |
| 200 | David Akers | .50 | .20 |
| 201 | Alex Smith QB RC | 10.00 | 4.00 |
| 202 | Aaron Rodgers RC | 20.00 | 8.00 |
| 203 | Ronnie Brown RC | 20.00 | 8.00 |
| 204 | Cadillac Williams RC | 12.00 | 5.00 |
| 205 | Braylon Edwards RC | 20.00 | 8.00 |
| 206 | Antrel Rolle RC | 6.00 | 2.50 |
| 207 | Cedric Benson RC | 6.00 | 2.50 |
| 208 | Troy Williamson RC | 6.00 | 2.50 |
| 209 | Mark Clayton RC | 6.00 | 2.50 |
| 210 | Matt Jones RC | 10.00 | 4.00 |
| 211 | Reggie Brown RC | 6.00 | 2.50 |
| 212 | Charlie Frye RC | 6.00 | 2.50 |
| 213 | Heath Miller RC | 12.00 | 5.00 |
| 214 | Vincent Jackson RC | 6.00 | 2.50 |
| 215 | Andrew Walter RC | 6.00 | 2.50 |
| 216 | Roddy White RC | 8.00 | 3.00 |
| 217 | Adam Jones RC | 6.00 | 2.50 |
| 218 | J.J. Arrington RC | 6.00 | 2.50 |
| 219 | Eric Shelton RC | 5.00 | 2.00 |
| 220 | Terrence Murphy RC | 4.00 | 1.50 |
| 221 | Frank Gore RC | 15.00 | 6.00 |
| 222 | Roscoe Parrish RC | 5.00 | 2.00 |
| 223 | Jason Campbell RC | 12.00 | 5.00 |
| 224 | Carlos Rogers RC | 6.00 | 2.50 |
| 225 | Mike Williams RC | 6.00 | 2.50 |
| 226 | Erasmus James RC | 1.50 | .60 |
| 227 | Travis Johnson RC | 1.25 | .60 |
| 228 | Dan Cody RC | 2.00 | .75 |
| 229 | Thomas Davis RC | 1.50 | .60 |
| 230 | David Pollack RC | 1.50 | .60 |
| 231 | David Greene RC | 1.50 | .60 |
| 232 | Alex Smith TE RC | 2.00 | .75 |
| 233 | Ryan Moats RC | 2.00 | .75 |
| 234 | Ciatrick Fason RC | 1.50 | .60 |
| 235 | Vernand Morency RC | 2.00 | .75 |
| 236 | Fred Gibson RC | 1.50 | .60 |
| 237 | Craphonso Thorpe RC | 1.50 | .60 |
| 238 | Kevin Everett RC | 2.00 | .75 |
| 239 | Kyle Orton RC | 2.50 | 1.00 |
| 240 | Derek Anderson RC | 3.00 | 1.25 |
| 241 | Derrick Johnson RC | 2.00 | .75 |
| 242 | Mark Bradley RC | 2.00 | .75 |
| 243 | Chris Henry RC | 2.00 | .75 |
| 244 | DeMarcus Ware RC | 3.00 | 1.25 |
| 245 | Luis Castillo RC | 2.00 | .75 |
| 246 | Mike Patterson RC | 1.50 | .60 |
| 247 | Brodney Pool RC | 1.50 | .60 |
| 248 | Barrett Ruud RC | 2.00 | .75 |
| 249 | Darren Sproles RC | 2.50 | 1.00 |
| 250 | Stefan LeFors RC | 1.50 | .60 |
| 251 | Josh Bullocks RC | 2.00 | .75 |
| 252 | Kevin Burnett RC | 1.50 | .60 |
| 253 | Lofa Tatupu RC | 2.50 | 1.00 |
| 254 | Matt Roth RC | 2.00 | .75 |
| 255 | Shaun Cody RC | 1.50 | .60 |
| 256 | Shawne Merriman RC | 3.00 | 1.25 |
| 257 | Corey Webster RC | 2.00 | .75 |
| 258 | Channing Crowder RC | 1.50 | .60 |
| 259 | Justin Miller RC | 1.50 | .60 |
| 260 | Eric Green RC | 1.25 | .50 |
| 261 | Marcus Spears RC | 2.00 | .75 |
| 262 | Marlin Jackson RC | 1.50 | .60 |
| 263 | Odell Thurman RC | 2.00 | .75 |
| 264 | Mike Nugent RC | 1.50 | .60 |

| | | |
|---|---|---|
| ☐ 265 Marion Barber RC | 6.00 | 2.50 |
| ☐ 266 Antraj Hawthorne RC | 1.50 | .60 |
| ☐ 267 Dan Orlovsky RC | 2.00 | .75 |
| ☐ 268 Fabian Washington RC | 2.00 | .75 |
| ☐ 269 Justin Tuck RC | 2.50 | 1.00 |
| ☐ 270 Jerome Mathis RC | 2.00 | .75 |
| ☐ 271 Ronald Bartell RC | 1.50 | .60 |
| ☐ 272 Kirk Morrison RC | 2.00 | .75 |
| ☐ 273 Adrian McPherson RC | 1.50 | .60 |
| ☐ 274 Matt Cassel RC | 5.00 | 2.00 |
| ☐ 275 Maurice Clarett RC | 1.50 | .60 |

## 2006 Upper Deck

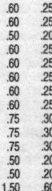

| | | |
|---|---|---|
| ☐ COMP.SET w/o RC's (200) | 30.00 | 12.00 |
| ☐ 1 Larry Fitzgerald | .75 | .30 |
| ☐ 2 Anquan Boldin | .60 | .25 |
| ☐ 3 J.J. Arrington | .60 | .25 |
| ☐ 4 Kurt Warner | .60 | .25 |
| ☐ 5 Neil Rackers | .50 | .20 |
| ☐ 6 Edgerrin James | .60 | .25 |
| ☐ 7 Michael Vick | .75 | .30 |
| ☐ 8 Alge Crumpler | .60 | .25 |
| ☐ 9 Warrick Dunn | .60 | .25 |
| ☐ 10 Michael Jenkins | .50 | .20 |
| ☐ 11 Roddy White | .50 | .20 |
| ☐ 12 DeAngelo Hall | .60 | .25 |
| ☐ 13 Jamal Lewis | .60 | .25 |
| ☐ 14 Derrick Mason | .60 | .25 |
| ☐ 15 Todd Heap | .60 | .25 |
| ☐ 16 Kyle Boller | .60 | .25 |
| ☐ 17 Ray Lewis | .75 | .30 |
| ☐ 18 Ed Reed | .60 | .25 |
| ☐ 19 Willis McGahee | .75 | .30 |
| ☐ 20 Lee Evans | .60 | .25 |
| ☐ 21 J.P. Losman | .60 | .25 |
| ☐ 22 Rashad Baker | .60 | .25 |
| ☐ 23 Takeo Spikes | .50 | .20 |
| ☐ 24 Aaron Schobel | .50 | .20 |
| ☐ 25 Steve Smith | .75 | .30 |
| ☐ 26 Jake Delhomme | .60 | .25 |
| ☐ 27 DeShaun Foster | .60 | .25 |
| ☐ 28 Keary Colbert | .60 | .25 |
| ☐ 29 Julius Peppers | .60 | .25 |
| ☐ 30 Ma'Ake Kemoeatu | .50 | .20 |
| ☐ 31 Rex Grossman | .75 | .30 |
| ☐ 32 Muhsin Muhammad | .60 | .25 |
| ☐ 33 Brian Urlacher | .75 | .30 |
| ☐ 34 Thomas Jones | .60 | .25 |
| ☐ 35 Cedric Benson | .60 | .25 |
| ☐ 36 Nathan Vasher | .60 | .25 |
| ☐ 37 Rudi Johnson | .60 | .25 |
| ☐ 38 Chad Johnson | .60 | .25 |
| ☐ 39 T.J. Houshmandzadeh | .60 | .25 |
| ☐ 40 Chris Henry | .60 | .25 |
| ☐ 41 Deltha O'Neal | .50 | .20 |
| ☐ 42 Odell Thurman | .60 | .25 |
| ☐ 43 Carson Palmer | .75 | .30 |
| ☐ 44 Charlie Frye | .60 | .25 |
| ☐ 45 Reuben Droughns | .60 | .25 |
| ☐ 46 Braylon Edwards | .75 | .30 |
| ☐ 47 Kellen Winslow Jr. | .75 | .30 |
| ☐ 48 Steve Heiden | .60 | .25 |
| ☐ 49 Joe Jurevicius | .60 | .25 |
| ☐ 50 Drew Bledsoe | .75 | .30 |
| ☐ 51 Julius Jones | .75 | .30 |
| ☐ 52 Terrell Owens | .75 | .30 |
| ☐ 53 Terry Glenn | .60 | .25 |

| | | |
|---|---|---|
| ☐ 54 Jason Witten | .60 | .25 |
| ☐ 55 DeMarcus Ware | .60 | .25 |
| ☐ 56 Roy Williams S | .60 | .25 |
| ☐ 57 Jake Plummer | .60 | .25 |
| ☐ 58 Tatum Bell | .60 | .25 |
| ☐ 59 Al Wilson | .50 | .20 |
| ☐ 60 Rod Smith | .60 | .25 |
| ☐ 61 Ashley Lelie | .60 | .25 |
| ☐ 62 Champ Bailey | .60 | .25 |
| ☐ 63 Javon Walker | .60 | .25 |
| ☐ 64 Jon Kitna | .60 | .25 |
| ☐ 65 Kevin Jones | .75 | .30 |
| ☐ 66 Roy Williams WR | .75 | .30 |
| ☐ 67 Mike Williams | .75 | .30 |
| ☐ 68 Marcus Pollard | .50 | .20 |
| ☐ 69 Dre Bly | .50 | .20 |
| ☐ 70 Brett Favre | 1.50 | .60 |
| ☐ 71 Ahman Green | .60 | .25 |
| ☐ 72 Donald Driver | .60 | .25 |
| ☐ 73 Robert Ferguson | .50 | .20 |
| ☐ 74 Bubba Franks | .60 | .25 |
| ☐ 75 Kabeer Gbaja-Biamila | .60 | .25 |
| ☐ 76 David Carr | .60 | .25 |
| ☐ 77 Domanick Davis | .60 | .25 |
| ☐ 78 Andre Johnson | .60 | .25 |
| ☐ 79 Eric Moulds | .60 | .25 |
| ☐ 80 Jeb Putzier | .50 | .20 |
| ☐ 81 Dunta Robinson | .60 | .25 |
| ☐ 82 Peyton Manning | 1.25 | .50 |
| ☐ 83 Dominic Rhodes | .60 | .25 |
| ☐ 84 Reggie Wayne | .60 | .25 |
| ☐ 85 Marvin Harrison | .75 | .30 |
| ☐ 86 Dallas Clark | .60 | .25 |
| ☐ 87 Dwight Freeney | .60 | .25 |
| ☐ 88 Bob Sanders | .60 | .25 |
| ☐ 89 Byron Leftwich | .60 | .25 |
| ☐ 90 Fred Taylor | .60 | .25 |
| ☐ 91 Greg Jones | .50 | .20 |
| ☐ 92 Ernest Wilford | .60 | .25 |
| ☐ 93 John Henderson | .50 | .20 |
| ☐ 94 Matt Jones | .60 | .25 |
| ☐ 95 Trent Green | .60 | .25 |
| ☐ 96 Larry Johnson | .60 | .25 |
| ☐ 97 Priest Holmes | .60 | .25 |
| ☐ 98 Eddie Kennison | .50 | .20 |
| ☐ 99 Tony Gonzalez | .60 | .25 |
| ☐ 100 Dante Hall | .60 | .25 |
| ☐ 101 Daunte Culpepper | .75 | .30 |
| ☐ 102 Ronnie Brown | .75 | .30 |
| ☐ 103 Marty Booker | .50 | .20 |
| ☐ 104 Chris Chambers | .60 | .25 |
| ☐ 105 Randy McMichael | .50 | .20 |
| ☐ 106 Zach Thomas | .75 | .30 |
| ☐ 107 Brad Johnson | .60 | .25 |
| ☐ 108 Chester Taylor | .60 | .25 |
| ☐ 109 Antoine Winfield | .50 | .20 |
| ☐ 110 Koren Robinson | .50 | .20 |
| ☐ 111 Travis Taylor | .50 | .20 |
| ☐ 112 Darren Sharper | .50 | .20 |
| ☐ 113 Tom Brady | 1.25 | .50 |
| ☐ 114 Corey Dillon | .60 | .25 |
| ☐ 115 Deion Branch | .60 | .25 |
| ☐ 116 Reche Caldwell | .50 | .20 |
| ☐ 117 Ben Watson | .50 | .20 |
| ☐ 118 Tedy Bruschi | .75 | .30 |
| ☐ 119 Rodney Harrison | .50 | .20 |
| ☐ 120 Drew Brees | .75 | .30 |
| ☐ 121 Deuce McAllister | .60 | .25 |
| ☐ 122 Joe Horn | .60 | .25 |
| ☐ 123 Donte Stallworth | .60 | .25 |
| ☐ 124 Devery Henderson | .50 | .20 |
| ☐ 125 Will Smith | .50 | .20 |
| ☐ 126 Eli Manning | 1.00 | .40 |
| ☐ 127 Tiki Barber | .75 | .30 |
| ☐ 128 Plaxico Burress | .60 | .25 |
| ☐ 129 Amani Toomer | .60 | .25 |
| ☐ 130 Jeremy Shockey | .75 | .30 |
| ☐ 131 Michael Strahan | .60 | .25 |
| ☐ 132 Osi Umenyiora | .60 | .25 |
| ☐ 133 Chad Pennington | .60 | .25 |
| ☐ 134 Curtis Martin | .75 | .30 |
| ☐ 135 Justin McCareins | .50 | .20 |
| ☐ 136 Laveranues Coles | .60 | .25 |
| ☐ 137 Jonathan Vilma | .60 | .25 |

| | | |
|---|---|---|
| ☐ 138 Shaun Ellis | .50 | .20 |
| ☐ 139 Aaron Brooks | .60 | .25 |
| ☐ 140 LaMont Jordan | .60 | .25 |
| ☐ 141 Randy Moss | .75 | .30 |
| ☐ 142 Jerry Porter | .60 | .25 |
| ☐ 143 Doug Gabriel | .50 | .20 |
| ☐ 144 Derrick Burgess | .50 | .20 |
| ☐ 145 Donovan McNabb | .75 | .30 |
| ☐ 146 Brian Westbrook | .60 | .25 |
| ☐ 147 Jevon Kearse | .60 | .25 |
| ☐ 148 Reggie Brown | .60 | .25 |
| ☐ 149 L.J. Smith | .50 | .20 |
| ☐ 150 Brian Dawkins | .60 | .25 |
| ☐ 151 Ben Roethlisberger | 1.25 | .50 |
| ☐ 152 Willie Parker | 1.00 | .40 |
| ☐ 153 Hines Ward | .75 | .30 |
| ☐ 154 Cedrick Wilson | .50 | .20 |
| ☐ 155 Heath Miller | .60 | .25 |
| ☐ 156 Joey Porter | .50 | .20 |
| ☐ 157 Troy Polamalu | 1.00 | .40 |
| ☐ 158 Philip Rivers | .75 | .30 |
| ☐ 159 LaDainian Tomlinson | 1.00 | .40 |
| ☐ 160 Keenan McCardell | .60 | .25 |
| ☐ 161 Eric Parker | .50 | .20 |
| ☐ 162 Antonio Gates | .75 | .30 |
| ☐ 163 Shawne Merriman | .60 | .25 |
| ☐ 164 Donnie Edwards | .50 | .20 |
| ☐ 165 Alex Smith QB | .75 | .30 |
| ☐ 166 Frank Gore | .75 | .30 |
| ☐ 167 Antonio Bryant | .50 | .20 |
| ☐ 168 Eric Johnson | .50 | .20 |
| ☐ 169 Arnaz Battle | .50 | .20 |
| ☐ 170 Bryant Young | .50 | .20 |
| ☐ 171 Matt Hasselbeck | .60 | .25 |
| ☐ 172 Shaun Alexander | .75 | .30 |
| ☐ 173 Darrell Jackson | .60 | .25 |
| ☐ 174 Etric Pruitt | .50 | .20 |
| ☐ 175 Julian Peterson | .60 | .25 |
| ☐ 176 Lofa Tatupu | .60 | .25 |
| ☐ 177 Marc Bulger | .60 | .25 |
| ☐ 178 Steven Jackson | .75 | .30 |
| ☐ 179 Torry Holt | .60 | .25 |
| ☐ 180 Kevin Curtis | .60 | .25 |
| ☐ 181 Isaac Bruce | .60 | .25 |
| ☐ 182 Leonard Little | .50 | .20 |
| ☐ 183 Chris Simms | .60 | .25 |
| ☐ 184 Cadillac Williams | .75 | .30 |
| ☐ 185 Joey Galloway | .60 | .25 |
| ☐ 186 Michael Clayton | .60 | .25 |
| ☐ 187 Derrick Brooks | .60 | .25 |
| ☐ 188 Ronde Barber | .60 | .25 |
| ☐ 189 Billy Volek | .50 | .20 |
| ☐ 190 Chris Brown | .60 | .25 |
| ☐ 191 Drew Bennett | .60 | .25 |
| ☐ 192 Ben Troupe | .50 | .20 |
| ☐ 193 David Givens | .60 | .25 |
| ☐ 194 Adam Jones | .50 | .20 |
| ☐ 195 Mark Brunell | .60 | .25 |
| ☐ 196 Clinton Portis | .75 | .30 |
| ☐ 197 Santana Moss | .60 | .25 |
| ☐ 198 Chris Cooley | .60 | .25 |
| ☐ 199 Antwaan Randle El | .60 | .25 |
| ☐ 200 Sean Taylor | .60 | .25 |
| ☐ 201 A.J. Hawk RC | 12.00 | 5.00 |
| ☐ 202 Anthony Fasano RC | 6.00 | 2.50 |
| ☐ 203 Brian Calhoun RC | 5.00 | 2.00 |
| ☐ 204 Chad Greenway RC | 6.00 | 2.50 |
| ☐ 205 Chad Jackson RC | 5.00 | 2.00 |
| ☐ 206 DeAngelo Williams RC | 10.00 | 4.00 |
| ☐ 207 D'Brickashaw Ferguson RC | 6.00 | 2.50 |
| ☐ 208 Brodie Croyle RC | 8.00 | 3.00 |
| ☐ 209 Haloti Ngata RC | 6.00 | 2.50 |
| ☐ 210 Jay Cutler RC | 25.00 | 10.00 |
| ☐ 211 Joseph Addai RC | 20.00 | 8.00 |
| ☐ 212 Laurence Maroney RC | 15.00 | 6.00 |
| ☐ 213 LenDale White RC | 12.00 | 5.00 |
| ☐ 214 Maurice Drew RC | 12.00 | 5.00 |
| ☐ 215 Mario Williams RC | 10.00 | 4.00 |
| ☐ 216 Matt Leinart RC | 20.00 | 8.00 |
| ☐ 217 Maurice Stovall RC | 6.00 | 2.50 |
| ☐ 218 Michael Huff RC | 6.00 | 2.50 |
| ☐ 219 Reggie Bush RC | 25.00 | 10.00 |
| ☐ 220 Santonio Holmes RC | 15.00 | 6.00 |
| ☐ 221 Sinorice Moss RC | 6.00 | 2.50 |

| | | |
|---|---|---|
| ❏ 222 Kellen Clemens RC | 8.00 | 3.00 |
| ❏ 223 Tarvaris Jackson RC | 6.00 | 2.50 |
| ❏ 224 Vernon Davis RC | 6.00 | 2.50 |
| ❏ 225 Vince Young RC | 20.00 | 8.00 |
| ❏ 226 Donte Whitner RC | 2.50 | 1.00 |
| ❏ 227 Antonio Cromartie RC | 2.50 | 1.00 |
| ❏ 228 Ashton Youboty RC | 2.50 | 1.00 |
| ❏ 229 Bobby Carpenter RC | 2.50 | 1.00 |
| ❏ 230 Brad Smith RC | 2.50 | 1.00 |
| ❏ 231 Brandon Williams RC | 2.50 | 1.00 |
| ❏ 232 Dominique Byrd RC | 2.00 | .75 |
| ❏ 233 Brodrick Bunkley RC | 2.50 | 1.00 |
| ❏ 234 Charlie Whitehurst RC | 2.50 | 1.00 |
| ❏ 235 Demetrius Williams RC | 2.50 | 1.00 |
| ❏ 236 Cory Rodgers RC | 2.50 | 1.00 |
| ❏ 237 Daniel Bullocks RC | 2.50 | 1.00 |
| ❏ 238 Manny Lawson RC | 2.50 | 1.00 |
| ❏ 239 Darrell Hackney RC | 2.00 | .75 |
| ❏ 240 Darryl Tapp RC | 2.00 | .75 |
| ❏ 241 David Thomas RC | 2.50 | 1.00 |
| ❏ 242 DeMeco Ryans RC | 3.00 | 1.25 |
| ❏ 243 Derek Hagan RC | 2.50 | 1.00 |
| ❏ 244 Devin Hester RC | 5.00 | 2.00 |
| ❏ 245 D'Qwell Jackson RC | 2.00 | .75 |
| ❏ 246 Brandon Marshall RC | 3.00 | 1.25 |
| ❏ 247 Ernie Sims RC | 2.50 | 1.00 |
| ❏ 248 Gabe Watson RC | 2.00 | .75 |
| ❏ 249 Jason Allen RC | 2.50 | 1.00 |
| ❏ 250 Greg Jennings RC | 4.00 | 1.50 |
| ❏ 251 Marcus Vick RC | 2.00 | .75 |
| ❏ 252 Jason Avant RC | 2.00 | .75 |
| ❏ 253 Jeremy Bloom RC | 2.00 | .75 |
| ❏ 254 Jerome Harrison RC | 2.50 | 1.00 |
| ❏ 255 Joe Klopfenstein RC | 2.00 | .75 |
| ❏ 256 Johnathan Joseph RC | 2.00 | .75 |
| ❏ 257 Jimmy Williams RC | 2.50 | 1.00 |
| ❏ 258 Kamerion Wimbley RC | 2.50 | 1.00 |
| ❏ 259 Leon Washington RC | 2.50 | 1.00 |
| ❏ 260 Marcedes Lewis RC | 2.50 | 1.00 |
| ❏ 261 Marcus McNeill RC | 2.00 | .75 |
| ❏ 262 Mathias Kiwanuka RC | 3.00 | 1.25 |
| ❏ 263 Leonard Pope RC | 2.50 | 1.00 |
| ❏ 264 Tamba Hali RC | 2.50 | 1.00 |
| ❏ 265 Mike Hass RC | 2.50 | 1.00 |
| ❏ 266 Omar Jacobs RC | 2.00 | .75 |
| ❏ 267 Jerious Norwood RC | 3.00 | 1.25 |
| ❏ 268 Owen Daniels RC | 2.50 | 1.00 |
| ❏ 269 P.J. Daniels RC | 2.00 | .75 |
| ❏ 270 Ray Edwards RC | 2.00 | .75 |
| ❏ 271 Michael Robinson RC | 2.50 | 1.00 |
| ❏ 272 Rocky McIntosh RC | 2.50 | 1.00 |
| ❏ 273 Travis Wilson RC | 2.50 | 1.00 |
| ❏ 274 Tye Hill RC | 2.50 | 1.00 |
| ❏ 275 Thomas Howard RC | 2.50 | 1.00 |

## 2007 Upper Deck

| | | |
|---|---|---|
| ❏ 1 Karlos Dansby | .50 | .20 |
| ❏ 2 Edgerrin James | .60 | .25 |
| ❏ 3 Matt Leinart | .75 | .30 |
| ❏ 4 Larry Fitzgerald | .75 | .30 |
| ❏ 5 Anquan Boldin | .60 | .25 |
| ❏ 6 Joe Horn | .60 | .25 |
| ❏ 7 Michael Jenkins | .60 | .25 |
| ❏ 8 Michael Vick | .75 | .30 |
| ❏ 9 Warrick Dunn | .60 | .25 |
| ❏ 10 Alge Crumpler | .60 | .25 |
| ❏ 11 Derrick Mason | .50 | .20 |

| | | |
|---|---|---|
| ❏ 12 Ed Reed | .60 | .25 |
| ❏ 13 Willis McGahee | .60 | .25 |
| ❏ 14 Steve McNair | .60 | .25 |
| ❏ 15 Mark Clayton | .60 | .25 |
| ❏ 16 Todd Heap | .50 | .20 |
| ❏ 17 Ray Lewis | .75 | .30 |
| ❏ 18 J.P. Losman | .50 | .20 |
| ❏ 19 Peerless Price | .50 | .20 |
| ❏ 20 Lee Evans | .60 | .25 |
| ❏ 21 Anthony Thomas | .50 | .20 |
| ❏ 22 David Carr | .60 | .25 |
| ❏ 23 DeAngelo Williams | .75 | .30 |
| ❏ 24 Julius Peppers | .60 | .25 |
| ❏ 25 Jake Delhomme | .60 | .25 |
| ❏ 26 DeShaun Foster | .50 | .20 |
| ❏ 27 Steve Smith | .60 | .25 |
| ❏ 28 Muhsin Muhammad | .60 | .25 |
| ❏ 29 Rex Grossman | .60 | .25 |
| ❏ 30 Desmond Clark | .50 | .20 |
| ❏ 31 Devin Hester | .75 | .30 |
| ❏ 32 Cedric Benson | .60 | .25 |
| ❏ 33 Bernard Berrian | .50 | .20 |
| ❏ 34 Brian Urlacher | .75 | .30 |
| ❏ 35 Justin Smith | .50 | .20 |
| ❏ 36 T.J. Houshmandzadeh | .60 | .25 |
| ❏ 37 Carson Palmer | .75 | .30 |
| ❏ 38 Rudi Johnson | .60 | .25 |
| ❏ 39 Chad Johnson | .60 | .25 |
| ❏ 40 Kamerion Wimbley | .50 | .20 |
| ❏ 41 Charlie Frye | .60 | .25 |
| ❏ 42 Tim Carter | .50 | .20 |
| ❏ 43 Jamal Lewis | .60 | .25 |
| ❏ 44 Kellen Winslow | .60 | .25 |
| ❏ 45 Braylon Edwards | .60 | .25 |
| ❏ 46 Roy Williams S | .60 | .25 |
| ❏ 47 Marion Barber | .75 | .30 |
| ❏ 48 Jason Witten | .60 | .25 |
| ❏ 49 Terry Glenn | .60 | .25 |
| ❏ 50 Demarcus Ware | .60 | .25 |
| ❏ 51 Tony Romo | 1.50 | .60 |
| ❏ 52 Julius Jones | .60 | .25 |
| ❏ 53 Terrell Owens | .75 | .30 |
| ❏ 54 Mike Bell | .60 | .25 |
| ❏ 55 John Lynch | .60 | .25 |
| ❏ 56 Rod Smith | .60 | .25 |
| ❏ 57 Travis Henry | .60 | .25 |
| ❏ 58 Jay Cutler | .75 | .30 |
| ❏ 59 Javon Walker | .60 | .25 |
| ❏ 60 Champ Bailey | .60 | .25 |
| ❏ 61 Tatum Bell | .50 | .20 |
| ❏ 62 Mike Furrey | .60 | .25 |
| ❏ 63 Jon Kitna | .60 | .25 |
| ❏ 64 Kevin Jones | .50 | .20 |
| ❏ 65 Roy Williams WR | .60 | .25 |
| ❏ 66 Bubba Franks | .50 | .20 |
| ❏ 67 Charles Woodson | .60 | .25 |
| ❏ 68 Brett Favre | 1.50 | .60 |
| ❏ 69 Donald Driver | .60 | .25 |
| ❏ 70 A.J. Hawk | .75 | .30 |
| ❏ 71 Ahman Green | .60 | .25 |
| ❏ 72 DeMeco Ryans | .60 | .25 |
| ❏ 73 Matt Schaub | .60 | .25 |
| ❏ 74 Andre Johnson | .60 | .25 |
| ❏ 75 Mario Williams | .60 | .25 |
| ❏ 76 Ron Dayne | .60 | .25 |
| ❏ 77 Dwight Freeney | .60 | .25 |
| ❏ 78 Dallas Clark | .60 | .25 |
| ❏ 79 Peyton Manning | 1.25 | .50 |
| ❏ 80 Marvin Harrison | .75 | .30 |
| ❏ 81 Reggie Wayne | .60 | .25 |
| ❏ 82 Joseph Addai | .75 | .30 |
| ❏ 83 Matt Jones | .60 | .25 |
| ❏ 84 David Garrard | .60 | .25 |
| ❏ 85 Ernest Wilford | .60 | .25 |
| ❏ 86 Reggie Williams | .60 | .25 |
| ❏ 87 Maurice Jones-Drew | .75 | .30 |
| ❏ 88 Fred Taylor | .60 | .25 |
| ❏ 89 Byron Leftwich | .60 | .25 |
| ❏ 90 Eddie Kennison | .50 | .20 |
| ❏ 91 Samie Parker | .50 | .20 |
| ❏ 92 Derrick Johnson | .50 | .20 |
| ❏ 93 Trent Green | .60 | .25 |
| ❏ 94 Larry Johnson | .60 | .25 |
| ❏ 95 Tony Gonzalez | .60 | .25 |

| | | |
|---|---|---|
| ❏ 96 Damon Huard | .60 | .25 |
| ❏ 97 Zach Thomas | .60 | .25 |
| ❏ 98 Daunte Culpepper | .60 | .25 |
| ❏ 99 Ronnie Brown | .60 | .25 |
| ❏ 100 Jason Taylor | .50 | .20 |
| ❏ 101 Chris Chambers | .60 | .25 |
| ❏ 102 Antoine Winfield | .50 | .20 |
| ❏ 103 Ryan Longwell | .50 | .20 |
| ❏ 104 Chester Taylor | .50 | .20 |
| ❏ 105 Tarvaris Jackson | .60 | .25 |
| ❏ 106 Troy Williamson | .50 | .20 |
| ❏ 107 Rodney Harrison | .50 | .20 |
| ❏ 108 Randy Moss | .75 | .30 |
| ❏ 109 Stephen Gostkowski | .50 | .20 |
| ❏ 110 Donte Stallworth | .60 | .25 |
| ❏ 111 Tom Brady | 1.50 | .60 |
| ❏ 112 Laurence Maroney | .75 | .30 |
| ❏ 113 Ben Watson | .50 | .20 |
| ❏ 114 Tedy Bruschi | .75 | .30 |
| ❏ 115 Charles Grant | .50 | .20 |
| ❏ 116 Michael Lewis | .50 | .20 |
| ❏ 117 Drew Brees | .60 | .25 |
| ❏ 118 Marques Colston | .75 | .30 |
| ❏ 119 Reggie Bush | 1.00 | .40 |
| ❏ 120 Deuce McAllister | .60 | .25 |
| ❏ 121 Amani Toomer | .60 | .25 |
| ❏ 122 Reuben Droughns | .60 | .25 |
| ❏ 123 Michael Strahan | .60 | .25 |
| ❏ 124 Plaxico Burress | .60 | .25 |
| ❏ 125 Osi Umenyiora | .50 | .20 |
| ❏ 126 Eli Manning | .75 | .30 |
| ❏ 127 Jeremy Shockey | .60 | .25 |
| ❏ 128 Brandon Jacobs | .60 | .25 |
| ❏ 129 Jonathan Vilma | .60 | .25 |
| ❏ 130 Jerricho Cotchery | .50 | .20 |
| ❏ 131 Chris Baker | .50 | .20 |
| ❏ 132 Chad Pennington | .60 | .25 |
| ❏ 133 Leon Washington | .60 | .25 |
| ❏ 134 Laveranues Coles | .60 | .25 |
| ❏ 135 Nnamdi Asomugha | .50 | .20 |
| ❏ 136 Dominic Rhodes | .60 | .25 |
| ❏ 137 Warren Sapp | .50 | .20 |
| ❏ 138 Justin Fargas | .50 | .20 |
| ❏ 139 Ronald Curry | .60 | .25 |
| ❏ 140 Brian Dawkins | .60 | .25 |
| ❏ 141 L.J. Smith | .50 | .20 |
| ❏ 142 Mike Patterson | .50 | .20 |
| ❏ 143 Brian Westbrook | .60 | .25 |
| ❏ 144 Reggie Brown | .60 | .25 |
| ❏ 145 Donovan McNabb | .75 | .30 |
| ❏ 146 Hines Ward | .75 | .30 |
| ❏ 147 James Farrior | .50 | .20 |
| ❏ 148 Ike Taylor | .50 | .20 |
| ❏ 149 Santonio Holmes | .60 | .25 |
| ❏ 150 Ben Roethlisberger | 1.00 | .40 |
| ❏ 151 Willie Parker | .75 | .30 |
| ❏ 152 Troy Polamalu | .75 | .30 |
| ❏ 153 Michael Turner | .60 | .25 |
| ❏ 154 Vincent Jackson | .50 | .20 |
| ❏ 155 Nate Kaeding | .50 | .20 |
| ❏ 156 Philip Rivers | .75 | .30 |
| ❏ 157 Antonio Gates | .60 | .25 |
| ❏ 158 Shawne Merriman | .60 | .25 |
| ❏ 159 LaDainian Tomlinson | 1.00 | .40 |
| ❏ 160 Amaz Battle | .50 | .20 |
| ❏ 161 Nate Clements | .50 | .20 |
| ❏ 162 Ashley Lelie | .60 | .25 |
| ❏ 163 Alex Smith QB | .75 | .30 |
| ❏ 164 Frank Gore | .75 | .30 |
| ❏ 165 Vernon Davis | .60 | .25 |
| ❏ 166 Mack Strong | .50 | .20 |
| ❏ 167 Lofa Tatupu | .60 | .25 |
| ❏ 168 Maurice Morris | .50 | .20 |
| ❏ 169 Bobby Engram | .50 | .20 |
| ❏ 170 Matt Hasselbeck | .60 | .25 |
| ❏ 171 Shaun Alexander | .60 | .25 |
| ❏ 172 Deion Branch | .60 | .25 |
| ❏ 173 Leonard Little | .50 | .20 |
| ❏ 174 Pisa Tinoisamoa | .50 | .20 |
| ❏ 175 Drew Bennett | .50 | .20 |
| ❏ 176 Steven Jackson | .75 | .30 |
| ❏ 177 Marc Bulger | .60 | .25 |
| ❏ 178 Torry Holt | .60 | .25 |
| ❏ 179 Isaac Bruce | .60 | .25 |

|  |  | | |
|---|---|---|---|
| 180 | Ronde Barber | .50 | .20 |
| 181 | Chris Simms | .50 | .20 |
| 182 | Mike Alstott | .60 | .25 |
| 183 | Derrick Brooks | .60 | .25 |
| 184 | Cadillac Williams | .60 | .25 |
| 185 | Michael Clayton | .60 | .25 |
| 186 | Joey Galloway | .60 | .25 |
| 187 | Brandon Jones | .50 | .20 |
| 188 | Keith Bulluck | .50 | .20 |
| 189 | Nick Harper | .50 | .20 |
| 190 | David Givens | .50 | .20 |
| 191 | Vince Young | .75 | .30 |
| 192 | LenDale White | .60 | .25 |
| 193 | Mark Brunell | .60 | .25 |
| 194 | Sean Taylor | .50 | .20 |
| 195 | Chris Cooley | .50 | .20 |
| 196 | Brandon Lloyd | .60 | .25 |
| 197 | Jason Campbell | .60 | .25 |
| 198 | Clinton Portis | .60 | .25 |
| 199 | Santana Moss | .60 | .25 |
| 200 | Antwaan Randle El | .50 | .20 |
| 201 | Levi Brown RC | 4.00 | 1.50 |
| 202 | Alan Branch RC | 3.00 | 1.25 |
| 203 | Buster Davis RC | 3.00 | 1.25 |
| 204 | Steve Breaston RC | 4.00 | 1.50 |
| 205 | Justin Blalock RC | 2.50 | 1.00 |
| 206 | Chris Houston RC | 3.00 | 1.25 |
| 207 | Laurent Robinson RC | 3.00 | 1.25 |
| 208 | Ben Grubbs RC | 3.00 | 1.25 |
| 209 | Troy Smith RC | 5.00 | 2.00 |
| 210 | Yamon Figurs RC | 4.00 | 1.50 |
| 211 | Le'Ron McClain RC | 6.00 | 2.50 |
| 212 | Trent Edwards RC | 10.00 | 4.00 |
| 213 | Dwayne Wright RC | 3.00 | 1.25 |
| 214 | Jon Beason RC | 4.00 | 1.50 |
| 215 | Ryan Kalil RC | 3.00 | 1.25 |
| 216 | Dan Bazuin RC | 3.00 | 1.25 |
| 217 | Garrett Wolfe RC | 4.00 | 1.50 |
| 218 | Michael Okwo RC | 3.00 | 1.25 |
| 219 | Chris Leak RC | 3.00 | 1.25 |
| 220 | Leon Hall RC | 3.00 | 1.25 |
| 221 | Jeff Rowe RC | 3.00 | 1.25 |
| 222 | Eric Wright RC | 4.00 | 1.50 |
| 223 | Isaiah Stanback RC | 4.00 | 1.50 |
| 224 | Anthony Spencer RC | 4.00 | 1.50 |
| 225 | Jarvis Moss RC | 4.00 | 1.50 |
| 226 | Tim Crowder RC | 3.00 | 1.25 |
| 227 | Ikaika Alama-Francis RC | 4.00 | 1.50 |
| 228 | Justin Harrell RC | 4.00 | 1.50 |
| 230 | James Jones RC | 4.00 | 1.50 |
| 231 | Jacoby Jones RC | 4.00 | 1.50 |
| 232 | Tony Ugoh RC | 3.00 | 1.25 |
| 233 | Daymeion Hughes RC | 3.00 | 1.25 |
| 234 | Reggie Nelson RC | 3.00 | 1.25 |
| 235 | Justin Durant RC | 3.00 | 1.25 |
| 236 | Turk McBride RC | 3.00 | 1.25 |
| 237 | DeMarcus Tank Tyler RC | 3.00 | 1.25 |
| 239 | Lorenzo Booker RC | 4.00 | 1.50 |
| 240 | Marcus McCauley RC | 3.00 | 1.25 |
| 241 | Brandon Meriweather RC | 4.00 | 1.50 |
| 242 | Antonio Pittman RC | 4.00 | 1.50 |
| 243 | Usama Young RC | 3.00 | 1.25 |
| 244 | Aaron Ross RC | 4.00 | 1.50 |
| 245 | Zak DeOssie RC | 4.00 | 1.50 |
| 246 | Darrelle Revis RC | 4.00 | 1.50 |
| 247 | David Harris RC | 3.00 | 1.25 |
| 248 | Zach Miller RC | 2.50 | 1.00 |
| 249 | Johnnie Lee Higgins RC | 3.00 | 1.25 |
| 250 | Michael Bush RC | 4.00 | 1.50 |
| 251 | Quentin Moses RC | 3.00 | 1.25 |
| 252 | Victor Abiamiri RC | 4.00 | 1.50 |
| 253 | Tony Hunt RC | 4.00 | 1.50 |
| 254 | Stewart Bradley RC | 4.00 | 1.50 |
| 255 | Lawrence Timmons RC | 4.00 | 1.50 |
| 256 | LaMarr Woodley RC | 4.00 | 1.50 |
| 257 | Matt Spaeth RC | 4.00 | 1.50 |
| 258 | Eric Weddle RC | 3.00 | 1.25 |
| 259 | Scott Chandler RC | 3.00 | 1.25 |
| 260 | Anthony Waters RC | 3.00 | 1.25 |
| 261 | Joe Staley RC | 3.00 | 1.25 |
| 262 | Jason Hill RC | 4.00 | 1.50 |
| 263 | Josh Wilson RC | 3.00 | 1.25 |
| 264 | Brandon Mebane RC | 3.00 | 1.25 |
| 265 | Adam Carriker RC | 3.00 | 1.25 |
| 266 | Jonathan Wade RC | 3.00 | 1.25 |
| 267 | Arron Sears RC | 3.00 | 1.25 |
| 268 | Sabby Piscitelli RC | 4.00 | 1.50 |
| 269 | Quincy Black RC | 4.00 | 1.50 |
| 270 | Michael Griffin RC | 4.00 | 1.50 |
| 271 | Chris Henry RB RC | 4.00 | 1.50 |
| 272 | Paul Williams RC | 3.00 | 1.25 |
| 273 | Chris Davis RC | 3.00 | 1.25 |
| 274 | H.B. Blades RC | 3.00 | 1.25 |
| 275 | Jordan Palmer RC | 3.00 | 1.25 |
| 276 | JaMarcus Russell RC | 10.00 | 4.00 |
| 277 | Calvin Johnson RC | 10.00 | 4.00 |
| 278 | Brady Quinn RC | 12.00 | 5.00 |
| 279 | Adrian Peterson RC | 30.00 | 12.00 |
| 280 | Marshawn Lynch RC | 8.00 | 3.00 |
| 281 | Ted Ginn Jr. RC | 6.00 | 2.50 |
| 282 | LaRon Landry RC | 5.00 | 2.00 |
| 283 | Jamaal Anderson RC | 3.00 | 1.25 |
| 284 | Amobi Okoye RC | 4.00 | 1.50 |
| 285 | Dwayne Bowe RC | 8.00 | 3.00 |
| 286 | Greg Olsen RC | 5.00 | 2.00 |
| 287 | Gaines Adams RC | 4.00 | 1.50 |
| 288 | Patrick Willis RC | 8.00 | 3.00 |
| 289 | Drew Stanton RC | 4.00 | 1.50 |
| 290 | Kevin Kolb RC | 6.00 | 2.50 |
| 291 | John Beck RC | 4.00 | 1.50 |
| 292 | Anthony Gonzalez RC | 6.00 | 2.50 |
| 294 | Robert Meachem RC | 4.00 | 1.50 |
| 295 | Joe Thomas RC | 4.00 | 1.50 |
| 296 | Dwayne Jarrett RC | 4.00 | 1.50 |
| 297 | Kenny Irons RC | 4.00 | 1.50 |
| 298 | Brian Leonard RC | 4.00 | 1.50 |
| 299 | Craig Buster Davis RC | 4.00 | 1.50 |
| 300 | Steve Smith USC RC | 5.00 | 2.00 |

## 2008 Upper Deck

| | | | |
|---|---|---|---|
| COMPLETE SET (325) | | 250.00 | 125.00 |
| COMP.SET w/o SP's (300) | | 50.00 | 25.00 |
| COMP.SET w/o RC's (200) | | 10.00 | 10.00 |
| 1 | Edgerrin James | .50 | .20 |
| 2 | Matt Leinart | .60 | .25 |
| 3 | Larry Fitzgerald | .60 | .25 |
| 4 | Anquan Boldin | .50 | .20 |
| 5 | Antrel Rolle | .40 | .15 |
| 6 | Joe Horn | .50 | .20 |
| 7 | Warrick Dunn | .50 | .20 |
| 8 | Alge Crumpler | .50 | .20 |
| 9 | Jerious Norwood | .50 | .20 |
| 10 | Michael Jenkins | .40 | .15 |
| 11 | Derrick Mason | .40 | .15 |
| 13 | Willis McGahee | .50 | .20 |
| 14 | Steve McNair | .50 | .20 |
| 15 | Todd Heap | .40 | .15 |
| 16 | Ray Lewis | .60 | .25 |
| 17 | Terrell Suggs | .40 | .15 |
| 18 | Trent Edwards | .60 | .25 |
| 19 | Lee Evans | .50 | .20 |
| 20 | Roscoe Parrish | .40 | .15 |
| 21 | Marshawn Lynch | .60 | .25 |
| 22 | Stacy Andrews | .40 | .15 |
| 23 | DeAngelo Williams | .50 | .20 |
| 24 | Julius Peppers | .50 | .20 |
| 25 | Steve Smith | .50 | .20 |
| 26 | Jake Delhomme | .50 | .20 |
| 27 | Lance Briggs | .40 | .15 |
| 28 | Rex Grossman | .50 | .20 |
| 29 | Devin Hester | .60 | .25 |
| 30 | Bernard Berrian | .50 | .20 |
| 31 | Brian Urlacher | .60 | .25 |
| 32 | Cedric Benson | .40 | .15 |
| 33 | Greg Olsen | .50 | .20 |
| 34 | T.J. Houshmandzadeh | .50 | .20 |
| 35 | Carson Palmer | .60 | .25 |
| 36 | Rudi Johnson | .50 | .20 |
| 37 | Chad Johnson | .60 | .25 |
| 38 | Kurt Warner | .60 | .25 |
| 39 | Kamerion Wimbley | .40 | .15 |
| 40 | Josh Cribbs | .50 | .20 |
| 41 | Jamal Lewis | .50 | .20 |
| 42 | Kellen Winslow | .50 | .20 |
| 43 | Braylon Edwards | .50 | .20 |
| 44 | Eric Wright | .40 | .15 |
| 45 | Anthony Henry | .40 | .15 |
| 46 | Roy Williams S | .50 | .20 |
| 47 | Marion Barber | .60 | .25 |
| 48 | Jason Witten | .50 | .20 |
| 49 | DeMarcus Ware | .50 | .20 |
| 50 | Tony Romo | 1.00 | .40 |
| 51 | Julius Jones | .50 | .20 |
| 52 | Terrell Owens | .60 | .25 |
| 53 | Greg Ellis | .40 | .15 |
| 54 | Patrick Crayton | .40 | .15 |
| 55 | John Lynch | .50 | .20 |
| 56 | Brandon Marshall | .50 | .20 |
| 57 | Travis Henry | .50 | .20 |
| 58 | Jay Cutler | .60 | .25 |
| 59 | De Bly | .40 | .15 |
| 60 | Javon Walker | .50 | .20 |
| 61 | Champ Bailey | .40 | .15 |
| 62 | Tatum Bell | .40 | .15 |
| 63 | Calvin Johnson | .60 | .25 |
| 64 | Jon Kitna | .50 | .20 |
| 65 | Roy Williams WR | .50 | .20 |
| 66 | Ernie Sims | .40 | .15 |
| 67 | Aaron Kampman | .40 | .15 |
| 68 | Bubba Franks | .40 | .15 |
| 69 | Charles Woodson | .50 | .20 |
| 70 | Brett Favre | 1.50 | .60 |
| 71 | Donald Driver | .50 | .20 |
| 72 | A.J. Hawk | .50 | .20 |
| 73 | Ahman Green | .50 | .20 |
| 74 | DeMeco Ryans | .50 | .20 |
| 75 | Andre Johnson | .50 | .20 |
| 76 | Mario Williams | .50 | .20 |
| 77 | Ron Dayne | .50 | .20 |
| 78 | Dwight Freeney | .50 | .20 |
| 79 | Dallas Clark | .50 | .20 |
| 80 | Peyton Manning | 1.00 | .40 |
| 81 | Marvin Harrison | .60 | .25 |
| 82 | Reggie Wayne | .60 | .25 |
| 83 | Joseph Addai | .60 | .25 |
| 84 | Matt Jones | .50 | .20 |
| 85 | David Garrard | .50 | .20 |
| 86 | Ernest Wilford | .40 | .15 |
| 87 | Reggie Williams | .50 | .20 |
| 88 | Maurice Jones-Drew | .50 | .20 |
| 89 | Fred Taylor | .60 | .25 |
| 90 | Reggie Nelson | .40 | .15 |
| 91 | Dwayne Bowe | .50 | .20 |
| 92 | Samie Parker | .40 | .15 |
| 93 | Derrick Johnson | .50 | .20 |
| 94 | Larry Johnson | .50 | .20 |
| 95 | Brodie Croyle | .60 | .25 |
| 96 | Tony Gonzalez | .50 | .20 |
| 97 | Jared Allen | .50 | .20 |
| 98 | Zach Thomas | .50 | .20 |
| 99 | Ronnie Brown | .50 | .20 |
| 100 | Jason Taylor | .50 | .20 |
| 101 | Ted Ginn Jr. | .60 | .25 |
| 102 | John Beck | .40 | .15 |
| 103 | Antoine Winfield | .40 | .15 |
| 104 | Adrian Peterson | 1.25 | .50 |
| 105 | Bob Sanders | .50 | .20 |
| 106 | Sidney Rice | .50 | .20 |
| 107 | Chester Taylor | .40 | .15 |
| 108 | Wes Welker | .60 | .25 |
| 109 | Rodney Harrison | .40 | .15 |
| 110 | Randy Moss | .60 | .25 |
| 111 | Donte Stallworth | .50 | .20 |
| 112 | Tom Brady | 1.00 | .40 |

| | | |
|---|---|---|
| ❏ 113 Laurence Maroney | .50 | .20 |
| ❏ 114 Ben Watson | .40 | .15 |
| ❏ 115 Tedy Bruschi | .60 | .25 |
| ❏ 116 Mike Vrabel | .40 | .15 |
| ❏ 117 Charles Grant | .40 | .15 |
| ❏ 118 Drew Brees | .60 | .25 |
| ❏ 119 Marques Colston | .50 | .20 |
| ❏ 120 Reggie Bush | .60 | .25 |
| ❏ 121 Deuce McAllister | .50 | .20 |
| ❏ 122 Mike McKenzie | .40 | .15 |
| ❏ 123 Amani Toomer | .50 | .20 |
| ❏ 124 Michael Strahan | .50 | .20 |
| ❏ 125 Plaxico Burress | .50 | .20 |
| ❏ 126 Osi Umenyiora | .40 | .15 |
| ❏ 127 Eli Manning | .60 | .25 |
| ❏ 128 Jeremy Shockey | .50 | .20 |
| ❏ 129 Brandon Jacobs | .50 | .20 |
| ❏ 130 Antonio Pierce | .40 | .15 |
| ❏ 131 Jonathan Vilma | .40 | .15 |
| ❏ 132 Jerricho Cotchery | .40 | .15 |
| ❏ 133 Kellen Clemens | .40 | .15 |
| ❏ 134 Leon Washington | .40 | .15 |
| ❏ 135 Thomas Jones | .50 | .20 |
| ❏ 136 Kirk Morrison | .40 | .15 |
| ❏ 137 Nnamdi Asomugha | .40 | .15 |
| ❏ 138 Derrick Burgess | .40 | .15 |
| ❏ 139 Justin Fargas | .40 | .15 |
| ❏ 140 Ronald Curry | .50 | .20 |
| ❏ 141 JaMarcus Russell | .60 | .25 |
| ❏ 142 Brian Dawkins | .50 | .20 |
| ❏ 143 Brian Westbrook | .50 | .20 |
| ❏ 144 Reggie Brown | .50 | .20 |
| ❏ 145 Donovan McNabb | .60 | .25 |
| ❏ 146 Hines Ward | .60 | .25 |
| ❏ 147 Santonio Holmes | .50 | .20 |
| ❏ 148 Ben Roethlisberger | .75 | .30 |
| ❏ 149 Willie Parker | .50 | .20 |
| ❏ 150 Troy Polamalu | .60 | .25 |
| ❏ 151 James Farrior | .40 | .15 |
| ❏ 152 Heath Miller | .40 | .15 |
| ❏ 153 Chris Chambers | .50 | .20 |
| ❏ 154 Philip Rivers | .50 | .20 |
| ❏ 155 Antonio Gates | .50 | .20 |
| ❏ 156 Shawne Merriman | .50 | .20 |
| ❏ 157 LaDainian Tomlinson | .75 | .30 |
| ❏ 158 Antonio Cromartie | .40 | .15 |
| ❏ 159 Shaun Phillips | .40 | .15 |
| ❏ 160 Jamal Williams | .40 | .15 |
| ❏ 161 Amaz Battle | .40 | .15 |
| ❏ 162 Nate Clements | .50 | .20 |
| ❏ 163 Alex Smith QB | .50 | .20 |
| ❏ 164 Frank Gore | .50 | .20 |
| ❏ 165 Vernon Davis | .40 | .15 |
| ❏ 166 Patrick Willis | .50 | .20 |
| ❏ 167 Lofa Tatupu | .50 | .20 |
| ❏ 168 Patrick Kerney | .40 | .15 |
| ❏ 169 Bobby Engram | .40 | .15 |
| ❏ 170 Matt Hasselbeck | .50 | .20 |
| ❏ 171 Shawn Andrews | .40 | .15 |
| ❏ 172 Deion Branch | .50 | .20 |
| ❏ 173 D.J. Hackett | .40 | .15 |
| ❏ 174 Leonard Little | .40 | .15 |
| ❏ 175 Pisa Tinoisamoa | .40 | .15 |
| ❏ 176 Steven Jackson | .60 | .25 |
| ❏ 177 Marc Bulger | .50 | .20 |
| ❏ 178 Torry Holt | .50 | .20 |
| ❏ 179 Isaac Bruce | .50 | .20 |
| ❏ 180 Randy McMichael | .40 | .15 |
| ❏ 181 Ronde Barber | .40 | .15 |
| ❏ 182 Cadillac Williams | .50 | .20 |
| ❏ 183 Derrick Brooks | .50 | .20 |
| ❏ 184 Michael Clayton | .40 | .15 |
| ❏ 185 Jeff Garcia | .50 | .20 |
| ❏ 186 Joey Galloway | .50 | .20 |
| ❏ 187 Gaines Adams | .40 | .15 |
| ❏ 188 Keith Bulluck | .40 | .15 |
| ❏ 189 Nick Harper | .40 | .15 |
| ❏ 190 David Givens | .40 | .15 |
| ❏ 191 Vince Young | .60 | .25 |
| ❏ 192 LenDale White | .50 | .20 |
| ❏ 193 Eric Moulds | .50 | .20 |
| ❏ 194 Jason Campbell | .50 | .20 |
| ❏ 195 Randall Godfrey | .40 | .15 |
| ❏ 196 Chris Cooley | .50 | .20 |

| | | |
|---|---|---|
| ❏ 197 Brandon Lloyd | .40 | .15 |
| ❏ 198 Clinton Portis | .50 | .20 |
| ❏ 199 Santana Moss | .50 | .20 |
| ❏ 200 London Fletcher | .40 | .15 |
| ❏ 201 Will Franklin RC | 2.00 | .75 |
| ❏ 202 Jerome Felton RC | 1.25 | .50 |
| ❏ 203 Adrian Arrington RC | 1.50 | .60 |
| ❏ 204 Alex Brink RC | 2.00 | .75 |
| ❏ 205 Allen Patrick RC | 1.50 | .60 |
| ❏ 206 Andre Caldwell RC | 1.50 | .60 |
| ❏ 207 Anthony Morelli RC | 2.00 | .75 |
| ❏ 208 Antoine Cason RC | 2.00 | .75 |
| ❏ 209 Aqib Talib RC | 2.00 | .75 |
| ❏ 210 Ben Moffitt RC | 1.25 | .50 |
| ❏ 211 Caleb Campbell RC | 2.00 | .75 |
| ❏ 212 T.C. Ostrander RC | 1.50 | .60 |
| ❏ 213 Bruce Davis RC | 2.00 | .75 |
| ❏ 214 Calais Campbell RC | 1.50 | .60 |
| ❏ 215 Chris Williams RC | 1.50 | .60 |
| ❏ 216 Chad Henne RC | 3.00 | 1.25 |
| ❏ 217 Chevis Jackson RC | 1.50 | .60 |
| ❏ 218 Chris Ellis RC | 1.50 | .60 |
| ❏ 219 Chris Johnson RC | 5.00 | 2.00 |
| ❏ 220 Cory Boyd RC | 1.50 | .60 |
| ❏ 221 Craig Steltz RC | 1.50 | .60 |
| ❏ 222 DJ Hall RC | 2.00 | .75 |
| ❏ 223 Chauncey Washington RC | 1.50 | .60 |
| ❏ 224 Darius Reynaud RC | 1.50 | .60 |
| ❏ 225 Davone Bess RC | 2.50 | 1.00 |
| ❏ 226 DeJuan Tribble RC | 1.25 | .50 |
| ❏ 227 DeMario Pressley RC | 1.50 | .60 |
| ❏ 228 Dennis Keyes RC | 1.25 | .50 |
| ❏ 229 Derrick Harvey RC | 1.50 | .60 |
| ❏ 230 Donnie Avery RC | 2.50 | 1.00 |
| ❏ 231 Xavier Olmon RC | 2.00 | .75 |
| ❏ 232 Dre Moore RC | 1.50 | .60 |
| ❏ 233 Dustin Keller RC | 2.00 | .75 |
| ❏ 234 Earl Bennett RC | 2.00 | .75 |
| ❏ 235 Erik Ainge RC | 2.00 | .75 |
| ❏ 236 Erin Henderson RC | 1.50 | .60 |
| ❏ 237 Curtis Lofton RC | 2.00 | .75 |
| ❏ 238 Felix Jones RC | 5.00 | 2.00 |
| ❏ 239 Josh Barrett RC | 1.25 | .50 |
| ❏ 240 Gosder Cherilus RC | 1.50 | .60 |
| ❏ 241 Harry Douglas RC | 2.00 | .75 |
| ❏ 242 Colt Brennan RC | 5.00 | 2.00 |
| ❏ 243 J Leman RC | 1.50 | .60 |
| ❏ 244 Jack Ikegwuonu RC | 1.50 | .60 |
| ❏ 245 Jacob Hester RC | 2.00 | .75 |
| ❏ 246 Jacob Tamme RC | 2.00 | .75 |
| ❏ 247 Jamaal Charles RC | 2.50 | 1.00 |
| ❏ 248 James Hardy RC | 2.00 | .75 |
| ❏ 249 Jermichael Finley RC | 2.00 | .75 |
| ❏ 250 Jerod Mayo RC | 3.00 | 1.25 |
| ❏ 251 Joe Flacco RC | 6.00 | 2.50 |
| ❏ 252 John Carlson RC | 2.00 | .75 |
| ❏ 253 John David Booty RC | 2.50 | 1.00 |
| ❏ 254 Jonathan Goff RC | 1.50 | .60 |
| ❏ 255 Jonathan Hefney RC | 1.50 | .60 |
| ❏ 256 Jordon Dizon RC | 2.00 | .75 |
| ❏ 257 Jordy Nelson RC | 2.50 | 1.00 |
| ❏ 258 Josh Johnson RC | 2.00 | .75 |
| ❏ 259 Justin Forsett RC | 2.00 | .75 |
| ❏ 260 Kalvin McRae RC | 1.50 | .60 |
| ❏ 261 Keenan Burton RC | 1.50 | .60 |
| ❏ 262 Kellen Davis RC | 1.25 | .50 |
| ❏ 263 Kentwan Balmer RC | 1.50 | .60 |
| ❏ 264 Keon Lattimore RC | 1.50 | .60 |
| ❏ 265 Kevin O'Connell RC | 2.50 | 1.00 |
| ❏ 266 Kevin Smith RC | 3.00 | 1.25 |
| ❏ 267 Thomas DeCoud RC | 1.25 | .50 |
| ❏ 268 Malcolm Kelly RC | 2.00 | .75 |
| ❏ 269 Marcus Monk RC | 2.00 | .75 |
| ❏ 270 Mario Manningham RC | 2.00 | .75 |
| ❏ 271 Mario Urrutia RC | 1.50 | .60 |
| ❏ 272 Martellus Bennett RC | 2.00 | .75 |
| ❏ 273 Martin Rucker RC | 1.50 | .60 |
| ❏ 274 Matt Flynn RC | 2.50 | 1.00 |
| ❏ 275 Matt Forte RC | 5.00 | 2.00 |
| ❏ 276 Owen Schmitt RC | 2.00 | .75 |
| ❏ 277 Paul Hubbard RC | 1.50 | .60 |
| ❏ 278 Paul Smith RC | 2.00 | .75 |
| ❏ 279 Philip Wheeler RC | 1.50 | .60 |
| ❏ 280 Quentin Groves RC | 1.50 | .60 |

| | | |
|---|---|---|
| ❏ 281 Quintin Demps RC | 1.50 | .60 |
| ❏ 282 Rashard Mendenhall RC | 4.00 | 1.50 |
| ❏ 283 Ray Rice RC | 2.50 | 1.00 |
| ❏ 284 Ryan Clady RC | 2.00 | .75 |
| ❏ 285 Ryan Grice-Mullen RC | 2.00 | .75 |
| ❏ 286 Ryan Torain RC | 2.00 | .75 |
| ❏ 287 Spencer Larsen RC | 1.25 | .50 |
| ❏ 288 Marcus Thomas RC | 1.50 | .60 |
| ❏ 289 Shawn Crable RC | 2.00 | .75 |
| ❏ 290 Frank Okam RC | 1.50 | .60 |
| ❏ 291 Tashard Choice RC | 2.00 | .75 |
| ❏ 292 Terrell Thomas RC | 1.50 | .60 |
| ❏ 293 Thomas Brown RC | 2.00 | .75 |
| ❏ 294 Tom Zbikowski RC | 2.50 | 1.00 |
| ❏ 295 Simeon Castille RC | 2.00 | .75 |
| ❏ 296 Trevor Laws RC | 2.00 | .75 |
| ❏ 297 Vernon Gholston RC | 2.00 | .75 |
| ❏ 298 Vince Hall RC | 1.25 | .50 |
| ❏ 299 Xavier Adibi RC | 1.50 | .60 |
| ❏ 300 Yvenson Bernard RC | 2.00 | .75 |
| ❏ 301 Andre Woodson SP RC | 6.00 | 2.50 |
| ❏ 302 Brian Brohm SP RC | 8.00 | 3.00 |
| ❏ 303 Devin Thomas SP RC | 6.00 | 2.50 |
| ❏ 304 Dennis Dixon SP RC | 6.00 | 2.50 |
| ❏ 305 Matt Ryan SP RC | 25.00 | 10.00 |
| ❏ 306 Darren McFadden SP RC | 15.00 | 6.00 |
| ❏ 307 Jonathan Stewart SP RC | 15.00 | 6.00 |
| ❏ 308 Mike Hart SP RC | 8.00 | 3.00 |
| ❏ 309 DeSean Jackson SP RC | 12.00 | 5.00 |
| ❏ 310 Early Doucet SP RC | 6.00 | 2.50 |
| ❏ 311 Lavelle Hawkins SP RC | 5.00 | 2.00 |
| ❏ 312 Limas Sweed SP RC | 8.00 | 3.00 |
| ❏ 313 Jake Long SP RC | 8.00 | 3.00 |
| ❏ 314 Sam Baker SP RC | 4.00 | 1.50 |
| ❏ 315 Glenn Dorsey SP RC | 8.00 | 3.00 |
| ❏ 316 Sedrick Ellis SP RC | 6.00 | 2.50 |
| ❏ 317 Chris Long SP RC | 6.00 | 2.50 |
| ❏ 318 Lawrence Jackson SP RC | 5.00 | 2.00 |
| ❏ 319 Ali Highsmith SP RC | 4.00 | 1.50 |
| ❏ 320 Dan Connor SP RC | 6.00 | 2.50 |
| ❏ 321 Kenny Phillips SP RC | 6.00 | 2.50 |
| ❏ 322 Keith Rivers SP RC | 6.00 | 2.50 |
| ❏ 323 Justin King SP RC | 5.00 | 2.00 |
| ❏ 324 Mike Jenkins SP RC | 6.00 | 2.50 |
| ❏ 325 Fred Davis SP RC | 6.00 | 2.50 |

## 2008 Upper Deck Draft Edition

| | | |
|---|---|---|
| ❏ 1 Anthony Morelli RC | 1.25 | .50 |
| ❏ 2 Adarius Bowman RC | 1.00 | .40 |
| ❏ 3 Ali Highsmith RC | .75 | .30 |
| ❏ 4 Andre Woodson RC | 1.25 | .50 |
| ❏ 5 Allen Patrick RC | 1.00 | .40 |
| ❏ 6 Antoine Cason RC | 1.25 | .50 |
| ❏ 7 Aqib Talib RC | 1.25 | .50 |
| ❏ 8 Ben Moffitt RC | .75 | .30 |
| ❏ 9 Gosder Cherilus RC | 1.00 | .40 |
| ❏ 10 Brian Brohm RC | 1.50 | .60 |
| ❏ 11 Calais Campbell RC | 1.00 | .40 |
| ❏ 12 Chad Henne RC | 2.00 | .75 |
| ❏ 13 Chevis Jackson RC | 1.00 | .40 |
| ❏ 14 Davone Bess RC | 1.50 | .60 |
| ❏ 15 Justin Forsett RC | 1.25 | .50 |
| ❏ 16 Chris Ellis RC | 1.00 | .40 |
| ❏ 17 Chris Long RC | 1.50 | .60 |
| ❏ 18 Colt Brennan RC | 3.00 | 1.25 |

| | | |
|---|---|---|
| 19 Craig Steltz RC | 1.00 | .40 |
| 20 DJ Hall RC | 1.25 | .50 |
| 21 Dan Connor RC | 1.25 | .50 |
| 22 Darren McFadden RC | 3.00 | 1.25 |
| 23 DeMarco Pressley RC | 1.00 | .40 |
| 24 Dennis Dixon RC | 1.25 | .50 |
| 25 Derrick Harvey RC | 1.00 | .40 |
| 26 DeSean Jackson RC | 2.50 | 1.00 |
| 27 D.Rodgers-Cromartie RC | 1.25 | .50 |
| 28 Donnie Avery RC | 1.50 | .60 |
| 29 Dorien Bryant RC | 1.00 | .40 |
| 30 Dre Moore RC | 1.00 | .40 |
| 31 Kellen Davis RC | .75 | .30 |
| 33 DaJuan Morgan RC | 1.00 | .40 |
| 34 Earl Bennett RC | 1.25 | .50 |
| 35 Kentwan Balmer RC | 1.00 | .40 |
| 36 Erik Ainge RC | 1.25 | .50 |
| 37 Felix Jones RC | 3.00 | 1.25 |
| 38 Frank Okam RC | 1.00 | .40 |
| 39 Fred Davis RC | 1.25 | .50 |
| 40 Glenn Dorsey RC | 1.50 | .60 |
| 41 Harry Douglas RC | 1.25 | .50 |
| 42 Jack Ikegwuonu RC | 1.00 | .40 |
| 43 Bruce Davis RC | 1.25 | .50 |
| 44 Jacob Tamme RC | 1.25 | .50 |
| 45 Jake Long RC | 1.50 | .60 |
| 46 Jamaal Charles RC | 1.50 | .60 |
| 47 James Hardy RC | 1.25 | .50 |
| 48 Erin Henderson RC | 1.00 | .40 |
| 49 J Leman RC | 1.00 | .40 |
| 50 Joe Flacco RC | 4.00 | 1.50 |
| 51 John Carlson RC | 1.25 | .50 |
| 52 John David Booty RC | 1.50 | .60 |
| 53 Jonathan Hefney RC | 1.00 | .40 |
| 54 Jonathan Stewart RC | 3.00 | 1.25 |
| 55 Jordy Nelson RC | 1.50 | .60 |
| 56 Josh Johnson RC | 1.25 | .50 |
| 57 Jacob Hester RC | 1.25 | .50 |
| 58 Keenan Burton RC | 1.00 | .40 |
| 59 Keith Rivers RC | 1.25 | .50 |
| 60 Kenny Phillips RC | 1.25 | .50 |
| 61 Kevin Smith RC | 2.00 | .75 |
| 62 Lavelle Hawkins RC | 1.00 | .40 |
| 63 Lawrence Jackson RC | 1.00 | .40 |
| 64 Limas Sweed RC | 1.50 | .60 |
| 65 Adrian Arrington RC | 1.00 | .40 |
| 66 Malcolm Kelly RC | 1.25 | .50 |
| 67 Martellus Bennett RC | 1.25 | .50 |
| 68 Marcus Monk RC | 1.25 | .50 |
| 69 Mario Manningham RC | 1.25 | .50 |
| 70 Mario Urrutia RC | 1.00 | .40 |
| 71 Martin Rucker RC | 1.00 | .40 |
| 72 Matt Flynn RC | 1.50 | .60 |
| 73 Matt Forte RC | 3.00 | 1.25 |
| 74 Matt Ryan RC | 5.00 | 2.00 |
| 75 Mike Hart RC | 1.50 | .60 |
| 76 Mike Jenkins RC | 1.25 | .50 |
| 77 Vernon Gholston RC | 1.25 | .50 |
| 78 Owen Schmitt RC | 1.25 | .50 |
| 79 Jonathan Goff RC | 1.00 | .40 |
| 80 Shawn Crable RC | 1.25 | .50 |
| 81 Justin King RC | 1.00 | .40 |
| 82 Philip Wheeler RC | 1.25 | .50 |
| 83 Paul Smith RC | 1.25 | .50 |
| 84 Rashard Mendenhall RC | 2.50 | 1.00 |
| 85 Ray Rice RC | 1.50 | .60 |
| 86 Ryan Clady RC | 1.25 | .50 |
| 87 Ryan Torain RC | 1.25 | .50 |
| 88 Sam Baker RC | .75 | .30 |
| 89 Quintin Demps RC | 1.00 | .40 |
| 90 Sam Keller RC | 1.25 | .50 |
| 91 Phillip Merling RC | 1.00 | .40 |
| 92 Steve Slaton RC | 2.50 | 1.00 |
| 93 Tashard Choice RC | 1.25 | .50 |
| 94 Terrell Thomas RC | 1.00 | .40 |
| 95 Thomas Brown RC | 1.25 | .50 |
| 96 Tom Zbikowski RC | 1.50 | .60 |
| 97 DeJuan Tribble RC | .75 | .30 |
| 98 Trevor Laws RC | 1.25 | .50 |
| 99 Vince Hall RC | .75 | .30 |
| 100 Xavier Adibi RC | 1.00 | .40 |
| 101 Edgerrin James | .60 | .25 |
| 102 Matt Leinart | .75 | .30 |
| 103 Larry Fitzgerald | .75 | .30 |
| 104 Joe Horn | .60 | .25 |
| 105 Warrick Dunn | .60 | .25 |
| 106 Jerious Norwood | .60 | .25 |
| 107 Ed Reed | .60 | .25 |
| 108 Willis McGahee | .60 | .25 |
| 109 Steve McNair | .60 | .25 |
| 110 Ray Lewis | .75 | .30 |
| 111 J.P. Losman | .50 | .20 |
| 112 Lee Evans | .60 | .25 |
| 113 Marshawn Lynch | .75 | .30 |
| 114 Eric Moulds | .60 | .25 |
| 115 Julius Peppers | .60 | .25 |
| 116 Steve Smith | .60 | .25 |
| 117 DeShaun Foster | .60 | .25 |
| 118 Devin Hester | .75 | .30 |
| 119 Bernard Berrian | .60 | .25 |
| 120 Cedric Benson | .50 | .20 |
| 121 Thomas Jones | .60 | .25 |
| 122 T.J. Houshmandzadeh | .60 | .25 |
| 123 Carson Palmer | .75 | .30 |
| 124 Chad Johnson | .60 | .25 |
| 125 Derek Anderson | .60 | .25 |
| 126 Kellen Winslow | .60 | .25 |
| 127 Braylon Edwards | .60 | .25 |
| 128 Anthony Henry | .50 | .20 |
| 129 Marion Barber | .75 | .30 |
| 130 DeMarcus Ware | .60 | .25 |
| 131 Tony Romo | 1.25 | .50 |
| 132 Brandon Marshall | .60 | .25 |
| 133 Jay Cutler | .75 | .30 |
| 134 Champ Bailey | .50 | .20 |
| 135 Tatum Bell | .50 | .20 |
| 136 Calvin Johnson | .75 | .30 |
| 137 Jon Kitna | .60 | .25 |
| 138 Ernie Sims | .50 | .20 |
| 139 Aaron Kampman | .50 | .20 |
| 140 Charles Woodson | .60 | .25 |
| 141 A.J. Hawk | .60 | .25 |
| 142 DeMeco Ryans | .60 | .25 |
| 143 Andre Johnson | .60 | .25 |
| 144 Mario Williams | .60 | .25 |
| 145 Dwight Freeney | .60 | .25 |
| 146 Dallas Clark | .60 | .25 |
| 147 Joseph Addai | .75 | .30 |
| 148 David Garrard | .60 | .25 |
| 149 Reggie Nelson | .50 | .20 |
| 150 Maurice Jones-Drew | .60 | .25 |
| 151 Dwayne Bowe | .60 | .25 |
| 152 Derrick Johnson | .50 | .20 |
| 153 Brodie Croyle | .75 | .30 |
| 154 Ronnie Brown | .60 | .25 |
| 155 Ted Ginn Jr. | .60 | .25 |
| 156 Channing Crowder | .50 | .20 |
| 157 Antoine Winfield | .50 | .20 |
| 158 Adrian Peterson | 1.50 | .60 |
| 159 Sidney Rice | .60 | .25 |
| 160 Wes Welker | .75 | .30 |
| 161 Laurence Maroney | .60 | .25 |
| 162 Ben Watson | .60 | .25 |
| 163 Drew Brees | .75 | .30 |
| 164 Reggie Bush | .75 | .30 |
| 165 Marques Colston | .60 | .25 |
| 166 Amani Toomer | .60 | .25 |
| 167 Osi Umenyiora | .50 | .20 |
| 168 Eli Manning | .75 | .30 |
| 169 Jonathan Vilma | .60 | .25 |
| 170 Kellen Clemens | .60 | .25 |
| 171 Kirk Morrison | .60 | .25 |
| 172 Nnamdi Asomugha | .50 | .20 |
| 173 JaMarcus Russell | .75 | .30 |
| 174 Brian Westbrook | .60 | .25 |
| 175 Reggie Brown | .60 | .25 |
| 176 Brian Dawkins | .60 | .25 |
| 177 Hines Ward | .75 | .30 |
| 178 Santonio Holmes | .60 | .25 |
| 179 Ben Roethlisberger | 1.00 | .40 |
| 180 Shawne Merriman | .60 | .25 |
| 181 LaDainian Tomlinson | 1.00 | .40 |
| 182 Antonio Cromartie | .50 | .20 |
| 183 Shaun Phillips | .50 | .20 |
| 184 Patrick Willis | .60 | .25 |
| 185 Alex Smith QB | .60 | .25 |
| 186 Frank Gore | .60 | .25 |
| 187 Lofa Tatupu | .60 | .25 |
| 188 Bobby Engram | .50 | .20 |
| 189 Deion Branch | .60 | .25 |
| 190 Steven Jackson | .75 | .30 |
| 191 Pisa Tinoisamoa | .50 | .20 |
| 192 Torry Holt | .60 | .25 |
| 193 Cadillac Williams | .60 | .25 |
| 194 Michael Clayton | .50 | .20 |
| 195 Gaines Adams | .50 | .20 |
| 196 Vince Young | .75 | .30 |
| 197 LenDale White | .60 | .25 |
| 198 Chris Cooley | .60 | .25 |
| 199 Clinton Portis | .60 | .25 |
| 200 Santana Moss | .60 | .25 |
| 201 B.Brohm/M.Urrutia | 2.00 | .75 |
| 202 D.McFadden/F.Jones | 4.00 | 1.50 |
| 203 D.Tribble/M.Ryan | 6.00 | 2.50 |
| 204 E.Doucet/G.Dorsey | 2.00 | .75 |
| 205 J.Long/M.Hart | 2.00 | .75 |
| 206 C.Brennan/D.Bess | 4.00 | 1.50 |
| 207 J.Booty/F.Davis | 2.00 | .75 |
| 208 D.Anderson/S.Jackson | 2.00 | .75 |
| 209 T.Brady/B.Edwards | 3.00 | 1.25 |
| 210 R.Bush/M.Leinart | 2.00 | .75 |
| 211 A.Highsmith/J.Leman | 1.25 | .50 |
| 212 A.Cason/D.Tribble | 1.50 | .60 |
| 213 C.Brennan/D.Dixon | 4.00 | 1.50 |
| 214 D.McFadden/M.Hart | 2.00 | .75 |
| 215 F.Davis/M.Rucker | 1.50 | .60 |
| 216 J.Hefney/C.Steltz | 1.25 | .50 |
| 217 L.Sweed/M.Manningham | 2.00 | .75 |
| 218 S.Baker/J.Long | 2.00 | .75 |
| 219 K.Balmer/G.Dorsey | 1.50 | .50 |
| 220 S.Slaton/R.Rice | 3.00 | 1.25 |
| 221 A.Highsmith/D.Connor | 1.50 | .60 |
| 222 A.Cason/T.Thomas | 1.50 | .60 |
| 223 B.Brohm/A.Woodson | 2.00 | .75 |
| 224 C.Long/G.Groves | 1.50 | .60 |
| 225 C.Steltz/K.Phillips | 1.50 | .60 |
| 226 F.Davis/J.Carlson | 1.50 | .60 |
| 227 G.Dorsey/S.Ellis | 2.00 | .75 |
| 228 J.Long/S.Baker | 2.00 | .75 |
| 229 L.Sweed/E.Doucet | 1.50 | .60 |
| 230 T.Choice/D.McFadden | 4.00 | 1.50 |
| 231 A.Highsmith/C.Jackson | 1.25 | .50 |
| 232 C.Henne/M.Manningham | 2.50 | 1.00 |
| 233 L.Hawkins/D.Jackson | 3.00 | 1.25 |
| 234 E.Henderson/D.Moore | 1.25 | .50 |
| 235 M.Kelly/A.Patrick | 1.50 | .60 |
| 236 M.Urrutia/H.Douglas | 1.50 | .60 |
| 237 M.Rucker/A.Spieker | 1.25 | .50 |
| 238 F.Jones/P.Hillis | 4.00 | 1.50 |
| 239 J.Hefney/E.Ainge | 1.25 | .50 |
| 240 V.Hall/X.Adibi | 1.25 | .50 |
| 241 C.Brennan/D.Lowery | 4.00 | 1.50 |
| 242 D.Dixon/K.Rivers | 1.50 | .60 |
| 243 H.Douglas/M.Jenkins | 1.50 | .60 |
| 244 J.Hester/K.Phillips | 1.50 | .60 |
| 245 J.Hefney/D.Hall | 1.50 | .60 |
| 246 M.Kelly/F.Okam | 1.50 | .60 |
| 247 J.Leman/M.Manningham | 1.50 | .60 |
| 248 M.Ryan/C.Long | 6.00 | 2.50 |
| 249 J.Booty/A.Cason | 2.00 | .75 |
| 250 S.Keller/A.Patrick | 1.50 | .60 |

## 2007 Upper Deck First Edition

| | | |
|---|---|---|
| ❏ 1 Matt Leinart | .40 | .15 |
| ❏ 2 Larry Fitzgerald | .40 | .15 |
| ❏ 3 Anquan Boldin | .30 | .12 |
| ❏ 4 Michael Vick | .30 | .12 |
| ❏ 5 Warrick Dunn | .30 | .15 |
| ❏ 6 Alge Crumpler | .30 | .12 |
| ❏ 7 Steve McNair | .30 | .12 |
| ❏ 8 Mark Clayton | .30 | .12 |
| ❏ 9 Todd Heap | .25 | .08 |
| ❏ 10 Ray Lewis | .40 | .15 |
| ❏ 11 J.P. Losman | .25 | .10 |
| ❏ 12 Lee Evans | .30 | .12 |
| ❏ 13 Anthony Thomas | .30 | .12 |
| ❏ 14 Jake Delhomme | .30 | .12 |
| ❏ 15 DeShaun Foster | .30 | .12 |
| ❏ 16 Steve Smith | .30 | .12 |
| ❏ 17 Cedric Benson | .30 | .12 |
| ❏ 18 Bernard Berrian | .25 | .10 |
| ❏ 19 Brian Urlacher | .40 | .15 |
| ❏ 20 Carson Palmer | .40 | .15 |
| ❏ 21 Rudi Johnson | .30 | .12 |
| ❏ 22 Chad Johnson | .30 | .12 |
| ❏ 23 Kellen Winslow | .30 | .12 |
| ❏ 24 Braylon Edwards | .30 | .12 |
| ❏ 25 Tony Romo | .75 | .30 |
| ❏ 26 Julius Jones | .30 | .12 |
| ❏ 27 Terrell Owens | .40 | .15 |
| ❏ 28 Jay Cutler | .40 | .15 |
| ❏ 29 Javon Walker | .30 | .12 |
| ❏ 30 Champ Bailey | .30 | .12 |
| ❏ 31 Jon Kitna | .25 | .10 |
| ❏ 32 Kevin Jones | .25 | .10 |
| ❏ 33 Roy Williams WR | .30 | .12 |
| ❏ 34 Brett Favre | .75 | .30 |
| ❏ 35 Donald Driver | .30 | .12 |
| ❏ 36 A.J. Hawk | .40 | .15 |
| ❏ 37 Andre Johnson | .30 | .12 |
| ❏ 38 Mario Williams | .30 | .12 |
| ❏ 39 Ron Dayne | .30 | .12 |
| ❏ 40 Peyton Manning | .60 | .25 |
| ❏ 41 Marvin Harrison | .40 | .15 |
| ❏ 42 Reggie Wayne | .30 | .12 |
| ❏ 43 Joseph Addai | .40 | .15 |
| ❏ 44 Maurice Jones-Drew | .40 | .15 |
| ❏ 45 Fred Taylor | .30 | .12 |
| ❏ 46 Byron Leftwich | .30 | .12 |
| ❏ 47 Larry Johnson | .30 | .12 |
| ❏ 48 Tony Gonzalez | .30 | .12 |
| ❏ 49 Damon Huard | .30 | .12 |
| ❏ 50 Ronnie Brown | .30 | .12 |
| ❏ 51 Jason Taylor | .25 | .10 |
| ❏ 52 Chris Chambers | .25 | .10 |
| ❏ 53 Chester Taylor | .25 | .10 |
| ❏ 54 Tarvaris Jackson | .25 | .10 |
| ❏ 55 Troy Williamson | .25 | .10 |
| ❏ 56 Tom Brady | .75 | .30 |
| ❏ 57 Laurence Maroney | .40 | .15 |
| ❏ 58 Ben Watson | .30 | .12 |
| ❏ 59 Asante Samuel | .25 | .10 |
| ❏ 60 Chad Pennington | .30 | .12 |
| ❏ 61 Leon Washington | .30 | .12 |
| ❏ 62 Laveranues Coles | .30 | .12 |
| ❏ 63 Eli Manning | .40 | .15 |
| ❏ 64 Jeremy Shockey | .30 | .12 |
| ❏ 65 Brandon Jacobs | .30 | .12 |
| ❏ 66 Drew Brees | .30 | .12 |
| ❏ 67 Marques Colston | .40 | .15 |
| ❏ 68 Reggie Bush | .50 | .20 |
| ❏ 69 Deuce McAllister | .30 | .12 |
| ❏ 70 Jerry Porter | .30 | .12 |
| ❏ 71 Justin Fargas | .25 | .10 |
| ❏ 72 Randy Moss | .40 | .15 |
| ❏ 73 Brian Westbrook | .30 | .12 |
| ❏ 74 Reggie Brown | .30 | .12 |
| ❏ 75 Donovan McNabb | .40 | .15 |
| ❏ 76 Ben Roethlisberger | .50 | .20 |
| ❏ 77 Willie Parker | .40 | .15 |
| ❏ 78 Troy Polamalu | .40 | .15 |
| ❏ 79 Antonio Gates | .30 | .12 |
| ❏ 80 Shawne Merriman | .30 | .12 |
| ❏ 81 LaDainian Tomlinson | .50 | .20 |
| ❏ 82 Alex Smith QB | .40 | .15 |
| ❏ 83 Frank Gore | .40 | .15 |
| ❏ 84 Vernon Davis | .30 | .12 |

| | | |
|---|---|---|
| ❏ 85 Steven Jackson | .40 | .15 |
| ❏ 86 Marc Bulger | .30 | .12 |
| ❏ 87 Torry Holt | .30 | .12 |
| ❏ 88 Isaac Bruce | .30 | .12 |
| ❏ 89 Matt Hasselbeck | .30 | .12 |
| ❏ 90 Shaun Alexander | .30 | .12 |
| ❏ 91 Deion Branch | .30 | .12 |
| ❏ 92 Cadillac Williams | .30 | .12 |
| ❏ 93 Michael Clayton | .30 | .12 |
| ❏ 94 Joey Galloway | .30 | .12 |
| ❏ 95 Vince Young | .40 | .15 |
| ❏ 96 LenDale White | .30 | .12 |
| ❏ 97 Jason Campbell | .30 | .12 |
| ❏ 98 Clinton Portis | .30 | .12 |
| ❏ 99 Santana Moss | .30 | .12 |
| ❏ 100 Antwaan Randle El | .25 | .10 |
| ❏ 101 JaMarcus Russell RC | 4.00 | 1.50 |
| ❏ 102 Brady Quinn RC | 5.00 | 2.00 |
| ❏ 103 Calvin Johnson RC | 4.00 | 1.50 |
| ❏ 104 Adrian Peterson RC | 12.00 | 5.00 |
| ❏ 105 Joe Thomas RC | 1.50 | .60 |
| ❏ 106 Levi Brown RC | 1.50 | .60 |
| ❏ 107 Gaines Adams RC | 1.50 | .60 |
| ❏ 108 Adam Carriker RC | 1.25 | .50 |
| ❏ 109 Ted Ginn Jr. RC | 2.50 | 1.00 |
| ❏ 110 Anthony Gonzalez RC | 2.50 | 1.00 |
| ❏ 111 Troy Smith RC | 2.00 | .75 |
| ❏ 112 Leon Hall RC | 1.25 | .50 |
| ❏ 113 LaMarr Woodley RC | 1.50 | .60 |
| ❏ 114 Alan Branch RC | 1.25 | .50 |
| ❏ 115 Patrick Willis RC | 3.00 | 1.25 |
| ❏ 116 Reggie Nelson RC | 1.25 | .50 |
| ❏ 117 Paul Posluszny RC | 2.00 | .75 |
| ❏ 118 Dwayne Bowe RC | 3.00 | 1.25 |
| ❏ 119 Steve Smith RC | 2.00 | .75 |
| ❏ 120 Dwayne Jarrett RC | 1.50 | .60 |
| ❏ 121 Marshawn Lynch RC | 3.00 | 1.25 |
| ❏ 122 Darius Walker RC | 1.50 | .60 |
| ❏ 123 Daymeion Hughes RC | 1.25 | .50 |
| ❏ 124 LaRon Landry RC | 2.00 | .75 |
| ❏ 125 Jon Beason RC | 1.50 | .60 |
| ❏ 126 Lawrence Timmons RC | 1.50 | .60 |
| ❏ 127 Drew Stanton RC | 1.50 | .60 |
| ❏ 128 Trent Edwards RC | 4.00 | 1.50 |
| ❏ 129 John Beck RC | 1.50 | .60 |
| ❏ 130 Kevin Kolb RC | 2.50 | 1.00 |
| ❏ 131 Amobi Okoye RC | 1.50 | .60 |
| ❏ 132 Michael Bush RC | 1.50 | .60 |
| ❏ 133 Darrelle Revis RC | 1.50 | .60 |
| ❏ 134 H.B. Blades RC | 1.25 | .50 |
| ❏ 135 Jamaal Anderson RC | 1.50 | .60 |
| ❏ 136 Robert Meachem RC | 1.50 | .60 |
| ❏ 137 Craig Davis RC | 1.50 | .60 |
| ❏ 138 Paul Williams RC | 1.25 | .50 |
| ❏ 139 Greg Olsen RC | 2.00 | .75 |
| ❏ 141 Jarvis Moss RC | 1.50 | .60 |
| ❏ 142 Justin Harrell RC | 1.50 | .60 |
| ❏ 143 DeMarcus Tank Tyler RC | 1.25 | .50 |
| ❏ 144 Aaron Ross RC | 1.50 | .60 |
| ❏ 145 Chris Houston RC | 1.25 | .50 |
| ❏ 146 Brandon Meriweather RC | 1.50 | .60 |
| ❏ 147 Eric Weddle RC | 1.25 | .50 |
| ❏ 148 Lorenzo Booker RC | 1.50 | .60 |
| ❏ 149 Buster Davis RC | 1.25 | .50 |
| ❏ 150 Antonio Pittman RC | 1.50 | .60 |
| ❏ 151 Chris Henry RC | 1.50 | .60 |
| ❏ 152 Kenny Irons RC | 1.50 | .60 |
| ❏ 154 Tony Hunt RC | 1.50 | .60 |
| ❏ 155 Brian Leonard RC | 1.50 | .60 |
| ❏ 156 Garrett Wolfe RC | 1.50 | .60 |
| ❏ 157 Yamon Figurs RC | 1.50 | .60 |
| ❏ 158 Johnnie Lee Higgins RC | 1.25 | .50 |
| ❏ 159 Jordan Palmer RC | 1.50 | .60 |
| ❏ 160 Chris Leak RC | 1.25 | .50 |
| ❏ 161 Rhema McKnight RC | 1.25 | .50 |
| ❏ 162 Dwayne Wright RC | 1.25 | .50 |
| ❏ 164 Jeff Rowe RC | 1.25 | .50 |
| ❏ 165 Zach Miller RC | 1.00 | .40 |
| ❏ 166 Ben Patrick RC | 1.25 | .50 |
| ❏ 167 Joe Staley RC | 1.25 | .50 |
| ❏ 168 Eric Wright RC | 1.25 | .50 |
| ❏ 169 Aundrae Allison RC | 1.25 | .50 |
| ❏ 170 Steve Breaston RC | 1.50 | .60 |
| ❏ 171 David Harris RC | 1.25 | .50 |

| | | |
|---|---|---|
| ❏ 172 Brandon Siler RC | 1.25 | .50 |
| ❏ 173 Tim Shaw RC | 1.25 | .50 |
| ❏ 174 Selvin Young RC | 2.50 | 1.00 |
| ❏ 175 Michael Griffin RC | 1.50 | .60 |
| ❏ 176 Kenneth Darby RC | 1.50 | .60 |
| ❏ 177 Anthony Spencer RC | 1.50 | .60 |
| ❏ 178 Charles Johnson RC | 1.00 | .40 |
| ❏ 179 Quentin Moses RC | 1.25 | .50 |
| ❏ 180 DeShawn Wynn RC | 1.50 | .60 |
| ❏ 181 Scott Chandler RC | 1.25 | .50 |
| ❏ 182 Stewart Bradley RC | 1.50 | .60 |
| ❏ 183 Ahmad Bradshaw RC | 2.00 | .75 |
| ❏ 184 Matt Spaeth RC | 1.50 | .60 |
| ❏ 185 Ray McDonald RC | 1.25 | .50 |
| ❏ 186 Ben Grubbs RC | 1.25 | .50 |
| ❏ 187 Jon Abbate RC | 1.00 | .40 |
| ❏ 188 Victor Abiamiri RC | 1.50 | .60 |
| ❏ 189 Courtney Taylor RC | 1.25 | .50 |
| ❏ 190 A.J. Davis RC | 1.00 | .40 |
| ❏ 191 Nate Harris RC | 1.25 | .50 |
| ❏ 192 Jonathan Wade RC | 1.25 | .50 |
| ❏ 193 Tim Crowder RC | 1.50 | .60 |
| ❏ 194 Legedu Naanee RC | 1.50 | .60 |
| ❏ 195 Quinn Pitcock RC | 1.25 | .50 |
| ❏ 196 Marcus McCauley RC | 1.50 | .60 |
| ❏ 197 Sabby Piscitelli RC | 1.50 | .60 |
| ❏ 198 Tanard Jackson RC | 1.50 | .60 |
| ❏ 199 Josh Gattis RC | 1.00 | .40 |
| ❏ 200 Rufus Alexander RC | 1.50 | .60 |

## 2008 Upper Deck First Edition

| | | |
|---|---|---|
| ❏ 1 Edgerrin James | .30 | .12 |
| ❏ 2 Matt Leinart | .40 | .15 |
| ❏ 3 Larry Fitzgerald | .40 | .15 |
| ❏ 4 Anquan Boldin | .30 | .12 |
| ❏ 5 Antrel Rolle | .25 | .10 |
| ❏ 6 Joe Horn | .30 | .12 |
| ❏ 7 Warrick Dunn | .30 | .12 |
| ❏ 8 Jerious Norwood | .30 | .12 |
| ❏ 9 Michael Jenkins | .25 | .10 |
| ❏ 10 Ed Reed | .30 | .12 |
| ❏ 11 Willis McGahee | .30 | .12 |
| ❏ 12 Steve McNair | .30 | .12 |
| ❏ 13 Todd Heap | .25 | .10 |
| ❏ 14 Ray Lewis | .40 | .15 |
| ❏ 15 Terrell Suggs | .25 | .10 |
| ❏ 16 Trent Edwards | .40 | .15 |
| ❏ 17 Lee Evans | .30 | .12 |
| ❏ 18 Roscoe Parrish | .25 | .10 |
| ❏ 19 Marshawn Lynch | .40 | .15 |
| ❏ 20 DeAngelo Williams | .30 | .12 |
| ❏ 21 Julius Peppers | .30 | .12 |
| ❏ 22 Steve Smith | .30 | .12 |
| ❏ 23 Cedric Benson | .25 | .10 |
| ❏ 24 Greg Olsen | .30 | .12 |
| ❏ 25 Lance Briggs | .25 | .10 |
| ❏ 26 Rex Grossman | .30 | .12 |
| ❏ 27 Devin Hester | .40 | .15 |
| ❏ 28 Brian Urlacher | .40 | .15 |
| ❏ 29 T.J. Houshmandzadeh | .30 | .12 |
| ❏ 30 Carson Palmer | .40 | .15 |
| ❏ 31 Rudi Johnson | .30 | .12 |
| ❏ 32 Chad Johnson | .30 | .12 |
| ❏ 33 Chris Henry | .25 | .10 |
| ❏ 34 Kamerion Wimbley | .25 | .10 |

| | | |
|---|---|---|
| ❑ 35 Joshua Cribbs | .30 | .12 |
| ❑ 36 Jamal Lewis | .30 | .12 |
| ❑ 37 Kellen Winslow | .30 | .12 |
| ❑ 38 Braylon Edwards | .30 | .12 |
| ❑ 39 Marion Barber | .40 | .15 |
| ❑ 40 Jason Witten | .30 | .12 |
| ❑ 41 DeMarcus Ware | .30 | .12 |
| ❑ 42 Tony Romo | .60 | .25 |
| ❑ 43 Terrell Owens | .40 | .15 |
| ❑ 44 John Lynch | .30 | .12 |
| ❑ 45 Brandon Marshall | .30 | .12 |
| ❑ 46 Jay Cutler | .40 | .15 |
| ❑ 47 Dre Bly | .25 | .10 |
| ❑ 48 Champ Bailey | .25 | .10 |
| ❑ 49 Tatum Bell | .25 | .10 |
| ❑ 50 Calvin Johnson | .40 | .15 |
| ❑ 51 Jon Kitna | .30 | .12 |
| ❑ 52 Roy Williams WR | .30 | .12 |
| ❑ 53 Ernie Sims | .25 | .10 |
| ❑ 54 Aaron Kampman | .30 | .12 |
| ❑ 55 Charles Woodson | .30 | .12 |
| ❑ 56 Brett Favre | 1.00 | .40 |
| ❑ 57 Donald Driver | .30 | .12 |
| ❑ 58 A.J. Hawk | .30 | .12 |
| ❑ 59 DeMeco Ryans | .30 | .12 |
| ❑ 60 Andre Johnson | .30 | .12 |
| ❑ 61 Mario Williams | .30 | .12 |
| ❑ 62 Ron Dayne | .30 | .12 |
| ❑ 63 Dwight Freeney | .30 | .12 |
| ❑ 64 Dallas Clark | .30 | .12 |
| ❑ 65 Peyton Manning | .60 | .25 |
| ❑ 66 Marvin Harrison | .40 | .15 |
| ❑ 67 Reggie Wayne | .30 | .12 |
| ❑ 68 Matt Jones | .30 | .12 |
| ❑ 69 David Garrard | .30 | .12 |
| ❑ 70 Reggie Williams | .30 | .12 |
| ❑ 71 Maurice Jones-Drew | .30 | .12 |
| ❑ 72 Fred Taylor | .30 | .12 |
| ❑ 73 Dwayne Bowe | .30 | .12 |
| ❑ 74 Derrick Johnson | .25 | .10 |
| ❑ 75 Larry Johnson | .30 | .12 |
| ❑ 76 Tony Gonzalez | .30 | .12 |
| ❑ 77 Ronnie Brown | .30 | .12 |
| ❑ 78 Jason Taylor | .30 | .12 |
| ❑ 79 Ted Ginn Jr. | .30 | .12 |
| ❑ 80 John Beck | .25 | .10 |
| ❑ 81 Adrian Peterson | .75 | .30 |
| ❑ 82 Sidney Rice | .30 | .12 |
| ❑ 83 Chester Taylor | .25 | .10 |
| ❑ 84 Bernard Berrian | .30 | .12 |
| ❑ 85 Wes Welker | .40 | .15 |
| ❑ 86 Randy Moss | .40 | .15 |
| ❑ 87 Tom Brady | .60 | .25 |
| ❑ 88 Laurence Maroney | .30 | .12 |
| ❑ 89 Mike Vrabel | .25 | .10 |
| ❑ 90 Drew Brees | .40 | .15 |
| ❑ 91 Marques Colston | .30 | .12 |
| ❑ 92 Reggie Bush | .40 | .15 |
| ❑ 93 Mike McKenzie | .25 | .10 |
| ❑ 94 Michael Strahan | .30 | .12 |
| ❑ 95 Plaxico Burress | .30 | .12 |
| ❑ 96 Eli Manning | .40 | .15 |
| ❑ 97 Jeremy Shockey | .30 | .12 |
| ❑ 98 Brandon Jacobs | .30 | .12 |
| ❑ 99 Jerricho Cotchery | .25 | .10 |
| ❑ 100 Kellen Clemens | .25 | .10 |
| ❑ 101 Leon Washington | .25 | .10 |
| ❑ 102 Thomas Jones | .30 | .12 |
| ❑ 103 Kirk Morrison | .25 | .10 |
| ❑ 104 Nnamdi Asomugha | .25 | .10 |
| ❑ 105 Derrick Burgess | .25 | .10 |
| ❑ 106 Ronald Curry | .25 | .10 |
| ❑ 107 JaMarcus Russell | .40 | .15 |
| ❑ 108 Brian Dawkins | .30 | .12 |
| ❑ 109 Brian Westbrook | .30 | .12 |
| ❑ 110 Reggie Brown | .25 | .10 |
| ❑ 111 Donovan McNabb | .40 | .15 |
| ❑ 112 Hines Ward | .40 | .15 |
| ❑ 113 Santonio Holmes | .30 | .12 |
| ❑ 114 Ben Roethlisberger | .50 | .20 |
| ❑ 115 Willie Parker | .30 | .12 |
| ❑ 116 Troy Polamalu | .40 | .15 |
| ❑ 117 Philip Rivers | .40 | .15 |
| ❑ 118 Antonio Gates | .30 | .12 |

| | | |
|---|---|---|
| ❑ 119 Shawne Merriman | .30 | .12 |
| ❑ 120 LaDainian Tomlinson | .50 | .20 |
| ❑ 121 Antonio Cromartie | .25 | .10 |
| ❑ 122 Alex Smith QB | .30 | .12 |
| ❑ 123 Frank Gore | .30 | .12 |
| ❑ 124 Vernon Davis | .25 | .10 |
| ❑ 125 Patrick Willis | .30 | .12 |
| ❑ 126 Lofa Tatupu | .30 | .12 |
| ❑ 127 Patrick Kerney | .25 | .10 |
| ❑ 128 Bobby Engram | .25 | .10 |
| ❑ 129 Matt Hasselbeck | .30 | .12 |
| ❑ 130 Deion Branch | .30 | .12 |
| ❑ 131 Pisa Tinoisamoa | .25 | .10 |
| ❑ 132 Steven Jackson | .40 | .15 |
| ❑ 133 Marc Bulger | .30 | .12 |
| ❑ 134 Torry Holt | .30 | .12 |
| ❑ 135 Randy McMichael | .25 | .10 |
| ❑ 136 Ronde Barber | .25 | .10 |
| ❑ 137 Cadillac Williams | .30 | .12 |
| ❑ 138 Joey Galloway | .30 | .12 |
| ❑ 139 Jeff Garcia | .30 | .12 |
| ❑ 140 Gaines Adams | .25 | .10 |
| ❑ 141 Keith Bulluck | .25 | .10 |
| ❑ 142 Nick Harper | .25 | .10 |
| ❑ 143 Vince Young | .40 | .15 |
| ❑ 144 LenDale White | .30 | .12 |
| ❑ 145 Alge Crumpler | .30 | .12 |
| ❑ 146 Jason Campbell | .30 | .12 |
| ❑ 147 Chris Cooley | .30 | .12 |
| ❑ 148 Brandon Lloyd | .25 | .10 |
| ❑ 149 Clinton Portis | .30 | .12 |
| ❑ 150 Santana Moss | .30 | .12 |
| ❑ 151 Alex Brink RC | 1.50 | .60 |
| ❑ 152 Anthony Morelli RC | 1.50 | .60 |
| ❑ 153 Antoine Cason RC | 1.50 | .60 |
| ❑ 154 Aqib Talib RC | 1.50 | .60 |
| ❑ 155 Calais Campbell RC | 1.25 | .50 |
| ❑ 156 Erin Henderson RC | 1.25 | .50 |
| ❑ 157 Chris Johnson RC | 4.00 | 1.50 |
| ❑ 158 DJ Hall RC | 1.50 | .60 |
| ❑ 159 DeJuan Tribble RC | 1.00 | .40 |
| ❑ 160 Derrick Harvey RC | 1.25 | .50 |
| ❑ 161 Mike Jenkins RC | 1.50 | .60 |
| ❑ 162 Dustin Keller RC | 1.50 | .60 |
| ❑ 163 Erik Ainge RC | 1.50 | .60 |
| ❑ 164 Felix Jones RC | 4.00 | 1.50 |
| ❑ 165 Gosder Cherilus RC | 1.25 | .50 |
| ❑ 166 Jack Ikegwuonu RC | 1.25 | .50 |
| ❑ 167 Jacob Hester RC | 1.50 | .60 |
| ❑ 168 Chauncey Washington RC | 1.25 | .50 |
| ❑ 169 J Leman RC | 1.25 | .50 |
| ❑ 170 Joe Flacco RC | 5.00 | 2.00 |
| ❑ 171 John David Booty RC | 2.00 | .75 |
| ❑ 172 Jordy Nelson RC | 2.00 | .75 |
| ❑ 173 Josh Johnson RC | 1.50 | .60 |
| ❑ 174 Kenny Phillips RC | 1.50 | .60 |
| ❑ 175 Malcolm Kelly RC | 1.50 | .60 |
| ❑ 176 Marcus Monk RC | 1.50 | .60 |
| ❑ 177 Mario Manningham RC | 1.50 | .60 |
| ❑ 178 Mario Urrutia RC | 1.25 | .50 |
| ❑ 179 Martin Rucker RC | 1.25 | .50 |
| ❑ 180 Matt Flynn RC | 2.00 | .75 |
| ❑ 181 Matt Forte RC | 4.00 | 1.50 |
| ❑ 182 Jerome Felton RC | 1.00 | .40 |
| ❑ 183 Owen Schmitt RC | 1.50 | .60 |
| ❑ 184 Ryan Grice-Mullen RC | 1.50 | .60 |
| ❑ 185 Paul Hubbard RC | 1.25 | .50 |
| ❑ 186 Quentin Groves RC | 1.25 | .50 |
| ❑ 187 Ray Rice RC | 2.00 | .75 |
| ❑ 188 Ryan Clady RC | 1.50 | .60 |
| ❑ 189 Ryan Torain RC | 1.50 | .60 |
| ❑ 190 Adrian Arrington RC | 1.25 | .50 |
| ❑ 191 Shawn Crable RC | 1.50 | .60 |
| ❑ 192 Allen Patrick RC | 1.25 | .50 |
| ❑ 193 Tashard Choice RC | 1.50 | .60 |
| ❑ 194 Terrell Thomas RC | 1.25 | .50 |
| ❑ 195 Thomas Brown RC | 1.50 | .60 |
| ❑ 196 Tom Zbikowski RC | 2.00 | .75 |
| ❑ 197 Jermichael Finley RC | 1.50 | .60 |
| ❑ 198 Trevor Laws RC | 1.50 | .60 |
| ❑ 199 Vince Hall RC | 1.00 | .40 |
| ❑ 200 Xavier Adibi RC | 1.25 | .50 |
| ❑ 201 Ali Highsmith RC | 1.00 | .40 |
| ❑ 202 Andre Woodson RC | 1.50 | .60 |

| | | |
|---|---|---|
| ❑ 203 Brian Brohm RC | 2.00 | .75 |
| ❑ 204 Chad Henne RC | 2.50 | 1.00 |
| ❑ 205 Chris Long RC | 2.00 | .75 |
| ❑ 206 Colt Brennan RC | 4.00 | 1.50 |
| ❑ 207 Dan Connor RC | 1.50 | .60 |
| ❑ 208 Darren McFadden RC | 4.00 | 1.50 |
| ❑ 209 Dennis Dixon RC | 1.50 | .60 |
| ❑ 210 DeSean Jackson RC | 3.00 | 1.25 |
| ❑ 211 Early Doucet RC | 1.50 | .60 |
| ❑ 212 Fred Davis RC | 1.50 | .60 |
| ❑ 213 Glenn Dorsey RC | 2.00 | .75 |
| ❑ 214 Jake Long RC | 2.00 | .75 |
| ❑ 215 Jonathan Stewart RC | 4.00 | 1.50 |
| ❑ 216 Justin King RC | 1.25 | .50 |
| ❑ 217 Keith Rivers RC | 1.50 | .60 |
| ❑ 218 Lavelle Hawkins RC | 1.25 | .50 |
| ❑ 219 Lawrence Jackson RC | 1.25 | .50 |
| ❑ 220 Limas Sweed RC | 2.00 | .75 |
| ❑ 221 Matt Ryan RC | 6.00 | 2.50 |
| ❑ 222 Mike Hart RC | 2.00 | .75 |
| ❑ 223 Earl Bennett RC | 1.50 | .60 |
| ❑ 224 Sam Baker RC | 1.00 | .40 |
| ❑ 225 Sedrick Ellis RC | 1.50 | .60 |

## 2008 Upper Deck Heroes

| | | |
|---|---|---|
| ❑ 1 Adrian Peterson | 1.50 | .60 |
| ❑ 2 Adrian Peterson | 1.50 | .60 |
| ❑ 3 Adrian Peterson | 1.50 | .60 |
| ❑ 4 Adrian Peterson | 1.50 | .60 |
| ❑ 5 Brett Favre | 2.00 | .75 |
| ❑ 6 Brett Favre | 2.00 | .75 |
| ❑ 7 Brett Favre | 2.00 | .75 |
| ❑ 8 Brett Favre | 2.00 | .75 |
| ❑ 9 Braylon Edwards | .60 | .25 |
| ❑ 10 Braylon Edwards | .60 | .25 |
| ❑ 11 Braylon Edwards | .60 | .25 |
| ❑ 12 Braylon Edwards | .60 | .25 |
| ❑ 13 Brodie Croyle | .75 | .30 |
| ❑ 14 Brodie Croyle | .75 | .30 |
| ❑ 15 Brodie Croyle | .75 | .30 |
| ❑ 16 Brodie Croyle | .75 | .30 |
| ❑ 17 Bob Sanders | .60 | .25 |
| ❑ 18 Bob Sanders | .60 | .25 |
| ❑ 19 Bob Sanders | .60 | .25 |
| ❑ 20 Bob Sanders | .60 | .25 |
| ❑ 21 Chad Johnson | .60 | .25 |
| ❑ 22 Chad Johnson | .60 | .25 |
| ❑ 23 Chad Johnson | .60 | .25 |
| ❑ 24 Chad Johnson | .60 | .25 |
| ❑ 25 DeMarcus Ware | .60 | .25 |
| ❑ 26 DeMarcus Ware | .60 | .25 |
| ❑ 27 DeMarcus Ware | .60 | .25 |
| ❑ 28 DeMarcus Ware | .60 | .25 |
| ❑ 29 Derek Anderson | .60 | .25 |
| ❑ 30 Derek Anderson | .60 | .25 |
| ❑ 31 Derek Anderson | .60 | .25 |
| ❑ 32 Derek Anderson | .60 | .25 |
| ❑ 33 Devin Hester | .75 | .30 |
| ❑ 34 Devin Hester | .75 | .30 |
| ❑ 35 Devin Hester | .75 | .30 |
| ❑ 36 Devin Hester | .75 | .30 |
| ❑ 37 Dwayne Bowe | .60 | .25 |
| ❑ 38 Dwayne Bowe | .60 | .25 |
| ❑ 39 Dwayne Bowe | .60 | .25 |
| ❑ 40 Dwayne Bowe | .60 | .25 |
| ❑ 41 Eli Manning | .75 | .30 |
| ❑ 42 Eli Manning | .75 | .30 |

| | | | |
|---|---|---:|---:|
| ☐ 43 | Eli Manning | .75 | .30 |
| ☐ 44 | Eli Manning | .75 | .30 |
| ☐ 45 | Jason Campbell | .60 | .25 |
| ☐ 46 | Jason Campbell | .60 | .25 |
| ☐ 47 | Jason Campbell | .60 | .25 |
| ☐ 48 | Jason Campbell | .60 | .25 |
| ☐ 49 | Joseph Addai | .75 | .30 |
| ☐ 50 | Joseph Addai | .75 | .30 |
| ☐ 51 | Joseph Addai | .75 | .30 |
| ☐ 52 | Joseph Addai | .75 | .30 |
| ☐ 53 | LenDale White | .60 | .25 |
| ☐ 54 | LenDale White | .60 | .25 |
| ☐ 55 | LenDale White | .60 | .25 |
| ☐ 56 | LenDale White | .60 | .25 |
| ☐ 57 | LaDainian Tomlinson | 1.00 | .40 |
| ☐ 58 | LaDainian Tomlinson | 1.00 | .40 |
| ☐ 59 | LaDainian Tomlinson | 1.00 | .40 |
| ☐ 60 | LaDainian Tomlinson | 1.00 | .40 |
| ☐ 61 | Marion Barber | .75 | .30 |
| ☐ 62 | Marion Barber | .75 | .30 |
| ☐ 63 | Marion Barber | .75 | .30 |
| ☐ 64 | Marion Barber | .75 | .30 |
| ☐ 65 | Marshawn Lynch | .75 | .30 |
| ☐ 66 | Marshawn Lynch | .75 | .30 |
| ☐ 67 | Marshawn Lynch | .75 | .30 |
| ☐ 68 | Marshawn Lynch | .75 | .30 |
| ☐ 69 | Greg Jennings | .60 | .25 |
| ☐ 70 | Greg Jennings | .60 | .25 |
| ☐ 71 | Greg Jennings | .60 | .25 |
| ☐ 72 | Greg Jennings | .60 | .25 |
| ☐ 73 | Patrick Willis | .60 | .25 |
| ☐ 74 | Patrick Willis | .60 | .25 |
| ☐ 75 | Patrick Willis | .60 | .25 |
| ☐ 76 | Patrick Willis | .60 | .25 |
| ☐ 77 | Peyton Manning | 1.25 | .50 |
| ☐ 78 | Peyton Manning | 1.25 | .50 |
| ☐ 79 | Peyton Manning | 1.25 | .50 |
| ☐ 80 | Peyton Manning | 1.25 | .50 |
| ☐ 81 | David Garrard | .60 | .25 |
| ☐ 82 | David Garrard | .60 | .25 |
| ☐ 83 | David Garrard | .60 | .25 |
| ☐ 84 | David Garrard | .60 | .25 |
| ☐ 85 | Ryan Grant | .75 | .30 |
| ☐ 86 | Ryan Grant | .75 | .30 |
| ☐ 87 | Ryan Grant | .75 | .30 |
| ☐ 88 | Ryan Grant | .75 | .30 |
| ☐ 89 | Tony Romo | 1.25 | .50 |
| ☐ 90 | Tony Romo | 1.25 | .50 |
| ☐ 91 | Tony Romo | 1.25 | .50 |
| ☐ 92 | Tony Romo | 1.25 | .50 |
| ☐ 93 | Wes Welker | .75 | .30 |
| ☐ 94 | Wes Welker | .75 | .30 |
| ☐ 95 | Wes Welker | .75 | .30 |
| ☐ 96 | Wes Welker | .75 | .30 |
| ☐ 97 | Willie Parker | .60 | .25 |
| ☐ 98 | Willie Parker | .60 | .25 |
| ☐ 99 | Willie Parker | .60 | .25 |
| ☐ 100 | Willie Parker | .60 | .25 |
| ☐ 101 | Adarius Bowman RC | 1.00 | .40 |
| ☐ 102 | Adarius Bowman RC | 1.00 | .40 |
| ☐ 103 | Ali Highsmith RC | .75 | .30 |
| ☐ 104 | Ali Highsmith RC | .75 | .30 |
| ☐ 106 | Andre Woodson RC | 1.25 | .50 |
| ☐ 107 | Antoine Cason RC | 1.25 | .50 |
| ☐ 108 | Antoine Cason RC | 1.25 | .50 |
| ☐ 109 | Aqib Talib RC | 1.25 | .50 |
| ☐ 110 | Aqib Talib RC | 1.25 | .50 |
| ☐ 111 | Ben Moffitt RC | .75 | .30 |
| ☐ 112 | Ben Moffitt RC | .75 | .30 |
| ☐ 113 | Brian Brohm RC | 1.50 | .60 |
| ☐ 114 | Brian Brohm RC | 1.50 | .60 |
| ☐ 115 | Calais Campbell RC | 1.00 | .40 |
| ☐ 116 | Calais Campbell RC | 1.00 | .40 |
| ☐ 117 | Chad Henne RC | 2.00 | .75 |
| ☐ 118 | Chad Henne RC | 2.00 | .75 |
| ☐ 119 | Chevis Jackson RC | 1.00 | .40 |
| ☐ 120 | Chevis Jackson RC | 1.00 | .40 |
| ☐ 121 | Chris Long RC | 1.50 | .60 |
| ☐ 122 | Chris Long RC | 1.50 | .60 |
| ☐ 123 | Colt Brennan RC | 3.00 | 1.25 |
| ☐ 124 | Colt Brennan RC | 3.00 | 1.25 |
| ☐ 125 | Craig Steltz RC | 1.00 | .40 |
| ☐ 126 | Craig Steltz RC | 1.00 | .40 |
| ☐ 127 | DJ Hall RC | 1.25 | .50 |
| ☐ 128 | DJ Hall RC | 1.25 | .50 |
| ☐ 129 | Dan Connor RC | 1.25 | .50 |
| ☐ 130 | Dan Connor RC | 1.25 | .50 |
| ☐ 131 | Darren McFadden RC | 3.00 | 1.25 |
| ☐ 132 | Darren McFadden RC | 3.00 | 1.25 |
| ☐ 133 | Dennis Dixon RC | 1.25 | .50 |
| ☐ 134 | Dennis Dixon RC | 1.25 | .50 |
| ☐ 135 | Derrick Harvey RC | 1.00 | .40 |
| ☐ 136 | Derrick Harvey RC | 1.00 | .40 |
| ☐ 137 | DeSean Jackson RC | 2.50 | 1.00 |
| ☐ 138 | DeSean Jackson RC | 2.50 | 1.00 |
| ☐ 139 | Dwight Lowery RC | .75 | .30 |
| ☐ 140 | Dwight Lowery RC | .75 | .30 |
| ☐ 141 | Early Doucet RC | 1.25 | .50 |
| ☐ 142 | Early Doucet RC | 1.25 | .50 |
| ☐ 143 | Felix Jones RC | 3.00 | 1.25 |
| ☐ 144 | Felix Jones RC | 3.00 | 1.25 |
| ☐ 145 | Fred Davis RC | 1.25 | .50 |
| ☐ 146 | Fred Davis RC | 1.25 | .50 |
| ☐ 147 | Glenn Dorsey RC | 1.50 | .60 |
| ☐ 148 | Glenn Dorsey RC | 1.50 | .60 |
| ☐ 149 | Jacob Tamme RC | 1.25 | .50 |
| ☐ 150 | Jacob Tamme RC | 1.25 | .50 |
| ☐ 151 | Jake Long RC | 1.50 | .60 |
| ☐ 152 | Jake Long RC | 1.50 | .60 |
| ☐ 153 | Shawn Crable RC | 1.25 | .50 |
| ☐ 154 | Shawn Crable RC | 1.25 | .50 |
| ☐ 155 | J Leman RC | 1.00 | .40 |
| ☐ 156 | J Leman RC | 1.00 | .40 |
| ☐ 157 | Joe Flacco RC | 4.00 | 1.50 |
| ☐ 158 | Joe Flacco RC | 4.00 | 1.50 |
| ☐ 159 | John Carlson RC | 1.25 | .50 |
| ☐ 160 | John Carlson RC | 1.25 | .50 |
| ☐ 161 | Jonathan Hefney RC | 1.00 | .40 |
| ☐ 162 | Jonathan Hefney RC | 1.00 | .40 |
| ☐ 163 | Jonathan Stewart RC | 3.00 | 1.25 |
| ☐ 164 | Jonathan Stewart RC | 3.00 | 1.25 |
| ☐ 165 | Keith Rivers RC | 1.25 | .50 |
| ☐ 166 | Keith Rivers RC | 1.25 | .50 |
| ☐ 167 | Lavelle Hawkins RC | 1.00 | .40 |
| ☐ 168 | Lavelle Hawkins RC | 1.00 | .40 |
| ☐ 169 | Lawrence Jackson RC | 1.00 | .40 |
| ☐ 170 | Lawrence Jackson RC | 1.00 | .40 |
| ☐ 171 | Limas Sweed RC | 1.50 | .60 |
| ☐ 172 | Limas Sweed RC | 1.50 | .60 |
| ☐ 173 | Justin King RC | 1.00 | .40 |
| ☐ 174 | Justin King RC | 1.00 | .40 |
| ☐ 175 | Malcolm Kelly RC | 1.25 | .50 |
| ☐ 176 | Malcolm Kelly RC | 1.25 | .50 |
| ☐ 177 | Mario Manningham RC | 1.25 | .50 |
| ☐ 178 | Mario Manningham RC | 1.25 | .50 |
| ☐ 179 | Matt Ryan RC | 5.00 | 2.00 |
| ☐ 180 | Matt Ryan RC | 5.00 | 2.00 |
| ☐ 181 | Mike Hart RC | 1.50 | .60 |
| ☐ 182 | Mike Hart RC | 1.50 | .60 |
| ☐ 183 | Mike Jenkins RC | 1.25 | .50 |
| ☐ 184 | Mike Jenkins RC | 1.25 | .50 |
| ☐ 185 | Ray Rice RC | 1.50 | .60 |
| ☐ 186 | Ray Rice RC | 1.50 | .60 |
| ☐ 187 | Rashard Mendenhall RC | 2.50 | 1.00 |
| ☐ 188 | Rashard Mendenhall RC | 2.50 | 1.00 |
| ☐ 189 | Sam Baker RC | .75 | .30 |
| ☐ 190 | Sam Baker RC | .75 | .30 |
| ☐ 191 | Sedrick Ellis RC | 1.25 | .50 |
| ☐ 192 | Sedrick Ellis RC | 1.25 | .50 |
| ☐ 193 | Tashard Choice RC | 1.25 | .50 |
| ☐ 194 | Tashard Choice RC | 1.25 | .50 |
| ☐ 195 | Terrell Thomas RC | 1.00 | .40 |
| ☐ 196 | Terrell Thomas RC | 1.00 | .40 |
| ☐ 197 | Tom Zbikowski RC | 1.50 | .60 |
| ☐ 198 | Tom Zbikowski RC | 1.50 | .60 |
| ☐ 199 | Xavier Adibi RC | 1.00 | .40 |
| ☐ 200 | Xavier Adibi RC | 1.00 | .40 |
| ☐ 201 | Barry Sanders | 2.00 | .75 |
| ☐ 202 | Barry Sanders | 2.00 | .75 |
| ☐ 203 | Barry Sanders | 2.00 | .75 |
| ☐ 204 | Billy Sims | 1.00 | .40 |
| ☐ 205 | Billy Sims | 1.00 | .40 |
| ☐ 206 | Billy Sims | 1.00 | .40 |
| ☐ 207 | Bo Jackson | 2.00 | .75 |
| ☐ 208 | Bo Jackson | 2.00 | .75 |
| ☐ 209 | Bo Jackson | 2.00 | .75 |
| ☐ 210 | Dan Marino | 2.50 | 1.00 |
| ☐ 211 | Dan Marino | 2.50 | 1.00 |
| ☐ 212 | Dan Marino | 2.50 | 1.00 |
| ☐ 213 | Fran Tarkenton | 1.25 | .50 |
| ☐ 214 | Fran Tarkenton | 1.25 | .50 |
| ☐ 215 | Fran Tarkenton | 1.25 | .50 |
| ☐ 216 | Franco Harris | 1.25 | .50 |
| ☐ 217 | Franco Harris | 1.25 | .50 |
| ☐ 218 | Franco Harris | 1.25 | .50 |
| ☐ 219 | Mel Blount | 1.00 | .40 |
| ☐ 220 | Mel Blount | 1.00 | .40 |
| ☐ 221 | Mel Blount | 1.00 | .40 |
| ☐ 222 | Paul Hornung | 1.25 | .50 |
| ☐ 223 | Paul Hornung | 1.25 | .50 |
| ☐ 224 | Paul Hornung | 1.25 | .50 |
| ☐ 225 | Jim Brown | 1.50 | .60 |
| ☐ 226 | Jim Brown | 1.50 | .60 |
| ☐ 227 | Jim Brown | 1.50 | .60 |
| ☐ 228 | Jim McMahon | 1.25 | .50 |
| ☐ 229 | Jim McMahon | 1.25 | .50 |
| ☐ 230 | Jim McMahon | 1.25 | .50 |
| ☐ 231 | John Elway | 2.00 | .75 |
| ☐ 232 | John Elway | 2.00 | .75 |
| ☐ 233 | John Elway | 2.00 | .75 |
| ☐ 234 | Ken Stabler | 1.25 | .50 |
| ☐ 235 | Ken Stabler | 1.25 | .50 |
| ☐ 236 | Ken Stabler | 1.25 | .50 |
| ☐ 237 | Ken Anderson | 1.00 | .40 |
| ☐ 238 | Ken Anderson | 1.00 | .40 |
| ☐ 239 | Ken Anderson | 1.00 | .40 |
| ☐ 240 | Roger Craig | 1.00 | .40 |
| ☐ 241 | Roger Craig | 1.00 | .40 |
| ☐ 242 | Roger Craig | 1.00 | .40 |
| ☐ 243 | Gale Sayers | 1.50 | .60 |
| ☐ 244 | Gale Sayers | 1.50 | .60 |
| ☐ 245 | Gale Sayers | 1.50 | .60 |
| ☐ 246 | Michael Johnson | 1.00 | .40 |
| ☐ 247 | Michael Johnson | 1.00 | .40 |
| ☐ 248 | Michael Johnson | 1.00 | .40 |
| ☐ 249 | Steve Vai | 1.00 | .40 |
| ☐ 250 | Steve Vai | 1.00 | .40 |
| ☐ 251 | Steve Vai | 1.00 | .40 |
| ☐ 252 | Tom Morello | 1.00 | .40 |
| ☐ 253 | Tom Morello | 1.00 | .40 |
| ☐ 254 | Tom Morello | 1.00 | .40 |
| ☐ 255 | Justin Hayward | 2.00 | .75 |
| ☐ 256 | Justin Hayward | 2.00 | .75 |
| ☐ 257 | Justin Hayward | 2.00 | .75 |
| ☐ 258 | Rulon Gardner | 1.00 | .40 |
| ☐ 259 | Rulon Gardner | 1.00 | .40 |
| ☐ 260 | Rulon Gardner | 1.00 | .40 |
| ☐ 264 | Tony Iommi | 1.00 | .40 |
| ☐ 265 | Tony Iommi | 1.00 | .40 |
| ☐ 266 | Tony Iommi | 1.00 | .40 |
| ☐ 267 | Jackie Joyner-Kersee | 1.00 | .40 |
| ☐ 268 | Jackie Joyner-Kersee | 1.00 | .40 |
| ☐ 269 | Jackie Joyner-Kersee | 1.00 | .40 |

## 2008 Upper Deck Icons

| | | | |
|---|---|---:|---:|
| ☐ 1 | Edgerrin James | .60 | .25 |
| ☐ 2 | Larry Fitzgerald | .75 | .30 |
| ☐ 3 | Matt Leinart | .75 | .30 |
| ☐ 4 | Jamal Lewis | .60 | .25 |
| ☐ 5 | Aaron Rodgers | .75 | .30 |
| ☐ 6 | Steve McNair | .60 | .25 |
| ☐ 7 | Ray Lewis | .75 | .30 |
| ☐ 8 | Todd Heap | .50 | .20 |
| ☐ 9 | Willis McGahee | .60 | .25 |
| ☐ 10 | Marshawn Lynch | .75 | .30 |

| | | |
|---|---|---|
| ❑ 11 Roscoe Parrish | .50 | .20 |
| ❑ 12 Trent Edwards | .75 | .30 |
| ❑ 13 DeShaun Foster | .60 | .25 |
| ❑ 14 Julius Peppers | .60 | .25 |
| ❑ 15 Thomas Jones | .60 | .25 |
| ❑ 16 Brian Urlacher | .75 | .30 |
| ❑ 17 Devin Hester | .75 | .30 |
| ❑ 18 Rex Grossman | .60 | .25 |
| ❑ 19 Carson Palmer | .75 | .30 |
| ❑ 20 T.J. Houshmandzadeh | .60 | .25 |
| ❑ 21 Rudi Johnson | .60 | .25 |
| ❑ 22 Derek Anderson | .60 | .25 |
| ❑ 23 Kellen Winslow | .60 | .25 |
| ❑ 24 Braylon Edwards | .60 | .25 |
| ❑ 25 Tony Romo | 1.25 | .50 |
| ❑ 26 Terrell Owens | .75 | .30 |
| ❑ 27 Marion Barber | .75 | .30 |
| ❑ 28 Brandon Marshall | .60 | .25 |
| ❑ 29 Travis Henry | .60 | .25 |
| ❑ 30 Champ Bailey | .50 | .20 |
| ❑ 31 Calvin Johnson | .75 | .30 |
| ❑ 32 Joseph Addai | .75 | .30 |
| ❑ 33 Jon Kitna | .60 | .25 |
| ❑ 34 Brett Favre | 2.00 | .75 |
| ❑ 35 Donald Driver | .60 | .25 |
| ❑ 36 Ryan Grant | .75 | .30 |
| ❑ 37 Greg Jennings | .60 | .25 |
| ❑ 38 DeMeco Ryans | .60 | .25 |
| ❑ 39 Andre Johnson | .60 | .25 |
| ❑ 40 Matt Schaub | .60 | .25 |
| ❑ 41 Peyton Manning | 1.25 | .50 |
| ❑ 42 Reggie Wayne | .60 | .25 |
| ❑ 43 Bob Sanders | .60 | .25 |
| ❑ 44 David Garrard | .60 | .25 |
| ❑ 45 Maurice Jones-Drew | .60 | .25 |
| ❑ 46 Matt Jones | .60 | .25 |
| ❑ 47 Fred Taylor | .60 | .25 |
| ❑ 48 Tony Gonzalez | .60 | .25 |
| ❑ 49 Derrick Johnson | .50 | .20 |
| ❑ 50 Dwayne Bowe | .60 | .25 |
| ❑ 51 Larry Johnson | .60 | .25 |
| ❑ 52 Ronnie Brown | .60 | .25 |
| ❑ 53 Ted Ginn Jr. | .60 | .25 |
| ❑ 54 Jason Taylor | .60 | .25 |
| ❑ 55 Tarvaris Jackson | .60 | .25 |
| ❑ 56 Adrian Peterson | 1.50 | .60 |
| ❑ 57 Ben Roethlisberger | 1.00 | .40 |
| ❑ 58 Tom Brady | 1.25 | .50 |
| ❑ 59 Randy Moss | .75 | .30 |
| ❑ 60 Laurence Maroney | .60 | .25 |
| ❑ 61 Wes Welker | .75 | .30 |
| ❑ 62 Drew Brees | .75 | .30 |
| ❑ 63 Marques Colston | .60 | .25 |
| ❑ 64 Reggie Bush | .75 | .30 |
| ❑ 65 Eli Manning | .75 | .30 |
| ❑ 66 Antonio Pierce | .50 | .20 |
| ❑ 67 Plaxico Burress | .60 | .25 |
| ❑ 68 Jeremy Shockey | .60 | .25 |
| ❑ 69 Jonathan Vilma | .60 | .25 |
| ❑ 70 JaMarcus Russell | .75 | .30 |
| ❑ 71 Kirk Morrison | .50 | .20 |
| ❑ 72 Ronald Curry | .60 | .25 |
| ❑ 73 Brian Westbrook | .60 | .25 |
| ❑ 74 Brian Dawkins | .60 | .25 |
| ❑ 75 Donovan McNabb | .75 | .30 |
| ❑ 76 Santonio Holmes | .60 | .25 |
| ❑ 77 Willie Parker | .60 | .25 |
| ❑ 78 Troy Polamalu | .75 | .30 |
| ❑ 79 LaDainian Tomlinson | 1.00 | .40 |
| ❑ 80 Shawne Merriman | .60 | .25 |
| ❑ 81 Antonio Cromartie | .50 | .20 |
| ❑ 82 Antonio Gates | .60 | .25 |
| ❑ 83 Alex Smith QB | .60 | .25 |
| ❑ 84 Frank Gore | .60 | .25 |
| ❑ 85 Patrick Willis | .60 | .25 |
| ❑ 86 Matt Hasselbeck | .60 | .25 |
| ❑ 87 Shaun Alexander | .60 | .25 |
| ❑ 88 Deion Branch | .60 | .25 |
| ❑ 89 Steven Jackson | .75 | .30 |
| ❑ 90 Torry Holt | .60 | .25 |
| ❑ 91 Marc Bulger | .60 | .25 |
| ❑ 92 Jeff Garcia | .60 | .25 |
| ❑ 93 Cadillac Williams | .60 | .25 |
| ❑ 94 Joey Galloway | .60 | .25 |

| | | |
|---|---|---|
| ❑ 95 Vince Young | .75 | .30 |
| ❑ 96 LenDale White | .60 | .25 |
| ❑ 97 Albert Haynesworth | .50 | .20 |
| ❑ 98 Jason Campbell | .60 | .25 |
| ❑ 99 Chris Cooley | .60 | .25 |
| ❑ 100 Clinton Portis | .60 | .25 |
| ❑ 101 Earl Bennett RC | 3.00 | 1.25 |
| ❑ 102 Adrian Arrington RC | 2.50 | 1.00 |
| ❑ 103 Ali Highsmith RC | 2.00 | .75 |
| ❑ 104 Allen Patrick RC | 2.50 | 1.00 |
| ❑ 105 Andre Caldwell RC | 2.50 | 1.00 |
| ❑ 106 Andre Woodson RC | 3.00 | 1.25 |
| ❑ 107 Antoine Cason RC | 3.00 | 1.25 |
| ❑ 108 Aqib Talib RC | 3.00 | 1.25 |
| ❑ 109 Ben Moffitt RC | 2.00 | .75 |
| ❑ 110 Brian Brohm RC | 4.00 | 1.50 |
| ❑ 111 Bruce Davis RC | 3.00 | 1.25 |
| ❑ 112 Calais Campbell RC | 2.50 | 1.00 |
| ❑ 113 Chad Henne RC | 5.00 | 2.00 |
| ❑ 114 Chevis Jackson RC | 2.50 | 1.00 |
| ❑ 115 Chris Ellis RC | 2.50 | 1.00 |
| ❑ 116 Chris Johnson RC | 8.00 | 3.00 |
| ❑ 117 Chris Long RC | 4.00 | 1.50 |
| ❑ 118 Colt Brennan RC | 8.00 | 3.00 |
| ❑ 119 Craig Steltz RC | 2.50 | 1.00 |
| ❑ 120 DJ Hall RC | 3.00 | 1.25 |
| ❑ 121 Dan Connor RC | 3.00 | 1.25 |
| ❑ 122 Darren McFadden RC | 8.00 | 3.00 |
| ❑ 123 Davone Bess RC | 4.00 | 1.50 |
| ❑ 124 DeMario Pressley RC | 2.50 | 1.00 |
| ❑ 125 Dennis Dixon RC | 3.00 | 1.25 |
| ❑ 126 DeSean Jackson RC | 6.00 | 2.50 |
| ❑ 127 Donnie Avery RC | 4.00 | 1.50 |
| ❑ 128 Jerome Simpson RC | 2.50 | 1.00 |
| ❑ 129 Dre Moore RC | 2.50 | 1.00 |
| ❑ 130 Dwight Lowery RC | 2.00 | .75 |
| ❑ 131 Early Doucet RC | 3.00 | 1.25 |
| ❑ 132 Erik Ainge RC | 3.00 | 1.25 |
| ❑ 133 Felix Jones RC | 8.00 | 3.00 |
| ❑ 134 Fred Davis RC | 3.00 | 1.25 |
| ❑ 135 Glenn Dorsey RC | 4.00 | 1.50 |
| ❑ 136 Harry Douglas RC | 3.00 | 1.25 |
| ❑ 137 Eddie Royal RC | 6.00 | 2.50 |
| ❑ 138 Jack Ikegwuonu RC | 2.50 | 1.00 |
| ❑ 139 Jacob Hester RC | 3.00 | 1.25 |
| ❑ 140 Jacob Tamme RC | 2.50 | 1.00 |
| ❑ 141 Jake Long RC | 4.00 | 1.50 |
| ❑ 142 Jamaal Charles RC | 4.00 | 1.50 |
| ❑ 143 James Hardy RC | 3.00 | 1.25 |
| ❑ 144 J Leman RC | 2.50 | 1.00 |
| ❑ 145 Joe Flacco RC | 10.00 | 4.00 |
| ❑ 146 John Carlson RC | 3.00 | 1.25 |
| ❑ 147 John David Booty RC | 4.00 | 1.50 |
| ❑ 148 Jonathan Goff RC | 2.50 | 1.00 |
| ❑ 149 Jonathan Hefney RC | 2.50 | 1.00 |
| ❑ 150 Jonathan Stewart RC | 8.00 | 3.00 |
| ❑ 151 Jordy Nelson RC | 4.00 | 1.50 |
| ❑ 152 Josh Johnson RC | 3.00 | 1.25 |
| ❑ 153 Justin Forsett RC | 3.00 | 1.25 |
| ❑ 154 Justin King RC | 2.50 | 1.00 |
| ❑ 155 Keenan Burton RC | 2.50 | 1.00 |
| ❑ 156 Keith Rivers RC | 3.00 | 1.25 |
| ❑ 157 Kenny Phillips RC | 3.00 | 1.25 |
| ❑ 158 Kentwan Balmer RC | 2.50 | 1.00 |
| ❑ 159 Kevin O'Connell RC | 4.00 | 1.50 |
| ❑ 160 Kevin Smith RC | 5.00 | 2.00 |
| ❑ 161 Alex Brink RC | 3.00 | 1.25 |
| ❑ 162 Lavelle Hawkins RC | 2.50 | 1.00 |
| ❑ 163 Lawrence Jackson RC | 2.50 | 1.00 |
| ❑ 164 Limas Sweed RC | 4.00 | 1.50 |
| ❑ 165 Malcolm Kelly RC | 3.00 | 1.25 |
| ❑ 166 Marcus Monk RC | 2.50 | 1.00 |
| ❑ 167 Mario Manningham RC | 3.00 | 1.25 |
| ❑ 168 Mario Urrutia RC | 2.50 | 1.00 |
| ❑ 169 Martellus Bennett RC | 3.00 | 1.25 |
| ❑ 170 Martin Rucker RC | 2.50 | 1.00 |
| ❑ 171 Matt Flynn RC | 4.00 | 1.50 |
| ❑ 172 Matt Forte RC | 8.00 | 3.00 |
| ❑ 173 Matt Ryan RC | 12.00 | 5.00 |
| ❑ 174 Mike Hart RC | 4.00 | 1.50 |
| ❑ 175 Mike Jenkins RC | 3.00 | 1.25 |
| ❑ 176 Owen Schmitt RC | 3.00 | 1.25 |
| ❑ 177 Paul Smith RC | 3.00 | 1.25 |
| ❑ 178 Philip Wheeler RC | 3.00 | 1.25 |

| | | |
|---|---|---|
| ❑ 179 Quentin Groves RC | 2.50 | 1.00 |
| ❑ 180 Quintin Demps RC | 2.50 | 1.00 |
| ❑ 181 Rashard Mendenhall RC | 6.00 | 2.50 |
| ❑ 182 Ray Rice RC | 4.00 | 1.50 |
| ❑ 183 Ryan Clady RC | 3.00 | 1.25 |
| ❑ 184 Ryan Torain RC | 3.00 | 1.25 |
| ❑ 185 Sam Baker RC | 2.00 | .75 |
| ❑ 186 Anthony Morelli RC | 3.00 | 1.25 |
| ❑ 187 Sedrick Ellis RC | 3.00 | 1.25 |
| ❑ 188 Dexter Jackson RC | 3.00 | 1.25 |
| ❑ 189 Shawn Crable RC | 3.00 | 1.25 |
| ❑ 190 Steve Slaton RC | 6.00 | 2.50 |
| ❑ 191 Tashard Choice RC | 3.00 | 1.25 |
| ❑ 192 Terrell Thomas RC | 2.50 | 1.00 |
| ❑ 193 Thomas Brown RC | 3.00 | 1.25 |
| ❑ 194 Tom Zbikowski RC | 4.00 | 1.50 |
| ❑ 195 Gosder Cherilus RC | 2.50 | 1.00 |
| ❑ 196 Trevor Laws RC | 3.00 | 1.25 |
| ❑ 197 Vernon Gholston RC | 3.00 | 1.25 |
| ❑ 198 Vince Hall RC | 2.00 | .75 |
| ❑ 199 Xavier Adibi RC | 2.50 | 1.00 |
| ❑ 200 Yvenson Bernard RC | 3.00 | 1.25 |
| ❑ 201 Jerome Felton RC | 2.00 | .75 |
| ❑ 202 Simeon Castille RC | 3.00 | 1.25 |
| ❑ 203 Craig Stevens RC | 2.50 | 1.00 |
| ❑ 204 Barry Richardson RC | 2.00 | .75 |
| ❑ 205 Beau Bell RC | 2.50 | 1.00 |
| ❑ 206 Caleb Campbell RC | 3.00 | 1.25 |
| ❑ 207 T.C. Ostrander RC | 3.00 | 1.25 |
| ❑ 208 Brad Cottam RC | 3.00 | 1.25 |
| ❑ 209 Brandon Flowers RC | 3.00 | 1.25 |
| ❑ 211 Chauncey Washington RC | 2.50 | 1.00 |
| ❑ 212 Chris Williams RC | 2.50 | 1.00 |
| ❑ 213 Cory Boyd RC | 2.50 | 1.00 |
| ❑ 214 Will Franklin RC | 2.50 | 1.00 |
| ❑ 215 Jo-Lonn Dunbar RC | 2.50 | 1.00 |
| ❑ 216 Xavier Omon RC | 2.50 | 1.00 |
| ❑ 217 Darius Reynaud RC | 2.50 | 1.00 |
| ❑ 218 Dantrell Savage RC | 3.00 | 1.25 |
| ❑ 219 DeJuan Tribble RC | 2.00 | .75 |
| ❑ 220 Dennis Keyes RC | 2.00 | .75 |
| ❑ 221 Devin Thomas RC | 3.00 | 1.25 |
| ❑ 222 Marcus Griffin RC | 2.00 | .75 |
| ❑ 223 Drew Radovich RC | 2.50 | 1.00 |
| ❑ 224 Marcus Thomas RC | 2.50 | 1.00 |
| ❑ 225 Frank Okam RC | 2.00 | .75 |
| ❑ 226 Brian Bonner RC | 2.00 | .75 |
| ❑ 227 Jamie Silva RC | 2.50 | 1.00 |
| ❑ 228 Jehuu Caulcrick RC | 2.50 | 1.00 |
| ❑ 229 Jermichael Finley RC | 3.00 | 1.25 |
| ❑ 230 Jerod Mayo RC | 5.00 | 2.00 |
| ❑ 231 Brandon McAnderson RC | 2.50 | 1.00 |
| ❑ 232 Jordon Dizon RC | 3.00 | 1.25 |
| ❑ 233 Josh Barrett RC | 2.00 | .75 |
| ❑ 234 Kalvin McRae RC | 2.50 | 1.00 |
| ❑ 235 Kellen Davis RC | 2.00 | .75 |
| ❑ 236 Keon Lattimore RC | 2.50 | 1.00 |
| ❑ 237 Leodis McKelvin RC | 3.00 | 1.25 |
| ❑ 239 Curtis Lofton RC | 3.00 | 1.25 |
| ❑ 240 Paul Hubbard RC | 2.50 | 1.00 |
| ❑ 241 Titus Brown RC | 2.00 | .75 |
| ❑ 242 Ryan Grice-Mullen RC | 3.00 | 1.25 |
| ❑ 243 Spencer Larsen RC | 2.00 | .75 |
| ❑ 244 Thomas DeCoud RC | 2.00 | .75 |
| ❑ 245 Erin Henderson RC | 2.50 | 1.00 |
| ❑ 246 Tracy Porter RC | 2.50 | 1.00 |
| ❑ 247 Trae Williams RC | 2.00 | .75 |
| ❑ 248 Trevor Scott RC | 2.50 | 1.00 |
| ❑ 249 Wesley Woodyard RC | 2.50 | 1.00 |
| ❑ 250 Xavier Lee RC | 2.50 | 1.00 |

## 2005 Upper Deck Rookie Premiere

| | | |
|---|---|---|
| ❑ COMPLETE SET (30) | 20.00 | 10.00 |
| ❑ 1 Ciatrick Fason | .60 | .25 |
| ❑ 2 Alex Smith QB | 1.25 | .50 |
| ❑ 3 Antrel Rolle | .75 | .30 |
| ❑ 4 Cadillac Williams | 1.50 | .60 |
| ❑ 5 Ronnie Brown | 2.50 | 1.00 |
| ❑ 6 Charlie Frye | .75 | .30 |
| ❑ 7 Roddy White | 1.00 | .40 |
| ❑ 8 Braylon Edwards | 2.50 | 1.00 |
| ❑ 9 Mark Bradley | .75 | .30 |

| | | |
|---|---|---|
| ❑ 10 Vincent Jackson | .75 | .30 |
| ❑ 11 Matt Jones | 1.25 | .50 |
| ❑ 12 Stefan LeFors | .60 | .25 |
| ❑ 13 Kyle Orton | 1.00 | .40 |
| ❑ 14 Troy Williamson | .75 | .30 |
| ❑ 15 Mark Clayton | .75 | .30 |
| ❑ 16 Aaron Rodgers | 2.50 | 1.00 |
| ❑ 17 Cedric Benson | .75 | .30 |
| ❑ 18 Mike Williams | .75 | .30 |
| ❑ 19 Adam Jones | .75 | .30 |
| ❑ 20 Reggie Brown | .75 | .30 |
| ❑ 21 J.J. Arrington | .75 | .30 |
| ❑ 22 Andrew Walter | .75 | .30 |
| ❑ 23 David Greene | .60 | .25 |
| ❑ 24 Roscoe Parrish | .60 | .25 |
| ❑ 25 Terrence Murphy | .50 | .20 |
| ❑ 26 Jason Campbell | 1.50 | .60 |
| ❑ 27 Maurice Clarett | .60 | .25 |
| ❑ 28 Frank Gore | 2.00 | .75 |
| ❑ 29 Ryan Moats | .75 | .30 |
| ❑ 30 Checklist Card | .75 | .30 |

## 2006 Aspire

| | | |
|---|---|---|
| ❑ COMPLETE SET (36) | 25.00 | 10.00 |
| ❑ 1 Reggie Bush | 4.00 | 1.50 |
| ❑ 2 Matt Leinart | 3.00 | 1.25 |
| ❑ 3 Vince Young | 3.00 | 1.25 |
| ❑ 4 Mario Williams | 1.50 | .60 |
| ❑ 5 Michael Huff | 1.00 | .40 |
| ❑ 6 Vernon Davis | 1.00 | .40 |
| ❑ 7 LenDale White | 2.00 | .75 |
| ❑ 8 Brodie Croyle | 1.25 | .50 |
| ❑ 9 Drew Olson | .75 | .30 |
| ❑ 10 Maurice Drew | 2.00 | .75 |
| ❑ 11 Tye Hill | 1.00 | .40 |
| ❑ 12 Michael Robinson | 1.00 | .40 |
| ❑ 13 Joseph Addai | 3.00 | 1.25 |
| ❑ 14 Paul Pinegar | .75 | .30 |
| ❑ 15 Jimmy Williams | 1.00 | .40 |
| ❑ 16 D.J. Shockley | 1.00 | .40 |
| ❑ 17 Mike Hass | 1.00 | .40 |
| ❑ 18 Demetrius Williams | 1.00 | .40 |
| ❑ 19 Reggie McNeal | .75 | .30 |
| ❑ 20 Charlie Whitehurst | 1.00 | .40 |
| ❑ 21 Maurice Stovall | 1.00 | .40 |
| ❑ 22 Sinorice Moss | 1.00 | .40 |
| ❑ 23 Jason Avant | 1.00 | .40 |
| ❑ 24 Omar Jacobs | .75 | .30 |
| ❑ 25 Laurence Maroney | 2.50 | 1.00 |
| ❑ 26 Martin Nance | .75 | .30 |

| | | |
|---|---|---|
| ❑ 27 Leonard Pope | 1.00 | .40 |
| ❑ 28 Rodrique Wright | .50 | .20 |
| ❑ 29 David Thomas | 1.00 | .40 |
| ❑ 30 Will Blackmon | 1.00 | .40 |
| ❑ 31 Dominique Byrd | .75 | .30 |
| ❑ 32 D'Brickashaw Ferguson | 1.00 | .40 |
| ❑ 33 Reggie Bush | 4.00 | 1.50 |
| ❑ 34 Matt Leinart | 3.00 | 1.25 |
| ❑ 35 Vince Young | 3.00 | 1.25 |
| ❑ 36 Jay Cutler | 4.00 | 1.50 |

## 2007 Aspire

| | | |
|---|---|---|
| ❑ 1 JaMarcus Russell | 2.50 | 1.00 |
| ❑ 2 Brady Quinn | 3.00 | 1.25 |
| ❑ 3 Drew Stanton | 1.00 | .40 |
| ❑ 4 John Beck | 1.00 | .40 |
| ❑ 5 Trent Edwards | 2.50 | 1.00 |
| ❑ 6 Troy Smith | 1.25 | .50 |
| ❑ 7 Kevin Kolb | 1.50 | .60 |
| ❑ 8 Jared Zabransky | 1.00 | .40 |
| ❑ 9 Jordan Palmer | 1.00 | .40 |
| ❑ 10 Chris Leak | .75 | .30 |
| ❑ 11 Adrian Peterson | 8.00 | 3.00 |
| ❑ 12 Marshawn Lynch | 2.00 | .75 |
| ❑ 13 Brian Leonard | 1.00 | .40 |
| ❑ 14 Antonio Pittman | 1.00 | .40 |
| ❑ 15 Kenny Irons | 1.00 | .40 |
| ❑ 16 Michael Bush | 1.00 | .40 |
| ❑ 17 Darius Walker | 1.00 | .40 |
| ❑ 18 Calvin Johnson | 2.50 | 1.00 |
| ❑ 19 Robert Meachem | 1.00 | .40 |
| ❑ 20 Dwayne Bowe | 2.00 | .75 |
| ❑ 21 Sidney Rice | 1.00 | .40 |
| ❑ 22 Craig Buster Davis | 1.00 | .40 |
| ❑ 23 Steve Smith USC | .75 | .30 |
| ❑ 24 Anthony Gonzalez | 1.50 | .60 |
| ❑ 25 Greg Olsen | 1.25 | .50 |
| ❑ 26 Zach Miller | .60 | .25 |
| ❑ 27 Levi Brown | 1.00 | .40 |
| ❑ 28 Gaines Adams | 1.00 | .40 |
| ❑ 29 Leon Hall | .75 | .30 |
| ❑ 30 Ted Ginn Jr. | 1.50 | .60 |
| ❑ 31 Patrick Willis | 1.50 | .60 |
| ❑ 32 Adam Carriker | .75 | .30 |
| ❑ 33 Aaron Ross | 1.00 | .40 |

## 2008 Aspire

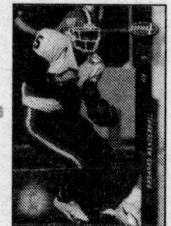

| | | |
|---|---|---|
| ❑ 1 Matt Ryan | 4.00 | 1.50 |
| ❑ 2 Brian Brohm | 1.25 | .50 |
| ❑ 3 Chad Henne | 1.50 | .60 |

| | | |
|---|---|---|
| ❑ 4 Joe Flacco | 3.00 | 1.25 |
| ❑ 5 John David Booty | 1.25 | .50 |
| ❑ 6 Josh Johnson | 1.00 | .40 |
| ❑ 7 Erik Ainge | 1.00 | .40 |
| ❑ 8 Dennis Dixon | 1.00 | .40 |
| ❑ 9 Darren McFadden | 2.50 | 1.00 |
| ❑ 10 Rashard Mendenhall | 2.00 | .75 |
| ❑ 11 Jonathan Stewart | 2.50 | 1.00 |
| ❑ 12 Jamaal Charles | 1.25 | .50 |
| ❑ 13 Felix Jones | 2.50 | 1.00 |
| ❑ 14 Ray Rice | 1.25 | .50 |
| ❑ 15 Kevin Smith | 1.50 | .60 |
| ❑ 16 Steve Slaton | 2.00 | .75 |
| ❑ 17 Mike Hart | 1.25 | .50 |
| ❑ 18 Malcolm Kelly | 1.00 | .40 |
| ❑ 19 DeSean Jackson | 2.00 | .75 |
| ❑ 20 Limas Sweed | 1.25 | .50 |
| ❑ 21 Early Doucet | 1.00 | .40 |
| ❑ 22 Andre Caldwell | .75 | .30 |
| ❑ 23 Devin Thomas | 1.00 | .40 |
| ❑ 24 James Hardy | 1.00 | .40 |
| ❑ 25 Fred Davis | 1.00 | .40 |
| ❑ 26 Jake Long | 1.25 | .50 |
| ❑ 27 Sedrick Ellis | 1.00 | .40 |
| ❑ 28 Vernon Gholston | 1.00 | .40 |
| ❑ 29 Keith Rivers | 1.00 | .40 |
| ❑ 30 Mike Jenkins | 1.00 | .40 |
| ❑ 31 Derrick Harvey | .75 | .30 |
| ❑ 32 Dan Connor | 1.00 | .40 |
| ❑ 33 Leodis McKelvin | 1.00 | .40 |

## 1996 Press Pass

| | | |
|---|---|---|
| ❑ COMPLETE SET (55) | 20.00 | 7.50 |
| ❑ 1 Keyshawn Johnson | 1.50 | .60 |
| ❑ 2 Jonathan Ogden | .60 | .25 |
| ❑ 3 Duane Clemons | .20 | .07 |
| ❑ 4 Kevin Hardy | .20 | .07 |
| ❑ 5 Eddie George | 2.50 | 1.00 |
| ❑ 6 Karim Abdul-Jabbar | .60 | .25 |
| ❑ 7 Terry Glenn | .60 | .25 |
| ❑ 8 Leeland McElroy | .40 | .15 |
| ❑ 9 Simeon Rice | .75 | .30 |
| ❑ 10 Roman Oben | .20 | .07 |
| ❑ 11 Daryl Gardener | .20 | .07 |
| ❑ 12 Marcus Coleman | .20 | .07 |
| ❑ 13 Christian Peter | .20 | .07 |
| ❑ 14 Tim Biakabutuka | .60 | .25 |
| ❑ 15 Eric Moulds | 1.50 | .60 |
| ❑ 16 Chris Darkins | .20 | .07 |
| ❑ 17 Andre Johnson | .20 | .07 |
| ❑ 18 Lawyer Milloy | .60 | .25 |
| ❑ 19 Jon Runyan | .20 | .07 |
| ❑ 20 Mike Alstott | 1.50 | .60 |
| ❑ 21 Jeff Hartings | .60 | .25 |
| ❑ 22 Amani Toomer | 1.25 | .50 |
| ❑ 23 Danny Kanell | .60 | .25 |
| ❑ 24 Marco Battaglia | .20 | .07 |
| ❑ 25 Stephen Davis | 1.50 | .60 |
| ❑ 26 Johnny McWilliams | .20 | .07 |
| ❑ 27 Israel Ifeanyi | .20 | .07 |
| ❑ 28 Scott Slutzker | .20 | .07 |
| ❑ 29 Bryant Mix | .20 | .07 |
| ❑ 30 Brian Roche | .20 | .07 |
| ❑ 31 Stanley Pritchett | .20 | .07 |
| ❑ 32 Jerome Woods | .20 | .07 |
| ❑ 33 Tommie Frazier | .40 | .15 |
| ❑ 34 Stepfret Williams | .20 | .07 |

| | | |
|---|---|---|
| ☐ 35 Ray Mickens | .20 | .07 |
| ☐ 36 Alex Van Dyke | .20 | .07 |
| ☐ 37 Bobby Hoying | .60 | .25 |
| ☐ 38 Tony Brackens | .60 | .25 |
| ☐ 39 Dietrich Jells | .20 | .07 |
| ☐ 40 Jason Odom | .20 | .07 |
| ☐ 41 Randall Godfrey | .20 | .07 |
| ☐ 42 Willie Anderson | .20 | .07 |
| ☐ 43 Tony Banks | .60 | .25 |
| ☐ 44 Michael Cheever | .20 | .07 |
| ☐ 45 Je'Rod Cherry | .20 | .07 |
| ☐ 46 Chris Doering | .20 | .07 |
| ☐ 47 Steve Taneyhill | .20 | .07 |
| ☐ 48 Kyle Wachholtz | .20 | .07 |
| ☐ 49 Dusty Zeigler | .20 | .07 |
| ☐ 50 Derrick Mayes | .40 | .15 |
| ☐ 51 Orpheus Roye | .20 | .07 |
| ☐ 52 Sedric Clark | .20 | .07 |
| ☐ 53 Richard Huntley | .40 | .15 |
| ☐ 54 Donnie Edwards | .60 | .25 |
| ☐ 55 Zach Thomas CL | .60 | .25 |
| ☐ RED Lawrence Phillips | 6.00 | 2.50 |
| ☐ P1 Tim Biakabutuka Promo | 1.00 | .40 |

## 1997 Press Pass

| | | |
|---|---|---|
| ☐ COMPLETE SET (49) | 20.00 | 7.50 |
| ☐ 1 Orlando Pace | .50 | .20 |
| ☐ 2 Warrick Dunn | 1.25 | .50 |
| ☐ 3 Danny Wuerffel | .50 | .20 |
| ☐ 4 Darnell Autry | .20 | .07 |
| ☐ 5 Troy Davis | .20 | .07 |
| ☐ 6 Jake Plummer | 2.00 | .75 |
| ☐ 7 Corey Dillon | 2.50 | 1.00 |
| ☐ 8 Reidel Anthony | .50 | .20 |
| ☐ 9 Byron Hanspard | .30 | .10 |
| ☐ 10 Tiki Barber | 2.50 | 1.00 |
| ☐ 11 Ike Hilliard | .50 | .20 |
| ☐ 12 Rae Carruth | .20 | .07 |
| ☐ 13 Yatil Green | .30 | .10 |
| ☐ 14 Peter Boulware | .50 | .20 |
| ☐ 15 Jim Druckenmiller | .30 | .10 |
| ☐ 16 Pat Barnes | .20 | .07 |
| ☐ 17 Trevor Pryce | .50 | .20 |
| ☐ 18 Kevin Lockett | .20 | .07 |
| ☐ 19 Koy Detmer | .20 | .07 |
| ☐ 20 Bryant Westbrook | .20 | .07 |
| ☐ 21 Darrell Russell | .20 | .07 |
| ☐ 22 Tony Gonzalez | 1.25 | .50 |
| ☐ 23 Shawn Springs | .30 | .10 |
| ☐ 24 Chris Canty | .20 | .07 |
| ☐ 25 David LaFleur | .20 | .07 |
| ☐ 26 Dwayne Rudd | .20 | .07 |
| ☐ 27 Bob Sapp | .50 | .20 |
| ☐ 28 Mike Vrabel | 2.00 | .75 |
| ☐ 29 Antowain Smith | 1.00 | .40 |
| ☐ 30 Keith Poole | .20 | .07 |
| ☐ 31 Sedrick Shaw | .30 | .10 |
| ☐ 32 Tremain Mack | .20 | .07 |
| ☐ 33 Matt Russell | .20 | .07 |
| ☐ 34 Reinard Wilson | .30 | .10 |
| ☐ 35 Marc Edwards | .30 | .10 |
| ☐ 36 Greg Jones | .20 | .07 |
| ☐ 37 Michael Booker | .20 | .07 |
| ☐ 38 James Farrior | .50 | .20 |
| ☐ 39 Danny Wuerffel HL | .30 | .10 |
| ☐ 40 Troy Davis HL | .20 | .07 |
| ☐ 41 Corey Dillon HL | 1.00 | .40 |
| ☐ 42 Jake Plummer HL | .75 | .30 |
| ☐ 43 Peter Boulware HL | .30 | .10 |
| ☐ 44 Eddie Robinson CO | .50 | .20 |
| ☐ 45 Bobby Bowden CO | .75 | .30 |
| ☐ 46 Steve Spurrier CO | 1.25 | .50 |
| ☐ 47 Gary Barnett CO | .20 | .07 |
| ☐ 48 Joe Paterno CO | 50.00 | 20.00 |
| ☐ 49 Tom Osborne CO | 1.25 | .50 |
| ☐ 50 Jarrett Irons CL | .20 | .07 |

## 1998 Press Pass

| | | |
|---|---|---|
| ☐ COMPLETE SET (50) | 20.00 | 7.50 |
| ☐ 1 Peyton Manning | 8.00 | 3.00 |
| ☐ 2 Ryan Leaf | .50 | .20 |
| ☐ 3 Charles Woodson | .75 | .30 |
| ☐ 4 Andre Wadsworth | .30 | .10 |
| ☐ 5 Randy Moss | 5.00 | 2.00 |
| ☐ 6 Curtis Enis | .25 | .08 |
| ☐ 7 Tra Thomas | .25 | .08 |
| ☐ 8 Flozell Adams | .25 | .08 |
| ☐ 9 Jason Peter | .25 | .08 |
| ☐ 10 Brian Simmons | .30 | .10 |
| ☐ 11 Takeo Spikes | .50 | .20 |
| ☐ 12 Michael Myers | .25 | .08 |
| ☐ 13 Kevin Dyson | .50 | .20 |
| ☐ 14 Grant Wistrom | .30 | .10 |
| ☐ 15 Fred Taylor | 1.25 | .50 |
| ☐ 16 Germane Crowell | .30 | .10 |
| ☐ 17 Sam Cowart | .30 | .10 |
| ☐ 18 Anthony Simmons LB | .30 | .10 |
| ☐ 19 Robert Edwards | .30 | .10 |
| ☐ 20 Shaun Williams | .30 | .10 |
| ☐ 21 Phil Savoy | .25 | .08 |
| ☐ 22 Leonard Little | .50 | .20 |
| ☐ 23 Saladin McCullough | .25 | .08 |
| ☐ 24 Duane Starks | .30 | .10 |
| ☐ 25 John Avery | .30 | .10 |
| ☐ 26 Vonnie Holliday | .50 | .20 |
| ☐ 27 Tim Dwight | .50 | .20 |
| ☐ 28 Donovin Darius | .25 | .08 |
| ☐ 29 Alonzo Mayes | .25 | .08 |
| ☐ 30 Jerome Pathon | .50 | .20 |
| ☐ 31 Brian Kelly | .30 | .10 |
| ☐ 32 Hines Ward | 2.50 | 1.25 |
| ☐ 33 Jacquez Green | .30 | .10 |
| ☐ 34 Marcus Nash | .25 | .08 |
| ☐ 35 Ahman Green | 1.50 | .60 |
| ☐ 36 Joe Jurevicius | .50 | .20 |
| ☐ 37 Tavian Banks | .30 | .10 |
| ☐ 38 Donald Hayes | .30 | .10 |
| ☐ 39 Robert Holcombe | .30 | .10 |
| ☐ 40 E.G. Green | .30 | .10 |
| ☐ 41 John Dutton | .25 | .08 |
| ☐ 42 Skip Hicks | .30 | .10 |
| ☐ 43 Pat Johnson | .30 | .10 |
| ☐ 44 Keith Brooking | .50 | .20 |
| ☐ 45 Alan Faneca | 1.00 | .40 |
| ☐ 46 Steve Spurrier CO | 1.00 | .40 |
| ☐ 47 Mike Price CO | .25 | .08 |
| ☐ 48 Bobby Bowden CO | .30 | .10 |
| ☐ 49 Tom Osborne CO | 1.00 | .40 |
| ☐ 50 Peyton Manning CL | 1.50 | .60 |
| ☐ P1 Randy Moss Promo | 4.00 | 1.50 |

## 1999 Press Pass

| | | |
|---|---|---|
| ☐ COMPLETE SET (45) | 20.00 | 7.50 |
| ☐ 1 Ricky Williams | 1.25 | .50 |
| ☐ 2 Tim Couch | .60 | .25 |
| ☐ 3 Champ Bailey | 1.00 | .40 |
| ☐ 4 Chris Claiborne | .30 | .10 |
| ☐ 5 Donovan McNabb | 3.00 | 1.25 |
| ☐ 6 Edgerrin James | 2.50 | 1.00 |
| ☐ 7 Akili Smith | 1.00 | .40 |
| ☐ 8 John Tait | .30 | .10 |
| ☐ 9 Javon Kearse | 1.50 | .60 |
| ☐ 10 Torry Holt | 1.50 | .60 |
| ☐ 11 Troy Edwards | .40 | .15 |
| ☐ 12 Chris McAlister | .40 | .15 |
| ☐ 13 Daunte Culpepper | 2.50 | 1.00 |
| ☐ 14 Andy Katzenmoyer | .40 | .15 |
| ☐ 15 David Boston | .60 | .25 |
| ☐ 16 Ebenezer Ekuban | .40 | .15 |
| ☐ 17 Peerless Price | .60 | .25 |
| ☐ 18 Shaun King | .60 | .25 |
| ☐ 19 Joe Germaine | .40 | .15 |
| ☐ 20 Brock Huard | .60 | .25 |
| ☐ 21 Michael Bishop | .60 | .25 |
| ☐ 22 Amos Zereoue | .60 | .25 |
| ☐ 23 Sedrick Irvin | .30 | .10 |
| ☐ 24 Autry Denson | .40 | .15 |
| ☐ 25 Kevin Faulk | .60 | .25 |
| ☐ 26 James Johnson | .40 | .15 |
| ☐ 27 D'Wayne Bates | .40 | .15 |
| ☐ 28 Kevin Johnson | 1.00 | .40 |
| ☐ 29 Tai Streets | .40 | .15 |
| ☐ 30 Craig Yeast | .40 | .15 |
| ☐ 31 Dre' Bly | .60 | .25 |
| ☐ 32 Anthony Poindexter | .30 | .10 |
| ☐ 33 Jared DeVries | .30 | .10 |
| ☐ 34 Rob Konrad | .60 | .25 |
| ☐ 35 Dat Nguyen | .60 | .25 |
| ☐ 36 Cade McNown | .40 | .15 |
| ☐ 37 Scott Covington | .60 | .25 |
| ☐ 38 Jon Jansen | .30 | .10 |
| ☐ 39 Rufus French | .30 | .10 |
| ☐ 40 Mike Rucker | .60 | .25 |
| ☐ 41 Aaron Gibson | .30 | .10 |
| ☐ 42 Kris Farris | .30 | .10 |
| ☐ 43 Anthony McFarland | .30 | .10 |
| ☐ 44 Matt Stinchcomb | .40 | .15 |
| ☐ 45 Dee Miller CL | .30 | .10 |

## 2000 Press Pass

❑ COMPLETE SET (45) 25.00 10.00
❑ 1 Peter Warrick .50 .20
❑ 2 Travis Claridge .25 .08
❑ 3 Courtney Brown .60 .25
❑ 4 Plaxico Burress 1.00 .40
❑ 5 Chad Pennington 1.00 .40
❑ 6 Thomas Jones .75 .30
❑ 7 Ron Dayne .50 .20
❑ 8 Brian Urlacher 2.00 .75
❑ 9 Corey Simon .60 .25
❑ 10 Chris Samuels .40 .15
❑ 11 Stockar McDougle .25 .08
❑ 12 Deon Grant .40 .15
❑ 13 Cosey Coleman .25 .08
❑ 14 Sylvester Morris .40 .15
❑ 15 Shyrone Stith .40 .15
❑ 16 Shaun Alexander 1.50 .60
❑ 17 Dez White .50 .20
❑ 18 John Engelberger .40 .15
❑ 19 Tim Rattay .50 .20
❑ 20 Todd Pinkston .50 .20
❑ 21 John Abraham .50 .20
❑ 22 R.Jay Soward .40 .15
❑ 23 Shaun Ellis .50 .20
❑ 24 Keith Bulluck .50 .20
❑ 25 Jerry Porter .60 .25
❑ 26 Darren Howard .40 .15
❑ 27 Joe Hamilton .40 .15
❑ 28 Deltha O'Neal .50 .20
❑ 29 Chris Redman .40 .15
❑ 30 Deon Dyer .40 .15
❑ 31 Jamal Lewis 1.00 .40
❑ 32 Chris Hovan .40 .15
❑ 33 Raynoch Thompson .40 .15
❑ 34 Travis Taylor .50 .20
❑ 35 Sebastian Janikowski .50 .20
❑ 36 Travis Prentice .40 .15
❑ 37 Tom Brady 20.00 10.00
❑ 38 Tee Martin .50 .20
❑ 39 J.R. Redmond .40 .15
❑ 40 Dennis Northcutt .50 .20
❑ 41 Laveranues Coles .60 .25
❑ 42 Danny Farmer .40 .15
❑ 43 Darrell Jackson 1.00 .40
❑ 44 Chris McIntosh .25 .08
❑ 45 Peter Warrick CL .50 .20
❑ P1 Peter Warrick Promo 2.00 .75

## 2001 Press Pass

❑ COMPLETE SET (50) 25.00 10.00
❑ COMP.FACTORY SET (46) 25.00 10.00
❑ COMP.SET w/o SP's (45) 20.00 7.50
❑ 1 Michael Vick CL 1.00 .40
❑ 2 Drew Brees 3.00 1.25
❑ 3 Michael Vick 2.00 .75
❑ 4 Chris Weinke .75 .30
❑ 5 Marques Tuiasosopo .75 .30
❑ 6 Josh Booty .75 .30
❑ 7 Josh Heupel .75 .30
❑ 8 Sage Rosenfels .75 .30
❑ 9 Mike McMahon .75 .30
❑ 10 Deuce McAllister .75 .30
❑ 11 LaDainian Tomlinson 12.00 5.00
❑ 12 LaMont Jordan 1.50 .60
❑ 13 James Jackson .75 .30
❑ 14 Travis Henry .75 .30
❑ 15 Anthony Thomas .75 .30

❑ 16 Travis Minor .60 .25
❑ 17 Michael Bennett .75 .30
❑ 18 Kevan Barlow .75 .30
❑ 19 Rudi Johnson 1.50 .60
❑ 20 Santana Moss 1.50 .60
❑ 21 Quincy Morgan .75 .30
❑ 22 Rod Gardner .75 .30
❑ 23 David Terrell .75 .30
❑ 24 Chris Chambers 1.50 .60
❑ 25 Reggie Wayne 2.00 .75
❑ 26 Ken-Yon Rambo .60 .25
❑ 27 Chad Johnson 2.00 .75
❑ 28 Snoop Minnis .60 .25
❑ 29 Freddie Mitchell .75 .30
❑ 30 Koren Robinson .75 .30
❑ 31 Bobby Newcombe .60 .25
❑ 32 Robert Ferguson .75 .30
❑ 33 Todd Heap .75 .30
❑ 34 Steve Hutchinson .60 .25
❑ 35 Leonard Davis .60 .25
❑ 36 Kenyatta Walker .40 .15
❑ 37 Justin Smith .75 .30
❑ 38 Jamal Reynolds .75 .30
❑ 39 Richard Seymour .75 .30
❑ 40 Shaun Rogers .75 .30
❑ 41 Gerard Warren .75 .30
❑ 42 Jamar Fletcher .60 .25
❑ 43 Gary Baxter .60 .25
❑ 44 Nate Clements .75 .30
❑ 45 Derrick Gibson .60 .25
❑ 46 Drew Brees PP 6.00 2.50
❑ 47 Michael Vick PP 4.00 1.50
❑ 48 Deuce McAllister PP 4.00 1.50
❑ 49 LaDainian Tomlinson PP 15.00 6.00
❑ 50 David Terrell PP 1.00 .40

## 2002 Press Pass

❑ COMPLETE SET (50) 40.00 15.00
❑ COMP.SET w/o SP's (45) 25.00 10.00
❑ 1 David Carr 1.50 .60
❑ 2 Eric Crouch 1.00 .40
❑ 3 Rohan Davey 1.00 .40
❑ 4 David Garrard 2.00 .75
❑ 5 Joey Harrington 1.25 .50
❑ 6 Kurt Kittner .75 .30
❑ 7 David Neill .75 .30
❑ 8 Patrick Ramsey 1.00 .40
❑ 9 Antwaan Randle El 1.25 .50
❑ 10 Damien Anderson .75 .30
❑ 11 T.J. Duckett 1.00 .40
❑ 12 DeShaun Foster 1.00 .40
❑ 13 Lamar Gordon 1.00 .40
❑ 14 William Green 1.00 .40
❑ 15 Leonard Henry .75 .30
❑ 16 Adrian Peterson 1.25 .50
❑ 17 Clinton Portis 4.00 1.50
❑ 18 Jonathan Wells 1.00 .40
❑ 19 Brian Westbrook 2.50 1.00
❑ 20 Antonio Bryant 1.00 .40
❑ 21 Reche Caldwell 1.00 .40
❑ 22 Kelly Campbell .75 .30
❑ 23 Andre Davis .75 .30
❑ 24 Jabar Gaffney 1.00 .40
❑ 25 Ron Johnson .75 .30
❑ 26 Ashley Lelie 2.00 .75
❑ 27 Josh Reed 1.00 .40
❑ 28 Cliff Russell .75 .30

❑ 29 Donte Stallworth 1.50 .60
❑ 30 Javon Walker 1.50 .60
❑ 31 Marquise Walker .75 .30
❑ 32 Daniel Graham 1.00 .40
❑ 33 Jeremy Shockey 2.00 .75
❑ 34 Bryant McKinnie .75 .30
❑ 35 Mike Pearson .50 .20
❑ 36 Mike Williams .75 .30
❑ 37 Phillip Buchanon 1.00 .40
❑ 38 Quentin Jammer 1.00 .40
❑ 39 Kalimba Edwards 1.00 .40
❑ 40 Julius Peppers 2.00 .75
❑ 41 Wendell Bryant .50 .20
❑ 42 John Henderson 1.00 .40
❑ 43 Ryan Sims 1.00 .40
❑ 44 Roy Williams 2.00 .75
❑ 45 David Carr CL .60 .25
❑ 46 David Carr PP 4.00 1.50
❑ 47 Joey Harrington PP 3.00 1.25
❑ 48 T.J. Duckett PP 2.00 .75
❑ 49 Donte Stallworth PP 4.00 1.50
❑ 50 William Green PP 2.50 1.00

## 2003 Press Pass

❑ COMPLETE SET (50) 50.00 20.00
❑ COMP.SET w/o SP's (45) 25.00 10.00
❑ 1 Brad Banks .75 .30
❑ 2 Kyle Boller 1.00 .40
❑ 3 Ken Dorsey .75 .30
❑ 4 Jason Gesser .75 .30
❑ 5 Rex Grossman 2.50 1.00
❑ 6 Kliff Kingsbury .75 .30
❑ 7 Byron Leftwich 1.50 .60
❑ 8 Carson Palmer 4.00 1.50
❑ 9 Dave Ragone .60 .25
❑ 10 Chris Simms 1.00 .40
❑ 11 Brian St.Pierre 1.00 .40
❑ 12 Chris Brown 1.00 .40
❑ 13 Avon Cobourne .60 .25
❑ 14 Dahrran Diedrick .60 .25
❑ 15 Justin Fargas 1.00 .40
❑ 16 Earnest Graham 1.00 .40
❑ 17 Larry Johnson 2.50 1.00
❑ 18 Willis McGahee 2.50 1.00
❑ 19 Musa Smith .75 .30
❑ 20 Onterrio Smith .75 .30
❑ 21 Lee Suggs .75 .30
❑ 22 Anquan Boldin 2.50 1.00
❑ 23 Talman Gardner .60 .25
❑ 24 Taylor Jacobs .75 .30
❑ 25 Andre Johnson 2.00 .75
❑ 26 Bryant Johnson 1.00 .40
❑ 27 Brandon Lloyd 1.00 .40
❑ 28 Charles Rogers .75 .30
❑ 29 Kelley Washington .75 .30
❑ 30 Teyo Johnson .75 .30
❑ 31 Bennie Joppru .60 .25
❑ 32 Jason Witten 2.00 .75
❑ 33 Andrew Pinnock .75 .30
❑ 34 Jordan Gross .60 .25
❑ 35 Kwame Harris .60 .25
❑ 36 Eric Steinbach .60 .25
❑ 37 Brett Williams .60 .25
❑ 38 Terence Newman 1.25 .50
❑ 39 Marcus Trufant 1.00 .40
❑ 40 Andre Woolfolk .75 .30
❑ 41 Terrell Suggs 1.25 .50

❏ 42 Jimmy Kennedy .75 .30
❏ 43 Boss Bailey .75 .30
❏ 44 Mike Doss 1.00 .40
❏ 45 Carson Palmer CL 1.50 .60
❏ 46 Carson Palmer PP 8.00 3.00
❏ 47 Byron Leftwich PP 3.00 1.25
❏ 48 Charles Rogers PP 1.50 .60
❏ 49 Kyle Boller PP 2.00 .75
❏ 50 Andre Johnson PP 4.00 1.50

## 2004 Press Pass

❏ COMPLETE SET (50) 50.00 20.00
❏ COMP.SET w/o SP's (45) 30.00 12.50
❏ 1 Casey Clausen .75 .30
❏ 2 Craig Krenzel 1.00 .40
❏ 3 J.P. Losman 1.25 .50
❏ 4 Eli Manning 6.00 2.50
❏ 5 Luke McCown 1.00 .40
❏ 6 John Navarre .75 .30
❏ 7 Cody Pickett .75 .30
❏ 8 Philip Rivers 3.00 1.25
❏ 9 Ben Roethlisberger 8.00 3.00
❏ 10 Matt Schaub 3.00 1.25
❏ 11 Cedric Cobbs .75 .30
❏ 12 Steven Jackson 3.00 1.25
❏ 13 Kevin Jones 1.00 .40
❏ 14 Greg Jones 1.00 .40
❏ 15 Julius Jones 2.50 1.00
❏ 16 Jarrett Payton .75 .30
❏ 17 Chris Perry .75 .30
❏ 18 Michael Turner 2.00 .75
❏ 19 Quincy Wilson .75 .30
❏ 20 Jason Wright .60 .25
❏ 21 Bernard Berrian 1.00 .40
❏ 22 Michael Clayton 1.00 .40
❏ 23 Devard Darling .75 .30
❏ 24 Lee Evans 1.25 .50
❏ 25 Larry Fitzgerald 3.00 1.25
❏ 26 Devery Henderson 1.00 .40
❏ 27 Michael Jenkins 1.00 .40
❏ 28 Darius Watts .75 .30
❏ 29 Mike Williams .75 .30
❏ 30 Roy Williams WR 2.50 1.00
❏ 31 Rashaun Woods .60 .25
❏ 32 Ben Troupe .75 .30
❏ 33 Shawn Andrews .75 .30
❏ 34 Robert Gallery .75 .30
❏ 35 Tommie Harris 1.00 .40
❏ 36 Vince Wilfork 1.00 .40
❏ 37 Will Smith .75 .30
❏ 38 Teddy Lehman .75 .30
❏ 39 Jonathan Vilma 1.00 .40
❏ 40 D.J. Williams 1.00 .40
❏ 41 DeAngelo Hall 1.00 .40
❏ 42 Dunta Robinson .75 .30
❏ 43 Derrick Strait .75 .30
❏ 44 Keith Smith .60 .25
❏ 45 Eli Manning CL 3.00 1.25
❏ 46 Eli Manning PP 10.00 4.00
❏ 47 Ben Roethlisberger PP 12.00 5.00
❏ 48 Larry Fitzgerald PP 5.00 2.00
❏ 49 Roy Williams PP 4.00 1.50
❏ 50 Philip Rivers PP 5.00 2.00

## 2005 Press Pass

❏ COMPLETE SET (50) 50.00 25.00
❏ COMP.SET w/o PP'S (45) 30.00 12.50
❏ POWER PICK STATED ODDS 1:14 H/R
❏ UNPRICED HOBBY SOLO PRINT RUN 1 SET
❏ 1 Derek Anderson 1.50 .60
❏ 2 Brock Berlin .75 .30
❏ 3 Charlie Frye 1.00 .40
❏ 4 Gino Guidugli .60 .25
❏ 5 David Greene .75 .30
❏ 6 Stefan LeFors .75 .30
❏ 7 Dan Orlovsky 1.00 .40
❏ 8 Kyle Orton 1.25 .50
❏ 9 Aaron Rodgers 3.00 1.25
❏ 10 Alex Smith QB 1.50 .60
❏ 11 Andrew Walter 1.00 .40
❏ 12 Jason White 1.00 .40
❏ 13 J.J. Arrington 1.00 .40
❏ 14 Ronnie Brown 3.00 1.25
❏ 15 Anthony Davis .75 .30
❏ 16 Kay-Jay Harris .75 .30
❏ 17 T.A. McLendon .60 .25
❏ 18 Ryan Moats 1.00 .40
❏ 19 Vernand Morency 1.00 .40
❏ 20 Cadillac Williams 2.00 .75
❏ 21 Mark Bradley 1.00 .40
❏ 22 Reggie Brown 1.00 .40
❏ 23 Mark Clayton 1.00 .40
❏ 24 Braylon Edwards 3.00 1.25
❏ 25 Fred Gibson .75 .30
❏ 26 Terrence Murphy .60 .25
❏ 27 J.R. Russell .60 .25
❏ 28 Craphonso Thorpe .75 .30
❏ 29 Roddy White 1.25 .50
❏ 30 Mike Williams 1.00 .40
❏ 31 Troy Williamson 1.00 .40
❏ 32 Heath Miller 2.00 .75
❏ 33 Alex Smith TE 1.00 .40
❏ 34 Khalil Barnes .60 .25
❏ 35 Jammal Brown .75 .30
❏ 36 Brandon Browner .60 .25
❏ 37 Marlin Jackson .75 .30
❏ 38 Carlos Rogers 1.00 .40
❏ 39 Antrel Rolle 1.00 .40
❏ 40 Dan Cody 1.00 .40
❏ 41 Erasmus James .75 .30
❏ 42 David Pollack .75 .30
❏ 43 Anttaj Hawthorne .75 .30
❏ 44 Derrick Johnson 1.00 .40
❏ 45 Ronnie Brown CL 1.50 .60
❏ 46 Cadillac Williams PP 4.00 1.50
❏ 47 Aaron Rodgers PP 6.00 2.50
❏ 48 Alex Smith QB PP 3.00 1.25
❏ 49 Braylon Edwards PP 6.00 2.50
❏ 50 Mike Williams PP 2.00 .75

## 2006 Press Pass

❏ COMPLETE SET (50) 50.00 20.00
❏ COMP.SET w/o SP's (45) 25.00 10.00
❏ POWER PICK ODDS 1:14
❏ UNPRICED SOLO SER.#'d TO 1
❏ 1 Brodie Croyle 1.25 .50
❏ 2 Jay Cutler 4.00 1.50
❏ 3 Omar Jacobs .75 .30
❏ 4 Matt Leinart 3.00 1.25
❏ 5 Drew Olson .75 .30

❏ 6 Michael Robinson 1.00 .40
❏ 7 D.J. Shockley 1.00 .40
❏ 8 Brad Smith 1.00 .40
❏ 9 Marcus Vick .75 .30
❏ 10 Charlie Whitehurst 1.00 .40
❏ 11 Vince Young 3.00 1.25
❏ 12 Joseph Addai 3.00 1.25
❏ 13 Reggie Bush 4.00 1.50
❏ 14 Jerome Harrison 1.00 .40
❏ 15 Laurence Maroney 2.50 1.00
❏ 16 Leon Washington 1.00 .40
❏ 17 LenDale White 2.00 .75
❏ 18 DeAngelo Williams 1.50 .60
❏ 19 Jason Avant 1.00 .40
❏ 20 Derek Hagan 1.00 .40
❏ 21 Chris Hannon .75 .30
❏ 22 Santonio Holmes 2.50 1.00
❏ 23 Chad Jackson .75 .30
❏ 24 Greg Lee .75 .30
❏ 25 Sinorice Moss 1.00 .40
❏ 26 Martin Nance .75 .30
❏ 27 Maurice Stovall 1.00 .40
❏ 28 Travis Wilson 1.00 .40
❏ 29 Dominique Byrd .75 .30
❏ 30 Vernon Davis 1.00 .40
❏ 31 Marcedes Lewis 1.00 .40
❏ 32 Leonard Pope 1.00 .40
❏ 33 Jimmy Williams 1.00 .40
❏ 34 Darnell Bing 1.00 .40
❏ 35 Michael Huff 1.00 .40
❏ 36 Mathias Kiwanuka 1.25 .50
❏ 37 Mario Williams 1.50 .60
❏ 38 Haloti Ngata 1.00 .40
❏ 39 Gabe Watson .75 .30
❏ 40 Rodrigue Wright .50 .20
❏ 41 D'Brickashaw Ferguson 1.00 .40
❏ 42 Chad Greenway 1.00 .40
❏ 43 A.J. Hawk 2.50 1.00
❏ 44 DeMeco Ryans 1.25 .50
❏ 45 Reggie Bush CL 2.00 .75
❏ 46 Reggie Bush PP 8.00 3.00
❏ 47 Matt Leinart PP 6.00 2.50
❏ 48 Vince Young PP 6.00 2.50
❏ 49 A.J. Hawk PP 5.00 2.00
❏ 50 DeAngelo Williams PP 3.00 1.25

## 2007 Press Pass

❏ COMPLETE SET (105) 60.00 25.00
❏ COMP.SET w/o SP's (100) 40.00 15.00
❏ 101-105 POWER PICK ODDS 1:14

| | | |
|---|---|---|
| ❏ UNPRICED SOLO SER.#'d TO 1 | | |
| ❏ 1 Chris Leak | | .25 |
| ❏ 2 Brady Quinn | .60 | .25 |
| ❏ 3 JaMarcus Russell | 2.00 | .75 |
| ❏ 4 Troy Smith | 1.00 | .40 |
| ❏ 5 Drew Stanton | .75 | .30 |
| ❏ 6 Michael Bush | .75 | .30 |
| ❏ 7 Tony Hunt | .75 | .30 |
| ❏ 8 Kenny Irons | .75 | .30 |
| ❏ 9 Brandon Jackson | .75 | .30 |
| ❏ 10 Marshawn Lynch | 1.50 | .60 |
| ❏ 11 Adrian Peterson | 6.00 | 2.50 |
| ❏ 12 Antonio Pittman | .75 | .30 |
| ❏ 13 Brian Leonard | .75 | .30 |
| ❏ 14 Dwayne Bowe | 1.50 | .60 |
| ❏ 15 Ted Ginn Jr. | 1.25 | .50 |
| ❏ 16 Anthony Gonzalez | 1.25 | .50 |
| ❏ 17 Dwayne Jarrett | .75 | .30 |
| ❏ 18 Calvin Johnson | 2.00 | .75 |
| ❏ 19 Robert Meachem | .75 | .30 |
| ❏ 20 Sidney Rice | .75 | .30 |
| ❏ 21 Garrett Wolfe | .75 | .30 |
| ❏ 22 Leon Hall | | .25 |
| ❏ 23 Gaines Adams | .75 | .30 |
| ❏ 24 Jamaal Anderson | | .25 |
| ❏ 25 Alan Branch | .60 | .25 |
| ❏ 26 Amobi Okoye | .75 | .30 |
| ❏ 27 Paul Posluszny | 1.00 | .40 |
| ❏ 28 Lawrence Timmons | .75 | .30 |
| ❏ 29 LaRon Landry | 1.00 | .40 |
| ❏ 30 Reggie Nelson | .60 | .25 |
| ❏ 31 John Beck | .75 | .30 |
| ❏ 32 Trent Edwards | 2.00 | .75 |
| ❏ 33 Kevin Kolb | 1.25 | .50 |
| ❏ 34 Jordan Palmer | .75 | .30 |
| ❏ 35 Lorenzo Booker | .75 | .30 |
| ❏ 36 Darius Walker | .75 | .30 |
| ❏ 37 Dwayne Wright | .60 | .25 |
| ❏ 38 DeShawn Wynn | .75 | .30 |
| ❏ 39 Zach Miller | .50 | .20 |
| ❏ 40 Greg Olsen | 1.00 | .40 |
| ❏ 41 Aundrae Allison | .60 | .25 |
| ❏ 42 Dallas Baker | .60 | .25 |
| ❏ 43 Jason Hill | .75 | .30 |
| ❏ 44 Steve Smith USC | 1.00 | .40 |
| ❏ 45 Darrelle Revis | .75 | .30 |
| ❏ 46 Aaron Ross | .75 | .30 |
| ❏ 47 Adam Carriker | .60 | .25 |
| ❏ 48 Charles Johnson | .50 | .20 |
| ❏ 49 Jarvis Moss | .75 | .30 |
| ❏ 50 Patrick Willis | 1.50 | .60 |
| ❏ 51 John Beck LDR | .75 | .30 |
| ❏ 52 JaMarcus Russell LDR | 2.00 | .75 |
| ❏ 53 Troy Smith LDR | 1.00 | .40 |
| ❏ 54 Jordan Palmer LDR | .75 | .30 |
| ❏ 55 Kevin Kolb LDR | 1.25 | .50 |
| ❏ 56 Brady Quinn LDR | 2.50 | 1.00 |
| ❏ 57 Garrett Wolfe LDR | .75 | .30 |
| ❏ 58 Dwayne Wright LDR | .60 | .25 |
| ❏ 59 Ahmad Bradshaw LDR | 1.00 | .40 |
| ❏ 60 Johnnie Lee Higgins LDR | .60 | .25 |
| ❏ 61 Robert Meachem LDR | .75 | .30 |
| ❏ 62 Rhema McKnight LDR | .60 | .25 |
| ❏ 63 Calvin Johnson LDR | 2.00 | .75 |
| ❏ 64 Joel Filani LDR | .60 | .25 |
| ❏ 65 Dwayne Bowe LDR | 1.50 | .60 |
| ❏ 66 Dagmeion Hughes LDR | .60 | .25 |
| ❏ 67 Reggie Nelson LDR | .60 | .25 |
| ❏ 68 LaMarr Woodley TC | .75 | .30 |
| ❏ 69 Troy Smith TC | 1.00 | .40 |
| ❏ 70 Brady Quinn TC | 2.50 | 1.00 |
| ❏ 71 Calvin Johnson TC | 2.00 | .75 |
| ❏ 72 Paul Posluszny TC | 1.00 | .40 |
| ❏ 73 Aaron Ross TC | .75 | .30 |
| ❏ 74 Patrick Willis TC | 1.50 | .60 |
| ❏ 75 Troy Smith AA | 1.00 | .40 |
| ❏ 76 Marshawn Lynch AA | 1.50 | .60 |
| ❏ 77 Johnnie Lee Higgins AA | .60 | .25 |
| ❏ 78 Dwayne Jarrett AA | .75 | .30 |
| ❏ 79 Calvin Johnson AA | 2.00 | .75 |
| ❏ 80 Robert Meachem AA | .75 | .30 |
| ❏ 81 Zach Miller AA | .50 | .20 |
| ❏ 82 Gaines Adams AA | .75 | .30 |
| ❏ 83 Paul Posluszny AA | 1.00 | .40 |
| ❏ 84 Leon Hall AA | .60 | .25 |
| ❏ 85 LaRon Landry AA | 1.00 | .40 |
| ❏ 86 Reggie Nelson AA | .60 | .25 |
| ❏ 87 Aaron Ross AA | .75 | .30 |
| ❏ 88 M.Lynch/D.Hughes TM | 1.50 | .60 |
| ❏ 89 C.Leak/R.Nelson TM | .60 | .25 |
| ❏ 90 L.Booker/L.Thomas TM | .75 | .30 |
| ❏ 91 J.Russell/D.Bowe TM | 2.00 | .75 |
| ❏ 92 B.Jackson/A.Carriker TM | .75 | .30 |
| ❏ 93 B.Quinn/D.Walker TM | .75 | .30 |
| ❏ 94 T.Smith/A.Pittman TM | 1.00 | .40 |
| ❏ 95 T.Ginn Jr./A.Gonzalez TM | 1.25 | .50 |
| ❏ 96 T.Hunt/P.Posluszny TM | .75 | .30 |
| ❏ 97 D.Jarrett/S.Smith TM | 1.00 | .40 |
| ❏ 98 Joseph Addai SS | 1.50 | .60 |
| ❏ 99 Reggie Bush SS | 2.00 | .75 |
| ❏ 100 Vince Young SS | 1.50 | .60 |
| ❏ 101 Brady Quinn PP | 6.00 | 2.50 |
| ❏ 102 JaMarcus Russell PP | 5.00 | 2.00 |
| ❏ 103 Adrian Peterson PP | 15.00 | 6.00 |
| ❏ 104 Calvin Johnson PP | 5.00 | 2.00 |
| ❏ 105 Ted Ginn Jr. PP | 3.00 | 1.25 |

## 2008 Press Pass

| | | |
|---|---|---|
| ❏ COMPLETE SET (105) | 60.00 | 25.00 |
| ❏ COMP.SET w/o SP'S (100) | 40.00 | 15.00 |
| ❏ 101-105 POWER PICK ODDS 1:14 | | |
| ❏ 1 Glenn Dorsey | 1.00 | .40 |
| ❏ 2 Chris Long | 1.00 | .40 |
| ❏ 3 Dan Connor | .75 | .30 |
| ❏ 4 Aqib Talib | .75 | .30 |
| ❏ 5 Kenny Phillips | .75 | .30 |
| ❏ 6 Erik Ainge | .75 | .30 |
| ❏ 7 John David Booty | 1.00 | .40 |
| ❏ 8 Colt Brennan | 2.00 | .75 |
| ❏ 9 Brian Brohm | 1.00 | .40 |
| ❏ 10 Joe Flacco | 2.50 | 1.00 |
| ❏ 11 Chad Henne | 1.25 | .50 |
| ❏ 12 Matt Ryan | 3.00 | 1.25 |
| ❏ 13 Andre Woodson | .75 | .30 |
| ❏ 14 Jamaal Charles | 1.00 | .40 |
| ❏ 15 Matt Forte | 2.00 | .75 |
| ❏ 16 Mike Hart | .75 | .30 |
| ❏ 17 Jacob Hester | .75 | .30 |
| ❏ 18 Chris Johnson | 2.00 | .75 |
| ❏ 19 Felix Jones | 2.00 | .75 |
| ❏ 20 Darren McFadden | 3.00 | 1.25 |
| ❏ 21 Rashard Mendenhall | 1.50 | .60 |
| ❏ 22 Ray Rice | 1.00 | .40 |
| ❏ 23 Steve Slaton | 1.50 | .60 |
| ❏ 24 Kevin Smith | 1.25 | .50 |
| ❏ 25 Jonathan Stewart | 2.00 | .75 |
| ❏ 26 Fred Davis | .75 | .30 |
| ❏ 27 Adrian Arrington | .60 | .25 |
| ❏ 28 Earl Bennett | .75 | .30 |
| ❏ 29 Adarius Bowman | .60 | .25 |
| ❏ 30 Early Doucet | .75 | .30 |
| ❏ 31 James Hardy | .75 | .30 |
| ❏ 32 DJ Hall | .75 | .30 |
| ❏ 33 DeSean Jackson | 1.50 | .60 |
| ❏ 34 Malcolm Kelly | .75 | .30 |
| ❏ 35 Mario Manningham | .75 | .30 |
| ❏ 36 Limas Sweed | 1.00 | .40 |
| ❏ 37 Devin Thomas | .75 | .30 |
| ❏ 38 Lavelle Hawkins | .60 | .25 |
| ❏ 39 Andre Caldwell | .60 | .25 |
| ❏ 40 Vernon Gholston | .75 | .30 |
| ❏ 41 Derrick Harvey | .60 | .25 |
| ❏ 42 Keith Rivers | .75 | .30 |
| ❏ 43 Mike Jenkins | .75 | .30 |
| ❏ 44 Leodis McKelvin | .75 | .30 |
| ❏ 45 Dennis Dixon | .75 | .30 |
| ❏ 46 Josh Johnson | .75 | .30 |
| ❏ 47 Tashard Choice | .60 | .25 |
| ❏ 48 Chauncey Washington | .75 | .30 |
| ❏ 49 John Carlson | 1.00 | .40 |
| ❏ 50 Donnie Avery | 1.00 | .40 |
| ❏ 51 Darren McFadden TC | 2.00 | .75 |
| ❏ 52 Matt Ryan TC | 3.00 | 1.25 |
| ❏ 53 Glenn Dorsey TC | 1.00 | .40 |
| ❏ 54 Dan Connor TC | .75 | .30 |
| ❏ 55 Fred Davis TC | .75 | .30 |
| ❏ 56 Chris Long TC | 1.00 | .40 |
| ❏ 57 Dennis Dixon COL | 2.00 | .75 |
| ❏ 58 Colt Brennan COL | 2.00 | .75 |
| ❏ 59 Matt Ryan COL | 3.00 | 1.25 |
| ❏ 60 Brian Brohm COL | 1.00 | .40 |
| ❏ 61 Andre Woodson COL | 1.00 | .40 |
| ❏ 62 Erik Ainge COL | .75 | .30 |
| ❏ 63 Kevin Smith COL | 1.25 | .50 |
| ❏ 64 Matt Forte COL | 2.00 | .75 |
| ❏ 65 Darren McFadden COL | 2.00 | .75 |
| ❏ 66 Jonathan Stewart COL | 2.00 | .75 |
| ❏ 67 Rashard Mendenhall COL | 1.50 | .60 |
| ❏ 68 Ray Rice COL | 1.00 | .40 |
| ❏ 69 Jamaal Charles COL | 1.00 | .40 |
| ❏ 70 Chris Johnson COL | 2.00 | .75 |
| ❏ 71 Jordy Nelson COL | 1.00 | .40 |
| ❏ 72 Davone Bess COL | 1.00 | .40 |
| ❏ 73 Donnie Avery COL | 1.00 | .40 |
| ❏ 74 Devin Thomas COL | .75 | .30 |
| ❏ 75 Mario Manningham COL | .75 | .30 |
| ❏ 76 Dan Connor AA | .75 | .30 |
| ❏ 77 Glenn Dorsey AA | 1.00 | .40 |
| ❏ 78 Mike Jenkins AA | .75 | .30 |
| ❏ 79 J Leman AA | .60 | .25 |
| ❏ 80 Chris Long AA | 1.00 | .40 |
| ❏ 81 Darren McFadden AA | 2.00 | .75 |
| ❏ 82 Jordy Nelson AA | 1.00 | .40 |
| ❏ 83 Martin Rucker AA | .75 | .30 |
| ❏ 84 Matt Ryan AA | 3.00 | 1.25 |
| ❏ 85 Kevin Smith AA | 1.25 | .50 |
| ❏ 86 Aqib Talib AA | .75 | .30 |
| ❏ 87 Steve Slaton AA | 1.50 | .60 |
| ❏ 88 Jonathan Stewart AA | 2.00 | .75 |
| ❏ 89 DeSean Jackson AA | 1.50 | .60 |
| ❏ 90 Woodson/K.Burton TM | .60 | .25 |
| ❏ 91 G.Dorsey/J.Hester TM | .75 | .30 |
| ❏ 92 B.Brohm/H.Douglas TM | .75 | .30 |
| ❏ 93 Henne/Manningham TM | 1.00 | .40 |
| ❏ 94 J.Charles/L.Sweed TM | .75 | .30 |
| ❏ 95 J.Booty/Washington TM | .75 | .30 |
| ❏ 96 J.Forsett/D.Jackson TM | 1.25 | .50 |
| ❏ 97 M.Flynn/E.Doucet TM | .75 | .30 |
| ❏ 98 M.Hart/A.Arrington TM | .75 | .30 |
| ❏ 99 D.Dixon/J.Stewart TM | 1.50 | .60 |
| ❏ 100 McFadden/Jones TM | 1.50 | .60 |
| ❏ 101 Darren McFadden PP | 5.00 | 2.00 |
| ❏ 102 Matt Ryan PP | 8.00 | 3.00 |
| ❏ 103 Brian Brohm PP | 2.50 | 1.00 |
| ❏ 104 Jonathan Stewart PP | 5.00 | 2.00 |
| ❏ 105 Malcolm Kelly PP | 2.00 | .75 |

## 2002 Press Pass JE

| | | |
|---|---|---|
| ❏ COMPLETE SET (45) | 25.00 | 10.00 |
| ❏ 1 David Carr | 1.50 | .60 |
| ❏ 2 Julius Peppers | 2.00 | .75 |
| ❏ 3 Joey Harrington | 1.25 | .50 |
| ❏ 4 Mike Williams | .75 | .30 |
| ❏ 5 Quentin Jammer | 1.00 | .40 |
| ❏ 6 Ryan Sims | 1.00 | .40 |
| ❏ 7 Bryant McKinnie | .75 | .30 |
| ❏ 8 Roy Williams | 2.00 | .75 |
| ❏ 9 John Henderson | 1.00 | .40 |
| ❏ 10 Wendell Bryant | .50 | .20 |
| ❏ 11 Donte Stallworth | 1.50 | .60 |
| ❏ 12 Jeremy Shockey | 2.00 | .75 |
| ❏ 13 William Green | 1.00 | .40 |
| ❏ 14 Phillip Buchanon | 1.00 | .40 |
| ❏ 15 T.J. Duckett | 1.00 | .40 |
| ❏ 16 Ashley Lelie | 2.00 | .75 |
| ❏ 17 Javon Walker | 1.50 | .60 |
| ❏ 18 Daniel Graham | 1.00 | .40 |
| ❏ 19 Jeramy Stevens | 1.00 | .40 |
| ❏ 20 Patrick Ramsey | 1.00 | .40 |
| ❏ 21 Jabar Gaffney | 1.00 | .40 |
| ❏ 22 DeShaun Foster | 1.00 | .40 |
| ❏ 23 Kalimba Edwards | 1.00 | .40 |
| ❏ 24 Josh Reed | 1.00 | .40 |
| ❏ 25 Mike Pearson | .50 | .20 |
| ❏ 26 Andre Davis | .75 | .30 |
| ❏ 27 Reche Caldwell | 1.00 | .40 |
| ❏ 28 Clinton Portis | 4.00 | 1.50 |
| ❏ 29 Maurice Morris | 1.00 | .40 |
| ❏ 30 Ladell Betts | 1.00 | .40 |
| ❏ 31 Antwaan Randle El | 1.25 | .50 |
| ❏ 32 Antonio Bryant | 1.00 | .40 |
| ❏ 33 Josh McCown | 1.25 | .50 |
| ❏ 34 Lamar Gordon | .75 | .30 |
| ❏ 35 Marquise Walker | .75 | .30 |
| ❏ 36 Cliff Russell | .75 | .30 |
| ❏ 37 Brian Westbrook | 2.50 | 1.00 |
| ❏ 38 Eric Crouch | 1.00 | .40 |
| ❏ 39 Jonathan Wells | 1.00 | .40 |
| ❏ 40 David Garrard | 2.00 | .75 |
| ❏ 41 Rohan Davey | 1.00 | .40 |
| ❏ 42 Ron Johnson | .75 | .30 |
| ❏ 43 Kurt Kittner | .75 | .30 |
| ❏ 44 Andre Peterson | 1.25 | .50 |
| ❏ 45 David Carr CL | .75 | .30 |

### 2003 Press Pass JE

| | | |
|---|---|---|
| ❏ COMPLETE SET (45) | 25.00 | 10.00 |
| ❏ 1 Boss Bailey | .75 | .30 |
| ❏ 2 Brad Banks | .75 | .30 |
| ❏ 3 Anquan Boldin | 2.50 | 1.00 |
| ❏ 4 Kyle Boller | 1.00 | .40 |
| ❏ 5 Chris Brown | 1.00 | .40 |
| ❏ 6 Avon Cobourne | .60 | .25 |
| ❏ 7 Ken Dorsey | .75 | .30 |
| ❏ 8 Justin Fargas | 1.00 | .40 |
| ❏ 9 Talman Gardner | .60 | .25 |
| ❏ 10 Jason Gesser | .75 | .30 |
| ❏ 11 Earnest Graham | 1.00 | .40 |
| ❏ 12 Jordon Gross | .60 | .25 |
| ❏ 13 Rex Grossman | 2.50 | 1.00 |
| ❏ 14 Kwame Harris | .60 | .25 |
| ❏ 15 Taylor Jacobs | .75 | .30 |
| ❏ 16 Larry Johnson | 2.50 | 1.00 |
| ❏ 17 Bryant Johnson | 1.00 | .40 |
| ❏ 18 Andre Johnson | 2.00 | .75 |
| ❏ 19 Teyo Johnson | .75 | .30 |
| ❏ 20 William Joseph | .60 | .25 |
| ❏ 21 Bennie Joppru | .60 | .25 |
| ❏ 22 Jimmy Kennedy | .75 | .30 |
| ❏ 23 Kliff Kingsbury | .75 | .30 |
| ❏ 24 Byron Leftwich | 1.50 | .60 |
| ❏ 25 Brandon Lloyd | 1.00 | .40 |
| ❏ 26 Jerome McDougle | .60 | .25 |
| ❏ 27 Willis McGahee | 2.50 | 1.00 |
| ❏ 28 Terence Newman | 1.25 | .50 |
| ❏ 29 Carson Palmer | 4.00 | 1.50 |
| ❏ 30 Terry Pierce | .60 | .25 |
| ❏ 31 Dave Ragone | .60 | .25 |
| ❏ 32 DeWayne Robertson | .75 | .30 |
| ❏ 33 Charles Rogers | .75 | .30 |
| ❏ 34 Chris Simms | 1.00 | .40 |
| ❏ 35 Musa Smith | .75 | .30 |
| ❏ 36 Onterrio Smith | .75 | .30 |
| ❏ 37 Brian St.Pierre | 1.00 | .40 |
| ❏ 38 Lee Suggs | .75 | .30 |
| ❏ 39 Terrell Suggs | 1.25 | .50 |
| ❏ 40 Marcus Trufant | 1.00 | .40 |
| ❏ 41 Seneca Wallace | 1.00 | .40 |
| ❏ 42 Kelley Washington | .75 | .30 |
| ❏ 43 Jason Witten | 2.00 | .75 |
| ❏ 44 Andre Woolfolk | .75 | .30 |
| ❏ 45 Byron Leftwich CL | .60 | .25 |

### 2006 Press Pass Legends

| | | |
|---|---|---|
| ❏ COMP.SET w/o SP's (90) | 40.00 | 20.00 |
| ❏ UNPRICED PLATINUM PRINT RUN 1 | | |
| ❏ UNPRICED PRINT PLATES SER.#'d TO 1 | | |
| ❏ UNPRICED RED PRINT RUN 5 | | |
| ❏ 1 Brodie Croyle | 1.50 | .60 |
| ❏ 2 Tarvaris Jackson | 1.25 | .50 |
| ❏ 3 Derek Hagan | 1.25 | .50 |
| ❏ 4 Devin Aromashodu | 1.00 | .40 |
| ❏ 5 Mathias Kiwanuka | 1.50 | .60 |
| ❏ 6 Omar Jacobs | 1.00 | .40 |
| ❏ 7 Tye Hill | 1.25 | .50 |
| ❏ 8 Charlie Whitehurst | 1.25 | .50 |
| ❏ 9 Joe Klopfenstein | 1.00 | .40 |
| ❏ 10 Chad Jackson | 1.00 | .40 |
| ❏ 11 Leon Washington | 1.25 | .50 |
| ❏ 12 Ernie Sims | 1.25 | .50 |
| ❏ 13 Leonard Pope | 1.25 | .50 |
| ❏ 14 D.J. Shockley | 1.25 | .50 |
| ❏ 15 Joseph Addai | 4.00 | 1.50 |
| ❏ 16 Vernon Davis | 1.25 | .50 |
| ❏ 17 DeAngelo Williams | 2.00 | .75 |
| ❏ 18 Sinorice Moss | 1.25 | .50 |
| ❏ 19 Martin Nance | 1.00 | .40 |
| ❏ 20 Jason Avant | 1.25 | .50 |
| ❏ 21 Laurence Maroney | 3.00 | 1.25 |
| ❏ 22 Brad Smith | 1.25 | .50 |
| ❏ 23 Mario Williams | 2.00 | .75 |
| ❏ 24 Brett Basanez | 1.25 | .50 |
| ❏ 25 Anthony Fasano | 1.25 | .50 |
| ❏ 26 Maurice Stovall | 1.25 | .50 |
| ❏ 27 Bobby Carpenter | 1.25 | .50 |
| ❏ 28 A.J. Hawk | 3.00 | 1.25 |
| ❏ 29 Santonio Holmes | 3.00 | 1.25 |
| ❏ 30 Ashton Youboty | 1.25 | .50 |
| ❏ 31 Travis Wilson | 1.25 | .50 |
| ❏ 32 Haloti Ngata | 1.25 | .50 |
| ❏ 33 Demetrius Williams | 1.25 | .50 |
| ❏ 34 Mike Hass | 1.25 | .50 |
| ❏ 35 Michael Robinson | 1.25 | .50 |
| ❏ 36 Greg Lee | 1.00 | .40 |
| ❏ 37 Cory Rodgers | 1.25 | .50 |
| ❏ 38 Michael Huff | 1.25 | .50 |
| ❏ 39A Vince Young Clr | 4.00 | 1.50 |
| ❏ 39B Vince Young B&W | 6.00 | 2.50 |
| ❏ 40 Reggie McNeal | 1.00 | .40 |
| ❏ 41 Bruce Gradkowski | 1.25 | .50 |
| ❏ 42 Darrell Hackney | 1.00 | .40 |
| ❏ 43 Maurice Drew | 2.50 | 1.00 |
| ❏ 44 Marcedes Lewis | 1.25 | .50 |
| ❏ 45 Drew Olson | 1.00 | .40 |
| ❏ 46 Darnell Bing | 1.25 | .50 |
| ❏ 47A Reggie Bush Clr | 5.00 | 2.00 |
| ❏ 47B Reggie Bush B&W | 8.00 | 3.00 |
| ❏ 48 Dominique Byrd | 1.00 | .40 |
| ❏ 49A Matt Leinart Clr | 4.00 | 1.50 |
| ❏ 49B Matt Leinart B&W | 6.00 | 2.50 |
| ❏ 50 LenDale White | 2.50 | 1.00 |
| ❏ 51A Jay Cutler Clr | 5.00 | 2.00 |
| ❏ 51B Jay Cutler B&W | 8.00 | 3.00 |
| ❏ 52 D'Brickashaw Ferguson | 1.25 | .50 |
| ❏ 53 Marcus Vick | 1.00 | .40 |
| ❏ 54 Jimmy Williams | 1.25 | .50 |
| ❏ 55 Jerome Harrison | 1.25 | .50 |
| ❏ 56 Ozzie Newsome | 1.25 | .50 |
| ❏ 57 Ken Stabler | 2.00 | .75 |
| ❏ 58A Bo Jackson B&W | 2.00 | .75 |
| ❏ 58B Bo Jackson Clr | 3.00 | 1.25 |
| ❏ 59 Steve Spurrier | 2.00 | .75 |
| ❏ 60 Charlie Ward | 1.25 | .50 |
| ❏ 61 Fran Tarkenton | 2.00 | .75 |
| ❏ 62 Herschel Walker | 1.25 | .50 |
| ❏ 63 Billy Cannon | 1.25 | .50 |
| ❏ 64 Y.A. Tittle | 1.50 | .60 |
| ❏ 65 Roger Craig | 1.50 | .60 |
| ❏ 66 Tommie Frazier | 1.25 | .50 |
| ❏ 67 Rocky Bleier | 1.50 | .60 |
| ❏ 68A Tim Brown B&W | 1.50 | .60 |
| ❏ 68B Tim Brown Clr | 2.50 | 1.00 |
| ❏ 69 Paul Hornung | 1.50 | .60 |
| ❏ 70 Joe Theismann | 1.50 | .60 |
| ❏ 71 Howard Cassady | 1.25 | .50 |
| ❏ 72 Archie Griffin | 1.00 | .40 |
| ❏ 73 Jack Tatum | 1.00 | .40 |
| ❏ 74 Paul Warfield | 1.50 | .60 |
| ❏ 75 Brian Bosworth | 1.50 | .60 |
| ❏ 76 Billy Sims | 1.25 | .50 |
| ❏ 77A Barry Sanders B&W | 2.50 | 1.00 |
| ❏ 77B Barry Sanders Clr | 4.00 | 1.50 |
| ❏ 78 Thurman Thomas | 1.25 | .50 |
| ❏ 79 Jack Ham | 1.25 | .50 |
| ❏ 80 Franco Harris | 1.50 | .60 |
| ❏ 81A Dan Marino B&W | 3.00 | 1.25 |
| ❏ 81B Dan Marino Clr | 5.00 | 2.00 |
| ❏ 82 Len Dawson | 1.50 | .60 |
| ❏ 83 Jim Plunkett | 1.25 | .50 |
| ❏ 84 Bob Lilly | 1.25 | .50 |
| ❏ 85 Steve Largent | 1.50 | .60 |
| ❏ 86 Ronnie Lott | 1.50 | .60 |
| ❏ 87 Bobby Bowden | 1.50 | .60 |
| ❏ 88 Bo Schembechler | 1.00 | .40 |
| ❏ 89 Darrell Royal | 1.25 | .50 |
| ❏ 90 Ara Parseghian | 1.25 | .50 |
| ❏ 91 Johnny Lattner SP | 5.00 | 2.00 |
| ❏ 92 Desmond Howard SP | 6.00 | 2.50 |

### 2007 Press Pass Legends

| | | |
|---|---|---|
| ❏ 1 Kenneth Darby | 1.25 | .50 |
| ❏ 2 Chris Henry | 1.25 | .50 |
| ❏ 3 Zach Miller | .75 | .30 |
| ❏ 4 Jamaal Anderson | 1.00 | .40 |
| ❏ 5 Kenny Irons | 1.25 | .50 |
| ❏ 6 Courtney Taylor | 1.00 | .40 |
| ❏ 7 John Beck | 1.25 | .50 |
| ❏ 8 Daymeion Hughes | 1.00 | .40 |
| ❏ 9 Marshawn Lynch | 2.50 | 1.00 |
| ❏ 10 Gaines Adams | 1.25 | .50 |
| ❏ 11 Chansi Stuckey | 1.00 | .40 |
| ❏ 12 Aundrae Allison | 1.00 | .40 |
| ❏ 13 Dallas Baker | 1.00 | .40 |
| ❏ 14 Chris Leak | 1.25 | .50 |
| ❏ 15 Jarvis Moss | 1.25 | .50 |
| ❏ 16 Reggie Nelson | 1.00 | .40 |

| | | |
|---|---|---|
| ❑ 17 DeShawn Wynn | 1.25 | .50 |
| ❑ 18 Paul Williams | 1.00 | .40 |
| ❑ 19 Dwayne Wright | 1.00 | .40 |
| ❑ 20 Lorenzo Booker | 1.25 | .50 |
| ❑ 21 Buster Davis | 1.00 | .40 |
| ❑ 22 Lawrence Timmons | 1.25 | .50 |
| ❑ 23 Quentin Moses | 1.00 | .40 |
| ❑ 24 Calvin Johnson | 3.00 | 1.25 |
| ❑ 25 Kevin Kolb | 2.00 | .75 |
| ❑ 26 Michael Bush | 1.25 | .50 |
| ❑ 27 Amobi Okoye | 1.25 | .50 |
| ❑ 28 Kolby Smith | 1.25 | .50 |
| ❑ 29 Joseph Addai | 1.25 | .50 |
| ❑ 30 Dwayne Bowe | 2.50 | 1.00 |
| ❑ 31 Craig Buster Davis | 1.25 | .50 |
| ❑ 32 LaRon Landry | 1.50 | .60 |
| ❑ 33 JaMarcus Russell | 3.00 | 1.25 |
| ❑ 34 Greg Olsen | 1.50 | .60 |
| ❑ 35 Alan Branch | 1.00 | .40 |
| ❑ 36 Leon Hall | 1.00 | .40 |
| ❑ 37 Drew Stanton | 1.25 | .50 |
| ❑ 38 Adam Carriker | 1.00 | .40 |
| ❑ 39 Brandon Jackson | 1.25 | .50 |
| ❑ 40 Jeff Rowe | 1.00 | .40 |
| ❑ 41 Garrett Wolfe | 1.25 | .50 |
| ❑ 42 Brady Quinn | 4.00 | 1.50 |
| ❑ 43 Ted Ginn Jr. | 2.00 | .75 |
| ❑ 44 Anthony Gonzalez | 2.00 | .75 |
| ❑ 45 Antonio Pittman | 1.25 | .50 |
| ❑ 46 Troy Smith | 1.50 | .60 |
| ❑ 47 Adrian Peterson | 10.00 | 4.00 |
| ❑ 48 Patrick Willis | 2.50 | 1.00 |
| ❑ 49 Tony Hunt | 1.25 | .50 |
| ❑ 50 Paul Posluszny | 1.50 | .60 |
| ❑ 51 Darrelle Revis | 1.25 | .50 |
| ❑ 52 Brian Leonard | 1.25 | .50 |
| ❑ 53 Sidney Rice | 1.25 | .50 |
| ❑ 54 Trent Edwards | 3.00 | 1.25 |
| ❑ 55 Robert Meachem | 1.25 | .50 |
| ❑ 56 Michael Griffin | 1.25 | .50 |
| ❑ 57 Aaron Ross | 1.25 | .50 |
| ❑ 58 Vince Young | 1.25 | .50 |
| ❑ 59 Joel Filani | 1.00 | .40 |
| ❑ 60 Dwayne Jarrett | 1.25 | .50 |
| ❑ 61 Steve Smith USC | 1.50 | .60 |
| ❑ 62 Johnnie Lee Higgins | 1.00 | .40 |
| ❑ 63 Jordan Palmer | 1.25 | .50 |
| ❑ 64 David Clowney | 1.00 | .40 |
| ❑ 65 Jason Hill | 1.25 | .50 |
| ❑ 66 Ozzie Newsome | 1.25 | .50 |
| ❑ 67 Ken Stabler | 2.00 | .75 |
| ❑ 68 Bart Starr | 2.50 | 1.00 |
| ❑ 69 Pat Sullivan | 1.00 | .40 |
| ❑ 70 Doug Flutie | 1.50 | .60 |
| ❑ 71 Ty Detmer | 1.00 | .40 |
| ❑ 72 Danny Wuerffel | 1.00 | .40 |
| ❑ 73 Jack Youngblood | 1.25 | .50 |
| ❑ 74 Fred Biletnikoff | 1.50 | .60 |
| ❑ 75 Herschel Walker | 1.25 | .50 |
| ❑ 76 Dick Butkus | 2.00 | .75 |
| ❑ 77 Y.A. Tittle | 1.50 | .60 |
| ❑ 78 Randy White | 1.25 | .50 |
| ❑ 79 Jerry Rice | 2.50 | 1.00 |
| ❑ 80 Joe Bellino | 1.00 | .40 |
| ❑ 81 Tommie Frazier | 1.25 | .50 |
| ❑ 82 Tom Osborne | 1.25 | .50 |
| ❑ 83 Tom Rathman | 1.00 | .40 |

| | | |
|---|---|---|
| ❑ 84 Johnny Rodgers | 1.00 | .40 |
| ❑ 85 Mike Rozier | 1.00 | .40 |
| ❑ 86 Jerome Bettis | 1.50 | .60 |
| ❑ 87 Paul Hornung | 1.50 | .60 |
| ❑ 88 Alan Page | 1.00 | .40 |
| ❑ 89 Rudy Ruettiger | 1.50 | .60 |
| ❑ 90 Joe Theismann | 1.50 | .60 |
| ❑ 91 Archie Griffin | 1.00 | .40 |
| ❑ 92 Brian Bosworth | 1.50 | .60 |
| ❑ 93 Steve Owens | 1.00 | .40 |
| ❑ 94 Billy Sims | 1.25 | .50 |
| ❑ 95 Archie Manning | 1.50 | .60 |
| ❑ 96 Raymond Berry | 1.25 | .50 |
| ❑ 97 James Lofton | 1.00 | .40 |
| ❑ 98 Marcus Allen | 1.50 | .60 |
| ❑ 99 John Hannah | 1.00 | .40 |
| ❑ 100 Dick Butkus CL | 1.25 | .50 |

## 2008 Press Pass Legends Bowl Edition

| | | |
|---|---|---|
| ❑ 1 Troy Aikman | 6.00 | 2.50 |
| ❑ 2 Tedy Bruschi | 4.00 | 1.50 |
| ❑ 3 Earl Campbell | 5.00 | 2.00 |
| ❑ 4 Cris Collinsworth | 4.00 | 1.50 |
| ❑ 5 Bill Cowher | 5.00 | 2.00 |
| ❑ 6 Eric Dickerson | 4.00 | 1.50 |
| ❑ 7 Glenn Dorsey | 3.00 | 1.25 |
| ❑ 8 Brett Favre | 10.00 | 4.00 |
| ❑ 9 Joe Flacco | 8.00 | 3.00 |
| ❑ 10 Matt Forte | 6.00 | 2.50 |
| ❑ 11 Tommie Frazier | 4.00 | 1.50 |
| ❑ 12 DeSean Jackson | 5.00 | 2.00 |
| ❑ 13 Chris Johnson | 6.00 | 2.50 |
| ❑ 14 Jimmy Johnson | 4.00 | 1.50 |
| ❑ 15 Felix Jones | 6.00 | 2.50 |
| ❑ 16 Lee Roy Jordan | 4.00 | 1.50 |
| ❑ 17 Jim Kelly | 5.00 | 2.00 |
| ❑ 18 Jack Lambert | 5.00 | 2.00 |
| ❑ 19 Chris Long | 3.00 | 1.25 |
| ❑ 20 Darren McFadden | 6.00 | 2.50 |
| ❑ 21 Rashard Mendenhall | 5.00 | 2.00 |
| ❑ 22 Joe Montana | 12.00 | 5.00 |
| ❑ 23 Warren Moon | 6.00 | 2.50 |
| ❑ 24 Ray Rice | 3.00 | 1.25 |
| ❑ 25 Eddie Royal | 5.00 | 2.00 |
| ❑ 26 Matt Ryan | 10.00 | 4.00 |
| ❑ 27 Gale Sayers | 6.00 | 2.50 |
| ❑ 28 Mike Singletary | 5.00 | 2.00 |
| ❑ 29 Steve Slaton | 5.00 | 2.00 |
| ❑ 30 Kevin Smith | 4.00 | 1.50 |
| ❑ 31 Chris Spielman | 4.00 | 1.50 |
| ❑ 32 Ken Stabler | 4.00 | 1.50 |
| ❑ 33 Jonathan Stewart | 6.00 | 2.50 |
| ❑ 34 Barry Switzer | 4.00 | 1.50 |
| ❑ 35 Herschel Walker | 4.00 | 1.50 |
| ❑ 36 Steve Young | 6.00 | 2.50 |
| ❑ 37 Derrick Brooks | 3.00 | 1.25 |
| ❑ 38 Joey Galloway | 3.00 | 1.25 |
| ❑ 39 Frank Gore | 4.00 | 1.50 |
| ❑ 40 Paul Hornung | 5.00 | 2.00 |
| ❑ 41 Sonny Jurgensen | 4.00 | 1.50 |
| ❑ 42 Ray Lewis | 4.00 | 1.50 |
| ❑ 43 George Rogers | 3.00 | 1.25 |
| ❑ 44 Dick Butkus | 6.00 | 2.50 |
| ❑ 45 Cris Carter | 5.00 | 2.00 |
| ❑ 46 Bob Griese | 5.00 | 2.00 |

| | | |
|---|---|---|
| ❑ 47 Bo Jackson | 6.00 | 2.50 |
| ❑ 48 Billy Kilmer | 4.00 | 1.50 |
| ❑ 49 Floyd Little | 3.00 | 1.25 |
| ❑ 50 Tommy McDonald | 4.00 | 1.50 |
| ❑ 51 Tom Rathman | 4.00 | 1.50 |
| ❑ 52 Billy Sims | 4.00 | 1.50 |
| ❑ 53 Steve Spurrier | 5.00 | 2.00 |
| ❑ 54 Aaron Kampman | 3.00 | 1.25 |
| ❑ 55 Mike Rozier | 3.00 | 1.25 |
| ❑ 56 Y.A. Tittle | 5.00 | 2.00 |
| ❑ 57 Craig Morton | 3.00 | 1.25 |
| ❑ 58 Hugh McElhenny | 5.00 | 2.00 |
| ❑ 59 Roger Craig | 4.00 | 1.50 |
| ❑ 60 Ty Detmer | 3.00 | 1.25 |
| ❑ 61 Craig James | 4.00 | 1.50 |
| ❑ 62 Tommy Nobis | 3.00 | 1.25 |
| ❑ 63 Pat Sullivan | 3.00 | 1.25 |
| ❑ 64 Joe Theismann | 5.00 | 2.00 |
| ❑ 65 Zach Thomas | 3.00 | 1.25 |
| ❑ 66 Danny Wuerffel | 4.00 | 1.50 |
| ❑ 67 Raymond Berry | 4.00 | 1.50 |
| ❑ 68 Rocky Bleier | 4.00 | 1.50 |
| ❑ 69 Billy Cannon | 3.00 | 1.25 |
| ❑ 70 Anthony Carter | 3.00 | 1.25 |
| ❑ 71 John Jefferson | 3.00 | 1.25 |
| ❑ 72 Johnny Rodgers | 3.00 | 1.25 |
| ❑ 73 Charles White | 3.00 | 1.25 |
| ❑ 74 Sam Huff | 4.00 | 1.50 |
| ❑ 75 Paul Warfield | 4.00 | 1.50 |
| ❑ 76 Donnie Avery | 3.00 | 1.25 |
| ❑ 77 Davone Bess | 3.00 | 1.25 |
| ❑ 78 John David Booty | 3.00 | 1.25 |
| ❑ 79 Colt Brennan | 6.00 | 2.50 |
| ❑ 80 Jamaal Charles | 3.00 | 1.25 |
| ❑ 81 Harry Douglas | 2.50 | 1.00 |
| ❑ 82 Chad Henne | 4.00 | 1.50 |
| ❑ 83 Malcolm Kelly | 2.50 | 1.00 |
| ❑ 84 Josh Morgan | 2.50 | 1.00 |
| ❑ 85 Jordy Nelson | 3.00 | 1.25 |
| ❑ 86 Limas Sweed | 3.00 | 1.25 |
| ❑ 87 Devin Thomas | 2.50 | 1.00 |
| ❑ 88 James Lofton | 3.00 | 1.25 |
| ❑ 89 Donnie Avery | 3.00 | 1.25 |
| ❑ 90 Joe Flacco | 6.00 | 2.50 |
| ❑ 91 Matt Forte | 6.00 | 2.50 |
| ❑ 92 DeSean Jackson | 5.00 | 2.00 |
| ❑ 93 Chris Johnson | 6.00 | 2.50 |
| ❑ 94 Felix Jones | 6.00 | 2.50 |
| ❑ 95 Darren McFadden | 6.00 | 2.50 |
| ❑ 96 Eddie Royal | 5.00 | 2.00 |
| ❑ 97 Matt Ryan | 10.00 | 4.00 |
| ❑ 98 Steve Slaton | 5.00 | 2.00 |
| ❑ 99 Kevin Smith | 4.00 | 1.50 |
| ❑ 100 Jonathan Stewart | 4.00 | 1.50 |

## 2001 Press Pass SE

| | | |
|---|---|---|
| ❑ COMPLETE SET (45) | 40.00 | 20.00 |
| ❑ 1 Michael Vick | 2.00 | .75 |
| ❑ 2 Drew Brees | 3.00 | 1.25 |
| ❑ 3 Quincy Carter | .75 | .30 |
| ❑ 4 Marques Tuiasosopo | .75 | .30 |
| ❑ 5 Chris Weinke | .75 | .30 |
| ❑ 6 Sage Rosenfels | .75 | .30 |
| ❑ 7 Jesse Palmer | .75 | .30 |
| ❑ 8 Mike McMahon | .75 | .30 |
| ❑ 9 Josh Booty | .75 | .30 |
| ❑ 10 Josh Heupel | .75 | .30 |

❑ 11 LaDainian Tomlinson 10.00 4.00
❑ 12 Deuce McAllister 2.00 .75
❑ 13 Michael Bennett .75 .30
❑ 14 Anthony Thomas .75 .30
❑ 15 LaMont Jordan 1.50 .60
❑ 16 Travis Henry .75 .30
❑ 17 James Jackson .75 .30
❑ 18 Kevan Barlow .60 .25
❑ 19 Travis Minor .60 .25
❑ 20 Rudi Johnson 1.50 .60
❑ 21 David Terrell .75 .30
❑ 22 Koren Robinson .75 .30
❑ 23 Rod Gardner .75 .30
❑ 24 Santana Moss 1.50 .60
❑ 25 Freddie Mitchell .75 .30
❑ 26 Reggie Wayne 2.00 .75
❑ 27 Quincy Morgan .75 .30
❑ 28 Chris Chambers 1.50 .60
❑ 29 Robert Ferguson .75 .30
❑ 30 Chad Johnson 2.00 .75
❑ 31 Snoop Minnis .60 .25
❑ 32 Todd Heap .75 .30
❑ 33 Steve Hutchinson .60 .25
❑ 34 Leonard Davis .60 .25
❑ 35 Kenyatta Walker .40 .15
❑ 36 Justin Smith .75 .30
❑ 37 Andre Carter .75 .30
❑ 38 Jamal Reynolds .75 .30
❑ 39 Gerard Warren .75 .30
❑ 40 Richard Seymour .75 .30
❑ 41 Damione Lewis .60 .25
❑ 42 Jamar Fletcher .60 .25
❑ 43 Nate Clements .75 .30
❑ 44 Derrick Gibson .60 .25
❑ 45 David Terrell CL .60 .25

## 2004 Press Pass SE

❑ COMPLETE SET (40) 30.00 15.00
❑ 1 Shawn Andrews .75 .30
❑ 2 Casey Clausen .75 .30
❑ 3 Michael Clayton 1.00 .40
❑ 4 Cedric Cobbs .75 .30
❑ 5 Devard Darling .75 .30
❑ 6 Lee Evans 1.25 .50
❑ 7 Larry Fitzgerald 3.00 1.25
❑ 8 Robert Gallery 1.00 .40
❑ 9 DeAngelo Hall 1.00 .40
❑ 10 Tommie Harris 1.00 .40
❑ 11 Ben Hartsock .75 .30
❑ 12 Devery Henderson 1.00 .40
❑ 13 Steven Jackson 3.00 1.25
❑ 14 Michael Jenkins 1.00 .40
❑ 15 Greg Jones .75 .30
❑ 16 Kevin Jones 1.00 .40
❑ 17 Teddy Lehman .75 .30
❑ 18 J.P. Losman 1.25 .50
❑ 19 Eli Manning 6.00 2.50
❑ 20 Mewelde Moore 1.00 .40
❑ 21 John Navarre .75 .30
❑ 22 Jarrett Payton .75 .30
❑ 23 Chris Perry 1.00 .40
❑ 24 Cody Pickett .75 .30
❑ 25 Philip Rivers 3.00 1.25
❑ 26 Ben Roethlisberger 8.00 3.00
❑ 27 Matt Schaub 3.00 1.25
❑ 28 Will Smith .75 .30
❑ 29 Ben Troupe .75 .30

❑ 30 Michael Turner 2.00 .75
❑ 31 Ben Watson 1.00 .40
❑ 32 Darius Watts .75 .30
❑ 33 Vince Wilfork 1.00 .40
❑ 34 Mike Williams .75 .30
❑ 35 Reggie Williams 1.00 .40
❑ 36 Roy Williams WR 2.50 1.00
❑ 37 Quincy Wilson .75 .30
❑ 38 Rashaun Woods .60 .25
❑ 39 Jason Wright .60 .25
❑ 40 Eli Manning CL 3.00 1.25
❑ NNO Eli Manning Mini Helmet 120.00 60.00

## 2005 Press Pass SE

❑ COMPLETE SET (40) 25.00 10.00
❑ 1 Charlie Frye 1.00 .40
❑ 2 David Greene .75 .30
❑ 3 Gino Guidugli .60 .25
❑ 4 Stefan LeFors .75 .30
❑ 5 Dan Orlovsky 1.00 .40
❑ 6 Kyle Orton 1.25 .50
❑ 7 Aaron Rodgers 3.00 1.25
❑ 8 Alex Smith QB 1.50 .60
❑ 9 Andrew Walter 1.00 .40
❑ 10 Jason White 1.00 .40
❑ 11 J.J. Arrington 1.00 .40
❑ 12 Marion Barber 3.00 1.25
❑ 13 Ronnie Brown 3.00 1.25
❑ 14 Anthony Davis .75 .30
❑ 15 Ciatrick Fason .75 .30
❑ 16 T.A. McLendon .60 .25
❑ 17 Vernand Morency 1.00 .40
❑ 18 Walter Reyes .60 .25
❑ 19 Cadillac Williams 2.00 .75
❑ 20 Mark Bradley 1.00 .40
❑ 21 Reggie Brown 1.00 .40
❑ 22 Mark Clayton 1.00 .40
❑ 23 Braylon Edwards 3.00 1.25
❑ 24 Fred Gibson .75 .30
❑ 25 Chris Henry 1.00 .40
❑ 26 Terrence Murphy .60 .25
❑ 27 J.R. Russell .60 .25
❑ 28 Craphonso Thorpe .75 .30
❑ 29 Roddy White 1.25 .50
❑ 30 Mike Williams 1.00 .40
❑ 31 Troy Williamson 1.00 .40
❑ 32 Heath Miller 2.00 .75
❑ 33 Alex Smith TE 1.00 .40
❑ 34 Jammal Brown 1.00 .40
❑ 35 Marlin Jackson .75 .30
❑ 36 Antrel Rolle 1.00 .40
❑ 37 Dan Cody 1.00 .40
❑ 38 Derrick Johnson 1.00 .40
❑ 39 Thomas Davis .75 .30
❑ 40 Aaron Rodgers CL 1.50 .60

## 2006 Press Pass SE

❑ COMPLETE SET (40) 30.00 12.50
❑ 1 Joseph Addai 3.00 1.25
❑ 2 Jason Avant 1.00 .40
❑ 3 Reggie Bush 4.00 1.50
❑ 4 Dominique Byrd .75 .30
❑ 5 Brodie Croyle 1.25 .50
❑ 6 Jay Cutler 4.00 1.50
❑ 7 Vernon Davis 1.00 .40
❑ 8 Maurice Drew 2.00 .75
❑ 9 Anthony Fasano 1.00 .40

❑ 10 D'Brickashaw Ferguson 1.00 .40
❑ 11 Bruce Gradkowski 1.00 .40
❑ 12 Darrell Hackney .75 .30
❑ 13 Derek Hagan 1.00 .40
❑ 14 Jerome Harrison 1.00 .40
❑ 15 A.J. Hawk 2.00 .75
❑ 16 Santonio Holmes 2.50 1.00
❑ 17 Michael Huff 1.00 .40
❑ 18 Chad Jackson .75 .30
❑ 19 Omar Jacobs .75 .30
❑ 20 Matt Leinart 3.00 1.25
❑ 21 Marcedes Lewis 1.00 .40
❑ 22 Laurence Maroney 2.50 1.00
❑ 23 Reggie McNeal .75 .30
❑ 24 Sinorice Moss 1.00 .40
❑ 25 Martin Nance .75 .30
❑ 26 Haloti Ngata 1.00 .40
❑ 27 Leonard Pope 1.00 .40
❑ 28 Michael Robinson 1.00 .40
❑ 29 D.J. Shockley 1.00 .40
❑ 30 Maurice Stovall 1.00 .40
❑ 31 Marcus Vick .75 .30
❑ 32 Leon Washington 1.00 .40
❑ 33 LenDale White 2.00 .75
❑ 34 Charlie Whitehurst 1.00 .40
❑ 35 Jimmy Williams 1.00 .40
❑ 36 Mario Williams 1.50 .60
❑ 37 DeAngelo Williams 1.50 .60
❑ 38 Demetrius Williams 1.00 .40
❑ 39 Vince Young 3.00 1.25
❑ 40 Vince Young CL 1.50 .60

## 2007 Press Pass SE

❑ 1 Reggie Nelson .75 .30
❑ 2 Patrick Willis 2.00 .75
❑ 3 Brian Leonard 1.00 .40
❑ 4 Sidney Rice 1.00 .40
❑ 5 Robert Meachem 1.00 .40
❑ 6 Chris Leak .75 .30
❑ 7 Calvin Johnson 2.50 1.00
❑ 8 Charles Johnson .60 .25
❑ 9 Kevin Kolb 1.50 .60
❑ 10 Drew Stanton 1.00 .40
❑ 11 Antonio Pittman 1.00 .40
❑ 12 Troy Smith 1.25 .50
❑ 13 Steve Smith USC 1.25 .50
❑ 14 Leon Hall .75 .30
❑ 15 Brandon Jackson 1.00 .40
❑ 16 Ted Ginn Jr. 1.50 .60
❑ 17 Aundrae Allison .75 .30

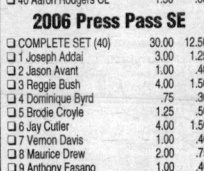

| | | |
|---|---|---|
| ❑ 18 DeShawn Wynn | 1.00 | .40 |
| ❑ 19 Dwayne Wright | .75 | .30 |
| ❑ 20 Michael Bush | 1.00 | .40 |
| ❑ 21 Dwayne Bowe | 2.00 | .75 |
| ❑ 22 Adam Carriker | .75 | .30 |
| ❑ 23 Paul Posluszny | 1.25 | .50 |
| ❑ 24 Aaron Ross | 1.00 | .40 |
| ❑ 25 Lorenzo Booker | 1.00 | .40 |
| ❑ 26 Jamaal Anderson | .75 | .30 |
| ❑ 27 Zach Miller | .60 | .25 |
| ❑ 28 Dallas Baker | .75 | .30 |
| ❑ 29 Adrian Peterson | 8.00 | 3.00 |
| ❑ 30 Dwayne Jarrett | 1.00 | .40 |
| ❑ 31 Greg Olsen | 1.25 | .50 |
| ❑ 32 Darius Walker | 1.00 | .40 |
| ❑ 33 Alan Branch | .75 | .30 |
| ❑ 34 Marshawn Lynch | 2.00 | .75 |
| ❑ 35 JaMarcus Russell | 2.50 | 1.00 |
| ❑ 36 Anthony Gonzalez | 1.50 | .60 |
| ❑ 37 Gaines Adams | 1.00 | .40 |
| ❑ 38 Craig Buster Davis | 1.00 | .40 |
| ❑ 39 Jason Hill | 1.00 | .40 |
| ❑ 40 Kenny Irons | 1.00 | .40 |
| ❑ 41 John Beck | 1.00 | .40 |
| ❑ 42 Lawrence Timmons | 1.00 | .40 |
| ❑ 43 Trent Edwards | 2.50 | 1.00 |
| ❑ 44 Tony Hunt | 1.00 | .40 |
| ❑ 45 Darrelle Revis | 1.00 | .40 |
| ❑ 46 Jarvis Moss | 1.00 | .40 |
| ❑ 47 LaRon Landry | 1.25 | .50 |
| ❑ 48 Brady Quinn | 3.00 | 1.25 |
| ❑ 49 Jordan Palmer | 1.00 | .40 |
| ❑ 50 Rhema McKnight | .75 | .30 |

### 1999 SAGE

| | | |
|---|---|---|
| ❑ COMPLETE SET (50) | 30.00 | 15.00 |
| ❑ 1 Rahim Abdullah | .60 | .25 |
| ❑ 2 Jerry Azumah | .60 | .25 |
| ❑ 3 Champ Bailey | 1.25 | .50 |
| ❑ 4 D'Wayne Bates | .60 | .25 |
| ❑ 5 Michael Bishop | 1.00 | .40 |
| ❑ 6 David Boston | 1.00 | .40 |
| ❑ 7 Fernando Bryant | .60 | .25 |
| ❑ 8 Tony Bryant | .60 | .25 |
| ❑ 9 Chris Claiborne | .40 | .15 |
| ❑ 10 Mike Cloud | .60 | .25 |
| ❑ 11 Cecil Collins | .40 | .15 |
| ❑ 12 Tim Couch | 1.00 | .40 |
| ❑ 13 Daunte Culpepper | 4.00 | 1.50 |
| ❑ 14 Jared DeVries | .60 | .25 |
| ❑ 15 Adrian Dingle | .60 | .25 |
| ❑ 16 Antuan Edwards | .60 | .25 |
| ❑ 17 Troy Edwards | .60 | .25 |
| ❑ 18 Kevin Faulk | 1.00 | .40 |
| ❑ 19 Rufus French | .40 | .15 |
| ❑ 20 Martin Gramatica | .40 | .15 |
| ❑ 21 Torry Holt | 2.50 | 1.00 |
| ❑ 22 Sedrick Irvin | .40 | .15 |
| ❑ 23 Edgerrin James | 4.00 | 1.50 |
| ❑ 24 Jon Jansen | .40 | .15 |
| ❑ 25 Andy Katzenmoyer | .60 | .25 |
| ❑ 26 Jevon Kearse | 2.50 | 1.00 |
| ❑ 27 Patrick Kerney | 1.00 | .40 |
| ❑ 28 Lamar King | .60 | .25 |

| | | |
|---|---|---|
| ❑ 29 Shaun King | .60 | .25 |
| ❑ 30 Jim Kleinsasser | 1.00 | .40 |
| ❑ 31 Rob Konrad | 1.00 | .40 |
| ❑ 32 Brian Kuklick | .60 | .25 |
| ❑ 33 Chris McAllister | .60 | .25 |
| ❑ 34 Darnell McDonald | .60 | .25 |
| ❑ 35 Reggie McGrew | .60 | .25 |
| ❑ 36 Donovan McNabb | 5.00 | 2.00 |
| ❑ 37 Cade McNown | 1.00 | .40 |
| ❑ 38 Dat Nguyen | 1.00 | .40 |
| ❑ 39 Solomon Page | .40 | .15 |
| ❑ 40 Mike Peterson | 1.00 | .40 |
| ❑ 41 Anthony Poindexter | .60 | .25 |
| ❑ 42 Peerless Price | 1.00 | .40 |
| ❑ 43 Mike Rucker | 1.00 | .40 |
| ❑ 44 L.J. Shelton | .40 | .15 |
| ❑ 45 Akili Smith | 1.50 | .60 |
| ❑ 46 John Tait | .40 | .15 |
| ❑ 47 Fred Vinson | .60 | .25 |
| ❑ 48 Al Wilson | 1.00 | .40 |
| ❑ 49 Antoine Winfield | .60 | .25 |
| ❑ 50 Damien Woody | .60 | .25 |

### 2000 SAGE

| | | |
|---|---|---|
| ❑ COMPLETE SET (50) | 15.00 | 6.00 |
| ❑ 1 John Abraham | .75 | .30 |
| ❑ 2 Shaun Alexander | 2.50 | 1.00 |
| ❑ 3 LaVar Arrington | 1.50 | .60 |
| ❑ 4 Courtney Brown | 1.00 | .40 |
| ❑ 5 Keith Bulluck | .75 | .30 |
| ❑ 6 Plaxico Burress | 1.50 | .60 |
| ❑ 7 Giovanni Carmazzi | .40 | .15 |
| ❑ 8 Kwame Cavil | .40 | .15 |
| ❑ 9 Cosey Coleman | .40 | .15 |
| ❑ 10 Laveranues Coles | 1.00 | .40 |
| ❑ 11 Tim Couch | .75 | .30 |
| ❑ 12 Ron Dayne | .75 | .30 |
| ❑ 13 Reuben Droughns | 1.00 | .40 |
| ❑ 14 Shaun Ellis | .60 | .25 |
| ❑ 15 John Engelberger | .60 | .25 |
| ❑ 16 Danny Farmer | .60 | .25 |
| ❑ 17 Dwayne Goodrich | .75 | .30 |
| ❑ 18 Deon Grant | .60 | .25 |
| ❑ 19 Chris Hovan | .60 | .25 |
| ❑ 20 Darren Howard | .60 | .25 |
| ❑ 21 Todd Husak | .75 | .30 |
| ❑ 22 Thomas Jones | 1.25 | .50 |
| ❑ 23 Curtis Keaton | .60 | .25 |
| ❑ 24 Jamal Lewis | 1.50 | .60 |
| ❑ 25 Anthony Lucas | .40 | .15 |
| ❑ 26 Tee Martin | .75 | .30 |
| ❑ 27 Stockar McDougle | .40 | .15 |
| ❑ 28 Corey Moore | .40 | .15 |
| ❑ 29 Rob Morris | .60 | .25 |
| ❑ 30 Sammy Morris | .75 | .30 |
| ❑ 31 Sylvester Morris | .60 | .25 |
| ❑ 32 Chad Pennington | 2.00 | .75 |
| ❑ 33 Todd Pinkston | .75 | .30 |
| ❑ 34 Ahmed Plummer | .75 | .30 |
| ❑ 35 Jerry Porter | 1.00 | .40 |
| ❑ 36 Travis Prentice | .60 | .25 |
| ❑ 37 Tim Rattay | .75 | .30 |
| ❑ 38 Chris Redman | .60 | .25 |
| ❑ 39 J.R. Redmond | .60 | .25 |

| | | |
|---|---|---|
| ❑ 40 Chris Samuels | .60 | .25 |
| ❑ 41 Brandon Short | .60 | .25 |
| ❑ 42 Corey Simon | 1.00 | .40 |
| ❑ 43 R.Jay Soward | .60 | .25 |
| ❑ 44 Shyrone Stith | .60 | .25 |
| ❑ 45 Raynoch Thompson | .60 | .25 |
| ❑ 46 Brian Urlacher | 3.00 | 1.25 |
| ❑ 47 Todd Wade | .40 | .15 |
| ❑ 48 Troy Walters | .75 | .30 |
| ❑ 49 Dez White | .75 | .30 |
| ❑ 50 Michael Wiley | .60 | .25 |

### 2001 SAGE

| | | |
|---|---|---|
| ❑ COMPLETE SET (50) | 20.00 | 7.50 |
| ❑ 1 Will Allen | .60 | .25 |
| ❑ 2 Adam Archuleta | .75 | .30 |
| ❑ 3 Jeff Backus | .60 | .25 |
| ❑ 4 Alex Bannister | .60 | .25 |
| ❑ 5 Gary Baxter | .60 | .25 |
| ❑ 6 Michael Bennett | .60 | .25 |
| ❑ 7 Josh Booty | .75 | .30 |
| ❑ 8 Drew Brees | 3.00 | 1.25 |
| ❑ 9 Correll Buckhalter | 1.00 | .40 |
| ❑ 10 Quincy Carter | .75 | .30 |
| ❑ 11 Chris Chambers | 1.50 | .60 |
| ❑ 12 Alge Crumpler | 1.00 | .40 |
| ❑ 13 Andre Dyson | .40 | .15 |
| ❑ 14 Robert Ferguson | .75 | .30 |
| ❑ 15 Jamar Fletcher | .60 | .25 |
| ❑ 16 Rod Gardner | .75 | .30 |
| ❑ 17 Reggie Germany | .60 | .25 |
| ❑ 18 Derrick Gibson | .60 | .25 |
| ❑ 19 Casey Hampton | .75 | .30 |
| ❑ 20 Tim Hasselbeck | .75 | .30 |
| ❑ 21 Todd Heap | .75 | .30 |
| ❑ 22 Travis Henry | .75 | .30 |
| ❑ 23 Josh Heupel | .75 | .30 |
| ❑ 24 Willie Howard | .60 | .25 |
| ❑ 25 Steve Hutchinson | .60 | .25 |
| ❑ 26 James Jackson | .75 | .30 |
| ❑ 27 Rudi Johnson | 1.50 | .60 |
| ❑ 28 LaMont Jordan | 1.50 | .60 |
| ❑ 29 Torrance Marshall | .75 | .30 |
| ❑ 30 Deuce McAllister | 2.00 | .75 |
| ❑ 31 Willie Middlebrooks | .60 | .25 |
| ❑ 32 Quincy Morgan | .75 | .30 |
| ❑ 33 Santana Moss | 1.50 | .60 |
| ❑ 34 Jesse Palmer | .75 | .30 |
| ❑ 35 Carlos Polk | .40 | .15 |
| ❑ 36 Ken-Yon Rambo | .60 | .25 |
| ❑ 37 Jamal Reynolds | .75 | .30 |
| ❑ 38 Koren Robinson | .75 | .30 |
| ❑ 39 Richard Seymour | .75 | .30 |
| ❑ 40 Justin Smith | .75 | .30 |
| ❑ 41 Fred Smoot | .75 | .30 |
| ❑ 42 Marcus Stroud | .75 | .30 |
| ❑ 43 David Terrell | .75 | .30 |
| ❑ 44 LaDainian Tomlinson | 10.00 | 4.00 |
| ❑ 45 Ja'Mar Toombs | .60 | .25 |
| ❑ 46 Michael Vick | 2.00 | .75 |
| ❑ 47 Kenyatta Walker | .40 | .15 |
| ❑ 48 Gerard Warren | .75 | .30 |
| ❑ 49 Reggie Wayne | 2.00 | .75 |
| ❑ 50 Jamie Winborn | .60 | .25 |

## 2002 SAGE

| | | |
|---|---|---|
| ❑ COMPLETE SET (45) | 40.00 | 15.00 |
| ❑ 1 Ladell Betts | 1.50 | .60 |
| ❑ 2 Antonio Bryant | 1.50 | .60 |
| ❑ 3 Reche Caldwell | 1.50 | .60 |
| ❑ 4 Kelly Campbell | 1.25 | .50 |
| ❑ 5 David Carr | 2.50 | 1.00 |
| ❑ 6 Tim Carter | 1.25 | .50 |
| ❑ 7 Eric Crouch | 1.50 | .60 |
| ❑ 8 Ronald Curr | 1.50 | .60 |
| ❑ 9 Rohan Davey | 1.50 | .60 |
| ❑ 10 Andre Davis | 1.25 | .50 |
| ❑ 11 T.J. Duckett | 1.50 | .60 |
| ❑ 12 Randy Fasani | 1.25 | .50 |
| ❑ 13 DeShaun Foster | 1.50 | .60 |
| ❑ 14 Dwight Freeney | 2.50 | 1.00 |
| ❑ 15 Jabar Gaffney | 1.50 | .60 |
| ❑ 16 Lamar Gordon | 1.50 | .60 |
| ❑ 17 Daniel Graham | 1.50 | .60 |
| ❑ 18 Joey Harrington | 2.00 | .75 |
| ❑ 19 Napoleon Harri | 1.50 | .60 |
| ❑ 20 Albert Haynesworth | 1.50 | .60 |
| ❑ 21 John Henderson | 5.00 | 2.00 |
| ❑ 22 Chad Hutchinson | 1.25 | .50 |
| ❑ 23 Quentin Jammer | 1.50 | .60 |
| ❑ 24 Ron Johnson | 1.25 | .50 |
| ❑ 25 Kurt Kittner | 1.25 | .50 |
| ❑ 26 Ashley Lelie | 3.00 | 1.25 |
| ❑ 27 Bryant McKinnie | 1.50 | .60 |
| ❑ 28 Maurice Morris | 1.50 | .60 |
| ❑ 29 David Neill | 1.25 | .50 |
| ❑ 30 J.T. O'Sullivan | 2.00 | .75 |
| ❑ 31 Brian Poli-Dixon | 1.25 | .50 |
| ❑ 32 Clinton Portis | 6.00 | 2.50 |
| ❑ 33 Patrick Ramsey | 1.50 | .60 |
| ❑ 34 Josh Reed | 1.50 | .60 |
| ❑ 35 Cliff Russell | 1.25 | .50 |
| ❑ 36 Lito Sheppard | 1.50 | .60 |
| ❑ 37 Jeremy Shockey | 3.00 | 1.25 |
| ❑ 38 Luke Staley | 1.25 | .50 |
| ❑ 39 Donte Stallworth | 2.50 | 1.00 |
| ❑ 40 Travis Stephens | 1.25 | .50 |
| ❑ 41 Chester Taylor | 2.50 | 1.00 |
| ❑ 42 Larry Tripplett | .75 | .30 |
| ❑ 43 Javon Walker | 2.50 | 1.00 |
| ❑ 44 Marquise Walker | 1.25 | .50 |
| ❑ 45 Jonathan Wells | 1.50 | .60 |

## 2003 SAGE

## 2004 SAGE

| | | |
|---|---|---|
| ❑ COMPLETE SET (46) | 30.00 | 12.50 |
| ❑ STATED PRINT RUN 3200 SETS | | |
| ❑ 1 Tatum Bell | 1.00 | .40 |
| ❑ 2 Bernard Berrian | 1.00 | .40 |
| ❑ 3 Michael Boulware | 1.00 | .40 |
| ❑ 4 Drew Carter | 1.00 | .40 |
| ❑ 5 Maurice Clarett | .75 | .30 |
| ❑ 6 Casey Clausen | .75 | .30 |
| ❑ 7 Michael Clayton | 1.00 | .40 |
| ❑ 8 Chris Collins | .60 | .25 |
| ❑ 9 Karlos Dansby | 1.00 | .40 |
| ❑ 10 Devard Darling | .75 | .30 |
| ❑ 11 Lee Evans | 1.25 | .50 |
| ❑ 12 Clarence Farmer | .60 | .25 |
| ❑ 13 Chris Gamble | .75 | .30 |
| ❑ 14 Jake Grove | .60 | .25 |
| ❑ 15 DeAngelo Hall | 1.25 | .50 |
| ❑ 16 Josh Harris | .60 | .25 |
| ❑ 17 Tommie Harris | 1.00 | .40 |

## 2005 SAGE

| | | |
|---|---|---|
| ❑ COMPLETE SET (45) | 25.00 | 10.00 |
| ❑ 1 Sam Aiken | 1.00 | .40 |
| ❑ 2 Boss Bailey | 1.00 | .40 |
| ❑ 3 Brad Banks | 1.00 | .40 |
| ❑ 4 Tully Banta-Cain | 1.25 | .50 |
| ❑ 5 Arnaz Battle | 1.25 | .50 |
| ❑ 6 Ronald Bellamy | 1.00 | .40 |
| ❑ 7 Kyle Boller | 1.25 | .50 |
| ❑ 8 Chris Brown | 1.25 | .50 |
| ❑ 9 Tyrone Calico | 1.00 | .40 |
| ❑ 10 Dallas Clark | 1.25 | .50 |
| ❑ 11 Kevin Curtis | 1.50 | .60 |
| ❑ 12 Sammy Davis | 1.00 | .40 |
| ❑ 13 Dahrran Diedrick | .75 | .30 |
| ❑ 14 Ken Dorsey | 1.00 | .40 |
| ❑ 15 Justin Fargas | 1.25 | .50 |
| ❑ 16 Justin Gage | 1.00 | .40 |
| ❑ 17 Jason Gesser | 1.00 | .40 |
| ❑ 18 Cie Grant | 1.00 | .40 |
| ❑ 19 Rex Grossman | 3.00 | 1.25 |
| ❑ 20 E.J. Henderson | 1.00 | .40 |
| ❑ 21 Taylor Jacobs | 1.00 | .40 |
| ❑ 22 Bryant Johnson | 1.25 | .50 |
| ❑ 23 Larry Johnson | 3.00 | 1.25 |
| ❑ 24 Teyo Johnson | 1.00 | .40 |
| ❑ 25 Kliff Kingsbury | 1.25 | .50 |
| ❑ 26 Brandon Lloyd | 1.25 | .50 |
| ❑ 27 Rashean Mathis | 1.00 | .40 |
| ❑ 28 Jerome McDougle | .75 | .30 |
| ❑ 29 Willis McGahee | 3.00 | 1.25 |
| ❑ 30 Billy McMullen | .75 | .30 |
| ❑ 31 Terence Newman | 1.50 | .60 |
| ❑ 32 Donnie Nickey | .75 | .30 |
| ❑ 33 Terry Pierce | .75 | .30 |
| ❑ 34 Dave Ragone | .75 | .30 |
| ❑ 35 Charles Rogers | 1.00 | .40 |
| ❑ 36 Chris Simms | 1.25 | .50 |
| ❑ 37 Musa Smith | 1.00 | .40 |
| ❑ 38 Lee Suggs | 1.25 | .50 |
| ❑ 39 Terrell Suggs | 1.50 | .60 |
| ❑ 40 Marcus Trufant | 1.25 | .50 |
| ❑ 41 Seneca Wallace | 1.25 | .50 |
| ❑ 42 Kelley Washington | 1.00 | .40 |
| ❑ 43 Matt Wilhelm | 1.00 | .40 |
| ❑ 44 Jason Witten | 2.50 | 1.00 |
| ❑ 45 George Wrighster | .75 | .30 |

| | | |
|---|---|---|
| ❑ 18 Devery Henderson | 1.00 | .40 |
| ❑ 19 Steven Jackson | 3.00 | 1.25 |
| ❑ 20 Michael Jenkins | 1.00 | .40 |
| ❑ 21 Greg Jones | 1.00 | .40 |
| ❑ 22 Kevin Jones | 1.00 | .40 |
| ❑ 23 Sean Jones | .75 | .30 |
| ❑ 24 Derrick Knight | .60 | .25 |
| ❑ 25 Craig Krenzel | 1.00 | .40 |
| ❑ 26 Jared Lorenzen | .75 | .30 |
| ❑ 27 Eli Manning | 6.00 | 2.50 |
| ❑ 28 John Navarre | .75 | .30 |
| ❑ 29 Chris Perry | 1.00 | .40 |
| ❑ 30 Cody Pickett | .75 | .30 |
| ❑ 31 Will Poole | 1.00 | .40 |
| ❑ 32 Philip Rivers | 3.00 | 1.25 |
| ❑ 33 Ell Roberson | 1.00 | .40 |
| ❑ 34 Dunta Robinson | .75 | .30 |
| ❑ 35 Ben Roethlisberger | 8.00 | 3.00 |
| ❑ 36 Rod Rutherford | .60 | .25 |
| ❑ 37 P.K. Sam | .60 | .25 |
| ❑ 38 Matt Schaub | 3.00 | 1.25 |
| ❑ 39 Will Smith | .75 | .30 |
| ❑ 40 Jeff Smoker | .75 | .30 |
| ❑ 41 Ben Troupe | .75 | .30 |
| ❑ 42 Ernest Wilford | 1.00 | .40 |
| ❑ 43 Reggie Williams | 1.00 | .40 |
| ❑ 44 Roy Williams WR | 2.50 | 1.00 |
| ❑ 45 Quincy Wilson | .75 | .30 |
| ❑ 46 Rashaun Woods | .60 | .25 |

| | | |
|---|---|---|
| ❑ COMPLETE SET (54) | 30.00 | 12.50 |
| ❑ 1 Derek Anderson | 2.00 | .75 |
| ❑ 2 J.J. Arrington | 1.25 | .50 |
| ❑ 3 Marion Barber | 4.00 | 1.50 |
| ❑ 4 Brock Berlin | 1.00 | .40 |
| ❑ 5 Jammal Brown | 1.25 | .50 |
| ❑ 6 Reggie Brown | 1.25 | .50 |
| ❑ 7 Ronnie Brown | 4.00 | 1.50 |
| ❑ 8 Jason Campbell | 2.50 | 1.00 |
| ❑ 9 Mark Clayton | 1.25 | .50 |
| ❑ 10 Channing Crowder | 1.00 | .40 |
| ❑ 11 Anthony Davis | 1.00 | .40 |
| ❑ 12 Josh Davis | .75 | .30 |
| ❑ 13 Thomas Davis | 1.00 | .40 |
| ❑ 14 Ciatrick Fason | 1.00 | .40 |
| ❑ 15 Ryan Fitzpatrick | 1.25 | .50 |
| ❑ 16 Charlie Frye | 1.25 | .50 |
| ❑ 17 Fred Gibson | 1.00 | .40 |
| ❑ 18 Johnathan Goddard | 1.00 | .40 |
| ❑ 19 Frank Gore | 3.00 | 1.25 |
| ❑ 20 David Greene | 1.00 | .40 |
| ❑ 21 Kay-Jay Harris | 1.00 | .40 |
| ❑ 22 Marlin Jackson | 1.00 | .40 |
| ❑ 23 Brandon Jacobs | 1.50 | .60 |
| ❑ 24 Derrick Johnson | 1.25 | .50 |
| ❑ 25 Matt Jones | 2.00 | .75 |
| ❑ 26 T.A. McLendon | .75 | .30 |
| ❑ 27 Adrian McPherson | 1.00 | .40 |
| ❑ 28 Justin Miller | 1.00 | .40 |
| ❑ 29 Vernand Morency | 1.25 | .50 |
| ❑ 30 Terrence Murphy | .75 | .30 |
| ❑ 31 Dan Orlovsky | 1.25 | .50 |
| ❑ 32 Kyle Orton | 1.50 | .60 |
| ❑ 33 Roscoe Parrish | 1.00 | .40 |
| ❑ 34 Brodney Pool | 1.00 | .40 |
| ❑ 35 Dante Ridgeway | .75 | .30 |

**2006 SAGE (continued)**

|  |  | | |
|---|---|---|---|
| 36 | Chris Rix | 1.00 | .40 |
| 37 | Aaron Rodgers | 4.00 | 1.50 |
| 38 | Carlos Rogers | 1.25 | .50 |
| 39 | J.R. Russell | .75 | .30 |
| 40 | Alex Smith TE | 1.25 | .50 |
| 41 | Alex Smith QB | 2.00 | .75 |
| 42 | Taylor Stubblefield | .75 | .30 |
| 43 | Craphonso Thorpe | 1.00 | .40 |
| 44 | Andrew Walter | 1.25 | .50 |
| 45 | DeMarcus Ware | 2.00 | .75 |
| 46 | Fabian Washington | 1.25 | .50 |
| 47 | Corey Webster | 1.25 | .50 |
| 48 | Jason White | 1.25 | .50 |
| 49 | Roddy White | 1.50 | .60 |
| 50 | Cadillac Williams | 2.50 | 1.00 |
| 51 | Troy Williamson | 1.25 | .50 |
| 52 | Maurice Clarett | 1.00 | .40 |
| 53 | Ben Roethlisberger | 3.00 | 1.25 |
| 54 | Antrel Rolle | 1.25 | .50 |
| 47 | Dwayne Slay | 1.00 | .40 |
| 48 | Maurice Stovall | 1.25 | .50 |
| 49 | David Thomas | 1.25 | .50 |
| 50 | Leon Washington | 1.25 | .50 |
| 51 | Pat Watkins | 1.25 | .50 |
| 52 | LenDale White | 2.50 | 1.00 |
| 53 | Charlie Whitehurst | 1.25 | .50 |
| 54 | Demetrius Williams | 1.25 | .50 |
| 55 | Jimmy Williams | 1.25 | .50 |
| 56 | Mario Williams | 2.00 | .75 |
| 57 | Rodrique Wright | .60 | .25 |
| 58 | Ashton Youboty | 1.25 | .50 |
| 59 | Vince Young | 4.00 | 1.50 |
| 60 | Alan Zemaitis | 1.25 | .50 |
| 48 | Kolby Smith | 1.25 | .50 |
| 49 | Steve Smith USC | 1.50 | .60 |
| 50 | Troy Smith | 1.50 | .60 |
| 51 | Jason Snelling | 1.00 | .40 |
| 52 | Isaiah Stanback | 1.25 | .50 |
| 53 | Drew Stanton | 1.25 | .50 |
| 54 | Courtney Taylor | 1.00 | .40 |
| 55 | Lawrence Timmons | 1.25 | .50 |
| 56 | DeMarcus Tank Tyler | 1.00 | .40 |
| 57 | Darius Walker | 1.25 | .50 |
| 58 | Paul Williams | 1.00 | .40 |
| 59 | Patrick Willis | 2.00 | .75 |
| 60 | Garrett Wolfe | 1.25 | .50 |
| 61 | LaMarr Woodley | 1.25 | .50 |
| 62 | Jared Zabransky | 1.25 | .50 |

## 2006 SAGE

|  |  | | |
|---|---|---|---|
| 1 | Joseph Addai | 4.00 | 1.50 |
| 2 | Devin Aromashodu | 1.00 | .40 |
| 3 | Jason Avant | 1.25 | .50 |
| 4 | Hank Baskett | 1.25 | .50 |
| 5 | Mike Bell | 1.25 | .50 |
| 6 | Will Blackmon | 1.25 | .50 |
| 7 | Daniel Bullocks | 1.25 | .50 |
| 8 | Reggie Bush | 5.00 | 2.00 |
| 9 | Dominique Byrd | 1.00 | .40 |
| 10 | Brian Calhoun | 1.00 | .40 |
| 11 | Bobby Carpenter | 1.25 | .50 |
| 12 | Antonio Cromartie | 1.25 | .50 |
| 13 | Brodie Croyle | 1.50 | .60 |
| 14 | Jay Cutler | 5.00 | 2.00 |
| 15 | Vernon Davis | 1.25 | .50 |
| 16 | Anthony Fasano | 1.25 | .50 |
| 17 | D'Brickashaw Ferguson | 1.25 | .50 |
| 18 | Charles Gordon | 1.00 | .40 |
| 19 | Bruce Gradkowski | 1.25 | .50 |
| 20 | Skyler Green | 1.25 | .50 |
| 21 | Jerome Harrison | 1.25 | .50 |
| 22 | Mike Hass | 1.25 | .50 |
| 23 | Taurean Henderson | 1.25 | .50 |
| 24 | Devin Hester | 2.50 | 1.00 |
| 25 | Tye Hill | 1.25 | .50 |
| 26 | Michael Huff | 1.25 | .50 |
| 27 | Tarvaris Jackson | 1.25 | .50 |
| 28 | Omar Jacobs | 1.00 | .40 |
| 29 | Maurice Drew | 2.50 | 1.00 |
| 30 | Winston Justice | 1.25 | .50 |
| 31 | Matt Leinart | 4.00 | 1.50 |
| 32 | Laurence Maroney | 3.00 | 1.25 |
| 33 | Reggie McNeal | 1.00 | .40 |
| 34 | Marcus McNeill | .60 | .25 |
| 35 | Erik Meyer | 1.00 | .40 |
| 36 | Sinorice Moss | 1.25 | .50 |
| 37 | Martin Nance | 1.00 | .40 |
| 38 | Drew Olson | 1.00 | .40 |
| 39 | Jonathan Orr | 1.00 | .40 |
| 40 | Paul Pinegar | 1.25 | .50 |
| 41 | Leonard Pope | 1.25 | .50 |
| 42 | Gerald Riggs Jr. | 1.25 | .50 |
| 43 | Michael Robinson | 1.25 | .50 |
| 44 | DeMeco Ryans | 1.50 | .60 |
| 45 | D.J. Shockley | 1.25 | .50 |
| 46 | Ernie Sims | 1.25 | .50 |

## 2007 SAGE

|  |  | | |
|---|---|---|---|
| 1 | Gaines Adams | 1.25 | .50 |
| 2 | Aundrae Allison | 1.00 | .40 |
| 3 | Dallas Baker | 1.00 | .40 |
| 4 | David Ball | .75 | .30 |
| 5 | John Beck | 1.25 | .50 |
| 6 | Dwayne Bowe | 2.50 | 1.00 |
| 7 | Alan Branch | 1.00 | .40 |
| 8 | Steve Breaston | 1.25 | .50 |
| 9 | Levi Brown | 1.25 | .50 |
| 10 | Michael Bush | 1.25 | .50 |
| 11 | Adam Carriker | 1.00 | .40 |
| 12 | David Clowney | 1.00 | .40 |
| 13 | Ken Darby | 1.25 | .50 |
| 14 | Craig Buster Davis | 1.25 | .50 |
| 15 | Trent Edwards | 3.00 | 1.25 |
| 16 | Earl Everett | 1.00 | .40 |
| 17 | Yamon Figurs | 1.25 | .50 |
| 18 | Joel Filani | 1.00 | .40 |
| 19 | Ted Ginn Jr. | 2.00 | .75 |
| 20 | Anthony Gonzalez | 2.00 | .75 |
| 21 | Michael Griffin | 1.25 | .50 |
| 22 | Leon Hall | 1.00 | .40 |
| 23 | Chris Henry | 1.25 | .50 |
| 24 | Johnnie Lee Higgins | 1.00 | .40 |
| 25 | Jason Hill | 1.25 | .50 |
| 26 | David Irons | .75 | .30 |
| 27 | Kenny Irons | 1.25 | .50 |
| 28 | Calvin Johnson | 3.00 | 1.25 |
| 29 | Ryan Kalil | 1.00 | .40 |
| 30 | Kevin Kolb | 2.00 | .75 |
| 31 | Chris Leak | 1.00 | .40 |
| 32 | Brian Leonard | 1.25 | .50 |
| 33 | Marshawn Lynch | 2.50 | 1.00 |
| 34 | Robert Meachem | 1.25 | .50 |
| 35 | Brandon Meriweather | 1.25 | .50 |
| 36 | Zach Miller | .75 | .30 |
| 37 | Jarvis Moss | 1.25 | .50 |
| 38 | Greg Olsen | 1.50 | .60 |
| 39 | Tyler Palko | 1.25 | .50 |
| 40 | Jordan Palmer | 1.25 | .50 |
| 41 | Adrian Peterson | 10.00 | 4.00 |
| 42 | Antonio Pittman | 1.25 | .50 |
| 43 | Brady Quinn | 4.00 | 1.50 |
| 44 | Sidney Rice | 1.25 | .50 |
| 45 | Aaron Ross | 1.25 | .50 |
| 46 | Jeff Rowe | 1.00 | .40 |
| 47 | JaMarcusÂ Russell | 3.00 | 1.25 |

## 2008 SAGE

|  |  | | |
|---|---|---|---|
| | COMPLETE SET (60) | 40.00 | 20.00 |
| 1 | Erik Ainge | 1.25 | .50 |
| 2 | Adrian Arrington | 1.00 | .40 |
| 3 | Donnie Avery | 1.50 | .60 |
| 4 | Sam Baker | .75 | .30 |
| 5 | John David Booty | 1.50 | .60 |
| 6 | Adarius Bowman | 1.00 | .40 |
| 7 | Brian Brohm | 1.50 | .60 |
| 8 | Keenan Burton | 1.00 | .40 |
| 9 | Andre Caldwell | 1.00 | .40 |
| 10 | John Carlson | 1.25 | .50 |
| 11 | Antoine Cason | 1.25 | .50 |
| 12 | Jamaal Charles | 1.50 | .60 |
| 13 | Tashard Choice | 1.25 | .50 |
| 14 | Ryan Clady | 1.25 | .50 |
| 15 | Dan Connor | 1.25 | .50 |
| 16 | Fred Davis | 1.25 | .50 |
| 17 | Dennis Dixon | 1.25 | .50 |
| 19 | Sedrick Ellis | 1.25 | .50 |
| 20 | Joe Flacco | 4.00 | 1.50 |
| 21 | Brandon Flowers | 1.25 | .50 |
| 22 | Matt Flynn | 1.50 | .60 |
| 23 | Will Franklin | 1.25 | .50 |
| 25 | James Hardy | 1.25 | .50 |
| 26 | Mike Hart | 1.50 | .60 |
| 27 | Derrick Harvey | 1.00 | .40 |
| 28 | Lavelle Hawkins | 1.00 | .40 |
| 29 | Chad Henne | 2.00 | .75 |
| 30 | Jacob Hester | 1.25 | .50 |
| 31 | DeSean Jackson | 2.50 | 1.00 |
| 32 | Lawrence Jackson | 1.00 | .40 |
| 33 | Mike Jenkins | 1.25 | .50 |
| 34 | Josh Johnson | 1.25 | .50 |
| 35 | Felix Jones | 3.00 | 1.25 |
| 36 | Dustin Keller | 1.25 | .50 |
| 37 | Sam Keller | 1.25 | .50 |
| 38 | Malcolm Kelly | 1.25 | .50 |
| 39 | Jake Long | 1.50 | .60 |
| 40 | Darren McFadden | 3.00 | 1.25 |
| 41 | Leodis McKelvin | 1.25 | .50 |
| 42 | Rashard Mendenhall | 2.50 | 1.00 |
| 43 | Jordy Nelson | 1.50 | .60 |
| 44 | Kevin O'Connell | 1.50 | .60 |
| 45 | Allen Patrick | 1.00 | .40 |
| 46 | Kenny Phillips | 1.25 | .50 |
| 47 | Darius Reynaud | 1.00 | .40 |

| | | |
|---|---|---|
| ❏ 48 Ray Rice | 1.50 | .60 |
| ❏ 49 Jason Rivers | 1.25 | .50 |
| ❏ 51 Martin Rucker | 1.00 | .40 |
| ❏ 52 Matt Ryan | 5.00 | 2.00 |
| ❏ 53 Owen Schmitt | 1.25 | .50 |
| ❏ 54 Steve Slaton | 2.50 | 1.00 |
| ❏ 55 Kevin Smith | 2.00 | .75 |
| ❏ 56 Paul Smith | 1.25 | .50 |
| ❏ 57 Jonathan Stewart | 3.00 | 1.25 |
| ❏ 58 Limas Sweed | 1.50 | .60 |
| ❏ 59 Devin Thomas | 1.25 | .50 |
| ❏ 60 Tom Zbikowski | 1.50 | .60 |

## 2000 SAGE HIT

| | | |
|---|---|---|
| ❏ COMPLETE SET (50) | 25.00 | 10.00 |
| ❏ 1 Jerry Porter | 1.00 | .40 |
| ❏ 2 Tim Couch | .75 | .30 |
| ❏ 3 Chris Samuels | .60 | .25 |
| ❏ 4 Plaxico Burress | 1.50 | .60 |
| ❏ 5 Michael Wiley | .60 | .25 |
| ❏ 6 Thomas Jones | 1.25 | .50 |
| ❏ 7 Chris Redman | .60 | .25 |
| ❏ 8 Anthony Lucas | .40 | .15 |
| ❏ 9 Kwame Cavil | .40 | .15 |
| ❏ 10 Chad Pennington | 2.00 | .75 |
| ❏ 11 LaVar Arrington | 2.00 | .75 |
| ❏ 12 Giovanni Carmazzi | .40 | .15 |
| ❏ 13 Tim Rattay | .75 | .30 |
| ❏ 14 Laveranues Coles | 1.00 | .40 |
| ❏ 15 Mario Edwards | .60 | .25 |
| ❏ 16 John Engelberger | .60 | .25 |
| ❏ 17 Tee Martin | .75 | .30 |
| ❏ 18 R.Jay Soward | .60 | .25 |
| ❏ 19 Ahmed Plummer | .75 | .30 |
| ❏ 20 Na'il Diggs | .60 | .25 |
| ❏ 21 J.R. Redmond | .75 | .30 |
| ❏ 22 Dez White | .75 | .30 |
| ❏ 23 Reuben Droughns | 1.00 | .40 |
| ❏ 24 Sylvester Morris | .60 | .25 |
| ❏ 25 Cosey Coleman | .40 | .15 |
| ❏ 26 Corey Moore | .60 | .25 |
| ❏ 27 Curtis Keaton | .60 | .25 |
| ❏ 28 Danny Farmer | .60 | .25 |
| ❏ 29 Travis Claridge | .40 | .15 |
| ❏ 30 Troy Walters | .75 | .30 |
| ❏ 31 Jamal Lewis | 1.50 | .60 |
| ❏ 32 Shaun King | .40 | .15 |
| ❏ 33 Ron Dayne | .75 | .30 |
| ❏ 34 Keith Bulluck | .75 | .30 |
| ❏ 35 Corey Simon | 1.00 | .40 |
| ❏ 36 Deon Dyer | .60 | .25 |
| ❏ 37 Shaun Alexander | 2.50 | 1.00 |
| ❏ 38 Shyrone Stith | .60 | .25 |
| ❏ 39 Shaun Ellis | .75 | .30 |
| ❏ 40 Todd Pinkston | .75 | .30 |
| ❏ 41 Travis Prentice | .60 | .25 |
| ❏ 42 Chris Hovan | .60 | .25 |
| ❏ 43 Brandon Short | .60 | .25 |
| ❏ 44 Brian Urlacher | 3.00 | 1.25 |
| ❏ 45 Rob Morris | .75 | .30 |
| ❏ 46 Raynoch Thompson | .60 | .25 |
| ❏ 47 Deon Grant | .60 | .25 |
| ❏ 48 Stockar McDougle | .40 | .15 |

| | | |
|---|---|---|
| ❏ 49 Darren Howard | .60 | .25 |
| ❏ 50 Courtney Brown | 1.00 | .40 |

## 2001 SAGE HIT

| | | |
|---|---|---|
| ❏ COMPLETE SET (50) | 25.00 | 10.00 |
| ❏ 1 David Terrell | .75 | .30 |
| ❏ 2 Jamar Fletcher | .60 | .25 |
| ❏ 3 Koren Robinson | .75 | .30 |
| ❏ 4 Ken-Yon Rambo | .60 | .25 |
| ❏ 5 LaDainian Tomlinson | 8.00 | 4.00 |
| ❏ 6 Santana Moss | 1.50 | .60 |
| ❏ 7 Michael Vick | 2.00 | .75 |
| ❏ 8 Steve Hutchinson | .60 | .25 |
| ❏ 9 Robert Ferguson | .75 | .30 |
| ❏ 10 Torrance Marshall | .75 | .30 |
| ❏ 11 Scotty Anderson | .75 | .30 |
| ❏ 12 Derrick Gibson | .60 | .25 |
| ❏ 13 Marcus Stroud | .75 | .30 |
| ❏ 14 Josh Heupel | .75 | .30 |
| ❏ 15 Drew Brees | 3.00 | 1.25 |
| ❏ 16 Gerard Warren | .75 | .30 |
| ❏ 17 Quincy Carter | .75 | .30 |
| ❏ 18 Gary Baxter | .60 | .25 |
| ❏ 19 Alex Bannister | .60 | .25 |
| ❏ 21 Andre Dyson | .40 | .15 |
| ❏ 22 Deuce McAllister | 2.00 | .75 |
| ❏ 23 Rod Gardner | .75 | .30 |
| ❏ 24 Jamie Winborn | .60 | .25 |
| ❏ 25 Will Allen | .60 | .25 |
| ❏ 26 Kenyatta Walker | .40 | .15 |
| ❏ 27 Tim Hasselbeck | .75 | .30 |
| ❏ 28 Alge Crumpler | 1.00 | .40 |
| ❏ 30 LaMont Jordan | 1.50 | .60 |
| ❏ 31 Jeff Backus | .60 | .25 |
| ❏ 32 Rudi Johnson | 1.50 | .60 |
| ❏ 33 Willie Howard | .60 | .25 |
| ❏ 34 Josh Booty | .75 | .30 |
| ❏ 35 Todd Heap | .75 | .30 |
| ❏ 36 Correll Buckhalter | 1.00 | .40 |
| ❏ 37 Jesse Palmer | .75 | .30 |
| ❏ 38 Carlos Polk | .40 | .15 |
| ❏ 39 Richard Seymour | .75 | .30 |
| ❏ 40 Adam Archuleta | .75 | .30 |
| ❏ 41 James Jackson | .75 | .30 |
| ❏ 42 Willie Middlebrooks | .60 | .25 |
| ❏ 43 Ja'Mar Toombs | .60 | .25 |
| ❏ 44 Chris Chambers | 1.50 | .60 |
| ❏ 45 Reggie Germany | .60 | .25 |
| ❏ 46 Casey Hampton | .75 | .30 |
| ❏ 47 Reggie Wayne | 2.00 | .75 |
| ❏ 48 Jamal Reynolds | .75 | .30 |
| ❏ 49 Justin Smith | .75 | .30 |
| ❏ 50 Quincy Morgan | .75 | .30 |

## 2002 SAGE HIT

| | | |
|---|---|---|
| ❏ COMPLETE SET (48) | 30.00 | 12.50 |
| ❏ 1 John Henderson | 1.25 | .50 |
| ❏ 2 Tim Carter | 1.00 | .40 |
| ❏ 3 Joey Harrington | 1.50 | .60 |
| ❏ 4 Marquise Walker | 1.00 | .40 |
| ❏ 5 Quentin Jammer | 1.25 | .50 |
| ❏ 6 Rohan Davey | 1.25 | .50 |
| ❏ 7A Eric Crouch QB | 1.25 | .50 |
| ❏ 7B Eric Crouch RB | 1.25 | .50 |

| | | |
|---|---|---|
| ❏ 8 David Carr | 2.00 | .75 |
| ❏ 9 Maurice Morris | 1.25 | .50 |
| ❏ 10 Jabar Gaffney | 1.25 | .50 |
| ❏ 11 David Neill | 1.00 | .40 |
| ❏ 12 Randy Fasani | 1.00 | .40 |
| ❏ 13 Alex Brown | 1.25 | .50 |
| ❏ 14 J.T. O'Sullivan | 1.50 | .60 |
| ❏ 15 Kurt Kittner | 1.00 | .40 |
| ❏ 16 Ashley Lelie | 2.50 | 1.00 |
| ❏ 17 Reche Caldwell | 1.25 | .50 |
| ❏ 18 T.J. Duckett | 1.25 | .50 |
| ❏ 19 Chester Taylor | 2.50 | 1.00 |
| ❏ 20 Jonathan Wells | 1.25 | .50 |
| ❏ 21 Kelly Campbell | 1.00 | .40 |
| ❏ 22 Bryant McKinnie | 1.00 | .40 |
| ❏ 23 Lito Sheppard | 1.25 | .50 |
| ❏ 24 Donte Stallworth | 2.00 | .75 |
| ❏ 25 Josh Reed | 1.25 | .50 |
| ❏ 26 DeShaun Foster | 1.25 | .50 |
| ❏ 27 Patrick Ramsey | 1.25 | .50 |
| ❏ 28 Clinton Portis | 5.00 | 2.00 |
| ❏ 29 Albert Haynesworth | 1.25 | .50 |
| ❏ 30 Antonio Bryant | 1.25 | .50 |
| ❏ 31 Cliff Russell | 1.00 | .40 |
| ❏ 32 Luke Staley | 1.00 | .40 |
| ❏ 33 Ron Johnson | 1.00 | .40 |
| ❏ 34 Travis Stephens | 1.00 | .40 |
| ❏ 35 Chad Hutchinson | 1.00 | .40 |
| ❏ 36 Lamar Gordon | 1.25 | .50 |
| ❏ 37 Larry Tripplett | .60 | .25 |
| ❏ 38 Napoleon Harris | 1.25 | .50 |
| ❏ 39 Daniel Graham | 1.25 | .50 |
| ❏ 40 Antonio Bryant | 1.25 | .50 |
| ❏ 41 Javon Walker | 2.00 | .75 |
| ❏ 42 Brian Poli-Dixon | 1.00 | .40 |
| ❏ 43 Jeremy Shockey | 2.50 | 1.00 |
| ❏ 44 Andre Davis | 1.00 | .40 |
| ❏ 45 Ladell Betts | 1.25 | .50 |
| ❏ 46 Michael Vick | 1.25 | .50 |
| ❏ NNO David Carr CL | .75 | .30 |

## 2003 SAGE HIT

| | | |
|---|---|---|
| ❏ COMPLETE SET (48) | 25.00 | 10.00 |
| ❏ 1 Charles Rogers | .75 | .30 |
| ❏ 2 Willis McGahee | 2.50 | 1.00 |
| ❏ 3 Amaz Battle | 1.00 | .40 |
| ❏ 4 Terence Newman | 1.25 | .50 |
| ❏ 5 Larry Johnson | 2.50 | 1.00 |
| ❏ 6 Taylor Jacobs | .75 | .30 |
| ❏ 7 Kyle Boller | 1.00 | .40 |
| ❏ 8 Rex Grossman | 2.50 | 1.00 |

| | | |
|---|---|---|
| ❑ 9 Jerome McDougle | .60 | .25 |
| ❑ 10 Jason Witten | 2.00 | .75 |
| ❑ 11 Ken Dorsey | .75 | .30 |
| ❑ 12 Justin Gage | .75 | .30 |
| ❑ 13 Andy Groom | .60 | .25 |
| ❑ 14 Seneca Wallace | 1.00 | .40 |
| ❑ 15 Dave Ragone | .60 | .25 |
| ❑ 16 Kliff Kingsbury | .75 | .30 |
| ❑ 17 Jason Gesser | .75 | .30 |
| ❑ 18 George Wrighster | .60 | .25 |
| ❑ 19 Ronald Bellamy | .75 | .30 |
| ❑ 20 Donnie Nickey | .60 | .25 |
| ❑ 21 Billy McMullen | .60 | .25 |
| ❑ 22 Lee Suggs | .75 | .30 |
| ❑ 23 Chris Brown | 1.00 | .40 |
| ❑ 24 Bryant Johnson | 1.00 | .40 |
| ❑ 25 Justin Fargas | 1.00 | .40 |
| ❑ 26 Brandon Lloyd | 1.00 | .40 |
| ❑ 27 Tyrone Calico | .75 | .30 |
| ❑ 28 Sam Aiken | .75 | .30 |
| ❑ 29 Cie Grant | .75 | .30 |
| ❑ 30 Dahrran Diedrick | .60 | .25 |
| ❑ 31 Kelley Washington | .75 | .30 |
| ❑ 32 Musa Smith | .75 | .30 |
| ❑ 33 Kevin Curtis | 1.25 | .50 |
| ❑ 34 Terry Pierce | .60 | .25 |
| ❑ 35 Matt Wilhelm | .75 | .30 |
| ❑ 36 Rashean Mathis | .75 | .30 |
| ❑ 37 Brad Banks | .75 | .30 |
| ❑ 38 Tully Banta-Cain | 1.00 | .40 |
| ❑ 39 Sammy Davis | .75 | .30 |
| ❑ 40 Teyo Johnson | .75 | .30 |
| ❑ 41 Chris Simms | 1.00 | .40 |
| ❑ 42 E.J. Henderson | .75 | .30 |
| ❑ 43 Terrell Suggs | 1.25 | .50 |
| ❑ 44 Dallas Clark | 1.00 | .40 |
| ❑ 45 Marcus Trufant | 1.00 | .40 |
| ❑ 46 Boss Bailey | .75 | .30 |
| ❑ 47 David Carr | 1.00 | .40 |
| ❑ NNO Charles Rogers CL | .60 | .25 |

## 2004 SAGE HIT

STEVEN JACKSON

| | | |
|---|---|---|
| ❑ COMPLETE SET (46) | 30.00 | 12.50 |
| ❑ 1 Reggie Williams | 1.00 | .40 |
| ❑ 2 Bernard Berrian | 1.00 | .40 |
| ❑ 3 Lee Evans | 1.25 | .50 |
| ❑ 4 Roy Williams WR | 2.50 | 1.00 |
| ❑ 5 Josh Harris | .60 | .25 |
| ❑ 6 Greg Jones | 1.00 | .40 |
| ❑ 7 Ben Roethlisberger | 8.00 | 3.00 |
| ❑ 8 Drew Carter | 1.00 | .40 |
| ❑ 9 Devery Henderson | 1.00 | .40 |
| ❑ 10 Eli Manning | 6.00 | 2.50 |
| ❑ 11 Karlos Dansby | 1.00 | .40 |
| ❑ 12 Michael Jenkins | 1.00 | .40 |
| ❑ 13 Maurice Clarett | .75 | .30 |
| ❑ 14 Michael Clayton | 1.00 | .40 |
| ❑ 15 Casey Clausen | .75 | .30 |
| ❑ 16 John Navarre | .75 | .30 |
| ❑ 17 Philip Rivers | 3.00 | 1.25 |

| | | |
|---|---|---|
| ❑ 18 Jeff Smoker | .75 | .30 |
| ❑ 19 Ernest Wilford | 1.00 | .40 |
| ❑ 20 Derrick Knight | .60 | .25 |
| ❑ 21 Chris Gamble | .75 | .30 |
| ❑ 22 Jared Lorenzen | .75 | .30 |
| ❑ 23 Chris Perry | 1.00 | .40 |
| ❑ 24 Rod Rutherford | .60 | .25 |
| ❑ 25 Kevin Jones | 1.00 | .40 |
| ❑ 26 Michael Boulware | 1.00 | .40 |
| ❑ 27 Tatum Bell | 1.00 | .40 |
| ❑ 28 Will Poole | 1.00 | .40 |
| ❑ 29 Jake Grove | .60 | .25 |
| ❑ 30 Eli Roberson | 1.00 | .40 |
| ❑ 31 Devard Darling | .75 | .30 |
| ❑ 32 Dunta Robinson | .75 | .30 |
| ❑ 33 Cody Pickett | .75 | .30 |
| ❑ 34 Steven Jackson | 3.00 | 1.25 |
| ❑ 35 Matt Schaub | 3.00 | 1.25 |
| ❑ 36 Sean Jones | .75 | .30 |
| ❑ 37 Tommie Harris | 1.00 | .40 |
| ❑ 38 Chris Collins | .60 | .25 |
| ❑ 39 Will Smith | .75 | .30 |
| ❑ 40 DeAngelo Hall | 1.00 | .40 |
| ❑ 41 Rashaun Woods | .60 | .25 |
| ❑ 42 Ben Troupe | .75 | .30 |
| ❑ 43 Quincy Wilson | .75 | .30 |
| ❑ 44 P.K. Sam | .60 | .25 |
| ❑ 45 Clarence Farmer | .60 | .25 |
| ❑ NNO Eli Manning CL | 3.00 | 1.25 |
| ❑ EM Eli Manning SEC/30 | 50.00 | 20.00 |

## 2005 SAGE HIT

| | | |
|---|---|---|
| ❑ COMPLETE SET (50) | 25.00 | 10.00 |
| ❑ 1 Craphonso Thorpe | .75 | .30 |
| ❑ 2 Derrick Johnson | 1.00 | .40 |
| ❑ 3 Frank Gore SP | 3.00 | 1.25 |
| ❑ 4 Ciatrick Fason | .75 | .30 |
| ❑ 5 Charlie Frye | 1.00 | .40 |
| ❑ 6 Antrel Rolle | 1.00 | .40 |
| ❑ 7 Dan Orlovsky | 1.00 | .40 |
| ❑ 8 Aaron Rodgers | 3.00 | 1.25 |
| ❑ 9 Mark Clayton | 1.00 | .40 |
| ❑ 10 Thomas Davis | .75 | .30 |
| ❑ 11 Alex Smith QB | 1.50 | .60 |
| ❑ 12 Fred Gibson SP | 1.00 | .40 |
| ❑ 13 Maurice Clarett SP | 1.00 | .40 |
| ❑ 14 David Greene | .75 | .30 |
| ❑ 15 Carlos Rogers | 1.00 | .40 |
| ❑ 16 Andrew Walter | 1.00 | .40 |
| ❑ 17 Jason Campbell | 2.00 | .75 |
| ❑ 18 Jason White | 1.00 | .40 |
| ❑ 19 Matt Jones | 1.50 | .60 |
| ❑ 20 Braman Barber SP | 4.00 | 1.50 |
| ❑ 21 Taylor Stubblefield | .60 | .25 |
| ❑ 22 Jammal Brown SP | 1.25 | .50 |
| ❑ 23 Ronnie Brown | 3.00 | 1.25 |
| ❑ 24 Cadillac Williams | 2.00 | .75 |
| ❑ 25 Kay-Jay Harris | .75 | .30 |
| ❑ 26 Reggie Brown | 1.00 | .40 |
| ❑ 27 Troy Williamson | 1.00 | .40 |

| | | |
|---|---|---|
| ❑ 28 Anthony Davis | .75 | .30 |
| ❑ 29 Josh Davis SP | .75 | .30 |
| ❑ 30 J.J. Arrington | 1.00 | .40 |
| ❑ 31 Alex Smith TE | 1.00 | .40 |
| ❑ 32 Corey Webster SP | 1.25 | .50 |
| ❑ 33 Vernand Morency | 1.00 | .40 |
| ❑ 34 Derek Anderson | 1.50 | .60 |
| ❑ 35 DeMarcus Ware | 2.00 | .75 |
| ❑ 36 Kyle Orton | 1.25 | .50 |
| ❑ 37 Brock Berlin | .75 | .30 |
| ❑ 38 Marlin Jackson | .75 | .30 |
| ❑ 39 Channing Crowder | .75 | .30 |
| ❑ 40 Roddy White | 1.25 | .50 |
| ❑ 41 Roscoe Parrish | .75 | .30 |
| ❑ 42 Adrian McPherson | .75 | .30 |
| ❑ 43 Brodney Pool | .75 | .30 |
| ❑ 44 T.A. McLendon | .60 | .25 |
| ❑ 45 Terrence Murphy | .60 | .25 |
| ❑ 46 Chris Rix | .75 | .30 |
| ❑ 47 Ben Roethlisberger SP | 3.00 | 1.25 |
| ❑ 48 Dante Ridgeway SP | .75 | .30 |
| ❑ 49 Justin Miller | .75 | .30 |
| ❑ 50 Johnathan Goddard SP | 1.00 | .40 |
| ❑ ROY Roethlisberger ROY/100 | 20.00 | 7.50 |

## 2006 SAGE HIT

MATT LEINART

| | | |
|---|---|---|
| ❑ COMPLETE SET (55) | 25.00 | 10.00 |
| ❑ #56 ISSUED AT 2006 ANAHEIM NATIONAL | | |
| ❑ 1 Reggie McNeal | .75 | .30 |
| ❑ 2 Jimmy Williams SP | 1.00 | .40 |
| ❑ 3 D.J. Shockley SP | 1.00 | .40 |
| ❑ 4 Omar Jacobs | .75 | .30 |
| ❑ 5 Reggie Bush | 4.00 | 1.50 |
| ❑ 6 Charlie Whitehurst | 1.00 | .40 |
| ❑ 7 Michael Huff | 1.00 | .40 |
| ❑ 8 Tye Hill | 1.00 | .40 |
| ❑ 9 Mario Williams | 1.50 | .60 |
| ❑ 10 Vince Young | 3.00 | 1.25 |
| ❑ 11 Matt Leinart UER | 3.00 | 1.25 |
| ❑ 12 Brodie Croyle | 1.25 | .50 |
| ❑ 13 Paul Pinegar | .75 | .30 |
| ❑ 14 Drew Olson | .75 | .30 |
| ❑ 15 Martin Nance | .75 | .30 |
| ❑ 16 David Thomas | 1.00 | .40 |
| ❑ 17 Dwayne Slay SP | .75 | .30 |
| ❑ 18 Vernon Davis | 1.00 | .40 |
| ❑ 19 Taurean Henderson SP | 1.00 | .40 |
| ❑ 20 Maurice Drew | 2.00 | .75 |
| ❑ 21 LenDale White | 2.00 | .75 |
| ❑ 22 Laurence Maroney | 2.50 | 1.00 |
| ❑ 23 Leon Washington | 1.00 | .40 |
| ❑ 24 Erik Meyer SP | .75 | .30 |
| ❑ 25 Maurice Stovall | 1.00 | .40 |
| ❑ 26 Ashton Youboty | 1.00 | .40 |
| ❑ 27 Devin Aromashodu | .75 | .30 |
| ❑ 28 Mike Hass | 1.00 | .40 |
| ❑ 29 Jonathan Orr | .75 | .30 |
| ❑ 30 Joseph Addai | 3.00 | 1.25 |
| ❑ 31 Leonard Pope | 1.00 | .40 |
| ❑ 32 Michael Robinson | 1.00 | .40 |

| | | |
|---|---|---|
| ❑ 33 Mike Bell | 1.00 | .40 |
| ❑ 34 Ernie Sims SP | 1.00 | .40 |
| ❑ 35 Skyler Green | 1.00 | .40 |
| ❑ 36 Demetrius Williams | 1.00 | .40 |
| ❑ 37 Winston Justice | 1.00 | .40 |
| ❑ 38 Sinorice Moss | 1.00 | .40 |
| ❑ 39 Charles Gordon SP | .75 | .30 |
| ❑ 40 Gerald Riggs | 1.00 | .40 |
| ❑ 41 Jerome Harrison | 1.00 | .40 |
| ❑ 42 Bobby Carpenter | 1.00 | .40 |
| ❑ 43 Dominique Byrd | .75 | .30 |
| ❑ 44 Bruce Gradkowski | 1.00 | .40 |
| ❑ 45 Rodrique Wright | .50 | .20 |
| ❑ 46 D'Brickashaw Ferguson | 1.00 | .40 |
| ❑ 47 Daniel Bullocks SP | 1.00 | .40 |
| ❑ 48 Jason Avant | 1.00 | .40 |
| ❑ 49 Will Blackmon | 1.00 | .40 |
| ❑ 50 Devin Hester SP | 2.00 | .75 |
| ❑ 51 Alan Zemaitis SP | 1.00 | .40 |
| ❑ 52 Hank Baskett | 1.00 | .40 |
| ❑ 53 Cadillac Williams ROY SP | 3.00 | 1.25 |
| ❑ 54 Bush/Leinart CL SP | 3.00 | 1.25 |
| ❑ 55 Vince Young CL SP | 2.00 | .75 |
| ❑ 56 Jay Cutler | 4.00 | 1.50 |

## 2007 SAGE HIT

| | | |
|---|---|---|
| ❑ COMPLETE SET (64) | 25.00 | 10.00 |
| ❑ 1 Paul Williams | .75 | .30 |
| ❑ 2 JaMarcus Russell | 2.50 | 1.00 |
| ❑ 3 Robert Meachem | 1.00 | .40 |
| ❑ 4 Sidney Rice | 1.00 | .40 |
| ❑ 5 Drew Stanton | 1.00 | .40 |
| ❑ 6 Jeff Rowe | .75 | .30 |
| ❑ 7 Zach Miller | .60 | .25 |
| ❑ 8 Joel Filani | .75 | .30 |
| ❑ 9 Chris Henry | 1.00 | .40 |
| ❑ 10 Brady Quinn | 3.00 | 1.25 |
| ❑ 11 Anthony Gonzalez | 1.50 | .60 |
| ❑ 12 Chris Leak | .75 | .30 |
| ❑ 13 David Clowney | .75 | .30 |
| ❑ 14 Isaiah Stanback | 1.00 | .40 |
| ❑ 15 Steve Breaston | 1.00 | .40 |
| ❑ 16 Yamon Figurs | 1.00 | .40 |
| ❑ 17 Lawrence Timmons | 1.00 | .40 |
| ❑ 18 Greg Olsen | 1.25 | .50 |
| ❑ 19 Michael Bush | 1.00 | .40 |
| ❑ 20 Alan Branch | .75 | .30 |
| ❑ 21 Johnnie Lee Higgins | .75 | .30 |
| ❑ 22 Aundrae Allison | .75 | .30 |
| ❑ 23 Kenny Irons | .75 | .30 |
| ❑ 24 Marshawn Lynch | 2.00 | .75 |
| ❑ 25 Earl Everett | .75 | .30 |
| ❑ 26 Courtney Taylor | .75 | .30 |
| ❑ 27 Michael Griffin | 1.00 | .40 |
| ❑ 28 Adrian Peterson | 8.00 | 3.00 |
| ❑ 29 Leon Hall | .75 | .30 |
| ❑ 30 David Ball | .75 | .30 |
| ❑ 31 Aaron Ross | 1.00 | .40 |
| ❑ 32 John Beck | 1.00 | .40 |
| ❑ 33 Kolby Smith | 1.00 | .40 |

| | | |
|---|---|---|
| ❑ 34 Ken Darby | 1.00 | .40 |
| ❑ 35 Trent Edwards | 2.50 | 1.00 |
| ❑ 36 Craig Buster Davis | 1.00 | .40 |
| ❑ 37 Ryan Kalil | .75 | .30 |
| ❑ 38 Jason Snelling | .75 | .30 |
| ❑ 39 Tyler Palko | 1.00 | .40 |
| ❑ 40 Dwayne Bowe | 2.00 | .75 |
| ❑ 41 Dallas Baker | .75 | .30 |
| ❑ 42 Steve Smith USC | 1.25 | .50 |
| ❑ 43 Jason Hill | 1.00 | .40 |
| ❑ 44 Kevin Kolb | 1.50 | .60 |
| ❑ 45 Jared Zabransky | 1.00 | .40 |
| ❑ 46 Brian Leonard | 1.00 | .40 |
| ❑ 47 Darius Walker | 1.00 | .40 |
| ❑ 48 Adam Carriker | .75 | .30 |
| ❑ 49 Patrick Willis | 1.50 | .60 |
| ❑ 50 Troy Smith | 1.25 | .50 |
| ❑ 51 Brandon Meriweather | 1.00 | .40 |
| ❑ 52 Jarvis Moss | 1.00 | .40 |
| ❑ 53 Levi Brown | 1.00 | .40 |
| ❑ 54 David Irons | .60 | .25 |
| ❑ 55 Garrett Wolfe | 1.00 | .40 |
| ❑ 56 LaMarr Woodley | 1.00 | .40 |
| ❑ 57 DeMarcus Tank Tyler | .75 | .30 |
| ❑ 58 Jordan Palmer | 1.00 | .40 |
| ❑ 59 Antonio Pittman | 1.00 | .40 |
| ❑ 60 Gaines Adams | 1.00 | .40 |
| ❑ 61 Calvin Johnson | 2.50 | 1.00 |
| ❑ ML Matt Leinart | 1.50 | .60 |
| ❑ RB Reggie Bush | 2.00 | .75 |
| ❑ VY Vince Young | 1.50 | .60 |

## 2008 SAGE HIT

| | | |
|---|---|---|
| ❑ COMPLETE SET (100) | 40.00 | 15.00 |
| ❑ COMP.LOW SERIES (50) | 20.00 | 7.50 |
| ❑ COMP.HIGH SERIES (50) | 20.00 | 7.50 |
| ❑ 1 John David Booty | 1.25 | .50 |
| ❑ 2 Will Franklin | 1.00 | .40 |
| ❑ 3 Danny Woodhead | 1.50 | .60 |
| ❑ 4 Limas Sweed | 1.25 | .50 |
| ❑ 5 Joe Flacco | 3.00 | 1.25 |
| ❑ 6 Brian Brohm | 1.25 | .50 |
| ❑ 7 Chad Henne | 1.50 | .60 |
| ❑ 8 Marcus Thomas | .75 | .30 |
| ❑ 9 Early Doucet | 1.00 | .40 |
| ❑ 10 Dennis Dixon | 1.00 | .40 |
| ❑ 11 Xavier Adibi | .75 | .30 |
| ❑ 12 Matt Ryan | 4.00 | 1.50 |
| ❑ 13 T.C. Ostrander | .75 | .30 |
| ❑ 14 Bernard Morris | .75 | .30 |
| ❑ 15 Sam Baker | .60 | .25 |
| ❑ 16 Adrian Arrington | .75 | .30 |
| ❑ 17 Kevin O'Connell | 1.25 | .50 |
| ❑ 18 Jacob Hester | 1.00 | .40 |
| ❑ 19 Keenan Burton | .75 | .30 |
| ❑ 20 Darius Reynaud | .75 | .30 |
| ❑ 21 Keon Lattimore | .75 | .30 |
| ❑ 22 Tashard Choice | 1.00 | .40 |
| ❑ 23 Jake Long | 1.25 | .50 |
| ❑ 24 Paul Smith | 1.00 | .40 |

| | | |
|---|---|---|
| ❑ 25 Jamaal Charles | 1.25 | .50 |
| ❑ 26 Yvenson Bernard | 1.00 | .40 |
| ❑ 27 Alex Brink | 1.00 | .40 |
| ❑ 28 James Hardy | 1.00 | .40 |
| ❑ 29 Martin Rucker | .75 | .30 |
| ❑ 30 Steve Slaton | 2.00 | .75 |
| ❑ 31 Derrick Harvey | .75 | .30 |
| ❑ 32 Andre Callender | 1.00 | .40 |
| ❑ 33 Jabari Arthur | .75 | .30 |
| ❑ 34 Bruce Hocker | 1.00 | .40 |
| ❑ 35 Kelvin McRae | .75 | .30 |
| ❑ 36 Lawrence Jackson | .75 | .30 |
| ❑ 37 Tyrell Johnson | 1.00 | .40 |
| ❑ 38 Marcus Howard | 1.00 | .40 |
| ❑ 39 Sam Keller | 1.00 | .40 |
| ❑ 40 Keith Rivers | 1.00 | .40 |
| ❑ 41 Brandon Flowers | 1.00 | .40 |
| ❑ 42 Adarius Bowman | .75 | .30 |
| ❑ 43 Ricky Santos | 1.00 | .40 |
| ❑ 44 Jordon Dizon | 1.00 | .40 |
| ❑ 45 Robert Jordan | .75 | .30 |
| ❑ 46 Maurice Purify | 1.00 | .40 |
| ❑ 47 Lavelle Hawkins | .75 | .30 |
| ❑ 48 Jason Rivers | 1.00 | .40 |
| ❑ 49 John Carlson | 1.00 | .40 |
| ❑ 50 Vernon Gholston | 1.00 | .40 |
| ❑ 51 D.McFadden/F.Jones | 1.50 | .60 |
| ❑ 52 M.Ryan/A.Callender | 2.50 | 1.00 |
| ❑ 53 D.Jackson/M.Lynch | 1.25 | .50 |
| ❑ 54 M.Flynn/J.Russell | .75 | .30 |
| ❑ 55 B.Brohm/M.Bush | .75 | .30 |
| ❑ 56 C.Henne/M.Hart | 1.00 | .40 |
| ❑ 57 B.Quinn/J.Carlson | 2.00 | .75 |
| ❑ 58 J.Stewart/D.Dixon | 1.50 | .60 |
| ❑ 59 A.Peterson/M.Kelly | 2.50 | 1.00 |
| ❑ 60 R.Rice/B.Leonard | .75 | .30 |
| ❑ 61 J.Booty/F.Davis | .75 | .30 |
| ❑ 62 J.Charles/L.Sweed | .75 | .30 |
| ❑ 63 M.Ryan/B.Brohm | 2.50 | 1.00 |
| ❑ 64 D.McFadden/R.Mendenhall | 1.50 | .60 |
| ❑ 65 M.Kelly/D.Jackson | 1.25 | .50 |
| ❑ 66 J.Flacco/J.Johnson | 2.00 | .75 |
| ❑ 67 A.Peterson/P.Willis | 2.50 | 1.00 |
| ❑ 68 Devin Thomas | 1.00 | .40 |
| ❑ 69 Beau Bell | .75 | .30 |
| ❑ 70 Owen Schmitt | 1.00 | .40 |
| ❑ 71 Paul Raymond | .75 | .30 |
| ❑ 72 Jordy Nelson | 1.25 | .50 |
| ❑ 73 Ray Rice | 1.25 | .50 |
| ❑ 74 Darrell Strong | .75 | .30 |
| ❑ 75 Felix Jones | 2.50 | 1.00 |
| ❑ 76 Kevin Smith | 1.50 | .60 |
| ❑ 77 Justin Forsett | 1.00 | .40 |
| ❑ 78 Antoine Cason | 1.00 | .40 |
| ❑ 79 Ryan Clady | 1.00 | .40 |
| ❑ 80 Mike Hart | 1.25 | .50 |
| ❑ 81 Kenny Phillips | 1.00 | .40 |
| ❑ 82 Jonathan Stewart | 2.50 | 1.00 |
| ❑ 83 Fred Davis | 1.00 | .40 |
| ❑ 84 Malcolm Kelly | 1.00 | .40 |
| ❑ 85 Matt Flynn | 1.25 | .50 |
| ❑ 86 Allen Patrick | .75 | .30 |
| ❑ 87 Brent Miller | .75 | .30 |
| ❑ 88 Andre Caldwell | .75 | .30 |
| ❑ 89 Josh Johnson | 1.00 | .40 |
| ❑ 90 Erik Ainge | 1.00 | .40 |
| ❑ 91 Tom Zbikowski | 1.25 | .50 |
| ❑ 92 Dan Connor | 1.00 | .40 |
| ❑ 93 Leodis McKelvin | 1.25 | .50 |
| ❑ 94 Sedrick Ellis | 1.00 | .40 |
| ❑ 95 Rashard Mendenhall | 2.00 | .75 |
| ❑ 96 Mike Jenkins | 1.00 | .40 |
| ❑ 97 Dustin Keller | 1.00 | .40 |
| ❑ 98 Donnie Avery | 1.25 | .50 |
| ❑ 99 DeSean Jackson | 2.00 | .75 |
| ❑ 100 Darren McFadden | 2.50 | 1.00 |

# Acknowledgments

Every year we make active solicitations for expert input. We are particularly appreciative of the help (however extensive or cursory) provided for this volume. We receive many inquiries, comments, and questions regarding material within this book. In fact, each and every one is read and digested. Time constraints, however, prevent us from personally replying. But keep sharing your knowledge. Even though we cannot respond to each letter, you are making significant contributions to the hobby through your interest and comments.

The effort to continually refine and improve our books also involves a growing number of people and types of expertise on our home team. Our company boasts a substantial Sports Data Publishing team, which strengthens our ability to provide comprehensive analysis of the marketplace.

Our football analysts played a major part in compiling this year's book, traveling thousands of miles during the past year to attend sportscard shows and visit card shops around the United States and Canada. The Beckett Football specialists are Brian Fleischer and Dan Hitt (Senior Manager of SDP).

Dave Lee's input as Beckett Football editor this past year helped immeasurably; Rich Klein as research analyst and primary proofer also added many hours of painstaking work.

The effort was ably assisted by the rest of the SDP Team: Matt Brumley, Keith Hower, Grant Sandground (Senior Price Guide Editor), and Tim Trout.

The price-gathering and analytical talents of this fine group of hobbyists have helped make our Beckett team stronger, while making this guide and its companion monthly Price Guide more widely recognized as the hobby's most reliable and relied-upon source of pricing information.

In addition, Bill Sutherland and Soma Madhdhipitla contributed many programming improvements to make this process smoother. Also, this book could not be produced without the fine work of our prepress team. Under the leadership of Pete Adauto, Gean Paul Figari was responsible for the layout and general presentation of this book.

# $1 or less.

We've got over 2 million cards priced under a buck.

Collecting has never been so affordable.

BECKETT

B

MARKETPLACE

# The ALL-TIME Fan Favorite GRADING SPECIAL!

## 10-10-10

Submit 10 or more cards for grading at the 10-day service level and pay only $10 per card

### Save $40 or more!

*HURRY, this offer expires June 30, 2010*

PHOTO BY SHAUN BOTTERILL/GETTY IMAGES